# Encyclopedia of Business Information Sources

ISSN 0071-0210

# Encyclopedia of Business Information Sources

A Bibliographic Guide to Nearly 25,000 Citations Covering
Over 1,100 subjects of Interest to Business Personnel

Includes: Abstracts and Indexes, Almanacs and Yearbooks, Bibliographies,
Biographical Sources, CD-ROM Databases, Directories, E-Books, Encyclopedias
and Dictionaries, Financial Ratios, Handbooks and Manuals, Internet
Databases, Online Databases, Periodicals and Newsletters, Price Sources,
Research Centers and Institutes, Statistics Sources, Trade and
Professional Societies, and Other Sources of Information on Each Topic

## 32nd EDITION
### Volume 2

## Virgil L. Burton III

GALE
CENGAGE Learning·

Farmington Hills, Mich • San Francisco • New York • Waterville, Maine
Meriden, Conn • Mason, Ohio • Chicago

**Encyclopedia of Business Information
Sources 32nd Edition, Volume 2**

Project Editor: Virgil L. Burton III

Composition and Electronic Prepress: Gary
Leach

Manufacturing: Rita Wimberley

© 2015 Gale, Cengage Learning

WCN: 01-100-101

For product information and technology assistance, contact us at
**Gale Customer Support, 1-800-877-4253.**
For permission to use material from this text or product,
submit all requests online at **www.cengage.com/permissions.**
Further permissions questions can be emailed to
**permissionrequest@cengage.com**

While every effort has been made to ensure the reliability of the
information presented in this publication, Gale, a part of Cengage Learning,
does not guarantee the accuracy of the data contained herein. Gale accepts
no payment for listing; and inclusion in the publication of any organization,
agency, institution, publication, service, or individual does not imply
endorsement of the editors or publisher. Errors brought to the attention of
the publisher and verified to the satisfaction of the publisher will be
corrected in future editions.

EDITORIAL DATA PRIVACY POLICY: Does this product contain information
about you as an individual? If so, for more information about our editorial
data privacy policies, please see our Privacy Statement at
www.gale.cengage.com.

*Gale*
27500 Drake Rd.
Farmington Hills, MI, 48331-3535

ISBN-13: 978-1-57302-543-0 (2V SET)
ISBN-13: 978-1-57302-544-7 (V1)
ISBN-13: 978-1-57302-545-4 (V2)

ISSN 0071-0210

Printed in the United States of America
1 2 3 4 5     19 18 17 16 15

# Contents

**Volume 2**

As the information needs of business managers and information professionals continue to increase, timely and convenient access becomes more valuable. The *Encyclopedia of Business Information Sources (EBIS)* is designed to assist these individuals in locating material relevant to today's rapidly-changing business environment.

*EBIS* now includes nearly 25,000 citations, dealing with more than 1,100 business, financial, and industrial topics. The subjects cover a variety of business-related concerns. These include, for example:

- Business functions—Accounting; Administration; Personnel Management

- Computer-related subjects—Computer Graphics; Computer Software Industry; Local Area Networks

- Foreign trade—International Marketing; Latin American Markets; North American Free Trade Agreement (NAFTA)

- Information industry topics—Electronic Publishing; Internet; Multimedia

## Easy to Use

A convenient and accessible grouping of information sources is provided for each business topic. Within these topics, there is the additional convenience of type-of-material categories: directories, periodicals, handbooks, and so forth. An extensive *Outline of Contents* (see p. xiii) makes the exact heading for any subject easy to locate. Many cross-references provide additional assistance in finding needed information.

*EBIS* thus serves two kinds of information needs: for a quick survey of publications and organizations relating to a particular topic, and for reference to a specific source that will provide a single fact or statistic.

## "Sources Cited" Section

For users with a specific title, organization, or service in mind, an alphabetic list of sources follows the main text. This *Sources Cited* section repeats all entries from the main text, sorting them alphabetically by publication title or organization name. The *Sources Cited* section also includes complete contact information.

## Extensive Updating

Thousands of changes and additions were required to update this edition of *EBIS*. Information was verified through reliable sources and independent research of the editorial staff. Current editions of *Gale's Encyclopedia of Associations and Research Centers Directory* were used to update nonprint sources in the categories of "Trade Associations and Professional Societies" and "Research Centers and Institutes."

Standard business or economic compilations, such as the annual *Economic Report of the President* and *Risk Management Association's Annual Statement Studies,* have been carefully examined and entered under topics for which these publications contain significant data. Many out-of-print and discontinued items have been deleted from this edition of *EBIS,* although a few titles considered to be unique or of particular interest have been retained. Should it be desirable to consult these works, they may be available at local libraries.

New material for this edition has been collected in various ways. These include examining publishers' catalogs or brochures, reviewing material in business libraries, scanning lists of recommended titles, and discussing publications with business librarians. Publishers' Internet Web pages have also been useful.

## Available in Electronic Formats

The Directory is also available as part of the Gale Directory Library. For more information, call 1-800-877-GALE

## Suggestions Are Welcome

If you have suggestions, concerns, or comments about the *Encyclopedia of Business Information Sources,* please contact:

*Encyclopedia of Business Information Sources*

Gale, Cengage Learning

27500 Drake Road

Farmington Hills, MI 48331-3535

Phone: 248-699-4253

Toll-free: 800-877-GALE

Fax: 248-699-8070

## Primary Listings

In the main section of the *Encyclopedia of Business Information Sources (EBIS)*, entries are arranged alphabetically by ❙1❙ topic, and further subdivided by ❙2❙ type of source and ❙3❙ publication title or organization name. For example:

❙1❙ CORPORATE FINANCE

❙2❙ DIRECTORIES

❙3❙ *America's Corporate Finance Directory*. National Register Publishing Co., Reed Elsevier Inc. Annual. $730.00. A directory of financial information, covering 5,000 major U. S. corporations.

❙3❙ *Corporate Finance Sourcebook*. National Register Publishing Co., Reed Elsevier Inc. Annual. $650.00. Lists more than 3,700 organizations providing corporate capital.

❙2❙ ONLINE DATABASES

❙3❙ *ABI/INFORM*. Proquest Co. Provides online indexing to business-related material occurring in more than 1,000 periodicals from 1971 to the present. Inquire as to online cost and availability.

❙2❙ RESEARCH CENTERS AND INSTITUTES

❙3❙ Bendheim Center for Finance. Princeton University, Dept. of Economics, Princeton, NJ 08544. Phone: (609)258-4023. Fax: (609)258-6419.

## Locate Topics in the Outline of Contents Section

The *Encyclopedia of Business Information Sources* covers more than 1,100 topics. The efficient way to locate a particular topic is to scan the *Outline of Contents* section, which follows this *User's Guide*. The *Outline of Contents* lists topics alphabetically.

Users can determine at a glance the specific form of the subject term that has been employed. Numerous cross-references provide assistance where necessary. For instance, if the term being sought is Cellular Telephones, the *Outline of Contents* provides a cross-reference directing users to the heading "Mobile Telephone Industry," where information on cell phones may be found.

## 19 Kinds of Sources

Material under each topic is grouped according to the type of source or form in which the information is provided. A user can look under the topic of interest (Corporate Finance, for example) to find key information sources arranged as follows:

- Abstracts and Indexes
- Almanacs and Yearbooks
- Bibliographies
- Biographical Sources
- CD-ROM Databases
- Directories
- E-Books
- Encyclopedias and Dictionaries
- Financial Ratios
- General Works
- Handbooks and Manuals
- Internet Databases
- Online Databases
- Other Sources
- Periodicals and Newsletters
- Price Sources
- Research Centers and Institutes
- Statistics Sources
- Trade/Professional Associations

## Content of the Entries

The content of the entries is described here and illustrated in the sample that appears on the previous page.

Entries for publications and online databases list the title of the work, the name of the author (where applicable), the name of the publisher or provider, frequency or year of publication, and price. Brief descriptive notes are often added to clarify listings. Entries included in the "Internet Databases" category provide the name of the Web site, the name of the provider or host, telephone/fax numbers, E-mail address, the URL address, and information on content and cost (most are free).

Entries for trade associations and research centers provide the organization name, address, telephone/fax numbers, and Internet information where available. Many of these entries include a brief description of the organization.

## Sources Cited Section

*Arrangement*—In the Sources Cited section, all entries from the primary listings in *EBIS* are arranged alphabetically by publication title, database title, or organization name.

*Contact Information*—The Sources Cited section provides contact information—including URL addresses and e-mail in most instances—for print publishers and for publishers or providers of online databases.

*Many of the online databases referenced in EBIS are available through the widely used service providers listed below.*

## ONLINE DATABASE VENDORS

### DIALOG
Dialog/Thomson Corp.
11000 Regency Parkway, Suite 10
Cary, NC 27518
(800)334-2564 or (919)462-8600
Fax: (919)468-9890
http://www.dialog.com

### DIALOG DataStar
Dialog/Thomson Corp.
11000 Regency Parkway, Suite 10
Cary, NC 27518
(800)334-2564 or (919)462-8600
Fax: (919)468-9890
http://www.dialog.com/products/
datastar

### InfoTrac OneFile
Gale, Cengage Learning
27500 Drake Road

Farmington Hills, MI 48331-3535
(800)877-4253 or (248) 699-4253
Fax: (800) 414-5043 or (248)699-8096
gale.cengage.com

### LEXIS-NEXIS
Reed-Elsevier Inc.
P. O. Box 933
Dayton, OH 45401-0933
(800)227-4908 or (937)865-6800
Fax: (937)865-6909
http://www.lexisnexis.com

### OCLC FirstSearch
OCLC Online Computer Library
Center, Inc.
6565 Kilgour Place
Dublin, OH 43017-3395
(800)848-5878 or (614)764-6000
Fax: (614)764-6096
http://www.oclc.org/firstsearch

### Ovid Technologies, Inc.
333 Seventh Ave., 20th Floor
New York, NY10001
(800)950-2035 or (646)674-6300
Fax: (646)674-6301
http://www.ovid.com

### Questel-Orbit, Inc.
1725 Duke Street, Suite 625
Alexandria, VA22314
(800)456-7248 or (703)519-1820
Fax: (703)519-1821
http://www.questel.orbit.com

### WESTLAW
West Group
610 Opperman Drive
Saint Paul, MN 55123
(800)328-4880 or (651)687-7000
Fax: (651)687-7849
http://www.westlaw.com

# M

## MACARONI

### PRICE SOURCES

*Supermarket News: The Industry's Weekly Newspaper*. Fairchild Publications. • Weekly. Individuals, $196.00 per year; retailers, $45.00 per year; manufacturers, $89.00 per year.

### TRADE/PROFESSIONAL ASSOCIATIONS

National Pasta Association. 750 National Press Bldg., 529 14th St. NW, Washington, DC 20045. Phone: (202)591-2459; Fax: (202)591-2445; Email: info@ilovepasta.org • URL: http://www.ilovepasta. org • Manufacturers of pasta in the U.S. and suppliers to the industry. Seeks to improve manufacturer and supplier efficiency. Conducts agricultural and technical research programs. Sponsors U.S. pasta product public relations program and pasta/durum wheat technical course.

## MACHINE DESIGN

*See also* MECHANICAL ENGINEERING

### PERIODICALS AND NEWSLETTERS

*Advanced Manufacturing Technology: Monthly Report*. Technical Insights. • Monthly. $695 Institutions. Covers technological developments relating to robotics, computer graphics, automation, computer-integrated manufacturing, and machining.

*International Journal of Machine Tools and Manufacture: Design, Research and Application*. Elsevier. • $4,493 Institutions. 15 times a year.

*Mechanism and Machine Theory*. Elsevier. • Monthly. $4,537 Institutions /year. Provides a medium of communication between engineers and scientists engaged in research and development within the fields of knowledge embraced by IF-ToMM, the International Federation for the Promotion of Mechanism and Machine Science.

## MACHINE SHOPS

### DIRECTORIES

*Dun's Industrial Guide: The Metalworking Directory*. Dun & Bradstreet Inc. • Annual. Libraries, $485; commercial institutions, $795.00. Lease basis. Three volumes. Lists about 65,000 U. S. manufacturing plants using metal and suppliers of metalworking equipment and materials. Includes names and titles of key personnel. Products, purchases, and processes are indicated.

*Modern Machine Shop*. Gardner Business Media, Inc. • Monthly. $89 Individuals. Lists products and services for the metalworking industry. Formerly *Modern Machine Shop CNC and Software Guide*.

### FINANCIAL RATIOS

*Annual Statement Studies*. Risk Management Association. • Annual. Compiled from over 280,000 financial statements.

*Annual Statement Studies: Industry Default Probabilities and Cash Flow Measures*. Risk Management Association. • Annual. $405 Nonmembers. Serves as a companion volume to the original *Annual Statement Studies*. Gives probability of default estimates on a percentage scale for more than 450 industries. Includes changes in position year-by-year for eight financial statement line items and provides percentage measures of cash flow.

### PERIODICALS AND NEWSLETTERS

*Modern Machine Shop*. Gardner Business Media, Inc. • Monthly. $89 Individuals. Lists products and services for the metalworking industry. Formerly *Modern Machine Shop CNC and Software Guide*.

## MACHINE TOOL INDUSTRY

*See also* TOOL INDUSTRY

### ABSTRACTS AND INDEXES

*Cutting Technology*. Penton Media Inc. • Seven times a year. Free to qualified personnel; others, $55.00 per year. Provides abstracts of the international literature of metal cutting and machining. Formerly *Cutting Tool-Machine Digest*.

*NTIS Alerts: Manufacturing Technology*. U.S. Department of Commerce National Technical Information Service. • Biweekly. $130 per year. Covers computer-aided design and manufacturing (CAD/CAM), engineering materials, quality control, machine tools, robots, lasers, productivity, and related subjects.

### CD-ROM DATABASES

*OECD Statistical Compendium*. Organization for Economic Cooperation and Development. • Semiannual. $1,905.00 per year for 1 to 10 users. CD-ROM contains more than 730,000 monthly, quarterly, and annual time series for OECD countries, 1960 to date. Includes fully searchable data on agriculture, food, economic indicators, national accounts, employment, energy, finance, industry, technology, and foreign trade. Results can be displayed in various forms.

### DIRECTORIES

*Dun's Industrial Guide: The Metalworking Directory*. Dun & Bradstreet Inc. • Annual. Libraries, $485; commercial institutions, $795.00. Lease basis. Three volumes. Lists about 65,000 U. S. manufacturing plants using metal and suppliers of metalworking equipment and materials. Includes names and titles of key personnel. Products, purchases, and processes are indicated.

*Industrial Laser Solutions Buyer's Guide*. PennWell Corp., Advanced Technology Div. • Annual. Lists industrial laser suppliers by category and geographic location. (Included with subscription to *Industrial Laser Solutions*.).

*The International Directory of Importers--Machine Tools and Accessories Importers*. Interdata. • $220 Individuals print. Covers: 1,900 international firms importing machine tools and accessories. Entries include: Company name and address, contact person, email, number of employees, year established, phone and telefaxes, business activity, bank references, as well as a listing of machine tools and accessories currently being imported.

*Modern Machine Shop*. Gardner Business Media, Inc. • Monthly. $89 Individuals. Lists products and services for the metalworking industry. Formerly *Modern Machine Shop CNC and Software Guide*.

### FINANCIAL RATIOS

*Annual Statement Studies*. Risk Management Association. • Annual. Compiled from over 280,000 financial statements.

*Annual Statement Studies: Industry Default Probabilities and Cash Flow Measures*. Risk Management Association. • Annual. $405 Nonmembers. Serves as a companion volume to the original *Annual Statement Studies*. Gives probability of default estimates on a percentage scale for more than 450 industries. Includes changes in position year-by-year for eight financial statement line items and provides percentage measures of cash flow.

### INTERNET DATABASES

*Business 2.0 Web Guide to the Best Business Links*. Business 2.0 Media Inc. Phone: (415)293-4800; Email: support@business2.com • URL: http://www. business2.com/webguide • Web site presents an extensive, searchable directory of links to "the best, most informative, and authoritative web pages." Twenty main categories cover business, finance, career, company information, people, and technology topics, with thousands of subtopics, all linking to Web sites recommended by experienced business researchers. Fees: Free.

*Fedstats*. Federal Interagency Council on Statistical Policy. Phone: (202)395-7254 • URL: http://www. fedstats.gov • Web site features an efficient search facility for full-text statistics produced by more than 100 federal agencies, including the Census Bureau, the Bureau of Economic Analysis, and the Bureau of Labor Statistics. Boolean searches can be made within one agency or for all agencies combined.

Links are offered to international statistical bureaus, including the UN, IMF, OECD, UNESCO, Eurostat, and 20 individual countries. Fees: Free.

*FreeLunch.com.* Economy.com, Inc. Phone: (610)696-8700; Fax: (610)696-1678 • URL: http:// www.freelunch.com • Web site provides free access to more than 200 million economic and financial data series, covering industry, demographics, labor markets, prices, retail sales, government spending, trade, interest rates, housing starts, the stock market, etc. Data is available in either chart or table form. Searching is offered. Free, but registration required. Economy.com, Inc. also offers fee-based economic analysis at *The Dismal Scientist* site (www.dismal. com).

## PERIODICALS AND NEWSLETTERS

*Industrial Laser Solutions for Manufacturing.* PennWell Corp., Advanced Technology Div. • Monthly. $300.00 per year. Covers industrial laser technology, especially machine tool applications.

*International Journal of Machine Tools and Manufacture: Design, Research and Application.* Elsevier. • $4,493 Institutions. 15 times a year.

*Modern Machine Shop.* Gardner Business Media, Inc. • Monthly. $89 Individuals. Lists products and services for the metalworking industry. Formerly *Modern Machine Shop CNC and Software Guide.*

## RESEARCH CENTERS AND INSTITUTES

Advanced Manufacturing Engineering Institute. University of Hartford, College of Engineering, Technology, and Architecture, 200 Bloomfield Ave., West Hartford, CT 06117. Phone: 800-678-4844 or (860)768-4112; Fax: (860)768-5073; Email: shetty@mail.hartford.edu.

## STATISTICS SOURCES

*Survey of Current Business.* U. S. Government Printing Office. • Published by Bureau of Economic Analysis, U. S. Department of Commerce. Presents a wide variety of business and economic data.

## TRADE/PROFESSIONAL ASSOCIATIONS

ASM International. 9639 Kinsman Rd., Materials Park, OH 44073-0002. Phone: 800-336-5152 or (440)338-5151; Email: memberservicecenter@ asminternational.org • URL: http://www. asminternational.org • Metallurgists, materials engineers, executives in materials producing and consuming industries; teachers and students. Disseminates technical information about the manufacture, use, and treatment of engineered materials. Offers in-plant, home study, and intensive courses through Materials Engineering Institute.

National Tooling and Machining Association. 1357 Rockside Rd., Cleveland, OH 44134-2776. Phone: 800-248-6862; Fax: (216)264-2840; Email: info@ ntma.org • URL: http://www.ntma.org.

# MACHINE TRANSLATING

## PERIODICALS AND NEWSLETTERS

*Computational Linguistics.* Association for Computational Linguistics. The MIT Press. • Quarterly. Covers developments in research and applications of natural language processing.

## TRADE/PROFESSIONAL ASSOCIATIONS

Association for Computational Linguistics. 209 N Eighth St., Stroudsburg, PA 18360. Phone: (570)476-8006; Fax: (570)476-0860; Email: acl@ aclweb.org • URL: http://www.aclweb.org • Individuals interested in computational linguistics. Deals with algorithms, models, and computer systems or components of systems for research on language, applications (translation, documentation, and lexicography), and scholarly investigation (stylistics and content analysis).

# MACHINE VISION

*See also* AUTOMATION; ROBOTS

## ABSTRACTS AND INDEXES

*Applied Science and Technology Index.* EBSCO Publishing Inc. • 11/year. Indexes a wide variety of English language technical, industrial, and engineering periodicals.

*Computer and Information Systems Abstracts Journal: An Abstract Journal Pertaining to the Theory, Design, Fabrication and Application of Computer and Information Systems.* CSA. • Monthly. $1,750 per year.

*Computer Science Index.* EBSCO Publishing Inc. • Quarterly. $245 per year. Contains brief abstracts of book and periodical literature covering all phases of computing, including approximately 70 specific application areas.

*Engineering Index Monthly: Abstracting and Indexing Services Covering Sources ofthe World's Engineering Literature.* Engineering Information Inc. • Monthly. Institutions, $5,279.00 per year. Provides indexing and abstracting of the world's engineering and technical literature.

*Internet and Personal Computing Abstracts (print edition).* EBSCO Publishing Inc. • Quarterly. $269.00 per year, including cumulative index. Provides more than 10,000 abstracts annually from both trade and academic publications. Covers computer hardware, software, product reviews, Web topics, e-commerce, networks, corporate news, security, and related topics. Formerly *Microcomputer Abstracts.*

*Key Abstracts: Machine Vision.* Institution of Engineering and Technology. • Monthly. $1,138. Provides international coverage of journal and proceedings literature on optical noncontact sensing.

*NTIS Alerts: Computers, Control & Information Theory.* U.S. Department of Commerce National Technical Information Service. • Biweekly. $130 per year. Covers computer hardware, software, control systems, pattern recognition, image processing, and related subjects.

*NTIS Alerts: Manufacturing Technology.* U.S. Department of Commerce National Technical Information Service. • Biweekly. $130 per year. Covers computer-aided design and manufacturing (CAD/CAM), engineering materials, quality control, machine tools, robots, lasers, productivity, and related subjects.

## CD-ROM DATABASES

*Applied Science and Technology Abstracts.* EBSCO Publishing Inc. • Citations for more than 700 prominent scientific, technical, engineering, and industrial periodicals.

## DIRECTORIES

*Frontline Solutions Buyer's Guide.* Advanstar Communications. • Annual. $34.95 plus $3.50 shipping. Publication includes: List of manufacturers, suppliers, consultants, value added resellers, and dealers/distributors of automatic identification and data capture software, technology, equipment, and products for bar code, biometric identification, electronic data interchange, machine vision, magnetic stripe, optical character recognition, radio frequency data communications, radio frequency identification, smart cards, and voice data entry; also includes related organizations, and sources for industry standards. Entries include: Company name, address, phone, e-mail, web address, products or services.

*Manufacturing Systems: Buyers Guide.* Reed Elsevier Group plc Reed Business Information. • Annual. Price on application. Contains information on companies manufacturing or supplying materials handling systems, CAD/CAM systems, specialized software for manufacturing, programmable controllers, machine vision systems, and automatic identification systems.

## ONLINE DATABASES

*Applied Science and Technology Index Online.* H.W. Wilson Co. • Provides online indexing of 500 major scientific, technical, industrial, and engineering periodicals. Time period is 1983 to date. Monthly updates. Inquire as to online cost and availability.

*Computer Database.* Cengage Learning Inc. • Provides one year of full-text online for 150 leading computer-related publications. Also includes 70,000 product specifications and brief profiles of 13,000 computer product vendors and manufacturers. Inquire as to prices and availability.

*Current Contents Connect.* Thomson Reuters Intellectual Property and Science. • Provides online abstracts of articles listed in the tables of contents of about 7,500 journals. Coverage is very broad, including science, social science, life science, technology, engineering, industry, agriculture, the environment, economics, and arts and humanities. Time period is two years, with weekly updates. Inquire as to online cost and availability.

## PERIODICALS AND NEWSLETTERS

*IEEE Transactions on Visualization and Computer Graphics.* IEEE - Communications Society. • Monthly. Contains research on subjects related to computer graphics and visualization techniques, systems, software, hardware, and user interface issues.

*International Journal of Intelligent Systems.* John Wiley and Sons, Inc., Journals Div. • Monthly. $1,925.00 per year; with online edition, $2,022.00 per year.

*Sensors: Your Resource for Sensing, Communications, and Control.* Advanstar Communications. • Monthly. $70.00 per year. Edited for design, production, and manufacturing engineers involved with sensing systems. Emphasis is on emerging technology.

## RESEARCH CENTERS AND INSTITUTES

Carnegie Mellon University - Imaging Systems Laboratory. 5320 Wean Hall, Robotics Department, Pittsburgh, PA 15213. Phone: (412)268-5601 or (412)268-3824; Fax: (412)621-7068 or (412)683-3763; Email: rht@cs.cmu.edu • URL: http://www. cs.cmu.edu/afs/cs.cmu.edu/project/pcvision/www/ • Fields of research include computer vision and document interpretation.

Computer Vision Laboratory. University of Arizona, Department of Electrical and Computer Engineering, 1230 E Speedway Blvd., Tucson, AZ 85721. Phone: (520)621-2434; Fax: (520)621-8076; Email: strickland@ece.arizona.edu • Research areas include computer vision and speech synthesis.

Digital Image Analysis Laboratory. University of Arizona, Dept. of Electrical and Computer Engineering, 1230 E Speedway Blvd., Tucson, AZ 85721. Phone: (520)621-4554; Fax: (520)621-8076; Email: dial@ece.arizona.edu • URL: http://www. ece.arizona.edu • Research fields include image processing, computer vision, and artificial intelligence.

Imaging and Computer Vision Center. Drexel University, 3141 Chestnut St., Philadelphia, PA 19104. Phone: (215)895-2215; Fax: (215)895-4983; Email: icvc-support@cbis.ece.drexel.edu • URL: http://www.biomed.drexel.edu • Fields of research include computer vision, robot vision, and expert systems.

Massachusetts Institute of Technology - The Media Laboratory. Bldg. E15, 77 Massachusetts Ave., Cambridge, MA 02139-4307. Phone: (617)253-5960; Fax: (617)258-6264; Email: walter@media. mit.edu • URL: http://www.media.mit.edu • Research areas include electronic publishing, spatial imaging, human-machine interface, computer vision, and advanced television.

Worcester Polytechnic Institute - Department of

Computer Science - Image Science Research Group. 100 Institute Rd., Worcester, MA 01609-2280. Phone: (508)831-5671 or (508)831-5357; Fax: (508)831-5776; Email: matt@wpi.edu • URL: http://web.cs.wpi.edu/Research/isrg/ • Areas of research include image processing, computer graphics, and computational vision.

## TRADE/PROFESSIONAL ASSOCIATIONS

AIM Global. One Landmark N, 20399 Rte. 19, Ste. 203, Cranberry Township, PA 16066. Phone: (724)742-4473; Fax: (724)742-4476; Email: info@aim-na.org • URL: http://www.aimglobal.org • Serves as a trade association for the automatic identification data captures technology industry.

Automated Imaging Association. 900 Victors Way, Ste. 140, Ann Arbor, MI 48108. Phone: (734)994-6088; Email: dwhalls@robotics.org • URL: http://www.visiononline.org • Represents manufacturers of machine vision components and systems, users, system integrators, universities and non-profit research groups, and financial firms that track the machine vision industry. Promotes the use and understanding of image capture and analysis technology.

Machine Vision Association of the Society of Manufacturing Engineers. 1 SME Dr., Dearborn, MI 48128. Phone: 800-733-4763 or (313)425-3000; Fax: (313)425-3400; Email: service@sme.org • URL: http://www.sme.org • Members are professional engineers, managers, and students. Promotes the effective use of machine vision (optical sensing of actual scenes for use in machine control).

# MACHINERY

## ABSTRACTS AND INDEXES

*Applied Science and Technology Index.* EBSCO Publishing Inc. • 11/year. Indexes a wide variety of English language technical, industrial, and engineering periodicals.

## CD-ROM DATABASES

*OECD Statistical Compendium.* Organization for Economic Cooperation and Development. • Semiannual. $1,905.00 per year for 1 to 10 users. CD-ROM contains more than 730,000 monthly, quarterly, and annual time series for OECD countries, 1960 to date. Includes fully searchable data on agriculture, food, economic indicators, national accounts, employment, energy, finance, industry, technology, and foreign trade. Results can be displayed in various forms.

## DIRECTORIES

*Automatic Merchandising Machine Operation Directory.* InfoGroup Inc. • Annual. Number of listings: 11,954. Entries include: Name, address, phone, size of advertisement, name of owner or manager, number of employees, year first in "Yellow Pages." Compiled from telephone company "Yellow Pages," nationwide.

*Directory of African Importers of Construction Machinery and Equipment.* EXIM Infotek Private Ltd. • Covers: 120 African importers of caterpillar, concrete mixers, construction and building equipment, construction machinery, earthmoving equipment, excavating equipment, mixers and pavers, stone crusher, and street maintenance equipment. Entries include: Company name, postal address, telephone, fax, e-mail, website, contact person, designation, and product details.

*Directory of American Manufacturers & Exporters of Machinery for Chemicals & Pharma Industry.* EXIM Infotek Private Ltd. • $10 Individuals. Covers: 60 American manufacturers and exporters of chemical process equipment, petroleum chemical processing equipment. Entries include: Company name, postal address, city, country, phone, fax, e-mail and websites. contact person, designation, and product details.

*Directory of Australia and New Zealand Importers of Construction Machinery and Equipment.* EXIM Infotek Private Ltd. • $150 Individuals. Covers: 25 Australian and New Zealand importers of bulldozers, concrete machinery, concrete paving plant, concrete product plant, construction and building equipment, construction machinery, earthmoving equipment and machinery, excavating equipment, excavator parts, hot mix asphalt plant, hydraulic brake parts, parts for excavators and dozers, road construction machinery, scale model and construction kit, street maintenance equipment, and used construction equipment. Entries include: Company name, postal address, telephone, fax, e-mail, website, contact person, designation, and product details.

*Directory of Belgium Importers of Construction Machinery and Equipment.* EXIM Infotek Private Ltd. • Covers: 30 Belgium importers of construction, building equipment and parts, earthmoving equipment, excavating equipment, industrial and construction vehicles, scale model and construction kit, and street maintenance equipment. Entries include: Company name, postal address, telephone, fax, e-mail, website, contact person, designation, and product details.

*Directory of British Importers of Construction Machinery and Equipment.* EXIM Infotek Private Ltd. • $150 Individuals. Covers: 30 British importers of construction, building equipment and parts, excavating equipment, scale model and construction kit. Entries include: Company name, postal address, telephone, fax, e-mail, website, contact person, designation, and product details.

*Directory of Chinese Manufacturers and Exporters of Construction Machinery and Equipment.* EXIM Infotek Private Ltd. • $150 Individuals. Covers: 30 Chinese manufacturers and exporters of building machinery, construction equipment, construction machinery, crusher, dust collectors, and mixers. Entries include: Company name, postal address, telephone, fax, e-mail, website, contact person, designation, and product details.

*Directory of Danish Importers of Construction Machinery and Equipment.* EXIM Infotek Private Ltd. • $150 Individuals. Covers: 20 Danish importers of construction, building equipment and parts, industrial and construction vehicles, and snow removal equipment. Entries include: Company name, postal address, telephone, fax, e-mail, website, contact person, designation, and product details.

*Directory of French Importers of Construction Machinery and Equipment.* EXIM Infotek Private Ltd. • $150 Individuals. Covers: 40 French importers of construction, building equipment and parts, excavating equipment, industrial and construction vehicles, scale model and construction kit, and street maintenance equipment. Entries include: Company name, postal address, telephone, fax, e-mail, website, contact person, designation, and product details.

*Directory of Indian Importers of Construction Machinery and Equipment.* EXIM Infotek Private Ltd. • $200 Individuals. Covers: 50 Indian importers of construction and building equipment, construction machinery, earthmoving spare parts, excavating equipment, spare parts for earthmoving machinery, and spare parts for heavy construction machine. Entries include: Company name, postal address, telephone, fax, e-mail, website, contact person, designation, and product details.

*Directory of Japanese Importers of Construction Machinery and Equipment.* EXIM Infotek Private Ltd. • $250 Individuals. Covers: 80 Japanese importers of construction and building equipment, construction machinery, mixers and pavers, road rollers, scale model and construction kit, shovels, street maintenance equipment, and used construction equipment. Entries include: Company name, postal address, telephone, fax, e-mail, website, contact person, designation, and product details.

*Directory of Japanese Manufacturers and Exporters of Construction Machinery and Equipment.* EXIM Infotek Private Ltd. • $1,000 Individuals. Covers: 610 Japanese manufacturers and exporters of building machinery, bulldozers (new and used), construction equipment and spare parts, crushers, dust collectors, excavators (new and used), land machinery, mixers and pavers, used concrete mixer trucks, used cranes, used crawler cranes, used crawler dump, used crawler loader, used dump trucks, used earthmoving equipment, used heavy equipment, used hydraulic excavators and truck cranes, used loaders, used mechanical truck cranes, used miniexcavators, used mixer truck, used motor grader, used road rollers, used rough terrain cranes, used tire shovels, used truck crane, used vibratory road rollers, and used wheel loaders. Entries include: Company name, postal address, telephone, fax, e-mail, website, contact person, designation, and product details.

*Directory of Middle East Importers of Machinery for Glass and Ceramic Industry.* EXIM Infotek Private Ltd. • $150 Individuals. Covers: 20 Middle East importers of ceramic industry equipment, ceramic industry supplies, glass making machinery and equipment. Entries include: Company name, postal address, telephone, fax, e-mail, website, contact person, designation, and product details.

*Directory of SAARC Importers of Construction Machinery and Equipment.* EXIM Infotek Private Ltd. • $300 Individuals. Covers: 80 companies in member countries of the South Asian Association for Regional Cooperation (SAARC) that import asphalt mixing plants, asphalt paving equipment, bulldozers, chip spreaders, road sweepers, concrete breakers, chipping hammer, concrete machinery and mixer, concrete production equipment, construction equipment and spare parts, dumpers, earthmoving equipment, excavating equipment, heavy construction machinery, hoists for construction, hydraulic concrete mixer, mixers and pavers, plate compactors, prime movers, rammers, road rollers, used construction machinery, used hydraulic truck mounted cranes, vibrators, and vibrating and pneumatic rollers. Entries include: Company name, postal address, telephone, fax, e-mail, website, contact person, designation, and product details.

*Directory of South American Importers of Construction Machinery and Equipment.* EXIM Infotek Private Ltd. • $550 Individuals. Covers: 260 South American importers of building and construction materials, concrete production equipment, construction and building equipment, construction machinery, excavating equipment, mixers and pavers, new parquet machinery, scale models and construction kit, street maintenance equipment, and used construction equipment. Entries include: Company name, postal address, telephone, fax, e-mail, website, contact person, designation, and product details.

*Directory of South Korean Manufacturers and Exporters of Construction Machinery and Equipment.* EXIM Infotek Private Ltd. • $250 Individuals. Covers: 90 South Korean manufacturers and exporters of asphalt mixing plant, bridge and tunnel construction machinery, building machinery, cement production plant, cement and plaster making plant, clay tile and brick production plant, concrete elements production plant, concrete making machinery, construction equipment, cranes and construction platforms, earthmoving and road making machinery, harbor and canal construction machinery, heavy mechanical handling equipment, road maintenance machinery, road rollers, scaffoldings and ladders, used construction equipment, and used cranes. Entries include: Company name, postal address, telephone, fax, e-mail, website, contact person, designation, and product details.

*Directory of South Korean Manufacturers & Exporters of Machinery for Chemicals & Pharma Industry.* EXIM Infotek Private Ltd. • $10 Individuals. Covers: 60 South Korean manufacturers and exporters of crushers/pulverizers for chemical industries, dryers/evaporators/crystallizers for chemical industries, electrochemical and electrolytic plant equipment, electroplating plant machinery, glycerine production plant machinery, heaters/boilers/distillers for chemical industries, organic chemical production plant equipment, paint/varnish/enamel/ink production plant equipment, pharmaceutical/cosmetic production plant equipment, reactors for chemical industry, screeners/mixers/centrifuges for chemical industry, and technical gas production plant equipment. Entries include: Company name, postal address, city, country, phone, fax, e-mail and websites, contact person, designation, and product details.

*Directory of South Korean Manufacturers & Exporters of Machinery for Leather & Shoe Industry.* EXIM Infotek Private Ltd. • $5 Individuals. Covers: 20 South Korean manufacturers and exporters of boot and shoe making machinery/equipment, leather working and saddlery making equipment. Entries include: Company name, postal address, city, country, phone, fax, e-mail and websites, contact person, designation, and product details.

*Directory of South Korean Manufacturers & Exporters of Machinery for Paper & Pulp Industry.* EXIM Infotek Private Ltd. • $5 Individuals. Covers: 30 South Korean manufacturers and exporters of cardboard finishing/forming/cutting machinery/equipment, cardboard making machinery/equipment, paper finishing/converting machinery/equipment, paper making plant equipment, pulp and cellulose production plant equipment. Entries include: Company name, postal address, city, country, phone, fax, e-mail and websites, contact person, designation, and product details.

*Directory of South Korean Manufacturers & Exporters of Machinery for Textile and Knitting Industry.* EXIM Infotek Private Ltd. • $15 Individuals. Covers: 150 South Korean manufacturers and exporters of beam brakes and discs for textile machinery, belts/hoses/webbing-textile, bobbins for textile industry, carpet and tapestry looms, cotton preparation machinery and equipment, felt and non-woven fabric making machinery, knitting machinery and attachments, lace and net making machinery, man-made fiber production and processing plants, ribbon and trim making machinery, silk and schappe preparation machinery and equipment, sleeves and strips for spinning mills, textile dyeing and boiling machinery/equipment, textile finishing machinery and equipment, textile machinery, textile machinery parts, textile printing machinery and equipment, textile printings, textile spinning and twisting machinery, textile washing/mercerizing machinery and equipment, textile waste processing, textile waste processing machinery and equipment, textile weaving machinery parts/accessories, textile weaving machinery/looms, textile winding and reeling machinery, weaving machines, yarn preparation machinery/equipment, and yarn tensioners. Entries include: Company name, postal address, city, country, telephone, fax, e-mail and websites, contact person, designation, and product details.

*Directory of Taiwanese Manufacturers and Exporters of Construction Machinery and Equipment.* EXIM Infotek Private Ltd. • $350 Individuals. Covers: 150 Taiwanese manufacturers and exporters of bridge and tunnel construction machinery, building machinery and equipment, cement production plant, cement and plaster making plant, clay tile and brick production plant, concrete elements production plant, concrete making machinery, cranes and construction platform, crushing machinery, earth-moving and road making machinery, harbor and canal construction machinery, heavy mechanical handling equipment, mixers, railway track construction machinery, road rollers, scaffoldings and ladders. Entries include: Company name, postal address, telephone, fax, e-mail, website, contact person, designation, and product details.

*Directory of Taiwanese Manufacturers & Exporters of Machinery for Chemicals & Pharma Industry.* EXIM Infotek Private Ltd. • $25 Individuals. Covers: 290 Taiwanese manufacturers and exporters of crushers/pulverizers for chemical industries, dryers/evaporators/crystallizers for chemical industries, electrochemical and electrolytic plant equipment, electroplating plant machinery, essence/perfume production plant equipment, explosive/match production plant equipment, fertilizer production plant equipment, glue/gelatin making plant equipment, heaters/boilers/distillers for chemical industries, inorganic chemical production plant equipment, organic chemical production plant equipment, paint/varnish/enamel/ink production plant equipment, pharmaceutical/cosmetic production plant equipment, reactors for chemical industry, screeners/mixers/centrifuges for chemical industry, soap making equipment, technical gas production plant equipment. Entries include: Company name, postal address, city, country, phone, fax, e-mail and websites, contact person, designation, and product details.

*Dun's Industrial Guide: The Metalworking Directory.* Dun & Bradstreet Inc. • Annual. Libraries, $485; commercial institutions, $795.00. Lease basis. Three volumes. Lists about 65,000 U. S. manufacturing plants using metal and suppliers of metalworking equipment and materials. Includes names and titles of key personnel. Products, purchases, and processes are indicated.

*Machine Tool Reference Guide.* Machinery Dealers National Association. • $29.95 Individuals CD-ROM. Covers: Nearly 1,000 metalworking machine tool manufacturers; international coverage. Database includes: Information on mergers and sources of parts. Entries include: Company name, address, phone, fax, product/service provided.

*Machinery Buyers' Guide: The Annual Directory of Engineering and Products Services.* Findlay Publications Ltd. • Annual. About 6,000 firms offering machine tool, engineering products, machinery, industrial equipment and services worldwide.

*Used Equipment Directory.* Penton. • Monthly. $35 Individuals 1 year, 3rd class mail, (12 issues). Publication includes: List of 800 dealers in used metalworking, electrical, power, process, and material handling equipment, woodworking and machine tools. Entries include: Company name, address, phone; principal executive; types of equipment handled; description of machinery offered. Principal content is approximately 75,000 paid listings of used equipment for sale, classified by type.

## E-BOOKS

*Encyclopedia of American Industries.* Cengage Learning Inc. • 2011. $807.00. 6th edition. Three volumes. Volume one is Manufacturing Industries and volume two is Service and Non-Manufacturing Industries. Provides the history, development, and recent status of approximately 1,000 industries. Includes statistical graphs, with industry and general indexes. Also available as eBook.

## FINANCIAL RATIOS

*Annual Statement Studies.* Risk Management Association. • Annual. Compiled from over 280,000 financial statements.

*Annual Statement Studies: Industry Default Probabilities and Cash Flow Measures.* Risk Management Association. • Annual. $405 Nonmembers. Serves as a companion volume to the original *Annual Statement Studies.* Gives probability of default estimates on a percentage scale for more than 450 industries. Includes changes in position year-by-year for eight financial statement line items and provides percentage measures of cash flow.

## INTERNET DATABASES

*Business 2.0 Web Guide to the Best Business Links.* Business 2.0 Media Inc. Phone: (415)293-4800; Email: support@business2.com • URL: http://www.business2.com/webguide • Web site presents an extensive, searchable directory of links to "the best, most informative, and authoritative web pages." Twenty main categories cover business, finance, career, company information, people, and technology topics, with thousands of subtopics, all linking to Web sites recommended by experienced business researchers. Fees: Free.

*Fedstats.* Federal Interagency Council on Statistical Policy. Phone: (202)395-7254 • URL: http://www.fedstats.gov • Web site features an efficient search facility for full-text statistics produced by more than 100 federal agencies, including the Census Bureau, the Bureau of Economic Analysis, and the Bureau of Labor Statistics. Boolean searches can be made within one agency or for all agencies combined. Links are offered to international statistical bureaus, including the UN, IMF, OECD, UNESCO, Eurostat, and 20 individual countries. Fees: Free.

*FreeLunch.com.* Economy.com, Inc. Phone: (610)696-8700; Fax: (610)696-1678 • URL: http://www.freelunch.com • Web site provides free access to more than 200 million economic and financial data series, covering industry, demographics, labor markets, prices, retail sales, government spending, trade, interest rates, housing starts, the stock market, etc. Data is available in either chart or table form. Searching is offered. Free, but registration required. Economy.com, Inc. also offers fee-based economic analysis at *The Dismal Scientist* site (www.dismal.com).

## ONLINE DATABASES

*Applied Science and Technology Index Online.* H.W. Wilson Co. • Provides online indexing of 500 major scientific, technical, industrial, and engineering periodicals. Time period is 1983 to date. Monthly updates. Inquire as to online cost and availability.

*Thomas Register Online.* Thomas Publishing Company L.L.C. • Provides concise information on approximately 194,000 U. S. companies, mainly manufacturers, with over 50,000 product classifications. Indexes over 115,000 trade names. Information is updated semiannually. Inquire as to online cost and availability.

## PERIODICALS AND NEWSLETTERS

*Processing.* Putman Media Inc. • 14 times a year. $54.00 per year. Emphasis is on descriptions of new products for all areas of industrial processing, including valves, controls, filters, pumps, compressors, fluidics, and instrumentation.

## RESEARCH CENTERS AND INSTITUTES

National Center for Manufacturing Sciences. 3025 Boardwalk, Ann Arbor, MI 48108-3230. Phone: 800-222-6267 or (734)995-0300; Fax: (734)995-1150 or (734)995-4004; Email: info@ncms.org • Research areas include process technology and control, machine mechanics, sensors, testing methods, and quality assurance.

U.S. International Trade Commission - Minerals, Metals, Machinery, and Miscellaneous Manufacturers Division. 500 E St. SW, Washington, DC 20436. Phone: (202)205-3418; Fax: (202)205-2217; Email: brookhart@usitc.gov • URL: http://www.usitc.gov • Survey data related to international trade matters, including international competitiveness of U.S. industries, especially iron and steel products, industrial minerals and nonferrous metals, machinery and general manufactured products.

## STATISTICS SOURCES

*Survey of Current Business.* U. S. Government Printing Office. • Published by Bureau of Economic Analysis, U. S. Department of Commerce. Presents a wide variety of business and economic data.

*United States Census of Manufactures.* U.S. Department of Commerce U.S. Census Bureau. • Quinquennial. Results presented in reports, tape, CD-ROM, and Diskette files.

## TRADE/PROFESSIONAL ASSOCIATIONS

Japan Machinery Center for Trade and Investment. Kikai Shinkou Kaikan, 4th Fl., 3-8-5, Shiba Koen, Minato, Tokyo, Tokyo 105-0011, Japan. Phone: 81 3 34319507; Fax: 81 3 34366455 • URL: http://www. jmcti.org • Exporters of machinery. Seeks to establish and maintain a domestic and international business climate beneficial to the exportation of machinery. Represents members' interests; gathers and disseminates information.

Machinery Dealers National Association. 315 S Patrick St., Alexandria, VA 22314-3501. Phone: 800-872-7807 or (703)836-9300; Fax: (703)836-9303; Email: office@mdna.org • URL: http://www. mdna.org • Dealers in used, rebuilt, and reconditioned industrial machinery.

Manufacturers Alliance for Productivity and Innovation. 1600 Wilson Blvd., 11th Fl., Arlington, VA 22209-2594. Phone: (703)841-9000; Fax: (703)841-9514 • URL: http://www.mapi.net • Manufacturing and related business service companies. Membership concentrated in the following sectors: aerospace; automotive; scientific instruments; electronics; computers and telecommunication equipment; high technology; chemicals/pharmaceuticals; oil and oil-related equipment; electrical equipment farm, construction, food, material handling and other machinery; primary and fabricated metals. Provides member services through councils and research programs. Produces a variety of research, including economic, policy and benchmark work to assist members in their planning, compliance and process improvement efforts.

# MACHINERY, USED

*See* SURPLUS PRODUCTS

# MAGAZINES

*See* PERIODICALS

# MAGNESIUM INDUSTRY

## STATISTICS SOURCES

*Non-Ferrous Metal Data Yearbook.* American Bureau of Metal Statistics. • Annual. $405.00. Provides worldwide data on approximately about 200 statistical tables covering many nonferrous metals. Includes production, consumption, inventories, exports, imports, and other data.

*Nonferrous Castings.* U. S. Bureau of the Census. • Annual. (Current Industrial Reports MA-33E.).

# MAGNETIC RECORDS AND RECORDINGS

*See* SOUND RECORDERS AND RECORDING

# MAIL ORDER BUSINESS

*See also* DIRECT MAIL ADVERTISING

## CD-ROM DATABASES

*MediaFinder.* Oxbridge Communications Inc. • $1,295 per year. Online database with 77,000 magazines, catalogs, newspapers, and journals.

## DIRECTORIES

*Drop Shipping Source Directory of Major Consumer Product Lines.* Consolidated Marketing Services, Inc. • Irregular. $15.00. Lists over 700 firms of a wide variety of consumer products that can be drop shipped.

*The National Directory of Catalogs.* Oxbridge Communications Inc. • Annual. $995 Individuals print version. Describes over 12,000 United States and Canadian catalogs within 78 subject areas.

## FINANCIAL RATIOS

*Annual Statement Studies.* Risk Management Association. • Annual. Compiled from over 280,000 financial statements.

*Annual Statement Studies: Industry Default Probabilities and Cash Flow Measures.* Risk Management Association. • Annual. $405 Nonmembers. Serves as a companion volume to the original *Annual Statement Studies.* Gives probability of default estimates on a percentage scale for more than 450 industries. Includes changes in position year-by-year for eight financial statement line items and provides percentage measures of cash flow.

## INTERNET DATABASES

*Advance Monthly Retail Trade Report.* U. S. Census Bureau. Phone: 800-541-8345 or (301)457-4100 or (301)763-2713; Fax: (301)457-1296 or (301)457-3842; Email: naics@census.gov • URL: http://www. census.gov/epcd/www/naicstab.htm • Web pages provide monthly sales figures for a wide range of retail businesses. Advance, preliminary, and final statistics are provided for the latest month available in each case, with a previous-year comparison. Updates are monthly.

## PERIODICALS AND NEWSLETTERS

*Catalog Age.* PRIMEDIA Business Magazine and Media. • 13 times a year. Free to qualified personnel; others, $85.00 per year. Edited for catalog marketing and management personnel.

*Direct Marketing News.* Haymarket Media Group Ltd. • Monthly. $148 U.S. /year. Includes special feature issues on catalog marketing, telephone marketing, database marketing, and fundraising. Includes monthly supplements, *DM News International*, *DRTV News*, and *TeleServices*.

*Non Store Marketing Report.* Maxwell Sroge Company Inc. • Description: Source of analyses of key trends and key happeningsin the mail order, Internet, and interactive shopping business. order companies. Recurring features include an semiannual insert titled Trendwatch, which assesses the performance of publicly owned direct selling businesses, and company profiles on direct marketing businesses in the news.

## STATISTICS SOURCES

*Annual Benchmark Report for Retail Trade and Food Services..A Detailed Summary of Retail Sales, Purchases, Accounts Receivable, Inventories, and Food Service Sales.* U. S. Government Printing Office. • Annual. $13.00. Issued by the U.S. Census Bureau. Provides detailed annual and monthly retail statistics for the most recent 10 years. Includes data for various kinds of retail outlets, including automobiles, furniture, appliances, building supplies, grocery stores, drug stores, gasoline stations, clothing, sporting goods, department stores, and restaurants.

## TRADE/PROFESSIONAL ASSOCIATIONS

National Mail Order Association. 2807 Polk St. NE, Minneapolis, MN 55418-2954. Phone: (612)788-1673; Email: info@nmoa.org • URL: http://www.

nmoa.org • Provides education, information, and business contacts to those involved in direct marketing and mail order. Reports new and established product sources, ideas, techniques, developments, and services of value to mail marketers. Reviews and disseminates information on reports, government findings, new books and directories, mailing lists, and general data relating to developing maximum mail order sales.

# MAIL SERVICE

*See* POSTAL SERVICES

# MAILING LISTS

*See also* DIRECT MAIL ADVERTISING

## CD-ROM DATABASES

*MediaFinder.* Oxbridge Communications Inc. • $1,295 per year. Online database with 77,000 magazines, catalogs, newspapers, and journals.

## PERIODICALS AND NEWSLETTERS

*Database Marketer.* SIMBA Information Inc. • Monthly. $329.00 per year.

*Direct Marketing: Using Direct Response Advertising to Enhance Marketing Database.* Hoke Communications Inc. • Monthly. $65.00 per year. Direct marketing to consumers and business.

*Target Marketing: The Leading Magazine for Integrated Database Marketing.* North American Publishing Co. • Monthly. $65.00 per year. Dedicated to direct marketing excellence. Formerly *Zip Target Marketing.*

# MAINTENANCE OF BUILDINGS

*See also* BUILDING INDUSTRY

## DIRECTORIES

*ICS Cleaning Specialists Annual Trade Directory and Buying Guide.* Specialist Publications Inc. • Annual. $35. Lists about 6,000 manufacturers and distributors of floor covering installation and cleaning equipment. Formerly *Installation and Cleaning Specialists Trade Directory and Buying Guide.*

*Maintenance Supplies Buyers' Guide.* Cygnus Business Media Inc. • Approximately 1,000 manufacturers and associations for commercial, industrial, and institutional janitorial supplies; international coverage. Formerly *Maintenance Supplies Annual.*

## FINANCIAL RATIOS

*Annual Statement Studies.* Risk Management Association. • Annual. Compiled from over 280,000 financial statements.

*Annual Statement Studies: Industry Default Probabilities and Cash Flow Measures.* Risk Management Association. • Annual. $405 Nonmembers. Serves as a companion volume to the original *Annual Statement Studies.* Gives probability of default estimates on a percentage scale for more than 450 industries. Includes changes in position year-by-year for eight financial statement line items and provides percentage measures of cash flow.

## HANDBOOKS AND MANUALS

*Window Washing Service.* Entrepreneur Press. • Looseleaf. $59.50. A practical guide to starting a window cleaning business. Covers profit potential, start-up costs, market size evaluation, owner's time required, pricing, accounting, advertising, promotion, etc. (Start-Up Business Guide No. E1012.).

## PERIODICALS AND NEWSLETTERS

*Building Operating Management: The National Magazine for Commercial and Institutional Build-*

ings Construction, Renovation, Facility Management. Trade Press Media Group. • Monthly. Free to qualified personnel.

*Cleaning Business: Published Monthly for the Self-Employed Cleaning and Maintenance Professionals.* William R. Griffin, Publisher. • Monthly. $20. Formerly *Service Business.*

*ICS Cleaning Specialist.* BNP Media. • Monthly. Free to qualified personnel. Written for floor covering installers and cleaners. Formerly *Installation and Cleaning Specialist.*

*Industrial Maintenance and Plant Operation.* Reed Elsevier Group plc Reed Business Information. • Monthly. $95.99 per year.

*Plant Services.* Putman Media Inc. • Monthly.

*Sanitary Maintenance.* Trade Press Media Group. • Monthly. Original publication serving the distributors and wholesalers of sanitary supplies.

## TRADE/PROFESSIONAL ASSOCIATIONS

Building Service Contractors Association International. 330 N Wabash Ave., Ste. 2000, Chicago, IL 60611. Phone: 800-368-3414; Fax: (312)673-6735; Email: info@bscai.org • URL: http://www.bscai.org • Firms and corporations in 40 countries engaged in contracting building maintenance services including the provision of labor, purchasing materials and janitorial cleaning and maintenance of a building or its surroundings; associate members are manufacturers of cleaning supplies and equipment. Seeks to provide a unified voice for building service contractors and to promote increased recognition by government, property owners and the general business and professional public. Conducts continuing study and action, through committees and special task groups on areas such as public affairs, costs and ratios, uniform accounting, industrial relations and personnel, marketing and sales, contract improvement, research and planning, materials and supplies sources, group insurance, management training, statistics collection, safety and insurance costs. Has developed a certification program for building service executives and a registration program for building service managers.

International Janitorial Cleaning Services Association. 2011 Oak St., Wyandotte, MI 48192. Phone: (734)252-6189; Email: info@ijcsa.com • URL: http://www.ijcsanetwork.com • Represents the interests of the janitorial industry. Promotes professionalism and ethics in the janitorial and cleaning services field. Provides training and education for cleaning professionals.

# MALLS, SHOPPING

*See* SHOPPING CENTERS

# MALPRACTICE

*See* PROFESSIONAL LIABILITY

# MANAGEMENT, BANK

*See* BANK MANAGEMENT

# MANAGEMENT BY OBJECTIVES

*See* INDUSTRIAL MANAGEMENT

# MANAGEMENT CONSULTANTS

*See also* CONSULTANTS

## ABSTRACTS AND INDEXES

*Business Periodicals Index Retrospective.* EBSCO Publishing Inc. • 11/year. Quarterly and annual cumulations.

## BIBLIOGRAPHIES

*Management Consultant Books.* Kennedy Information Inc. • Annual. Free. Contains descriptions of selected books from various publishers on management consulting.

## DIRECTORIES

*Directory of Fund Raising and Nonprofit Management Consultants.* Taft Group. • $49. Covers: 1,500 consultants and training organizations for nonprofit groups. Entries include: Organization name, address, phone, fax, year founded, publications and videos, partners or executives, description of service.

*European Federation of Management Consultants Associations--European Directory: European Directory of Management Consultants.* European Federation of Management Consultants Associations. • Covers: 22 associations plus members. Entries include: Name, address, phone, fax; activities; date established; number of consultants.

*Harvard Business School Guide to Careers in Management Consulting.* Harvard Business Review Press. • $10.83 Individuals. Publication includes: Well-known consulting firms, a mailing list of recruiting contacts, and a selective bibliography of relevant books and directories compiled by the Harvard Business School.

*Institute of Management Consultants--Management Consultants Resource Guide.* Institute of Management Consultants USA. • Database covers: 2,800 individuals who practice management consulting as individuals or members of firms worldwide. Database includes: Name, firm, address, phone; fax; email; website; areas of competence for certified management consultants.

*Management Consultancy.* Jordans Ltd. • $50 plus 5 pounds shipping. Covers: management consultants in the United Kingdom. Database includes: Industry market profiles. Entries include: Company name, address, phone, name of chief executive, financial data for previous three years, corporate ownership, shareholder data, and business description.

*Management Consultants Directory.* InfoGroup Inc. • Annual. Number of listings: 51,839. Entries include: Name, address, phone, size of advertisement, name of owner or manager, number of employees, year first in "Yellow Pages." Compiled from telephone company "Yellow Pages," nationwide.

*Management Consulting: A Complete Guide to the Industry, 2nd Edition.* John Wiley & Sons Inc. • $60 Individuals hardcover. Covers: Top fifty consulting firms in the nation; complete game plan for novice management consultants trying to break into the business along with expert guidelines for veterans looking to expand their services.

## E-BOOKS

*CIO and Corporate Strategic Management: Changing Role of CIO to CEO.* Cengage Learning Inc. • Published by Information Science Reference. Provides analysis within theoretical frameworks and consulting recommendations, and starts with the demand side of CEO successions, specifically highlighting approaches in IT foundations, e-business development and IT sourcing decisions.

## FINANCIAL RATIOS

*Annual Statement Studies.* Risk Management Association. • Annual. Compiled from over 280,000 financial statements.

*Annual Statement Studies: Industry Default Probabilities and Cash Flow Measures.* Risk Management Association. • Annual. $405 Nonmembers.

Serves as a companion volume to the original *Annual Statement Studies.* Gives probability of default estimates on a percentage scale for more than 450 industries. Includes changes in position year-by-year for eight financial statement line items and provides percentage measures of cash flow.

## ONLINE DATABASES

*Wilson Business Abstracts Online.* H.W. Wilson Co. • Indexes and abstracts 600 major business periodicals, plus the *Wall Street Journal* and the business section of the *New York Times.* Indexing is from 1982, abstracting from 1990, with the two newspapers included from 1993. Updated weekly. Inquire as to online cost and availability. (*Business Periodicals Index* without abstracts is also available online.).

## PERIODICALS AND NEWSLETTERS

*Consultants News: Independent Commentary on Management Consulting Since 1970.* Kennedy Information Inc. • Monthly. $295.00 per year. Newsletter. News and ideas for management consultants.

## STATISTICS SOURCES

*U.S. Industry and Trade Outlook.* U.S. Department of Commerce National Technical Information Service. • Annual. Produced by the International Trade Administration, U.S. Department of Commerce, in a "public-private" partnership with DRI/McGraw-Hill and Standard & Poor's. Provides basic data, outlook for the current year, and "Long-Term Prospects" (five-year projections) for a wide variety of products and services. Includes high technology industries. Formerly *U.S. Industrial Outlook.*

## TRADE/PROFESSIONAL ASSOCIATIONS

Association of Certified Adizes Practitioners International. 1212 Mark Ave., Carpinteria, CA 93013. Phone: (805)565-2901; Fax: (805)565-0741; Email: paula@adizes.com • URL: http://www. adizes.com • Professional management consultants who are certified to practice the Adizes Method of management. (The Adizes method, devised by Dr. Ichak Adizes, is a comprehensive approach to creating and managing healthy change within a company.) Promotes organizational transformation (consulting) as a profession. Facilitates discussion of ideas and exchange of information among members. Conducts research and educational programs.

Association of Internal Management Consultants. 824 Caribbean Ct., Marco Island, FL 34145. Phone: (239)642-0580; Fax: (239)642-1119 • URL: http://www.aimc.org • Consists of internal management consultants. Seeks to develop and encourage the professional practice of internal management-consulting; establish high standards of professional performance; serve as a forum for the exchange of information and the sharing of professional methods and techniques; cooperate with commercial, educational, and governmental bodies on matters of common interest. Conducts educational seminars.

Association of Management Consulting Firms. 370 Lexington Ave., Ste. 2209, New York, NY 10017. Phone: (212)262-3055; Fax: (212)262-3054; Email: info@amcf.org • URL: http://www.amcf.org • Members are management consultants.

Association of Productivity Specialists. 521 5th Ave., Ste. 1700, New York, NY 10175. Email: inquire@apsworld.org • URL: http://www.apsworld. org • Firms and individuals engaged in the Productivity Specialist segment of the management consultant profession. Seeks to promote greater public knowledge of the productivity specialist profession (productivity specialists develop management systems to achieve business objectives in numerous areas, including production levels, quality performance, inventory costs, operating costs and manufacturing lead times); to improve professional capabilities of member firms by promoting educational and research and development programs; to cooperate with federal, state, and local government agencies on matters of interest to members; to help member firms improve, develop and review skills of their professional employees. Has established standards of ethics and competence for productivity specialists.

European Federation of Management Consultancies Associations. Kunstlaan Ave. des Arts 3-5, B-1210 Brussels, Belgium. Phone: 32 2 2500650 or 32 2 2500651; Email: feaco@feaco.org • URL: http://www.feaco.org • European associations of national management consultancy associations. Purposes are to: promote and develop the profession of management consultancy; foster high standards of professional practice and ethics; mediate the exchange of information and experience among member associations and companies and individuals within member associations; establish relations with other organizations interested in management practice. Upholds professional Guidelines for Business Ethics; studies, promotes, and protects the professional interests of members. Maintains liaison with other management consultancy organizations.

Expediting Management Association. c/o Patricia Murphy, Executive Administrator, 534 Bridlecreek Green SW, Calgary, AB, Canada T2Y 3P2. Phone: (403)201-6401; Fax: (403)201-6402 • URL: http://www.expedite.org • Expediting managers; associate members are organizations, firms, and other individuals involved in the profession. (Expeditors work to ensure the efficient delivery of goods and services within or between businesses.) Promotes high professional and ethical standards in expediting. Conducts training programs, seminars, and workshops. Certifies expediting managers and associates; offers courses. Conducts on-site programs for corporations and groups.

Institute of Certified Professional Managers. James Madison University, MSC 5504, Harrisonburg, VA 22807. Phone: (540)568-3247; Email: info@icm.biz • URL: http://icpm.biz • Seeks to raise competency and professionalism in the field of management through training and certification of individuals, management chapters, and corporate groups. Sets performance standards for managers worldwide, offers services in the areas of management education, academic assessment, and certification.

Institute of Management Consultants. 45 Glenferrie Rd., Ste. 999, Melbourne, VIC 3144, Australia. Phone: 800-800719 • URL: http://www.imc.org.au • Represents management consultants in Australia.

Institute of Management Consultants and Advisers. 19 Elgin Rd., Dublin 4, Dublin, Ireland. Phone: 353 1 6349636; Fax: 353 1 2815330; Email: info@imca.ie • URL: http://www.imca.ie • Aims to advance the management consultancy profession in Ireland. Provides Code of Professional Conduct to ensure that the members render the highest standards of performance and service.

Institute of Management Consultants USA. 2025 M St. NW, Ste. 800, Washington, DC 20036. Phone: (202)367-1261; Fax: (202)367-2134; Email: huchler@verizon.net • URL: http://www.imcusa.org • Individual management consultants who work privately or in consulting firms. Sets standards of professionalism and ethics for the management consulting profession.

Interim Management Association. Dorset House, 1st Fl., 27-45 Stamford St., London SE1 9NT, United Kingdom. • URL: http://www.interimmanagement.uk.com • Recruitment consultancies specializing in interim managers for industry and commerce at senior level.

Iran Management Consultant Association. Unit 3, No. 70, Mahdinejad Alley, 4th St., Tehran, Iran. Phone: 98 21 88246929 or 98 21 88248548; Fax: 98 21 88246929 or 98 21 88248548; Email: info@imca.ir • URL: http://en.imca.ir • Aims to protect the legal rights and interests of management consultants in Iran. Provides the means of propagating management culture to increase productivity, economic and social sustainable development.

Management Consultancies Association. 36-38 Cornhill, 5th Fl., London EC3V 3NG, United Kingdom. Phone: 44 20 76457950; Fax: 44 20 76457951; Email: info@mca.org.uk • URL: http://www.mca.org.uk • Enhances the consultancy management profession. Furthers the collective objectives and interests of its members. Acts as a focal point for individuals wishing to seek advice on management consultancy. Serves as a forum for members to discuss matters of current interest and future policy.

National Bureau of Certified Consultants. c/o Peter A. Land Associates, Inc., 4210 Lomac St., Montgomery, AL 36106. Phone: (334)271-2639 • URL: http://www.peteland.com/cpcm.htm • Promotes adherence to high standards of ethics and practice in the field of management consulting. Works to improve management consulting curricula.

National Executive Service Corps. 55 W 39th St., 12th Fl., New York, NY 10018. Phone: (212)269-1234; Fax: (212)269-0959; Email: info@nesc.org • URL: http://www.nesc.org • Provides management and business advisory services to non-profit educational, health care, social services, cultural, and religious organizations. Supplies services through experienced and senior-leveled business people who act as volunteer management consultants.

# MANAGEMENT DEVELOPMENT

*See* EXECUTIVE TRAINING AND DEVELOPMENT

# MANAGEMENT, FINANCIAL

*See* FINANCIAL MANAGEMENT

# MANAGEMENT GAMES

## PERIODICALS AND NEWSLETTERS

*Simulation & Gaming: An International Journal of Theory, Design and Research.* Pine Forge Press. • Quarterly. $156 Individuals. Served as a leading international forum for the exploration and development of simulation/gaming methodologies used in education, training, consultation, and research.

## TRADE/PROFESSIONAL ASSOCIATIONS

Association for Business Simulation and Experiential Learning. The Citadel, School of Business Administration, 171 Moultrie St., Charleston, SC 29409. Phone: (936)294-1975 or (530)898-6395 • URL: http://absel.org • Business professors and practitioners dedicated to the development and use of experiential teaching techniques, both computerized and noncomputerized, in business education. Assists potential users through informal dialogue with experienced members and through tutorial sessions at annual meetings.

# MANAGEMENT INFORMATION SYSTEMS

*See also* COMPUTERS; SYSTEMS IN MANAGEMENT

## ABSTRACTS AND INDEXES

*Business Periodicals Index Retrospective.* EBSCO Publishing Inc. • 11/year. Quarterly and annual cumulations.

*Internet and Personal Computing Abstracts (print edition).* EBSCO Publishing Inc. • Quarterly. $269.00 per year, including cumulative index. Provides more than 10,000 abstracts annually from both trade and academic publications. Covers computer hardware, software, product reviews, Web topics, e-commerce, networks, corporate news, security, and related topics. Formerly *Microcomputer Abstracts.*

## CD-ROM DATABASES

*Datapro on CD-ROM: Computer Systems Analyst.* Gartner Inc. • Monthly. Price on application. Includes detailed information on specific computer hardware and software products, such as peripherals, security systems, document imaging systems, and UNIX-related products.

## DIRECTORIES

*KMWorld Buyer's Guide.* Knowledge Asset Media Inc. • Semiannual. $2,395 (Basic Corporate Profile Package) One Issue — Spring 2014 Edition PLUS 6 Months Online. Controlled circulation as part of *KMWorld.* Contains corporate and product profiles related to various aspects of knowledge management and information systems. (Knowledge Asset Media is a an affiliate of Information Today, Inc.).

*Major Information Technology Companies of the World.* Cengage Learning Inc. • Annual. $1,460 Individuals. 2008. 11th edition. eBook. Published by Graham & Whiteside. Contains profiles of more than 8,250 leading information technology companies in various countries.

## ENCYCLOPEDIAS AND DICTIONARIES

*Encyclopedia of Business and Finance.* Cengage Learning Inc. • 2014. $485. 3rd edition. Two volumes. Published by Macmillan Reference USA. Contains articles on accounting, business administration, banking, finance, management information systems, and marketing.

## INTERNET DATABASES

*InfoTech Trends.* Data Analysis Group. Phone: (925)462-1202; Fax: (925)462-1225; Email: support@infotechtrends.com • URL: http://www.infotechtrends.com • Web site provides both free and fee-based market research data on the information technology industry, including computers, peripherals, telecommunications, the Internet, software, CD-ROM/DVD, e-commerce, and workstations. Fees: Free for current (most recent year) data; more extensive information has various fee structures. Formerly *Computer Industry Forecasts.*

## ONLINE DATABASES

*Computer Database.* Cengage Learning Inc. • Provides one year of full-text online for 150 leading computer-related publications. Also includes 70,000 product specifications and brief profiles of 13,000 computer product vendors and manufacturers. Inquire as to prices and availability.

*Wilson Business Abstracts Online.* H.W. Wilson Co. • Indexes and abstracts 600 major business periodicals, plus the *Wall Street Journal* and the business section of the *New York Times.* Indexing is from 1982, abstracting from 1990, with the two newspapers included from 1993. Updated weekly. Inquire as to online cost and availability. (*Business Periodicals Index* without abstracts is also available online.).

## PERIODICALS AND NEWSLETTERS

*CIO: The Magazine for Chief Information Officers.* CXO Media Inc. • Monthly. $129 per year. Edited for chief information officers. Includes a monthly "Web Business" section (incorporates the former *WebMaster* periodical) and a monthly "Enterprise" section for other company executives.

*Computer Economics Networking Strategies Report: Advising IT Decision Maker ractices and Current Trends.* Computer Economics Inc. •

Monthly. $395.00 per year. Newsletter. Edited for information technology managers. Covers news and trends relating to a variety of corporate computer network and management information systems topics. Emphasis is on costs. Formerly *Intranet and Networking Strategies Report.*

*Computer Economics Report: The Financial Advisor of Data Processing Users.* Computer Economics Inc. • Monthly. $695. Newsletter on lease/purchase decisions, prices, discounts, residual value forecasts, personnel allocation, cost control, and other corporate computer topics. Edited for information technology (IT) executives.

*Computerworld: Newsweekly for Information Technology Leaders.* ComputerWorld Inc. • Weekly. $190.00 per year.

*DM Review: The Premier Publication for Business Intelligence and Analytics.* SourceMedia Inc. • Monthly. $49.00 per year. Edited for corporate executives and information technology personnel. Covers data management, business intelligence, data warehousing, systems management, data integration, knowledge management, data mining, and related topics.

*Information and Management; International Journal of Information Systems Applications.* Elsevier. • Eight times a year. Institutions, $646.00 per year.

*Information Executive: A Monthly Publication for DPMA and the Information Systems Profession.* Association of Information Technology Professionals. • Monthly. $45.00 per year. Articles reporting developmental and technical aspects of EDP services, supplies, equipment, accessories and related contemporary trends and issues. Formerly *Inside DPMA.*

*Information Strategy: The Executive's Journal.* Auerbach Publications. • Quarterly. $195.00 per year.

*Information Systems Management.* Auerbach Publications. • Quarterly. $175 Individuals. Journal provides expert guidance in the innovative management of information systems resources. Formerly *Journal of Information Systems Management.*

*Information Systems; Data Bases: Their Creation, Management and Utilization.* Elsevier. • $250 Individuals. Eight times a year. Institutions, $1,554.00 per year.

*Information Week: Business Innovation Powered by Technology.* UBM L.L.C. • Weekly. $199.00 per year. The magazine for information systems management.

*IT Cost Management Strategies: The Planning Assistant for IT Directors.* Computer Economics Inc. • Monthly. $495.00 per year. Newsletter for information technology professionals. Covers data processing costs, budgeting, financial management, and related topics.

*MIS Quarterly.* University of Minnesota, School of Management. MIS Research Center, Carlson School of Management. • Quarterly. $175 Individuals 1-year subscription within US (print).

*Network Computing: Computing in a Network Environment.* UBM L.L.C. • Semimonthly. Free to qualified personnel.

*Report on Healthcare Information Management.* Capital Publications, Inc. • Monthly. $358.00 per year. Newsletter. Covers management information sytems for hospitals and physicicans' groups.

*Systems User.* Caulfield Publishing Ltd. • Monthly. $62.00 per year.

## RESEARCH CENTERS AND INSTITUTES

Massachusetts Institute of Technology - Sloan School of Management - Center for Information Systems Research. Bldg. NE25, 7th Fl., 5 Cambridge Ctr., Cambridge, MA 02142. Phone: (617)253-2348; Fax: (617)253-4424; Email: cisr@ mit.edu • URL: http://cisr.mit.edu • Defining, researching, and reporting on significant issues in the management of information technology, including the managerial use of computers and computer-based information, the management of the information systems (I/S) function, and the business value of information technology on organizations. Disseminates significant research findings to the information systems user community.

### TRADE/PROFESSIONAL ASSOCIATIONS

AFCOM. 9100 Chester Towne Centre Rd., West Chester, OH 45069. Phone: (714)643-8110 or (714)997-7966; Fax: (714)997-9743; Email: membership@afcom.com • URL: http://www. afcom.com • Data center, networking and enterprise systems management professionals from medium and large scale mainframe, midrange and client/server data centers worldwide. Works to meet the professional needs of the enterprise system management community. Provides information and support through educational events, research and assistance hotlines, and surveys.

Society for Advancement of Management. 6300 Ocean Dr., OCNR 330, Unit 5807, Corpus Christi, TX 78412. Phone: 888-827-6077 or (361)825-3045; Fax: (361)825-5609; Email: moustafa.abdelsamad@ tamucc.edu • URL: http://www.samnational.org • Represents management executives in industry commerce, government, and education. Fields of interest include management education, policy and strategy, MIS, international management, administration, budgeting, collective bargaining, distribution, incentives, materials handling, quality control, and training.

Society for Information Management. 15000 Commerce Pkwy., Ste. C, Mount Laurel, NJ 08054. Phone: 800-387-9746; Fax: (856)439-0525; Email: sim@simnet.org • URL: http://www.simnet.org • Provides a diverse membership with a sound infrastructure to pool insights resulting to access to international IT perspectives, continuing education opportunities and an elite network of peer resources through programs designed exclusively for the information management executive. Aims to support IT leaders by increasing the knowledge base of members and associates; giving back to local communities; being the voice of the IT community on critical issues and developing the next generation of effective IT leaders.

TechAmerica. 1001 19th St. N, 20th Fl., Arlington, VA 22209. Phone: (202)682-9110; Fax: (202)682-9111; Email: database@techamerica.org • URL: http://www.techamerica.org • A division of the Information Technology Association of America; software companies involved in the development or marketing of software for personal, midrange, and mainframe computers. Promotes the software industry and addresses specific problems of the industry. Represents the industry before various governmental units; provides educational programs to members; conducts research and makes available legal services. Develops standards.

# MANAGEMENT OF FACTORIES

*See* FACTORY MANAGEMENT

# MANAGEMENT, OPERATIONS

*See* OPERATIONS MANAGEMENT

# MANAGEMENT, PARTICIPATIVE

*See* PARTICIPATIVE MANAGEMENT

# MANAGEMENT, PRODUCTION

*See* OPERATIONS MANAGEMENT

# MANAGEMENT, SCIENTIFIC

*See* TIME AND MOTION STUDY

# MANAGEMENT SYSTEMS

*See* SYSTEMS IN MANAGEMENT

# MANAGEMENT THEORY

*See also* ADMINISTRATION

### ABSTRACTS AND INDEXES

*Business Periodicals Index Retrospective.* EBSCO Publishing Inc. • 11/year. Quarterly and annual cumulations.

*Social Sciences Citation Index.* Thomson Reuters Corp. • Weekly. Product is accessed via *Web of Science.*

*Social Sciences Index Retrospective: 1907-1983.* EBSCO Publishing Inc. • Indexing for 1,000,000 articles. Coverage includes international index and social sciences and humanities index.

### CD-ROM DATABASES

*Social Sciences Abstracts.* EBSCO Publishing Inc. • Provides indexing from 1983 and abstracting from 1994 of more than 750 periodicals covering economics, area studies, community health, public administration, public welfare, urban studies, and many other topics related to the social sciences.

*Social Sciences Citation Index.* Thomson Reuters Corp. • Weekly. Product is accessed via *Web of Science.*

### DIRECTORIES

*Management Training Buyer's Guide.* Training Information Network Ltd. • Annual. $25. Covers: Over 600 suppliers of management training courses, consultancy, videos, films, packages, and training aids throughout the United Kingdom. Entries include: Company name, address, phone, fax, name and title of contact, number of employees, geographical area served, branch office or subsidiary names and addresses, description.

### ENCYCLOPEDIAS AND DICTIONARIES

*Blackwell Encyclopedia of Management.* John Wiley & Sons Inc. Scientific, Technical, Medical, and Scholarly Div. (Wiley-Blackwell). • 2010. eBook. 2nd edition. Published by John Wiley & Sons. Divided into 12 individual subject volumes and an index. Volumes provide clear, concise, expert definitions and explanations of the key concepts in each area.

*Encyclopedia of Management (EoM).* Cengage Learning Inc. • $434 Individuals. 2012. 7th Edition. Contains 316 essays on business management topics. eBook available. Inquire for pricing.

### ONLINE DATABASES

*Wilson Business Abstracts Online.* H.W. Wilson Co. • Indexes and abstracts 600 major business periodicals, plus the *Wall Street Journal* and the business section of the *New York Times.* Indexing is from 1982, abstracting from 1990, with the two newspapers included from 1993. Updated weekly. Inquire as to online cost and availability. (*Business Periodicals Index* without abstracts is also available online.).

*Wilson Social Sciences Abstracts Online.* H.W. Wilson Co. • Provides online abstracting and indexing of more than 500 periodicals covering area studies, community health, public administration, public welfare, urban studies, and many other social science topics. Time period is 1994 to date for abstracts and 1983 to date for indexing, with updates weekly. Inquire as to online cost and availability.

## PERIODICALS AND NEWSLETTERS

*Academy of Management Journal.* Academy of Management. • Bimonthly. $180 /year for individuals and academic libraries (print only). Presents research papers on management-related topics.

*Academy of Management Perspectives.* Academy of Management. • Quarterly. $130 /year for individuals in U.S. (print only). Contains articles relating to the practical application of management principles and theory.

*Academy of Management Review.* Academy of Management. • Quarterly. $350 Individuals print + online. A scholarly journal concerned with the theory of management and organizations.

*Administrative Science Quarterly.* Cornell University, Johnson Graduate School of Management. • Quarterly. $299 Institutions combined (print & e-access).

*Chief Executive Magazine.* Chief Executive Group, LLC. • Monthly. $99 per year.

*Harvard Business Review.* Harvard University, Graduate School of Business Administration. Harvard Business School Publishing. • 10/year.

*The Journal of Business.* The University of Chicago Press, Journals Div. • Quarterly. Individuals, $31.00 per year; institutions, $125.00 per year; students, $25.00 per year.

*MIT Sloan Management Review.* Sloan Management Review Association. Massachusetts Institute of Technology Department of Urban Studies and Planning Community Innovators Lab. • Quarterly. $69. A business journal that bridges the gap between management research and practice.

*Organizational Dynamics: A Quarterly Review of Organizational Behavior for Management Executives.* American Management Association. • Quarterly. Individuals, $77.00 per year; institutions, $171.00 per year. Covers the application of behavioral sciences to business management.

## RESEARCH CENTERS AND INSTITUTES

Board of Research. Babson College, 204 Babson, Babson Park, MA 02457-0310. Phone: (781)235-1200; Fax: (718)239-6416; Email: chern@babson. edu • URL: http://www.babson.edu/bor • Research areas include management, entrepreneurial characteristics, and multi-product inventory analysis.

Executive Education. University of Wisconsin-Madison, School of Business, 601 University Ave., Madison, WI 53706-1035. Phone: 800-292-8964 or (608)441-7357; Fax: (608)441-7133; Email: info@exed.wisc.edu • URL: http://exed.wisc.edu.

University of Illinois at Urbana-Champaign - Bureau of Economic and Business Research. 430 Wohlers Hall, Office of Research, College of Business, 1206 S 6th St., Champaign, IL 61820. Phone: (217)333-2330; Fax: (217)333-7410; Email: lhuff@uiuc.edu • URL: http://business.illinois.edu/research • Economics and business, including studies in business expectations, health economics, forecasting and planning, innovation, entrepreneurship, consumer behavior, poverty problems, small business operations and problems, investment and growth, productivity, research methodology, organizational behavior, and international business and banking.

University of Pennsylvania - Wharton School - SEI Center for Advanced Studies in Management. 700 Jon M. Huntsman Hall, 3730 Walnut St., Philadelphia, PA 19104-6340. Phone: (215)898-8267 or (215)898-6848; Email: windj@wharton. upenn.edu • URL: http://seicenter.wharton.upenn.

edu • Conducts interdisciplinary management studies.

## TRADE/PROFESSIONAL ASSOCIATIONS

Academy of Management. PO Box 3020, Briarcliff Manor, NY 10510-8020. Phone: (914)923-2607; Fax: (914)923-2615; Email: membership@aom.org • URL: http://www.aom.org • Professors in accredited universities and colleges who teach management; selected business executives who have made significant written contributions to the literature in the field of management and organization. Offers placement service.

American Management Association. 1601 Broadway, New York, NY 10019-7420. Phone: 877-566-9441 or (212)586-8100 or (518)891-5510; Fax: (212)903-8168 or (518)891-0368; Email: customerservice@amanet.org • URL: http://www. amanet.org • Provides educational forums worldwide where members and their colleagues learn superior, practical business skills and explore best practices of world-class organizations through interaction with each other and expert faculty practitioners. Maintains a publishing program providing tools individuals use to extend learning beyond the classroom in a process of life-long professional growth and development through education.

American Society for Competitiveness. 664 Pratt Dr., 304 Eberly, IUP, Indiana, PA 15705. Phone: (724)357-5928; Fax: (724)357-7768; Email: office. asc2@gmail.com • URL: http://www.eberly.iup.edu/ASCWeb • Seeks to foster education and knowledge in subjects related to competitiveness by: facilitating exchange of information and ideas among educators, policy makers, and business people, and by encouraging and assisting research activities which advance knowledge of competitiveness practices and increase the available body of teaching and practice materials. Seeks to serve the needs of entrepreneurial scholars and intellectual managers. Specifically through its conferences and publications, intends to effectively serve the needs of academicians interested in the practical application of organizational theory and practicing managers interested in the intellectual development of the discipline.

Asia Academy of Management. Chinese University of Hong Kong, Faculty of Business Administration, Shatin, New Territories, Hong Kong, Hong Kong, China. Fax: 852 2603 6840; Email: asia-aom@cuhk. edu.hk • URL: http://www.baf.cuhk.edu.hk/asia-aom • Seeks to advance management theory, research, and education relevant to Asia. Encourages members to contribute to global management scholarship.

Asian Association of Management Organisations. Rua de Xangai No. 175, Edif. ACM, 9 Andar, Macau, Macao, China. Phone: 853 28323283; Fax: 853 28323267 • URL: http://www.aamo.net • Organization representing the national management organizations of Asian countries. Seeks to advance management practice; promotes continuing professional development of managers. Facilitates exchange of information among members; conducts research and educational programs.

Asian Institute of Management. Eugenio Lopez Foundation Bldg., Joseph R. McMicking Campus, 123 Paseo de Roxas Ave., Makati City 1229, Philippines. Phone: 63 2 8924011 or 63 2 8924023; Fax: 63 2 8672114 or 63 2 8179240; Email: enrollment@aim.edu • URL: http://www.aim.edu • Managers and business and management educators. Seeks to advance the theory and practice of business and organizational management. Sponsors research and educational programs.

Association of Certified Adizes Practitioners International. 1212 Mark Ave., Carpinteria, CA 93013. Phone: (805)565-2901; Fax: (805)565-0741; Email: paula@adizes.com • URL: http://www.

adizes.com • Professional management consultants who are certified to practice the Adizes Method of management. (The Adizes method, devised by Dr. Ichak Adizes, is a comprehensive approach to creating and managing healthy change within a company.) Promotes organizational transformation (consulting) as a profession. Facilitates discussion of ideas and exchange of information among members. Conducts research and educational programs.

Australian Institute of Management. 380 La Trobe St., Level 20, Melbourne, VIC 3000, Australia. Phone: 61 3 95348181; Fax: 61 3 95345050; Email: enquiry@aimvic.com.au • URL: http://www.aim. com.au • Promotes growth in management and leadership. Provides management training and consultancy services.

Beta Gamma Sigma. 125 Weldon Pkwy., Maryland Heights, MO 63043. Phone: 800-337-4677 or (314)432-5650; Fax: (314)432-7083; Email: bgshonors@betagammasigma.org • URL: http://www.betagammasigma.org • International honor society. For students in business and management at business programs accredited by AACSB International. Supports the advancement of business thought and practice to encourage lifelong learning.

Beyster Institute. 9500 Gilman Dr. Otterson Hall S, Fourth Fl., La Jolla, CA 92093-0553. Phone: (858)246-0654; Email: beysterinfo@rady.ucsd.edu • URL: http://beysterinstitute.ucsd.edu • Helps business leaders build successful companies worldwide through training, education and outreach. Serves entrepreneurs by teaching them how to be effective managers and showing them how employee ownership can be adapted to fit their individual companies.

Canadian Institute of Management. Lower Level, 15 Collier St., Barrie, ON, Canada L4M 1G5. Phone: (705)725-8926; Fax: (705)725-8196; Email: office@cim.ca • URL: http://www.cim.ca • Management personnel. Seeks to advance the practice of business management; promotes continuing professional development of members. Serves as a clearinghouse on management and related topics; facilitates exchange of information among members; makes available educational and training programs.

Canadian Management Centre. 150 York St., 5th Fl., Toronto, ON, Canada M5H 3S5. Phone: 877-262-2519; Fax: (416)214-6047; Email: cmcinfo@cmcoutperform.com • URL: http://cmcoutperform. com • Managers of corporations and organizations. Promotes excellence in management. Conducts educational and training programs for management personnel.

Central Asian Foundation for Management Development. Abai Ave., No. 52, 480008 Almaty, Kazakhstan. Phone: 7 3272 423545; Fax: 7 3272 509228; Email: caman@iab.almaty.kz • URL: http://caman-kz.euro.ru • Aims to promote formation and development of business education in the region. Promotes management and management education development and improvement in the Central Asian region.

Chartered Management Institute. 2 Savoy Ct., Strand, London WC2R OEZ, United Kingdom. Phone: 44 20 74970580; Fax: 44 20 74970463; Email: enquiries@managers.org.uk • URL: http://www.managers.org.uk • Promotes the development, exercise and recognition of professional management. Provides services in the areas of management development, management advice, management information and management networks.

Delhi Management Association. India Habitat Ctre., Core 6A, 1st Fl., Lodi Rd., New Delhi 110 003, Delhi, India. Phone: 91 11 24649552; Fax: 91 11 24649553; Email: dmadelhi@sify.com • URL: http://www.dmadelhi.org • Unites to participate in an exciting venture of institution-building, evolving a unique equation of synergy within the India

Habitat Centre complex. Shares common concern for habitat.

European Finance Association. Pl. de Brouckere Plein 31, B-1000 Brussels, Belgium. Phone: 32 2 2266660 or 32 2 2266665; Fax: 32 2 5121929; Email: kannel@eiasm.be • URL: http://www.efa-online.org/r/default.asp?iId=ILGLJ • Academics and practitioners interested in financial management and theory and application. Fosters dissemination and exchange of information; provides forum for presentation of research results in the areas of company finance, investment, financial markets, and banking.

European Foundation for Management Development. Rue Gachard 88, 1050 Brussels, Belgium. Phone: 32 2 6290810; Fax: 32 2 6290811 • URL: http://www.efmd.org • Corporations, educational institutions, employers associations, management consultants, and individuals in 45 countries with an interest in management development, training, and education. Seeks to identify, research, and address leading management development issues. Fosters development of professional competence of those responsible for management development within companies and educational institutions; promotes education, development, and research in the field through working groups, seminars and conferences. Strives to organize effective interaction among all those involved in the management development process.

European International Business Academy. c/o EI-ASM, Hotel Metropole, 2nd Fl., Pl. de Brouckere Plein, 31, B-1000 Brussels, Belgium. Phone: 32 2 2266660; Fax: 32 2 5121929 • URL: http://www.eiba-online.org • Individuals and associations involved in international business. Encourages exchange of ideas; fosters communication among members; serves as an information clearinghouse for those interested in education and research of international business.

European Women's Management Development International Network. Geisbergweg 6c, 65205 Wiesbaden, Germany. • URL: http://www.ewmd.org • Strives to improve management by developing women's managerial skills, and raising the professional profile of women as managers. Disseminates and exchange knowledge and experience in establishing best practices for management development.

Graduate Management Admission Council. 11921 Freedom Dr., Ste. 300, Reston, VA 20190. Phone: 866-505-6559 or (703)668-9600; Fax: (703)668-9601; Email: customercare@gmac.com • URL: http://www.gmac.com • Graduate schools of management and business administration. Works to establish criteria for use in admission to graduate management programs. Provides professional development for academic administrators and seminars for admissions officers. Maintains Graduate Management Admission Search Service, a program that provides institutions with the names of qualified students with desirable characteristics. Employs Educational Testing Service to develop and administer the Graduate Management Admission Test. Conducts research on student selection issues and political and social issues related to graduate management education.

Graduate Management Association of Australia. PO Box 6328, Melbourne, VIC 8008, Australia. Phone: 61 3 95363109; Fax: 61 3 95253656; Email: service@gmaa.com.au • URL: http://www.gmaa.asn.au • Promotes the standing graduate schools and postgraduate management. Enhances the value of graduate management qualifications. Contributes to the development of Australia and its managerial resources. Provides a forum for the interaction of members and students from various management schools. Pursues the regular exchange of ideas and knowledge between members and leaders in industry and management education.

Hong Kong Management Association. W Haking Management Development Ctre., 14th Fl. Fairmont House, 8 Cotton Tree Dr., Central, Hong Kong, Hong Kong, China. Phone: 852 25266516; Fax: 852 28684387; Email: hkma@hkma.org.hk • URL: http://www.hkma.org.hk • Business managers and administrators. Promotes efficient and successful business management. Conducts management education and training courses.

Hrvatsko Udruženje Menadžera I Poduzetnik. Ban Josip Jelacic Square 15 / II., HR-10000 Zagreb, Croatia. Phone: 385 1 4838709; Fax: 385 1 4811787 • URL: http://www.croma.hr • Works to foster professional management practices in Croatian business and industry. Offers educational programs and business related information.

Institute of Administrative Management. Halesfield 7, Coppice House, Telford TF7 4NA, United Kingdom. Phone: 44 20 70912600 or 44 20 70912606; Fax: 44 20 70917340; Email: info@instam.org • URL: http://www.instam.org • Seeks to promote and develop, for the public benefit, the science of administrative management in all branches; encourage the attainment of professional academic qualifications. Provides the latest techniques and developments in the field of administrative management via conferences, seminars, meetings and publications.

Institute of Directors - Zimbabwe. 1 Grantchester Close, Northwood, Mt. Pleasant, Harare, Zimbabwe. Phone: 263 4 301866 or 263 4 301136 • URL: http://www.iodzim.com • Individuals employed as directors either in a managerial or administrative capacity or as a non-executive director by corporations in Zimbabwe. Promotes the interests of domestic businesses; works to develop management techniques particularly suited to local needs. Facilitates communication among members. Conducts research and educational programs.

Institute of Leadership and Management. Stowe House, Netherstowe, Lichfield WS13 6TJ, United Kingdom. Phone: 44 1543 266886 or 44 1543 266867; Fax: 44 1543 266811 or 44 1543 266893; Email: customer@i-l-m.com • URL: http://www.i-l-m.com • Fellows, Members and Associates - Corporate grades; Affiliates and Students Non-corporate grades. Aims to encourage and develop the science and practice of management and gain recognition of management as a profession.

Institute of Management Services. Brooke House, 24 Dam St., Staffordshire, Lichfield WS13 6AA, United Kingdom. Phone: 44 1543 266909; Fax: 44 1543 257848; Email: admin@ims-stowe.fsnet.co.uk • URL: http://www.ims-productivity.com • Represents industry, commerce and the public sector including armed services and police. Serves as professional, qualifying body whose main activities are to provide qualifications and education and to disseminate knowledge in the field of management services. Investigates, advises and carries out solutions to management and organizational problems.

International Academy of Management. 21 Pearson Ave., 08034 Barcelona, Spain. Phone: 34 93 2534200; Email: epy@iese.edu • URL: http://theiam.ws • Leaders in management from 32 countries who have been elected fellows of the IAM in recognition for their contributions to the field. Seeks to: provide a body to safeguard the objectivity and precision of management and the disciplined integration of new/progressive managerial trends; stimulate intellectual interests in management.

International Association for Chinese Management Research. Kogod School of Business, 4400 Massachusetts Ave. NW, Washington, DC 20016. Phone: (316)978-6788; Fax: (316)978-3349; Email: iacmrus@gmail.com • URL: http://www.iacmr.org • Promotes scholarly studies of organization and management of firms in the Chinese context. Fosters the development of management research capabilities in and on China. Facilitates international collaboration between management researchers from around the globe.

International Farm Management Association. c/o Tony King, Honorary Secretary, 38 West End, Cambridge CB22 4LX, United Kingdom. Phone: 44 1223 832527; Email: honsecretary@ifmaonline.org • URL: http://www.ifmaonline.org • Farmers, extension workers, academics, resource use planners, and managers in 68 countries concerned with the planning, production, and marketing in agriculture. Furthers the knowledge and understanding of farm business management and fosters the exchange of ideas and information about farm management theory and practice worldwide.

International Project Management Association. PO Box 7905, 1008 AC Amsterdam, Netherlands. Phone: 31 33 2473430; Fax: 31 33 2460470; Email: info@ipma.ch • URL: http://www.ipma.ch • National project management associations in 43 countries. Liaises the international exchange of project management information and promotes the advancement of project management methods, systems, and practical application techniques. Encourages the development of and cooperates with national organizations with common interests; provides for individual participation in countries without national societies.

IQNet Association - International Certification Network. Bollwerk 31, CH-3000 Bern, Switzerland. Phone: 41 31 3102440; Fax: 41 31 3102449; Email: headoffice@iqnet.ch • URL: http://www.iqnet-certification.com • National management systems certification bodies. Seeks to advance the practice of corporate and organizational management and business excellence. Evaluates management systems and bestows certification upon qualified organizations; serves as a clearinghouse on management systems.

Irish Management Institute. Sandyford Rd., Dublin 16, Dublin, Ireland. Phone: 353 1 2955147 or 353 1 2078513; Email: programmeadvisors@imi.ie • URL: http://www.imi.ie • Works with individuals and organisations to improve the practice of management in Ireland.

Japan Management Association. Convention Div., 3-1-22 Shiba-koen, Minato-ku, Tokyo 105-8522, Japan. Phone: 81 3 34346211 or 81 334 341246; Fax: 81 3 34341087 or 81 334 340269; Email: global@jma.or.jp • URL: http://www.jma.or.jp • Japanese corporations and individuals. Management education organization working to develop and conduct public business education and training programs including seminars, conferences, symposia, and overseas study tours. Makes available correspondence courses, audiovisual and computer-assisted instruction programs, in-company training programs, and cruise seminars. Conducts research and disseminates information on topics including white-collar productivity in Japan, creativity development in business and industry, and globally oriented management reform. Maintains liaison with similar organizations worldwide. Organizes conferences and exhibitions for trade associations. Maintains 14 interdisciplinary divisions and 13 supporting departments. Provides management consulting service; operates speakers' bureau.

Kenya Institute of Management. PO Box 43706, Nairobi, Kenya. Phone: 254 20 2445600 or 254 20 2445555; Email: kim@kim.ac.ke • URL: http://www.kim.ac.ke • Individuals and businesses in Kenya. Works to increase and disseminate information on the science of management; stimulates interest in effective management; formulates standards for professional conduct, experience, and training; encourages education in the principles and practices of management by establishing and promoting training courses, scholarships, and grants; conducts examinations and awards certificates and diplomas; provides facilities for research into management problems; organizes management seminars for professional training and small business creation.

New Zealand Institute of Management. Level 7, Lumley House, 3-11 Hunter St., Wellington 6140, New Zealand. Phone: 64 4 4958300; Email: enquiries@nzim.co.nz • URL: http://www.nzim.co.nz • Managers and managerial personnel. Promotes improved management of businesses in New Zealand. Conducts continuing professional education programs; maintains information center.

Organization Design Forum. 5016 E Mulberry Dr., Phoenix, AZ 85018-6525. Phone: (602)510-9105; Email: info@organizationdesignforum.org • URL: http://organizationdesignforum.org • Academics, practitioners, consultants, and human resource professionals. Works to promote the knowledge and practice of organizational design. Focuses on the effect organization structure and processes have on the performance of individuals, groups, and the organization itself. Offers basic and advanced training in organization design techniques.

Society for Advancement of Management. 6300 Ocean Dr., OCNR 330, Unit 5807, Corpus Christi, TX 78412. Phone: 888-827-6077 or (361)825-3045; Fax: (361)825-5609; Email: moustafa.abdelsamad@tamucc.edu • URL: http://www.samnational.org • Represents management executives in industry commerce, government, and education. Fields of interest include management education, policy and strategy, MIS, international management, administration, budgeting, collective bargaining, distribution, incentives, materials handling, quality control, and training.

Southern Africa Institute for Management Services. PO Box 7045, Centurion, Tshwane 0046, South Africa. Phone: 27 79 4979183; Fax: 27 86 5587183; Email: saimas@global.co.za • URL: http://www.saimas.org.za • Maintains professional standards for the management services practice. Seeks to improve professional expertise. Promotes the education and training of persons who enter, or intend to enter the field of management services.

Swiss Management Association. Zeltweg 48, 8032 Zurich, Switzerland. Phone: 41 44 2022325; Fax: 41 44 2699001; Email: office@smg.ch • URL: http://www.smg.ch • Acts as an umbrella association of personalities from economy, science, administration; deals with and takes into transdisciplinary consideration the complex terms related to decision making; promotes exchange of capabilities and knowledge, ideas and questions, and experience and aims of leadership and management.

Workflow Management Coalition. 759 CJC Hwy., Ste. No. 363, Cohasset, MA 02025-2115. Phone: (781)719-9209; Fax: (781)735-0491; Email: nathaniel@wfmc.org • URL: http://www.wfmc.org • Represents adopters, developers, consultants, analysts, university and research groups engaged in workflow and Business Process Management (BPM). Seeks to expand the BPM market by promoting the business value of process management. Strives to decrease the risk of using BPM and workflow products through interoperability standards.

World Confederation of Productivity Science. c/o Linda Carbone, Executive Secretary, 500 Sherbrooke St. W, Ste. 900, Montreal, QC, Canada H3A 3C6. Email: secretariat@wcps.info • URL: http://www.wcps.info • Fraternal association of manufacturing and commercial enterprises and employees, government agencies, professional institutions, and researchers. Goals are to promote productivity science, advance management techniques, and improve the quality of working life and environment.

# MANPOWER

*See* LABOR SUPPLY

# MANUALS, PROCEDURE

*See* PROCEDURE MANUALS

# MANUFACTURED HOUSING

*See* PREFABRICATED HOUSE INDUSTRY

# MANUFACTURERS' AGENTS

## DIRECTORIES

*American Companies' Hong Kong Agents and Distributors.* American Chamber of Commerce in Hong Kong. • $500 Nonmembers. Covers: Over 1,000 U.S. companies represented by 120 agents and distributors from Hong Kong.

*Manufacturers' Agents National Association - Directory of Manufacturers' Sales Agencies.* Manufacturers' Agents National Association. • Lists over 4,000 independent agents and firms. Price includes one year subscription to Agency Sales Magazines. Formerly *Manufacturers' Agents National Association-Directory of Members.*

## HANDBOOKS AND MANUALS

*Sales Representative Law Guide.* Wolters Kluwer Law & Business CCH. • $195.00 per year. Looseleaf service. Semiannual updates. Covers state laws on independent sales representation. Includes checklists and forms.

## PERIODICALS AND NEWSLETTERS

*Agency Sales: The Marketing Magazine for Manufacturers' Agencies and Their Principals.* Manufacturers' Agents National Association. • Monthly. $79 Individuals.

*Rep-Letter.* Manufacturers' Agents National Association. • Monthly. $37.50. A bound-in monthly feature of *Agency Sales Magazine.*

## TRADE/PROFESSIONAL ASSOCIATIONS

American Association of Inside Sales Professionals. 14530 Florissant Path, Apple Valley, MN 55124. Phone: 800-604-7085; Email: info@aa-isp.org • URL: http://www.aa-isp.org • Serves as an authoritative resource to leaders and individual sales representatives. Aims to perfect the skills of inside sale professionals. Conducts leadership and career development trainings, member forums and networking, conferences, education and accreditation programs that will help advance the inside sales profession.

Manufacturers' Agents National Association. 6321 W Dempster St., Ste. 110, Morton Grove, IL 60053. Phone: 877-626-2776 or (949)859-4040; Fax: (949)855-2973; Email: mana@manaonline.org • URL: http://www.manaonline.org • Manufacturers' agents in all fields representing two or more manufacturers on a commission basis; associate members are manufacturers and others interested in improving the agent-principal relationship. Maintains code of ethics and rules of business and professional conduct; issues model standard form of agreement.

# MANUFACTURING

*See* INDUSTRY

# MAPS

## ABSTRACTS AND INDEXES

*Geographical Abstracts: Human and Physical Geography.* Elsevier. • Monthly. Institutions,

$4,213.00 per year. *Human Geography,* $1,822.00 per year. Annual cumulation. *Physical Geography,* $2,391.00 per year. Annual cumulation.

## OTHER SOURCES

*Atlas & Gazetteer Series.* DeLorme. • Consists of 50 volumes covering all areas of the U. S. Includes detailed maps, as well as descriptions of attractions, natural areas, and historic sites.

*Lloyd's Maritime Atlas.* Informa P.L.C. Informa Sports Group. • Biennial. $119.00. Contains more than 70 pages of world, ocean, regional, and port maps in color. Provides additional information for the planning of world shipping routes, including data on distances, port facilities, recurring weather hazards at sea, international load line zones, and sailing times.

*Maps On File.* InfoBase Holdings Inc. • Annual. $75 2012 Update. Up to 500 reproducable maps.

## PERIODICALS AND NEWSLETTERS

*Cartography and Geographic Information Science.* American Congress on Surveying and Mapping. • 5/year. $229 Institutions.

*Surveying and Land Information Systems: Devoted to the Advancement of the Sciences of Surveying and Mapping.* American Congress on Surveying and Mapping. • Quarterly. Free to members; nonmembers, $110.00 per year. Formerly *Surveying and Mapping.*

# MARBLE

*See also* QUARRYING

## PERIODICALS AND NEWSLETTERS

*Building Stone Magazine.* Building Stone Institute. • Quarterly. $20 Individuals /year. Information on the natural stone industry.

## TRADE/PROFESSIONAL ASSOCIATIONS

Marble Institute of America. 28901 Clemens Rd., Ste. 100, Cleveland, OH 44145-1166. Phone: (440)250-9222; Fax: (440)250-9223; Email: miainfo@marble-institute.com • URL: http://www.marble-institute.com • Quarriers, exporters, fabricators, importers, wholesalers, finishers, suppliers and installing contractors of dimension stone for interior and exterior application; persons involved in the refinishing and restoration of dimension stone. Promotes the uses of dimension stone to architects, engineers, designers and other specifying authorities. Sponsors visual aid projects; works with ASTM in developing standard specifications for the use of dimension stone in construction. Compiles statistics. Distributes consumer information. Publishes technical guidelines, advisories and manuals.

# MARGARINE INDUSTRY

## DIRECTORIES

*Major Food and Drink Companies of the World.* Cengage Learning Inc. • 12th edition. eBook. Published by Graham & Whiteside. Contains profiles and trade names for more than 9,200 important food and beverage companies in various countries. In addition to foods, includes both alcoholic and nonalcoholic drink products.

## INTERNET DATABASES

*USDA.* U.S. National Institute of Standards and Technology. 100 Bureau Dr., Gaithersburg, MD 20899-1070. Phone: 800-877-8339 or (301)975-6478 or (202)720-2791; Fax: (301)975-8295; Email: inquiries@nist.gov • URL: http://www.nist.gov • The USDA home page has six sections: News and Information; What's New; About USDA; Agencies; Opportunities; Search and Help. Keyword searching is offered from the USDA home page and from various individual agency home pages. Agencies are the Economic Research Service, Agricultural Marketing Service, National Agricultural Statistics Service, National Agricultural Library, and about 12 others. Updating varies. Fees: Free.

## ONLINE DATABASES

*Food Science and Technology Abstracts (online).* IFIS North American Desk. • Produced by International Food Information Service. Provides about 500,000 online citations, with abstracts, to the international literature of food science, technology, commodities, engineering, and processing. Approximately 2,000 periodicals are covered. Time period is 1969 to date, with monthly updates. Inquire as to online cost and availability.

## STATISTICS SOURCES

*Agricultural Statistics.* U.S. Department of Agriculture National Agricultural Statistics Service. • Annual. $46 Individuals. Provides a wide variety of statistical data relating to agricultural production, supplies, consumption, prices/price-supports, foreign trade, costs, and returns, as well as farm labor, loans, income, and population. In many cases, historical data is shown annually for 10 years. In addition to farm data, includes detailed fishery statistics.

## TRADE/PROFESSIONAL ASSOCIATIONS

National Association of Margarine Manufacturers. 1156 15th St. NW, Ste. 900, Washington, DC 20005. Phone: (202)785-3232; Fax: (202)223-9741; Email: namm@kellencompany.com • URL: http://www.margarine.org • Margarine manufacturers, distributors and industry suppliers. Represents members' legislative and regulatory interests. Develops and disseminates information about margarine and margarine products to the public.

# MARINAS

## ABSTRACTS AND INDEXES

*Fluid Abstracts: Civil Engineering.* Elsevier. • Monthly. $3,804 Institutions print. Monthly. Institutions, $1,709.00 per year. Includes annual cumulation. Includes the literature of coastal structures. Published in England by Elsevier Science Publishing Ltd. Formerly *Civil Engineering Hydraulics Abstracts.*

*Oceanic Abstracts.* CSA. • Monthly. $1,645.00 per year. Includes print and online editions. Covers oceanography, marine biology, ocean shipping, and a wide range of other marine-related subject areas.

*Readers' Guide to Periodical Literature.* EBSCO Publishing Inc. • Provides indexing for over 400 periodicals dating back to 1983.

## CD-ROM DATABASES

*Readers' Guide to Periodical Literature.* EBSCO Publishing Inc. • Provides indexing for over 400 periodicals dating back to 1983.

## DIRECTORIES

*Waterway Guide--The Yachtman's Bible.* Argus Press Inc. • $36.95 postpaid. Covers: inland and coastal waterways in the eastern half of the United States; published in three editions. Northern edition covers coastal waterways from the Delaware Bay to the U.S.-Canadian border; plus New York canals, Champlain Waterways, and St. Lawrence River; Middle Atlantic edition covers waterways from the Chesapeake Bay to the Florida-Georgia line; Southern edition covers intracoastal waterways from the Florida-Georgia line to the Texas-Mexico border and the Bahamas. Entries include: Name of marine facility, location, navigation information and courses, points of interest, anchorages.

## RESEARCH CENTERS AND INSTITUTES

National Ports and Waterways Institute. University of New Orleans, 2300 Claredon Blvd., Ste. 300,

Arlington, VA 22201. Phone: (703)276-7101; Fax: (703)276-7102; Email: npwi@seas.gwu.edu • URL: http://www.members.tripod.com/npwi.

# MARINE ENGINEERING

## ABSTRACTS AND INDEXES

*NTIS Alerts: Ocean Sciences and Technology.* U.S. Department of Commerce National Technical Information Service. • Biweekly. $130 per year. Provides descriptions of government-sponsored research reports and software, with ordering information.

## DIRECTORIES

*Fairplay World Shipping Directory.* Fairplay Publications Ltd. • Daily. Covers: More than 76,000 companies worldwide engaged in some aspect of shipping, including over 10,000 ship-owners with fleets totaling over 45,000 vessels, shipbuilders and repairers, marine insurance shipping finance, protection and indemnity associations, marine equipment suppliers, and towing, salvage, and dredging; also lists marine organizations, shipbrokers, and consulting engineers and surveyors. Entries include: Company name, address, phone, fax, e-mail, URL, names of directors and executives, brief description of business; listings may also include associated and subsidiary companies and financial data.

*Lloyd's Marine Equipment Buyers' Guide.* Informa Group PLC. • Annual. $270.00. Published in the UK by Lloyd's List (www.lloydslist.com). Lists more than 6,000 companies worldwide supplying over 2,000 types of marine products and services, including offshore equipment.

*Lloyd's Maritime Directory.* Informa P.L.C. Informa Sports Group. • Annual. Covers: Over 40,000 shipowners, managers, and operators with 75,000 vessels. Also includes Marine consultants; towing, salvage, solicitors, P&I clubs; ship building and repair firms; general maritime organizations, banking and finance and more. Entries include: Firm name, address, phone, fax, e-mail, Internet; branch offices; names of principal executives; agents; parent and associated companies; and, for shipowners and lines, detailed information on ships owned, type, or capacity, etc. The former second volume of 'International Shipping and Shipbuilding Directory' is now published separately with the title 'Lloyd's List Marine Equipment Buyers' Guide' (see separate entry).

*Motorship Directory of Shipowners and Shipbuilders.* Reed Elsevier Group plc Reed Business Information. • Formerly *Directory of Shipowners and Shipbuilders.*

## PERIODICALS AND NEWSLETTERS

*Journal of Offshore Technology.* Institute of Marine Engineering, Science and Technology. • Bimonthly. Free to members; non-members, £52.00 per year. Covers the latest technological developments and trends for senior offshore engineers.

*Maritime IT & Electronics.* Institute of Marine Engineering, Science and Technology. • Bimonthly. £58.00 per year. Covers modern electronic technology as applied to all areas of the maritime industry. Includes navigation systems, communications, control systems, monitoring, diagnostics, and software.

*Naval Engineers Journal.* American Society of Naval Engineers. • Quarterly. $233 Individuals Print and Online. Contains technical papers in the field of naval engineering. It also contains schedules of meetings, symposia, and other events, news, notes, and membership information.

*Satellite News.* Access Intelligence L.L.C. • Description: Provides business insights and analysis into the commercial satellite industry including new satellite applications, developing technologies, and unfold-

ing partnerships. Recurring features include columns titled Satellite Spotlight, DBS News, Satellite News, Newsmaker Interiews, Satellite Circuit, and Satellite News Financial Ticker.

*Workboat.* Diversified Business Communications Inc. • Monthly. Provides in-depth reporting on topics including offshore services, shipbuilding and repair, port security, marine electronics, environmental regulations and more.

## TRADE/PROFESSIONAL ASSOCIATIONS

American Society of Naval Engineers. 1452 Duke St., Alexandria, VA 22314. Phone: (703)836-6727; Fax: (703)836-7491; Email: asnehq@navalengineers.org • URL: http://www.navalengineers.org • Professional civilian and Navy engineers interested in naval engineering including ordnance, navigation, aeronautics, propulsion, hull, electrical and electronic, naval architecture, ocean engineering, space systems, logistics, and related subjects.

Marine Technology Society. 1100 H St. NW, Ste. LL100, Washington, DC 20005. Phone: (202)717-8705; Fax: (202)347-4302; Email: membership@mtsociety.org • URL: http://www.mtsociety.org • Scientists, engineers, educators, and others with professional interest in the marine sciences or related fields; includes institutional and corporate members. Disseminates marine scientific and technical information, including institutional, environmental, physical, and biological aspects; fosters a deeper understanding of the world's seas and attendant technologies. Maintains 13 sections and 29 professional committees. Conducts tutorials.

# MARINE INSURANCE

## BIBLIOGRAPHIES

*Insurance and Employee Benefits Literature.* Special Libraries Association. • Bimonthly. $15.00 per year. Lists a wide variety of literature in all branches of the insurance industry. Includes annotations.

## DIRECTORIES

*Fairplay World Shipping Directory.* Fairplay Publications Ltd. • Daily. Covers: More than 76,000 companies worldwide engaged in some aspect of shipping, including over 10,000 ship-owners with fleets totaling over 45,000 vessels, shipbuilders and repairers, marine insurance shipping finance, protection and indemnity associations, marine equipment suppliers, and towing, salvage, and dredging; also lists marine organizations, shipbrokers, and consulting engineers and surveyors. Entries include: Company name, address, phone, fax, e-mail, URL, names of directors and executives, brief description of business; listings may also include associated and subsidiary companies and financial data.

*Lloyd's Maritime Directory.* Informa P.L.C. Informa Sports Group. • Annual. Covers: Over 40,000 shipowners, managers, and operators with 75,000 vessels. Also includes Marine consultants; towing, salvage, solicitors, P&I clubs; ship building and repair firms; general maritime organizations, banking and finance and more. Entries include: Firm name, address, phone, fax, e-mail, Internet; branch offices; names of principal executives; agents; parent and associated companies; and, for shipowners and lines, detailed information on ships owned, type, or capacity, etc. The former second volume of 'International Shipping and Shipbuilding Directory' is now published separately with the title 'Lloyd's List Marine Equipment Buyers' Guide' (see separate entry).

## ONLINE DATABASES

*I.I.I. Data Base Search.* Insurance Information Institute. • Provides online citations and abstracts of insurance-related literature in magazines, newspapers, trade journals, and books. Emphasis is on property and casualty insurance issues, including highway safety, product safety, and environmental liability. Inquire as to online cost and availability.

## PERIODICALS AND NEWSLETTERS

*Business Insurance: News Magazine for Corporate Risk, Employee Benefit and Financial Executives.* Crain Communications Inc. • Weekly. $95.00 per year. Covers a wide variety of business insurance topics, including risk management, employee benefits, workers compensation, marine insurance, and casualty insurance.

## STATISTICS SOURCES

*Property-Casualty Insurance Facts.* Insurance Information Institute. • Annual. $22.50. Formerly *Insurance Facts.*

## TRADE/PROFESSIONAL ASSOCIATIONS

American Institute of Marine Underwriters. 14 Wall St., Ste. 820, New York, NY 10005-2101. Phone: (212)233-0550; Fax: (212)227-5102; Email: aimu@aimu.org • URL: http://www.aimu.org/contactus.html • Marine insurance companies authorized to conduct business in one or more states of the U.S. Services to members includes: referral information on legislative and regulatory questions; training and educational programs; analysis of international conventions and agreements affecting the business of marine insurance; access to offices of correspondents worldwide; development of forms and clauses to meet changing maritime requirements; information-gathering assistance. Sponsors educational programs.

# MARINE LAW

*See* MARITIME LAW AND REGULATION

# MARITIME INDUSTRY

*See* SHIPS, SHIPPING AND SHIPBUILDING

# MARITIME LAW AND REGULATION

## ABSTRACTS AND INDEXES

*Index to Legal Periodicals and Books.* H.W. Wilson Co. • Monthly. $490.00 per year. Quarterly and annual cumulations.

## BIBLIOGRAPHIES

*Law of the Sea: A Select Bibliography.* United Nations Publications. • Annual. $17.00. Includes 23 subject categories.

*Law of the Sea Bulletin.* United Nations Publications. • Three times per year.

## DIRECTORIES

*Capital for Shipping.* Informa Publishing Group. • Annual. $128.00. Published in the UK by Lloyd's List (www.lloydslist.com). Consists of a "Financial Directory" and a "Legal Directory," listing international ship finance providers and international law firms specializing in shipping. Included with subscription to *Lloyd's Shipping Economist.*

*Fairplay World Shipping Directory.* Fairplay Publications Ltd. • Daily. Covers: More than 76,000 companies worldwide engaged in some aspect of shipping, including over 10,000 ship-owners with fleets totaling over 45,000 vessels, shipbuilders and repairers, marine insurance shipping finance, protection and indemnity associations, marine equipment suppliers, and towing, salvage, and dredging; also lists marine organizations, shipbrokers, and consulting engineers and surveyors. Entries include: Company name, address, phone, fax, e-mail, URL, names of directors and executives, brief description

of business; listings may also include associated and subsidiary companies and financial data.

*Lloyd's Maritime Directory.* Informa P.L.C. Informa Sports Group. • Annual. Covers: Over 40,000 shipowners, managers, and operators with 75,000 vessels. Also includes Marine consultants; towing, salvage, solicitors, P&I clubs; ship building and repair firms; general maritime organizations, banking and finance and more. Entries include: Firm name, address, phone, fax, e-mail, Internet; branch offices; names of principal executives; agents; parent and associated companies; and, for shipowners and lines, detailed information on ships owned, type, or capacity, etc. The former second volume of 'International Shipping and Shipbuilding Directory' is now published separately with the title 'Lloyd's List Marine Equipment Buyers' Guide' (see separate entry).

## OTHER SOURCES

*Benedict on Admiralty.* Matthew Bender and Company Inc. • Three times a year. $3,138.00. 27 looseleaf volumes. Periodic supplementation. Covers American law of the sea and shipping.

## PERIODICALS AND NEWSLETTERS

*Ocean Development and International Law.* Taylor & Francis Group Journals. • Quarterly. $440 Individuals print. Peer-reviewed law journal.

*Tulane Maritime Law Journal.* Tulane University School of Law. • Semiannual. $28.00 per year. Formerly *Maritime Lawyer.*

*United States Coast Guard Marine Safety Council Proceedings.* U.S. Department of Homeland Security U.S. Coast Guard. • Bimonthly.

## TRADE/PROFESSIONAL ASSOCIATIONS

Maritime Law Association of the U.S. c/o Robert B. Parrish, President, 501 W Bay St., Jacksonville, FL 32202-4428. Phone: (904)421-8436; Fax: (904)421-8437 • URL: http://www.mlaus.org • Lawyers and others interested in maritime law. Provides advisers to government and industry officials. Maintains microfiche collection.

# MARKET RESEARCH

*See also* CONSUMER SURVEYS; INTERVIEWING; MARKET STATISTICS; MARKETING; STATISTICS SOURCES; SURVEY METHODS

## ALMANACS AND YEARBOOKS

*Research Alert Yearbook: Vital Facts on Consumer Behavior and Attitudes.* EPM Communications Inc. • Annual. $349 Individuals Single user (PDF) or Print. Provides summaries of consumer market research from the newsletters *Research Alert, Youth Markets Alert,* and *Minority Markets Alert.* Includes tables, charts, graphs, and textual summaries for 41 subject categories. Sources include reports, studies, polls, and focus groups.

*Research in Marketing: An Annual Compilation of Research.* Jagdish N. Sheth, editor. Elsevier. • Annual. Price on application.

## CD-ROM DATABASES

*OECD Statistical Compendium.* Organization for Economic Cooperation and Development. • Semiannual. $1,905.00 per year for 1 to 10 users. CD-ROM contains more than 730,000 monthly, quarterly, and annual time series for OECD countries, 1960 to date. Includes fully searchable data on agriculture, food, economic indicators, national accounts, employment, energy, finance, industry, technology, and foreign trade. Results can be displayed in various forms.

## DIRECTORIES

*Data Sources for Business and Market Analysis.* Hoover's Inc. • $54.95. Covers: Sources of business

information from providers including the federal government, regional and local governments, foreign sources, universities, research centers, and professional and trade associations.

*Findex: The Worldwide Directory of Market Research Reports, Studies, and Surveys.* MarketResearch.com. • Annual. Provides brief annotations of market research reports and related publications from about 1,000 publishers, arranged by topic. Back of book includes Report Titles by Publisher, Publishers/Distributors Directory, Subject Index, Geography Index, and Company Index. (Formerly published by Cambridge Information Group.).

*GreenBook.* New York American Marketing Association. • Annual. Contains information on companies offering focus group facilities, including recruiting, moderating, and transcription services.

*GreenBook Worldwide Directory of Marketing Research Companies and Services.* New York AMA - Green Book. • Annual. Contains information in 300 categories on more than 2,500 market research companies, consultants, field services, computer services, survey research companies, etc. Indexed by specialty, industry, company, computer program, and personnel. Available online. Formerly *Greenbook Worldwide International Directory of Marketing Research Companies and Services.*

*The Guide: A Practical Handbook of Marketing Research Sources in the United Kingdom and Western Europe.* Key Note Publications Ltd. • $165. Covers: Sources of marketing research in the United Kingdom and Western Europe, including business information sources, market research sources, advertising organizations, periodicals, newspapers, magazines, official statistical sources, online databases, and libraries. Entries include: For databases--Database name, host, producer, contents, frequency of updates. For others--Name, address, phone, fax, description.

*IAL Directory of European Industrial and Business Market Reports.* IAL Consultants. • Irregular. $250 postpaid. Covers: publishers and producers of market reports, statistical summaries, and other data; includes government and non-government organizations, libraries, press, and international sources in Europe, including the socialist states of Eastern Europe. Entries include: Publisher name and address, title and subject of report, language, number of pages, price.

*Marketing Surveys Index.* Marketing Answers Ltd. • $380 per year. Covers: about 8,000 recently-published market research and business reports from around the world. Entries include: Report title; publisher name, address, phone, fax, e-mail and contact name; countries covered by report, publication date, number of pages, price, description of report.

*Medical and Healthcare Marketplace Guide.* IDD Inc. • Annual. $595.00. Two volumes. Provides market survey summaries for about 500 specific product and service categories (volume one: "Research Reports"). Contains profiles of nearly 5,500 pharmaceutical, medical product, and healthcare service companies (volume two: "Company Profiles").

*Researching Markets, Industries, & Business Opportunities.* MarketResearch.com. • Irregular. $245. Publication includes: Lists of sources of business and market information. Entries include: Source name, address, phone, description. Principal content of publication is discussion of methods for studying markets and industries.

## E-BOOKS

*Branding Your Business.* Cengage Learning Inc. • 2010. eBook. Details what a brand is and what it is not, how to conduct a 'DIY' brand audit and how to use marketing NLP and psychology principles to create a powerful brand.

## INTERNET DATABASES

*Business 2.0 Web Guide to the Best Business Links.* Business 2.0 Media Inc. Phone: (415)293-4800; Email: support@business2.com • URL: http://www.business2.com/webguide • Web site presents an extensive, searchable directory of links to "the best, most informative, and authoritative web pages." Twenty main categories cover business, finance, career, company information, people, and technology topics, with thousands of subtopics, all linking to Web sites recommended by experienced business researchers. Fees: Free.

*Factiva.* Dow Jones Reuters Business Interactive, LLC. Phone: 800-369-7466 or (609)452-1511; Fax: (609)520-5770; Email: solutions@factiva.com • URL: http://www.factiva.com • Fee-based Web site provides "global news and business information through Web sites and content integration solutions." Includes Dow Jones and Reuters newswires, The Wall Street Journal, and more than 7,000 other sources of current news, historical articles, market research reports, and investment analysis. Content includes 96 major U. S. newspapers, 900 non-English sources, trade publications, media transcripts, country profiles, news photos, etc.

*InSite 2.* Intelligence Data/Thomson Financial. Phone: 800-654-0393 or (617)856-1890; Fax: (617)737-3182; Email: intelligence.data@tfn.com • URL: http://www.insite2.gale.com/ • Fee-based Web site consolidates information in a "Base Pack" consisting of Business InSite, Market InSite, and Company InSite. Optional databases are Consumer InSite, Health and Wellness InSite, Newsletter InSite, and Computer InSite. Includes fulltext content from more than 2,500 trade publications, journals, newsletters, newspapers, analyst reports, and other sources. Continuous updating. Formerly produced by The Gale Group.

*Intelligence Data.* Thomson Financial. Phone: 800-654-0393; Fax: (617)824-2477 • URL: http://www.intelligencedata.com • Fee-based Web site provides a wide variety of information relating to competitive intelligence, strategic planning, business development, mergers, acquisitions, sales, and marketing. "Intelliscope" feature offers searching of other Thomson units, such as Investext, MarkIntel, InSite 2, and Industry Insider. Weekly updating.

## ONLINE DATABASES

*Market Research Monitor.* Euromonitor International Inc. • Contains full-text reports online from *Market Research Europe, Market Research Great Britain, Market Research International, and Retail Monitor International.* Time period is 1995 to date, with monthly updates. Inquire as to online cost and availability.

*Market Research Reports.* MarketResearch.com. • Provides online full text of market research reports produced by FIND/SVP, Packaged Facts, Specialists in Business Information and others. Contains market data for a wide variety of industries, products, and services, including market size, forecasts, trends, structure, and opportunities. Inquire as to online cost and availability.

*MarkIntel.* Thomson Financial. • Provides the current full text online of more than 50,000 market research reports covering 54 industries, from 85 leading research firms worldwide. Reports include extensive forecasts and market analysis. Inquire as to online cost and availability.

## PERIODICALS AND NEWSLETTERS

*American Demographics: Consumer Trends for Business Leaders.* Media Central. • Monthly. $58.00 per year.

*Brandweek: The Newsweekly of Marketing Communications.* Nielsen Business Media Inc. • 46 times a year. $149.00 per year. Includes articles and case studies on mass marketing and mass media. Formerly *Adweek's Marketing Week.*

*Database Marketer.* SIMBA Information Inc. • Monthly. $329.00 per year.

*The Information Advisor: Tips and Techniques for Smart Information Users.* MarketResearch.com. • Monthly. $159.00 per year. Newsletter. Evaluates and discusses online, CD-ROM, and published sources of business, financial, and market research information.

*Marketing to the Emerging Minorities.* EPM Communications Inc. • Monthly. $295 /year. Newsletter on market research relating to African American, Asian American, and U. S. Hispanic populations.

*Research Alert: A Bi-Weekly Report of Consumer Marketing Studies.* EPM Communications Inc. • Biweekly. $389 /year. Provides descriptions (abstracts) of new, consumer market research reports from private, government, and academic sources. Includes sample charts and tables.

*Youth Markets Alert.* EPM Communications Inc. • Description: Features information and research results related to young consumers from elementary school through high school.

## RESEARCH CENTERS AND INSTITUTES

Aalborg University - Center for Labor Market Research. Fibigerstraede 1, 9220 Alborg, Denmark. Phone: 45 99409940; Fax: 45 98155346 • URL: http://www.dps.aau.dk/forskningsenheder/carma-english • Work organization, technology developments, cooperation and management styles, collective bargaining, wage and personnel policies in private enterprises and public institutions.

Aalto University - Center for Markets in Transition. PO Box 21230, FIN-00076 Aalto, Finland. Phone: 358 9 403538149; Fax: 358 9 47038706; Email: riitta.kosonen@aalto.fi • URL: http://cemat.aalto.fi/en • Markets and economies in transition in Central and Eastern Europe. Research focuses on economic development in Northwest Russia, strategies of foreign enterprises in Russia and the Baltic States, post-socialist transformation on enterprise and industry level, business cultures and norms around the Baltic Sea, Russian raw materials as a business, and tourism development.

Economic Research Service - Cattle and Beef. 355 E St. SW, Washington, DC 20024-3221. Phone: 800-999-6779 or (202)694-5183; Email: kmathews@ers.usda.gov • URL: http://ers.usda.gov/topics/animal-products/cattle-beef.aspx#.U5Eq73I2aDg • Market analysis and research on the U.S. cattle and beef sectors, including domestic supply and utilization, live cattle and retail beef prices, and international trade.

Mongolian National Chamber of Commerce and Industry - Economic and Market Research Center. Government Bldg. 11, Rm. 711, J. Sambuu St. 11, Ulaanbaatar, Mongolia. Phone: 976 11 327176; Fax: 976 324620; Email: chamber@mongolchamber.mn • URL: http://www.mongolchamber.mn/en/index.php • Economics, market research, trade and business promotion, consultancy, and training.

University of Nebraska—Omaha - Nebraska Business Development Center. Mammel Hall, Ste. 200, College of Business Administration, 6708 Pine St., Omaha, NE 68182. Phone: (402)554-2521; Fax: (402)554-3473; Email: rbernier@unomaha.edu • URL: http://nbdc.unomaha.edu • Sustainable development, technology commercialization, management education, market research, marketing plans, strategic planning, financial planning, cash flow budgeting, capital budgeting, loan packaging, and rural development.

University of Wollongong - Centre for Social Marketing Research. Bldg. 19, Rm. 1034a, Faculty of Commerce, Northfields Ave., Wollongong, NSW 2522, Australia. Phone: 61 2 42215994; Fax: 61 2 42213257; Email: csmr@uow.edu.au • URL: http:// www.uow.edu.au/commerce/smm/mark/academics/ UOW010679.htm • Social marketing, including commercial marketing, nonprofit marketing, and issues of corporate social responsibility.

## TRADE/PROFESSIONAL ASSOCIATIONS

American Marketing Association. 311 S Wacker Dr., Ste. 5800, Chicago, IL 60606. Phone: 800-AMA-1150 or (312)542-9000; Fax: (312)542-9001 • URL: http://www.marketingpower.com • Serves as a professional society of marketing and market research executives, sales and promotion managers, advertising specialists, academics, and others interested in marketing. Fosters research; sponsors seminars, conferences, and student marketing clubs; provides educational placement service and doctoral consortium.

Marketing Research Association. 1156 15th St. NW, Ste. 302, Washington, DC 20005. Phone: 888-512-1050 or (202)800-2545; Fax: (888)512-1050; Email: membership@marketingresearch.org • URL: http:// www.marketingresearch.org • Companies and individuals involved in any area of opinion and marketing research, such as data collection, research, or as an end-user.

# MARKET STATISTICS

*See also* BUSINESS STATISTICS; MARKET RESEARCH; MARKETING; PURCHASING POWER; STATISTICS SOURCES

## ALMANACS AND YEARBOOKS

*World Development Report.* World Bank Group. • Annual. Covers history, conditions, and trends relating to economic globalization and localization. Includes selected data from *World Development Indicators* for 132 countries or economies. Key indicators are provided for 78 additional countries or economies.

## BIBLIOGRAPHIES

*Statistics Sources.* Cengage Learning Inc. • $874 Individuals. 2012. $836.00. 37th edition. Lists sources of statistical information for more than 20,000 topics.

## CD-ROM DATABASES

*Sourcebooks America CD-ROM.* CACI Marketing Systems. • Annual. $1,250.00. Provides the CD-ROM version of *The Sourcebook of ZIP Code Demographics: Census Edition* and *The Sourcebook of County Demographics: Census Edition.*

*World Development Report.* World Bank Group. • Annual. Covers history, conditions, and trends relating to economic globalization and localization. Includes selected data from *World Development Indicators* for 132 countries or economies. Key indicators are provided for 78 additional countries or economies.

## DIRECTORIES

*Consumer USA: 2010.* Euromonitor International Business Reference Div. • Annual. $995 Individuals U.S.D. An analytical overview of the U.S. market. Provides historic and forecast volume and value sales statistics on over 330 consumer product sectors. Database includes: Company and brand share data.

*Editor & Publisher Market Guide.* Editor and Publisher Company Inc. • Annual. $150 Individuals. Market data for more than 1,600 cities and 3,096 counties.

*Market Share Reporter (MSR).* Cengage Learning Inc. • $777 Individuals. 2013. $740.00. Published by Gale. Provides consumer market share data for leading companies. Also available as eBook.

*Sectores.* Databank S.p.A. • Annual. $1,300 per report. A series of reports on 100 industrial sectors in Spain. Each report includes a description of the industry, trends, size of market and market shares of individual companies, and financial data in addition to a list of names and addresses of industry suppliers.

*SourceGuide to Industrial Market Data.* London Business School Information Service. • $100. Covers: Directories, yearbooks, journals, statistical sources, market reports, trade and research associations, libraries and information services, and databases that provide data on 14 industrial market sectors in the U.K. Entries include: Source name, address, phone, description, evaluation.

*SourceGuide to Market Share and Business Ranking Tables.* London Business School Information Service. • $100. Covers: Key U.K., Pan European, and international business ranking and market share information published in 1989 or later and available in U.K. commercial libraries; includines newspapers, journals, directories, and databases. Entries include: Source name, address, phone, description.

*World Market Share Reporter.* Cengage Learning Inc. • $572 Individuals. Compilation of global market share data from periodical literature. Covers nearly 1,670 entries in 360 geographic worldwide locations of companies and products and services.

## ONLINE DATABASES

*Industry Insider.* Thomson Financial. • Contains full-text online industry research reports from more than 200 leading trade associations, covering 50 specific industries. Reports include extensive statistics and market research data. Inquire as to online cost and availability.

## STATISTICS SOURCES

*European Marketing Data and Statistics.* Cengage Learning Inc. • 2013. $475.00. Published by Euromonitor International. Presents essential marketing data, including demographics and consumer expenditure patterns for 44 European countries. Also available as eBook.

*International Marketing Data and Statistics.* Cengage Learning Inc. • 2013. $475.00. Published by Euromonitor International. Contains statistics on population, economic factors, energy, consumer expenditures, prices, and other items affecting marketing in 160 non-European countries of the world. Also available as eBook.

*Market Share Reporter (MSR).* Cengage Learning Inc. • $777 Individuals. 2013. $740.00. Published by Gale. Provides consumer market share data for leading companies. Also available as eBook.

*Sales and Marketing Management Survey of Buying Power.* Nielsen Business Media Inc. • Annual. $150.00.

*World Economic Factbook.* Cengage Learning Inc. • Annual. $475 Individuals E-book. Published by Euromonitor International. Presents key economic facts and figures for each of 204 countries worldwide, including details of chief industries, export-import trade, currency, political risk, household expenditures, and the economic situation in general.

*World Economic Prospects.* Cengage Learning Inc. • 2010. $650.00. 8th edition. Published by Euromonitor International. Ranks countries by specific economic characteristics, such as gross domestic product (GDP) per capita and short term growth prospects. Discusses the economic situation, prospects, and market potential of each of the countries.

*World Market Share Reporter.* Cengage Learning Inc. • $572 Individuals. Compilation of global market share data from periodical literature. Covers nearly 1,670 entries in 360 geographic worldwide locations of companies and products and services.

# MARKETING

*See also* CHAIN STORES; DISTRIBUTION; MARKET RESEARCH; MARKET STATISTICS; SALESMEN AND SALESMAN-SHIP

## ABSTRACTS AND INDEXES

*Business Periodicals Index Retrospective.* EBSCO Publishing Inc. • 11/year. Quarterly and annual cumulations.

*NTIS Alerts: Business & Economics.* U.S. Department of Commerce National Technical Information Service. • Biweekly. $130 per year. Covers consumer affairs, minority enterprises, marketing and economics, international commerce, banking, and finance.

*What's New in Advertising and Marketing.* Special Libraries Association - Advertising and Marketing Div. • Quarterly. Non-profit organizations, $20.00 per year; corporations, $30.00 per year. Lists and briefly describes a wide variety of free or inexpensive material relating to advertising, marketing, and media.

## CD-ROM DATABASES

*Business Abstracts with Full Text.* EBSCO Publishing Inc. • Includes full text articles from more than 460 business publications from 1982 to present. Indexing for nearly 880 publications.

## DIRECTORIES

*American and Common Market Club Directory.* American and Common Market Club. • Annual. Entries include: name, address, phone, fax.

*Dun's 50,000--Spain's Largest Companies.* Dun & Bradstreet Inc. • Annual. £438. Covers: 50,000 of the largest marketing companies in Spain. Entries include: Company name, address, operation information, key marketing information, key financial information.

*International Directory of Marketing Information Sources.* Euromonitor International Business Reference Div. • Irregular. $650. Covers: Marketing sources in major non-European industrialized countries. Entries include: Over 6,000 contacts, services, and publications.

*Internet Resources and Services for International Marketing and Advertising: A Global Guide.* Greenwood Electronic Media. • $75 Individuals hardcover. Covers: Over 2,000 Web sites with information pertaining to marketing and advertising in more than 150 countries.

*Marketing for Dummies.* John Wiley & Sons Inc. • $24.95 Individuals paperback. Publication includes: Marketing web sites, marketing consultants, trade associations, market researchers, and other experts. Entries include: Individual or company name, address, phone number, web site address (where applicable). Principal content of publication is articles on marketing strategies.

*The Marketing Managers Yearbook.* AP Information Services Ltd. • Annual. £229 Single issue. Covers: Approximately 10,500 private and public sector companies in the U.K., as well as 6,000 companies providing marketing related products and services, including advertising agencies, public relations firms, consultancies, research experts, hospitality industry companies, media outlets, software producers, professional associations, and other organizations. Database includes: Articles written by marketing professionals; statistical tables; list of forthcoming exhibitions. Entries include: For major companies--Name, address, phone, fax, names and titles of key personnel, number of employees, number of sales employees, line of business, brand/product names, parent company, Standard Industrial Classification (SIC) codes. For service companies--Name, address, phone, fax, year established, name and title of contact, names and titles of key person-

nel, fields of specialization, number of employees, associated firms, major clients, subsidiary and branch names and locations.

*World Directory of Marketing Information Sources.* Euromonitor International Business Reference Div. • Irregular. $590. Covers: 6,000 market research organizations, libraries and information services, information databases, business and marketing associations, business and marketing journals, statistical offices, chambers of commerce, embassies, and foreign trade departments in Europe. Entries include: Organization, agency, or association name, contact name and address, type of data offered, publications.

## E-BOOKS

*Advances in Electronic Marketing.* Cengage Learning Inc. • 2006. eBook. Published by Information Science Reference. Examines the challenges that organizations face today within three major themes: the global environment, the strategic/technological realm, and the buyer behavior of online consumers.

*Branding Your Business.* Cengage Learning Inc. • 2010. eBook. Details what a brand is and what it is not, how to conduct a 'DIY' brand audit and how to use marketing NLP and psychology principles to create a powerful brand.

*Business Applications and Computational Intelligence.* Cengage Learning Inc. • 2005. eBook. Addresses the need for a compact overview of the diversity of applications in a number of business disciplines, and consists of chapters written by leading international researchers. Chapters cover most fields of business, including: marketing, data mining, e-commerce, production and operations, finance, decision-making, and general management.

*Contemporary Research in E-Branding.* Cengage Learning Inc. • 2009. eBook. Published by Information Science Reference. Provides research on the emergent issue of the Internet as a central organizing platform for integrating marketing communications.

*Develop Your Marketing Skills.* Cengage Learning Inc. • 2010. eBook. Published by Kogan Page. S user-friendly guide appropriate for business people for whom implementation is the key issue. It outlines the key concepts and principles which govern the subject of marketing, such as product management, market research, communications, market coverage, creating a marketing plan and pricing perspectives. It also gives key insights into how theories and tools work in actual business scenarios, shows you how to improve customer satisfaction and highlights contemporary issues, such as sustainability.

*E-Marketing in Developed and Developing Countries: Emerging Practices.* Cengage Learning Inc. • 2013. eBook. Highlights the strategies and applications used in both developed and developing countries; proving to be beneficial for entrepreneurs, policy makers, researchers, and students wishing to expand their comprehensive knowledge in this field.

*How to Market Your Business.* • 2009. eBook. Published by Kogan Page. Covers market research, advertising, promotion, selling techniques, product launches, and use of the internet - everything you need to ensure your product reaches your market successfully.

*Starting a Successful Business.* Cengage Learning Inc. • 2009. eBook. Published by Kogan Page. Covers topics such as franchises, marketing, publicity, e-business, financial management, business law, recruitment, taxation, insurance, business planning and development.

## ENCYCLOPEDIAS AND DICTIONARIES

*Encyclopedia of American Business.* Cengage Learning Inc. • 2013. eBook. 2 volumes. 800 essays. A guide to the nuts and bolts of business jargon. Difficult ideas are explained in straightforward language to help non-specialists, students, and general readers understand the complex and sometimes confusing concepts and terms that are used in business. Five general areas of business are covered: accounting, banking, finance, marketing, and management.

*Encyclopedia of Business and Finance.* Cengage Learning Inc. • 2014. $485. 3rd edition. Two volumes. Published by Macmillan Reference USA. Contains articles on accounting, business administration, banking, finance, management information systems, and marketing.

*Encyclopedia of Global Brands.* Cengage Learning Inc. • 2013. $735. 2 volumes. Contains 270 entries, written in case-study style, that highlight details including how a product originated and was first marketed, how it developed commercially and how it fares today compared with its competitors and its own history. eBook available. Contact for pricing.

*Encyclopedia of Major Marketing Strategies.* Cengage Learning Inc. • $500 Individuals. Covers 100 major marketing strategies for some of the top global and emerging brands from 2011-2012.

## HANDBOOKS AND MANUALS

*Gale Business Insights Handbook Of.* Cengage Learning Inc. • $627 Individuals. Examines the questions "What is social media marketing" and "How can it be used in my business?".

*Promotional Marketing.* Entrepreneur Press. • Looseleaf. $59.50. A practical guide to sales promotion and marketing for small businesses. (Start-Up Business Guide No. E1111.).

## INTERNET DATABASES

*EBSCO Information Services.* EBSCO Publishing Inc. 10 Estes St., Ipswich, MA 01938-2106. Phone: 800-653-2726 or (978)356-6500; Fax: (978)356-6565; Email: information@ebscohost.com • URL: http://www.ebscohost.com • Fee-based Web site providing Internet access to a wide variety of databases, including business-related material. Full text is available for many periodical titles, with daily updates. Fees: Apply.

*InSite 2.* Intelligence Data/Thomson Financial. Phone: 800-654-0393 or (617)856-1890; Fax: (617)737-3182; Email: intelligence.data@tfn.com • URL: http://www.insite2.gale.com/ • Fee-based Web site consolidates information in a "Base Pack" consisting of Business InSite, Market InSite, and Company InSite. Optional databases are Consumer InSite, Health and Wellness InSite, Newsletter InSite, and Computer InSite. Includes fulltext content from more than 2,500 trade publications, journals, newsletters, newspapers, analyst reports, and other sources. Continuous updating. Formerly produced by The Gale Group.

*ProQuest.* ProQuest L.L.C. 789 E Eisenhower Pkwy., Ann Arbor, MI 48106-1346. Phone: 800-521-0600 or (734)761-4700; Fax: (734)662-4554; Email: info@proquest.com • URL: http://www.proquest.com • Fee-based Web site providing Internet access to more than 3,000 periodicals, newspapers, and other publications. Many items are available full-text, with daily updates. Includes extensive corporate and financial information. Fees: Apply.

## ONLINE DATABASES

*Wilson Business Abstracts Online.* H.W. Wilson Co. • Indexes and abstracts 600 major business periodicals, plus the *Wall Street Journal* and the business section of the *New York Times.* Indexing is from 1982, abstracting from 1990, with the two newspapers included from 1993. Updated weekly. Inquire as to online cost and availability. (*Business Periodicals Index* without abstracts is also available online.).

## OTHER SOURCES

*Marketing the Law Firm: Business Development Techniques.* ALM Media Properties LLC. • Looseleaf. $510.00. Updated as needed. Covers client surveys, brochures, direct mail, Web sites, seminars, newsletters, proposals, trade shows, and other marketing avenues for both large and small law firms. (Law Journal Press).

## PERIODICALS AND NEWSLETTERS

*Adweek Magazines' Technology Marketing.* Nielsen Business Media Inc. • Monthly. $55.00 per year. Edited for marketing executives in high technology industries. Covers both advertising and marketing. Formerly *MC Technology Marketing Intelligence.*

*The Business to Business Marketer.* Business Marketing Association. • 10/year Quarterly. $59/year for nonmembers. Magazine reporting on marketing and communications including database marketing, telemarketing, international marketing, direct marketing, and high-tech marketing.

*Database Marketer.* SIMBA Information Inc. • Monthly. $329.00 per year.

*Green Data Centers and Internet Business.* Information Gatekeepers Inc. • Monthly. $695 U.S. and Canada print. Provides marketing and technology information on new developments in the internet telephone industry on a worldwide basis.

*Incentive: Managing and Marketing Through Motivation.* Nielsen Business Media Inc. • Monthly. $59.00 per year.

*Interactive Marketing and P R News: News and Practical Advice on Using Interactive Advertising and Marketing to Sell Your Products.* Access Intelligence L.L.C. • Biweekly. $495.00 per year. Newsletter. Provides information and guidance on merchandising via CD-ROM ("multimedia catalogs"), the Internet, and interactive TV. Topics include "cybermoney," addresses for e-mail marketing, "virtual malls," and other interactive subjects. Formerly *Interactive Marketing News.*

*Internet Marketing Report: News and Advice to Help Companies Harness the Power of the Internet to Achieve Business Objectives.* American Future Systems Inc. • Semimonthly. $299.00 per year. Newsletter. Covers Internet marketing strategy, site traffic, success stories, technology, cost control, and other Web site advertising and marketing topics.

*Journal of Internet Commerce.* Taylor & Francis Ltd. • Quarterly. $115 Individuals print and online. Presents scholarly articles on marketing and other aspects of electronic commerce.

*The Licensing Letter (TLL).* EPM Communications Inc. • Description: Concerned with all aspects of licensed merchandising, "the business of associating someone's name, likeness or creation with someone else&'s product or service, for a consideration." Recurring features include statistics, research, events, mechanics, available properties, and identification of licensors, licensing agents, and licensees.

*Marketing Business.* Chartered Institute of Marketing. • Monthly. £35 for nonmembers and non-students in Europe. Provides information about the new technologies and marketing techniques that are being faced by today's marketers.

*Marketing the Law Firm.* ALM Media Properties LLC. • Monthly. $475. Focuses on actions that lawyers can take to find more clients and do more business. (A Law Journal Newsletter, formerly published by Leader Publications under the title *Marketing for Lawyers* ).

*Marketplace Magazine: Northeast Wisconsin's Business Magazine.* Marketplace Magazine. • Semimonthly. $48. Business magazine (tabloid).

*The Packer: The Business Newspaper of the Produce Industry.* Vance Publishing Corp. • Weekly. $99 Individuals. Newspaper on produce marketing.

*Potentials: Ideas and Products that Motivate.* Nielsen Business Media Inc. • Monthly. $59.00 per year. Covers incentives, premiums, awards, and gifts as related to promotional activities. Formerly *Potentials in Marketing.*

*PROMO: Promotion Marketing Worldwide.* Primedia Business Magazines and Media. • Monthly. $65.00 per year. Edited for companies and agencies that utilize couponing, point-of-purchase advertising, special events, games, contests, premiums, product samples, and other unique promotional items.

*Psychology and Marketing.* John Wiley and Sons, Inc., Journals Div. • Monthly. $2,179 Institutions. Spots the latest social, economic, and cultural trends that affect marketing decisions.

*Sales and Marketing Management.* Nielsen Business Media Inc. • Monthly. $48.00 per year.

*Schmalenbach Business Review.* Verlagsgruppe Handelsblatt GmbH. • Quarterly. $135 Institutions.

## RESEARCH CENTERS AND INSTITUTES

U.S. Food and Drug Administration - Center for Drug Evaluation and Research - Office of Prescription Drug Promotion. Bldg. 51, Rm. 3200, 10903 New Hampshire Ave., Silver Spring, MD 20993-0002. Phone: (301)796-1200; Fax: (301)847-8445; Email: thomas.abrams@fda.hhs.gov • URL: http://www.fda.gov/AboutFDA/CentersOffices/OfficeofMedicalProductsandTobacco/CDER/ucm090142.htm • Industry-wide marketing practices of the pharmaceutical industry and improvement of drug communications between FDA, health professionals, and the public. Specific research areas include prescription drugs, marketing practices, and health communications.

University of Wollongong - Centre for Social Marketing Research. Bldg. 19, Rm. 1034a, Faculty of Commerce, Northfields Ave., Wollongong, NSW 2522, Australia. Phone: 61 2 42215994; Fax: 61 2 42213257; Email: csmr@uow.edu.au • URL: http://www.uow.edu.au/commerce/smm/mark/academics/UOW010679.htm • Social marketing, including commercial marketing, nonprofit marketing, and issues of corporate social responsibility.

## TRADE/PROFESSIONAL ASSOCIATIONS

American Marketing Association. 311 S Wacker Dr., Ste. 5800, Chicago, IL 60606. Phone: 800-AMA-1150 or (312)542-9000; Fax: (312)542-9001 • URL: http://www.marketingpower.com • Serves as a professional society of marketing and market research executives, sales and promotion managers, advertising specialists, academics, and others interested in marketing. Fosters research; sponsors seminars, conferences, and student marketing clubs; provides educational placement service and doctoral consortium.

Canadian Agri-Marketing Association - Manitoba. 3336 Portage Ave., Ste. 509, Winnipeg, MB, Canada R3K 2H9. Phone: (204)782-6618 or (204)837-2853; Email: camamb@mymts.net • URL: http://www.cama.org/manitoba/ManitobaHome.aspx • Represents and supports individuals involved in agricultural marketing.

Canadian Agri-Marketing Association - Ontario. c/o Mary Thornly, Executive Director, 22 Guyers Dr., RR 3, Port Elgin, ON, Canada N0H 2C7. Phone: (519)389-6552; Email: camaont@bmts.com • URL: http://www.cama.org/Ontario/OntarioHome.aspx • Represents and supports individuals involved in agricultural marketing.

European Financial Management and Marketing Association. 8, rue Bayen, F-75017 Paris, France. Phone: 33 1 47425272; Fax: 33 1 47425676; Email: info@efma.com • URL: http://www.efma.com • European financial organizations in 17 countries. Goals are to: establish communication among individuals working with European financial organizations and supporting the concept of marketing; encourage innovation in the field; foster initiation of financial marketing research projects; represent the interests of European financial marketing. Sponsors seminars and professional training sessions. Maintains documentation center. Compiles data on credit card systems.

Information Technology Services Marketing Association. 91 Hartwell Ave., Lexington, MA 02421-3137. Phone: (781)862-8500; Fax: (781)674-1366; Email: info@itsma.com • URL: http://www.itsma.com • Supports marketing executives who market and sell technology-related services and solutions. Provides research, consulting and training to the world's leading technology, communications, and professional services providers. Facilitates peer sharing and networking opportunities among members.

Personal Injury Lawyers Marketing and Management Association. 607 Briarwood Dr., Ste. 4, Myrtle Beach, SC 29572. Phone: 800-497-1890 or (843)361-1700; Fax: (866)859-8126; Email: info@pilmma.org • URL: http://www.pilmma.org • Represents personal injury lawyers and disability attorneys. Provides members with the necessary tools, information and education to help grow and manage a successful contingency-based injury and disability law practice. Seeks to fulfill the marketing and management needs of members by granting access to sources of credible information and educational events.

# MARKETING, BANK

*See* BANK MARKETING

# MARKETING, CHEMICAL

*See* CHEMICAL MARKETING

# MARKETING, DIRECT

*See* DIRECT MARKETING

# MARKETING, INDUSTRIAL

*See* INDUSTRIAL MARKETING

# MARKETING, INTERNATIONAL

*See* INTERNATIONAL MARKETING

# MARKETING, MULTILEVEL

*See* MULTILEVEL MARKETING

# MARKING MACHINES

## DIRECTORIES

*Marking Products and Equipment Buyer's Guide.* Marking Devices Publishing Co. • Annual. Included in subscription to *Marking Industry Magazine.*

# MASONRY

## DIRECTORIES

*Masonry Buyer's Guide.* Mason Contractors Association of America. • Lists manufacturers or suppliers of products and services related to masonry construction.

## FINANCIAL RATIOS

*Annual Statement Studies.* Risk Management Association. • Annual. Compiled from over 280,000 financial statements.

*Annual Statement Studies: Industry Default Probabilities and Cash Flow Measures.* Risk Management Association. • Annual. $405 Nonmembers. Serves as a companion volume to the original *Annual Statement Studies.* Gives probability of default estimates on a percentage scale for more than 450 industries. Includes changes in position year-by-year for eight financial statement line items and provides percentage measures of cash flow.

## PERIODICALS AND NEWSLETTERS

*Masonry Design West.* Pleasanton Publishing Co. • Bimonthly. Price on application.

## TRADE/PROFESSIONAL ASSOCIATIONS

Mason Contractors Association of America. 1481 Merchant Dr., Algonquin, IL 60102. Phone: 800-536-2225 or (224)678-9709; Fax: (224)678-9714 • URL: http://www.masoncontractors.org • Masonry construction firms. Conducts specialized education and research programs. Compiles statistics.

National Concrete Masonry Association. 13750 Sunrise Valley Dr., Herndon, VA 20171. Phone: (703)713-1900; Fax: (703)713-1910; Email: info@ncma.org • URL: http://www.ncma.org • Manufacturers of concrete masonry units (concrete blocks), segmental retaining wall units and paving block; associate members are machinery, cement and aggregate manufacturers. Conducts testing and research on masonry units and masonry assemblies. Compiles statistics.

# MASS MEDIA

*See also* ADVERTISING MEDIA; MEDIA RESEARCH

## ABSTRACTS AND INDEXES

*Business Periodicals Index Retrospective.* EBSCO Publishing Inc. • 11/year. Quarterly and annual cumulations.

*Communication Abstracts: An International Information Service.* Pine Forge Press. • Bimonthly. Institutions, $1,150.00 per year. Provides broad coverage of the literature of communications, including broadcasting and advertising.

*Readers' Guide to Periodical Literature.* EBSCO Publishing Inc. • Provides indexing for over 400 periodicals dating back to 1983.

*What's New in Advertising and Marketing.* Special Libraries Association - Advertising and Marketing Div. • Quarterly. Non-profit organizations, $20.00 per year; corporations, $30.00 per year. Lists and briefly describes a wide variety of free or inexpensive material relating to advertising, marketing, and media.

## BIBLIOGRAPHIES

*Communication Booknotes Quarterly : Recent Titles in Telecommunications, Informaation, and Media.* Lawrence Erlbaum Associates Inc. • Quarterly. Contains descriptive reviews of new publications.

## CD-ROM DATABASES

*ABI/INFORM.* ProQuest L.L.C. • Monthly. Provides CD-ROM indexing and abstracting of worldwide business literature. Archival discs are available from 1971. Formerly *ABI/INFORM OnDisc.*

*Applied Science & Business Periodicals Retrospective.* EBSCO Publishing Inc. • Includes citations for more than 3 million articles detailing events, issues, and trends in business and industry.

*Authority Computer and Telecommunications Law Library.* Matthew Bender and Company Inc. • Quarterly. Price on request. Full text CD-ROM

provides cases, analysis, sample agreements, and other information relating to computer law, telecommunications regulation (cable, broadcasting, satellite, Internet), international computer law, and computer contracts.

*PAIS International.* ProQuest L.L.C. • Monthly. $1,995.00 per year. Contains over 650,000 citations to the literature of contemporary social, political, and economic issues.

*Readers' Guide to Periodical Literature.* EBSCO Publishing Inc. • Provides indexing for over 400 periodicals dating back to 1983.

## DIRECTORIES

*Advertising & Press Annual in Africa.* International Publications Service. • Annual. Covers: African newspapers, magazines, radio and television stations, annuals, poster and transportation advertising and exhibits and shows; leading advertisers and professionals in the field in Africa; associations involved in a variety of fields of advertising and publicity in Africa.

*Burrelle's Media Directory: Broadcast Media.* BurrelleLuce. • Annual. $550.00. Approximately 48,000 print and electronic media in North America. Provides detailed descriptions, including programming and key personnel.

*Burrelle's Media Directory: Magazines and Newsletters.* BurrellesLuce. • Annual. $550.00. Provides detailed descriptions of more than 13,500 magazines and newsletters published in the U.S., Canada, and Mexico. Categories are professional, consumer, trade, and college. Semiannual *Updates.* Includes CD-ROM.

*Burrelle's Media Directory: Newspapers and Related Media.* BurrellesLuce. • Annual. $550.00. *Daily Newspapers* volume lists more than 2,200 daily publications in the U. S., Canada, and Mexico. *Non-Daily Newspapers* volume lists more than 10,400 items published no more than three times a week. Provides detailed descriptions, including key personnel.

*Burrelle's New Jersey Media Directory.* BurrellesLuce. • Annual. $60 plus $4.00 shipping. Covers: Over 1,200 New Jersey periodicals, newspapers, college publications, radio and television stations, and cable television systems. Also includes New York City and Philadelphia daily newspapers. Entries include: For publications-- Title, publisher name, address, phone, names and titles of key personnel, frequency, circulation, geographical area covered, advertising and editorial deadlines. For others--Call letters and/or company name and address, names and titles of key personnel, markets covered.

*Media Rates & Data.* Media-Daten AG. • Biennial. Covers: National and international newspapers, journals, trade press and local Swiss newsletters, radio and television. Entries include: Publications name, address, phone, rates, schedules.

*Mississippi News Media Directory.* News Media Directories. • Annual. $45 Individuals. Covers: Newspapers, periodicals, radio and television broadcasting stations, and press services operating in Mississippi. Entries include: Publisher or company name, address, phone, names and titles of key personnel, publication title, call letters, hours of operation, and frequency.

*VNU Business Media.* ADWEEK Media. • Annual. $100.00. Presents cost, circulation, and audience statistics for various mass media segments, including television, radio, magazines, newspapers, telephone yellow pages, and cinema.

*Washington: A Comprehensive Directory of the Key Institutions and Leaders in th e National Capitol Area.* Columbia Books Inc. • Annual. $149.00. Provides information on about 5,000 Washington, DC key businesses, government offices, non-profit organizations, and cultural institutions, with the

---

**For publishers' addresses, refer to SOURCES CITED section at the back of the book.**

names of about 25,000 principal executives. Includes Washington media, law offices, foundations, labor unions, international organizations, clubs, etc.

## ENCYCLOPEDIAS AND DICTIONARIES

*Encyclopedia of Communication and Information.* Cengage Learning Inc. • 2003. eBook. Published by Macmillan Reference USA. Provides an overview of universal modes of communication. Inquire about price and availability.

*World Press Encyclopedia.* Cengage Learning Inc. • 2003. $572.00. Second edition. Two volumes. Comprehensive essays cover the background and economic framework of newspapers and other news media in about 200 countries. Covers relevant legal issues, censorship, government relations, education in journalism, status of news agencies, cable, Internet, and other media topics. eBook also available.

## INTERNET DATABASES

*Pew Research Center for the People and the Press.* Pew Charitable Trusts. Phone: (202)293-3126; Fax: (202)293-2569; Email: mailprc@people-press.org • URL: http://www.people-press.org • Free Web site includes public opinion poll "Reports by Topic." Five broad subject areas cover business, social issues, foreign policy, news media, and politics. Searching is offered within each of these broad areas, and there are links to other major sources of public opinion poll results ("FYI Other Polls").

*Wired News.* Lycos Inc. 400-2 Totten Pond Rd., Waltham, MA 02451-2053. Phone: (781)370-2700 or (415)276-8400; Fax: (781)370-2600 or (415)276-8500; Email: press@lycos.com • URL: http://www.lycos.com • Provides summaries and full-text of "Top Stories" relating to the Internet, computers, multimedia, telecommunications, and the electronic information industry in general. These news stories are placed in the broad categories of Politics, Business, Culture, and Technology. Affiliated with *Wired* magazine. Fees: Free.

## ONLINE DATABASES

*Wilson Business Abstracts Online.* H.W. Wilson Co. • Indexes and abstracts 600 major business periodicals, plus the *Wall Street Journal* and the business section of the *New York Times.* Indexing is from 1982, abstracting from 1990, with the two newspapers included from 1993. Updated weekly. Inquire as to online cost and availability. (*Business Periodicals Index* without abstracts is also available online.).

## PERIODICALS AND NEWSLETTERS

*Brandweek: The Newsweekly of Marketing Communications.* Nielsen Business Media Inc. • 46 times a year. $149.00 per year. Includes articles and case studies on mass marketing and mass media. Formerly *Adweek's Marketing Week.*

*Media Industry Newsletter.* Access Intelligence L.L.C. • Description: Covers the media industry, including advertising, marketing, publishing, radio, and television. Recurring features include weekly box scores of advertising pages in major magazines, salaries of top executives, earnings reports, and news of people in the industry.

*Mediaweek: The News Magazine of the Media.* Nielsen Business Media Inc. • Published for advertising media buyers and managers.

*NewsInc.: The Business of the Newspaper Business.* The Cole Group. • Biweekly. $425 Individuals. Reports on trends in mass media, especially with regard to newspaper publishing. Articles on cable TV and other competitive media are included.

## RESEARCH CENTERS AND INSTITUTES

Marquette University - Center for Mass Media Research. 1250 W Wisconsin Ave., Milwaukee, WI 53233. Phone: (414)288-6787 or (414)288-3453; Fax: (414)288-3099; Email: robert.griffin@

marquette.edu • URL: http://news.marquette.edu/experts/center-for-mass-media-research • Conducts social scientific research into the roles, processes, uses, and effects of mass communication among individuals and in society. Applies social science communication theory and research to the investigation and solution of social problems, especially those involving environment, energy, health risks, science, and technology.

University of Southern California - Integrated Media Systems Center. 306 Powell Hall of Engineering, 3737 Watt Way, Los Angeles, CA 90089-0272. Phone: (213)740-8945; Fax: (213)740-2539; Email: shahabi@usc.edu • URL: http://imsc.usc.edu • Media areas for research include education, mass communication, and entertainment.

University of Wisconsin—Madison - Mass Communications Research Center. 5115 Vilas Hall, 821 University Ave., Madison, WI 53706. Phone: (608)262-3690 or (608)263-3381; Fax: (608)262-1361; Email: dshah@wisc.edu • URL: http://mcrc.journalism.wisc.edu • Mass communication, including mass media institutions, processes and effects generally and in a number of specific contexts. Current research specializations include political communication, communication campaigns, health communication, uses and effects of new communication technologies, cognitive and attention processes, advertising and persuasion, history of mass communication, framing, minorities, international and intercultural communication, community, geographic contexts, risk and science communication, and methodological studies.

Vanderbilt University - First Amendment Center. 1207 18th Ave. S, Nashville, TN 37212. Phone: (615)727-1600; Fax: (615)727-1319; Email: info@fac.org • URL: http://www.firstamendmentcenter.org • Research fields include mass communication and technological change, including mass media and the public trust.

## TRADE/PROFESSIONAL ASSOCIATIONS

Association for Education in Journalism and Mass Communication. 234 Outlet Pointe Blvd., Ste. A, Columbia, SC 29210-5667. Phone: (803)798-0271; Fax: (803)772-3509; Email: aejmchq@aol.com • URL: http://www.aejmc.org • Professional organization of college and university journalism and communication teachers. Works to improve methods and standards of teaching and stimulate research. Compiles statistics on enrollments and current developments in journalism education. Maintains a listing of journalism and communication teaching positions available and teaching positions wanted, revised bimonthly.

# MATERIALS

## ABSTRACTS AND INDEXES

*Engineered Materials Abstracts.* Cambridge Information Group. • Monthly. $995.00 per year. Provides citations to the technical and engineering literature of plastic, ceramic, and composite materials.

*Key Abstracts: Advanced Materials.* Institution of Engineering and Technology. • $790 per year. Provides international coverage of journal and proceedings literature, including publications on ceramics and composite materials.

*NTIS Alerts: Manufacturing Technology.* U.S. Department of Commerce National Technical Information Service. • Biweekly. $130 per year. Covers computer-aided design and manufacturing (CAD/CAM), engineering materials, quality control, machine tools, robots, lasers, productivity, and related subjects.

*NTIS Alerts: Materials Sciences.* U.S. Department of Commerce National Technical Information Service. • Biweekly. $130 per year. Covers ceram-

ics, glass, coatings, composite materials, alloys, plastics, wood, paper, adhesives, fibers, lubricants, and related subjects.

## ALMANACS AND YEARBOOKS

*Progress in Materials Science: An International Review Journal.* Elsevier. • $2,793 Individuals Print. Publishes authoritative reviews of recent advances in the science of materials and their exploitation in engineering.

## BIBLIOGRAPHIES

*ASTM List of Publications.* ASTM International. • Annual.

## CD-ROM DATABASES

*METADEX Materials Collection: Metals-Polymers-Ceramics.* Cambridge Scientific Abstracts L.P. • Quarterly. Provides CD-ROM citations to the worldwide literature of materials science and metallurgy. Corresponds to *Metals Abstracts, Alloys Index, Steels Alert, Nonferrous Alert, Polymers/Ceramics/Composites Alert,* and *Engineered Materials Abstracts*. (Formerly produced by ASM International.).

*Plastics Digest on CD-ROM.* IHS Standards Store. • Semiannual. CD-ROM index version (technical data only), $695.00 per year or $495.00 per disc. CD-ROM image version (technical data and specification sheet images), $1,295.00 per year or $995.00 per disc. Provides detailed information on the properties of 20,000 types of plastic, both current and obsolete. Time period is 1977 to date. Includes trade names and supplier names and addresses.

## DIRECTORIES

*Materials Research Centres: A World Directory of Organizations and Programmes in Materials Science.* Specialist Journals. • Biennial. $445.00. Profiles of research centers in 75 countries. Materials include plastics, metals, fibers, etc.

## ONLINE DATABASES

*Engineered Materials Abstracts (online).* Cambridge Scientific Abstracts L.P. • Provides online citations to the technical and engineering literature of plastic, ceramic, and composite materials. Time period is 1986 to date, with monthly updates. (Formerly produced by ASM International.) Inquire as to online cost and availability.

## PERIODICALS AND NEWSLETTERS

*High-Tech Materials Alert: Advanced Materials: Their Uses and Manufacture.* Technical Insights. • Monthly. Institutions, $695.00 per year. Newsletter on technical developments relating to high-performance materials, including metals and ceramics. Includes market forecasts.

*International Materials Review.* ASM International. • $1,801 Nonmembers online. Bimonthly. Provides technical and research coverage of metals, alloys, and advanced materials. Formerly *International Metals Review.*

*Journal of Advanced Materials.* Society for the Advancement of Material and Process Engineering. • Quarterly. Individuals, $60.00 per year; institutions, $150.00 per year. Contains technical and research articles. Formerly *SAMPE Quarterly.*

*Materials Evaluation.* American Society for Nondestructive Testing. • Monthly. $135 Individuals. Provides up-to-date information about NDT applications and technical articles addressing nondestructive testing applications.

*Materials Performance: Articles on Corrosion Science and Engineering Solutions for Corrosion Problems.* National Association of Corrosion Engineers. NACE International: The Corrosion Society. • Monthly. $115 Nonmembers 1-year subscription. Covers the protection and performance of materials in corrosive environments. Includes information on new materials and industrial coatings.

*Metallurgical and Materials Transactions A: Physical Metallurgy and Materials Science.* ASM International. • Monthly. $3,640 Members 1-year subscription. Formerly *Metallurgical Transactions A- Physical Metallurgy and Materials Science.* Publishes contributions on all aspects of physical metallurgy and materials science, with a special emphasis on relationships among the processing, structure, and properties of materials.

*SAMPE Journal.* Society for the Advancement of Material and Process Engineering. • Bimonthly. $125 Individuals print and online. Magazine covering materials and process engineering.

## RESEARCH CENTERS AND INSTITUTES

Brown University - Center for Advanced Materials Research. Box M, Providence, RI 02912. Phone: (401)863-2859; Fax: (401)863-6701; Email: nitin_padture@brown.edu • URL: http://brown.edu/research/institute-molecular-nanoscale-innovation/research/center-advanced-materials-research • Fundamental and applied research in study of technologically important international materials issues of the 21st century embracing materials science, including studies of electronic and mechanical properties of semiconductor microstructures, fundamentals of plasticity and fracture, microscopic basis of glass formation, and physics and engineering of conductor/nonconductor interfaces. Collaborate with investigators from several universities.

Massachusetts Institute of Technology - Materials Processing Center. 77 Massachusetts Ave., Cambridge, MA 02139-4301. Phone: (617)253-5179; Fax: (617)258-6900; Email: cthomp@mit.edu • URL: http://mpc-web.mit.edu • Conducts processing, engineering, and economic research in ferrous and nonferrous metals, ceramics, polymers, photonic materials, superconductors, welding, composite materials, and other materials.

## TRADE/PROFESSIONAL ASSOCIATIONS

ASM International. 9639 Kinsman Rd., Materials Park, OH 44073-0002. Phone: 800-336-5152 or (440)338-5151; Email: memberservicecenter@asminternational.org • URL: http://www.asminternational.org • Metallurgists, materials engineers, executives in materials producing and consuming industries; teachers and students. Disseminates technical information about the manufacture, use, and treatment of engineered materials. Offers in-plant, home study, and intensive courses through Materials Engineering Institute.

Materials Research Society. 506 Keystone Dr., Warrendale, PA 15086-7573. Phone: (724)779-3003 or (724)779-3004; Fax: (724)779-8313; Email: info@mrs.org • URL: http://www.mrs.org • Represents the interests of materials researchers from academia, industry, and government that promotes communication for the advancement of interdisciplinary materials research to improve the quality of life. Fosters interaction among researchers working on different classes of inorganic and organic materials and to promote interdisciplinary basic research on materials. Provides forum for industry, government, and university cooperation; conducts technical conferences, tutorial lectures. Maintains speakers' bureau.

The Minerals, Metals, and Materials Society. 184 Thorn Hill Rd., Warrendale, PA 15086-7514. Phone: 800-759-4867 or (724)776-9000; Fax: (724)776-3770; Email: webmaster@tms.org • URL: http://www.tms.org/TMSHome.aspx • Members are metallurgists, metallurgical engineers, and materials scientists. Divisions include Light Metals and Electronic, Magnetic, and Photonic Materials. Formerly The Metallurigical Society.

National Research Council - Division on Engineering and Physical Sciences - National Materials and Manufacturing Board. The National Academies, 500 5th St. NW, Washington, DC 20001-2736. Phone: (202)334-3505; Fax: (202)334-3575; Email: nmmb@nas.edu • URL: http://sites.nationalacademies.org/DEPS/NMMB/index.htm • Represents members of the board and its committees and panels appointed by the chairman of the National Research Council; industry, universities, research institutes, and government. Promotes the advancement of materials science and engineering in the national interest. Conducts studies on materials problem, potential approaches, and policy issues.

# MATERIALS, BUILDING

*See* BUILDING MATERIALS INDUSTRY

# MATERIALS, COMPOSITE

*See* COMPOSITE MATERIALS

# MATERIALS HANDLING

## ABSTRACTS AND INDEXES

*Key Abstracts: Factory Automation.* Institution of Engineering and Technology. • Monthly. $1,138. Provides international coverage of journal and proceedings literature, including publications on CAD/CAM, materials handling, robotics, and factory management.

## CD-ROM DATABASES

*OECD Statistical Compendium.* Organization for Economic Cooperation and Development. • Semiannual. $1,905.00 per year for 1 to 10 users. CD-ROM contains more than 730,000 monthly, quarterly, and annual time series for OECD countries, 1960 to date. Includes fully searchable data on agriculture, food, economic indicators, national accounts, employment, energy, finance, industry, technology, and foreign trade. Results can be displayed in various forms.

## DIRECTORIES

*Directory of African Importers of Material Handling Equipment & Supplies.* EXIM Infotek Private Ltd. • $250 Individuals. Covers: 60 African importers of conveyors, cranes and hoists, elevators and lifts, forklifts, lifting machinery and equipment, liquid handling equipment, loading and unloading equipment, material handling systems for garment industries, and monorail materials handling equipment. Entries include: Company name, postal address, telephone, fax, e-mail, website, contact person, designation, and product details.

*Directory of American Manufacturers & Exporters of Material Handling Equipment.* EXIM Infotek Private Ltd. • $850 Individuals. Covers: 480 American manufacturers and exporters of airport baggage handling equipment, bag openers, bulk bag loading and unloading equipment, bulk handling systems, bulk materials handling equipment, carts, chain and cable conveyors, conveyor chains, conveyor bands, conveyor systems, cranes, endless conveyor belts, forklift trucks, hand trucks, hoists, hydraulic cranes, lift trucks, liquid handling products, lumber materials handling equipment, material handling booms, mining and construction equipment, non-powered materials handling equipment, pallet racks, platforms, pneumatic conveying systems, restraint equipment, turntables, weigh belt feeders, winches, and hoists.

*Directory of Asian Importers of Material Handling Equipment & Supplies.* EXIM Infotek Private Ltd. • Covers: 300 Asian importers of aerial lifts and platforms, backhoe loaders, chain hoist, conveying machine, conveyor systems, crane equipment, hoists, crawler crane, electric hoist, elevator lifts, elevators, escalators, forklift parts and accessories, hand pallet truck, hoisting blocks chipping machine and spares, liebherr tower cranes, liquid handling equipment, loaders, loading and unloading equipment, materials handling containers and equipment materials handling and lifting system, mobile cranes, monorail materials handling equipment, pallet truck, pulley, roller chain, used conveyor belts, used excavators, used forklift, wheel loaders, and winch. Entries include: Company name, postal address, telephone, fax, e-mail, website, contact person, designation, and product details.

*Directory of Australia & New Zealand Importers of Material Handling Equipment.* EXIM Infotek Private Ltd. • $150 Individuals. Covers: 35 Australian and New Zealand importers of chain hoist, chip conveyer, conveyor products, conveyor systems, crane equipment, cranes and hoists, electric hoist, elevators lifts, escalators, forklifts, forklift parts and accessories, forklift trucks, freight and shipping containers, grain handling equipment, hand trolleys, industrial brake equipment, lifting equipment, liquid handling equipment, loaders, loading and unloading equipment, materials handling equipment and hardware, monorail materials handling equipment, pulley, and winches. Entries include: Company name, postal address, telephone, fax, e-mail, website, contact person, designation, and product details.

*Directory of Belgium Importers of Materials Handling Equipment.* EXIM Infotek Private Ltd. • $150 Individuals. Covers: 35 companies in Belgium that import conveyors, cranes and hoisting equipment, fork lifts, liquid handling equipment, loading and unloading equipment, materials handling equipment and parts, winches, and pulleys. Entries include: Company name, postal address, telephone, fax, e-mail, website, contact person, designation, and product details.

*Directory of British Importers of Material Handling Equipment.* EXIM Infotek Private Ltd. • $200 Individuals. Covers: 45 British importers of conveyors, cranes and hoisting equipment, elevators lifts, forklifts, liquid handling equipment, loading and unloading equipment, materials handling equipment and parts, monorail materials handling equipment, winches, and pulleys. Entries include: Company name, postal address, telephone, fax, e-mail, website, contact person, designation, and product details.

*Directory of Chinese Manufacturers & Exporters of Material Handling Equipment.* EXIM Infotek Private Ltd. • $150 Individuals. Covers: 40 Chinese manufacturers and exporters of conveyors, cranes, electric hoist, elevators, escalators, forklift trucks, hand trucks, handling tools, hoisting machine, lifting equipment, lifts, materials handling equipment, pallets, containers, and pulleys. Entries include: Company name, postal address, telephone, fax, e-mail, website, contact person, designation, and product details.

*Directory of European Importers of Material Handling Equipment & Supplies.* EXIM Infotek Private Ltd. • Covers: 450 European importers of conveyors, cranes and hoisting equipment, elevating work platforms, elevators lifts, elevators, lifts and escalators, forklifts, handling equipment, lifting and hoisting tools, lifting equipment, liquid handling equipment, loading and unloading equipment, material handling systems for garment industries, monorail materials handling equipment, winches, and pulleys. Entries include: Company name, postal address, telephone, fax, e-mail, website, contact person, designation, and product details.

*Directory of French Importers of Material Handling Equipment.* EXIM Infotek Private Ltd. • $250 Individuals. Covers: 70 French importers of conveyors, cranes and hoisting equipment, elevators lifts, forklifts, liquid handling equipment, loading and unloading equipment, materials handling equipment and parts, winches, and pulleys. Entries include: Company name, postal address, telephone, fax, e-mail, website, contact person, designation, and product details.

*Directory of Indian Importers of Material Handling Equipment & Supplies.* EXIM Infotek Private Ltd. • $150 Individuals. Covers: 20 Indian importers of loading equipment, unloading equipment, and materials handling equipment. Entries include: Company name, postal address, telephone, fax, e-mail, website, contact person, designation, and product details.

*Directory of Japanese Importers of Material Handling Equipment.* EXIM Infotek Private Ltd. • $150 Individuals. Covers: 40 Japanese importers of conveying machine, conveyors, cranes and hoists, elevators lifts, elevators, lifts and escalators, forklifts, loading and unloading equipment, materials handling equipment and parts. Entries include: Company name, postal address, telephone, fax, e-mail, website, contact person, designation, and product details.

*Directory of Japanese Manufacturers & Exporters of Material Handling Equipment.* EXIM Infotek Private Ltd. • $250 Individuals. Covers: 80 Japanese manufacturers and exporters of conveying machines, conveyors, cranes, escalators, forklifts, hand trolleys, hand trucks, materials handling equipment, used forklift trucks, and warehousing equipment. Entries include: Company name, postal address, telephone, fax, e-mail, website, contact person, designation, and product details.

*Directory of Middle East Importers of Material Handling Equipment & Supplies.* EXIM Infotek Private Ltd. • Covers: 320 Middle East importers of conveying equipment and supplies, conveyors, crane overload indicators, cranes and hoists, elevators and lifts, escalators, forklifts, electric and hydraulic lifts, liquid handling equipment, loading and unloading equipment, materials handling systems for garment industries, monorail materials handling equipment, road construction handling equipment, winches, and pulleys. Entries include: Company name, postal address, telephone, fax, e-mail, website, contact person, designation, and product details.

*Directory of North American Importers of Material Handling Equipment & Supplies.* EXIM Infotek Private Ltd. • Covers: 120 North American importers of cargo handling equipment, conveyors, cranes and hoists, elevators and lifts, forklift parts, liquid handling equipment and supplies, loading and unloading equipment, materials handling equipment and parts, and winches. Entries include: Company name, postal address, telephone, fax, e-mail, website, contact person, designation, and product details.

*Directory of SAARC Importers of Material Handling Equipment.* EXIM Infotek Private Ltd. • Covers: 45 companies in member countries of the South Asian Association for Regional Cooperation (SAARC) that import backhoe loaders, cargo hooks, cement factory chains, chain for conveyors, container handling equipment, conveyors, crane lorries, cranes and hoists, crawler crane, electric chain block, elevators lifts, escalators, forklift parts and accessories, hand pallet truck, hoisting blocks chipping machine and spares, electrical and manual hoists, hydraulic excavators, loaders, loading and unloading equipment, materials handling containers and equipment, material handling systems, material lifting system, mobile cranes, mop carts, pallet truck, pulley, roller and accumulating conveyors, rough terrain crane, and wheel loaders. Entries include: Company name, postal address, telephone, fax, e-mail, website, contact person, designation, and product details.

*Directory of South American Importers of Material Handling Equipment & Supplies.* EXIM Infotek Private Ltd. • Covers: 140 South American import-

ers of conveyors, cranes and hoists, elevator parts, elevators and lifts, escalators, forklifts, loading and unloading equipment, materials handling equipment and parts, monorail material handling equipment, winches, and pulleys. Entries include: Company name, postal address, telephone, fax, e-mail, website, contact person, designation, and product details.

*Directory of South Korean Manufacturers & Exporters of Material Handling Equipment.* EXIM Infotek Private Ltd. • $400 Individuals. Covers: 170 South Korean manufacturers and exporters of automated handling and storage equipment, barrows, trolleys, carts, conveyors and elevators, cranes, hoists, winches, forklift trucks, handling equipment parts and accessories, ice crushers, lifts, mobile cranes, overhead conveyors, pallets and containers, pneumatic handling equipment, pulleys, and cable wheels. Entries include: Company name, postal address, telephone, fax, e-mail, website, contact person, designation, and product details.

*Directory of Taiwanese Manufacturers & Exporters of Material Handling Equipment.* EXIM Infotek Private Ltd. • $750 Individuals. Covers: 400 Taiwanese manufacturers and exporters of automated handling storage equipment, barrows, trolleys, carts, conveyors, elevators, cranes, hoists, winches, forklift trucks, handling equipment parts and accessories, hydraulic dump hoists, lifts, elevators, mobile cranes, overhead conveyors, pallets and containers, pneumatic handling equipment, pulleys, and cable wheels. Entries include: Company name, postal address, telephone, fax, e-mail, website, contact person, designation, and product details.

*Manufacturing Systems: Buyers Guide.* Reed Elsevier Group plc Reed Business Information. • Annual. Price on application. Contains information on companies manufacturing or supplying materials handling systems, CAD/CAM systems, specialized software for manufacturing, programmable controllers, machine vision systems, and automatic identification systems.

*Modern Materials Handling Casebook Directory.* Reed Elsevier Group plc Reed Business Information. • Annual. Lists about 2,300 manufacturers of equipment and supplies in the materials handling industry. Supplement to *Modern Materials Handling.*

## INTERNET DATABASES

*Business 2.0 Web Guide to the Best Business Links.* Business 2.0 Media Inc. Phone: (415)293-4800; Email: support@business2.com • URL: http://www.business2.com/webguide • Web site presents an extensive, searchable directory of links to "the best, most informative, and authoritative web pages." Twenty main categories cover business, finance, career, company information, people, and technology topics, with thousands of subtopics, all linking to Web sites recommended by experienced business researchers. Fees: Free.

*Fedstats.* Federal Interagency Council on Statistical Policy. Phone: (202)395-7254 • URL: http://www.fedstats.gov • Web site features an efficient search facility for full-text statistics produced by more than 100 federal agencies, including the Census Bureau, the Bureau of Economic Analysis, and the Bureau of Labor Statistics. Boolean searches can be made within one agency or for all agencies combined. Links are offered to international statistical bureaus, including the UN, IMF, OECD, UNESCO, Eurostat, and 20 individual countries. Fees: Free.

*FreeLunch.com.* Economy.com, Inc. Phone: (610)696-8700; Fax: (610)696-1678 • URL: http://www.freelunch.com • Web site provides free access to more than 200 million economic and financial data series, covering industry, demographics, labor markets, prices, retail sales, government spending, trade, interest rates, housing starts, the stock market, etc. Data is available in either chart or table form.

Searching is offered. Free, but registration required. Economy.com, Inc. also offers fee-based economic analysis at *The Dismal Scientist* site (www.dismal.com).

## PERIODICALS AND NEWSLETTERS

*Material Handling Management: Educating Industry on Product Handling, Flow Strategies, and Automation Technology.* Penton Media Inc. • 13 times a year. Free to qualified personnel; others, $50.00 per year. Formerly *Material Handling Engineering.*

*Modern Materials Handling.* Reed Elsevier Group plc Reed Business Information. • 14 times a year. $99.90 per year. For managers and engineers who buy or specify equipment used to move, store, control and protect products throughout the manufacturing and warehousing cycles. Includes *Casebook Directory* and *Planning Guide.* Also includes *ADC News and Solutions.*

## STATISTICS SOURCES

*Survey of Current Business.* U. S. Government Printing Office. • Published by Bureau of Economic Analysis, U. S. Department of Commerce. Presents a wide variety of business and economic data.

## TRADE/PROFESSIONAL ASSOCIATIONS

Material Handling Equipment Distributors Association. 201 US Hwy. 45, Vernon Hills, IL 60061-2398. Phone: (847)680-3500; Fax: (847)362-6989; Email: connect@mheda.org • URL: http://www.mheda.org • Distributors and manufacturers of material handling equipment. Aims to improve the proficiency of independent material handling distributors.

Material Handling Industry. 8720 Red Oak Blvd., Ste. 201, Charlotte, NC 28217-3996. Phone: 800-345-1815 or (704)676-1190; Fax: (704)676-1199; Email: jnofsinger@mhia.org • URL: http://www.mhia.org • Formerly Material Handling Industry.

Materials Handling Industry of America. 8720 Red Oak Blvd., Ste. 201, Charlotte, NC 28217-3996. Phone: (704)676-1190; Fax: (704)676-1199 • URL: http://www.mhi.org • Formerly Materials Handling and Management Society.

# MATERIALS, HAZARDOUS

*See HAZARDOUS MATERIALS*

# MATHEMATICAL STATISTICS

*See STATISTICAL METHODS*

# MATHEMATICS, BUSINESS

*See BUSINESS MATHEMATICS*

# MATURE CONSUMER MARKET

## ABSTRACTS AND INDEXES

*Business Periodicals Index Retrospective.* EBSCO Publishing Inc. • 11/year. Quarterly and annual cumulations.

*Readers' Guide to Periodical Literature.* EBSCO Publishing Inc. • Provides indexing for over 400 periodicals dating back to 1983.

## CD-ROM DATABASES

*ABI/INFORM.* ProQuest L.L.C. • Monthly. Provides CD-ROM indexing and abstracting of worldwide business literature. Archival discs are available from 1971. Formerly *ABI/INFORM OnDisc.*

*Applied Science & Business Periodicals Retrospective.* EBSCO Publishing Inc. • Includes citations for more than 3 million articles detailing events, issues, and trends in business and industry.

*Readers' Guide to Periodical Literature.* EBSCO Publishing Inc. • Provides indexing for over 400 periodicals dating back to 1983.

## ENCYCLOPEDIAS AND DICTIONARIES

*Encyclopedia of Aging.* David J. Ekerdt, editor. Cengage Learning Inc. • $770. Includes articles relating to the financial aspects of aging, such as housing, long-term care insurance, pensions, social security, individual retirement accounts, savings, and retirement planning. eBook also available. Inquire for pricing.

## ONLINE DATABASES

*Ageline.* AARP. • Provides indexing and abstracting of the literature of social gerontology, including consumer aspects, financial planning, employment, housing, health care services, mental health, social security, and retirement. Time period is 1978 to date. Inquire as to online cost and availability.

*Wilson Business Abstracts Online.* H.W. Wilson Co. • Indexes and abstracts 600 major business periodicals, plus the *Wall Street Journal* and the business section of the *New York Times*. Indexing is from 1982, abstracting from 1990, with the two newspapers included from 1993. Updated weekly. Inquire as to online cost and availability. (*Business Periodicals Index* without abstracts is also available online.).

## PERIODICALS AND NEWSLETTERS

*Selling to Seniors.* Community Development Services, Inc. CD Publications. • Monthly. $329.00 per year. Newsletter on effective ways to reach the "over 50" market.

## RESEARCH CENTERS AND INSTITUTES

Consumer Research Center. The Conference Board, 845 3rd Ave., New York, NY 10022. Phone: (212)339-0232; Fax: (212)836-9754; Email: crc@conference-board.org • URL: http://www.conference-board.org/economics/crc.cfm • Conducts research on the consumer market, including elderly and working women segments.

Georgia State University - Center for Mature Consumer Studies. J. Mack Robinson College of Business, 35 Broad St. NW, Atlanta, GA 30303. Phone: (404)413-7670 or (404)413-7650; Fax: (404)413-7699; Email: gmoschis@gsu.edu • URL: http://marketing.robinson.gsu.edu/research-centers-roundtables/cmcs • Serves as an information resource, assisting in strategy development for reaching the mature consumer market.

# MEASURES

*See* WEIGHTS AND MEASURES

# MEAT INDUSTRY

*See also* CATTLE INDUSTRY; LIVESTOCK INDUSTRY; SHEEP INDUSTRY; SWINE INDUSTRY

## ABSTRACTS AND INDEXES

*Food Science and Technology Abstracts.* Ovid Technologies Inc. • Monthly. $1,780.00 per year. Provides worldwide coverage of the literature of food technology and food production.

*Foods Adlibra: Key to the World's Food Literature.* General Mills, Inc. Foods Adlibra Publications. • Semimonthly. $240.00 per year. Provides journal citations and abstracts to the literature of food technology and packaging.

## CD-ROM DATABASES

*OECD Statistical Compendium.* Organization for Economic Cooperation and Development. Semiannual. $1,905.00 per year for 1 to 10 users. CD-ROM contains more than 730,000 monthly, quarterly, and annual time series for OECD countries, 1960 to date. Includes fully searchable data on agriculture, food, economic indicators, national accounts, employment, energy, finance, industry, technology, and foreign trade. Results can be displayed in various forms.

## DIRECTORIES

*Directory of Chinese Manufacturers & Exporters of Meat & Meat Products.* EXIM Infotek Private Ltd. • $5 Individuals. Covers: 30 Chinese manufacturers and exporters of chicken meat, crabs and crabmeat, frozen beef, lean meat products, meat, meat and meat products, pork meat, walnut meat. Entries include: Company name, postal address, city, country, phone, fax, e-mail and websites, contact person, designation, and product details.

*Directory of Japanese Manufacturers & Exporters of Meat Products.* EXIM Infotek Private Ltd. • $5 Individuals. Covers: 20 Japanese manufacturers and exporters of fresh and frozen meat, meat, salmon, and salmon products. Entries include: Company name, postal address, city, country, phone, fax, e-mail and websites, contact person, designation, and product details.

*Directory of South Korean Manufacturers & Exporters of Meat & Meat Products.* EXIM Infotek Private Ltd. • $5 Individuals. Covers: 20 South Korean manufacturers and exporters of meat and game-processed/preserved, meat and meat products, meat-dried, and sausage casings. Entries include: Company name, postal address, city, country, phone, fax, e-mail and websites, contact person, designation, and product details.

*Directory of Taiwanese Manufacturers & Exporters of Meat & Meat Products.* EXIM Infotek Private Ltd. • $5 Individuals. Covers: 30 Taiwanese manufacturers and exporters of meat and game-processed/preserved, meat and meat products, meat-dried. Entries include: Company name, postal address, city, country, phone, fax, e-mail and websites, contact person, designation, and product details.

*Major Food and Drink Companies of the World.* Cengage Learning Inc. • 12th edition. eBook. Published by Graham & Whiteside. Contains profiles and trade names for more than 9,200 important food and beverage companies in various countries. In addition to foods, includes both alcoholic and nonalcoholic drink products.

*Meat, Poultry and Egg Inspection Directory.* U.S. Department of Agriculture. U.S. Department of Agriculture. • Monthly. Lists companies that produce meat, poultry and egg products.

*Meat Processing-Buyer's Guide-North American Edition.* Watt Publishing. • Annual. $12.00. In-depth statistical review of the meat, poultry, and seafood industries with graphs and tables; governmental phonebook; listing of meat associations, list of suppliers to the industry; list of equipment, services, and supplies, list of meat processors and their respective products.

## FINANCIAL RATIOS

*Annual Statement Studies.* Risk Management Association. • Annual. Compiled from over 280,000 financial statements.

*Annual Statement Studies: Industry Default Probabilities and Cash Flow Measures.* Risk Management Association. • Annual. $405 Nonmembers. Serves as a companion volume to the original *Annual Statement Studies.* Gives probability of default estimates on a percentage scale for more than 450 industries. Includes changes in position year-by-year for eight financial statement line items and provides percentage measures of cash flow.

## INTERNET DATABASES

*BEEF.* National Cattlemen's Beef Association. Phone: (303)694-0305; Fax: (303)694-2851; Email: cows@beef.org • URL: http://www.beef.org • Web site provides detailed information from the "Cattle and Beef Handbook," including "Beef Economics" (production, sales, consumption, retail value, foreign competition, etc.). Text of monthly newsletter is also available: "The Beef Brief-Issues & Trends in the Cattle Industry." Keyword searching is offered. Fees: Free.

*Business 2.0 Web Guide to the Best Business Links.* Business 2.0 Media Inc. Phone: (415)293-4800; Email: support@business2.com • URL: http://www.business2.com/webguide • Web site presents an extensive, searchable directory of links to "the best, most informative, and authoritative web pages." Twenty main categories cover business, finance, career, company information, people, and technology topics, with thousands of subtopics, all linking to Web sites recommended by experienced business researchers. Fees: Free.

*Fedstats.* Federal Interagency Council on Statistical Policy. Phone: (202)395-7254 • URL: http://www.fedstats.gov • Web site features an efficient search facility for full-text statistics produced by more than 100 federal agencies, including the Census Bureau, the Bureau of Economic Analysis, and the Bureau of Labor Statistics. Boolean searches can be made within one agency or for all agencies combined. Links are offered to international statistical bureaus, including the UN, IMF, OECD, UNESCO, Eurostat, and 20 individual countries. Fees: Free.

*FreeLunch.com.* Economy.com, Inc. Phone: (610)696-8700; Fax: (610)696-1678 • URL: http://www.freelunch.com • Web site provides free access to more than 200 million economic and financial data series, covering industry, demographics, labor markets, prices, retail sales, government spending, trade, interest rates, housing starts, the stock market, etc. Data is available in either chart or table form. Searching is offered. Free, but registration required. Economy.com, Inc. also offers fee-based economic analysis at *The Dismal Scientist* site (www.dismal.com).

*USDA.* U.S. National Institute of Standards and Technology. 100 Bureau Dr., Gaithersburg, MD 20899-1070. Phone: 800-877-8339 or (301)975-6478 or (202)720-2791; Fax: (301)975-8295; Email: inquiries@nist.gov • URL: http://www.nist.gov • The USDA home page has six sections: News and Information; What's New; About USDA; Agencies; Opportunities; Search and Help. Keyword searching is offered from the USDA home page and from various individual agency home pages. Agencies are the Economic Research Service, Agricultural Marketing Service, National Agricultural Statistics Service, National Agricultural Library, and about 12 others. Updating varies. Fees: Free.

## ONLINE DATABASES

*Food Science and Technology Abstracts (online).* IFIS North American Desk. • Produced by International Food Information Service. Provides about 500,000 online citations, with abstracts, to the international literature of food science, technology, commodities, engineering, and processing. Approximately 2,000 periodicals are covered. Time period is 1969 to date, with monthly updates. Inquire as to online cost and availability.

## PERIODICALS AND NEWSLETTERS

*Deli News.* Delicatessen Council of Southern California, Inc. Pacific Rim Publishing Co. • Monthly. $25.00 per year. Includes product news and comment related to cheeses, lunch meats, packaged fresh meats, kosher foods, gourmet-specialty items, and bakery products.

*Food Distribution Magazine.* Phoenix Media Network Inc. • Monthly. $49.00 per year. Edited for marketers and buyers of domestic and imported, specialty or gourmet food products, including ethnic foods, seasonings, and bakery items.

*Meat and Poultry: The Business Journal of the Meat and Poultry Industry.* Sosland Publishing Co. • Monthly. $85 Out of country print (digital access is free).

*Meat Business Magazine.* Record Printing. • Monthly. $20. Monthly publication for small to medium meat processors.

*Meat Processing: North American Edition.* Watt Publishing. • Monthly. $54.00 per year.

## PRICE SOURCES

*The National Provisioner: Serving Meat, Poultry, and Seafood Processors.* BNP Media. • Monthly. $85.04 Individuals. *Buyer's Guide* available. Meat, poultry and seafood newsletter.

## STATISTICS SOURCES

*Agricultural Statistics.* U.S. Department of Agriculture National Agricultural Statistics Service. • Annual. $46 Individuals. Provides a wide variety of statistical data relating to agricultural production, supplies, consumption, prices/price-supports, foreign trade, costs, and returns, as well as farm labor, loans, income, and population. In many cases, historical data is shown annually for 10 years. In addition to farm data, includes detailed fishery statistics.

*Survey of Current Business.* U. S. Government Printing Office. • Published by Bureau of Economic Analysis, U. S. Department of Commerce. Presents a wide variety of business and economic data.

## TRADE/PROFESSIONAL ASSOCIATIONS

American Meat Institute. 1150 Connecticut Ave. NW, 12th Fl., Washington, DC 20036. Phone: (202)587-4200; Fax: (202)587-4300 • URL: http://www.meatami.com • Represents the interests of packers and processors of beef, pork, lamb, veal, and turkey products and their suppliers throughout North America. Provides legislative, regulatory, and public relations services. Conducts scientific research. Offers marketing and technical assistance. Sponsors educational programs.

Fullblood Simmental Fleckvieh Federation. PO Box 321, Cisco, TX 76437. Phone: 855-353-2584; Fax: (855)638-2582; Email: info@fleckvieh.com • URL: http://www.fleckvieh.com • Aims to develop and promote Fullblood Simmental and Fullblood Fleckvieh cattle. Seeks to educate beef producers on the economic traits of Fullblood Simmental and Fullblood Fleckvieh cattle. Strives to promote the use of Fullblood Simmental and Fullblood Fleckvieh beef cattle genetics and to preserve and market the breeds in North America and worldwide to both purebred and commercial beef producers.

National Cattlemen's Beef Association. 9110 E Nichols Ave., Ste. 300, Centennial, CO 80112. Phone: (303)694-0305; Fax: (303)694-2851; Email: information@beef.org • URL: http://www.beefusa. org • Represents 149 organizations of livestock marketers, growers, meat packers, food retailers, and food service firms. Conducts extensive program of promotion, education and information about beef, veal, and associated meat products. Conducts projects such as recipe testing and development, food demonstrations, food photography, educational service to colleges, experimental meat cutting methods, merchandising programs, and preparation of materials for newspapers, magazines, radio, and television.

North American Meat Processors Association. 1910 Association Dr., Reston, VA 20191. Phone: 800-368-3043 or (703)758-1900; Fax: (703)758-8001; Email: info@namp.com • URL: http://www.namp. com • Represents wholesalers of meats and meat products to hotels, restaurants, schools, hospitals, and institutions. Conducts technical seminars.

# MEAT PACKING INDUSTRY

*See* MEAT INDUSTRY

# MECHANICAL DRAWING

## PERIODICALS AND NEWSLETTERS

*Engineering Design Graphics Journal.* American Society for Engineering Education. • Three times a year. Free to members; Non-members, $24.00 per year. Concerned with engineering graphics, computer graphics, geometric modeling, computer-aided drafting, etc.

## TRADE/PROFESSIONAL ASSOCIATIONS

American Design Drafting Association. 105 E Main St., Newbern, TN 38059. Phone: (731)627-0802; Fax: (731)627-9321; Email: corporate@adda.org • URL: http://www.adda.org • Designers, drafters, drafting managers, chief drafters, supervisors, administrators, instructors, and students of design and drafting. Encourages a continued program of education for self-improvement and professionalism in design and drafting and computer-aided design/drafting. Informs members of effective techniques and materials used in drawings and other graphic presentations. Evaluates curriculum of educational institutions through certification program; sponsors drafter certification program.

# MECHANICAL ENGINEERING

*See also* MACHINE DESIGN

## ABSTRACTS AND INDEXES

*Applied Mechanics Reviews: An Assessment of World Literature in Engineering Sciences.* ASME International. • Bimonthly. $129 print and online.

*Engineering Index Monthly: Abstracting and Indexing Services Covering Sources of the World's Engineering Literature.* Engineering Information Inc. • Monthly. Institutions, $5,279.00 per year. Provides indexing and abstracting of the world's engineering and technical literature.

*Mechanical Engineering Abstracts.* Cambridge Scientific Abstracts L.P. • Quarterly. $1,620 Individuals print + web edition (includes shipping). Database covering international literature on mechanical engineering, engineering management, and production engineering, including specific and theoretical applications. Formerly *ISMEC - Mechanical Engineering Abstracts.*

## BIOGRAPHICAL SOURCES

*Who's Who in Science and Engineering.* Marquis Who's Who L.L.C. • Biennial. $249.00. Provides concise biographical information on 33,545 prominent engineers and scientists. International coverage, with geographical and professional indexes.

## PERIODICALS AND NEWSLETTERS

*International Journal of Mechanical Sciences.* Elsevier. • $4,702 Institutions. Monthly. Qualified personnel, $228.00 per year.

*Journal of Applied Mechanics.* ASME International. • $129 Members. Bimonthly. Subscription includes online edition.

*Mechanical Engineering.* ASME International. • Monthly. $25 Members /year. The official monthly publication of the ASME.

## RESEARCH CENTERS AND INSTITUTES

Engineering Dean's Office. University of California at Berkeley, 320 McLaughlin Hall, Berkeley, CA 94720-1700. Phone: (510)642-5771; Fax: (510)642-9178; Email: sastry@coe.berkeley.edu • URL: http://www.coe.berkeley.edu • Research fields

include civil, electrical, industrial, mechanical, and other types of engineering.

## TRADE/PROFESSIONAL ASSOCIATIONS

ASME International. 2 Park Ave., New York, NY 10016-5990. Phone: 800-843-2763 or (973)882-1170; Fax: (973)882-1717; Email: customercare@asme.org • URL: http://www.asme.org • Technical society of mechanical engineers and students. Conducts research; develops boiler, pressure vessel, and power test codes. Develops safety codes and standards for equipment. Conducts short course programs, and Identifying Research Needs Program. Maintains 19 research committees and 38 divisions.

# MEDIA, INTERACTIVE

*See* INTERACTIVE MEDIA

# MEDIA, MASS

*See* MASS MEDIA

# MEDIA RESEARCH

*See also* ADVERTISING RESEARCH; MASS MEDIA

## ABSTRACTS AND INDEXES

*Business Periodicals Index Retrospective.* EBSCO Publishing Inc. • 11/year. Quarterly and annual cumulations.

*Communication Abstracts: An International Information Service.* Pine Forge Press. • Bimonthly. Institutions, $1,150.00 per year. Provides broad coverage of the literature of communications, including broadcasting and advertising.

*Electronics and Communications Abstracts Journal: Comprehensive Coverage of Essential Scientific Literature.* CSA. • Monthly. $1,665.00 per year. Includes print and online editions.

## DIRECTORIES

*Gale Directory of Publications and Broadcast Media (GDPBM).* Cengage Learning Inc. • Annual. $1,362 Individuals. Covers approximately 57,000 publications and broadcasting stations, including newspapers, magazines, journals, radio stations, television stations, radio/television/cable networks, syndicates and cable systems in the U.S. and Canada. Newsletters and directories are excluded.

*Top 30 U.S. Business Media.* • Semiannual. $49. More than 900 editors, reporters, producers, and bookers at 30 major business media outlets.

*VNU Business Media.* ADWEEK Media. • Annual. $100.00. Presents cost, circulation, and audience statistics for various mass media segments, including television, radio, magazines, newspapers, telephone yellow pages, and cinema.

## GENERAL WORKS

*Journal of Media Business Studies.* Joenkoeping International Business School, Media Management and Transformation Centre. • Quarterly. $65 Individuals. Peer-reviewed journal devoted to research on business aspects of media including strategic, organizational, financial, marketing, and entrepreneurial issues and practices.

## INTERNET DATABASES

*Pew Research Center for the People and the Press.* Pew Charitable Trusts. Phone: (202)293-3126; Fax: (202)293-2569; Email: mailprc@people-press.org • URL: http://www.people-press.org • Free Web site includes public opinion poll "Reports by Topic." Five broad subject areas cover business, social issues, foreign policy, news media, and politics. Searching is offered within each of these broad areas, and there are links to other major sources of public opinion poll results ("FYI Other Polls").

## ONLINE DATABASES

*Wilson Business Abstracts Online.* H.W. Wilson Co. • Indexes and abstracts 600 major business periodicals, plus the *Wall Street Journal* and the business section of the *New York Times*. Indexing is from 1982, abstracting from 1990, with the two newspapers included from 1993. Updated weekly. Inquire as to online cost and availability. (*Business Periodicals Index* without abstracts is also available online.).

## PERIODICALS AND NEWSLETTERS

*American Demographics: Consumer Trends for Business Leaders.* Media Central. • Monthly. $58.00 per year.

*Journal of Advertising Research.* Advertising Research Foundation. • Quarterly. $365 Individuals standard subscription. Journal of advertising, marketing, and media research.

*Journal of Applied Communication Research.* National Communication Association. • Quarterly. $110.00 per year.

*Mediaweek: The News Magazine of the Media.* Nielsen Business Media Inc. • Published for advertising media buyers and managers.

## RESEARCH CENTERS AND INSTITUTES

Center for Media and Public Affairs. 933 N Kenmore St., Ste. 405, Arlington, VA 22201. Phone: (571)319-0029; Fax: (571)319-0034; Email: mail@cmpa.com • URL: http://www.cmpa.com • Analyzes scientifically how the media treat social and political issues. Conducts surveys to determine media impact on public opinion. Performs rapid response media analyses, enabling the impact of media coverage to be determined as it occurs.

University of Southern California - Integrated Media Systems Center. 306 Powell Hall of Engineering, 3737 Watt Way, Los Angeles, CA 90089-0272. Phone: (213)740-8945; Fax: (213)740-2539; Email: shahabi@usc.edu • URL: http://imsc.usc.edu • Media areas for research include education, mass communication, and entertainment.

University of Wisconsin—Madison - Center for Communication Research. Department of Communication Arts, College of Letters & Science, 821 University Ave., Madison, WI 53706. Phone: (608)262-2543; Fax: (608)262-9953; Email: xenos@wisc.edu • URL: http://ccr.commarts.wisc.edu • Media effects, including prosocial programming's effects on children, the effects of media violence on children's aggression and fears, and aging and media use. Political communication, including the framing of issues, political advertising, and the representation of nation-states on TV. Interpersonal communication, including group processes, information sharing, and group memory. Conflict and miscommunication.

University of Wisconsin—Madison - Mass Communications Research Center. 5115 Vilas Hall, 821 University Ave., Madison, WI 53706. Phone: (608)262-3690 or (608)263-3381; Fax: (608)262-1361; Email: dshah@wisc.edu • URL: http://mcrc.journalism.wisc.edu • Mass communication, including mass media institutions, processes and effects generally and in a number of specific contexts. Current research specializations include political communication, communication campaigns, health communication, uses and effects of new communication technologies, cognitive and attention processes, advertising and persuasion, history of mass communication, framing, minorities, international and intercultural communication, community, geographic contexts, risk and science communication, and methodological studies.

## TRADE/PROFESSIONAL ASSOCIATIONS

American Marketing Association. 311 S Wacker Dr., Ste. 5800, Chicago, IL 60606. Phone: 800-AMA-1150 or (312)542-9000; Fax: (312)542-9001 • URL: http://www.marketingpower.com • Serves as a professional society of marketing and market research executives, sales and promotion managers, advertising specialists, academics, and others interested in marketing. Fosters research; sponsors seminars, conferences, and student marketing clubs; provides educational placement service and doctoral consortium.

Marketing Research Association. 1156 15th St. NW, Ste. 302, Washington, DC 20005. Phone: 888-512-1050 or (202)800-2545; Fax: (888)512-1050; Email: membership@marketingresearch.org • URL: http://www.marketingresearch.org • Companies and individuals involved in any area of opinion and marketing research, such as data collection, research, or as an end-user.

# MEDIATION

*See* ARBITRATION

# MEDICAL CARE INDUSTRY

*See* HEALTH CARE INDUSTRY

# MEDICAL ECONOMICS (PRACTICE MANAGEMENT)

*See also* GROUP MEDICAL PRACTICE; HEALTH CARE INDUSTRY

## BIBLIOGRAPHIES

*Medical & Health Care Books & Serials in Print.* Grey House Publishing. • $645 Individuals Hardcover. Provides immediate access to the highly specialized publishing activity in the health sciences and allied health fields.

## DIRECTORIES

*Directory of Physician Groups and Networks.* Dorland Healthcare Information. • Annual. $495.00. Available only online. Approximately 8,000 independent practice associations (IPAs), physician hospital organizations (PHOs), management service organizations (MSOs), physician practice management companies (PPMCs), and group practices having 20 or more physicians.

## FINANCIAL RATIOS

*Annual Statement Studies.* Risk Management Association. • Annual. Compiled from over 280,000 financial statements.

*Annual Statement Studies: Industry Default Probabilities and Cash Flow Measures.* Risk Management Association. • Annual. $405 Nonmembers. Serves as a companion volume to the original *Annual Statement Studies.* Gives probability of default estimates on a percentage scale for more than 450 industries. Includes changes in position year-by-year for eight financial statement line items and provides percentage measures of cash flow.

*Industry Norms and Key Business Ratios.* Dun & Bradstreet Inc. • Annual. Five volumes. Covers over 800 kinds of businesses, arranged by Standard Industrial Classification number. More detailed editions covering longer periods of time are also available.

## PERIODICALS AND NEWSLETTERS

*Dental Economics.* PennWell Publishing Co. • Monthly. $132 Individuals. Magazine featuring business-related articles for dentists.

*Dental Practice and Finance.* MEDEC Dental Communications. • Bimonthly. $55.00 per year. Covers practice management and financial topics for dentists. Includes investment advice.

*Group Practice Journal.* American Medical Group Association. • 10/year. $75 Institutions.

*Health Care Strategic Management: The Newsletter for Hospital Strategies.* The Business Word. • Monthly. $284.00 per year. Planning, marketing and resource allocation.

*Health Marketing Quarterly.* The Haworth Press Inc. • Quarterly. $580.00 per year.

*HME News: The Business Newspaper for Home Medical Equipment Providers.* HME News. • Monthly. Business newspaper for home medical equipment providers. Editorial coverage focuses on industry news, mergers and acquisitions, governmental and regulatory impact on the HME industry, as well as product reviews and industry trend coverage.

*Medesthetics: Business Education for Medical Practitioners.* Creative Age Publications Inc. • Bimonthly. Trade magazine for medical practitioners.

*Medical Economics.* Advanstar Medical. • Semimonthly. $109 /year. Covers the financial, economic, insurance, administrative, and other non-clinical aspects of private medical practice. Provides investment and estate planning advice.

*Medical Economics General Surgery-Orthopedic Surgery.* Thomson Medical Economics. • Monthly. $65.00 per year. Provides information and advice on practice management (non-clinical) for surgeons. Formerly *Medical Economics for Surgeons.*

*Medicare Compliance Alert.* UCG Holdings L.P. • $489 24 issues. Description: Provides news and guidance to help keep health care practices on the right side of fraud and abuse laws and regulations.

*MGMA Connexion.* Medical Group Management Association. • 10/year. $95 Individuals /year. Formerly *Medical Group Management Journal.* Provides in-depth coverage of key industry topics and advice for group practice professionals.

*Modern Physician: Essential Business News for the Executive Physician.* Crain Communications Inc. • Monthly. $45.00. Edited for physicians responsible for business decisions at hospitals, clinics, HMOs, and other health groups. Includes special issues on managed care, practice management, legal issues, and finance.

*Nursing Economics: The Journal for Health Care Leaders.* Jannetti Publications Inc. • Bimonthly. Individuals, $80.00 per year; institutions, $100.00 per year.

*Nursing Management.* Springhouse Corp. Lippincott Williams & Wilkins. • Monthly. Individuals, $83.00 per year; institutions, $397.00 per year. Non-clinical subject matter.

*Optometric Management: The Business and Marketing Magazine for Optometry.* Boucher Communications, Inc. • Monthly. $37.00 per year. Provides information and advice for optometrists on practice management and marketing.

*Physicians & Computers.* Moorhead Publications Inc. • Monthly. $40.00 per year. Includes material on computer diagnostics, online research, medical and non-medical software, computer equipment, and practice management.

*Physician's Marketing and Management.* AHC Media. • Monthly. Individuals, $299.00 per year; institutions, $323.00 per year. Newsletter. Formerly *Physician's Marketing.*

*Podiatry Management.* Kane Communications Inc. • 9/year. $38. Non-clinical subject matter.

*Private Practice.* Congress of County Medical Societies (CCMS) Publishing Co. • Monthly. $18.00 per year.

---

*Resident and Staff Physician.* Romaine Pierson Publishers Inc. • Monthly. Individuals, $83.00 per year institutions, $149.00 per year; students, $50.00 per year.

## TRADE/PROFESSIONAL ASSOCIATIONS

American College of Medical Practice Executives. 104 Inverness Terr. E, Englewood, CO 80112-5306. Phone: 877-275-6462 or (303)799-1111; Fax: (303)643-4439; Email: acmpe@mgma.com • URL: http://www.mgma.com/about/default.aspx?id=242 • Formerly American College of Medical Group Administrators.

American Medical Association. AMA Plaza, 330 N Wabash Ave., Chicago, IL 60611. Phone: 800-621-8335 or (312)464-4430; Fax: (312)464-5226; Email: amalibrary@ama-assn.org • URL: http://www.ama-assn.org • Represents county medical societies and physicians. Disseminates scientific information to members and the public. Informs members on significant medical and health legislation on state and national levels and represents the profession before Congress and governmental agencies. Cooperates in setting standards for medical schools, hospitals, residency programs, and continuing medical education courses. Offers physician placement service and counseling on practice management problems. Operates library that lends material and provides specific medical information to physicians. Maintains Ad-hoc committees for such topics as health care planning and principles of medical ethics.

American Medical Group Association. 1 Prince St., Alexandria, VA 22314-3318. Phone: (703)838-0033; Fax: (703)548-1890; Email: dfisher@amga.org • URL: http://www.amga.org • Represents the interests of medical groups. Advocates for the medical groups and patients through innovation and information sharing, benchmarking, developing leadership, and improving patient care. Provides political advocacy, educational and networking programs and publications, benchmarking data services, and financial and operations assistance.

American Professional Practice Association. Association Member Service Center, Hillsboro Executive Center N, 550 Fairway Dr., Ste. 107, Deerfield Beach, FL 33441-1834. Phone: 800-221-2168; Fax: (954)571-8582; Email: membership@assnservices.com • URL: http://www.appa-assn.com • Provides physicians with economic benefits and financial services including the following: unsecured loan plans, mortgage loans, group insurance discounts, accounts receivable collections, office supplies, wealth protection and a vision and dental plan.

Medical Group Management Association. 104 Inverness Terr. E, Englewood, CO 80112-5306. Phone: 877-275-6462 or (303)799-1111; Fax: (303)643-4439; Email: service@mgma.com • URL: http://www.mgma.com • Represents professionals involved in the management of medical group practices and administration of other ambulatory healthcare facilities. Provides products and services that includes education, benchmarking, surveys, national advocacy and networking opportunities for members.

# MEDICAL ELECTRONICS

*See also* MEDICAL TECHNOLOGY

## ABSTRACTS AND INDEXES

*Applied Science and Technology Index.* EBSCO Publishing Inc. • 11/year. Indexes a wide variety of English language technical, industrial, and engineering periodicals.

*Excerpta Medica: Biophysics, Bioengineering, and Medical Instrumentation.* Elsevier. • $7,353 Institutions print journal. 16 times a year. Institutions, $2,859 per year. Section 27 of *Excerpta Medica.*

*NTIS Alerts: Biomedical Technology & Human Factor Engineering.* U.S. Department of Commerce National Technical Information Service. • Biweekly. $130 per year. Covers biotechnology, ergonomics, bionics, artificial intelligence, prosthetics, and related subjects.

## CD-ROM DATABASES

*Applied Science and Technology Abstracts.* EBSCO Publishing Inc. • Citations for more than 700 prominent scientific, technical, engineering, and industrial periodicals.

*Health Devices Journals.* ECRI Institute. • Monthly. $285 each.

## DIRECTORIES

*Medical Product Manufacturing News Buyers Guide.* Canon Communications LLC. • A directory of over 3,000 medical device and medical electronic equipment. Formerly *Medical Product Manufacturing News-Buyer's Guide and Designer's Sourcebook.*

## INTERNET DATABASES

*Manufacturing Profiles.* U. S. Bureau of the Census. Phone: (301)763-4636 or (301)763-4100; Fax: (301)763-4794; Email: webmaster@census.gov • URL: http://www.census.gov/prod/www/abs/mfg-prof.html • The Census Bureau makes available free on PDF (Portable Document Format) an annual consolidation of the entire Current Industrial Report series, presenting "all the data compiled." Contains statistics on production, shipments, inventories, consumption, exports, imports, and orders for a wide variety of manufactured products.

## ONLINE DATABASES

*Applied Science and Technology Index Online.* H.W. Wilson Co. • Provides online indexing of 500 major scientific, technical, industrial, and engineering periodicals. Time period is 1983 to date. Monthly updates. Inquire as to online cost and availability.

*Current Contents Connect.* Thomson Reuters Intellectual Property and Science. • Provides online abstracts of articles listed in the tables of contents of about 7,500 journals. Coverage is very broad, including science, social science, life science, technology, engineering, industry, agriculture, the environment, economics, and arts and humanities. Time period is two years, with weekly updates. Inquire as to online cost and availability.

*F-D-C Reports.* Elsevier Business Intelligence. • An online version of "The Gray Sheet" (medical devices), "The Pink Sheet" (pharmaceuticals), "The Rose Sheet" (cosmetics), "The Blue Sheet" (biomedical), and "The Tan Sheet" (nonprescription). Contains full-text information on legal, technical, corporate, financial, and marketing developments from 1987 to date, with weekly updates. Inquire as to online cost and availability.

*INSPEC.* Institution of Electrical Engineers. • Provides online citations, with abstracts, to the world literature of electrical engineering, electronics, optoelectronics, telecommunications, industrial controls, instrumentation, computer technology, information technology, and physics. Coverage includes more than 4,000 technical and scientific journals from 1969 to date, with weekly updating. (INSPEC is Information Services in Physics, Electronics, and Computing.) Inquire as to online cost and availability.

## PERIODICALS AND NEWSLETTERS

*Health Devices Alerts: A Summary of Reported Problems, Hazards, Recalls, and Updates.* ECRI Institute. • Weekly. $3,649.40 per year. Looseleaf service. Contains reviews of health equipment problems. Includes *Health Devices Alerts Action Items, Health Devices Alerts Abstracts, Health Devices Alerts FDA Data, Health Devices Alerts Implants, Health Devices Alerts Hazards Bulletin.*

*Medical Laser Report.* PennWell Corp. • Description: Presents news on the medical laser industry, technology, research, and markets. Recurring features include news of research, business news and product introductions.

*Medical Product Manufacturing News.* Canon Communications LLC. • 5/year. Directed at manufacturers of medical devices and medical electronic equipment. Covers industry news, service news, and new products.

*MEEN Diagnostic and Invasive Technology.* Reilly Communications Group. • $90 Canada and Mexico. Bimonthly. Free to qualified personnel. Provides medical electronics industry news and new product information. Formerly *Medical Electronics and Equipment News.*

*Physicians & Computers.* Moorhead Publications Inc. • Monthly. $40.00 per year. Includes material on computer diagnostics, online research, medical and non-medical software, computer equipment, and practice management.

## RESEARCH CENTERS AND INSTITUTES

Laboratory of Electronics. Rockefeller University, 1230 York Ave., New York, NY 10065. Phone: (212)327-8000; Fax: (212)327-7613; Email: ros@rockvax.rockefeller.edu • URL: http://www.rockefeller.edu • Studies the application of computer engineering and electronics to biomedicine.

University of Wisconsin—Madison - Medical Electronics Laboratory. 1300 University Ave., Rm. 80, Madison, WI 53706. Phone: (608)262-1326; Email: yee@physiology.wisc.edu • URL: http://www.mel.wisc.edu • Develops electronic instrumentation for medical and biological research.

## STATISTICS SOURCES

*U.S. Industry and Trade Outlook.* U.S. Department of Commerce National Technical Information Service. • Annual. Produced by the International Trade Administration, U.S. Department of Commerce, in a "public-private" partnership with DRI/McGraw-Hill and Standard & Poor's. Provides basic data, outlook for the current year, and "Long-Term Prospects" (five-year projections) for a wide variety of products and services. Includes high technology industries. Formerly *U.S. Industrial Outlook.*

## TRADE/PROFESSIONAL ASSOCIATIONS

Association for the Advancement of Medical Instrumentation. 4301 N Fairfax Dr., Ste. 301, Arlington, VA 22203-1633. Phone: 800-332-2264 or (703)525-4890 or (240)646-7031; Fax: (703)276-0793 or (301)206-9789; Email: customerservice@aami.org • URL: http://www.aami.org • Members are engineers, technicians, physicians, manufacturers, and others with an interest in medical instrumentation.

# MEDICAL INSURANCE

*See* HEALTH INSURANCE

# MEDICAL LABORATORIES

*See* CLINICAL LABORATORY INDUSTRY

# MEDICAL LIABILITY

*See* PROFESSIONAL LIABILITY

# MEDICAL SERVICE, INDUSTRIAL

*See* INDUSTRIAL MEDICINE

# MEDICAL TECHNOLOGY

*See also* MEDICAL TECHNOLOGY; SURGI-
CAL INSTRUMENTS INDUSTRY; X-RAY
EQUIPMENT INDUSTRY

## ABSTRACTS AND INDEXES

*Excerpta Medica: Biophysics, Bioengineering, and
Medical Instrumentation.* Elsevier. • $7,353 Institu-
tions print journal. 16 times a year. Institutions,
$2,859 per year. Section 27 of *Excerpta Medica.*

## CD-ROM DATABASES

*NTIS Database.* Ovid Technologies Inc. • Quarterly.
$2,850.00 per year. Guide to over 2 million
bibliographic entries. Compiled by the U.S. National
Technical Information Service.

## DIRECTORIES

*International Directory of Importers--Medical,
Hospital, and Surgical Equipment and Supplies.*
International Directory of Importers. • Annual. $295
Individuals print. Covers: 5,000 worldwide
manufacturers, importers, and firms trading in medical, hospital, and surgical equipment and supplies.
Entries include: Company name, address, phone,
fax, email address when available, importing
manager, year established.

*Medical and Healthcare Marketplace Guide.* IDD
Inc. • Annual. $595.00. Two volumes. Provides
market survey summaries for about 500 specific
product and service categories (volume one:
"Research Reports"). Contains profiles of nearly
5,500 pharmaceutical, medical product, and healthcare service companies (volume two: "Company
Profiles").

## FINANCIAL RATIOS

*Industry Norms and Key Business Ratios.* Dun &
Bradstreet Inc. • Annual. Five volumes. Covers over
800 kinds of businesses, arranged by Standard
Industrial Classification number. More detailed editions covering longer periods of time are also
available.

## HANDBOOKS AND MANUALS

*Physicians' Desk Reference for Ophthalmology.*
Medical Economics Co. • Annual. $49.95. Provides
detailed descriptions of ophthalmological
instrumentation, equipment, supplies, lenses, and
prescription drugs. Indexed by manufacturer,
product name, product category, active drug ingredi-
ent, and instrumentation. Editorial discussion is
included.

## INTERNET DATABASES

*National Library of Medicine.* National Institutes of
Health. 9000 Rockville Pke., Bethesda, MD 20892.
Phone: (301)496-4000; Email: nihinfo@od.nih.gov
• URL: http://www.nih.gov • NLM Web site offers
free access through MEDLINE ("PubMed") to about
nine million references to articles appearing in some
4,000 biomedical journals, with abstracts. Search
interfaces range from "simple keywords to advanced
Boolean expressions." The NLM site offers many
links to other sources of biomedical and technical
information (the National Center for Biotechnology
Information, for example). Fees: Free.

## ONLINE DATABASES

*F-D-C Reports.* Elsevier Business Intelligence. • An
online version of "The Gray Sheet" (medical
devices), "The Pink Sheet" (pharmaceuticals), "The
Rose Sheet" (cosmetics), "The Blue Sheet"
(biomedical), and "The Tan Sheet"
(nonprescription). Contains full-text information on
legal, technical, corporate, financial, and marketing
developments from 1987 to date, with weekly
updates. Inquire as to online cost and availability.

## OTHER SOURCES

*Pharmaceutical Litigation Reporter: The National
Journal of Record of Pharmaceutical Litigation.* An-

drews Publications. • Monthly. $775.00 per year.
Newsletter. Reports on a wide variety of legal cases
involving the pharmaceutical and medical device
industries. Includes product liability lawsuits.

## PERIODICALS AND NEWSLETTERS

*Administrative Radiology Journal: The Journal of
Medical Imaging Business, Management &
Administration.* Glendale Publishing Corp. •
Monthly. $96 Individuals. Monthly Journal of Imag-
ing Administration for Chief Imaging M.D.'s, Imag-
ing Department Managers, Radiation Oncology
Directors, and Healthcare Administrators.

*The Gray Sheet Reports: Medical Devices,
Diagnostics and Instrumentation.* Elsevier Business
Intelligence. • Weekly. Institutions, $1,172.00 per
year. Newsletter. Provides industry and financial
news, including a medical sector stock index. Monitors regulatory developments at the Center for
Devices and Radiological Health of the U. S. Food
and Drug Administration.

*Health Devices Alerts: A Summary of Reported
Problems, Hazards, Recalls, and Updates.* ECRI
Institute. • Weekly. $3,649.40 per year. Looseleaf
service. Contains reviews of health equipment
problems. Includes *Health Devices Alerts Action
Items, Health Devices Alerts Abstracts, Health
Devices Alerts FDA Data, Health Devices Alerts
Implants, Health Devices Alerts Hazards Bulletin.*

*Health News Daily.* Elsevier Business Intelligence. •
Description: Tracks developments in health care
policy, legislation and regulation, insurance,
pharmaceuticals, delivery, manufacturing, technology and treatment, funding, and research.

*HME News.* HME News. • Monthly. Covers the
home medical equipment business for dealers and
manufacturers. Provides information on a wide
variety of home health care supplies and equipment.

*IEEE Pulse.* IEEE - Communications Society. •
Bimonthly. Published for biomedical engineers.

*Medical Device and Diagnostic Industry.* Canon
Communications LLC. • Monthly. Focused on the
medical technology industry.

*Medical Device Technology.* Elsevier. • $143.94
print and e-book. Provides undergraduate engineering students with an introduction to commonly
manufactured medical devices.

*Medical Product Manufacturing News.* Canon Communications LLC. • 5/year. Directed at manufacturers of medical devices and medical electronic
equipment. Covers industry news, service news, and
new products.

*Medical Technology Stock Letter.* Medical Technology Stock Letter. • Description: Specializes in
investments in biotechnology companies. Offers
news of the industry and recommendations for buying, selling, and holding stocks. Recurring features
include news of research, a model portfolio reflecting the editors' investment strategy, and columns
titled Pulse of the Market and Industry Scan.
**Remarks:** Also available through e-mail.

*MEEN Diagnostic and Invasive Technology.* Reilly
Communications Group. • $90 Canada and Mexico.
Bimonthly. Free to qualified personnel. Provides
medical electronics industry news and new product
information. Formerly *Medical Electronics and
Equipment News.*

*MX--Business Strategies for Medical Technology
Executives: Business Strategies for Medical
Technology Executives.* UBM Canon. • Semiannual.
$50 Single issue. Trade magazine covering medical
device technology for executives in the industry.

*Pharmaceutical and Medical Device Law Bulletin.*
ALM Media Properties LLC. • Monthly. $199.00
per year. Newsletter. Edited for lawyers concerned
with drug product or medical device litigation.
Contains industry news items of special interest,
reports on new products, legal case summaries, Food

and Drug Administration actions, patent issues, and
related news reports. (A Law Journal Newsletter,
formerly published by Leader Publications).

*Seminars in Ultrasound, CT and MRI.* Elsevier Inc.
• Bimonthly. $357 Individuals online + print.
Journal reviewing current techniques and equipment
used in ultrasound, CT, and MRI.

*Surgical Products.* Advantage Business Media
L.L.C. • Monthly. $41.90 per year. Covers new
Technology and products for surgeons and operation
rooms.

## RESEARCH CENTERS AND INSTITUTES

ECRI: Emergency Care Research Institute. 5200
Butler Pike, Plymouth Meeting, PA 19462-1298.
Phone: (610)825-6000; Fax: (610)834-1275; Email:
info@ecri.org • URL: http://www.ecri.org • Major
research area is health care technology.

University of Wisconsin—Madison - Medical
Electronics Laboratory. 1300 University Ave., Rm.
80, Madison, WI 53706. Phone: (608)262-1326;
Email: yee@physiology.wisc.edu • URL: http://
www.mel.wisc.edu • Develops electronic
instrumentation for medical and biological research.

University of Wisconsin—Madison - Medical
Instrumentation Laboratory. 1550 Engineering Dr.,
Madison, WI 53706. Phone: (608)263-1574; Fax:
(608)265-9239; Email: webster@engr.wisc.edu •
URL: http://www.engr.wisc.edu • Research subjects
include medical electrodes, medical amplifiers, bioimpedance techniques, and miniature tactile pressure sensors.

## TRADE/PROFESSIONAL ASSOCIATIONS

American Institute for Medical and Biological
Engineering. 1701 K St. NW, Ste. 510, Washington,
DC 20006. Phone: (202)496-9660; Email: info@
aimbe.org • URL: http://www.aimbe.org •
Represents individuals with an interest in medical
and biological engineering. Fosters exchange of
ideas and information among members; works to
establish a clear identity for the field and improve
public awareness of members' activities; serves as
liaison between members and government agencies.
Conducts educational programs; promotes public
interest in science and science education.

Association for the Advancement of Medical
Instrumentation. 4301 N Fairfax Dr., Ste. 301,
Arlington, VA 22203-1633. Phone: 800-332-2264 or
(703)525-4890 or (240)646-7031; Fax: (703)276-
0793 or (301)206-9789; Email: customerservice@
aami.org • URL: http://www.aami.org • Members
are engineers, technicians, physicians, manufacturers, and others with an interest in medical
instrumentation.

# MEDICARE

*See also* HEALTH CARE INDUSTRY;
HEALTH INSURANCE; SOCIAL SECURITY

## ABSTRACTS AND INDEXES

*NTIS Alerts: Health Care.* U.S. Department of Commerce National Technical Information Service. •
Biweekly. $130 per year. Covers a wide variety of
health care topics, including quality assurance,
delivery organization, economics (costs), technology, and legislation.

*Readers' Guide to Periodical Literature.* EBSCO
Publishing Inc. • Provides indexing for over 400
periodicals dating back to 1983.

## CD-ROM DATABASES

*Authority Health Care Law Library.* Matthew
Bender and Company Inc. • Periodic updates. Price
on request. Full text CD-ROM provides legal
information, case law, and analysis relating to health
care facilities, health insurance, longterm care,
Medigap, and Medicare.

*Readers' Guide to Periodical Literature.* EBSCO Publishing Inc. • Provides indexing for over 400 periodicals dating back to 1983.

### DIRECTORIES

*Geriatric Care Directory.* InfoGroup Inc. • Annual. Number of listings: 5,059. Entries include: Name, address, phone, size of advertisement, name of owner or manager, number of employees, year first in "Yellow Pages." Compiled from telephone company "Yellow Pages," nationwide.

*The National Managed Care Leadership Directory.* HealthQuest Publishers from MCOL. • $249 Individuals print. Covers: 844 companies and 7,020 executive listings in the managed care industry including health plans, provider networks, PBMs, administrative organizations (quality improvement organizations, utilizations and disease management organizations, and TPAs) and specialty organizations (dental, vision and behavioral).

### HANDBOOKS AND MANUALS

*Medicare and Coordinated Care Plans.* Consumer Information Center. • Free. Published by the U. S. Department of Health and Human Services. Contains detailed information on services to Medicare beneficiaries from health maintenance organizations (HMOs).

*Medicare: Employer Health Plans.* Consumer Information Center. • Free. Published by the U. S. Department of Health and Human Services. Explains the special rules that apply to Medicare beneficiaries who have employer group health plan coverage. (Publication No. 520-Y.).

*Medicare Explained.* Wolters Kluwer Law & Business CCH. • Annual. $67.95.

*Medicare Handbook.* U. S. Government Printing Office. • Annual. $3.00. Issued by the Health Care Financing Administration, U. S. Department of Health and Human Services. Provides information on Medicare hospital insurance and medical insurance, including benefits, options, and rights. Discusses the functions of Medigap insurance, managed care plans, peer review organizations, and Medicare insurance carriers. Formerly *Medicare Handbook.*

*Nursing Home Regulations Manual.* Thompson Publishing Group Inc. • $295.00 per year. Looseleaf service. Includes monthly updates, newsletters and internet access. Serves as a comprehensive guide to the Nursing Home Reform Act, federal regulations, resident assessment, deficiency findings, Medicare, Medicaid, Health Care Financing Administration (HCFA) policies, and related topics for nursing home and assisted living facility owners and managers.

*Social Security & Medicare Facts.* • Annual. $110.00.

*Social Security Handbook.* U. S. Government Printing Office. • Annual. $53.00. Issued by the Social Security Administration (www.ssa.gov). Provides detailed information about social security programs, including Medicare, with brief descriptions of related programs administered by agencies other than the Social Security Administration.

### INTERNET DATABASES

*Free Insurance Advice.* InsWeb, Inc. 2868 Prospect Park Dr., Ste. 650, Rancho Cordova, CA 95670. Phone: (916)853-3300; Fax: (916)853-3300; Email: customercare@insweb.com • URL: http://www.insweb.com • Web site offers a wide variety of advice and information on automobile, life, health, and "other" insurance. Includes glossaries of insurance terms, Standard & Poor's ratings of individual insurance companies, and "Financial Needs Estimators." Searching is available. Fees: Free.

*Medicare: The Official U. S. Government Site for Medicare Information.* Centers for Medicare and Medicaid Services. Phone: (202)690-6726 • URL:

http://www.medicare.gov • Web site provides extensive information on Medicare health plans, publications, fraud, nursing homes, top 20 questions and answers, etc. Includes access to the National Nursing Home Database, providing summary compliance information on "every Medicare and Medicaid certified nursing home in the country. "Online searching is offered. Fees: Free.

*Social Security Online: The Official Web Site of the Social Security Administration.* U. S. Social Security Administration. Phone: 800-772-1213 or (410)965-7700 • URL: http://www.ssa.gov • Web site provides a wide variety of online information relating to social security and Medicare. Topics include benefits, disability, employer wage reporting, personal earnings statements, statistics, government financing, social security law, and public welfare reform legislation.

### PERIODICALS AND NEWSLETTERS

*American Health Care Association: Provider.* American Health Care Association. • Monthly. $48.00 per year. Formerly *American Health Care Association Journal.*

*Health Care Financing Review.* U. S. Government Printing Office. • Quarterly. $48 Individuals. Issued by the Health Care Financing Administration, U. S. Department of Health and Human Services. Presents articles by professionals in the areas of health care costs and financing.

*Health Policy and Biomedical Research: The Blue Sheet.* Elsevier Business Intelligence. • 51 times a year. $716.00 per year. Newsletter. Emphasis is on news of medical research agencies and institutions, especially the National Institutes of Health (NIH).

*Home Health Line: The Home Care Industry's National Independent Newsletter.* • 48 times per year. $527.00 per year. Newsletter on legislation and regulations affecting the home health care industry, with an emphasis on federal funding and Medicare programs.

*Medical Benefits.* Wolters Kluwer Law and Business. • Description: Focuses on key developments, statistics, and studies relating to the health care system. Covers eight major topic areas: cost containment, employee benefits, employee health/wellness, quality of care, delivery systems, government in health care, legal issues, and health care expenditure data.

*Medicare Compliance Alert.* UCG Holdings L.P. • $489 24 issues. Description: Procvides news and guidance to help keep health care practices on the right side of fraud and abuse laws and regulations.

*Older Americans Report.* Business Publishers Inc. • Bimonthly. $449 Individuals. Description: Features brief articles on legislative, judicial, and federal agency activities concerning older Americans. Covers news of developments in such areas as Social Security, social services, Medicare, programs for retirement and pension funds, research projects, and the Older Americans Act. Recurring features include book reviews and a calendar of events.

### RESEARCH CENTERS AND INSTITUTES

Center for the Study of Aging. University of Bridgeport, Carlson Hall, 303 University Ave., Division of Counseling and Human Resources, Bridgeport, CT 06601. Phone: (203)576-4175; Fax: (203)576-4200; Email: kaplin@bridgeport.edu • Research activities include the study of Medicare and Medicaid.

Johns Hopkins University Bloomberg School of Public Health - Center for Health Services and Outcomes Research. Hampton House, 6th Fl., Department of Health Policy & Management, 624 N Broadway, Baltimore, MD 21205-1901. Phone: (410)955-6567; Fax: (410)955-0470; Email: awu@jhsph.edu • URL: http://www.jhsph.edu/research/centers-and-institutes/health-services-outcomes-research/index.html • Health services, including

determinants of health outcomes; the impacts of alternative health care systems on cost and quality; effective strategies for health promotion and disease prevention; and methods of meeting the needs of high risk populations such as the poor, elderly, mentally ill, disabled, and children.

Malcolm Wiener Center for Social Policy. Harvard University, John F. Kennedy School of Government, 79 John F. Kennedy St., Cambridge, MA 02138. Phone: (617)495-1100; Fax: (617)496-9053; Email: mwcenter@harvaard.edu • URL: http://www.hks.harvard.edu • Does multidisciplinary research on health care access and financing.

National Center for Policy Analysis. 14180 Dallas Pkwy., Ste. 350, Dallas, TX 75254. Phone: (972)386-6272; Email: media@ncpa.org • URL: http://www.ncpa.org • Includes studies on medicare.

Thomas A. Roe Institute for Economic Policy Studies. Heritage Foundation, 214 Massachusetts Ave. NE, Washington, DC 20002-4999. Phone: (202)546-4400 or (202)675-1761; Fax: (202)546-8328; Email: info@heritage.org • URL: http://www.heritage.org • Concerned with the financing of Medicare.

Stratis Health. 2901 Metro Dr., Ste. 400, Bloomington, MN 55425-1525. Phone: 877-787-2847 or (952)854-3306; Fax: (952)853-8503; Email: info@stratishealth.org • URL: http://www.stratishealth.org • Physicians interested in ensuring the availability of quality health care at reasonable costs. Evaluates health care services at hospitals, retirement homes, and other facilities. Develops health care standards for hospitals and offers consultation services to operators of health care facilities to improve efficiency in services. Conducts research and development on latest treatments and medical technologies. Tests new medical technologies.

University of Chicago. 947 E 58th St., MC0926, Chicago, IL 60637-5416. Phone: (773)702-6371 or (773)702-1234; Fax: (773)702-1216 or (773)702-7222; Email: info@ssa.uchicago.edu • URL: http://pps.bsd.uchicago.edu/.

Wayne State University - College of Nursing - Office of Health Research. Cohn Bldg., Rm. 319, 5557 Cass Ave., Detroit, MI 48202. Phone: (313)577-4135; Fax: (313)577-5777; Email: n.artinian@wayne.edu • URL: http://www.nursing.wayne.edu/faculty/health-research.php • Studies innovation in health care organization and financing.

### TRADE/PROFESSIONAL ASSOCIATIONS

National Association for Home Care and Hospice. 228 7th St. SE, Washington, DC 20003. Phone: (202)547-7424; Fax: (202)547-3540; Email: exec@nahc.org • URL: http://www.nahc.org • Promotes high standards of patient care in home care services. Members are durable medical providers, medical equipment and oxygen suppliers, mainly for home health care.

National Committee to Preserve Social Security and Medicare. 10 G St. NE, Ste. 600, Washington, DC 20002-4253. Phone: 800-966-1935 or (202)216-0420 or (202)216-8378; Fax: (202)216-0446; Email: memberservices@ncpssm.org • URL: http://www.ncpssm.org • Members are individuals concerned with Medicare and social security programs. Formerly National Committee to Preserve Social Security.

# MEDICINE, INDUSTRIAL

*See* INDUSTRIAL MEDICINE

# MEETING MANAGEMENT

### ABSTRACTS AND INDEXES

*Business Periodicals Index Retrospective.* EBSCO Publishing Inc. • 11/year. Quarterly and annual cumulations.

## CD-ROM DATABASES

*ABI/INFORM*. ProQuest L.L.C. • Monthly. Provides CD-ROM indexing and abstracting of worldwide business literature. Archival discs are available from 1971. Formerly *ABI/INFORM OnDisc*.

*Applied Science & Business Periodicals Retrospective*. EBSCO Publishing Inc. • Includes citations for more than 3 million articles detailing events, issues, and trends in business and industry.

## HANDBOOKS AND MANUALS

*Seminar Promoting*. Entrepreneur Press. • Looseleaf. $59.50. A practical guide to starting a seminar promotion business. Covers profit potential, start-up costs, market size evaluation, owner's time required, site selection, pricing, accounting, advertising, promotion, etc. (Start-Up Business Guide No. E1071.).

## INTERNET DATABASES

*Trade Show Center*. Global Sources/Trade Media Holdings Ltd. Phone: (656)574-2800; Email: service@globalsources.com • URL: http://www.globalsources.com/TRADESHW/TRDSHFRM.HTM • Free Web site provides current, detailed information on more than 1,000 major trade shows worldwide, including events in the U. S., but with an emphasis on "Asia and Greater China." Searching is offered by product, supplier, country, and month of year. Includes links to "Trade Information.".

## ONLINE DATABASES

*Wilson Business Abstracts Online*. H.W. Wilson Co. • Indexes and abstracts 600 major business periodicals, plus the *Wall Street Journal* and the business section of the *New York Times*. Indexing is from 1982, abstracting from 1990, with the two newspapers included from 1993. Updated weekly. Inquire as to online cost and availability. (*Business Periodicals Index* without abstracts is also available online.).

## PERIODICALS AND NEWSLETTERS

*Harvard Management Communication Letter*. Harvard Business School Publishing. • Description: Provides information and techniques for managers on effective communication.

*Meeting and Conference Executives Alert*. MCEA. • Monthly. $99.00 per year. Newsletter. Formerly *Meeting Planners Alert*.

*The Meeting Professional*. Meeting Professionals International. • Monthly. $99 Nonmembers. Published for professionals in the meeting and convention industry. Contains news, features, and how-to's for domestic and international meetings management. Formerly *Meeting Manager*.

# MEETINGS

See CONFERENCES, WORKSHOPS, AND SEMINARS

# MEETINGS, SALES

See SALES CONVENTIONS

# MEN'S CLOTHING INDUSTRY

## CD-ROM DATABASES

*OECD Statistical Compendium*. Organization for Economic Cooperation and Development. • Semiannual. $1,905.00 per year for 1 to 10 users. CD-ROM contains more than 730,000 monthly, quarterly, and annual time series for OECD countries, 1960 to date. Includes fully searchable data on agriculture, food, economic indicators, national accounts, employment, energy, finance,

industry, technology, and foreign trade. Results can be displayed in various forms.

## FINANCIAL RATIOS

*Annual Statement Studies*. Risk Management Association. • Annual. Compiled from over 280,000 financial statements.

*Annual Statement Studies: Industry Default Probabilities and Cash Flow Measures*. Risk Management Association. • Annual. $405 Nonmembers. Serves as a companion volume to the original *Annual Statement Studies*. Gives probability of default estimates on a percentage scale for more than 450 industries. Includes changes in position year-by-year for eight financial statement line items and provides percentage measures of cash flow.

## INTERNET DATABASES

*Advance Monthly Retail Trade Report*. U. S. Census Bureau. Phone: 800-541-8345 or (301)457-4100 or (301)763-2713; Fax: (301)457-1296 or (301)457-3842; Email: naics@census.gov • URL: http://www.census.gov/epcd/www/naicstab.htm • Web pages provide monthly sales figures for a wide range of retail businesses. Advance, preliminary, and final statistics are provided for the latest month available in each case, with a previous-year comparison. Updates are monthly.

*Business 2.0 Web Guide to the Best Business Links*. Business 2.0 Media Inc. Phone: (415)293-4800; Email: support@business2.com • URL: http://www.business2.com/webguide • Web site presents an extensive, searchable directory of links to "the best, most informative, and authoritative web pages." Twenty main categories cover business, finance, career, company information, people, and technology topics, with thousands of subtopics, all linking to Web sites recommended by experienced business researchers. Fees: Free.

*Fedstats*. Federal Interagency Council on Statistical Policy. Phone: (202)395-7254 • URL: http://www.fedstats.gov • Web site features an efficient search facility for full-text statistics produced by more than 100 federal agencies, including the Census Bureau, the Bureau of Economic Analysis, and the Bureau of Labor Statistics. Boolean searches can be made within one agency or for all agencies combined. Links are offered to international statistical bureaus, including the UN, IMF, OECD, UNESCO, Eurostat, and 20 individual countries. Fees: Free.

*FreeLunch.com*. Economy.com, Inc. Phone: (610)696-8700; Fax: (610)696-1678 • URL: http://www.freelunch.com • Web site provides free access to more than 200 million economic and financial data series, covering industry, demographics, labor markets, prices, retail sales, government spending, trade, interest rates, housing starts, the stock market, etc. Data is available in either chart or table form. Searching is offered. Free, but registration required. Economy.com, Inc. also offers fee-based economic analysis at *The Dismal Scientist* site (www.dismal.com).

*Manufacturing Profiles*. U. S. Bureau of the Census. Phone: (301)763-4636 or (301)763-4100; Fax: (301)763-4794; Email: webmaster@census.gov • URL: http://www.census.gov/prod/www/abs/mfg-prof.html • The Census Bureau makes available free on PDF (Portable Document Format) an annual consolidation of the entire Current Industrial Report series, presenting "all the data compiled." Contains statistics on production, shipments, inventories, consumption, exports, imports, and orders for a wide variety of manufactured products.

## PERIODICALS AND NEWSLETTERS

*DNR: The Men's Fashion Retail Textile Authority*. Fairchild Publications. • Daily. $85.00 per year. Formerly *Daily News Record*.

*GQ: Gentleman's Quarterly for Men*. Conde Nast Publications. • Monthly. $15 Individuals.

*Tobe Report*. Tobe Associates Inc. • Monthly. Edited for fashion retailers. Provides detailed information and analysis relating to current trends in the women's, children's, and men's apparel and accessories markets.

## STATISTICS SOURCES

*Annual Benchmark Report for Retail Trade and Food Services..A Detailed Summary of Retail Sales, Purchases, Accounts Receivable, Inventories, and Food Service Sales*. U. S. Government Printing Office. • Annual. $13.00. Issued by the U.S. Census Bureau. Provides detailed annual and monthly retail statistics for the most recent 10 years. Includes data for various kinds of retail outlets, including automobiles, furniture, appliances, building supplies, grocery stores, drug stores, gasoline stations, clothing, sporting goods, department stores, and restaurants.

*Survey of Current Business*. U. S. Government Printing Office. • Published by Bureau of Economic Analysis, U. S. Department of Commerce. Presents a wide variety of business and economic data.

## TRADE/PROFESSIONAL ASSOCIATIONS

Clothing Manufacturers Association of the U.S.A. 730 Broadway, 10th Fl., New York, NY 10003. Phone: (212)529-0823; Fax: (212)529-1739 or (212)529-1443; Email: kaplancma730@hotmail.com.

# MENTAL HEALTH

*See also* INDUSTRIAL PSYCHOLOGY

## ABSTRACTS AND INDEXES

*Psychological Abstracts*. American Psychological Association. • Monthly. Members, $815.00 per year; individuals and institutions, $1,207.00 per year. Covers the international literature of psychology and the behavioral sciences. Includes journals, technical reports, dissertations, and other sources.

## CD-ROM DATABASES

*Consumer Health Complete*. EBSCO Publishing Inc. • Full text of more than 250 health references, health diagrams, videos, pamphlets.

## DIRECTORIES

*Child Therapists Directory*. InfoGroup Inc. • Annual. Number of listings: 41,340. Entries include: Name, address, phone, size of advertisement, name of owner or manager, number of employees, year first in "Yellow Pages." Compiled from telephone company "Yellow Pages," nationwide.

*Complete Mental Health Directory*. Grey House Publishing. • $165 Individuals. Covers: mental health resources including government agencies, professional meetings and seminars, clinic and hospital management companies, and pharmaceutical companies and their mental health product lines.

## ENCYCLOPEDIAS AND DICTIONARIES

*Gale Encyclopedia of Psychology*. Cengage Learning Inc. • 2000. $267.00. Second edition. Includes bibliographies arranged by topic and a glossary. More than 650 topics are covered.

## GENERAL WORKS

*Journal of Business and Psychology*. Business Psychology Research Institute. Springer Science-Business Media LLC. • Quarterly. $614 Institutions print. An international outlet publishing high quality research designed to advance organizational science and practice.

## HANDBOOKS AND MANUALS

*PDR Drug Guide for Mental Health Professionals*. Thomson Medical Economics. • Annual. $39.95. Contains detailed profiles of more than 70 "common psychotropic drugs organized by brand name." Also contains information on the psychological side effects of about 1,000 other prescription drugs.

## INTERNET DATABASES

*National Library of Medicine.* National Institutes of Health. 9000 Rockville Pke., Bethesda, MD 20892. Phone: (301)496-4000; Email: nihinfo@od.nih.gov • URL: http://www.nih.gov • NLM Web site offers free access through MEDLINE ("PubMed") to about nine million references to articles appearing in some 4,000 biomedical journals, with abstracts. Search interfaces range from "simple keywords to advanced Boolean expressions." The NLM site offers many links to other sources of biomedical and technical information (the National Center for Biotechnology Information, for example). Fees: Free.

## PERIODICALS AND NEWSLETTERS

*Journal of Behavioral Health Services and Research.* Association of Behaviorial Healthcare Management. Lippincott Williams & Wilkins. • Quarterly. Individuals, $81.95 per year; institutions, $231.95 per year. Pertains to the financing and organization of behavioral health services. Formerly *Journal of Mental Health Administration.*

*Journal of Business and Psychology.* Business Psychology Research Institute. Springer Science-Business Media LLC. • Quarterly. $614 Institutions print. An international outlet publishing high quality research designed to advance organizational science and practice.

*Journal of Workplace Behavior Health.* The Haworth Press Inc. • Quarterly. $160 Individuals print + online. An academic and practical journal focusing on employee alcoholism and mental health problems. Formerly *Labor-Management Alcoholism Journal.*

*Mental Health Law Reporter.* Business Publishers Inc. • Monthly. $290 Individuals. Description: Provides news and coverage of court cases pertaining to legal issues affecting mental health professionals.

*Occupational Therapy in Mental Health: A Journal of Psychosocial Practice and Research.* The Haworth Press Inc. • Quarterly. Institutions, $385.00 per year.

*Psychology Today.* Sussex Publishers Inc. • $19.97 6 issues.

## RESEARCH CENTERS AND INSTITUTES

Hungarian Academy of Sciences - Institute of Cognitive Neuroscience and Psychology. PO Box 398, H-1394 Budapest, Hungary. Phone: 36 1 2396726; Fax: 36 1 2396727; Email: info@mtapi.hu • URL: http://www.mtapi.hu • Elementary cognitive psychology, cognitive psychophysiology, social information processing, and organization of personal and social identity.

## TRADE/PROFESSIONAL ASSOCIATIONS

American Mental Health Counselors Association. 801 N Fairfax St., Ste. 304, Alexandria, VA 22314. Phone: 800-326-2642 or (703)548-6002; Fax: (703)548-4775 • URL: http://www.amhca.org • Professional counselors employed in mental health services; students. Aims to: deliver quality mental health services to children, youth, adults, families, and organizations; improve the availability and quality of counseling services through licensure and certification, training standards, and consumer advocacy. Supports specialty and special interest networks. Fosters communication among members. A division of the American Counseling Association.

Mental Health America. 2000 N Beauregard St., 6th Fl., Alexandria, VA 22311. Phone: 800-969-6642 or (703)684-7722; Fax: (703)684-5968 • URL: http://www.mentalhealthamerica.net • Addresses all aspects of mental health and mental illness and is dedicated to improving mental health, preventing mental disorders, and achieving victory over mental illnesses. Accomplishes its mission through advocacy, public education, research, and service in partnership with more than 340 affiliates across the country.

# MENTAL INSTITUTIONS

## ABSTRACTS AND INDEXES

*Psychological Abstracts.* American Psychological Association. • Monthly. Members, $815.00 per year; individuals and institutions, $1,207.00 per year. Covers the international literature of psychology and the behavioral sciences. Includes journals, technical reports, dissertations, and other sources.

## CD-ROM DATABASES

*Authority Health Care Law Library.* Matthew Bender and Company Inc. • Periodic updates. Price on request. Full text CD-ROM provides legal information, case law, and analysis relating to health care facilities, health insurance, longterm care, Medigap, and Medicare.

## DIRECTORIES

*AHA Integrated Delivery Network Directory: U.S. Health Care Systems, Networks, and Alliances.* American Hospital Association. • Annual. $250.00. Provides information about a wide variety of U.S. health care groups and affiliations, including hospitals, nursing homes, rehabilitation centers, psychiatric facilities, home health care agencies, clinical laboratories, outpatient facilities, and diagnostic imaging centers. Includes names of more than 8,000 key executives.

## PERIODICALS AND NEWSLETTERS

*AHA News.* American Hospital Association. HealthForum. • Description: Highlights major news affecting hospitals and the health care field. Reports on legislation and regulation, court cases, surveys, and federal programs. Carries information on individual hospitals and allied hospital associations.

*Health Facilities Management.* American Hospital Association. Health Forum L.L.C. • Covers building maintenance and engineering for hospitals and nursing homes.

## TRADE/PROFESSIONAL ASSOCIATIONS

National Association of Psychiatric Health System. 900 17th St. NW, Ste. 420, Washington, DC 20006-2507. Phone: (202)393-6700; Fax: (202)783-6041; Email: naphs@naphs.org • URL: http://www.naphs.org • Formerly National Association of Private Psychiatric Hospitals.

National Association of State Mental Health Program Directors. 66 Canal Ctr. Plz., Ste. 302, Alexandria, VA 22314. Phone: (703)739-9333; Fax: (703)548-9517 • URL: http://www.nasmhpd.org • Promotes cooperation of state government agencies in delivery of services to people with severe mental illnesses; fosters the exchange of scientific and programmatic information in the administration of public mental health programs including treatment programs, community and hospital care of persons with mental illness, mental retardation, or substance abuse disorders. Monitors state and federal and congressional activities; gathers and analyzes information on organization, structure, funding, and programming of state government mental health programs. Operates under a cooperative agreement with the National Governors' Association.

# MERCHANT MARINE

*See* SHIPS, SHIPPING AND SHIPBUILDING

# MERCHANTS

*See* RETAIL TRADE

# MERGERS AND ACQUISITIONS

*See also* LEVERAGED BUYOUTS

## ALMANACS AND YEARBOOKS

*Merger Yearbook.* SourceMedia Inc. • Annual. $595.00. Provides detailed information on mergers and acquisitions announced or completed during the year. Includes many charts.

## CD-ROM DATABASES

*Buyout Financing Sources/M & A Intermediaries.* SourceMedia Inc. • Annual. $895.00. Provides the CD-ROM combination of *Directory of Buyout Financing Sources* and *Directory of M & A Intermediaries.* Contains information on more than 1,000 financing sources (banks, insurance companies, venture capital firms, etc.) and 850 intermediaries (corporate acquirers, valuation firms, lawyers, accountants, etc.). Also includes back issues of *Buyouts Newsletter* and *Mergers & Acquisitions Report.* Fully searchable.

## DIRECTORIES

*The Buyouts Directory of Mergers & Acquisition Intermediaries.* Securities Data Publishing. • Annual. $195. Covers: 600 U.S. and Canadian business brokers, as well as other merger and acquisition intermediaries. Database includes: Five articles explaining the role of acquisition intermediaries. Entries include: Company name, address, phone, profiles of commercial, merchant and investment banks.

*DealBase II: An Electronic Database of Acquisition Opportunities.* Business Publications Inc. • Monthly. $425 per year. Diskette. Database covers: Over 675 of middle market companies, currently available for acquisition, with annual revenues between 3 and 75 million dollars. Database includes: Company name, location, description, revenues, profitability, purchase price, industry, contact information, merger/acquisition data.

*Food Business Mergers & Acquisitions.* Food Institute. • Annual. $295 Individuals print version and disk. Covers: Companies involved in food industry company mergers or take-overs, including import-export, banking, and advertising firms. Database includes: Ratings and financial information for selected firms from Moody's Investors Service. Entries include: Acquiring company name, location; acquired company name, location, products, number of units or stores.

*Fortune--Deals of the Year Issue.* Time Inc. • $5. Publication includes: 50 largest United States corporate financial transactions, including mergers, acquisitions, leveraged buyouts, and debt and equity offerings. Entries include: Companies involved, value (value and percent of book value), date and type of transaction, type of industry, financial intermediary, fee charged.

*International M & A Review.* Euromoney Institutional Investor P.L.C. • $375 Individuals. Covers: Merger and acquisition advising companies in Europe and U.S. Database includes: Country profiles and reviews of mergers and acquisitions by industry. Entries include: Name, address, phone, fax, names and titles of key personnel, year founded, description of business activities.

*Merger and Acquisition Sourcebook.* NVST Inc. • Annual. $450 Single issue discounted price. Publication includes: Profiles of companies most active in mergers and acquisitions in the previous year. Entries include: Company name, address, phone, financial data, history of transactions. Principal content of publication is summary and analysis of merger, acquisition, and divestiture activity in the previous year; company reorganizations; and terminated financial transactions.

626

For publishers' addresses, refer to SOURCES CITED section at the back of the book.

*The Merger Yearbook.* Cambridge Corp. • Annual. $490 plus $5.00 shipping. Publication includes: About 15,000 mergers and joint ventures announced during preceding year, including lists of largest mergers, firms participating most frequently in acquisitions or joint ventures, active acquirers and divesters, acquisitions by foreign firms, and leveraged buyouts, mergers, and joint ventures in preceding year. Principal content of pubication is information on corporate mergers and acquisitions. Entries include: Company names, locations, and announced terms and prices; many listings include financial or other data.

*Mergers & Acquisitions Magazine--Rosters.* MLR Publishing Co. • Bimonthly. $70 per issue. Each issue includes a roster in three sections: "Mergers & Acquisitions," covering major deals concluded between American firms; "Foreign Investment in the U.S.," covering foreign firms which acquired companies in the United States; and "U.S. Investment Abroad," covering acquisitions by United States firms in other countries. Additional information on pending and completed deals, cancellations, and sell-offs is given in news sections. Entries include: Names and locations of participants, sales and net income of each, terms, lines of business of each participant, and effective date of transaction.

*Mergerstat Transaction Roster.* FactSet Mergerstat L.L.C. • Annual. $299.00. A directory of all U. S. companies that were involved in merger and acquisition activity during the year covered. Includes details of each transaction.

*Spain-Portugal Mergers and Acquisitions Directory.* S.p.A • Biennial. Covers: 200 banks, brokers, auditors, lawyers of the mergers and acquisitions sector with the names of the principals in Spain and Portugal. Entries include: Company name, names and titles of key personnel, number of employees, financial data, branch office name and address, description, services provided.

*World M&A Network.* NVST Inc. • Monthly Quarterly. $395 U.S.. Lists companies for sale, companies seeking to purchase other companies, and sources of acquisition financing.

### INTERNET DATABASES

*InSite 2.* Intelligence Data/Thomson Financial. Phone: 800-654-0393 or (617)856-1890; Fax: (617)737-3182; Email: intelligence.data@tfn.com • URL: http://www.insite2.gale.com/ • Fee-based Web site consolidates information in a "Base Pack" consisting of Business InSite, Market InSite, and Company InSite. Optional databases are Consumer InSite, Health and Wellness InSite, Newsletter InSite, and Computer InSite. Includes fulltext content from more than 2,500 trade publications, journals, newsletters, newspapers, analyst reports, and other sources. Continuous updating. Formerly produced by The Gale Group.

*Intelligence Data.* Thomson Financial. Phone: 800-654-0393; Fax: (617)824-2477 • URL: http://www.intelligencedata.com • Fee-based Web site provides a wide variety of information relating to competitive intelligence, strategic planning, business development, mergers, acquisitions, sales, and marketing. "Intelliscope" feature offers searching of other Thomson units, such as Investext, MarkIntel, InSite 2, and Industry Insider. Weekly updating.

### OTHER SOURCES

*Acquisitions and Mergers: Negotiated and Contested Transactions.* Joy M. Bryan and Simone M. Lorne. Thomson West. • $342 Individuals per month. Includes legal forms and documents. (Securities Law Series).

*Business Strategies.* Wolters Kluwer Law & Business CCH. • Semimonthly. $795.00 per year. Four looseleaf volumes. Semimonthly updates. Legal, tax, and accounting aspects of business planning and decision-making. Provides information on start-ups,

forms of ownership (partnerships, corporations), failing businesses, reorganizations, acquisitions, and so forth. Includes *Business Strategies Bulletin,* a monthly newsletter.

*Capital Changes Reports.* Wolters Kluwer Law & Business CCH. • Weekly. $1,395.00. Six looseleaf volumes. Arranged alphabetically by company. This service presents a chronological capital history that includes reorganizations, mergers and consolidations. Recent actions are found in Volume One - "New Matters.".

*Mergers & Acquisitions.* Glasser LegalWorks. • Looseleaf. $225.00, including CD-ROM version. Periodic Supplementation. Includes explanations of M & A legal procedures, with annotated forms. (Emerging Growth Companies Series.)

*Savings Institutions: Mergers, Acquisitions, and Conversions.* ALM Media Properties LLC. • $560. Provides detailed information on the legal complexities of mergers and acquisitions involving savings institutions. (Law Journal Press).

### PERIODICALS AND NEWSLETTERS

*Acquisitions Monthly.* Thomson Financial Inc. • Monthly. $790.00 per year. Published in London. Provides detailed information, commentary, and statistics on merger, acquisition, and buyout activity in Europe, the U.S., and Asia.

*Business and Acquisition Newsletter.* Newsletters International, Inc. • Monthly. $300.00 per year. Information about firms that want to buy or sell companies, divisions, subsidiaries, product lines, patents, etc.

*Mergers & Acquisitions Report.* SourceMedia Inc. • Weekly. $1,295.00 per year. Newsletter. Covers pending and ongoing mergers, acquisitions, restructurings, and bankruptcies.

*Mergers & Acquisitions: The Dealmaker's Journal.* SourceMedia Inc. • Bimonthly. $475.00 per year. Provides articles on various aspects of M & A, including valuation, pricing, taxes, and strategy. Current M & A deals are listed and described.

*Mergerstat Quarterly Reports.* Houlihan Lokey Inc. • Quarterly. $100.00 per year. Newsletter. Provides details and analysis of recent corporate merger activity. Includes "Top deals year-to-date" and rankings of financial and legal advisors.

### TRADE/PROFESSIONAL ASSOCIATIONS

Alliance of Merger and Acquisition Advisors. 200 E Randolph St., 24th Fl., Chicago, IL 60601. Phone: 877-844-2535; Fax: (312)729-9800; Email: info@ amaaonline.org • URL: http://www.amaaonline.com • Serves the educational and resource needs of mergers and acquisitions professionals. Helps members improve their level of knowledge to better market and deliver their advisory services. Maintains the highest recognized standards of professional excellence for corporate advisory and transaction services.

International Association of Merger and Acquisition Professionals. 6000 Cattleridge Dr., Ste. 300, Sarasota, FL 34232. Phone: (941)378-5500; Email: info@imap.com • URL: http://www.imap.com • Firms with experience in the merger/acquisition field that meet the association's criteria of professional background and financial ability (primarily specialists in selling, buying, and merging medium-sized businesses with sales in the range of 1 to 100 million dollars); allied members include individuals and firms that provide auxiliary services for the completion of merger/acquisition transactions. Purposes are: promotion of the science of merger/ acquisition consultancy; encouragement of educational and training material in the field; enhancement of the image and professional standing of industry specialists; expeditious but confidential distribution of business information on available merger or acquisition prospects.

## MERIT RATING

*See* RATING OF EMPLOYEES

## METAL FINISHING

### ABSTRACTS AND INDEXES

*The Surface Treatment & Finishing of Aluminium & its Alloys.* Finishing Publications Ltd. • $390 6th Edition. Over 12,000 abstracts. Collection of almost 12,000 abstracts from 1960 to date, relating to the surface treatment of aluminium, incl. papers, patents, books.

### DIRECTORIES

*Dun's Industrial Guide: The Metalworking Directory.* Dun & Bradstreet Inc. • Annual. Libraries, $485; commercial institutions, $795.00. Lease basis. Three volumes. Lists about 65,000 U. S. manufacturing plants using metal and suppliers of metalworking equipment and materials. Includes names and titles of key personnel. Products, purchases, and processes are indicated.

*Metal Finishing Guidebook and Directory.* Elsevier. • Included with subscription to Metal Finishing. Lists manufacturers and suppliers to the industry.

### PERIODICALS AND NEWSLETTERS

*Finishers' Management.* Publication Management Inc. • 10 times a year. $35.00 per year.

*Industrial Paint and Powder: Coatings Manufacturing and Application.* Reed Elsevier Group plc Reed Business Information. • Monthly. $72.90 per year. Supplement available, *Annual Buyer's Guide.* Formerly *Industrial Finishing.*

*Metal Finishing: Devoted Exclusively to Metallic Surface Treatments.* Elsevier. • Monthly. Institutions, $190.00 per year. Includes annual *Metal Finishing Guidebook and Directory.*

*Modern Metals.* • Monthly. $85.00 per year. Covers management and production for plants that fabricate and finish metals of various kinds.

*Plating and Surface Finishing: Electroplating, Finishing of Metals, Organic Finishing.* American Electroplaters and Surface Finishers Society. • Monthly. Members, $16.00 per year; non-members, $60.00 per year.

*Products Finishing.* Gardner Business Media, Inc. • Monthly. Covers the latest news and trends of industrial plating, painting, powder coating, cleaning, pretreatment and mechanical finishing.

### TRADE/PROFESSIONAL ASSOCIATIONS

National Association for Surface Finishing. 1155 15th St. NW, Ste. 500, Washington, DC 20005. Phone: (202)457-8404 or (703)887-7235; Fax: (202)530-0659; Email: passante@nasf.org • URL: http://www.nasf.org • Members are management personnel of metal and plastic finishing companies. Finishing includes plating, coating, polishing, rust-proofing, and other processes.

## METAL INDUSTRY

### ABSTRACTS AND INDEXES

*Metals Abstracts.* CSA. • Monthly. $3,575.00 per year. Includes print and online editions.

### CD-ROM DATABASES

*OECD Statistical Compendium.* Organization for Economic Cooperation and Development. • Semiannual. $1,905.00 per year for 1 to 10 users. CD-ROM contains more than 730,000 monthly, quarterly, and annual time series for OECD countries, 1960 to date. Includes fully searchable data on agriculture, food, economic indicators, national accounts, employment, energy, finance, industry, technology, and foreign trade. Results can be displayed in various forms.

## DIRECTORIES

*Directory of Linkage Industries.* Hong Kong Productivity Council. • Annual. $220 pick up at HKPC Office. Covers: Major jobshops and suppliers in the metal industry in Hong Kong as well as their operations in Mainland China including mold and tool making, surface finishing, industrial machinery repair and maintenance, and hot and cold working and metal machinery.

*Dun's Industrial Guide: The Metalworking Directory.* Dun & Bradstreet Inc. • Annual. Libraries, $485; commercial institutions, $795.00. Lease basis. Three volumes. Lists about 65,000 U. S. manufacturing plants using metal and suppliers of metalworking equipment and materials. Includes names and titles of key personnel. Products, purchases, and processes are indicated.

*Materials Research Centres: A World Directory of Organizations and Programmes in Materials Science.* Specialist Journals. • Biennial. $445.00. Profiles of research centers in 75 countries. Materials include plastics, metals, fibers, etc.

*Metal & Steel Traders of the World.* Metal Bulletin Ltd. • Annual. $995 Individuals. Covers: 2,000 steel traders worldwide, including exporters, importers, merchants, producers, sales companies, and agents. Entries include: Company name, address, phone, e-mail and web addresses where possible, executives, date founded, parent and subsidiary companies, products.

*Metal Products: Industry Sector Profile.* Philippine-German Export Development Project Philippine Bureau of Export Trade Promotion. • Publication includes: Companies exporting metal products from the Philippines. Entries include: Company name, address, phone, fax, name and title of contact, type of business, year established, subsidiary and branch names and locations, financial data, number of employees, government registrations, professional memberships, bank references, supply capability, export experience, business plan. Principal content of publication is an overview of the business environment and metal products industry in the Philippines.

*North American Scrap Metals Directory.* Recycling Today Media Group. • Annual. $95.20 Individuals discounted price. Covers: Suppliers of scrap metal materials in North America. Entries include: Contact information.

*Swiss Foundry and Metalworks.* Verlag fur Internationale Wirtschaftsliteratur Ltd. • Biennial. $60. Covers: Manufacturers, associations, and importers in the metal, iron, foundry and metal working industries. Entries include: Company or association name, address, phone.

## E-BOOKS

*Encyclopedia of American Industries.* Cengage Learning Inc. • 2011. $807.00. 6th edition. Three volumes. Volume one is Manufacturing Industries and volume two is Service and Non-Manufacturing Industries. Provides the history, development, and recent status of approximately 1,000 industries. Includes statistical graphs, with industry and general indexes. Also available as eBook.

## INTERNET DATABASES

*Business 2.0 Web Guide to the Best Business Links.* Business 2.0 Media Inc. Phone: (415)293-4800; Email: support@business2.com • URL: http://www. business2.com/webguide • Web site presents an extensive, searchable directory of links to "the best, most informative, and authoritative web pages." Twenty main categories cover business, finance, career, company information, people, and technology topics, with thousands of subtopics, all linking to Web sites recommended by experienced business researchers. Fees: Free.

*Fedstats.* Federal Interagency Council on Statistical Policy. Phone: (202)395-7254 • URL: http://www.

fedstats.gov • Web site features an efficient search facility for full-text statistics produced by more than 100 federal agencies, including the Census Bureau, the Bureau of Economic Analysis, and the Bureau of Labor Statistics. Boolean searches can be made within one agency or for all agencies combined. Links are offered to international statistical bureaus, including the UN, IMF, OECD, UNESCO, Eurostat, and 20 individual countries. Fees: Free.

*FreeLunch.com.* Economy.com, Inc. Phone: (610)696-8700; Fax: (610)696-1678 • URL: http:// www.freelunch.com • Web site provides free access to more than 200 million economic and financial data series, covering industry, demographics, labor markets, prices, retail sales, government spending, trade, interest rates, housing starts, the stock market, etc. Data is available in either chart or table form. Searching is offered. Free, but registration required. Economy.com, Inc. also offers fee-based economic analysis at *The Dismal Scientist* site (www.dismal. com).

## PERIODICALS AND NEWSLETTERS

*Advanced Materials and Processes.* ASM International. • Monthly. $325 Institutions. Incorporates *Metal Progress.*Technical information and reports on new developments in the technology of engineered materials and manufacturing processes.

*JOM: The Member Journal of the Minerals, Metals and Materials Society.* The Minerals, Metals, and Materials Society. • Four times a year. Membership. A scholarly journal covering all phases of metals and metallurgy.

*Metal Bulletin.* Metal Bulletin Inc. • Daily. £1,395 1-year standard subscription. Provides news of international trends, prices, and market conditions for both steel and non-ferrous metal industries. (Published in England.).

*Metal Bulletin Monthly.* Metal Bulletin Inc. • Monthly. Edited for international metal industry business executives and senior technical personnel. Covers business, economic, and technical developments. (Published in England.).

*Metal Center News.* Sackett Business Media Inc. • Monthly. $109 U.S. 1-year subscription (12 MCN magazine plus 1 annual directory). The trade magazine of the metals distribution industry: the service centers that warehouse, process and distribute carbon and stainless steels, aluminum and copper and brass.

*Modern Metals.* • Monthly. $85.00 per year. Covers management and production for plants that fabricate and finish metals of various kinds.

*33 Metalproducing: For Primary Producers of Steel, Aluminum, and Copper-Base Alloys.* Penton Media Inc. • Monthly. $65.00 per year. Covers metal production technology and methods and industry news. Includes a bimonthly *Nonferrous Supplement.*

## PRICE SOURCES

*Platt's Metals Week.* Platts Global Energy. • Weekly. $770 Individuals.

## STATISTICS SOURCES

*Non-Ferrous Metal Data Yearbook.* American Bureau of Metal Statistics. • Annual. $405.00. Provides worldwide data on approximately about 200 statistical tables covering many nonferrous metals. Includes production, consumption, inventories, exports, imports, and other data.

*Standard & Poor's Industry Surveys.* Standard & Poor's Financial Services L.L.C. • Semiannual. $1,800.00. Two looseleaf volumes. Includes monthly *Supplements.* Provides detailed, individual surveys of 52 major industry groups. Each survey is revised on a semiannual basis. Also includes "Monthly Investment Review" (industry group investment analysis) and monthly "Trends & Projections" (economic analysis).

*Survey of Current Business.* U. S. Government Printing Office. • Published by Bureau of Economic Analysis, U. S. Department of Commerce. Presents a wide variety of business and economic data.

## TRADE/PROFESSIONAL ASSOCIATIONS

ASM International. 9639 Kinsman Rd., Materials Park, OH 44073-0002. Phone: 800-336-5152 or (440)338-5151; Email: memberservicecenter@ asminternational.org • URL: http://www. asminternational.org • Metallurgists, materials engineers, executives in materials producing and consuming industries; teachers and students. Disseminates technical information about the manufacture, use, and treatment of engineered materials. Offers in-plant, home study, and intensive courses through Materials Engineering Institute.

Palladium Alliance International. PO Box 81511, Billings, MT 59108. Phone: 877-473-7873; Email: info@luxurypalladium.com • URL: http://www. luxurypalladium.com • Represents experts who work with retailers, producers and manufacturers all over the world. Focuses on establishing palladium as a luxurious, precious and distinctive metal. Provides education, marketing and technical support and a vision for the advancement of palladium.

# METAL INDUSTRY, NONFERROUS

*See* NONFERROUS METAL INDUSTRY

# METAL PLATING

*See* METAL FINISHING

# METAL POWDERS

*See* POWDER METALLURGY INDUSTRY

# METAL WORKING INDUSTRY

*See also* MACHINE TOOL INDUSTRY

## ABSTRACTS AND INDEXES

*Cutting Technology.* Penton Media Inc. • Seven times a year. Free to qualified personnel; others, $55.00 per year. Provides abstracts of the international literature of metal cutting and machining. Formerly *Cutting Tool-Machine Digest.*

*Metalforming Digest.* CSA. • Monthly. Price on application. Provides abstracts of the international literature of metal forming, including powder metallurgy, stamping, extrusion, forging, etc.

## DIRECTORIES

*Dun's Industrial Guide: The Metalworking Directory.* Dun & Bradstreet Inc. • Annual. Libraries, $485; commercial institutions, $795.00. Lease basis. Three volumes. Lists about 65,000 U. S. manufacturing plants using metal and suppliers of metalworking equipment and materials. Includes names and titles of key personnel. Products, purchases, and processes are indicated.

*Machine Tool Reference Guide.* Machinery Dealers National Association. • $29.95 Individuals CD-ROM. Covers: Nearly 1,000 metalworking machine tool manufacturers; international coverage. Database includes: Information on mergers and sources of parts. Entries include: Company name, address, phone, fax, product/service provided.

*Who's Who in Metal Forming and Fabricating.* Fabricators and Manufacturers Association International. • Annual. $200 for nonmembers. Lists members of the Fabricators and Manufacturers Association (FMA), International; and members of the Tube and Pipe Association. Includes five indexes. Formerly *FMA Member Resource Directory*.

## INTERNET DATABASES

*Manufacturing Profiles*. U. S. Bureau of the Census. Phone: (301)763-4636 or (301)763-4100; Fax: (301)763-4794; Email: webmaster@census.gov • URL: http://www.census.gov/prod/www/abs/mfg-prof.html • The Census Bureau makes available free on PDF (Portable Document Format) an annual consolidation of the entire Current Industrial Report series, presenting "all the data compiled." Contains statistics on production, shipments, inventories, consumption, exports, imports, and orders for a wide variety of manufactured products.

## PERIODICALS AND NEWSLETTERS

*Production Technology News*. Reed Elsevier Group plc Reed Business Information. • Monthly. $57.99 /year. Formerly *Metalworking Digest*. Premier resource for the latest information on new technology, services, systems and products.

## RESEARCH CENTERS AND INSTITUTES

Advanced Manufacturing Engineering Institute. University of Hartford, College of Engineering, Technology, and Architecture, 200 Bloomfield Ave., West Hartford, CT 06117. Phone: 860-678-4844 or (860)768-4112; Fax: (860)768-5073; Email: shetty@mail.hartford.edu.

## STATISTICS SOURCES

*U.S. Industry and Trade Outlook*. U.S. Department of Commerce National Technical Information Service. • Annual. Produced by the International Trade Administration, U.S. Department of Commerce, in a "public-private" partnership with DRI/ McGraw-Hill and Standard & Poor's. Provides basic data, outlook for the current year, and "Long-Term Prospects" (five-year projections) for a wide variety of products and services. Includes high technology industries. Formerly *U.S. Industrial Outlook*.

## TRADE/PROFESSIONAL ASSOCIATIONS

Precision Metalforming Association. 6363 Oak Tree Blvd., Independence, OH 44131-2556. Phone: (216)901-8800; Fax: (216)901-9190; Email: pma@ pma.org • URL: http://www.metalform.com • Represents the metalforming industry of North America; the industry that creates precision metal products using stamping, fabricating and other value-added processes. Its member companies include metal stampers, fabricators, spinners, slide formers and roll formers, as well as suppliers of equipment, materials and services to the industry. Members are located in 30 countries, with the majority found in North America; in 41 states of the United States as well as Canada and Mexico. Conducts technical and educational programs, compiles statistics, offers training systems, and provides legislative and regulatory assistance to members.

# METALLURGY

*See also* METAL INDUSTRY; POWDER METALLURGY INDUSTRY

## ABSTRACTS AND INDEXES

*Alloys Index*. CSA. • Monthly. $775 print and online.

*Applied Science and Technology Index*. EBSCO Publishing Inc. • 11/year. Indexes a wide variety of English language technical, industrial, and engineering periodicals.

*Metals Abstracts*. CSA. • Monthly. $3,575.00 per year. Includes print and online editions.

*NTIS Alerts: Materials Sciences*. U.S. Department of Commerce National Technical Information Service. • Biweekly. $130 per year. Covers ceram-

ics, glass, coatings, composite materials, alloys, plastics, wood, paper, adhesives, fibers, lubricants, and related subjects.

## CD-ROM DATABASES

*METADEX Materials Collection: Metals-Polymers-Ceramics*. Cambridge Scientific Abstracts L.P. • Quarterly. Provides CD-ROM citations to the worldwide literature of materials science and metallurgy. Corresponds to *Metals Abstracts, Alloys Index, Steels Alert, Nonferrous Alert, Polymers/ Ceramics/Composites Alert*, and *Engineered Materials Abstracts*. (Formerly produced by ASM International.).

## ONLINE DATABASES

*Applied Science and Technology Index Online*. H.W. Wilson Co. • Provides online indexing of 500 major scientific, technical, industrial, and engineering periodicals. Time period is 1983 to date. Monthly updates. Inquire as to online cost and availability.

## PERIODICALS AND NEWSLETTERS

*High-Tech Materials Alert: Advanced Materials: Their Uses and Manufacture*. Technical Insights. • Monthly. Institutions, $695.00 per year. Newsletter on technical developments relating to high-performance materials, including metals and ceramics. Includes market forecasts.

*International Materials Review*. ASM International. • $1,801 Nonmembers online. Bimonthly. Provides technical and research coverage of metals, alloys, and advanced materials. Formerly *International Metals Review*.

*JOM: The Member Journal of the Minerals, Metals and Materials Society*. The Minerals, Metals, and Materials Society. • Four times a year. Membership. A scholarly journal covering all phases of metals and metallurgy.

*Metallurgia, The Journal of Metals Technology, Metal Forming and Thermal Processing*. British Forging Industry Association. DMG World Media Ltd. • Monthly. $157.00 per year.

*Metallurgical and Materials Transactions A: Physical Metallurgy and Materials Science*. ASM International. • Monthly. $3,640 Members 1-year subscription. Formerly *Metallurgical Transactions A- Physical Metallurgy and Materials Science*. Publishes contributions on all aspects of physical metallurgy and materials science, with a special emphasis on relationships among the processing, structure, and properties of materials.

*Metallurgical and Materials Transactions B: Process Metallurgy and Materials Processing Science*. ASM International. • Bimonthly. $2,856 /year. Formerly *Metallurgical Transactions B: Process Metallurgy*. Focused on process metallurgy and materials processing science, contains only original, critically reviewed research on primary manufacturing processes, from extractive metallurgy to the making of a shape.

*Scripta Materialia*. Acta Metallurgica, Inc. Elsevier. • Semimonthly. $2,472 Institutions. Provides a forum for the rapid publication of short communications on the relationship between the structure and the properties of inorganic materials.

## RESEARCH CENTERS AND INSTITUTES

Basic Metals Processing Research Institute. University of Pittsburgh, Swanson School of Engineering, 151 Benedum Hall, Pittsburgh, PA 15261. Phone: (412)624-9800; Fax: (412)624-9808; Email: ssoeadm@pitt.edu • URL: http://www. engineering.pitt.edu/Research/Facilities/Basic_ Metals_Processing_Research_Institute_ (BAMPRI)/#.

Cooperative Program in Metallurgy. Pennsylvania State University, Dept. of Materials and Engineering, 124 Steidle Bldg., University Park, PA 16802. Phone: (814)865-3760; Fax: (814)865-2917; Email:

rx7@psu.edu • URL: http://www.matse.psu.edu.

Massachusetts Institute of Technology - Materials Processing Center. 77 Massachusetts Ave., Cambridge, MA 02139-4301. Phone: (617)253-5179; Fax: (617)258-6900; Email: cthomp@mit.edu • URL: http://mpc-web.mit.edu • Conducts processing, engineering, and economic research in ferrous and nonferrous metals, ceramics, polymers, photonic materials, superconductors, welding, composite materials, and other materials.

## TRADE/PROFESSIONAL ASSOCIATIONS

ASM International. 9639 Kinsman Rd., Materials Park, OH 44073-0002. Phone: 800-336-5152 or (440)338-5151; Email: memberservicecenter@ asminternational.org • URL: http://www. asminternational.org • Metallurgists, materials engineers, executives in materials producing and consuming industries; teachers and students. Disseminates technical information about the manufacture, use, and treatment of engineered materials. Offers in-plant, home study, and intensive courses through Materials Engineering Institute.

The Minerals, Metals, and Materials Society. 184 Thorn Hill Rd., Warrendale, PA 15086-7514. Phone: 800-759-4867 or (724)776-9000; Fax: (724)776-3770; Email: webmaster@tms.org • URL: http:// www.tms.org/TMSHome.aspx • Members are metallurgists, metallurgical engineers, and materials scientists. Divisions include Light Metals and Electronic, Magnetic, and Photonic Materials. Formerly The Metallurigical Society.

Mining and Metallurgical Society of America. PO Box 810, Boulder, CO 80306-0810. Phone: (303)444-6032; Fax: (415)899-0262; Email: contactmmsa@mmsa.net • URL: http://www.mmsa. net • Works for the conservation of mineral resources, the advancement of mining and metallurgical industries, the better protection of mine investors and mine workers, the increase of scientific knowledge, and the encouragement of high professional ideals and ethics.

# METALS, RARE EARTH

*See* RARE EARTH METALS

# METEOROLOGY

*See* WEATHER AND WEATHER FORECASTING

# METRIC SYSTEM

*See* WEIGHTS AND MEASURES

# MEXICO

*See* LATIN AMERICAN MARKETS

# MICROCOMPUTERS AND MINICOMPUTERS

*See also* ARTIFICIAL INTELLIGENCE; COMPUTER COMMUNICATIONS; COMPUTER CRIME AND SECURITY; COMPUTER PERIPHERALS AND ACCESSORIES; COMPUTER SOFTWARE INDUSTRY; COMPUTERS; COMPUTERS IN EDUCATION; DESKTOP PUBLISHING; OPTICAL DISK STORAGE DEVICES; PORTABLE COMPUTERS; WORD PROCESSING

## ABSTRACTS AND INDEXES

*Applied Science and Technology Index.* EBSCO Publishing Inc. • 11/year. Indexes a wide variety of English language technical, industrial, and engineering periodicals.

*Business Periodicals Index Retrospective.* EBSCO Publishing Inc. • 11/year. Quarterly and annual cumulations.

*Computer and Information Systems Abstracts Journal: An Abstract Journal Pertaining to the Theory, Design, Fabrication and Application of Computer and Information Systems.* CSA. • Monthly. $1,750 per year.

*Computer Science Index.* EBSCO Publishing Inc. • Quarterly. $245 per year. Contains brief abstracts of book and periodical literature covering all phases of computing, including approximately 70 specific application areas.

*Current Contents: Engineering, Computing and Technology.* Thomson Reuters Intellectual Property and Science. • Weekly. $730 per year. Reproductions of contents pages of technical journals. Includes *Author Index, Address Directory, Current Book Contents,* and *Title Word Index.* Formerly *Current Contents: Engineering, Technology and Applied Sciences.*

*Inspec Direct.* Institution of Engineering and Technology. • Monthly. $2,400 per year. Section C of *Science Abstracts.*

*Internet and Personal Computing Abstracts (print edition).* EBSCO Publishing Inc. • Quarterly. $269.00 per year, including cumulative index. Provides more than 10,000 abstracts annually from both trade and academic publications. Covers computer hardware, software, product reviews, Web topics, e-commerce, networks, corporate news, security, and related topics. Formerly *Microcomputer Abstracts.*

*Science Citation Index.* Thomson Reuters Intellectual Property and Science. • Weekly. Includes *Source Index, Citation Index, Permuterm Subject Index,* and *Corporate Index.* Provides researchers, administrators, faculty, and students with quick, powerful access to the bibliographic and citation information they need to find research data, analyze trends, journals and researchers, and share their findings.

## ALMANACS AND YEARBOOKS

*Information Technology Outlook.* Organisation for Economic Co-operation and Development Publications and Information Center. • Biennial. A review of recent developments in international markets for computer hardware, software, and services. Also examines current legal provisions for information systems security and privacy in OECD countries.

## CD-ROM DATABASES

*Business Abstracts with Full Text.* EBSCO Publishing Inc. • Includes full text articles from more than 460 business publications from 1982 to present. Indexing for nearly 880 publications.

*Datapro on CD-ROM: Computer Systems Hardware and Software.* Gartner Inc. • Monthly. Price on application. CD-ROM provides product specifications, product reports, user surveys, and market forecasts for a wide range of computer hardware and software.

*Science Citation Index.* Thomson Reuters Intellectual Property and Science. • Weekly. Includes *Source Index, Citation Index, Permuterm Subject Index,* and *Corporate Index.* Provides researchers, administrators, faculty, and students with quick, powerful access to the bibliographic and citation information they need to find research data, analyze trends, journals and researchers, and share their findings.

## ENCYCLOPEDIAS AND DICTIONARIES

*Encyclopedia of Microcomputers.* Allen Kent and James G. Williams, editors. Taylor & Francis Online. • 27 volumes. $5,265.00. $195.00 per volume. Dates vary. Contains scholarly articles written by microcomputer experts. Includes bibliographies.

## FINANCIAL RATIOS

*Industry Norms and Key Business Ratios.* Dun & Bradstreet Inc. • Annual. Five volumes. Covers over 800 kinds of businesses, arranged by Standard Industrial Classification number. More detailed editions covering longer periods of time are also available.

## INTERNET DATABASES

*InfoTech Trends.* Data Analysis Group. Phone: (925)462-1202; Fax: (925)462-1225; Email: support@infotechtrends.com • URL: http://www.infotechtrends.com • Web site provides both free and fee-based market research data on the information technology industry, including computers, peripherals, telecommunications, the Internet, software, CD-ROM/DVD, e-commerce, and workstations. Fees: Free for current (most recent year) data; more extensive information has various fee structures. Formerly *Computer Industry Forecasts.*

*Wired News.* Lycos Inc. 400-2 Totten Pond Rd., Waltham, MA 02451-2053. Phone: (781)370-2700 or (415)276-8400; Fax: (781)370-2600 or (415)276-8500; Email: press@lycos.com • URL: http://www.lycos.com • Provides summaries and full-text of "Top Stories" relating to the Internet, computers, multimedia, telecommunications, and the electronic information industry in general. These news stories are placed in the broad categories of Politics, Business, Culture, and Technology. Affiliated with *Wired* magazine. Fees: Free.

## ONLINE DATABASES

*Applied Science and Technology Index Online.* H.W. Wilson Co. • Provides online indexing of 500 major scientific, technical, industrial, and engineering periodicals. Time period is 1983 to date. Monthly updates. Inquire as to online cost and availability.

*Computer Database.* Cengage Learning Inc. • Provides one year of full-text online for 150 leading computer-related publications. Also includes 70,000 product specifications and brief profiles of 13,000 computer product vendors and manufacturers. Inquire as to prices and availability.

*Wilson Business Abstracts Online.* H.W. Wilson Co. • Indexes and abstracts 600 major business periodicals, plus the *Wall Street Journal* and the business section of the *New York Times.* Indexing is from 1982, abstracting from 1990, with the two newspapers included from 1993. Updated weekly. Inquire as to online cost and availability. (*Business Periodicals Index* without abstracts is also available online.).

## PERIODICALS AND NEWSLETTERS

*Computer Shopper: The Computer Magazine for Direct Buyers.* Media Inc. • Nationwide marketplace for computer equipment.

*Computerworld: Newsweekly for Information Technology Leaders.* ComputerWorld Inc. • Weekly. $190.00 per year.

*EDP Weekly: The Leading Weekly Computer News Summary.* Computer Age and EDP News Services. • Weekly. $495.00 per year. Newsletter. Summarizes news from all areas of the computer and microcomputer industries.

*IEEE Micro.* IEEE - Communications Society. • Bimonthly. Contains high-quality technical articles from designers, systems integrators, and users discussing the design, performance, or application of microcomputer and microprocessor systems.

*InfoWorld: Defining Technology for Business.* Info-

World Publishing. • Weekly. $195.00 per year. For personal computing professionals.

*Microprocessor Report: The Insiders' Guide to Microprocessor Hardware.* Reed Elsevier Group plc Reed Business Information. • 12 times a year. $695.00 per year. Newsletter. Covers the technical aspects of microprocessors from Intel, IBM, Cyrix, Motorola, and others.

*Online Libraries and Microcomputers.* Information Intelligence Inc. • Ten times a year. Individuals $43.75 per year; libraries. $62.50 per year. Newsletter. Covers library automation and electronic information (online, CD-ROM). Reviews or describes new computer hardware and software for library use.

*PC Magazine: The Independent Guide to Personal Computing and the Internet.* Media Inc. • Biweekly. $49.97 per year.

*PC World: The No. 1 Source for Definitive How-to-Buy, How-to-Use Advice on Personal Computing Systems and Software.* IDG Communications Inc. • Monthly. $29.90 per year.

*PlugIn Datamation: Profit and Value from Information Technology.* EarthWeb. • Monthly. Price on application. Technical, semi-technical and general news covering EDP topics.

*Release 1.0 Esther Dysons Monthly Report.* EDventure Holdings Inc. • Description: Reports on technology, communications, and the Internet. Reviews and analyzes the technology business. Recurring features include a calendar of events.

*Smart Computing.* Sandhills Publishing Co. • Monthly. $29.00 per year. Provides basic computer advice "in plain English." Includes reviews of hardware and software.

*Software Magazine.* Wiesner Publishing, Inc. • Monthly. Free to qualified personnel; others, $42.00 per year.

## PRICE SOURCES

*Computer Price Guide: The Blue Book of Used IBM Computer Prices.* Computer Economics Inc. • Quarterly. $140.00 per year. Provides average prices of used IBM computer equipment, including "complete lists of obsolete IBM equipment." Includes a newsletter on trends in the used computer market. Edited for dealers, leasing firms, and business computer buyers.

## RESEARCH CENTERS AND INSTITUTES

Carnegie Mellon Research Institute-The Robotics Institute. 5000 Forbes Ave., Pittsburgh, PA 15213. Phone: (412)268-3818; Fax: (412)268-6436; Email: robotics@ri.cmu.edu • URL: http://www.ri.cmu.edu • Multidisciplinary research activities include expert systems applications, minicomputer and microcomputer systems design, genetic engineering, and transportation systems analysis.

Columbia University - Center for Advanced Information Management. 650 W 168th St., Black Bldg. - 130, New York, NY 10032. Phone: (212)305-2944 or (212)305-5334; Fax: (212)305-0196 or (212)305-3302; Email: tomaselli@cat.columbia.edu • URL: http://www.cat.columbia.edu • Biomedical informatics, computer science, computational and systems biology, biomedical imaging.

Department of Electrical and Microelectronic Engineering. Rochester Institute of Technology, Kate Gleason College of Engineering, 77 Lomb Memorial Dr., Rochester, NY 14623. Phone: (585)475-2165; Fax: (585)475-5845; Email: eme@rit.edu • URL: http://www.rit.edu/kgcoe/eme • Facilities include digital computer organization/microcomputer laboratory.

Technology Based Learning and Research. Arizona State University, College of Education, Phoenix, AZ 85069. Phone: (602)543-6358; Fax: (602)543-6900; Email: ps@asu.edu • URL: http://tblr.asu.edu •

Research activities are related to computer literacy.

## STATISTICS SOURCES

*Standard & Poor's Industry Surveys.* Standard & Poor's Financial Services L.L.C. • Semiannual. $1,800.00. Two looseleaf volumes. Includes monthly *Supplements.* Provides detailed, individual surveys of 52 major industry groups. Each survey is revised on a semiannual basis. Also includes "Monthly Investment Review" (industry group investment analysis) and monthly "Trends & Projections" (economic analysis).

*U.S. Industry and Trade Outlook.* U.S. Department of Commerce National Technical Information Service. • Annual. Produced by the International Trade Administration, U.S. Department of Commerce, in a "public-private" partnership with DRI/McGraw-Hill and Standard & Poor's. Provides basic data, outlook for the current year, and "Long-Term Prospects" (five-year projections) for a wide variety of products and services. Includes high technology industries. Formerly *U.S. Industrial Outlook.*

## TRADE/PROFESSIONAL ASSOCIATIONS

Computing Technology Industry Association. 3500 Lacey Rd., Ste. 100, Downers Grove, IL 60515. Phone: (630)678-8300; Fax: (630)678-8384; Email: membership@comptia.org • URL: http://www.comptia.org • Trade association of more than 19,000 companies and professional IT members in the rapidly converging computing and communications market. Has members in more than 89 countries and provides a unified voice for the industry in the areas of e-commerce standards, vendor-neutral certification, service metrics, public policy and workforce development. Serves as information clearinghouse and resource for the industry; sponsors educational programs.

# MICROFICHE

*See* MICROFORMS

# MICROFILM

*See* MICROFORMS

# MICROFORMS

*See also* DOCUMENT IMAGING

## CD-ROM DATABASES

*LISA Plus.* Cambridge Scientific Abstracts L.P. • Quarterly. $2,000 per year. CD-ROM version of Library Information and Science Abstracts, providing abstracting and indexing of the world's library and information science literature, 1969 to date. Contains more than 180,000 citations.

## DIRECTORIES

*AIIM Buying Guide.* Association for Information and Image Management International Headquarters. • Annual. $64. Publication includes: List of approximately 460 manufacturers, software developers, suppliers, service companies, consultants, and system integrators in the document management industry. Entries include: Company name, address, phone, product/service provided, product or sales contact, business descriptions, number of employees. Organization was formerly called National Micrographics Association.

*Microcosm.* Dun & Bradstreet Inc. • Microfiche. Covers: Over 150 separate editions list companies in local business areas throughout the U.S. Entries include: Company name, address, phone, number of employees, Standard Industrial Classification (SIC) code, sales volume, principal officer name and title, DUNS number.

## OTHER SOURCES

*Information and Image Management: The State of the Industry.* Association for Information and Image Management International. • Annual. $130.00. Market data with five-year forecasts. Covers electronic imaging, micrographics supplies and equipment, software, and records management services.

## PERIODICALS AND NEWSLETTERS

*InForm.* Victor O. Schinnerer and Company Inc. • Description: Reports national and state developments affecting architects and engineers.

*Microform and Imaging Review.* R.R. Bowker L.L.C. • Quarterly. $198.00 per year. Evaluates scholarly micropublications for libraries. Includes articles on microform management. Text in German.

*Micrographics and Hybrid Imaging Systems Newsletter: Monthly Report for Busines Excutives Who Use of Market Microfilm Services and Hybrid Imaging Services and Equipment.* Microfilm Publishing Inc. • Monthly. $198.00 per year. A report for business executives who use or market microfilm services and equipment. Formerly *Micrographics Newsletter.*

## TRADE/PROFESSIONAL ASSOCIATIONS

Association for Information and Image Management International. 1100 Wayne Ave., Ste. 1100, Silver Spring, MD 20910. Phone: 800-477-2446 or (301)587-8202; Fax: (301)587-2711; Email: aiim@aiim.org • URL: http://www.aiim.org • Manufacturers, vendors and individual users of information and image management equipment, products and services. Holds special meetings for trade members and companies. Maintains speakers' bureau. Operates resource center. Compiles statistics.

# MICROGRAPHICS

*See* MICROFORMS

# MICROPHOTOGRAPHY

*See* MICROFORMS

# MICROPROCESSORS

*See* MICROCOMPUTERS AND MINICOMPUTERS

# MICROWAVES

## ABSTRACTS AND INDEXES

*Key Abstracts: Microwave Technology.* Institution of Engineering and Technology. • Monthly. $1,138. Provides international coverage of journal and proceedings literature.

## DIRECTORIES

*Microwaves and RF Product Data Directory.* Penton. • Lists a large number of reputable, reliable firms specializing in the product categories under which they are listed.

## PERIODICALS AND NEWSLETTERS

*Microwave and Optical Technology Letters.* John Wiley and Sons, Inc., Journals Div. • Monthly. Provides quick publication (3 to 6 month turnaround) of the most recent findings and achievements in high frequency technology, from RF to optical spectrum.

*Microwave Journal.* Horizon House Publications Inc. • Monthly. Source for the latest product announcements, industry news, catalogs, and vendor information for the RF and microwave industry.

## STATISTICS SOURCES

*U.S. Industry and Trade Outlook.* U.S. Department of Commerce National Technical Information Service. • Annual. Produced by the International Trade Administration, U.S. Department of Commerce, in a "public-private" partnership with DRI/McGraw-Hill and Standard & Poor's. Provides basic data, outlook for the current year, and "Long-Term Prospects" (five-year projections) for a wide variety of products and services. Includes high technology industries. Formerly *U.S. Industrial Outlook.*

# MIGRATION

*See* IMMIGRATION AND EMIGRATION

# MIGRATION OF INDUSTRY

*See* LOCATION OF INDUSTRY

# MILITARY ASSOCIATIONS

## OTHER SOURCES

*Adjutants General Association of the United States.* • Adjutants General (National Guard) of the states and territories.

*American Military Society.* • Active or retired members of the armed services (Army, Navy, Air Force, Marine Corps, and Coast Guard), and civilians. Develops and supports activities which promote the general well-being of the members; upholds and defends the Constitution; supports national defense; and preserves the memories and traditions of the Armed Forces.

*National Guard Executive Directors Association.* • Provides a forum for the exchange of information of common interest to members and the organizations they represent; encourages states to organize and maintain a National Guard association; participates in improving the operational readiness, training and image of the National Guard on both state and national levels.

*Society of the Fifth Division.* • Works to perpetuate and memorialize the valiant acts and patriotic deeds of the Fifth Division.

## TRADE/PROFESSIONAL ASSOCIATIONS

Air Force Association. 1501 Lee Hwy., Arlington, VA 22209-1198. Phone: 800-727-3337 or (703)247-5800; Fax: (703)247-5853; Email: membership@afa.org • URL: http://www.afa.org • Promotes public understanding of aerospace power and the pivotal role it plays in the security of the nation.

Air Force Sergeants Association. 5211 Auth Rd., Suitland, MD 20746-4339. Phone: 800-638-0594 or (301)899-3500; Fax: (301)899-8136 • URL: http://www.hqafsa.org//AM/Template.cfm?Section=Home • Any enlisted man or woman, active or retired, in the Air Force, Air National Guard, Air Force Reserve, Army Air Corps, or Army Air Forces; women auxiliaries. Works to: promote, preserve, and uphold fair and equitable legislation as it pertains to the welfare of the airmen who served and are serving in the U.S.A.F.; maintain the highest professional standards and integrity among members; promote the interests of members, the U.S., and the rest of the "free world"; promote religious, educational, and recreational activities among members, in order to develop a better understanding and mutual respect. Sponsors educational seminars, Air Force training, JOBCAP, a job placement service, and programs for retired members. Provides congressional representation, insurance, and other services.

American Retirees Association. PO Box 2333, Redlands, CA 92373-0781. Phone: (909)557-0107 or (505)856-2080; Fax: (909)335-2711; Email:

contactara@rocketmail.com • URL: http://www. americanretirees.org • Active, reserve, and retired members of the uniformed military services of the United States. Seeks to address what the group feels are inequities in the Uniformed Services Former Spouses' Protection Act (USFSPA). Provides advisory services to military retirees and second families adversely affected by these laws; lobbies for amendments to the USFSPA.

Armed Forces Hostess Association. The Pentagon, Rm. 1E541, 6604 Army Pentagon, Washington, DC 20310. Phone: (703)614-0350 or (703)614-0485; Fax: (703)697-5542 • URL: http://sswafha.hqda. pentagon.mil • Information office operated by volunteer wives of the armed forces. Assists in welcoming service families to the Washington, DC area; provides information on living conditions at all U.S. installations in the U.S. and overseas. Maintains information files on topics ranging from animal care and camps to universities and local vacation areas.

Army Nurse Corps Association. PO Box 39235, San Antonio, TX 78218-1235. Phone: (210)650-3534; Fax: (210)650-3494; Email: membership@e-anca. org • URL: http://e-anca.org • Army Nurse Corps officers from active, or retiree status or those serving honorably for shorter periods, or reserve duty. Provides educational and social opportunities for members; disseminates information to the public. Seeks to preserve history of the U.S. Army Nurse Corps.

Association of Graduates of the United States Air Force Academy. 3116 Academy Dr., USAF Academy, CO 80840-4475. Phone: (719)472-0300; Fax: (719)333-4194; Email: aog@aogusafa.org • URL: http://www.usafa.org • Graduates and friends of the U.S. Air Force Academy. Promotes interest in and dedication to the mission, ideals, objectives, activities, and history of the Academy; encourages young people to attend the Academy; encourages and supports fundraising for the Academy; fosters camaraderie among Academy graduates and U.S. armed forces officer corps; professional development of the armed forces officer corps. Sponsors annual class reunions/homecomings. Offers scholarships to graduates of the academy and their dependents; provides placement service. Operates charitable program, including humanitarian support for next-of-kin of academy graduates. Compiles statistics.

Association of Military Colleges and Schools of the United States. 12332 Washington Brice Rd., Fairfax, VA 22033. Phone: (703)272-8406; Email: amcsus@cox.net • URL: http://www.amcsus.org • Comprises of military colleges and secondary schools.

Association of Military Surgeons of the U.S. 9320 Old Georgetown Rd., Bethesda, MD 20814-1653. Phone: 800-761-9320 or (301)897-8800; Fax: (301)530-5446; Email: amsus@amsus.org • URL: http://www.amsus.org • Physicians, dentists, veterinarians, nurses, pharmacists, dietitians, therapists, and others of commissioned rank (or grades E5 through E9) or equivalent in the Army, Navy, Air Force, Public Health Service, and Veterans Administration; Reserve and National Guard officers are also eligible for membership. Advances all phases of federal medicine and allied sciences related to federal health services. Provides group insurance.

Association of NROTC Colleges and Universities. University of Rochester, 575 Mt. Hope Ave., Rochester, NY 14620. Phone: (585)273-1765; Fax: (585)275-8531; Email: scott.verrenti@rochester.edu • URL: http://www.conferences.rochester.edu/ NROTCconstitution.html • Representatives from colleges and universities that have Naval Reserve Officers Training Corps units on their campuses. Promotes NROTC training and coordinates the ef-

forts of institutions offering this service.

Chief Warrant and Warrant Officers Association. 200 V St. SW, Washington, DC 20024-3321. Phone: 800-792-8447 or (202)554-7753; Fax: (202)484-0641; Email: cwoauscg@verizon.net • URL: http:// www.cwoauscg.org • Individuals who currently hold or once held the rank of Warrant Officer or Chief Warrant Officer on the active, retired, and reserve rolls of the U.S. Coast Guard. Works to aid members in advancing their professional abilities. Seeks to enhance their value, loyalty, and devotion to the service; promotes its unity and morale through social association.

Civil Affairs Association. 6689 Kodiak Dr., Fayetteville, NC 28304. Email: civilaffairs@ civilaffairsassoc.org • URL: http://www. civilaffairsassoc.org • U.S. Army active and reserve officers and enlisted personnel serving in Army or Marine Corps civil affairs units or in civil affairs staff positions in major military headquarters, and international members. Advocates and promotes a strong U.S. military civil affairs capability.

Enlisted Association of National Guard of the United States. 3133 Mt. Vernon Ave., Alexandria, VA 22305-2640. Phone: 800-234-3264 or (703)519-3846; Fax: (703)519-3849; Email: eangus@eangus. org • URL: http://www.eangus.org • Active and retired members of the U.S. National Guard. Conducts educational, legislative and charitable programs.

Judge Advocates Association. PO Box 30380, Alexandria, VA 22310-8380. • URL: http://jaa.org • Active, reserve, retired and former Judge Advocates of the Army, Navy, Air Force, Marine Corps, Coast Guard and practitioners of military and veterans law. Assists in the development of military law and an efficient military and veterans legal and judicial system.

Marine Corps Association. 715 Broadway St., Quantico, VA 22134. Phone: 800-336-0291 or (703)640-6161; Fax: (703)640-0823 • URL: http://www.mca-marines.org • Represents active duty, reserve, retired, Fleet Reserve, honorably discharged Marines, and members of other services who have served with Marine Corps units. Disseminates information about the military arts and sciences to members; assists members' professional advancement; fosters the spirit and works to preserve the traditions of the United States Marine Corps. Maintains discount book service and group insurance plan for members. Association founded by members of the Second Provisional Marine Brigade at Guantanamo Bay, Cuba.

Marine Corps Aviation Association. 715 Broadway St., Quantico, VA 22134. Phone: 800-280-3001 or (703)630-1903; Fax: (703)630-2713; Email: mcaa@ flymcaa.org • URL: http://www.flymcaa.org • Members and former members of U.S. Marine aviation units and others with an interest in Marine Corps aviation; aerospace corporations. Aims to: perpetuate camaraderie in marine aviation; foster and encourage professional excellence and recognize important achievements in marine aviation. Conducts charitable programs.

Marine Corps Reserve Association. 8626 Lee Hwy., Ste. 205, Fairfax, VA 22031-2135. Phone: (703)289-1204; Email: usmcra1926@gmail.com • URL: http://www.usmcra.org • Marines who have served on active duty in peace or war. Seeks to: advance the professional skills of marines; represent and assist individual members; promote the interests of the U.S. Marine Corps in order to advance the welfare and preserve the security of the United States. Maintains speakers' bureau and placement service.

Military Impacted Schools Association. 6327 S 196th St., Omaha, NE 68135-3806. Phone: 800-291-6472 • URL: http:// militaryimpactedschoolsassociation.org • Provides the educational needs of military families, including

quality of life initiatives, community and school district support, and aid funding.

Military Vehicle Preservation Association. 3305 Blue Ridge Cut Off, Independence, MO 64055-6101. Phone: 800-365-5798 or (816)833-6872; Fax: (816)833-5115; Email: hq@mvpa.org • URL: http:// www.mvpa.org • Represents individuals and groups interested in the preservation, restoration, safe operation, maintenance, and enjoyment of historic military vehicles. Informs the public of the historical value of collectible military vehicles; serves as a clearinghouse for technical and historical information.

Montford Point Marine Association. PO Box 1070, Sharon Hill, PA 19079. Email: info@ montfordpointmarines.org • URL: http://www. montfordpointmarines.com • Represents veterans and active members of all branches of the U.S. Armed Forces. Aims to support educational assistance programs, veterans programs and promotion of community services. Works to improve the social conditions of veterans, local families, youth and the growing population of senior citizens; named after Montford Point, New River, Camp Lejeune, NC, the only base in America used for the recruit or "Boot Camp" training of black Marines, 1942-49.

National Association for Uniformed Services. 5535 Hempstead Way, Springfield, VA 22151. Phone: 800-842-3451 or (703)750-1342; Email: info@naus. org • URL: http://www.naus.org • Members of the uniformed military services, active, retired or reserve, veteran, enlisted and officers, and their spouses or widows. Develops and supports legislation that upholds the security of the U.S., sustains the morale of the uniformed services, and provides fair and equitable consideration for all service people. Protects and improves compensation, entitlements, and benefits. Provides discount rates on travel, insurance, auto rentals, charge cards, prescription medicine, and legal services.

National Association of Superintendents of U.S. Naval Shore Establishments. 89 Pine Legde Dr., Wells, ME 04090. Phone: (207)646-7316; Email: admin@nasnse.org • URL: http://nasnse.org • Superintendents of production, maintenance, and public works branches of naval shore establishments. Promotes the general welfare of members professionally, intellectually, and socially; cultivates high standards of professional ethics.

National Guard Association of the United States. 1 Massachusetts Ave. NW, Washington, DC 20001-1401. Phone: (202)789-0031; Fax: (202)682-9358; Email: ngaus@ngaus.org • URL: http://www.ngaus. org • Active and Retired Officers and Warrant Officers of the Army National Guard and Air National Guard of the States, Commonwealth of Puerto Rico, the District of Columbia, Guam, and the Virgin Islands. Goals include: adequate national security and a strong Army National Guard and Air National Guard of the United States as components of the armed forces. Sponsors public affairs competition for National Guard personnel. Maintains the Museum of the National Guard, containing rare art and artifacts relating to the militia and National Guard.

National Naval Officers Association. PO Box 10871, Alexandria, VA 22310-0871. Phone: (703)231-8554 • URL: http://nnoa.memberclicks.net • Active, reserve, and retired Navy, Marine, and Coast Guard officers and students in college and military sea service programs. Promotes and assists recruitment, retention, and career development of minority officers in the naval service. Conducts specialized education; maintains counseling, referral, and mentorship. Makes available non-ROTC grants-in-aid. Sponsors competitions; operates charitable program.

Naval Enlisted Reserve Association. 6703 Farragut Ave., Falls Church, VA 22042-2189. Phone: 800-

776-9020 • URL: http://www.nera.org • Enlisted personnel of the U.S. Naval Reserve, Marine Corps Reserve, and Coast Guard Reserve on active duty, inactive duty, or retired. Works to promote career enlisted service in the "sea-going" branches of the armed services; concerned with the readiness, training, morale, and well-being of all Reservists; obtains fair and proper recognition of the contributions made by Reservists to the national defense and to obtain protection and extension of benefits and entitlements for those Reservists who are currently serving and for those who have already served satisfactorily and have retired. Works with Congress and military leaders for legislation and proposals designed to improve and enhance the effectiveness of Reserve programs; also works to provide a communications link with the public.

Naval Reserve Association. 1619 King St., Alexandria, VA 22314-2793. Phone: 877-628-9411; Fax: (866)683-3647 • URL: http://www.ausn.org • Naval officers on active or inactive duty or retired. Maintains involvement with legislation affecting U.S. Navy and Naval Reserve. Provides Naval Officer Promotion Record Reviews. Sponsors Naval Reserve Junior Officer of the Year Programs. Offers professional education; sponsors competitions; maintains speakers' bureau.

Non Commissioned Officers Association of the United States of America. 9330 Corporate Dr., Ste. 701, Selma, TX 78154-1257. Phone: 800-662-2620 or (210)653-6161; Fax: (210)637-3337 • URL: http://www.ncoausa.org • Noncommissioned and petty officers of the United States military serving in grades E1 through E9 from all five branches of the U.S. Armed Forces; includes active duty and retired personnel, members of the Reserve and National Guard components, and personnel who held the rank of NCO/PO at the time of separation from active duty under honorable conditions. Formed for patriotic, fraternal, social, and benevolent purposes. Offers veterans job assistance, legislative representation, and grants. Conducts charitable programs.

Reserve Officers Association of the United States. 1 Constitution Ave. NE, Washington, DC 20002-5618. Phone: 800-809-9448 or (202)479-2200; Fax: (202)547-1641 • URL: http://www.roa.org • Represents reserve members of the seven United States Uniformed Services-Army, Navy, Air Force, Marines, Coast Guard, Public Health Service, and National Oceanic and Atmospheric Administration Corps. Aims to "support and promote the development and execution of a military policy for the United States that will provide adequate National Security."

State Guard Association of the United States. 36 Thorn Oak, Ste. 200, Dove Canyon, CA 92679. Phone: (949)888-5792; Fax: (949)888-4799; Email: info@sgaus.org • URL: http://www.sgaus.org • Active and retired officers and enlisted personnel of State Defense Forces (SDF) including State Guard, State Military Reserve, National Reserve, Defense Force, Guard Reserve, and other militia. Promotes the SDF in states where they exist; lobbies on behalf of SDF before state and federal governments; fosters exchange among states to keep members abreast of changes in laws pertaining to the SDF. Seeks to educate the public and disseminates information on the history and mission of the militia and to advocate a viable state militia system.

Tailhook Association. 9696 Businesspark Ave., San Diego, CA 92131-1643. Phone: 800-322-4665 or (858)689-9223; Fax: (858)578-8839 • URL: http://www.tailhook.net • Individuals who have been designated as Naval Aviators or Naval Flight Officers and have made carrier landings; other individuals who have made carrier landings or who have the background and interest to support the objectives of the association. Seeks to foster, develop, study, and

support U.S. aircraft carriers and aircrews, and their role in the nation's defense system.

U.S. Armor Association. PO Box 607, Fort Knox, KY 40121-0607. Phone: (502)942-8624; Fax: (502)942-6219 • URL: http://www.cavalryandarmor.com • U.S. Army officers, noncommissioned officers, enlisted men, and veterans of all components. Disseminates professional knowledge of military art and science, especially mobile ground warfare.

United States Army Warrant Officers Association. 462 Herndon Pkwy., Ste. 207, Herndon, VA 20170-5235. Phone: (703)742-7727; Fax: (703)742-7728 • URL: http://www.usawoa.org • Active duty, National Guard, Reserve, and retired U.S. Army warrant officers. Promotes the technical and social welfare of warrant officers. Recommends Army improvement programs. Circulates professional information among warrant officers. Stimulates patriotism, devotion to duty, and comradeship among members.

United States Marine Corps Drill Instructors Association. PO Box 5117, Parris Island, SC 29905. Phone: (828)757-0968 • URL: http://www.parrisislanddi.org • Present and former U.S. Marine Corps drill instructors. Fosters a spirit of comradery through social and recreational activities. Promotes the welfare of elderly, disabled, and needy veterans; sponsors patriotic, charitable, and educational programs. Maintains living memorial monument fund; conducts blood drives and active participants' toys 4 tots.

# MILITARY COMMISSARIES

*See* POST EXCHANGES

# MILITARY MARKET

*See also* DEFENSE INDUSTRIES

## BIBLIOGRAPHIES

*Defense and Security.* U. S. Government Printing Office. • Annual. Free. Issued by the Superintendent of Documents. A list of government publications on defense and related topics. Formerly *Defense Supply and Logistics.* (Subject Bibliography No. 153.).

## DIRECTORIES

*Directory of Middle East Importers of Military & Police Equipment & Supplies.* EXIM Infotek Private Ltd. • $200 Individuals. Covers: 45 Middle East importers of ammunition, military electronic equipment, military equipment and supplies, police equipment, surplus military equipment and supplies, traffic control systems and equipment. Entries include: Company name, postal address, telephone, fax, e-mail, website, contact person, designation, and product details.

*International Directory for Selling Military Products and Services.* DIANE Publishing Co. • $50 Individuals Paperback. Covers: Procurement policies and procedures for 13 European countries plus Australia, Canada, Egypt and Israel. Entries include: Points of contact, getting started, access to technical documents, procurement methods, types of contracts, contract provisions, pre-award surveys, classified information, restrictions on foreign competition, contract administration.

*Military Retailing Directory.* Military Retailing Publisher. • Annual. Edited for use by military commissaries in making purchasing decisions. Lists sources of goods and sevices, with official military department and retail order numbers.

## FINANCIAL RATIOS

*Industry Norms and Key Business Ratios.* Dun & Bradstreet Inc. • Annual. Five volumes. Covers over

800 kinds of businesses, arranged by Standard Industrial Classification number. More detailed editions covering longer periods of time are also available.

## ONLINE DATABASES

*Aerospace America Magazine.* American Institute of Aeronautics and Astronautics. • Monthly. $200 Institutions non member, domestic. Covers aeronautics and space technology with special attention to aerospace defense, design, and electronics.

*Aerospace Database.* American Institute of Aeronautics and Astronautics. • Contains abstracts of literature covering all aspects of the aerospace and aircraft industry 1983 to date. Monthly updates. Inquire as to online cost and availability.

## OTHER SOURCES

*Jane's All the World's Aircraft.* Jane's Information Group, Inc. • Annual. $630.00; CD-ROM edition, $1,455.00; online edition, $1,566.00; microfiche edition, $3,075.00. Lists civil and military aircraft, helicopters, airships, and aero engines.

## PERIODICALS AND NEWSLETTERS

*Aerospace America Magazine.* American Institute of Aeronautics and Astronautics. • Monthly. $200 Institutions non member, domestic. Covers aeronautics and space technology with special attention to aerospace defense, design, and electronics.

*Defense Electronics.* RentPath Inc. • Monthly.

*Defense Systems Review and Military Communications.* Cosgriff-Martin Publishing Group, Inc. • Monthly. $35.00 per year.

*Flight International.* Reed Business Information Ltd. • Weekly. $140.00 per year. Technical aerospace coverage.

*Inside R and D: A Weekly Report on Technical Innovation.* Technical Insights. • Weekly. Institutions, $840.00 per year. Concentrates on new and significant developments. Formerly *Technology Transfer Week.*

*Interservice.* American Logistics Association. • Quarterly. $20.00 per year. Official Journal of the American Logistics Association.

*Military Grocer.* Downey Communications Inc. • Five times a year. $30.00 per year. Edited for managers and employees of supermarkets on military bases. (These are supermarkets administered by the Defense Commissary Agency.).

*National Defense: NDIA's Business and Technology Magazine.* National Defense Industrial Association. • 10 times a year. $35.00 per year.

*Navy Supply Corps Newsletter.* U. S. Government Printing Office. • Bimonthly. $31 U.S.. Newsletter issued by U. S. Navy Supply Systems Command. Provides news of Navy supplies and stores activities.

## TRADE/PROFESSIONAL ASSOCIATIONS

American Institute of Aeronautics and Astronautics. 1801 Alexander Bell Dr., Ste. 500, Reston, VA 20191-4344. Phone: 800-639-2422 or (703)264-7500; Fax: (703)264-7551; Email: custserv@aiaa.org • URL: http://www.aiaa.org • Represents scientists and engineers in the field of aeronautics and astronautics. Facilitates interchange of technological information through publications and technical meetings in order to foster overall technical progress in the field and increase the professional competence of members. Operates Public Policy program to provide federal decision-makers with the technical information and policy guidance needed to make effective policy on aerospace issues. Public Policy program activities include congressional testimony, position papers, section public policy activities, and workshops. Offers placement assistance; compiles statistics; offers educational programs. Provides abstracting services through its AIAA Access.

---

American Logistics Association. 1101 Vermont Ave. NW, Ste. 1002, Washington, DC 20005. Phone: (202)466-2520; Fax: (202)296-4419 • URL: http://www.ala-national.org • Promotes, protects and ensures the continued viability of the military resale (Commissary and Exchange Benefits) and Morale, Welfare and Recreations (MWR Benefits) industries. Acts as liaison between manufacturers and the Armed Forces' purchasing agencies. Promotes cooperation between the Congress, Defense Department and the industries which it conducts business.

National Defense Industrial Association. 2111 Wilson Blvd., Ste. 400, Arlington, VA 22201. Phone: (703)522-1820 or (703)247-2548; Email: bprokuski@ndia.org • URL: http://www.ndia.org • Concerned citizens, military and government personnel, and defense-related industry workers interested in industrial preparedness for the national defense of the United States. Operates Technology Services that provides a forum for discussion of defense industry programs and issues. Conducts 55 technical meetings per year.

Research and Development Associates for Military Food and Packaging Systems. 16607 Blanco Rd., Ste. 501, San Antonio, TX 78232. Phone: (210)493-8024; Fax: (210)493-8036; Email: hqs@militaryfood.org • URL: http://militaryfood.org/newsite • Industrial firms, educational institutions and related groups engged in food, food service, distribution and container research and development.

# MILK INDUSTRY

*See* DAIRY INDUSTRY

# MILLERS AND MILLING

*See* FLOUR INDUSTRY

# MILLINERY INDUSTRY

## HANDBOOKS AND MANUALS
*Women's Accessories Store.* Entrepreneur Press. • Looseleaf. $59.50. A practical guide to starting a women's clothing accessories shop. Covers profit potential, start-up costs, market size evaluation, owner's time required, site selection, lease negotiation, pricing, accounting, advertising, promotion, etc. (Start-Up Business Guide No. E1333.).

# MILLWORK

*See* WOODWORKING INDUSTRIES

# MINERALOGY

*See also* METALLURGY; MINES AND MINERAL RESOURCES

## PERIODICALS AND NEWSLETTERS
*Rocks & Minerals.* Routledge. • Bimonthly. $213 Institutions print and online. Six issues per year.

## TRADE/PROFESSIONAL ASSOCIATIONS
American Federation of Mineralogical Societies. PO Box 302, Glyndon, MD 21071-0302. Phone: (410)833-7926; Email: central_office@amfed.org • URL: http://www.amfed.org • Aims to further the earth sciences and the education of the public regarding earth sciences.

Mineralogical Society of America. 3635 Concorde Pkwy., Ste. 500, Chantilly, VA 20151-1110. Phone: (703)652-9950; Fax: (703)652-9951; Email:

business@minsocam.org • URL: http://www.minsocam.org.

The Minerals, Metals, and Materials Society. 184 Thorn Hill Rd., Warrendale, PA 15086-7514. Phone: 800-759-4867 or (724)776-9000; Fax: (724)776-3770; Email: webmaster@tms.org • URL: http://www.tms.org/TMSHome.aspx • Members are metallurgists, metallurgical engineers, and materials scientists. Divisions include Light Metals and Electronic, Magnetic, and Photonic Materials. Formerly The Metallurigical Society.

# MINES AND MINERAL RESOURCES

*See also* MINERALOGY; NATURAL RESOURCES

## BIOGRAPHICAL SOURCES
*Mining Engineering.* Society for Mining, Metallurgy, and Exploration. • Monthly. $245 per year, includes full print and online access.

## CD-ROM DATABASES
*Environment Abstracts on CD-ROM.* University Publications of America. • Quarterly. $1,295.00 per year. Contains the following CD-ROM databases: *Environment Abstracts, Energy Abstracts,* and *Acid Rain Abstracts.* Length of coverage varies.

*OECD Statistical Compendium.* Organization for Economic Cooperation and Development. • Semiannual. $1,905.00 per year for 1 to 10 users. CD-ROM contains more than 730,000 monthly, quarterly, and annual time series for OECD countries, 1960 to date. Includes fully searchable data on agriculture, food, economic indicators, national accounts, employment, energy, finance, industry, technology, and foreign trade. Results can be displayed in various forms.

## DIRECTORIES
*Agricultural and Mineral Commodities Year Book.* Routledge Reference. • $420 Individuals Hardback. Publication includes: List of international commodity organizations. Entries include: Name, address, phone, fax, e-mail, URL, publications, name of the chairperson, and description. Principal content of publication is a gathering of information about 40 commodities traded internationally, including barley, phosphates, soybeans, wool, zinc, lead, and natural gas.

*Caribbean Countries Mineral Industry Handbook.* International Business Publications, USA. • $99.95 Individuals hardcopy, E-book and CD-ROM. Covers: strategic information and contacts on mining and mineral industry of the Caribbean countries.

*Directory of American Manufacturers & Exporters of Minerals.* EXIM Infotek Private Ltd. • $10 Individuals. Covers: 70 American manufacturers and exporters of calcium carbonate, carbonate magnesium, crushed lime, dolomitic quicklime, high calcium lime, hydrated lime, lime and limestone, magnesia chemicals, magnesium, mica, minerals, oxide magnesium, pulverized lime, quartz, stearate magnesium, and talc. Entries include: Company name, postal address, city, country, phone, fax, e-mail and websites, contact person, designation, and product details.

*Directory of Asian Importers of Minerals.* EXIM Infotek Private Ltd. • $800 Individuals. Covers: 370 Asian importers of acid phosphoric mineral, bauxite, borax, carbon and graphite products, copper mineral, crucibles made of alumina or quartz, faucets, ferrites, floruspar, fossils, graphite, gypsum, industrial minerals, iron ore, iron oxide, lead, limestone, magnesium oxide, manganese ore, metals and minerals, mica, mineral oil, mineral products and raw materials, mineral raw materials, ores, phosphoric acid, rare earth minerals, rare metal

minerals, rare metals, rock phosphate, silica sand, soil, sulfur, zinc, zircon sand, zirconic, and zirconium sand. Entries include: Company name, postal address, telephone, fax, e-mail, website, contact person, designation, and product details.

*Directory of Chinese Importers of Minerals.* EXIM Infotek Private Ltd. • $150 Individuals. Covers: 25 Chinese importers of copper mineral, iron ore, iron oxide, metals, and minerals. Entries include: Company name, postal address, telephone, fax, e-mail, website, contact person, designation, and product details.

*Directory of Chinese Manufacturers & Exporters of Minerals.* EXIM Infotek Private Ltd. • $15 Individuals. Covers: 170 Chinese manufacturers and exporters of alumina products, carbon graphite, dolomite, faucet, feldspar, graphite, graphite-natural, iron oxide red, magnesium sulphate, mica and mecanite products, mineral products, minerals, natural quartz powder, non-metallic minerals, phosphate, phosphoric acid, phosphorous acid, phosphorous yellow, phosphorus products, quartz, rare earths, rare metals, and sulphate. Entries include: Company name, postal address, city, country, phone, fax, e-mail and websites, contact person, designation, and product details.

*Directory of Indian Importers of Minerals.* EXIM Infotek Private Ltd. • Covers: 80 Indian Importers of borax, graphite, iron ore, lead, mica, mineral oil, minerals, ores, sulfur, zinc, and zirconium sand. Entries include: Company name, postal address, telephone, fax, e-mail, website, contact person, designation, and product details.

*Directory of Japanese Importers of Minerals.* EXIM Infotek Private Ltd. • Covers: 150 Japanese importers of carbon and graphite products, crucibles made of alumina or quartz, graphite, gypsum, iron ore, limestone, manganese ore, mica, mineral oil, mineral products and raw materials, minerals, ores, rare metal minerals, silica sand, soil, sulfur, and zinc. Entries include: Company name, postal address, telephone, fax, e-mail, website, contact person, designation, and product details.

*Directory of Japanese Manufacturers & Exporters of Minerals.* EXIM Infotek Private Ltd. • $5 Individuals. Covers: 20 Japanese manufacturers and exporters of graphite, limestones, mineral products, phosphate, and rare metals. Entries include: Company name, postal address, city, country, phone, fax, e-mail and websites, contact person, designation, and product details.

*Directory of Middle East Importers of Minerals.* EXIM Infotek Private Ltd. • $250 Individuals. Covers: 60 Middle East importers of aluminum alloy ingot, clay, lead, mica, minerals, ores, titanium dioxide, zinc, zinc concentrate, zinc ingot, and zinc ingueat. Entries include: Company name, postal address, telephone, fax, e-mail, website, contact person, designation, and product details.

*Directory of North American Importers of Minerals.* EXIM Infotek Private Ltd. • $200 Individuals. Covers: 50 North American importers of alabaster, clay, graphite, industrial minerals, limestone, magnesium, mica, minerals, and ores. Entries include: Company name, postal address, telephone, fax, e-mail, website, contact person, designation, and product details.

*Directory of SAARC Importers of Minerals.* EXIM Infotek Private Ltd. • Covers: 20 companies in member countries of the South Asian Association for Regional Cooperation (SAARC) that import borax, faucets, graphite, gypsum, lead, magnesium oxide, manganese ore, mica, mineral products, rock phosphate, silica base, soil, sulfur, and zinc. Entries include: Company name, postal address, telephone, fax, e-mail, website, contact person, designation, and product details.

*Directory of South Korean Manufacturers & Export-*

*ers of Minerals.* EXIM Infotek Private Ltd. • $10 Individuals. Covers: 70 South Korean manufacturers and exporters of clays, graphite and clay bonded graphite products, graphite-natural, gypsum and anhydrite, gypsum/plaster and lime, gypsum/plaster and stucco products, limestones, magnesium minerals, mica and mecanite products, quartz and silica electro thermic products, quartzite of crystal, silicon minerals, slate products, and steatite and pyrophillite. Entries include: Company name, postal address, city, country, phone, fax, e-mail and websites, contact person, designation, and product details.

*Directory of Taiwanese Manufacturers & Exporters of Minerals.* EXIM Infotek Private Ltd. • $5 Individuals. Covers: 30 Taiwanese manufacturers and exporters of clays, gypsum/plaster and stucco products, limestones, magnesium minerals, mica and mecanite products, quartz and silica electro thermic products, quartzite of crystal, silicon minerals, slate products. Entries include: Company name, postal address, city, country, phone, fax, e-mail and websites, contact person, designation, and product details.

*Directory of the Coal Industry of the Former Soviet Union.* Flegon Press. • $150. Covers: Over 450 coal mines and companies associated with the industry of the former Soviet Union, including collieries, machinery manufacturing, equipment repair, and associations. Database includes: Full coal specifications and import requests. Entries include: Company national, telex, and names of managing personnel.

*Engineering and Mining Journal Annual Buyers' Guide.* Primedia Business Magazines and Media. • Annual. Free to qualified subscribers; others, $69.00. List of manufacturers and suppliers of mining equipment; international coverage. Formerly *Engineering and Mining Journal Buying Directory.*

*Kompass.* Kompass Deutschland Verlags- und Vertriebsgesellschaft, mbH. • Annual. $88. Covers: German products and companies specializing in coal extraction, ore mining, quarries, cement industry, glass and ceramics.

*Middle East Countries Mineral Industry Handbook.* International Business Publications, USA. • $99.95 Individuals hardcopy, e-book, CD-ROM. Covers: Strategic information and contacts on mining resources and mineral industry on Middle East Countries.

*South America Mineral Industry Handbook.* International Business Publications, USA. • $99.95 Individuals hardcopy, e-book, CD-ROM. Covers: Strategic information and contacts on mining resources and mineral industry on South America.

*Western European Countries Mineral Industry Handbook.* International Business Publications, USA. • $99.95 Individuals Hardbound. Covers: strategic information and contacts on mining and mineral industry of the Western European countries.

*Wyoming Directory of Manufacturing and Mining.* Wyoming Business Council. • Biennial. $15. Covers: About 790 companies in mining and manufacturing; state and local organizations and government agencies that provide business assistance. Entries include: For businesses--Name of firm, address, phone, name of key executive, product or activity, parent company (if any), codes for number of employees and geographic scope, Standard Industrial Classification (SIC) code. For organizations and agencies--Name of agency or organization, address, phone, contact name or official.

## FINANCIAL RATIOS

*Quarterly Financial Report for Manufacturing, Mining, Trade, and Selected Service Industries.* U.S. Federal Trade Commission and U.S. Securities and Exchange Commission. U.S. Census Bureau Foreign Trade Division. • Quarterly. Quarterly.

Report on financial results of U.S. corporations.

## INTERNET DATABASES

*Business 2.0 Web Guide to the Best Business Links.* Business 2.0 Media Inc. Phone: (415)293-4800; Email: support@business2.com • URL: http://www.business2.com/webguide • Web site presents an extensive, searchable directory of links to "the best, most informative, and authoritative web pages." Twenty main categories cover business, finance, career, company information, people, and technology topics, with thousands of subtopics, all linking to Web sites recommended by experienced business researchers. Fees: Free.

*Fedstats.* Federal Interagency Council on Statistical Policy. Phone: (202)395-7254 • URL: http://www.fedstats.gov • Web site features an efficient search facility for full-text statistics produced by more than 100 federal agencies, including the Census Bureau, the Bureau of Economic Analysis, and the Bureau of Labor Statistics. Boolean searches can be made within one agency or for all agencies combined. Links are offered to international statistical bureaus, including the UN, IMF, OECD, UNESCO, Eurostat, and 20 individual countries. Fees: Free.

*FreeLunch.com.* Economy.com, Inc. Phone: (610)696-8700; Fax: (610)696-1678 • URL: http://www.freelunch.com • Web site provides free access to more than 200 million economic and financial data series, covering industry, demographics, labor markets, prices, retail sales, government spending, trade, interest rates, housing starts, the stock market, etc. Data is available in either chart or table form. Searching is offered. Free, but registration required. Economy.com, Inc. also offers fee-based economic analysis at *The Dismal Scientist* site (www.dismal.com).

*Manufacturing Profiles.* U. S. Bureau of the Census. Phone: (301)763-4636 or (301)763-4100; Fax: (301)763-4794; Email: webmaster@census.gov • URL: http://www.census.gov/prod/www/abs/mfg-prof.html • The Census Bureau makes available free on PDF (Portable Document Format) an annual consolidation of the entire Current Industrial Report series, presenting "all the data compiled." Contains statistics on production, shipments, inventories, consumption, exports, imports, and orders for a wide variety of manufactured products.

*NMA.* National Mining Association. Phone: (202)463-2600; Fax: (202)463-2666 • URL: http://www.nma.org • Web site provides information on the U. S. coal and mineral industries. Includes "Salient Statistics of the Mining Industry," showing a wide variety of annual data (six years) for coal and non-fuel minerals. Publications of the National Mining Association are described and links are provided to other sites. (National Mining Association formerly known as National Coal Association.) Fees: Free.

## OTHER SOURCES

*American Law of Mining.* Rocky Mountain Mineral Law Institute. Matthew Bender and Company Inc. • $768.00. Six looseleaf volumes. Periodic supplementation.

## PERIODICALS AND NEWSLETTERS

*Canadian Resources and PennyMines Analyst: The Canadian Newsletter for Penny-Mines Investors Who Insist on Geological Value.* MPL Communications Inc. • Weekly. $145.00 per year. Newsletter. Mainly on Canadian gold mine stocks. Formerly *Canadian PennyMines Analyst.*

*Colorado School of Mines Quarterly Review.* Colorado School of Mines Press. • Quarterly. $65.00 per year.

*Earth and Mineral Sciences.* College of Earth and Mineral Sciences. Pennsylvania State University. • Semiannual. Free. Current research in material science, mineral engineering, geosciences, meteorol-

ogy, geography and mineral economics.

*Mines Magazine.* Colorado School of Mines Alumni Association and the Colorado School of Mines. • Quarterly. $50. A critical communication serving the Colorado School of Mines community.

*The Mining Record.* Howell International Enterprises. • Monthly. $85 Individuals second class mail. Description: Discusses a myriad of issues within the mining industry, particularly exploration, development, production, and milling.

*Mining Week.* National Mining Association. • Weekly. Covers legislative, business, research, and other developments of interest to the mining industry.

*The Northern Miner: Devoted to the Mineral Resources Industry of Canada.* Scott's Directories. • Weekly. $114 per year.

## RESEARCH CENTERS AND INSTITUTES

Colorado School of Mines - Mesoscopic Physics Laboratory. Department of Physics, 1500 Illinois St., Golden, CO 80401. Phone: 800-446-9488 or (303)273-3850 or (303)273-3000; Fax: (303)273-3919 or (303)273-3244; Email: jscales@mines.edu • URL: http://mesoscopic.mines.edu/ • Mesoscopic phenomena, millimeter wave physics, quantum chaos, wave propagation in random media, rock physics.

U.S. International Trade Commission - Minerals, Metals, Machinery, and Miscellaneous Manufacturers Division. 500 E St. SW, Washington, DC 20436. Phone: (202)205-3418; Fax: (202)205-2217; Email: brookhart@usitc.gov • URL: http://www.usitc.gov • Survey data related to international trade matters, including international competitiveness of U.S. industries, especially iron and steel products, industrial minerals and nonferrous metals, machinery and general manufactured products.

## STATISTICS SOURCES

*Quarterly Mining Review.* National Mining Association. • Quarterly. $300.00 per year. Contains detailed data on production, shipments, consumption, stockpiles, and trade for coal and various minerals. (Publisher formerly National Coal Association.).

*Statistical Yearbook.* United Nations Publications. • Annual. $125.00. Contains statistics for about 200 countries on a wide variety of economic, industrial, and demographic topics. Compiled by United Nations Statistical Office.

*Survey of Current Business.* U. S. Government Printing Office. • Published by Bureau of Economic Analysis, U. S. Department of Commerce. Presents a wide variety of business and economic data.

*United States Census of Mineral Industries.* Bureau of the Census, U.S. Department of Commerce. U. S. Government Printing Office. • Quinquennial.

## TRADE/PROFESSIONAL ASSOCIATIONS

Mining and Metallurgical Society of America. PO Box 810, Boulder, CO 80306-0810. Phone: (303)444-6032; Fax: (415)899-0262; Email: contactmmsa@mmsa.net • URL: http://www.mmsa.net • Works for the conservation of mineral resources, the advancement of mining and metallurgical industries, the better protection of mine investors and mine workers, the increase of scientific knowledge, and the encouragement of high professional ideals and ethics.

# MINICOMPUTERS

*See* MICROCOMPUTERS AND MINICOMPUTERS

# MINING

*See* MINES AND MINERAL RESOURCES

# MINISTERS OF STATE

*See* DIPLOMATIC AND CONSULAR
SERVICE

# MINORITY BUSINESS

## ABSTRACTS AND INDEXES

*NTIS Alerts: Business & Economics.* U.S. Department of Commerce National Technical Information Service. • Biweekly. $130 per year. Covers consumer affairs, minority enterprises, marketing and economics, international commerce, banking, and finance.

## BIOGRAPHICAL SOURCES

*Who's Who Among African Americans.* Cengage Learning Inc. • Annual. Includes biographical details on over 20,000 notable African Americans. eBook also available. Contact for pricing.

## DIRECTORIES

*Afro-Brazilian Organization Directory.* Universal Publishers Inc. • Covers: Listings of Black entities and organizations in Brazil.

*Asian Business League of San Francisco Membership Directory.* Asian Business League of San Francisco. • Includes contact information for both Asian-Pacific Americans and non-Asian Pacific Amercians with an interest in expanding leadership skills.

*Black Enterprise--Black Engineering Firms Issue.* Earl Graves Publishing Co. • Irregular. $3.50. Covers: U.S. companies owned or controlled by African Americans. Entries include: Name, address, phone.

*The Business of Supplier Diversity: A Handbook of Essential Contacts and Information for Navigating the Industry.* Diversity Information Resources. • Annual. $129 Individuals. Covers: Business opportunity fairs, seminars, and workshops; National Supplier Development Council regional offices; Small Business Administration and Minority Business Development Administration offices; minority and women-owned business directories; and other resources for minority and women-owned businesses. Database includes: Summaries of legislation affecting minority businesses; glossary.

*Coalition for Minority Business Development Resource Directory.* Indianapolis Chamber of Commerce. • Annual. $25 Nonmembers. Covers: Agencies and organizations in Indiana devoted to aiding minority-owned businesses and entrepreneurs. Entries include: Organization name, address, phone.

*Directory of Certified Local, Small, and Disadvantaged Business Enterprises.* District of Columbia Local Business Opportunity Commission. • Annual. Covers about 700 suppliers of professional, commercial, and industrial products and services, and construction services, all firms in which minority ownership and control has been certified by the District of Columbia Local Business Opportunity Commission in accordance with D.C. Law I-95.

*Directory of Minority & Women-Owned Businesses.* Business Service Div. Birmingham Area Chamber of Commerce. • Covers: Approximately 1,200 businesses in Birmingham, Alabama, that are owned by women or minorities. Entries include: Company name, address, phone, name and title of contact, Standard Industrial Classification (SIC) code.

*Directory of Minority and Women Owned Businesses.* Louisiana Office of Minority and Women's Business Enterprise Department of Economic Development. • Quarterly. Contains information on minority and women-owned businesses.

*LGBT Friendly Directory.* VCS Gay Pride Rockland. • Covers: Businesses, services, and community organizations. Entries include: Company name, address, contact information, e-mail, and website.

*London Black Business and Professionals Directory.* Smart Choice Communications Inc. • Professionals, businesses, and community entities serving and working with the black community.

*Minority and Women-Owned Business Resource Guide.* Dallas Regional Chamber. • Annual. $15 Members. Covers: Minority and women-owned businesses in the greater Dallas area. Entries include: Company name, address, phone; business classification.

*National Directory of Minority-Owned Business Firms.* Business Research Services Inc. • $295 Individuals paperback. Provides access to minority business enterprises. Detailed entries furnish up to 17 points of data about each firm, including complete address, contact name, minority type, date founded, certification status, trading area, business description, number of employees and sales volume.

*National Minority and Women-Owned Business Directory.* Diversity Information Resources. • Annual. $169 Individuals print. Covers: Information regarding minority and women-owned business directories to acquaint major corporations and government purchasing agents with the products and services of minority and women-owned firms. Covers approximately 7000 minority-owned firms. Entries include: Company name, address, phone, fax, e-mail, Web site, number of employees, year established, products or services, certification status, minority identification, annual sales, NAICS code.

*Northeast Texas Buyers Guide to Minority Business.* Dallas/Fort Worth Minority Business Development Council. • Annual. Covers about 730 private firms offering professional, commercial, and industrial products and services, and in which more than 50% of company ownership is held by minority group members.

*Northwest Native American Business Directory.* ONABEN - Native American Business Network. • $19.95 Individuals. Covers: 350 native businesses, casinos, tribes, Native American chambers, and business associations in the Northwest.

*Wisconsin Minority-Owned Business Directory.* Wisconsin Department of Commerce. • Annual. Covers approximately 750 non-retail minority firms.

## INTERNET DATABASES

*MBDA: Minority Business Development Agency.* U. S. Department of Commerce. Phone: 800-786-9199 or (703)308-4357; Fax: (703)305-7786; Email: help@mbda.gov • URL: http://www.uspto.gov • Web site provides links to a wide variety of advice and information for minority businesses. Main headings are Access to Markets, Access to Capital, Management & Technical Assistance, and Education & Training. An MBDA Resource Locator helps to locate sources of assistance in specific cities. Fees: Free. (Additional "business contracting and assistance tools" are offered to those who register with the site.)

*MBEMAG.* Minority Business Entrepreneur Magazine. Phone: (310)540-9398; Fax: (310)792-8263; Email: webmaster@mbemag.com • URL: http://www.mbemag.com • Web site's main feature is the "MBE Business Resources Directory." This provides complete mailing addresses, phone, fax, and Web site addresses (URL) for more than 40 organizations and government agencies having information or assistance for ethnic minority and women business owners. Some other links are "Current Events," "Calendar of Events," and "Business Opportunities." Updating is bimonthly. Fees: Free.

## PERIODICALS AND NEWSLETTERS

*MBI: The National Report on Minority, Women-Owned and Disadvantaged Business.* Community Development Services, Inc. CD Publications. • Semimonthly. $379.00 per year. Newsletter. Provides news of affirmative action, government contracts, minority business employment, and education/training for minorities in business. Formerly *Minorities in Business.*

*Minority Business Entrepreneur.* Minority Business Entrepreneur. • Bimonthly. $25 Individuals print amd digital. Reports on issues "critical to the growth and development of minority and women-owned firms." Provides information on relevant legislation and profiles successful women and minority entrepreneurs.

## TRADE/PROFESSIONAL ASSOCIATIONS

Airport Minority Advisory Council. 2001 Jefferson Davis Hwy., Ste. 500, Arlington, VA 22202. Phone: (703)414-2622; Fax: (703)414-2686; Email: amac. info@amac-org.com • URL: http://www.amac-org. com • Advocates for equal opportunity for minorities and women in airport contracting and employment.

Alliance of Supplier Diversity Professionals. PO Box 782049, Orlando, FL 32878-2049. Phone: 877-405-6565; Email: info@asdp.us • URL: http://www. asdp.us • Represents supplier diversity professionals throughout the United States. Offers education and professional development opportunities, certification for professionals within management, supplier diversity, procurement and similar career paths. Provides a forum for members to exchange information on all aspects of the supplier diversity profession.

American Indian Business Leaders. Gallagher Business Bldg., Ste. 366, Missoula, MT 59812. Phone: 877-245-2425; Fax: (406)243-2086 • URL: http:// www.aibl.org • Provides a support system for American Indian students interested in learning the skills necessary to acquire a job, design their own business, raise capital, and network with successful American Indian business people. Provides career development opportunities for members as well as opportunities to develop strong work ethics and gain professional experience.

Armenian American Chamber of Commerce. 225 E Broadway, Ste. 313C, Glendale, CA 91205. Phone: (818)247-0196; Fax: (818)247-7668; Email: aacc@ armenianchamber.com • URL: http://www. armenianchamber.org • Aims to serve the needs of the business community in the United States and abroad. Assists its members, which consist of business persons, professionals and scholars in business development and networking. Advances the industrial, commercial, professional and public interests of the Armenian American community.

Asian Business League of San Francisco. PO Box 191345, San Francisco, CA 94119-1345. Phone: (415)670-9022; Email: info@ablsf.org • URL: http://www.ablsf.org • Seeks to promote and further the success of Asian Americans in business. Provides its members with seminars and opportunities to meet with other business leaders in the community, to participate in the advocacy to issues important to Asian Americans and to learn and share pertinent information about the current economic and business climate on both local and international level.

Association of African American Financial Advisors. PO Box 4853, Capitol Heights, MD 20791. Phone: (240)396-2530; Fax: (888)392-5702; Email: info@aaafainc.cm • URL: http://aaafainc. com • Seeks to develop and foster professional relationships among African American professionals working in the financial advisory industry. Provides assistance and nurturing for those families that seek to improve their opportunities for participating and prospering financially in an economically progressive society. Strives to create support networks for minority financial professionals. Provides a forum for further education, training and visibility of its members.

**Association of Latino Administrators and Superintendents.** PO Box 65204, Washington, DC 20035. Phone: (202)466-0808; Email: contact@alasedu.org • URL: http://www.alasedu.net • Represents the interests of Latino superintendents and administrators. Provides professional development programs to strengthen the skills of superintendents, principals and other administrators. Advocates for policies to ensure the quality of the public education system.

**Association of Moroccan Professionals in America.** PO Box 77254, San Francisco, CA 94107. Fax: (801)996-6334; Email: jaridati@amp-usa.org • URL: http://www.amp-usa.org • Promotes networking opportunities among Moroccan professionals. Advances the social and professional development of Moroccan professionals. Encourages bilateral commercial exchanges between the U.S. and Morocco. Provides community service and education initiatives in Morocco.

**Canadian Council for Aboriginal Business.** 2 Berkeley St., Ste. 310, Toronto, ON, Canada M5A 4J5. Phone: (416)961-8663; Fax: (416)961-3995; Email: info@ccab.com • URL: http://www.ccab.com • Promotes the full participation of aboriginal people in the Canadian economy. Seeks to connect aboriginal and non-aboriginal people and companies with the opportunities required to achieve personal and business success. Develops and operates the Progressive Aboriginal Relations (PAR) benchmarking and hallmarking program. Administers the Canadian Aboriginal Business Hall of Fame.

**Coalition of Asian American Business Organizations.** 255 Rex Blvd., Auburn Hills, MI 48326. Phone: (248)760-5125; Fax: (248)853-0606; Email: mming66@caabo.org • URL: http://www.caabo.org • Aims to promote cooperation and growth among Asian businesses. Serves as a collective voice for Asian American businesses and entrepreneurs. Educates and advocates on local, state, regional and national issues that impact Asian business organizations. Provides leadership training, mentorship and scholarship programs to members.

**Council of Supplier Diversity Professionals.** PO Box 70226, Rochester, MI 48307. Email: info@ncsdp.com • URL: http://www.ncsdp.com • Aims to assist in the growth and development of the supplier diversity profession. Provides a forum to share information, ideas and issues concerning supplier diversity. Offers career-development strategies for supplier diversity professionals.

**Diversity Information Resources.** 2105 Central Ave. NE, Minneapolis, MN 55418. Phone: (612)781-6819; Fax: (612)781-0109; Email: info@diversityinforesources.com • URL: http://www.diversityinforesources.com • Promotes businesses with minority, women, veteran, service-disabled veteran and HUBZone ownership. Compiles and publishes minority and women-owned business directories to acquaint major corporations and government purchasing agents with the products and services of minority and women-owned firms. Sponsors national supplier diversity seminars.

**Executive Leadership Council.** 1001 N Fairfax St., Ste. 300, Alexandria, VA 22314. Phone: (703)706-5200; Email: elcinfo@elcinfo.com • URL: http://www.elcinfo.com • Provides senior African-American corporate executives with a network and leadership forum that adds perspective and direction to the achievement of excellence in business, economic and public policies for the African-American community and its corporations, and the community at large. Conducts educational and research programs.

**Korean American Society of Entrepreneurs.** 2882 Sand Hill Rd., Ste. 100, Menlo Park, CA 94025. Email: ben@kase.org • URL: http://www.kase.org • Brings together entrepreneurs, engineers, corporate executives, venture capitalists, and other professionals with roots or interests in Korea. Fosters and supports network of Korean Americans interested in starting or playing key roles in companies in the United States. Facilitates the professional development, networking, and mentoring of its members. Provides information on all areas related to its members' interests.

**Latin American Venture Capital Association.** 589 8th Ave., 18th Fl., New York, NY 10018. Phone: (646)315-6735; Fax: (646)349-1047; Email: info@lavca.org • URL: http://www.lavca.org • Promotes the growth of the private equity and venture capital industry in Latin America and the Caribbean. Advocates on behalf of the industry by disseminating information to the media, promoting the region to investors and supporting efforts to improve the regulatory framework. Conducts research on industry trends, performance and policy environment. Develops model documents, industry guides and standards.

**Latin Business Association.** 120 S San Pedro St., Ste. 530, Los Angeles, CA 90012. Phone: (213)628-8510; Fax: (213)628-8519 • URL: http://www.lbausa.com • Latino business owners and corporations. Assists Latino business owners to develop their businesses.

**National Association of Minority Automobile Dealers.** 9745 Lottsford Rd., Ste. 150, Largo, MD 20774. Phone: (301)306-1614; Fax: (301)306-1493 • URL: http://www.namad.org • Automobile dealers. Acts as liaison between membership, the federal government, the community, and industry representatives; seeks to better the business conditions of its members on an ongoing basis. Serves as a confidential spokesperson for dealers. Offers business analysis, financial counseling, and short- and long-term management planning. Conducts research programs; compiles statistics.

**National Association of Minority Government Contractors.** PO Box 44609, Washington, DC 20026. Email: info@namgc.org • URL: http://www.namgc.org • Focuses on enhancing diversification in the workplace. Provides opportunities for the federal, state and local government sector to find key resources in order to engage in contracting opportunities. Provides members with networking, information and services which will connect them with federal, state and local government contracting opportunities.

**National Association of Professional Asian American Women.** 304 Oak Knoll Terr., Rockville, MD 20850. Phone: (301)785-8585; Email: napaw@comcast.net • URL: http://www.napaw.org • Represents the professional interests of Asian-American women. Promotes continued personal and professional development; works to enhance career opportunities. Encourages greater visibility of Asian-American women in public decision-making. Conducts educational programs.

**National Black Business Council.** 600 Corporate Pointe, Ste. 1010, Culver City, CA 90230. Phone: (310)585-6222; Email: info@nbbc.org • URL: http://www.nbbc.org • Aims to create and advance black businesses; advocates for expansion of black business procurement.

**National Black Chamber of Commerce.** 4400 Jenifer St. NW, Ste. 331, Washington, DC 20015-2133. Phone: (202)466-6888; Fax: (202)466-4918; Email: info@nationalbcc.org • URL: http://www.nationalbcc.org • Works for the issues of economics and entrepreneurship in the African-American community.

**National Black MBA Association.** 1 E Wacker Ste. 3500, Chicago, IL 60601. Phone: (312)236-2622; Fax: (312)236-0390; Email: info@nbmbaa.org • URL: http://www.nbmbaa.org • Creates educational opportunities to form professional and economic growth of African-Americans. Develops partnerships to its members and provides educational programs to increase the awareness on business field.

**National Council of Asian American Business Associations.** 475 N Whisman Rd., Ste. 200, Mountain View, CA 94043. Phone: (650)303-6164; Fax: (650)350-1545; Email: info@national-caaba.org • URL: http://www.national-caaba.org • Serve as the voice of Asian Pacific American business owners in the United States. Works to effect positive change in the areas of economic development, public contracting and private procurement, and public and fiscal policies that impact Asian Pacific American businesses and communities at large. Seeks to create opportunities in the social, political, and economic sectors for the Asian Pacific American business community.

**National Council of Minorities in Energy.** 1725 I St. NW, Ste. 300, Washington, DC 20006. Phone: 866-663-9045; Fax: (866)663-8007; Email: contact@minoritiesinenergy.org • URL: http://www.minoritiesinenergy.org • Advocates for development and utilization of minority and women-owned businesses in the energy sector and energy-related industries across the United States and in international markets. Provides information regarding opportunities in the energy industry. Advocates on regulatory and legislative issues at the federal, state and local levels. Presents methodologies to help implement access to capital and credit facilitation.

**National Latina Business Women Association.** 11664 National Blvd., Ste. 283, Los Angeles, CA 90064. Phone: 888-MY-NLBWA; Email: info@nlbwa.org • URL: http://nlbwa.org • Strives to promote, develop, and support the growth of Latina business owners and professionals. Seeks to create networking and mentoring opportunities for members.

**National Minority Business Council.** 1633 Broadway, 30th Fl., New York, NY 10019. Phone: (347)289-7620 or (212)245-2652; Email: info@nmbc.org • URL: http://nmbc.org • Represents minority businesses in all areas of industry and commerce. Seeks to increase profitability by developing marketing, sales, and management skills in minority businesses. Acts as an informational source for the national minority business community. Includes programs such as: legal services plan that provides free legal services to members in such areas as sales contracts, copyrights, estate planning, and investment agreement; business referral service that develops potential customer leads; international trade assistance program that provides technical assistance in developing foreign markets; executive banking program that teaches members how to package a business loan for bank approval; procurement outreach program for minority and women business owners. Conducts continuing management education and provides assistance in teaching youth the free enterprise system.

**National Minority Supplier Development Council.** 1359 Broadway, 10th Fl., Ste. 1000, New York, NY 10018. Phone: (212)768-0430; Email: info@nmsdc.org • URL: http://www.nmsdc.org • Provides a direct link between its 3,500 corporate members and minority-owned businesses (Black, Hispanic, Asian and Native American) and increases procurement and business opportunities for minority businesses of all sizes.

**National Society of Hispanic MBAs.** 450 E John Carpenter Fwy., Irving, TX 75062. Phone: 877-467-4622 or (214)596-9338; Fax: (214)596-9325 • URL: http://www.nshmba.org • Hispanic MBA professional business network dedicated to economic and philanthropic advancement.

**National Utilities Diversity Council.** 1017 L St., Sacramento, CA 95814. Phone: (916)492-9163;

---

Fax: (916)473-9444; Email: mpl@cpuc.ca.gov • Promotes diversity in the utility industry in the areas of governance, employment, procurement, language access/customer service and philanthropy. Serves as a resource that promotes the inclusion of women, racial and ethnic minorities, service disabled veterans and other organized groups in utility corporate governance, philanthropy, employment, procurement, language access and customer service.

Native American Finance Officers Association. 1101 30th St. NW, Ste. 500, Washington, DC 20007. Phone: (202)631-2003 • URL: http://www.nafoa.org • Improves the quality of financial and business management of Native American governments and businesses. Promotes tribal sovereignty through sound financial management. Develops scholarship training and internship program for Native American students and tribal employees.

Turkish American Business Connection. 2784 Homestead Rd., No. 118, Santa Clara, CA 95051. Phone: (408)404-5208; Fax: (408)404-5208; Email: info@tabc-us.org • URL: http://www.tabc-us.org • Brings together Turkish-American entrepreneurs, professionals and business people. Advances the interests of Turkish-American businessmen, entrepreneurs and professionals from all industries. Promotes professional networking opportunities for and among its members.

# MINORITY MARKETS

## ALMANACS AND YEARBOOKS

*Research Alert Yearbook: Vital Facts on Consumer Behavior and Attitudes.* EPM Communications Inc. • Annual. $349 Individuals Single user (PDF) or Print. Provides summaries of consumer market research from the newsletters *Research Alert, Youth Markets Alert,* and *Minority Markets Alert.* Includes tables, charts, graphs, and textual summaries for 41 subject categories. Sources include reports, studies, polls, and focus groups.

## PERIODICALS AND NEWSLETTERS

*Marketing to the Emerging Minorities.* EPM Communications Inc. • Monthly. $295 /year. Newsletter on market research relating to African American, Asian American, and U. S. Hispanic populations.

## TRADE/PROFESSIONAL ASSOCIATIONS

National Hispanic Corporate Council. 1050 Connecticut Ave. NW, Fl. 10, Washington, DC 20036-5334. Phone: (202)772-1100; Fax: (202)772-3101; Email: info@nhcchq.org • URL: http://www.nhcchq.org • Corporate think tank serving Fortune 1000 companies and their representatives as a principal resource for information, expertise and counsel about Hispanic issues affecting corporate objectives, and to advocate for increased employment, leadership and business opportunities for Hispanics in corporate America.

National Minority Supplier Development Council. 1359 Broadway, 10th Fl., Ste. 1000, New York, NY 10018. Phone: (212)768-0430; Email: info@nmsdc. org • URL: http://www.nmsdc.org • Provides a direct link between its 3,500 corporate members and minority-owned businesses (Black, Hispanic, Asian and Native American) and increases procurement and business opportunities for minority businesses of all sizes.

Native American Coalition for Healthy Alternatives. 1038 E Tallent St., Rapid City, SD 57701. Phone: (605)877-4650 • URL: http://nacha501c.org • Strives to enhance the quality of life for the underrepresented by providing various services related to financial literacy.

# MINORITY NEWSPAPERS

## CD-ROM DATABASES

*Newspaper Abstracts Ondisc.* ProQuest L.L.C. • Monthly. $2,950.00 per year (covers 1989 to date;

archival discs are available for 1985-88). Provides cover-to-cover CD-ROM indexing and abstracting of 19 major newspapers, including the *New York Times, Wall Street Journal, Washington Post, Chicago Tribune,* and *Los Angeles Times.*

## DIRECTORIES

*Hispanic Media & Market Source.* Kantar Media SRDS. • Quarterly. $445 per year. Provides detailed information on the following Hispanic advertising media in the U.S.: TV, radio, newspapers, magazines, direct mail, outdoor, and special events.

# MISSILE INDUSTRY

*See* ROCKET INDUSTRY

# MOBILE HOME INDUSTRY

*See also* PREFABRICATED HOUSE INDUSTRY; RECREATIONAL VEHICLE INDUSTRY

## CD-ROM DATABASES

*OECD Statistical Compendium.* Organization for Economic Cooperation and Development. • Semiannual. $1,905.00 per year for 1 to 10 users. CD-ROM contains more than 730,000 monthly, quarterly, and annual time series for OECD countries, 1960 to date. Includes fully searchable data on agriculture, food, economic indicators, national accounts, employment, energy, finance, industry, technology, and foreign trade. Results can be displayed in various forms.

*Sourcebooks America CD-ROM.* CACI Marketing Systems. • Annual. $1,250.00. Provides the CD-ROM version of *The Sourcebook of ZIP Code Demographics: Census Edition* and *The Sourcebook of County Demographics: Census Edition.*

## FINANCIAL RATIOS

*Annual Statement Studies.* Risk Management Association. • Annual. Compiled from over 280,000 financial statements.

*Annual Statement Studies: Industry Default Probabilities and Cash Flow Measures.* Risk Management Association. • Annual. $405 Nonmembers. Serves as a companion volume to the original *Annual Statement Studies.* Gives probability of default estimates on a percentage scale for more than 450 industries. Includes changes in position year-by-year for eight financial statement line items and provides percentage measures of cash flow.

## INTERNET DATABASES

*Business 2.0 Web Guide to the Best Business Links.* Business 2.0 Media Inc. Phone: (415)293-4800; Email: support@business2.com • URL: http://www.business2.com/webguide • Web site presents an extensive, searchable directory of links to "the best, most informative, and authoritative web pages." Twenty main categories cover business, finance, career, company information, people, and technology topics, with thousands of subtopics, all linking to Web sites recommended by experienced business researchers. Fees: Free.

*Fedstats.* Federal Interagency Council on Statistical Policy. Phone: (202)395-7254 • URL: http://www.fedstats.gov • Web site features an efficient search facility for full-text statistics produced by more than 100 federal agencies, including the Census Bureau, the Bureau of Economic Analysis, and the Bureau of Labor Statistics. Boolean searches can be made within one agency or for all agencies combined. Links are offered to international statistical bureaus, including the UN, IMF, OECD, UNESCO, Eurostat, and 20 individual countries. Fees: Free.

*FreeLunch.com.* Economy.com, Inc. Phone: (610)696-8700; Fax: (610)696-1678 • URL: http://

www.freelunch.com • Web site provides free access to more than 200 million economic and financial data series, covering industry, demographics, labor markets, prices, retail sales, government spending, trade, interest rates, housing starts, the stock market, etc. Data is available in either chart or table form. Searching is offered. Free, but registration required. Economy.com, Inc. also offers fee-based economic analysis at *The Dismal Scientist* site (www.dismal. com).

## PRICE SOURCES

*NADA Appraisal Guides.* National Automobile Dealers Association. • Prices and frequencies vary. Guides to prices of used cars, old used cars, motorcycles, mobile homes, recreational vehicles, and mopeds.

## STATISTICS SOURCES

*Survey of Current Business.* U. S. Government Printing Office. • Published by Bureau of Economic Analysis, U. S. Department of Commerce. Presents a wide variety of business and economic data.

## TRADE/PROFESSIONAL ASSOCIATIONS

Manufactured Housing Institute. 1655 N Fort Myer Dr., Ste. 104, Arlington, VA 22209-3108. Phone: (703)558-0400; Fax: (703)558-0401 • URL: http://www.manufacturedhousing.org • Manufacturers of manufactured homes; suppliers of equipment, components, furnishings and services, financial services companies, state association organizations, retailers and community owners. Promotes sales of manufactured homes through programs and services in six key areas: government relations, technical activities, financing, public relations, site development and community operations. Conducts research and educational programs; provides statistics.

# MOBILE TELEPHONE INDUSTRY

## ABSTRACTS AND INDEXES

*Applied Science and Technology Index.* EBSCO Publishing Inc. • 11/year. Indexes a wide variety of English language technical, industrial, and engineering periodicals.

## DIRECTORIES

*Major Telecommunications Companies of the World.* Cengage Learning Inc. • Annual. $1,360 Individuals. Published by Graham & Whiteside. Contains detailed information and trade names for more than 5,950 important telecommunications companies in various countries.

*RCR and Global Wireless' International Database.* Crain Communications Inc. • Annual. $950. Covers: Worldwide cellular and PCS carriers.

*Telecommunications Directory.* Cengage Learning Inc. • Annual. $993 Individuals. Two volumes: North America and International. Cover national and international voice and data communications networks, electronic mail services, teleconferencing facilities and services, facsimile services, Internet access providers, videotex and teletext operations, transactional services, local area networks, audiotex services, microwave systems/networkers, satellite facilities, and others involved in telecommunications, including related consultants, advertisers/marketers; associations, regulatory bodies, and publishers. Available as eBook.

## ONLINE DATABASES

*Applied Science and Technology Index Online.* H.W. Wilson Co. • Provides online indexing of 500 major scientific, technical, industrial, and engineering periodicals. Time period is 1983 to date. Monthly updates. Inquire as to online cost and availability.

## PERIODICALS AND NEWSLETTERS

*Convergence: The Journal of Research Into New Media Technologies.* Reed Elsevier Group plc Reed

Business Information. • Monthly. Individuals, $40.00 per year; institutions, $160.00 per year. Covers the merging of communications technologies. Includes telecommunications networks, interactive TV, multimedia, wireless phone service, and electronic information services.

*Handheld Computing: The Number One Guide to Handheld Devices.* Mobile Media Group. • 9/year. Covers handheld devices for consumers, including PDAs, cell phones, digital cameras, MP3 players, tablet PCs, accessories, and software. Includes product reviews.

*Laptop Magazine.* Bedford Communications Inc. • Monthly. Consumer magazine containing articles and product reviews for notebook/laptop computers, handheld computers, tablet devices, cell phones, digital cameras, and other consumer electronic products.

*Mobile PC.* Future Network USA. • Monthly. $20.00 per year. Provides information and detailed product reviews for consumers. Covers notebook/laptop computers, personal digital assistants (PDAs), wireless network equipment, cell phones, digital cameras, and other electronic products.

*PICA Bulletin: News and Analysis for the Personal Communication Industry.* PCIA - The Wireless Infrastucture Association. • Weekly. $550.00 per year.

*RCR Wireless News: The Newspaper for the Wireless Communications Industry.* Crain Communications. • Weekly. $64.00 per year. Covers news of the wireless communications industry, including business and financial developments. Formerly *RCR*.

## STATISTICS SOURCES

*U.S. Industry and Trade Outlook.* U.S. Department of Commerce National Technical Information Service. • Annual. Produced by the International Trade Administration, U.S. Department of Commerce, in a "public-private" partnership with DRI/McGraw-Hill and Standard & Poor's. Provides basic data, outlook for the current year, and "Long-Term Prospects" (five-year projections) for a wide variety of products and services. Includes high technology industries. Formerly *U.S. Industrial Outlook*.

## TRADE/PROFESSIONAL ASSOCIATIONS

CTIA - The Wireless Association. 1400 16th St. NW, Ste. 600, Washington, DC 20036. Phone: (202)736-3200 or (202)785-0081; Fax: (202)785-0721 • URL: http://www.ctia.org • Individuals and organizations actively engaged in cellular radiotelephone communications, including: telephone companies and corporations providing radio communications; lay firms; engineering firms; consultants and manufacturers. (A cellular radiotelephone is a mobile communications device. An area is geographically divided into low frequency cells monitored by a computer that switches callers from one frequency to another as they move from cell to cell.) Objectives are to: promote, educate, and facilitate the professional interests, needs, and concerns of members with respect to the development and commercial applications of cellular technology; provide an opportunity for exchanging experience and concerns; broaden the understanding and importance of cellular communication technology. Conducts discussions, studies, and courses.

PCIA - The Wireless Infrastucture Association. 500 Montgomery St., Ste. 500, Alexandria, VA 22314. Phone: (703)535-7492; Fax: (703)836-1608; Email: membership@pcia.com • URL: http://www.pcia.com • Promotes development of industry standards for mobile telephone systems. Also concerned with the advertising and marketing of mobile telephones. Formerly National Mobile Radio System.

# MODEMS

*See* COMPUTER COMMUNICATIONS

# MODULAR CONSTRUCTION

*See* PREFABRICATED HOUSE INDUSTRY

# MOLASSES INDUSTRY

## DIRECTORIES

*Directory of Asian Importers of Honey and Syrup.* EXIM Infotek Private Ltd. • $150 Individuals. Covers: 35 Asian importers of honey, syrups, and honey products. Entries include: Company name, postal address, telephone, fax, e-mail, website, contact person, designation, and product details.

*Directory of Middle East Importers of Honey and Syrup.* EXIM Infotek Private Ltd. • $150 Individuals. Covers: 20 Middle East importers of honey and syrups. Entries include: Company name, postal address, telephone, fax, e-mail, website, contact person, designation, and product details.

## INTERNET DATABASES

*USDA.* U.S. National Institute of Standards and Technology. 100 Bureau Dr., Gaithersburg, MD 20899-1070. Phone: 800-877-8339 or (301)975-6478 or (202)720-2791; Fax: (301)975-8295; Email: inquiries@nist.gov • URL: http://www.nist.gov • The USDA home page has six sections: News and Information; What's New; About USDA; Agencies; Opportunities; Search and Help. Keyword searching is offered from the USDA home page and from various individual agency home pages. Agencies are the Economic Research Service, Agricultural Marketing Service, National Agricultural Statistics Service, National Agricultural Library, and about 12 others. Updating varies. Fees: Free.

## PERIODICALS AND NEWSLETTERS

*Molasses Market News.* Livestock and Seed Div. • Description: Provides the market news on molasses and its import and export.

## PRICE SOURCES

*Feedstuffs.* Miller Publishing Co. • Weekly. $144 Individuals.

## STATISTICS SOURCES

*Agricultural Statistics.* U.S. Department of Agriculture National Agricultural Statistics Service. • Annual. $46 Individuals. Provides a wide variety of statistical data relating to agricultural production, supplies, consumption, prices/price-supports, foreign trade, costs, and returns, as well as farm labor, loans, income, and population. In many cases, historical data is shown annually for 10 years. In addition to farm data, includes detailed fishery statistics.

*Sugar and Sweetener Situation and Outlook.* U. S. Government Printing Office. • Three times per year. $18.00 per year. Issued by Economic Research Service, U. S. Department of Agriculture. Provides current statistical information on supply, demand, and prices.

# MONEY

*See also* COINS AS AN INVESTMENT; FOREIGN EXCHANGE; INFLATION; INTEREST; PAPER MONEY

## ABSTRACTS AND INDEXES

*Business Periodicals Index Retrospective.* EBSCO Publishing Inc. • 11/year. Quarterly and annual cumulations.

## CD-ROM DATABASES

*EconLit.* Ovid Technologies Inc. • Updated monthly. Lists journal articles, book reviews, disserations of economic literature. Over 1,400 journals covered.

*OECD Statistical Compendium.* Organization for Economic Cooperation and Development. • Semiannual. $1,905.00 per year for 1 to 10 users. CD-ROM contains more than 730,000 monthly, quarterly, and annual time series for OECD countries, 1960 to date. Includes fully searchable data on agriculture, food, economic indicators, national accounts, employment, energy, finance, industry, technology, and foreign trade. Results can be displayed in various forms.

## DIRECTORIES

*Futures Magazine SourceBook: The Most Complete List of Exchanges, Companies, Regulators, Organizations, etc., Offering Products and Services to the Futures and Options Industry.* Futures Magazine Inc. • Annual. $19.50. Provides information on commodity futures brokers, trading method services, publications, and other items of interest to futures traders and money managers.

*Major Financial Institutions of the World.* Cengage Learning Inc. • $1,460 Individuals. 2012. 16th edition. eBook. Published by Graham & Whiteside. Contains detailed information on more than 10,000 important financial institutions in various countries. Includes banks, investment companies, and insurance companies.

*Money Market Directory of Pension Funds and Their Investment Managers.* Standard & Poors Money Market Directories. • Institutional funds and managers.

## HANDBOOKS AND MANUALS

*Monetary Policy and Reserve Requirements Handbook.* U.S. Federal Reserve System Board of Governors Publications Services. • $75 U.S.. Includes regulations A and D.

## INTERNET DATABASES

*BanxQuote Banking, Mortgage, and Finance Center.* BanxQuote, Inc. Phone: (914)722-1600; Fax: (914)722-6630; Email: info@banx.com • URL: http://www.banx.com • Daily. Web site quotes interest rates paid by banks around the country on various savings products, as well as rates paid by consumers for automobile loans, mortgages, credit cards, home equity loans, and personal loans. Also provided: stock quotes, indexes, stock options, futures trading data, economic indicators, and links to many other financial sites.

*Bureau of Economic Analysis.* U. S. Department of Commerce, Bureau of Economic Analysis. Phone: (202)606-9900; Fax: (202)606-5310; Email: webmaster@bea.doc.gov • URL: http://www.bea.doc.gov • Web site includes "News Release Information" covering national, regional, and international economic estimates from the BEA. Highlights of releases appear online the same day, complete text and tables appear the next day. "Recent News Releases" section provides titles for past nine months, with links. "BEA Data and Methodology" includes "Frequently Requested NIPA Data" (national income and product accounts, such as gross domestic product and personal income). Other statistics are available. Fees: Free.

*Business 2.0 Web Guide to the Best Business Links.* Business 2.0 Media Inc. Phone: (415)293-4800; Email: support@business2.com • URL: http://www.business2.com/webguide • Web site presents an extensive, searchable directory of links to "the best, most informative, and authoritative web pages." Twenty main categories cover business, finance, career, company information, people, and technology topics, with thousands of subtopics, all linking to Web sites recommended by experienced business researchers. Fees: Free.

*Factiva.* Dow Jones Reuters Business Interactive, LLC. Phone: 800-369-7466 or (609)452-1511; Fax: (609)520-5770; Email: solutions@factiva.com • URL: http://www.factiva.com • Fee-based Web site provides "global news and business information through Web sites and content integration solutions." Includes Dow Jones and Reuters newswires, The Wall Street Journal, and more than 7,000 other sources of current news, historical articles, market research reports, and investment analysis. Content includes 96 major U. S. newspapers, 900 non-English sources, trade publications, media transcripts, country profiles, news photos, etc.

*Federal Reserve Board Publications and Education Resources.* Board of Governors of the Federal Reserve System. Phone: (202)452-3000; Fax: (202)452-3819 • URL: http://www.federalreserve.gov/publications.htm • Web site provides access to statistics, surveys, and research from the Federal Reserve Board. *Federal Reserve Bulletin* articles are available as abstracts or full text (PDF) currently or from six-year archives. The link "Statistics: Releases and Historical Data" offers daily, weekly, monthly, quarterly, and annual data in great detail for interest rates, foreign exchange, consumer credit, money stock measures, industrial production indexes, bank reserves, and other items. Historical tabulations are available for various time periods. Free.

*Fedstats.* Federal Interagency Council on Statistical Policy. Phone: (202)395-7254 • URL: http://www.fedstats.gov • Web site features an efficient search facility for full-text statistics produced by more than 100 federal agencies, including the Census Bureau, the Bureau of Economic Analysis, and the Bureau of Labor Statistics. Boolean searches can be made within one agency or for all agencies combined. Links are offered to international statistical bureaus, including the UN, IMF, OECD, UNESCO, Eurostat, and 20 individual countries. Fees: Free.

*The Financial Post.* National Post Online. Phone: 800-805-1184 or (244)383-2300; Fax: (416)383-2443 • URL: http://www.nationalpost.com/financialpost/ • Provides a broad range of Canadian business news online, with daily updates. Includes news, opinion, and special reports, as well as "Investing," "Money Rates," "Market Watch," and "Daily Mutual Funds." Allows advanced searching (Boolean operators), with links to various other sites. Fees: Free.

*FreeLunch.com.* Economy.com, Inc. Phone: (610)696-8700; Fax: (610)696-1678 • URL: http://www.freelunch.com • Web site provides free access to more than 200 million economic and financial data series, covering industry, demographics, labor markets, prices, retail sales, government spending, trade, interest rates, housing starts, the stock market, etc. Data is available in either chart or table form. Searching is offered. Free, but registration required. Economy.com, Inc. also offers fee-based economic analysis at *The Dismal Scientist* site (www.dismal.com).

*Futures Online.* Futures Magazine Inc. Phone: (312)846-4600; Fax: (312)846-4638 • URL: http://www.futuresmag.com • Web site presents updates of *Futures* magazine and links to other futures-related sites.

*Nexis.com.* Lexis-Nexis Group. Phone: 800-227-4908 or (937)865-6800; Fax: (937)865-6909; Email: webmaster@prod.lexis-nexis.com • URL: http://www.nexis.com • Fee-based Web site offers searching of about 2.8 billion documents in some 30,000 news, business, and legal information sources. Features include a subject directory covering 1,200 topics in 34 categories and a Company Dossier containing information on more than 500,000 public and private companies. Boolean searching is offered.

*Wall Street Journal Interactive Edition.* Dow Jones & Co., Inc. 1211 Avenue of the Americas, New York, NY 10036. Phone: 800-369-5663; Email: service@dowjones.com • URL: http://new.dowjones.com • Fee-based Web site providing online searching of worldwide information from *The Wall Street Journal.* Includes "Company Snapshots," "The Journal's Greatest Hits," "Index to Market Data," "Journal Links," etc. Financial price quotes are available. Fees: $49.00 per year; $29.00 per year to print subscribers.

## ONLINE DATABASES

*Banking Information Source.* ProQuest L.L.C. • Provides indexing and abstracting of periodical and other literature from 1982 to date, with weekly updates. Covers the financial services industry: banks, savings institutions, investment houses, credit unions, insurance companies, and real estate organizations. Emphasis is on marketing and management. Inquire as to online cost and availability. (Formerly *FINIS: Financial Industry Information Service.*).

*Wilson Business Abstracts Online.* H.W. Wilson Co. • Indexes and abstracts 600 major business periodicals, plus the *Wall Street Journal* and the business section of the *New York Times.* Indexing is from 1982, abstracting from 1990, with the two newspapers included from 1993. Updated weekly. Inquire as to online cost and availability. (*Business Periodicals Index* without abstracts is also available online.).

## OTHER SOURCES

*Money Fund Monitor.* iMoneyNet Inc. • Provides daily and weekly performance information and rankings. Contact for pricing.

*Money Fund Report.* iMoneyNet Inc. • Weekly. $1,095.00 per year. Looseleaf. Contains detailed information on about 1,000 U.S. money market funds, including portfolios and yields.

## PERIODICALS AND NEWSLETTERS

*American Banker: The Financial Services Daily.* SourceMedia Inc. • Daily. $895.00 per year. Provides news of banking, investment products, mortgages, credit unions, finance, bank technology, and legal developments.

*Financial Markets, Institutions, and Instruments.* New York University, Salomon Center. Blackwell Publishing Inc. • Five times a year. Institutions, $338.00 per year. Includes online edition. Edited to "bridge the gap between the academic and professional finance communities." Special fifth issue each year provides surveys of developments in four areas: money and banking, derivative securities, corporate finance, and fixed-income securities.

*Financial Times (London).* The Financial Times, Inc. • Daily, except Sunday. $572.88 per year. An international business and financial newspaper, featuring news from London, Paris, Frankfurt, New York, and Tokyo. Includes worldwide stock and bond market data, commodity market data, and monetary/currency exchange information.

*Futures: News, Analysis, and Strategies for Futures, Options, and Derivatives Traders.* Futures Magazine Inc. • Monthly. $39 Individuals. Edited for institutional money managers and traders, brokers, risk managers, and individual investors or speculators. Includes special feature issues on interest rates, technical indicators, currencies, charts, precious metals, hedge funds, and derivatives. Supplements available.

*Grant's Interest Rate Observer.* Grant's Financial Publishing Inc. • Biweekly. $1,025 Individuals. Newsletter containing detailed analysis of money-related topics, including interest rate trends, global credit markets, fixed-income investments, bank loan policies, and international money markets.

*IMF Survey.* International Monetary Fund. • Description: Timely news on topics of general interest in the fields of international finance, country economics, trade, and commodities. Contains information on the IMF's activities, including press releases, major management speeches, and lending activity data rates.

*International Bank Credit Analyst.* BCA Publications Ltd. • Monthly. $795.00 per year. "A monthly forecast and analysis of currency movements, interest rates, and stock market developments in the principal countries, based on a continuous appraisal of money and credit trends worldwide." Includes many charts and graphs providing international coverage of money, credit, and securities.

*International Currency Review.* World Reports Ltd. • Quarterly. $475.00 per year.

*International Market Alert.* UCG Holdings L.P. • Description: Provides a fax service covering financial markets, world economy developments, foreign exchange, and U.S. interest rates.

*InvesTech Market Analyst: Technical and Monetary Investment Analysis.* Investech Research. • Every three weeks. $190.00 per year. Newsletter. Provides interpretation of monetary statistics and Federal Reserve actions, especially as related to technical analysis of stock market price trends.

*Money.* • 13 times a year. $19.95 per year. Covers all aspects of family finance; investments, careers, shopping, taxes, insurance, consumerism, etc.

*Money Reporter: The Insider's Letter for Investors Whose Interest is More Interest.* MPL Communications Inc. • Semimonthly. $227 /year. Supplement available, *Monthly Key Investment.* Canadian interest-bearing deposits and investments.

*Moneyletter.* Agora Inc. • Description: Provides assertive, do-it-yourself, individual investors with a unique market timing system, specific buy and sell recommendations, and portfolio allocation advice on no-load mutual funds. Features updates on economic and financial market, fund profiles, and articles on non-mutual fund financial planning issues.

*One Hundred Highest Yields.* Bankrate Inc. • Weekly. $124.00 per year. Newsletter. List CD's and money markets offered by federally insured banks. National coverage.

*Powell Monetary Analyst.* Larson M. Powell, editor. Reserve Research Ltd. • Description: Offers investment advice concentrating on precious metals, gold coins, currencies, and mining stocks.

*U.S. Banker.* SourceMedia Inc. • Monthly. $65.00 per year. Edited for bank executives and managers. Covers a wide variety of banking and financial topics.

## RESEARCH CENTERS AND INSTITUTES

Ludwig von Mises Institute for Austrian Economics. 518 W Magnolia Ave., Auburn, AL 36832. Phone: (334)321-2100; Fax: (334)321-2119; Email: contact@mises.org • URL: http://www.mises.org.

University of Pennsylvania - The Wharton School - Rodney L. White Center for Financial Research. 3254 Steinberg Hall-Dietrich Hall, Philadelphia, PA 19104-6367. Phone: (215)898-7616; Fax: (215)573-8084; Email: rlwctr@finance.wharton.upenn.edu • URL: http://rodneywhitecenter.wharton.upenn.edu • Research areas include financial management, money markets, real estate finance, and international finance.

## STATISTICS SOURCES

*The AIER Chart Book.* AIER Research Staff. American Institute for Economic Research. • Annual. $4 Individuals. A compact compilation of long-range charts ("Purchasing Power of the Dollar," for example, goes back to 1780) covering various aspects of the U. S. economy. Includes inflation, interest rates, debt, gold, taxation, stock prices, etc. (Economic Education Bulletin.).

*Selected Interest Rates.* U.S. Federal Reserve System Board of Governors Publications Services. • Weekly release, $20.00 per year.

*Survey of Current Business.* U. S. Government Printing Office. • Published by Bureau of Economic Analysis, U. S. Department of Commerce. Presents a wide variety of business and economic data.

*Treasury Bulletin.* U. S. Government Printing Office. • Quarterly. $51 List Price. Issued by the Financial Management Service, U. S. Treasury Department. Provides data on the federal budget, government securities and yields, the national debt, and the financing of the federal government in general.

# MONEY MARKET

*See* MONEY

# MONEY MARKET FUNDS

*See* INVESTMENT COMPANIES

# MONEY RATES

*See* INTEREST

# MONOPOLIES

*See* ANTITRUST ACTIONS

# MORALE, INDUSTRIAL

*See* HUMAN RELATIONS

# MORTALITY

*See* VITAL STATISTICS

# MORTGAGE BANKS

*See also* MORTGAGES

## PERIODICALS AND NEWSLETTERS

*Crittenden Report: Real Estate Financing.* Crittenden Research Inc. • Semimonthly. Newsletter on real estate lending and mortgages. Includes semiannual *Crittenden Directory of Real Estate Financing.*

*Mortgage Banking: The Magazine of Real Estate Finance Managers and Employees.* Mortgage Bankers Association. • Monthly. $45.00 per year.

*Origination News: For Mortgage Brokers, Correspondents, Lenders, and Wholesalers.* SourceMedia Inc. • Monthly. $78.00 per year. Edited for executives responsible for the origination and subsequent sale of mortgage loans.

## TRADE/PROFESSIONAL ASSOCIATIONS

Mortgage Bankers Association. 1919 M St. NW, 5th Fl., Washington, DC 20036. Phone: 800-793-6222 or (202)557-2700; Email: membership@mba.org • URL: http://www.mbaa.org • Principal lending and investor interests in the mortgage finance field, including mortgage banking firms, commercial banks, life insurance companies, title companies, and savings and loan associations. Seeks to improve methods of originating, servicing, and marketing loans of residential and income-producing properties through industry education and cooperation with federal agencies and the Congress. Holds clinics on all aspects of the mortgage finance business. Sponsors School of Mortgage Banking, and correspondence courses and web-based training on mortgage subjects for member personnel. Collects statistics and conducts research on the industry.

National Association of Mortgage Processors. 1250 Connecticut Ave. NW, Ste. 200, Washington, DC 20036. Phone: 800-977-1197 or (202)261-6505;

Fax: (202)318-0655; Email: contact@mortgageprocessor.org • URL: http://www.mortgageprocessor.org • Represents mortgage processors. Assists contract loan processors as well as in-house mortgage loan processors in all aspects of their businesses. Offers services such as training classes, blog cafe, community discussion, certification programs and download library.

# MORTGAGES

*See also* MORTGAGE BANKS; REAL ESTATE INVESTMENTS

## CD-ROM DATABASES

*OECD Statistical Compendium.* Organization for Economic Cooperation and Development. • Semiannual. $1,905.00 per year for 1 to 10 users. CD-ROM contains more than 730,000 monthly, quarterly, and annual time series for OECD countries, 1960 to date. Includes fully searchable data on agriculture, food, economic indicators, national accounts, employment, energy, finance, industry, technology, and foreign trade. Results can be displayed in various forms.

## HANDBOOKS AND MANUALS

*Monthly Payment Direct Reduction Loan Schedules.* Financial Publishing Co. • $75 13th edition. Loan amortization schedules, showing equal monthly payments necessary to amortize a loan of $1,000. Also shows the amount of interest and principal in each payment, and the balance outstanding at any time during the life of the loan.

*Mortgage Loan Disclosure Handbook: A Step-by-Step Guide with Forms.* Thomson West. • Annual. $363.00. Covers disclosure requirements that lenders must meet under federal laws and regulations. Discusses the Truth-in-Lending Act, RESPA (Real Estate Settlement Procedures Act), the Equal Credit Opportunity Act, and the Fair Credit Reporting Act. (Real Property Law Series).

*Practical Guide to Real Estate Taxation.* David F. Windish. Wolters Kluwer Law & Business CCH. • $150 1-4 Copies. Date not set. Serves as a guide to the federal tax consequences of real estate ownership and operation. Covers mortgages, rental agreements, interest, landlord income, forms of ownership, and other tax-oriented topics.

## INTERNET DATABASES

*BanxQuote Banking, Mortgage, and Finance Center.* BanxQuote, Inc. Phone: (914)722-1600; Fax: (914)722-6630; Email: info@banx.com • URL: http://www.banx.com • Daily. Web site quotes interest rates paid by banks around the country on various savings products, as well as rates paid by consumers for automobile loans, mortgages, credit cards, home equity loans, and personal loans. Also provided: stock quotes, indexes, stock options, futures trading data, economic indicators, and links to many other financial sites.

*Business 2.0 Web Guide to the Best Business Links.* Business 2.0 Media Inc. Phone: (415)293-4800; Email: support@business2.com • URL: http://www.business2.com/webguide • Web site presents an extensive, searchable directory of links to "the best, most informative, and authoritative web pages." Twenty main categories cover business, finance, career, company information, people, and technology topics, with thousands of subtopics, all linking to Web sites recommended by experienced business researchers. Fees: Free.

*Business Week Online.* McGraw-Hill. Phone: (212)512-2511; Fax: (684)842-6101 • URL: http://www.businessweek.com • Web site provides complete contents of current issue of *Business Week* plus "BW Daily" with additonal business news, financial market quotes, and corporate information from Standard & Poor's. Includes various features,

such as "Banking Center" with mortgage and interest data, and "Interactive Computer Buying Guide." The "Business Week Archive" is fully searchable back to 1996.

*Fedstats.* Federal Interagency Council on Statistical Policy. Phone: (202)395-7254 • URL: http://www.fedstats.gov • Web site features an efficient search facility for full-text statistics produced by more than 100 federal agencies, including the Census Bureau, the Bureau of Economic Analysis, and the Bureau of Labor Statistics. Boolean searches can be made within one agency or for all agencies combined. Links are offered to international statistical bureaus, including the UN, IMF, OECD, UNESCO, Eurostat, and 20 individual countries. Fees: Free.

*FreeLunch.com.* Economy.com, Inc. Phone: (610)696-8700; Fax: (610)696-1678 • URL: http://www.freelunch.com • Web site provides free access to more than 200 million economic and financial data series, covering industry, demographics, labor markets, prices, retail sales, government spending, trade, interest rates, housing starts, the stock market, etc. Data is available in either chart or table form. Searching is offered. Free, but registration required. Economy.com, Inc. also offers fee-based economic analysis at *The Dismal Scientist* site (www.dismal.com).

## OTHER SOURCES

*Real Estate Financing, with Forms on Disk.* ALM Media Properties LLC. • $560 print + online + ebook. Includes forms on two diskettes. Covers loan modifications, wraparound mortgage loans, loans for condos, co-ops, and time shares, saleleasebacks, installment sales, sales of mortgage loans, and various related topics. (Law Journal Press).

## PERIODICALS AND NEWSLETTERS

*Affordable Housing Finance.* Alexander & Edwards Publishing. • 10/year. $119 Individuals. Provides advice and information on obtaining financing for lower-cost housing. Covers both government and private sources.

*Broker: The Sales and Management Resource for Mortgage Originators.* SourceMedia Inc. • Bimonthly. $48.00 per year. Edited for mortgage brokers. Emphasis is on marketing, leads to new business, and profitability.

*Crittenden Report: Real Estate Financing.* Crittenden Research Inc. • Semimonthly. Newsletter on real estate lending and mortgages. Includes semiannual *Crittenden Directory of Real Estate Financing.*

*Housing Affairs Letter: The Weekly Washington Report on Housing.* Community Development Services, Inc. CD Publications. • Weekly. $624 print and online, 12 months. Covers mortgage activity news, including forecasts of mortgage rates.

*Mortgage and Real Estate Executives Report.* Thomson West. • Source of ideas and new updates. Covers the latest opportunities and developments.

*Mortgage-Backed Securities Letter.* Securities Data Publishing. • Description: Covers developments in the structured finance markets. Analyzes transactions and their collateral; follows litigation, refinancing opportunities, and market conditions.

*Mortgage Servicing News: For Residential amd Commercial Servicers.* SourceMedia Inc. • Monthly. $98.00 per year. Edited for personnel involved with processing and handling of mortgage loan payments and disbursements for such items as insurance and taxes.

*Mortgage Technology.* SourceMedia Inc. • Eight times a year. $78.00 per year. Covers the use of computers, software, automation, and technology in the mortgage industry. Includes reviews of new hardware and software products.

*Real Estate Finance.* Institutional Investor Inc. Journals Group. • Bimonthly. $350.00 per year. Covers real estate for professional investors. Provides information on complex financing, legalities, and industry trends.

*Real Estate Finance and Investment.* Institutional Investor Inc. Journals Group. • Weekly. $2,275.00 per year. Includes print and online editions. Newsletter for professional investors in commercial real estate. Includes information on financing, restructuring, strategy, and regulation.

## RESEARCH CENTERS AND INSTITUTES

University of California, Los Angeles - Richard S. Ziman Center for Real Estate. Gold Hall, Ste. B100, 110 Westwood Plz., Los Angeles, CA 90095-1481. Phone: (310)206-9424 or (213)825-3977; Fax: (310)267-5391 or (310)206-5455; Email: stuart. gabriel@anderson.ucla.edu • URL: http://www. anderson.ucla.edu/centers/ziman • Secondary mortgage markets, housing finance, growth management, infrastructure, corporate finance issues, and development industry.

## STATISTICS SOURCES

*American Housing Survey for the United States in (year).* U. S. Government Printing Office. • Biennial. $51.00. Issued by the U. S. Census Bureau (www. census.gov). Covers both owner-occupied and renter-occupied housing. Includes data on such factors as condition of building, type of mortgage, utility costs, and housing occupied by minorities. (Current Housing Reports, H150.).

*Statistical Information on the Financial Services Industry.* American Bankers Association. • Annual. Members, $150.00; non-members, $275.00. Presents a wide variety of data relating to banking and financial services, including consumer economics, personal finance, credit, government loans, capital markets, and international banking.

*Survey of Current Business.* U. S. Government Printing Office. • Published by Bureau of Economic Analysis, U. S. Department of Commerce. Presents a wide variety of business and economic data.

*Survey of Mortgage Lending Activity.* U.S. Department of Housing and Urban Development. • Monthly.

## TRADE/PROFESSIONAL ASSOCIATIONS

Mortgage Insurance Companies of America. 1425 K St. NW, Ste. 210, Washington, DC 20005. Phone: (202)682-2683 or (202)393-5566; Fax: (202)842-9252; Email: doug@micadc.org • URL: http://www. micanews.com • U.S. and Australian mortgage insurance companies united to provide a forum for discussion of industrywide standards, and for representation before Congress and federal and state regulatory agencies that reviews housing-related legislation. Compiles statistics.

# MOTEL INDUSTRY

*See* HOTEL AND MOTEL INDUSTRY

# MOTION PICTURE CAMERAS

*See* CAMERA INDUSTRY

# MOTION PICTURE INDUSTRY

*See also* MOTION PICTURE
PHOTOGRAPHY; MOTION PICTURE
THEATERS

## ALMANACS AND YEARBOOKS

*International Motion Picture Almanac: Reference Tool of the Film Industry.* Quigley Publishing Co. •

Annual. $275 print. Reference covering the motion picture industry.

*Magill's Cinema Annual.* Cengage Learning Inc. • $228 Individuals. Annual. $208.00. Provides reviews and facts for new films released each year in the United States. Typically covers about 300 movies, with nine indexes to title, director, screenwriter, actor, music, etc. Includes awards, obituaries, and "up-and- coming" performers of the year.

*Motion Picture Credits Database.* Academy of Motion Picture Arts and Sciences. • Annual. $50. Gathered credits from films hoping to qualify for awards.

*The Motion Picture Guide Annual.* CineBooks. • Annual. $99.95. Provides detailed information on every domestic and foreign film released theatrically in the U. S. during the year covered. Includes annual Academy Award listings and film industry obituaries. Yearly volumes are available for older movies, beginning with the 1987 edition for films of 1986.

## BIBLIOGRAPHIES

*Films and Audiovisual Information.* U. S. Government Printing Office. • Annual. Free. Issued by the Superintendent of Documents. A list of government publications on motion picture and audiovisual topics. Formerly *Motion Pictures, Films and Audiovisual Information.* (Subject Bibliography No. 73.).

## CD-ROM DATABASES

*Bowker's Complete Video Directory on Disc.* Bowker Electronic Publishing. • Quarterly. $520.00 per year. An extensive CD-ROM directory of video tapes and laserdisks. Includes film reviews from *Variety.*

## DIRECTORIES

*Films and Videos on Photography.* A and C Black Publishers Ltd. • $15 Individuals. Covers: Films and videos dealing with photography. Entries include: Title, length, whether in color or black-and-white, format, release date, country in which produced, language, name of director, names of producing agency and distributors, synopsis, series note, review citations, and awards; distributors' name and address given in a separate list.

*Hollywood Creative Directory: Below-the-Line Talent.* IFILMpro. • Annual. $80.00. Lists more than 6,000 cinematographers, production designers, costume designers, film editors, set decorators, and art directors and their associated 15,000 film titles.

*Hollywood Creative Directory: Film Writers.* IFILMpro. • Annual. $85.00. Lists more than 8,000 screenwriters and their associated 35,000 film titles. Includes projects in development and unsold screenplays.

*Hollywood Creative Directory: The Phone Book to Hollywood.* IFILM Publishing. • Semiannual. $149.95 per year. Three issues per year. Single issue, $59.95. Lists about 9,900 talent agents, personal managers, and casting directors.

*Index to AV Producers and Distributors.* National Information Center for Educational Media. Plexus Publishing Inc. • Biennial. $89.00. A directory listing about 23,300 producers and distributors of all types of audiovisual educational materials.

*Producers Directory.* Hollywood Creative Directory. • Covers: over 1,700 film and TV production companies, studios, networks, and TV shows, and over 7,700 creative executives within those companies. Majority of listings are located in Los Angeles and New York. Entries include: Company name, staff names and titles, address, phone, fax, e-mail address, web site address, company type, studio deals, and select credits.

*The Ultimate Directory of Film Technicians: A Necrology of Dates and Places of Births and Deaths*

*of More than 9,000 Producers, Directors, Screenwriters, Composers, Cinematographers...* The Scarecrow Press Inc. • $70 Individuals Hardback. Covers: Film technicians from the beginning of the film industry to the present, including executives, producers, directors, screenwriters, cinematographers, set and costume designers, composers, art directors, choreographers, publicists, and editors. Entries include: Birth and death dates and career information.

*Variety International Film Guide.* Peter Cowie, editor. Silman-James Press. • Annual. $24.95. Covers the "who, what, where, and when of the international film scene." Includes information from 70 countries on film festivals, top-grossing films, awards, schools, etc.

## E-BOOKS

*The Business of Entertainment.* Cengage Learning Inc. • 2010. eBook. Covers movies popular music, and television. Includes information on the nuts and bolts of daily life in the industry, including the challenges of digitizing content, globalization, promoting stars and shows, protecting intellectual property, and developing talent.

## FINANCIAL RATIOS

*Annual Statement Studies.* Risk Management Association. • Annual. Compiled from over 280,000 financial statements.

*Annual Statement Studies: Industry Default Probabilities and Cash Flow Measures.* Risk Management Association. • Annual. $405 Nonmembers. Serves as a companion volume to the original *Annual Statement Studies.* Gives probability of default estimates on a percentage scale for more than 450 industries. Includes changes in position year-by-year for eight financial statement line items and provides percentage measures of cash flow.

## OTHER SOURCES

*Videolog.* Muze, Inc. • Annual. $250.00. Five volumes. Provides detailed information on more than 170,000 VHS and DVD video titles. Includes a "Directory of Stars and Directors" and 13 category sections.

*Westlaw Journal Entertainment Industry.* Thomson Reuters Westlaw. • Monthly. *Sports and Entertainment Litigation Reporter.* Provides concise, unbiased coverage of litigation involving such issues as breach of contract, First Amendment, invasion of privacy, unfair competition, misappropriation of funds, and copyright and trademark issues.

## PERIODICALS AND NEWSLETTERS

*Boxoffice Magazine: The Business Magazine of The Global Motion Picture Industry.* Media Enterprises L.P. • Monthly. $59.95 Individuals. Trade magazine for the motion picture exhibition industry; including news of film distribution and exhibition, film reviews, and technical articles.

*Daily Variety.* Variety Media Publications. • Daily. $199 Individuals. Covers entire scope of the entertainment business on the East and West coast.

*Entertainment Law and Finance.* ALM Media Properties LLC. • Monthly. $485 print and online. Covers contracts, royalties, litigation, copyright, taxation, etc., for the music industry, motion pictures, broadcasting, publishing, video, and related media. (A Law Journal Newsletter, formerly published by Leader Publications.).

*Film Journal International.* Nielsen Business Media Inc. • Monthly. $65.00 per year. Formerly *Film Journal.*

*Film Quarterly: Quarterly of Film, Radio and Television.* University of California Press - Journals and Digital Publishing Division. • Quarterly. Review of radio, tv, and fim.

*The Hollywood Reporter.* Daily. $199.00 per year. Covers the latest news in film, TV, cable, multimedia, music, and theatre. Includes box office grosses and entertainment industry financial data.

*SMPTE Motion Imaging Journal.* Society of Motion Picture and Television Engineers. • Monthly. $125 Nonmembers. Peer-reviewed journal containing articles pertaining to new developments in motion picture and television technology; standards and recommended practices; general news of the industry. Formerly *SMPTE Journal.*

*Variety: The International Entertainment Weekly.* Reed Elsevier Group plc Reed Business Information. • Weekly. $199 Individuals print + online. Contains national and international news of show business, with emphasis on motion pictures and television. Includes *Market* and *Special Focus* issues.

### RESEARCH CENTERS AND INSTITUTES

University of Wisconsin - Madison - Wisconsin Historical Society - Wisconsin Center for Film and Theater Research. 816 State St., Madison, WI 53706-1417. Phone: (608)264-6466 or (608)264-6467; Fax: (608)264-6472; Email: askmovies@ wisconsinhistory.org • URL: http://www. wisconsinhistory.org/Content. aspx?dsNav=N:4294963828-4294963805&dsRecordDetails=R:CS4075 • Studies the performing arts in America, including theater, cinema, radio, and television.

### STATISTICS SOURCES

*Standard & Poor's Industry Surveys.* Standard & Poor's Financial Services L.L.C. • Semiannual. $1,800.00. Two looseleaf volumes. Includes monthly *Supplements.* Provides detailed, individual surveys of 52 major industry groups. Each survey is revised on a semiannual basis. Also includes "Monthly Investment Review" (industry group investment analysis) and monthly "Trends & Projections" (economic analysis).

*U.S. Industry and Trade Outlook.* U.S. Department of Commerce National Technical Information Service. • Annual. Produced by the International Trade Administration, U.S. Department of Commerce, in a "public-private" partnership with DRI/ McGraw-Hill and Standard & Poor's. Provides basic data, outlook for the current year, and "Long-Term Prospects" (five-year projections) for a wide variety of products and services. Includes high technology industries. Formerly *U.S. Industrial Outlook.*

### TRADE/PROFESSIONAL ASSOCIATIONS

Association of Cinema and Video Laboratories. 1833 Centinela Ave., Santa Monica, CA 90404. Phone: (310)828-1098; Fax: (310)828-9737; Email: lab@ntaudio.com • URL: http://www.acvl.org • Motion picture film or video transfer laboratories; non-laboratory firms with allied interests. Provides a forum for the exchange of ideas in connection with the technical, administrative and managerial problems of the motion picture and video laboratory industry. Concerns include: government relations; public and industry relations; product specifications; improvement of technical practices and procedures; other areas of interest to film and video laboratories.

Directors Guild of America. 7920 Sunset Blvd., Los Angeles, CA 90046. Phone: 800-421-4173 or (310)289-2000; Email: dgawebsupport@dga.org • URL: http://www.dga.org • Negotiates agreements for members.

Motion Picture Association of America. 1600 Eye St. NW, Washington, DC 20006. Phone: (202)293-1966; Fax: (202)296-7410; Email: contactus@ mpaa.org • URL: http://www.mpaa.org • Affiliated with Alliance of Motion Picture and Television Producers and the Motion Picture Association. Formerly Motion Picture Producers and Distributors of America.

Producers Guild of America. 8530 Wilshire Blvd., Ste. 400, Beverly Hills, CA 90211. Phone:

(310)358-9020; Fax: (310)358-9520; Email: info@ producersguild.org • URL: http://www. producersguild.org • Represents, protects and promotes the interests of members of the producing team in film, television and new media.

# MOTION PICTURE PHOTOGRAPHY

*See also* CAMERA INDUSTRY; PHOTOGRAPHIC INDUSTRY

### ABSTRACTS AND INDEXES

*Art Index.* EBSCO Publishing Inc. • Quarterly. Annual cumulations. Price varies. Subject and author index to periodicals in art, architecture, industrial design, city planning, photography, and various related topics.

### BIBLIOGRAPHIES

*Films and Audiovisual Information.* U. S. Government Printing Office. • Annual. Free. Issued by the Superintendent of Documents. A list of government publications on motion picture and audiovisual topics. Formerly *Motion Pictures, Films and Audiovisual Information.* (Subject Bibliography No. 73.).

### DIRECTORIES

*Hollywood Creative Directory: Below-the-Line Talent.* IFILMpro. • Annual. $80.00. Lists more than 6,000 cinematographers, production designers, costume designers, film editors, set decorators, and art directors and their associated 15,000 film titles.

### ONLINE DATABASES

*Art Index Online.* H.W. Wilson Co. • Indexes a wide variety of art-related periodicals, 1984 to date. Monthly updates. Inquire as to online cost and availability.

### PERIODICALS AND NEWSLETTERS

*SHOOT: The Leading Newsweekly for Commercial Production and Postproduction.* Nielsen Business Media Inc. • Weekly. $125 /year. Covers animation, music, sound design, computer graphics, visual effects, cinematography, and other aspects of television and motion picture production, with emphasis on TV commercials.

*SMPTE Motion Imaging Journal.* Society of Motion Picture and Television Engineers. • Monthly. $125 Nonmembers. Peer-reviewed journal containing articles pertaining to new developments in motion picture and television technology; standards and recommended practices; general news of the industry. Formerly *SMPTE Journal.*

### TRADE/PROFESSIONAL ASSOCIATIONS

American Society of Cinematographers. 1782 N Orange Dr., Hollywood, CA 90078. Phone: 800-448-0145; Fax: (323)882-6391 • URL: http://www. theasc.com • Professional directors of photography in motion picture and television photography and others affiliated with cinematography.

# MOTION PICTURE THEATERS

### DIRECTORIES

*Cinemas Directory.* InfoGroup Inc. • Annual. Number of listings: 9,544. Entries include: Name, address, phone, size of advertisement, name of owner or manager, number of employees, year first in "Yellow Pages." Compiled from telephone company "Yellow Pages," nationwide.

*Motion Picture TV and Theatre Directory: For Services and Products.* Motion Picture Enterprises Publications Inc. • Semiannual. $16.20. Companies providing products and services to the motion picture and television industries.

*The Theatre Listing: A Directory of Professional Theatre in Canada.* Professional Association of Canadian Theatres. • Covers: Over 300 English-language professional theatres in Canada. Entries include: Theatre name, address, phone, fax, e-mail, internet sites, contacts, key personnel, budget, mandates, facilities, submissions, repertoire, play development and other programs, affiliations.

### FINANCIAL RATIOS

*Annual Statement Studies.* Risk Management Association. • Annual. Compiled from over 280,000 financial statements.

*Annual Statement Studies: Industry Default Probabilities and Cash Flow Measures.* Risk Management Association. • Annual. $405 Nonmembers. Serves as a companion volume to the original *Annual Statement Studies.* Gives probability of default estimates on a percentage scale for more than 450 industries. Includes changes in position year-by-year for eight financial statement line items and provides percentage measures of cash flow.

### PERIODICALS AND NEWSLETTERS

*Boxoffice: The Business Magazine of the Global Motion Picture Industry.* RLD Communication. • Monthly. $40.00 per year. Provides national and local news about theater management and operations, industry trends about film production and distribution.

*Film Journal International.* Nielsen Business Media Inc. • Monthly. $65.00 per year. Formerly *Film Journal.*

### TRADE/PROFESSIONAL ASSOCIATIONS

National Association of Theatre Owners. 750 1st St. NE, Ste. 1130, Washington, DC 20002. Phone: (202)962-0054; Fax: (202)962-0370; Email: nato@ natodc.com • URL: http://www.natoonline.org • Owners, operators and executives of motion picture theaters. Provides services to assist theater owners in successfully operating their theaters including monitoring legislative and technological advancements; compiles statistics.

# MOTION PICTURES IN EDUCATION

*See* AUDIOVISUAL AIDS IN EDUCATION

# MOTION PICTURES IN INDUSTRY

*See* AUDIOVISUAL AIDS IN INDUSTRY

# MOTION STUDY

*See* TIME AND MOTION STUDY

# MOTIVATION (PSYCHOLOGY)

*See also* INDUSTRIAL PSYCHOLOGY

### ABSTRACTS AND INDEXES

*Psychological Abstracts.* American Psychological Association. • Monthly. Members, $815.00 per year; individuals and institutions, $1,207.00 per year. Covers the international literature of psychology and the behavioral sciences. Includes journals, technical reports, dissertations, and other sources.

### PERIODICALS AND NEWSLETTERS

*Incentive: Managing and Marketing Through Motivation.* Nielsen Business Media Inc. • Monthly. $59.00 per year.

*Motivation and Emotion.* Springer. • Publishes theoretical papers and original research reports either a basic or applied nature that focus on motivation and emotion.

*Teamwork: Your Personal Guide to Working Successfully with People.* Dartnell Corp. • Monthly. $249 Individuals Print and Online - Annual. Offers your employees practical tips and techniques that help them work together as a cohesive unit, improve relations with other teams, and motivate themselves.

# MOTIVATION PAMPHLETS

*See* PAMPHLETS

# MOTOR BUSES

*See also* TRANSPORTATION INDUSTRY

## FINANCIAL RATIOS

*Annual Statement Studies.* Risk Management Association. • Annual. Compiled from over 280,000 financial statements.

*Annual Statement Studies: Industry Default Probabilities and Cash Flow Measures.* Risk Management Association. • Annual. $405 Nonmembers. Serves as a companion volume to the original *Annual Statement Studies.* Gives probability of default estimates on a percentage scale for more than 450 industries. Includes changes in position year-by-year for eight financial statement line items and provides percentage measures of cash flow.

## ONLINE DATABASES

*TRIS: Transportation Research Information Service.* The National Academies National Research Council. • Contains abstracts and citations to a wide range of transportation literature, 1968 to present, with monthly updates. Includes references to the literature of air transportation, highways, ships and shipping, railroads, trucking, and urban mass transportation. Formerly *TRIS-ON-LINE.* Inquire as to online cost and availability.

## PERIODICALS AND NEWSLETTERS

*BUSRide.* Power Trade Media L.L.C. • Monthly. $39 U.S.. Magazine covering all aspects of transit and motorcoach industry.

*Commercial Carrier Journal.* Randall-Reilly Publishing Company L.L.C. • Monthly.

*Fleet Owner.* Primedia Business Magazines and Media. • Monthly. $45.00 per year.

*School Bus Fleet.* Bobit Business Media. • Monthly. $25.00 per year. Includes *Factbook.*

## STATISTICS SOURCES

*Rural Transit Fact Book.* American Public Transportation Association. • Annual. Serves as a national resource for statistics and information on rural transit in America.

# MOTOR CARS

*See* AUTOMOBILES

# MOTOR TRANSPORT

*See* TRUCKING INDUSTRY

# MOTOR TRUCK INDUSTRY

*See* TRUCKING INDUSTRY

# MOTOR TRUCK TRAILERS

*See* TRUCK TRAILERS

# MOTOR VEHICLE EQUIPMENT INDUSTRY

*See* AUTOMOBILE EQUIPMENT INDUSTRY

# MOTOR VEHICLE LAW AND REGULATION

*See also* INTERSTATE COMMERCE

## ABSTRACTS AND INDEXES

*Current Law Index.* Cengage Learning Inc. • $1,332 Individuals. Monthly. $1269.00 per year. Produced in cooperation with the American Association of Law Libraries. Indexes more than 900 law journals, legal newspapers, and specialty publications from the U.S., Canada, U.K., Ireland, Australia, and New Zealand.

## INTERNET DATABASES

*Lexis.com Research System.* Lexis-Nexis Group. Phone: 800-227-4908 or (937)865-6800; Fax: (937)865-6909; Email: webmaster@prod.lexis-nexis.com • URL: http://www.nexis.com • Fee-based Web site offers extensive searching of a wide variety of legal sources. Additional features include Daily Opinion Service, lexis.com Bookstore, Career Center, CLE Center, Law Schools, and Practice Pages ("Pages specific to areas of specialty").

## PERIODICALS AND NEWSLETTERS

*AAMVA Bulletin.* American Association of Motor Vehicle Administrators. • Description: Provides news and legislative information for motor vehicle administrators. Recurring features include news of research, announcements, and legislative information.

*Motor Vehicle Regulation: State Capitals.* Wakeman/Walworth Inc. • 50 times a year. $245.00 per year; print and online editions, $350.00 per year. Formerly *From the State Capitals: Motor Vehicle Regulation.*

## TRADE/PROFESSIONAL ASSOCIATIONS

National Committee on Uniform Traffic Laws and Ordinances. 107 S West St., No. 110, Alexandria, VA 22314-2824. Phone: 800-807-5290; Fax: (540)465-5383; Email: twogen2@yahoo.com • URL: http://www.ncutlo.org • Formerly National Conference on Street and Highway Safety.

# MOTOR VEHICLE LICENSES

*See* MOTOR VEHICLE LAW AND REGULATION

# MOTOR VEHICLE PARKING

*See* PARKING

# MOTOR VEHICLE PARTS INDUSTRY

*See* AUTOMOBILE EQUIPMENT INDUSTRY

# MOTOR VEHICLES, FOREIGN

*See* FOREIGN AUTOMOBILES

# MOTOR VEHICLES, USED

*See* USED CAR INDUSTRY

# MOTORCYCLES

## DIRECTORIES

*Directory of Chinese Manufacturers & Exporters of Motorcycles, Parts & Accessories.* EXIM Infotek Private Ltd. • $10 Individuals. Covers: 50 Chinese manufacturers and exporters of bikes, motor bike accessories, motorcycle bulbs, motorcycle fittings, motorcycle locks, motorcycle parts, motorcycle starting motors, motorcycles, and scooters. Entries include: Company name, postal address, city, country, phone, fax, e-mail and websites, contact person, designation, and product details.

*Directory of Japanese Manufacturers & Exporters of Motorcycles, Parts & Accessories.* EXIM Infotek Private Ltd. • $20 Individuals. Covers: 280 Japanese manufacturers and exporters of motorcycle parts, motorcycles, motorcycles and accessories, used motorcycles and parts, used scooters. Entries include: Company name, postal address, city, country, phone, fax, e-mail and websites, contact person, designation, and product details.

*Directory of Taiwanese Manufacturers & Exporters of Motorcycles, Parts & Accessories.* EXIM Infotek Private Ltd. • $10 Individuals. Covers: 50 Taiwanese manufacturers and exporters of motorcycle mirrors, motorcycle parts, motorcycles and mopeds. Entries include: Company name, postal address, city, country, phone, fax, e-mail and websites, contact person, designation, and product details.

*The International Directory of Importers--Bicycles, Mopeds and Motorcycles Importers.* Interdata. • $200 Individuals print. Covers: 800 international firms importing bicycles, mopeds and motorcycles. Entries include: Company name and address, contact person, email, number of employees, year established, phone and telefaxes, business activity, bank references, as well as a listing of bicycles, mopeds and motorcycles currently being imported.

*Motorcycle & Powersports News Buyers Guide.* A.B. Publications Inc. • Provides information on companies related to the motorcycle business. Formerly *Motorcycle Product News Trade Directory.*

## PERIODICALS AND NEWSLETTERS

*Cycle World.* Bonnier Corp. • Monthly. $22 Individuals 2 years. Magazine on street, dirt, dual-purpose, and all-terrain motorcylces. Covering tests, aftermarket products, parts and accessories, competition, personalities, travel, and nostalgia.

*Dealernews: The Voice of Powersports Retailers.* Advantstar Communications. • News concerning the power sports motor vehicle industry.

*Motorcycle Product News.* Athletic Business Publications Inc. • Monthly. $55.00 per year. Edited for wholesalers and retailers of motorcycles and supplies.

*Motorcycle Shopper: The Source for Motorcycles, Parts, Accessories, Sidecars, Tools, Clubs, Events, and More.* Payne Corp. • Monthly. $19.95 per year. Contains consumer advertisements for buying, selling, and trading motorcycles and parts.

*Motorcyclist.* PRIMEDIA Inc. • Monthly. $10.00 per year.

*Robb Report Motorcycling.* CurtCo Robb Media. • Semiannual. Price on application. Contains reviews of the "newest high-quality motorcycles.".

## PRICE SOURCES

*NADA Appraisal Guides.* National Automobile Dealers Association. • Prices and frequencies vary. Guides to prices of used cars, old used cars, motorcycles, mobile homes, recreational vehicles, and mopeds.

## STATISTICS SOURCES

*U.S. Industry and Trade Outlook.* U.S. Department of Commerce National Technical Information

Service. • Annual. Produced by the International Trade Administration, U.S. Department of Commerce, in a "public-private" partnership with DRI/ McGraw-Hill and Standard & Poor's. Provides basic data, outlook for the current year, and "Long-Term Prospects" (five-year projections) for a wide variety of products and services. Includes high technology industries. Formerly *U.S. Industrial Outlook*.

### TRADE/PROFESSIONAL ASSOCIATIONS

American Motorcyclist Association. 13515 Yarmouth Dr., Pickerington, OH 43147. Phone: 800-262-5646 or (614)856-1900; Fax: (614)856-1920 • URL: http://www.americanmotorcyclist.com • Represents motorcycle enthusiasts. Acts as a rule-making body for motorcycle competition. Promotes highway safety. Maintains museum and hall of fame.

Motorcycle Industry Council. 2 Jenner St., Ste. 150, Irvine, CA 92618-3806. Phone: (949)727-4211; Fax: (949)727-3313 • URL: http://www.mic.org • Manufacturers and distributors of motorcycles and allied industries. Maintains liaison with state and federal governments. Operates collection of research documents, federal and state government documents, and trade publications. Compiles statistics.

# MOTORS

*See* ENGINES

# MOVING OF EMPLOYEES

*See* RELOCATION OF EMPLOYEES

# MOVING PICTURE INDUSTRY

*See* MOTION PICTURE INDUSTRY

# MULTILEVEL MARKETING

### ABSTRACTS AND INDEXES

*Business Periodicals Index Retrospective*. EBSCO Publishing Inc. • 11/year. Quarterly and annual cumulations.

### ONLINE DATABASES

*Wilson Business Abstracts Online*. H.W. Wilson Co. • Indexes and abstracts 600 major business periodicals, plus the *Wall Street Journal* and the business section of the *New York Times*. Indexing is from 1982, abstracting from 1990, with the two newspapers included from 1993. Updated weekly. Inquire as to online cost and availability. (*Business Periodicals Index* without abstracts is also available online.).

# MULTIMEDIA

*See also* ELECTRONIC PUBLISHING; INTERACTIVE MEDIA; OPTICAL DISK STORAGE DEVICES

### ABSTRACTS AND INDEXES

*Business Periodicals Index Retrospective*. EBSCO Publishing Inc. • 11/year. Quarterly and annual cumulations.

*Computer Science Index*. EBSCO Publishing Inc. • Quarterly. $245 per year. Contains brief abstracts of book and periodical literature covering all phases of computing, including approximately 70 specific application areas.

*F & S Index: United States*. Cengage Learning Inc. • $2,659 Individuals. Monthly. $2,532.00 per year, including quarterly and annual cumulations. Provides annotated citations to marketing, business,

financial, and industrial literature. Coverage of U.S. business activity includes trade journals, financial magazines, business newspapers, and special reports.

*Internet and Personal Computing Abstracts (print edition)*. EBSCO Publishing Inc. • Quarterly. $269.00 per year, including cumulative index. Provides more than 10,000 abstracts annually from both trade and academic publications. Covers computer hardware, software, product reviews, Web topics, e-commerce, networks, corporate news, security, and related topics. Formerly *Microcomputer Abstracts*.

*Library Literature and Information Science Index*. H.W. Wilson Co. • Quarterly. Annual cumulation. Price varies.

*Readers' Guide to Periodical Literature*. EBSCO Publishing Inc. • Provides indexing for over 400 periodicals dating back to 1983.

### CD-ROM DATABASES

*Business Abstracts with Full Text*. EBSCO Publishing Inc. • Includes full text articles from more than 460 business publications from 1982 to present. Indexing for nearly 880 publications.

*Readers' Guide to Periodical Literature*. EBSCO Publishing Inc. • Provides indexing for over 400 periodicals dating back to 1983.

*WILSONDISC: Library Literature and Information Science Index*. H.W. Wilson Co. • Quarterly. Includes unlimited access to the online version of *Library Literature*. Provides CD-ROM indexing of about 400 periodicals, covering a wide range of topics having to do with libraries, library management, and the information industry.

### DIRECTORIES

*AV Market Place: The Complete Business Directory of Audio, Audio Visual, Computer Systems, Film, Video, and Programming, with Industry Yellow Pages*. Information Today, Inc. • Annual. $279.50 Individuals list price. Provides information on "more than 7,500 companies that create, apply, or distribute AV equipment and services for business, education, science, and government." Multimedia, virtual reality, presentation software, and interactive video are among the categories. Formerly published by R. R. Bowker.

*KMWorld Buyer's Guide*. Knowledge Asset Media Inc. • Semiannual. $2,395 (Basic Corporate Profile Package) One Issue — Spring 2014 Edition PLUS 6 Months Online. Controlled circulation as part of *KMWorld*. Contains corporate and product profiles related to various aspects of knowledge management and information systems. (Knowledge Asset Media is a an affiliate of Information Today, Inc.).

*Music Technology Buyer's Guide*. United Entertainment Media. • $6.95. Annual. Lists more than 4,000 hardware and software music production products from 350 manufacturers. Includes synthesizers, MIDI hardware and software, mixers, microphones, music notation software, etc. Produced by the editorial staffs of *Keyboard* and *EQ* magazines.

*SRDS Interactive Advertising Source*. Kantar Media SRDS. • Quarterly. $569.00 per year. Provides descriptive profiles, rates, audience, personnel, etc., for producers of various forms of interactive or multimedia advertising: online/Internet, CD-ROM, interactive TV, interactive cable, interactive telephone, interactive kiosk, and others.

### HANDBOOKS AND MANUALS

*Trade Secret Protection in an Information Age*. Gale R. Peterson. Glasser LegalWorks. • Looseleaf. $149. 00, including sample forms on disk. Periodic supplementation available. Covers trade secret law relating to computer software, online databases, and multimedia products. Explanations are based on more than 1,000 legal cases. Sample forms on disk

include work-for-hire examples and covenants not to compete.

### INTERNET DATABASES

*InfoTech Trends*. Data Analysis Group. Phone: (925)462-1202; Fax: (925)462-1225; Email: support@infotechtrends.com • URL: http://www. infotechtrends.com • Web site provides both free and fee-based market research data on the information technology industry, including computers, peripherals, telecommunications, the Internet, software, CD-ROM/DVD, e-commerce, and workstations. Fees: Free for current (most recent year) data; more extensive information has various fee structures. Formerly *Computer Industry Forecasts*.

*Wired News*. Lycos Inc. 400-2 Totten Pond Rd., Waltham, MA 02451-2053. Phone: (781)370-2700 or (415)276-8400; Fax: (781)370-2600 or (415)276-8500; Email: press@lycos.com • URL: http://www. lycos.com • Provides summaries and full-text of "Top Stories" relating to the Internet, computers, multimedia, telecommunications, and the electronic information industry in general. These news stories are placed in the broad categories of Politics, Business, Culture, and Technology. Affiliated with *Wired* magazine. Fees: Free.

### ONLINE DATABASES

*Computer Database*. Cengage Learning Inc. • Provides one year of full-text online for 150 leading computer-related publications. Also includes 70,000 product specifications and brief profiles of 13,000 computer product vendors and manufacturers. Inquire as to prices and availability.

*Wilson Business Abstracts Online*. H.W. Wilson Co. • Indexes and abstracts 600 major business periodicals, plus the *Wall Street Journal* and the business section of the *New York Times*. Indexing is from 1982, abstracting from 1990, with the two newspapers included from 1993. Updated weekly. Inquire as to online cost and availability. (*Business Periodicals Index* without abstracts is also available online.).

### OTHER SOURCES

*Keyboard: The World's Leading Music Technology Magazine*. United Entertainment Media. • Monthly. $25.95 per year. Emphasis is on recording systems, keyboard technique, and computer-assisted music (MIDI) systems.

### PERIODICALS AND NEWSLETTERS

*Advanced Imaging: Solutions for the Electronic Imaging Professional*. Cygnus Business Media. • Monthly. $60.00 per year Covers document-based imaging technologies, products, systems, and services. Coverage is also devoted to multimedia and electronic printing and publishing.

*Computer Music Journal*. The MIT Press. • Quarterly. Covers digital soound and the musical applications of computers.

*Desktop Video Communications*. BCR Enterprises, Inc,. • Bimonthly. Free per year. Covers multimedia technologies, with emphasis on video conferencing and the "virtual office."

*Digital Imaging: The Magazine for the Imaging Professional*. Cygnus Business Media Inc. • Bimonthly. $24.95 per year. Edited for business and professional users of electronic publishing products and services. Topics covered include document imaging, CD-ROM publishing, digital video, and multimedia services. Formerly *Micro Publishing News*.

*DV Magazine*. UBM L.L.C. • Monthly. Edited for producers and creators of digital media. Includes topics relating to video, audio, animation, multimedia, interactive design, and special effects. Covers both hardware and software, with product reviews. Formerly *Digital Video Magazine*.

*EContent: Digital Content Strategies and*

*Resources.* Online Inc. • Monthly. $110.00 per year. Emphasis is on the business management and financial aspects of the digital content industry. (Formerly published by Online, Inc.).

*Educational Marketer: The Educational Publishing Industry's Voice of Authority Since 1968.* SIMBA Information Inc. • Biweekly. $695 Individuals Online download. Edited for suppliers of educational materials to schools and colleges at all levels. Covers print and electronic publishing, software, audiovisual items, and multimedia. Includes corporate news and educational statistics.

*Electronic Information Report: Empowering Industry Decision Makers Since 1979.* SIMBA Information Inc. • 46 times a year. $649.00 per year. Newsletter. Provides business and financial news and trends for online services, electronic publishing, storage media, multimedia, and voice services. Includes information on relevant IPOs (initial public offerings) and mergers. Formerly *Electronic Information Week*.

*eMedia: The Digital Studio Magazine.* Online Inc. • Monthly. $98.00 per year. Covers video production equipment, digital video editing, electronic publishing, digital content streaming, encoding, and other topics related to digital content creation and multimedia. (Formerly published by Online, Inc.).

*IEEE Multimedia Magazine.* Institute of Electrical and Electronic Engineers. • Quarterly. $39 print only. Provides a wide variety of technical information relating to multimedia systems and applications. Articles cover research, advanced applications, working systems, and theory.

*Interactive Content: Consumer Media Strategies Monthly.* Jupitermedia Corp. • Monthly. $675.00 per year; with online edition, $775.00 per year. Newsletter. Covers the broad field of providing content (information, news, entertainment) for the Internet/World Wide Web.

*Maximum PC.* Imagine Media, Inc. • Quarterly. $29.95 per year. Provides articles and reviews relating to multimedia hardware and software. Each issue includes a CD-ROM sampler (emphasis is on games). Formed by the merger of Home PC and Boot.

*Media Device Report.* Jon Peddie Associates. • Description: Covers media and electronic devices and companies, as well as business information for those devices and companies. Recurring features include a company profile, editorial articles, technology briefs, IPO's, stocks, and stock indices.

*Multimedia Schools: A Practical Journal of Technology for Education including Multimedia, CD-ROM, Online and Internet and Hardware in K-12.* Information Today, Inc. • Six times a year. $39.95 per year. Edited for school librarians, media center directors, computer coordinators, and others concerned with educational multimedia. Coverage includes the use of CD-ROM sources, the Internet, online services, and library technology.

*Sound & Vision: Home Theater- Audio- Video- MultimediaMovies- Music.* Bonnier AB. • 10/year. $12.97 10 issues. Popular magazine providing explanatory articles and critical reviews of equipment and media (CD-ROM, DVD, etc.). Supplement available *Stereo Review's Sound and Vision Buyers Guide.* Replaces *Stereo Review* and *Video Magazine*.

*Video Librarian: The Video Review Magazine.* Video Librarian. • Bimonthly. $64. Edited for public and school libraries. Each issue includes reviews of hundreds of video DVDs or cassettes, in various subject areas.

## RESEARCH CENTERS AND INSTITUTES

Boston University - Multimedia Communications Laboratory. Department of Electrical & Computer Engineering, 8 Saint Mary's St., Boston, MA 02215. Phone: (617)353-9877; Fax: (617)353-6440; Email:

tdcl@bu.edu • URL: http://hulk.bu.edu • Research areas include interactive multimedia applications.

Carnegie Mellon University - College of Fine Arts - Studio for Creative Inquiry. 5000 Forbes Ave., Rm. 111, Pittsburgh, PA 15213-3890. Phone: (412)268-3451; Fax: (412)268-2829; Email: mmbm@andrew.cmu.edu • URL: http://studioforcreativeinquiry.org • Research areas include artificial intelligence, virtual reality, hypermedia, multimedia, and telecommunications, in relation to the arts.

International Data Corp. 5 Speen St., Ste. 1, Framingham, MA 01701-4674. Phone: 800-343-4935 or (508)872-8200; Fax: (508)935-4015 or (508)935-4271; Email: idcinfo@idc.com • URL: http://www.idc.com • Private research firm specializing in market research related to computers, multimedia, and telecommunications.

Massachusetts Institute of Technology - The Media Laboratory. Bldg. E15, 77 Massachusetts Ave., Cambridge, MA 02139-4307. Phone: (617)253-5960; Fax: (617)258-6264; Email: walter@media.mit.edu • URL: http://www.media.mit.edu • Research areas include electronic publishing, spatial imaging, human-machine interface, computer vision, and advanced television.

U.S. Department of Energy - Office of Energy Efficiency and Renewable Energy - Industrial Technologies Program - Industrial Assessment Center. School of Engineering, San Francisco State University, 1600 Holloway Ave., San Francisco, CA 94132. Phone: (415)338-6218 or (415)338-7736; Fax: (415)338-3086; Email: iac@sfsu.edu • URL: http://www.sfsu.edu/iac • Research areas include multimedia, computerized experimental arts processes, and digital sound.

University of Illinois at Chicago - Electronic Visualization Laboratory. Department of Computer Science, Rm. 1120, MC 152, 851 S Morgan St., Chicago, IL 60607-7053. Phone: (312)996-3002; Fax: (312)413-7585; Email: spiff@uic.edu • URL: http://www.evl.uic.edu • Research areas include computer graphics, virtual reality, multimedia, and interactive techniques.

University of Southern California - Integrated Media Systems Center. 306 Powell Hall of Engineering, 3737 Watt Way, Los Angeles, CA 90089-0272. Phone: (213)740-8945; Fax: (213)740-2539; Email: shahabi@usc.edu • URL: http://imsc.usc.edu • Media areas for research include education, mass communication, and entertainment.

# MULTINATIONAL CORPORATIONS

*See also* CORPORATIONS; INTERNATIONAL BUSINESS; INTERNATIONAL TAXATION

## ABSTRACTS AND INDEXES

*Business Periodicals Index Retrospective.* EBSCO Publishing Inc. • 11/year. Quarterly and annual cumulations.

## CD-ROM DATABASES

*InvesText.* Thomson Financial. • Monthly. Contains full text on CD-ROM of investment research reports from about 630 sources, including leading brokers and investment bankers. Reports are available on both U. S. and international publicly traded corporations. Separate industry reports cover more than 50 industries. Time span is 1982 to date.

*Newspaper Abstracts Ondisc.* ProQuest L.L.C. • Monthly. $2,950.00 per year (covers 1989 to date; archival discs are available for 1985-88). Provides cover-to-cover CD-ROM indexing and abstracting of 19 major newspapers, including the *New York Times*, *Wall Street Journal*, *Washington Post*, *Chicago Tribune*, and *Los Angeles Times*.

## DIRECTORIES

*American Big Businesses Directory.* InfoGroup Inc. • Annual. $295. Covers: 218,000 U.S. businesses with more than 100 employees, and 500,000 key executives and directors. CD-ROM version contains 160,000 top firms and 431,000 key executives. Entries include: Name, address, phone, names and titles of key personnel, number of employees, sales volume, Standard Industrial Classification (SIC) codes, subsidiaries and parent company names, stock exchanges on which traded.

*America's Corporate Families.* Dun & Bradstreet Inc. • Annual. Covers approximately 12,700 U.S. corporations. Ultimate companies must meet all of the following criteria for inclusion: two or more business locations, 250 or more employees at that location or in excess of $25 million in sales volume or a tangible net worth greater than $500,000, and controlling interest in one or more subsidiary company.

*Database, Directory of MNCs Companies in India.* NIIR Project Consultancy Services. • $100 U.S. CD-ROM. Covers: Multinational companies in India. Entries include: Name, address, country of origin, phone, fax, e-mail, website, CEO name.

*Directory of Multinationals.* Macmillan Publishers Ltd. Nature Publishing Group. • Irregular. $595 plus s/h. Approximately 450 multinational corporations with sales of $1 billion during 1996 and significant foreign investments.

*Foreign Representatives in the U. S. Yellow Book: Who's Who in the U. S. Offices of Foreign Corporations, Foreign Nations, the Foreign Press, and Intergovernmental Organizations.* Leadership Directories Inc. • Semiannual. $465 per year. Lists executives located in the U. S. for 1,200 foreign companies, 300 foreign banks and other financial institutions, 175 embassies and consulates, and 375 foreign press outlets. Includes five indexes.

*Hoover's Handbook of World Business.* Dun & Bradstreet Inc. Hoover's Inc. • Annual. $225 Individuals Hardcover. Covers: Hundreds of companies headquartered outside the U.S., including many with substantial activity in the U.S.; global enterprises, businesses that dominate their respective industries, and representative companies from all major industries. Entries include: Company name, overview, history, exchange and stock symbols, fiscal year-end date, names and titles of key personnel, name of auditors, number of employees, headquarters address, phone, fax, description of where the company does business, specific products/services/brand names produced, key competitors, 10 years of key financial data.

*Macmillan Directory of Multinationals.* Palgrave Macmillan. • Biennial. $295 plus 9 for shipping. Covers over 400 multinational industrial companies with consolidated sales of over $1 billion.

*Market Share Reporter (MSR).* Cengage Learning Inc. • $777 Individuals. 2013. $740.00. Published by Gale. Provides consumer market share data for leading companies. Also available as eBook.

*Morningstar American Depositary Receipts.* Morningstar Inc. • Biweekly. Looseleaf. Provides detailed profiles of 700 foreign companies having shares traded in the U. S. through American Depositary Receipts (ADRs).

*Multinational Companies in Argentina.* Business Monitor International Ltd. • Annual. $995 Individuals CD-ROM. Covers: 4,470 senior executive contacts on 1,650 leading US, European and Asian multinational companies across 34 industry sectors in Argentina. Entries include: Full company name, address, phone and fax numbers, email and web addresses, and key contact names and titles.

*Multinational Companies in Bahrain.* Business Monitor International Ltd. • Annual. $995 Individuals CD-ROM. Covers: 2,040 senior executive contacts on 640 leading US, European and Asian multinational companies across 34 industry sectors in Bahrain. Entries include: Full company name, address, phone and fax numbers, email and web addresses, and key contact names and titles.

*Multinational Companies in Brazil.* Business Monitor International Ltd. • Annual. $995 Individuals CD-ROM. Covers: 9,520 senior executive contacts on 3,880 leading US, European and Asian multinational companies across 34 industry sectors in Brazil. Entries include: Full company name, address, phone and fax numbers, email and web addresses, and key contact names and titles.

*Multinational Companies in Chile.* Business Monitor International Ltd. • Annual. $995 Individuals CD-ROM. Covers: 3,530 senior executive contacts on 1,080 leading US, European and Asian multinational companies across 34 industry sectors in Chile. Entries include: Full company name, address, phone and fax numbers, email and web addresses, and key contact names and titles.

*Multinational Companies in Colombia.* Business Monitor International Ltd. • Annual. $995 Individuals CD-ROM. Covers: 2,200 senior executive contacts on 830 leading US, European and Asian multinational companies across 34 industry sectors in Colombia. Entries include: Full company name, address, phone and fax numbers, email and web addresses, and key contact names and titles.

*Multinational Companies in Egypt.* Business Monitor International Ltd. • Annual. $995 Individuals CD-ROM. Covers: 4,630 senior executive contacts on 1,520 leading US, European and Asian multinational companies across 37 industry sectors in Egypt. Entries include: full company name, address, phone and fax numbers, email and web addresses, and key contact names and titles.

*Multinational Companies in Estonia.* Business Monitor International Ltd. • Annual. $995 Individuals CD-ROM. Covers: 1,310 senior executive contacts on 400 leading US, European and Asian multinational companies across 34 industry sectors in Estonia. Entries include: Full company name, address, phone and fax numbers, email and web addresses, and key contact names and titles.

*Multinational Companies in Greece.* Business Monitor International Ltd. • Annual. $1,660 Individuals CD-ROM. Covers: 5,330 senior executive contacts on 2,070 leading US, European and Asian multinational companies across 34 industry sectors in Greece. Entries include: Full company name, address, phone and fax numbers, email and web addresses, and key contact names and titles.

*Multinational Companies in Hungary.* Business Monitor International Ltd. • Annual. $1,660 Individuals CD-ROM. Covers: 4,630 senior executive contacts on 1,450 leading US, European and Asian multinational companies 34 industry sectors in Hungary. Entries include: Full company name, address, phone and fax numbers, email and web addresses, and key contact names and titles.

*Multinational Companies in Iran.* Business Monitor International Ltd. • Annual. $995 Individuals CD-ROM. Covers: 2,910 senior executive contacts on 1,940 leading US, European and Asian multinational companies across 34 industry sectors in Iran. Entries include: Full company name, address, phone and fax numbers, email and web addresses, and key contact names and titles.

*Multinational Companies in Jordan, Lebanon & Syria.* Business Monitor International Ltd. • Annual. $1,110 Individuals. Covers: 3,860 senior executive contacts on 1,150 foreign company subsidiaries across 34 industry sectors in Jordan, Lebanon, and Syria. Entries include: Full company name, address, phone and fax numbers, email and web addresses, and key contact names and titles.

*Multinational Companies in Kuwait.* Business Monitor International Ltd. • $995 Individuals. Covers: 2,110 senior executive contacts on 610 leading US, European and Asian multinational companies across 34 industry sectors in Kuwait. Entries include: Full company name, address, phone and fax numbers, email and web addresses, and key contact names and titles.

*Multinational Companies in Latvia.* Business Monitor International Ltd. • Annual. $995 Individuals. Covers: 1,340 senior executive contacts on 460 leading US, European and Asian multinational companies across 34 industry sectors in Latvia. Entries include: Full company name, address, phone and fax numbers, email and web addresses, and key contact names and titles.

*Multinational Companies in Lithuania.* Business Monitor International Ltd. • Annual. $995 Individuals. Covers: 1,000 senior executive contacts on 450 leading US, European and Asian multinational companies across 34 industry sectors in Lithuania. Entries include: Full company name, address, phone and fax numbers, email and web addresses, and key contact names and titles.

*Multinational Companies in Macedonia.* Business Monitor International Ltd. • Annual. $1,110 Individuals USA. Covers: 900 senior executive contacts on 290 leading US, European and Asian multinational companies across 34 industry sectors in Macedonia. Entries include: Full company name, address, phone and fax numbers, email and web addresses, and key contact names and titles.

*Multinational Companies in Mexico.* Business Monitor International Ltd. • Annual. $995 Individuals. Covers: 5,990 senior executive contacts on 2,030 leading US, European and Asian multinational companies across 34 industry sectors in Mexico. Entries include: Full company name, address, phone and fax numbers, email and web addresses, and key contact names and titles.

*Multinational Companies in Peru.* Business Monitor International Ltd. • Annual. $995 Individuals. Covers: 2,260 senior executive contacts on 720 leading US, European and Asian multinational companies across 37 industry sectors in Peru. Entries include: Full company name, address, phone and fax numbers, email and web addresses, and key contact names and titles.

*Multinational Companies in Poland.* Business Monitor International Ltd. • Annual. $1,660 Individuals. Covers: 5,340 senior executive contacts on 2,030 leading US, European and Asian multinational companies across 37 industry sectors in Poland. Entries include: Full company name, address, phone and fax numbers, email and web addresses, and key contact names and titles.

*Multinational Companies in Qatar.* Business Monitor International Ltd. • Annual. $995 Individuals. Covers: 1,690 senior executive contacts on 640 leading US, European and Asian multinational across 34 industry sectors in Qatar. Entries include: Full company name, address, phone and fax numbers, email and web addresses, and key contact names and titles.

*Multinational Companies in Romania.* Business Monitor International Ltd. • Annual. $1,110 Individuals. Covers: 3,190 senior executive contacts on 1,190 leading US, European and Asian multinational companies across 34 industry sectors in Romania. Entries include: Full company name, address, phone and fax numbers, email and web addresses, and key contact names and titles.

*Multinational Companies in Russia.* Business Monitor International Ltd. • Annual. $1,660 Individuals. Covers: 6,150 senior executive contacts on 2,560 leading US, European and Asian multinational companies across 34 industry sectors in Russia. Entries include: Full company name, address, phone

and fax numbers, email and web addresses, and key contact names and titles.

*Multinational Companies in Saudi Arabia.* Business Monitor International Ltd. • Annual. $1,660 Individuals. Covers: 6,730 senior executive contacts on 1,650 leading US, European and Asian multinational companies across 34 industry sectors in Saudi Arabia. Entries include: Full company name, address, phone and fax numbers, email and web addresses, and key contact names and titles.

*Multinational Companies in Serbia.* Business Monitor International Ltd. • Annual. $1,110 Individuals. Covers: 2,230 senior executive contacts on 760 leading US, European and Asian multinational companies across 34 industry sectors in Serbia. Entries include: Full company name, address, phone and fax numbers, email and web addresses, and key contact names and titles.

*Multinational Companies in Slovakia.* Business Monitor International Ltd. • Annual. $995 Individuals. Covers: 2,610 senior executive contacts on 830 leading US, European and Asian multinational companies across 34 industry sectors in Slovakia. Entries include: Full company name, address, phone and fax numbers, email and web addresses, and key contact names and titles.

*Multinational Companies in Slovenia.* Business Monitor International Ltd. • Annual. $1,110 Individuals. Covers: 2,290 senior executive contacts on 620 leading US, European and Asian multinational companies across 34 industry sectors in Slovenia. Entries include: Full company name, address, phone and fax numbers, email and web addresses, and key contact names and titles.

*Multinational Companies in Southern Africa.* Business Monitor International Ltd. • Annual. $1,110 Individuals. Covers: 2,960 senior executive contacts on 1,890 leading US, European and Asian multinational companies across 34 industry sectors in Southern Africa. Entries include: Full company name, address, phone and fax numbers, email and web addresses, and key contact names and titles.

*Multinational Companies in the Caribbean.* Business Monitor International Ltd. • Annual. $995 Individuals CDR. Covers: 7,000 senior executive contacts on 2,120 leading US, European and Asian multinational companies across 34 industry sectors in the Caribbean. Entries include: full company name, address, phone and fax numbers, email and web addresses, and key contact names and titles.

*Multinational Companies in the Philippines: Yearbook 2010.* Business Monitor International Ltd. • $995 Individuals CD. Covers: 4,910 senior executive contacts at 1,220 leading US, European and Asian multinational companies across 34 industry sectors in the Philippines. Entries include: Name, location, description, phone, ownership status and parentage.

*Multinational Companies in the UAE.* Business Monitor International Ltd. • Annual. $2,215 Individuals. Covers: 12,010 senior executive contacts on 3,970 leading US, European and Asian multinational companies across 34 industry sectors in United Arab Emirates. Entries include: Full company name, address, phone and fax numbers, email and web addresses, and key contact names and titles.

*Multinational Companies in Turkey.* Business Monitor International Ltd. • Annual. $1,660 Individuals. Covers: 5,960 senior executive contacts on 2,150 leading US, European and Asian multinational companies across 34 industry sectors in Turkey. Entries include: Full company name, address, phone and fax numbers, email and web addresses, and key contact names and titles.

*Multinational Companies in Ukraine.* Business Monitor International Ltd. • Annual. $1,110 Individuals. Covers: 2,420 senior executive contacts on 850 leading US, European and Asian multinational companies across 34 industry sectors in Ukraine. Entries include: Full company name, address, phone and fax numbers, email and web addresses, and key contact names and titles.

*Multinational Companies in Venezuela.* Business Monitor International Ltd. • Annual. $1,150 Individuals. Covers: 1,658 senior executive contacts on 568 foreign company subsidiaries across 34 industry sectors in Venezuela. Entries include: Full company name, address, phone and fax numbers, email and web addresses, and key contact names and titles.

*Multinational Food & Drink Companies in Emerging Europe Directory.* Aroq Ltd. • $577.46 with CD-ROM. Covers: 1,577 decision makers and 559 multinational food and drink companies in Europe.

*World Leading Global Brand Owners.* Euromonitor International Business Reference Div. • $1,495 Individuals Hardcopy. Covers: Profiles of the top 200 multinationals worldwide operating in key consumer markets. Entries include: Detailed corporate and financial information and analysis, information on the global market share and significant subsidiaries, strengths, weaknesses, opportunities and threats, main brands, product range, and full operational data.

*The World's Major Companies.* Euromonitor International Business Reference Div. • $550. Covers: Approximately 4,000 major multinational companies. Entries include: Company name, address, phone, telex, names and titles of key personnel, number of employees, financial data, subsidiary and branch names and locations, description.

*World's Major Multinationals.* Euromonitor International Business Reference Div. • Covers: List of major multinational companies. Entries include: Company name, address, phone; performance analysis; list of subsidiaries; market share; net profit and turnover; leading brands; and merger and acquisition information.

### INTERNET DATABASES

*EBSCO Information Services.* EBSCO Publishing Inc. 10 Estes St., Ipswich, MA 01938-2106. Phone: 800-653-2726 or (978)356-6500; Fax: (978)356-6565; Email: information@ebscohost.com • URL: http://www.ebscohost.com • Fee-based Web site providing Internet access to a wide variety of databases, including business-related material. Full text is available for many periodical titles, with daily updates. Fees: Apply.

*Ebusiness Forum: Global Business Intelligence for the Digital Age.* Economist Intelligence Unit (EIU), Economist Group. Phone: 800-938-4685 or (212)554-0600; Fax: (212)586-0248; Email: newyork@eiu.com • URL: http://www.ebusinessforum.com • Web site provides information relating to multinational business, with an emphasis on activities in specific countries. Includes rankings of countries for "e-business readiness," additional data on the political, economic, and business environment in 180 nations ("Doing Business in" and "Today's News Analysis.") Fees: Free, but registration is required for access to all content. Daily updates.

*Factiva.* Dow Jones Reuters Business Interactive, LLC. Phone: 800-369-7466 or (609)452-1511; Fax: (609)520-5770; Email: solutions@factiva.com • URL: http://www.factiva.com • Fee-based Web site provides "global news and business information through Web sites and content integration solutions." Includes Dow Jones and Reuters newswires, The Wall Street Journal, and more than 7,000 other sources of current news, historical articles, market research reports, and investment analysis. Content includes 96 major U. S. newspapers, 900 non-English sources, trade publications, media transcripts, country profiles, news photos, etc.

*InSite 2.* Intelligence Data/Thomson Financial. Phone: 800-654-0393 or (617)856-1890; Fax: (617)737-3182; Email: intelligence.data@tfn.com • URL: http://www.insite2.gale.com/ • Fee-based Web site consolidates information in a "Base Pack" consisting of Business InSite, Market InSite, and Company InSite. Optional databases are Consumer InSite, Health and Wellness InSite, Newsletter InSite, and Computer InSite. Includes fulltext content from more than 2,500 trade publications, journals, newsletters, newspapers, analyst reports, and other sources. Continuous updating. Formerly produced by The Gale Group.

*Nexis.com.* Lexis-Nexis Group. Phone: 800-227-4908 or (937)865-6800; Fax: (937)865-6909; Email: webmaster@prod.lexis-nexis.com • URL: http://www.nexis.com • Fee-based Web site offers searching of about 2.8 billion documents in some 30,000 news, business, and legal information sources. Features include a subject directory covering 1,200 topics in 34 categories and a Company Dossier containing information on more than 500,000 public and private companies. Boolean searching is offered.

*ProQuest.* ProQuest L.L.C. 789 E Eisenhower Pkwy., Ann Arbor, MI 48106-1346. Phone: 800-521-0600 or (734)761-4700; Fax: (734)662-4554; Email: info@proquest.com • URL: http://www.proquest.com • Fee-based Web site providing Internet access to more than 3,000 periodicals, newspapers, and other publications. Many items are available full-text, with daily updates. Includes extensive corporate and financial information. Fees: Apply.

### ONLINE DATABASES

*InvesText.* Thomson Financial. • Provides full text online of investment research reports from more than 600 sources, including leading brokers and investment bankers. Reports are available on approximately 60,000 U. S. and international corporations. Separate industry reports cover 54 industries. Time span is 1982 to date, with daily updates. Inquire as to online cost and availability.

*Wilson Business Abstracts Online.* H.W. Wilson Co. • Indexes and abstracts 600 major business periodicals, plus the *Wall Street Journal* and the business section of the *New York Times.* Indexing is from 1982, abstracting from 1990, with the two newspapers included from 1993. Updated weekly. Inquire as to online cost and availability. (*Business Periodicals Index* without abstracts is also available online.).

### OTHER SOURCES

*World Investment Report.* United Nations Publications. • Annual. Concerned with foreign direct investment, economic development, regional trends, transnational corporations, and globalization.

### PERIODICALS AND NEWSLETTERS

*Business Week International: The World's Only International Newsweekly of Business.* McGraw Hill Financial Inc. • Weekly. $95.00 per year.

*Canadian Business.* Canadian Business Media. • Biweekly. $20 per year. Edited for corporate managers and executives, this is a major periodical in Canada covering a variety of business, economic, and financial topics. Emphasis is on the top 500 Canadian corporations.

*Chief Executive Magazine.* Chief Executive Group, LLC. • Monthly. $99 per year.

*CTC Reporter.* United Nations Conference on Trade and Development. United Nations, Department of Public Information. • Semiannual. $20. Reports on both governmental and non-governmental aspects of multinational corporations. Issued by the United Nations Centre on Transnational Corporations (UNCTC). Formerly *CTC Reporter.*

*Financial Times (London).* The Financial Times, Inc. • Daily, except Sunday. $572.88 per year. An international business and financial newspaper, featuring news from London, Paris, Frankfurt, New York, and Tokyo. Includes worldwide stock and bond market data, commodity market data, and monetary/currency exchange information.

*Fortune Magazine.* Time Inc., Business Information Group. • Biweekly. $19.99 all access. Edited for top executives and upper-level managers.

*Harvard Business Review.* Harvard University, Graduate School of Business Administration. Harvard Business School Publishing. • 10/year.

*International Trade and Investment Letter: Trends in U.S Policies, Trade Finance and Trading Operations.* International Business Affairs Corp. • Monthly. $240.00 per year. Newsletter.

*Multinational Monitor.* Essential Information. • Monthly. $19.95 Individuals for new subscribers. Tracks the activities of multinational corporations and their effects on the Third World, labor and the environment.

*The New Information Report: The International Industry Dossier.* Washington Researchers Ltd. • Looseleaf service. $160.00 per year. Monthly updates. Formerly *The International Information Report.*

### RESEARCH CENTERS AND INSTITUTES

University of Pennsylvania - Center for Human Resources. 204 Steinberg Hall/Dietrich Hall, The Wharton School, 3620 Locust Walk, Philadelphia, PA 19104-6302. Phone: (215)898-5606; Fax: (215)898-5908; Email: cappelli@wharton.upenn.edu • URL: http://chr.wharton.upenn.edu • U.S. and international manpower issues, labor-management relations, human resources management and related areas.

### STATISTICS SOURCES

*Market Share Reporter (MSR).* Cengage Learning Inc. • $777 Individuals. 2013. $740.00. Published by Gale. Provides consumer market share data for leading companies. Also available as eBook.

# MUNICIPAL BONDS

*See also* BONDS; MUNICIPAL FINANCE

### CD-ROM DATABASES

*OECD Statistical Compendium.* Organization for Economic Cooperation and Development. • Semiannual. $1,905.00 per year for 1 to 10 users. CD-ROM contains more than 730,000 monthly, quarterly, and annual time series for OECD countries, 1960 to date. Includes fully searchable data on agriculture, food, economic indicators, national accounts, employment, energy, finance, industry, technology, and foreign trade. Results can be displayed in various forms.

### DIRECTORIES

*Mergent Municipal and Government Manual.* Mergent Inc. • Covers all U.S. taxing jurisdictions and agencies with total long-term rated debt of $25,000,000 or over.

### INTERNET DATABASES

*Business 2.0 Web Guide to the Best Business Links.* Business 2.0 Media Inc. Phone: (415)293-4800; Email: support@business2.com • URL: http://www.business2.com/webguide • Web site presents an extensive, searchable directory of links to "the best, most informative, and authoritative web pages." Twenty main categories cover business, finance, career, company information, people, and technology topics, with thousands of subtopics, all linking to Web sites recommended by experienced business researchers. Fees: Free.

*ETF Connect.* Nuveen Investments. Phone: 800-257-8787 • URL: http://www.etfconnect.com • Free Web site makes available extensive, searchable information on individual closed-end investment funds, preferred share funds, and exchange-traded index funds. Information on a particular fund is available by name or as part of a classification (high yield, investment grade, municipal, emerging markets, global equity, etc.). Fund charts are available for various time periods, as is data concerning premiums or discounts, dividends, annualized total return, credit quality, "Top 10 Holdings," and so forth.

*Factiva.* Dow Jones Reuters Business Interactive, LLC. Phone: 800-369-7466 or (609)452-1511; Fax: (609)520-5770; Email: solutions@factiva.com • URL: http://www.factiva.com • Fee-based Web site provides "global news and business information through Web sites and content integration solutions." Includes Dow Jones and Reuters newswires, The Wall Street Journal, and more than 7,000 other sources of current news, historical articles, market research reports, and investment analysis. Content includes 96 major U. S. newspapers, 900 non-English sources, trade publications, media transcripts, country profiles, news photos, etc.

*Fedstats.* Federal Interagency Council on Statistical Policy. Phone: (202)395-7254 • URL: http://www.fedstats.gov • Web site features an efficient search facility for full-text statistics produced by more than 100 federal agencies, including the Census Bureau, the Bureau of Economic Analysis, and the Bureau of Labor Statistics. Boolean searches can be made within one agency or for all agencies combined. Links are offered to international statistical bureaus, including the UN, IMF, OECD, UNESCO, Eurostat, and 20 individual countries. Fees: Free.

*FreeLunch.com.* Economy.com, Inc. Phone: (610)696-8700; Fax: (610)696-1678 • URL: http://www.freelunch.com • Web site provides free access to more than 200 million economic and financial data series, covering industry, demographics, labor markets, prices, retail sales, government spending, trade, interest rates, housing starts, the stock market, etc. Data is available in either chart or table form. Searching is offered. Free, but registration required. Economy.com, Inc. also offers fee-based economic analysis at *The Dismal Scientist* site (www.dismal.com).

*Nexis.com.* Lexis-Nexis Group. Phone: 800-227-4908 or (937)865-6800; Fax: (937)865-6909; Email: webmaster@prod.lexis-nexis.com • URL: http://www.nexis.com • Fee-based Web site offers searching of about 2.8 billion documents in some 30,000 news, business, and legal information sources. Features include a subject directory covering 1,200 topics in 34 categories and a Company Dossier containing information on more than 500,000 public and private companies. Boolean searching is offered.

*Wall Street Journal Interactive Edition.* Dow Jones & Co., Inc. 1211 Avenue of the Americas, New York, NY 10036. Phone: 800-369-5663; Email: service@dowjones.com • URL: http://new.dowjones.com • Fee-based Web site providing on-line searching of worldwide information from *The Wall Street Journal.* Includes "Company Snapshots," "The Journal's Greatest Hits," "Index to Market Data," "Journal Links," etc. Financial price quotes are available. Fees: $49.00 per year; $29.00 per year to print subscribers.

### ONLINE DATABASES

*Fitch Ratings Delivery Service.* Fitch. • Daily. Provides online delivery of Fitch financial ratings in three sectors: "Corporate Finance" (corporate bonds, insurance companies), "Structured Finance" (asset-backed securities), and "U.S. Public Finance" (municipal bonds).

### OTHER SOURCES

*Blue List of Current Municipal and Corporate Offerings.* Standard & Poor's Financial Services L.L.C. • Daily. $940.00 per year. Compendium of municipal and corporate bond offers.

*Fitch Insights.* Fitch Investors Service, Inc. • Biweekly. $1,040.00 per year. Includes bond rating actions and explanation of actions. Provides commentary and Fitch's view of the financial markets.

### PERIODICALS AND NEWSLETTERS

*CreditWeek.* Standard & Poor's Financial Services L.L.C. • Weekly. Price on application. Provides news and analysis of the municipal bond market, including information on new issues.

*The Lynch Municipal Bond Advisory.* James F. Lynch., editor. The Lynch Municipal Bond Advisory. • Monthly. Description: Addresses the municipal bond market.

### PRICE SOURCES

*Bank and Quotation Record.* William B. Dana Co. • Monthly. $130.00 per year.

### STATISTICS SOURCES

*S & P's Municipal Bond Book, with Notes, Commercial Paper, & IRBs.* Standard & Poor's Financial Services L.L.C. • Bimonthly. $965.00 per year. Includes ratings and statistical information for about 20,000 municipal bonds, notes, commercial paper issues, and industrial revenue bonds (IRBs). The creditworthiness ("Rationales") of 200 selected municipalities and other issuers is discussed. Securities "under surveillance" by S & P are listed.

*Statistical Annual: Interest Rates, Metals, Stock Indices, Options on Financial Futures, Options on Metals Futures.* Chicago Board of Trade. • Annual. Includes historical data on GNMA CDR Futures, Cash-Settled GNMA Futures, U. S. Treasury Bond Futures, U. S. Treasury Note Futures, Options on Treasury Note Futures, NASDAQ-100 Futures, Major Market Index Futures, Major Market Index MAXI Futures, Municipal Bond Index Futures, 1,000-Ounce Silver Futures, Options on Silver Futures, and Kilo Gold Futures.

*Survey of Current Business.* U. S. Government Printing Office. • Published by Bureau of Economic Analysis, U. S. Department of Commerce. Presents a wide variety of business and economic data.

## MUNICIPAL FINANCE

*See also* MUNICIPAL BONDS; MUNICIPAL GOVERNMENT; PUBLIC FINANCE

### PERIODICALS AND NEWSLETTERS

*Government Finance Review.* Government Finance Officers Association of United States and Canada. • Bimonthly. $35 Individuals.

*Municipal Finance Journal.* Civic Research Institute. • Quarterly. $359 Individuals Print and Online. Recent tax and legal trends affecting both large and small state municipalities.

*Nation's Cities Weekly.* National League of Cities. • Weekly. $96 Nonmembers. Description: Presents news on the latest developments in Congress, the White House, federal agencies, and other public interest groups which may affect the nation's cities.

*Project Finance: The Magazine for Global Development.* American Educational Systems. • 11 times a year. $740.00 per year. Includes print and online editions. Provides articles on the financing of the infrastructure (transportation, utilities, communications, the environment, etc.) Coverage is international. Supplements available *World Export Credit Guide* and *Project Finance Book of Lists.* Formed by the merger of *Infrastructure Finance* and *Project and Trade Finance.*

*Public Finance Review.* Pine Forge Press. • Bimonthly. $1,223 Institutions print & e-access. Public economy journal. Formerly *Public Finance Quarterly.*

### RESEARCH CENTERS AND INSTITUTES

University of Tennessee at Knoxville - Municipal Technical Advisory Service Library. 600 Henley St.,

Ste. 120, Knoxville, TN 37996-4105. Phone: (865)974-0411; Fax: (865)974-0423; Email: steve.thompson@tennessee.edu • URL: http://www.mtas.tennessee.edu/web2012.nsf/Web/Home • Research areas include municipal finance, police administration, and public works.

### STATISTICS SOURCES

*S & P's Municipal Bond Book, with Notes, Commercial Paper, & IRBs.* Standard & Poor's Financial Services L.L.C. • Bimonthly. $965.00 per year. Includes ratings and statistical information for about 20,000 municipal bonds, notes, commercial paper issues, and industrial revenue bonds (IRBs). The creditworthiness ("Rationales") of 200 selected municipalities and other issuers is discussed. Securities "under surveillance" by S & P are listed.

### TRADE/PROFESSIONAL ASSOCIATIONS

Association of Government Accountants. 2208 Mt. Vernon Ave., Alexandria, VA 22301-1314. Phone: 800-AGA-7211 or (703)684-6931; Fax: (703)548-9367; Email: agamembers@agacgfm.org • URL: http://www.agacgfm.org • Members are employed by federal, state, county, and city government agencies. Includes accountants, auditors, budget officers, and other government finance administrators and officials.

## MUNICIPAL GOVERNMENT

*See also* CITIES AND TOWNS; CITY PLANNING; COUNTY GOVERNMENT; PUBLIC ADMINISTRATION

### ABSTRACTS AND INDEXES

*Social Sciences Citation Index.* Thomson Reuters Corp. • Weekly. Product is accessed via *Web of Science.*

*Social Sciences Index Retrospective: 1907-1983.* EBSCO Publishing Inc. • Indexing for 1,000,000 articles. Coverage includes international index and social sciences and humanities index.

### BIOGRAPHICAL SOURCES

*Who's Who in American Politics.* Marquis Who's Who L.L.C. • Biennial. $349 Individuals. Contains about 27,000 biographical sketches of local, state, and national elected or appointed individuals.

### CD-ROM DATABASES

*Social Sciences Abstracts.* EBSCO Publishing Inc. • Provides indexing from 1983 and abstracting from 1994 of more than 750 periodicals covering economics, area studies, community health, public administration, public welfare, urban studies, and many other topics related to the social sciences.

*Social Sciences Citation Index.* Thomson Reuters Corp. • Weekly. Product is accessed via *Web of Science.*

### DIRECTORIES

*Carroll's Municipal/County Directory.* Caroll Publishing. • Semiannual. $500 Individuals. Provides listings of about 90,000 city, town, and county officials in the U. S.

*Carroll's Municipal Directory.* Caroll Publishing. • Annual. $500 Individuals. Covers: About 51,000 officials in more than 7,900 cities towns and villages: includes top elected council or elected board members. Entries include: Name, county name, locator phone, address, population; officials' names, titles, addresses, and phone numbers.

*Directory of Private Sector Services to Cities.* Texas Municipal League. • Annual. $10. Covers: about 300 firms providing services to city governments in Texas, including attorneys, accountants, architects, auditors, construction managers, engineers, inspectors, real estate appraisers and counselors, and water resource and supply companies. Entries include: Firm name, address, phone, name and title of contact, services, geographical area served.

*Government Phone Book USA: Your Comprehensive Guide to Federal, State, County, and Local Government Offices in the United States.* Omnigraphics Inc. • Annual. $265.00. Contains more than 270,000 listings of federal, state, county, and local government offices and personnel, including legislatures. Formerly *Government Directory of Addresses and Phone Numbers.*

*Mayors of America's Principal Cities.* United States Conference of Mayors. • Semiannual. About 1,000 mayors of cities with populations of 30,000 or more.

*Mergent Municipal and Government Manual.* Mergent Inc. • Covers all U.S. taxing jurisdictions and agencies with total long-term rated debt of $25,000,000 or over.

*Municipal Yellow Book: Who's Who in the Leading City and County Governments and Local Authorities.* Leadership Directories Inc. • Annual. $465 /year. Lists approximately 30,000 key personnel in city and county departments, agencies, subdivisions, and branches.

## HANDBOOKS AND MANUALS

*Municipal Management Series.* International City/County Management Association. • 14 volumes. Various dates, 1968 to 1988. Finance, planning, training, public relations, and other subjects.

## ONLINE DATABASES

*Wilson Social Sciences Abstracts Online.* H.W. Wilson Co. • Provides online abstracting and indexing of more than 500 periodicals covering area studies, community health, public administration, public welfare, urban studies, and many other social science topics. Time period is 1994 to date for abstracts and 1983 to date for indexing, with updates weekly. Inquire as to online cost and availability.

## OTHER SOURCES

*Local Government Law.* Chester J. Antieau. Matthew Bender and Company Inc. • $2,619 Print. States the principle of law for all types of local governments, and backs those principles with case citations from all jurisdictions. Examines the laws and their impact in three primary cases.

## PERIODICALS AND NEWSLETTERS

*American City and County: Administration, Engineering and Operations in Relation to Local Government.* RentPath Inc. • Monthly. Free to qualified personnel. Edited for mayors, city managers, and other local officials. Emphasis is on equipment and basic services.

*Current Municipal Problems.* Thomson West. • Full text journal articles on municipal law and administration. Indexing included.

*Governing: The States and Localities.* • Monthly. $39.95 per year. Edited for state and local government officials. Covers finance, office management, computers, telecommunications, environmental concerns, etc.

*Government Technology: Solutions for State and Local Government in the Information Age.* e.Republic Inc. • Monthly.

*ICMA Newsletter.* International City/County Management Association. • Description: Discusses local government, professional management, and federal regulation. Publishes news of Association activities. Recurring features include news of members; reports of publications, educational workshops, positions open in public management; and two main supplements titled Nuts & Bolts and ICMA University.

*National Civic Review.* National Civic League, Inc. Jossey-Bass. • Quarterly. $252 Institutions Online or Print only. Presents civic strategies for improving local government operations and community life.

*Nation's Cities Weekly.* National League of Cities. •

Weekly. $96 Nonmembers. Description: Presents news on the latest developments in Congress, the White House, federal agencies, and other public interest groups which may affect the nation's cities.

*Public Management: Devoted to the Conduct of Local Government.* International City/County Management Association. • 11/year. $46 U.S. for nonmembers.

*Public Risk.* Public Risk Management Association. • Monthly. $130 Individuals. Covers risk management for state and local governments, including various kinds of liabilities.

*U.S. Mayor.* United States Conference of Mayors. • Description: Provides a national forum for issues that affect cities in the U.S. Contains ideas in public programs and coverage of innovative projects. Recurring features include letters to the editor, interviews, a calendar of events, and reports of meetings.

## TRADE/PROFESSIONAL ASSOCIATIONS

Association of Governmental Risk Pools. 9 Cornell Rd., Latham, NY 12110. Phone: (518)389-2782; Email: info@agrip.org • URL: http://www.agrip.org • Works to promote risk pooling as a practical extension of a public entity's obligation to be a good steward of public funds. Aims to act as an advocate for the advancement of intergovernmental pooling as the most appropriate risk financing mechanism for most public entities. Seeks to provide meaningful and significant educational and professional support for the governing bodies and employees of intergovernmental risk pools.

National Civic League. 6000 E Evans Ave., Ste. 3-012, Denver, CO 80222. Phone: (303)571-4343 • URL: http://www.ncl.org • Community leaders, civic leaders, educators, public officials, civic organizations, libraries, nonprofits and businesses interested in community building, transforming democratic institutions and developing techniques of citizen action and participation. Serves as a clearinghouse for information on healthy communities, community renewal, local campaign, finance reform, All-American cities, city and county charters, election systems and techniques of citizen participation.

National League of Cities. 1301 Pennsylvania Ave. NW, Ste. 550, Washington, DC 20004-1747. Phone: 877-827-2385 or (202)626-3000; Email: memberservices@nlc.org • URL: http://www.nlc.org • Formerly American Municipal Association.

Public Risk Management Association. 700 S Washington St., Ste. 218, Alexandria, VA 22314. Phone: (703)528-7701; Fax: (703)739-0200; Email: info@primacentral.org • URL: http://www.primacentral.org • Public agency risk, insurance, human resources, attorneys, and/or safety managers from cities, counties, villages, towns, school boards, and other related areas. Provides an information clearinghouse and communications network for public risk managers to share resources, ideas, and experiences. Offers information on risk, insurance, and safety management. Monitors state and federal legislative actions and court decisions that deal with immunity, tort liability, and intergovernmental risk pools. Maintains library containing current reports from governmental units on their insurance procedures, self-insurance plans, and loss control and safety programs; and copies of policy statements, job descriptions, contractual arrangements, and indemnification clauses.

# MUSHROOM INDUSTRY

## INTERNET DATABASES

*USDA.* U.S. National Institute of Standards and Technology. 100 Bureau Dr., Gaithersburg, MD 20899-1070. Phone: 800-877-8339 or (301)975-6478 or (202)720-2791; Fax: (301)975-8295; Email:

inquiries@nist.gov • URL: http://www.nist.gov • The USDA home page has six sections: News and Information; What's New; About USDA; Agencies; Opportunities; Search and Help. Keyword searching is offered from the USDA home page and from various individual agency home pages. Agencies are the Economic Research Service, Agricultural Marketing Service, National Agricultural Statistics Service, National Agricultural Library, and about 12 others. Updating varies. Fees: Free.

## PERIODICALS AND NEWSLETTERS

*Mushroom Journal.* Mushroom Growers Association. • Monthly. Membership.

*Mushroom News.* American Mushroom Institute. • Monthly. $300 Individuals. Articles range from general interest to the latest technical innovations.

## STATISTICS SOURCES

*Agricultural Statistics.* U.S. Department of Agriculture National Agricultural Statistics Service. • Annual. $46 Individuals. Provides a wide variety of statistical data relating to agricultural production, supplies, consumption, prices/price-supports, foreign trade, costs, and returns, as well as farm labor, loans, income, and population. In many cases, historical data is shown annually for 10 years. In addition to farm data, includes detailed fishery statistics.

## TRADE/PROFESSIONAL ASSOCIATIONS

American Mushroom Institute. 1 Massachusetts Ave. NW, Ste. 800, Washington, DC 20001. Phone: (202)842-4344; Fax: (202)408-7763; Email: ami@mwmlaw.com • URL: http://www.americanmushroom.org • Mushroom growers, processors, suppliers, and researchers united to promote the growing and marketing of cultivated mushrooms. Aims to: increase cultivated mushroom consumption; develop better and more economical methods of growing and marketing mushrooms; collect and disseminate the latest statistics and other information; foster research programs beneficial to the industry; aid members with any problems. Supports a short course on mushroom science at Penn State University and an international congress on mushroom science.

# MUSIC INDUSTRY

*See also* MUSICAL INSTRUMENTS INDUSTRY; PHONOGRAPH AND PHONOGRAPH RECORD INDUSTRIES

## ABSTRACTS AND INDEXES

*Music Index: A Subject-Author Guide to Music Periodical Literature.* Harmonie Park Press. • Quarterly. $2,195.00 per year. Annual cummulation. Supplement available: *Music Index Subject Heading List.* Guide to current periodicals. Entries are in language of country issuing the index.

## BIOGRAPHICAL SOURCES

*Contemporary Musicians.* Cengage Learning Inc. • $188 Individuals. Annual. $171.00 per volume. 75 volumes. Provides biographical information on more than 3,600 musical figures in a variety of genres. Also available in eBook format. Contact for pricing.

## DIRECTORIES

*Billboard's International Buyer's Guide.* Nielsen Co. • Annual. $135 $6.00 s/h. Covers: record companies; music publishers; record and tape wholesalers; services and supplies for the music-record-tape-video industry; record and tape dealer accessories, fixtures, and merchandising products; includes United States and over 65 other countries. Entries include: Company name, address, phone, names of principal executives, trade and brand names and/or list of products and services.

*The Fono Directory.* CMP Information Ltd. • $66. Covers: Radio, record labels, television stations, artist management, and retail organizations in Europe including the United Kingdom and Ireland for those interested in the music industry. Entries include: Name, address, phone, fax.

*The Grey House Performing Arts Directory.* Grey House Publishing. • Annual. $250 Individuals Softcover. Covers: More than 8,500 dance companies, instrumental music programs, opera companies, choral groups, theatre companies, performing arts series, and performing arts facilities. Database includes: Information resources section covering hundreds of performing arts associations, publications, and Web sites. Entries include: Mailing address, telephone and fax numbers, e-mail addresses, Web sites, mission statement, key management contacts, and facility information such as capacity, season, and attendance.

*Instrumentalist--Directory of Summer Music Camps, Clinics, and Workshops Issue.* Instrumentalist Co. • Annual. Publication includes: List of nearly 250 summer music camps, clinics, and workshops in the United States; limited Canadian and foreign coverage. Entries include: Camp name, location, name of director, opening and closing dates, tuition fees, courses offered.

*Music Technology Buyer's Guide.* United Entertainment Media. • $6.95. Annual. Lists more than 4,000 hardware and software music production products from 350 manufacturers. Includes synthesizers, MIDI hardware and software, mixers, microphones, music notation software, etc. Produced by the editorial staffs of *Keyboard* and *EQ* magazines.

*The Music Week International Directory.* CMP Information Ltd. • Annual. $80. Covers: Music companies worldwide operating in over 20 sectors including record companies, distributors, publishers, manufacturers, promoters, and studios. Entries include: Name, address, phone, fax, e-mail address, and URL.

*Musical America International Directory of the Performing Arts.* UBM Global Trade. • Annual. $115.00. Covers United States and Canada.

*National Association of Schools of Music-- Directory.* National Association of Schools of Music. • Annual. $20 Individuals. Covers: Approximately 630 college and university departments of music and music conservatories accredited by the association. Entries include: School name, address, type of membership, description of music program, name of chief administrator, phone, degree or other study programs offered in music.

*Recording Industry Sourcebook.* Cardinal Business Media. • Annual. $71.99 Individuals. Covers: 14,000 contacts in the music industry in over 65 categories, including record producers, publishers, promoters, attorneys, major and independent record labels, and music production facilities. Entries include: Name, address, phone, fax, name and title of contact, subsidiary and branch names and locations, background information, email, web address.

### E-BOOKS

*The Business of Entertainment.* Cengage Learning Inc. • 2010. eBook. Covers movies popular music, and television. Includes information on the nuts and bolts of daily life in the industry, including the challenges of digitizing content, globalization, promoting stars and shows, protecting intellectual property, and developing talent.

### GENERAL WORKS

*Nashville Music Business Directory.* Nashville Area Chamber of Commerce. • $15 Nonmembers. Lists record publisher, distributors, recording companies, talent agencies and management companies in the Nashville music industry.

### OTHER SOURCES

*Keyboard: The World's Leading Music Technology Magazine.* United Entertainment Media. • Monthly. $25.95 per year. Emphasis is on recording systems, keyboard technique, and computer-assisted music (MIDI) systems.

*Lindey on Entertainment, Publishing and the Arts.* Alexander Lindey, editor. Thomson West. • $1,582.86 Full Set. Provides basic forms, applicable law, and guidance.

*Phonolog.* Muze, Inc. • Annual. $550.00. 10 volumes. Provides detailed information on more than 370,000 titles of commercially available and out-of-print music recordings. Includes popular, jazz, and classical titles.

### PERIODICALS AND NEWSLETTERS

*Cash Box: The International Music-Record Weekly.* Cash Box Publishing Co., Inc. • Weekly. $185.00 per year.

*Computer Music Journal.* The MIT Press. • Quarterly. Covers digital soound and the musical applications of computers.

*DownBeat.* Maher Publications Inc. • Monthly. $32.99 print or print and online. Information on contemporary music.

*Entertainment Law and Finance.* ALM Media Properties LLC. • Monthly. $485 print and online. Covers contracts, royalties, litigation, copyright, taxation, etc., for the music industry, motion pictures, broadcasting, publishing, video, and related media. (A Law Journal Newsletter, formerly published by Leader Publications.).

*Mix Magazine: Professional Recording, Sound, and Music Production.* Primedia Business Magazine and Media. • Monthly. $35.99 U.S. print and digital access. Professional audio and music production periodical.

*Music Inc.* Maher Publications Inc. • 11 times a year. $16.00. per year. Music and sound retailing. Formerly *Up Beat Monthly.*

*Music Journal.* Incorporated Society of Musicians. • Bimonthly. Contains news from our members, advice from our team, features and opinion pieces from experts in the music profession.

*Music Reference Services Quarterly.* The Haworth Press Inc. • Quarterly. Institutions, $95.00 per year. An academic journal for music librarians.

*Music Trades.* Music Trades Corp. • Monthly. $16 Individuals. Music trade magazine. Includes *Purchaser's Guide to the Music Industries.*

*Sound & Vision: Home Theater- Audio- Video- MultimediaMovies- Music.* Bonnier AB. • 10/year. $12.97 10 issues. Popular magazine providing explanatory articles and critical reviews of equipment and media (CD-ROM, DVD, etc.). Supplement available *Stereo Review's Sound and Vision Buyers Guide.* Replaces *Stereo Review* and *Video Magazine.*

### STATISTICS SOURCES

*U.S. Industry and Trade Outlook.* U.S. Department of Commerce National Technical Information Service. • Annual. Produced by the International Trade Administration, U.S. Department of Commerce, in a "public-private" partnership with DRI/ McGraw-Hill and Standard & Poor's. Provides basic data, outlook for the current year, and "Long-Term Prospects" (five-year projections) for a wide variety of products and services. Includes high technology industries. Formerly *U.S. Industrial Outlook.*

### TRADE/PROFESSIONAL ASSOCIATIONS

American Society of Composers, Authors and Publishers. 1900 Broadway, New York, NY 10023. Phone: 800-952-7227 or (212)621-6000; Fax: (212)621-8453 • URL: http://www.ascap.com • Composers, lyricists, and publishers. Serves as a clearinghouse in the field of music performing rights. Grants licenses and distributes royalties for the public performance of the copyrighted musical works of its members by broadcasters, symphony orchestras, and other users.

NAMM - The International Music Products Association. 5790 Armada Dr., Carlsbad, CA 92008-4608. Phone: 800-767-6266 or (760)438-8001; Fax: (760)438-7327; Email: info@namm.org • URL: http://www.namm.org • Retailers of musical instruments and allied products, manufacturers, distributors, jobbers, wholesalers and publishers of print music. Holds several professional development seminars in various locations around the country and 2 major trade shows.

# MUSICAL INSTRUMENTS INDUSTRY

*See also* MUSIC INDUSTRY

### DIRECTORIES

*Musical Merchandise Review: Directory of Musical Instrument Dealers.* Larkin Publications. • Annual. $125.00. Lists retailers of musical instruments and supplies.

*Musical Merchandise Review: Music Industry Directory.* Larkin Publications. • Annual. $25.00. Lists about 1,500 manufacturers and distributors of musical instruments and supplies. Includes indexes to products and trade names.

### FINANCIAL RATIOS

*Annual Statement Studies.* Risk Management Association. • Annual. Compiled from over 280,000 financial statements.

*Annual Statement Studies: Industry Default Probabilities and Cash Flow Measures.* Risk Management Association. • Annual. $405 Nonmembers. Serves as a companion volume to the original *Annual Statement Studies.* Gives probability of default estimates on a percentage scale for more than 450 industries. Includes changes in position year-by-year for eight financial statement line items and provides percentage measures of cash flow.

### PERIODICALS AND NEWSLETTERS

*Electronic Musician.* Primedia Business Magazines and Media. • Monthly. $23.97 per year.

*Instrumentalist: A Magazine for School and College Band and Orchestra Directors, Professional Instrumentalist, Teacher-Training Specialists in Instrumental Music Education and Instrumental Teachers.* Instrumentalist Co. • Monthly. $21 Individuals. Professional journal for school band and orchestra directors and teachers of instruments in those ensembles.

*Music Trades.* Music Trades Corp. • Monthly. $16 Individuals. Music trade magazine. Includes *Purchaser's Guide to the Music Industries.*

### PRICE SOURCES

*Guitars and Musical Instruments.* Orion Research Corp. • Annual. $179 Individuals. List of manufacturers of guitars and musical instruments. Original list prices and years of manufacture are also shown.

### STATISTICS SOURCES

*U.S. Industry and Trade Outlook.* U.S. Department of Commerce National Technical Information Service. • Annual. Produced by the International Trade Administration, U.S. Department of Commerce, in a "public-private" partnership with DRI/ McGraw-Hill and Standard & Poor's. Provides basic data, outlook for the current year, and "Long-Term Prospects" (five-year projections) for a wide variety of products and services. Includes high technology industries. Formerly *U.S. Industrial Outlook.*

### TRADE/PROFESSIONAL ASSOCIATIONS

International Band and Orchestra Products Association. 262 W. 38th St., Room 1506, New

York, NY 10018-5815. Phone: (212)302-0801; Fax: (212)302-0783; Email: assnhdqs@earthlink.net.

Music Distributors Association. 14070 Proton Rd., Ste. 100, LB 9, Dallas, TX 75244. Phone: (972)233-9107; Fax: (972)490-4219; Email: office@musicdistributors.org • URL: http://www.musicdistributors.org • International distributors and suppliers of musical instruments, sheet music, and allied merchandise; manufacturers of musical merchandise.

NAMM - The International Music Products Association. 5790 Armada Dr., Carlsbad, CA 92008-4608. Phone: 800-767-6266 or (760)438-8001; Fax: (760)438-7327; Email: info@namm.org • URL: http://www.namm.org • Retailers of musical instruments and allied products, manufacturers, distributors, jobbers, wholesalers and publishers of print music. Holds several professional development seminars in various locations around the country and 2 major trade shows.

# MUTUAL FUNDS

*See* INVESTMENT COMPANIES

# MUTUAL SAVINGS BANKS

*See* SAVINGS BANKS

# N

## NAFTA

*See* NORTH AMERICAN FREE TRADE AGREEMENT

## NARCOTICS

*See also* DRUG ABUSE AND TRAFFIC; PHARMACEUTICAL INDUSTRY

### CD-ROM DATABASES

*International Pharmaceutical Abstracts.* Ovid Technologies Inc. • Quarterly. International pharmaceutical literature from 1970 to date.

### ENCYCLOPEDIAS AND DICTIONARIES

*Encyclopedia of Drugs, Alcohol, and Addictive Behavior.* Cengage Learning Inc. • $820 Individuals. 2009. 3rd Edition. eBook. Published by Macmillan Reference USA. Covers the social, economic, political, and medical aspects of addiction. Inquire for price and availability.

### GENERAL WORKS

*Drugs, Alcohol & Tobacco: Learning About Addictive Behavior.* Edited by Rosalyn Carson-Dewitt, M.D. Cengage Learning Inc. • $512. Three volumes. Contains 200 articles on various aspects of addiction. Includes color illustrations, a glossary, and comprehensive indexing. Macmillan Reference USA imprint. eBook also available. Inquire for pricing.

### ONLINE DATABASES

*Toxline.* National Library of Medicine. • Weekly. Abstracting service covering human and animal toxicity studies, 1965 to present (older studies available in *Toxback* file). Weekly updates. Inquire as to online cost and availability.

### PERIODICALS AND NEWSLETTERS

*Bulletin on Narcotics.* United Nations Publications. • Quarterly. $10.00 per issue. Editions in Chinese, French, Russian and Spanish.

### STATISTICS SOURCES

*Psychotropic Substances.* United Nations Publications. • Annual. $50.00.

## NATIONAL ACCOUNTING

*See also* ECONOMIC POLICY; ECONOMIC STATISTICS; ECONOMICS

### ABSTRACTS AND INDEXES

*Social Sciences Citation Index.* Thomson Reuters Corp. • Weekly. Product is accessed via *Web of Science.*

*Social Sciences Index Retrospective: 1907-1983.* EBSCO Publishing Inc. • Indexing for 1,000,000 articles. Coverage includes international index and social sciences and humanities index.

### ALMANACS AND YEARBOOKS

*National Accounts Statistics: Main Aggregates and Detailed Tables.* United Nations Publications. • Annual.

### CD-ROM DATABASES

*EconLit.* Ovid Technologies Inc. • Updated monthly. Lists journal articles, book reviews, disserations of economic literature. Over 1,400 journals covered.

*OECD Statistical Compendium.* Organization for Economic Cooperation and Development. • Semiannual. $1,905.00 per year for 1 to 10 users. CD-ROM contains more than 730,000 monthly, quarterly, and annual time series for OECD countries, 1960 to date. Includes fully searchable data on agriculture, food, economic indicators, national accounts, employment, energy, finance, industry, technology, and foreign trade. Results can be displayed in various forms.

*Social Sciences Abstracts.* EBSCO Publishing Inc. • Provides indexing from 1983 and abstracting from 1994 of more than 750 periodicals covering economics, area studies, community health, public administration, public welfare, urban studies, and many other topics related to the social sciences.

*Social Sciences Citation Index.* Thomson Reuters Corp. • Weekly. Product is accessed via *Web of Science.*

### INTERNET DATABASES

*Business 2.0 Web Guide to the Best Business Links.* Business 2.0 Media Inc. Phone: (415)293-4800; Email: support@business2.com • URL: http://www.business2.com/webguide • Web site presents an extensive, searchable directory of links to "the best, most informative, and authoritative web pages." Twenty main categories cover business, finance, career, company information, people, and technology topics, with thousands of subtopics, all linking to Web sites recommended by experienced business researchers. Fees: Free.

*Fedstats.* Federal Interagency Council on Statistical Policy. Phone: (202)395-7254 • URL: http://www.fedstats.gov • Web site features an efficient search facility for full-text statistics produced by more than 100 federal agencies, including the Census Bureau, the Bureau of Economic Analysis, and the Bureau of Labor Statistics. Boolean searches can be made within one agency or for all agencies combined. Links are offered to international statistical bureaus, including the UN, IMF, OECD, UNESCO, Eurostat, and 20 individual countries. Fees: Free.

*FreeLunch.com.* Economy.com, Inc. Phone: (610)696-8700; Fax: (610)696-1678 • URL: http://www.freelunch.com • Web site provides free access to more than 200 million economic and financial data series, covering industry, demographics, labor markets, prices, retail sales, government spending, trade, interest rates, housing starts, the stock market, etc. Data is available in either chart or table form. Searching is offered. Free, but registration required. Economy.com, Inc. also offers fee-based economic analysis at *The Dismal Scientist* site (www.dismal.com).

*U.S. Census Bureau: The Official Statistics.* U. S. Bureau of the Census. Phone: (301)763-4636 or (301)763-4100; Fax: (301)763-4794; Email: webmaster@census.gov • URL: http://www.census.gov/prod/www/abs/mfg-prof.html • Web site is "Your Source for Social, Demographic, and Economic Information." Contains "Current U. S. Population Count," "Current Economic Indicators," and a wide variety of data under "Other Official Statistics." Keyword searching is provided. Fees: Free.

### ONLINE DATABASES

*Wilson Social Sciences Abstracts Online.* H.W. Wilson Co. • Provides online abstracting and indexing of more than 500 periodicals covering area studies, community health, public administration, public welfare, urban studies, and many other social science topics. Time period is 1994 to date for abstracts and 1983 to date for indexing, with updates weekly. Inquire as to online cost and availability.

### STATISTICS SOURCES

*Quarterly National Accounts.* Organisation for Economic Co-operation and Development Publications and Information Center. • Quarterly. $125.00 per year. National accounts data of OECD countries.

*Statistical Abstract of the United States.* U. S. Government Printing Office. • Annual. $44.00. Issued by the U. S. Bureau of the Census.

*Statistical Yearbook.* United Nations Publications. • Annual. $125.00. Contains statistics for about 200 countries on a wide variety of economic, industrial, and demographic topics. Compiled by United Nations Statistical Office.

*Survey of Current Business.* U. S. Government Printing Office. • Published by Bureau of Economic Analysis, U. S. Department of Commerce. Presents a wide variety of business and economic data.

## NATIONAL BRANDS

*See* TRADEMARKS AND TRADE NAMES

# NATIONAL DEBT

*See also* FEDERAL BUDGET

## ABSTRACTS AND INDEXES

*Business Periodicals Index Retrospective.* EBSCO Publishing Inc. • 11/year. Quarterly and annual cumulations.

*Readers' Guide to Periodical Literature.* EBSCO Publishing Inc. • Provides indexing for over 400 periodicals dating back to 1983.

## CD-ROM DATABASES

*International Development Statistics.* Organization for Economic Cooperation and Development. • Annual. $71.00. Issued by the OECD Development Assistance Committee. CD-ROM contains data on aid to more than 180 recipient countries, including amount, origin, type, and recipients' external debt.

*OECD Statistical Compendium.* Organization for Economic Cooperation and Development. • Semiannual. $1,905.00 per year for 1 to 10 users. CD-ROM contains more than 730,000 monthly, quarterly, and annual time series for OECD countries, 1960 to date. Includes fully searchable data on agriculture, food, economic indicators, national accounts, employment, energy, finance, industry, technology, and foreign trade. Results can be displayed in various forms.

*Readers' Guide to Periodical Literature.* EBSCO Publishing Inc. • Provides indexing for over 400 periodicals dating back to 1983.

## INTERNET DATABASES

*Business 2.0 Web Guide to the Best Business Links.* Business 2.0 Media Inc. Phone: (415)293-4800; Email: support@business2.com • URL: http://www.business2.com/webguide • Web site presents an extensive, searchable directory of links to "the best, most informative, and authoritative web pages." Twenty main categories cover business, finance, career, company information, people, and technology topics, with thousands of subtopics, all linking to Web sites recommended by experienced business researchers. Fees: Free.

*Fedstats.* Federal Interagency Council on Statistical Policy. Phone: (202)395-7254 • URL: http://www.fedstats.gov • Web site features an efficient search facility for full-text statistics produced by more than 100 federal agencies, including the Census Bureau, the Bureau of Economic Analysis, and the Bureau of Labor Statistics. Boolean searches can be made within one agency or for all agencies combined. Links are offered to international statistical bureaus, including the UN, IMF, OECD, UNESCO, Eurostat, and 20 individual countries. Fees: Free.

*FreeLunch.com.* Economy.com, Inc. Phone: (610)696-8700; Fax: (610)696-1678 • URL: http://www.freelunch.com • Web site provides free access to more than 200 million economic and financial data series, covering industry, demographics, labor markets, prices, retail sales, government spending, trade, interest rates, housing starts, the stock market, etc. Data is available in either chart or table form. Searching is offered. Free, but registration required. Economy.com, Inc. also offers fee-based economic analysis at *The Dismal Scientist* site (www.dismal.com).

## ONLINE DATABASES

*Wilson Business Abstracts Online.* H.W. Wilson Co. • Indexes and abstracts 600 major business periodicals, plus the *Wall Street Journal* and the business section of the *New York Times.* Indexing is from 1982, abstracting from 1990, with the two newspapers included from 1993. Updated weekly. Inquire as to online cost and availability. (*Business Periodicals Index* without abstracts is also available online.).

## PERIODICALS AND NEWSLETTERS

*OMB Watcher.* O M B Watch. • Bimonthly. Individuals, $35.00 per year. Monitors operations of the federal Office of Management and Budget.

## RESEARCH CENTERS AND INSTITUTES

League of Women Voters Education Fund. 1730 M St. NW, Ste. 1000, Washington, DC 20036-4508. Phone: (202)429-1965; Fax: (202)429-0854 • URL: http://www.lwv.org/education-fund • Research fields include federal deficit issues.

## STATISTICS SOURCES

*The AIER Chart Book.* AIER Research Staff. American Institute for Economic Research. • Annual. $4 Individuals. A compact compilation of long-range charts ("Purchasing Power of the Dollar," for example, goes back to 1780) covering various aspects of the U. S. economy. Includes inflation, interest rates, debt, gold, taxation, stock prices, etc. (Economic Education Bulletin.).

*Survey of Current Business.* U. S. Government Printing Office. • Published by Bureau of Economic Analysis, U. S. Department of Commerce. Presents a wide variety of business and economic data.

*Treasury Bulletin.* U. S. Government Printing Office. • Quarterly. $51 List Price. Issued by the Financial Management Service, U. S. Treasury Department. Provides data on the federal budget, government securities and yields, the national debt, and the financing of the federal government in general.

## TRADE/PROFESSIONAL ASSOCIATIONS

Committee for a Responsible Federal Budget. 1899 L St. NW, Ste. 225, Washington, DC 20036. Phone: (202)596-3597; Fax: (202)986-3696; Email: crfb@crfb.org • URL: http://crfb.org • Members are corporations and others seeking to improve the federal budget process.

Private Sector Council. Partnership for Public Service, 1100 New York Ave. NW, Ste. 200 E, Washington, DC 20005. Phone: (202)292-1020 or (202)775-9111; Fax: (202)775-8885 • URL: http://ourpublicservice.org/OPS/programs/psc • Serves as a nonpartisan, public service organization dedicated to improving the productivity, efficiency, and management of the federal government through a cooperative sharing of knowledge between the public and private sectors.

# NATIONAL HOLIDAYS

*See* ANNIVERSARIES AND HOLIDAYS

# NATIONAL LABOR GROUP

## OTHER SOURCES

*Democracy International.* • Seeks to build a movement of individuals dedicated to practical action on behalf of common commitments to human rights and pluralistic democracy including freedom of speech and press, religious liberty, free political parties, and the right to contest elections. Works to develop political and economic self-determination of citizens allowing them to control their resources, choose their social systems, and end discrimination. Aims to: revive democracy where it has been destroyed; encourage and sustain democrats trying to bring democracy to dictatorships. Calls upon democracies to: increase help for democratic leaders and politicians in the Third World; provide economic sustenance to relieve human suffering; strengthen democracy where it exists. Provides a forum for democrats to express solidarity and to help each other; encourages membership in an effort to build an international force of people working to make the cause of democracy an enduring ideal. Publicizes the efforts of democratic movements in dictatorships; attempts to increase the amount of uncensored information to closed societies.

# NATIONAL LABOR ORGANIZATION

## OTHER SOURCES

*UAW - Community Action Program.* • Serves as a program of the International Union, United Automobile, Aerospace and Agricultural Implement Workers of America. Informs UAW members through political education programs on topics including lobbying, the relationship between collective bargaining and the ballot box, and voluntary fundraising for political contributions. Maintains speakers' bureau; compiles statistics.

# NATIONAL PLANNING

*See* ECONOMIC POLICY

# NATIONAL PRODUCT

*See* GROSS NATIONAL PRODUCT

# NATIONS, LAW OF

*See* INTERNATIONAL LAW AND REGULATION

# NATURAL GAS

*See also* GAS INDUSTRY; PETROLEUM INDUSTRY; PROPANE AND BUTANE GAS INDUSTRY

## ONLINE DATABASES

*Tulsa.* Information Services. • Worldwide literature in the petroleum and natural gas areas, 1965 to present. Inquire as to online cost and availability. Includes petroleum exploration patents. Updated weekly.

## PERIODICALS AND NEWSLETTERS

*American Gas: The Monthly Magazine of the American Gas Association.* American Gas Association. • Monthly. $59 Nonmembers U.S. & Canada. Magazine for gas distribution and transmission industry senior and mid-level executives focusing on business, legislative, regulatory, and technical issues.

*Energy & Fuels.* American Chemical Society. • Bimonthly. $1,537 Institutions. An interdisciplinary technical journal covering non-nuclear energy sources: petroleum, gas, synthetic fuels, etc.

*Gas Digest: The Magazine of Gas Operations.* T-P Graphics. • Quarterly. Free. Articles and data relating to operations and management phases of natural gas operations.

*Gas Utility Manager.* James Informational Media Inc. • Monthly. $95 Free to qualified subscribers USA. Trade magazine covering the natural gas market for industry professionals. Formerly *Gas Utility and Pipeline Industries.*

*Natural Gas and Electricity: The Monthly Journal for Producers, Marketers, Pipels and End Users.* John Wiley & Sons Inc. • Monthly. $1,994 Institutions Online or Print only. Covers business, economic, regulatory, and high-technology news relating to the natural gas industry.

*Natural Gas Week.* Energy Intelligence Group. • Weekly. Covers natural gas economics, news, and analysis of gas/electric convergence.

*The Oilman Weekly Newsletter.* PennWell Corp., Petroleum Div. • Weekly. $1,990.00 per year. Newsletter. Provides news of developments concerning the North Sea and European oil and gas businesses. Each issue contains four pages of statistical data.

## PRICE SOURCES

*AGA Rate Service.* American Gas Association. • Semiannual. $175 Members. Looseleaf service.

*Energy Prices and Taxes.* International Energy Agency. Organisation for Economic Co-operation and Development Publications and Information Center. • Quarterly. $385 Individuals. Compiled by the International Energy Agency. Provides data on prices and taxation of petroleum products, natural gas, coal, and electricity. Diskette edition, $800.00. (Published in Paris).

## STATISTICS SOURCES

*Annual Energy Outlook, with Projections to (year).* U. S. Government Printing Office. • Annual. $39.00. Issued by the Energy Information Administration, U. S. Department of Energy (www.eia.doe.gov). Contains detailed statistics and 20-year projections for electricity, oil, natural gas, coal, and renewable energy. Text provides extensive discussion of energy issues and "Market Trends.".

*Annual Energy Review.* U. S. Government Printing Office. • Annual. $59.00. Issued by the Energy Information Administration, Office of Energy Markets and End Use, U. S. Department of Energy. Presents long-term historical as well as recent data on production, consumption, stocks, imports, exports, and prices of the principal energy commodities in the U. S.

*Petroleum Supply Annual.* U. S. Government Printing Office. • Annual. $78.00. Two volumes. Produced by the Energy Information Administration, U. S. Department of Energy. Contains worldwide data on the petroleum industry and petroleum products.

*Petroleum Supply Monthly.* U. S. Government Printing Office. • Monthly. Produced by the Energy Information Administration, U. S. Department of Energy. Provides worldwide statistics on a wide variety of petroleum products. Covers production, supplies, exports and imports, transportation, refinery operations, and other aspects of the petroleum industry.

*Standard & Poor's Industry Surveys.* Standard & Poor's Financial Services L.L.C. • Semiannual. $1,800.00. Two looseleaf volumes. Includes monthly *Supplements.* Provides detailed, individual surveys of 52 major industry groups. Each survey is revised on a semiannual basis. Also includes "Monthly Investment Review" (industry group investment analysis) and monthly "Trends & Projections" (economic analysis).

*U.S. Industry and Trade Outlook.* U.S. Department of Commerce National Technical Information Service. • Annual. Produced by the International Trade Administration, U.S. Department of Commerce, in a "public-private" partnership with DRI/McGraw-Hill and Standard & Poor's. Provides basic data, outlook for the current year, and "Long-Term Prospects" (five-year projections) for a wide variety of products and services. Includes high technology industries. Formerly *U.S. Industrial Outlook.*

## TRADE/PROFESSIONAL ASSOCIATIONS

American Gas Association. 400 N Capitol St. NW, Washington, DC 20001. Phone: (202)824-7000; Email: ggardner@aga.org • URL: http://www.aga.org • Advocates for local natural gas utility companies; provides a broad range of programs and services for member natural gas pipelines, marketers, gatherers, international gas companies and industry associates.

Natural Energy Services Association. 17515 Spring Cypress Rd., Ste. C-327, Cypress, TX 77429-2688. Phone: (713)856-6525; Fax: (713)856-6199 • URL: http://www.nesanet.org.

# NATURAL RESOURCES

*See also* FOREST PRODUCTS; GAS INDUSTRY; MINES AND MINERAL RESOURCES; PETROLEUM INDUSTRY; RECYCLING

## CD-ROM DATABASES

*Environment Abstracts on CD-ROM.* University Publications of America. • Quarterly. $1,295.00 per year. Contains the following CD-ROM databases: *Environment Abstracts, Energy Abstracts,* and *Acid Rain Abstracts.* Length of coverage varies.

## DIRECTORIES

*Biomass Industry Profile Directory.* DIANE Publishing Co. • $40 Individuals Paperback. Publication includes: Lists of all businesses and agencies involved in biomass energy in the Western United States.

## ENCYCLOPEDIAS AND DICTIONARIES

*Environmental Encyclopedia.* Cengage Learning Inc. • $327 Individuals. 2011. $298.00. 4th edition. Provides over 1,300 articles on all aspects of the environment. Written in non-technical style. eBook also available. Inquire for pricing.

## INTERNET DATABASES

*U.S. Census Bureau: The Official Statistics.* U. S. Bureau of the Census. Phone: (301)763-4636 or (301)763-4100; Fax: (301)763-4794; Email: webmaster@census.gov • URL: http://www.census.gov/prod/www/abs/mfg-prof.html • Web site is "Your Source for Social, Demographic, and Economic Information." Contains "Current U. S. Population Count," "Current Economic Indicators," and a wide variety of data under "Other Official Statistics." Keyword searching is provided. Fees: Free.

## PERIODICALS AND NEWSLETTERS

*Environmental Business Journal: Strategic Information for a Changing Industry.* Environmental Business International Inc. • Monthly. $250 Single issue. Includes both industrial and financial information relating to individual companies and to the environmental industry in general. Covers air pollution, wat es, U.S. Department of Health and Human Services. Provides conference, workshop, and symposium proceedings, as well as extensive reviews of environmental prospects.

*The Natural Resources Journal.* University of New Mexico School of Law. • Semiannual. Published by the University of New Mexico School of Law and is an international, interdisciplinary forum devoted to the study of natural and environmental resources.

*Resources Policy; The International Journal on the Economics, Planning and Use of Non-Renewable Resources.* Elsevier. • Quarterly. $246 Individuals.

## STATISTICS SOURCES

*Statistical Abstract of the United States.* U. S. Government Printing Office. • Annual. $44.00. Issued by the U. S. Bureau of the Census.

## TRADE/PROFESSIONAL ASSOCIATIONS

Australian Marine Conservation Society. 4/145 Melbourne St., Brisbane, QLD 4101, Australia. Phone: 61 7 38466777; Fax: 61 7 38466788; Email: amcs@amcs.org.au • URL: http://www.marineconservation.org.au • Aims to conserve the waterways, oceans and coasts of Australia by focusing on protecting the oceans from threats of pollution, habitat loss, unsustainable fisheries, coastal zone degradation and climate change. Acts as a resource on marine environmental issues for government agencies, politicians, media and the public.

Clean Technology and Sustainable Industries Organization. 3925 W Braker Ln., Austin, TX 78759. Email: community@ct-si.org • URL: http://www.ct-si.org • Advances the commercialization

and global adoption of clean technologies and sustainable industry practices. Promotes clean technology development. Establishes programs and advocacy for clean technologies and global integration of sustainable industry practices.

The Conservation Campaign. 10 Milk St., Ste. 810, Boston, MA 02108. Phone: (617)371-0526; Email: tcc@conservationcampaign.org • URL: http://www.conservationcampaign.org • Provides practical and operational support to local and statewide voter campaigns and legislative lobbying efforts. Strives to help towns, cities, counties, special districts and states create the funding they need to preserve and enhance their landscapes, whether it is wilderness and natural areas, urban parks and playgrounds or working forests and farmlands. Promotes grassroots movements to gain public funding for conservation funding.

Geode Resource, Conservation, and Development. 308 N 3rd St., Burlington, IA 52601. Phone: (319)752-6395; Fax: (319)752-0106 • URL: http://geodercd.org • Provides rural development services in natural resources in such areas as water quality, crop diversification, grant writing, community facilities or services, and planning resource economic development projects for an administration cost.

National Wildlife Federation. 11100 Wildlife Center Dr., Reston, VA 20190. Phone: 800-822-9919 or (703)438-6000 • URL: http://www.nwf.org • Serves as a member-supported conservation group, with over four million members and supporters. Federation of state and territorial affiliates, associate members and individual conservationist-contributors. Seeks to educate, inspire and assist individuals and organizations of diverse cultures to conserve wildlife and other natural resources and to protect the earth's environment in order to achieve a peaceful, equitable and sustainable future. Encourages the intelligent management of the life-sustaining resources of the earth and promotes greater appreciation of wild places, wildlife and the natural resources shared by all. Publishes educational materials and conservation periodicals.

Women Organizing for Change in Agriculture and Natural Resource Management. 1775 K St. NW, Ste. 410, Washington, DC 20006. Phone: (202)331-9099; Fax: (202)331-9366 • URL: http://www.wocan.org • Builds leadership among women and men in agriculture and natural resource management towards gender equality. Seeks to empower women as leaders and agents in adapting to, mitigating and reducing the adverse effects of climate change. Creates global awareness campaigns on the impact of climate change in women. Conducts and publishes gender-specific climate change research.

# NAVAL LAW

*See* MARITIME LAW AND REGULATION

# NAVAL STORES

## PERIODICALS AND NEWSLETTERS

*Pine Chemicals Review.* Kriedt Enterprises Ltd. • Bimonthly. $110 Individuals. Formerly *Forest Chemicals Review.*

# NAVY

## DIRECTORIES

*Carroll's Federal & Federal Regional Directory.* Caroll Publishing. • Semiannual. $500 Individuals. Lists more than 23,000 U. S. government officials throughout the country, including military installations.

*Carroll's Federal Regional Directory.* Caroll

Publishing. • Annual. $500 Individuals. Covers: Over 32,000 officials in federal congressional, judicial, and executive branch departments and agencies outside the District of Columbia. Database includes: Regional maps showing states covered in each federal region and Federal Information Centers. Entries include: Organization or agency name; names, addresses, and phone numbers of key personnel.

*Federal Regional Yellow Book: Who's Who in the Federal Government's Departments, Agencies, Military Installations, and Service Academies Outside of Washington, DC.* Leadership Directories Inc. • Semiannual. $465 Individuals annual. Lists over 35,000 federal officials and support staff at 8,000 regional offices.

## PERIODICALS AND NEWSLETTERS

*Naval Affairs: In the Interest of the Enlisted Active Duty Reserve, and Retired Personnel of the U.S. Navy, Marine Corps and Coast Guard.* Fleet Reserve Association. • Free to members; non-members, $7.00 per year.

*Naval Aviation News.* Chief of Naval Operations Bureau of Aeronautics. U. S. Government Printing Office. • Quarterly. $8 U.S. Single copy. Articles on all phases on Navy and Marine activity.

*Naval Engineers Journal.* American Society of Naval Engineers. • Quarterly. $233 Individuals Print and Online. Contains technical papers in the field of naval engineering. It also contains schedules of meetings, symposia, and other events, news, notes, and membership information.

*Naval Research Logistics: An International Journal.* John Wiley & Sons Inc. • 8/year. $2,868 Institutions Online or Print Only. Peer-reviewed journal in operations research, applied statistics, and general quantitative modeling, with special interest in applications covering the full spectrum of logistics problems.

*Naval Review: Annual Review of World Seapower.* United States Naval Institute. • Annual. Price on application. Covers the previous year's events. May issue of *U.S. Naval Institute Proceedings.*

*Navy Supply Corps Newsletter.* U. S. Government Printing Office. • Bimonthly. $31 U.S.. Newsletter issued by U. S. Navy Supply Systems Command. Provides news of Navy supplies and stores activities.

*Navy Times: Marine Corps, Navy, Coast Guard.* Gannett Government Media Corp. • Weekly. $52.00 per year. In two editions: Domestic and International. *Supplement available.*

*Seapower.* Navy League of the United States. • Monthly. $58 Nonmembers 1 year. Magazine covering America's seapower and the role of the sea services in defense.

## STATISTICS SOURCES

*Annual Report of the Secretary of Defense.* U.S. Department of Defense - Office of the Secretary. • Annual.

## TRADE/PROFESSIONAL ASSOCIATIONS

Naval Historical Foundation. 1306 Dahlgren Ave. SE, Washington Navy Yard, Washington, DC 20374-5109. Phone: 888-880-0102 or (202)678-4333; Fax: (202)889-3565; Email: nhfwny@navyhistory.org • URL: http://www.navyhistory.org • Dedicated to preserving and promoting the Navy's proud heritage, including the principal donation point for personal papers relating to naval history, a dynamic nationwide oral history program, a means for supporting the Navy's historical collections and programs, especially the Navy Museum. Provides historic research, and document and photo reproduction services.

Navy Club of the United States of America. c/o Tom Minchin, National Executive Secretary, 304 Sarheim Rd., Harrisburg, PA 17112-2234. Phone:

(717)884-1900; Email: ncusa1940@gmail.com • URL: http://www.navyclubusa.org • Persons who are, or have been, in the active service of the U.S. Navy, Naval Reserve, Marine Corps, Marine Corps Reserve, and Coast Guard. Promotes and encourages further public interest in the U.S. Navy and its history and to uphold the spirit and ideals of the U.S. Navy. Acts as public forum for members' views on national defense. Assists Navy Recruiting Command. Conducts charitable activities.

Navy League of the United States. 2300 Wilson Blvd., Ste. 200, Arlington, VA 22201-5424. Phone: 800-356-5760 or (703)528-1775; Fax: (703)528-2333 • URL: http://navyleague.org • Civilian organization that supports U.S. capability to keep the sea lanes open through a strong, viable Navy, Marine Corps, Coast Guard, and Merchant Marine. Seeks to awaken interest and cooperation of U.S. citizens in matters serving to aid, improve, and develop the efficiency of U.S. naval and maritime forces and equipment; acquires and disseminates information concerning the conditions of U.S. naval and maritime forces and equipment.

# NEGOTIATION

### See also INDUSTRIAL RELATIONS

## ABSTRACTS AND INDEXES

*Index to Legal Periodicals and Books.* H.W. Wilson Co. • Monthly. $490.00 per year. Quarterly and annual cumulations.

## HANDBOOKS AND MANUALS

*Negotiating to Settlement in Divorce.* Sanford N. Katz, editor. Wolters Kluwer Law and Business. • $75.00. Looseleaf service. Periodic supplementation.

## OTHER SOURCES

*Strategic Sales Negotiations.* American Management Association Extension Institute. • $1,895 Members (2) days seminar. Details tools and techniques of successful negotiation.

## PERIODICALS AND NEWSLETTERS

*Inside Negotiations.* EFR Corp. • Monthly. $98.00 per year. Newsletter. Labor negotiations.

*Negotiation Journal: On the Process of Dispute Settlement.* Program on Negotiation. Blackwell Publishing Inc. • Quarterly. $495 Individuals.

## RESEARCH CENTERS AND INSTITUTES

Massey University - Dispute Resolution Centre. College of Business, Private Bag 11222, Palmerston North, New Zealand. Phone: 64 6 3505799; Fax: 64 6 3505809; Email: dispute@massey.ac.nz • URL: http://www.massey.ac.nz/massey/learning/colleges/college-business/international-students/specialisation/dispute-resolution.cfm • Negotiation, mediation, and arbitration.

Rutgers University - Center for Negotiation and Conflict Resolution. Bloustein School of Planning & Public Policy, 33 Livingston Ave., New Brunswick, NJ 08901-1985. Phone: (848)932-2896; Fax: (732)932-2493; Email: cncr@rci.rutgers.edu • URL: http://policy.rutgers.edu/CNCR • Seeks to expand and improve conflict resolution within a context that fosters greater theoretical understanding.

University of Maryland at College Park - International Communications and Negotiations Simulations. 0145 Tydings Hall, Department of Government & Politics, College Park, MD 20742. Phone: (301)405-4172; Fax: (301)314-9301; Email: dfridl@umd.edu • URL: http://www.icons.umd.edu • Focuses on the critical connections between international issues and the perspectives that different cultures bring to negotiations. Also teaches cross cultural negotiation and develops international economic, environmental, and political scenarios/

curriculum materials for university and high school students.

# NEW ISSUES (FINANCE)

## HANDBOOKS AND MANUALS

*Securities: Public and Private Offerings,* 2d. William W. Prifti. Thomson West. • Semiannual. $1,383 Individuals Binder/Looseleaf - Full Set. How to issue securities. (Securities Law Series).

## INTERNET DATABASES

*Business Week Online.* McGraw-Hill. Phone: (212)512-2511; Fax: (684)842-6101 • URL: http://www.businessweek.com • Web site provides complete contents of current issue of *Business Week* plus "BW Daily" with additonal business news, financial market quotes, and corporate information from Standard & Poor's. Includes various features, such as "Banking Center" with mortgage and interest data, and "Interactive Computer Buying Guide." The "Business Week Archive" is fully searchable back to 1996.

*IPOfn.* IPO Financial Network. Phone: (973)379-5100; Fax: (973)379-1696; Email: info@ipofinancial.com • URL: http://www.ipofinancial.com • Web site provides free information on initial public offerings: "Pricing Recap" (price performance), "Calendar Update" (weekly listing of new offerings), "Company Roster" (Web sites), "Stock Brokers" (IPO dealers), and "Brokerage Firms" (underwriters). Fees: Basic data is free. Extensive analysis and recommendations are available through fee-based telephone, fax, and database services. Daily updates.

## OTHER SOURCES

*Going Public and the Public Corporation.* Harold S. Bloomenthal and Samuel Wolff. Thomson West. • Semiannual. $1,827.75 full set. Includes legal forms and documents. (Securities Law Series).

*Initial Public Offerings.* Glasser LegalWorks. • Looseleaf. $225.00, including CD-ROM version. Periodic Supplementation. Includes explanations of legal procedures for IPOs, with annotated forms. (Emerging Growth Companies Series.).

## PERIODICALS AND NEWSLETTERS

*Investment Dealers' Digest.* SourceMedia Inc. • Weekly. $750.00 per year. Covers financial news, trends, new products, people, private placements, new issues of securities, and other aspects of the investment business. Includes feature stories.

*Medical Technology Stock Letter.* Medical Technology Stock Letter. • Description: Specializes in investments in biotechnology companies. Offers news of the industry and recommendations for buying, selling, and holding stocks. Recurring features include news of research, a model portfolio reflecting the editors' investment strategy, and columns titled Pulse of the Market and Industry Scan. **Remarks:** Also available through e-mail.

## TRADE/PROFESSIONAL ASSOCIATIONS

Financial Industry Regulatory Authority. 1735 K St., Washington, DC 20006. Phone: (301)590-6500; Fax: (202)293-6260; Email: francine.lee@finra.org • URL: http://www.finra.org • Formerly National Association of Securities Dealers.

# NEW PRODUCTS

### See also INVENTIONS; PATENTS

## INTERNET DATABASES

*InSite 2.* Intelligence Data/Thomson Financial. Phone: 800-654-0393 or (617)856-1890; Fax: (617)737-3182; Email: intelligence.data@tfn.com • URL: http://www.insite2.gale.com/ • Fee-based Web site consolidates information in a "Base Pack" consisting of Business InSite, Market InSite, and Company InSite. Optional databases are Consumer InSite, Health and Wellness InSite, Newsletter In-Site, and Computer InSite. Includes fulltext content from more than 2,500 trade publications, journals, newsletters, newspapers, analyst reports, and other sources. Continuous updating. Formerly produced by The Gale Group.

## PERIODICALS AND NEWSLETTERS

*Industrial Equipment News.* Thomas Publishing Company L.L.C. • Monthly. Contains new product information for manufacturing industries.

*International New Product Newsletter.* International New Product Newsletter. • Monthly. $25 per issue. Description: Provides "advance news of new products and processes, primarily from sources outside the U.S." Emphasizes new products which can cut costs and improve efficiency. Recurring features include the column Special Licensing Opportunities which lists new products and processes that are available for manufacture under license, or are for sale or import.

*New Equipment Digest.* Intertec Publishing. • Monthly. Magazine (tabloid) showcasing new or improved equipment, products, materials, and components. Formerly *Material Handling Engineering.*

*New Equipment Reporter: New Products Industrial News.* DeRoche Publications. • Monthly. Controlled circulation.

*Potentials: Ideas and Products that Motivate.* Nielsen Business Media Inc. • Monthly. $59.00 per year. Covers incentives, premiums, awards, and gifts as related to promotional activities. Formerly *Potentials in Marketing.*

*Product Design and Development.* Advantage Business Media L.L.C. • 9/year.

## TRADE/PROFESSIONAL ASSOCIATIONS

Product Development and Management Association. 330 N Wabash Ave., Ste. 2000, Chicago, IL 60611. Phone: 800-232-5241 or (312)321-5145; Fax: (312)673-6885; Email: pdma@pdma.org • URL: http://www.pdma.org • Managers working in product innovation; teachers and researchers in the areas of product innovation management, product planning and development, and new product marketing; government regulators and facilitators involved in the product development process; product innovation consultants; market research firms; new product institutes; advertising agencies and media; testing companies; trade associations. Promotes improved product innovation management by drawing upon members' resources. Encourages research designed to make product innovation management more effective and efficient; Provides forum for the exchange of ideas and findings among universities, industry, government and related sectors.

# NEW YORK STOCK EXCHANGE

*See* STOCK EXCHANGES

# NEWSLETTERS

*See also* INVESTMENT ADVISORY SERVICES; PERIODICALS

## CD-ROM DATABASES

*MediaFinder.* Oxbridge Communications Inc. • $1,295 per year. Online database with 77,000 magazines, catalogs, newspapers, and journals.

## DIRECTORIES

*Burrelle's Media Directory: Magazines and Newsletters.* BurrellesLuce. • Annual. $550.00.

Provides detailed descriptions of more than 13,500 magazines and newsletters published in the U.S., Canada, and Mexico. Categories are professional, consumer, trade, and college. Semiannual *Updates.* Includes CD-ROM.

## GENERAL WORKS

*Creating Excellence: Vermont's Journal for people in growing businesses.* New World Publishing Inc. • Bimonthly. $12. Magazine featuring successful Vermont business people and emphasizing personal development.

## HANDBOOKS AND MANUALS

*Newsletter Publishing.* Entrepreneur Press. • Looseleaf. $59.50. A practical guide to starting a newsletter. Covers profit potential, start-up costs, market size evaluation, pricing, accounting, advertising, promotion, etc. (Start-Up Business Guide No. E1067.).

## INTERNET DATABASES

*PubList.com: The Internet Directory of Publications.* Bowes & Associates, Inc. Phone: (781)792-0999; Fax: (781)792-0988; Email: info@publist.com • URL: http://www.publist.com • "The premier online global resource for information about print and electronic publications." Provides online searching for information on more than 150,000 magazines, journals, newsletters, e-journals, and monographs. Database entries generally include title, publisher, format, address, editor, circulation, subject, and International Standard Serial Number (ISSN). Fees: Free.

*Ulrichsweb.com.* R.R. Bowker L.L.C. 630 Central Ave, New Providence, NJ 07974. Phone: 888-269-5372 or (908)286-1090; Email: info@bowker.com • URL: http://www.bowker.com • Web site provides fee-based access to about 250,000 serials records from the *Ulrich's International Periodicals Directory* database. Includes periodical evaluations from *Library Journal* and *Magazines for Libraries.* Monthly updates.

## PERIODICALS AND NEWSLETTERS

*Blair Business Mirror.* Blair County Chamber of Commerce. • Monthly. Features chamber news, stories of chamber members and notices of upcoming programs and events.

*Buffalo Business First.* American City Business Journals, Inc. • $96 Individuals print + online. Contains the full text of Buffalo Business First, a business tabloid covering Buffalo, New York.

*Business Performance Management.* Intertec Publishing. • Magazine for business managers. Covers organizing, automating, and analyzing of business methodologies and processes.

*Cincinnati Business Courier.* American City Business Journals, Inc. • Contains the full text of Cincinnati Business Courier, a business tabloid covering Cincinnati, Ohio.

*Circulation Management.* Media Central. • Monthly. $39.00 per year. Edited for circulation professionals in the magazine and newsletter publishing industry. Covers marketing, planning, promotion, management, budgeting, and related topics.

*Columbus Business First.* American City Business Journals, Inc. • Contains the full text of Columbus Business First, a business tabloid covering Columbus, Ohio.

*Dallas Business Journal.* American City Business Journals, Inc. • Weekly. $95 Individuals print + online. Metro business journal.

*Hulbert Financial Digest.* Hulbert Financial Digest. • Monthly. Description: Provides performance ratings on more than 400 portfolios recommended by more than 145 financial newsletters, calculated on the basis of model portfolios constructed according to each newsletter's advice. Includes a timing scoreboard, analysis of newsletter performance, list of

mutual funds most frequently recommended for sale or purchase, a stock market sentiment index, and a question and answer section.

*Ideas Unlimited: For Editors.* OmniPrint Inc. • Monthly. $195.00 per year. Includes CD-Rom. Contains fillers for company newsletters: articles, cartoons, jokes, seasonal items, etc.

*Northern Business Journal.* Northern Business Journal. • Magazine presenting business articles related to northeastern Ontario, Canada.

*The Perspective: Main Street Perspective (Business in the Southwest).* Cheallaigh Shamrock. • Biweekly. Magazine.

# NEWSPAPER CLIPPINGS

*See* CLIPPING SERVICES

# NEWSPAPER MARKET RESEARCH

*See also* MARKET RESEARCH

## DIRECTORIES

*Editor & Publisher Market Guide.* Editor and Publisher Company Inc. • Annual. $150 Individuals. Market data for more than 1,600 cities and 3,096 counties.

# NEWSPAPER WORK

*See* JOURNALISM

# NEWSPAPERS

*See also* COLLEGE AND SCHOOL NEWSPAPERS; FOREIGN LANGUAGE PRESS AND NEWSPAPERS; JOURNALISM; MINORITY NEWSPAPERS

## ABSTRACTS AND INDEXES

*Newsbank.* NewsBank Inc. • Monthly. Price varies. Quarterly and annual cumulations. Index to articles of current interest from over 500 U.S. newspapers.

## ALMANACS AND YEARBOOKS

*Editor & Publisher International Yearbook: Encyclopedia of the Newspaper Industry.* Editor and Publisher Company Inc. • Annual. $150.00. Daily and Sunday newspapers in the United States and Canada.

## CD-ROM DATABASES

*MediaFinder.* Oxbridge Communications Inc. • $1,295 per year. Online database with 77,000 magazines, catalogs, newspapers, and journals.

*Newspaper Abstracts Ondisc.* ProQuest L.L.C. • Monthly. $2,950.00 per year (covers 1989 to date; archival discs are available for 1985-88). Provides cover-to-cover CD-ROM indexing and abstracting of 19 major newspapers, including the *New York Times, Wall Street Journal, Washington Post, Chicago Tribune,* and *Los Angeles Times.*

## DIRECTORIES

*ANR National Directory of Community Newspapers.* American Newspaper Representatives Inc. • Annual. $125 Individuals. Covers more than 10,000 newspapers.

*Burrelle's Media Directory: Newspapers and Related Media.* BurrellesLuce. • Annual. $550.00. *Daily Newspapers* volume lists more than 2,200 daily publications in the U. S., Canada, and Mexico. *Non-Daily Newspapers* volume lists more than 10,400 items published no more than three times a week. Provides detailed descriptions, including key personnel.

*Business and Financial News Media.* Larriston Communications. • Annual. $99 book. Covers: over 300 daily newspapers with at least 50,000 in circulation and a business or finance correspondent; television stations and all-news radio stations in the largest 40 markets; periodicals of general or business and finance interest; syndicated business and financial columnists and newswriters; news and wire services; and free-lance writers whose specialties include business and financial topics. Entries include: Outlet name, address, phone, names and titles of contacts who cover business, finance, or economic news; news services used; circulation or audience figures.

*Compuserve Companion: Finding Newspapers and Magazines Online.* BiblioData. • $29.95. Covers: More than 3,200 newspapers, newsletters, and magazines that are available for full text searching on CompuServe. Database includes: Introductory chapter of searching tips. Entries include: Publication name, dates of coverage, lag times, and appropriate "Go" commands.

*International Media Guide: Newspapers Worldwide.* Kantar Media SRDS. • $553 Individuals online; 1 year. Covers over 3,400 papers in every major city in the world.

*Media Rates & Data.* Media-Daten AG. • Biennial. Covers: National and international newspapers, journals, trade press and local Swiss newsletters, radio and television. Entries include: Publications name, address, phone, rates, schedules.

*Newspapers Online.* BiblioData. • Irregular. $99. Covers: Approximately 150 daily newspapers available online. Entries include: Name, address, phone, editor name, details on geographical area served; description; list of regional newsmaking companies/people/topics; circulation figures; electronic availability and coverage; electronic searching tips; name and phone of contact for database assistance.

*Working Press of the Nation.* R.R. Bowker L.L.C. • Annual. $530.00. $295.00 per volume. Three volumes: (1) *Newspaper Directory*; (2) *Magazine and Internal Publications Directory*; (3) *Radio and Television Directory*. Includes names of editors and other personnel.

## ENCYCLOPEDIAS AND DICTIONARIES

*World Press Encyclopedia.* Cengage Learning Inc. • 2003. $572.00. Second edition. Two volumes. Comprehensive essays cover the background and economic framework of newspapers and other news media in about 200 countries. Covers relevant legal issues, censorship, government relations, education in journalism, status of news agencies, cable, Internet, and other media topics. eBook also available.

## FINANCIAL RATIOS

*Annual Statement Studies.* Risk Management Association. • Annual. Compiled from over 280,000 financial statements.

*Annual Statement Studies: Industry Default Probabilities and Cash Flow Measures.* Risk Management Association. • Annual. $405 Nonmembers. Serves as a companion volume to the original *Annual Statement Studies*. Gives probability of default estimates on a percentage scale for more than 450 industries. Includes changes in position year-by-year for eight financial statement line items and provides percentage measures of cash flow.

## GENERAL WORKS

*Baltimore Business Journal.* American City Business Journal. • Weekly. $88 Individuals print + online. Newspaper reporting Baltimore business news.

*Brampton Business Times.* Metroland Media Group. • Community business-to-business newspaper.

*Lafayette Business Digest.* Kapp Crowell Communications. • Weekly. $43.50 Individuals. Newspaper covering local business.

*Northumberland Business Times.* Metroland Media Group. • Monthly. Community newspaper bringing messages for and about local business.

## INTERNET DATABASES

*Factiva.* Dow Jones Reuters Business Interactive, LLC. Phone: 800-369-7466 or (609)452-1511; Fax: (609)520-5770; Email: solutions@factiva.com • URL: http://www.factiva.com • Fee-based Web site provides "global news and business information through Web sites and content integration solutions." Includes Dow Jones and Reuters newswires, The Wall Street Journal, and more than 7,000 other sources of current news, historical articles, market research reports, and investment analysis. Content includes 96 major U. S. newspapers, 900 non-English sources, trade publications, media transcripts, country profiles, news photos, etc.

*Nexis.com.* Lexis-Nexis Group. Phone: 800-227-4908 or (937)865-6800; Fax: (937)865-6909; Email: webmaster@prod.lexis-nexis.com • URL: http://www.nexis.com • Fee-based Web site offers searching of about 2.8 billion documents in some 30,000 news, business, and legal information sources. Features include a subject directory covering 1,200 topics in 34 categories and a Company Dossier containing information on more than 500,000 public and private companies. Boolean searching is offered.

*Wall Street Journal Interactive Edition.* Dow Jones & Co., Inc. 1211 Avenue of the Americas, New York, NY 10036. Phone: 800-369-5663; Email: service@dowjones.com • URL: http://new.dowjones.com • Fee-based Web site providing online searching of worldwide information from *The Wall Street Journal.* Includes "Company Snapshots," "The Journal's Greatest Hits," "Index to Market Data," "Journal Links," etc. Financial price quotes are available. Fees: $49.00 per year; $29.00 per year to print subscribers.

## ONLINE DATABASES

*Albany Business Review.* American City Business Journals, Inc. • $86 Individuals print + online. Contains the full text of The Business Review, a local business tabloid covering news in the Albany, New York, area.

*Business Insurance.* Crain Communications Inc. • Weekly. $799 Individuals data + print and digital. Contains the complete text of *Business Insurance,* a newspaper providing information on the purchase and administration of corporate insurance and self-insurance programs, including property and liability insurance, reinsurance, and employee benefit and risk management programs.

## OTHER SOURCES

*Little River News: The Oldest Business Institution in Little River County.* Little River News. • Weekly (Thurs.). $35 Individuals in Ashdown, Foreman, Wilton, Ogden, Horatio, Ben, Lomond, De Queen and Lockesburg. Newspaper with Democratic orientation.

## PERIODICALS AND NEWSLETTERS

*Territorial Newspapers..*

*Albuquerque Business First.* American City Business Journals, Inc. • Weekly. $81 Individuals print and digital. Local business newspaper.

*Boulder County Business Report (BCBR).* Boulder County Business Report. • Biweekly. $44.97 Individuals. Local business newspaper.

*Business.* Chamber of Commerce and Industry of Tirana. • Monthly. Contains information on business and economics.

*Business Day.* BDFM Publishers Ltd. • Daily. R 1,700 Individuals. Business newspaper.

*The Business Examiner.* Business Examiner Newspaper Group. • Biweekly. $50 Individuals. Local business newspaper.

*Business First of Buffalo: Western New York's Busi-* ness Newspaper. American City Business Journals, Inc. • Weekly. $100 Individuals. Business Newspaper.

*Business Gazette.* Post-Newsweek Media Inc. • Weekly (Fri.). Community business newspaper.

*Business Monthly.* • Monthly. $9 Individuals. Local business newspaper.

*Business West.* Hagen Marketing & Communication. • Quarterly. $20 Individuals. Magazine featuring Pacific Rim business news for Californians.

*Business World.* BusinessWorld Publishing Corp. • Daily. Business and financial newspaper.

*Cape Business News.* Cape Business News. • Monthly. R 172 Individuals print. Business newspaper.

*Caspian Business News.* Caspian Business News. • Weekly. Local business newspaper.

*Charleston Regional Business Journal.* SC Biz News. • Contains the full text of Charleston Regional Business Journal, a business tabloid covering the Charleston, South Carolina and surrounding region.

*Charlotte Business Journal.* American City Business Journals, Inc. • Weekly. $92 Individuals print + online. Newspaper for the business community of Charlotte and the surrounding thirteen-county area.

*Crain's Detroit Business.* Crain Communications Inc. • Weekly (Mon.). $59 Individuals print edition. Local business tabloid covering Wayne, Macomb, Oakland, Livingston, and Washtenaw counties.

*The Daily Record: Business and Legal News of Maryland.* The Daily Record CPN. • Mon.-Sat.. $269 Individuals print and online. Daily Business Newspaper reporting news and features on business, real estate, technology, healthcare and law.

*The Delmarva Farmer: The Agribusiness Newspaper of the Mid-Atlantic Region.* American Farm Publications Inc. • Biweekly. $31 Individuals /year. Newspaper (tabloid) featuring news of interest to agricultural concerns in Maryland, Delaware, Virginia, New Jersey, and Pennsylvania.

*Denver Business Journal.* American City Business Journals. • Weekly. $100 Individuals print and digital. Local business newspaper.

*Durham Business Times.* Metroland Media Group. • Community newspaper covering issues affecting Durham businesses.

*Editor and Publisher - The Newsmagazine of the Fourth Estate Since 1894.* Editor & Publisher Magazine. • Weekly. $79 Individuals Total Access - Print and Digital. Trade journal of the newspaper industry.

*Edmonton and Homersham Commerce & Industry: Report on Business.* Edmonton and Homersham Commerce & Industry. • Monthly. $5. Business newspaper.

*GSA Business.* GSA Business. • Biweekly. $49.95 Individuals /year. Local business newspaper.

*Hindu Business Line.* Kasturi & Sons Ltd. • Daily. Rs 1,496 Individuals all days. Newspaper covering business, economics, banks and banking.

*Inside Tucson Business.* Territorial Newspapers. • Weekly. $50 Individuals. Newspaper featuring business news.

*Kansas City Business Journal.* American City Business Journal. • Weekly Weekly (Fri.). $50 Individuals print and digital - 52 weeks. Local business newspaper.

*Las Colinas Business News.* Dallas-Fort Worth Suburban Newspapers Inc. • Weekly (Wed.). Community newspaper.

*The Los Angeles Business Journal.* The Los Angeles Business Journal. • Weekly (Mon.). $129.95 Individuals. Newspaper (tabloid) covering local business news, business trends, executive profiles, and information for the Los Angeles area executive.

*Louisville Business First: The Weekly Business Newspaper of Greater Louisville.* American City Business Journals, Inc. • Weekly. $80 Individuals. Weekly Business Newspaper.

*Nashville Business Journal.* American City Business Journals, Inc. • Weekly. $91 Individuals print and digital. Regional business newspaper.

*National Small Business Journal: The information newspaper for small & growing businesses.* TWG Publishing Co. • $15 annual. Newspaper containing articles geared toward small businesses and their interests.

*New Orleans CityBusiness.* New Orleans CityBusiness. • Weekly. $129 Individuals print + online. Business newspaper (Tabloid).

*NewsInc.: The Business of the Newspaper Business.* The Cole Group. • Biweekly. $425 Individuals. Reports on trends in mass media, especially with regard to newspaper publishing. Articles on cable TV and other competitive media are included.

*Newspaper Financial Executives Journal.* International Newspaper Financial Executives. • Quarterly. $100.00. Provides financially related information to newspaper executives.

*The Northern Colorado Business Report.* The Northern Colorado Business Report. • Biweekly. $44.97 Individuals. Business newspaper.

*Observer of Business and Politics.* Anthony Jasudasan. • Daily. Newspaper focusing on business and economics.

*Philadelphia Business Journal.* Philadelphia Business Journal. • Weekly. $105 Individuals print and digital. Regional and general business newspaper.

*Publishers' Auxiliary.* National Newspaper Association..

*St. Louis Business Journal.* American City Business Journals, Inc. • Weekly. $89 Individuals print + online. Business newspaper.

*San Diego Business Journal.* San Diego Business Journal. • Weekly (Mon.). $99 Individuals. Metropolitan business newspaper specializing in investigative and enterprise reporting on San Diego County businesses and related issues.

*South Carolina Business Journal.* South Carolina Chamber of Commerce. • Monthly. $25. Business newspaper.

*Toronto Business Journal.* Toronto Business Journal. • Weekly. $93 By mail. Newspaper covering local business.

*Uptown San Diego Examiner: Business News.* Uptown Examiner Group. • Semiweekly (Wed. and Fri.). $35 Individuals. Community newspaper.

## RESEARCH CENTERS AND INSTITUTES

Northwestern University - Media Management Center. 1801 Maple Ave., Ste. 5316, Evanston, IL 60208-2101. Phone: (847)491-4900; Fax: (847)491-5619; Email: mediamanagement@mmc. northwestern.edu • URL: http://www. mediamanagementcenter.org • Research areas are related to various business aspects of the newspaper industry: management, marketing, personnel, planning, accounting, and finance. A joint activity of the J. L. Kellogg Graduate School of Management and the Medill School of Journalism.

## STATISTICS SOURCES

*U.S. Industry and Trade Outlook.* U.S. Department of Commerce National Technical Information Service. • Annual. Produced by the International Trade Administration, U.S. Department of Commerce, in a "public-private" partnership with DRI/McGraw-Hill and Standard & Poor's. Provides basic data, outlook for the current year, and "Long-Term Prospects" (five-year projections) for a wide variety of products and services. Includes high technology industries. Formerly *U.S. Industrial Outlook.*

## TRADE/PROFESSIONAL ASSOCIATIONS

American Society of News Editors. Missouri School of Journalism, 209 Reynolds Journalism Inst., Columbia, MO 65211. Phone: (573)884-2405 or (703)453-1133 • URL: http://www.asne.org • Consists of leaders of multimedia news organizations, deans and endowed chairs at accredited journalism schools. Focuses on open government and the First Amendment, journalism education, leadership and diversity.

Media Financial Management Association. 550 W Frontage Rd., Ste. 3600, Northfield, IL 60093. Phone: (847)716-7000; Fax: (847)716-7004; Email: info@mediafinance.org • URL: http://www. mediafinance.org • Members are accountants and other financial personnel in the radio and television broadcasting industries. Formerly Broadcast Financial Management Association.

National Federation of Press Women. 200 Little Falls St., Ste. 405, Falls Church, VA 22046. Phone: 800-780-2715 or (703)237-9804 or (703)534-2500; Fax: (703)237-9808; Email: presswomen@aol.com • URL: http://www.nfpw.org • Serves as federal of state associations of professional women and men in all phases of communications on a full-time or freelance basis. Seeks to: encourage the highest standards of professionalism in journalism; provide for exchange of ideas, knowledge, and experience. Offers specialized education programs.

National Newspaper Association. PO Box 7540, Columbia, MO 65205-7540. Phone: (573)777-4980; Fax: (573)777-4985 or (573)237-9808 • URL: http://nnaweb.org • Protects, promotes and enhances community newspapers. Represents community newspapers across America. Promotes quality journalism and business practices at its annual convention, through its various contests and awards and various other educational programs.

National Press Club. National Press Bldg., 529 14th St. NW, 13th Fl., Washington, DC 20045. Phone: (202)662-7500 or (202)662-7505; Fax: (202)662-7512 • URL: http://press.org • Reporters, writers and news people employed by newspapers, wire services, magazines, radio and television stations and other forms of news media. Sponsors sports, travel and cultural events, rap sessions with news figures and authors and newsmaker breakfasts and luncheons. Offers monthly training.

The Newspaper Guild. 501 3rd St. NW, Washington, DC 20001-2760. Phone: (202)434-7177; Fax: (202)434-1472; Email: guild@cwa-union.org • URL: http://www.newsguild.org • AFL-CIO; Canadian Labour Congress, and International Federation of Journalists. Sponsors Newspaper Guild International Pension Fund that provides retirement benefits to persons employed in the news industry.

# NEWSPAPERS, SCHOOL

*See* COLLEGE AND SCHOOL NEWSPAPERS

# NEWSPRINT PAPER INDUSTRY

*See* PAPER INDUSTRY

# NICKEL INDUSTRY

*See* METAL INDUSTRY

# NOISE CONTROL

## ABSTRACTS AND INDEXES

*Environment Abstracts.* University Publications of America. • Monthly. Price varies. Provides multidis-

ciplinary coverage of the world's environmental literature. Incorporates *Acid Rain Abstracts.*

*Environment Abstracts Annual: A Guide to the Key Environmental Literature of the Year.* University Publications of America. • Annual. $495.00. A yearly cumulation of *Environment Abstracts.*

*Excerpta Medica: Environmental Health and Pollution Control.* Elsevier. • 16 times a year. Institutions, $3,246.00 per year. Section 46 of *Excerpta Medica.* Covers air, water, and land pollution and noise control.

*NTIS Alerts: Environmental Pollution & Control.* U.S. Department of Commerce National Technical Information Service. • Biweekly. $130 per year. Covers the following categories of environmental pollution: air, water, solid wastes, radiation, pesticides, and noise.

*Pollution Abstracts.* Cambridge Information Group. • Monthly. $1,390.00 per year. Includes print and online editions; with index, $1,515.00 per year.

## CD-ROM DATABASES

*Environment Abstracts on CD-ROM.* University Publications of America. • Quarterly. $1,295.00 per year. Contains the following CD-ROM databases: *Environment Abstracts, Energy Abstracts,* and *Acid Rain Abstracts.* Length of coverage varies.

## DIRECTORIES

*Sound and Vibration Buyer's Guide.* • Annual. Free to qualified personnel. Lists of manufacturers of products for noise and vibration control, dynamic measurements instrumentation, and dynamic testing equipment.

## ENCYCLOPEDIAS AND DICTIONARIES

*Pollution A to Z.* Cengage Learning Inc. • 2003.Two volumes. Provides encyclopedic coverage of many aspects of environmental pollution, including air, water, noise, and soil. Inquire as to price and availability.

## PERIODICALS AND NEWSLETTERS

*Acoustical Society of America Journal.* Acoustical Society of America. • Monthly. Institutions, $1,325.00 per year. Includes print and online editions.

*Noise Control Engineering Journal.* Institute of Noise Control Engineering. • Bimonthly. $90 Individuals.

*Noise Regulation Report: The Nation's Only Noise Control Publication.* Great Circle Communications LLC. • Monthly. $487 Individuals. Covers federal and state rules and regulations for the control of excessive noise.

*Sound and Vibration.* Sound and Vibration. • Monthly. $60 Other countries 12 issues - 1 year. Monthly. Free to qualified personnel; others, $60.00 per year.

## RESEARCH CENTERS AND INSTITUTES

Joint Institute for Advancement of Flight Sciences. 725 23rd St. NW, 227 Hunting Ave., Washington, DC 20052. Phone: (202)994-6080; Fax: (202)994-3394; Email: jiafs@seas.gwu.edu • Conducts research in aeronautics, astronautics, and acoustics (flight-produced noise).

Pennsylvania State University - College of Engineering - Center for Acoustics and Vibration. 229 Hammond Bldg., University Park, PA 16802. Phone: (814)863-0103 or (814)865-2761; Fax: (814)865-5965 or (814)863-7222; Email: gal4@psu. edu • URL: http://www.cav.psu.edu • Comprised of eight technical groups researching aspects of acoustics and vibration: Acoustic Characterization of Materials; Active Structures and Noise Control; Flow Induced Noise; Machinery Prognostics and Condition Monitoring; Propagation and Radiation; Quiet Product Design; Rotorcraft Acoustics and Dynamics; and Structural Vibration and Acoustics.

and structural response induced by turbulent separation, noise control in automotive HVAC systems, and aeroacoustic radiation from automotive alternators. Materials Evaluation studies physical acoustics in composites and other advanced materials, acoustic microscopy and microstructural features, X-ray radiography to study residual stress, sensors for materials process monitoring and control, nondestructive evaluation of advanced materials, optical, fiberoptical and laser ultrasonic techniques for materials evaluation, and infrared thermography. Propagation and Radiation technical group researches generation and propagation of sound waves, response, fuzzy dynamics, mechanical and thermal internal fields, chains, belts, and gear vibrations, and chassis dynamics modeling.

# NON-FOODS MERCHANDISERS

*See* RACK JOBBERS

# NONFERROUS METAL INDUSTRY

*See also* METAL INDUSTRY

## ABSTRACTS AND INDEXES

*Applied Science and Technology Index.* EBSCO Publishing Inc. • 11/year. Indexes a wide variety of English language technical, industrial, and engineering periodicals.

*F & S Index: United States.* Cengage Learning Inc. • $2,659 Individuals. Monthly. $2,532.00 per year, including quarterly and annual cumulations. Provides annotated citations to marketing, business, financial, and industrial literature. Coverage of U.S. business activity includes trade journals, financial magazines, business newspapers, and special reports.

## CD-ROM DATABASES

*Applied Science and Technology Abstracts.* EBSCO Publishing Inc. • Citations for more than 700 prominent scientific, technical, engineering, and industrial periodicals.

## DIRECTORIES

*North American Scrap Metals Directory.* Recycling Today Media Group. • Annual. $95.20 Individuals discounted price. Covers: Suppliers of scrap metal materials in North America. Entries include: Contact information.

## INTERNET DATABASES

*Manufacturing Profiles.* U. S. Bureau of the Census. Phone: (301)763-4636 or (301)763-4100; Fax: (301)763-4794; Email: webmaster@census.gov • URL: http://www.census.gov/prod/www/abs/mfg-prof.html • The Census Bureau makes available free on PDF (Portable Document Format) an annual consolidation of the entire Current Industrial Report series, presenting "all the data compiled." Contains statistics on production, shipments, inventories, consumption, exports, imports, and orders for a wide variety of manufactured products.

## ONLINE DATABASES

*Applied Science and Technology Index Online.* H.W. Wilson Co. • Provides online indexing of 500 major scientific, technical, industrial, and engineering periodicals. Time period is 1983 to date. Monthly updates. Inquire as to online cost and availability.

## PERIODICALS AND NEWSLETTERS

*Foundry Management and Technology.* Penton Media Inc. • Monthly. $50 others. Coverage includes nonferrous casting technology and production.

*JOM: The Member Journal of the Minerals, Metals*

*and Materials Society.* The Minerals, Metals, and Materials Society. • Four times a year. Membership. A scholarly journal covering all phases of metals and metallurgy.

*Metal Bulletin.* Metal Bulletin Inc. • Daily. £1,395 1-year standard subscription. Provides news of international trends, prices, and market conditions for both steel and non-ferrous metal industries. (Published in England).

*Metal Bulletin Monthly.* Metal Bulletin Inc. • Monthly. Edited for international metal industry business executives and senior technical personnel. Covers business, economic, and technical developments. (Published in England.).

*Modern Metals.* • Monthly. $85.00 per year. Covers management and production for plants that fabricate and finish metals of various kinds.

*33 Metalproducing: For Primary Producers of Steel, Aluminum, and Copper-Base Alloys.* Penton Media Inc. • Monthly. $65.00 per year. Covers metal production technology and methods and industry news. Includes a bimonthly *Nonferrous Supplement.*

## RESEARCH CENTERS AND INSTITUTES

Massachusetts Institute of Technology - Materials Processing Center. 77 Massachusetts Ave., Cambridge, MA 02139-4301. Phone: (617)253-5179; Fax: (617)258-6900; Email: cthomp@mit.edu • URL: http://mpc-web.mit.edu • Conducts processing, engineering, and economic research in ferrous and nonferrous metals, ceramics, polymers, photonic materials, superconductors, welding, composite materials, and other materials.

Pennsylvania State University - College of Engineering - Harold and Inge Marcus Department of Industrial and Manufacturing Engineering - Metal Casting Laboratory. 221 Leonard Bldg., University Park, PA 16802. Phone: (814)863-7290 or (814)863-5640; Fax: (814)863-4745; Email: rcv2@psu.edu • URL: http://www.ie.psu.edu • Properties and processing of cast metals and alloys, dimensional control of castings, environmental solutions for the metal casting industry.

U.S. International Trade Commission - Minerals, Metals, Machinery, and Miscellaneous Manufacturers Division. 500 E St. SW, Washington, DC 20436. Phone: (202)205-3418; Fax: (202)205-2217; Email: brookhart@usitc.gov • URL: http://www.usitc.gov • Survey data related to international trade matters, including international competitiveness of U.S. industries, especially iron and steel products, industrial minerals and nonferrous metals, machinery and general manufactured products.

University of Wisconsin-Madison - Cast Metals Laboratory. University of Wisconsin-Madison, Dept. of Materials Science & Engineering, 276 Materials Science & Engineering Bldg., 1509 University Ave., Madison, WI 53706-1595. Phone: (608)262-3732 or (608)262-2562; Fax: (608)262-8353; Email: msaedept@engr.wisc.edu • URL: http://www.engr.wisc.edu/mse.

## STATISTICS SOURCES

*Non-Ferrous Metal Data Yearbook.* American Bureau of Metal Statistics. • Annual. $405.00. Provides worldwide data on approximately about 200 statistical tables covering many nonferrous metals. Includes production, consumption, inventories, exports, imports, and other data.

*Nonferrous Castings.* U. S. Bureau of the Census. • Annual. (Current Industrial Reports MA-33E.).

## TRADE/PROFESSIONAL ASSOCIATIONS

The Minerals, Metals, and Materials Society. 184 Thorn Hill Rd., Warrendale, PA 15086-7514. Phone: 800-759-4867 or (724)776-9000; Fax: (724)776-3770; Email: webmaster@tms.org • URL: http://www.tms.org/TMSHome.aspx • Members are metallurgists, metallurgical engineers, and materials scientists. Divisions include Light Metals and

Electronic, Magnetic, and Photonic Materials. Formerly The Metallurigical Society.

Non-Ferrous Founders' Society. 1480 Renaissance Dr., Ste. 310, Park Ridge, IL 60068. Phone: (847)299-0950; Fax: (847)299-3598; Email: nffstaff@nffs.org • URL: http://www.nffs.org • Manufacturers of brass, bronze, aluminum, and other nonferrous castings.

Non-Ferrous Metals Producers Committee. 2030 M St. NW, Ste. 800, Washington, DC 20036. Phone: (202)466-7720; Fax: (202)466-2710 • URL: http://www.arcat.com/arcatcos/cos37/arc37679.cfm • Represents domestic copper, lead, and zinc producers. Promotes the interests of copper, lead, and zinc mining and metal industries in the U.S. with emphasis on tariffs, laws, regulations, and government policies affecting international trade and foreign imports.

# NONPRESCRIPTION DRUG INDUSTRY

*See also* PHARMACEUTICAL INDUSTRY

## CD-ROM DATABASES

*Pharmacopeia of Herbs.* CME Inc. • $149.00. Frequently updated CD-ROM provides searchable data on a wide variety of herbal medicines, vitamins, and amino acids. Includes information on clinical studies, contraindications, side-effects, phytoactivity, and 534 therapeutic use categories. Contains a 1,000 word glossary.

## DIRECTORIES

*Drug Facts and Comparisons.* Wolters Kluwer Health. • $565 Individuals Loose-leaf. Provides detailed information on more than 20,000 prescription drugs and 6000 over-the-counter products. Arrangement is according to 13 therapeutic categories. Includes charts and tables.

*Drug Interaction Facts.* Wolters Kluwer Health. • Contains data on the interactions of some 20,000 prescription drugs. Interactions are rated according to magnitude and likelihood of effects, from one (most severe) to five (least severe). Includes drug/drug and drug/food interactions.

*PDR for Nutritional Supplements.* Medical Economics Co. • $59.95 Individuals. Includes trade names, usage, adverse reactions, dosage, and other information about vitamins and minerals.

*Red Book.* American Monument Association. • Annual. $60. Covers: 7,000 retail monument dealers, suppliers of granite and marble, wholesalers, quarriers, funeral homes and cemeteries. Entries include: company; name, address, phone, fax; trade classification, names of owner or corporate officers and their titles. Available only to members of The American Monument Association.

## ONLINE DATABASES

*F-D-C Reports.* Elsevier Business Intelligence. • An online version of "The Gray Sheet" (medical devices), "The Pink Sheet" (pharmaceuticals), "The Rose Sheet" (cosmetics), "The Blue Sheet" (biomedical), and "The Tan Sheet" (nonprescription). Contains full-text information on legal, technical, corporate, financial, and marketing developments from 1987 to date, with weekly updates. Inquire as to online cost and availability.

## PERIODICALS AND NEWSLETTERS

*Chain Drug Review: The Reporter for the Chain Drug Store Industry.* Racher Press Inc. • $199 Institutions. Covers news and trends of concern to the chain drug store industry. Includes special articles on OTC (over-the-counter) drugs.

*Journal of Dietary Supplements.* The Haworth Press Inc. • Quarterly. $175.00 per year to libraries; $50.00 per year to individuals. Edited with a view to both academic research and industry concerns. Sections are dedicated to health professionals, educators, and dieticians. Includes book reviews and short reviews of research appearing elsewhere. Formerly *Journal of Nutraceuticals, Functional & Medical Foods.*

*Natural Products Marketplace.* Virgo Publishing L.L.C. • Monthly. $50.00 per year. Covers all aspects of the vitamin and health supplement market, including new products. Includes an annual buyer's guide, an annual compilation of industry statistics, and annual guides to vitamins and herbs.

*Nutrition Industry Executive.* Vitamin Retailer Magazine, Inc. • 10 times a year. $50.00 per year. Edited for manufacturers of vitamins and other dietary supplements. Covers marketing, new products, industry trends, regulations, manufacturing procedures, and related topics. Includes a directory of suppliers to the industry.

*The Tan Sheet: Nonprescription Pharmaceuticals and Nutritionals.* Elsevier Business Intelligence. • Weekly. $1,220.00 per year. Newsletter covering over-the-counter drugs and vitamin supplements. Emphasis is on regulatory activities of the U. S. Food and Drug Administration (FDA).

## TRADE/PROFESSIONAL ASSOCIATIONS

Consumer Healthcare Products Association. 900 19th St. NW, Ste. 700, Washington, DC 20006. Phone: (202)429-9260; Fax: (202)223-6835; Email: melville@chpa-info.org • URL: http://www.chpa-info.org • Marketers of nonprescription medicines and dietary supplements, which are packaged and available over-the-counter; associate members include suppliers, consultants, research and testing laboratories, advertising agencies and media. Obtains and disseminates business, legislative, regulatory and scientific information; conducts voluntary labeling review service to assist members in complying with laws and regulations.

# NONPROFIT CORPORATIONS

*See also* ASSOCIATIONS; FOUNDATIONS

## BIBLIOGRAPHIES

*Catalog of Nonprofit Literature.* • Dates vary. Covers the literature of philanthropy, foundations, nonprofit organizations, fund-raising, and federal aid.

*Resource Center Product Catalog.* Society for Nonprofit Organizations. • Included in subscription to *Non-profit World.*

## DIRECTORIES

*Directory of Fund Raising and Nonprofit Management Consultants.* Taft Group. • $49. Covers: 1,500 consultants and training organizations for nonprofit groups. Entries include: Organization name, address, phone, fax, year founded, publications and videos, partners or executives, description of service.

*Guide to Federal Funding for Governments and Nonprofits.* Thompson Publishing Group Inc. • Updated continuously; printed on request. $399. Contains detailed descriptions of federal grant programs in economic development, housing, transportation, social services, science, etc.

*Non-Profit Organizations Directory.* InfoGroup Inc. • Annual. Number of listings: 80,335. Entries include: Name, address, phone, size of advertisement, name of owner or manager, number of employees, year first in "Yellow Pages." Compiled from telephone company "Yellow Pages," nationwide.

*Nonprofit Management Resources Directory.* Global Ties U.S. • Covers: Nonprofit organizations. Entries include: Name, address, phone, fax, email, and website address.

## GENERAL WORKS

*The NonProfit Times: The Leading Business Publication For Nonprofit Management.* NPT Publishing Group Inc. • $49.95 Individuals print. Trade journal serving nonprofit organizations.

## OTHER SOURCES

*Charitable Giving and Solicitation.* Thomson RIA. • $495.00 per year. Looseleaf service. Updates 13 times a year. Bulletin discusses federal tax rules pertaining to charitable contributions.

## PERIODICALS AND NEWSLETTERS

*Charitable Business Magazine: Canada's Non-Profit Management Magazine.* Momentum Media Management. • Bimonthly. $15. Magazine for Canadian executives, administrators, purchasing and operations personnel at charitable and non-profit organizations.

*Non-Profit Legal and Tax Letter.* Organization Management Inc. • $235 Individuals. Covers fund raising, taxation, management, postal regulations, and other topics for nonprofit organizations.

*Nonprofit Counsel.* John Wiley and Sons, Inc., Journals Div. • Monthly. $399 Institutions.

*Nonprofit Issues.* Donald W. Kramer. • Description: Presents legal information for nonprofit executives and their professional advisors.

*Nonprofit Management and Leadership.* Jossey-Bass. • Quarterly. $160 Institutions.

*Nonprofit World: The National Bi-Monthly Nonprofit Leadership and Management Journal.* Society for Nonprofit Organizations. • Bimonthly.

## TRADE/PROFESSIONAL ASSOCIATIONS

Alliance for Nonprofit Management. 12 Middlesex Rd., Chestnut Hill, MA 02467. Phone: 888-776-2434; Email: info@allianceonline.org • URL: http://www.allianceonline.org • Members are devoted to building the capacity of nonprofit organizations in order to increase their effectiveness.

Broadsource. 750 9th St. NW, Ste. 650, Washington, DC 20001-4793. Phone: 877-892-6273 or (202)349-2500; Fax: (202)349-2599 • URL: http://www.boardsource.org • Seeks to improve the effectiveness of nonprofit boards of trustees. Formerly National Center for Nonprofit Boards.

Business Volunteers Unlimited. 1300 E 9th St., Ste. 1805, Cleveland, OH 44114-1509. Phone: (216)736-7711; Fax: (216)736-7710; Email: bvu@bvuvolunteers.org • URL: http://www.bvuvolunteers.org • Works to promote effective volunteerism and strong leadership. Provides consulting, education and volunteer referral services to nonprofit and businesses. Trains business executives for leadership roles on nonprofit boards.

Council of Institutional Investors. 888 17th St. NW, Ste. 500, Washington, DC 20006. Phone: (202)822-0800; Fax: (202)822-0801; Email: info@cii.org • URL: http://www.cii.org • Members are nonprofit organization pension plans and other nonprofit institutional investors.

DMA Nonprofit Federation. 1615 L St. NW, Ste. 1100, Washington, DC 20036. Phone: (202)861-2427; Fax: (202)628-4383; Email: aosgood@the-dma.org • URL: http://www.nonprofitfederation.org • Trade and lobbying group for non-profit organizations that use direct and online marketing to raise funds and communicate with members. Sponsors professional development conferences and seminars, lobbies on state and federal legislation, regulation, and standards related to direct marketing and related issues. Provides information about and participants in litigation affecting non-profits. Promotes the overall welfare of non-profits. Represents health care charities, social service agencies, religious groups, colleges and universities and fraternal organizations.

Lesotho Council of Non-Governmental Organizations. Private Bag A445, Maseru 100, Lesotho. Phone: 266 223 17205 or 266 223 25798; Fax: 266 223 10412; Email: admin@lcn.org.ls • URL: http://www.lcn.org.ls • Promotes sustainable management of natural resources, socioeconomic development and social justice in Lesotho. Offers and provides support to the NGO community. Stimulates, promotes and builds capacity within Lesotho NGOs.

National Center on Nonprofit Enterprise. 205 S Patrick St., Alexandria, VA 22314. Phone: (703)548-7978 or (757)214-5084; Fax: (501)637-2807; Email: richard@nationalcne.org • URL: http://www.nationalcne.org • Represents academic researchers, business leaders, consultants and non-profit practitioners supporting a comprehensive program of educational activities and services addressing economic and business decision-making issues facing the non-profit sector.

National Executive Service Corps. 55 W 39th St., 12th Fl., New York, NY 10018. Phone: (212)269-1234; Fax: (212)269-0959; Email: info@nesc.org • URL: http://www.nesc.org • Provides management and business advisory services to non-profit educational, health care, social services, cultural, and religious organizations. Supplies services through experienced and senior-leveled business people who act as volunteer management consultants.

Nonprofit Academic Centers Council. 2121 Euclid Ave., Cleveland, OH 44115-2214. Phone: (216)687-9221 • URL: http://nonprofit-academic-centers-council.org • Provides leadership to strengthen existing centers and supports the establishment of new centers. Fosters collaboration among programs and centers. Develops creative approaches to researcher-practitioner collaborations.

Nonprofit Australia. c/o Netregistry Pty Ltd., PO Box 270, Sydney, NSW 2007, Australia. • URL: http://www.nonprofitaustralia.org.au • Improves the viability of nonprofit organizations for the benefit of Australian society. Increases the capabilities of nonprofit leadership teams and board members. Reduces the operating costs and increases the financial capacity of the sector. Develops targeted services and projects that provide new or improved solutions to the challenges faced by different sectors of Australian society.

Nonprofit VOTE. 89 South St., Ste. 203, Boston, MA 02111-2750. Phone: (617)357-8683; Email: info@nonprofitvote.org • URL: http://www.nonprofitvote.org • Aims to expand the role of America's nonprofits in voting and elections. Provides resources and support to 501(c)(3) nonprofit voter participation initiatives that work year-round to increase the number of nonprofits integrating voter engagement activities into their ongoing work. Seeks to sustain the increasing voter participation in the country.

Turnaround Management Association. 150 N Wacker Dr., Ste. 1900, Chicago, IL 60606. Phone: (312)578-6900; Fax: (312)578-8336; Email: info@turnaround.org • URL: http://www.turnaround.org/Default.aspx • Practitioners (interim managers, consultants, corporate managers and professional advisors), academics, students, attorneys and judges, commercial lenders and legislative personnel. Promotes the image and credibility of the turnaround profession; fosters professional development and networking opportunities for turnaround executives; serves as a clearinghouse of information and research pertinent to the profession. Conducts networking forums; offers educational and credentialing programs.

# NONWOVEN FABRICS INDUSTRY

*See also* INDUSTRIAL FABRICS INDUSTRY

## ABSTRACTS AND INDEXES

*Applied Science and Technology Index*. EBSCO Publishing Inc. • 11/year. Indexes a wide variety of English language technical, industrial, and engineering periodicals.

*Textile Technology Index™*. EBSCO Publishing Inc. • Monthly. $545 Individuals. Includes indexing and abstracts for more than 470 periodicals.

## DIRECTORIES

*International Directory of the Nonwoven Fabrics Industry*. INDA, Association of the Nonwoven Fabrics Industry. • $100 Nonmembers. Lists more than 2,200 manufacturers of nonwoven fabrics and suppliers of raw material and equipment.

## ONLINE DATABASES

*Textile Technology Index™*. EBSCO Publishing Inc. • Monthly. $545 Individuals. Includes indexing and abstracts for more than 470 periodicals.

*World Textiles*. Elsevier. • Provides abstracting and indexing from 1970 of worldwide textile literature (periodicals, books, pamphlets, and reports). Includes U. S., European, and British patent information. Updating is monthly. Inquire as to online cost and availability.

## PERIODICALS AND NEWSLETTERS

*International Textile Bulletin: Nonwovens and Industrial Textiles Edition*. ITS Publishing, International Textile Service. • Quarterly. $170.00 per year. Editions in Chinese, English, French, German, Italian and Spanish.

*Nonwovens Industry: The International Magazine for the Nonwoven Fabrics and Disposable Soft Goods Industry*. Rodman Publications. • Monthly. $48 Individuals.

## RESEARCH CENTERS AND INSTITUTES

Fibrous Materials Research Center. Drexel University, Dept. of Materials Engineering, 3141 Chestnut St., Philadelphia, PA 19104. Phone: (215)895-2323; Fax: (215)895-6760; Email: materials@coe.drexel.edu • URL: http://www.materials.drexel.edu • Research fields include computer-aided design of nonwoven fabrics and design curves for industrial fibers.

Textile Materials Technology. Philadelphia University, 4201 Henry Ave., Philadelphia, PA 19144. Phone: (215)951-2700; Fax: (215)951-2651; Email: admissions@philau.edu • URL: http://www.philau.edu/textilemat • Many research areas, including industrial and nonwoven textiles.

# NORTH AMERICAN FREE TRADE AGREEMENT

*See also* LATIN AMERICAN MARKETS

## ABSTRACTS AND INDEXES

*Business Periodicals Index Retrospective*. EBSCO Publishing Inc. • 11/year. Quarterly and annual cumulations.

*PAIS International*. ProQuest L.L.C. • Monthly. $850.00 per year; cumulations three times a year. Provides topical citations to the worldwide literature of public affairs, economics, demographics, sociology, and trade. Text in English; indexed materials in English, French, German, Italian, Portuguese and Spanish.

*Readers' Guide to Periodical Literature*. EBSCO Publishing Inc. • Provides indexing for over 400 periodicals dating back to 1983.

## CD-ROM DATABASES

*Business Abstracts with Full Text*. EBSCO Publishing Inc. • Includes full text articles from more than 460 business publications from 1982 to present. Indexing for nearly 880 publications.

*PAIS International*. ProQuest L.L.C. • Monthly. $1,995.00 per year. Contains over 650,000 citations to the literature of contemporary social, political, and economic issues.

*Readers' Guide to Periodical Literature*. EBSCO Publishing Inc. • Provides indexing for over 400 periodicals dating back to 1983.

## DIRECTORIES

*NAFTA Register*. Global Contact Inc. • Annual. Covers: Companies within the NAFTA region interested in exporting their products/services. Entries include: Company name, address, phone, fax, e-mail and Internet addresses, name and title of contact, list of products/services offered.

## ONLINE DATABASES

*Wilson Business Abstracts Online*. H.W. Wilson Co. • Indexes and abstracts 600 major business periodicals, plus the *Wall Street Journal* and the business section of the *New York Times*. Indexing is from 1982, abstracting from 1990, with the two newspapers included from 1993. Updated weekly. Inquire as to online cost and availability. (*Business Periodicals Index* without abstracts is also available online.).

## RESEARCH CENTERS AND INSTITUTES

Claremont McKenna College - Lowe Institute of Political Economy. Bauer Ctr. 322, 500 E 9th St., Claremont, CA 91711-6400. Phone: (909)621-8012; Fax: (909)607-8008; Email: marc.weidenmier@cmc.edu • URL: http://www.claremontmckenna.edu/lowe • Research topics include NAFTA.

# NOTARIES

## PERIODICALS AND NEWSLETTERS

*The National Notary*. National Notary Association. • Bimonthly. $45 Members includes magazine & bulletin. Legal trade magazine.

## TRADE/PROFESSIONAL ASSOCIATIONS

American Society of Notaries. PO Box 5707, Tallahassee, FL 32314-5707. Phone: (850)671-5164; Fax: (850)671-5165 • URL: http://www.asnnotary.org • Notaries Public. Provides members with educational services and technical support. Promotes high ethical standards for notaries. Seeks to increase public awareness of the valuable contribution of notaries.

National Notary Association. 9350 DeSoto Ave., Chatsworth, CA 91313-2402. Phone: 800-876-6827 • URL: http://www.nationalnotary.org • Notaries public (officers empowered to witness the signing of documents, identify the signers, take acknowledgments, and administer oaths). Works to teach notaries public in the U.S. their duties, powers, limitations, liabilities, and obligations. Keeps members informed of changes in notary law; offers various services, supplies, and insurance plans to members. Maintains speakers' bureau.

# NOTEBOOK COMPUTERS

*See* PORTABLE COMPUTERS

# NOTIONS

*See* GIFT BUSINESS

# NUCLEAR ENERGY

*See also* ENERGY SOURCES

## ABSTRACTS AND INDEXES

*Applied Science and Technology Index*. EBSCO Publishing Inc. • 11/year. Indexes a wide variety of English language technical, industrial, and engineering periodicals.

*NTIS Alerts: Energy*. U.S. Department of Commerce National Technical Information Service. • Biweekly. $130 per year. Covers electric power, batteries, fuels, geothermal energy, heating/cooling systems, nuclear technology, solar energy, energy policy, and related subjects.

*Science Citation Index*. Thomson Reuters Intellectual Property and Science. • Weekly. Includes *Source Index*, *Citation Index*, *Permuterm Subject Index*, and *Corporate Index*. Provides researchers, administrators, faculty, and students with quick, powerful access to the bibliographic and citation information they need to find research data, analyze trends, journals and researchers, and share their findings.

## ALMANACS AND YEARBOOKS

*Annual Review of Nuclear and Particle Science*. Annual Reviews. • Annual. $99 Individuals online only.

## BIBLIOGRAPHIES

*Nuclear Power*. U. S. Government Printing Office. • Annual. Free. Lists government publications. GPO Subject Bibliography Number 200.

## CD-ROM DATABASES

*Science Citation Index*. Thomson Reuters Intellectual Property and Science. • Weekly. Includes *Source Index*, *Citation Index*, *Permuterm Subject Index*, and *Corporate Index*. Provides researchers, administrators, faculty, and students with quick, powerful access to the bibliographic and citation information they need to find research data, analyze trends, journals and researchers, and share their findings.

## DIRECTORIES

*Platt's Directory of Electric Power Producers and Distributors*. Platts Global Energy. • Annual. $495 hardcopy. Over 3,500 investor-owned, municipal, rural cooperative and government electric utility systems in the U.S. and Canada. Formerly *Directory of Electric Power Producers and Distributors*.

*World Energy and Nuclear Directory*. Specialist Journals. • Biennial. $385.00. Lists 5,000 public and private, international research and development organizations functioning in a wide variety of areas related to energy.

## E-BOOKS

*Macmillan Encyclopedia of Energy*. Cengage Learning Inc. • 2003. eBook. Published by Macmillan Reference USA. Covers the business, technology, and history of a wide variety of energy sources. Inquire as to price and availability.

## HANDBOOKS AND MANUALS

*Mergent's Public Utility Manual*. Mergent Inc. • Annual. $1,995.00. Updated weekly online. Contains financial and other information concerning publicly-held utility companies (electric, gas, telephone, water).

## OTHER SOURCES

*Major Energy Companies of the World*. Cengage Learning Inc. • Annual. $1,460 Individuals. 2008. 12th edition. eBook. Published by Graham & Whiteside. Contains detailed information on more than 4,850 important energy companies in various countries. Industries include electricity generation, coal, natural gas, nuclear energy, petroleum, fuel distribution, and equipment for energy production.

## PERIODICALS AND NEWSLETTERS

*Bulletin of the Atomic Scientists: The Magazine of Global Security News and Analysis*. Bulletin of the Atomic Scientists. • Bimonthly. $56.00 per year.

*DOE This Month*. U. S. Government Printing Office. • Monthly. $22 per year. Describes the U.S. Department of Energy's research and development activities and DOE publications. Includes information on nuclear energy, renewable energy sources, and synthetic fuels.

*INIS Newsletter.* International Atomic Energy Agency, Division of Publications. • Irregular. Free. Newsletter of the International Nuclear Information System (INIS).

*Journal of Energy Engineering: The International Journal.* Architectural Engineering Institute of ASCE. • Quarterly. $350 Individuals Online only. Contains reports on the development of scientific and engineering knowledge in the planning, management, and generation of electrical power.

*Nuclear Engineering International.* Wilmington Publishers Ltd. • Monthly. $341.00 per year. Text in English; summaries in French and German.

*Nuclear Fuel.* Platts Global Energy. • Biweekly. $3,270.00 per year. Newsletter.

*Nuclear News.* American Nuclear Society. • Monthly. $510 Individuals online only. Magazine focusing on applications of nuclear energy. Includes *Nuclear News Buyers Guide* and three special issues.

*Nuclear Plant Journal.* International Nuclear Power Industry. EQES Inc. • Bimonthly. $120.00 per year.

*Nuclear Science and Engineering: Research and Development Related to Peaceful Utilization of Nuclear Energy.* American Nuclear Society. • Nine times per year. Institutions, $1,725.00 per year. Includes online edition.

*Nuclear Standards News.* American Nuclear Society. • Semimonthly. Description: Provides current information on nuclear standards, U.S. Nuclear Regulatory Commission (NRC) regulations and licensing issues, and developments in the domestic and international nuclear standards field. Recurring features include a calendar of standards meetings and notices of pertinent publications.

*Nuclear Technology.* American Nuclear Society. • Monthly. $2,260 Individuals print only. Nuclear power; science and engineering.

*Nucleonics Week.* Platts Global Energy. • Weekly. $3,000 basic. Description: Provides an overview of all international developments relating to commercial nuclear power. Offers coverage of plant construction, low-level waste issues, government policies, plant performance, services, and decommissioning, as well as "comprehensive statistical coverage of plant production and the economics of nuclear power." Recurring features include a monthly listing of nuclear power electric generation worldwide. **Remarks:** Also available in electronic format.

*Power.* The McGraw-Hill Companies Inc. • Description: Covers design, operation, construction, and maintenance of power plants for utilities, process industries, and manufacturers.

*Russian Nuclear Industry Business Opportunities Handbook.* International Business Publications, USA. • $99.95 Individuals. Strategic and business information on Russian nuclear industry, research on nuclear reactors, and contact information for major industrial and research facilities.

## RESEARCH CENTERS AND INSTITUTES

Massachusetts Institute of Technology - Laboratory for Nuclear Science. Bldg. 26-505, 77 Massachusetts Ave., Cambridge, MA 02139. Phone: (617)253-2395; Email: milner@mit.edu • URL: http://web.mit.edu/lns • High energy, medium energy, relativistic heavy-ion, and neutrino physics, elementary particle and nuclear theory, plus applications of nuclear techniques.

U.S. Department of Energy - Bioenergy Feedstock Development Program - Oak Ridge National Laboratory. 1 Bethel Valley Rd., Oak Ridge, TN 37831-6006. Phone: 800-541-1625 or (865)574-4160; Fax: (865)574-0595 or (865)574-2232; Email:

ighotline@hq.doe.gov • URL: http://www.ornl.gov.

U.S. Department of Energy - National Nuclear Security Administration - Los Alamos National Security, LLC - Los Alamos National Laboratory. PO Box 1663, Los Alamos, NM 87545. Phone: (505)667-5061 or (505)667-7000; Fax: (505)667-2997 or (505)665-4411; Email: mcmillan1@lanl. gov • URL: http://www.lanl.gov • Nuclear, high-energy, plasma, low temperature, and cryogenic physics, earth and space sciences, engineering and environmental sciences, life sciences, inorganic chemistry, metallurgy, cryogenic engineering, molecular biology, mesons, mathematics, biomedicine, energy, and national security, including research and development programs relating to nuclear and thermonuclear weapons, use of nuclear energy for production of power, energy lasers, controlled release of thermonuclear energy, and thermionic conversion.

University of California, San Diego - Center for Energy Research. 9500 Gilman Dr., MC 0417, La Jolla, CA 92093-0417. Phone: (858)534-6527 or (858)534-4285; Fax: (858)534-7716; Email: faw@ames.ucsd.edu • URL: http://cer.ucsd.edu • Stable, secure, and affordable energy supplies that have minimal impact on the environment.

University of Michigan Energy Institute. Michigan Memorial Phoenix Laboratory, 2301 Bonisteel Blvd., Ann Arbor, MI 48109-2100. Phone: (734)763-7401; Fax: (734)763-9232; Email: umichenergy@umich.edu • URL: http://www. energy.umich.edu • Conducts research in peaceful uses of nuclear energy.

## STATISTICS SOURCES

*Annual Energy Outlook, with Projections to (year).* U. S. Government Printing Office. • Annual. $39.00. Issued by the Energy Information Administration, U. S. Department of Energy (www.eia.doe.gov). Contains detailed statistics and 20-year projections for electricity, oil, natural gas, coal, and renewable energy. Text provides extensive discussion of energy issues and "Market Trends.".

*Annual Energy Review.* U. S. Government Printing Office. • Annual. $59.00. Issued by the Energy Information Administration, Office of Energy Markets and End Use, U. S. Department of Energy. Presents long-term historical as well as recent data on production, consumption, stocks, imports, exports, and prices of the principal energy commodities in the U. S.

*OECD Nuclear Energy Data.* Organization for Economic Cooperation and Development. Organisation for Economic Co-operation and Development Publications and Information Center. • Annual. $58. 00. Produced by the OECD Nuclear Energy Agency. Provides a yearly compilation of basic statistics on electricity generation and nuclear power in OECD member countries. Text in English and French.

## TRADE/PROFESSIONAL ASSOCIATIONS

American Nuclear Insurers. 95 Glastonbury Blvd., Ste. 300, Glastonbury, CT 06033-4412. Phone: (860)682-1301; Fax: (860)659-0002; Email: info@ nuclearinsurance.com • URL: http://www.amnucins. com • Domestic property/casualty nuclear insurance companies. Strives to ensure safe and secure insurance capacity for customers. Audits financial performance of all member companies annually, ensures compliance with guidelines.

American Nuclear Society. 555 N Kensington Ave., La Grange Park, IL 60526. Phone: 800-323-3044 or (708)352-6611; Fax: (708)352-0499; Email: nuclear@ans.org • URL: http://www.ans.org • Physicists, chemists, educators, mathematicians, life scientists, engineers, metallurgists, managers, and administrators with professional experience in nuclear science or nuclear engineering. Works to advance science and engineering in the nuclear industry. Disseminates information; promotes

research; conducts meetings devoted to scientific and technical papers; works with government agencies, educational institutions, and other organizations dealing with nuclear issues.

Bulletin of the Atomic Scientists. 1155 E 60th St., Chicago, IL 60637. Phone: (772)702-6301 • URL: http://thebulletin.org • Works to inform polic leaders and the public about risks to humanity from nuclear weapons, nuclear energy, climate change, and biotechnology.

Nuclear Energy Institute. 1201 F St. NW, Ste. 1100, Washington, DC 20004-1218. Phone: (202)739-8000; Fax: (202)785-4019; Email: webmasterp@ nei.org • URL: http://www.nei.org • Represents Electric utilities, manufacturers, industrial firms, research and service organizations, educational institutions, labor groups, and governmental agencies engaged in development and utilization of nuclear energy, especially nuclear-produced electricity, and other energy matters. Maintains speakers' bureau; compiles statistics and public attitude data.

Nuclear Information and Records Management Association. 10 Almas Rd., Windham, NH 03087-1105. Phone: (603)432-6476; Fax: (603)432-3024; Email: nirma@nirma.org • URL: http://www.nirma. org • Concerned with the maintenance of nuclear industry corporate records. Formerly Nuclear Records Management Association.

Nuclear Information and Resource Service. 6930 Carroll Ave., Ste. 340, Takoma Park, MD 20912. Phone: (301)270-6477; Fax: (301)270-4291; Email: nirsnet@nirs.org • URL: http://www.nirs.org • Promotes alternatives to nuclear power. Affiliated with World Information Service on Energy.

Nuclear Suppliers Association. PO Box 1354, Westerly, RI 02891. Phone: (401)637-4224; Fax: (401)637-4822; Email: nsanews@charter.net • URL: http://www.nuclearsuppliers.org • Companies involved in the manufacture or distribution of products and services for the nuclear industry. Promotes nuclear power and the interests of the nuclear industry.

Oak Ridge Institute for Science and Education. 130 Badger Ave., OAB-44, Oak Ridge, TN 37831-0117. Phone: (865)576-3000 or (865)576-3146; Fax: (865)241-2923 or (615)576-9522; Email: communications@orau.org • URL: http://www. orise.orau.gov • Represents private, not-for-profit corporations and a consortium of 91 doctoral-granting colleges and universities. Serves the government, academia, and the private sector in important areas of science and technology. Manages and operates the Oak Ridge Institute for Science and Education (ORISE) for the U.S. Department of Energy. ORISE undertakes national and international programs in education, training, health, and the environment.

Professional Reactor Operator Society. PO Box 484, Byron, IL 61010-0484. Phone: 800-422-2725 or (815)234-8140; Fax: (800)422-2725; Email: theprosoffice@aol.com • URL: http://nucpros.com • Plenary members are licensed and certified nuclear reactor operators; associate members include equipment manufacturers and utility companies. Aims to develop a communication network between nuclear reactor operators and government agencies, Congress, and industry in order to promote safety and efficiency in nuclear facilities. Believes that the education, experience, and training of nuclear facility operators have not been fairly considered in the formation of regulations, guidelines, and decisions that affect their careers. Areas of concern include educational requirements and job stress. Plans to survey the views and concerns of members and other involved parties; also plans personal presentations of members' views, supported by scientific data, to persons in the decision-making process. Offers direct mailing service to members from advertisers

---

and placement agencies. Compiles statistics.

# NUMERICAL CONTROL OF MACHINERY (NC) )

*See* COMPUTER-AIDED

# NUMISMATICS

*See* COINS AS AN INVESTMENT

# NURSERIES (HORTICULTURAL)

*See also* FLORIST SHOPS

## ABSTRACTS AND INDEXES

*Horticultural Science Abstracts.* CABI Publishing North America. • Updated weekly online; also available in print, delivered monthly.

*NTIS Alerts: Agriculture & Food.* U.S. Department of Commerce National Technical Information Service. • Biweekly. $130 per year. Covers agricultural economics, horticulture, fisheries, veterinary medicine, food technology, and related subjects.

## DIRECTORIES

*Andersen Horticultural Library's Source List of Plants and Seeds.* Andersen Horticultural Library. • Irregular. $39.95 Individuals postpaid. Covers: More than 600 nurseries that offer over 70,000 different plants. Entries include: Company name, address, phone.

## ONLINE DATABASES

*CAB Abstracts.* CABI. • Contains 46 specialized abstract collections covering over 10,000 journals and monographs in the areas of agriculture, horticulture, forest products, farm products, nutrition, dairy science, poultry, grains, animal health, entomology, etc. Time period is 1972 to date, with monthly updates. Inquire as to online cost and availability. *CAB Abstracts on CD-ROM* also available, with annual updating.

## PERIODICALS AND NEWSLETTERS

*Canadian Florist Greenhouse & Nursery: The National Horticulural Business Publication.* Horticulture Publications. • Monthly. $18. Magazine for commercial florists, greenhouse growers, nurseries, garden centers, interior landscapers, and craft and hobby retailers.

*Greenhouse Grower.* Meister Media. • $37.45 Individuals. Concerned with all crops grown under glass or plastic.

*Horticulture: Gardening at its Best.* Krause Publications Inc. • Bimonthly. $19.95 per year.

*Nursery Business Retailer.* Brantwood Publications Inc. • Bimonthly. Price on application.

## STATISTICS SOURCES

*Nursery Business Retailer--Top 100 Retailer Report.* Brantwood Publications Inc. • Annual. $15. Lists the largest 100 garden centers and retail nurseries based on sales.

# NURSERY SCHOOLS

*See* DAY CARE CENTERS

# NURSING HOMES

*See also* LONG-TERM CARE INSURANCE; RETIREMENT COMMUNITIES

## CD-ROM DATABASES

*Authority Health Care Law Library.* Matthew Bender and Company Inc. • Periodic updates. Price on request. Full text CD-ROM provides legal information, case law, and analysis relating to health care facilities, health insurance, longterm care, Medigap, and Medicare.

## DIRECTORIES

*AHA Integrated Delivery Network Directory: U.S. Health Care Systems, Networks, and Alliances.* American Hospital Association. • Annual. $250.00. Provides information about a wide variety of U.S. health care groups and affiliations, including hospitals, nursing homes, rehabilitation centers, psychiatric facilities, home health care agencies, clinical laboratories, outpatient facilities, and diagnostic imaging centers. Includes names of more than 8,000 key executives.

*Homes for the Aged Directory.* InfoGroup Inc. • Annual. Number of listings: 5,059. Entries include: Name, address, phone, size of advertisement, name of owner or manager, number of employees, year first in "Yellow Pages." Compiled from telephone company "Yellow Pages," nationwide.

*Homes--Nursing--Directory.* InfoGroup Inc. • Annual. Number of listings: 22,509. Entries include: Name, address, phone, size of advertisement, name of owner or manager, number of employees, year first in "Yellow Pages." Compiled from telephone company "Yellow Pages," nationwide.

*National Directory of Adult Day Care Centers.* Health Resources Publishing. • Irregular. $145 Individuals. Covers: Over 3,200 centers and programs providing adult day care; 1,100 are described in detail. Database includes: Bibliography of resources; aging services suppliers' guide. Entries include: Center or program name, address, phone, director or coordinator name; detailed listings include programs, providing sponsor information, geographic area served, fees, number of clients and staff, hours and days of operation, client eligibility criteria, services and activities offered.

## FINANCIAL RATIOS

*Annual Statement Studies.* Risk Management Association. • Annual. Compiled from over 280,000 financial statements.

*Annual Statement Studies: Industry Default Probabilities and Cash Flow Measures.* Risk Management Association. • Annual. $405 Nonmembers. Serves as a companion volume to the original *Annual Statement Studies.* Gives probability of default estimates on a percentage scale for more than 450 industries. Includes changes in position year-by-year for eight financial statement line items and provides percentage measures of cash flow.

## HANDBOOKS AND MANUALS

*Nursing Home Regulations Manual.* Thompson Publishing Group Inc. • $295.00 per year. Looseleaf service. Includes monthly updates, newsletters and internet access. Serves as a comprehensive guide to the Nursing Home Reform Act, federal regulations, resident assessment, deficiency findings, Medicare, Medicaid, Health Care Financing Administration (HCFA) policies, and related topics for nursing home and assisted living facility owners and managers.

## INTERNET DATABASES

*Medicare: The Official U. S. Government Site for Medicare Information.* Centers for Medicare and Medicaid Services. Phone: (202)690-6726 • URL: http://www.medicare.gov • Web site provides extensive information on Medicare health plans, publications, fraud, nursing homes, top 20 questions and answers, etc. Includes access to the National Nursing Home Database, providing summary compliance information on "every Medicare and Medicaid certified nursing home in the country.

"Online searching is offered. Fees: Free.

## PERIODICALS AND NEWSLETTERS

*AHA News.* American Hospital Association. HealthForum. • Description: Highlights major news affecting hospitals and the health care field. Reports on legislation and regulation, court cases, surveys, and federal programs. Carries information on individual hospitals and allied hospital associations.

*American Health Care Association: Provider.* American Health Care Association. • Monthly. $48.00 per year. Formerly *American Health Care Association Journal.*

*Contemporary Longterm Care.* Leisure Publications Inc. • Monthly. Free to qualified personnel. Edited for the long term health care industry, including retirement centers with life care, continuing care communities, and nursing homes.

*Continuing Care News: Supporting the Transition into Post Hospital Care.* Stevenson Publishing Corp. • Monthly. $99.00 per year. Topics include insurance, legal issues, health business news, ethics, and case management. Includes annual *Buyer's Guide.*

*Geriatric Care.* Eymann Publications Inc. • Monthly. $87.50 Individuals.

*Health Facilities Management.* American Hospital Association. Health Forum L.L.C. • Covers building maintenance and engineering for hospitals and nursing homes.

*Housing the Elderly Report.* Community Development Services, Inc. CD Publications. • Monthly. $249.00 per year. Newsletter. Edited for retirement communities, apartment projects, and nursing homes. Covers news relative to business and property management issues.

*McKnight's Long Term Care News.* Thomson Medical Economics. • Monthly. Edited for retirement housing directors and nursing home administrators.

*Modern Healthcare: The Newsmagazine for Administrators and Managers in Hospitals and Other Healthcare Institutions.* Crain Communications Inc. • $159 Premium Access (Web + Data + Digital Edition).

*Nursing Homes: Long Term Care Management.* Medquest Communications, LLC. • Monthly. $95.00 per year. Covers business, finance, and management topics for nursing home directors and administrators.

*Older Americans Report.* Business Publishers Inc. • Bimonthly. $449 Individuals. Description: Features brief articles on legislative, judicial, and federal agency activities concerning older Americans. Covers news of developments in such areas as Social Security, social services, Medicare, programs for retirement and pension funds, research projects, and the Older Americans Act. Recurring features include book reviews and a calendar of events.

*Provider: For Long Term Care Professionals.* American Health Care Association. • Monthly. $48 /year for nonmembers and libraries. Edited for medical directors, administrators, owners, and others concerned with extended care facilities and nursing homes. Covers business management, legal issues, financing, reimbursement, care planning, ethics, human resources, etc. Includes *Buyers' Guide.*

## STATISTICS SOURCES

*Standard & Poor's Industry Surveys.* Standard & Poor's Financial Services L.L.C. • Semiannual. $1,800.00. Two looseleaf volumes. Includes monthly *Supplements.* Provides detailed, individual surveys of 52 major industry groups. Each survey is revised on a semiannual basis. Also includes "Monthly Investment Review" (industry group investment analysis) and monthly "Trends & Projections" (economic analysis).

## TRADE/PROFESSIONAL ASSOCIATIONS

American College of Health Care Administrators. 1321 Duke St., Ste. 400, Alexandria, VA 22314.

**For publishers' addresses, refer to SOURCES CITED section at the back of the book.**

Phone: (202)536-5120; Fax: (866)874-1585; Email: mgrachek@achca.org • URL: http://www.achca.org • Formerly American College of Nursing Home Administrators.

American Health Care Association. 1201 L St. NW, Washington, DC 20005. Phone: (202)842-4444; Fax: (202)842-3860 • URL: http://www.ahcancal. org/Pages/Default.aspx • Federation of state associations of long-term health care facilities. Promotes standards for professionals in long-term health care delivery and quality care for patients and residents in a safe environment. Focuses on issues of availability, quality, affordability, and fair payment. Operates as liaison with governmental agencies, Congress, and professional associations. Compiles statistics.

# NUT INDUSTRY

## ABSTRACTS AND INDEXES

*Food Science and Technology Abstracts.* Ovid Technologies Inc. • Monthly. $1,780.00 per year. Provides worldwide coverage of the literature of food technology and food production.

*Foods Adlibra: Key to the World's Food Literature.* General Mills, Inc. Foods Adlibra Publications. • Semimonthly. $240.00 per year. Provides journal citations and abstracts to the literature of food technology and packaging.

## DIRECTORIES

*Directory of Chinese Manufacturers & Exporters of Nuts & Dried Fruits.* EXIM Infotek Private Ltd. • $5 Individuals. Covers: 30 Chinese manufacturers and exporters of chestnuts, dried fruits, dry fruits, nuts-dried, peanut kernels, walnuts. Entries include: Company name, postal address, city, country, phone, fax, e-mail and websites, contact person, designation, and product details.

*Major Food and Drink Companies of the World.* Cengage Learning Inc. • 12th edition. eBook. Published by Graham & Whiteside. Contains profiles and trade names for more than 9,200 important food and beverage companies in various countries. In addition to foods, includes both alcoholic and nonalcoholic drink products.

## INTERNET DATABASES

*USDA.* U.S. National Institute of Standards and Technology. 100 Bureau Dr., Gaithersburg, MD 20899-1070. Phone: 800-877-8339 or (301)975-6478 or (202)720-2791; Fax: (301)975-8295; Email: inquiries@nist.gov • URL: http://www.nist.gov • The USDA home page has six sections: News and Information; What's New; About USDA; Agencies; Opportunities; Search and Help. Keyword searching is offered from the USDA home page and from various individual agency home pages. Agencies are the Economic Research Service, Agricultural Marketing Service, National Agricultural Statistics Service, National Agricultural Library, and about 12 others. Updating varies. Fees: Free.

## ONLINE DATABASES

*Food Science and Technology Abstracts (online).* IFIS North American Desk. • Produced by International Food Information Service. Provides about 500,000 online citations, with abstracts, to the international literature of food science, technology, commodities, engineering, and processing. Approximately 2,000 periodicals are covered. Time period is 1969 to date, with monthly updates. Inquire as to online cost and availability.

## PERIODICALS AND NEWSLETTERS

*The Nutshell.* Northern Nut Growers Association. • Quarterly. Description: Brings information to amateur and expert nut growers on cultural practices, new developments in propagation, and knowledge of new and better cultivars and where to get them. Contains supplements of reports on the latest practices, experiments in progress, and storage of nuts. Recurring features include letters to the editor, interviews, news of research, a calendar of events, reports of meetings, book reviews, and notices of publications available.

*Peanut Journal and Nut World.* Virginia-Carolina Peanut Association. Peanut Journal Publishing Co. • Monthly. $8.00 per year.

## RESEARCH CENTERS AND INSTITUTES

College of Tropical Agriculture and Human Resources. University of Hawaii at Manoa, 2515 Campus Rd., Miller Hall 110, Honolulu, HI 96822. Phone: (808)956-8234; Fax: (808)956-9105; Email: gallom@ctahr.hawaii.edu • URL: http://www.ctahr. hawaii.edu • Concerned with the production and marketing of tropical food and ornamental plant products, including pineapples, bananas, coffee, and macadamia nuts.

## STATISTICS SOURCES

*Agricultural Statistics.* U.S. Department of Agriculture National Agricultural Statistics Service. • Annual. $46 Individuals. Provides a wide variety of statistical data relating to agricultural production, supplies, consumption, prices/price-supports, foreign trade, costs, and returns, as well as farm labor, loans, income, and population. In many cases, historical data is shown annually for 10 years. In addition to farm data, includes detailed fishery statistics.

## TRADE/PROFESSIONAL ASSOCIATIONS

Northern Nut Growers Association. PO Box 6216, Hamden, CT 06517-0216. Fax: (203)974-8502; Email: icomserve@aol.com • URL: http://www. northernnutgrowers.org • Consists of nut tree culturists, farmers, amateur and commercial nut tree growers, experiment station workers, horticultural teachers, scientists, nut tree breeders, nursery people, and foresters. Conducts visits to amateur and commercial orchards, experimental and research sites, nurseries and nut processing plants.

# NUTRITION

*See* DIET

# NYLON

*See* SYNTHETIC TEXTILE FIBER
INDUSTRY

# O

## OBSOLETE SECURITIES

### OTHER SOURCES

*Capital Changes Reports.* Wolters Kluwer Law & Business CCH. • Weekly. $1,395.00. Six looseleaf volumes. Arranged alphabetically by company. This service presents a chronological capital history that includes reorganizations, mergers and consolidations. Recent actions are found in Volume One - "New Matters.".

### PERIODICALS AND NEWSLETTERS

*Financial History: Chronicling the History of America's Capital Markets.* Museum of American Finance. • Quarterly. Membership. Contains articles on early stock and bond markets and trading in the U. S., with photographs and other illustrations. Current trading in rare and unusual, obsolete stock and bond certificates is featured. Formerly *Friends of Financial History.*

### PRICE SOURCES

*National Bond Summary.* OTC Markets Group Inc. • Monthly, with semiannual cumulations. $504.00 per year. Includes price quotes for both active and inactive issues, with transfer agents, market makers (brokers), capital changes, name changes, and other corporate information. Formerly published by the National Quotation Bureau.

*National Stock Summary.* OTC Markets Group Inc. • Monthly, with semiannual cumulations. $576.00 per year. Includes price quotes for both active and inactive issues, with transfer agents, market makers (brokers), capital changes, name changes, and other corporate information. Pink Sheets LLC also provides daily and weekly stock price services. Formerly published by the National Quotation Bureau.

## OCCUPATIONAL HEALTH

*See* INDUSTRIAL HYGIENE

## OCCUPATIONAL SAFETY

*See* INDUSTRIAL SAFETY

## OCCUPATIONAL THERAPY

### ABSTRACTS AND INDEXES

*Psychological Abstracts.* American Psychological Association. • Monthly. Members, $815.00 per year; individuals and institutions, $1,207.00 per year. Covers the international literature of psychology and the behavioral sciences. Includes journals, technical reports, dissertations, and other sources.

### PERIODICALS AND NEWSLETTERS

*Occupational Therapy in Health Care: A Journal of Contemporary Practice.* The Haworth Press Inc. • Quarterly. $275.00 per year.

*Occupational Therapy in Mental Health: A Journal of Psychosocial Practice and Research.* The Haworth Press Inc. • Quarterly. Institutions, $385.00 per year.

### TRADE/PROFESSIONAL ASSOCIATIONS

American Occupational Therapy Association. 4720 Montgomery Ln., Ste. 200, Bethesda, MD 20814-3449. Phone: 800-SAY-AOTA or (301)652-6611; Fax: (301)652-7711; Email: members@aota.org • URL: http://www.aota.org • Occupational therapists and occupational therapy assistants. Provides services to people whose lives have been disrupted by physical injury or illness, developmental problems, the aging process, or social or psychological difficulties. Occupational therapy focuses on the active involvement of the patient in specially designed therapeutic tasks and activities to improve function, performance capacity, and the ability to cope with demands of daily living.

## OCCUPATIONS

*See also* EMPLOYMENT; JOB DESCRIPTIONS; JOB RESUMES; VOCATIONAL EDUCATION; VOCATIONAL GUIDANCE

### BIBLIOGRAPHIES

*Job Hunter's Sourcebook.* Cengage Learning Inc. • $243 Individuals. 2012. $231.00. 12th edition. Covers over 200 professions and occupations.

### CD-ROM DATABASES

*Sourcebooks America CD-ROM.* CACI Marketing Systems. • Annual. $1,250.00. Provides the CD-ROM version of *The Sourcebook of ZIP Code Demographics: Census Edition* and *The Sourcebook of County Demographics: Census Edition.*

### DIRECTORIES

*Career Information Center.* Glencoe Publishing Co. • Biennial. $778 Individuals. Organized into 13 occupational clusters (comprising 13 volumes and an index volume). Each volume includes a section listing accredited occupational educational and vocational institutions. A second section lists more than 700 occupational profiles and over 3,000 organizations with jobs in the field of work with which the volume is concerned. Database includes: Job summary chart; industry snapshots that summarize major developments; photographs; overview of the job market; job hunting information and tips.

Entries include: For institutions--Name, address, programs and degrees offered. For organizations--Name, address.

### HANDBOOKS AND MANUALS

*Occupational Outlook Handbook.* Bureau of Labor Statistics, U.S. Department of Labor. U. S. Government Printing Office. • Biennial. $22 Individuals. Issued as one of the Bureau's Bulletin series and kept up to date by *Occupational Outlook Quarterly.*

### OTHER SOURCES

*Chronicle Occupational Briefs.* Chronicle Guidance Publications Inc. • $5.50 e-mailed, single title. Approximately 600 pamphlets about various occupations.

### PERIODICALS AND NEWSLETTERS

*Career World.* Weekly Reader Corp. • Six times a year. $33.95. per year. Up-to-the-minute, important career and vocational news for students in grades 7 thru 12.

*Occupational Outlook Quarterly.* U.S. Department of Labor Bureau of Labor Statistics. • Quarterly. $30 Two years. Magazine providing occupational and employment information.

*ReCareering Newsletter: An Idea and Resource Guide to Second Career and Relocation Planning.* Publications Plus, Inc. • Monthly. $59.00 per year. Edited for "downsized managers, early retirees, and others in career transition after leaving traditional employment." Offers advice on second careers, franchises, starting a business, finances, education, training, skills assessment, and other matters of interest to the newly unemployed.

*TECHniques.* Informix Software. • Eight times a year. Free to members; non-members, $45.00 per year. Formerly *Vocational Educational Journal.*

### STATISTICS SOURCES

*Occupational Projections and Training Data.* U. S. Government Printing Office. • Biennial. $31.50. Issued by Bureau of Labor Statistics, U. S. Department of Labor. Contains projections of employment change and job openings over the next 15 years for about 500 specific occupations. Also includes the number of associate, bachelor's, master's, doctoral, and professional degrees awarded in a recent year for about 900 specific fields of study.

*Statistics on Occupational Wages and Hours of Work and on Food Prices.* International Labor Organization. • Annual. Provides international data on wages and hours for 159 occupations within 49 industries. Includes retail prices for 93 food items.

### TRADE/PROFESSIONAL ASSOCIATIONS

Association for Career and Technical Education. 1410 King St., Alexandria, VA 22314. Phone: 800-

826-9972; Fax: (703)683-7424; Email: acte@
acteonline.org • URL: http://www.acteonline.org
• Represents teachers, supervisors, administrators,
and others interested in the development and
improvement of vocational, Technical, and practical
arts education. Areas of interest include: secondary,
postsecondary, and adult vocational education;
education for special population groups; cooperative education. Works with such government agencies as: Bureau of Apprenticeship in Department of
Labor; Office of Vocational Rehabilitation in
Department of Health and Human Services;
Veterans Administration; Office of Vocational and
Adult Education of the Department of Education.
Maintains hall of fame.

# OCEAN LINERS

*See* STEAMSHIP LINES

# OCEANOGRAPHIC INDUSTRIES

*See also* MARINE ENGINEERING

## ABSTRACTS AND INDEXES

*Applied Science and Technology Index.* EBSCO
Publishing Inc. • 11/year. Indexes a wide variety of
English language technical, industrial, and engineer-
ing periodicals.

*Meteorological & Geoastrophysical Abstracts
(MGA).* American Meteorological Society.
American Meteorological Society. • Monthly.
$1,605 print. Journal presenting abstrcts of current
world literature in meteorology, climatology,
aeronomy, planetary atmospheres, solar-terrestrial
relations, hydrology, oceanography, glaciology.

*NTIS Alerts: Ocean Sciences and Technology.* U.S.
Department of Commerce National Technical
Information Service. • Biweekly. $130 per year.
Provides descriptions of government-sponsored
research reports and software, with ordering
information.

*Oceanic Abstracts.* CSA. • Monthly. $1,645.00 per
year. Includes print and online editions. Covers
oceanography, marine biology, ocean shipping, and
a wide range of other marine-related subject areas.

## ALMANACS AND YEARBOOKS

*Earth Almanac: An Annual Geophysical Review of
the State of the Planet.* Natalie Goldstein.
Greenwood Publishing Group Inc. • $91.95.
Provides background information, statistics, and a
summary of major events relating to the atmosphere,
oceans, land, and fresh water.

## DIRECTORIES

*Sea Technology Buyers Guide/Directory.* • Annual.
$56 U.S. priority mail. Covers: Manufacturing,
service, research and development, engineering,
construction, drilling, equipment lease and rental
firms, and testing organizations providing goods and
services to the oceanographic, offshore, marine sciences, and undersea defense industries. Eight
informational sections. Entries include: Company
name, contact information, executives' names, list
of products and/or services.

## ONLINE DATABASES

*Applied Science and Technology Index Online.* H.W.
Wilson Co. • Provides online indexing of 500 major
scientific, technical, industrial, and engineering
periodicals. Time period is 1983 to date. Monthly
updates. Inquire as to online cost and availability.

*Aqualine.* Cambridge Scientific Abstracts L.P. •
Provides online citations and abstracts to a wide
variety of literature relating to the aquatic environment, including 400 journals, from 1960 to date.

Updating is monthly. Inquire as to online cost and
availability.

## PERIODICALS AND NEWSLETTERS

*Ocean Development and International Law.* Taylor
& Francis Group Journals. • Quarterly. $440
Individuals print. Peer-reviewed law journal.

*Ocean Engineering: An International Journal of
Research and Development.* Elsevier. • 18 times a
year. Qualified personnel, $261.00 per year; institu-
tions, $4,074.00 per year.

*Progress in Oceanography.* Elsevier. • $225
Individuals.

*Sea Technology.* Compass Publications Inc. •
Monthly. $60 U.S.. Marine industry's recognized
authority for ocean design, engineering and application of equipment and services in the global ocean
community.

## TRADE/PROFESSIONAL ASSOCIATIONS

Marine Technology Society. 1100 H St. NW, Ste.
LL100, Washington, DC 20005. Phone: (202)717-
8705; Fax: (202)347-4302; Email: membership@
mtsociety.org • URL: http://www.mtsociety.org •
Scientists, engineers, educators, and others with
professional interest in the marine sciences or
related fields; includes institutional and corporate
members. Disseminates marine scientific and technical information, including institutional,
environmental, physical, and biological aspects;
fosters a deeper understanding of the world's seas
and attendant technologies. Maintains 13 sections
and 29 professional committees. Conducts tutorials.

National Ocean Industries Association. 1120 G St.
NW, Ste. 900, Washington, DC 20005. Phone:
(202)347-6900; Fax: (202)347-8650; Email:
rmyers@noia.org • URL: http://www.noia.org •
Corporations organized to promote the common
business interests of the offshore and ocean-oriented
industries by: increasing public understanding of the
ocean's use and its relation to the economy;
encouraging interest in industrial, scientific,
recreational, research, and educational activities in
the field of ocean enterprise; encouraging the
development and use of the resources of the ocean
consistent with environmental practices and
safeguards; encouraging compatible use of ocean
resources; improving communication between
industry and the federal government. Supports
legislation and other governmental action favorable
to the offshore and ocean industry and counsels
against such action when it is not favorable. Seeks
to expand the role of the free enterprise system in the
development of ocean resources.

# OECD

*See* ORGANIZATION FOR ECONOMIC
COOPERATION AND DEVELOPMENT

# OFF-PRICE RETAILERS

*See* DISCOUNT HOUSES

# OFFICE APPLIANCES

*See* OFFICE EQUIPMENT AND SUPPLIES

# OFFICE AUTOMATION

*See also* DESKTOP PUBLISHING;
FACSIMILE SYSTEMS; MICROCOMPUT-
ERS AND MINICOMPUTERS; WORD
PROCESSING

## ABSTRACTS AND INDEXES

*Business Periodicals Index Retrospective.* EBSCO
Publishing Inc. • 11/year. Quarterly and annual
cumulations.

*Computer and Information Systems Abstracts
Journal: An Abstract Journal Pertaining to the
Theory, Design, Fabrication and Application of
Computer and Information Systems.* CSA. •
Monthly. $1,750 per year.

*Computer Science Index.* EBSCO Publishing Inc. •
Quarterly. $245 per year. Contains brief abstracts of
book and periodical literature covering all phases of
computing, including approximately 70 specific application areas.

*Inspec Direct.* Institution of Engineering and
Technology. • Monthly. $2,400 per year. Section C
of *Science Abstracts.*

*Key Abstracts: Business Automation.* Institution of
Engineering and Technology. • Monthly. $1,138.
Provides international coverage of journal and
proceedings literature.

## ONLINE DATABASES

*Wilson Business Abstracts Online.* H.W. Wilson Co.
• Indexes and abstracts 600 major business
periodicals, plus the *Wall Street Journal* and the
business section of the *New York Times.* Indexing is
from 1982, abstracting from 1990, with the two
newspapers included from 1993. Updated weekly.
Inquire as to online cost and availability. (*Business
Periodicals Index* without abstracts is also available
online.).

## PERIODICALS AND NEWSLETTERS

*EDP Weekly: The Leading Weekly Computer News
Summary.* Computer Age and EDP News Services. •
Weekly. $495.00 per year. Newsletter. Summarizes
news from all areas of the computer and
microcomputer industries.

*Law Technology News: Products, Systems, and
Services for Legal Professionals.* ALM Media
Properties LLC. • Monthly. 115 Dh. Features
descriptions of new technology products and
services of interest to the legal profession.

*Office Products Analyst: A Monthly Report Devoted
to the Analysis of Office Products.* Industry Analysts
Inc. • Monthly. $350.00 per year. Newsletter.
Includes user ratings of office automation
equipment.

## RESEARCH CENTERS AND INSTITUTES

University of Michigan - Collaboratory for Research
on Electronic Work. School of Information N, Rm.
2226, 1075 Beal Ave., Ann Arbor, MI 48109-2112.
Phone: (734)764-6131; Fax: (734)647-8045; Email:
finholt@umich.edu • URL: http://www.crew.umich.
edu/about.html • Concerned with the design and use
of computer-based tools for thinking and planning
in the professional office.

# OFFICE BUILDINGS

## PERIODICALS AND NEWSLETTERS

*Building Operating Management: The National
Magazine for Commercial and Institutional Build-
ings Construction, Renovation, Facility
Management.* Trade Press Media Group. • Monthly.
Free to qualified personnel.

*Business Facilities: The Location Advisor.* Group C
Media Inc. • Monthly. Free to qualified personnel;
others, $30.00 per year. Facility planning and site
selection.

*Commercial Building: Tranforming Plans into
Buildings.* Stamats Communications Inc. •
Bimonthly. $48.00 per year. Edited for building
contractors, engineers, and architects. Includes
special features on new products, climate control,
plumbing, and vertical transportation.

*National Real Estate Investor.* Penton. • Bimonthly.
Magazine on commercial real estate investment,
development and management. Includes annual
*Directory.* Market surveys by city.

*Office Relocation Magazine.* ORM Group. •

Bimonthly. $39.00 per year. Provides articles on the relocation of office facilities.

*Real Estate Economics: Journal of the American Real Estate and Urban Economics Association.* The MIT Press. • Quarterly. Covers a wide range of issues, from tax rules to brokers' commissions to corporate real estate including housing and urban economics, and the financial economics of real estate development and investment.

## PRICE SOURCES

*National Real Estate Index.* CB Richard Ellis Group Inc. • Price and frequency on application. Provides reports on commercial real estate prices, rents, capitalization rates, and trends in more than 65 metropolitan areas. Time span is 12 years. Includes urban office buildings, suburban offices, warehouses, retail properties, and apartments.

## STATISTICS SOURCES

*ULI Market Profiles: North America.* Urban Land Institute. • Annual. Members, $249.95; non-members, $299.95. Provides real estate marketing data for residential, retail, office, and industrial sectors. Covers 76 U. S. metropolitan areas and 13 major foreign metropolitan areas.

## TRADE/PROFESSIONAL ASSOCIATIONS

American Real Estate and Urban Economics Association. The Center for Real State Education and Research, 821 Academic Way, 223 RBB, Tallahassee, FL 32306-1110. Phone: 866-273-8321 or (850)644-7898; Fax: (850)644-4077; Email: areuea@areuea.org • URL: http://www.areuea.org • Members are real estate teachers, researchers, economists, and others concerned with urban real estate and investment.

British Council for Offices. 78-79 Leadenhall St., London EC3A 3DH, United Kingdom. Phone: 44 20 7283 0125; Fax: 44 20 7626 1553; Email: mail@ bco.org.uk • URL: http://www.bco.org.uk • Seeks to research, develop and communicate best practice in all aspects of the office sector. Provides a forum for the discussion and debate of issues affecting office sector. Advances understanding of effective office space.

Building Owners and Managers Association International. 1101 15th St. NW, Ste. 800, Washington, DC 20005-5021. Phone: 800-426-6292 or (202)408-2662; Fax: (202)326-6377; Email: info@boma.org • URL: http://www.boma.org • Formerly National Association of Building Owners and Managers.

National Association of Industrial and Office Properties. 2201 Cooperative Way, Ste. 300, Herndon, VA 20171-3034. Phone: (703)904-7100; Fax: (703)904-7942 • URL: http://www.naiop.org • Members are owners and developers of business, industrial, office, and retail properties. Formerly The Association of Commercial Real Estate.

## OFFICE DESIGN

### DIRECTORIES

*The SOURCE: Commercial Buildings Products Guide.* Stamats Business Media. • Annual. Lists sources of surface materials, furniture, lighting, etc., for interior designers. Formerly the annual buyers guide.

### PERIODICALS AND NEWSLETTERS

*Interiors and Sources.* L.C. Clark Publishing Company Inc. • Bimonthly. $27.00 per year. Promotes professionalism for interior designers and design firms. Includes special features on office systems, work stations, and office furniture.

*Today's Facility Manager: The Magazine of Facilities-Interior Planning Team.* Group C Media Inc. • Monthly. $30.00 per year. Covers office design, furnishings, and furniture, including open plan systems. Formerly *Business Interiors.*

*Tradeline Exclusive Reports.* Tradeline Inc. • Monthly. $120.00 per year. Newsletter. Covers the planning, design, construction, and renovation of of a variety of corporate facilities. Formerly *FM Data Monthly.*

## RESEARCH CENTERS AND INSTITUTES

Organizational Systems Research Association. Morehead State University, 150 University Blvd., Box 2478, Morehead, KY 40351-1689. Phone: (606)783-2718; Fax: (606)783-5025; Email: d.everett@moreheadstate.edu • URL: http://ais.site-ym.com/members/group_content_view. asp?group=89777&id=170352&terms=sigosra • Research areas include the analysis, design, and administration of office systems. Formerly Office Systems Research Association.

# OFFICE EQUIPMENT AND SUPPLIES

*See also* COMPUTERS; OFFICE FURNITURE INDUSTRY; WORD PROCESSING

## DIRECTORIES

*Annuaire Bureautique--Informatique.* Alphamedian Louis Johanet. • Annual. Covers: manufacturers and suppliers of office machinery in France.

*Australian Newsagent & Stationer Buyer's Guide.* Thorpe-Bowker. • Annual. $45. Covers: manufacturers and suppliers of office supplies in Australia; some foreign office supply manufacturers with their Australian agents; related organizations in Australia. Entries include: Manufacturer, supplier, agent, or organization name, address, phone.

*BPIA Directory and Buyer's Guide.* Independent Office Products and Furniture Dealers Association. • Annual. $100 payment must accompany order. Covers: Approximately 3,000 manufacturers, wholesalers, retailers, and sales and marketing representatives in the office products industry. Entries include: Company name, address, phone, principal executives, number of employees, branch stores, and products or services.

*BTA Membership Directory.* Business Technology Association. • Annual. $125 for members. Publication includes: List of 3,000 retailers and 500 manufacturers of typewriters, calculators, word processors, computers, dictation equipment, copying machines, mailing equipment, network equipment, and other office machines. Entries include: Company name, address, phone, fax, e-mail, website, names of executives; dealer listings include codes showing products handled.

*Computers & Office Equipment Importers & Buyers Directory.* BD International. • $132 Individuals. Covers: 8,000 importers, buyers, wholesalers, and distributors of computers and office equipment. Entries include: Name, address, phone, fax, contact person, nature of business, website, and e-mail.

*Dictating Machines & Supplies Wholesale Directory.* InfoGroup Inc. • Updated continuously; printed on request. Number of listings: 585. Entries include: Name, address, phone, size of advertisement, name of owner or manager, number of employees, year first in "Yellow Pages." Compiled from telephone company "Yellow Pages," nationwide.

*Directory of American Manufacturers & Exporters of Stationery Articles & Education Supplies.* EXIM Infotek Private Ltd. • $15 Individuals. Covers: 180 American manufacturers and exporters of address books, air brush colors, appointment books, ball pens, ball point pens, artists' brush, card and passport cases, clip boards, desk pads and accessories, desk pens, desk sets, desk top accessories, envelopes, felt tip, files, filing folders, fluorescent,

hobby brushes, ink, letter openers, markers, nibs, organizers, paper clips, parker pens, pencils, lead and mechanical pencils, non-mechanical pencils, steel pens, refills, rulers, scrapbooks, stationery products, stationery specialties, stationery supplies, stencil, and writing instruments. Entries include: Company name, postal address, telephone, fax, e-mail, website, contact person, designation, and product details.

*Directory of Computer and Point-of-Sale Systems for Office Products and Furniture Dealers.* Independent Office Products and Furniture Dealers Association. • Irregular. $60. Covers: Approximately 45 manufacturers and distributors of computer, point-of-sale, and contract furniture systems for the office products industry. Entries include: Company name, address, phone, description of product or service.

*Directory of Danish Importers of Office Equipment & Supplies.* EXIM Infotek Private Ltd. • $10 Individuals. Covers: 50 Danish importers of accounting and bookkeeping equipment, addressing and mailing equipment, banking equipment and supplies, calculators, cash registers, copying machines and supplies, fax and duplicating papers, office equipment and supplies, office machines, time recorders and timers, and typewriters. Entries include: Company name, postal address, telephone, fax, e-mail, website, contact person, designation, and product details.

*Directory of South Korean Manufacturers & Exporters of Stationery Articles & Education Supplies.* EXIM Infotek Private Ltd. • $250 Individuals. Covers: 70 South Korean manufacturers and exporters of drawing and mathematical instruments, filing systems, inks and artists colors, pencil cases, pens, pencils, rubber stamps and pads, staplers, stationeries, stationery and greeting cards, stationery articles, writing and drawing equipment. Entries include: Company name, postal address, telephone, fax, e-mail, website, contact person, designation, and product details.

*Directory of Wholesale Printing & Office Supplies Sources.* Gordon Press Publishers. • Irregular. $260. 95.

*Facilities Design & Management--Directory Issue.* Bpi Communications Inc. • $10. Publication includes: List of about 2,000 suppliers of office furnishings, equipment, services; professional associations. Entries include: For suppliers--Company name, address, phone, products or services. For associations--Name, address.

*France Environment.* Editions Louis Johanet. • Annual. Covers: 8,000 office machinery and supply manufacturers, wholesalers, and distributors in France. Entries include: Company name, address, phone, telex number.

*Government Product News--Buyers Guide for Office Equipment Issue.* Intertec Publishing. • Annual. $5. Publication includes: List of over 1,000 manufacturers of office equipment. Entries include: Company name, address, phone, name and title of contact.

*Imaging Supplies Annual.* Forrester Research Inc. • Annual. $125. Publication includes: List of over 300 service companies, suppliers and manufacturers of products such as ribbons, ink jet ink, toner, photo conductors, technology-specific papers and print elements for computer printers, typewriters, copiers, and other office equipment. Entries include: Company name, address, phone, fax, telex, name and title of contact, products, services, coding to indicate distribution method. Principal content of publication is articles about the imaging supplies industry.

*The International Directory of Importers - Office Equipment, Stationery and Supplies Importers.* Interdata. • Annual. $320 Individuals print. Covers: 7,100 international firms importing office equipment, stationery and supplies. Entries include: Company name and address, contact person, email, number of employees, year established, phone and telefaxes, business activity, bank references, as well as a listing of office equipment, stationery and supplies currently being imported.

*Office--Czech Republic.* I.S.M.C. Information Systems and Marketing Contacts Ltd. • $75. Covers: Companies in the office furnishment and office equipment industries in the Czech Republic.

*Office Equipment, Stationery & Supplies, Packaging Importer Directory.* Biz Focus Company Ltd. • $320 Individuals. Covers: 8,596 importers of accounting and invoicing machine, calculating machine, packaging and bottling machinery accessories, mailing and postal machinery and equipment, office machinery and equipment, and plastic articles for office use. Entries include: Company name, contact person, contact address, telephone number, fax number, e-mail, URL, and import products.

*Office Products Dealer--Product Buying Guide and Industry Directory Issue.* Hitchcock Publishing Co. • Annual. $15 plus $3.00 shipping. Publication includes: Lists of manufacturers, wholesalers, and distributors of furniture, machines, computer and word processing systems, and office products and equipment; manufacturers' representatives, and national industry associations that serve retail office products dealers.

*Office Products Representatives Alliance-- Membership Directory.* Office Products Representatives Alliance. • Annual. $50 Nonmembers. Covers: nearly 120 independent office product and office furniture distribution firms. Entries include: Firm name, address, phone, product and service provided.

*Office Supplies Directory.* InfoGroup Inc. • Annual. Lists companies that offer office supplies and equipment.

*Orion Blue Book--Copier.* Orion Research Corp. • Annual. $130 Individuals hardbound or CD. Publication includes: List of manufacturers of copiers and other office equipment. Entries include: Company name, address, phone. Principal content of publication is a listing of 3,091 office equipment products with the original retail value, value paid to customer on trade-in when in mint condition, and average value paid to customer on trade-in.

*Paper Shredding Machines Directory.* InfoGroup Inc. • Updated continuously; printed on request. Number of listings: 700. Entries include: Name, address, phone, size of advertisement, name of owner or manager, number of employees, year first in "Yellow Pages." Compiled from telephone company "Yellow Pages," nationwide.

*Smart/Utilize Catalog Index.* Property Management Systems Corp. • Bimonthly. Database covers: about 20,000 manufacturers of over 250,000 models of electronic, computer, office, and machine tool equipment; limited international coverage. Database includes: Company name, address, phone, subsidiary and branch names and locations, description of products with model number and performance specifications, trade/brand names, merger/buyout audit trail.

## OTHER SOURCES

*Business Automation Reference Service: Office Equipment.* Alltech Publishing Co. • Monthly. $100.00 per year. Looseleaf service.

*Business Consumers's Network.* Buyers Laboratory L.L.C. • Monthly. $795.00 per year. Looseleaf service. Tests office equipment and issues reports. Formerly *Buyers Laboratory Report on Office Products.*

## PERIODICALS AND NEWSLETTERS

*Business Consumer's Advisor.* Buyers Laboratory L.L.C. • Description: Focuses on office equipment and supplies, offering purchasing advice and explor-

ing methods of increasing office productivity through appropriate management of the equipment and its operators. Offers readers a chance to share their experiences, evaluate products and equipment, and gives results of Buyers Laboratory's testing.

## PRICE SOURCES

*Copier.* Orion Research Corp. • Annual. $39 Individuals. Quotes retail and wholesale prices of used office equipment. Original list prices and years of manufacture are also shown.

## TRADE/PROFESSIONAL ASSOCIATIONS

Business Technology Association. 12411 Wornall Rd., Ste. 200, Kansas City, MO 64145. Phone: 800-869-6688 or (816)941-3100; Fax: (816)941-4843 or (816)941-2829 • URL: http://www.bta.org • Dealers and resellers of office equipment and networking products and services. Offers 60 seminars on management, service, technology, and business systems. Conducts research, provides business-supporting services and benefits, including insurance, and legal counsel.

Independent Office Products and Furniture Dealers Association. 3601 E Joppa Rd., Baltimore, MD 21234. Phone: (410)930-8100; Fax: (410)931-8111; Email: cbates@nopanet.org • URL: http://www.iopfda.org • Formerly Office Furniture Dealers Alliance.

# OFFICE FORMS

*See* FORMS AND BLANKS

# OFFICE FURNITURE INDUSTRY

## DIRECTORIES

*BPIA Directory and Buyer's Guide.* Independent Office Products and Furniture Dealers Association. • Annual. $100 payment must accompany order. Covers: Approximately 3,000 manufacturers, wholesalers, retailers, and sales and marketing representatives in the office products industry. Entries include: Company name, address, phone, principal executives, number of employees, branch stores, and products or services.

*FDM--The Source--Woodworking Industry Directory.* Reed Elsevier Group plc Reed Business Information. • Annual. $25. Publication includes: List of over 1,800 suppliers to secondary woodworking industry; coverage includes Canada. Entries include: Company name, address, phone, fax, product lines.

*Office Products Representatives Alliance-- Membership Directory.* Office Products Representatives Alliance. • Annual. $50 Nonmembers. Covers: nearly 120 independent office product and office furniture distribution firms. Entries include: Firm name, address, phone, product and service provided.

## FINANCIAL RATIOS

*Annual Statement Studies.* Risk Management Association. • Annual. Compiled from over 280,000 financial statements.

*Annual Statement Studies: Industry Default Probabilities and Cash Flow Measures.* Risk Management Association. • Annual. $405 Nonmembers. Serves as a companion volume to the original *Annual Statement Studies.* Gives probability of default estimates on a percentage scale for more than 450 industries. Includes changes in position year-by-year for eight financial statement line items and provides percentage measures of cash flow.

## PERIODICALS AND NEWSLETTERS

*Contract: The Business Magazine of Commercial and Institutional Interior Design, and Architecture, Planning and Construction.* Nielsen Business Media

Inc. • Monthly. $94.00 per year. Firms engaged in specifying furniture and furnishings for commercial installations. Formerly *Contract Design.*

*FDM: For Builders of Cabinets, Fixtures, Furniture, Millwork Furniture Design a nd Manufacturing.* Chartwell Communications, Inc. • Monthly. Free to qualified personnel. Edited for furniture executives, production managers, and designers. Covers the manufacturing of household, office, and institutional furniture, store fixtures, and kitchen and bathroom cabinets.

*Office World News.* BUS Publications. • Monthly. Free to qualified personnel; others, $50.00 per year. Formerly *Office Products News.*

## TRADE/PROFESSIONAL ASSOCIATIONS

Business and Institutional Furniture Manufacturer's Association. 678 Front Ave. NW, Ste. 150, Grand Rapids, MI 49504-5368. Phone: (616)285-3963; Fax: (616)285-3765 • URL: http://www.bifma.org • Organized group of furniture manufacturers and suppliers addressing issues of common concern to the contract furnishings industry. Works to develop, expand, and promote work environments that enhance the productivity and comfort of customers.

# OFFICE IN THE HOME

*See* SELF-EMPLOYMENT

# OFFICE MACHINES

*See* OFFICE EQUIPMENT AND SUPPLIES

# OFFICE MANAGEMENT

*See also* ADMINISTRATION; SYSTEMS IN MANAGEMENT; WORD PROCESSING

## ABSTRACTS AND INDEXES

*Business Periodicals Index Retrospective.* EBSCO Publishing Inc. • 11/year. Quarterly and annual cumulations.

## CD-ROM DATABASES

*Business Abstracts with Full Text.* EBSCO Publishing Inc. • Includes full text articles from more than 460 business publications from 1982 to present. Indexing for nearly 880 publications.

## ONLINE DATABASES

*Wilson Business Abstracts Online.* H.W. Wilson Co. • Indexes and abstracts 600 major business periodicals, plus the *Wall Street Journal* and the business section of the *New York Times.* Indexing is from 1982, abstracting from 1990, with the two newspapers included from 1993. Updated weekly. Inquire as to online cost and availability. (*Business Periodicals Index* without abstracts is also available online.).

## PERIODICALS AND NEWSLETTERS

*Hard at Work.* Professional Training Associates Inc. • Monthly. $89.00 per year. Newsletter on common personnel problems of supervisors and office managers. Formerly *Practical Supervision.*

*Nine to Five Newsletter.* 9 to 5, National Association of Working Women. • 5/year. $25 Individuals. A newsletter dealing with the rights and concerns of women office workers.

## TRADE/PROFESSIONAL ASSOCIATIONS

British Council for Offices. 78-79 Leadenhall St., London EC3A 3DH, United Kingdom. Phone: 44 20 7283 0125; Fax: 44 20 7626 1553; Email: mail@bco.org.uk • URL: http://www.bco.org.uk • Seeks to research, develop and communicate best practice in all aspects of the office sector. Provides a forum for the discussion and debate of issues affecting office sector. Advances understanding of effective office space.

Nine to Five: National Association of Working Women. 207 E Buffalo St., Ste.211, Milwaukee, WI 53202. Phone: 800-522-0925 or (414)274-0925; Fax: (414)272-2870; Email: 9to5@9to5.org • URL: http://www.feminist.com/9to5.htm • Members are women office workers. Strives for the improvement of office working conditions for women and the elimination of sex and race discrimination.

## OFFICE PRACTICE

*See also* WORD PROCESSING

### HANDBOOKS AND MANUALS

*Secretarial/Word Processing Service*. Entrepreneur Press. • Looseleaf. $59.50. A practical guide to starting a secretarial and word processing business. Covers profit potential, start-up costs, market size evaluation, owner's time required, site selection, pricing, accounting, advertising, promotion, etc. (Start-Up Business Guide No. E1136.).

### PERIODICALS AND NEWSLETTERS

*Administrative Assistant's Update*. MPL Communications Inc. • Monthly. $189 Individuals Annual. Description: Offers useful news, information, and suggestions to administrative assistants. Features articles on aspects of secretarial work, including items on problem-solving, office automation, computerization, and grammar and vocabulary development.

*OfficePro*. Stratton Publishing and Marketing Inc. • Nine times a year. $25.00 per year. Provides statistics and other information about secretaries and office trends. Formerly *Secretary*.

*The Take-Charge Assistant*. American Management Association. • Monthly. Description: Features career and professional guidance, tips, and problem solving.

### TRADE/PROFESSIONAL ASSOCIATIONS

International Association of Administrative Professionals. 10502 N Ambassador Dr., Ste. 100, Kansas City, MO 64153. Phone: (816)891-6600; Fax: (816)891-9118; Email: jay.donohue@iaap-hq.org • URL: http://www.iaap-hq.org • Formerly Professional Secretaries International.

## OFFICE SUPPLIES

*See* OFFICE EQUIPMENT AND SUPPLIES

## OFFICIAL PUBLICATIONS

*See* GOVERNMENT PUBLICATIONS

## OFFICIALS AND EMPLOYEES

*See* GOVERNMENT EMPLOYEES

## OFFSHORE PETROLEUM INDUSTRY

*See also* PETROLEUM INDUSTRY

### ABSTRACTS AND INDEXES

*Applied Science and Technology Index*. EBSCO Publishing Inc. • 11/year. Indexes a wide variety of English language technical, industrial, and engineering periodicals.

### DIRECTORIES

*Lloyd's Marine Equipment Buyers' Guide*. Informa Group PLC. • Annual. $270.00. Published in the UK by Lloyd's List (www.lloydslist.com). Lists more than 6,000 companies worldwide supplying over 2,000 types of marine products and services, including offshore equipment.

*Worldwide Offshore Petroleum Directory*. PennWell Corp., Petroleum Div. • Annual. $135.00. Lists about 5,800 companies.

### PERIODICALS AND NEWSLETTERS

*Journal of Offshore Technology*. Institute of Marine Engineering, Science and Technology. • Bimonthly. Free to members; non-members, £52.00 per year. Covers the latest technological developments and trends for senior offshore engineers.

*Maritime IT & Electronics*. Institute of Marine Engineering, Science and Technology. • Bimonthly. £58.00 per year. Covers modern electronic technology as applied to all areas of the maritime industry. Includes navigation systems, communications, control systems, monitoring, diagnostics, and software.

*Ocean Oil Weekly Report: News, Analysis, and Market Trends of the Worldwide Offshore Oil and Gas Industry*. PennWell Corp., Petroleum Div. • Weekly. $495.00 per year. Newsletter with emphasis on the Gulf of Mexico offshore oil industry. Includes statistics.

*Offshore: Incorporating The Oilman*. PennWell Corp., Industrial Div. • Monthly. $75.00 per year.

*The Oilman Weekly Newsletter*. PennWell Corp., Petroleum Div. • Weekly. $1,990.00 per year. Newsletter. Provides news of developments concerning the North Sea and European oil and gas businesses. Each issue contains four pages of statistical data.

### RESEARCH CENTERS AND INSTITUTES

University of Texas at Austin - Geotechnical Engineering Center. Department of Civil, Architectural and Environmental Engineering, Cockrell School of Engineering, 1 University Station, C1792, Austin, TX 78712-0280. Phone: (512)232-3682; Fax: (512)471-6548; Email: k.stokoe@mail.utexas.edu • URL: http://www.ce.utexas.edu/dept/area/geotech/index.html • Areas of research include offshore complexes.

### TRADE/PROFESSIONAL ASSOCIATIONS

American Petroleum Institute. 1220 L St. NW, Washington, DC 20005-4070. Phone: (202)682-8000 • URL: http://www.api.org • Corporations in the petroleum and allied industries, including producers, refiners, marketers, and transporters of crude oil, lubricating oil, gasoline and natural gas. Provides public policy development, advocacy, research, and technical services to enhance the ability of the petroleum industry to fulfill its mission: meeting the nation's energy needs; enhancing the environmental, health, and safety performance of the industry; conducting research to advance petroleum technology, equipment, and standards; Consensus policies and collective action on issues impacting its members; and works collaboratively with all industry oil and gas associations, and other organizations, to enhance industry unity and effectiveness in its advocacy. Also provides the opportunity for standards development, technical cooperation and other activities to improve the industry's competitiveness through sponsorship of self-supporting programs.

Deep Draft Lubricant Association. c/o Shawn Konrad, Director, Belle Chasse Marine Transportation, 5813 Citrus Blvd., Harahan, LA 70123-5810. Phone: (504)837-3125; Email: information@ddla.org • URL: http://www.ddla.org • Promotes the interests of persons and firms engaged in the delivery of petroleum lubricants to deep draft vessels in the waters of the United States. Strives to create awareness of the individual operators, their suppliers and the industry of operational efficiencies and environmental regulations. Works to develop and improve performance standards and business methods.

Offshore Marine Service Association. 935 Graver St., Ste. 2040, New Orleans, LA 70112. Phone: (504)528-9411; Fax: (504)528-9415 • URL: http://www.offshoremarine.org • Owners, operators, suppliers and crews of vessels servicing offshore oil and mineral installations. Seeks to advance the industry worldwide; monitors legislation and governmental regulations affecting the construction of offshore oil marine equipment and the operation of these specialized vessels, used primarily to supply and service offshore oil and gas operations worldwide. Conducts educational and personnel development and training programs; disseminates information on insurance and legal issues affecting offshore vessel operations. Maintains numerous committees representing all types of vessels engaged in the support of offshore installations.

## OIL AND FATS INDUSTRY

### ABSTRACTS AND INDEXES

*Food Science and Technology Abstracts*. Ovid Technologies Inc. • Monthly. $1,780.00 per year. Provides worldwide coverage of the literature of food technology and food production.

*Foods Adlibra: Key to the World's Food Literature*. General Mills, Inc. Foods Adlibra Publications. • Semimonthly. $240.00 per year. Provides journal citations and abstracts to the literature of food technology and packaging.

### CD-ROM DATABASES

*OECD Statistical Compendium*. Organization for Economic Cooperation and Development. • Semiannual. $1,905.00 per year for 1 to 10 users. CD-ROM contains more than 730,000 monthly, quarterly, and annual time series for OECD countries, 1960 to date. Includes fully searchable data on agriculture, food, economic indicators, national accounts, employment, energy, finance, industry, technology, and foreign trade. Results can be displayed in various forms.

### DIRECTORIES

*Directory of Chinese Manufacturers & Exporters of Oil & Fats--Cooking & Vegetable*. EXIM Infotek Private Ltd. • $5 Individuals. Covers: 30 Chinese manufacturers and exporters of cooking oil, edible oil, oils and fats-edible, peanut oil, pine oils, rapeseed, soybean oil, vegetable oil. Entries include: Company name, postal address, city, country, phone, fax, e-mail and websites, contact person, designation, and product details.

*Directory of South Korean Manufacturers & Exporters of Oil & Fats--Cooking & Vegetable*. EXIM Infotek Private Ltd. • $5 Individuals. Covers: 20 South Korean manufacturers and exporters of oils and fats-edible. Entries include: Company name, postal address, city, country, phone, fax, e-mail and websites, contact person, designation, and product details.

*Directory of Taiwanese Manufacturers & Exporters of Oil & Fats--Cooking & Vegetable*. EXIM Infotek Private Ltd. • $5 Individuals. Covers: 20 South Korean manufacturers and exporters of oils and fats-edible. Entries include: Company name, postal address, city, country, phone, fax, e-mail and websites, contact person, designation, and product details.

*Major Food and Drink Companies of the World*. Cengage Learning Inc. • 12th edition. eBook. Published by Graham & Whiteside. Contains profiles and trade names for more than 9,200 important food and beverage companies in various countries. In addition to foods, includes both alcoholic and nonalcoholic drink products.

## INTERNET DATABASES

*Business 2.0 Web Guide to the Best Business Links.* Business 2.0 Media Inc. Phone: (415)293-4800; Email: support@business2.com • URL: http://www.business2.com/webguide • Web site presents an extensive, searchable directory of links to "the best, most informative, and authoritative web pages." Twenty main categories cover business, finance, career, company information, people, and technology topics, with thousands of subtopics, all linking to Web sites recommended by experienced business researchers. Fees: Free.

*Fedstats.* Federal Interagency Council on Statistical Policy. Phone: (202)395-7254 • URL: http://www.fedstats.gov • Web site features an efficient search facility for full-text statistics produced by more than 100 federal agencies, including the Census Bureau, the Bureau of Economic Analysis, and the Bureau of Labor Statistics. Boolean searches can be made within one agency or for all agencies combined. Links are offered to international statistical bureaus, including the UN, IMF, OECD, UNESCO, Eurostat, and 20 individual countries. Fees: Free.

*FreeLunch.com.* Economy.com, Inc. Phone: (610)696-8700; Fax: (610)696-1678 • URL: http://www.freelunch.com • Web site provides free access to more than 200 million economic and financial data series, covering industry, demographics, labor markets, prices, retail sales, government spending, trade, interest rates, housing starts, the stock market, etc. Data is available in either chart or table form. Searching is offered. Free, but registration required. Economy.com, Inc. also offers fee-based economic analysis at *The Dismal Scientist* site (www.dismal.com).

*Manufacturing Profiles.* U. S. Bureau of the Census. Phone: (301)763-4636 or (301)763-4100; Fax: (301)763-4794; Email: webmaster@census.gov • URL: http://www.census.gov/prod/www/abs/mfg-prof.html • The Census Bureau makes available free on PDF (Portable Document Format) an annual consolidation of the entire Current Industrial Report series, presenting "all the data compiled." Contains statistics on production, shipments, inventories, consumption, exports, imports, and orders for a wide variety of manufactured products.

*USDA.* U.S. National Institute of Standards and Technology. 100 Bureau Dr., Gaithersburg, MD 20899-1070. Phone: 800-877-8339 or (301)975-6478 or (202)720-2791; Fax: (301)975-8295; Email: inquiries@nist.gov • URL: http://www.nist.gov • The USDA home page has six sections: News and Information; What's New; About USDA; Agencies; Opportunities; Search and Help. Keyword searching is offered from the USDA home page and from various individual agency home pages. Agencies are the Economic Research Service, Agricultural Marketing Service, National Agricultural Statistics Service, National Agricultural Library, and about 12 others. Updating varies. Fees: Free.

## ONLINE DATABASES

*CAB Abstracts.* CABI. • Contains 46 specialized abstract collections covering over 10,000 journals and monographs in the areas of agriculture, horticulture, forest products, farm products, nutrition, dairy science, poultry, grains, animal health, entomology, etc. Time period is 1972 to date, with monthly updates. Inquire as to online cost and availability. *CAB Abstracts on CD-ROM* also available, with annual updating.

*Food Science and Technology Abstracts (online).* IFIS North American Desk. • Produced by International Food Information Service. Provides about 500,000 online citations, with abstracts, to the international literature of food science, technology, commodities, engineering, and processing. Approximately 2,000 periodicals are covered. Time period is 1969 to date, with monthly updates. Inquire as to online cost and availability.

## PERIODICALS AND NEWSLETTERS

*Inform: International News on Fats, Oils, and Related Materials.* American Oil Chemists Society. AOCS Press. • Monthly. Individuals, $120.00 per year; institutions, $360.00 per year. Covers a wide range of technical and business topics relating to the processing and utilization of edible oils, essential oils, and oilseeds.

## STATISTICS SOURCES

*Agricultural Statistics.* U.S. Department of Agriculture National Agricultural Statistics Service. • Annual. $46 Individuals. Provides a wide variety of statistical data relating to agricultural production, supplies, consumption, prices/price-supports, foreign trade, costs, and returns, as well as farm labor, loans, income, and population. In many cases, historical data is shown annually for 10 years. In addition to farm data, includes detailed fishery statistics.

*Survey of Current Business.* U. S. Government Printing Office. • Published by Bureau of Economic Analysis, U. S. Department of Commerce. Presents a wide variety of business and economic data.

## TRADE/PROFESSIONAL ASSOCIATIONS

American Oil Chemists' Society. 2710 S Boulder, Urbana, IL 61803-7190. Phone: (217)359-2344; Fax: (217)351-8091; Email: general@aocs.org • URL: http://www.aocs.org • Chemists, biochemists, chemical engineers, research directors, plant personnel, and others in laboratories and chemical process industries concerned with animal, marine, and vegetable oils and fats, and their extraction, refining, safety, packaging, quality control, and use in consumer and industrial products such as foods, drugs, paints, waxes, lubricants, soaps, and cosmetics. Sponsors short courses; certifies referee chemists; distributes cooperative check samples; sells official reagents. Maintains 100 committees. Operates job placement service for members only.

National Cottonseed Products Association. 866 Willow Tree Cir., Cordova, TN 38018. Phone: (901)682-0800; Fax: (901)682-2856; Email: info@cottonseed.com • URL: http://www.cottonseed.com • Oil mills, refiners, dealers, brokers, chemists, and others interested in margarine, cooking fats, soaps, lubricants, cattle feed, and fertilizer. Maintains uniform trading rules covering the buying, selling, weighing, sampling, and analysis of cottonseed and its products; supports extensive research program to increase processing efficiency and to improve the quality and usefulness of cottonseed products. Conducts research programs and market development activities.

National Institute of Oilseed Products. 750 National Press Bldg., 529 14th St. NW, Washington, DC 20045. Phone: (202)591-2461 or (202)785-3232; Fax: (202)223-9741; Email: niop@kellencompany.com • URL: http://www.oilseed.org • Shippers, brokers, growers, manufacturers, refiners, transportation, end users--anything to do with oilseeds. Establishes and maintains trading rules.

National Renderers Association. 500 Montgomery St., Ste. 310, Alexandria, VA 22314. Phone: (703)683-0155; Fax: (571)970-2279; Email: renderers@nationalrenderers.com • URL: http://nationalrenderers.org • Producers of tallow and grease products (for use in soap and lubricants), and meat meal (for use in animal feeds), obtained as by-products of the meat-packing industry. Conducts research and educational programs; provides international and domestic market development services and legislative representation.

## OIL BURNER INDUSTRY

*See* FUEL OIL INDUSTRY

## OIL FIELD MACHINERY

*See* PETROLEUM EQUIPMENT INDUSTRY

## OIL FUEL INDUSTRY

*See* FUEL OIL INDUSTRY

## OIL INDUSTRY

*See* PETROLEUM INDUSTRY

## OIL MARKETING

*See* PETROLEUM MARKETING

## OIL TANKERS

*See* TANK SHIPS

## OILSEED INDUSTRY

*See* OIL AND FATS INDUSTRY

## OLD AGE

*See* RETIREMENT

## OLD AGE AND SURVIVORS INSURANCE

*See* SOCIAL SECURITY

## OLD AGE HOMES

*See* NURSING HOMES

## OLDER CONSUMERS

*See* MATURE CONSUMER MARKET

## OLDER WORKERS

*See* EMPLOYMENT OF OLDER WORKERS

## OLEOMARGARINE INDUSTRY

*See* MARGARINE INDUSTRY

## OLIVE OIL INDUSTRY

### DIRECTORIES

*Major Food and Drink Companies of the World.* Cengage Learning Inc. • 12th edition. eBook. Published by Graham & Whiteside. Contains profiles and trade names for more than 9,200 important food and beverage companies in various countries. In addition to foods, includes both alcoholic and nonalcoholic drink products.

### INTERNET DATABASES

*USDA.* U.S. National Institute of Standards and Technology. 100 Bureau Dr., Gaithersburg, MD 20899-1070. Phone: 800-877-8339 or (301)975-6478 or (202)720-2791; Fax: (301)975-8295; Email: inquiries@nist.gov • URL: http://www.nist.gov •

**For publishers' addresses, refer to SOURCES CITED section at the back of the book.**

The USDA home page has six sections: News and Information; What's New; About USDA; Agencies; Opportunities; Search and Help. Keyword searching is offered from the USDA home page and from various individual agency home pages. Agencies are the Economic Research Service, Agricultural Marketing Service, National Agricultural Statistics Service, National Agricultural Library, and about 12 others. Updating varies. Fees: Free.

## ONLINE DATABASES

*Food Science and Technology Abstracts (online).* IFIS North American Desk. • Produced by International Food Information Service. Provides about 500,000 online citations, with abstracts, to the international literature of food science, technology, commodities, engineering, and processing. Approximately 2,000 periodicals are covered. Time period is 1969 to date, with monthly updates. Inquire as to online cost and availability.

## STATISTICS SOURCES

*Agricultural Statistics.* U.S. Department of Agriculture National Agricultural Statistics Service. • Annual. $46 Individuals. Provides a wide variety of statistical data relating to agricultural production, supplies, consumption, prices/price-supports, foreign trade, costs, and returns, as well as farm labor, loans, income, and population. In many cases, historical data is shown annually for 10 years. In addition to farm data, includes detailed fishery statistics.

## TRADE/PROFESSIONAL ASSOCIATIONS

Association of Food Industries. 3301 Rte. 66, Ste. 205, Bldg. C, Neptune, NJ 07753. Phone: (732)922-3008; Fax: (732)922-3590; Email: info@afius.org • URL: http://www.afius.org • Food processors, importers, and import agents nationally; food brokers in the New York metropolitan market and overseas food exporters. Maintains arbitration tribunal, government relations, and information services.

# ON-THE-JOB TRAINING

*See* TRAINING OF EMPLOYEES

# ONION INDUSTRY

## INTERNET DATABASES

*USDA.* U.S. National Institute of Standards and Technology. 100 Bureau Dr., Gaithersburg, MD 20899-1070. Phone: 800-877-8339 or (301)975-6478 or (202)720-2791; Fax: (301)975-8295; Email: inquiries@nist.gov • URL: http://www.nist.gov • The USDA home page has six sections: News and Information; What's New; About USDA; Agencies; Opportunities; Search and Help. Keyword searching is offered from the USDA home page and from various individual agency home pages. Agencies are the Economic Research Service, Agricultural Marketing Service, National Agricultural Statistics Service, National Agricultural Library, and about 12 others. Updating varies. Fees: Free.

## PERIODICALS AND NEWSLETTERS

*National Onion Association--Newsletter.* National Onion Association. • Quarterly. Description: Provides information on the onion industry.

## STATISTICS SOURCES

*Agricultural Statistics.* U.S. Department of Agriculture National Agricultural Statistics Service. • Annual. $46 Individuals. Provides a wide variety of statistical data relating to agricultural production, supplies, consumption, prices/price-supports, foreign trade, costs, and returns, as well as farm labor, loans, income, and population. In many cases, historical data is shown annually for 10 years. In ad-

dition to farm data, includes detailed fishery statistics.

## TRADE/PROFESSIONAL ASSOCIATIONS

National Onion Association. 822 7th St., Ste. 510, Greeley, CO 80631-3941. Phone: (970)353-5895; Fax: (970)353-5897; Email: info@onions-usa.org • URL: http://www.onions-usa.org • Growers, brokers, grower-shippers, shippers, suppliers, and support professionals engaged in the onion industry. Promotes the onion industry. Compiles monthly statistical report of stocks-on-hand, acreage, yield, and production of onions in the U.S. Lobbies issues of importance to national onion industry.

# ONLINE COMMERCE

*See* ELECTRONIC COMMERCE

# ONLINE INFORMATION SYSTEMS

*See also* COMPUTER COMMUNICATIONS; INFORMATION INDUSTRY; INTERNET

## ABSTRACTS AND INDEXES

*Computer and Information Systems Abstracts Journal: An Abstract Journal Pertaining to the Theory, Design, Fabrication and Application of Computer and Information Systems.* CSA. • Monthly. $1,750 per year.

*Computer Science Index.* EBSCO Publishing Inc. • Quarterly. $245 per year. Contains brief abstracts of book and periodical literature covering all phases of computing, including approximately 70 specific application areas.

*Information Science Abstracts.* American Society for Information Science. Information Today, Inc. • Nine times a year. $725.00 per year.

*Internet and Personal Computing Abstracts (print edition).* EBSCO Publishing Inc. • Quarterly. $269.00 per year, including cumulative index. Provides more than 10,000 abstracts annually from both trade and academic publications. Covers computer hardware, software, product reviews, Web topics, e-commerce, networks, corporate news, security, and related topics. Formerly *Microcomputer Abstracts.*

*Library Literature and Information Science Index.* H.W. Wilson Co. • Quarterly. Annual cumulation. Price varies.

*LISA: Library and Information Science Abstracts.* R.R. Bowker L.L.C. • 13 times a year. $1,055.00 per year; includes print and online editions.

## ALMANACS AND YEARBOOKS

*Annual Society for Information Science and Technology, Information and Business Div.* Martha E. Williams, editor. Information Today, Inc. • Annual. $79.95 Members. Published on behalf of the American Society for Information Science (ASIS). Covers trends in planning, basic techniques, applications, and the information profession in general.

*Business-Professional Online Markets.* SIMBA Information Inc. • Annual. $1,995 print. Provides a review of current conditions in the online information industry. Profiles of major database producers and online services are included.

## CD-ROM DATABASES

*LISA Plus.* Cambridge Scientific Abstracts L.P. • Quarterly. $2,000 per year. CD-ROM version of Library Information and Science Abstracts, providing abstracting and indexing of the world's library and information science literature, 1969 to date. Contains more than 180,000 citations.

*WILSONDISC: Library Literature and Information*

*Science Index.* H.W. Wilson Co. • Quarterly. Includes unlimited access to the online version of *Library Literature.* Provides CD-ROM indexing of about 400 periodicals, covering a wide range of topics having to do with libraries, library management, and the information industry.

## DIRECTORIES

*ABC/Dienstverleners.* ABC Business Directories BV. • Quarterly. Database covers: 24,000 Dutch service companies, including accounting firms, law firms, car leasing firms, audiovisual consultants, transport companies, advertising agencies, hotels, and restaurants. Entries include: Company name, address, phone, fax, telex; executive names; capital; bank affiliation; year founded; number of employees; product information.

*ABC Netherlands.* ABC voor Handel en Industries C.V. • Quarterly. Database covers: 120,000 profiles of Dutch companies in all lines of business. Entries include: Company name, address, management, products, number of employees, sales, founding year, parent companies, subsidiaries, branches and offices abroad, export/import activities.

*ABC voor Handel en Industrie.* ABC voor Handel en Industries C.V. • Quarterly. Database covers: Approximately 120,000 profiles of Dutch manufacturers, importers, import agents and service providers and their products/services; also includes some 46,000 foreign houses' representatives in Holland. Entries include: Company name, address, phone, fax, telex; executive names; capital; bank affiliation; year founded; number of employees.

*ADVERTISE.* Deutscher Sparkassenverlag GmbH. • Weekly. Database covers: Worldwide cooperative venture offers and requests, covering product import and export, technology transfer, joint ventures, and related ventures. Emphasis is on opportunities for small and medium-sized European companies. Entries include: Company name, address, phone; company profile; descriptors and codes for products and services; type of cooperation sought; dates of entry and validity.

*All India Directory/Database of Automobile Components/Parts Manufacturers, Exporters, Dealers, Suppliers.* NIIR Project Consultancy Services. • $250 Individuals CD-ROM. Covers: 11,000 automobile components/parts manufacturers and exporters, dealers, suppliers in India. Entries include: Company name, addresses, pin, city, phone, mobile (wherever available), fax (wherever available), e-mail (wherever available), website (wherever available), products details.

*American Business Database.* Mailer's Software. • Covers: More than 1.2 million listings of all the companies and organizations in the U.S. that possess their own unique ZIP Plus 4 code. Entries include: Company name, phone, complete mailing address with ZIP Plus 4 and Carrier Route Codes; state and county FIPS Codes; Standard Industrial Classification (SIC) code.

*Analyse Major Databases from European Sources.* Bureau van Dijk S.A. • Annual. Covers: 150,000 of the top companies in Europe. Entries include: Company name, address, phone, fax, telex; date of incorporation.

*Analysis.* FT Analysis. • Daily. Database covers: all U.K. publicly quoted and Unlisted Securities Market (USM) companies. Database includes: Company name, address, phone, principal activities, names and titles of key personnel, business history, major holdings, capital structure, and share prices, key ratios, dividend data, balance sheets, and profit and loss summaries for the most recent five years. Also includes complete text of recent company announcements filed with the London Stock Exchange, complete text of more than 7,000 stockbroker research reports, and complete text of U.K. annual reports.

*Asian Company Profiles.* Asian Company Profiles Ltd. • Bimonthly. Database covers: over 500,000 Asian-based companies (including companies in China, Malaysia, Singapore, Indonesia, Korea, Hong Kong, Philippines, Thailand, Vietnam, Australia, New Zealand, Laos, Cambodia, Taiwan, and Papua New Guinea). Database includes: Company name, address, phone, fax, E-mail, products, Standard Industrial Classification (SIC) codes and Harmonized codes, year established, number of employees, issued capital, names and titles of key personnel, company type, subsidiaries and affiliates, organizational chart, factory description and size, product descriptions, related companies, financial data, importers' agencies, trade statistics. Expanded coverage to include companies of other Asian nations is planned.

*ASTREE: L'Annuaire Commercial Electronique.* Bureau van Dijk S.A. • Quarterly. Database covers: Company reports on 800,000 French companies. Entries include: Company name, address, date of incorporation, company type, type of activity, managers, turnover, export, profit, shareholders' funds, debt, number of employees, shareholders, and subsidiaries.

*ATTILA Business Database.* Ost-West Direkt Werbegesellschaft mbH. • Quarterly. Database covers: over 2.6 million companies in Bulgaria, Poland, the Czech Republic, Hungary, Lithuania, and the Slovak Republic. Database includes: Company name, address, phone, fax, legal status, ownership, foundation date/capital, registration court, governmental district, contact person, number of employees, products, line of business.

*Austrian Companies Database.* Hoppenstedt Produktinformationen GmbH. • Semiannual. €2,318. Database covers: 15,000 major companies (or those which bill at least 70 million annually and/or have at least 100 employees) and 55,000 business executives in Austria. Entries include: Name, address, phone, fax, management names, range of products or services, number of employees, revenue and equity.

*Automated Sources of Information in the Department of Commerce.* U.S. Department of Commerce National Technical Information Service. • $25 plus $5 handling fee (PB88-132568AHT). Diskette. Covers: Agencies of the United States Department of Commerce that produce or support online databases, electronic bulletin boards, information centers, and publications. Database includes: Agency name, address, phone, name and title of contact, information system content, titles of principal publications.

*BISNES Plus.* INFOTRADE N.V. • Daily. Database covers: Financial and descriptive information on more than one million Belgian companies and private businesses. Entries include: Name, address, name and title of contact, commercial registration numbers, data and form of incorporation, bank accounts, association memberships, principal language, number of employees, names of management personnel, activities and products, trademarks, trading partners, financial statements for the most recent three years.

*Bottin Entreprises.* Bottin S.A. • Annual. Database covers: about 100,000 French companies. Database includes: Company name, address, phone, telex, type of business, capital, legal incorporation, formal structure, branches or other locations, if any; some include names of directors, financial turnover (period specified), number of employees.

*BPO, Call Center IT, Telecom, Computer Software & Hardware Companies Database, Directory of India.* NIIR Project Consultancy Services. • $200 Individuals CD-ROM. Covers: BPO, call center, telecom, computer software and hardware companies in India. Entries include: Name of companies, address, city, pin code, phone, fax, 2,250

e-mail, 2,350 website and contact person with designation.

*British Export Interactive Website.* Reed Business Information. • Database covers: 17,000 companies in the United Kingdom, as well as the products and services they actively export. Database includes: Full electronic commerce.

*Brokers.* IZUM Information Service. • Quarterly. Database covers: Approximately 22 databases currently available on information providers and/or database producers in Slovenia. Part of the INFORS database. Entries include: Database name, acronym, date status, topic, language, number of records, update frequency, source of data, host, vendor, and producer.

*Browning Database Review.* Browning Associates. • Irregular. $50 payment with order. Covers: over 125 databases providing Canadian business information. Entries include: Database name and acronym, content, scope, time span, frequency of update, size, percentage of Canadian content, connect rates and requirements; name, address, and phone of producer and of the Canadian and/or United States distributor.

*BUSINESS.* BUSINESS Datenbanken GmbH. • Monthly. Database covers: About 35,000 manufacturers, importers and exporters, research establishments, chambers of commerce, trade promotion agencies, banks and investment companies offering or seeking business opportunities worldwide. Database includes: Name of company, address, type of opportunity or business, product and country codes.

*Business Database Finder.* The Information Advisor. • Annual. $99. Covers: Business databases and online hosts. Database includes: Comparative charts/tables showing features and costs of databases. Entries include: Name of database, description of product/service.

*Business Directory for Americans Abroad.* TeleDiplomacy Inc. • Database covers: Businesses and immigration, import, and export issues of interest to U.S. Citizens travelling abroad. Entries include: Contact information.

*Business Directory for Diplomats.* TeleDiplomacy Inc. • Database covers: Businesses and immigration, import, and export issues of interest to diplomats in the Washington, DC, area. Entries include: Contact information.

*Business Directory for Educators.* TeleDiplomacy Inc. • Database covers: Items of interest to educators on business trips abroad. Entries include: Contact information.

*Business Directory for Foreign Visitors.* TeleDiplomacy Inc. • Database covers: Businesses and immigration, import, and export issues of interest to visitors to the United States. Entries include: Contact information.

*The Business Information Report.* Dun & Bradstreet Inc. • Continuous. Database covers: More than 9 million public and private U.S. Companies. Database includes: Company name, address, history, financial and sales data, number of employees, selling terms, products/services.

*Business Litigation Database.* Trans Union Credit Information Co. • Continuous. Database covers: 8 million court records on companies from New York and New Jersey, including suits, judgments, satisfactions, bankruptcies, foreclosures (for New Jersey only), and federal, state, and city tax liens. Entries include: Defendant name and address, plaintiff name and address, court of filing, filing date, docket number, dollar amount of action, type of action.

*Business: Your Partner in China Plus.* Computing Center of the Ministry of Foreign Trade and Economic Cooperation. • $650. Database covers: Listings concerning China's foreign trade, including customs, commodity inspection agencies, insurance agencies, and banks. Database includes:

International transport information, animal quarantine laws, and travel agencies.

*Camerdata.* Camerdata S.A. • Monthly. Database covers: Approximately 2 million Spanish business firms. Database includes: Company name, address, number of employees, sector of activity.

*Canadian Federal Corporations and Directors.* Postmedia Network Inc. • Monthly. Covers: About 400,000 federally incorporated Canadian companies. Database includes: Company name, address, date incorporated, parent or subsidiary companies, financial data for two years, names and home addresses of directors.

*Canadian Financial Database.* Globe Interactive. • Database covers: about 500 of the leading Canadian corporations. Database includes: Company name, address, phone, names and titles of key personnel, financial data.

*CCN Business Information Database.* CCN Business Information Ltd. • Continuous. Database covers: Approximately 3 million companies in the U.K. Database includes: Company name, address, phone, registration number, date and legal form of incorporation, holding company, directors, auditor, number of employees, prinicpal activities, financial data.

*China's Machine & Electric Enterprises and Products Database.* Computing Center of the Ministry of Foreign Trade and Economic Cooperation. • $1,600. Database covers: 100,000 Chinese machine and electric companies. Entries include: Contact information, office hours, executives, bankers, number of employees, contact person, registered capital, sales, list of products.

*China's Manufacturers and Products Database.* Computing Center of the Ministry of Foreign Trade and Economic Cooperation. • $3,600. Database covers: 50,000 manufacturers in China. Entries include: Contact information, office hours, executives, bankers, number of employees, contact person, registered capital, sales, list of products.

*CINFOLINK Directory of Information Services and the Internet in China.* CINFOLINK Services. • Biennial. $20 U.S. plus airmail postage within North America $2.50. Covers: nearly 400 electronic databases and information networks, approximately 225 related publication and information sources (including associations, research institutes of the Chinese Academy of Sciences, universities and colleges, and libraries), and 150 current Internet sources in China and Hong Kong. Entries include: For database services--Name, description, type of data, language, size, updating frequency, timespan; producer name and address; contact name, phone, fax; other formats, subject(s), status, price, etc. For publication sources--Name, address, phone, fax, titles produced, description.

*CIS-States Companies.* COMMIT GmbH. • Quarterly. Database covers: companies in the nations of the Commonwealth of Independent States. Database includes: Company name, address, legal status, products, number of employees.

*Commodity Price Statistics.* United Nations Publications. • Database covers: Free-market prices and price indices for selected commodities that concern commodity-dependant countries. Price indices are provided for commodity groups (including food, tropical beverages, vegetable oilseeds and oils, agricultural raw materials, minerals, ores and metals), and for all groups in current dollars and SDRs.

*Companies in Greenland at Randburg.* Randburg.com. • Database covers: Companies in Greenland. Entries include: Company name, address, phone, fax, description.

*Company Intelligence.* Information Access Co. Gale Group Inc. • Daily. Database covers: over 160,000 private and public U.S. companies, and 30,000 international companies. Database includes: Company name, address, phone, variant company name, description of business, Standard Industrial Classification (SIC) codes, year founded, special features, ultimate and immediate parent companies, number of employees, information sources, names and titles of key personnel, financial data; ten most recent citations about the company from articles in over 5,000 publications indexed by Information Access Company.

*Corridor Directory.* Miller Freeman UK Ltd. • Database covers: More than 10,000 UK manufacturers, retailers, agents, wholesalers, service suppliers, and associations in the furniture and furnishings industry. Entries include: Company information.

*Creditreform-Datenbank.* Verband der Vereine Creditreform e.V. • Daily. Database covers: Credit information on more than 3,100,000 million joint stock and individual trading companies in Austria and Germany. Entries include: Company name, address, legal form, dates of formation or reformation, capital, partners, number of employees, product line, financial indicators covering capital, obligations, annual income, property and equipment, warehouse stocks, loan payment record, liabilities, credit rating, biographical information on company principal officials.

*D & B-Dun's Market Identifiers.* Dun & Bradstreet Inc. • Quarterly. Covers 7.5 million public and private companies with at least five employees or $1 million in sales.

*DASH: Directors and Shareholdings.* Bureau van Dijk S.A. • Database covers: One million limited companies and two million directors combined with details on individual and corporate shareholders in the United Kingdom. Entries include: Company name, address, phone, fax, activity, employee range, legal form, status, capital, turnover, holding companies and corporate shareholders; director name, date of birth, address, marital status, nationality, occupation, qualification, appointment date.

*Database, Directory of MNCs Companies in India.* NIIR Project Consultancy Services. • $100 U.S. CD-ROM. Covers: Multinational companies in India. Entries include: Name, address, country of origin, phone, fax, e-mail, website, CEO name.

*Database of World Wide General Traders.* NIIR Project Consultancy Services. • $200 Individuals CD-ROM. Covers: Worldwide general traders (exporters and importers). Entries include: Company name, postal address, city, state, pin code, phone, fax and email (2,100,000+).

*DealBase II: An Electronic Database of Acquisition Opportunities.* Business Publications Inc. • Monthly. $425 per year. Diskette. Database covers: Over 675 of middle market companies, currently available for acquisition, with annual revenues between 3 and 75 million dollars. Database includes: Company name, location, description, revenues, profitability, purchase price, industry, contact information, merger/acquisition data.

*Der Runde Herold.* Herold Business Data GmbH. • Annual. Database covers: Approximately 225,000 Austrian companies. Entries include: Company name, address, phone, type of business, region, and postal code. For the 10,000 largest companies, includes turnover figures, number of employees, and key personnel.

*Dial-A-Fax Business Directory: World's Largest Resources of Fax Services.* Dial-A-Fax Directories Corp. • $289 plus 4.95 postage. Database covers: Approximately 1,400,000 companies in the United States. Entries include: Name, city, state, phone, fax, Standard Industrial Classification (SIC) code.

*DIALOG Business Connection.* The Dialog Corp. • Continuous. Database covers: 10,000,000 private and public companies in the United States; over 1,000,000 companies in Canada and Europe.

Database includes: Company name, address, phone, corporate affiliations, key officers, names of directors, products or services, revenue, sales volume, market share, financial information, number of employees, merger activities, new equipment or facility purchases. This online service provides access to 25 databases already available on DIALOG as individual files, including "D&B--Dun's Market Identifiers," "D&B--Dun's Financial Records," "Disclosure," "Media General Databank," and "BusinessWire." The database provides the ability to conduct corporate intelligence, financial screening, and sales prospecting; to locate information on products and markets; to gain access to the latest news; and to set up an electronic clipping service.

*Direct Mail Service.* Information Resource Group. • Continuous. $150 per thousand names. Company maintains a database of about 1,200,000 Information Technology (IT) and corporate professionals at 200,000 companies throughout the United States and Canada; with more than 400 functional job titles to choose from. Database includes: Company name, address, names and titles of key personnel, number of employees, geographical area served, financial data, Standard Industrial Classification (SIC) code, type of hardware system and software utilized.

*Directory, Database of Small & Medium Enterprise (SMEs) in India.* NIIR Project Consultancy Services. • $250 Individuals CD-ROM. Covers: 250,000+ small & medium enterprises (SME's) in India. Entries include: Name, full postal address, postal code, phone, contact person, company name, address, city, pin code, fax, e-mail, website, products details.

*Directory of Automated Criminal Justice Information Systems.* U.S. Bureau of Justice Statistics. • $60. Covers: Over 1,870 computerized information systems serving over 700 police, courts, state and local government judicial and correctional agencies. Entries include: Description of system or agency; acronym; type of system; functions; hardware and software configuration; function names, addresses, and phone numbers of agency contact.

*Disclosure SEC Database.* Disclosure Inc. • Weekly. Database covers: Approximately 11,000 public companies that have at least 500 shareholders of one class of stock and a minimum of five million dollars in assets, and have filed a 10K, 20F, or Registration Statement with the Securities and Exchange Commission within the preceding 18 months. Database includes: Company name, address, phone, names and titles of key personnel and directors, state in which incorporated; Standard Industrial Classification (SIC) code; Fortune, Forbes, CUSIP, DUNS numbers; auditors, subsidiaries; annual and quarterly balance sheets and income statements; five-year financial summary; sources and uses of funds, price/earnings data, stock transfer agent, text of management discussion and President's letter, and other information. Institutional holdings, 5% ownership holdings, and ownership by insiders for 5,000 companies are reported in "Disclosure/Spectrum Ownership," updated quarterly; detailed data list of specific institutions and individuals, their relationship to the company, their holdings, and their most recent trades. Full text of documents available in print and on microfiche.

*Dun & Bradstreet Germany.* Dun & Bradstreet Inc. • €70 Individuals. Database covers: Over 160 million companies in Germany. Database includes: Company name, address, phone, names and titles of key personnel, number of employees, turnover, financial data, SIC code.

*Dun & Bradstreet Italy.* CRIBIS D & B Ltd. • Database covers: Approximately 473,000 companies in Italy. Database includes: Company name, address, names and titles of key personnel, number of employees, turnover, financial data, line of business, SIC code.

*Dun & Bradstreet Swiss Company Information.* Dun & Bradstreet AG. • Monthly. Database covers: more than 180,000 businesses in Switzerland and Liechtenstein. Database includes: Company name, address, phone, headquarter and subsidiary, name and title of contact, year founded, SIC code, business activities, number of employees, senior executive name, sales volume, accounting and banking firm, DUNS number.

*Dun & Bradstreet United States.* Dun & Bradstreet Canada Ltd. • Quarterly. Database covers: 1.1 million U.S. businesses with 10 or more employees. Database includes: Company name, address, phone, chief executive officer, type of business, DUNS number, company status, subsidiary, manufacturing activity, language preference, geographic code, SIC codes, year current control of company established, date record was updated, number of employees at listed location, number of employees total, total sales volume for listed location.

*Dundsdata.* Dun & Bradstreet France S.A. • Database covers: more than 9 million European businesses, with emphasis on France. Database includes: Company name, address, product trade name, capital, net value, financial data, affiliates and subsidiaries, principal directors.

*Dun's Business Update.* Dun & Bradstreet Inc. • Biweekly. Database covers: more than 600,000 business establishments in the U.S. Database includes: Company name, address, phone, line of business, chief executive officer, number of employees, corporation affiliation, company status, sales.

*Dun's Electronic Business Directory.* Dun & Bradstreet Inc. • Quarterly. Database covers: about 9 million U.S. financial services, professionals, hospitals and other medical facilities, wholesalers, retailers, construction firms, business services, government agencies, manufacturers, agriculture and mining companies, transportation firms, and utilities. Database includes: For businesses--Name, address, phone, county, Standard Industrial Classification (SIC) code, description of business, population of city, number of employees, type of advertising in yellow pages, whether a company, a corporation, or an individual.

*Dun's Financial Reference Plus.* Dun & Bradstreet Inc. • $5,275 3 years. Database covers: over 1,500,000 public and private U.S. companies. Database includes: For all companies--Company name, address, phone, D-U-N-S company number, Standard Industrial Classification (SIC) code, year established, number of employees, name of principal and owners, executive profiles, business activities, subsidiary and branch names and locations. For 750,000 businesses--Up to three-year detailed spreadsheet analysis of financial statements, including 14 key performance ratios, and balance sheet, income statement, and other financial data.

*Dunsmarketing.* Dun & Bradstreet France S.A. • Database covers: over 240,000 French companies with more than 10 employees or annual turnover exceeding 10 million French Francs. Database includes: Company name, address, phone, year founded, executive officer name and title, number of employees, sector of activity, SIC code, business and import/export volume, affiliate and subsidiary companies, financial data.

*DunsPrint Worldwide.* Dun & Bradstreet Inc. • Continuous. Database covers: Approximately 16 million companies worldwide. Database includes: Company name, address, phone, legal structure, products and services, SIC code, number of employees, branch offices, officer name, parent and subsidiary companies, company history, operation summary, legal suits against company, financial data, stock issues, projected sales, payment history, DUNS number.

*DunsScope.* Dun & Bradstreet France S.A. • Daily.

Database covers: Approximately 2 million French businesses and 18 million businesses in other countries. Database includes: Company name, address, phone, legal structure, products/services, SIC code, number of employees, officer name and title, parent and subsidiary companies, branch offices, company history, operations summary, legal suits against company, financial data, stock issues and mergers, dividends, review of payment history, credit rating, company's bank.

*Eastern Europe: A Directory and Sourcebook.* Euromonitor International Business Reference Div. • $440. Publication includes: Lists of publishers of private research, journals and newsletters, online databases, consultants, and abstracts and indexes providing information on eastern Europe. Database includes: Economic and demographic data, analysis of business practices, markets, investment opportunities, and rankings.

*EMMA: Easy Mailing and Marketing Applications.* Bureau van Dijk S.A. • Quarterly. Database covers: More than 1,000,000 companies in the United Kingdom. Entries include: Company name, address, date of incorporation, company type, activity, directors, holding companies, turnover, net assets, pretax profit, number of employees.

*Euroretailnet.* Corporate Intelligence Group. • Database covers: Approximately 3,000 retailers in 17 European countries, including U.S. and Japanese companies doing business in Europe. Entries include: Company name, address, phone, fax, names and titles of key personnel, geographical area served; number of employees, financial data, subsidiary and branch names and locations; description; promotional activity; distribution system; information technology utilized.

*Export/Import Markets: Puerto Rico Edition.* Direct Marketing & Media Group Inc. • $30. Covers: about 1,000 firms located in Puerto Rico and engaged in exporting, importing, and supplying services to international trade (including steamship lines and agents, banks, rental firms, freight forwarders, and custom house brokers). Entries include: For steamship lines and agents--Firm name, address, phone, fax, telex, name of firms represented. For others--Company name, address, phone, fax, telex, names and titles of key personnel, number of employees, product/service.

*Fairfax County Business Database.* Fairfax County Economic Development Authority. • Description: Database cover approximately 7,000 Fairfax County-located businesses, including high-tech firms, financial and legal firms, retail, and personal services. Government agencies are not included. Entries include: Company name, address, phone, fax, e-mail (if available), name and title of contact; number of employees, occupied space in square feet, and geographical submarket of county. Formerly available in print edition; latest edition 1990.

*Family Tree.* Dun & Bradstreet Inc. • Continuous. Database covers: About 200,000 corporations and their subsidiaries and branch companies. Database includes: Company name, address, phone, corporate standing (whether parent or holding company, subsidiary, or other), Standard Industrial Classification (SIC) code, names and titles of key personnel, sales volume, financial information, Dun & Bradstreet rating.

*Finnish Export Companies.* FINPRO. • Database covers: over 2,500 Finnish export companies. Database includes: Company name, address, names and titles of key personnel, products.

*Foreign Direct Investment Database.* United Nations Conference on Trade and Development. • $80 Individuals. Database covers: Statistics on foreign direct investment for 196 countries. The FDI database presents aggregate inflows, outflows, inward stocks and outward stocks of foreign direct investment.

*FP500 Database.* International Press Publications Inc. • $139 Individuals for subscribers of National Post. Publication includes: Company contact information, revenue, assets, net income, return on investment capital and officer information. Principal content of publication is 1,000 Canadian corporations, including Canada's top 500 private and public companies plus 300 additional corporations.

*France Business Directory, Database.* NIIR Project Consultancy Services. • $100 Individuals CD-ROM. Covers: 40,000 categorized listings of French business companies. Entries include: Company name, phone, fax, email, website address, details of business/services provided.

*French Companies Full Financials.* RENCOM S&W. • Monthly. Database covers: Over 100,000 French companies in various sectors of industry and commerce. Entries include: Name, address, phone, senior management personnel, legal status, year founded, line of business, products, financial information.

*FUND ME! Sources.* IGW Canada Inc. • Quarterly. $495. CD-ROM, diskette. Database covers: over 2,000 programs, grants, and subsidies for research and business available in Canada from a variety of sources, including government agencies and departments, private foundations, international associations, banks, and venture capital companies. Entries include: Program title, sponsoring organization name, address, phone, areas of interest, program criteria and description, funding amount and type.

*FUNDED!.* IGW Canada Inc. • CD-ROM. Database covers: over 500 researchers, companies, and projects that have been awarded funds by public sector agencies and selected private sector organizations.

*Gale Directory of Databases (GDD).* Cengage Learning Inc. • Semiannual. $723 Individuals in 6 volumes. Offers comprehensive coverage of the electronic database industry with profiles for more than 15,000 databases and more than 3,000 producers, online services, and vendors.

*GATEWAYS.* IZUM Information Service. • Monthly. Database covers: 10 databases currently available online on records on the Internet and other networks providers in Slovenia. Entries include: Database name, acronym, date status, topic, language, number of records, update frequency, source of data, host, vendor, and producer.

*Holden's Annual Directory 1811.* S&N British Data Archive Ltd. • £16.95 Individuals. Database covers: Professions, trades, and residents in London and other towns in Great Britain. Entries include: Name and address.

*Hungarian Companies.* S2UV Rt. Computing and Management Services. • Continuous. Database covers: Approximately 30,000 companies in Hungary. Database includes: Company name, address, phone, management, official tax and company registration numbers, industry activity codes, year founded, number of employees.

*ICC UK Company Financial Database.* Dun & Bradstreet U.K. ICC Information. • Weekly. Database covers: Comprehensive analysis on 2.2 million companies with limited liability in the UK--large, medium, and small, quoted and non-quoted, public and private, from all sectors on industry and commerce. Provides data for all types of company research, providing extended profit and loss accounts and balance sheet information, new cash flow items, together with new auditors' qualification reference data, comprehensive business ratios, industrial comparisons, growth rates, and an improved credit rating system. Access to complete database of U.K. Directors with over 5 million directorships covered exact images of alt company accounts and annual returns.

*Indian Exporters Directory, Database.* NIIR Project

Consultancy Services. • $200 U.S. CD-ROM. Covers: 43,000+ Indian exporters. Entries include: Company name, contact person name and designation, full postal address, phone, fax, email (wherever available), website address (wherever available), activity.

*Indian Importers Directory, Database.* NIIR Project Consultancy Services. • $150 Individuals CD-ROM. Covers: 20,000+ Indian importers. Entries include: Company name, contact person name and designation, full postal address, phone, fax, email (wherever available), website address (wherever available), activity.

*Indiana All-Business Database.* Harris InfoSource. • Database covers: 21,000 manufacturing and service companies throughout Indiana.

*Industrial Market Location.* Market Location Ltd. • Database covers: about 150,000 manufacturing and distribution firms and commercial businesses in the United Kingdom. Database includes: Company name, address, phone, names and titles of key personnel, number of employees, description of product/service, Standard Industrial Classification (SIC) code.

*Infotel--The Electronic Directory of Companies from Romania.* Chamber of Commerce and Industry of Romania. • Covers: More than 500,00 Romanian companies. Entries include: Company name, headquarters address, telephone and fax number, registration, statistical and fiscal codes, profile, equity, shareholders, number of employees, gross profit.

*INFOTRADE Belgian Company Financial Data.* INFOTRADE N.V. • Daily. Database covers: More than 1,000,000 descriptive and financial profiles of Belgian companies and private businesses. Entries include: Company name, address, name and title of contact; commercial registration numbers; date and form of incorporation; bank accounts; association memberships; principal language; number of employees; names of management personnel; activities and products; trademarks; trading partners; financial statements for the most recent three years.

*International Business Opportunities Database.* NIIR Project Consultancy Services. • $100 Individuals CD-ROM. Covers: 180,000+ global importers, exporters, agents, representatives, business opportunity seekers, various trade opportunities. Entries include: Company name, address, phone and fax, email, and websites.

*International Stocks Database Directory.* Vision Information Inc. • Monthly. Database covers: publicly traded companies listed on various stock exchanges globally. Database includes: Company name; contact data; exchanges on which traded; financial, business, and news information.

*Internet Ships Register.* IHS Global Ltd. Lloyd's Register--Fairplay Ltd. • $1,350 Individuals single user. Database covers: Over 180,000 shipowners, operators, managers, and builders. Entries include: Name, address, phone. Database also includes details on over 83,000 commercial vessels with photographs. Fixture information also available at an additional cost.

*IT Companies Database.* NIIR Project Consultancy Services. • $100 Individuals CD-ROM. Covers: 5,000+ contacts of IT companies in India. Entries include: Company name, address, phone, fax, e-mail and website, contact person and product details.

*ITALI.* SEAT. • Monthly. Database covers: Over 260,000 Italian companies in all lines of business.

*Japan Business Directory, Database.* NIIR Project Consultancy Services. • $100 Individuals CD-ROM. Covers: 12,800 categorized listings of Japanese business companies. Entries include: Company name, phone, fax, email, website address, details of business/services provided.

*The Job-Seeker's Guide to On-line Resources.*

Kennedy Information Inc. • $14.95 plus $4 shipping. Covers: Approximately 140 candidate databases, job-posting services, and related resources with introductory text containing tips for novices. Entries include: On-line name, address, phone, fax; e-mail address, description.

*Kelly's Industrial Directory--CD.* Reed Business Information. • Annual. Database of UK industrial companies. Database covers: 200,000 companies under 17,000 headings.

*Key British Enterprises Financial Performance.* Dun & Bradstreet Inc. • Monthly. Database covers: Approximately 50,000 of the largest companies in the United Kingdom. Database includes: Company name, address, director name, parent company, product trade name, annual and export sales, number of employees, export markets, trade description, trade awards, Companies Registration Office number, pre-tax profit, net worth, total assets, current assets, current liabilities, working capital, long-term debt, return on capital, profit margin, current ratio, profit per employee, U.S. and U.K. SIC code.

*Kompass.* AffarsData. • Quarterly. Database covers: Approximately 400,000 manufacturers and distributors of approximately 70,000 products and services in Sweden, Norway, Denmark, Germany, United Kingdom, Switzerland, Netherlands, Belgium, Luxemberg, France, Spain, Italy, and Finland. Database includes: Company name, address, phone, products and services, turnover, share capital, year of establishment, export areas, and managing director.

*Kompass Asia/Pacific.* Kompass International Management Corp. • Annual. Database covers: over 260,000 Asian and Pacific companies in Japan, Korea, Hong Kong, Taiwan, China, Singapore, Malaysia, Thailand, Indonesia, Philippines, Brunei/Darussalem, India, Australia, and New Zealand. Database includes: Company name, address, phone, names and titles of key personnel, foreign trade status, number of employees, languages spoken, business descriptions, industry and product listings.

*Kompass-Benelux.* Kompass Belgium Products. • Database covers: 50,000 companies in the Benelux countries, which includes Belgium, the Netherlands, and Luxembourg. Entries include: Company name, address, product list, directors and management, turnover, number of employees.

*Kompass Finance.* Kompass France. • Annual. $1,650. Database covers: Financial information for approximately 50,000 French industrial and commercial firms. Database includes: Company name, address, phone, products and services; financial data and alliances.

*Kompass Poland.* EUROSTART Sp. z o.o. • Semiannual. Database covers: 25,000 Polish companies. Entries include: Company name, address, name and title of contact; general manager's name; rate of turnover; employment information; details of products and services offered.

*KOOPERACJA.* EUROSTART Sp. z o.o. • Semiannual. Database covers: small and medium-sized businesses in Poland. Database includes: Company name, address, phone, line of business, products.

*Korea Business Directory, Database.* NIIR Project Consultancy Services. • $100 Individuals CD-ROM. Covers: 85,000 categorized listings of Korean business companies. Entries include: Company name, phone, fax, email, website address, details of business/services provided.

*Les Pages Pro.* Bureau van Dijk S.A. • Annual. Database covers: Business to business directory of France Telecom with more than 300,000 subscribers. Entries include: Name, SIRET identification number, telephone number, type of number, full address, activity, employee range.

*Library Journal: Reference: Print, CD-ROM, On-line (year).* Reed Elsevier Group plc Reed Business Information. • Annual. Issued in November as a supplement to *Library Journal.* Lists new and updated reference material, including general and trade print titles, directories, annuals, CD-ROM titles, and online sources. Includes material from more than 200 publishers, arranged by company name, with an index by subject.

*Library Journal Sourcebook: The Reference For Library Products & Services.* Reed Elsevier Group plc Reed Business Information. • Annual. Publication includes: List of over 600 suppliers of products and services used by libraries from abstracting to word processing equipment. Entries include: Company name, address, phone, list of products or services. Complete listings for more than 100 architectural firms; Disaster planning for librarians.

*Lithuanian Companies.* Litauisches Informationsinstitut. • Quarterly. Database covers: companies in Lithuania. Database includes: Company name, address, legal status, products, number of employees.

*Major Companies on CD-ROM.* Graham & Whiteside. • $7,845 Individuals individual countries sold separately; inquire for. Database covers: 55,000 companies outside North America, including Europe, the Far East and Australia, Middle East, Africa, Latin America, Central Europe, Eastern Europe, the CIS, and Southwest Asia. Entries include: Company name, address, phone, fax, number of employees, sales, assets, profits, date established, SIC codes, parent and subsidiary companies, name and title of contact.

*Major Information Technology Companies of the World.* Cengage Learning Inc. • Annual. $1,460 Individuals. 2008. 11th edition. eBook. Published by Graham & Whiteside. Contains profiles of more than 8,250 leading information technology companies in various countries.

*Major Telecommunications Companies of the World.* Cengage Learning Inc. • Annual. $1,360 Individuals. Published by Graham & Whiteside. Contains detailed information and trade names for more than 5,950 important telecommunications companies in various countries.

*Marketing Address Data.* Herold Business Data GmbH. • Annual. Database covers: More than 246,000 businesses in Austria. Entries include: Company name, address, phone, fax, line of business.

*MarketPlace.* Dun and Bradstreet Sales and Marketing Solutions. • Quarterly. $850 list price. Database covers: Over 11 million U.S. businesses. Database includes: four quarterly updates of databases and software along with 1000 meter credits. Entries include: Company name, address, phone, name and title of contact, type of business, annual sales, number of employees, year founded, type of site, ownership, Standard Industrial Classification (SIC) code, DUNS number, latitude/longitude, firmographic and industry specific data.

*MARKUS: Marketinguntersuchungen.* Bureau van Dijk S.A. • Quarterly. Database covers: More than 900,000 German and Austrian companies. Entries include: Company name, address, date of incorporation, company type, register number, managers, shareholders, banks, WZ activity codes, trade description, number of employees, turnover, shareholders' funds.

*MASTER: Marketing Strategy and Efficient Research.* Bureau van Dijk S.A. • Quarterly. Database covers: More than 700,000 companies and business entities in Belgium. Entries include: Company name, address, date of incorporation, company type, activity, management, turnover, shareholders' funds, profit, debt, number of employees.

*Michigan Site Network.* Michigan Economic Development Corporation. • Database covers: Available buildings, land parcels, and brownfield sites in Michigan. Database includes: Name, address or location, facilities, transportation access; name, address, and phone of contact; locational maps; pictures.

*National Solid Waste Grants Database.* RCRA Research Library. • Database covers: More than 500 grant and loan providers as well as venture capitalists interested in recycling, reuse and solid waste management. Database includes: Contact information for some Northeastern U.S. firms.

*Net Jobs.* Hoover's Inc. • $12.95. Covers: Internet sites and online sources dealing with employment, including resume writing tips, interviewing advice, and classified listings. Entries include: Name, location/host.

*Newspapers Online.* BiblioData. • Irregular. $99. Covers: Approximately 150 daily newspapers available online. Entries include: Name, address, phone, editor name, details on geographical area served; description; list of regional newsmaking companies/people/topics; circulation figures; electronic availability and coverage; electronic searching tips; name and phone of contact for database assistance.

*OCREFO Creditreform Companies.* Verband der Vereine Creditreform e.V. • Quarterly. Database covers: over 20,000 profiles of companies registered in the new German states. Database includes: Company name, address, phone, legal status, year founded, registration data, owner, capital, management description, industry classification code, number of employees, annual sales.

*OFERES.* Instituto Espanol de Comercio Exterior. • Weekly. Database covers: Approximately 100,000 export companies in Spain. Database includes: Company name, address, phone, fax, number of employees, export representative, languages, activity, current annual and total export volume, product sector, trademarks and brand names, trade partners.

*On-Line Job Search Companion.* Hoover's Inc. • $14.95. Covers: Online sources of employment opportunities. Database includes: Information on selecting a career path. Entries include: Name, location/host.

*Online Business Link.* InfoGroup Inc. • Monthly. Database covers: More than 14 million United States businesses listed in "Yellow Pages" phone books nationwide, 551,000 manufacturers, and 4.3 million high-income consumers. Database includes: For businesses--Company name, address, phone, Standard Industrial Classification (SIC) code, brand and speciality information. For manufacturers--Company name, address, phone, name and title of chief officer, number of employees, sales volume, Standard Industrial Classification (SIC) code. For consumers--Name, address, phone, whether under or over 50 years of age. For company profiles--Company name, address, phone, Standard Industrial Classification (SIC) code, "Yellow Pages" category, as size, year listing first appeared in "Yellow Pages" (tracking began in 1985), franchise, brand or professional speciality. Business listings only were previously available under the title "Instant Yellow Page Service." A print version is available for each of the business categories listed in the "Yellow Pages" (use "Yellow Pages" categories to locate separate entries).

*OPAC Directory: An Annual Guide to Internet-Accessible Online Public Access Catalogs.* Mecklermedia Corp. • Annual. $70. Covers: Approximately 1,000 online public access catalogs (OPACs) and other locally mounted databases form hundreds of libraries worldwide. Database includes: Accessing Online Bibliographic Databases--annotated entries on over 700 Internet-accessible OPACs worldwide. Entries include: Description, access, search methods.

*PhoneDisc New York & New England.* PhoneDisc USA Corp. • Monthly. CD-Rom. Database covers:

Over 12 million residences and businesses in New York and New England. Database includes: Individual or company name, address, phone, Standard Industrial Classification (SIC) code. Includes residential, business, and government listings supplied by New York and New England telephone companies, along with independent telephone companies within the region.

*PhoneDisc QuickRef.* PhoneDisc USA Corp. • Annual. $69. CD-Rom. Database covers: 100,000 businesses; state, federal, and local governments; libraries; colleges and universities; embassies; law firms; industrial manufacturers; associations; organizations; etc. Database includes: Company or organization name, address, phone, Standard Industrial Classification (SIC) code, annual sales, billings, number of employees. Information is extracted from the "National Directory of Addresses and Telephone Numbers" (see separate entry).

*Polish Companies.* Informationsvermittlungsagentur Waldemar Kubanski. • Quarterly. Database covers: Polish companies. Entries include: Company name, address, phone, fax, industrial sector, legal status.

*Procurement Automated Source System.* U.S. Small Business Administration. • Annual. Online database. Database covers: More than 180,000 small businesses (including some 29,000 minority-owned, 44,000 woman-owned, and 51,000 veteran-owned businesses) seeking government procurement contracts. Database includes: Company name, address, phone, name and title of contact, employer identification number, number of employees, year established, geographical area served, whether veteran-, minority-, or woman-owned, whether interested in international trade, Standard Industrial Classification (SIC) code, Federal Supply Code (FSC), quality assurance information. Capability statement used by contracting officials of federal agencies and prime contractors to locate firms which can provide needed goods and services. For more info call: (800)231-PASS.

*ProFile Canada.* Micromedia ProQuest. • Quarterly. Database covers: Approximately 17,000 Canadian companies and organizations. Entries include: Legal company name, trade name, address, phone, fax, e-mail, URL, number of employees, benefits, pension information, and number of branches. Some listings include sales range, size of customer base, Standard Industrial Classification (SIC) code, import/export activity, Canadian Business 500 ranking, Financial Post 500 ranking, and key personnel.

*RCR and Global Wireless' International Database.* Crain Communications Inc. • Annual. $950. Covers: Worldwide cellular and PCS carriers.

*REACH: Review and Analysis of Companies in Holland.* Bureau van Dijk S.A. • Bimonthly. Database covers: 150,000 company reports, including top 7,000 companies in Holland. Entries include: Company name, address, phone, fax, company history, description, historical annual accounts, financial ratios, directors and officers, names of holdings and subsidiaries, stock data.

*Report on Business Corporate Database.* Globe Information Services Info Globe Online. • Weekly. Database covers: Current and historical information on over 3,000 Canadian companies, taken from their quarterly and annual reports. Database includes: Company name, address, phone, description of business, financial data, officers, general corporate information.

*SANI.* CERVED S.p.A. • Daily. Database covers: about 4 million Italian industrial, commercial, agricultural, and trade companies. Database includes: Company name, address, date and type of incorporation, incorporation capital, product/service, names and titles of key personnel. CERVED stands for Centri Elettronici Reteconnessi Valutazione Elaborazione Dati.

*Seibt - Umwelttechnikprodukte: Buyer's Guide for Environmental Technology.* Seibt Verlag GmbH. • Semiannual. €33. Database covers: German manufacturers, wholesalers, importers, exporters, and service firms that supply products for industry and international trade; German companies involved in the manufacturing and supply of medical and pharmaceutical equipment and supplies.

*Singapore Exporters Database.* NIIR Project Consultancy Services. • $100 Individuals CD-ROM. Covers: 3,641 Singapore exporters. Entries include: Company name, full postal address, phone, fax, email (wherever available), website (wherever available), telex (wherever available).

*SIRENE.* France Institut National de la Statistique et des Etudes Economiques. • Daily. Database covers: Approximately 2.5 million French industrial and commercial firms. Entries include: Firm name, address, type of incorporation, national identification code, sector of activity, number of salaried employees, quarterly business volume.

*Smart/Utilize Catalog Index.* Property Management Systems Corp. • Bimonthly. Database covers: about 20,000 manufacturers of over 250,000 models of electronic, computer, office, and machine tool equipment; limited international coverage. Database includes: Company name, address, phone, subsidiary and branch names and locations, description of products with model number and performance specifications, trade/brand names, merger/buyout audit trail.

*SRDS Interactive Advertising Source.* Kantar Media SRDS. • Quarterly. $569.00 per year. Provides descriptive profiles, rates, audience, personnel, etc., for producers of various forms of interactive or multimedia advertising: online/Internet, CD-ROM, interactive TV, interactive cable, interactive telephone, interactive kiosk, and others.

*STOR-TELE.* AffarsData. • Database covers: Approximately 100,000 Swedish companies. Database includes: Company name, address, phone, products and services.

*TelCor America Classified Directory.* TelCor America. • Continuous. Database covers: All types of businesses in the United States. Database includes: Company name, address, phone; product/service; geographical area served. The telephone number for accessing the computer is (216)835-4550.

*Teleselekt.* Austrian Federal Economic Chamber. • Semiannual. Database covers: 10,000 Austrian exporters and importers and 18,000 products. Entries include: Company name and address, management, number of employees, turnover, shares, commodities, services, and product information.

*Top European Companies Database.* European Business Press Group N.V. • Annual. Diskette. Covers 500 major companies in Europe. Entries include: Company name, address, phone, names and titles of key personnel, financial data.

*Top 500 MBS Investors.* Inside Mortgage Finance Publications Inc. • $500. Database covers: The top 500 thrift, commercial bank, and federal credit unions in terms of their mortgage-related securities holdings. Entries include: Name, address, phone.

*Top 900 Blue Chip Indian Companies Database.* NIIR Project Consultancy Services. • $200 Individuals CD-ROM. Covers: 900 Blue chip Indian companies. Entries include: Company name, name of CEO, postal address, city, state, pin code, phone, fax and the stock exchanges on which they are listed.

*Toyo Keizai Company Information.* Toyo Keizai Inc. • Daily. Database covers: Japanese companies.

*Trademarkscan--International Register.* Thomson CompuMark Americas. • Semimonthly. Database covers: Over 445,000 active registered trademarks

on file at the World Intellectual Property Organization. Also included are inactive records from the last 3 years. Entries include: Trademark word and/or design reference, current status, international class(es), description of product/service, registration number, publication details, owner name/location.

*TRW Trade Payment Guide.* TRW Business Credit Services. • Quarterly. Database covers: About 2,500,000 credit active business locations. Database includes: Company name, address, phone; Standard Industrial Classification (SIC) code; public record filings indicator; TRW days beyond terms credit store/history.

*UNCTAD-Trade Analysis and Information System.* United Nations Conference on Trade and Development. • Database covers: Indicators of trade control measures (tariff, para-tariff and non-tariff measures), as well as imports by suppliers at each harmonized system 6-digit level for over 160 countries. It also provides country notes of trade regimes for some 40 developing countries, describing market access conditions according to the UNCTAD coding system of Trade control measures.

*Wer Liefert Was? Central Europe: Business-to-Business Directory.* Wer liefert was GmbH. • Annual. Database covers: Over 45,000 companies in the Czech Republic, Slovenia, Slovakia, and Croatia. Entries include: Name, address, phone, fax, description of products/services offered.

*Wer Liefert Was? Online.* Wer liefert was GmbH. • Database covers: Products and services from over 307,356 companies in Germany, Austria, Switzerland, the Netherlands, Belgium, Luxembourg, the Czech Republic, Slovakia, Slovenia, Croatia, the UK, France, and Italy. Entries include: Company name, address, phone, product/service, managers, ISO certification, e-mail/internet address.

*Western Manufacturers Database Prospect System.* Harris InfoSource. • $3,125. Database covers: Manufacturers covering the western U.S. Entries include: Company number of employees, annual sales, plant size, year established, names and titles for up to 10 executives, SIC codes.

*World Database of Business Information Sources on the Internet.* Euromonitor International Business Reference Div. • $690. Covers: Over 35,000 business information sources worldwide, including 12,000 organizations, 13,000 publications, 2,000 exhibitions, and 700 online databases. Entries include: Source name, contact information, description.

*World Databases in Company Information.* K.G. Saur Verlag KG. • Covers: Electronically published databases and their vendors, worldwide.

*Worldscope Fundamentals.* Thomson Reuters Corp. • Daily. Database covers: profiles, company financial statement data, ratios, and stock performance of approximately 20,000 companies listed on leading stock exchanges worldwide. Database includes: Company name, address, phone, names and titles of key personnel, products, number of employees, major shareholders, geographic and product segment, financial data.

## E-BOOKS

*Encyclopedia of Emerging Industries.* Cengage Learning Inc. • $546 6th edition. Provides detailed information on 140 "newly flourishing" industries. Includes historical background, organizational structure, significant individuals, current conditions, major companies, work force, technology trends, research developments, and other industry facts.

## ENCYCLOPEDIAS AND DICTIONARIES

*Encyclopedia of Communication and Information.* Cengage Learning Inc. • 2003. eBook. Published by Macmillan Reference USA. Provides an overview of universal modes of communication. Inquire about price and availability.

## INTERNET DATABASES

*InfoTech Trends.* Data Analysis Group. Phone: (925)462-1202; Fax: (925)462-1225; Email: support@infotechtrends.com • URL: http://www.infotechtrends.com • Web site provides both free and fee-based market research data on the information technology industry, including computers, peripherals, telecommunications, the Internet, software, CD-ROM/DVD, e-commerce, and workstations. Fees: Free for current (most recent year) data; more extensive information has various fee structures. Formerly *Computer Industry Forecasts.*

*Search Engine Watch.* Internet.com Corp. Phone: (203)662-2800; Fax: (203)655-4686 • URL: http://www.searchenginewatch.com • Web site offers information on various aspects of search engines, including new developments, indexing systems, technology, ratings and reviews of major operators, specialty services, tutorials, news, history, "Search Engine EKGs," "Facts and Fun," etc. Online searching is provided. Formerly *A Webmaster's Guide to Search Engines.*

*Wired News.* Lycos Inc. 400-2 Totten Pond Rd., Waltham, MA 02451-2053. Phone: (781)370-2700 or (415)276-8400; Fax: (781)370-2600 or (415)276-8500; Email: press@lycos.com • URL: http://www.lycos.com • Provides summaries and full-text of "Top Stories" relating to the Internet, computers, multimedia, telecommunications, and the electronic information industry in general. These news stories are placed in the broad categories of Politics, Business, Culture, and Technology. Affiliated with *Wired* magazine. Fees: Free.

## ONLINE DATABASES

*Computer Database.* Cengage Learning Inc. • Provides one year of full-text online for 150 leading computer-related publications. Also includes 70,000 product specifications and brief profiles of 13,000 computer product vendors and manufacturers. Inquire as to prices and availability.

## OTHER SOURCES

*E-Business, Internet, and Online Transactions.* Michael L. Taviss and others. Glasser LegalWorks. • Looseleaf. $225.00, including CD-ROM version. Periodic Supplementation. Covers the legal aspects of online content, marketing, advertising, domain names, software licensing, and other Internet issues. Includes many sample forms. (Emerging Growth Companies Series.).

*Home Banking Report.* Jupitermedia Corp. • Annual. $695.00. Market research report. Covers banking from home by phone or online, with projections of growth in future years.

*World Online Markets.* Jupitermedia Corp. • Annual. $1,895.00. Market research report. Provides broad coverage of worldwide Internet and online information business activities, including country-by-country data. Includes company profiles and five-year forecasts or trend projections.

## PERIODICALS AND NEWSLETTERS

*Electronic Information Report: Empowering Industry Decision Makers Since 1979.* SIMBA Information Inc. • 46 times a year. $649.00 per year. Newsletter. Provides business and financial news and trends for online services, electronic publishing, storage media, multimedia, and voice services. Includes information on relevant IPOs (initial public offerings) and mergers. Formerly *Electronic Information Week.*

*InfoAlert: Your Expert Guide to Online Business Information.* Economics Press Inc. • Monthly. $129.00 per year. Newsletter. Provides information on recommended World Wide Web sites in various business, marketing, industrial, and financial areas.

*Information Hotline.* Science Associates/

International Inc. • Monthly. $150. Description: "The oldest, most respected, continuously published newsletter." Devoted to objective coverage of trends, policy, analysis, and opinion in the information field.

*Information Outlook: The Monthly Magazine of the Special Libraries Association.* Special Libraries Association. • Monthly. $65.00 per year. Topics include information technology, the Internet, copyright, research techniques, library management, and professional development. Replaces *Special Libraries* and *SpeciaList.*

*Information Processing and Management: An International Journal.* Elsevier. • $327 Individuals. Bimonthly. Qualified personnel, $301.00 per year; institutions, $1,196.00 per year. Text in English, French, German and Italian.

*Information Retrieval and Library Automation.* Lomond Publications. • Monthly. $75.00 per year. Summarizes research events and literature worldwide.

*Information Sciences; An International Journal.* Elsevier. • $161 Individuals. 36 times a year. Individuals, $106.00 per year; institutions, $3,557.00 per year. Three sections, A: Informatics and Computer Science, B: Intelligent Systems, C: Applications.

*Information Systems; Data Bases: Their Creation, Management and Utilization.* Elsevier. • $250 Individuals. Eight times a year. Institutions, $1,554.00 per year.

*Information Today: The Newspaper for Users and Producers of Electronic Information Services.* Information Today, Inc. • 11 times a year. $68.95 per year.

*Innovative Publisher: Publishing Strategies for New Markets.* Emmelle Publishing Co., Inc. • Biweekly. $69.00 per year. Provides articles and news on electronic publishing (CD-ROM or online) and desktop publishing.

*Internet Reference Services Quarterly: A Journal of Innovative Information Practice, Technologies, and Resources.* The Haworth Press Inc. • Quarterly. $110.00 per year. Covers both theoretical research and practical applications.

*Journal of Electronic Resources in Medical Libraries.* The Haworth Press Inc. • Quarterly. $240.00 per year to libraries; $75.00 per year to individuals.

*Law Technology News: Products, Systems, and Services for Legal Professionals.* ALM Media Properties LLC. • Monthly. 115 Dh. Features descriptions of new technology products and services of interest to the legal profession.

*Multimedia Schools: A Practical Journal of Technology for Education including Multimedia, CD-ROM, Online and Internet and Hardware in K-12.* Information Today, Inc. • Six times a year. $39.95 per year. Edited for school librarians, media center directors, computer coordinators, and others concerned with educational multimedia. Coverage includes the use of CD-ROM sources, the Internet, online services, and library technology.

*Online Libraries and Microcomputers.* Information Intelligence Inc. • Ten times a year. Individuals $43.75 per year; libraries $62.50 per year. Newsletter. Covers library automation and electronic information (online, CD-ROM). Reviews or describes new computer hardware and software for library use.

*Online Newsletter.* Information Intelligence Inc. • Description: Tracks developments in the fields of CD-ROM and online services. Contains news of online/CD-ROM developments and events, mergers and acquisitions, personnel movements, telecommunications and networks, new equipment and developments, microcomputer hardware and software, new and forthcoming databases, forthcom-

ing meetings, and publications and user aids.

*Online Searcher.* Information Today, Inc. • Bimonthly. $139 U.S. One year subscription. Covers a wide range of topics relating to online database searching.

*Online Searcher.* Information Today, Inc. • Bimonthly. $139.00 per year. Edited for librarians, Webmasters, site designers, content managers, and others concerned with knowledge/information management. Includes critical reviews of Web sites, software, search engines, and information services. (Formerly published by Online, Inc.).

*Physicians & Computers.* Moorhead Publications Inc. • Monthly. $40.00 per year. Includes material on computer diagnostics, online research, medical and non-medical software, computer equipment, and practice management.

*WebFinance.* SourceMedia Inc. • Semimonthly. $995.00 per year. Newsletter (also available online at www.webfinance.net). Covers the Internet-based provision of online financial services by banks, online brokers, mutual funds, and insurance companies. Provides news stories, analysis, and descriptions of useful resources.

## RESEARCH CENTERS AND INSTITUTES

Massachusetts Institute of Technology - Computer Science and Artificial Intelligence Laboratory. The Stata Ctr., Bldg. 32, 32 Vassar St., Cambridge, MA 02139. Phone: (617)253-5851; Fax: (617)258-8682; Email: rus@csail.mit.edu • URL: http://www.csail.mit.edu • Research is in four areas: Intelligent Systems; Parallel Systems; Systems, Languages, and Networks; and Theory. Emphasis is on the application of online computing.

Nerac Inc. 1 Technology Dr., Tolland, CT 06084-3900. Phone: (860)872-7000; Fax: (860)875-1749; Email: info@nerac.com • URL: http://www.nerac.com.

University of Southern California - Information Sciences Institute. 4676 Admiralty Way, Ste. 1001, Marina del Rey, CA 90292. Phone: (310)822-1511; Fax: (310)823-6714; Email: vcomms@usc.edu • URL: http://www.isi.edu/home • Research fields include online information and computer science, with emphasis on the World Wide Web.

## TRADE/PROFESSIONAL ASSOCIATIONS

American Society for Information Science and Technology. 8555 16th St., Ste. 850, Silver Spring, MD 20910. Phone: (301)495-0900; Fax: (301)495-0810; Email: asis@asis.org • URL: http://www.asis.org • Members are information managers, scientists, librarians, and others who are interested in the storage, retrieval, and use of information.

Electronic Frontier Foundation. 815 Eddy St., San Francisco, CA 94109. Phone: (415)436-9333; Fax: (415)436-9993; Email: info@eff.org • URL: http://www.eff.org • Promotes the creation of legal and structural approaches to help ease the assimilation of new technologies by society. Seeks to: help policymakers develop a better understanding of issues underlying telecommunications; increase public understanding of the opportunities and challenges posed by computing and telecommunications fields. Fosters awareness of civil liberties issues arising from the advancements in new computer-based communications media and supports litigation to preserve, protect, and extend First Amendment rights in computing and telecommunications technology. Maintains speakers' bureau; conducts educational programs. Encourages and supports the development of tools to endow non-technical users with access to computer-based telecommunications.

Library and Information Technology Association. 50 E Huron St., Chicago, IL 60611-2795. Phone: 800-545-2433; Fax: (312)280-3257; Email: lita@ala.org • URL: http://www.ala.org/lita • Affiliated with the American Library Association. Formerly Information Science and Automation Division of ALA.

---

National Federation of Advanced Information Services. c/o Jill O'Neill, Director, 1518 Walnut St., Ste. 1004, Philadelphia, PA 19102-3403. Phone: (215)893-1561; Fax: (215)893-1564 • URL: http://nfais.org • Formerly National Federation of Abstracting and Indexing Services.

Reference and User Services Association of the American Library Association. 50 E Huron St., Chicago, IL 60611. Phone: 800-545-2433 or (312)280-4395; Fax: (312)280-5273; Email: rusa@ala.org • URL: http://www.ala.org/rusa • Affiliated with American Library Association. Formerly Reference and Adult Services Division of American Library Association.

## OPERATING RATIOS

*See* FINANCIAL RATIOS

## OPERATIONS MANAGEMENT

### DIRECTORIES

*China Logistics Directory.* SinoMedia Ltd. • $80 Individuals book. Covers: 2,300 logistics companies operating in China across 12 industry sectors including airlines, airport, harbor & station operators, associations & consultants, construction companies, express forwarders, IT resources, land transportation, logistics equipment suppliers, logistics industrial parks, logistics services (custom brokers, air carriers and service companies), non-vessel operating common carriers, shipping companies, warehousing, third party logistics & supply chain solution. Entries include: English and Chinese names, address, headquarters location, phone and faxes, emails, key contact individuals, website.

*Malaysia Logistics Directory (MLD).* Marshall Cavendish Business Information Private Ltd. • $30 Individuals local, foreign and other countries. Covers: information and contacts on Malaysian logistics industry, freight forwarders, transport companies, airlines and other cargo related supporting industries.

### PERIODICALS AND NEWSLETTERS

*Fee Income Growth Strategies.* Siefer Consultants Inc. • Description: Discusses the role of fees and service charges for money orders, cashier's checks, nonsufficient funds, loans, automatic teller machine cards, and other ancillary services in the profitability of financial institutions.

*Operations Management.* Institutional Investor Inc. Journals Group. • Weekly. $2,105.00 per year. Includes print and online editions. Newsletter. Edited for managers of securities clearance and settlement at financial institutions. Covers new products, technology, legalities, management practices, and other topics related to securities processing.

*Production and Operations Management.* Production and Operations Management Society. • Quarterly 6/year. $70 Individuals per year.

### RESEARCH CENTERS AND INSTITUTES

African Development Bank. BP 1387, Rue Joseph Anoma, Abidjan, Côte d'Ivoire. Phone: 225 20 20 44 44; Fax: 225 20 20 49 59; Email: afdb@afdb.org • URL: http://www.afdb.org • Representatives of national financial institutions. Seeks to further economic development of member states. Serves as a clearinghouse on national and regional economic development. Provides financial support and consulting services to development programs and agencies. Sponsors research and educational programs.

### TRADE/PROFESSIONAL ASSOCIATIONS

AFCOM. 9100 Chester Towne Centre Rd., West Chester, OH 45069. Phone: (714)643-8110 or (714)997-7966; Fax: (714)997-9743; Email: membership@afcom.com • URL: http://www.afcom.com • Data center, networking and enterprise systems management professionals from medium and large scale mainframe, midrange and client/server data centers worldwide. Works to meet the professional needs of the enterprise system management community. Provides information and support through educational events, research and assistance hotlines, and surveys.

Construction Management Association of America. 7926 Jones Branch Dr., Ste. 800, McLean, VA 22102. Phone: (703)356-2622; Fax: (703)356-6388; Email: info@cmaanet.org • URL: http://cmaanet.org • Promotes the growth and development of construction management as a professional service; encourages high professional standards. Conducts conferences and forums on construction management topics. Sponsors a professional certification program.

European Operations Management Association. c/o EIASM, Pl. de Brouckere Plein 31, B-1000 Brussels, Belgium. Phone: 32 2 2266660; Fax: 32 2 5121929; Email: euroma@eiasm.be • URL: http://www.euroma-online.org • Advances operations management in both manufacturing and service through research, education and practice.

Institute for Operations Research and the Management Sciences. 5521 Research Park Dr., Ste. 200, Catonsville, MD 21228. Phone: 800-446-3676 or (443)757-3500; Fax: (443)757-3515; Email: informs@informs.org • URL: http://www.informs.org • International scientific society dedicated to improving operational processes, decision-making and management through the application of methods from science and mathematics. Represents operations researchers, management scientists and those working in related fields within engineering and the information, decision, mathematical and social sciences.

Production and Operations Management Society. The University of Texas at Dallas, School of Management, 2601 N Floyd Rd., Richardson, TX 75080. Phone: (972)883-4047; Fax: (972)883-5834; Email: poms@utdallas.edu • URL: http://www.poms.org • Members are professionals and educators in fields related to operations management and production.

Production Managers Association. Ealing Studios, Ealing Green, Ealing, London W5 5EP, United Kingdom. Phone: 44 20 87588699; Email: pma@pma.org.uk • URL: http://www.pma.org.uk • Professional organization representing over 180 production managers working in film, television and multimedia.

## OPERATIONS RESEARCH

*See also* AUTOMATION; SYSTEMS IN MANAGEMENT

### ABSTRACTS AND INDEXES

*International Abstracts in Operations Research.* International Federation of Operational Research Societies. Palgrave Macmillan. • Bimonthly. Institutions, $980.00 per year. Includes print and online editions.

### PERIODICALS AND NEWSLETTERS

*Operations Research.* INFORMS. • Bimonthly. Individuals, $110.00 per year; institutions, $612.00 per year.

*Operations Research Letters.* Elsevier. • 8 times a year. Institutions, $1,068.00 per year.

## OPHTHALMIC INDUSTRY

*See also* CONTACT LENS AND INTRAOCULAR LENS INDUSTRIES

### ABSTRACTS AND INDEXES

*Index Medicus.* U.S. National Library of Medicine. U. S. Government Printing Office. • Monthly. $522 Individuals. Bibliographic listing of references to current articles from approximately 3,000 of the world's biomedical journals.

*Science Citation Index.* Thomson Reuters Intellectual Property and Science. • Weekly. Includes *Source Index, Citation Index, Permuterm Subject Index,* and *Corporate Index.* Provides researchers, administrators, faculty, and students with quick, powerful access to the bibliographic and citation information they need to find research data, analyze trends, journals and researchers, and share their findings.

### BIBLIOGRAPHIES

*Medical & Health Care Books & Serials in Print.* Grey House Publishing. • $645 Individuals Hardcover. Provides immediate access to the highly specialized publishing activity in the health sciences and allied health fields.

### CD-ROM DATABASES

*Science Citation Index.* Thomson Reuters Intellectual Property and Science. • Weekly. Includes *Source Index, Citation Index, Permuterm Subject Index,* and *Corporate Index.* Provides researchers, administrators, faculty, and students with quick, powerful access to the bibliographic and citation information they need to find research data, analyze trends, journals and researchers, and share their findings.

### DIRECTORIES

*Eyeglasses Directory.* InfoGroup Inc. • Annual. Number of listings: 18,811. Entries include: Name, address, phone, size of advertisement, name of owner or manager, number of employees, year first in "Yellow Pages." Compiled from telephone company "Yellow Pages," nationwide.

### FINANCIAL RATIOS

*Annual Statement Studies.* Risk Management Association. • Annual. Compiled from over 280,000 financial statements.

*Annual Statement Studies: Industry Default Probabilities and Cash Flow Measures.* Risk Management Association. • Annual. $405 Nonmembers. Serves as a companion volume to the original *Annual Statement Studies.* Gives probability of default estimates on a percentage scale for more than 450 industries. Includes changes in position year-by-year for eight financial statement line items and provides percentage measures of cash flow.

### HANDBOOKS AND MANUALS

*Physicians' Desk Reference for Ophthalmology.* Medical Economics Co. • Annual. $49.95. Provides detailed descriptions of ophthalmological instrumentation, equipment, supplies, lenses, and prescription drugs. Indexed by manufacturer, product name, product category, active drug ingredient, and instrumentation. Editorial discussion is included.

### ONLINE DATABASES

*Embase.* Elsevier. • Worldwide medical literature, 1974 to present. Weekly updates. Inquire as to online cost and availability.

### PERIODICALS AND NEWSLETTERS

*Eyecare Business: The Magazine for Progressive Dispensing.* Boucher Communications, Inc. • Monthly. Individuals, $75.00 per year. Covers the business side of optometry and optical retailing. Each issue features "Frames and Fashion.".

*Ophthalmology.* American Academy of Opthalmology. American Academy of Ophthalmology. • Monthly. $404 Individuals online or print. Journal publishing original, peer-reviewed reports of research in ophthalmology, including basic science investigations and clinical studies.

*Ophthalmology Times: All the Clinical News in Sight.* Advanstar Communications Inc. • Semimonthly. $263 Individuals other countries. Magazine for ophthalmic community.

*Optometric Management: The Business and Marketing Magazine for Optometry.* Boucher Communications, Inc. • Monthly. $37.00 per year. Provides information and advice for optometrists on practice management and marketing.

## RESEARCH CENTERS AND INSTITUTES

Department of Ophthalmology. Icahn School of Medicine at Mount Sinai, 1 Gustave L. Levy Pl., Box 1183, New York, NY 10029. Phone: (212)241-0939; Fax: (212)987-1799 • URL: http://icahn. mssm.edu/departments-and-institutes/ ophthalmology.

Ophthalmic Research Institute. 6110 Executive Blvd., Ste. 506, Rockville, MD 20852. Phone: (301)984-4735; Fax: (301)984-4737.

Section of Ophthalmology and Visual Science. University of Chicago, 5841 S Maryland Ave. -MC2114, Chicago, IL 60637. Phone: (773)702-3937; Fax: (773)702-1000; Email: jernest@midway. uchicago.edu • URL: http://surgery.uchicago.edu/ specialties/ovs.

University of California, San Francisco - Francis I. Proctor Foundation for Research in Ophthalmology. 95 Kirkham St., San Francisco, CA 94143-0944. Phone: (415)476-1442; Fax: (415)476-2521; Email: todd.margolis@ucsf.edu • URL: http://proctor.ucsf. edu • Infectious and inflammatory diseases of the eye with particular emphasis on chlamydial infections, trachoma, herpetic eye infections, dry eye conditions, and uveitis.

## STATISTICS SOURCES

*U.S. Industry and Trade Outlook.* U.S. Department of Commerce National Technical Information Service. • Annual. Produced by the International Trade Administration, U.S. Department of Commerce, in a "public-private" partnership with DRI/ McGraw-Hill and Standard & Poor's. Provides basic data, outlook for the current year, and "Long-Term Prospects" (five-year projections) for a wide variety of products and services. Includes high technology industries. Formerly *U.S. Industrial Outlook.*

## TRADE/PROFESSIONAL ASSOCIATIONS

American Academy of Optometry. 2909 Fairgreen St., Orlando, FL 32803. Phone: 800-969-4226 or (321)710-3937; Fax: (407)893-9890; Email: aaoptom@aaoptom.org • URL: http://www.aaopt. org • Optometrists, educators and scientists interested in optometric education and standards of care in visual problems.

American Optometric Association. 243 N Lindbergh Blvd., Fl. 1, Saint Louis, MO 63141-7881. Phone: 800-365-2219 or (314)991-4100; Fax: (314)991-4101; Email: ilamo@aoa.org • URL: http://www.aoa.org • Professional association of optometrists, students of optometry, and paraoptometric assistants and technicians. Purposes are: to improve the quality, availability, and accessibility of eye and vision care; to represent the optometric profession; to help members conduct their practices; to promote the highest standards of patient care. Monitors and promotes legislation concerning the scope of optometric practice, alternate health care delivery systems, health care cost containment, Medicare, and other issues relevant to eye/vision care. Supports the International Library, Archives and Museum of Optometry which includes references on ophthalmic and related sciences with emphasis on the history and socioeconomic aspects of optometry. Operates Vision U.S.A. program, which provides free eye care to the working poor, and the InfantSEE program, which provides free vision assessments for infants between six and twelve

months of age. Conducts specialized education programs; operates placement service; compiles statistics. Maintains museum. Conducts Seal of Acceptance Program.

Better Vision Institute. Vision Council of America, 225 Reinekers Ln., Ste. 700, Alexandria, VA 22314. Phone: (703)548-4560; Fax: (703)548-4580; Email: ezb@thevisioncouncil.org • URL: http://www. thevisioncouncil.org/bvi • Advisory council of the Vision Council of America. Carried out in consultation with a board of eye care professionals who inform the public of the need for more adequate vision care.

National Academy of Opticianry. 8401 Corporate Dr., Ste. 605, Landover, MD 20785. Phone: 800-229-4828; Fax: (301)577-3880; Email: ctucker@ nao.org • URL: http://www.nao.org • Offers review courses for national certification and state licensure examinations to members. Maintains speakers' bureau and Career Progression Program.

National Optometric Association. 5009 Beatties Ford Rd., Ste. 107, No. 278, Charlotte, NC 28216. Phone: 877-394-2020 or (704)918-1809; Email: mainoffice@natoptassoc.org • URL: http:// nationaloptometricassociation.com • Represents optometrists dedicated to increasing awareness of the status of eye/vision health in the minority community and the national community at-large. Strives to make known the impact of the eye/vision dysfunction on the effectiveness and productivity of citizens and the academic proficiency of students. Conducts national minority recruiting programs, job placement, assistance programs for graduates, practitioners, and optometric organizations, and the promotion of delivery of care. Maintains speakers' bureau. Offers specialized education program.

Opticians Association of America. 4064 E Fir Hill Dr., Lakeland, TN 38002. Phone: (901)388-2423; Fax: (901)388-2348; Email: oaa@oaa.org • URL: http://www.oaa.org • Formerly Guild of Prescription Opticians of America.

Vision Council - Optical Lab Division. 225 Reinekers Ln., Ste. 700, Alexandria, VA 22314. Phone: 866-826-0290 or (703)548-4560; Fax: (703)548-4580; Email: info@thevisioncouncil.org • URL: http://www.thevisioncouncil.org/ola • Represents independent, wholesale ophthalmic laboratories and suppliers serving the ophthalmic field.

# OPIATES

*See* NARCOTICS

# OPINION POLLS

*See* PUBLIC OPINION

# OPTICAL DISK STORAGE DEVICES

*See also* INFORMATION INDUSTRY; MICROCOMPUTERS AND MINICOMPUTERS; MULTIMEDIA

## ABSTRACTS AND INDEXES

*Applied Science and Technology Index.* EBSCO Publishing Inc. • 11/year. Indexes a wide variety of English language technical, industrial, and engineering periodicals.

*Business Periodicals Index Retrospective.* EBSCO Publishing Inc. • 11/year. Quarterly and annual cumulations.

*Computer and Information Systems Abstracts Journal: An Abstract Journal Pertaining to the Theory, Design, Fabrication and Application of*

*Computer and Information Systems.* CSA. • Monthly. $1,750 per year.

*Current Contents: Engineering, Computing and Technology.* Thomson Reuters Intellectual Property and Science. • Weekly. $730 per year. Reproductions of contents pages of technical journals. Includes *Author Index, Address Directory, Current Book Contents,* and *Title Word Index.* Formerly *Current Contents: Engineering, Technology and Applied Sciences.*

*Electronics and Communications Abstracts Journal: Comprehensive Coverage of Essential Scientific Literature.* CSA. • Monthly. $1,665.00 per year. Includes print and online editions.

*Inspec Direct.* Institution of Engineering and Technology. • Monthly. $2,400 per year. Section C of *Science Abstracts.*

*Key Abstracts: Computer Communications and Storage.* Institution of Engineering and Technology. • Monthly. $1,138. Provides international coverage of journal and proceedings literature, including material on optical disks and networks.

*Library Literature and Information Science Index.* H.W. Wilson Co. • Quarterly. Annual cumulation. Price varies.

## CD-ROM DATABASES

*LISA Plus.* Cambridge Scientific Abstracts L.P. • Quarterly. $2,000 per year. CD-ROM version of Library Information and Science Abstracts, providing abstracting and indexing of the world's library and information science literature, 1969 to date. Contains more than 180,000 citations.

*WILSONDISC: Library Literature and Information Science Index.* H.W. Wilson Co. • Quarterly. Includes unlimited access to the online version of *Library Literature.* Provides CD-ROM indexing of about 400 periodicals, covering a wide range of topics having to do with libraries, library management, and the information industry.

## DIRECTORIES

*Broadcast Engineering--Equipment Reference Manual.* Penton. • Annual. Publication includes: List of more than 1,400 manufacturers and distributors of communications equipment for radio, television, and recording applications. Database includes: Specifications for major brands of professional broadcast hardware. Entries include: For manufacturers--Company name, address. For distributors and dealers--Company name, address, phone, product or service provided, geographic area covered.

*Business & Legal CD-ROMs in Print.* Mecklermedia Corp. • Annual. $55. Covers: Approximately 600 business and legal CD-ROMs. Entries include: Title, producer name, address, phone.

*CD-ROM EEKOD.* Promar Ltd. • Annual. $2,500. Covers: More than 246,500 company profiles in Eastern Europe, including Austria, Czech Republic, Croatia, Latvia, Lithuania, Hungary, Poland, Slovenia, Azerbaidjan, Slovakia, Belarus, Estonia, Romania, Moldavia, Russia, Ukraine, and Yugoslavia.

*Compact Disc Monaci.* Guida Monaci S.p.A. • Semiannual. Covers: 110,000 companies and agencies of the public and private sector in Italy, along with 200,000 business professionals. Entries include: For individuals--Name, address, position, qualifications.

*Compact Disc of the National Bank of Belgium.* Banque Nationale de Belgique S.A. • Quarterly. $284.94 CD-ROM. CD-ROM. Database covers: About 260,000 Belgian companies. Database includes: Company name, address, national number, financial data, activity, juridical form, and juridical situation.

*Corporate Affiliations Plus.* LexisNexis. • Quarterly. $2,595 Individuals 12 month single-user license

*Encyclopedia of Business Information Sources • 32nd Edition, Vol. 2*

(database). CD-ROM. Covers corporate statistics and current financial information on over 30,000 domestic and foreign parent companies and their 145,000 subsidiaries, as well as 306,000 key executives. Entries include: Sales, assets, liabilities, ownership percentage.

*Dafsaliens Database of Ownership Links--France.* Dafsaliens. • Monthly. Covers: More than 120,000 companies worldwide. Entries include: Company names, registration number, form of incorporation, addresses, telephone, fax, description of business, shareholders subsidiaries and cross holdings, and financial data. CD-ROM includes historical data to trace changing structures and current and former directors and officers.

*DealBase II: An Electronic Database of Acquisition Opportunities.* Business Publications Inc. • Monthly. $425 per year. Diskette. Database covers: Over 675 of middle market companies, currently available for acquisition, with annual revenues between 3 and 75 million dollars. Database includes: Company name, location, description, revenues, profitability, purchase price, industry, contact information, merger/acquisition data.

*EEKOD--East European Kompass on Disc.* Kompass Deutschland Verlags- und Vertriebsgesellschaft, mbH. • €1,789.52 Individuals includes print, data export, and 1 update. Covers: Approximately 464,498 East European company profiles, including Austria, Azerbaidjan, Belarus, Boznia-Herzegovina, Bulgaria, Croatia, Czech Republic, Estonia, Hungary, Latvia, Lithuania, Moldavia, Poland, Romania, Russia, Slovakia, Slovenia, Ukraina, and Yugoslavia.

*The Expert Marketplace.* Dun & Bradstreet Inc. • Database covers: More than 200,000 business consulting firms, business case studies and business improvement articles. Entries include: Consulting firm name, address, phone, fax, services, areas of expertise, executive name and title, staff, e-mail address, client list.

*The Fax Banque.* InterCom Projects Ltd. • Quarterly. Diskette. Covers: Over 16,000 businesses in Central America and Miami, Florida. Entries include: Company name, address, phone, fax, description of commercial activity.

*FUND ME! Sources.* IGW Canada Inc. • Quarterly. $495. CD-ROM, diskette. Database covers: over 2,000 programs, grants, and subsidies for research and business available in Canada from a variety of sources, including government agencies and departments, private foundations, international associations, banks, and venture capital companies. Entries include: Program title, sponsoring organization name, address, phone, areas of interest, program criteria and description, funding amount and type.

*FUNDED!.* IGW Canada Inc. • CD-ROM. Database covers: over 500 researchers, companies, and projects that have been awarded funds by public sector agencies and selected private sector organizations.

*German Business CD-ROM.* Datamedia GmbH. • Description: CD-ROM. Database covers: approximately 1.8 businesses in Germany. Entries include: Company name, address, phone, fax, classification information.

*Hoover's Company Capsules on CD-ROM.* Hoover's Inc. • Quarterly. $399.95. CD-ROM contains information on approximately 11,000 U.S. companies and over 30,000 CEOs and CFOs. Database includes: Built-in mailing label capability. Entries include: Company name, address, phone, fax, operations overview, web site address, CEO, CFO, sales, employment size, ticker symbol, stock exchange, industry, fiscal year end.

*Hoover's Company Profiles on CD-ROM.* Hoover's Inc. • Quarterly. $324.95 per year. CD-ROM. Contains over 1,200 in-depth company profiles and

approximately 200 detailed industry profiles of U.S., international, and private companies. Database includes: 200 industry profiles from the U.S. Department of Commerce. Entries include: Operations, strategies, histories, products and brand names, officers, competitors, locations, and financial informtion.

*Idaho Manufacturers Directory and Industrial Database.* Manufacturers' News Inc. • Annual. $89 Individuals print. Covers: 2,560 manufacturers in Idaho. Entries include: Company name, address, phone, names and titles of key personnel, year established, number of employees, plant square footage, services, Standard Industry Classification (SIC) code, parent and subsidiary company information, type of in-house computer system, URL, e-mail address.

*International Communications and Business Database on CD-ROM.* Jaeger and Waldmann. • Annual. $440. Covers: Extensive list of companies located in approximately 220 countries. Entries include: Company name, address, phone; products and services; various data.

*J W CD-ROM Fax Directory.* Telex-Verlag Jaeger + Waldmann GmbH. • Annual. $690. Covers: Nearly 95,000 Canadian businesses and other institutions and organizations owning fax machines. Also includes some listings for North and South America, Asia, Africa, and Australia. Entries include: Company or organization name, address, phone, fax, telex, and information on product/service, J+W trade codes.

*J W Communications CD International and J W Business CD International.* Telex-Verlag Jaeger + Waldmann GmbH. • Annual. $440. Covers: Six million companies worldwide. Entries include: Company name and address, communications data, and products and services code. Country database includes dialing codes, products and services, and trade classification in four languages.

*Library Journal: Reference: Print, CD-ROM, Online (year).* Reed Elsevier Group plc Reed Business Information. • Annual. Issued in November as a supplement to *Library Journal.* Lists new and updated reference material, including general and trade print titles, directories, annuals, CD-ROM titles, and online sources. Includes material from more than 200 publishers, arranged by company name, with an index by subject.

*Library Journal Sourcebook: The Reference For Library Products & Services.* Reed Elsevier Group plc Reed Business Information. • Annual. Publication includes: List of over 600 suppliers of products and services used by libraries from abstracting to word processing equipment. Entries include: Company name, address, phone, list of products or services. Complete listings for more than 100 architectural firms; Disaster planning for librarians.

*Maine Manufacturers Register and Industrial Database.* Manufacturers' News Inc. • Annual. $92 Individuals print. Covers: 2,683 manufacturers in Maine. Entries include: Company name, address, phone, names and titles of key personnel, year established, number of employees, plant square footage, services, Standard Industry Classification (SIC) code, parent and subsidiary company information, type of in-house computer system, URL, e-mail address.

*Major Companies on CD-ROM.* Graham & Whiteside. • $7,845 Individuals individual countries sold separately; inquire for. Database covers: 55,000 companies outside North America, including Europe, the Far East and Australia, Middle East, Africa, Latin America, Central Europe, Eastern Europe, the CIS, and Southwest Asia. Entries include: Company name, address, phone, fax, number of employees, sales, assets, profits, date established, SIC codes, parent and subsidiary companies, name and title of contact.

*Massachusetts Manufacturers Register and Industrial Database.* Manufacturers' News Inc. • Annual. $141 Individuals print. Covers: 9,577 manufacturers in Massachusetts. Entries include: Company name, address, phone, names and titles of key personnel, year established, number of employees, plant square footage, services, Standard Industry Classification (SIC) code, parent and subsidiary company information, type of in-house computer system, URL, e-mail address.

*MBA Track's Directory of Employers on Diskette.* Hoover's Inc. • $99.95. Database covers: 2,500 companies employing the greatest number of MBAs in the U.S. Entries include: Company name, address, phone, fax, human resources director, industry type.

*Nevada Manufacturers Directory and Industrial Database.* Manufacturers' News Inc. • Annual. $86 Individuals print. Covers: 2,104 manufacturers in Nevada. Entries include: Company name, address, phone, names and titles of key personnel, year established, number of employees, plant square footage, services, Standard Industry Classification (SIC) code, parent and subsidiary company information, type of in-house computer system, URL, e-mail address.

*New Hampshire Manufacturers Register and Industrial Database.* Manufacturers' News Inc. • Annual. $93 Individuals print. Covers: 2,963 manufacturers in New Hampshire. Entries include: Company name, address, phone, names and titles of key personnel, year established, number of employees, plant square footage, services, Standard Industry Classification (SIC) code, parent and subsidiary company information, type of in-house computer system, URL, e-mail address.

*Oregon Manufacturers Directory and Industrial Database.* Manufacturers' News Inc. • Annual. $114 Individuals print. Covers: 6,835 manufacturers in Oregon. Entries include: Company name, address, phone, names and titles of key personnel, year established, number of employees, plant square footage, services, Standard Industry Classification (SIC) code, parent and subsidiary company information, type of in-house computer system, URL, e-mail address.

*OZ on Disc--Top 25,000.* Read Only Memory Proprietary Ltd. • Quarterly. $4,950 per year. CD-ROM. Covers over 25,000 companies in Australia. Entries include: Company name, address, phone, fax, names and titles of key personnel, number of employees, Standard Industrial Classification (SIC) codes and descriptions, gross sales, related companies, banker.

*Recording Industry Sourcebook.* Cardinal Business Media. • Annual. $71.99 Individuals. Covers: 14,000 contacts in the music industry in over 65 categories, including record producers, publishers, promoters, attorneys, major and independent record labels, and music production facilities. Entries include: Name, address, phone, fax, name and title of contact, subsidiary and branch names and locations, background information, email, web address.

*SRDS Interactive Advertising Source.* Kantar Media SRDS. • Quarterly. $569.00 per year. Provides descriptive profiles, rates, audience, personnel, etc., for producers of various forms of interactive or multimedia advertising: online/Internet, CD-ROM, interactive TV, interactive cable, interactive telephone, interactive kiosk, and others.

*Top European Companies Database.* European Business Press Group N.V. • Annual. Diskette. Covers 500 major companies in Europe. Entries include: Company name, address, phone, names and titles of key personnel, financial data.

*Utah Manufacturers Directory and Industrial Database.* Manufacturers' News Inc. • Annual. $102 Individuals print. Covers: 4,504 manufacturers in

Utah. Entries include: Company name, address, phone, names and titles of key personnel, year established, number of employees, plant square footage, services, Standard Industry Classification (SIC) code, parent and subsidiary company information, type of in-house computer system, URL, e-mail address.

*VenCap Data Quest.* Reference Press Inc. • $89.95 Eastern version. Diskette. Contains over 750 venture capital firms in the eastern and western U.S. Entries include: Company name, address, phone, fax, officers, partners, type of fund, number of years providing funding, dollars under management, industries covered and geographical preferences, preferred low- and high-average investments, preferred maturity stages, and product description of portfolio companies.

*The Venture Capital Directory on CD-ROM.* Infon Corp. • Covers: over 500 venture capital firms and over 2,000 investors. Entries include: venture capital firms--investment size, location, and industry; investors--education and experience.

*Vermont Manufacturers Register and Industrial Database.* Manufacturers' News Inc. • Annual. $82 Individuals print. Covers: 1,698 manufacturers in Vermont. Entries include: Company name, address, phone, names and titles of key personnel, year established, number of employees, plant square footage, services, Standard Industry Classification (SIC) code, parent and subsidiary company information, type of in-house computer system, URL, e-mail address.

*Washington Manufacturers Directory and Industrial Database.* Manufacturers' News Inc. • Annual. $118 Individuals print. Covers: 7,834 manufacturers in Washington State. Entries include: Company name, address, phone, names and titles of key personnel, year established, number of employees, plant square footage, services, Standard Industry Classification (SIC) code, parent and subsidiary company information, type of in-house computer system, URL, e-mail address.

*Which Business CD-ROM?.* Bowker-Saur. • Annual. $259 plus $30.00 shipping.. Publication includes: List of major CD-ROM publishers in the field of business; coverage includes the U.K. and Europe, with limited U.S. listings. Principal content of publication is information significant CD-ROM titles in various business fields, such as company directories, company accounts, mergers/ acquisitions, business news, legislation/regulations, market research, industries, economics and finance, international trade, and business management literature. Entries include: Publisher name, address, phone.

## INTERNET DATABASES

*InfoTech Trends.* Data Analysis Group. Phone: (925)462-1202; Fax: (925)462-1225; Email: support@infotechtrends.com • URL: http://www. infotechtrends.com • Web site provides both free and fee-based market research data on the information technology industry, including computers, peripherals, telecommunications, the Internet, software, CD-ROM/DVD, e-commerce, and workstations. Fees: Free for current (most recent year) data; more extensive information has various fee structures. Formerly *Computer Industry Forecasts.*

## ONLINE DATABASES

*Applied Science and Technology Index Online.* H.W. Wilson Co. • Provides online indexing of 500 major scientific, technical, industrial, and engineering periodicals. Time period is 1983 to date. Monthly updates. Inquire as to online cost and availability.

*Wilson Business Abstracts Online.* H.W. Wilson Co. • Indexes and abstracts 600 major business periodicals, plus the *Wall Street Journal* and the business section of the *New York Times.* Indexing is from 1982, abstracting from 1990, with the two

newspapers included from 1993. Updated weekly. Inquire as to online cost and availability. (*Business Periodicals Index* without abstracts is also available online.).

## PERIODICALS AND NEWSLETTERS

*CD-ROM Information Products: The Evaluative Guide.* Ashgate Publishing Co. • Quarterly. $110.00 per year. Provides detailed evaluations of new CD-ROM information products.

*Computer Music Journal.* The MIT Press. • Quarterly. Covers digital soound and the musical applications of computers.

*Digital Imaging: The Magazine for the Imaging Professional.* Cygnus Business Media Inc. • Bimonthly. $24.95 per year. Edited for business and professional users of electronic publishing products and services. Topics covered include document imaging, CD-ROM publishing, digital video, and multimedia services. Formerly *Micro Publishing News.*

*EDP Weekly: The Leading Weekly Computer News Summary.* Computer Age and EDP News Services. • Weekly. $495.00 per year. Newsletter. Summarizes news from all areas of the computer and microcomputer industries.

*Innovative Publisher: Publishing Strategies for New Markets.* Emmelle Publishing Co., Inc. • Biweekly. $69.00 per year. Provides articles and news on electronic publishing (CD-ROM or online) and desktop publishing.

*Interactive Marketing and P R News: News and Practical Advice on Using Interactive Advertising and Marketing to Sell Your Products.* Access Intelligence L.L.C. • Biweekly. $495.00 per year. Newsletter. Provides information and guidance on merchandising via CD-ROM ("multimedia catalogs"), the Internet, and interactive TV. Topics include "cybermoney," addresses for e-mail marketing, "virtual malls," and other interactive subjects. Formerly *Interactive Marketing News.*

*Mass Storage News: Opportunities and Trends in Data Storage and Retrieval.* Jameson Publishing. • Biweekly. $597.00 per year. Newsletter. Provides descriptions of products and systems using optical storage. Formerly *Optical Memory News.*

*Maximum PC.* Imagine Media, Inc. • Quarterly. $29.95 per year. Provides articles and reviews relating to multimedia hardware and software. Each issue includes a CD-ROM sampler (emphasis is on games). Formed by the merger of Home PC and Boot.

*Online Searcher.* Information Today, Inc. • Bimonthly. $139 U.S. One year subscription. Covers a wide range of topics relating to online database searching.

*Sound & Vision: Home Theater- Audio- Video-MultimediaMovies- Music.* Bonnier AB. • 10/year. $12.97 10 issues. Popular magazine providing explanatory articles and critical reviews of equipment and media (CD-ROM, DVD, etc.). Supplement available *Stereo Review's Sound and Vision Buyers Guide.* Replaces *Stereo Review* and *Video Magazine.*

*Tape/Disc Business.* Access Intelligence L.L.C. • Monthly. $74. Magazine for dealers, manufacturers, and users of magnetic and optical media.

## RESEARCH CENTERS AND INSTITUTES

Communications and Information Processing Group. Rensselaer Polytechnic Institute, 7010 JEC, 110 Eighth St., Troy, NY 12180-3590. Phone: (518)276-6823; Fax: (518)276-6261; Email: modestin@ipl.rpi.edu • URL: http://www.ecse.rpi. edu • Includes Optical Signal Processing Laboratory and Speech Processing Laboratory.

## TRADE/PROFESSIONAL ASSOCIATIONS

Association for Information and Image Management International. 1100 Wayne Ave., Ste. 1100,

Silver Spring, MD 20910. Phone: 800-477-2446 or (301)587-8202; Fax: (301)587-2711; Email: aiim@ aiim.org • URL: http://www.aiim.org • Manufacturers, vendors and individual users of information and image management equipment, products and services. Holds special meetings for trade members and companies. Maintains speakers' bureau. Operates resource center. Compiles statistics.

# OPTICAL ENGINEERING

*See* OPTICS INDUSTRY

# OPTICAL FIBERS

*See* FIBER OPTICS INDUSTRY

# OPTICAL PUBLISHING SYSTEMS

*See* OPTICAL DISK STORAGE DEVICES

# OPTICS INDUSTRY

*See also* FIBER OPTICS INDUSTRY

## ABSTRACTS AND INDEXES

*Science Citation Index.* Thomson Reuters Intellectual Property and Science. • Weekly. Includes *Source Index, Citation Index, Permuterm Subject Index,* and *Corporate Index.* Provides researchers, administrators, faculty, and students with quick, powerful access to the bibliographic and citation information they need to find research data, analyze trends, journals and researchers, and share their findings.

## CD-ROM DATABASES

*Science Citation Index.* Thomson Reuters Intellectual Property and Science. • Weekly. Includes *Source Index, Citation Index, Permuterm Subject Index,* and *Corporate Index.* Provides researchers, administrators, faculty, and students with quick, powerful access to the bibliographic and citation information they need to find research data, analyze trends, journals and researchers, and share their findings.

## DIRECTORIES

*The International Directory of Importers - Optical Goods & Instruments Importers.* Interdata. • $220 Individuals print. Covers: 2,100 international firms importing optical goods and instruments. Entries include: Company name and address, contact person, email, number of employees, year established, phone and telefaxes, business activity, bank references, as well as a listing of optical goods and instruments currently being imported.

*Optical Goods Manufacturers Directory.* InfoGroup Inc. • Annual. Number of listings: 1,197. Entries include: Name, address, phone, size of advertisement, name of owner or manager, number of employees, year first in "Yellow Pages." Compiled from telephone company "Yellow Pages," nationwide.

## PERIODICALS AND NEWSLETTERS

*Fiber Optics News.* Access Intelligence L.L.C. • Weekly. $797.00 per year. Newsletter.

*Optical Engineering.* SPIE. • Monthly. Members $45.00 per year; institutions, $815.00 per year. Technical papers and letters.

*Optical Prism: Canada's Optical Business Magazine Since 1983.* Nusand Publishing Inc. • 8/year. $45 Other countries. An independent magazine providing practical information on practice management as well as coverage of Canada's optical industry to Canadian optometrists and their suppliers.

*Optical Society of America Journal.* Optical Society of America. • Monthly. Part A, $2,173.00 per year; Part B, $2,173.00 per year.

*Photonics Spectra.* Laurin Publishing Company Inc. • Monthly. Serves as a network among engineers, scientists and end users who develop, commercialize and buy photonics products. Provides both technical and practical information for every aspect of the global industry, integrating all segments of photonics.

### RESEARCH CENTERS AND INSTITUTES

Optical Sciences Center. University of Arizona, 1630 E University Blvd., Tucson, AZ 85721. Phone: (520)621-6997; Fax: (520)621-9613 • URL: http://www.optics.arizona.edu.

University of Rochester - Institute of Optics. Wilmot Bldg., 275 Hutchison Rd., Rochester, NY 14627-0186. Phone: (585)275-2322; Fax: (585)244-4936; Email: xi-cheng.zhang@rochester.edu • URL: http://www.optics.rochester.edu • Fourier optics, quantum optics, electro- and acousto-optics, geometrical optics, optoelectronics, fiber optics, image processing, image-forming systems, holography, optical processing, laser engineering, ultra-high resolutive dye laser spectroscopy, integrated optics, automatic lens design, testing, and fabrication, optical and electronic properties of solids, thin films, gradient index optics, and nonlinear optics.

### TRADE/PROFESSIONAL ASSOCIATIONS

Optical Society of America. 2010 Massachusetts Ave. NW, Washington, DC 20036-1023. Phone: 800-766-405A or (202)223-8130; Fax: (202)223-1096; Email: info@osa.org • URL: http://www.osa.org • Persons interested in any branch of optics: research, instruction, optical applications, manufacture, distribution of optical equipment, and physiological optics. Sponsors topical meetings.

Vision Council - Optical Lab Division. 225 Reinekers Ln., Ste. 700, Alexandria, VA 22314. Phone: 866-826-0290 or (703)548-4560; Fax: (703)548-4580; Email: info@thevisioncouncil.org • URL: http://www.thevisioncouncil.org/ola • Represents independent, wholesale ophthalmic laboratories and suppliers serving the ophthalmic field.

# OPTIONS (PUTS AND CALLS)

*See* STOCK OPTION CONTRACTS

# OPTOELECTRONICS

*See also* ELECTRONICS INDUSTRY; OPTICS INDUSTRY; PHOTONICS

### ABSTRACTS AND INDEXES

*Applied Science and Technology Index.* EBSCO Publishing Inc. • 11/year. Indexes a wide variety of English language technical, industrial, and engineering periodicals.

*Key Abstracts: Optoelectronics.* Institution of Engineering and Technology. • Monthly. $1,138. Provides international coverage of journal and proceedings literature relating to fiber optics, lasers, and optoelectronics in general.

*NTIS Alerts: Electrotechnology.* U.S. Department of Commerce National Technical Information Service. • Biweekly. $130 per year. Covers electronic components, semiconductors, antennas, circuits, optoelectronic devices, and related subjects.

*Science Citation Index.* Thomson Reuters Intellectual Property and Science. • Weekly. Includes *Source Index, Citation Index, Permuterm Subject Index,* and *Corporate Index.* Provides researchers,

administrators, faculty, and students with quick, powerful access to the bibliographic and citation information they need to find research data, analyze trends, journals and researchers, and share their findings.

### CD-ROM DATABASES

*Science Citation Index.* Thomson Reuters Intellectual Property and Science. • Weekly. Includes *Source Index, Citation Index, Permuterm Subject Index,* and *Corporate Index.* Provides researchers, administrators, faculty, and students with quick, powerful access to the bibliographic and citation information they need to find research data, analyze trends, journals and researchers, and share their findings.

### DIRECTORIES

*Frontline Solutions Buyer's Guide.* Advanstar Communications. • Annual. $34.95 plus $3.50 shipping. Publication includes: List of manufacturers, suppliers, consultants, value added resellers, and dealers/distributors of automatic identification and data capture software, technology, equipment, and products for bar code, biometric identification, electronic data interchange, machine vision, magnetic stripe, optical character recognition, radio frequency data communications, radio frequency identification, smart cards, and voice data entry; also includes related organizations, and sources for industry standards. Entries include: Company name, address, phone, e-mail, web address, products or services.

### ONLINE DATABASES

*INSPEC.* Institution of Electrical Engineers. • Provides online citations, with abstracts, to the world literature of electrical engineering, electronics, optoelectronics, telecommunications, industrial controls, instrumentation, computer technology, information technology, and physics. Coverage includes more than 4,000 technical and scientific journals from 1969 to date, with weekly updating. (INSPEC is Information Services in Physics, Electronics, and Computing.) Inquire as to online cost and availability.

### PERIODICALS AND NEWSLETTERS

*Microwave and Optical Technology Letters.* John Wiley and Sons, Inc., Journals Div. • Monthly. Provides quick publication (3 to 6 month turnaround) of the most recent findings and achievements in high frequency technology, from RF to optical spectrum.

*Optical Engineering.* SPIE. • Monthly. Members $45.00 per year; institutions, $815.00 per year. Technical papers and letters.

*Photonics Spectra.* Laurin Publishing Company Inc. • Monthly. Serves as a network among engineers, scientists and end users who develop, commercialize and buy photonics products. Provides both technical and practical information for every aspect of the global industry, integrating all segments of photonics.

### RESEARCH CENTERS AND INSTITUTES

Fiber and Electro Optics Research Center. Virginia Polytechnic Institute and State University, Dept. of Electrical Engineering, 106 Plantation Rd., Blacksburg, VA 24061. Phone: (540)231-7203; Fax: (540)231-4561; Email: roclaus@vt.edu • URL: http://www.unirel.vt.edu/history/extension_outreach_research/technology_development_centers.html.

University of Central Florida - Center for Research and Education in Optics and Lasers. College of Optics & Photonics, 4000 Central Florida Blvd., Orlando, FL 32816-2700. Phone: (407)823-6800; Fax: (407)823-6880; Email: creol@creol.ucf.edu • URL: http://www.creol.ucf.edu • Photonics, nanophotonics, biophotonics, optical switching,

nonlinear optics fiber optics, laser propagation, waveguides, growth of nonlinear and laser host materials, optical scattering, laser-produced plasmas, free electron lasers, opto-electronics, quantum electronics, optical sensors, correlation techniques, laser-induced damage, optical power limiting, ultra-fast phenomena (femtosecond laser interactions), nonlinear optical spectroscopy, diffractive optics, liquid crystal optics, spatial solitons, image understanding, thin film optics, X-ray lasers, diode pumped lasers, micro-lasers, and classical optics. Applications include the following: optical telecommunications, new laser sources, detection, surveillance, reconnaissance, command and control, counter and counter-counter measures, intelligence collection, and the development of improved optical components, sensor protection, optical computing, and medical lasers.

University of Florida - College of Engineering - Department of Electrical & Computer Engineering - Photonics Research Laboratory. 216 Larsen Hall, Gainesville, FL 32611-6200. Phone: (352)392-0911 or (352)392-9265; Fax: (352)392-8671; Email: rakov@ece.ufl.edu • URL: http://old.ece.ufl.edu/research/labs/photonics.html • Integrated optics, optoelectronic integration, high-speed electro-optic guided-wave modulators, modulators with linearized transfer curves, wavelength-selective filters, waveguide structures in ferroelectric crystals with domain reversals, waveguide lasers/amplifiers.

University of Rochester - Institute of Optics. Wilmot Bldg., 275 Hutchison Rd., Rochester, NY 14627-0186. Phone: (585)275-2322; Fax: (585)244-4936; Email: xi-cheng.zhang@rochester.edu • URL: http://www.optics.rochester.edu • Fourier optics, quantum optics, electro- and acousto-optics, geometrical optics, optoelectronics, fiber optics, image processing, image-forming systems, holography, optical processing, laser engineering, ultra-high resolutive dye laser spectroscopy, integrated optics, automatic lens design, testing, and fabrication, optical and electronic properties of solids, thin films, gradient index optics, and nonlinear optics.

# OPTOMETRIC INDUSTRY

*See* OPHTHALMIC INDUSTRY

# ORANGE INDUSTRY

*See* CITRUS FRUIT INDUSTRY

# ORDNANCE MARKET

*See* MILITARY MARKET

# ORGANIZATION

*See* INDUSTRIAL MANAGEMENT

# ORGANIZATION FOR ECONOMIC COOPERATION AND DEVELOPMENT

*See also* FOREIGN TRADE

### BIBLIOGRAPHIES

*OECD Catalogue of Publications.* Organization for Economic Cooperation and Development. Organisation for Economic Co-operation and Development Publications and Information Center. • Online only. No print edition.

### CD-ROM DATABASES

*OECD Statistical Compendium.* Organization for Economic Cooperation and Development. •

Semiannual. $1,905.00 per year for 1 to 10 users. CD-ROM contains more than 730,000 monthly, quarterly, and annual time series for OECD countries, 1960 to date. Includes fully searchable data on agriculture, food, economic indicators, national accounts, employment, energy, finance, industry, technology, and foreign trade. Results can be displayed in various forms.

## PERIODICALS AND NEWSLETTERS

*Central Banking: Policy, Markets, Supervision.* European Business Publications Inc. • Quarterly. $260.00 per year, including annual *Central Banking Directory.* Published in England by Central Banking Publications. Reports and comments on the activities of central banks around the world. Also provides discussions of the International Monetary Fund (IMF), the Organization for Economic Cooperation and Development (OECD), the Bank for International Settlements (BIS), and the World Bank.

*News from OECD.* Organisation for Economic Co-operation and Development Publications and Information Center. • Monthly.

*OECD Observer.* Organisation for Economic Co-operation and Development Publications and Information Center. • Bimonthly. $101 Individuals print + online. Magazine on economic affairs, science, and technology.

## TRADE/PROFESSIONAL ASSOCIATIONS

Asian Clearing Union. 47, 7th Negarestan Alley, Pasdaran Ave., Tehran, Iran. Phone: 98 21 2842076 or 98 21 2854509; Fax: 98 21 2847677; Email: acusecret@cbi.ir • URL: http://www. asianclearingunion.org • Central banks, monetary authorities, and treasuries of Asian countries. Works to economize on the use of exchange reserves; promotes shifting of national banking services to domestic banks; seeks to enhance economic, financial, and commercial cooperation among Asian nations. Provides short-term credit facilities.

German-Chinese Business Association. Unter Sachsenhausen 10-26, D-50667 Cologne, Germany. Phone: 49 221 120370; Fax: 49 221 120417; Email: info@dcw-ev.de • URL: http://www.dcw-ev.de • Promotes mutual co-operation in the economic sphere, particularly between medium-sized Chinese and German companies. Supports intensive exchange of thoughts and experiences between all institutions and companies interested in doing business in China. Organizes information seminars on a regular basis in various cities.

Organisation for Economic Co-Operation and Development. 2, rue Andre Pascal, F-75775 Paris, France. Phone: 33 1 45248200; Fax: 1 45248500; Email: webmaster@oecd.org • URL: http://www. oecd.org.

# ORGANIZATION FOR EUROPEAN ECONOMIC COOPERATION

*See* ORGANIZATION FOR ECONOMIC COOPERATION AND DEVELOPMENT

# ORGANIZATION THEORY

*See* MANAGEMENT THEORY

# ORGANIZATIONS

*See* ASSOCIATIONS

# ORGANIZED LABOR

*See* LABOR UNIONS

# ORIENTAL RUG INDUSTRY

## PERIODICALS AND NEWSLETTERS

*Oriental Rug Review.* Oriental Rug Auction Review Inc. • Bimonthly. $48.00 per year.

## TRADE/PROFESSIONAL ASSOCIATIONS

Oriental Rug Importers Association. 100 Park Plaza Dr., Secaucus, NJ 07094. Phone: (201)866-5054; Fax: (201)866-6169; Email: oria@oria.org • URL: http://rugknot.com/oria-members-section/contact-about-us/ • Represents wholesalers and importers of Oriental rugs. Fosters ethical business practices and promotes the best interests of the Oriental Rug Trade in the United States and in countries that produce Oriental rugs.

# ORTHOPEDIC APPLIANCE INDUSTRY

*See* PROSTHETICS INDUSTRY

# OUTDOOR ADVERTISING

*See also* SIGNS AND SIGN BOARDS

## FINANCIAL RATIOS

*Annual Statement Studies.* Risk Management Association. • Annual. Compiled from over 280,000 financial statements.

*Annual Statement Studies: Industry Default Probabilities and Cash Flow Measures.* Risk Management Association. • Annual. $405 Nonmembers. Serves as a companion volume to the original *Annual Statement Studies.* Gives probability of default estimates on a percentage scale for more than 450 industries. Includes changes in position year-by-year for eight financial statement line items and provides percentage measures of cash flow.

## PERIODICALS AND NEWSLETTERS

*Signs of the Times.* ST Media Group International Inc. • 13 times a year. For designers and manufacturers of all types of signs. Features how-to-tips.

## TRADE/PROFESSIONAL ASSOCIATIONS

Outdoor Advertising Association of America. 1850 M St. NW, Ste. 1040, Washington, DC 20036. Phone: (202)833-5566; Fax: (202)833-1522; Email: nfletcher@oaaa.org • URL: http://www.oaaa.org • Firms owning, erecting and maintaining standardized poster panels and painted display advertising facilities. Absorbed Shelter Advertising Association.

# OUTDOOR AMUSEMENTS

*See* AMUSEMENT INDUSTRY

# OUTPLACEMENT CONSULTANTS

*See* EMPLOYMENT AGENCIES AND SERVICES

# OVER-THE-COUNTER DRUGS

*See* NONPRESCRIPTION DRUG INDUSTRY

# OVER-THE-COUNTER SECURITIES INDUSTRY

*See also* SECURITIES; STOCK BROKERS; STOCKS

## DIRECTORIES

*Institutional Buyers of Small-Cap Stocks.* bigdough. com Inc. • Annual. $295.00. Provides detailed profiles of more than 837 institutional buyers of small capitalization stocks. Includes names of financial analysts and portfolio managers.

*Mergent OTC Industrial Manual.* Mergent Inc. • Annual. $1,995 including 'News Reports.' Covers over 2,500 companies whose stock is traded over the counter. Includes biweekly *Moody's OTC Industrial News Report.*

## HANDBOOKS AND MANUALS

*Mergent OTC Industrial Manual.* Mergent Inc. • Annual. $1,995 including 'News Reports.' Covers over 2,500 companies whose stock is traded over the counter. Includes biweekly *Moody's OTC Industrial News Report.*

*Mergent OTC Unlisted Manual.* Mergent. • Annual, $1,995.00 per year. Includes supplement *Moody's OTC Unlisted News Report.*

*N A S D Manual.* National Association of Securities Dealers, Inc. Wolters Kluwer Law & Business CCH. • Quarterly. $452.00 per year. CD-Rom, $459.00.

## INTERNET DATABASES

*Factiva.* Dow Jones Reuters Business Interactive, LLC. Phone: 800-369-7466 or (609)452-1511; Fax: (609)520-5770; Email: solutions@factiva.com • URL: http://www.factiva.com • Fee-based Web site provides "global news and business information through Web sites and content integration solutions." Includes Dow Jones and Reuters newswires, The Wall Street Journal, and more than 7,000 other sources of current news, historical articles, market research reports, and investment analysis. Content includes 96 major U. S. newspapers, 900 non-English sources, trade publications, media transcripts, country profiles, news photos, etc.

*Nexis.com.* Lexis-Nexis Group. Phone: 800-227-4908 or (937)865-6800; Fax: (937)865-6909; Email: webmaster@prod.lexis-nexis.com • URL: http:// www.nexis.com • Fee-based Web site offers searching of about 2.8 billion documents in some 30,000 news, business, and legal information sources. Features include a subject directory covering 1,200 topics in 34 categories and a Company Dossier containing information on more than 500,000 public and private companies. Boolean searching is offered.

*TheStreet.com: Your Insider's Look at Wall Street.* TheStreet.com, Inc. Phone: 800-562-9571 or (212)321-5000; Fax: (212)321-5016 • URL: http:// www.thestreet.com • Daily. Iconoclastic advice and comment on the stock market, but premium service displays a more comprehensive selection of news and analysis.

*Wall Street Journal Interactive Edition.* Dow Jones & Co., Inc. 1211 Avenue of the Americas, New York, NY 10036. Phone: 800-369-5663; Email: service@dowjones.com • URL: http://new. dowjones.com • Fee-based Web site providing online searching of worldwide information from *The Wall Street Journal.* Includes "Company Snapshots," "The Journal's Greatest Hits," "Index to Market Data," "Journal Links," etc. Financial price quotes are available. Fees: $49.00 per year; $29.00 per year to print subscribers.

## ONLINE DATABASES

*EdgarPlus: SEC Basic Filings.* Thomson Reuters Markets. • Online service provides full text of about 60,000 documents that have been filed with the U.S. Securities and Exchange Commission, 1987 to date, with daily updates. Filings include 6-K, 8-K, 10-K, 10-C, 10-Q, 20-F, and proxy statements. Inquire as to online cost and availability.

## PERIODICALS AND NEWSLETTERS

*Equities: Investment News of Promising Public Companies.* Equities Magazine LLC. • Bimonthly. $21.00 per year. Formerly *OTC Review.*

*Financial Sentinel: Your Beacon to the World of Investing.* Gulf Atlantic Publish, Inc. • Monthly. $29.95 per year. Provides "The only complete listing of all OTC Bulletin Board stocks traded, with all issues listed on the Nasdaq SmallCap Market, the Toronto, and Vancouver Stock Exchanges." Also includes investment advice and recommendations of small capitalization stocks.

*The Penny Fortune Newsletter.* James M. Fortune, editor. Phoenix Communications Group Ltd. • Description: Instructs small investors on how to invest modest sums of money every two weeks to build a portfolio of stocks and mutual funds.

*Special Situations Newsletter: In-Depth Survey of Under-Valued Stocks.* Charles Howard Kaplan. • Monthly. $75.00 per year. Newsletter. Principal content is "This Month's Recommendation," a detailed analysis of one special situation stock.

*Standard & Poor's SmallCap 600 Guide.* McGraw Hill Financial Inc. • Monthly. $24.95. Contains detailed profiles of the companies included in Standard & Poor's SmallCap 600 Index of stock prices. Includes income and balance sheet data for up to 10 years, with growth and stability rankings for 600 small capitalization corporations.

### PRICE SOURCES

*Bank and Quotation Record.* William B. Dana Co. • Monthly. $130.00 per year.

*National Bond Summary.* OTC Markets Group Inc. • Monthly, with semiannual cumulations. $504.00 per year. Includes price quotes for both active and inactive issues, with transfer agents, market makers (brokers), capital changes, name changes, and other corporate information. Formerly published by the National Quotation Bureau.

*National Stock Summary.* OTC Markets Group Inc. • Monthly, with semiannual cumulations. $576.00 per year. Includes price quotes for both active and inactive issues, with transfer agents, market makers (brokers), capital changes, name changes, and other corporate information. Pink Sheets LLC also provides daily and weekly stock price services. Formerly published by the National Quotation Bureau.

### TRADE/PROFESSIONAL ASSOCIATIONS

Financial Industry Regulatory Authority. 1735 K St., Washington, DC 20006. Phone: (301)590-6500; Fax: (202)293-6260; Email: francine.lee@finra.org • URL: http://www.finra.org • Formerly National Association of Securities Dealers.

# OVERSEAS EMPLOYMENT

*See* EMPLOYMENT IN FOREIGN COUNTRIES

# OXYACETYLENE WELDING

*See* WELDING

# OYSTER INDUSTRY

*See also* SEAFOOD INDUSTRY; SHELLFISH INDUSTRY

### PERIODICALS AND NEWSLETTERS

*Seafood Business.* Diversified Business Communications Inc. • $57 U.S.. Edited for a wide range of seafood buyers, including distributors, restaurants, supermarkets, and institutions. Special issues feature information on specific products, such as salmon or lobster.

### TRADE/PROFESSIONAL ASSOCIATIONS

Molluscan Shellfish Institute. c/o Lisa Wedding, National Fisheries Institute, 7918 Jones Branch Dr., Ste. 700, McLean, VA 22102. Phone: (703)752-8880; Fax: (703)752-7583 • URL: http://www.aboutseafood.com • A division of the National Fisheries Institute. Shellfish producers, processors, distributors, growers, and suppliers to the industry. Works to promote, protect, and advance the interests of the shellfish industry. Cooperates with federal, state, and municipal authorities in matters of legislation, sanitation standards, controls, and conservation.

National Shellfisheries Association. c/o Linda Kallansrude, 14 Carter Ln., East Quogue, NY 11942-4335. Phone: (631)653-6327; Fax: (631)653-6327; Email: secretariat@shellfish.org • URL: http://www.shellfish.org • Biologists, hydrographers, public health workers, shellfish producers, and fishery administrators. Encourages research on mollusks and crustaceans, with emphasis on those forms of economic importance known as shellfish.

Pacific Coast Shellfish Growers Association. 120 State Ave. NE, No. 142, Olympia, WA 98501. Phone: (360)754-2744; Fax: (360)754-2743; Email: pcsga@pcsga.org • URL: http://www.pcsga.org • Oyster, clam, mussel, scallop, geoduck growers, openers, packers and shippers in Alaska, California, Oregon, Washington, Hawaii and Mexico.

# P

## PACKAGING

*See also* CONTAINER INDUSTRY; PAPER BOX AND PAPER CONTAINER INDUSTRIES; PAPERBOARD AND PAPERBOARD PACKAGING INDUSTRIES

### ABSTRACTS AND INDEXES

*Foods Adlibra: Key to the World's Food Literature.* General Mills, Inc. Foods Adlibra Publications. • Semimonthly. $240.00 per year. Provides journal citations and abstracts to the literature of food technology and packaging.

### BIOGRAPHICAL SOURCES

*Who's Who in Packaging.* Institute of Packaging Professionals. • Annual. Covers information on the packaging industry. Formerly *Who's Who and What's What in Packaging.*

### DIRECTORIES

*Directory of Chinese Importers of Packaging Materials & Supplies.* EXIM Infotek Private Ltd. • Covers: 35 Chinese importers of bopp film, cardboard, packaging materials, and wrapping paper. Entries include: Company name, postal address, telephone, fax, e-mail, website, contact person, designation, and product details.

*Directory of Packaging and Allied Industries.* NIIR Project Consultancy Services. • $100 Individuals. Covers: 1,000 companies/industries (manufacturers and suppliers) of packaging industries, packaging raw material, packaging machineries in India. Entries include: Company name, full postal address, phone, fax, email (wherever available), website address (wherever available).

*Household and Personal Products Industry Buyers Guide.* Rodman Publications. • Annual. Lists of suppliers to manufacturers of cosmetics, toiletries, soaps, detergents, and related household and personal products.

*Household and Personal Products Industry Contract Manufacturing/Private Label Directory.* Rodman Publications. • Annual. Provides information for about 450 companies offering private label or contract packaged household and personal care products, such as detergents, cosmetics, polishes, insecticides, and various aerosol items.

### OTHER SOURCES

*Food Law Reports.* Wolters Kluwer Law & Business CCH. • Weekly. $1,459.00 per year. Six looseleaf volumes. Covers regulation of adulteration, packaging, labeling, and additives. Formerly *Food Drug Cosmetic Law Reports.*

### PERIODICALS AND NEWSLETTERS

*Household and Personal Products Industry: The Magazine for the Detergent, Soap, Cosmetic and Toiletry, Wax, Polish and Aerosol Industries.* Rodman Publications. • Monthly. Covers marketing, packaging, production, technical innovations, private label developments, and aerosol packaging for soap, detergents, cosmetics, insecticides, and a variety of other household products.

*Packaging Digest.* Reed Elsevier Group plc Reed Business Information. • 13 times a year. $119.90 per year.

*Packaging Technology and Science.* John Wiley and Sons, Inc., Journals Div. • Eight times a year. Individuals, $650.00 per year; institutions, $3,152.00 per year. Provides international coverage of subject matter. Published in England by John Wiley & Sons Ltd.

### RESEARCH CENTERS AND INSTITUTES

Institute of Food Science. Cornell University, 114 Stocking Hall, Ithaca, NY 14853-7201. Phone: (607)255-7900; Fax: (607)254-4868; Email: ddm2@cornell.edu • URL: http://www.nysaes.cornell.edu/cifs • Research areas include the chemistry and processing of food commodities, food processing engineering, food packaging, and nutrition.

Michigan State University - Institute for Food Laws and Regulations. G.M. Trout Food Science and Human Nutrition Bldg., 469 Wilson Rd., Ste. 139, East Lansing, MI 48824. Phone: (517)355-8295; Fax: (517)432-1492; Email: iflr@msu.edu • URL: http://www.iflr.msu.edu • Conducts research on the food industry, including processing, packaging, marketing, and new products.

## PACKAGING LABELS

*See* LABELS AND LABELING

## PACKAGING MACHINERY

### PERIODICALS AND NEWSLETTERS

*Packaging Digest.* Reed Elsevier Group plc Reed Business Information. • 13 times a year. $119.90 per year.

### STATISTICS SOURCES

*U.S. Industry and Trade Outlook.* U.S. Department of Commerce National Technical Information Service. • Annual. Produced by the International Trade Administration, U.S. Department of Commerce, in a "public-private" partnership with DRI/McGraw-Hill and Standard & Poor's. Provides basic data, outlook for the current year, and "Long-Term Prospects" (five-year projections) for a wide variety of products and services. Includes high technology industries. Formerly *U.S. Industrial Outlook.*

### TRADE/PROFESSIONAL ASSOCIATIONS

Packaging Machinery Manufacturers Institute. 1191 Freedom Dr., Ste. 600, Reston, VA 20190. Phone: (571)612-3200; Fax: (703)243-8556 • URL: http://www.pmmi.org • Represents manufacturers of machinery used for all packaging operations including filling, capping, labeling, wrapping, cartoning, case loading, blister packaging, aerosol, check weighing, coding, counting, form-fill-seal, and bagging.

## PACKAGING, PRESSURE

*See* PRESSURE PACKAGING

## PACKING INDUSTRY

*See* MEAT INDUSTRY

## PAINT AND PAINTING

*See also* INDUSTRIAL COATINGS; VARNISH AND VARNISHING

### ABSTRACTS AND INDEXES

*CPI Digest: Key to World Literature Serving the Coatings, Plastics, Fibers, Adhesives, and Related Industries.* CPI Information Services. • Monthly. $397.00 per year. Abstracts of business and technical articles for polymer-based, chemical process industries. Includes a monthly list of relevant U. S. patents. International coverage.

*World Surface Coatings Abstracts.* PRA Coatings Technology Centre. • Monthly. Available in print or online.

### CD-ROM DATABASES

*OECD Statistical Compendium.* Organization for Economic Cooperation and Development. • Semiannual. $1,905.00 per year for 1 to 10 users. CD-ROM contains more than 730,000 monthly, quarterly, and annual time series for OECD countries, 1960 to date. Includes fully searchable data on agriculture, food, economic indicators, national accounts, employment, energy, finance, industry, technology, and foreign trade. Results can be displayed in various forms.

### DIRECTORIES

*Directory of American Manufacturers & Exporters of Paints, Varnishes & Allied Products.* EXIM Infotek Private Ltd. • $30 Individuals. Covers: 450 American manufacturers and exporters of abrasion resistant coatings, agricultural/horticultural foliar applied coatings, anodizing, anti-slip paints and coatings, buffing compound applicators, chartek intumescent epoxy for structural steel, coatings, coatings and coating materials, coatings-abrasion resistant, coatings-anti- graffiti, coatings-anti-skid, coatings-asphalt, coatings-ceramic, coatings-corrosion resistant, coatings-floor, coatings-heat resistant, coatings-metal, coatings-metallic, coatings-pipeline, coatings-ultraviolet, corrosion resistant, corrosion resistant coatings, custom coatings, decorative coatings, easels, electrically conductive coatings, encapsulating resins, epoxy coatings, flexible bright metallic coatings for auto wheels, trims, high performance coatings, industrial coatings, lacquers coatings, military specification coatings, optical coatings, paint brushes, paints, paper coatings, permanent protective coatings, pipe coatings, plastic coatings, polyester coatings, polyester resins and coatings, polyurethane coatings, primers coatings, refractory coatings, self locking coating for screws and studs, solvents, urethane coatings, waterproof, waterproofing coatings, wear and corrosion resistant, and wood coatings. Entries include: Company name, postal address, city, country, telephone, fax, e-mail and websites, contact person, designation, and product details.

*Directory of Chinese Manufacturers & Exporters of Paints, Varnishes & Allied Products.* EXIM Infotek Private Ltd. • $10 Individuals. Covers: 70 Chinese manufacturers and exporters of absorbent resin, coating materials, coating raw materials, coating-automobiles, coating-fire proof, coating-water proof, lacquer, latex paints, paint, paint brushes, paint mixers, paint rollers, paints, polyester paints, polyurethane resins, powder coatings, and wall paints. Entries include: Company name, postal address, city, country, phone, fax, e-mail and websites, contact person, designation, and product details.

*Directory of Japanese Manufacturers & Exporters of Paints, Varnishes & Allied Products.* EXIM Infotek Private Ltd. • $5 Individuals. Covers: 20 Japanese manufacturers and exporters of paint, paints, polyurethane resin coatings, powder coatings, and synthetic resins for paint. Entries include: Company name, postal address, city, country, phone, fax, e-mail and websites, contact person, designation, and product details.

*Directory of South Korean Manufacturers & Exporters of Paints, Varnishes & Allied Products.* EXIM Infotek Private Ltd. • $5 Individuals. Covers: 40 South Korean manufacturers and exporters of anti-corrosion products, lacquers and paints-primers, varnishes and stains-distempers, and vitreous colors/enamels and glazes. Entries include: Company name, postal address, city, country, phone, fax, e-mail and websites, contact person, designation, and product details.

*Directory of Taiwanese Manufacturers & Exporters of Paints, Varnishes & Allied Products.* EXIM Infotek Private Ltd. • $10 Individuals. Covers: 60 Taiwanese manufacturers and exporters of anti-corrosion products, lacquers and paints-primers, mastics/putties and sealing compounds, varnishes and stains-distempers, and vitreous colors/enamels and glazes. Entries include: Company name, postal address, city, country, phone, fax, e-mail and websites, contact person, designation, and product details.

## FINANCIAL RATIOS

*Annual Statement Studies.* Risk Management Association. • Annual. Compiled from over 280,000 financial statements.

*Annual Statement Studies: Industry Default Probabilities and Cash Flow Measures.* Risk Management Association. • Annual. $405 Nonmembers. Serves as a companion volume to the original *Annual Statement Studies.* Gives probability of default estimates on a percentage scale for more than 450

industries. Includes changes in position year-by-year for eight financial statement line items and provides percentage measures of cash flow.

## INTERNET DATABASES

*Business 2.0 Web Guide to the Best Business Links.* Business 2.0 Media Inc. Phone: (415)293-4800; Email: support@business2.com • URL: http://www.business2.com/webguide • Web site presents an extensive, searchable directory of links to "the best, most informative, and authoritative web pages." Twenty main categories cover business, finance, career, company information, people, and technology topics, with thousands of subtopics, all linking to Web sites recommended by experienced business researchers. Fees: Free.

*Fedstats.* Federal Interagency Council on Statistical Policy. Phone: (202)395-7254 • URL: http://www.fedstats.gov • Web site features an efficient search facility for full-text statistics produced by more than 100 federal agencies, including the Census Bureau, the Bureau of Economic Analysis, and the Bureau of Labor Statistics. Boolean searches can be made within one agency or for all agencies combined. Links are offered to international statistical bureaus, including the UN, IMF, OECD, UNESCO, Eurostat, and 20 individual countries. Fees: Free.

*FreeLunch.com.* Economy.com, Inc. Phone: (610)696-8700; Fax: (610)696-1678 • URL: http://www.freelunch.com • Web site provides free access to more than 200 million economic and financial data series, covering industry, demographics, labor markets, prices, retail sales, government spending, trade, interest rates, housing starts, the stock market, etc. Data is available in either chart or table form. Searching is offered. Free, but registration required. Economy.com, Inc. also offers fee-based economic analysis at *The Dismal Scientist* site (www.dismal.com).

*Manufacturing Profiles.* U. S. Bureau of the Census. Phone: (301)763-4636 or (301)763-4100; Fax: (301)763-4794; Email: webmaster@census.gov • URL: http://www.census.gov/prod/www/abs/mfg-prof.html • The Census Bureau makes available free on PDF (Portable Document Format) an annual consolidation of the entire Current Industrial Report series, presenting "all the data compiled." Contains statistics on production, shipments, inventories, consumption, exports, imports, and orders for a wide variety of manufactured products.

## ONLINE DATABASES

*World Surface Coatings Abstracts (Online).* Paint Research Association of Great Britain. • Indexing and abstracting of the literature of paint and surface coatings, 1976 to present. Monthly updates. Inquire as to online cost and availability.

## PERIODICALS AND NEWSLETTERS

*Modern Paint and Coatings.* Chemical Week Associates. • Monthly. $52.00 per year. A comprehensive publication highlighting formulators and suppliers to the Paint, Coatings and Ink Industry.

*Paint and Coatings Industry.* BNP Media. • Monthly. Free to members, non-members, $55.00 per year. Includes annual *Raw Material and Equipment Directory and Buyers Guide.*

*Paint and Decorating Retailer.* Paint and Decorating Retailers Association. • Monthly. $45.00 per year. Formerly *Decorating Retailer.*

## RESEARCH CENTERS AND INSTITUTES

Emulsion Polymers Institute. Lehigh University, Iacocca Hall, Rm. D-325, 111 Research Dr., Bethlehem, PA 18015. Phone: (610)758-3602; Fax: (610)758-5880; Email: eric.daniels@lehigh.edu • URL: http://www.lehigh.edu/inemuls/epi/ • Includes latex paint research.

## STATISTICS SOURCES

*Paint, Varnish, and Lacquer.* U. S. Bureau of the Census. • Quarterly and annual. Provides data on

shipments: value, quantity, imports, and exports. Includes paint, varnish, lacquer, product finishes, and special purpose coatings. (Current Industrial Reports, MQ-28F.).

*Survey of Current Business.* U. S. Government Printing Office. • Published by Bureau of Economic Analysis, U. S. Department of Commerce. Presents a wide variety of business and economic data.

## TRADE/PROFESSIONAL ASSOCIATIONS

American Coatings Association. 1500 Rhode Island Ave. NW, Washington, DC 20005. Phone: (202)462-6272; Fax: (202)462-8549 • URL: http://www.paint.org • Formerly National Paint and Coatings Association.

Painting and Decorating Contractors of America. 2316 Millpark Dr., Maryland Heights, MO 63043. Phone: 800-332-7322 or (314)514-7322; Fax: (314)890-2068; Email: rbright@pdca.org • URL: http://www.pdca.org • Painting and wallcovering contractors.

Professional Decorative Painters Association. PO Box 13427, Denver, CO 80201-3427. Email: admin@pdpa.org • URL: http://www.pdpa.org • Promotes the advancement of professional decorative painting worldwide. Provides a forum for the industry's stakeholders, craftspersons, students, and manufacturers to improve the level of practice and relationship design in the field. Offers resources to foster growth and professionalism within the industry.

# PAMPHLETS

## ABSTRACTS AND INDEXES

*Vertical File Index: Guide to Pamphlets and References to Current Topics.* H.W. Wilson Co. • 11 times a year. $115.00 per year. A subject and title index to selected pamphlet material.

# PAPER BAG INDUSTRY

## PERIODICALS AND NEWSLETTERS

*Paper, Film and Foil Converter.* Primedia Business Magazines and Media. • Monthly. $88.00 per year.

## TRADE/PROFESSIONAL ASSOCIATIONS

Paper Shipping Sack Manufacturers' Association. 5050 Blue Church Rd., Coopersburg, PA 18036. Phone: (610)282-6845; Fax: (610)282-1577; Email: admin@pssma.org • URL: http://www.pssma.com • Manufacturers of multi-wall (3-4-5-6 walls) paper shipping sacks designed for packaging and shipping products in domestic and export commerce.

# PAPER BOARD INDUSTRY

*See* PAPERBOARD AND PAPERBOARD PACKAGING INDUSTRIES

# PAPER BOX AND PAPER CONTAINER INDUSTRIES

*See also* BOX INDUSTRY; CONTAINER INDUSTRY; PAPERBOARD AND PAPERBOARD PACKAGING INDUSTRIES

## DIRECTORIES

*Paperboard Packaging Council Member Directory.* Paperboard Packaging Council. • Annual.

## STATISTICS SOURCES

*U.S. Industry and Trade Outlook.* U.S. Department of Commerce National Technical Information Service. • Annual. Produced by the International Trade Administration, U.S. Department of Commerce, in a "public-private" partnership with DRI/McGraw-Hill and Standard & Poor's. Provides basic data, outlook for the current year, and "Long-Term Prospects" (five-year projections) for a wide variety of products and services. Includes high technology industries. Formerly *U.S. Industrial Outlook.*

# PAPER CONTAINERS

*See* PAPER BOX AND PAPER CONTAINER INDUSTRIES

# PAPER INDUSTRY

*See also* PAPERBOARD AND PAPERBOARD PACKAGING INDUSTRIES; WOODPULP INDUSTRY

## ABSTRACTS AND INDEXES

*Abstract Bulletin of Paper Science and Technology.* Engineering Information Inc. • Monthly. Institutions, $1,874.00 per year. Worldwide coverage of the scientific and technical literature of interest to the pulp and paper industry.

*NTIS Alerts: Materials Sciences.* U.S. Department of Commerce National Technical Information Service. • Biweekly. $130 per year. Covers ceramics, glass, coatings, composite materials, alloys, plastics, wood, paper, adhesives, fibers, lubricants, and related subjects.

## CD-ROM DATABASES

*OECD Statistical Compendium.* Organization for Economic Cooperation and Development. • Semiannual. $1,905.00 per year for 1 to 10 users. CD-ROM contains more than 730,000 monthly, quarterly, and annual time series for OECD countries, 1960 to date. Includes fully searchable data on agriculture, food, economic indicators, national accounts, employment, energy, finance, industry, technology, and foreign trade. Results can be displayed in various forms.

## DIRECTORIES

*Directory of African Importers of Machinery for Paper & Pulp Industry.* EXIM Infotek Private Ltd. • Covers: 20 African importers of envelope making machinery, exercise book making machinery, paper making machinery and toilet paper making machines. Entries include: Company name, postal address, telephone, fax, e-mail, website, contact person, designation, and product details.

*Directory of American Manufacturers & Exporters of Paper & Paper Products.* EXIM Infotek Private Ltd. • $5 Individuals. Covers: 40 American manufacturers and exporters of bags-paper lined, carbon papers, collect and process paper for recycling, computer paper products, fax paper, paper, and white paper recycling. Entries include: Company name, postal address, city, country, phone, fax, e-mail and websites, contact person, designation, and product details.

*Directory of Australia & New Zealand Importers of Paper & Paper Products.* EXIM Infotek Private Ltd. • $150 Individuals. Covers: 30 Australian and New Zealand importers of cardboard vases, coated paper, colored copy paper, construction paper in rolls, graphic papers, greaseproof paper, kraft paper, label papers, newsprint paper, paper products, paper bags, paper cups and plates, paper napkins, paper waste, photocopy paper, printing paper, recycled paper, rice paper, specialty papers, tissue paper products, and toilet paper rolls. Entries include: Company name, postal address, telephone, fax, e-mail, website, contact person, designation, and product details.

*Directory of Chinese Importers of Paper & Paper Products.* EXIM Infotek Private Ltd. • $150 Individuals. Covers: 40 Chinese importers of newsprint, paper, wood pulp, paper products, paper waste, printing paper, pulp, and specialty paper. Entries include: Company name, postal address,

telephone, fax, e-mail, website, contact person, designation, and product details.

*Directory of Chinese Manufacturers & Exporters of Paper & Paper Products.* EXIM Infotek Private Ltd. • $10 Individuals. Covers: 60 Chinese manufacturers and exporters of cardboard, disposable paper products, craft paper tapes, napkins, paper, paper products, paper pulp, paperboard, and tissue papers. Entries include: Company name, postal address, city, country, phone, fax, e-mail and websites, contact person, designation, and product details.

*Directory of European Importers of Paper & Paper Products.* EXIM Infotek Private Ltd. • Covers: 480 European importers of coated paper, envelopes, handmade paper and products, newsprint, office goods of paper and cardboard, office papers, paper and paper products, wood pulp, paper bags, paper cups and plates, paper waste, photographic paper, printing paper, sanitary and toilet paper goods, sanitary napkins, specialty papers, sugarcane paper, tissue paper, and wrapping articles. Entries include: Company name, postal address, telephone, fax, e-mail, website, contact person, designation, and product details.

*Directory of Indian Importers of Paper & Paper Products.* EXIM Infotek Private Ltd. • $450 Individuals. Covers: 200 Indian importers of absorbent tissue, art paper, base paper, coated paper, decorative paper, kraft paper, newsprints paper, paper and paper boards, paper products, wood pulp, paper bags, paper waste, printing paper, sanitary and toilet paper goods, sanitary napkins, specialty paper, thermal paper reels for fax, and tissue paper. Entries include: Company name, postal address, telephone, fax, e-mail, website, contact person, designation, and product details.

*Directory of Japanese Importers of Paper & Paper Products.* EXIM Infotek Private Ltd. • Covers: 120 Japanese importers of base paper for coatings, corrugated paper, foreign paper, kraft paper, paper and paper boards, paper products, wood pulp, paper bags, paper boards, paper lantern, paper napkins, paper pulp products article, paperboards, printing paper, pulp, screen paper, special paper, specialty paper, tissue paper, and waste paper. Entries include: Company name, postal address, telephone, fax, e-mail, website, contact person, designation, and product details.

*Directory of Japanese Manufacturers & Exporters of Paper & Paper Products.* EXIM Infotek Private Ltd. • $10 Individuals. Covers: 50 Japanese manufacturers and exporters of copying paper, corrugated paper and board, decorative laminating paper, foreign paper, craft paper, paper, paper cups, paper napkins, paper pulp products articles, paperboard, plain paper for copying machines, printing paper, pulp, screen paper, sensitized paper for blue printing machines, special paper, stencil paper, thermal paper, and wood pulp. Entries include: Company name, postal address, city, country, phone, fax, e-mail and websites, contact person, designation, and product details.

*Directory of Middle East Importers of Machinery for Paper & Pulp Industry.* EXIM Infotek Private Ltd. • Covers: 30 Middle East importers of paper bag manufacturing machinery and paper making machinery. Entries include: Company name, postal address, telephone, fax, e-mail, website, contact person, designation, and product details.

*Directory of North American Importers of Paper & Paper Products.* EXIM Infotek Private Ltd. • Covers: 210 North American importers of copier paper, decorative paper, fax and duplicating paper, gift wrap, gold foil paper, handmade paper, handmade paper materials, kraft paper, newsprint, paper and paper products, wood pulp, paper bags, paper cups, paper goods, paper napkins, paper plates, paper waste, printing paper, recycled paper, sanitary and toilet paper goods, specialty paper, and tissue paper.

Entries include: Company name, postal address, telephone, fax, e-mail, website, contact person, designation, and product details.

*Directory of South American Importers of Machinery for Paper & Pulp Industry.* EXIM Infotek Private Ltd. • Covers: 40 South American importers of paper and pulp mill machinery and equipment and paper making machinery. Entries include: Company name, postal address, telephone, fax, e-mail, website, contact person, designation, and product details.

*Directory of South Korean Manufacturers & Exporters of Machinery for Paper & Pulp Industry.* EXIM Infotek Private Ltd. • $5 Individuals. Covers: 30 South Korean manufacturers and exporters of cardboard finishing/forming/cutting machinery/equipment, cardboard making machinery/equipment, paper finishing/converting machinery/equipment, paper making plant equipment, pulp and cellulose production plant equipment. Entries include: Company name, postal address, city, country, phone, fax, e-mail and websites, contact person, designation, and product details.

*Directory of South Korean Manufacturers & Exporters of Paper & Paper Products.* EXIM Infotek Private Ltd. • $20 Individuals. Covers: 280 South Korean manufacturers and exporters of base and backing paper, cardboard, cardboard/corrugated-packaging, coated and laminated paper/board, corrugated paper and board, paper and cardboard tubes, paper and paper rolls for technical use, paper and paper rolls printed for writing/technical, paper article-diecut/embossed, paper packaging/bags and sacks, photographic paper/board/film, printing and drawing paper/board, pulp mechanical and chemicals, reinforced cardboard and vulcanized fiber products, reinforced cardboard products, tissue paper and cellulose wadding, wallpaper and paper backed wallcoverings, wrapping/crepe paper. Entries include: Company name, postal address, city, country, phone, fax, e-mail and websites, contact person, designation, and product details.

*Directory of Taiwanese Manufacturers & Exporters of Machinery for Paper & Pulp Industry.* EXIM Infotek Private Ltd. • $10 Individuals. Covers: 120 Taiwanese manufacturers and exporters of cardboard finishing/forming/cutting machinery/equipment, cardboard making machinery/equipment, paper finishing/converting machinery/equipment, paper making plant equipment, pulp and cellulose production plant equipment. Entries include: Company name, postal address, city, country, phone, fax, e-mail and websites, contact person, designation, products detail.

*Directory of Taiwanese Manufacturers & Exporters of Paper & Paper Products.* EXIM Infotek Private Ltd. • $20 Individuals. Covers: 240 Taiwanese manufacturers and exporters of base and backing paper, cardboard, cardboard articles-diecut/embossed, cardboard/corrugated-packaging, coated and laminated paper/board, corrugated paper and board, heat transfer printing paper, paper and cardboard tubes, paper and paper rolls for technical use, paper and paper rolls printed for writing/technical, paper articles-diecut/embossed, paper packaging/bags and sacks, printing and drawing paper/board, pulp mechanical and chemicals, recycled paper pulp, reinforced cardboard products, tissue paper and cellulose wadding, wallpaper and paper backed wallcoverings, and wrapping/crepe paper. Entries include: Company name, postal address, city, country, phone, fax, e-mail and websites, contact person, designation, and product details.

*The International Directory of Importers - Paper, Paper Goods and Stationery Products Importers.* Interdata. • $295 Individuals print version. Covers: 4,400 international firms importing paper, paper goods and stationery products. Entries include: Company name and address, contact person, email, number of employees, year established, phone and telefaxes, business activity, bank references, as well as a listing of paper, paper goods and stationery products currently being imported.

*Lockwood-Post's Directory of the Pulp, Paper and Allied Trades.* Miller Freeman Inc. • Annual. $257 Individuals add shipping & handling regular ed. Covers almost 1,000 U.S. and Canadian pulp and paper companies and their mills; 4,000 paper converters; 3,000 paper merchants; and industry associations. Formerly *Lockwood's Directory of the Paper and Allied Trades.*

*Paper Manufacturers Directory.* InfoGroup Inc. • Annual. Number of listings: 1,832. Entries include: Name, address, phone, size of advertisement, name of owner or manager, number of employees, year first in "Yellow Pages." Compiled from telephone company "Yellow Pages," nationwide.

*Walden's ABC Guide.* Walden-Mott Corp. • Annual. $245 Individuals full online access and free print edition. Covers: Over 10,000 firms which manufacture, convert, and sell paper products and their suppliers. Entries include: Company name, address, phone, names of executives, and products and services offered.

### E-BOOKS

*Encyclopedia of American Industries.* Cengage Learning Inc. • 2011. $807.00. 6th edition. Three volumes. Volume one is Manufacturing Industries and volume two is Service and Non-Manufacturing Industries. Provides the history, development, and recent status of approximately 1,000 industries. Includes statistical graphs, with industry and general indexes. Also available as eBook.

### INTERNET DATABASES

*Business 2.0 Web Guide to the Best Business Links.* Business 2.0 Media Inc. Phone: (415)293-4800; Email: support@business2.com • URL: http://www.business2.com/webguide • Web site presents an extensive, searchable directory of links to "the best, most informative, and authoritative web pages." Twenty main categories cover business, finance, career, company information, people, and technology topics, with thousands of subtopics, all linking to Web sites recommended by experienced business researchers. Fees: Free.

*Fedstats.* Federal Interagency Council on Statistical Policy. Phone: (202)395-7254 • URL: http://www.fedstats.gov • Web site features an efficient search facility for full-text statistics produced by more than 100 federal agencies, including the Census Bureau, the Bureau of Economic Analysis, and the Bureau of Labor Statistics. Boolean searches can be made within one agency or for all agencies combined. Links are offered to international statistical bureaus, including the UN, IMF, OECD, UNESCO, Eurostat, and 20 individual countries. Fees: Free.

*FreeLunch.com.* Economy.com, Inc. Phone: (610)696-8700; Fax: (610)696-1678 • URL: http://www.freelunch.com • Web site provides free access to more than 200 million economic and financial data series, covering industry, demographics, labor markets, prices, retail sales, government spending, trade, interest rates, housing starts, the stock market, etc. Data is available in either chart or table form. Searching is offered. Free, but registration required. Economy.com, Inc. also offers fee-based economic analysis at *The Dismal Scientist* site (www.dismal.com).

### PERIODICALS AND NEWSLETTERS

*Paper Age.* Global Publications. • 10 times a year. $20.00 per year.

*Pulp and Paper.* Paperloop. • 11 times a year. $135.00 per year.

*Pulp and Paper Week.* Paperloop. • Weekly. $1,450 /year.

*Solutions! The Official Publication of TAPPI and*

*PIMA.* Technical Association of the Pulp & Paper Industry. • Monthly. Membership. Formerly *TAPPI Journal.*

### STATISTICS SOURCES

*The Pulp and Paper Industry in OECD Member Countries.* Organization for Economic Cooperation and Development. Organisation for Economic Co-operation and Development Publications and Information Center. • Annual. $31.00. Presents annual data on production, consumption, capacity, utilization, and foreign trade. Covers 33 pulp and paper products in OECD countries. Text in English and French.

*Standard & Poor's Industry Surveys.* Standard & Poor's Financial Services L.L.C. • Semiannual. $1,800.00. Two looseleaf volumes. Includes monthly *Supplements*. Provides detailed, individual surveys of 52 major industry groups. Each survey is revised on a semiannual basis. Also includes "Monthly Investment Review" (industry group investment analysis) and monthly "Trends & Projections" (economic analysis).

*Statistics of Paper, Paperboard and Wood Pulp.* American Forest and Paper Association. • Annual. $395.00. Formerly *Statistics of Paper and Paperboard.*

*Survey of Current Business.* U. S. Government Printing Office. • Published by Bureau of Economic Analysis, U. S. Department of Commerce. Presents a wide variety of business and economic data.

### TRADE/PROFESSIONAL ASSOCIATIONS

American Forest and Paper Association. 1101 K St., NW, Ste. 700, Washington, DC 20005. Phone: (202)463-2700; Fax: (202)463-2785; Email: info@afandpa.org • URL: http://www.afandpa.org • National trade association of the forest, pulp, paper, paperboard and wood products industry. Represents approximately 400 member companies and related trade associations that grow, harvest, and process wood and wood fiber, manufacture pulp, paper and paperboard from both virgin and recycled fiber, and produce solid wood products.

Japan Paper Exporters' Association. Kami Parupu Bldg., 3-9-11, Ginza, Chuo-ku, Tokyo, Tokyo 104-8139, Japan. Phone: 81 3 32484831; Fax: 81 3 32484834; Email: info@jpeta.or.jp • URL: http://www.jpeta.or.jp • Exporters of paper and related products. Seeks to establish and maintain a domestic and international business climate beneficial to the paper trade. Represents members' interests; gathers and disseminates information.

Japan Paper Importers' Association. Kami Papuru Bldg., 3-9-11, Ginza, Chuo-ku, Tokyo, Tokyo 104-8139, Japan. Phone: 81 3 32484831; Fax: 81 3 32484834 • URL: http://www.jpeta.or.jp • Importers of paper and related products. Seeks to establish and maintain a domestic and international business climate beneficial to the paper trade. Represents members' interests; gathers and disseminates information.

NPTA Alliance. 330 N Wabash Ave., Ste. 2000, Chicago, IL 60611. Phone: 800-355-NPTA or (312)321-4092 or (631)777-2223; Fax: (312)673-6736; Email: npta@gonpta.com • URL: http://www.gonpta.com • Wholesale distributors and suppliers of paper, plastics and allied products.

Paper Industry Management Association. 15 Technology Pkwy. S, Norcross, GA 30092. Phone: (770)209-7230; Fax: (770)209-7359 • URL: http://www.pima-online.org • Professional organization of pulp, paper mill, and paper-converting production executives.

## PAPER MONEY

*See also* MONEY

### PERIODICALS AND NEWSLETTERS

*Paper Money.* Society of Paper Money Collectors. • Bimonthly. Membership.

## PAPERBACK BOOKS

*See* PAPERBOUND BOOK INDUSTRY

## PAPERBOARD AND PAPERBOARD PACKAGING INDUSTRIES

*See also* CONTAINER INDUSTRY; PAPER BOX AND PAPER CONTAINER INDUSTRIES; PAPER INDUSTRY

### CD-ROM DATABASES

*OECD Statistical Compendium.* Organization for Economic Cooperation and Development. • Semiannual. $1,905.00 per year for 1 to 10 users. CD-ROM contains more than 730,000 monthly, quarterly, and annual time series for OECD countries, 1960 to date. Includes fully searchable data on agriculture, food, economic indicators, national accounts, employment, energy, finance, industry, technology, and foreign trade. Results can be displayed in various forms.

### FINANCIAL RATIOS

*Annual Statement Studies.* Risk Management Association. • Annual. Compiled from over 280,000 financial statements.

*Annual Statement Studies: Industry Default Probabilities and Cash Flow Measures.* Risk Management Association. • Annual. $405 Nonmembers. Serves as a companion volume to the original *Annual Statement Studies*. Gives probability of default estimates on a percentage scale for more than 450 industries. Includes changes in position year-by-year for eight financial statement line items and provides percentage measures of cash flow.

### INTERNET DATABASES

*Business 2.0 Web Guide to the Best Business Links.* Business 2.0 Media Inc. Phone: (415)293-4800; Email: support@business2.com • URL: http://www.business2.com/webguide • Web site presents an extensive, searchable directory of links to "the best, most informative, and authoritative web pages." Twenty main categories cover business, finance, career, company information, people, and technology topics, with thousands of subtopics, all linking to Web sites recommended by experienced business researchers. Fees: Free.

*Fedstats.* Federal Interagency Council on Statistical Policy. Phone: (202)395-7254 • URL: http://www.fedstats.gov • Web site features an efficient search facility for full-text statistics produced by more than 100 federal agencies, including the Census Bureau, the Bureau of Economic Analysis, and the Bureau of Labor Statistics. Boolean searches can be made within one agency or for all agencies combined. Links are offered to international statistical bureaus, including the UN, IMF, OECD, UNESCO, Eurostat, and 20 individual countries. Fees: Free.

*FreeLunch.com.* Economy.com, Inc. Phone: (610)696-8700; Fax: (610)696-1678 • URL: http://www.freelunch.com • Web site provides free access to more than 200 million economic and financial data series, covering industry, demographics, labor markets, prices, retail sales, government spending, trade, interest rates, housing starts, the stock market, etc. Data is available in either chart or table form. Searching is offered. Free, but registration required. Economy.com, Inc. also offers fee-based economic analysis at *The Dismal Scientist* site (www.dismal.com).

## PERIODICALS AND NEWSLETTERS

*Paperboard Packaging Worldwide.* Advantar Communications. • Monthly. $39.00 per year.

## PRICE SOURCES

*Official Board Markets: "The Yellow Sheet".* Mark Arzoumanian. Advantar Communications. • Weekly. $160.00 per year. Covers the corrugated container, folding carton, rigid box and waste paper industries.

## STATISTICS SOURCES

*Statistics of Paper, Paperboard and Wood Pulp.* American Forest and Paper Association. • Annual. $395.00. Formerly *Statistics of Paper and Paperboard.*

*Survey of Current Business.* U. S. Government Printing Office. • Published by Bureau of Economic Analysis, U. S. Department of Commerce. Presents a wide variety of business and economic data.

## TRADE/PROFESSIONAL ASSOCIATIONS

Paperboard Packaging Council. 1350 Main St., Ste. 1508, Springfield, MA 01103-1628. Phone: (413)686-9191; Fax: (413)747-7777; Email: ben@ paperbox.org • URL: http://www.paperbox.org • Represents manufacturers of paperboard packaging. Sponsors public relations activities, safety programs, and biannual human resource seminars. Conducts overall industry statistical studies, marketing surveys, product reviews, and labor relations and bargaining agreement studies. Provides active technical and production service.

# PAPERBOUND BOOK INDUSTRY

*See also* BOOK INDUSTRY; PUBLISHING INDUSTRY

## ALMANACS AND YEARBOOKS

*The Library and Book Trade Almanac.* Information Today, Inc. • $209 Individuals Hardbound. Reviews key trends and events and provides basic statistical information. Includes financial averages: library expenditures, salaries, and book prices. Contains lists of "best books, literary prizes, winners, and bestsellers." Formerly published by R. R. Bowker.

## DIRECTORIES

*American Book Trade Directory (ABD).* Information Today, Inc. • Annual. $379.50 Individuals softbound. Covers: Nearly 20,000 retail and antiquarian book dealers, plus 1,200 book and magazine wholesalers, distributors, and jobbers-in all 50 states and U.S. territories. Also included are sections of auctioneers of literary property, exporters/importers, booktrade associations, foreign language book dealers, book and literary appraisers, and rental library chains. Entries include: Bookstore name, address, phone, owner or manager, types and subjects of books stocked, specialty, sidelines, year established, SAN (Standard Address Number), number of volumes stocked, square footage.

*International Literary Market Place: The Directory of the International Book Publishing Industry.* Information Today, Inc. • Annual. $299 Individuals softbound. Covers more than 180 countries. Listings include publishers, literary agents, major booksellers, book clubs, literary prizes, distributors, trade associations, etc. Formerly published by R. R. Bowker.

*Literary Market Place: The Directory of the American Book Publishing Industry.* Information Today, Inc. • Annual. $399 Individuals 2-volume set/ softbound plus $25 shipping/handling. Listings include publishers, agents, ad agencies, associations, distributors, events, key executives, services, and suppliers (50 directory sections in all). Formerly published by R. R. Bowker.

## ONLINE DATABASES

*Books in Print Online.* Bowker Electronic Publishing. • The online version of *Books in Print, Forthcoming Books, Paperbound Books in Print* and other Bowker bibliographic publications: lists the books of over 50,000 U.S. publishers. Includes books recently declared out-of-print. Updated monthly. Inquire as to online cost and availability.

## PERIODICALS AND NEWSLETTERS

*Publishers Weekly: The International News Magazine of Book Publishing.* Reed Elsevier Group plc Reed Business Information. • Weekly. $20.95 print and online; monthly. The international news magazine of book publishing.

# PARKING

## DIRECTORIES

*Parking Products & Services Directory: Parking Magazine.* National Parking Association. • Annual. $125 Individuals print and online. Covers: About 300 firms supplying products and services to the parking industry, including about 52 parking consultants. Entries include: Company name, address, phone, fax, product/service descriptions.

## PERIODICALS AND NEWSLETTERS

*Downtown Idea Exchange: Essential Information for Downtown Research and Development Center.* Downtown Research and Development Center. Alexander Communications Group Inc. • Monthly. $227 Individuals. Newsletter for those concerned with central business districts. Provides news and other information on planning, development, parking, mass transit, traffic, funding, and other topics.

*Parking: The Magazine of the Parking Industry.* National Parking Association. • 10 times a year. $125.00 per year. Includes *Product and Services Directory.*

## TRADE/PROFESSIONAL ASSOCIATIONS

National Parking Association. 1112 16th St. NW, Ste. 840, Washington, DC 20036. Phone: 800-647-7275 or (202)296-4336; Fax: (202)296-3102; Email: info@npapark.org • URL: http://www.npapark.org • Owners and operators of off-street parking facilities; architects, traffic engineers, equipment suppliers and manufacturers, colleges, universities, municipalities, airport authorities; others with an interest in downtown parking. Provides specialized education programs; offers scholarship program through the Parking Industry Institute.

# PARKS

*See also* AMUSEMENT INDUSTRY

## ABSTRACTS AND INDEXES

*Environment Abstracts.* University Publications of America. • Monthly. Price varies. Provides multidisciplinary coverage of the world's environmental literature. Incorporates *Acid Rain Abstracts.*

*Environment Abstracts Annual: A Guide to the Key Environmental Literature of the Year.* University Publications of America. • Annual. $495.00. A yearly cumulation of *Environment Abstracts.*

## CD-ROM DATABASES

*Environment Abstracts on CD-ROM.* University Publications of America. • Quarterly. $1,295.00 per year. Contains the following CD-ROM databases: *Environment Abstracts, Energy Abstracts,* and *Acid Rain Abstracts.* Length of coverage varies.

## OTHER SOURCES

*Atlas & Gazetteer Series.* DeLorme. • Consists of 50 volumes covering all areas of the U. S. Includes detailed maps, as well as descriptions of attractions, natural areas, and historic sites.

## TRADE/PROFESSIONAL ASSOCIATIONS

National Association of County Park and Recreation Officials. c/o Brenda Adams-Weyant, Association Manager, PO Box 74, Marienville, PA 16239. Phone: (814)927-8212; Fax: (814)927-6659 • URL: http://www.nacpro.org • Members are elected or appointed county government officials with parks and/or recreation advisory, administrative, or policy-making authority. Stimulates interest in county park and recreation resources and works to obtain more effective use of public and privately owned land and water areas.

National Recreation and Park Association. 22377 Belmont Ridge Rd., Ashburn, VA 20148-4501. Phone: 800-262-6772 or (703)858-0784; Email: customerservice@nrpa.org • URL: http://www.nrpa. org • Formerly National Conference on State Parks.

# PARLIAMENTARY PROCEDURE

## ABSTRACTS AND INDEXES

*Current Law Index.* Cengage Learning Inc. • $1,332 Individuals. Monthly. $1269.00 per year. Produced in cooperation with the American Association of Law Libraries. Indexes more than 900 law journals, legal newspapers, and specialty publications from the U.S., Canada, U.K., Ireland, Australia, and New Zealand.

## INTERNET DATABASES

*Lexis.com Research System.* Lexis-Nexis Group. Phone: 800-227-4908 or (937)865-6800; Fax: (937)865-6909; Email: webmaster@prod.lexis-nexis.com • URL: http://www.nexis.com • Fee-based Web site offers extensive searching of a wide variety of legal sources. Additional features include Daily Opinion Service, lexis.com Bookstore, Career Center, CLE Center, Law Schools, and Practice Pages ("Pages specific to areas of specialty").

## PERIODICALS AND NEWSLETTERS

*National Parliamentarian.* National Association of Parliamentarians. • Quarterly. Provides readers with insightful, up-to-date information on parliamentary procedure and how it is applied to a variety of situations and needs.

*Parliamentary Journal.* American Institute of Parliamentarians. • Quarterly. Journal presenting organizational problems and solutions that are parliamentary in nature.

## TRADE/PROFESSIONAL ASSOCIATIONS

American Institute of Parliamentarians. 550M Ritchie Hwy., No. 271, Severna Park, MD 21146. Phone: 888-664-0428; Fax: (410)544-4640; Email: aip@aipparl.org • URL: http://www.aipparl.org • Parliamentarians and others interested in parliamentary procedure. Promotes the preparation and use of parliamentary literature. Conducts certification program qualifying members in two classes: Certified Parliamentarian and Certified Professional Parliamentarian. Encourages teaching of and provides speakers on parliamentary procedure in universities, colleges, and high schools. Conducts research. Sponsors practicum (four-day seminars in different parts of the country; scholarships available). Offers correspondence courses.

National Association of Parliamentarians. 213 S Main St., Independence, MO 64050-3808. Phone: 888-627-2929 or (816)833-3892; Fax: (816)833-3893; Email: hq@nap2.org • URL: http://www. parliamentarians.org • Represents persons interested in parliamentary procedure. Works to study, teach, promote, and disseminate the democratic principles of parliamentary law and procedure. Conducts examination and awards title of Registered Parliamentarian. Maintains referral service of Professional Registered Parliamentarians.

---

# PART-TIME EMPLOYEES

*See* TEMPORARY EMPLOYEES

# PARTICIPATIVE MANAGEMENT

## PERIODICALS AND NEWSLETTERS

*IPA Magazine.* Involvement and Participation Association. • Quarterly. $66 outside the United Kingdom. Magazine covering human development. Formerly *Involvement of Participation.*

*New Horizons.* Horticultural Research Institute. • Semiannual. Description: Explores research of the science and art of nursery, retail garden center, and landscape plant production, marketing, and care.

*Team Leader.* LRP Publications Library. • Description: Keeps business team leaders up to date on team-leading techniques and provides solutions to team-oriented issues.

## RESEARCH CENTERS AND INSTITUTES

University of California, Berkeley - Institute for Business Innovation. F402 Haas School of Business, No. 1930, Berkeley, CA 94720-1930. Phone: (510)642-4041; Fax: (510)642-2826; Email: teece@ haas.berkeley.edu • URL: http://businessinnovation. berkeley.edu • Research areas include a wide range of business management functions.

## TRADE/PROFESSIONAL ASSOCIATIONS

IdeasAmerica. PO Box 210863, Auburn Hills, MI 48321. Phone: (248)961-2674; Fax: (248)253-9252; Email: ia@ideas-america.org • URL: http://www. ideas-america.org • Represents finance, commerce, industry, and government professionals. Dedicated to the worth, contributions, and benefits of employee suggestion systems and other employee involvement processes. Supports communication between employees and employer for the purpose of exchanging ideas.

# PARTNERSHIP

## ABSTRACTS AND INDEXES

*Current Law Index.* Cengage Learning Inc. • $1,332 Individuals. Monthly. $1269.00 per year. Produced in cooperation with the American Association of Law Libraries. Indexes more than 900 law journals, legal newspapers, and specialty publications from the U.S., Canada, U.K., Ireland, Australia, and New Zealand.

## HANDBOOKS AND MANUALS

*Business Taxpayer Information Publications.* U. S. Government Printing Office. • Annual. $66 U.S. Looseleaf. Two volumes, consisting of *Circular E, Employer's Tax Guide* and *Employer's Supplemental Tax Guide.* Issued by the Internal Revenue Service (http://www.irs.ustreas.gov). Includes a variety of business-related tax information, including withholding tables, tax calendars, self-employment issues, partnership matters, corporation topics, depreciation, and bankruptcy.

## INTERNET DATABASES

*Lexis.com Research System.* Lexis-Nexis Group. Phone: 800-227-4908 or (937)865-6800; Fax: (937)865-6909; Email: webmaster@prod.lexis-nexis.com • URL: http://www.nexis.com • Fee-based Web site offers extensive searching of a wide variety of legal sources. Additional features include Daily Opinion Service, lexis.com Bookstore, Career Center, CLE Center, Law Schools, and Practice Pages ("Pages specific to areas of specialty").

## OTHER SOURCES

*Business Strategies.* Wolters Kluwer Law & Business CCH. • Semimonthly. $795.00 per year. Four looseleaf volumes. Semimonthly updates. Legal,

tax, and accounting aspects of business planning and decision-making. Provides information on start-ups, forms of ownership (partnerships, corporations), failing businesses, reorganizations, acquisitions, and so forth. Includes *Business Strategies Bulletin,* a monthly newsletter.

## PERIODICALS AND NEWSLETTERS

*Law Firm Partnership and Benefits Report.* ALM Media Properties LLC. • Monthly. $499 per year. Covers personnel issues for law firms, including compensation, partnership agreements, malpractice, employment discrimination, training, health insurance, pension plans, and other matters relating to human resources management. (A Law Journal Newsletter, formerly published by Leader Publications).

*Stanger Report: A Guide to Partnership Investing.* Robert A. Stanger & Company Inc. • Quarterly. $447 Individuals Annual. Includes overall statistics on the size of the current market, quarterly fundraising, current distribution rates and coverage and latest valuation reports for closed non-traded REITs, market updates on new registrations, newly-effective issues and fund closings, secondary market transactions, and more.

# PARTY PLAN SELLING

*See* DIRECT MARKETING

# PASTA INDUSTRY

## ABSTRACTS AND INDEXES

*Food Science and Technology Abstracts.* Ovid Technologies Inc. • Monthly. $1,780.00 per year. Provides worldwide coverage of the literature of food technology and food production.

*Foods Adlibra: Key to the World's Food Literature.* General Mills, Inc. Foods Adlibra Publications. • Semimonthly. $240.00 per year. Provides journal citations and abstracts to the literature of food technology and packaging.

## DIRECTORIES

*Major Food and Drink Companies of the World.* Cengage Learning Inc. • 12th edition. eBook. Published by Graham & Whiteside. Contains profiles and trade names for more than 9,200 important food and beverage companies in various countries. In addition to foods, includes both alcoholic and nonalcoholic drink products.

## INTERNET DATABASES

*I Love Pasta.* National Pasta Association. Phone: (202)637-5888; Fax: (202)223-9741; Email: npa@ ilovepasta.org • URL: http://www.ilovepasta.org • Web site provides a wide variety of information about pasta and the pasta industry. Includes 300 pasta recipes, pasta FAQs, and nutritional data. Industry statistics can be displayed, including data on imports, production, and per capita use in various countries. Extensive durum wheat data is provided.

## ONLINE DATABASES

*Food Science and Technology Abstracts (online).* IFIS North American Desk. • Produced by International Food Information Service. Provides about 500,000 online citations, with abstracts, to the international literature of food science, technology, commodities, engineering, and processing. Approximately 2,000 periodicals are covered. Time period is 1969 to date, with monthly updates. Inquire as to online cost and availability.

## PERIODICALS AND NEWSLETTERS

*Fancy Food and Culinary Products.* Talcott Communications Corp. • Monthly. $34.00 per year. Emphasizes new specialty food products and the business management aspects of the specialty food

and confection industries. Includes special issues on wine, cheese, candy, "upscale" cookware, and gifts. Formerly (Fancy Foods).

*National Pasta Association FYI Newsletter.* National Pasta Association. • Weekly. Membership.

*Pasta Journal.* National Pasta Association. • Bimonthly. $35.00 per year.

## TRADE/PROFESSIONAL ASSOCIATIONS

National Pasta Association. 750 National Press Bldg., 529 14th St. NW, Washington, DC 20045. Phone: (202)591-2459; Fax: (202)591-2445; Email: info@ilovepasta.org • URL: http://www.ilovepasta. org • Manufacturers of pasta in the U.S. and suppliers to the industry. Seeks to improve manufacturer and supplier efficiency. Conducts agricultural and technical research programs. Sponsors U.S. pasta product public relations program and pasta/durum wheat technical course.

# PATENTS

*See also* INVENTIONS; NEW PRODUCTS; TECHNOLOGY TRANSFER

## ABSTRACTS AND INDEXES

*CPI Digest: Key to World Literature Serving the Coatings, Plastics, Fibers, Adhesives, and Related Industries.* CPI Information Services. • Monthly. $397.00 per year. Abstracts of business and technical articles for polymer-based, chemical process industries. Includes a monthly list of relevant U. S. patents. International coverage.

*World Patent Information.* European Commission BEL. Elsevier. • Quarterly. $1,030 Institutions up to 5 authorized users. Contains papers concerned with all aspects of Industrial Property information and documentation.

## CD-ROM DATABASES

*Authority Intellectual Property Library.* Matthew Bender and Company Inc. • Quarterly. Price on request. CD-ROM contains updated full text of *Intellectual Property Counseling and Litigation, Computer Law, International Computer Law, Nimmer on Copyright, Milgrim on Trade Secrets, Patent Litigation, Patent Licensing Transactions, Trademark Protection and Practice,* and other Matthew Bender publications relating to the law of intellectual property.

*CASSIS.* U.S. Patent and Trademark Office - Office of Electronic Information Products. • CD-ROM products include *Trademarks ASSIGN* (assignment deeds, bimonthly), *Trademarks ASSIST* (search tools, single- disc), *Trademarks PENDING* (applications on file, bimonthly), *Trademarks REGISTERED* (active trademarks, 1884 to date).

*PatentWeb.* Micropatent L.L.C. • Over 50 million full-text records.

## DIRECTORIES

*Patent's Handbook: A Guide for Inventors and Researchers to Searching Patent Documents and Preparing and Making an Application.* McFarland & CPI, Publishers. • $39.95 Individuals softcover. Publication includes: List of information sources for researching patents and inventorship. Principal content of publication is an overview of the patent system in the United States. Database includes: Diagrams, facsimiles, appendix.

## ENCYCLOPEDIAS AND DICTIONARIES

*Attorney's Dictionary of Patent Claims: Legal Materials and Practice Commentaries.* Irwin M. Aisenberg. Matthew Bender and Company Inc. • $607.00. Three looseleaf volumes. Periodic supplementation. Operational guidance for bank officers, with analysis of statutory law and agency regulations.

## HANDBOOKS AND MANUALS

*Antitrust-Intellectual Property Handbook.* Alan J. Weinschel. Glasser LegalWorks. • Looseleaf. $175.00. Periodic supplementation. Covers patent licensing, patent antitrust issues, innovation markets, intervention by government agencies, standard-setting activities, royalty arrangements, and related intellectual property/antitrust topics. Provides explanations, legal guidance, and historical background.

*Intellectual Property Primary Law Sourcebook.* Matthew Bender and Company Inc. • $175 print only. Provides federal copyright, patent, and trademark statutes, as well as the Leahy-Smith America Invents Act.

*Patent Law Basics.* Thomson West. • $498.50 full set. Covers Patent and Trademark Office applications, patent ownership, rights, protection, infringement, litigation, and other fundamentals of patent law.

*Patent Law Handbook.* Thomson West. • Annual. $1,025 book-softbound. Contains detailed information on patent law.

*Protecting Trade Secrets, Patents, Copyrights, and Trademarks.* Robert C. Dorr and Christopher H. Munch. Aspen Publishers, Inc. • $165.00. Looseleaf service.

## INTERNET DATABASES

*Delphion Research.* Thomson Delphion. Phone: 800-411-4811 or (630)799-0600; Fax: (630)799-0688; Email: support@delphion.com • URL: http://www.delphion.com • Fee-based Web site provides more than 40 million records of full-text patent information from the U. S. Patent and Trademark Office and from about 70 foreign countries. Corporate and individual subscriptions are available.

*United States Patent and Trademark Office.* U. S. Department of Commerce. Phone: 800-786-9199 or (703)308-4357; Fax: (703)305-7786; Email: help@mbda.gov • URL: http://www.uspto.gov • Web site provides extensive information about patents and trademarks, with advanced search facilities for specific documents or names. "Special Pages" are available for "How to Search," "Trademarks-Logos-Brands," "Inventor Resources," and other topics. A complete fee schedule is available for filing applications, appeals, copies, etc.

## ONLINE DATABASES

*CLAIMS.* IFI/Plenum Data Corp. • Includes seven separate databases: *CLAIMS/Citation, CLAIMS/ Compound Registry, CLAIMS/Comprehensive Data Base, CLAIMS/Reassignment & Reexamination, CLAIMS/Reference, CLAIMS/U.S. Patent Abstracts,* and *CLAIMS/Uniterm.* Provides extensive current and historical information on U.S. Patents. Inquire as to online cost and availability.

*Derwent U. S. Patents.* Derwent Patent Agency. • Provides citations and abstracts for more then one million U. S. patents issued since 1971. Weekly updates. Inquire as to online cost and availability.

*Derwent World Patents Index.* Derwent Patent Agency. • Contains abstracts of more than 20 million patent documents from many countries. Time span varies. Weekly updates. Inquire as to online cost and availability.

*U.S. Patents Fulltext.* DIALOG. • Contains complete text of patents issued by the U. S. Patent and Trademark Office since 1971. Weekly updates. Inquire as to online cost and availability.

## OTHER SOURCES

*Chisum on Patents.* Matthew Bender and Company Inc. • 5/year. $5,864. 16 looseleaf volumes. An analysis of patent law in the U. S. Includes bibliography and glossary.

*Intellectual Property and Antitrust Law.* William C. Holmes. Thomson West. • Semiannual. $1,347 full set. Includes patent, trademark, and copyright practices.

## PERIODICALS AND NEWSLETTERS

*Intellectual Property Today.* • Monthly. $96.00 per year. Covers legal developments in copyright, patents, trademarks, and licensing. Emphasizes the effect of new technology on intellectual property. Formerly *Law Works.*

*Les Nouvelles.* Licensing Executives Society. • Quarterly. Description: Concerned with technological licensing and related subjects. Covers technology, patents, trademarks, and licensing "know-how" world-wide.

*Official Gazette of the United States Patent and Trademark Office: Patents.* U. S. Government Printing Office. • Weekly. Contains the Patents, Patent Office Notices, and Designs issued each week (www.uspto.gov). Annual indexes are sold separately.

*Patent and Trademark Office Society Journal.* Patent and Trademark Office Society. • Individuals, $20.00 per year.

*Patent Strategy and Management.* ALM Media Properties LLC. • Monthly. $225.00 per year. Newsletter. Provides news of recent legal and business trends in the area of patent issuance and litigation. (A Law Journal Newsletter, formerly published by Leader Publications).

## TRADE/PROFESSIONAL ASSOCIATIONS

American Intellectual Property Law Association. 241 18th St. S, Ste. 700, Arlington, VA 22202. Phone: (703)415-0780; Fax: (703)415-0786; Email: aipla@aipla.org • URL: http://www.aipla.org/Pages/default.aspx • Voluntary bar association of lawyers practicing in the fields of patents, trademarks, copyrights, and trade secrets. Aids in the operation and improvement of U.S. patent, trademark, and copyright systems, including the laws by which they are governed and rules and regulations under which federal agencies administer those laws. Sponsors moot court and legal writing competitions.

# PAYROLL ADMINISTRATION

*See* WAGES AND SALARIES

# PEACH INDUSTRY

*See also* FRUIT INDUSTRY

## DIRECTORIES

*Major Food and Drink Companies of the World.* Cengage Learning Inc. • 12th edition. eBook. Published by Graham & Whiteside. Contains profiles and trade names for more than 9,200 important food and beverage companies in various countries. In addition to foods, includes both alcoholic and nonalcoholic drink products.

## INTERNET DATABASES

*USDA.* U.S. National Institute of Standards and Technology. 100 Bureau Dr., Gaithersburg, MD 20899-1070. Phone: 800-877-8339 or (301)975-6478 or (202)720-2791; Fax: (301)975-8295; Email: inquiries@nist.gov • URL: http://www.nist.gov • The USDA home page has six sections: News and Information; What's New; About USDA; Agencies; Opportunities; Search and Help. Keyword searching is offered from the USDA home page and from various individual agency home pages. Agencies are the Economic Research Service, Agricultural Marketing Service, National Agricultural Statistics Service, National Agricultural Library, and about 12 others. Updating varies. Fees: Free.

## ONLINE DATABASES

*Food Science and Technology Abstracts (online).* IFIS North American Desk. • Produced by International Food Information Service. Provides about 500,000 online citations, with abstracts, to the international literature of food science, technology, commodities, engineering, and processing. Approximately 2,000 periodicals are covered. Time period is 1969 to date, with monthly updates. Inquire as to online cost and availability.

## PERIODICALS AND NEWSLETTERS

*Peach-Times.* National Peach Council. • Quarterly. Membership.

## STATISTICS SOURCES

*Agricultural Statistics.* U.S. Department of Agriculture National Agricultural Statistics Service. • Annual. $46 Individuals. Provides a wide variety of statistical data relating to agricultural production, supplies, consumption, prices/price-supports, foreign trade, costs, and returns, as well as farm labor, loans, income, and population. In many cases, historical data is shown annually for 10 years. In addition to farm data, includes detailed fishery statistics.

# PEANUT AND PEANUT OIL INDUSTRIES

*See also* NUT INDUSTRY; OIL AND FATS INDUSTRY

## DIRECTORIES

*American Peanut Council--Membership Directory: Peanut Industry Directory.* American Peanut Council. • Annual. Covers: About 250 growers, shellers, processors, manufacturers, brokers, and allied businesses providing goods and services to the peanut industry. Entries include: Company name, address, phone, fax, telex, e-mail, names of principal executives, subsidiary and branch names and locations, products.

*Major Food and Drink Companies of the World.* Cengage Learning Inc. • 12th edition. eBook. Published by Graham & Whiteside. Contains profiles and trade names for more than 9,200 important food and beverage companies in various countries. In addition to foods, includes both alcoholic and nonalcoholic drink products.

## INTERNET DATABASES

*USDA.* U.S. National Institute of Standards and Technology. 100 Bureau Dr., Gaithersburg, MD 20899-1070. Phone: 800-877-8339 or (301)975-6478 or (202)720-2791; Fax: (301)975-8295; Email: inquiries@nist.gov • URL: http://www.nist.gov • The USDA home page has six sections: News and Information; What's New; About USDA; Agencies; Opportunities; Search and Help. Keyword searching is offered from the USDA home page and from various individual agency home pages. Agencies are the Economic Research Service, Agricultural Marketing Service, National Agricultural Statistics Service, National Agricultural Library, and about 12 others. Updating varies. Fees: Free.

## ONLINE DATABASES

*Food Science and Technology Abstracts (online).* IFIS North American Desk. • Produced by International Food Information Service. Provides about 500,000 online citations, with abstracts, to the international literature of food science, technology, commodities, engineering, and processing. Approximately 2,000 periodicals are covered. Time period is 1969 to date, with monthly updates. Inquire as to online cost and availability.

## PERIODICALS AND NEWSLETTERS

*The Peanut Farmer: For Commercial Growers of Peanuts and Related Agribusiness.* SpecComm International Inc. • Seven times a year. $15.00 per year.

*Peanut Journal and Nut World.* Virginia-Carolina

Peanut Association. Peanut Journal Publishing Co. • Monthly. $8.00 per year.

*Peanut Science.* American Peanut Research and Education Society. • Semiannual. $9.00 per issue.

## STATISTICS SOURCES

*Agricultural Statistics.* U.S. Department of Agriculture National Agricultural Statistics Service. • Annual. $46 Individuals. Provides a wide variety of statistical data relating to agricultural production, supplies, consumption, prices/price-supports, foreign trade, costs, and returns, as well as farm labor, loans, income, and population. In many cases, historical data is shown annually for 10 years. In addition to farm data, includes detailed fishery statistics.

## TRADE/PROFESSIONAL ASSOCIATIONS

American Peanut Council. 1500 King St., Ste. 301, Alexandria, VA 22314-2737. Phone: (703)838-9500; Email: info@peanutsusa.com • URL: http://www.peanutsusa.com • Growers, shellers, brokers, processors, and manufacturers; allied businesses providing goods and services to the peanut industry. Encourages research to improve quality of peanuts.

American Peanut Research and Education Society. PO Box 15825, College Station, TX 77841. Phone: (979)845-8278 or (229)329-2949 • URL: http://www.apresinc.com • Federal, state, and private company employees involved in the peanut industry. Works to improve the welfare of all segments of the peanut industry. Provides for exchange of information, cooperative planning, and review of all phases of peanut research and extension being carried on by government agencies and private industry.

Peanut and Tree Nut Processors Association. PO Box 2660, Alexandria, VA 22301. Phone: (301)365-2521; Email: jhodges@ptnpa.org • URL: http://www.ptnpa.org • Formerly Peanut Butter Manufacturers and NutSalters Association.

# PEAR INDUSTRY

*See also* FRUIT INDUSTRY

## DIRECTORIES

*Major Food and Drink Companies of the World.* Cengage Learning Inc. • 12th edition. eBook. Published by Graham & Whiteside. Contains profiles and trade names for more than 9,200 important food and beverage companies in various countries. In addition to foods, includes both alcoholic and nonalcoholic drink products.

## INTERNET DATABASES

*USDA.* U.S. National Institute of Standards and Technology. 100 Bureau Dr., Gaithersburg, MD 20899-1070. Phone: 800-877-8339 or (301)975-6478 or (202)720-2791; Fax: (301)975-8295; Email: inquiries@nist.gov • URL: http://www.nist.gov • The USDA home page has six sections: News and Information; What's New; About USDA; Agencies; Opportunities; Search and Help. Keyword searching is offered from the USDA home page and from various individual agency home pages. Agencies are the Economic Research Service, Agricultural Marketing Service, National Agricultural Statistics Service, National Agricultural Library, and about 12 others. Updating varies. Fees: Free.

## ONLINE DATABASES

*Food Science and Technology Abstracts (online).* IFIS North American Desk. • Produced by International Food Information Service. Provides about 500,000 online citations, with abstracts, to the international literature of food science, technology, commodities, engineering, and processing. Approximately 2,000 periodicals are covered. Time period is 1969 to date, with monthly updates. Inquire as to online cost and availability.

## STATISTICS SOURCES

*Agricultural Statistics.* U.S. Department of Agriculture National Agricultural Statistics Service. • Annual. $46 Individuals. Provides a wide variety of statistical data relating to agricultural production, supplies, consumption, prices/price-supports, foreign trade, costs, and returns, as well as farm labor, loans, income, and population. In many cases, historical data is shown annually for 10 years. In addition to farm data, includes detailed fishery statistics.

# PECAN INDUSTRY

*See also* NUT INDUSTRY

## DIRECTORIES

*Major Food and Drink Companies of the World.* Cengage Learning Inc. • 12th edition. eBook. Published by Graham & Whiteside. Contains profiles and trade names for more than 9,200 important food and beverage companies in various countries. In addition to foods, includes both alcoholic and nonalcoholic drink products.

## INTERNET DATABASES

*USDA.* U.S. National Institute of Standards and Technology. 100 Bureau Dr., Gaithersburg, MD 20899-1070. Phone: 800-877-8339 or (301)975-6478 or (202)720-2791; Fax: (301)975-8295; Email: inquiries@nist.gov • URL: http://www.nist.gov • The USDA home page has six sections: News and Information; What's New; About USDA; Agencies; Opportunities; Search and Help. Keyword searching is offered from the USDA home page and from various individual agency home pages. Agencies are the Economic Research Service, Agricultural Marketing Service, National Agricultural Statistics Service, National Agricultural Library, and about 12 others. Updating varies. Fees: Free.

## ONLINE DATABASES

*Food Science and Technology Abstracts (online).* IFIS North American Desk. • Produced by International Food Information Service. Provides about 500,000 online citations, with abstracts, to the international literature of food science, technology, commodities, engineering, and processing. Approximately 2,000 periodicals are covered. Time period is 1969 to date, with monthly updates. Inquire as to online cost and availability.

## PERIODICALS AND NEWSLETTERS

*Pecan South.* Texas Pecan Growers Association. • Monthly. $18.00 per year.

## STATISTICS SOURCES

*Agricultural Statistics.* U.S. Department of Agriculture National Agricultural Statistics Service. • Annual. $46 Individuals. Provides a wide variety of statistical data relating to agricultural production, supplies, consumption, prices/price-supports, foreign trade, costs, and returns, as well as farm labor, loans, income, and population. In many cases, historical data is shown annually for 10 years. In addition to farm data, includes detailed fishery statistics.

## TRADE/PROFESSIONAL ASSOCIATIONS

National Pecan Shellers Association. 1100 Johnson Ferry Rd., Ste. 300, Atlanta, GA 30342. Phone: (678)298-1189; Email: npsa@kellencompany.com • URL: http://www.ilovepecans.org • Shellers and processors of pecans. Promotes the welfare and interests of the pecan shelling and processing industry.

# PENCILS

*See* WRITING INSTRUMENTS

# PENNY STOCKS

*See* OVER-THE-COUNTER SECURITIES INDUSTRY

# PENS

*See* WRITING INSTRUMENTS

# PENSIONS

*See also* EMPLOYEE BENEFIT PLANS; ESTATE PLANNING; TRUSTS AND TRUSTEES; Individual Retirement Accounts

## ABSTRACTS AND INDEXES

*Insurance Periodicals Index.* Specials Libraries Association, Insurance and Employees Benefits Div. NILS Publishing Co. • Annual. $250.00. Compiled by the Insurance and Employee Benefits Div., Special Libraries Association. A yearly index of over 15,000 articles from about 35 insurance periodicals. Arrangement is by subject, with an index to authors.

## BIBLIOGRAPHIES

*Insurance and Employee Benefits Literature.* Special Libraries Association. • Bimonthly. $15.00 per year. Lists a wide variety of literature in all branches of the insurance industry. Includes annotations.

## DIRECTORIES

*America's Corporate Finance Directory.* LexisNexis. • Annual. $1,399 Individuals print. Covers: Financial personnel and outside financial services relationships of 5,000 leading United States corporations and their wholly-owned United States subsidiaries. Entries include: Company name, address, phone, fax, telex, e-mail addresses, stock exchange information, earnings, total assets, size of pension/profit-sharing fund portfolio, number of employees, description of business, wholly-owned U.S. Subsidiaries of parent company; name and title of key executives; outside suppliers of financial services.

*Money Market Directory of Pension Funds and Their Investment Managers.* Standard & Poors Money Market Directories. • Institutional funds and managers.

*National Directory of Pension Funds That Invest in Real Estate Investments and Mortgages.* Communication Network International Inc. • Irregular. $750 payment must accompany order. Covers: 1,300 pension funds. Entries include: Fund name, manager's name, address, phone, amount of investment.

*Nelson Information's Directory of Pension Fund Consultants.* Nelson Information. • Annual. $995. Covers the pension plan sponsor industry. More than 325 worldwide consulting firms are described. Formerly *Nelson's Guide to Pension Fund Consultants.*

*Nelson Information's Directory of Plan Sponsors.* Nelson Information. • Annual. Approximately 19,000 plan sponsors (corporate, union, public/government, endowment, foundation, and hospital) of investments (pensions, endowments) funds with assets over $10 million. Formerly *Nelson's Directory of Plan Sponsors and Tax-Exempt Funds.*

## ENCYCLOPEDIAS AND DICTIONARIES

*Encyclopedia of Aging.* David J. Ekerdt, editor. Cengage Learning Inc. • $770. Includes articles relating to the financial aspects of aging, such as housing, long-term care insurance, pensions, social security, individual retirement accounts, savings, and retirement planning. eBook also available. Inquire for pricing.

## HANDBOOKS AND MANUALS

*Pension and Employee Benefits: Code-ERISA and Regulations.* Wolters Kluwer Law & Business CCH. • $123.00. Two volumes.

*Pension and Profit Sharing Plans for Small or Medium Size Businesses.* Aspen Publishers, Inc. • Monthly. $191.50 per year. Newsletter. Topics of interest and concern to professionals who serve small and medium size pension and profit sharing plans.

*Pension Plan Fix-It Handbook.* Thompson Publishing Group Inc. • Two looseleaf volumes. $529.00 per year. Two looseleaf volumes. Monthly updates and newsletters. Serves as a comprehensive guide to pension plan administration, taxation, and federal regulation. Includes both defined benefit and defined contribution plans.

*Retirement Benefits Tax Guide.* Wolters Kluwer Law & Business CCH. • $199.00. Looseleaf service.

*U.S. Master Pension Guide.* Wolters Kluwer Law & Business CCH. • Annual. $99.95 1 - 4 (quantity). Explains IRS rules and regulations applying to 401(k) plans, 403(k) plans, ESOPs (employee stock ownership plans), IRAs, SEPs (simplified employee pension plans), Keogh plans, and nonqualified plans.

## INTERNET DATABASES

*EBSCO Information Services.* EBSCO Publishing Inc. 10 Estes St., Ipswich, MA 01938-2106. Phone: 800-653-2726 or (978)356-6500; Fax: (978)356-6565; Email: information@ebscohost.com • URL: http://www.ebscohost.com • Fee-based Web site providing Internet access to a wide variety of databases, including business-related material. Full text is available for many periodical titles, with daily updates. Fees: Apply.

*Free Insurance Advice.* InsWeb, Inc. 2868 Prospect Park Dr., Ste. 650, Rancho Cordova, CA 95670. Phone: (916)853-3300; Fax: (916)853-3300; Email: customercare@insweb.com • URL: http://www.insweb.com • Web site offers a wide variety of advice and information on automobile, life, health, and "other" insurance. Includes glossaries of insurance terms, Standard & Poor's ratings of individual insurance companies, and "Financial Needs Estimators." Searching is available. Fees: Free.

*InSite 2.* Intelligence Data/Thomson Financial. Phone: 800-654-0393 or (617)856-1890; Fax: (617)737-3182; Email: intelligence.data@tfn.com • URL: http://www.insite2.gale.com/ • Fee-based Web site consolidates information in a "Base Pack" consisting of Business InSite, Market InSite, and Company InSite. Optional databases are Consumer InSite, Health and Wellness InSite, Newsletter InSite, and Computer InSite. Includes fulltext content from more than 2,500 trade publications, journals, newsletters, newspapers, analyst reports, and other sources. Continuous updating. Formerly produced by The Gale Group.

*ProQuest.* ProQuest L.L.C. 789 E Eisenhower Pkwy., Ann Arbor, MI 48106-1346. Phone: 800-521-0600 or (734)761-4700; Fax: (734)662-4554; Email: info@proquest.com • URL: http://www.proquest.com • Fee-based Web site providing Internet access to more than 3,000 periodicals, newspapers, and other publications. Many items are available full-text, with daily updates. Includes extensive corporate and financial information. Fees: Apply.

*Small Business Retirement Savings Advisor.* U. S. Department of Labor. Phone: (202)219-8921 • URL: http://www.dol.gov/elaws/pwbaplan.htm • Web site provides "answers to a variety of commonly asked questions about retirement saving options for small business employers." Includes a comparison chart and detailed descriptions of various plans: 401(k), SEP-IRA, SIMPLE-IRA, Payroll Deduction IRA, Keogh Profit-Sharing, Keogh Money Purchase, and Defined Benefit. Searching is offered. Fees: Free.

## OTHER SOURCES

*BNA Pension and Benefits Reporter.* Bloomberg BNA. • Weekly. $996.00 per year. Three looseleaf volumes. Legal developments affecting pensions. Formerly *BNA Pension Reporter.*

*Individual Retirement Plans Guide.* Wolters Kluwer Law & Business CCH. • $540.00 per year. Looseleaf service. Monthly updates. Covers IRA plans (Individual Retirement Accounts), SEP plans (Simplified Employee Pensions), and Keogh plans (self-employed retirement accounts).

*Lieber on Pensions.* William M. Lieber. Wolters Kluwer Law and Business. • $595.00. Five volumes. Looseleaf service. Periodic supplementation. Organizes, describes, and analyzes ERISA and IRS pension rules. Topical arrangement.

*Pension Fund Litigation Reporter.* Andrews Publications. • Semimonthly. $750.00 per year. Newsletter. Contains reports on legal cases involving pension fund fiduciaries (trustees).

## PERIODICALS AND NEWSLETTERS

*Contingencies: The Magazine of the Actuarial Profession.* American Academy of Actuaries. • Bimonthly. $24 Nonmembers. Provides non-technical articles on the actuarial aspects of insurance, employee benefits, and pensions.

*Employee Benefit Plan Review.* Charles D. Spencer and Associates, Inc. • $395 Individuals. Monthly. Provides a review of recent events affecting the administration of employee benefit programs.

*Money Management Letter: Bi-Weekly Newsletter Covering the Pensions and Money Maagement Industry.* Institutional Investor Inc. Journals Group. • Biweekly. $2,440.00 per year. Newsletter. Includes print and online editions. Edited for pension fund investment managers.

*Older Americans Report.* Business Publishers Inc. • Bimonthly. $449 Individuals. Description: Features brief articles on legislative, judicial, and federal agency activities concerning older Americans. Covers news of developments in such areas as Social Security, social services, Medicare, programs for retirement and pension funds, research projects, and the Older Americans Act. Recurring features include book reviews and a calendar of events.

*Pensions and Investments: The Newspaper of Corporate and Institutional Investing.* Crain Communications Inc. • Biweekly. $325.00 per year. Formerly *Pensions and Investment Age.*

*Retirement Plans Bulletin: Practical Explanations for the IRA and Retirement Plan Professional.* Universal Pensions Inc. • Monthly. $99.00 per year. Newsletter. Provides information on the rules and regulations governing qualified (tax-deferred) retirement plans.

## RESEARCH CENTERS AND INSTITUTES

Center for Pension and Retirement Research. Miami University, Department of Economics, 109E Laws Hall, Oxford, OH 45056. Phone: (513)529-2850; Fax: (513)529-3308; Email: swilliamson@eh.net • Research areas include pension economics, pension plans, and retirement decisions.

Pension Research Council. The Wharton School of the University of Pennsylvania, 3620 Locust Walk, 3000 Steinberg Hall - Dietrich Hall, Philadelphia, PA 19104-6302. Phone: (215)898-7620; Fax: (215)573-3418; Email: prc@wharton.upenn.edu • URL: http://www.pensionresearchcouncil.org • Research areas include various types of private sector and public employee pension plans.

## STATISTICS SOURCES

*EBRI Pension Investment Report.* Employee Benefit Research Institute. • Periodic Quarterly. $500 /issue for nonmembers. Irregular. Membership.

*Pension Facts.* American Council of Life Insurance. • Biennial. Free.

## TRADE/PROFESSIONAL ASSOCIATIONS

American Benefits Council. 1501 M St. NW, Ste. 600, Washington, DC 20005-1775. Phone: (202)289-6700; Fax: (202)289-4582; Email: info@abcstaff.org • URL: http://www.americanbenefitscouncil.org • Serves as national trade association for companies concerned about federal legislation and regulations affecting all aspects of the employee benefits system. Represents the entire spectrum of the private employee benefits community and sponsors or administers retirement and health plans covering more than one hundred million Americans.

American Society of Pension Professionals and Actuaries. 4245 N Fairfax Dr., Ste. 750, Arlington, VA 22203. Phone: (703)516-9300; Fax: (703)516-9308; Email: customercare@asppa.org • URL: http://www.asppa.org • Members are involved in the pension and insurance aspects of employee benefits. Includes an Insurance and Risk Management Committee, and sponsors an annual 401(k) Workshop.

Association of Canadian Pension Management. 1255 Bay St., Ste. 304, Toronto, ON, Canada M5R 2A9. Phone: (416)964-1260; Fax: (416)964-0567; Email: info@acpm.com • URL: http://www.acpm.com/aboutACPM.aspx • Works to improve the health and growth of the Canadian public and private retirement income systems. Advocates clarity, good governance and administration and balanced consideration of shareholder interests to federal and provincial legislators and regulators on behalf of the Canadian pension industry.

Council of Institutional Investors. 888 17th St. NW, Ste. 500, Washington, DC 20006. Phone: (202)822-0800; Fax: (202)822-0801; Email: info@cii.org • URL: http://www.cii.org • Members are nonprofit organization pension plans and other nonprofit institutional investors.

Japanese Society of Certified Pension Actuaries. Mita NN Bldg., B1F, 4-1-23 Shiba, Minato-ku, Tokyo, Tokyo 108-0014, Japan. Phone: 81 3 54420208; Fax: 81 3 54420700 • URL: http://www.jscpa.or.jp/english • Maintains and upholds standards of practice for certified pension actuaries.

# PEPPER INDUSTRY

*See* SPICE INDUSTRY

# PERFORMANCE EVALUATION

*See* RATING OF EMPLOYEES

# PERFORMING ARTS

*See* SHOW BUSINESS

# PERFUME INDUSTRY

*See also* COSMETICS INDUSTRY

## DIRECTORIES

*Directory of American Manufacturers & Exporters of Essential Oils.* EXIM Infotek Private Ltd. • $10 Individuals. Covers: 90 American manufacturers & exporters of essential oil of peppermint & spearmint, essential oils, fragrance, massage oils. Entries include: Company name, postal address, city, country, phone, fax, e-mail & websites, contact person, designation, products detail.

*Fragrance and Olfactory Dictionary.* Fragrance Foundation. • Irregular. $5 for members. Principal content of publication definitions of fragrance and olfactory terms.

*Who's Who Membership Directory.* Personal Care Product Council. • Annual. Available on website. Lists 600 member companies, with key personnel, products, and services.

*World Cosmetics and Toiletries Marketing Directory.* Cengage Learning Inc. • 2010. $475.00. 6th edition. Published by Euromonitor. Provides detailed descriptions of the world's cosmetics and toiletries companies. Includes consumers market research data.

## ONLINE DATABASES

*F-D-C Reports.* Elsevier Business Intelligence. • An online version of "The Gray Sheet" (medical devices), "The Pink Sheet" (pharmaceuticals), "The Rose Sheet" (cosmetics), "The Blue Sheet" (biomedical), and "The Tan Sheet" (nonprescription). Contains full-text information on legal, technical, corporate, financial, and marketing developments from 1987 to date, with weekly updates. Inquire as to online cost and availability.

## PERIODICALS AND NEWSLETTERS

*Executive Update.* Personal Care Product Council. • Monthly newsletter for members.

*Perfumer and Flavorist.* Allured Business Media. • Monthly. $135.00 per year. Provides information on the art and technology of flavors and fragrances, including essential oils, aroma chemicals, and spices.

*The Rose Sheet: Toiletries, Fragrances and Skin Care.* Elsevier Business Intelligence. • 51 times a year. $1,910.00 online only. Newsletter. Provides industry news, regulatory news, market data, and a "Weekly Trademark Review" for the cosmetics industry.

## STATISTICS SOURCES

*Synthetic Organic Chemicals: United States Production and Sales.* International Trade Commission. U. S. Government Printing Office. • Annual.

## TRADE/PROFESSIONAL ASSOCIATIONS

Personal Care Products Council. 1620 L St. NW, Ste. 1200, Washington, DC 20036. Phone: (202)331-1770; Fax: (202)331-1969 • URL: http://www.personalcarecouncil.org • Formerly Cosmetic, Toiletry and Fragrance Association.

# PERIODICALS

*See also* HOUSE ORGANS; NEWSLETTERS; NEWSPAPERS; TRADE JOURNALS

## ABSTRACTS AND INDEXES

*Applied Science and Technology Index.* EBSCO Publishing Inc. • 11/year. Indexes a wide variety of English language technical, industrial, and engineering periodicals.

*Business Periodicals Index Retrospective.* EBSCO Publishing Inc. • 11/year. Quarterly and annual cumulations.

*Government Periodicals Index.* ProQuest L.L.C. • An index to approximately 180 periodicals issued by various agencies of the federal government.

*Humanities Index.* H.W. Wilson Co. • Quarterly. Annual cumulation. Price varies.

*Readers' Guide to Periodical Literature.* EBSCO Publishing Inc. • Provides indexing for over 400 periodicals dating back to 1983.

*Social Sciences Citation Index.* Thomson Reuters Corp. • Weekly. Product is accessed via *Web of Science.*

*Social Sciences Index Retrospective: 1907-1983.* EBSCO Publishing Inc. • Indexing for 1,000,000 articles. Coverage includes international index and social sciences and humanities index.

## BIBLIOGRAPHIES

*U.S. Government Subscriptions.* U. S. Government Printing Office. • Quarterly. Free. Includes agency and subject indexes.

## CD-ROM DATABASES

*MediaFinder.* Oxbridge Communications Inc. • $1,295 per year. Online database with 77,000 magazines, catalogs, newspapers, and journals.

*Readers' Guide to Periodical Literature.* EBSCO Publishing Inc. • Provides indexing for over 400 periodicals dating back to 1983.

*Serials Directory.* EBSCO Publishing Inc. • Contains data from more than 108,000 worldwide publishers.

*Social Sciences Abstracts.* EBSCO Publishing Inc. • Provides indexing from 1983 and abstracting from 1994 of more than 750 periodicals covering economics, area studies, community health, public administration, public welfare, urban studies, and many other topics related to the social sciences.

*Social Sciences Citation Index.* Thomson Reuters Corp. • Weekly. Product is accessed via *Web of Science.*

## DIRECTORIES

*Burrelle's Media Directory: Magazines and Newsletters.* BurrellesLuce. • Annual. $550.00. Provides detailed descriptions of more than 13,500 magazines and newsletters published in the U.S., Canada, and Mexico. Categories are professional, consumer, trade, and college. Semiannual *Updates.* Includes CD-ROM.

*Business Education Forum--Professional Leadership Roster Issue.* National Business Education Association. • Quarterly. Publication includes: List of key personnel in business education, including officers of national, regional, and state associations and state and local supervisory personnel in business education. Entries include: Institution or association name, names of officers and board members, addresses, phone, and Internet address.

*Business Finland.* Helsinki Media. • Annual. Publication includes: Lists of 250 major exporters and the 50 largest business groups in Finland. Principal content of publication is information on Finnish business and economic issues. Entries include: Company or organization name, address, phone, name and title of contact, number of employees, financial data, description, Standard Industrial Classification (SIC) code.

*Business Week--Survey of Executive Compensation Issue.* The McGraw-Hill Companies Inc. • Weekly. $46.95 for 1 year. Publication includes: Executives in major industries of the United States and their compensation in salary, bonuses, stock options, stock appreciation rights. Entries include: Company name, sales, and return on equity; names and titles of chief executives, salary, and total of salary and bonus with percentage of change from prior year, long term compensation, one-year and three-year pay to performance analysis.

*Cabell's Directory of Publishing Opportunities in Economics and Finance.* Cabell Publishing Inc. • Irregular. Covers: Over 860 scholarly periodicals in economics and finance. Entries include: Publication name, address, subject interests, editorial guidelines and style, submission procedures, audience and circulation of the publication, and reviewer acceptance rate data.

*Cabell's Directory of Publishing Opportunities in Management.* Cabell Publishing Inc. • Irregular. $244.95 Individuals. Covers: Over 1,180 scholarly periodicals in management. Entries include: Publication name, address, subject interests, editorial guidelines and style, submission procedures, audience and circulation of the publication, and reviewer acceptance rate data.

*Compuserve Companion: Finding Newspapers and Magazines Online.* BiblioData. • $29.95. Covers: More than 3,200 newspapers, newsletters, and magazines that are available for full text searching on CompuServe. Database includes: Introductory

chapter of searching tips. Entries include: Publication name, dates of coverage, lag times, and appropriate "Go" commands.

*Corporate Philanthropy in New England.* Development and Technical Assistance Center Inc. • Irregular. $80 Connecticut. Corporations in New England that have gross sales of over $10 million or at least 200 employees and an office in the state and that have given grants or have other funding programs; separate editions available for Connecticut, Maine, New Hampshire, Rhode Island, and Vermont.

*Dance Magazine College Guide.* Dance Magazine Inc. • Annual. $46.95 Individuals. Covers: Approximately 600 college-level dance programs. Entries include: College name, address, phone, and name of contact for dance department; degrees offered; degree requirements; facilities; special programs; admission requirements; tuition and fees; financial aid available. Also includes articles on issues in dance education.

*Facilities Design & Management--Directory Issue.* Bpi Communications Inc. • $10. Publication includes: List of about 2,000 suppliers of office furnishings, equipment, services; professional associations. Entries include: For suppliers--Company name, address, phone, products or services. For associations--Name, address.

*Florida Trend--Directory of Public Companies Issue.* Trend Book Div. • Annual. $3.95. Publication includes: List of 250 publicly owned companies headquartered in Florida. Entries include: Name, address, phone, name of chief executive, financial keys, product or service.

*Forbes--Chief Executive Compensation Survey Issue.* Forbes Inc. • Annual. $4.95. Publication includes: List of 800 firms. Entries include: (In tabular form) Company name, name of chief executive officer, age, rank, compensation in salary and bonus, other remuneration, stock gains, total remuneration, years with company, years as chief executive, place of birth, educational and business background.

*Fortune--Deals of the Year Issue.* Time Inc. • $5. Publication includes: 50 largest United States corporate financial transactions, including mergers, acquisitions, leveraged buyouts, and debt and equity offerings. Entries include: Companies involved, value (value and percent of book value), date and type of transaction, type of industry, financial intermediary, fee charged.

*Grey House Directory of Special Issues: A Guide to Business Magazines.* Grey House Publishing. • $175 Softcover. Covers: 4,000 business magazines with special issues as well as industry-specific magazines targeting researchers. Entries include: Publisher name, address, phone, fax, e-mail, brief description of content or audience.

*Imaging Supplies Annual.* Forrester Research Inc. • Annual. $125. Publication includes: List of over 300 service companies, suppliers and manufacturers of products such as ribbons, ink jet ink, toner, photo conductors, technology-specific papers and print elements for computer printers, typewriters, copiers, and other office equipment. Entries include: Company name, address, phone, fax, telex, name and title of contact, products, services, coding to indicate distribution method. Principal content of publication is articles about the imaging supplies industry.

*Importing for the Small Business: The Daily Telegraph Guide.* Kogan Page, Limited. • Irregular. $8.99. Publication includes: List of organizations able to help small businesses in the United Kingdom. Entries include: Organization name, address. Principal contents are articles on ordering, transport, payment, customs, and related aspects of importing for small businesses.

*International Directory of Little Magazines and Small Presses.* Dustbooks. • Annual. $65 Individuals CD-ROM (3 directories). Over 4,000 small, independent magazines, presses, and papers.

*Los Angeles Business Journal--Book of Lists.* LABJ Inc. • Annual. $395. Covers: major companies, foundations, government officials, utilities, newspapers, radio and television stations, airlines, hospitals, financial institutions, shopping centers, resorts, and prominent individuals in Los Angeles County, California. Incorporates information in "Los Angeles Business Journal--Consultants Directory," now discontinued.

*The Merger Yearbook.* Cambridge Corp. • Annual. $490 plus $5.00 shipping. Publication includes: About 15,000 mergers and joint ventures announced during preceding year, including lists of largest mergers, firms participating most frequently in acquisitions or joint ventures, active acquirers and divesters, acquisitions by foreign firms, and leveraged buyouts, mergers, and joint ventures in preceding year. Principal content of pubication is information on corporate mergers and acquisitions. Entries include: Company names, locations, and announced terms and prices; many listings include financial or other data.

*Mergers & Acquisitions Magazine--Rosters.* MLR Publishing Co. • Bimonthly. $70 per issue. Each issue includes a roster in three sections: "Mergers & Acquisitions," covering major deals concluded between American firms; "Foreign Investment in the U.S.," covering foreign firms which acquired companies in the United States; and "U.S. Investment Abroad," covering acquisitions by United States firms in other countries. Additional information on pending and completed deals, cancellations, and sell-offs is given in news sections. Entries include: Names and locations of participants, sales and net income of each, terms, lines of business of each participant, and effective date of transaction.

*Office Products Dealer--Product Buying Guide and Industry Directory Issue.* Hitchcock Publishing Co. • Annual. $15 plus $3.00 shipping. Publication includes: Lists of manufacturers, wholesalers, and distributors of furniture, machines, computer and word processing systems, and office products and equipment; manufacturers' representatives, and national industry associations that serve retail office products dealers.

*Plant Shutdowns Monitor.* DataCenter. • Monthly. $450 per year for profit organizations. Provides monthly listings of United States plant and business closures, layoffs, corporate downsizing and moves, organized by company involved; includes event location, industry, number of workers involved, explanatory notes.

*Researching Markets, Industries, & Business Opportunities.* MarketResearch.com. • Irregular. $245. Publication includes: Lists of sources of business and market information. Entries include: Source name, address, phone, description. Principal content of publication is discussion of methods for studying markets and industries.

*Serials Directory: An International Reference Book.* EBSCO Publishing Inc. • Quarterly. $525. Covers: Over 185,000 current and ceased periodicals and serials worldwide. Entries include: Serial title, publisher, address, phone, price, ISSN; Library of Congress, Dewey Decimal, National Library of Medicine, and Universal Decimal classification numbers; CODEN designations, description of editorial content; whether publication is peer reviewed; name of advertising manager; registration at the Copyright Clearance Center. Other format availabilities (CD-Rom), indexing and abstracting information.

*Signs of the Times Magazine--Buyers' Guide Issue.* ST Media Group International Inc. • Annual. Publication includes: List of more than 600 manufacturers and distributors of equipment and supplies for the sign industry; trade associations, consultants, trade shows, and other related organizations. Entries include: For manufacturers and distributors--Company name, address, phone, name of sales contact; manufacturer listings also include product lines. For others--Organization name, address, phone; trade show listings include dates.

*Signs of the Times Magazine--Sign Erection and Maintenance Directory Section.* ST Media Group International Inc. • Monthly. Publication includes: List of over 750 companies that erect or maintain electrical signs. Entries include: Company name, address, phone, services.

*Signs of the Times Magazine--Sign Supply Distributors Directory Section.* ST Media Group International Inc. • Monthly. $39 per year -13 issues. Publication includes: List of more than 80 suppliers of products and services used by sign companies; all listings are paid. Entries include: Name of firm, address, phone, code indicating type of product.

*Standard Periodical Directory.* Oxbridge Communications Inc. • Annual. $1,995 Individuals print version. Covers: 63,000 magazines, journals, newsletters, directories, house organs, association publications, etc., in the United States and Canada. Entries include: Publication current and former title; publisher name, address, phone; names and titles of key personnel; circulation and advertising rates; description of contents; ISSN, year founded, frequency; subscription rates, print method, page size, number of pages.

*Starting a Successful Small Business.* Kogan Page, Limited. • Irregular. $8.99. Publication includes: List of organizations of assistance to those starting small businesses. Entries include: Organization name, address. Principal content of publication is a discussion of how to set up a successful small business, including marketing, finances, legal questions, employment, and insurance.

*Swap Meet Magazine.* Forum Publishing Co. • Monthly. $29.97 Individuals 1 year (12 issues). Covers: Over 5,000 manufacturers and importers of jewelry, electronics, clothing, cosmetics, watches, novelties, and other items that are sold to merchandise retailers and flee market vendors at wholesale prices. Entries include: Company name, address, phone, products or services.

*Ulrich's Periodicals Directory: International Periodicals Information Since 1932.* R.R. Bowker L.L.C. • Annual. $1,260 Individuals Hardcover, 4 volumes. Covers: Nearly 200,000 current periodicals and newspapers published worldwide. Entries include: In main list--Publication title; Dewey Decimal Classification number, Library of Congress Classification Number (where applicable), CODEN designation (for sci-tech serials), British Library Document Supply Centre shelfmark number, country code, ISSN; subtitle, language(s) of text, year first published, frequency, subscription prices, sponsoring organization, publishing company name, address, phone, fax, e-mail and website addresses, editor and publisher names; regular features (reviews, advertising, abstracts, bibliographies, trade literature, etc. ), indexes, circulation, format, brief description of content; availability of microforms and reprints; whether refereed; CD-ROM availability with vendor name; online availability with service name; services that index or abstract the periodical, with years covered; advertising rates and contact; right and permissions contact name and phone; availability through document deliver.

*Working Press of the Nation.* R.R. Bowker L.L.C. • Annual. $530.00. $295.00 per volume. Three volumes: (1) *Newspaper Directory*; (2) *Magazine and Internal Publications Directory*; (3) *Radio and Television Directory.* Includes names of editors and other personnel.

## FINANCIAL RATIOS

*Annual Statement Studies.* Risk Management Association. • Annual. Compiled from over 280,000 financial statements.

*Annual Statement Studies: Industry Default Probabilities and Cash Flow Measures.* Risk Management Association. • Annual. $405 Nonmembers. Serves as a companion volume to the original *Annual Statement Studies*. Gives probability of default estimates on a percentage scale for more than 450 industries. Includes changes in position year-by-year for eight financial statement line items and provides percentage measures of cash flow.

## INTERNET DATABASES

*EBSCO Information Services.* EBSCO Publishing Inc. 10 Estes.St., Ipswich, MA 01938-2106. Phone: 800-653-2726 or (978)356-6500; Fax: (978)356-6565; Email: information@ebscohost.com • URL: http://www.ebscohost.com • Fee-based Web site providing Internet access to a wide variety of databases, including business-related material. Full text is available for many periodical titles, with daily updates. Fees: Apply.

*ProQuest.* ProQuest L.L.C. 789 E Eisenhower Pkwy., Ann Arbor, MI 48106-1346. Phone: 800-521-0600 or (734)761-4700; Fax: (734)662-4554; Email: info@proquest.com • URL: http://www.proquest.com • Fee-based Web site providing Internet access to more than 3,000 periodicals, newspapers, and other publications. Many items are available full-text, with daily updates. Includes extensive corporate and financial information. Fees: Apply.

*PubList.com: The Internet Directory of Publications.* Bowes & Associates, Inc. Phone: (781)792-0999; Fax: (781)792-0988; Email: info@publist.com • URL: http://www.publist.com • "The premier online global resource for information about print and electronic publications." Provides online searching for information on more than 150,000 magazines, journals, newsletters, e-journals, and monographs. Database entries generally include title, publisher, format, address, editor, circulation, subject, and International Standard Serial Number (ISSN). Fees: Free.

*Ulrichsweb.com.* R.R. Bowker L.L.C. 630 Central Ave, New Providence, NJ 07974. Phone: 888-269-5372 or (908)286-1090; Email: info@bowker.com • URL: http://www.bowker.com • Web site provides fee-based access to about 250,000 serials records from the *Ulrich's International Periodicals Directory* database. Includes periodical evaluations from *Library Journal* and *Magazines for Libraries*. Monthly updates.

*WilsonWeb Periodicals Databases.* H.W. Wilson Co. 950 University Ave., Bronx, NY 10452-4224. Phone: 800-367-6770 or (718)588-8400 or (718)558-8400; Fax: (718)590-1617 or (800)590-1617; Email: custserv@hwwilson.com • URL: http://www.hwwilson.com • Web sites provide fee-based access to *Wilson Business Full Text, Applied Science & Technology Full Text, Biological & Agricultural Index, Library Literature & Information Science Full Text*, and *Readers' Guide Full Text, Mega Edition*. Daily updates.

## ONLINE DATABASES

*CPI.Q.* Cengage Learning Inc. • Electronic version of the *Canadian Periodical Index*. Provides citations from 1988 to date for English and French language periodicals. Indexing from 1980 to present. Inquire as to price and availability.

*Ulrich's International Periodicals Directory Online.* Bowker Electronic Publishing. • $2,175 Individuals hardcover. Includes over 275,000 periodicals currently published worldwide and publications discontinued. Corresponds to *Ulrich's International Periodcals Directory, Irregular Serials and Annuals, Bowker International Serials Database Update,* and *Sources of Serials.*

*Wilson Social Sciences Abstracts Online.* H.W. Wilson Co. • Provides online abstracting and indexing of more than 500 periodicals covering area studies, community health, public administration, public welfare, urban studies, and many other social science topics. Time period is 1994 to date for abstracts and 1983 to date for indexing, with updates weekly. Inquire as to online cost and availability.

## OTHER SOURCES

*Bacon's Newspaper and Magazine Directories.* Cision US Inc. • Annual. $325.00 per year. Two volumes: Magazines and Newspapers. Covers print media in the United States and Canada. Formerly *Bacon's Publicity Checker.*

## PERIODICALS AND NEWSLETTERS

*Circulation Management.* Media Central. • Monthly. $39.00 per year. Edited for circulation professionals in the magazine and newsletter publishing industry. Covers marketing, planning, promotion, management, budgeting, and related topics.

*Folio: The New Dynamics of Magazine Publishing.* Penton. • Monthly. $96.00 per year.

*The Serials Librarian.* The Haworth Press Inc. • Quarterly. Two volumes.

*Serials Review.* Reed Elsevier N.V. • Quarterly. $288 Institutions all countries except Europe & Japan. Journal primarily concerned with serials information and management. Occasionally contains topical reviews of serial literature.

## STATISTICS SOURCES

*U.S. Industry and Trade Outlook.* U.S. Department of Commerce National Technical Information Service. • Annual. Produced by the International Trade Administration, U.S. Department of Commerce, in a "public-private" partnership with DRI/McGraw-Hill and Standard & Poor's. Provides basic data, outlook for the current year, and "Long-Term Prospects" (five-year projections) for a wide variety of products and services. Includes high technology industries. Formerly *U.S. Industrial Outlook.*

## TRADE/PROFESSIONAL ASSOCIATIONS

American Society of Magazine Editors. c/o Nina Fortuna, Director, 757 3rd Ave., 11th Fl., New York, NY 10017-2194. Phone: (212)872-3700 or (212)872-3737; Fax: (212)906-0128 • URL: http://www.magazine.org/asme • Represents magazine editors. Sponsors annual editorial internship program for college juniors and the National Magazine Awards.

Audit Bureau of Circulations. 48 W Seegers Rd., Arlington Heights, IL 60005-3913. Phone: (224)366-6939 or (224)366-6500; Fax: (224)366-6949; Email: service@accessabc.com • URL: http://www.accessabc.com • Verifies newspaper and periodical circulation statements. Includes a Business Publications Industry Committee and a Magazine Directors Advisory Committee.

BPA Worldwide. 100 Beard Sawmill Rd., 6th Fl., Shelton, CT 06484. Phone: (203)447-2800; Fax: (203)447-2900; Email: ghansen@bpaww.com • URL: http://www.bpaww.com • Verifies business and consumer periodical circulation statements. Includes a Circulation Managers Committee. Formerly Business Publications Audit of Circulation.

MPA - The Association of Magazine Media. 757 3rd Ave., 11th Fl., New York, NY 10017. Phone: (212)872-3700 or (212)872-3745; Email: mpa@magazine.org • URL: http://www.magazine.org • Members are publishers of consumer and other periodicals. Affiliated with American Society of Magazine Editors; Media Credit Association;

Publishers Information Bureau. Formerly Magazine Publishers Association.

Publishers Information Bureau. 810 7th Ave., 24th Fl., New York, NY 10019. Phone: (212)872-3700 or (212)872-3722; Email: weadie@magazine.org • URL: http://www.magazine.org • Measures the amount and type of advertising in magazines and reports this information monthly through printed and electronic formats; service prepared by TNSMI/Competitive Media Reporting (contracting agent).

# PERIODICALS, BUSINESS

*See* TRADE JOURNALS

# PERSONAL CARE PRODUCTS

*See* COSMETICS INDUSTRY

# PERSONAL FINANCE

*See also* ESTATE PLANNING; FINANCIAL PLANNING; HOME OWNERSHIP; INVESTMENTS; LIFE INSURANCE; PENSIONS; TAX SHELTERS

## ABSTRACTS AND INDEXES

*Readers' Guide to Periodical Literature.* EBSCO Publishing Inc. • Provides indexing for over 400 periodicals dating back to 1983.

## CD-ROM DATABASES

*Newspaper Abstracts Ondisc.* ProQuest L.L.C. • Monthly. $2,950.00 per year (covers 1989 to date; archival discs are available for 1985-88). Provides cover-to-cover CD-ROM indexing and abstracting of 19 major newspapers, including the *New York Times, Wall Street Journal, Washington Post, Chicago Tribune,* and *Los Angeles Times.*

*Readers' Guide to Periodical Literature.* EBSCO Publishing Inc. • Provides indexing for over 400 periodicals dating back to 1983.

## DIRECTORIES

*Plunkett's On-Line Trading, Finance, and Investment Web Sites Almanac.* Plunkett Research Ltd. • Annual. $149.99. Provides profiles and usefulness rankings of financial Web sites. Sites are rated from 1 to 5 for specific uses. Includes CD-ROM.

## ENCYCLOPEDIAS AND DICTIONARIES

*Everyday Finance: Economics, Personal Money Management, and Entrepreneurship.* Cengage Learning Inc. • $258 Individuals. 2008. 2 volumes. Contains 300 topical entries that are organized into 3 units: How the Economy Works; Personal Finance: Buying, Borrowing, Saving, and Insuring; and The World of Business. eBook available. Inquire for pricing.

## INTERNET DATABASES

*BanxQuote Banking, Mortgage, and Finance Center.* BanxQuote, Inc. Phone: (914)722-1600; Fax: (914)722-6630; Email: info@banx.com • URL: http://www.banx.com • Daily. Web site quotes interest rates paid by banks around the country on various savings products, as well as rates paid by consumers for automobile loans, mortgages, credit cards, home equity loans, and personal loans. Also provided: stock quotes, indexes, stock options, futures trading data, economic indicators, and links to many other financial sites.

## ONLINE DATABASES

*Banking Information Source.* ProQuest L.L.C. • Provides indexing and abstracting of periodical and other literature from 1982 to date, with weekly updates. Covers the financial services industry:

banks, savings institutions, investment houses, credit unions, insurance companies, and real estate organizations. Emphasis is on marketing and management. Inquire as to online cost and availability. (Formerly *FINIS: Financial Industry Information Service.*).

## OTHER SOURCES

*Financial Planning and Financial Planning Ideas.* Prentice Hall PTR. • Two looseleaf volumes. Periodic supplementation. Price on application.

*Individual Retirement Plans Guide.* Wolters Kluwer Law & Business CCH. • $540.00 per year. Looseleaf service. Monthly updates. Covers IRA plans (Individual Retirement Accounts), SEP plans (Simplified Employee Pensions), and Keogh plans (self-employed retirement accounts).

## PERIODICALS AND NEWSLETTERS

*American Banker: The Financial Services Daily.* SourceMedia Inc. • Daily. $895.00 per year. Provides news of banking, investment products, mortgages, credit unions, finance, bank technology, and legal developments.

*Estate Planner's Alert.* Thomson RIA. • Monthly. $290 Individuals Print. Covers the tax aspects of personal finance, including home ownership, investments, insurance, retirement planning, and charitable giving. Formerly *Estate and Financial Planners Alert.*

*Family Economics and Nutrition Review.* U. S. Government Printing Office. • Semi-annual. $13.00 per year. Issued by the Consumer and Food Economics Institute, U. S. Department of Agriculture. Provides articles on consumer expenditures and budgeting for food, clothing, housing, energy, education, etc.

*Financial Counseling and Planning (JFCP).* Association for Financial Counseling and Planning Education. • Semiannual. Disseminates scholarly research relating to finacial planning and counseling.

*Forbes.* Forbes Inc. • Biweekly. $29.99 Individuals. Magazine reporting on industry, business and finance management.

*Investment News: The Weekly Newspaper for Financial Advisers.* Crain Communications Inc. • Weekly. $29.00 per year. Edited for both personal and institutional investment advisers, planners, and managers.

*The Investment Reporter.* MPL Communications Inc. • Description: Profiles specific companies and market trends and developments, making recommendations to assist in formulating investment strategies. Includes short articles offering advice on investment decisions.

*Money.* • 13 times a year. $19.95 per year. Covers all aspects of family finance; investments, careers, shopping, taxes, insurance, consumerism, etc.

*Personal Finance.* KCI Communications Inc. • Description: Contains articles on subjects of interest to those investigating personal finance strategies. Provides news, information, and suggestions on investment decisions. Covers stock and growth stock activity, individual retirement accounts, market trends and developments, and real estate. Recurring features include columns titled Capsule Advisory and Answers to Your Money Questions.

*Predictions: Specific Investment Forecasts and Recommendations from the World's Top Financial Experts.* Lee Euler, editor. Agora Inc. • Monthly. $78.00 per year. Newsletter.

*Private Asset Management.* Institutional Investor Inc. Journals Group. • Biweekly. $2,335.00 per year. Newsletter. Includes print and online editions. Edited for managers investing the private assets of wealthy ("high-net-worth") individuals. Includes marketing, taxation, regulation, and fee topics.

*U.S. Banker.* SourceMedia Inc. • Monthly. $65.00 per year. Edited for bank executives and managers.

Covers a wide variety of banking and financial topics.

## RESEARCH CENTERS AND INSTITUTES

American Institute for Economic Research. 250 Division St., Great Barrington, MA 01230-1000. Phone: 888-528-1216; Fax: (413)528-0103; Email: info@aier.org • URL: http://www.aier.org • Through research and publications, provides "information on economic and financial subjects that is useful and completely independent of special interests." Sponsors a fellowship program for graduate study of economics at the institute and in absentia.

Center for Financial Responsibility. Texas Tech University, Lubbock, TX 79409-11210. Phone: (806)742-5050; Fax: (806)742-5033 • URL: http://www.depts.ttu.edu/cfr • Research areas include financial preparation for retirement, financial education, determinants of financial satisfaction, risk tolerance, and the career preparation of retirement industry professionals.

New York University - C.V. Starr Center for Applied Economics. 19 W 4th St., 6th Fl., New York, NY 10012. Phone: (212)998-8936; Fax: (212)995-3932; Email: sydney.ludvigson@nyu.edu • URL: http://cvstarrnyu.org • Economic issues of social and economic consequence. Also develops analytical tools to facilitate economic decision making for the future.

## STATISTICS SOURCES

*Statistical Information on the Financial Services Industry.* American Bankers Association. • Annual. Members, $150.00; non-members, $275.00. Presents a wide variety of data relating to banking and financial services, including consumer economics, personal finance, credit, government loans, capital markets, and international banking.

*Statistics of Income Bulletin.* U. S. Government Printing Office. • Quarterly. $44. Current data compiled from tax returns relating to income, assets, and expenses of individuals and businesses. (U. S. Internal Revenue Service.).

## TRADE/PROFESSIONAL ASSOCIATIONS

Association for Financial Counseling and Planning Education. 1940 Duke St., Ste. 200, Alexandria, VA 22314-3452. Phone: (703)684-4484; Fax: (703)684-4485 • URL: http://www.afcpe.org • Members are researchers, academics, financial counselors and financial planners.

Conference on Consumer Finance Law. Oklahoma City University School of Law, 2501 N Blackwelder Ave., Oklahoma City, OK 73106. Phone: (405)208-5198 or (405)208-5363 • URL: http://www.ccflonline.org • Formerly Conference on Personal Finance Law.

Institute of Consumer Financial Education. PO Box 34070, San Diego, CA 92163-4070. Phone: (619)239-1401; Fax: (619)923-3284; Email: info@icfe.info • URL: http://www.financial-education-icfe.org • Aims to encourage Americans to improve spending, saving, investing, insuring, and financial planning habits to lessen their dependence on Social Security, welfare, or other individuals. Provides financial education courses to junior high and high school. Maintains a resource section of videos, books and home study courses in personal finance.

JumpStart Coalition for Personal Financial Literacy. 919 18th St. NW, Ste. 300, Washington, DC 20006. Phone: 888-45-EDUCATE; Fax: (202)223-0321 • URL: http://www.jumpstartcoalition.org • Aims to improve the financial literacy of kindergarten through college-age youth. Seeks to prepare youth for life-long, successful financial decision-making. Provides advocacy, research, standards, and educational resources.

Junior Achievement. 1 Education Way, Colorado Springs, CO 80906. Phone: (719)540-8000; Fax: (719)540-6299; Email: newmedia@ja.org • URL:

http://www.juniorachievement.org/web/ja-usa/home • Aims to educate students in grades K-12 about entrepreneurship, work readiness, and financial literacy through experiential, hands-on programs. Helps prepare young people for the "real world" by showing them how to generate wealth and effectively manage it, how to create jobs which make their communities more robust, and how to apply entrepreneurial thinking to the workplace. Encourages students to apply lessons into action, and learn the value of contributing to their communities.

National Association of Blessed Billionaires. Presbyterian Church of Mt. Vernon, 199 N Columbus Ave., Mount Vernon, NY 10553. Phone: (914)633-4417 or (347)933-3000; Email: nabb10m@aol.com • URL: http://blessedbillionaires.org • Aims to build self-esteem and good moral character among young people. Helps young men and women gain the skills they need to become successful and responsible adults. Provides a vehicle for inner-city youth to learn about and participate in the competitive market through leadership and entrepreneurial training. Conducts training on all aspects of business and money management.

Native American Coalition for Healthy Alternatives. 1038 E Tallent St., Rapid City, SD 57701. Phone: (605)877-4650 • URL: http://nacha501c.org • Strives to enhance the quality of life for the underrepresented by providing various services related to financial literacy.

# PERSONAL FINANCE COMPANIES

*See* FINANCE COMPANIES

# PERSONNEL CLASSIFICATION

*See* JOB ANALYSIS

# PERSONNEL INTERVIEWING

*See* INTERVIEWING

# PERSONNEL MANAGEMENT

*See also* HUMAN RELATIONS; INDUSTRIAL RELATIONS

## ABSTRACTS AND INDEXES

*Business Periodicals Index Retrospective.* EBSCO Publishing Inc. • 11/year. Quarterly and annual cumulations.

## ALMANACS AND YEARBOOKS

*Research in Personnel and Human Resources Management.* Gerald D. Ferris, editor. Elsevier. • Dates vary. $78.50. 21 volumes.

## CD-ROM DATABASES

*Business Abstracts with Full Text.* EBSCO Publishing Inc. • Includes full text articles from more than 460 business publications from 1982 to present. Indexing for nearly 880 publications.

## ENCYCLOPEDIAS AND DICTIONARIES

*BLR Job Descriptions Encyclopedia.* Business & Legal Resources, Inc. • $299 Individuals. $299.00. Two volumes. More than 700 prewritten job descriptions.

## HANDBOOKS AND MANUALS

*Personnel Management: Communications.* Prentice Hall PTR. • Looseleaf. Periodic supplementation. Price on application. Includes how to write ef-

fectively and how to prepare employee publications.

*Personnel Management: Compensation.* Prentice Hall PTR. • Looseleaf. Periodic supplementation. Price on application.

*Personnel Management: Labor Relations Guide.* Prentice Hall PTR. • Three looseleaf volumes. Periodic supplementation. Price on application.

*Personnel Management: Policies and Practices.* Prentice Hall PTR. • Looseleaf. Periodic supplementation. Price on application.

## INTERNET DATABASES

*Wageweb: Salary Survey Data On-Line.* HRPDI: Human Resources Programs Development and Improvement. Phone: (804)363-1792; Fax: (804)594-3721; Email: salaries@wageweb.com • URL: http://www.wageweb.com • Web site provides salary information for more than 170 benchmark positions, including (for example) 29 information management jobs. Data shows average minimum, median, and average maximum compensation for each position, based on salary surveys. Fees: Free for national salary data; $169.00 per year for more detailed information (geographic, organization size, specific industries).

## ONLINE DATABASES

*Wilson Business Abstracts Online.* H.W. Wilson Co. • Indexes and abstracts 600 major business periodicals, plus the *Wall Street Journal* and the business section of the *New York Times.* Indexing is from 1982, abstracting from 1990, with the two newspapers included from 1993. Updated weekly. Inquire as to online cost and availability. (*Business Periodicals Index* without abstracts is also available online.).

## OTHER SOURCES

*BNA Policy and Practice Series.* Bloomberg BNA. • Weekly. $1,965.00 per year. Three looseleaf volumes. Includes personnel management, labor relations, fair employment practice, compensation, and wage-hour laws.

*Employment Forms and Policies.* Matthew Bender and Company Inc. • $150 print and e-book. Periodic supplementation available. Contains more than 300 forms, policies, and checklists for use by small or medium-sized businesses. Covers such topics as employee selection, payroll issues, benefits, performance appraisal, dress codes, and employee termination.

*Fundamentals of Human Resources.* American Management Association Extension Institute. • Looseleaf. $139.00. Self-study course on a wide range of personnel topics. Emphasis is on practical explanations, examples, and problem solving. Quizzes and a case study are included.

*Human Resources Management Whole.* Wolters Kluwer Law & Business CCH. • Nine looseleaf volumes. $1,572 per year. Includes monthly updates. Components are *Ideas and Trends Newsletter, Employment Relations, Compensation, Equal Employment Opportunity, Personnel Practices/Communications* and *OSHA Compliance.* Components are available separately.

## PERIODICALS AND NEWSLETTERS

*Employment Law Strategist.* Law Journal Newsletter. • $439 per year. Covers employment law topics, including immigration laws, repetitive stress claims, workplace violence, liability of actions of intoxicated employees, record keeping, liability for fetal injury, independent contractor, and employee issues. Monthly. 229 individuals electronic edition. Description: Reports on legal strategy and substantive developments in the area of matrimonial law, including such topics as tax considerations, custody, visitation, division of property, and valuation. Recurring features include litigation roundup and a legislative update.

---

*HR Magazine (Human Resources): Strategies and Solutions for Human Resource Professionals.* Society for Human Resource Management. • Monthly. $70. Formerly *Personnel Administrator.*

*HRfocus: The Hands-On Tool for Human Resources Professionals.* American Management Association. IOMA Inc. • Monthly. Covers "all aspects of HR management," including corporate culture, the impact of technology, recruiting strategies, and training. Formerly *Personnel.*

*Human Resource Executive.* LRP Publications Library. • 16 times a year. $89.95 per year. Edited for directors of corporate human resource departments. Special issues emphasize training, benefits, retirement planning, recruitment, outplacement, workers' compensation, legal pitfalls, and oes emphasize training, benefits, retirement planning, recruitment, outplacement, workers' compensation, legal pitfalls, and other personnel topics.

*Law Firm Partnership and Benefits Report.* ALM Media Properties LLC. • Monthly. $499 per year. Covers personnel issues for law firms, including compensation, partnership agreements, malpractice, employment discrimination, training, health insurance, pension plans, and other matters relating to human resources management. (A Law Journal Newsletter, formerly published by Leader Publications).

*People & Strategy.* HR People and Strategy. • Quarterly. $150 Nonmembers print only. Contains current theory, research and practice in strategic human resource management.

*People to People.* American Public Power Association. • Description: Reports on public sector labor and personnel issues, especially those concerning the electric utility industry. Summarizes case studies in public labor relations.

*Personnel Psychology.* Personnel Psychology Inc. • Quarterly. $98.00 per year. Publishes research articles and book reviews.

*Perspective.* Magna Publications Inc. • Description: Provides administrators with guidelines for keeping their schools out of court. Examines current trends in law related to higher education, as well as past and future legal issues affecting students, faculty, administrators and the public. Recurring features include columns titled Key Case Review, Follow-Up, Resources, Legislative Note, Outside the Courts, Cross-Examination, and Cases Noted.

*Public Personnel Management.* International Personnel Management Association. • Quarterly. $273 Institutions. Contains trends, case studies, and the latest research by top human resource scholars and industry experts.

## RESEARCH CENTERS AND INSTITUTES

Brandeis University - Center for Youth and Communities. Heller Bldg., 3rd Fl., MS 035, 415 S St., Waltham, MA 02454. Phone: (781)736-4835 or (781)736-3729; Fax: (781)736-3773; Email: curnan@brandeis.edu • URL: http://cyc.brandeis.edu • Formerly Center for Human Resources.

## TRADE/PROFESSIONAL ASSOCIATIONS

Asia Catalyst. 39 W 32nd St., Ste. 1602, New York, NY 10001. Phone: (212)967-2123; Email: info@asiacatalyst.org • URL: http://www.asiacatalyst.org • Provides support services to non-governmental organizations (NGOs). Facilitates capacity-building training in personnel and financial management. Conducts fundraising, advocacy, and media outreach activities. Fosters research on human rights issues that are of direct concern to NGOs.

Catalyst. 120 Wall St., 5th Fl., New York, NY 10005-3904. Phone: (212)514-7600; Fax: (212)514-8470; Email: info@catalyst.org • URL: http://www.catalyst.org • Works to advance women in Business and the professions. Serves as a source of information on women in business for past four decades.

Helps companies and women maximize their potential. Holds current statistics, print media, and research materials on issues related to women in business.

Central and East European Management Development Association. Presernova cesta 33, 4260 Bled, Slovenia. Phone: 386 4 5792505 or 386 4 5792570; Email: info@ceeman.org • URL: http://www.ceeman.org • Specialists in business education and management personnel in commercial business, industry, professional, and technical fields from 42 countries. Seeks to improve the quality of management education throughout central and Eastern Europe. Provides a forum for discussion and exchange among individuals teaching, practicing, or studying management; provides IQA accreditation.

Employers Group. 4000 Continental Blvd., Ste. 300, El Segundo, CA 90245. Phone: 800-748-8484 or (213)765-3989; Fax: (213)742-0301; Email: serviceone@employersgroup.com • URL: http://www.employersgroup.com • Provides human resources management services including wage, salary, and benefit surveys; personnel practices surveys; management counseling; management education programs; litigation surveillance; government relations; and research library service. Provides customized human resources services including employee opinion surveys and employee communications programs through its subsidiary, The Employers Group Service Corp. Offers unemployment insurance services, workers' compensation programs, and in-house management training programs. Conducts research and educational programs; maintains speakers' bureau.

European Association for Personnel Management. c/o Chartered Institute of Personnel and Development, 151 The Broadway, Wimbledon, London SW19 1JQ, United Kingdom. Phone: 44 20 86126200; Fax: 44 20 86126201 • URL: http://www.eapm.org • Represents national personnel management associations. Seeks to maintain professional standards of personnel management and act as representative for personnel management associations in Europe. Disseminates information.

HR People and Strategy. 1800 Duke St., Alexandria, VA 22314. Phone: 888-602-3270; Fax: (703)535-6490; Email: info@hrps.org • URL: http://www.hrps.org • Human resource planning professionals representing 160 corporations and 3,000 individual members, including strategic human resources planning and development specialists, staffing analysts, business planners, line managers, and others who function as business partners in the application of strategic human resource management practices. Seeks to increase the impact of human resource planning and management on business and organizational performance. Sponsors program of professional development in human resource planning concepts, techniques, and practices. Offers networking opportunities.

Institute of Personnel Management of Zimbabwe. Union Ave., Harare, Zimbabwe. Phone: 263 4755241 or 263 4 755241; Fax: 263 4721454 or 263 4 755244; Email: ipmz@ecoweb.co.zw • URL: http://www.ipmz.org.zw • Works as a professional association of personnel workers in Zimbabwe. Promotes the profession of personnel training labor human resource management. Works to improve commercial and industrial productivity through people management.

Irish Institute of Training and Development. Millennium Business Park, 4 Sycamore House, Naas, Kildare, Ireland. Phone: 353 45 881166; Fax: 353 45 881192; Email: info@iitd.com • URL: http://www.iitd.ie • Individuals working in human resource development in Ireland. Fosters communication among members. Conducts educational programs.

National Human Resources Association. PO Box 5455, Manchester, NH 03108-5455. Phone: 866-

523-4417; Fax: (603)718-3124; Email: info@humanresources.org • URL: http://www.humanresources.org • Represents human resource executives in business, industry, education and government. Established to expand and improve the professionalism of those in human resource management.

# PERSONNEL MANUALS

*See PROCEDURE MANUALS*

# PERSONNEL RECRUITMENT

*See RECRUITMENT OF PERSONNEL*

# PEST CONTROL INDUSTRY

*See also PESTICIDE INDUSTRY*

## ABSTRACTS AND INDEXES

*Biological and Agricultural Index.* H.W. Wilson Co. • 11 times a year. Annual and quarterly cumulations. Price varies.

*Entomology Abstracts.* CSA. • Monthly. 11 times a year. $1,570.00 per year. Includes print and online editions.

## CD-ROM DATABASES

*Biological & Agricultural Index Plus.* EBSCO Publishing Inc. • Full text of literature in biology and agriculture. Also includes podcasts, indexing and abstracts.

## INTERNET DATABASES

*PestWeb: The Pest Control Industry Website.* Univar USA. Phone: 800-888-4897 or (425)889-3400; Email: webmaster@pestweb.com • URL: http://www.pestweb.com • Web site provides a wide variety of information on pest control products, manufacturers, associations, news, and education. Includes "Insects and Other Organisms," featuring details on 27 different kinds of pests, from ants to wasps. Online searching is offered. Fees: Free.

## ONLINE DATABASES

*Biological Sciences Database.* Cambridge Scientific Abstracts L.P. • Includes online versions of *Biotechnology Research Abstracts, Entomology Abstracts, Genetics Abstracts,* and about 20 other abstract collections. Time period is 1978 to date, with monthly updates. Inquire as to online cost and availability.

*CAB Abstracts.* CABI. • Contains 46 specialized abstract collections covering over 10,000 journals and monographs in the areas of agriculture, horticulture, forest products, farm products, nutrition, dairy science, poultry, grains, animal health, entomology, etc. Time period is 1972 to date, with monthly updates. Inquire as to online cost and availability. *CAB Abstracts on CD-ROM* also available, with annual updating.

## PERIODICALS AND NEWSLETTERS

*Pest Control.* Advantstar Communications. • Monthly. $44.00 per year.

*Pest Control Technology.* Group Interest Enterprises. GIE Media, Inc. • Monthly. $32.00 per year. Provides technical and business management information for pest control personnel.

## RESEARCH CENTERS AND INSTITUTES

Ohio State University - Laboratory for Pest Control Application Technology. Ohio Agricultural Research & Development Ctr., 1680 Madison Ave., Wooster, OH 44691. Phone: (330)263-3931; Fax: (330)263-3686; Email: downer.2@osu.edu • URL: http://www.oardc.ohio-state.edu/lpcat • Conducts pest control research in cooperation with the U. S.

     **For publishers' addresses, refer to SOURCES CITED section at the back of the book.**

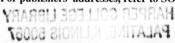

Department of Agriculture.

Purdue University - Center for Urban and Industrial Pest Management. Department of Entomology, 901 W State St., West Lafayette, IN 47907. Phone: (765)494-4564; Fax: (765)494-0535; Email: gbennett@purdue.edu • URL: http://extension.entm. purdue.edu/urban/home.html • Conducts research on the control of household and structural insect pests.

## TRADE/PROFESSIONAL ASSOCIATIONS

National Pest Management Association International. 10460 N St., Fairfax, VA 22030. Phone: 800-678-6722 or (703)352-6762; Fax: (703)352-3031; Email: npmateam@ vaultcommunications.com • URL: http://www. pestworld.org • Represents firms engaged in control of insects, rodents, birds, and other pests, in or around structures, through use of insecticides, rodenticides, miticides, fumigants, and non-chemical methods. Provides advisory services on control procedures, new products, and safety and business administration practices. Promotes June as National Pest Control Month. Sponsors research, periodic technical and management seminars.

# PESTICIDE INDUSTRY

*See also* AGRICULTURAL CHEMICALS; PEST CONTROL INDUSTRY

## ABSTRACTS AND INDEXES

*NTIS Alerts: Environmental Pollution & Control.* U.S. Department of Commerce National Technical Information Service. • Biweekly. $130 per year. Covers the following categories of environmental pollution: air, water, solid wastes, radiation, pesticides, and noise.

*Review of Agricultural Entomology: Consisting of Abstracts of Reviews of Current Literature on Applied Entomology Throughout the World.* CABI Publishing North America. • Monthly. Institutions, $1,505.00 per year. Print and online edition, $1,505.00 per year. Published in England by CABI Publishing. Provides worldwide coverage of the literature. (Formerly *Review of Applied Entomology, Series A: Agricultural.*).

*Review of Medical and Veterinary Entomology.* CAB International. • Monthly. Provides worldwide coverage of the literature. Formerly *Review of Applied Entomology, Series B: Medical and Veterinary.*

## CD-ROM DATABASES

*AGRICOLA on SilverPlatter.* Ovid Technologies Inc. • Updated monthly. Price varies. Produced by the National Agricultural Library. Provides over 4 million citations to the literature of agriculture, agricultural economics, animal sciences, entomology, fertilizer, food, forestry, nutrition, pesticides, plant science, water resources, and other topics.

## DIRECTORIES

*The Agrochemical Companies Fact File.* Hemming Information Services. • $695. Covers: 300 agrochemical manufacturers; formulators; biopesticide manufacturers, and agrochemical trading companies worldwide. Entries include: Details on key executives, financial data, operating locations, main markets, products, subsidiaries, joint ventures, and portfolios.

*Directory of Chinese Manufacturers & Exporters of Agro Chemicals, Fertilizers, Pesticides, Insecticides.* EXIM Infotek Private Ltd. • $20 Individuals. Covers: 210 Chinese manufacturers and exporters of agricultural chemical products, agricultural chemicals, agrochemicals, biochemical products, biological pesticides, bio-pesticides, chemical fertilizers, farm chemicals, fertilizers, herbicides, insecticide, nitrogen fertilizer, pesticide intermediates, pesticides, and phosphate fertilizers.

Entries include: Company name, postal address, city, country, phone, fax, e-mail and websites, contact person, designation, and product details.

*Household and Personal Products Industry Buyers Guide.* Rodman Publications. • Annual. Lists of suppliers to manufacturers of cosmetics, toiletries, soaps, detergents, and related household and personal products.

*Household and Personal Products Industry Contract Manufacturing/Private Label Directory.* Rodman Publications. • Annual. Provides information for about 450 companies offering private label or contract packaged household and personal care products, such as detergents, cosmetics, polishes, insecticides, and various aerosol items.

*Major Chemical and Petrochemical Companies of the World.* Cengage Learning Inc. • Annual. $1,460 Individuals. 2008. 12th edition. eBook. Published by Graham & Whiteside. Contains profiles of more than 8,500 important chemical and petrochemical companies in various countries. Subject areas include general chemicals, specialty chemicals, agricultural chemicals, petrochemicals, industrial gases, and fertilizers.

## HANDBOOKS AND MANUALS

*Defending Pesticides in Litigation.* David Whitacre and Shane Anderson. Thomson West. • Annual. $1,155 book-softbound. Discusses liability and other legal issues related to the manufacture and use of pesticides. Includes a guide to FIFRA (Federal Insecticide, Fungicide, and Rodenticide Act). (Environmental Law Series).

## ONLINE DATABASES

*Derwent Crop Protection File.* Derwent Information Ltd. • Provides citations to the international journal literature of agricultural chemicals and pesticides from 1968 to date, with updating eight times per year. Formerly *PESTDOC.* Inquire as to online cost and availability.

## PERIODICALS AND NEWSLETTERS

*Dealer Progress: How Smart Agribusiness is Growing.* The Fertilizer Institute. • Bimonthly. Free to qualified personnel; others, $40.00 per year. Published in association with the Fertilizer Institute. Includes information on fertilizers and agricultural chemicals, including farm pesticides. Formerly *Progress.*

*Household and Personal Products Industry: The Magazine for the Detergent, Soap, Cosmetic and Toiletry, Wax, Polish and Aerosol Industries.* Rodman Publications. • Monthly. Covers marketing, packaging, production, technical innovations, private label developments, and aerosol packaging for soap, detergents, cosmetics, insecticides, and a variety of other household products.

*Pest Control.* Advanstar Communications. • Monthly. $44.00 per year.

*Pest Control Technology.* Group Interest Enterprises. GIE Media, Inc. • Monthly. $32.00 per year. Provides technical and business management information for pest control personnel.

*Pesticide Biochemistry and Physiology: An International Journal.* Elsevier. • Nine times a year. Individuals, $487.00 per year; institutions, $1,819.00 per year; students, $89.00 per year.

## STATISTICS SOURCES

*Synthetic Organic Chemicals: United States Production and Sales.* International Trade Commission. U. S. Government Printing Office. • Annual.

## TRADE/PROFESSIONAL ASSOCIATIONS

Association of American Pesticide Control Officials. PO Box 466, Milford, DE 19963-0466. Phone: (302)422-8152; Fax: (302)422-2435; Email: info@ aapco.org • URL: http://www.aapco.org • State agencies controlling the sale, use, and distribution of

pesticides. Promotes uniform laws, regulations, and policies of enforcement.

National Pest Management Association International. 10460 N St., Fairfax, VA 22030. Phone: 800-678-6722 or (703)352-6762; Fax: (703)352-3031; Email: npmateam@ vaultcommunications.com • URL: http://www. pestworld.org • Represents firms engaged in control of insects, rodents, birds, and other pests, in or around structures, through use of insecticides, rodenticides, miticides, fumigants, and non-chemical methods. Provides advisory services on control procedures, new products, and safety and business administration practices. Promotes June as National Pest Control Month. Sponsors research, periodic technical and management seminars.

# PET FOOD

*See* PET INDUSTRY

# PET INDUSTRY

*See also* VETERINARY PRODUCTS

## DIRECTORIES

*American Veterinary Medical Association-- Directory and Resource Manual: AVMA Membership Directory and Resource Manual.* American Veterinary Medical Association. • Annual. $150 Nonmembers in USA and their territories. Covers: AVMA members; code of ethics, AVMA bylaws. Database includes: Extensive list of veterinary medical and related associations, veterinary schools, related government agencies. Entries include: Name, spouse's name, address, email, phones and codes for practice activity, type of employer, institution granting degree, and year received.

*Food Chemicals News Directory.* Food Chemical News. CRC Press. • Semiannual. $497.00. Over 2,000 subsidiaries belonging to nearly 250 corporate parents plus an additional 3,000 independent processors. Formerly *Hereld's 1,500.*

*Pet Hospitals and Clinics Directory.* InfoGroup Inc. • Annual. Number of listings: 14,050. Entries include: Name, address, phone, size of advertisement, name of owner or manager, number of employees, year first in "Yellow Pages." Compiled from telephone company "Yellow Pages," nationwide.

## HANDBOOKS AND MANUALS

*Pet Shop.* Entrepreneur Press. • $19.95. Looseleaf. $59.50. A practical guide to starting a pet store. Covers profit potential, start-up costs, market size evaluation, owner's time required, site selection, lease negotiation, pricing, accounting, advertising, promotion, etc. (Start-Up Business Guide No. E1007.).

## PERIODICALS AND NEWSLETTERS

*Pet Age: The Magazine for the Professional Retailer.* Michelle Maskaly, editor. H.H. Backer Associates Inc. • Monthly. $160 Other countries. Covers news and feature articles about human and animal relationships.

*Pet Product News.* I-5 Publishing LLC. • Free to qualified personnel; others, $118.00 per year. Supplement available *Pet Product News Buyer's Guide.*

*Petfood Industry.* Watt Publishing. • Bimonthly. $96.

## TRADE/PROFESSIONAL ASSOCIATIONS

American Pet Products Association. 255 Glenville Rd., Greenwich, CT 06831. Phone: 800-452-1225 or (203)532-0000; Fax: (203)532-0551 • URL: http:// www.americanpetproducts.org • U.S. Manufacturers and importers of pet products. Provides public relations program to promote pet ownership and pet care. Sponsors the association's annual National Pet Products Trade Show; publishes the National Pet Owner's Survey, the association's research study in the pet industry.

Pet Food Institute. 2025 M St. NW, Ste. 800, Washington, DC 20036-2422. Phone: (202)367-1120; Fax: (202)367-2120; Email: info@petfoodinstitute.org • URL: http://www.petfoodinstitute.org • Represents the manufacturers of 97% of the commercial pet food produced in the United States. Serves as the voice of the industry before legislative and regulatory bodies at both the federal and state levels.

Pet Industry Distributors Association. 3465 Box Hill Corporate Center Dr., Ste. H, Abingdon, MD 21009. Phone: (443)640-1060; Fax: (443)640-1086; Email: pida@kingmgmt.org • URL: http://www.pida.org • Strives to enhance the well-being of the pet product wholesaler-distributor. Promotes partnerships between suppliers and customers. Fosters the human-companion animal bond.

Pet Industry Joint Advisory Council. 1146 19th St. NW, Ste. 350, Washington, DC 20036-3746. Phone: 800-553-7387 or (202)452-1525; Fax: (202)452-1516; Email: info@pijac.org • URL: http://www.pijac.org • Pet retailers, manufacturers and distributors; companion animal suppliers; pet industry trade associations. Works to monitor federal and state regulations and legislation affecting the industry. Sponsors research projects and industry-related educational programs.

# PETROCHEMICAL INDUSTRY

*See also* CHEMICAL INDUSTRIES; PETROLEUM INDUSTRY

## ABSTRACTS AND INDEXES

*Applied Science and Technology Index.* EBSCO Publishing Inc. • 11/year. Indexes a wide variety of English language technical, industrial, and engineering periodicals.

## BIOGRAPHICAL SOURCES

*Who's Who in World Petrochemicals and Plastics.* Reed Elsevier Group plc Reed Business Information. • Annual. $175.00. Names, addresses, telephone numbers, and company affiliations of individuals active in the petrochemical business. Formerly *Who's Who in World Petrochemicals.*

## DIRECTORIES

*Major Chemical and Petrochemical Companies of the World.* Cengage Learning Inc. • Annual. $1,460 Individuals. 2008. 12th edition. eBook. Published by Graham & Whiteside. Contains profiles of more than 8,500 important chemical and petrochemical companies in various countries. Subject areas include general chemicals, specialty chemicals, agricultural chemicals, petrochemicals, industrial gases, and fertilizers.

## FINANCIAL RATIOS

*Industry Norms and Key Business Ratios.* Dun & Bradstreet Inc. • Annual. Five volumes. Covers over 800 kinds of businesses, arranged by Standard Industrial Classification number. More detailed editions covering longer periods of time are also available.

## PERIODICALS AND NEWSLETTERS

*Hydrocarbon Processing.* Gulf Publishing Co. • $239 Individuals. Contains practical analysis and insight into the latest technological advances in the refining, petrochemical and natural gas/LNG industries.

*Oil, Gas and Petrochem Equipment.* PennWell Corp., Industrial Div. • Monthly. $35.00 per year.

*PetroChemical News: A Weekly News Service in*

*English Devoted to the Worldwide Petrochemical Industry.* William F. Bland Co. • Weekly. $897. Report of current and significant news about the petrochemical business worldwide.

## TRADE/PROFESSIONAL ASSOCIATIONS

American Chemical Society. 1155 16th St. NW, Washington, DC 20036. Phone: 800-227-5558 or (202)872-4600; Email: help@acs.org • URL: http://www.acs.org • Scientific and educational society of chemists and chemical engineers. Conducts: studies and surveys; special programs for disadvantaged persons; legislation monitoring, analysis, and reporting; courses for graduate chemists and chemical engineers; radio and television programming. Offers career guidance counseling; administers the Petroleum Research Fund and other grants and fellowship programs. Operates Employment Clearing Houses. Compiles statistics. Maintains speakers' bureau and 33 divisions.

# PETROLEUM EQUIPMENT INDUSTRY

## FINANCIAL RATIOS

*Annual Statement Studies.* Risk Management Association. • Annual. Compiled from over 280,000 financial statements.

*Annual Statement Studies: Industry Default Probabilities and Cash Flow Measures.* Risk Management Association. • Annual. $405 Nonmembers. Serves as a companion volume to the original *Annual Statement Studies.* Gives probability of default estimates on a percentage scale for more than 450 industries. Includes changes in position year-by-year for eight financial statement line items and provides percentage measures of cash flow.

## PERIODICALS AND NEWSLETTERS

*Hart's E and P.* Hart Energy. • Monthly. Edited for "decision makers" in petroleum exploration and production. Emphasis is on technology. Formerly *Petroleum Engineer International.*

*Oil, Gas and Petrochem Equipment.* PennWell Corp., Industrial Div. • Monthly. $35.00 per year.

## STATISTICS SOURCES

*Standard & Poor's Industry Surveys.* Standard & Poor's Financial Services L.L.C. • Semiannual. $1,800.00. Two looseleaf volumes. Includes monthly *Supplements.* Provides detailed, individual surveys of 52 major industry groups. Each survey is revised on a semiannual basis. Also includes "Monthly Investment Review" (industry group investment analysis) and monthly "Trends & Projections" (economic analysis).

*U.S. Industry and Trade Outlook.* U.S. Department of Commerce National Technical Information Service. • Annual. Produced by the International Trade Administration, U.S. Department of Commerce, in a "public-private" partnership with DRI/McGraw-Hill and Standard & Poor's. Provides basic data, outlook for the current year, and "Long-Term Prospects" (five-year projections) for a wide variety of products and services. Includes high technology industries. Formerly *U.S. Industrial Outlook.*

## TRADE/PROFESSIONAL ASSOCIATIONS

Petroleum Equipment Institute. PO Box 2380, Tulsa, OK 74101-2380. Phone: (918)494-9696; Fax: (918)491-9895; Email: info@pei.org • URL: http://www.pei.org • Distributors and manufacturers of equipment used in service stations, bulk plants and other petroleum marketing operations.

Petroleum Equipment Suppliers Association. 1240 Blalock Rd., Ste. 110, Houston, TX 77055. Phone: (713)932-0168; Fax: (713)932-0497; Email: info@pesa.org • URL: http://www.pesa.org/index.php/home/c/home • Promotes improvement of the petroleum equipment, service, and supply industries.

Represents members' interests; cooperates with the federal government in matters of national concern; gathers and disseminates information. Conducts educational programs.

# PETROLEUM INDUSTRY

*See also* FUEL OIL INDUSTRY; GASOLINE INDUSTRY; OFFSHORE PETROLEUM INDUSTRY; PETROCHEMICAL INDUSTRY; PETROLEUM EQUIPMENT INDUSTRY; PETROLEUM MARKETING; PIPELINE INDUSTRY; PROPANE AND BUTANE GAS INDUSTRY

## ABSTRACTS AND INDEXES

*Fuel and Energy Abstracts: A Summary of World Literature on All Scientific, Technical, Commercial and Environmental Aspects of Fuel and Energy.* Elsevier. • Bimonthly. $3,287 Institutions.

*NTIS Alerts: Energy.* U.S. Department of Commerce National Technical Information Service. • Biweekly. $130 per year. Covers electric power, batteries, fuels, geothermal energy, heating/cooling systems, nuclear technology, solar energy, energy policy, and related subjects.

*Petroleum Abstracts.* University of Tulsa. • 50 times a year. Service basis. Worldwide literature related to petroleum exploration and production.

*Petroleum-Energy Business News Index Elsevier Engineering Information, Inc.* Elsevier. • Monthly. Members, $475.00 per year; non-members, $950.00 per year.

## CD-ROM DATABASES

*OECD Statistical Compendium.* Organization for Economic Cooperation and Development. • Semiannual. $1,905.00 per year for 1 to 10 users. CD-ROM contains more than 730,000 monthly, quarterly, and annual time series for OECD countries, 1960 to date. Includes fully searchable data on agriculture, food, economic indicators, national accounts, employment, energy, finance, industry, technology, and foreign trade. Results can be displayed in various forms.

## DIRECTORIES

*Directory of American Manufacturers & Exporters of Petroleum Products.* EXIM Infotek Private Ltd. • $10 Individuals. Covers: 120 American manufacturers & exporters of additives for engines, brake & transmission fluid, gas, gear lubricants, hydraulic oils, industrial oil, lubricants, lubricating oil & greases, oils-cutting & drawing, oils-hardening, tempering & quenching, petroleum & chemical industry, synthetic oil, water soluble oils. Entries include: Company name, postal address, city, country, phone, fax, e-mail & websites, contact person, designation, products detail.

*Directory of Chinese Manufacturers & Exporters of Petroleum Products.* EXIM Infotek Private Ltd. • $10 Individuals. Covers: 50 Chinese manufacturers and exporters of coal tar, fuel, lubricating oil, natural gases, petrochemicals, petroleum chemicals, and petroleum products. Entries include: Company name, postal address, city, country, phone, fax, e-mail and websites, contact person, designation, and product details.

*Directory of Japanese Manufacturers & Exporters of Petroleum Products.* EXIM Infotek Private Ltd. • $5 Individuals. Covers: 20 Japanese manufacturers and exporters of fuel, mineral oils and greases, petrochemical industries, petroleum hydrocarbon resins, petroleum products, and petroleum utensils. Entries include: Company name, postal address, city, country, phone, fax, e-mail and websites, contact person, designation, and product details.

*Directory of South American Importers of Petroleum Products.* EXIM Infotek Private Ltd. • $350

Individuals. Covers: 120 South American importers of crude oil, fuel products, hydraulic fluid, lubricants, oil, grease and petroleum products, propane gas, and specialty lubricants. Entries include: Company name, postal address, telephone, fax, e-mail, website, contact person, designation, and product details.

*Directory of South Korean Manufacturers & Exporters of Petroleum Products.* EXIM Infotek Private Ltd. • $10 Individuals. Covers: 60 South Korean manufacturers and exporters of mineral oils and greases, natural oils and greases for technical use, petroleum products/fuels and lubricants, solvents-petroleum based, tar and bituminous products, tar and resin distillation products. Entries include: Company name, postal address, city, country, phone, fax, e-mail and websites, contact person, designation, and product details.

*Directory of Taiwanese Manufacturers & Exporters of Petroleum Products.* EXIM Infotek Private Ltd. • $10 Individuals. Covers: 50 Taiwanese manufacturers and exporters of mineral oils and greases, natural gases, natural oils and greases for technical use, petroleum products/fuels and lubricants, tar and bituminous products, and tar and resin distillation products. Entries include: Company name, postal address, city, country, phone, fax, e-mail and websites, contact person, designation, products detail.

*Emerging Europe Oil and Gas Directory.* Business Monitor International Ltd. • $895 Individuals. Covers: 698 top oil and gas executives on 234 leading oil and gas companies from Emerging Europe. Entries include: Parent company head offices, full company name, address, phone and fax numbers, email and website address, senior oil and gas contact personnel, company description and profile, nationality, and ownership status.

*Hart's Oil and Gas Finance Sourcebook.* Hart Energy. • Annual. $495 Individuals. Covers: More than 3,500 oil and gas companies in eight categories: drilling risk capital, reserve purchasers, downstream risk capital, financial institutions, and intermediaries. Entries include: Company name, address, phone, fax, telex, e-mail address, website, names and titles of key personnel, geographic and operating preferences, deal criteria, total assets, recent deal history, number of wells owned and/or participating in, total annual production figures, primary contact for proposals, proposal turn around time.

*Institutional Buyers of Energy Stocks.* bigdough. com Inc. • Annual. $645.00. Provides detailed profiles 555 institutional buyers of petroleum-related and other energy stocks. Includes names of financial analysts and portfolio managers.

*Latin America & Caribbean Oil and Gas Directory.* Business Monitor International Ltd. • $995 Individuals CD. Covers: 828 top oil and gas executives on 309 leading oil and gas companies from Latin America. Entries include: parent company head offices, full company name, address, phone and fax numbers, email and website address, senior contact personnel, company description and profile, nationality, and ownership status.

*Middle East and Africa Oil and Gas Directory.* Business Monitor International Ltd. • $975 Individuals CD. Covers: 1,126 top oil and gas executives on 424 leading oil and gas companies from Middle East and Africa. Entries include: Parent company head offices, full company name, address, phone and fax numbers, email and website address, senior contact personnel, company description and profile, nationality, and ownership status.

*Oil and Gas Asia Business Directory.* AP Energy Business Publications Private Ltd. • Annual. Drilling and production companies, pipeline contractors and operators, refinery, petrochemical and gas processing operators, equipment and service companies.

## E-BOOKS

*Encyclopedia of American Industries.* Cengage Learning Inc. • 2011. $807.00. 6th edition. Three volumes. Volume one is Manufacturing Industries and volume two is Service and Non-Manufacturing Industries. Provides the history, development, and recent status of approximately 1,000 industries. Includes statistical graphs, with industry and general indexes. Also available as eBook.

*Macmillan Encyclopedia of Energy.* Cengage Learning Inc. • 2003. eBook. Published by Macmillan Reference USA. Covers the business, technology, and history of a wide variety of energy sources. Inquire as to price and availability.

## ENCYCLOPEDIAS AND DICTIONARIES

*Manual of Oil and Gas Terms.* Matthew Bender and Company Inc. • $148.00. 15th edition. Defines technical, legal, and tax terms relating to the oil and gas industry.

## HANDBOOKS AND MANUALS

*Summers on Oil and Gas.* Thomson West. • Annual. $1,101 Individuals book - hardbound - full set. Legal aspects of the petroleum industry.

## INTERNET DATABASES

*Business 2.0 Web Guide to the Best Business Links.* Business 2.0 Media Inc. Phone: (415)293-4800; Email: support@business2.com • URL: http://www.business2.com/webguide • Web site presents an extensive, searchable directory of links to "the best, most informative, and authoritative web pages." Twenty main categories cover business, finance, career, company information, people, and technology topics, with thousands of subtopics, all linking to Web sites recommended by experienced business researchers. Fees: Free.

*Fedstats.* Federal Interagency Council on Statistical Policy. Phone: (202)395-7254 • URL: http://www.fedstats.gov • Web site features an efficient search facility for full-text statistics produced by more than 100 federal agencies, including the Census Bureau, the Bureau of Economic Analysis, and the Bureau of Labor Statistics. Boolean searches can be made within one agency or for all agencies combined. Links are offered to international statistical bureaus, including the UN, IMF, OECD, UNESCO, Eurostat, and 20 individual countries. Fees: Free.

*FreeLunch.com.* Economy.com, Inc. Phone: (610)696-8700; Fax: (610)696-1678 • URL: http://www.freelunch.com • Web site provides free access to more than 200 million economic and financial data series, covering industry, demographics, labor markets, prices, retail sales, government spending, trade, interest rates, housing starts, the stock market, etc. Data is available in either chart or table form. Searching is offered. Free, but registration required. Economy.com, Inc. also offers fee-based economic analysis at *The Dismal Scientist* site (www.dismal.com).

## ONLINE DATABASES

*Tulsa.* Information Services. • Worldwide literature in the petroleum and natural gas areas, 1965 to present. Inquire as to online cost and availability. Includes petroleum exploration patents. Updated weekly.

## OTHER SOURCES

*Federal Taxation of Oil and Gas Transactions.* Matthew Bender and Company Inc. • $771 book. Covers the depletion deduction; tax treament of costs incurred in drilling; oil and gas partnerships; equipment depreciation, and more.

*Major Energy Companies of the World.* Cengage Learning Inc. • Annual. $1,460 Individuals. 2008. 12th edition. eBook. Published by Graham & Whiteside. Contains detailed information on more than 4,850 important energy companies in various countries. Industries include electricity generation, coal, natural gas, nuclear energy, petroleum, fuel distribution, and equipment for energy production.

*Oil Price Information Service.* UCG Holdings L.P. • Weekly. $545 Individuals. Quotes wholesale terminal prices for various petroleum products.

## PERIODICALS AND NEWSLETTERS

*Energy & Fuels.* American Chemical Society. • Bimonthly. $1,537 Institutions. An interdisciplinary technical journal covering non-nuclear energy sources: petroleum, gas, synthetic fuels, etc.

*Energy Compass.* Energy Intelligence Group. • Description: Focuses on worldwide geopolitical developments and their impact on the oil industry. Also includes marketing and trading information, political risk assessment, and current events and trends. **Remarks:** Available via fax, e-mail, or online.

*Hart's E and P.* Hart Energy. • Monthly. Edited for "decision makers" in petroleum exploration and production. Emphasis is on technology. Formerly *Petroleum Engineer International.*

*International Journal of Energy Research.* John Wiley and Sons, Inc., Journals Div. • 15 times a year. Individuals, $2,685.00 per year; institutions, $3,500.00 per year. Published in England by John Wiley & Sons Ltd.

*International Oil News.* William F. Bland Co. • Description: Covers "timely and significant developments in the international oil business, including exploration, production, transportation, refining, and marketing.".

*Lundberg Letter.* Lundberg Survey Inc. • Description: Provides statistics and analysis of U.S. oil marketing primary data. Includes an in-depth single-subject profile of a development in the petroleum market in each issue. Discusses such topics as retail/wholesale pricing, market shares, and station characteristics nationwide and regionally.

*Oil and Gas Investor.* Hart Energy. • Monthly. $297.00 per year.

*Oil and Gas Journal.* PennWell Corp., Industrial Div. • Weekly. $84.00 per year.

*Oil Daily: Daily Newspaper of the Petroleum Industry.* Energy Intelligence Group. • Daily. Email, $1,595.00 per year; fax, $2,395.00 per year, online, $1,495.00 per year. Newspaper for the petroleum industry.

*Oil, Gas and Energy Quarterly.* Matthew Bender and Company Inc. • Quarterly. $474.00 per year. Covers latest tax ideas, techniques, and practice pointers in oil and gas taxation and accounting features.

*The Oilman Weekly Newsletter.* PennWell Corp., Petroleum Div. • Weekly. $1,990.00 per year. Newsletter. Provides news of developments concerning the North Sea and European oil and gas businesses. Each issue contains four pages of statistical data.

*PetroChemical News: A Weekly News Service in English Devoted to the Worldwide Petrochemical Industry.* William F. Bland Co. • Weekly. $897. Report of current and significant news about the petrochemical business worldwide.

*Petroleum Intelligence Weekly.* Energy Intelligence Group. • Description: Provides a "concise weekly summary and analysis of key developments in world oil and natural gas markets." Supplies highlights in petroleum news on an international scale. Concerned with OPEC (Organization of Petroleum Exporting Countries) and non-OPEC production levels, coverage of OPEC meetings and policy decisions, and quarterly demand and oil trade figures. Recurring features include analyses of emerging trends in oil and gas markets, notices of publications available, and columns titled Marketview (a weekly wrap-up of crude oil trading) and What's New Around the World (news briefs relating to the petroleum industry and market).

*Petroleum Management: The International Business Magazine for the Oil and Gas Industry.* Management Publishing Services. • Monthly. $36. Trade magazine.

## PRICE SOURCES

*Energy Prices and Taxes.* International Energy Agency. Organisation for Economic Co-operation and Development Publications and Information Center. • Quarterly. $385 Individuals. Compiled by the International Energy Agency. Provides data on prices and taxation of petroleum products, natural gas, coal, and electricity. Diskette edition, $800.00. (Published in Paris).

*Platt's Oilgram Price Report: an International Daily Oil-Gas Price and Marketing Letter.* Platts Global Energy. • Daily. $19,995 Individuals. Prices and marketing intelligence for petroleum products. Includes weekly statistical summaries. Worldwide coverage.

## STATISTICS SOURCES

*Annual Energy Outlook, with Projections to (year).* U. S. Government Printing Office. • Annual. $39.00. Issued by the Energy Information Administration, U. S. Department of Energy (www.eia.doe.gov). Contains detailed statistics and 20-year projections for electricity, oil, natural gas, coal, and renewable energy. Text provides extensive discussion of energy issues and "Market Trends.".

*Annual Energy Review.* U. S. Government Printing Office. • Annual. $59.00. Issued by the Energy Information Administration, Office of Energy Markets and End Use, U. S. Department of Energy. Presents long-term historical as well as recent data on production, consumption, stocks, imports, exports, and prices of the principal energy commodities in the U. S.

*OECD Oil and Gas Information.* Organisation for Economic Co-operation and Development Publications and Information Center. • Annual. Price varies. Data on oil and gas balances, supplies, consumption by end use sector and trade of OECD countries. Text in English and French.

*The Oil and Natural Gas Producing Industry in Your State.* Independent Petroleum Association of America. Petroleum Independent Publishers, Inc. • Annual. Free to members; non-members, $75.00. Statistical issue of *Petroleum Independent*.

*Oil/Energy Statistics Bulletin: And Canadian Oil Reports.* Oil Statistics Company Inc. • Biweekly. $185.00 per year.

*Petroleum Supply Annual.* U. S. Government Printing Office. • Annual. $78.00. Two volumes. Produced by the Energy Information Administration, U. S. Department of Energy. Contains worldwide data on the petroleum industry and petroleum products.

*Petroleum Supply Monthly.* U. S. Government Printing Office. • Monthly. Produced by the Energy Information Administration, U. S. Department of Energy. Provides worldwide statistics on a wide variety of petroleum products. Covers production, supplies, exports and imports, transportation, refinery operations, and other aspects of the petroleum industry.

*Reserves of Crude Oil, Natural Gas Liquids and Natural Gas in the United States and Canada and United States Productive Capacity.* American Gas Association. • Annual. Price on application.

*Short-Term Energy Outlook: Quarterly Projections.* U. S. Government Printing Office. • Semiannual. Issued by Energy Information Administration, U. S. Department of Energy. Contains forecasts of U. S. energy supply, demand, and prices.

*Standard & Poor's Industry Surveys.* Standard & Poor's Financial Services L.L.C. • Semiannual. $1,800.00. Two looseleaf volumes. Includes

monthly *Supplements.* Provides detailed, individual surveys of 52 major industry groups. Each survey is revised on a semiannual basis. Also includes "Monthly Investment Review" (industry group investment analysis) and monthly "Trends & Projections" (economic analysis).

*Survey of Current Business.* U. S. Government Printing Office. • Published by Bureau of Economic Analysis, U. S. Department of Commerce. Presents a wide variety of business and economic data.

*Weekly Petroleum Status Report.* Energy Information Administration. U. S. Government Printing Office. • Weekly. Current statistics in the context of both historical information and selected prices and forecasts.

## TRADE/PROFESSIONAL ASSOCIATIONS

American Fuel and Petrochemical Manufacturers. 1667 K St. NW, Ste. 700, Washington, DC 20006. Phone: (202)457-0480; Fax: (202)457-0486; Email: info@afpm.org • URL: http://www.afpm.org • Formerly National Petrochemical and Refiners Association.

American Petroleum Institute. 1220 L St. NW, Washington, DC 20005-4070. Phone: (202)682-8000 • URL: http://www.api.org • Corporations in the petroleum and allied industries, including producers, refiners, marketers, and transporters of crude oil, lubricating oil, gasoline and natural gas. Provides public policy development, advocacy, research, and technical services to enhance the ability of the petroleum industry to fulfill its mission: meeting the nation's energy needs; enhancing the environmental, health, and safety performance of the industry; conducting research to advance petroleum technology, equipment, and standards; Consensus policies and collective action on issues impacting its members; and works collaboratively with all industry oil and gas associations, and other organizations, to enhance industry unity and effectiveness in its advocacy. Also provides the opportunity for standards development, technical cooperation and other activities to improve the industry's competitiveness through sponsorship of self-supporting programs.

Deep Draft Lubricant Association. c/o Shawn Konrad, Director, Belle Chasse Marine Transportation, 5813 Citrus Blvd., Harahan, LA 70123-5810. Phone: (504)837-3125; Email: information@ddla.org • URL: http://www.ddla.org • Promotes the interests of persons and firms engaged in the delivery of petroleum lubricants to deep draft vessels in the waters of the United States. Strives to create awareness of the individual operators, their suppliers and the industry of operational efficiencies and environmental regulations. Works to develop and improve performance standards and business methods.

International Energy Credit Association. 1500 Commerce Pkwy., Ste. C, Mount Laurel, NJ 08054. Phone: (856)380-6854; Fax: (856)439-0525 • URL: http://www.ieca.net • Credit executives of petroleum and energy related companies and vendors to the field. Conducts educational seminars.

International Petroleum Industry Environmental Conservation Association. 209-215 Blackfriars Rd., 5th Fl., London SE1 8NL, United Kingdom. Phone: 44 20 76332388; Fax: 44 20 76332389; Email: info@ipieca.org • URL: http://www.ipieca.org • Represents 52% of worldwide oil and gas production drawn from 26 private and state-owned companies as well as 12 national, regional, international associations. Represents both upstream and downstream of the oil and gas industry on key global environmental issues, including oil spill preparedness and response, global climate change, health, fuel quality, biodiversity and social responsibility.

National Petroleum Council. 1625 K St. NW, Ste.

600, Washington, DC 20006. Phone: (202)393-6100; Fax: (202)331-8539; Email: info@npc.org • URL: http://www.npc.org • Advisory council to the Secretary of Energy on matters relating to oil and gas.

# PETROLEUM INDUSTRY, OFFSHORE

*See* OFFSHORE PETROLEUM INDUSTRY

# PETROLEUM MARKETING

*See also* PETROLEUM INDUSTRY

## FINANCIAL RATIOS

*Industry Norms and Key Business Ratios.* Dun & Bradstreet Inc. • Annual. Five volumes. Covers over 800 kinds of businesses, arranged by Standard Industrial Classification number. More detailed editions covering longer periods of time are also available.

## HANDBOOKS AND MANUALS

*World Crude Oil Data.* Energy Intelligence Group. • Annual. An overview covers "The Inner Workings of Crude Oil Markets," including a glossary of terms. Reference sections contain detailed profiles of 44 "key producing countries," legal terms, crude oil sales contracts, prices, and other information.

## PERIODICALS AND NEWSLETTERS

*Oil and Gas Journal.* PennWell Corp., Industrial Div. • Weekly. $84.00 per year.

*Oil Daily: Daily Newspaper of the Petroleum Industry.* Energy Intelligence Group. • Daily. Email, $1,595.00 per year; fax, $2,395.00 per year, online, $1,495.00 per year. Newspaper for the petroleum industry.

*Oil Express: Inside Report on Trends in Petroleum Marketing Without the Influence of Advertising.* UCG Holdings L.P. • 50 times a year. $337.00 per year. Newsletter. Provides news of trends in petroleum marketing and convenience store operations. Includes *U.S. Oil Week's Price Monitor* (petroleum product prices) and *C-Store Digest* (news concerning convenience stores operated by the major oil companies) and *Fuel Oil Update.* Formerly *U.S. Oil Week.*

*Oil Market Intelligence.* Energy Intelligence Group. • Description: Provides analysis and statistics on worldwide oil markets and leading regional markets, including both the Atlantic Basin (Europe and the Americas) and Pacific Basins (East of Suez and the Far East). Covers futures and options markets and furnishes a monthly scorecard of prices for key products and crudes.

*The Oil Marketing Bulletin.* UCG Holdings L.P. • Weekly. $695.00 per year. Newsletter. Marketing information service.

*Platt's Oilgram News.* The McGraw-Hill Companies Inc. • Daily. $3,990 basic. Description: Monitors the latest developments in the politics and economics of petroleum. Covers exploration, production, supply and transportation, refining, and marketing. Recurring features include interviews, news of research, and reports of meetings. Coverage is global in scope.

## STATISTICS SOURCES

*Petroleum Marketing Monthly.* U. S. Government Printing Office. • Monthly. Current information and statistics relating to a wide variety of petroleum products. (Office of Oil and Gas, Energy Information Administration, U. S. Department of Energy.).

*Standard & Poor's Industry Surveys.* Standard & Poor's Financial Services L.L.C. • Semiannual. $1,800.00. Two looseleaf volumes. Includes monthly *Supplements*. Provides detailed, individual surveys of 52 major industry groups. Each survey is revised on a semiannual basis. Also includes "Monthly Investment Review" (industry group investment analysis) and monthly "Trends & Projections" (economic analysis).

*Standard & Poor's Statistical Service. Current Statistics.* Standard & Poor's Financial Services L.L.C. • Monthly. $688.00 per year. Includes 10 *Basic Statistics* sections, *Current Statistics Supplements* and *Annual Security Price Index Record*.

## TRADE/PROFESSIONAL ASSOCIATIONS

American Petroleum Institute. 1220 L St. NW, Washington, DC 20005-4070. Phone: (202)682-8000 • URL: http://www.api.org • Corporations in the petroleum and allied industries, including producers, refiners, marketers, and transporters of crude oil, lubricating oil, gasoline and natural gas. Provides public policy development, advocacy, research, and technical services to enhance the ability of the petroleum industry to fulfill its mission: meeting the nation's energy needs; enhancing the environmental, health, and safety performance of the industry; conducting research to advance petroleum technology, equipment, and standards; Consensus policies and collective action on issues impacting its members; and works collaboratively with all industry oil and gas associations, and other organizations, to enhance industry unity and effectiveness in its advocacy. Also provides the opportunity for standards development, technical cooperation and other activities to improve the industry's competitiveness through sponsorship of self-supporting programs.

# PHARMACEUTICAL INDUSTRY

*See also* DRUG STORES; GENERIC DRUG INDUSTRY; NONPRESCRIPTION DRUG INDUSTRY

## ABSTRACTS AND INDEXES

*Applied Science and Technology Index.* EBSCO Publishing Inc. • 11/year. Indexes a wide variety of English language technical, industrial, and engineering periodicals.

*International Pharmaceutical Abstracts: Key to the World's Literature of Pharmacy.* American Society of Health-System Pharmacists. • Semimonthly. $565.50 per year.

*Science Citation Index.* Thomson Reuters Intellectual Property and Science. • Weekly. Includes *Source Index, Citation Index, Permuterm Subject Index,* and *Corporate Index.* Provides researchers, administrators, faculty, and students with quick, powerful access to the bibliographic and citation information they need to find research data, analyze trends, journals and researchers, and share their findings.

## ALMANACS AND YEARBOOKS

*Annual Review of Pharmacology and Toxicology.* Annual Reviews. • Annual. $99 Individuals online only.

## BIBLIOGRAPHIES

*Medical & Health Care Books & Serials in Print.* Grey House Publishing. • $645 Individuals Hardcover. Provides immediate access to the highly specialized publishing activity in the health sciences and allied health fields.

## CD-ROM DATABASES

*International Pharmaceutical Abstracts.* Ovid Technologies Inc. • Quarterly. International pharmaceutical literature from 1970 to date.

*Mosby's GenRx (year).* CME Inc. • Quarterly. $250.00. CD-ROM contains detailed monographs for more than 45,000 generic and brand name prescription drugs. Includes color pill images and customizable patient education handouts.

*Science Citation Index.* Thomson Reuters Intellectual Property and Science. • Weekly. Includes *Source Index, Citation Index, Permuterm Subject Index,* and *Corporate Index.* Provides researchers, administrators, faculty, and students with quick, powerful access to the bibliographic and citation information they need to find research data, analyze trends, journals and researchers, and share their findings.

## DIRECTORIES

*Asia Pacific Pharmaceuticals and Healthcare Directory.* Business Monitor International Ltd. • $895 Individuals. Covers: 3,353 top pharmaceutical executives at 1,120 leading pharmaceutical companies from China, Hong Kong, India, Indonesia, Malaysia, the Philippines, Singapore, South Korea, Taiwan, Thailand and Vietnam. Entries include: Company name and address; phone, fax, email and website address; senior contact personnel; full description of company activity; local company profile; nationality; and ownership status and parentage.

*California Bioscience Directory.* San Diego Regional Chamber of Commerce. • $345 Members. Covers: 1,700 California companies and over 6,000 key managers in biotechnology, biomedical, pharmaceutical, bioresearch, and medical device firms.

*Directory of American Manufacturers & Exporters of Pharmaceutical Products.* EXIM Infotek Private Ltd. • $5 Individuals. Covers: 30 American manufacturers and exporters of animal health products, dental medicaments, dental pharmaceuticals, generic pharmaceuticals, nuclear medicine, pharmaceuticals. Entries include: Company name, postal address, city, country, phone, fax, e-mail and websites, contact person, designation, and product details.

*Directory of Chinese Manufacturers & Exporters of Pharmaceutical Products.* EXIM Infotek Private Ltd. • $25 Individuals. Covers: 330 Chinese manufacturers and exporters of antibiotics, biopharmaceuticals, bulk drugs, capsules, drugs, eye drops, intermediate for medicines, medicaments, medicines, medicines for animals, paracetamol, pharmaceutical materials, pharmaceutical products, pharmaceuticals, veterinary medicines. Entries include: Company name, postal address, city, country, phone, fax, e-mail and websites, contact person, designation, and product details.

*Directory of Chinese Manufacturers & Exporters of Pharmaceutical Raw Materials.* EXIM Infotek Private Ltd. • $10 Individuals. Covers: 80 Chinese manufacturers and exporters of amino-acid, enzymes, medicine industrial chemicals, pharmaceutical chemicals, pharmaceutical intermediates, pharmaceutical raw material, raw material for medicines, and vitamins/hormones and organ extracts. Entries include: Company name, postal address, city, country, phone, fax, e-mail and websites, contact person, designation, and product details.

*Directory of Japanese Manufacturers & Exporters of Machinery for Chemicals & Pharma Industry.* EXIM Infotek Private Ltd. • $5 Individuals. Covers: 20 Japanese manufacturers and exporters of chemical equipment, chemical industrial equipment, chemical industries machinery, chemical machinery, chemical plant equipment, and pharmaceutical plant equipment. Entries include: Company name, postal address, city, country, phone, fax, e-mail and websites, contact person, designation, and product details.

*Directory of Japanese Manufacturers & Exporters of Pharmaceutical Products.* EXIM Infotek Private Ltd. • $10 Individuals. Covers: 120 Japanese manufacturers & exporters of hygienic-pharmaceutical goods, medicaments, medicines, pharmaceutical materials, pharmaceuticals. Entries include: Company name, postal address, city, country, phone, fax, e-mail & websites, contact person, designation, products detail.

*Directory of South Korean Manufacturers & Exporters of Pharmaceutical Products.* EXIM Infotek Private Ltd. • $10 Individuals. Covers: 120 South Korean manufacturers & exporters of antibiotics, microencapsulated pharmaceuticals, ophthalmic preparations, pharmaceutical preparations for cardio-vascular, pharmaceutical preparations, veterinary preparations-general, vitamin preparations. Entries include: Company name, postal address, city, country, phone, fax, e-mail & websites, contact person, designation, products detail.

*Directory of South Korean Manufacturers & Exporters of Pharmaceutical Raw Materials.* EXIM Infotek Private Ltd. • $5 Individuals. Covers: 20 South Korean manufacturers and exporters of gelatins for pharmaceuticals, hypodermoclysis and phleboclysis solutions, pharmaceutical base and suppository compounds, vitamins/hormones and organ extracts. Entries include: Company name, postal address, city, country, phone, fax, e-mail and websites, contact person, designation, and product details.

*Directory of Taiwanese Manufacturers & Exporters of Pharmaceutical Products.* EXIM Infotek Private Ltd. • $20 Individuals. Covers: 250 Taiwanese manufacturers and exporters of antibiotics, microencapsulated pharmaceuticals, ophthalmic preparations, pharmaceutical preparations for cardio-vascular, pharmaceutical preparations, veterinary preparations-general, vitamin preparations. Entries include: Company name, postal address, city, country, phone, fax, e-mail and websites, contact person, designation, and product details.

*Directory of Taiwanese Manufacturers & Exporters of Pharmaceutical Raw Materials.* EXIM Infotek Private Ltd. • $20 Individuals. Covers: 190 Taiwanese manufacturers and exporters of gelatins for pharmaceuticals, hypodermoclysis and phleboclysis solution, pharmaceutical base and suppository compounds, vitamins/hormones and organ extracts. Entries include: Company name, postal address, city, country, phone, fax, e-mail and websites, contact person, designation, and product details.

*Drug Facts and Comparisons.* Wolters Kluwer Health. • $565 Individuals Loose-leaf. Provides detailed information on more than 20,000 prescription drugs and 6000 over-the-counter products. Arrangement is according to 13 therapeutic categories. Includes charts and tables.

*Drug Interaction Facts.* Wolters Kluwer Health. • Contains data on the interactions of some 20,000 prescription drugs. Interactions are rated according to magnitude and likelihood of effects, from one (most severe) to five (least severe). Includes drug/drug and drug/food interactions.

*Emerging Europe Pharmaceuticals and Healthcare Directory.* Business Monitor International Ltd. • $895 Individuals. Covers: 2,212 top pharmaceutical executives at 794 leading pharmaceutical companies from Bosnia, Bulgaria, Croatia, the Czech Republic, Estonia, Hungary, Latvia, Lithuania, Macedonia, Poland, Romania, Russia, Serbia, Slovakia, Slovenia and the Ukraine. Entries include: Parent company head offices, full company name, address, phone and fax numbers, email and website address, senior contact personnel, company description and profile, nationality, and ownership status.

*The International Directory of Importers--Drugs and Pharmaceuticals Importers.* Interdata. • Annual. $260 Individuals print. Covers: 2,900 international firms importing drugs and pharmaceuticals. Entries include: Company name and address, contact person, email, number of employees, year established, phone and telefaxes, business activity, bank references, as well as a listing of drugs and pharmaceuticals currently being imported.

*Latin America and Caribbean Pharmaceuticals and Healthcare Directory.* Business Monitor International Ltd. • $995 Individuals CD. Covers: 1,908 top pharmaceutical executives at 598 leading pharmaceutical companies from Argentina, Brazil, Chile, Colombia, Mexico, Peru, Venezuela and the Caribbean. Entries include: parent company head offices, full company name, address, phone and fax numbers, email and website address, senior contact personnel, company description and profile, nationality, and ownership status.

*Major Pharmaceutical & Biotechnology Companies of the World.* Cengage Learning Inc. • Contains directory information on more than 4070 of the world's largest pharmaceutical companies, providing essential business profiles of the international leaders in the industry.

*Medical and Healthcare Marketplace Guide.* IDD Inc. • Annual. $595.00. Two volumes. Provides market survey summaries for about 500 specific product and service categories (volume one: "Research Reports"). Contains profiles of nearly 5,500 pharmaceutical, medical product, and healthcare service companies (volume two: "Company Profiles").

*Middle East and Africa Pharmaceuticals and Healthcare Directory.* Business Monitor International Ltd. • $975 Individuals CD. Covers: 2,032 top pharmaceutical executives on 615 leading pharmaceutical companies from Algeria, Bahrain, Botswana, Egypt, Greece, Iran, Jordan, Kuwait, Lebanon, Libya, Morocco, Mozambique, Namibia, Oman, Qatar, Saudi Arabia, South Africa, Syria, Tunisia, Turkey, UAE, Yemen, Zambia and Zimbabwe. Entries include: Parent company head offices, full company name, address, phone and fax numbers, email and website address, senior contact personnel, company description and profile, nationality, and ownership status.

*Pharmaceutical Strategic Alliances: The Complete Drug and Biotech Alliances Reference Guide.* Windhover Information Inc. • Annual. $2,495 Single issue volume XVII (print). Covers: Pharmaceutical industry strategic alliances, including joint ventures, research and development collaborations, marketing/licensing agreements, and equity investments. Entries include: Company name, address, phone, names and titles of key personnel, financial data, description of transaction, terms, valuations, product information including therapeutic categories, clinical phase of development, geographic marketing rights, statistical charts.

*Red Book.* American Monument Association. • Annual. $60. Covers: 7,000 retail monument dealers, suppliers of granite and marble, wholesalers, quarriers, funeral homes and cemeteries. Entries include: company; name, address, phone, fax; trade classification, names of owner or corporate officers and their titles. Available only to members of The American Monument Association.

*Scott's Canadian Pharmacists Directory.* Scott's Directories. • Biennial. $229 Individuals Web pinpointer. Covers: Approximately 18,000 pharmacists, university pharmacy faculty members, pharmacy suppliers, and drug and poison information centers in Canada, chain drug stores, independent. Entries include: Name, address, phone, names and titles of key personnel, biographical data (for pharmacists), geographical area served.

## ENCYCLOPEDIAS AND DICTIONARIES

*American Drug Index.* Wolters Kluwer Health. • Annual. $99.95 Individuals. Lists over 20,000 drug entries in dictionary style.

*USAN and the USP Dictionary of Drug Names.*

United States Pharmacopeial Convention. • Annual. Adopted names, brand names, compendial and other generic names, CAS Registry Numbers, molecular weights, and other information.

## FINANCIAL RATIOS

*Annual Statement Studies.* Risk Management Association. • Annual. Compiled from over 280,000 financial statements.

*Annual Statement Studies: Industry Default Probabilities and Cash Flow Measures.* Risk Management Association. • Annual. $405 Nonmembers. Serves as a companion volume to the original *Annual Statement Studies.* Gives probability of default estimates on a percentage scale for more than 450 industries. Includes changes in position year-by-year for eight financial statement line items and provides percentage measures of cash flow.

*Quarterly Financial Report for Manufacturing, Mining, Trade, and Selected Service Industries.* U.S. Federal Trade Commission and U.S. Securities and Exchange Commission. U.S. Census Bureau Foreign Trade Division. • Quarterly. Quarterly. Report on financial results of U.S. corporations.

## HANDBOOKS AND MANUALS

*Approved Drug Products, with Therapeutic Equivalence Evaluations.* U. S. Government Printing Office. • $273 U.S.. Issued by the Food and Drug Administration, U. S. Department of Health and Human Services. Lists prescription drugs that have been approved by the FDA. Includes therapeutic equivalents to aid in containment of health costs and to serve State drug selection laws.

*PDR Drug Guide for Mental Health Professionals.* Thomson Medical Economics. • Annual. $39.95. Contains detailed profiles of more than 70 "common psychotropic drugs organized by brand name." Also contains information on the psychological side effects of about 1,000 other prescription drugs.

*PDR Guide to Drug Interactions, Side Effects, Indications.* American Medical Association. Medical Economics Co. • Annual. $48.95. Includes a list of prescription drugs by "precise clinical situation.".

*Physicians' Desk Reference.* Medical Economics Co. • Annual. $82.95. Generally known as "PDR." Provides detailed descriptions, effects, and adverse reactions for about 4,000 prescription drugs. Includes data on more than 250 drug manufacturers, with brand name and generic name indexes and drug identification photographs. Discontinued drugs are also listed.

*Physicians' Desk Reference for Ophthalmology.* Medical Economics Co. • Annual. $49.95. Provides detailed descriptions of ophthalmological instrumentation, equipment, supplies, lenses, and prescription drugs. Indexed by manufacturer, product name, product category, active drug ingredient, and instrumentation. Editorial discussion is included.

*United States Pharmacopeia National Formulary.* United States Pharmacopeial Convention. • Annual. $850. Contains standards for (chemical and biological drug substances, dosage forms, and compounded preparations), excipients, medical devices, and dietary supplements.

## INTERNET DATABASES

*Manufacturing Profiles.* U. S. Bureau of the Census. Phone: (301)763-4636 or (301)763-4100; Fax: (301)763-4794; Email: webmaster@census.gov • URL: http://www.census.gov/prod/www/abs/mfg-prof.html • The Census Bureau makes available free on PDF (Portable Document Format) an annual consolidation of the entire Current Industrial Report series, presenting "all the data compiled." Contains statistics on production, shipments, inventories, consumption, exports, imports, and orders for a wide variety of manufactured products.

*National Library of Medicine.* National Institutes of

Health. 9000 Rockville Pke., Bethesda, MD 20892. Phone: (301)496-4000; Email: nihinfo@od.nih.gov • URL: http://www.nih.gov • NLM Web site offers free access through MEDLINE ("PubMed") to about nine million references to articles appearing in some 4,000 biomedical journals, with abstracts. Search interfaces range from "simple keywords to advanced Boolean expressions." The NLM site offers many links to other sources of biomedical and technical information (the National Center for Biotechnology Information, for example). Fees: Free.

*Rx List: The Internet Drug Index.* WebMD Health Corp. 111 8th Ave., New York, NY 10011. Phone: (212)624-3700 • URL: http://www.wbmd.com • Web site features detailed information (cost, usage, dosage, side effects, etc.) from Mosby, Inc. for about 300 major pharmaceutical products, representing two thirds of prescriptions filled in the U. S. (3,700 other products are listed). The "Top 200" drugs are ranked by number of prescriptions filled. Keyword searching is provided. Fees: Free.

## ONLINE DATABASES

*Derwent Drug File.* Derwent Information Ltd. • Provides indexing and abstracting of the world's pharmaceutical journal literature since 1964, with weekly updates. Formerly *RINGDOC.* Inquire as to online cost and availability.

*Drug Information Fulltext (DIF).* American Society of Health-System Pharmacists. • Provides full text monographs from the *American Hospital Formulary Service* and the *Handbook On Injectable Drugs.* Inquire as to online cost and availability.

*F-D-C Reports.* Elsevier Business Intelligence. • An online version of "The Gray Sheet" (medical devices), "The Pink Sheet" (pharmaceuticals), "The Rose Sheet" (cosmetics), "The Blue Sheet" (biomedical), and "The Tan Sheet" (nonprescription). Contains full-text information on legal, technical, corporate, financial, and marketing developments from 1987 to date, with weekly updates. Inquire as to online cost and availability.

*Gale Group PharmaBiomed Business Journals.* Cengage Learning Inc. • Contains international coverage of full-text articles from trade journals on pharmaceuticals, biotechnology, and healthcare, including information on methods and techniques, business practices, new products, companies, markets, market share, research and development, regulations, and applied technologies in these fields.

## OTHER SOURCES

*Food Law Reports.* Wolters Kluwer Law & Business CCH. • Weekly. $1,459.00 per year. Six looseleaf volumes. Covers regulation of adulteration, packaging, labeling, and additives. Formerly *Food Drug Cosmetic Law Reports.*

*Pharmaceutical Litigation Reporter: The National Journal of Record of Pharmaceutical Litigation.* Andrews Publications. • Monthly. $775.00 per year. Newsletter. Reports on a wide variety of legal cases involving the pharmaceutical and medical device industries. Includes product liability lawsuits.

## PERIODICALS AND NEWSLETTERS

*Biotech Business Week.* NewsRX. • Weekly. $2,295 Other countries. Publication that provides news and information from pharmaceutical and biotechnology companies, with a focus on business trends and analysis.

*Community Pharmacist: Meeting the Professional and Educational Needs of Today's Practitioner.* ELF Publicatons, Inc. • Bimonthly. $25.00 per year. Edited for retail pharmacists in various settings, whether independent or chain-operated. Covers both pharmaceutical and business topics.

*Drug Benefit Trends: For Pharmacy Managers and Managed HealthCare Professionals.* Cliggott Publishing Co. • Monthly. Individuals, $95.00 per year; libraries, $120.00 per year; students, $40.00

per year. Covers the business of managed care drug benefits.

*Drug Development Research.* John Wiley & Sons Inc. • Monthly. $8,040 U.S., Canada, and Mexico Online only - institution.

*Drug Topics.* Thomson Medical Economics. • Monthly. Edited for retail pharmacists, hospital pharmacists, pharmacy chain store executives, wholesalers, buyers, and others concerned with drug dispensing and drug store management. Provides information on new products, including personal care items and cosmetics.

*FDA Consumer.* U. S. Government Printing Office. • Bimonthly. $14.00 per year. Issued by the U. S. Food and Drug Administration. Provides consumer information about FDA regulations and product safety.

*The Green Sheet.* Elsevier Business Intelligence. • Weekly. $109.00 per year. Newsletter for retailers and wholesalers of pharmaceutical products. Includes pricing developments and new drug announcements.

*Health News Daily.* Elsevier Business Intelligence. • Description: Tracks developments in health care policy, legislation and regulation, insurance, pharmaceuticals, delivery, manufacturing, technology and treatment, funding, and research.

*Healthcare Distributor: The Industry's Multi-Market Information Resource.* ELF Publications Inc. • Bimonthly. Formerly *Wholesale Drugs Magazine.*

*Hospital Pharmacist Report.* Thomson Medical Economics. • Monthly. $39.00 per year. Covers both business and clinical topics for hospital pharmacists.

*Med Ad News.* Engel Publishing Partners. • Monthly. $225.00 per year. Covers the field of pharmaceutical advertising and marketing.

*The Medical Letter on Drugs and Therapeutics.* Medical Letter. • Biweekly. $98 Individuals per year. Provides critical evaluation of new drugs, including effectiveness, toxicity, cost, and possible alternatives.

*Medical Marketing and Media.* Haymarket Media, Inc. • Monthly. $148 U.S. 1-year subscription. Contains articles on marketing, direct marketing, advertising media, and sales personnel for the healthcare and pharmaceutical industries.

*Pharma Business: The International Magazine of Pharmaceutical Business and Marketing.* Engel Publishing Partners. • Six times a year. $235.00 per year. Circulated mainly in European countries. Coverage includes worldwide industry news, new drug products, regulations, and research developments.

*The Pharma Letter.* The Pharma Letter. • Fifty times a year. $720.00 per year. Newsletter. Formerly *Marketletter.*

*Pharmaceutical and Medical Device Law Bulletin.* ALM Media Properties LLC. • Monthly. $199.00 per year. Newsletter. Edited for lawyers concerned with drug product or medical device litigation. Contains industry news items of special interest, reports on new products, legal case summaries, Food and Drug Administration actions, patent issues, and related news reports. (A Law Journal Newsletter, formerly published by Leader Publications).

*Pharmaceutical Engineering.* International Society for Pharmaceutical Engineering. • Bimonthly. Feature articles provide practical application and specification information on the design, construction, supervision and maintenance of process equipment, plant systems, instrumentation and pharmaceutical facilities.

*Pharmaceutical Executive: For Global Business and Marketing Leaders.* Advanstar Communications. • Monthly. Covers fresh ideas about sales, regulations, finance, meetings and IT.

*Pharmaceutical Processing.* Advantage Business Media L.L.C. • 10/year. Includes *Buyers' Guide.* Formerly *Pharmaceutical and Cosmetic Equipment.*

*Pharmaceutical Representative.* McKnight's Long-Term Care News. • Monthly. $37.95 per year. Edited for drug company salespeople and sales managers.

*Pharmaceutical Technology.* Advanstar Communications. • Monthly. Practical hands on information about the manufacture of pharmaceutical products, focusing on applied technology.

*Pharmacopeial Forum.* United States Pharmacopeial Convention. • Bimonthly. $469 Individuals. Journal on drug standards.

*The Pink Sheet: Prescription Pharmaceuticals and Biotechnology.* Elsevier Business Intelligence. • 51 times a year. Institutions, $1,431.00 per year. Newsletter covering business and regulatory developments affecting the pharmaceutical and biotechnology industries. Provides information on generic drug approvals and includes a drug sector stock index.

*The Tan Sheet: Nonprescription Pharmaceuticals and Nutritionals.* Elsevier Business Intelligence. • Weekly. $1,220.00 per year. Newsletter covering over-the-counter drugs and vitamin supplements. Emphasis is on regulatory activities of the U. S. Food and Drug Administration (FDA).

## RESEARCH CENTERS AND INSTITUTES

Pharmacology Research Laboratory. c/o David Flockhart, Division Chief, Indiana University School of Medicine, Division of Clinical Pharmacology, 950 W Walnut St., Rm. 402, Indianapolis, IN 46202. Phone: (317)274-2810 or (317)274-2820 • URL: http://medicine.iupui.edu/clinpharm

Tufts University - Tufts Center for the Study of Drug Development. 75 Kneeland St., Ste. 1100, Boston, MA 02111. Phone: (617)636-2170; Fax: (617)636-2425; Email: csdd@tufts.edu • URL: http://csdd.tufts.edu • Provides strategic information to help drug developers, regulators, and policy makers improve the quality and efficiency of pharmaceutical development, review, and utilization; focuses on: research & development, economic, and performance issues; regulatory policies and initiatives; biotechnology product development; drug development operational processes; public policy, healthcare financing, and law.

U.S. Food and Drug Administration - Center for Drug Evaluation and Research - Office of Prescription Drug Promotion. Bldg. 51, Rm. 3200, 10903 New Hampshire Ave., Silver Spring, MD 20993-0002. Phone: (301)796-1200; Fax: (301)847-8445; Email: thomas.abrams@fda.hhs.gov • URL: http://www.fda.gov/AboutFDA/CentersOffices/OfficeofMedicalProductsandTobacco/CDER/ucm090142.htm • Industry-wide marketing practices of the pharmaceutical industry and improvement of drug communications between FDA, health professionals, and the public. Specific research areas include prescription drugs, marketing practices, and health communications.

University of Mississippi - Center for Pharmaceutical Marketing and Management. Faser Hall Rms. 128-136, School of Pharmacy, University, MS 38677. Phone: (662)915-5352 or (662)915-5948; Fax: (662)915-5262; Email: benb3@olemiss.edu • URL: http://www.pharmacy.olemiss.edu/cpmm • Proprietary and in-house marketing and management studies relating to pharmaceutical products, including formulary decision factors, generic substitution, reimbursement issues, medication compliance and consumer preferences. Conducts mail surveys, telephone interviews, focus groups, internet surveys, consumer reaction panels, and surveys of professionals at national and state meetings.

## STATISTICS SOURCES

*Pharmaceutical Research Manufacturers Association Annual Fact Book.* Pharmaceutical Research and Manufacturers Association. • Annual.

*Standard & Poor's Industry Surveys.* Standard & Poor's Financial Services L.L.C. • Semiannual. $1,800.00. Two looseleaf volumes. Includes monthly *Supplements.* Provides detailed, individual surveys of 52 major industry groups. Each survey is revised on a semiannual basis. Also includes "Monthly Investment Review" (industry group investment analysis) and monthly "Trends & Projections" (economic analysis).

*Standard & Poor's Statistical Service. Current Statistics.* Standard & Poor's Financial Services L.L.C. • Monthly. $688.00 per year. Includes 10 *Basic Statistics* sections, *Current Statistics Supplements* and *Annual Security Price Index Record.*

*U.S. Industry and Trade Outlook.* U.S. Department of Commerce National Technical Information Service. • Annual. Produced by the International Trade Administration, U.S. Department of Commerce, in a "public-private" partnership with DRI/McGraw-Hill and Standard & Poor's. Provides basic data, outlook for the current year, and "Long-Term Prospects" (five-year projections) for a wide variety of products and services. Includes high technology industries. Formerly *U.S. Industrial Outlook.*

## TRADE/PROFESSIONAL ASSOCIATIONS

American College of Apothecaries. 2830 Summer Oaks Dr., Bartlett, TN 38134. Phone: (901)383-8119; Fax: (901)473-8187; Email: info@acainfo.org • URL: http://acainfo.org • A professional society of pharmacists.

American Society of Health-System Pharmacists. 7272 Wisconsin Ave., Bethesda, MD 20814. Phone: 866-279-0681 or (301)664-8700 or (301)657-3000; Fax: (301)657-1251; Email: custserv@ashp.org • URL: http://www.ashp.org • Affiliated with American Hospital Association and American Nurses Association.

APhA Academy of Pharmacy Practice and Management. 2215 Constitution Ave. NW, Washington, DC 20037. Phone: 800-237-APHA or (202)628-4410 or (202)429-7557; Fax: (202)783-2351; Email: infocenter@aphanet.org • URL: http://www.pharmacist.com/apha-appm • Pharmacists concerned with rendering professional services directly to the public, without regard for status of employment or environment of practice. Formerly Academy of Pharmacy Practice and Management.

Drug, Chemical and Associated Technologies Association. One Washington Blvd., Ste. 7, Robbinsville, NJ 08691-3162. Phone: 800-640-3228 or (609)448-1000; Fax: (609)448-1944 • URL: http://www.dcat.org • Formerly Drug, Chemical and Allied Trades Section of the New York Board of Trade.

Drug Information Association. 800 Enterprise Rd., Ste. 200, Horsham, PA 19044-3595. Phone: (215)442-6100; Fax: (215)442-6199; Email: dia@diahome.org • URL: http://www.diahome.org • Provides neutral, global forum promoting exchange of information critical to professional performance and achievement in the discovery, development, regulation, surveillance, or marketing of pharmaceuticals or related products.

Healthcare Distribution Management Association. 901 N Glebe Rd., Ste. 1000, Arlington, VA 22203. Phone: (703)787-0000; Fax: (703)812-5282 • URL: http://www.healthcaredistribution.org • Wholesalers and manufacturers of drug and health care products and industry service providers. Seeks to secure safe and effective distribution of healthcare products, create and exchange industry knowledge affecting the future of distribution management, and influence standards and business processes that produce efficient health care commerce. Compiles statistics;

sponsors research and specialized education programs.

INFARMA - Employers' Union of Innovative Pharmaceutical Companies. Pulawska 17 St., PL-02-515 Warsaw, Poland. Phone: 48 22 8528230; Fax: 48 22 8528231; Email: biuro@infarma.pl • URL: http://www.infarma.pl • Foreign-based pharmaceutical manufacturing companies maintaining operations in Poland. Promotes creation of a business climate favorable to members. Represents members' interests before government agencies and trade organizations; conducts educational and charitable programs.

National Association of Boards of Pharmacy. 1600 Feehanville Dr., Mount Prospect, IL 60056. Phone: (847)391-4406; Fax: (847)391-4502; Email: custserv@nabp.net • URL: http://www.nabp.net • Pharmacy boards of several states, District of Columbia, Puerto Rico, Virgin Islands, several Canadian provinces, the states of Victoria, Australia, and New South Wales, the Pharmaceutical Society of New Zealand, and the South African Pharmacy Council. Provides for inter-state reciprocity in pharmaceutical licensure based upon a uniform minimum standard of pharmaceutic education and uniform legislation; improves the standards of pharmaceutical education licensure and practice. Provides legislative information; sponsors uniform licensure examination; also provides information on accredited school and college requirements. Maintains pharmacy and drug law statistics.

National Association of Chain Drug Stores. 1776 Wilson Blvd., Ste. 200, Arlington, VA 22209. Phone: (703)549-3001; Fax: (703)836-4869; Email: contactus@nacds.org • URL: http://www.nacds.org • Represents the concerns of community pharmacies in Washington, in state capitals, and across the country. Members are more than 210 chain community pharmacy companies. Collectively, community pharmacy comprises the largest component of pharmacy practice with over 107,000 FTE pharmacists.

National Association of Pharmaceutical Sales Representatives. 2020 Pennsylvania Ave. NW, Ste. 5050, Washington, DC 20006-1811. Phone: 800-284-1060; Email: contact@napsronline.org • URL: http://www.napsronline.org • Represents sales representatives, sales managers and sales trainers who work in the pharmaceutical industry. Provides Continuing Medical Education to members as well as candidates who wish to start a pharmaceutical sales career. Aims to educate, train, create standards and provide current information for professional pharmaceutical sales representatives as well as for individuals who want to gain entry into the industry.

National Council for Prescription Drug Programs. 9240 E Raintree Dr., Scottsdale, AZ 85260-7518. Phone: (480)477-1000; Fax: (480)767-1042; Email: ncpdp@ncpdp.org • URL: http://www.ncpdp.org • Concerned with standardization of third party prescription drug programs.

National Pharmaceutical Association. 107 Kilmayne Dr., Ste. C, Cary, NC 27511. Phone: 877-215-2091; Fax: (919)469-5858; Email: npha@npha.net • URL: http://npha.net • State and local associations of professional minority pharmacists. Provides a means whereby members may "contribute to their common improvement, share their experiences, and contribute to the public good."

National Pharmaceutical Council. 1717 Pennsylvania Ave. NW, Ste. 800, Washington, DC 20006. Phone: (202)827-2100; Fax: (202)827-0314; Email: info@npcnow.org • URL: http://www.npcnow.org • Pharmaceutical manufacturers producing high-quality prescription medication and other pharmaceutical products. Generates research; conducts specialized educational programs and forums.

Pharmaceutical Research and Manufacturers Association. 950 F St. NW, Ste. 300, Washington, DC 20004. Phone: (202)835-3400 • URL: http://www.phrma.org • Formerly Pharmaceutical Manufacturers Association.

# PHARMACIES

*See* DRUG STORES

# PHILANTHROPY

## ABSTRACTS AND INDEXES

*Index to Legal Periodicals and Books.* H.W. Wilson Co. • Monthly. $490.00 per year. Quarterly and annual cumulations.

## BIBLIOGRAPHIES

*Catalog of Nonprofit Literature.* • Dates vary. Covers the literature of philanthropy, foundations, nonprofit organizations, fund-raising, and federal aid.

## DIRECTORIES

*Corporate 500: Directory of Corporate Philanthropy.* Public Management Institute. • Annual. $375 plus $10.00 shipping. Covers: 554 major corporations with philanthropic programs. Entries include: Corporation name, corporate foundation name (if applicable), address, philanthropic interests and priorities, policy statement, contribution committee members, financial profile, activities eligible for funding, contact person, sample grants, application procedures, analysis of giving patterns.

*Corporate Giving Directory.* Information Today, Inc. • Annual. $699.50 Individuals softbound; plus $20 shipping and handling. Covers: Top 1,000 major corporation- and company-sponsored foundations and direct-giving programs. Database includes: Appendix to abridged entries of more than 2,000 additional funders. Entries include: Giving program's sponsoring company name, address, phone, fax, e-mail, website; names and biographies of living officers, and contact person; grants data, including types, average amounts, sample grants; application procedures; analysis of giving priorities; and information on the company, including products, Fortune rank, sales, ticker symbol/stock exchange information, operating locations, number of employees, information on employee-matching gifts (including restrictions and ratio), and nonmonetary support.

*Corporate Giving Yellow Pages: Guide to Corporate Giving Contacts.* Taft Group. • $99. Covers: more than 3,500 corporate contact persons with information on corporate charitable giving. Entries include: Company name, address, phone, fax, name and title of contact, name of company foundation (if any).

*Directory of Catholic Charities USA Directories.* Catholic Charities USA. • Annual. $25 Individuals. Covers: Nearly 1,200 Catholic community and social service agencies. Listings include diocesan agencies, state Catholic conferences. Entries include: Organization name, address, name and title of director, phone, fax.

*Directory of Corporate and Foundation Givers.* Taft Group. • $270. Covers: 8,000 private foundations, corporate foundations, and companies that give money to nonprofit organizations. Entries include: Foundation name, sponsoring company name, address, phone, fax, e-mail, URL, contact name; financial summary, including assets and amounts given for up to previous three years; Employer Identification Number; summary of contributions, including typical recipients, grant types, nonmonetary support types, geographic distribution; names and titles of key personnel; application procedures; grants summary including total grants, highest grant,

typical grant range, and list of recent grants, giving amounts and names of recipients.

*Directory of International Corporate Giving in America and Abroad.* Taft Group. • $215. Covers: 443 foreign-owned companies that support nonprofit organizations in the U.S., and 170 U.S. companies that support organizations overseas. Entries include: Corporation name, foundation name; name, title, and phone of contact; location of U.S. headquarters, number of employees, total foundation assets, name and address of overseas parent company; summary of grant support, including amounts given, geographical area and types of activities preferred, and recently funded programs.

*Directory of Japanese Giving.* Corporate Citizen. • $190. Covers: Approximately 190 Japanese firms that participate in philanthropic activities in the U.S. Entries include: Company; name, address, phone; telex, names and titles of key personnel; description of policies, programs, and foundations; history of giving and volunteer activities in the U.S.; U.S. nonprofit organizations funded, geographical area served.

*Educators' Guide to Corporate Support.* Information Interface Institute. • $375 per year. Covers: Approximately 450 corporations, 300 associations, 200 government agencies, and 100 foundations that provide support to educational concerns. Entries include: Sponsoring organization name, address, phone, programs and teaching aids, contact person, geographic preferences for funding, program preferences, and grade levels supported.

*Guide to UK Company Giving.* The Directory of Social Change. • Biennial. $75 Individuals. Covers: Over 600 largest corporate donors in the United Kingdom. Entries include: Company name, address, phone, name and title of contact, financial data, including donation figures (additional information given for companies donating in excess of 500 million Ls per year).

*Hollis Sponsorship & Donations Yearbook.* Hobsons PLC. • Annual. £145 Individuals. Covers: Companies in the United Kingdom offering commercial sponsorships and donations to arts, charity, educational, media, and sports organizations; organizations looking for sponsorships and donations; sponsorship consultants; providers of services such as speakers, caterers, lawyers, insurance, and suppliers of promotional merchandise. Over 3,000 companies and organizations are listed. Entries include: Company or organization name, address, phone, fax, name and title of contact; sponsors list projects sponsored, sponsorship budget and date set, preferred areas of support, total donations; organizations seeking sponsors list projects needing aid, amount of funding required, benefits to the sponsoring company; consultants list number of employees, main interests.

*International Directory of Corporate Philanthropy.* Taylor & Francis Group. • Annual. $250.00. Published by Europa Publications (www. europapublications.com). Contains profiles of about 1,000 corporate foundations and "co-ordinating organizations" in various countries of the world. Provides details of charitable activities and philanthropic expenditures.

*The Major Companies Guide: The Charitable and Community Support of the UK's Leading Companies.* The Directory of Social Change. • Biennial. $16.95. Covers: about 400 companies in the United Kingdom with 160 millions Ls in cash donations and 100 millions Ls in community contributions. Entries include: Company name, address, phone, names and titles of key personnel, financial data, amount of donations annually, donation policy and practice, number of employees, employee involvement, branch office or subsidiary names, descriptions of product/service, type of business, community support programs.

*National Directory of Corporate Giving.* • Annual. $195 Individuals. Provides information on nearly 4,400 company-sponsored foundations and corporate giving programs.

*Wise Giving Guide.* Better Business Bureau - Wise Giving Alliance. • Three times per year. Full year available via contribution. Evaluates national charities against a set of standards concerning management, government and budget.

## INTERNET DATABASES

*ACGA: Partners in Philanthropy.* American Council on Gift Annuities. Phone: (317)269-6271; Fax: (317)269-6276; Email: acga@acga-web.org • URL: http://www.acga-web.org • Web site provides detailed information on gift annuities, including suggested charitable gift annuity rates for use by charities and their donors. Rates for immediate and deferred annuities are presented in the form of tables for ages 20 to 90 (and over), for both "Single Life" and "Two Lives - Joint and Survivor." Other items covered include the philosophy of gift annuities, state regulations, "What's New," and a search site. Fees: Free.

*Welcome to the Foundation Center.* Foundation Center. Phone: (212)620-4230 or (212)807-3679; Fax: (212)807-3677; Email: mfn@fdncenter.org • URL: http://www.fdncenter.org • Web site provides a wide variety of information about foundations, grants, and philanthropy, with links to philanthropic organizations. "Grantmaker Information" link furnishes descriptions of available funding.

## PERIODICALS AND NEWSLETTERS

*Chronicle of Philanthropy:The Newspaper of the Non-Profit World.* The Chronicle of Higher Education. • Biweekly. $77 per year.

*Foundation News & Commentary.* Council on Foundations. • Bimonthly. Bimonthly. $48.00 per year. Formerly *Foundation News.*

*Nonprofit Issues.* Donald W. Kramer. • Description: Presents legal information for nonprofit executives and their professional advisors.

*Trusts and Estates.* RentPath Inc. • Monthly. $139.00 per year. Includes annual *Directory.*

## RESEARCH CENTERS AND INSTITUTES

Boston College - Center for Corporate Citizenship. Carroll School of Management, 55 Lee Rd., Chestnut Hill, MA 02467-3942. Phone: (617)552-4545; Fax: (617)552-8499; Email: kv.smith@bc.edu • URL: http://www.bcccc.net • Areas of study include corporate images within local communities, corporate community relations, social vision, and philanthropy. Formerly Center for Corporate Community Relations.

Boston College - Center on Wealth and Philanthropy. 142 Beacon St., Chestnut Hill, MA 02467. Phone: (617)552-4070; Fax: (617)552-3903; Email: paul.schervish@bc.edu • URL: http://www.bc.edu/research/cwp • Spirituality, wealth, philanthropy and other aspects of cultural life in an age of affluence. Projects explore the association among philanthropy, income, and wealth; the organizational and moral determinants of giving and volunteering; and the implications for fundraising and philanthropy.

## STATISTICS SOURCES

*The Corporate Contributions Plan: From Strategy to Budget.* The Conference Board. • Annual. Members, $30.00, non-members, $120.00.

## TRADE/PROFESSIONAL ASSOCIATIONS

Association of Fundraising Professionals. 4300 Wilson Blvd., Ste. 300, Arlington, VA 22203. Phone: 800-666-3863 or (703)684-0410; Fax: (703)684-0540; Email: afp@afpnet.org • URL: http://www.afpnet.org • Formerly National Society of Fundraising Executives.

BBB Wise Giving Council. 3033 Wilson Blvd., Ste.

600, Arlington, VA 22201. Phone: (703)276-0100; Fax: (703)525-8277; Email: info@bbb.org • URL: http://www.bbb.org • Sets accountability standards and provides information for nonprofit organizations that solicit contributions from the public. Formerly National Charities Information Bureau.

Better Business Bureau - Wise Giving Alliance. 3033 Wilson Blvd., Ste. 600, Arlington, VA 22201. Phone: (703)276-0100; Fax: (703)525-8277; Email: info@bbb.org • URL: http://www.bbb.org • Supported by companies and local Better Business Bureaus operated autonomously in the United States and Puerto Rico, which are in turn supported by 270,000 local business members. Seeks to promote and foster the highest ethical relationship between businesses and the public through voluntary self-regulation, consumer and business education, and service excellence. Provides support to local Better Business Bureaus. Administers the advertising industry's self-regulatory program that monitors and investigates the truth and accuracy of national advertising claims; monitors and pre-screens advertising directed towards children. Develops information on national charitable organizations and whether they meet voluntary ethical standards for soliciting organizations. Provides information to help consumers and businesses make informed purchasing decisions and avoid costly scams and frauds; and settles consumer complaints through arbitration and other means. Operates BBB AUTO LINE, a national mediation and arbitration service providing an independent forum to resolve consumer complaints involving 32 participating auto manufacturers; Local Better Business Bureaus respond to more than 23 million requests for service annually, fielding 20 million pre-purchase inquiries and 3 million complaints.

Council on Foundations. 2121 Crystal Dr., Ste. 700, Arlington, VA 22202-3706. Phone: 800-673-9036 or (703)879-0600; Email: membership@cof.org • URL: http://www.cof.org • Formerly National Council on Community Foundations.

National Association of State Charity Officials. c/o Alissa Gardenswartz, 1300 Broadway, 7th Fl., Denver, CO 80203. • URL: http://www.nasconet.org • Members are state officials responsible for the administration of charitable solicitation laws.

National Committee for Responsive Philanthropy. 1331 H St. NW, Ste. 200, Washington, DC 20005-4706. Phone: (202)387-9177; Fax: (202)332-5084; Email: info@ncrp.org • URL: http://www.ncrp.org • Promotes charitable giving to new organizations working for social change or controversial issues. Formerly Committee for Responsive Philanthropy.

Nonprofit Academic Centers Council. 2121 Euclid Ave., Cleveland, OH 44115-2214. Phone: (216)687-9221 • URL: http://nonprofit-academic-centers-council.org • Provides leadership to strengthen existing centers and supports the establishment of new centers. Fosters collaboration among programs and centers. Develops creative approaches to researcher-practitioner collaborations.

# PHILATELY

*See STAMPS AS AN INVESTMENT*

# PHONOGRAPH AND PHONOGRAPH RECORD INDUSTRIES

*See also HIGH FIDELITY/STEREO; SOUND RECORDERS AND RECORDING*

## ABSTRACTS AND INDEXES

*Music Library Association Notes: Quarterly Journal of the Music Library Association.* Music Library

Association. • Quarterly. Individuals, $70.00 per year; institutions, $80.00 per year. Indexes record reviews (classical).

## DIRECTORIES

*Billboard's International Buyer's Guide.* Nielsen Co. • Annual. $135 $6.00 s/h. Covers: record companies; music publishers; record and tape wholesalers; services and supplies for the music-record-tape-video industry; record and tape dealer accessories, fixtures, and merchandising products; includes United States and over 65 other countries. Entries include: Company name, address, phone, names of principal executives, trade and brand names and/or list of products and services.

*Record Retailing Directory.* • Annual. $215 Individuals magazine. Covers: Over 5,000 independent and chain store record retailers (including audiobooks and online) in the U.S., American Samoa, Guam, and Puerto Rico. Entries include: For independents--Name, address, phone, store owner. For chain stores--Name, address, phone, fax, corporate management staff, number of outlets, year founded, corporate headquarters address and phone.

## OTHER SOURCES

*Phonolog.* Muze, Inc. • Annual. $550.00. 10 volumes. Provides detailed information on more than 370,000 titles of commercially available and out-of-print music recordings. Includes popular, jazz, and classical titles.

## PERIODICALS AND NEWSLETTERS

*Cash Box: The International Music-Record Weekly.* Cash Box Publishing Co., Inc. • Weekly. $185.00 per year.

*Dealerscope: Product and Strategy for Consumer Technology Retailing.* North American Publishing Co. • Monthly. $79 /year. Formerly *Dealerscope Consumer Electronices Marketplace.* Provides product information and valuable strategy for consumer technology retailers.

## PRICE SOURCES

*Audio.* Orion Research Corp. • Annual. $179 Individuals. Quotes retail and wholesale prices of used audio equipment. Original list prices and years of manufacture are also shown.

## TRADE/PROFESSIONAL ASSOCIATIONS

Music Business Association. 1 Eves Dr., Ste. 138, Marlton, NJ 08053. Phone: (856)596-2221; Fax: (856)596-7299 • URL: http://www.musicbiz.org • Serves the music and other prerecorded entertainment software industry as a forum for insight and dialogue; members include retailers, wholesalers, distributors, entertainment software suppliers, and suppliers of related products and services.

Recording Industry Association of America. 1025 F St. NW, 10th Fl., Washington, DC 20004. Phone: (202)775-0101 • URL: http://www.riaa.com • Formerly Record Industry Association of America.

# PHOTOCOPYING INDUSTRY

*See COPYING MACHINE INDUSTRY*

# PHOTOENGRAVING

*See also PRINTING AND PRINTING EQUIPMENT INDUSTRIES*

## PERIODICALS AND NEWSLETTERS

*Prepress Bulletin.* Bessie Halfacre, editor. International Prepress Association. • Bimonthly. $20.00 per year. Provides management and technical information on the graphic arts prepress industry.

# PHOTOGRAPHIC INDUSTRY

*See also CAMERA INDUSTRY; COMMERCIAL PHOTOGRAPHY; GRAPHIC ARTS INDUSTRY; MOTION PICTURE PHOTOGRAPHY*

## ABSTRACTS AND INDEXES

*Art Index.* EBSCO Publishing Inc. • Quarterly. Annual cumulations. Price varies. Subject and author index to periodicals in art, architecture, industrial design, city planning, photography, and various related topics.

*Imaging Abstracts.* Royal Photographic Society of Great Britain, Imaging Science and Technology Group. Elsevier. • Bimonthly. $860.00 per year. Formerly *Photographic Abstracts.*

## CD-ROM DATABASES

*Bodyshots - Business.* Digital Wisdom Inc. • Provides designers and desktop publishers with a comprehensive photographic stock collection of high-resolution images of people in a variety of everyday situations and activities.

## DIRECTORIES

*Directory of African Importers of Photographic Equipment and Supplies.* EXIM Infotek Private Ltd. • $300 Individuals. Covers: 95 African importers of cameras and videos, lens and accessories, photographic chemicals, motion picture and theater equipment, digital camera, microfilm and blueprint equipment, photographic equipment and supplies, photographic goods, photographic materials and hardware, photographic processing supplies, and video cameras. Entries include: Company name, postal address, telephone, fax, e-mail, website, contact person, designation, and product details.

*Directory of Asian Importers of Photographic Equipment and Supplies.* EXIM Infotek Private Ltd. • $500 Individuals. Covers: 170 Asian importers of cameras, lens and accessories, photographic chemicals, motion picture and theater equipment, colored film, black and white film, digital camera, plate and photographic papers, graphic films, microfilm and blueprint equipment, motion picture films, photo film, photo finishing equipment, photo finishing paper and chemicals, photographic equipment, photographic goods, photographic materials, photographic paper, and tripod. Entries include: Company name, postal address, telephone, fax, e-mail, website, contact person, designation, and product details.

*Directory of Australia and New Zealand Importers of Photographic Equipment.* EXIM Infotek Private Ltd. • $150 Individuals. Covers: 20 Australian and New Zealand importers of camera bags and cases, camera lenses, photographic chemicals, motion picture and theater equipment, digital camera, film, plate and photographic papers, infrared cameras, infrared camera accessories, photo film, photo process equipment, photographic equipment and supplies. Entries include: Company name, postal address, telephone, fax, e-mail, website, contact person, designation, and product details.

*Directory of European Importers of Photographic Equipment and Supplies.* EXIM Infotek Private Ltd. • $600 Individuals. Covers: 300 European importers of cameras, lens and accessories, photographic chemicals, motion picture and theater equipment, digital still camera, film, plates and photographic papers, microfilm and blueprint equipment, motion picture films, photo films, photo processing and developing equipment, photocameras, photographic chemicals and papers, photographic equipment and supplies, photographic films for offset reproduction, photographic processing equipment, and thermographic camera. Entries include: Company name, postal address, telephone, fax, e-mail, website, contact person, designation, and product details.

*Directory of French Importers of Photographic Equipment and Supplies.* EXIM Infotek Private Ltd. • $150 Individuals. Covers: 25 French importers of cameras, lenses and accessories, photographic chemicals motion picture and theater equipment, film, plate photographic papers, microfilm and blueprint equipment, photo processing and develop-

ing equipment, photographic equipment and supplies. Entries include: Company name, postal address, telephone, fax, e-mail, website, contact person, designation, and product details.

*Directory of German Importers of Photographic Equipment and Supplies.* EXIM Infotek Private Ltd. • $150 Individuals. Covers: 25 German importers of cameras, lens and accessories, motion picture and theater equipment, film, plate and photographic papers, photographic equipment and supplies. Entries include: Company name, postal address, telephone, fax, e-mail, website, contact person, designation, and product details.

*Directory of North American Importers of Photographic Equipment and Supplies.* EXIM Infotek Private Ltd. • $300 Individuals. Covers: 130 North American importers of camera film, cameras, lens and accessories, motion picture and theater equipment, digital camera, disposable flash camera, film, plates and photographic papers, graphic art supplies, graphic arts equipment, microfilm equipment, motion picture film, photographic equipment and supplies, photographic goods, photographic papers, photographic products, professional motion picture equipment, and slide projectors. Entries include: Company name, postal address, telephone, fax, e-mail, website, contact person, designation, and product details.

*Directory of South American Importers of Photographic Equipment and Supplies.* EXIM Infotek Private Ltd. • $350 Individuals. Covers: 130 South American importers of cameras, lens and accessories, cinema, motion picture equipment, theater equipment and supplies, film, plates and photographic papers, microfilm and blueprint equipment, photographic equipment and supplies, and photographic processing equipment. Entries include: Company name, postal address, telephone, fax, e-mail, website, contact person, designation, and product details.

*The International Directory of Importers-- Photographic Equipment and Supplies Importers.* Interdata. • $200 Individuals print version. Covers: 1,700 international firms importing photographic equipment and supplies. Entries include: Company name and address, contact person, email, number of employees, year established, phone and telefaxes, business activity, bank references, as well as a listing of photographic equipment and supplies currently being imported.

## FINANCIAL RATIOS

*Cost of Doing Business Survey.* Professional School Photographers Association International. • Biennial. $99. Emphasis is on photographic retailing.

## HANDBOOKS AND MANUALS

*One-Hour Photo Processing Lab.* Entrepreneur Press. • Looseleaf. $59.50. A practical guide to starting a film developing and printing business. Covers profit potential, start-up costs, market size evaluation, owner's time required, site selection, lease negotiation, pricing, accounting, advertising, promotion, etc. (Start-Up Business Guide No. E1209.).

## ONLINE DATABASES

*Art Index Online.* H.W. Wilson Co. • Indexes a wide variety of art-related periodicals, 1984 to date. Monthly updates. Inquire as to online cost and availability.

## PERIODICALS AND NEWSLETTERS

*Photo Marketing.* Professional School Photographers Association International. • Monthly. Membership.

*Shutterbug.* Source Interlink Media L.L.C. • Monthly. $17.95 Individuals. Articles about new equipment, test reports on film accessories, how-to articles, etc.

## PRICE SOURCES

*Camera.* Orion Research Corp. • Annual. $144 Individuals. Quotes retail and wholesale prices of used cameras and equipment. Original list prices and years of manufacture are also shown.

## STATISTICS SOURCES

*U.S. Industry and Trade Outlook.* U.S. Department of Commerce National Technical Information Service. • Annual. Produced by the International Trade Administration, U.S. Department of Commerce, in a "public-private" partnership with DRI/McGraw-Hill and Standard & Poor's. Provides basic data, outlook for the current year, and "Long-Term Prospects" (five-year projections) for a wide variety of products and services. Includes high technology industries. Formerly *U.S. Industrial Outlook.*

## TRADE/PROFESSIONAL ASSOCIATIONS

International Imaging Industry Association. 2001 L St., NW Ste. 700, Washington, DC 20036-4928. Phone: 800-272-6657 or (202)371-0101; Fax: (202)728-9614; Email: help@computer.org • URL: http://www.ieee.org • Develops and promotes the adoption of open industry standards, addressing environmental issues and providing a voice for the industry that will benefit all users. Promotes environment, health and safety concerns; works with various government agencies including the EPA, TSA, and WTO to ensure the best interests of the imaging industry are represented.

Photographic Society of America. 8421 S Walker Ave., Ste. 104, Oklahoma City, OK 73139. Phone: 855-772-4636 or (405)843-1437; Email: hq@psa-photo.org • URL: http://www.psa-photo.org • Camera clubs; amateur, advanced amateur photographers. Sponsors competitions. Conducts slide and print contests, provides instruction slide sets, slide analysis, print portfolios, and other technical services.

Photoimaging Manufacturers and Distributors Association. 7600 Jericho Tpke., Ste. 301, Woodbury, NY 11797. Phone: (516)802-0895; Fax: (516)364-0140 • URL: http://www.pmda.com • Formerly Photographic Manufacturers and Distributors Association.

Professional School Photographers Association International. 3000 Picture Pl., Jackson, MI 49201. Phone: 800-762-9287 or (517)788-8100; Fax: (517)788-8371; Email: m.bell@bellphoto.com • URL: http://www.pmai.org • Retailers of photo and video equipment, film, and supplies; firms developing and printing film. Maintains hall of fame. Compiles statistics; conducts research and educational programs.

Stock Artists Alliance. 229 Peachtree St., Ste. 2200, Atlanta, GA 30303. Phone: 888-722-1334; Fax: (404)614-6405; Email: admin@stockartistsalliance.org • URL: http://www.stockartistsalliance.org • Aims to support and protect the business interests of professional stock photographers worldwide. Provides information resources and promotes the use of equitable business models, fair contracts and ethical practices at all levels of the stock industry. Strengthens solidarity among stock artists.

# PHOTOGRAPHY, COMMERCIAL

*See* COMMERCIAL PHOTOGRAPHY

# PHOTOGRAPHY, INDUSTRIAL

*See* COMMERCIAL PHOTOGRAPHY

# PHOTOMECHANICAL PROCESSES

*See* GRAPHIC ARTS INDUSTRY

# PHOTONICS

*See also* OPTOELECTRONICS

## ABSTRACTS AND INDEXES

*Applied Science and Technology Index.* EBSCO Publishing Inc. • 11/year. Indexes a wide variety of English language technical, industrial, and engineering periodicals.

## ONLINE DATABASES

*Applied Science and Technology Index Online.* H.W. Wilson Co. • Provides online indexing of 500 major scientific, technical, industrial, and engineering periodicals. Time period is 1983 to date. Monthly updates. Inquire as to online cost and availability.

## PERIODICALS AND NEWSLETTERS

*Optics and Photonics News.* Optical Society of America. • Monthly. $99.00 per year. Includes print and online editions.

*Photonics Spectra.* Laurin Publishing Company Inc. • Monthly. Serves as a network among engineers, scientists and end users who develop, commercialize and buy photonics products. Provides both technical and practical information for every aspect of the global industry, integrating all segments of photonics.

## RESEARCH CENTERS AND INSTITUTES

Center for Advanced Phototonic and Electronic Materials. State University of New York at Buffalo, Fronczak Hall, Rm. 227-229, N Campus, Buffalo, NY 14260. Phone: (716)645-2422; Fax: (716)645-5964; Email: ub-capem@acsu.buffalo.edu • URL: http://www.grad.buffalo.edu • Does integrated optics research, including photonic circuitry.

Communications and Information Processing Group. Rensselaer Polytechnic Institute, 7010 JEC, 110 Eighth St., Troy, NY 12180-3590. Phone: (518)276-6823; Fax: (518)276-6261; Email: modestin@ipl.rpi.edu • URL: http://www.ecse.rpi.edu • Includes Optical Signal Processing Laboratory and Speech Processing Laboratory.

Massachusetts Institute of Technology - Materials Processing Center. 77 Massachusetts Ave., Cambridge, MA 02139-4301. Phone: (617)253-5179; Fax: (617)258-6900; Email: cthomp@mit.edu • URL: http://mpc-web.mit.edu • Conducts processing, engineering, and economic research in ferrous and nonferrous metals, ceramics, polymers, photonic materials, superconductors, welding, composite materials, and other materials.

Mediphotonics Laboratory. City College of City University of New York, 160 Convent Ave., New York, NY 10031. Phone: (212)650-7760; Fax: (212)650-5530 • URL: http://www.cuny.edu.

Polytechnic University - Center for Advanced Technology in Telecommunications. 2 MetroTech Ctr., 9th Fl., Brooklyn, NY 11201. Phone: (718)260-3050; Fax: (718)260-3074; Email: info@catt.poly.edu • URL: http://catt.poly.edu • Research fields include active media for optical communication.

University of Florida - College of Engineering - Department of Electrical & Computer Engineering - Photonics Research Laboratory. 216 Larsen Hall, Gainesville, FL 32611-6200. Phone: (352)392-0911 or (352)392-9265; Fax: (352)392-8671; Email: rakov@ece.ufl.edu • URL: http://old.ece.ufl.edu/research/labs/photonics.html • Integrated optics, optoelectronic integration, high-speed electro-optic guided-wave modulators, modulators with linearized transfer curves, wavelength-selective filters, waveguide structures in ferroelectric crystals with domain reversals, waveguide lasers/amplifiers.

## TRADE/PROFESSIONAL ASSOCIATIONS

The Minerals, Metals, and Materials Society. 184 Thorn Hill Rd., Warrendale, PA 15086-7514. Phone: 800-759-4867 or (724)776-9000; Fax: (724)776-3770; Email: webmaster@tms.org • URL: http://www.tms.org/TMSHome.aspx • Members are metallurgists, metallurgical engineers, and materials scientists. Divisions include Light Metals and Electronic, Magnetic, and Photonic Materials. Formerly The Metallurigical Society.

Optical Society of America. 2010 Massachusetts Ave. NW, Washington, DC 20036-1023. Phone: 800-766-405A or (202)223-8130; Fax: (202)223-1096; Email: info@osa.org • URL: http://www.osa.org • Persons interested in any branch of optics: research, instruction, optical applications, manufacture, distribution of optical equipment, and physiological optics. Sponsors topical meetings.

# PHYSICAL DISTRIBUTION

*See* DISTRIBUTION

# PHYSICAL FITNESS INDUSTRY

*See* FITNESS INDUSTRY

# PICKETING

*See* STRIKES AND LOCKOUTS

# PIERS

*See* PORTS

# PIG INDUSTRY

*See* SWINE INDUSTRY

# PIGGYBACK TRANSPORT

*See* TRUCK TRAILERS

# PILOTS

*See* AIR PILOTS

# PINEAPPLE INDUSTRY

*See also* FRUIT INDUSTRY

## RESEARCH CENTERS AND INSTITUTES

College of Tropical Agriculture and Human Resources. University of Hawaii at Manoa, 2515 Campus Rd., Miller Hall 110, Honolulu, HI 96822. Phone: (808)956-8234; Fax: (808)956-9105; Email: gallom@ctahr.hawaii.edu • URL: http://www.ctahr.hawaii.edu • Concerned with the production and marketing of tropical food and ornamental plant products, including pineapples, bananas, coffee, and macadamia nuts.

# PIPE

*See also* PLUMBING INDUSTRY

## CD-ROM DATABASES

*OECD Statistical Compendium.* Organization for Economic Cooperation and Development. • Semiannual. $1,905.00 per year for 1 to 10 users. CD-ROM contains more than 730,000 monthly, quarterly, and annual time series for OECD countries, 1960 to date. Includes fully searchable data on agriculture, food, economic indicators, national accounts, employment, energy, finance, industry, technology, and foreign trade. Results can be displayed in various forms.

## DIRECTORIES

*HPAC Engineering Info-Dex.* Penton Media Inc. • Annual. $30. Industry directory of products, manufacturers, and trade names and a composite of catalog data for mechanical systems engineering professionals.

*Who's Who in Metal Forming and Fabricating.* Fabricators and Manufacturers Association International. • Annual. $200 for nonmembers. Lists members of the Fabricators and Manufacturers Association (FMA), International; and members of the Tube and Pipe Association. Includes five indexes. Formerly *FMA Member Resource Directory.*

## FINANCIAL RATIOS

*Annual Statement Studies.* Risk Management Association. • Annual. Compiled from over 280,000 financial statements.

*Annual Statement Studies: Industry Default Probabilities and Cash Flow Measures.* Risk Management Association. • Annual. $405 Nonmembers. Serves as a companion volume to the original *Annual Statement Studies.* Gives probability of default estimates on a percentage scale for more than 450 industries. Includes changes in position year-by-year for eight financial statement line items and provides percentage measures of cash flow.

## INTERNET DATABASES

*Business 2.0 Web Guide to the Best Business Links.* Business 2.0 Media Inc. Phone: (415)293-4800; Email: support@business2.com • URL: http://www.business2.com/webguide • Web site presents an extensive, searchable directory of links to "the best, most informative, and authoritative web pages." Twenty main categories cover business, finance, career, company information, people, and technology topics, with thousands of subtopics, all linking to Web sites recommended by experienced business researchers. Fees: Free.

*Fedstats.* Federal Interagency Council on Statistical Policy. Phone: (202)395-7254 • URL: http://www.fedstats.gov • Web site features an efficient search facility for full-text statistics produced by more than 100 federal agencies, including the Census Bureau, the Bureau of Economic Analysis, and the Bureau of Labor Statistics. Boolean searches can be made within one agency or for all agencies combined. Links are offered to international statistical bureaus, including the UN, IMF, OECD, UNESCO, Eurostat, and 20 individual countries. Fees: Free.

*FreeLunch.com.* Economy.com, Inc. Phone: (610)696-8700; Fax: (610)696-1678 • URL: http://www.freelunch.com • Web site provides free access to more than 200 million economic and financial data series, covering industry, demographics, labor markets, prices, retail sales, government spending, trade, interest rates, housing starts, the stock market, etc. Data is available in either chart or table form. Searching is offered. Free, but registration required. Economy.com, Inc. also offers fee-based economic analysis at *The Dismal Scientist* site (www.dismal.com).

## PERIODICALS AND NEWSLETTERS

*Heating/Piping/Air Conditioning Engineering: The Magazine of Mechanical Systems Engineering.* Penton Media Inc. • Monthly. Covers design, specification, installation, operation, and maintenance for systems in industrial, commercial, and institutional buildings. Formerly (Heating, Piping and Air Conditioning).

## STATISTICS SOURCES

*American Iron and Steel Annual Statistical Report.* American Iron and Steel Institute. • Annual. $100 Individuals.

---

*Survey of Current Business*. U. S. Government Printing Office. • Published by Bureau of Economic Analysis, U. S. Department of Commerce. Presents a wide variety of business and economic data.

## TRADE/PROFESSIONAL ASSOCIATIONS

Ductile Iron Pipe Research Association. 1322 Riverhaven Pl., Birmingham, AL 35244-2560. Phone: (205)402-8700; Email: info@dipra.org • URL: http://www.dipra.org • Provides engineering information about cast iron and ductile iron pipe to utility and construction engineers.

Manufacturers Standardization Society. 127 Park St. NE, Vienna, VA 22180. Phone: (703)281-6613; Fax: (703)281-6671; Email: info@mss-hq.com • URL: http://www.mss-hq.com • Members are valve and fitting companies. Publishes standards and specifications.

National Certified Pipe Welding Bureau. 1385 Piccard Dr., Rockville, MD 20850. Phone: 800-556-3653 or (301)869-5800; Fax: (301)990-9690 • URL: http://www.mcaa.org/ncpwb • Contractors in the piping field. Conducts research on development in the field of certified welding for the piping industry; establishes uniform welding procedures for pipe welding; provides for interchange of records of qualified welders.

National Clay Pipe Institute. N6369 US Hwy. 12, Ste. A, Elkhorn, WI 53121. Phone: (262)742-2904; Fax: (360)242-9094; Email: info@ncpi.org • URL: http://www.ncpi.org • Manufacturers of vitrified clay sewer pipe and fittings. Promotes use of clay pipe for sanitary sewer systems. Provides engineering advisory services; conducts scientific research; acts as government liaison.

National Corrugated Steel Pipe Association. 14070 Proton Rd., Ste. 100, LB 9, Dallas, TX 75244. Phone: (972)850-1907; Fax: (972)490-4219 • URL: http://www.ncspa.org • Represents firms fabricating corrugated steel drainage pipe and structures; steel mills; allied industries. Provides engineering service in design and installation of drainage products and systems. Conducts research programs.

Plastics Pipe Institute. 105 Decker Ct., Ste. 825, Irving, TX 75062. Phone: (469)499-1044; Fax: (469)499-1063 • URL: http://plasticpipe.org • Manufacturers of plastic pipe and fittings and suppliers of plastic pipe raw materials. Develops technical reports and promotes trade and user acceptance. Compiles statistics; offers research programs. Conducts periodic training seminar on plastic piping.

## PIPELINE INDUSTRY

### ABSTRACTS AND INDEXES

*NTIS Alerts: Transportation*. U.S. Department of Commerce National Technical Information Service. • Biweekly. $130 per year. Covers air, marine, highway, inland waterway, pipeline, and railroad transportation.

### PERIODICALS AND NEWSLETTERS

*Pipe Line and Gas Industry: Crude Oil and Products Pipelines, Gas Transmission and Gas Distribution*. Gulf Publishing Co. • Monthly. Free to qualified personnel; others, $29.00 per year. International edition available.

*Pipeline and Gas Journal: Energy Construction, Transportation and Distribution*. Oildom Publishing Company of Texas Inc. • Monthly. $33.00 per year. Covers engineering and operating methods on cross-country pipelines that transport crude oil products and natural gas. Includes *Energy Management Report*. Incorporates *Pipeline*.

### TRADE/PROFESSIONAL ASSOCIATIONS

Association of Oil Pipe Lines. 1808 Eye St. NW, Ste. 300, Washington, DC 20006. Phone: (202)408-7970; Fax: (202)280-1949 • URL: http://www.aopl.org • Oil pipeline companies, most of which are regulated common carriers. Assembles statistical and other data relating to the pipeline industry for presentation to congress, governmental departments, agencies and commissions, trade associations, and the public.

Pipe Line Contractors Association. 1700 Pacific Ave., Ste. 4100, Dallas, TX 75201-4675. Phone: (214)969-2700; Email: plca@plca.org • URL: http://www.plca.org • Contractors of mainline cross-country pipeline. Associate members are equipment manufacturers, suppliers, and dealers. Represents the industry in labor negotiations.

## PIPES (SMOKING)

*See* TOBACCO AND TOBACCO INDUSTRY

## PISTOLS

*See* FIREARMS INDUSTRY

## PLACEMENT BUREAUS

*See* COLLEGE PLACEMENT BUREAUS

## PLANNED ECONOMY

*See* ECONOMIC POLICY

## PLANNING

### ABSTRACTS AND INDEXES

*Social Sciences Citation Index*. Thomson Reuters Corp. • Weekly. Product is accessed via *Web of Science*.

*Social Sciences Index Retrospective: 1907-1983*. EBSCO Publishing Inc. • Indexing for 1,000,000 articles. Coverage includes international index and social sciences and humanities index.

### CD-ROM DATABASES

*Business Abstracts with Full Text*. EBSCO Publishing Inc. • Includes full text articles from more than 460 business publications from 1982 to present. Indexing for nearly 880 publications.

*Social Sciences Abstracts*. EBSCO Publishing Inc. • Provides indexing from 1983 and abstracting from 1994 of more than 750 periodicals covering economics, area studies, community health, public administration, public welfare, urban studies, and many other topics related to the social sciences.

*Social Sciences Citation Index*. Thomson Reuters Corp. • Weekly. Product is accessed via *Web of Science*.

### DIRECTORIES

*Planning Your Future: Resources on Careers and Higher Education*. AMIDEAST Publications. • Irregular. $29.95 Individuals first class mail. Covers: over 1,000 printed and electronic sources of information on education and training for approximately 150 careers, including accredited programs, nontraditional education, internships, and disabled student services. Entries include: Title name, date of publication, order address.

### INTERNET DATABASES

*Intelligence Data*. Thomson Financial. Phone: 800-654-0393; Fax: (617)824-2477 • URL: http://www.intelligencedata.com • Fee-based Web site provides a wide variety of information relating to competitive intelligence, strategic planning, business development, mergers, acquisitions, sales, and marketing. "Intelliscope" feature offers searching of other Thomson units, such as Investext, MarkIntel, InSite 2, and Industry Insider. Weekly updating.

### ONLINE DATABASES

*Wilson Business Abstracts Online*. H.W. Wilson Co. • Indexes and abstracts 600 major business periodicals, plus the *Wall Street Journal* and the business section of the *New York Times*. Indexing is from 1982, abstracting from 1990, with the two newspapers included from 1993. Updated weekly. Inquire as to online cost and availability. (*Business Periodicals Index* without abstracts is also available online.).

*Wilson Social Sciences Abstracts Online*. H.W. Wilson Co. • Provides online abstracting and indexing of more than 500 periodicals covering area studies, community health, public administration, public welfare, urban studies, and many other social science topics. Time period is 1994 to date for abstracts and 1983 to date for indexing, with updates weekly. Inquire as to online cost and availability.

### OTHER SOURCES

*Business Strategies*. Wolters Kluwer Law & Business CCH. • Semimonthly. $795.00 per year. Four looseleaf volumes. Semimonthly updates. Legal, tax, and accounting aspects of business planning and decision-making. Provides information on start-ups, forms of ownership (partnerships, corporations), failing businesses, reorganizations, acquisitions, and so forth. Includes *Business Strategies Bulletin*, a monthly newsletter.

*How to Write a Business Plan*. American Management Association Extension Institute. • Looseleaf. $159.00. Self-study course. Emphasis is on practical explanations, examples, and problem solving. Quizzes and a case study are included.

*Macroeconomics and Company Planning*. Continuing Professional Education Div. American Institute of Certified Public Accountants. • Looseleaf. Self-study course.

### PERIODICALS AND NEWSLETTERS

*Futures; The Journal of Forecasting, Planning and Policy*. Elsevier. • 10/year. $1,618 Institutions.

*Journal of Business Strategy*. SourceMedia Inc. • Bimonthly. $98.00 per year. Covers management planning techniques and corporate strategy for senior executives.

*Planning*. American Planning Association. • Monthly. $85 Nonmembers.

*strategy business*. • Quarterly. $38.00 per year.

### RESEARCH CENTERS AND INSTITUTES

African Development Bank. BP 1387, Rue Joseph Anoma, Abidjan, Côte d'Ivoire. Phone: 225 20 20 44 44; Fax: 225 20 20 49 59; Email: afdb@afdb.org • URL: http://www.afdb.org • Representatives of national financial institutions. Seeks to further economic development of member states. Serves as a clearinghouse on national and regional economic development. Provides financial support and consulting services to development programs and agencies. Sponsors research and educational programs.

Cornell University - Program in International Studies in Planning. 106 W Sibley Hall, Ithaca, NY 14853-3901. Phone: (607)255-4331 or (607)255-4613; Fax: (607)255-1971; Email: wwg1@cornell.edu • URL: http://aap.cornell.edu/crp/programs/grad/internation-studies.cfm • Research activities are related to international urban and regional planning, with emphasis on developing areas.

Pennsylvania State University at Harrisburg - Institute of State and Regional Affairs - Pennsylvania State Data Center. 777 W Harrisburg Pike, Middletown, PA 17057-4898. Phone: (717)948-6336; Fax: (717)948-6754; Email: pasdc@psu.edu • URL: http://www.pasdc.hbg.psu.edu • Conducts research in environmental, general, and socioeconomic planning. Zoning is included.

## TRADE/PROFESSIONAL ASSOCIATIONS

American Planning Association. 205 N Michigan Ave., Ste. 1200, Chicago, IL 60601. Phone: (312)431-9100; Fax: (312)786-6700; Email: customerservice@planning.org • URL: http://www. planning.org • Public and private planning agency officials, professional planners, planning educators, elected and appointed officials, and other persons involved in urban and rural planning. Works to foster the best techniques and decisions for the planned development of communities and regions. Provides extensive professional services and publications to professionals and laypeople in planning and related fields; serves as a clearinghouse for information. Through Planning Advisory Service, a research and inquiry-answering service, provides, on an annual subscription basis, advice on specific inquiries and a series of research reports on planning, zoning, and environmental regulations. Supplies information on job openings and makes definitive studies on salaries and recruitment of professional planners. Conducts research; collaborates in joint projects with local, national, and international organizations.

# PLANT ENGINEERING

*See* FACTORY MANAGEMENT

# PLANT LOCATION

*See* LOCATION OF INDUSTRY

# PLANT MAINTENANCE

*See* MAINTENANCE OF BUILDINGS

# PLANT MANAGEMENT

*See* FACTORY MANAGEMENT

# PLANT PROTECTION

*See* INDUSTRIAL SECURITY PROGRAMS

# PLANT SITES

*See* LOCATION OF INDUSTRY

# PLASTER AND PLASTERING

## FINANCIAL RATIOS

*Annual Statement Studies.* Risk Management Association. • Annual. Compiled from over 280,000 financial statements.

*Annual Statement Studies: Industry Default Probabilities and Cash Flow Measures.* Risk Management Association. • Annual. $405 Nonmembers. Serves as a companion volume to the original *Annual Statement Studies.* Gives probability of default estimates on a percentage scale for more than 450 industries. Includes changes in position year-by-year for eight financial statement line items and provides percentage measures of cash flow.

## PERIODICALS AND NEWSLETTERS

*ENR: Connecting the Industry Worldwide.* McGraw Hill Financial Inc. • Weekly. $74.00 per year.

## TRADE/PROFESSIONAL ASSOCIATIONS

Association of the Wall and Ceiling Industries International. 513 W Broad St., Ste. 210, Falls Church, VA 22046. Phone: (703)538-1600; Fax: (703)534-8307 • URL: http://www.awci.org • Acoustical tile, drywall, demountable partitions, lathing and plastering, fireproofing, light-gauge steel framing, stucco and exterior insulation finish systems contractors, suppliers and manufacturers.

# PLASTIC CONTAINERS

*See* CONTAINER INDUSTRY

# PLASTICS INDUSTRY

*See also* COMPOSITE MATERIALS

## ABSTRACTS AND INDEXES

*Applied Science and Technology Index.* EBSCO Publishing Inc. • 11/year. Indexes a wide variety of English language technical, industrial, and engineering periodicals.

*CPI Digest: Key to World Literature Serving the Coatings, Plastics, Fibers, Adhesives, and Related Industries.* CPI Information Services. • Monthly. $397.00 per year. Abstracts of business and technical articles for polymer-based, chemical process industries. Includes a monthly list of relevant U. S. patents. International coverage.

*Engineered Materials Abstracts.* Cambridge Information Group. • Monthly. $995.00 per year. Provides citations to the technical and engineering literature of plastic, ceramic, and composite materials.

*NTIS Alerts: Materials Sciences.* U.S. Department of Commerce National Technical Information Service. • Biweekly. $130 per year. Covers ceramics, glass, coatings, composite materials, alloys, plastics, wood, paper, adhesives, fibers, lubricants, and related subjects.

*The Polymer Library.* Rubber and Plastics Research Association of Great Britian. Smithers Rapra Technology. • Monthly. $2,700.00 per year. Up-to-date survey of current international information relevant to the rubber, plastics and associated industries.

## CD-ROM DATABASES

*METADEX Materials Collection: Metals-Polymers-Ceramics.* Cambridge Scientific Abstracts L.P. • Quarterly. Provides CD-ROM citations to the worldwide literature of materials science and metallurgy. Corresponds to *Metals Abstracts, Alloys Index, Steels Alert, Nonferrous Alert, Polymers/Ceramics/Composites Alert,* and *Engineered Materials Abstracts.* (Formerly produced by ASM International.).

*OECD Statistical Compendium.* Organization for Economic Cooperation and Development. • Semiannual. $1,905.00 per year for 1 to 10 users. CD-ROM contains more than 730,000 monthly, quarterly, and annual time series for OECD countries, 1960 to date. Includes fully searchable data on agriculture, food, economic indicators, national accounts, employment, energy, finance, industry, technology, and foreign trade. Results can be displayed in various forms.

*Plastics Digest on CD-ROM.* IHS Standards Store. • Semiannual. CD-ROM index version (technical data only), $695.00 per year or $495.00 per disc. CD-ROM image version (technical data and specification sheet images), $1,295.00 per year or $995.00 per disc. Provides detailed information on the properties of 20,000 types of plastic, both current and obsolete. Time period is 1977 to date. Includes trade names and supplier names and addresses.

## DIRECTORIES

*Chemicals, Plastics & Rubber Yearbook.* George Warman Publications Ltd. • Biennial. $45. Covers: Chemical, plastics and rubber products, manufacturers, associations, and colleges/universities in South Africa. Entries include: Company name, address, phone, brand name, specifications, statistics, services, suppliers of machinery and instrumentation.

*Directory of African Importers of Plastic Scrap and Raw Materials.* EXIM Infotek Private Ltd. • $300 Individuals. Covers: 90 African importers of plastic raw materials, plastic scrap and waste, polyethylene raw materials, PVC compounds, low-density polyethylene (LDPE) raw material, PF raw materials, molding powder, polester chips raw materials, PP/PVC/PE raw materials, PVC resins raw materials, and plasticizers. Entries include: Company name, postal address, telephone, fax, e-mail, website, contact person, designation, and product details.

*Directory of Australia and New Zealand Importers of Plastic Scrap and Raw Materials.* EXIM Infotek Private Ltd. • $5 Individuals. Covers: 20 Australian and New Zealand importers of fiberglass resins, high-density polyethylene (HDPE), HMS scrap, industrial polyurethane, nylon resin, plastic raw materials, plastic scrap and waste, poly propylene, polyethylene resin, polymers, polyurethane chemicals, polyurethane form, polyurethane products, and polypropylene raw materials. Entries include: Company name, postal address, telephone, fax, e-mail, website, contact person, designation, and product details.

*Directory of Chinese Importers of Plastic Scrap and Raw Materials.* EXIM Infotek Private Ltd. • $200 Individuals. Covers: 60 Chinese importers of ABS scrap, high-density polyethylene (HDPE), pet bottle scrap in flakes and PVC waste, plastic raw materials, plastic resins, plastic scrap and waste, plastic additives, and polypropylene. Entries include: Company name, postal address, telephone, fax, e-mail, website, contact person, designation, and product details.

*Directory of European Importers of Plastic Scrap and Raw Materials.* EXIM Infotek Private Ltd. • $550 Individuals. Covers: 260 European importers of acrylic polymers, fiberglass resins, low-density polyethylene (LDPE), pet scrap and waste, plastic granules, plastic raw materials, plastic scrap and waste, polymer and plastic raw materials, polymers for textile and plastic, polypropylene, polyvinyl chloride, polypropylene raw material, ABS/PC and pet raw materials, HDPE and pet raw materials, PVC raw materials, and reagents. Entries include: Company name, postal address, telephone, fax, e-mail, website, contact person, designation, and product details.

*Directory of French Importers of Plastics Scrap and Raw Materials.* EXIM Infotek Private Ltd. • $150 Individuals. Covers: 20 French importers of plastic raw materials and reagents. Entries include: Company name, postal address, telephone, fax, e-mail, website, contact person, designation, and product details.

*Directory of Indian Importers of Plastic Scrap and Raw Materials.* EXIM Infotek Private Ltd. • $600 Individuals. Covers: 200 Indian importers of ABS scrap, acrylamide, butyl acrylate, granules, HD, high-density polyethylene (HDPE), HDPE granules, HMS scrap, low-density polyethylene (LDPE), LDPE granules, linear low-density polyethylene (LLDPE), master batches, plastic granules, plastic raw materials, plastic scrap and waste, polycarbonate, polypropylene, polymers, polypropylene scraps, polypropylene granules, polyurethane chemicals, polyurethane resin, polyvinyl alcohol, polytetrafluoroethylene (PTFE) products, PVC compound, PVC resin, raw materials, and styrene monomer. Entries include: Company name, postal address, telephone, fax, e-mail, website, contact person, designation, and product details.

*Directory of Japanese Importers of Plastic Scrap and Raw Materials.* EXIM Infotek Private Ltd. • $200 Individuals. Covers: 30 Japanese importers of plastic raw materials, plastic resins, plasticizers, plastics, and plastic additives. Entries include: Company name, postal address, telephone, fax, e-mail, website, contact person, designation, and product details.

*Directory of Middle East Importers of Plastic Scrap and Raw Materials.* EXIM Infotek Private Ltd. • $450 Individuals. Covers: 180 Middle East importers of fiberglass resins, high-density polyethylene (HDPE), LDPE scrap, phenol formaldehyde resin, plastic materials, plastic raw materials, plastic scrap and waste, polyester powder, polymer, polypropylene, PVC (granule), and waste plastic. Entries include: Company name, postal address, telephone, fax, e-mail, website, contact person, designation, and product details.

*Directory of North American Importers of Plastic Scrap and Raw Materials.* EXIM Infotek Private Ltd. • $250 Individuals. Covers: 80 North American importers of high-density polyethylene (HDPE), low-density polyethylene (LDPE), phenolic, plastic raw materials, plastic resins, plastic scrap and waste, polyester, polyvinyl alcohol, and polypropylene (PP). Entries include: Company name, postal address, telephone, fax, e-mail, website, contact person, designation, and product details.

*Directory of Plastics Industry.* Hong Kong Productivity Council. • Annual. $300 pick up at HKPC office. Covers: Over 3,000 companies from plastic manufacturers in Hong Kong as well as their operations in mainland China. Entries include: Name, address, phone, fax, e-mail, URL, number of employees, turnover, and products/name brands.

*Directory of SAARC Importers of Plastic Scrap and Raw Materials.* EXIM Infotek Private Ltd. • $300 Individuals. Covers: 95 SAARC Countries importers of ABS scrap, acrylic thickener, granules, high-density polyethylene (HDPE), HDPE film grade granules, low-density polyethylene (LDPE), linear low density polythylene (LLDPE), pet resin, plastic granules, plastic molding compounds, plastic raw materials and semi-finished products, plastic scrap and waste, polycarbonate, polyethylene granules, polypropylene and waste, polyvinyl alcohol, PP and PE resins for rope making, PP granules, PVC compound, PVC resin, PVC scrap, raw materials for polyurethane form, raw materials for printed laminate, soft PVC scrap, and transparent PVC scrap. Entries include: Company name, postal address, telephone, fax, e-mail, website, contact person, designation, and product details.

*Directory of South American Importers of Plastic Scrap and Raw Materials.* EXIM Infotek Private Ltd. • $300 Individuals. Covers: 110 South American importers of pet resins, plastic raw materials, plastic scrap and waste, polyester resins, and PVC compounds. Entries include: Company name, postal address, telephone, fax, e-mail, website, contact person, designation, and product details.

*Directory of South Korean Manufacturers & Exporters of Plastics & Plastic Products.* EXIM Infotek Private Ltd. • $600 Individuals. Covers: 300 South Korean manufacturers and exporters of doors, windows, skylights, glass fiber reinforced plastic products, haberdasher articles, laminating roll film, offlets drain channels, plastic articles for shops, plastic films, plastic injection molding products, plastic laminated sheets, plastic products for agricultural industry, building industry, chemical industry, pharmaceutical industry, cosmetic industry, electrical and electronics industry, mechanical engineering industry, optical and photographic industry, surgical and orthopedic use, textile industry, food and beverage industry; plastic semi-finished products-bars/rods/shapes, plastic semi-finished products-plates/sheets/film/tape, plastic-

injection molding, polyester film, and sponges.

*The International Directory of Importers--Plastics & Plastic Products Importers.* Interdata. • $295 Individuals print. Covers: 4,400 international firms importing plastics and plastic products. Entries include: Company name and address, contact person, email, number of employees, year established, phone and telefaxes, business activity, bank references, as well as a listing of plastics and plastic products currently being imported.

*International Plastics Directory.* Verlag fur Internationale Wirtschaftsliteratur Ltd. • 64. $600. Covers: Plastics producers and processors worldwide. Entries include: Company name, address, phone, description, production line, trademarks, number of machines, associated companies.

*Materials Research Centres: A World Directory of Organizations and Programmes in Materials Science.* Specialist Journals. • Biennial. $445.00. Profiles of research centers in 75 countries. Materials include plastics, metals, fibers, etc.

*Surface Coating Resin Index.* European Resin Manufacturers' Association. • Triennial. $5. Covers: Manufacturers, products and trade names of surface coating resins in the United Kingdom. Entries include: Manufacturer name, address, phone, products, trade names.

## E-BOOKS

*Encyclopedia of American Industries.* Cengage Learning Inc. • 2011. $807.00. 6th edition. Three volumes. Volume one is Manufacturing Industries and volume two is Service and Non-Manufacturing Industries. Provides the history, development, and recent status of approximately 1,000 industries. Includes statistical graphs, with industry and general indexes. Also available as eBook.

*Encyclopedia of Emerging Industries.* Cengage Learning Inc. • $546 6th edition. Provides detailed information on 140 "newly flourishing" industries. Includes historical background, organizational structure, significant individuals, current conditions, major companies, work force, technology trends, research developments, and other industry facts.

## FINANCIAL RATIOS

*Annual Statement Studies.* Risk Management Association. • Annual. Compiled from over 280,000 financial statements.

*Annual Statement Studies: Industry Default Probabilities and Cash Flow Measures.* Risk Management Association. • Annual. $405 Nonmembers. Serves as a companion volume to the original *Annual Statement Studies.* Gives probability of default estimates on a percentage scale for more than 450 industries. Includes changes in position year-by-year for eight financial statement line items and provides percentage measures of cash flow.

## GENERAL WORKS

*Plastics Hot Line: The Nation's Marketplace for Plastics Processing Equipment & Materials, Business and Employment Opportunities.* IMS L.L.C. • Monthly. Trade magazine.

## INTERNET DATABASES

*Business 2.0 Web Guide to the Best Business Links.* Business 2.0 Media Inc. Phone: (415)293-4800; Email: support@business2.com • URL: http://www.business2.com/webguide • Web site presents an extensive, searchable directory of links to "the best, most informative, and authoritative web pages." Twenty main categories cover business, finance, career, company information, people, and technology topics, with thousands of subtopics, all linking to Web sites recommended by experienced business researchers. Fees: Free.

*Fedstats.* Federal Interagency Council on Statistical Policy. Phone: (202)395-7254 • URL: http://www.fedstats.gov • Web site features an efficient search

facility for full-text statistics produced by more than 100 federal agencies, including the Census Bureau, the Bureau of Economic Analysis, and the Bureau of Labor Statistics. Boolean searches can be made within one agency or for all agencies combined. Links are offered to international statistical bureaus, including the UN, IMF, OECD, UNESCO, Eurostat, and 20 individual countries. Fees: Free.

*FreeLunch.com.* Economy.com, Inc. Phone: (610)696-8700; Fax: (610)696-1678 • URL: http://www.freelunch.com • Web site provides free access to more than 200 million economic and financial data series, covering industry, demographics, labor markets, prices, retail sales, government spending, trade, interest rates, housing starts, the stock market, etc. Data is available in either chart or table form. Searching is offered. Free, but registration required. Economy.com, Inc. also offers fee-based economic analysis at *The Dismal Scientist* site (www.dismal.com).

## ONLINE DATABASES

*Applied Science and Technology Index Online.* H.W. Wilson Co. • Provides online indexing of 500 major scientific, technical, industrial, and engineering periodicals. Time period is 1983 to date. Monthly updates. Inquire as to online cost and availability.

*Engineered Materials Abstracts (online).* Cambridge Scientific Abstracts L.P. • Provides online citations to the technical and engineering literature of plastic, ceramic, and composite materials. Time period is 1986 to date, with monthly updates. (Formerly produced by ASM International.) Inquire as to online cost and availability.

## PERIODICALS AND NEWSLETTERS

*Advances in Polymer Technology.* Polymer Processing Institute. John Wiley & Sons Inc. • Quarterly. $950 Institutions.

*Journal of Applied Polymer Science.* John Wiley and Sons, Inc., Journals Div. • Semimonthly. $14,495.00 per year; with online edition, $15,220.00, four volumes.

*Plastics Engineering.* Society of Plastics Engineers. • 10/year. $142 Nonmembers. Plastics trade magazine.

*Plastics News.* Crain Communications, Inc. • Weekly. $89 per year. Features articles regarding commercial, financial, legislative and market-related developments worldwide that affect North American plastic product manufacturers and their suppliers and customers.

*Plastics Technology: The Only Magazine for Plastics Processors.* Nielsen Business Media Inc. • 13 times a year. Free to qualified personnel; others, $89.00 per year.

*Plastics Week: The Global Newsletter.* McGraw Hill Financial Inc. • Weekly. $530.00 per year. Newsletter. Covers international trends in plastics production, technology, research, and legislation.

*Polymer Engineering and Science.* Society of Plastics Engineers. • Monthly. $822 Individuals. Contains proceedings of symposia on such diverse topics as polyblends, mechanics of plastics and polymer welding.

*Urethanes Technology.* Crain Communications Ltd. • Bimonthly. $108 Individuals. Covers the international polyurethane industry.

## RESEARCH CENTERS AND INSTITUTES

Massachusetts Institute of Technology - Materials Processing Center. 77 Massachusetts Ave., Cambridge, MA 02139-4301. Phone: (617)253-5179; Fax: (617)258-6900; Email: cthomp@mit.edu • URL: http://mpc-web.mit.edu • Conducts processing, engineering, and economic research in ferrous and nonferrous metals, ceramics, polymers, photonic materials, superconductors, welding, composite materials, and other materials.

Plastics Institute of America. 1 University Ave.,

Lowell, MA 01854. Phone: (978)934-2575; Fax: (978)934-3089; Email: contactus@plasticsinstitute.org • URL: http://www.plasticsinstitute.org • Serves as an educational and research organization supported on a cooperative basis by companies in the plastics and allied industries. Conducts fundamental research in plastics science and engineering and supports educational activities at the graduate school level in these fields. Provides comprehensive technical information to its members. Conducts a graduate level program of education for plastics scientists and engineers, in cooperation with major U.S. universities and colleges involved in polymer science and engineering.

## STATISTICS SOURCES

*Standard & Poor's Industry Surveys.* Standard & Poor's Financial Services L.L.C. • Semiannual. $1,800.00. Two looseleaf volumes. Includes monthly *Supplements.* Provides detailed, individual surveys of 52 major industry groups. Each survey is revised on a semiannual basis. Also includes "Monthly Investment Review" (industry group investment analysis) and monthly "Trends & Projections" (economic analysis).

*Survey of Current Business.* U. S. Government Printing Office. • Published by Bureau of Economic Analysis, U. S. Department of Commerce. Presents a wide variety of business and economic data.

# PLATING

*See* METAL FINISHING

# PLATINUM INDUSTRY

## PERIODICALS AND NEWSLETTERS

*Johnson Matthey Technology Review.* Johnson Matthey PLC. • Quarterly. Covers research on the science and technology of the platinum group metals and developments in their application in industry.

## STATISTICS SOURCES

*Non-Ferrous Metal Data Yearbook.* American Bureau of Metal Statistics. • Annual. $405.00. Provides worldwide data on approximately about 200 statistical tables covering many nonferrous metals. Includes production, consumption, inventories, exports, imports, and other data.

*Standard & Poor's Industry Surveys.* Standard & Poor's Financial Services L.L.C. • Semiannual. $1,800.00. Two looseleaf volumes. Includes monthly *Supplements.* Provides detailed, individual surveys of 52 major industry groups. Each survey is revised on a semiannual basis. Also includes "Monthly Investment Review" (industry group investment analysis) and monthly "Trends & Projections" (economic analysis).

# PLUMBING INDUSTRY

*See also* HEATING AND VENTILATION

## DIRECTORIES

*Directory of Listed Plumbing Products.* International Association of Plumbing and Mechanical Officials. • Bimonthly. $118 Members per year. Covers: About 1,500 manufacturers of approximately 10,000 plumbing products and appliances. Entries include: Manufacturer name, address, product name, model number, product description.

*The International Directory of Importers-- Plumbing, Sanitary Ware, Pipes & Fittings Importers.* Interdata. • $260 Individuals print. Covers: 3,700 international firms importing plumbing, sanitary ware, pipes and fittings. Entries include: Company name and address, contact person, email,

number of employees, year established, phone and telefaxes, business activity, bank references, as well as a listing of plumbing, sanitary ware, pipes and fittings currently being imported.

*Plumbing Engineer--Product Directory Issue: Engineered Plumbing Systems Directory.* TMB Publishing Inc. • Monthly. $50 Individuals one year. Covers: Over 400 plumbing products from approximately 250 manufacturers. Database includes: List of American Society of Plumbing Engineers (ASPE) national officers, industry associations. Entries include: Company name, phone, fax, website, and e-mail; name of engineering contact with the firm.

## FINANCIAL RATIOS

*American Supply Association Operating Performance Report.* American Supply Association. • Annual. $399 Members. Report provides details on operating performance.

*Annual Statement Studies.* Risk Management Association. • Annual. Compiled from over 280,000 financial statements.

*Annual Statement Studies: Industry Default Probabilities and Cash Flow Measures.* Risk Management Association. • Annual. $405 Nonmembers. Serves as a companion volume to the original *Annual Statement Studies.* Gives probability of default estimates on a percentage scale for more than 450 industries. Includes changes in position year-by-year for eight financial statement line items and provides percentage measures of cash flow.

## INTERNET DATABASES

*Manufacturing Profiles.* U. S. Bureau of the Census. Phone: (301)763-4636 or (301)763-4100; Fax: (301)763-4794; Email: webmaster@census.gov • URL: http://www.census.gov/prod/www/abs/mfg-prof.html • The Census Bureau makes available free on PDF (Portable Document Format) an annual consolidation of the entire Current Industrial Report series, presenting "all the data compiled." Contains statistics on production, shipments, inventories, consumption, exports, imports, and orders for a wide variety of manufactured products.

## PERIODICALS AND NEWSLETTERS

*Plumbing Business Owner.* Cahaba Media Group. • Monthly. Business magazine for plumbers.

*Plumbing Systems and Design.* American Society of Plumbing Engineers. • 10 times per year.

## STATISTICS SOURCES

*Plumbing Fixtures.* U. S. Bureau of the Census. • Quarterly and annual. Provides data on shipments: value, quantity, imports, and exports. Includes both metal and plastic fixtures. (Current Industrial Reports, MQ-34E.).

*U.S. Industry and Trade Outlook.* U.S. Department of Commerce National Technical Information Service. • Annual. Produced by the International Trade Administration, U.S. Department of Commerce, in a "public-private" partnership with DRI/ McGraw-Hill and Standard & Poor's. Provides basic data, outlook for the current year, and "Long-Term Prospects" (five-year projections) for a wide variety of products and services. Includes high technology industries. Formerly *U.S. Industrial Outlook.*

## TRADE/PROFESSIONAL ASSOCIATIONS

American Society of Plumbing Engineers. 6400 Shafer Ct., Ste. 350, Rosemont, IL 60018. Phone: (847)296-0002; Fax: (847)296-2963; Email: info@ aspe.org • URL: http://aspe.org • Represents engineers and designers involved in the design and specification of plumbing systems; manufacturers, governmental officials, and contractors related to the industry may become members on a limited basis. Seeks to resolve professional problems in plumbing engineering; advocates greater cooperation among members and plumbing officials, contractors, labor-

ers, and the public. Code committees examine regulatory codes pertaining to the industry and submit proposed revisions to code writing authorities to simplify, standardize, and modernize all codes. Sponsors American Society of Plumbing Engineers Research Foundation; operates certification program.

American Supply Association. 1200 N Arlington Heights Rd., Ste. 150, Itasca, IL 60143. Phone: (630)467-0000; Fax: (630)467-0001; Email: info@ asa.net • URL: http://www.asa.net • Represents wholesale, distributors, and manufacturers of plumbing and heating, cooling, pipes, valves, and fittings. Compiles statistics on operating costs and makes occasional studies of compensation, fringe benefits, wages, and salaries. Conducts research studies and forecasting surveys. Offers group insurance. Maintains management institutes, home study courses under the ASA Education Foundation and Endowment program, provides technology and produces a CD-ROM and internet catalogue of manufacturers.

Decorative Plumbing and Hardware Association. 7508 Wisconsin Ave., 4th Fl., Bethesda, MD 20814-3561. Phone: (301)657-3642; Fax: (301)907-9326; Email: info@dpha.net • URL: http://www.dpha.net • Advances the business and professional development of independent dealers, manufacturers, representatives and others involved in the decorative plumbing and hardware industry. Offers educational programs to train staff, create career paths and provide recognition.

National Association of Plumbing, Heating, Cooling Contractors. 180 S Washington St., Ste. 100, Falls Church, VA 22046. Phone: 800-533-7694 or (703)237-8100; Fax: (703)237-7442; Email: naphcc@naphcc.org • URL: http://www.phccweb. org • Federation of state and local associations of plumbing, heating, and cooling contractors. Seeks to advance sanitation, encourage sanitary laws, and generally improve the plumbing, heating, ventilating, and air conditioning industries. Conducts apprenticeship training programs, workshops, seminars, political action committee, educational and research programs.

Plumbing and Drainage Institute. 800 Turnpike St., Ste. 300, North Andover, MA 01845. Phone: 800-589-8956 or (978)557-0720; Email: pdi@pdionline. org • URL: http://www.pdionline.org • Formerly Plumbing and Drainage Manufacturers Association.

# PLYWOOD INDUSTRY

*See also* LUMBER INDUSTRY

## ABSTRACTS AND INDEXES

*Forest Products Abstracts.* CABI Publishing North America. • Weekly updates.

## DIRECTORIES

*Directory of Belgium Importers of Lumber, Timber, Plywood and Hardboards.* EXIM Infotek Private Ltd. • $150 Individuals. Covers: 25 Belgium importers of doors, windows, hardwood flooring, floor tiles, hardwood lumber, softwood lumber, plywood, veneer, poles, wood, pilings and logs. Entries include: Company name, postal address, telephone, fax, e-mail, website, contact person, designation, and product details.

## PERIODICALS AND NEWSLETTERS

*ENR: Connecting the Industry Worldwide.* McGraw Hill Financial Inc. • Weekly. $74.00 per year.

*Panel World.* Hatton-Brown Publishers Inc. • Bimonthly. Business magazine serving the worldwide veneer, plywood, and panel board industry. Formerly *Plywood and Panel World.*

## STATISTICS SOURCES

*U.S. Industry and Trade Outlook.* U.S. Department of Commerce National Technical Information

Service. • Annual. Produced by the International Trade Administration, U.S. Department of Commerce, in a "public-private" partnership with DRI/McGraw-Hill and Standard & Poor's. Provides basic data, outlook for the current year, and "Long-Term Prospects" (five-year projections) for a wide variety of products and services. Includes high technology industries. Formerly *U.S. Industrial Outlook*.

## TRADE/PROFESSIONAL ASSOCIATIONS

APA: The Engineered Wood Association. 7011 S 19th St., Tacoma, WA 98466. Phone: (253)565-6600 or (253)620-7400; Fax: (253)565-7265; Email: help@apawood.org • URL: http://www.apawood.org • Manufacturers of structural panel products, oriented strand board and composites. Conducts trade promotion through advertising, publicity, merchandising, and field promotion. Maintains quality supervision in accordance with U.S. product standards, APA performance standards, and APA trademarking. Conducts research to improve products, applications, and manufacturing techniques. Sponsors Engineered Wood Research Foundation; compiles statistics.

Engineered Wood Technology Association. APA - The Engineered Wood Association, 7011 S 19th St., Tacoma, WA 98466-5333. Phone: (253)620-7237 or (253)565-6600; Fax: (253)565-7265 • URL: http://www.apawood.org/ewrf_level_b.cfm?content=srv_sup_about • Represents manufacturers of construction and industrial panels and related products; associate members. Sponsors research programs on improvement in panel production processes and techniques.

Hardwood Federation. 1111 19th St. NW, Ste. 800, Washington, DC 20036. Phone: (202)463-2452; Fax: (202)463-4702 • URL: http://www.hardwoodfederation.wildapricot.org • Represents organizations engaged in the manufacturing, wholesaling or distribution of North American hardwood lumber, veneer, plywood, flooring and related products. Seeks to promote and represent the common business interests of and improve business conditions among members of the hardwood industry. Strives to maintain a healthy business environment for family businesses and small companies in the hardwood community.

# POINT-OF-PURCHASE ADVERTISING

*See also* DISPLAY OF MERCHANDISE

## PERIODICALS AND NEWSLETTERS

*P-O-P Design (Point-of-Purchase): Products and News for High-Volume Pro ducers and Designers of Displays, Signs and Fixtures.* Hoyt Publishing. • Nine times a year. $59.00 per year.

*PROMO: Promotion Marketing Worldwide.* Primedia Business Magazines and Media. • Monthly. $65.00 per year. Edited for companies and agencies that utilize couponing, point-of-purchase advertising, special events, games, contests, premiums, product samples, and other unique promotional items.

## TRADE/PROFESSIONAL ASSOCIATIONS

Point-of-Purchase Advertising International. 440 N Wells St., Ste. 740, Chicago, IL 60654. Phone: (312)863-2900; Fax: (312)229-1152; Email: info@popai.de • URL: http://www.popai.com • Producers and suppliers of point-of-purchase advertising signs and displays and national and regional advertisers and retailers interested in use and effectiveness of signs, displays and other point-of-purchase media. Conducts student education programs; maintains speakers' bureau.

# POINT-OF-SALE SYSTEMS (POS)

*See also* AUTOMATIC IDENTIFICATION SYSTEMS

## DIRECTORIES

*Cash Registers and Supplies-Wholesale Directory.* InfoGroup Inc. • Annual. Number of listings: 2,539. Entries include: Name, address, phone (including area code), size of advertisement, year first in "Yellow Pages," name of owner or manager, number of employees. Compiled from telephone company "Yellow Pages," nationwide.

*Directory of Computer and Point-of-Sale Systems for Office Products and Furniture Dealers.* Independent Office Products and Furniture Dealers Association. • Irregular. $60. Covers: Approximately 45 manufacturers and distributors of computer, point-of-sale, and contract furniture systems for the office products industry. Entries include: Company name, address, phone, description of product or service.

*Frontline Solutions Buyer's Guide.* Advanstar Communications. • Annual. $34.95 plus $3.50 shipping. Publication includes: List of manufacturers, suppliers, consultants, value added resellers, and dealers/distributors of automatic identification and data capture software, technology, equipment, and products for bar code, biometric identification, electronic data interchange, machine vision, magnetic stripe, optical character recognition, radio frequency data communications, radio frequency identification, smart cards, and voice data entry; also includes related organizations, and sources for industry standards. Entries include: Company name, address, phone, e-mail, web address, products or services.

## PERIODICALS AND NEWSLETTERS

*Corporate EFT Report.* Phillips International, Inc. • Biweekly. $695.00 per year. Newsletter on subject of electronic funds transfer.

## STATISTICS SOURCES

*Statistical Information on the Financial Services Industry.* American Bankers Association. • Annual. Members, $150.00; non-members, $275.00. Presents a wide variety of data relating to banking and financial services, including consumer economics, personal finance, credit, government loans, capital markets, and international banking.

## TRADE/PROFESSIONAL ASSOCIATIONS

Electronic Funds Transfer Association. 4000 Legato Rd., Ste. 1100, Fairfax, VA 22033. Phone: (571)318-5556; Fax: (571)318-5557; Email: dennisambach@efta.org • URL: http://www.efta.org • Financial institutions, credit card companies, ATM owners, networks and processors, hardware and software manufacturers and e-commerce companies dedicated to the advancement of electronic payment systems and commerce.

# POLICE EQUIPMENT

*See* LAW ENFORCEMENT INDUSTRIES

# POLICY MANUALS

*See* PROCEDURE MANUALS

# POLITICAL ACTION COMMITTEE

## DIRECTORIES

*National Directory of Corporate Public Affairs.* Columbia Books and Information Services. • Annual. $249 Individuals. Covers: About 17,000 corporations that have PACs foundations or other public affairs activities; over 14,000 corporate public affairs personnel. Database includes: List of contract lobbyists serving corporations at the state level; membership directory of the Public Affairs Council. Entries include: Company name, headquarters address, Washington, DC, address (if any), names of political action committees, PAC funds contributed, names of principal recipients; name of corporate foundation; total grants per year, assets; giving priorities; names and titles of public affairs personnel. For personnel--Name, title, affiliation, address, phone; if a lobbyist, where registered.

## OTHER SOURCES

*American Medical Political Action Committee.* • Represents physicians, their spouses, and others interested in political action and participation in public affairs. Seeks to further political knowledge of its members and to provide them with means for concerted political action.

*Business-Industry Political Action Committee.* • Works as independent, bipartisan organization that works to elect pro-business candidates to Congress; has group's Business Institute for Political Analysis that carries out extensive programs of political analysis, research, and communication on campaigns and elections, and fosters business participation in the political process.

*UAW - Community Action Program.* • Serves as a program of the International Union, United Automobile, Aerospace and Agricultural Implement Workers of America. Informs UAW members through political education programs on topics including lobbying, the relationship between collective bargaining and the ballot box, and voluntary fundraising for political contributions. Maintains speakers' bureau; compiles statistics.

## TRADE/PROFESSIONAL ASSOCIATIONS

National Association of Business Political Action Committees. 101 Constitution Ave. NW, Ste. L-110, Washington, DC 20001-2115. Phone: (202)341-3780; Fax: (202)478-0342; Email: nabpac@nabpac.org • URL: http://www.nabpac.org • Political action professionals and government affairs representatives interested in campaign finance reform issues and innovations in political action committee management.

Trust Companies' Association of Japan. Nippon Kaikan, 6th Fl., 2-6-2, Otemachi, Chiyoda, Tokyo 100-0004, Japan. Phone: 81 3 3241-7135; Fax: 81 3 3241-7200 • URL: http://www.shintaku-kyokai.or.jp • Works on the promotion, protection, and advancement of the interests of closed-ended investment trust companies and their shareholders by influencing developments in legislation and practice affecting investors, companies and the stock market, by political lobbying and by promotion of their merits, in particular to private investors and independent financial advisers.

# POLITICAL ACTION ORGANIZATION

## OTHER SOURCES

*AIDS United.* • Serves as a representative in Washington, DC, of community-based AIDS service organizations. Advocates, at the federal level, for more effective AIDS policy, legislation, and funding. Works collaboratively with AIDS Action Foundation, a national public policy research organization.

*American Renewal Foundation.* • Explores opportunities for renewal; seeks to provide a voice in the national conversation as well as the vision of the nation's founders, through research and promotion of Christian, ethical solutions to national and global issues. Broadcasts a daily radio news show, The World from Washington, and a weekly radio show for teens called SpeakOut. Runs the web newspaper, Page One Daily. Maintains a large student program; new members are always invited to apply. Provides internship opportunities.

*Business Alliance for Commerce in Hemp.* • Businesses, consumers, and other individuals and organizations with an interest in hemp and hemp products. Promotes "full and unrestricted restoration of hemp as a sustainable farm crop and industrial resource"; seeks to legalize therapeutic use of marijuana and regulate adult consumption. Conducts lobbying, community organization, and outreach activities supporting hemp producers and consumers; consulting services; disseminates information on the commercial and industrial uses of hemp and the therapeutic benefits of marijuana.

*Campaign for Working Families.* • Represents the interests and values of America's traditional families in the political arena. Works on electing pro-family, pro-life and pro-free enterprise candidates to federal and state offices. Conducts extensive media campaigns and distribution of literature.

*Common Cause.* • Nonpartisan citizens' lobby. Dedicated to fighting for open, honest, and accountable government at the national, state, and local levels. Gathers and disseminates information on the effects of money in politics; lobbies for political finance and other campaign reforms.

*Democracy International.* • Seeks to build a movement of individuals dedicated to practical action on behalf of common commitments to human rights and pluralistic democracy including freedom of speech and press, religious liberty, free political parties, and the right to contest elections. Works to develop political and economic self-determination of citizens allowing them to control their resources, choose their social systems, and end discrimination. Aims to: revive democracy where it has been destroyed; encourage and sustain democrats trying to bring democracy to dictatorships. Calls upon democracies to: increase help for democratic leaders and politicians in the Third World; provide economic sustenance to relieve human suffering; strengthen democracy where it exists. Provides a forum for democrats to express solidarity and to help each other; encourages membership in an effort to build an international force of people working to make the cause of democracy an enduring ideal. Publicizes the efforts of democratic movements in dictatorships; attempts to increase the amount of uncensored information to closed societies.

*EMILY's List.* • Political network for Democratic women. Seeks to raise campaign funds for the election of pro-choice Democratic women to political office.

*FreedomWorks.* • Devoted to ensuring that government actions foster growth, economic well being and individual responsibility. Sponsors an internship program, introducing its participants to the Washington policy world, giving them a broader base of knowledge about the organization and its inner operations.

*International Action Center.* • Opposes U.S. militarism. Organizes opposition to U.S. intervention abroad and to racism and political repression at home. Sponsors educational activities and research.

*League of Revolutionaries for a New America.* • Works toward a vision of a cooperative world where the full potential of all can contribute to the good of everyone.

*Military Toxics Project.* • Promotes clean up of military pollution, safeguards transportation of hazardous materials, advances development of preventative solutions to toxic, radioactive pollution from military activities.

*Naval Sea Cadet Corps.* • Youths aged 11-17 years interested in the Navy, Marine Corps, Coast Guard, and Merchant Marines. Works to instill good citizenship and patriotism in youth. Encourages qualities such as personal neatness, loyalty, obedience, dependability, and responsibility to others. Offers courses in physical fitness and military drill, first aid, water safety, basic seamanship, and naval history and traditions.

*Project on Government Oversight.* • Promotes accountability in government; monitors governmental agencies; exposes abuses of power, and waste and fraud committed by the government and its contractors.

*Social Democrats, U.S.A.* • Serves as political action and education organization of young people, students, and trade unionists. Supports Independent and Democratic liberal-labor candidates for public office. Seeks realignment of the major political parties in the U.S. Maintains speakers' bureau. Supports "greater democratic decision-making over the social forces that control our everyday economic lives." Recommends democratic economic planning to ease pains of the economic crisis and to allocate resources in the public interest. Favors public aid to education and increased public investment in such areas as national health care, mass transit, low-cost housing, and new sources of energy. Supports trade unionism. Believes in foreign policy that supports democratic movements and governments.

*Society of the 3rd Infantry Division.* • Past and present members of the 3rd Infantry Division of the U.S. Army and attached and supporting units; families of veterans of the division. Fosters and strengthens associations and friendships formed during service with the Third Infantry Division. Honors the Third Infantry Division War Dead and perpetuates their memory. Encourages and achieves the mutual benefit and support resulting from a close and cooperative alliance between the Society and the Third Infantry Division, U.S. Army. Supports the government of the United States. Assists in the maintenance of monuments dedicated to the Third Infantry Division. Organizes and conducts wreath laying and memorial ceremonies.

*U.S.-English.* • Aims to preserve the common bond by making English the official language of government in the U.S. Promotes opportunities for people living here to learn English.

*Women Against Military Madness.* • Advocates for a radical shift in the nation's priorities away from militarism, military spending, arms trade, military intervention and the militarization of schools.

## RESEARCH CENTERS AND INSTITUTES

Free Congress Foundation. 901 N Washington, Ste. 206, Alexandria, VA 22314-1535. Email: contact@freecongress.org • URL: http://www.freecongress.org • Brings messages of traditional values, conservative government, and institutional reform to America through publications and TV programs on America's Voice network. Includes projects such as: Judicial Selection Monitoring Project, "Taking Back Our Constitution" seminar services and the Center for Technology Policy's privacy papers.

## TRADE/PROFESSIONAL ASSOCIATIONS

Better Government Association. 223 W Jackson Blvd., Ste. 900, Chicago, IL 60606. Phone: (312)427-8330; Fax: (312)821-9038; Email: info@bettergov.org • URL: http://www.bettergov.org • Individuals and corporations concerned with major public policy questions and dedicated to promoting efficient use of tax dollars and high standards of public service. Encourages a responsive and economical government by improving government institutions' performance and maintaining high ethical standards among public officials. Uses official documents, on-the-record interviews, undercover operations, and sophisticated techniques of investigative reporting to uncover corruption. Works closely with national and local media to expose waste, inefficiency, and corruption and to educate the public on the inner workings of the government. Sponsors intern programs for students in law and investigative research.

Canadian Council of Chief Executives. 99 Bank St., Ste. 1001, Ottawa, ON, Canada K1P 6B9. Phone: (613)238-3727; Fax: (613)238-3247; Email: info@ceocouncil.ca • URL: http://www.ceocouncil.ca • Businesses and trade organizations. Promotes a healthy national economy. Conducts research; lobbies for legislation favorable to business; represents members' interests.

# POLITICAL ECONOMY

*See* ECONOMICS

# POLLS, OPINION

*See* PUBLIC OPINION

# POLLUTION OF AIR

*See* AIR POLLUTION

# POLLUTION OF WATER

*See* WATER POLLUTION

# POPCORN INDUSTRY

*See* SNACK FOOD INDUSTRY

# POPULATION

*See also* CENSUS REPORTS; VITAL STATISTICS

## ABSTRACTS AND INDEXES

*PAIS International.* ProQuest L.L.C. • Monthly. $850.00 per year; cumulations three times a year. Provides topical citations to the worldwide literature of public affairs, economics, demographics, sociology, and trade. Text in English; indexed materials in English, French, German, Italian, Portuguese and Spanish.

*Social Sciences Citation Index.* Thomson Reuters Corp. • Weekly. Product is accessed via *Web of Science.*

*Social Sciences Index Retrospective: 1907-1983.* EBSCO Publishing Inc. • Indexing for 1,000,000 articles. Coverage includes international index and social sciences and humanities index.

## ALMANACS AND YEARBOOKS

*Research in Population Economics.* Elsevier. • Irregular. $90.25. Volumes 4-9.

*Vital Signs: The Trends That Are Shaping Our Future (year).* Worldwatch Institute. • Annual. $19.95. Provides access to selected indicators showing social, economic, and environmental trends throughout the world. Includes data relating to food, energy, transportation, finance, population, and other topics.

*World Development Report.* World Bank Group. • Annual. Covers history, conditions, and trends relating to economic globalization and localization. Includes selected data from *World Development Indicators* for 132 countries or economies. Key indicators are provided for 78 additional countries or economies.

## BIBLIOGRAPHIES

*Monthly Product Announcement.* U. S. Bureau of the Census. • Monthly. Lists Census Bureau publications and products that became available during the previous month.

*U.S. Census Bureau Catalog and Guide.* U. S. Government Printing Office. • Annual. Lists publications and electronic media products currently available from the U. S. Bureau of the Census, along with some out of print items. Includes comprehensive title and subject indexes. Formerly *Bureau of the Census Catalog.*

## CD-ROM DATABASES

*OECD Statistical Compendium.* Organization for Economic Cooperation and Development. • Semiannual. $1,905.00 per year for 1 to 10 users. CD-ROM contains more than 730,000 monthly, quarterly, and annual time series for OECD countries, 1960 to date. Includes fully searchable data on agriculture, food, economic indicators, national accounts, employment, energy, finance, industry, technology, and foreign trade. Results can be displayed in various forms.

*PAIS International.* ProQuest L.L.C. • Monthly. $1,995.00 per year. Contains over 650,000 citations to the literature of contemporary social, political, and economic issues.

*Social Sciences Abstracts.* EBSCO Publishing Inc. • Provides indexing from 1983 and abstracting from 1994 of more than 750 periodicals covering economics, area studies, community health, public administration, public welfare, urban studies, and many other topics related to the social sciences.

*Social Sciences Citation Index.* Thomson Reuters Corp. • Weekly. Product is accessed via *Web of Science.*

*Sourcebooks America CD-ROM.* CACI Marketing Systems. • Annual. $1,250.00. Provides the CD-ROM version of *The Sourcebook of ZIP Code Demographics: Census Edition* and *The Sourcebook of County Demographics: Census Edition.*

*World Development Report.* World Bank Group. • Annual. Covers history, conditions, and trends relating to economic globalization and localization. Includes selected data from *World Development Indicators* for 132 countries or economies. Key indicators are provided for 78 additional countries or economies.

## E-BOOKS

*Social Trends & Indicators USA.* Monique D. Magee, editor. Cengage Learning Inc. • Includes data on labor, economics, the health care industry, crime, leisure, population, education, social security, and many other topics. Sources include various government agencies and major publications. Inquire for pricing.

## ENCYCLOPEDIAS AND DICTIONARIES

*Encyclopedia of Population.* Cengage Learning Inc. • 2003. $443.00. Two volumes. Published by Macmillan Reference USA. Formerly *Macmillan's International Encyclopedia of Population.* Covers a broad range of topics in demography and neighboring disciplines. Emphasis is on developments in population research during the past 20 years. eBook also available.

## INTERNET DATABASES

*Business 2.0 Web Guide to the Best Business Links.* Business 2.0 Media Inc. Phone: (415)293-4800; Email: support@business2.com • URL: http://www.business2.com/webguide • Web site presents an extensive, searchable directory of links to "the best, most informative, and authoritative web pages." Twenty main categories cover business, finance, career, company information, people, and technology topics, with thousands of subtopics, all linking to Web sites recommended by experienced business researchers. Fees: Free.

*Fedstats.* Federal Interagency Council on Statistical Policy. Phone: (202)395-7254 • URL: http://www.fedstats.gov • Web site features an efficient search facility for full-text statistics produced by more than 100 federal agencies, including the Census Bureau, the Bureau of Economic Analysis, and the Bureau of Labor Statistics. Boolean searches can be made within one agency or for all agencies combined. Links are offered to international statistical bureaus, including the UN, IMF, OECD, UNESCO, Eurostat, and 20 individual countries. Fees: Free.

*FreeLunch.com.* Economy.com, Inc. Phone: (610)696-8700; Fax: (610)696-1678 • URL: http://www.freelunch.com • Web site provides free access to more than 200 million economic and financial data series, covering industry, demographics, labor markets, prices, retail sales, government spending, trade, interest rates, housing starts, the stock market, etc. Data is available in either chart or table form. Searching is offered. Free, but registration required. Economy.com, Inc. also offers fee-based economic analysis at *The Dismal Scientist* site (www.dismal.com).

## ONLINE DATABASES

*Wilson Social Sciences Abstracts Online.* H.W. Wilson Co. • Provides online abstracting and indexing of more than 500 periodicals covering area studies, community health, public administration, public welfare, urban studies, and many other social science topics. Time period is 1994 to date for abstracts and 1983 to date for indexing, with updates weekly. Inquire as to online cost and availability.

## PERIODICALS AND NEWSLETTERS

*American Demographics: Consumer Trends for Business Leaders.* Media Central. • Monthly. $58.00 per year.

*Demography.* Population Association of America. • Quarterly. $295 Institutions incl. free access or e-only. Scientific journal covering demographic research, including social sciences, geography, history, biology, statistics, business epidemiology and public health.

*Population Bulletin.* Population Reference Bureau. • Quarterly. $3.50 Single issue. Covers population issues, country/regional studies, and health issues.

*The Reporter.* Population Connection. • Quarterly. Description: Reports on population growth and related social, environmental, and economic issues. Tracks legislative developments. Recurring features include interviews, news of research, book reviews, and regular columns.

*World Watch: Working for a Sustainable Future.* Worldwatch Institute. • Bimonthly. $25.00 per year. Emphasis is on environmental trends, including developments in population growth, climate change, human behavior, the role of government, and other factors.

## RESEARCH CENTERS AND INSTITUTES

Harvard University - Center for Population and Development Studies. 9 Bow St., Cambridge, MA 02138. Phone: (617)495-2021; Fax: (617)495-5418; Email: lberkman@hsph.harvard.edu • URL: http://www.hsph.harvard.edu/population-development • Demography, human ecology, and economic, social, and environmental determinants and consequences of population changes in developing countries, including studies of public health aspects of fertility and the balance between populations and their resources, theories of population dynamics and their implications for public policy, political and ethical aspects of population, and the effect of nutrition and exercise on female reproduction.

McMaster University - Research Institute for Quantitative Studies in Economics and Population. Kenneth Taylor Hall, Rm. 426, 1280 Main St. W, Hamilton, ON, Canada L8S 4M4. Phone: (905)525-9140; Fax: (905)521-8232; Email: qsep@

mcmaster.ca • URL: http://socserv.mcmaster.ca/qsep • Broad-based studies in quantitative economics, demography, and related social science areas.

RAND - Labor and Population Program. 1700 Main St., Santa Monica, CA 90407-2138. Phone: (310)393-0411 • URL: http://www.rand.org/labor • United States labor markets, demography of families and children, social welfare policy and family and child well being, social and economic functioning of the elderly, economic and social change in developing countries.

U.S. Census Bureau Demographic Programs - Demographic Surveys Division. 4600 Silver Hill Rd., Washington, DC 20233. Phone: (301)763-2071 • URL: http://www.census.gov/aboutus/sur_demo.html • Survey and data collection on demographics in such areas as income, education, health, employment, unemployment, crime, expenditures, and housing. Division is also responsible for contracting with other federal agencies for survey work to be completed by divisions in the Bureau.

University of Chicago - Center for Population Economics. 5807 S Woodlawn Ave., Chicago, IL 60637. Phone: (773)702-7709; Fax: (773)702-2901; Email: rwf@cpe.uchicago.edu • URL: http://www.cpe.uchicago.edu • Analysis of long-term structural changes in the economy at the microeconomic level, including studies on the economics of mortality in North America (1650-1910), nutrition, labor welfare, labor productivity, distribution of wealth, economic mobility, patterns and determinants of internal migration, and savings and investments by households.

University of Minnesota - Minnesota Population Center. 50 Willey Hall, 225 - 19th Ave. S, Minneapolis, MN 55455. Phone: (612)624-5818; Fax: (612)626-8375; Email: mpc@umn.edu • URL: http://www.pop.umn.edu • Historical demography, population geography, economics, public health, and family and life course demography.

University of North Carolina at Chapel Hill - Carolina Population Center. University Sq., CB 8120, 123 W Franklin St., Chapel Hill, NC 27516-2524. Phone: (919)966-2157 or (919)966-2152; Fax: (919)966-6638; Email: pmorgan@unc.edu • URL: http://www.cpc.unc.edu • Coordinates on a University-wide basis, an interdisciplinary program in population research and research training. Activities encompass social, behavioral and health sciences, including anthropology, biostatistics, city and regional planning, economics, epidemiology, family medicine, geography, health behavior and education, maternal and child health, nutrition, obstetrics and gynecology, political science, psychology, health policy and administration, sociology, business administration, and journalism. Serves as a link between the university and related institutions and agencies in the U.S. and abroad.

## STATISTICS SOURCES

*Population and Vital Statistics Report.* United Nations Publications. • Semiannual. $40.00 per year. Contains worldwide demographic statistics.

*Quarterly Labour Force Statistics.* Organization for Economic Cooperation and Development. Organisation for Economic Co-operation and Development Publications and Information Center. • Quarterly. $90.00 per year. Provides current data for OECD member countries on population, employment, unemployment, civilian labor force, armed forces, and other labor factors.

*Statistical Abstract of the United States.* U. S. Government Printing Office. • Annual. $44.00. Issued by the U. S. Bureau of the Census.

*Statistical Yearbook.* United Nations Publications. • Annual. $125.00. Contains statistics for about 200 countries on a wide variety of economic, industrial, and demographic topics. Compiled by United Nations Statistical Office.

*United States Census of Population and Housing.* Bureau of the Census, U.S. Department of Commerce. U. S. Government Printing Office. • Quinquennial.

## TRADE/PROFESSIONAL ASSOCIATIONS

Population Action International. 1300 19th St. NW, Ste. 200, Washington, DC 20036-1624. Phone: (202)557-3400; Fax: (202)728-4177; Email: pai@popact.org • URL: http://www.populationaction.org • Seeks to advance policies and programs that slow population growth in order to enhance the quality of life for all ages. Advocates expansion of voluntary family planning, other reproductive health services, and educational and economic opportunities for girls and women.

Population Association of America. 8630 Fenton St., Ste. 722, Silver Spring, MD 20910-3812. Phone: (301)565-6710; Fax: (301)565-7850; Email: lmbrown@popassoc.org • URL: http://www.populationassociation.org • Individuals interested in demography and its scientific aspects.

Population Council. 1 Dag Hammarskjold Plz., New York, NY 10017. Phone: 877-339-0500 or (212)339-0500 or (212)237-9434; Fax: (212)755-6052; Email: pubinfo@popcouncil.org • URL: http://www.popcouncil.org • Seeks to improve the well-being and reproductive health of current and future generations around the world. Helps achieve a humane, equitable, and sustainable balance between people and resources. Conducts research in three areas: HIV and AIDS; poverty, gender, and youth; and reproductive health.

Population Reference Bureau. 1875 Connecticut Ave. NW, Ste. 520, Washington, DC 20009-5728. Phone: 800-877-9881; Fax: (202)328-3937; Email: popref@prb.org • URL: http://www.prb.org • Gathers, interprets, and disseminates information on the facts and implications of national and world population trends.

# PORCELAIN INDUSTRY

*See* POTTERY INDUSTRY

# PORK

*See* SWINE INDUSTRY

# PORT AUTHORITIES

*See* PORTS

# PORTABLE COMPUTERS

## ABSTRACTS AND INDEXES

*Business Periodicals Index Retrospective.* EBSCO Publishing Inc. • 11/year. Quarterly and annual cumulations.

*Computer and Information Systems Abstracts Journal: An Abstract Journal Pertaining to the Theory, Design, Fabrication and Application of Computer and Information Systems.* CSA. • Monthly. $1,750 per year.

*Computer Science Index.* EBSCO Publishing Inc. • Quarterly. $245 per year. Contains brief abstracts of book and periodical literature covering all phases of computing, including approximately 70 specific application areas.

*Internet and Personal Computing Abstracts (print edition).* EBSCO Publishing Inc. • Quarterly. $269.00 per year, including cumulative index. Provides more than 10,000 abstracts annually from

both trade and academic publications. Covers computer hardware, software, product reviews, Web topics, e-commerce, networks, corporate news, security, and related topics. Formerly *Microcomputer Abstracts.*

## CD-ROM DATABASES

*ABI/INFORM.* ProQuest L.L.C. • Monthly. Provides CD-ROM indexing and abstracting of worldwide business literature. Archival discs are available from 1971. Formerly *ABI/INFORM OnDisc.*

*Business Abstracts with Full Text.* EBSCO Publishing Inc. • Includes full text articles from more than 460 business publications from 1982 to present. Indexing for nearly 880 publications.

## INTERNET DATABASES

*InfoTech Trends.* Data Analysis Group. Phone: (925)462-1202; Fax: (925)462-1225; Email: support@infotechtrends.com • URL: http://www.infotechtrends.com • Web site provides both free and fee-based market research data on the information technology industry, including computers, peripherals, telecommunications, the Internet, software, CD-ROM/DVD, e-commerce, and workstations. Fees: Free for current (most recent year) data; more extensive information has various fee structures. Formerly *Computer Industry Forecasts.*

*Wired News.* Lycos Inc. 400-2 Totten Pond Rd., Waltham, MA 02451-2053. Phone: (781)370-2700 or (415)276-8400; Fax: (781)370-2600 or (415)276-8500; Email: press@lycos.com • URL: http://www.lycos.com • Provides summaries and full-text of "Top Stories" relating to the Internet, computers, multimedia, telecommunications, and the electronic information industry in general. These news stories are placed in the broad categories of Politics, Business, Culture, and Technology. Affiliated with *Wired* magazine. Fees: Free.

## ONLINE DATABASES

*Computer Database.* Cengage Learning Inc. • Provides one year of full-text online for 150 leading computer-related publications. Also includes 70,000 product specifications and brief profiles of 13,000 computer product vendors and manufacturers. Inquire as to prices and availability.

*Wilson Business Abstracts Online.* H.W. Wilson Co. • Indexes and abstracts 600 major business periodicals, plus the *Wall Street Journal* and the business section of the *New York Times.* Indexing is from 1982, abstracting from 1990, with the two newspapers included from 1993. Updated weekly. Inquire as to online cost and availability. (*Business Periodicals Index* without abstracts is also available online.).

## PERIODICALS AND NEWSLETTERS

*Handheld Computing: The Number One Guide to Handheld Devices.* Mobile Media Group. • 9/year. Covers handheld devices for consumers, including PDAs, cell phones, digital cameras, MP3 players, tablet PCs, accessories, and software. Includes product reviews.

*Laptop Magazine.* Bedford Communications Inc. • Monthly. Consumer magazine containing articles and product reviews for notebook/laptop computers, handheld computers, tablet devices, cell phones, digital cameras, and other consumer electronic products.

*Mobile PC.* Future Network USA. • Monthly. $20.00 per year. Provides information and detailed product reviews for consumers. Covers notebook/laptop computers, personal digital assistants (PDAs), wireless network equipment, cell phones, digital cameras, and other electronic products.

## STATISTICS SOURCES

*U.S. Industry and Trade Outlook.* U.S. Department of Commerce National Technical Information Service. • Annual. Produced by the International

Trade Administration, U.S. Department of Commerce, in a "public-private" partnership with DRI/McGraw-Hill and Standard & Poor's. Provides basic data, outlook for the current year, and "Long-Term Prospects" (five-year projections) for a wide variety of products and services. Includes high technology industries. Formerly *U.S. Industrial Outlook.*

## TRADE/PROFESSIONAL ASSOCIATIONS

Computing Technology Industry Association. 3500 Lacey Rd., Ste. 100, Downers Grove, IL 60515. Phone: (630)678-8300; Fax: (630)678-8384; Email: membership@comptia.org • URL: http://www.comptia.org • Trade association of more than 19,000 companies and professional IT members in the rapidly converging computing and communications market. Has members in more than 89 countries and provides a unified voice for the industry in the areas of e-commerce standards, vendor-neutral certification, service metrics, public policy and workforce development. Serves as information clearinghouse and resource for the industry; sponsors educational programs.

# PORTABLE DATABASES

*See* OPTICAL DISK STORAGE DEVICES

# PORTFOLIO MANAGEMENT

*See* INSTITUTIONAL INVESTMENTS

# PORTLAND CEMENT

*See* CEMENT INDUSTRY

# PORTS

## DIRECTORIES

*Ports and Terminals Guide.* IHS Global Ltd. Lloyd's Register--Fairplay Ltd. • Biennial. $895 Individuals. Covers: Over 23,000 ports and service providers and details on over 10,000 ports. Also includes port conditions and news and ship index of 58,000 vessels. Database includes: Over 4,000 plans, maps, and port photographs. Entries include: For ports and service providers--Name, address, phone; for ports--location, general overview, load line zone, and maximum vessel size.

*U.S. Custom House Guide.* UBM Global Trade. • Annual. $899 online access. Publication includes: List of ports having customs facilities, customs officials, port authorities, chambers of commerce, embassies and consulates, foreign trade zones, and other organizations; related trade services. Entries include: For each principal port--Name of organization or agency, address, phone, fax, names and titles of key personnel; description and limitations of port facilities. For service firms--Company name, address, phone, fax. Principal content is U.S. tariff schedules and customs regulations, and a "How to Import" manual.

## OTHER SOURCES

*Lloyd's Maritime Atlas.* Informa P.L.C. Informa Sports Group. • Biennial. $119.00. Contains more than 70 pages of world, ocean, regional, and port maps in color. Provides additional information for the planning of world shipping routes, including data on distances, port facilities, recurring weather hazards at sea, international load line zones, and sailing times.

## RESEARCH CENTERS AND INSTITUTES

National Ports and Waterways Institute. University of New Orleans, 2300 Claredon Blvd., Ste. 300, Arlington, VA 22201. Phone: (703)276-7101; Fax:

(703)276-7102; Email: npwi@seas.gwu.edu • URL: http://www.members.tripod.com/npwi.

**TRADE/PROFESSIONAL ASSOCIATIONS**
Federation of European Private Port Operators. Ave. des Arts 3-4-5, B-1210 Brussels, Belgium. Phone: 32 2 7367552; Fax: 32 2 7323149; Email: info@ feport.be • URL: http://www.feport.be • European Private port operators. Represents members' interests.

# POSITION EVALUATION

*See* JOB ANALYSIS

# POSITIONS

*See* OCCUPATIONS

# POST EXCHANGES

**PERIODICALS AND NEWSLETTERS**
*Exchange and Commissary News.* Executive Business Media Inc. • Monthly. $95.00 per year.

*Navy Supply Corps Newsletter.* U. S. Government Printing Office. • Bimonthly. $31 U.S.. Newsletter issued by U. S. Navy Supply Systems Command. Provides news of Navy supplies and stores activities.

# POSTAL SERVICES

**BIBLIOGRAPHIES**
*Postal Service.* U. S. Government Printing Office. • Annual. Free. Issued by the Superintendent of Documents. A list of government publications on mail services and the post office. (Subject Bibliography No. 169.).

**DIRECTORIES**
*National Five-Digit Zip Code and Post Office Directory.* United States Postal Service - National Customer Support Center. • Annual. Two volumes. Formerly National Zip Code and Post Office Directory-.

**INTERNET DATABASES**
*United States Postal Service: Make Your Mark.* U.S. Postal Service. Phone: (202)268-2000; Email: webmaster@email.usps.com • URL: http://www. usps.com • Web site contains detailed information on U. S. mail services and post offices, including ZIP codes, postage rates, stamps, addressing, Express Mail tracking, and consumer postal information in general. Links are provided to the State Department for passport procedures and to the IRS for tax forms.

**OTHER SOURCES**
*Bullinger's Postal and Shippers Guide for the United States and Canada.* Alber Leland Inc. • Annual. $375.00. Approximately 260,000 communities in the United States and Canada.

**PERIODICALS AND NEWSLETTERS**
*Postal Bulletin.* U. S. Government Printing Office. • Biweekly. $163. Issued by the United States Postal Service. Contains orders, instructions, and information relating to U. S. mail service.

*Postal World.* UCG Holdings L.P. • Description: Disseminates information to help readers run a more efficient mail operation. "Discusses how to trim postage costs, speed delivery, improve mailroom productivity, and plan for rate increases." Recurring features include an annual salary survey and periodic special reports.

**STATISTICS SOURCES**
*Annual Report of Postmaster General.* United States Postal Service. • Annual.

*U.S. Postal Service Revenue and Cost Analysis Report.* United States Postal Service. • Annual.

**TRADE/PROFESSIONAL ASSOCIATIONS**
Parcel Shippers Association. 1800 Diagonal Rd., Ste. 320, Alexandria, VA 22314. Phone: (571)257-7617; Fax: (571)257-7613; Email: psa@ parcelshippers.org • URL: http://www. parcelshippers.org • Wholesalers, retailers, mail order houses, and other firms using parcel post service for distribution of products. Promotes the efficient and economical distribution of small package shipments.

# POSTERS

*See* ART IN INDUSTRY; COMMERCIAL ART; SIGNS AND SIGN BOARDS

# POTASH INDUSTRY

*See also* FERTILIZER INDUSTRY

**DIRECTORIES**
*Major Chemical and Petrochemical Companies of the World.* Cengage Learning Inc. • Annual. $1,460 Individuals. 2008. 12th edition. eBook. Published by Graham & Whiteside. Contains profiles of more than 8,500 important chemical and petrochemical companies in various countries. Subject areas include general chemicals, specialty chemicals, agricultural chemicals, petrochemicals, industrial gases, and fertilizers.

**PRICE SOURCES**
*Green Markets.* Pike and Fischer Inc. • Weekly. $915.00 per year. Newsletter including prices for potash and other agricultural chemicals.

**TRADE/PROFESSIONAL ASSOCIATIONS**
International Plant Nutrition Institute. 3500 Parkway Ln., Ste. 550, Norcross, GA 30092-2844. Phone: (770)447-0335; Fax: (770)448-0439; Email: info@ ipni.net • URL: http://www.ipni.net • Formerly Potash and Phosphate Institute.

# POTATO INDUSTRY

*See also* SWEET POTATO INDUSTRY; VEGETABLE INDUSTRY

**ABSTRACTS AND INDEXES**
*Field Crop Abstracts.* CABI Publishing North America. • Monthly. Published in England by CABI Publishing, formerly Commonwealth Agricultural Bureaux.

*Potato Abstracts.* CABI Publishing North America. • Quarterly. Institutions, $610.00 per year. Online edition available, $640.00 per year. Includes single site internet access. Published in England by CABI Publishing. Provides worldwide coverage of the literature.

**DIRECTORIES**
*Major Food and Drink Companies of the World.* Cengage Learning Inc. • 12th edition. eBook. Published by Graham & Whiteside. Contains profiles and trade names for more than 9,200 important food and beverage companies in various countries. In addition to foods, includes both alcoholic and nonalcoholic drink products.

**INTERNET DATABASES**
*USDA.* U.S. National Institute of Standards and Technology. 100 Bureau Dr., Gaithersburg, MD 20899-1070. Phone: 800-877-8339 or (301)975-6478 or (202)720-2791; Fax: (301)975-8295; Email: inquiries@nist.gov • URL: http://www.nist.gov • The USDA home page has six sections: News and Information; What's New; About USDA; Agencies;

Opportunities; Search and Help. Keyword searching is offered from the USDA home page and from various individual agency home pages. Agencies are the Economic Research Service, Agricultural Marketing Service, National Agricultural Statistics Service, National Agricultural Library, and about 12 others. Updating varies. Fees: Free.

**ONLINE DATABASES**
*CAB Abstracts.* CABI. • Contains 46 specialized abstract collections covering over 10,000 journals and monographs in the areas of agriculture, horticulture, forest products, farm products, nutrition, dairy science, poultry, grains, animal health, entomology, etc. Time period is 1972 to date, with monthly updates. Inquire as to online cost and availability. *CAB Abstracts on CD-ROM* also available, with annual updating.

*Food Science and Technology Abstracts (online).* IFIS North American Desk. • Produced by International Food Information Service. Provides about 500,000 online citations, with abstracts, to the international literature of food science, technology, commodities, engineering, and processing. Approximately 2,000 periodicals are covered. Time period is 1969 to date, with monthly updates. Inquire as to online cost and availability.

**PERIODICALS AND NEWSLETTERS**
*Potato Grower of Idaho.* Harris Publishing Inc. • Monthly. $24 per year.

**STATISTICS SOURCES**
*Agricultural Statistics.* U.S. Department of Agriculture National Agricultural Statistics Service. • Annual. $46 Individuals. Provides a wide variety of statistical data relating to agricultural production, supplies, consumption, prices/price-supports, foreign trade, costs, and returns, as well as farm labor, loans, income, and population. In many cases, historical data is shown annually for 10 years. In addition to farm data, includes detailed fishery statistics.

*Vegetables and Specialties Situation and Outlook.* U. S. Government Printing Office. • Three times a year. Issued by the Economic Research Service of the U. S. Department of Agriculture. Provides current statistical information on supply, demand, and prices.

**TRADE/PROFESSIONAL ASSOCIATIONS**
National Potato Council. 1300 L St. NW, Ste. 910, Washington, DC 20005. Phone: (202)682-9456; Fax: (202)682-0333; Email: spudinfo@ nationalpotatocouncil.org • URL: http:// nationalpotatocouncil.org • Commercial potato growers. Takes action on national potato legislative, regulatory, and environmental issues.

Potato Association of America. University of Maine, 5719 Crossland Hall, Rm. 220, Orono, ME 04469-5719. Phone: (207)581-3042; Fax: (207)581-3015; Email: umpotato@maine.edu • URL: http:// potatoassociation.org • Represents breeders, entomologists, horticulturists, plant pathologists, soil and fertilizer specialists, food technologists, producers, and handlers.

# POTATOES, SWEET

*See* SWEET POTATO INDUSTRY

# POTTERY INDUSTRY

*See also* CERAMICS INDUSTRY; GLASSWARE INDUSTRY

**PERIODICALS AND NEWSLETTERS**
*Giftware News: The International Magazine for Gifts, China and Glass, Stationery and Home*

*Accessories.* Talcott Communications Corp. • Monthly.

# POULTRY INDUSTRY

*See also* TURKEY INDUSTRY

## ABSTRACTS AND INDEXES

*Food Science and Technology Abstracts.* Ovid Technologies Inc. • Monthly. $1,780.00 per year. Provides worldwide coverage of the literature of food technology and food production.

*Foods Adlibra: Key to the World's Food Literature.* General Mills, Inc. Foods Adlibra Publications. • Semimonthly. $240.00 per year. Provides journal citations and abstracts to the literature of food technology and packaging.

*Poultry Abstracts.* CABI Publishing North America. • Monthly. Institutions, $760.00 per year. Online edition available. Single site internet access, $735.00 per year. Published in England by CABI Publishing. Provides worldwide coverage of the literature.

## CD-ROM DATABASES

*OECD Statistical Compendium.* Organization for Economic Cooperation and Development. • Semiannual. $1,905.00 per year for 1 to 10 users. CD-ROM contains more than 730,000 monthly, quarterly, and annual time series for OECD countries, 1960 to date. Includes fully searchable data on agriculture, food, economic indicators, national accounts, employment, energy, finance, industry, technology, and foreign trade. Results can be displayed in various forms.

## DIRECTORIES

*Major Food and Drink Companies of the World.* Cengage Learning Inc. • 12th edition. eBook. Published by Graham & Whiteside. Contains profiles and trade names for more than 9,200 important food and beverage companies in various countries. In addition to foods, includes both alcoholic and nonalcoholic drink products.

*Meat, Poultry and Egg Inspection Directory.* U.S. Department of Agriculture. U.S. Department of Agriculture. • Monthly. Lists companies that produce meat, poultry and egg products.

## FINANCIAL RATIOS

*Annual Statement Studies.* Risk Management Association. • Annual. Compiled from over 280,000 financial statements.

*Annual Statement Studies: Industry Default Probabilities and Cash Flow Measures.* Risk Management Association. • Annual. $405 Nonmembers. Serves as a companion volume to the original *Annual Statement Studies.* Gives probability of default estimates on a percentage scale for more than 450 industries. Includes changes in position year-by-year for eight financial statement line items and provides percentage measures of cash flow.

## INTERNET DATABASES

*Business 2.0 Web Guide to the Best Business Links.* Business 2.0 Media Inc. Phone: (415)293-4800; Email: support@business2.com • URL: http://www.business2.com/webguide • Web site presents an extensive, searchable directory of links to "the best, most informative, and authoritative web pages." Twenty main categories cover business, finance, career, company information, people, and technology topics, with thousands of subtopics, all linking to Web sites recommended by experienced business researchers. Fees: Free.

*Fedstats.* Federal Interagency Council on Statistical Policy. Phone: (202)395-7254 • URL: http://www.fedstats.gov • Web site features an efficient search facility for full-text statistics produced by more than 100 federal agencies, including the Census Bureau,

the Bureau of Economic Analysis, and the Bureau of Labor Statistics. Boolean searches can be made within one agency or for all agencies combined. Links are offered to international statistical bureaus, including the UN, IMF, OECD, UNESCO, Eurostat, and 20 individual countries. Fees: Free.

*FreeLunch.com.* Economy.com, Inc. Phone: (610)696-8700; Fax: (610)696-1678 • URL: http://www.freelunch.com • Web site provides free access to more than 200 million economic and financial data series, covering industry, demographics, labor markets, prices, retail sales, government spending, trade, interest rates, housing starts, the stock market, etc. Data is available in either chart or table form. Searching is offered. Free, but registration required. Economy.com, Inc. also offers fee-based economic analysis at *The Dismal Scientist* site (www.dismal.com).

*USDA.* U.S. National Institute of Standards and Technology. 100 Bureau Dr., Gaithersburg, MD 20899-1070. Phone: 800-877-8339 or (301)975-6478 or (202)720-2791; Fax: (301)975-8295; Email: inquiries@nist.gov • URL: http://www.nist.gov • The USDA home page has six sections: News and Information; What's New; About USDA; Agencies; Opportunities; Search and Help. Keyword searching is offered from the USDA home page and from various individual agency home pages. Agencies are the Economic Research Service, Agricultural Marketing Service, National Agricultural Statistics Service, National Agricultural Library, and about 12 others. Updating varies. Fees: Free.

## ONLINE DATABASES

*CAB Abstracts.* CABI. • Contains 46 specialized abstract collections covering over 10,000 journals and monographs in the areas of agriculture, horticulture, forest products, farm products, nutrition, dairy science, poultry, grains, animal health, entomology, etc. Time period is 1972 to date, with monthly updates. Inquire as to online cost and availability. *CAB Abstracts on CD-ROM* also available, with annual updating.

*Food Science and Technology Abstracts (online).* IFIS North American Desk. • Produced by International Food Information Service. Provides about 500,000 online citations, with abstracts, to the international literature of food science, technology, commodities, engineering, and processing. Approximately 2,000 periodicals are covered. Time period is 1969 to date, with monthly updates. Inquire as to online cost and availability.

## PERIODICALS AND NEWSLETTERS

*Egg Industry: Covering Egg Production, Processing and Marketing.* Watt Publishing. • Monthly. Free to qualified personnel; others, $36.00 per year. Newsletter. Formerly *Poultry Tribune.*

*Poultry and Egg Marketing: The Bi-Monthly News Magazine of the Poultry Marketing Industry.* Poultry & Egg News Inc. Franklin Publishing. • Bimonthly. Free to qualified personnel; others, $6.00 per year. Processing and marketing of eggs and poultry products.

*Poultry Science.* Poultry Science Association. • Monthly. $540 Individuals online. Contains articles on how to advance the scientific study of poultry.

*Poultry Times.* Poultry & Egg News Inc. Franklin Publishing. • Biweekly. Directed to grow-out operations for the egg and poultry business.

*Poultry USA.* Watt Publishing. • Bimonthly. $28.00 per year. Incorporates *Broiler Industry.*

## STATISTICS SOURCES

*Agricultural Statistics.* U.S. Department of Agriculture National Agricultural Statistics Service. • Annual. $46 Individuals. Provides a wide variety of statistical data relating to agricultural production, supplies, consumption, prices/price-supports, foreign trade, costs, and returns, as well as farm

labor, loans, income, and population. In many cases, historical data is shown annually for 10 years. In addition to farm data, includes detailed fishery statistics.

*Survey of Current Business.* U. S. Government Printing Office. • Published by Bureau of Economic Analysis, U. S. Department of Commerce. Presents a wide variety of business and economic data.

## TRADE/PROFESSIONAL ASSOCIATIONS

American Egg Board. 1460 Renaissance Dr., Ste. 301, Park Ridge, IL 60068. Phone: (847)296-7043; Fax: (847)296-7007; Email: aeb@aeb.org • URL: http://www.aeb.org • Board of American egg producers appointed by the Secretary of Agriculture. Offers advertising, educational, research, and promotional programs designed to increase consumption of eggs and egg products. Conducts consumer educators and food-service seminars, and food safety education programs.

American Poultry Association. PO Box 306, Burgettstown, PA 15021-0306. Phone: (724)729-3459; Email: secretaryapa@comcast.net • URL: http://www.amerpoultryassn.com • Poultry industry. Strives to protect and promote the standard-bred poultry industry in all of its phases.

National Chicken Council. 1152 15th St. NW, Ste. 430, Washington, DC 20005-2622. Phone: (202)296-2622; Fax: (202)293-4005; Email: ncc@chickenusa.org • URL: http://www.nationalchickencouncil.org • Membership includes producers/processors of broiler chickens; distributors and allied industry. Sponsors National Chicken Cooking Contest and National Chicken Month. Compiles statistics; conducts generic promotion program for chicken; provides government relations services for member companies and the broiler industry.

Poultry Science Association. 1800 S Oak St., Ste. 100, Champaign, IL 61820-6974. Phone: (217)356-5285 or (217)356-3182; Fax: (217)398-4119; Email: psa@assochq.org • URL: http://www.poultryscience.org • Aims to advance the poultry industry. Promotes discovery, application and dissemination of knowledge. Creates a forum for the exchange of information among various segments of the poultry industry.

# POVERTY

*See* PUBLIC WELFARE

# POWDER METALLURGY INDUSTRY

## ABSTRACTS AND INDEXES

*Metal Powder Report.* Elsevier. • $759 Institutions. 11 times a year. Technical articles, company reports, up-to-date news and book reviews cover powder metallurgy worldwide.

*Metalforming Digest.* CSA. • Monthly. Price on application. Provides abstracts of the international literature of metal forming, including powder metallurgy, stamping, extrusion, forging, etc.

## PERIODICALS AND NEWSLETTERS

*International Journal of Powder Metallurgy.* American Powder Metallurgy Institute. APMI International. • Quarterly. Individuals, $85.00 per year; institutions, $180.00 per year.

*Powder Metallurgy.* Institute of Materials, Minerals and Mining. • Five issues per year. $1048.00 per year.

## TRADE/PROFESSIONAL ASSOCIATIONS

Metal Powder Industries Federation. 105 College Rd. E, Princeton, NJ 08540. Phone: 888-546-8676 or (609)452-7700; Fax: (609)987-8523; Email:

info@mpif.org • URL: http://www.mpif.org • Manufacturers of metal powders, powder metallurgy processing equipment and tools, powder metallurgy products, and refractory and reactive metals. Member associations are: Metal Injection Molding Association; Metal Powder Producers Association; Advanced Particulate Materials Association; Powder Metallurgy Equipment Association; Powder Metallurgy Parts Association; Refractory Metals Association. Promotes the science and industry of powder metallurgy and metal powder application through: sponsorship of technical meetings, seminars, and exhibits; establishment of standards; compilation of statistics; public relations; publications. Maintains speakers' bureau and placement service; conducts research.

# POWER (MECHANICAL)

*See also* FUEL; MECHANICAL ENGINEERING

## DIRECTORIES

*Directory of African Importers of Energy and Power Equipment.* EXIM Infotek Private Ltd. • $150 Individuals. Covers: 30 African importers of power transmission equipment and supplies, solar energy equipment, solar panels, solar water heaters, and wind energy equipment. Entries include: Company name, postal address, telephone, fax, e-mail, website, contact person, designation, and product details.

*Directory of American Manufacturers and Exporters of Energy and Power Equipment.* EXIM Infotek Private Ltd. • $200 Individuals. Covers: 50 American manufacturers and exporters of solar control film, power systems and components, battery-free solar equipment, solar battery charge regulators, solar control equipment, solar electric (photovoltaics), solar energy equipment, solar modules, solar panels, and solar photovoltics. Entries include: Company name, postal address, telephone, fax, e-mail, website, contact person, designation, and product details.

*Directory of Australia and New Zealand Importers of Energy and Power Equipment.* EXIM Infotek Private Ltd. • $150 Individuals. Covers: 20 Australian and New Zealand importers of energy conservation products, industrial power system, industrial transmission products, power transmission equipment supplies, power transmission products, solar cells, solar charge controller and modules, solar energy equipment, solar pool heating, transmission and allied equipment. Entries include: Company name, postal address, telephone, fax, e-mail, website, contact person, designation, and product details.

*Directory of European Importers of Energy and Power Equipment.* EXIM Infotek Private Ltd. • Covers: 180 European importers of alternative energy equipment, energy saving equipment, nuclear equipment and materials, power transmission component, power transmission equipment and supplies, power transmission equipment, solar energy equipment, and wind energy equipment. Entries include: Company name, postal address, telephone, fax, e-mail, website, contact person, designation, and product details.

*Directory of Major Manufacturers of T&D Equipment.* NRG Expert. • Covers: More than 1,500 international manufacturers of equipment used in the power sector, including switchgear, HV transformers, insulated cables, uninsulated lines, insulators, bushings, and fittings. Entries include: Company name, address, telephone and fax numbers.

*Directory of Middle East Importers of Energy and Power Equipment.* EXIM Infotek Private Ltd. • $300 Individuals. Covers: 100 Middle East import-

ers of alternative energy equipment, nuclear equipment and material, power generation equipment, power transmission equipment and supplies, solar energy equipment, wind energy equipment, and transmission and allied equipment. Entries include: Company name, postal address, telephone, fax, e-mail, website, contact person, designation, and product details.

*Directory of North American Importers of Energy and Power Equipment.* EXIM Infotek Private Ltd. • Covers: 100 North American importers of alternative energy equipment, power supply system, power transmission component, power transmission equipment and supplies, solar cell products, solar energy equipment, and wind energy equipment. Entries include: Company name, postal address, telephone, fax, e-mail, website, contact person, designation, and product details.

*Directory of South American Importers of Energy and Power Equipment.* EXIM Infotek Private Ltd. • $250 Individuals. Covers: 70 South American importers of power transmission equipment and supplies, solar energy equipment, wind energy equipment, transmission and allied equipment. Entries include: Company name, postal address, telephone, fax, e-mail, website, contact person, designation, and product details.

*Directory of South Korean Manufacturers and Exporters of Energy and Power Equipment.* EXIM Infotek Private Ltd. • Covers: 30 South Korean manufacturers and exporters of nuclear engineering plants, nuclear protection and detection instruments, power distribution equipment for various uses, power relays, and solar energy equipment. Entries include: Company name, postal address, telephone, fax, e-mail, website, contact person, designation, and product details.

*Directory of Taiwanese Manufacturers and Exporters of Energy and Power Equipment.* EXIM Infotek Private Ltd. • $250 Individuals. Covers: 80 Taiwanese manufacturers and exporters of fuel and elements for nuclear energy industry, nuclear engineering plants, nuclear protection and detection instruments, nuclear reactors, power distribution equipment for various uses, and solar energy equipment. Entries include: Company name, postal address, telephone, fax, e-mail, website, contact person, designation, and product details.

## HANDBOOKS AND MANUALS

*Motion Systems Handbook.* Penton Media Inc. • Annual. $30.00.

## PERIODICALS AND NEWSLETTERS

*IEEE Industry Applications Magazine.* IEEE - Communications Society. • Bimonthly. Covers new industrial applications of power conversion, drives, lighting, and control. Emphasis is on the petroleum, chemical, rubber, plastics, textile, and mining industries.

*Power Engineering International.* PennWell Corp., Industrial Div. • Monthly.

## TRADE/PROFESSIONAL ASSOCIATIONS

Mechanical Power Transmission Association. 5672 Strand Ct., Ste. 2, Naples, FL 34110. Phone: (239)514-3441; Fax: (239)514-3470; Email: bob@mpta.org • URL: http://www.mpta.org • Manufacturers of multiple V-belt drive sheaves and elastomeric couplings for mechanical power transmission machinery.

National Association of Power Engineers. 1 Springfield St., Chicopee, MA 01013. Phone: (413)592-6273; Fax: (413)592-1998; Email: nape@powerengineers.com • URL: http://www.powerengineers.com • Professional society of power and stationary engineers; associate members are sales engineers and teachers of any phase of engineering. Areas of interest include air conditioning, compressed air, electric power, refrigeration,

steam, and water. Promotes education in the power engineering areas. Secures and enforces engineers' license laws to prevent the destruction of life and property in the generation and transmission of power and for the conservation of fuel resources of the nation.

Power-Motion Technology Representatives Association. 5353 Wayzata Blvd., Ste. 350, Minneapolis, MN 55416-1300. Phone: 888-817-7872; Fax: (949)252-8096; Email: ptrahq@ptra.org • URL: http://www.ptra.org • Manufacturers and independent manufacturers representatives in the power transmission industry. Seeks to provide a channel of communication between manufacturers' independent representatives and their principals and other manufacturers within the industry by allowing interchange of sound business management ideas and by offering consultation on solving operational problems. Provides information and referral; compiles surveys. Offers training programs that include panels, table talk discussions and seminars on special topics.

Power Transmission Distributors Association. 230 W Monroe St., Ste. 1410, Chicago, IL 60606-4802. Phone: (312)516-2100; Fax: (312)516-2101; Email: ptda@ptda.org • URL: http://www.ptda.org • Distributors and manufacturers of power transmission/motion and position control equipment. Maintains business management and continuing education resources; conducts educational programs; compiles statistics; sponsors industry summit; conducts research; cosponsors industry tradeshows.

# POWER COMPANIES

*See* ELECTRIC UTILITIES

# POWER PLANTS, ELECTRIC

*See* ELECTRIC POWER PLANTS

# POWER TOOL INDUSTRY

*See also* TOOL INDUSTRY

## ABSTRACTS AND INDEXES

*Engineering Index Monthly: Abstracting and Indexing Services Covering Sources ofthe World's Engineering Literature.* Engineering Information Inc. • Monthly. Institutions, $5,279.00 per year. Provides indexing and abstracting of the world's engineering and technical literature.

*Mechanical Engineering Abstracts.* Cambridge Scientific Abstracts L.P. • Quarterly. $1,620 Individuals print + web edition (includes shipping). Database covering international literature on mechanical engineering, engineering management, and production engineering, including specific and theoretical applications. Formerly *ISMEC - Mechanical Engineering Abstracts.*

*NTIS Alerts: Manufacturing Technology.* U.S. Department of Commerce National Technical Information Service. • Biweekly. $130 per year. Covers computer-aided design and manufacturing (CAD/CAM), engineering materials, quality control, machine tools, robots, lasers, productivity, and related subjects.

## DIRECTORIES

*Assembly Buyers Guide.* Reed Elsevier Group plc Reed Business Information. • Annual. $68.00. Lists manufacturers and suppliers of equipment relating to assembly automation, fasteners, adhesives, robotics, and power tools.

*ProSales Buyer's Guide.* DoveTale Publishers. • Annual. Price on application. A directory of equipment for professional builders.

*Tools of the Trade Annual Buyers Guide.* DoveTale Publishers. • Annual. Price on application. A directory of tools for the construction industry.

## PERIODICALS AND NEWSLETTERS

*Building Material Dealer.* National Lumber and Building Material Dealers Association. • Monthly. $48.00 per year. Includes special feature issues on hand and power tools, lumber, roofing, kitchens, flooring, windows and doors, and insulation. Formerly *Builder Material Retailer.*

*Hardware Age.* Reed Elsevier Group plc Reed Business Information. • Monthly. $75.00 per year.

*National Home Center News: News and Analysis for the Home Improvement, Building Material Industry.* Lebhar-Friedman Inc. • 22 times a year. $99.00 per year. Includes special feature issues on hardware and tools, building materials, millwork, electrical supplies, lighting, and kitchens.

*ProSales: For Dealers and Distributors Serving the Professional Contractor.* DoveTale Publishers. • Includes special feature issues on selling, credit, financing, and the marketing of power tools.

## STATISTICS SOURCES

*U.S. Industry and Trade Outlook.* U.S. Department of Commerce National Technical Information Service. • Annual. Produced by the International Trade Administration, U.S. Department of Commerce, in a "public-private" partnership with DRI/McGraw-Hill and Standard & Poor's. Provides basic data, outlook for the current year, and "Long-Term Prospects" (five-year projections) for a wide variety of products and services. Includes high technology industries. Formerly *U.S. Industrial Outlook.*

## TRADE/PROFESSIONAL ASSOCIATIONS

Power Tool Institute. 1300 Sumner Ave., Cleveland, OH 44115-2851. Phone: (216)241-7333; Fax: (216)241-0105; Email: pti@powertoolinstitute.com • URL: http://www.powertoolinstitute.com • Represents manufacturers of portable and stationary tools, both electric and battery operated. Distributes publications and videos on power tool safety. Offers educational programs.

# PRECIOUS STONES

*See* GEMS AND GEMSTONES

# PREFABRICATED HOUSE INDUSTRY

*See also* BUILDING INDUSTRY; MOBILE HOME INDUSTRY

## DIRECTORIES

*Automated Builder Annual Buyers' Guide.* • Annual. $12.00. Over 250 manufacturers and suppliers to the manufactured and pre-fabricated housing industry.

## STATISTICS SOURCES

*U.S. Industry and Trade Outlook.* U.S. Department of Commerce National Technical Information Service. • Annual. Produced by the International Trade Administration, U.S. Department of Commerce, in a "public-private" partnership with DRI/McGraw-Hill and Standard & Poor's. Provides basic data, outlook for the current year, and "Long-Term Prospects" (five-year projections) for a wide variety of products and services. Includes high technology industries. Formerly *U.S. Industrial Outlook.*

## TRADE/PROFESSIONAL ASSOCIATIONS

Manufactured Housing Institute. 1655 N Fort Myer Dr., Ste. 104, Arlington, VA 22209-3108. Phone: (703)558-0400; Fax: (703)558-0401 • URL: http://www.manufacturedhousing.org • Manufacturers of

manufactured homes; suppliers of equipment, components, furnishings and services, financial services companies, state association organizations, retailers and community owners. Promotes sales of manufactured homes through programs and services in six key areas: government relations, technical activities, financing, public relations, site development and community operations. Conducts research and educational programs; provides statistics.

National Association of Home Builders - Systems Builder Council. 1201 15th St. NW, Washington, DC 20005. Phone: 800-368-5242 or (202)266-8200; Fax: (202)266-8400 • URL: http://www.nahb.org/reference_list.aspx?sectionID=815 • Formerly Home Manufacturers Councils of NAHB.

# PREMIUMS

*See also* ADVERTISING SPECIALTIES

## DIRECTORIES

*PROMO Annual SourceBook: The Only Guide to the $70 Billion Promotion Industry.* Primedia Business Magazines and Media. • Annual. $49.95. Lists service and supply companies for the promotion industry. Includes annual salary survey and award winning campaigns.

## HANDBOOKS AND MANUALS

*Specialty Advertising.* Entrepreneur Press. • Looseleaf. $59.50. A practical guide to starting a business dealing in advertising specialties. Covers profit potential, market size evaluation, start-up costs, pricing, accounting, advertising, promotion, etc. (Start-Up Business Guide No. E1292.).

## OTHER SOURCES

*Idea Source Guide; A Monthly Report to Executives in Advertising, Merchandising and Sales Promotion.* Bramlee, Inc. • Monthly. $150.00 per year. Lists new premiums and novelty products.

## PERIODICALS AND NEWSLETTERS

*Incentive: Managing and Marketing Through Motivation.* Nielsen Business Media Inc. • Monthly. $59.00 per year.

*Potentials: Ideas and Products that Motivate.* Nielsen Business Media Inc. • Monthly. $59.00 per year. Covers incentives, premiums, awards, and gifts as related to promotional activities. Formerly *Potentials in Marketing.*

*PROMO: Promotion Marketing Worldwide.* Primedia Business Magazines and Media. • Monthly. $65.00 per year. Edited for companies and agencies that utilize couponing, point-of-purchase advertising, special events, games, contests, premiums, product samples, and other unique promotional items.

# PREPARED FOODS

*See* PROCESSED FOOD INDUSTRY

# PRESIDENTS OF COMPANIES

*See* EXECUTIVES

# PRESS CLIPPINGS

*See* CLIPPING SERVICES

# PRESSURE GROUPS

## ALMANACS AND YEARBOOKS

*Congressional Quarterly Almanac.* CQ Press. • Annual. $549 print. Offers exclusive insight into the

forces that drove action on legislation.

## DIRECTORIES

*Government Affairs Yellow Book: Who's Who in Government Affairs.* Leadership Directories Inc. • Semiannual. $465 per year. Includes in-house lobbyists of corporations and organizations, Political Action Committees (PACs), congressional liaisons, and independent lobbying firms.

*Lobbyists Directory.* InfoGroup Inc. • Annual. Number of listings: 1,107. Entries include: Name, address, phone, size of advertisement, name of owner or manager, number of employees, year first in "Yellow Pages." Compiled from telephone company "Yellow Pages," nationwide.

## PERIODICALS AND NEWSLETTERS

*Congressional Record.* U.S. Congress. U. S. Government Printing Office. • Daily. Daily. Indexes give names, subjects, and history of bills. Texts of bills not included.

*Influence: Clients' Guide to the Business of Lobbying.* ALM Media Properties LLC. • Monthly. $349.00 per year. Newsletter. Provides influence-related news about "lobby shops," companies, associations, and the government. Covers grass-roots campaigns, public relations strategies, new client signings, and fresh registrations. Edited for government relations personnel, public affairs professionals, and lawyers. (Legal Times).

*Legal Times: Law and Lobbying in the Nation's Capital.* ALM Media Properties LLC. • Weekly. $318.00 per year. Published in Washington, DC. Provides news relating to lawyers and the federal government. Special features cover a variety of topics relating to law firm administration.

## TRADE/PROFESSIONAL ASSOCIATIONS

Association of Government Relations Professionals. 2121 Eisenhower Ave., Ste. 110, Alexandria, VA 22314-2530. Phone: 888-712-1357 or (703)960-3011; Email: info@agrp.org • URL: http://grprofessionals.org • Registered lobbyists and other professionals interested in the lobbying profession.

# PRESSURE PACKAGING

*See also* PACKAGING

## PERIODICALS AND NEWSLETTERS

*Spray Technology and Marketing: The Magazine of Spray Pressure Packaging.* Industry Publications Inc. • Monthly. $30.00 per year. Formerly *Aerosol Age.*

# PRESSURE SENSITIVE TAPE INDUSTRY

*See* ADHESIVES

# PRETZEL INDUSTRY

*See* SNACK FOOD INDUSTRY

# PRICES AND PRICING

*See also* CONSUMER PRICE INDEXES; INFLATION

## CD-ROM DATABASES

*OECD Statistical Compendium.* Organization for Economic Cooperation and Development. • Semiannual. $1,905.00 per year for 1 to 10 users. CD-ROM contains more than 730,000 monthly, quarterly, and annual time series for OECD countries, 1960 to date. Includes fully searchable data on agriculture, food, economic indicators, national accounts, employment, energy, finance, industry, technology, and foreign trade. Results can be displayed in various forms.

## DIRECTORIES

*Printworld Directory of Contemporary Prints and Prices.* Printworld International Inc. • Irregular. $229 Individuals regular price. Biographical data on 5,000 international artists in contemporary print-making; thousands of galleries who handle prints and hundreds of print publishers, and 600,000 print/price listings.

## INTERNET DATABASES

*Bureau of Economic Analysis.* U. S. Department of Commerce, Bureau of Economic Analysis. Phone: (202)606-9900; Fax: (202)606-5310; Email: webmaster@bea.doc.gov • URL: http://www.bea.doc.gov • Web site includes "News Release Information" covering national, regional, and international economic estimates from the BEA. Highlights of releases appear online the same day, complete text and tables appear the next day. "Recent News Releases" section provides titles for past nine months, with links. "BEA Data and Methodology" includes "Frequently Requested NIPA Data" (national income and product accounts, such as gross domestic product and personal income). Other statistics are available. Fees: Free.

*Business 2.0 Web Guide to the Best Business Links.* Business 2.0 Media Inc. Phone: (415)293-4800; Email: support@business2.com • URL: http://www.business2.com/webguide • Web site presents an extensive, searchable directory of links to "the best, most informative, and authoritative web pages." Twenty main categories cover business, finance, career, company information, people, and technology topics, with thousands of subtopics, all linking to Web sites recommended by experienced business researchers. Fees: Free.

*CRB Market Overview.* Commodity Research Bureau. Phone: 800-621-5271 or (312)554-8456; Fax: (312)939-4135; Email: info@crbtrader.com • URL: http://www.crbtrader.com/data/ • Web site provides free, detailed, current price quotes for about 100 futures contracts, covering Currencies, Energies, Financials, Grains, Meats, Metals, "Softs" (orange juice, coffee, etc.) and stock price indexes. Includes contract specifications and detailed prices of options on futures.

*Fedstats.* Federal Interagency Council on Statistical Policy. Phone: (202)395-7254 • URL: http://www.fedstats.gov • Web site features an efficient search facility for full-text statistics produced by more than 100 federal agencies, including the Census Bureau, the Bureau of Economic Analysis, and the Bureau of Labor Statistics. Boolean searches can be made within one agency or for all agencies combined. Links are offered to international statistical bureaus, including the UN, IMF, OECD, UNESCO, Eurostat, and 20 individual countries. Fees: Free.

*FreeLunch.com.* Economy.com, Inc. Phone: (610)696-8700; Fax: (610)696-1678 • URL: http://www.freelunch.com • Web site provides free access to more than 200 million economic and financial data series, covering industry, demographics, labor markets, prices, retail sales, government spending, trade, interest rates, housing starts, the stock market, etc. Data is available in either chart or table form. Searching is offered. Free, but registration required. Economy.com, Inc. also offers fee-based economic analysis at *The Dismal Scientist* site (www.dismal.com).

*Summary of Commentary on Current Economic Conditions by Federal Reserve District.* Board of Governors of the Federal Reserve System. Phone: (202)452-3000; Fax: (202)452-3819 • URL: http://www.federalreserve.gov/publications.htm • 8/year. Free Web site provides current "anecdotal information" eight times a year on economic conditions

within each of the 12 Federal Reserve Districts, plus an extensive national *Summary*. Text is based on the opinions of bank officials, business executives, economists, financial market experts, and others. Typically contains views of consumer spending, manufacturing, services, credit, employment, prices, wages, and the economy in general. Usually referred to as the Beige Book.

## PRICE SOURCES

*CPI Detailed Report: Consumer Price Index.* U. S. Government Printing Office. • Monthly. $45 Individuals. Cost of living data.

*Monthly Commodity Price Bulletin.* United Nations Publications. • Monthly. $125.00 per year. Provides monthly average prices for the previous 12 months for a wide variety of commodities traded internationally.

*PPI Detailed Report.* Periodical covering business. Bureau of Labor Statistics, U.S. Department of Labor. U. S. Government Printing Office. • Monthly. $55 Individuals.

## RESEARCH CENTERS AND INSTITUTES

U.S. Bureau of Labor Statistics - Office of Prices and Living Conditions. 2 Massachusetts Ave. NE, Rm. 3120, Washington, DC 20212. Phone: (202)691-5200; Fax: (202)691-7890; Email: greenless.john@bls.gov • URL: http://www.bls.gov/bls/inflation.htm • Prices in retail and primary markets; conducts research to improve the measurement of price change. Areas of interest include consumer price indexes; producer price indexes; export and import price indexes for U.S. foreign trade; and consumer expenditures, income, assets, and liabilities of all U.S. families. Office comprises: the Consumer Expenditure Surveys Division; Consumer Prices and Price Indexes Division, which provides measures of price change for a specified market basket of consumer goods and services; Industrial Prices and Price Indexes Division, which provides measures of change in prices received by producers at the level of the first commercial transaction for many commodities and some services; International Prices Division, which measures change in the prices of commodities and some services imported to and exported from the United States; Price and Index Number Research Division; and Price Statistical Methods Division.

## STATISTICS SOURCES

*Bulletin of Labour Statistics: Supplementing the Annual Data Presented in the Year Book of Labour Statistics.* International Labor Ofice. • Quarterly. $84.00 per year. Includes five Supplements. A supplement to *Yearbook of Labour Statistics.* Provides current labor and price index statistics for over 130 countries. Generally includes data for the most recent four years. Text in English, French and Spanish.

*Prices and Earnings Around the Globe.* Union Bank of Switzerland. • Triennial. Free. Published in Zurich. Compares prices and purchasing power in 48 major cities of the world. Wages and hours are also compared.

*Statistical Yearbook.* United Nations Publications. • Annual. $125.00. Contains statistics for about 200 countries on a wide variety of economic, industrial, and demographic topics. Compiled by United Nations Statistical Office.

*Statistics on Occupational Wages and Hours of Work and on Food Prices.* International Labor Organization. • Annual. Provides international data on wages and hours for 159 occupations within 49 industries. Includes retail prices for 93 food items.

*Survey of Current Business.* U. S. Government Printing Office. • Published by Bureau of Economic Analysis, U. S. Department of Commerce. Presents a wide variety of business and economic data.

# PRIME RATE

*See* INTEREST

# PRINTING AND PRINTING EQUIPMENT INDUSTRIES

*See also* COPYING MACHINE INDUSTRY; GRAPHIC ARTS INDUSTRY; PHOTOENGRAVING; TYPESETTING

## CD-ROM DATABASES

*OECD Statistical Compendium.* Organization for Economic Cooperation and Development. • Semiannual. $1,905.00 per year for 1 to 10 users. CD-ROM contains more than 730,000 monthly, quarterly, and annual time series for OECD countries, 1960 to date. Includes fully searchable data on agriculture, food, economic indicators, national accounts, employment, energy, finance, industry, technology, and foreign trade. Results can be displayed in various forms.

## DIRECTORIES

*Directory of Asian Importers of Calendars, Greeting, Prints and Lithographs.* EXIM Infotek Private Ltd. • $300 Individuals. Covers: 105 Asian importers of calendars, greeting cards, postcards, diaries, posters, prints, lithographs, etching, serigraphs, original painting, smart cards, vinyl flooring, visiting cards, and wedding cards. Entries include: Company name, postal address, telephone, fax, e-mail, website, contact person, designation, and product details.

*Directory of Middle East Importers of Calendars, Greeting, Prints and Lithographs.* EXIM Infotek Private Ltd. • $200 Individuals. Covers: 55 Middle East importers of calendars, greeting cards, postcards, Christmas cards, greeting cards, morals, pictures, etchings, posters, prints, and lithographs. Entries include: Company name, postal address, telephone, fax, e-mail, website, contact person, designation, and product details.

*Directory of North American Importers of Calendars, Greeting, Prints and Lithographs.* EXIM Infotek Private Ltd. • $300 Individuals. Covers: 110 North American importers of art prints, cards, calendars, greeting cards, postcards, pictures, posters, prints, lithograph and etching, printing and graphic arts. Entries include: Company name, postal address, telephone, fax, e-mail, website, contact person, designation, and product details.

*Directory of Printing and Allied Industries.* NIIR Project Consultancy Services. • $100 Individuals CD-ROM. Covers: 1,000 companies/industries (manufacturers and suppliers), printing inks, printing machineries, printing raw material in India. Entries include: Company name, full postal address, phone, fax, email (wherever available), website address (wherever available).

*In-Plant Printer Buyer's Guide.* Innes Publishing Co. • Annual. $10.00. Manufacturers of equipment for the in-plant and grahic arts industry. Formerly *In-Plant Printer and Electronic Publisher Buyer's Guide.*

*The International Directory of Importers--Printing and Graphic Arts Equipment and Supplies Importers.* Interdata. • $220 Individuals print. Covers: 2,500 international firms importing printing and graphic arts equipment and supplies. Entries include: Company name and address, contact person, email, number of employees, year established, phone and telefaxes, business activity, bank references, as well as a listing of printing and graphic arts equipment and supplies currently being imported.

*Malaysia Printing and Supporting Industries Directory (MPSID).* Marshall Cavendish Business

Information Private Ltd. • $30 Individuals local, foreign and other countries. Covers: information on the printing industry of Malaysia. Entries include: corporate profiles, contact details on printing and publishing companies, equipment, supplies and accessories.

*Print Solutions--Buyers' Guide Issue*. Print Services and Distribution Association. • Annual. $49 Individuals. Publication includes: List of about 600 suppliers of business forms and other business printing, such as ad specialties, bar-coded forms & labels, commercial printing calendars, tags, cards, labels, and printed stationery. Entries include: name, address, phone, fax, capabilities, product/service.

*Printworld Directory of Contemporary Prints and Prices*. Printworld International Inc. • Irregular. $229 Individuals regular price. Biographical data on 5,000 international artists in contemporary printmaking; thousands of galleries who handle prints and hundreds of print publishers, and 600,000 print/ price listings.

*Screen Printing--Buyer's Guide Issue*. ST Media Group International Inc. • Annual. Publication includes: List of about 500 manufacturers and distributors of products and equipment used in the screen printing industry. Database includes: Calendar of trade events; lists of industry associations, colleges and universities, reference guides. Entries include: Company name, address, phone; branch office locations, phone number, name of sales contact, product lines, geographic area served.

*Screen Printing--Distributor/Dealer Directory Section*. ST Media Group International Inc. • Monthly. $5 per issue. Publication includes: Listings of over 135 dealers and distributors of screen printing equipment, materials, and services. Entries include: Company name, address, phone, fax, name and title of contact, geographical area served, and product/service.

### FINANCIAL RATIOS

*Printing Industries of America Ratios*. Printing Industries of America - Center for Technology and Research. • Annual. $750 Members Full Set (volume 1-16). Annual financial benchmarking study.

### INTERNET DATABASES

*Business 2.0 Web Guide to the Best Business Links*. Business 2.0 Media Inc. Phone: (415)293-4800; Email: support@business2.com • URL: http://www. business2.com/webguide • Web site presents an extensive, searchable directory of links to "the best, most informative, and authoritative web pages." Twenty main categories cover business, finance, career, company information, people, and technology topics, with thousands of subtopics, all linking to Web sites recommended by experienced business researchers. Fees: Free.

*Fedstats*. Federal Interagency Council on Statistical Policy. Phone: (202)395-7254 • URL: http://www. fedstats.gov • Web site features an efficient search facility for full-text statistics produced by more than 100 federal agencies, including the Census Bureau, the Bureau of Economic Analysis, and the Bureau of Labor Statistics. Boolean searches can be made within one agency or for all agencies combined. Links are offered to international statistical bureaus, including the UN, IMF, OECD, UNESCO, Eurostat, and 20 individual countries. Fees: Free.

*FreeLunch.com*. Economy.com, Inc. Phone: (610)696-8700; Fax: (610)696-1678 • URL: http:// www.freelunch.com • Web site provides free access to more than 200 million economic and financial data series, covering industry, demographics, labor markets, prices, retail sales, government spending, trade, interest rates, housing starts, the stock market, etc. Data is available in either chart or table form. Searching is offered. Free, but registration required. Economy.com, Inc. also offers fee-based economic

analysis at *The Dismal Scientist* site (www.dismal. com).

### PERIODICALS AND NEWSLETTERS

*Color Publishing*. PennWell Corp., Advanced Technology Div. • Bimonthly. $29.70 per year.

*Graphic Arts Monthly: The Magazine of the Printing Industry*. Reed Elsevier Group plc Reed Business Information. • Monthly. Free to qualified personnel; others, $142.99 per year.

*In-Plant Printer: The In-Plant Management Magazine*. Innes Publishing Co. • Bimonthly. $75.00 per year. Formerly *In-Plant Printer and Electronic Publisher*.

*Printing Impressions*. North American Publishing Co. • *Master Specifier*.

*Quick Printing: The Information Source for Commercial Copyshops and Printshops*. Cygnus Business Media. • Monthly.

### RESEARCH CENTERS AND INSTITUTES

Rochester Institute of Technology - Chester F. Carlson Center for Imaging Science. 54 Lomb Memorial Dr., Rochester, NY 14623. Phone: (585)475-5944; Fax: (585)475-5988; Email: baum@cis.rit.edu • URL: http://www.cis.rit.edu • Imaging sciences, including remote sensing, digital image processing, color science, optics, medical diagnostic imaging, visual perception, sensor development, printing technology, and astronomical imaging.

### STATISTICS SOURCES

*Survey of Current Business*. U. S. Government Printing Office. • Published by Bureau of Economic Analysis, U. S. Department of Commerce. Presents a wide variety of business and economic data.

### TRADE/PROFESSIONAL ASSOCIATIONS

National Association for Printing Leadership. 1 Meadowlands Plz., Ste. 1511, East Rutherford, NJ 07073. Phone: 800-642-6275 or (201)634-9600; Fax: (201)634-0324 or (201)986-2976; Email: jtruncale@napl.org • URL: http://www.napl.org • Text: Formerly National Association of Printers and Lithographers.

National Association of Quick Printers. c/o Mitch Evans, Chairman, Mitch Evans Consulting, 8 Driftwood Cottage Ln., Daufuskie Island, SC 29915. Phone: (561)351-6950; Email: mitch@ mitchevansconsulting.com • URL: http://napl.org/ naqp • Independent printers and printing franchise businesses; industry suppliers. Seeks to bring recognition, improved quality, and increased profits to the entire quick printing field. Provides services to members; works to advance the collective interests of the printing industries at the national and international levels.

NPES-The Association for Suppliers of Printing and Publishing and Converting Technologies. 1899 Preston White Dr., Reston, VA 20191-4326. Phone: (703)264-7200; Fax: (703)620-0994; Email: npes@ npes.org • URL: http://www.npes.org • Formerly Association for Suppliers of Printing and Publishing and Converting Technologies.

Print Alliance Credit Exchange. 1100 Main St., Buffalo, NY 14209. Fax: (716)878-0479 • URL: http:// www.gopace.com • Manufacturers or designers of business forms or graphic media, selling to dealers, distributors, office supply, copy stores, or end users. Promotes the collection, computation, and exchange of factual ledger experience information by members. Compiles statistics.

Printing Industries of America - Center for Technology and Research. 200 Deer Run Rd., Sewickley, PA 15143-2600. Phone: 800-910-4283 or (412)741-6860; Fax: (412)741-2311; Email: printingind@ printing.org • URL: http://www.printing.org/ctr • Affiliated with Printing Industries of America.

# PRINTING INDUSTRY

## GENERAL WORKS

*Business Documents: For Professional Buyers of Forms, Labels and Electronic Systems*. Penton. • Quarterly. $24 Individuals.

# PRINTING INK INDUSTRY

## ABSTRACTS AND INDEXES

*CPI Digest: Key to World Literature Serving the Coatings, Plastics, Fibers, Adhesives, and Related Industries*. CPI Information Services. • Monthly. $397.00 per year. Abstracts of business and technical articles for polymer-based, chemical process industries. Includes a monthly list of relevant U. S. patents. International coverage.

## DIRECTORIES

*Directory of Printing and Allied Industries*. NIIR Project Consultancy Services. • $100 Individuals CD-ROM. Covers: 1,000 companies/industries (manufacturers and suppliers), printing inks, printing machineries, printing raw material in India. Entries include: Company name, full postal address, phone, fax, email (wherever available), website address (wherever available).

## RESEARCH CENTERS AND INSTITUTES

Rochester Institute of Technology - Chester F. Carlson Center for Imaging Science. 54 Lomb Memorial Dr., Rochester, NY 14623. Phone: (585)475-5944; Fax: (585)475-5988; Email: baum@cis.rit.edu • URL: http://www.cis.rit.edu • Imaging sciences, including remote sensing, digital image processing, color science, optics, medical diagnostic imaging, visual perception, sensor development, printing technology, and astronomical imaging.

## TRADE/PROFESSIONAL ASSOCIATIONS

National Association of Printing Ink Manufacturers. 15 Technology Pkwy. S, Peachtree Corners, GA 30092. Phone: (770)209-7289; Fax: (678)680-4920 • URL: http://www.napim.org • Formerly National Association of Printing Ink Makers.

# PRINTING STYLE MANUALS

## PERIODICALS AND NEWSLETTERS

*Copy Editor: Language News for the Publishing Profession*. McMurry Newsletters. • Bimonthly. Newsletter for professional copy editors and proofreaders. Includes such items as "Top Ten Resources for Copy Editors.".

# PRISONS

*See* LAW ENFORCEMENT INDUSTRIES

# PRIVATE COMPANIES

*See also* CLOSELY HELD CORPORATIONS

## ABSTRACTS AND INDEXES

*Business Periodicals Index Retrospective*. EBSCO Publishing Inc. • 11/year. Quarterly and annual cumulations.

## CD-ROM DATABASES

*D & B Business Locator*. Dun & Bradstreet Inc. • Quarterly. $2,495.00 per year. CD-ROM provides concise information on more than 10 million U. S. companies or businesses. Includes data on number of employees.

*Standard & Poor's Corporations*. Dialog OnDisc. • Monthly. Price on application. Produced by Standard & Poor's. Contains three CD-ROM files: Executives, Private Companies, and Public Companies, providing detailed information on more than 70,000 business executives, 55,000 private companies, and 12,000 publicly-traded corporations.

## DIRECTORIES

*American Big Businesses Directory.* InfoGroup Inc. • Annual. $295. Covers: 218,000 U.S. businesses with more than 100 employees, and 500,000 key executives and directors. CD-ROM version contains 160,000 top firms and 431,000 key executives. Entries include: Name, address, phone, names and titles of key personnel, number of employees, sales volume, Standard Industrial Classification (SIC) codes, subsidiaries and parent company names, stock exchanges on which traded.

*American Manufacturers Directory.* InfoGroup Inc. • Annual. $295. Covers: more than 150,000 manufacturing companies with 20 or more employees. CD-ROM version lists all 531,000 U.S. manufacturers, in all employee size ranges. Entries include: Company name, address, phone, contact name, Standard Industrial Classification (SIC) codes, number of employees, sales volume code, credit rating scores.

*The Book of Lists.* • Annual. $125 Individuals Zip file download. Covers: Leading employers and private companies located in Orange County, California. Entries include: Company name, address, phone, names and titles of key personnel; product/service, financial data, number of employees.

*Crawford's Directory of City Connections.* AP Information Services Ltd. • $325. Covers: Approximately 3,500 private and public sector companies in the U.K., as well as advisers to the financial sector, including stockholders, solicitors, auditors, and insurance advisers. Entries include: Name, address, phone, names and titles of key personnel.

*D & B Million Dollar Directory.* Dun & Bradstreet Inc. • Annual. Covers 1,600,000 public and private businesses with either a net worth of $500,000 or more, 250 or more employees at that location, or $25,000,000 or more in sales volume; includes industrial corporations, utilities, transportation companies, bank and trust companies, stock brokers, mutual and stock insurance companies, wholesalers, retailers, and domestic subsidiaries of foreign corporations.

*Directory of Private Sector Services to Cities.* Texas Municipal League. • Annual. $10. Covers: about 300 firms providing services to city governments in Texas, including attorneys, accountants, architects, auditors, construction managers, engineers, inspectors, real estate appraisers and counselors, and water resource and supply companies. Entries include: Firm name, address, phone, name and title of contact, services, geographical area served.

*Growth Companies Register.* Financial Publishing Ltd. • Annual. $175. Covers: Private companies in Britain with profits of 50,000 or more. Entries include: Financial data, company profile, name of company directors, SIC codes, addresses.

*Hoover's Handbook of American Business.* Dun & Bradstreet Inc. Hoover's Inc. • Annual. $245 Individuals hardcover. Provides detailed profiles of more than 750 large public and private companies, including history, executives, brand names, key competitors, and up to 10 years of financial data. Includes indexes by industry, location, executive name, company name, and brand name.

*Hoover's Handbook of Private Companies.* Dun & Bradstreet Inc. Hoover's Inc. • Annual. $245. Contains profiles of 900 private companies and organizations. Includes indexes by industry, location, executive name, and product.

*How to Find Information about Private Companies.* MarketResearch.com. • Irregular. $59. Covers: Organizations, publications, and individuals that collect information on private companies. Database

includes: Corporate research tips. Entries include: Name, address, phone.

*Internet Access Providers: An International Resource Directory.* Mecklermedia Corp. • $30. Covers: 150 private companies, electronic bulletin board systems, and regional networks that offer dial-in access to the Internet. Entries include: Description.

*Owners and Officers of Private Companies.* Taft Group. • Annual. $320. Covers over 128,000 key executives who own and operate America's 48,000 private companies with annual sales over $3 million.

*Sibbald Guide to Every Public and the Top 100 Private Companies in Missouri.* Acorn Press Inc. • Annual. $80 per year, plus $5.00 shipping; payment must accompany order. Covers: 205 public and privately-held corporations and financial institutions in Missouri. Entries include: Company name, address, phone; brief company history and description, names and titles of officers and directors; return on beginning equity, return on sales/revenues; condensed balance sheet, income statement for past five years, auditors, transfer agent, legal counsel, stock exchange.

*Sibbald Guide to the Texas Top 250 Public Companies and Top 250 Private Companies.* Acorn Press Inc. • Annual. $102.50 per year, plus $5.00 shipping; payment must accompany order.. Covers: 500 public and privately-held corporations and financial institutions in Texas. Entries include: Company name, address, phone; brief company history and description, names and titles of officers and directors; return on beginning equity, return on sales/revenues; condensed balance sheet, income statement for past five years, auditors, transfer agent, legal counsel, stock exchange.

*Ward's Business Directory of U.S. Private and Public Companies.* Cengage Learning Inc. • Annual. $3,627 Individuals five-volume set. Eight volumes. Ward's contains basic information on about 115,000 business firms, of which 90 percent are private companies. Volumes available individually.

## INTERNET DATABASES

*EBSCO Information Services.* EBSCO Publishing Inc. 10 Estes St., Ipswich, MA 01938-2106. Phone: 800-653-2726 or (978)356-6500; Fax: (978)356-6565; Email: information@ebscohost.com • URL: http://www.ebscohost.com • Fee-based Web site providing Internet access to a wide variety of databases, including business-related material. Full text is available for many periodical titles, with daily updates. Fees: Apply.

*Factiva.* Dow Jones Reuters Business Interactive, LLC. Phone: 800-369-7466 or (609)452-1511; Fax: (609)520-5770; Email: solutions@factiva.com • URL: http://www.factiva.com • Fee-based Web site provides "global news and business information through Web sites and content integration solutions." Includes Dow Jones and Reuters newswires, The Wall Street Journal, and more than 7,000 other sources of current news, historical articles, market research reports, and investment analysis. Content includes 96 major U. S. newspapers, 900 non-English sources, trade publications, media transcripts, country profiles, news photos, etc.

*Hoover's Online.* Hoover's Inc. 5800 Airport Blvd., Austin, TX 78752-4204. Phone: 866-443-3939 or (512)374-4500 or (866)281-5969; Fax: (512)374-4501; Email: salesteam@hoovers.com • URL: http://www.hoovers.com • Web site provides stock quotes, lists of companies, and a variety of business information at no charge. In-depth company profiles are available.

*InSite 2.* Intelligence Data/Thomson Financial. Phone: 800-654-0393 or (617)856-1890; Fax: (617)737-3182; Email: intelligence.data@tfn.com • URL: http://www.insite2.gale.com/ • Fee-based Web site consolidates information in a "Base Pack"

consisting of Business InSite, Market InSite, and Company InSite. Optional databases are Consumer InSite, Health and Wellness InSite, Newsletter InSite, and Computer InSite. Includes fulltext content from more than 2,500 trade publications, journals, newsletters, newspapers, analyst reports, and other sources. Continuous updating. Formerly produced by The Gale Group.

*Nexis.com.* Lexis-Nexis Group. Phone: 800-227-4908 or (937)865-6800; Fax: (937)865-6909; Email: webmaster@prod.lexis-nexis.com • URL: http://www.nexis.com • Fee-based Web site offers searching of about 2.8 billion documents in some 30,000 news, business, and legal information sources. Features include a subject directory covering 1,200 topics in 34 categories and a Company Dossier containing information on more than 500,000 public and private companies. Boolean searching is offered.

*ProQuest.* ProQuest L.L.C. 789 E Eisenhower Pkwy., Ann Arbor, MI 48106-1346. Phone: 800-521-0600 or (734)761-4700; Fax: (734)662-4554; Email: info@proquest.com • URL: http://www.proquest.com • Fee-based Web site providing Internet access to more than 3,000 periodicals, newspapers, and other publications. Many items are available full-text, with daily updates. Includes extensive corporate and financial information. Fees: Apply.

*Switchboard.* Switchboard, Inc. Phone: (508)898-8000; Fax: (508)898-1755; Email: webmaster@switchboard.com • URL: http://www.switchboard.com • Web site provides telephone numbers and street addresses for more than 100 million business locations and residences in the U. S. Broad industry categories are available. Fees: Free.

## ONLINE DATABASES

*American Business Directory.* InfoGroup Inc. • Provides brief online information on more than 10 million U. S. companies, including individual plants and branches. Entries typically include address, phone number, industry classification code, and contact name. Updating is quarterly. Inquire as to online cost and availability.

*TRW Business Credit Profiles.* Experian Information Solutions Inc. • Provides credit history (trade payments, payment trends, payment totals, payment history, etc.) for public and private U. S. companies. Key facts and banking information are also given. Updates are weekly. Inquire as to online cost and availability.

*Wilson Business Abstracts Online.* H.W. Wilson Co. • Indexes and abstracts 600 major business periodicals, plus the *Wall Street Journal* and the business section of the *New York Times.* Indexing is from 1982, abstracting from 1990, with the two newspapers included from 1993. Updated weekly. Inquire as to online cost and availability. (*Business Periodicals Index* without abstracts is also available online.).

## OTHER SOURCES

*Going Private.* ALM Media Properties LLC. • $560 print + online + ebook. Discusses the legal ramifications of a publicly-owned company "going private" by way of a sale, leveraged buyout, reverse stock split, or merger. (Law Journal Press).

## PERIODICALS AND NEWSLETTERS

*Inc.: The Magazine for Growing Companies.* INC. • 10/year. $10 U.S. /year for two subscription. Edited for small office and home businesses with one to 25 employees. Covers management, office technology, and lifestyle. Incorporates *Self-Employed Professional.*

## RESEARCH CENTERS AND INSTITUTES

Baylor University - Center for Private Enterprise. PO Box 98003, Waco, TX 76798. Phone: (254)710-2263 or (254)710-6898; Fax: (254)710-1092; Email: kimberly_mencken@baylor.edu • URL: http://www.

baylor.edu/business • Includes studies of entrepreneurship and women entrepreneurs.

Lehigh University - Martindale Center for the Study of Private Enterprise. 621 Taylor St., Ste. 350, Bethlehem, PA 18015. Phone: (610)758-4771; Fax: (610)758-6549; Email: jra1@lehigh.edu • URL: http://martindale.cc.lehigh.edu • Business and economics, including financial condition and future of public pension plans, labor markets, investment opportunities in Eastern Europe and Latin America, microfinance trends, health economics and U.S.-Canadian free trade.

## TRADE/PROFESSIONAL ASSOCIATIONS

Business Council of Papua New Guinea. PO Box 404, Konedobu, Papua New Guinea. Phone: 675 3200700; Fax: 675 3200701; Email: executive@bcpng.org.pg • URL: http://www.bcpng.org.pg • Represents the interests of the private sector to the government and public institutions. Promotes the importance and role of economic growth, freedom and enterprise. Fosters dialogue and debate between the public sector, the private sector and academia.

Center for International Private Enterprise. 1155 15th St. NW, Ste. 700, Washington, DC 20005. Phone: (202)721-9200; Fax: (202)721-9250; Email: info@cipe.org • URL: http://www.cipe.org • Members are people involved in small businesses.

Center for International Private Enterprise - Egypt Office. Fayoum St., No. 1, Off Cleopatra St., Heliopolis, Fl. 8, Ste. 8003, Cairo 11341, Egypt. Phone: 20 2 4143282; Fax: 20 2 4143295; Email: rzoghbi@cipe-egypt.org • URL: http://www.cipe.org • Encourages the growth of voluntary business organizations and private enterprise systems, such as chambers of commerce, trade associations, employers' organizations, and business-oriented research groups, particularly in developing countries. Creates exchanges among business leaders and institutions to strengthen the international private enterprise system. Offers leadership training for association executives.

Confederation of Bolivian Private Entrepreneurs. Calle Mendez Arcos No. 117, Plz. Espana, La Paz, Bolivia. Phone: 591 2 2420999 or 591 2421254; Fax: 591 2 2421272; Email: cepb@cepb.org.bo • URL: http://www.cepb.org.bo • Represents the interests of the private entrepreneurs in Bolivia.

High Council for Private Enterprise. Las Colinas, Calle Alta, Casa N 12, Detras De Gasolinera Puma, Managua, Nicaragua. Phone: 505 2276-3333 or 505 2276-2708; Fax: 505 2276-1666; Email: relacionespublicas@cosep.org.ni • URL: http://www.cosep.org.ni • Promotes the establishment of the democracy in terms of economic, political and social aspects of Nicaragua through programs and actions.

Honduran Private Enterprise Council. apdo. 3240, Tegucigalpa, Honduras. Phone: 504 2 2353336; Fax: 504 2 2353345 • URL: http://www.cohep.com/l • Acts in the defense of the principles and indoctrinates of the free company. Works for the enterprise development, economic and social growth of Honduras.

Industrial Society. Av. Andres Bello 2777, Piso 3, Las Condes, Santiago, Chile. Phone: 56 2 3913100; Fax: 56 2 3913200; Email: sofofa@sofofa.cl • URL: http://web.sofofa.cl • Represents the views and interests of Chilean industry and business. Promotes the advancement and expansion of the private sector.

National Association of Private Enterprise. Blvd. del Hipodromo 542 Col. San Benito, San Salvador, El Salvador. Phone: 503 2209-8300; Fax: 503 2209-8317; Email: comunicaciones@anep.org.sv • URL: http://www.anep.org.sv • Promotes the enterprise sector of El Salvador.

National Council of Private Enterprises - Panama. Apartado 0816-07197, Zone 1, Panama City, Panama. Phone: 507 2 112672 or 507 2 112677; Fax:

507 2 112694; Email: conep1@cwpanama.net • URL: http://www.conep.org.pa • Promotes members' interest.

Representative of German Industry and Trade. 1776 I St. NW, Ste. 1000, Washington, DC 20006. Phone: (202)659-4777; Fax: (202)659-4779; Email: info@rgit-usa.com • URL: http://www.rgit-usa.com • Organizations representing 95% of private industry in Germany. Provides data concerning economic developments and the economic environment in Germany.

# PRIVATE LABEL PRODUCTS

## ABSTRACTS AND INDEXES

*Business Periodicals Index Retrospective.* EBSCO Publishing Inc. • 11/year. Quarterly and annual cumulations.

## CD-ROM DATABASES

*ABI/INFORM.* ProQuest L.L.C. • Monthly. Provides CD-ROM indexing and abstracting of worldwide business literature. Archival discs are available from 1971. Formerly *ABI/INFORM OnDisc.*

*Business Abstracts with Full Text.* EBSCO Publishing Inc. • Includes full text articles from more than 460 business publications from 1982 to present. Indexing for nearly 880 publications.

## DIRECTORIES

*Household and Personal Products Industry Buyers Guide.* Rodman Publications. • Annual. Lists of suppliers to manufacturers of cosmetics, toiletries, soaps, detergents, and related household and personal products.

*Household and Personal Products Industry Contract Manufacturing/Private Label Directory.* Rodman Publications. • Annual. Provides information for about 450 companies offering private label or contract packaged household and personal care products, such as detergents, cosmetics, polishes, insecticides, and various aerosol items.

*International Private Label Directory.* E.W. Williams Publications Co. • Annual. Provides information on over 2,000 suppliers of a wide variety of private label and generic products: food, over-the-counter health products, personal care items, and general merchandise.

*Private Label Directory.* E.W. Williams Publications Co. • Annual. $75 U.S. and Canada. Covers: Over 1,400 suppliers of food, health and beauty care, household supplies, general merchandise and service and supplies, with private and generic labels; international coverage. Entries include: Company name, address, phone, fax, e-mail, internet, names and titles of key personnel, products.

## ONLINE DATABASES

*Wilson Business Abstracts Online.* H.W. Wilson Co. • Indexes and abstracts 600 major business periodicals, plus the *Wall Street Journal* and the business section of the *New York Times.* Indexing is from 1982, abstracting from 1990, with the two newspapers included from 1993. Updated weekly. Inquire as to online cost and availability. (*Business Periodicals Index* without abstracts is also available online.).

## PERIODICALS AND NEWSLETTERS

*Household and Personal Products Industry: The Magazine for the Detergent, Soap, Cosmetic and Toiletry, Wax, Polish and Aerosol Industries.* Rodman Publications. • Monthly. Covers marketing, packaging, production, technical innovations, private label developments, and aerosol packaging for soap, detergents, cosmetics, insecticides, and a variety of other household products.

*Private Label Buyer.* Stagnito Communcitions, Inc. • 8/year. Covers new private label product develop-

ments for chain stores. Formerly *Private Label News.*

*Private Label International: The Magazine for Store Labels (Own Brands) and Generics.* E.W. Williams Publications Co. • Semiannual. Edited for large chain store buyers and for manufacturers of private label products. Text in English; summaries in French and German.

*Private Label: The Magazine for House Brands and Generics.* E.W. Williams Publications Co. • Bimonthly. Edited for buyers of private label, controlled packer, and generic-labeled products. Concentrates on food, health and beauty aids, and general merchandise.

## TRADE/PROFESSIONAL ASSOCIATIONS

Private Label Manufacturers Association. 630 3rd Ave., New York, NY 10017. Phone: (212)972-3131; Fax: (212)983-1382; Email: info@plma.com • URL: http://plma.com • Membership consists of manufacturers, brokers, suppliers, and consultants. Educates consumers on the quality and value of private label or store brand products; promotes private label industry. Compiles statistics; conducts research programs for members.

# PRIVATE SCHOOLS

*See also* SCHOOLS

## CD-ROM DATABASES

*ERIC SilverPlatter.* U.S. Department of Education Institute of Education Sciences Education Resources Information Center. • Opinion papers, evaluations, speeches.

## DIRECTORIES

*Schools (Dancing) Directory.* InfoGroup Inc. • Annual. Number of listings: 14,474. Entries include: Name, address, phone, size of advertisement, name of owner or manager, number of employees, year first in "Yellow Pages." Compiled from telephone company "Yellow Pages," nationwide.

## ONLINE DATABASES

*ERIC.* U.S. Department of Education Institute of Education Sciences Educational Resources Information Center. • Funded by the U.S. Department of Education, Institute of Education Sciences (formerly Office of Educational Research and Improvement). Provides access to more than one million online records covering education-related journal and report literature, 1966 to date. Updating is monthly. Inquire as to online cost and availability.

## PERIODICALS AND NEWSLETTERS

*Independent School.* National Association of Independent Schools. • 3/year. $54 Nonmembers. An open forum for exchange of information about elementary and secondary education in general, and independent education in particular.

## TRADE/PROFESSIONAL ASSOCIATIONS

National Association of Independent Schools. 1129 20th St. NW, Ste. 800, Washington, DC 20036-3425. Phone: (202)973-9700; Fax: (888)316-3862 or (202)973-9790; Email: info@nais.org • URL: http://www.nais.org • Independent elementary and secondary school members; regional associations of independent schools and related associations. Provides curricular and administrative research and services. Conducts educational programs; compiles statistics.

# PRIVATIZATION

## ABSTRACTS AND INDEXES

*Index to Legal Periodicals and Books.* H.W. Wilson Co. • Monthly. $490.00 per year. Quarterly and annual cumulations.

---

**For publishers' addresses, refer to SOURCES CITED section at the back of the book.**

## TRADE/PROFESSIONAL ASSOCIATIONS

Citizens for a Sound Economy. 1250 H St. NW, Ste. 700, Washington, DC 20005-3908. Phone: 888-564-6273 or (202)783-3870 or (202)942-7649; Fax: (202)783-4687; Email: cse@cse.org • URL: http://www.cse.org • Absorbed Council for a Competitive Economy and Tax Foundation.

National Council for Public-Private Partnerships. 2000 15th St. NW, Ste. 200, Washington, DC 20005. Phone: (202)962-0555; Fax: (202)289-7499; Email: ncppp@ncppp.org • URL: http://www.ncppp.org • Promotes private ownership of public services. Formerly Privitization Council, Inc.

# PRIZES

*See* CONTESTS, PRIZES, AND AWARDS

# PROCEDURE MANUALS

*See also* TECHNICAL WRITING

## ENCYCLOPEDIAS AND DICTIONARIES

*BLR Job Descriptions Encyclopedia.* Business & Legal Resources, Inc. • $299 Individuals. $299.00. Two volumes. More than 700 prewritten job descriptions.

## PERIODICALS AND NEWSLETTERS

*Technical Communication.* Society for Technical Communication. • Quarterly. Includes articles about the practical application of technical communication.

# PROCESS CONTROL EQUIPMENT

*See* CONTROL EQUIPMENT INDUSTRY

# PROCESSED FOOD INDUSTRY

*See also* FOOD INDUSTRY

## ABSTRACTS AND INDEXES

*Food Science and Technology Abstracts.* Ovid Technologies Inc. • Monthly. $1,780.00 per year. Provides worldwide coverage of the literature of food technology and food production.

*Foods Adlibra: Key to the World's Food Literature.* General Mills, Inc. Foods Adlibra Publications. • Semimonthly. $240.00 per year. Provides journal citations and abstracts to the literature of food technology and packaging.

*NTIS Alerts: Agriculture & Food.* U.S. Department of Commerce National Technical Information Service. • Biweekly. $130 per year. Covers agricultural economics, horticulture, fisheries, veterinary medicine, food technology, and related subjects.

## ALMANACS AND YEARBOOKS

*Almanac of the Canning, Freezing, Preserving Industries.* Food Institute. • Annual. $110 Individuals Hard Copy mail delivery or pdf email from publisher. Contains U.S. food laws and regulations and detailed production statistics.

## DIRECTORIES

*Food Processing Guide and Directory.* Putman Media Inc. • Annual. $90. Lists over 5,390 food ingredient and equipment manufacturers.

*Major Food and Drink Companies of the World.* Cengage Learning Inc. • 12th edition. eBook. Published by Graham & Whiteside. Contains profiles and trade names for more than 9,200

important food and beverage companies in various countries. In addition to foods, includes both alcoholic and nonalcoholic drink products.

*Plunkett's Food Industry Almanac.* Plunkett Research Ltd. • $349.99 Individuals print + online. Covers: 340 leading companies in the global food industry. Entries include: Name, address, phone, fax, and key executives. Also includes analysis and information on trends, technology, and statistics in the field.

*World Food Marketing Directory.* Euromonitor International Business Reference Div. • $475 Individuals. Covers: Over 2,000 retailers and wholesalers, 1,500 manufacturers, over 2,000 international and European organizations, statistical agencies, trade journals and associations, databases, and trade fairs in the grocery and food industries worldwide. Entries include: Company name, address, phone, telex, names of parent company and subsidiaries, number of employees, financial data, products and brand names handled; retailers and wholesalers include type of outlet, names and titles of key personnel.

## ONLINE DATABASES

*Food Science and Technology Abstracts (online).* IFIS North American Desk. • Produced by International Food Information Service. Provides about 500,000 online citations, with abstracts, to the international literature of food science, technology, commodities, engineering, and processing. Approximately 2,000 periodicals are covered. Time period is 1969 to date, with monthly updates. Inquire as to online cost and availability.

## PERIODICALS AND NEWSLETTERS

*Food Manufacturing.* Advantage Business Media L.L.C. • 9/year. $54 Individuals. Edited for food processing operations managers and food engineering managers. Includes end-of-year *Food Products and Equipment Literature Review.*

*Food Processing.* Putman Media Inc. • Monthly. $89 others. Edited for executive and operating personnel in the food processing industry.

*Food Processing Newsletter.* Putman Media Inc. • Weekly. $100 Individuals. Covers food processing industry news and trends.

*National Packing News.* National Packing News. • Description: Discusses topics that affect the food processing industry in the nation, including production, marketing, new developments and products, new plants and plant expansions, and professional appointments. Recurring features include news of research, statistics, book reviews, and obituaries. **Remarks:** Incorporates the former Eastern Packing News and Western Packing News.

*Prepared Foods.* BNP Media. • Monthly. Edited for food manufacturing management, marketing, and operations personnel.

## RESEARCH CENTERS AND INSTITUTES

Food Industries Center. Ohio State University, 110 Parker Food Science & Technology Bldg., 2015 Fyffe Rd., Columbus, OH 43210. Phone: (614)292-6281; Fax: (614)292-0218; Email: fst@osu.edu • URL: http://www.fst.ohio-state.edu.

Institute of Food Science. Cornell University, 114 Stocking Hall, Ithaca, NY 14853-7201. Phone: (607)255-7900; Fax: (607)254-4868; Email: ddm2@cornell.edu • URL: http://www.nysaes.cornell.edu/cifs • Research areas include the chemistry and processing of food commodities, food processing engineering, food packaging, and nutrition.

Michigan State University - Institute for Food Laws and Regulations. G.M. Trout Food Science and Human Nutrition Bldg., 469 Wilson Rd., Ste. 139, East Lansing, MI 48824. Phone: (517)355-8295; Fax: (517)432-1492; Email: iflr@msu.edu • URL: http://www.iflr.msu.edu • Conducts research on the food

industry, including processing, packaging, marketing, and new products.

National Food Processors Association Research Foundation. 1350 I (Eye) St. NW, Ste. 300, Washington, DC 20005. Phone: (202)639-5900; Fax: (202)639-5932; Email: nfpa@gmaonline.org • URL: http://www.gmaonline.org • Conducts research on food processing engineering, chemistry, microbiology, sanitation, preservation aspects, and public health factors.

# PROCUREMENT, GOVERNMENT

*See* GOVERNMENT PURCHASING

# PRODUCE INDUSTRY

*See* VEGETABLE INDUSTRY

# PRODUCT DESIGN

*See* DESIGN IN INDUSTRY

# PRODUCT DEVELOPMENT

*See* NEW PRODUCTS

# PRODUCT LIABILITY

*See* PRODUCT SAFETY AND LIABILITY

# PRODUCT MANAGEMENT

*See* MARKETING

# PRODUCT QUALITY

*See* QUALITY OF PRODUCTS

# PRODUCT RATING RESEARCH

*See* QUALITY OF PRODUCTS

# PRODUCT SAFETY AND LIABILITY

## ABSTRACTS AND INDEXES

*Applied Science and Technology Index.* EBSCO Publishing Inc. • 11/year. Indexes a wide variety of English language technical, industrial, and engineering periodicals.

*Index to Legal Periodicals and Books.* H.W. Wilson Co. • Monthly. $490.00 per year. Quarterly and annual cumulations.

## CD-ROM DATABASES

*Consumer Health Complete.* EBSCO Publishing Inc. • Full text of more than 250 health references, health diagrams, videos, pamphlets.

## DIRECTORIES

*Product Safety Consultants Directory.* InfoGroup Inc. • Annual. Number of listings: 2,727. Entries include: Name, address, phone, size of advertisement, name of owner or manager, number of employees, year first in "Yellow Pages." Compiled from telephone company "Yellow Pages," nationwide.

728

For publishers' addresses, refer to SOURCES CITED section at the back of the book.

## ONLINE DATABASES

*I.I.I. Data Base Search.* Insurance Information Institute. • Provides online citations and abstracts of insurance-related literature in magazines, newspapers, trade journals, and books. Emphasis is on property and casualty insurance issues, including highway safety, product safety, and environmental liability. Inquire as to online cost and availability.

## OTHER SOURCES

*Pharmaceutical Litigation Reporter: The National Journal of Record of Pharmaceutical Litigation.* Andrews Publications. • Monthly. $775.00 per year. Newsletter. Reports on a wide variety of legal cases involving the pharmaceutical and medical device industries. Includes product liability lawsuits.

*Product Liability.* ALM Media Properties LLC. • $515. Covers product liability litigation as viewed by both the plaintiff and the defendant. Provides detailed discussion of pre-trial and trial procedures. (Law Journal Press).

## PERIODICALS AND NEWSLETTERS

*Business Products Industry Report.* Independent Office Products and Furniture Dealers Association. • Semimonthly. $95 Nonmembers. Magazine serving the business products industry.

*Consumer Product Safety Review.* U. S. Government Printing Office. • Quarterly. $18.00 per year. Issued by the U. S. Consumer Product Safety Commission.

*FDA Consumer.* U. S. Government Printing Office. • Bimonthly. $14.00 per year. Issued by the U. S. Food and Drug Administration. Provides consumer information about FDA regulations and product safety.

*Pharmaceutical and Medical Device Law Bulletin.* ALM Media Properties LLC. • Monthly. $199.00 per year. Newsletter. Edited for lawyers concerned with drug product or medical device litigation. Contains industry news items of special interest, reports on new products, legal case summaries, Food and Drug Administration actions, patent issues, and related news reports. (A Law Journal Newsletter, formerly published by Leader Publications).

*Product Liability Law and Strategy.* ALM Media Properties LLC. • Monthly. $475. Contains product liability verdict and settlement reports, legislative proposal analysis, and strategies for both the plaintiff's counsel and the defendant's counsel. (A Law Journal Newsletter, formerly published by Leader Publications).

*Product Safety Letter.* Washington Business Information Inc. • Description: Follows the actions of the Consumer Product Safety Commission and other regulatory agencies and monitors developments and trends in the manufacturing industry. Offers "inside information about major regulatory trends, actions, opinions, and ideas." Spotlights stringent new rules which affect the production and sale of many common items. Recurring features include news of research and reports of meetings.

## RESEARCH CENTERS AND INSTITUTES

George Mason University - Law and Economics Center. School of Law, Hazel Hall, Ste. 440, 3301 Fairfax Dr., Arlington, VA 22201. Phone: (703)993-8040; Fax: (703)993-8181 or (703)993-8088; Email: hnbutler@gmu.edu • URL: http://www.masonlec.org • Research fields include product liability law.

## TRADE/PROFESSIONAL ASSOCIATIONS

International Board of Certification of Safety Managers. 173 Tucker Rd., Ste. 202, Helena, AL 35080. Phone: (205)664-8412; Fax: (205)663-9541; Email: info@ibfcsm.org • URL: http://www.ibfcsm.org • Evaluates qualifications of product safety managers. Formerly International Product Safety Management Certification Board.

The Product Liability Alliance. National Associa-

tion of Wholesaler-Distributors, 1325 G St. NW, Ste. 1000, Washington, DC 20005. Phone: (202)872-0885; Fax: (202)785-0586; Email: naw@naw.org • Seeks enactment of federal product liability tort reform legislation. Supports and coordinates members' efforts in gaining passage of a product liability law. Coalition of trade associations, manufacturers, and nonmanufacturing product sellers. Works with the business community to develop suggestions and guidelines for such a law.

# PRODUCT TESTING

*See* QUALITY OF PRODUCTS

# PRODUCTION CONTROL

*See also* INVENTORY CONTROL; QUALITY CONTROL

## PERIODICALS AND NEWSLETTERS

*Production.* Gardner Business Media, Inc. • Covers the latest manufacturing management issues. Discusses the strategic and financial implications of various tecnologies as they impact factory management, quality and competitiveness.

*Production and Inventory Management Journal.* APICS. • Quarterly.

## TRADE/PROFESSIONAL ASSOCIATIONS

APICS. 8430 W Bryn Mawr Ave., Ste. 1000, Chicago, IL 60631. Phone: 800-444-2742 or (773)867-1777; Fax: (773)639-3000; Email: service@apics.org • URL: http://www.apics.org • Members are professional resource managers.

Global Sourcing Council. 750 Third Ave., 11th Fl., New York, NY 10017. Phone: (631)398-3366; Email: sanjaysrr@gmail.com • URL: http://www.gscouncil.org • Supports people and organizations with an interest in the social and economic effects of sourcing. Serves as a forum for the discussion of the social and economic impacts of global sourcing. Provides opportunities for professional networking and business development. Addresses issues relevant to any company involved in global business operations.

# PRODUCTION ENGINEERING

*See* INDUSTRIAL ENGINEERING

# PRODUCTION MANAGEMENT

*See* OPERATIONS MANAGEMENT

# PRODUCTIVITY

## ABSTRACTS AND INDEXES

*NTIS Alerts: Manufacturing Technology.* U.S. Department of Commerce National Technical Information Service. • Biweekly. $130 per year. Covers computer-aided design and manufacturing (CAD/CAM), engineering materials, quality control, machine tools, robots, lasers, productivity, and related subjects.

## E-BOOKS

*Different Thinking.* Cengage Learning Inc. • 2009. eBook. Published by Kogan Page. Presents practical tools and strategies your company can use to help you drastically increase productivity and earning power. The authors show you how you can question your strategies, create new markets, give your

products a radical makeover, and invent innovative new price and profit models to give you a competitive advantage over your rivals.

## INTERNET DATABASES

*Summary of Commentary on Current Economic Conditions by Federal Reserve District.* Board of Governors of the Federal Reserve System. Phone: (202)452-3000; Fax: (202)452-3819 • URL: http://www.federalreserve.gov/publications.htm • 8/year. Free Web site provides current "anecdotal information" eight times a year on economic conditions within each of the 12 Federal Reserve Districts, plus an extensive national *Summary.* Text is based on the opinions of bank officials, business executives, economists, financial market experts, and others. Typically contains views of consumer spending, manufacturing, services, credit, employment, prices, wages, and the economy in general. Usually referred to as the Beige Book.

## PERIODICALS AND NEWSLETTERS

*Lean Manufacturing Advisor: Techniques and Technologies Supporting Lean Manufacturing and TPM.* Productivity Inc. • Monthly. $167.00 per year. Formerly Productivity.

## RESEARCH CENTERS AND INSTITUTES

Center for Quality and Productivity. University of North Texas, College of Business Administration, 1155 Union Cir., No. 311160, Denton, TX 76203. Phone: (940)369-8476; Email: prybutok@unt.edu • URL: http://www.coba.unt.edu • Fields of research include the management of quality systems and statistical methodology.

U.S. Bureau of Labor Statistics - Office of Productivity and Technology - Foreign Labor Statistics Division. 2 Massachusetts Ave. NE, Ste. 2150, Washington, DC 20212-0001. Phone: (202)691-5654; Fax: (202)691-5679 • URL: http://www.bls.gov/fls/ • Labor conditions and developments abroad. Research involves the development of internationally comparable economic-statistical measures covering the labor force and unemployment, productivity, and labor costs. This information is used to assess current economic trends abroad that may affect U.S. performance; inform government and private officials of foreign developments that might affect U.S. policy; review foreign experience for possible application domestically; aid in the appraisal of U.S. competitiveness in foreign and domestic markets; and provide labor information to individuals, corporations, labor unions, and others concerned with foreign investment and development.

University of Wisconsin—Madison - Center for Quality and Productivity Improvement. 3130 Engineering Centers Bldg., 1550 Engineering Dr., Madison, WI 53706. Phone: (608)263-2520; Fax: (608)263-1425; Email: carayon@ie.engr.wisc.edu • URL: http://cqpi.engr.wisc.edu • Research areas include quality management and industrial engineering.

W.E. Upjohn Institute for Employment Research. 300 S Westnedge Ave., Kalamazoo, MI 49007-4686. Phone: 888-227-8569 or (269)343-5541; Fax: (269)343-7310; Email: communications@upjohn.org • URL: http://www.upjohninstitute.org • Research fields include unemployment, unemployment insurance, worker's compensation, labor productivity, profit sharing, the labor market, economic development, earnings, training, and other areas related to employment.

## STATISTICS SOURCES

*Report on the American Workforce.* U. S. Government Printing Office. • Annual. Issued by the U. S. Department of Labor (www.dol.gov). Appendix contains tabular statistics, including employment, unemployment, price indexes, consumer expenditures, employee benefits (retirement, insurance, vacation, etc.), wages, productivity, hours of work, and occupational injuries. Annual figures are shown for up to 50 years.

## TRADE/PROFESSIONAL ASSOCIATIONS

APQC. 123 N Post Oak Ln., Houston, TX 77024. Phone: 800-776-9676 or (713)681-4020; Fax: (713)681-8578; Email: apqcinfo@apqc.org • URL: http://www.apqc.org • Resource for process and performance improvement. Helps organizations adapt to rapidly changing environments, build new and better ways to work, and succeed in a competitive marketplace. Focuses on productivity, knowledge management, benchmarking, and quality improvement initiatives. Works with member organizations to identify best practices, discover effective methods of improvement, broadly disseminate findings, and connect individuals with one another and the knowledge and tools they need to succeed. Serves approximately 500 organizations worldwide in all sectors of business, education, and government.

Association of Productivity Specialists. 521 5th Ave., Ste. 1700, New York, NY 10175. Email: inquire@apsworld.org • URL: http://www.apsworld. org • Firms and individuals engaged in the Productivity Specialist segment of the management consultant profession. Seeks to promote greater public knowledge of the productivity specialist profession (productivity specialists develop management systems to achieve business objectives in numerous areas, including production levels, quality performance, inventory costs, operating costs and manufacturing lead times); to improve professional capabilities of member firms by promoting educational and research and development programs; to cooperate with federal, state, and local government agencies on matters of interest to members; to help member firms improve, develop and review skills of their professional employees. Has established standards of ethics and competence for productivity specialists.

China Productivity Center. 2F, No. 79 Xintai 5th Rd., Section 1, Xizhi District, Taipei 221, Taiwan. Phone: 886 2 2698-2989; Fax: 886 2 2698-2976; Email: service@cpc.org.tw • URL: http://www.cpc. org.tw.

Hong Kong Productivity Council. HKPC Bldg., 78 Tat Chee Ave., Hong Kong, Hong Kong, China. Phone: 852 27885678; Fax: 852 27885900 • URL: http://www.hkpc.org • Representatives of management, labor, academia, the professions, and government agencies. Promotes productivity excellence through the provision of integrated support across the value chain of Hong Kong firms. Defines productivity as "the effective use of innovation and resources to increase the value-added content of products and services." Provides services in four major areas: manufacturing technologies, management systems, information technologies, and environmental technologies.

National Productivity and Competitiveness Council. 4th Fl. Alexander House, Cybercity, Ebene City, Mauritius. Phone: 230 4677700; Fax: 230 4673838; Email: natpro@intnet.mu • URL: http://www. npccmauritius.com • Generating consensus and building innovation capacity to move to a higher growth path. Hosts seminars and assemblies.

National Productivity Council. Utpadakta Bhavan, 5-6 Institutional Area, Lodhi Rd., New Delhi 110 003, Delhi, India. Phone: 91 11 24690331; Fax: 91 11 24615002; Email: npcinfo@npcindia.gov.in • URL: http://www.npcindia.gov.in • Represents professionals in the field of productivity. Promotes increased efficiency in all aspects of Indian economic activity. Conducts research, gathers and disseminates information.

Productivity Association of Pakistan. Natl. Productivity Organization, Ministry of Industries, Software Technology Park, 2nd Fl., Constitution Ave., Islamabad, Pakistan. Phone: 92 51 2823304 or 92 51 2823305; Fax: 92 51 2823309; Email: info@ npo.gov.pk • URL: http://www.npo.gov.pk/ productivity-association • Seeks to promote and increase productivity by utilizing the knowledge, experience, expertise and resources of members. Aims to strengthen networking activities with public and private sector organizations. Provides a platform for the exchange of information and knowledge that are of strategic importance to research and development.

Singapore Productivity Association. 11 Eunos Rd. 8, No. 08-01, Singapore 408601, Singapore. Phone: 65 62783344; Fax: 65 62725095; Email: customersvc@spa.org.sg • URL: http://www.spa. org.sg • Promotes the active involvement of organizations and individuals in the productivity movement. Encourages the spread of productivity and techniques.

The Work Foundation. Peter Runge House, 3 Carlton House Ter., London SW1Y 5DG, United Kingdom. Phone: 44 870 1656700 or 44 20 79763565; Email: customercentre@ theworkfoundation.com • URL: http://www. theworkfoundation.com • Works to improve the quality and productivity of U.K. work life, offers clients innovative solutions through research, consultancy, leadership and coaching programs.

World Confederation of Productivity Science. c/o Linda Carbone, Executive Secretary, 500 Sherbrooke St. W, Ste. 900, Montreal, QC, Canada H3A 3C6. Email: secretariat@wcps.info • URL: http:// www.wcps.info • Fraternal association of manufacturing and commercial enterprises and employees, government agencies, professional institutions, and researchers. Goals are to promote productivity science, advance management techniques, and improve the quality of working life and environment.

# PRODUCTS, NEW

*See* NEW PRODUCTS

# PRODUCTS, QUALITY OF

*See* QUALITY OF PRODUCTS

# PROFESSIONAL ASSOCIATIONS

*See* ASSOCIATIONS

# PROFESSIONAL CORPORATIONS

*See also* CORPORATIONS

## ABSTRACTS AND INDEXES

*Index to Legal Periodicals and Books.* H.W. Wilson Co. • Monthly. $490.00 per year. Quarterly and annual cumulations.

## HANDBOOKS AND MANUALS

*Professional Corporations and Associations.* Berrien C. Eaton. Matthew Bender and Company Inc. • Semiannual. $3,211 ebook. Detailed information on forming, operating and changing a professional corporation or association.

## OTHER SOURCES

*Business Strategies.* Wolters Kluwer Law & Business CCH. • Semimonthly. $795.00 per year. Four looseleaf volumes. Semimonthly updates. Legal, tax, and accounting aspects of business planning and decision-making. Provides information on start-ups, forms of ownership (partnerships, corporations), failing businesses, reorganizations, acquisitions, and so forth. Includes *Business Strategies Bulletin*, a monthly newsletter.

# PROFESSIONAL LIABILITY

## ABSTRACTS AND INDEXES

*Current Law Index.* Cengage Learning Inc. • $1,332 Individuals. Monthly. $1269.00 per year. Produced in cooperation with the American Association of Law Libraries. Indexes more than 900 law journals, legal newspapers, and specialty publications from the U.S., Canada, U.K., Ireland, Australia, and New Zealand.

*Index to Legal Periodicals and Books.* H.W. Wilson Co. • Monthly. $490.00 per year. Quarterly and annual cumulations.

## CD-ROM DATABASES

*Authority Health Care Law Library.* Matthew Bender and Company Inc. • Periodic updates. Price on request. Full text CD-ROM provides legal information, case law, and analysis relating to health care facilities, health insurance, longterm care, Medigap, and Medicare.

*Index to Legal Periodicals and Books.* EBSCO Publishing Inc. • Contains indexing of more than 1,400 English language legal periodicals from 1981 to date and 2,500 books.

## DIRECTORIES

*Insurance Marketplace: The Agents and Brokers Guide to Non-Standard and Special ty Lines, Aviation, Marine and International Insurance.* The Rough Notes Company Inc. • Annual. Lists specialty, excess, and surplus insurance lines.

## HANDBOOKS AND MANUALS

*Accountants' Liability.* Practising Law Institute. • $335 free shipping. Covers all aspects of accountants' professional liability issues, including depositions and court cases.

## INTERNET DATABASES

*Lexis.com Research System.* Lexis-Nexis Group. Phone: 800-227-4908 or (937)865-6800; Fax: (937)865-6909; Email: webmaster@prod.lexisnexis.com • URL: http://www.nexis.com • Fee-based Web site offers extensive searching of a wide variety of legal sources. Additional features include Daily Opinion Service, lexis.com Bookstore, Career Center, CLE Center, Law Schools, and Practice Pages ("Pages specific to areas of specialty").

## ONLINE DATABASES

*LegalTrac.* Cengage Learning Inc. • Online database. Provides indexing for approximately 875 titles of periodical literature relating to legal matters from 1980 to date. Corresponds to online *Legal Resource Index.* Inquire as to price and availability.

## OTHER SOURCES

*Andrews' Professional Liability Litigation Reporter.* Andrews Publications. • Monthly. $550.00 per year. Provides reports on lawsuits against attorneys, accountants, and investment professionals.

*Citation: Current Legal Developments Relating to Medicine and Allied Professions.* American Medical Association, Health Law Div. Citation Publishing Corp. • Semimonthly. $130.00 per year. Newsletter. Contains summaries of lawsuits affecting medical personnel or hospitals.

*Directors and Officers Liability: Prevention, Insurance, and Indemnification.* ALM Media Properties LLC. • $530 per year. Covers the legal risks faced by corporate directors and officers. (Law Journal Press).

*Hospital Liability.* ALM Media Properties LLC. • $550. Written for attorneys representing either hospitals or patients of hospitals. Covers a wide variety of legal topics relating to hospital/physician malpractice, including the expansion of HMO liability. (Law Journal Press).

## PERIODICALS AND NEWSLETTERS

*Healthcare Risk Management.* AHC Media. • Description: Analyzes specific legal cases and trends relevant to healthcare liability. Discusses malpractice, liability for patients, staff and visitor injury, injury prevention, biomedical engineering, and medical staff credentials. Also covers high-risk areas of hospitals, hospital-owned home health and physician practices, accreditation, Medicare reimbursement, physician liability, medical records, and claims management. Recurring features include interviews, statistics, news of research, guest columns, legal briefs, and commentaries.

*Medical Economics.* Advanstar Medical. • Semimonthly. $109 /year. Covers the financial, economic, insurance, administrative, and other non-clinical aspects of private medical practice. Provides investment and estate planning advice.

*Medical Economics General Surgery-Orthopedic Surgery.* Thomson Medical Economics. • Monthly. $65.00 per year. Provides information and advice on practice management (non-clinical) for surgeons. Formerly *Medical Economics for Surgeons.*

*Medical Malpractice Law and Strategy.* ALM Media Properties LLC. • Monthly. $479 per year. Covers malpractice legal issues for lawyers representing physicians and for lawyers representing patients. Includes news of judicial, legislative, and medical developments affecting malpractice strategies. (A Law Journal Newsletter, formerly published by Leader Publications).

*Professional Negligence Law Reporter.* American Association for Justice. • Description: Covers professional negligence cases, including verdicts, settlements, and court opinions. Coverage focuses on health care providers, accountants, lawyers, engineers, insurance brokers and nursing homes, among other areas. Recurring features include by-lined articles, bibliographies, and indexes.

## TRADE/PROFESSIONAL ASSOCIATIONS

Defense Research Institute. 55 W Monroe St., Ste. 2000, Chicago, IL 60603-5121. Phone: (312)795-1101; Fax: (312)795-0749 • URL: http://www.dri.org • Lawyers, claims people, adjusters, insurance companies, trade associations, corporations, and "target" defendants in civil litigation, such as doctors, pharmacists, engineers, manufacturers, and other professional and skilled personnel. Seeks to increase the knowledge and improve the skills of defense lawyers and to improve the adversary system of justice. Maintains research facilities, including files of speeches, briefs, and names of expert witnesses in various fields. Maintains Expert Witness Index.

Physician Insurers Association of America. 2275 Research Blvd., Ste. 250, Rockville, MD 20850. Phone: (301)947-9000; Fax: (301)947-9090 • URL: http://www.piaa.us • Members are cooperative physicians' professional liability insurers affiliated with state medical societies.

## PROFESSIONS

*See* OCCUPATIONS

## PROFESSORS AND INSTRUCTORS

*See* COLLEGE FACULTIES

## PROFIT SHARING

*See also* EMPLOYEE BENEFIT PLANS

## HANDBOOKS AND MANUALS

*Pension and Profit Sharing Plans for Small or Medium Size Businesses.* Aspen Publishers, Inc. • Monthly. $191.50 per year. Newsletter. Topics of interest and concern to professionals who serve small and medium size pension and profit sharing plans.

## PERIODICALS AND NEWSLETTERS

*Profit Sharing.* Plan Sponsor Council of America. • Bimonthly. Membership.

## RESEARCH CENTERS AND INSTITUTES

W.E. Upjohn Institute for Employment Research. 300 S Westnedge Ave., Kalamazoo, MI 49007-4686. Phone: 888-227-8569 or (269)343-5541; Fax: (269)343-7310; Email: communications@upjohn.org • URL: http://www.upjohninstitute.org • Research fields include unemployment, unemployment insurance, worker's compensation, labor productivity, profit sharing, the labor market, economic development, earnings, training, and other areas related to employment.

## TRADE/PROFESSIONAL ASSOCIATIONS

Plan Sponsor Council of America. 20 N Wacker Dr., Ste. 3700, Chicago, IL 60606. Phone: (312)419-1863; Fax: (312)419-1864; Email: psca@psca.org • URL: http://www.psca.org • Members are business firms with profit sharing and/or 401(K) plans. Affiliated with the Profit Sharing/401(K) Education Foundation. Formerly Profit Sharing Council of America.

## PROGRAMMED LEARNING

### PERIODICALS AND NEWSLETTERS

*Educational Technology: The Magazine for Managers of Change in Education.* Educational Technology Publications, Inc. • Bimonthly. $139.00 per year.

*Innovations in Education and Training International.* Association for Education and Training Technology. Routledge. • Quarterly. Individuals, $81.00 per year; libraries and other institutions, $290.00 per year. Provides up-to-date coverage of educational and training technologies. Formerly *Educational and Training Technology International.*

## PROGRAMMING, COMPUTER

*See* COMPUTER SOFTWARE INDUSTRY

## PROGRAMMING, LINEAR

*See* LINEAR PROGRAMMING

## PROGRAMS, TELEVISION

*See* TELEVISION PROGRAMS

## PROJECT MANAGEMENT

*See also* INDUSTRIAL MANAGEMENT

### CD-ROM DATABASES

*Applied Science & Business Periodicals Retrospective.* EBSCO Publishing Inc. • Includes citations for more than 3 million articles detailing events, issues, and trends in business and industry.

*Bibliography on the Project Manager and Project Oragnization.* Project Management Institute. • $15.

### ONLINE DATABASES

*Wilson Business Abstracts Online.* H.W. Wilson Co. • Indexes and abstracts 600 major business

periodicals, plus the *Wall Street Journal* and the business section of the *New York Times.* Indexing is from 1982, abstracting from 1990, with the two newspapers included from 1993. Updated weekly. Inquire as to online cost and availability. (*Business Periodicals Index* without abstracts is also available online.).

### PERIODICALS AND NEWSLETTERS

*Project Management Journal.* Project Management Institute. • 6/year Quarterly. $465 Institutions. Contains technical articles dealing with the interests of the field of project management.

### STATISTICS SOURCES

*Project Management Salary Survey.* Project Management Institute. • Annual. $200.00. Gives compensation data for key project management positions in North America, according to job title, level of responsibility, number of employees supervised, and various other factors. Includes data on retirement plans and benefits.

### TRADE/PROFESSIONAL ASSOCIATIONS

Association for Project Management. Ibis House, Regent Park, Summerleys Rd., Princes Risborough HP27 9LE, United Kingdom. Email: info@apm.org.uk • URL: http://www.apm.org.uk • Strives to develop and promote the professional disciplines of project and programme management for the public benefit.

Association for Project Management Hong Kong. c/o Agee Leung, 35/F Central Plaza, 18 Harbour Rd., Wan Chai, Hong Kong, China. Phone: 852 51810371; Email: agee.leung@apm.org.uk • URL: http://www.apm.org.uk/group/apm-hong-kong-branch • Aims to establish project management as the recognized profession essential for managing beneficial change in every type of business. Provides career development to project and management professionals.

Australian Institute of Project Management. Level 9, 139 Macquarie St., Sydney, NSW 2000, Australia. Phone: 61 2 82888700; Fax: 61 2 82888711; Email: info@aipm.com.au • URL: http://www.aipm.com.au • Works to promote the progress of the profession of project management.

BPM-Focus. 3640-B3 N Federal Hwy., No. 421, Lighthouse Point, FL 33064. Phone: (954)688-4922; Fax: (954)758-7219; Email: info@bpmfocus.org • URL: http://www.bpmfocus.org • Identifies and clarifies issues that are common to users of workflow, electronic commerce, knowledge management and those who are in the process of re-engineering their organizations.

College of Performance Management. 101 S Whiting St., Ste. 320, Alexandria, VA 22304. Phone: (703)370-7885; Fax: (703)370-1757 • URL: http://www.mycpm.org • Serves as a forum for the exchange of information on project management and performance measurement in business. Conducts educational programs.

International Project Management Association. PO Box 7905, 1008 AC Amsterdam, Netherlands. Phone: 31 33 2473430; Fax: 31 33 2460470; Email: info@ipma.ch • URL: http://www.ipma.ch • National project management associations in 43 countries. Liaises the international exchange of project management information and promotes the advancement of project management methods, systems, and practical application techniques. Encourages the development of and cooperates with national organizations with common interests; provides for individual participation in countries without national societies.

Iranian Institute of Project and Process Management. Jalale-Ale-Ahmad 87, Tehran, Iran. Phone: 98 21 8826 8881; Fax: 98 21 8826 8881; Email: info@ippma.ir • Works to promote project management.

Project Management Institute. 14 Campus Blvd., Newtown Square, PA 19073-3299. Phone: 855-746-4849 or (610)356-4600; Fax: (610)482-9971; Email: customercare@pmi.org • URL: http://www.pmi.org • Corporations and individuals engaged in the practice of project management; project management students and educators. Seeks to advance the study, teaching and practice of project management. Establishes project management standards; conducts educational and professional certification courses; bestows Project Management Professional credential upon qualified individuals. Offers educational seminars and global congresses.

# PROMOTION

*See* SALES PROMOTION

# PROMOTIONAL MERCHANDISE

*See* PREMIUMS

# PROOFREADING

*See* PRINTING STYLE MANUALS

# PROPANE AND BUTANE GAS INDUSTRY

*See also* NATURAL GAS; PETROLEUM INDUSTRY

## CD-ROM DATABASES

*Environment Abstracts on CD-ROM.* University Publications of America. • Quarterly. $1,295.00 per year. Contains the following CD-ROM databases: *Environment Abstracts, Energy Abstracts,* and *Acid Rain Abstracts.* Length of coverage varies.

## FINANCIAL RATIOS

*Annual Statement Studies.* Risk Management Association. • Annual. Compiled from over 280,000 financial statements.

*Annual Statement Studies: Industry Default Probabilities and Cash Flow Measures.* Risk Management Association. • Annual. $405 Nonmembers. Serves as a companion volume to the original *Annual Statement Studies.* Gives probability of default estimates on a percentage scale for more than 450 industries. Includes changes in position year-by-year for eight financial statement line items and provides percentage measures of cash flow.

## PERIODICALS AND NEWSLETTERS

*Butane-Propane News.* Butane-Propane News Inc. • Monthly. Qualified personnel, $30.00 per year.

*Oil Daily: Daily Newspaper of the Petroleum Industry.* Energy Intelligence Group. • Daily. Email, $1,595.00 per year; fax, $2,395.00 per year, online, $1,495.00 per year. Newspaper for the petroleum industry.

## STATISTICS SOURCES

*Petroleum Supply Annual.* U. S. Government Printing Office. • Annual. $78.00. Two volumes. Produced by the Energy Information Administration, U. S. Department of Energy. Contains worldwide data on the petroleum industry and petroleum products.

*Petroleum Supply Monthly.* U. S. Government Printing Office. • Monthly. Produced by the Energy Information Administration, U. S. Department of Energy. Provides worldwide statistics on a wide variety of petroleum products. Covers production, supplies, exports and imports, transportation,

refinery operations, and other aspects of the petroleum industry.

## TRADE/PROFESSIONAL ASSOCIATIONS

National Propane Gas Association. 1899 L St. NW, Ste. 350, Washington, DC 20036-4623. Phone: (202)466-7200; Fax: (202)466-7205; Email: info@npga.org • URL: http://www.npga.org/i4a/pages/index.cfm?pageid=1 • Represents the propane industry, including small businesses and large corporations engaged in the retail marketing of propane gas and appliances, producers and wholesalers of propane gas and equipment, manufacturers and fabricators of propane gas cylinders and tanks, propane transporters, and manufacturer's representatives. Works to promote the safe and increased use of propane; advocates in Congress and federal regulatory agencies for favorable environment for production, distributing, and marketing of propane gas. Develops safety standards and training materials for the safe use and distribution of propane gas.

# PROPERTY AND LIABILITY INSURANCE

*See also* CASUALTY INSURANCE; FIRE INSURANCE; MARINE INSURANCE; PROFESSIONAL LIABILITY; RISK MANAGEMENT

## ABSTRACTS AND INDEXES

*Insurance Periodicals Index.* Specials Libraries Association, Insurance and Employees Benefits Div. NILS Publishing Co. • Annual. $250.00. Compiled by the Insurance and Employee Benefits Div., Special Libraries Association. A yearly index of over 15,000 articles from about 35 insurance periodicals. Arrangement is by subject, with an index to authors.

## BIBLIOGRAPHIES

*Insurance and Employee Benefits Literature.* Special Libraries Association. • Bimonthly. $15.00 per year. Lists a wide variety of literature in all branches of the insurance industry. Includes annotations.

## ONLINE DATABASES

*I.I.I. Data Base Search.* Insurance Information Institute. • Provides online citations and abstracts of insurance-related literature in magazines, newspapers, trade journals, and books. Emphasis is on property and casualty insurance issues, including highway safety, product safety, and environmental liability. Inquire as to online cost and availability.

## OTHER SOURCES

*Best's Insurance Reports: Property-Casualty.* A.M. Best Company Inc. • Annual. $750.00. Guide to over 3,200 major property/casualty companies.

*Fire and Casualty Insurance Law Reports.* Wolters Kluwer Law & Business CCH. • $870.00 per year. Looseleaf service. Semimonthly updates.

*The Law of Liability Insurance.* Matthew Bender and Company Inc. • $395. Five looseleaf volumes. Periodic supplementation. Explains the terms and phases essential for a general understanding of liability insurance, and discusses injuries to both persons and property.

## PERIODICALS AND NEWSLETTERS

*Chartered Property and Casualty Underwriters eJournal.* Society of Chartered Property and Casualty Underwriters. • Monthly. Published by the Chartered Property and Casualty Underwriters Society (CPCU). Edited for professional insurance underwriters and agents.

*Fire, Casualty and Surety Bulletin.* • Monthly. $420.00 per year. Five looseleaf volumes.

*Insurance and Technology.* UBM L.L.C. • Monthly. $65.00 per year. Covers information technology and

systems management as applied to the operation of life, health, casualty, and property insurance companies.

*Insurance Coverage Law Bulletin.* ALM Media Properties LLC. • Monthly. $510. Provides news of property insurance claims management and coverage disputes. Edited for both legal and non-legal insurance professionals. (A Law Journal Newsletter, formerly published by Leader Publications).

*The John Liner Letter.* Standard Publishing Corp. • $245 /year. Description: Provides risk management and technical insurance advice for business firms, such as broadening coverage, cutting costs, and anticipating special insurance problems.

*National Underwriter, Property and Casualty Edition.* • Weekly. $92.00 per year.

*Risk Management.* Risk and Insurance Management Society. Risk and Insurance Management Society. • 10/year. $115 Individuals. Magazine featuring analysis, insight, and news for corporate risk managers.

*Rough Notes.* The Rough Notes Company Inc. • Monthly. $25 Individuals.

## RESEARCH CENTERS AND INSTITUTES

University of Pennsylvania - S.S. Huebner Foundation. 3000 Steinberg Hall-Dietrich Hall, 3620 Locust Walk, Philadelphia, PA 19104-6302. Phone: (215)898-9631; Fax: (215)573-2218; Email: huebner_foundation@wharton.upenn.edu • URL: http://www.huebnergeneva.org/huebner • Awards grants for research in various areas of insurance.

## STATISTICS SOURCES

*Property-Casualty Insurance Facts.* Insurance Information Institute. • Annual. $22.50. Formerly *Insurance Facts.*

*Standard & Poor's Industry Surveys.* Standard & Poor's Financial Services L.L.C. • Semiannual. $1,800.00. Two looseleaf volumes. Includes monthly *Supplements.* Provides detailed, individual surveys of 52 major industry groups. Each survey is revised on a semiannual basis. Also includes "Monthly Investment Review" (industry group investment analysis) and monthly "Trends & Projections" (economic analysis).

*U.S. Industry and Trade Outlook.* U.S. Department of Commerce National Technical Information Service. • Annual. Produced by the International Trade Administration, U.S. Department of Commerce, in a "public-private" partnership with DRI/McGraw-Hill and Standard & Poor's. Provides basic data, outlook for the current year, and "Long-Term Prospects" (five-year projections) for a wide variety of products and services. Includes high technology industries. Formerly *U.S. Industrial Outlook.*

## TRADE/PROFESSIONAL ASSOCIATIONS

American Institute for CPCU. 720 Providence Rd., Ste. 100, Malvern, PA 19355-3433. Phone: 800-644-2101 or (610)644-2100; Fax: (610)640-9576 • URL: http://www.aicpcu.org • Determines qualifications for professional certification of insurance personnel; conducts examinations and awards designation of Chartered Property Casualty Underwriter (CPCU).

American Insurance Association. 2101 L St. NW, Ste. 400, Washington, DC 20037. Phone: (202)828-7100; Fax: (202)293-1219 • URL: http://www.aiadc.org/aiapub • Represents companies providing property and casualty insurance and suretyship. Monitors and reports on economic, political, and social trends; serves as a clearinghouse for ideas, advice, and technical information. Represents members' interests before state and federal legislative and regulatory bodies; coordinates members' litigation.

National Association of Professional Insurance Agents. 400 N Washington St., Alexandria, VA 22314. Phone: (703)836-9340; Fax: (703)836-1279; Email: web@pianet.org • URL: http://www.pianet.

com • Members are independent agents in various fields of insurance. Formerly National Association of Mutual Insurance Agents.

Risk and Insurance Management Society. 1065 Ave. of the Americas, 13th Fl., New York, NY 10018. Phone: 800-713-7467 or (212)286-9292; Fax: (212)986-9716; Email: lists@rims.org • URL: http://www.rims.org • Formerly American Society of Insurance Management.

# PROPERTY MANAGEMENT

*See also* REAL ESTATE BUSINESS

## DIRECTORIES

*Property Management Association--Directory.* Property Management Association. • Annual. $50 Nonmembers. Covers: Over 539 property managers and 336 related supplier firms. Entries include: For property managers--Name, firm name, address, phone, fax, specialty. For supplier firms--Company name, name of contact, address, phone, fax.

*U.S. Real Estate Register.* Barry Inc. • Annual. $95 Individuals. Covers: Real estate departments of large national companies, industrial economic/ development organizations, utilities, real estate brokers, and railroads involved in commercial and industrial real estate development. Entries include: Company or organization name, address; many listings include name of contact.

## PERIODICALS AND NEWSLETTERS

*Building Operating Management: The National Magazine for Commercial and Institutional Buildings Construction, Renovation, Facility Management.* Trade Press Media Group. • Monthly. Free to qualified personnel.

*Buildings: The Source for Facilities Decision-Makers.* Stamats Communications Inc. • Monthly. $70.00 per year. Serves professional building ownership/management organizations.

*Housing the Elderly Report.* Community Development Services, Inc. CD Publications. • Monthly. $249.00 per year. Newsletter. Edited for retirement communities, apartment projects, and nursing homes. Covers news relative to business and property management issues.

*Managing Housing Letter.* Community Development Services, Inc. CD Publications. • Description: Provides news and advice for owners and managers of rental housing--public, private, and subsidized--including news from Washington and practical management tips. Recurring features include news of research.

*Properties.* Properties Magazine, Inc. • Monthly. $24.95 Individuals. News and features of interest to income property owners managers and related industries in Northeastern Ohio.

*Real Estate Forum.* • Ten times a year. $35.00 per year. Formerly *Better Buildings*.

## RESEARCH CENTERS AND INSTITUTES

University of California, Los Angeles - Richard S. Ziman Center for Real Estate. Gold Hall, Ste. B100, 110 Westwood Plz., Los Angeles, CA 90095-1481. Phone: (310)206-9424 or (213)825-3977; Fax: (310)267-5391 or (310)206-5455; Email: stuart. gabriel@anderson.ucla.edu • URL: http://www. anderson.ucla.edu/centers/ziman • Secondary mortgage markets, housing finance, growth management, infrastructure, corporate finance issues, and development industry.

## TRADE/PROFESSIONAL ASSOCIATIONS

Building Owners and Managers Association International. 1101 15th St. NW, Ste. 800, Washington, DC 20005-5021. Phone: 800-426-6292 or (202)408-2662; Fax: (202)326-6377; Email: info@boma.org • URL: http://www.boma.org •

Formerly National Association of Building Owners and Managers.

Community Associations Institute. 6402 Arlington Blvd., Ste. 500, Falls Church, VA 22042. Phone: 888-224-4321 or (703)970-9220; Fax: (703)970-9558; Email: cai-info@caionline.org • URL: http://www.caionline.org • Condominium and homeowner associations, cooperatives, and association-governed planned communities of all sizes and architectural types; community or property managers and management firms; individual homeowners; community association managers and management firms; public officials; and lawyers, accountants, engineers, reserve specialists, builder/developers and other providers of professional services and products for CAs. Seeks to educate and represent America's 250,000 residential condominium, cooperative and homeowner associations and related professionals and service providers. Aims to foster vibrant, responsive, competent community associations that promote harmony, community and responsible leadership.

National Apartment Association. 4300 Wilson Blvd., Ste. 400, Arlington, VA 22203. Phone: (703)518-6141; Fax: (703)248-9440; Email: webmaster@ naahq.org • URL: http://www.naahq.org • Federation of 155 state and local associations of industry professionals engaged in all aspects of the multifamily housing industry, including owners, builders, investors, developers, managers, and allied service representatives. Provides education and certification for property management executives, on-site property managers, maintenance personnel, property supervisors, and leasing agents. Offers a nationwide legislative network concerned with governmental decisions at the federal, state, and local levels.

National Property Management Association. 4025 Tampa Rd., Ste. 1203, Oldsmar, FL 34677. Phone: (813)475-6998; Fax: (813)749-0812; Email: hq@ npma.org • URL: http://www.npma.org • Aims to build leadership by educating, training and promoting standards of competency and ethical behavior in the asset management of personal property. Serves property professionals throughout the United States; members represent companies and organizations in both the public and private sectors, including scientific laboratories, universities, hospitals, public school systems, and local, state and federal government agencies.

Property Council of Australia. 11 Barrack St., Level 1, Sydney, NSW 2000, Australia. Phone: 61 2 90331900; Fax: 61 2 90331967; Email: info@ propertyoz.com.au • URL: http://www.propertyoz. com.au • Institutional investors, pension funds, property trusts, financial organizations, private investors, and developers. Represents the interests of the property sector in Australia. Seeks to increase property into an internationally competitive asset class. Participates in lobbying and advocacy activities. Offers educational programs. Conducts research; compiles statistics.

Property Management Association. 7508 Wisconsin Ave., 4th Fl., Bethesda, MD 20814. Phone: (301)657-9200; Fax: (301)907-9326; Email: info@ pma-dc.org • URL: http://www.pma-dc.org • Property management professionals who own and operate multifamily residential, commercial, retail, industrial and other income-producing properties and firms that provide goods and services used in real property management. Works to enhance the interests and welfare of property owners, managers, supervisory employees and contractors involved in the management of multifamily residential and commercial property. Provides education and a forum for exchange of ideas on efficient methods of operation and progressive policies of management.

# PROPERTY TAX

*See also* INDUSTRIAL REAL ESTATE; TAX SHELTERS

## ABSTRACTS AND INDEXES

*Index to Legal Periodicals and Books.* H.W. Wilson Co. • Monthly. $490.00 per year. Quarterly and annual cumulations.

## DIRECTORIES

*International Association of Assessing Officers Membership Directory.* International Association of Assessing Officers. • Annual. Lists about 8,500 state and local officials concerned with valuation of property tax.

## HANDBOOKS AND MANUALS

*Practical Guide to Real Estate Taxation.* David F. Windish. Wolters Kluwer Law & Business CCH. • $150 1-4 Copies. Date not set. Serves as a guide to the federal tax consequences of real estate ownership and operation. Covers mortgages, rental agreements, interest, landlord income, forms of ownership, and other tax-oriented topics.

*U.S. Master Property Tax Guide.* Wolters Kluwer Law & Business CCH. • Annual. $130.90 Quantity: 1 -4. Provides state-by-state coverage of "key property tax issues and concepts," including exemptions, assessments, taxpayer remedies, and property tax calendars.

## OTHER SOURCES

*Manufacturers' Tax Alert.* Wolters Kluwer Law & Business CCH. • Monthly $297.00 per year. Newsletter. Covers the major tax issues affecting manufacturing companies. Includes current developments in various kind of federal, state, and international taxes: sales, use, franchise, property, and corporate income.

## PERIODICALS AND NEWSLETTERS

*Property Tax Alert.* State Taxation Institute. • Description: Features updates on property tax issues. Recurring features include a calendar of events and notices of publications available.

*Real Estate Finance.* Institutional Investor Inc. Journals Group. • Bimonthly. $350.00 per year. Covers real estate for professional investors. Provides information on complex financing, legalities, and industry trends.

## RESEARCH CENTERS AND INSTITUTES

University of Illinois at Urbana-Champaign - Office of Real Estate Research. 140A Wohlers Hall, 1206 S 6th St., Champaign, IL 61820. Phone: (217)333-2278; Fax: (217)244-3102; Email: orer@illinois. edu • URL: http://business.illinois.edu/orer • Ongoing and contract studies on real estate issues, including appraisal and valuation, marketing and brokerage, environmental issues, land markets, municipal finance, property management, real estate investment, real estate financial markets, tenure choice, law, and public policy issues such as property rights, rent control, taxation, eminent domain, impact fees, etc.

University of Michigan - Stephen M. Ross School of Business - Office of Tax Policy Research. 701 Tappan St., Rm. R5380, Ann Arbor, MI 48109-1234. Phone: (734)763-3068; Fax: (734)763-4032; Email: jslemrod@umich.edu • URL: http://www.bus. umich.edu/OTPR/ • Tax policy, including compliance, capital gains, reform, international taxation, and income dynamics.

# PROPOSALS, BUSINESS

*See* BUSINESS START-UP PLANS AND PROPOSALS

---

# PROSTHETICS INDUSTRY

## ABSTRACTS AND INDEXES

*NTIS Alerts: Biomedical Technology & Human Factor Engineering.* U.S. Department of Commerce National Technical Information Service. • Biweekly. $130 per year. Covers biotechnology, ergonomics, bionics, artificial intelligence, prosthetics, and related subjects.

## FINANCIAL RATIOS

*Annual Statement Studies.* Risk Management Association. • Annual. Compiled from over 280,000 financial statements.

*Annual Statement Studies: Industry Default Probabilities and Cash Flow Measures.* Risk Management Association. • Annual. $405 Nonmembers. Serves as a companion volume to the original *Annual Statement Studies.* Gives probability of default estimates on a percentage scale for more than 450 industries. Includes changes in position year-by-year for eight financial statement line items and provides percentage measures of cash flow.

## TRADE/PROFESSIONAL ASSOCIATIONS

American Orthotic and Prosthetic Association. 330 John Carlyle St., Ste. 200, Alexandria, VA 22314. Phone: (571)431-0876; Fax: (571)431-0899; Email: info@aopanet.org • URL: http://www.aopanet.org • Represents more than 1,400 member companies that custom fit or manufacture componentry for patients with prostheses (artificial limbs) and orthoses (braces).

# PROTECTIVE SERVICES

*See* INDUSTRIAL SECURITY PROGRAMS

# PSYCHOLOGICAL TESTING

*See also* INDUSTRIAL PSYCHOLOGY; RATING OF EMPLOYEES

## ABSTRACTS AND INDEXES

*Psychological Abstracts.* American Psychological Association. • Monthly. Members, $815.00 per year; individuals and institutions, $1,207.00 per year. Covers the international literature of psychology and the behavioral sciences. Includes journals, technical reports, dissertations, and other sources.

## ALMANACS AND YEARBOOKS

*Mental Measurements Yearbook.* University of Nebraska-Lincoln Buros Institute. • Biennial. $210. Includes timely, consumer-oriented test reviews, providing evaluative information to promote and encourage informed test selection.

## BIBLIOGRAPHIES

*Tests in Print.* Linda L. Murphy and others. University of Nebraska-Lincoln Buros Institute of Mental Measurements. • Price varies. Two volumes. Lists over 4,000 testing instruments.

## DIRECTORIES

*Tests.* Cengage Learning Inc. • 2008. $105.00. 6th edition. List nearly 200 publishers for over 2,000 tests. Published by Pro-Ed Inc.

## ENCYCLOPEDIAS AND DICTIONARIES

*Gale Encyclopedia of Psychology.* Cengage Learning Inc. • 2000. $267.00. Second edition. Includes bibliographies arranged by topic and a glossary. More than 650 topics are covered.

## GENERAL WORKS

*Journal of Business and Psychology.* Business Psychology Research Institute. Springer Science-Business Media LLC. • Quarterly. $614 Institutions print. An international outlet publishing high quality

research designed to advance organizational science and practice.

## PERIODICALS AND NEWSLETTERS

*Educational and Psychological Measurement: Devoted to the Development and Application of Measures of Individual Differences.* Pine Forge Press. • Bimonthly. $1,235 Institutions Print & E-access. Offers the most current theoretical and applied papers in the measurement field.

*Journal of Business and Psychology.* Business Psychology Research Institute. Springer Science-Business Media LLC. • Quarterly. $614 Institutions print. An international outlet publishing high quality research designed to advance organizational science and practice.

*Measurement and Evaluation in Counseling and Development.* Association for Measurement and Evaluation in Counseling. American Counseling Association. • Quarterly. Free to members; nonmembers, $60.00 per year.

## TRADE/PROFESSIONAL ASSOCIATIONS

American Counseling Association. 5999 Stevenson Ave., Alexandria, VA 22304. Phone: 800-347-6647; Fax: (703)823-0252; Email: membership@counseling.org • URL: http://www.counseling.org • Counseling professionals in elementary and secondary schools, higher education, community agencies and organizations, rehabilitation programs, government, industry, business, private practice, career counseling, and mental health counseling. Conducts professional development institutes and provides liability insurance. Maintains Counseling and Human Development Foundation to fund counseling projects.

# PSYCHOLOGY, INDUSTRIAL

*See* INDUSTRIAL PSYCHOLOGY

# PUBLIC ACCOUNTANTS

*See* CERTIFIED PUBLIC ACCOUNTANTS

# PUBLIC ADMINISTRATION

*See also* CIVIL SERVICE; COMPUTERS IN GOVERNMENT; MUNICIPAL GOVERNMENT; STATE GOVERNMENT

## ABSTRACTS AND INDEXES

*PAIS International.* ProQuest L.L.C. • Monthly. $850.00 per year; cumulations three times a year. Provides topical citations to the worldwide literature of public affairs, economics, demographics, sociology, and trade. Text in English; indexed materials in English, French, German, Italian, Portuguese and Spanish.

*Sage Public Administration Abstracts.* EBSCO Publishing Inc. • Titles include Journal of Public Economics, Public Administration, and Public Administration Review.

*Social Sciences Citation Index.* Thomson Reuters Corp. • Weekly. Product is accessed via *Web of Science.*

*Social Sciences Index Retrospective: 1907-1983.* EBSCO Publishing Inc. • Indexing for 1,000,000 articles. Coverage includes international index and social sciences and humanities index.

## CD-ROM DATABASES

*PAIS International.* ProQuest L.L.C. • Monthly. $1,995.00 per year. Contains over 650,000 citations to the literature of contemporary social, political, and economic issues.

*Social Sciences Abstracts.* EBSCO Publishing Inc. •

Provides indexing from 1983 and abstracting from 1994 of more than 750 periodicals covering economics, area studies, community health, public administration, public welfare, urban studies, and many other topics related to the social sciences.

*Social Sciences Citation Index.* Thomson Reuters Corp. • Weekly. Product is accessed via *Web of Science.*

## ONLINE DATABASES

*Wilson Social Sciences Abstracts Online.* H.W. Wilson Co. • Provides online abstracting and indexing of more than 500 periodicals covering area studies, community health, public administration, public welfare, urban studies, and many other social science topics. Time period is 1994 to date for abstracts and 1983 to date for indexing, with updates weekly. Inquire as to online cost and availability.

## PERIODICALS AND NEWSLETTERS

*Administration and Society.* Pine Forge Press. • 9/year. $1,546 Institutions print. Scholarly journal concerned with public administration and the effects of bureaucracy.

*Administrative Science Quarterly.* Cornell University, Johnson Graduate School of Management. • Quarterly. $299 Institutions combined (print & e-access).

*Governing: The States and Localities.* • Monthly. $39.95 per year. Edited for state and local government officials. Covers finance, office management, computers, telecommunications, environmental concerns, etc.

*Public Administration and Development: An International Journal of Training, Research and Practice.* John Wiley and Sons, Inc., Journals Div. • 5/year. $2,038 Institutions. Focuses on administrative practice at the local, regional and national levels. International coverage. Published in England by John Wiley and Sons Ltd.

*Public Administration Review (PAR).* American Society for Public Administration. • Bimonthly. $539 Institutions U.S., print + online. Serves governmental administrators, public officials, educators, research workers, and others interested in the public management profession. Includes online edition.

*Public Risk.* Public Risk Management Association. • Monthly. $130 Individuals. Covers risk management for state and local governments, including various kinds of liabilities.

## RESEARCH CENTERS AND INSTITUTES

Cleveland State University - Center for Public Management. Urban Bldg., Rm. 120, 2121 Euclid Ave., Cleveland, OH 44115-2214. Phone: (216)687-9221; Email: k.e.obrien@csuohio.edu • URL: http://urban.csuohio.edu/publicmanagement • Finance and economics, Ohio's revenue and tax systems, economic development, and historic preservation (including tax credit support).

Louisiana State University - Public Administration Institute. Business Education Complex, Rm. 2000, Baton Rouge, LA 70803. Phone: (225)578-6743; Fax: (225)578-9078; Email: pai@lsu.edu • URL: http://business.lsu.edu/Public-Administration-Institute/Pages/About.aspx • Public administration, including studies on health policy, minority health care, economics and taxes, state and local governments, and public finance.

## TRADE/PROFESSIONAL ASSOCIATIONS

American Society for Public Administration. 1301 Pennsylvania Ave. NW, Ste. 700, Washington, DC 20004-1716. Phone: (202)393-7878; Fax: (202)638-4952; Email: info@aspanet.org • URL: http://www.aspanet.org/public • Promotes excellence in public service, including government, non-profit and private sectors, and academic community.

Public Risk Management Association. 700 S

Washington St., Ste. 218, Alexandria, VA 22314. Phone: (703)528-7701; Fax: (703)739-0200; Email: info@primacentral.org • URL: http://www. primacentral.org • Public agency risk, insurance, human resources, attorneys, and/or safety managers from cities, counties, villages, towns, school boards, and other related areas. Provides an information clearinghouse and communications network for public risk managers to share resources, ideas, and experiences. Offers information on risk, insurance, and safety management. Monitors state and federal legislative actions and court decisions that deal with immunity, tort liability, and intergovernmental risk pools. Maintains library containing current reports from governmental units on their insurance procedures, self-insurance plans, and loss control and safety programs; and copies of policy statements, job descriptions, contractual arrangements, and indemnification clauses.

# PUBLIC ASSISTANCE

*See* PUBLIC WELFARE

# PUBLIC DOCUMENTS

*See* GOVERNMENT PUBLICATIONS

# PUBLIC FINANCE

*See also* COUNTY FINANCE; FEDERAL BUDGET; MUNICIPAL FINANCE; TAXATION

## ABSTRACTS AND INDEXES

*PAIS International*. ProQuest L.L.C. • Monthly. $850.00 per year; cumulations three times a year. Provides topical citations to the worldwide literature of public affairs, economics, demographics, sociology, and trade. Text in English; indexed materials in English, French, German, Italian, Portuguese and Spanish.

*Social Sciences Citation Index*. Thomson Reuters Corp. • Weekly. Product is accessed via *Web of Science*.

*Social Sciences Index Retrospective: 1907-1983*. EBSCO Publishing Inc. • Indexing for 1,000,000 articles. Coverage includes international index and social sciences and humanities index.

## CD-ROM DATABASES

*OECD Statistical Compendium*. Organization for Economic Cooperation and Development. • Semiannual. $1,905.00 per year for 1 to 10 users. CD-ROM contains more than 730,000 monthly, quarterly, and annual time series for OECD countries, 1960 to date. Includes fully searchable data on agriculture, food, economic indicators, national accounts, employment, energy, finance, industry, technology, and foreign trade. Results can be displayed in various forms.

*PAIS International*. ProQuest L.L.C. • Monthly. $1,995.00 per year. Contains over 650,000 citations to the literature of contemporary social, political, and economic issues.

*Social Sciences Abstracts*. EBSCO Publishing Inc. • Provides indexing from 1983 and abstracting from 1994 of more than 750 periodicals covering economics, area studies, community health, public administration, public welfare, urban studies, and many other topics related to the social sciences.

*Social Sciences Citation Index*. Thomson Reuters Corp. • Weekly. Product is accessed via *Web of Science*.

## FINANCIAL RATIOS

*Financial Report of the United States Government*. U. S. Government Printing Office. • Annual. $21.00.

Issued by the U. S. Treasury Department (www. treas.gov). Presents information about the financial condition and operations of the federal government. Program accounting systems of various government agencies provide data for the report.

## INTERNET DATABASES

*Business 2.0 Web Guide to the Best Business Links*. Business 2.0 Media Inc. Phone: (415)293-4800; Email: support@business2.com • URL: http://www. business2.com/webguide • Web site presents an extensive, searchable directory of links to "the best, most informative, and authoritative web pages." Twenty main categories cover business, finance, career, company information, people, and technology topics, with thousands of subtopics, all linking to Web sites recommended by experienced business researchers. Fees: Free.

*Fedstats*. Federal Interagency Council on Statistical Policy. Phone: (202)395-7254 • URL: http://www. fedstats.gov • Web site features an efficient search facility for full-text statistics produced by more than 100 federal agencies, including the Census Bureau, the Bureau of Economic Analysis, and the Bureau of Labor Statistics. Boolean searches can be made within one agency or for all agencies combined. Links are offered to international statistical bureaus, including the UN, IMF, OECD, UNESCO, Eurostat, and 20 individual countries. Fees: Free.

*FreeLunch.com*. Economy.com, Inc. Phone: (610)696-8700; Fax: (610)696-1678 • URL: http:// www.freelunch.com • Web site provides free access to more than 200 million economic and financial data series, covering industry, demographics, labor markets, prices, retail sales, government spending, trade, interest rates, housing starts, the stock market, etc. Data is available in either chart or table form. Searching is offered. Free, but registration required. Economy.com, Inc. also offers fee-based economic analysis at *The Dismal Scientist* site (www.dismal. com).

## ONLINE DATABASES

*Wilson Social Sciences Abstracts Online*. H.W. Wilson Co. • Provides online abstracting and indexing of more than 500 periodicals covering area studies, community health, public administration, public welfare, urban studies, and many other social science topics. Time period is 1994 to date for abstracts and 1983 to date for indexing, with updates weekly. Inquire as to online cost and availability.

## PERIODICALS AND NEWSLETTERS

*American Banker: The Financial Services Daily*. SourceMedia Inc. • Daily. $895.00 per year. Provides news of banking, investment products, mortgages, credit unions, finance, bank technology, and legal developments.

*Journal of Government Financial Management*. Association of Government Accountants. • Quarterly. $95 Individuals. *Government Accountants Journal*.

*Project Finance: The Magazine for Global Development*. American Educational Systems. • 11 times a year. $740.00 per year. Includes print and online editions. Provides articles on the financing of the infrastructure (transportation, utilities, communications, the environment, etc). Coverage is international. Supplements available *World Export Credit Guide* and *Project Finance Book of Lists*. Formed by the merger of *Infrastructure Finance* and *Project and Trade Finance*.

*Public Finance Review*. Pine Forge Press. • Bimonthly. $1,223 Institutions print & e-access. Public economy journal. Formerly *Public Finance Quarterly*.

*U.S. Banker*. SourceMedia Inc. • Monthly. $65.00 per year. Edited for bank executives and managers. Covers a wide variety of banking and financial topics.

## STATISTICS SOURCES

*Revenue Statistics*. Organisation for Economic Cooperation and Development Publications and Information Center. • Annual. $65.00. Presents data on government revenues in OECD countries, classified by type of tax and level of government. Text in English and French.

*Statistical Information on the Financial Services Industry*. American Bankers Association. • Annual. Members, $150.00; non-members, $275.00. Presents a wide variety of data relating to banking and financial services, including consumer economics, personal finance, credit, government loans, capital markets, and international banking.

*Survey of Current Business*. U. S. Government Printing Office. • Published by Bureau of Economic Analysis, U. S. Department of Commerce. Presents a wide variety of business and economic data.

*Treasury Bulletin*. U. S. Government Printing Office. • Quarterly. $51 List Price. Issued by the Financial Management Service, U. S. Treasury Department. Provides data on the federal budget, government securities and yields, the national debt, and the financing of the federal government in general.

## TRADE/PROFESSIONAL ASSOCIATIONS

Argentine Fiscal Associations. IFLYSIB Calle 59, 789, CC 565, B19 00BTE La Plata, Argentina. Phone: 54 221 4254904; Fax: 54 221 4257317; Email: afa@iflysib.unlp.edu.ar • URL: http://www2. ib.edu.ar/afa • Promotes the study and advancement of international and comparative law with regards to public finance, specifically international, comparative fiscal law and the financial and economic aspects of taxation.

Association of Government Accountants. 2208 Mt. Vernon Ave., Alexandria, VA 22301-1314. Phone: 800-AGA-7211 or (703)684-6931; Fax: (703)548-9367; Email: agamembers@agacgfm.org • URL: http://www.agacgfm.org • Members are employed by federal, state, county, and city government agencies. Includes accountants, auditors, budget officers, and other government finance administrators and officials.

Citizens for a Sound Economy. 1250 H St. NW, Ste. 700, Washington, DC 20005-3908. Phone: 888-564-6273 or (202)783-3870 or (202)942-7649; Fax: (202)783-4687; Email: cse@cse.org • URL: http:// www.cse.org • Absorbed Council for a Competitive Economy and Tax Foundation.

European Organisation of Supreme Audit Institutions. c/o Ramon Alvarez de Miranda, Secretary General, Fuencarral 81, 28004 Madrid, Spain. Phone: 34 91 446 04 66; Fax: 34 91 593 38 94; Email: eurosai@tcu.es • URL: http://www. eurosai.org • Promotes professional and technical understanding of audit and public finance; works to secure unification of terminology in the field of audit of public finance.

# PUBLIC HOUSING

*See* HOUSING

# PUBLIC LIBRARIES

*See* LIBRARIES

# PUBLIC OPINION

## ABSTRACTS AND INDEXES

*Business Periodicals Index Retrospective*. EBSCO Publishing Inc. • 11/year. Quarterly and annual cumulations.

*PAIS International*. ProQuest L.L.C. • Monthly. $850.00 per year; cumulations three times a year.

Provides topical citations to the worldwide literature of public affairs, economics, demographics, sociology, and trade. Text in English; indexed materials in English, French, German, Italian, Portuguese and Spanish.

*Social Sciences Citation Index.* Thomson Reuters Corp. • Weekly. Product is accessed via *Web of Science.*

*Social Sciences Index Retrospective: 1907-1983.* EBSCO Publishing Inc. • Indexing for 1,000,000 articles. Coverage includes international index and social sciences and humanities index.

### CD-ROM DATABASES

*PAIS International.* ProQuest L.L.C. • Monthly. $1,995.00 per year. Contains over 650,000 citations to the literature of contemporary social, political, and economic issues.

*Social Sciences Abstracts.* EBSCO Publishing Inc. • Provides indexing from 1983 and abstracting from 1994 of more than 750 periodicals covering economics, area studies, community health, public administration, public welfare, urban studies, and many other topics related to the social sciences.

*Social Sciences Citation Index.* Thomson Reuters Corp. • Weekly. Product is accessed via *Web of Science.*

### INTERNET DATABASES

*Pew Research Center for the People and the Press.* Pew Charitable Trusts. Phone: (202)293-3126; Fax: (202)293-2569; Email: mailprc@people-press.org • URL: http://www.people-press.org • Free Web site includes public opinion poll "Reports by Topic." Five broad subject areas cover business, social issues, foreign policy, news media, and politics. Searching is offered within each of these broad areas, and there are links to other major sources of public opinion poll results ("FYI Other Polls").

### ONLINE DATABASES

*Wilson Business Abstracts Online.* H.W. Wilson Co. • Indexes and abstracts 600 major business periodicals, plus the *Wall Street Journal* and the business section of the *New York Times.* Indexing is from 1982, abstracting from 1990, with the two newspapers included from 1993. Updated weekly. Inquire as to online cost and availability. (*Business Periodicals Index* without abstracts is also available online.).

*Wilson Social Sciences Abstracts Online.* H.W. Wilson Co. • Provides online abstracting and indexing of more than 500 periodicals covering area studies, community health, public administration, public welfare, urban studies, and many other social science topics. Time period is 1994 to date for abstracts and 1983 to date for indexing, with updates weekly. Inquire as to online cost and availability.

### PERIODICALS AND NEWSLETTERS

*AAPOR Newsletter.* American Association for Public Opinion Research. • Semiannual Quarterly. Description: Publishes news of the Association. Recurring features include a president's column, new member list, and personal notes.

*Polling Report: An Independent Survey of Trends Affecting Elections, Government, and Business.* Polling Report Inc. • Biweekly. $195 Individuals. Reports on the results of a wide variety of public opinion polls.

*Public Opinion Quarterly.* American Association for Public Opinion Research. The University of Chicago Press, Journals Div. • Quarterly. $53 Individuals.

*Public Pulse: Roper's Authoritative Report on What Americans are Thinking, Doing, and Buying.* GfK SE. • Monthly. $297.00. Newsletter. Contains news of surveys of American attitudes, values, and behavior. Each issue includes a research supplement giving "complete facts and figures behind each survey question.".

*World Opinion Update.* Survey Research Consultants International, Inc. Survey Research Consultants International Inc. • Description: Gives tabular results of recent public opinion polls conducted in many countries on international public affairs subjects: sociological, political, economic, military, and religious. Recurring features include statistics.

### RESEARCH CENTERS AND INSTITUTES

Rutgers University - Eagleton Institute of Politics - Eagleton Center for Public Interest Polling. 191 Ryders Ln., New Brunswick, NJ 08901. Phone: (732)932-9384; Fax: (732)932-6778; Email: redlawsk@rutgers.edu • URL: http://eagletonpoll.rutgers.edu • Provides survey research and program evaluation services.

### TRADE/PROFESSIONAL ASSOCIATIONS

National Council on Public Polls. 1425 Broad St., Ste. 7, Clifton, NJ 07013. Phone: 800-786-8000 or (973)857-8500; Fax: (973)857-8578; Email: info@ncpp.org • URL: http://www.ncpp.org • Members are public opinion polling organizations.

# PUBLIC RELATIONS AND PUBLICITY

*See also* ADVERTISING

### INTERNET DATABASES

*EBSCO Information Services.* EBSCO Publishing Inc. 10 Estes St., Ipswich, MA 01938-2106. Phone: 800-653-2726 or (978)356-6500; Fax: (978)356-6565; Email: information@ebscohost.com • URL: http://www.ebscohost.com • Fee-based Web site providing Internet access to a wide variety of databases, including business-related material. Full text is available for many periodical titles, with daily updates. Fees: Apply.

*InSite 2.* Intelligence Data/Thomson Financial. Phone: 800-654-0393 or (617)856-1890; Fax: (617)737-3182; Email: intelligence.data@tfn.com • URL: http://www.insite2.gale.com/ • Fee-based Web site consolidates information in a "Base Pack" consisting of Business InSite, Market InSite, and Company InSite. Optional databases are Consumer InSite, Health and Wellness InSite, Newsletter InSite, and Computer InSite. Includes fulltext content from more than 2,500 trade publications, journals, newsletters, newspapers, analyst reports, and other sources. Continuous updating. Formerly produced by The Gale Group.

*ProQuest.* ProQuest L.L.C. 789 E Eisenhower Pkwy., Ann Arbor, MI 48106-1346. Phone: 800-521-0600 or (734)761-4700; Fax: (734)662-4554; Email: info@proquest.com • URL: http://www.proquest.com • Fee-based Web site providing Internet access to more than 3,000 periodicals, newspapers, and other publications. Many items are available full-text, with daily updates. Includes extensive corporate and financial information. Fees: Apply.

### PERIODICALS AND NEWSLETTERS

*Communication Briefings: A Monthly Idea Source for Decision Makers.* Briefings Publishing Group. • Monthly. $97. Presents useful ideas for communication, public relations, customer service, human resources, and employee training.

*Communication World: The Magazine for Communication Professionals.* International Association of Business Communicators. • Emphasis is on public relations, media relations, corporate communication, and writing.

*PR News.* Access Intelligence L.L.C. • Weekly. $1,049 Individuals. Provides information and knowledge to handle any program with the best tools and insights at hand.

*Public Relations.* Access Intelligence L.L.C. •

Biweekly. $397.00 per year. Newsletter on public relations and client communications for the healthcare industry. Incorporates (Healthcare PR and Marketing News).

*Public Relations Quarterly.* Hudson Associates. • Quarterly. $65.00 per year. Opinion articles and case studies on the theory and practice of public relations for and by leading practitioners and academicians.

*Public Relations Review: Journal of Research and Comment.* Elsevier. • 5/year. $228 Individuals. Contains articles based on empirical research undertaken by professionals and academics in the field of public relations.

*Public Relations Strategist: Issues and Trends That Affect Management.* Public Relations Society of America. • Quarterly. $150 U.S.. Provides public relations advice for corporate and government executives.

### TRADE/PROFESSIONAL ASSOCIATIONS

Public Relations Society of America. 33 Maiden Ln., 11th Fl., New York, NY 10038-5150. Phone: (212)460-1400; Fax: (212)995-0757 or (212)995-5024; Email: hq@prsa.org • URL: http://www.prsa.org • Absorbed American Public Relations Association and National Communication Council for Human Services.

# PUBLIC SERVICE CORPORATIONS

*See* PUBLIC UTILITIES

# PUBLIC SPEAKING

*See also* DEBATES AND DEBATING; TOASTS

### HANDBOOKS AND MANUALS

*American Speaker: Your Guide to Successful Speaking.* Briefings Publishing Group. • Bimonthly. $399.00. Newsletter. Provides practical advice on public speaking.

### TRADE/PROFESSIONAL ASSOCIATIONS

Corporate Speech Pathology Network. 10 Glenlake Pkwy., Ste. 130, Atlanta, GA 30328. Phone: (678)592-0052 • URL: http://www.corspan.org • Represents the interests of corporate speech pathologists and other individuals and corporations exploring speech training. Seeks to promote and improve speech in the business and corporate settings. Encourages members to share information and ideas.

National Speakers Association. 1500 S Priest Dr., Tempe, AZ 85281. Phone: (480)968-2552; Email: info@gettingtothefinishline.com • URL: http://www.nsaspeaker.org • Professional speakers. Works to increase public awareness of the speaking profession, advance the integrity and visibility of professional speakers, and provide a learning and communication vehicle to professional speakers. Sponsors workshops, conventions, and labs.

# PUBLIC TRANSPORTATION

*See also* MOTOR BUSES; RAILROADS; TRANSPORTATION INDUSTRY

### ABSTRACTS AND INDEXES

*NTIS Alerts: Transportation.* U.S. Department of Commerce National Technical Information Service. • Biweekly. $130 per year. Covers air, marine, highway, inland waterway, pipeline, and railroad transportation.

*Readers' Guide to Periodical Literature.* EBSCO Publishing Inc. • Provides indexing for over 400 periodicals dating back to 1983.

## CD-ROM DATABASES

*OECD Statistical Compendium.* Organization for Economic Cooperation and Development. • Semiannual. $1,905.00 per year for 1 to 10 users. CD-ROM contains more than 730,000 monthly, quarterly, and annual time series for OECD countries, 1960 to date. Includes fully searchable data on agriculture, food, economic indicators, national accounts, employment, energy, finance, industry, technology, and foreign trade. Results can be displayed in various forms.

*Readers' Guide to Periodical Literature.* EBSCO Publishing Inc. • Provides indexing for over 400 periodicals dating back to 1983.

## DIRECTORIES

*Mass Transit: Consultants.* Cygnus Business Media Inc. • Annual. $64.00. Listings for over 300 urban transportation architects, designers, engineers, planners, consultants and other specialists serving the urban transportation industry.

*Mass Transit: Supplier's Guide.* Cygnus Business Media Inc. • Directory of over 800 manufacturers and distributors serving the urban transportation industry.

## INTERNET DATABASES

*Business 2.0 Web Guide to the Best Business Links.* Business 2.0 Media Inc. Phone: (415)293-4800; Email: support@business2.com • URL: http://www. business2.com/webguide • Web site presents an extensive, searchable directory of links to "the best, most informative, and authoritative web pages." Twenty main categories cover business, finance, career, company information, people, and technology topics, with thousands of subtopics, all linking to Web sites recommended by experienced business researchers. Fees: Free.

*Fedstats.* Federal Interagency Council on Statistical Policy. Phone: (202)395-7254 • URL: http://www. fedstats.gov • Web site features an efficient search facility for full-text statistics produced by more than 100 federal agencies, including the Census Bureau, the Bureau of Economic Analysis, and the Bureau of Labor Statistics. Boolean searches can be made within one agency or for all agencies combined. Links are offered to international statistical bureaus, including the UN, IMF, OECD, UNESCO, Eurostat, and 20 individual countries. Fees: Free.

*FreeLunch.com.* Economy.com, Inc. Phone: (610)696-8700; Fax: (610)696-1678 • URL: http:// www.freelunch.com • Web site provides free access to more than 200 million economic and financial data series, covering industry, demographics, labor markets, prices, retail sales, government spending, trade, interest rates, housing starts, the stock market, etc. Data is available in either chart or table form. Searching is offered. Free, but registration required. Economy.com, Inc. also offers fee-based economic analysis at *The Dismal Scientist* site (www.dismal. com).

## ONLINE DATABASES

*TRIS: Transportation Research Information Service.* The National Academies National Research Council. • Contains abstracts and citations to a wide range of transportation literature, 1968 to present, with monthly updates. Includes references to the literature of air transportation, highways, ships and shipping, railroads, trucking, and urban mass transportation. Formerly *TRIS-ON-LINE.* Inquire as to online cost and availability.

## PERIODICALS AND NEWSLETTERS

*Downtown Idea Exchange: Essential Information for Downtown Research and Development Center.* Downtown Research and Development Center. Alexander Communications Group Inc. • Monthly. $227 Individuals. Newsletter for those concerned

with central business districts. Provides news and other information on planning, development, parking, mass transit, traffic, funding, and other topics.

*Mass Transit: Better Transit Through Better Management.* Cygnus Business Media Inc. • Bimonthly. 48.00 per year.

*Metro.* Bobit Business Media. • Nine times a year. $40.00 per year. Subject matter is the management of public transportationsystems. Includes Factbook.

*Nation's Cities Weekly.* National League of Cities. • Weekly. $96 Nonmembers. Description: Presents news on the latest developments in Congress, the White House, federal agencies, and other public interest groups which may affect the nation's cities.

*Passenger Transport: The Weekly Newspaper of the Public Transportation Industry.* American Public Transportation Association. • Weekly. $75 Individuals. Covers current events and trends in mass transportation.

*Urban Transport News: Management-Funding Terrorism-Ridership-Technology.* Business Publishers Inc. • 25 times a year. $437.00 per year. Newsletter. Provides current news from Capitol Hill, the White House, the Dept. of Transportation, as well as transit operations and industries across the country.

## RESEARCH CENTERS AND INSTITUTES

Carnegie Mellon Research Institute-The Robotics Institute. 5000 Forbes Ave., Pittsburgh, PA 15213. Phone: (412)268-3818; Fax: (412)268-6436; Email: robotics@ri.cmu.edu • URL: http://www.ri.cmu.edu • Multidisciplinary research activities include expert systems applications, minicomputer and microcomputer systems design, genetic engineering, and transportation systems analysis.

Massachusetts Institute of Technology - Center for Transportation and Logistics. 77 Massachusetts Ave., E40-276, Cambridge, MA 02139. Phone: (617)253-5320; Fax: (617)253-4560; Email: sheffi@mit.edu • URL: http://ctl.mit.edu • Transportation and logistics, with emphasis on problem-oriented, interdisciplinary, and multi-model studies, including studies on innovative urban transportation systems, transport technology innovations, railroad systems operations, trucking, energy policies, regional transportation planning and programming, highway location and design, flight transportation, ocean shipping, transportation systems analysis, logistics, supply chain management, logistics organizations, shipper/carrier relationships and logistics information technology.

Texas A&M University - Texas Transportation Institute. 3135 TAMU, College Station, TX 77843-3135. Phone: (979)845-1713; Fax: (979)845-9356; Email: dennis-c@tamu.edu • URL: http://tti.tamu. edu • Concerned with all forms and modes of transportation. Research areas include transportation economics, highway construction, traffic safety, public transportation, and highway engineering.

University of Central Florida - Transportation Systems Institute. Department of Civil, Environmental, and Construction Engineering, 12800 Pegasus Dr., Ste. 211, Orlando, FL 32816-2450. Phone: (407)823-2988; Fax: (407)823-3315; Email: haitham.al-deek@ucf.edu • URL: http://tsi. cecs.ucf.edu • Research areas include mass transportation systems.

University of Florida - Transportation Research Center. 512 Weil Hall, Gainesville, FL 32611. Phone: 800-226-1013 or (352)392-9537 or (352)392-7575; Fax: (352)392-3394 or (352)392-3224; Email: elefter@ce.ufl.edu • URL: http://trc.ce. ufl.edu • Traffic operations, traffic simulation, traffic signal control, congestion pricing, network modeling, optimization, transportation planning, land use planning, older driver issues.

University of Missouri—St. Louis - Center for Business and Industrial Studies. 220 Express Scripts

Hall, 1 University Dr., Saint Louis, MO 63121-4499. Phone: (314)516-6108 or (314)516-5451; Email: ldsmith@umsl.edu • URL: http://www.umsl. edu/divisions/business/ncbis/index.html • Research fields include inventory and management control. Specific projects also include development of computer software for operations in public transit systems.

University of Wisconsin—Milwaukee - Center for Urban Transportation Studies. PO Box 784, Milwaukee, WI 53201. Phone: (414)229-5787; Fax: (414)229-6958; Email: cuts@csd.uwm.edu • URL: http://www4.uwm.edu/cuts • Transportation engineering and planning, mass transit, outreach, and technology transfer. Studies include alternative methods of organizing transportation planning; transit sensitive land use design; highway projects effects on land use; intelligent transportation systems; investigations of transport improvement, evaluation, and methodologies through private financing; the use of microcomputers for transportation planning; improved methods of transport management; and transit innovations.

## STATISTICS SOURCES

*Survey of Current Business.* U. S. Government Printing Office. • Published by Bureau of Economic Analysis, U. S. Department of Commerce. Presents a wide variety of business and economic data.

## TRADE/PROFESSIONAL ASSOCIATIONS

American Disabled for Attendant Program Today. 1208 S Logan St., Denver, CO 80210. Phone: (303)733-9324 or (512)442-0252; Fax: (303)733-6211; Email: adapt@adapt.org • URL: http://www. adapt.org • Members are disabled individuals promoting wheelchair accessibility in all forms of public transportation.

American Public Transportation Association. 1666 K St. NW, Ste. 1100, Washington, DC 20006. Phone: (202)496-4800; Fax: (202)496-4324; Email: info@apta.com • URL: http://www.apta.com • Motor bus and rapid transit systems; organizations responsible for planning, designing, constructing, financing and operating transit systems; business organizations which supply products and services to transit, academic institutions and state associations and departments of transportation. Represents the public interest in improving transit. Encourages cooperation among its members, their employees, the general public and compliance with the letter and spirit of equal opportunity principles. Seeks to: collect information relative to public transit; assist in the training, education and professional development of all persons involved in public transit; and engage in activities which promote public transit. Provides a medium for exchange of experiences, discussion, and a comparative study of public transit affairs; Promotes research.

# PUBLIC UTILITIES

*See also* ELECTRIC UTILITIES; ENERGY SOURCES; GAS INDUSTRY; TELEPHONE INDUSTRY; WATER SUPPLY

## CD-ROM DATABASES

*Environment Abstracts on CD-ROM.* University Publications of America. • Quarterly. $1,295.00 per year. Contains the following CD-ROM databases: *Environment Abstracts, Energy Abstracts*, and *Acid Rain Abstracts.* Length of coverage varies.

*OECD Statistical Compendium.* Organization for Economic Cooperation and Development. • Semiannual. $1,905.00 per year for 1 to 10 users. CD-ROM contains more than 730,000 monthly, quarterly, and annual time series for OECD countries, 1960 to date. Includes fully searchable data on agriculture, food, economic indicators, national accounts, employment, energy, finance, industry, technology, and foreign trade. Results can be displayed in various forms.

## HANDBOOKS AND MANUALS

*Mergent's Public Utility Manual.* Mergent Inc. • Annual. $1,995.00. Updated weekly online. Contains financial and other information concerning publicly-held utility companies (electric, gas, telephone, water).

## INTERNET DATABASES

*Bureau of Economic Analysis.* U. S. Department of Commerce, Bureau of Economic Analysis. Phone: (202)606-9900; Fax: (202)606-5310; Email: webmaster@bea.doc.gov • URL: http://www.bea. doc.gov • Web site includes "News Release Information" covering national, regional, and international economic estimates from the BEA. Highlights of releases appear online the same day, complete text and tables appear the next day. "Recent News Releases" section provides titles for past nine months, with links. "BEA Data and Methodology" includes "Frequently Requested NIPA Data" (national income and product accounts, such as gross domestic product and personal income). Other statistics are available. Fees: Free.

*Business 2.0 Web Guide to the Best Business Links.* Business 2.0 Media Inc. Phone: (415)293-4800; Email: support@business2.com • URL: http://www. business2.com/webguide • Web site presents an extensive, searchable directory of links to "the best, most informative, and authoritative web pages." Twenty main categories cover business, finance, career, company information, people, and technology topics, with thousands of subtopics, all linking to Web sites recommended by experienced business researchers. Fees: Free.

*Fedstats.* Federal Interagency Council on Statistical Policy. Phone: (202)395-7254 • URL: http://www. fedstats.gov • Web site features an efficient search facility for full-text statistics produced by more than 100 federal agencies, including the Census Bureau, the Bureau of Economic Analysis, and the Bureau of Labor Statistics. Boolean searches can be made within one agency or for all agencies combined. Links are offered to international statistical bureaus, including the UN, IMF, OECD, UNESCO, Eurostat, and 20 individual countries. Fees: Free.

*FreeLunch.com.* Economy.com, Inc. Phone: (610)696-8700; Fax: (610)696-1678 • URL: http:// www.freelunch.com • Web site provides free access to more than 200 million economic and financial data series, covering industry, demographics, labor markets, prices, retail sales, government spending, trade, interest rates, housing starts, the stock market, etc. Data is available in either chart or table form. Searching is offered. Free, but registration required. Economy.com, Inc. also offers fee-based economic analysis at *The Dismal Scientist* site (www.dismal. com).

## OTHER SOURCES

*Utilities Industry Litigation Reporter: National Coverage of the Many Types of Litigation Stemming From the Transmission and Distribution of Energy By Publicly and Privately Owned Utilities.* Andrews Publications. • Monthly. $775.00 per year. Newsletter. Reports on legal cases involving the generation or distribution of energy.

## PERIODICALS AND NEWSLETTERS

*Public Utilities Fortnightly.* Public Utilities Reports Inc. • Monthly. $287 Individuals. Management magazine for utility executives in electric, gas, telecommunications and water industries.

## RESEARCH CENTERS AND INSTITUTES

Institute of Public Utilities. Michigan State University, Owen Graduate Hall, 735 E Shaw Ln., Rm. W157, East Lansing, MI 48825-1109. Phone: (517)355-1876; Fax: (517)355-1854; Email: ipu@

msu.edu • URL: http://www.ipu.msu.edu • Represents the interests of privately and publicly owned utility companies in energy, telecommunications and water. Facilitates research and discussion of problems currently faced by public utility industry. Conducts educational programs in conjunction with National Association of Regulatory Utility Commissioners. Holds periodic seminars and special training programs.

## STATISTICS SOURCES

*American Housing Survey for the United States in (year).* U. S. Government Printing Office. • Biennial. $51.00. Issued by the U. S. Census Bureau (www. census.gov). Covers both owner-occupied and renter-occupied housing. Includes data on such factors as condition of building, type of mortgage, utility costs, and housing occupied by minorities. (Current Housing Reports, H150.).

*Survey of Current Business.* U. S. Government Printing Office. • Published by Bureau of Economic Analysis, U. S. Department of Commerce. Presents a wide variety of business and economic data.

## TRADE/PROFESSIONAL ASSOCIATIONS

National Association of Regulatory Utility Commissioners. 1101 Vermont Ave. NW, Ste. 200, Washington, DC 20005-3553. Phone: (202)898-2200; Fax: (202)898-2213; Email: admin@naruc. org • URL: http://www.naruc.org • Formerly National Association of Railway and Utility Commissioners.

National Utilities Diversity Council. 1017 L St., Sacramento, CA 95814. Phone: (916)492-9163; Fax: (916)473-9444; Email: mpl@cpuc.ca.gov • Promotes diversity in the utility industry in the areas of governance, employment, procurement, language access/customer service and philanthropy. Serves as a resource that promotes the inclusion of women, racial and ethnic minorities, service disabled veterans and other organized groups in utility corporate governance, philanthropy, employment, procurement, language access and customer service.

Retail Energy Supply Association. PO Box 6089, Harrisburg, PA 17112. Phone: (717)566-5405; Email: tmccormick@resausa.org • URL: http:// www.resausa.org • Represents the interests of retail energy suppliers. Promotes the development and furthering of retail energy markets in the United States. Sponsors social and networking opportunities for members.

Utility Industry Group. Southern California Edison Co., Bldg. 3-2 MD3, 4910 Rivergrade Rd., Irwindale, CA 91706. Phone: (626)543-6291; Fax: (626)302-5332 • URL: http://www.uig.org • Represents the interests of the utility industry including distribution companies, energy suppliers, service providers and their customers, supply chain participants and other interested parties. Promotes effective implementation of electronic commerce to standards committees, governmental bodies and other appropriate organizations involved in the standards setting process. Provides a forum for the exchange of ideas and solutions related to electronic commerce and its influence on the business needs of the utility industry.

Utility Supply Management Alliance. PO Box 6608, Pine Bluff, AR 71611. Phone: (913)768-7005; Fax: (913)397-0901; Email: parbuckle4@comcast.net • URL: http://www.usma.com • Reduces overall supply chain costs by providing a forum for utilities and suppliers. Advocates for aggressive and responsible leadership, responsiveness to customer needs and continuous improvement in supply chain management. Improves the service and profitability of utilities and suppliers.

# PUBLIC WELFARE

## ABSTRACTS AND INDEXES

*PAIS International.* ProQuest L.L.C. • Monthly. $850.00 per year; cumulations three times a year. Provides topical citations to the worldwide literature of public affairs, economics, demographics, sociology, and trade. Text in English; indexed materials in English, French, German, Italian, Portuguese and Spanish.

*Readers' Guide to Periodical Literature.* EBSCO Publishing Inc. • Provides indexing for over 400 periodicals dating back to 1983.

*Social Sciences Citation Index.* Thomson Reuters Corp. • Weekly. Product is accessed via *Web of Science.*

*Social Sciences Index Retrospective: 1907-1983.* EBSCO Publishing Inc. • Indexing for 1,000,000 articles. Coverage includes international index and social sciences and humanities index.

## CD-ROM DATABASES

*Newspaper Abstracts Ondisc.* ProQuest L.L.C. • Monthly. $2,950.00 per year (covers 1989 to date; archival discs are available for 1985-88). Provides cover-to-cover CD-ROM indexing and abstracting of 19 major newspapers, including the *New York Times, Wall Street Journal, Washington Post, Chicago Tribune,* and *Los Angeles Times.*

*PAIS International.* ProQuest L.L.C. • Monthly. $1,995.00 per year. Contains over 650,000 citations to the literature of contemporary social, political, and economic issues.

*Readers' Guide to Periodical Literature.* EBSCO Publishing Inc. • Provides indexing for over 400 periodicals dating back to 1983.

*Social Sciences Abstracts.* EBSCO Publishing Inc. • Provides indexing from 1983 and abstracting from 1994 of more than 750 periodicals covering economics, area studies, community health, public administration, public welfare, urban studies, and many other topics related to the social sciences.

*Social Sciences Citation Index.* Thomson Reuters Corp. • Weekly. Product is accessed via *Web of Science.*

## DIRECTORIES

*Government Assistance Almanac: The Guide to Federal, Domestic, Financial and Other Programs Covering Grants, Loans, Insurance, Personal Payments and Benefits.* Omnigraphics Inc. • Annual. $275 print. Gives users updated information on all available federal domestic assistance programs. These programs represent nearly $2 trillion worth of federal assistance earmarked for distribution to consumers, children, parents, veterans, senior citizens, students, businesses, civic groups, state and local agencies, and others.

*Public Human Services Directory.* American Public Human Services Association. • Annual. $225 Individuals. Covers: Federal, state, territorial, county, and major municipal public human service agencies. Database includes: Information on all major human service programs, such as child welfare, child support enforcement. Medicaid eligibility and claims, interstate compacts, and other programs. Entries include: Agency name, address, phone, fax, e-mail address, web site address, names of key personnel, program area.

## E-BOOKS

*Social Trends & Indicators USA.* Monique D. Magee, editor. Cengage Learning Inc. • Includes data on labor, economics, the health care industry, crime, leisure, population, education, social security, and many other topics. Sources include various government agencies and major publications. Inquire for pricing.

**For publishers' addresses, refer to SOURCES CITED section at the back of the book.**

## HANDBOOKS AND MANUALS

*Social Security Handbook.* U. S. Government Printing Office. • Annual. $53.00. Issued by the Social Security Administration (www.ssa.gov). Provides detailed information about social security programs, including Medicare, with brief descriptions of related programs administered by agencies other than the Social Security Administration.

## INTERNET DATABASES

*FedWorld: A Program of the United States Department of Commerce.* National Technical Information Service. Phone: 800-553-NTIS or (703)605-6000; Fax: (703)605-6900; Email: webmaster@fedworld. gov • URL: http://www.fedworld.gov • Web site offers "a comprehensive central access point for searching, locating, ordering, and acquiring government and business information." Emphasis is on searching the Web pages, databases, and government reports of a wide variety of federal agencies. Fees: Free.

*FirstGov: Your First Click to the U. S. Government.* General Services Administration. Phone: 800-333-4636 or (202)501-0705; Email: public.affairs@gsa. gov • URL: http://www.gsa.gov • Free Web site provides extensive links to federal agencies covering a wide variety of topics, such as agriculture, business, consumer safety, education, the environment, government jobs, grants, health, social security, statistics sources, taxes, technology, travel, and world affairs. Also provides links to federal forms, including IRS tax forms. Searching is offered, both keyword and advanced.

*Social Security Online: The Official Web Site of the Social Security Administration.* U. S. Social Security Administration. Phone: 800-772-1213 or (410)965-7700 • URL: http://www.ssa.gov • Web site provides a wide variety of online information relating to social security and Medicare. Topics include benefits, disability, employer wage reporting, personal earnings statements, statistics, government financing, social security law, and public welfare reform legislation.

*U.S. Census Bureau: The Official Statistics.* U. S. Bureau of the Census. Phone: (301)763-4636 or (301)763-4100; Fax: (301)763-4794; Email: webmaster@census.gov • URL: http://www.census. gov/prod/www/abs/mfg-prof.html • Web site is "Your Source for Social, Demographic, and Economic Information." Contains "Current U. S. Population Count," "Current Economic Indicators," and a wide variety of data under "Other Official Statistics." Keyword searching is provided. Fees: Free.

## ONLINE DATABASES

*Wilson Social Sciences Abstracts Online.* H.W. Wilson Co. • Provides online abstracting and indexing of more than 500 periodicals covering area studies, community health, public administration, public welfare, urban studies, and many other social science topics. Time period is 1994 to date for abstracts and 1983 to date for indexing, with updates weekly. Inquire as to online cost and availability.

## OTHER SOURCES

*Resist.* • Provides grants to small progressive groups in all parts of the country; has aided groups that have organized for reproductive rights for women, gay rights, nuclear disarmament, the rights of Third World people, and work for social and economic justice.

## PERIODICALS AND NEWSLETTERS

*Journal of Poverty: Innovations on Social, Political, and Economic Inequalities.* The Haworth Press Inc. • Quarterly. $180.00 per year to libraries; $50.00 per year to individuals. Covers the social, emotional, and economic consequences of public assistance. Topics include welfare policy, immigrants' rights, hiring practices, managed healthcare, child support,

disabilities, food programs, and affirmative action. (See also www.journalofpoverty.org).

*Policy and Practice of Public Human Services.* American Public Human Services Association. • Quarterly. $75 /year for nonmembers. Contains articles, research reports, and book reviews about human services and public policy. Formerly *Public Welfare.*

*Public Assistance and Welfare Trends: State Capitals.* Wakeman/Walworth Inc. • 50 times a year. $245.00 per year; print and online editions, $350.00 per year. Newsletter. Formerly *From the State Capitals: Public Assistance and Welfare Trends.*

*Review of Social Economy.* Association for Social Economics. Taylor & Francis Ltd. • Quarterly. $152 Individuals Print and Online. Quarterly. Subject matter is concerned with the relationships between social values and economics. Includes articles on income distribution, poverty, labor, and class.

## STATISTICS SOURCES

*Social Security Bulletin.* Social Security Administration. U. S. Government Printing Office. • Quarterly. $27.00 per year. Annual statistical supplement.

*Statistical Abstract of the United States.* U. S. Government Printing Office. • Annual. $44.00. Issued by the U. S. Bureau of the Census.

## TRADE/PROFESSIONAL ASSOCIATIONS

American Public Human Services Association. 1133 19th St. NW, Ste. 400, Washington, DC 20036. Phone: (202)682-0100; Fax: (202)289-6555; Email: pubs@aphsa.org • URL: http://www.aphsa.org • Public human service agencies, their professional staff members, and others interested in public human services. Works to develop, promote and implement human service policies that improve the health and well-being of families, children and adults.

Corporate Voices for Working Families. 1020 19th St. NW, Ste. 750, Washington, DC 20036. Phone: (202)467-8130; Fax: (202)467-8140; Email: dklein@corporatevioces.org • URL: http://www. cvworkingfamilies.org • Represents the private sector on public policy issues involving working families. Aims to improve the lives of working families and the competitiveness of American businesses. Facilitates research and provides solutions to legislators and businesses on issues important to America's working families.

# PUBLIC WORKS

*See also* BUILDING CONTRACTS; BUILDING INDUSTRY

## ABSTRACTS AND INDEXES

*PAIS International.* ProQuest L.L.C. • Monthly. $850.00 per year; cumulations three times a year. Provides topical citations to the worldwide literature of public affairs, economics, demographics, sociology, and trade. Text in English; indexed materials in English, French, German, Italian, Portuguese and Spanish.

## CD-ROM DATABASES

*PAIS International.* ProQuest L.L.C. • Monthly. $1,995.00 per year. Contains over 650,000 citations to the literature of contemporary social, political, and economic issues.

## DIRECTORIES

*Public Works Manual.* Public Works Journal Corp. • Annual. $45. Publication includes: List of about 3,500 manufacturers and distributors of equipment, materials, services, computers, and software used in the design, construction, maintenance, and operation of streets and highways, water systems, wastewater and solid wastes processing, and recreation areas. Entries include: Company name,

address, products. Principal content is technical articles on public works topics.

## PERIODICALS AND NEWSLETTERS

*ENR: Connecting the Industry Worldwide.* McGraw Hill Financial Inc. • Weekly. $74.00 per year.

*Project Finance: The Magazine for Global Development.* American Educational Systems. • 11 times a year. $740.00 per year. Includes print and online editions. Provides articles on the financing of the infrastructure (transportation, utilities, communications, the environment, etc). Coverage is international. Supplements available *World Export Credit Guide* and *Project Finance Book of Lists.* Formed by the merger of *Infrastructure Finance* and *Project and Trade Finance.*

*Public Works: City, County and State.* Public Works Journal Corp. • Monthly. Includes *Public Works Manual.*

## RESEARCH CENTERS AND INSTITUTES

University of Tennessee at Knoxville - Municipal Technical Advisory Service Library. 600 Henley St., Ste. 120, Knoxville, TN 37996-4105. Phone: (865)974-0411; Fax: (865)974-0423; Email: steve. thompson@tennessee.edu • URL: http://www.mtas. tennessee.edu/web2012.nsf/Web/Home • Research areas include municipal finance, police administration, and public works.

## STATISTICS SOURCES

*United States Census of Construction Industries.* U.S. Department of Commerce U.S. Census Bureau. • Quinquennial. Results presented in reports, tape, and CD-ROM files.

## TRADE/PROFESSIONAL ASSOCIATIONS

American Public Works Association. 1275 K St. NW, Ste. 750, Washington, DC 20005. Phone: 800-848-APWA or (202)408-9541; Fax: (202)408-9542; Email: apwa@apwa.net • URL: http://www.apwa. net • Chief administrators, commissioners, and directors of public works, city engineers, superintendents, and department heads of transportation, water, waste water, solid waste, equipment services, and buildings and grounds; federal, provincial, and state administrators and engineers; consultants and educators; associate members are equipment manufacturers' representatives, utility company officials, and contractors; student members are engineering and public administration students interested in the theory and practice of the design, construction, maintenance, administration, and operation of public works facilities and services. Conducts historical research on public works subjects and demonstrates applicability of history to current public works problems and issues through Public Works Historical Society. Sponsors research and education foundations.

# PUBLICITY

*See* PUBLIC RELATIONS AND PUBLICITY

# PUBLISHERS, COLLEGE

*See* UNIVERSITY PRESSES

# PUBLISHING, DESKTOP

*See* DESKTOP PUBLISHING

# PUBLISHING, ELECTRONIC

*See* ELECTRONIC PUBLISHING

---

# PUBLISHING INDUSTRY

*See also* BIBLIOGRAPHY; BOOK
CATALOGS; BOOK INDUSTRY; BOOKSEL-
LING; ELECTRONIC PUBLISHING;
PAPERBOUND BOOK INDUSTRY;
UNIVERSITY PRESSES

## ABSTRACTS AND INDEXES

*Book Review Digest: An Index to Reviews of Current Books.* H.W. Wilson Co. • 10 times a year. Quarterly and annual cumulation. Price varies.

## BIBLIOGRAPHIES

*American Book Publishing Record: Arranged by Dewey Decimal Classification and Indexed by Author, Title, and Subject.* R.R. Bowker L.L.C. • Monthly. $365 Individuals Annual. Offers access to the newest cataloging records from the Library of Congress.

*Booklist.* Library and Information Technology Association. • Biweekly. $147.50 U.S. and Canada /year. Reviews library materials for school and public libraries. Incorporates *Reference Books Bulletin.*

*Books in Print.* R.R. Bowker L.L.C. • Combines the trusted and authoritative source of bibliographic information with powerful search, discovery and collection development tools designed specifically to streamline the book discovery and acquisition process.

*Forthcoming Books.* R.R. Bowker L.L.C. • Quarterly. $375 Individuals Annual. Reference database listing forthcoming publications and new issues, editions, or volumes of previously published books or serials. Supplement to *Books in Print.*

## CD-ROM DATABASES

*LISA Plus.* Cambridge Scientific Abstracts L.P. • Quarterly. $2,000 per year. CD-ROM version of Library Information and Science Abstracts, providing abstracting and indexing of the world's library and information science literature, 1969 to date. Contains more than 180,000 citations.

## DIRECTORIES

*Advertising & Press Annual in Africa.* International Publications Service. • Annual. Covers: African newspapers, magazines, radio and television stations, annuals, poster and transportation advertising and exhibits and shows; leading advertisers and professionals in the field in Africa; associations involved in a variety of fields of advertising and publicity in Africa.

*African Publishers Network Consultants Register.* Bellagio Publishing Network. • Covers: 66 publishing consultants in Africa with specializations in bookselling, children's books, copyright, design, distribution, electronic publishing, finance, editing, librarianship, management, marketing, printing, production, training, scholarly publishing, translation, and writing.

*Asia: A Directory and Sourcebook.* Euromonitor International Business Reference Div. • Irregular. $430. Publication includes: Regional overview, major companies, information sources statistical datafile. Entries include: Name of organization, firm, or agency, address, statistical data, purpose or service.

*Books--Publishing & Printing Directory.* InfoGroup Inc. • Annual. Number of listings: 1,224. Entries include: Name, address, phone, size of advertisement, name of owner or manager, number of employees, year first in "Yellow Pages." Compiled from telephone company "Yellow Pages," nationwide.

*Business and Legal Forms for Authors and Self-publishers.* Allworth Press. • $24.99 Single issue paperback. Publication includes: Contact information for volunteer lawyers for the arts. Principal content of publication is instruction and use of business and legal forms for authors and self-publishers.

*Business Researchers Network.* Penny Hill Press. • Monthly. $195 per year. Publication includes: Listing of sources of critical data and insights on foreign competition, political risks, and new export markets. Entries include: Name, address, phone, description of information available.

*Compuserve Companion: Finding Newspapers and Magazines Online.* BiblioData. • $29.95. Covers: More than 3,200 newspapers, newsletters, and magazines that are available for full text searching on CompuServe. Database includes: Introductory chapter of searching tips. Entries include: Publication name, dates of coverage, lag times, and appropriate "Go" commands.

*Datapro Reports.* Datapro Information Services Group. • Monthly. $495 minimum cost per year, depending on service. Datapro produces sixty information services covering products, vendors, markets, and technologies in large systems, microcomputers, telecommunications, data communications, word processing, software, office automation systems, copiers and duplicators, information security systems, retail automation equipment, banking automation equipment, personal computer communications, communications alternatives, and electronic publishing systems. Reports generally include descriptions and analyses of each equipment model offered by each manufacturer in the field, comparison charts, and lists of suppliers, associations, consultants, etc., with addresses and phone numbers. Individual descriptions include a summary and detailed reports on technical characteristics and operation. Reports are on looseleaf pages.

*Directory of Canadian Information Sources.* Browning Associates. • Covers: approximately 1,500 directories, market surveys, trade guides, association publications, and special periodical issues that are sources of Canadian information. Entries include: Publication title, publisher name, address, phone, frequency, price, scope of coverage, description of contents and arrangement, whether advertising is accepted, other details.

*Eastern Europe: A Directory and Sourcebook.* Euromonitor International Business Reference Div. • $440. Publication includes: Lists of publishers of private research, journals and newsletters, online databases, consultants, and abstracts and indexes providing information on eastern Europe. Database includes: Economic and demographic data, analysis of business practices, markets, investment opportunities, and rankings.

*Encyclopedia of Business Information Sources.* Cengage Learning Inc. • Annual. $626 Individuals. Contains bibliographic information on more than 35,000 live, print, and electronic sources of information covering more than 1,100 subjects of interest to business personnel. Includes abstracts and indexes, almanacs and yearbooks, bibliographies, online databases, research centers and institutes, and more. Available as eBook.

*Engineering Index Annual.* Elsevier Engineering Information. • Annual. $7,720 Individuals for all countries except Europe, JPN and IRN. Publication includes: Authors and publishers of engineering literature worldwide. Entries include: Author Biographical data and Company name. Principal content of publication is bibliographic citations and abstracts.

*Global Business and Industrial Directories Publishers Directory.* International Business Publications, USA. • $99.95 Individuals. Covers: Largest business and industrial directories publishers worldwide.

*Goff's Business Travellers' Guide.* Adprint. • Annual. $1.95. Covers: about 200 hotels in the United Kingdom. Entries include: Hotel name, address, phone, telex, fax, location, proximity of major city and airport, description of facilities, rates, whether credit cards are accepted, restaurants, symbols for amenities.

*Government Product News--Buyers Guide for Office Equipment Issue.* Intertec Publishing. • Annual. $5. Publication includes: List of over 1,000 manufacturers of office equipment. Entries include: Company name, address, phone, name and title of contact.

*IAL Directory of European Industrial and Business Market Reports.* IAL Consultants. • Irregular. $250 postpaid. Covers: publishers and producers of market reports, statistical summaries, and other data; includes government and non-government organizations, libraries, press, and international sources in Europe, including the socialist states of Eastern Europe. Entries include: Publisher name and address, title and subject of report, language, number of pages, price.

*International Literary Market Place: The Directory of the International Book Publishing Industry.* Information Today, Inc. • Annual. $299 Individuals softbound. Covers more than 180 countries. Listings include publishers, literary agents, major booksellers, book clubs, literary prizes, distributors, trade associations, etc. Formerly published by R. R. Bowker.

*Library Journal: Reference: Print, CD-ROM, Online (year).* Reed Elsevier Group plc Reed Business Information. • Annual. Issued in November as a supplement to *Library Journal.* Lists new and updated reference material, including general and trade print titles, directories, annuals, CD-ROM titles, and online sources. Includes material from more than 200 publishers, arranged by company name, with an index by subject.

*Library Journal Sourcebook: The Reference For Library Products & Services.* Reed Elsevier Group plc Reed Business Information. • Annual. Publication includes: List of over 600 suppliers of products and services used by libraries from abstracting to word processing equipment. Entries include: Company name, address, phone, list of products or services. Complete listings for more than 100 architectural firms; Disaster planning for librarians.

*Literary Market Place: The Directory of the American Book Publishing Industry.* Information Today, Inc. • Annual. $399 Individuals 2-volume set/ softbound plus $25 shipping/handling. Listings include publishers, agents, ad agencies, associations, distributors, events, key executives, services, and suppliers (50 directory sections in all). Formerly published by R. R. Bowker.

*Los Angeles Business Journal--Book of Lists.* LABJ Inc. • Annual. $395. Covers: major companies, foundations, government officials, utilities, newspapers, radio and television stations, airlines, hospitals, financial institutions, shopping centers, resorts, and prominent individuals in Los Angeles County, California. Incorporates information in "Los Angeles Business Journal--Consultants Directory," now discontinued.

*Media Rates & Data.* Media-Daten AG. • Biennial. Covers: National and international newspapers, journals, trade press and local Swiss newsletters, radio and television. Entries include: Publications name, address, phone, rates, schedules.

*Publishers' Catalogues.* Northern Lights Internet Solutions Ltd. • Covers: Publishing companies worldwide. Entries include: Company name, address, phone, fax, titles.

*Publishers Directory.* Cengage Learning Inc. • Annual. $756 Individuals print. Contains detailed information on more than 30,000 U.S. and Canadian publishers as well as small, independent presses.

*Publishers' International ISBN Directory.* Walter de Gruyter GmbH & Co. KG. • Annual. Covers: About 620,000 publishers in the United States and 200 other countries, of which about 555,000 have been assigned International Standard Book Numbers (IS-BNs) by one of 140 ISBN Group Agencies. Entries include: For publishers--Name, address, phone, fax, telex, e-mail, ISBN, group, and prefix numbers. For agencies--Name, address, phone, fax, e-mail, group number, names and titles of key personnel in charge of ISBN matters. Publication is a merger of "International ISBN Publishers' Directory" and "Publishers' International Directory.".

*VNU Business Media.* ADWEEK Media. • Annual. $100.00. Presents cost, circulation, and audience statistics for various mass media segments, including television, radio, magazines, newspapers, telephone yellow pages, and cinema.

*Which Business CD-ROM?.* Bowker-Saur. • Annual. $259 plus $30.00 shipping.. Publication includes: List of major CD-ROM publishers in the field of business; coverage includes the U.K. and Europe, with limited U.S. listings. Principal content of publication is information significant CD-ROM titles in various business fields, such as company directories, company accounts, mergers/ acquisitions, business news, legislation/regulations, market research, industries, economics and finance, international trade, and business management literature. Entries include: Publisher name, address, phone.

*Who Knows Who: Networking through Corporate Boards.* Who Knows Who Publishers. • Annual. $165. Publication includes: List of over 1,000 companies noted by either Fortune magazine or Forbes magazine, or both; over 120 major foundations. Entries include: Company or foundation name, address, phone, boards of directors. Principal content of publication is lists of the companies and their boards of directors showing relationships among the companies by showing which of the board members sit on several of the companies' boards, i.e. interlocking directorates.

*Writer's Guide to Book Editors, Publishers, and Literary Agents, Who They Are, What They Want, and How to Win Them Over.* Prima Publishing Inc. • Annual. $27.95; with CD-ROM, $49.95. Directory for authors includes information on publishers' response times and pay rates.

## FINANCIAL RATIOS

*Annual Statement Studies.* Risk Management Association. • Annual. Compiled from over 280,000 financial statements.

*Annual Statement Studies: Industry Default Probabilities and Cash Flow Measures.* Risk Management Association. • Annual. $405 Nonmembers. Serves as a companion volume to the original *Annual Statement Studies.* Gives probability of default estimates on a percentage scale for more than 450 industries. Includes changes in position year-by-year for eight financial statement line items and provides percentage measures of cash flow.

## INTERNET DATABASES

*Publishers' Catalogues Home Page.* EBSCO Publishing Inc. 10 Estes St., Ipswich, MA 01938-2106. Phone: 800-653-2726 or (978)356-6500; Fax: (978)356-6565; Email: information@ebscohost. com • URL: http://www.ebscohost.com • Provides links to the Web home pages of about 1,700 U. S. publishers (including about 80 University presses) and publishers in 48 foreign countries. "International/Multinational Publishers" are included, such as the International Monetary Fund, the World Bank, and the World Trade Organization. Publishers are arranged in convenient alphabetical lists. Searching is offered. Fees: Free.

## ONLINE DATABASES

*Books in Print Online.* Bowker Electronic Publishing. • The online version of *Books in Print, Forthcoming Books, Paperbound Books in Print* and other Bowker bibliographic publications: lists the

books of over 50,000 U.S. publishers. Includes books recently declared out-of-print. Updated monthly. Inquire as to online cost and availability.

## OTHER SOURCES

*Huenefeld Report: For Managers and Planners in Modest-Sized Book Publishing Houses.* John Huenefeld, editor. The Huenefeld Company Inc. • Biweekly. $88.00 per year.

*Lindey on Entertainment, Publishing and the Arts.* Alexander Lindey, editor. Thomson West. • $1,582.86 Full Set. Provides basic forms, applicable law, and guidance.

## PERIODICALS AND NEWSLETTERS

*Choice Magazine: Current Reviews for Academic Libraries.* Association of College Research Libraries. Library and Information Technology Association. • Monthly. $415. A publication of the Association of College and Research Libraries. Contains book reviews, primarily for college and university libraries.

*Color Publishing.* PennWell Corp., Advanced Technology Div. • Bimonthly. $29.70 per year.

*Copy Editor: Language News for the Publishing Profession.* McMurry Newsletters. • Bimonthly. Newsletter for professional copy editors and proofreaders. Includes such items as "Top Ten Resources for Copy Editors.".

*Educational Marketer: The Educational Publishing Industry's Voice of Authority Since 1968.* SIMBA Information Inc. • Biweekly. $695 Individuals On-line download. Edited for suppliers of educational materials to schools and colleges at all levels. Covers print and electronic publishing, software, audiovisual items, and multimedia. Includes corporate news and educational statistics.

*Independent Publisher: Leading the World of Book Selling in New Directions.* Jenkins Group Inc. • Bimonthly. Free. Covers business, finance, production, marketing, and other management topics for small publishers, including college presses. Emphasis is on book publishing.

*Innovative Publisher: Publishing Strategies for New Markets.* Emmelle Publishing Co., Inc. • Biweekly. $69.00 per year. Provides articles and news on electronic publishing (CD-ROM or online) and desktop publishing.

*Publishers Weekly: The International News Magazine of Book Publishing.* Reed Elsevier Group plc Reed Business Information. • Weekly. $20.95 print and online; monthly. The international news magazine of book publishing.

*The SIMBA Report on Directory Publishing.* SIMBA Information Inc. • Monthly. Newsletter.

## STATISTICS SOURCES

*Standard & Poor's Industry Surveys.* Standard & Poor's Financial Services L.L.C. • Semiannual. $1,800.00. Two looseleaf volumes. Includes monthly *Supplements.* Provides detailed, individual surveys of 52 major industry groups. Each survey is revised on a semiannual basis. Also includes "Monthly Investment Review" (industry group investment analysis) and monthly "Trends & Projections" (economic analysis).

*U.S. Industry and Trade Outlook.* U.S. Department of Commerce National Technical Information Service. • Annual. Produced by the International Trade Administration, U.S. Department of Commerce, in a "public-private" partnership with DRI/ McGraw-Hill and Standard & Poor's. Provides basic data, outlook for the current year, and "Long-Term Prospects" (five-year projections) for a wide variety of products and services. Includes high technology industries. Formerly *U.S. Industrial Outlook.*

## TRADE/PROFESSIONAL ASSOCIATIONS

Association of American Publishers. 71 5th Ave., 2nd Fl., New York, NY 10003-3004. Phone:

(212)255-0200; Fax: (212)255-7007; Email: info@ publishers.org • URL: http://www.publishers.org • Represents the major commercial publishers in the United States as well as smaller and non-profit publishers, university presses and scholarly societies. Helps in the protection of intellectual property rights in all media. Promotes reading and literacy and the freedom to publish at home and abroad. Conducts seminars and workshops on various publishing topics including rights and permission, sales, and educational publishing. Compiles statistics.

Association of American University Presses. 28 W 36th St., Ste. 602, New York, NY 10018. Phone: (212)989-1010; Fax: (212)989-0275 or (212)989-0975; Email: info@aaupnet.org • URL: http://www. aaupnet.org • Helps university presses do their work more economically, creatively, and effectively through its own activities in education-training, fundraising and development, statistical research and analysis, and community and institutional relations.

Association of Learned and Professional Society Publishers. 1-3 Ship St., Shoreham-by-Sea, West Sussex BN43 5DH, United Kingdom. Phone: 44 1442 828928 or 44 190 3 871686; Fax: 44 190 3 871457; Email: audrey.mcculloch@alpsp.org • URL: http://www.alpsp.org.

Book Industry Study Group. 145 W 45th St., Ste. 601, New York, NY 10036. Phone: (646)336-7141; Fax: (646)336-6214; Email: info@bisg.org • URL: http://www.bisg.org • Represents publishers, manufacturers, suppliers, wholesalers, retailers, librarians, and other engaged in the business of print and electronic media.

Financial Publishers Association. 15430 Endeavor Dr., Jupiter, FL 33478-6402. Phone: (561)515-8555; Fax: (561)282-4509; Email: support@ financialpublishers.org • URL: http://www. financialpublishers.org • Aims to enhance the financial publishing industry's reputation for excellence. Shares knowledge of business best practices to help members. Provides financial information to guide investors.

# PULPWOOD INDUSTRY

*See* WOODPULP INDUSTRY

# PUMPS AND COMPRESSORS

## ABSTRACTS AND INDEXES

*Applied Science and Technology Index.* EBSCO Publishing Inc. • 11/year. Indexes a wide variety of English language technical, industrial, and engineering periodicals.

*Current Contents: Engineering, Computing and Technology.* Thomson Reuters Intellectual Property and Science. • Weekly. $730 per year. Reproductions of contents pages of technical journals. Includes *Author Index, Address Directory, Current Book Contents,* and *Title Word Index.* Formerly *Current Contents: Engineering, Technology and Applied Sciences.*

*Fluid Abstracts: Process Engineering.* Elsevier. • Monthly. Institutions, $1,709.00 per year. Includes annual cumulation. Formerly *Pumps and Other Fluids Machinery: Abstracts.*

## DIRECTORIES

*Fluid Power Handbook and Directory.* Penton Media Inc. • Biennial. Over 1,500 manufacturers and 3,000 distributors of fluid power products in the United States and Canada.

*The International Directory of Importers--Pumps & Compressors Importers.* Interdata. • $220 Individuals print. Covers: 2,200 international firms importing pumps and compressors. Entries include: Company name and address, contact person, email, number of employees, year established, phone and telefaxes, business activity, bank references, as well as a listing of pumps and compressors currently being imported.

## INTERNET DATABASES

*Manufacturing Profiles.* U. S. Bureau of the Census. Phone: (301)763-4636 or (301)763-4100; Fax: (301)763-4794; Email: webmaster@census.gov • URL: http://www.census.gov/prod/www/abs/mfg-prof.html • The Census Bureau makes available free on PDF (Portable Document Format) an annual consolidation of the entire Current Industrial Report series, presenting "all the data compiled." Contains statistics on production, shipments, inventories, consumption, exports, imports, and orders for a wide variety of manufactured products.

## ONLINE DATABASES

*Applied Science and Technology Index Online.* H.W. Wilson Co. • Provides online indexing of 500 major scientific, technical, industrial, and engineering periodicals. Time period is 1983 to date. Monthly updates. Inquire as to online cost and availability.

*FLUIDEX.* Elsevier. • Produced in the Netherlands by Elsevier Science B.V. Provides indexing and abstracting of the international literature of fluid engineering and technology, 1973 to date, with monthly updates. Also known as *Fluid Engineering Abstracts.* Inquire as to online cost and availability.

*Thomas Register Online.* Thomas Publishing Company L.L.C. • Provides concise information on approximately 194,000 U. S. companies, mainly manufacturers, with over 50,000 product classifications. Indexes over 115,000 trade names. Information is updated semiannually. Inquire as to online cost and availability.

## PERIODICALS AND NEWSLETTERS

*Hydraulics and Pneumatics: The Magazine of Fluid Power and Motion Control Systems.* Penton Media Inc..

*Industrial Equipment News.* Thomas Publishing Company L.L.C. • Monthly. Contains new product information for manufacturing industries.

*New Equipment Digest.* Intertec Publishing. • Monthly. Magazine (tabloid) showcasing new or improved equipment, products, materials, and components. Formerly *Material Handling Engineering.*

*New Equipment Reporter: New Products Industrial News.* DeRoche Publications. • Monthly. Controlled circulation.

*Plant Engineering.* CFE Media LLC. • Monthly. $145. Includes *Plant Engineering Product Supplier Guide.*

*Processing.* Putman Media Inc. • 14 times a year. $54.00 per year. Emphasis is on descriptions of new products for all areas of industrial processing, including valves, controls, filters, pumps, compressors, fluidics, and instrumentation.

## RESEARCH CENTERS AND INSTITUTES

Purdue University - Ray W. Herrick Laboratories. School of Mechanical Engineering, 140 S Martin Jischke Dr., West Lafayette, IN 47907-2031. Phone: (765)494-2132; Fax: (765)494-0787; Email: rhlab@ecn.purdue.edu • URL: http://engineering.purdue.edu/Herrick/index.html • Mechanical engineering, including studies on heating, air conditioning, and refrigeration equipment and systems, engineering acoustics, noise and vibration control (including vehicle and engine noise), sound quality, positive displacement compressor technology, mechanical reliability, precision measurements, mechanics of materials, tribology, noise control materials, electro-hydraulic and engine controls, emissions, and automatic control.

## STATISTICS SOURCES

*Pumps and Compressors.* U. S. Bureau of the Census. • Annual. Provides data on value of manufacturers' shipments, quantity, exports, imports, etc. (Current Industrial Reports, MA-35P.).

## TRADE/PROFESSIONAL ASSOCIATIONS

Contractors Pump Bureau. 6737 W Washington St., Ste. 2400, Milwaukee, WI 53214-5647. Phone: (414)272-0943; Fax: (414)272-1170; Email: aem@aem.org • URL: http://www.aem.org/Groups/Groups/Group.asp?G=22 • A bureau of the Association of Equipment Manufacturers. Manufacturers of pumping machinery and engines for the construction industry; suppliers to the manufacturers. Works toward the standardization of sizes and capacities of contractors' pumps.

# PURCHASING

## ABSTRACTS AND INDEXES

*Business Periodicals Index Retrospective.* EBSCO Publishing Inc. • 11/year. Quarterly and annual cumulations.

## CD-ROM DATABASES

*Business Abstracts with Full Text.* EBSCO Publishing Inc. • Includes full text articles from more than 460 business publications from 1982 to present. Indexing for nearly 880 publications.

## ONLINE DATABASES

*Thomas Register Online.* Thomas Publishing Company L.L.C. • Provides concise information on approximately 194,000 U. S. companies, mainly manufacturers, with over 50,000 product classifications. Indexes over 115,000 trade names. Information is updated semiannually. Inquire as to online cost and availability.

*Wilson Business Abstracts Online.* H.W. Wilson Co. • Indexes and abstracts 600 major business periodicals, plus the *Wall Street Journal* and the business section of the *New York Times.* Indexing is from 1982, abstracting from 1990, with the two newspapers included from 1993. Updated weekly. Inquire as to online cost and availability. (*Business Periodicals Index* without abstracts is also available online.).

## PERIODICALS AND NEWSLETTERS

*Business & Industry--Who's Who in Purchasing Issue.* Business Magazine Inc. • Annual. $5 postpaid. Contains rosters for 19 purchasing manager associations in Minnesota, Iowa, Nebraska, North and South Dakota, and Wisconsin.

*Business Consumer's Advisor.* Buyers Laboratory L.L.C. • Description: Focuses on office equipment and supplies, offering purchasing advice and exploring methods of increasing office productivity through appropriate management of the equipment and its operators. Offers readers a chance to share their experiences, evaluate products and equipment, and gives results of Buyers Laboratory's testing.

*Healthcare Purchasing News: A Magazine for Hospital Materials Management Central Service, Infection Control Practitioners.* Thomson Medical Economics. • Monthly. $72. Edited for personnel responsible for the purchase of medical, surgical, and hospital equipment and supplies. Features new purchasing techniques and new products. Includes news of the activities of two major purchasing associations, Health Care Material Management Society and International Association of Healthcare Central Service Materiel Management.

*Industrial Purchasing Agent.* Publications for Industry. • Description: Covers new product releases pertaining to the industrial manufacturing industry. Recurring features include by-line spreads, news of research, and new literature releases.

*Purchasing: The Magazine of Total Supply Chain*

*Management.* Reed Elsevier Group plc Reed Business Information. • 24 times a year. $109.90 per year. Includes *Guide and Directory.*

## TRADE/PROFESSIONAL ASSOCIATIONS

Alliance of Supplier Diversity Professionals. PO Box 782049, Orlando, FL 32878-2049. Phone: 877-405-6565; Email: info@asdp.us • URL: http://www.asdp.us • Represents supplier diversity professionals throughout the United States. Offers education and professional development opportunities, certification for professionals within management, supplier diversity, procurement and similar career paths. Provides a forum for members to exchange information on all aspects of the supplier diversity profession.

Association for Healthcare Resource and Materials Management. 155 N Wacker Dr., Chicago, IL 60606. Phone: (312)422-3840; Fax: (312)422-4573; Email: ahrmm@aha.org • URL: http://www.ahrmm.org • Members are involved with the purchasing and distribution of supplies and equipment for hospitals and other healthcare establishments. Formerly American Society for Healthcare Materials Management.

Council of Supplier Diversity Professionals. PO Box 70226, Rochester, MI 48307. Email: info@ncsdp.com • URL: http://www.ncsdp.com • Aims to assist in the growth and development of the supplier diversity profession. Provides a forum to share information, ideas and issues concerning supplier diversity. Offers career-development strategies for supplier diversity professionals.

Institute for Supply Management. 2055 E Centennial Cir., Tempe, AZ 85284-1898. Phone: 800-888-6276 or (480)752-6276; Fax: (480)752-7890; Email: custsvc@ism.ws • URL: http://www.ism.ws • Represents industrial, commercial and utility firms; educational institutions and government agencies. Disseminates information on procurement. Works to develop more efficient supply management methods. Conducts program for certification as a supply manager. Cosponsors executive purchasing management institutes at Michigan State University and Arizona State University. Provides in-company training. Maintains speakers' bureau and reference service.

Utility Supply Management Alliance. PO Box 6608, Pine Bluff, AR 71611. Phone: (913)768-7005; Fax: (913)397-0901; Email: parbuckle4@comcast.net • URL: http://www.usma.com • Reduces overall supply chain costs by providing a forum for utilities and suppliers. Advocates for aggressive and responsible leadership, responsiveness to customer needs and continuous improvement in supply chain management. Improves the service and profitability of utilities and suppliers.

## PURCHASING AGENTS

*See* PURCHASING

## PURCHASING POWER

*See also* CONSUMER ECONOMICS; INCOME; MARKET STATISTICS

## DIRECTORIES

*Editor & Publisher Market Guide.* Editor and Publisher Company Inc. • Annual. $150 Individuals. Market data for more than 1,600 cities and 3,096 counties.

*Marketing Economics Key Plants: Guide to Industrial Purchasing Power.* Marketing Economics Institute Ltd. • Biennial. $136 national edition. Covers: more than 40,000 key manufacturing plants with 100 or more employees (SIC 2011-3999); there are also editions for New England, Middle Atlantic, East North Central, West North Central, South Atlantic, East South Central, West South Central, and Mountain/Pacific regions. Entries include: Company name, address, number of employees, phone, SIC numbers.

## STATISTICS SOURCES

*The AIER Chart Book.* AIER Research Staff. American Institute for Economic Research. • Annual. $4 Individuals. A compact compilation of long-range charts ("Purchasing Power of the Dollar," for example, goes back to 1780) covering various aspects of the U. S. economy. Includes inflation, interest rates, debt, gold, taxation, stock prices, etc. (Economic Education Bulletin.).

*Prices and Earnings Around the Globe.* Union Bank of Switzerland. • Triennial. Free. Published in Zurich. Compares prices and purchasing power in 48 major cities of the world. Wages and hours are also compared.

*Sales and Marketing Management Survey of Buying Power.* Nielsen Business Media Inc. • Annual. $150. 00.

# PUTS AND CALLS

*See* STOCK OPTION CONTRACTS

---

# Q

## QUALITY CONTROL

*See also* PRODUCTION CONTROL; STANDARDIZATION

### ABSTRACTS AND INDEXES

*NTIS Alerts: Manufacturing Technology.* U.S. Department of Commerce National Technical Information Service. • Biweekly. $130 per year. Covers computer-aided design and manufacturing (CAD/CAM), engineering materials, quality control, machine tools, robots, lasers, productivity, and related subjects.

### PERIODICALS AND NEWSLETTERS

*Quality and Reliability Engineering International.* John Wiley and Sons, Inc., Journals Div. • 8/year. $3,503 Institutions. Designed to bridge the gap between existing theoretical methods and scientific research on the one hand, and current industrial practices on the other. Published in England by John Wiley and Sons Ltd.

*Quality Management Journal.* American Society for Quality. • Quarterly. $65 Members. Emphasizes research in quality control and management.

*Quality Progress.* American Society for Quality. • Monthly. $70 Members. Covers developments in quality improvement throughout the world.

### RESEARCH CENTERS AND INSTITUTES

National Center for Manufacturing Sciences. 3025 Boardwalk, Ann Arbor, MI 48108-3230. Phone: 800-222-6267 or (734)995-0300; Fax: (734)995-1150 or (734)995-4004; Email: info@ncms.org • Research areas include process technology and control, machine mechanics, sensors, testing methods, and quality assurance.

Techsolve Inc. 6705 Steger Dr., Cincinnati, OH 45237. Phone: 800-345-4482 or (513)948-2000; Fax: (513)948-2109 or (800)345-4482; Email: perkins@techsolve.org • URL: http://www.techsolve.org • Fields of research include quality improvement, computer-aided design, artificial intelligence, and employee training.

### TRADE/PROFESSIONAL ASSOCIATIONS

American Society for Quality. PO Box 3005, Milwaukee, WI 53201-3005. Phone: 800-248-1946 or (414)272-8575; Email: help@asq.org • URL: http://asq.org • Individuals and organizations dedicated to the ongoing development, advancement, and promotion of quality concepts, principles, and technologies. Through its Education Development Department, offers courses in quality engineering, reliability engineering, managing for quality, management of quality costs, quality audit-development and administration, management of the inspection function, probability and statistics for engineers and scientists, and product liability and prevention.

## QUALITY OF PRODUCTS

*See also* CONSUMER EDUCATION; STANDARDIZATION

### CD-ROM DATABASES

*Consumer Health Complete.* EBSCO Publishing Inc. • Full text of more than 250 health references, health diagrams, videos, pamphlets.

### PERIODICALS AND NEWSLETTERS

*Consumer Reports.* Consumers Union of United States. • Monthly. $30 Individuals. Magazine featuring analyses and investigative reporting of products. Includes *Annual Buying Guide.*

*Consumer's Research Magazine: Analyzing Consumer Issues.* Consumers' Research. • Monthly. $24.00 per year.

*NDT and E International; The Independent Journal of Non-Destructive Testing.* Elsevier. • 8/year. $1,315 Institutions.

### TRADE/PROFESSIONAL ASSOCIATIONS

American National Standards Institute. 1899 L St. NW, 11th Fl., Washington, DC 20036-3807. Phone: (202)293-8020; Fax: (202)293-9287; Email: info@ansi.org • URL: http://www.ansi.org • Industrial firms, trade associations, technical societies, labor organizations, consumer organizations, and government agencies. Serves as clearinghouse for nationally coordinated voluntary standards for fields ranging from information technology to building construction. Gives status as American National Standards to standards developed by agreement from all groups concerned, in such areas as: definitions, terminology, symbols, and abbreviations; materials, performance characteristics, procedure, and methods of rating; methods of testing and analysis; size, weight, volume, and rating; practice, safety, health, and building construction. Provides information on foreign standards and represents United States interests in international standardization work.

Consumers Union of United States. 101 Truman Ave., Yonkers, NY 10703-1057. Phone: (914)378-2000 • URL: http://www.consumersunion.org • Testing, rating, and reporting organization providing information on competing brands of appliances, automobiles, food products, and household equipment. Aims to provide consumers with information and advice on consumer goods and services; to give information and assistance on all financial matters affecting consumers; to initiate and to cooperate with individual and group efforts seeking to create, maintain, and enhance the quality of life for consumers. Regional offices represent consumer interests in the legislature, courts, and administrative agencies. Derives income from sale of its publication, *Consumer Reports,* and other publications. All subscribers may become members. Produces a syndicated radio program, Report to Consumers; a syndicated newspaper column, *From Consumer Reports*; and television series for cable television, Consumer Reports Presents.

## QUARRYING

*See also* CLAY INDUSTRY; LIMESTONE INDUSTRY; MARBLE

### DIRECTORIES

*Gravel Directory--Wholesalers.* InfoGroup Inc. • Annual. Number of listings: 12,943. Entries include: Name, address, phone, size of advertisement, name of owner or manager, number of employees, year first in "Yellow Pages." Compiled from telephone company "Yellow Pages," nationwide.

*Kompass.* Kompass Deutschland Verlags- und Vertriebsgesellschaft, mbH. • Annual. $88. Covers: German products and companies specializing in coal extraction, ore mining, quarries, cement industry, glass and ceramics.

### FINANCIAL RATIOS

*Annual Statement Studies.* Risk Management Association. • Annual. Compiled from over 280,000 financial statements.

*Annual Statement Studies: Industry Default Probabilities and Cash Flow Measures.* Risk Management Association. • Annual. $405 Nonmembers. Serves as a companion volume to the original *Annual Statement Studies.* Gives probability of default estimates on a percentage scale for more than 450 industries. Includes changes in position year-by-year for eight financial statement line items and provides percentage measures of cash flow.

### PERIODICALS AND NEWSLETTERS

*Building Stone Magazine.* Building Stone Institute. • Quarterly. $20 Individuals /year. Information on the natural stone industry.

*Pit and Quarry.* Advanstar Communications. • Monthly. Covers crushed stone, sand and gravel, etc.

*Rock Products: The Aggregate Industry's Journal of Applied Technology.* Primedia Business Magazines and Media. • Monthly. $56.00 per year.

### STATISTICS SOURCES

*United States Census of Mineral Industries.* Bureau of the Census, U.S. Department of Commerce. U. S.

Government Printing Office. • Quinquennial.

## TRADE/PROFESSIONAL ASSOCIATIONS

Building Stone Institute. 5 Riverside Dr., Bldg. 2, Chestertown, NY 12817. Phone: 866-786-6313 or (518)803-4336; Fax: (518)803-6313 or (518)803-4338 • URL: http://www.buildingstoneinstitute.org • Represents natural stone quarriers, fabricators, installers, dealers, importers, expo and restorers. Serves as a clearinghouse of information for architects, contractors, and masons. Promotes the use of natural stone.

National Building Granite Quarries Association. 1220 L St. NW, Ste. 100-167, Washington, DC 20005. Phone: 800-557-2848 • URL: http://www.nbgqa.com • Represents quarriers and manufacturers of building granites. Provides specifications for designers.

National Stone, Sand and Gravel Association. 1605 King St., Alexandria, VA 22314-2726. Phone: 800-342-1415 or (703)525-8788 or (703)526-1098; Fax: (703)525-7782; Email: info@nssga.org • URL: http://www.nssga.org • Formerly National Stone Association.

# R

## RACK JOBBERS

### HANDBOOKS AND MANUALS

*Progressive Grocer Guidebook.* Trade Dimensions. • Annual. $375.00. Over 800 major chain and independent food retailers and wholesalers in the United States and Canada; also includes food brokers, rack jobbers, candy and tobacco distributors, and magazine distributors.

### PERIODICALS AND NEWSLETTERS

*Non-Foods Management: The Annual Supermarket State of the Industry Report.* Millennium Media Corp. • Annual. $45.00. Written for top management and non-foods decision makers and executives at supermarkets.

### TRADE/PROFESSIONAL ASSOCIATIONS

Music Business Association. 1 Eves Dr., Ste. 138, Marlton, NJ 08053. Phone: (856)596-2221; Fax: (856)596-7299 • URL: http://www.musicbiz.org • Serves the music and other prerecorded entertainment software industry as a forum for insight and dialogue; members include retailers, wholesalers, distributors, entertainment software suppliers, and suppliers of related products and services.

## RADIO AND TELEVISION ADVERTISING

*See also* ADVERTISING; ADVERTISING MEDIA; RADIO BROADCASTING INDUSTRY; TELEVISION BROADCASTING INDUSTRY

### DIRECTORIES

*RAB Co-op Directory.* Radio Advertising Bureau. • Annual. Database covers: Over 5,000 manufacturers that provide cooperative allowances for radio advertising. Database includes: Company name, address, name of contact, phone, fax, allowance, accrual rate, whether plan is administered by distributor, and expiration dates.

*VNU Business Media.* ADWEEK Media. • Annual. $100.00. Presents cost, circulation, and audience statistics for various mass media segments, including television, radio, magazines, newspapers, telephone yellow pages, and cinema.

### ONLINE DATABASES

*Arbitron Radio County Coverage.* Arbitron Inc. • Ratings of radio and TV stations plus audience measurement data, updated frequently. Inquire as to online cost and availability.

### PERIODICALS AND NEWSLETTERS

*Broadcasting and Cable.* NewBay Media, LLC. • 51 times a year. $179.00 per year; includes print and online editions. Formerly *Broadcasting.*

*SHOOT: The Leading Newsweekly for Commercial Production and Postproduction.* Nielsen Business Media Inc. • Weekly. $125 /year. Covers animation, music, sound design, computer graphics, visual effects, cinematography, and other aspects of television and motion picture production, with emphasis on TV commercials.

### STATISTICS SOURCES

*Radio Facts: The Voice of Urban Culture.* RadioMan Publishing Inc. • Annual. $50.00.

*Television and Cable Factbook.* Warren Communications News Inc. • Annual. $595. Commercial and noncommercial television stations and networks.

### TRADE/PROFESSIONAL ASSOCIATIONS

Radio Advertising Bureau. 1320 Greenway Dr., Ste. 500, Irving, TX 75038-2587. Phone: 800-232-3131 or (972)753-6786 or (516)753-6782; Fax: (972)753-6727 or (212)753-6727; Email: efarber@rab.com • URL: http://www.rab.com • Includes radio stations, radio networks, station sales representatives, and allied industry services, such as producers, research firms, schools, and consultants. Calls on advertisers and agencies to promote the sale of radio time as an advertising medium. Sponsors program to increase professionalism of radio salespeople, awarding Certified Radio Marketing Consultant designation to those who pass examination. Sponsors regional marketing conferences. Conducts extensive research program into all phases of radio sales. Issues reports on use of radio by national, regional, and local advertisers. Speaks before conventions and groups to explain benefits of radio advertising. Sponsors Radio Creative Fund. Compiles statistics.

## RADIO AND TELEVISION REPAIR INDUSTRY

### PERIODICALS AND NEWSLETTERS

*Electronic Servicing & Technology: The How-To Magazine of Electronics.* CQ Communications. • Monthly. Free to qualified personnel; others, $26.95 per year. Provides how-to technical information to technicians who service consumer electronics equipment.

*Poptronics.* Gernsback Publications, Inc. • Monthly. $19.99 per year. Incorporates *Electronics Now.*

### STATISTICS SOURCES

*United States Census of Service Industries.* U.S. Department of Commerce U.S. Census Bureau. • Quinquennial. Various reports available.

### TRADE/PROFESSIONAL ASSOCIATIONS

National Electronics Service Dealers Association. 3608 Pershing Ave., Fort Worth, TX 76107-4527. Phone: 800-797-9197 or (817)921-9061; Fax: (817)921-3741; Email: mack@nesda.com • URL: http://www.nesda.com • Local and state electronic service associations and companies. Supplies technical service information on business management training to electronic service dealers. Offers certification and training programs through International Society of Certified Electronics Technicians. Conducts technical service and business management seminars.

## RADIO BROADCASTING INDUSTRY

*See also* RADIO AND TELEVISION ADVERTISING; RADIO EQUIPMENT INDUSTRY; TELEVISION BROADCASTING INDUSTRY

### ABSTRACTS AND INDEXES

*Communication Abstracts: An International Information Service.* Pine Forge Press. • Bimonthly. Institutions, $1,150.00 per year. Provides broad coverage of the literature of communications, including broadcasting and advertising.

### DIRECTORIES

*BIA's Radio Yearbook.* BIA/Kelsey. • Annual. $240 Individuals. U.S. Radio stations, radio equipment manufacturers, and related service providers and trade associations.

*Burrelle's Media Directory: Broadcast Media.* BurrellesLuce. • Annual. $550.00. Approximately 48,000 print and electronic media in North America. Provides detailed descriptions, including programming and key personnel.

*Investing in Radio Market Report.* BIA/Kelsey. • Quarterly. $1,475 Individuals. Covers: U.S. Radio industry markets and inclusive stations. Database includes: Market data, including revenues, demographics, and economic indicators. Entries include: For stations--Call letters, technical attributes, format, estimated revenues, owner, last acquisition date and price, ratings for eight books.

*Working Press of the Nation.* R.R. Bowker L.L.C. • Annual. $530.00. $295.00 per volume. Three volumes: (1) *Newspaper Directory*; (2) *Magazine and Internal Publications Directory*; (3) *Radio and Television Directory*. Includes names of editors and other personnel.

### FINANCIAL RATIOS

*Annual Statement Studies.* Risk Management Association. • Annual. Compiled from over 280,000 financial statements.

*Annual Statement Studies: Industry Default Prob-*

For publishers' addresses, refer to SOURCES CITED section at the back of the book.

747

*abilities and Cash Flow Measures.* Risk Management Association. • Annual. $405 Nonmembers. Serves as a companion volume to the original *Annual Statement Studies.* Gives probability of default estimates on a percentage scale for more than 450 industries. Includes changes in position year-by-year for eight financial statement line items and provides percentage measures of cash flow.

## OTHER SOURCES

*FCC Record.* U. S. Government Printing Office. • Semimonthly. $813 U.S. 1 year. Produced by the Federal Communications Commission (www.fcc. gov). An inclusive compilation of decisions, reports, public notices, and other documents of the FCC.

## PERIODICALS AND NEWSLETTERS

*Broadcast Engineering: Journal of Broadcast Technology.* Penton. • 10 times a year. Free to qualified personnel; others, $65.00 per year. Technical magazine for the broadcast industry.

*Broadcast Investor: Newsletter on Radio-TV Station Finance.* Paul Kagan Associates, Inc. • Monthly. $925.00 per year. Newsletter for investors in publicly held radio and television broadcasting companies.

*Broadcasting and Cable.* NewBay Media, LLC. • 51 times a year. $179.00 per year; includes print and online editions. Formerly *Broadcasting.*

*Entertainment Law and Finance.* ALM Media Properties LLC. • Monthly. $485 print and online. Covers contracts, royalties, litigation, copyright, taxation, etc., for the music industry, motion pictures, broadcasting, publishing, video, and related media. (A Law Journal Newsletter, formerly published by Leader Publications.).

*Journal of Broadcasting and Electronic Media.* Broadcast Education Association. • Quarterly. $40 Nonmembers /year in U.S.. Scholarly articles about developments, trends and research.

*Radio World.* IMAS Publishing Group. • Biweekly. Free. Emphasis is on radio broadcast engineeri and equipment. Text in English, Portuguese and Spanish.

## STATISTICS SOURCES

*Standard & Poor's Industry Surveys.* Standard & Poor's Financial Services L.L.C. • Semiannual. $1,800.00. Two looseleaf volumes. Includes monthly *Supplements.* Provides detailed, individual surveys of 52 major industry groups. Each survey is revised on a semiannual basis. Also includes "Monthly Investment Review" (industry group investment analysis) and monthly "Trends & Projections" (economic analysis).

## TRADE/PROFESSIONAL ASSOCIATIONS

American Sportscasters Association. 225 Broadway, Ste. 2030, New York, NY 10007. Phone: (212)227-8080; Fax: (212)571-0556; Email: inquiry@ americansportscastersonline.com • URL: http:// www.americansportscastersonline.com • Radio and television sportscasters. Sponsors seminars, clinics, and symposia for aspiring announcers and sportscasters. Compiles statistics. Operates speakers' bureau, placement service, hall of fame, and biographical archives. Maintains American Sportscaster Hall of Fame Trust. Is currently implementing Hall of Fame Museum, Community Programs.

Broadcast Education Association. 1771 N St. NW, Washington, DC 20036-2891. Phone: (202)429-5355 or (202)429-3935; Fax: (202)775-2981; Email: beamemberservices@nab.org • URL: http://www. beaweb.org • Universities and colleges; faculty and students; promotes improvement of curriculum and teaching methods, broadcasting research, television and radio production, and programming teaching on the college level.

National Association of Broadcasters. 1771 N St. NW, Washington, DC 20036. Phone: 800-342-2460

or (202)429-5300 or (202)429-5490; Email: nab@ nab.org • URL: http://www.nab.org • Formerly National Association of Radio and Television Broadcasters.

# RADIO EQUIPMENT INDUSTRY

*See also* COMMUNICATION SYSTEMS; HIGH FIDELITY/STEREO; TELEVISION APPARATUS INDUSTRY

## ABSTRACTS AND INDEXES

*NTIS Alerts: Communication.* U.S. Department of Commerce National Technical Information Service. • Biweekly. $130 Individuals per year; domestic/ foreign. Covers common carriers, satellites, radio/TV equipment, telecommunication regulations, and related subjects.

## DIRECTORIES

*Broadcast Engineering--Equipment Reference Manual.* Penton. • Annual. Publication includes: List of more than 1,400 manufacturers and distributors of communications equipment for radio, television, and recording applications. Database includes: Specifications for major brands of professional broadcast hardware. Entries include: For manufacturers--Company name, address. For distributors and dealers--Company name, address, phone, product or service provided, geographic area covered.

## FINANCIAL RATIOS

*Annual Statement Studies.* Risk Management Association. • Annual. Compiled from over 280,000 financial statements.

*Annual Statement Studies: Industry Default Probabilities and Cash Flow Measures.* Risk Management Association. • Annual. $405 Nonmembers. Serves as a companion volume to the original *Annual Statement Studies.* Gives probability of default estimates on a percentage scale for more than 450 industries. Includes changes in position year-by-year for eight financial statement line items and provides percentage measures of cash flow.

## PERIODICALS AND NEWSLETTERS

*Broadcast Engineering: Journal of Broadcast Technology.* Penton. • 10 times a year. Free to qualified personnel; others, $65.00 per year. Technical magazine for the broadcast industry.

*Poptronics.* Gernsback Publications, Inc. • Monthly. $19.99 per year. Incorporates *Electronics Now.*

*RCR Wireless News: The Newspaper for the Wireless Communications Industry.* Crain Communications. • Weekly. $64.00 per year. Covers news of the wireless communications industry, including business and financial developments. Formerly *RCR.*

*Sound and Communications.* Testa Communications. • Monthly. $15.00 per year. A business, news and technical journal for contractors, consultants, engineers and system managers who design, install and purchase sound and communications equipment. Provides important industry information, also serves as a communicator for the various elements that comprise this strong and dynamic market.

## TRADE/PROFESSIONAL ASSOCIATIONS

North American Retail Dealers Association. 222 S Riverside Plz., Ste. 2100, Chicago, IL 60606. Phone: 800-621-0298 or (312)648-0649; Fax: (312)648-1212; Email: nardasvc@narda.com • URL: http:// www.narda.com • Firms engaged in the retailing of electronic and electrical devices and components. Promotes and represents members' interests. Makes available services to members including: legal and technical consulting; employee screening; bank card

processing; long-distance phone discounts; financial statements analysis; in-store promotion kits; customer check authorization. Advocates for members' interests before federal regulatory bodies; disseminates information on new regulations affecting members. Conducts educational programs.

# RADIO STATIONS

*See* RADIO BROADCASTING INDUSTRY

# RADIOISOTOPES

*See* ISOTOPES

# RADIOLOGICAL EQUIPMENT

*See* X-RAY EQUIPMENT INDUSTRY

# RADIOS

*See* RADIO EQUIPMENT INDUSTRY

# RAILROAD EQUIPMENT INDUSTRY

## CD-ROM DATABASES

*OECD Statistical Compendium.* Organization for Economic Cooperation and Development. • Semiannual. $1,905.00 per year for 1 to 10 users. CD-ROM contains more than 730,000 monthly, quarterly, and annual time series for OECD countries, 1960 to date. Includes fully searchable data on agriculture, food, economic indicators, national accounts, employment, energy, finance, industry, technology, and foreign trade. Results can be displayed in various forms.

## DIRECTORIES

*Directory of Taiwanese Manufacturers & Exporters of Railway Equipment & Supplies.* EXIM Infotek Private Ltd. • $5 Individuals. Covers: 20 Taiwanese manufacturers and exporters of locomotives/railcars and tramcars, railway equipments, railways and tram carriage/wagons. Entries include: Company name, postal address, city, country, phone, fax, e-mail and websites, contact person, designation, and product details.

## INTERNET DATABASES

*Business 2.0 Web Guide to the Best Business Links.* Business 2.0 Media Inc. Phone: (415)293-4800; Email: support@business2.com • URL: http://www. business2.com/webguide • Web site presents an extensive, searchable directory of links to "the best, most informative, and authoritative web pages." Twenty main categories cover business, finance, career, company information, people, and technology topics, with thousands of subtopics, all linking to Web sites recommended by experienced business researchers. Fees: Free.

*Fedstats.* Federal Interagency Council on Statistical Policy. Phone: (202)395-7254 • URL: http://www. fedstats.gov • Web site features an efficient search facility for full-text statistics produced by more than 100 federal agencies, including the Census Bureau, the Bureau of Economic Analysis, and the Bureau of Labor Statistics. Boolean searches can be made within one agency or for all agencies combined. Links are offered to international statistical bureaus, including the UN, IMF, OECD, UNESCO, Eurostat, and 20 individual countries. Fees: Free.

*FreeLunch.com.* Economy.com, Inc. Phone: (610)696-8700; Fax: (610)696-1678 • URL: http://

www.freelunch.com • Web site provides free access to more than 200 million economic and financial data series, covering industry, demographics, labor markets, prices, retail sales, government spending, trade, interest rates, housing starts, the stock market, etc. Data is available in either chart or table form. Searching is offered. Free, but registration required. Economy.com, Inc. also offers fee-based economic analysis at *The Dismal Scientist* site (www.dismal. com).

## ONLINE DATABASES

*Thomas Register Online*. Thomas Publishing Company L.L.C. • Provides concise information on approximately 194,000 U. S. companies, mainly manufacturers, with over 50,000 product classifications. Indexes over 115,000 trade names. Information is updated semiannually. Inquire as to online cost and availability.

## PERIODICALS AND NEWSLETTERS

*Railway Track and Structures*. Simmons-Boardman Publishing Corp. • Monthly.

## STATISTICS SOURCES

*Railroad Facts*. Association of American Railroads. • $5 Nonmembers. Annual.

*Survey of Current Business*. U. S. Government Printing Office. • Published by Bureau of Economic Analysis, U. S. Department of Commerce. Presents a wide variety of business and economic data.

## TRADE/PROFESSIONAL ASSOCIATIONS

American Railway Car Institute. c/o Edward Whalen, Chairman, FreightCar America Inc., 2 N Riverside Plz., Ste. 1300, Chicago, IL 60606. Phone: (202)347-4664; Fax: (312)928-0890 • URL: http:// rsiweb.org/about/rsi-committees/arci • Conducts research and standardization activities, particularly in freight car design and container standards. Provides for exchange of data on new devices used in freight cars. Compiles statistics on orders, deliveries, and backlogs of railroad cars with Association of American Railroads.

American Railway Engineering and Maintenance of Way Association. 10003 Derekwood Ln., Ste. 210, Lanham, MD 20706-4875. Phone: (301)459-3200; Fax: (301)459-8077 • URL: http://www.arema.org • Professional organization of railway and transit officials concerned with design, construction, and maintenance of bridges, buildings, water service facilities, communications and signals systems, and other railway structures; engineering professors, editors, and government and private timber specialists.

Railway Engineering-Maintenance Suppliers Association. 500 New Jersey Ave. NW, Ste. 400, Washington, DC 20001. Phone: (202)715-2921; Fax: (202)204-5753; Email: info@remsa.org • URL: http://www.remsa.org • Provides global business development opportunities to members. Works to transfer knowledge about markets, products and the industry to members and their customers. Supports government initiatives that advance the North American railroad industry.

Railway Systems Suppliers. 9306 New LaGrange Rd., Ste. 100, Louisville, KY 40242. Phone: (502)327-7774; Fax: (502)327-0541; Email: rssi@ rssi.org • URL: http://rssi.org • Corporations, partnerships, and individuals engaged in the manufacture, sale, and service of products, appliances, apparatus, and devices used in railway signals, controls, and communications; engineers and contractors engaged in construction or maintenance of any such product. Collects and disseminates information of interest to members.

## RAILROADS

*See also* TRANSPORTATION INDUSTRY

## ABSTRACTS AND INDEXES

*NTIS Alerts: Transportation*. U.S. Department of Commerce National Technical Information Service. • Biweekly. $130 per year. Covers air, marine, highway, inland waterway, pipeline, and railroad transportation.

## CD-ROM DATABASES

*OECD Statistical Compendium*. Organization for Economic Cooperation and Development. • Semiannual. $1,905.00 per year for 1 to 10 users. CD-ROM contains more than 730,000 monthly, quarterly, and annual time series for OECD countries, 1960 to date. Includes fully searchable data on agriculture, food, economic indicators, national accounts, employment, energy, finance, industry, technology, and foreign trade. Results can be displayed in various forms.

## INTERNET DATABASES

*Business 2.0 Web Guide to the Best Business Links*. Business 2.0 Media Inc. Phone: (415)293-4800; Email: support@business2.com • URL: http://www. business2.com/webguide • Web site presents an extensive, searchable directory of links to "the best, most informative, and authoritative web pages." Twenty main categories cover business, finance, career, company information, people, and technology topics, with thousands of subtopics, all linking to Web sites recommended by experienced business researchers. Fees: Free.

*Fedstats*. Federal Interagency Council on Statistical Policy. Phone: (202)395-7254 • URL: http://www. fedstats.gov • Web site features an efficient search facility for full-text statistics produced by more than 100 federal agencies, including the Census Bureau, the Bureau of Economic Analysis, and the Bureau of Labor Statistics. Boolean searches can be made within one agency or for all agencies combined. Links are offered to international statistical bureaus, including the UN, IMF, OECD, UNESCO, Eurostat, and 20 individual countries. Fees: Free.

*FreeLunch.com*. Economy.com, Inc. Phone: (610)696-8700; Fax: (610)696-1678 • URL: http:// www.freelunch.com • Web site provides free access to more than 200 million economic and financial data series, covering industry, demographics, labor markets, prices, retail sales, government spending, trade, interest rates, housing starts, the stock market, etc. Data is available in either chart or table form. Searching is offered. Free, but registration required. Economy.com, Inc. also offers fee-based economic analysis at *The Dismal Scientist* site (www.dismal. com).

## ONLINE DATABASES

*TRIS: Transportation Research Information Service*. The National Academies National Research Council. • Contains abstracts and citations to a wide range of transportation literature, 1968 to present, with monthly updates. Includes references to the literature of air transportation, highways, ships and shipping, railroads, trucking, and urban mass transportation. Formerly *TRIS-ON-LINE*. Inquire as to online cost and availability.

## OTHER SOURCES

*Consumers United for Rail Equity*. • Coalition of railroad shippers that are captive to a single railroad for their transportation needs.

## PERIODICALS AND NEWSLETTERS

*International Railway Journal: The First International Railway and Rapid Transit Journal*. Simmons-Boardman Publishing Corp. • Monthly. $72.00 per year. Formerly *International Railway Journal and Rapid Transit Review*. Text in English; summaries in French, German and Spanish.

*Progressive Railroading*. Trade Press Media Group. • Monthly. Provides feature articles, news, new product information, etc. Relative to the railroad and rail transit industry.

*Railway Age*. Simmons-Boardman Publishing Corp. • Monthly.

*Trains; The Magazine of Railroading*. Kalmbach Publishing Co. • Monthly. $39.95 per year.

*U.S. Rail News*. Business Publishers Inc. • Description: Reports developments in all aspects of the rail transportation industry. Covers topics such as deregulation, mergers and acquisitions, labor relations, and financial management. Recurring features include news briefs and a calendar of related conferences and meetings.

## STATISTICS SOURCES

*Railroad Facts*. Association of American Railroads. • $5 Nonmembers. Annual.

*Survey of Current Business*. U. S. Government Printing Office. • Published by Bureau of Economic Analysis, U. S. Department of Commerce. Presents a wide variety of business and economic data.

## TRADE/PROFESSIONAL ASSOCIATIONS

Association of American Railroads. 425 3rd St. SW, Washington, DC 20024. Phone: (202)639-2100 or (202)639-2345; Fax: (202)639-2558; Email: media@aari.org • URL: http://www.aar.org • Coordinating and research agency of the American freight railway industry. Fields of interest include railroad operation and maintenance, statistics, research, public relations, communications, signals, car exchange rules, safety, police and security matters, and testing and standards of railroad equipment. Operates Transportation Technology Center in Pueblo, CO and Railinc in Cary, NC.

National Association of Railroad Passengers. 505 Capitol Ct. NE, Ste. 300, Washington, DC 20002-7706. Phone: (202)408-8362; Fax: (202)408-8287; Email: narp@narprail.org • URL: http://www. narprail.org • Users of rail passenger service, other concerned individuals, and organizations wishing to improve and expand rail passenger service. Seeks to increase public awareness and understanding of rail passenger service and its benefits. Works for fair and equal treatment for rail passenger service by government, in relation to other forms of transportation, and in the areas of defense transportation, mail transportation, taxation and user charges, and research and development expenditures. Seeks the establishment of a national transportation policy that includes rail passenger service as an essential element; initiates specific rail passenger improvements with appropriate government and transportation officials.

National Association of Railway Business Women. c/o Amy Schapp, Membership Chairperson, 5109 S 194th St., Omaha, NE 68135. Email: narbwinfo@ narbw.org • URL: http://www.narbw.org • Formerly Railway Business Women's Association.

Railway Supply Institute. 425 3rd St. SW, Ste. 920, Washington, DC 20024. Phone: (202)347-4664; Fax: (202)347-0047 • URL: http://rsiweb.org • Formerly Railway Progress Institute.

## RAISIN INDUSTRY

*See* FRUIT INDUSTRY

## RARE BOOKS

*See* BOOK COLLECTING

## RARE EARTH METALS

## PERIODICALS AND NEWSLETTERS

*Rare Earth Bulletin*. Multi-Science Publishing Company Ltd. • Bimonthly. Contains informative and concise summaries of scientific/technical papers, written in straightforward style by qualified experts.

*RIC News.* Rare-Earth Information Center. • Quarterly. Contains items of current interest concerning the science and technology of the rare earth.

# RATING OF EMPLOYEES

*See also* INDUSTRIAL PSYCHOLOGY; PERSONNEL MANAGEMENT; PSYCHOLOGICAL TESTING

## TRADE/PROFESSIONAL ASSOCIATIONS
College of Performance Management. 101 S Whiting St., Ste. 320, Alexandria, VA 22304. Phone: (703)370-7885; Fax: (703)370-1757 • URL: http://www.mycpm.org • Serves as a forum for the exchange of information on project management and performance measurement in business. Conducts educational programs.

# RATIO ANALYSIS

*See* FINANCIAL RATIOS

# REAL ESTATE APPRAISAL

*See* REAL PROPERTY VALUATION

# REAL ESTATE BUSINESS

*See also* APARTMENT HOUSES; BUILDING INDUSTRY; CONDOMINIUMS; HOUSING; MORTGAGES; OFFICE BUILDINGS; REAL ESTATE INVESTMENTS; REAL PROPERTY VALUATION; TAX SHELTERS

## DIRECTORIES
*Directory of Real Estate Development & Related Education Programs.* Urban Land Institute. • Biennial. $24.95 Individuals paperback. Covers: over 60 real estate development education programs currently being offered at colleges and universities. Entries include: College or university name, address, list of faculty members, curriculum, tuition, length of program, degrees offered, financial aid information, job placement services, international programs, e-mail addresses.

*Guide to Business and Real Estate Loan Sources.* International Wealth Success, Inc. • Annual. $25 Individuals. Covers: Several hundred financial institutions that lend money for real estate investment. Entries include: Institution name, address, phone.

*Real Estate Software Directory and Catalog.* Z-Law Software Inc. • Semiannual. Publication includes: Listings of producers of real estate related software programs and ordering information. Principal content of publication is product name, description, specifications, requirements. Database includes: Applications for landlords, realtors, investors, property managers, lenders, contractors, attorneys, developers, and appraisers.

*Triangle Business Journal's Book of Lists.* Greater Raleigh Chamber of Commerce. • $45 Members. Provides 25 listings for 75 different business sectors in Raleigh and Durham area including advertising agencies, architects, banks, real estate agencies, hotels, accountants, and golf courses.

*U.S. Residential Real Estate Investment Guide for Foreigners.* International Business Publications, USA. • $99.95 Individuals hardcopy, E-book and CD-ROM. Covers: basic and contact information for buying and selling real estate in the US.

## FINANCIAL RATIOS
*Annual Statement Studies.* Risk Management Association. • Annual. Compiled from over 280,000 financial statements.

*Annual Statement Studies: Industry Default Probabilities and Cash Flow Measures.* Risk Management Association. • Annual. $405 Nonmembers. Serves as a companion volume to the original *Annual Statement Studies.* Gives probability of default estimates on a percentage scale for more than 450 industries. Includes changes in position year-by-year for eight financial statement line items and provides percentage measures of cash flow.

## GENERAL WORKS
*Business Opportunities Journal.* Business Service Corp. • Monthly. Newspaper covering businesses for sale.

*Business Valuations: Businesses, Securities, and Real Estate.* American CPE Inc. • Contains detailed training information covering the valuation of businesses and other instruments and property related to businesses, including bonds, securities, preferred and common stock, and real estate.

*Business Ventures.* Business Service Corp. • Monthly. Journal covering franchising, real estate, and investments. Also lists businesses for sale by owner.

## HANDBOOKS AND MANUALS
*Complete Guide to Your Real Estate Closing: Answers to All Your Questions from Opening Escrow to Negotiating Fees to Signing Closing Papers.* Sandy Gadow. McGraw Hill Financial Inc. • Date not set. $19.95. Includes sample forms and work sheets, with specific real estate closing information for all 50 states. (Teach Yourself Series).

*Practical Guide to Real Estate Taxation.* David F. Windish. Wolters Kluwer Law & Business CCH. • $150 1-4 Copies. Date not set. Serves as a guide to the federal tax consequences of real estate ownership and operation. Covers mortgages, rental agreements, interest, landlord income, forms of ownership, and other tax-oriented topics.

## ONLINE DATABASES
*Banking Information Source.* ProQuest L.L.C. • Provides indexing and abstracting of periodical and other literature from 1982 to date, with weekly updates. Covers the financial services industry: banks, savings institutions, investment houses, credit unions, insurance companies, and real estate organizations. Emphasis is on marketing and management. Inquire as to online cost and availability. (Formerly *FINIS: Financial Industry Information Service.*).

## OTHER SOURCES
*The Law of Distressed Real Estate: Foreclosure, Workouts, and Procedures.* Thomson West. • $1,934.25 full set. Five looseleaf volumes. Periodic supplementation. (Real Property LawSeries).

*Real Estate Financing, with Forms on Disk.* ALM Media Properties LLC. • $560 print + online + ebook. Includes forms on two diskettes. Covers loan modifications, wraparound mortgage loans, loans for condos, co-ops, and time shares, sale-leasebacks, installment sales, sales of mortgage loans, and various related topics. (Law Journal Press).

## PERIODICALS AND NEWSLETTERS
*American Banker: The Financial Services Daily.* SourceMedia Inc. • Daily. $895.00 per year. Provides news of banking, investment products, mortgages, credit unions, finance, bank technology, and legal developments.

*Commercial Leasing Law and Strategy.* ALM Media Properties LLC. • Monthly. $489 per year. Covers commercial real estate leasing developments relating to large retailers, tenant inducements, tax

consequences, unbilled rent obligations, and other matters. (A Law Journal Newsletter, formerly published by Leader Publications).

*Heartland Real Estate Business.* France Publications Inc. • Monthly. $65 Individuals. Magazine that covers the latest news, developments and trends in commercial real estate in the Midwest.

*Maddux Business Report: The Business of Tampa Bay.* Maddux Publishing L.C. • Monthly. $35 Individuals online. Magazine on business and real estate activities in the seven-county Tampa Bay region.

*National Real Estate Investor.* Penton. • Bimonthly. Magazine on commercial real estate investment, development and management. Includes annual *Directory.* Market surveys by city.

*The Practical Real Estate Lawyer.* Committee on Continuing Professional Education. American Law Institute - Committee on Continuing Professional Education. • Bimonthly. $99 per year. Frequently includes legal forms for use in real estate practice.

*Real Estate Forum: America's Premier Real Estate Business Magazine.* Real Estate Media Inc. • 10/year. Emphasis on corporate and industrial real estate.

*Real Estate Issues.* Counselors of Real Estate. • 3/year. $60 Individuals. Contains incisive, dynamic articles that respond to current trends and practices in the real estate industry.

*Real Estate Review.* Thomson West. • Gives inside information on the latest ideas in real estate. Provides advice from the leaders of the real estate field.

*Realtor Magazine.* National Association of Realtors. • Monthly. Free to members; non-members, $54.00 per year. Provides industry news and trends for realtors. Special features include Annual Compensation Survey, Annual Technology Survey, Annual All Stars, and The Year in Real Estate.

*Realtor Magazine: The Business tool for Real Estate Professionals.* National Association of Realtors. • Monthly. $56 Nonmembers U.S. Real estate magazine.

*Realty and Building.* Realty and Building Inc. • Biweekly. $54.00 per year.

*Relocation Journal and Real Estate News.* Mobility Services International. • Monthly. Free. Newsletter for real estate, building, financing and investing. Formed by the merger of *Real Estate News* and *Relocation Journal.*

*The Residential Specialist.* Council of Residential Specialists. • Bimonthly Quarterly. $29.95 Nonmembers. Covers sales techniques, communication and brokerage management, residential sales associates and brokers.

*Texas Real Estate Business.* France Publications Inc. • Monthly. $64 Individuals. Magazine that covers the latest news, developments and trends in commercial real estate in Texas.

*U.S. Banker.* SourceMedia Inc. • Monthly. $65.00 per year. Edited for bank executives and managers. Covers a wide variety of banking and financial topics.

*Western Real Estate Business: Connecting Real Estate in the West.* France Publications Inc. • Monthly. $67 Individuals. Magazine that covers the latest news, developments and trends in commercial real estate in the western states.

## RESEARCH CENTERS AND INSTITUTES
Northwestern University - Guthrie Center for Real Estate Research. Kellogg School, 2001 Sheridan Rd., Rm. 401, Evanston, IL 60208. Phone: (847)491-3564; Fax: (847)491-5719; Email: tsm@kellogg.northwestern.edu • URL: http://www.kellogg.northwestern.edu/departments/real-estate/faculty-research/guthrie-center.aspx • Tax, real

estate, and urban development and economics.

**Samuel Zell and Robert Lurie Real Estate Center.**
The Wharton School, University of Pennsylvania,
Steinberg Hall-Dietrich Hall, 3620 Locust Walk,
Ste. 1400, Philadelphia, PA 19104-6302. Phone:
(215)898-9687; Fax: (215)573-2220; Email:
frostr@wharton.upenn.edu • URL: http://realestate.
wharton.upenn.edu.

**University of California, Los Angeles - Richard S.
Ziman Center for Real Estate.** Gold Hall, Ste. B100,
110 Westwood Plz., Los Angeles, CA 90095-1481.
Phone: (310)206-9424 or (213)825-3977; Fax:
(310)267-5391 or (310)206-5455; Email: stuart.
gabriel@anderson.ucla.edu • URL: http://www.
anderson.ucla.edu/centers/ziman • Secondary
mortgage markets, housing finance, growth management, infrastructure, corporate finance issues, and
development industry.

**University of Illinois at Urbana-Champaign -
Bureau of Economic and Business Research.** 430
Wohlers Hall, Office of Research, College of Business, 1206 S 6th St., Champaign, IL 61820. Phone:
(217)333-2330; Fax: (217)333-7410; Email: lhuff@
uiuc.edu • URL: http://business.illinois.edu/research
• Economics and business, including studies in business expectations, health economics, forecasting and
planning, innovation, entrepreneurship, consumer
behavior, poverty problems, small business operations and problems, investment and growth,
productivity, research methodology, organizational
behavior, and international business and banking.

## STATISTICS SOURCES

*ULI Market Profiles: North America.* Urban Land
Institute. • Annual. Members, $249.95; non-
members, $299.95. Provides real estate marketing
data for residential, retail, office, and industrial
sectors. Covers 76 U. S. metropolitan areas and 13
major foreign metropolitan areas.

*U.S. Housing Markets.* DoveTale Publishers. •
Monthly. $345.00 per year. Includes eight interim
reports. Provides data on residential building
permits, apartment building completions, rental
vacancy rates, sales of existing homes, average
home prices, housing affordability, etc. All major U.
S. cities and areas are covered.

## TRADE/PROFESSIONAL ASSOCIATIONS

**Counselors of Real Estate.** 430 N Michigan Ave.,
Chicago, IL 60611-4089. Phone: (312)329-8427 or
(312)329-8429; Fax: (312)329-8881; Email: info@
cre.org • URL: http://www.cre.org • Formerly
American Society of Real Estate Counselors.

**National Association of Independent Real Estate
Brokers.** 7102 Mardyke Ln., Indianapolis, IN 46226.
Phone: (317)547-4679; Email: director@
nationalrealestatebrokers.org • URL: http://
nationalrealestatebrokers.org • Aims to educate
independent real estate brokers and real estate
agents. Promotes the value of independent real
estate brokers and real estate agents nationwide
through national promotional campaigns. Works to
introduce the general public to independent real
estate brokers and real estate agents, their real estate
companies and the benefits they offer.

**National Association of Real Estate Brokers.** 9831
Greenbelt Rd., Lanham, MD 20706. Phone:
(301)552-9340; Fax: (301)552-9216; Email: info@
nareb.com • URL: http://www.nareb.com •
Members of the real estate industry. Research,
educational and certification programs include: Real
Estate Management Brokers Institute; National
Society of Real Estate Appraisers; Real Estate
Brokerage Institute; United Developers Council.
Encourages unity among those who are engaged in
real estate. Promotes and maintains high standards
of conduct. Protects the public against unethical,
improper, or fraudulent practices connected with the
real estate business. Conducts research; compiles
statistics on productivity, marketing and

development. Gives members license to use "Realtist" symbol. Sponsors educational seminars.
Maintains Willis E. Carson Library.

**National Association of Real Estate Consultants.**
404 4th Ave., Lewiston, ID 83501. Phone: (208)746-
7963; Fax: (208)746-4760 • URL: http://www.narec.
com • Works to assist real estate professionals in reframing their focus as real estate consultants to
better meet the needs of today's savvy consumer.
Helps promote alternative or fee-for-service real
estate business models.

**National Association of Realtors.** 430 N Michigan
Ave., Chicago, IL 60611-4087. Phone: 800-874-
6500; Email: infocentral@realtors.org • URL: http://
www.realtor.org • Federation of 54 state and territory associations and 1,860 local real estate boards
whose members are real estate brokers and agents;
terms are registered by the association in the U.S.
Patent and Trademark Office and in the states.
Promotes education, high professional standards and
modern techniques in specialized real estate work
such as brokerage, appraisal, property management,
land development, industrial real estate, farm
brokerage and counseling. Conducts research
programs.

# REAL ESTATE, INDUSTRIAL

*See* INDUSTRIAL REAL ESTATE

# REAL ESTATE INVESTMENT TRUSTS

*See also* REAL ESTATE INVESTMENTS

## DIRECTORIES

*Institutional Buyers of REIT Securities.* bigdough.
com Inc. • Semiannual. $995.00 per year. Provides
detailed profiles of about 500 institutional buyers of
REIT securities. Includes names of financial
analysts and portfolio managers.

## PERIODICALS AND NEWSLETTERS

*National Real Estate Investor.* Penton. • Bimonthly.
Magazine on commercial real estate investment,
development and management. Includes annual
*Directory.* Market surveys by city.

## STATISTICS SOURCES

*Realty Stock Review.* • Semimonthly. $325.00 per
year. Looseleaf service.

## TRADE/PROFESSIONAL ASSOCIATIONS

**National Association of Real Estate Investment
Trusts.** 1875 I St. NW, Ste. 600, Washington, DC
20006-5413. Phone: 800-362-7348 or (202)739-
9400; Fax: (202)739-9401; Email: baiken@nareit.
com • URL: http://www.reit.com • Formerly
National Association of Real Estste Investment
Funds.

# REAL ESTATE INVESTMENTS

*See also* REAL ESTATE BUSINESS; REAL
ESTATE INVESTMENT TRUSTS

## DIRECTORIES

*Directory of Foreign Investors That Invest in U.S.A.
Property and Real Estate.* Communication Network
International Inc. • Biennial. $650. Covers: more
than 3,500 investors. Entries include: Personal
name, address; United States representative name,
address, phone; approximate dollar amount of U.S.
investments.

*Japanese Investment in U.S. and Canadian Real
Estate Directory.* Mead Ventures Inc. • Annual.
$295. Covers: about 550 Japanese investors,

brokers, lenders, consultants, and developers in the
United States and Canada; and about 275 companies
in Japan. Entries include: Company name, address,
phone, fax, telex, name and title of contact,
geographical area served, services provided and
description of projects and services.

*Nelson Information's Directory of Institutional Real
Estate.* Nelson Information. • Annual. Includes real
estate investment managers, service firms, consultants, real estate investment trusts (REITs), and various institutional investors in real estate. Formerly
*Nelson's Directory of Real Estate Investments.*

*U.S. Residential Real Estate Investment Guide for
Foreigners.* International Business Publications,
USA. • $99.95 Individuals hardcopy, E-book and
CD-ROM. Covers: basic and contact information for
buying and selling real estate in the US.

## OTHER SOURCES

*Federal Taxes Affecting Real Estate.* Matthew
Bender and Company Inc. • Semiannual. $573 book.
Explains and illustrates the most important federal
tax principles applying to daily real estate
transactions.

## PERIODICALS AND NEWSLETTERS

*Crittenden Report: Real Estate Financing.* Crittenden Research Inc. • Semimonthly. Newsletter on
real estate lending and mortgages. Includes semiannual *Crittenden Directory of Real Estate Financing.*

*National Real Estate Investor.* Penton. • Bimonthly.
Magazine on commercial real estate investment,
development and management. Includes annual
*Directory.* Market surveys by city.

*Real Estate Economics: Journal of the American
Real Estate and Urban Economics Association.* The
MIT Press. • Quarterly. Covers a wide range of issues, from tax rules to brokers' commissions to
corporate real estate including housing and urban
economics, and the financial economics of real
estate development and investment.

*Real Estate Finance.* Institutional Investor Inc.
Journals Group. • Bimonthly. $350.00 per year. Cov-
ers real estate for professional investors. Provides
information on complex financing, legalities, and
industry trends.

*Real Estate Finance and Investment.* Institutional
Investor Inc. Journals Group. • Weekly. $2,275.00
per year. Includes print and online editions. Newsletter for professional investors in commercial real
estate. Includes information on financing, restructuring, strategy, and regulation.

*Real Estate Tax Digest.* LexisNexis. • Description:
Features articles on and analyses of legislation,
Treasury regulations, federal court and Tax Court
decisions, Revenue Rulings, Revenue Procedures,
and selected Letter Rulings of the Internal Revenue
Service pertaining to federal taxation affecting real
estate activities. Includes columns titled Special
Topic, New Developments, Practitioner's Corner,
and Inside Washington.

*The Residential Specialist.* Council of Residential
Specialists. • Bimonthly Quarterly. $29.95
Nonmembers. Covers sales techniques, communication and brokerage management, residential sales associates and brokers.

*Stanger Report: A Guide to Partnership Investing.*
Robert A. Stanger & Company Inc. • Quarterly.
$447 Individuals Annual. Includes overall statistics
on the size of the current market, quarterly fundraising, current distribution rates and coverage and latest valuation reports for closed non-traded REITs,
market updates on new registrations, newly-
effective issues and fund closings, secondary market
transactions, and more.

## PRICE SOURCES

*National Real Estate Index.* CB Richard Ellis Group
Inc. • Price and frequency on application. Provides
reports on commercial real estate prices, rents,

capitalization rates, and trends in more than 65 metropolitan areas. Time span is 12 years. Includes urban office buildings, suburban offices, warehouses, retail properties, and apartments.

### RESEARCH CENTERS AND INSTITUTES

University of Pennsylvania - The Wharton School - Rodney L. White Center for Financial Research. 3254 Steinberg Hall-Dietrich Hall, Philadelphia, PA 19104-6367. Phone: (215)898-7616; Fax: (215)573-8084; Email: rlwctr@finance.wharton.upenn.edu • URL: http://rodneywhitecenter.wharton.upenn.edu • Research areas include financial management, money markets, real estate finance, and international finance.

### TRADE/PROFESSIONAL ASSOCIATIONS

American Real Estate and Urban Economics Association. The Center for Real State Education and Research, 821 Academic Way, 223 RBB, Tallahassee, FL 32306-1110. Phone: 866-273-8321 or (850)644-7898; Fax: (850)644-4077; Email: areuea@areuea.org • URL: http://www.areuea.org • Members are real estate teachers, researchers, economists, and others concerned with urban real estate and investment.

Association of Real Estate Funds. 65 Kingsway, London WC2B 6TD, United Kingdom. Phone: 44 20 72694677; Email: info@aref.org.uk • URL: http://www.aref.org.uk • Aims to raise awareness of Real Estate Funds and demonstrate the advantages of these funds as effective real estate investment vehicles. Represents its members' interests on legislative, regulatory and fiscal matters affecting the real estate industry.

Building Owners and Managers Association International. 1101 15th St. NW, Ste. 800, Washington, DC 20005-5021. Phone: 800-426-6292 or (202)408-2662; Fax: (202)326-6377; Email: info@boma.org • URL: http://www.boma.org • Formerly National Association of Building Owners and Managers.

## REAL ESTATE MANAGEMENT

*See* PROPERTY MANAGEMENT

## REAL PROPERTY VALUATION

*See also* REAL ESTATE BUSINESS; VALUATION

### DIRECTORIES

*Boat Appraisers Directory.* InfoGroup Inc. • Annual. Number of listings: 17,331. Entries include: Name, address, phone, size of advertisement, name of owner or manager, number of employees, year first in "Yellow Pages." Compiled from telephone company "Yellow Pages," nationwide.

### TRADE/PROFESSIONAL ASSOCIATIONS

American Society of Appraisers. 11107 Sunset Hills Rd., Ste. 310, Reston, VA 20190. Phone: 800-272-8258 or (703)478-2228; Fax: (703)742-8471; Email: asainfo@appraisers.org • URL: http://www.appraisers.org • Professional appraisal educator, testing, and accrediting society. Sponsors mandatory recertification program for all members. Offers a consumer information service to the public.

Appraisal Institute. 200 W Madison St., Ste. 1500, Chicago, IL 60606. Phone: 888-756-4624 or (312)335-4401 or (312)335-4100; Fax: (312)335-4415; Email: aiservice@appraisalinstitute.org • URL: http://www.appraisalinstitute.org • General appraisers who hold the MAI designation, and residential members who hold the SRA designation.

Enforces Code of Professional Ethics and Standards of Professional Appraisal Practice. Confers one general designation, the MAI, and one residential designation, the SRA. Provides training in valuation of residential and income properties, market analysis, and standards of professional appraisal practice. Sponsors courses in preparation for state certification and licensing; offers continuing education programs for designated members.

Association of Appraiser Regulatory Officials. c/o Larry Disney, President, 135 W Irvin St., Ste. 301, Richmond, KY 40475. Phone: (605)773-4608; Fax: (605)773-5369 • URL: http://www.aaro.net • Represents real estate appraiser licensing agencies in the United States and its territories. Seeks to improve the administration and enforcement of real estate appraisal laws. Provides education, research, communication and cooperation among appraiser regulatory officials.

National Association of Real Estate Appraisers. 810 N Farrell Dr., Palm Springs, CA 92262. Phone: 877-743-6806; Fax: (760)327-5631; Email: info@narea-assoc.org • URL: http://www.narea-assoc.org • Real estate appraisers. Aims to make available the services of the most highly qualified real estate appraisers. Offers certification to members.

## RECESSIONS

*See* BUSINESS CYCLES

## RECORDS MANAGEMENT

### OTHER SOURCES

*Information and Image Management: The State of the Industry.* Association for Information and Image Management International. • Annual. $130.00. Market data with five-year forecasts. Covers electronic imaging, micrographics supplies and equipment, software, and records management services.

### PERIODICALS AND NEWSLETTERS

*The Infomation Management Journal: The Journal for the Information Management Professionals.* A R M A International. • Quarterly. Free to members; non-members, $95.00 per year; institutions and libraries, $53.00 per year. Formerly *Records Management Quarterly.*

*InForm.* Victor O. Schinnerer and Company Inc. • Description: Reports national and state developments affecting architects and engineers.

### TRADE/PROFESSIONAL ASSOCIATIONS

ARMA International - The Association of Information Management Professionals. 11880 College Blvd., Ste. 450, Overland Park, KS 66210. Phone: 800-422-2762 or (913)341-3808; Fax: (913)341-3742; Email: headquarters@armaintl.org • URL: http://www.arma.org • Formerly ARMA International-The Information Management Professionals.

Society of Corporate Secretaries and Governance Professionals. 240 W 35th St., Ste. 400, New York, NY 10001. Phone: (212)681-2000; Fax: (212)681-2005 • URL: http://www.governanceprofessionals.org • Corporate secretaries, assistant secretaries, officers and executives of corporations and others interested in corporate practices and procedures. Conducts surveys and research. Sponsors educational programs for members. Maintains a central information and reference service.

## RECORDS, PHONOGRAPH

*See* PHONOGRAPH AND PHONOGRAPH RECORD INDUSTRIES

## RECREATION, INDUSTRIAL

*See* INDUSTRIAL RECREATION

## RECREATION INDUSTRY

*See also* AMUSEMENT INDUSTRY; INDUSTRIAL RECREATION; PARKS; SPORTING GOODS INDUSTRY; SPORTS BUSINESS

### ABSTRACTS AND INDEXES

*Leisure, Recreation and Tourism Abstracts.* CABI Publishing North America. • Quarterly. Members, $280.00 per year; Institutions, $610.00 per year. Includes single site internet access. Provides coverage of the worldwide literature of travel, recreation, sports, and the hospitality industry.

### DIRECTORIES

*Accreditation Process Guide.* American Camping Association. • Annual. Lists camp standards for camps undergoing on-site accreditation visits.

*Frontier West/Great Plains & Mountain Region Campground Guide.* Woodall Publications Corp. • Annual. $4.95 Individuals discounted price. Covers: Campground site listings for Colorado, Montana, Nebraska, North Dakota, South Dakota, Utah, and Wyoming. Entries include: Site name, address, phone, facility description, driving directions, camping fees, attractions and seasonal events. It also includes, new for 2004, "Discover Outdoor RV Adventures" and Woodall's Guide to Seasonal Sites.

*New York/New England & Eastern Canada Campground Guide.* Woodall Publications Corp. • Annual. $10.95 retail price. Covers: Campground site listings for New England states, including Maine, Connecticut, Massachusetts, New Hampshire, New York, Rhode Island, Vermont, and Ontario. Entries include: Site name, address, phone, facility description, driving directions, camping fees, attractions and seasonal events.

*Trailer Life Campground and RV Services Directory.* Trailer Life Publishing Company Inc. • Annual. $19.95. Describes and rates over 18,000 RV campgrounds, service centers and tourist attractions.

*Woodall's Canada Campground Guide.* Woodall Publications Corp. • $8.96 Individuals discounted. Covers: Campground site listings for all Canadian provinces. Entries include: Site name, address, phone, facility description, driving directions, camping fees, attractions and seasonal events.

*Woodall's Far West Campground Guide.* Woodall Publications Corp. • Annual. $4.95 Individuals. Covers: Campground site listings for the Far West U.S., including Alaska, Arizona, California, Idaho, Nevada, Oregon, Washington, and British Columbia, Mexico, and the Yukon. Entries include: Site name, address, phone, facility description, driving directions, camping fees, attractions and seasonal events.

*Woodall's Frontier West/Great Plains & Mountain Region Campground Guide.* Woodall Publications Corp. • $4.95 Individuals. Covers: Campground site listings for Arkansas, Kansas, Missouri, New Mexico, Oklahoma, Texas, and Mexico. Entries include: Site name, address, phone, facility description, driving directions, camping fees, attractions and seasonal events.

*Woodall's Great Lakes Campground Guide.* Woodall Publications Corp. • Annual. $4.95 Individuals. Covers: Campground site listings for Great Lakes states, including Illinois, Indiana, Iowa, Michigan, Minnesota, Ohio, and Wisconsin. Entries include: Site name, address, phone, facility description, driving directions, camping fees, attractions and seasonal events.

*Woodall's Mid-Atlantic Campground Guide.* Woodall Publications Corp. • Annual. $4.95 Individuals. Covers: Campground site listings for Mid-Atlantic states, including Delaware, District of Columbia, Maryland, New Jersey, Pennsylvania, Virginia, and West Virginia. Entries include: Site name, address, phone, facility description, driving directions, camping fees, attractions and seasonal events.

*Woodall's South Campground Guide*. Woodall Publications Corp. • Annual. $10.95 Individuals Retail price. Covers: Campground site listings for the 9 Southern U.S. states, including Alabama, Florida, Georgia, Kentucky, Louisiana, Mississippi, North Carolina, South Carolina, and Tennessee. Entries include: Site name, address, phone, facility description, driving directions, camping fees, attractions and seasonal events.

### E-BOOKS

*Social Trends & Indicators USA*. Monique D. Magee, editor. Cengage Learning Inc. • Includes data on labor, economics, the health care industry, crime, leisure, population, education, social security, and many other topics. Sources include various government agencies and major publications. Inquire for pricing.

### PERIODICALS AND NEWSLETTERS

*Campground Management: Business Publication for Profitable Outdoor Recreation*. Woodall Publications Corp. • Monthly. $24.95 per year.

*Camping Magazine*. American Camping Association. • Bimonthly. $29.95 per year. Contains recent trends and latest research in the camp industry.

*Employee Services Management: The Journal of Employee Services Recreation, Heal th and Education*. Employee Services Management. • Bimonthly. Free to members; non-members, $52.00 per year.

### STATISTICS SOURCES

*Outlook for Travel and Tourism*. U.S. Travel Association. • Annual. Members, $100.00; non-members, $175.00. Contains forecasts of the performance of the U. S. travel industry, including air travel, business travel, recreation (attractions), and accomodations.

*Statistical Abstract of the United States*. U. S. Government Printing Office. • Annual. $44.00. Issued by the U. S. Bureau of the Census.

### TRADE/PROFESSIONAL ASSOCIATIONS

Amusement Industry Manufacturers and Suppliers International. 3026 S Orange, Santa Ana, CA 92707. Phone: (714)425-5747; Fax: (714)276-9666; Email: info@aimsintl.org • URL: http://www.aimsintl.org • Represents manufacturers and suppliers of amusement riding devices and equipment used by amusement parks, carnivals, and traveling amusement companies. Exchanges information on safety, maintenance, state laws, transportation, and credit. Works to develop safety programs and codes at the federal and state levels; carries out public relations activities; and cooperates with the ASTM to develop voluntary standards for amusement rides and devices.

Employee Morale and Recreation Association. PO Box 10517, Rockville, MD 20849. • URL: http://employeemorale.org • Corporations and governmental agencies that sponsor recreation, fitness, and service programs for their employees; associate members are manufacturers and suppliers in the employee recreation market and distributors of consumer products and services. Serves as an information resource network for members nationwide. Implements and maintains a diverse range of employee services; believes that employee services, as practical solutions to work/life issues, are essential to sound business management. Conducts programs that improves relations between employees and management, increases overall

productivity, boosts morale, and reduces absenteeism and turnover.

International Amusement and Leisure Defense Association. PO Box 4563, Louisville, KY 40204. Phone: (502)473-0956; Fax: (502)473-7352; Email: info@ialda.org • URL: http://www.ialda.org • Promotes and protects the interests of the amusement and leisure industries. Encourages members to exchange information, share experiences and develop litigation strategies regarding the amusement and leisure industry. Serves as a clearinghouse for speakers and authors on industry-specific topics.

National Association of RV Parks and Campgrounds. 9085 E Mineral Cir., Ste. 200, Centennial, CO 80112. Phone: (303)681-0401; Fax: (303)681-0426; Email: info@arvc.org • URL: http://www.arvc.org • Formerly National Campground Owners Association.

# RECREATIONAL VEHICLE INDUSTRY

*See also* MOBILE HOME INDUSTRY

### ABSTRACTS AND INDEXES

*Trailer Life*. Good Sam Club. Affinity Group Inc., T L Enterprises. • Monthly. $15.97 /year.

### DIRECTORIES

*Recreation Vehicle Industry Association-- Membership Directory and Industry Buyer's Guide*. Recreation Vehicle Industry Association. • Annual. Covers: Approximately 500 member recreation vehicle manufacturers, component parts suppliers, and associate firms; RV-related state and regional associations. Entries include: For businesses-- Company name, address, phone, fax, name of contact, subsidiary and branch names and locations, product provided. For associations--Association name, address, phone.

*RV Business--RV Industry Directory Issue*. Affinity Group Inc. • Annual. $19.95 Individuals 1-4 copies. Publication includes: About 250 recreational vehicle manufacturers, 700 suppliers, and 600 distributors, wholesalers, manufacturers' representatives, and others in the industry; limited international coverage. Entries include: For manufacturers-- Company name, address, phone, fax, names of key personnel, location of branch plants, types of vehicles made, brand names. For suppliers, and distributors--Company name, address, phone, fax, names of key personnel, products. For representatives--Company name, address, phone, fax, names and titles of key personnel, companies represented.

*The RVDA Membership Directory and Resource Guide*. Recreation Vehicle Dealers Association of North America. • Annual. Covers: Over 900 retail sales firms handling travel trailers, camping trailers, truck campers, and motor homes in the United States and Canada that are open for business twelve months of the year. Entries include: Company name, address, phone, and owner's or manager's name.

### PERIODICALS AND NEWSLETTERS

*Highways*. Good Sam club. Affinity Group Inc., T L Enterprises. • 11 times a year. Membership. Five regional editions. Formerly *Good Sam's Hi-Way Herald*.

*MH/RV Builders News: The Magazine for Builders of Manufactured-Mobile-Modular-Marine Homes and Recreational Vehicles*. Patrick Finn, editor. Dan Kamrow and Associates, Inc. • Bimonthly. Controlled circulation.

*RV Business*. Affinity Group Inc. • Monthly. Includes news about the entire recreational vehicle industry in the U.S.

### PRICE SOURCES

*NADA Appraisal Guides*. National Automobile Dealers Association. • Prices and frequencies vary.

Guides to prices of used cars, old used cars, motorcycles, mobile homes, recreational vehicles, and mopeds.

### TRADE/PROFESSIONAL ASSOCIATIONS

Recreation Vehicle Dealers Association of North America. 3930 University Dr., Fairfax, VA 22030-2515. Phone: (703)591-7130; Fax: (703)359-0152; Email: jnewhouse@rvda.org • URL: http://www.rvda.org.

Recreation Vehicle Industry Association. 1896 Preston White Dr., Reston, VA 20191. Phone: 800-336-0154 or (703)620-6003; Fax: (703)620-5071; Email: rvia@rvia.org • URL: http://www.rvia.org • Recreation vehicle manufacturers, manufacturers' representatives, and suppliers of accessories and equipment used by manufacturers. Seeks to provide a unified recreation vehicle organization for manufacturers and component parts suppliers of motor homes, travel trailers, fifth wheel trailers, horse trailer conversions, sport-utility trailers, truck campers and folding camping trailers. Promotes and represents the growth and concerns of the industry to federal and state government departments, the media, and the public. Collects shipment statistics, technical data, and consumer and media information. Monitors industry compliance with safety standards and the activities of federal and state governments that affect the RV industry. Provides legal and public relations services. Sponsors market research.

# RECRUITMENT OF PERSONNEL

*See also* COLLEGE PLACEMENT BUREAUS; PERSONNEL MANAGEMENT

### BIBLIOGRAPHIES

*Executive Search Books*. Kennedy Information Inc. • Annual. Free. Contains descriptions of selected books from various publishers on executive recruitment.

### DIRECTORIES

*U.K. Directory of Talent Management*. Executive Grapevine International Ltd. • $239 Individuals. Covers: 700 top U.K. executive recruitment and interim management providers and over 3,000 consultant biographies. Entries include: Company profile, consultant biographies, salary range of assignments, function, fees, and major clients.

### PERIODICALS AND NEWSLETTERS

*Affirmative Action Register: The E E O Recruitment Publication*. INSIGHT Into Diversity. • Monthly. $15 Individuals. "The *Affirmative Action Register* is the only nationwide publication that provides for systematic distribution to mandated minorities, females, handicapped, veterans, and Native Americans." Each issue consists of recruitment advertisements placed by equal opportunity employers (institutions and companies).

*Human Resource Executive*. LRP Publications Library. • 16 times a year. $89.95 per year. Edited for directors of corporate human resource departments. Special issues emphasize training, benefits, retirement planning, recruitment, outplacement, workers' compensation, legal pitfalls, and oes emphasize training, benefits, retirement planning, recruitment, outplacement, workers' compensation, legal pitfalls, and other personnel topics.

*People & Strategy*. HR People and Strategy. • Quarterly. $150 Nonmembers print only. Contains current theory, research and practice in strategic human resource management.

*Recruiting Trends: The Monthly Newsletter for the Recruiting Executive*. Kennedy Information Inc. • Monthly. $179.00 per year.

---

## TRADE/PROFESSIONAL ASSOCIATIONS

Association of Executive Search Consultants. 425 5thAve., 4th Fl., New York, NY 10016. Phone: (212)398-9556; Email: info@bluesteps.com • URL: http://www.aesc.org/eweb/StartPage.aspx • Represents executive search consulting firms worldwide, establishes professional and ethical standards for its members, and serves to broaden public understanding of the executive search process. Specialized form of management consulting, conducted through an exclusive engagement with a client organization.

# RECYCLING

*See also* NATURAL RESOURCES; SURPLUS PRODUCTS; WASTE PRODUCTS

## ABSTRACTS AND INDEXES

*Environment Abstracts.* University Publications of America. • Monthly. Price varies. Provides multidisciplinary coverage of the world's environmental literature. Incorporates *Acid Rain Abstracts.*

*Environment Abstracts Annual: A Guide to the Key Environmental Literature of the Year.* University Publications of America. • Annual. $495.00. A yearly cumulation of *Environment Abstracts.*

## CD-ROM DATABASES

*Environment Abstracts on CD-ROM.* University Publications of America. • Quarterly. $1,295.00 per year. Contains the following CD-ROM databases: *Environment Abstracts, Energy Abstracts,* and *Acid Rain Abstracts.* Length of coverage varies.

## DIRECTORIES

*Asphalt Recycling & Reclaiming Association-- Membership Directory.* Asphalt Recycling and Reclaiming Association. • Annual. Covers: About 200 contractors, manufacturers, consulting engineers, and public works officials involved in asphalt reclaiming and recycling. Entries include: Name of company, address, phone; key personnel; type of organization or company; product line, or contact person.

*North American Scrap Metals Directory.* Recycling Today Media Group. • Annual. $95.20 Individuals discounted price. Covers: Suppliers of scrap metal materials in North America. Entries include: Contact information.

*Recycling and Waste Management Guide to the Internet.* Government Institutes. • $72 Individuals. Covers: More than 350 web sites, discussion lists, and news groups on the internet covering waste management and recycling issues. Entries include: Site name, address, subject, site summary, contact name and e-mail.

## ENCYCLOPEDIAS AND DICTIONARIES

*Environmental Encyclopedia.* Cengage Learning Inc. • $327 Individuals. 2011. $298.00. 4th edition. Provides over 1,300 articles on all aspects of the environment. Written in non-technical style. eBook also available. Inquire for pricing.

## PERIODICALS AND NEWSLETTERS

*EM: A&WMA's Environmental Solutions That Make Good Business Sense.* Air and Waste Management Association. • Monthly. Institutions, $299.00 per year; nonprofit and government agencies, $199.00 per year. Newsletter. Provides news of regulations, legislation, and technology relating to the environment, recycling, and waste control. Formerly *Environmental Manager.*

*Environmental Business Journal: Strategic Information for a Changing Industry.* Environmental Business International Inc. • Monthly. $250 Single issue. Includes both industrial and financial information relating to individual companies and to the environmental industry in general. Covers air pollu-

tion, wat es, U. S. Department of Health and Human Services. Provides conference, workshop, and symposium proceedings, as well as extensive reviews of environmental prospects.

*Recycling Today.* Group Interest Enterprises. GIE Media, Inc. • Monthly. Serves the recycling industry in all areas.

*Resources, Conservation and Recycling.* Elsevier. • Monthly. $392 Individuals. Emphasizes the transformation processes involved in a transition toward more sustainable production and consumption systems.

*Reuse/Recycle.* Rowman & Littlefield Education. • Description: Contains information on "new processes, machinery, and uses for both industrial and municipal recycling." Publishes news of waste-to-energy and waste-to-materials processes, markets for recycled materials, recycling processing, plants, equipment and case history of successful projects and programs in the U.S. and Europe. Focuses on large-scale post-consumer, post-commercial and post-industrial waste recycling. Recurring features include a calendar of events.

*Scrap.* Institute of Scrap Recycling Industries. • Bimonthly. $48 Individuals companies. Magazine for the scrap processing and recycling industry. Formerly *Scrap Processing and Recycling.*

*Solid Waste Report: Resource Recovery-Recycling-Collection-Disposal.* Business Publishers Inc. • Weekly. $627.00 per year. Newsletter. Covers regulation, business news, technology, and international events relating to solid waste management.

## STATISTICS SOURCES

*U.S. Industry and Trade Outlook.* U.S. Department of Commerce National Technical Information Service. • Annual. Produced by the International Trade Administration, U.S. Department of Commerce, in a "public-private" partnership with DRI/ McGraw-Hill and Standard & Poor's. Provides basic data, outlook for the current year, and "Long-Term Prospects" (five-year projections) for a wide variety of products and services. Includes high technology industries. Formerly *U.S. Industrial Outlook.*

## TRADE/PROFESSIONAL ASSOCIATIONS

Battery Recycling Association of North America. 12505 N Main St., Ste. 212, Rancho Cucamonga, CA 91739. • URL: http://www.brana-online.org • Represents companies that handle, recycle, transport and manage portable power batteries. Seeks to establish guidance and training on the proper methods and regulations governing the safe handling of batteries. Fosters dialogue with battery handlers, recyclers, manufacturers and the regulatory community.

Electronics TakeBack Coalition. 4200 Park Blvd. No. 228, Oakland, CA 94602-1312. Phone: (510)614-0110; Email: info@etakeback.org • URL: http://www.electronicstakeback.com • Promotes green design and responsible recycling in the electronics industry. Aims to protect the health and well being of electronics users, workers, and the communities where electronics are produced and discarded. Encourages electronics manufacturers to offer programs to take back and recycle old electronics.

# REDEVELOPMENT, URBAN

*See* URBAN DEVELOPMENT

# REFERENCE SOURCES

*See* INFORMATION SOURCES

# REFINERIES

*See* PETROLEUM INDUSTRY

# REFRACTORIES

*See also* CERAMICS INDUSTRY; CLAY INDUSTRY

## INTERNET DATABASES

*Manufacturing Profiles.* U. S. Bureau of the Census. Phone: (301)763-4636 or (301)763-4100; Fax: (301)763-4794; Email: webmaster@census.gov • URL: http://www.census.gov/prod/www/abs/mfg-prof.html • The Census Bureau makes available free on PDF (Portable Document Format) an annual consolidation of the entire Current Industrial Report series, presenting "all the data compiled." Contains statistics on production, shipments, inventories, consumption, exports, imports, and orders for a wide variety of manufactured products.

## STATISTICS SOURCES

*Refractories.* U. S. Bureau of the Census. • Annual. Provides data on value of manufacturers' shipments, quantity, exports, imports, etc. (Current Industrial Reports, MA-32C.).

## TRADE/PROFESSIONAL ASSOCIATIONS

The Refractories Institute. PO Box 8439, Pittsburgh, PA 15218. Phone: (412)244-1880; Fax: (412)244-1881; Email: info@refractoriesinstitute.org • URL: http://www.refractoriesinstitute.org • Members are producers of fire brick and other refactory materials.

# REFRIGERATION INDUSTRY

*See also* AIR CONDITIONING INDUSTRY

## DIRECTORIES

*Air Conditioning & Heating & Refrigeration Equipment Directory.* InfoGroup Inc. • Annual. Number of listings: 689. Entries include: Name, address, phone, size of advertisement, name of owner or manager, number of employees, year first in "Yellow Pages." Compiled from telephone company "Yellow Pages," nationwide.

*Directory of Asian Importers of Refrigeration Equipment and Supplies.* EXIM Infotek Private Ltd. • $400 Individuals. Covers: 180 Asian importers of air cooled water chillers, centrifugal chillers, chest freezers, cold rooms, cooling towers, deep freezers, freezers, ice cream display, refrigeration and air conditioning equipment, refrigeration parts and supplies, refrigeration spare parts, refrigeration and air conditioning servicing accessories, commercial refrigeration, and industrial refrigeration. Entries include: Company name, postal address, telephone, fax, e-mail, website, contact person, designation, and product details.

*Directory of French Importers of Refrigeration Equipment and Supplies.* EXIM Infotek Private Ltd. • Covers: 20 French importers of freezers, refrigerators, and refrigeration equipment. Entries include: Company name, postal address, telephone, fax, e-mail, website, contact person, designation, and product details.

*Directory of Japanese Manufacturers and Exporters of Refrigeration Equipment and Supplies.* EXIM Infotek Private Ltd. • Covers: 20 Japanese manufacturers and exporters of fluorocarbon refrigerants, refrigeration equipment, and used refrigerators. Entries include: Company name, postal address, telephone, fax, e-mail, website, contact person, designation, and product details.

*Directory of North American Importers of Refrigeration Equipment and Supplies.* EXIM Infotek Private Ltd. • $300 Individuals. Covers: 110 North American importers of freezer, refrigeration and air conditioning equipment, and refrigerator parts. Entries include: Company name, postal address, telephone, fax, e-mail, website, contact person, designation, and product details.

*Grocery Headquarters: The Newspaper for the Food Industry.* Trend Publishing Inc. • Monthly. $80. Covers the sale and distribution of food products and other items sold in supermarkets and grocery stores. Edited mainly for retailers and wholesalers. Incorporates (Grocery Distribution).

*The International Directory of Importers - Refrigeration, Ventilation and Heating Equipment Importers.* Interdata. • $260 Individuals print. Covers: 3,300 international firms importing refrigeration, ventilation and heating equipment. Entries include: Company name and address, contact person, email, number of employees, year established, phone and telefaxes, business activity, bank references, as well as a listing of refrigeration, ventilation and heating equipment currently being imported.

## INTERNET DATABASES

*Manufacturing Profiles.* U. S. Bureau of the Census. Phone: (301)763-4636 or (301)763-4100; Fax: (301)763-4794; Email: webmaster@census.gov • URL: http://www.census.gov/prod/www/abs/mfg-prof.html • The Census Bureau makes available free on PDF (Portable Document Format) an annual consolidation of the entire Current Industrial Report series, presenting "all the data compiled." Contains statistics on production, shipments, inventories, consumption, exports, imports, and orders for a wide variety of manufactured products.

## PERIODICALS AND NEWSLETTERS

*Air Conditioning, Heating, and Refrigeration News: The HVACR Contractor's Weekly Newsmagazine.* BNP Media. • Weekly. $87.00 per year. Includes *Supplement.*

*International Journal of Refrigeration.* Elsevier. • Monthly. $2,048 Institutions. Qualified personnel, $99.00 per year. Text in English and French.

*Refrigeration.* John W. Yopp Publications, Inc. • Monthly. $30.00 per year.

## RESEARCH CENTERS AND INSTITUTES

Purdue University - Ray W. Herrick Laboratories. School of Mechanical Engineering, 140 S Martin Jischke Dr., West Lafayette, IN 47907-2031. Phone: (765)494-2132; Fax: (765)494-0787; Email: rhlab@ecn.purdue.edu • URL: http://engineering.purdue.edu/Herrick/index.html • Mechanical engineering, including studies on heating, air conditioning, and refrigeration equipment and systems, engineering acoustics, noise and vibration control (including vehicle and engine noise), sound quality, positive displacement compressor technology, mechanical reliability, precision measurements, mechanics of materials, tribology, noise control materials, electro-hydraulic and engine controls, emissions, and automatic control.

## STATISTICS SOURCES

*Refrigeration, Air Conditioning, and Warm Air Heating Equipment.* U. S. Bureau of the Census. • Annual. Provides data on quantity and value of shipments by manufacturers. Formerly *Air Conditioning and Refrigeration Equipment.* (Current Industrial Reports, MA-333M.).

*U.S. Industry and Trade Outlook.* U.S. Department of Commerce National Technical Information Service. • Annual. Produced by the International Trade Administration, U.S. Department of Commerce, in a "public-private" partnership with DRI/McGraw-Hill and Standard & Poor's. Provides basic data, outlook for the current year, and "Long-Term Prospects" (five-year projections) for a wide variety of products and services. Includes high technology industries. Formerly *U.S. Industrial Outlook.*

## TRADE/PROFESSIONAL ASSOCIATIONS

American Society of Heating, Refrigerating and Air-Conditioning Engineers. 1791 Tullie Cir. NE, Atlanta, GA 30329. Phone: 800-527-4723 or (404)636-8400; Fax: (404)321-5478; Email: ashrae@ashrae.org • URL: http://www.ashrae.org • Represents Technical society of heating, ventilating, refrigeration, and air-conditioning engineers. Sponsors numerous research programs in cooperation with universities, research laboratories, and government agencies on subjects such as human and animal environmental studies, effects of air-conditioning, quality of inside air, heat transfer, flow, and cooling processes. Conducts professional development seminars. Writes method of test standards and other standards addressing energy conservation in buildings, indoor air quality, and refrigerants. Publishes extensive literature and electronic products.

Refrigerating Engineers and Technicians Association. PO Box 1819, Salinas, CA 93902. Phone: (831)455-8783; Fax: (831)455-7856; Email: info@reta.com • URL: http://www.reta.com • Formerly National Association Practical Refrigerating Engineers.

# REFUSE DISPOSAL

*See* SANITATION INDUSTRY

# REGIONAL AIRLINES

*See* AIRLINE INDUSTRY

# REGIONAL PLANNING

*See also* CITY PLANNING; ZONING

## ABSTRACTS AND INDEXES

*Journal of Planning Literature.* Ohio State University, Dept. of City and Regional Planning. Pine Forge Press. • Quarterly. $1,380 Institutions Print and E-access. Provides reviews and abstracts of city and regional planning lierature.

*PAIS International.* ProQuest L.L.C. • Monthly. $850.00 per year; cumulations three times a year. Provides topical citations to the worldwide literature of public affairs, economics, demographics, sociology, and trade. Text in English; indexed materials in English, French, German, Italian, Portuguese and Spanish.

*Social Sciences Citation Index.* Thomson Reuters Corp. • Weekly. Product is accessed via *Web of Science.*

*Social Sciences Index Retrospective: 1907-1983.* EBSCO Publishing Inc. • Indexing for 1,000,000 articles. Coverage includes international index and social sciences and humanities index.

## CD-ROM DATABASES

*PAIS International.* ProQuest L.L.C. • Monthly. $1,995.00 per year. Contains over 650,000 citations to the literature of contemporary social, political, and economic issues.

*Social Sciences Abstracts.* EBSCO Publishing Inc. • Provides indexing from 1983 and abstracting from 1994 of more than 750 periodicals covering economics, area studies, community health, public administration, public welfare, urban studies, and many other topics related to the social sciences.

*Social Sciences Citation Index.* Thomson Reuters Corp. • Weekly. Product is accessed via *Web of Science.*

## DIRECTORIES

*AICP Membership Directory.* Association of Independent Commercial Producers. • $45 Nonmembers. Covers: General member companies that specialize in producing commercials on various media, including film, video, and computer, for advertisers and agencies. Associate member companies listed serve the industry, such as post-production and editorial houses, equipment and prop suppliers, casting agencies and others. AMP members are music production shops; press members are those in the press who cover the industry. Entries include: Company name, address, phone, fax, e-mail, URL, contact names, and names of people represented.

## HANDBOOKS AND MANUALS

*Zoning and Planning Deskbook, 2d.* Katherine Kmiec Turner and Douglas W. Kmiec, authors. Thomson West. • Annual. $530.60 book - softbound; full set. Emphasis is on legal issues. Examines the latest developments in land use control, discussing procedural and substantive considerations, remedies, strategies, and state and federal litigation.

## ONLINE DATABASES

*Wilson Social Sciences Abstracts Online.* H.W. Wilson Co. • Provides online abstracting and indexing of more than 500 periodicals covering area studies, community health, public administration, public welfare, urban studies, and many other social science topics. Time period is 1994 to date for abstracts and 1983 to date for indexing, with updates weekly. Inquire as to online cost and availability.

## PERIODICALS AND NEWSLETTERS

*Planning.* American Planning Association. • Monthly. $85 Nonmembers.

*Planning and Zoning News.* Planning & Zoning Center Inc. • Monthly. $185 per year. Newsletter on planning and zoning issues in the United States.

## RESEARCH CENTERS AND INSTITUTES

Federal University of Mines Gerais - Center for Regional Development and Planning. Av. Antonio Carlos, 6627, 31270-901 Belo Horizonte, MT, Brazil. Phone: 55 31 34097100; Fax: 55 31 34097203 • URL: http://web.face.ufmg.br/cedeplar/site/ • Regional economics, especially the intersection of economics and demography with other disciplines, particularly health and the environment.

## TRADE/PROFESSIONAL ASSOCIATIONS

American Planning Association. 205 N Michigan Ave., Ste. 1200, Chicago, IL 60601. Phone: (312)431-9100; Fax: (312)786-6700; Email: customerservice@planning.org • URL: http://www.planning.org • Public and private planning agency officials, professional planners, planning educators, elected and appointed officials, and other persons involved in urban and rural development. Works to foster the best techniques and decisions for the planned development of communities and regions. Provides extensive professional services and publications to professionals and laypeople in planning and related fields; serves as a clearinghouse for information. Through Planning Advisory Service, a research and inquiry-answering service, provides, on an annual subscription basis, advice on specific inquiries and a series of research reports on planning, zoning, and environmental regulations. Supplies information on job openings and makes definitive studies on salaries and recruitment of professional planners. Conducts research; collaborates in joint projects with local, national, and international organizations.

Regional Science Association International. University of Azores, Ofícce 155-156, Rua Capitao Joao D'Avila, Angra do Heroismo, 9700-042 Ponta Delgada, Portugal. • URL: http://www.regionalscience.org • Represents community of scholars interested in the regional impacts of national or global processes of economic and social change.

# REGISTRATION OF TRADEMARKS

*See* TRADEMARKS AND TRADE NAMES

---

# REGULATION OF INDUSTRY

*See also* LAWS

## ABSTRACTS AND INDEXES

*Current Law Index.* Cengage Learning Inc. • $1,332 Individuals. Monthly. $1269.00 per year. Produced in cooperation with the American Association of Law Libraries. Indexes more than 900 law journals, legal newspapers, and specialty publications from the U.S., Canada, U.K., Ireland, Australia, and New Zealand.

*Index to Legal Periodicals and Books.* H.W. Wilson Co. • Monthly. $490.00 per year. Quarterly and annual cumulations.

*PAIS International.* ProQuest L.L.C. • Monthly. $850.00 per year; cumulations three times a year. Provides topical citations to the worldwide literature of public affairs, economics, demographics, sociology, and trade. Text in English; indexed materials in English, French, German, Italian, Portuguese and Spanish.

*Social Sciences Citation Index.* Thomson Reuters Corp. • Weekly. Product is accessed via *Web of Science.*

*Social Sciences Index Retrospective: 1907-1983.* EBSCO Publishing Inc. • Indexing for 1,000,000 articles. Coverage includes international index and social sciences and humanities index.

## ALMANACS AND YEARBOOKS

*Advertising Law Guide.* Wolters Kluwer Law & Business CCH. • Monthly. $2,115. Contains full-text reporting of state and federal laws as well as federal regulations.

*American Law Yearbook.* Cengage Learning Inc. • $308 Individuals. Annual. $280.00. Serves as a yearly supplement to *West's Encyclopedia of American Lawa.* Describes new legal developments in many subject areas.

*Securities, Commodities, and Federal Banking: 1999 in Review.* Wolters Kluwer Law & Business CCH. • Irregular. $57.00. Summarizes the year's significant legal and regulatory developments.

## CD-ROM DATABASES

*Business Abstracts with Full Text.* EBSCO Publishing Inc. • Includes full text articles from more than 460 business publications from 1982 to present. Indexing for nearly 880 publications.

*Index to Legal Periodicals and Books.* EBSCO Publishing Inc. • Contains indexing of more than 1,400 English language legal periodicals from 1981 to date and 2,500 books.

*Newspaper Abstracts Ondisc.* ProQuest L.L.C. • Monthly. $2,950.00 per year (covers 1989 to date; archival discs are available for 1985-88). Provides cover-to-cover CD-ROM indexing and abstracting of 19 major newspapers, including the *New York Times, Wall Street Journal, Washington Post, Chicago Tribune,* and *Los Angeles Times.*

*PAIS International.* ProQuest L.L.C. • Monthly. $1,995.00 per year. Contains over 650,000 citations to the literature of contemporary social, political, and economic issues.

*Social Sciences Abstracts.* EBSCO Publishing Inc. • Provides indexing from 1983 and abstracting from 1994 of more than 750 periodicals covering economics, area studies, community health, public administration, public welfare, urban studies, and many other topics related to the social sciences.

*Social Sciences Citation Index.* Thomson Reuters Corp. • Weekly. Product is accessed via *Web of Science.*

## DIRECTORIES

*Federal Regional Yellow Book: Who's Who in the Federal Government's Departments, Agencies, Military Installations, and Service Academies*

*Outside of Washington, DC.* Leadership Directories Inc. • Semiannual. $465 Individuals annual. Lists over 35,000 federal officials and support staff at 8,000 regional offices.

*United States Government Manual.* Office of the Federal Register. • Annual. $29 Individuals. Provides information on the agencies of the executive, judicial, and legislative branches of the Federal government. Contains a section on terminated or transferred agencies. Database includes: Includes boards, commissions, committees and quasi-official agencies and organizations in which US participates.

## ENCYCLOPEDIAS AND DICTIONARIES

*Encyclopedia of Governmental Advisory Organizations.* Cengage Learning Inc. • Annual. $1,178 Individuals print. Contains more than 7,300 entries describing activities and personnel. Complete contact information.

*West's Encyclopedia of American Law.* Cengage Learning Inc. • 2004. eBook. Second edition. Covers a wide variety of legal topics for the general reader. Inquire for pricing.

## HANDBOOKS AND MANUALS

*ADA Compliance Guide.* Thompson Publishing Group Inc. • $499 print only. Provides detailed information for employers and others on complying with the Americans With Disabilities Act (ADA). Includes material on employment discrimination, transportation accessibility, accessibility in public accommodations, and state disability laws.

*United States Export Administration Regulations.* U. S. Government Printing Office. • $199 U.S. Looseleaf. Includes supplements.. Includes basic manual and supplementary bulletins for one year. Issued by the Bureau of Export Administration, U. S. Department of Commerce (www.doc.gov). Consists of export licensing rules and regulations.

## INTERNET DATABASES

*Factiva.* Dow Jones Reuters Business Interactive, LLC. Phone: 800-369-7466 or (609)452-1511; Fax: (609)520-5770; Email: solutions@factiva.com • URL: http://www.factiva.com • Fee-based Web site provides "global news and business information through Web sites and content integration solutions." Includes Dow Jones and Reuters newswires, The Wall Street Journal, and more than 7,000 other sources of current news, historical articles, market research reports, and investment analysis. Content includes 96 major U. S. newspapers, 900 non-English sources, trade publications, media transcripts, country profiles, news photos, etc.

*FedWorld: A Program of the United States Department of Commerce.* National Technical Information Service. Phone: 800-553-NTIS or (703)605-6000; Fax: (703)605-6900; Email: webmaster@fedworld. gov • URL: http://www.fedworld.gov • Web site offers "a comprehensive central access point for searching, locating, ordering, and acquiring government and business information." Emphasis is on searching the Web pages, databases, and government reports of a wide variety of federal agencies. Fees: Free.

*FirstGov: Your First Click to the U. S. Government.* General Services Administration. Phone: 800-333-4636 or (202)501-0705; Email: public.affairs@gsa. gov • URL: http://www.gsa.gov • Free Web site provides extensive links to federal agencies covering a wide variety of topics, such as agriculture, business, consumer safety, education, the environment, government jobs, grants, health, social security, statistics sources, taxes, technology, travel, and world affairs. Also provides links to federal forms, including IRS tax forms. Searching is offered, both keyword and advanced.

*GPO Access.* U. S. Government Printing Office Sales Program, Bibliographic Systems Branch. Phone: (888)293-6498 or (202)512-1530; Fax:

(202)512-1262; Email: gpoaccess@gpo.gov • URL: http://www.access.gpo.gov • Web site provides searching of the GPO's Sales Product Catalog (SPC), also known as Publications Reference File (PRF). Covers all "Government information products currently offered for sale by the Superintendent of Documents." There are also specialized search pages for individual databases, such as the *Code of Federal Regulations,* the *Federal Register,* and *Commerce Business Daily.* Updated daily. Fees: Free.

*Lexis.com Research System.* Lexis-Nexis Group. Phone: 800-227-4908 or (937)865-6800; Fax: (937)865-6909; Email: webmaster@prod.lexis-nexis.com • URL: http://www.nexis.com • Fee-based Web site offers extensive searching of a wide variety of legal sources. Additional features include Daily Opinion Service, lexis.com Bookstore, Career Center, CLE Center, Law Schools, and Practice Pages ("Pages specific to areas of specialty").

*Nexis.com.* Lexis-Nexis Group. Phone: 800-227-4908 or (937)865-6800; Fax: (937)865-6909; Email: webmaster@prod.lexis-nexis.com • URL: http://www.nexis.com • Fee-based Web site offers searching of about 2.8 billion documents in some 30,000 news, business, and legal information sources. Features include a subject directory covering 1,200 topics in 34 categories and a Company Dossier containing information on more than 500,000 public and private companies. Boolean searching is offered.

*U.S. Business Advisor.* Small Business Administration. Phone: (202)205-6600; Fax: (202)205-7064 • URL: http://www.sba.gov • Web site provides "a one-stop electronic link to all the information and services government provides for the business community." Covers about 60 federal agencies that exist to assist or regulate business. Detailed information is provided on financial assistance, workplace issues, taxes, regulations, international trade, and other business topics. Searching is offered. Fees: Free.

## ONLINE DATABASES

*Wilson Business Abstracts Online.* H.W. Wilson Co. • Indexes and abstracts 600 major business periodicals, plus the *Wall Street Journal* and the business section of the *New York Times.* Indexing is from 1982, abstracting from 1990, with the two newspapers included from 1993. Updated weekly. Inquire as to online cost and availability. (*Business Periodicals Index* without abstracts is also available online.).

*Wilson Social Sciences Abstracts Online.* H.W. Wilson Co. • Provides online abstracting and indexing of more than 500 periodicals covering area studies, community health, public administration, public welfare, urban studies, and many other social science topics. Time period is 1994 to date for abstracts and 1983 to date for indexing, with updates weekly. Inquire as to online cost and availability.

## OTHER SOURCES

*ADA Compliance Manual for Employers.* Matthew Bender and Company Inc. • Looseleaf. $95.00. Periodic supplementation available. "Every business with more than 15 employees must comply with the Amricans with Disabilities Act." This guide provides practical advice on job requirements, accessibility, employee selection, reasonable accomodations, termination issues, and other matters.

*Chemical Regulation Reporter: A Weekly Review of Activity Affecting Chemical Users and Manufacturers.* Bloomberg BNA. • Weekly. $2,226 per year. Looseleaf service.

*FCC Record.* U. S. Government Printing Office. • Semimonthly. $813 U.S. 1 year. Produced by the Federal Communications Commission (www.fcc. gov). An inclusive compilation of decisions, reports, public notices, and other documents of the FCC.

*Occupational Safety and Health Handbook: An*

*Employer's Guide to OSHA Laws.* Matthew Bender and Company Inc. • $128. Periodic supplementation available. Covers inspections, violations, the citation process, ergonomics, hazards, equipment, and other topics relating to the law enforced by the federal Occupational Safety and Health Administration (OSHA).

*Practical Guide to the Occupational Safety and Health Act.* ALM Media Properties LLC. • $545 print + online + ebook. Covers the practical aspects of doing business while complying with OSHA regulations. Covers inspections, enforcement, rights of employees, the possibility of criminal prosecution, and related issues. (Law Journal Press).

## PERIODICALS AND NEWSLETTERS

*Europe and Eurasia Business Committee Dispatch.* Hungarian-U.S. Business Council. • Weekly. $350 /year for nonmembers. Provides information on regulations, legislation and specific industries for Central/Eastern Europe, New Independent States, Turkey and Iran.

*FCC Report: An Exclusive Report on Domestic and International Telecommunications Policy and Regulation.* Warren Communications News Inc. • 26 times a year. $670.00 per year. Newsletter concerned principally with Federal Communications Commission reglations and policy.

*Federal Register.* Office of the Federal Register. U. S. Government Printing Office. • Daily except Saturday and Sunday. $764.00 per year. Publishes regulations and legal notices issued by federal agencies, including executive orders and presidential proclamations. Issued by the National Archives and Records Administration (www.nara.gov).

*Regulation: Cato Review of Business & Government.* Cato Institute. • Quarterly. $20 Individuals. Magazine publishing articles on goverment regulation.

## RESEARCH CENTERS AND INSTITUTES

Georgia State University - Center for the Study of Regulated Industry. Department of Finance, Robinson College of Business, Atlanta, GA 30302-3989. Phone: (404)413-7310; Fax: (404)413-7312; Email: profmorin@msn.com • URL: http://robinson.gsu.edu/faculty/csri.html • Energy consumption and the regulation of public utilities.

Rutgers University - Center for Research in Regulated Industries. Rutgers Business School, 1 Washington Park, Rm. 1104, Newark, NJ 07102-3122. Phone: (973)353-5761; Fax: (973)353-1348; Email: crri@business.rutgers.edu • URL: http://www.crri.rutgers.edu • Regulated industries, especially economics and finance of such institutions, governance mechanisms, and price structures.

University of Manchester - Centre on Regulation and Competition. Harold Hankins Bldg., Precinct Ctr., Institute for Development Policy & Management, School of Environment & Development, Oxford Rd., Manchester M13 9QH, United Kingdom. Phone: 44 161 2752798; Fax: 44 161 2750808; Email: paul.cook@manchester.ac.uk • URL: http://www.competition-regulation.org.uk/ • Economic regulation and policy; regulatory impact assessment; competition, innovation and development; competition policy and development; institutional innovation in regulatory governance; regulations, politics and poverty.

## STATISTICS SOURCES

*Property-Casualty Insurance Facts.* Insurance Information Institute. • Annual. $22.50. Formerly *Insurance Facts.*

## TRADE/PROFESSIONAL ASSOCIATIONS

Community Financial Services Association. 515 King St., Ste. 300, Alexandria, VA 22314. Phone: 888-572-9329; Fax: (703)684-1219; Email: info@cfsaa.com • URL: http://cfsaa.com • Works to promote laws and regulations that balance the interests of the payday advance industry with consumers. Supports and encourages responsible industry practices.

CropLife Australia. AMP Bldg., Level 2, 1 Hobart Pl., Locked Bag 916, Canberra, ACT 2601, Australia. Phone: 61 2 62306399; Fax: 61 2 62306355 • URL: http://www.croplifeaustralia.org.au • Works for a fair, science-based regulatory system, encourages research and development.

# REGULATION OF SECURITIES

*See* SECURITIES LAW AND REGULATION

# REHABILITATION, VOCATIONAL

*See* VOCATIONAL REHABILITATION

# REIT'S

*See* REAL ESTATE INVESTMENT TRUSTS

# RELOCATION OF EMPLOYEES

## ABSTRACTS AND INDEXES

*Business Periodicals Index Retrospective.* EBSCO Publishing Inc. • 11/year. Quarterly and annual cumulations.

## ONLINE DATABASES

*Wilson Business Abstracts Online.* H.W. Wilson Co. • Indexes and abstracts 600 major business periodicals, plus the *Wall Street Journal* and the business section of the *New York Times.* Indexing is from 1982, abstracting from 1990, with the two newspapers included from 1993. Updated weekly. Inquire as to online cost and availability. (*Business Periodicals Index* without abstracts is also available online.).

## PERIODICALS AND NEWSLETTERS

*Direction: For the Moving and Storage Industry.* American Moving and Storage Association. • Monthly. $35.00 per year. Newsletter on developments affecting the household goods movingindustry. Formerly *American Mover.*

*Insulation Outlook: Business Solutions for Expanding or Relocating Companies.* National Insulation Association. • $98.00 per year. Covers site selection and related topics.

*Mobility.* Employee Relocation Council. • Monthly. $48 /year. Covers various aspects of the moving of corporate employees.

*Office Relocation Magazine.* ORM Group. • Bimonthly. $39.00 per year. Provides articles on the relocation of office facilities.

*Runzheimer Reports on Relocation.* Runzheimer International. • Monthly. $354.00 per year. Newsletter.

## STATISTICS SOURCES

*Survey and Analysis of Employee Relocation Policies and Costs.* Runzheimer International. • Annual. Based on surveys of relocation administrators.

## TRADE/PROFESSIONAL ASSOCIATIONS

American Moving and Storage Association. 1611 Duke St., Alexandria, VA 22314-3406. Phone: 888-849-2672 or (703)683-7410; Fax: (703)683-7527 or (703)548-1845; Email: amconf@amconf.org • URL: http://www.promover.org • Members are household

goods movers, storage companies, and trucking firms.

Worldwide ERC. 4401 Wilson Blvd., Ste. 510, Arlington, VA 22203. Phone: (703)842-3400; Fax: (703)527-1552; Email: customercare@worldwideerc.org • URL: http://www.worldwideerc.org/Pages/index.aspx • Members are major corporations seeking efficiency and minimum disruption when employee transfers take place. Formerly Employee Relocation Real Estate Advisory Council.

# REMODELING

*See* HOME IMPROVEMENT INDUSTRY

# RENTAL, EQUIPMENT

*See* EQUIPMENT LEASING

# RENTAL SERVICES

*See also* AUTOMOBILE LEASE AND RENTAL SERVICES; EQUIPMENT LEASING

## DIRECTORIES

*Houseboats Directory--Rentals.* InfoGroup Inc. • Annual. Number of listings: 5274. Entries include: Name, address, phone, size of advertisement, name of owner or manager, number of employees, year first in "Yellow Pages." Compiled from telephone company "Yellow Pages," nationwide.

*Leasing Sourcebook: The Directory of the U. S. Capital Equipment Leasing Industry.* Bibliotechnology Systems and Publishing Co. • Every 12-18 months. $135.00. Lists approximately 5,200 capital equipment leasing companies.

## FINANCIAL RATIOS

*Annual Statement Studies.* Risk Management Association. • Annual. Compiled from over 280,000 financial statements.

*Annual Statement Studies: Industry Default Probabilities and Cash Flow Measures.* Risk Management Association. • Annual. $405 Nonmembers. Serves as a companion volume to the original *Annual Statement Studies.* Gives probability of default estimates on a percentage scale for more than 450 industries. Includes changes in position year-by-year for eight financial statement line items and provides percentage measures of cash flow.

*NARDA's Cost of Doing Business Survey.* North American Retail Dealers Association. • $50 Members. Provides insight into revenue and costs, warranty information, expenses, and asset/liability information.

## PERIODICALS AND NEWSLETTERS

*Equipment Leasing and Finance.* Equipment Leasing and Finance Association. • 10 times a year. $100.00 per year. Edited for equipment leasing companies. Covers management, funding, marketing, etc.

*Rental.* Cygnus Business Media Inc. • Annual. Product rental management trade magazine.

*Rental Equipment Register.* Penton. • Monthly.

*Rental Management.* American Rental Association. • Monthly. Covers all market segments of the equipment rental industry.

## STATISTICS SOURCES

*Survey of Industry Activity.* Equipment Leasing and Finance Association. • Annual. Provides financial and statistical data on the equipment leasing industry. Price on application.

*U.S. Industry and Trade Outlook.* U.S. Department of Commerce National Technical Information Service. • Annual. Produced by the International

---

**For publishers' addresses, refer to SOURCES CITED section at the back of the book.**

Trade Administration, U.S. Department of Commerce, in a "public-private" partnership with DRI/ McGraw-Hill and Standard & Poor's. Provides basic data, outlook for the current year, and "Long-Term Prospects" (five-year projections) for a wide variety of products and services. Includes high technology industries. Formerly *U.S. Industrial Outlook.*

### TRADE/PROFESSIONAL ASSOCIATIONS

American Rental Association. 1900 19th St., Moline, IL 61265-4179. Phone: 800-334-2177 or (309)764-2475; Fax: (309)764-1533 • URL: http:// www.ararental.org • Firms engaged in the rental of event and party equipment, tools, machinery, and other products; includes independent, franchised, and chain store operators. Associates are suppliers of equipment, merchandise, and other items. Seeks to foster better business methods; promote study of economic trends in the rental industry.

Canadian Finance and Leasing Association. 15 Toronto St., Ste. 301, Toronto, ON, Canada M5C 2E3. Phone: 877-213-7373 or (416)860-1133; Fax: (416)860-1140; Email: info@cfla-acfl.ca • URL: http://www.cfla-acfl.ca • Providers of financing and rental and leasing services. Promotes adherence to high standards of ethics and practice by members; seeks to advance the financing, renting, and leasing industries. Represents members' commercial and regulatory interests; conducts promotional and advocacy campaigns.

## RENTAL SERVICES, AUTOMOBILE

*See* AUTOMOBILE LEASE AND RENTAL SERVICES

## REPORT WRITING

*See also* TECHNICAL WRITING

### DIRECTORIES

*Datapro Reports.* Datapro Information Services Group. • Monthly. $495 minimum cost per year, depending on service. Datapro produces sixty information services covering products, vendors, markets, and technologies in large systems, microcomputers, telecommunications, data communications, word processing, software, office automation systems, copiers and duplicators, information security systems, retail automation equipment, banking automation equipment, personal computer communications, communications alternatives, and electronic publishing systems. Reports generally include descriptions and analyses of each equipment model offered by each manufacturer in the field, comparison charts, and lists of suppliers, associations, consultants, etc., with addresses and phone numbers. Individual descriptions include a summary and detailed reports on technical characteristics and operation. Reports are on looseleaf pages.

### PERIODICALS AND NEWSLETTERS

*Harvard Management Communication Letter.* Harvard Business School Publishing. • Description: Provides information and techniques for managers on effective communication.

## RESEARCH, ADVERTISING

*See* ADVERTISING RESEARCH

## RESEARCH AND DEVELOPMENT

*See also* BUSINESS RESEARCH; ECONOMIC RESEARCH; INDUSTRIAL RESEARCH; LABORATORIES; MARKET RESEARCH; SCIENTIFIC APPARATUS AND INSTRUMENT INDUSTRIES; TECHNOLOGY

### ABSTRACTS AND INDEXES

*Applied Science and Technology Index.* EBSCO Publishing Inc. • 11/year. Indexes a wide variety of English language technical, industrial, and engineering periodicals.

*Science Citation Index.* Thomson Reuters Intellectual Property and Science. • Weekly. Includes *Source Index, Citation Index, Permuterm Subject Index,* and *Corporate Index.* Provides researchers, administrators, faculty, and students with quick, powerful access to the bibliographic and citation information they need to find research data, analyze trends, journals and researchers, and share their findings.

### ALMANACS AND YEARBOOKS

*Science and Technology Almanac.* Greenwood Publishing Group Inc. • $99.95 Individuals hardcover. Provides the most comprehensive source for the significant science news of 2001 and for scientific information in general.

### BIOGRAPHICAL SOURCES

*American Men & Women of Science (AMWS).* Cengage Learning Inc. • 2013. $1508.00. 31st edition. Over 135,000 scientists active in the physical, biological, mathematical, computer science and engineering fields in the United States and Canada.

*Who's Who in Science and Engineering.* Marquis Who's Who L.L.C. • Biennial. $249.00. Provides concise biographical information on 33,545 prominent engineers and scientists. International coverage, with geographical and professional indexes.

### CD-ROM DATABASES

*Applied Science and Technology Abstracts.* EBSCO Publishing Inc. • Citations for more than 700 prominent scientific, technical, engineering, and industrial periodicals.

*NTIS Database.* Ovid Technologies Inc. • Quarterly. $2,850.00 per year. Guide to over 2 million bibliographic entries. Compiled by the U.S. National Technical Information Service.

*Science Citation Index.* Thomson Reuters Intellectual Property and Science. • Weekly. Includes *Source Index, Citation Index, Permuterm Subject Index,* and *Corporate Index.* Provides researchers, administrators, faculty, and students with quick, powerful access to the bibliographic and citation information they need to find research data, analyze trends, journals and researchers, and share their findings.

### DIRECTORIES

*Directory of Belgian Research Centers with Libraries or Documentation Services.* National Center for Scientific & Technical Documentation Royal Library. • Annual. $1,000. Covers: 1,090 research centers, including universities and companies, in Belgium. Entries include: Center name, address, phone, databases, uses of information.

*European Sources of Scientific and Technical Information.* Cartermill International. • Irregular. $225. Covers: over 1,500 patents and standards offices, national offices of information, and organizations active in scientific fields in Europe, including former Soviet bloc nations. Provides English-language version of foreign terminology. Entries include: Organization name, address, phone, fax, e-mail and website addresses, year founded, name of contact, parent company, subject(s) covered, publications, library facilities, and information, consulting, and training services.

*Materials Research Centres: A World Directory of Organizations and Programmes in Materials Science.* Specialist Journals. • Biennial. $445.00. Profiles of research centers in 75 countries. Materials include plastics, metals, fibers, etc.

*Medical Research Centres: A World Directory of*

*Organizations and Programmes.* Informa Group PLC. • Biennial. $470.00. Two volumes. Contains profiles of more than 7,000 medical research facilities around the world. Includes medical, dental, nursing, pharmaceutical, psychiatric, and surgical research centers.

*Plunkett's Engineering and Research Industry Almanac.* Plunkett Research Ltd. • Annual. $349.99. Contains detailed profiles of major engineering and technology corporations. Includes CD-ROM.

*Register of Development Research Projects in Latin America.* OECD Publishing. • Irregular. $75. Covers: 1,304 development research projects in 16 Latin American countries concerned with economic and social development, including economic policy, institutional framework, demography, labor, culture, and education. Entries include: Project title, institution name and address, researcher names, financial sponsor names and addresses, dates, description of project, planned output.

*Research Centers Directory.* Cengage Learning Inc. • Annual. $1,071 Individuals paperback. 2012. 42nd edition. Covers university, government, and other nonprofit research organizations established on a permanent basis to carry on continuing research programs in all areas of study; includes research institutes, laboratories, experiment stations, research parks, technology transfer centers, and other facilities and activities; coverage includes Canada. eBook also available.

*World Energy and Nuclear Directory.* Specialist Journals. • Biennial. $385.00. Lists 5,000 public and private, international research and development organizations functioning in a wide variety of areas related to energy.

### E-BOOKS

*Encyclopedia of Emerging Industries.* Cengage Learning Inc. • $546 6th edition. Provides detailed information on 140 "newly flourishing" industries. Includes historical background, organizational structure, significant individuals, current conditions, major companies, work force, technology trends, research developments, and other industry facts.

### FINANCIAL RATIOS

*Annual Statement Studies.* Risk Management Association. • Annual. Compiled from over 280,000 financial statements.

*Annual Statement Studies: Industry Default Probabilities and Cash Flow Measures.* Risk Management Association. • Annual. $405 Nonmembers. Serves as a companion volume to the original *Annual Statement Studies.* Gives probability of default estimates on a percentage scale for more than 450 industries. Includes changes in position year-by-year for eight financial statement line items and provides percentage measures of cash flow.

### INTERNET DATABASES

*FedWorld: A Program of the United States Department of Commerce.* National Technical Information Service. Phone: 800-553-NTIS or (703)605-6000; Fax: (703)605-6900; Email: webmaster@fedworld. gov • URL: http://www.fedworld.gov • Web site offers "a comprehensive central access point for searching, locating, ordering, and acquiring government and business information." Emphasis is on searching the Web pages, databases, and government reports of a wide variety of federal agencies. Fees: Free.

### ONLINE DATABASES

*Applied Science and Technology Index Online.* H.W. Wilson Co. • Provides online indexing of 500 major scientific, technical, industrial, and engineering periodicals. Time period is 1983 to date. Monthly updates. Inquire as to online cost and availability.

*Current Contents Connect.* Thomson Reuters Intellectual Property and Science. • Provides online abstracts of articles listed in the tables of contents of about 7,500 journals. Coverage is very broad, including science, social science, life science, technology, engineering, industry, agriculture, the environment, economics, and arts and humanities. Time period is two years, with weekly updates. Inquire as to online cost and availability.

## OTHER SOURCES

*Army AL&T: Professional Publication of the AL&T Community.* U. S. Government Printing Office. • Quarterly. $21 U.S.. Produced by the U.S. Army Materiel Command (www.amc.army.mil). Reports on Army research, development, and acquisition. Formerly *Army RD&A.*

## PERIODICALS AND NEWSLETTERS

*DOE This Month.* U. S. Government Printing Office. • Monthly. $22 per year. Describes the U.S. Department of Energy's research and development activities and DOE publications. Includes information on nuclear energy, renewable energy sources, and synthetic fuels.

*Inside R and D: A Weekly Report on Technical Innovation.* Technical Insights. • Weekly. Institutions, $840.00 per year. Concentrates on new and significant developments. Formerly *Technology Transfer Week.*

*International Journal of Economics and Business Modeling.* Bioinfo Publications. • Peer-reviewed journal publishing information in areas of business modeling, management and applied research.

*Research and Development: The Voice of the Research and Development Community.* Reed Elsevier Group plc Reed Business Information. • 13 times a year. $81.90 per year.

*The Scientist.* • Biweekly. Individuals, $29.00 per year; institutions, $58.00 per year. Contains news for scientific, research, and technical personnel.

## RESEARCH CENTERS AND INSTITUTES

Federal Highway Administration - Office of Transportation Policy Studies. 1200 New Jersey Ave. SE, 8th Fl., Washington, DC 20590. Phone: (202)366-9232; Fax: (202)366-3297; Email: mary. tischer@dot.gov • URL: http://www.fhwa.dot.gov/policy/otps • Formulation of highway policy and legislative initiatives. Principal areas of research interest are highway use, performance, and requirements and the relationship of these factors to commercial highway transport; truck sizes and weights; cost allocations; transportation user charge substructures, taxing policies and subsidy issues, and the effects of these issues upon various public and private groups; and the economic characteristics of specific industries (as necessary for the formulation of highway program policy).

Hawaii Department of Business, Economic Development, and Tourism - Research and Economic Analysis Division. No. 1 Capitol District Bldg., 250 S Hotel St., Honolulu, HI 96813. Phone: (808)586-2355 • URL: http://dbedt.hawaii.gov/economic • Business, economic development, tourism.

Michigan State University College of Human Medicine - Office of Medical Education Research and Development. E Fee Hall, Rm. A-202, 965 Fee Rd., East Lansing, MI 48824-1316. Phone: (517)353-2037 or (517)353-7791; Fax: (517)432-1798; Email: mavis@msu.edu • URL: http://omerad.msu.edu • Improvement in medical education and related service programs, through program evaluation, performance assessment, faculty development, and the application of technology to improve instruction.

Monash University - Centre for Research in Accounting and Finance. Wellington Rd., Bldg. 11E, Clayton, VIC 3168, Australia. Phone: 61 3 99052389; Fax: 61 3 99055475; Email: kim. langfield-smith@buseco.monash.edu.au • URL: http://www.buseco.monash.edu.au/aaf/research/ • Accounting and finance.

Small Business Administration - Office of Technology. 409 3rd St. SW, Washington, DC 20416. Phone: (202)205-6450; Fax: (202)481-1518; Email: edsel.brown@sba.gov • URL: http://archive. sba.gov/aboutsba/sbaprograms/sbir/index.html • Provides policy for the Small Business Innovation Research Program (SBIR). SBIR is a federal procurement system that provides qualified small business concerns with opportunities to compete for federal research and development awards. Also oversees the Small Business Technology Transfer (STTR) Program. STTR coordinates cooperative research and development activities between small business STTR awardee, nonprofit research institutions, or federally funded research and development centers.

Small Business Innovation Research Program - Small Business Technology Transfer Program. Germantown Bldg., SC-29, 1000 Independence Ave. SW, Washington, DC 20585. Phone: (301)903-5707; Fax: (301)903-5488; Email: sbir-sttr@science.doe.gov • URL: http://science.energy.gov/sbir • Private sector commercialization of energy-related innovations derived from Federal research and development; technological innovation; the use small business to meet Federal research and development needs; Phase I funding up to $100,000 for a period of approximately nine months; further funding (up to $750,000 for not more than 24 months) to continue development of promising programs initiated in Phase I; and, finally, follow-on funding for commercial applications of the research or development pursued by small business with non-federal capital, or alternatively, follow-on non-SBIR federal contracts for products or processes desired by the government. to $100,000 for a period of approximately six months; further funding (up to $750,000 for not more than 24 months) to continue development of promising programs initiated in Phase I; and, finally, follow-on funding for commercial applications of the research or development pursued by small business with nonfederal capital, or alternatively, follow-on non-SBIR federal contracts for products or processes desired by the government.

SOAS, University of London - Centre for Development Policy and Research. Russell Sq., Thornhaught St., London WC1H 0XG, United Kingdom. Phone: 44 20 798984316; Fax: 44 20 74363844 • URL: http://www.soas.ac.uk/cdpr • Economies in transition, stabilization and structural adjustment programs, illicit drugs and development, development assistance.

Texas Tech University - Center for Healthcare Innovation, Education and Research. Rawls College of Business Administration, Lubbock, TX 79409. Phone: (806)742-1236; Fax: (806)742-3434; Email: tim.huerta@ttu.edu • URL: http://chier.ba.ttu.edu/index.asp • Interdisciplinary approaches to studying healthcare safety issues and addition of electronic medical records.

U.S. Bureau of Labor Statistics - Office of Prices and Living Conditions. 2 Massachusetts Ave. NE, Rm. 3120, Washington, DC 20212. Phone: (202)691-5200; Fax: (202)691-7890; Email: greenless.john@bls.gov • URL: http://www.bls.gov/bls/inflation.htm • Prices in retail and primary markets; conducts research to improve the measurement of price change. Areas of interest include consumer price indexes; producer price indexes; export and import price indexes for U.S. foreign trade; and consumer expenditures, income, assets, and liabilities of all U.S. families. Office comprises: the Consumer Expenditure Surveys Division; Consumer Prices and Price Indexes Division, which provides measures of price change for a specified market basket of consumer goods and services; Industrial Prices and Price Indexes Division, which provides measures of change in prices received by producers at the level of the first commercial transaction for many commodities and some services; International Prices Division, which measures change in the prices of commodities and some services imported to and exported from the United States; Price and Index Number Research Division; and Price Statistical Methods Division.

U.S. Bureau of Labor Statistics - Office of Productivity and Technology - Foreign Labor Statistics Division. 2 Massachusetts Ave. NE, Ste. 2150, Washington, DC 20212-0001. Phone: (202)691-5654; Fax: (202)691-5679 • URL: http://www.bls.gov/fls/ • Labor conditions and developments abroad. Research involves the development of internationally comparable economic-statistical measures covering the labor force and unemployment, productivity, and labor costs. This information is used to assess current economic trends abroad that may affect U.S. performance; inform government and private officials of foreign developments that might affect U.S. policy; review foreign experience for possible application domestically; aid in the appraisal of U.S. competitiveness in foreign and domestic markets; and provide labor information to individuals, corporations, labor unions, and others concerned with foreign investment and development.

U.S. Customs and Border Protection - Office of Field Operations - Laboratories and Scientific Services Division - Research Laboratory. 7501 Boston Blvd., Ste. 113, Springfield, VA 22153. Phone: (703)921-7200; Fax: (703)921-7155; Email: cbp.labresearch@dhs.gov • URL: http://www.cbp. gov/xp/cgov/import/operations_support/labs_scientific_svcs/ • Provides technical services in support of the U.S. Customs mission in tariff and trade and in enforcement. Principal area of interest is analytical chemistry (instrumentation and methodology). Laboratory supports a field laboratory system, with affiliated laboratories in New York City, Savannah, New Orleans, Los Angeles, San Francisco, Chicago, and San Juan.

U.S. Environmental Protection Agency - Office of Research and Development. 1200 Pennsylvania Ave. NW, MC 8101R, Washington, DC 20460. Phone: (202)564-6620 or (202)564-6825; Email: kadeli. lek@epa.gov • URL: http://www2.epa.gov/aboutepa/about-office-research-and-development-ord • Provides research support and management and production of technical information.

U.S. Food and Drug Administration - Center for Drug Evaluation and Research - Office of Prescription Drug Promotion. Bldg. 51, Rm. 3200, 10903 New Hampshire Ave., Silver Spring, MD 20993-0002. Phone: (301)796-1200; Fax: (301)847-8445; Email: thomas.abrams@fda.hhs.gov • URL: http://www.fda.gov/AboutFDA/CentersOffices/OfficeofMedicalProductsandTobacco/CDER/ucm090142.htm • Industry-wide marketing practices of the pharmaceutical industry and improvement of drug communications between FDA, health professionals, and the public. Specific research areas include prescription drugs, marketing practices, and health communications.

## TRADE/PROFESSIONAL ASSOCIATIONS

Accounting and Finance Benchmarking Consortium. 4606 FM 1960 W, Ste. 250, Houston, TX 77069-9949. Phone: (281)440-5044 • URL: http://www.afbc.org • Accounting and finance managers of corporations with an interest in benchmarking. Promotes the use of benchmarking, wherein businesses compare their processes with those of their competitors, as a means of improving corporate efficiency and profitability. Facilitates exchange of information among members; conducts target operations, procurement, development, and maintenance studies; identifies model business practices.

Agricultural Economics Society. Holtwood, Red Lion St., Cropredy, Banbury OX17 1PD, United Kingdom. Phone: 44 1295 750182 • URL: http://www.aes.ac.uk • Agricultural economists in the UK, students of agricultural economics, and interested individuals. Promotes the study and teaching of all disciplines relevant to agricultural economics. Areas of interest include agricultural industry; food and related industries; rural communities. Conducts studies in fields of economics, statistics, marketing, business management, politics, history, and sociology.

Asia Academy of Management. Chinese University of Hong Kong, Faculty of Business Administration, Shatin, New Territories, Hong Kong, Hong Kong, China. Phone: 852 2603 6840; Email: asia-aom@cuhk.edu.hk • URL: http://www.baf.cuhk.edu.hk/asia-aom • Seeks to advance management theory, research, and education relevant to Asia. Encourages members to contribute to global management scholarship.

Asian Association of Management Organisations. Rua de Xangai No. 175, Edif. ACM, 9 Andar, Macau, Macao, China. Phone: 853 28323283; Fax: 853 28323267 • URL: http://www.aamo.net • Organization representing the national management organizations of Asian countries. Seeks to advance management practice; promotes continuing professional development of managers. Facilitates exchange of information among members; conducts research and educational programs.

Asian Institute of Management. Eugenio Lopez Foundation Bldg., Joseph R. McMicking Campus, 123 Paseo de Roxas Ave., Makati City 1229, Philippines. Phone: 63 2 8924011 or 63 2 8924023; Fax: 63 2 8672114 or 63 2 8179240; Email: enrollment@aim.edu • URL: http://www.aim.edu • Managers and business and management educators. Seeks to advance the theory and practice of business and organizational management. Sponsors research and educational programs.

Asset Based Finance Association. 3rd Fl., 20 Hill Rise, Surrey, Richmond TW10 6UA, United Kingdom. Phone: 44 20 8332 9955; Fax: 44 20 8332 2585 • URL: http://www.abfa.org.uk • Brokers, business agents, and factors in the United Kingdom. Promotes and protects members' interests in the fields of factoring and invoice discounting. Conducts educational and research programs. Maintains a code of conduct; fosters the advancement of knowledge and experience; awards diplomas to students. Disseminates information; compiles statistics.

Association for Enterprise Information. 2111 Wilson Blvd., Ste. 400, Arlington, VA 22201. Phone: (703)247-9474 or (703)247-2597; Fax: (703)522-3192; Email: dchesebrough@afei.org • URL: http://www.afei.org/Pages/default.aspx • Strives to advance enterprise integration and electronic business practices for industries and governments.

Auto Suppliers Benchmarking Association. 4606 FM 1960 W, Ste. 250, Houston, TX 77069-9949. Phone: (281)440-5044; Fax: (281)440-6677 • URL: http://www.asbabenchmarking.com • Automotive supplier firms with an interest in benchmarking. Promotes the use of benchmarking, wherein businesses compare their processes with those of their competitors, as a means of improving corporate efficiency and profitability. Facilitates exchange of information among members; conducts target operations, procurement, development, and maintenance studies; identifies model business practices.

British Crop Protection Council. c/o Chris Todd, Manager, 7 Omni Business Centre, Omega Park, Alton GU34 2QD, United Kingdom. Phone: 44 1420 593 200 or 44 1420 593200; Fax: 44 1420 593 209 or 44 1420 593209; Email: md@bcpc.org • URL:

http://www.bcpc.org • Promotes the knowledge and understanding of crop protection/production through conferences, publications, teaching resources for schools, training manuals, identifying R&D needs for policy makers.

Conference Board - Europe. Chaussee de la Hulpe 178, 6th Fl., B-1170 Brussels, Belgium. Phone: 32 2 675 5405; Email: brussels@conferenceboard.org • URL: http://www.conference-board.org • Promotes management and the marketplace to help businesses strengthen their performance and better serve society. Conducts research, makes forecasts, assesses trends, publishes information and analysis, and brings executives together for exchange of ideas.

CropLife Australia. AMP Bldg., Level 2, 1 Hobart Pl., Locked Bag 916, Canberra, ACT 2601, Australia. Phone: 61 2 62306399; Fax: 61 2 62306355 • URL: http://www.croplifeaustralia.org.au • Works for a fair, science-based regulatory system, encourages research and development.

European Foundation for Management Development. Rue Gachard 88, 1050 Brussels, Belgium. Phone: 32 2 6290810; Fax: 32 2 6290811 • URL: http://www.efmd.org • Corporations, educational institutions, employers associations, management consultants, and individuals in 45 countries with an interest in management development, training, and education. Seeks to identify, research, and address leading management development issues. Fosters development of professional competence of those responsible for management development within companies and educational institutions; promotes education, development, and research in the field through working groups, seminars and conferences. Strives to organize effective interaction among all those involved in the management development process.

European International Business Academy. c/o EI-ASM, Hotel Metropole, 2nd Fl., Pl. de Brouckere Plein, 31, B-1000 Brussels, Belgium. Phone: 32 2 2266660; Fax: 32 2 5121929 • URL: http://www.eiba-online.org • Individuals and associations involved in international business. Encourages exchange of ideas; fosters communication among members; serves as an information clearinghouse for those interested in education and research of international business.

European Marketing Academy. Pl. de Brouckere Plein, 31, B-1000 Brussels, Belgium. Phone: 32 2 2266660; Fax: 32 2 5121929; Email: emac@eiasm.be • URL: http://www.emac-online.org/r/default.asp?iId=FLFDIE • Persons involved or interested in teaching or research in the field of marketing. Serves as forum for exchange of information concerning marketing; fosters improved dissemination of information; promotes international exchange in the field of marketing.

Finance Sector Union of Australia. 341 Queen St., Melbourne, VIC 3000, Australia. Fax: 61 39 1300366378 or 61 39 1300307943; Email: fsuinfo@fsunion.org.au • URL: http://www.fsunion.org.au • Employees of private and public sector financial services companies. Works to enhance members' welfare and conditions of employment. Conducts union organization training and insurance industry research.

French Society of Agricultural Economics. 19 Av. du Maine, F-75732 Paris, France. Phone: 33 1 45498840; Fax: 33 1 45498841; Email: sfer.asso@orange.fr • URL: http://www.sfer.asso.fr • Educators, social scientists, civil servants, and other interested persons. Promotes research and instruction in the economic, political, and social applications of agriculture and rural space. Acts as a forum for the exchange of ideas and information. Conducts colloquia.

Institute of Directors - Zimbabwe. 1 Grantchester Close, Northwood, Mt. Pleasant, Harare, Zimbabwe.

Phone: 263 4 301866 or 263 4 301136 • URL: http://www.iodzim.com • Individuals employed as directors either in a managerial or administrative capacity or as a non-executive director by corporations in Zimbabwe. Promotes the interests of domestic businesses; works to develop management techniques particularly suited to local needs. Facilitates communication among members. Conducts research and educational programs.

International Contact Center Benchmarking Consortium. The Benchmarking Network, 4606 FM 1960 W, Ste. 250, Houston, TX 77069-9949. Phone: (281)440-5044; Fax: (281)440-6677; Email: info@iccbc.org • URL: http://www.iccbc.org • Corporations that manage call centers. Promotes the use of benchmarking, wherein businesses compare their processes with those of their competitors, as a means of improving corporate efficiency and profitability. Facilitates exchange of information among members; conducts target operations, procurement, development, and maintenance studies; identifies model business practices.

Japan Association of Corporate Executives. 1-4-6, Marunouchi, Chiyoda-ku, Tokyo 100-0005, Japan. Phone: 81 3 32111271 or 81 3 32840220; Fax: 81 3 32132946 or 81 3 32123774; Email: kdcontact1207@doyukai.or.jp • URL: http://www.doyukai.or.jp • Businesspersons in Japan. Formulates social, economic, policy proposals through research and discussion among members.

Kenya Institute of Management. PO Box 43706, Nairobi, Kenya. Phone: 254 20 2445600 or 254 20 2445555; Email: kim@kim.ac.ke • URL: http://www.kim.ac.ke • Individuals and businesses in Kenya. Works to increase and disseminate information on the science of management; stimulates interest in effective management; formulates standards for professional conduct, experience, and training; encourages education in the principles and practices of management by establishing and promoting training courses, scholarships, and grants; conducts examinations and awards certificates and diplomas; provides facilities for research into management problems; organizes management seminars for professional training and small business creation.

The National Academies - National Research Council. 500 5th St. NW, Washington, DC 20001. Phone: (202)334-2000 • URL: http://www.nationalacademies.org/nrc/ • Scientists, engineers, and other professionals serving pro bono on approximately 900 study committees. Serves as an independent adviser to the federal government on scientific and technical questions of national importance; is jointly administered by the National Academy of Sciences, National Academy of Engineering, and Institute of Medicine. Carries out objectives through conferences, technical committees, surveys, collection and analysis of scientific and technical data, and administration of public and private funds for research projects and fellowships.

Netherlands Society for Industry and Trade. Jan Van Nassaustraat 75, NL-2596 BP The Hague, Netherlands. Phone: 31 70 3141940; Fax: 31 70 3247515; Email: info@de-maatschappij.nl • URL: http://www.de-maatschappij.nl • Association of businesses and industries in the Netherlands. Promotes trade and investment. Conducts research.

Processors' and Growers' Research Organisation. The Research Station, Great North Rd., Thornhaugh, Peterborough PE8 6HJ, United Kingdom. Phone: 44 1780 782585; Fax: 44 1780 783993; Email: info@pgro.org • URL: http://www.pgro.org • Farmers, food processors, merchant seedsmen, agro-chemical companies, higher education institutes and research stations. Provides research, evaluation and advice on the growing, harvesting and usage of different types of peas and beans. This includes the evaluation of new varieties, crop protection products and growing and harvesting techniques. Provides technical services including seed and soil testing and instrument calibration.

**Property Council of Australia.** 11 Barrack St., Level 1, Sydney, NSW 2000, Australia. Phone: 61 2 90331900; Fax: 61 2 90331967; Email: info@ propertyoz.com.au • URL: http://www.propertyoz. com.au • Institutional investors, pension funds, property trusts, financial organizations, private investors, and developers. Represents the interests of the property sector in Australia. Seeks to increase property into an internationally competitive asset class. Participates in lobbying and advocacy activities. Offers educational programs. Conducts research; compiles statistics.

**Society of Medical Banking Excellence.** The Medical Banking Project, 401 Pond View Ct., Franklin, TN 37064. Phone: (615)794-2009; Fax: (615)468-7606; Email: info@mbproject.org • Seeks to advance the creation of digital infrastructures to be used to test and implement EDI processing techniques and analytics in medical payment channels.

**World Association for Small and Medium Enterprises.** Plot No. 4, Institutional Area, Sector 16A, Noida 201301, Uttar Pradesh, India. Fax: 91 120 4216283; Email: bds@wasmeinfo.org • URL: http://www.wasmeinfo.org • Works to undertake research programmes and incisive studies on various issues of small businesses; arranges placement of counsellors, specialists and trainers to facilitate flow of knowledge and expertise in specific fields.

**World Confederation of Productivity Science.** c/o Linda Carbone, Executive Secretary, 500 Sherbrooke St. W, Ste. 900, Montreal, QC, Canada H3A 3C6. Email: secretariat@wcps.info • URL: http:// www.wcps.info • Fraternal association of manufacturing and commercial enterprises and employees, government agencies, professional institutions, and researchers. Goals are to promote productivity science, advance management techniques, and improve the quality of working life and environment.

# RESEARCH, BUSINESS

*See* BUSINESS RESEARCH

# RESEARCH, ECONOMIC

*See* ECONOMIC RESEARCH

# RESEARCH, INDUSTRIAL

*See* INDUSTRIAL RESEARCH

# RESEARCH, LIBRARY

*See* LIBRARY RESEARCH

# RESEARCH, MARKETING

*See* MARKET RESEARCH

# RESELLERS, COMPUTER

*See* COMPUTER RETAILING

# RESOURCES

*See* NATURAL RESOURCES

# RESTAURANTS, LUNCHROOMS, ETC.

*See also* CATERERS AND CATERING; DRIVE-IN AND CURB SERVICES; EMPLOYEE LUNCHROOMS AND CAFETERIAS; FOOD SERVICE INDUSTRY

## CD-ROM DATABASES

*OECD Statistical Compendium.* Organization for Economic Cooperation and Development. • Semiannual. $1,905.00 per year for 1 to 10 users. CD-ROM contains more than 730,000 monthly, quarterly, and annual time series for OECD countries, 1960 to date. Includes fully searchable data on agriculture, food, economic indicators, national accounts, employment, energy, finance, industry, technology, and foreign trade. Results can be displayed in various forms.

## DIRECTORIES

*Council on Hotel, Restaurant and Institutional Education--Member Directory and Resource Guide.* International Council on Hotel, Restaurant, and Institutional Education. • Biennial. Covers: Over 2,000 educational programs and institutions in the hotel, restaurant, and tourism industries. Entries include: Name, address, phone, fax.

*Directory of High Volume Independent Restaurants.* Chain Store Guide. • Annual. $1,375 Individuals online pro plus. Approximately 4,200 independently owned restaurants with annual sales of at least $1 million.

## FINANCIAL RATIOS

*Annual Statement Studies.* Risk Management Association. • Annual. Compiled from over 280,000 financial statements.

*Annual Statement Studies: Industry Default Probabilities and Cash Flow Measures.* Risk Management Association. • Annual. $405 Nonmembers. Serves as a companion volume to the original *Annual Statement Studies.* Gives probability of default estimates on a percentage scale for more than 450 industries. Includes changes in position year-by-year for eight financial statement line items and provides percentage measures of cash flow.

*Restaurant Industry Operations Report.* National Restaurant Association. • Annual. $100 Members. Presents operating results as amounts per restaurant seat and as ratios to total sales.

## HANDBOOKS AND MANUALS

*Pizzeria.* Entrepreneur Press. • Looseleaf. $59.50. A practical guide to starting a pizza shop. Covers profit potential, start-up costs, market size evaluation, owner's time required, site selection, lease negotiation, pricing, accounting, advertising, promotion, etc. (Start-Up Business Guide No. E1006.).

*Restaurant Start-Up.* Entrepreneur Press. • $19.95. Looseleaf. $59.50. A practical guide to starting a restaurant. Covers profit potential, start-up costs, market size evaluation, owner's time required, site selection, lease negotiation, pricing, accounting, advertising, promotion, etc. (Start-Up Business Guide No. E1279.).

*Sandwich Shop/Deli.* Entrepreneur Press. • Looseleaf. $59.50. A practical guide to starting a sandwich shop and delicatessen. Covers profit potential, start-up costs, market size evaluation, owner's time required, site selection, lease negotiation, pricing, accounting, advertising, promotion, etc. (Start-Up Business Guide No. E1156.).

## INTERNET DATABASES

*Advance Monthly Retail Trade Report.* U. S. Census Bureau. Phone: 800-541-8345 or (301)457-4100 or (301)763-2713; Fax: (301)457-1296 or (301)457-3842; Email: naics@census.gov • URL: http://www. census.gov/epcd/www/naicstab.htm • Web pages provide monthly sales figures for a wide range of retail businesses. Advance, preliminary, and final statistics are provided for the latest month available in each case, with a previous-year comparison. Updates are monthly.

*Business 2.0 Web Guide to the Best Business Links.* Business 2.0 Media Inc. Phone: (415)293-4800; Email: support@business2.com • URL: http://www. business2.com/webguide • Web site presents an extensive, searchable directory of links to "the best, most informative, and authoritative web pages." Twenty main categories cover business, finance, career, company information, people, and technology topics, with thousands of subtopics, all linking to Web sites recommended by experienced business researchers. Fees: Free.

*Fedstats.* Federal Interagency Council on Statistical Policy. Phone: (202)395-7254 • URL: http://www. fedstats.gov • Web site features an efficient search facility for full-text statistics produced by more than 100 federal agencies, including the Census Bureau, the Bureau of Economic Analysis, and the Bureau of Labor Statistics. Boolean searches can be made within one agency or for all agencies combined. Links are offered to international statistical bureaus, including the UN, IMF, OECD, UNESCO, Eurostat, and 20 individual countries. Fees: Free.

*FreeLunch.com.* Economy.com, Inc. Phone: (610)696-8700; Fax: (610)696-1678 • URL: http:// www.freelunch.com • Web site provides free access to more than 200 million economic and financial data series, covering industry, demographics, labor markets, prices, retail sales, government spending, trade, interest rates, housing starts, the stock market, etc. Data is available in either chart or table form. Searching is offered. Free, but registration required. Economy.com, Inc. also offers fee-based economic analysis at *The Dismal Scientist* site (www.dismal. com).

## PERIODICALS AND NEWSLETTERS

*Bottomline.* Hospitality Financial and Technology Professionals. • Bimonthly. Free to members, educational institutions and libraries; non-members, $50.00 per year. Contains articles on accounting, finance, information technology, and management for hotels, resorts, casinos, clubs, and other hospitality businesses.

*Chef.* Aktiebolaget Electrolux. • Monthly. $24.00 per year. Edited for executive chefs, food and beverage directors, caterers, banquet and club managers, and others responsible for food buying and food service. Special coverage of regional foods is provided.

*Cooking for Profit.* CP Publishing Inc. • Monthly. $25.00 per year. The challenge of operations management in the food service industry.

*The Cornell Hotel and Restaurant Administration Quarterly.* Cornell University School of Hotel Administration. Pine Forge Press. • Bimonthly. Individuals, $113.00 per year; institutions, $319.00 per year.

*Foodservice and Hospitality Magazine: Canada's Hospitality Business Magazine.* Kostuch Publications Ltd. • Monthly. $55 Canada. Magazine for restaurant and hotel operators.

*Foodservice Equipment and Supplies.* Reed Elsevier Group plc Reed Business Information. • $106.90 Individuals.

*Hospitality Technology: Guiding High-Growth Businesses to Best-Choice IT Solutions.* Edgell Communications Inc. • 10/year. Covers information technology, computer communications, and software for foodservice and lodging enterprises.

*Nation's Restaurant News: The Newspaper of the Food Service Industry.* Lebhar-Friedman Inc. • $49.95 Individuals All access. 50 times a year.

---

*Restaurant Hospitality.* Penton Media Inc. • Monthly.

*Restaurants and Institutions.* Reed Elsevier Group plc Reed Business Information. • Semimonthly. $149.00 per year. Features news, new products, recipes, menu concepts and merchandising ideas from the most successful foodservice operations around the U.S.

## STATISTICS SOURCES

*Annual Benchmark Report for Retail Trade and Food Services..A Detailed Summary of Retail Sales, Purchases, Accounts Receivable, Inventories, and Food Service Sales.* U. S. Government Printing Office. • Annual. $13.00. Issued by the U.S. Census Bureau. Provides detailed annual and monthly retail statistics for the most recent 10 years. Includes data for various kinds of retail outlets, including automobiles, furniture, appliances, building supplies, grocery stores, drug stores, gasoline stations, clothing, sporting goods, department stores, and restaurants.

*Standard & Poor's Industry Surveys.* Standard & Poor's Financial Services L.L.C. • Semiannual. $1,800.00. Two looseleaf volumes. Includes monthly *Supplements.* Provides detailed, individual surveys of 52 major industry groups. Each survey is revised on a semiannual basis. Also includes "Monthly Investment Review" (industry group investment analysis) and monthly "Trends & Projections" (economic analysis).

*Survey of Current Business.* U. S. Government Printing Office. • Published by Bureau of Economic Analysis, U. S. Department of Commerce. Presents a wide variety of business and economic data.

## TRADE/PROFESSIONAL ASSOCIATIONS

National Restaurant Association. 2055 L St. NW, Ste. 700, Washington, DC 20036. Phone: 800-424-5156 or (202)331-5900; Fax: (202)331-2429 • URL: http://www.restaurant.org • Represents restaurants, cafeterias, clubs, contract foodservice management, drive-ins, caterers, institutional food services and other members of the foodservice industry; also represents establishments belonging to non-affiliated state and local restaurant associations in governmental affairs. Supports foodservice education and research in several educational institutions. Is affiliated with the Educational Foundation of the National Restaurant Association to provide training and education for operators, food and equipment manufacturers, distributors and educators. Has 300,000 member locations.

Restaurant Facility Management Association. 5600 Tennyson Pkwy., Ste. 280, Plano, TX 75024. Phone: (972)805-0905; Fax: (972)805-0906; Email: tracy@rfmaonline.com • URL: http://www.rfmaonline.com • Aims to promote the advancement of the restaurant facility management profession. Maintains professional and ethical standards among members. Provides networking to share knowledge and exchange information.

# RESTRAINT OF TRADE

*See* ANTITRUST ACTIONS

# RESUMES

*See* JOB RESUMES

# RETAIL SELLING

*See* SALESMEN AND SALESMANSHIP

# RETAIL TRADE

*See also* CHAIN STORES; DEPARTMENT STORES; DISCOUNT HOUSES

## CD-ROM DATABASES

*OECD Statistical Compendium.* Organization for Economic Cooperation and Development. • Semiannual. $1,905.00 per year for 1 to 10 users. CD-ROM contains more than 730,000 monthly, quarterly, and annual time series for OECD countries, 1960 to date. Includes fully searchable data on agriculture, food, economic indicators, national accounts, employment, energy, finance, industry, technology, and foreign trade. Results can be displayed in various forms.

## DIRECTORIES

*American Big Businesses Directory.* InfoGroup Inc. • Annual. $295. Covers: 218,000 U.S. businesses with more than 100 employees, and 500,000 key executives and directors. CD-ROM version contains 160,000 top firms and 431,000 key executives. Entries include: Name, address, phone, names and titles of key personnel, number of employees, sales volume, Standard Industrial Classification (SIC) codes, subsidiaries and parent company names, stock exchanges on which traded.

*American Manufacturers Directory.* InfoGroup Inc. • Annual. $295. Covers: more than 150,000 manufacturing companies with 20 or more employees. CD-ROM version lists all 531,000 U.S. manufacturers, in all employee size ranges. Entries include: Company name, address, phone, contact name, Standard Industrial Classification (SIC) codes, number of employees, sales volume code, credit rating scores.

*Blinds-Venetian & Vertical- Retail Directory.* InfoGroup Inc. • Annual. Number of listings: 8,244. Entries include: Name, address, phone, size of advertisement, name of owner or manager, number of employees, year first in "Yellow Pages." Compiled from telephone company "Yellow Pages," nationwide.

*Cameras Directory--Retail Companies.* InfoGroup Inc. • Annual. Number of listings: 5,303. Entries include: Name, address, phone, size of advertisement, name of owner or manager, number of employees, year first in "Yellow Pages." Compiled from telephone company "Yellow Pages," nationwide.

*Denver Merchandise Mart Directory.* Denver Merchandise Mart. • Annual. Covers: About 4,000 manufacturers, importers, and wholesale distributors of men's, women's, and children's clothing, western apparel, shoes, gifts, gourmet items, bath accessories, jewelry, resort merchandise, and home furnishings who are represented in the Denver Merchandise Mart. Entries include: Firm name, mart address; alphabetical listings include phone.

*Electronic Equipment & Supplies--Retail Directory.* InfoGroup Inc. • Annual. Number of listings: 13,108. Entries include: Name, address, phone, size of advertisement, name of owner or manager, number of employees, year first in "Yellow Pages." Compiled from telephone company "Yellow Pages," nationwide.

*Health & Beauty Aids--Retail Directory.* InfoGroup Inc. • Annual. Number of listings: 18,716. Entries include: Name, address, phone, size of advertisement, name of owner or manager, number of employees, year first in "Yellow Pages." Compiled from telephone company "Yellow Pages," nationwide.

*Mass Merchandisers & Off-Price Apparel Buyers.* Communication Publications & Resources. • Annual. $329 Individuals directory price. Covers: 7,900 buyers and 3,400 companies in mass merchandise and off-price apparel industry. Entries include: Company name, address, phone, fax, e-mail, URL, names and titles of key personnel, geographical area served, branch office or subsidiary names and addresses, products and/or services provided, sales volume, parent company name.

*Retail Shops Directory.* InfoGroup Inc. • Annual. Number of listings: 7,325. Entries include: Name, address, phone, size of advertisement, name of owner or manager, number of employees, year first in "Yellow Pages." Compiled from telephone company "Yellow Pages," nationwide.

## E-BOOKS

*Encyclopedia of American Industries.* Cengage Learning Inc. • 2011. $807.00. 6th edition. Three volumes. Volume one is Manufacturing Industries and volume two is Service and Non-Manufacturing Industries. Provides the history, development, and recent status of approximately 1,000 industries. Includes statistical graphs, with industry and general indexes. Also available as eBook.

## FINANCIAL RATIOS

*Cost of Doing Business Survey.* National Sporting Goods Association. • Biennial. Includes income statements, balance sheets, sales per employee, sales per square foot, inventory turnover, etc.

## INTERNET DATABASES

*Advance Monthly Retail Trade Report.* U. S. Census Bureau. Phone: 800-541-8345 or (301)457-4100 or (301)763-2713; Fax: (301)457-1296 or (301)457-3842; Email: naics@census.gov • URL: http://www.census.gov/epcd/www/naicstab.htm • Web pages provide monthly sales figures for a wide range of retail businesses. Advance, preliminary, and final statistics are provided for the latest month available in each case, with a previous-year comparison. Updates are monthly.

*Bureau of Economic Analysis.* U. S. Department of Commerce, Bureau of Economic Analysis. Phone: (202)606-9900; Fax: (202)606-5310; Email: webmaster@bea.doc.gov • URL: http://www.bea.doc.gov • Web site includes "News Release Information" covering national, regional, and international economic estimates from the BEA. Highlights of releases appear online the same day, complete text and tables appear the next day. "Recent News Releases" section provides titles for past nine months, with links. "BEA Data and Methodology" includes "Frequently Requested NIPA Data" (national income and product accounts, such as gross domestic product and personal income). Other statistics are available. Fees: Free.

*Business 2.0 Web Guide to the Best Business Links.* Business 2.0 Media Inc. Phone: (415)293-4800; Email: support@business2.com • URL: http://www.business2.com/webguide • Web site presents an extensive, searchable directory of links to "the best, most informative, and authoritative web pages." Twenty main categories cover business, finance, career, company information, people, and technology topics, with thousands of subtopics, all linking to Web sites recommended by experienced business researchers. Fees: Free.

*Fedstats.* Federal Interagency Council on Statistical Policy. Phone: (202)395-7254 • URL: http://www.fedstats.gov • Web site features an efficient search facility for full-text statistics produced by more than 100 federal agencies, including the Census Bureau, the Bureau of Economic Analysis, and the Bureau of Labor Statistics. Boolean searches can be made within one agency or for all agencies combined. Links are offered to international statistical bureaus, including the UN, IMF, OECD, UNESCO, Eurostat, and 20 individual countries. Fees: Free.

*FreeLunch.com.* Economy.com, Inc. Phone: (610)696-8700; Fax: (610)696-1678 • URL: http://www.freelunch.com • Web site provides free access to more than 200 million economic and financial data series, covering industry, demographics, labor markets, prices, retail sales, government spending, trade, interest rates, housing starts, the stock market, etc. Data is available in either chart or table form. Searching is offered. Free, but registration required. Economy.com, Inc. also offers fee-based economic analysis at *The Dismal Scientist* site (www.dismal.com).

## ONLINE DATABASES

*American Business Directory.* InfoGroup Inc. • Provides brief online information on more than 10 million U. S. companies, including individual plants and branches. Entries typically include address, phone number, industry classification code, and contact name. Updating is quarterly. Inquire as to online cost and availability.

*Market Research Monitor.* Euromonitor International Inc. • Contains full-text reports online from *Market Research Europe, Market Research Great Britain, Market Research International, and Retail Monitor International.* Time period is 1995 to date, with monthly updates. Inquire as to online cost and availability.

## PERIODICALS AND NEWSLETTERS

*Catalogue & E-business.* Catalogue & e-business. • Monthly. £65 Individuals. Trade magazine covering catalog, mail order, and electronic commerce.

*Internet Retailer: E-Business Strategies.* Thomson Financial Inc. • 10 times a year. $98.00 per year. Trade journal on the selling of retail merchandise through the Internet. Provides information on pricing, payment systems, order management, fraud, digital imaging, advertising, Web trends, and other topics.

*NSGA Now Magazine.* National Sporting Goods Association. • Bimonthly. $50 for nonmembers. Bimonthy. Membership. Covers news and marketing trends for sporting goods retailers. Formerly *NSGA Sports Retailer.*

*Retailing Today.* Robert Kahn and Associates. • Description: Focuses on general merchandise, apparel, furniture, hardware, automotive, and food retailing. Offers "original research, comments on current trends and conditions, recommendations for company policy, and emphasis on ethical conduct in business.".

*Retailing Today: The Newspaper of Discount Retailing; The News Source for Power Retailing.* Lebhar-Friedman Inc. • Semimonthly. $119 Individuals. Retailing business industry news and information.

*Stores.* National Retail Federation. NRF Enterprises Inc. • Monthly. Offers an insider's view of the entire retail industry by featuring the latest trends, hottest ideas, current technologies and consumer attitudes.

*Value Retail News: The Journal of Outlet and Off-Price Retail and Development.* Off-Price Specialists, Inc. Value Retail News. • Monthly. $99 Members. Provides news of the off-price and outlet store industry. Emphasis is on real estate for outlet store centers.

## PRICE SOURCES

*CPI Detailed Report: Consumer Price Index.* U. S. Government Printing Office. • Monthly. $45 Individuals. Cost of living data.

## RESEARCH CENTERS AND INSTITUTES

Northwestern University - Center for Retail Management. Kellogg School of Management, 2001 Sheridan Rd., Evanston, IL 60208. Phone: (847)467-3600; Fax: (847)467-3620; Email: r-blattberg@kellogg.northwestern.edu • URL: http://www.kellogg.northwestern.edu/research/retail/ • Conducts research related to retail marketing and management.

Texas A&M University - Center for Retailing Studies. Wehner Bldg., Ste. 201, Mays Business School, 4112 TAMU, College Station, TX 77843-4112. Phone: (979)845-0325; Fax: (979)845-5117 or (979)845-5230; Email: c-bridges@mays.tamu.edu • URL: http://www.crstamu.org • Research areas include retailing issues and consumer economics.

## STATISTICS SOURCES

*Annual Benchmark Report for Retail Trade and Food Services..A Detailed Summary of Retail Sales, Purchases, Accounts Receivable, Inventories, and Food Service Sales.* U. S. Government Printing Office. • Annual. $13.00. Issued by the U.S. Census Bureau. Provides detailed annual and monthly retail statistics for the most recent 10 years. Includes data for various kinds of retail outlets, including automobiles, furniture, appliances, building supplies, grocery stores, drug stores, gasoline stations, clothing, sporting goods, department stores, and restaurants.

*Manufacturing & Distribution USA.* Cengage Learning Inc. • Biennial. $631 Individuals three-volume set. 2012. 7th edition. eBook. Three volumes. Presents statistics and projections relating to economic activity in more than 600 business classifications.

*Standard & Poor's Industry Surveys.* Standard & Poor's Financial Services L.L.C. • Semiannual. $1,800.00. Two looseleaf volumes. Includes monthly *Supplements.* Provides detailed, individual surveys of 52 major industry groups. Each survey is revised on a semiannual basis. Also includes "Monthly Investment Review" (industry group investment analysis) and monthly "Trends & Projections" (economic analysis).

*Survey of Current Business.* U. S. Government Printing Office. • Published by Bureau of Economic Analysis, U. S. Department of Commerce. Presents a wide variety of business and economic data.

*ULI Market Profiles: North America.* Urban Land Institute. • Annual. Members, $249.95; nonmembers, $299.95. Provides real estate marketing data for residential, retail, office, and industrial sectors. Covers 76 U. S. metropolitan areas and 13 major foreign metropolitan areas.

*United States Census of Retail Trade.* U.S. Department of Commerce U.S. Census Bureau. • Quinquennial.

## TRADE/PROFESSIONAL ASSOCIATIONS

Dublin City Business Association. 21 Dawson St., Dublin 2, Dublin, Ireland. Phone: 353 1 6622995; Email: info@dcba.ie • URL: http://www.dcba.ie • Retail Federation in the city of Dublin. Promotes a sustainable city centre that is attractive to live, work, visit, and shop in.

Italian Confederation of Retailers, Commerce, Tourism and Service. Via Nazionale, 60, I-00184 Rome, Italy. Phone: 39 6 47251; Fax: 39 6 4746886; Email: confes@confesercenti.it • URL: http://www.confesercenti.it • Small and mid-sized enterprises in the commercial, tourist, and service sectors in Italy. Represents and promotes the retailing, tourism, service and other commercial industries.

National Retail Federation. 325 7th St. NW, Ste. 1100, Washington, DC 20004. Phone: 800-673-4692 or (202)783-7971 or (202)347-1932; Fax: (202)737-2849; Email: bookinquiries@nrf.com • URL: http://www.nrf.com • Represents state retail associations, several dozen national retail associations, as well as large and small corporate members representing the breadth and diversity of the retail industry's establishment and employees. Conducts informational and educational conferences related to all phases of retailing including financial planning and cash management, taxation, economic forecasting, expense planning, shortage control, credit, electronic data processing, telecommunications, merchandise management, buying, traffic, security, supply, materials handling, store planning and construction, personnel administration, recruitment and training, and advertising and display.

# RETAILERS, COMPUTER

*See* COMPUTER RETAILING

# RETAILERS, OFF-PRICE

*See* DISCOUNT HOUSES

# RETIREE MARKET

*See* MATURE CONSUMER MARKET

# RETIREMENT

*See also* EMPLOYMENT OF OLDER WORKERS; MATURE CONSUMER MARKET; PENSIONS; RETIREMENT COMMUNITIES; SOCIAL SECURITY

## CD-ROM DATABASES

*Authority Tax and Estate Planning Library.* Matthew Bender and Company Inc. • Periodic revisions. Price on request. CD contains updated full text of *Bender's Payroll Tax Guide, Depreciation Handbook, Federal Income Taxation of Corporations, Tax Planning for Corporations, Modern Estate Planning, Planning for Large Estates, Murphy's Will Clauses, Tax & Estate Planning for the Elderly,* and 12 other Matthew Bender publications. The Internal Revenue Code is also included.

## ENCYCLOPEDIAS AND DICTIONARIES

*Encyclopedia of Aging.* David J. Ekerdt, editor. Cengage Learning Inc. • $770. Includes articles relating to the financial aspects of aging, such as housing, long-term care insurance, pensions, social security, individual retirement accounts, savings, and retirement planning. eBook also available. Inquire for pricing.

## HANDBOOKS AND MANUALS

*Planning for Your Retirement: IRA and Keogh Plans.* Wolters Kluwer Law & Business CCH. • Annual.

*Retirement Benefits Tax Guide.* Wolters Kluwer Law & Business CCH. • $199.00. Looseleaf service.

## INTERNET DATABASES

*Free Insurance Advice.* InsWeb, Inc. 2868 Prospect Park Dr., Ste. 650, Rancho Cordova, CA 95670. Phone: (916)853-3300; Fax: (916)853-3300; Email: customercare@insweb.com • URL: http://www.insweb.com • Web site offers a wide variety of advice and information on automobile, life, health, and "other" insurance. Includes glossaries of insurance terms, Standard & Poor's ratings of individual insurance companies, and "Financial Needs Estimators." Searching is available. Fees: Free.

*Small Business Retirement Savings Advisor.* U. S. Department of Labor. Phone: (202)219-8921 • URL: http://www.dol.gov/elaws/pwbaplan.htm • Web site provides "answers to a variety of commonly asked questions about retirement saving options for small business employers." Includes a comparison chart and detailed descriptions of various plans: 401(k), SEP-IRA, SIMPLE-IRA, Payroll Deduction IRA, Keogh Profit-Sharing, Keogh Money Purchase, and Defined Benefit. Searching is offered. Fees: Free.

## ONLINE DATABASES

*Ageline.* AARP. • Provides indexing and abstracting of the literature of social gerontology, including consumer aspects, financial planning, employment, housing, health care services, mental health, social security, and retirement. Time period is 1978 to date. Inquire as to online cost and availability.

## OTHER SOURCES

*Individual Retirement Plans Guide.* Wolters Kluwer Law & Business CCH. • $540.00 per year. Looseleaf service. Monthly updates. Covers IRA plans (Individual Retirement Accounts), SEP plans (Simplified Employee Pensions), and Keogh plans (self-employed retirement accounts).

## PERIODICALS AND NEWSLETTERS

*AARP Bulletin.* AARP. • Monthly. Description: Monitors issues and events affecting Americans aged 50 and over. Covers medical benefits and other services of interest. Recurring features include Association news, editorials, and columns titled As We See It, Bulletin Board, Washingtonwatch, Stateswatch, and Reader Forum.

*Estate Planner's Alert.* Thomson RIA. • Monthly. $290 Individuals Print. Covers the tax aspects of personal finance, including home ownership, investments, insurance, retirement planning, and charitable giving. Formerly *Estate and Financial Planners Alert.*

*Financial Planning: The Magazine for Financial Service Professionals.* SourceMedia Inc. • Monthly. $79.00 per year. Edited for independent financial planners and insurance agents. Covers retirement planning, estate planning, tax planning, and insurance, including long-term healthcare considerations. Special features include a Retirement Planning Issue, Mutual Fund Performance Survey, and Variable Life and Annuity Survey.

*Journal of Aging and Social Policy: A Journal Devoted to Aging and Social Policy.* The Haworth Press Inc. • Quarterly. $415.00 per year.

*Kiplinger's Retirement Report.* Kiplinger Washington Editors Inc. • $39.95 /year. Description: Offers information for the retired and soon-to-be-retired. Discusses such topics as money management, estate planning, health, travel and what's going on in Washington DC.

*Older Americans Report.* Business Publishers Inc. • Bimonthly. $449 Individuals. Description: Features brief articles on legislative, judicial, and federal agency activities concerning older Americans. Covers news of developments in such areas as Social Security, social services, Medicare, programs for retirement and pension funds, research projects, and the Older Americans Act. Recurring features include book reviews and a calendar of events.

*ReCareering Newsletter: An Idea and Resource Guide to Second Career and Relocation Planning.* Publications Plus, Inc. • Monthly. $59.00 per year. Edited for "downsized managers, early retirees, and others in career transition after leaving traditional employment." Offers advice on second careers, franchises, starting a business, finances, education, training, skills assessment, and other matters of interest to the newly unemployed.

*Retirement Letter: The Money Newsletter for Mature People.* Peter A. Dickinson, editor. Access Intelligence L.L.C. • Monthly. $49.00 per year.

*Retirement Life.* Manpower Education Institute. • Quarterly. Information for retirees.

*Retirement Plans Bulletin: Practical Explanations for the IRA and Retirement Plan Professional.* Universal Pensions Inc. • Monthly. $99.00 per year. Newsletter. Provides information on the rules and regulations governing qualified (tax-deferred) retirement plans.

## RESEARCH CENTERS AND INSTITUTES

Case Western Reserve University - Elderly Care Research Center. Mather Memorial Bldg., Rm. 231B, 10900 Euclid Ave., Cleveland, OH 44106-1712. Phone: (216)368-2704; Fax: (216)368-1078; Email: exk@case.edu • URL: http://www.case.edu/artsci/soci/ecrc • Aging, health, and mental health, including public policy issues, predictors of wellness and vulnerability, environmental and social influences on well-being of the elderly, cross-national and cross-cultural comparisons, and health and mental health outcomes of stress, coping, and adaptation.

Center for Financial Responsibility. Texas Tech University, Lubbock, TX 79409-11210. Phone: (806)742-5050; Fax: (806)742-5033 • URL: http://

www.depts.ttu.edu/cfr • Research areas include financial preparation for retirement, financial education, determinants of financial satisfaction, risk tolerance, and the career preparation of retirement industry professionals.

Center for Pension and Retirement Research. Miami University, Department of Economics, 109E Laws Hall, Oxford, OH 45056. Phone: (513)529-2850; Fax: (513)529-3308; Email: swilliamson@eh.net • Research areas include pension economics, pension plans, and retirement decisions.

Retirement Research Foundation. 8765 W Higgins Rd., Ste. 430, Chicago, IL 60631-4172. Phone: (773)714-8080; Fax: (773)714-8089; Email: info@rrf.org • URL: http://www.rrf.org • Works to promote aging and retirement issues. Supports efforts that improve care for the aging, and enable older adults to live at home or in residential settings that facilitate independent living.

## STATISTICS SOURCES

*Social Security Bulletin.* Social Security Administration. U. S. Government Printing Office. • Quarterly. $27.00 per year. Annual statistical supplement.

## TRADE/PROFESSIONAL ASSOCIATIONS

National Active and Retired Federal Employees Association. 606 N Washington St., Alexandria, VA 22314. Phone: 800-627-3394 or (703)838-7760; Fax: (703)838-7785 • URL: http://www.narfe.org/departments/home/index.cfm • Formerly National Association of Retired Civil Employees.

# RETIREMENT AGE

*See* EMPLOYMENT OF OLDER WORKERS

# RETIREMENT COMMUNITIES

*See also* NURSING HOMES

## ABSTRACTS AND INDEXES

*PAIS International.* ProQuest L.L.C. • Monthly. $850.00 per year; cumulations three times a year. Provides topical citations to the worldwide literature of public affairs, economics, demographics, sociology, and trade. Text in English; indexed materials in English, French, German, Italian, Portuguese and Spanish.

*Readers' Guide to Periodical Literature.* EBSCO Publishing Inc. • Provides indexing for over 400 periodicals dating back to 1983.

## CD-ROM DATABASES

*PAIS International.* ProQuest L.L.C. • Monthly. $1,995.00 per year. Contains over 650,000 citations to the literature of contemporary social, political, and economic issues.

*Readers' Guide to Periodical Literature.* EBSCO Publishing Inc. • Provides indexing for over 400 periodicals dating back to 1983.

## DIRECTORIES

*National Directory of Adult Day Care Centers.* Health Resources Publishing. • Irregular. $145 Individuals. Covers: Over 3,200 centers and programs providing adult day care; 1,100 are described in detail. Database includes: Bibliography of resources; aging services suppliers' guide. Entries include: Center or program name, address, phone, director or coordinator name; detailed listings include programs, providing sponsor information, geographic area served, fees, number of clients and staff, hours and days of operation, client eligibility criteria, services and activities offered.

## PERIODICALS AND NEWSLETTERS

*American Health Care Association: Provider.* American Health Care Association. • Monthly.

$48.00 per year. Formerly *American Health Care Association Journal.*

*Contemporary Longterm Care.* Leisure Publications Inc. • Monthly. Free to qualified personnel. Edited for the long term health care industry, including retirement centers with life care, continuing care communities, and nursing homes.

*Housing the Elderly Report.* Community Development Services, Inc. CD Publications. • Monthly. $249.00 per year. Newsletter. Edited for retirement communities, apartment projects, and nursing homes. Covers news relative to business and property management issues.

*McKnight's Long Term Care News.* Thomson Medical Economics. • Monthly. Edited for retirement housing directors and nursing home administrators.

*Retirement Community Business.* Great River Publishing, Inc. • Quarterly. $15.00 per year. Contains articles on management, marketing, legal concerns, development, construction, and other business-related topics.

## TRADE/PROFESSIONAL ASSOCIATIONS

American College of Health Care Administrators. 1321 Duke St., Ste. 400, Alexandria, VA 22314. Phone: (202)536-5120; Fax: (866)874-1585; Email: mgrachek@achca.org • URL: http://www.achca.org • Formerly American College of Nursing Home Administrators.

Community Associations Institute. 6402 Arlington Blvd., Ste. 500, Falls Church, VA 22042. Phone: 888-224-4321 or (703)970-9220; Fax: (703)970-9558; Email: cai-info@caionline.org • URL: http://www.caionline.org • Condominium and homeowner associations, cooperatives, and association-governed planned communities of all sizes and architectural types; community or property managers and management firms; individual homeowners; community association managers and management firms; public officials; and lawyers, accountants, engineers, reserve specialists, builder/developers and other providers of professional services and products for CAs. Seeks to educate and represent America's 250,000 residential condominium, cooperative and homeowner associations and related professionals and service providers. Aims to foster vibrant, responsive, competent community associations that promote harmony, community and responsible leadership.

National Institute of Senior Housing. National Council on Aging, 1901 L St. NW, 4th Fl., Washington, DC 20036. Phone: (202)479-1200; Fax: (202)479-0735 • URL: http://www.ncoa.org • Members are organizations and individuals concerned with the housing needs of older persons. Provides information on the development and management of housing suitable for the elderly. Affiliated with National Council on Aging.

# REVENUE SHARING

*See* FEDERAL AID

# REVIEWS

*See* BOOK REVIEWS

# RICE INDUSTRY

## ABSTRACTS AND INDEXES

*Biological and Agricultural Index.* H.W. Wilson Co. • 11 times a year. Annual and quarterly cumulations. Price varies.

*Rice Abstracts.* CABI Publishing North America. • Quarterly. Published in England by CABI Publishing. Provides worldwide coverage of the literature.

## CD-ROM DATABASES

*OECD Statistical Compendium.* Organization for Economic Cooperation and Development. • Semiannual. $1,905.00 per year for 1 to 10 users. CD-ROM contains more than 730,000 monthly, quarterly, and annual time series for OECD countries, 1960 to date. Includes fully searchable data on agriculture, food, economic indicators, national accounts, employment, energy, finance, industry, technology, and foreign trade. Results can be displayed in various forms.

## DIRECTORIES

*Major Food and Drink Companies of the World.* Cengage Learning Inc. • 12th edition. eBook. Published by Graham & Whiteside. Contains profiles and trade names for more than 9,200 important food and beverage companies in various countries. In addition to foods, includes both alcoholic and nonalcoholic drink products.

## INTERNET DATABASES

*Business 2.0 Web Guide to the Best Business Links.* Business 2.0 Media Inc. Phone: (415)293-4800; Email: support@business2.com • URL: http://www. business2.com/webguide • Web site presents an extensive, searchable directory of links to "the best, most informative, and authoritative web pages." Twenty main categories cover business, finance, career, company information, people, and technology topics, with thousands of subtopics, all linking to Web sites recommended by experienced business researchers. Fees: Free.

*Fedstats.* Federal Interagency Council on Statistical Policy. Phone: (202)395-7254 • URL: http://www. fedstats.gov • Web site features an efficient search facility for full-text statistics produced by more than 100 federal agencies, including the Census Bureau, the Bureau of Economic Analysis, and the Bureau of Labor Statistics. Boolean searches can be made within one agency or for all agencies combined. Links are offered to international statistical bureaus, including the UN, IMF, OECD, UNESCO, Eurostat, and 20 individual countries. Fees: Free.

*FreeLunch.com.* Economy.com, Inc. Phone: (610)696-8700; Fax: (610)696-1678 • URL: http:// www.freelunch.com • Web site provides free access to more than 200 million economic and financial data series, covering industry, demographics, labor markets, prices, retail sales, government spending, trade, interest rates, housing starts, the stock market, etc. Data is available in either chart or table form. Searching is offered. Free, but registration required. Economy.com, Inc. also offers fee-based economic analysis at *The Dismal Scientist* site (www.dismal. com).

*USDA.* U.S. National Institute of Standards and Technology. 100 Bureau Dr., Gaithersburg, MD 20899-1070. Phone: 800-877-8339 or (301)975-6478 or (202)720-2791; Fax: (301)975-8295; Email: inquiries@nist.gov • URL: http://www.nist.gov • The USDA home page has six sections: News and Information; What's New; About USDA; Agencies; Opportunities; Search and Help. Keyword searching is offered from the USDA home page and from various individual agency home pages. Agencies are the Economic Research Service, Agricultural Marketing Service, National Agricultural Statistics Service, National Agricultural Library, and about 12 others. Updating varies. Fees: Free.

## ONLINE DATABASES

*CAB Abstracts.* CABI. • Contains 46 specialized abstract collections covering over 10,000 journals and monographs in the areas of agriculture, horticulture, forest products, farm products, nutrition, dairy science, poultry, grains, animal health, entomology, etc. Time period is 1972 to date, with monthly updates. Inquire as to online cost and availability. *CAB Abstracts on CD-ROM* also available, with annual updating.

*Food Science and Technology Abstracts (online).* IFIS North American Desk. • Produced by International Food Information Service. Provides about 500,000 online citations, with abstracts, to the international literature of food science, technology, commodities, engineering, and processing. Approximately 2,000 periodicals are covered. Time period is 1969 to date, with monthly updates. Inquire as to online cost and availability.

## PERIODICALS AND NEWSLETTERS

*Rice Farming.* Vance Publishing Corp. • Six times a year. $30.00 per year.

*Rice Journal: For Commerical Growers of Rice and Related Agribusiness.* SpecComm International Inc. • Seven times a year. $15.00 per year.

## STATISTICS SOURCES

*Agricultural Statistics.* U.S. Department of Agriculture National Agricultural Statistics Service. • Annual. $46 Individuals. Provides a wide variety of statistical data relating to agricultural production, supplies, consumption, prices/price-supports, foreign trade, costs, and returns, as well as farm labor, loans, income, and population. In many cases, historical data is shown annually for 10 years. In addition to farm data, includes detailed fishery statistics.

*Survey of Current Business.* U. S. Government Printing Office. • Published by Bureau of Economic Analysis, U. S. Department of Commerce. Presents a wide variety of business and economic data.

## TRADE/PROFESSIONAL ASSOCIATIONS

Rice Millers' Association. USA Rice Federation, 2101 Wilson Blvd., Ste. 610, Arlington, VA 22201. Phone: (703)236-2300; Fax: (703)236-2301; Email: riceinfo@usarice.com • URL: http://www.usarice. com/index.php?option=com_ content&view=article&id=139&Itemid=441 • Represents independent and farmer-cooperative rice milling operators. Provides economic and statistical information on production, milling, and distribution of rice. Promotes research aimed at new uses for rice products and improvements in processing, packaging, storing, and distributing rice. Maintains liaison with U.S. and foreign government agencies, congress, and foreign buyers of U.S. rice.

# RIFLES

*See* FIREARMS INDUSTRY

# RISK MANAGEMENT

*See also* INSURANCE

## ABSTRACTS AND INDEXES

*Insurance Periodicals Index.* Specials Libraries Association, Insurance and Employees Benefits Div. NILS Publishing Co. • Annual. $250.00. Compiled by the Insurance and Employee Benefits Div., Special Libraries Association. A yearly index of over 15,000 articles from about 35 insurance periodicals. Arrangement is by subject, with an index to authors.

## BIBLIOGRAPHIES

*Insurance and Employee Benefits Literature.* Special Libraries Association. • Bimonthly. $15.00 per year. Lists a wide variety of literature in all branches of the insurance industry. Includes annotations.

## CD-ROM DATABASES

*OECD Statistical Compendium.* Organization for Economic Cooperation and Development. • Semiannual. $1,905.00 per year for 1 to 10 users. CD-ROM contains more than 730,000 monthly, quarterly, and annual time series for OECD countries, 1960 to date. Includes fully searchable data on agriculture, food, economic indicators,

national accounts, employment, energy, finance, industry, technology, and foreign trade. Results can be displayed in various forms.

## E-BOOKS

*Managing Business Risk.* Cengage Learning Inc. • 2009. eBook. Published by Kogan Page. A guide that can help in identifying potential areas of risk within a business. Examines the five key areas of risk you need to consider in today's complex and competitive business market. Drawing on expert advice from leading risk consultants, lawyers and regulatory authorities, it shows you how to protect your business against a rising tide of business risks.

## GENERAL WORKS

*International Journal of Business Continuity and Risk Management (IJBCRM).* Inderscience Enterprises Limited. • Quarterly. €520 Individuals print. Peer-reviewed journal covering risk management and business continuity.

## INTERNET DATABASES

*Business 2.0 Web Guide to the Best Business Links.* Business 2.0 Media Inc. Phone: (415)293-4800; Email: support@business2.com • URL: http://www. business2.com/webguide • Web site presents an extensive, searchable directory of links to "the best, most informative, and authoritative web pages." Twenty main categories cover business, finance, career, company information, people, and technology topics, with thousands of subtopics, all linking to Web sites recommended by experienced business researchers. Fees: Free.

*Derivatives.* Imagine Software Inc. 233 Broadway, 17th Fl., New York, NY 10279. Phone: (212)317-7600; Fax: (212)317-7601 • URL: http://www. derivatives.com • Web site mainly promotes proprietary software for the use of derivatives in risk management, but also provides free access to articles on a variety of derivatives-related topics.

## ONLINE DATABASES

*I.I.I. Data Base Search.* Insurance Information Institute. • Provides online citations and abstracts of insurance-related literature in magazines, newspapers, trade journals, and books. Emphasis is on property and casualty insurance issues, including highway safety, product safety, and environmental liability. Inquire as to online cost and availability.

## OTHER SOURCES

*Managing Financial Risk with Forwards, Futures, Options, and Swaps.* American Management Association Extension Institute. • Looseleaf. $159.00. Self-study course. Emphasis is on practical explanations, examples, and problem solving. Quizzes and a case study are included.

## PERIODICALS AND NEWSLETTERS

*Business Insurance: News Magazine for Corporate Risk, Employee Benefit and Financial Executives.* Crain Communications Inc. • Weekly. $95.00 per year. Covers a wide variety of business insurance topics, including risk management, employee benefits, workers compensation, marine insurance, and casualty insurance.

*Claims.* • Monthly. $46.00 per year. Edited for insurance adjusters, risk managers, and claims professionals. Covers investigation, fraud, insurance law, and other claims-related topics.

*Collections and Credit Risk: The Authority for Commercial and Consumer Credit Professionals.* SourceMedia Inc. • Monthly. $95.00 per year. Contains articles on the technology and business management of credit and collection functions. Includes coverage of bad debts, bankruptcy, and credit risk management.

*CSO: The Resource for Security Executives.* CXO Media Inc. • 10/year. $70 U.S. and Canada. Edited for corporate chief security officers (CSOs). Covers a wide variety of business security issues, including computer security, identity theft, spam, physical security, loss prevention, risk management, privacy, and investigations.

*D & O Advisor: Risk Management for Directors and Officers.* ALM Media Properties LLC. • Quarterly. $125.00 per year. Covers a wide range of legal topics of concern to corporate boards and key executives.

*Healthcare Risk Management.* AHC Media. • Description: Analyzes specific legal cases and trends relevant to healthcare liability. Discusses malpractice, liability for patients, staff and visitor injury, injury prevention, biomedical engineering, and medical staff credentials. Also covers high-risk areas of hospitals, hospital-owned home health and physician practices, accreditation, Medicare reimbursement, physician liability, medical records, and claims management. Recurring features include interviews, statistics, news of research, guest columns, legal briefs, and commentaries.

*Public Risk.* Public Risk Management Association. • Monthly. $130 Individuals. Covers risk management for state and local governments, including various kinds of liabilities.

*Risk and Insurance.* LRP Publications Library. • Monthly. Price on application. Topics include risk management, workers' compensation, reinsurance, employee benefits, and managed care.

*Risk Management.* Risk and Insurance Management Society. Risk and Insurance Management Society. • 10/year. $115 Individuals. Magazine featuring analysis, insight, and news for corporate risk managers.

*Treasury and Risk Management.* Wicks Business Information. • 10 times a year. $64.00 per year. Covers risk management tools and techniques. Incorporates *Treasury.*

### RESEARCH CENTERS AND INSTITUTES

Georgia State University - Center for Risk Management and Insurance Research. PO Box 4036, Atlanta, GA 30302-4036. Phone: (404)413-7515 or (404)413-7500; Fax: (404)413-7516 or (404)413-7499; Email: rwklein@gsu.edu • URL: http://rmictr.gsu.edu • Insurance, finance, and economics. Provides technical materials and policy research in the areas of health care financing, international issues, law and regulation, corporate finance, retirement financing, risk, risk management, insurance, finance, economics. Research focuses on risk management and insurance including insurance markets, catastrophe risk, financial instruments, social insurance, health care financing, retirement, law, public policy, and regulation.

RAND - Center for Terrorism Risk Management Policy. 1200 S Hayes St., Arlington, VA 22202-5050. Phone: (703)413-1100; Email: ctrmp@rand.org • URL: http://www.rand.org/multi/ctrmp.html • Terrorist threats and their affect on economic security. Research focuses on terrorism risk insurance, terrorism liability, compensation, security, and terrorism risk management.

### TRADE/PROFESSIONAL ASSOCIATIONS

American Risk and Insurance Association. 716 Providence Rd., Malvern, PA 19355-3402. Phone: (610)640-1997; Fax: (610)725-1007; Email: aria@theinstitutes.org • URL: http://www.aria.org • Promotes education and research in the science of risk and insurance.

American Society of Pension Professionals and Actuaries. 4245 N Fairfax Dr., Ste. 750, Arlington, VA 22203. Phone: (703)516-9300; Fax: (703)516-9308; Email: customercare@asppa.org • URL: http://www.asppa.org • Members are involved in the pension and insurance aspects of employee benefits. Includes an Insurance and Risk Management Committee, and sponsors an annual 401(k) Workshop.

Association of Certified Treasury Managers. 52, Na-

garjuna Hills, Hyderabad 500 082, Telangana, India. Phone: 91 40 23435368 or 91 40 23435374; Fax: 91 40 23352521; Email: info@actmindia.org • URL: http://www.qfinance.com/information-sources/association-of-certified-treasury-managers-india • Develops and regulates the growth of the treasury management profession. Organizes seminars, workshops, and training programs in treasury management, foreign exchange management, risk management, and allied areas. Provides placement assistance to members and students.

Association of Governmental Risk Pools. 9 Cornell Rd., Latham, NY 12110. Phone: (518)389-2782; Email: info@agrip.org • URL: http://www.agrip.org • Works to promote risk pooling as a practical extension of a public entity's obligation to be a good steward of public funds. Aims to act as an advocate for the advancement of intergovernmental pooling as the most appropriate risk financing mechanism for most public entities. Seeks to provide meaningful and significant educational and professional support for the governing bodies and employees of intergovernmental risk pools.

Federation of European Risk Management Associations. Ave. de Tervuren, 237 B-12, B-1150 Brussels, Belgium. Phone: 32 2 7619432; Fax: 32 2 7718720; Email: info@ferma.eu • URL: http://www.ferma.eu • Exists to widen and raise the culture of Risk Management throughout Europe to its members and to the risk management and insurance community.

North American Security Products Organization. 204 E St. NE, Washington, DC 20002. Phone: (202)608-1322; Fax: (202)547-6348; Email: smc@naspo.info • URL: http://www.naspo.info • Aims to combat fraud within the areas of brand protection, finance and identity. Fosters the development of security risk management standards to reduce financial fraud, identify document fraud and dilution of brand integrity. Enables security product firms to classify and validate their ability to deliver high, medium or basic levels of security assurance throughout their operations.

Public Risk Management Association. 700 S Washington St., Ste. 218, Alexandria, VA 22314. Phone: (703)528-7701; Fax: (703)739-0200; Email: info@primacentral.org • URL: http://www.primacentral.org • Public agency risk, insurance, human resources, attorneys, and/or safety managers from cities, counties, villages, towns, school boards, and other related areas. Provides an information clearinghouse and communications network for public risk managers to share resources, ideas, and experiences. Offers information on risk, insurance, and safety management. Monitors state and federal legislative actions and court decisions that deal with immunity, tort liability, and intergovernmental risk pools. Maintains library containing current reports from governmental units on their insurance procedures, self-insurance plans, and loss control and safety programs; and copies of policy statements, job descriptions, contractual arrangements, and indemnification clauses.

Risk and Insurance Management Society. 1065 Ave. of the Americas, 13th Fl., New York, NY 10018. Phone: 800-713-7467 or (212)286-9292; Fax: (212)986-9716; Email: lists@rims.org • URL: http://www.rims.org • Formerly American Society of Insurance Management.

Security Analysis and Risk Management Association. PO Box 100284, Arlington, VA 22210. Phone: (703)635-7906; Fax: (703)635-7935; Email: info@sarma.org • URL: http://sarma.org • Aims to further the development, standardization and professionalization of the security analysis and risk management discipline. Provides leadership, education and certification for security analysis and risk management professionals. Serves as a forum to share information, ideas and methodologies to

improve the development and application of the security analysis and risk management profession. TechAssure Association. 1550 17th St., Ste. 600, Denver, CO 80202. Phone: (888)208-8670 • Provides training and education services for risk management professionals that specialize in technology, life sciences and digital media industries. Works with insurance companies to customize policy forms and to improve the underwriting process. Encourages members to share best practices and to discuss ideas and experiences.

# ROAD MAPS

*See* MAPS

# ROAD SIGNS

*See* SIGNS AND SIGN BOARDS

# ROADS AND HIGHWAYS

*See also* TOLL ROADS

### ABSTRACTS AND INDEXES

*NTIS Alerts: Transportation.* U.S. Department of Commerce National Technical Information Service. • Biweekly. $130 per year. Covers air, marine, highway, inland waterway, pipeline, and railroad transportation.

### BIBLIOGRAPHIES

*Road Construction and Safety.* U. S. Government Printing Office. • Annual. Free. Issued by the Superintendent of Documents. A list of government publications on highway construction and traffic safety. Formerly *Highway Construction, Safety and Traffic.* (Subject Bibliography No. 3.).

### CD-ROM DATABASES

*OECD Statistical Compendium.* Organization for Economic Cooperation and Development. • Semiannual. $1,905.00 per year for 1 to 10 users. CD-ROM contains more than 730,000 monthly, quarterly, and annual time series for OECD countries, 1960 to date. Includes fully searchable data on agriculture, food, economic indicators, national accounts, employment, energy, finance, industry, technology, and foreign trade. Results can be displayed in various forms.

### DIRECTORIES

*Better Roads--Annual Winter Maintenance Equipment & Materials Issue: Federal State County Township Road & Municipalities.* James Informational Media Inc. • Annual. $95 Individuals per year prepaid. Publication includes: List of manufacturers of equipment and suppliers of materials and services for winter roads maintenance. Also features information on road agencies, construction/maintenance, and safety. Entries include: Company name, address.

*Public Works Manual.* Public Works Journal Corp. • Annual. $45. Publication includes: List of about 3,500 manufacturers and distributors of equipment, materials, services, computers, and software used in the design, construction, maintenance, and operation of streets and highways, water systems, wastewater and solid wastes processing, and recreation areas. Entries include: Company name, address, products. Principal content is technical articles on public works topics.

### HANDBOOKS AND MANUALS

*Standard Highway Signs, as Specified in the Manual on Uniform Traffic Control Devices.* U. S. Government Printing Office. • Looseleaf. $153.00. Issued by the U. S. Department of Transportation (www.dot.gov). Includes basic manual, with updates for an indeterminate period. Contains illustrations of typical standard signs approved for use on streets and highways, and provides information on dimensions and placement of symbols.

## INTERNET DATABASES

*Business 2.0 Web Guide to the Best Business Links.* Business 2.0 Media Inc. Phone: (415)293-4800; Email: support@business2.com • URL: http://www.business2.com/webguide • Web site presents an extensive, searchable directory of links to "the best, most informative, and authoritative web pages." Twenty main categories cover business, finance, career, company information, people, and technology topics, with thousands of subtopics, all linking to Web sites recommended by experienced business researchers. Fees: Free.

*Fedstats.* Federal Interagency Council on Statistical Policy. Phone: (202)395-7254 • URL: http://www.fedstats.gov • Web site features an efficient search facility for full-text statistics produced by more than 100 federal agencies, including the Census Bureau, the Bureau of Economic Analysis, and the Bureau of Labor Statistics. Boolean searches can be made within one agency or for all agencies combined. Links are offered to international statistical bureaus, including the UN, IMF, OECD, UNESCO, Eurostat, and 20 individual countries. Fees: Free.

*FreeLunch.com.* Economy.com, Inc. Phone: (610)696-8700; Fax: (610)696-1678 • URL: http://www.freelunch.com • Web site provides free access to more than 200 million economic and financial data series, covering industry, demographics, labor markets, prices, retail sales, government spending, trade, interest rates, housing starts, the stock market, etc. Data is available in either chart or table form. Searching is offered. Free, but registration required. Economy.com, Inc. also offers fee-based economic analysis at *The Dismal Scientist* site (www.dismal.com).

## ONLINE DATABASES

*TRIS: Transportation Research Information Service.* The National Academies National Research Council. • Contains abstracts and citations to a wide range of transportation literature, 1968 to present, with monthly updates. Includes references to the literature of air transportation, highways, ships and shipping, railroads, trucking, and urban mass transportation. Formerly *TRIS-ON-LINE.* Inquire as to online cost and availability.

## PERIODICALS AND NEWSLETTERS

*ENR: Connecting the Industry Worldwide.* McGraw Hill Financial Inc. • Weekly. $74.00 per year.

*Highway Financing and Construction: State Capitals.* Wakeman/Walworth Inc. • 50 times a year. $345.00 per year.; print and online editions, $490.00 per year. Newsletter. Formerly *From the State Capitals: Highway Financing and Construction.*

*Public Roads: A Journal of Highway Research and Development.* U. S. Government Printing Office. • Bimonthly. $31 U.S.. Contains articles relating to highway research, engineering, safety on the highways, surfacing, and other subjects.

*Roads & Bridges.* Scranton Gillette Communications Inc. • Monthly. Provides information on the planning/design, administration/management, engineering and contract execution for the road and bridge industry.

*Transportation Builder.* American Road and Transportation Builders Association. Heartland Custom Publishers Group. • Monthly. $50.00 per year.

## RESEARCH CENTERS AND INSTITUTES

Massachusetts Institute of Technology - Center for Transportation and Logistics. 77 Massachusetts Ave., E40-276, Cambridge, MA 02139. Phone: (617)253-5320; Fax: (617)253-4560; Email:

sheffi@mit.edu • URL: http://ctl.mit.edu • Transportation and logistics, with emphasis on problem-oriented, interdisciplinary, and multi-model studies, including studies on innovative urban transportation systems, transport technology innovations, railroad systems operations, trucking, energy policies, regional transportation planning and programming, highway location and design, flight transportation, ocean shipping, transportation systems analysis, logistics, supply chain management, logistics organizations, shipper/carrier relationships and logistics information technology.

Northwestern University - Transportation Center. 600 Foster St., Evanston, IL 60208-4055. Phone: (847)491-7287; Fax: (847)491-3090; Email: masmah@northwestern.edu • URL: http://transportation.northwestern.edu • Transportation, including information technology, air, rail, motor carrier, ocean and inland shipping, pipeline, telecommunications, and public transit. Focuses on the movement of materials, people, energy, and information. Emphasizes development of advanced models in logistics (vehicle routing, scheduling, inventory management, facility location), analyses of safety in the motor carrier and airline industries, evaluation of the impact of delivery restrictions in congested areas, use of advanced information technologies as competitive weapons in transportation management, studies of the impact of regulatory reform on industry economy, models of intercity travel behavior and suburban congestion, transportation planning.

Texas A&M University - Texas Transportation Institute. 3135 TAMU, College Station, TX 77843-3135. Phone: (979)845-1713; Fax: (979)845-9356; Email: dennis-c@tamu.edu • URL: http://tti.tamu.edu • Concerned with all forms and modes of transportation. Research areas include transportation economics, highway construction, traffic safety, public transportation, and highway engineering.

University of Michigan - Transportation Research Institute. 2901 Baxter Rd., Ann Arbor, MI 48109-2150. Phone: (734)764-6504; Fax: (734)936-1081; Email: umtri-director@umich.edu • URL: http://www.umtri.umich.edu • Research areas include highway safety, transportation systems, and shipbuilding.

University of Texas at Austin - Center for Transportation Research. 1616 Guadalupe St., Ste. 4.202, MC D9300, Austin, TX 78701. Phone: (512)232-3100; Fax: (512)232-3153; Email: bhat@mail.utexas.edu • URL: http://www.utexas.edu/research/ctr • Coordinates and develops highway, air, rail, pipeline, waterway, intermodal and transportation policy, and mass transportation research activities at the University. Emphasizes improvement of local and state transportation, including studies on optimizing traffic flow, transportation planning and policy, computer methods of structural design, foundation design, alternative fuels, multimodal transportation investment, pavement design, drainage, dynamics of highway loading, safety, and highway structures. Operates a cooperative research program with the Texas Department of Transportation.

## STATISTICS SOURCES

*Survey of Current Business.* U. S. Government Printing Office. • Published by Bureau of Economic Analysis, U. S. Department of Commerce. Presents a wide variety of business and economic data.

## TRADE/PROFESSIONAL ASSOCIATIONS

American Concrete Pavement Association. 500 New Jersey Ave. NW, 7th Fl., Washington, DC 20001. Phone: (202)638-2272; Fax: (202)638-2688; Email: acpa@pavement.com • URL: http://www.pavement.com • Contractors, cement companies, equipment manufacturers, material service suppliers, ready mixed concrete producers, consultants, trucking companies/material haulers and others allied with

the concrete pavement industry. Advocates the use of concrete pavement for highways, airports, streets, and roads.

American Highway Users Alliance. 1101 14th St. NW, Ste. 750, Washington, DC 20005. Phone: (202)857-1200; Fax: (202)857-1220; Email: info@highways.org • URL: http://www.highways.org • Broad-based consumers group for American motorists, truckers and businesses. Employs lobbying, media, communications and grassroots advocacy, promotes public policy that devotes highway use taxes to investments in safe and uncongested national highway systems.

American Road and Transportation Builders Association. 1219 28th St. NW, Washington, DC 20007-3389. Phone: (202)289-4434; Fax: (202)289-4435; Email: general@artba.org • URL: http://www.artba.org • Promotes on-the-job training programs.

Associated General Contractors of America. 2300 Wilson Blvd., Ste. 400, Arlington, VA 22201. Phone: 800-242-1767 or (703)548-3118 or (703)837-5319; Fax: (703)548-3119 or (703)837-5407; Email: info@agc.org • URL: http://www.agc.org • General construction contractors; subcontractors; industry suppliers; service firms. Provides market services through its divisions. Conducts special conferences and seminars designed specifically for construction firms. Compiles statistics on job accidents reported by member firms. Maintains 65 committees, including joint cooperative committees with other associations and liaison committees with federal agencies.

National Asphalt Pavement Association. 5100 Forbes Blvd., Lanham, MD 20706. Phone: 888-468-6499 or (301)731-4748; Fax: (301)731-4621; Email: napa@hotmix.org • URL: http://www.hotmix.org • Manufacturers and producers of scientifically proportioned Hot Mix Asphalt for use in all paving, including highways, airfields, and environmental usages. Membership includes hot mix producers, paving contractors, equipment manufacturers, engineering consultants, and others. Supports research and publishes information on: producing, stockpiling, and feeding of the aggregate to the manufacturing facility; drying; methods of screening, storing, and proportioning in the manufacturing facility; production of the hot mix asphalt; transporting mix to paver; lay down procedure and rolling; general workmanship; and related construction practices and materials. Commits to product quality, environmental control, safety and health, and energy conservation. Conducts training programs on a variety of technical and managerial topics for industry personnel. Maintains speakers' bureau and Hot Mix Asphalt Hall of Fame.

The Road Information Program. 3000 Connecticut Ave. NW, Ste. 208, Washington, DC 20008. Phone: (202)466-6706 • URL: http://www.tripnet.org • Conducts public education programs for the highway industry. Promotes transportation policies that relieve traffic congestion, improve air quality, make highway travel safer and enhance economic productivity.

## ROADS, TOLL

*See* TOLL ROADS

## ROBOTS

*See also* ARTIFICIAL INTELLIGENCE; AUTOMATION; MACHINE VISION

## ABSTRACTS AND INDEXES

*Applied Science and Technology Index.* EBSCO Publishing Inc. • 11/year. Indexes a wide variety of English language technical, industrial, and engineering periodicals.

*Current Contents: Engineering, Computing and Technology.* Thomson Reuters Intellectual Property and Science. • Weekly. $730 per year. Reproductions of contents pages of technical journals. Includes *Author Index, Address Directory, Current Book Contents,* and *Title Word Index.* Formerly *Current Contents: Engineering, Technology and Applied Sciences.*

*Engineering Index Monthly: Abstracting and Indexing Services Covering Sources of the World's Engineering Literature.* Engineering Information Inc. • Monthly. Institutions, $5,279.00 per year. Provides indexing and abstracting of the world's engineering and technical literature.

*Key Abstracts: Factory Automation.* Institution of Engineering and Technology. • Monthly. $1,138. Provides international coverage of journal and proceedings literature, including publications on CAD/CAM, materials handling, robotics, and factory management.

*Key Abstracts: Machine Vision.* Institution of Engineering and Technology. • Monthly. $1,138. Provides international coverage of journal and proceedings literature on optical noncontact sensing.

*Key Abstracts: Robotics and Control.* Institution of Engineering and Technology. • Monthly. $1,138. Provides international coverage of journal and proceedings literature.

*NTIS Alerts: Manufacturing Technology.* U.S. Department of Commerce National Technical Information Service. • Biweekly. $130 per year. Covers computer-aided design and manufacturing (CAD/CAM), engineering materials, quality control, machine tools, robots, lasers, productivity, and related subjects.

*Science Citation Index.* Thomson Reuters Intellectual Property and Science. • Weekly. Includes *Source Index, Citation Index, Permuterm Subject Index,* and *Corporate Index.* Provides researchers, administrators, faculty, and students with quick, powerful access to the bibliographic and citation information they need to find research data, analyze trends, journals and researchers, and share their findings.

## BIBLIOGRAPHIES

*Automation.* U. S. Government Printing Office. • Annual. Free. Issued by the Superintendent of Documents. A list of government publications on automation, computers, and related topics. Formerly *Computers and Data Processing.* (Subject Bibliography No. 51.).

## CD-ROM DATABASES

*Science Citation Index.* Thomson Reuters Intellectual Property and Science. • Weekly. Includes *Source Index, Citation Index, Permuterm Subject Index,* and *Corporate Index.* Provides researchers, administrators, faculty, and students with quick, powerful access to the bibliographic and citation information they need to find research data, analyze trends, journals and researchers, and share their findings.

## DIRECTORIES

*Assembly Buyers Guide.* Reed Elsevier Group plc Reed Business Information. • Annual. $68.00. Lists manufacturers and suppliers of equipment relating to assembly automation, fasteners, adhesives, robotics, and power tools.

## ONLINE DATABASES

*Applied Science and Technology Index Online.* H.W. Wilson Co. • Provides online indexing of 500 major scientific, technical, industrial, and engineering periodicals. Time period is 1983 to date. Monthly updates. Inquire as to online cost and availability.

## PERIODICALS AND NEWSLETTERS

*Advanced Manufacturing Technology: Monthly Report.* Technical Insights. • Monthly. $695

Institutions. Covers technological developments relating to robotics, computer graphics, automation, computer-integrated manufacturing, and machining.

*International Journal of Robotics Research.* Pine Forge Press. • $2,494 Institutions print and e-access. Offers incisive and thought-provoking original research papers and articles, perceptive reviews, and lively editorials on ground-breaking trends issues, technical developments, and theories in robotics by the outstanding scholars and practitioners in the field.

## RESEARCH CENTERS AND INSTITUTES

Carnegie Mellon University - Robotics Institute. 5000 Forbes Ave., Pittsburgh, PA 15213-3890. Phone: (412)268-3818; Fax: (412)268-6436; Email: matt.mason@cs.cmu.edu • URL: http://www.ri.cmu.edu • Robotics and artificial intelligence as they relate to the fields of computer science, electrical engineering, mechanical engineering, and operations research. Areas of research and development include robotics in hazardous environments, robots for work in unstructured environments, robotics for the factory of the future, and basic robotic technologies.

Center for Automation and Robotics Research. University of Rhode Island, Kirk Bldg., Kingston, RI 02881. Phone: (401)874-2514; Fax: (401)874-2355 • URL: http://mcise.uri.edu/datseris/robotics/index.htm.

General Robotics, Automation, Sensing & Perception. University of Pennsylvania, GRASP Laboratory, Levine Hall, 4th Fl., 3330 Walnut St., Philadelphia, PA 19104-6228. Phone: (215)898-5814; Fax: (215)573-2048; Email: betsy@central.cis.upenn.edu • URL: http://www.cis.upenn.edu/grasp/.

Imaging and Computer Vision Center. Drexel University, 3141 Chestnut St., Philadelphia, PA 19104. Phone: (215)895-2215; Fax: (215)895-4983; Email: icvc-support@cbis.ece.drexel.edu • URL: http://www.biomed.drexel.edu • Fields of research include computer vision, robot vision, and expert systems.

Purdue University - Robot Vision Laboratory. Electrical Engineering Bldg., School of Electrical and Computer Engineering, 465 Northwestern Ave., West Lafayette, IN 47907-2035. Phone: (765)494-4600 or (765)494-3456; Fax: (765)494-6440; Email: kak@purdue.edu • URL: http://engineering.purdue.edu/RVL • Advanced automation with robotics and artificial intelligence, including studies in sensory feedback for intelligent robot manipulation and fundamental research in computer vision.

University of Florida - Center for Intelligent Machines and Robotics. Department of Mechanical Engineering, Gainesville, FL 32611. Phone: (352)392-9461; Fax: (352)392-1071; Email: ccrane@ufl.edu • URL: http://cimar.mae.ufl.edu/CIMAR/index.html • Robotics and artificial intelligence, including studies in industrial robotics, nuclear reactor maintenance, interactive animated display of man-controlled and autonomous robots, light machinery, hazardous area manipulation, and human augmentation.

University of Maryland at College Park - Center for Automation Research. A.V. Williams Bldg. 115, Rm. 4413, College Park, MD 20742-3275. Phone: (301)405-4526; Fax: (301)314-9115; Email: lsd@umiacs.umd.edu • URL: http://www.cfar.umd.edu • Automation, including computer vision, graphics, robotics, and perceptual interfaces.

University of Toronto - Robotics and Automation Laboratory. Department of Mechanical Engineering, 5 King's College Rd., Toronto, ON, Canada M5S 3G8. Phone: (416)978-5745; Fax: (416)978-7753; Email: golden@mie.utoronto.ca • URL: http://www.mie.utoronto.ca/labs/ral.

## STATISTICS SOURCES

*U.S. Industry and Trade Outlook.* U.S. Department of Commerce National Technical Information Service. • Annual. Produced by the International Trade Administration, U.S. Department of Commerce, in a "public-private" partnership with DRI/McGraw-Hill and Standard & Poor's. Provides basic data, outlook for the current year, and "Long-Term Prospects" (five-year projections) for a wide variety of products and services. Includes high technology industries. Formerly *U.S. Industrial Outlook.*

## TRADE/PROFESSIONAL ASSOCIATIONS

Association for Unmanned Vehicle Systems International. 2700 S Quincy St., Ste. 400, Arlington, VA 22206. Phone: (703)845-9671; Fax: (703)845-9679; Email: info@auvsi.org • URL: http://www.auvsi.org • Concerned with the development of unmanned systems and robotics technologies.

Robotic Industries Association. 900 Victors Way, Ste. 140, Ann Arbor, MI 48108. Phone: (734)994-6088; Fax: (734)994-3338; Email: webmaster@robotics.org • URL: http://www.robotics.org • Represents the interests of the robotics industry. Member companies include robot manufacturers, users, system integrators, component suppliers, research groups, and consulting firms. Sponsors the biennial International Robots and Vision Show, develops the ANSI/RIA national robot safety standard, collects and reports robotics industry statistics.

Robotics International of the Society of Manufacturing Engineers. 1 SME Dr., Dearborn, MI 48128. Phone: 800-733-4763 or (313)425-3000; Fax: (313)425-3400; Email: service@sme.org • URL: http://www.sme.org • Engineers, managers, educators and government officials in 50 countries working or interested in the field of robotics. Affiliated with the Society of Manufacturing Engineers.

# ROCK PRODUCTS

*See* QUARRYING

# ROCKET INDUSTRY

*See also* AEROSPACE INDUSTRY

## ABSTRACTS AND INDEXES

*International Aerospace Abstracts.* American Institute of Aeronautics and Astronautics, Inc. CSA. • 11 times a year. $2,260.00 per year. Includes print and online editions.

## ALMANACS AND YEARBOOKS

*Progress in Aerospace Sciences: An International Journal.* Elsevier. • $2,631 Individuals Print. Aerospace journal. Text in English, French and German.

## GENERAL WORKS

*History of Rocketry and Astronautics.* American Astronautical Society. Univelt Inc. • $95. Various volumes and prices. Covers the history of rocketry and astronautics since 1880. Prices vary. (AAS History Series).

*Space Sciences: Macmillan Science Library.* Cengage Learning Inc. • $690 Individuals. 2012. $629.00. Four volumes. Includes business and economic aspects of aerospace technology. (Macmillan Reference USA imprint, Macmillan Science Library). eBook also available.

## OTHER SOURCES

*Advances in the Astronautical Sciences.* American Astronautical Society. Univelt Inc. • $215 Individuals. Price varies. Volumes in this series cover the proceedings of various astronautical conferences and symposia.

## PERIODICALS AND NEWSLETTERS

*Aerospace Daily.* McGraw Hill Financial Inc. • Description: Reports on developments in the aerospace industry in the U.S. and overseas. Covers related political decisions. **Remarks:** Available in print, e-mail, and URL format.

*Journal of Astronautical Sciences.* American Astronautical Society. • Quarterly. $189 Institutions 1-year subscription. An archival publication devoted to the sciences and technology of astronautics.

## RESEARCH CENTERS AND INSTITUTES

California Institute of Technology. Caltech 17-6, 1200 E Califoria Blvd., Pasadena, CA 91125. Phone: 800-514-2665 or (626)395-6811 or (818)395-6811; Fax: (818)393-4218 or (626)395-5768; Email: feefback@jpl.nasa.gov • URL: http://www.caltech.edu.

Joint Institute for Advancement of Flight Sciences. 725 23rd St. NW, 227 Hunting Ave., Washington, DC 20052. Phone: (202)994-6080; Fax: (202)994-3394; Email: jiafs@seas.gwu.edu • Conducts research in aeronautics, astronautics, and acoustics (flight-produced noise).

## STATISTICS SOURCES

*Aerospace Facts and Figures.* Aerospace Industries Association of America. • Annual. $35 Individuals. Includes financial data for the aerospace industries.

*U.S. Industry and Trade Outlook.* U.S. Department of Commerce National Technical Information Service. • Annual. Produced by the International Trade Administration, U.S. Department of Commerce, in a "public-private" partnership with DRI/McGraw-Hill and Standard & Poor's. Provides basic data, outlook for the current year, and "Long-Term Prospects" (five-year projections) for a wide variety of products and services. Includes high technology industries. Formerly *U.S. Industrial Outlook.*

## TRADE/PROFESSIONAL ASSOCIATIONS

National Association of Rocketry. PO Box 407, Marion, IA 52302-0407. Phone: 800-262-4872; Fax: (319)373-8910; Email: nar-hq@nar.org • URL: http://www.nar.org • Model rockets. Formerly Model Missile Association.

# ROLLER BEARINGS

*See* BEARINGS AND BALL BEARINGS

# ROOFING INDUSTRY

*See also* BUILDING INDUSTRY; BUILDING MATERIALS INDUSTRY

## DIRECTORIES

*Low-Slope Roofing Materials Guide.* National Roofing Contractors Association. • Covers: Approximately 250 manufacturers and suppliers of low-slope roof membrane, metal roof panels, cements and coatings, insulation board, and roof fastener products for commercial, industrial, and institutional purposes. Entries include: Company name, location, phone, name and title of contact, description of products, warranty information.

*Roofing Contractor--Single Ply Systems Index Issue.* BNP Media. • Annual. Publication includes: List of manufacturers of single ply roofing products. Entries include: Company name, address, phone, products.

*Roofing Service Consultants Directory.* InfoGroup Inc. • Annual. Number of listings: 1,225. Entries include: Name, address, phone, size of advertisement, name of owner or manager, number of employees, year first in "Yellow Pages." Compiled from telephone company "Yellow Pages," nationwide.

## FINANCIAL RATIOS

*Annual Statement Studies.* Risk Management Association. • Annual. Compiled from over 280,000 financial statements.

*Annual Statement Studies: Industry Default Probabilities and Cash Flow Measures.* Risk Management Association. • Annual. $405 Nonmembers. Serves as a companion volume to the original *Annual Statement Studies.* Gives probability of default estimates on a percentage scale for more than 450 industries. Includes changes in position year-by-year for eight financial statement line items and provides percentage measures of cash flow.

## PERIODICALS AND NEWSLETTERS

*Building Material Dealer.* National Lumber and Building Material Dealers Association. • Monthly. $48.00 per year. Includes special feature issues on hand and power tools, lumber, roofing, kitchens, flooring, windows and doors, and insulation. Formerly *Builder Material Retailer.*

*Roofing, Siding, Insulation.* Advanstar Communications. • Monthly. $44.00 per year.

## TRADE/PROFESSIONAL ASSOCIATIONS

Asphalt Roofing Manufacturers Association. 750 National Press Bldg., 529 14th St. NW, Washington, DC 20045. Phone: (202)591-2450; Fax: (202)591-2445; Email: rhitchcock@kellencompany.com • URL: http://www.asphaltroofing.org • Manufacturers of asphalt shingles, rollgoods, built-up roofing systems (BUR) and modified bitumen roofing systems. Compiles statistics.

National Roofing Contractors Association. 10255 W Higgins Rd., Ste. 600, Rosemont, IL 60018-5607. Phone: (847)299-9070; Fax: (847)299-1183 • URL: http://www.nrca.net • Roofing, roof deck, and waterproofing contractors and industry-related associate members. Assists members to successfully satisfy their customers through technical support, testing and research, education, marketing, government relations, and consultation.

# ROPE AND TWINE INDUSTRY

## TRADE/PROFESSIONAL ASSOCIATIONS

Cordage Institute. 994 Old Eagle School Rd., Ste. 1019, Wayne, PA 19087. Phone: (610)971-4854; Fax: (610)971-4859; Email: info@cordageinstitute.com • URL: http://www.ropecord.com • Represents manufacturers of natural and synthetic fiber cordage, in constructions, industry suppliers, consultants, and machinery manufacturers. Offers standard technical information and educational programs. Operates speakers' bureau. Compiles statistics.

# RUBBER AND RUBBER GOODS INDUSTRIES

*See also* PLASTICS INDUSTRY; TIRE INDUSTRY

## ABSTRACTS AND INDEXES

*CPI Digest: Key to World Literature Serving the Coatings, Plastics, Fibers, Adhesives, and Related Industries.* CPI Information Services. • Monthly. $397.00 per year. Abstracts of business and technical articles for polymer-based, chemical process industries. Includes a monthly list of relevant U. S. patents. International coverage.

*The Polymer Library.* Rubber and Plastics Research Association of Great Britian. Smithers Rapra Technology. • Monthly. $2,700.00 per year. Up-to-date survey of current international information relevant to the rubber, plastics and associated industries.

## CD-ROM DATABASES

*OECD Statistical Compendium.* Organization for Economic Cooperation and Development. • Semiannual. $1,905.00 per year for 1 to 10 users. CD-ROM contains more than 730,000 monthly, quarterly, and annual time series for OECD countries, 1960 to date. Includes fully searchable data on agriculture, food, economic indicators, national accounts, employment, energy, finance, industry, technology, and foreign trade. Results can be displayed in various forms.

## DIRECTORIES

*Chemicals, Plastics & Rubber Yearbook.* George Warman Publications Ltd. • Biennial. $45. Covers: Chemical, plastics and rubber products, manufacturers, associations, and colleges/universities in South Africa. Entries include: Company name, address, phone, brand name, specifications, statistics, services, suppliers of machinery and instrumentation.

*Directory of American Manufacturers & Exporters of Machinery for Rubber Industry.* EXIM Infotek Private Ltd. • Covers: 25 American manufacturers and exporters of machinery for rubber, tire retreading equipment and supplies, tire spreaders, and inspection machines. Entries include: Company name, postal address, telephone, fax, e-mail, website, contact person, designation, and product details.

*Directory of Asian Importers of Machinery for Rubber Industry.* EXIM Infotek Private Ltd. • Covers: 30 Asian importers of rubber industry equipment and supplies and rubber processing machinery. Entries include: Company name, postal address, telephone, fax, e-mail, website, contact person, designation, and product details.

*Directory of European Importers of Machinery for Rubber Industry.* EXIM Infotek Private Ltd. • Covers: 35 European importers of industrial equipment tires and rubber industry equipment and supplies. Entries include: Company name, postal address, telephone, fax, e-mail, website, contact person, designation, and product details.

*Directory of Taiwanese Manufacturers & Exporters of Machinery for Rubber Industry.* EXIM Infotek Private Ltd. • $250 Individuals. Covers: 80 Taiwanese manufacturers and exporters of bicycle tire building machine, raw rubber processing and vulcanizing machine and equipment, rubber injection molding machine, rubber products, and tire making machinery. Entries include: Company name, postal address, telephone, fax, e-mail, website, contact person, designation, and product details.

## E-BOOKS

*Encyclopedia of American Industries.* Cengage Learning Inc. • 2011. $807.00. 6th edition. Three volumes. Volume one is Manufacturing Industries and volume two is Service and Non-Manufacturing Industries. Provides the history, development, and recent status of approximately 1,000 industries. Includes statistical graphs, with industry and general indexes. Also available as eBook.

## INTERNET DATABASES

*Business 2.0 Web Guide to the Best Business Links.* Business 2.0 Media Inc. Phone: (415)293-4800; Email: support@business2com • URL: http://www.business2.com/webguide • Web site presents an extensive, searchable directory of links to "the best, most informative, and authoritative web pages." Twenty main categories cover business, finance, career, company information, people, and technology topics, with thousands of subtopics, all linking to Web sites recommended by experienced business researchers. Fees: Free.

*Fedstats.* Federal Interagency Council on Statistical Policy. Phone: (202)395-7254 • URL: http://www.fedstats.gov • Web site features an efficient search

---

facility for full-text statistics produced by more than 100 federal agencies, including the Census Bureau, the Bureau of Economic Analysis, and the Bureau of Labor Statistics. Boolean searches can be made within one agency or for all agencies combined. Links are offered to international statistical bureaus, including the UN, IMF, OECD, UNESCO, Eurostat, and 20 individual countries. Fees: Free.

*FreeLunch.com.* Economy.com, Inc. Phone: (610)696-8700; Fax: (610)696-1678 • URL: http://www.freelunch.com • Web site provides free access to more than 200 million economic and financial data series, covering industry, demographics, labor markets, prices, retail sales, government spending, trade, interest rates, housing starts, the stock market, etc. Data is available in either chart or table form. Searching is offered. Free, but registration required. Economy.com, Inc. also offers fee-based economic analysis at *The Dismal Scientist* site (www.dismal.com).

## PERIODICALS AND NEWSLETTERS

*Rubber & Plastics News.* Crain Communications Inc. • Biweekly. $99 Individuals. Written for rubber product manufacturers.

*Rubber Chemistry & Technology.* American Chemical Society - Rubber Division. • Four times per year.

*Rubber World.* Lippincott. • Monthly. $34 /year. Provides plant engineering personnel with the latest equipment and production technology.

## RESEARCH CENTERS AND INSTITUTES

University of Southern California - Tlargi Rubber Technology Foundation., Los Angeles, CA 90089-1211. Phone: (213)740-2225; Fax: (213)740-8053; Email: salove@almaak.usc.edu.

## STATISTICS SOURCES

*Rubber Statistical Bulletin.* International Rubber Study Group. • Quarterly. S$3,000.00 per year. S$1,500.00 per issue.

*Survey of Current Business.* U. S. Government Printing Office. • Published by Bureau of Economic Analysis, U. S. Department of Commerce. Presents a wide variety of business and economic data.

# RUG INDUSTRY

*See* FLOOR COVERINGS

# RUGS, ORIENTAL

*See* ORIENTAL RUG INDUSTRY

# RULES OF ORDER

*See* PARLIAMENTARY PROCEDURE

# RUM INDUSTRY

*See* DISTILLING INDUSTRY

# RURAL COMMUNITY DEVELOPMENT

*See* COMMUNITY DEVELOPMENT

# RURAL CREDIT

*See* AGRICULTURAL CREDIT

# RURAL ELECTRIFICATION

## CD-ROM DATABASES

*Environment Abstracts on CD-ROM.* University Publications of America. • Quarterly. $1,295.00 per year. Contains the following CD-ROM databases: *Environment Abstracts, Energy Abstracts,* and *Acid Rain Abstracts.* Length of coverage varies.

## PERIODICALS AND NEWSLETTERS

*R E Magazine.* National Rural Electric Cooperative Association. • Monthly. $43 Members. News and information about the rural electric utility industry. Formerly *Rural Electrification.*

## TRADE/PROFESSIONAL ASSOCIATIONS

National Rural Electric Cooperative Association. 4301 Wilson Blvd., Arlington, VA 22203. Phone: (703)907-5500 or (703)907-5732; Fax: (703)907-5517; Email: michael.lynch@nreca.coop • URL: http://www.nreca.coop/Pages/default.aspx • Rural electric cooperative systems, public power districts and public utility districts in 46 states. Conducts activities such as: legislative representation; energy and regulatory; management institutes; professional conferences; training and consulting services; insurance and safety programs; international program; wage and salary surveys.

National Rural Utilities Cooperative Finance Corp. 20701 Cooperative Way, Dulles, VA 20166. Phone: 800-424-2954 or (703)709-6700 or (703)467-1800; Fax: (703)467-5175; Email: publicrelations@nrucfc.coop • URL: http://www.nrucfc.coop.

# RYE INDUSTRY

*See also* GRAIN INDUSTRY

## ABSTRACTS AND INDEXES

*Biological and Agricultural Index.* H.W. Wilson Co. • 11 times a year. Annual and quarterly cumulations. Price varies.

*Wheat, Barley and Triticale Abstracts.* CABI. • Updated weekly. Published in England by CABI Publishing. Provides worldwide coverage of the literature of wheat, barley, and rye.

## CD-ROM DATABASES

*OECD Statistical Compendium.* Organization for Economic Cooperation and Development. • Semiannual. $1,905.00 per year for 1 to 10 users. CD-ROM contains more than 730,000 monthly, quarterly, and annual time series for OECD countries, 1960 to date. Includes fully searchable data on agriculture, food, economic indicators, national accounts, employment, energy, finance, industry, technology, and foreign trade. Results can be displayed in various forms.

## INTERNET DATABASES

*Business 2.0 Web Guide to the Best Business Links.* Business 2.0 Media Inc. Phone: (415)293-4800; Email: support@business2.com • URL: http://www.business2.com/webguide • Web site presents an extensive, searchable directory of links to "the best,

most informative, and authoritative web pages." Twenty main categories cover business, finance, career, company information, people, and technology topics, with thousands of subtopics, all linking to Web sites recommended by experienced business researchers. Fees: Free.

*Fedstats.* Federal Interagency Council on Statistical Policy. Phone: (202)395-7254 • URL: http://www.fedstats.gov • Web site features an efficient search facility for full-text statistics produced by more than 100 federal agencies, including the Census Bureau, the Bureau of Economic Analysis, and the Bureau of Labor Statistics. Boolean searches can be made within one agency or for all agencies combined. Links are offered to international statistical bureaus, including the UN, IMF, OECD, UNESCO, Eurostat, and 20 individual countries. Fees: Free.

*FreeLunch.com.* Economy.com, Inc. Phone: (610)696-8700; Fax: (610)696-1678 • URL: http://www.freelunch.com • Web site provides free access to more than 200 million economic and financial data series, covering industry, demographics, labor markets, prices, retail sales, government spending, trade, interest rates, housing starts, the stock market, etc. Data is available in either chart or table form. Searching is offered. Free, but registration required. Economy.com, Inc. also offers fee-based economic analysis at *The Dismal Scientist* site (www.dismal.com).

*USDA.* U.S. National Institute of Standards and Technology. 100 Bureau Dr., Gaithersburg, MD 20899-1070. Phone: 800-877-8339 or (301)975-6478 or (202)720-2791; Fax: (301)975-8295; Email: inquiries@nist.gov • URL: http://www.nist.gov • The USDA home page has six sections: News and Information; What's New; About USDA; Agencies; Opportunities; Search and Help. Keyword searching is offered from the USDA home page and from various individual agency home pages. Agencies are the Economic Research Service, Agricultural Marketing Service, National Agricultural Statistics Service, National Agricultural Library, and about 12 others. Updating varies. Fees: Free.

## ONLINE DATABASES

*CAB Abstracts.* CABI. • Contains 46 specialized abstract collections covering over 10,000 journals and monographs in the areas of agriculture, horticulture, forest products, farm products, nutrition, dairy science, poultry, grains, animal health, entomology, etc. Time period is 1972 to date, with monthly updates. Inquire as to online cost and availability. *CAB Abstracts on CD-ROM* also available, with annual updating.

## STATISTICS SOURCES

*Agricultural Statistics.* U.S. Department of Agriculture National Agricultural Statistics Service. • Annual. $46 Individuals. Provides a wide variety of statistical data relating to agricultural production, supplies, consumption, prices/price-supports, foreign trade, costs, and returns, as well as farm labor, loans, income, and population. In many cases, historical data is shown annually for 10 years. In addition to farm data, includes detailed fishery statistics.

*Survey of Current Business.* U. S. Government Printing Office. • Published by Bureau of Economic Analysis, U. S. Department of Commerce. Presents a wide variety of business and economic data.

# S

## SAFE DEPOSITS (BANKING)

*See also* BANKS AND BANKING

### PERIODICALS AND NEWSLETTERS

*The Safe Deposit Bulletin.* New York State Safe Deposit Association. • Description: Discusses topics on safe and sound business practice for safe deposit organizations. Recurring features include news of research, notices of publications available, a calendar of events, news of educational opportunities, Association news, current legal and regulatory changes, current practices and procedures and Q&A section.

## SAFETY

*See also* ACCIDENTS; FIRE PROTECTION; INDUSTRIAL HYGIENE; INDUSTRIAL SAFETY

### ABSTRACTS AND INDEXES

*Health and Safety Science Abstracts.* Institute of Safety and Systems Management. Cambridge Information Group. • Monthly. Provides coverage of world literature on general safety, environmental and ecological safety, industrial hygiene and occupational safety, transportation safety, aviation and aerospace safety, and medical safety. Formerly *Safety Science Abstracts Journal.*

### CD-ROM DATABASES

*OSH-ROM: Occupational Safety and Health Information on CD-ROM.* SilverPlatter Information Inc. • Price and frequency on application. Produced in Geneva by the International Occupational Safety and Health Information Centre, International Labour Organization (www.ilo.org). Provides about two million citations and abstracts to the worldwide literature of industrial safety, industrial hygiene, hazardous materials, and accident prevention. Material is included from journals, technical reports, books, government publications, and other sources. Time span varies.

### DIRECTORIES

*European System for Security and Cooperation Handbook.* International Business Publications, USA. • $99.95 Individuals hardcover, e-book, CD-ROM. Covers: U.S. security strategic materials and contacts.

### PERIODICALS AND NEWSLETTERS

*EHS Today.* Penton Media Inc. • Monthly. $55.00 per year. Industrial safety and security management.

*Professional Safety.* American Society of Safety Engineers. • Monthly. $60 U.S., Canada, and Mexico. Emphasis is on research and technology in the field of accident prevention.

*Safety and Health.* National Safety Council. • Monthly. Qualified professionals may receive free for one year.

### RESEARCH CENTERS AND INSTITUTES

Indiana University - School of Public Health - Department of Applied Health Science. 1025 E 7th St., Ste. 111, Bloomington, IN 47405. Phone: (812)855-1561 • URL: http://www.publichealth. indiana.edu/departments/applied-health-science/ index.shtml • Health behavior, quantitative and qualitative evaluation of instructional materials, and human behavior and attitudes relating to safety and driver education, including studies on industrial safety, health and safety practices in industry and recreational settings, childhood accident prevention and injury control, nutrition, family life, and human development.

Lawrence Berkeley National Laboratory - Environment, Health and Safety Division - Safety Advisory Committee. 1 Cyclotron Rd., MS 90R1140, Berkeley, CA 94720-8128. Phone: (510)486-7653; Fax: (510)486-7488; Email: paseidl@lbl.gov • URL: http://www.lbl.gov/ehs/sac/ • Development and implementation of environment, safety, and health policy, guidelines, codes, and regulatory interpretation of the Lawrence Berkeley National Laboratory.

### STATISTICS SOURCES

*Injury Facts.* National Safety Council. • Annual. $109.85 Nonmembers.

### TRADE/PROFESSIONAL ASSOCIATIONS

American Society of Safety Engineers. 1800 E Oakton St., Des Plaines, IL 60018. Phone: (847)699-2929; Fax: (847)768-3434; Email: customerservice@asse.org • URL: http://www.asse. org • Professional society of safety engineers, safety directors, and others concerned with accident prevention, environmental protection and safety and health programs. Sponsors National Safety Month and conducts research and educational programs. Develops/publishes ANSI safety-related standards and other technical literature. Compiles statistics; maintains job placement service.

Building Security Council. 1801 Alexander Bell Dr., Reston, VA 20191. Phone: (703)295-6314; Fax: (703)295-6415; Email: jschmid@burnsmcd.com • Aims to improve the security of state, municipal and privately owned buildings. Enhances public safety by promoting building security. Administers and maintains rating systems that enable building owners and operators to evaluate and improve the security of their facilities.

Coalition to Insure Against Terrorism. 1875 Eye St. NW, Ste. 600, Washington, DC 20006-5413. Phone: (202)739-9454; Email: info@ insureagainstterrorism.org • URL: http://www. insureagainstterrorism.org • Represents organizations in the transportation, real estate, manufacturing, construction, entertainment and retail sectors. Seeks the passage of legislation that will enable the nation's insurers to provide holders with comprehensive terrorism coverage. Supports the passage of the Terrorism Risk Insurance Revision and Extension Act (TRIREA).

Industry Council for Emergency Response Technologies. PO Box 42563, Washington, DC 20015-2604. Phone: (240)398-3065; Email: george. rice@theindustrycouncil.org • URL: http://www. theindustrycouncil.org • Represents the emergency communications industry in the development of emergency technology infrastructure and policy for the good of public safety and the public it serves. Conducts scientifically credible and objective research to support innovation in the 9-1-1 industry for the benefit of the public. Brings together industry leaders in order to maximize the value of research and development investment.

International Air Filtration Certifiers Association. c/o Michael Alleman, 129 S Gallatin, Liberty, MO 64068. Phone: 888-679-1904; Fax: (816)792-8105 • URL: http://www.iafca.com • Promotes professionalism in the biological safety cabinet industry. Establishes and maintains certification program for biological safety cabinet certifiers. Provides information and guidance to legislative and regulatory agencies with regard to laws and standards affecting the industry.

Security Analysis and Risk Management Association. PO Box 100284, Arlington, VA 22210. Phone: (703)635-7906; Fax: (703)635-7935; Email: info@sarma.org • URL: http://sarma.org • Aims to further the development, standardization and professionalization of the security analysis and risk management discipline. Provides leadership, education and certification for security analysis and risk management professionals. Serves as a forum to share information, ideas and methodologies to improve the development and application of the security analysis and risk management profession.

## SAFETY APPLIANCES

*See* INDUSTRIAL SAFETY

## SAFETY EDUCATION

*See* SAFETY

---

# SAFETY, INDUSTRIAL

*See* INDUSTRIAL SAFETY

# SAFETY, PRODUCT

*See* PRODUCT SAFETY AND LIABILITY

# SALAD OIL INDUSTRY

*See* OIL AND FATS INDUSTRY

# SALE OF BUSINESS ENTERPRISES

*See* BUSINESS ENTERPRISES, SALE OF

# SALES AUCTION

*See* AUCTIONS

# SALES CONTESTS

*See* SALES PROMOTION

# SALES CONVENTIONS

*See also* CONFERENCES, WORKSHOPS, AND SEMINARS; CONVENTIONS; SALES MANAGEMENT

## DIRECTORIES

*Trade Shows Worldwide.* Cengage Learning Inc. • 2013. $645.00. 31st edition. Provides detailed information from over 75 countries on more than 10,000 trade shows and exhibitions. Separate sections are provided for trade shows/exhibitions, for sponsors/organizers, and for services, facilities, and information sources. Indexing is by date, location, subject, name, and keyword.

## INTERNET DATABASES

*Trade Show Center.* Global Sources/Trade Media Holdings Ltd. Phone: (656)574-2800; Email: service@globalsources.com • URL: http://www. globalsources.com/TRADESHW/TRDSHFRM. HTM • Free Web site provides current, detailed information on more than 1,000 major trade shows worldwide, including events in the U. S., but with an emphasis on "Asia and Greater China." Searching is offered by product, supplier, country, and month of year. Includes links to "Trade Information.".

## PERIODICALS AND NEWSLETTERS

*Successful Meetings: The Authority on Meetings and Incentive Travel Management.* Nielsen Business Media Inc. • Monthly. Monthly. $79.00 per year.

# SALES FINANCE COMPANIES

*See* FINANCE COMPANIES

# SALES MANAGEMENT

*See also* MARKETING; SALESMEN AND SALESMANSHIP

## E-BOOKS

*Winning New Business.* Cengage Learning Inc. • 2009. eBook. Published by Kogan Page. Offers information to those who seek the skills of success-

ful selling but lack the training - or the courage - to sell effectively.

## PERIODICALS AND NEWSLETTERS

*Journal of Personal Selling and Sales Management (JPSSM).* M.E. Sharpe Inc. • Quarterly. $84 Individuals. An academic journal containing peer-reviewed articles. Includes "Selling and Sales Management Abstracts" (summaries of relevant articles appearing in various publications).

*Sales and Marketing Management.* Nielsen Business Media Inc. • Monthly. $48.00 per year.

*Selling: The Front Line of Business.* Dartnell Corp. • Monthly. $79 Individuals. Magazine covering information for sales professionals in all areas.

## TRADE/PROFESSIONAL ASSOCIATIONS

Gift Sales Manager Association. 14710 Quaker Bottom Rd., Sparks, MD 21152. Phone: (410)472-3593; Email: ldcolson@comcast.net • URL: http:// www.giftsalesmanagers.org • Represents the interests of sales managers in the gift and home decor industry. Works to improve company operations and increase sales. Serves as a forum to exchange information and ideas among members.

# SALES PROMOTION

*See also* ADVERTISING; MARKETING; PREMIUMS; PUBLIC RELATIONS AND PUBLICITY; SALES MANAGEMENT

## DIRECTORIES

*PROMO Annual SourceBook: The Only Guide to the $70 Billion Promotion Industry.* Primedia Business Magazines and Media. • Annual. $49.95. Lists service and supply companies for the promotion industry. Includes annual salary survey and award winning campaigns.

## ENCYCLOPEDIAS AND DICTIONARIES

*Encyclopedia of Major Marketing Strategies.* Cengage Learning Inc. • $500 Individuals. Covers 100 major marketing strategies for some of the top global and emerging brands from 2011-2012.

## HANDBOOKS AND MANUALS

*Promotional Marketing.* Entrepreneur Press. • Looseleaf. $59.50. A practical guide to sales promotion and marketing for small businesses. (Start-Up Business Guide No. E1111.).

## OTHER SOURCES

*Idea Source Guide; A Monthly Report to Executives in Advertising, Merchandising and Sales Promotion.* Bramlee, Inc. • Monthly. $150.00 per year. Lists new premiums and novelty products.

## PERIODICALS AND NEWSLETTERS

*Database Marketer.* SIMBA Information Inc. • Monthly. $329.00 per year.

*Incentive: Managing and Marketing Through Motivation.* Nielsen Business Media Inc. • Monthly. $59.00 per year.

*The Licensing Letter (TLL).* EPM Communications Inc. • Description: Concerned with all aspects of licensed merchandising, "the business of associating someone's name, likeness or creation with someone else&'s product or service, for a consideration." Recurring features include statistics, research, events, mechanics, available properties, and identification of licensors, licensing agents, and licensees.

*PROMO: Promotion Marketing Worldwide.* Primedia Business Magazines and Media. • Monthly. $65.00 per year. Edited for companies and agencies that utilize couponing, point-of-purchase advertising, special events, games, contests, premiums, product samples, and other unique promotional items.

## TRADE/PROFESSIONAL ASSOCIATIONS

Marketing Agencies Association Worldwide. 60 Peachcroft Dr., Bernardsville, NJ 07924. Phone: (908)428-4300; Fax: (908)766-1277; Email: simon. mahoney@maaw.org • URL: http://www.maaw.org • Represents the interests of CEOs, presidents, managing directors and principals of top marketing services agencies. Provides opportunity for marketing professionals to meet with peers, raise company profile on both a national and a global platform, and influence the future of industry. Fosters networking through conferences.

# SALES REPRESENTATIVES

*See* MANUFACTURERS' AGENTS

# SALES TAX

*See also* STATE LAW

## HANDBOOKS AND MANUALS

*U.S. Master Sales and Use Tax Guide.* Wolters Kluwer Law & Business CCH. • Annual. $129.95 1 - 4 (quantity). Contains concise information on sales and use taxes in all states and the District of Columbia.

## OTHER SOURCES

*Manufacturers' Tax Alert.* Wolters Kluwer Law & Business CCH. • Monthly $297.00 per year. Newsletter. Covers the major tax issues affecting manufacturing companies. Includes current developments in various kind of federal, state, and international taxes: sales, use, franchise, property, and corporate income.

*Multistate Sales Tax Guide.* Wolters Kluwer Law & Business CCH. • Monthly. $1,349 /year. Looseleaf service. Nine volumes.. Formerly *All State Sales Tax Reports.* Gives in-depth state sales tax law coverage on a wide variety of tax-related issues.

## PERIODICALS AND NEWSLETTERS

*E-Commerce Tax Alert.* Wolters Kluwer Law & Business CCH. • Description: Print and online newsletter covering e-commerce taxation issues, including compliance and sourcing, e-cash implications, the Internet tax debate, and other topics.

## RESEARCH CENTERS AND INSTITUTES

University of Michigan - Stephen M. Ross School of Business - Office of Tax Policy Research. 701 Tappan St., Rm. R5380, Ann Arbor, MI 48109-1234. Phone: (734)763-3068; Fax: (734)763-4032; Email: jslemrod@umich.edu • URL: http://www.bus. umich.edu/OTPR/ • Tax policy, including compliance, capital gains, reform, international taxation, and income dynamics.

# SALESMEN AND SALESMANSHIP

*See also* SALES MANAGEMENT

## CD-ROM DATABASES

*Business Abstracts with Full Text.* EBSCO Publishing Inc. • Includes full text articles from more than 460 business publications from 1982 to present. Indexing for nearly 880 publications.

## DIRECTORIES

*Directory of Chinese and Foreign Management and Sales Personnel.* Standards Press of China. • Biennial. $30. Covers: 8,700 companies, organizations, and individuals in business, industry, and other professionals. Entries include: Name, address, phone, telex, name and title of contact, names and titles of key personnel, geographical area covered, description of activities.

*Plunkett's Retail Industry Almanac: Complete Profiles on the Retail 500: The Leading Firms in Retail Stores, Services, Catalogs, and On-Line Sales.* Plunkett Research Ltd. • Annual. $349.99 Individuals print. Covers: 500 of the largest retail stores, services, catalogs, and on-line sales companies. Entries include: Firm name, address, phone, fax; description; and leading executives with their titles, addresses, phone numbers, fax numbers, E-mail addresses, and Web sites.

## ONLINE DATABASES

*Wilson Business Abstracts Online.* H.W. Wilson Co. • Indexes and abstracts 600 major business periodicals, plus the *Wall Street Journal* and the business section of the *New York Times.* Indexing is from 1982, abstracting from 1990, with the two newspapers included from 1993. Updated weekly. Inquire as to online cost and availability. (*Business Periodicals Index* without abstracts is also available online.).

## PERIODICALS AND NEWSLETTERS

*Journal of Personal Selling and Sales Management (JPSSM).* M.E. Sharpe Inc. • Quarterly. $84 Individuals. An academic journal containing peer-reviewed articles. Includes "Selling and Sales Management Abstracts" (summaries of relevant articles appearing in various publications).

*Pharmaceutical Representative.* McKnight's Long-Term Care News. • Monthly. $37.95 per year. Edited for drug company salespeople and sales managers.

## TRADE/PROFESSIONAL ASSOCIATIONS

American Association of Inside Sales Professionals. 14530 Florissant Path, Apple Valley, MN 55124. Phone: 800-604-7085; Email: info@aa-isp.org • URL: http://www.aa-isp.org • Serves as an authoritative resource to leaders and individual sales representatives. Aims to perfect the skills of inside sale professionals. Conducts leadership and career development trainings, member forums and networking, conferences, education and accreditation programs that will help advance the inside sales profession.

# SALMON INDUSTRY

*See also* FISH INDUSTRY; SEAFOOD INDUSTRY

## ABSTRACTS AND INDEXES

*Oceanic Abstracts.* CSA. • Monthly. $1,645.00 per year. Includes print and online editions. Covers oceanography, marine biology, ocean shipping, and a wide range of other marine-related subject areas.

## PERIODICALS AND NEWSLETTERS

*Seafood Business.* Diversified Business Communications Inc. • $57 U.S.. Edited for a wide range of seafood buyers, including distributors, restaurants, supermarkets, and institutions. Special issues feature information on specific products, such as salmon or lobster.

# SAND AND GRAVEL INDUSTRY

*See* QUARRYING

# SANITATION INDUSTRY

*See also* AIR POLLUTION; CLEANING COMPOSITIONS; PUBLIC WORKS; RECYCLING; WASTE MANAGEMENT; WATER POLLUTION; WATER SUPPLY

## ABSTRACTS AND INDEXES

*Environment Abstracts.* University Publications of America. • Monthly. Price varies. Provides multidis-

ciplinary coverage of the world's environmental literature. Incorporates *Acid Rain Abstracts.*

*Environment Abstracts Annual: A Guide to the Key Environmental Literature of the Year.* University Publications of America. • Annual. $495.00. A yearly cumulation of *Environment Abstracts.*

*NTIS Alerts: Environmental Pollution & Control.* U.S. Department of Commerce National Technical Information Service. • Biweekly. $130 per year. Covers the following categories of environmental pollution: air, water, solid wastes, radiation, pesticides, and noise.

*Pollution Abstracts.* Cambridge Information Group. • Monthly. $1,390.00 per year. Includes print and on-line editions; with index, $1,515.00 per year.

## CD-ROM DATABASES

*Environment Abstracts on CD-ROM.* University Publications of America. • Quarterly. $1,295.00 per year. Contains the following CD-ROM databases: *Environment Abstracts, Energy Abstracts,* and *Acid Rain Abstracts.* Length of coverage varies.

## DIRECTORIES

*Directory of Asian Importers of Waste Disposal & Recycling Equipment.* EXIM Infotek Private Ltd. • $300 Individuals. Covers: 100 Asian importers of compactors, garbage disposals and compactors, incinerators, incubators, sand and recycles use, sewage systems, syringe and needle destroyers, waste disposal equipment, waste management, waste recycling equipment, waste water treatment equipment, and water treatment systems. Entries include: Company name, postal address, telephone, fax, e-mail, website, contact person, designation, and product details.

*Public Works Manual.* Public Works Journal Corp. • Annual. $45. Publication includes: List of about 3,500 manufacturers and distributors of equipment, materials, services, computers, and software used in the design, construction, maintenance, and operation of streets and highways, water systems, wastewater and solid wastes processing, and recreation areas. Entries include: Company name, address, products. Principal content is technical articles on public works topics.

## PERIODICALS AND NEWSLETTERS

*Environmental Regulation: State Capitals.* Wakeman/Walworth Inc. • 50 times a year. $245.00 per year; print and online editions, $350.00 per year. Newsletter. Formerly *From the State Capitals: Environmental Regulation.*

*OSHA Required Safety Training for Supervisors.* Occupational Safety and Health Administration. Business & Legal Resources, Inc. • Monthly. $99.00 per year. Newsletter. Formerly *Safetyworks for Supervisors.*

*Public Works: City, County and State.* Public Works Journal Corp. • Monthly. Includes *Public Works Manual.*

*Sanitary Maintenance.* Trade Press Media Group. • Monthly. Original publication serving the distributors and wholesalers of sanitary supplies.

*Sludge Newsletter: The Newsletter on Municipal Wastewater and Biosolids.* Business Publishers Inc. • Biweekly. $409.00 per year. per year. Newsletter. Monitors sludge management developments in Washington and around the country.

*Solid Waste Report: Resource Recovery-Recycling-Collection-Disposal.* Business Publishers Inc. • Weekly. $627.00 per year. Newsletter. Covers regulation, business news, technology, and international events relating to solid waste management.

## TRADE/PROFESSIONAL ASSOCIATIONS

American Public Works Association. 1275 K St. NW, Ste. 750, Washington, DC 20005. Phone: 800-848-APWA or (202)408-9541; Fax: (202)408-9542;

Email: apwa@apwa.net • URL: http://www.apwa. net • Chief administrators, commissioners, and directors of public works, city engineers, superintendents, and department heads of transportation, water, waste water, solid waste, equipment services, and buildings and grounds; federal, provincial, and state administrators and engineers; consultants and educators; associate members are equipment manufacturers' representatives, utility company officials, and contractors; student members are engineering and public administration students interested in the theory and practice of the design, construction, maintenance, administration, and operation of public works facilities and services. Conducts historical research on public works subjects and demonstrates applicability of history to current public works problems and issues through Public Works Historical Society. Sponsors research and education foundations.

American Society of Sanitary Engineering. 18927 Hickory Creek Dr., Ste. 220, Mokena, IL 60448. Phone: (708)995-3019; Fax: (708)479-6139 • URL: http://www.asse-plumbing.org • Plumbing officials, sanitary engineers, plumbers, plumbing contractors, building officials, architects, engineers, designing engineers, physicians, and others interested in health. Conducts research on plumbing and sanitation, and develops performance standards for components of the plumbing system. Sponsors disease research program and other studies of waterborne epidemics.

NSF International. 789 N Dixboro Rd., Ann Arbor, MI 48113. Phone: 800-673-6275 or (734)769-8010; Fax: (734)769-0109; Email: info@nsf.org • URL: http://www.nsf.org • Specializes in the areas of public health and environmental quality focusing on water quality, food safety, indoor air health and the environment. Develops standards, operates product certification and listings programs for products that meet or exceed public health safety standards. Maintains a worldwide network of auditors who conduct unannounced inspections of manufacturer facilities to ensure compliance and to protect the integrity of the NSF Certification Mark. Provides special research and testing services to industry, government, and foundations.

# SATELLITE COMMUNICATIONS

*See* COMMUNICATIONS SATELLITES

# SAVINGS AND LOAN ASSOCIATIONS

*See also* SAVINGS BANKS

## BIBLIOGRAPHIES

*Financial Institutions.* U. S. Government Printing Office. • Annual. Free. Lists government publications. Formerly *Banks and Banking.* GPO Subject Bibliography No. 128.

## CD-ROM DATABASES

*OECD Statistical Compendium.* Organization for Economic Cooperation and Development. • Semiannual. $1,905.00 per year for 1 to 10 users. CD-ROM contains more than 730,000 monthly, quarterly, and annual time series for OECD countries, 1960 to date. Includes fully searchable data on agriculture, food, economic indicators, national accounts, employment, energy, finance, industry, technology, and foreign trade. Results can be displayed in various forms.

## DIRECTORIES

*The Savings Directory.* Accuity Inc. • Semiannual. $570 Individuals. Covers: Nearly 2,000 savings institutions and their 13,000 branch offices. Database includes: Lists of top 500 companies ranked by assets, deposits, and loans; savings institution routing numbers in numeric sequence; and discontinued or changed institution names. Entries include: Institution name, address, phone, fax, type, identification of mutual or stock ownership, type of insurance, routing number, number of employees, names and titles of key personnel, branch office locations, financial and operational data.

## INTERNET DATABASES

*BanxQuote Banking, Mortgage, and Finance Center.* BanxQuote, Inc. Phone: (914)722-1600; Fax: (914)722-6630; Email: info@banx.com • URL: http://www.banx.com • Daily. Web site quotes interest rates paid by banks around the country on various savings products, as well as rates paid by consumers for automobile loans, mortgages, credit cards, home equity loans, and personal loans. Also provided: stock quotes, indexes, stock options, futures trading data, economic indicators, and links to many other financial sites.

*The Bauer Group: Reporting On and Analyzing the Performance of U. S. Banks, Thrifts, and Credit Unions.* Bauer Financial Reports, Inc. Phone: 800-388-6686 or (305)445-9500; Fax: (305)445-6775 or (800)230-9569 • URL: http://www.bauerfinancial. com • Web site provides ratings (0 to 5 stars) of individual banks and credit unions, based on capital ratios and other financial criteria. Online searching for bank or credit union names is offered. Fees: Free.

*Business 2.0 Web Guide to the Best Business Links.* Business 2.0 Media Inc. Phone: (415)293-4800; Email: support@business2.com • URL: http://www. business2.com/webguide • Web site presents an extensive, searchable directory of links to "the best, most informative, and authoritative web pages." Twenty main categories cover business, finance, career, company information, people, and technology topics, with thousands of subtopics, all linking to Web sites recommended by experienced business researchers. Fees: Free.

*Fedstats.* Federal Interagency Council on Statistical Policy. Phone: (202)395-7254 • URL: http://www. fedstats.gov • Web site features an efficient search facility for full-text statistics produced by more than 100 federal agencies, including the Census Bureau, the Bureau of Economic Analysis, and the Bureau of Labor Statistics. Boolean searches can be made within one agency or for all agencies combined. Links are offered to international statistical bureaus, including the UN, IMF, OECD, UNESCO, Eurostat, and 20 individual countries. Fees: Free.

*FreeLunch.com.* Economy.com, Inc. Phone: (610)696-8700; Fax: (610)696-1678 • URL: http:// www.freelunch.com • Web site provides free access to more than 200 million economic and financial data series, covering industry, demographics, labor markets, prices, retail sales, government spending, trade, interest rates, housing starts, the stock market, etc. Data is available in either chart or table form. Searching is offered. Free, but registration required. Economy.com, Inc. also offers fee-based economic analysis at *The Dismal Scientist* site (www.dismal. com).

## ONLINE DATABASES

*Banking Information Source.* ProQuest L.L.C. • Provides indexing and abstracting of periodical and other literature from 1982 to date, with weekly updates. Covers the financial services industry: banks, savings institutions, investment houses, credit unions, insurance companies, and real estate organizations. Emphasis is on marketing and management. Inquire as to online cost and availability. (Formerly *FINIS: Financial Industry Information Service.*).

## OTHER SOURCES

*Savings Institutions: Mergers, Acquisitions, and Conversions.* ALM Media Properties LLC. • $560. Provides detailed information on the legal complexities of mergers and acquisitions involving savings institutions. (Law Journal Press).

## PERIODICALS AND NEWSLETTERS

*American Banker: The Financial Services Daily.* SourceMedia Inc. • Daily. $895.00 per year. Provides news of banking, investment products, mortgages, credit unions, finance, bank technology, and legal developments.

*Fee Income Growth Strategies.* Siefer Consultants Inc. • Description: Discusses the role of fees and service charges for money orders, cashier's checks, nonsufficient funds, loans, automatic teller machine cards, and other ancillary services in the profitability of financial institutions.

*Guide to Banks and Thrifts: A Quarterly Compilation of Financial Institutions Ratings and Analysis.* Weiss Research Inc. • Quarterly. $438.00 per year. Emphasis is on rating of financial safety and relative risk. Includes annual summary.

*Jumbo Rate News.* BauerFinancial Inc. • Description: Reports on high-yielding, insured Jumbo CD (Certificate of Deposit) rates nationwide. Analyzes each institution by current credit-worthiness, and lists current assets and capital ratios. Provides phone numbers, contacts, methods of computation, and information on how interest is paid. Also contains financial news, insights, and commentary of interest to Jumbo CD investors. Recurring features include editorials and news of interest.

*One Hundred Highest Yields.* Bankrate Inc. • Weekly. $124.00 per year. Newsletter. List CD's and money markets offered by federally insured banks. National coverage.

*Recommended Bank and Thrift Report.* BauerFinancial Inc. • Quarterly. $585.00 per year. Newsletter provides information on "safe, financially sound" commercial banks, savings banks, and savings and loan institutions. Various factors are considered, including tangible capital ratios and total risk-based capital ratios. (Six regional editions are also available at $150.00 per edition per year.).

*Safe Money Report.* Weiss Research Inc. • Monthly. $99.00 per year. Newsletter. Provides financial advice and current safety ratings of various banks, savings and loan companies, insurance companies, and securities dealers.

*Treasury Manager's Report: Strategic Information for the Financial Executive.* Access Intelligence L.L.C. • Biweekly. $630.00. Newsletter reporting on legal developments affecting the operations of banks, savings institutions, and other financial service organizations. Formerly *Financial Services Law Report.*

*Troubled and Problematic Bank and Thrift Report.* BauerFinancial Inc. • Quarterly. $225.00 per year. Newsletter provides information on seriously undercapitalized ("Troubled") banks and savings institutions, as defined by a federal Prompt Corrective Action Rule. "Problematic" banks and thrifts are those meeting regulatory capital levels, but showing negative trends.

*U.S. Banker.* SourceMedia Inc. • Monthly. $65.00 per year. Edited for bank executives and managers. Covers a wide variety of banking and financial topics.

## STATISTICS SOURCES

*Standard & Poor's Industry Surveys.* Standard & Poor's Financial Services L.L.C. • Semiannual. $1,800.00. Two looseleaf volumes. Includes monthly *Supplements.* Provides detailed, individual surveys of 52 major industry groups. Each survey is revised on a semiannual basis. Also includes "Monthly Investment Review" (industry group investment analysis) and monthly "Trends & Projections" (economic analysis).

*Statistical Information on the Financial Services Industry.* American Bankers Association. • Annual. Members, $150.00; non-members, $275.00. Presents a wide variety of data relating to banking and financial services, including consumer economics, personal finance, credit, government loans, capital markets, and international banking.

*Survey of Current Business.* U. S. Government Printing Office. • Published by Bureau of Economic Analysis, U. S. Department of Commerce. Presents a wide variety of business and economic data.

# SAVINGS BANKS

*See also* SAVINGS AND LOAN ASSOCIATIONS

## BIBLIOGRAPHIES

*Financial Institutions.* U. S. Government Printing Office. • Annual. Free. Lists government publications. Formerly *Banks and Banking.* GPO Subject Bibliography No. 128.

## DIRECTORIES

*The Savings Directory.* Accuity Inc. • Semiannual. $570 Individuals. Covers: Nearly 2,000 savings institutions and their 13,000 branch offices. Database includes: Lists of top 500 companies ranked by assets, deposits, and loans; savings institution routing numbers in numeric sequence; and discontinued or changed institution names. Entries include: Institution name, address, phone, fax, type, identification of mutual or stock ownership, type of insurance, routing number, number of employees, names and titles of key personnel, branch office locations, financial and operational data.

*Savings Institutions--Top 200.* Savings & Commerce Bankers-America. • Annual. $5. Covers: 200 leading savings institutions as determined by their assets and savings. Entries include: Contact information.

## HANDBOOKS AND MANUALS

*U.S. Master Bank Tax Guide.* Wolters Kluwer Law & Business CCH. • Annual. $389.95 Individuals book-softcover. Summarizes and explains federal tax rules affecting financial institutions.

## INTERNET DATABASES

*BanxQuote Banking, Mortgage, and Finance Center.* BanxQuote, Inc. Phone: (914)722-1600; Fax: (914)722-6630; Email: info@banx.com • URL: http://www.banx.com • Daily. Web site quotes interest rates paid by banks around the country on various savings products, as well as rates paid by consumers for automobile loans, mortgages, credit cards, home equity loans, and personal loans. Also provided: stock quotes, indexes, stock options, futures trading data, economic indicators, and links to many other financial sites.

## OTHER SOURCES

*Savings Institutions: Mergers, Acquisitions, and Conversions.* ALM Media Properties LLC. • $560. Provides detailed information on the legal complexities of mergers and acquisitions involving savings institutions. (Law Journal Press).

## PERIODICALS AND NEWSLETTERS

*Operations Alert.* America's Community Bankers. • Description: Reviews recent regulatory and product developments that affect community bank operations.

*Recommended Bank and Thrift Report.* BauerFinancial Inc. • Quarterly. $585.00 per year. Newsletter provides information on "safe, financially sound" commercial banks, savings banks, and savings and loan institutions. Various factors are considered, including tangible capital ratios and total risk-based capital ratios. (Six regional editions are also available at $150.00 per edition per year.).

# SAVINGS BONDS

*See* GOVERNMENT BONDS

# SAW INDUSTRY

*See also* HARDWARE INDUSTRY; TOOL INDUSTRY; WOODWORKING INDUSTRIES

## DIRECTORIES

*ProSales Buyer's Guide.* DoveTale Publishers. • Annual. Price on application. A directory of equipment for professional builders.

*Tools of the Trade Annual Buyers Guide.* DoveTale Publishers. • Annual. Price on application. A directory of tools for the construction industry.

## PERIODICALS AND NEWSLETTERS

*Hardware Age.* Reed Elsevier Group plc Reed Business Information. • Monthly. $75.00 per year.

*Power Equipment Trade.* Hatton-Brown Publishers Inc. • 10/year. Formerly *Chain Saw Age and Power Equipment Trade.*

# SAWMILLS

*See* LUMBER INDUSTRY

# SCHOLARSHIPS AND STUDENT AID

*See also* STUDY ABROAD

## ABSTRACTS AND INDEXES

*Readers' Guide to Periodical Literature.* EBSCO Publishing Inc. • Provides indexing for over 400 periodicals dating back to 1983.

## CD-ROM DATABASES

*Readers' Guide to Periodical Literature.* EBSCO Publishing Inc. • Provides indexing for over 400 periodicals dating back to 1983.

## DIRECTORIES

*Government Assistance Almanac: The Guide to Federal, Domestic, Financial and Other Programs Covering Grants, Loans, Insurance, Personal Payments and Benefits.* Omnigraphics Inc. • Annual. $275 print. Gives users updated information on all available federal domestic assistance programs. These programs represent nearly $2 trillion worth of federal assistance earmarked for distribution to consumers, children, parents, veterans, senior citizens, students, businesses, civic groups, state and local agencies, and others.

*Scholarships, Fellowships & Loans.* Cengage Learning Inc. • $369 Individuals. 2013. $353.00. 30th edition. Describes more than 7,300 scholarships, fellowships, loans, and other educational funding sources available to U.S. and Canadian undergraduate and graduate students. eBook also available.

## E-BOOKS

*The College Blue Book.* Cengage Learning Inc. • Annual. $572 Individuals. Published by Macmillan Reference USA. Provides detailed information on programs, degrees, and financial aid sources in the U.S. and Canada.

## HANDBOOKS AND MANUALS

*The Student Guide: Financial Aid.* U.S. Dept. of Education - Federal Student Aid Information Center. • Annual. Describes financial aid for college and vocational school students. Available online.

## ONLINE DATABASES

*ERIC.* U.S. Department of Education Institute of Education Sciences Educational Resources Information Center. • Funded by the U.S. Department of Education, Institute of Education Sciences (formerly Office of Educational Research and Improvement). Provides access to more than one million online records covering education-related journal and report literature, 1966 to date. Updating is monthly. Inquire as to online cost and availability.

## PERIODICALS AND NEWSLETTERS

*Student Aid News: The Independent Biweekly News Service on Student Financial Assistance Programs.* Wolters Kluwer Law and Business. • Biweekly. $383.00 per year. Newsletter on federal student aid programs.

## TRADE/PROFESSIONAL ASSOCIATIONS

Coalition of Higher Education Assistance Organizations. 1101 Vermont Ave. NW, Ste. 400, Washington, DC 20005-3586. Phone: (202)289-3910 or (202)289-3903; Fax: (202)371-0197 • URL: http://www.coheao.com • Purpose is to support student loan programs and monitor regulations.

National Association of Student Financial Aid Administrators. 1101 Connecticut Ave. NW, Ste. 1100, Washington, DC 20036-4312. Phone: (202)785-0453; Fax: (202)785-1487; Email: web@nasfaa.org • URL: http://www.nasfaa.org • Serves as a national forum for matters related to student aid.

National Council of Higher Education Resources. 1100 Connecticut Ave. NW, Ste. 1200, Washington, DC 20036-4110. Phone: (202)822-2106; Fax: (202)822-2143; Email: info@ncher.us • URL: http://www.ncher.us • Attempts to coordinate federal, state, and private functions in the student loan program.

# SCHOOL COMPUTERS

*See* COMPUTERS IN EDUCATION

# SCHOOL JOURNALISM

*See* COLLEGE AND SCHOOL NEWSPAPERS

# SCHOOLS

*See also* BUSINESS EDUCATION; COLLEGES AND UNIVERSITIES; PRIVATE SCHOOLS; STUDY ABROAD; VOCATIONAL EDUCATION

## ABSTRACTS AND INDEXES

*Education Index.* H.W. Wilson Co. • 10 times a year. Quarterly and annual cumulations. Price varies.

*Educational Administration Abstracts.* Pine Forge Press. • Quarterly. $722 Institutions.

## ALMANACS AND YEARBOOKS

*Educational Media and Technology Yearbook.* Libraries Unlimited. • Annual. $80 print.

*National Society for the Study of Education Yearbook.* National Society for the Study of Education. The University of Chicago Press. • Annual. Membership. Two volumes per year.

## BIOGRAPHICAL SOURCES

*Who's Who in American Education.* Marquis Who's Who L.L.C. • Biennial. $159.95. Contains over 27,000 concise biographies of teachers, administrators, and other individuals involved in all levels of American education.

## CD-ROM DATABASES

*Education Index Retrospective: 1929-1983.* EBSCO Publishing Inc. • Provides indexing of education-related literature from 1983 to date.

*ERIC SilverPlatter.* U.S. Department of Education Institute of Education Sciences Education Resources Information Center. • Opinion papers, evaluations, speeches.

*Newspaper Abstracts Ondisc.* ProQuest L.L.C. • Monthly. $2,950.00 per year (covers 1989 to date; archival discs are available for 1985-88). Provides cover-to-cover CD-ROM indexing and abstracting of 19 major newspapers, including the *New York Times, Wall Street Journal, Washington Post, Chicago Tribune,* and *Los Angeles Times.*

## DIRECTORIES

*Business Schools Directory.* InfoGroup Inc. • Annual. Number of listings: 5,329. Entries include: Name, address, phone, size of advertisement, name of owner or manager, number of employees, year first in "Yellow Pages." Compiled from telephone company "Yellow Pages," nationwide.

*Educational Dealer--Buyers' Guide Issue.* Fahy-Williams Publishing Inc. • Annual. Publication includes: List of approximately 2,000 suppliers of educational materials and equipment. Entries include: Company name, address, phone, products or services.

*Educators Resource Directory.* Grey House Publishing. • Annual. $145 Individuals softcover. Covers: Publishing opportunities, state by state information on enrollment, funding and grant resources, associations and conferences, teaching jobs abroad all geared toward elementary and secondary school professionals. Also covers online databases, textbook publishers, school suppliers, plus state and federal agencies. Entries include: Contact name, address, phone, fax, description, publications. A unique compilation of over 6,500 educational resources and over 130 tables and charts of education statistics and rankings.

*National Association of Schools of Music--Directory.* National Association of Schools of Music. • Annual. $20 Individuals. Covers: Approximately 630 college and university departments of music and music conservatories accredited by the association. Entries include: School name, address, type of membership, description of music program, name of chief administrator, phone, degree or other study programs offered in music.

*School Business Affairs--Association of School Business Officials Official Membership Directory Issue.* Association of School Business Officials International..

## E-BOOKS

*Social Trends & Indicators USA.* Monique D. Magee, editor. Cengage Learning Inc. • Includes data on labor, economics, the health care industry, crime, leisure, population, education, social security, and many other topics. Sources include various government agencies and major publications. Inquire for pricing.

*21st Century Management: A Reference Handbook.* Cengage Learning Inc. • 2008. eBook. Published by Sage Publications. Highlights the topics, issues, questions and debates that any student obtaining a degree in the field of management must master to be effective in today's business world.

## INTERNET DATABASES

*FedWorld: A Program of the United States Department of Commerce.* National Technical Information Service. Phone: 800-553-NTIS or (703)605-6000; Fax: (703)605-6900; Email: webmaster@fedworld.gov • URL: http://www.fedworld.gov • Web site offers "a comprehensive central access point for searching, locating, ordering, and acquiring government and business information." Emphasis is on searching the Web pages, databases, and government reports of a wide variety of federal agencies. Fees: Free.

*FirstGov: Your First Click to the U. S. Government.* General Services Administration. Phone: 800-333-4636 or (202)501-0705; Email: public.affairs@gsa.gov • URL: http://www.gsa.gov • Free Web site provides extensive links to federal agencies covering a wide variety of topics, such as agriculture, business, consumer safety, education, the environment, government jobs, grants, health, social security, statistics sources, taxes, technology, travel, and world affairs. Also provides links to federal forms, including IRS tax forms. Searching is offered, both keyword and advanced.

*U.S. Census Bureau: The Official Statistics.* U. S. Bureau of the Census. Phone: (301)763-4636 or (301)763-4100; Fax: (301)763-4794; Email: webmaster@census.gov • URL: http://www.census.gov/prod/www/abs/mfg-prof.html • Web site is "Your Source for Social, Demographic, and Economic Information." Contains "Current U. S. Population Count," "Current Economic Indicators," and a wide variety of data under "Other Official Statistics." Keyword searching is provided. Fees: Free.

## ONLINE DATABASES

*Education Index Online.* H.W. Wilson Co. • Indexes a wide variety of periodicals related to schools, colleges, and education, 1984 to date. Monthly updates. Inquire as to online cost and availability.

*ERIC.* U.S. Department of Education Institute of Education Sciences Educational Resources Information Center. • Funded by the U.S. Department of Education, Institute of Education Sciences (formerly Office of Educational Research and Improvement). Provides access to more than one million online records covering education-related journal and report literature, 1966 to date. Updating is monthly. Inquire as to online cost and availability.

## PERIODICALS AND NEWSLETTERS

*Chicago Business.* Chicago Business. • Semimonthly. $15 Individuals. Collegiate business school publication.

*Education Week: American Education's Newspaper of Record.* Editorial Projects in Education. • $39 Individuals 20 printed and online access. 43 times a year.

*Educational Administration Quarterly.* University Council for Educational Administratiotion. Pine Forge Press. • 5/year. $956 Institutions Print & E-access. Publishes prominent empirical and conceptual articles focused on timely and critical leadership and policy issues of educational organizations.

*Educational Marketer: The Educational Publishing Industry's Voice of Authority Since 1968.* SIMBA Information Inc. • Biweekly. $695 Individuals On-line download. Edited for suppliers of educational materials to schools and colleges at all levels. Covers print and electronic publishing, software, audiovisual items, and multimedia. Includes corporate news and educational statistics.

*School Business Affairs.* Association of School Business Officials. ASBO International. • Monthly. Published 11 times per year. Available to members.

*School Planning & Management.* Peter Li Inc. • Monthly. Contains articles about facility planning, safety and security, maintenance and operations, business, technology and finance issues.

*Taxes-Property: State Capitals.* Wakeman/Walworth Inc. • 50 times a year. $345.00 per year; print and online edition, $490.00. Formerly *From the State Capitals: Taxes-Property.*

## RESEARCH CENTERS AND INSTITUTES

Australian National University - Research School of Social Sciences., Canberra, ACT 0200, Australia. Phone: 61 2 252257; Fax: 61 2 250502; Email: adam.graycar@anu.edu.au • URL: http://rsss.anu.edu.au • Demography and sociology, economics,

law, history, philosophy, political science, sociology, social and political theory, research evaluation and policy, immigration and multicultural studies.

University of California, Los Angeles - Institute for the Study of Educational Entrepreneurship. Moore Hall, Box 951521, Los Angeles, CA 90095. Phone: (310)825-2297; Email: isee@gseis.ucla.edu • URL: http://isee.gseis.ucla.edu • Relationships between private for-profit, private not-for-profit, and public organizations and their potential to advance public education reform.

## STATISTICS SOURCES

*School Enrollment, Social and Economic Characteristics of Students.* U. S. Government Printing Office. • Annual. $2.50. Issued by the U. S. Bureau of the Census. Presents detailed tabulations of data on school enrollment of the civilian noninstitutional population three years old and over. Covers nursery school, kindergarten, elementary school, high school, college, and graduate school. Information is provided on age, race, sex, family income, marital status, employment, and other characteristics.

*Statistical Abstract of the United States.* U. S. Government Printing Office. • Annual. $44.00. Issued by the U. S. Bureau of the Census.

## TRADE/PROFESSIONAL ASSOCIATIONS

Association of School Business Officials International. 11401 N Shore Dr., Reston, VA 20190-4232. Phone: 866-682-2729 or (703)478-0405; Fax: (703)708-7060 or (703)478-0205; Email: asboreq@asbointl.org • URL: http://asbointl.org • School business managers; assistant superintendents in charge of business; supervisors of accounting; directors of transportation, maintenance, food service, data processing, and operations; office managers; school business officials, school board members, and others interested in school business management. Business associates are vendors providing products and/or services to schools. Promotes improvement and advancement of school business management. Provides a forum for the exchange of information and ideas among professionals; keeps legislative bodies, governmental agencies, and members of the educational community informed of key issues relating to the administration of educational facilities. Maintains professional registration program, insurance and continuing education program, certificate of excellence program in financial reporting and meritorious budget awards program. Maintains 17 committees.

National Education Association. 1201 16th St. NW, Washington, DC 20036-3290. Phone: 800-229-4200 or (202)822-7200; Fax: (202)822-7974; Email: highered@nea.org • URL: http://www.nea.org • Professional organization and union of elementary and secondary school teachers, college and university professors, administrators, principals, counselors, and others concerned with education.

National School Boards Association. 1680 Duke St., Alexandria, VA 22314-3493. Phone: (703)838-6722 or (703)838-6731; Fax: (703)683-7590; Email: info@nsba.org • URL: http://www.nsba.org • Federation of state school boards associations, the Board of Education of the District of Columbia and the Virgin Islands Board of Education. Advocates equity and quality education for primary and secondary public school children through legal counsel, research studies, legislative advocacy programs, and services for members, conferences, and magazines. Provides information on topics affecting K-12 public education and school policy. Maintains library and specialized clearinghouses.

National School Supply and Equipment Association. 8380 Colesville Rd., Ste. 250, Silver Spring, MD 20910. Phone: 800-395-5550 or (301)495-0240; Fax: (301)495-3330; Email: customerservice@nssea.org • URL: http://www.nssea.org • Absorbed

Education Industries Association. Formerly National School Service Institute.

# SCHOOLS, PRIVATE

*See* PRIVATE SCHOOLS

# SCIENTIFIC APPARATUS AND INSTRUMENT INDUSTRIES

*See also* LABORATORIES

## ABSTRACTS AND INDEXES

*Applied Science and Technology Index.* EBSCO Publishing Inc. • 11/year. Indexes a wide variety of English language technical, industrial, and engineering periodicals.

*Key Abstracts: Electronic Instrumentation.* The Insititution of Engineering and Technology. • Monthly. $1,138. Provides international coverage of journal and proceedings literature. Published in England by the Institution of Electrical Engineers (IEE).

*Science Citation Index.* Thomson Reuters Intellectual Property and Science. • Weekly. Includes *Source Index, Citation Index, Permuterm Subject Index,* and *Corporate Index.* Provides researchers, administrators, faculty, and students with quick, powerful access to the bibliographic and citation information they need to find research data, analyze trends, journals and researchers, and share their findings.

## BIOGRAPHICAL SOURCES

*Who's Who in Science and Engineering.* Marquis Who's Who L.L.C. • Biennial. $249.00. Provides concise biographical information on 33,545 prominent engineers and scientists. International coverage, with geographical and professional indexes.

## CD-ROM DATABASES

*Science Citation Index.* Thomson Reuters Intellectual Property and Science. • Weekly. Includes *Source Index, Citation Index, Permuterm Subject Index,* and *Corporate Index.* Provides researchers, administrators, faculty, and students with quick, powerful access to the bibliographic and citation information they need to find research data, analyze trends, journals and researchers, and share their findings.

## DIRECTORIES

*Australian Scientific and Laboratory Exports.* Peter Isaacson Publications. • Annual. $80. Covers: Scientific and medical products and services available for export from Australia.

*Directory of African Importers of Laboratory & Scientific Instruments & Supplies.* EXIM Infotek Private Ltd. • Covers: 250 African importers of binoculars, microscopes, telescopes, laboratory and scientific glass, laboratory and scientific instruments, laboratory chemicals, laboratory equipment, laboratory glassware, laboratory reagents, magnifiers, scientific equipment, and testing equipment. Entries include: Company name, postal address, telephone, fax, e-mail, website, contact person, designation, and product details.

*Directory of Asian Importers of Biological Products.* EXIM Infotek Private Ltd. • $250 Individuals. Covers: 20 Asian importers of biological products and molecular biology. Entries include: Company name, postal address, telephone, fax, e-mail, website, contact person, designation, and product details.

*Directory of Asian Importers of Laboratory & Scientific Instruments and Supplies.* EXIM Infotek Private Ltd. • $1,400 Individuals. Covers: 620 Asian importers of analysis equipment, analytical instruments, anatomical models, binoculars, microscopes, telescopes, biotechnology instruments, borosilicate glass tubing, educational scientific equipment, electrical test equipment, glass tubular vial and ampoules, gyrocompass, laboratory equipment, laboratory and scientific glass, laboratory supplies, laboratory glassware, laboratory instruments, laboratory reagents, non-contact infrared thermometers, non-destructive testing equipment, radiology equipment, scientific instruments, testing and measuring equipment, testing instruments, testing machines, thermometers, and barometers. Entries include: Company name, postal address, telephone, fax, e-mail, website, contact person, designation, and product details.

*Directory of Belgium Importers of Laboratory & Scientific Instruments & Supplies.* EXIM Infotek Private Ltd. • $250 Individuals. Covers: 50 Belgium importers of binoculars, microscopes, telescopes, scientific and laboratory instrument, and testing equipment. Entries include: Company name, postal address, telephone, fax, e-mail, website, contact person, designation, and product details.

*Directory of British Importers of Laboratory & Scientific Instruments & Supplies.* EXIM Infotek Private Ltd. • $300 Individuals. Covers: 120 British importers of binoculars, microscopes, telescopes, laboratory and scientific glass, scientific and laboratory instrument, and testing equipment. Entries include: Company name, postal address, telephone, fax, e-mail, website, contact person, designation, and product details.

*Directory of European Importers of Laboratory & Scientific Instruments & Supplies.* EXIM Infotek Private Ltd. • Covers: 1,300 European importers of binoculars, microscopes, telescopes, evaporators, laboratory and scientific glass, laboratory diagnostic equipment and supplies, laboratory instruments, reagents for laboratories, scientific instrument, and testing equipment. Entries include: Company name, postal address, telephone, fax, e-mail, website, contact person, designation, and product details.

*Directory of French Importers of Laboratory & Scientific Instruments & Supplies.* EXIM Infotek Private Ltd. • Covers: 110 French importers of binoculars, microscopes, binoculars, telescopes, scientific and laboratory instruments, and testing equipment. Entries include: Company name, postal address, telephone, fax, e-mail, website, contact person, designation, and product details.

*Directory of German Importers of Laboratory & Scientific Instruments & Supplies.* EXIM Infotek Private Ltd. • $250 Individuals. Covers: 50 German importers of binoculars, microscopes, telescopes, scientific and laboratory instrument, and testing equipment. Entries include: Company name, postal address, telephone, fax, e-mail, website, contact person, designation, and product details.

*Directory of Indian Importers of Laboratory & Scientific Instruments & Supplies.* EXIM Infotek Private Ltd. • $300 Individuals. Covers: 120 Indian importers of binoculars, microscope, telescopes, borosilicate glass tubing, educational scientific equipment, laboratory equipment, laboratory glassware, laboratory instruments, scientific instruments, testing and measuring equipment, testing instruments, thermometers, and barometers. Entries include: Company name, postal address, telephone, fax, e-mail, website, contact person, designation, and product details.

*Directory of Japanese Importers of Laboratory & Scientific Instruments & Supplies.* EXIM Infotek Private Ltd. • $450 Individuals. Covers: 200 Japanese importers of analytical instruments, binoculars, microscopes, telescopes, laboratory and scientific glass, laboratory instruments, laboratory reagents, scientific and laboratory equipment, scientific instruments, testing and measuring equip-

ment, testing instruments, testing machines, thermometers, and barometers. Entries include: Company name, postal address, telephone, fax, e-mail, website, contact person, designation, and product details.

*Directory of Middle East Importers of Laboratory & Scientific Instruments & Supplies.* EXIM Infotek Private Ltd. • Covers: 510 Middle East importers of analysis equipment, binoculars, microscopes, telescopes, laboratory and scientific glass ware, laboratory and scientific instruments, laboratory equipment, material testing equipment, microscopes, scientific and laboratory instruments, scientific equipment, scientific instruments, soil testing equipment, and testing equipment. Entries include: Company name, postal address, telephone, fax, e-mail, website, contact person, designation, and product details.

*Directory of North American Importers of Laboratory & Scientific Instruments and Supplies.* EXIM Infotek Private Ltd. • Covers: 150 North American importers of binoculars, microscope, telescopes, laboratory equipment, laboratory and scientific glass, laboratory apparatus, magnifiers, microscope accessories, microscopes, scientific instruments, soil testing equipment, and testing equipment. Entries include: Company name, postal address, telephone, fax, e-mail, website, contact person, designation, and product details.

*Directory of South American Importers of Laboratory & Scientific Instruments & Supplies.* EXIM Infotek Private Ltd. • Covers: 480 South American importers of binoculars, microscopes, telescopes, laboratory and scientific instruments, laboratory articles and equipment, laboratory glassware, laboratory products, and testing equipment. Entries include: Company name, postal address, telephone, fax, e-mail, website, contact person, designation, and product details.

*ISA Directory of Automation.* International Society of Automation. • Over 2,400 manufacturers of control and instrumentation equipment, over 1,000 manufacturers' representatives, and several hundred service companies; coverage includes Canada.

## E-BOOKS

*SAGE Sourcebook of Modern Biomedical Devices Business Environments in a Global Market.* Cengage Learning Inc. • 2007. eBook. Published by Sage Publications. A source of information that presents and quantifies the commercial success of numerous types of biomedical devices available in the global market.

## ONLINE DATABASES

*Applied Science and Technology Index Online.* H.W. Wilson Co. • Provides online indexing of 500 major scientific, technical, industrial, and engineering periodicals. Time period is 1983 to date. Monthly updates. Inquire as to online cost and availability.

*INSPEC.* Institution of Electrical Engineers. • Provides online citations, with abstracts, to the world literature of electrical engineering, electronics, optoelectronics, telecommunications, industrial controls, instrumentation, computer technology, information technology, and physics. Coverage includes more than 4,000 technical and scientific journals from 1969 to date, with weekly updating. (INSPEC is Information Services in Physics, Electronics, and Computing.) Inquire as to online cost and availability.

## PERIODICALS AND NEWSLETTERS

*Control Engineering: Covering Control, Instrumentation and Automation Systems Worldwide.* Reed Elsevier Group plc Reed Business Information. • Monthly. $109.90 per year.

*Instrumentation and Automation News: Instruments, Controls, Manufacturing Software, Electronic and Mechanical Components.* Reed

Elsevier Group plc Reed Business Information. • Monthly. $61.90 per year.

*INTECH: The International Journal of Instrumentation and Control.* ISA Services Inc. • Monthly. $72.00 per year.

*ISA Transactions.* ISA-The Instrumentation, Systems and Automation Society. American Institute of Physics. • Quarterly. $310.00 per year.

*Measurements and Control.* Measurements and Data Corp. • Bimonthly. $24.00 per year. Supplement available: *M & C: Measurement and Control News.*

*Review of Scientific Instruments.* American Institute of Physics. • Monthly. $90 /year for members of AIP and its affiliates. Includes information on scientific instruments, apparatus, and techniques.

*Today's Chemist at Work.* American Chemical Society. • Monthly. Institutions, $200.00 per year; others, price on application. Provide pracrtical information for chemists on day-to-day operations. Product coverage includes chemicals, equipment, apparatus, instruments, and supplies.

## STATISTICS SOURCES

*Selected Instruments and Related Products.* U.S. Department of Commerce U.S. Census Bureau. • Annual. (Current Industrial Reports, MA-334B.).

*U.S. Industry and Trade Outlook.* U.S. Department of Commerce National Technical Information Service. • Annual. Produced by the International Trade Administration, U.S. Department of Commerce, in a "public-private" partnership with DRI/ McGraw-Hill and Standard & Poor's. Provides basic data, outlook for the current year, and "Long-Term Prospects" (five-year projections) for a wide variety of products and services. Includes high technology industries. Formerly *U.S. Industrial Outlook.*

## TRADE/PROFESSIONAL ASSOCIATIONS

International Air Filtration Certifiers Association. c/o Michael Alleman, 129 S Gallatin, Liberty, MO 64068. Phone: 888-679-1904; Fax: (816)792-8105 • URL: http://www.iafca.com • Promotes professionalism in the biological safety cabinet industry. Establishes and maintains certification program for biological safety cabinet certifiers. Provides information and guidance to legislative and regulatory agencies with regard to laws and standards affecting the industry.

# SCIENTIFIC LABORATORIES

*See* LABORATORIES

# SCIENTIFIC RESEARCH

*See* RESEARCH AND DEVELOPMENT

# SCRAP

*See* WASTE PRODUCTS

# SCRAP METAL

*See* IRON AND STEEL SCRAP METAL INDUSTRY

# SCREW MACHINE INDUSTRY

*See* MACHINE TOOL INDUSTRY

# SEAFOOD INDUSTRY

*See also* FISH INDUSTRY; OYSTER INDUSTRY; SHELLFISH INDUSTRY

---

**For publishers' addresses, refer to SOURCES CITED section at the back of the book.**

## ABSTRACTS AND INDEXES

*Food Science and Technology Abstracts.* Ovid Technologies Inc. • Monthly. $1,780.00 per year. Provides worldwide coverage of the literature of food technology and food production.

*Foods Adlibra: Key to the World's Food Literature.* General Mills, Inc. Foods Adlibra Publications. • Semimonthly. $240.00 per year. Provides journal citations and abstracts to the literature of food technology and packaging.

*NTIS Alerts: Agriculture & Food.* U.S. Department of Commerce National Technical Information Service. • Biweekly. $130 per year. Covers agricultural economics, horticulture, fisheries, veterinary medicine, food technology, and related subjects.

*Oceanic Abstracts.* CSA. • Monthly. $1,645.00 per year. Includes print and online editions. Covers oceanography, marine biology, ocean shipping, and a wide range of other marine-related subject areas.

## DIRECTORIES

*Directory of Chinese Manufacturers & Exporters of Seafood & Fish.* EXIM Infotek Private Ltd. • $10 Individuals. Covers: 50 Chinese manufacturers and exporters of Alaska pollack fillets, asparagus-frozen, canned asparagus, fish, fish fillets, frozen cooked crawfish, frozen fillets, frozen fish, frozen octopus, frozen seafood products, marine products, scallops, seafood, seaweed, shrimps and prawns. Entries include: Company name, postal address, city, country, phone, fax, e-mail and websites, contact person, designation, and product details.

*Directory of South Korean Manufacturers & Exporters of Sea Food & Fish.* EXIM Infotek Private Ltd. • $400 Individuals. Covers: 160 South Korean manufacturers and exporters of crustaceans, fish and shelfish by-products, fish roes, fish (canned/bottled), fish, processed fish, saltwater fish, frozen sea food products, marine algae and plankton, mollusks, shelfish and seaweed (canned/bottled), shrimps and prawns. Entries include: Company name, postal address, telephone, fax, e-mail, website, contact person, designation, and product details.

*Major Food and Drink Companies of the World.* Cengage Learning Inc. • 12th edition. eBook. Published by Graham & Whiteside. Contains profiles and trade names for more than 9,200 important food and beverage companies in various countries. In addition to foods, includes both alcoholic and nonalcoholic drink products.

## ONLINE DATABASES

*ASFA Aquaculture Abstracts (Online).* Cambridge Scientific Abstracts L.P. • Indexing and abstracting of the literature of marine life, 1984 to present. Inquire as to online cost and availability.

*Food Science and Technology Abstracts (online).* IFIS North American Desk. • Produced by International Food Information Service. Provides about 500,000 online citations, with abstracts, to the international literature of food science, technology, commodities, engineering, and processing. Approximately 2,000 periodicals are covered. Time period is 1969 to date, with monthly updates. Inquire as to online cost and availability.

## PERIODICALS AND NEWSLETTERS

*Fishermen's News.* Fishermen's News, Inc. • Monthly. $15.00 per year.

*National Fisherman.* Diversified Business Communications Inc. • Monthly. $14.95 Individuals 1 year. American fishing industry and boat building trade.

*Seafood Business.* Diversified Business Communications Inc. • $57 U.S. Edited for a wide range of seafood buyers, including distributors, restaurants, supermarkets, and institutions. Special issues feature information on specific products, such as salmon or lobster.

## STATISTICS SOURCES

*U.S. Industry and Trade Outlook.* U.S. Department of Commerce National Technical Information Service. • Annual. Produced by the International Trade Administration, U.S. Department of Commerce, in a "public-private" partnership with DRI/McGraw-Hill and Standard & Poor's. Provides basic data, outlook for the current year, and "Long-Term Prospects" (five-year projections) for a wide variety of products and services. Includes high technology industries. Formerly *U.S. Industrial Outlook.*

## TRADE/PROFESSIONAL ASSOCIATIONS

Southeastern Fisheries Association. 1118-B Thomasville Rd., Tallahassee, FL 32303. Phone: (850)224-0612; Fax: (850)222-3663; Email: info@sfaonline.org • URL: http://www.sfaonline.org/ • Producers, distributors and suppliers of seafood in the South Atlantic and Gulf of Mexico areas. Disseminates information on legislation, both proposed and implemented, that affects fishermen in that area. Promotes and represents commercial fishermen's interests in legislative, industrial and environmental matters. Provides HAACP training onsite.

Sustainable Fishery Advocates. 303 Potrero St., Ste. 201, Santa Cruz, CA 95060. Phone: (831)427-1707; Fax: (309)213-4688; Email: t.ish@sustainablefishery.org • URL: http://www.sustainablefishery.org • Aims to improve the sustainability and financial performance of seafood retailers, distributors and producers. Provides innovative, market-based tools to promote the health and recovery of ocean ecosystems. Supports sustainability in the seafood industry through environmentally responsible business practices.

# SEALANTS

*See* ADHESIVES

# SEAPORTS

*See* PORTS

# SECRETARIAL PRACTICE

*See* OFFICE PRACTICE

# SECRETARIES

*See* OFFICE PRACTICE

# SECURITIES

*See also* BONDS; CLOSED-END FUNDS; CONVERTIBLE SECURITIES; DERIVATIVE SECURITIES; DIVIDENDS; FINANCIAL ANALYSIS; GOVERNMENT BONDS; INVESTMENT COMPANIES; INVESTMENTS; MUNICIPAL BONDS; OBSOLETE SECURITIES; OVER-THE-COUNTER SECURITIES INDUSTRY; REAL ESTATE INVESTMENT TRUSTS; SECURITIES LAW AND REGULATION

## BIOGRAPHICAL SOURCES

*Who's Who in the Securities Industry.* Economist Publishing Co. • Annual. $15.00. Lists about 1,000 investment bankers.

## CD-ROM DATABASES

*OECD Statistical Compendium.* Organization for Economic Cooperation and Development. • Semiannual. $1,905.00 per year for 1 to 10 users. CD-ROM contains more than 730,000 monthly, quarterly, and annual time series for OECD

countries, 1960 to date. Includes fully searchable data on agriculture, food, economic indicators, national accounts, employment, energy, finance, industry, technology, and foreign trade. Results can be displayed in various forms.

## DIRECTORIES

*HedgeWorld Annual Compendium: The Hedge Fund Industry's Definitive Reference Guide.* HedgeWorld. • Annual. $499.00. Contains profiles of 500 domestic and offshore hedge funds with more than $50 million in assets under management. Includes articles on "The Basics of Investing in Hedge Funds," "Beyond the Basics," and other information.

*HedgeWorld Service Provider League Tables & Analyses.* HedgeWorld. • Annual. $595.00. Provides quantitative and qualitative information on firms providing services to hedge funds: accountants/auditors, administrators, custodians, legal counsel, and prime brokers. Detailed categories cover banks, clearing services, consultants, derivatives business, investment companies, wealth management services, etc.

*Mergent International Manual and News Reports.* Mergent Inc. • Financial and other information about 13,000 companies in 100 countries. Formerly *Moody's International Manual and News Reports.*

*Morningstar American Depository Receipts.* Morningstar Inc. • Biweekly. Looseleaf. Provides detailed profiles of 700 foreign companies having shares traded in the U. S. through American Depositary Receipts (ADRs).

*Securities Industry Yearbook.* Securities Industry and Financial Markets Association. • Annual. $110 Members. Covers: over 600 member securities firms, with about 480 of them covered in detail. Entries include: For firms covered in detail--Company name, name of parent company, address, phone, capital position and rank, number of offices and type, number of employees, area of specialization, names and titles of key personnel, number of registered representatives, departments with name of department head, dollar volume of underwriting and syndication by type, other financial data. For other firms--Company name, address, name of delegated liaison to the association.

## HANDBOOKS AND MANUALS

*Mergent OTC Unlisted Manual.* Mergent. • Annual, $1,995.00 per year. Includes supplement *Moody's OTC Unlisted News Report.*

*Mergent's Manuals.* Mergent Inc. • Annual. Looseleaf supplements. Prices on application.

*Securities: Public and Private Offerings, 2d.* William W. Prifti. Thomson West. • Semiannual. $1,383 Individuals Binder/Looseleaf - Full Set. How to issue securities. (Securities Law Series).

## INTERNET DATABASES

*Business 2.0 Web Guide to the Best Business Links.* Business 2.0 Media Inc. Phone: (415)293-4800; Email: support@business2.com • URL: http://www.business2.com/webguide • Web site presents an extensive, searchable directory of links to "the best, most informative, and authoritative web pages." Twenty main categories cover business, finance, career, company information, people, and technology topics, with thousands of subtopics, all linking to Web sites recommended by experienced business researchers. Fees: Free.

*Business Week Online.* McGraw-Hill. Phone: (212)512-2511; Fax: (684)842-6101 • URL: http://www.businessweek.com • Web site provides complete contents of current issue of *Business Week* plus "BW Daily" with additonal business news, financial market quotes, and corporate information from Standard & Poor's. Includes various features, such as "Banking Center" with mortgage and interest data, and "Interactive Computer Buying Guide." The "Business Week Archive" is fully searchable back to 1996.

*Factiva.* Dow Jones Reuters Business Interactive, LLC. Phone: 800-369-7466 or (609)452-1511; Fax: (609)520-5770; Email: solutions@factiva.com • URL: http://www.factiva.com • Fee-based Web site provides "global news and business information through Web sites and content integration solutions." Includes Dow Jones and Reuters newswires, The Wall Street Journal, and more than 7,000 other sources of current news, historical articles, market research reports, and investment analysis. Content includes 96 major U. S. newspapers, 900 non-English sources, trade publications, media transcripts, country profiles, news photos, etc.

*Fedstats.* Federal Interagency Council on Statistical Policy. Phone: (202)395-7254 • URL: http://www.fedstats.gov • Web site features an efficient search facility for full-text statistics produced by more than 100 federal agencies, including the Census Bureau, the Bureau of Economic Analysis, and the Bureau of Labor Statistics. Boolean searches can be made within one agency or for all agencies combined. Links are offered to international statistical bureaus, including the UN, IMF, OECD, UNESCO, Eurostat, and 20 individual countries. Fees: Free.

*FreeLunch.com.* Economy.com, Inc. Phone: (610)696-8700; Fax: (610)696-1678 • URL: http://www.freelunch.com • Web site provides free access to more than 200 million economic and financial data series, covering industry, demographics, labor markets, prices, retail sales, government spending, trade, interest rates, housing starts, the stock market, etc. Data is available in either chart or table form. Searching is offered. Free, but registration required. Economy.com, Inc. also offers fee-based economic analysis at *The Dismal Scientist* site (www.dismal.com).

*Nexis.com.* Lexis-Nexis Group. Phone: 800-227-4908 or (937)865-6800; Fax: (937)865-6909; Email: webmaster@prod.lexis-nexis.com • URL: http://www.nexis.com • Fee-based Web site offers searching of about 2.8 billion documents in some 30,000 news, business, and legal information sources. Features include a subject directory covering 1,200 topics in 34 categories and a Company Dossier containing information on more than 500,000 public and private companies. Boolean searching is offered.

*Wall Street Journal Interactive Edition.* Dow Jones & Co., Inc. 1211 Avenue of the Americas, New York, NY 10036. Phone: 800-369-5663; Email: service@dowjones.com • URL: http://new.dowjones.com • Fee-based Web site providing on-line searching of worldwide information from *The Wall Street Journal.* Includes "Company Snapshots," "The Journal's Greatest Hits," "Index to Market Data," "Journal Links," etc. Financial price quotes are available. Fees: $49.00 per year; $29.00 per year to print subscribers.

## ONLINE DATABASES

*Fitch Ratings Delivery Service.* Fitch. • Daily. Provides online delivery of Fitch financial ratings in three sectors: "Corporate Finance" (corporate bonds, insurance companies), "Structured Finance" (asset-backed securities), and "U.S. Public Finance" (municipal bonds).

*Value Line Convertible Data Base.* Value Line Inc. • Provides online data for about 600 convertible bonds and other convertible securities: price, yield, premium, issue size, liquidity, and maturity. Information is current, with weekly updates. Inquire as to online cost and availability.

*Vickers On-Line.* Vickers Stock Research Corp. • Provides detailed online information relating to insider trading and the securities holdings of institutional investors. Daily updates. Inquire as to online cost and availability.

## OTHER SOURCES

*Capital Changes Reports.* Wolters Kluwer Law & Business CCH. • Weekly. $1,395.00. Six looseleaf

volumes. Arranged alphabetically by company. This service presents a chronological capital history that includes reorganizations, mergers and consolidations. Recent actions are found in Volume One - "New Matters.".

*Fitch Insights.* Fitch Investors Service, Inc. • Biweekly. $1,040.00 per year. Includes bond rating actions and explanation of actions. Provides commentary and Fitch's view of the financial markets.

## PERIODICALS AND NEWSLETTERS

*Financial Analysts Journal.* CFA Institute. • Bimonthly. $50 Members print and online. Contains important topics related to the investment industry.

*Financial Markets, Institutions, and Instruments.* New York University, Salomon Center. Blackwell Publishing Inc. • Five times a year. Institutions, $338.00 per year. Includes online edition. Edited to "bridge the gap between the academic and professional finance communities." Special fifth issue each year provides surveys of developments in four areas: money and banking, derivative securities, corporate finance, and fixed-income securities.

*Financial Times (London).* The Financial Times, Inc. • Daily, except Sunday. $572.88 per year. An international business and financial newspaper, featuring news from London, Paris, Frankfurt, New York, and Tokyo. Includes worldwide stock and bond market data, commodity market data, and monetary/currency exchange information.

*Institutional Investor: The Premier of Professional Magazine Finance.* Institutional Investor Inc. Journals Group. • Monthly. $445.00 per year. Includes print and online editions. Edited for portfolio managers and other investment professionals. Special feature issues include "Country Credit Ratings," "Fixed Income Trading Ranking," "All-America Research Team," and "Global Banking Ranking.".

*International Bank Credit Analyst.* BCA Publications Ltd. • Monthly. $795.00 per year. "A monthly forecast and analysis of currency movements, interest rates, and stock market developments in the principal countries, based on a continuous appraisal of money and credit trends worldwide." Includes many charts and graphs providing international coverage of money, credit, and securities.

*Investment Dealers' Digest.* SourceMedia Inc. • Weekly. $750.00 per year. Covers financial news, trends, new products, people, private placements, new issues of securities, and other aspects of the investment business. Includes feature stories.

*Investor's Business Daily.* Investor's Business Daily, Inc. • Daily. $329 Individuals print. Business and financial newspaper.

*Mortgage-Backed Securities Letter.* Securities Data Publishing. • Description: Covers developments in the structured finance markets. Analyzes transactions and their collateral; follows litigation, refinancing opportunities, and market conditions.

*Operations Management.* Institutional Investor Inc. Journals Group. • Weekly. $2,105.00 per year. Includes print and online editions. Newsletter. Edited for managers of securities clearance and settlement at financial institutions. Covers new products, technology, legalities, management practices, and other topics related to securities processing.

*Private Equity Week.* Thomson Financial Inc. • Weekly. $1,495.00 per year. Provides detailed information on both prospective and completed private equity transactions. Includes news, data, commentary, trends, developments, and analysis.

*Private Placement Letter: The Weekly for Privately Placed Fixed-Income Securities.* SourceMedia Inc. • Weekly. $1,495 per year. Newsletter. Provides information on private financing of debt and convertible securities.

*SEC News Digest.* U.S. Securities and Exchange Commission, Public Reference Room. • Daily. Provides information on Commission actions.

*Securities Technology Monitor.* SourceMedia Inc. • Newsletter covers securities dealing and processing, including regulatory compliance, shareholder services, human resources, transaction clearing, and technology.

*Securities Week.* McGraw-Hill Financial Services Co. • Description: Acts as a trade publication for Wall Street executives, publishing news stories on pertinent events and developments within the industry including those related to legislative and regulatory activity, major stock exchanges, investment banking and retail firms, institutional trading, and new products. Recurring features include reports on research departments and a column titled Financial Futures/Commodities Report.

## PRICE SOURCES

*Bank and Quotation Record.* William B. Dana Co. • Monthly. $130.00 per year.

*National Bond Summary.* OTC Markets Group Inc. • Monthly, with semiannual cumulations. $504.00 per year. Includes price quotes for both active and inactive issues, with transfer agents, market makers (brokers), capital changes, name changes, and other corporate information. Formerly published by the National Quotation Bureau.

*National Stock Summary.* OTC Markets Group Inc. • Monthly, with semiannual cumulations. $576.00 per year. Includes price quotes for both active and inactive issues, with transfer agents, market makers (brokers), capital changes, name changes, and other corporate information. Pink Sheets LLC also provides daily and weekly stock price services. Formerly published by the National Quotation Bureau.

## RESEARCH CENTERS AND INSTITUTES

Princeton University - Bendheim Center for Finance. Department of Economics, 26 Prospect Ave., Princeton, NJ 08540-5296. Phone: (609)258-0770; Fax: (609)258-0771; Email: jessicab@princeton.edu • URL: http://www.princeton.edu/bcf • Research areas include securities markets, portfolio analysis, credit markets, and corporate finance. Emphasis is on quantitative and mathematical perspectives.

University of Chicago - Booth School of Business - Center for Research in Security Prices. 105 W Adams St., Ste. 1700, Chicago, IL 60603. Phone: (312)263-6400; Fax: (312)263-6430; Email: subscriptions@crsp.chicagobooth.edu • URL: http://www.crsp.com • Historical financial data.

## STATISTICS SOURCES

*Standard & Poor's Stock Reports: NASDAQ and Regional Exchanges.* Standard & Poor's Financial Services L.L.C. • Irregular. $1,100.00 per year. Looseleaf service. Provides two pages of financial details and other information for each corporation included.

*Standard & Poor's Stock Reports: New York Stock Exchange.* Standard & Poor's Financial Services L.L.C. • Irregular. $1,295.00 per year. Looseleaf service. Provides two pages of financial details and other information for each corporation with stock listed on the N. Y. Stock Exchange.

*Statistical Information on the Financial Services Industry.* American Bankers Association. • Annual. Members, $150.00; non-members, $275.00. Presents a wide variety of data relating to banking and financial services, including consumer economics, personal finance, credit, government loans, capital markets, and international banking.

*Stocks, Bonds, Bills, and Inflation Classic Yearbook.* Ibbotson Associates. • Annual. $185. Provides detailed data from 1926 to the present on inflation and the returns from various kinds of financial investments, such as small-cap stocks and long-term government bonds.

*Survey of Current Business.* U. S. Government Printing Office. • Published by Bureau of Economic Analysis, U. S. Department of Commerce. Presents a wide variety of business and economic data.

*United States Securities and Exchange Commission Annual Report.* U. S. Government Printing Office. • Annual. The Commission maintains a Web site at www.sec.gov.

## TRADE/PROFESSIONAL ASSOCIATIONS

Association for Financial Markets in Europe. St. Michael's House, 1 George Yard, London EC3V 9DH, United Kingdom. Phone: 44 207 7439300; Fax: 44 207 7439301 • URL: http://www.afme.eu • Principal trade association in the UK for firms active in the investment banking and securities industry. Represents the interests of its members on all aspects of their business and promotes their views to the authorities in the UK, the European Union, and elsewhere.

CFA Institute. 560 Ray C. Hunt Dr., Charlottesville, VA 22903-2981. Phone: 800-247-8132 or (434)951-5499; Fax: (434)951-5262; Email: info@cfainstitute.org • URL: http://www.cfainstitute.org/pages/index.aspx • Formerly Association for Investment Management and Research.

Financial Industry Regulatory Authority. 1735 K St., Washington, DC 20006. Phone: (301)590-6500; Fax: (202)293-6260; Email: francine.lee@finra.org • URL: http://www.finra.org • Formerly National Association of Securities Dealers.

Japan Securities Dealers' Association. 1-5-8, Kayaba-cho Nihonbashi, Chuo, Tokyo 103-0025, Japan. Phone: 81 3 3667-8537; Email: international@wan.jsda.or.jp • URL: http://www.jsda.or.jp/en • Represents securities companies and registered financial institutions. Aims to protect investors by ensuring fair and smooth trading in securities and other transactions by members of the association. Promotes the implementation of policy measures for the revitalization of the Japanese securities markets in order to contribute to the growth and development of the Japanese economy.

# SECURITIES AND EXCHANGE COMMISSION

*See* SECURITIES LAW AND REGULATION

# SECURITIES, CONVERTIBLE

*See* CONVERTIBLE SECURITIES

# SECURITIES, DERIVATIVE

*See* DERIVATIVE SECURITIES

# SECURITIES LAW AND REGULATION

## ABSTRACTS AND INDEXES

*Current Law Index.* Cengage Learning Inc. • $1,332 Individuals. Monthly. $1269.00 per year. Produced in cooperation with the American Association of Law Libraries. Indexes more than 900 law journals, legal newspapers, and specialty publications from the U.S., Canada, U.K., Ireland, Australia, and New Zealand.

*Index to Legal Periodicals and Books.* H.W. Wilson Co. • Monthly. $490.00 per year. Quarterly and annual cumulations.

## ALMANACS AND YEARBOOKS

*American Law Yearbook.* Cengage Learning Inc. • $308 Individuals. Annual. $280.00. Serves as a

yearly supplement to *West's Encyclopedia of American Lawa.* Describes new legal developments in many subject areas.

*Emerging Trends in Securities Law.* Thomson West. • Annual. $536.90. Presents a detailed chronicle of events and analysis of evolving trends.(Securities Law Handbook Series).

*Securities, Commodities, and Federal Banking: 1999 in Review.* Wolters Kluwer Law & Business CCH. • Irregular. $57.00. Summarizes the year's significant legal and regulatory developments.

*Securities Law Review.* Thomson West. • $1,144 Individuals Print. Helps you stay on top of current critical thinking in securities regulation, as well as recent judicial, legislative and regulatory decisions.

## CD-ROM DATABASES

*Compact D/SEC.* Thomson Reuters Corp. • Monthly. Provides 200 financial data items for 12,000 U. S. publicly-held corporations filing reports with the Securities and Exchange Commission. Includes company profiles.

*Index to Legal Periodicals and Books.* EBSCO Publishing Inc. • Contains indexing of more than 1,400 English language legal periodicals from 1981 to date and 2,500 books.

## DIRECTORIES

*Bullseye Ownership Report.* CDA/Equity Intelligence. • Weekly. $800. Covers: over 1,300 institutions that have filed statements of company ownership with the Securities and Exchange Commission, including 13D and 13G five-percent beneficial ownership, 14D-1 tender offers, 13(f) institutional common stock holdings, 13(f) institutional convertible holdings, U.S. investment company holdings, foreign investment company holdings. Entries include: Company name, value held, change in shares, going back five consecutive quarters, money center, turnover, investment style, type of institute, investment discretion, voting authority, filing date and percent of shares outstanding.

## ENCYCLOPEDIAS AND DICTIONARIES

*West's Encyclopedia of American Law.* Cengage Learning Inc. • 2004. eBook. Second edition. Covers a wide variety of legal topics for the general reader. Inquire for pricing.

## HANDBOOKS AND MANUALS

*Money Manager's Compliance Guide.* Thompson Publishing Group Inc. • $739.00 per year. Two looseleaf volumes. Monthly updates and newletters. Edited for investment advisers and investment companies to help them be in compliance with governmental regulations, including SEC rules, restrictions based on the Employee Retirement Income Security Act (ERISA), and regulations issued by the Commodity Futures Trading Commission (CFTC).

*Responsibilities of Corporate Officers and Directors Under Federal Securities Law.* Wolters Kluwer Law & Business CCH. • Annual. $132 paperback. Includes discussions of indemnification, "D & O" insurance, corporate governance, and insider liability.

*SEC Accounting Rules.* Wolters Kluwer Law & Business CCH. • $448.00. Looseleaf service.

*SEC Financial Reporting: Annual Reports to Shareholders, Form 10-K, and Quarterly Financial Reporting.* Matthew Bender and Company Inc. • Annual. $254.00. Looseleaf service. Coverage of aspects of financial reporting with GAAP disclosure and Regulation S-X preparation Step-by-step procedures for preparing information for Form 10-K and annual shareholders reports.

*SEC Handbook: Rules and Forms for Financial Statements and Related Disclosures.* Wolters Kluwer Law & Business CCH. • Annual. $59.00.

Contains full text of rules and requirements set by the Securities and Exchange Commisssion for preparation of corporate financial statements.

*Securities Crimes.* Thomson West. • Annual. $798 full set. Analyzes the enfo of federal securities laws from the viewpoint of the defendant. Discusses Securities and Exchange Commission (SEC) investigations and federal sentencing guidelines. (Securities Law Series).

*Securities Law Handbook.* Thomson West. • $966 Individuals Book - softbound - Full set. Provides in-depth coverage of basic and specialized issues, including types of offerings, registration, reporting, potential violations, and enforcement.

*Securities: Public and Private Offerings, 2d.* William W. Prifti. Thomson West. • Semiannual. $1,383 Individuals Binder/Looseleaf - Full Set. How to issue securities. (Securities Law Series).

## INTERNET DATABASES

*Factiva.* Dow Jones Reuters Business Interactive, LLC. Phone: 800-369-7466 or (609)452-1511; Fax: (609)520-5770; Email: solutions@factiva.com • URL: http://www.factiva.com • Fee-based Web site provides "global news and business information through Web sites and content integration solutions." Includes Dow Jones and Reuters newswires, The Wall Street Journal, and more than 7,000 other sources of current news, historical articles, market research reports, and investment analysis. Content includes 96 major U. S. newspapers, 900 non-English sources, trade publications, media transcripts, country profiles, news photos, etc.

*Lexis.com Research System.* Lexis-Nexis Group. Phone: 800-227-4908 or (937)865-6800; Fax: (937)865-6909; Email: webmaster@prod.lexis-nexis.com • URL: http://www.nexis.com • Fee-based Web site offers extensive searching of a wide variety of legal sources. Additional features include Daily Opinion Service, lexis.com Bookstore, Career Center, CLE Center, Law Schools, and Practice Pages ("Pages specific to areas of specialty").

*Nexis.com.* Lexis-Nexis Group. Phone: 800-227-4908 or (937)865-6800; Fax: (937)865-6909; Email: webmaster@prod.lexis-nexis.com • URL: http://www.nexis.com • Fee-based Web site offers searching of about 2.8 billion documents in some 30,000 news, business, and legal information sources. Features include a subject directory covering 1,200 topics in 34 categories and a Company Dossier containing information on more than 500,000 public and private companies. Boolean searching is offered.

*Rutgers Accounting Web.* Rutgers University Accounting Research Center. Phone: (973)353-5172; Fax: (973)353-1283 • URL: http://www.rutgers.edu/accounting • RAW Web site provides extensive links to sources of national and international accounting information, such as the Big Six accounting firms, the Financial Accounting Standards Board (FASB), SEC filings (EDGAR), journals, publishers, software, the International Accounting Network, and "Internet's largest list of accounting firms in USA." Searching is offered. Fees: Free.

*U.S. Securities and Exchange Commission.* 100 F St. NE, Washington, DC 20549. Phone: 800-732-0330 or (202)942-8080; Fax: (202)942-9634; Email: webmaster@sec.gov • URL: http://www.sec.gov • SEC Web site offers free access through EDGAR to text of official corporate filings, such as annual reports (10-K), quarterly reports (10-Q), and proxies. (EDGAR is "Electronic Data Gathering, Analysis, and Retrieval System.") An example is given of how to obtain executive compensation data from proxies. Text of the daily *SEC News Digest* is offered, as are links to other government sites, non-government market regulators, and U. S. stock exchanges. Search facilities are extensive. Fees: Free.

## ONLINE DATABASES

*EdgarPlus: SEC Basic Filings.* Thomson Reuters Markets. • Online service provides full text of about 60,000 documents that have been filed with the U.S. Securities and Exchange Commission, 1987 to date, with daily updates. Filings include 6-K, 8-K, 10-K, 10-C, 10-Q, 20-F, and proxy statements. Inquire as to online cost and availability.

## OTHER SOURCES

*Blue Sky Law Reports.* Joseph C. Long. Wolters Kluwer Law & Business CCH. • Looseleaf service. $1,130.00 per year. Periodic supplementation. Semimonthly updates.

*Blue Sky Regulation.* Matthew Bender and Company Inc. • $2,448 per book. Four looseleaf volumes. Periodic supplementation. Covers state securities laws and regulations.

*BNA's Banking Report: Legal and Regulatory Developments in the Financial Services Industry.* Bloomberg BNA. • Weekly. $1,221.00 per year. Two looseleaf volumes. Emphasis on federal regulations.

*Formation and Financing of Emerging Companies.* Daniel E. O'Connor and others. Glasser LegalWorks. • $499 Individuals Binder/Looseleaf (Full set). Periodic Supplementation. Covers incorporation, bylaws, indemnification, intellectual property, financing sources, venture capital, due diligence, bridge loans, investor rights, compliance, and other legal issues associated with company formation. (Emerging Growth Companies Series.).

*Fund Governance: Legal Duties of Investment Company Directors.* ALM Media Properties LLC. • $580 print and online + ebook. Covers the legal obligations of directors of mutual funds and closed-end funds. (Law Journal Press).

*Going Private.* ALM Media Properties LLC. • $560 print + online + ebook. Discusses the legal ramifications of a publicly-owned company "going private" by way of a sale, leveraged buyout, reverse stock split, or merger. (Law Journal Press).

*International Capital Markets and Securities Regulation.* Harold S. Bloomenthal. Thomson West. • $3,876 full set. Nine looseleaf volumes. Periodic supplementation. Securities regulation in industrialized nations. (Securities Law Series).

*Taxation of Securities Transactions.* Matthew Bender and Company Inc. • Semiannual. $653. Looseleaf service. Covers taxation of a wide variety of securities transactions, including those involving stocks, bonds, options, short sales, new issues, mutual funds, dividend distributions, foreign securities, and annuities.

*White Collar Crime: Business and Regulatory Offenses.* ALM Media Properties LLC. • $740 print + online + ebook. Covers such legal matters as criminal tax cases, securities fraud, computer crime, mail fraud, bank embezzlement, criminal antitrust activities, extortion, perjury, the criminal liability of corporations, and RICO (Racketeer Influenced and Corrupt Organization Act). (Law Journal Press).

## PERIODICALS AND NEWSLETTERS

*Compliance Reporter.* Institutional Investor Inc. Journals Group. • Newsletter for investment dealers and others on complying with securities laws and regulations.

*The Review of Securities and Commodities Regulations: An Analysis of Current Laws, Regulations Affecting the Securities and Futures Industries.* Standard & Poor's Financial Services L.L.C. • 22 times a year. $350.00 per year.

*SEC News Digest.* U.S. Securities and Exchange Commission, Public Reference Room. • Daily. Provides information on Commission actions.

*SEC Today.* Washington Service Bureau Inc. • Daily. Includes the official *SEC News Digest* from the Securities and Exchange Commission and reports on public company filing activity.

*Securities and Federal Corporate Law Report.* Thomson West. • Features articles on securities and corporate law topics, providing highlights of significant cases, administrative policy, staff guidelines, and other important news and trends.

*Securities Arbitration Commentator.* Richard P. Ryder. • Monthly. $695.00 per year. Newsletter. Edited for attorneys and other professionals concerned with securities arbitration.

*Securities Week.* McGraw-Hill Financial Services Co. • Description: Acts as a trade publication for Wall Street executives, publishing news stories on pertinent events and developments within the industry including those related to legislative and regulatory activity, major stock exchanges, investment banking and retail firms, institutional trading, and new products. Recurring features include reports on research departments and a column titled Financial Futures/Commodities Report.

## TRADE/PROFESSIONAL ASSOCIATIONS

North American Securities Administrators Association. 750 1st St. NE, Ste. 1140, Washington, DC 20002-8034. Phone: (202)737-0900; Fax: (202)783-3571; Email: ri@nasaa.org • URL: http://www.nasaa.org • Represents the interests of the state, provincial and territorial securities administrators in the U.S., Canada, Mexico and Puerto Rico. Provides support to its members in government relations and with federal regulators, industry SROs and other groups.

# SECURITIES, OBSOLETE

*See* OBSOLETE SECURITIES

# SECURITIES, TAX EXEMPT

*See* MUNICIPAL BONDS

# SECURITY ANALYSIS

*See* FINANCIAL ANALYSIS

# SECURITY, COMPUTER

*See* COMPUTER CRIME AND SECURITY

# SECURITY DEALERS

*See* STOCK BROKERS

# SECURITY, INDUSTRIAL

*See* INDUSTRIAL SECURITY PROGRAMS

# SECURITY SYSTEMS, ELECTRONIC

*See* ELECTRONIC SECURITY SYSTEMS

# SEED INDUSTRY

## ABSTRACTS AND INDEXES

*Biological and Agricultural Index.* H.W. Wilson Co. • 11 times a year. Annual and quarterly cumulations. Price varies.

*Seed Abstracts.* CABI. • Available monthly in print; updated weekly online. Provides fully searchable abstracts.

## DIRECTORIES

*Directory of American Manufacturers & Exporters of Seeds & Bulbs--Flowers & Vegetables.* EXIM Infotek Private Ltd. • $10 Individuals. Covers: 80 American manufacturers and exporters of agricultural vegetable seeds, alfalfa seeds, cotton seeds, edible seeds, field seeds, flower seeds, forage seeds, grass seeds, hybrid sunflower seeds, livestock forage, rice seeds, seeds, sorghum seeds, soybeans seeds, sunflower seeds, turf seeds, vegetable seeds, and wheat seeds. Entries include: Company name, postal address, city, country, phone, fax, e-mail and websites, contact person, designation, and product details.

*Global Seed Guide: World Reference Source for the Commercial Seed Industry.* Ball Publishing. • Annual. $40.00. Includes company listings, type of business, type of seed, research centers, industry data, events calendar, and associations.

## FINANCIAL RATIOS

*Annual Statement Studies.* Risk Management Association. • Annual. Compiled from over 280,000 financial statements.

*Annual Statement Studies: Industry Default Probabilities and Cash Flow Measures.* Risk Management Association. • Annual. $405 Nonmembers. Serves as a companion volume to the original *Annual Statement Studies.* Gives probability of default estimates on a percentage scale for more than 450 industries. Includes changes in position year-by-year for eight financial statement line items and provides percentage measures of cash flow.

## ONLINE DATABASES

*CAB Abstracts.* CABI. • Contains 46 specialized abstract collections covering over 10,000 journals and monographs in the areas of agriculture, horticulture, forest products, farm products, nutrition, dairy science, poultry, grains, animal health, entomology, etc. Time period is 1972 to date, with monthly updates. Inquire as to online cost and availability. *CAB Abstracts on CD-ROM* also available, with annual updating.

## PERIODICALS AND NEWSLETTERS

*Journal of New Seeds: Innovations in Production, Biotechnology, Quality, and Marketing.* The Haworth Press Inc. • Quarterly. $240.00 per year to libraries; $65.00 per year to individuals. Covers research and development for a new generation of seeds having a high degree of quality and productivity. Topics relating to global seed production include marketing, economics, and intellectual property rights.

*Seed Business Magazine.* Australian Seed Federation. • Quarterly.

*The Seed Technologist Newsletter.* Society of Commercial Seed Technologists. • 3/year. $35. Includes annual proceedings.

*Seed World.* Scranton Gillette Communications Inc. • *Seed Trade Buyer's Guide.*

## TRADE/PROFESSIONAL ASSOCIATIONS

American Seed Research Foundation. 1701 Duke St., Ste. 275, Alexandria, VA 22314. Phone: (703)837-8140; Fax: (703)837-9365 • URL: http://www.seedresearch.org • Breeders, producers, and distributors of seeds. Seeks to advance seed technology by supporting research on seeds.

American Seed Trade Association. 1701 Duke St., Ste. 275, Alexandria, VA 22314-3415. Phone: 888-890-7333 or (703)837-8140; Fax: (703)837-9365; Email: info@amseed.org • URL: http://www.amseed.org • Breeders, growers, assemblers, conditioners, wholesalers, and retailers of grain, grass, vegetable, flower, and other seed for planting purposes.

Association of American Seed Control Officials. c/o Fawad Shah, Legislation and Labeling Committee

Member, 801 Summit Crossing Pl., Ste. C, Gastonia, NC 28054-2194. Phone: (704)810-8884; Fax: (704)852-4109 • URL: http://www.seedcontrol.org • Officials who administer U.S. federal and state, and Dominion of Canada seed laws. Promotes uniformity in seed laws, rules and regulations, and in the administration of laws relative to the sale and distribution of seeds; furthers the exchange of constructive ideas among administrators of seed laws; seeks to study and suggest improvements in proposed seed legislation; cooperates with administrators of state, federal, and Canadian seed laws; promotes a general appreciation of the benefits of seed control to farmers, seedsmen, and the public by encouraging the marketing and use of correctly labeled seed of high quality.

National Council of Commercial Plant Breeders. c/o Ann Jorss, Secretary-Treasurer, 1701 Duke St., Ste. 275, Alexandria, VA 22314. Phone: (703)837-8140; Fax: (703)837-9365 • URL: http://www.nccpb.org • Commercial seed firms. Engages in plant research and breeding programs in order to develop and market new and improved seeds and plants. Promotes and seeks to protect the interests of private industry in seed development, processing, and marketing. Monitors legislative matters pertaining to the seed industry and public agency programs as they affect private firms engaged in plant breeding.

# SELENIUM INDUSTRY

## ABSTRACTS AND INDEXES

*CA Selects: Selenium and Tellurium Chemistry.* American Chemical Society. American Chemical Society Chemical Abstracts Service. • Semiweekly. Members, $92.00 per year; non-members, $305.00 per year. Looseleaf service. Incorporates *Selenium and Tellurium Abstracts.*

## STATISTICS SOURCES

*Non-Ferrous Metal Data Yearbook.* American Bureau of Metal Statistics. • Annual. $405.00. Provides worldwide data on approximately about 200 statistical tables covering many nonferrous metals. Includes production, consumption, inventories, exports, imports, and other data.

# SELF-EMPLOYMENT

*See also* ENTREPRENEURS AND INTRA-PRENEURS; KEOGH PLANS; SMALL BUSINESS

## DIRECTORIES

*Greater Phoenix Chamber Membership List--Home-Based Businesses.* Greater Phoenix Chamber of Commerce. • $295 Members. Covers: 67 home-based businesses in the greater Phoenix, Arizona area. Entries include: Contact details.

## ENCYCLOPEDIAS AND DICTIONARIES

*Encyclopedia of Small Business.* Cengage Learning Inc. • $763 Individuals. 2010. $696.00. 4th edition. Two volumes. Contains about 600 informative entries on a wide variety of topics affecting small business. Arrangement is alphabetical. eBook also available. Inquire for pricing.

## HANDBOOKS AND MANUALS

*Business Taxpayer Information Publications.* U. S. Government Printing Office. • Annual. $66 U.S. Looseleaf. Two volumes, consisting of *Circular E, Employer's Tax Guide* and *Employer's Supplemental Tax Guide.* Issued by the Internal Revenue Service (http://www.irs.ustreas.gov). Includes a variety of business-related tax information, including withholding tables, tax calendars, self-employment issues, partnership matters, corporation topics, depreciation, and bankruptcy.

*CCH Guide to Car, Travel, Entertainment, and*

*Home Office Deductions.* Wolters Kluwer Law & Business CCH. • Annual. Explains how to claim maximum tax deductions for common business expenses. Includes automobile depreciation tables, lease value tables, worksheets, and examples of filled-in tax forms.

## INTERNET DATABASES

*Small Business Retirement Savings Advisor.* U. S. Department of Labor. Phone: (202)219-8921 • URL: http://www.dol.gov/elaws/pwbaplan.htm • Web site provides "answers to a variety of commonly asked questions about retirement saving options for small business employers." Includes a comparison chart and detailed descriptions of various plans: 401(k), SEP-IRA, SIMPLE-IRA, Payroll Deduction IRA, Keogh Profit-Sharing, Keogh Money Purchase, and Defined Benefit. Searching is offered. Fees: Free.

## PERIODICALS AND NEWSLETTERS

*Home Office Connections: A Monthly Journal of News, Ideas, Opportunities, and Savings for Those Who Work at Home.* Home Office Association of America. • Monthly. Free to members; non-members, $49.00 per year.

*HomeOffice: The Homebased Office Authority.* Entrepreneur Press. • Bimonthly. $11.97 per year. Contains advice for operating a business in the home.

*Inc.: The Magazine for Growing Companies.* INC. • 10/year. $10 U.S. /year for two subscription. Edited for small office and home businesses with one to 25 employees. Covers management, office technology, and lifestyle. Incorporates *Self-Employed Professional.*

*ReCareering Newsletter: An Idea and Resource Guide to Second Career and Relocation Planning.* Publications Plus, Inc. • Monthly. $59.00 per year. Edited for "downsized managers, early retirees, and others in career transition after leaving traditional employment." Offers advice on second careers, franchises, starting a business, finances, education, training, skills assessment, and other matters of interest to the newly unemployed.

*Self-Employed.* National Association for the Self-Employed. • Bimonthly. Provides articles on marketing, management, motivation, accounting, taxes, and other topics for businesses having fewer than 15 employees.

*Small Business Tax News.* Inside Mortgage Finance Publications. • Monthly. $139 Online. Contains latest news on tax changes, as well as detailed analysis of guidances from the IRS.

*The Small Business Tax Review.* A/N Group Inc. • Description: Reports tax news on such topics as new laws, court cases, IRS rulings, fringe benefits, and business and individual taxes, with emphasis on smaller businesses. Advises on financial planning and technical aspects of small business management.

*SOHO Journal.* National Association for the Cottage Industry. • Members, $25.00 per year; libraries, $35.00 per year. Newsletter on home businesses. Formerly *Mind Your Own Business at Home.*

## RESEARCH CENTERS AND INSTITUTES

Cooperative State Research, Education, and Extension Service - Small and Home-Based Business. 4435 Waterfront Ctr., 800 9th St. SW, Washington, DC 20250. Phone: (202)720-5997; Fax: (202)690-2975; Email: amclaren@csrees.usda.gov • URL: http://www.csrees.usda.gov/smallhomebasedbusiness.cfm • Women-owned and operated farms and ranches, rural entrepreneurship, small and home-based businesses.

National Institute on Disability and Rehabilitation Research - Self-Employment Technology Transfer. 52 Corbin Hall, Rural Institute on Disabilities, University of Montana, Missoula, MT 59812. Phone: 800-732-0320 or (406)268-2743; Fax:

(406)243-4730; Email: nancy@ruralinstitute.umt. edu • URL: http://rtc.ruralinstitute.umt.edu/SelEm/ RuSelfEm.htm • Vocational rehabilitation research, specifically, self-employment for people with disabilities.

## TRADE/PROFESSIONAL ASSOCIATIONS

American Home Business Association. 53 W 9000 S, Sandy, UT 84070. Phone: 866-396-7773 or (801)273-2350; Fax: (866)396-7773 or (801)273-2399; Email: info@homebusinessworks.com • URL: http://www.homebusinessworks.com • Offers benefits and services dedicated to supporting the needs of home business, small business and entrepreneurs. Benefits include health-auto-home insurance, legal, low long distance and 800 numbers, business line of credit, merchant accounts, tax programs, office supply and travel discounts and more. Seeks to provide members access to the best traditional benefits and timely information that is critical to conduct a successful home, small or Internet business.

Home-Based Working Moms. PO Box 1628, Spring, TX 77383-1628. Phone: (281)757-2207 • URL: http://www.hbwm.com • Individuals who work at home or would like to. Promotes working at home as an option for people in applicable positions; seeks to enhance the careers of members currently working at home. Serves as a forum for exchange of information among members. Makes available member matching service. Advocates for creation of more work-at-home opportunities by American businesses.

Mothers' Home Business Network. PO Box 423, East Meadow, NY 11554. Phone: (516)997-7394; Fax: (516)997-0839; Email: momhomebiz@mhbn. com • URL: http://www.homeworkingmom.com • Mothers choosing to work at home so they can earn income, maintain careers, and remain the primary caretakers of their children. Offers advice and support services on how to begin a successful business at home; helps members communicate with others who have chosen the same career option. Provides information on home business products and services, including home furnishings, raw materials and office supplies, and publications. Consults with corporations and manufacturers on reaching the home-based market. Refers media to potential interviewees and writers specializing in home business topics.

National Association for the Self-Employed. PO Box 241, Annapolis Junction, MD 20701-0241. Phone: 800-232-6273; Email: advocacy@nase.org • URL: http://www.nase.org • Members are very small businesses and the self-employed. Acts as an advocacy group at the state and federal levels.

National Association of Home Based Businesses. 5432 Price Ave., Baltimore, MD 21215. Phone: (410)367-5308 or (410)367-5309; Email: nahbb@ msn.com • URL: http://www.usahomebusiness.com • Affiliated with International Association for Business Organizations and the Small Business Network.

National Federation of Independent Business. 53 Century Blvd., Ste. 250, Nashville, TN 37214. Phone: (202)554-9000 or (615)874-5288; Email: web_membership@nfib.org • URL: http://www. nfib.com/ • Members are independent business and professional people.

Support Services Alliance. 2457 State Rte. 7, Ste. 1, Cobleskill, NY 12043. Phone: 800-909-2772; Email: info@ssamembers.com • URL: http://www. ssamembers.com • Represents small businesses (less than 50 employees), the self-employed, and associations of such individuals. Provides services and programs such as group purchasing discounts, health coverage, legislative advocacy, and business and financial support services.

# SELLING

*See* SALESMEN AND SALESMANSHIP

# SELLING A BUSINESS

*See* BUSINESS ENTERPRISES, SALE OF

# SELLING BY TELEPHONE

*See* TELEPHONE SELLING

# SEMICONDUCTOR INDUSTRY

*See also* MICROCOMPUTERS AND MINICOMPUTERS; SUPERCONDUCTORS

## ABSTRACTS AND INDEXES

*Applied Science and Technology Index.* EBSCO Publishing Inc. • 11/year. Indexes a wide variety of English language technical, industrial, and engineering periodicals.

*Business Periodicals Index Retrospective.* EBSCO Publishing Inc. • 11/year. Quarterly and annual cumulations.

*Current Contents: Engineering, Computing and Technology.* Thomson Reuters Intellectual Property and Science. • Weekly. $730 per year. Reproductions of contents pages of technical journals. Includes *Author Index, Address Directory, Current Book Contents,* and *Title Word Index.* Formerly *Current Contents: Engineering, Technology and Applied Sciences.*

*Key Abstracts: Semiconductor Devices.* Institution of Engineering and Technology. • Monthly. $1,138. Provides international coverage of journal and proceedings literature.

*NTIS Alerts: Electrotechnology.* U.S. Department of Commerce National Technical Information Service. • Biweekly. $130 per year. Covers electronic components, semiconductors, antennas, circuits, optoelectronic devices, and related subjects.

*Solid State and Superconductivity Abstracts.* Cambridge Scientific Abstracts L.P. • Monthly. Covers chemistry, physics, metallurgy, resonance, materials, measurement, and superconductivity theories, applications, and problem areas. Formerly *Solid State Abstracts Journal.*

## DIRECTORIES

*IC Master (Integrated circuits): The Electronics Industry's Leading Source of ICInformation.* IC Master. • Annual. $195.00. Semiannual supplements. Product information on 120,000 commercially available integrated circuits.

*Semiconductor International--Semi Source.* Reed Elsevier Group plc Reed Business Information. • Annual. Publication includes: Lists of companies associated with the design, processing, assembly, packaging, and testing of semiconductor devices, integrated circuits, and hybrid circuits. Database includes: Specifications from industry equipment and material suppliers. Entries include: Company name, address, phone, fax, products.

## FINANCIAL RATIOS

*Industry Norms and Key Business Ratios.* Dun & Bradstreet Inc. • Annual. Five volumes. Covers over 800 kinds of businesses, arranged by Standard Industrial Classification number. More detailed editions covering longer periods of time are also available.

## INTERNET DATABASES

*Manufacturing Profiles.* U. S. Bureau of the Census. Phone: (301)763-4636 or (301)763-4100; Fax:

(301)763-4794; Email: webmaster@census.gov • URL: http://www.census.gov/prod/www/abs/mfg-prof.html • The Census Bureau makes available free on PDF (Portable Document Format) an annual consolidation of the entire Current Industrial Report series, presenting "all the data compiled." Contains statistics on production, shipments, inventories, consumption, exports, imports, and orders for a wide variety of manufactured products.

## ONLINE DATABASES

*Applied Science and Technology Index Online.* H.W. Wilson Co. • Provides online indexing of 500 major scientific, technical, industrial, and engineering periodicals. Time period is 1983 to date. Monthly updates. Inquire as to online cost and availability.

*INSPEC.* Institution of Electrical Engineers. • Provides online citations, with abstracts, to the world literature of electrical engineering, electronics, optoelectronics, telecommunications, industrial controls, instrumentation, computer technology, information technology, and physics. Coverage includes more than 4,000 technical and scientific journals from 1969 to date, with weekly updating. (INSPEC is Information Services in Physics, Electronics, and Computing.) Inquire as to online cost and availability.

*Wilson Business Abstracts Online.* H.W. Wilson Co. • Indexes and abstracts 600 major business periodicals, plus the *Wall Street Journal* and the business section of the *New York Times.* Indexing is from 1982, abstracting from 1990, with the two newspapers included from 1993. Updated weekly. Inquire as to online cost and availability. (*Business Periodicals Index* without abstracts is also available online.).

## PERIODICALS AND NEWSLETTERS

*Computer.* Institute of Electrical and Electronic Engineers. • Monthly. Covers all aspects of computer science.

*ECN Literature News.* Reed Elsevier Group plc Reed Business Information. • Bimonthly. Price on application.

*IEEE Micro.* IEEE - Communications Society. • Bimonthly. Contains high-quality technical articles from designers, systems integrators, and users discussing the design, performance, or application of microcomputer and microprocessor systems.

*Inside Chips Ventures: The Global Report with Executive Perspective.* HTE Research Inc. • Monthly. $595.00 per year. Tracks the activities of semiconductor firms worldwide. Formerly *Semiconductor Industry and Business Survey Newsletter.*

*Integrated Circuits International: An International Bulletin for Suppliers and Users of Integrated Circuits.* Elsevier. • Monthly. $541.00 per year. For suppliers and users of integrated circuits.

*Microprocessor Report: The Insiders' Guide to Microprocessor Hardware.* Reed Elsevier Group plc Reed Business Information. • 12 times a year. $695.00 per year. Newsletter. Covers the technical aspects of microprocessors from Intel, IBM, Cyrix, Motorola, and others.

*Semiconductor International: The Industry Sourcebook for Processing, Assembly and Testing.* Reed Electronics Group. • Monthly. $131.99 per year. Devoted to processing, assembly and testing techniques.

*Solid State Technology.* PennWell Corp., Advanced Technology Div. • 8/year. $258 Individuals. Covers the technical and business aspects of semiconductor and integrated circuit production. Includes *Buyers Guide.*

## RESEARCH CENTERS AND INSTITUTES

Arizona State University - Center for Solid State Electronics Research. PO Box 876206, Tempe, AZ 85287-6206. Phone: (480)965-3708; Fax: (480)965-

8118; Email: trevor.thornton@asu.edu • URL: http://more.engineering.asu.edu/nanofab • Fabrication and modeling of nanostructures, heterostructures, molecular beam epitaxy, integrated optoelectronics, and silicon integrated circuits, bio-molecular electronics, bio-mems, nano-fluids, high-k dielectrics.

Massachusetts Institute of Technology - Lincoln Laboratory. 244 Wood St., Lexington, MA 02420-9108. Phone: (781)981-5500; Fax: (781)981-7086; Email: llnews@ll.mit.edu • URL: http://www.ll.mit.edu • Multidisciplinary off-campus research unit. Research fields include solid state devices.

Microelectronics Laboratory. c/o Mark Brenner, Manager, Ohio State University, 310 Caldwell Laboratory, 2015 Neil Ave., Columbus, OH 43210-1272. Phone: (614)292-2306; Fax: (614)292-7596 • URL: http://cleanroom.ece.ohio-state.edu.

Semiconductor Device Laboratory. Department of Electrical and Computing Engineering, University of Virginia, 351 McCormick, Thornton Hall, Rm. C210, Charlottesville, VA 22904. Phone: (424)924-3960; Fax: (424)924-8818; Email: rcandler@ee.ucla.edu • URL: http://www.ece.virginia.edu.

Semiconductor Research Laboratory. Duke University, Dept. of Electrical and Computer Engineering, Durham, NC 27708. Phone: (919)660-5252; Fax: (919)660-5293; Email: abrown@ee.duke.edu • URL: http://www.ee.duke.edu.

Solid-State Device and Materials Research Laboratory. School of Electrical and Computer Engineering, Purdue University, 465 Northwestern Ave., West Lafayette, IN 47907. Phone: (765)494-3540; Fax: (765)494-6441; Email: miller@ecn.purdue.edu • URL: http://www.ece.purdue.edu.

Stanford University - Center for Integrated Systems. Paul G. Allen Bldg., MS 4070, 420 Via Palou Mall, Stanford, CA 94305-4070. Phone: (650)725-3621; Fax: (650)725-0991; Email: rdasher@cis.stanford.edu • URL: http://cis.stanford.edu • Research programs include manufacturing science, design science, computer architecture, semiconductor technology, and telecommunications.

## STATISTICS SOURCES

*Semiconductors, Printed Circuit Boards, and Other Electronic Components.* U. S. Bureau of the Census. • Annual. Provides data on shipments: value, quantity, imports, and exports. (Current Industrial Reports, MA-36Q.).

*Standard & Poor's Industry Surveys.* Standard & Poor's Financial Services L.L.C. • Semiannual. $1,800.00. Two looseleaf volumes. Includes monthly *Supplements.* Provides detailed, individual surveys of 52 major industry groups. Each survey is revised on a semiannual basis. Also includes "Monthly Investment Review" (industry group investment analysis) and monthly "Trends & Projections" (economic analysis).

*U.S. Industry and Trade Outlook.* U.S. Department of Commerce National Technical Information Service. • Annual. Produced by the International Trade Administration, U.S. Department of Commerce, in a "public-private" partnership with DRI/McGraw-Hill and Standard & Poor's. Provides basic data, outlook for the current year, and "Long-Term Prospects" (five-year projections) for a wide variety of products and services. Includes high technology industries. Formerly *U.S. Industrial Outlook.*

## TRADE/PROFESSIONAL ASSOCIATIONS

JEDEC. 3103 N 10th St., Ste. 240-S, Arlington, VA 22201-2107. Phone: (703)907-7515 • URL: http://www.jedec.org • Affiliated with Electronic Industries Alliance. Formerly Joint Electron Device Engineering Council.

North America Chinese Clean-tech and Semiconductor Association. 809 Cuesta Dr., Ste. 208B, Mountain View, CA 94040-3666. • URL:

http://www.nacsa.com • Represents the interests of professionals dedicated to the advancement of Chinese professionals in high-tech industries. Strengthens networking among professionals. Fosters entrepreneurship among ethnic Chinese. Promotes the exchange in the global semiconductor and information technology industries.

# SEMINARS

*See* CONFERENCES, WORKSHOPS, AND SEMINARS

# SENATE

*See* UNITED STATES CONGRESS

# SENSORS, INDUSTRIAL

*See* CONTROL EQUIPMENT INDUSTRY

# SERIAL PUBLICATIONS

*See* PERIODICALS

# SERVICE, CUSTOMER

*See* CUSTOMER SERVICE

# SERVICE INDUSTRIES

## CD-ROM DATABASES

*Business Abstracts with Full Text.* EBSCO Publishing Inc. • Includes full text articles from more than 460 business publications from 1982 to present. Indexing for nearly 880 publications.

*OECD Statistical Compendium.* Organization for Economic Cooperation and Development. • Semiannual. $1,905.00 per year for 1 to 10 users. CD-ROM contains more than 730,000 monthly, quarterly, and annual time series for OECD countries, 1960 to date. Includes fully searchable data on agriculture, food, economic indicators, national accounts, employment, energy, finance, industry, technology, and foreign trade. Results can be displayed in various forms.

## DIRECTORIES

*ABC/Dienstverleners.* ABC Business Directories BV. • Quarterly. Database covers: 24,000 Dutch service companies, including accounting firms, law firms, car leasing firms, audiovisual consultants, transport companies, advertising agencies, hotels, and restaurants. Entries include: Company name, address, phone, fax, telex; executive names; capital; bank affiliation; year founded; number of employees; product information.

*American Big Businesses Directory.* InfoGroup Inc. • Annual. $295. Covers: 218,000 U.S. businesses with more than 100 employees, and 500,000 key executives and directors. CD-ROM version contains 160,000 top firms and 431,000 key executives. Entries include: Name, address, phone, names and titles of key personnel, number of employees, sales volume, Standard Industrial Classification (SIC) codes, subsidiaries and parent company names, stock exchanges on which traded.

*American Manufacturers Directory.* InfoGroup Inc. • Annual. $295. Covers: more than 150,000 manufacturing companies with 20 or more employees. CD-ROM version lists all 531,000 U.S. manufacturers, in all employee size ranges. Entries include: Company name, address, phone, contact name, Standard Industrial Classification (SIC)

codes, number of employees, sales volume code, credit rating scores.

*Directory of California Wholesalers and Service Companies.* Harris InfoSource. • Annual. $210 Individuals hardcover. Covers: Approximately 225,200 wholesalers, distributors, and other service firms in California. Includes key executives. Database includes: Statistical data, trade show calendar. Entries include: Company name, address, parent name/location, telephone, fax and 800 numbers, web site address (on CD-ROM only), number of employees, year established, annual revenue, plant size, business description, Standard Industrial Classification (SIC) code, executive names/titles, public ownership, legal structure, import/export designators, and female/minority ownership.

*Directory of Service Companies.* Dun & Bradstreet Inc. • Annual. Covers: Management consulting services; executive search services; public relations, engineering, and architectural services; business services; accounting, auditing, and bookkeeping services; consumer services; health services; legal services; social services; research services; repair services; and hospitality, motion picture, amusement, and recreation services.

*Dun's Regional Directory of Service Companies--Canada.* Dun & Bradstreet Inc. • Covers: more than 10,000 service enterprises in Canada with eight or more employees and from Standard Industrial Classification (SIC) codes 07, 47, 60-80, and 82-89. Entries include: Company name, address, phone, SIC codes, parent company, number of employees, names and titles of key personnel, DUNS number.

*Illinois Services Directory.* Manufacturers' News Inc. • Annual. $209 Individuals Print (Hardcover); plus Shipping and Handling. Covers: Over 26,548 wholesalers, jobbers, contractors, retailers, services, and 76,898 executives in Illinois. Entries include: Company name, address, phone; names, titles, and functions of key personnel; year established, number of employees, office square footage, services, Standard Industrial Classification (SIC) code, net worth, parent company and subsidiary company information, type of in-house computer system, email address, fax, web address.

*Massachusetts Service Directory.* George D. Hall Company Inc. • $69 plus $4.95 shipping. Covers: over 12,700 non-manufacturing companies with five or more employees. Entries include: Company name, address, phone, names of key executives, number of employees, product or service, Standard Industrial Classification (SIC) code.

*National Services Directory.* Dun & Bradstreet Inc. • $495. Covers: Approximately 20,000 service companies in Canada. Entries include: Name, address, phone, fax.

*Tennessee Business Services Directory.* Nashville Area Chamber of Commerce. • $121 Members. Covers: 7,500 Tennessee businesses in the service industry with 20 employees and in the restaurant industry with 50 employees. Entries include: Name, address, phone, and fax.

*Vault Guide to the Top Business Services Employers.* Vault.com Inc. • $19.95 Individuals Online. Covers: Top business service companies in United States. Entries include: Company name, contact person, location, address, phone and fax numbers, zip code, statistics, hiring process and email.

*Wisconsin Business Services Directory.* WMC Foundation. • Annual. $199 Individuals. Covers: Over 10,700 business service companies with 25 or more employees in Wisconsin. Entries include: Company name, address, phone, fax, number of employees, SIC codes, names and titles of key personnel, services offered, product descriptions,

ownership status, import/export activity, parent company.

*Wisconsin Services Directory.* Harris InfoSource. • Annual. $98 members/libraries. Covers: 16,000 business service companies in Wisconsin and over 24,000 key contact personnel. Entries include: Company name, address, phone, fax, name and title of contact, names and titles of key personnel, number of employees, geographical area served, financial data, subsidiary and branch names and locations, product/service, Standard Industrial Classification (SIC) code, computer used, year established, import/export information, web and e-mail address, first month of fiscal year, export countries.

## E-BOOKS

*Encyclopedia of American Industries.* Cengage Learning Inc. • 2011. $807.00. 6th edition. Three volumes. Volume one is Manufacturing Industries and volume two is Service and Non-Manufacturing Industries. Provides the history, development, and recent status of approximately 1,000 industries. Includes statistical graphs, with industry and general indexes. Also available as eBook.

## INTERNET DATABASES

*Business 2.0 Web Guide to the Best Business Links.* Business 2.0 Media Inc. Phone: (415)293-4800; Email: support@business2.com • URL: http://www.business2.com/webguide • Web site presents an extensive, searchable directory of links to "the best, most informative, and authoritative web pages." Twenty main categories cover business, finance, career, company information, people, and technology topics, with thousands of subtopics, all linking to Web sites recommended by experienced business researchers. Fees: Free.

*Fedstats.* Federal Interagency Council on Statistical Policy. Phone: (202)395-7254 • URL: http://www.fedstats.gov • Web site features an efficient search facility for full-text statistics produced by more than 100 federal agencies, including the Census Bureau, the Bureau of Economic Analysis, and the Bureau of Labor Statistics. Boolean searches can be made within one agency or for all agencies combined. Links are offered to international statistical bureaus, including the UN, IMF, OECD, UNESCO, Eurostat, and 20 individual countries. Fees: Free.

*FreeLunch.com.* Economy.com, Inc. Phone: (610)696-8700; Fax: (610)696-1678 • URL: http://www.freelunch.com • Web site provides free access to more than 200 million economic and financial data series, covering industry, demographics, labor markets, prices, retail sales, government spending, trade, interest rates, housing starts, the stock market, etc. Data is available in either chart or table form. Searching is offered. Free, but registration required. Economy.com, Inc. also offers fee-based economic analysis at *The Dismal Scientist* site (www.dismal.com).

*Summary of Commentary on Current Economic Conditions by Federal Reserve District.* Board of Governors of the Federal Reserve System. Phone: (202)452-3000; Fax: (202)452-3819 • URL: http://www.federalreserve.gov/publications.htm • 8/year. Free Web site provides current "anecdotal information" eight times a year on economic conditions within each of the 12 Federal Reserve Districts, plus an extensive national *Summary*. Text is based on the opinions of bank officials, business executives, economists, financial market experts, and others. Typically contains views of consumer spending, manufacturing, services, credit, employment, prices, wages, and the economy in general. Usually referred to as the Beige Book.

## ONLINE DATABASES

*American Business Directory.* InfoGroup Inc. • Provides brief online information on more than 10 million U. S. companies, including individual plants and branches. Entries typically include address, phone number, industry classification code, and contact name. Updating is quarterly. Inquire as to online cost and availability.

*Wilson Business Abstracts Online.* H.W. Wilson Co. • Indexes and abstracts 600 major business periodicals, plus the *Wall Street Journal* and the business section of the *New York Times.* Indexing is from 1982, abstracting from 1990, with the two newspapers included from 1993. Updated weekly. Inquire as to online cost and availability. (*Business Periodicals Index* without abstracts is also available online.).

### PERIODICALS AND NEWSLETTERS

*Cleaning Business: Published Monthly for the Self-Employed Cleaning and Maintenance Professionals.* William R. Griffin, Publisher. • Monthly. $20. Formerly *Service Business.*

*Hotels: The Magazine of the Worldwide Hotel Industry.* International Hotel Association. Reed Elsevier Group plc Reed Business Information. • Contains critical information on all aspects of the worldwide hotel industry including design, food & beverage, finance, development marketing and technology.

### STATISTICS SOURCES

*Statistics on International Trade in Services.* Organization for Economic Cooperation and Development. Organisation for Economic Co-operation and Development Publications and Information Center. • Annual. $126.00. Presents a compilation and assessment of data on OECD member countries' international trade in services. Covers four major categories for 20 years: travel, transportation, government services, and other services.

*Survey of Current Business.* U. S. Government Printing Office. • Published by Bureau of Economic Analysis, U. S. Department of Commerce. Presents a wide variety of business and economic data.

*United States Census of Service Industries.* U.S. Department of Commerce U.S. Census Bureau. • Quinquennial. Various reports available.

### TRADE/PROFESSIONAL ASSOCIATIONS

Italian Confederation of Retailers, Commerce, Tourism and Service. Via Nazionale, 60, I-00184 Rome, Italy. Phone: 39 6 47251; Fax: 39 6 4746886; Email: confes@confesercenti.it • URL: http://www.confesercenti.it • Small and mid-sized enterprises in the commercial, tourist, and service sectors in Italy. Represents and promotes the retailing, tourism, service and other commercial industries.

National Association of Service Managers. PO Box 250796, Milwaukee, WI 53225-6512. Phone: (414)466-6060 or (414)847-1200; Fax: (414)466-0840; Email: kenc@kencook.com • URL: http://www.nasm.com • Absorbed Service Managers of America.

# SERVICE INDUSTRY, FOOD

*See* FOOD SERVICE INDUSTRY

# SERVICE MEN, DISCHARGED

*See* VETERANS

# SERVICE MERCHANDISERS

*See* RACK JOBBERS

# SERVICE STATIONS

*See* GASOLINE SERVICE STATIONS

# SEVERANCE PAY

*See* WAGES AND SALARIES

# SEWAGE DISPOSAL

*See* SANITATION INDUSTRY

# SEWING MACHINE INDUSTRY

*See also* TEXTILE MACHINERY

### DIRECTORIES

*Directory of African Importers of Sewing Machines and Parts.* EXIM Infotek Private Ltd. • $250 Individuals. Covers: 80 African importers of embroidery machine, garment industry machinery and equipment, industrial sewing machine and parts, and pleating machine. Entries include: Company name, postal address, telephone, fax, e-mail, website, contact person, designation, and product details.

*Directory of Asian Importers of Sewing Machines and Parts.* EXIM Infotek Private Ltd. • $450 Individuals. Covers: 125 Asian importers of embroidery machinery, garment industry equipment and accessories, household sewing machine, industrial sewing machine, industrial sewing machine parts, new and reconditioned sewing machine, sewing machine and spare parts, sewing machine repairs, domestic sewing machine, sewing needles, stitch machine, and used embroidery machine. Entries include: Company name, postal address, telephone, fax, e-mail, website, contact person, designation, and product details.

*Directory of European Importers of Sewing Machines & Parts.* EXIM Infotek Private Ltd. • $10 Individuals. Covers: 60 European importers of industrial sewing machines and parts, knitting equipment parts and articles, knitting machine needles, and sewing machine needles. Entries include: Company name, postal address, telephone, fax, e-mail, website, contact person, designation, and product details.

*Directory of Middle East Importers of Sewing Machines and Parts.* EXIM Infotek Private Ltd. • $250 Individuals. Covers: 70 Middle East importers of embroidery machinery, garment industry equipment, industrial sewing machine and parts, new and used industrial sewing machine and spare parts, and domestic sewing machine. Entries include: Company name, postal address, telephone, fax, e-mail, website, contact person, designation, and product details.

*Directory of North American Importers of Sewing Machines and Parts.* EXIM Infotek Private Ltd. • $250 Individuals. Covers: 60 North American importers of embroidery machinery, industrial sewing machine and parts, sewing machine and sewing accessories, domestic sewing machine, and sewing machine needles. Entries include: Company name, postal address, telephone, fax, e-mail, website, contact person, designation, and product details.

*Directory of SAARC Importers of Sewing Machines and Parts.* EXIM Infotek Private Ltd. • $200 Individuals. Covers: 55 SAARC countries importers of buttonholer and button covering machine, compact fusing press M/C, embroidery machinery, garment industry equipment and accessories, household sewing machine and parts, sewing machine equipment, sewing machine repairs, domestic and industrial sewing machine, sewing needles, stitch machine, thread trimmers, used embroidery machine, and used schiffli embroidery. Entries include: Company name, postal address, telephone, fax, e-mail, website, contact person,

designation, and product details.

*Directory of South American Importers of Sewing Machines and Parts.* EXIM Infotek Private Ltd. • $350 Individuals. Covers: 110 South American importers of garment industry equipment, sewing machine and parts (domestic and industrial), and sewing machine needles. Entries include: Company name, postal address, telephone, fax, e-mail, website, contact person, designation, and product details.

# SEXUAL HARASSMENT IN THE WORKPLACE

### ABSTRACTS AND INDEXES

*Business Periodicals Index Retrospective.* EBSCO Publishing Inc. • 11/year. Quarterly and annual cumulations.

*Index to Legal Periodicals and Books.* H.W. Wilson Co. • Monthly. $490.00 per year. Quarterly and annual cumulations.

*PAIS International.* ProQuest L.L.C. • Monthly. $850.00 per year; cumulations three times a year. Provides topical citations to the worldwide literature of public affairs, economics, demographics, sociology, and trade. Text in English; indexed materials in English, French, German, Italian, Portuguese and Spanish.

*Readers' Guide to Periodical Literature.* EBSCO Publishing Inc. • Provides indexing for over 400 periodicals dating back to 1983.

*Social Sciences Citation Index.* Thomson Reuters Corp. • Weekly. Product is accessed via *Web of Science.*

*Social Sciences Index Retrospective: 1907-1983.* EBSCO Publishing Inc. • Indexing for 1,000,000 articles. Coverage includes international index and social sciences and humanities index.

### CD-ROM DATABASES

*ABI/INFORM.* ProQuest L.L.C. • Monthly. Provides CD-ROM indexing and abstracting of worldwide business literature. Archival discs are available from 1971. Formerly *ABI/INFORM OnDisc.*

*Business Abstracts with Full Text.* EBSCO Publishing Inc. • Includes full text articles from more than 460 business publications from 1982 to present. Indexing for nearly 880 publications.

*Index to Legal Periodicals and Books.* EBSCO Publishing Inc. • Contains indexing of more than 1,400 English language legal periodicals from 1981 to date and 2,500 books.

*Newspaper Abstracts Ondisc.* ProQuest L.L.C. • Monthly. $2,950.00 per year (covers 1989 to date; archival discs are available for 1985-88). Provides cover-to-cover CD-ROM indexing and abstracting of 19 major newspapers, including the *New York Times, Wall Street Journal, Washington Post, Chicago Tribune,* and *Los Angeles Times.*

*PAIS International.* ProQuest L.L.C. • Monthly. $1,995.00 per year. Contains over 650,000 citations to the literature of contemporary social, political, and economic issues.

*Readers' Guide to Periodical Literature.* EBSCO Publishing Inc. • Provides indexing for over 400 periodicals dating back to 1983.

*Social Sciences Abstracts.* EBSCO Publishing Inc. • Provides indexing from 1983 and abstracting from 1994 of more than 750 periodicals covering economics, area studies, community health, public administration, public welfare, urban studies, and many other topics related to the social sciences.

*Social Sciences Citation Index.* Thomson Reuters Corp. • Weekly. Product is accessed via *Web of Science.*

### HANDBOOKS AND MANUALS

*Women and the Law.* Carol H. Lefcourt, editor. Thomson West. • Annual. $691.60 Individuals book -

softbound. Covers such topics as employment discrimination, pay equity (comparable worth), sexual harassment in the workplace, property rights, and child custody issues.

## ONLINE DATABASES

*Contemporary Women's Issues.* Cengage Learning Inc. • Provides full-text articles online from 150 periodicals and a wide variety of additional sources relating to economic, legal, social, political, education, health, and other women's issues. Time span is 1992 to date. Weekly updates. Inquire as to online cost and availability.

*LegalTrac.* Cengage Learning Inc. • Online database. Provides indexing for approximately 875 titles of periodical literature relating to legal matters from 1980 to date. Corresponds to online *Legal Resource Index.* Inquire as to price and availability.

*Wilson Business Abstracts Online.* H.W. Wilson Co. • Indexes and abstracts 600 major business periodicals, plus the *Wall Street Journal* and the business section of the *New York Times.* Indexing is from 1982, abstracting from 1990, with the two newspapers included from 1993. Updated weekly. Inquire as to online cost and availability. (*Business Periodicals Index* without abstracts is also available online.).

*Wilson Social Sciences Abstracts Online.* H.W. Wilson Co. • Provides online abstracting and indexing of more than 500 periodicals covering area studies, community health, public administration, public welfare, urban studies, and many other social science topics. Time period is 1994 to date for abstracts and 1983 to date for indexing, with updates weekly. Inquire as to online cost and availability.

## OTHER SOURCES

*Sex Discrimination and Sexual Harassment in the Work Place.* ALM Media Properties LLC. • $565. Considers both sides: the point of view of employers and the point of view of employees filing complaints. Coverage includes sexual harassment statutes, the Family Medical Leave Act, the Equal Pay Act, "glass ceiling" issues, pregnancy discrimination, childcare issues, reinstatement after a leave, and other legal matters. (Law Journal Press).

## PERIODICALS AND NEWSLETTERS

*Nine to Five Newsletter.* 9 to 5, National Association of Working Women. • 5/year. $25 Individuals. A newsletter dealing with the rights and concerns of women office workers.

## RESEARCH CENTERS AND INSTITUTES

Center for Women Policy Studies. 1776 Massachusetts Ave. NW, Ste. 450, Washington, DC 20036. Phone: (202)872-1770; Fax: (202)296-8962; Email: cwps@centerwomenpolicy.org • URL: http://www.centerwomenpolicy.org • Conducts research on the policy issues that affect the legal, economic, educational, and social status of women, including sexual harassment in the workplace, and women and AIDS.

## TRADE/PROFESSIONAL ASSOCIATIONS

Legal Momentum. 5 Hanover Sq., Ste. 1502, New York, NY 10004. Phone: (212)925-6635; Email: info@legalmomentum.org • URL: http://www.legalmomentum.org • Formerly NOW Legal Defense and Education Fund.

National Partnership for Women & Families. 1875 Connecticut Ave. NW, Ste. 650, Washington, DC 20009. Phone: (202)986-2600; Fax: (202)986-2539; Email: info@nationalpartnership.org • URL: http://www.nationalpartnership.org • Formerly Women's Legal Defense Fund.

National Women's Law Center. 11 Dupont Cir. NW, Ste. 800, Washington, DC 20036-1209. Phone: (202)588-5180; Fax: (202)588-5185; Email: info@nwlc.org • URL: http://www.nwlc.org • Uses the law in all its forms: getting new laws on the books;

litigating ground-breaking lawsuits all the way to the Supreme Court; and educating the public about how to make the law and public policies work for women and their families. "Takes on the issues that cut to the core of women's and girls' lives" in health, education, employment, and family economic security, with special priority given to the needs of low-income women and their families.

Nine to Five: National Association of Working Women. 207 E Buffalo St., Ste.211, Milwaukee, WI 53202. Phone: 800-522-0925 or (414)274-0925; Fax: (414)272-2870; Email: 9to5@9to5.org • URL: http://www.feminist.com/9to5.htm • Members are women office workers. Strives for the improvement of office working conditions for women and the elimination of sex and race discrimination.

# SHAREHOLDERS

*See* STOCKHOLDERS

# SHARES OF STOCK

*See* STOCKS

# SHEEP INDUSTRY

*See also* LIVESTOCK INDUSTRY; WOOL AND WORSTED INDUSTRY

## INTERNET DATABASES

*USDA.* U.S. National Institute of Standards and Technology. 100 Bureau Dr., Gaithersburg, MD 20899-1070. Phone: 800-877-8339 or (301)975-6478 or (202)720-2791; Fax: (301)975-8295; Email: inquiries@nist.gov • URL: http://www.nist.gov • The USDA home page has six sections: News and Information; What's New; About USDA; Agencies; Opportunities; Search and Help. Keyword searching is offered from the USDA home page and from various individual agency home pages. Agencies are the Economic Research Service, Agricultural Marketing Service, National Agricultural Statistics Service, National Agricultural Library, and about 12 others. Updating varies. Fees: Free.

## PERIODICALS AND NEWSLETTERS

*Sheep Breeder.* Mead Livestock Services Inc. • Monthly.

## PRICE SOURCES

*The National Provisioner: Serving Meat, Poultry, and Seafood Processors.* BNP Media. • Monthly. $85.04 Individuals. *Buyer's Guide* available. Meat, poultry and seafood newsletter.

## STATISTICS SOURCES

*Agricultural Statistics.* U.S. Department of Agriculture National Agricultural Statistics Service. • Annual. $46 Individuals. Provides a wide variety of statistical data relating to agricultural production, supplies, consumption, prices/price-supports, foreign trade, costs, and returns, as well as farm labor, loans, income, and population. In many cases, historical data is shown annually for 10 years. In addition to farm data, includes detailed fishery statistics.

## TRADE/PROFESSIONAL ASSOCIATIONS

American Sheep Industry Association. 9785 Maroon Cir., Ste. 360, Englewood, CO 80112. Phone: (303)771-3500; Fax: (303)771-8200; Email: info@sheepusa.org • URL: http://www.sheepusa.org • Producers of sheep and wool. Goal is to advance the standards and profitability of the sheep industry. Conducts lobbying activities to promote legislation beneficial to the industry.

# SHEET METAL INDUSTRY

*See also* AIR CONDITIONING INDUSTRY; HEATING AND VENTILATION; ROOFING INDUSTRY

## DIRECTORIES

*HPAC Engineering Info-Dex.* Penton Media Inc. • Annual. $30. Industry directory of products, manufacturers, and trade names and a composite of catalog data for mechanical systems engineering professionals.

*Who's Who in Metal Forming and Fabricating.* Fabricators and Manufacturers Association International. • Annual. $200 for nonmembers. Lists members of the Fabricators and Manufacturers Association (FMA), International; and members of the Tube and Pipe Association. Includes five indexes. Formerly *FMA Member Resource Directory.*

## FINANCIAL RATIOS

*Annual Statement Studies.* Risk Management Association. • Annual. Compiled from over 280,000 financial statements.

*Annual Statement Studies: Industry Default Probabilities and Cash Flow Measures.* Risk Management Association. • Annual. $405 Nonmembers. Serves as a companion volume to the original *Annual Statement Studies.* Gives probability of default estimates on a percentage scale for more than 450 industries. Includes changes in position year-by-year for eight financial statement line items and provides percentage measures of cash flow.

## PERIODICALS AND NEWSLETTERS

*Heating/Piping/Air Conditioning Engineering: The Magazine of Mechanical Systems Engineering.* Penton Media Inc. • Monthly. Covers design, specification, installation, operation, and maintenance for systems in industrial, commercial, and institutional buildings. Formerly (Heating, Piping and Air Conditioning).

*Snips.* BNP Media. • Monthly. $18.00 per year. Provides information for heating, air conditioning, sheet metal and ventilating contractors, wholesalers, manufacturers representatives and manufacturers.

# SHELLFISH INDUSTRY

*See also* FISH INDUSTRY; LOBSTER INDUSTRY; OYSTER INDUSTRY; SEAFOOD INDUSTRY

## DIRECTORIES

*Major Food and Drink Companies of the World.* Cengage Learning Inc. • 12th edition. eBook. Published by Graham & Whiteside. Contains profiles and trade names for more than 9,200 important food and beverage companies in various countries. In addition to foods, includes both alcoholic and nonalcoholic drink products.

## ONLINE DATABASES

*Food Science and Technology Abstracts (online).* IFIS North American Desk. • Produced by International Food Information Service. Provides about 500,000 online citations, with abstracts, to the international literature of food science, technology, commodities, engineering, and processing. Approximately 2,000 periodicals are covered. Time period is 1969 to date, with monthly updates. Inquire as to online cost and availability.

## PERIODICALS AND NEWSLETTERS

*Commercial Fisheries News.* Compass Publications, Fisheries Division. • Monthly. $21.95 print only. Covers the commercial fishing industry in New England. Includes news of marine technology, boat-building, fish and lobster prices, business trends, government regulation, and other topics.

*Seafood Business.* Diversified Business Communications Inc. • $57 U.S.. Edited for a wide range of seafood buyers, including distributors, restaurants, supermarkets, and institutions. Special issues feature information on specific products, such as salmon or lobster.

## TRADE/PROFESSIONAL ASSOCIATIONS

Molluscan Shellfish Institute. c/o Lisa Wedding, National Fisheries Institute, 7918 Jones Branch Dr., Ste. 700, McLean, VA 22102. Phone: (703)752-8880; Fax: (703)752-7583 • URL: http://www.aboutseafood.com • A division of the National Fisheries Institute. Shellfish producers, processors, distributors, growers, and suppliers to the industry. Works to promote, protect, and advance the interests of the shellfish industry. Cooperates with federal, state, and municipal authorities in matters of legislation, sanitation standards, controls, and conservation.

National Shellfisheries Association. c/o Linda Kallansrude, 14 Carter Ln., East Quogue, NY 11942-4335. Phone: (631)653-6327; Fax: (631)653-6327; Email: secretariat@shellfish.org • URL: http://www.shellfish.org • Biologists, hydrographers, public health workers, shellfish producers, and fishery administrators. Encourages research on mollusks and crustaceans, with emphasis on those forms of economic importance known as shellfish.

# SHELTERS, TAX

*See* TAX SHELTERS

# SHIPBUILDING

*See* SHIPS, SHIPPING AND SHIPBUILDING

# SHIPPING

*See* SHIPS, SHIPPING AND SHIPBUILDING

# SHIPS, SHIPPING AND SHIPBUILDING

*See also* BOAT INDUSTRY; EXPORT-IMPORT TRADE; FREIGHT TRANSPORT; MARINE ENGINEERING; OCEANOGRAPHIC INDUSTRIES; PORTS; STEAMSHIP LINES; TANK SHIPS; TRANSPORTATION INDUSTRY

## ABSTRACTS AND INDEXES

*NTIS Alerts: Ocean Sciences and Technology.* U.S. Department of Commerce National Technical Information Service. • Biweekly. $130 per year. Provides descriptions of government-sponsored research reports and software, with ordering information.

*NTIS Alerts: Transportation.* U.S. Department of Commerce National Technical Information Service. • Biweekly. $130 per year. Covers air, marine, highway, inland waterway, pipeline, and railroad transportation.

*Oceanic Abstracts.* CSA. • Monthly. $1,645.00 per year. Includes print and online editions. Covers oceanography, marine biology, ocean shipping, and a wide range of other marine-related subject areas.

## ALMANACS AND YEARBOOKS

*American Bureau of Shipping International Directory of Offices.* American Bureau Of Shipping Inc. • Annual. $520. ABS Employee and office listings.

## DIRECTORIES

*Capital for Shipping.* Informa Publishing Group. • Annual. $128.00. Published in the UK by Lloyd's

List (www.lloydslist.com). Consists of a "Financial Directory" and a "Legal Directory," listing international ship finance providers and international law firms specializing in shipping. Included with subscription to *Lloyd's Shipping Economist.*

*Fairplay World Shipping Directory.* Fairplay Publications Ltd. • Daily. Covers: More than 76,000 companies worldwide engaged in some aspect of shipping, including over 10,000 ship-owners with fleets totaling over 45,000 vessels, shipbuilders and repairers, marine insurance shipping finance, protection and indemnity associations, marine equipment suppliers, and towing, salvage, and dredging; also lists marine organizations, shipbrokers, and consulting engineers and surveyors. Entries include: Company name, address, phone, fax, e-mail, URL, names of directors and executives, brief description of business; listings may also include associated and subsidiary companies and financial data.

*Guide to Shipbuilding, Repair, and Maintenance.* Informa Marine and Transport. • Annual. Price on application. Provides worldwide coverage of shipbuilding, repair, and maintenance facilities and marine equipment suppliers for the maritime industry. Included with subscription to *Lloyd's Ship Manager.*

*Internet Ships Register.* IHS Global Ltd. Lloyd's Register--Fairplay Ltd. • $1,350 Individuals single user. Database covers: Over 180,000 shipowners, operators, managers, and builders. Entries include: Name, address, phone. Database also includes details on over 83,000 commercial vessels with photographs. Fixture information also available at an additional cost.

*List of Shipowners, Managers, and Managing Agents.* Lloyd's Register of Shipping. • Annual. $350.00, including 10 updates per year. Published in the UK by Lloyd's Register-Fairplay Ltd. Lists 40,000 shipowners, managers, and agents worldwide. Cross-referenced with *Lloyd's Register of Ships.*

*Lloyd's Marine Equipment Buyers' Guide.* Informa Group PLC. • Annual. $270.00. Published in the UK by Lloyd's List (www.lloydslist.com). Lists more than 6,000 companies worldwide supplying over 2,000 types of marine products and services, including offshore equipment.

*Lloyd's Maritime Directory.* Informa P.L.C. Informa Sports Group. • Annual. Covers: Over 40,000 shipowners, managers, and operators with 75,000 vessels. Also includes Marine consultants; towing, salvage, solicitors, P&I clubs; ship building and repair firms; general maritime organizations, banking and finance and more. Entries include: Firm name, address, phone, fax, e-mail, Internet; branch offices; names of principal executives; agents; parent and associated companies; and, for shipowners and lines, detailed information on ships owned, type, or capacity, etc. The former second volume of 'International Shipping and Shipbuilding Directory' is now published separately with the title 'Lloyd's List Marine Equipment Buyers' Guide' (see separate entry).

*Newbuildings Register.* IHS Global Ltd. Lloyd's Register--Fairplay Ltd. • Monthly. $2,850 Individuals CD-ROM. Covers: Shipowners and builders of new commercial ships. Entries include: Name, address, phone.

*PC Register.* IHS Global Ltd. Lloyd's Register--Fairplay Ltd. • $7,600 Individuals CD-ROM; single user; quarterly updates. Covers: Shipbuilder and owner information for over 170,000 vessels of 100 GT and above. Entries include: Name, address, phone.

*Sea-web Directory.* IHS Global Ltd. Lloyd's Register--Fairplay Ltd. • $1,175 Individuals Online. Covers: Over entries including 178,000 companies

in the shipping industry, 129,000 ship operators details and 52,000 contact names. Maritime organizations, ship brokers, marine insurance companies, and maritime schools are among the groups included. Entries include: Name, address, phone, fax.

## INTERNET DATABASES

*CDC Vessel Sanitation Program (VSP): Charting a Healthier Course.* U. S. Centers for Disease Control and Prevention. Phone: (770)488-7070; Fax: (888)232-6789; Email: vsp@cdc.gov • URL: http://www.cdc.gov/nceh/vsp/ • Annual. Web site provides details of unannounced sanitation inspections of individual cruise ships arriving at U. S. ports. Includes detailed results of the most recent inspection of each ship and results of inspections taking place in years past. There are lists of "Ships Inspected Past 2 Months" and "Ships with Not Satisfactory Scores" (passing grade is 85). CDC standards cover drinking water, food, and general cleanliness. Online searching is possible by ship name, inspection date, and numerical scores. Fees: Free.

## ONLINE DATABASES

*TRIS: Transportation Research Information Service.* The National Academies National Research Council. • Contains abstracts and citations to a wide range of transportation literature, 1968 to present, with monthly updates. Includes references to the literature of air transportation, highways, ships and shipping, railroads, trucking, and urban mass transportation. Formerly *TRIS-ON-LINE.* Inquire as to online cost and availability.

## OTHER SOURCES

*Lloyd's Maritime Atlas.* Informa P.L.C. Informa Sports Group. • Biennial. $119.00. Contains more than 70 pages of world, ocean, regional, and port maps in color. Provides additional information for the planning of world shipping routes, including data on distances, port facilities, recurring weather hazards at sea, international load line zones, and sailing times.

## PERIODICALS AND NEWSLETTERS

*International Trade Reporter Export Reference Manual.* Bloomberg BNA. • Biweekly. $874.00 per year. Looseleaf service.

*JOC Shipping Digest: For Export and Transportation Executives.* Shipper Group. • Weekly.

*Maritime IT & Electronics.* Institute of Marine Engineering, Science and Technology. • Bimonthly. £58.00 per year. Covers modern electronic technology as applied to all areas of the maritime industry. Includes navigation systems, communications, control systems, monitoring, diagnostics, and software.

*Ocean Navigator: Marine Navigation and Ocean Voyaging.* Navigator Publishing L.L.C. • Bimonthly. $27.95 per year.

## RESEARCH CENTERS AND INSTITUTES

University of Michigan - Transportation Research Institute. 2901 Baxter Rd., Ann Arbor, MI 48109-2150. Phone: (734)764-6504; Fax: (734)936-1081; Email: umtri-director@umich.edu • URL: http://www.umtri.umich.edu • Research areas include highway safety, transportation systems, and shipbuilding.

## STATISTICS SOURCES

*Review of Maritime Transport.* United Nations Conference on Trade and Development. United Nations Publications. • Annual. $95.00.

*U.S. Industry and Trade Outlook.* U.S. Department of Commerce National Technical Information Service. • Annual. Produced by the International Trade Administration, U.S. Department of Commerce, in a "public-private" partnership with DRI/McGraw-Hill and Standard & Poor's. Provides basic data, outlook for the current year, and "Long-Term Prospects" (five-year projections) for a wide variety of products and services. Includes high technology industries. Formerly *U.S. Industrial Outlook*.

## TRADE/PROFESSIONAL ASSOCIATIONS

International Maritime Industries Forum. c/o The Baltic Exchange, 38 St. Mary Axe, London EC3A 8BH, United Kingdom. Phone: 44 20 79296429; Fax: 44 20 79296430; Email: info@imif.org • URL: http://www.imif.org • Shipowners and builders, shipbreakers, oil companies, insurance companies, classification societies, and bankers in 25 countries. Seeks to: maintain a healthy commercial and financial climate for all sectors of shipping, including ownership, operation, construction, and international trade; encourage discussions of mutual interest; foster change and stimulate action to benefit the maritime industry. Strives to upgrade the standards of ships, port state control and to establish shipbreaking plants in the Third World to promote its large market for rerolled and recycled ship scrap.

National Association of Marine Services. 5458 Wagon Master Dr., Colorado Springs, CO 80917. Phone: (719)573-5946; Fax: (719)573-5952; Email: nams@namsshipchandler.com • URL: http://www. namsshipchandler.com • Affiliated with International Ship Suppliers Association. Formerly National Associated Marine Suppliers.

National Association of Waterfront Employers. 919 18th St. NW, Ste. 901, Washington, DC 20006. Phone: (202)587-4800; Fax: (202)587-4888; Email: mto@nawe.us • URL: http://www.nawe.us • Formerly National Association of Stevedoves.

# SHOE INDUSTRY

*See also* LEATHER INDUSTRY

## CD-ROM DATABASES

*OECD Statistical Compendium*. Organization for Economic Cooperation and Development. • Semiannual. $1,905.00 per year for 1 to 10 users. CD-ROM contains more than 730,000 monthly, quarterly, and annual time series for OECD countries, 1960 to date. Includes fully searchable data on agriculture, food, economic indicators, national accounts, employment, energy, finance, industry, technology, and foreign trade. Results can be displayed in various forms.

## DIRECTORIES

*American Shoemaking Directory*. Shoe Trades Publishing Co. Research Services. • Annual. $60 Individuals. Covers: Shoe manufacturers in the United States, Puerto Rico, and Canada. Entries include: Company name, address, phone, fax, names of executives, product information brand names. Also key personnel; Plant output, trade sold, and sales offices included.

*Directory of American Manufacturers & Exporters of Zippers, Garment & Shoe Accessories*. EXIM Infotek Private Ltd. • $5 Individuals. Covers: 40 American manufacturers and exporters of bar code labels, belts-buckles, buckles, buttons, metal snap fasteners, metal zippers, nylon molded zippers, and zippers. Entries include: Company name, postal address, city, country, phone, fax, e-mail and websites, contact person, designation, and product details.

*Directory of Apparel Specialty Stores*. Chain Store Guide. • Annual. $495 Individuals Directory. Covers 4,700 apparel and sporting goods specialty stores in the United States and Canada, operating more than 80,000 stores. Include company name, phone and fax numbers, company e-mail and web addresses and other information.

*Directory of British Footwear Exporters*. British Footwear Association. • Biennial. Covers: Manufacturers of footwear who export products.

Entries include: Company name, address, phone, telex, trade name.

*Directory of Chinese Manufacturers & Exporters of Shoes & Footwears*. EXIM Infotek Private Ltd. • $20 Individuals. Covers: 260 Chinese manufacturers and exporters of baby shoes, boots-rubber, boots, canvas shoes, casual shoes, children's shoes, footwear, jogging shoes, ladies leather shoes, leather shoes, plastic sandals, plastic slippers, up shoes, rubber boots, rubber shoes, sandals, school shoes, shoes, slippers, snow boots. Entries include: Company name, postal address, city, country, phone, fax, e-mail and websites, contact person, designation, and product details.

*Directory of Chinese Manufacturers & Exporters of Zipper, Garment & Shoe Accessories*. EXIM Infotek Private Ltd. • $10 Individuals. Covers: 80 Chinese manufacturers and exporters of apparel accessories, belt buckles, buttons, buttons-resin, clothing accessories, fashion garment accessories, garment accessories, hooks, lining cloths, metal buckles, metal zippers, needles, plastic zipper, sewing kits, sewing needles, tailoring accessories, zipper products, and zippers. Entries include: Company name, postal address, city, country, phone, fax, e-mail and websites, contact person, designation, and product details.

*Directory of South Korean Manufacturers & Exporters of Shoes & Footwears*. EXIM Infotek Private Ltd. • $10 Individuals. Covers: 90 South Korean manufacturers & exporters of boots-rubber, footwear soles/components, footwear-industrial/ protective, footwear-sports, footwear-standard. Entries include: Company name, postal address, city, country, phone, fax, e-mail & websites, contact person, designation, products detail.

*Directory of Taiwanese Manufacturers & Exporters of Shoes & Footwears*. EXIM Infotek Private Ltd. • $30 Individuals. Covers: 430 Taiwanese manufacturers and exporters of baby shoes, footwear soles/components, footwear-industrial/ protective, footwear-sports, footwear-standard, footwear-wooden, shoes, and shoes materials. Entries include: Company name, postal address, city, country, phone, fax, e-mail and websites, contact person, designation, and product details.

*Directory of Taiwanese Manufacturers & Exporters of Zippers, Garment & Shoe Accessories*. EXIM Infotek Private Ltd. • $15 Individuals. Covers: 140 Taiwanese manufacturers and exporters of apparel accessories, belt buckles, buttons, elastic band accessories, elastic braid, elastic cords, elastic ribbons, elastic yarn and fabrics, eyelets, garment accessories, hooks, loop fasteners, metal buttons, patches, plastic buckles, sewing kits, sewing notions, shoe buckles, woven labels, zipper products, and zippers. Entries include: Company name, postal address, city, country, phone, fax, e-mail and websites, contact person, designation, and product details.

*Shoe Factory Buyer's Guide*. Shoe Trades Publishing Co. Research Services. • Annual. $59 Individuals. Covers: Over 600 suppliers and their representatives to the shoe manufacturing industries in the United States and Canada. Entries include: Company name, address, phone, fax, trade and brand names, list of products or services.

## FINANCIAL RATIOS

*Annual Statement Studies*. Risk Management Association. • Annual. Compiled from over 280,000 financial statements.

*Annual Statement Studies: Industry Default Probabilities and Cash Flow Measures*. Risk Management Association. • Annual. $405 Nonmembers. Serves as a companion volume to the original *Annual Statement Studies*. Gives probability of default estimates on a percentage scale for more than 450 industries. Includes changes in position year-by-year for eight financial statement line items and provides percentage measures of cash flow.

## HANDBOOKS AND MANUALS

*Shoe Stats*. Footwear Distributors and Retailers of America. • Annual. Free to members; non-members, $350.00; libraries, $225.00. Includes *Statistical Reporter*.

## INTERNET DATABASES

*Advance Monthly Retail Trade Report*. U. S. Census Bureau. Phone: 800-541-8345 or (301)457-4100 or (301)763-2713; Fax: (301)457-1296 or (301)457-3842; Email: naics@census.gov • URL: http://www. census.gov/epcd/www/naicstab.htm • Web pages provide monthly sales figures for a wide range of retail businesses. Advance, preliminary, and final statistics are provided for the latest month available in each case, with a previous-year comparison. Updates are monthly.

*Business 2.0 Web Guide to the Best Business Links*. Business 2.0 Media Inc. Phone: (415)293-4800; Email: support@business2.com • URL: http://www. business2.com/webguide • Web site presents an extensive, searchable directory of links to "the best, most informative, and authoritative web pages." Twenty main categories cover business, finance, career, company information, people, and technology topics, with thousands of subtopics, all linking to Web sites recommended by experienced business researchers. Fees: Free.

*Fedstats*. Federal Interagency Council on Statistical Policy. Phone: (202)395-7254 • URL: http://www. fedstats.gov • Web site features an efficient search facility for full-text statistics produced by more than 100 federal agencies, including the Census Bureau, the Bureau of Economic Analysis, and the Bureau of Labor Statistics. Boolean searches can be made within one agency or for all agencies combined. Links are offered to international statistical bureaus, including the UN, IMF, OECD, UNESCO, Eurostat, and 20 individual countries. Fees: Free.

*FreeLunch.com*. Economy.com, Inc. Phone: (610)696-8700; Fax: (610)696-1678 • URL: http:// www.freelunch.com • Web site provides free access to more than 200 million economic and financial data series, covering industry, demographics, labor markets, prices, retail sales, government spending, trade, interest rates, housing starts, the stock market, etc. Data is available in either chart or table form. Searching is offered. Free, but registration required. Economy.com, Inc. also offers fee-based economic analysis at *The Dismal Scientist* site (www.dismal. com).

*Manufacturing Profiles*. U. S. Bureau of the Census. Phone: (301)763-4636 or (301)763-4100; Fax: (301)763-4794; Email: webmaster@census.gov • URL: http://www.census.gov/prod/www/abs/mfg-prof.html • The Census Bureau makes available free on PDF (Portable Document Format) an annual consolidation of the entire Current Industrial Report series, presenting "all the data compiled." Contains statistics on production, shipments, inventories, consumption, exports, imports, and orders for a wide variety of manufactured products.

## PERIODICALS AND NEWSLETTERS

*Footwear News*. Fairchild Publications. • Weekly. $72 Individuals.

## STATISTICS SOURCES

*Annual Benchmark Report for Retail Trade and Food Services..A Detailed Summary of Retail Sales, Purchases, Accounts Receivable, Inventories, and Food Service Sales*. U. S. Government Printing Office. • Annual. $13.00. Issued by the U.S. Census Bureau. Provides detailed annual and monthly retail statistics for the most recent 10 years. Includes data for various kinds of retail outlets, including automobiles, furniture, appliances, building supplies, grocery stores, drug stores, gasoline stations, clothing, sporting goods, department stores, and restaurants.

*Standard & Poor's Industry Surveys*. Standard &

Poor's Financial Services L.L.C. • Semiannual. $1,800.00. Two looseleaf volumes. Includes monthly *Supplements*. Provides detailed, individual surveys of 52 major industry groups. Each survey is revised on a semiannual basis. Also includes "Monthly Investment Review" (industry group investment analysis) and monthly "Trends & Projections" (economic analysis).

*Survey of Current Business.* U. S. Government Printing Office. • Published by Bureau of Economic Analysis, U. S. Department of Commerce. Presents a wide variety of business and economic data.

**TRADE/PROFESSIONAL ASSOCIATIONS**
National Shoe Retailers Association. 7386 N La Cholla Blvd., Tucson, AZ 85741-2305. Phone: 800-673-8446 or (520)209-1710; Fax: (520)209-5595; Email: info@nsra.org • URL: http://www.nsra.org • Proprietors of independent shoe stores and stores with major shoe departments. Provides business services and professional development programs including bankcard processing, shipping, freight discounts, free website listing, employee training; conducts research; monitors legislation.

# SHOP PRACTICE

*See* MACHINE SHOPS

# SHOPLIFTING

*See* CRIME AND CRIMINALS

# SHOPPING CENTERS

*See also* RETAIL TRADE

**DIRECTORIES**
*Canadian Directory of Shopping Centres.* Rogers Publishing Ltd. • Annual Periodic. $1,125 1-year on-line subscription plus 3-volume print set. (Eastern Canada and Western Canada). Describes about 2,200 shopping centers and malls, including those under development.

**HANDBOOKS AND MANUALS**
*Shopping Center and Store Leases.* Emanuel B. Halper. ALM Media Properties LLC. • $375 Individuals print. Contains detailed information on supermarket and fast-food restaurants and includes an annotated sample lease form. Also provides expert guidance and insights on negotiating use and exclusive clauses, covering 26 distinct categories of tenants.

**PERIODICALS AND NEWSLETTERS**
*Chain Store Age: The NewsMagazine for Retail Executives.* Lebhar-Friedman Inc. • 9/year. Formerly *Chain Store Age Executive with Shopping Center Age.*

*Retail Traffic.* Penton. • Monthly. $74. Provides coverage of all phases of the shopping center industry. Formerly *Shopping Center World.*

*Value Retail News: The Journal of Outlet and Off-Price Retail and Development.* Off-Price Specialists, Inc. Value Retail News. • Monthly. $99 Members. Provides news of the off-price and outlet store industry. Emphasis is on real estate for outlet store centers.

# SHORTHAND

*See* OFFICE PRACTICE

# SHORTHAND REPORTING

**TRADE/PROFESSIONAL ASSOCIATIONS**
National Court Reporters Association. 8224 Old Courthouse Rd., Vienna, VA 22182-3808. Phone: 800-272-6272 or (703)556-6272; Fax: (703)556-6291; Email: president@ncrahq.org • URL: http://www.ncra.org • Represents Independent state, regional, and local associations. Verbatim court reporters who work as official reporters for courts and government agencies, as freelance reporters for independent contractors, and as captioners for television programming; retired reporters, teachers of court reporting, and school officials; student court reporters.

# SHOW BUSINESS

*See also* AMUSEMENT INDUSTRY

**ABSTRACTS AND INDEXES**
*Communication Abstracts: An International Information Service.* Pine Forge Press. • Bimonthly. Institutions, $1,150.00 per year. Provides broad coverage of the literature of communications, including broadcasting and advertising.

*Readers' Guide to Periodical Literature.* EBSCO Publishing Inc. • Provides indexing for over 400 periodicals dating back to 1983.

**BIOGRAPHICAL SOURCES**
*Contemporary Theatre, Film & Television.* Cengage Learning Inc. • $338 Individuals. 2012. $308.00 per volume. Previous volumes available. Provides detailed biographical and career information on more than 20,000 currently popular performers, directors, writers, producers, designers, managers, choreographers, technicians, composers, executives, dancers, and critics. eBook also available. Contact for pricing.

**CD-ROM DATABASES**
*Readers' Guide to Periodical Literature.* EBSCO Publishing Inc. • Provides indexing for over 400 periodicals dating back to 1983.

**DIRECTORIES**
*Entertainment Sourcebook: An Insider's Guide on Where to Find Everything.* Applause Theatre & Cinema Books. • Annual. $45.00. Compiled by the Association of Theatrical Artists and Craftspeople (www.entertainmentsourcebook.com/ATAC.htm). Lists more than 5,000 sources of theatrical and entertainment supplies and services, such as props, costumes, publicity agencies, scenic shops, amusement park equipment, audio/video products, balloons, wigs, make-up, magic supplies, etc.

*The Grey House Performing Arts Directory.* Grey House Publishing. • Annual. $250 Individuals Softcover. Covers: More than 8,500 dance companies, instrumental music programs, opera companies, choral groups, theatre companies, performing arts series, and performing arts facilities. Database includes: Information resources section covering hundreds of performing arts associations, publications, and Web sites. Entries include: Mailing address, telephone and fax numbers, e-mail addresses, Web sites, mission statement, key management contacts, and facility information such as capacity, season, and attendance.

**OTHER SOURCES**
*Westlaw Journal Entertainment Industry.* Thomson Reuters Westlaw. • Monthly. *Sports and Entertainment Litigation Reporter.* Provides concise, unbiased coverage of litigation involving such issues as breach of contract, First Amendment, invasion of privacy, unfair competition, misappropriation of funds, and copyright and trademark issues.

**PERIODICALS AND NEWSLETTERS**
*Daily Variety.* Variety Media Publications. • Daily. $199 Individuals. Covers entire scope of the entertainment business on the East and West coast.

*Entertainment Design: The Art and Technology of Show Business.* Primedia Business Magazines. • Monthly. $34.97 per year. Contains material on performing arts management, staging, scenery, costuming, etc. Supersedes *TCI - Theatre Crafts International.*

*Entertainment Law and Finance.* ALM Media Properties LLC. • Monthly. $485 print and online. Covers contracts, royalties, litigation, copyright, taxation, etc., for the music industry, motion pictures, broadcasting, publishing, video, and related media. (A Law Journal Newsletter, formerly published by Leader Publications.).

*The Hollywood Reporter.* • Daily. $199.00 per year. Covers the latest news in film, TV, cable, multimedia, music, and theatre. Includes box office grosses and entertainment industry financial data.

*Performing Arts Forum.* International Society for the Performing Arts Foundation. • Description: Directed toward producers, managers, promoters, and representatives of artists and performing arts events in the U.S. and other countries. Discusses techniques and problems involved with the development and administration of the performing arts. Recurring features include items from readers, news of research, Society reports, and notes on members.

*Theatre Journal.* Association for Theatre in Higher Education. Johns Hopkins University Press. • Quarterly. $81 Individuals print (2 years). Quarterly. Individuals, $35.00 per year; institutions, $108.00 per year. Contains material on theatre history, theatre news, and reviews of books and plays.

*Variety: The International Entertainment Weekly.* Reed Elsevier Group plc Reed Business Information. • Weekly. $199 Individuals print + online. Contains national and international news of show business, with emphasis on motion pictures and television. Includes *Market* and *Special Focus* issues.

**RESEARCH CENTERS AND INSTITUTES**
University of Wisconsin - Madison - Wisconsin Historical Society - Wisconsin Center for Film and Theater Research. 816 State St., Madison, WI 53706-1417. Phone: (608)264-6466 or (608)264-6467; Fax: (608)264-6472; Email: askmovies@wisconsinhistory.org • URL: http://www.wisconsinhistory.org/Content.aspx?dsNav=N:4294963828-4294963805&dsRecordDetails=R:CS4075 • Studies the performing arts in America, including theater, cinema, radio, and television.

**STATISTICS SOURCES**
*United States Census of Service Industries.* U.S. Department of Commerce U.S. Census Bureau. • Quinquennial. Various reports available.

**TRADE/PROFESSIONAL ASSOCIATIONS**
Association of Theatrical Artists and Craftspeople. 48 Fairway St., Bloomfield, NJ 07003-5515. Phone: (212)234-9001 • URL: http://www.atacbiz.com • Members are artists and craftspeople working in theatre, film, TV, and advertising. Areas of expertise include props, costumes, millinery, puppetry, display, and special effects.

# SHOW WINDOWS

*See* DISPLAY OF MERCHANDISE

# SICKNESS INSURANCE

*See* HEALTH INSURANCE

# SIGNS AND SIGN BOARDS

*See also* COMMERCIAL ART; DISPLAY OF MERCHANDISE; OUTDOOR ADVERTISING; POSTERS

---

## DIRECTORIES

*Advertising (Signs) Directory.* InfoGroup Inc. • Annual. Number of listings: 28,945. Entries include: Name, address, phone, size of advertisement, name of owner or manager, number of employees, year first in "Yellow Pages." Compiled from telephone company "Yellow Pages," nationwide.

## FINANCIAL RATIOS

*Annual Statement Studies.* Risk Management Association. • Annual. Compiled from over 280,000 financial statements.

*Annual Statement Studies: Industry Default Probabilities and Cash Flow Measures.* Risk Management Association. • Annual. $405 Nonmembers. Serves as a companion volume to the original *Annual Statement Studies.* Gives probability of default estimates on a percentage scale for more than 450 industries. Includes changes in position year-by-year for eight financial statement line items and provides percentage measures of cash flow.

## HANDBOOKS AND MANUALS

*Standard Highway Signs, as Specified in the Manual on Uniform Traffic Control Devices.* U. S. Government Printing Office. • Looseleaf. $153.00. Issued by the U. S. Department of Transportation (www. dot.gov). Includes basic manual, with updates for an indeterminate period. Contains illustrations of typical standard signs approved for use on streets and highways, and provides information on dimensions and placement of symbols.

## PERIODICALS AND NEWSLETTERS

*Signs of the Times.* ST Media Group International Inc. • 13 times a year. For designers and manufacturers of all types of signs. Features how-to-tips.

## TRADE/PROFESSIONAL ASSOCIATIONS

Professional Lighting and Sign Management Companies of America. 1100-H Brandywine Blvd., Zanesville, OH 43701-7303. Phone: (740)452-4541 • URL: http://plasmalighting.org • Represents independently owned service providers offering lighting and signage services, workmanship and expertise. Seeks to uphold the standards of practice within the lighting and sign management industry. Promotes and protects the interests of members.

# SILK INDUSTRY

*See also* TEXTILE INDUSTRY

## ABSTRACTS AND INDEXES

*Textile Technology Index*™. EBSCO Publishing Inc. • Monthly. $545 Individuals. Includes indexing and abstracts for more than 470 periodicals.

## DIRECTORIES

*Directory of Chinese Manufacturers & Exporters of Cotton, Silk, Wool Raw and Waste.* EXIM Infotek Private Ltd. • $10 Individuals. Covers: 50 Chinese manufacturers and exporters of cotton, cotton products, cotton pulp, goat's wool, mulberry silk, wool, wool and wool products. Entries include: Company name, postal address, city, country, phone, fax, e-mail and websites, contact person, designation, and product details.

## ONLINE DATABASES

*Textile Technology Index*™. EBSCO Publishing Inc. • Monthly. $545 Individuals. Includes indexing and abstracts for more than 470 periodicals.

*World Textiles.* Elsevier. • Provides abstracting and indexing from 1970 of worldwide textile literature (periodicals, books, pamphlets, and reports). Includes U. S., European, and British patent information. Updating is monthly. Inquire as to online cost and availability.

## PERIODICALS AND NEWSLETTERS

*Journal of Natural Fibers.* The Haworth Press Inc. • Quarterly. $400.00 per year to libraries; $45.00 per

year to individuals. Covers applications, technology, research, and world markets relating to fibers from silk, wool, cotton, flax, hemp, jute, etc. Previously *Natural Fibres,* published annually.

# SILVER INDUSTRY

*See also* COINS AS AN INVESTMENT; METAL INDUSTRY; MONEY

## CD-ROM DATABASES

*METADEX Materials Collection: Metals-Polymers-Ceramics.* Cambridge Scientific Abstracts L.P. • Quarterly. Provides CD-ROM citations to the worldwide literature of materials science and metallurgy. Corresponds to *Metals Abstracts, Alloys Index, Steels Alert, Nonferrous Alert, Polymers/Ceramics/Composites Alert,* and *Engineered Materials Abstracts.* (Formerly produced by ASM International.).

## STATISTICS SOURCES

*Non-Ferrous Metal Data Yearbook.* American Bureau of Metal Statistics. • Annual. $405.00. Provides worldwide data on approximately about 200 statistical tables covering many nonferrous metals. Includes production, consumption, inventories, exports, imports, and other data.

*Standard & Poor's Industry Surveys.* Standard & Poor's Financial Services L.L.C. • Semiannual. $1,800.00. Two looseleaf volumes. Includes monthly *Supplements.* Provides detailed, individual surveys of 52 major industry groups. Each survey is revised on a semiannual basis. Also includes "Monthly Investment Review" (industry group investment analysis) and monthly "Trends & Projections" (economic analysis).

*Statistical Annual: Interest Rates, Metals, Stock Indices, Options on Financial Futures, Options on Metals Futures.* Chicago Board of Trade. • Annual. Includes historical data on GNMA CDR Futures, Cash-Settled GNMA Futures, U. S. Treasury Bond Futures, U. S. Treasury Note Futures, Options on Treasury Note Futures, NASDAQ-100 Futures, Major Market Index Futures, Major Market Index MAXI Futures, Municipal Bond Index Futures, 1,000-Ounce Silver Futures, Options on Silver Futures, and Kilo Gold Futures.

*United States Census of Mineral Industries.* Bureau of the Census, U.S. Department of Commerce. U. S. Government Printing Office. • Quinquennial.

# SILVERWARE

*See* TABLEWARE

# SKIP TRACERS

*See* COLLECTING OF ACCOUNTS

# SLOT MACHINES

*See* VENDING MACHINES

# SMALL ARMS

*See* FIREARMS INDUSTRY

# SMALL BUSINESS

*See also* BUSINESS; BUSINESS ENTERPRISES, SALE OF; BUSINESS START-UP PLANS AND PROPOSALS; FRANCHISES; SELF-EMPLOYMENT; SMALL BUSINESS INVESTMENT COMPANIES; VENTURE CAPITAL

## BIBLIOGRAPHIES

*Small Business Sourcebook.* Cengage Learning Inc. • Annual. $747 Individuals print. Contains over 340 profiles on small businesses as well as nearly 100 small business topics.

## CD-ROM DATABASES

*OECD Statistical Compendium.* Organization for Economic Cooperation and Development. • Semiannual. $1,905.00 per year for 1 to 10 users. CD-ROM contains more than 730,000 monthly, quarterly, and annual time series for OECD countries, 1960 to date. Includes fully searchable data on agriculture, food, economic indicators, national accounts, employment, energy, finance, industry, technology, and foreign trade. Results can be displayed in various forms.

## DIRECTORIES

*Alliance of Area Business Publications--Membership Directory.* Alliance of Area Business Publications. • Annual. Covers over 70 local, state, and regional member business publications in the United States, Canada, Australia and Puerto Rico.

*American Small Business Coalition--Membership Directory.* American Small Business Council. • Quarterly. Covers individual professionals and companies doing business in support of government agency requirements.

*Business Capital Sources.* International Wealth Success, Inc. • Annual. $20 Individuals. Covers: About 1,500 banks, insurance and mortgage companies, commercial finance, leasing, and venture capital firms that lend money for business investment. Entries include: Company or institution name, address, phone.

*Chelsea Area Chamber of Commerce Community Profile & Business Directory.* Chelsea Area Chamber of Commerce. • Covers businesses in Chelsea, Michigan.

*Classified Directory of Products & Services.* SMC Business Councils. • Biennial. Covers: over 5,000 small business concerns in central and western Pennsylvania. Entries include: Company name, address, phone, e-mail address, URL, contact name, description of products or services provided, Standard Industrial Classification (SIC) code.

*Colstrip Chamber of Commerce--Business Directory.* Colstrip Chamber of Commerce. • Covers businesses in Colstrip, Montana.

*Crawley Business Guide and Directory.* Crawley Borough Council. • Covers businesses in Crawley, United Kingdom.

*Directory, Database of Small & Medium Enterprise (SMEs) in India.* NIIR Project Consultancy Services. • $250 Individuals CD-ROM. Covers: 250,000+ small & medium enterprises (SME's) in India. Entries include: Name, full postal address, postal code, phone, contact person, company name, address, city, pin code, fax, e-mail, website, products details.

*Free Money from the Federal Government for Small Businesses and Entrepreneurs.* John Wiley and Sons Inc. Technical Insights. • $18.95 Individuals. Covers: Approximately 1,500 grants and funding programs from 52 government agencies. Database includes: Bibliography. Entries include: Program name, description, contact information.

*Hanover Association of Business and Chamber of Commerce--Business Directory.* Hanover Association of Business and Chamber of Commerce. • Annual. List of businesses in Hanover. Also provides information for companies and families moving to Hanover county and the town of Ashland.

*Importing for the Small Business: The Daily Telegraph Guide.* Kogan Page, Limited. • Irregular. $8.99. Publication includes: List of organizations able to help small businesses in the United Kingdom. Entries include: Organization name, address. Principal contents are articles on ordering, transport, payment, customs, and related aspects of importing for small businesses.

*Iran Business Database.* Faust Information GmbH. • $539 Individuals CD-ROM. Covers 30,000 companies in Iran.

*Jamaica Hills Association--Business Directory.* Jamaica Hills Association. • Covers entrepreneurs, businesses, and artists in Jamaica Plain, Massachusetts.

*Katy Business Association--Directory.* Katy Business Association. • List of businesses in Katy, Texas.

*Management Services and Technical Assistance: Small Business Resource.* Metro Atlanta Chamber of Commerce. • $8. Covers: Resources available to small businesses in the metropolitan Atlanta area. Entries include: Organization name, address, phone, description.

*Nisku Business Directory.* Nisku Business Association. • Annual. $30 Nonmembers book or CD. Lists companies located in Nisku Business Park and Edmonton International Airport.

*Oakdale Business and Professional Association--Directory of Members.* Oakdale Business and Professional Association. • List of business members in Oakdale, Minnesota.

*Rowlett Business Directory.* Business Directories of Texas. • List of businesses in Rowlett, Texas.

*SBIC Directory and Handbook of Small Business Finance.* International Wealth Success Inc. • Annual. $15 payment with order. Covers: over 400 small business investment companies (SBIC's) that lend money for periods from 5 to 20 years to small businesses. Entries include: Company name, address, amount and type of financing.

*Small Business Reference Guide.* Bluechip Books. • Irregular. $14.95. Covers: over 350 firms, associations, and government agencies offering products and services of assistance to small businesses. Entries include: Organization name, address, phone; most listings also include description of services, products, or activities.

*Small Business Sources of Capital Handbook.* Metro Atlanta Chamber of Commerce. • $8. Covers: Sources of capital available to small businesses in the metropolitan Atlanta area. Entries include: Source name, address, phone, description.

*South Carroll Business Association--Directory.* South Carroll Business Association. • Covers local business owners and managers in South Caroll county.

*Starting a Successful Small Business.* Kogan Page, Limited. • Irregular. $8.99. Publication includes: List of organizations of assistance to those starting small businesses. Entries include: Organization name, address. Principal content of publication is a discussion of how to set up a successful small business, including marketing, finances, legal questions, employment, and insurance.

*Strathalbyn District Commerce Association--Business Directory.* Strathalbyn District Commerce Association. • Covers local businesses in Strathalbyn, South Australia.

*Vero Beach Christian Business Association--Directory.* Vero Beach Christian Business Association. • Covers Christian business leaders in Vero Beach, Florida.

*Who's Who in Alexandria Business.* Alexandria Chamber of Commerce. • Annual. Covers businesses in Alexandria, Virginia.

*Wilton Manors Business Association--Directory.* Wilton Manors Business Association. • Covers 200 businesses in Wilton Manors.

### E-BOOKS

*Entrepreneur's Showcase: Market Research for Small Businesses and the Woman Entrepreneur's Guide to Financing a Business.* Cengage Learning Inc. • 2006. eBook. Published by Know!Books Press. Provides information on multiple aspects of entrepreneurship, focusing on market research for small business as well as on more gender-specific topics involved in starting a business.

*Global Electronic Business Research: Opportunities and Directions.* Cengage Learning Inc. • 2006. eBook. Published by Information Science Reference. Encourages researchers and professionals interested in SMEs (small to medium-sized enterprises) and e-commerce to address the next phase in this field. This book points to some of the impending issues concerning e-commerce in SMEs, and highlights the need to do something in order to bridge the existing divide between the two. Global Electronic Business Research raises the importance of addressing the e-commerce phenomenon in SMEs at a global level.

*How to Market Your Business.* • 2009. eBook. Published by Kogan Page. Covers market research, advertising, promotion, selling techniques, product launches, and use of the internet - everything you need to ensure your product reaches your market successfully.

*How to Value and Sell Your Business.* Cengage Learning Inc. • 2009. eBook. Published by Kogan Page. Provides in-depth commentary and advice on the valuation and sale of a small- to medium-sized business, developing an exit strategy, tax and legal issues, marketing your business, managing the sale process, etc, in order to ensure maximum profit.

*Start Up and Run Your Own Business.* Cengage Learning Inc. • 2010. eBook. Published by Kogan Page. Offers a complete information resource for those looking to set up their own business, including raising finance, taxation, IT, market research and employment issues.

*Starting a Business from Home.* Cengage Learning Inc. • 2009. eBook. Published by Kogan Page. Offers information about running a profitable and successful business from your own home with particular emphasis on opportunities provided by the internet.

*Starting a Successful Business.* Cengage Learning Inc. • 2009. eBook. Published by Kogan Page. Covers topics such as franchises, marketing, publicity, e-business, financial management, business law, recruitment, taxation, insurance, business planning and development.

### ENCYCLOPEDIAS AND DICTIONARIES

*Encyclopedia of Small Business.* Cengage Learning Inc. • $763 Individuals. 2010. $696.00. 4th edition. Two volumes. Contains about 600 informative entries on a wide variety of topics affecting small business. Arrangement is alphabetical. eBook also available. Inquire for pricing.

### GENERAL WORKS

*Area Business Councils/Small Business Update.* Greater San Antonio Chamber of Commerce. • Weekly.

*Homemade Money: How to Select, Start, Manage, Market and Multiply the Profits of a Business at Home.* Rowman and Littlefield Publishers Inc. • $24.95 Individuals book 1 and 2. Provides information on beginning and developing a home-based business.

*How to Organize and Run a Small Business.* American CPE Inc. • Contains detailed training information covering the basics of creating, organizing, and running a small business.

*Not Too Small to Care: Small Businesses and Child Care.* Child Care Action Campaign. • $15 for members. Profiles 29 small businesses that have implemented child care benefits: on-or-near-site child care centers, employee subsidies, and parental leave.

*Small Business Barometer.* Small Business Association of Michigan. • Contains surveys of Michigan business owners and reports on their economic outlook.

### HANDBOOKS AND MANUALS

*SBA Loan Guide.* Entrepreneur Meida, Inc. • Looseleaf. $59.50. A practical guide to obtaining loans through the Small Business Administration. (Start-Up Business Guide No. E1315.).

*Standard Business Forms for the Entrepreneur.* Entrepreneur Press. • Looseleaf. $59.50. A practical collection of forms useful to entrepreneurial small businesses. (Start-Up Business Guide No. E1319.).

*Start-Up Business Guides.* Entrepreneur Press. • Looseleaf. $59.50 each. Practical guides to starting a wide variety of small businesses.

### INTERNET DATABASES

*Business 2.0 Web Guide to the Best Business Links.* Business 2.0 Media Inc. Phone: (415)293-4800; Email: support@business2.com • URL: http://www.business2.com/webguide • Web site presents an extensive, searchable directory of links to "the best, most informative, and authoritative web pages." Twenty main categories cover business, finance, career, company information, people, and technology topics, with thousands of subtopics, all linking to Web sites recommended by experienced business researchers. Fees: Free.

*MBEMAG.* Minority Business Entrepreneur Magazine. Phone: (310)540-9398; Fax: (310)792-8263; Email: webmaster@mbemag.com • URL: http://www.mbemag.com • Web site's main feature is the "MBE Business Resources Directory." This provides complete mailing addresses, phone, fax, and Web site addresses (URL) for more than 40 organizations and government agencies having information or assistance for ethnic minority and women business owners. Some other links are "Current Events," "Calendar of Events," and "Business Opportunities." Updating is bimonthly. Fees: Free.

*Small Business Retirement Savings Advisor.* U. S. Department of Labor. Phone: (202)219-8921 • URL: http://www.dol.gov/elaws/pwbaplan.htm • Web site provides "answers to a variety of commonly asked questions about retirement saving options for small business employers." Includes a comparison chart and detailed descriptions of various plans: 401(k), SEP-IRA, SIMPLE-IRA, Payroll Deduction IRA, Keogh Profit-Sharing, Keogh Money Purchase, and Defined Benefit. Searching is offered. Fees: Free.

*Switchboard.* Switchboard, Inc. Phone: (508)898-8000; Fax: (508)898-1755; Email: webmaster@switchboard.com • URL: http://www.switchboard.com • Web site provides telephone numbers and street addresses for more than 100 million business locations and residences in the U. S. Broad industry categories are available. Fees: Free.

*U.S. Business Advisor.* Small Business Administration. Phone: (202)205-6600; Fax: (202)205-7064 • URL: http://www.sba.gov • Web site provides "a one-stop electronic link to all the information and services government provides for the business community." Covers about 60 federal agencies that exist to assist or regulate business. Detailed information is provided on financial assistance, workplace issues, taxes, regulations, international trade, and other business topics. Searching is offered. Fees: Free.

### ONLINE DATABASES

*American Business Directory.* InfoGroup Inc. • Provides brief online information on more than 10 million U. S. companies, including individual plants and branches. Entries typically include address, phone number, industry classification code, and contact name. Updating is quarterly. Inquire as to online cost and availability.

*Gale BusinessForms.* Cengage Learning Inc. •

Contains professionally drafted state-specific documents and forms for businesses. Covers dozens of topics, including arbitration, bills of sale, collections, confidentiality and nondisclosure, distributorships, guaranty, liens, limited liability companies, power of attorney, and technology.

*Small Business Resource Center.* Cengage Learning Inc. • Covers all major areas of starting and operating a business including financing, management, marketing, human resources, franchising, accounting and taxes.

## OTHER SOURCES

*Start-Up and Emerging Companies: Planning, Financing, and Operating the Successful Business, with Forms on Disk.* ALM Media Properties LLC. • $925 print + online + ebook. Covers a wide variety of business and legal topics relating to new enterprises. Provides information on venture financing, formation of corporations, tax laws, limited liability companies, employee benefits, contracts, and accounting. Includes a CD-ROM containing more than 75 sample legal forms, clauses, agreements, organizational resolutions, and checklists. (Law Journal Press).

## PERIODICALS AND NEWSLETTERS

*Business Digest of Lehigh Valley.* Business Digest of Lehigh Valley. • Monthly. Small business magazine (tabloid).

*Business Start-Ups: Smart Ideas for Your Small Business.* Entrepreneur Press. • Monthly. $14.97 per year. Provides advice for starting a small business. Includes business trends, new technology, E-commerce, and case histories ("real-life stories").

*Business Trends.* Quebecor Media Inc. • Monthly. $24 Individuals Canadian (GST included). Magazine featuring local business-related articles for the Sarnia, Ontario area in Canada.

*Entrepreneur: The Small Business Authority.* Entrepreneur Press. • Monthly. $19.97 per year. Contains advice for small business owners and prospective owners. Includes numerous franchise advertisements.

*Entrepreneurship: Theory and Practice.* Blackwell Publishing Inc. • Bimonthly. $590 Institutions Online or Print only.

*The Home Business Report.* The Kerner Group Inc. • Provides information on how to operate a home-based business or work from home. Features real life success stories, how-to articles on marketing, and strategies to keep focused on goals. Recurring features include letters to the editor, interviews, news of research, job listings, book reviews, and notices of publications available.

*Home Office Connections: A Monthly Journal of News, Ideas, Opportunities, and Savings for Those Who Work at Home.* Home Office Association of America. • Monthly. Free to members; nonmembers, $49.00 per year.

*HomeOffice: The Homebased Office Authority.* Entrepreneur Press. • Bimonthly. $11.97 per year. Contains advice for operating a business in the home.

*In Business: The Magazine for Environmental Entrepreneuring.* The JG Press Inc. • Bimonthly. $33.00 per year. Magazine for environmental entrepreneuring.

*Inc.: The Magazine for Growing Companies.* INC. • 10/year. $10 U.S. /year for two subscription. Edited for small office and home businesses with one to 25 employees. Covers management, office technology, and lifestyle. Incorporates *Self-Employed Professional.*

*International Wealth Success Newsletter: The Monthly Newsletter of Worldwide Wealth Opportunities.* Tyler G. Hicks, editor. International Wealth Success, Inc. • Monthly. $24.00 per year. Newsletter. Provides information on a variety of

small business topics, including financing, mail order, foreign opportunities, licensing, and franchises.

*Minority Business Entrepreneur.* Minority Business Entrepreneur. • Bimonthly. $25 Individuals print amd digital. Reports on issues "critical to the growth and development of minority and women-owned firms." Provides information on relevant legislation and profiles successful women and minority entrepreneurs.

*National Small Business Journal: The information newspaper for small & growing businesses.* TWG Publishing Co. • $15 annual. Newspaper containing articles geared toward small businesses and their interests.

*The Small Business Advisor.* Small Business Advisors Inc. • Monthly. $45 print or soft copy. Seeks to help emerging growth companies increase profits. Considers small business issues, including marketing sales, finance, taxes, organizing, competition, management, and human resources. Recurring features include letters to the editor, interviews, and columns titled Info Bank, In the Mail Box, Taxes, Human Resources, Marketing, Insurance, and Law. Remarks: Publication suspended in 1980; resumed publication Fall 1993.

## RESEARCH CENTERS AND INSTITUTES

Babson College - Arthur M. Blank Center for Entrepreneurship. 231 Forest St., Wellesley Hills, MA 02481-6834. Phone: (781)233-5023; Fax: (781)239-4178; Email: jstrimaitis@babson.edu • URL: http://www.babson.edu/Academics/centers/blank-center/Pages/home.aspx • Sponsors annual Babson College Entrepreneurship Research Conference.

Cooperative State Research, Education, and Extension Service - Small and Home-Based Business. 4435 Waterfront Ctr., 800 9th St. SW, Washington, DC 20250. Phone: (202)720-5997; Fax: (202)690-2975; Email: amclaren@csrees.usda.gov • URL: http://www.csrees.usda.gov/smallhomebasedbusiness.cfm • Women-owned and operated farms and ranches, rural entrepreneurship, small and home-based businesses.

The Darla Moore School of Business - Division of Research. University of South Carolina at Columbia, 1705 College St., Columbia, SC 29208. Phone: (803)777-2510; Fax: (803)777-2510; Email: steel@moore.sc.edu • URL: http://www.mooreschool.sc.edu.

East Tennessee State University - Tennessee Small Business Development Center. College of Business & Technology, 2109 W Market St., Johnson City, TN 37604. Phone: (423)439-8505; Fax: (423)439-8506; Email: bjustice@mail.tsbdc.org • URL: http://www.tsbdc.org • Small business assistance in the areas of business plans and strategies, financial forecasts, feasibility studies, financial statement analysis, credit establishment and collection policies, inventory control analysis, marketing plans, accounting and record-keeping systems, licenses, permits, tax authorities, organizational structure, management succession, professional development, and buying and selling.

Grand Valley State University - Michigan Small Business and Technology Development Center. 1020-L William Seidman Center, 50 Front Ave. SW, Grand Rapids, MI 49504. Phone: (616)331-7480; Fax: (616)331-7485; Email: sbtdchq@gvsu.edu • URL: http://misbtdc.org • Manufacturing, financing, and international business information (particularly the export process) for small businesses. Resources for the export process includes determining and detailing international feasibility, foreign market entry plans, and responding to international inquiries. Foreign market information includes business etiquette and negotiating, country demographics, detailed tax information, financing sources,

industry specific information, intellectual property rights, market contracts, rules and regulations, specific market information, and tariff reduction schedules.

Lehigh University - Small Business Development Center. 125 Goodman Dr., Bethlehem, PA 18015. Phone: (610)758-3980; Fax: (610)758-5205; Email: insbdc@lehigh.edu • URL: http://www.lehigh.edu/insbdc/index.html • Problems faced by small businesses, the impact of the general economy on the formation and operation of small business, and characteristics on entrepreneurs.

Massey University - New Zealand Centre for Small and Medium Enterprise Research. Private Box 756, Wellington, New Zealand. Phone: 64 4 8015799; Fax: 64 4 8020290; Email: d.deakins@massey.ac.nz • URL: http://www.massey.ac.nz/massey/learning/departments/centres-research/new-zealand-centre-for-sme-research/nzsmerc.cfm • Micro-enterprises, small enterprises, and medium enterprises.

Small Business Administration - Office of Technology. 409 3rd St. SW, Washington, DC 20416. Phone: (202)205-6450; Fax: (202)481-1518; Email: edsel.brown@sba.gov • URL: http://archive.sba.gov/aboutsba/sbaprograms/sbir/index.html • Provides policy for the Small Business Innovation Research Program (SBIR). SBIR is a federal procurement system that provides qualified small business concerns with opportunities to compete for federal research and development awards. Also oversees the Small Business Technology Transfer (STTR) Program. STTR coordinates cooperative research and development activities between small business STTR awardee, nonprofit research institutions, or federally funded research and development centers.

Small Business Innovation Research Program - Small Business Technology Transfer Program. Germantown Bldg., SC-29, 1000 Independence Ave. SW, Washington, DC 20585. Phone: (301)903-5707; Fax: (301)903-5488; Email: sbir-sttr@science.doe.gov • URL: http://science.energy.gov/sbir • Private sector commercialization of energy-related innovations derived from Federal research and development; technological innovation; the use small business to meet Federal research and development needs; Phase I funding up to $100,000 for a period of approximately nine months; further funding (up to $750,000 for not more than 24 months) to continue development of promising programs initiated in Phase I; and, finally, follow-on funding for commercial applications of the research or development pursued by small business with nonfederal capital, or alternatively, follow-on non-SBIR federal contracts for products or processes desired by the government. to $100,000 for a period of approximately six months; further funding (up to $750,000 for not more than 24 months) to continue development of promising programs initiated in Phase I; and, finally, follow-on funding for commercial applications of the research or development pursued by small business with nonfederal capital, or alternatively, follow-on non-SBIR federal contracts for products or processes desired by the government.

U.S. Small Business Administration - Office of Advocacy - Research and Statistics - Office of Economic Research. 409 3rd St., 7th Fl., Washington, DC 20416. Phone: (202)205-6533 or (202)205-6973; Fax: (202)206-6928 or (202)205-6928; Email: advocacy@sba.gov • URL: http://www.sba.gov/advo/research • Economic research and analysis pertaining to small business economic issues and statistics. Of particular interest are projects that are policy-oriented to develop alternative approaches to solving small business problems. Proposals may be submitted by any individual or firm (including small businesses).

University of Missouri—Columbia - Business

Research and Information Development Group. 410 S 6th St., 200 Engineering N, Columbia, MO 65211. Phone: (573)882-8855; Fax: (573)884-4297; Email: schmidtdc@missouri.edu • URL: http://www.bridg. org • Entrepreneurship, small business development and growth.

University of Quebec at Trois-Rivieres - Research Institute for Small and Medium-Sized Enterprises. Pavillon Desjardins-Hydro-Quebec, 3351, Blvd. des Forges, Trois-Rivieres, QC, Canada G9A 5H7. Phone: (819)376-5235; Fax: (819)376-5138; Email: inrpme@uqtr.ca • URL: http://oraprdnt.uqtr. uquebec.ca/pls/public/gscw030?owa_no_site=861 • Small business and entrepreneurship, including management, strategy, finance, operation, marketing, information systems innovation, regional sciences, and economics.

## TRADE/PROFESSIONAL ASSOCIATIONS

American Home Business Association. 53 W 9000 S, Sandy, UT 84070. Phone: 866-396-7773 or (801)273-2350; Fax: (866)396-7773 or (801)273-2399; Email: info@homebusinessworks.com • URL: http://www.homebusinessworks.com • Offers benefits and services dedicated to supporting the needs of home business, small business and entrepreneurs. Benefits include health-auto-home insurance, legal, low long distance and 800 numbers, business line of credit, merchant accounts, tax programs, office supply and travel discounts and more. Seeks to provide members access to the best traditional benefits and timely information that is critical to conduct a successful home, small or Internet business.

American Small Business Coalition. 6700 Alexander Bell Dr., Ste. 200, Columbia, MD 21046. Phone: (410)381-7378; Email: sponsor@theasbc. org • URL: http://www.theasbc.org • Focuses on supporting the development of relationships, best practices and market intelligence for companies doing business in the government sector. Seeks to augment industry education and outreach efforts as a resource partner to agencies of the U.S. Government. Assists in the ongoing development and growth of member companies who support agency mission requirements through their direct and indirect provisioning of goods and services. Provides industry education, relationship development and strategy alignment assistance to member companies new to government contracting. Supports the success of government contractors designated "other than small business" who seek assistance with identifying viable small business partners in multiple industry domains.

American Small Manufacturers Coalition. PO Box 15289, Washington, DC 20003. Phone: (202)341-7066; Fax: (202)315-3906 • URL: http://www. smallmanufacturers.org • Strives to help small manufacturers to succeed. Improves the innovativeness and productivity of America's manufacturing community. Advocates for legislative and programmatic resources to allow small manufacturers to compete in the global marketplace.

BEST Employers Association. 2505 McCabe Way, Irvine, CA 92614. Phone: 866-706-2225; Email: bestassoc@bestlife.com • URL: http://www. beassoc.org • Provides small independent businesses with managerial, economic, financial and sales information helpful for business improvement. Organizes and sponsors healthcare alliances for small employers. (The acronym BEST stands for Beneficial Employees Security Trust).

Central Association of Women Entrepreneurs. Kaisaniemenkatu 1 B a 74, FIN-00100 Helsinki, Finland. Phone: 358 40 5222252; Email: toimisto@ yrittajanaiset.fi • URL: http://www.yrittajanaiset.fi • Women entrepreneurs in Finland. Promotes the participation of women in Finland's economic structure. Assists women in small business development.

European Association of Craft, Small and Medium-Sized Enterprises. Rue Jacques de Lalaingstraat 4, B-1040 Brussels, Belgium. Phone: 32 2 230 75 99; Fax: 32 2 2 230 78 61; Email: info@ueapme.com • URL: http://www.ueapme.com • Represents the interests, at the European level, of crafts, trades and SMEs in the European Union and countries applying for accession to the European Union.

Mountains and Plains Independent Booksellers Association. 3278 Big Spruce Way, Park City, UT 84098. Phone: (435)649-6079; Fax: (435)649-6105; Email: info@mountainsplains.org • URL: http:// www.mountainsplains.org • Supports independent bookstores; promotes literacy and defends freedom of speech and of the press.

National Association of Entrepreneurial Parents. PO Box 320722, Fairfield, CT 06825. Phone: (203)371-6212; Fax: (203)371-6212 • URL: http://www.en-parent.com • Seeks to assist "parents who are looking to balance work and family on their own terms." Facilitates networking among entrepreneurial parents; provides ad opportunities for members; organizes support groups for members; makes available discount programs and services to members.

National Association of Small Business Contractors. 700 12th St. NW, Ste. 700, Washington, DC 20005. Phone: 888-861-9290 • URL: http://www.nasbc.org • Serves and advances the interests of small business contractors. Seeks to establish opportunities for small business owners to meet with state and federal agencies, prime contractors, potential teaming partners and procurement experts. Strives to create a strong and respected voice for advocacy in support of small business' interests.

National Federation of Independent Business. 53 Century Blvd., Ste. 250, Nashville, TN 37214. Phone: (202)554-9000 or (615)874-5288; Email: web_membership@nfib.org • URL: http://www. nfib.com/ • Members are independent business and professional people.

National Small Business Association. 1156 15th St. NW, Ste. 1100, Washington, DC 20005. Phone: 800-345-6728 or (202)293-8830; Fax: (202)872-8543; Email: info@nsba.biz • URL: http://www.nsba.biz • Small businesses including manufacturing, wholesale, retail, service, and other firms. Works to advocate at the federal level on behalf of smaller businesses.

Organization for Competitive Markets. PO Box 6486, Lincoln, NE 68506. Phone: (402)817-4443 • URL: http://www.competitivemarkets.com • Works for increased competition and protection for the agricultural marketplace. Works against "abuse of corporate power and consolidation of the agricultural market."

Small Business Service Bureau. 554 Main St., Worcester, MA 01615-0014. Phone: 800-343-0939; Email: info@sbsb.com • URL: http://www.sbsb. com • Represents businesses with less than 100 employees. Offers planning and strategy programs to aid businesspersons in starting, improving, or expanding small businesses. Disseminates guides, manuals and other materials on small business operations. Offers trade assistance to the People's Republic of China.

Small Firms Association. Confederation House, 84-86 Lower Baggot St., Dublin 2, Dublin, Ireland. Phone: 353 1 6051500 or 353 1 6051602; Fax: 353 1 353 1 6381602; Email: info@sfa.ie • URL: http:// www.sfa.ie • Represents the small enterprises in Ireland. Provides economic, commercial, employee relations and social affairs advice and assistance.

Support Services Alliance. 2457 State Rte. 7, Ste. 1, Cobleskill, NY 12043. Phone: 800-909-2772; Email: info@ssamembers.com • URL: http://www. ssamembers.com • Represents small businesses (less than 50 employees), the self-employed, and associations of such individuals. Provides services and

programs such as group purchasing discounts, health coverage, legislative advocacy, and business and financial support services.

World Association for Small and Medium Enterprises. Plot No. 4, Institutional Area, Sector 16A, Noida 201301, Uttar Pradesh, India. Fax: 91 120 4216283; Email: bds@wasmeinfo.org • URL: http://www.wasmeinfo.org • Works to undertake research programmes and incisive studies on various issues of small businesses; arranges placement of counsellors, specialists and trainers to facilitate flow of knowledge and expertise in specific fields.

# SMALL BUSINESS INVESTMENT COMPANIES

## DIRECTORIES

*American Small Business Coalition--Membership Directory.* American Small Business Council. • Quarterly. Covers individual professionals and companies doing business in support of government agency requirements.

## HANDBOOKS AND MANUALS

*Moody's Bank and Finance Manual.* Mergent. • Annual. $1,750 Four volumes.. Includes biweekly supplements in *Moody's Bank and Finance News Report.*

## STATISTICS SOURCES

*Small Business Administration. Annual Report.* U. S. Government Printing Office. • Annual. Two volumes.

## TRADE/PROFESSIONAL ASSOCIATIONS

National Association of Small Business Contractors. 700 12th St. NW, Ste. 700, Washington, DC 20005. Phone: 888-861-9290 • URL: http://www.nasbc.org • Serves and advances the interests of small business contractors. Seeks to establish opportunities for small business owners to meet with state and federal agencies, prime contractors, potential teaming partners and procurement experts. Strives to create a strong and respected voice for advocacy in support of small business' interests.

Small Business Investor Alliance. 1100 H St. NW, Ste. 610, Washington, DC 20005. Phone: (202)628-5055; Email: membership@sbia.org • URL: http:// www.sbia.org • Affiliated with Small Business Investor Alliance.

# SMALL LOAN COMPANIES

*See* FINANCE COMPANIES

# SMOKING POLICY

*See also* TOBACCO AND TOBACCO INDUSTRY

## ABSTRACTS AND INDEXES

*Readers' Guide to Periodical Literature.* EBSCO Publishing Inc. • Provides indexing for over 400 periodicals dating back to 1983.

## CD-ROM DATABASES

*Readers' Guide to Periodical Literature.* EBSCO Publishing Inc. • Provides indexing for over 400 periodicals dating back to 1983.

## GENERAL WORKS

*Drugs, Alcohol & Tobacco: Learning About Addictive Behavior.* Edited by Rosalyn Carson-Dewitt, M.D. Cengage Learning Inc. • $512. Three volumes. Contains 200 articles on various aspects of addiction. Includes color illustrations, a glossary, and comprehensive indexing. Macmillan Reference USA imprint. eBook also available. Inquire for pricing.

## RESEARCH CENTERS AND INSTITUTES

University of Kentucky - College of Agriculture, Food and Environment - Kentucky Tobacco Research and Development Center. Cooper & University Drs., Lexington, KY 40546-0236. Phone: (859)257-5798; Fax: (859)323-1077; Email: ochamb@uky.edu • URL: http://www2.ca.uky.edu/ktrdc/index.html • Application of biotechnology for the development of new crops based on tobacco and other plants. Development of new medicinal and industrial applications for plant natural products. Development of new crops from native plants and adaptation of existing crops for more efficient production of plant-made pharmaceuticals, plant-made industrial products, and plant natural products.

# SNACK FOOD INDUSTRY

*See also* BAKING INDUSTRY; FOOD INDUSTRY

## DIRECTORIES

*Baking/Snack Directory & Buyer's Guide.* Sosland Publishing Co. • Annual. $205 Individuals S&H for ea. additional copy is $2 reg., $16 prior.. Covers: Wholesale bakers of bread, cake, cookies, crackers, pasta; manufacturers of snack foods, mixes, and frozen dough; licensors of proprietary brands; manufacturers of equipment and products and suppliers of services used in wholesale baking. For bakers--Company name, address, phone, principal headquarters and plant personnel, principal products, sales volume, production method, and number of employees. For manufacturers--Company name, address, phone, name and title of contact. Entries include: Company name, address, phone, executive name.

*Major Food and Drink Companies of the World.* Cengage Learning Inc. • 12th edition. eBook. Published by Graham & Whiteside. Contains profiles and trade names for more than 9,200 important food and beverage companies in various countries. In addition to foods, includes both alcoholic and nonalcoholic drink products.

## ONLINE DATABASES

*Food Science and Technology Abstracts (online).* IFIS North American Desk. • Produced by International Food Information Service. Provides about 500,000 online citations, with abstracts, to the international literature of food science, technology, commodities, engineering, and processing. Approximately 2,000 periodicals are covered. Time period is 1969 to date, with monthly updates. Inquire as to online cost and availability.

## PERIODICALS AND NEWSLETTERS

*Confectioner: The Magazine.* BNP Media. • Bimonthly. $70.17 per year. Covers a wide variety of topics relating to the distribution and retailing of candy and snacks.

*Food Distribution Magazine.* Phoenix Media Network Inc. • Monthly. $49.00 per year. Edited for marketers and buyers of domestic and imported, specialty or gourmet food products, including ethnic foods, seasonings, and bakery items.

*Snack Food and Wholesale Bakery: The Magazine That Defines the Snack Food Industry.* BNP Media. • Monthly. Monthly. Free to qualified personnel; others, $85.06 per year. Provides information for producers of pretzels, potato chips, cookies, crackers, nuts, and other snack foods. Includes *Annual Buyers Guide* and *State of Industry Report.*

## TRADE/PROFESSIONAL ASSOCIATIONS

Biscuit and Cracker Manufacturers Association. 6325 Woodside Ct., Ste. 125, Columbia, MD 21046. Phone: (443)545-1645; Fax: (410)290-8585 • URL: http://www.thebcma.org • Members are bakers of crackers and cookies. Formerly Biscuit Bakers Institute.

Cookie and Snack Bakers Association. c/o Craig Parrish, Executive Director, 1128 Maple Dr. NW, Cleveland, TN 37312. Phone: (423)280-8056; Email: csparrish@bellsouth.net • URL: http://www.casba.us • Members are bakers of snacks and cookies.

Peanut and Tree Nut Processors Association. PO Box 2660, Alexandria, VA 22301. Phone: (301)365-2521; Email: jhodges@ptnpa.org • URL: http://www.ptnpa.org • Formerly Peanut Butter Manufacturers and NutSalters Association.

Popcorn Board. 330 N Wabash Ave., Ste. 2000, Chicago, IL 60611. Phone: (312)644-6610; Email: info@popcorn.org • URL: http://www.popcorn.org • Represents companies engaged in popcorn processing and trade management activities as well as government relations. Provides a platform for discussion on the popcorn industry. Maintains hall of fame for retired members who have made contributions to the industry.

# SNUFF

*See* TOBACCO AND TOBACCO INDUSTRY

# SOAPS AND DETERGENTS

*See* CLEANING PRODUCTS INDUSTRY

# SOCIAL ACCOUNTING

*See* NATIONAL ACCOUNTING

# SOCIAL CLUB

## OTHER SOURCES

*Arnold Air Society.* • Honorary professional fraternity within AFROTC. Organizes community service projects. Sponsors Silver Wings, a nonmilitary campus service organization.

*The Creative Coalition.* • Actors, writers, directors and other arts and entertainment professionals. Aims to educate members about social and political issues, particularly in the areas of the First Amendment, arts advocacy and public education.

*National Society of Pershing Rifles.* • Members range from military to civilian, male to female. Seeks to foster a spirit of friendship and cooperation among men and women in the military department and to maintain a highly efficient drill company.

*National Society of Scabbard and Blade.* • Honorary and recognition fraternity - men and women, military; advanced ROTC; junior ROTC, and all-Service. Maintains speakers' bureau.

*Navy Club of the United States of America Auxiliary.* • Women relatives of men who have served in the United States Navy, Marine Corps, Coast Guard, and component reserve services; women who are eligible in their own right for membership in the Navy Club of the United States of America. Provides assistance to the Navy Club; promotes fraternal love and sociability; encourages interest in the U.S. Navy and its history. Activities include veterans' service, rehabilitation programs, child welfare assistance, handicapped services, and overseas relief, memorials, and community service. Supports U.S. Navy special services. Maintains museum.

# SOCIAL RESPONSIBILITY

*See also* BUSINESS ETHICS; COMMUNITY RELATIONS

## ABSTRACTS AND INDEXES

*PAIS International.* ProQuest L.L.C. • Monthly. $850.00 per year; cumulations three times a year. Provides topical citations to the worldwide literature of public affairs, economics, demographics, sociology, and trade. Text in English; indexed materials in English, French, German, Italian, Portuguese and Spanish.

*Social Sciences Citation Index.* Thomson Reuters Corp. • Weekly. Product is accessed via *Web of Science.*

*Social Sciences Index Retrospective: 1907-1983.* EBSCO Publishing Inc. • Indexing for 1,000,000 articles. Coverage includes international index and social sciences and humanities index.

## ALMANACS AND YEARBOOKS

*Research in Corporate Social Performance and Policy: An Annual Compilation of Research.* Elsevier. • Dates vary. $78.50. 15 volumes.

## CD-ROM DATABASES

*Newspaper Abstracts Ondisc.* ProQuest L.L.C. • Monthly. $2,950.00 per year (covers 1989 to date; archival discs are available for 1985-88). Provides cover-to-cover CD-ROM indexing and abstracting of 19 major newspapers, including the *New York Times, Wall Street Journal, Washington Post, Chicago Tribune,* and *Los Angeles Times.*

*PAIS International.* ProQuest L.L.C. • Monthly. $1,995.00 per year. Contains over 650,000 citations to the literature of contemporary social, political, and economic issues.

*Social Sciences Abstracts.* EBSCO Publishing Inc. • Provides indexing from 1983 and abstracting from 1994 of more than 750 periodicals covering economics, area studies, community health, public administration, public welfare, urban studies, and many other topics related to the social sciences.

*Social Sciences Citation Index.* Thomson Reuters Corp. • Weekly. Product is accessed via *Web of Science.*

## ONLINE DATABASES

*Wilson Social Sciences Abstracts Online.* H.W. Wilson Co. • Provides online abstracting and indexing of more than 500 periodicals covering area studies, community health, public administration, public welfare, urban studies, and many other social science topics. Time period is 1994 to date for abstracts and 1983 to date for indexing, with updates weekly. Inquire as to online cost and availability.

## PERIODICALS AND NEWSLETTERS

*Business and Society: A Journal of Interdisciplinary Exploration.* International Association for Business and Society Research Committee. Pine Forge Press. • Quarterly. $402.00 per year.

*Business and Society Review: Journal of the Center for Business Ethics at Bentley College.* Blackwell Publishing Inc. • Quarterly. Institutions, $359.00 per year. Includes online edition.

*Review of Social Economy.* Association for Social Economics. Taylor & Francis Ltd. • Quarterly. $152 Individuals Print and Online. Quarterly. Subject matter is concerned with the relationships between social values and economics. Includes articles on income distribution, poverty, labor, and class.

## RESEARCH CENTERS AND INSTITUTES

Boston College - Center for Corporate Citizenship. Carroll School of Management, 55 Lee Rd., Chestnut Hill, MA 02467-3942. Phone: (617)552-4545; Fax: (617)552-8499; Email: kv.smith@bc.edu • URL: http://www.bcccc.net • Areas of study include corporate images within local communities, corporate community relations, social vision, and philanthropy. Formerly Center for Corporate Community Relations.

Clinical Research Institute of Montreal - Centre for

Bioethics. 110 Pine Ave. W, Montreal, QC, Canada H2W 1R7. Phone: (514)987-5617; Fax: (514)987-5695; Email: david.roy@ircm.qc.ca • URL: http://www.ircm.qc.ca/bioethique/ • Works to identify and resolve ethical issues in medical practice and research. Monitors legal and policy issues such as "do not resuscitate" protocols and human experimentation. Facilitates exchange of information among physicians, medical scientists, and other health professionals. Conducts research and educational programs.

Johns Hopkins University - Johns Hopkins Berman Institute of Bioethics. Deering Hall, 1809 Ashland Ave., Baltimore, MD 21205. Phone: (410)614-5550; Email: bioethics@jhu.edu • URL: http://www.bioethicsinstitute.org • Moral and policy issues in biomedical science, health care, and health policy, and the development of thoughtful solutions for the benefit of society.

San Jose State University - Institute for Social Responsibility, Ethics, and Education. 1 Washington Sq., San Jose, CA 95192-0096. Phone: (408)924-5563; Fax: (408)924-4527; Email: lawrence.quill@sjsu.edu • URL: http://www.sjsu.edu/isree • Social responsibility, including professional and business ethics.

University of Bath - School of Management - Centre for Business Organisations and Society., Bath BA2 7AY, United Kingdom. Phone: 44 1225 384974 • URL: http://www.bath.ac.uk/cbos • Relationship between corporations and the societies in which they operate, the ethical position of modern corporations in different societal contexts, and the study of corporate social responsibility as a strategic phenomenon.

University of Pennsylvania - Center for Bioethics. c/o Dr. Arthur L. Caplan, Director, 3401 Market St., Philadelphia, PA 19104-3318. Fax: (215)573-3036 • URL: http://www.pennmedicine.org/lung/research/centers-institutes/center-for-bioethics.html • Works as an interdisciplinary unit of the University of Pennsylvania Health System; seeks to advance scholarly and public understanding of ethical, legal, social and public policy issues in healthcare. Conducts research aimed at improving the practice and delivery of medical care. Offers degree programs. Maintains speakers' bureau.

University of Pittsburgh - Business, Government, and Society Research Institute. School of Business, Mervis Hall, Pittsburgh, PA 15260. Phone: (412)648-1555; Fax: (412)648-1693; Email: mitnick@pitt.edu.

University of Wollongong - Centre for Social Marketing Research. Bldg. 19, Rm. 1034a, Faculty of Commerce, Northfields Ave., Wollongong, NSW 2522, Australia. Phone: 61 2 42215994; Fax: 61 2 42213257; Email: csmr@uow.edu.au • URL: http://www.uow.edu.au/commerce/smm/mark/academics/UOW010679.htm • Social marketing, including commercial marketing, nonprofit marketing, and issues of corporate social responsibility.

## TRADE/PROFESSIONAL ASSOCIATIONS

Business and Community Foundation. 1D, 1st Fl., Shahpur Jat, New Delhi 110049, Delhi, India. Phone: 91 11 3253-6392 • URL: http://www.bcfindia.org • Promotes awareness and practice of good corporate citizenship as a business operation; promotes businesses to become an integral part of the societal process whereby people have access and control over resources to make informed choices and decisions towards a more humane, compassionate and just society in India.

Business for Social Responsibility. 88 Kearny St., 12th Fl., San Francisco, CA 94108. Phone: (415)984-3200; Fax: (415)984-3201; Email: connect@bsr.org • URL: http://www.bsr.org • Large, small, and medium-sized businesses. Promotes responsible business behavior and serves as a

resource to companies striving to make ethical business decisions.

Corporate Social Responsibility Association. 155 E Boardwalk Dr., No. 544, Fort Collins, CO 80525. Phone: (303)944-4225; Fax: (303)496-0437; Email: jhall@csrassn.com • URL: http://csrassn.com • Promotes information gathering, networking and implementation of corporate social responsibility. Works to integrate ethical, social and environmental concerns in business. Supports best management practices in consolidating corporate social responsibility.

Economic Justice Institute. University of Wisconsin Law School, 975 Bascom Mall, Madison, WI 53706-1399. Phone: (608)262-2240 • URL: http://law.wisc.edu/eji • Provides advocate services for consumers and low-income families through education, research, training and representation. Aims to educate and empower consumers by providing services and information.

Executives Without Borders. 281 Summer St., 5th Fl., Boston, MA 02210. Phone: 800-790-6134; Email: contactus@execwb.org • URL: http://www.executiveswithoutborders.org • Encourages businessmen and businesswomen to use their leadership positions to foster the growth of business in developing countries. Provides humanitarian aid to alleviate the effects of natural and economic disasters. Promotes cooperation and works with research institutions to find sustainable business solutions.

Global Grassroots. 1950 Lafayette Rd., Ste. 200, Portsmouth, NH 03801-8663. Phone: (603)643-0400; Email: info@globalgrassroots.org • URL: http://www.globalgrassroots.org/index.htm • Works to empower, unite, and support relief of poor, distressed and underprivileged women worldwide. Benefits women by establishing a global network of leading entrepreneurs. Raises awareness of critical issues facing women worldwide, especially sexual and gender-based violence during conflict.

Local Initiatives Support Corporation. 501 7th Ave., New York, NY 10018-5903. Phone: (212)455-9800; Fax: (212)682-5929; Email: info@lisc.org • URL: http://www.lisc.org • Seeks to help independent community-based organizations in deteriorated areas to improve local, physical, and economic conditions while strengthening their own management and financial capabilities. Matches funds contributed by local corporations and foundations with those provided by national donors and investors; offers loans and grants to local organizations and projects. Administers national community development loan programs in cooperation with major financial institutions.

Mananga Management Centre. PO Box 5100, Mbabane, Swaziland. Email: info@mananga.sz • URL: http://www.mananga.sz • Development organizations and individuals with an interest in development issues. Promotes more effective management of development projects. Sponsors training courses for development administrators; initiates programs in areas including agricultural development, women's rights, rural development, environmental protection, water supply and sanitation, and vocational education.

New Rules for Global Finance Coalition. 2000 M St. NW, Ste. 720, Washington, DC 20036-3327. Phone: (202)277-9390; Fax: (202)280-1141 • URL: http://www.new-rules.org • Represents the interests of development, human rights, labor, environmental, and religious organizations and scholars. Aims to reform the global financial architecture to prevent financial crises. Works to stabilize the world economy, reduce poverty and inequality, uphold fundamental rights, and protect the environment.

Work for Progress. 1543 Wazee St., Ste. 440, Denver, CO 80202-1450. Phone: (303)623-4900; Fax: (720)306-3699; Email: info@workforprogress.

org • URL: http://www.workforprogress.org • Focuses on strengthening organizations that work for social change. Recruits job-seekers to work with the nation's nonprofit organizations and progressive campaigns for social justice, consumer protection and the environment. Helps activist-minded job-seekers to connect with progressive campaigns and organizations that are working across the country on progressive issues.

# SOCIAL SECURITY

*See also* MEDICARE

## ABSTRACTS AND INDEXES

*Readers' Guide to Periodical Literature.* EBSCO Publishing Inc. • Provides indexing for over 400 periodicals dating back to 1983.

*Social Sciences Citation Index.* Thomson Reuters Corp. • Weekly. Product is accessed via *Web of Science.*

*Social Sciences Index Retrospective: 1907-1983.* EBSCO Publishing Inc. • Indexing for 1,000,000 articles. Coverage includes international index and social sciences and humanities index.

## CD-ROM DATABASES

*Readers' Guide to Periodical Literature.* EBSCO Publishing Inc. • Provides indexing for over 400 periodicals dating back to 1983.

*Social Sciences Abstracts.* EBSCO Publishing Inc. • Provides indexing from 1983 and abstracting from 1994 of more than 750 periodicals covering economics, area studies, community health, public administration, public welfare, urban studies, and many other topics related to the social sciences.

*Social Sciences Citation Index.* Thomson Reuters Corp. • Weekly. Product is accessed via *Web of Science.*

*SSA Publications on CD-ROM.* U. S. Government Printing Office. • Monthly. Provides updated text of three Social Security Administration publications: *Program Operations Manual; Social Security Handbook;* and *Social Security Rulings.*

## DIRECTORIES

*Government Assistance Almanac: The Guide to Federal, Domestic, Financial and Other Programs Covering Grants, Loans, Insurance, Personal Payments and Benefits.* Omnigraphics Inc. • Annual. $275 print. Gives users updated information on all available federal domestic assistance programs. These programs represent nearly $2 trillion worth of federal assistance earmarked for distribution to consumers, children, parents, veterans, senior citizens, students, businesses, civic groups, state and local agencies, and others.

## E-BOOKS

*Social Trends & Indicators USA.* Monique D. Magee, editor. Cengage Learning Inc. • Includes data on labor, economics, the health care industry, crime, leisure, population, education, social security, and many other topics. Sources include various government agencies and major publications. Inquire for pricing.

## HANDBOOKS AND MANUALS

*Medicare Explained.* Wolters Kluwer Law & Business CCH. • Annual. $67.95.

*Social Security Benefits, Including Medicare.* Wolters Kluwer Law & Business CCH. • Annual. $11.00.

*Social Security Explained.* Wolters Kluwer Law & Business CCH. • Annual. $37.00.

*Social Security Handbook.* U. S. Government Printing Office. • Annual. $53.00. Issued by the Social Security Administration (www.ssa.gov). Provides detailed information about social security programs, including Medicare, with brief descriptions of related programs administered by agencies other than the Social Security Administration.

*Social Security Manual.* • Annual. $22.95.

*Social Security Practice Guide.* Matthew Bender and Company Inc. • Irregular. $1,839 Individuals Book. Periodic supplementation. Complete, practical guide on all substantive and procedural aspects of social security practice. Prepared under the supervision of the National Organization of Social Security Claimants' Representatives (NOSSCR).

*Social Security Programs Throughout the World.* U. S. Government Printing Office. • Annual. $35.70 Individuals International List price - paperback. Issued by the Social Security Administration (www. ssa.gov). Presents basic information on more than 170 social security systems around the world.

### INTERNET DATABASES

*Social Security Online: The Official Web Site of the Social Security Administration.* U. S. Social Security Administration. Phone: 800-772-1213 or (410)965-7700 • URL: http://www.ssa.gov • Web site provides a wide variety of online information relating to social security and Medicare. Topics include benefits, disability, employer wage reporting, personal earnings statements, statistics, government financing, social security law, and public welfare reform legislation.

### ONLINE DATABASES

*Ageline.* AARP. • Provides indexing and abstracting of the literature of social gerontology, including consumer aspects, financial planning, employment, housing, health care services, mental health, social security, and retirement. Time period is 1978 to date. Inquire as to online cost and availability.

*Wilson Social Sciences Abstracts Online.* H.W. Wilson Co. • Provides online abstracting and indexing of more than 500 periodicals covering area studies, community health, public administration, public welfare, urban studies, and many other social science topics. Time period is 1994 to date for abstracts and 1983 to date for indexing, with updates weekly. Inquire as to online cost and availability.

### PERIODICALS AND NEWSLETTERS

*Journal of Aging and Social Policy: A Journal Devoted to Aging and Social Policy.* The Haworth Press Inc. • Quarterly. $415.00 per year.

*Older Americans Report.* Business Publishers Inc. • Bimonthly. $449 Individuals. Description: Features brief articles on legislative, judicial, and federal agency activities concerning older Americans. Covers news of developments in such areas as Social Security, social services, Medicare, programs for retirement and pension funds, research projects, and the Older Americans Act. Recurring features include book reviews and a calendar of events.

### STATISTICS SOURCES

*Social Security Bulletin.* Social Security Administration. U. S. Government Printing Office. • Quarterly. $27.00 per year. Annual statistical supplement.

*Statistical Abstract of the United States.* U. S. Government Printing Office. • Annual. $44.00. Issued by the U. S. Bureau of the Census.

### TRADE/PROFESSIONAL ASSOCIATIONS

National Conference of State Social Security Administrators. c/o Joe L. Lancaster, Jr., Secretary, PO Box 639, Frankfort, KY 40602-0639. Email: secretary@ncsssa.org • URL: http://www.ncssa.org • Formerly Conference of State Social Security Administrators.

## SOCIAL WELFARE

*See* PUBLIC WELFARE

## SOCIETY AND BUSINESS

*See* SOCIAL RESPONSIBILITY

## SOFT DRINK INDUSTRY

### DIRECTORIES

*Beverage Marketing Directory.* Beverage Marketing Corp. • Annual. $995 Individuals print. Covers: Over 25,500 beer wholesalers, wine and spirits wholesalers, soft drink bottlers and franchisors, breweries, wineries, distilleries, alcoholic beverage importers, bottled water companies; and trade associations, government agencies, micro breweries, juice, coffee, tea, milk companies, and others concerned with the beverage and bottling industries; coverage includes Canada. Entries include: Beverage and bottling company listings contain company name, address, phone, names of key executives, number of employees, brand names, and other information, including number of franchisees, number of delivery trucks, sales volume. Suppliers and related companies and organizations listings include similar but less detailed information.

*European Drinks Marketing Directory.* Euromonitor International Business Reference Div. • Irregular Biennial. $215. Covers: The European drinks industry, including marketing, retailers, wholesalers, leading companies, market trends, and industry details. Entries include: Name, address, phone, fax, telex.

*Major Food and Drink Companies of the World.* Cengage Learning Inc. • 12th edition. eBook. Published by Graham & Whiteside. Contains profiles and trade names for more than 9,200 important food and beverage companies in various countries. In addition to foods, includes both alcoholic and nonalcoholic drink products.

### FINANCIAL RATIOS

*Annual Statement Studies.* Risk Management Association. • Annual. Compiled from over 280,000 financial statements.

*Annual Statement Studies: Industry Default Probabilities and Cash Flow Measures.* Risk Management Association. • Annual. $405 Nonmembers. Serves as a companion volume to the original *Annual Statement Studies.* Gives probability of default estimates on a percentage scale for more than 450 industries. Includes changes in position year-by-year for eight financial statement line items and provides percentage measures of cash flow.

*Industry Norms and Key Business Ratios.* Dun & Bradstreet Inc. • Annual. Five volumes. Covers over 800 kinds of businesses, arranged by Standard Industrial Classification number. More detailed editions covering longer periods of time are also available.

### PERIODICALS AND NEWSLETTERS

*Soft Drink Letter.* Whitaker Newsletters Inc. • Description: Covers news pertaining to the beverage industry with emphasis on soft drinks, mixers, and bottled water. Includes reports on new products and federal/state regulations, interviews with leading industry executives, marketing trends, and advertising and marketing research.

### STATISTICS SOURCES

*U.S. Industry and Trade Outlook.* U.S. Department of Commerce National Technical Information Service. • Annual. Produced by the International Trade Administration, U.S. Department of Commerce, in a "public-private" partnership with DRI/McGraw-Hill and Standard & Poor's. Provides basic data, outlook for the current year, and "Long-Term Prospects" (five-year projections) for a wide variety of products and services. Includes high technology industries. Formerly *U.S. Industrial Outlook.*

### TRADE/PROFESSIONAL ASSOCIATIONS

American Beverage Association. 1101 16th St. NW, Washington, DC 20036. Phone: (202)463-6732 or (202)463-6770; Fax: (202)659-5349; Email: info@ameribev.org • URL: http://www.ameribev.org • Active members are bottlers and distributors of soft drinks and franchise companies; associate members are suppliers of materials and services. Conducts government affairs activities on the national and state levels, discussion of industry problems, and general improvement of operating procedures. Conducts research on beverage laws.

## SOFTWARE INDUSTRY, COMPUTER

*See* COMPUTER SOFTWARE INDUSTRY

## SOLAR ENERGY

### ABSTRACTS AND INDEXES

*Applied Science and Technology Index.* EBSCO Publishing Inc. • 11/year. Indexes a wide variety of English language technical, industrial, and engineering periodicals.

*NTIS Alerts: Energy.* U.S. Department of Commerce National Technical Information Service. • Biweekly. $130 per year. Covers electric power, batteries, fuels, geothermal energy, heating/cooling systems, nuclear technology, solar energy, energy policy, and related subjects.

*Science Citation Index.* Thomson Reuters Intellectual Property and Science. • Weekly. Includes *Source Index, Citation Index, Permuterm Subject Index,* and *Corporate Index.* Provides researchers, administrators, faculty, and students with quick, powerful access to the bibliographic and citation information they need to find research data, analyze trends, journals and researchers, and share their findings.

### BIBLIOGRAPHIES

*Solar Energy.* U. S. Government Printing Office. • Annual. Free. Lists government publications. GPO Subject Bibliography Number 9.

### CD-ROM DATABASES

*Science Citation Index.* Thomson Reuters Intellectual Property and Science. • Weekly. Includes *Source Index, Citation Index, Permuterm Subject Index,* and *Corporate Index.* Provides researchers, administrators, faculty, and students with quick, powerful access to the bibliographic and citation information they need to find research data, analyze trends, journals and researchers, and share their findings.

### DIRECTORIES

*Directory of SRCC Certified Collectors and Solar Water Heating Systems Ratings.* Solar Rating and Certification Corporation. • Irregular. Covers: Nearly 20 manufacturers of solar collectors and water heaters certified by the organization. Entries include: Company name, address, system model and description, including technical specifications, thermal performance ratings, etc., for one or more systems.

*Energy User News: Energy Technology Buyers Guide.* BNP Media. • Annual. $10.00. List of about 400 manufacturers, manufacturers' representatives, dealers, and distributors of energy management equipment. *Annual Review* and *Forecast* issue.

### E-BOOKS

*Macmillan Encyclopedia of Energy.* Cengage Learning Inc. • 2003. eBook. Published by Macmillan Reference USA. Covers the business, technology, and history of a wide variety of energy sources. Inquire as to price and availability.

## ONLINE DATABASES

*Photovoltaic Module Retail Businesses in the World.* Momentum Technologies L.L.C. • Contains 811 directory listings of retail businesses throughout the world that supply photovoltaic modules and associated energy equipment. Includes business name, address, phone number, fax number, e-mail address, and web site address. Includes brief descriptions of product lines, services offered, and business type. Provides keyword search functions.

*Solar Energy Businesses in the World.* Momentum Technologies L.L.C. • Contains detailed directory listings and contact information for more than 16,302 solar energy businesses in operation throughout the world. Includes business name, address, phone and fax numbers, and online contact addresses. Includes brief descriptions of product lines, services offered, and business type. Covers businesses manufacturing, selling, or distributing solar electric power systems, solar heating systems, photovoltaic modules, solar water pumping systems, and more. Searchable by product, location, business type, company name, and keyword.

## OTHER SOURCES

*Major Energy Companies of the World.* Cengage Learning Inc. • Annual. $1,460 Individuals. 2008. 12th edition. eBook. Published by Graham & Whiteside. Contains detailed information on more than 4,850 important energy companies in various countries. Industries include electricity generation, coal, natural gas, nuclear energy, petroleum, fuel distribution, and equipment for energy production.

## PERIODICALS AND NEWSLETTERS

*Alternative Energy Retailer.* Zackin Publications Inc. • Monthly. $32.00 per year.

*Independent Energy: The Power Industry's Business Magazine.* PennWell Corp., Industrial Div. • 10 times a year. $127.00 per year. Covers non-utility electric power plants (cogeneration) and other alternative sources of electric energy.

*Journal of Energy Engineering: The International Journal.* Architectural Engineering Institute of ASCE. • Quarterly. $350 Individuals Online only. Contains reports on the development of scientific and engineering knowledge in the planning, management, and generation of electrical power.

*Renewable Energy: An International Journal.* Elsevier. • Monthly. $3,799 Institutions.

*Solar Energy: International Journal for Scientists, Engineers and Technologists Energy and Its Application.* International Solar Energy Society. Elsevier..

## RESEARCH CENTERS AND INSTITUTES

Solar Energy and Energy Conversion Laboratory. University of Florida, Dept. of Mechanical Engineering, 231 MAE-A, Gainesville, FL 32611. Phone: (352)392-0961; Fax: (352)392-7303; Email: solar@cimar.me.ufl.edu • URL: http://www.mse.ufl.edu.

University of Hawaii at Manoa - Hawaii Natural Energy Institute. 1680 E West Rd., Post 109, Honolulu, HI 96822. Phone: (808)956-8890; Fax: (808)956-2336; Email: hnei@hawaii.edu • URL: http://www.hnei.hawaii.edu • Research areas include geothermal, wind, solar, hydroelectric, and other energy sources.

University of Oregon - Solar Energy Center. Department of Physics, 1274 University of Oregon, Eugene, OR 97403-1274. Phone: (541)346-4745 or (541)346-3656; Fax: (541)346-5861 • URL: http://uocatalog.uoregon.edu/graduatestudies/research%20institutes%20and%20centers • Solar resource monitoring and assessment, and analysis of climate in terms of architectural response.

## STATISTICS SOURCES

*Annual Energy Outlook, with Projections to (year).* U. S. Government Printing Office. • Annual. $39.00.

Issued by the Energy Information Administration, U. S. Department of Energy (www.eia.doe.gov). Contains detailed statistics and 20-year projections for electricity, oil, natural gas, coal, and renewable energy. Text provides extensive discussion of energy issues and "Market Trends.".

*U.S. Industry and Trade Outlook.* U.S. Department of Commerce National Technical Information Service. • Annual. Produced by the International Trade Administration, U.S. Department of Commerce, in a "public-private" partnership with DRI/McGraw-Hill and Standard & Poor's. Provides basic data, outlook for the current year, and "Long-Term Prospects" (five-year projections) for a wide variety of products and services. Includes high technology industries. Formerly *U.S. Industrial Outlook.*

## TRADE/PROFESSIONAL ASSOCIATIONS

International Photovoltaic Equipment Association. PO Box 771507, Orlando, FL 32877. Phone: (407)856-9100; Email: ekus@ipvea.com • URL: http://www.ipvea.org • Represents manufacturers and suppliers of photovoltaic (PV) fabrication equipment and related raw materials used in PV ingot, wafer, cell and panel manufacturing. Fosters the development of the photovoltaic equipment manufacturing industry. Provides members with a forum for information, discussion and exchange of ideas to develop business opportunities and strategic partnerships.

Sustainable Buildings Industry Council. 1090 Vermont Ave. NW, Ste. 700, Washington, DC 20005. Phone: (202)289-7800; Fax: (202)289-1092; Email: nibs@nibs.org • URL: http://www.nibs.org/?page=sbic • Works to advance the design, affordability, energy performance, and environmental soundness of commercial, institutional, and residential buildings nationwide. Offers professional training, consumer education, and energy analysis tools. Provides accurate, easy-to-use guidelines, software, and general information about energy conservation measures, energy efficient equipment and appliances, daylighting, and sustainable architecture. Active in presenting workshops and seminars geared toward improving building energy performance in cities and towns throughout the nation.

# SOLE PROPRIETORSHIP

*See* SELF-EMPLOYMENT

# SOLID STATE DEVICES

*See* SEMICONDUCTOR INDUSTRY

# SOLID WASTE TREATMENT

*See* SANITATION INDUSTRY

# SOUND RECORDERS AND RECORDING

*See also* HIGH FIDELITY/STEREO; PHONOGRAPH AND PHONOGRAPH RECORD INDUSTRIES

## DIRECTORIES

*Music Technology Buyer's Guide.* United Entertainment Media. • $6.95. Annual. Lists more than 4,000 hardware and software music production products from 350 manufacturers. Includes synthesizers, MIDI hardware and software, mixers, microphones, music notation software, etc. Produced by the editorial staffs of *Keyboard* and *EQ* magazines.

*Recording Industry Sourcebook.* Cardinal Business

Media. • Annual. $71.99 Individuals. Covers: 14,000 contacts in the music industry in over 65 categories, including record producers, publishers, promoters, attorneys, major and independent record labels, and music production facilities. Entries include: Name, address, phone, fax, name and title of contact, subsidiary and branch names and locations, background information, email, web address.

## OTHER SOURCES

*Keyboard: The World's Leading Music Technology Magazine.* United Entertainment Media. • Monthly. $25.95 per year. Emphasis is on recording systems, keyboard technique, and computer-assisted music (MIDI) systems.

## PERIODICALS AND NEWSLETTERS

*Computer Music Journal.* The MIT Press. • Quarterly. Covers digital soound and the musical applications of computers.

*Mix Magazine: Professional Recording, Sound, and Music Production.* Primedia Business Magazine and Media. • Monthly. $35.99 U.S. print and digital access. Professional audio and music production periodical.

*Pro Audio Review: The Industry's Equipment Authority.* IMAS Publishing Group. • Monthly. $24.95 /year. Provides critical product reviews of professional audio equipment and recording gear, including bench tests and user reports.

*SHOOT: The Leading Newsweekly for Commercial Production and Postproduction.* Nielsen Business Media Inc. • Weekly. $125 /year. Covers animation, music, sound design, computer graphics, visual effects, cinematography, and other aspects of television and motion picture production, with emphasis on TV commercials.

*Sound & Vision: Home Theater- Audio- Video-MultimediaMovies- Music.* Bonnier AB. • 10/year. $12.97 10 issues. Popular magazine providing explanatory articles and critical reviews of equipment and media (CD-ROM, DVD, etc.). Supplement available *Stereo Review's Sound and Vision Buyers Guide.* Replaces *Stereo Review* and *Video Magazine.*

## PRICE SOURCES

*Audio.* Orion Research Corp. • Annual. $179 Individuals. Quotes retail and wholesale prices of used audio equipment. Original list prices and years of manufacture are also shown.

*Guitars and Musical Instruments.* Orion Research Corp. • Annual. $179 Individuals. List of manufacturers of guitars and musical instruments. Original list prices and years of manufacture are also shown.

## RESEARCH CENTERS AND INSTITUTES

Computer Graphics Laboratory. New York Institute of Technology, Fine Arts, Old Westbury, NY 11568. Phone: (516)686-7542; Fax: (516)686-7428; Email: pvoci@nyit.edu • URL: http://www.nyit.edu • Research areas include computer graphics, computer animation, and digital sound.

U.S. Department of Energy - Office of Energy Efficiency and Renewable Energy - Industrial Technologies Program - Industrial Assessment Center. School of Engineering, San Francisco State University, 1600 Holloway Ave., San Francisco, CA 94132. Phone: (415)338-6218 or (415)338-7736; Fax: (415)338-3086; Email: iac@sfsu.edu • URL: http://www.sfsu.edu/iac • Research areas include multimedia, computerized experimental arts processes, and digital sound.

# SOUTH AMERICA

*See* LATIN AMERICAN MARKETS

---

# SOYBEAN INDUSTRY

*See also* COMMODITY FUTURES TRADING;
OIL AND FATS INDUSTRY

## ABSTRACTS AND INDEXES

*Field Crop Abstracts.* CABI Publishing North America. • Monthly. Published in England by CABI Publishing, formerly Commonwealth Agricultural Bureaux.

*Soybean Abstracts.* CABI Publishing North America. • Weekly. Searchable database of soybean research. Provides worldwide coverage of the literature.

## DIRECTORIES

*Major Food and Drink Companies of the World.* Cengage Learning Inc. • 12th edition. eBook. Published by Graham & Whiteside. Contains profiles and trade names for more than 9,200 important food and beverage companies in various countries. In addition to foods, includes both alcoholic and nonalcoholic drink products.

## INTERNET DATABASES

*USDA.* U.S. National Institute of Standards and Technology. 100 Bureau Dr., Gaithersburg, MD 20899-1070. Phone: 800-877-8339 or (301)975-6478 or (202)720-2791; Fax: (301)975-8295; Email: inquiries@nist.gov • URL: http://www.nist.gov • The USDA home page has six sections: News and Information; What's New; About USDA; Agencies; Opportunities; Search and Help. Keyword searching is offered from the USDA home page and from various individual agency home pages. Agencies are the Economic Research Service, Agricultural Marketing Service, National Agricultural Statistics Service, National Agricultural Library, and about 12 others. Updating varies. Fees: Free.

## ONLINE DATABASES

*CAB Abstracts.* CABI. • Contains 46 specialized abstract collections covering over 10,000 journals and monographs in the areas of agriculture, horticulture, forest products, farm products, nutrition, dairy science, poultry, grains, animal health, entomology, etc. Time period is 1972 to date, with monthly updates. Inquire as to online cost and availability. *CAB Abstracts on CD-ROM* also available, with annual updating.

*Food Science and Technology Abstracts (online).* IFIS North American Desk. • Produced by International Food Information Service. Provides about 500,000 online citations, with abstracts, to the international literature of food science, technology, commodities, engineering, and processing. Approximately 2,000 periodicals are covered. Time period is 1969 to date, with monthly updates. Inquire as to online cost and availability.

## PERIODICALS AND NEWSLETTERS

*Consensus: National Futures and Financial Weekly.* Consensus Inc. • Weekly. $365.00 per year. Newspaper. Contains news, statistics, and special reports relating to agricultural, industrial, and financial futures markets. Features daily basis price charts, reprints of market advice, and "The Consensus Index of Bullish Market Opinion" (charts show percent bullish of advisors for various futures).

*Corn and Soybean Digest.* American Soybean Association. Penton. • Weekly. 11 times a year. $25.00 per year. Provides high acreage farmers who grow soy beans in rotation with other crops timely production, marketing and management information.

*Soya and Oilseed Bluebook.* Soyatech, Inc. • Annual. $70.00. Includes quarterly *Bluebook Update.* Formerly *Soya Bluebook Plus.* Contains more than 3,300 company listings and references to over 400 individual products, supplies, equipment systems or services.

## STATISTICS SOURCES

*Agricultural Statistics.* U.S. Department of Agriculture National Agricultural Statistics Service. • Annual. $46 Individuals. Provides a wide variety of statistical data relating to agricultural production, supplies, consumption, prices/price-supports, foreign trade, costs, and returns, as well as farm labor, loans, income, and population. In many cases, historical data is shown annually for 10 years. In addition to farm data, includes detailed fishery statistics.

*Statistical Annual: Grains, Options on Agricultural Futures.* Chicago Board of Trade. • Annual. Includes historical data on Wheat Futures, Options on Wheat Futures, Corn Futures, Options on Corn Futures, Oats Futures, Soybean Futures, Options on Soybean Futures, Soybean Oil Futures, Soybean Meal Futures.

## TRADE/PROFESSIONAL ASSOCIATIONS

American Soybean Association. 12125 Woodcrest Executive Dr., Ste. 100, Saint Louis, MO 63141-5009. Phone: 800-688-7692 or (314)576-1770; Fax: (314)576-2786; Email: membership@soy.org • URL: http://soygrowers.com • Develops and implements policies to increase the profitability of its members and the entire soybean industry.

National Oilseed Processors Association. 1300 L St. NW, Ste. 1020, Washington, DC 20005-4168. Phone: (202)842-0463; Fax: (202)842-9126; Email: nopa@nopa.org • URL: http://www.nopa.org • Represents processors of oilseeds.

# SPECIAL DAYS AND WEEKS

*See* ANNIVERSARIES AND HOLIDAYS

# SPECIAL EVENT PLANNING

## PERIODICALS AND NEWSLETTERS

*IEG's Sponsorship Report: The International Newsletter of Event Sponsorship and Lifestyle Marketing.* IEG LLC. • $499 multi-user subscription. Newsletter reporting on corporate sponsorship of special events: sports, music, festivals, and the arts. Edited for event producers, directors, and marketing personnel.

*PROMO: Promotion Marketing Worldwide.* Primedia Business Magazines and Media. • Monthly. $65.00 per year. Edited for companies and agencies that utilize couponing, point-of-purchase advertising, special events, games, contests, premiums, product samples, and other unique promotional items.

*The Special Event Magazine.* Penton. • Monthly. $48.00 per year. Edited for professionals concerned with parties, meetings, galas, and special events of all kinds and sizes. Provides practical ideas for event planning. Formerly *Special Events.*

## TRADE/PROFESSIONAL ASSOCIATIONS

Bridal Show Producers International. 2701 Del Paso Rd. 130-343, Sacramento, CA 95835. Fax: (800)573-6070 • URL: http://www.bspibridalshows.com • Represents and promotes the bridal show industry. Maintains and enhances the quality of bridal shows. Increases communications and integrity among exhibitors and producers. Fosters mutual support and camaraderie among members.

# SPECIAL LIBRARIES

*See also* LIBRARIES

## ABSTRACTS AND INDEXES

*Library Literature and Information Science Index.* H.W. Wilson Co. • Quarterly. Annual cumulation. Price varies.

*Social Sciences Citation Index.* Thomson Reuters Corp. • Weekly. Product is accessed via *Web of Science.*

## ALMANACS AND YEARBOOKS

*The Library and Book Trade Almanac.* Information Today, Inc. • $209 Individuals Hardbound. Reviews key trends and events and provides basic statistical information. Includes financial averages: library expenditures, salaries, and book prices. Contains lists of "best books, literary prizes, winners, and bestsellers." Formerly published by R. R. Bowker.

## CD-ROM DATABASES

*LISA Plus.* Cambridge Scientific Abstracts L.P. • Quarterly. $2,000 per year. CD-ROM version of Library Information and Science Abstracts, providing abstracting and indexing of the world's library and information science literature, 1969 to date. Contains more than 180,000 citations.

*Social Sciences Citation Index.* Thomson Reuters Corp. • Weekly. Product is accessed via *Web of Science.*

*WILSONDISC: Library Literature and Information Science Index.* H.W. Wilson Co. • Quarterly. Includes unlimited access to the online version of *Library Literature.* Provides CD-ROM indexing of about 400 periodicals, covering a wide range of topics having to do with libraries, library management, and the information industry.

## DIRECTORIES

*American Library Directory (ALD).* Information Today, Inc. • Annual. $369.50 Individuals hardbound; plus $25 shipping and handling. Covers: Over 36,000 U.S. and Canadian academic, public, county, provincial, and regional libraries; library systems; medical, law, and other special libraries; and libraries for the blind and physically handicapped. Separate section lists over 350 library networks and consortia and 220 accredited and unaccredited library school programs. Entries include: For libraries--Name, supporting or affiliated institution or firm name, address, phone, fax, electronic mail address, Standard Address Number (SANs), names of librarian and department heads, income, collection size, special collections, computer hardware, automated functions, and type of catalog. For library systems--Name, location. For library schools--Name, address, phone, fax, electronic mail address, director, type of training and degrees, admission requirements, tuition, faculty size. For networks and consortia--Name, address, phone, names of affiliates, name of director, function.

*Directory of Special Libraries and Information Centers.* Cengage Learning Inc. • Annual. $966 Individuals. 2010. 38th edition. eBook. Provides detailed contact and descriptive information on subject-specific resource collections maintained by government agencies, businesses, publishers, educational and nonprofit organizations, and associations worldwide.

## ONLINE DATABASES

*American Library Directory Online.* Information Today, Inc. • Provides information on more than 30,000 public, college, and special libraries in the U.S. and Canada, with annual updates. Includes library networks, consortia, organizations, and schools. Inquire as to online cost and availability.

## OTHER SOURCES

*Legal Research and Law Library Management.* ALM Media Properties LLC. • $565. Covers the planning and operation of libraries for law firms, including personnel selection and selection of books, periodicals, online services, microforms, and other materials. (Law Journal Press).

## PERIODICALS AND NEWSLETTERS

*Business and Finance Division Bulletin.* Special Libraries Association. • Quarterly. $12.00 per year.

*Information Outlook: The Monthly Magazine of the Special Libraries Association.* Special Libraries Association. • Monthly. $65.00 per year. Topics include information technology, the Internet, copyright, research techniques, library management, and professional development. Replaces *Special Libraries* and *SpeciaList.*

*Journal of Agricultural and Food Information.* The Haworth Press Inc. • Quarterly. Institutions, $95.00 per year. A journal for librarians and others concerned with the acquisition of information on food and agriculture.

*Journal of Business and Finance Librarianship.* The Haworth Press Inc. • Quarterly. $165.00 per year.

*Journal of Electronic Resources in Medical Libraries.* The Haworth Press Inc. • Quarterly. $240.00 per year to libraries; $75.00 per year to individuals.

*Medical Reference Services Quarterly.* The Haworth Press Inc. • Quarterly. Institutions, $275.00 per year. An academic and practical journal for medical reference librarians.

*Music Reference Services Quarterly.* The Haworth Press Inc. • Quarterly. Institutions, $95.00 per year. An academic journal for music librarians.

*The One-Person Library: A Newsletter for Librarians and Management.* Information Bridges International Inc. • Monthly. $85.00 per year. Newsletter for librarians working alone or with minimal assistance. Contains reports on library literature, management advice, case studies, book reviews, and general information.

*Science & Technology Libraries.* Routledge Journals Taylor & Francis Group. • Quarterly. $121 Individuals online only. Peer-reviewed professional journal providing instructive material prepared for the science and technology librarian.

## STATISTICS SOURCES

*SLA Annual Salary Survey.* Special Libraries Association. • Annual. Members, $75.00; nonmembers, $150.00. Provides data on salaries for special librarians in the U. S. and Canada, according to location, job title, industry, budget, and years of experience.

# SPECIALISTS

*See* CONSULTANTS

# SPECIALTY FOOD INDUSTRY

*See also* FOOD INDUSTRY

## ABSTRACTS AND INDEXES

*Food Science and Technology Abstracts.* Ovid Technologies Inc. • Monthly. $1,780.00 per year. Provides worldwide coverage of the literature of food technology and food production.

*Foods Adlibra: Key to the World's Food Literature.* General Mills, Inc. Foods Adlibra Publications. • Semimonthly. $240.00 per year. Provides journal citations and abstracts to the literature of food technology and packaging.

## DIRECTORIES

*Major Food and Drink Companies of the World.* Cengage Learning Inc. • 12th edition. eBook. Published by Graham & Whiteside. Contains profiles and trade names for more than 9,200 important food and beverage companies in various countries. In addition to foods, includes both alcoholic and nonalcoholic drink products.

## ONLINE DATABASES

*Food Science and Technology Abstracts (online).* IFIS North American Desk. • Produced by

International Food Information Service. Provides about 500,000 online citations, with abstracts, to the international literature of food science, technology, commodities, engineering, and processing. Approximately 2,000 periodicals are covered. Time period is 1969 to date, with monthly updates. Inquire as to online cost and availability.

## PERIODICALS AND NEWSLETTERS

*Deli News.* Delicatessen Council of Southern California, Inc. Pacific Rim Publishing Co. • Monthly. $25.00 per year. Includes product news and comment related to cheeses, lunch meats, packaged fresh meats, kosher foods, gourmet-specialty items, and bakery products.

*Fancy Food and Culinary Products.* Talcott Communications Corp. • Monthly. $34.00 per year. Emphasizes new specialty food products and the business management aspects of the specialty food and confection industries. Includes special issues on wine, cheese, candy, "upscale" cookware, and gifts. Formerly (Fancy Foods).

*Food Distribution Magazine.* Phoenix Media Network Inc. • Monthly. $49.00 per year. Edited for marketers and buyers of domestic and imported, specialty or gourmet food products, including ethnic foods, seasonings, and bakery items.

*Gourmet News: The Business Newspaper for the Gourmet Industry.* HME News. • Monthly. $60.00 per year. Provides news of the gourmet food industry, including specialty food stores, upscale cookware shops, and gift shops.

*Gourmet Retailer.* Nielsen Business Media Inc. • Monthly. Free to qualified personnel; others, $75.00 per year. Covers upscale food and housewares, including confectionery items, bakery operations, and coffee.

## TRADE/PROFESSIONAL ASSOCIATIONS

National Association for the Specialty Food Trade. 136 Madison Ave., 12th Fl., New York, NY 10016. Phone: (212)482-6440 or (212)921-1690; Fax: (212)921-1898 • URL: http://www.specialtyfood.com • Members are manufacturers, processors, importers, retailers, and brokers of specialty and gourmet food items.

Sustainable Food Trade Association. 49 Race St., New Castle, VA 24127-6397. Phone: (413)624-6678; Email: info@sustainablefoodtrade.org • URL: http://www.sustainablefoodtrade.org • Works to foster sustainable business practices in the organic food trade. Collaborates with businesses in the organic and natural foods trade to align their day-to-day business practices with sustainability principles. Provides education, research, and networking for industry leaders to create opportunities for cross-supply chain innovation and best practices.

# SPECULATION

## DIRECTORIES

*Futures Magazine SourceBook: The Most Complete List of Exchanges, Companies, Regulators, Organizations, etc., Offering Products and Services to the Futures and Options Industry.* Futures Magazine Inc. • Annual. $19.50. Provides information on commodity futures brokers, trading method services, publications, and other items of interest to futures traders and money managers.

## INTERNET DATABASES

*Futures Online.* Futures Magazine Inc. Phone: (312)846-4600; Fax: (312)846-4638 • URL: http://www.futuresmag.com • Web site presents updates of *Futures* magazine and links to other futures-related sites.

*TheStreet.com: Your Insider's Look at Wall Street.* TheStreet.com, Inc. Phone: 800-562-9571 or (212)321-5000; Fax: (212)321-5016 • URL: http://

www.thestreet.com • Daily. Iconoclastic advice and comment on the stock market, but premium service displays a more comprehensive selection of news and analysis.

## PERIODICALS AND NEWSLETTERS

*The Cheap Investor: The Investor's Guide to Microcap and Turn Around Stocks Under $5 Per Share.* Mathews and Associates Inc. • Monthly. $697 per year. Gives three to six buy recommendations, updates on precious recommendations and investment tips on quality stock under $5.00.

*Financial Sentinel: Your Beacon to the World of Investing.* Gulf Atlantic Publish, Inc. • Monthly. $29.95 per year. Provides "The only complete listing of all OTC Bulletin Board stocks traded, with all issues listed on the Nasdaq SmallCap Market, the Toronto, and Vancouver Stock Exchanges." Also includes investment advice and recommendations of small capitalization stocks.

*Futures: News, Analysis, and Strategies for Futures, Options, and Derivatives Traders.* Futures Magazine Inc. • Monthly. $39 Individuals. Edited for institutional money managers and traders, brokers, risk managers, and individual investors or speculators. Includes special feature issues on interest rates, technical indicators, currencies, charts, precious metals, hedge funds, and derivatives. Supplements available.

*The Low Priced Stock Survey.* Horizon Publishing Co. • Weekly. Description: Reviews and analyzes stocks offered at a price of $20 or less. Analysis is divided into sections: Emerging Growth Opportunities, The Fundamentalist, Bargain Spotlight, Stock of the Month, and Master List Highlights. Includes weekly closes of the Dow Jones Industrials and NASDAQ, and statistics.

*The Penny Fortune Newsletter.* James M. Fortune, editor. Phoenix Communications Group Ltd. • Description: Instructs small investors on how to invest modest sums of money every two weeks to build a portfolio of stocks and mutual funds.

*The Prudent Speculator.* Al Frank Asset Management Inc. • Description: Presents a fundamental approach to stock selection and buying strategies for long-term capital gains appreciation. Provides technical analysis to aid market timing for both speculators and conservative investors. Reviews editor's personal common stock portfolio in comparison with the Dow Jones Industrials and New York Stock Exchange Composite Index. Recurring features include a column titled Currently Recommended Stocks with follow-up reviews.

*SFO: Stocks, Futures & Options.* W and A Publishing. • Subtitle: *Official Journal for Personal Investing in Stocks, Futures, and Options.* Covers mainly speculative techniques for stocks, commodity futures, financial futures, stock index futures, foreign exchange, short selling, and various kinds of options.

*Special Situations Newsletter: In-Depth Survey of Under-Valued Stocks.* Charles Howard Kaplan. • Monthly. $75.00 per year. Newsletter. Principal content is "This Month's Recommendation," a detailed analysis of one special situation stock.

## RESEARCH CENTERS AND INSTITUTES

University of Chicago - Booth School of Business - Center for Research in Security Prices. 105 W Adams St., Ste. 1700, Chicago, IL 60603. Phone: (312)263-6400; Fax: (312)263-6430; Email: subscriptions@crsp.chicagobooth.edu • URL: http://www.crsp.com • Historical financial data.

University of Pennsylvania - The Wharton School - Rodney L. White Center for Financial Research. 3254 Steinberg Hall-Dietrich Hall, Philadelphia, PA 19104-6367. Phone: (215)898-7616; Fax: (215)573-8084; Email: rlwctr@finance.wharton.upenn.edu • URL: http://rodneywhitecenter.wharton.upenn.edu • Research areas include financial management,

---

**For publishers' addresses, refer to SOURCES CITED section at the back of the book.**

money markets, real estate finance, and international finance.

# SPEECH RECOGNITION

*See* VOICE RECOGNITION

# SPEECHES

*See* PUBLIC SPEAKING

# SPICE INDUSTRY

## DIRECTORIES

*Directory of Chinese Manufacturers & Exporters of Spices, Seasonings & Flavorings.* EXIM Infotek Private Ltd. • $5 Individuals. Covers: 30 Chinese manufacturers and exporters of chili, dried chili, dried ginger, garlic powder, pepper, salt, seasonings, spices. Entries include: Company name, postal address, city, country, phone, fax, e-mail and websites, contact person, designation, and product details.

*Directory of Japanese Manufacturers & Exporters of Spices, Seasoning & Flavourings.* EXIM Infotek Private Ltd. • $5 Individuals. Covers: 20 Japanese manufacturers and exporters of seasonings. Entries include: Company name, postal address, city, country, phone, fax, e-mail and websites, contact person, designation, and product details.

*Major Food and Drink Companies of the World.* Cengage Learning Inc. • 12th edition. eBook. Published by Graham & Whiteside. Contains profiles and trade names for more than 9,200 important food and beverage companies in various countries. In addition to foods, includes both alcoholic and nonalcoholic drink products.

## ONLINE DATABASES

*Food Science and Technology Abstracts (online).* IFIS North American Desk. • Produced by International Food Information Service. Provides about 500,000 online citations, with abstracts, to the international literature of food science, technology, commodities, engineering, and processing. Approximately 2,000 periodicals are covered. Time period is 1969 to date, with monthly updates. Inquire as to online cost and availability.

## PERIODICALS AND NEWSLETTERS

*Perfumer and Flavorist.* Allured Business Media. • Monthly. $135.00 per year. Provides information on the art and technology of flavors and fragrances, including essential oils, aroma chemicals, and spices.

## TRADE/PROFESSIONAL ASSOCIATIONS

American Spice Trade Association. 1101 17th St. NW, Ste. 700, Washington, DC 20036. Phone: (202)331-2460; Fax: (202)463-8998 • URL: http://www.astaspice.org • Works to foment the export of American spices. Promotes the interests of the American spice industry.

# SPORTING GOODS INDUSTRY

*See also* RECREATION INDUSTRY

## DIRECTORIES

*Directory of African Importers of Sporting Goods.* EXIM Infotek Private Ltd. • $350 Individuals. Covers: 125 African importers of diving equipment, golf equipment and supplies, scuba and diving equipment and supply, sports equipment, sporting goods and toys, tennis and badminton equipment and supplies, and watersports equipment. Entries include: Company name, postal address, telephone, fax,

e-mail, website, contact person, designation, and product details.

*Directory of Asian Importers of Sporting Goods.* EXIM Infotek Private Ltd. • $1,050 Individuals. Covers: 460 Asian importers of badminton, badminton rackets, baseball and golf caps, baseball supplies, basketball, billiard game table and equipment, billiard pool equipment, bowling equipment and supplies, cricket and hockey goods, firearms, football tools, golf accessories, golf ball, golf carts, golf club and bags, hobby and do-it-yourself articles, leisure and sports goods, playground equipment, equipment for sauna, spa, and swimming pool, shuttlecocks, ski equipment and supplies, snow sports goods, sports bags, sports wear, sports gloves, stadium equipment, table tennis equipment and accessories, tennis equipment and supplies, tennis rackets, volley balls, water sports equipment and supplies, windsurfing and surfing products.

*Directory of Australia & New Zealand Importers of Sporting Goods.* EXIM Infotek Private Ltd. • $300 Individuals. Covers: 95 Australian and New Zealand importers of adventure sporting goods, baseball supplies, basketball equipment, beach accessories, firearms, footballs, golf ball, golf carts, golf course accessories, golf equipment, golf tools, handballs, hobby and do-it-yourself articles, judo accessories, motorcycle boots, mountaineering equipment and supplies, net balls, rugby balls, skates and accessories, ski equipment, ski gloves, ski sports goods, snow sports goods, snowboards, soccer balls, sports bags, sports gloves, sports water equipment, string for rackets, surfing products, volley balls, water sports equipment and supplies, wind surfing accessories and equipment, winter sports equipment and goods.

*Directory of Chinese Manufacturers & Exporters of Sporting Goods.* EXIM Infotek Private Ltd. • Covers: 170 Chinese manufacturers and exporters of athletic sports equipment, badminton rackets, basket balls, bowling equipment, camping goods, fishing accessories, fishing nets, fishing tackle, football, golf accessories, golf carts and vans, golf goods, gymnasium and exercise equipment, handball, leisure goods, mountaineering products, outdoor products, ruck sack, shuttle cock, skate scooters, sporting goods, sports bags, sports equipment, sports goods, sports shoes, sports suits, sportswear, tennis rackets, and volleyball. Entries include: Company name, postal address, telephone, fax, e-mail, website, contact person, designation, and product details.

*Directory of European Importers of Sporting Goods.* EXIM Infotek Private Ltd. • $1,350 Individuals. Covers: 610 European importers of balls, baseball supplies, billiard pool equipment and supplies, bowling equipment and supplies, climbing equipment and supplies, footwear, golf equipment and supplies, hiking accessories, uniforms and accessories, mountaineering equipment and supplies, playground equipment, scuba and diving equipment and supply, ski equipment and supplies, ski bindings, snow sports goods, snowmobiles and accessories, soccer training ball, sporting goods and toys, sporting guns and rifles, sports bags, sports gloves, sports inventory, stadium equipment, surfboards, tennis and badminton equipment and supplies, water ski equipment and supplies, water sports equipment and supplies, windsurfing accessories, windsurfing equipment and supplies, and wintersports goods.

*Directory of French Importers of Sporting Goods.* EXIM Infotek Private Ltd. • $250 Individuals. Covers: 80 French importers of firearms, golf equipment and supplies, playground equipment, scuba and diving equipment and supply, ski equipment and supplies, sporting goods and toys, sporting goods, tennis and badminton equipment and supplies, water sports equipment and supplies. Entries include: Company name, postal address, telephone, fax,

e-mail, website, contact person, designation, and product details.

*Directory of German Importers of Sporting Goods.* EXIM Infotek Private Ltd. • Covers: 40 German importers of golf equipment and supplies, mountaineering equipment and supplies, scuba and diving equipment and supply, ski equipment and supplies, sporting goods and toys, sporting goods, tennis and badminton equipment and supplies, water ski equipment and supplies, and water sports equipment and supplies. Entries include: Company name, postal address, telephone, fax, e-mail, website, contact person, designation, and product details.

*Directory of Japanese Importers of Camping and Backpacking Equipments and Supplies.* EXIM Infotek Private Ltd. • $150 Individuals. Covers: 40 Japanese importers of camping and backpacking equipment, camping goods, mountaineering equipment, and outdoor goods. Entries include: Company name, postal address, telephone, fax, e-mail, website, contact person, designation, and product details.

*Directory of Japanese Importers of Fishing & Hunting Equipment & Supplies.* EXIM Infotek Private Ltd. • Covers: 35 Japanese importers of fishing and hunting equipment, fishing supplies, fishing nets and floats, and fishing tackles. Entries include: Company name, postal address, telephone, fax, e-mail, website, contact person, designation, and product details.

*Directory of Japanese Manufacturers & Exporters of Sporting Goods.* EXIM Infotek Private Ltd. • Covers: 30 Japanese manufacturers and exporters of fishing nets, fishing nets and floats, golf bags, leisure goods, ski carrier and roof racks, sporting goods, sports goods, sports shoes, and sportswear. Entries include: Company name, postal address, telephone, fax, e-mail, website, contact person, designation, and product details.

*Directory of Middle East Importers of Sporting Goods.* EXIM Infotek Private Ltd. • Covers: 280 Middle East importers of billiard, pool equipment and supplies, bowling equipment and supplies, diving equipment, firearms, golf equipment and supplies, hiking accessories, mountain climbing equipment, playground equipment, ski boots, skiing accessories, sporting goods and toys, sporting goods, sporting guns and cartridges, sports goods, stadium equipment, tennis and badminton equipment and supplies, turf maintenance equipment, water ski equipment and supplies, water sports equipment and supplies, and windsurfing goods. Entries include: Company name, postal address, telephone, fax, e-mail, website, contact person, designation, and product details.

*Directory of North American Importers of Camping and Backpacking Equipment and Supplies.* EXIM Infotek Private Ltd. • $300 Individuals. Covers: 100 North American importers of awnings, backpack, backsacks, backpacking equipment and supplies, camping equipment, outdoor recreational equipment and tents. Entries include: Company name, postal address, telephone, fax, e-mail, website, contact person, designation, and product details.

*Directory of North American Importers of Sporting Goods.* EXIM Infotek Private Ltd. • Covers: 440 North American importers of baseball caps, baseball supplies, billiard, pool equipment and supplies, climbing equipment, climbing gear, exercise equipment, firearms, golf ball, golf caps, golf cart accessories, golf course accessories and tools, golf equipment and supplies, martial arts supplies, medals, mountain climbing equipment, playground equipment, polo seats, scuba and diving equipment, skateboards and accessories, ski equipment and supplies, snowboard, soccer balls, soccer equipment, soccer games, sport bags, sporting goods, toys, sports bags, sports footwear, tennis and badminton equipment, trekking wear, water ski equipment and supplies, water sports equipment and supplies, and windsurfing accessories.

*Directory of SAARC Importers of Sporting Goods.* EXIM Infotek Private Ltd. • Covers: 50 companies in member countries of the South Asian Association for Regional Cooperation (SAARC) that import cricket and hockey goods, rafting equipment, equipment for sauna, spa, swimming pool, shuttlecocks, sporting goods, sports gloves, swimming accessories, tennis and badminton equipment and supplies, tennis balls, and trekking equipment. Entries include: Company name, postal address, telephone, fax, e-mail, website, contact person, designation, and product details.

*Directory of South American Importers of Sporting Goods.* EXIM Infotek Private Ltd. • Covers: 140 South American importers of bowling equipment and supplies, fire arms, golf equipment and supplies, hiking accessories, mountaineering equipment and supplies, play ground equipment, riding accessories, skating equipment, ski boots, skiing accessories, sporting goods and toys, sporting goods, tennis and badminton equipment and supplies, and water sports equipment and supplies. Entries include: Company name, postal address, telephone, fax, e-mail, website, contact person, designation, and product details.

*Directory of South Korean Manufacturers & Exporters of Sporting Goods.* EXIM Infotek Private Ltd. • $250 Individuals. Covers: 90 South Korean manufacturers and exporters of ball sports equipment, billiard table sets/cues, camping equipment, fishing tackle, golf carts and van, golf club and badminton shafts, gymnasium and exercise equipment, sports equipment, winter and mountaineering sports equipment. Entries include: Company name, postal address, telephone, fax, e-mail, website, contact person, designation, and product details.

*Directory of Taiwanese Manufacturers & Exporters of Fishing & Hunting Equipment & Supplies.* EXIM Infotek Private Ltd. • $250 Individuals. Covers: 70 Taiwanese manufacturers and exporters of fish farming equipment, fishing lure, knotted nets, and nettings. Entries include: Company name, postal address, telephone, fax, e-mail, website, contact person, designation, and product details.

*The International Directory of Importers--Sporting Goods and Toys Importers.* Interdata. • Annual. $295 Individuals print. Covers: 4,700 international firms importing sporting goods and toys. Entries include: Company name and address, contact person, email, number of employees, year established, phone and telefaxes, business activity, bank references, as well as a listing of sporting goods and toys currently being imported.

*Lacrosse Equipment & Suppliers Directory.* Info-Group Inc. • Annual. Number of listings: 22,706. Entries include: Name, address, phone, size of advertisement, name of owner or manager, number of employees, year first in "Yellow Pages." Compiled from telephone company "Yellow Pages," nationwide.

*Pool Table Equipment and Supplies Directory.* Info-Group Inc. • Annual. Number of listings: 22,706. Entries include: Name, address, phone, size of advertisement, name of owner or manager, number of employees, year first in "Yellow Pages." Compiled from telephone company "Yellow Pages," nationwide.

*SIA Snow Sports Directory.* SnowSports Industries America. • Annual. Covers: 1,000 manufacturers, distributors, and suppliers of ski, snowboard, on-snow, and in-line skate apparel, equipment, and accessories who are members of SIA and who exhibit at the SIA show. Entries include: Company name, address, phone, names of management, sales representatives, and products (including trade or brand names).

## FINANCIAL RATIOS

*Annual Statement Studies.* Risk Management Association. • Annual. Compiled from over 280,000 financial statements.

*Annual Statement Studies: Industry Default Probabilities and Cash Flow Measures.* Risk Management Association. • Annual. $405 Nonmembers. Serves as a companion volume to the original *Annual Statement Studies.* Gives probability of default estimates on a percentage scale for more than 450 industries. Includes changes in position year-by-year for eight financial statement line items and provides percentage measures of cash flow.

*Cost of Doing Business Survey.* National Sporting Goods Association. • Biennial. Includes income statements, balance sheets, sales per employee, sales per square foot, inventory turnover, etc.

## GENERAL WORKS

*Archery Business: The Voice of the Archery Industry.* Grand View Media Group Inc. • Bimonthly. Trade magazine covering the business side of archery and bowhunting.

## HANDBOOKS AND MANUALS

*Sporting Goods Store.* Entrepreneur Press. • Looseleaf. $59.50. A practical guide to starting a retail sporting goods business. Covers profit potential, start-up costs, market size evaluation, owner's time required, site selection, lease negotiation, pricing, accounting, advertising, promotion, etc. (Start-Up Business Guide No. E1286.).

## INTERNET DATABASES

*Advance Monthly Retail Trade Report.* U. S. Census Bureau. Phone: 800-541-8345 or (301)457-4100 or (301)763-2713; Fax: (301)457-1296 or (301)457-3842; Email: naics@census.gov • URL: http://www.census.gov/epcd/www/naicstab.htm • Web pages provide monthly sales figures for a wide range of retail businesses. Advance, preliminary, and final statistics are provided for the latest month available in each case, with a previous-year comparison. Updates are monthly.

## PERIODICALS AND NEWSLETTERS

*NSGA Now Magazine.* National Sporting Goods Association. • Bimonthly. $50 for nonmembers. Bimonthly. Membership. Covers news and marketing trends for sporting goods retailers. Formerly *NSGA Sports Retailer.*

*SHOT Business.* Bonnier Corp. • Magazine featuring shooting sports industry.

*Sporting Goods Business: The National Newsmagazine of the Sporting Goods Industry.* Nielsen Business Media Inc. • 16 times a year. Free to qualified personnel; others, $65.00 per year. The national news magazine of the sporting goods industry.

*Sports Trend.* Shore Communications Inc. • Monthly. $60 Individuals. Magazine serving sporting goods retailers and mass merchandisers with sporting goods departments; covering products related to every major sport.

*TransWorld Business.* Bonnier Corp. • Magazine featuring board-sports news and information.

## STATISTICS SOURCES

*Annual Benchmark Report for Retail Trade and Food Services..A Detailed Summary of Retail Sales, Purchases, Accounts Receivable, Inventories, and Food Service Sales.* U. S. Government Printing Office. • Annual. $13.00. Issued by the U.S. Census Bureau. Provides detailed annual and monthly retail statistics for the most recent 10 years. Includes data for various kinds of retail outlets, including automobiles, furniture, appliances, building supplies, grocery stores, drug stores, gasoline stations, clothing, sporting goods, department stores, and restaurants.

*U.S. Industry and Trade Outlook.* U.S. Department

of Commerce National Technical Information Service. • Annual. Produced by the International Trade Administration, U.S. Department of Commerce, in a "public-private" partnership with DRI/McGraw-Hill and Standard & Poor's. Provides basic data, outlook for the current year, and "Long-Term Prospects" (five-year projections) for a wide variety of products and services. Includes high technology industries. Formerly *U.S. Industrial Outlook.*

## TRADE/PROFESSIONAL ASSOCIATIONS

National Association of Sporting Goods Wholesalers. 1833 Centre Point Cir., Ste. 123, Naperville, IL 60563. Phone: (630)596-9006; Fax: (630)544-5055; Email: info@nasgw.org • URL: http://www.nasgw.org • Represents wholesalers and manufacturers of primarily fishing tackle and shooting equipment.

National Sporting Goods Association. 1601 Feehanville Dr., Ste. 300, Mount Prospect, IL 60056. Phone: 800-815-5422; Fax: (847)391-9827; Email: info@nsga.org • URL: http://www.nsga.org • Provides services, education and information to assist member to profit in a competitive marketplace.

# SPORTS BUSINESS

*See also* GOLF INDUSTRY; RECREATION INDUSTRY

## ABSTRACTS AND INDEXES

*Leisure, Recreation and Tourism Abstracts.* CABI Publishing North America. • Quarterly. Members, $280.00 per year; Institutions, $610.00 per year. Includes single site internet access. Provides coverage of the worldwide literature of travel, recreation, sports, and the hospitality industry.

*Readers' Guide to Periodical Literature.* EBSCO Publishing Inc. • Provides indexing for over 400 periodicals dating back to 1983.

## CD-ROM DATABASES

*Readers' Guide to Periodical Literature.* EBSCO Publishing Inc. • Provides indexing for over 400 periodicals dating back to 1983.

## DIRECTORIES

*Athletic Business--Professional Directory Section.* Athletic Business Publications Inc. • Monthly. $8 per issue. Publication includes: List of architects, engineers, contractors, and consultants in athletic facility planning and construction; all listings are paid. Entries include: Company name, address, phone, fax and short description of company.

*Baseball Batting Ranges Directory.* InfoGroup Inc. • Annual. Number of listings: 1,050. Entries include: Name, address, phone, size of advertisement, name of owner or manager, number of employees, year first in "Yellow Pages." Compiled from telephone company "Yellow Pages," nationwide.

## E-BOOKS

*The Business of Sports.* Cengage Learning Inc. • 2010. eBook. Covers the spectrum of topics and issues relating to the management and promotion of organized sports.

## GENERAL WORKS

*Club Business International (CBI).* International Health, Racquet and Sportsclub Association. • Monthly. $25 Members U.S.. Features the quality and profitability of commercial health, racquet, and sports clubs.

*Sport, Business and Management.* Emerald Group Publishing Ltd. • Peer-reviewed journal covering the development of coherent, high-quality body of work in sport, business and management.

## OTHER SOURCES

*Law of Professional and Amateur Sports.* Thomson West. • Annual. $624 full set. Covers agent-player agreements, collective bargaining, negotiation of player contracts, taxation, and other topics.

## PERIODICALS AND NEWSLETTERS

*Media Sports Business.* SNL Kagan. • Description: Discusses the economics of national and regional cable and pay TV sports. Includes semiannual census of cable and pay sports channels, coverage of values of sports media rights, and news of other developments in the field. **Remarks:** Also available via e-mail and fax.

*Powersports Business.* Ehlert Publishing Group Inc. • $96 Other countries. Powersports trade magazine.

*Sport Business.* Sport Business International. • Monthly. $270 Individuals. Professional magazine covering the business of sports worldwide.

*Sports Industry News: Management and Finance, Regulation and Litigation, Media and Marketing.* Gamepoint Publishing. • Weekly. $244.00 per year. Newsletter. Covers ticket promotions, TV rights, player contracts, concessions, endorsements, etc.

## RESEARCH CENTERS AND INSTITUTES

Marquette University - Law School - National Sports Law Institute. 1215 W Michigan St., Milwaukee, WI 53233. Phone: (414)288-5816; Fax: (414)288-5818; Email: paul.anderson@marquette. edu • URL: http://law.marquette.edu/national-sports-law-institute/welcome • Promotes ethical practices in amateur and professional sports activities.

Northeastern University - Center for the Study of Sport in Society. Richards Hall, Ste. 350, 360 Huntington Ave., Boston, MA 02115. Phone: (617)373-4025; Fax: (617)373-8574; Email: sportinsociety@neu.edu • URL: http://www. northeastern.edu/sportinsociety • Research fields include sport sociology, sport journalism, and sport business.

## STATISTICS SOURCES

*United States Census of Service Industries.* U.S. Department of Commerce U.S. Census Bureau. • Quinquennial. Various reports available.

## TRADE/PROFESSIONAL ASSOCIATIONS

American Sportscasters Association. 225 Broadway, Ste. 2030, New York, NY 10007. Phone: (212)227-8080; Fax: (212)571-0556; Email: inquiry@ americansportscastersonline.com • URL: http:// www.americansportscastersonline.com • Radio and television sportscasters. Sponsors seminars, clinics, and symposia for aspiring announcers and sportscasters. Compiles statistics. Operates speakers' bureau, placement service, hall of fame, and biographical archives. Maintains American Sportscaster Hall of Fame Trust. Is currently implementing Hall of Fame Museum, Community Programs.

National Sportscasters and Sportswriters Association. PO Box 1545, Salisbury, NC 28145. Phone: (704)633-4275; Fax: (704)633-2027 • URL: http://nssafame.com • Members are sportswriters and radio/TV sportscasters.

# SPOT RADIO ADVERTISING

*See* RADIO AND TELEVISION ADVERTIS-
ING

# SPOT WELDING

*See* WELDING

# STAFF MAGAZINES

*See* HOUSE ORGANS

# STAINLESS STEEL

*See* IRON AND STEEL INDUSTRY

# STAMPS AS AN INVESTMENT

## DIRECTORIES

*Stamp Exchangers Directory.* Levine Publications. • Annual. $35. Covers: over 1000 people who are interested in exchanging stamps, coins, and other collectibles with Americans; international coverage. Entries include: Name, address, item collected.

## PERIODICALS AND NEWSLETTERS

*Scott Stamp Monthly.* Scott Publishing Company Inc. • Monthly. $19.99 per year.

*Stamp Collector.* Krause Publications Inc. • Biweekly. $32.98 per year. Newspaper.

*Stamps: The Weekly Magazine of Philately.* American Publishing Co. of New York. • Weekly. $23.50 per year.

## TRADE/PROFESSIONAL ASSOCIATIONS

American Philatelic Society. 100 Match Factory Pl., Bellefonte, PA 16823. Phone: (814)933-3803; Fax: (814)933-6128; Email: webmaster@stamps.org • URL: http://www.stamps.org • Collectors of postage and revenue stamps, first day covers, postal history, and related philatelic items. Helps members buy and sell stamps; operates expertise service; offers stamp insurance program; circulates slide programs. Maintains hall of fame; offers correspondence courses; accredits judges for philatelic competitions. Conducts philatelic seminars.

American Stamp Dealers Association. PO Box 692, Leesport, PA 19533-0692. Phone: 800-369-8207; Email: asda@americanstampdealer.com • URL: http://www.asdaonline.com • Dealers and wholesalers of stamps, albums and other philatelic materials. Sponsors National Stamp Collecting Week in November.

Philatelic Foundation. 341 W 38th St., 5th Fl., New York, NY 10018-9692. Phone: (212)221-6555; Fax: (212)221-6208; Email: philatelicfoundation@ verizon.net • URL: http://www.philatelicfoundation. org • Educational institution chartered by New York State Department of Education for philatelic study and research. Offers philatelic slide programs as an educational aid for schools, organized youth groups, and stamp clubs. Renders opinions on stamps and other philatelic material. Prepares exhibitions for stamp shows.

# STANDARD INDUSTRIAL CLASSIFICATION

*See* INDUSTRY

# STANDARDIZATION

*See also* MATERIALS; QUALITY CONTROL

## ABSTRACTS AND INDEXES

*Index and Directory of Industry Standards.* IHS Energy Group. • Annual. $395.00 Seven volumes. Covers approximately 20,000 international and 35,000 U.S. industrial standards as well as 362 industrial organizations.

## BIBLIOGRAPHIES

*Publications of the National Institute of Standards and Technology.* U. S. Government Printing Office. • Annual. Keyword and author indexes.

## E-BOOKS

*Information Communication Technology Standardization for E-Business Sectors: Integrating*

*Supply and Demand Factors.* Cengage Learning Inc. • Published by Information Science Reference. Explores aspects affecting the nature, relevance, and quality of standards, and the impact they have on businesses.

## PERIODICALS AND NEWSLETTERS

*ANSI Standards Action.* American National Standards Institute. • Weekly. Description: Lists new and proposed American National Standards and draft international standards of the International Organization for Standardization (ISO), International Electrotechnical Commission (IEC), European Committee for Standardization (CEN), and European Committee for Electrotechnical Standardization (CENELEC). Lists proposed foreign government regulations from countries that signed the General Agreement on Tariffs and Trade (GATT) Standards Code. Provides listing for registration of organization names in the United States. **Remarks:** Subscription includes ANSI Reporter (see separate listing).

*ISO Management Systems.* American National Standards Institute. • Bimonthly. Price on application. Newsletter on quality standards. Published by the International Organization for Standardization (ISO). Text in English. Formerly *ISO 9000 and ISO 14000 News.*

*Standards Engineering.* Standards Engineering Society. • Bimonthly. $45.00 per year.

## TRADE/PROFESSIONAL ASSOCIATIONS

American National Standards Institute. 1899 L St. NW, 11th Fl., Washington, DC 20036-3807. Phone: (202)293-8020; Fax: (202)293-9287; Email: info@ ansi.org • URL: http://www.ansi.org • Industrial firms, trade associations, technical societies, labor organizations, consumer organizations, and government agencies. Serves as clearinghouse for nationally coordinated voluntary standards for fields ranging from information technology to building construction. Gives status as American National Standards to standards developed by agreement from all groups concerned, in such areas as: definitions, terminology, symbols, and abbreviations; materials, performance characteristics, procedure, and methods of rating; methods of testing and analysis; size, weight, volume, and rating; practice, safety, health, and building construction. Provides information on foreign standards and represents United States interests in international standardization work.

Chartered Alternative Investment Analyst Association. 100 University Dr., Amherst, MA 01002-2357. Phone: (413)253-7373; Fax: (413)253-4494; Email: info@caia.org • URL: http://caia.org • Seeks to establish the Chartered Alternative Investment Analyst designation as the educational standard for the alternative investment industry. Advocates for high standards of professional conduct in the field of alternative investment analysis. Promotes professional development through continuous education. Facilitates communication among industry professionals.

Group Underwriters Association of America. c/o Roland Birkner, Co-Chairperson, 233 S Wacker Dr., Ste. 2000, Chicago, IL 60606. Phone: (312)288-7206; Email: roland.birkner@willis.com • URL: http://www.guaa.com • Promotes the study, analysis, and discussion pertaining to all matters of mutual interest in underwriting group products. Seeks to uphold the standards of practices within the group insurance industry. Provides its members the opportunities for professional development, networking and information gathering.

Korean Standards Association. Korean Technology Ctr., 701-7, Yeoksam-Dong, Gangnam-Gu, Seoul 135-513, South Korea. Phone: 82 2 60094513; Fax: 82 2 69194006; Email: ksaicd@ksa.or.kr • URL: http://www.ksa.or.kr/eng • Provides industrial research and survey, education and training on quality and standardization; serves as the national KS certification body; promotes globalization of local enterprises.

NCSL International. 2995 Wilderness Pl., Ste. 107, Boulder, CO 80301-5404. Phone: (303)440-3339 or (206)544-4885; Fax: (303)440-3384; Email: info@ncsli.org • URL: http://www.ncsli.org • Representatives of measurements standards and calibration laboratories; organizations with related interests. Seeks cost reduction or solution of problems, both technical and administrative, that besiege all measurement activities in the physical sciences, engineering, and technology. Conducts conferences and meetings for presentation of papers and discussions pertaining to technical and managerial problems, operating practices, and policies for measurement standards laboratories. Works with educational organizations to develop programs for training technical personnel and professional metrologists.

# START-UP PLANS

*See* BUSINESS START-UP PLANS AND PROPOSALS

# STATE EMPLOYEES

*See* GOVERNMENT EMPLOYEES

# STATE FINANCE

*See* PUBLIC FINANCE

# STATE GOVERNMENT

*See also* PUBLIC ADMINISTRATION

## ABSTRACTS AND INDEXES

*Current Law Index.* Cengage Learning Inc. • $1,332 Individuals. Monthly. $1269.00 per year. Produced in cooperation with the American Association of Law Libraries. Indexes more than 900 law journals, legal newspapers, and specialty publications from the U.S., Canada, U.K., Ireland, Australia, and New Zealand.

## ALMANACS AND YEARBOOKS

*Suggested State Legislation (SSL).* Chief Officers of State Library Agencies. • Annual. A source of legislative ideas and drafting assistance for state government officials.

## BIOGRAPHICAL SOURCES

*Who's Who in American Politics.* Marquis Who's Who L.L.C. • Biennial. $349 Individuals. Contains about 27,000 biographical sketches of local, state, and national elected or appointed individuals.

## CD-ROM DATABASES

*Newspaper Abstracts Ondisc.* ProQuest L.L.C. • Monthly. $2,950.00 per year (covers 1989 to date; archival discs are available for 1985-88). Provides cover-to-cover CD-ROM indexing and abstracting of 19 major newspapers, including the *New York Times, Wall Street Journal, Washington Post, Chicago Tribune,* and *Los Angeles Times.*

*OECD Statistical Compendium.* Organization for Economic Cooperation and Development. • Semiannual. $1,905.00 per year for 1 to 10 users. CD-ROM contains more than 730,000 monthly, quarterly, and annual time series for OECD countries, 1960 to date. Includes fully searchable data on agriculture, food, economic indicators, national accounts, employment, energy, finance, industry, technology, and foreign trade. Results can be displayed in various forms.

## DIRECTORIES

*Carroll's State Directory.* Caroll Publishing. • Annual. $500 Individuals 3 issues per year. Covers: About 70,000 state government officials in all branches of government; officers, committees and members of state legislatures; managers of boards and authorities. Entries include: Name, address, phone, fax, title.

*Carroll's State Directory: CD-ROM Edition.* Caroll Publishing. • Three times a year. $325.00 per year. Provides CD-ROM listings of about 43,000 state officials, plus the text of all state constitutions and biographies of all governors. Also available online.

*CSG State Directories I: State Elective Officials.* Chief Officers of State Library Agencies. • Annual. $65 Individuals. Covers: About 8,000 state legislators, elected state executive branch officials, and state supreme court judges. Database includes: Miscellaneous state facts and term limit information. Entries include: Name, title, address, district, party affiliation, fax and facts about each state-motto, flower, bird, nickname, capitol address, bill status phone, land area, population, D. C. Liaison, term limits, election and session dates.

*Das Grosse Einkaufs 1x1 der Deutschen Wirtschaft: Band 3: Deutsche Wirtschafts-Standorte.* Deutscher Adressbuch-Verlag fur Wirtschaft und Verkehr GmbH. • Annual. $200 prepaid. Covers: federal and state govermental agencies of the Federal Republic of Germany; approximately 220,000 German industrial, retail, wholesale, and service companies; national and regional trade organizations. Database includes: List of place names with former names and geographical location; maps. Entries include: Agency, organization, or company name, address, phone; headquarters office location for branch companies.

*Government Phone Book USA: Your Comprehensive Guide to Federal, State, County, and Local Government Offices in the United States.* Omnigraphics Inc. • Annual. $265.00. Contains more than 270,000 listings of federal, state, county, and local government offices and personnel, including legislatures. Formerly *Government Directory of Addresses and Phone Numbers.*

*Judicial Yellow Book: Who's Who in Federal and State Courts.* Leadership Directories Inc. • Semiannual. $465 /year. Lists more than 3,200 judges and staffs in various federal courts and 1,200 judges and staffs in state courts. Includes biographical profiles of judges.

*Rhode Island Directory of Human Service Agencies & Government Agencies.* Travelers Aid Society of Rhode Island. • Biennial. Covers: about 1,200 public and private nonprofit human service agencies and organizations in Rhode Island. Entries include: Agency name, address, phone, name of contact or director; description of services; hours open; eligibility requirements; ages and geographic area served; fee for service; funding.

## INTERNET DATABASES

*Business 2.0 Web Guide to the Best Business Links.* Business 2.0 Media Inc. Phone: (415)293-4800; Email: support@business2.com • URL: http://www.business2.com/webguide • Web site presents an extensive, searchable directory of links to "the best, most informative, and authoritative web pages." Twenty main categories cover business, finance, career, company information, people, and technology topics, with thousands of subtopics, all linking to Web sites recommended by experienced business researchers. Fees: Free.

*Fedstats.* Federal Interagency Council on Statistical Policy. Phone: (202)395-7254 • URL: http://www.fedstats.gov • Web site features an efficient search facility for full-text statistics produced by more than 100 federal agencies, including the Census Bureau, the Bureau of Economic Analysis, and the Bureau of Labor Statistics. Boolean searches can be made within one agency or for all agencies combined. Links are offered to international statistical bureaus, including the UN, IMF, OECD, UNESCO, Eurostat, and 20 individual countries. Fees: Free.

*FreeLunch.com.* Economy.com, Inc. Phone: (610)696-8700; Fax: (610)696-1678 • URL: http://www.freelunch.com • Web site provides free access to more than 200 million economic and financial data series, covering industry, demographics, labor markets, prices, retail sales, government spending, trade, interest rates, housing starts, the stock market, etc. Data is available in either chart or table form. Searching is offered. Free, but registration required. Economy.com, Inc. also offers fee-based economic analysis at *The Dismal Scientist* site (www.dismal.com).

*Lexis.com Research System.* Lexis-Nexis Group. Phone: 800-227-4908 or (937)865-6800; Fax: (937)865-6909; Email: webmaster@prod.lexis-nexis.com • URL: http://www.nexis.com • Fee-based Web site offers extensive searching of a wide variety of legal sources. Additional features include Daily Opinion Service, lexis.com Bookstore, Career Center, CLE Center, Law Schools, and Practice Pages ("Pages specific to areas of specialty").

## OTHER SOURCES

*Government Discrimination: Equal Protection Law and Litigation.* James A. Kushner. Thomson West. • Semiannual. $708.75 full set. Covers discrimination in employment, housing, and other areas by local, state, and federal offices or agencies. (Civil Rights Series).

## PERIODICALS AND NEWSLETTERS

*Governing: The States and Localities.* • Monthly. $39.95 per year. Edited for state and local government officials. Covers finance, office management, computers, telecommunications, environmental concerns, etc.

*Government Technology: Solutions for State and Local Government in the Information Age.* e.Republic Inc. • Monthly.

*Public Risk.* Public Risk Management Association. • Monthly. $130 Individuals. Covers risk management for state and local governments, including various kinds of liabilities.

*Spectrum: Journal of State Government.* Chief Officers of State Library Agencies. • Quarterly. $49.99 Individuals. State government journal. Formerly *Journal of State Government.*

*State Capitals.* Wakeman/Walworth Inc. • Irregular. Prices may vary. A group of 39 newsletters, with each publication having its own subtitle and topic of relevance to state government.

*State Government News: The Monthly Magazine Covering All Facets of State Government.* Chief Officers of State Library Agencies. • Monthly. $39.00 per year.

*State Legislative Report.* National Conference of State Legislatures. • Description: Contains briefings on topics of state legislative concerns covering a broad range of policy issues.

*State Legislatures.* National Conference of State Legislatures. • Description: Provides a national perspective on government and policy in the each state. Features articles on public policy issues.

## STATISTICS SOURCES

*Almanac of the Fifty States: Basic Data Profiles with Comparative Tables.* Information Publications Inc. • Annual. $65.00.

*Survey of Current Business.* U. S. Government Printing Office. • Published by Bureau of Economic Analysis, U. S. Department of Commerce. Presents a wide variety of business and economic data.

## TRADE/PROFESSIONAL ASSOCIATIONS

Association of Governmental Risk Pools. 9 Cornell Rd., Latham, NY 12110. Phone: (518)389-2782; Email: info@agrip.org • URL: http://www.agrip.org • Works to promote risk pooling as a practical extension of a public entity's obligation to be a good steward of public funds. Aims to act as an advocate for the advancement of intergovernmental pooling as the most appropriate risk financing mechanism for most public entities. Seeks to provide meaningful and significant educational and professional support for the governing bodies and employees of intergovernmental risk pools.

Chief Officers of State Library Agencies. 201 E Main St., Ste. 1405, Lexington, KY 40507. Phone: 800-800-1910 or (859)514-9151 or (859)244-8000; Fax: (859)514-9166 or (859)244-8001; Email: lsinger@amrms.com • URL: http://www.cosla.org • Supersedes American Legislator Association.

National Association of State Budget Officers. Hall of the States Bldg., 444 N Capitol St. NW, Ste. 642, Washington, DC 20001-1556. Phone: (202)624-5382 or (202)624-8804; Fax: (202)624-7745; Email: nasbo-direct@nasbo.org • URL: http://www.nasbo.org • Budget directors, their deputies, and superior officers of the states and territories. Seeks to encourage study and research in state budgeting and promote cooperation and efficiency in budget programs. Conducts budget and legislative briefing every spring and four to five educational seminars each year.

National Association of State Procurement Officials. 201 E Main St., Ste. 1405, Lexington, KY 40507-2004. Phone: (859)514-9159; Fax: (859)514-9166; Email: headquarters@naspo.org • URL: http://www.naspo.org • Purchasing officials of the states and territories. Formerly National Association of State Purchasing Officials.

National Conference of State Legislatures. 7700 E 1st Pl., Denver, CO 80230-7143. Phone: (303)364-7700; Fax: (303)364-7800; Email: ncslnet-admin@ncsl.org • URL: http://www.ncsl.org • Affiliated with Council of State Governments.

National Governors' Association. Hall of the States, 444 N Capitol St. NW, Ste. 267, Washington, DC 20001-1512. Phone: (202)624-5300; Fax: (202)624-5313 • URL: http://www.nga.org/cms/home.html • Governors of the 50 states, Guam, American Samoa, the Virgin Islands, the Northern Mariana Islands, and Puerto Rico. Serves as vehicle through which governors influence the development and implementation of national policy and apply creative leadership to state problems. Keeps the federal establishment informed of the needs and perceptions of states. Through its Center for Best Practices, it provides a vehicle for sharing information on innovative programs among the states and providing technical assistance to governors on a wide range of issues.

Public Risk Management Association. 700 S Washington St., Ste. 218, Alexandria, VA 22314. Phone: (703)528-7701; Fax: (703)739-0200; Email: info@primacentral.org • URL: http://www.primacentral.org • Public agency risk, insurance, human resources, attorneys, and/or safety managers from cities, counties, villages, towns, school boards, and other related areas. Provides an information clearinghouse and communications network for public risk managers to share resources, ideas, and experiences. Offers information on risk, insurance, and safety management. Monitors state and federal legislative actions and court decisions that deal with immunity, tort liability, and intergovernmental risk pools. Maintains library containing current reports from governmental units on their insurance procedures, self-insurance plans, and loss control and safety programs; and copies of policy statements, job descriptions, contractual arrangements, and indemnification clauses.

# STATE INCOME TAX

*See* STATE TAXES

# STATE LAW

*See also* SALES TAX

## ABSTRACTS AND INDEXES

*Index to Legal Periodicals and Books.* H.W. Wilson Co. • Monthly. $490.00 per year. Quarterly and annual cumulations.

## ALMANACS AND YEARBOOKS

*Suggested State Legislation (SSL).* Chief Officers of State Library Agencies. • Annual. A source of legislative ideas and drafting assistance for state government officials.

## HANDBOOKS AND MANUALS

*National Survey of State Laws.* Cengage Learning Inc. • 2007. eBook. 6th edition. Provides concise state-by-state comparisons of current state laws on a wide variety of topics. Includes references to specific codes or statutes. Inquire for pricing.

## OTHER SOURCES

*Labor Relations.* Wolters Kluwer Law & Business CCH. • $2,589.00 per year. Seven looseleaf volumes. Weekly updates. Covers labor relations, wages and hours, state labor laws, and employment practices. Supplement available, *Labor Law Reports.* Summary Newsletter.

## PERIODICALS AND NEWSLETTERS

*State Legislative Report.* National Conference of State Legislatures. • Description: Contains briefings on topics of state legislative concerns covering a broad range of policy issues.

## RESEARCH CENTERS AND INSTITUTES

Czech Republic Academy of Sciences - Institute of State and Law. Narodni 18, 116 00 Prague, Czech Republic. Phone: 420 221 990711; Fax: 420 221 933056; Email: ilaw@ilaw.cas.cz • URL: http://www.ilaw.cas.cz • Theory of state and law; selected issues of constitutional law; legal ramifications of the transition to a market economy; legal issues in environmental protection; problems with international law, especially law in the European Community and harmonization with Czech law with these systems; and legal informatics.

University of Illinois at Springfield - Center for State Policy and Leadership. Public Affairs Ctr., Rm. 409, 1 University Plz., MS PAC 409, Springfield, IL 62703-5407. Phone: (217)206-8417; Fax: (217)206-6542; Email: draci2@uis.edu • URL: http://cspl.uis.edu • Public problems and policies, focusing on applied research on the Illinois government, the judicial system, and state administrative agencies. Specific areas of study include social services, health policy, Illinois budgeting, public law and administrative rule making, law and public policy, patronage, capital punishment, abortion, and campaign and school financing. Also evaluates the effectiveness of government programs.

## TRADE/PROFESSIONAL ASSOCIATIONS

Chief Officers of State Library Agencies. 201 E Main St., Ste. 1405, Lexington, KY 40507. Phone: 800-800-1910 or (859)514-9151 or (859)244-8000; Fax: (859)514-9166 or (859)244-8001; Email: lsinger@amrms.com • URL: http://www.cosla.org • Supersedes American Legislator Association.

National Association of Attorneys General. 2030 M St. NW, 8th Fl., Washington, DC 20036-3306. Phone: (202)326-6000 or (202)326-6027; Fax: (202)331-1427 • URL: http://www.naag.org • Attorneys general of the 50 states, District of Columbia, American Samoa, Guam, Puerto Rico, Virgin Islands, and Northern Mariana Islands. Sponsors legal education seminars on consumer protection, environmental protection, antitrust, corrections, insurance, charitable trusts and solicitations, and Supreme Court practice.

National Conference of Commissioners on Uniform State Laws. 111 N Wabash Ave., Ste. 1010, Chicago, IL 60602-1917. Phone: (312)450-6600 or (312)450-6603; Fax: (312)450-6601 or (312)915-0187 • URL: http://www.uniformlaws.org • Judges, law school deans and professors, and practicing attorneys appointed by state governors. Promotes uniformity in state law on subjects where uniformity is deemed desirable and practicable. Also promotes uniformity of judicial decisions throughout the U.S. Drafts uniform and model acts on subjects suitable for interstate compact and subjects in which uniformity will make more effective the exercise of state powers and promote interstate cooperation.

National Conference of State Legislatures. 7700 E 1st Pl., Denver, CO 80230-7143. Phone: (303)364-7700; Fax: (303)364-7800; Email: ncslnet-admin@ncsl.org • URL: http://www.ncsl.org • Affiliated with Council of State Governments.

North American Securities Administrators Association. 750 1st St. NE, Ste. 1140, Washington, DC 20002-8034. Phone: (202)737-0900; Fax: (202)783-3571; Email: ri@nasaa.org • URL: http://www.nasaa.org • Represents the interests of the state, provincial and territorial securities administrators in the U.S., Canada, Mexico and Puerto Rico. Provides support to its members in government relations and with federal regulators, industry SROs and other groups.

# STATE TAXES

*See also* TAXATION

## CD-ROM DATABASES

*The Tax Directory.* Tax Analysts. • Quarterly. $499 Individuals both volumes, web, CD or print. Updated quarterly on CD-ROM and in print; updated continually online. Covering federal, state, and international tax officials, tax practitioners, and corporate tax executives.

## DIRECTORIES

*The Tax Directory.* Tax Analysts. • Quarterly. $499 Individuals both volumes, web, CD or print. Updated quarterly on CD-ROM and in print; updated continually online. Covering federal, state, and international tax officials, tax practitioners, and corporate tax executives.

## HANDBOOKS AND MANUALS

*All States Tax Handbook.* Thomson RIA. • Annual. $89. Tax structures for fifty states.

*State Tax Actions.* National Conference of State Legislatures. • Annual. $35 Individuals List price. Summarizes yearly tax changes by type and by state. Features state-by state-details about tax actions taken during regular and special legislative sessions.

*U.S. Master Multistate Corporate Tax Guide.* Wolters Kluwer Law & Business CCH. • Annual. $136.75 Quantiy: 1 - 4. Provides corporate income tax information for 47 states, New York City, and the District of Columbia.

*U.S. Master Property Tax Guide.* Wolters Kluwer Law & Business CCH. • Annual. $130.90 Quantity: 1 -4. Provides state-by-state coverage of "key property tax issues and concepts," including exemptions, assessments, taxpayer remedies, and property tax calendars.

*U.S. Master Sales and Use Tax Guide.* Wolters Kluwer Law & Business CCH. • Annual. $129.95 1 - 4 (quantity). Contains concise information on sales and use taxes in all states and the District of Columbia.

## INTERNET DATABASES

*Rutgers Accounting Web.* Rutgers University Accounting Research Center. Phone: (973)353-5172; Fax: (973)353-1283 • URL: http://www.rutgers.edu/accounting • RAW Web site provides extensive links to sources of national and international accounting information, such as the Big Six accounting firms, the Financial Accounting Standards Board (FASB), SEC filings (EDGAR), journals, publishers, software, the International Accounting Network, and "Internet's largest list of accounting firms in USA." Searching is offered. Fees: Free.

## ONLINE DATABASES

*Accounting and Tax Database.* ProQuest L.L.C. • Provides indexing and abstracting of the literature of accounting, taxation, and financial management, 1971 to date. Updating is weekly. Especially covers accounting, auditing, banking, bankruptcy, employee compensation and benefits, cash management, financial planning, and credit. Inquire as to online cost and availability.

## OTHER SOURCES

*All States Tax Guide.* Prentice Hall PTR. • Looseleaf. Periodic supplementation. Price on application. One volume summary of taxes for all states.

*Manufacturers' Tax Alert.* Wolters Kluwer Law & Business CCH. • Monthly $297.00 per year. Newsletter. Covers the major tax issues affecting manufacturing companies. Includes current developments in various kind of federal, state, and international taxes: sales, use, franchise, property, and corporate income.

*Multistate Sales Tax Guide.* Wolters Kluwer Law & Business CCH. • Monthly. $1,349 /year. Looseleaf service. Nine volumes.. Formerly *All State Sales Tax Reports.* Gives in-depth state sales tax law coverage on a wide variety of tax-related issues.

## PERIODICALS AND NEWSLETTERS

*E-Commerce Tax Alert.* Wolters Kluwer Law & Business CCH. • Description: Print and online newsletter covering e-commerce taxation issues, including compliance and sourcing, e-cash implications, the Internet tax debate, and other topics.

*Highlights and Documents.* Tax Analysts. • Daily. $2,599.95 Individuals. Provides daily coverage of IRS, congressional, judicial, state, and international tax developments. Includes abstracts and citations for "all tax documents released within the previous 24 to 48 hours." Annual compilation available *Highlights and Documents on Microfiche.*

*Interstate Tax Insights.* Interstate Tax Corporation. • Monthly. $100 for 6 issues. In-depth analyses, tax savings ideas, and updates for state tax practitioners.

*State Income Tax Alert.* State Taxation Institute. • Description: Features updates on state income tax issues. Recurring features include a calendar of events, book reviews, and news of educational opportunities.

*State Tax Notes.* Tax Analysts. • Weekly. $949.00 per year, including annual CD-ROM. Newsletter. Covers tax developments in all states. Provides state tax document summaries and citations.

## RESEARCH CENTERS AND INSTITUTES

University of Michigan - Stephen M. Ross School of Business - Office of Tax Policy Research. 701 Tappan St., Rm. R5380, Ann Arbor, MI 48109-1234. Phone: (734)763-3068; Fax: (734)763-4032; Email: jslemrod@umich.edu • URL: http://www.bus.umich.edu/OTPR/ • Tax policy, including compliance, capital gains, reform, international taxation, and income dynamics.

## STATISTICS SOURCES

*Statistical Abstract of the United States.* U. S. Government Printing Office. • Annual. $44.00. Issued by the U. S. Bureau of the Census.

---

# STATIONERY INDUSTRY

*See* OFFICE EQUIPMENT AND SUPPLIES

# STATISTICAL METHODS

*See also* BUSINESS MATHEMATICS; BUSINESS STATISTICS; ECONOMIC STATISTICS; MARKET STATISTICS

## ABSTRACTS AND INDEXES

*Current Index to Statistics: Applications, Methods, and Theory.* American Statistical Association. • Annual. An index to journal articles on statistical applications and methodology.

*Institute of Mathematical Statistics Bulletin.* Institute of Mathematical Statistics. • Bimonthly. $82 /year for institutions. Contains meeting programs, calendar of events, faculty recruitment advertising, book reviews, and abstracts of printed papers.

*Science Citation Index.* Thomson Reuters Intellectual Property and Science. • Weekly. Includes *Source Index*, *Citation Index*, *Permuterm Subject Index*, and *Corporate Index*. Provides researchers, administrators, faculty, and students with quick, powerful access to the bibliographic and citation information they need to find research data, analyze trends, journals and researchers, and share their findings.

*Statistical Theory and Method Abstracts.* International Association for Official Statistics. • Available as a component of Zentralblatt MATH (ZBMATH), referred to as STMA-Z. Contact for pricing.

## CD-ROM DATABASES

*MathSciNet.* American Mathematical Society. • Electronic resource with citations, abstracts, and reviews to the literature of mathematics, statistics, and computer science, 1940 to date.

*Science Citation Index.* Thomson Reuters Intellectual Property and Science. • Weekly. Includes *Source Index*, *Citation Index*, *Permuterm Subject Index*, and *Corporate Index*. Provides researchers, administrators, faculty, and students with quick, powerful access to the bibliographic and citation information they need to find research data, analyze trends, journals and researchers, and share their findings.

## GENERAL WORKS

*Applied Stochastic Models in Business and Industry.* John Wiley & Sons Inc. • Bimonthly. $2,744 Institutions, other countries print only. Journal covering applications and problem-solving techniques of applied probability and data analysis.

## PERIODICALS AND NEWSLETTERS

*JASA.* American Statistical Association. • Quarterly. $652 Individuals. Statistics information.

*Journal of Business and Economic Statistics.* American Statistical Association. • Quarterly. $62 for members. Emphasis is on statistical measurement and applications for business and economics.

*Mathematical Finance: An International Journal of Mathematics, Statistics, and Financial Economics.* Blackwell Publishing Inc. • Quarterly. $1,453 Institutions print only. Covers the use of sophisticated mathematical tools in financial research and practice.

*The Review of Economics and Statistics.* The MIT Press. • 5/year. $567 Institutions Online. Journal of applied economics, published some of the most important articles in empirical economics.

## RESEARCH CENTERS AND INSTITUTES

Center for Mathematical Studies in Economics and Management Science. Northwestern University, 580

---

Leverone Hall, 2001 Sheridan Rd., Evanston, IL 60208-2014. Phone: (847)491-3527; Fax: (847)491-2530; Email: cms-ems@kellogg.northwestern.edu • URL: http://www.kellogg.northwestern.edu/research/math.

Center for Quality and Productivity. University of North Texas, College of Business Administration, 1155 Union Cir., No. 311160, Denton, TX 76203. Phone: (940)369-8476; Email: prybutok@unt.edu • URL: http://www.coba.unt.edu • Fields of research include the management of quality systems and statistical methodology.

University of Michigan - Center for Statistical Consultation and Research. 3550 Rackham, 915 E Washington St., Ann Arbor, MI 48109-1070. Phone: (734)764-7828; Fax: (734)647-2440; Email: cscar@umich.edu • URL: http://cscar.research.umich.edu • Statistical analysis and statistical computing techniques. Provides statistical consulting service and data analysis for graduate students and faculty of the University. Also provides statistical software support.

## TRADE/PROFESSIONAL ASSOCIATIONS

American Statistical Association. 732 N Washington St., Alexandria, VA 22314-1943. Phone: 888-231-3473 or (703)684-1221; Fax: (703)684-2037; Email: asainfo@amstat.org • URL: http://www.amstat.org • Professional society of persons interested in the theory, methodology, and application of statistics to all fields of human endeavor.

# STATISTICS, BUSINESS

*See* BUSINESS STATISTICS

# STATISTICS, MATHEMATICAL

*See* STATISTICAL METHODS

# STATISTICS SOURCES

*See also* BUSINESS STATISTICS; ECONOMIC STATISTICS; MARKET STATISTICS

## ALMANACS AND YEARBOOKS

*The Statesman's Yearbook: Statistical and Historical Annual of the States of the World.* St. Martin's Press. • Annual. £220 Individuals Hardcover. presents a political, economic and social account of every country of the world together with facts and analysis.

*The World Almanac and Book of Facts.* The World Almanac and Book of Facts. • Annual. $11.95.

*World Development Report.* World Bank Group. • Annual. Covers history, conditions, and trends relating to economic globalization and localization. Includes selected data from *World Development Indicators* for 132 countries or economies. Key indicators are provided for 78 additional countries or economies.

## BIBLIOGRAPHIES

*Statistics Sources.* Cengage Learning Inc. • $874 Individuals. 2012. $836.00. 37th edition. Lists sources of statistical information for more than 20,000 topics.

## CD-ROM DATABASES

*OECD Statistical Compendium.* Organization for Economic Cooperation and Development. • Semiannual. $1,905.00 per year for 1 to 10 users. CD-ROM contains more than 730,000 monthly, quarterly, and annual time series for OECD countries, 1960 to date. Includes fully searchable

---

**For publishers' addresses, refer to SOURCES CITED section at the back of the book.**

data on agriculture, food, economic indicators, national accounts, employment, energy, finance, industry, technology, and foreign trade. Results can be displayed in various forms.

*World Development Report.* World Bank Group. • Annual. Covers history, conditions, and trends relating to economic globalization and localization. Includes selected data from *World Development Indicators* for 132 countries or economies. Key indicators are provided for 78 additional countries or economies.

## DIRECTORIES

*The Internet Blue Pages: The Guide to Federal Government Web Sites.* Information Today, Inc. • Annual. $34.95. Provides information on more than 1,800 Web sites used by various agencies of the federal government. Includes indexes to agencies and topics. Links to all Web sites listed are available at www.fedweb.com. (CyberAge Books.).

*World Directory of Non-Official Statistical Sources.* Euromonitor International Business Reference Div. • $750 Individuals U.S.D. Covers: Over 2,800 titles, serials, and statistical data services produced by associations, business schools, trade journals, market research companies, banks, insurance companies, employers' organizations, and building societies in the world. Entries include: Source title, publisher or producer name, address, phone, fax, description.

## INTERNET DATABASES

*Business 2.0 Web Guide to the Best Business Links.* Business 2.0 Media Inc. Phone: (415)293-4800; Email: support@business2.com • URL: http://www.business2.com/webguide • Web site presents an extensive, searchable directory of links to "the best, most informative, and authoritative web pages." Twenty main categories cover business, finance, career, company information, people, and technology topics, with thousands of subtopics, all linking to Web sites recommended by experienced business researchers. Fees: Free.

*Fedstats.* Federal Interagency Council on Statistical Policy. Phone: (202)395-7254 • URL: http://www.fedstats.gov • Web site features an efficient search facility for full-text statistics produced by more than 100 federal agencies, including the Census Bureau, the Bureau of Economic Analysis, and the Bureau of Labor Statistics. Boolean searches can be made within one agency or for all agencies combined. Links are offered to international statistical bureaus, including the UN, IMF, OECD, UNESCO, Eurostat, and 20 individual countries. Fees: Free.

*FedWorld: A Program of the United States Department of Commerce.* National Technical Information Service. Phone: 800-553-NTIS or (703)605-6000; Fax: (703)605-6900; Email: webmaster@fedworld.gov • URL: http://www.fedworld.gov • Web site offers "a comprehensive central access point for searching, locating, ordering, and acquiring government and business information." Emphasis is on searching the Web pages, databases, and government reports of a wide variety of federal agencies. Fees: Free.

*FirstGov: Your First Click to the U. S. Government.* General Services Administration. Phone: 800-333-4636 or (202)501-0705; Email: public.affairs@gsa.gov • URL: http://www.gsa.gov • Free Web site provides extensive links to federal agencies covering a wide variety of topics, such as agriculture, business, consumer safety, education, the environment, government jobs, grants, health, social security, statistics sources, taxes, technology, travel, and world affairs. Also provides links to federal forms, including IRS tax forms. Searching is offered, both keyword and advanced.

*FreeLunch.com.* Economy.com, Inc. Phone: (610)696-8700; Fax: (610)696-1678 • URL: http://www.freelunch.com • Web site provides free access to more than 200 million economic and financial data series, covering industry, demographics, labor markets, prices, retail sales, government spending, trade, interest rates, housing starts, the stock market, etc. Data is available in either chart or table form. Searching is offered. Free, but registration required. Economy.com, Inc. also offers fee-based economic analysis at *The Dismal Scientist* site (www.dismal.com).

*InSite 2.* Intelligence Data/Thomson Financial. Phone: 800-654-0393 or (617)856-1890; Fax: (617)737-3182; Email: intelligence.data@tfn.com • URL: http://www.insite2.gale.com/ • Fee-based Web site consolidates information in a "Base Pack" consisting of Business InSite, Market InSite, and Company InSite. Optional databases are Consumer InSite, Health and Wellness InSite, Newsletter InSite, and Computer InSite. Includes fulltext content from more than 2,500 trade publications, journals, newsletters, newspapers, analyst reports, and other sources. Continuous updating. Formerly produced by The Gale Group.

*U.S. Census Bureau: The Official Statistics.* U. S. Bureau of the Census. Phone: (301)763-4636 or (301)763-4100; Fax: (301)763-4794; Email: webmaster@census.gov • URL: http://www.census.gov/prod/www/abs/mfg-prof.html • Web site is "Your Source for Social, Demographic, and Economic Information." Contains "Current U. S. Population Count," "Current Economic Indicators," and a wide variety of data under "Other Official Statistics." Keyword searching is provided. Fees: Free.

## OTHER SOURCES

*Business Rankings Annual (BRA).* Cengage Learning Inc. • Annual. $584 Individuals. A guide to lists and rankings appearing in major business publications. The top ten names are listed in each case.

## PERIODICALS AND NEWSLETTERS

*Internet Connection: Your Guide to Government Resources.* Glasser LegalWorks. • 10 times a year. $89.00 per year. Newsletter (print) devoted to finding free or low-cost U. S. Government information on the Internet. Provides detailed descriptions of government Web sites.

## RESEARCH CENTERS AND INSTITUTES

Brazil Ministry of Planning - Brazilian Institute of Geography and Statistics. Avda. Franklin Roosevelt 166/10 andar, Castelo, 20021-120 Rio de Janeiro, RJ, Brazil. Phone: 55 21 21424501; Fax: 55 21 424933; Email: webmaster@ibge.gov.br • URL: http://www.ibge.gov.br • Main research activities include: periodical censuses and continuous surveys on prices, industrial, agricultural and services activities and the national accounts; population and household censuses and yearly household surveys; systematic mapping of the Brazilian territory, geodesy and thematic studies on environment and natural resources.

Humboldt University of Berlin - Center for Applied Statistics and Economics. Spandauer Str. 1, 10178 Berlin, Germany. Phone: 49 30 20935630; Fax: 49 30 20935649; Email: stat@wiwi.hu-berlin.de • URL: http://www.case.hu-berlin.de • Statistics and economics.

National Institute of Statistics and Economic Studies - Center for Research in Economics and Statistics. 15 Blvd. Gabriel Péri, F-92245 Malakoff, France. Phone: 33 1 41176081; Fax: 33 1 41176029 • URL: http://www.insee.fr/en/insee-statistique-publique/default.asp?page=connaitre/genes.htm • Economic and social modeling; conception and implementation of statistical methods.

Social Security Administration - Office of Research, Evaluation, and Statistics. 6401 Security Blvd., Baltimore, MD 21235. Phone: (410)965-2841 • URL: http://www.ssa.gov/policy/about/ORES.html • Social security programs. Activities include: conducting policy studies mandated by Congress; conducting policy studies intended to support the legislative development process, such as research on the relationship between social security and the U.S. economy, descriptions of the effects of specific program provisions, and analysis of the role of social security in providing for the economic security of the aged and disabled; tabulating basic statistics on the beneficiary population from administrative records and surveys; maintaining and enhancing databases used to conduct these activities; evaluating the effectiveness of enacted legislation, legislative proposals, and current law provisions, and providing statistical and methodological support to aid other SSA components.

## STATISTICS SOURCES

*Statistical Abstract of the United States.* U. S. Government Printing Office. • Annual. $44.00. Issued by the U. S. Bureau of the Census.

*Statistical Yearbook.* United Nations Publications. • Annual. $125.00. Contains statistics for about 200 countries on a wide variety of economic, industrial, and demographic topics. Compiled by United Nations Statistical Office.

*Survey of Current Business.* U. S. Government Printing Office. • Published by Bureau of Economic Analysis, U. S. Department of Commerce. Presents a wide variety of business and economic data.

## TRADE/PROFESSIONAL ASSOCIATIONS

Irish Business and Employers' Confederation. Confederation House, 84-86 Lower Baggot St., Dublin IRL-2, Dublin, Ireland. Phone: 353 1 6051500; Fax: 353 1 6381500; Email: info@ibec.ie • URL: http://www.ibec.ie • Firms: industrial, commercial, and public sector firms that manufacture products or provide services. Promotes the growth and development of Irish industry and commercial activity. Advises the government and represents interests of industry on relevant legislative issues. Maintains the Irish Business Bureau in conjunction with Irish Business and Employers Confederation and the Chambers of Commerce of Ireland. Develops public awareness of the role of industry in national development through press, radio, television, and public meetings. Monitors technological developments; compiles statistics; provides advice and assistance to members; maintains speakers' bureau.

# STATISTICS, VITAL

*See* VITAL STATISTICS

# STATUTES

*See* LAWS

# STEAM HEATING

*See* HEATING AND VENTILATION

# STEAMSHIP LINES

*See also* SHIPS, SHIPPING AND SHIPBUILD-ING

## DIRECTORIES

*List of Shipowners, Managers, and Managing Agents.* Lloyd's Register of Shipping. • Annual. $350.00, including 10 updates per year. Published in the UK by Lloyd's Register-Fairplay Ltd. Lists 40,000 shipowners, managers, and agents worldwide. Cross-referenced with *Lloyd's Register of Ships.*

*Plunkett's Airline, Hotel, and Travel Industry*

*Almanac.* Plunkett Research Ltd. • Annual. $349.99. Contains profiles of 300 leading companies, including airlines, hotels, travel agencies, theme parks, cruise lines, casinos, and car rental companies.

### INTERNET DATABASES

*CDC Vessel Sanitation Program (VSP): Charting a Healthier Course.* U. S. Centers for Disease Control and Prevention. Phone: (770)488-7070; Fax: (888)232-6789; Email: vsp@cdc.gov • URL: http://www.cdc.gov/nceh/vsp/ • Annual. Web site provides details of unannounced sanitation inspections of individual cruise ships arriving at U. S. ports. Includes detailed results of the most recent inspection of each ship and results of inspections taking place in years past. There are lists of "Ships Inspected Past 2 Months" and "Ships with Not Satisfactory Scores" (passing grade is 85). CDC standards cover drinking water, food, and general cleanliness. Online searching is possible by ship name, inspection date, and numerical scores. Fees: Free.

### PERIODICALS AND NEWSLETTERS

*Cruise Travel.* World Publishing Co. • Bimonthly. $38.95 /year.

*Summary of Sanitation Inspections of International Cruise Ships.* Centers for Disease Control and Prevention. • Biweekly. Apply. "All passenger cruise ships arriving at U. S. ports are subject to unannounced inspection.to achieve levels of sanitation that will minimize the potential for gastrointestinal disease outbreaks on these ships." Individual ships are listed, with sanitation rating and date of inspection. (CDC Document No. 510051.).

*Travel Weekly.* Northstar Travel Media L.L.C. • Weekly. $266.00 per year. Includes cruise guides, a weekly "Business Travel Update," and special issues devoted to particular destinations and areas. Edited mainly for travel agents and tour operators.

# STEEL FOUNDRIES

*See* FOUNDRIES

# STEEL INDUSTRY

*See* IRON AND STEEL INDUSTRY

# STENOGRAPHERS

*See* OFFICE PRACTICE

# STENOGRAPHY

*See* SHORTHAND

# STEREOPHONIC SOUND

*See* HIGH FIDELITY/STEREO

# STOCK AND STOCK BREEDING

*See* LIVESTOCK INDUSTRY

# STOCK BROKERS

### BIOGRAPHICAL SOURCES

*Who's Who in Finance and Business.* Marquis Who's Who L.L.C. • Biennial. $349 Individuals. Provides over 21,000 concise biographies of business leaders in all fields.

### DIRECTORIES

*Major Financial Institutions of the World.* Cengage Learning Inc. • $1,460 Individuals. 2012. 16th edition. eBook. Published by Graham & Whiteside. Contains detailed information on more than 10,000 important financial institutions in various countries. Includes banks, investment companies, and insurance companies.

*Plunkett's On-Line Trading, Finance, and Investment Web Sites Almanac.* Plunkett Research Ltd. • Annual. $149.99. Provides profiles and usefulness rankings of financial Web sites. Sites are rated from 1 to 5 for specific uses. Includes CD-ROM.

*Who's Who in Finance and Business.* Marquis Who's Who L.L.C. • Biennial. $349 Individuals. Provides over 21,000 concise biographies of business leaders in all fields.

*Zacks Analyst Directory.* Zacks Investment Research Inc. • Updated daily. Lists stockbroker investment analysts and gives the names of major U.S. corporations covered by those analysts.

### HANDBOOKS AND MANUALS

*N A S D Manual.* National Association of Securities Dealers, Inc. Wolters Kluwer Law & Business CCH. • Quarterly. $452.00 per year. CD-Rom, $459.00.

*Securities Crimes.* Thomson West. • Annual. $798 full set. Analyzes the enfo of federal securities laws from the viewpoint of the defendant. Discusses Securities and Exchange Commission (SEC) investigations and federal sentencing guidelines. (Securities Law Series).

### OTHER SOURCES

*Andrews' Professional Liability Litigation Reporter.* Andrews Publications. • Monthly. $550.00 per year. Provides reports on lawsuits against attorneys, accountants, and investment professionals.

*Broker-Dealer Regulation.* David A. Lipton. Thomson West. • Semiannual. $114 per month. Focuses on the basics of stockbroker license application procedure, registration, regulation, and responsibilities. (Securities Law Series).

### PERIODICALS AND NEWSLETTERS

*Investment Dealers' Digest.* SourceMedia Inc. • Weekly. $750.00 per year. Covers financial news, trends, new products, people, private placements, new issues of securities, and other aspects of the investment business. Includes feature stories.

*Investment Management Mandate Pipeline.* SourceMedia Inc. • Weekly. $1,295.00 per year. Newsletter. Edited for money managers and other investment professionals. Covers personnel news, investment strategies, and industry trends.

*Investment News: The Weekly Newspaper for Financial Advisers.* Crain Communications Inc. • Weekly. $29.00 per year. Edited for both personal and institutional investment advisers, planners, and managers.

*On Wall Street.* SourceMedia Inc. • Monthly. $96.00 per year. Edited for securities dealers. Includes articles on financial planning, retirement planning, variable annuities, and money management, with special coverage of 401(k) plans and IRAs.

*Operations Management.* Institutional Investor Inc. Journals Group. • Weekly. $2,105.00 per year. Includes print and online editions. Newsletter. Edited for managers of securities clearance and settlement at financial institutions. Covers new products, technology, legalities, management practices, and other topics related to securities processing.

*Registered Representative.* Intertec Publishing. • Monthly.

*Safe Money Report.* Weiss Research Inc. • Monthly. $99.00 per year. Newsletter. Provides financial advice and current safety ratings of various banks,

savings and loan companies, insurance companies, and securities dealers.

*Securities Arbitration Commentator.* Richard P. Ryder. • Monthly. $695.00 per year. Newsletter. Edited for attorneys and other professionals concerned with securities arbitration.

*Securities Technology Monitor.* SourceMedia Inc. • Newsletter covers securities dealing and processing, including regulatory compliance, shareholder services, human resources, transaction clearing, and technology.

*Traders Magazine.* SourceMedia Inc. • Monthly. $60.00 per year. Edited for institutional buy side and sell side equity traders. Covers industry news, market trends, regulatory developments, and personnel news. Serves as the official publication of the Security Traders Association.

### STATISTICS SOURCES

*Standard & Poor's Industry Surveys.* Standard & Poor's Financial Services L.L.C. • Semiannual. $1,800.00. Two looseleaf volumes. Includes monthly *Supplements.* Provides detailed, individual surveys of 52 major industry groups. Each survey is revised on a semiannual basis. Also includes "Monthly Investment Review" (industry group investment analysis) and monthly "Trends & Projections" (economic analysis).

*U.S. Industry and Trade Outlook.* U.S. Department of Commerce National Technical Information Service. • Annual. Produced by the International Trade Administration, U.S. Department of Commerce, in a "public-private" partnership with DRI/McGraw-Hill and Standard & Poor's. Provides basic data, outlook for the current year, and "Long-Term Prospects" (five-year projections) for a wide variety of products and services. Includes high technology industries. Formerly *U.S. Industrial Outlook.*

*United States Securities and Exchange Commission Annual Report.* U. S. Government Printing Office. • Annual. The Commission maintains a Web site at www.sec.gov.

### TRADE/PROFESSIONAL ASSOCIATIONS

Financial Industry Regulatory Authority. 1735 K St., Washington, DC 20006. Phone: (301)590-6500; Fax: (202)293-6260; Email: francine.lee@finra.org • URL: http://www.finra.org • Formerly National Association of Securities Dealers.

# STOCK DIVIDENDS

*See* DIVIDENDS

# STOCK EXCHANGES

*See also* STOCKS

### DIRECTORIES

*All Ordinaries Index Companies Handbook.* Australian Stock Exchange Ltd. Exchange Centre. • $29.95 plus $10.00 postage and handling. Covers: approximately 314 companies that comprise the Australian All Ordinaries Index as of September of the year issued, plus Health-Biotechnology and Telecommunications Index companies that are not included in the All Ordinaries Companies Index. Entries include: Company name, address, phone, names and titles of key personnel, key business summary, financial data, description of product/service, list of major shareholders, share price chart.

*Australia's Top 100.* Australian Stock Exchange Ltd. Exchange Centre. • Annual. $20 plus 10 dollars shipping. Covers: top 100 listed companies on the Australian Stock Exchange ranked by market capitalization. Entries include: Company name, address, phone, fax, telex, names and titles of key personnel, financial data, company history, description of products and activities.

*The Dow Jones Guide to the World Stock Market.* Reference Press Inc. • Annual. $39.95. Covers: 2,600 companies in 20 countries that form the Dow Jones World Stock Index. Database includes: A ranking of the companies listed by country, market value, industry, and other factors. Entries include: Company name, address, phone, description, main lines of business, history, sales, earnings, dividends, and financial performance.

*Handbook of World Stock and Commodity Exchanges.* Blackwell Publishing Inc. • Annual. $265.00. Provides detailed information on over 200 stock and commodity exchanges in more than 50 countries.

*NASDAQ BX Guide.* Wolters Kluwer Law & Business CCH. • Annual. Covers: Members and member organizations, constitution & rules of the Exchange. Database includes: List of stocks and bonds admitted to trading on the exchange, arranged alphabetically by name of issuing company, and including description and class of stock or bond, trading code, trading post, and par value. Entries include: Name, affiliation, address, date of admission to exchange.

*NASDAQ PHLX Guide.* Wolters Kluwer Law & Business CCH. • Annual. $794 Individuals print. Covers: Members, associate members, and member organizations of the stock exchange in Philadelphia, Pennsylvania. Database includes: Directory and Constitution rules published for the Exchange. Entries include: Name, affiliation, address, date of admission to exchange.

*New York Stock Exchange Guide.* Commerce Clearing House Inc. • Monthly. $485 per year, postpaid; payment with order. Covers: about 1,380 member companies listed as traders with the New York Stock Exchange, and exchange and floor officials. Entries include: Company name, address, date admitted, representatives.

*Profile's Stock Exchange Handbook.* Profile Media. • Quarterly. R 155 Individuals. Covers: About 650 companies whose stock is traded on the Johannesburg, South Africa, stock exchange. Entries include: Company name, address, names and titles of key personnel, line of business, names of associated and subsidiary companies, capital, dates of dividend payments, five-year financial data, five-year comparison of high and low share prices and volumes traded.

*The Stock Exchange of Hong Kong--Fact Book.* The Stock Exchange of Hong Kong Corporate Communications Department. • Annual. Publication includes: List of companies listed on the Stock Exchange of Hong Kong. Principal content of publication is stock price index movement, trading value and volume, market capitalization, dividend yields and P/E ratios, and listed companies' activities and statistical records. Principal content of publication is a picture of the Hong Kong stock market for the year.

*The Stock Exchange of Hong Kong--List of Exchange Participants and Holders of Stock Exchange Trading Rights.* The Stock Exchange of Hong Kong Corporate Communications Department. • Quarterly. $134. Covers: Hong Kong stock exchange, including lists of exchange participants, holders of stock exchange trading rights, dealing directors, options exchange participants, and registered branch offices. Entries include: Name, address, phone.

*Trade Directory of Mexico.* Hoover's Inc. • Annual. $99.95. Published by IMF Editora. Contains profiles of 6,000 Mexican companies involved in foreign trade. Includes profile of Mexico and of the individual states.

*Yearbook of the Athens Stock Exchange.* Athens Stock Exchange. • Annual. €20 plus postage. Covers: About 196 companies quoted on the Athens

Stock Exchange; list of stockbrokers. Database includes: List of business loans available, with description and financial data; financial statistics. Entries include: For companies--Name, address, phone, telex, year established, year first listed, line of business, number of shareholders, board of directors, number of employees, financial data. For brokers--Name, address, phone.

## HANDBOOKS AND MANUALS

*N A S D Manual.* National Association of Securities Dealers, Inc. Wolters Kluwer Law & Business CCH. • Quarterly. $452.00 per year. CD-Rom, $459.00.

## INTERNET DATABASES

*Factiva.* Dow Jones Reuters Business Interactive, LLC. Phone: 800-369-7466 or (609)452-1511; Fax: (609)520-5770; Email: solutions@factiva.com • URL: http://www.factiva.com • Fee-based Web site provides "global news and business information through Web sites and content integration solutions." Includes Dow Jones and Reuters newswires, The Wall Street Journal, and more than 7,000 other sources of current news, historical articles, market research reports, and investment analysis. Content includes 96 major U. S. newspapers, 900 non-English sources, trade publications, media transcripts, country profiles, news photos, etc.

*Nexis.com.* Lexis-Nexis Group. Phone: 800-227-4908 or (937)865-6800; Fax: (937)865-6909; Email: webmaster@prod.lexis-nexis.com • URL: http:// www.nexis.com • Fee-based Web site offers searching of about 2.8 billion documents in some 30,000 news, business, and legal information sources. Features include a subject directory covering 1,200 topics in 34 categories and a Company Dossier containing information on more than 500,000 public and private companies. Boolean searching is offered.

*U.S. Securities and Exchange Commission.* 100 F St. NE, Washington, DC 20549. Phone: 800-732-0330 or (202)942-8088; Fax: (202)942-9634; Email: webmaster@sec.gov • URL: http://www.sec.gov • SEC Web site offers free access through EDGAR to text of official corporate filings, such as annual reports (10-K), quarterly reports (10-Q), and proxies. (EDGAR is "Electronic Data Gathering, Analysis, and Retrieval System.") An example is given of how to obtain executive compensation data from proxies. Text of the daily *SEC News Digest* is offered, as are links to other government sites, non-government market regulators, and U. S. stock exchanges. Search facilities are extensive. Fees: Free.

*Wall Street Journal Interactive Edition.* Dow Jones & Co., Inc. 1211 Avenue of the Americas, New York, NY 10036. Phone: 800-369-5663; Email: service@dowjones.com • URL: http://new. dowjones.com • Fee-based Web site providing on-line searching of worldwide information from *The Wall Street Journal.* Includes "Company Snapshots," "The Journal's Greatest Hits," "Index to Market Data," "Journal Links," etc. Financial price quotes are available. Fees: $49.00 per year; $29.00 per year to print subscribers.

## PERIODICALS AND NEWSLETTERS

*Financial History: Chronicling the History of America's Capital Markets.* Museum of American Finance. • Quarterly. Membership. Contains articles on early stock and bond markets and trading in the U. S., with photographs and other illustrations. Current trading in rare and unusual, obsolete stock and bond certificates is featured. Formerly *Friends of Financial History.*

*Financial Sentinel: Your Beacon to the World of Investing.* Gulf Atlantic Publish, Inc. • Monthly. $29.95 per year. Provides "The only complete listing of all OTC Bulletin Board stocks traded, with all issues listed on the Nasdaq SmallCap Market, the Toronto, and Vancouver Stock Exchanges." Also includes investment advice and recommendations of

small capitalization stocks.

## STATISTICS SOURCES

*American Stock Exchange Weekly Bulletin.* Nasdaq-AMEX Market Group. • Weekly. $20.00 per year. Looseleaf service.

*NASDAQ-AMEX Market Group Fact Book.* NASD MediaSource. • Annual. $20.00. Published by the American Stock Exchange, Inc. Contains statistical data relating to the American Stock Exchange. Also provides the address and phone number for each company listed on the Exchange. Formerly *American Stock Exchange Fact Book.*

*SRC Green Book of 5 Trend 35-Year Charts.* Securities Research Co. • Annual. $150.00. Chart book presents statistical information on the stocks of 400 leading companies over a 35-year period. Each full page chart is in semi-log format to avoid visual distortion. Also includes charts of 12 leading market averages or indexes and 39 major industry groups.

## TRADE/PROFESSIONAL ASSOCIATIONS

Chicago Stock Exchange Inc. 440 S LaSalle St., Chicago, IL 60605-1028. Phone: (312)663-2222; Fax: (312)663-2231; Email: info@chx.com • URL: http://www.chx.com • Brokers and dealers in local and national securities. Wholly-owned subsidiaries: Midwest Securities Trust Company; Midwest Clearing Corp.; Mortgage Backed Securities Clearing Corporation. Provides an auction market for purchase and sale of equity securities.

# STOCK INDEX TRADING

*See also* FINANCIAL FUTURES TRADING

## ABSTRACTS AND INDEXES

*Business Periodicals Index Retrospective.* EBSCO Publishing Inc. • 11/year. Quarterly and annual cumulations.

## DIRECTORIES

*Futures Magazine SourceBook: The Most Complete List of Exchanges, Companies, Regulators, Organizations, etc., Offering Products and Services to the Futures and Options Industry.* Futures Magazine Inc. • Annual. $19.50. Provides information on commodity futures brokers, trading method services, publications, and other items of interest to futures traders and money managers.

## INTERNET DATABASES

*BanxQuote Banking, Mortgage, and Finance Center.* BanxQuote, Inc. Phone: (914)722-1600; Fax: (914)722-6630; Email: info@banx.com • URL: http://www.banx.com • Daily. Web site quotes interest rates paid by banks around the country on various savings products, as well as rates paid by consumers for automobile loans, mortgages, credit cards, home equity loans, and personal loans. Also provided: stock quotes, indexes, stock options, futures trading data, economic indicators, and links to many other financial sites.

*CRB Market Overview.* Commodity Research Bureau. Phone: 800-621-5271 or (312)554-8456; Fax: (312)939-4135; Email: info@crbtrader.com • URL: http://www.crbtrader.com/data/ • Web site provides free, detailed, current price quotes for about 100 futures contracts, covering Currencies, Energies, Financials, Grains, Meats, Metals, "Softs" (orange juice, coffee, etc.) and stock price indexes. Includes contract specifications and detailed prices of options on futures.

*ETF Connect.* Nuveen Investments. Phone: 800-257-8787 • URL: http://www.etfconnect.com • Free Web site makes available extensive, searchable information on individual closed-end investment funds, preferred share funds, and exchange-traded index funds. Information on a particular fund is available by name or as part of a classification (high yield, investment grade, municipal, emerging markets, global equity, etc.). Fund charts are available for various time periods, as is data concerning premiums or discounts, dividends, annualized total return, credit quality, "Top 10 Holdings," and so forth.

*Futures Online.* Futures Magazine Inc. Phone: (312)846-4600; Fax: (312)846-4638 • URL: http://www.futuresmag.com • Web site presents updates of *Futures* magazine and links to other futures-related sites.

### ONLINE DATABASES

*Wilson Business Abstracts Online.* H.W. Wilson Co. • Indexes and abstracts 600 major business periodicals, plus the *Wall Street Journal* and the business section of the *New York Times.* Indexing is from 1982, abstracting from 1990, with the two newspapers included from 1993. Updated weekly. Inquire as to online cost and availability. (*Business Periodicals Index* without abstracts is also available online.).

### PERIODICALS AND NEWSLETTERS

*Futures: News, Analysis, and Strategies for Futures, Options, and Derivatives Traders.* Futures Magazine Inc. • Monthly. $39 Individuals. Edited for institutional money managers and traders, brokers, risk managers, and individual investors or speculators. Includes special feature issues on interest rates, technical indicators, currencies, charts, precious metals, hedge funds, and derivatives. Supplements available.

*SFO: Stocks, Futures & Options.* W and A Publishing. • Subtitle: *Official Journal for Personal Investing in Stocks, Futures, and Options.* Covers mainly speculative techniques for stocks, commodity futures, financial futures, stock index futures, foreign exchange, short selling, and various kinds of options.

*Technical Analysis of Stocks & Commodities: The Traders Magazine.* Technical Analysis Inc. • $89.99 Individuals Annual. 13 times a year. Covers use of personal computers for stock trading, price movement analysis by means of charts, and other technical trading methods.

### RESEARCH CENTERS AND INSTITUTES

University of Chicago - Booth School of Business - Center for Research in Security Prices. 105 W Adams St., Ste. 1700, Chicago, IL 60603. Phone: (312)263-6400; Fax: (312)263-6430; Email: subscriptions@crsp.chicagobooth.edu • URL: http://www.crsp.com • Historical financial data.

### STATISTICS SOURCES

*Statistical Annual: Interest Rates, Metals, Stock Indices, Options on Financial Futures, Options on Metals Futures.* Chicago Board of Trade. • Annual. Includes historical data on GNMA CDR Futures, Cash-Settled GNMA Futures, U. S. Treasury Bond Futures, U. S. Treasury Note Futures, Options on Treasury Note Futures, NASDAQ-100 Futures, Major Market Index Futures, Major Market Index MAXI Futures, Municipal Bond Index Futures, 1,000-Ounce Silver Futures, Options on Silver Futures, and Kilo Gold Futures.

### TRADE/PROFESSIONAL ASSOCIATIONS

Financial Industry Regulatory Authority. 1735 K St., Washington, DC 20006. Phone: (301)590-6500; Fax: (202)293-6260; Email: francine.lee@finra.org • URL: http://www.finra.org • Formerly National Association of Securities Dealers.

# STOCK MARKET

*See* STOCK EXCHANGES

# STOCK OPTION CONTRACTS

### DIRECTORIES

*Futures Magazine SourceBook: The Most Complete List of Exchanges, Companies, Regulators, Organizations, etc., Offering Products and Services to the Futures and Options Industry.* Futures Magazine Inc. • Annual. $19.50. Provides information on commodity futures brokers, trading method services, publications, and other items of interest to futures traders and money managers.

### INTERNET DATABASES

*BanxQuote Banking, Mortgage, and Finance Center.* BanxQuote, Inc. Phone: (914)722-1600; Fax: (914)722-6630; Email: info@banx.com • URL: http://www.banx.com • Daily. Web site quotes interest rates paid by banks around the country on various savings products, as well as rates paid by consumers for automobile loans, mortgages, credit cards, home equity loans, and personal loans. Also provided: stock quotes, indexes, stock options, futures trading data, economic indicators, and links to many other financial sites.

*Futures Online.* Futures Magazine Inc. Phone: (312)846-4600; Fax: (312)846-4638 • URL: http://www.futuresmag.com • Web site presents updates of *Futures* magazine and links to other futures-related sites.

### OTHER SOURCES

*Managing Financial Risk with Forwards, Futures, Options, and Swaps.* American Management Association Extension Institute. • Looseleaf. $159.00. Self-study course. Emphasis is on practical explanations, examples, and problem solving. Quizzes and a case study are included.

### PERIODICALS AND NEWSLETTERS

*Futures: News, Analysis, and Strategies for Futures, Options, and Derivatives Traders.* Futures Magazine Inc. • Monthly. $39 Individuals. Edited for institutional money managers and traders, brokers, risk managers, and individual investors or speculators. Includes special feature issues on interest rates, technical indicators, currencies, charts, precious metals, hedge funds, and derivatives. Supplements available.

*Option Advisor.* Investment Research Institute Inc. • Monthly. $199.00 per year. Newsletter. Provides specific advice and recommendations for trading in stock option contracts (puts and calls).

*SFO: Stocks, Futures & Options.* W and A Publishing. • Subtitle: *Official Journal for Personal Investing in Stocks, Futures, and Options.* Covers mainly speculative techniques for stocks, commodity futures, financial futures, stock index futures, foreign exchange, short selling, and various kinds of options.

### TRADE/PROFESSIONAL ASSOCIATIONS

Chicago Board Options Exchange Inc. 400 S LaSalle St., Chicago, IL 60605. Phone: 877-843-2263 or (312)786-5600; Fax: (312)786-7409; Email: help@cboe.com • URL: http://www.cboe.com • Individuals, institutions and firms engaged in the buying and selling of various products including stock options, cash-settled index options, options on HOLDRs, options on Exchange Traded Funds and Structured Products.

# STOCKBROKERS

*See* STOCK BROKERS

# STOCKHOLDERS

*See also* INSIDER TRADING

### ABSTRACTS AND INDEXES

*Business Periodicals Index Retrospective.* EBSCO Publishing Inc. • 11/year. Quarterly and annual cumulations.

### INTERNET DATABASES

*U.S. Securities and Exchange Commission.* 100 F St. NE, Washington, DC 20549. Phone: 800-732-0330 or (202)942-8088; Fax: (202)942-9634; Email: webmaster@sec.gov • URL: http://www.sec.gov • SEC Web site offers free access through EDGAR to text of official corporate filings, such as annual reports (10-K), quarterly reports (10-Q), and proxies. (EDGAR is "Electronic Data Gathering, Analysis, and Retrieval System.") An example is given of how to obtain executive compensation data from proxies. Text of the daily *SEC News Digest* is offered, as are links to other government sites, non-government market regulators, and U. S. stock exchanges. Search facilities are extensive. Fees: Free.

### ONLINE DATABASES

*Wilson Business Abstracts Online.* H.W. Wilson Co. • Indexes and abstracts 600 major business periodicals, plus the *Wall Street Journal* and the business section of the *New York Times.* Indexing is from 1982, abstracting from 1990, with the two newspapers included from 1993. Updated weekly. Inquire as to online cost and availability. (*Business Periodicals Index* without abstracts is also available online.).

### PERIODICALS AND NEWSLETTERS

*Investor Relations Business.* SourceMedia Inc. • Semimonthly. $495.00 per year. Covers the issues affecting stockholder relations, corporate public relations, and institutional investor relations.

*Pensions and Investments: The Newspaper of Corporate and Institutional Investing.* Crain Communications Inc. • Biweekly. $325.00 per year. Formerly *Pensions and Investment Age.*

*Securities Technology Monitor.* SourceMedia Inc. • Newsletter covers securities dealing and processing, including regulatory compliance, shareholder services, human resources, transaction clearing, and technology.

*Trusts and Estates.* RentPath Inc. • Monthly. $139.00 per year. Includes annual *Directory.*

# STOCKINGS

*See* HOSIERY INDUSTRY

# STOCKS

*See also* DIVIDENDS; INVESTMENT ADVISORY SERVICES; INVESTMENTS; OVER-THE-COUNTER SECURITIES INDUSTRY; STOCK EXCHANGES

### CD-ROM DATABASES

*OECD Statistical Compendium.* Organization for Economic Cooperation and Development. • Semiannual. $1,905.00 per year for 1 to 10 users. CD-ROM contains more than 730,000 monthly, quarterly, and annual time series for OECD countries, 1960 to date. Includes fully searchable data on agriculture, food, economic indicators, national accounts, employment, energy, finance, industry, technology, and foreign trade. Results can be displayed in various forms.

### DIRECTORIES

*American Stock Exchange Guide.* Wolters Kluwer Law & Business CCH. • Annual. $896 Individuals print. Covers: About 1,275 member companies listed as traders with the American Stock Exchange, and exchange and floor officials. Entries include:

Company name, address, date admitted, names of representatives.

*China Stock Directory.* China Economic Review. • $75 Individuals. Covers: 1,800 mainland-listed companies on the Shanghai and Shenzhen markets. Publication includes: Information about a company history, business operations, share price range, shareholders, key executives, contact details, complete financials top shareholders, their share types and percentage stakes.

*FII Annual Guide to Stocks.* Financial Information Inc. • Annual. $2,250. Two volumes. Formerly *Financial Stock Guide Service: Directory of Active Stocks.*

*Financial Annual Registrars Service.* Extel Financial Ltd. • Annual. $110. Covers: United Kingdom companies listed on one of the UK stock exchanges. Entries include: Company name, registrar's name, address, phone, fax, telex, types of stocks and shares, nominal value.

*Insiders' Chronicle.* American Banker Newsletters. • Covers: publicly held companies in whose securities there has been significant buying or selling by executive officers, directors, and those who hold 10% or more of its shares. Database includes: Market news, quotations, and statistics. Entries include: Company name, name and title of person involved, number of shares held, number of shares bought or sold, price per share, date of transaction.

*Institutional Buyers of Small-Cap Stocks.* bigdough. com Inc. • Annual. $295.00. Provides detailed profiles of more than 837 institutional buyers of small capitalization stocks. Includes names of financial analysts and portfolio managers.

*Major French Companies.* DAFSA. • Annual. Covers: Companies with shares traded on the stock exchange in France. Entries include: Company name, address, phone, officers, directors, executives, banking information, financial institutions, broker-trading.

*Midwest Stock Exchange Guide.* Wolters Kluwer Law & Business CCH. • Annual. $395 per year. Covers: members, associate members, and member organizations. Database includes: List of stocks and bonds traded on the exchange, arranged alphabetically by name of issuing company, trading code, trading post, and par value; rules of exchange. Entries include: Name, affiliation, address, date of admission to exchange.

*Morningstar American Depositary Receipts.* Morningstar Inc. • Biweekly. Looseleaf. Provides detailed profiles of 700 foreign companies having shares traded in the U. S. through American Depositary Receipts (ADRs).

*Nordic Stock Guide.* Delphi Economics AB. • $34.95 plus $3.50 shipping. Covers: nearly 250 public companies in Denmark, Finland, Norway, and Sweden. Database includes: Interest rate histories, exchange rates, and commodities prices for each country. Entries include: Company name, address, phone, names and titles of key personnel, overview of company operations, stock and financial data for previous six years.

*Quarterly Report on Companies whose Stocks are Quoted on the Stock Markets.* Bolsas de Comercio de Madrid, Bilbao, Barcelona, Valencia. • Quarterly. Covers: Companies on the stock exchange in Spain. Entries include: Company name, address, phone, financial and economic data.

*Quoted Companies on the Brussels and Antwerp Stock Exchange.* DAFSA - Belgique S.A. • Annual. Covers: Companies with shares traded on the Antwerp and Brussels stock exchanges. Entries include: Company name, address, phone, officers, directors, executives, banks, brokers.

*Stocks, Bonds, Options & Derivatives: Symbol Book.* American Stock Exchange Inc. • Quarterly. $8 per edition. Covers: Ticker symbols, corporate

names, cusip numbers, and other information on stocks, bonds, options, and derivative products listed on the American Stock Exchange.

*Thailand: The MFC Investment Handbook.* Hoover's Inc. • Annual. $46.95 plus $3.50 shipping. Covers: over 340 companies listed on the Stock Exchange of Thailand; 23 unit trusts. Entries include: Company name, address, phone, fax, stock symbol, company overview, price per share, trading volume, net income, capital, financial ratios, foreign holdings, limits on foreign ownership, list of major shareholders, names and titles of key personnel.

*Walker's Manual of Community Bank Stocks.* Walker's Manual Inc. • $95. Covers 502 community banks in the United States--community banks are financed with less than $10 million and usually serve a limited geographic area.

*Who Owns Corporate America.* Taft Group. • Annual. $285. Covers: nearly 75,000 officers, directors, and 10% principal stockholders who own securities registered with the Securities and Exchange Commission. Entries include: Name, company, stock symbol, number of shares held, date of last stock transaction, class of security held, type of ownership, relationship of stockholder to the company, market value of holdings.

*Zacks Analyst Directory.* Zacks Investment Research Inc. • Updated daily. Lists stockbroker investment analysts and gives the names of major U.S. corporations covered by those analysts.

*Zacks Analyst Guide.* Zacks Investment Research Inc. • Ranks analysts within more than 70 industry groups.

## GENERAL WORKS

*Business Valuations: Businesses, Securities, and Real Estate.* American CPE Inc. • Contains detailed training information covering the valuation of businesses and other instruments and property related to businesses, including bonds, securities, preferred and common stock, and real estate.

## HANDBOOKS AND MANUALS

*Mergent Handbook of Common Stocks.* Mergent Inc. • Quarterly. Price on application. Facts, performance trends and financial summaries on nearly 1,000 New York Stock Exchange companies. Formerly *Moody's Handbook of Common Stocks.*

## INTERNET DATABASES

*BanxQuote Banking, Mortgage, and Finance Center.* BanxQuote, Inc. Phone: (914)722-1600; Fax: (914)722-6630; Email: info@banx.com • URL: http://www.banx.com • Daily. Web site quotes interest rates paid by banks around the country on various savings products, as well as rates paid by consumers for automobile loans, mortgages, credit cards, home equity loans, and personal loans. Also provided: stock quotes, indexes, stock options, futures trading data, economic indicators, and links to many other financial sites.

*Business 2.0 Web Guide to the Best Business Links.* Business 2.0 Media Inc. Phone: (415)293-4800; Email: support@business2.com • URL: http://www. business2.com/webguide • Web site presents an extensive, searchable directory of links to "the best, most informative, and authoritative web pages." Twenty main categories cover business, finance, career, company information, people, and technology topics, with thousands of subtopics, all linking to Web sites recommended by experienced business researchers. Fees: Free.

*Business Week Online.* McGraw-Hill. Phone: (212)512-2511; Fax: (684)842-6101 • URL: http:// www.businessweek.com • Web site provides complete contents of current issue of *Business Week* plus "BW Daily" with additonal business news, financial market quotes, and corporate information from Standard & Poor's. Includes various features, such as "Banking Center" with mortgage and inter-

est data, and "Interactive Computer Buying Guide." The "Business Week Archive" is fully searchable back to 1996.

*CANOE: Canadian Online Explorer.* Canoe Limited Partnership. Phone: (416)947-2154; Fax: (416)947-2209 • URL: http://www.canoe.ca • Web site provides a wide variety of Canadian news and information, including business and financial data. Includes "Money," "Your Investment," "Technology," and "Stock Quotes." Allows keyword searching, with links to many other sites. Daily updating. Fees: Free.

*Factiva.* Dow Jones Reuters Business Interactive, LLC. Phone: 800-369-7466 or (609)452-1511; Fax: (609)520-5770; Email: solutions@factiva.com • URL: http://www.factiva.com • Fee-based Web site provides "global news and business information through Web sites and content integration solutions." Includes Dow Jones and Reuters newswires, The Wall Street Journal, and more than 7,000 other sources of current news, historical articles, market research reports, and investment analysis. Content includes 96 major U. S. newspapers, 900 non-English sources, trade publications, media transcripts, country profiles, news photos, etc.

*Fedstats.* Federal Interagency Council on Statistical Policy. Phone: (202)395-7254 • URL: http://www. fedstats.gov • Web site features an efficient search facility for full-text statistics produced by more than 100 federal agencies, including the Census Bureau, the Bureau of Economic Analysis, and the Bureau of Labor Statistics. Boolean searches can be made within one agency or for all agencies combined. Links are offered to international statistical bureaus, including the UN, IMF, OECD, UNESCO, Eurostat, and 20 individual countries. Fees: Free.

*The Financial Post.* National Post Online. Phone: 800-805-1184 or (244)383-2300; Fax: (416)383-2443 • URL: http://www.nationalpost.com/ financialpost/ • Provides a broad range of Canadian business news online, with daily updates. Includes news, opinion, and special reports, as well as "Investing," "Money Rates," "Market Watch," and "Daily Mutual Funds." Allows advanced searching (Boolean operators), with links to various other sites. Fees: Free.

*FreeLunch.com.* Economy.com, Inc. Phone: (610)696-8700; Fax: (610)696-1678 • URL: http:// www.freelunch.com • Web site provides free access to more than 200 million economic and financial data series, covering industry, demographics, labor markets, prices, retail sales, government spending, trade, interest rates, housing starts, the stock market, etc. Data is available in either chart or table form. Searching is offered. Free, but registration required. Economy.com, Inc. also offers fee-based economic analysis at *The Dismal Scientist* site (www.dismal. com).

*Hoover's Online.* Hoover's Inc. 5800 Airport Blvd., Austin, TX 78752-4204. Phone: 866-443-3939 or (512)374-4500 or (866)281-5969; Fax: (512)374-4501; Email: salesteam@hoovers.com • URL: http://www.hoovers.com • Web site provides stock quotes, lists of companies, and a variety of business information at no charge. In-depth company profiles are available.

*Mergent Online.* Mergent Inc. 580 Kingsley Park Dr., Fort Mill, SC 29715. Phone: 800-937-1398 or (704)527-2700 or (704)559-7601; Fax: (704)559-6837 or (704)559-6960; Email: customerservice@ mergent.com • URL: http://www.mergent.com • Fee-based Web site provides detailed information on 20,000 publicly-owned companies in 100 foreign countries, as well as more than 10,000 corporations listed on the New York Stock Exchange, American Stock Exchange, NASDAQ, and U.S. regional exchanges. Searching is offered on many financial variables and text fields. Weekly updating. Formerly *FIS Online.*

*Morningstar.com: Your First Second Opinion.* Morningstar Inc. 22 W Washington St., Chicago, IL 60602. Phone: 800-735-0700 or (312)696-6000; Fax: (312)696-6001; Email: newsroom@ morningstar.com • URL: http://www.corporate. morningstar.com • Annual. $199 Premium membership. Web site provides a broad selection of information and advice on both mutual funds and individual stocks, including financial news and articles on investment fundamentals.

*Nexis.com.* Lexis-Nexis Group. Phone: 800-227-4908 or (937)865-6800; Fax: (937)865-6909; Email: webmaster@prod.lexis-nexis.com • URL: http:// www.nexis.com • Fee-based Web site offers searching of about 2.8 billion documents in some 30,000 news, business, and legal information sources. Features include a subject directory covering 1,200 topics in 34 categories and a Company Dossier containing information on more than 500,000 public and private companies. Boolean searching is offered.

*TheStreet.com: Your Insider's Look at Wall Street.* TheStreet.com, Inc. Phone: 800-562-9571 or (212)321-5000; Fax: (212)321-5016 • URL: http:// www.thestreet.com • Daily. Iconoclastic advice and comment on the stock market, but premium service displays a more comprehensive selection of news and analysis.

## ONLINE DATABASES

*EdgarPlus: SEC Basic Filings.* Thomson Reuters Markets. • Online service provides full text of about 60,000 documents that have been filed with the U.S. Securities and Exchange Commission, 1987 to date, with daily updates. Filings include 6-K, 8-K, 10-K, 10-C, 10-Q, 20-F, and proxy statements. Inquire as to online cost and availability.

*First Call Consensus Earnings Estimates.* Thomson Financial Inc. • Online service provides corporate earnings estimates for more than 2,500 U. S. companies, based on data from leading brokerage firms. Weekly updates. Inquire as to online cost and availability.

*Zacks Earnings Estimates.* Zacks Investment Research Inc. • Provides online earnings projections for about 6,000 U. S. corporations, based on investment analysts' reports. Data is mainly from 200 major brokerage firms. Time span varies according to online provider, with daily or weekly updates. Inquire as to online cost and availability.

## OTHER SOURCES

*Blue Book of Stock Reports.* MPL Communications Inc. • Biweekly. $260.00 per year. Canadian Business Service reports on over 250 Canadian companies.

*Chartcraft Monthly NYSE and ASE Chartbook.* Chartcraft Inc. • Monthly. $402.00 per year. Includes all common stocks on New York and American Stock Exchanges.

*Chartcraft Over-the-Counter Chartbook.* Chartcraft Inc. • Quarterly. $114.00 per year. Includes more than 1,000 unlisted stocks. Long term charts.

*Granville Market Letter.* Joseph Granville, editor. • 46 times a year. $250.00 per year.

*Mansfield Stock Chart Service.* R.W. Mansfield Co. • Weekly. Price varies. Newsletter. Covers New York Stock Exchange, American Stock Exchange, OTC exchange, international stocks and industry groups. Partial subscriptions available.

*Mergent's Annual Dividend Record.* Mergent Inc. • Annual. Provides detailed dividend data, including tax information, for 12,000 stocks and 18,000 mutual funds. Covers the most recent year. Formerly *Moody's Annual Dividend Record.*

*The Value Line Investment Survey.* Value Line Inc. • Weekly. $598 U.S. /year. Provides detailed information and ratings for 1,700 stocks actively-traded in the U. S.

## PERIODICALS AND NEWSLETTERS

*Canadian Resources and PennyMines Analyst: The Canadian Newsletter for Penny-Mines Investors Who Insist on Geological Value.* MPL Communications Inc. • Weekly. $145.00 per year. Newsletter. Mainly on Canadian gold mine stocks. Formerly *Canadian PennyMines Analyst.*

*Dow Theory Forecasts.* Horizon Publishing Co. • Weekly. Provides information and advice on blue chip and income stocks.

*Dow Theory Letters.* Dow Theory Letters, Inc. • Triweekly. $300 /year. Newsletter on stock market trends, investing, and economic conditions.

*DRIP Investor: Your Guide to Buying Stocks Without a Broker.* Horizon Publishing Co. • Monthly. $89.00 per year. Newsletter covering the dividend reinvestment plans (DRIPs) of various publicly-owned corporations. Includes model portfolios and *Directory of Dividend Reinvestment Plans.*

*Emerging Growth.* Navellier and Associates Inc. • Monthly. $275.00 per year. Newsletter. Provides specific stock selection and model portfolio advice (conservative, moderately aggressive, and aggressive) based on quantitative analysis and modern portfolio theory.

*The Financial Post: Canadian's Business Voice.* Financial Post Datagroup. • Daily. $200.00 per year. Provides Canadian business, economic, financial, and investment news. Features extensive price quotes from all major Canadian markets: stocks, bonds, mutual funds, commodities, and currencies. Supplement available: *Financial Post 500.* Includes annual supplement.

*Financial Sentinel: Your Beacon to the World of Investing.* Gulf Atlantic Publish, Inc. • Monthly. $29.95 per year. Provides "The only complete listing of all OTC Bulletin Board stocks traded, with all issues listed on the Nasdaq SmallCap Market, the Toronto, and Vancouver Stock Exchanges." Also includes investment advice and recommendations of small capitalization stocks.

*Financial Times (London).* The Financial Times, Inc. • Daily, except Sunday. $572.88 per year. An international business and financial newspaper, featuring news from London, Paris, Frankfurt, New York, and Tokyo. Includes worldwide stock and bond market data, commodity market data, and monetary/currency exchange information.

*Forbes.* Forbes Inc. • Biweekly. $29.99 Individuals. Magazine reporting on industry, business and finance management.

*Growth Stock Outlook.* Charles Allmon, editor. Growth Stock Outlook Inc. • Description: Provides data on stock earnings, sales, price-earnings ratios, dividends, book values, returns on shareholder equity, and institutional holdings. Recommends specific companies for long-term investment. Recurring features include a stock selection guide, and a $10,000 supervised portfolio. **Remarks:** Subscription includes the supplements Junior Growth Stocks, New Issue Digest, and (see separate listings); also includes access to a telephone hotline.

*InvesTech Market Analyst: Technical and Monetary Investment Analysis.* Investech Research. • Every three weeks. $190.00 per year. Newsletter. Provides interpretation of monetary statistics and Federal Reserve actions, especially as related to technical analysis of stock market price trends.

*Investment Guide (IG).* American Investment Services Inc. • Monthly. $59 printed version. Description: Contains analyses of stock market activity and strategies for investment. Recurring features include market statistics, Dow high-yield stock investing.

*The Investment Reporter.* MPL Communications Inc. • Description: Profiles specific companies and market trends and developments, making recom-

mendations to assist in formulating investment strategies. Includes short articles offering advice on investment decisions.

*Investor's Business Daily.* Investor's Business Daily, Inc. • Daily. $329 Individuals print. Business and financial newspaper.

*Investors Intelligence.* Michael Burke, editor. Chartcraft Inc. • Description: Serves as a "comprehensive and authoritative Stock Market Advisory Service dedicated to bringing the investor facts, original projections, and a cross section of the recommendations of other leading Services.".

*The Low Priced Stock Survey.* Horizon Publishing Co. • Weekly. Description: Reviews and analyzes stocks offered at a price of $20 or less. Analysis is divided into sections: Emerging Growth Opportunities, The Fundamentalist, Bargain Spotlight, Stock of the Month, and Master List Highlights. Includes weekly closes of the Dow Jones Industrials and NASDAQ, and statistics.

*Medical Technology Stock Letter.* Medical Technology Stock Letter. • Description: Specializes in investments in biotechnology companies. Offers news of the industry and recommendations for buying, selling, and holding stocks. Recurring features include news of research, a model portfolio reflecting the editors' investment strategy, and columns titled Pulse of the Market and Industry Scan. **Remarks:** Also available through e-mail.

*The Moneypaper.* Temper of the Times Communications, Inc. Temper of the Times Communications Inc. • Description: Contains strategies to minimize stock sales costs and articles on investing and market trends. Includes a summary of monthly financial news drawn from over 70 financial publications and advisory services. Recurring features include columns titled Summing Up, Market Outlook, and Stocktrack.

*Richard C. Young's Intelligence Report.* Access Intelligence L.L.C. • Description: Provides information for "serious, conservative investors (buy and hold as opposed to active traders)." Features investing advice and recommendations for best funds, stocks, and bonds for current or retirement income.

*SFO: Stocks, Futures & Options.* W and A Publishing. • Subtitle: *Official Journal for Personal Investing in Stocks, Futures, and Options.* Covers mainly speculative techniques for stocks, commodity futures, financial futures, stock index futures, foreign exchange, short selling, and various kinds of options.

*Special Situations Newsletter: In-Depth Survey of Under-Valued Stocks.* Charles Howard Kaplan. • Monthly. $75.00 per year. Newsletter. Principal content is "This Month's Recommendation," a detailed analysis of one special situation stock.

*Standard & Poor's SmallCap 600 Guide.* McGraw Hill Financial Inc. • Monthly. $24.95. Contains detailed profiles of the companies included in Standard & Poor's SmallCap 600 Index of stock prices. Includes income and balance sheet data for up to 10 years, with growth and stability rankings for 600 small capitalization corporations.

*The Wall Street Digest.* Donald H. Rowe The Wall Street Digest. • Description: Covers major investment areas, including stocks and bonds; foreign currencies; gold, silver, and other precious metals; real estate; tax shelters; and estate planning. Recurring features include "a digest of the month's best" investment and financial seminars, newsletter reviews, and statistics.

## PRICE SOURCES

*National Stock Summary.* OTC Markets Group Inc. • Monthly, with semiannual cumulations. $576.00 per year. Includes price quotes for both active and inactive issues, with transfer agents, market makers (brokers), capital changes, name changes, and other corporate information. Pink Sheets LLC also provides daily and weekly stock price services. Formerly published by the National Quotation Bureau.

*Standard and Poor's Daily Stock Price Records.* Standard & Poor's Financial Services L.L.C. • Quarterly. $420 New York Stock Exchange.

## RESEARCH CENTERS AND INSTITUTES

University of Chicago - Booth School of Business - Center for Research in Security Prices. 105 W Adams St., Ste. 1700, Chicago, IL 60603. Phone: (312)263-6400; Fax: (312)263-6430; Email: subscriptions@crsp.chicagobooth.edu • URL: http://www.crsp.com • Historical financial data.

## STATISTICS SOURCES

*Advance-Decline Album.* Dow Theory Letters, Inc. • Annual. Contains one page for each year since 1931. Includes charts of the New York Stock Exchange advance-decline ratio and the Dow Jones industrial average.

*The AIER Chart Book.* AIER Research Staff. American Institute for Economic Research. • Annual. $4 Individuals. A compact compilation of long-range charts ("Purchasing Power of the Dollar," for example, goes back to 1780) covering various aspects of the U. S. economy. Includes inflation, interest rates, debt, gold, taxation, stock prices, etc. (Economic Education Bulletin.).

*Security Owner's Stock Guide.* Standard & Poor's Financial Services L.L.C. • Monthly. $125.00 per year.

*SRC Green Book of 5 Trend 35-Year Charts.* Securities Research Co. • Annual. $150.00. Chart book presents statistical information on the stocks of 400 leading companies over a 35-year period. Each full page chart is in semi-log format to avoid visual distortion. Also includes charts of 12 leading market averages or indexes and 39 major industry groups.

*Standard & Poor's Stock Reports: NASDAQ and Regional Exchanges.* Standard & Poor's Financial Services L.L.C. • Irregular. $1,100.00 per year. Looseleaf service. Provides two pages of financial details and other information for each corporation included.

*Standard & Poor's Stock Reports: New York Stock Exchange.* Standard & Poor's Financial Services L.L.C. • Irregular. $1,295.00 per year. Looseleaf service. Provides two pages of financial details and other information for each corporation with stock listed on the N. Y. Stock Exchange.

*Stocks, Bonds, Bills, and Inflation Classic Yearbook.* Ibbotson Associates. • Annual. $185. Provides detailed data from 1926 to the present on inflation and the returns from various kinds of financial investments, such as small-cap stocks and long-term government bonds.

*Survey of Current Business.* U. S. Government Printing Office. • Published by Bureau of Economic Analysis, U. S. Department of Commerce. Presents a wide variety of business and economic data.

## TRADE/PROFESSIONAL ASSOCIATIONS

Federation of Euro-Asian Stock Exchanges. Borsa Istanbul Bldg., Emirgan, TR-34467 Istanbul, Turkey. Phone: 90 212 298 2160; Fax: 90 212 298 2209; Email: secretariat@feas.org • URL: http://www.feas.org • Committed to a fair, efficient and transparent market environment. Works to eliminate trade barriers, and to promote development of the Euro-Asian stock markets. Provides cross listing and trading opportunities for securities issued within member countries.

Financial Industry Regulatory Authority. 1735 K St., Washington, DC 20006. Phone: (301)590-6500; Fax: (202)293-6260; Email: francine.lee@finra.org • URL: http://www.finra.org • Formerly National Association of Securities Dealers.

# STONE INDUSTRY

*See* QUARRYING

# STORAGE

*See* WAREHOUSES

# STORE DISPLAYS

*See* DISPLAY OF MERCHANDISE

# STORES (RETAIL TRADE)

*See* RETAIL TRADE

# STORES, CONVENIENCE

*See* CONVENIENCE STORES

# STORES, DEPARTMENT

*See* DEPARTMENT STORES

# STRATEGIC PLANNING

*See* PLANNING

# STRATEGY, BUSINESS

*See* BUSINESS STRATEGY

# STREET LIGHTING

*See* LIGHTING

# STREET MAPS

*See* MAPS

# STRESS (ANXIETY)

*See also* INDUSTRIAL PSYCHOLOGY; MENTAL HEALTH

## ABSTRACTS AND INDEXES

*Psychological Abstracts.* American Psychological Association. • Monthly. Members, $815.00 per year; individuals and institutions, $1,207.00 per year. Covers the international literature of psychology and the behavioral sciences. Includes journals, technical reports, dissertations, and other sources.

## CD-ROM DATABASES

*Consumer Health Complete.* EBSCO Publishing Inc. • Full text of more than 250 health references, health diagrams, videos, pamphlets.

## ENCYCLOPEDIAS AND DICTIONARIES

*Gale Encyclopedia of Psychology.* Cengage Learning Inc. • 2000. $267.00. Second edition. Includes bibliographies arranged by topic and a glossary. More than 650 topics are covered.

## GENERAL WORKS

*Journal of Business and Psychology.* Business Psychology Research Institute. Springer Science-Business Media LLC. • Quarterly. $614 Institutions print. An international outlet publishing high quality research designed to advance organizational science and practice.

## OTHER SOURCES

*Personal Strategies for Managing Stress.* American Management Association Extension Institute. • $139.00. Self-study course. Emphasis is on practical explanations, examples, and problem solving. Quizzes and a case study are included.

## PERIODICALS AND NEWSLETTERS

*Journal of Business and Psychology.* Business Psychology Research Institute. Springer Science-Business Media LLC. • Quarterly. $614 Institutions print. An international outlet publishing high quality research designed to advance organizational science and practice.

*Stress and Health.* John Wiley and Sons, Inc., Journals Div. • $1,204 Institutions, other countries print. A forum for discussion of all aspects of stress, which affect the individual in both health and disease. Provides international coverage. Formerly *Stress Medicine.*

## RESEARCH CENTERS AND INSTITUTES

American Institute of Stress. 9112 Camp Bowie West Blvd., No. 228, Fort Worth, TX 76116. Phone: (682)239-6823; Fax: (817)394-0593; Email: info@stress.org • URL: http://www.stress.org • Explores personal and social consequences of stress. Compiles research data on occupational stress and executive stress or "burn out."

# STRIKES AND LOCKOUTS

*See also* ARBITRATION; COLLECTIVE BARGAINING; LABOR; LABOR LAW AND REGULATION; LABOR UNIONS

## CD-ROM DATABASES

*OECD Statistical Compendium.* Organization for Economic Cooperation and Development. • Semiannual. $1,905.00 per year for 1 to 10 users. CD-ROM contains more than 730,000 monthly, quarterly, and annual time series for OECD countries, 1960 to date. Includes fully searchable data on agriculture, food, economic indicators, national accounts, employment, energy, finance, industry, technology, and foreign trade. Results can be displayed in various forms.

## ENCYCLOPEDIAS AND DICTIONARIES

*St. James Encyclopedia of Labor History Worldwide.* Cengage Learning Inc. • $484. 2003. Two volumes. Cover 300 key events, national and international, that took place in labor history over the past 200 years. Includes illustrations, maps, a glossary, a bibliography, and indexes. St. James Press imprint. eBook also available. Inquire for pricing.

## INTERNET DATABASES

*Business 2.0 Web Guide to the Best Business Links.* Business 2.0 Media Inc. Phone: (415)293-4800; Email: support@business2.com • URL: http://www.business2.com/webguide • Web site presents an extensive, searchable directory of links to "the best, most informative, and authoritative web pages." Twenty main categories cover business, finance, career, company information, people, and technology topics, with thousands of subtopics, all linking to Web sites recommended by experienced business researchers. Fees: Free.

*Fedstats.* Federal Interagency Council on Statistical Policy. Phone: (202)395-7254 • URL: http://www.fedstats.gov • Web site features an efficient search facility for full-text statistics produced by more than 100 federal agencies, including the Census Bureau, the Bureau of Economic Analysis, and the Bureau of Labor Statistics. Boolean searches can be made within one agency or for all agencies combined. Links are offered to international statistical bureaus, including the UN, IMF, OECD, UNESCO, Eurostat, and 20 individual countries. Fees: Free.

*FreeLunch.com.* Economy.com, Inc. Phone: (610)696-8700; Fax: (610)696-1678 • URL: http://www.freelunch.com • Web site provides free access to more than 200 million economic and financial data series, covering industry, demographics, labor markets, prices, retail sales, government spending, trade, interest rates, housing starts, the stock market, etc. Data is available in either chart or table form. Searching is offered. Free, but registration required. Economy.com, Inc. also offers fee-based economic analysis at *The Dismal Scientist* site (www.dismal.com).

**PERIODICALS AND NEWSLETTERS**

*Union Labor Report.* Bloomberg BNA. • Biweekly. Description: Covers legal, legislative, and regulatory developments and trends affecting management and labor in the workplace.

**STATISTICS SOURCES**

*Survey of Current Business.* U. S. Government Printing Office. • Published by Bureau of Economic Analysis, U. S. Department of Commerce. Presents a wide variety of business and economic data.

# STRUCTURAL MATERIALS

*See* BUILDING MATERIALS INDUSTRY

# STUDENT AID

*See* SCHOLARSHIPS AND STUDENT AID

# STUDY ABROAD

**ABSTRACTS AND INDEXES**

*Education Index.* H.W. Wilson Co. • 10 times a year. Quarterly and annual cumulations. Price varies.

*Readers' Guide to Periodical Literature.* EBSCO Publishing Inc. • Provides indexing for over 400 periodicals dating back to 1983.

**CD-ROM DATABASES**

*Education Index Retrospective: 1929-1983.* EBSCO Publishing Inc. • Provides indexing of education-related literature from 1983 to date.

*ERIC SilverPlatter.* U.S. Department of Education Institute of Education Sciences Education Resources Information Center. • Opinion papers, evaluations, speeches.

*Readers' Guide to Periodical Literature.* EBSCO Publishing Inc. • Provides indexing for over 400 periodicals dating back to 1983.

**DIRECTORIES**

*IIEPassport: Academic Year Abroad.* Institute of International Education. • Annual. $54.95 Individuals. Covers: Almost 6,000 undergraduate and graduate study-abroad programs conducted worldwide during the academic year by United States and foreign colleges and universities and other organizations in 80 countries. Entries include: Program name, sponsoring institution, contact person, address, phone, e-mail, website, pertinent dates, orientation, subjects offered, credits, housing, scholarships, language of instruction, related travel, teaching methods, tuition and other costs, prerequisites, work-study or internship opportunities, etc. Not to be confused with 'Academic Year and Summer Programs Abroad,' described separately.

*Vacation Study Abroad: The Complete Guide to Summer and Short-Term Study.* Institute of International Education. • Annual. Covers: More than 2,200 college-level and adult education summer and short-term courses sponsored by the United States and foreign colleges, language schools, and private and public organizations. Courses run from

as briefly as two weeks to three months. Entries include: Name of institution or other sponsor, inclusive dates, subjects offered, orientation information, language of instruction, whether United States college credit is offered and how much, related travel, housing, costs, scholarships, work-study or internship opportunities, deadline, phone, fax, e-mail, website and address for application.

**ONLINE DATABASES**

*Education Index Online.* H.W. Wilson Co. • Indexes a wide variety of periodicals related to schools, colleges, and education, 1984 to date. Monthly updates. Inquire as to online cost and availability.

*ERIC.* U.S. Department of Education Institute of Education Sciences Educational Resources Information Center. • Funded by the U.S. Department of Education, Institute of Education Sciences (formerly Office of Educational Research and Improvement). Provides access to more than one million online records covering education-related journal and report literature, 1966 to date. Updating is monthly. Inquire as to online cost and availability.

**PERIODICALS AND NEWSLETTERS**

*NAFSA Newsletter.* • Description: Concerned with international educational interchange. Reports on English as a second language, foreign admissions, study abroad, foreign student advising, community programming, and other subjects. Recurring features include government news, book reviews, news of members, Association news, and columns titled News and Briefs and From the Front Lines of Advocacy.

*Transitions Abroad: The Guide to Learning, Living, and Working Overseas.* Transitions Abroad Publishing. • Bimonthly. Provides practical information and advice on foreign education and employment. Supplement available *Overseas Travel Planner.*

**TRADE/PROFESSIONAL ASSOCIATIONS**

The College Board. 45 Columbus Ave., New York, NY 10023-6917. Phone: (212)713-8000; Email: aces@info.collegeboard.org • URL: http://www.collegeboard.org • Represents the schools, colleges, universities, and other educational organizations that seek to connect members to success and opportunity. Serves students, parents, high schools, and colleges through major programs and services in college admission, guidance, assessment, financial aid, enrollment, and teaching and learning.

Council on International Educational Exchange USA. 300 Fore St., Portland, ME 04101. Phone: 800-407-8839 or (207)553-4000; Fax: (207)553-4299; Email: contact@ciee.org • URL: http://www.ciee.org • Members are educational institutions and agencies that promote and sponsor international education exchange. Formerly Council on Student Travel.

EF Foundation for Foreign Study. 1 Education St., Cambridge, MA 02141. Phone: 800-447-4273; Fax: (617)619-1401; Email: exchangeyear@ef.com • URL: http://www.effoundation.org • Seeks to further international understanding through cultural and academic exchange. Sponsors academic homestay programs, such as High School Year in Europe. Formerly EF Educational Foundation for Foreign Study.

NAFSA: Association of International Educators. 1307 New York Ave. NW, 8th Fl., Washington, DC 20005-4701. Phone: 800-836-4994 or (202)737-3699; Fax: (202)737-3657; Email: inbox@nafsa.org • URL: http://www.nafsa.org • Members are individuals, organizations, and institutions involved with international educational interchange, including foreign student advisors, overseas educational advisers, foreign student admission officers, and U. S. students abroad. Formerly National Association for Foreign Student Affairs.

National Registration Center for Study Abroad. 207 E Buffalo St., Ste. 610, Milwaukee, WI 53202-5712. Phone: (414)278-0631 or (414)278-7410; Fax: (414)271-8884; Email: study@nrcsa.com • URL: http://www.nrcsa.com • Members are foreign universities, foreign language institutions, and other institutions or organizations offering foreign study programs designed for North Americans.

# STYLE MANUALS

*See* PRINTING STYLE MANUALS

# SUBJECT HEADINGS

*See* INDEXING

# SUBLIMINAL ADVERTISING

*See* ADVERTISING

# SUBURBAN SHOPPING CENTERS

*See* SHOPPING CENTERS

# SUGAR INDUSTRY

**CD-ROM DATABASES**

*OECD Statistical Compendium.* Organization for Economic Cooperation and Development. • Semiannual. $1,905.00 per year for 1 to 10 users. CD-ROM contains more than 730,000 monthly, quarterly, and annual time series for OECD countries, 1960 to date. Includes fully searchable data on agriculture, food, economic indicators, national accounts, employment, energy, finance, industry, technology, and foreign trade. Results can be displayed in various forms.

**DIRECTORIES**

*Major Food and Drink Companies of the World.* Cengage Learning Inc. • 12th edition. eBook. Published by Graham & Whiteside. Contains profiles and trade names for more than 9,200 important food and beverage companies in various countries. In addition to foods, includes both alcoholic and nonalcoholic drink products.

**INTERNET DATABASES**

*Business 2.0 Web Guide to the Best Business Links.* Business 2.0 Media Inc. Phone: (415)293-4800; Email: support@business2.com • URL: http://www.business2.com/webguide • Web site presents an extensive, searchable directory of links to "the best, most informative, and authoritative web pages." Twenty main categories cover business, finance, career, company information, people, and technology topics, with thousands of subtopics, all linking to Web sites recommended by experienced business researchers. Fees: Free.

*Fedstats.* Federal Interagency Council on Statistical Policy. Phone: (202)395-7254 • URL: http://www.fedstats.gov • Web site features an efficient search facility for full-text statistics produced by more than 100 federal agencies, including the Census Bureau, the Bureau of Economic Analysis, and the Bureau of Labor Statistics. Boolean searches can be made within one agency or for all agencies combined. Links are offered to international statistical bureaus, including the UN, IMF, OECD, UNESCO, Eurostat, and 20 individual countries. Fees: Free.

*FreeLunch.com.* Economy.com, Inc. Phone: (610)696-8700; Fax: (610)696-1678 • URL: http://www.freelunch.com • Web site provides free access to more than 200 million economic and financial data series, covering industry, demographics, labor markets, prices, retail sales, government spending, trade, interest rates, housing starts, the stock market, etc. Data is available in either chart or table form. Searching is offered. Free, but registration required. Economy.com, Inc. also offers fee-based economic analysis at *The Dismal Scientist* site (www.dismal. com).

*USDA.* U.S. National Institute of Standards and Technology. 100 Bureau Dr., Gaithersburg, MD 20899-1070. Phone: 800-877-8339 or (301)975-6478 or (202)720-2791; Fax: (301)975-8295; Email: inquiries@nist.gov • URL: http://www.nist.gov • The USDA home page has six sections: News and Information; What's New; About USDA; Agencies; Opportunities; Search and Help. Keyword searching is offered from the USDA home page and from various individual agency home pages. Agencies are the Economic Research Service, Agricultural Marketing Service, National Agricultural Statistics Service, National Agricultural Library, and about 12 others. Updating varies. Fees: Free.

### ONLINE DATABASES

*CAB Abstracts.* CABI. • Contains 46 specialized abstract collections covering over 10,000 journals and monographs in the areas of agriculture, horticulture, forest products, farm products, nutrition, dairy science, poultry, grains, animal health, entomology, etc. Time period is 1972 to date, with monthly updates. Inquire as to online cost and availability. *CAB Abstracts on CD-ROM* also available, with annual updating.

*Food Science and Technology Abstracts (online).* IFIS North American Desk. • Produced by International Food Information Service. Provides about 500,000 online citations, with abstracts, to the international literature of food science, technology, commodities, engineering, and processing. Approximately 2,000 periodicals are covered. Time period is 1969 to date, with monthly updates. Inquire as to online cost and availability.

### PERIODICALS AND NEWSLETTERS

*Sugar Bulletin.* American Sugar Cane League of the U.S.A. • Monthly. Free to members; non-members, $15.00 per year.

*Sugar Journal: Covering the World's Sugar Industry.* Kriedt Enterprises Ltd. • Monthly. $50 U.S. 12 issues. A monthly technical publication designed to inform sugar beet and cane farms, factories, and refineries throughout the world about the latest developments in the sugar industry.

*Sugar Producer: Representing the Sugar Beet Industry in the United States.* Harris Publishing Inc. • 9/year. $20 Individuals. Seven times a year. $10.95 per year. Supplies sugar beet growers with information to assist them in production of quality sugar beet crops.

*Sugar y Azucar.* RUSPAM Communications Inc. • Monthly. $75.00 per year. Text in English and Spanish.

### STATISTICS SOURCES

*Agricultural Statistics.* U.S. Department of Agriculture National Agricultural Statistics Service. • Annual. $46 Individuals. Provides a wide variety of statistical data relating to agricultural production, supplies, consumption, prices/price-supports, foreign trade, costs, and returns, as well as farm labor, loans, income, and population. In many cases, historical data is shown annually for 10 years. In addition to farm data, includes detailed fishery statistics.

*Sugar and Sweetener Situation and Outlook.* U. S. Government Printing Office. • Three times per year. $18.00 per year. Issued by Economic Research Service, U. S. Department of Agriculture. Provides current statistical information on supply, demand, and prices.

*Survey of Current Business.* U. S. Government Printing Office. • Published by Bureau of Economic Analysis, U. S. Department of Commerce. Presents a wide variety of business and economic data.

### TRADE/PROFESSIONAL ASSOCIATIONS

American Sugar Alliance. 2111 Wilson Blvd., Ste. 600, Arlington, VA 22201. Phone: (703)351-5055; Fax: (703)351-6698; Email: info@sugaralliance.org • URL: http://www.sugaralliance.org • Domestic producers, processors, and refiners of sugar beets, and sugarcane; labor organizations; allied organizations that supply goods and services to the domestic sweetener producing industry. Works to increase public awareness of the international economic and political factors influencing sweetener production; seeks increased support from consumers and the government for a U.S. sugar policy that is favorable to domestic sugar and sweetener producers; strives to maintain among domestic producers the ability to meet the sweetener needs of the U.S.

American Sugar Cane League. 206 E Bayou Rd., Thibodaux, LA 70301. Phone: (985)448-3707; Fax: (985)448-3722 • URL: http://www.amscl.org • Louisiana sugar cane growers and processors.

# SUGGESTION SYSTEMS

### PERIODICALS AND NEWSLETTERS

*New Horizons.* Horticultural Research Institute. • Semiannual. Description: Explores research of the science and art of nursery, retail garden center, and landscape plant production, marketing, and care.

### TRADE/PROFESSIONAL ASSOCIATIONS

IdeasAmerica. PO Box 210863, Auburn Hills, MI 48321. Phone: (248)961-2674; Fax: (248)253-9252; Email: ia@ideas-america.org • URL: http://www. ideas-america.org • Represents finance, commerce, industry, and government professionals. Dedicated to the worth, contributions, and benefits of employee suggestion systems and other employee involvement processes. Supports communication between employees and employer for the purpose of exchanging ideas.

# SULPHUR INDUSTRY

*See also* CHEMICAL INDUSTRIES

### CD-ROM DATABASES

*OECD Statistical Compendium.* Organization for Economic Cooperation and Development. • Semiannual. $1,905.00 per year for 1 to 10 users. CD-ROM contains more than 730,000 monthly, quarterly, and annual time series for OECD countries, 1960 to date. Includes fully searchable data on agriculture, food, economic indicators, national accounts, employment, energy, finance, industry, technology, and foreign trade. Results can be displayed in various forms.

### DIRECTORIES

*Major Chemical and Petrochemical Companies of the World.* Cengage Learning Inc. • Annual. $1,460 Individuals. 2008. 12th edition. eBook. Published by Graham & Whiteside. Contains profiles of more than 8,500 important chemical and petrochemical companies in various countries. Subject areas include general chemicals, specialty chemicals, agricultural chemicals, petrochemicals, industrial gases, and fertilizers.

### INTERNET DATABASES

*Business 2.0 Web Guide to the Best Business Links.* Business 2.0 Media Inc. Phone: (415)293-4800; Email: support@business2.com • URL: http://www. business2.com/webguide • Web site presents an extensive, searchable directory of links to "the best, most informative, and authoritative web pages."

Twenty main categories cover business, finance, career, company information, people, and technology topics, with thousands of subtopics, all linking to Web sites recommended by experienced business researchers. Fees: Free.

*Fedstats.* Federal Interagency Council on Statistical Policy. Phone: (202)395-7254 • URL: http://www. fedstats.gov • Web site features an efficient search facility for full-text statistics produced by more than 100 federal agencies, including the Census Bureau, the Bureau of Economic Analysis, and the Bureau of Labor Statistics. Boolean searches can be made within one agency or for all agencies combined. Links are offered to international statistical bureaus, including the UN, IMF, OECD, UNESCO, Eurostat, and 20 individual countries. Fees: Free.

*FreeLunch.com.* Economy.com, Inc. Phone: (610)696-8700; Fax: (610)696-1678 • URL: http:// www.freelunch.com • Web site provides free access to more than 200 million economic and financial data series, covering industry, demographics, labor markets, prices, retail sales, government spending, trade, interest rates, housing starts, the stock market, etc. Data is available in either chart or table form. Searching is offered. Free, but registration required. Economy.com, Inc. also offers fee-based economic analysis at *The Dismal Scientist* site (www.dismal. com).

### PERIODICALS AND NEWSLETTERS

*Sulphur: Covers All Aspects of World Sulphur and Sulphuric Acid Industry.* British Sulphur Publishing. • Bimonthly. $520.00 per year.

### STATISTICS SOURCES

*Survey of Current Business.* U. S. Government Printing Office. • Published by Bureau of Economic Analysis, U. S. Department of Commerce. Presents a wide variety of business and economic data.

# SULPHURIC ACID

*See* SULPHUR INDUSTRY

# SUN, ENERGY FROM

*See* SOLAR ENERGY

# SUPERCONDUCTORS

*See also* SEMICONDUCTOR INDUSTRY

### ABSTRACTS AND INDEXES

*Applied Science and Technology Index.* EBSCO Publishing Inc. • 11/year. Indexes a wide variety of English language technical, industrial, and engineering periodicals.

*Key Abstracts: High Temperature Superconductors.* Institution of Engineering and Technology. • Monthly. $1,138. Approximately 250 summaries on superconductors.

*Solid State and Superconductivity Abstracts.* Cambridge Scientific Abstracts L.P. • Monthly. Covers chemistry, physics, metallurgy, resonance, materials, measurement, and superconductivity theories, applications, and problem areas. Formerly *Solid State Abstracts Journal.*

### ONLINE DATABASES

*Applied Science and Technology Index Online.* H.W. Wilson Co. • Provides online indexing of 500 major scientific, technical, industrial, and engineering periodicals. Time period is 1983 to date. Monthly updates. Inquire as to online cost and availability.

### OTHER SOURCES

*Superconductor Week: The Newsletter of Record in the Field of Superconductivity.* WestTech. • $450

Individuals Internet Only. Covers applications of superconductivity and cryogenics, including new markets and products.

## PERIODICALS AND NEWSLETTERS

*Superconductor and Cyroelectronics.* WestTech. • Quarterly. $22.00 per year.

## RESEARCH CENTERS AND INSTITUTES

Massachusetts Institute of Technology - Materials Processing Center. 77 Massachusetts Ave., Cambridge, MA 02139-4301. Phone: (617)253-5179; Fax: (617)258-6900; Email: cthomp@mit.edu • URL: http://mpc-web.mit.edu • Conducts processing, engineering, and economic research in ferrous and nonferrous metals, ceramics, polymers, photonic materials, superconductors, welding, composite materials, and other materials.

Stanford University - Edward L. Ginzton Laboratory. Spilker Engineering and Applied Sciences, 348 Via Pueblo Mall, Stanford, CA 94305. Phone: (650)724-2765; Fax: (650)725-2533; Email: solgaard@stanford.edu • URL: http://www.stanford. edu/group/ginzton • Research fields include low-temperature physics and superconducting electronics.

## STATISTICS SOURCES

*U.S. Industry and Trade Outlook.* U.S. Department of Commerce National Technical Information Service. • Annual. Produced by the International Trade Administration, U.S. Department of Commerce, in a "public-private" partnership with DRI/ McGraw-Hill and Standard & Poor's. Provides basic data, outlook for the current year, and "Long-Term Prospects" (five-year projections) for a wide variety of products and services. Includes high technology industries. Formerly *U.S. Industrial Outlook.*

# SUPERMARKETS

*See also* CHAIN STORES; GROCERY BUSINESS

## DIRECTORIES

*Grocery Headquarters: The Newspaper for the Food Industry.* Trend Publishing Inc. • Monthly. $80. Covers the sale and distribution of food products and other items sold in supermarkets and grocery stores. Edited mainly for retailers and wholesalers. Incorporates (Grocery Distribution).

*Plunkett's Food Industry Almanac.* Plunkett Research Ltd. • $349.99 Individuals print + online. Covers: 340 leading companies in the global food industry. Entries include: Name, address, phone, fax, and key executives. Also includes analysis and information on trends, technology, and statistics in the field.

*Trade Dimensions' Market Scope: The Desktop Guide to Supermarket Share.* Trade Dimensions. • Annual. Covers: Market share for over 1,400 supermarket chains and wholesalers. Entries include: Company name, location, number of stores in the area, market share. Syndicated market areas include 52 AC Nielsen Scantrack markets, all 64 IRI InfoScan markets, all 205 DMAs (Designated Market Areas) and 100 MSAs (government-defined), plus 48 Trade Dimensions markets.

## FINANCIAL RATIOS

*FMI Annual Financial Review.* Food Marketing Institute. • Annual. $150 Members. Provides financial data on the supermarket industry.

*Food Retailing Industry Speaks.* Food Marketing Institute. • Annual. Members, $150; non-members, $350. Provides data on overall food industry marketing performance, including retail distribution and store operations.

*Operating Results of Independent Supermarkets.* Food Marketing Institute. • Annual. Members, $50;

non-members, $150. Includes data on gross margins, inventory turnover, expenses, etc.

## HANDBOOKS AND MANUALS

*Progressive Grocer Guidebook.* Trade Dimensions. • Annual. $375.00. Over 800 major chain and independent food retailers and wholesalers in the United States and Canada; also includes food brokers, rack jobbers, candy and tobacco distributors, and magazine distributors.

## PERIODICALS AND NEWSLETTERS

*Military Grocer.* Downey Communications Inc. • Five times a year. $30.00 per year. Edited for managers and employees of supermarkets on military bases. (These are supermarkets administered by the Defense Commissary Agency.).

*Progressive Grocer.* Nielsen Business Media Inc. • 18 times a year. $129.00 per year. Formerly *Supermarket Business.*

*Progressive Grocer: The Magazine of Supermarketing.* Nielsen Business Media Inc..

## PRICE SOURCES

*Supermarket News: The Industry's Weekly Newspaper.* Fairchild Publications. • Weekly. Individuals, $196.00 per year; retailers, $45.00 per year; manufacturers, $89.00 per year.

## STATISTICS SOURCES

*Standard & Poor's Industry Surveys.* Standard & Poor's Financial Services L.L.C. • Semiannual. $1,800.00. Two looseleaf volumes. Includes monthly *Supplements.* Provides detailed, individual surveys of 52 major industry groups. Each survey is revised on a semiannual basis. Also includes "Monthly Investment Review" (industry group investment analysis) and monthly "Trends & Projections" (economic analysis).

## TRADE/PROFESSIONAL ASSOCIATIONS

National Grocers Association. 1005 N Glebe Rd., Ste. 250, Arlington, VA 22201-5758. Phone: (703)516-0700; Fax: (703)516-0115; Email: feedback@nationalgrocers.org • URL: http://www. nationalgrocers.org • Independent food retailers; wholesale food distributors servicing 29,000 food stores. Promotes industry interests and works to advance understanding, trade and cooperation among all sectors of the food industry. Represents members' interests before the government. Aids in the development of programs designed to improve the productivity and efficiency of the food distribution industry. Offers services in areas such as store planning and engineering, personnel selection and training, operations and advertising. Sponsors seminars and in-house training. Maintains liaison with Women Grocers of America, which serves as an advisory arm.

# SURGICAL INSTRUMENTS INDUSTRY

*See also* DENTAL SUPPLY INDUSTRY; HOSPITAL EQUIPMENT; MEDICAL TECHNOLOGY

## ABSTRACTS AND INDEXES

*Excerpta Medica: Biophysics, Bioengineering, and Medical Instrumentation.* Elsevier. • $7,353 Institutions print journal. 16 times a year. Institutions, $2,859 per year. Section 27 of *Excerpta Medica.*

## CD-ROM DATABASES

*Health Devices Journals.* ECRI Institute. • Monthly. $285 each.

## DIRECTORIES

*The International Directory of Importers - Medical, Hospital and Surgical Equipment and Supplies Importers.* Interdata. • $295 Individuals print. Cov-

ers: 4,400 international firms importing medical, hospital and surgical equipment and supplies. Entries include: Company name and address, contact person, email, number of employees, year established, phone and telefaxes, business activity, bank references, as well as a listing of medical, hospital and surgical equipment and supplies currently being imported.

## FINANCIAL RATIOS

*Annual Statement Studies.* Risk Management Association. • Annual. Compiled from over 280,000 financial statements.

*Annual Statement Studies: Industry Default Probabilities and Cash Flow Measures.* Risk Management Association. • Annual. $405 Nonmembers. Serves as a companion volume to the original *Annual Statement Studies.* Gives probability of default estimates on a percentage scale for more than 450 industries. Includes changes in position year-by-year for eight financial statement line items and provides percentage measures of cash flow.

## INTERNET DATABASES

*National Library of Medicine.* National Institutes of Health. 9000 Rockville Pke., Bethesda, MD 20892. Phone: (301)496-4000; Email: nihinfo@od.nih.gov • URL: http://www.nih.gov • NLM Web site offers free access through MEDLINE ("PubMed") to about nine million references to articles appearing in some 4,000 biomedical journals, with abstracts. Search interfaces range from "simple keywords to advanced Boolean expressions." The NLM site offers many links to other sources of biomedical and technical information (the National Center for Biotechnology Information, for example). Fees: Free.

## ONLINE DATABASES

*Embase.* Elsevier. • Worldwide medical literature, 1974 to present. Weekly updates. Inquire as to online cost and availability.

*F-D-C Reports.* Elsevier Business Intelligence. • An online version of "The Gray Sheet" (medical devices), "The Pink Sheet" (pharmaceuticals), "The Rose Sheet" (cosmetics), "The Blue Sheet" (biomedical), and "The Tan Sheet" (nonprescription). Contains full-text information on legal, technical, corporate, financial, and marketing developments from 1987 to date, with weekly updates. Inquire as to online cost and availability.

## PERIODICALS AND NEWSLETTERS

*The Gray Sheet Reports: Medical Devices, Diagnostics and Instrumentation.* Elsevier Business Intelligence. • Weekly. Institutions, $1,172.00 per year. Newsletter. Provides industry and financial news, including a medical sector stock index. Monitors regulatory developments at the Center for Devices and Radiological Health of the U. S. Food and Drug Administration.

*Health Devices Alerts: A Summary of Reported Problems, Hazards, Recalls, and Updates.* ECRI Institute. • Weekly. $3,649.40 per year. Looseleaf service. Contains reviews of health equipment problems. Includes *Health Devices Alerts Action Items, Health Devices Alerts Abstracts, Health Devices Alerts FDA Data, Health Devices Alerts Implants, Health Devices Alerts Hazards Bulletin.*

*Health Industry Today: The Market Letter for Health Care Industry Vendors.* The Business Word. • Monthly. $360.00 per year; online edition, $420.00 per year.

*Healthcare Products Today Magazine.* Health Industry Distribution Association. Communication Publications & Resources. • 10 times a year. $49.95 per year. Formerly *Medical Product Sales.*

*Healthcare Purchasing News: A Magazine for Hospital Materials Management Central Service, Infection Control Practitioners.* Thomson Medical Economics. • Monthly. $72. Edited for personnel responsible for the purchase of medical, surgical, and hospital equipment and supplies. Features new purchasing techniques and new products. Includes news of the activities of two major purchasing associations, Health Care Material Management Society and International Association of Healthcare Central Service Materiel Management.

*Medical Product Manufacturing News.* Canon Communications LLC. • 5/year. Directed at manufacturers of medical devices and medical electronic equipment. Covers industry news, service news, and new products.

*MEEN Diagnostic and Invasive Technology.* Reilly Communications Group. • $90 Canada and Mexico. Bimonthly. Free to qualified personnel. Provides medical electronics industry news and new product information. Formerly *Medical Electronics and Equipment News.*

*Pharmaceutical and Medical Device Law Bulletin.* ALM Media Properties LLC. • Monthly. $199.00 per year. Newsletter. Edited for lawyers concerned with drug product or medical device litigation. Contains industry news items of special interest, reports on new products, legal case summaries, Food and Drug Administration actions, patent issues, and related news reports. (A Law Journal Newsletter, formerly published by Leader Publications).

*Surgical Products.* Advantage Business Media L.L.C. • Monthly. $41.90 per year. Covers new Technology and products for surgeons and operation rooms.

## STATISTICS SOURCES

*Standard & Poor's Industry Surveys.* Standard & Poor's Financial Services L.L.C. • Semiannual. $1,800.00. Two looseleaf volumes. Includes monthly *Supplements.* Provides detailed, individual surveys of 52 major industry groups. Each survey is revised on a semiannual basis. Also includes "Monthly Investment Review" (industry group investment analysis) and monthly "Trends & Projections" (economic analysis).

*U.S. Industry and Trade Outlook.* U.S. Department of Commerce National Technical Information Service. • Annual. Produced by the International Trade Administration, U.S. Department of Commerce, in a "public-private" partnership with DRI/McGraw-Hill and Standard & Poor's. Provides basic data, outlook for the current year, and "Long-Term Prospects" (five-year projections) for a wide variety of products and services. Includes high technology industries. Formerly *U.S. Industrial Outlook.*

## TRADE/PROFESSIONAL ASSOCIATIONS

Association for Healthcare Resource and Materials Management. 155 N Wacker Dr., Chicago, IL 60606. Phone: (312)422-3840; Fax: (312)422-4573; Email: ahrmm@aha.org • URL: http://www.ahrmm.org • Members are involved with the purchasing and distribution of supplies and equipment for hospitals and other healthcare establishments. Formerly American Society for Healthcare Materials Management.

Association for the Advancement of Medical Instrumentation. 4301 N Fairfax Dr., Ste. 301, Arlington, VA 22203-1633. Phone: 800-332-2264 or (703)525-4890 or (240)646-7031; Fax: (703)276-0793 or (301)206-9789; Email: customerservice@aami.org • URL: http://www.aami.org • Members are engineers, technicians, physicians, manufacturers, and others with an interest in medical instrumentation.

# SURPLUS FARM PRODUCE

*See* FARM PRODUCE

# SURPLUS PRODUCTS

*See also* RECYCLING; WASTE PRODUCTS

## DIRECTORIES

*Used Equipment Directory.* Penton. • Monthly. $35 Individuals 1 year, 3rd class mail, (12 issues). Publication includes: List of 800 dealers in used metalworking, electrical, power, process, and material handling equipment, woodworking and machine tools. Entries include: Company name, address, phone; principal executive; types of equipment handled; description of machinery offered. Principal content is approximately 75,000 paid listings of used equipment for sale, classified by type.

## PERIODICALS AND NEWSLETTERS

*Surplus Record: Machinery and Equipment Directory.* Surplus Record Inc. • Monthly. $33.00 per year. Lists over 46,000 items of used and surplus machine tools, chemical processing and electrical equipment.

## TRADE/PROFESSIONAL ASSOCIATIONS

Associated Surplus Dealers. 6255 W Sunset Blvd., 19th Fl., Los Angeles, CA 90028. Phone: 800-421-4511 or (323)817-2200; Fax: (310)481-1900; Email: camille.candella@nielsen.com • URL: http://www.asdonline.com • Represents surplus, general merchandise, and close-out dealers, manufacturers, manufacturers' representatives, and others. Promotes trade shows; provides liaison with government agencies; offers group life insurance coverage.

Machinery Dealers National Association. 315 S Patrick St., Alexandria, VA 22314-3501. Phone: 800-872-7807 or (703)836-9300; Fax: (703)836-9303; Email: office@mdna.org • URL: http://www.mdna.org • Dealers in used, rebuilt, and reconditioned industrial machinery.

# SURVEY METHODS

*See also* MARKET RESEARCH

## ABSTRACTS AND INDEXES

*Current Index to Statistics: Applications, Methods, and Theory.* American Statistical Association. • Annual. An index to journal articles on statistical applications and methodology.

## DIRECTORIES

*GreenBook.* New York American Marketing Association. • Annual. Contains information on companies offering focus group facilities, including recruiting, moderating, and transcription services.

*GreenBook Worldwide Directory of Marketing Research Companies and Services.* New York AMA - Green Book. • Annual. Contains information in 300 categories on more than 2,500 market research companies, consultants, field services, computer services, survey research companies, etc. Indexed by specialty, industry, company, computer program, and personnel. Available online. Formerly *Greenbook Worldwide International Directory of Marketing Research Companies and Services.*

## GENERAL WORKS

*RICS Business.* Royal Institution of Chartered Surveyors. • 10/year. Delivers news, features, analysis and interviews from the surveying profession.

## PERIODICALS AND NEWSLETTERS

*Journal of Business and Economic Statistics.* American Statistical Association. • Quarterly. $62 for members. Emphasis is on statistical measurement and applications for business and economics.

*Survey Research.* University of Illinois at Chicago - Survey Research Laboratory. • 3/year. $15 Individuals. Description: Contains "descriptions of current survey research projects by academic and not-for-profit survey research organizations; news from survey research centers; descriptions of recent methodological publications on survey research."; Recurring features include news of research and

columns titled Current Research, Personnel Notes, and New Methodological Publications.

## RESEARCH CENTERS AND INSTITUTES

University of Illinois at Chicago - Survey Research Laboratory. 412 S Peoria St., 6th Fl., Chicago, IL 60607. Phone: (312)996-5300; Fax: (312)996-3358 or (312)413-3358; Email: tjohnson@srl.uic.edu • URL: http://www.srl.uic.edu • Research areas include survey methodology and sampling techniques.

## TRADE/PROFESSIONAL ASSOCIATIONS

American Statistical Association. 732 N Washington St., Alexandria, VA 22314-1943. Phone: 888-231-3473 or (703)684-1221; Fax: (703)684-2037; Email: asainfo@amstat.org • URL: http://www.amstat.org • Professional society of persons interested in the theory, methodology, and application of statistics to all fields of human endeavor.

Council of American Survey Research Organizations. 170 N Country Rd., Ste. 4, Port Jefferson, NY 11777. Phone: (631)928-6954; Fax: (631)928-6041; Email: casro@casro.org • URL: http://www.casro.org • Members are survey research companies. Various committees are concerned with standards, survey research quality, and technology.

# SURVEYS, CONSUMER

*See* CONSUMER SURVEYS

# SWEET POTATO INDUSTRY

*See also* POTATO INDUSTRY

## INTERNET DATABASES

*USDA.* U.S. National Institute of Standards and Technology. 100 Bureau Dr., Gaithersburg, MD 20899-1070. Phone: 800-877-8339 or (301)975-6478 or (202)720-2791; Fax: (301)975-8295; Email: inquiries@nist.gov • URL: http://www.nist.gov • The USDA home page has six sections: News and Information; What's New; About USDA; Agencies; Opportunities; Search and Help. Keyword searching is offered from the USDA home page and from various individual agency home pages. Agencies are the Economic Research Service, Agricultural Marketing Service, National Agricultural Statistics Service, National Agricultural Library, and about 12 others. Updating varies. Fees: Free.

## STATISTICS SOURCES

*Agricultural Statistics.* U.S. Department of Agriculture National Agricultural Statistics Service. • Annual. $46 Individuals. Provides a wide variety of statistical data relating to agricultural production, supplies, consumption, prices/price-supports, foreign trade, costs, and returns, as well as farm labor, loans, income, and population. In many cases, historical data is shown annually for 10 years. In addition to farm data, includes detailed fishery statistics.

*Vegetables and Specialties Situation and Outlook.* U. S. Government Printing Office. • Three times a year. Issued by the Economic Research Service of the U. S. Department of Agriculture. Provides current statistical information on supply, demand, and prices.

# SWEETENER INDUSTRY

*See* SUGAR INDUSTRY

# SWIMMING POOL INDUSTRY

## DIRECTORIES

*Swimming Pool/Spa Age--Product Directory.* Primedia Business. • Annual. $47.95 payment must accompany order. Covers: about 2,000 manufacturers of swimming pool and spa equipment and supplies, and suppliers of services for the industry; manufacturers of spas and hot tubs; distributors and manufacturers' representatives; and pool industry associations. Entries include: Company or association name, address, phone, name and title of contact, branch offices.

## FINANCIAL RATIOS

*Annual Statement Studies.* Risk Management Association. • Annual. Compiled from over 280,000 financial statements.

*Annual Statement Studies: Industry Default Probabilities and Cash Flow Measures.* Risk Management Association. • Annual. $405 Nonmembers. Serves as a companion volume to the original *Annual Statement Studies.* Gives probability of default estimates on a percentage scale for more than 450 industries. Includes changes in position year-by-year for eight financial statement line items and provides percentage measures of cash flow.

## GENERAL WORKS

*The Business of Swimming.* Institute of Sport and Recreation Management. • £125 for members. Features information on consumer perspective and behavior in swimming pools.

## PERIODICALS AND NEWSLETTERS

*Pool and Spa News: The National Trade Magazine for the Swimming Poool & Spa Industry.* DoveTale Publishers. • Semimonthly. $19.97. Covers news, product information, business tips, technical information and design ideas for professionals in the pool and spa industry.

## TRADE/PROFESSIONAL ASSOCIATIONS

Association of Pool and Spa Professionals. 2111 Eisenhower Ave., Ste. 500, Alexandria, VA 22314. Phone: (703)838-0083; Fax: (703)549-0493; Email: memberservices@apsp.org • URL: http://www.apsp.org • Formerly National Spa and Pool Institute.

## SWINE INDUSTRY

*See also* LIVESTOCK INDUSTRY; MEAT INDUSTRY

## INTERNET DATABASES

*USDA.* U.S. National Institute of Standards and Technology. 100 Bureau Dr., Gaithersburg, MD 20899-1070. Phone: 800-877-8339 or (301)975-6478 or (202)720-2791; Fax: (301)975-8295; Email: inquiries@nist.gov • URL: http://www.nist.gov • The USDA home page has six sections: News and Information; What's New; About USDA; Agencies; Opportunities; Search and Help. Keyword searching is offered from the USDA home page and from various individual agency home pages. Agencies are the Economic Research Service, Agricultural Marketing Service, National Agricultural Statistics Service, National Agricultural Library, and about 12 others. Updating varies. Fees: Free.

## ONLINE DATABASES

*CAB Abstracts.* CABI. • Contains 46 specialized abstract collections covering over 10,000 journals and monographs in the areas of agriculture, horticulture, forest products, farm products, nutrition, dairy science, poultry, grains, animal health, entomology, etc. Time period is 1972 to date, with monthly updates. Inquire as to online cost and availability. *CAB Abstracts on CD-ROM* also available, with annual updating.

## PERIODICALS AND NEWSLETTERS

*National Hog Farmer.* Primedia Business Magazines and Media. • Monthly. $39 Individuals 1 year. Provides professional pork producers with breaking news, business management guidance, and timely production information needed to keep

modern pork production systems competitive and profitable.

## STATISTICS SOURCES

*Agricultural Statistics.* U.S. Department of Agriculture National Agricultural Statistics Service. • Annual. $46 Individuals. Provides a wide variety of statistical data relating to agricultural production, supplies, consumption, prices/price-supports, foreign trade, costs, and returns, as well as farm labor, loans, income, and population. In many cases, historical data is shown annually for 10 years. In addition to farm data, includes detailed fishery statistics.

## TRADE/PROFESSIONAL ASSOCIATIONS

National Pork Producers Council. 122 C St. NW, Ste. 875, Washington, DC 20001. Phone: (202)347-3600; Fax: (202)347-5265 • URL: http://www.nppc.org • Federation of state pork producer associations. Promotes the pork industry through research programs, consumer education, and lobbying activities. Compiles statistics; maintains speakers' bureau and hall of fame.

National Swine Registry - United Duroc Swine Registry. 2639 Yeager Rd., West Lafayette, IN 47996-2417. Phone: (765)463-3594; Fax: (765)497-2959; Email: nsr@nationalswine.com • URL: http://www.nationalswine.com • Promotes the Duroc swine breed in the U.S.

## SYNTHETIC FUELS

*See also* FUEL

## ABSTRACTS AND INDEXES

*Applied Science and Technology Index.* EBSCO Publishing Inc. • 11/year. Indexes a wide variety of English language technical, industrial, and engineering periodicals.

*NTIS Alerts: Energy.* U.S. Department of Commerce National Technical Information Service. • Biweekly. $130 per year. Covers electric power, batteries, fuels, geothermal energy, heating/cooling systems, nuclear technology, solar energy, energy policy, and related subjects.

## CD-ROM DATABASES

*Environment Abstracts on CD-ROM.* University Publications of America. • Quarterly. $1,295.00 per year. Contains the following CD-ROM databases: *Environment Abstracts, Energy Abstracts,* and *Acid Rain Abstracts.* Length of coverage varies.

## E-BOOKS

*Macmillan Encyclopedia of Energy.* Cengage Learning Inc. • 2003. eBook. Published by Macmillan Reference USA. Covers the business, technology, and history of a wide variety of energy sources. Inquire as to price and availability.

## OTHER SOURCES

*Major Energy Companies of the World.* Cengage Learning Inc. • Annual. $1,460 Individuals. 2008. 12th edition. eBook. Published by Graham & Whiteside. Contains detailed information on more than 4,850 important energy companies in various countries. Industries include electricity generation, coal, natural gas, nuclear power, petroleum, fuel distribution, and equipment for energy production.

## PERIODICALS AND NEWSLETTERS

*DOE This Month.* U. S. Government Printing Office. • Monthly. $22 per year. Describes the U.S. Department of Energy's research and development activities and DOE publications. Includes information on nuclear energy, renewable energy sources, and synthetic fuels.

*Energy & Fuels.* American Chemical Society. • Bimonthly. $1,537 Institutions. An interdisciplinary technical journal covering non-nuclear energy

sources: petroleum, gas, synthetic fuels, etc.

*Journal of Energy Engineering: The International Journal.* Architectural Engineering Institute of ASCE. • Quarterly. $350 Individuals Online only. Contains reports on the development of scientific and engineering knowledge in the planning, management, and generation of electrical power.

*Power Generation Technology and Markets.* Pasha Publishing Inc. • Weekly. $790.00 per year. Newsletter. Formerly *Coal and Synfuels Technology.*

## RESEARCH CENTERS AND INSTITUTES

University of Oklahoma - Mewbourne College of Earth and Energy - Energy Institute of the Americas. Sarkeys Energy Ctr., Rm. 1510, 100 E Boyd, Norman, OK 73019-1006. Phone: (405)325-4753 or (405)325-3821; Fax: (405)325-3180 or (405)325-6621; Email: ywalschap@ou.edu • URL: http://www.ou.edu/content/mcee/international_programs/energy_instituteoftheamericas.html • Energy resources and related environmental issues in the Americas. Recognizing the interdependence of the Americas with respect to energy resources, development, technology and supply, the institute engages in activities that promote energy sector growth that is economically and environmentally sound. The institute also seeks to further greater hemispheric self-sufficiency through dependable and competitively priced energy, expand national, integrated economies and increase the quality of life for the peoples of the Americas.

## SYNTHETIC TEXTILE FIBER INDUSTRY

*See also* FIBER INDUSTRY; TEXTILE INDUSTRY

## ABSTRACTS AND INDEXES

*CPI Digest: Key to World Literature Serving the Coatings, Plastics, Fibers, Adhesives, and Related Industries.* CPI Information Services. • Monthly. $397.00 per year. Abstracts of business and technical articles for polymer-based, chemical process industries. Includes a monthly list of relevant U. S. patents. International coverage.

*Textile Technology Index™.* EBSCO Publishing Inc. • Monthly. $545 Individuals. Includes indexing and abstracts for more than 470 periodicals.

*World Textile Abstracts.* Elsevier. • $2,609 Institutions, other countries. Digests of articles published in the world's textile literature. Includes subscription to *World Textile Digest.*

## CD-ROM DATABASES

*OECD Statistical Compendium.* Organization for Economic Cooperation and Development. • Semiannual. $1,905.00 per year for 1 to 10 users. CD-ROM contains more than 730,000 monthly, quarterly, and annual time series for OECD countries, 1960 to date. Includes fully searchable data on agriculture, food, economic indicators, national accounts, employment, energy, finance, industry, technology, and foreign trade. Results can be displayed in various forms.

## DIRECTORIES

*World Directory of Manufactured Fiber Producers.* Fiber Economics Bureau. • Annual. $395 CD-ROM, 2014 issue. Provides information on 2,000 fiber producers in 75 countries. (Fiber Economics Bureau is a subsidiary of the American Fiber Manufacturers Association.).

## GENERAL WORKS

*Manufactured Fiber Fact Book.* Fiber Economics Bureau. • Biennial. $10.00. Provides a general review of the history and development of the synthetic fiber industry. (Fiber Economics Bureau is a subsidiary of the American Fiber Manufacturers Association.).

## INTERNET DATABASES

*Business 2.0 Web Guide to the Best Business Links.* Business 2.0 Media Inc. Phone: (415)293-4800; Email: support@business2.com • URL: http://www.business2.com/webguide • Web site presents an extensive, searchable directory of links to "the best, most informative, and authoritative web pages." Twenty main categories cover business, finance, career, company information, people, and technology topics, with thousands of subtopics, all linking to Web sites recommended by experienced business researchers. Fees: Free.

*Fedstats.* Federal Interagency Council on Statistical Policy. Phone: (202)395-7254 • URL: http://www.fedstats.gov • Web site features an efficient search facility for full-text statistics produced by more than 100 federal agencies, including the Census Bureau, the Bureau of Economic Analysis, and the Bureau of Labor Statistics. Boolean searches can be made within one agency or for all agencies combined. Links are offered to international statistical bureaus, including the UN, IMF, OECD, UNESCO, Eurostat, and 20 individual countries. Fees: Free.

*FreeLunch.com.* Economy.com, Inc. Phone: (610)696-8700; Fax: (610)696-1678 • URL: http://www.freelunch.com • Web site provides free access to more than 200 million economic and financial data series, covering industry, demographics, labor markets, prices, retail sales, government spending, trade, interest rates, housing starts, the stock market, etc. Data is available in either chart or table form. Searching is offered. Free, but registration required. Economy.com, Inc. also offers fee-based economic analysis at *The Dismal Scientist* site (www.dismal.com).

## ONLINE DATABASES

*Textile Technology Index™.* EBSCO Publishing Inc. • Monthly. $545 Individuals. Includes indexing and abstracts for more than 470 periodicals.

*World Textiles.* Elsevier. • Provides abstracting and indexing from 1970 of worldwide textile literature (periodicals, books, pamphlets, and reports). Includes U. S., European, and British patent information. Updating is monthly. Inquire as to online cost and availability.

## PERIODICALS AND NEWSLETTERS

*DNR: The Men's Fashion Retail Textile Authority.* Fairchild Publications. • Daily. $85.00 per year. Formerly *Daily News Record.*

*Fiber Organon: Featuring Manufactured Fibers.* Fiber Economics Bureau. • Monthly. $300.00 per year. Summarizes "confidential producer information on the U.S. manufactured fiber market." Provides detailed statistics on production, shipments, exports, and capacity. Special issues cover worldwide data and specific end use products. (Fiber Economics Bureau is a subsidiary of the American Fiber Manufacturers Association.).

*International Fiber Journal.* International Media Group Inc. • $125 print delivery. Bimonthly. Covers manmade fiber technology and manufacturing.

*Manufactured Fiber Review.* Fiber Economics Bureau. • Monthly. $350 Individuals. Provides a "quick-release four-page monthly review of the latest U.S. data on manufactured fiber." Coverage includes production, shipments, exports, and utilization rates. (Fiber Economics Bureau is a subsidiary of the American Fiber Manufacturers Association.).

## STATISTICS SOURCES

*Survey of Current Business.* U. S. Government Printing Office. • Published by Bureau of Economic Analysis, U. S. Department of Commerce. Presents a wide variety of business and economic data.

## TRADE/PROFESSIONAL ASSOCIATIONS

American Fiber Manufacturers Association. 1530 Wilson Blvd., Ste. 690, Arlington, VA 22209-2418. Phone: (703)875-0432; Fax: (703)875-0907 • URL: http://www.fibersource.com/afma/afma.htm • Producers of manufactured fibers used in apparel, household goods, industrial materials, and other types of products. Represents the industry in educational, governmental, and foreign trade matters. Distributes a video depicting production and end uses of manufactured fibers.

# SYSTEMS ENGINEERING

*See* INDUSTRIAL ENGINEERING

# SYSTEMS IN MANAGEMENT

*See also* COMPUTERS; MANAGEMENT INFORMATION SYSTEMS; OFFICE MANAGEMENT; WORD PROCESSING

## ABSTRACTS AND INDEXES

*Key Abstracts: Software Engineering.* Institution of Engineering and Technology. • Monthly. $1,138. Provides international coverage of journal and proceedings literature.

## PERIODICALS AND NEWSLETTERS

*Computertalk: For Contemporary Pharmacy Management.* ComputerTalk Associates Inc. • Bimonthly. $50.00 per year. Provides detailed advice and information on computer systems for pharmacies, including a buyers' guide issue.

*Insurance and Technology.* UBM L.L.C. • Monthly. $65.00 per year. Covers information technology and systems management as applied to the operation of life, health, casualty, and property insurance companies.

*PlugIn Datamation: Profit and Value from Information Technology.* EarthWeb. • Monthly. Price on application. Technical, semi-technical and general news covering EDP topics.

*Software Economics Letter: Maximizing Your Return on Corporate Software.* Computer Economics Inc. • Monthly. $395.00 per year. Newsletter for information systems managers. Contains data on business software trends, vendor licensing policies, and other corporate software management issues.

## TRADE/PROFESSIONAL ASSOCIATIONS

IQNet Association - International Certification Network. Bollwerk 31, CH-3000 Bern, Switzerland. Phone: 41 31 3102440; Fax: 41 31 3102449; Email: headoffice@iqnet.ch • URL: http://www.iqnet-certification.com • National management systems certification bodies. Seeks to advance the practice of corporate and organizational management and business excellence. Evaluates management systems and bestows certification upon qualified organizations; serves as a clearinghouse on management systems.

# SYSTEMS INTEGRATION

## ABSTRACTS AND INDEXES

*Applied Science and Technology Index.* EBSCO Publishing Inc. • 11/year. Indexes a wide variety of English language technical, industrial, and engineering periodicals.

*Business Periodicals Index Retrospective.* EBSCO Publishing Inc. • 11/year. Quarterly and annual cumulations.

*Computer and Information Systems Abstracts Journal: An Abstract Journal Pertaining to the Theory, Design, Fabrication and Application of Computer and Information Systems.* CSA. • Monthly. $1,750 per year.

*Computer Science Index.* EBSCO Publishing Inc. • Quarterly. $245 per year. Contains brief abstracts of book and periodical literature covering all phases of computing, including approximately 70 specific application areas.

*Internet and Personal Computing Abstracts (print edition).* EBSCO Publishing Inc. • Quarterly. $269.00 per year, including cumulative index. Provides more than 10,000 abstracts annually from both trade and academic publications. Covers computer hardware, software, product reviews, Web topics, e-commerce, networks, corporate news, security, and related topics. Formerly *Microcomputer Abstracts.*

## CD-ROM DATABASES

*ABI/INFORM.* ProQuest L.L.C. • Monthly. Provides CD-ROM indexing and abstracting of worldwide business literature. Archival discs are available from 1971. Formerly *ABI/INFORM OnDisc.*

*Applied Science and Technology Abstracts.* EBSCO Publishing Inc. • Citations for more than 700 prominent scientific, technical, engineering, and industrial periodicals.

*Business Abstracts with Full Text.* EBSCO Publishing Inc. • Includes full text articles from more than 460 business publications from 1982 to present. Indexing for nearly 880 publications.

## DIRECTORIES

*Manufacturing Systems: Buyers Guide.* Reed Elsevier Group plc Reed Business Information. • Annual. Price on application. Contains information on companies manufacturing or supplying materials handling systems, CAD/CAM systems, specialized software for manufacturing, programmable controllers, machine vision systems, and automatic identification systems.

## E-BOOKS

*Encyclopedia of Emerging Industries.* Cengage Learning Inc. • $546 6th edition. Provides detailed information on 140 "newly flourishing" industries. Includes historical background, organizational structure, significant individuals, current conditions, major companies, work force, technology trends, research developments, and other industry facts.

## INTERNET DATABASES

*InfoTech Trends.* Data Analysis Group. Phone: (925)462-1202; Fax: (925)462-1225; Email: support@infotechtrends.com • URL: http://www.infotechtrends.com • Web site provides both free and fee-based market research data on the information technology industry, including computers, peripherals, telecommunications, the Internet, software, CD-ROM/DVD, e-commerce, and workstations. Fees: Free for current (most recent year) data; more extensive information has various fee structures. Formerly *Computer Industry Forecasts.*

## ONLINE DATABASES

*Applied Science and Technology Index Online.* H.W. Wilson Co. • Provides online indexing of 500 major scientific, technical, industrial, and engineering periodicals. Time period is 1983 to date. Monthly updates. Inquire as to online cost and availability.

*Computer Database.* Cengage Learning Inc. • Provides one year of full-text online for 150 leading computer-related publications. Also includes 70,000 product specifications and brief profiles of 13,000 computer product vendors and manufacturers. Inquire as to prices and availability.

*Wilson Business Abstracts Online.* H.W. Wilson Co. • Indexes and abstracts 600 major business periodicals, plus the *Wall Street Journal* and the business section of the *New York Times.* Indexing is from 1982, abstracting from 1990, with the two newspapers included from 1993. Updated weekly. Inquire as to online cost and availability. (*Business Periodicals Index* without abstracts is also available online.).

## PERIODICALS AND NEWSLETTERS

*Advanced Manufacturing Technology: Monthly Report.* Technical Insights. • Monthly. $695 Institutions. Covers technological developments relating to robotics, computer graphics, automation, computer-integrated manufacturing, and machining.

## RESEARCH CENTERS AND INSTITUTES

Stanford University - Center for Integrated Systems. Paul G. Allen Bldg., MS 4070, 420 Via Palou Mall, Stanford, CA 94305-4070. Phone: (650)725-3621; Fax: (650)725-0991; Email: rdasher@cis.stanford. edu • URL: http://cis.stanford.edu • Research programs include manufacturing science, design science, computer architecture, semiconductor technology, and telecommunications.

## TRADE/PROFESSIONAL ASSOCIATIONS

AIM Global. One Landmark N, 20399 Rte. 19, Ste. 203, Cranberry Township, PA 16066. Phone: (724)742-4473; Fax: (724)742-4476; Email: info@ aim-na.org • URL: http://www.aimglobal.org • Serves as a trade association for the automatic identification data captures technology industry.

NaSPA. 7044 S 13th St., Oak Creek, WI 53154. Phone: (414)908-4945 or (414)768-8000; Fax: (414)768-8001; Email: customercare@naspa.com • URL: http://www.naspa.com • Members are systems programmers, communications analysts, database administrators, and other technical management personnel.

# T

## TABLEWARE

### DIRECTORIES

*Gifts & Tablewares--Directory Issue*. Scott's Directories. • Annual. $52.95 Individuals. Publication includes: List of approximately 1,000 manufacturers and suppliers of gift, home decor, stationery, and tableware items in Canada. Database includes: Calendar of Canadian, American, European, and Asian trade shows. Entries include: Company name, address, phone, fax, name, address, and phone of branches and showrooms; description of products and services; email and web sites.

*Jewelers' Circular/Keystone-Jewelers' Directory*. Reed Elsevier Group plc Reed Business Information. • About 8,500 manufacturers, importers and wholesale jewelers providing merchandise and supplies to the jewelry retailing industry; and related trade organizations. Included with subscription to *Jewelers' Circular Keystone*.

### PERIODICALS AND NEWSLETTERS

*Gifts and Decorative Accessories: The International Business Magazine of Gifts, Tabletop, Gourmet, Home Accessories, Greeting Card and Social Stationery*. Reed Elsevier Group plc Reed Business Information. • Monthly. $53.95 per year. Includes *Annual Directory*.

*Giftware News: The International Magazine for Gifts, China and Glass, Stationery and Home Accessories*. Talcott Communications Corp. • Monthly.

*Jewelers' Circular Keystone (JCK)*. Reed Elsevier Group plc Reed Business Information. • Monthly. $90.00 per year.

## TAILORING

*See also* CLOTHING INDUSTRY; FASHION INDUSTRY; MEN'S CLOTHING INDUSTRY

### DIRECTORIES

*Alteration Contractors Directory*. InfoGroup Inc. • Annual. Number of listings: 22,248. Entries include: Name, address, phone, size of advertisement, name of owner or manager, number of employees, year first in "Yellow Pages." Compiled from telephone company "Yellow Pages," nationwide.

### PERIODICALS AND NEWSLETTERS

*Custom Tailor*. Custom Tailors and Designers Association. • Three times a year. $50.00 per year. Controlled circulation.

### TRADE/PROFESSIONAL ASSOCIATIONS

Custom Tailors and Designers Association. 42732 Ridgeway Dr., Broadlands, VA 20148. Phone: 888-248-2832; Fax: (866)661-1240; Email: info@ctda. com • URL: http://www.ctda.com • Formerly Merchant Tailors and Designers Association of America.

## TALL OIL INDUSTRY

*See also* OIL AND FATS INDUSTRY

### ALMANACS AND YEARBOOKS

*CRB Commodity Yearbook*. Commodity Research Bureau. CRB. • Annual. $179 plus $10.00 shipping cost. The single most comprehensive source of commodity and futures market information available.

### DIRECTORIES

*Directory of North American Importers of Oil Seeds*. EXIM Infotek Private Ltd. • Covers: 30 North American importers of mustard, oil seeds, peanut, sesame seeds, soybeans, and sunflower seeds. Entries include: Company name, postal address, telephone, fax, e-mail, website, contact person, designation, and product details.

### TRADE/PROFESSIONAL ASSOCIATIONS

Pine Chemicals Association. PO Box 17136, Fernandina Beach, FL 32035. Phone: (404)994-6267 • URL: http://www.pinechemicals.org • Represents manufacturers of chemical products (other than pulp, paper and paper products) produced by, or from, wood pulp industry products. Sponsors educational and management meetings. Collects statistical data.

## TANK SHIPS

*See also* SHIPS, SHIPPING AND SHIPBUILD-ING

### DIRECTORIES

*Fairplay World Shipping Directory*. Fairplay Publications Ltd. • Daily. Covers: More than 76,000 companies worldwide engaged in some aspect of shipping, including over 10,000 ship-owners with fleets totaling over 45,000 vessels, shipbuilders and repairers, marine insurance shipping finance, protection and indemnity associations, marine equipment suppliers, and towing, salvage, and dredging; also lists marine organizations, shipbrokers, and consulting engineers and surveyors. Entries include: Company name, address, phone, fax, e-mail, URL, names of directors and executives, brief description of business; listings may also include associated and subsidiary companies and financial data.

*List of Shipowners, Managers, and Managing Agents*. Lloyd's Register of Shipping. • Annual.

$350.00, including 10 updates per year. Published in the UK by Lloyd's Register-Fairplay Ltd. Lists 40,000 shipowners, managers, and agents worldwide. Cross-referenced with *Lloyd's Register of Ships*.

*Lloyd's Maritime Directory*. Informa P.L.C. Informa Sports Group. • Annual. Covers: Over 40,000 shipowners, managers, and operators with 75,000 vessels. Also includes Marine consultants; towing, salvage, solicitors, P&I clubs; ship building and repair firms; general maritime organizations, banking and finance and more. Entries include: Firm name, address, phone, fax, e-mail, Internet; branch offices; names of principal executives; agents; parent and associated companies; and, for shipowners and lines, detailed information on ships owned, type, or capacity, etc. The former second volume of 'International Shipping and Shipbuilding Directory' is now published separately with the title 'Lloyd's List Marine Equipment Buyers' Guide' (see separate entry).

*Tanker Register*. Clarkson Research Studies. • Annual. $522 Individuals. Covers: More than 5,820 tankers and combined carriers throughout the world having deadweight tonnage exceeding 10,000, and their owners and managers. Entries include: Ship name, owner or manager, where registered, when and where built, tonnage, draft, capacity, engines, etc.

### PRICE SOURCES

*American Tanker Rate Schedule*. Association of Ship Brokers and Agents U.S.A. • Biennial Annual. $3,400 Two years. Contains tanker freight rates.

### TRADE/PROFESSIONAL ASSOCIATIONS

Association of Ship Brokers and Agents. 510 Sylvan Ave., Ste. 201, Englewood Cliffs, NJ 07632. Phone: (201)569-2882; Fax: (201)569-9082; Email: asba@ asba.org • URL: http://www.asba.org • Includes a Tanker Committee.

## TANK TRUCKS

*See* TRUCKING INDUSTRY

## TANKERS

*See* TANK SHIPS

## TANNING INDUSTRY

*See also* LEATHER INDUSTRY

## DIRECTORIES

*American Leather Chemists Association--Membership Directory.* American Leather Chemists Association. • Annual. Covers: About 500 chemists, leather technologists, and educators concerned with the tanning and leather industry. Entries include: Personal name, address; company name, address, phone, fax.

## PERIODICALS AND NEWSLETTERS

*Newsbreak.* Leather Industries of America. • Free to members and other qualified personnel. Reports on issues and events in the luggage industry.

*Society of Leather Technologists and Chemists Journal.* Society of Leather Technologies and Chemists. • Bimonthly. Bimonthly. $75.00 per year. Scientific, technical, historical and commercial papers on leather and allied industries. Contains papers covering all topics of associated interest with other sections devoted to news of new products/processes, news of members, meeting reports, notes on relevant publications and our own Axel's Agony Column which deals with topical subjects.

## TRADE/PROFESSIONAL ASSOCIATIONS

American Leather Chemists Association. 1314 50th St., Ste. 103, Lubbock, TX 79412-2940. Phone: (806)741-1798; Fax: (806)744-1785; Email: alca@ leatherchemists.org • URL: http://www.leatherchemists.org • Chemists, leather technologists, and educators concerned with the tanning and leather industry. Works to devise and perfect methods for the analysis and testing of leathers and materials used in leather manufacture. Promotes advancement of chemistry and other sciences, especially their application to problems confronting the leather industry.

Leather Industries of America. 3050 K St. NW, Ste. 400, Washington, DC 20007. Phone: (202)342-8497; Fax: (202)342-8583; Email: info@leatherusa. com • URL: http://www.leatherusa.com • Formerly Tanners' Council of America.

# TARIFF

## DIRECTORIES

*U.S. Custom House Guide.* UBM Global Trade. • Annual. $899 Individuals online access. Publication includes: List of ports having customs facilities, customs officials, port authorities, chambers of commerce, embassies and consulates, foreign trade zones, and other organizations; related trade services. Entries include: For each principal port-- Name of organization or agency, address, phone, fax, names and titles of key personnel; description and limitations of port facilities. For service firms-- Company name, address, phone, fax. Principal content is U.S. tariff schedules and customs regulations, and a "How to Import" manual.

## OTHER SOURCES

*Worldtariff Guidebook on Customs Tariff Schedules of Import Duties.* Worldtariff Division, Morse Agri-Energy Associates. • Looseleaf. Over 60 volumes. Prices vary. Consists generally of volumes for individual countries and volumes for broad classes of products, such as clothing. (Country volumes are typically $500.00 each.).

# TAX ADMINISTRATION

*See also* TAXATION

## GENERAL WORKS

*Getting Cash Out of Your Business.* American CPE Inc. • Contains detailed training information covering methods of minimizing tax burdens and maximizing owner benefits and opportunities to draw cash from businesses.

## ONLINE DATABASES

*Accounting and Tax Database.* ProQuest L.L.C. • Provides indexing and abstracting of the literature of accounting, taxation, and financial management, 1971 to date. Updating is weekly. Especially covers accounting, auditing, banking, bankruptcy, employee compensation and benefits, cash management, financial planning, and credit. Inquire as to online cost and availability.

## OTHER SOURCES

*Internal Revenue Manual: Audit and Administration.* Wolters Kluwer Law & Business CCH. • Irregular. $1,254.00. Six looseleaf volumes. Reproduces IRS tax administration provisions and procedures.

## PERIODICALS AND NEWSLETTERS

*Accounting Today: The Business Newspaper for the Tax & Accounting Community.* SourceMedia Inc. • Biweekly. $99.00 per year. Covers news affecting tax and accounting professionals.

*Tax Administrators News.* Federation of Tax Administrators. • Description: Focuses on state tax legislation and administration. Covers research results and federal legislation that affects state taxation. Recurring features include state-by-state news of tax changes and innovations in administration, announcements of conferences and meetings, profiles of state revenue commissioners, and special sections on motor fuel taxes and technology in tax administration.

*The Tax Executive.* Tax Executives Institute. • Bimonthly. $22 Single issue.

## RESEARCH CENTERS AND INSTITUTES

Harvard Law School International Tax Program. Harvard Law School, 1563 Massachusetts Ave., 1563 Massachusetts Ave., Cambridge, MA 02138. Phone: (617)495-3100 or (617)495-4406; Fax: (617)495-1110; Email: sfs@law.harvard.edu • URL: http://www.law.harvard.edu/programs/index.html • Studies the worldwide problems of taxation, including tax law and tax administration.

# TAX, ESTATE

*See* INHERITANCE TAX

# TAX, EXCISE

*See* EXCISE TAX

# TAX EXEMPT SECURITIES

*See* MUNICIPAL BONDS

# TAX, GIFT

*See* GIFT TAX

# TAX, INCOME

*See* INCOME TAX

# TAX, INHERITANCE

*See* INHERITANCE TAX

# TAX LAW AND REGULATION

*See also* INCOME TAX; STATE TAXES; TAXATION

## ABSTRACTS AND INDEXES

*Current Law Index.* Cengage Learning Inc. • $1,332 Individuals. Monthly. $1269.00 per year. Produced in cooperation with the American Association of Law Libraries. Indexes more than 900 law journals, legal newspapers, and specialty publications from the U.S., Canada, U.K., Ireland, Australia, and New Zealand.

*Index to Legal Periodicals and Books.* H.W. Wilson Co. • Monthly. $490.00 per year. Quarterly and annual cumulations.

## ALMANACS AND YEARBOOKS

*Tax Year in Review.* Wolters Kluwer Law & Business CCH. • Annual. Covers the year's "major new legislative and regulatory changes.".

## CD-ROM DATABASES

*Authority Tax and Estate Planning Library.* Matthew Bender and Company Inc. • Periodic revisions. Price on request. CD contains updated full text of *Bender's Payroll Tax Guide, Depreciation Handbook, Federal Income Taxation of Corporations, Tax Planning for Corporations, Modern Estate Planning, Planning for Large Estates, Murphy's Will Clauses, Tax & Estate Planning for the Elderly,* and 12 other Matthew Bender publications. The Internal Revenue Code is also included.

*Federal Tax Products.* U. S. Government Printing Office. • Annual. $27.00. CD-ROM issued by the Internal Revenue Service (www.irs.treas.gov/forms_pubs/). Provides current tax forms, instructions, and publications. Also includes older tax forms beginning with 1991.

*Index to Legal Periodicals and Books.* EBSCO Publishing Inc. • Contains indexing of more than 1,400 English language legal periodicals from 1981 to date and 2,500 books.

## DIRECTORIES

*Global Tax Guide Handbook.* International Business Publications, USA. • $149. Basic tax guide for over 80 countries.

## GENERAL WORKS

*Tax Policy and the Economy.* The MIT Press. • Annual. $25. Reviews "issues in the current tax debate.".

## HANDBOOKS AND MANUALS

*Business Taxation Manual.* Business SA. • $418 Nonmembers. Contains information on taxation obligations for businesses.

*U.S. Master Bank Tax Guide.* Wolters Kluwer Law & Business CCH. • Annual. $389.95 Individuals book-softcover. Summarizes and explains federal tax rules affecting financial institutions.

## INTERNET DATABASES

*CCH Essentials: An Internet Tax Research and Primary Source Library.* CCH, Inc. Phone: 800-248-3248 or (773)866-6000; Fax: (773)866-3608 or (800)224-8299; Email: cust_serv@cch.com • URL: http://tax.cch.com/essentials • Fee-based Web site provides full-text coverage of federal tax law and regulations, including rulings, procedures, tax court decisions, and IRS publications, announcements, notices, and penalties. Includes explanation, analysis, tax planning guides, and a daily tax news service. Searching is offered, including citation search.

*Court Filings.* ProQuest LLC. 2250 Perimeter Park Dr., Ste. 300, Morrisville, NC 27560. Phone: 800-334-2564 or (919)804-6400; Fax: (919)804-6410; Email: contact@dialog.com • URL: http://www.dialog.com • The three main sections of Tax Analysts home page are "Tax News" (Today's Tax News, Feature of the Week, Tax Snapshots, Tax Calendar); "Products & Services" (Product Catalog, Press Releases); and "Public Interest" (Discussion Groups, Tax Clinic, Tax History Project). Fees: Free for coverage of current tax events; fee-based for comprehensive information. Daily updating.

*Factiva*. Dow Jones Reuters Business Interactive, LLC. Phone: 800-369-7466 or (609)452-1511; Fax: (609)520-5770; Email: solutions@factiva.com • URL: http://www.factiva.com • Fee-based Web site provides "global news and business information through Web sites and content integration solutions." Includes Dow Jones and Reuters newswires, The Wall Street Journal, and more than 7,000 other sources of current news, historical articles, market research reports, and investment analysis. Content includes 96 major U. S. newspapers, 900 non-English sources, trade publications, media transcripts, country profiles, news photos, etc.

*Internal Revenue Service IRS.gov*. Internal Revenue Service. Phone: 800-829-1040 or (202)622-5000; Fax: (202)622-5844 • URL: http://www.irs.gov • Web site provides a wide variety of tax information, including IRS forms and publications. Searching is available. Fees: Free.

*Lexis.com Research System*. Lexis-Nexis Group. Phone: 800-227-4908 or (937)865-6800; Fax: (937)865-6909; Email: webmaster@prod.lexis-nexis.com • URL: http://www.nexis.com • Fee-based Web site offers extensive searching of a wide variety of legal sources. Additional features include Daily Opinion Service, lexis.com Bookstore, Career Center, CLE Center, Law Schools, and Practice Pages ("Pages specific to areas of specialty").

*Nexis.com*. Lexis-Nexis Group. Phone: 800-227-4908 or (937)865-6800; Fax: (937)865-6909; Email: webmaster@prod.lexis-nexis.com • URL: http://www.nexis.com • Fee-based Web site offers searching of about 2.8 billion documents in some 30,000 news, business, and legal information sources. Features include a subject directory covering 1,200 topics in 34 categories and a Company Dossier containing information on more than 500,000 public and private companies. Boolean searching is offered.

*Rutgers Accounting Web*. Rutgers University Accounting Research Center. Phone: (973)353-5172; Fax: (973)353-1283 • URL: http://www.rutgers.edu/accounting • RAW Web site provides extensive links to sources of national and international accounting information, such as the Big Six accounting firms, the Financial Accounting Standards Board (FASB), SEC filings (EDGAR), journals, publishers, software, the International Accounting Network, and "Internet's largest list of accounting firms in USA." Searching is offered. Fees: Free.

**OTHER SOURCES**

*Foreign Tax and Trade Briefs*. Matthew Bender and Company Inc. • Quarterly. $1,054 book. The latest tax and trade information for over 100 foreign countries.

*White Collar Crime: Business and Regulatory Offenses*. ALM Media Properties LLC. • $740 print + online + ebook. Covers such legal matters as criminal tax cases, securities fraud, computer crime, mail fraud, bank embezzlement, criminal antitrust activities, extortion, perjury, the criminal liability of corporations, and RICO (Racketeer Influenced and Corrupt Organization Act). (Law Journal Press).

**PERIODICALS AND NEWSLETTERS**

*Daily Tax Report*. Bloomberg BNA. • Daily. Monitors tax legislation, hearings, rulings, and court decisions.

*E-Commerce Tax Alert*. Wolters Kluwer Law & Business CCH. • Description: Print and online newsletter covering e-commerce taxation issues, including compliance and sourcing, e-cash implications, the Internet tax debate, and other topics.

*Highlights and Documents*. Tax Analysts. • Daily. $2,599.95 Individuals. Provides daily coverage of IRS, congressional, judicial, state, and international tax developments. Includes abstracts and citations for "all tax documents released within the previous

24 to 48 hours." Annual compilation available *Highlights and Documents on Microfiche*.

*Internal Revenue Bulletin*. Thomson RIA. • Weekly. Description: Presents new treasury and IRS releases in full official text. Contains rulings and decisions, releases on treaties, tax legislation, administrative and procedural releases, disbarment and suspensions.

*Internal Revenue Cumulative Bulletin*. U. S. Government Printing Office. • Semiannual. Issued by the Internal Revenue Service. Cumulates all items of a "permanent nature" appearing in the weekly *Internal Revenue Bulletin*.

*The Kiplinger Tax Letter*. Kiplinger Washington Editors Inc. • Description: Reports new tax regulations, changes, decisions, and pending legislation. Includes coverage of the House Ways and Means and Senate Committees, federal monetary and fiscal policy, securities, finance, and social security.

*The Practical Tax Lawyer*. Committee on Continuing Professional Education. American Law Institute - Committee on Continuing Professional Education. • Quarterly. $89 Members per year. Contains advice on how to solve tax problems of every company's clients.

*Tax Notes: The Weekly Tax Service*. Tax Analysts. • Weekly. Weekly. $1,699.00 per year. Includes an *Annual* and compilations of previous years. Newsletter. Covers "tax news from all federal sources," including congressional committees, tax courts, and the Internal Revenue Service. Each issue contains "summaries of every document that pertains to federal tax law," with citations. Commentary is provided.

*Tax Practice*. Tax Analysts. • Weekly. $199.00 per year. Newsletter. Covers news affecting tax practitioners and litigators, with emphasis on federal court decisions, rules and regulations, and tax petitions. Provides a guide to Internal Revenue Service audit issues.

*Taxation and Revenue Policies: State Capitals*. Wakeman/Walworth Inc. • 50 times a year. $345.00 per year; print and online edition, $490.00 per year. Formerly *From the State Capitals: Taxation and Revenue Policies*.

*Taxes-Property: State Capitals*. Wakeman/Walworth Inc. • 50 times a year. $345.00 per year; print and online edition, $490.00. Formerly *From the State Capitals: Taxes-Property*.

*Taxes: The Tax Magazine*. Wolters Kluwer Law & Business CCH. • Monthly. $420 Individuals. Provides its readers with cogent, innovative and practice-oriented analyses of federal, state and international tax issues.

**RESEARCH CENTERS AND INSTITUTES**

Harvard Law School International Tax Program. Harvard Law School, 1563 Massachusetts Ave., 1563 Massachusetts Ave., Cambridge, MA 02138. Phone: (617)495-3100 or (617)495-4406; Fax: (617)495-1110; Email: sfs@law.harvard.edu • URL: http://www.law.harvard.edu/programs/index.html • Studies the worldwide problems of taxation, including tax law and tax administration.

University of Michigan - Stephen M. Ross School of Business - Office of Tax Policy Research. 701 Tappan St., Rm. R5380, Ann Arbor, MI 48109-1234. Phone: (734)763-3068; Fax: (734)763-4032; Email: jslemrod@umich.edu • URL: http://www.bus.umich.edu/OTPR/ • Tax policy, including compliance, capital gains, reform, international taxation, and income dynamics.

# TAX MANAGEMENT

*See* TAXATION

# TAX PLANNING

*See also* ESTATE PLANNING; FINANCIAL PLANNING; INCOME TAX

**ABSTRACTS AND INDEXES**

*Business Periodicals Index Retrospective*. EBSCO Publishing Inc. • 11/year. Quarterly and annual cumulations.

**CD-ROM DATABASES**

*Authority Tax and Estate Planning Library*. Matthew Bender and Company Inc. • Periodic revisions. Price on request. CD contains updated full text of *Bender's Payroll Tax Guide, Depreciation Handbook, Federal Income Taxation of Corporations, Tax Planning for Corporations, Modern Estate Planning, Planning for Large Estates, Murphy's Will Clauses, Tax & Estate Planning for the Elderly*, and 12 other Matthew Bender publications. The Internal Revenue Code is also included.

**HANDBOOKS AND MANUALS**

*CCH Analysis of Top Tax Issues*. Wolters Kluwer Law & Business CCH. • Annual. $49.00. Covers yearly tax changes affecting business and personal transactions, planning, and returns.

*CCH Guide to Car, Travel, Entertainment, and Home Office Deductions*. Wolters Kluwer Law & Business CCH. • Annual. Explains how to claim maximum tax deductions for common business expenses. Includes automobile depreciation tables, lease value tables, worksheets, and examples of filled-in tax forms.

*Essentials of Federal Income Taxation for Individuals and Business*. Wolters Kluwer Law & Business CCH. • Annual. $165. Covers basic tax planning and tax reduction strategies as affected by tax law changes and IRS interpretations. Includes sample filled-in forms.

*Retirement Benefits Tax Guide*. Wolters Kluwer Law & Business CCH. • $199.00. Looseleaf service.

*Tax Planning for Highly Compensated Individuals*. RIA Group. • $235.00. Looseleaf service. Biennial supplementation.

**INTERNET DATABASES**

*CCH Essentials: An Internet Tax Research and Primary Source Library*. CCH, Inc. Phone: 800-248-3248 or (773)866-6000; Fax: (773)866-3608 or (800)224-8299; Email: cust_serv@cch.com • URL: http://tax.cch.com/essentials • Fee-based Web site provides full-text coverage of federal tax law and regulations, including rulings, procedures, tax court decisions, and IRS publications, announcements, notices, and penalties. Includes explanation, analysis, tax planning guides, and a daily tax news service. Searching is offered, including citation search.

**ONLINE DATABASES**

*Wilson Business Abstracts Online*. H.W. Wilson Co. • Indexes and abstracts 600 major business periodicals, plus the *Wall Street Journal* and the business section of the *New York Times*. Indexing is from 1982, abstracting from 1990, with the two newspapers included from 1993. Updated weekly. Inquire as to online cost and availability. (*Business Periodicals Index* without abstracts is also available online.).

**PERIODICALS AND NEWSLETTERS**

*Financial Planning: The Magazine for Financial Service Professionals*. SourceMedia Inc. • Monthly. $79.00 per year. Edited for independent financial planners and insurance agents. Covers retirement planning, estate planning, tax planning, and insurance, including long-term healthcare considerations. Special features include a Retirement Planning Issue, Mutual Fund Performance Survey, and Variable Life and Annuity Survey.

*Money.* • 13 times a year. $19.95 per year. Covers all aspects of family finance; investments, careers, shopping, taxes, insurance, consumerism, etc.

*Retirement Plans Bulletin: Practical Explanations for the IRA and Retirement Plan Professional.* Universal Pensions Inc. • Monthly. $99.00 per year. Newsletter. Provides information on the rules and regulations governing qualified (tax-deferred) retirement plans.

*The Tax Adviser.* American Institute of Certified Public Accountants. • Monthly. $106.25 Individuals. Newsletter about federal tax issues.

*Tax Management Weekly Report.* Tax Management Inc. • Weekly. Description: Covers developments affecting taxation and the tax aspects of accounting. Includes summaries of federal cases including the U.S. Tax Court, synopses of IRS general counsel and technical advice memoranda, analysis of selected IRS revenue rulings, procedures and private letter rulings, and status reports of Treasury Department actions on pending regulations. Covers topics in financial planning, including memoranda on current financial and tax planning strategies.

*Taxes: The Tax Magazine.* Wolters Kluwer Law & Business CCH. • Monthly. $420 Individuals. Provides its readers with cogent, innovative and practice-oriented analyses of federal, state and international tax issues.

## RESEARCH CENTERS AND INSTITUTES

American Institute for Economic Research. 250 Division St., Great Barrington, MA 01230-1000. Phone: 888-528-1216; Fax: (413)528-0103; Email: info@aier.org • URL: http://www.aier.org • Through research and publications, provides "information on economic and financial subjects that is useful and completely independent of special interests." Sponsors a fellowship program for graduate study of economics at the institute and in absentia.

## TRADE/PROFESSIONAL ASSOCIATIONS

American Society of Cost Segregation Professionals. 1101 Pennsylvania Ave. NW, 6th Fl., Washington, DC 20004. Phone: (203)671-7372; Fax: (203)745-0724; Email: info@ascsp.org • URL: http://www.ascsp.org • Seeks to address the growing need for credentials, educational programs, technical standards and a code of ethics for the cost segregation industry. Establishes a measurable standard by which cost segregation consultants will be evaluated. Develops benchmark technical standards for reporting that are aligned with the IRS Audit Techniques Guide for Cost Segregation.

National Association of Tax Professionals. PO Box 8002, Appleton, WI 54914-8002. Phone: 800-558-3402; Fax: (800)747-0001; Email: natp@natptax. com • URL: http://www.natptax.com/Pages/default. aspx • Promotes high professional standards for tax practitioners. Formerly National Association for Tax Practitioners.

## TAX, PROPERTY

*See* PROPERTY TAX

## TAX SHELTERS

*See also* INCOME TAX; INDUSTRIAL REAL ESTATE; INTERNATIONAL TAXATION; KEOGH PLANS; PROPERTY TAX; REAL ESTATE INVESTMENTS

## ABSTRACTS AND INDEXES

*Business Periodicals Index Retrospective.* EBSCO Publishing Inc. • 11/year. Quarterly and annual cumulations.

*Index to Legal Periodicals and Books.* H.W. Wilson Co. • Monthly. $490.00 per year. Quarterly and annual cumulations.

## HANDBOOKS AND MANUALS

*Tax Planning for Highly Compensated Individuals.* RIA Group. • $235.00. Looseleaf service. Biennial supplementation.

## ONLINE DATABASES

*Wilson Business Abstracts Online.* H.W. Wilson Co. • Indexes and abstracts 600 major business periodicals, plus the *Wall Street Journal* and the business section of the *New York Times.* Indexing is from 1982, abstracting from 1990, with the two newspapers included from 1993. Updated weekly. Inquire as to online cost and availability. (*Business Periodicals Index* without abstracts is also available online.).

## OTHER SOURCES

*Federal Taxes Affecting Real Estate.* Matthew Bender and Company Inc. • Semiannual. $573 book. Explains and illustrates the most important federal tax principles applying to daily real estate transactions.

## PERIODICALS AND NEWSLETTERS

*Money.* • 13 times a year. $19.95 per year. Covers all aspects of family finance; investments, careers, shopping, taxes, insurance, consumerism, etc.

*Personal Finance.* KCI Communications Inc. • Description: Contains articles on subjects of interest to those investigating personal finance strategies. Provides news, information, and suggestions on investment decisions. Covers stock and growth stock activity, individual retirement accounts, market trends and developments, and real estate. Recurring features include columns titled Capsule Advisory and Answers to Your Money Questions.

*Real Estate Tax Digest.* LexisNexis. • Description: Features articles on and analyses of legislation, Treasury regulations, federal court and Tax Court decisions, Revenue Rulings, Revenue Procedures, and selected Letter Rulings of the Internal Revenue Service pertaining to federal taxation affecting real estate activities. Includes columns titled Special Topic, New Developments, Practitioner's Corner, and Inside Washington.

*Stanger Report: A Guide to Partnership Investing.* Robert A. Stanger & Company Inc. • Quarterly. $447 Individuals Annual. Includes overall statistics on the size of the current market, quarterly fundraising, current distribution rates and coverage and latest valuation reports for closed non-traded REITs, market updates on new registrations, newly-effective issues and fund closings, secondary market transactions, and more.

*Tax-Advantaged Securities Law Report.* Robert J. Haft. Thomson West. • Description: Devotes each issue to one or two articles on federal or major state law concerning tax-advantaged securities. Presents explanation and analysis of new decisions, laws, rulings, and regulations. Gives practical advice and cautions for selected tax investments.

## RESEARCH CENTERS AND INSTITUTES

University of Michigan - Stephen M. Ross School of Business - Office of Tax Policy Research. 701 Tappan St., Rm. R5380, Ann Arbor, MI 48109-1234. Phone: (734)763-3068; Fax: (734)763-4032; Email: jslemrod@umich.edu • URL: http://www.bus. umich.edu/OTPR/ • Tax policy, including compliance, capital gains, reform, international taxation, and income dynamics.

## TAXATION

## ABSTRACTS AND INDEXES

*Accounting and Tax Index.* ProQuest L.L.C. • Quarterly. Indexes accounting, auditing, and taxation literature appearing in journals, books, pamphlets, conference proceedings, and newsletters.

*Index to Federal Tax Articles.* Thomson RIA. •

Quarterly. $1,565. Bibliographic listing of every significant article on federal income, estate and gift taxation since 1913. Lists over 36,000 articles.

## ALMANACS AND YEARBOOKS

*National Tax Association Proceedings of the Annual Conference on Taxation.* National Tax Association-Tax Institute of America. • Annual. Members, $85. 00; individuals, $70.00; libraries, $90.00; corporations, $130.00.

*New York University Annual Institute on Federal Taxation.* Melvin Cornfield. Matthew Bender and Company Inc. • Annual. $518 Individuals Book or Electronic version. Includes extensive index, table of revenue rulings, Code section reference table, table of Treasury regulations and more.

## CD-ROM DATABASES

*Authority Tax and Estate Planning Library.* Matthew Bender and Company Inc. • Periodic revisions. Price on request. CD contains updated full text of *Bender's Payroll Tax Guide, Depreciation Handbook, Federal Income Taxation of Corporations, Tax Planning for Corporations, Modern Estate Planning, Planning for Large Estates, Murphy's Will Clauses, Tax & Estate Planning for the Elderly,* and 12 other Matthew Bender publications. The Internal Revenue Code is also included.

*Business Abstracts with Full Text.* EBSCO Publishing Inc. • Includes full text articles from more than 460 business publications from 1982 to present. Indexing for nearly 880 publications.

*EconLit.* Ovid Technologies Inc. • Updated monthly. Lists journal articles, book reviews, dissertations of economic literature. Over 1,400 journals covered.

*Newspaper Abstracts Ondisc.* ProQuest L.L.C. • Monthly. $2,950.00 per year (covers 1989 to date; archival discs are available for 1985-88). Provides cover-to-cover CD-ROM indexing and abstracting of 19 major newspapers, including the *New York Times, Wall Street Journal, Washington Post, Chicago Tribune,* and *Los Angeles Times.*

*OECD Statistical Compendium.* Organization for Economic Cooperation and Development. • Semiannual. $1,905.00 per year for 1 to 10 users. CD-ROM contains more than 730,000 monthly, quarterly, and annual time series for OECD countries, 1960 to date. Includes fully searchable data on agriculture, food, economic indicators, national accounts, employment, energy, finance, industry, technology, and foreign trade. Results can be displayed in various forms.

*The Tax Directory.* Tax Analysts. • Quarterly. $499 Individuals both volumes, web, CD or print. Updated quarterly on CD-ROM and in print; updated continually online. Covering federal, state, and international tax officials, tax practitioners, and corporate tax executives.

*U.S. Master Tax Guide.* Wolters Kluwer Law & Business CCH. • Annual. $93.50.

## DIRECTORIES

*The Tax Directory.* Tax Analysts. • Quarterly. $499 Individuals both volumes, web, CD or print. Updated quarterly on CD-ROM and in print; updated continually online. Covering federal, state, and international tax officials, tax practitioners, and corporate tax executives.

## E-BOOKS

*Start Up and Run Your Own Business.* Cengage Learning Inc. • 2010. eBook. Published by Kogan Page. Offers a complete information resource for those looking to set up their own business, including raising finance, taxation, IT, market research and employment issues.

## GENERAL WORKS

*Tax Policy and the Economy.* The MIT Press. • Annual. $25. Reviews "issues in the current tax debate.".

## HANDBOOKS AND MANUALS

*CCH Analysis of Top Tax Issues.* Wolters Kluwer Law & Business CCH. • Annual. $49.00. Covers yearly tax changes affecting business and personal transactions, planning, and returns.

*RIA Federal Tax Handbook.* Thomson RIA. • Annual. $95.75 book or e-book. Provides quick and easy access to critical tax questions, the RIA Federal Tax Handbook offers comprehensive, insightful guidance on federal tax law, including the latest regulations, rulings, and revenue procedures as well as precise explanations about changes that could impact your business or your clients.

*Tax Guide for Small Business.* U.S. Department of the Treasury, Internal Revenue Service. U. S. Government Printing Office. • Annual. $11 Individuals USA List price. Contains tax information for small business owners.

*U.S. Master Estate and Gift Tax Guide.* Wolters Kluwer Law & Business CCH. • Annual. $103 Quantity: 1 - 4. Covers federal estate and gift taxes, including generation-skipping transfer tax plans. Includes tax tables and sample filled-in tax return forms.

*U.S. Master Tax Guide.* Wolters Kluwer Law & Business CCH. • Annual. $93.50.

## INTERNET DATABASES

*Business 2.0 Web Guide to the Best Business Links.* Business 2.0 Media Inc. Phone: (415)293-4800; Email: support@business2.com • URL: http://www.business2.com/webguide • Web site presents an extensive, searchable directory of links to "the best, most informative, and authoritative web pages." Twenty main categories cover business, finance, career, company information, people, and technology topics, with thousands of subtopics, all linking to Web sites recommended by experienced business researchers. Fees: Free.

*CCH Essentials: An Internet Tax Research and Primary Source Library.* CCH, Inc. Phone: 800-248-3248 or (773)866-6000; Fax: (773)866-3608 or (800)224-8299; Email: cust_serv@cch.com • URL: http://tax.cch.com/essentials • Fee-based Web site provides full-text coverage of federal tax law and regulations, including rulings, procedures, tax court decisions, and IRS publications, announcements, notices, and penalties. Includes explanation, analysis, tax planning guides, and a daily tax news service. Searching is offered, including citation search.

*Court Filings.* ProQuest LLC. 2250 Perimeter Park Dr., Ste. 300, Morrisville, NC 27560. Phone: 800-334-2564 or (919)804-6400; Fax: (919)804-6410; Email: contact@dialog.com • URL: http://www.dialog.com • The three main sections of Tax Analysts home page are "Tax News" (Today's Tax News, Feature of the Week, Tax Snapshots, Tax Calendar); "Products & Services" (Product Catalog, Press Releases); and "Public Interest" (Discussion Groups, Tax Clinic, Tax History Project). Fees: Free for coverage of current tax events; fee-based for comprehensive information. Daily updating.

*Factiva.* Dow Jones Reuters Business Interactive, LLC. Phone: 800-369-7466 or (609)452-1511; Fax: (609)520-5770; Email: solutions@factiva.com • URL: http://www.factiva.com • Fee-based Web site provides "global news and business information through Web sites and content integration solutions." Includes Dow Jones and Reuters newswires, The Wall Street Journal, and more than 7,000 other sources of current news, historical articles, market research reports, and investment analysis. Content includes 96 major U. S. newspapers, 900 non-English sources, trade publications, media transcripts, country profiles, news photos, etc.

*Fedstats.* Federal Interagency Council on Statistical Policy. Phone: (202)395-7254 • URL: http://www.fedstats.gov • Web site features an efficient search facility for full-text statistics produced by more than 100 federal agencies, including the Census Bureau, the Bureau of Economic Analysis, and the Bureau of Labor Statistics. Boolean searches can be made within one agency or for all agencies combined. Links are offered to international statistical bureaus, including the UN, IMF, OECD, UNESCO, Eurostat, and 20 individual countries. Fees: Free.

*FedWorld: A Program of the United States Department of Commerce.* National Technical Information Service. Phone: 800-553-NTIS or (703)605-6000; Fax: (703)605-6900; Email: webmaster@fedworld.gov • URL: http://www.fedworld.gov • Web site offers "a comprehensive central access point for searching, locating, ordering, and acquiring government and business information." Emphasis is on searching the Web pages, databases, and government reports of a wide variety of federal agencies. Fees: Free.

*FirstGov: Your First Click to the U. S. Government.* General Services Administration. Phone: 800-333-4636 or (202)501-0705; Email: public.affairs@gsa.gov • URL: http://www.gsa.gov • Free Web site provides extensive links to federal agencies covering a wide variety of topics, such as agriculture, business, consumer safety, education, the environment, government jobs, grants, health, social security, statistics sources, taxes, technology, travel, and world affairs. Also provides links to federal forms, including IRS tax forms. Searching is offered, both keyword and advanced.

*FreeLunch.com.* Economy.com, Inc. Phone: (610)696-8700; Fax: (610)696-1678 • URL: http://www.freelunch.com • Web site provides free access to more than 200 million economic and financial data series, covering industry, demographics, labor markets, prices, retail sales, government spending, trade, interest rates, housing starts, the stock market, etc. Data is available in either chart or table form. Searching is offered. Free, but registration required. Economy.com, Inc. also offers fee-based economic analysis at *The Dismal Scientist* site (www.dismal.com).

*Nexis.com.* Lexis-Nexis Group. Phone: 800-227-4908 or (937)865-6800; Fax: (937)865-6909; Email: webmaster@prod.lexis-nexis.com • URL: http://www.nexis.com • Fee-based Web site offers searching of about 2.8 billion documents in some 30,000 news, business, and legal information sources. Features include a subject directory covering 1,200 topics in 34 categories and a Company Dossier containing information on more than 500,000 public and private companies. Boolean searching is offered.

*TAXNET.PRO.* Carswell. Phone: 800-387-5164 or (416)609-3800; Fax: (416)298-5082; Email: orders@carswell.com • URL: http://www.carswell.com/taxnetpro.asp • Fee-based Web site provides complete coverage of Canadian tax law and regulation, including income tax, provincial taxes, accounting, and payrolls. Daily updates. Base price varies according to product.

## ONLINE DATABASES

*Accounting and Tax Database.* ProQuest L.L.C. • Provides indexing and abstracting of the literature of accounting, taxation, and financial management, 1971 to date. Updating is weekly. Especially covers accounting, auditing, banking, bankruptcy, employee compensation and benefits, cash management, financial planning, and credit. Inquire as to online cost and availability.

*Wilson Business Abstracts Online.* H.W. Wilson Co. • Indexes and abstracts 600 major business periodicals, plus the *Wall Street Journal* and the business section of the *New York Times.* Indexing is from 1982, abstracting from 1990, with the two newspapers included from 1993. Updated weekly. Inquire as to online cost and availability. (*Business Periodicals Index* without abstracts is also available online.).

## OTHER SOURCES

*All States Tax Guide.* Prentice Hall PTR. • Looseleaf. Periodic supplementation. Price on application. One volume summary of taxes for all states.

*Federal Taxation of Income, Estates and Gifts.* Warren, Gorham & Lamont/RIA. • 3/year. $1,950 print. Five looseleaf volumes. Updates three times a year. Covers aspects of income taxation of individuals, corporations, partnerships, estates, and gifts. Clear analysis to exact answers to tax questions.

*Federal Taxes Citator.* MacMillan Publishing Co. • $550.00 per year. Two looseleaf volumes. Monthly supplements.

*Taxation of Securities Transactions.* Matthew Bender and Company Inc. • Semiannual. $653. Looseleaf service. Covers taxation of a wide variety of securities transactions, including those involving stocks, bonds, options, short sales, new issues, mutual funds, dividend distributions, foreign securities, and annuities.

## PERIODICALS AND NEWSLETTERS

*Daily Tax Report.* Bloomberg BNA. • Daily. Monitors tax legislation, hearings, rulings, and court decisions.

*E-Commerce Tax Alert.* Wolters Kluwer Law & Business CCH. • Description: Print and online newsletter covering e-commerce taxation issues, including compliance and sourcing, e-cash implications, the Internet tax debate, and other topics.

*Highlights and Documents.* Tax Analysts. • Daily. $2,599.95 Individuals. Provides daily coverage of IRS, congressional, judicial, state, and international tax developments. Includes abstracts and citations for "all tax documents released within the previous 24 to 48 hours." Annual compilation available *Highlights and Documents on Microfiche.*

*International Tax Report: Maximizing Tax Opportunities Worldwide.* Informa Group PLC. • Monthly. $1,100.00 per year.

*The Kiplinger Tax Letter.* Kiplinger Washington Editors Inc. • Description: Reports new tax regulations, changes, decisions, and pending legislation. Includes coverage of the House Ways and Means and Senate Committees, federal monetary and fiscal policy, securities, finance, and social security.

*National Tax Journal.* National Tax Association-Tax Institute of America. • Quarterly. Membership. Topics of current interest in the field of taxation and public finance in the U.S. and foreign countries.

*The Practical Accountant: Providing the Competitive Edge.* SourceMedia Inc. • Monthly. $65.00 per year. Covers tax planning, financial planning, practice management, client relationships, and related topics.

*Schmalenbach Business Review.* Verlagsgruppe Handelsblatt GmbH. • Quarterly. $135 Institutions.

*Tax Notes: The Weekly Tax Service.* Tax Analysts. • Weekly. Weekly. $1,699.00 per year. Includes an *Annual* and compilations of previous years. Newsletter. Covers "tax news from all federal sources," including congressional committees, tax courts, and the Internal Revenue Service. Each issue contains "summaries of every document that pertains to federal tax law," with citations. Commentary is provided.

*Tax Practice.* Tax Analysts. • Weekly. $199.00 per year. Newsletter. Covers news affecting tax practitioners and litigators, with emphasis on federal court decisions, rules and regulations, and tax petitions. Provides a guide to Internal Revenue Service audit issues.

*Taxes on Parade.* Wolters Kluwer Law & Business CCH. • Weekly. $129.00 per year. Newsletter.

*Taxes: The Tax Magazine.* Wolters Kluwer Law & Business CCH. • Monthly. $420 Individuals. Provides its readers with cogent, innovative and practice-oriented analyses of federal, state and international tax issues.

## RESEARCH CENTERS AND INSTITUTES

Congressional Budget Office - Tax Analysis Division. Ford House Office Bldg., 4th Fl., 2nd & D Sts. SW, Washington, DC 20515-6925. Phone: (202)226-2602; Fax: (202)226-2714 • URL: http://www.cbo.gov/about/our-organization-and-people#tad • Responsible for estimating tax revenues, analyzing tax expenditures, and preparing tax-policy studies. Division analyzes the U.S. tax structure and changes to that structure, focusing on such issues as the effect of changing economic conditions on tax revenues, consumption taxes, and the distribution of tax burdens.

Harvard Law School International Tax Program. Harvard Law School, 1563 Massachusetts Ave., 1563 Massachusetts Ave., Cambridge, MA 02138. Phone: (617)495-3100 or (617)495-4406; Fax: (617)495-1110; Email: sfs@law.harvard.edu • URL: http://www.law.harvard.edu/programs/index.html • Studies the worldwide problems of taxation, including tax law and tax administration.

University of Michigan - Stephen M. Ross School of Business - Office of Tax Policy Research. 701 Tappan St., Rm. R5380, Ann Arbor, MI 48109-1234. Phone: (734)763-3068; Fax: (734)763-4032; Email: jslemrod@umich.edu • URL: http://www.bus.umich.edu/OTPR/ • Tax policy, including compliance, capital gains, reform, international taxation, and income dynamics.

## STATISTICS SOURCES

*The AIER Chart Book.* AIER Research Staff. American Institute for Economic Research. • Annual. $4 Individuals. A compact compilation of long-range charts ("Purchasing Power of the Dollar," for example, goes back to 1780) covering various aspects of the U. S. economy. Includes inflation, interest rates, debt, gold, taxation, stock prices, etc. (Economic Education Bulletin.).

*Revenue Statistics.* Organisation for Economic Co-operation and Development Publications and Information Center. • Annual. $65.00. Presents data on government revenues in OECD countries, classified by type of tax and level of government. Text in English and French.

*Statistics of Income Bulletin.* U. S. Government Printing Office. • Quarterly. $44. Current data compiled from tax returns relating to income, assets, and expenses of individuals and businesses. (U. S. Internal Revenue Service.).

*Survey of Current Business.* U. S. Government Printing Office. • Published by Bureau of Economic Analysis, U. S. Department of Commerce. Presents a wide variety of business and economic data.

## TRADE/PROFESSIONAL ASSOCIATIONS

Citizens for a Sound Economy. 1250 H St. NW, Ste. 700, Washington, DC 20005-3908. Phone: 888-564-6273 or (202)783-3870 or (202)942-7649; Fax: (202)783-4687; Email: cse@cse.org • URL: http://www.cse.org • Absorbed Council for a Competitive Economy and Tax Foundation.

National Tax Association-Tax Institute of America. 725 15th St. NW, Ste. 600, Washington, DC 20005-2109. Phone: (202)737-3325 or (202)261-5577; Fax: (202)737-7308; Email: natltax@aol.com • URL: http://www.ntanet.org.

National Taxpayers Union. 108 N Alfred St., Alexandria, VA 22314-3053. Phone: (703)683-5700; Fax: (703)683-5722; Email: ntu@ntu.org • URL: http://www.ntu.org • Seeks to: reduce government spending; cut taxes; protect the rights of taxpayers. Claims to have helped generate federal budget cuts of over 120 billion dollars. Activities include research programs and an intense lobbying campaign in Washington, DC; has been a leader in the fights against government ventures such as:

social security tax; guaranteed income; congressional and bureaucratic pay raises; federal subsidies; foreign aid; national health insurance. Works for a balanced federal budget/tax limitation constitutional amendment; federal pension reform; reduction of capital gains and personal income tax; social security reform. Has worked for airline deregulation; indexing of federal income tax, California's Proposition 13, Massachusetts Proposition 2 1/2, and other state tax cutting initiatives. Conducts annual voting study of congressmen and senators, rating their votes on spending and tax issues and presenting awards for best and worst records.

# TAXATION, INTERNATIONAL

*See* INTERNATIONAL TAXATION

# TAXES, STATE

*See* STATE TAXES

# TAXICABS

## PERIODICALS AND NEWSLETTERS

*Taxi and Livery Management.* International Taxicab and Livery Association. • Quarterly. $16.00 per year.

# TAYLOR SYSTEM OF SHOP MANAGEMENT

*See* TIME AND MOTION STUDY

# TEA INDUSTRY

*See also* COFFEE INDUSTRY

## ALMANACS AND YEARBOOKS

*CRB Commodity Yearbook.* Commodity Research Bureau. CRB. • Annual. $179 plus $10.00 shipping cost. The single most comprehensive source of commodity and futures market information available.

## DIRECTORIES

*Directory of Chinese Manufacturers & Exporters of Tea & Coffee.* EXIM Infotek Private Ltd. • $10 Individuals. Covers: 50 Chinese manufacturers and exporters of black tea, Chinese tea, coffee, green tea, jasmine tea, oolong tea, and organic tea. Entries include: Company name, postal address, city, country, phone, fax, e-mail and websites, contact person, designation, and product details.

*Directory of Taiwanese Manufacturers & Exporters of Tea & Coffee.* EXIM Infotek Private Ltd. • $5 Individuals. Covers: 20 Taiwanese manufacturers and exporters of Chinese tea, cocoa and chocolate products, coffee and coffee substitutes. Entries include: Company name, postal address, city, country, phone, fax, e-mail and websites, contact person, designation, and product details.

## INTERNET DATABASES

*USDA.* U.S. National Institute of Standards and Technology. 100 Bureau Dr., Gaithersburg, MD 20899-1070. Phone: 800-877-8339 or (301)975-6478 or (202)720-2791; Fax: (301)975-8295; Email: inquiries@nist.gov • URL: http://www.nist.gov • The USDA home page has six sections: News and Information; What's New; About USDA; Agencies; Opportunities; Search and Help. Keyword searching is offered from the USDA home page and from various individual agency home pages. Agencies are the Economic Research Service, Agricultural Marketing Service, National Agricultural Statistics Service, National Agricultural Library, and about 12 others.

Updating varies. Fees: Free.

## PERIODICALS AND NEWSLETTERS

*Fancy Food and Culinary Products.* Talcott Communications Corp. • Monthly. $34.00 per year. Emphasizes new specialty food products and the business management aspects of the specialty food and confection industries. Includes special issues on wine, cheese, candy, "upscale" cookware, and gifts. Formerly (Fancy Foods).

*Sri Lanka Journal of Tea Science.* Tea Research Institute of Sri Lanka. • Semiannual. $20. Journal covering the tea industry. Text in English. Formerly *Tea Quarterly.*

*Tea and Coffee Trade Journal.* Lockwood Publications Inc. • Monthly. $49 Individuals. Current trends in coffee roasting and tea packing industry.

## STATISTICS SOURCES

*Agricultural Statistics.* U.S. Department of Agriculture National Agricultural Statistics Service. • Annual. $46 Individuals. Provides a wide variety of statistical data relating to agricultural production, supplies, consumption, prices/price-supports, foreign trade, costs, and returns, as well as farm labor, loans, income, and population. In many cases, historical data is shown annually for 10 years. In addition to farm data, includes detailed fishery statistics.

# TEA ROOMS

*See* RESTAURANTS, LUNCHROOMS, ETC.

# TECHNICAL ANALYSIS (FINANCE)

*See also* COMPUTERS IN FINANCE; DOW THEORY; FINANCIAL ANALYSIS

## DIRECTORIES

*Futures Magazine SourceBook: The Most Complete List of Exchanges, Companies, Regulators, Organizations, etc., Offering Products and Services to the Futures and Options Industry.* Futures Magazine Inc. • Annual. $19.50. Provides information on commodity futures brokers, trading method services, publications, and other items of interest to futures traders and money managers.

## INTERNET DATABASES

*Futures Online.* Futures Magazine Inc. Phone: (312)846-4600; Fax: (312)846-4638 • URL: http://www.futuresmag.com • Web site presents updates of *Futures* magazine and links to other futures-related sites.

## OTHER SOURCES

*Mansfield Stock Chart Service.* R.W. Mansfield Co. • Weekly. Price varies. Newsletter. Covers New York Stock Exchange, American Stock Exchange, OTC exchange, international stocks and industry groups. Partial subscriptions available.

## PERIODICALS AND NEWSLETTERS

*Dow Theory Letters.* Dow Theory Letters, Inc. • Triweekly. $300 /year. Newsletter on stock market trends, investing, and economic conditions.

*Futures: News, Analysis, and Strategies for Futures, Options, and Derivatives Traders.* Futures Magazine Inc. • Monthly. $39 Individuals. Edited for institutional money managers and traders, brokers, risk managers, and individual investors or speculators. Includes special feature issues on interest rates, technical indicators, currencies, charts, precious metals, hedge funds, and derivatives. Supplements available.

*InvesTech Market Analyst: Technical and Monetary Investment Analysis.* Investech Research. • Every three weeks. $190.00 per year. Newsletter. Provides interpretation of monetary statistics and Federal Reserve actions, especially as related to technical analysis of stock market price trends.

*SFO: Stocks, Futures & Options.* W and A Publishing. • Subtitle: *Official Journal for Personal Investing in Stocks, Futures, and Options.* Covers mainly speculative techniques for stocks, commodity futures, financial futures, stock index futures, foreign exchange, short selling, and various kinds of options.

*Technical Analysis of Stocks & Commodities: The Traders Magazine.* Technical Analysis Inc. • $89.99 Individuals Annual. 13 times a year. Covers use of personal computers for stock trading, price movement analysis by means of charts, and other technical trading methods.

*Technical Trends: The Indicator Accuracy Service.* Technical Trends Inc. • 40 times a year. $147.00 per year. Technical investment newsletter.

## PRICE SOURCES

*CRB Futures Perspective: Agricultural Edition.* Commodity Research Bureau. • Weekly. $230.00 per year. Service provides comprehensive price charts for more than 20 agricultural commodity futures, from cocoa to wheat (includes lumber). Also provides technical analysis of price movements and market commentary. Formerly part of *CRB Futures Chart Service.*

*CRB Futures Perspective: Financial Edition.* Commodity Research Bureau. • Weekly. $275.00 per year. Service provides comprehensive price charts for more than 50 financial futures, from Australian Bills to Swiss Francs (includes precious metals and oil). Also provides technical analysis of price movements and market commentary. Formerly part of *CRB Futures Chart Service.*

## RESEARCH CENTERS AND INSTITUTES

Research Foundation of CFA Institute. c/o Walter V. Haslett, Jr., Executive Director, 477 Madison Ave., 21st Fl., New York, NY 10022. Phone: (856)780-5349; Email: info@cfainstitute.org • URL: http://www.cfainstitute.org/learning/foundation/Pages/index.aspx • Affiliated with Financial Analysts Federation.

University of Chicago - Booth School of Business - Center for Research in Security Prices. 105 W Adams St., Ste. 1700, Chicago, IL 60603. Phone: (312)263-6400; Fax: (312)263-6430; Email: subscriptions@crsp.chicagobooth.edu • URL: http://www.crsp.com • Historical financial data.

University of Pennsylvania - The Wharton School - Rodney L. White Center for Financial Research. 3254 Steinberg Hall-Dietrich Hall, Philadelphia, PA 19104-6367. Phone: (215)898-7616; Fax: (215)573-8084; Email: rlwctr@finance.wharton.upenn.edu • URL: http://rodneywhitecenter.wharton.upenn.edu • Research areas include financial management, money markets, real estate finance, and international finance.

## STATISTICS SOURCES

*Advance-Decline Album.* Dow Theory Letters, Inc. • Annual. Contains one page for each year since 1931. Includes charts of the New York Stock Exchange advance-decline ratio and the Dow Jones industrial average.

*SRC Green Book of 5 Trend 35-Year Charts.* Securities Research Co. • Annual. $150.00. Chart book presents statistical information on the stocks of 400 leading companies over a 35-year period. Each full page chart is in semi-log format to avoid visual distortion. Also includes charts of 12 leading market averages or indexes and 39 major industry groups.

## TRADE/PROFESSIONAL ASSOCIATIONS

American Association of Professional Technical Analysts. 10621 Big Canoe, 5516 Red Fox Dr., Big Canoe, GA 30143. Phone: 800-222-7636; Email: membership@aapta.com • URL: http://www.aapta.com • Aims to promote the use of technical analysis. Provides a forum for members to share ideas, information, research and analytical techniques. Encourages the highest professional ethics and competence among technical analysts.

CFA Institute. 560 Ray C. Hunt Dr., Charlottesville, VA 22903-2981. Phone: 800-247-8132 or (434)951-5499; Fax: (434)951-5262; Email: info@cfainstitute.org • URL: http://www.cfainstitute.org/pages/index.aspx • Formerly Association for Investment Management and Research.

International Function Point Users Group. 191 Clarksville Rd., Princeton Junction, NJ 08550. Phone: (609)799-4900; Fax: (609)799-7032; Email: ifpug@ifpug.org • URL: http://www.ifpug.org • Works to increase the "effectiveness of its members' information technology environments through the applications of function point analysis and other software measurement techniques."

Technical Analysis Society of St. Lucia. PO Box 1764, Castries 00110-5000, Saint Lucia. • URL: http://www.tasstlucia.com • Promotes technical analysis for the study and self-directed investments in the financial markets. Fosters excellence in the theory and practice of technical analysis. Provides a local forum for St. Lucian traders and investors to share ideas, news, and experiences.

# TECHNICAL ASSISTANCE

*See also* DEVELOPING AREAS

## DIRECTORIES

*Technical Services in the United Kingdom.* Financial Times Healthcare. • Irregular. $400. Covers: 2,000 public and private companies offering technical services and facilities for hire in the United Kingdom. Entries include: Company name, address, phone, type of service, facilities.

## TRADE/PROFESSIONAL ASSOCIATIONS

Finance Project. 1150 18th St. NW, Ste. 325, Washington, DC 20036-3856. Phone: (202)628-4200; Fax: (202)628-1293; Email: info@financeproject.org • URL: http://www.financeproject.org • Develops and disseminates information, knowledge, tools, technical assistance for improved policies, programs, financing strategies that will benefit children, families and communities.

# TECHNICAL BOOKS

*See* TECHNOLOGY

# TECHNICAL EDUCATION

*See also* VOCATIONAL EDUCATION

## ABSTRACTS AND INDEXES

*Education Index.* H.W. Wilson Co. • 10 times a year. Quarterly and annual cumulations. Price varies.

*Vocational Education and Training Abstracts.* Taylor & Francis Ltd. • Annual. $1,622 Institutions print + online. Journal providing information needs of those engaged in technical or vocational education.Published in England. Formerly *Technical Education Abstracts.*

## CD-ROM DATABASES

*ERIC SilverPlatter.* U.S. Department of Education Institute of Education Sciences Education Resources Information Center. • Opinion papers, evaluations, speeches.

## DIRECTORIES

*American Trade Schools Directory.* Croner Publications Inc. • $120 base and supplements; plus $9.95 shipping, payment with order. Covers: over 12,000 private and public trade, technical, and vocational schools. Entries include: School name, address, phone, contact person, year school founded, private or public, accrediting agencies, whether approved by state or Veterans Administration, home study courses offered.

## ONLINE DATABASES

*Education Index Online.* H.W. Wilson Co. • Indexes a wide variety of periodicals related to schools, colleges, and education, 1984 to date. Monthly updates. Inquire as to online cost and availability.

*ERIC.* U.S. Department of Education Institute of Education Sciences Educational Resources Information Center. • Funded by the U.S. Department of Education, Institute of Education Sciences (formerly Office of Educational Research and Improvement). Provides access to more than one million online records covering education-related journal and report literature, 1966 to date. Updating is monthly. Inquire as to online cost and availability.

## PERIODICALS AND NEWSLETTERS

*Technical Education News.* Glencoe/McGraw-Hill. • Semiannual. Free to qualified personnel.

## TRADE/PROFESSIONAL ASSOCIATIONS

American Technical Education Association. Dunwoody College of Technology, 818 Dunwoody Blvd., Minneapolis, MN 55403. Phone: (612)381-3315; Email: info@ateaonline.org • URL: http://www.ateaonline.org • Dedicated to excellence in the quality of post-secondary technical education with emphasis on professional development.

Association of Private Sector Colleges and Universities. 1101 Connecticut Ave. NW, Ste. 900, Washington, DC 20036. Phone: 866-711-8574 or (202)336-6700; Fax: (202)336-6828; Email: apscu@apscu.org • URL: http://www.career.org • Represents private post-secondary schools, institutes, colleges and universities that provide career-specific educational programs.

# TECHNICAL LITERATURE

*See* TECHNOLOGY

# TECHNICAL SOCIETIES

*See* ASSOCIATIONS

# TECHNICAL WRITING

*See also* PROCEDURE MANUALS

## PERIODICALS AND NEWSLETTERS

*Technical Communication.* Society for Technical Communication. • Quarterly. Includes articles about the practical application of technical communication.

# TECHNOLOGICAL UNEMPLOYMENT

*See* UNEMPLOYMENT

# TECHNOLOGY

*See also* RESEARCH AND DEVELOPMENT

## ABSTRACTS AND INDEXES

*Applied Science and Technology Index.* EBSCO Publishing Inc. • 11/year. Indexes a wide variety of English language technical, industrial, and engineering periodicals.

*Current Contents: Engineering, Computing and Technology.* Thomson Reuters Intellectual Property and Science. • Weekly. $730 per year. Reproductions of contents pages of technical journals. Includes *Author Index, Address Directory, Current Book Contents,* and *Title Word Index.* Formerly *Current Contents: Engineering, Technology and Applied Sciences.*

*Engineering Index Monthly: Abstracting and Indexing Services Covering Sources ofthe World's Engineering Literature.* Engineering Information Inc. • Monthly. Institutions, $5,279.00 per year. Provides indexing and abstracting of the world's engineering and technical literature.

*NTIS Alerts: Manufacturing Technology.* U.S. Department of Commerce National Technical Information Service. • Biweekly. $130 per year. Covers computer-aided design and manufacturing (CAD/CAM), engineering materials, quality control, machine tools, robots, lasers, productivity, and related subjects.

## ALMANACS AND YEARBOOKS

*McGraw-Hill Yearbook of Science and Technology.* McGraw Hill Financial Inc. • Annual. $145.00.

*Research in Philosophy and Technology.* Elsevier. • Dates vary. Price varies. 21 volumes.

*Research on Technological Innovation, Management and Policy.* Richard S. Rosenbloom and Robert A. Burgelman, editors. Elsevier. • Dates vary. Prices vary. Seven volumes.

*Science and Technology Almanac.* Greenwood Publishing Group Inc. • $99.95 Individuals hardcover. Provides the most comprehensive source for the significant science news of 2001 and for scientific information in general.

## BIBLIOGRAPHIES

*New Technical Books: A Selective List With Descriptive Annotations.* New York Public Library, Science and Technology Research Center. • Bimonthly. $30.00 per year.

*Reference Reviews.* Information Today, Inc. • Eight times a year. Price on application. Published in London by Aslib: The Association for Information Management. Incorporates *Aslib Book Guide.*

## BIOGRAPHICAL SOURCES

*American Men & Women of Science (AMWS).* Cengage Learning Inc. • 2013. $1508.00. 31st edition. Over 135,000 scientists active in the physical, biological, mathematical, computer science and engineering fields in the United States and Canada.

*Who's Who in Science and Engineering.* Marquis Who's Who L.L.C. • Biennial. $249.00. Provides concise biographical information on 33,545 prominent engineers and scientists. International coverage, with geographical and professional indexes.

## CD-ROM DATABASES

*Applied Science and Technology Abstracts.* EBSCO Publishing Inc. • Citations for more than 700 prominent scientific, technical, engineering, and industrial periodicals.

*NTIS Database.* Ovid Technologies Inc. • Quarterly. $2,850.00 per year. Guide to over 2 million bibliographic entries. Compiled by the U.S. National Technical Information Service.

*OECD Statistical Compendium.* Organization for Economic Cooperation and Development. • Semiannual. $1,905.00 per year for 1 to 10 users. CD-ROM contains more than 730,000 monthly, quarterly, and annual time series for OECD

countries, 1960 to date. Includes fully searchable data on agriculture, food, economic indicators, national accounts, employment, energy, finance, industry, technology, and foreign trade. Results can be displayed in various forms.

## DIRECTORIES

*Advanced Manufacturing Technology.* John Wiley & Sons Inc. Scientific, Technical, Medical, and Scholarly Div. (Wiley-Blackwell). • Monthly. Publication includes: List of companies involved in developing advanced manufacturing technologies such as robotics, artificial intelligence in computers, ultrasonics, lasers, and waterjet cutters; also lists sources of information and education on high-technology. Entries include: Company or organization name, address, phone, name of contact; description of process, product, or service. Principal content is articles and analysis of advanced manufacturing technology.

*Directory of California Technology Companies.* San Francisco Chamber of Commerce. • $161 Members. Covers: 12,000 California-based technology manufacturers, wholesalers, and software and service companies working in fields such as research and development, aerospace, software, biotech, aerospace and others. Entries include: Contact details.

*Directory of Colorado Manufacturers--Information, Science, & Technology.* University of Colorado at Boulder Leeds School of Business Business Research Division. • $25 clearance price. Covers: More than 1,600 Colorado manufacturers in the information, science and technology fields. Entries include: Plant address, mailing address, telephone number, e-mail, Web address, names and titles of key personnel, NAICS code numbers, number of employees, branch and subsidiary details, area of distribution.

*Directory of ICT Companies in Mauritius.* National Computer Board. • Annual. Covers: 300 companies operating in the ICT sector in Mauritius in a wide range of activities including software development, call centre, BPO, web-enabled activities, training, hardware assembly and sales, networking and other support services. Entries include: Company name, address, phone, fax, e-mail, website, directors, contact person, number of employees, company profile, competencies, export markets, products, and services.

*EMPRESAS.* Brazilian Institute for Information in Science and Technology. • Monthly. Database covers: companies that sell publicly available software programs. Entries include: Name of firm, address, phone, telex, products and services.

*A Guide to China's New and High-Tech Development Zone Enterprises.* Social Sciences Documentation Publishing House. • $75. Covers: 5,000 high-tech enterprises in China. Entries include: Contact information, administrative person, revenues, fixed assets, number of employees, product names.

*High-Tech Materials Alert.* John Wiley & Sons Inc. Scientific, Technical, Medical, and Scholarly Div. (Wiley-Blackwell). • Monthly. Publication includes: List of manufacturers and suppliers of high performance alloys, metals, ceramics, plastics, graphite, and other materials. Entries include: Company name, address, phone. Principal content is articles and analyses of new materials for industrial processes.

*Industrial & Technology-Based Firms Directory.* Charleston Metro Chamber of Commerce. • $150 Members. Covers: 1,500 plus manufacturing, distribution, and technology-based firms operating in the tri-county area. Technology-based firms included are not only from certain manufacturing sectors but also from the information technology, engineering, biotech, research and development, and other sciences sectors. Entries include: Company

name, address, county, phone, web site if known, NAICS code, number of local employees, primary products or services, year established locally, and names of the top officer on site, human resource representative and purchasing agent where applicable.

*IT Companies Database.* NIIR Project Consultancy Services. • $100 Individuals CD-ROM. Covers: 5,000+ contacts of IT companies in India. Entries include: Company name, address, phone, fax, e-mail and website, contact person and product details.

*IT Legal Guide.* VNU Business Publications Ltd. • Annual. $45 plus 4 postage. Covers: More than 400 manufacturers, distributors, and consultants in the United Kingdom specializing with information on 300 technology products and services for the legal profession. Database includes: List of pertinent information sources. Entries include: Name, address, phone, fax, description of products/services.

*Northern California High Technology.* Rich's Business Directories Inc. • $935 Individuals database download. Covers: Over 9,104 high technology firms in Northern California. Publication includes: Over 38,839 contact names. Entries include: Company name, address, web address, stock symbol, headquarters, year established, product type.

*Plunkett's Engineering and Research Industry Almanac.* Plunkett Research Ltd. • Annual. $349.99. Contains detailed profiles of major engineering and technology corporations. Includes CD-ROM.

*Science et Technologie au Quebec.* Quebec Dans Le Monde. • Biennial. $52.95 Individuals. Covers: over 1,150 scientific associations, periodicals, research and development facilities, and research centers in Quebec. Entries include: Organization name, address, phone, fax, toll-free phone, description of services.

*South Central High Technology Firms.* Rich's Business Directories Inc. • $199 Individuals 1 year premium online. Covers: Approximately 2,221 high tech research, manufacturing, and development firms in south central United States (Arkansas, Louisiana, and Oklahoma). Entries include: Company name, address, phone, names and titles of key personnel, year established, number of employees, type of ownership, annual sales volume, product service provided, SIC code.

*Tech Directions--Annual Buyers' Guide: A Directory of Suppliers.* Prakken Publications Inc. • Annual. Publication includes: Directory of manufacturers and suppliers of equipment and materials to industrial and vocational/technical schools, community colleges, and universities. Entries include: Company name, address, phone, fax, logo, e-mail, web address, product descriptions.

## E-BOOKS

*Encyclopedia of American Industries.* Cengage Learning Inc. • 2011. $807.00. 6th edition. Three volumes. Volume one is Manufacturing Industries and volume two is Service and Non-Manufacturing Industries. Provides the history, development, and recent status of approximately 1,000 industries. Includes statistical graphs, with industry and general indexes. Also available as eBook.

*Encyclopedia of Emerging Industries.* Cengage Learning Inc. • $546 6th edition. Provides detailed information on 140 "newly flourishing" industries. Includes historical background, organizational structure, significant individuals, current conditions, major companies, work force, technology trends, research developments, and other industry facts.

*Selected Readings on Information Technology and Business Systems Management.* Cengage Learning Inc. • 2009. eBook. Published by Information Science Reference. Focuses on key issues concerning technology in business. Contains selected readings in areas such as e-business, mobile marketing, and information resources management.

## GENERAL WORKS

*How Products Are Made.* Cengage Learning Inc. • $211 Individuals. 2007. Volume 7. $192. Provides easy-to-read, step-by-step descriptions of how approximately 100 different products are manufactured. eBook also available.

## INTERNET DATABASES

*FedWorld: A Program of the United States Department of Commerce.* National Technical Information Service. Phone: 800-553-NTIS or (703)605-6000; Fax: (703)605-6900; Email: webmaster@fedworld. gov • URL: http://www.fedworld.gov • Web site offers "a comprehensive central access point for searching, locating, ordering, and acquiring government and business information." Emphasis is on searching the Web pages, databases, and government reports of a wide variety of federal agencies. Fees: Free.

*InSite 2.* Intelligence Data/Thomson Financial. Phone: 800-654-0393 or (617)856-1890; Fax: (617)737-3182; Email: intelligence.data@tfn.com • URL: http://www.insite2.gale.com/ • Fee-based Web site consolidates information in a "Base Pack" consisting of Business InSite, Market InSite, and Company InSite. Optional databases are Consumer InSite, Health and Wellness InSite, Newsletter InSite, and Computer InSite. Includes fulltext content from more than 2,500 trade publications, journals, newsletters, newspapers, analyst reports, and other sources. Continuous updating. Formerly produced by The Gale Group.

*WilsonWeb Periodicals Databases.* H.W. Wilson Co. 950 University Ave., Bronx, NY 10452-4224. Phone: 800-367-6770 or (718)588-8400 or (718)558-8400; Fax: (718)590-1617 or (800)590-1617; Email: custserv@hwwilson.com • URL: http://www.hwwilson.com • Web sites provide fee-based access to *Wilson Business Full Text, Applied Science & Technology Full Text, Biological & Agricultural Index, Library Literature & Information Science Full Text,* and *Readers' Guide Full Text, Mega Edition.* Daily updates.

## ONLINE DATABASES

*Aerospace America Magazine.* American Institute of Aeronautics and Astronautics. • Monthly. $200 Institutions non member, domestic. Covers aeronautics and space technology with special attention to aerospace defense, design, and electronics.

*Aerospace Database.* American Institute of Aeronautics and Astronautics. • Contains abstracts of literature covering all aspects of the aerospace and aircraft industry 1983 to date. Monthly updates. Inquire as to online cost and availability.

*Applied Science and Technology Index Online.* H.W. Wilson Co. • Provides online indexing of 500 major scientific, technical, industrial, and engineering periodicals. Time period is 1983 to date. Monthly updates. Inquire as to online cost and availability.

*Current Contents Connect.* Thomson Reuters Intellectual Property and Science. • Provides online abstracts of articles listed in the tables of contents of about 7,500 journals. Coverage is very broad, including science, social science, life science, technology, engineering, industry, agriculture, the environment, economics, and arts and humanities. Time period is two years, with weekly updates. Inquire as to online cost and availability.

*INSPEC.* Institution of Electrical Engineers. • Provides online citations, with abstracts, to the world literature of electrical engineering, electronics, optoelectronics, telecommunications, industrial controls, instrumentation, computer technology, information technology, and physics. Coverage includes more than 4,000 technical and scientific journals from 1969 to date, with weekly updating. (INSPEC is Information Services in Physics,

Electronics, and Computing.) Inquire as to online cost and availability.

## OTHER SOURCES

*Survey of Advanced Technology: A Strategic Analysis of Today's Leading-edge Information Technologies.* I.T. Works. • Annual. $795.00. Surveys the corporate use (or neglect) of advanced computer technology. Topics include major technology trends and emerging technologies.

## PERIODICALS AND NEWSLETTERS

*Adweek Magazines' Technology Marketing.* Nielsen Business Media Inc. • Monthly. $55.00 per year. Edited for marketing executives in high technology industries. Covers both advertising and marketing. Formerly *MC Technology Marketing Intelligence.*

*Aerospace America Magazine.* American Institute of Aeronautics and Astronautics. • Monthly. $200 Institutions non member, domestic. Covers aeronautics and space technology with special attention to aerospace defense, design, and electronics.

*African Review of Business and Technology.* Alain Charles Publishing Ltd. • Magazine covering technology and business information about Africa.

*Asian Review of Business and Technology.* Alain Charles Publishing Ltd. • Bimonthly. $78 Individuals. Magazine covering technology and business in Asia.

*Green Data Centers and Internet Business.* Information Gatekeepers Inc. • Monthly. $695 U.S. and Canada print. Provides marketing and technology information on new developments in the internet telephone industry on a worldwide basis.

*High Technology Business.* Infotechnology Publishing Corp. • Monthly. $60 Individuals. Magazine containing information on current trends and developments in the full range of high technology industries. Material is directed toward business people in the high technology field.

*Internet Marketing and Technology Report: Advising Marketing, Sales, and Corporate Executives on Online Opportunities.* Computer Economics Inc. • Monthly. $387.00 per year. Newsletter. Covers strategic marketing, sales, advertising, public relations, and corporate communications, all in relation to the Internet. Includes information on "cutting-edge technology" for the Internet.

*J@pan Inc Magazine: Business Technology People.* Japan Incorporated Communications K.K. • Monthly. English language magazine covering business and technology in Japan for professionals worldwide.

*Laptop: Mobile Solutions for Business & Life.* Bedford Communications Inc. • Magazine covering the innovation of advance technology.

*Technological Forecasting and Social Change: An International Journal of the Dragon Project.* Elsevier. • Nine times a year. Individuals, $131.00 per year; institutions, $839.00 per year.

*Technology Forecasts and Technology Surveys.* Technology Forecasts. • Monthly. $192.00 per year. Newsletter. Information on major breakthroughs in advanced technologies along with forecasts of effects on future applications and markets.

*Technology in Society: An International Journal.* Elsevier. • Quarterly. Individuals, $233.00 per year; institutions, $981.00 per year.

*Technology Review: MITs National Magazine of Technology and Policy.* Massachusetts Institute of Technology Department of Urban Studies and Planning Community Innovators Lab. • Ten times a year. $30.00 per year. Examines current technological issues facing society.

*21.C: Scanning the Future: A Magazine of Culture, Technology, and Science.* International Publishers Distributors. • Quarterly. $24.00 per year. Contains multidisciplinary articles relating to the 21st century.

## RESEARCH CENTERS AND INSTITUTES

Arizona State University - Sandra Day O'Connor College of Law - Center for Law, Science and Innovation. Armstrong Hall, 1100 S McAllister Ave., Tempe, AZ 85287. Phone: (480)965-6181 • URL: http://www.law.asu.edu/lsi • Studies the development of legal frameworks for new technologies and advancing the use of science in legal decision making.

Carnegie Mellon University - Center for Analytical Research in Technology. 5000 Forbes Ave., Tepper School of Business, Pittsburgh, PA 15213. Phone: (412)268-6903; Fax: (412)268-7357; Email: holgers@andrew.cmu.edu • URL: http://www.tepper.cmu.edu/faculty-research/research-centers/center-for-analyticalresearch-in-technology-cart/index.aspx • Business and technology.

Columbia University - Columbia Center for Excellence in E-Business. Corporate & Foundation Relations, Columbia Business School, 33 W 60th St., 7th Fl., New York, NY 10023-7905. Phone: (212)854-3427; Fax: (212)678-0825; Email: ejj3@columbia.edu • URL: http://www4.gsb.columbia.edu/cebiz • Business, information technology, and e-commerce.

Dartmouth College - Glassmeyer/McNamee Center for Digital Strategies. 100 Tuck Hall, Hanover, NH 03755-9000. Phone: (603)646-0899; Fax: (603)646-0900; Email: digital.strategies@dartmouth.edu • URL: http://digitalstrategies.tuck.dartmouth.edu • Impact of information technologies on the ability of businesses to integrate and collaborate with customers and supply chain partners.

Massachusetts Institute of Technology - Department of Urban Studies and Planning - Community Innovators Lab. Department of Urban Studies and Planning, Bldg./Rm. 9-419, 77 Massachusetts Ave., Cambridge, MA 02139. Phone: (617)253-3216; Fax: (617)258-6515; Email: colab-info@mit.edu • URL: http://web.mit.edu/colab • Provides opportunity for minority community activists and local governmental officials (10 to 12 per year) to spend a year of reflection, study, and research at the Massachusetts Institute of Technology. The Program is being redesigned to capture the potential of new information technologies for poor communities and communities of color.

National Institute of Standards and Technology - Advanced Technology Program - Economic Assessment Office. 100 Bureau Dr., MS 4710, Gaithersburg, MD 20899-4710. Phone: (301)975-8978; Fax: (301)975-4776; Email: stephanie.shipp@nist.gov • URL: http://www.atp.nist.gov/eao/eao_main.htm • Seeks to evaluate how private-public partnerships in technology development interact with commercial markets and to assess their impact on the economy and society.

Secretary of Agriculture and Supply - Institute of Food Technology. Avda. Brasil 2880, Caixa Postal 139, 13070-178 Campinas, SP, Brazil. Phone: 55 19 37431700; Fax: 55 19 37431799; Email: rh@ital.sp.gov.br • URL: http://www.ital.sp.gov.br • Food science, engineering and technology, including dehydrated foods, grain storage, juices and beverages, biotechnology, meat and meat products, postharvest physiology of fruit and vegetable, food packaging, equipment design, flours and bakery products, milk and dairy products, marketing and economics, edible oils, seafood resources, and physical, chemical, biochemical, microbiological, and sensory evaluation of food products.

Simon Fraser University - Centre for Policy Research on Science and Technology. 8888 University Dr., Burnaby, BC, Canada V5A 1S6. Phone: (778)782-5114; Fax: (778)782-5239; Email: smith@sfu.ca • URL: http://www.sfu.ca/cprost/ • Focuses on the relationship between public policy and technology. Specific areas of public policy research include: innovation metrics, innovation policy; management of technological change;

indicators of science and technology and innovation; disaster mitigation; and valuation of information services.

Small Business Administration - Office of Technology. 409 3rd St. SW, Washington, DC 20416. Phone: (202)205-6450; Fax: (202)481-1518; Email: edsel.brown@sba.gov • URL: http://archive. sba.gov/aboutsba/sbaprograms/sbir/index.html • Provides policy for the Small Business Innovation Research Program (SBIR). SBIR is a federal procurement system that provides qualified small business concerns with opportunities to compete for federal research and development awards. Also oversees the Small Business Technology Transfer (STTR) Program. STTR coordinates cooperative research and development activities between small business STTR awardee, nonprofit research institutions, or federally funded research and development centers.

Small Business Innovation Research Program - Small Business Technology Transfer Program. Germantown Bldg., SC-29, 1000 Independence Ave. SW, Washington, DC 20585. Phone: (301)903-5707; Fax: (301)903-5488; Email: sbir-sttr@ science.doe.gov • URL: http://science.energy.gov/ sbir • Private sector commercialization of energy-related innovations derived from Federal research and development; technological innovation; the use small business to meet Federal research and development needs; Phase I funding up to $100,000 for a period of approximately nine months; further funding (up to $750,000 for not more than 24 months) to continue development of promising programs initiated in Phase I; and, finally, follow-on funding for commercial applications of the research or development pursued by small business with non-federal capital, or alternatively, follow-on non-SBIR federal contracts for products or processes desired by the government. to $100,000 for a period of approximately six months; further funding (up to $750,000 for not more than 24 months) to continue development of promising programs initiated in Phase I; and, finally, follow-on funding for commercial applications of the research or development pursued by small business with nonfederal capital, or alternatively, follow-on non-SBIR federal contracts for products or processes desired by the government.

Stanford University - U.S.-Asia Technology Management Center. School of Engineering, 450 Serra Mall, Stanford, CA 94305. Phone: (650)724-0096; Fax: (650)725-9974; Email: rdasher@ stanford.edu • URL: http://asia.stanford.edu • Business and technology trends in advanced electronics, information technology, supply chain management, entrepreneurship in Asia, optoelectronics, nanotechnologies, semiconductor chips, packaging, etc.

Tel Aviv University - Interdisciplinary Center for Technology Analysis and Forecasting. Ramat Aviv, 69978 Tel Aviv, Israel. Phone: 972 3 6407571; Email: tsofer@eng.tau.ac.il • URL: http://ictaf.tau. ac.il/index.asp?lang=eng • Center assists decision makers through forecasting studies on issues of national interest as well as high-tech strategy, and translates findings into short-term decisions. Areas of interest include systems analysis, chemistry, economics, physics, mechanical engineering, electronics, operations research, sociology, statistics, business administration, production engineering, information science, science policy, high-tech strategy, urban planning, space and remote sensing.

U.S. Bureau of Labor Statistics - Office of Productivity and Technology - Foreign Labor Statistics Division. 2 Massachusetts Ave. NE, Ste. 2150, Washington, DC 20212-0001. Phone: (202)691-5654; Fax: (202)691-5679 • URL: http:// www.bls.gov/fls/ • Labor conditions and developments abroad. Research involves the development of

internationally comparable economic-statistical measures covering the labor force and unemployment, productivity, and labor costs. This information is used to assess current economic trends abroad that may affect U.S. performance; inform government and private officials of foreign developments that might affect U.S. policy; review foreign experience for possible application domestically; aid in the appraisal of U.S. competitiveness in foreign and domestic markets; and provide labor information to individuals, corporations, labor unions, and others concerned with foreign investment and development.

University of Alabama - Enterprise Integration Laboratory. Culverhouse College of Commerce & Business Administration, Tuscaloosa, AL 35487-0226. Phone: (205)348-5525; Fax: (205)348-6327; Email: dhale@cba.ua.edu • URL: http://old.cba.ua. edu/mis/research/eil • Sharing, managing, controlling, and coordinating business data, work practices, and networks.

University of Edinburgh - Arts and Humanities Research Council - Research Centre for Studies in Intellectual Property and Technology Law. School of Law, Old College, S Bridge, Edinburgh EH8 9YL, United Kingdom. Phone: 44 131 6502014; Fax: 44 131 6506317; Email: itandip@ed.ac.uk • URL: http://www.law.ed.ac.uk/ahrc/aboutus.aspx • Intellectual property, copyright, patents, technology, commerce, society, information technology, genetics, and medical jurisprudence and ethics.

University of London - Centre for the History of Science, Technology and Medicine. Department of Humanities, Imperial College, S Kensington Campus, London SW7 2AZ, United Kingdom. Phone: 44 20 75945220; Fax: 44 20 75949353; Email: a.warwick@imperial.ac.uk • URL: http:// www3.imperial.ac.uk/historyofscience • History of science, technology, and medicine.

University of Quebec at Montreal - Centre for Interdisciplinary Research on Science and Technology. Succursale Centre-Ville, C.P. 8888, Montreal, QC, Canada H3C 3P8. Phone: (514)987-4018; Fax: (514)987-7726; Email: doray.pierre@ uqam.ca • URL: http://www.cirst.uqam.ca • Economics, management, policy, and history of science and technology.

Washington University in St. Louis - Center for Security Technologies. 1 Brookings Dr., Box 1127, Saint Louis, MO 63130. Phone: (314)935-4767; Fax: (314)935-7500; Email: rsi@wustl.edu • URL: http://www.cst.wustl.edu/ • Systems that provide judgment and control critical to the security of people, objects, and intellectual assets, while considering key factors such as privacy, public policy, and economic impact.

## STATISTICS SOURCES

*Standard & Poor's Industry Surveys.* Standard & Poor's Financial Services L.L.C. • Semiannual. $1,800.00. Two looseleaf volumes. Includes monthly *Supplements.* Provides detailed, individual surveys of 52 major industry groups. Each survey is revised on a semiannual basis. Also includes "Monthly Investment Review" (industry group investment analysis) and monthly "Trends & Projections" (economic analysis).

*U.S. Industry and Trade Outlook.* U.S. Department of Commerce National Technical Information Service. • Annual. Produced by the International Trade Administration, U.S. Department of Commerce, in a "public-private" partnership with DRI/ McGraw-Hill and Standard & Poor's. Provides basic data, outlook for the current year, and "Long-Term Prospects" (five-year projections) for a wide variety of products and services. Includes high technology industries. Formerly *U.S. Industrial Outlook.*

## TRADE/PROFESSIONAL ASSOCIATIONS

Alpha Iota Delta. University of Detroit Mercy, 4001 W McNichols Rd., Detroit, MI 48221. Phone: (313)993-1219; Fax: (313)993-1052; Email: ulfertgw@udmercy.edu • URL: http://www. alphaiotadelta.com • Serves as honor society for men and women in decision sciences and information systems.

Australian Institute of Agricultural Science and Technology. PO Box 576, Sydney, NSW 1585, Australia. Phone: 61 2 94318657; Fax: 61 2 94318677; Email: admin@aginstitute.com.au • URL: http://www.aginstitute.com.au • Provides expert services to its clients and the community, together with ways that these are enhanced through professional development, networking, and representation of the interests of agricultural industries.

BC Innovation Council. 1188 W Georgia St., 9th Fl., Vancouver, BC, Canada V6E 4A2. Phone: 800-665-7222 or (604)683-2724; Fax: (604)683-6567; Email: info@bcic.ca • URL: http://www.bcic.ca • Provides support and access to companies and institutions by using research results, development projects and programs to further enhance in creating innovations.

Clean Technology and Sustainable Industries Organization. 3925 W Braker Ln., Austin, TX 78759. Email: community@ct-si.org • URL: http:// www.ct-si.org • Advances the commercialization and global adoption of clean technologies and sustainable industry practices. Promotes clean technology development. Establishes programs and advocacy for clean technologies and global integration of sustainable industry practices.

Electronic Industry Citizenship Coalition. 1155 15th St. NW, Ste. 500, Washington, DC 20005. Email: info@eicc.info • URL: http://www.eicc.info • Represents global ICT companies and their suppliers. Aims to promote a common code of conduct for the electronics, information and communications technology (ICT) industry. Works to improve environmental and worker conditions.

Energy Storage Council. 3963 Flora Pl., 2nd Fl., Saint Louis, MO 63110. Phone: (314)495-4545; Email: info@energystoragecouncil.org • URL: http://www.energystoragecouncil.org • Promotes research, development and deployment of storage technologies within the energy storage industry. Raises awareness of the importance of storage for the future of America's electricity supply and energy security. Develops policies on key legislative and regulatory issues affecting the energy storage industry.

Environmental Industries Commission. Alliance House, 12 Caxton St., London SW1H 0QL, United Kingdom. Phone: 44 207 2224148 or 44 207 6549942; Email: info@eic-uk.co.uk • URL: http:// www.eic-uk.co.uk • Provides environmental technology equipment and services suppliers with a strong and effective voice to influence the debate on the future of the industry among policy makers in Westminster, Whitehall and Brussels. Promotes constructive cooperation between the regulated, the regulators and the UK's environmental technology suppliers.

Hong Kong Productivity Council. HKPC Bldg., 78 Tat Chee Ave., Hong Kong, Hong Kong, China. Phone: 852 27885678; Fax: 852 27885900 • URL: http://www.hkpc.org • Representatives of management, labor, academia, the professions, and government agencies. Promotes productivity excellence through the provision of integrated support across the value chain of Hong Kong firms. Defines productivity as "the effective use of innovation and resources to increase the value-added content of products and services." Provides services in four major areas: manufacturing technologies, management systems, information technologies, and environmental technologies.

Hospitality Financial and Technology Professionals. 11709 Boulder Ln., Ste. 110, Austin, TX 78726. Phone: 800-646-4387 or (512)249-5333; Fax: (512)249-1533; Email: membership@hftp.org • URL: http://www.hftp.org • Accountants, financial officers and MIS managers in 50 countries working in hotels, resorts, casinos, restaurants, and clubs. Develops uniform system of accounts. Conducts education, training, and certification programs; offers placement service; maintains hall of fame.

Hotel Technology Next Generation. 650 E Algonquin Rd., Ste. 207, Schaumburg, IL 60173. Phone: (847)303-5560; Email: info@htng.org • URL: http://www.htng.org • Promotes collaboration and partnership among hoteliers and technology providers. Serves as the voice of the global hotel community and facilitates the development of technology models for the hospitality industry. Works to increase the effectiveness and efficiency of hotels and creates a healthy ecosystem of technology suppliers.

Information Technology Alliance. 23940 N 73rd Pl., Scottsdale, AZ 85255. Phone: (480)515-2003; Fax: (602)294-2399 • URL: http://www.italliance.com • Represents mid-market technology professionals, consultants, and product/service providers in North America. Aims to create a community where members share information and build relationships that improve the way they do business with their clients. Protects the quality of the profession and promotes public welfare.

Information Technology Services Marketing Association. 91 Hartwell Ave., Lexington, MA 02421-3137. Phone: (781)862-8500; Fax: (781)674-1366; Email: info@itsma.com • URL: http://www.itsma.com • Supports marketing executives who market and sell technology-related services and solutions. Provides research, consulting and training to the world's leading technology, communications, and professional services providers. Facilitates peer sharing and networking opportunities among members.

Israel Advanced Technologies Industries. PO Box 12591, 46733 Herzliya, Israel. Phone: 972 73 7136313; Fax: 972 73 7136314; Email: orit@iati.co.il • URL: http://www.iati.co.il • Promotes the development of the venture capital industry in Israel. Supports and enhances the growth of Israeli high-technology industries. Secures special conditions and privileges for members from service organizations in Israel and abroad.

I.T. Financial Management Association. PO Box 30188, Santa Barbara, CA 93130. Phone: (805)687-7390; Fax: (805)687-7382; Email: info@itfma.com • URL: http://www.itfma.com • Individuals and corporations interested in the financial management of information technology (IT) organizations. Works for the education and improvement of members and the industry. Offers certification in IT financial management. Conducts peer studies, in-house seminars, and chargeback system reviews. Operates educational programs.

TechAssure Association. 1550 17th St., Ste. 600, Denver, CO 80202. Phone: (888)208-8670 • Provides training and education services for risk management professionals that specialize in technology, life sciences and digital media industries. Works with insurance companies to customize policy forms and to improve the underwriting process. Encourages members to share best practices and to discuss ideas and experiences.

Women's High Tech Coalition. c/o MaryClare Fitzgerald, Chief Executive Officer, Dutko Grayling, 100 M St. SE, No. 500, Washington, DC 20003. Phone: (202)479-7141 • URL: http://www.womenshightech.org • Provides resources and opportunities for professional women in the technology industry. Works to create an atmosphere that generates sincere discussions and access to industry leaders both in the private and public sector.

# TECHNOLOGY TRANSFER

## ABSTRACTS AND INDEXES

*Business Periodicals Index Retrospective.* EBSCO Publishing Inc. • 11/year. Quarterly and annual cumulations.

## ONLINE DATABASES

*Wilson Business Abstracts Online.* H.W. Wilson Co. • Indexes and abstracts 600 major business periodicals, plus the *Wall Street Journal* and the business section of the *New York Times.* Indexing is from 1982, abstracting from 1990, with the two newspapers included from 1993. Updated weekly. Inquire as to online cost and availability. (*Business Periodicals Index* without abstracts is also available online.).

## PERIODICALS AND NEWSLETTERS

*Technology Forecasts and Technology Surveys.* Technology Forecasts. • Monthly. $192.00 per year. Newsletter. Information on major breakthroughs in advanced technologies along with forecasts of effects on future applications and markets.

*Technology Transfer Highlights.* Argonne National Laboratory Industrial Technology Development Div. • Description: Provides information on federally-developed technology available for transfer and commercialization.

*Telecom Business.* Primedia Business Magazines. • Monthly. Professional magazine covering the telecommunications industry for carriers, resellers and next generation networks.

## RESEARCH CENTERS AND INSTITUTES

Argonne National Laboratory - Office of Technology Transfer. 9700 S Cass Ave., Bldg. 201, Lemont, IL 60439-4832. Phone: 800-627-2596; Fax: (630)252-5230; Email: partners@anl.gov • URL: http://www.anl.gov/technology/technology-development-and-commercialization • Formerly Industrial Technology Development Center.

California Institute of Technology - Office of Sponsored Research. 1200 E California Blvd., MC 231-15, Pasadena, CA 91125. Phone: (626)395-6219 or (626)395-6073; Fax: (626)795-4571; Email: david.mayo@caltech.edu • URL: http://researchadministration.caltech.edu/osr • Responsible for administrative and financial aspects of extramurally sponsored research conducted by faculty members and graduate students of the Institute.

George Washington University - Center for International Science and Technology Policy. Elliott School of International Affairs, 1957 E St. NW, Ste. 403, Washington, DC 20052. Phone: (202)994-7292; Fax: (202)994-1639; Email: space1@gwu.edu • URL: http://www.gwu.edu/cistp • Research areas include technology transfer.

Massachusetts Institute of Technology - Office of Sponsored Programs. Bldg. E19-750, 77 Massachusetts Ave., Cambridge, MA 02139. Phone: (617)324-9022; Fax: (617)253-4734; Email: mchristy@mit.edu • URL: http://osp.mit.edu • Administers sponsored research program of the Institute, negotiating research contracts, taking care of business and contractual obligations, and serving as liaison with research sponsors.

Office for Sponsored Research. Harvard University, Holyoke Ctr., Rm. 620, 1350 Massachusetts Ave., Cambridge, MA 02138. Phone: (617)495-5501; Fax: (617)496-2524 • URL: http://osp.fad.harvard.edu.

Princeton University - Princeton Forrestal Center. 105 College Rd. E, Princeton, NJ 08540. Phone: (609)452-7720; Fax: (609)452-7485; Email: picus@picusassociates.com • URL: http://www.princetonforrestalcenter.com • Designed to create an interdependent mix of academia and business enterprise.

Rensselaer Polytechnic Institute. Rensselaer Union, 110 8th St., Troy, NY 12180-3590. Phone: (518)276-6000 or (518)276-6344; Fax: (518)276-8728 or (518)276-4887; Email: ads@poly.rpi.edu • URL: http://www.rpi.edu • Serves as a conduit for research interactions between Rensselaer Polytechnic Institute and private companies.

Stanford University - Stanford Research Park. Real Estate Office, Ste. 200, 3160 Porter Dr., Palo Alto, CA 94304. Phone: (650)497-9797; Fax: (650)724-5059; Email: tgriego@stanford.edu • URL: http://lbre.stanford.edu/realestate/research_park • Links research resources of Stanford University with private enterprise.

University of Pennsylvania - Office of Research Services. 3451 Walnut St., Rm. P-221, Philadelphia, PA 19104-6205. Phone: (215)898-7293; Fax: (215)898-9708; Email: epeloso@upenn.edu • URL: http://www.upenn.edu/researchservices • Administers extramurally sponsored research for all departments and research units of the University and handles processing of research applications, financial reporting, and indirect cost proposal preparation.

# TEENAGE MARKET

*See* YOUTH MARKET

# TELECOMMUNICATIONS

*See also* COMMUNICATION SYSTEMS; COMPUTER COMMUNICATIONS; TELEPHONE INDUSTRY

## ABSTRACTS AND INDEXES

*Communication Abstracts: An International Information Service.* Pine Forge Press. • Bimonthly. Institutions, $1,150.00 per year. Provides broad coverage of the literature of communications, including broadcasting and advertising.

*Electronics and Communications Abstracts Journal: Comprehensive Coverage of Essential Scientific Literature.* CSA. • Monthly. $1,665.00 per year. Includes print and online editions.

*Key Abstracts: Telecommunications.* The Institution of Engineering and Technology. • Monthly. $1,138. Provides international coverage of journal and proceedings literature. Published in England by the Institution of Electrical Engineers (IEE).

*NTIS Alerts: Communication.* U.S. Department of Commerce National Technical Information Service. • Biweekly. $130 Individuals per year; domestic/foreign. Covers common carriers, satellites, radio/TV equipment, telecommunication regulations, and related subjects.

## ALMANACS AND YEARBOOKS

*OECD Communications Outlook.* Organisation for Economic Co-operation and Development Publications and Information Center. • Biennial. Provides international coverage of yearly telecommunications activity. Includes charts, graphs, and maps.

## CD-ROM DATABASES

*Authority Computer and Telecommunications Law Library.* Matthew Bender and Company Inc. • Quarterly. Price on request. Full text CD-ROM provides cases, analysis, sample agreements, and other information relating to computer law, telecommunications regulation (cable, broadcasting, satellite, Internet), international computer law, and computer contracts.

*Datapro on CD-ROM: Communications Analyst.* Gartner Inc. • Monthly. Price on application. Provides detailed information on products and services for communications systems, including local area networks and voice systems.

*OECD Statistical Compendium.* Organization for Economic Cooperation and Development. • Semiannual. $1,905.00 per year for 1 to 10 users. CD-ROM contains more than 730,000 monthly, quarterly, and annual time series for OECD countries, 1960 to date. Includes fully searchable data on agriculture, food, economic indicators, national accounts, employment, energy, finance, industry, technology, and foreign trade. Results can be displayed in various forms.

## DIRECTORIES

*African Telecommunications Directory.* Information Gatekeepers Inc. • $495 Individuals. Publication includes: Lists of service providers and equipment providers in 36 African countries in the fields of fiber optics, optical networks, WDM, ADSL, ATM, Internet, high-speed local area networks, wireless, and the emerging telecom markets.

*Asia Pacific Telecommunications Directory.* Business Monitor International Ltd. • $895 Individuals. Covers: 2,438 top telecommunications executives at 893 leading telecommunications companies from Asia Pacific. Entries include: company name and address; phone, fax, email and website address; senior contact personnel; full description of company activity; local company profile; nationality; and ownership status and parentage.

*BPO, Call Center IT, Telecom, Computer Software & Hardware Companies Database, Directory of India.* NIIR Project Consultancy Services. • $200 Individuals CD-ROM. Covers: BPO, call center, telecom, computer software and hardware companies in India. Entries include: Name of companies, address, city, pin code, phone, fax, 2,250 e-mail, 2,350 website and contact person with designation.

*Definitive Directory of Competitive Telecommunications Service Providers.* Advanstar Communications Inc. • Annual. $275 Nonmembers plus $6 shipping. Covers: Hundreds of new and existing competitive telecommunications service providers. Entries include: Name, address, phone, fax, statistical data, company profiles, market research on revenues, services, operating territories.

*Dial-A-Fax Business Directory: World's Largest Resources of Fax Services.* Dial-A-Fax Directories Corp. • $289 plus 4.95 postage. Database covers: Approximately 1,400,000 companies in the United States. Entries include: Name, city, state, phone, fax, Standard Industrial Classification (SIC) code.

*Emerging Europe Telecommunications Directory.* Business Monitor International Ltd. • $895 Individuals. Covers: 1,333 top telecommunications executives at 445 leading telecommunications companies from Emerging Europe. Entries include: parent company head offices, full company name, address, phone and fax numbers, email and website address, senior contact personnel, company description and profile, nationality, and ownership status.

*Kenya Telecom Industry Investment Guide.* International Business Publications, USA. • $99.95 Individuals hardcopy, e-book, CD-ROM. Covers: Kenya Telecom Industry. Entries include: Investment opportunities, regulations, and contacts.

*Latin America and Caribbean Telecommunications Directory.* Business Monitor International Ltd. • $995 Individuals CD. Covers: 2,506 top telecommunications executives at 808 leading telecommunications companies from Latin America and Caribbean. Entries include: parent company head offices, full company name, address, phone and fax numbers, email and website address, senior contact personnel, company description and profile, nationality, and ownership status.

*Long Distance Telephone Services Directory.* InfoGroup Inc. • Annual. Number of listings: 2,403.

Entries include: Name, address, phone, size of advertisement, name of owner or manager, number of employees, year first in "Yellow Pages." Compiled from telephone company "Yellow Pages," nationwide.

*Major Telecommunications Companies of Europe.* Graham & Whiteside. • Annual. $245 softback. Covers: Over 1,500 telecommunications companies in Austria, Belgium, Bulgaria, Croatia, Cyprus, Czech Republic, Denmark, Eire, Estonian Republic, Finland, France, Germany, Greece, Hungary, Israel, Italy, Latvian Republic, Lithuanian Republic, Luxembourg, Netherlands, Norway, Poland, Portugal, Romania, Slovakia, Slovenia, Spain, Sweden, Switzerland, and the United Kingdom involved in the telecommunications industry, including telecommunications companies, equipment suppliers, and Internet companies. Entries include: Company name, address, phone and names and titles of key personnel.

*Major Telecommunications Companies of the Far East & Australasia.* Graham & Whiteside. • Annual. $245 softback. Covers: Over 1,000 telecommunications companies in Australia, Brunei, Cambodia, China, Hong Kong, Indonesia, Japan, Laos, Malaysia, New Zealand, Philippines, Singapore, South Korea, Taiwan, Thailand, and Vietnam involved in the telecommunications industry, including telecommunications companies, equipment suppliers, and Internet companies. Entries include: Company name, address, phone and names and titles of key personnel.

*Major Telecommunications Companies of the World.* Cengage Learning Inc. • Annual. $1,360 Individuals. Published by Graham & Whiteside. Contains detailed information and trade names for more than 5,950 important telecommunications companies in various countries.

*Middle East and Africa Telecommunications Directory.* Business Monitor International Ltd. • $995 Individuals CD. Covers: 1,402 top telecommunications executives on 450 leading telecommunications companies from Middle East and Africa. Entries include: Parent company head offices, full company name, address, phone and fax numbers, email and website address, senior contact personnel, company description and profile, nationality, and ownership status.

*Phone Communication Services Directory.* InfoGroup Inc. • Annual. Number of listings: 5473. Entries include: Name, address, phone, size of advertisement, name of owner or manager, number of employees, year first in "Yellow Pages." Compiled from telephone company "Yellow Pages," nationwide.

*Plunkett's E-Commerce and Internet Business Almanac.* Plunkett Research Ltd. • Annual. $349.99. Contains detailed profiles of 250 large companies engaged in various areas of Internet commerce, including e-business Web sites, communications equipment manufacturers, and Internet service providers. Includes CD-ROM.

*Plunkett's Telecommunications Industry Almanac: Your Reference Source to All Facets of the Telecom Business.* Plunkett Research Ltd. • Biennial. $349.99 Individuals eBook, print and CD-ROM. Covers: 500 of the largest companies involved in telecommunications. Entries include: Name, address, phone, fax, names and titles of key personnel, subsidiary and branch names and locations, financial data, salaries and benefits, description of products/ services, overview of company culture/activities.

*President's Club! Presidents of Computer and Telecommunications Companies Directory.* Ex-IBM Corp. • $95 per issue. Covers: over 2,200 presidents of companies, organizations, or associations involved in the computer and telecommunications industries. Entries include: Company, organization,

or association name, president's name, address, and phone.

*Russian Encyclopedia of Information and Telecommunications: Information on Information.* International Bureau for Information and Telecommunications. • $30. Covers: Approximately 1,500 organizations, 2,500 managers and senior employees in information and telecommunications in Russia. Also includes detailed descriptions of 1,700 electronic databases, 150 telecommunication networks, hosts, and their information resource. Entries include: Company, organization or personal name, address, phone, e-mail, website address, names and titles of key personnel, biographical data for individuals, number of employees, financial data, branch office or subsidiary names and addresses, products or services provided, key data, title of database.

*Telecommunications Directory.* Cengage Learning Inc. • Annual. $993 Individuals. Two volumes: North America and International. Cover national and international voice and data communications networks, electronic mail services, teleconferencing facilities and services, facsimile services, Internet access providers, videotex and teletext operations, transactional services, local area networks, audiotex services, microwave systems/networkers, satellite facilities, and others involved in telecommunications, including related consultants, advertisers/ marketers; associations, regulatory bodies, and publishers. Available as eBook.

*Telehealth Buyer's Guide.* Miller Freeman Inc. • Annual. $10.00. Lists sources of telecommunications and information technology products and services for the health care industry.

*TIA Directory and Desk Reference.* Telecommunications Industry Association. • Lists manufacturers and suppliers of interconnect telephone equipment. Formerly *Multimedia Telecommunications Sourcebook.*

## E-BOOKS

*Encyclopedia of Emerging Industries.* Cengage Learning Inc. • $546 6th edition. Provides detailed information on 140 "newly flourishing" industries. Includes historical background, organizational structure, significant individuals, current conditions, major companies, work force, technology trends, research developments, and other industry facts.

## ENCYCLOPEDIAS AND DICTIONARIES

*Encyclopedia of Communication and Information.* Cengage Learning Inc. • 2003. eBook. Published by Macmillan Reference USA. Provides an overview of universal modes of communication. Inquire about price and availability.

*The Froehlich-Kent Encyclopedia of Telecommunications.* Fritz E. Froehlich and Allen Kent, editors. Taylor & Francis Online. • 18 volumes. $3,510.00. $195.00 per volume. Dates vary. Contains scholarly articles written by telecommunications experts. Includes bibliographies.

## GENERAL WORKS

*tC teleCommunication: Magazine for Business, Technical and Politics.* tC teleCommunication Publishing Group Ltd. • Monthly. €61.03 Individuals. Journal covering economic and political events in the telecommunications market in Germany and worldwide.

## INTERNET DATABASES

*Business 2.0 Web Guide to the Best Business Links.* Business 2.0 Media Inc. Phone: (415)293-4800; Email: support@business2.com • URL: http://www. business2.com/webguide • Web site presents an extensive, searchable directory of links to "the best, most informative, and authoritative web pages." Twenty main categories cover business, finance, career, company information, people, and technology topics, with thousands of subtopics, all linking to Web sites recommended by experienced business researchers. Fees: Free.

*InfoTech Trends.* Data Analysis Group. Phone: (925)462-1202; Fax: (925)462-1225; Email: support@infotechtrends.com • URL: http://www. infotechtrends.com • Web site provides both free and fee-based market research data on the information technology industry, including computers, peripherals, telecommunications, the Internet, software, CD-ROM/DVD, e-commerce, and workstations. Fees: Free for current (most recent year) data; more extensive information has various fee structures. Formerly *Computer Industry Forecasts.*

*Wired News.* Lycos Inc. 400-2 Totten Pond Rd., Waltham, MA 02451-2053. Phone: (781)370-2700 or (415)276-8400; Fax: (781)370-2600 or (415)276-8500; Email: press@lycos.com • URL: http://www. lycos.com • Provides summaries and full-text of "Top Stories" relating to the Internet, computers, multimedia, telecommunications, and the electronic information industry in general. These news stories are placed in the broad categories of Politics, Business, Culture, and Technology. Affiliated with *Wired* magazine. Fees: Free.

## ONLINE DATABASES

*INSPEC.* Institution of Electrical Engineers. • Provides online citations, with abstracts, to the world literature of electrical engineering, electronics, optoelectronics, telecommunications, industrial controls, instrumentation, computer technology, information technology, and physics. Coverage includes more than 4,000 technical and scientific journals from 1969 to date, with weekly updating. (INSPEC is Information Services in Physics, Electronics, and Computing.) Inquire as to online cost and availability.

## OTHER SOURCES

*Telecommunications Regulation: Cable, Broadcasting, Satellite, and the Internet.* Matthew Bender and Company Inc. • Semiannual. $1,747. Four looseleaf volumes. Covers local, state, and federal regulation, with emphasis on the Telecommunications Act of 1996. Includes regulation of television, telephone, cable, satellite, computer communication, and online services. Formerly *Cable Television Law.*

## PERIODICALS AND NEWSLETTERS

*Business Communications Review.* Key3Media Group, Inc. • Monthly. $45.00 per year. Edited for communications managers in large end-user companies and institutions. Includes special feature issues on intranets and network management.

*Communications Daily: The Authoritative News Service of Electronic Communications.* Warren Communications News Inc. • Covers telecommunications, including the telephone industry, broadcasting, cable TV, satellites, data communications, and electronic publishing. Features corporate and industry news.

*Communications News.* Nelson Publishing Inc. • Monthly.

*Communications News: Solutions for Today's Networking Decision Managers.* Nelson Publishing Inc. • Monthly. Free to qualified personnel; others, $84.00 per year. Includes coverage of "Internetworking" and "Intranetworking." Emphasis is on emerging telecommunications technologies.

*Convergence: The Journal of Research Into New Media Technologies.* Reed Elsevier Group plc Reed Business Information. • Monthly. Individuals, $40.00 per year; institutions, $160.00 per year. Covers the merging of communications technologies. Includes telecommunications networks, interactive TV, multimedia, wireless phone service, and electronic information services.

*Electronic Information Report: Empowering Industry Decision Makers Since 1979.* SIMBA Information Inc. • 46 times a year. $649.00 per year.

Newsletter. Provides business and financial news and trends for online services, electronic publishing, storage media, multimedia, and voice services. Includes information on relevant IPOs (initial public offerings) and mergers. Formerly *Electronic Information Week.*

*FCC Report: An Exclusive Report on Domestic and International Telecommunications Policy and Regulation.* Warren Communications News Inc. • 26 times a year. $670.00 per year. Newsletter concerned principally with Federal Communications Commission regulations and policy.

*Fiber Optics and Communications.* Information Gatekeepers Inc. • Monthly. $695.00. Emphasis on the use of fiber optics in telecommunications.

*Harvard Management Communication Letter.* Harvard Business School Publishing. • Description: Provides information and techniques for managers on effective communication.

*Interactive Home: Consumer Technology Monthly.* Jupiter Communications. • Monthly. $625.00 per year; with online edition, $725.00 per year. Newsletter on devices to bring the Internet into the average American home. Covers TV set-top boxes, game devices, telephones with display screens, handheld computer communication devices, the usual PCs, etc.

*International Journal of Communication Systems.* John Wiley and Sons, Inc., Journals Div. • Monthly. $3,378 Institutions. Published in England by John Wiley and Sons Ltd. Formerly *International Journal of Digital and Analog Communication Systems.*

*RCR Wireless News: The Newspaper for the Wireless Communications Industry.* Crain Communications. • Weekly. $64.00 per year. Covers news of the wireless communications industry, including business and financial developments. Formerly *RCR.*

*State and Local Communications Report.* Wolters Kluwer Law and Business. • Biweekly. $645.00 per year. Newsletter. Formerly *Telecommunications Week.*

*Telecommunications.* • Monthly. Free to qualified personnel; others, $145.00 per year. International coverage.

*Telecommunications Policy.* Elsevier. • 11/year. $1,973 Institutions.

*Telecommunications Reports.* • Twice monthly. $2,039.00 per year.

*Teleconferencing Business Magazine: Annual Directory of Teleconferencing Products & Services.* Business Teleconferencing. • Annual. $36. Magazine for news on the industry of teleconferencing.

## RESEARCH CENTERS AND INSTITUTES

Carnegie Mellon University - College of Fine Arts - Studio for Creative Inquiry. 5000 Forbes Ave., Rm. 111, Pittsburgh, PA 15213-3890. Phone: (412)268-3451; Fax: (412)268-2829; Email: mmbm@andrew. cmu.edu • URL: http://studioforcreativeinquiry.org • Research areas include artificial intelligence, virtual reality, hypermedia, multimedia, and telecommunications, in relation to the arts.

International Data Corp. 5 Speen St., Ste. 1, Framingham, MA 01701-4674. Phone: 800-343-4935 or (508)872-8200; Fax: (508)935-4015 or (508)935-4271; Email: idcinfo@idc.com • URL: http://www.idc.com • Private research firm specializing in market research related to computers, multimedia, and telecommunications.

Stanford University - Center for Integrated Systems. Paul G. Allen Bldg., MS 4070, 420 Via Palou Mall, Stanford, CA 94305-4070. Phone: (650)725-3621; Fax: (650)725-0991; Email: rdasher@cis.stanford. edu • URL: http://cis.stanford.edu • Research programs include manufacturing science, design science, computer architecture, semiconductor technology, and telecommunications.

## STATISTICS SOURCES

*Standard & Poor's Industry Surveys.* Standard & Poor's Financial Services L.L.C. • Semiannual. $1,800.00. Two looseleaf volumes. Includes monthly *Supplements.* Provides detailed, individual surveys of 52 major industry groups. Each survey is revised on a semiannual basis. Also includes "Monthly Investment Review" (industry group investment analysis) and monthly "Trends & Projections" (economic analysis).

*U.S. Industry and Trade Outlook.* U.S. Department of Commerce National Technical Information Service. • Annual. Produced by the International Trade Administration, U.S. Department of Commerce, in a "public-private" partnership with DRI/McGraw-Hill and Standard & Poor's. Provides basic data, outlook for the current year, and "Long-Term Prospects" (five-year projections) for a wide variety of products and services. Includes high technology industries. Formerly *U.S. Industrial Outlook.*

## TRADE/PROFESSIONAL ASSOCIATIONS

Competitive Telecommunications Association. 1200 G St., NW, Ste. 350, Washington, DC 20005. Phone: 800-468-7022 or (202)296-6650; Fax: (202)296-7585; Email: rhaisman@comptel.org • URL: http:// www.comptel.org • Formerly Association of Long Distance Telephone Companies.

International Contact Center Benchmarking Consortium. The Benchmarking Network, 4606 FM 1960 W, Ste. 250, Houston, TX 77069-9949. Phone: (281)440-5044; Fax: (281)440-6677; Email: info@ iccbc.org • URL: http://www.iccbc.org • Corporations that manage call centers. Promotes the use of benchmarking, wherein businesses compare their processes with those of their competitors, as a means of improving corporate efficiency and profitability. Facilitates exchange of information among members; conducts target operations, procurement, development, and maintenance studies; identifies model business practices.

# TELECOMMUTING

*See also* COMPUTER COMMUNICATIONS

## CD-ROM DATABASES

*OECD Statistical Compendium.* Organization for Economic Cooperation and Development. • Semiannual. $1,905.00 per year for 1 to 10 users. CD-ROM contains more than 730,000 monthly, quarterly, and annual time series for OECD countries, 1960 to date. Includes fully searchable data on agriculture, food, economic indicators, national accounts, employment, energy, finance, industry, technology, and foreign trade. Results can be displayed in various forms.

## E-BOOKS

*Handbook of Research in Mobile Business: Technical, Methodological, and Social Perspectives.* Cengage Learning Inc. • 2011. eBook. 2 volumes. 2nd edition. Published by Information Science Reference. Provides research and scientific findings in the constantly expanding field of mobile business. 63 chapters.

*Handbook of Research on Virtual Workplaces and the New Nature of Business Practices.* Cengage Learning Inc. • 2008. eBook. Published by Information Science Reference. Compiles authoritative research from 51 scholars from 17 countries, covering the issues surrounding the influx of information technology to the office environment, from choice and effective use of technologies to necessary participants in the virtual workplace.

## INTERNET DATABASES

*Business 2.0 Web Guide to the Best Business Links.* Business 2.0 Media Inc. Phone: (415)293-4800; Email: support@business2.com • URL: http://www.

business2.com/webguide • Web site presents an extensive, searchable directory of links to "the best, most informative, and authoritative web pages." Twenty main categories cover business, finance, career, company information, people, and technology topics, with thousands of subtopics, all linking to Web sites recommended by experienced business researchers. Fees: Free.

*Telecommuting, Teleworking, and Alternative Officing.* Gil Gordon Associates. Phone: (732)329-2266; Fax: (732)329-2703 • URL: http://www.gilgordon.com • Web site includes "About Telecommuting" (questions and answers), "Worldwide Resources" (news groups, publications, conferences), and "Technology" (virtual office, intranets, groupware). Other features include monthly updates and an extensive list of telecommuting/telework related books. Fees: Free.

### PERIODICALS AND NEWSLETTERS

*Desktop Video Communications.* BCR Enterprises, Inc,. • Bimonthly. Free per year. Covers multimedia technologies, with emphasis on video conferencing and the "virtual office."

*The Home Business Report.* The Kerner Group Inc. • Provides information on how to operate a home-based business or work from home. Features real life success stories, how-to articles on marketing, and strategies to keep focused on goals. Recurring features include letters to the editor, interviews, news of research, job listings, book reviews, and notices of publications available.

*Home Office Connections: A Monthly Journal of News, Ideas, Opportunities, and Savings for Those Who Work at Home.* Home Office Association of America. • Monthly. Free to members; non-members, $49.00 per year.

*InterActive Consumers.* MarketResearch.com. • Monthly. $395.00 per year. Newsletter. Covers the emerging markets for digital content, products, and services. Includes market information on telecommuting, online services, the Internet, online investing, and other areas of electronic commerce.

*Telecons.* Applied Business Telecommunications. • Bimonthly. $30.00 per year. Topics include teleconferencing, videoconferencing, distance learning, telemedicine, and telecommuting.

*TeleTrends.* International Telework Association Council. • Quarterly. Newsletter. Price on application.

### RESEARCH CENTERS AND INSTITUTES

Computerized Conferencing and Communications Center. New Jersey Institute of Technology, University Heights, Newark, NJ 07102-1982. Phone: (973)596-3000 • URL: http://www.njit.edu • Research areas include computer conferencing software and computer-mediated communication systems.

# TELEGRAPH

*See* TELECOMMUNICATIONS

# TELEMARKETING

*See also* TELEPHONE SELLING

### ABSTRACTS AND INDEXES

*Business Periodicals Index Retrospective.* EBSCO Publishing Inc. • 11/year. Quarterly and annual cumulations.

### ONLINE DATABASES

*Wilson Business Abstracts Online.* H.W. Wilson Co. • Indexes and abstracts 600 major business periodicals, plus the *Wall Street Journal* and the business section of the *New York Times.* Indexing is

from 1982, abstracting from 1990, with the two newspapers included from 1993. Updated weekly. Inquire as to online cost and availability. (*Business Periodicals Index* without abstracts is also available online.).

### OTHER SOURCES

*Telemarketing Law Guide.* Wolters Kluwer Law & Business CCH. • Contains detailed information on federal do-not-call legislation, various state laws, court decisions, and penalties.

### PERIODICALS AND NEWSLETTERS

*Call Center.* UBM L.L.C. • Monthly. Free to qualified personnel. Emphasis is on telemarketing, selling, and customer service. Includes articles on communication technology. Formerly *Call Center Solutions.*

*CC News: The Business Newspaper for Call Center and Customer Care Professionals.* HME News. • Monthly. Free to qualified personnel; others, $60.00 per year. Includes news of call center technical developments.

*Direct Marketing News.* Haymarket Media Group Ltd. • Monthly. $148 U.S. /year. Includes special feature issues on catalog marketing, telephone marketing, database marketing, and fundraising. Includes monthly supplements, *DM News International*, *DRTV News*, and *TeleServices.*

*Target Marketing: The Leading Magazine for Integrated Database Marketing.* North American Publishing Co. • Monthly. $65.00 per year. Dedicated to direct marketing excellence. Formerly *Zip Target Marketing.*

*Telemarketer.* Actel Marketing. • Semimonthly. $285.00 per year. Newsletter.

*Telephone Selling Report: Providing Proven Sales Ideas You Can Use.* Art Sobczak, editor. Business by Phone Inc. • Bimonthly. $69.00 per year. Newsletter. How-to newsletter providing proven ideas, tips, and techniques for telephone prospecting and selling.

### TRADE/PROFESSIONAL ASSOCIATIONS

Professional Association for Customer Engagement. 8500 Keystone Crossing, Ste. 480, Indianapolis, IN 46240. Phone: (317)816-9336 • URL: http://paceassociation.com • Businesses involved in teleservices, telephone marketing sales, including suppliers, distributors, users, and hardware and software manufacturers; educators and teleservice businesses. Provides for the specific needs of the total telephone services community; assists in understanding and using telephone communications for marketing purposes; sponsors educational programs.

# TELEPHONE ANSWERING SERVICE

### HANDBOOKS AND MANUALS

*Telephone Answering Service.* Entrepreneur Press. • Looseleaf. $59.50. A practical guide to starting a telephone answering service. Covers profit potential, start-up costs, market size evaluation, owner's time required, pricing, accounting, advertising, promotion, etc. (Start-Up Business Guide No. E1148).

### PERIODICALS AND NEWSLETTERS

*TeleCommunicator.* Association of TeleServices International. • Bimonthly. Description: Contains news concerning telephone company, legislative and governmental actions, and Association activities.

### STATISTICS SOURCES

*United States Census of Service Industries.* U.S. Department of Commerce U.S. Census Bureau. • Quinquennial. Various reports available.

### TRADE/PROFESSIONAL ASSOCIATIONS

Association of TeleServices International. 222 S Westmonte Dr., Ste. 101, Altamonte Springs, FL

32714. Phone: 866-896-ATSI; Fax: (407)774-6440; Email: admin@atsi.org • URL: http://www.atsi.org • An organization of telephone answering and voice message services.

# TELEPHONE EQUIPMENT INDUSTRY

### ABSTRACTS AND INDEXES

*Applied Science and Technology Index.* EBSCO Publishing Inc. • 11/year. Indexes a wide variety of English language technical, industrial, and engineering periodicals.

*Science Citation Index.* Thomson Reuters Intellectual Property and Science. • Weekly. Includes *Source Index, Citation Index, Permuterm Subject Index,* and *Corporate Index.* Provides researchers, administrators, faculty, and students with quick, powerful access to the bibliographic and citation information they need to find research data, analyze trends, journals and researchers, and share their findings.

### CD-ROM DATABASES

*Science Citation Index.* Thomson Reuters Intellectual Property and Science. • Weekly. Includes *Source Index, Citation Index, Permuterm Subject Index,* and *Corporate Index.* Provides researchers, administrators, faculty, and students with quick, powerful access to the bibliographic and citation information they need to find research data, analyze trends, journals and researchers, and share their findings.

### DIRECTORIES

*Directory of Asian Importers of Telephone Instruments and Accessories.* EXIM Infotek Private Ltd. • $600 Individuals. Covers: 300 Asian importers of caller ID telephone instruments, CDMA phone, cellular phone accessories and parts, cordless telephone, EPABX systems, GSM mobile phone, handphone accessories, headphone, intercom systems, microphone, microwave components, PABX and intercom equipment, pager alphanumberic, pagers, beepers, telefax equipment, telephone accessories, telephone answering equipment, telephone electronic components, telephone (cables), and used cellular phone. Entries include: Company name, postal address, telephone, fax, e-mail, website, contact person, designation, and product details.

*Directory of European Importers of Telephone Instruments and Accessories.* EXIM Infotek Private Ltd. • $600 Individuals. Covers: 320 European importers of cellular phone, mobile phone accessories, faces for mobile phone, GSM cellular phone, microphone, headphone, wireless phone, Nokia phone, pagers, beepers, telefax equipment, telephone answering equipment, telephone housing, telephonic switching apparatus, wires and cables. Entries include: Company name, postal address, telephone, fax, e-mail, website, contact person, designation, and product details.

*Directory of German Importers of Telephone Instruments and Accessories.* EXIM Infotek Private Ltd. • $200 Individuals. Covers: 40 German importers of mobile phone, cellular phone accessories, microphone, Nokia phone, telefax equipment, and telephone answering equipment. Entries include: Company name, postal address, telephone, fax, e-mail, website, contact person, designation, and product details.

*Directory of SAARC Importers of Telephone Instruments and Accessories.* EXIM Infotek Private Ltd. • $200 Individuals. Covers: 55 SAARC Countries importers of cellular phone accessories and parts, cordless telephone, digital telephone systems, EPABX systems, headphone, intercom systems, PABX and intercom equipment, pagers, beepers, telecommunication products, telefax equipment, telephone accessories, telephone answering equipment, telephone (cables), used auto phone set, and VHF/SSB radio telephone. Entries include: Company name, postal address, telephone, fax, e-mail, website, contact person, designation, and product details.

*Major Telecommunications Companies of the World.* Cengage Learning Inc. • Annual. $1,360 Individuals. Published by Graham & Whiteside. Contains detailed information and trade names for more than 5,950 important telecommunications companies in various countries.

*Plunkett's Telecommunications Industry Almanac: Your Reference Source to All Facets of the Telecom Business.* Plunkett Research Ltd. • Biennial. $349.99 Individuals eBook, print and CD-ROM. Covers: 500 of the largest companies involved in telecommunications. Entries include: Name, address, phone, fax, names and titles of key personnel, subsidiary and branch names and locations, financial data, salaries and benefits, description of products/ services, overview of company culture/activities.

*Telecommunications Directory.* Cengage Learning Inc. • Annual. $993 Individuals. Two volumes: North America and International. Cover national and international voice and data communications networks, electronic mail services, teleconferencing facilities and services, facsimile services, Internet access providers, videotex and teletext operations, transactional services, local area networks, audiotex services, microwave systems/networkers, satellite facilities, and others involved in telecommunications, including related consultants, advertisers/ marketers; associations, regulatory bodies, and publishers. Available as eBook.

*TIA Directory and Desk Reference.* Telecommunications Industry Association. • Lists manufacturers and suppliers of interconnect telephone equipment. Formerly *Multimedia Telecommunications Sourcebook.*

## FINANCIAL RATIOS

*Annual Statement Studies.* Risk Management Association. • Annual. Compiled from over 280,000 financial statements.

*Annual Statement Studies: Industry Default Probabilities and Cash Flow Measures.* Risk Management Association. • Annual. $405 Nonmembers. Serves as a companion volume to the original *Annual Statement Studies.* Gives probability of default estimates on a percentage scale for more than 450 industries. Includes changes in position year-by-year for eight financial statement line items and provides percentage measures of cash flow.

## INTERNET DATABASES

*Manufacturing Profiles.* U. S. Bureau of the Census. Phone: (301)763-4636 or (301)763-4100; Fax: (301)763-4794; Email: webmaster@census.gov • URL: http://www.census.gov/prod/www/abs/mfg-prof.html • The Census Bureau makes available free on PDF (Portable Document Format) an annual consolidation of the entire Current Industrial Report series, presenting "all the data compiled." Contains statistics on production, shipments, inventories, consumption, exports, imports, and orders for a wide variety of manufactured products.

## PERIODICALS AND NEWSLETTERS

*Communications News.* Nelson Publishing Inc. • Monthly.

*Communications News: Solutions for Today's Networking Decision Managers.* Nelson Publishing Inc. • Monthly. Free to qualified personnel; others, $84.00 per year. Includes coverage of "Internetworking" and "Intranetworking." Emphasis is on emerging telecommunications technologies.

*IEEE Communications Magazine.* IEEE - Communications Society. • Monthly. Covers all areas of

communications such as lightwave telecommunications, high-speed data communications, personal communications systems (PCS), ISDN, and more.

*T W I C E: This Week in Consumer Electronics.* Reed Elsevier Group plc Reed Business Information. • 29 times a year. $129.90 per year. Contains marketing and manufacturing news relating to a wide variety of consumer electronic products, including video, audio, telephone, and home office equipment.

*Telephony: Intelligence for the Broadband Economy.* Primedia Business Magazines and Media. • Biweekly. $114.00 per year.

## STATISTICS SOURCES

*Standard & Poor's Industry Surveys.* Standard & Poor's Financial Services L.L.C. • Semiannual. $1,800.00. Two looseleaf volumes. Includes monthly *Supplements.* Provides detailed, individual surveys of 52 major industry groups. Each survey is revised on a semiannual basis. Also includes "Monthly Investment Review" (industry group investment analysis) and monthly "Trends & Projections" (economic analysis).

## TRADE/PROFESSIONAL ASSOCIATIONS

Telecommunications Industry Association. 1320 N Courthouse Rd., Ste. 200, Arlington, VA 22201. Phone: (703)907-7700; Fax: (703)907-7727; Email: gseiffert@tiaonline.org • URL: http://www.tiaonline.org • Serves the communications and IT industry, with proven strengths in standards development, domestic and international public policy, and trade shows. Facilitates business development and opportunities and a competitive market environment; provides a forum for member companies, the manufacturers and suppliers of products and services used in global communications. Represents the communications sector of the Electronic Industries Alliance.

# TELEPHONE INDUSTRY

*See also* TELECOMMUNICATIONS

## DIRECTORIES

*Directory of African Importers of Telephone Instruments and Accessories.* EXIM Infotek Private Ltd. • $400 Individuals. Covers: 120 African Importers of mobile phone, cordless telephone, fax machine, GSM cellular handset, GSM mobile phone, headphone, mobile accessories, telefax equipment, telephone equipment, and telephone systems. Entries include: Company name, postal address, telephone, fax, e-mail, website, contact person, designation, and product details.

*Directory of Australia and New Zealand Importers of Telephone Instruments and Accessories.* EXIM Infotek Private Ltd. • $150 Individuals. Covers: 20 Australian and New Zealand importers of cellular phone accessories and parts, cellular phone camera lens, EPABX systems, GSM phones, handphone accessories, intercom systems, microphones, microwave components, pagers, beepers, telephone headsets, telephone systems, and used mobile phones. Entries include: Company name, postal address, telephone, fax, e-mail, website, contact person, designation, and product details.

*Directory of Middle East Importers of Telephone Instruments and Accessories.* EXIM Infotek Private Ltd. • $350 Individuals. Covers: 110 Middle East importers of mobile phone, microphone, mobile accessories, pagers, beepers, telefax equipment, telephone control unit, and telephone index. Entries include: Company name, postal address, telephone, fax, e-mail, website, contact person, designation, and product details.

*Directory of North American Importers of Telephone Instruments and Accessories.* EXIM Infotek Private

Ltd. • $300 Individuals. Covers: 100 North American importers of beepers, cellular accessories, cellular mobile phone, cellular phone, cordless telephone, GSM phones, headphone, microphone, Nokia phone, pagers, telephone accessories, telephone answering equipment, telephone equipment, and used cellphone. Entries include: Company name, postal address, telephone, fax, e-mail, website, contact person, designation, and product details.

*Directory of South American Importers of Telephone Instruments and Accessories.* EXIM Infotek Private Ltd. • $300 Individuals. Covers: 110 South American importers of mobile phone, mobile phone accessories, microphone, headphone, pagers, telecommunication equipment, telefax equipment, and telephone equipment. Entries include: Company name, postal address, telephone, fax, e-mail, website, contact person, designation, and product details.

*Telecommunications Directory.* Cengage Learning Inc. • Annual. $993 Individuals. Two volumes: North America and International. Cover national and international voice and data communications networks, electronic mail services, teleconferencing facilities and services, facsimile services, Internet access providers, videotex and teletext operations, transactional services, local area networks, audiotex services, microwave systems/networkers, satellite facilities, and others involved in telecommunications, including related consultants, advertisers/ marketers; associations, regulatory bodies, and publishers. Available as eBook.

*The Telephone Industry Directory.* Access Intelligence L.L.C. • $249 U.S., Canada, and Mexico. Covers: 7,000 companies and 14,000 contacts in the telephone industry.

## FINANCIAL RATIOS

*Annual Statement Studies.* Risk Management Association. • Annual. Compiled from over 280,000 financial statements.

*Annual Statement Studies: Industry Default Probabilities and Cash Flow Measures.* Risk Management Association. • Annual. $405 Nonmembers. Serves as a companion volume to the original *Annual Statement Studies.* Gives probability of default estimates on a percentage scale for more than 450 industries. Includes changes in position year-by-year for eight financial statement line items and provides percentage measures of cash flow.

*Industry Norms and Key Business Ratios.* Dun & Bradstreet Inc. • Annual. Five volumes. Covers over 800 kinds of businesses, arranged by Standard Industrial Classification number. More detailed editions covering longer periods of time are also available.

## HANDBOOKS AND MANUALS

*Mergent's Public Utility Manual.* Mergent Inc. • Annual. $1,995.00. Updated weekly online. Contains financial and other information concerning publicly-held utility companies (electric, gas, telephone, water).

## INTERNET DATABASES

*Switchboard.* Switchboard, Inc. Phone: (508)898-8000; Fax: (508)898-1755; Email: webmaster@switchboard.com • URL: http://www.switchboard.com • Web site provides telephone numbers and street addresses for more than 100 million business locations and residences in the U. S. Broad industry categories are available. Fees: Free.

## PERIODICALS AND NEWSLETTERS

*Communications News.* Nelson Publishing Inc. • Monthly.

*Communications News: Solutions for Today's Networking Decision Managers.* Nelson Publishing Inc. • Monthly. Free to qualified personnel; others,

$84.00 per year. Includes coverage of "Internetworking" and "Intrenetworking." Emphasis is on emerging telecommunications technologies.

*FCC Report: An Exclusive Report on Domestic and International Telecommunications Policy and Regulation.* Warren Communications News Inc. • 26 times a year. $670.00 per year. Newsletter concerned principally with Federal Communications Commission reglations and policy.

*Telco Business Report: Executive Briefings on the Bell Operating Companies, Regional Holding Companies and Independent Telcos.* Briefings Publishing Group. • 26 times a year. $759.00 per year. Newsletter. Covers long-distance markets, emerging technologies, strategies of Bell operating companies, and other telephone business topics.

*Telecommunications.* • Monthly. Free to qualified personnel; others, $145.00 per year. International coverage.

*Telecommunications Reports.* • Twice monthly. $2,039.00 per year.

*Telephone Management Strategist.* Buyers Laboratory L.L.C. • Monthly. $125.00 per year. Newsletter. Information on business telecommunications.

*Telephony: Intelligence for the Broadband Economy.* Primedia Business Magazines and Media. • Biweekly. $114.00 per year.

### RESEARCH CENTERS AND INSTITUTES

National Regulatory Research Institute. 8611 2nd Ave., Ste. 2C, Silver Spring, MD 20910. Phone: (301)588-5383 or (301)588-5384; Email: nrri.admin@nrri.org • URL: http://www.nrri.org • Electric, natural gas, water, and telephone utility regulation procedures. Specific topics include gas wellhead price deregulation, power pooling, gas marginal cost pricing, utility operating efficiency, regulatory incentives, retail wheeling, pricing wheeled power, funding nuclear decommissioning, measured rate telephone service, telecommunications competition, small water utility regulation, and electric utility subsidiaries.

### STATISTICS SOURCES

*Annual Statistical Reports of Independent Telephone Companies.* Federal Communications Commission Wireless Telecommunications Bureau. • Annual.

*Phonefacts.* United States Telecom Association. • Annual. Members, $5.00; non-members, $10.00. Presents basic statistics on the independent telephone industry in the U. S.

*Quarterly Operating Data of 68 Telephone Carriers.* Federal Communications Commission Wireless Telecommunications Bureau. • Quarterly.

*Standard & Poor's Statistical Service. Current Statistics.* Standard & Poor's Financial Services L.L.C. • Monthly. $688.00 per year. Includes 10 *Basic Statistics* sections, *Current Statistics Supplements* and *Annual Security Price Index Record.*

*TPG Briefing on Local Exchange Statistics.* Warren Communication News. • Annual. $325.00. Contains statistics on local telephone companies: revenues, expenses, debt, income, advertising, access lines, network usage, etc. Provides "Current Information on Major Competitors.".

*U.S. Industry and Trade Outlook.* U.S. Department of Commerce National Technical Information Service. • Annual. Produced by the International Trade Administration, U.S. Department of Commerce, in a "public-private" partnership with DRI/McGraw-Hill and Standard & Poor's. Provides basic data, outlook for the current year, and "Long-Term Prospects" (five-year projections) for a wide variety of products and services. Includes high technology industries. Formerly *U.S. Industrial Outlook.*

### TRADE/PROFESSIONAL ASSOCIATIONS

Competitive Telecommunications Association. 1200 G St., NW, Ste. 350, Washington, DC 20005. Phone:

800-468-7022 or (202)296-6650; Fax: (202)296-7585; Email: rhaisman@comptel.org • URL: http://www.comptel.org • Formerly Association of Long Distance Telephone Companies.

NCTA: The Rural Broadband Association. 4121 Wilson Blvd., Ste. 1000, Arlington, VA 22203. Phone: (703)351-2000 or (703)351-2030; Fax: (703)351-2001; Email: sbloomfield@ntca.org • URL: http://www.ntca.org • Members are telephone cooperatives and statewide associations.

Organization for the Promotion and Advancement of Small Telecommunications Companies. 2020 K St. NW, 7th Fl., Washington, DC 20006. Phone: (202)659-5990; Email: mks@opastco.org • URL: http://www.opastco.org • Members are small telephone companies serving rural areas. Formerly Organization for the Protection and Advancement of Small Telephone Companies.

Power and Communication Contractors Association. 1908 Mt. Vernon Ave., 2nd Fl., Alexandria, VA 22301. Phone: 800-542-7222 or (703)212-7734; Fax: (703)548-3733; Email: info@pccaweb.org • URL: http://www.pccaweb.org • Contractors engaged in electrical power and communication line construction.

Telecommunications Industry Association. 1320 N Courthouse Rd., Ste. 200, Arlington, VA 22201. Phone: (703)907-7700; Fax: (703)907-7727; Email: gseiffert@tiaonline.org • URL: http://www.tiaonline.org • Serves the communications and IT industry, with proven strengths in standards development, domestic and international public policy, and trade shows. Facilitates business development and opportunities and a competitive market environment; provides a forum for member companies, the manufacturers and suppliers of products and services used in global communications. Represents the communications sector of the Electronic Industries Alliance.

## TELEPHONE SELLING

*See also* TELEMARKETING

### PERIODICALS AND NEWSLETTERS

*Call Center.* UBM L.L.C. • Monthly. Free to qualified personnel. Emphasis is on telemarketing, selling, and customer service. Includes articles on communication technology. Formerly *Call Center Solutions.*

## TELEPHONES

*See* TELEPHONE EQUIPMENT INDUSTRY

## TELEPHONES, MOBILE

*See* MOBILE TELEPHONE INDUSTRY

## TELESCOPES

*See also* OPTICS INDUSTRY

### PERIODICALS AND NEWSLETTERS

*Sky and Telescope: The Essential Guide to Astronomy.* Sky Publishing Corp. • Monthly. $37.95/year. Reports astronomy and space science for amateurs and professionals. Many "how to" features.

## TELETEXT

*See* VIDEOTEX/TELETEXT

## TELEVISION ADVERTISING

*See* RADIO AND TELEVISION ADVERTISING

## TELEVISION APPARATUS INDUSTRY

*See also* TELEVISION ENGINEERING; VIDEO RECORDING INDUSTRY

### DIRECTORIES

*Broadcast Engineering--Equipment Reference Manual.* Penton. • Annual. Publication includes: List of more than 1,400 manufacturers and distributors of communications equipment for radio, television, and recording applications. Database includes: Specifications for major brands of professional broadcast hardware. Entries include: For manufacturers--Company name, address. For distributors and dealers--Company name, address, phone, product or service provided, geographic area covered.

*DV Buyer's Guide.* UBM L.L.C. • Annual. $10.00. A directory of professional video products, including digital cameras, monitors, editing systems, and software.

*EIA Publications Index/EIA Trade Directory.* Electronic Industries Alliance. • Annual. Free.

*Interactive TV Investor Buyer's Guide and Directory.* Paul Kagan Associates, Inc. • Annual. Price on application. (A special issue of the periodical *Convergence*.).

### E-BOOKS

*Encyclopedia of Emerging Industries.* Cengage Learning Inc. • $546 6th edition. Provides detailed information on 140 "newly flourishing" industries. Includes historical background, organizational structure, significant individuals, current conditions, major companies, work force, technology trends, research developments, and other industry facts.

### FINANCIAL RATIOS

*Annual Statement Studies.* Risk Management Association. • Annual. Compiled from over 280,000 financial statements.

*Annual Statement Studies: Industry Default Probabilities and Cash Flow Measures.* Risk Management Association. • Annual. $405 Nonmembers. Serves as a companion volume to the original *Annual Statement Studies.* Gives probability of default estimates on a percentage scale for more than 450 industries. Includes changes in position year-by-year for eight financial statement line items and provides percentage measures of cash flow.

*NARDA's Cost of Doing Business Survey.* North American Retail Dealers Association. • $50 Members. Provides insight into revenue and costs, warranty information, expenses, and asset/liability information.

### INTERNET DATABASES

*Manufacturing Profiles.* U. S. Bureau of the Census. Phone: (301)763-4636 or (301)763-4100; Fax: (301)763-4794; Email: webmaster@census.gov • URL: http://www.census.gov/prod/www/abs/mfg-prof.html • The Census Bureau makes available free on PDF (Portable Document Format) an annual consolidation of the entire Current Industrial Report series, presenting "all the data compiled." Contains statistics on production, shipments, inventories, consumption, exports, imports, and orders for a wide variety of manufactured products.

### PERIODICALS AND NEWSLETTERS

*Convergence: The Journal of Research Into New Media Technologies.* Reed Elsevier Group plc Reed Business Information. • Monthly. Individuals, $40.00 per year; institutions, $160.00 per year. Covers the merging of communications technologies. Includes telecommunications networks, interactive TV, multimedia, wireless phone service, and electronic information services.

*Dealerscope: Product and Strategy for Consumer*

**For publishers' addresses, refer to SOURCES CITED section at the back of the book.**

*Technology Retailing.* North American Publishing Co. • Monthly. $79 /year. Formerly *Dealerscope Consumer Electronices Marketplace.* Provides product information and valuable strategy for consumer technology retailers.

*Robb Report Home Entertaining & Design.* CurtCo Robb Media. • Monthly. $65. Covers "high end" home theaters, audio, video, wireless home networks, and custom installations.

*Smart TV and Sound: Interactive Television and DVD-MP3-Internet Audio and Video-Satellite Television.* York Publishing Inc. • Semiannual. $14.97 per year. Consumer magazine covering WebTV, PC/TV appliances, DVD players, "Smart TV," and other topics relating to interactive television, the Internet, and multimedia. Formerly *Smart TV.*

*Video Technology News.* Access Intelligence L.L.C. • Description: Reports on video technologies from a business point of view. Provides industry analyses and forecasts, reports on new products and emerging media trends. Covers legal and regulatory developments. **Remarks:** Incorporates the former FutureHome Technology News, merged December 1992.

## PRICE SOURCES

*Video and Television.* Orion Research Corp. • Annual. $144 Individuals. Quotes retail and wholesale prices of used video and TV equipment. Original list prices and years of manufacture are also shown.

## STATISTICS SOURCES

*Standard & Poor's Industry Surveys.* Standard & Poor's Financial Services L.L.C. • Semiannual. $1,800.00. Two looseleaf volumes. Includes monthly *Supplements.* Provides detailed, individual surveys of 52 major industry groups. Each survey is revised on a semiannual basis. Also includes "Monthly Investment Review" (industry group investment analysis) and monthly "Trends & Projections" (economic analysis).

## TRADE/PROFESSIONAL ASSOCIATIONS

LCD TV Association. 16055 SW Walker Rd., Ste. 264, Beaverton, OR 97006-4942. Phone: (215)206-6506; Email: membership@lcdtvassociation.org • URL: http://www.lcdtvassociation.org • Aims to help the LCD TV supply chain and retail channel as well as the end customer. Creates and promotes new features and functions for the industry. Provides methods to improve members' products and services.

North American Retail Dealers Association. 222 S Riverside Plz., Ste. 2100, Chicago, IL 60606. Phone: 800-621-0298 or (312)648-0649; Fax: (312)648-1212; Email: nardasvc@narda.com • URL: http://www.narda.com • Firms engaged in the retailing of electronic and electrical devices and components. Promotes and represents members' interests. Makes available services to members including: legal and technical consulting; employee screening; bank card processing; long-distance phone discounts; financial statements analysis; in-store promotion kits; customer check authorization. Advocates for members' interests before federal regulatory bodies; disseminates information on new regulations affecting members. Conducts educational programs.

# TELEVISION BROADCASTING INDUSTRY

*See also* CABLE TELEVISION INDUSTRY; TELEVISION APPARATUS INDUSTRY; TELEVISION ENGINEERING

## ABSTRACTS AND INDEXES

*Communication Abstracts: An International Information Service.* Pine Forge Press. • Bimonthly.

Institutions, $1,150.00 per year. Provides broad coverage of the literature of communications, including broadcasting and advertising.

## BIOGRAPHICAL SOURCES

*Contemporary Theatre, Film & Television.* Cengage Learning Inc. • $338 Individuals. 2012. $308.00 per volume. Previous volumes available. Provides detailed biographical and career information on more than 20,000 currently popular performers, directors, writers, producers, designers, managers, choreographers, technicians, composers, executives, dancers, and critics. eBook also available. Contact for pricing.

## DIRECTORIES

*BIA's Television Yearbook.* BIA/Kelsey. • Annual. $250 Individuals. U.S. Television markets and their inclusive stations, television equipment manufacturers, and related service providers and trade associations.

*Burrelle's Media Directory: Broadcast Media.* BurrellesLuce. • Annual. $550.00. Approximately 48,000 print and electronic media in North America. Provides detailed descriptions, including programming and key personnel.

*Producers Directory.* Hollywood Creative Directory. • Covers: over 1,700 film and TV production companies, studios, networks, and TV shows, and over 7,700 creative executives within those companies. Majority of listings are located in Los Angeles and New York. Entries include: Company name, staff names and titles, address, phone, fax, e-mail address, web site address, company type, studio deals, and select credits.

*Top 30 U.S. Business Media.* • Semiannual. $49. More than 900 editors, reporters, producers, and bookers at 30 major business media outlets.

*Working Press of the Nation.* R.R. Bowker L.L.C. • Annual. $530.00. $295.00 per volume. Three volumes: (1) *Newspaper Directory*; (2) *Magazine and Internal Publications Directory*; (3) *Radio and Television Directory.* Includes names of editors and other personnel.

*World Radio TV Handbook: The Directory of Global Broadcasting.* World Radio TV Handbook. • Annual. Covers: 25,000 radio and television stations worldwide; national regulatory bodies. Database includes: Maps; essays on international broadcasting, list of English-language broadcasts. Entries include: For stations--Name, frequency, address, phone, telex, name and title of contact and key personnel, description of programming. For agencies--Name, address, phone.

## E-BOOKS

*The Business of Entertainment.* Cengage Learning Inc. • 2010. eBook. Covers movies popular music, and television. Includes information on the nuts and bolts of daily life in the industry, including the challenges of digitizing content, globalization, promoting stars and shows, protecting intellectual property, and developing talent.

## FINANCIAL RATIOS

*Annual Statement Studies.* Risk Management Association. • Annual. Compiled from over 280,000 financial statements.

*Annual Statement Studies: Industry Default Probabilities and Cash Flow Measures.* Risk Management Association. • Annual. $405 Nonmembers. Serves as a companion volume to the original *Annual Statement Studies.* Gives probability of default estimates on a percentage scale for more than 450 industries. Includes changes in position year-by-year for eight financial statement line items and provides percentage measures of cash flow.

*Industry Norms and Key Business Ratios.* Dun & Bradstreet Inc. • Annual. Five volumes. Covers over 800 kinds of businesses, arranged by Standard

Industrial Classification number. More detailed editions covering longer periods of time are also available.

## OTHER SOURCES

*FCC Record.* U. S. Government Printing Office. • Semimonthly. $813 U.S. 1 year. Produced by the Federal Communications Commission (www.fcc.gov). An inclusive compilation of decisions, reports, public notices, and other documents of the FCC.

*Telecommunications Regulation: Cable, Broadcasting, Satellite, and the Internet.* Matthew Bender and Company Inc. • Semiannual. $1,747. Four looseleaf volumes. Covers local, state, and federal regulation, with emphasis on the Telecommunications Act of 1996. Includes regulation of television, telephone, cable, satellite, computer communication, and on-line services. Formerly *Cable Television Law.*

*Westlaw Journal Entertainment Industry.* Thomson Reuters Westlaw. • Monthly. *Sports and Entertainment Litigation Reporter.* Provides concise, unbiased coverage of litigation involving such issues as breach of contract, First Amendment, invasion of privacy, unfair competition, misappropriation of funds, and copyright and trademark issues.

## PERIODICALS AND NEWSLETTERS

*Broadcast Investor: Newsletter on Radio-TV Station Finance.* Paul Kagan Associates, Inc. • Monthly. $925.00 per year. Newsletter for investors in publicly held radio and television broadcasting companies.

*Broadcasting and Cable.* NewBay Media, LLC. • 51 times a year. $179.00 per year; includes print and online editions. Formerly *Broadcasting.*

*Call Sheet.* Nielsen Business Media Inc. • 10 times per year. $59.00. per year. Directory, production and casting guide, designed for actors and writers. Formerly *Ross Reports Television.*

*Entertainment Law and Finance.* ALM Media Properties LLC. • Monthly. $485 print and online. Covers contracts, royalties, litigation, copyright, taxation, etc., for the music industry, motion pictures, broadcasting, publishing, video, and related media. (A Law Journal Newsletter, formerly published by Leader Publications.).

*The Hollywood Reporter.* • Daily. $199.00 per year. Covers the latest news in film, TV, cable, multimedia, music, and theatre. Includes box office grosses and entertainment industry financial data.

*International Radio and Television Society Newsletter.* International Radio and Television Society Foundation. • Quarterly.

*Television Digest with Consumer Electronics.* Warren Communications News Inc. • Weekly. $944.00 per year. Newsletter featuring new consumer entertainment products utilizing electronics. Also covers the television broadcasting and cable TV industries, with corporate and industry news.

*Television Quarterly.* Academy of Television Arts and Sciences. • Quarterly. Individuals, $30.00 per year; students, $22.00 per year.

*Television Week.* Crain Communications Inc. • Weekly. $119.00 per year. Formerly *Electronic Media.*

*TV Technology.* IMAS Publishing Group. • Biweekly. $75.00 per year. International coverage available.

*Variety: The International Entertainment Weekly.* Reed Elsevier Group plc Reed Business Information. • Weekly. $199 Individuals print + online. Contains national and international news of show business, with emphasis on motion pictures and television. Includes *Market* and *Special Focus* issues.

## RESEARCH CENTERS AND INSTITUTES

Institute for Telecommunications Studies. School of Telecommunication, 9 S College St., Athens, OH

45701. Phone: (740)593-4866; Fax: (740)593-9184; Email: don.flournoy@ohio.edu • URL: http://www. mediaschool.ohiou.edu • International telecommunications, social impact of mass communication, economic and management aspects of cable, wireless, satellite, broadcast and Internet industries, emerging telecommunication technologies, computer applications, multimedia TV, and training.

Marquette University - Center for Mass Media Research. 1250 W Wisconsin Ave., Milwaukee, WI 53233. Phone: (414)288-6787 or (414)288-3453; Fax: (414)288-3099; Email: robert.griffin@ marquette.edu • URL: http://news.marquette.edu/ experts/center-for-mass-media-research • Conducts social scientific research into the roles, processes, uses, and effects of mass communication among individuals and in society. Applies social science communication theory and research to the investigation and solution of social problems, especially those involving environment, energy, health risks, science, and technology.

## STATISTICS SOURCES

*Standard & Poor's Industry Surveys.* Standard & Poor's Financial Services L.L.C. • Semiannual. $1,800.00. Two looseleaf volumes. Includes monthly *Supplements.* Provides detailed, individual surveys of 52 major industry groups. Each survey is revised on a semiannual basis. Also includes "Monthly Investment Review" (industry group investment analysis) and monthly "Trends & Projections" (economic analysis).

*Television and Cable Factbook.* Warren Communications News Inc. • Annual. $595. Commercial and noncommercial television stations and networks.

*United States Census of Service Industries.* U.S. Department of Commerce U.S. Census Bureau. • Quinquennial. Various reports available.

## TRADE/PROFESSIONAL ASSOCIATIONS

Academy of Television Arts and Sciences. 5220 Lankershim Blvd., North Hollywood, CA 91601. Phone: (818)754-2800 • URL: http://www.emmys. com • Professionals in the television and film industry. Aims to advance the arts and sciences of television through services to the industry in education, preservation of television programs, and information and community relations; to foster creative leadership in the television industry. Sponsors Television Academy Hall of Fame. Maintains library on television credits and historical material, the Television Academy Archives, and archives at UCLA of over 35,000 television programs. Offers internships to students. Holds luncheon and speakers series and meetings on problems of the various crafts.

Alliance for Women in Media. 1760 Old Meadow Rd., Ste. 500, McLean, VA 22102. Phone: (703)506-3290; Fax: (703)506-3266; Email: info@ allwomeninmedia.org • URL: http:// allwomeninmedia.org • Formerly known as the American Women in Radio and Television.

American Sportscasters Association. 225 Broadway, Ste. 2030, New York, NY 10007. Phone: (212)227-8080; Fax: (212)571-0556; Email: inquiry@ americansportscastersonline.com • URL: http:// www.americansportscastersonline.com • Radio and television sportscasters. Sponsors seminars, clinics, and symposia for aspiring announcers and sportscasters. Compiles statistics. Operates speakers' bureau, placement service, hall of fame, and biographical archives. Maintains American Sportscaster Hall of Fame Trust. Is currently implementing Hall of Fame Museum, Community Programs.

Association of Public Television Stations. 2100 Crystal Dr., Ste. 700, Arlington, VA 22202. Phone: (202)654-4200; Fax: (202)654-4236; Email: pbutler@apts.org • URL: http://www.apts.org •

Public television licensees whose goal is to organize efforts of public television stations in areas of planning and research and in representation before the government. Maintains current information on the public television system including such areas as licensee characteristics, financing and industry trends; makes projections on system growth and income. Monitors social, economic and demographic trends that have an impact on public television services. Prepares and disseminates general information about public television to policymaking agencies, the press, and the public.

Corporation for Public Broadcasting. 401 9th St. NW, Washington, DC 20004. Phone: 800-272-2190 or (202)879-9600; Fax: (202)879-9699; Email: oigemail@cpb.org • URL: http://www.cpb.org • Promotes and finances the growth and development of noncommercial radio and television. Makes grants to local public television and radio stations, program producers, and program distribution networks; studies emerging technologies; works to provide adequate long-range financing from the U.S. government and other sources for public broadcasting. Supports children's services; compiles statistics; sponsors training programs.

Media Financial Management Association. 550 W Frontage Rd., Ste. 3600, Northfield, IL 60093. Phone: (847)716-7000; Fax: (847)716-7004; Email: info@mediafinance.org • URL: http://www. mediafinance.org • Members are accountants and other financial personnel in the radio and television broadcasting industries. Formerly Broadcast Financial Management Association.

Media Rating Council. 420 Lexington Ave., Ste. 343, New York, NY 10170. Phone: (212)972-0300; Fax: (212)972-2786; Email: staff@ mediaratingcouncil.org • URL: http://www. mediaratingcouncil.org • Broadcast and cable trade associations, media owners, advertising agencies, cable networks, and national networks including National Association of Broadcasters, Television Bureau of Advertising, Radio Advertising Bureau, Cable Advertising Bureau. Establishes minimum standards for electronic media ratings surveys. Commissions audits by CPA firms of the collection and processing of data gathered by audience measurement services, including A.C. Nielsen, Arbitron, Statistical Research Inc., and Mediafax.

National Association of Black Owned Broadcasters. 1201 Connecticut Ave. NW, Ste. 200, Washington, DC 20036. Phone: (202)463-8970; Fax: (202)429-0657; Email: nabobinfo@nabob.org • URL: http:// www.nabob.org • Black broadcast station owners; black formatted stations not owned or controlled by blacks; organizations having an interest in the black consumer market or black broadcast industry; individuals interested in becoming owners; and communications schools, departments and professional groups and associations. Represents the interests of existing and potential black radio and television stations. Works with the Office of Federal Procurement Policy to determine which government contracting major advertisers and advertising agencies are complying with government initiatives to increase the amount of advertising dollars received by minority-owned firms. Conducts lobbying activities; provides legal representation for the protection of minority ownership policies. Sponsors annual Communications Awards Dinner each March. Conducts workshops; compiles statistics.

National Association of Broadcasters. 1771 N St. NW, Washington, DC 20036. Phone: 800-342-2460 or (202)429-5300 or (202)429-5490; Email: nab@ nab.org • URL: http://www.nab.org • Formerly National Association of Radio and Television Broadcasters.

National Association of Television Program Executives. Phone: (310)857-1621 • URL: http:// www.natpe.org • Formerly National Association of

Television Program Executives.

National Sportscasters and Sportswriters Association. PO Box 1545, Salisbury, NC 28145. Phone: (704)633-4275; Fax: (704)633-2027 • URL: http://nssafame.com • Members are sportswriters and radio/TV sportscasters.

PROMAXBDA. 1522e Cloverfield Blvd., Santa Monica, CA 90404. Phone: (310)788-7600; Fax: (310)788-7616 • URL: http://www.promaxbda.org • Advertising, public relations, and promotion managers of cable, radio, and television stations, systems and networks; syndicators. Seeks to: advance the role and increase the effectiveness of promotion and marketing within the industry, related industries, and educational communities. Conducts workshops and weekly fax service for members. Operates employment service. Maintains speakers' bureau, hall of fame, and resource center with print, audio, and visual materials.

## TELEVISION, CABLE

*See* CABLE TELEVISION INDUSTRY

## TELEVISION ENGINEERING

*See also* TELEVISION APPARATUS INDUSTRY

### DIRECTORIES

*Broadcast Engineering--Equipment Reference Manual.* Penton. • Annual. Publication includes: List of more than 1,400 manufacturers and distributors of communications equipment for radio, television, and recording applications. Database includes: Specifications for major brands of professional broadcast hardware. Entries include: For manufacturers--Company name, address. For distributors and dealers--Company name, address, phone, product or service provided, geographic area covered.

### PERIODICALS AND NEWSLETTERS

*Broadcast Engineering: Journal of Broadcast Technology.* Penton. • 10 times a year. Free to qualified personnel; others, $65.00 per year. Technical magazine for the broadcast industry.

*SHOOT: The Leading Newsweekly for Commercial Production and Postproduction.* Nielsen Business Media Inc. • Weekly. $125 /year. Covers animation, music, sound design, computer graphics, visual effects, cinematography, and other aspects of television and motion picture production, with emphasis on TV commercials.

*SMPTE Motion Imaging Journal.* Society of Motion Picture and Television Engineers. • Monthly. $125 Nonmembers. Peer-reviewed journal containing articles pertaining to new developments in motion picture and television technology; standards and recommended practices; general news of the industry. Formerly *SMPTE Journal.*

*Video Technology News.* Access Intelligence L.L.C. • Description: Reports on video technologies from a business point of view. Provides industry analyses and forecasts, reports on new products and emerging media trends. Covers legal and regulatory developments. **Remarks:** Incorporates the former FutureHome Technology News, merged December 1992.

## TELEVISION, FOREIGN

*See* FOREIGN RADIO AND TELEVISION

## TELEVISION PROGRAMS

### PERIODICALS AND NEWSLETTERS

*Multichannel News.* Reed Elsevier Group plc Reed Business Information. • 51 times a year. $139.00 per year. Covers the business, programming, market and technology concerns of cable television operators and their suppliers.

*The TV Guide.* Gemstar-TV Guide International. • Weekly. $46.28 per year.

**TRADE/PROFESSIONAL ASSOCIATIONS**

National Association of Television Program Executives. Phone: (310)857-1621 • URL: http://www.natpe.org • Formerly National Association of Television Program Executives.

## TELEVISION RECORDING

See VIDEO RECORDING INDUSTRY

## TELEVISION REPAIR INDUSTRY

See RADIO AND TELEVISION REPAIR INDUSTRY

## TELEVISION, SATELLITE

See COMMUNICATIONS SATELLITES

## TELEVISION STATIONS

See TELEVISION BROADCASTING INDUSTRY

## TELLER MACHINES

See BANK AUTOMATION

## TEMPORARY EMPLOYEES

**ABSTRACTS AND INDEXES**

*Business Periodicals Index Retrospective.* EBSCO Publishing Inc. • 11/year. Quarterly and annual cumulations.

**FINANCIAL RATIOS**

*Annual Statement Studies.* Risk Management Association. • Annual. Compiled from over 280,000 financial statements.

*Annual Statement Studies: Industry Default Probabilities and Cash Flow Measures.* Risk Management Association. • Annual. $405 Nonmembers. Serves as a companion volume to the original *Annual Statement Studies.* Gives probability of default estimates on a percentage scale for more than 450 industries. Includes changes in position year-by-year for eight financial statement line items and provides percentage measures of cash flow.

**HANDBOOKS AND MANUALS**

*Temporary Help Service.* Entrepreneur Press. • Looseleaf. $59.50. A practical guide to starting an employment agency for temporary workers. Covers profit potential, start-up costs, market size evaluation, owner's time required, site selection, lease negotiation, pricing, accounting, advertising, promotion, etc. (Start-Up Business Guide No. E1189.).

**ONLINE DATABASES**

*Wilson Business Abstracts Online.* H.W. Wilson Co. • Indexes and abstracts 600 major business periodicals, plus the *Wall Street Journal* and the business section of the *New York Times.* Indexing is from 1982, abstracting from 1990, with the two newspapers included from 1993. Updated weekly. Inquire as to online cost and availability. (*Business*

*Periodicals Index* without abstracts is also available online.).

**OTHER SOURCES**

*Contingent Workforce: Business and Legal Strategies.* ALM Media Properties LLC. • $550 print and online. Covers the legal, employee benefit, and taxation aspects of alternative work arrangements (temporary employees, independent contractors, outsourcing). (Law Journal Press).

**PERIODICALS AND NEWSLETTERS**

*Working Options.* Association of Part-Time Professionals. • Bimonthly. Description: Advocates alternative work schedules, particularly part-time employment for professionals. Topics include job sharing, older workers, personnel policies, employee benefits, insurance, chapter news, and legislative news. Also provides how-to information on part-time employment and profiles employees and employers who have used flexible work schedules and part-time employment to their advantage. Recurring features include news about the Association and a column titled Point of View, the Executive Director's Corner and Members' Mail Box.

**TRADE/PROFESSIONAL ASSOCIATIONS**

American Staffing Association. 277 S Washington St., Ste. 200, Alexandria, VA 22314-3675. Phone: (703)253-2020; Fax: (703)253-2053; Email: asa@americanstaffing.net • URL: http://www.americanstaffing.net/index.cfm • Promotes and represents the staffing industry through legal and legislative advocacy, public relations, education, and the establishment of high standards of ethical conduct.

## TENNIS INDUSTRY

**PERIODICALS AND NEWSLETTERS**

*Tennis Industry.* Tennis Industry Association. • Bimonthly. $22.00 per year. Edited for retailers serving the "serious tennis enthusiast." Provides news of apparel, rackets, equipment, and court construction.

## TERMINATION OF EMPLOYMENT

See DISMISSAL OF EMPLOYEES

## TESTING OF PRODUCTS

See QUALITY OF PRODUCTS

## TEXTILE DESIGN

See also TEXTILE INDUSTRY

**ABSTRACTS AND INDEXES**

*Textile Technology Index™.* EBSCO Publishing Inc. • Monthly. $545 Individuals. Includes indexing and abstracts for more than 470 periodicals.

**DIRECTORIES**

*Oferta Exportable del Sector Textil de la Confeccion, Colombia.* The Export Promotion Fund, Proexpo. • Covers: Textiles and clothing manufacturers in Columbia. Entries include: Company name, address, phone, number of employees, type of product exported, export capacity, name of contact person.

**ONLINE DATABASES**

*Textile Technology Index™.* EBSCO Publishing Inc. • Monthly. $545 Individuals. Includes indexing and abstracts for more than 470 periodicals.

*World Textiles.* Elsevier. • Provides abstracting and indexing from 1970 of worldwide textile literature

(periodicals, books, pamphlets, and reports). Includes U. S., European, and British patent information. Updating is monthly. Inquire as to online cost and availability.

## TEXTILE FIBERS, SYNTHETIC

See SYNTHETIC TEXTILE FIBER INDUSTRY

## TEXTILE INDUSTRY

**ABSTRACTS AND INDEXES**

*AATCC Review.* American Association of Textile Chemists and Colorists. • Monthly. $650 Individuals print + online. Monthly magazine for professionals in the textile wet processing and dyestuff industries. Formerly Textile Chemist and Colorist and American Dyestuff Reporter.

*Textile Technology Index™.* EBSCO Publishing Inc. • Monthly. $545 Individuals. Includes indexing and abstracts for more than 470 periodicals.

*World Textile Abstracts.* Elsevier. • $2,609 Institutions, other countries. Digests of articles published in the world's textile literature. Includes subscription to *World Textile Digest.*

**CD-ROM DATABASES**

*OECD Statistical Compendium.* Organization for Economic Cooperation and Development. • Semiannual. $1,905.00 per year for 1 to 10 users. CD-ROM contains more than 730,000 monthly, quarterly, and annual time series for OECD countries, 1960 to date. Includes fully searchable data on agriculture, food, economic indicators, national accounts, employment, energy, finance, industry, technology, and foreign trade. Results can be displayed in various forms.

**DIRECTORIES**

*All India Textile Exporters and Manufacturers.* NIIR Project Consultancy Services. • $100 Individuals CD-ROM. Covers: 4,000 textile exporters and manufacturers in India. Entries include: Company name, contact person name, email (wherever available).

*Directory of American Manufacturers & Exporters of Machinery for Textile & Knitting Industry.* EXIM Infotek Private Ltd. • $10 Individuals. Covers: 110 American manufacturers & exporters of dyeing machinery, knitting & braiding machinery, man-made fiber toe cutters, textile & printing machinery, textile machinery, weaving machinery. Entries include: Company name, postal address, city, country, phone, fax, e-mail & websites, contact person, designation, products detail.

*Directory of Chinese Manufacturers & Exporters of Textiles & Fabrics.* EXIM Infotek Private Ltd. • $30 Individuals. Covers: 380 Chinese manufacturers and exporters of acrylic fabric, cloth, cotton fabrics, cotton textiles, dyed fabrics, fabrics-blended, fabrics-grey, fabrics, fabrics for industrial use, fabrics-denim, fabrics-silk, garment fabrics, industrial cloths, jacquard fabrics, knitted fabrics, linens, non-woven fabrics, polyester cloth, polyester fabrics, printed fabrics, pure silk, rayon products, silk, silk products, silk velvet, spinning fabrics, synthetic textiles, textile fabrics, textile materials, textile products, textile raw material and products, textiles, textiles accessories, tricot fabrics, woolen fabric garments, woolen fabrics, worsted fabrics, and woven fabrics. Entries include: Company name, postal address, city, country, phone, fax, e-mail and websites, contact person, designation, and product details.

*Directory of Japanese Manufacturers & Exporters of Cotton, Silk, Wool Raw & Waste.* EXIM Infotek Private Ltd. • $5 Individuals. Covers: 20 Japanese manufacturers and exporters of cotton, cotton products, felt, wool and wool products. Entries include: Company name, postal address, city, country, phone, fax, e-mail and websites, contact person, designation, and product details.

*Directory of Japanese Manufacturers & Exporters of Textile & Fabrics.* EXIM Infotek Private Ltd. • $10 Individuals. Covers: 80 Japanese manufacturers and exporters of chenille, clothing and textile products, cords and tassels, core fabrics, dyed fabrics, fabrics, knitted fabrics, net and tulle, non woven fabrics, PTFE coated glass fiber fabrics, silk, silk products, textile and its articles, textile piece goods, textile products, textiles, and woven fabrics. Entries include: Company name, postal address, city, country, phone, fax, e-mail and websites, contact person, designation, and product details.

*Directory of SAARC Importers of Zipper and Garment Accessories.* EXIM Infotek Private Ltd. • $250 Individuals. Covers: 90 SAARC Countries importers of badges and crests, buckles, buttons, eyelets, fusing multiflexible, garment accessories, labels (textile), ladies garment accessories, leather hardware, needles, sewing notions/zippers/buttons, shirt clips, stitching needles, and zipper. Entries include: Company name, postal address, telephone, fax, e-mail, website, contact person, designation, and product details.

*Directory of South Korean Manufacturers & Exporters of Machinery for Textile and Knitting Industry.* EXIM Infotek Private Ltd. • $15 Individuals. Covers: 150 South Korean manufacturers and exporters of beam brakes and discs for textile machinery, belts/hoses/webbing-textile, bobbins for textile industry, carpet and tapestry looms, cotton preparation machinery and equipment, felt and non-woven fabric making machinery, knitting machinery and attachments, lace and net making machinery, manmade fiber production and processing plants, ribbon and trim making machinery, silk and schappe preparation machinery and equipment, sleeves and strips for spinning mills, textile dyeing and boiling machinery/equipment, textile finishing machinery and equipment, textile machinery, textile machinery parts, textile printing machinery and equipment, textile printings, textile spinning and twisting machinery, textile washing/mercerizing machinery and equipment, textile waste processing, textile waste processing machinery and equipment, textile weaving machinery parts/accessories, textile weaving machinery/looms, textile winding and reeling machinery, weaving machines, yarn preparation machinery/equipment, and yarn tensioners. Entries include: Company name, postal address, city, country, telephone, fax, e-mail and websites, contact person, designation, and product details.

*Directory of South Korean Manufacturers & Exporters of Textile & Fabrics.* EXIM Infotek Private Ltd. • $30 Individuals. Covers: 390 South Korean manufacturers and exporters of dyeing and finishing for fabrics and textile goods, fabric-cotton for furnishing, fabrics for industrial use, fabrics-cotton, fabrics-hemp/jute/paper, fabric-silk, fabrics-knitted, fabrics-linen, fabrics-manmade fiber, fabrics-non woven, felts/felted fabrics, net and tulle, textiles, velvet items, wadding and flock textile for industrial use, and woolen fabrics. Entries include: Company name, postal address, city, country, phone, fax, e-mail and websites, contact person, designation, and product details.

*Directory of Taiwanese Manufacturers & Exporters of Cotton, Silk, Wool Raw & Waste.* EXIM Infotek Private Ltd. • $5 Individuals. Covers: 20 Taiwanese manufacturers and exporters of raw cotton and vegetable textile fiber, raw wool and other animal fibers. Entries include: Company name, postal address, city, country, phone, fax, e-mail and websites, contact person, designation, and product details.

*Directory of Taiwanese Manufacturers & Exporters*

*of Textile & Fabrics.* EXIM Infotek Private Ltd. • $30 Individuals. Covers: 410 Taiwanese manufacturers and exporters of clothing and textile products, cotton fabrics, dyeing and finishing for fabrics and textile goods, fabric-cotton for furnishing, fabrics, fabrics for industrial use, fabrics-cotton, fabrics-hemp/jute/paper, fabric-silk, fabrics-knitted, fabrics-linen, fabrics-manmade fiber, fabrics-non woven, felts/felted fabrics, garment fabrics, knitted fabrics, knitted fabrics-pile/plush, net and tulle, non woven fabrics, polyester cloth, reflective fabrics, textiles, wadding and flock textiles for industrial use, and woolen fabrics. Entries include: Company name, postal address, city, country, phone, fax, e-mail and websites, contact person, designation, and product details.

*The International Directory of Importers--Textiles & Fabrics Importers.* Interdata. • $260 Individuals print. Covers: 3,600 international firms importing textiles and fabrics. Entries include: Company name and address, contact person, email, number of employees, year established, phone and telefaxes, business activity, bank references, as well as a listing of textiles and fabrics currently being imported.

*Textile World Blue Book.* RentPath Inc. • Annual. $160.00. Provides information on more than 5,200 textile mills in the U.S., Canada, and Mexico, including number of employees and names of about 17,000 key personnel. Also provides data on 2,500 suppliers of equipment and products for textile mills. Also known as *Official North American Textile World Blue Book,* formerly *Textile Red Book.*

## E-BOOKS

*Encyclopedia of American Industries.* Cengage Learning Inc. • 2011. $807.00. 6th edition. Three volumes. Volume one is Manufacturing Industries and volume two is Service and Non-Manufacturing Industries. Provides the history, development, and recent status of approximately 1,000 industries. Includes statistical graphs, with industry and general indexes. Also available as eBook.

## FINANCIAL RATIOS

*Quarterly Financial Report for Manufacturing, Mining, Trade, and Selected Service Industries.* U.S. Federal Trade Commission and U.S. Securities and Exchange Commission. U.S. Census Bureau Foreign Trade Division. • Quarterly. Quarterly. Report on financial results of U.S. corporations.

## INTERNET DATABASES

*Business 2.0 Web Guide to the Best Business Links.* Business 2.0 Media Inc. Phone: (415)293-4800; Email: support@business2.com • URL: http://www.business2.com/webguide • Web site presents an extensive, searchable directory of links to "the best, most informative, and authoritative web pages." Twenty main categories cover business, finance, career, company information, people, and technology topics, with thousands of subtopics, all linking to Web sites recommended by experienced business researchers. Fees: Free.

*Fedstats.* Federal Interagency Council on Statistical Policy. Phone: (202)395-7254 • URL: http://www.fedstats.gov • Web site features an efficient search facility for full-text statistics produced by more than 100 federal agencies, including the Census Bureau, the Bureau of Economic Analysis, and the Bureau of Labor Statistics. Boolean searches can be made within one agency or for all agencies combined. Links are offered to international statistical bureaus, including the UN, IMF, OECD, UNESCO, Eurostat, and 20 individual countries. Fees: Free.

*FreeLunch.com.* Economy.com, Inc. Phone: (610)696-8700; Fax: (610)696-1678 • URL: http://www.freelunch.com • Web site provides free access to more than 200 million economic and financial data series, covering industry, demographics, labor markets, prices, retail sales, government spending, trade, interest rates, housing starts, the stock market,

etc. Data is available in either chart or table form. Searching is offered. Free, but registration required. Economy.com, Inc. also offers fee-based economic analysis at *The Dismal Scientist* site (www.dismal.com).

*Manufacturing Profiles.* U. S. Bureau of the Census. Phone: (301)763-4636 or (301)763-4100; Fax: (301)763-4794; Email: webmaster@census.gov • URL: http://www.census.gov/prod/www/abs/mfg-prof.html • The Census Bureau makes available free on PDF (Portable Document Format) an annual consolidation of the entire Current Industrial Report series, presenting "all the data compiled." Contains statistics on production, shipments, inventories, consumption, exports, imports, and orders for a wide variety of manufactured products.

## ONLINE DATABASES

*Textile Technology Index™.* EBSCO Publishing Inc. • Monthly. $545 Individuals. Includes indexing and abstracts for more than 470 periodicals.

*World Textiles.* Elsevier. • Provides abstracting and indexing from 1970 of worldwide textile literature (periodicals, books, pamphlets, and reports). Includes U. S., European, and British patent information. Updating is monthly. Inquire as to on-line cost and availability.

## PERIODICALS AND NEWSLETTERS

*DNR: The Men's Fashion Retail Textile Authority.* Fairchild Publications. • Daily. $85.00 per year. Formerly *Daily News Record.*

*EMB: Embroidery/Monogram Business.* EMB. • Monthly. Trade magazine for the embroidery industry.

*International Dyer.* World Textile Publications Ltd. • Monthly. $90.00 per year.

*International Textile Bulletin: Dyeing-Printing-Finishing Edition.* ITS Publishing, International Textile Service. • Quarterly. $170.00 per year. Editions in Chinese, English, French, German, Italian and Spanish.

*International Textile Bulletin: Nonwovens and Industrial Textiles Edition.* ITS Publishing, International Textile Service. • Quarterly. $170.00 per year. Editions in Chinese, English, French, German, Italian and Spanish.

*International Textile Bulletin: Yarn and Fabric Forming Edition.* ITS Publishing, International Textile Service. • Quarterly. $170.00 per year. Editions in Chinese, English, French, German, Italian and Spanish.

*International Textiles: Information and Inspiration.* Textile Institute. Benjamin Dent & Company Ltd. • 10 times a year. $220.00 per year. Text in English, French and German; supplement in Japanese.

*Journal of Natural Fibers.* The Haworth Press Inc. • Quarterly. $400.00 per year to libraries; $45.00 per year to individuals. Covers applications, technology, research, and world markets relating to fibers from silk, wool, cotton, flax, hemp, jute, etc. Previously *Natural Fibres,* published annually.

*Textile Horizons: Providing Essential Reading for All Present and Future Decision Makers in Textiles and Fashion Worldwide.* World Textile Publications Ltd. • Bimonthly. $115.00 per year.

*Textile Research Journal.* TRI/Princeton. • Monthly. Individuals, $325.00 per year; college and university libraries, $500.00 per year.

*Textile World.* Biilian Publishing Inc. • Monthly. Free to qualified personnel.

## RESEARCH CENTERS AND INSTITUTES

Department of Science and Technology - Philippine Textile Research Institute. General Santos Ave., Bicutan, Taguig City, Philippines. Phone: 63 2 8371325; Fax: 63 2 8371325; Email: carlos@dost.gov.ph • URL: http://www.ptri.dost.gov.ph • Applied research and development on textiles focusing on judicious utilization of fibrous materials and auxiliaries from indigenous resources, improving and/or inventing textile machinery, processes, and production methods for the Philippine textile, garment and allied industry. Areas of study include indigenous fibers, natural dyes, sericulture, processes, tool and machine development.

Institute of Textile Technology. College of Textiles, Box 8301, N Carolina State University, 2401 Research Dr., Raleigh, NC 27695-8301. Phone: (919)513-7583; Fax: (888)348-3512; Email: wgoneal@itt.edu • URL: http://www.itt.edu • Textile materials, processes, and technology, with an emphasis on processing, instrumentation, statistical quality control, and testing of raw materials and finished products. Special attention given to yarn manufacture, carding, finishing operations, operations research applications, computer applications to manufacturing, techniques for evaluation of fiber quality, chemical treatment of raw materials, mechanical blending of fibers, environmental and energy conservation, methods of improving fabric finishes, applications of statistical methods, simulation, expert systems, processing, and interrelation of production, costs, and quality in yarn and fabric manufacture.

Textile Materials Technology. Philadelphia University, 4201 Henry Ave., Philadelphia, PA 19144. Phone: (215)951-2700; Fax: (215)951-2651; Email: admissions@philau.edu • URL: http://www.philau.edu/textilemat • Many research areas, including industrial and nonwoven textiles.

## STATISTICS SOURCES

*Survey of Current Business.* U. S. Government Printing Office. • Published by Bureau of Economic Analysis, U. S. Department of Commerce. Presents a wide variety of business and economic data.

# TEXTILE MACHINERY

*See also* MACHINERY; TEXTILE INDUSTRY

## DIRECTORIES

*Directory of Chinese Manufacturers & Exporters of Machinery for Textile & Knitting Industry.* EXIM Infotek Private Ltd. • $5 Individuals. Covers: 40 Chinese manufacturers and exporters of arrow-shaft looms, drying machines, knitting machines, textile machinery, and textile machinery parts. Entries include: Company name, postal address, city, country, phone, fax, e-mail and websites, contact person, designation, and product details.

*Directory of Japanese Manufacturers & Exporters of Machinery for Textile & Knitting Industry.* EXIM Infotek Private Ltd. • $5 Individuals. Covers: 20 Japanese manufacturers and exporters of dyeing machines, knitting machines, knitting needles, spindle machines, textile machinery, and textile machinery parts. Entries include: Company name, postal address, city, country, phone, fax, e-mail and websites, contact person, designation, and product details.

*Textile Month.* Reed Business Information. • Biennial. $4. Covers: United Kingdom companies representing overseas manufacturers of textile machinery. Entries include: Company name, address, phone, telex, key personnel, overseas contacts, types of machinery handled.

## RESEARCH CENTERS AND INSTITUTES

Institute of Textile Technology. College of Textiles, Box 8301, N Carolina State University, 2401 Research Dr., Raleigh, NC 27695-8301. Phone: (919)513-7583; Fax: (888)348-3512; Email: wgoneal@itt.edu • URL: http://www.itt.edu • Textile materials, processes, and technology, with an emphasis on processing, instrumentation, statistical quality control, and testing of raw materials and

finished products. Special attention given to yarn manufacture, carding, finishing operations, operations research applications, computer applications to manufacturing, techniques for evaluation of fiber quality, chemical treatment of raw materials, mechanical blending of fibers, environmental and energy conservation, methods of improving fabric finishes, applications of statistical methods, simulation, expert systems, processing, and interrelation of production, costs, and quality in yarn and fabric manufacture.

## STATISTICS SOURCES

*U.S. Industry and Trade Outlook.* U.S. Department of Commerce National Technical Information Service. • Annual. Produced by the International Trade Administration, U.S. Department of Commerce, in a "public-private" partnership with DRI/McGraw-Hill and Standard & Poor's. Provides basic data, outlook for the current year, and "Long-Term Prospects" (five-year projections) for a wide variety of products and services. Includes high technology industries. Formerly *U.S. Industrial Outlook.*

## TRADE/PROFESSIONAL ASSOCIATIONS

American Textile Machinery Association. 201 Park Washington Ct., Falls Church, VA 22046. Phone: (703)538-1789; Email: info@atmanet.org • URL: http://www.atmanet.org • Manufacturers of capital equipment for textile manufacture and interested individuals from academia, industry, banking, transportation, insurance, engineering, textiles, and other industries.

# TEXTILE MILLS

*See* TEXTILE INDUSTRY

# TEXTILES, HOME

*See* LINEN INDUSTRY

# TEXTILES, INDUSTRIAL

*See* INDUSTRIAL FABRICS INDUSTRY

# TEXTILES, NONWOVEN

*See* NONWOVEN FABRICS INDUSTRY

# THEATER MANAGEMENT

## DIRECTORIES

*Entertainment Sourcebook: An Insider's Guide on Where to Find Everything.* Applause Theatre & Cinema Books. • Annual. $45.00. Compiled by the Association of Theatrical Artists and Craftspeople (www.entertainmentsourcebook.com/ATAC.htm). Lists more than 5,000 sources of theatrical and entertainment supplies and services, such as props, costumes, publicity agencies, scenic shops, amusement park equipment, audio/video products, balloons, wigs, make-up, magic supplies, etc.

*The Grey House Performing Arts Directory.* Grey House Publishing. • Annual. $250 Individuals Softcover. Covers: More than 8,500 dance companies, instrumental music programs, opera companies, choral groups, theatre companies, performing arts series, and performing arts facilities. Database includes: Information resources section covering hundreds of performing arts associations, publications, and Web sites. Entries include: Mailing address, telephone and fax numbers, e-mail addresses, Web sites, mission statement, key management contacts, and facility information such as capacity, season, and attendance.

## GENERAL WORKS

*Business in the Arts Award Brochures.* Business Committee for the Arts. • $4 plus shipping and handling. Presents highlights of theatre-support programs developed by businesses receiving the national Business in the Arts Awards.

## PERIODICALS AND NEWSLETTERS

*Entertainment Design: The Art and Technology of Show Business.* Primedia Business Magazines. • Monthly. $34.97 per year. Contains material on performing arts management, staging, scenery, costuming, etc. Supersedes *TCI - Theatre Crafts International.*

*Facility Manager.* International Association of Venue Managers. • Quarterly. Free to members; non-members, $55.00 per year.

*In Focus.* Lighthouse International. • Description: Reaches visually handicapped children through stories, poems, and drawings contributed by young readers. Covers subjects of interest to youngsters, especially those related to their experiences and hopes for the future. Also includes puzzles, contests, and items of interest to parents and educators, such as new book and symposium announcements.

## RESEARCH CENTERS AND INSTITUTES

City University of New York - Martin E. Segal Theatre Center. 365 5th Ave., New York, NY 10016-4309. Phone: (212)817-1860; Fax: (212)817-1562; Email: mestc@gc.cuny.edu • URL: http://thesegalcenter.org • Theatre arts, including studies of theatre, dance, and film as independent and inter-related arts. Current projects focus on publishing journals on American, Slavic, Russian, Western European, and East European theatre, drama, and film; and translations of foreign plays into English.

International Theatre Studies Center. University of Kansas, 339 Murphy Hall, 1530 Naismith Dr., Rm. 356, Lawrence, KS 66045. Phone: (785)864-3511.

Ohio State University - Jerome Lawrence and Robert E. Lee Theatre Research Institute. 119 Thompson Library, 1858 Neil Ave. Mall, Columbus, OH 43210-1230. Phone: (614)292-6614 or (614)292-9606; Fax: (614)688-8417; Email: theatreinst@osu.edu • URL: http://library.osu.edu/find/collections/theatre-research-institute • Theatrical activities in western Europe from 15th-19th centuries, especially festivals, theater architecture and machinery designs, costume designs, commedia dell'arte materials from 19th and 20th centuries, American and English promptbooks, and general theater and dance material from 19th, 20th and 21st centuries. Archives of American Theatre Companies and individual playwrights. Provides primary materials to students and scholars for research and publication, including doctoral work. Arranges exhibitions of materials.

University of Wisconsin - Madison - Wisconsin Historical Society - Wisconsin Center for Film and Theater Research. 816 State St., Madison, WI 53706-1417. Phone: (608)264-6466 or (608)264-6467; Fax: (608)264-6472; Email: askmovies@wisconsinhistory.org • URL: http://www.wisconsinhistory.org/Content.aspx?dsNav=N:4294963828-4294963805&dsRecordDetails=R:CS4075 • Studies the performing arts in America, including theater, cinema, radio, and television.

## TRADE/PROFESSIONAL ASSOCIATIONS

Association of Theatrical Artists and Craftspeople. 48 Fairway St., Bloomfield, NJ 07003-5515. Phone: (212)234-9001 • URL: http://www.atacbiz.com • Members are artists and craftspeople working in theatre, film, TV, and advertising. Areas of expertise include props, costumes, millinery, puppetry, display, and special effects.

Association of Theatrical Press Agents and Managers. Penn Plz., Ste. 1703, 225 W 34th St.,

New York, NY 10122. Phone: (212)719-3666; Fax: (212)302-1585; Email: info@atpam.com • URL: http://www.atpam.com • A labor union for theater managers and press agents. Affiliated with AFL-CIO.

Broadway League. 729 7th Ave., 5th Fl., New York, NY 10019. Phone: (212)764-1122 or (212)703-0200; Fax: (212)944-2136; Email: league@broadway.org • URL: http://www.broadwayleague.com • Members are legitimate theater producers and owners and operators of legitimate theaters. Formerly League of American Theatres and Producers.

National Association of Theatre Owners. 750 1st St. NE, Ste. 1130, Washington, DC 20002. Phone: (202)962-0054; Fax: (202)962-0370; Email: nato@natodc.com • URL: http://www.natoonline.org • Owners, operators and executives of motion picture theaters. Provides services to assist theater owners in successfully operating their theaters including monitoring legislative and technological advancements; compiles statistics.

## THEATERS, MOTION PICTURE

*See* MOTION PICTURE THEATERS

## THESES

*See* DISSERTATIONS

## THIRD WORLD NATIONS

*See* DEVELOPING AREAS

## TILE INDUSTRY

### FINANCIAL RATIOS

*Industry Norms and Key Business Ratios.* Dun & Bradstreet Inc. • Annual. Five volumes. Covers over 800 kinds of businesses, arranged by Standard Industrial Classification number. More detailed editions covering longer periods of time are also available.

### PERIODICALS AND NEWSLETTERS

*Tile and Decorative Surfaces: The Voice of America's Tile Market.* Dialysis Inc. • Monthly. $50.00 per year.

*Tile Design and Installation.* BNP Media. • Quarterly. $55.00 per year. Formerly *Tile World.*

### STATISTICS SOURCES

*U.S. Industry and Trade Outlook.* U.S. Department of Commerce National Technical Information Service. • Annual. Produced by the International Trade Administration, U.S. Department of Commerce, in a "public-private" partnership with DRI/McGraw-Hill and Standard & Poor's. Provides basic data, outlook for the current year, and "Long-Term Prospects" (five-year projections) for a wide variety of products and services. Includes high technology industries. Formerly *U.S. Industrial Outlook.*

### TRADE/PROFESSIONAL ASSOCIATIONS

Ceramic Tile Distributors Association. 800 Roosevelt Rd., Bldg. C, Ste. 312, Glen Ellyn, IL 60137. Phone: (630)545-9415; Fax: (630)790-3095; Email: info@ctdahome.org • URL: http://www.ctdahome.org • Wholesale distributors and manufacturers of ceramic tile and related products. Promotes the increase of sales volumes in the ceramic tile industry through educational programs and networking. Promotes independent ceramic tile distributors and represents their interests. Provides technical information; compiles statistics. Sponsors

competitions. Maintains insurance program for members and speakers' bureau.

Resilient Floor Covering Institute. 115 Broad St., Ste. 201, Lagrange, GA 30240. Phone: (706)882-3833; Fax: (706)882-3880 • URL: http://www.rfci.com • Supports the manufacturers of vinyl composition tile, solid vinyl tile, or sheet vinyl and rubber tile and people who use its products. Provides technical information and data regarding the resilient flooring industry.

Tile Roofing Institute. 23607 Hwy. 99, Ste. 2C, Edmonds, WA 98026. Phone: (425)778-6162; Fax: (425)771-9588; Email: info@tileroofing.org • URL: http://www.tileroofing.org • Members are producers of clay and concrete tile roofing. Formerly National Tile Roofing Manufacturers Association.

## TIMBER INDUSTRY

*See* LUMBER INDUSTRY

## TIME AND MOTION STUDY

### TRADE/PROFESSIONAL ASSOCIATIONS

MTM Association for Standards and Research. 1111 E Touhy Ave., Des Plaines, IL 60018. Phone: (847)299-1111; Fax: (847)299-3509; Email: webmaster@mtm.org • URL: http://www.mtm.org • Persons interested in the fields of industrial engineering, industrial psychology, and human engineering. Conducts research at accredited institutions on human motion (the physical movement of body and limb), with emphasis on examining: internal velocity, acceleration, tension, and control characteristics of a given motion under several conditions; external regularities of given groups of motion as they vary under several conditions of performance; the proper use of motion information in measuring, controlling, and improving manual activities. Also studies ergonomics and the effects of workplace environment on productivity. Provides information on fatigue, optimum methods of performance, the effect of practice on motion performance, and the use of motion information for determining allowances and predicting total performance time. Has developed computer programs for the application of Methods Time Measurement (MTM) and MTM-based work measurement systems. Conducts training courses and testing for certification of practitioners and instructors in all Association MTM Systems. Develops and makes available specialized productivity management services.

## TIN INDUSTRY

### ALMANACS AND YEARBOOKS

*CRB Commodity Yearbook.* Commodity Research Bureau. CRB. • Annual. $179 plus $10.00 shipping cost. The single most comprehensive source of commodity and futures market information available.

### CD-ROM DATABASES

*OECD Statistical Compendium.* Organization for Economic Cooperation and Development. • Semiannual. $1,905.00 per year for 1 to 10 users. CD-ROM contains more than 730,000 monthly, quarterly, and annual time series for OECD countries, 1960 to date. Includes fully searchable data on agriculture, food, economic indicators, national accounts, employment, energy, finance, industry, technology, and foreign trade. Results can be displayed in various forms.

### DIRECTORIES

*Dun's Industrial Guide: The Metalworking Directory.* Dun & Bradstreet Inc. • Annual. Libraries, $485; commercial institutions, $795.00. Lease

basis. Three volumes. Lists about 65,000 U. S. manufacturing plants using metal and suppliers of metalworking equipment and materials. Includes names and titles of key personnel. Products, purchases, and processes are indicated.

### INTERNET DATABASES

*Business 2.0 Web Guide to the Best Business Links.* Business 2.0 Media Inc. Phone: (415)293-4800; Email: support@business2.com • URL: http://www.business2.com/webguide • Web site presents an extensive, searchable directory of links to "the best, most informative, and authoritative web pages." Twenty main categories cover business, finance, career, company information, people, and technology topics, with thousands of subtopics, all linking to Web sites recommended by experienced business researchers. Fees: Free.

*Fedstats.* Federal Interagency Council on Statistical Policy. Phone: (202)395-7254 • URL: http://www.fedstats.gov • Web site features an efficient search facility for full-text statistics produced by more than 100 federal agencies, including the Census Bureau, the Bureau of Economic Analysis, and the Bureau of Labor Statistics. Boolean searches can be made within one agency or for all agencies combined. Links are offered to international statistical bureaus, including the UN, IMF, OECD, UNESCO, Eurostat, and 20 individual countries. Fees: Free.

*FreeLunch.com.* Economy.com, Inc. Phone: (610)696-8700; Fax: (610)696-1678 • URL: http://www.freelunch.com • Web site provides free access to more than 200 million economic and financial data series, covering industry, demographics, labor markets, prices, retail sales, government spending, trade, interest rates, housing starts, the stock market, etc. Data is available in either chart or table form. Searching is offered. Free, but registration required. Economy.com, Inc. also offers fee-based economic analysis at *The Dismal Scientist* site (www.dismal.com).

### PERIODICALS AND NEWSLETTERS

*The Northern Miner: Devoted to the Mineral Resources Industry of Canada.* Scott's Directories. • Weekly. $114 per year.

*Tin International.* Tin Magazines Ltd. • Monthly. $215.00 per year. News and analysis for the international tin industry.

### PRICE SOURCES

*Platt's Metals Week.* Platts Global Energy. • Weekly. $770 Individuals.

### STATISTICS SOURCES

*Non-Ferrous Metal Data Yearbook.* American Bureau of Metal Statistics. • Annual. $405.00. Provides worldwide data on approximately about 200 statistical tables covering many nonferrous metals. Includes production, consumption, inventories, exports, imports, and other data.

*Survey of Current Business.* U. S. Government Printing Office. • Published by Bureau of Economic Analysis, U. S. Department of Commerce. Presents a wide variety of business and economic data.

## TIRE INDUSTRY

*See also* RUBBER AND RUBBER GOODS INDUSTRIES

### ABSTRACTS AND INDEXES

*The Polymer Library.* Rubber and Plastics Research Association of Great Britian. Smithers Rapra Technology. • Monthly. $2,700.00 per year. Up-to-date survey of current international information relevant to the rubber, plastics and associated industries.

### ALMANACS AND YEARBOOKS

*Tire and Rim Association Year Book.* Tire and Rim Association. • $119 Individuals. Contains all TRA

Standards and related information approved by the Association for tires, rims and allied parts for ground vehicles.

## CD-ROM DATABASES

*OECD Statistical Compendium.* Organization for Economic Cooperation and Development. • Semiannual. $1,905.00 per year for 1 to 10 users. CD-ROM contains more than 730,000 monthly, quarterly, and annual time series for OECD countries, 1960 to date. Includes fully searchable data on agriculture, food, economic indicators, national accounts, employment, energy, finance, industry, technology, and foreign trade. Results can be displayed in various forms.

## DIRECTORIES

*Directory of American Manufacturers & Exporters of Tyres & Tubes.* EXIM Infotek Private Ltd. • $10 Individuals. Covers: 70 American manufacturers and exporters of tire repair materials, tires, tires and tubes, and tires for trucks and heavy equipment. Entries include: Company name, postal address, city, country, phone, fax, e-mail and websites, contact person, designation, and product details.

*Directory of Chinese Manufacturers & Exporters of Tyres & Tubes.* EXIM Infotek Private Ltd. • $10 Individuals. Covers: 60 Chinese manufacturers and exporters of automobile tires and tubes, inner tubes for tires, rubber tires and tubes, tires and tubes, tires for truck, vehicle tires and inner tubes. Entries include: Company name, postal address, city, country, phone, fax, e-mail and websites, contact person, designation, and product details.

*Directory of Japanese Manufacturers & Exporters of Tyres & Tubes.* EXIM Infotek Private Ltd. • $10 Individuals. Covers: 70 Japanese manufacturers and exporters of automobile tires and tubes, rubber tires and tubes, tires, tires and tubes, tires-used, used truck tires, and used tires. Entries include: Company name, postal address, city, country, phone, fax, e-mail and websites, contact person, designation, and product details.

*Directory of South Korean Manufacturers & Exporters of Tyres & Tubes.* EXIM Infotek Private Ltd. • $5 Individuals. Covers: 20 South Korean manufacturers and exporters of tires-remolded, vehicle tires and inner tubes. Entries include: Company name, postal address, city, country, phone, fax, e-mail and websites, contact person, designation, and product details.

*Directory of Taiwanese Manufacturers & Exporters of Tyres & Tubes.* EXIM Infotek Private Ltd. • $10 Individuals. Covers: 110 Taiwanese manufacturers & exporters of tire repair materials, tires, tires-remolded, vehicle tires & inner tubes. Entries include: Company name, postal address, city, country, phone, fax, e-mail & websites, contact person, designation, products detail.

*The International Directory of Importers--Tires and Tubes Importers: Auto, Cycle, Truck.* Interdata. • $200 Individuals print. Covers: 1,300 international firms importing tires and tubes (auto/cycle/truck). Entries include: Company name and address, contact person, email, number of employees, year established, phone and telefaxes, business activity, bank references, as well as a listing of tires and tubes (auto/cycle/truck) currently being imported.

*Modern Tire Dealer: Facts/Directory.* Nielsen Business Media Inc. • Directories of tire and car service suppliers, tire shop jobbers, and national state associations.

*Modern Tire Dealer--Facts/Directory Issue.* Bobit Business Media. • Annual. Publication includes: Directories of tire and car service suppliers, tire shop jobbers, and national and state associations. Entries include: Generally, listings show company or organization name, address, phone, names and titles of key personnel. Listings for manufacturers include products.

*Tire Review--Sourcebook & Directory Issue.* Babcox. • Annual. Publication includes: About 850 suppliers of tires, repair equipment, and automotive service supplies and equipment to tire dealers and retreaders. Entries include: Company name, address, phone, name and title of contact, products, brand names, email and website addresses.

## INTERNET DATABASES

*Business 2.0 Web Guide to the Best Business Links.* Business 2.0 Media Inc. Phone: (415)293-4800; Email: support@business2.com • URL: http://www.business2.com/webguide • Web site presents an extensive, searchable directory of links to "the best, most informative, and authoritative web pages." Twenty main categories cover business, finance, career, company information, people, and technology topics, with thousands of subtopics, all linking to Web sites recommended by experienced business researchers. Fees: Free.

*Fedstats.* Federal Interagency Council on Statistical Policy. Phone: (202)395-7254 • URL: http://www.fedstats.gov • Web site features an efficient search facility for full-text statistics produced by more than 100 federal agencies, including the Census Bureau, the Bureau of Economic Analysis, and the Bureau of Labor Statistics. Boolean searches can be made within one agency or for all agencies combined. Links are offered to international statistical bureaus, including the UN, IMF, OECD, UNESCO, Eurostat, and 20 individual countries. Fees: Free.

*FreeLunch.com.* Economy.com, Inc. Phone: (610)696-8700; Fax: (610)696-1678 • URL: http://www.freelunch.com • Web site provides free access to more than 200 million economic and financial data series, covering industry, demographics, labor markets, prices, retail sales, government spending, trade, interest rates, housing starts, the stock market, etc. Data is available in either chart or table form. Searching is offered. Free, but registration required. Economy.com, Inc. also offers fee-based economic analysis at *The Dismal Scientist* site (www.dismal.com).

## PERIODICALS AND NEWSLETTERS

*Dealernews: The Voice of Powersports Retailers.* Advanstar Communications. • News concerning the power sports motor vehicle industry.

*Modern Tire Dealer.* • Monthly. $65.00 per year. Serves independent tire dealers. Cover automotive service and dealership management topics.

*Tire Business.* Crain Communications, Inc. • Biweekly. $79.00 per year. Edited for independent tire retailers and wholesalers.

*Tire Review: The Authority on Tire Dealer Profitability.* Babcox Publications Inc. • Monthly. $64.00. Includes *LiftGuide, Custom Wheel and Tire Style Guide, Sourcebook and Directory and NTDRA Show.*

## STATISTICS SOURCES

*Survey of Current Business.* U. S. Government Printing Office. • Published by Bureau of Economic Analysis, U. S. Department of Commerce. Presents a wide variety of business and economic data.

# TITANIUM INDUSTRY

*See also* METAL INDUSTRY; MINES AND MINERAL RESOURCES

## ALMANACS AND YEARBOOKS

*CRB Commodity Yearbook.* Commodity Research Bureau. CRB. • Annual. $179 plus $10.00 shipping cost. The single most comprehensive source of commodity and futures market information available.

## DIRECTORIES

*International Titanium Association Buyers Guide.* International Titanium Association. • Annual.

## ONLINE DATABASES

*CA Search.* American Chemical Society Chemical Abstracts Service. • Guide to chemical literature, 1967 to present. Inquire as to online cost and availability.

## PERIODICALS AND NEWSLETTERS

*33 Metalproducing: For Primary Producers of Steel, Aluminum, and Copper-Base Alloys.* Penton Media Inc. • Monthly. $65.00 per year. Covers metal production technology and methods and industry news. Includes a bimonthly *Nonferrous Supplement.*

*Titanium Newsletter.* Titanium Development Association. • Description: Presents news on the titanium industry. Covers corporate and Association activities, personnel changes, and legislative news. Recurring features include news of research, news of members, a calendar of events, product information, and columns titled Ti News Pipeline and Ti Reference Library.

## PRICE SOURCES

*Platt's Metals Week.* Platts Global Energy. • Weekly. $770 Individuals.

## STATISTICS SOURCES

*Non-Ferrous Metal Data Yearbook.* American Bureau of Metal Statistics. • Annual. $405.00. Provides worldwide data on approximately about 200 statistical tables covering many nonferrous metals. Includes production, consumption, inventories, exports, imports, and other data.

*Titanium: A Statistical Review.* International Titanium Association. • Annual. $75.

*U.S. Industry and Trade Outlook.* U.S. Department of Commerce National Technical Information Service. • Annual. Produced by the International Trade Administration, U.S. Department of Commerce, in a "public-private" partnership with DRI/McGraw-Hill and Standard & Poor's. Provides basic data, outlook for the current year, and "Long-Term Prospects" (five-year projections) for a wide variety of products and services. Includes high technology industries. Formerly *U.S. Industrial Outlook.*

# TITLE INSURANCE

## PERIODICALS AND NEWSLETTERS

*Title News.* American Land Title Association. • Monthly. Description: Provides information for title companies and property investors.

## TRADE/PROFESSIONAL ASSOCIATIONS

American Land Title Association. 1828 L St. NW, Ste. 705, Washington, DC 20036-5104. Phone: 800-787-2582 or (202)296-3671; Fax: (202)223-5843 or (800)329-2582; Email: service@alta.org • URL: http://www.alta.org • Represents the abstracters, title insurance companies, and attorneys specializing in real property law.

# TITLES OF DEGREES

*See* ACADEMIC DEGREES

# TOASTS

*See also* PUBLIC SPEAKING

## PERIODICALS AND NEWSLETTERS

*The Toastmaster: For Better Listening, Thinking, Speaking.* Suzanne Frey, editor. Toastmasters International. • Monthly. Membership. Provides information and "how-to" articles on communication and leadership.

# TOBACCO AND TOBACCO INDUSTRY

*See also* CIGAR AND CIGARETTE INDUSTRY; SMOKING POLICY

## ABSTRACTS AND INDEXES

*Tobacco Abstracts.* North Carolina State University North Carolina Agricultural Research Service. • Monthly. Bimonthly.

## ALMANACS AND YEARBOOKS

*Tobacco Retailers Almanac.* International Premium Cigar and Pipe Retailers. • Annual. Lists virtually every tobacco related product available (including cigars, cigarettes, pipes, tobacco, lighters and gift items).

## CD-ROM DATABASES

*OECD Statistical Compendium.* Organization for Economic Cooperation and Development. • Semiannual. $1,905.00 per year for 1 to 10 users. CD-ROM contains more than 730,000 monthly, quarterly, and annual time series for OECD countries, 1960 to date. Includes fully searchable data on agriculture, food, economic indicators, national accounts, employment, energy, finance, industry, technology, and foreign trade. Results can be displayed in various forms.

## DIRECTORIES

*Directory of American Manufacturers & Exporters of Tobacco & Tobacco Products.* EXIM Infotek Private Ltd. • Covers: 20 American manufacturers and exporters of cigarettes. Entries include: Company name, postal address, telephone, fax, e-mail, website, contact person, designation, and product details.

## FINANCIAL RATIOS

*Quarterly Financial Report for Manufacturing, Mining, Trade, and Selected Service Industries.* U.S. Federal Trade Commission and U.S. Securities and Exchange Commission. U.S. Census Bureau Foreign Trade Division. • Quarterly. Quarterly. Report on financial results of U.S. corporations.

## GENERAL WORKS

*Drugs, Alcohol & Tobacco: Learning About Addictive Behavior.* Edited by Rosalyn Carson-Dewitt, M.D. Cengage Learning Inc. • $512. Three volumes. Contains 200 articles on various aspects of addiction. Includes color illustrations, a glossary, and comprehensive indexing. Macmillan Reference USA imprint. eBook also available. Inquire for pricing.

## INTERNET DATABASES

*Business 2.0 Web Guide to the Best Business Links.* Business 2.0 Media Inc. Phone: (415)293-4800; Email: support@business2.com • URL: http://www.business2.com/webguide • Web site presents an extensive, searchable directory of links to "the best, most informative, and authoritative web pages." Twenty main categories cover business, finance, career, company information, people, and technology topics, with thousands of subtopics, all linking to Web sites recommended by experienced business researchers. Fees: Free.

*Fedstats.* Federal Interagency Council on Statistical Policy. Phone: (202)395-7254 • URL: http://www.fedstats.gov • Web site features an efficient search facility for full-text statistics produced by more than 100 federal agencies, including the Census Bureau, the Bureau of Economic Analysis, and the Bureau of Labor Statistics. Boolean searches can be made within one agency or for all agencies combined. Links are offered to international statistical bureaus, including the UN, IMF, OECD, UNESCO, Eurostat, and 20 individual countries. Fees: Free.

*FreeLunch.com.* Economy.com, Inc. Phone: (610)696-8700; Fax: (610)696-1678 • URL: http://www.freelunch.com • Web site provides free access to more than 200 million economic and financial data series, covering industry, demographics, labor markets, prices, retail sales, government spending, trade, interest rates, housing starts, the stock market, etc. Data is available in either chart or table form.

Searching is offered. Free, but registration required. Economy.com, Inc. also offers fee-based economic analysis at *The Dismal Scientist* site (www.dismal.com).

*USDA.* U.S. National Institute of Standards and Technology. 100 Bureau Dr., Gaithersburg, MD 20899-1070. Phone: 800-877-8339 or (301)975-6478 or (202)720-2791; Fax: (301)975-8295; Email: inquiries@nist.gov • URL: http://www.nist.gov • The USDA home page has six sections: News and Information; What's New; About USDA; Agencies; Opportunities; Search and Help. Keyword searching is offered from the USDA home page and from various individual agency home pages. Agencies are the Economic Research Service, Agricultural Marketing Service, National Agricultural Statistics Service, National Agricultural Library, and about 12 others. Updating varies. Fees: Free.

## OTHER SOURCES

*Westlaw Journal Tobacco Industry.* Thomson Reuters Westlaw. • $2,988.96. Reports on major lawsuits brought against tobacco companies.

## PERIODICALS AND NEWSLETTERS

*Bureau of Alcohol, Tobacco, and Firearms Quarterly Bulletin.* Bureau of Alcohol, Tobacco, and Firearms, U.S. Department of the Treasury. U. S. Government Printing Office. • Quarterly. $25.00 per year. Laws and regulations.

*Smokeshop.* • Bimonthly. $24.00 per year.

*Tobacco International.* Lockwood Publications Inc. • Weekly. $32.00 per year.

*Tobacco Reporter: Devoted to All Segments of the International Tobacco Trade Processing, Trading, Manufacturing.* SpecComm International Inc. • Monthly. $36.00 per year.

## RESEARCH CENTERS AND INSTITUTES

U.S. Department of the Treasury - Alcohol and Tobacco Tax and Trade Bureau - Scientific Services Division - Compliance Laboratory. 490 N Wiget Ln., Walnut Creek, CA 94598. Phone: (513)684-3356; Email: compliance.laboratory@ttb.gov • URL: http://www.ttb.gov/ssd/compliance_monitoring_lab.shtml • Monitoring of regulatory compliance of both beverage and nonbeverage alcohol products.

University of Kentucky - College of Agriculture, Food and Environment - Kentucky Tobacco Research and Development Center. Cooper & University Drs., Lexington, KY 40546-0236. Phone: (859)257-5798; Fax: (859)323-1077; Email: ochamb@uky.edu • URL: http://www2.ca.uky.edu/ktrdc/index.html • Application of biotechnology for the development of new crops based on tobacco and other plants. Development of new medicinal and industrial applications for plant natural products. Development of new crops from native plants and adaptation of existing crops for more efficient production of plant-made pharmaceuticals, plant-made industrial products, and plant natural products.

University of Toronto - Ontario Tobacco Research Unit. 33 Russell St., Toronto, ON, Canada M5S 2S1. Phone: (416)595-6888; Fax: (416)595-6068; Email: info@otru.org • URL: http://otru.org • Tobacco control, including epidemiology of tobacco use and cessation, tobacco and youth, gender issues in tobacco use, ethnicity and tobacco use, economic factors in tobacco use, tobacco policy attitudes, policy and program evaluation, community interventions, and environmental tobacco smoke.

## STATISTICS SOURCES

*Agricultural Statistics.* U.S. Department of Agriculture National Agricultural Statistics Service. • Annual. $46 Individuals. Provides a wide variety of statistical data relating to agricultural production, supplies, consumption, prices/price-supports, foreign trade, costs, and returns, as well as farm labor, loans, income, and population. In many cases, historical data is shown annually for 10 years. In addition to farm data, includes detailed fishery statistics.

*Standard & Poor's Industry Surveys.* Standard & Poor's Financial Services L.L.C. • Semiannual. $1,800.00. Two looseleaf volumes. Includes monthly *Supplements.* Provides detailed, individual surveys of 52 major industry groups. Each survey is revised on a semiannual basis. Also includes "Monthly Investment Review" (industry group investment analysis) and monthly "Trends & Projections" (economic analysis).

*Survey of Current Business.* U. S. Government Printing Office. • Published by Bureau of Economic Analysis, U. S. Department of Commerce. Presents a wide variety of business and economic data.

## TRADE/PROFESSIONAL ASSOCIATIONS

American Wholesale Marketers Association. 2750 Prosperity Ave., Ste. 530, Fairfax, VA 22031. Phone: 800-482-2962; Fax: (703)573-5738 • URL: http://www.awmanet.org • Represents the interests of distributors of convenience-related products. Its members include wholesalers, retailers, manufacturers, brokers and allied organizations from across the U.S. and abroad. Programs include strong legislative representation in Washington and a broad spectrum of targeted education, business and information services. Sponsors the country's largest show for candy and convenience related products in conjunction with its semi-annual convention.

International Premium Cigar and Pipe Retailers. No. 4 Bradley Park Ct., Ste. 2-H, Columbus, GA 31904-3637. Phone: (706)494-1143; Fax: (706)494-1893; Email: info@ipcpr.org • URL: http://www.ipcpr.org • Formerly Retail Tobacco Dealers of America.

# TOLL ROADS

*See also* ROADS AND HIGHWAYS

## BIBLIOGRAPHIES

*Road Construction and Safety.* U. S. Government Printing Office. • Annual. Free. Issued by the Superintendent of Documents. A list of government publications on highway construction and traffic safety. Formerly *Highway Construction, Safety and Traffic.* (Subject Bibliography No. 3.).

## ONLINE DATABASES

*TRIS: Transportation Research Information Service.* The National Academies National Research Council. • Contains abstracts and citations to a wide range of transportation literature, 1968 to present, with monthly updates. Includes references to the literature of air transportation, highways, ships and shipping, railroads, trucking, and urban mass transportation. Formerly *TRIS-ON-LINE.* Inquire as to online cost and availability.

## PERIODICALS AND NEWSLETTERS

*Tollways.* International Bridge, Tunnel and Turnpike Association. • Monthly. Description: Focuses on trends, developments, and news about the worldwide toll industry for members.

# TOMATO INDUSTRY

*See also* VEGETABLE INDUSTRY

## DIRECTORIES

*Major Food and Drink Companies of the World.* Cengage Learning Inc. • 12th edition. eBook. Published by Graham & Whiteside. Contains profiles and trade names for more than 9,200 important food and beverage companies in various countries. In addition to foods, includes both alcoholic and nonalcoholic drink products.

**For publishers' addresses, refer to SOURCES CITED section at the back of the book.**

## INTERNET DATABASES

*USDA.* U.S. National Institute of Standards and Technology. 100 Bureau Dr., Gaithersburg, MD 20899-1070. Phone: 800-877-8339 or (301)975-6478 or (202)720-2791; Fax: (301)975-8295; Email: inquiries@nist.gov • URL: http://www.nist.gov • The USDA home page has six sections: News and Information; What's New; About USDA; Agencies; Opportunities; Search and Help. Keyword searching is offered from the USDA home page and from various individual agency home pages. Agencies are the Economic Research Service, Agricultural Marketing Service, National Agricultural Statistics Service, National Agricultural Library, and about 12 others. Updating varies. Fees: Free.

## ONLINE DATABASES

*Food Science and Technology Abstracts (online).* IFIS North American Desk. • Produced by International Food Information Service. Provides about 500,000 online citations, with abstracts, to the international literature of food science, technology, commodities, engineering, and processing. Approximately 2,000 periodicals are covered. Time period is 1969 to date, with monthly updates. Inquire as to online cost and availability.

## STATISTICS SOURCES

*Agricultural Statistics.* U.S. Department of Agriculture National Agricultural Statistics Service. • Annual. $46 Individuals. Provides a wide variety of statistical data relating to agricultural production, supplies, consumption, prices/price-supports, foreign trade, costs, and returns, as well as farm labor, loans, income, and population. In many cases, historical data is shown annually for 10 years. In addition to farm data, includes detailed fishery statistics.

*Vegetables and Specialties Situation and Outlook.* U. S. Government Printing Office. • Three times a year. Issued by the Economic Research Service of the U. S. Department of Agriculture. Provides current statistical information on supply, demand, and prices.

# TOOL INDUSTRY

*See also* HARDWARE INDUSTRY; MACHINE TOOL INDUSTRY; POWER TOOL INDUSTRY

## ABSTRACTS AND INDEXES

*Engineering Index Monthly: Abstracting and Indexing Services Covering Sources ofthe World's Engineering Literature.* Engineering Information Inc. • Monthly. Institutions, $5,279.00 per year. Provides indexing and abstracting of the world's engineering and technical literature.

*Mechanical Engineering Abstracts.* Cambridge Scientific Abstracts L.P. • Quarterly. $1,620 Individuals print + web edition (includes shipping). Database covering international literature on mechanical engineering, engineering management, and production engineering, including specific and theoretical applications. Formerly *ISMEC - Mechanical Engineering Abstracts.*

## DIRECTORIES

*Directory of American Manufacturers & Exporters of Handtools.* EXIM Infotek Private Ltd. • $30 Individuals. Covers: 400 American manufacturers and exporters of copper and aluminum press sleeve swagers, cutting tools, diamond saw blades, fixtures tools, flange spreaders, grinder tools, grooving and proofing tools, hacksaw, hand tools-electric and air, hand tools-files, hand tools-hammers, hand tools-modeling, hand tools-pillers, hand tools-power, hand tools, hand tools-shovels, hand tools-utica, hand tools-wrenches, high speed steel, hydraulic maintenance tools, jewelry, landscaping tools, miniature tools, non-sparking safety tools, nut splitters, pneumatic tools, pocket knives, power tool accessories, precision miniature tools, precision tools, reamers, rivet setting machines, safety tools, screwdrivers, serrated blades, sheet metal hand tools, sledges, pry bars and railroad track tools, socket sets, special tools-custom, special tools, tool holders, tooling, tools, torque tools, torque wrenches, tube tools, wire tools, and wrenches. Entries include: Company name, postal address, city, country, telephone, fax, e-mail and websites, contact person, designation, and product details.

*Directory of Chinese Manufacturers & Exporters of Handtools.* EXIM Infotek Private Ltd. • $10 Individuals. Covers: 70 Chinese manufacturers and exporters of air tools, electric power tools, hammers, hand tools, hardware tools, pliers/clamps and similar tools, screwdrivers, tool cabinets, tool cases, and tools. Entries include: Company name, postal address, city, country, phone, fax, e-mail and websites, contact person, designation, and product details.

*Directory of Japanese Manufacturers & Exporters of Handtools.* EXIM Infotek Private Ltd. • $10 Individuals. Covers: 60 Japanese manufacturers and exporters of air tools, hand tools, tools, and turning tools. Entries include: Company name, postal address, city, country, phone, fax, e-mail and websites, contact person, designation, and product details.

*Directory of South Korean Manufacturers & Exporters of Handtools.* EXIM Infotek Private Ltd. • $10 Individuals. Covers: 70 South Korean manufacturers and exporters of box-tool, builders tools, carbide tools, chisels/taps/dies and similar tools, electric and electro-magnetic tools, hammers/mallets and similar tools, metal hand and diamond tools, pliers/clamps and similar tools, roofers and decorators tools, and screwdrivers/wrenches. Entries include: Company name, postal address, city, country, phone, fax, e-mail and websites, contact person, designation, and product details.

*Directory of Taiwanese Manufacturers & Exporters of Handtools.* EXIM Infotek Private Ltd. • $35 Individuals. Covers: 510 Taiwanese manufacturers and exporters of builders tools, carbide tools, chisels/taps/dies and similar tools, electric and electro-magnetic tools, files/rasps and similar tools, hammers/mallets and similar tools, hand tools, handy sealer, metal hand and diamond tools, multipurpose tools, pliers/clamps and similar tools, roofers and decorators tools, screwdrivers/wrenches, tagging guns, tool cases, and tools for powerline maintenance. Entries include: Company name, postal address, city, country, phone, fax, e-mail and websites, contact person, designation, and product details.

*Dun's Industrial Guide: The Metalworking Directory.* Dun & Bradstreet Inc. • Annual. Libraries, $485; commercial institutions, $795.00. Lease basis. Three volumes. Lists about 65,000 U. S. manufacturing plants using metal and suppliers of metalworking equipment and materials. Includes names and titles of key personnel. Products, purchases, and processes are indicated.

*The International Directory of Importers - Hand Tools and Power Tools Importers.* Interdata. • $260 Individuals print. Covers: 3,000 international firms importing hand tools and power tools. Entries include: Company name and address, contact person, email, number of employees, year established, phone and telefaxes, business activity, bank references, as well as a listing of hand tools and power tools currently being imported.

## ONLINE DATABASES

*Thomas Register Online.* Thomas Publishing Company L.L.C. • Provides concise information on approximately 194,000 U. S. companies, mainly manufacturers, with over 50,000 product classifications. Indexes over 115,000 trade names.

Information is updated semiannually. Inquire as to online cost and availability.

## PERIODICALS AND NEWSLETTERS

*Cutting Tool Engineering.* CTE Publications Inc. • Monthly. $75 U.S. One year subscription (free to qualified subscribers within the U.S.). Serves manufacturers involved in cutting and grinding metals and other materials.

*Die Casting Engineer.* North American Die Casting Association. • Bimonthly. $60 U.S., Canada, and Mexico. Bimonthly. Included with membership.

## STATISTICS SOURCES

*U.S. Industry and Trade Outlook.* U.S. Department of Commerce National Technical Information Service. • Annual. Produced by the International Trade Administration, U.S. Department of Commerce, in a "public-private" partnership with DRI/McGraw-Hill and Standard & Poor's. Provides basic data, outlook for the current year, and "Long-Term Prospects" (five-year projections) for a wide variety of products and services. Includes high technology industries. Formerly *U.S. Industrial Outlook.*

## TRADE/PROFESSIONAL ASSOCIATIONS

National Tooling and Machining Association. 1357 Rockside Rd., Cleveland, OH 44134-2776. Phone: 800-248-6862; Fax: (216)264-2840; Email: info@ntma.org • URL: http://www.ntma.org.

North American Die Casting Association. 3250 N Arlington Heights Rd., Ste. 101, Arlington Heights, IL 60004. Phone: (847)279-0001; Fax: (847)279-0002; Email: nadca@diecasting.org • URL: http://www.diecasting.org • Represents producers of die castings and suppliers to the industry, product and die designers, metallurgists, and students. Develops product standards; compiles trade statistics on metal consumption trends; conducts promotional activities; provides information on chemistry, mechanics, engineering, and other arts and sciences related to die casting. Provides training materials and short, intensive courses in die casting. Maintains speakers' bureau.

# TOOLS, POWER

*See* POWER TOOL INDUSTRY

# TOTAL QUALITY MANAGEMENT (TQM)

*See also* QUALITY CONTROL

## ABSTRACTS AND INDEXES

*Business Periodicals Index Retrospective.* EBSCO Publishing Inc. • 11/year. Quarterly and annual cumulations.

## CD-ROM DATABASES

*ABI/INFORM.* ProQuest L.L.C. • Monthly. Provides CD-ROM indexing and abstracting of worldwide business literature. Archival discs are available from 1971. Formerly *ABI/INFORM OnDisc.*

*Business Abstracts with Full Text.* EBSCO Publishing Inc. • Includes full text articles from more than 460 business publications from 1982 to present. Indexing for nearly 880 publications.

## ONLINE DATABASES

*Wilson Business Abstracts Online.* H.W. Wilson Co. • Indexes and abstracts 600 major business periodicals, plus the *Wall Street Journal* and the business section of the *New York Times.* Indexing is from 1982, abstracting from 1990, with the two newspapers included from 1993. Updated weekly. Inquire as to online cost and availability. (*Business Periodicals Index* without abstracts is also available online.).

## PERIODICALS AND NEWSLETTERS

*ISO Management Systems.* American National Standards Institute. • Bimonthly. Price on application. Newsletter on quality standards. Published by the International Organization for Standardization (ISO). Text in English. Formerly *ISO 9000 and ISO 14000 News.*

*Quality Management Journal.* American Society for Quality. • Quarterly. $65 Members. Emphasizes research in quality control and management.

*Quality Progress.* American Society for Quality. • Monthly. $70 Members. Covers developments in quality improvement throughout the world.

## RESEARCH CENTERS AND INSTITUTES

Center for Quality and Productivity. University of North Texas, College of Business Administration, 1155 Union Cir., No. 311160, Denton, TX 76203. Phone: (940)369-8476; Email: prybutok@unt.edu • URL: http://www.coba.unt.edu • Fields of research include the management of quality systems and statistical methodology.

University of Wisconsin—Madison - Center for Quality and Productivity Improvement. 3130 Engineering Centers Bldg., 1550 Engineering Dr., Madison, WI 53706. Phone: (608)263-2520; Fax: (608)263-1425; Email: carayon@ie.engr.wisc.edu • URL: http://cqpi.engr.wisc.edu • Research areas include quality management and industrial engineering.

## TRADE/PROFESSIONAL ASSOCIATIONS

American Society for Quality. PO Box 3005, Milwaukee, WI 53201-3005. Phone: 800-248-1946 or (414)272-8575; Email: help@asq.org • URL: http://asq.org • Individuals and organizations dedicated to the ongoing development, advancement, and promotion of quality concepts, principles, and technologies. Through its Education Development Department, offers courses in quality engineering, reliability engineering, managing for quality, management of quality costs, quality audit-development and administration, management of the inspection function, probability and statistics for engineers and scientists, and product liability and prevention.

# TOURIST INDUSTRY

*See* TRAVEL INDUSTRY

# TOWN GOVERNMENT

*See* MUNICIPAL GOVERNMENT

# TOWN PLANNING

*See* CITY PLANNING

# TOWNS AND CITIES

*See* CITIES AND TOWNS

# TOXIC SUBSTANCES

*See* HAZARDOUS MATERIALS

# TOXICOLOGY, INDUSTRIAL

*See* INDUSTRIAL HYGIENE

# TOY INDUSTRY

## DIRECTORIES

*Directory of American Manufacturers & Exporters of Toys & Games.* EXIM Infotek Private Ltd. • $15

Individuals. Covers: 170 American manufacturers and exporters of arts and craft kits, baby cribs, balloons, carnival toys, children's toys, coin operated games, dolls, educational toys, games, infant toys, inflatable, joke novelties, juvenile furniture, kite reels, magic tricks, outdoor games, outdoor toys, pedal cars, plastic playing cards, plastic toys, playing cards and children's games, plush toys, pools, preschool toys, puzzles, ride-on toys, slot machines, sports memorabilia, stuffed toys, toy parts-plastic, toys, toys and games, and video games. Entries include: Company name, postal address, city, country, phone, fax, e-mail and websites, contact person, designation, and product details.

*Directory of Chinese Manufacturers & Exporters of Toys & Games.* EXIM Infotek Private Ltd. • $20 Individuals. Covers: 240 Chinese manufacturers and exporters of baby care products, baby carriages, baby products, baby strollers, babyware, chess sets, child bicycles, children's toys, children's vehicles, cloth toys, craft toys, dolls, electric toys, electrical toys (a/c), electronic toys, firecrackers, fireworks, games, masks, plastic toys, playing cards, plush toys, porcelain toys, remote control toys, rubber toys, stuffed toys, toy fireworks, toy guns, toys, toy parts, toys-intelligent-adults, waterguns, wooden puzzles, and wooden toys. Entries include: Company name, postal address, city, country, phone, fax, e-mail and websites, contact person, designation, and product details.

*Directory of Japanese Manufacturers & Exporters of Toys & Games.* EXIM Infotek Private Ltd. • $10 Individuals. Covers: 80 Japanese manufacturers and exporters of baby chairs, battery operated toys, board games, cloth toys, dolls, educational toys, electronic toys, games, general toys, hobbies, hobby crafts, inflatable vinyl toys, jigsaw puzzles, metal and plastic toys, plastic toys, pre-school toys, puzzles, radio controlled cars, ride on toys, shadow masks, stuffed toys, stuffed animals, toys, trading cards, vehicles for children, and wooden toys. Entries include: Company name, postal address, city, country, phone, fax, e-mail and websites, contact person, designation, and product details.

*Directory of South Korean Manufacturers & Exporters of Toys & Games.* EXIM Infotek Private Ltd. • $10 Individuals. Covers: 90 South Korean manufacturers & exporters of animal toys, dolls & puppets, model aircrafts, musical articles & toys, party & educational games, plush toys, stuffed toys, toys & games-electric/electronic, toys & games-mechanical, toys & games-plastic, toys & games-rubber, toys & games-wooden. Entries include: Company name, postal address, city, country, phone, fax, e-mail & websites, contact person, designation, products detail.

*Directory of Taiwanese Manufacturers & Exporters of Toys & Games.* EXIM Infotek Private Ltd. • $40 Individuals. Covers: 670 Taiwanese manufacturers and exporters of aircraft models, baby buggies, baby carriages, baby music potties, baby prams and cycles, baby tricycles and bicycles, baby walkers, cots, cradles and prams, dart game sets, dolls and puppets, educational toys, jumping balls, model aircrafts, music planes, musical articles and toys, party and educational games, plastic sporting games, puzzles/jigsaw puzzles, stuffed toys, talking planes, toys, toys and games-electric/electronic, toys and games-mechanical, toys and games-plastic, toys and games-rubber, toys and games-wooden, and video game machines. Entries include: Company name, postal address, city, country, phone, fax, e-mail and websites, contact person, designation, and product details.

*The International Directory of Importers--Sporting Goods and Toys Importers.* Interdata. • Annual. $295 Individuals print. Covers: 4,700 international firms importing sporting goods and toys. Entries include: Company name and address, contact person, email,

number of employees, year established, phone and telefaxes, business activity, bank references, as well as a listing of sporting goods and toys currently being imported.

*The Official American International Toy Fair Directory.* Toy Industry Association. • Annual. Covers: About 1,500 toy, game, and holiday decoration manufacturers and their representatives. Entries include: Company name, address, phone, e-mail, fax, website, booth number or location at Toy Fair, products, name of representative.

*Toy Trader Year Book.* Turret-Wheatland Ltd. • Annual. Covers: Toy and toy supplier manufacturers, importers, wholesalers, retailers, and agents in the U.K. Entries include: Company name, address, phone, products, brand names.

*Toys & Games--Buyer's Guide Issue.* Chelsie Communications Inc. • Annual. Publication includes: List of about 400 Canadian manufacturers and distributors of toys and games for children; trade associations, trade show organizers, and licensors. Entries include: For manufacturers and distributors--Company name, address, phone, key officials, branches, name of firm represented, key to line of business. For associations--Name, address, phone, contact name, property/show represented.

*World Directory of Toys & Games.* World-Wide Market-Link. • Irregular. $35. Covers: 1,700 toy and game importers and wholesalers in 60 countries. Entries include: Company name, address, phone.

## FINANCIAL RATIOS

*Annual Statement Studies.* Risk Management Association. • Annual. Compiled from over 280,000 financial statements.

*Annual Statement Studies: Industry Default Probabilities and Cash Flow Measures.* Risk Management Association. • Annual. $405 Nonmembers. Serves as a companion volume to the original *Annual Statement Studies.* Gives probability of default estimates on a percentage scale for more than 450 industries. Includes changes in position year-by-year for eight financial statement line items and provides percentage measures of cash flow.

## PERIODICALS AND NEWSLETTERS

*Playthings: For Today's Merchandiser of Toys, Hobbies and Crafts.* Reed Elsevier Group plc Reed Business Information. • Monthly. $39.95 per year. Includes annual *Directory.* Covers the major toy and hobby categories, industry news and news products.

# TRACTORS

*See* AGRICULTURAL MACHINERY

# TRADE ASSOCIATIONS

*See* ASSOCIATIONS

# TRADE, BOARDS OF

*See* CHAMBERS OF COMMERCE

# TRADE CATALOGS

*See* CATALOGS AND DIRECTORIES

# TRADE DIRECTORIES

*See* CATALOGS AND DIRECTORIES

# TRADE JOURNALS

*See also* PERIODICALS

## ABSTRACTS AND INDEXES

*Business Periodicals Index Retrospective.* EBSCO Publishing Inc. • 11/year. Quarterly and annual cumulations.

## CD-ROM DATABASES

*MediaFinder.* Oxbridge Communications Inc. • $1,295 per year. Online database with 77,000 magazines, catalogs, newspapers, and journals.

## DIRECTORIES

*Burrelle's Media Directory: Magazines and Newsletters.* BurrellesLuce. • Annual. $550.00. Provides detailed descriptions of more than 13,500 magazines and newsletters published in the U.S., Canada, and Mexico. Categories are professional, consumer, trade, and college. Semiannual *Updates.* Includes CD-ROM.

*International Media Guide: Business-Professional: Asia/Pacific, Middle East, Africa.* Kantar Media SRDS. • $553 Individuals online; 1 year. Provides information on 3,800 trade publications "from Africa to the Pacific Rim," including advertising rates and circulation data.

*International Media Guide Business-Professional Publications: Europe.* Kantar Media SRDS. • $553 Individuals online; 1 year. Describes 8,800 trade journals from Eastern and Western Europe, with advertising rates and circulation data.

*International Media Guide: Business/Professional Publications: The Americas.* Kantar Media SRDS. • $553 Individuals online; 1 year. Describes over 4,400 trade publications from North, South, and Central America, with advertising rates and circulation data.

## HANDBOOKS AND MANUALS

*Gulf Business Development Handbook.* National United States-Arab Chamber of Commerce. • $5 for members. Includes public and private trade resources.

## INTERNET DATABASES

*EBSCO Information Services.* EBSCO Publishing Inc. 10 Estes St., Ipswich, MA 01938-2106. Phone: 800-653-2726 or (978)356-6500; Fax: (978)356-6565; Email: information@ebscohost.com • URL: http://www.ebscohost.com • Fee-based Web site providing Internet access to a wide variety of databases, including business-related material. Full text is available for many periodical titles, with daily updates. Fees: Apply.

*InSite 2.* Intelligence Data/Thomson Financial. Phone: 800-654-0393 or (617)856-1890; Fax: (617)737-3182; Email: intelligence.data@tfn.com • URL: http://www.insite2.gale.com/ • Fee-based Web site consolidates information in a "Base Pack" consisting of Business InSite, Market InSite, and Company InSite. Optional databases are Consumer InSite, Health and Wellness InSite, Newsletter InSite, and Computer InSite. Includes fulltext content from more than 2,500 trade publications, journals, newsletters, newspapers, analyst reports, and other sources. Continuous updating. Formerly produced by The Gale Group.

*ProQuest.* ProQuest L.L.C. 789 E Eisenhower Pkwy., Ann Arbor, MI 48106-1346. Phone: 800-521-0600 or (734)761-4700; Fax: (734)662-4554; Email: info@proquest.com • URL: http://www.proquest.com • Fee-based Web site providing Internet access to more than 3,000 periodicals, newspapers, and other publications. Many items are available full-text, with daily updates. Includes extensive corporate and financial information. Fees: Apply.

*PubList.com: The Internet Directory of Publications.* Bowes & Associates, Inc. Phone: (781)792-0999; Fax: (781)792-0988; Email: info@publist.com • URL: http://www.publist.com • "The premier online global resource for information about

print and electronic publications." Provides online searching for information on more than 150,000 magazines, journals, newsletters, e-journals, and monographs. Database entries generally include title, publisher, format, address, editor, circulation, subject, and International Standard Serial Number (ISSN). Fees: Free.

*Ulrichsweb.com.* R.R. Bowker L.L.C. 630 Central Ave, New Providence, NJ 07974. Phone: 888-269-5372 or (908)286-1090; Email: info@bowker.com • URL: http://www.bowker.com • Web site provides fee-based access to about 250,000 serials records from the *Ulrich's International Periodicals Directory* database. Includes periodical evaluations from *Library Journal* and *Magazines for Libraries.* Monthly updates.

*WilsonWeb Periodicals Databases.* H.W. Wilson Co. 950 University Ave., Bronx, NY 10452-4224. Phone: 800-367-6770 or (718)588-8400 or (718)558-8400; Fax: (718)590-1617 or (800)590-1617; Email: custserv@hwwilson.com • URL: http://www.hwwilson.com • Web sites provide fee-based access to *Wilson Business Full Text, Applied Science & Technology Full Text, Biological & Agricultural Index, Library Literature & Information Science Full Text,* and *Readers' Guide Full Text, Mega Edition.* Daily updates.

## ONLINE DATABASES

*CPI.Q.* Cengage Learning Inc. • Electronic version of the *Canadian Periodical Index.* Provides citations from 1988 to date for English and French language periodicals. Indexing from 1980 to present. Inquire as to price and availability.

## PERIODICALS AND NEWSLETTERS

*Folio: The New Dynamics of Magazine Publishing.* Penton. • Monthly. $96.00 per year.

*SI: Special Issues.* Trip Wyckoff, editor. Hoover's Inc. • Bimonthly. $149.95 per year. Newsletter. Serves as a supplement to *Directory of Business Periodical Special Issues.* Provides information on trade journal special issues and editorial calendars.

## TRADE/PROFESSIONAL ASSOCIATIONS

American Society of Business Publications Editors. 214 N Hale St., Wheaton, IL 60187. Phone: (603)510-4588; Fax: (603)510-4501; Email: info@asbpe.org • URL: http://www.asbpe.org.

BPA Worldwide. 100 Beard Sawmill Rd., 6th Fl., Shelton, CT 06484. Phone: (203)447-2800; Fax: (203)447-2900; Email: ghansen@bpaww.com • URL: http://www.bpaww.com • Verifies business and consumer periodical circulation statements. Includes a Circulation Managers Committee. Formerly Business Publications Audit of Circulation.

# TRADE NAMES

*See* TRADEMARKS AND TRADE NAMES

# TRADE SECRETS

*See also* INTELLECTUAL PROPERTY

## ABSTRACTS AND INDEXES

*Business Periodicals Index Retrospective.* EBSCO Publishing Inc. • 11/year. Quarterly and annual cumulations.

*Index to Legal Periodicals and Books.* H.W. Wilson Co. • Monthly. $490.00 per year. Quarterly and annual cumulations.

## HANDBOOKS AND MANUALS

*Protecting Trade Secrets, Patents, Copyrights, and Trademarks.* Robert C. Dorr and Christopher H. Munch. Aspen Publishers, Inc. • $165.00. Looseleaf service.

*Trade Secret Protection in an Information Age.* Gale R. Peterson. Glasser LegalWorks. • Looseleaf. $149.00, including sample forms on disk. Periodic supplementation available. Covers trade secret law relating to computer software, online databases, and multimedia products. Explanations are based on more than 1,000 legal cases. Sample forms on disk include work-for-hire examples and covenants not to compete.

*Worldwide Trade Secrets Law.* Melvin Jager, author. Thomson West. • Annual. $2,560 3 volume looseleaf (Full set). Covers the pure trade secret license, the pure patent license, hybrid patents, and trade secret licenses.

## ONLINE DATABASES

*Wilson Business Abstracts Online.* H.W. Wilson Co. • Indexes and abstracts 600 major business periodicals, plus the *Wall Street Journal* and the business section of the *New York Times.* Indexing is from 1982, abstracting from 1990, with the two newspapers included from 1993. Updated weekly. Inquire as to online cost and availability. (*Business Periodicals Index* without abstracts is also available online.).

## OTHER SOURCES

*Trade Secrets.* ALM Media Properties LLC. • $520. Covers the legal protection of trade secrets, including information on the Economic Espionage Act of 1996. Includes a CD-ROM with samples of applicable legal forms. (Law Journal Press).

## PERIODICALS AND NEWSLETTERS

*Security Management.* ASIS International. • Monthly. $60 Nonmembers print and online. Included in membership. Articles cover the protection of corporate assets, including personnel property and information security.

## TRADE/PROFESSIONAL ASSOCIATIONS

ASIS International. 1625 Prince St., Alexandria, VA 22314. Phone: (703)519-6200; Fax: (703)519-6299; Email: asis@asisonline.org • URL: http://www.asisonline.org/Pages/default.aspx • ASIS is the world's largest organization dedicated to security professionals. Presents seminars and exhibits and offers a variety of educational programs on security issues in a number of fields including communications.

# TRADE SHOWS

*See also* CONVENTIONS

## ABSTRACTS AND INDEXES

*Business Periodicals Index Retrospective.* EBSCO Publishing Inc. • 11/year. Quarterly and annual cumulations.

## DIRECTORIES

*Canadian National Business Directory.* Todd Publications. • $250. Covers: 200,000 businesses, including tradeshows, exhibitions, and meetings. Database includes: Glossary of Internet terms; list of products and services online. Entries include: Address and phone number.

*Exhibitor: Best Practices in Trade Shows and Events.* Exhibitor Publications Inc. • Annual. $18/year; print or online. Covers about 200 manufacturers of trade show exhibit equipment. Formerly *Buyer's Guide to Trade Show Displays.*

*Global Trade & Business Show Directory.* International Business Publications, USA. • $99.95 Individuals paperback. Covers: Approximately 1,000 largest trade, business, and professional shows and exhibitions in the U.S. and other countries.

*MediaMap/High-Tech Trade Show Report.* Cision US Inc. • Annual. $495. Covers: 350 domestic and international high-tech trade shows. Entries include: Name, address, phone, fax; contact persons; show dates, focus and technology profile; exhibitor and attendee figures; attendee demographics; booth space rates.

*Trade Shows Worldwide.* Cengage Learning Inc. • 2013. $645.00. 31st edition. Provides detailed information from over 75 countries on more than 10,000 trade shows and exhibitions. Separate sections are provided for trade shows/exhibitions, for sponsors/organizers, and for services, facilities, and information sources. Indexing is by date, location, subject, name, and keyword.

### INTERNET DATABASES

*Trade Show Center.* Global Sources/Trade Media Holdings Ltd. Phone: (656)574-2800; Email: service@globalsources.com • URL: http://www.globalsources.com/TRADESHW/TRDSHFRM.HTM • Free Web site provides current, detailed information on more than 1,000 major trade shows worldwide, including events in the U. S., but with an emphasis on "Asia and Greater China." Searching is offered by product, supplier, country, and month of year. Includes links to "Trade Information.".

### ONLINE DATABASES

*Wilson Business Abstracts Online.* H.W. Wilson Co. • Indexes and abstracts 600 major business periodicals, plus the *Wall Street Journal* and the business section of the *New York Times.* Indexing is from 1982, abstracting from 1990, with the two newspapers included from 1993. Updated weekly. Inquire as to online cost and availability. (*Business Periodicals Index* without abstracts is also available online.).

### PERIODICALS AND NEWSLETTERS

*Exhibit Builder.* Exhibit Builder. • Seven timees a year. $40.00 per year. For designers and builders of trade show exhibits.

*Facility Manager.* International Association of Venue Managers. • Quarterly. Free to members; nonmembers, $55.00 per year.

*Successful Meetings: The Authority on Meetings and Incentive Travel Management.* Nielsen Business Media Inc. • Monthly. Monthly. $79.00 per year.

*Tradeshow and Exhibit Manager.* Goldstein & Associates. • Bimonthly. $80.00 per year. Edited for exhibit, tradeshow, and exposition managers. Covers design trends, site selection, shipping problems, industry news, etc. Supplement available *Tradeshow Directory.*

*Tradeshow Week: Since 1971, the Only Weekly Source of News and Statistics on the Tradeshow Industry.* Reed Elsevier Group plc Reed Business Information. • 50 times a year. $419.00 per year; includes 18 *Supplements and 7 Websites.* Edited for corporate and association trade show and exhibit managers. Includes show calendars and labor rates.

### TRADE/PROFESSIONAL ASSOCIATIONS

Center for Exhibition Industry Research. 12700 Park Central Dr., Ste. 308, Dallas, TX 75251. Phone: (972)687-9242; Fax: (972)692-6020; Email: info@ceir.org • URL: http://www.ceir.org • Promotes the trade show as a marketing device. Formerly Trade Show Bureau.

# TRADE UNIONS

*See* LABOR UNIONS

# TRADEMARKS AND TRADE NAMES

*See also* COPYRIGHT; PATENTS

### CD-ROM DATABASES

*Authority Intellectual Property Library.* Matthew Bender and Company Inc. • Quarterly. Price on request. CD-ROM contains updated full text of *Intellectual Property Counseling and Litigation, Computer Law, International Computer Law, Nimmer on Copyright, Milgrim on Trade Secrets, Patent Litigation, Patent Licensing Transactions, Trademark Protection and Practice,* and other Matthew Bender publications relating to the law of intellectual property.

*CASSIS.* U.S. Patent and Trademark Office - Office of Electronic Information Products. • CD-ROM products include *Trademarks ASSIGN* (assignment deeds, bimonthly), *Trademarks ASSIST* (search tools, single- disc), *Trademarks PENDING* (applications on file, bimonthly), *Trademarks REGISTERED* (active trademarks, 1884 to date).

*TRADEMARKSCAN - Federal.* EBSCOhost. • Updated weekly. Contains information for more than 5 million records.

*TRADEMARKSCAN - U.S. State.* EBSCOhost. • Updated weekly. Provides information for more than 1.4 million trademarks registered with the Office of the Secretary of State in all 50 states and in Puerto Rico.

### DIRECTORIES

*Brands and Their Companies (BTC).* Cengage Learning Inc. • Annual. Coverage of more than 426,000 entries on trade names, trademarks, and brand names of consumer-oriented products and their 115,000 manufacturers, importers, marketers, or distributors. Formerly Trade Names Dictionary.

*European Drinks Marketing Directory.* Euromonitor International Business Reference Div. • Irregular Biennial. $215. Covers: The European drinks industry, including marketing, retailers, wholesalers, leading companies, market trends, and industry details. Entries include: Name, address, phone, fax, telex.

*Plunkett's Food Industry Almanac.* Plunkett Research Ltd. • $349.99 Individuals print + online. Covers: 340 leading companies in the global food industry. Entries include: Name, address, phone, fax, and key executives. Also includes analysis and information on trends, technology, and statistics in the field.

*Trademarkscan--International Register.* Thomson CompuMark Americas. • Semimonthly. Database covers: Over 445,000 active registered trademarks on file at the World Intellectual Property Organization. Also included are inactive records from the last 3 years. Entries include: Trademark word and/or design reference, current status, international class(es), description of product/ service, registration number, publication details, owner name/location.

*World Database of Consumer Brands and Their Owners.* Euromonitor International Business Reference Div. • Annual. $995. Covers: Descriptive information on the owning companies of approximately 56,000 brands across 1,000 consumer sectors in 85 countries.

*World Food Marketing Directory.* Euromonitor International Business Reference Div. • $475 Individuals. Covers: Over 2,000 retailers and wholesalers, 1,500 manufacturers, over 2,000 international and European organizations, statistical agencies, trade journals and associations, databases, and trade fairs in the grocery and food industries worldwide. Entries include: Company name, address, phone, telex, names of parent company and subsidiaries, number of employees, financial data, products and brand names handled; retailers and wholesalers include type of outlet, names and titles of key personnel.

### HANDBOOKS AND MANUALS

*Gilson Trademark Protection and Practice.* Jerome Gilson. Matthew Bender and Company Inc. • 3/year. $2,579 Individuals Book. Periodic supplementation. Covers U.S. trademark practice.

*Intellectual Property Primary Law Sourcebook.* Matthew Bender and Company Inc. • $175 print only. Provides federal copyright, patent, and trademark statutes, as well as the Leahy-Smith America Invents Act.

*Trademark Manual of Examining Procedure.* U. S. Government Printing Office. • $70 Individuals looseleaf binding. Covers "practices and procedures" relating to the processing of applications to register trademarks in the U. S. Patent and Trademark Office.

*World Trademark Law and Practice.* Matthew Bender and Company Inc. • $1,864 print. Five looseleaf volumes. Periodic supplementation. A guide to international trademark practice with detailed coverage of 35 major jurisdictions and summary coverage for over 100.

### INTERNET DATABASES

*SAEGIS Internet Search.* Thomson & Thomson. Phone: 800-692-8833 or (617)479-1600; Fax: (617)786-8273; Email: support@thomson-thomson.com • URL: http://www.thomson-thomson.com • Fee-based Web site provides extensive, common law screening of the World Wide Web for trademarks. Searches are performed offline, with final report delivered to user's "SAEGIS Inbox." Context of trademark within each relevant Web site is indicated, and links are provided.

*United States Patent and Trademark Office.* U. S. Department of Commerce. Phone: 800-786-9199 or (703)308-4357; Fax: (703)305-7786; Email: help@mbda.gov • URL: http://www.uspto.gov • Web site provides extensive information about patents and trademarks, with advanced search facilities for specific documents or names. "Special Pages" are available for "How to Search," "Trademarks-Logos-Brands," "Inventor Resources," and other topics. A complete fee schedule is available for filing applications, appeals, copies, etc.

### ONLINE DATABASES

*Thomas Register Online.* Thomas Publishing Company L.L.C. • Provides concise information on approximately 194,000 U. S. companies, mainly manufacturers, with over 50,000 product classifications. Indexes over 115,000 trade names. Information is updated semiannually. Inquire as to online cost and availability.

*TRADEMARKSCAN: International Register.* Thomson CompuMark Americas. • Supplies current information on more than 400,000 trademarks registered with the World Intellectual Property Organization. Updates are monthly. Inquire as to online cost and availability. (TRADEMARKSCAN also maintains extensive databases for individual countries: Canada, U. K., Germany, Italy, France, and others.).

*TRADEMARKSCAN: U. S. Federal.* Thomson CompuMark Americas. • Provides information on more than two million trademarks registered and pending at the U. S. Patent and Trademark Office. Time period is 1884 to date for active trademarks, with updates twice a week. Graphic images are show. Inquire as to online cost and availability.

*TRADEMARKSCAN: U. S. State.* Thomson CompuMark Americas. • Contains information on more than 970,000 trademarks registered with the Office of the Secretary of State in all 50 states and in Puerto Rico. Time period is 1900 to date for active trademarks, with weekly updates. Inquire as to online cost and availability.

### OTHER SOURCES

*Callmann on Unfair Competition, Trademarks and Monopolies.* Louis Altman and Rudolf Callmann. Thomson West. • Semiannual. $2,973. Covers various aspects of anti-competitive behavior.

*Intellectual Property and Antitrust Law.* William C. Holmes. Thomson West. • Semiannual. $1,347 full set. Includes patent, trademark, and copyright practices.

## PERIODICALS AND NEWSLETTERS

*Intellectual Property Today.* • Monthly. $96.00 per year. Covers legal developments in copyright, patents, trademarks, and licensing. Emphasizes the effect of new technology on intellectual property. Formerly *Law Works.*

*Les Nouvelles.* Licensing Executives Society. • Quarterly. Description: Concerned with technological licensing and related subjects. Covers technology, patents, trademarks, and licensing "know-how" world-wide.

*Official Gazette of the United States Patent and Trademark Office: Trademarks.* U. S. Government Printing Office. • Weekly. $1,229.00 per year by first class mail. Contains Trademarks, Trademark Notices, Marks Published for Opposition, Trademark Registrations Issued, and Index of Registrants (www.uspto.gov).

*The Trademark Reporter.* International Trademark Association. • Bimonthly. $80 Members. Contains articles on trademark developments, trademark law, and the use of trademarks.

*The Trademarker Reporter.* International Trademark Association. • Bimonthly. Publishes works of high-quality legal scholarship by trademark practitioners and professionals, academic faculty and law students.

# TRADES

*See* OCCUPATIONS

# TRADING

*See* BARTER AND COUNTERTRADE

# TRADING STAMPS

*See* PREMIUMS

# TRAFFIC ACCIDENTS AND TRAFFIC SAFETY

*See also* ACCIDENTS

## ABSTRACTS AND INDEXES

*Highway Safety Literature.* • Annual. $80.00.

*Transportation Research Information Services ((TRIS)).* Transportation Research Board, Highway Research Information. • Part of the TRID database, which contains more than 900,000 research records.

## BIBLIOGRAPHIES

*Road Construction and Safety.* U. S. Government Printing Office. • Annual. Free. Issued by the Superintendent of Documents. A list of government publications on highway construction and traffic safety. Formerly *Highway Construction, Safety and Traffic.* (Subject Bibliography No. 3.).

## ONLINE DATABASES

*I.I.I. Data Base Search.* Insurance Information Institute. • Provides online citations and abstracts of insurance-related literature in magazines, newspapers, trade journals, and books. Emphasis is on property and casualty insurance issues, including highway safety, product safety, and environmental liability. Inquire as to online cost and availability.

*TRIS: Transportation Research Information Service.* The National Academies National Research Council. • Contains abstracts and citations to a wide range of transportation literature, 1968 to present, with monthly updates. Includes references to the literature of air transportation, highways, ships and shipping, railroads, trucking, and urban mass

transportation. Formerly *TRIS-ON-LINE.* Inquire as to online cost and availability.

## PERIODICALS AND NEWSLETTERS

*Insurance Institute for Highway Safety, Status Report.* Insurance Institute for Highway Safety. • 10 times a year. Free.

## RESEARCH CENTERS AND INSTITUTES

Insurance Institute for Highway Safety. 1005 N Glebe Rd., Ste. 800, Arlington, VA 22201. Phone: (703)247-1500; Fax: (703)247-1588 • URL: http://www.iihs.org • Studies highway safety, including seat belt use, air bags, property damage, vehicle recalls, and the role of alcohol and drugs.

Texas A&M University - Texas Transportation Institute. 3135 TAMU, College Station, TX 77843-3135. Phone: (979)845-1713; Fax: (979)845-9356; Email: dennis-c@tamu.edu • URL: http://tti.tamu.edu • Concerned with all forms and modes of transportation. Research areas include transportation economics, highway construction, traffic safety, public transportation, and highway engineering.

University of Michigan - Transportation Research Institute. 2901 Baxter Rd., Ann Arbor, MI 48109-2150. Phone: (734)764-6504; Fax: (734)936-1081; Email: umtri-director@umich.edu • URL: http://www.umtri.umich.edu • Research areas include highway safety, transportation systems, and shipbuilding.

## STATISTICS SOURCES

*Injury Facts.* National Safety Council. • Annual. $109.85 Nonmembers.

## TRADE/PROFESSIONAL ASSOCIATIONS

American Driver and Traffic Safety Education Association. Highway Safety Services, LLC, 1434 Trim Tree Rd., Indiana, PA 15701. Phone: 877-485-7172 or (724)801-8246; Fax: (724)349-5042; Email: office@adtsea.org • URL: http://www.adtsea.org • Professional organization of teachers and supervisors interested in improving driver and traffic safety education in colleges and secondary and elementary schools. Awards honorary memberships to retired persons distinguished in the field. Provides assistance to state departments of education, colleges and universities, state associations, and local school districts.

American Highway Users Alliance. 1101 14th St. NW, Ste. 750, Washington, DC 20005. Phone: (202)857-1200; Fax: (202)857-1220; Email: info@highways.org • URL: http://www.highways.org • Broad-based consumers group for American motorists, truckers and businesses. Employs lobbying, media, communications and grassroots advocacy, promotes public policy that devotes highway use taxes to investments in safe and uncongested national highway systems.

Center for Auto Safety. 1825 Connecticut Ave. NW, Ste. 330, Washington, DC 20009-5708. Phone: (202)328-7700 • URL: http://www.autosafety.org • Seeks to "reduce the human and economic losses wrought by the automobile and the auto industry." As an auto and highway safety advocate, the center monitors government agencies charged with regulation of the industry, supports safety standards, participates in the rule-making procedures of the National Highway Traffic Safety Administration and the Federal Highway Administration, and occasionally institutes legal action. Collects literature and statistics on automobile safety and analyzes developments in the field. Letters are being coded by auto make, 2nd model, year.

# TRAFFIC ENGINEERING

*See also* TOLL ROADS; TRANSPORTATION INDUSTRY

## ABSTRACTS AND INDEXES

*Transportation Research Information Services ((TRIS)).* Transportation Research Board, Highway Research Information. • Part of the TRID database, which contains more than 900,000 research records.

## PERIODICALS AND NEWSLETTERS

*ITE Journal.* Institute of Transportation Engineers. • Monthly. $75 U.S., Canada, and Mexico. Technical magazine focusing on the plan, design, and operation of surface transportation systems. Formerly *Transportation Engineering.*

*Traffic Engineering and Control: The International Journal of Traffic Management and Transportation Planning.* Printerhall Ltd. • Monthly. $120.00 per year. Provides authoritative articles on planning, engineering and management of highways for safe and efficient operation.

*Traffic World: The Logistics News Weekly n.* Journal of Commerce, Inc. • Weekly. $174.00 per year.

*Transportation Quarterly: An Independent Journal for Better Transportation Policy.* Eno Transportation Foundation. • Quarterly. $55.00 per year. To qualify a written request must be submitted.

## TRADE/PROFESSIONAL ASSOCIATIONS

American Road and Transportation Builders Association. 1219 28th St. NW, Washington, DC 20007-3389. Phone: (202)289-4434; Fax: (202)289-4435; Email: general@artba.org • URL: http://www.artba.org • Promotes on-the-job training programs.

# TRAFFIC MANAGEMENT (INDUSTRIAL)

*See also* DISTRIBUTION; TRANSPORTATION INDUSTRY

## PERIODICALS AND NEWSLETTERS

*Chilton's Distribution: The Transportation and Business Logistics Magazine.* Reed Elsevier Group plc Reed Business Information. • Monthly. $65.00 per year.

*Traffic World: The Logistics News Weekly n.* Journal of Commerce, Inc. • Weekly. $174.00 per year.

*Transportation and Distribution: Integrating Logistics in Supply Chain Management.* Penton Media Inc. • Monthly. Free to qualified personnel; others, $50.00 per year. Essential information on transportation and distribution practices in domestic and international trade.

*Transportation Journal.* American Society of Transportation and Logistics. • Quarterly. $128 Individuals print or online. Covers research findings and original writings on transportation, logistics, and related fields.

## TRADE/PROFESSIONAL ASSOCIATIONS

American Society of Transportation and Logistics. 8430 W Bryn Mawr Ave., Ste. 1000, Chicago, IL 60631. Phone: (773)355-4900; Fax: (773)355-4888; Email: info@astl.org • URL: http://www.astl.org • Persons engaged in transportation, traffic, logistics, or physical distribution management. Works to establish standards of knowledge, technical training, experience, conduct, and ethics, and to encourage high standards of education and technical training requisite for the proper performance of traffic, transportation, logistics, and physical distribution management. Conducts extensive educational programs.

National Industrial Transportation League. 1700 N Moore St., Ste. 1900, Arlington, VA 22209. Phone: (703)524-5011; Fax: (703)524-5017; Email: info@nitl.org • URL: http://www.nitl.org • Seeks to promote adequate national and international transportation; encourages the exchange of ideas and information concerning traffic and transportation; and cooperates with regulatory agencies and other transportation companies in developing an understanding of legislation.

# TRAFFIC MANAGEMENT (STREETS AND HIGHWAYS)

*See also* TRAFFIC ENGINEERING; TRANSPORTATION INDUSTRY

## ABSTRACTS AND INDEXES

*Transportation Research Information Services ((TRIS)).* Transportation Research Board, Highway Research Information. • Part of the TRID database, which contains more than 900,000 research records.

## BIBLIOGRAPHIES

*Road Construction and Safety.* U. S. Government Printing Office. • Annual. Free. Issued by the Superintendent of Documents. A list of government publications on highway construction and traffic safety. Formerly *Highway Construction, Safety and Traffic.* (Subject Bibliography No. 3.).

## DIRECTORIES

*Jane's Road Traffic Management and ITS.* Jane's Information Group, Inc. • Annual. $470.00. A directory of traffic control equipment and services. Includes detailed product descriptions.

## HANDBOOKS AND MANUALS

*Standard Highway Signs, as Specified in the Manual on Uniform Traffic Control Devices.* U. S. Government Printing Office. • Looseleaf. $153.00. Issued by the U. S. Department of Transportation (www. dot.gov). Includes basic manual, with updates for an indeterminate period. Contains illustrations of typical standard signs approved for use on streets and highways, and provides information on dimensions and placement of symbols.

## ONLINE DATABASES

*TRIS: Transportation Research Information Service.* The National Academies National Research Council. • Contains abstracts and citations to a wide range of transportation literature, 1968 to present, with monthly updates. Includes references to the literature of air transportation, highways, ships and shipping, railroads, trucking, and urban mass transportation. Formerly *TRIS-ON-LINE.* Inquire as to online cost and availability.

## PERIODICALS AND NEWSLETTERS

*Downtown Idea Exchange: Essential Information for Downtown Research and Development Center.* Downtown Research and Development Center. Alexander Communications Group Inc. • Monthly. $227 Individuals. Newsletter for those concerned with central business districts. Provides news and other information on planning, development, parking, mass transit, traffic, funding, and other topics.

*Public Roads: A Journal of Highway Research and Development.* U. S. Government Printing Office. • Bimonthly. $31 U.S.. Contains articles relating to highway research, engineering, safety on the highways, surfacing, and other subjects.

*Transportation Journal.* American Society of Transportation and Logistics. • Quarterly. $128 Individuals print or online. Covers research findings and original writings on transportation, logistics, and related fields.

## RESEARCH CENTERS AND INSTITUTES

Northwestern University - Center for Public Safety. 1801 Maple Ave., Evanston, IL 60201-3149. Phone: 800-323-4011 or (847)491-5476; Fax: (847)491-5270; Email: nucps@northwestern.edu • URL: http://nucps.northwestern.edu • Police management, traffic law enforcement, criminal justice, accident investigation, and highway safety in all areas of traffic and transportation engineering, including highway and street design, traffic operations, use of

computer tools, site development, and transit planning and operation.

## TRADE/PROFESSIONAL ASSOCIATIONS

American Society of Transportation and Logistics. 8430 W Bryn Mawr Ave., Ste. 1000, Chicago, IL 60631. Phone: (773)355-4900; Fax: (773)355-4888; Email: info@astl.org • URL: http://www.astl.org • Persons engaged in transportation, traffic, logistics, or physical distribution management. Works to establish standards of knowledge, technical training, experience, conduct, and ethics, and to encourage high standards of education and technical training requisite for the proper performance of traffic, transportation, logistics, and physical distribution management. Conducts extensive educational programs.

# TRAINING OF EMPLOYEES

*See also* EXECUTIVE TRAINING AND DEVELOPMENT

## DIRECTORIES

*ATD Buyer's Guide.* ASTD. • Annual. Database covers: Businesses and individual consultants offering products, services, and equipment for sale to persons in corporate training and human resource development. Entries include: Company name, contact information and name, profile, list of products and services.

## ENCYCLOPEDIAS AND DICTIONARIES

*Encyclopedia of E-Leadership, Counseling and Training.* Cengage Learning Inc. • Offers an in-depth description of key terms and concepts related to different themes, issues, and trends in educational leadership, counseling, and technology integration in modern universities and organizations worldwide.

## PERIODICALS AND NEWSLETTERS

*Human Resource Executive.* LRP Publications Library. • 16 times a year. $89.95 per year. Edited for directors of corporate human resource departments. Special issues emphasize training, benefits, retirement planning, recruitment, outplacement, workers' compensation, legal pitfalls, and oes emphasize training, benefits, retirement planning, recruitment, outplacement, workers' compensation, legal pitfalls, and other personnel topics.

*T and D Magazine.* ASTD. • Monthly. Free to members; non-members, $85.00 per year.

*Team Leader.* LRP Publications Library. • Description: Keeps business team leaders up to date on team-leading techniques and provides solutions to team-oriented issues.

*Training: The Magazine of Covering the Human Side of Business.* Nielsen Business Media Inc. • Monthly. $78.00 per year.

## RESEARCH CENTERS AND INSTITUTES

FHI 360 - National Institute for Work and Learning. 1825 Connecticut Ave. NW, Washington, DC 20009. Phone: (202)884-8184; Fax: (202)884-8422; Email: icharner@fhi360.org • URL: http://www.niwl.org • Research areas include adult education, training, unemployment insurance, and career development.

Middle Tennessee State University - Tennessee Center for Labor-Management Relations. 1313 Old Ft. Pky., Ste. 300, Murfreesboro, TN 37129. Phone: (615)895-4166; Fax: (615)895-9389 • URL: http://www.tnlabormgmt.org • Steward training, leadership, supervisor training, labor-management cooperation, stress management, negotiation, health and safety, worker participation, mediation, alternate dispute resolution, and diversity.

Princeton University - Industrial Relations Section. Firestone Library, A-18-J, 1 Washington Rd., Princeton, NJ 08544. Phone: (609)258-4040; Fax: (609)258-2907; Email: c6789@princeton.edu •

URL: http://www.irs.princeton.edu • Fields of research include labor supply, manpower training, unemployment, and equal employment opportunity.

Techsolve Inc. 6705 Steger Dr., Cincinnati, OH 45237. Phone: 800-345-4482 or (513)948-2000; Fax: (513)948-2109 or (800)345-4482; Email: perkins@techsolve.org • URL: http://www. techsolve.org • Fields of research include quality improvement, computer-aided design, artificial intelligence, and employee training.

W.E. Upjohn Institute for Employment Research. 300 S Westnedge Ave., Kalamazoo, MI 49007-4686. Phone: 888-227-8569 or (269)343-5541; Fax: (269)343-7310; Email: communications@upjohn. org • URL: http://www.upjohninstitute.org • Research fields include unemployment, unemployment insurance, worker's compensation, labor productivity, profit sharing, the labor market, economic development, earnings, training, and other areas related to employment.

## STATISTICS SOURCES

*Occupational Projections and Training Data.* U. S. Government Printing Office. • Biennial. $31.50. Issued by Bureau of Labor Statistics, U. S. Department of Labor. Contains projections of employment change and job openings over the next 15 years for about 500 specific occupations. Also includes the number of associate, bachelor's, master's, doctoral, and professional degrees awarded in a recent year for about 900 specific fields of study.

## TRADE/PROFESSIONAL ASSOCIATIONS

American Technical Education Association. Dunwoody College of Technology, 818 Dunwoody Blvd., Minneapolis, MN 55403. Phone: (612)381-3315; Email: info@ateaonline.org • URL: http:// www.ateaonline.org • Dedicated to excellence in the quality of post-secondary technical education with emphasis on professional development.

Asia Catalyst. 39 W 32nd St., Ste. 1602, New York, NY 10001. Phone: (212)967-2123; Email: info@ asiacatalyst.org • URL: http://www.asiacatalyst.org • Provides support services to non-governmental organizations (NGOs). Facilitates capacity-building training in personnel and financial management. Conducts fundraising, advocacy, and media outreach activities. Fosters research on human rights issues that are of direct concern to NGOs.

ASTD. 1640 King St., Alexandria, VA 22314-2746. Phone: 800-628-2783 or (703)683-8100; Fax: (703)683-1523; Email: customercare@astd.org • URL: http://www.astd.org • Represents workplace learning and performance professionals.

Eastern and Southern Africa Management Institute. PO Box 3030, Arusha, Tanzania. Phone: 255 27 2508384 or 255 27 2508385; Fax: 255 27 2508285; Email: esamihq@esamihq.ac.tz • URL: http://www. esami-africa.org • Management personnel and vocational training programs. Seeks to advance the practice of business and organizational administration. Facilitates exchange of information among members; makes available educational and training programs.

Edexcel International. 190 High Holborn, London WC1V 7BH, United Kingdom. Phone: 44 1204 770696; Email: internationaleo@pearson.com • URL: http://www.edexcel.com/international/europe • Approves academic and work-related programmes of study including GNVQs, NVQs and GCSEs, A levels and A/S levels throughout England, Wales and Northern Ireland, and overseas and awards qualifications to students who successfully complete these and HND programmes.

Finance Sector Union of Australia. 341 Queen St., Melbourne, VIC 3000, Australia. Fax: 61 39 1300366378 or 61 39 1300307943; Email: fsuinfo@ fsunion.org.au • URL: http://www.fsunion.org.au • Employees of private and public sector financial services companies. Works to enhance members' welfare and conditions of employment. Conducts union organization training and insurance industry research.

Irish Institute of Training and Development. Millennium Business Park, 4 Sycamore House, Naas, Kildare, Ireland. Phone: 353 45 881166; Fax: 353 45 881192; Email: info@iitd.com • URL: http://www.iitd.ie • Individuals working in human resource development in Ireland. Fosters communication among members. Conducts educational programs.

Manpower Education Institute. 1835 Charles Ave., Lancaster, SC 29720-1512. Phone: (718)548-4200; Email: info@meipublishing.com • URL: http://www.manpower-education.org • Individuals from the fields of business, labor, and education who develop educational film series for the U.S. labor force. Series includes: Ready or Not (pre-retirement planning), Your Future Is Now (high school equivalency programs), Read Your Way Up (reading skills improvement), Out of Work (for the unemployed), If You Don't Come In Sunday, Don't Come In Monday (history of the American labor movement), Plug Us In (to assist workers reentering the labor market), and Where Do I Fit In (new worker orientation).

Ohio State University - College of Education and Human Ecology - Center on Education and Training for Employment. 1900 Kenny Rd., Columbus, OH 43210-1016. Phone: 800-848-4815 or (614)292-8008; Fax: (614)292-1260; Email: kelsey.28@osu.edu • URL: http://cete.osu.edu • Formerly National Center for Research in Vocational Education.

# TRAINS

*See* RAILROADS

# TRANSDUCERS, INDUSTRIAL

*See* CONTROL EQUIPMENT INDUSTRY

# TRANSISTORS

*See* SEMICONDUCTOR INDUSTRY

# TRANSLATING MACHINES

*See* MACHINE TRANSLATING

# TRANSLATIONS AND TRANSLATORS

*See also* MACHINE TRANSLATING

## ABSTRACTS AND INDEXES
*Transdex Index.* ProQuest L.L.C. • Provides access to materials originally published outside the United States and translated into English.

## TRADE/PROFESSIONAL ASSOCIATIONS
American Translators Association. 225 Reinekers Ln., Ste. 590, Alexandria, VA 22314. Phone: (703)683-6100; Fax: (703)683-6122; Email: ata@atanet.org • URL: http://www.atanet.org • Fosters the professional development of translators and interpreters and promotes the translation and interpretation professions.

# TRANSPORTATION EQUIPMENT INDUSTRY

## FINANCIAL RATIOS
*Industry Norms and Key Business Ratios.* Dun & Bradstreet Inc. • Annual. Five volumes. Covers over

800 kinds of businesses, arranged by Standard Industrial Classification number. More detailed editions covering longer periods of time are also available.

*Quarterly Financial Report for Manufacturing, Mining, Trade, and Selected Service Industries.* U.S. Federal Trade Commission and U.S. Securities and Exchange Commission. U.S. Census Bureau Foreign Trade Division. • Quarterly. Quarterly. Report on financial results of U.S. corporations.

## ONLINE DATABASES
*TRIS: Transportation Research Information Service.* The National Academies National Research Council. • Contains abstracts and citations to a wide range of transportation literature, 1968 to present, with monthly updates. Includes references to the literature of air transportation, highways, ships and shipping, railroads, trucking, and urban mass transportation. Formerly *TRIS-ON-LINE.* Inquire as to online cost and availability.

## PERIODICALS AND NEWSLETTERS
*ITE Journal.* Institute of Transportation Engineers. • Monthly. $75 U.S., Canada, and Mexico. Technical magazine focusing on the plan, design, and operation of surface transportation systems. Formerly *Transportation Engineering.*

# TRANSPORTATION INDUSTRY

## ABSTRACTS AND INDEXES
*NTIS Alerts: Transportation.* U.S. Department of Commerce National Technical Information Service. • Biweekly. $130 per year. Covers air, marine, highway, inland waterway, pipeline, and railroad transportation.

## ALMANACS AND YEARBOOKS
*Research in Transportation Economics.* Elsevier. • $727 Individuals Print. Covers a wide variety of topics relating to the economic aspects of transportation, government regulatory policies regarding transportation, and issues of concern to transportation industry planners.

## CD-ROM DATABASES
*Business Abstracts with Full Text.* EBSCO Publishing Inc. • Includes full text articles from more than 460 business publications from 1982 to present. Indexing for nearly 880 publications.

*OECD Statistical Compendium.* Organization for Economic Cooperation and Development. • Semiannual. $1,905.00 per year for 1 to 10 users. CD-ROM contains more than 730,000 monthly, quarterly, and annual time series for OECD countries, 1960 to date. Includes fully searchable data on agriculture, food, economic indicators, national accounts, employment, energy, finance, industry, technology, and foreign trade. Results can be displayed in various forms.

## DIRECTORIES
*Movers Directory.* InfoGroup Inc. • Annual. Number of listings: 15,712. Entries include: Name, address, phone, size of advertisement, name of owner or manager, number of employees, year first in "Yellow Pages." Compiled from telephone company "Yellow Pages," nationwide.

*The Transportation Leader--Buyer's Guide Issue.* Taxicab, Limousine and Paratransit Association. • Annual. Publication includes: List of manufacturers of taxicabs, minibuses, vans, limousines, parts, service equipment, wheelchair lifts, communications systems; also includes consultants, insurance agencies, advertising services, propane or natural gas systems; dealers in used vehicles, two-way radios, and meters; and other companies servicing the for-hire vehicle fleet industry (taxicabs,

limousines, vans, and minibuses). Entries include: Company name, address, phone, contact person, and brief description of product or service.

*Transportation Telephone Tickler.* Journal of Commerce Group. • Annual. $199 Individuals free shipping and handling. Covers: 24,000 companies and agents in North American port districts which provide transportation services ranging from air freight forwarding to warehousing. Published in a four-volume national edition and 7 regional editions. Entries include: Company name, headquarters and branch addresses, phone and fax numbers, names of key personnel, e-mail and web addresses.

## E-BOOKS
*Encyclopedia of American Industries.* Cengage Learning Inc. • 2011. $807.00. 6th edition. Three volumes. Volume one is Manufacturing Industries and volume two is Service and Non-Manufacturing Industries. Provides the history, development, and recent status of approximately 1,000 industries. Includes statistical graphs, with industry and general indexes. Also available as eBook.

## GENERAL WORKS
*Airline Business.* Dagens Industri. • Monthly. Publication covering the transportation industry.

*Transportation Business.* Baxter Publications Inc. • Biweekly. Publication covering all aspects of the transportation industry.

## INTERNET DATABASES
*Bureau of Economic Analysis.* U. S. Department of Commerce, Bureau of Economic Analysis. Phone: (202)606-9900; Fax: (202)606-5310; Email: webmaster@bea.doc.gov • URL: http://www.bea.doc.gov • Web site includes "News Release Information" covering national, regional, and international economic estimates from the BEA. Highlights of releases appear online the same day, complete text and tables appear the next day. "Recent News Releases" section provides titles for past nine months, with links. "BEA Data and Methodology" includes "Frequently Requested NIPA Data" (national income and product accounts, such as gross domestic product and personal income). Other statistics are available. Fees: Free.

*Business 2.0 Web Guide to the Best Business Links.* Business 2.0 Media Inc. Phone: (415)293-4800; Email: support@business2.com • URL: http://www.business2.com/webguide • Web site presents an extensive, searchable directory of links to "the best, most informative, and authoritative web pages." Twenty main categories cover business, finance, career, company information, people, and technology topics, with thousands of subtopics, all linking to Web sites recommended by experienced business researchers. Fees: Free.

*Fedstats.* Federal Interagency Council on Statistical Policy. Phone: (202)395-7254 • URL: http://www.fedstats.gov • Web site features an efficient search facility for full-text statistics produced by more than 100 federal agencies, including the Census Bureau, the Bureau of Economic Analysis, and the Bureau of Labor Statistics. Boolean searches can be made within one agency or for all agencies combined. Links are offered to international statistical bureaus, including the UN, IMF, OECD, UNESCO, Eurostat, and 20 individual countries. Fees: Free.

*FreeLunch.com.* Economy.com, Inc. Phone: (610)696-8700; Fax: (610)696-1678 • URL: http://www.freelunch.com • Web site provides free access to more than 200 million economic and financial data series, covering industry, demographics, labor markets, prices, retail sales, government spending, trade, interest rates, housing starts, the stock market, etc. Data is available in either chart or table form. Searching is offered. Free, but registration required. Economy.com, Inc. also offers fee-based economic analysis at *The Dismal Scientist* site (www.dismal.com).

## ONLINE DATABASES

*TRIS: Transportation Research Information Service.* The National Academies National Research Council. • Contains abstracts and citations to a wide range of transportation literature, 1968 to present, with monthly updates. Includes references to the literature of air transportation, highways, ships and shipping, railroads, trucking, and urban mass transportation. Formerly *TRIS-ON-LINE.* Inquire as to online cost and availability.

*Wilson Business Abstracts Online.* H.W. Wilson Co. • Indexes and abstracts 600 major business periodicals, plus the *Wall Street Journal* and the business section of the *New York Times.* Indexing is from 1982, abstracting from 1990, with the two newspapers included from 1993. Updated weekly. Inquire as to online cost and availability. (*Business Periodicals Index* without abstracts is also available online.).

## PERIODICALS AND NEWSLETTERS

*Defense Transportation Journal.* National Defense Transportation Association. • Bimonthly. $35 in U.S.. Bimonthly. Free to members.

*ITE Journal.* Institute of Transportation Engineers. • Monthly. $75 U.S., Canada, and Mexico. Technical magazine focusing on the plan, design, and operation of surface transportation systems. Formerly *Transportation Engineering.*

*Modern Bulk Transporter.* Primedia Business Magazines and Media. • Monthly. Information for bulk logisitcs.

*Passenger Transport: The Weekly Newspaper of the Public Transportation Industry.* American Public Transportation Association. • Weekly. $75 Individuals. Covers current events and trends in mass transportation.

*Research on Transport Economics.* Organisation for Economic Co-operation and Development Publications and Information Center. • Annual. Quarterly $138.00. Text in French.

*Transportation Journal.* American Society of Transportation and Logistics. • Quarterly. $128 Individuals print or online. Covers research findings and original writings on transportation, logistics, and related fields.

*Transportation Research Part E: Logistics and Transportation Review.* University of British Columbia Centre for Transportation Studies. Elsevier. • Bimonthly. Individuals, $213.00 per year; institutions, $897.00 per year.

*Transportation Science.* INFORMS. • Quarterly. Individuals, $155.00 per year. Includes print and on-line editions. Institutions, $221.00 per year. Includes print and online editions.

*Urban Transport News: Management-Funding Terrorism-Ridership-Technology.* Business Publishers Inc. • 25 times a year. $437.00 per year. Newsletter. Provides current news from Capitol Hill, the White House, the Dept. of Transportation, as well as transit operations and industries across the country.

## RESEARCH CENTERS AND INSTITUTES

Federal Highway Administration - Office of Transportation Policy Studies. 1200 New Jersey Ave. SE, 8th Fl., Washington, DC 20590. Phone: (202)366-9232; Fax: (202)366-3297; Email: mary.tischer@dot.gov • URL: http://www.fhwa.dot.gov/policy/otps • Formulation of highway policy and legislative initiatives. Principal areas of research interest are highway use, performance, and requirements and the relationship of these factors to commercial highway transport; truck sizes and weights; cost allocations; transportation user charge substructures, taxing policies and subsidy issues, and the effects of these issues upon various public and private groups; and the economic characteristics of specific industries (as necessary for the formula-

tion of highway program policy).

Massachusetts Institute of Technology - Center for Transportation and Logistics. 77 Massachusetts Ave., E40-276, Cambridge, MA 02139. Phone: (617)253-5320; Fax: (617)253-4560; Email: sheffi@mit.edu • URL: http://ctl.mit.edu • Transportation and logistics, with emphasis on problem-oriented, interdisciplinary, and multi-model studies, including studies on innovative urban transportation systems, transport technology innovations, railroad systems operations, trucking, energy policies, regional transportation planning and programming, highway location and design, flight transportation, ocean shipping, transportation systems analysis, logistics, supply chain management, logistics organizations, shipper/carrier relationships and logistics information technology.

Northwestern University - Transportation Center. 600 Foster St., Evanston, IL 60208-4055. Phone: (847)491-7287; Fax: (847)491-3090; Email: masmah@northwestern.edu • URL: http://transportation.northwestern.edu • Transportation, including information technology, air, rail, motor carrier, ocean and inland shipping, pipeline, telecommunications, and public transit. Focuses on the movement of materials, people, energy, and information. Emphasizes development of advanced models in logistics (vehicle routing, scheduling, inventory management, facility location), analyses of safety in the motor carrier and airline industries, evaluation of the impact of delivery restrictions in congested areas, use of advanced information technologies as competitive weapons in transportation management, studies of the impact of regulatory reform on industry economy, models of intercity travel behavior and suburban congestion, transportation planning.

Texas A&M University - Texas Transportation Institute. 3135 TAMU, College Station, TX 77843-3135. Phone: (979)845-1713; Fax: (979)845-9356; Email: dennis-c@tamu.edu • URL: http://tti.tamu.edu • Concerned with all forms and modes of transportation. Research areas include transportation economics, highway construction, traffic safety, public transportation, and highway engineering.

University of Florida - Transportation Research Center. 512 Weil Hall, Gainesville, FL 32611. Phone: 800-226-1013 or (352)392-9537 or (352)392-7575; Fax: (352)392-3394 or (352)392-3224; Email: elefter@ce.ufl.edu • URL: http://trc.ce.ufl.edu • Traffic operations, traffic simulation, traffic signal control, congestion pricing, network modeling, optimization, transportation planning, land use planning, older driver issues.

University of Michigan - Transportation Research Institute. 2901 Baxter Rd., Ann Arbor, MI 48109-2150. Phone: (734)764-6504; Fax: (734)936-1081; Email: umtri-director@umich.edu • URL: http://www.umtri.umich.edu • Research areas include highway safety, transportation systems, and shipbuilding.

## STATISTICS SOURCES

*Standard & Poor's Industry Surveys.* Standard & Poor's Financial Services L.L.C. • Semiannual. $1,800.00. Two looseleaf volumes. Includes monthly *Supplements.* Provides detailed, individual surveys of 52 major industry groups. Each survey is revised on a semiannual basis. Also includes "Monthly Investment Review" (industry group investment analysis) and monthly "Trends & Projections" (economic analysis).

*Statistical Yearbook.* United Nations Publications. • Annual. $125.00. Contains statistics for about 200 countries on a wide variety of economic, industrial, and demographic topics. Compiled by United Nations Statistical Office.

*Survey of Current Business.* U. S. Government Printing Office. • Published by Bureau of Economic

Analysis, U. S. Department of Commerce. Presents a wide variety of business and economic data.

*United States Census of Transportation.* Bureau of the Census, U.S. Department of Commerce. U. S. Government Printing Office. • Quinquennial.

*U.S. Industry and Trade Outlook.* U.S. Department of Commerce National Technical Information Service. • Annual. Produced by the International Trade Administration, U.S. Department of Commerce, in a "public-private" partnership with DRI/McGraw-Hill and Standard & Poor's. Provides basic data, outlook for the current year, and "Long-Term Prospects" (five-year projections) for a wide variety of products and services. Includes high technology industries. Formerly *U.S. Industrial Outlook.*

## TRADE/PROFESSIONAL ASSOCIATIONS

American Public Transportation Association. 1666 K St. NW, Ste. 1100, Washington, DC 20006. Phone: (202)496-4800; Fax: (202)496-4324; Email: info@apta.com • URL: http://www.apta.com • Motor bus and rapid transit systems; organizations responsible for planning, designing, constructing, financing and operating transit systems; business organizations which supply products and services to transit, academic institutions and state associations and departments of transportation. Represents the public interest in improving transit. Encourages cooperation among its members, their employees, the general public and compliance with the letter and spirit of equal opportunity principles. Seeks to: collect information relative to public transit; assist in the training, education and professional development of all persons involved in public transit; and engage in activities which promote public transit. Provides a medium for exchange of experiences, discussion, and a comparative study of public transit affairs; Promotes research.

American Society of Transportation and Logistics. 8430 W Bryn Mawr Ave., Ste. 1000, Chicago, IL 60631. Phone: (773)355-4900; Fax: (773)355-4888; Email: info@astl.org • URL: http://www.astl.org • Persons engaged in transportation, traffic, logistics, or physical distribution management. Works to establish standards of knowledge, technical training, experience, conduct, and ethics, and to encourage high standards of education and technical training requisite for the proper performance of traffic, transportation, logistics, and physical distribution management. Conducts extensive educational programs.

National Defense Transportation Association. 50 S Pickett St., Ste. 220, Alexandria, VA 22304-7296. Phone: (703)751-5011; Fax: (703)823-8761 • URL: http://www.ndtahq.com • Men and women in the field of transportation, travel logistics and related areas in the Armed Forces, federal government, private industry and the academic sector. Strives to foster a strong and efficient transportation system in support of national defense. Serves as link between government and industry on transportation matters. Operates a job placement service for members.

# TRANSPORTATION, PUBLIC

*See* PUBLIC TRANSPORTATION

# TRAVEL AGENCIES

*See also* TRAVEL INDUSTRY

## BIBLIOGRAPHIES

*Travel and Tourism.* U. S. Government Printing Office. • Annual. Free. Issued by the Superintendent of Documents. A list of government publications on the travel industry and tourism. Formerly *Mass Transit, Travel and Tourism.* (Subject Bibliography No. 302.).

## DIRECTORIES

*Plunkett's Airline, Hotel, and Travel Industry Almanac.* Plunkett Research Ltd. • Annual. $349.99. Contains profiles of 300 leading companies, including airlines, hotels, travel agencies, theme parks, cruise lines, casinos, and car rental companies.

## FINANCIAL RATIOS

*Annual Statement Studies.* Risk Management Association. • Annual. Compiled from over 280,000 financial statements.

*Annual Statement Studies: Industry Default Probabilities and Cash Flow Measures.* Risk Management Association. • Annual. $405 Nonmembers. Serves as a companion volume to the original *Annual Statement Studies.* Gives probability of default estimates on a percentage scale for more than 450 industries. Includes changes in position year-by-year for eight financial statement line items and provides percentage measures of cash flow.

## HANDBOOKS AND MANUALS

*Travel Agency.* Entrepreneur Press. • Looseleaf. $59.50. A practical guide to starting a travel agency. Covers profit potential, start-up costs, market size evaluation, owner's time required, site selection, lease negotiation, pricing, accounting, advertising, promotion, etc. (Start-Up Business Guide No. E1154.).

## OTHER SOURCES

*ICTA Travel Management Text Series.* Institute of Certified Travel Agents. • Four volumes. Volume one, *Business Management for Travel Agents*; volume two, *Personnel Management for Travel Agents*; volume three, *Marketing for Travel Agents*; volume four, *Domestic Leisure and International Tourism.*

## PERIODICALS AND NEWSLETTERS

*Travel Agent: The National Newsweekly Magazine of the Travel Industry.* Advanstar Communications. • 51 times a year. 250.00 per. year.

## TRADE/PROFESSIONAL ASSOCIATIONS

Association of Retail Travel Agents. 4320 N Miller Rd., Scottsdale, AZ 85251-3606. Phone: 866-369-8969 or (859)269-9739; Fax: (866)743-2087 • URL: http://www.arta.travel • Represents retail travel agents and agencies in North America. Promotes the interests of retail travel agents through representation on industry councils, testimony before Congress and participation government proceedings. Conducts joint marketing and educational programs; sponsors work-study program.

# TRAVEL, AIR

*See* AIR TRAVEL

# TRAVEL, BUSINESS

*See* BUSINESS TRAVEL

# TRAVEL INDUSTRY

*See also* AIR TRAVEL; BUSINESS TRAVEL; HOTEL AND MOTEL INDUSTRY; TRAVEL AGENCIES

## ABSTRACTS AND INDEXES

*Leisure, Recreation and Tourism Abstracts.* CABI Publishing North America. • Quarterly. Members, $280.00 per year; Institutions, $610.00 per year. Includes single site internet access. Provides coverage of the worldwide literature of travel, recreation, sports, and the hospitality industry.

## BIBLIOGRAPHIES

*Travel and Tourism.* U. S. Government Printing Office. • Annual. Free. Issued by the Superintendent of Documents. A list of government publications on the travel industry and tourism. Formerly *Mass Transit, Travel and Tourism.* (Subject Bibliography No. 302.).

## CD-ROM DATABASES

*OECD Statistical Compendium.* Organization for Economic Cooperation and Development. • Semiannual. $1,905.00 per year for 1 to 10 users. CD-ROM contains more than 730,000 monthly, quarterly, and annual time series for OECD countries, 1960 to date. Includes fully searchable data on agriculture, food, economic indicators, national accounts, employment, energy, finance, industry, technology, and foreign trade. Results can be displayed in various forms.

## DIRECTORIES

*Al-Batinah Tourist Guide.* Oman Chamber of Commerce and Industry. • Provides information and data on tourist sites, locations, services, and facilities they offer in Batinah Region. Entries include: Names and addresses of travel and tourism organizations and companies.

*Alternative Travel Directory: The Complete Guide to Traveling, Studying, and Living Overseas.* Transitions Abroad Publishing. • Annual. Covers: Over 2,000 sources of information on international employment, education, and specialty travel opportunities. Entries include: Source name, address, phone, description, cost dates.

*Australian Hospitality Directory.* Associated Media Group. • Annual. Provides business information on transport, food service, entertainment, equipment and supplies, education and management, furniture, bedding, and lighting.

*Bottin Touristique du Quebec.* Quebec Dans Le Monde. • Annual. $51.95 Individuals. Covers: Approximately 800 business, cultural and recreational travel agencies and agents in Quebec. Entries include: Company name, address, phone, fax, agent name, address, phone, fax, activities.

*Dakhiliya Region Tourist Guide.* Oman Chamber of Commerce and Industry. • Provides information and data on tourist sites, locations, services in Dakhiliya Region. Entries include: Names and addresses of travel and tourism organizations and companies.

*Minnesota Airport Directory & Travel Guide.* Minnesota Department of Transportation, Office of Aeronautics. • Annual. Covers: Airports and public seaplane bases in Minnesota. Database includes: Information on approaches, ditches, lights, nearby rivers, elevation, latitude and longitude, storage facilities and repair potential. Entries include: Address and telephone number.

*The Travel Book: Guide to the Travel Guides.* The Scarecrow Press Inc. • Covers: Travel guides from throughout the world.

*World of Information Business & Economic Europe Review.* Kogan Page, Limited. • Covers: Tourist and business information, including airlines, banks, hotels, ministries and associations in Europe. Entries include: Address.

## GENERAL WORKS

*ACTE Global Business Journal.* Association of Corporate Travel Executives. • Quarterly. Magazine covering corporate travel.

*Hong Kong for the Business Visitor.* Hong Kong Trade Development Council. • Annual. Journal of travel, tourism, business and economics.

*Tourism Economics: The Business and Finance of Tourism and Recreation.* IP Publishing Ltd. • Bimonthly. $530 Institutions. Journal covering the business and finance aspects of the tourism and recreation industry.

## HANDBOOKS AND MANUALS

*Health Information for International Travel.* U.S. Dept. of Health and Human Services - Centers for Disease Control and Prefabricated. • Annual. $38. Produced by the Centers for Disease Control and Prevention (CDC). Primarily edited for "healthcare providers who administer pre- and post-travel counseling and care." Also serves as a reference for airlines, cruise lines, and the travel industry in general. Covers such items as injuries during travel, motion sickness, disabilities, vaccines, insect repellents, and travel with children. Sometimes known as "The Yellow Book.".

## INTERNET DATABASES

*Business 2.0 Web Guide to the Best Business Links.* Business 2.0 Media Inc. Phone: (415)293-4800; Email: support@business2.com • URL: http://www.business2.com/webguide • Web site presents an extensive, searchable directory of links to "the best, most informative, and authoritative web pages." Twenty main categories cover business, finance, career, company information, people, and technology topics, with thousands of subtopics, all linking to Web sites recommended by experienced business researchers. Fees: Free.

*Fedstats.* Federal Interagency Council on Statistical Policy. Phone: (202)395-7254 • URL: http://www.fedstats.gov • Web site features an efficient search facility for full-text statistics produced by more than 100 federal agencies, including the Census Bureau, the Bureau of Economic Analysis, and the Bureau of Labor Statistics. Boolean searches can be made within one agency or for all agencies combined. Links are offered to international statistical bureaus, including the UN, IMF, OECD, UNESCO, Eurostat, and 20 individual countries. Fees: Free.

*FreeLunch.com.* Economy.com, Inc. Phone: (610)696-8700; Fax: (610)696-1678 • URL: http://www.freelunch.com • Web site provides free access to more than 200 million economic and financial data series, covering industry, demographics, labor markets, prices, retail sales, government spending, trade, interest rates, housing starts, the stock market, etc. Data is available in either chart or table form. Searching is offered. Free, but registration required. Economy.com, Inc. also offers fee-based economic analysis at *The Dismal Scientist* site (www.dismal.com).

## ONLINE DATABASES

*United States International Air Travel Statistics.* U. S. Department of Transportation, Center for Transportation Information. • Provides detailed statistics on air passenger travel between the U. S. and foreign countries for both scheduled and charter flights. Time period is 1975 to date, with monthly updates. Inquire as to online cost and availability.

## OTHER SOURCES

*Travel Law.* ALM Media Properties LLC. • $555. Emphasis is on the legal rights of travelers, including a consideration of class action suits. Includes such matters as tour operator liability, hotel responsibilities, overbooking by airlines, and frequent-flyer issues. (Law Journal Press).

## PERIODICALS AND NEWSLETTERS

*Business Travel Magazine.* Eco N.V. • Monthly. Business travel magazine covering destinations, suppliers and lifestyle.

*Business Travel News.* Nielsen Business Media Inc. • Weekly. Tabloid newspaper covering business travel.

*Business Travel Planner-North American Edition.* Northstar Travel Media L.L.C. • Quarterly. $169 Individuals online. Magazine covering business and leisure travel.

*Business Traveller.* BRT Reise Publishing GmbH. • Bimonthly. Consumer magazine covering business travel.

*Cruise Travel.* World Publishing Co. • Bimonthly. $38.95 /year.

*Journal of Quality Assurance in Hospitality and Tourism: Improvements in Marketing, Management, and Development.* The Haworth Press Inc. • Quarterly. $240.00 per year to libraries; $50.00 per year to individuals. Includes research papers, case studies, abstracts of dissertations, book reviews, conference reviews, and Web site reviews.

*Newsline: Research News from the U. S. Travel Data Center.* U.S. National Research Council. • Monthly. $55.00 per year. Newsletter. Covers trends in the U. S. travel industry.

*Passport Newsletter.* Remy Publishing Co. • Monthly. $89.00 per year. Formerly *Passport.*

*Resort Management and Operations: The Resort Resource.* Finan Publishing. • Bimonthly. Price on application. Edited for hospitality professionals at both large and small resort facilities.

*Summary of Health Information for International Travel.* U.S. Department of Health and Human Services. • Biweekly. Formerly *Weekly Summary of Health Information for International Travel.*

*Travel and Leisure.* American Express Publishing Corp. • Monthly. $39.00 per year. In three regional editions and one demographic edition.

*Travel Management Daily.* Cahners Business Information. • Description: E-mail and internet publication which offers news and advice for those who work in the travel industry.

*Travel Smart: Pay Less, Enjoy More.* Dunan Communications, Inc. • Monthly. $39.00 per year. Newsletter. Provides information and recommendations for travelers. Emphasis is on travel value and opportunities for bargains. Incorporates *Joy of Travel.*

*Travel Trade News Edition: The Business Paper of the Travel Industry.* Travel Trade Publications. • Weekly. $10.00 per year. Formerly *Travel Trade.*

*Travel Weekly.* Northstar Travel Media L.L.C. • Weekly. $266.00 per year. Includes cruise guides, a weekly "Business Travel Update," and special issues devoted to particular destinations and areas. Edited mainly for travel agents and tour operators.

## RESEARCH CENTERS AND INSTITUTES

Hawaii Department of Business, Economic Development, and Tourism - Research and Economic Analysis Division. No. 1 Capitol District Bldg., 250 S Hotel St., Honolulu, HI 96813. Phone: (808)586-2355 • URL: http://dbedt.hawaii.gov/economic • Business, economic development, tourism.

## STATISTICS SOURCES

*Outlook for Travel and Tourism.* U.S. Travel Association. • Annual. Members, $100.00; non-members, $175.00. Contains forecasts of the performance of the U. S. travel industry, including air travel, business travel, recreation (attractions), and accomodations.

*Statistics on International Trade in Services.* Organization for Economic Cooperation and Development. Organisation for Economic Cooperation and Development Publications and Information Center. • Annual. $126.00. Presents a compilation and assessment of data on OECD member countries' international trade in services. Covers four major categories for 20 years: travel, transportation, government services, and other services.

*Summary of International Travel to the United States.* International Trade Administration, Tourism Industries. U.S. Department of Commerce. • Monthly. Quarterly and annual versions available. Provides statistics on air travel to the U.S. from 90 countries. Formerly *Summary and Analysis of International Travel to the United States.*

*Survey of Current Business.* U. S. Government Printing Office. • Published by Bureau of Economic Analysis, U. S. Department of Commerce. Presents a wide variety of business and economic data.

*Tourism Policy and International Tourism in OECD Member Countries.* Organisation for Economic Cooperation and Development Publications and Information Center. • Annual. $50.00. Reviews developments in the international tourism industry in OECD member countries. Includes statistical information.

## TRADE/PROFESSIONAL ASSOCIATIONS

Binational Tourism Alliance. 143 Genesee St., Buffalo, NY 14203. Phone: 877-884-2736 or (716)856-6525; Fax: (716)856-6754; Email: arlene.white@btapartners.com • URL: http://www.btapartners.com • Promotes tourism products and services and supports tourism development in Canada and the United States. Seeks to improve business opportunities and growth potential of members. Provides industry research and information, training and professional development.

Italian Confederation of Retailers, Commerce, Tourism and Service. Via Nazionale, 60, I-00184 Rome, Italy. Phone: 39 6 47251; Fax: 39 6 4746886; Email: confes@confesercenti.it • URL: http://www.confesercenti.it • Small and mid-sized enterprises in the commercial, tourist, and service sectors in Italy. Represents and promotes the retailing, tourism, service and other commercial industries.

Jordan Information Bureau. 3504 International Dr. NW, Washington, DC 20008. Phone: (202)966-2664 or (202)265-1606; Fax: (202)966-3110; Email: hkjembassydc@jordanembassyus.org • URL: http://www.jordanembassyus.org • Provides cultural, economic, and travel information on Jordan.

National Tour Association. 101 Prosperous Pl., Ste. 350, Lexington, KY 40509. Phone: 800-682-8886 or (859)264-6540; Fax: (859)264-6570; Email: questions@ntastaff.com • URL: http://www.ntaonline.com • Formerly National Tour Brokers Association.

# TRAVEL TRAILERS

*See* RECREATIONAL VEHICLE INDUSTRY

# TREASURERS

*See* CORPORATE DIRECTORS AND OFFICERS

# TREASURY BONDS

*See* GOVERNMENT BONDS

# TRIALS AND JURIES

*See also* STATE LAW

## ABSTRACTS AND INDEXES

*Index to Legal Periodicals and Books.* H.W. Wilson Co. • Monthly. $490.00 per year. Quarterly and annual cumulations.

## DIRECTORIES

*International Academy of Trial Lawyers Roster.* International Academy of Trial Lawyers. • Biennial. Free. More than 2,400 trial lawyers board certified in civil and criminal trial advocacy; members of the board.

## GENERAL WORKS

*Great American Trials - Trials from 1637-2001.* Cengage Learning Inc. • 2001. $286.00. Second edition. Two volumes. Contains discussions and details of momentous American trials from 1637 to 2001.

## OTHER SOURCES

*The Law of Juries.* Nancy Gertner and Judith Mizner. Glasser LegalWorks. • Looseleaf. $124.00. Periodic supplementation. Topics include voir dire & juror selection, peremptory challenges, trial location (venue), jury structure, jury deliberation, and jury conduct or misconduct.

## PERIODICALS AND NEWSLETTERS

*Champion.* Carrefour Participacoes S.A. • 10 times a year. $25.00 per year.

*Trial.* American Association for Justice. • Monthly. $89 Individuals.

*Trial Lawyers Quarterly.* New York State Trial Lawyers Association. • Quarterly. $50.00 per year.

## TRADE/PROFESSIONAL ASSOCIATIONS

American Association for Justice. 777 6th St. NW, Ste. 200, Washington, DC 20001. Phone: 800-424-2725 or (202)965-3500; Fax: (202)625-7084; Email: membership@justice.org • URL: http://www.justice.org/cps/rde/xchg/justice/hs.xsl/default.htm • Concerned with the behavioral aspects of litigation.

American Judges Association. 300 Newport Ave., Williamsburg, VA 23185-4147. Phone: (757)259-1841; Fax: (757)259-1520; Email: aja@ncsc.dni.us • URL: http://aja.ncsc.dni.us • Seeks to improve administration of justice at all levels of the courts.

American Judicature Society. Center Building, 2014 Broadway, Ste. 100, Nashville, TN 37203. Phone: 800-626-4089 or (615)873-4675; Fax: (615)873-4671 • URL: http://www.ajs.org • Lawyers, judges, law teachers, government officials, and citizens interested in the effective administration of justice. Conducts research; presents educational programs; offers a consultation service; sponsors and organizes citizens' conferences on judicial improvement. Coordinates the work of states in judicial discipline and removal through its Center for Judicial Conduct Organizations.

Council for Court Excellence. 1111 14th St. NW, Ste. 500, Washington, DC 20005-5628. Phone: (202)785-5917; Email: info@courtexcellence.org • URL: http://www.courtexcellence.org • Lawyers, business leaders, and civic and judicial branch members. Aims to develop and advocate methods of improving the administration of justice in local and federal courts. Stimulates understanding and communication between citizens and the courts. Conducts educational workshops.

National Association for Court Management. National Center for State Courts, 300 Newport Ave., Williamsburg, VA 23185-4147. Phone: 800-616-6165 or (757)259-1841; Fax: (757)259-1520; Email: nacm@ncsc.org • URL: http://nacmnet.org • Court management professionals. Aims to foster communication among members. Conducts educational programs.

National Association of Criminal Defense Lawyers. 1660 L St. NW, 12th Fl., Washington, DC 20036. Phone: (202)872-8600; Fax: (202)872-8690; Email: assist@nacdl.org • URL: http://www.nacdl.org • Formerly National Association of Defense Lawyers in Criminal Cases.

National Center for State Courts. 300 Newport Ave., Williamsburg, VA 23185. Phone: 800-616-6164 or (757)259-1525 or (757)259-1826; Fax: (757)220-0449; Email: jcochet@ncsc.org • URL: http://www.ncsc.org • Provides assistance to state and local trial and appellate courts in improving their structure and administration. Furnishes consultant services; conducts national studies and projects; acts as a clearinghouse for exchange of information on court problems; coordinates activities of other organizations involved in judicial improvement, providing secretariat services for several. Conducts conferences and training courses. Compiles statistics on state court caseload and administrative operations. Research includes: appellate procedures, pretrial services, court delay, alternatives to incarceration, juvenile justice, rural court services, alternative dispute resolution, jury management, and sentencing and judicial information systems. Offers placement service.

# TRUCK TRAILERS

*See also* AUTOMOTIVE INDUSTRY; TRUCKING INDUSTRY

## CD-ROM DATABASES

*OECD Statistical Compendium.* Organization for Economic Cooperation and Development. • Semiannual. $1,905.00 per year for 1 to 10 users. CD-ROM contains more than 730,000 monthly, quarterly, and annual time series for OECD countries, 1960 to date. Includes fully searchable data on agriculture, food, economic indicators, national accounts, employment, energy, finance, industry, technology, and foreign trade. Results can be displayed in various forms.

## FINANCIAL RATIOS

*Annual Statement Studies.* Risk Management Association. • Annual. Compiled from over 280,000 financial statements.

*Annual Statement Studies: Industry Default Probabilities and Cash Flow Measures.* Risk Management Association. • Annual. $405 Nonmembers. Serves as a companion volume to the original *Annual Statement Studies.* Gives probability of default estimates on a percentage scale for more than 450 industries. Includes changes in position year-by-year for eight financial statement line items and provides percentage measures of cash flow.

## INTERNET DATABASES

*Business 2.0 Web Guide to the Best Business Links.* Business 2.0 Media Inc. Phone: (415)293-4800; Email: support@business2.com • URL: http://www. business2.com/webguide • Web site presents an extensive, searchable directory of links to "the best, most informative, and authoritative web pages." Twenty main categories cover business, finance, career, company information, people, and technology topics, with thousands of subtopics, all linking to Web sites recommended by experienced business researchers. Fees: Free.

*Fedstats.* Federal Interagency Council on Statistical Policy. Phone: (202)395-7254 • URL: http://www. fedstats.gov • Web site features an efficient search facility for full-text statistics produced by more than 100 federal agencies, including the Census Bureau, the Bureau of Economic Analysis, and the Bureau of Labor Statistics. Boolean searches can be made within one agency or for all agencies combined. Links are offered to international statistical bureaus, including the UN, IMF, OECD, UNESCO, Eurostat, and 20 individual countries. Fees: Free.

*FreeLunch.com.* Economy.com, Inc. Phone: (610)696-8700; Fax: (610)696-1678 • URL: http:// www.freelunch.com • Web site provides free access to more than 200 million economic and financial data series, covering industry, demographics, labor markets, prices, retail sales, government spending, trade, interest rates, housing starts, the stock market, etc. Data is available in either chart or table form. Searching is offered. Free, but registration required. Economy.com, Inc. also offers fee-based economic analysis at *The Dismal Scientist* site (www.dismal. com).

*Manufacturing Profiles.* U. S. Bureau of the Census. Phone: (301)763-4636 or (301)763-4100; Fax: (301)763-4794; Email: webmaster@census.gov • URL: http://www.census.gov/prod/www/abs/mfg-prof.html • The Census Bureau makes available free on PDF (Portable Document Format) an annual

consolidation of the entire Current Industrial Report series, presenting "all the data compiled." Contains statistics on production, shipments, inventories, consumption, exports, imports, and orders for a wide variety of manufactured products.

## PERIODICALS AND NEWSLETTERS

*Trailer Body Builders Buyers Guide.* Primedia Business Magazines and Media. • Annual. Controlled circulation. List of 8,000 products used by original equipment manufacturers of truck trailers and truck bodies.

## STATISTICS SOURCES

*Survey of Current Business.* U. S. Government Printing Office. • Published by Bureau of Economic Analysis, U. S. Department of Commerce. Presents a wide variety of business and economic data.

*Truck Trailers.* U. S. Bureau of the Census. • Monthly Annual. Provides data on shipments of truck trailers and truck trailer vans: value, quantity, imports, and exports. (Current Industrial Reports, M37L.).

## TRADE/PROFESSIONAL ASSOCIATIONS

North American Trailer Dealers Association. 111 2nd Ave. NE, Unit 1405, Saint Petersburg, FL 33701-3480. Phone: (727)360-0304; Fax: (727)231-8356; Email: info@natda.org • URL: http://natda. org • Supports the light and medium duty trailer dealers industry. Promotes financial strength, professional credibility and industry recognition for trailer dealers and manufacturers throughout the United States. Provides trailer dealers with benefits, programs and education.

# TRUCKING INDUSTRY

## ALMANACS AND YEARBOOKS

*Ward's Automotive Yearbook.* Ward's Communications. • Annual. $570 Single issue 2010 edition. Comprehensive statistical information on automotive production, sales, truck data and suppliers. Included with subscription to *Ward's Automotive Reports.*

## DIRECTORIES

*American Motor Carrier Directory.* UBM Global Trade. • Annual. Publication includes: Lists of all licensed Less Than Truckload (LTL) general commodity carriers in the United States; includes specialized motor carriers and related services; includes refrigerated carriers, heavy haulers, bulk haulers, riggers, and specified commodity carriers; state and federal regulatory bodies governing the trucking industry; tariff publishing bureaus; freight claim councils; industry associations, etc. Entries include: For carriers and services--Company name, address of headquarters and terminals, phones, tariffs followed, names of executives, insurance, and equipment information, services or commodities handled. Principal content of publication is listing of direct point-to-point services of LTL general commodity carriers throughout the United States and to Canada and Mexico.

*Heavy Duty Trucking--Council of Fleet Specialists Equipment Buyer's Guide & Services Directory.* Newport Communications Div. HIC Corp. • Annual. $45 included in subscription; free to equipment and maintenance managers. Covers: 500 Council of Fleet Specialists member manufacturers and wholesalers specializing in heavy-duty truck parts and repairs. Entries include: Company name, address, phone, names of executives, parts or services manufactured or available; wholesaler listings also show area served. A special section of 'Heavy Duty Trucking' magazine prepared by the Council of Fleet Specialists, 315 Delaware, Kansas City, MO 64105 (816-421-2600).

*Modern Bulk Transporter Buyers Guide.* Penton. • Contains key suppliers to the tank truck, tank

container and storage terminal industries.

*Motor Carrier Permit & Tax Update.* J.J. Keller and Associates Inc. • Monthly. $219 1 year; print or online. Provides regular updates on changes to permitting and reporting requirements.

*My Little Salesman Truck and Trailer Catalog.* My Little Salesman. • Monthly. Products serving the trucking industry. Central and Western editions.

*National Truck Equipment Association--Market Resource Guide.* National Truck Equipment Association. • Annual. $50 Nonmembers. Covers: Over 1,500 distributors who install commercial truck bodies and related equipment on chassis-cabs, truck body and equipment manufacturers, and associates. Entries include: Company name, address, phone, fax, e-mail, web site, name and title of contact; membership type and year began membership, products or services.

*Truck Frame & Axle Repair Association--Membership Directory.* Truck-frame & Axle Repair Association. • Biennial. Covers: About 150 regular and associate members that repair heavy-duty truck equipment or supply the industry. Database includes: Map showing locations of members. Entries include: Firm name, address, phone, key personnel, coding to indicate specialties.

## FINANCIAL RATIOS

*Annual Statement Studies.* Risk Management Association. • Annual. Compiled from over 280,000 financial statements.

*Annual Statement Studies: Industry Default Probabilities and Cash Flow Measures.* Risk Management Association. • Annual. $405 Nonmembers. Serves as a companion volume to the original *Annual Statement Studies.* Gives probability of default estimates on a percentage scale for more than 450 industries. Includes changes in position year-by-year for eight financial statement line items and provides percentage measures of cash flow.

## ONLINE DATABASES

*TRIS: Transportation Research Information Service.* The National Academies National Research Council. • Contains abstracts and citations to a wide range of transportation literature, 1968 to present, with monthly updates. Includes references to the literature of air transportation, highways, ships and shipping, railroads, trucking, and urban mass transportation. Formerly *TRIS-ON-LINE.* Inquire as to online cost and availability.

## PERIODICALS AND NEWSLETTERS

*Commercial Carrier Journal.* Randall-Reilly Publishing Company L.L.C. • Monthly.

*Fleet Owner.* Primedia Business Magazines and Media. • Monthly. $45.00 per year.

*Heavy Duty Trucking: The Business Magazine of Trucking.* H.I.C. Corp. • Monthly.

*Light & Medium Truck: The Business Magazine for Light & Medium Truck Operators.* TT Publishing. • Monthly. Magazine for users of pick-up and delivery trucks.

*Modern Bulk Transporter.* Primedia Business Magazines and Media. • Monthly. Information for bulk logisitcs.

*Transport Topics.* American Trucking Associations. • Description: Covers news of the trucking transportation industry.

## STATISTICS SOURCES

*American Trucking Trends.* American Trucking Associations. Trucking Information Services, Inc. • Annual. $95.00 for members, $200.00 for nonmembers.

*U.S. Industry and Trade Outlook.* U.S. Department of Commerce National Technical Information Service. • Annual. Produced by the International Trade Administration, U.S. Department of Commerce, in a "public-private" partnership with DRI/ McGraw-Hill and Standard & Poor's. Provides basic data, outlook for the current year, and "Long-Term Prospects" (five-year projections) for a wide variety of products and services. Includes high technology industries. Formerly *U.S. Industrial Outlook.*

### TRADE/PROFESSIONAL ASSOCIATIONS

American Moving and Storage Association. 1611 Duke St., Alexandria, VA 22314-3406. Phone: 888-849-2672 or (703)683-7410; Fax: (703)683-7527 or (703)548-1845; Email: amconf@amconf.org • URL: http://www.promover.org • Members are household goods movers, storage companies, and trucking firms.

American Trucking Associations. 950 N Glebe Rd., Ste. 210, Arlington, VA 22203-4181. Phone: (703)838-1700; Email: media@trucking.org • URL: http://www.truckline.com • Motor carriers, suppliers, state trucking associations, and national conferences of trucking companies. Works to influence the decisions of federal, state, and local government bodies; promotes increased efficiency, productivity, and competitiveness in the trucking industries; sponsors American Trucking Associations Foundation. Provides quarterly financial and operating statistics service. Offers comprehensive accounting service for all sizes of carriers. Promotes highway and driver safety; supports highway research projects; and studies technical and regulatory problems of the trucking industry. Sponsors competitions; compiles statistics. Maintains numerous programs and services including: Management Information Systems Directory; Compensation Survey; Electronic Data Interchange Standards.

National Motor Freight Traffic Association. 1001 N Fairfax St., Ste. 600, Alexandria, VA 22314. Phone: 866-411-6632 or (703)838-1810 or (703)683-6046; Fax: (703)683-6296; Email: customerservice@ nmfta.org • URL: http://www.nmfta.org • Motor common carriers of general commodities. Represents interests of membership before the Surface Transportation Board, the Congress, the courts and state regulatory agencies.

National Private Truck Council. 950 N Glebe Rd., Ste. 2300, Arlington, VA 22203-4183. Phone: (703)683-1300 or (703)838-8816; Fax: (703)683-1217; Email: info@nptc.org • URL: http://www. nptc.org • Represents private motor carrier truck fleets and their suppliers.

National Tank Truck Carriers. 950 N Glebe Rd., Ste. 520, Arlington, VA 22203. Phone: 800-441-1414 or (703)838-1960; Fax: (703)838-8860; Email: nttcstaff@tanktruck.org • URL: http://www. tanktruck.org • Common or contract "for-hire" tank truck carriers transporting liquid and dry bulk commodities, chemicals, food processing commodities, petroleum, and related products; allied industry suppliers. Promotes federal standards of construction, design, operation and use of tank trucks and equipment. Coordinates truck transportation system for shippers of bulk commodities. Secures improvements in tank specifications. Sponsors annual schools; conducts research.

## TRUCKS (MANUFACTURING)

*See also* AUTOMOTIVE INDUSTRY; TRANSPORTATION INDUSTRY; TRUCK TRAILERS; TRUCKING INDUSTRY

### CD-ROM DATABASES

*OECD Statistical Compendium.* Organization for Economic Cooperation and Development. • Semiannual. $1,905.00 per year for 1 to 10 users. CD-ROM contains more than 730,000 monthly, quarterly, and annual time series for OECD countries, 1960 to date. Includes fully searchable data on agriculture, food, economic indicators,

national accounts, employment, energy, finance, industry, technology, and foreign trade. Results can be displayed in various forms.

### DIRECTORIES

*Plunkett's Automobile Industry Almanac.* Plunkett Research Ltd. • $349.99 Individuals print + online; one-year subscription. Covers: 300 leading companies in the automotive industry. Entries include: Name, address, phone, fax, and key executives. Also includes analysis and information on trends, technology, and statistics in the field.

*Truck Cover and Tarp Association Membership Directory.* Industrial Fabrics Association International. • Annual. Publication includes: Listings of member companies that manufacture and supply material, equipment or services to the truck cover and tarpaulin industry. Entries include: name, address, phone, fax of company and names and titles of key personnel, along with descriptions of services and products.

### INTERNET DATABASES

*Business 2.0 Web Guide to the Best Business Links.* Business 2.0 Media Inc. Phone: (415)293-4800; Email: support@business2.com • URL: http://www. business2.com/webguide • Web site presents an extensive, searchable directory of links to "the best, most informative, and authoritative web pages." Twenty main categories cover business, finance, career, company information, people, and technology topics, with thousands of subtopics, all linking to Web sites recommended by experienced business researchers. Fees: Free.

*Fedstats.* Federal Interagency Council on Statistical Policy. Phone: (202)395-7254 • URL: http://www. fedstats.gov • Web site features an efficient search facility for full-text statistics produced by more than 100 federal agencies, including the Census Bureau, the Bureau of Economic Analysis, and the Bureau of Labor Statistics. Boolean searches can be made within one agency or for all agencies combined. Links are offered to international statistical bureaus, including the UN, IMF, OECD, UNESCO, Eurostat, and 20 individual countries. Fees: Free.

*FreeLunch.com.* Economy.com, Inc. Phone: (610)696-8700; Fax: (610)696-1678 • URL: http:// www.freelunch.com • Web site provides free access to more than 200 million economic and financial data series, covering industry, demographics, labor markets, prices, retail sales, government spending, trade, interest rates, housing starts, the stock market, etc. Data is available in either chart or table form. Searching is offered. Free, but registration required. Economy.com, Inc. also offers fee-based economic analysis at *The Dismal Scientist* site (www.dismal. com).

### ONLINE DATABASES

*Ward's AutoInfoBank.* Ward's Communications. • Provides weekly, monthly, quarterly, and annual statistical data from 1980 to date for U. S. and imported cars and trucks. Covers production, shipments, sales, inventories, optional equipment, etc. Updating varies by series. Inquire as to online cost and availability.

### PERIODICALS AND NEWSLETTERS

*Successful Dealer.* Kona Communications Inc. • Bimonthly. $50.00 per year. For truck and heavy duty equipment dealers.

### STATISTICS SOURCES

*Survey of Current Business.* U. S. Government Printing Office. • Published by Bureau of Economic Analysis, U. S. Department of Commerce. Presents a wide variety of business and economic data.

### TRADE/PROFESSIONAL ASSOCIATIONS

National Truck Equipment Association. 37400 Hills Tech Dr., Farmington Hills, MI 48331-3414. Phone: 800-441-NTEA or (248)489-7090; Fax: (248)489-

8590; Email: info@ntea.com • URL: http://www. ntea.com • Serves as a trade group for commercial truck, truck body, truck equipment, trailer and accessory manufacturers and distributors. Advises members of current federal regulations affecting the manufacturing and installation of truck bodies and equipment; works to enhance the professionalism of management and improve profitability in the truck equipment business.

## TRUSTS AND TRUSTEES

*See also* ESTATE PLANNING; FOUNDATIONS; INSTITUTIONAL INVESTMENTS; INVESTMENT COMPANIES

### ABSTRACTS AND INDEXES

*Accounting and Tax Index.* ProQuest L.L.C. • Quarterly. Indexes accounting, auditing, and taxation literature appearing in journals, books, pamphlets, conference proceedings, and newsletters.

*Current Law Index.* Cengage Learning Inc. • $1,332 Individuals. Monthly. $1269.00 per year. Produced in cooperation with the American Association of Law Libraries. Indexes more than 900 law journals, legal newspapers, and specialty publications from the U.S., Canada, U.K., Ireland, Australia, and New Zealand.

*Index to Legal Periodicals and Books.* H.W. Wilson Co. • Monthly. $490.00 per year. Quarterly and annual cumulations.

### ALMANACS AND YEARBOOKS

*American Law Yearbook.* Cengage Learning Inc. • $308 Individuals. Annual. $280.00. Serves as a yearly supplement to *West's Encyclopedia of American Lawa.* Describes new legal developments in many subject areas.

### CD-ROM DATABASES

*Index to Legal Periodicals and Books.* EBSCO Publishing Inc. • Contains indexing of more than 1,400 English language legal periodicals from 1981 to date and 2,500 books.

### DIRECTORIES

*Directory of Trust Banking.* Thomson Financial Publishing. • Annual. $344.00. Contains profiles of bank affiliated trust companies, independent trust companies, trust investment advisors, and trust fund managers. Provides contact information for professional personnel at more than 3,000 banking and other financial institutions.

*Money Market Directory of Pension Funds and Their Investment Managers.* Standard & Poors Money Market Directories. • Institutional funds and managers.

### ENCYCLOPEDIAS AND DICTIONARIES

*West's Encyclopedia of American Law.* Cengage Learning Inc. • 2004. eBook. Second edition. Covers a wide variety of legal topics for the general reader. Inquire for pricing.

### HANDBOOKS AND MANUALS

*Trust Administration and Taxation.* Matthew Bender and Company Inc. • Semiannual. $1,857 Individuals Book. A well-documented, practical text on the establishment, administration and taxation of trusts, covering revocable living trusts, charitable remainder trusts, and more.

*Trust Department Administration and Operations.* Matthew Bender and Company Inc. • Semiannual. $726 Individuals Book or Electronic version. Covers every aspect of setting up a trust department, day-to-day administration, asset management, operations, marketing, and internal management. A procedural manual, training guide and idea source.

### INTERNET DATABASES

*Lexis.com Research System.* Lexis-Nexis Group. Phone: 800-227-4908 or (937)865-6800; Fax:

(937)865-6909; Email: webmaster@prod.lexis-nexis.com • URL: http://www.nexis.com • Fee-based Web site offers extensive searching of a wide variety of legal sources. Additional features include Daily Opinion Service, lexis.com Bookstore, Career Center, CLE Center, Law Schools, and Practice Pages ("Pages specific to areas of specialty").

**ONLINE DATABASES**

*Banking Information Source.* ProQuest L.L.C. • Provides indexing and abstracting of periodical and other literature from 1982 to date, with weekly updates. Covers the financial services industry: banks, savings institutions, investment houses, credit unions, insurance companies, and real estate organizations. Emphasis is on marketing and management. Inquire as to online cost and availability. (Formerly *FINIS: Financial Industry Information Service.*).

**OTHER SOURCES**

*Fiduciary Tax Guide.* Wolters Kluwer Law & Business CCH. • Monthly. $478.00 per year. Looseleaf service. Covers federal income taxation of estates, trusts, and beneficiaries. Provides information on gift and generation- skipping taxation.

*Pension Fund Litigation Reporter.* Andrews Publications. • Semimonthly. $750.00 per year. Newsletter. Contains reports on legal cases involving pension fund fiduciaries (trustees).

**PERIODICALS AND NEWSLETTERS**

*American Banker: The Financial Services Daily.* SourceMedia Inc. • Daily. $895.00 per year. Provides news of banking, investment products, mortgages, credit unions, finance, bank technology, and legal developments.

*Bank Investment Consultant: Sales Strategies for the Financial Adviser.* SourceMedia Inc. • Monthly. Controlled circulation. Covers sales and marketing techniques for bank investment and asset management divisions. Formerly *Bank Investment Marketing.*

*Investment Management Mandate Pipeline.* Source-Media Inc. • Weekly. $1,295.00 per year. Newsletter. Edited for money managers and other investment professionals. Covers personnel news, investment strategies, and industry trends.

*Investment News: The Weekly Newspaper for Financial Advisers.* Crain Communications Inc. • Weekly. $29.00 per year. Edited for both personal and institutional investment advisers, planners, and managers.

*Private Asset Management.* Institutional Investor Inc. Journals Group. • Biweekly. $2,335.00 per year. Newsletter. Includes print and online editions. Edited for managers investing the private assets of wealthy ("high-net-worth") individuals. Includes marketing, taxation, regulation, and fee topics.

*Robb Report Worth: Wealth in Perspective.* CurtCo Robb Media. • Monthly. $54.95 per year. Glossy magazine featuring articles for the affluent on personal financial management, investments, estate planning, trusts, private bankers, taxes, travel, yachts, and lifestyle. Formerly *Worth: Financial Intelligence.*

*Trust Letter.* American Bankers Association. • Monthly. Description: Contains updates of national legislation and regulation that impacts the trust and investment businesses. Reports on significant industry happenings, important research, and provides coverage of ABA legislative/regulatory testimony and committee activities, especially in the areas of taxation, securities, and employee benefits.

*Trust Management Update.* American Bankers Association. • Bimonthly. $95.00 per year.

*Trusts and Estates.* RentPath Inc. • Monthly. $139.00 per year. Includes annual *Directory.*

*U.S. Banker.* SourceMedia Inc. • Monthly. $65.00 per year. Edited for bank executives and managers. Covers a wide variety of banking and financial topics.

**STATISTICS SOURCES**

*EBRI Pension Investment Report.* Employee Benefit Research Institute. • Periodic Quarterly. $500 /issue for nonmembers. Irregular. Membership.

**TRADE/PROFESSIONAL ASSOCIATIONS**

Trust Companies' Association of Japan. Nippon Kaikan, 6th Fl., 2-6-2, Otemachi, Chiyoda, Tokyo 100-0004, Japan. Phone: 81 3 3241-7135; Fax: 81 3 3241-7200 • URL: http://www.shintaku-kyokai.or.jp • Works on the promotion, protection, and advancement of the interests of closed-ended investment trust companies and their shareholders by influencing developments in legislation and practice affecting investors, companies and the stock market, by political lobbying and by promotion of their merits, in particular to private investors and independent financial advisers.

# TRUSTS, INVESTMENT

*See* INVESTMENT COMPANIES

# TUNA FISH INDUSTRY

*See also* FISH INDUSTRY

**ABSTRACTS AND INDEXES**

*Oceanic Abstracts.* CSA. • Monthly. $1,645.00 per year. Includes print and online editions. Covers oceanography, marine biology, ocean shipping, and a wide range of other marine-related subject areas.

**ALMANACS AND YEARBOOKS**

*Inter-American Tropical Tuna Commission Annual Report.* William H. Bayliff, editor. Inter-American Tropical Tuna Commission. • Annual. Summary of scientific research carried on during the year. Includes financial statements. Text in English and Spanish.

**PERIODICALS AND NEWSLETTERS**

*Inter-American Tropical Tuna Commission Bulletin.* Inter-American Tropical Tuna Commission. • Irregular. Price varies. Description of results of scientific studies. Text in English and Spanish.

*Seafood Business.* Diversified Business Communications Inc. • $57 U.S.. Edited for a wide range of seafood buyers, including distributors, restaurants, supermarkets, and institutions. Special issues feature information on specific products, such as salmon or lobster.

# TURKEY INDUSTRY

*See also* POULTRY INDUSTRY

**ALMANACS AND YEARBOOKS**

*CRB Commodity Yearbook.* Commodity Research Bureau. CRB. • Annual. $179 plus $10.00 shipping cost. The single most comprehensive source of commodity and futures market information available.

**INTERNET DATABASES**

*USDA.* U.S. National Institute of Standards and Technology. 100 Bureau Dr., Gaithersburg, MD 20899-1070. Phone: 800-877-8339 or (301)975-6478 or (202)720-2791; Fax: (301)975-8295; Email: inquiries@nist.gov • URL: http://www.nist.gov • The USDA home page has six sections: News and Information; What's New; About USDA; Agencies; Opportunities; Search and Help. Keyword searching is offered from the USDA home page and from various individual agency home pages. Agencies are the Economic Research Service, Agricultural Marketing Service, National Agricultural Statistics Service, National Agricultural Library, and about 12 others. Updating varies. Fees: Free.

**PRICE SOURCES**

*PPI Detailed Report.* Periodical covering business. Bureau of Labor Statistics, U.S. Department of Labor. U. S. Government Printing Office. • Monthly. $55 Individuals.

**STATISTICS SOURCES**

*Agricultural Statistics.* U.S. Department of Agriculture National Agricultural Statistics Service. • Annual. $46 Individuals. Provides a wide variety of statistical data relating to agricultural production, supplies, consumption, prices/price-supports, foreign trade, costs, and returns, as well as farm labor, loans, income, and population. In many cases, historical data is shown annually for 10 years. In addition to farm data, includes detailed fishery statistics.

**TRADE/PROFESSIONAL ASSOCIATIONS**

National Turkey Federation. 1225 New York Ave., Ste. 400, Washington, DC 20005. Phone: (202)898-0100; Fax: (202)898-0203; Email: info@turkeyfed.org • URL: http://www.eatturkey.com • Serves as the national advocate for all segments of the turkey industry. Provides services and conducts activities that increase demand for its members' products by protecting and enhancing their ability to profitably provide wholesome, high-quality, and nutritious products.

# TURNPIKES

*See* TOLL ROADS

# TURPENTINES AND RESINS

*See* NAVAL STORES

# TWINE INDUSTRY

*See* ROPE AND TWINE INDUSTRY

# TYPE AND TYPE FOUNDING

*See* PRINTING AND PRINTING EQUIPMENT INDUSTRIES; TYPESETTING

# TYPESETTING

**FINANCIAL RATIOS**

*Annual Statement Studies.* Risk Management Association. • Annual. Compiled from over 280,000 financial statements.

*Annual Statement Studies: Industry Default Probabilities and Cash Flow Measures.* Risk Management Association. • Annual. $405 Nonmembers. Serves as a companion volume to the original *Annual Statement Studies.* Gives probability of default estimates on a percentage scale for more than 450 industries. Includes changes in position year-by-year for eight financial statement line items and provides percentage measures of cash flow.

# U

## ULTRASONICS

### ABSTRACTS AND INDEXES

*Acoustics Abstracts*. Multi-Science Publishing Company Ltd. • Monthly. $600.

### PERIODICALS AND NEWSLETTERS

*Seminars in Ultrasound, CT and MRI*. Elsevier Inc. • Bimonthly. $357 Individuals online + print. Journal reviewing current techniques and equipment used in ultrasound, CT, and MRI.

*Sensors: Your Resource for Sensing, Communications, and Control*. Advanstar Communications. • Monthly. $70.00 per year. Edited for design, production, and manufacturing engineers involved with sensing systems. Emphasis is on emerging technology.

*Ultrasonic Imaging, An International Journal*. Dynamedia of America Inc. • Quarterly. $325.00 per year.

*Ultrasonics: The World's Leading Journal Covering the Science and Technology of Ultrasound*. Elsevier. • 10 times a year. Institutions, $131.00 per year; institutions, $1,461.00 per year.

*Ultrasound in Medicine and Biology (UMB)*. Elsevier. • Monthly. Institutions, $1,305.00 per year.

## UNDERTAKERS AND UNDERTAKING

*See* FUNERAL HOMES AND DIRECTORS

## UNDERWEAR INDUSTRY

*See also* KNIT GOODS INDUSTRY

### DIRECTORIES

*Body Fashions/Intimate Apparel Buyer's Guide: BFIA Buyers Guide*. Advanstar Communications. • Annual. Publication includes: List of suppliers and manufacturers within the intimate apparel and hosiery industry. Entries include: Company name, address, phone.

## UNDERWRITERS

*See* INSURANCE UNDERWRITERS

## UNEMPLOYMENT

*See also* DISMISSAL OF EMPLOYEES; EMPLOYMENT; UNEMPLOYMENT INSURANCE

### CD-ROM DATABASES

*OECD Statistical Compendium*. Organization for Economic Cooperation and Development. • Semiannual. $1,905.00 per year for 1 to 10 users. CD-ROM contains more than 730,000 monthly, quarterly, and annual time series for OECD countries, 1960 to date. Includes fully searchable data on agriculture, food, economic indicators, national accounts, employment, energy, finance, industry, technology, and foreign trade. Results can be displayed in various forms.

*Sourcebooks America CD-ROM*. CACI Marketing Systems. • Annual. $1,250.00. Provides the CD-ROM version of *The Sourcebook of ZIP Code Demographics: Census Edition* and *The Sourcebook of County Demographics: Census Edition*.

### INTERNET DATABASES

*Bureau of Economic Analysis*. U. S. Department of Commerce, Bureau of Economic Analysis. Phone: (202)606-9900; Fax: (202)606-5310; Email: webmaster@bea.doc.gov • URL: http://www.bea.doc.gov • Web site includes "News Release Information" covering national, regional, and international economic estimates from the BEA. Highlights of releases appear online the same day, complete text and tables appear the next day. "Recent News Releases" section provides titles for past nine months, with links. "BEA Data and Methodology" includes "Frequently Requested NIPA Data" (national income and product accounts, such as gross domestic product and personal income). Other statistics are available. Fees: Free.

*Business 2.0 Web Guide to the Best Business Links*. Business 2.0 Media Inc. Phone: (415)293-4800; Email: support@business2.com • URL: http://www.business2.com/webguide • Web site presents an extensive, searchable directory of links to "the best, most informative, and authoritative web pages." Twenty main categories cover business, finance, career, company information, people, and technology topics, with thousands of subtopics, all linking to Web sites recommended by experienced business researchers. Fees: Free.

*Fedstats*. Federal Interagency Council on Statistical Policy. Phone: (202)395-7254 • URL: http://www.fedstats.gov • Web site features an efficient search facility for full-text statistics produced by more than 100 federal agencies, including the Census Bureau, the Bureau of Economic Analysis, and the Bureau of Labor Statistics. Boolean searches can be made within one agency or for all agencies combined. Links are offered to international statistical bureaus, including the UN, IMF, OECD, UNESCO, Eurostat, and 20 individual countries. Fees: Free.

*FreeLunch.com*. Economy.com, Inc. Phone: (610)696-8700; Fax: (610)696-1678 • URL: http://

www.freelunch.com • Web site provides free access to more than 200 million economic and financial data series, covering industry, demographics, labor markets, prices, retail sales, government spending, trade, interest rates, housing starts, the stock market, etc. Data is available in either chart or table form. Searching is offered. Free, but registration required. Economy.com, Inc. also offers fee-based economic analysis at *The Dismal Scientist* site (www.dismal.com).

### OTHER SOURCES

*Foreign Labor Trends*. U. S. Government Printing Office. • Irregular (50 to 60 issues per year, each on an individual country). $95.00 per year. Prepared by various American Embassies. Issued by the Bureau of International Labor Affairs, U. S. Department of Labor. Covers labor developments in important foreign countries, including trends in wages, working conditions, labor supply, employment, and unemployment.

### RESEARCH CENTERS AND INSTITUTES

Princeton University - Industrial Relations Section. Firestone Library, A-18-J, 1 Washington Rd., Princeton, NJ 08544. Phone: (609)258-4040; Fax: (609)258-2907; Email: c6789@princeton.edu • URL: http://www.irs.princeton.edu • Fields of research include labor supply, manpower training, unemployment, and equal employment opportunity.

W.E. Upjohn Institute for Employment Research. 300 S Westnedge Ave., Kalamazoo, MI 49007-4686. Phone: 888-227-8569 or (269)343-5541; Fax: (269)343-7310; Email: communications@upjohn.org • URL: http://www.upjohninstitute.org • Research fields include unemployment, unemployment insurance, worker's compensation, labor productivity, profit sharing, the labor market, economic development, earnings, training, and other areas related to employment.

### STATISTICS SOURCES

*Bulletin of Labour Statistics: Supplementing the Annual Data Presented in the Year Book of Labour Statistics*. International Labor Ofice. • Quarterly. $84.00 per year. Includes five Supplements. A supplement to *Yearbook of Labour Statistics*. Provides current labor and price index statistics for over 130 countries. Generally includes data for the most recent four years. Text in English, French and Spanish.

*Quarterly Labour Force Statistics*. Organization for Economic Cooperation and Development. Organisation for Economic Co-operation and Development Publications and Information Center. • Quarterly. $90.00 per year. Provides current data for OECD member countries on population, employment, unemployment, civilian labor force, armed forces, and other labor factors.

*Report on the American Workforce*. U. S. Government Printing Office. • Annual. Issued by the U. S. Department of Labor (www.dol.gov). Appendix contains tabular statistics, including employment, unemployment, price indexes, consumer expenditures, employee benefits (retirement, insurance, vacation, etc.), wages, productivity, hours of work, and occupational injuries. Annual figures are shown for up to 50 years.

*Survey of Current Business*. U. S. Government Printing Office. • Published by Bureau of Economic Analysis, U. S. Department of Commerce. Presents a wide variety of business and economic data.

# UNEMPLOYMENT INSURANCE

## BIBLIOGRAPHIES

*Insurance and Employee Benefits Literature*. Special Libraries Association. • Bimonthly. $15.00 per year. Lists a wide variety of literature in all branches of the insurance industry. Includes annotations.

## CD-ROM DATABASES

*OECD Statistical Compendium*. Organization for Economic Cooperation and Development. • Semiannual. $1,905.00 per year for 1 to 10 users. CD-ROM contains more than 730,000 monthly, quarterly, and annual time series for OECD countries, 1960 to date. Includes fully searchable data on agriculture, food, economic indicators, national accounts, employment, energy, finance, industry, technology, and foreign trade. Results can be displayed in various forms.

## HANDBOOKS AND MANUALS

*Payroll Management Guide*. Wolters Kluwer Law & Business CCH. • Weekly Monthly. $1,159 Individuals. Covers the basics of payroll management, including employer obligations, recordkeeping, taxation, unemployment insurance, processing of new employees, and government penalties.

## INTERNET DATABASES

*Business 2.0 Web Guide to the Best Business Links*. Business 2.0 Media Inc. Phone: (415)293-4800; Email: support@business2.com • URL: http://www. business2.com/webguide • Web site presents an extensive, searchable directory of links to "the best, most informative, and authoritative web pages." Twenty main categories cover business, finance, career, company information, people, and technology topics, with thousands of subtopics, all linking to Web sites recommended by experienced business researchers. Fees: Free.

*Fedstats*. Federal Interagency Council on Statistical Policy. Phone: (202)395-7254 • URL: http://www. fedstats.gov • Web site features an efficient search facility for full-text statistics produced by more than 100 federal agencies, including the Census Bureau, the Bureau of Economic Analysis, and the Bureau of Labor Statistics. Boolean searches can be made within one agency or for all agencies combined. Links are offered to international statistical bureaus, including the UN, IMF, OECD, UNESCO, Eurostat, and 20 individual countries. Fees: Free.

*FreeLunch.com*. Economy.com, Inc. Phone: (610)696-8700; Fax: (610)696-1678 • URL: http:// www.freelunch.com • Web site provides free access to more than 200 million economic and financial data series, covering industry, demographics, labor markets, prices, retail sales, government spending, trade, interest rates, housing starts, the stock market, etc. Data is available in either chart or table form. Searching is offered. Free, but registration required. Economy.com, Inc. also offers fee-based economic analysis at *The Dismal Scientist* site (www.dismal. com).

## ONLINE DATABASES

*I.I.I. Data Base Search*. Insurance Information Institute. • Provides online citations and abstracts of insurance-related literature in magazines, newspapers, trade journals, and books. Emphasis is on property and casualty insurance issues, including highway safety, product safety, and environmental liability. Inquire as to online cost and availability.

## RESEARCH CENTERS AND INSTITUTES

FHI 360 - National Institute for Work and Learning. 1825 Connecticut Ave. NW, Washington, DC 20009. Phone: (202)884-8184; Fax: (202)884-8422; Email: icharner@fhi360.org • URL: http://www.niwl.org • Research areas include adult education, training, unemployment insurance, and career development.

## STATISTICS SOURCES

*Survey of Current Business*. U. S. Government Printing Office. • Published by Bureau of Economic Analysis, U. S. Department of Commerce. Presents a wide variety of business and economic data.

*Unemployment Insurance Weekly Claims Report*. U.S. Department of Labor, Employment and Training Administration. • Weekly.

## TRADE/PROFESSIONAL ASSOCIATIONS

Ledernes Hovedeorganisation. Vermlandsgade 65, DK-2300 Copenhagen, Denmark. Phone: 45 32833283; Email: lederne@lederne.dk • URL: http://www.lederne.dk • Business managers and executives. Represents members' interests before government agencies, industry associations, and the public. Manages unemployment insurance fund for members; makes available legal services; conducts continuing professional training programs.

# UNIFORM COMMERCIAL CODE

*See* BUSINESS LAW

# UNIFORMS

## DIRECTORIES

*LAW and ORDER Magazine*. Hendon Publishing Co. • Lists manufacturers, dealers, and distributors of equipment and services for police departments.

*Law Enforcement Technology Directory*. Cygnus Business Media Inc. • Annual. $60.00 per year. $6.00 per issue; a directory of products, equipment, services, and technology for police professionals. Includes weapons, uniforms, communications equipment, and software.

## PERIODICALS AND NEWSLETTERS

*NAUMD News*. National Association of Uniform Manufacturers and Distributors. • Description: Reports news that affects the uniform manufacturing and distributing industry. Also discusses Association programs and seminars, committee activities, and governmental trends and regulations.

## TRADE/PROFESSIONAL ASSOCIATIONS

North-American Association of Uniform Manufacturers and Distributors. 6800 Jericho Tpke., Ste. 120W, Syosset, NY 11791. Phone: (516)393-5838; Fax: (516)393-5878 • URL: http://www. naumd.com • Formerly Uniform Manufacturers Exchange.

# UNIONS

*See* LABOR UNIONS

# UNITED FUNDS

*See* COMMUNITY FUNDS

# UNITED NATIONS

*See also* INTERNATIONAL AGENCIES

## ABSTRACTS AND INDEXES

*Index to Proceedings of the Economic and Social Council*. United Nations Publications. • Irregular.

*United Nations Document Index*. United Nations Publications. • Quarterly. Annual cumulation. Text in English.

## ALMANACS AND YEARBOOKS

*National Accounts Statistics: Main Aggregates and Detailed Tables*. United Nations Publications. • Annual.

## BIBLIOGRAPHIES

*Monthly Bibliography*. United Nations Publications. • Monthly. $180 per year. Text in English and French.

## PERIODICALS AND NEWSLETTERS

*UN Chronicle*. United Nations Pulications. • 11 times a year. $25.00 per year. Editions in English, French and Spanish.

## STATISTICS SOURCES

*Statistical Yearbook*. United Nations Publications. • Annual. $125.00. Contains statistics for about 200 countries on a wide variety of economic, industrial, and demographic topics. Compiled by United Nations Statistical Office.

# UNITED STATES CONGRESS

*See also* LAWS

## ABSTRACTS AND INDEXES

*Congressional Index*. Wolters Kluwer Law & Business CCH. • Index to action on Public Bills from introduction to final disposition. Subject, author, and bill number indexes.

*Current Law Index*. Cengage Learning Inc. • $1,332 Individuals. Monthly. $1269.00 per year. Produced in cooperation with the American Association of Law Libraries. Indexes more than 900 law journals, legal newspapers, and specialty publications from the U.S., Canada, U.K., Ireland, Australia, and New Zealand.

## ALMANACS AND YEARBOOKS

*Congressional Quarterly Almanac*. CQ Press. • Annual. $549 print. Offers exclusive insight into the forces that drove action on legislation.

## BIBLIOGRAPHIES

*Congress in Print: The Weekly Catalog of Congressional Documents*. U. S. Government Printing Office. • Newsletter.

## BIOGRAPHICAL SOURCES

*Almanac of American Politics*. National Journal Group Inc. • Biennial. $60.73 Individuals hardcover. Biennial. Includes biographies of U.S. senators and representatives, with group ratings, key votes, and election results.

*Who's Who in American Politics*. Marquis Who's Who L.L.C. • Biennial. $349 Individuals. Contains about 27,000 biographical sketches of local, state, and national elected or appointed individuals.

## CD-ROM DATABASES

*Newspaper Abstracts Ondisc*. ProQuest L.L.C. • Monthly. $2,950.00 per year (covers 1989 to date; archival discs are available for 1985-88). Provides cover-to-cover CD-ROM indexing and abstracting of 19 major newspapers, including the *New York Times*, *Wall Street Journal*, *Washington Post*, *Chicago Tribune*, and *Los Angeles Times*.

## DIRECTORIES

*Carroll's Federal & Federal Regional Directory*. Caroll Publishing. • Semiannual. $500 Individuals.

Lists more than 23,000 U. S. government officials throughout the country, including military installations.

*Carroll's Federal Directory.* Caroll Publishing. • $550 Single issue 4 issues per year. Covers approximately 37,000 executive managers in federal government offices in Washington, DC, including executive, congressional and judicial branches; members of Congress and Congressional committees and staff.

*Washington Information Directory.* CQ Press. • Annual. $175 Individuals print cloth, standing order. Covers: 10,000 governmental agencies, congressional committees, and non-governmental associations considered competent sources of specialized information. Entries include: Name of agency, committee, or association; address, phone, fax, and Internet; annotation concerning function or activities of the office; and name of contact.

### GENERAL WORKS

*Congressional Investigations: Law and Practice.* John C. Grabow. Wolters Kluwer Law and Business. • $95.00. Looseleaf service. Periodic supplementation.

### HANDBOOKS AND MANUALS

*Senate Manual.* U. S. Government Printing Office. • Biennial. $57.00. Contains the standing rules, orders, laws, and resolutions affecting the Senate, as well as copies of historical U.S. documents, such as Jefferson's Manual, Declaration of Independence, Articles of Confederation, Constitution of the United States.

### INTERNET DATABASES

*FedWorld: A Program of the United States Department of Commerce.* National Technical Information Service. Phone: 800-553-NTIS or (703)605-6000; Fax: (703)605-6900; Email: webmaster@fedworld.gov • URL: http://www.fedworld.gov • Web site offers "a comprehensive central access point for searching, locating, ordering, and acquiring government and business information." Emphasis is on searching the Web pages, databases, and government reports of a wide variety of federal agencies. Fees: Free.

*FirstGov: Your First Click to the U. S. Government.* General Services Administration. Phone: 800-333-4636 or (202)501-0705; Email: public.affairs@gsa.gov • URL: http://www.gsa.gov • Free Web site provides extensive links to federal agencies covering a wide variety of topics, such as agriculture, business, consumer safety, education, the environment, government jobs, grants, health, social security, statistics sources, taxes, technology, travel, and world affairs. Also provides links to federal forms, including IRS tax forms. Searching is offered, both keyword and advanced.

*Lexis.com Research System.* Lexis-Nexis Group. Phone: 800-227-4908 or (937)865-6800; Fax: (937)865-6909; Email: webmaster@prod.lexis-nexis.com • URL: http://www.nexis.com • Fee-based Web site offers extensive searching of a wide variety of legal sources. Additional features include Daily Opinion Service, lexis.com Bookstore, Career Center, CLE Center, Law Schools, and Practice Pages ("Pages specific to areas of specialty").

### PERIODICALS AND NEWSLETTERS

*Congressional Monitor: Daily Listing of All Scheduled Congressional Committee Hearings with Witnesses.* Congressional Quarterly Inc. • Daily. $1,349.00 per year. Weekly *Supplements.*

*Congressional Record.* U.S. Congress. U. S. Government Printing Office. • Daily. Daily. Indexes give names, subjects, and history of bills. Texts of bills not included.

*National Journal: The Weekly on Politics and Government.* National Journal Group Inc. • Weekly.

$1,499 Individuals. Includes semiannual supplement *Capital Source.* A non-partisan weekly magazine on politics and government.

### TRADE/PROFESSIONAL ASSOCIATIONS

National Committee for an Effective Congress. 218 D St., SE, Fl. 3, Washington, DC 20003. Phone: (202)639-8300 • URL: http://www.ncec.org • Raises funds from private citizens and distributes them to its endorsed candidates for the United States Senate and House of Representatives.

# UNITED STATES CUSTOMS SERVICE

*See* CUSTOMS HOUSE, U.S. CUSTOMS SERVICE

# UNITED STATES GOVERNMENT BONDS

*See* GOVERNMENT BONDS

# UNITED STATES GOVERNMENT PUBLICATIONS

*See* GOVERNMENT PUBLICATIONS

# UNIVERSITIES

*See* COLLEGES AND UNIVERSITIES

# UNIVERSITY DEGREES

*See* ACADEMIC DEGREES

# UNIVERSITY LIBRARIES

*See* COLLEGE AND UNIVERSITY LIBRARIES

# UNIVERSITY PRESSES

*See also* PUBLISHING INDUSTRY

### CD-ROM DATABASES

*ERIC SilverPlatter.* U.S. Department of Education Institute of Education Sciences Education Resources Information Center. • Opinion papers, evaluations, speeches.

### INTERNET DATABASES

*Publishers' Catalogues Home Page.* EBSCO Publishing Inc. 10 Estes St., Ipswich, MA 01938-2106. Phone: 800-653-2726 or (978)356-6500; Fax: (978)356-6565; Email: information@ebscohost.com • URL: http://www.ebscohost.com • Provides links to the Web home pages of about 1,700 U. S. publishers (including about 80 University presses) and publishers in 48 foreign countries. "International/Multinational Publishers" are included, such as the International Monetary Fund, the World Bank, and the World Trade Organization. Publishers are arranged in convenient alphabetical lists. Searching is offered. Fees: Free.

### ONLINE DATABASES

*ERIC.* U.S. Department of Education Institute of Education Sciences Educational Resources Information Center. • Funded by the U.S. Department of Education, Institute of Education Sciences (formerly Office of Educational Research and Improvement).

Provides access to more than one million online records covering education-related journal and report literature, 1966 to date. Updating is monthly. Inquire as to online cost and availability.

### PERIODICALS AND NEWSLETTERS

*Independent Publisher: Leading the World of Book Selling in New Directions.* Jenkins Group Inc. • Bimonthly. Free. Covers business, finance, production, marketing, and other management topics for small publishers, including college presses. Emphasis is on book publishing.

### TRADE/PROFESSIONAL ASSOCIATIONS

Association of American University Presses. 28 W 36th St., Ste. 602, New York, NY 10018. Phone: (212)989-1010; Fax: (212)989-0275 or (212)989-0975; Email: info@aaupnet.org • URL: http://www.aaupnet.org • Helps university presses do their work more economically, creatively, and effectively through its own activities in education-training, fundraising and development, statistical research and analysis, and community and institutional relations.

Association of Learned and Professional Society Publishers. 1-3 Ship St., Shoreham-by-Sea, West Sussex BN43 5DH, United Kingdom. Phone: 44 1442 828928 or 44 190 3 871686; Fax: 44 190 3 871457; Email: audrey.mcculloch@alpsp.org • URL: http://www.alpsp.org.

# UNIX

*See also* COMPUTER SOFTWARE INDUSTRY

### ABSTRACTS AND INDEXES

*Computer Science Index.* EBSCO Publishing Inc. • Quarterly. $245 per year. Contains brief abstracts of book and periodical literature covering all phases of computing, including approximately 70 specific application areas.

*Internet and Personal Computing Abstracts (print edition).* EBSCO Publishing Inc. • Quarterly. $269.00 per year, including cumulative index. Provides more than 10,000 abstracts annually from both trade and academic publications. Covers computer hardware, software, product reviews, Web topics, e-commerce, networks, corporate news, security, and related topics. Formerly *Microcomputer Abstracts.*

*Key Abstracts: Software Engineering.* Institution of Engineering and Technology. • Monthly. $1,138. Provides international coverage of journal and proceedings literature.

### CD-ROM DATABASES

*Datapro on CD-ROM: Computer Systems Analyst.* Gartner Inc. • Monthly. Price on application. Includes detailed information on specific computer hardware and software products, such as peripherals, security systems, document imaging systems, and UNIX-related products.

### INTERNET DATABASES

*InfoTech Trends.* Data Analysis Group. Phone: (925)462-1202; Fax: (925)462-1225; Email: support@infotechtrends.com • URL: http://www.infotechtrends.com • Web site provides both free and fee-based market research data on the information technology industry, including computers, peripherals, telecommunications, the Internet, software, CD-ROM/DVD, e-commerce, and workstations. Fees: Free for current (most recent year) data; more extensive information has various fee structures. Formerly *Computer Industry Forecasts.*

### ONLINE DATABASES

*Computer Database.* Cengage Learning Inc. • Provides one year of full-text online for 150 leading computer-related publications. Also includes 70,000 product specifications and brief profiles of 13,000 computer product vendors and manufacturers. Inquire as to prices and availability.

## PERIODICALS AND NEWSLETTERS

*Dr. Dobb's Journal: Software Tools for the Professional Programmer.* UBM L.L.C. • Monthly. $34.95 per year. A technical publication covering software development, languages, operating systems, and applications.

*Information Week: Business Innovation Powered by Technology.* UBM L.L.C. • Weekly. $199.00 per year. The magazine for information systems management.

*Sys Admin: The Journal for Unix System Administrators.* UBM L.L.C. • Monthly. $39.00 per year. Provides technical information for managers of Unix systems.

# UNLISTED SECURITIES

*See* OVER-THE-COUNTER SECURITIES INDUSTRY

# UPHOLSTERY

## TRADE/PROFESSIONAL ASSOCIATIONS

National Association of Decorative Fabric Distributors. 1 Windsor Cove, Ste. 305, Columbia, SC 29223-1833. Phone: 800-445-8629 or (803)765-0860; Email: info@nadfd.com • URL: http://www.nadfd.com • Formerly National Association of Upholstery Fabric Distributors.

# URANIUM INDUSTRY

*See also* ATOMIC POWER; MINES AND MINERAL RESOURCES

## ALMANACS AND YEARBOOKS

*CRB Commodity Yearbook.* Commodity Research Bureau. CRB. • Annual. $179 plus $10.00 shipping cost. The single most comprehensive source of commodity and futures market information available.

## CD-ROM DATABASES

*Environment Abstracts on CD-ROM.* University Publications of America. • Quarterly. $1,295.00 per year. Contains the following CD-ROM databases: *Environment Abstracts, Energy Abstracts,* and *Acid Rain Abstracts.* Length of coverage varies.

## PERIODICALS AND NEWSLETTERS

*Nuclear Fuel.* Platts Global Energy. • Biweekly. $3,270.00 per year. Newsletter.

## STATISTICS SOURCES

*Non-Ferrous Metal Data Yearbook.* American Bureau of Metal Statistics. • Annual. $405.00. Provides worldwide data on approximately about 200 statistical tables covering many nonferrous metals. Includes production, consumption, inventories, exports, imports, and other data.

# URBAN AREAS

*See* CITIES AND TOWNS

# URBAN DEVELOPMENT

*See also* CITY PLANNING; COMMUNITY DEVELOPMENT; HOUSING

## ABSTRACTS AND INDEXES

*Index to Current Urban Documents.* Greenwood Publishing Group Inc. • Quarterly. $500.00 per year. Includes annual *Cumulation.*

*Social Sciences Citation Index.* Thomson Reuters Corp. • Weekly. Product is accessed via *Web of Science.*

*Social Sciences Index Retrospective: 1907-1983.* EBSCO Publishing Inc. • Indexing for 1,000,000 articles. Coverage includes international index and social sciences and humanities index.

*Urban Studies Abstracts.* EBSCO Publishing Inc. • Quarterly. $967 Institutions print only. Coverage includes community development, urban affairs, urban history.

## CD-ROM DATABASES

*Newspaper Abstracts Ondisc.* ProQuest L.L.C. • Monthly. $2,950.00 per year (covers 1989 to date; archival discs are available for 1985-88). Provides cover-to-cover CD-ROM indexing and abstracting of 19 major newspapers, including the *New York Times, Wall Street Journal, Washington Post, Chicago Tribune,* and *Los Angeles Times.*

*Social Sciences Abstracts.* EBSCO Publishing Inc. • Provides indexing from 1983 and abstracting from 1994 of more than 750 periodicals covering economics, area studies, community health, public administration, public welfare, urban studies, and many other topics related to the social sciences.

*Social Sciences Citation Index.* Thomson Reuters Corp. • Weekly. Product is accessed via *Web of Science.*

## HANDBOOKS AND MANUALS

*Zoning and Planning Law Handbook.* Patricia Salkin. Thomson West. • Annual. $601.30. Assembles the insights and guidance offered by the country's leading authorities in zoning law, land use planning, and conservation.

## ONLINE DATABASES

*Wilson Social Sciences Abstracts Online.* H.W. Wilson Co. • Provides online abstracting and indexing of more than 500 periodicals covering area studies, community health, public administration, public welfare, urban studies, and many other social science topics. Time period is 1994 to date for abstracts and 1983 to date for indexing, with updates weekly. Inquire as to online cost and availability.

## OTHER SOURCES

*American Land Planning Law.* John Taylor and Norma Williams. Thomson West. • $1,058 Individuals full set. Examines the changing priorities in zoning and land use practices, focusing on the relationship between private activity and governmental power, and analyzing over 15,000 cases from all 50 states.

## PERIODICALS AND NEWSLETTERS

*Downtown Idea Exchange: Essential Information for Downtown Research and Development Center.* Downtown Research and Development Center. Alexander Communications Group Inc. • Monthly. $227 Individuals. Newsletter for those concerned with central business districts. Provides news and other information on planning, development, parking, mass transit, traffic, funding, and other topics.

*Real Estate Economics: Journal of the American Real Estate and Urban Economics Association.* The MIT Press. • Quarterly. Covers a wide range of issues, from tax rules to brokers' commissions to corporate real estate including housing and urban economics, and the financial economics of real estate development and investment.

*Urban Affairs Review.* Pine Forge Press. • Bimonthly. $1,241 Institutions print & e-access. Urban studies journal. Formerly *Urban Affairs Quarterly.*

*Urban Land: News and Trends in Land Development.* Urban Land Institute. • Monthly.

## RESEARCH CENTERS AND INSTITUTES

University of California, Berkeley - Institute of Urban and Regional Development. 316 Wurster Hall, MC 1870, Berkeley, CA 94720-1870. Phone: (510)642-4874; Fax: (510)643-9576; Email: iurd@berkeley.edu • URL: http://iurd.berkeley.edu • Research topics include the effects of changing economic trends in urban areas.

University of Wisconsin—Milwaukee - Center for Urban Initiatives and Research. Engelmann Hall, Rm. B50, 2033 E Hartford Ave., Milwaukee, WI 53211. Phone: (414)229-5916; Fax: (414)229-3884; Email: cuir@uwm.edu • URL: http://www4.uwm.edu/cuir • Public policy with emphasis on metropolitan governance and economic revitalization, urban education, technological innovation and transfer, state and metropolitan public policy, health care organization and policy, employment and manpower, and housing and urban development. Also studies gangs and drug use in Midwestern cities.

Virginia Commonwealth University - Virginia Center for Urban Development. 919 W Franklin St., Richmond, VA 23284-3061. Phone: (804)828-7528; Fax: (804)828-6838; Email: bkinsey@vcu.edu • URL: http://www.vcu.edu/cppweb/urban • Economics, including impact analysis and forecasting.

## TRADE/PROFESSIONAL ASSOCIATIONS

American Real Estate and Urban Economics Association. The Center for Real State Education and Research, 821 Academic Way, 223 RBB, Tallahassee, FL 32306-1110. Phone: 866-273-8321 or (850)644-7898; Fax: (850)644-4077; Email: areuea@areuea.org • URL: http://www.areuea.org • Members are real estate teachers, researchers, economists, and others concerned with urban real estate and investment.

Dublin City Business Association. 21 Dawson St., Dublin 2, Dublin, Ireland. Phone: 353 1 6622995; Email: info@dcba.ie • URL: http://www.dcba.ie • Retail Federation in the city of Dublin. Promotes a sustainable city centre that is attractive to live, work, visit, and shop in.

International Downtown Association. 1025 Thomas Jefferson St. NW, Ste. 500W, Washington, DC 20007. Phone: (202)393-6801; Fax: (202)393-6869; Email: question@ida-downtown.org • URL: http://www.ida-downtown.org • Represents vital and livable urban centers. Works to build partnerships that anchor the well-being of towns, cities and regions throughout the world.

Mananga Management Centre. PO Box 5100, Mbabane, Swaziland. Email: info@mananga.sz • URL: http://www.mananga.sz • Development organizations and individuals with an interest in development issues. Promotes more effective management of development projects. Sponsors training courses for development administrators; initiates programs in areas including agricultural development, women's rights, rural development, environmental protection, water supply and sanitation, and vocational education.

National Aboriginal Lands Managers Association. 1024 Mississauga St., Curve Lake, ON, Canada K0L 1R0. Phone: 877-234-9813 or (705)657-7660; Fax: (705)657-7177; Email: info@nalma.ca • URL: http://www.nalma.ca • Advances the professional development and technical expertise in the field of land management. Provides a working environment to all First Nations Lands Managers. Creates opportunities for networking between land managers on land related issues. Creates a system that will assist First Nations interests in various land management functions.

National Association of Housing and Redevelopment Officials. 630 Eye St. NW, Washington, DC 20001-3736. Phone: 877-866-2476 or (202)289-3500; Fax: (202)289-8181; Email: nahro@nahro.org • URL: http://www.nahro.org • Formerly National Association of Housing Officials.

World Energy Cities Partnership. 901 Bagby,

Houston, TX 77002. Phone: (832)393-0829; Email: matthew.shailer@houstontx.gov • URL: http://www.energycities.org • Collaborates and assists cities around the world to support the local energy sectors. Encourages exchange of petroleum industry knowledge and economic and infrastructure development strategies. Provides a network of industry support services and resources.

# URBAN MANAGEMENT

*See* MUNICIPAL GOVERNMENT

# URBAN PLANNING

*See* CITY PLANNING

# USED CAR INDUSTRY

*See also* AUTOMOBILE DEALERS

## HANDBOOKS AND MANUALS

*Used-Car Rental Agency.* Entrepreneur Press. • Looseleaf. $59.50. A practical guide to starting a used-car rental business. Covers profit potential, start-up costs, market size evaluation, owner's time required, site selection, lease negotiation pricing, accounting, advertising, promotion, etc. (Start-Up Business Guide No. E1108.).

*Used Car Sales.* Entrepreneur Press. • Looseleaf. $59.50. A practical guide to getting started in the business of selling used cars. Covers profit potential, start-up costs, market size evaluation, owner's time required, site selection, lease negotiation, pricing, accounting, advertising, etc. (Start-Up Business Guide No. E2330.).

## INTERNET DATABASES

*Advance Monthly Retail Trade Report.* U. S. Census Bureau. Phone: 800-541-8345 or (301)457-4100 or (301)763-2713; Fax: (301)457-1296 or (301)457-3842; Email: naics@census.gov • URL: http://www.census.gov/epcd/www/naicstab.htm • Web pages provide monthly sales figures for a wide range of retail businesses. Advance, preliminary, and final statistics are provided for the latest month available in each case, with a previous-year comparison. Updates are monthly.

## PERIODICALS AND NEWSLETTERS

*Used Car Dealer.* National Independent Automobile Dealers Association. • Monthly. $80 /year for nonmembers. Association magazine for dealers who buy and sell used cars.

## PRICE SOURCES

*Automotive Market Report.* Automotive Auction Publishing Inc. • Biweekly. $130.00 Per Year. Current wholesale values of used vehicles.

*Edmund's Used Cars and Trucks, Prices and Ratings.* Edmund Publications Corp. • Quarterly. $39.96 Individuals. Lists American and foreign used car prices for the past 10 years.

*NADA Appraisal Guides.* National Automobile Dealers Association. • Prices and frequencies vary. Guides to prices of used cars, old used cars, motorcycles, mobile homes, recreational vehicles, and mopeds.

## STATISTICS SOURCES

*Annual Benchmark Report for Retail Trade and Food Services..A Detailed Summary of Retail Sales, Purchases, Accounts Receivable, Inventories, and Food Service Sales.* U. S. Government Printing Office. • Annual. $13.00. Issued by the U.S. Census Bureau. Provides detailed annual and monthly retail statistics for the most recent 10 years. Includes data for various kinds of retail outlets, including automobiles, furniture, appliances, building supplies, grocery stores, drug stores, gasoline stations, clothing, sporting goods, department stores, and restaurants.

## TRADE/PROFESSIONAL ASSOCIATIONS

National Auto Auction Association. 5320 Spectrum Dr., Ste. D, Frederick, MD 21703. Phone: (301)696-0400; Fax: (301)631-1359; Email: naaa@naaa.com • URL: http://www.naaa.com • Owners/operators of wholesale automobile and truck auctions; associate members are car and truck manufacturers, insurers of checks and titles, car and truck rental companies, publishers of auto price guide books, and others connected with the industry. Maintains hall of fame.

National Independent Automobile Dealers Association. 2521 Brown Blvd., Arlington, TX 76006. Phone: 800-682-3837 or (817)640-3838 or (434)983-2073; Fax: (817)649-5866; Email: info@niada.com • URL: http://www.niada.com • Individuals, companies, or corporations licensed by their states as dealers to buy and sell used motor vehicles; associate members are businesses related to or associated with the buying or selling of motor vehicles. Gathers and disseminates information relative to the used car industry; represents used car dealers before regulatory and legislative bodies; provides educational and other programs to help used car dealers understand their responsibilities; works for the betterment of the automobile industry. Works closely with local and state independent automobile dealers' associations and others concerning dealers and the public. Maintains code of fair dealing for members. Conducts seminars, meetings, and professional training programs. Maintains speakers' bureau, services for children, and charitable programs. Sponsors competitions; compiles statistics.

# USED PRODUCTS

*See* SURPLUS PRODUCTS

# UTENSILS, COOKING

*See* HOUSEWARES INDUSTRY

# UTILITIES, PUBLIC

*See* PUBLIC UTILITIES

# V

## VACUUM CLEANERS

### CD-ROM DATABASES

*OECD Statistical Compendium.* Organization for Economic Cooperation and Development. • Semiannual. $1,905.00 per year for 1 to 10 users. CD-ROM contains more than 730,000 monthly, quarterly, and annual time series for OECD countries, 1960 to date. Includes fully searchable data on agriculture, food, economic indicators, national accounts, employment, energy, finance, industry, technology, and foreign trade. Results can be displayed in various forms.

### INTERNET DATABASES

*Business 2.0 Web Guide to the Best Business Links.* Business 2.0 Media Inc. Phone: (415)293-4800; Email: support@business2.com • URL: http://www.business2.com/webguide • Web site presents an extensive, searchable directory of links to "the best, most informative, and authoritative web pages." Twenty main categories cover business, finance, career, company information, people, and technology topics, with thousands of subtopics, all linking to Web sites recommended by experienced business researchers. Fees: Free.

*Fedstats.* Federal Interagency Council on Statistical Policy. Phone: (202)395-7254 • URL: http://www.fedstats.gov • Web site features an efficient search facility for full-text statistics produced by more than 100 federal agencies, including the Census Bureau, the Bureau of Economic Analysis, and the Bureau of Labor Statistics. Boolean searches can be made within one agency or for all agencies combined. Links are offered to international statistical bureaus, including the UN, IMF, OECD, UNESCO, Eurostat, and 20 individual countries. Fees: Free.

*FreeLunch.com.* Economy.com, Inc. Phone: (610)696-8700; Fax: (610)696-1678 • URL: http://www.freelunch.com • Web site provides free access to more than 200 million economic and financial data series, covering industry, demographics, labor markets, prices, retail sales, government spending, trade, interest rates, housing starts, the stock market, etc. Data is available in either chart or table form. Searching is offered. Free, but registration required. Economy.com, Inc. also offers fee-based economic analysis at *The Dismal Scientist* site (www.dismal.com).

### STATISTICS SOURCES

*Survey of Current Business.* U. S. Government Printing Office. • Published by Bureau of Economic Analysis, U. S. Department of Commerce. Presents a wide variety of business and economic data.

## VALUATION

*See also* REAL PROPERTY VALUATION

### TRADE/PROFESSIONAL ASSOCIATIONS

American Society of Appraisers. 11107 Sunset Hills Rd., Ste. 310, Reston, VA 20190. Phone: 800-272-8258 or (703)478-2228; Fax: (703)742-8471; Email: asainfo@appraisers.org • URL: http://www.appraisers.org • Professional appraisal educator, testing, and accrediting society. Sponsors mandatory recertification program for all members. Offers a consumer information service to the public.

Appraisers Association of America. 212 W 35th St., 11th Fl. S, New York, NY 10001. Phone: (212)889-5404; Fax: (212)889-5503; Email: referrals@appraisersassociation.org • URL: http://www.appraisersassociation.org • Professional society of appraisers of personal property such as: Americana; antiques; armor; art objects; bibelot; books; bronzes; china and porcelain; clocks and watches; coins; crystal and glass; curios; diamonds and jewelry; enamels; etchings; fine art; firearms; furniture; furs; graphic art; guns; household furnishings; ivories; leather goods; lighting fixtures; linens and lace; miniatures; music; musical instruments; oriental art; paintings; pewter; pianos; primitive art; prints; rugs; sculpture; Sheffield plate; silver and silverware; stamps; steins and tankards; taxes; and woodcarvings.

Canadian Institute of Chartered Business Valuators. 277 Wellington St. W, Ste. 710, Toronto, ON, Canada M5V 3H2. Phone: (416)977-1117; Fax: (416)977-7066; Email: admin@cicbv.ca • URL: http://www.cicbv.ca • Chartered business valuators. Promotes excellence in the practice of business valuation. Serves as a forum for the exchange of information among members; makes available continuing professional development programs for business valuators.

## VALVES

### DIRECTORIES

*European Valves for Control, Isolation and Safety.* Roles & Associates Ltd. • Irregular. $96. Covers: suppliers of valves, actuators, auxiliary equipment, piping and connectors in Europe. Entries include: Company name, address, phone, descriptions of services, products provided.

### FINANCIAL RATIOS

*Annual Statement Studies.* Risk Management Association. • Annual. Compiled from over 280,000 financial statements.

*Annual Statement Studies: Industry Default Prob-* *abilities and Cash Flow Measures.* Risk Management Association. • Annual. $405 Nonmembers. Serves as a companion volume to the original *Annual Statement Studies.* Gives probability of default estimates on a percentage scale for more than 450 industries. Includes changes in position year-by-year for eight financial statement line items and provides percentage measures of cash flow.

### INTERNET DATABASES

*Manufacturing Profiles.* U. S. Bureau of the Census. Phone: (301)763-4636 or (301)763-4100; Fax: (301)763-4794; Email: webmaster@census.gov • URL: http://www.census.gov/prod/www/abs/mfg-prof.html • The Census Bureau makes available free on PDF (Portable Document Format) an annual consolidation of the entire Current Industrial Report series, presenting "all the data compiled." Contains statistics on production, shipments, inventories, consumption, exports, imports, and orders for a wide variety of manufactured products.

### PERIODICALS AND NEWSLETTERS

*Processing.* Putman Media Inc. • 14 times a year. $54.00 per year. Emphasis is on descriptions of new products for all areas of industrial processing, including valves, controls, filters, pumps, compressors, fluidics, and instrumentation.

### STATISTICS SOURCES

*U.S. Industry and Trade Outlook.* U.S. Department of Commerce National Technical Information Service. • Annual. Produced by the International Trade Administration, U.S. Department of Commerce, in a "public-private" partnership with DRI/McGraw-Hill and Standard & Poor's. Provides basic data, outlook for the current year, and "Long-Term Prospects" (five-year projections) for a wide variety of products and services. Includes high technology industries. Formerly *U.S. Industrial Outlook.*

### TRADE/PROFESSIONAL ASSOCIATIONS

Manufacturers Standardization Society. 127 Park St. NE, Vienna, VA 22180. Phone: (703)281-6613; Fax: (703)281-6671; Email: info@mss-hq.com • URL: http://www.mss-hq.com • Members are valve and fitting companies. Publishes standards and specifications.

## VARIABLE ANNUITIES

*See* ANNUITIES

## VARIETY STORES

*See also* RETAIL TRADE

## CD-ROM DATABASES

*OECD Statistical Compendium.* Organization for Economic Cooperation and Development. • Semiannual. $1,905.00 per year for 1 to 10 users. CD-ROM contains more than 730,000 monthly, quarterly, and annual time series for OECD countries, 1960 to date. Includes fully searchable data on agriculture, food, economic indicators, national accounts, employment, energy, finance, industry, technology, and foreign trade. Results can be displayed in various forms.

## FINANCIAL RATIOS

*Annual Statement Studies.* Risk Management Association. • Annual. Compiled from over 280,000 financial statements.

*Annual Statement Studies: Industry Default Probabilities and Cash Flow Measures.* Risk Management Association. • Annual. $405 Nonmembers. Serves as a companion volume to the original *Annual Statement Studies.* Gives probability of default estimates on a percentage scale for more than 450 industries. Includes changes in position year-by-year for eight financial statement line items and provides percentage measures of cash flow.

## INTERNET DATABASES

*Business 2.0 Web Guide to the Best Business Links.* Business 2.0 Media Inc. Phone: (415)293-4800; Email: support@business2.com • URL: http://www. business2.com/webguide • Web site presents an extensive, searchable directory of links to "the best, most informative, and authoritative web pages." Twenty main categories cover business, finance, career, company information, people, and technology topics, with thousands of subtopics, all linking to Web sites recommended by experienced business researchers. Fees: Free.

*Fedstats.* Federal Interagency Council on Statistical Policy. Phone: (202)395-7254 • URL: http://www. fedstats.gov • Web site features an efficient search facility for full-text statistics produced by more than 100 federal agencies, including the Census Bureau, the Bureau of Economic Analysis, and the Bureau of Labor Statistics. Boolean searches can be made within one agency or for all agencies combined. Links are offered to international statistical bureaus, including the UN, IMF, OECD, UNESCO, Eurostat, and 20 individual countries. Fees: Free.

*FreeLunch.com.* Economy.com, Inc. Phone: (610)696-8700; Fax: (610)696-1678 • URL: http:// www.freelunch.com • Web site provides free access to more than 200 million economic and financial data series, covering industry, demographics, labor markets, prices, retail sales, government spending, trade, interest rates, housing starts, the stock market, etc. Data is available in either chart or table form. Searching is offered. Free, but registration required. Economy.com, Inc. also offers fee-based economic analysis at *The Dismal Scientist* site (www.dismal. com).

## STATISTICS SOURCES

*Survey of Current Business.* U. S. Government Printing Office. • Published by Bureau of Economic Analysis, U. S. Department of Commerce. Presents a wide variety of business and economic data.

## VARNISH AND VARNISHING

*See also* PAINT AND PAINTING

## INTERNET DATABASES

*Manufacturing Profiles.* U. S. Bureau of the Census. Phone: (301)763-4636 or (301)763-4100; Fax: (301)763-4794; Email: webmaster@census.gov • URL: http://www.census.gov/prod/www/abs/mfg-prof.html • The Census Bureau makes available free on PDF (Portable Document Format) an annual consolidation of the entire Current Industrial Report

series, presenting "all the data compiled." Contains statistics on production, shipments, inventories, consumption, exports, imports, and orders for a wide variety of manufactured products.

## ONLINE DATABASES

*World Surface Coatings Abstracts (Online).* Paint Research Association of Great Britain. • Indexing and abstracting of the literature of paint and surface coatings, 1976 to present. Monthly updates. Inquire as to online cost and availability.

## PERIODICALS AND NEWSLETTERS

*Modern Paint and Coatings.* Chemical Week Associates. • Monthly. $52.00 per year. A comprehensive publication highlighting formulators and suppliers to the Paint, Coatings and Ink Industry.

## STATISTICS SOURCES

*Paint, Varnish, and Lacquer.* U. S. Bureau of the Census. • Quarterly and annual. Provides data on shipments: value, quantity, imports, and exports. Includes paint, varnish, lacquer, product finishes, and special purpose coatings. (Current Industrial Reports, MQ-28F.).

## TRADE/PROFESSIONAL ASSOCIATIONS

American Coatings Association. 1500 Rhode Island Ave. NW, Washington, DC 20005. Phone: (202)462-6272; Fax: (202)462-8549 • URL: http://www.paint. org • Formerly National Paint and Coatings Association.

## VCR

*See* VIDEO RECORDING INDUSTRY

## VEGETABLE INDUSTRY

## ABSTRACTS AND INDEXES

*Field Crop Abstracts.* CABI Publishing North America. • Monthly. Published in England by CABI Publishing, formerly Commonwealth Agricultural Bureaux.

*Food Science and Technology Abstracts.* Ovid Technologies Inc. • Monthly. $1,780.00 per year. Provides worldwide coverage of the literature of food technology and food production.

*Foods Adlibra: Key to the World's Food Literature.* General Mills, Inc. Foods Adlibra Publications. • Semimonthly. $240.00 per year. Provides journal citations and abstracts to the literature of food technology and packaging.

*Horticultural Science Abstracts.* CABI Publishing North America. • Updated weekly online; also available in print, delivered monthly.

## CD-ROM DATABASES

*AGRICOLA on SilverPlatter.* Ovid Technologies Inc. • Updated monthly. Price varies. Produced by the National Agricultural Library. Provides over 4 million citations to the literature of agriculture, agricultural economics, animal sciences, entomology, fertilizer, food, forestry, nutrition, pesticides, plant science, water resources, and other topics.

## DIRECTORIES

*American Vegetable Grower--Source Book.* Meister Media Worldwide. • Annual. Publication includes: Lists of suppliers of agricultural chemicals and manufacturers and suppliers of other agricultural products, equipment, and services including packaging equipment, transportation services, direct marketing suppliers, plants and seeds, etc. Entries include: Company name, address, phone, fax, e-mail.

*Directory of Chinese Manufacturers & Exporters of Fruits & Vegetables.* EXIM Infotek Private Ltd. • $15 Individuals. Covers: 150 Chinese manufacturers and exporters of apples, bamboo shoots, canned

fruits, canned mushrooms, canned pineapples, carrots, cherries, dehydrated vegetables, dried carrots, dried mushrooms, dried vegetables, frozen bamboo shoots, frozen carrots, frozen fruits, frozen vegetables, fruit, garlic, garlic sprouts, ginger, grapes, green beans, vermicelli, green vegetables, lychee, mushrooms, mushrooms and fungi, onion slices, onions, onions-Chinese, oranges, pea pods, salted vegetables, strawberries, vegetable products, vegetables, and vegetables-canned. Entries include: Company name, postal address, city, country, phone, fax, e-mail and websites, contact person, designation, and product details.

*Major Food and Drink Companies of the World.* Cengage Learning Inc. • 12th edition. eBook. Published by Graham & Whiteside. Contains profiles and trade names for more than 9,200 important food and beverage companies in various countries. In addition to foods, includes both alcoholic and nonalcoholic drink products.

*Western Growers Association--Membership Directory.* Western Growers Association. • Annual. Covers: 2,700 growers, shippers, packers, brokers, and distributors of fruits, vegetables, nuts, and allied industries in California and Arizona. Entries include: Company name, address, phone and fax, names of executives, list of commodities.

## ENCYCLOPEDIAS AND DICTIONARIES

*Encyclopedia of Food and Culture.* Cengage Learning Inc. • 2003. $657.00. Three volumes. Contains 600 articles covering various aspects of food and its place in society, from agronomy to zucchini. Includes illustrations and a detailed index. eBook also available, updated in 2004.

## INTERNET DATABASES

*USDA.* U.S. National Institute of Standards and Technology. 100 Bureau Dr., Gaithersburg, MD 20899-1070. Phone: 800-877-8339 or (301)975-6478 or (202)720-2791; Fax: (301)975-8295; Email: inquiries@nist.gov • URL: http://www.nist.gov • The USDA home page has six sections: News and Information; What's New; About USDA; Agencies; Opportunities; Search and Help. Keyword searching is offered from the USDA home page and from various individual agency home pages. Agencies are the Economic Research Service, Agricultural Marketing Service, National Agricultural Statistics Service, National Agricultural Library, and about 12 others. Updating varies. Fees: Free.

## ONLINE DATABASES

*Agricola.* U.S. National Agricultural Library World List of Agricultural Serials. • Covers worldwide agricultural literature. Over 3.3 million citations, 1970 to present, with monthly updates. Inquire as to online cost and availability.

*Food Science and Technology Abstracts (online).* IFIS North American Desk. • Produced by International Food Information Service. Provides about 500,000 online citations, with abstracts, to the international literature of food science, technology, commodities, engineering, and processing. Approximately 2,000 periodicals are covered. Time period is 1969 to date, with monthly updates. Inquire as to online cost and availability.

## PERIODICALS AND NEWSLETTERS

*Food Distribution Magazine.* Phoenix Media Network Inc. • Monthly. $49.00 per year. Edited for marketers and buyers of domestic and imported, specialty or gourmet food products, including ethnic foods, seasonings, and bakery items.

*The Grower: Profitable Business Strategies for Fruit and Vegetable Growers.* Vance Publishing Corp. • Monthly. $45 Individuals. Magazine providing management information for the commercial fruit and vegetable producer with emphasis on management, industry trends, effective marketing, chemicals, and legislative and regulatory environments.

*The Packer: Devoted to the Interest of Commericial Growers, Packers, Shippers, Receivers and Retailers of Fruits, Vegetables and Other Products.* Vance Publishing Corp., Produce Div. • Weekly. $65.00 per year. Supplements available: *Brand Directory and Fresh Trends, Packer's Produce Availability and Merchandising Guide* and *Produce Services Sourcebooks.*

*The Packer: The Business Newspaper of the Produce Industry.* Vance Publishing Corp. • Weekly. $99 Individuals. Newspaper on produce marketing.

*Produce Merchandising: The Packer's Retailing and Merchandising Magazine.* Vance Publishing Corp. • Monthly. $35.00 per year. Provides information and advice on the retail marketing and promotion of fresh fruits and vegetalbe.

*Produce News.* Zim-mer Trade Publications Inc. • Weekly. $35.00 per year.

*Western Grower and Shipper: The Business Magazine of the Western Product Industry.* Western Growers Association. • Monthly. $18.00 per year.

## STATISTICS SOURCES

*Agricultural Statistics.* U.S. Department of Agriculture National Agricultural Statistics Service. • Annual. $46 Individuals. Provides a wide variety of statistical data relating to agricultural production, supplies, consumption, prices/price-supports, foreign trade, costs, and returns, as well as farm labor, loans, income, and population. In many cases, historical data is shown annually for 10 years. In addition to farm data, includes detailed fishery statistics.

*Vegetables and Specialties Situation and Outlook.* U. S. Government Printing Office. • Three times a year. Issued by the Economic Research Service of the U. S. Department of Agriculture. Provides current statistical information on supply, demand, and prices.

# VEGETABLE OIL INDUSTRY

*See* OIL AND FATS INDUSTRY

# VENDING MACHINES

## DIRECTORIES

*Directory of European Importers of Vending and Coin Operated Machines.* EXIM Infotek Private Ltd. • $200 Individuals. Covers: 60 European importers of vending and coin operated machine. Entries include: Company name, postal address, telephone, fax, e-mail, website, contact person, designation, and product details.

*Directory of South American Importers of Vending and Coin Operated Machines.* EXIM Infotek Private Ltd. • $150 Individuals. Covers: 20 South American importers of vending and coin operated machinery. Entries include: Company name, postal address, telephone, fax, e-mail, website, contact person, designation, and product details.

*National Automatic Merchandising Association-Directory of Members.* National Automatic Merchandising Association. • Annual. Lists vending and food service management firms, along with vending machine manufacturers and distributors and producers of other equipment and food items.

## FINANCIAL RATIOS

*Annual Statement Studies.* Risk Management Association. • Annual. Compiled from over 280,000 financial statements.

*Annual Statement Studies: Industry Default Probabilities and Cash Flow Measures.* Risk Management Association. • Annual. $405 Nonmembers. Serves as a companion volume to the original *Annual Statement Studies.* Gives probability of default estimates on a percentage scale for more than 450

industries. Includes changes in position year-by-year for eight financial statement line items and provides percentage measures of cash flow.

## INTERNET DATABASES

*Manufacturing Profiles.* U. S. Bureau of the Census. Phone: (301)763-4636 or (301)763-4100; Fax: (301)763-4794; Email: webmaster@census.gov • URL: http://www.census.gov/prod/www/abs/mfg-prof.html • The Census Bureau makes available free on PDF (Portable Document Format) an annual consolidation of the entire Current Industrial Report series, presenting "all the data compiled." Contains statistics on production, shipments, inventories, consumption, exports, imports, and orders for a wide variety of manufactured products.

## PERIODICALS AND NEWSLETTERS

*Cash Box: The International Music-Record Weekly.* Cash Box Publishing Co., Inc. • Weekly. $185.00 per year.

*Vending Times: Vending-Feeding-Coffee Service-Music and Games.* Vending Times Inc. • Monthly. $50 Individuals. Incorporates *V-T Music and Games.*

## STATISTICS SOURCES

*Vending Machines.* U. S. Bureau of the Census. • Annual. Provides data on value of manufacturers' shipments, quantity, exports, imports, etc. (Current Industrial Reports, MA-35U.)

*Vending Times Census of the Industry.* Vending Times Inc. • Annual. $50 U.S. and Canada.

## TRADE/PROFESSIONAL ASSOCIATIONS

National Automatic Merchandising Association. 20 N Wacker Dr., Ste. 3500, Chicago, IL 60606-3102. Phone: 888-337-8363 or (312)346-0370; Fax: (312)704-4140; Email: dgary@vending.org • URL: http://www.vending.org • Manufacturing and operating companies in the automatic vending machine industry; food service management firms; office coffee machine operators; suppliers of products and services. Compiles industry statistics.

National Bulk Vendors Association. 1202 E Maryland Ave., Ste. 1K, Phoenix, AZ 85014-1342. Phone: 888-628-2872; Fax: (480)302-5108; Email: admin@nbva.org • URL: http://www.nbva.info • Manufacturers, distributors, and operators of bulk vending merchandise and equipment.

# VENEERS AND VENEERING

*See* LUMBER INDUSTRY; PLYWOOD INDUSTRY

# VENTURE CAPITAL

## ALMANACS AND YEARBOOKS

*National Venture Capital Association Yearbook.* Thomson Financial Inc. • Annual. $195.00. Provides a yearly review of the U.S. venture capital industry, including statistical data.

## DIRECTORIES

*Business Capital Sources.* International Wealth Success, Inc. • Annual. $20 Individuals. Covers: About 1,500 banks, insurance and mortgage companies, commercial finance, leasing, and venture capital firms that lend money for business investment. Entries include: Company or institution name, address, phone.

*China and Venture Capital & Private Equity Directory 500.* Zero2IPO. • Annual. $455 Individuals. Covers: 600 institutions specializing in venture capital and private equity investment in China. Entries include: Company contact information, executive team, criteria for investment, cases of investment, and amount of capital under the management.

*Directory of Venture Capital and Private Equity Firms.* Grey House Publishing. • $750 Individuals. Covers: 2,300 domestic and international venture capital and private equity firms. Entries include: Firm name, address, phone, fax, e-mail, URL, description of services, names and titles of key personnel.

*Directory of Venture Capital: 2nd Edition.* John Wiley & Sons Inc. • $59.95 Individuals paperback. Covers: More than 600 actively investing venture capital firms and funding sources. Database includes: Samples of standard agreements and contracts. Entries include: Company name, address, phone, types of investments, geographic preference.

*Gale Directory of Early Stage Investment.* Cengage Learning Inc. • $606 print only. Covers several types of early stage investors including: venture capitalists, business incubators, angel investors and angel groups, corporate investment divisions, crowdfunding and co-operative groups.

*Gold Book of Venture Capital Firms.* Todd Publications. • $75. Covers: 869 venture capital firms in 37 specialties. Database includes: Introduction on working with venture capital firms. Entries include: Firm name, names and titles of key personnel, specialty, preferred stage of financing.

*IVCI Directory of Domestic and International Venture Groups.* International Venture Capital Institute Inc. Baxter Associates Inc. • Annual. $9.95 per issue. Covers: over 200 venture capital clubs; international coverage. Entries include: Organization name, address, phone, name and title of contact.

*IVCI Directory of Venture Capital Seed and Early-Stage Funds.* International Venture Capital Institute Inc. Baxter Associates Inc. • Covers: Over 225 venture capital firms which do seed and/or early-stage joint ventures. Entries include: Contact information.

*Pratt's Guide to Venture Capital Sources.* Greenwood Electronic Media. • Annual. $249. Covers: Approximately 800 venture capital firms, principally in the United States; small business investment corporations (SBICs); corporate venture groups; and selected consultants and "deal men"; separate section for providers of professional services to venture capitalists. Database includes: Articles on raising venture capital. Entries include: Company name, address, phone, names of executives, investment preferences, and industry preferences.

*Vankirk's International Venture Capital Directory.* Online Publishing Inc. • Semiannual. $245. Covers: more than 350 companies and organizations providing capital to business ventures outside the U.S. Database includes: Articles on working with venture capitalists, trends and statistics, and how to develop an effective business plan; glossary. Entries include: Organization name, address, phone, fax, names and titles of key personnel, preferred stage of funding; preferred industries, geographic preference, minimum and maximum amounts invested, preferred size of investment, total capital under management, current activity level, total of recently made investments, compensation method, type of organization, year founded, staff size, trade association memberships, affiliated organizations and funds, corporate description.

*Vankirk's Venture Capital Investments Profiled.* Online Publishing Inc. • Semiannual. $245. Covers: more than 1,200 investments made by over 110 venture capital firms. Database includes: Statistics; glossary. Entries include: Investing firm name, address, phone, fax, names and titles of key personnel; recipient firm's name, location, description of product or service, amount of funding provided, stage of funding; industry, type of investment (debt, equity, etc.).

*VenCap Data Quest.* Reference Press Inc. • $89.95

Eastern version. Diskette. Contains over 750 venture capital firms in the eastern and western U.S. Entries include: Company name, address, phone, fax, officers, partners, type of fund, number of years providing funding, dollars under management, industries covered and geographical preferences, preferred low- and high-average investments, preferred maturity stages, and product description of portfolio companies.

*The Venture Capital Directory on CD-ROM.* Infon Corp. • Covers: over 500 venture capital firms and over 2,000 investors. Entries include: venture capital firms--investment size, location, and industry; investors--education and experience.

## OTHER SOURCES

*Formation and Financing of Emerging Companies.* Daniel E. O'Connor and others. Glasser LegalWorks. • $499 Individuals Binder/Looseleaf (Full set). Periodic Supplementation. Covers incorporation, bylaws, indemnification, intellectual property, financing sources, venture capital, due diligence, bridge loans, investor rights, compliance, and other legal issues associated with company formation. (Emerging Growth Companies Series.).

*Start-Up and Emerging Companies: Planning, Financing, and Operating the Successful Business, with Forms on Disk.* ALM Media Properties LLC. • $925 print + online + ebook. Covers a wide variety of business and legal topics relating to new enterprises. Provides information on venture financing, formation of corporations, tax laws, limited liability companies, employee benefits, contracts, and accounting. Includes a CD-ROM containing more than 75 sample legal forms, clauses, agreements, organizational resolutions, and checklists. (Law Journal Press).

## PERIODICALS AND NEWSLETTERS

*Corporate Financing Week: The Newsweekly of Corporate Finance, Investment Banking and M and A.* Institutional Investor Inc. Journals Group. • Weekly. $2,550.00 per year. Includes print and on-line editions. Newsletter for corporate finance officers. Emphasis is on debt and equity financing, mergers, leveraged buyouts, investment banking, and venture capital.

*Inc.: The Magazine for Growing Companies.* INC. • 10/year. $10 U.S. /year for two subscription. Edited for small office and home businesses with one to 25 employees. Covers management, office technology, and lifestyle. Incorporates *Self-Employed Professional.*

*Venture Capital Journal.* Thomson Venture Economics. • Description: Hard news, analysis and data on the North American private equity market.

## STATISTICS SOURCES

*U.S. Industry and Trade Outlook.* U.S. Department of Commerce National Technical Information Service. • Annual. Produced by the International Trade Administration, U.S. Department of Commerce, in a "public-private" partnership with DRI/McGraw-Hill and Standard & Poor's. Provides basic data, outlook for the current year, and "Long-Term Prospects" (five-year projections) for a wide variety of products and services. Includes high technology industries. Formerly *U.S. Industrial Outlook.*

## TRADE/PROFESSIONAL ASSOCIATIONS

African Private Equity and Venture Capital Association. The Banking Hall, Cropthorne Ct., 26 Maide Vale, London, United Kingdom. Phone: 44 20 3632 0408; Email: avca@avca-africa.org • URL: http://www.avcanet.com • Advances, develops and stimulates private equity and venture capital in Africa. Promotes high ethical standards of business conduct and professional competence in the private equity and venture capital industries.

American Council for Capital Formation. 1001 Connecticut Ave. NW, Ste. 620, Washington, DC 20036.

Phone: (202)293-5811; Fax: (202)785-8165; Email: info@accf.org • URL: http://accf.org • Supports capital formation as a general concept. Formerly American Council on Capitol Gain and Estate Taxation.

Associacao Brasileira de Private Equity and Venture Capital. Avenida Rio Branco, 123, Rm. 1505, 20040-005 Rio de Janeiro, RJ, Brazil. Phone: 55 21 39702432 • URL: http://www.abvcap.com.br • Promotes and develops the private equity and venture capital industry in Brazil. Represents the interests of the Brazilian private equity and venture capital community.

Australian Venture Capital Association Limited. Level 10, Kyle House, 27-31 Macquarie Pl., Sydney, NSW 2000, Australia. Phone: 61 2 82437000 or 61 2 82382600; Email: members@avcal.com.au • URL: http://www.avcal.com.au • Promotes the venture capital and private equity industry in Australia. Provides networking events for members, industry tools (non-disclosure agreement, valuation guidelines, Standard Industry Trust Deed and Standard VCLP), information for entrepreneurs seeking capital and employment database.

British Venture Capital Association. 5th Fl. E, Chancery House, 53-64 Chancery Ln., London WC2A 1QS, United Kingdom. Phone: 44 20 74920400; Fax: 44 20 74201801; Email: bvca@bvca.co.uk • URL: http://www.bvca.co.uk • Venture capital, private equity, and professional firms connected with the venture capital industry. Represents virtually every major source of venture capital in the UK. Provides information about members to entrepreneurs and investors; represents members' views in discussions with Government and other bodies; provides a forum for the exchange of views among members; develops and maintains the highest standards of professional practice and provides training for members' employees.

Canada's Venture Capital and Private Equity Association. 1201-372 Bay St., Toronto, ON, Canada M5H 2W9. Phone: (416)487-0519; Fax: (416)487-5899; Email: cvca@cvca.ca • URL: http://www.cvca.ca • Ventures and risks capital companies. Promotes economic growth through provision of capital to emerging businesses. Conducts research; facilitates exchange of information among members; represents the venture capital industry before government agencies, industrial and financial organizations, and the public.

China Venture Capital and Private Equity Association. Office Tower E1, 21/F, Rm. 2109, 1 E Chang An Ave., Beijing 100738, Hebei, China. Phone: 86 10 85183584; Fax: 86 10 85150835 • URL: http://www.cvca.com.cn • Promotes the interests and the development of venture capital and private equity industry in the Greater China Region. Fosters understanding of the importance of venture capital and private equity to the vitality of the Greater China economy and global economies.

German Private Equity and Venture Capital Association. Residenz Deutschen Theater, Reinhardtstrasse 27c, D-10117 Berlin, Germany. Phone: 49 30 3069820; Fax: 49 30 30698220; Email: bvk@bvkap.de • URL: http://www.bvkap.de • Represents the venture capital and private equity companies in Germany. Aims to create a favorable environment for the industry through publications and cooperation with other institutions.

Hong Kong Venture Capital and Private Equity Association. Rm. 2001, Wilson House, 19 - 27 Wyndham St., Central, Hong Kong, Hong Kong, China. Phone: 852 21677518; Fax: 852 21677530 ; Email: hkvca@hkvca.com.hk • URL: http://web.hkvca.com.hk/en • Promotes and protects the interests of the venture capital industry in Hong Kong. Educates enterprises about venture capital/private equity as a partner in creating value in the business. Seeks to improve the investment environ-

ment in Hong Kong and in the People's Republic of China.

Hungarian Venture Capital and Private Equity Association. 11 Pauler St., H-1013 Budapest, Hungary. Phone: 36 1 4750924; Email: hvca@hvca.hu • URL: http://www.hvca.hu • Promotes the interests and the development of the venture capital and private equity industry in Hungary. Creates a set of professional and ethical standards for member companies. Provides a regular forum for the exchange of ideas among members.

Indian Venture Capital Association. C-7, Pashchimi Marg, Vasant Vihar, New Delhi 110 057, Delhi, India. Phone: 91 11 46160389; Email: aakriti@indiavca.org • URL: http://www.indiavca.org • Facilitates the growth of venture capital and private equity activities in India. Encourages and assists in the creation of more venture capital and private equity funds in India. Works to increase the skills of India's entrepreneurs.

Investment Company Institute. 1401 H St. NW, Ste. 1200, Washington, DC 20005. Phone: (202)326-5800 or (202)371-5413; Fax: (202)326-5986; Email: chris@ici.org • URL: http://www.ici.org • Formerly American Association of Minority Enterprise Small Business Investment Companies.

Israel Advanced Technologies Industries. PO Box 12591, 46733 Herzliya, Israel. Phone: 972 73 7136313; Fax: 972 73 7136314; Email: orit@iati.co.il • URL: http://www.iati.co.il • Promotes the development of the venture capital industry in Israel. Supports and enhances the growth of Israeli high-technology industries. Secures special conditions and privileges for members from service organizations in Israel and abroad.

Italian Private Equity and Venture Capital Association. Via Pietro Mascagni n. 7, I-20122 Milan, Italy. Phone: 39 2 7607531; Fax: 39 2 76398044; Email: info@aifi.it • URL: http://www.aifi.it • Lobbies in the legislative and institutional process. Organizes symposia and seminars, educational programs and supports research activities.

Latin American Venture Capital Association. 589 8th Ave., 18th Fl., New York, NY 10018. Phone: (646)315-6735; Fax: (646)349-1047; Email: info@lavca.org • URL: http://www.lavca.org • Promotes the growth of the private equity and venture capital industry in Latin America and the Caribbean. Advocates on behalf of the industry by disseminating information to the media, promoting the region to investors and supporting efforts to improve the regulatory framework. Conducts research on industry trends, performance and policy environment. Develops model documents, industry guides and standards.

Latvian Venture Capital and Private Equity Association. Skolas St. 25-1, LV-1010 Riga, Latvia. Phone: 371 6 29477979 or 371 6 29265627; Email: info@lvca.lv • URL: http://www.lvca.lv • Promotes the development of the venture capital sector in Latvia. Informs businessmen and the society about venture capital financing possibilities. Promotes the exchange of information among members.

Malaysian Venture Capital and Private Equity Association. 54-3, Jalan 27/70A, Desa Sri Hartamas, 50480 Kuala Lumpur, Malaysia. Phone: 60 3 23006550; Fax: 60 3 62062484; Email: info@mvca.org.my • URL: http://www.mvca.org.my • Promotes, develops and maintains the venture capital industry in Malaysia as a source of equity financing for the start-up or development of small and medium-sized enterprises. Encourages the promotion, research, and analysis of venture capital in Malaysia and other countries. Serves as a forum for the exchange of views among members. Represents the members to all governmental institutions or public authorities.

National Development Council. 708 Third Ave., Ste.

710, New York, NY 10017. Phone: (212)682-1106 or (859)578-4850; Fax: (212)573-6118; Email: training@nationaldevelopmentcouncil.org • URL: http://www.nationaldevelopmentcouncil.org • Brings innovative economic development financing programs to urban and rural communities interested in local business and industrial growth, commercial revitalization, and permanent job creation. Finances professionals' work with cities, counties, and states to: build permanent systems for developing financing; train local staff; structure and negotiate financing for development projects, local business development, and industrial expansion. Conducts intensive training program for economic development professionals with courses in business credit analysis, real estate financing, loan packaging, federal financing, and program management and implementation; has provided advice to congress and federal agencies that has helped create lending programs for job creation and small business investment; has initiated and managed presidential programs for Presidents Nixon, Ford, Carter, and Reagan.

Polish Private Equity Association. ul. E Plater 53, 31 pietro, 00-113 Warsaw, Poland. Phone: 48 22 4588430; Fax: 48 22 4588555; Email: psik@psik. org.pl • URL: http://www.ppea.org.pl • Promotes and develops the private equity and venture capital industry in Poland. Represents the interests of the Polish private equity and venture capital community in Poland and abroad. Keeps members informed about significant initiatives and proposed changes to the legal, tax and regulatory environment.

Russian Venture Capital Association. ORm. 209, Bldg. 12B, prospekt Engelsa 27, 194156 Saint Petersburg, Russia. Phone: 7 812 3266180; Fax: 7 812 3266180; Email: rvca@rvca.ru • URL: http://www.rvca.ru • Promotes the development of the venture capital industry in Russia. Seeks to create a positive political and entrepreneurial environment for investment activities. Represents members' interests at the government level and in financial and industrial markets within the country and abroad.

Singapore Venture Capital and Private Equity Association. 14 Robinson Rd., No. 07-02A, Far East Finance Bldg., Singapore 048545, Singapore. Phone: 65 6 2247001; Fax: 65 6 2246772; Email: info@svca.org.sg • URL: http://www.svca.org.sg • Promotes, develops, and maintains local venture capital and private equity industry as a source of equity finance. Represents the local venture capital industry in dealing with parties from other countries. Fosters interaction among members, investors, and investees.

Slovak Venture Capital Association. Stefanikova 6a, 811 05 Bratislava, Slovakia. Phone: 421 2 754414356; Fax: 421 2 754431180; Email: slovca@slovca.sk • URL: http://www.slovca.sk • Provides information for people seeking venture capital for new and existing enterprises. Represents the interests of members before the government and other related institutions/agencies. Encourages the highest standards of business practice.

Small Business Investor Alliance. 1100 H St. NW, Ste. 610, Washington, DC 20005. Phone: (202)628-5055; Email: membership@sbia.org • URL: http://www.sbia.org • Affiliated with Small Business Investor Alliance.

South African Venture Capital and Private Equity Association. PO Box 1140, Houghton 2041, South Africa. Phone: 27 11 2680041; Fax: 27 11 2680527; Email: info@savca.co.za • URL: http://www.savca.co.za • Promotes the venture capital and private equity profession in Southern Africa. Develops and stimulates professional and transactional venture capital and private equity investments.

Taiwan Private Equity and Venture Capital Association. Rm. 133, 10th Fl., No. 133, Sect. C, Minsheng E Rd., Songshan Dist., Taipei 105,

Taiwan. Phone: 886 2 25450075; Fax: 886 2 25452752; Email: public@tvca.org.tw • URL: http://www.tvca.org.tw • Promotes awareness of the venture capital industry in Taiwan and its importance to the economy. Provides networking opportunity among members. Acts as a liaison between members and the government in order to update members of relevant investment regulations. Establishes professional venture capital information center in Taiwan in order to provide members with relevant local and international industry information. Promotes relevant business laws and regulations and economic policies.

Thai Venture Capital Association. 19/1 Bldg. 2, King Chamnan-aksorn, Phaholyothin Rd., Phayathai, Bangkok 10400, Thailand. Phone: 66 2 6617898; Fax: 66 2 6617899; Email: tvca@venturecapital.or.th • URL: http://www.venturecapital.or.th • Promotes venture capital and private equity businesses in Thailand. Supports and assists members in all problems related to venture capital businesses, including negotiations with any foreign parties. Promotes closer working relationships among members in order to exchange ideas and opinions regarding technical knowledge, news, economic research and financial information.

# VETERANS

## INTERNET DATABASES

*U.S. Census Bureau: The Official Statistics.* U. S. Bureau of the Census. Phone: (301)763-4636 or (301)763-4100; Fax: (301)763-4794; Email: webmaster@census.gov • URL: http://www.census.gov/prod/www/abs/mfg-prof.html • Web site is "Your Source for Social, Demographic, and Economic Information." Contains "Current U. S. Population Count," "Current Economic Indicators," and a wide variety of data under "Other Official Statistics." Keyword searching is provided. Fees: Free.

## PERIODICALS AND NEWSLETTERS

*Military Officer.* Military Officers Association. • Monthly. Serves the overall military community.

*VFW Magazine: Ensuring Rights, Recognition, and Remembrance.* Remembrance. • 11/year. $15 Nonmembers. Events and general features.

## STATISTICS SOURCES

*Annual Report of the Secretary of Veterans Affairs.* U.S. Department of Veterans Affairs. • Annual. Shows monies distributed and received by the Dept. of Veterans Affairs. Describes the activities of the Department during the fiscal year.

*Statistical Abstract of the United States.* U. S. Government Printing Office. • Annual. $44.00. Issued by the U. S. Bureau of the Census.

## TRADE/PROFESSIONAL ASSOCIATIONS

American Legion. 700 N Pennsylvania St., Indianapolis, IN 46206. Phone: 800-504-4098 or (317)630-1200; Fax: (317)630-1223; Email: acy@legion.org • URL: http://www.legion.org • Consists of honorably discharged wartime veterans of the U.S. armed forces. Provides a unified voice for veterans in Washington, DC. Offers free assistance with Veterans Administration claims and benefits. Sponsors American Legion baseball competition, national high school oratorical contest, and children's services; cosponsors National Education Week. Maintains museum.

Diversity Information Resources. 2105 Central Ave. NE, Minneapolis, MN 55418. Phone: (612)781-6819; Fax: (612)781-0109; Email: info@diversityinforesources.com • URL: http://www.diversityinforesources.com • Promotes businesses with minority, women, veteran, service-disabled veteran and HUBZone ownership. Compiles and publishes minority and women-owned business

directories to acquaint major corporations and government purchasing agents with the products and services of minority and women-owned firms. Sponsors national supplier diversity seminars.

Military Officers Association of America. 201 N Washington St., Alexandria, VA 22314-2537. Phone: 800-234-6622 or (703)549-2311; Email: msc@moaa.org • URL: http://www.moaa.org • Formerly The Retired Oficers Association.

National Association of State Directors of Veterans Affairs. 107 S West St., Ste. 550, Alexandria, VA 22314. Phone: (334)242-5075; Fax: (334)353-5072 • URL: http://www.nasdva.us • Directors of veterans' affairs for state governments. Serves as medium for exchange of ideas among state veterans' officers. Maintains liaison with all congressionally chartered veterans' organizations.

# VETERINARY PRODUCTS

*See also* PET INDUSTRY

## ABSTRACTS AND INDEXES

*Index Veterinarius: Comprehensive Monthly Subject and Author Index to the World's Veterinary Literature. Availabe in Print and on the Internet.* CABI Publishing North America. • Monthly. Institutions, $1,660.00 per year. Annual cumulation. Includes single site internet access. Published in England by CABI Publishing. Provides worldwide coverage of the literature.

*NTIS Alerts: Agriculture & Food.* U.S. Department of Commerce National Technical Information Service. • Biweekly. $130 per year. Covers agricultural economics, horticulture, fisheries, veterinary medicine, food technology, and related subjects.

*Review of Medical and Veterinary Entomology.* CAB International. • Monthly. Provides worldwide coverage of the literature. Formerly *Review of Applied Entomology, Series B: Medical and Veterinary*.

## ALMANACS AND YEARBOOKS

*Advances in Small Animal Medicine and Surgery.* Elsevier. • Monthly. $458 Institutions, other countries print. Contains abstracts from the field.

## BIOGRAPHICAL SOURCES

*AVMA Directory.* American Veterinary Medical Association. • Annual. $100.00. 62,500 veterinarians; not limited to AVMA members. Formerly *American Veterinary Medical Association Directory*.

## CD-ROM DATABASES

*AGRICOLA on SilverPlatter.* Ovid Technologies Inc. • Updated monthly. Price varies. Produced by the National Agricultural Library. Provides over 4 million citations to the literature of agriculture, agricultural economics, animal sciences, entomology, fertilizer, food, forestry, nutrition, pesticides, plant science, water resources, and other topics.

## ONLINE DATABASES

*CAB Abstracts.* CABI. • Contains 46 specialized abstract collections covering over 10,000 journals and monographs in the areas of agriculture, horticulture, forest products, farm products, nutrition, dairy science, poultry, grains, animal health, entomology, etc. Time period is 1972 to date, with monthly updates. Inquire as to online cost and availability. *CAB Abstracts on CD-ROM* also available, with annual updating.

*Derwent Veterinary Drug File.* Derwent Information Ltd. • Provides indexing and abstracting of the world's veterinary drug literature since 1968, with monthly updates. Formerly *VETDOC*. Inquire as to online cost and availability.

## PERIODICALS AND NEWSLETTERS

*DVM: The Newsmagazine of Veterinary Medicine.* Advanstar Communications, Healthcare Group. • Monthly. $39.00 per year. Includes new drugs and new products.

*Tack'n Togs Merchandising: The Monthly Business Magazine for Equine Retailers.* Farm Progress Companies Inc. • Monthly. International trade magazine for marketers of products for horse and rider.

*Veterinary Economics: Business Solutions for Practicing Veterinarians.* Thomson Veterinary Healthcare Communications. • Monthly. $42 Individuals. Provides business management and financial articles for veterinarians.

## TRADE/PROFESSIONAL ASSOCIATIONS

American Veterinary Medical Association. 1931 N Meacham Rd., Ste. 100, Schaumburg, IL 60173-4360. Phone: 800-248-2862 or (847)925-8070; Fax: (847)925-1329; Email: info@avma.org • URL: http://www.avma.org • Professional society of veterinarians. Conducts educational and research programs. Provides placement service. Sponsors American Veterinary Medical Association Foundation and Educational Commission for Foreign Veterinary Graduates. Compiles statistics. Accredits veterinary medical education programs and veterinary technician education programs.

# VICE

*See* CRIME AND CRIMINALS

# VIDEO CAMERAS

*See* VIDEO RECORDING INDUSTRY

# VIDEO RECORDING INDUSTRY

## ABSTRACTS AND INDEXES

*Applied Science and Technology Index.* EBSCO Publishing Inc. • 11/year. Indexes a wide variety of English language technical, industrial, and engineering periodicals.

*Business Periodicals Index Retrospective.* EBSCO Publishing Inc. • 11/year. Quarterly and annual cumulations.

*Communication Abstracts: An International Information Service.* Pine Forge Press. • Bimonthly. Institutions, $1,150.00 per year. Provides broad coverage of the literature of communications, including broadcasting and advertising.

*Current Contents: Engineering, Computing and Technology.* Thomson Reuters Intellectual Property and Science. • Weekly. $730 per year. Reproductions of contents pages of technical journals. Includes *Author Index, Address Directory, Current Book Contents,* and *Title Word Index.* Formerly *Current Contents: Engineering, Technology and Applied Sciences.*

*Electronics and Communications Abstracts Journal: Comprehensive Coverage of Essential Scientific Literature.* CSA. • Monthly. $1,665.00 per year. Includes print and online editions.

## BIBLIOGRAPHIES

*Films and Audiovisual Information.* U. S. Government Printing Office. • Annual. Free. Issued by the Superintendent of Documents. A list of government publications on motion picture and audiovisual topics. Formerly *Motion Pictures, Films and Audiovisual Information.* (Subject Bibliography No. 73.).

## CD-ROM DATABASES

*Bowker's Complete Video Directory on Disc.* Bowker Electronic Publishing. • Quarterly. $520.00

per year. An extensive CD-ROM directory of video tapes and laserdisks. Includes film reviews from *Variety.*

## DIRECTORIES

*AV Market Place: The Complete Business Directory of Audio, Audio Visual, Computer Systems, Film, Video, and Programming, with Industry Yellow Pages.* Information Today, Inc. • Annual. $279.50 Individuals list price. Provides information on "more than 7,500 companies that create, apply, or distribute AV equipment and services for business, education, science, and government." Multimedia, virtual reality, presentation software, and interactive video are among the categories. Formerly published by R. R. Bowker.

*Broadcast Engineering--Equipment Reference Manual.* Penton. • Annual. Publication includes: List of more than 1,400 manufacturers and distributors of communications equipment for radio, television, and recording applications. Database includes: Specifications for major brands of professional broadcast hardware. Entries include: For manufacturers--Company name, address. For distributors and dealers--Company name, address, phone, product or service provided, geographic area covered.

*DV Buyer's Guide.* UBM L.L.C. • Annual. $10.00. A directory of professional video products, including digital cameras, monitors, editing systems, and software.

*Film and Video Finder.* National Information Center for Educational Media. Plexus Publishing Inc. • Biennial. Contains 675,000 listings of film and video educational, technical and vocational children's programs and literary materials.

*Telecommunications Directory.* Cengage Learning Inc. • Annual. $993 Individuals. Two volumes: North America and International. Cover national and international voice and data communications networks, electronic mail services, teleconferencing facilities and services, facsimile services, Internet access providers, videotex and teletext operations, transactional services, local area networks, audiotex services, microwave systems/networkers, satellite facilities, and others involved in telecommunications, including related consultants, advertisers/marketers; associations, regulatory bodies, and publishers. Available as eBook.

## HANDBOOKS AND MANUALS

*Videocassette Rental Store.* Entrepreneur Press. • Looseleaf. $59.50. A practical guide to starting a videocassette rental store. Covers profit potential, start-up costs, market size evaluation, owner's time required, site selection, lease negotiation, pricing, accounting, advertising, promotion, etc. (Start-Up Business Guide No. E1192.).

## ONLINE DATABASES

*Applied Science and Technology Index Online.* H.W. Wilson Co. • Provides online indexing of 500 major scientific, technical, industrial, and engineering periodicals. Time period is 1983 to date. Monthly updates. Inquire as to online cost and availability.

*Wilson Business Abstracts Online.* H.W. Wilson Co. • Indexes and abstracts 600 major business periodicals, plus the *Wall Street Journal* and the business section of the *New York Times.* Indexing is from 1982, abstracting from 1990, with the two newspapers included from 1993. Updated weekly. Inquire as to online cost and availability. (*Business Periodicals Index* without abstracts is also available online.).

## OTHER SOURCES

*Videolog.* Muze, Inc. • Annual. $250.00. Five volumes. Provides detailed information on more than 170,000 VHS and DVD video titles. Includes a "Directory of Stars and Directors" and 13 category sections.

## PERIODICALS AND NEWSLETTERS

*DV Magazine.* UBM L.L.C. • Monthly. Edited for producers and creators of digital media. Includes topics relating to video, audio, animation, multimedia, interactive design, and special effects. Covers both hardware and software, with product reviews. Formerly *Digital Video Magazine.*

*EContent: Digital Content Strategies and Resources.* Online Inc. • Monthly. $110.00 per year. Emphasis is on the business management and financial aspects of the digital content industry. (Formerly published by Online, Inc.).

*eMedia: The Digital Studio Magazine.* Online Inc. • Monthly. $98.00 per year. Covers video production equipment, digital video editing, electronic publishing, digital content streaming, encoding, and other topics related to digital content creation and multimedia. (Formerly published by Online, Inc.).

*Entertainment Law and Finance.* ALM Media Properties LLC. • Monthly. $485 print and online. Covers contracts, royalties, litigation, copyright, taxation, etc., for the music industry, motion pictures, broadcasting, publishing, video, and related media. (A Law Journal Newsletter, formerly published by Leader Publications.).

*Presentations: Technology and Techniques for Effective Communication.* Nielsen Business Media Inc. • Monthly. Free to qualified personnel; others, $69.00 per year. Covers the use of presentation hardware and software, including audiovisual equipment and computerized display systems. Includes an annual *Buyers Guide to Presentation Products.*

*SHOOT: The Leading Newsweekly for Commercial Production and Postproduction.* Nielsen Business Media Inc. • Weekly. $125 /year. Covers animation, music, sound design, computer graphics, visual effects, cinematography, and other aspects of television and motion picture production, with emphasis on TV commercials.

*Smart TV and Sound: Interactive Television and DVD-MP3-Internet Audio and Video-Satellite Television.* York Publishing Inc. • Semiannual. $14.97 per year. Consumer magazine covering WebTV, PC/TV appliances, DVD players, "Smart TV," and other topics relating to interactive television, the Internet, and multimedia. Formerly *Smart TV.*

*Sound & Vision: Home Theater- Audio- Video-MultimediaMovies- Music.* Bonnier AB. • 10/year. $12.97 10 issues. Popular magazine providing explanatory articles and critical reviews of equipment and media (CD-ROM, DVD, etc.). Supplement available *Stereo Review's Sound and Vision Buyers Guide.* Replaces *Stereo Review* and *Video Magazine.*

*T W I C E: This Week in Consumer Electronics.* Reed Elsevier Group plc Reed Business Information. • 29 times a year. $129.90 per year. Contains marketing and manufacturing news relating to a wide variety of consumer electronic products, including video, audio, telephone, and home office equipment.

*Television Digest with Consumer Electronics.* Warren Communications News Inc. • Weekly. $944.00 per year. Newsletter featuring new consumer entertainment products utilizing electronics. Also covers the television broadcasting and cable TV industries, with corporate and industry news.

*Television Week.* Crain Communications Inc. • Weekly. $119.00 per year. Formerly *Electronic Media.*

*Video Business.* Chilton Publications. • Weekly. Magazine for retailers of pre-recorded video software and related goods and services.

*Video Investor.* SNL Kagan. • Description: Reports videocassette industry developments, including sales statistics and forecasts. Provides news of related conventions and events and focuses on sales and rentals of film product, performance of retail outlets, market shares of suppliers and distributors, the sale of chains and outlets, hardware revenues and sales, and laser disk technologies. **Remarks:** Also available via e-mail and fax.

*Video Librarian: The Video Review Magazine.* Video Librarian. • Bimonthly. $64. Edited for public and school libraries. Each issue includes reviews of hundreds of video DVDs or cassettes, in various subject areas.

## PRICE SOURCES
*Video and Television.* Orion Research Corp. • Annual. $144 Individuals. Quotes retail and wholesale prices of used video and TV equipment. Original list prices and years of manufacture are also shown.

## STATISTICS SOURCES
*Standard & Poor's Industry Surveys.* Standard & Poor's Financial Services L.L.C. • Semiannual. $1,800.00. Two looseleaf volumes. Includes monthly *Supplements.* Provides detailed, individual surveys of 52 major industry groups. Each survey is revised on a semiannual basis. Also includes "Monthly Investment Review" (industry group investment analysis) and monthly "Trends & Projections" (economic analysis).

*U.S. Industry and Trade Outlook.* U.S. Department of Commerce National Technical Information Service. • Annual. Produced by the International Trade Administration, U.S. Department of Commerce, in a "public-private" partnership with DRI/McGraw-Hill and Standard & Poor's. Provides basic data, outlook for the current year, and "Long-Term Prospects" (five-year projections) for a wide variety of products and services. Includes high technology industries. Formerly *U.S. Industrial Outlook.*

## TRADE/PROFESSIONAL ASSOCIATIONS
Association of Cinema and Video Laboratories. 1833 Centinela Ave., Santa Monica, CA 90404. Phone: (310)828-1098; Fax: (310)828-9737; Email: lab@ntaudio.com • URL: http://www.acvl.org • Motion picture film or video transfer laboratories; non-laboratory firms with allied interests. Provides a forum for the exchange of ideas in connection with the technical, administrative and managerial problems of the motion picture and video laboratory industry. Concerns include: government relations; public and industry relations; product specifications; improvement of technical practices and procedures; other areas of interest to film and video laboratories.

Consumer Electronics Association. 1919 S Eads St., Arlington, VA 22202. Phone: 866-858-1555 or (703)907-7600 or (703)907-7650; Fax: (703)907-7675 or (630)953-8957; Email: info@ce.org • URL: http://www.ce.org • Manufacturers of consumer technology and electronics products. Strives to aid members in growth through connections, education, exposure, and by providing information. Hosts workshops and educational programs.

National Association of Video Distributors. 16530 Ventura Blvd., Ste. 400, Encino, CA 91436. Phone: (818)385-1500; Fax: (818)385-1500 • URL: http://navdonline.org • Promotes the home video products industry. Conducts industry-wide programs in areas such as public, government, and industry relations.

# VIDEOCASSETTES
*See* VIDEO RECORDING INDUSTRY

# VIDEODISCS
*See* VIDEO RECORDING INDUSTRY

# VIDEOTAPE
*See* VIDEO RECORDING INDUSTRY

# VIDEOTEX/TELETEXT

## ALMANACS AND YEARBOOKS
*Interactive TV Investor.* Paul Kagan Associates, Inc. • Semimonthly. $895.00. Provides current information on interactive-TV applications and technical developments. Includes forecasts. Formerly *Interactive Television.*

## CD-ROM DATABASES
*LISA Plus.* Cambridge Scientific Abstracts L.P. • Quarterly. $2,000 per year. CD-ROM version of Library Information and Science Abstracts, providing abstracting and indexing of the world's library and information science literature, 1969 to date. Contains more than 180,000 citations.

## DIRECTORIES
*DV Buyer's Guide.* UBM L.L.C. • Annual. $10.00. A directory of professional video products, including digital cameras, monitors, editing systems, and software.

*Interactive TV Investor Buyer's Guide and Directory.* Paul Kagan Associates, Inc. • Annual. Price on application. (A special issue of the periodical *Convergence.*).

*SRDS Interactive Advertising Source.* Kantar Media SRDS. • Quarterly. $569.00 per year. Provides descriptive profiles, rates, audience, personnel, etc., for producers of various forms of interactive or multimedia advertising: online/Internet, CD-ROM, interactive TV, interactive cable, interactive telephone, interactive kiosk, and others.

*Telecommunications Directory.* Cengage Learning Inc. • Annual. $993 Individuals. Two volumes: North America and International. Cover national and international voice and data communications networks, electronic mail services, teleconferencing facilities and services, facsimile services, Internet access providers, videotex and teletext operations, transactional services, local area networks, audiotex services, microwave systems/networkers, satellite facilities, and others involved in telecommunications, including related consultants, advertisers/marketers; associations, regulatory bodies, and publishers. Available as eBook.

## PERIODICALS AND NEWSLETTERS
*Computer Video.* IMAS Publishing Group. • Bimonthly. $35.00 per year.

*Convergence: The Journal of Research Into New Media Technologies.* Reed Elsevier Group plc Reed Business Information. • Monthly. Individuals, $40.00 per year; institutions, $160.00 per year. Covers the merging of communications technologies. Includes telecommunications networks, interactive TV, multimedia, wireless phone service, and electronic information services.

*Digital Imaging: The Magazine for the Imaging Professional.* Cygnus Business Media Inc. • Bimonthly. $24.95 per year. Edited for business and professional users of electronic publishing products and services. Topics covered include document imaging, CD-ROM publishing, digital video, and multimedia services. Formerly *Micro Publishing News.*

*Interactive Home: Consumer Technology Monthly.* Jupiter Communications. • Monthly. $625.00 per year; with online edition, $725.00 per year. Newsletter on devices to bring the Internet into the average American home. Covers TV set-top boxes, game devices, telephones with display screens, handheld computer communication devices, the usual PCs, etc.

*Report on Electronic Commerce: Online Business, Financial and Consumer Strategies and Trends.* Wolters Kluwer Law and Business. • Biweekly. $1,789.00 per year. Newsletter. Includes *Daily Multimedia News Service.* Incorporates *Interactive Services Report.*

*Smart TV and Sound: Interactive Television and DVD-MP3-Internet Audio and Video-Satellite Television.* York Publishing Inc. • Semiannual. $14.97 per year. Consumer magazine covering WebTV, PC/TV appliances, DVD players, "Smart TV," and other topics relating to interactive television, the Internet, and multimedia. Formerly *Smart TV.*

*Telecons.* Applied Business Telecommunications. • Bimonthly. $30.00 per year. Topics include teleconferencing, videoconferencing, distance learning, telemedicine, and telecommuting.

*Telematics and Informatics: An International Journal on Telecommunications and Internet Technology.* Elsevier. • Four times a year. Institutions, $938.00 per year.

*Television Week.* Crain Communications Inc. • Weekly. $119.00 per year. Formerly *Electronic Media.*

## RESEARCH CENTERS AND INSTITUTES
Massachusetts Institute of Technology - The Media Laboratory. Bldg. E15, 77 Massachusetts Ave., Cambridge, MA 02139-4307. Phone: (617)253-5960; Fax: (617)258-6264; Email: walter@media.mit.edu • URL: http://www.media.mit.edu • Research areas include electronic publishing, spatial imaging, human-machine interface, computer vision, and advanced television.

# VIEWTEXT

*See* VIDEOTEX/TELETEXT

# VIRTUAL REALITY

*See also* COMPUTER ANIMATION

## ABSTRACTS AND INDEXES
*Internet and Personal Computing Abstracts (print edition).* EBSCO Publishing Inc. • Quarterly. $269.00 per year, including cumulative index. Provides more than 10,000 abstracts annually from both trade and academic publications. Covers computer hardware, software, product reviews, Web topics, e-commerce, networks, corporate news, security, and related topics. Formerly *Microcomputer Abstracts.*

## ALMANACS AND YEARBOOKS
*Virtual Reality Annual International Symposium.* IEEE - Computer Society. • Annual.

## DIRECTORIES
*AV Market Place: The Complete Business Directory of Audio, Audio Visual, Computer Systems, Film, Video, and Programming, with Industry Yellow Pages.* Information Today, Inc. • Annual. $279.50 Individuals list price. Provides information on "more than 7,500 companies that create, apply, or distribute AV equipment and services for business, education, science, and government." Multimedia, virtual reality, presentation software, and interactive video are among the categories. Formerly published by R. R. Bowker.

## E-BOOKS
*Encyclopedia of Emerging Industries.* Cengage Learning Inc. • $546 6th edition. Provides detailed information on 140 "newly flourishing" industries. Includes historical background, organizational structure, significant individuals, current conditions, major companies, work force, technology trends, research developments, and other industry facts.

## INTERNET DATABASES
*InfoTech Trends.* Data Analysis Group. Phone: (925)462-1202; Fax: (925)462-1225; Email: support@infotechtrends.com • URL: http://www.infotechtrends.com • Web site provides both free and

fee-based market research data on the information technology industry, including computers, peripherals, telecommunications, the Internet, software, CD-ROM/DVD, e-commerce, and workstations. Fees: Free for current (most recent year) data; more extensive information has various fee structures. Formerly *Computer Industry Forecasts.*

*Wired News.* Lycos Inc. 400-2 Totten Pond Rd., Waltham, MA 02451-2053. Phone: (781)370-2700 or (415)276-8400; Fax: (781)370-2600 or (415)276-8500; Email: press@lycos.com • URL: http://www.lycos.com • Provides summaries and full-text of "Top Stories" relating to the Internet, computers, multimedia, telecommunications, and the electronic information industry in general. These news stories are placed in the broad categories of Politics, Business, Culture, and Technology. Affiliated with *Wired* magazine. Fees: Free.

## ONLINE DATABASES

*Computer Database.* Cengage Learning Inc. • Provides one year of full-text online for 150 leading computer-related publications. Also includes 70,000 product specifications and brief profiles of 13,000 computer product vendors and manufacturers. Inquire as to prices and availability.

## PERIODICALS AND NEWSLETTERS

*IMAGES.* IMAGE Society. • Semiannual. $25. Newsletter Provides news of virtual reality developments and the IMAGE Society.

## RESEARCH CENTERS AND INSTITUTES

Carnegie Mellon University - College of Fine Arts - Studio for Creative Inquiry. 5000 Forbes Ave., Rm. 111, Pittsburgh, PA 15213-3890. Phone: (412)268-3451; Fax: (412)268-2829; Email: mmbm@andrew.cmu.edu • URL: http://studioforcreativeinquiry.org • Research areas include artificial intelligence, virtual reality, hypermedia, multimedia, and telecommunications, in relation to the arts.

University of Illinois at Chicago - Electronic Visualization Laboratory. Department of Computer Science, Rm. 1120, MC 152, 851 S Morgan St., Chicago, IL 60607-7053. Phone: (312)996-3002; Fax: (312)413-7585; Email: spiff@uic.edu • URL: http://www.evl.uic.edu • Research areas include computer graphics, virtual reality, multimedia, and interactive techniques.

# VIRUSES, COMPUTER

*See* COMPUTER CRIME AND SECURITY

# VISUAL EDUCATION

*See* AUDIOVISUAL AIDS IN EDUCATION

# VITAL STATISTICS

*See also* CENSUS REPORTS; POPULATION

## ALMANACS AND YEARBOOKS

*Vital Signs: The Trends That Are Shaping Our Future (year).* Worldwatch Institute. • Annual. $19.95. Provides access to selected indicators showing social, economic, and environmental trends throughout the world. Includes data relating to food, energy, transportation, finance, population, and other topics.

## BIBLIOGRAPHIES

*Health and Vital Statistics.* U. S. Government Printing Office. • Annual. Free. Lists government publications. (GPO Subject Bibliography Number 121).

## CD-ROM DATABASES

*OECD Statistical Compendium.* Organization for Economic Cooperation and Development. •

Semiannual. $1,905.00 per year for 1 to 10 users. CD-ROM contains more than 730,000 monthly, quarterly, and annual time series for OECD countries, 1960 to date. Includes fully searchable data on agriculture, food, economic indicators, national accounts, employment, energy, finance, industry, technology, and foreign trade. Results can be displayed in various forms.

## E-BOOKS

*Social Trends & Indicators USA.* Monique D. Magee, editor. Cengage Learning Inc. • Includes data on labor, economics, the health care industry, crime, leisure, population, education, social security, and many other topics. Sources include various government agencies and major publications. Inquire for pricing.

## INTERNET DATABASES

*Business 2.0 Web Guide to the Best Business Links.* Business 2.0 Media Inc. Phone: (415)293-4800; Email: support@business2.com • URL: http://www.business2.com/webguide • Web site presents an extensive, searchable directory of links to "the best, most informative, and authoritative web pages." Twenty main categories cover business, finance, career, company information, people, and technology topics, with thousands of subtopics, all linking to Web sites recommended by experienced business researchers. Fees: Free.

*Fedstats.* Federal Interagency Council on Statistical Policy. Phone: (202)395-7254 • URL: http://www.fedstats.gov • Web site features an efficient search facility for full-text statistics produced by more than 100 federal agencies, including the Census Bureau, the Bureau of Economic Analysis, and the Bureau of Labor Statistics. Boolean searches can be made within one agency or for all agencies combined. Links are offered to international statistical bureaus, including the UN, IMF, OECD, UNESCO, Eurostat, and 20 individual countries. Fees: Free.

*FreeLunch.com.* Economy.com, Inc. Phone: (610)696-8700; Fax: (610)696-1678 • URL: http://www.freelunch.com • Web site provides free access to more than 200 million economic and financial data series, covering industry, demographics, labor markets, prices, retail sales, government spending, trade, interest rates, housing starts, the stock market, etc. Data is available in either chart or table form. Searching is offered. Free, but registration required. Economy.com, Inc. also offers fee-based economic analysis at *The Dismal Scientist* site (www.dismal.com).

*National Center for Health Statistics: Monitoring the Nation's Health.* National Center for Health Statistics, Centers for Disease Control and Prevention. Phone: (301)458-4000; Email: nchsquery@cdc.gov • URL: http://www.cdc.gov/nchswww • Web site provides detailed data on diseases, vital statistics, and health care in the U. S. Includes a search facility and links to many other health-related Web sites. "Fastats A to Z" offers quick data on hundreds of topics from Accidents to Work-Loss Days, with links to Comprehensive Data and related sources. Frequent updates. Fees: Free.

*U.S. Census Bureau: The Official Statistics.* U. S. Bureau of the Census. Phone: (301)763-4636 or (301)763-4100; Fax: (301)763-4794; Email: webmaster@census.gov • URL: http://www.census.gov/prod/www/abs/mfg-prof.html • Web site is "Your Source for Social, Demographic, and Economic Information." Contains "Current U. S. Population Count," "Current Economic Indicators," and a wide variety of data under "Other Official Statistics." Keyword searching is provided. Fees: Free.

## PERIODICALS AND NEWSLETTERS

*World Watch: Working for a Sustainable Future.* Worldwatch Institute. • Bimonthly. $25.00 per year. Emphasis is on environmental trends, including

developments in population growth, climate change, human behavior, the role of government, and other factors.

## STATISTICS SOURCES

*Population and Vital Statistics Report.* United Nations Publications. • Semiannual. $40.00 per year. Contains worldwide demographic statistics.

*Statistical Abstract of the United States.* U. S. Government Printing Office. • Annual. $44.00. Issued by the U. S. Bureau of the Census.

*Statistical Yearbook.* United Nations Publications. • Annual. $125.00. Contains statistics for about 200 countries on a wide variety of economic, industrial, and demographic topics. Compiled by United Nations Statistical Office.

*The Universal Healthcare Almanac: A Complete Guide for the Healthcare Professional - Facts, Figures, Analysis.* Silver & Cherner, Ltd. • $195.00 per year. Looseleaf service. Quarterly updates. Includes a wide variety of health care statistics: national expenditures, hospital data, health insurance, health professionals, vital statistics, demographics, etc. Years of coverage vary, with long range forecasts provided in some cases.

*Vital Statistics of the United States.* Public Health Service, U.S. Dept. of Health and Human Services. Bernan Press. • Biennial. $110.

*Vital Statistics of the United States: Life Tables.* U. S. Government Printing Office. • Annual. $64. Produced by the National Center for Health Statistics, Public Health Service, U. S. Department of Health and Human Services. Provides detailed data on expectation of life by age, race, and sex. Historical data is shown annually from the year 1900. (Vital Statistics, volume 2.).

## TRADE/PROFESSIONAL ASSOCIATIONS

National Association for Public Health Statistics and Information Systems. 962 Wayne Ave., Ste. 701, Silver Spring, MD 20910. Phone: (301)563-6001; Fax: (301)563-6012; Email: hq@naphsis.org • URL: http://www.naphsis.org/Pages/home.aspx • Members are officials of state and local health agencies.

# VITAMINS

*See also* DIET; HEALTH FOOD INDUSTRY

## ABSTRACTS AND INDEXES

*Nutrition Abstracts and Reviews, Series A: Human and Experimental.* CABI Publishing North America. • Monthly. Institutions, $1,835.00 per year. Includes single site internet access. Published in England by CABI Publishing. Provides worldwide coverage of the literature.

## CD-ROM DATABASES

*International Pharmaceutical Abstracts.* Ovid Technologies Inc. • Quarterly. International pharmaceutical literature from 1970 to date.

*Pharmacopeia of Herbs.* CME Inc. • $149.00. Frequently updated CD-ROM provides searchable data on a wide variety of herbal medicines, vitamins, and amino acids. Includes information on clinical studies, contraindications, side-effects, phytoactivity, and 534 therapeutic use categories. Contains a 1,000 word glossary.

## DIRECTORIES

*PDR for Nutritional Supplements.* Medical Economics Co. • $59.95 Individuals. Includes trade names, usage, adverse reactions, dosage, and other information about vitamins and minerals.

## INTERNET DATABASES

*National Library of Medicine.* National Institutes of Health. 9000 Rockville Pke., Bethesda, MD 20892. Phone: (301)496-4000; Email: nihinfo@od.nih.gov

• URL: http://www.nih.gov • NLM Web site offers free access through MEDLINE ("PubMed") to about nine million references to articles appearing in some 4,000 biomedical journals, with abstracts. Search interfaces range from "simple keywords to advanced Boolean expressions." The NLM site offers many links to other sources of biomedical and technical information (the National Center for Biotechnology Information, for example). Fees: Free.

## ONLINE DATABASES

*Embase.* Elsevier. • Worldwide medical literature, 1974 to present. Weekly updates. Inquire as to online cost and availability.

## PERIODICALS AND NEWSLETTERS

*International Journal for Vitamin and Nutrition Research.* Hogrefe & Huber Publishers. • Quarterly. $202.00 per year.

*Journal of Dietary Supplements.* The Haworth Press Inc. • Quarterly. $175.00 per year to libraries; $50.00 per year to individuals. Edited with a view to both academic research and industry concerns. Sections are dedicated to health professionals, educators, and dieticians. Includes book reviews and short reviews of research appearing elsewhere. Formerly *Journal of Nutraceuticals, Functional & Medical Foods.*

*Natural Products Marketplace.* Virgo Publishing L.L.C. • Monthly. $50.00 per year. Covers all aspects of the vitamin and health supplement market, including new products. Includes an annual buyer's guide, an annual compilation of industry statistics, and annual guides to vitamins and herbs.

*Nutrition Industry Executive.* Vitamin Retailer Magazine, Inc. • 10 times a year. $50.00 per year. Edited for manufacturers of vitamins and other dietary supplements. Covers marketing, new products, industry trends, regulations, manufacturing procedures, and related topics. Includes a directory of suppliers to the industry.

*Prevention: The Magazine for Better Health.* Rodale Inc. • Monthly. $24 Individuals.

*The Tan Sheet: Nonprescription Pharmaceuticals and Nutritionals.* Elsevier Business Intelligence. • Weekly. $1,220.00 per year. Newsletter covering over-the-counter drugs and vitamin supplements. Emphasis is on regulatory activities of the U. S. Food and Drug Administration (FDA).

## TRADE/PROFESSIONAL ASSOCIATIONS

Natural Products Association. 1773 T St. NW, Washington, DC 20009. Phone: 800-966-6632 or (202)223-0101; Fax: (202)223-0250; Email: natural@npainfo.org • URL: http://www.npainfo.org • Represents retailers, wholesalers, brokers, distributors and manufacturers of natural, nutritional, dietetic foods, supplements, services and natural body and home care products.

# VITICULTURE

*See* GRAPE INDUSTRY

# VOCABULARY

## ENCYCLOPEDIAS AND DICTIONARIES

*Roget's International Thesaurus.* Barbara A. Kipfer, editor. • 2011. Seventh edition.

# VOCATIONAL EDUCATION

*See also* TECHNICAL EDUCATION; TRAINING OF EMPLOYEES

## ABSTRACTS AND INDEXES

*Education Index.* H.W. Wilson Co. • 10 times a year. Quarterly and annual cumulations. Price varies.

## CD-ROM DATABASES

*ERIC SilverPlatter.* U.S. Department of Education Institute of Education Sciences Education Resources Information Center. • Opinion papers, evaluations, speeches.

## DIRECTORIES

*American Trade Schools Directory.* Croner Publications Inc. • $120 base and supplements; plus $9.95 shipping, payment with order. Covers: over 12,000 private and public trade, technical, and vocational schools. Entries include: School name, address, phone, contact person, year school founded, private or public, accrediting agencies, whether approved by state or Veterans Administration, home study courses offered.

*Schools--Business & Vocational Directory.* Info-Group Inc. • Annual. Covers over 5,000 businesses and vocations.

## HANDBOOKS AND MANUALS

*Resume Writing and Career Counseling.* Entrepreneur Press. • Looseleaf. $59.50. A practical guide to starting a resume writing and career counseling service. Covers profit potential, start-up costs, market size evaluation, owner's time required, site selection, pricing, accounting, advertising, promotion, etc. (Start-Up Business Guide No. E1260.).

## ONLINE DATABASES

*Education Index Online.* H.W. Wilson Co. • Indexes a wide variety of periodicals related to schools, colleges, and education, 1984 to date. Monthly updates. Inquire as to online cost and availability.

*ERIC.* U.S. Department of Education Institute of Education Sciences Educational Resources Information Center. • Funded by the U.S. Department of Education, Institute of Education Sciences (formerly Office of Educational Research and Improvement). Provides access to more than one million online records covering education-related journal and report literature, 1966 to date. Updating is monthly. Inquire as to online cost and availability.

## PERIODICALS AND NEWSLETTERS

*TECHniques.* Informix Software. • Eight times a year. Free to members; non-members, $45.00 per year. Formerly Vocational Educational Journal.

## TRADE/PROFESSIONAL ASSOCIATIONS

Association for Career and Technical Education. 1410 King St., Alexandria, VA 22314. Phone: 800-826-9972; Fax: (703)683-7424; Email: acte@acteonline.org • URL: http://www.acteonline.org • Represents teachers, supervisors, administrators, and others interested in the development and improvement of vocational, Technical, and practical arts education. Areas of interest include: secondary, postsecondary, and adult vocational education; education for special population groups; cooperative education. Works with such government agencies as: Bureau of Apprenticeship in Department of Labor; Office of Vocational Rehabilitation in Department of Health and Human Services; Veterans Administration; Office of Vocational and Adult Education of the Department of Education. Maintains hall of fame.

Eastern and Southern Africa Management Institute. PO Box 3030, Arusha, Tanzania. Phone: 255 27 2508384 or 255 27 2508385; Fax: 255 27 2508285; Email: esamihq@esamihq.ac.tz • URL: http://www.esami-africa.org • Management personnel and vocational training programs. Seeks to advance the practice of business and organizational administration. Facilitates exchange of information among members; makes available educational and training programs.

Edexcel International. 190 High Holborn, London WC1V 7BH, United Kingdom. Phone: 44 1204 770696; Email: internationaleo@pearson.com •

URL: http://www.edexcel.com/international/europe • Approves academic and work-related programmes of study including GNVQs, NVQs and GCSEs, A levels and A/S levels throughout England, Wales and Northern Ireland, and overseas and awards qualifications to students who successfully complete these and HND programmes.

Ohio State University - College of Education and Human Ecology - Center on Education and Training for Employment. 1900 Kenny Rd., Columbus, OH 43210-1016. Phone: 800-848-4815 or (614)292-8008; Fax: (614)292-1260; Email: kelsey.28@osu.edu • URL: http://cete.osu.edu • Formerly National Center for Research in Vocational Education.

# VOCATIONAL GUIDANCE

*See also* COUNSELING; JOB HUNTING; OCCUPATIONS

## BIBLIOGRAPHIES

*Educators Guide to Free Guidance Materials.* Educators Progress Service Inc. • Annual. $37.95 Individuals. Lists free-loan films, filmstrips, audiotapes, videotapes and free printed materials on guidance.

*Job & Career Books.* Kennedy Information Inc. • Annual. Free. Contains descriptions of selected books from various publishers on job searching and choice of career.

## DIRECTORIES

*Careers in Focus--Business Managers.* InfoBase Holdings Inc. • $35 Individuals hardcover. Covers: An overview of business managers, followed by a selection of jobs profiled in detail, including the nature of the job, earnings, prospects for employment, what kind of training and skills it requires, and sources for further information. Database includes: Black and white photographs.

*Careers in Focus--Entrepreneurs.* InfoBase Holdings Inc. • $35 Individuals hardcover. Covers: An overview of entrepreneurship, followed by a selection of jobs profiled in detail, including the nature of the job, earnings, prospects for employment, what kind of training and skills it requires, and sources for further information. Database includes: Black and white photographs.

*Manager's Handbook: Everything You Need to Know about How Business and Management Work.* Pearson Learning Group. • $24.95. Publication includes: Business directory representing key areas of management in Canada and the United States. Principal content of publication is reference guide for new and experienced managers.

## HANDBOOKS AND MANUALS

*Occupational Outlook Handbook.* Bureau of Labor Statistics, U.S. Department of Labor. U. S. Government Printing Office. • Biennial. $22 Individuals. Issued as one of the Bureau's Bulletin series and kept up to date by *Occupational Outlook Quarterly.*

## PERIODICALS AND NEWSLETTERS

*Career Development Quarterly.* National Career Development Association. American Counseling Association. • Quarterly. $226 Institutions print or online. Features articles on career counseling, individual and organizational career development, work and leisure, career education, career coaching, and career management.

*Counseling and Values.* Association for Spiritual, Ethical and Religious Values in Counseling. American Counseling Association. • Semiannual. $107 Nonmembers print or online. Journal focusing on the role of values and religion in counseling and psychology.

*Occupational Outlook Quarterly.* U.S. Department of Labor Bureau of Labor Statistics. • Quarterly. $30

Two years. Magazine providing occupational and employment information.

## RESEARCH CENTERS AND INSTITUTES

FHI 360 - National Institute for Work and Learning. 1825 Connecticut Ave. NW, Washington, DC 20009. Phone: (202)884-8184; Fax: (202)884-8422; Email: icharner@fhi360.org • URL: http://www.niwl.org • Research areas include adult education, training, unemployment insurance, and career development.

## TRADE/PROFESSIONAL ASSOCIATIONS

American Counseling Association. 5999 Stevenson Ave., Alexandria, VA 22304. Phone: 800-347-6647; Fax: (703)823-0252; Email: membership@ counseling.org • URL: http://www.counseling.org • Counseling professionals in elementary and secondary schools, higher education, community agencies and organizations, rehabilitation programs, government, industry, business, private practice, career counseling, and mental health counseling. Conducts professional development institutes and provides liability insurance. Maintains Counseling and Human Development Foundation to fund counseling projects.

National Career Development Association. 305 N Beech Cir., Broken Arrow, OK 74012. Phone: 866-367-6232 or (918)663-7060; Fax: (918)663-7058; Email: webeditor@ncda.org • URL: http://www. ncda.org • Represents professionals and others interested in career development or counseling in various work environments. Supports counselors, education and training personnel, and allied professionals working in schools, colleges, business/ industry, community and government agencies, and in private practice. Provides publications, support for state and local activities, human equity programs, and continuing education and training for these professionals. Provides networking opportunities for career professionals in business, education, and government.

Total Attorneys. 25 E Washington St., Ste. 510, Chicago, IL 60602. Phone: 877-349-1307; Email: solutions@totalattorneys.com • URL: http://www. totalattorneys.com • Focuses on the advancement of attorneys, paralegals and other legal support staff. Offers solo practitioners and small law firms the tools, training and network needed to collaborate with peers, connect with experts and find better work-life balance. Coordinates workshops and conferences, educational resources, legal tools, affinity partnerships and community forums.

# VOCATIONAL REHABILITATION

## PERIODICALS AND NEWSLETTERS

*International Rehabilitation Review.* Rehabilitation International. • Triennial. $45 Individuals print. Description: Contains news and articles on international, national, and local developments in the fields of disability prevention and rehabilitation. Provides regular coverage of United Nations agencies, discusses the elimination of architectural and attitudinal barriers to disabled persons, and examines new trends in service delivery. Recurring features include news of research, book reviews, and a calendar of events.

## RESEARCH CENTERS AND INSTITUTES

Brunel University - Centre for Research in Rehabilitation. Mary Seacole Bldg. 301D, School of Health Sciences & Social Care, Uxbridge UB8 3PH, United Kingdom. Phone: 44 1895 274000; Fax: 44 1895 232806; Email: lorraine.desouza@brunel. ac.uk • URL: http://www.brunel.ac.uk/shssc/ research/crr • Enabling people with disabilities to fulfill their potential for health and personal development. Current issues include: promotion of health research to build evidence based practice;

development of research links between health care providers and academic researchers; evaluation of new and existing health technologies; and development of research that reflects clinical reality and that reduces the physical, psychological, and financial burden of care.

National Institute on Disability and Rehabilitation Research - Self-Employment Technology Transfer. 52 Corbin Hall, Rural Institute on Disabilities, University of Montana, Missoula, MT 59812. Phone: 800-732-0320 or (406)268-2743; Fax: (406)243-4730; Email: nancy@ruralinstitute.umt. edu • URL: http://rtc.ruralinstitute.umt.edu/SelEm/ RuSelfEm.htm • Vocational rehabilitation research, specifically, self-employment for people with disabilities.

Vecova Centre for Disability Services and Research. 3304 - 33rd St. NW, Calgary, AB, Canada T2L 2A6. Phone: (403)284-1121; Fax: (403)284-1146; Email: info@vecova.ca • URL: http://vecova.ca • Associated with University of Calgary.

## TRADE/PROFESSIONAL ASSOCIATIONS

American Medical Rehabilitation Providers Association. 1710 N St. NW, Washington, DC 20036. Phone: 888-346-4624 or (202)223-1920; Fax: (202)223-1925 • URL: http://www.amrpa.org • Rehabilitation facilities in the U.S. and Canada; agencies operating established medical, residential and vocational rehabilitation facilities. Promotes expansion and improvement of rehabilitation services to disabled persons as provided in rehabilitation facilities. Represents the concerns of rehabilitation providers before Congress and government agencies. Is concerned with quality operation of rehabilitation centers and facilities. Conducts research and development programs in national rehabilitation policy. Sponsors seminars and provides specialized education programs.

CARF International. 6951 E Southpoint Rd., Tucson, AZ 85756-9407. Phone: 888-281-6531 or (520)325-1044; Fax: (520)318-1129; Email: feedback@carf.org • URL: http://www.carf.org • Formerly Commission on Accreditation of Rehabilitation.

Council of State Administrators of Vocational Rehabilitation. 1 Research Ct., Ste. 450, Rockville, MD 20850. Phone: (301)519-8023 • URL: http:// www.rehabnetwork.org • Administrators of state vocational rehabilitation agencies. Serves as an advisory body to federal agencies and the public in the development of policies affecting rehabilitation of handicapped persons; acts as a forum for discussion on the provision of quality rehabilitation services. Compiles statistics.

National Rehabilitation Information Center. 8400 Corprate Dr., Ste. 500, Landover, MD 20785. Phone: 800-346-2742 or (301)459-5900; Fax: (301)459-4263; Email: naricinfo@heitechservices. com • URL: http://www.naric.com • Aims to improve delivery of information to the rehabilitation community. Disseminates the findings of programs funded by the National Institute on Disability and Rehabilitation Research; prepares custom bibliographies; helps locate answers to reference questions; searches for relevant materials in other commercially available databases.

Rehabilitation International. 25 E 21st St., 4th Fl., New York, NY 10010. Phone: (212)420-1500; Fax: (212)505-0871; Email: ri@riglobal.org • URL: http://rehab-international.org • Formerly International Society for Rehabilitation of the Disabled.

# VOCATIONS

*See OCCUPATIONS*

# VOICE RECOGNITION

*See also* COMPUTER COMMUNICATIONS; MICROCOMPUTERS AND MINICOMPUTERS

## ABSTRACTS AND INDEXES

*Applied Science and Technology Index.* EBSCO Publishing Inc. • 11/year. Indexes a wide variety of English language technical, industrial, and engineering periodicals.

*Business Periodicals Index Retrospective.* EBSCO Publishing Inc. • 11/year. Quarterly and annual cumulations.

*Communication Abstracts: An International Information Service.* Pine Forge Press. • Bimonthly. Institutions, $1,150.00 per year. Provides broad coverage of the literature of communications, including broadcasting and advertising.

*Computer and Information Systems Abstracts Journal: An Abstract Journal Pertaining to the Theory, Design, Fabrication and Application of Computer and Information Systems.* CSA. • Monthly. $1,750 per year.

*Computer Science Index.* EBSCO Publishing Inc. • Quarterly. $245 per year. Contains brief abstracts of book and periodical literature covering all phases of computing, including approximately 70 specific application areas.

*Current Contents: Engineering, Computing and Technology.* Thomson Reuters Intellectual Property and Science. • Weekly. $730 per year. Reproductions of contents pages of technical journals. Includes *Author Index, Address Directory, Current Book Contents,* and *Title Word Index.* Formerly *Current Contents: Engineering, Technology and Applied Sciences.*

*Electronics and Communications Abstracts Journal: Comprehensive Coverage of Essential Scientific Literature.* CSA. • Monthly. $1,665.00 per year. Includes print and online editions.

*Inspec Direct.* Institution of Engineering and Technology. • Monthly. $2,400 per year. Section C of *Science Abstracts.*

## DIRECTORIES

*Frontline Solutions Buyer's Guide.* Advanstar Communications. • Annual. $34.95 plus $3.50 shipping. Publication includes: List of manufacturers, suppliers, consultants, value added resellers, and dealers/distributors of automatic identification and data capture software, technology, equipment, and products for bar code, biometric identification, electronic data interchange, machine vision, magnetic stripe, optical character recognition, radio frequency data communications, radio frequency identification, smart cards, and voice data entry; also includes related organizations, and sources for industry standards. Entries include: Company name, address, phone, e-mail, web address, products or services.

*Telecommunications Directory.* Cengage Learning Inc. • Annual. $993 Individuals. Two volumes: North America and International. Cover national and international voice and data communications networks, electronic mail services, teleconferencing facilities and services, facsimile services, Internet access providers, videotex and teletext operations, transactional services, local area networks, audiotex services, microwave systems/networkers, satellite facilities, and others involved in telecommunications, including related consultants, advertisers/ marketers; associations, regulatory bodies, and publishers. Available as eBook.

## ONLINE DATABASES

*Applied Science and Technology Index Online.* H.W. Wilson Co. • Provides online indexing of 500 major scientific, technical, industrial, and engineering periodicals. Time period is 1983 to date. Monthly updates. Inquire as to online cost and availability.

*Wilson Business Abstracts Online.* H.W. Wilson Co. • Indexes and abstracts 600 major business periodicals, plus the *Wall Street Journal* and the business section of the *New York Times.* Indexing is from 1982, abstracting from 1990, with the two newspapers included from 1993. Updated weekly. Inquire as to online cost and availability. (*Business Periodicals Index* without abstracts is also available online.).

## PERIODICALS AND NEWSLETTERS

*EDP Weekly: The Leading Weekly Computer News Summary.* Computer Age and EDP News Services. • Weekly. $495.00 per year. Newsletter. Summarizes news from all areas of the computer and microcomputer industries.

## RESEARCH CENTERS AND INSTITUTES

Communications and Information Processing Group. Rensselaer Polytechnic Institute, 7010 JEC, 110 Eighth St., Troy, NY 12180-3590. Phone: (518)276-6823; Fax: (518)276-6261; Email: modestin@ipl.rpi.edu • URL: http://www.ecse.rpi. edu • Includes Optical Signal Processing Laboratory and Speech Processing Laboratory.

Computer Vision Laboratory. University of Arizona, Department of Electrical and Computer Engineering, 1230 E Speedway Blvd., Tucson, AZ 85721.

Phone: (520)621-2434; Fax: (520)621-8076; Email: strickland@ece.arizona.edu • Research areas include computer vision and speech synthesis.

Marquette University - Center for Intelligent Systems, Controls, and Signal Processing. College of Engineering, 1515 W Wisconsin Ave., Milwaukee, WI 53233. Phone: (414)288-3501; Fax: (414)288-5579; Email: ron.brown@marquette.edu • URL: http://www.marquette.edu • Intelligent controls, control systems, optimization, identification, time series modeling, multiple time-scale systems, digital signal processing, digital filtering, speech processing.

Massachusetts Institute of Technology - Computer Science and Artificial Intelligence Laboratory. The Stata Ctr., Bldg. 32, 32 Vassar St., Cambridge, MA 02139. Phone: (617)253-5851; Fax: (617)258-8682; Email: rus@csail.mit.edu • URL: http://www.csail. mit.edu • Research is in four areas: Intelligent Systems; Parallel Systems; Systems, Languages, and Networks; and Theory. Emphasis is on the application of online computing.

Michigan State University - Artificial Language Laboratory. 405 Computer Ctr., East Lansing, MI 48824-1042. Phone: (517)353-5399 or (517)353-0870; Fax: (517)353-4766; Email: artlang@pilot. msu.edu • URL: http://www.msu.edu/unit/artlang/ • Research areas include speech analysis and synthesis by computer.

Mind-Machine Interaction Research Center. University of Florida, Electrical and Computer Engineering Dept., 300 Weil Hall, Gainesville, FL 32611-6200. Phone: (352)392-6000; Fax: (352)392-9673; Email: info@eng.ufl.edu • URL: http://www. eng.ufl.edu.

Stanford University - Information Systems Laboratory. 350 Serra Mall, Department of Electrical Engineering, Stanford, CA 94305-9510. Phone: (650)723-3473; Fax: (650)723-8473; Email: abbas@ee.stanford.edu • URL: http://isl.stanford. edu • Research fields include speech coding and recognition.

## TRADE/PROFESSIONAL ASSOCIATIONS

The Institute of Financial Operations. 940 N Fern Creek Ave., Orlando, FL 32803. Phone: 877-885-4277 or (407)351-3322; Fax: (407)895-5031; Email: inquire@financialops.org • URL: http://www.tawpi. org • Members are companies that use or supply various recognition technologies equipment. Formerly The Association for Work Process Improvement.

# VOLUME FEEDING

*See* FOOD SERVICE INDUSTRY

# W

## WAGE DIFFERENTIALS

*See* WAGES AND SALARIES

## WAGE INCENTIVES

*See* WAGES AND SALARIES

## WAGE NEGOTIATIONS

*See* COLLECTIVE BARGAINING

## WAGES AND SALARIES

*See also* EXECUTIVE COMPENSATION;
INCOME

### CD-ROM DATABASES

*Authority Tax and Estate Planning Library.* Matthew Bender and Company Inc. • Periodic revisions. Price on request. CD contains updated full text of *Bender's Payroll Tax Guide, Depreciation Handbook, Federal Income Taxation of Corporations, Tax Planning for Corporations, Modern Estate Planning, Planning for Large Estates, Murphy's Will Clauses, Tax & Estate Planning for the Elderly,* and 12 other Matthew Bender publications. The Internal Revenue Code is also included.

*Business Abstracts with Full Text.* EBSCO Publishing Inc. • Includes full text articles from more than 460 business publications from 1982 to present. Indexing for nearly 880 publications.

*OECD Statistical Compendium.* Organization for Economic Cooperation and Development. • Semiannual. $1,905.00 per year for 1 to 10 users. CD-ROM contains more than 730,000 monthly, quarterly, and annual time series for OECD countries, 1960 to date. Includes fully searchable data on agriculture, food, economic indicators, national accounts, employment, energy, finance, industry, technology, and foreign trade. Results can be displayed in various forms.

*Sourcebooks America CD-ROM.* CACI Marketing Systems. • Annual. $1,250.00. Provides the CD-ROM version of *The Sourcebook of ZIP Code Demographics: Census Edition* and *The Sourcebook of County Demographics: Census Edition.*

### HANDBOOKS AND MANUALS

*Payroll Management Guide.* Wolters Kluwer Law & Business CCH. • Weekly Monthly. $1,159 Individuals. Covers the basics of payroll management, including employer obligations, recordkeep-ing, taxation, unemployment insurance, processing of new employees, and government penalties.

*Personnel Management: Compensation.* Prentice Hall PTR. • Looseleaf. Periodic supplementation. Price on application.

### INTERNET DATABASES

*Bureau of Economic Analysis.* U. S. Department of Commerce, Bureau of Economic Analysis. Phone: (202)606-9900; Fax: (202)606-5310; Email: webmaster@bea.doc.gov • URL: http://www.bea.doc.gov • Web site includes "News Release Information" covering national, regional, and international economic estimates from the BEA. Highlights of releases appear online the same day, complete text and tables appear the next day. "Recent News Releases" section provides titles for past nine months, with links. "BEA Data and Methodology" includes "Frequently Requested NIPA Data" (national income and product accounts, such as gross domestic product and personal income). Other statistics are available. Fees: Free.

*Business 2.0 Web Guide to the Best Business Links.* Business 2.0 Media Inc. Phone: (415)293-4800; Email: support@business2.com • URL: http://www.business2.com/webguide • Web site presents an extensive, searchable directory of links to "the best, most informative, and authoritative web pages." Twenty main categories cover business, finance, career, company information, people, and technology topics, with thousands of subtopics, all linking to Web sites recommended by experienced business researchers. Fees: Free.

*EBSCO Information Services.* EBSCO Publishing Inc. 10 Estes St., Ipswich, MA 01938-2106. Phone: 800-653-2726 or (978)356-6500; Fax: (978)356-6565; Email: information@ebscohost.com • URL: http://www.ebscohost.com • Fee-based Web site providing Internet access to a wide variety of databases, including business-related material. Full text is available for many periodical titles, with daily updates. Fees: Apply.

*Fedstats.* Federal Interagency Council on Statistical Policy. Phone: (202)395-7254 • URL: http://www.fedstats.gov • Web site features an efficient search facility for full-text statistics produced by more than 100 federal agencies, including the Census Bureau, the Bureau of Economic Analysis, and the Bureau of Labor Statistics. Boolean searches can be made within one agency or for all agencies combined. Links are offered to international statistical bureaus, including the UN, IMF, OECD, UNESCO, Eurostat, and 20 individual countries. Fees: Free.

*FreeLunch.com.* Economy.com, Inc. Phone: (610)696-8700; Fax: (610)696-1678 • URL: http://www.freelunch.com • Web site provides free access to more than 200 million economic and financial data series, covering industry, demographics, labor markets, prices, retail sales, government spending, trade, interest rates, housing starts, the stock market, etc. Data is available in either chart or table form. Searching is offered. Free, but registration required. Economy.com, Inc. also offers fee-based economic analysis at *The Dismal Scientist* site (www.dismal.com).

*InSite 2.* Intelligence Data/Thomson Financial. Phone: 800-654-0393 or (617)856-1890; Fax: (617)737-3182; Email: intelligence.data@tfn.com • URL: http://www.insite2.gale.com/ • Fee-based Web site consolidates information in a "Base Pack" consisting of Business InSite, Market InSite, and Company InSite. Optional databases are Consumer InSite, Health and Wellness InSite, Newsletter InSite, and Computer InSite. Includes fulltext content from more than 2,500 trade publications, journals, newsletters, newspapers, analyst reports, and other sources. Continuous updating. Formerly produced by The Gale Group.

*ProQuest.* ProQuest L.L.C. 789 E Eisenhower Pkwy., Ann Arbor, MI 48106-1346. Phone: 800-521-0600 or (734)761-4700; Fax: (734)662-4554; Email: info@proquest.com • URL: http://www.proquest.com • Fee-based Web site providing Internet access to more than 3,000 periodicals, newspapers, and other publications. Many items are available full-text, with daily updates. Includes extensive corporate and financial information. Fees: Apply.

*Summary of Commentary on Current Economic Conditions by Federal Reserve District.* Board of Governors of the Federal Reserve System. Phone: (202)452-3000; Fax: (202)452-3819 • URL: http://www.federalreserve.gov/publications.htm • 8/year. Free Web site provides current "anecdotal information" eight times a year on economic conditions within each of the 12 Federal Reserve Districts, plus an extensive national *Summary.* Text is based on the opinions of bank officials, business executives, economists, financial market experts, and others. Typically contains views of consumer spending, manufacturing, services, credit, employment, prices, wages, and the economy in general. Usually referred to as the Beige Book.

*Wageweb: Salary Survey Data On-Line.* HRPDI: Human Resources Programs Development and Improvement. Phone: (804)363-1792; Fax: (804)594-3721; Email: salaries@wageweb.com • URL: http://www.wageweb.com • Web site provides salary information for more than 170 benchmark positions, including (for example) 29 information management jobs. Data shows average minimum, median, and average maximum compensation for each position, based on salary surveys. Fees: Free

---

for national salary data; $169.00 per year for more detailed information (geographic, organization size, specific industries).

### ONLINE DATABASES

*Accounting and Tax Database.* ProQuest L.L.C. • Provides indexing and abstracting of the literature of accounting, taxation, and financial management, 1971 to date. Updating is weekly. Especially covers accounting, auditing, banking, bankruptcy, employee compensation and benefits, cash management, financial planning, and credit. Inquire as to online cost and availability.

*Wilson Business Abstracts Online.* H.W. Wilson Co. • Indexes and abstracts 600 major business periodicals, plus the *Wall Street Journal* and the business section of the *New York Times.* Indexing is from 1982, abstracting from 1990, with the two newspapers included from 1993. Updated weekly. Inquire as to online cost and availability. (*Business Periodicals Index* without abstracts is also available online.).

### OTHER SOURCES

*BNA Policy and Practice Series: Wages and Hours.* Bloomberg BNA. • Weekly. $938.00 per year. Looseleaf service.

*Business Rankings Annual (BRA).* Cengage Learning Inc. • Annual. $584 Individuals. A guide to lists and rankings appearing in major business publications. The top ten names are listed in each case.

*Foreign Labor Trends.* U. S. Government Printing Office. • Irregular (50 to 60 issues per year, each on an individual country). $95.00 per year. Prepared by various American Embassies. Issued by the Bureau of International Labor Affairs, U. S. Department of Labor. Covers labor developments in important foreign countries, including trends in wages, working conditions, labor supply, employment, and unemployment.

*Labor Relations.* Wolters Kluwer Law & Business CCH. • $2,589.00 per year. Seven looseleaf volumes. Weekly updates. Covers labor relations, wages and hours, state labor laws, and employment practices. Supplement available, *Labor Law Reports.* Summary Newsletter.

### PERIODICALS AND NEWSLETTERS

*Compensation and Benefits Review: The Journal of Total Compensation Strategies.* Pine Forge Press. • Bimonthly. $565 Individuals print only. Contains a summary of the latest compensation and benefits surveys, reports, and legal and regulatory developments.

*Paytech.* American Payroll Association. • Monthly. Membership. Covers the details and technology of payroll administration.

### RESEARCH CENTERS AND INSTITUTES

W.E. Upjohn Institute for Employment Research. 300 S Westnedge Ave., Kalamazoo, MI 49007-4686. Phone: 888-227-8569 or (269)343-5541; Fax: (269)343-7310; Email: communications@upjohn. org • URL: http://www.upjohninstitute.org • Research fields include unemployment, unemployment insurance, worker's compensation, labor productivity, profit sharing, the labor market, economic development, earnings, training, and other areas related to employment.

### STATISTICS SOURCES

*American Salaries and Wages Survey.* Cengage Learning Inc. • Annual. $342. Arranged alphabetically by occupational classifications. Provides salary data for different experience levels and in specific areas of the U.S. Includes cost of living data for metropolitan areas.

*Bulletin of Labour Statistics: Supplementing the Annual Data Presented in the Year Book of Labour Statistics.* International Labour Ofice. • Quarterly.

$84.00 per year. Includes five Supplements. A supplement to *Yearbook of Labour Statistics.* Provides current labor and price index statistics for over 130 countries. Generally includes data for the most recent four years. Text in English, French and Spanish.

*Occupational Earnings and Wage Trends in Metropolitan Areas.* U.S. Department of Labor Bureau of Labor Statistics. • Three times a year.

*Prices and Earnings Around the Globe.* Union Bank of Switzerland. • Triennial. Free. Published in Zurich. Compares prices and purchasing power in 48 major cities of the world. Wages and hours are also compared.

*Project Management Salary Survey.* Project Management Institute. • Annual. $200.00. Gives compensation data for key project management positions in North America, according to job title, level of responsibility, number of employees supervised, and various other factors. Includes data on retirement plans and benefits.

*Report on the American Workforce.* U. S. Government Printing Office. • Annual. Issued by the U. S. Department of Labor (www.dol.gov). Appendix contains tabular statistics, including employment, unemployment, price indexes, consumer expenditures, employee benefits (retirement, insurance, vacation, etc.), wages, productivity, hours of work, and occupational injuries. Annual figures are shown for up to 50 years.

*Statistics on Occupational Wages and Hours of Work and on Food Prices.* International Labor Organization. • Annual. Provides international data on wages and hours for 159 occupations within 49 industries. Includes retail prices for 93 food items.

*Survey of Current Business.* U. S. Government Printing Office. • Published by Bureau of Economic Analysis, U. S. Department of Commerce. Presents a wide variety of business and economic data.

### TRADE/PROFESSIONAL ASSOCIATIONS

American Payroll Association. 660 N Main Ave., Ste. 100, San Antonio, TX 78205-1217. Phone: (210)226-4600 or (210)224-6406; Fax: (210)226-4027 or (210)224-6038; Email: APA@ americanpayroll.org • URL: http://www. americanpayroll.org • Payroll employees. Works to increase members' skills and professionalism through education and mutual support. Represents the interest of members before legislative bodies. Conducts training courses. Operates speakers' bureau; conducts educational programs. Administers the certified payroll professional program of recognition.

Canadian Payroll Association. 250 Bloor St. E, Ste. 1600, Toronto, ON, Canada M4W 1E6. Phone: 800-387-4693 or (416)487-3380; Fax: (416)487-3384; Email: Membership@payroll.ca • URL: http://www. payroll.ca • Represents the payroll community in Canada; offers education programs, advocacy efforts, products and services to help members enhance and adapt payroll operations, meet new legislative requirements, address changing workplace needs and take advantage of emerging technologies.

WorldatWork. 14040 N Northsight Blvd., Scottsdale, AZ 85260. Phone: 866-816-2962 or (480)922-2020 or (480)951-9191; Fax: (480)483-8352 or (866)816-2962; Email: customerrelations@ worldatwork.org • URL: http://www.worldatwork. org • Dedicated to knowledge leadership in compensation, benefits and total rewards, focusing on disciplines associated with attracting, retaining and motivating employees. Offers CCP, CBP, and GRP certification and education programs, conducts surveys, research and provides networking opportunities.

# WALLPAPER INDUSTRY

### PERIODICALS AND NEWSLETTERS

*Paint and Decorating Retailer.* Paint and Decorating Retailers Association. • Monthly. $45.00 per year. Formerly *Decorating Retailer.*

### TRADE/PROFESSIONAL ASSOCIATIONS

Painting and Decorating Contractors of America. 2316 Millpark Dr., Maryland Heights, MO 63043. Phone: 800-332-7322 or (314)514-7322; Fax: (314)890-2068; Email: rbright@pdca.org • URL: http://www.pdca.org • Painting and wallcovering contractors.

# WAREHOUSES

### DIRECTORIES

*Grocery Headquarters: The Newspaper for the Food Industry.* Trend Publishing Inc. • Monthly. $80. Covers the sale and distribution of food products and other items sold in supermarkets and grocery stores. Edited mainly for retailers and wholesalers. Incorporates (Grocery Distribution).

*International Directory of Refrigerated Warehouses and Distribution Centers.* Global Cold Chain Alliance. • Continuous. Lists locations/services of 1,000 public refrigerated warehouses in 30 countries. Formerly *International Directory of Public Refrigerated Warehouses.*

*International Warehouse Logistics Association-- Roster of Members.* International Warehouse Logistics Association. • Annual. Covers: 550 warehouses, general storage facilities and distribution centers for non-refrigerated products in the US, Canada, Panama, Mexico, Venezuela, Puerto Rico, Dominican Republic and Costa Rica.

*Warehouse Management's Guide to Public Warehousing.* Reed Elsevier Group plc Reed Business Information. • Annual. $55.00. List of general merchandise,contract and refrigerated warehouses.

*Warehousing Distribution Directory.* UBM Global Trade. • Semiannual. Publication includes: List of about 800 warehousing and consolidation companies and firms offering trucking, trailer on flatcar, container on flatcar, and piggyback carrier services. Entries include: Name of firm, address, phone, name and title of contact, services, insurance provided, bank references, territory covered, restrictions, number of staff, and branches or subsidiaries with their locations.

### FINANCIAL RATIOS

*Annual Statement Studies.* Risk Management Association. • Annual. Compiled from over 280,000 financial statements.

*Annual Statement Studies: Industry Default Probabilities and Cash Flow Measures.* Risk Management Association. • Annual. $405 Nonmembers. Serves as a companion volume to the original *Annual Statement Studies.* Gives probability of default estimates on a percentage scale for more than 450 industries. Includes changes in position year-by-year for eight financial statement line items and provides percentage measures of cash flow.

### OTHER SOURCES

*How to Plan and Manage Warehouse Operations.* American Management Association Extension Institute. • Looseleaf. $159.00. Self-study course. Emphasis is on practical explanations, examples, and problem solving. Quizzes and a case study are included.

### PERIODICALS AND NEWSLETTERS

*Chilton's Distribution: The Transportation and Business Logistics Magazine.* Reed Elsevier Group plc Reed Business Information. • Monthly. $65.00 per year.

*Transportation and Distribution: Integrating*

*Logistics in Supply Chain Management.* Penton Media Inc. • Monthly. Free to qualified personnel; others, $50.00 per year. Essential information on transportation and distribution practices in domestic and international trade.

### TRADE/PROFESSIONAL ASSOCIATIONS

American Chain of Warehouses. 156 Flamingo Dr., Beecher, IL 60401. Phone: (708)946-9792; Fax: (708)946-9793; Email: bjurus@acwi.org • URL: http://www.acwi.org • Represents commercial warehouses. Provides national sales representation. Disseminates information.

American Moving and Storage Association. 1611 Duke St., Alexandria, VA 22314-3406. Phone: 888-849-2672 or (703)683-7410; Fax: (703)683-7527 or (703)548-1845; Email: amconf@amconf.org • URL: http://www.promover.org • Members are household goods movers, storage companies, and trucking firms.

# WARM AIR HEATING

*See* HEATING AND VENTILATION

# WASHING MACHINE INDUSTRY

*See* ELECTRIC APPLIANCE INDUSTRY

# WASTE DISPOSAL

*See* SANITATION INDUSTRY

# WASTE MANAGEMENT

*See also* HAZARDOUS MATERIALS

### ABSTRACTS AND INDEXES

*Applied Science and Technology Index.* EBSCO Publishing Inc. • 11/year. Indexes a wide variety of English language technical, industrial, and engineering periodicals.

### DIRECTORIES

*Directory of American Manufacturers & Exporters of Waste Disposal & Recycling Equipment.* EXIM Infotek Private Ltd. • Covers: 340 American manufacturers and exporters of advanced wash recycling systems, balers and recycling equipment, baling presses, compactors, decontamination waste disposable systems, garbage disposers, glass and can crushers, hazardous materials, hazardous waste disposal system, food waste disposers, indoor and outdoor steel and fiberglass receptacles, modern gas chlorinators, recycled wood and paper waste and fiber materials, recycling center equipment, aluminum can densors and flattener, sewage treatment systems, shredders, solid waste disposable systems, stump and wood waste disposable equipment, tire shredders, trash compactors, waste handling equipment, wastewater reclamation equipment, wastewater treatment systems, and wood waste recycling equipment.

*Directory of Middle East Importers of Waste Disposal & Recycling Equipment.* EXIM Infotek Private Ltd. • Covers: 55 Middle East importers of sewage equipment, waste disposal equipment, and waste recycling equipment. Entries include: Company name, postal address, telephone, fax, e-mail, website, contact person, designation, and product details.

*Directory of South American Importers of Waste Disposal & Recycling Equipment.* EXIM Infotek Private Ltd. • Covers: 40 South American importers of garbage disposals and compactors, waste disposal

equipment, and waste recycling equipment. Entries include: Company name, postal address, telephone, fax, e-mail, website, contact person, designation, and product details.

*Directory of Taiwanese Manufacturers and Exporters of Waste Disposal and Recycling Equipment.* EXIM Infotek Private Ltd. • $250 Individuals. Covers: 70 Taiwanese manufacturers and exporters of domestic refuse and waste incinerators. Entries include: Company name, postal address, telephone, fax, e-mail, website, contact person, designation, and product details.

*Hazardous Waste Consultant Directory of Commercial Hazardous Waste Management Facilities.* Elsevier. • Annual. $115.00. List of 170 facilities that process, store, and dispose of hazardous waste materials.

*National Solid Wastes Management Association: Member Companies.* National Waste and Recycling Association. • Annual. Lists waste management consulting firms. Available via website.

*Recycling and Waste Management Guide to the Internet.* Government Institutes. • $72 Individuals. Covers: More than 350 web sites, discussion lists, and news groups on the internet covering waste management and recycling issues. Entries include: Site name, address, subject, site summary, contact name and e-mail.

*Waste Age Buyers' Guide.* RentPath Inc. • Annual. Manufacturers of equipment and supplies for the waste management industry.

### ONLINE DATABASES

*Waste Treatment System Businesses in the World.* Momentum Technologies L.L.C. • Contains 250 directory listings of businesses throughout the world that manufacture or sell waste treatment systems and associated components. Includes business name, address, phone number, fax number, e-mail address, and web site address. Provides brief descriptions of product lines, services offered, and business type. Includes information on manufacturers, component makers, wholesalers, retailers, system designers, system installers, trade associations, and more. Searchable by location, business type, company name, and keyword.

### OTHER SOURCES

*Hazardous Waste Litigation Reporter: The National Journal of Record of Hazardous Waste-Related Litigation.* Andrews Publications. • Semimonthly. $875.00 per year. Newsletter. Reports on hazardous waste legal cases.

### PERIODICALS AND NEWSLETTERS

*Air and Waste Management Association Journal.* • Monthly. Individuals, $150.00 per year; institutions, $329.00 per year: nonprofit institutions, $229.00 per year. Includes annual *Directory of Governmental Air Pollution Agencies.*

*EM: A&WMA's Environmental Solutions That Make Good Business Sense.* Air and Waste Management Association. • Monthly. Institutions, $299.00 per year; nonprofit and government agencies, $199.00 per year. Newsletter. Provides news of regulations, legislation, and technology relating to the environment, recycling, and waste control. Formerly *Environmental Manager.*

*Environmental Regulation: State Capitals.* Wakeman/Walworth Inc. • 50 times a year. $245.00 per year; print and online editions, $350.00 per year. Newsletter. Formerly *From the State Capitals: Environmental Regulation.*

*Sludge Newsletter: The Newsletter on Municipal Wastewater and Biosolids.* Business Publishers Inc. • Biweekly. $409.00 per year. per year. Newsletter. Monitors sludge management developments in Washington and around the country.

*Solid Waste Report: Resource Recovery-Recycling-Collection-Disposal.* Business Publishers Inc. •

Weekly. $627.00 per year. Newsletter. Covers regulation, business news, technology, and international events relating to solid waste management.

*Waste Business West.* CHMM Inc. • Bimonthly. Magazine for waste-industry.

*Waste Treatment Technology News.* BCC Research. • Description: Profiles existing and developing industrial waste treatment techniques. Follows governmental action such as Superfund legislation and EPA (Environmental Protection Agency) activities. Focuses on the research and development of waste treatment technologies, listing recent patents in the field. Recurring features include news of research.

### RESEARCH CENTERS AND INSTITUTES

Atkinson Center for a Sustainable Future. Cornell University, 200 Rice Hall, Ithaca, NY 14853-5601. Phone: (607)255-7535; Fax: (607)255-6714; Email: fjd3@cornell.edu • URL: http://www. sustainablefuture.cornell.edu • Advances multidisciplinary research and cultivates innovative collaborations to foster a sustainable future.

Environmental Engineering Center. Michigan Technological University, 1400 Townsend Dr., Houghton, MI 49931. Phone: (906)487-2025; Fax: (906)487-3167; Email: biology@mtu.edu • URL: http://www.bio.mtu.edu/research • Applies biotechnological research to waste management and resource recovery.

University of Tennessee at Knoxville - Waste Management Research and Education Institute. Energy, Environment & Resources Ctr., 311 Conference Ctr. Bldg., Knoxville, TN 37996-4134. Phone: (865)974-4251 or (865)974-1000; Fax: (865)974-1838; Email: barkenbu@utk.edu • URL: http://eerc.ra.utk.edu/WMREI.html • Research fields include chemical, nuclear, and solid waste management, especially waste policy and environmental biotechnology studies.

# WASTE PRODUCTS

*See also* IRON AND STEEL SCRAP METAL INDUSTRY; RECYCLING; SANITATION INDUSTRY

### ABSTRACTS AND INDEXES

*Environment Abstracts.* University Publications of America. • Monthly. Price varies. Provides multidisciplinary coverage of the world's environmental literature. Incorporates *Acid Rain Abstracts.*

*Environment Abstracts Annual: A Guide to the Key Environmental Literature of the Year.* University Publications of America. • Annual. $495.00. A yearly cumulation of *Environment Abstracts.*

*Pollution Abstracts.* Cambridge Information Group. • Monthly. $1,390.00 per year. Includes print and online editions; with index, $1,515.00 per year.

### CD-ROM DATABASES

*Environment Abstracts on CD-ROM.* University Publications of America. • Quarterly. $1,295.00 per year. Contains the following CD-ROM databases: *Environment Abstracts, Energy Abstracts,* and *Acid Rain Abstracts.* Length of coverage varies.

### PERIODICALS AND NEWSLETTERS

*Scrap.* Institute of Scrap Recycling Industries. • Bimonthly. $48 Individuals companies. Magazine for the scrap processing and recycling industry. Formerly *Scrap Processing and Recycling.*

*Waste Treatment Technology News.* BCC Research. • Description: Profiles existing and developing industrial waste treatment techniques. Follows governmental action such as Superfund legislation and EPA (Environmental Protection Agency) activities. Focuses on the research and development of waste treatment technologies, listing recent patents in the field. Recurring features include news of research.

# WATCH INDUSTRY

*See* CLOCK AND WATCH INDUSTRY

# WATER POLLUTION

*See also* SANITATION INDUSTRY; WATER SUPPLY

## ABSTRACTS AND INDEXES

*Environment Abstracts.* University Publications of America. • Monthly. Price varies. Provides multidisciplinary coverage of the world's environmental literature. Incorporates *Acid Rain Abstracts.*

*Environment Abstracts Annual: A Guide to the Key Environmental Literature of the Year.* University Publications of America. • Annual. $495.00. A yearly cumulation of *Environment Abstracts.*

*Excerpta Medica: Environmental Health and Pollution Control.* Elsevier. • 16 times a year. Institutions, $3,246.00 per year. Section 46 of *Excerpta Medica.* Covers air, water, and land pollution and noise control.

*NTIS Alerts: Environmental Pollution & Control.* U.S. Department of Commerce National Technical Information Service. • Biweekly. $130 per year. Covers the following categories of environmental pollution: air, water, solid wastes, radiation, pesticides, and noise.

*Pollution Abstracts.* Cambridge Information Group. • Monthly. $1,390.00 per year. Includes print and online editions; with index, $1,515.00 per year.

## BIBLIOGRAPHIES

*Literature Review.* Water Environment Federation. • Annual. Provides a review of published books and articles on water quality topics from the previous year.

## CD-ROM DATABASES

*Environment Abstracts on CD-ROM.* University Publications of America. • Quarterly. $1,295.00 per year. Contains the following CD-ROM databases: *Environment Abstracts, Energy Abstracts,* and *Acid Rain Abstracts.* Length of coverage varies.

## ENCYCLOPEDIAS AND DICTIONARIES

*Environmental Encyclopedia.* Cengage Learning Inc. • $327 Individuals. 2011. $298.00. 4th edition. Provides over 1,300 articles on all aspects of the environment. Written in non-technical style. eBook also available. Inquire for pricing.

*Pollution A to Z.* Cengage Learning Inc. • 2003.Two volumes. Provides encyclopedic coverage of many aspects of environmental pollution, including air, water, noise, and soil. Inquire as to price and availability.

## ONLINE DATABASES

*Aqualine.* Cambridge Scientific Abstracts L.P. • Provides online citations and abstracts to a wide variety of literature relating to the aquatic environment, including 400 journals, from 1960 to date. Updating is monthly. Inquire as to online cost and availability.

## PERIODICALS AND NEWSLETTERS

*Environmental Business Journal: Strategic Information for a Changing Industry.* Environmental Business International Inc. • Monthly. $250 Single issue. Includes both industrial and financial information relating to individual companies and to the environmental industry in general. Covers air pollution, wat es, U. S. Department of Health and Human Services. Provides conference, workshop, and

symposium proceedings, as well as extensive reviews of environmental prospects.

*Environmental Regulation: State Capitals.* Wakeman/Walworth Inc. • 50 times a year. $245.00 per year; print and online editions, $350.00 per year. Newsletter. Formerly *From the State Capitals: Environmental Regulation.*

*Pollution Engineering: Magazine of Environmental Control.* BNP Media. • Monthly. Covers the air, water, waste and remediation environmental concerns in the Pollution Control field.

*Water and Environment Manager.* Chartered Institution of Water and Environmental Management. Terence Dalton Ltd. • 10 times a year. $90.00 per year. Formerly *Chartered Institution of Water and Environmental Management Newsletter.*

## STATISTICS SOURCES

*Standard & Poor's Industry Surveys.* Standard & Poor's Financial Services L.L.C. • Semiannual. $1,800.00. Two looseleaf volumes. Includes monthly *Supplements.* Provides detailed, individual surveys of 52 major industry groups. Each survey is revised on a semiannual basis. Also includes "Monthly Investment Review" (industry group investment analysis) and monthly "Trends & Projections" (economic analysis).

*U.S. Industry and Trade Outlook.* U.S. Department of Commerce National Technical Information Service. • Annual. Produced by the International Trade Administration, U.S. Department of Commerce, in a "public-private" partnership with DRI/McGraw-Hill and Standard & Poor's. Provides basic data, outlook for the current year, and "Long-Term Prospects" (five-year projections) for a wide variety of products and services. Includes high technology industries. Formerly *U.S. Industrial Outlook.*

## TRADE/PROFESSIONAL ASSOCIATIONS

Association of Clean Water Administrators. 1221 Connecticut Ave. NW, 2nd Fl., Washington, DC 20036. Phone: (202)756-0600; Fax: (202)756-0605.

European Union of National Associations of Water Suppliers and Waste Water Services. Rue du Luxembourg 47-51, B-1050 Brussels, Belgium. Phone: 32 2 7064080; Fax: 32 2 7064081 • URL: http://eureau.org • Represents water suppliers and waste water operators united to defend their common interests. Assesses and monitors water supply problems; reviews and discusses prospective legislation affecting the industry. Recommends practical and legislative solutions to problems with respect to differing technologies, climates, and geographical and economic situations in member states. Collaborates with other technical associations.

# WATER POWER

*See* HYDROELECTRIC INDUSTRY

# WATER SUPPLY

*See also* DESALINATION INDUSTRY; SANITATION INDUSTRY; WATER POLLUTION

## ABSTRACTS AND INDEXES

*Pollution Abstracts.* Cambridge Information Group. • Monthly. $1,390.00 per year. Includes print and online editions; with index, $1,515.00 per year.

## ALMANACS AND YEARBOOKS

*Earth Almanac: An Annual Geophysical Review of the State of the Planet.* Natalie Goldstein. Greenwood Publishing Group Inc. • $91.95. Provides background information, statistics, and a summary of major events relating to the atmosphere, oceans, land, and fresh water.

## CD-ROM DATABASES

*AGRICOLA on SilverPlatter.* Ovid Technologies Inc. • Updated monthly. Price varies. Produced by the National Agricultural Library. Provides over 4 million citations to the literature of agriculture, agricultural economics, animal sciences, entomology, fertilizer, food, forestry, nutrition, pesticides, plant science, water resources, and other topics.

## DIRECTORIES

*American Water Works Association--Sourcebook.* American Water Works Association. • Annual. Covers: Member suppliers and distributors of water supply products and services, contractors for water supply projects, and engineering consultants. Entries include: Company name, address, names of executives, trade and brand names, products and services offered.

*Water Conditioning & Purification--Buyers Guide Issue.* Publicom Inc. • Continuous. Publication includes: List of about 800 manufacturers and suppliers in the water treatment and purification industry. Entries include: Company name, address, phone, name of contact, line of business.

*Water Filtering and Purification System Businesses in the World.* Momentum Technologies L.L.C. • Contains 322 directory listings and contact information of businesses providing water filtering and purification systems throughout the world. Includes business name, address, phone number, fax number, e-mail address, and web site address. Provides brief descriptions of product lines, services offered, and business type. Includes information on manufacturers, component makers, wholesalers, retailers, system designers, system installers, trade associations, and more. Searchable by location, business type, company name, and keyword.

## ONLINE DATABASES

*Aqualine.* Cambridge Scientific Abstracts L.P. • Provides online citations and abstracts to a wide variety of literature relating to the aquatic environment, including 400 journals, from 1960 to date. Updating is monthly. Inquire as to online cost and availability.

## PERIODICALS AND NEWSLETTERS

*Environmental Regulation: State Capitals.* Wakeman/Walworth Inc. • 50 times a year. $245.00 per year; print and online editions, $350.00 per year. Newsletter. Formerly *From the State Capitals: Environmental Regulation.*

*Ground Water.* National Ground Water Association. National Ground Water Association. • Bimonthly. $19 Members.

*National Water Conditions.* U.S. Geological Survey - Water Resources Division. • Description: Describes the month's water conditions in the U.S. and Canada, compiling data on streamflow, ground water conditions, surface water, reservoirs, the flow of large rivers, water temperatures, and dissolved solids.

*Utility Business.* Penton. • Monthly. Trade magazine covering the utility industry for executives, managers and others in the electric, gas, water and telecommunications utility business.

## RESEARCH CENTERS AND INSTITUTES

University of Delaware - College of Agriculture and Natural Resources - Delaware Water Resources Center. 531 S College Ave., Newark, DE 19716. Phone: (302)831-2191 or (302)831-2698; Fax: (302)831-3651 or (302)831-6758; Email: jtsims@udel.edu • URL: http://ag.udel.edu/dwrc • Water and other resources that affect water, including basic and practical studies on supply, use, conservation, and reuse of water. Also studies wastewater reclamation, economic, governmental, and other social aspects of water resource development, groundwater flow, and water use efficiency in agriculture. Established under Water Resources Research Act of 1964, Public Law 88-379; authorized currently under Water Research Act of 1984, Public Law 98-242, to conduct and coordinate research activities to assure the state and surrounding region of a supply of water sufficient in quantity and quality to meet requirements of its expanding population and economy. Assists in training of scientists for research on water resources problems.

### TRADE/PROFESSIONAL ASSOCIATIONS

American Water Resources Association. PO Box 1626, Middleburg, VA 20118-1626. Phone: (540)687-8390; Fax: (540)687-8395; Email: info@awra.org • URL: http://www.awra.org • Engineers; natural, physical, and social scientists; other persons engaged in any aspect of the field of water resources; business concerns and other organizations; students in water resources. Includes members from 62 nations. Seeks to advance water resources research, planning, development, and management. Endeavors to collect and disseminate ideas and information relative to water resources science and technology via scientific journal, newsletter, conferences and symposia and published proceedings.

American Water Works Association. 6666 W Quincy Ave., Denver, CO 80235-3098. Phone: 800-926-7337 or (303)794-7711; Fax: (303)347-0804 • URL: http://www.awwa.org • Water utility managers, superintendents, engineers, chemists, bacteriologists, and other individuals interested in public water supply; municipal- and investor-owned water departments; boards of health; manufacturers of waterworks equipment; government officials and consultants interested in water supply. Develops standards and supports research programs in waterworks design, construction, operation, and management. Conducts in-service training schools and prepares manuals for waterworks personnel. Maintains hall of fame. Offers placement service via member newsletter; compiles statistics. Offers training; children's services; and information center on the water utilities industry, potable water, and water reuse.

European Union of National Associations of Water Suppliers and Waste Water Services. Rue du Luxembourg 47-51, B-1050 Brussels, Belgium. Phone: 32 2 7064080; Fax: 32 2 7064081 • URL: http://eureau.org • Represents water suppliers and waste water operators united to defend their common interests. Assesses and monitors water supply problems; reviews and discusses prospective legislation affecting the industry. Recommends practical and legislative solutions to problems with respect to differing technologies, climates, and geographical and economic situations in member states. Collaborates with other technical associations.

National Ground Water Association. 601 Dempsey Rd., Westerville, OH 43081. Phone: 800-551-7379 or (614)898-7791; Fax: (614)898-7786; Email: ngwa@ngwa.org • URL: http://www.ngwa.org • Ground water drilling contractors; manufacturers and suppliers of drilling equipment; ground water scientists such as geologists, engineers, public health officials, and others interested in the problems of locating, developing, preserving, and using ground water supplies. Conducts seminars, and continuing education programs. Encourages scientific education, research, and the development of standards; offers placement services; compiles market statistics. Offers charitable program. Maintains speakers' bureau.

## WATERFRONTS

*See* PORTS

## WATERWAYS

### ABSTRACTS AND INDEXES

*NTIS Alerts: Transportation.* U.S. Department of Commerce National Technical Information Service. • Biweekly. $130 per year. Covers air, marine, highway, inland waterway, pipeline, and railroad transportation.

*Oceanic Abstracts.* CSA. • Monthly. $1,645.00 per year. Includes print and online editions. Covers oceanography, marine biology, ocean shipping, and a wide range of other marine-related subject areas.

### DIRECTORIES

*Inland River Guide.* Waterways Journal Inc. • Annual. $73. Covers barge and towing companies operating on Mississippi River System, Warrior-Tom Bigbee System, and Gulf Intracoastal Waterwa: all inland and Gulf Coast shipyards; public and private terminals on waterway;: contracting and dredging firms; government agencies dealing with waterways.

*Waterway Guide--The Yachtman's Bible.* Argus Press Inc. • $36.95 postpaid. Covers: inland and coastal waterways in the eastern half of the United States; published in three editions. Northern edition covers coastal waterways from the Delaware Bay to the U.S.-Canadian border; plus New York canals, Champlain Waterways, and St. Lawrence River; Middle Atlantic edition covers waterways from the Chesapeake Bay to the Florida-Georgia line; Southern edition covers intracoastal waterways from the Florida-Georgia line to the Texas-Mexico border and the Bahamas. Entries include: Name of marine facility, location, navigation information and courses, points of interest, anchorages.

### TRADE/PROFESSIONAL ASSOCIATIONS

National Waterways Conference. 1100 N Glebe Rd., Ste. 1010, Arlington, VA 22201. Phone: (703)224-8007 or (703)243-4090; Fax: (866)371-1390 or (703)243-4155; Email: amy@waterways.org • URL: http://www.waterways.org • Petroleum, coal, chemical, electric power, building materials, iron and steel, and grain companies; industrial development agencies, port authorities, and other governmental bodies; water carriers; companies which build, repair, service, or insure vessels; water resource development associations, banks, chambers of commerce, and individuals. Seeks to promote a better understanding of the public value of the American waterways system. Conducts research on the economics of water transportation; sponsors an educational program to point up the diverse benefits of efficient water transport; keeps members and other waterway proponents posted on developments affecting national waterways policy.

## WATERWORKS

*See* WATER SUPPLY

## WEALTHY CONSUMERS

*See* AFFLUENT MARKET

## WEATHER AND WEATHER FORECASTING

*See also* CLIMATE

### ABSTRACTS AND INDEXES

*Meteorological & Geoastrophysical Abstracts (MGA).* American Meteorological Society. American Meteorological Society. • Monthly. $1,605 print. Journal presenting abstrcts of current world literature in meteorology, climatology,

aeronomy, planetary atmospheres, solar-terrestrial relations, hydrology, oceanography, glaciology.

### ALMANACS AND YEARBOOKS

*AMS Conference Proceedings.* American Meteorological Society. • Annual.

### E-BOOKS

*Weather Almanac.* Cengage Learning Inc. • 2004. eBook. 11th edition. Weather records for 108 major U.S. cities and a climatic overview of the country. Contact for pricing.

### ONLINE DATABASES

*Accu-Data.* Accu-Weather Inc. • Provides detailed, current weather conditions and weather forecasts for many U. S. and foreign cities and regions. Updating is continuous. Inquire as to online cost and availability.

### OTHER SOURCES

*Lloyd's Maritime Atlas.* Informa P.L.C. Informa Sports Group. • Biennial. $119.00. Contains more than 70 pages of world, ocean, regional, and port maps in color. Provides additional information for the planning of world shipping routes, including data on distances, port facilities, recurring weather hazards at sea, international load line zones, and sailing times.

### PERIODICALS AND NEWSLETTERS

*Daily Weather Maps.* U.S. Department of Commerce. • Weekly series.

*Hourly Precipitation Data.* U.S. National Climatic Data Center. • Monthly. Published separately for 41 states.

*Journal of Applied Meteorology and Climatology.* American Meteorological Society. • Monthly. $1,110 Members corporation and institution; online and print. Peer-reviewed journal exploring the applications of the atmospheric sciences to operational and practical goals.

*Monthly Climatic Data for the World.* U.S. National Climatic Data Center. • Monthly. Contains monthly mean temperature, pressure, precipitation, vapor pressure, and hours of sunshine for approximately 2,000 surface data collection stations worldwide and monthly mean upper air temperatures, dew point depressions, and wind velocities for approximately 500 observing sites.

*Monthly Weather Review.* American Meteorological Society. • Monthly. $1,600 Nonmembers online and print. Peer-reviewed journal presenting original research and survey papers concerned with weather analysis and forecasting.

*Storm Data.* U.S. National Climatic Data Center. • Monthly. Contains a chronological listing, by state, of hurricanes, tornadoes, thunderstorms, hail, floods, drought conditions, lightning, high winds, snow, temperature extremes and other weather phenomena.

### TRADE/PROFESSIONAL ASSOCIATIONS

American Meteorological Society. 45 Beacon St., Boston, MA 02108-3693. Phone: (617)227-2425 or (617)227-2426; Fax: (617)742-8718; Email: amsinfo@ametsoc.org • URL: http://www.ametsoc.org • Professional meteorologists, oceanographers, and hydrologists; interested students and nonprofessionals. Develops and disseminates information on the atmospheric and related oceanic and hydrospheric sciences; seeks to advance professional applications. Activities include guidance service, scholarship programs, career information, certification of consulting meteorologists, and a seal of approval program to recognize competence in radio and television weathercasting. Issues statements of policy to assist public understanding on subjects such as weather modification, forecasting, tornadoes, hurricanes, flash floods, and meteorological satellites. Provides abstracting services. Prepares educational films, filmstrips, and slides for a new curriculum in meteorology at the ninth grade level. Issues monthly announcements of job openings for meteorologists.

# WEAVING

*See also* TEXTILE INDUSTRY

## ABSTRACTS AND INDEXES

*Textile Technology Index*™. EBSCO Publishing Inc. • Monthly. $545 Individuals. Includes indexing and abstracts for more than 470 periodicals.

## ONLINE DATABASES

*Textile Technology Index*™. EBSCO Publishing Inc. • Monthly. $545 Individuals. Includes indexing and abstracts for more than 470 periodicals.

*World Textiles*. Elsevier. • Provides abstracting and indexing from 1970 of worldwide textile literature (periodicals, books, pamphlets, and reports). Includes U. S., European, and British patent information. Updating is monthly. Inquire as to online cost and availability.

## PERIODICALS AND NEWSLETTERS

*International Textile Bulletin: Yarn and Fabric Forming Edition*. ITS Publishing, International Textile Service. • Quarterly. $170.00 per year. Editions in Chinese, English, French, German, Italian and Spanish.

*Shuttle, Spindle & Dyepot*. Handweavers Guild of America. • Quarterly. Comprised of articles on fiber arts.

# WEEKLY NEWSPAPERS

*See* NEWSPAPERS

# WEIGHT CONTROL

*See* DIET

# WEIGHTS AND MEASURES

## ALMANACS AND YEARBOOKS

*International Society of Weighing and Measurement Membership Directory and Product Guide*. International Society of Weighing and Measurement. • Annual.

## DIRECTORIES

*The International Directory of Importers - Measuring Equipment and Scales Importers*. Interdata. • $220 Individuals print version. Covers: 1,900 international firms importing measuring equipment and scales. Entries include: Company name and address, contact person, email, number of employees, year established, phone and telefaxes, business activity, bank references, as well as a listing of measuring equipment and scales currently being imported.

## PERIODICALS AND NEWSLETTERS

*ISWM News*. International Society of Weighing and Measurement. • Description: Contains calendar of events, new product information, industry updates, technical articles, and association news.

*Metric Today*. U.S. Metric Association Inc. • Description: Provides news on metric system conversion in the U.S., Canada, and abroad. Covers metrication updates in industry, government, education, and consumer areas. Recurring features include news of members, metric book reviews, editorials, data on metric standards, and letters to the editor.

## TRADE/PROFESSIONAL ASSOCIATIONS

American National Metric Council. 1625 Massachusetts Ave. NW, Washington, DC 20036. Phone: (203)232-4545; Email: anmcmetric@pi-c.com • URL: http://lamar.colostate.edu/hillger/anmc.htm • Companies, organizations, and individuals interested in keeping up-to-date on all the latest information on the status of metric transition in the U.S. Aims to coordinate metric transition planning activities for all affected segments in the private sector of American society.

National Conference on Weights and Measures. 1135 M St., Ste. 110, Lincoln, NE 68508-2196. Phone: (402)434-4880; Fax: (402)434-4878; Email: info@ncwm.net • URL: http://www.ncwm.net • State and local weights and measures officials; representatives of manufacturers of weighing and measuring devices, trade associations, industry (users of devices), and representatives of federal government. Promotes uniformity in weights and measures laws, regulations, specifications and tolerances. Sponsored by National Institute of Standards and Technology.

# WELDING

## ABSTRACTS AND INDEXES

*Applied Science and Technology Index*. EBSCO Publishing Inc. • 11/year. Indexes a wide variety of English language technical, industrial, and engineering periodicals.

## ALMANACS AND YEARBOOKS

*Welding Research Council Yearbook*. Welding Research Council. • Annual. Lists the objectives and long-range plans of the Council and committee membership.

## DIRECTORIES

*Directory of European Importers of Welding Equipment and Supplies*. EXIM Infotek Private Ltd. • $350 Individuals. Covers: 130 European importers of arc welding equipment, electrodes, soldering equipment, welding equipment, and welding supplies. Entries include: Company name, postal address, telephone, fax, e-mail, website, contact person, designation, and product details.

*Directory of Middle East Importers of Welding Equipment and Supplies*. EXIM Infotek Private Ltd. • $350 Individuals. Covers: 140 Middle East importers of electrodes, soldering equipment, soldering supplies, welding equipment, welding products, and welding supplies. Entries include: Company name, postal address, telephone, fax, e-mail, website, contact person, designation, and product details.

*Directory of SAARC Importers of Welding Equipments and Supplies*. EXIM Infotek Private Ltd. • $150 Individuals. Covers: 30 SAARC Countries importers of crush electrodes, ferrosillicon and graphite electrodes, M.S. welding rods, soldering and earthing materials, welding equipment, welding electrodes, welding gases, welding generators, welding machine and materials, welding products, welding rods, and welding supplies. Entries include: Company name, postal address, telephone, fax, e-mail, website, contact person, designation, and product details.

*International Directory of Importers--Welding and Soldering Equipment Importers*. Interdata. • Annual. $200 Individuals print. Covers: 700 international firms importing welding and soldering equipment. Entries include: Company name and address, contact person, email, number of employees, year established, phone and telefaxes, business activity, bank references, as well as a listing of welding and soldering equipment currently being imported.

## FINANCIAL RATIOS

*Annual Statement Studies*. Risk Management Association. • Annual. Compiled from over 280,000 financial statements.

*Annual Statement Studies: Industry Default Probabilities and Cash Flow Measures*. Risk Manage-
ment Association. • Annual. $405 Nonmembers. Serves as a companion volume to the original *Annual Statement Studies*. Gives probability of default estimates on a percentage scale for more than 450 industries. Includes changes in position year-by-year for eight financial statement line items and provides percentage measures of cash flow.

## ONLINE DATABASES

*Applied Science and Technology Index Online*. H.W. Wilson Co. • Provides online indexing of 500 major scientific, technical, industrial, and engineering periodicals. Time period is 1983 to date. Monthly updates. Inquire as to online cost and availability.

*Weldasearch*. TWI World Centre for Materials Joining Technology. • Contains abstracts of international welding literature, 1967 to date. Inquire as to online cost and availability.

## PERIODICALS AND NEWSLETTERS

*The Gases and Welding Distributor*. Penton Media Inc. • Bimonthly. Free to qualified personnel; others, $55.00 per year. Formerly *Welding Distributor*.

## RESEARCH CENTERS AND INSTITUTES

Massachusetts Institute of Technology - Materials Processing Center. 77 Massachusetts Ave., Cambridge, MA 02139-4301. Phone: (617)253-5179; Fax: (617)258-6900; Email: cthomp@mit.edu • URL: http://mpc-web.mit.edu • Conducts processing, engineering, and economic research in ferrous and nonferrous metals, ceramics, polymers, photonic materials, superconductors, welding, composite materials, and other materials.

## STATISTICS SOURCES

*United States Census of Service Industries*. U.S. Department of Commerce U.S. Census Bureau. • Quinquennial. Various reports available.

*U.S. Industry and Trade Outlook*. U.S. Department of Commerce National Technical Information Service. • Annual. Produced by the International Trade Administration, U.S. Department of Commerce, in a "public-private" partnership with DRI/McGraw-Hill and Standard & Poor's. Provides basic data, outlook for the current year, and "Long-Term Prospects" (five-year projections) for a wide variety of products and services. Includes high technology industries. Formerly *U.S. Industrial Outlook*.

## TRADE/PROFESSIONAL ASSOCIATIONS

American Welding Society. 8669 Doral Blvd., Ste. 130, Miami, FL 33166. Phone: 800-443-9353 or (305)443-9353; Fax: (305)443-7559; Email: info@aws.org • URL: http://www.aws.org • One of several sponsors of the Welding Research Council and the Materials Properties Council. Professional engineering society in the field of welding. Sponsors seminars. Maintains over 130 technical and handbook committees, 171 sections, educational committees, and task forces.

Gases and Welding and Distributors Association. 8669 Doral Blvd., Ste. 130, Doral, FL 33166. Phone: 877-382-6440; Fax: (305)442-7451; Email: gawda@gawda.org • URL: http://www.gawda.org • Formerly National Welding Supply Association.

Resistance Welding Manufacturing Alliance. c/o Keila DeMoraes, 8669 Doral Blvd., Ste. 130, Doral, FL 33166. Phone: (305)443-9353; Email: rwma@aws.org • URL: http://www.aws.org/rwma • Manufacturers, suppliers, and users of resistance welding equipment and supplies. Conducts Resistance Welding School, an annual educational program. Compiles statistics. Offers VHS tape program on basics of resistance welding.

# WELFARE, PUBLIC

*See* PUBLIC WELFARE

# WELLNESS PROGRAMS

*See* EMPLOYEE WELLNESS PROGRAMS

# WHARVES

*See* PORTS

# WHEAT INDUSTRY

*See also* COMMODITY FUTURES TRADING;
FLOUR INDUSTRY; GRAIN INDUSTRY

## ABSTRACTS AND INDEXES

*Wheat, Barley and Triticale Abstracts.* CABI. •
Updated weekly. Published in England by CABI
Publishing. Provides worldwide coverage of the
literature of wheat, barley, and rye.

## ALMANACS AND YEARBOOKS

*CRB Commodity Yearbook.* Commodity Research
Bureau. CRB. • Annual. $179 plus $10.00 shipping
cost. The single most comprehensive source of commodity and futures market information available.

## CD-ROM DATABASES

*OECD Statistical Compendium.* Organization for
Economic Cooperation and Development. •
Semiannual. $1,905.00 per year for 1 to 10 users.
CD-ROM contains more than 730,000 monthly,
quarterly, and annual time series for OECD
countries, 1960 to date. Includes fully searchable
data on agriculture, food, economic indicators,
national accounts, employment, energy, finance,
industry, technology, and foreign trade. Results can
be displayed in various forms.

## INTERNET DATABASES

*Business 2.0 Web Guide to the Best Business Links.*
Business 2.0 Media Inc. Phone: (415)293-4800;
Email: support@business2.com • URL: http://www.
business2.com/webguide • Web site presents an
extensive, searchable directory of links to "the best,
most informative, and authoritative web pages."
Twenty main categories cover business, finance,
career, company information, people, and technology topics, with thousands of subtopics, all linking
to Web sites recommended by experienced business
researchers. Fees: Free.

*Fedstats.* Federal Interagency Council on Statistical
Policy. Phone: (202)395-7254 • URL: http://www.
fedstats.gov • Web site features an efficient search
facility for full-text statistics produced by more than
100 federal agencies, including the Census Bureau,
the Bureau of Economic Analysis, and the Bureau of
Labor Statistics. Boolean searches can be made
within one agency or for all agencies combined.
Links are offered to international statistical bureaus,
including the UN, IMF, OECD, UNESCO, Eurostat,
and 20 individual countries. Fees: Free.

*FreeLunch.com.* Economy.com, Inc. Phone:
(610)696-8700; Fax: (610)696-1678 • URL: http://
www.freelunch.com • Web site provides free access
to more than 200 million economic and financial
data series, covering industry, demographics, labor
markets, prices, retail sales, government spending,
trade, interest rates, housing starts, the stock market,
etc. Data is available in either chart or table form.
Searching is offered. Free, but registration required.
Economy.com, Inc. also offers fee-based economic
analysis at *The Dismal Scientist* site (www.dismal.
com).

*USDA.* U.S. National Institute of Standards and
Technology. 100 Bureau Dr., Gaithersburg, MD
20899-1070. Phone: 800-877-8339 or (301)975-
6478 or (202)720-2791; Fax: (301)975-8295; Email:
inquiries@nist.gov • URL: http://www.nist.gov •
The USDA home page has six sections: News and
Information; What's New; About USDA; Agencies;

Opportunities; Search and Help. Keyword searching
is offered from the USDA home page and from vari-
ous individual agency home pages. Agencies are the
Economic Research Service, Agricultural Marketing
Service, National Agricultural Statistics Service,
National Agricultural Library, and about 12 others.
Updating varies. Fees: Free.

## ONLINE DATABASES

*CAB Abstracts.* CABI. • Contains 46 specialized
abstract collections covering over 10,000 journals
and monographs in the areas of agriculture,
horticulture, forest products, farm products, nutrition, dairy science, poultry, grains, animal health,
entomology, etc. Time period is 1972 to date, with
monthly updates. Inquire as to online cost and
availability. *CAB Abstracts on CD-ROM* also available, with annual updating.

## PERIODICALS AND NEWSLETTERS

*Amber Waves.* Economic Research Service Hazard
Analysis and Critical Control Points. • Quarterly.
Replaces *Agricultural Outlook; Food Review;* and
*Rural America.* Provides research and analysis from
the U.S. Department of Agriculture's Economic
Research Service. Includes economic data on
agriculture, food, trade, and environmental factors.

*Oregon Wheat.* Oregon Wheat Growers League. •
Bi-monthly. Free to members; non-members, $15.00
per year. Deals with planting, weeds, and disease
warnings, storage and marketing of wheat and
barley. Specifically for Oregon growers.

*Western Farmer-Stockman.* Farm Progress
Companies Inc. • Monthly. $26.95 Individuals
1-year subscription. Formerly *Montana Farmer.*

## PRICE SOURCES

*Nebraska Farmer.* Farm Progress Companies Inc. •
$26.95 Individuals.

## STATISTICS SOURCES

*Agricultural Statistics.* U.S. Department of
Agriculture National Agricultural Statistics Service.
• Annual. $46 Individuals. Provides a wide variety
of statistical data relating to agricultural production,
supplies, consumption, prices/price-supports,
foreign trade, costs, and returns, as well as farm
labor, loans, income, and population. In many cases,
historical data is shown annually for 10 years. In addition to farm data, includes detailed fishery
statistics.

*Statistical Annual: Grains, Options on Agricultural
Futures.* Chicago Board of Trade. • Annual. Includes
historical data on Wheat Futures, Options on Wheat
Futures, Corn Futures, Options on Corn Futures,
Oats Futures, Soybean Futures, Options on Soybean
Futures, Soybean Oil Futures, Soybean Meal
Futures.

*Survey of Current Business.* U. S. Government Printing Office. • Published by Bureau of Economic
Analysis, U. S. Department of Commerce. Presents
a wide variety of business and economic data.

## TRADE/PROFESSIONAL ASSOCIATIONS

National Association of Wheat Growers. 415 2nd St.
NE, Ste. 300, Washington, DC 20002. Phone:
(202)547-7800; Email: wheatworld@wheatworld.
org • URL: http://www.wheatworld.org • Federation
of 19 state wheat growers associations. Represents
wheat grower interest in educational, legislative, and
regulatory projects and issues for wheat farmers in
Washington, DC. Sponsors research and transportation, and leadership conferences; conducts seminars.
Conducts charitable programs.

North American Millers' Association. 600 Maryland
Ave. SW, Ste. 825 W, Washington, DC 20024.
Phone: (202)484-2200 or (202)554-1618; Fax:
(202)488-7416; Email: generalinfo@namamillers.
org • URL: http://www.namamillers.org • Grain
milling companies that are processors of specially
blended corn, wheat, and sorghum foods that are

used primarily for overseas feeding programs. Millers of wheat, corn, oats, durum, and rye flour;
members' mill 95 percent of total United States
capacity.

# WHISKEY INDUSTRY

*See* DISTILLING INDUSTRY

# WHOLESALE TRADE

*See also* DISTRIBUTION; RACK JOBBERS

## CD-ROM DATABASES

*OECD Statistical Compendium.* Organization for
Economic Cooperation and Development. •
Semiannual. $1,905.00 per year for 1 to 10 users.
CD-ROM contains more than 730,000 monthly,
quarterly, and annual time series for OECD
countries, 1960 to date. Includes fully searchable
data on agriculture, food, economic indicators,
national accounts, employment, energy, finance,
industry, technology, and foreign trade. Results can
be displayed in various forms.

## DIRECTORIES

*Accounting and Bookkeeping Systems (Wholesale)
Directory.* InfoGroup Inc. • Annual. Number of listings: 547. Entries include: Name, address, phone,
size of advertisement, name of owner or manager,
number of employees, year first in "Yellow Pages."
Compiled from telephone company "Yellow Pages,"
nationwide.

*American Big Businesses Directory.* InfoGroup Inc.
• Annual. $295. Covers: 218,000 U.S. businesses
with more than 100 employees, and 500,000 key
executives and directors. CD-ROM version contains
160,000 top firms and 431,000 key executives.
Entries include: Name, address, phone, names and
titles of key personnel, number of employees, sales
volume, Standard Industrial Classification (SIC)
codes, subsidiaries and parent company names,
stock exchanges on which traded.

*American Book Trade Directory (ABD).* Information
Today, Inc. • Annual. $379.50 Individuals
softbound. Covers: Nearly 20,000 retail and
antiquarian book dealers, plus 1,200 book and
magazine wholesalers, distributors, and jobbers-in
all 50 states and U.S. territories. Also included are
sections of auctioneers of literary property,
exporters/importers, booktrade associations, foreign
language book dealers, book and literary appraisers,
and rental library chains. Entries include: Bookstore
name, address, phone, owner or manager, types and
subjects of books stocked, specialty, sidelines, year
established, SAN (Standard Address Number),
number of volumes stocked, square footage.

*American Manufacturers Directory.* InfoGroup Inc.
• Annual. $295. Covers: more than 150,000
manufacturing companies with 20 or more
employees. CD-ROM version lists all 531,000 U.S.
manufacturers, in all employee size ranges. Entries
include: Company name, address, phone, contact
name, Standard Industrial Classification (SIC)
codes, number of employees, sales volume code,
credit rating scores.

*American Wholesalers and Distributors Directory.*
Cengage Learning Inc. • Annual. $450 Individuals
print. Lists more than 27,000 national, regional,
state, and local wholesalesrs.

*Business Forms & Systems (Wholesale) Directory.*
InfoGroup Inc. • Annual. Number of listings: 7,565.
Entries include: Company name, address, phone
(including area code), size of advertisement, year
first in "Yellow Pages," name of owner or manager,
number of employees. Compiled from telephone
company "Yellow Pages," nationwide.

*Cash Registers and Supplies-Wholesale Directory.*

InfoGroup Inc. • Annual. Number of listings: 2,539. Entries include: Name, address, phone (including area code), size of advertisement, year first in "Yellow Pages," name of owner or manager, number of employees. Compiled from telephone company "Yellow Pages," nationwide.

*Clothes & Accessories (Women) Wholesale Directory.* InfoGroup Inc. • Annual. Number of listings: 4,468. Entries include: Name, address, phone, size of advertisement, name of owner or manager, number of employees, year first in "Yellow Pages." Compiled from telephone company "Yellow Pages," nationwide.

*Colombian Exportable Offer.* The Export Promotion Fund, Proexpo. • Covers: Manufacturers, distributors, and wholesalers in Colombia. Entries include: Contact information.

*Dictating Machines & Supplies Wholesale Directory.* InfoGroup Inc. • Updated continuously; printed on request. Number of listings: 585. Entries include: Name, address, phone, size of advertisement, name of owner or manager, number of employees, year first in "Yellow Pages." Compiled from telephone company "Yellow Pages," nationwide.

*Directory of California Wholesalers and Service Companies.* Harris InfoSource. • Annual. $210 Individuals hardcover. Covers: Approximately 225,200 wholesalers, distributors, and other service firms in California. Includes key executives. Database includes: Statistical data, trade show calendar. Entries include: Company name, address, parent name/location, telephone, fax and 800 numbers, web site address (on CD-ROM only), number of employees, year established, annual revenue, plant size, business description, Standard Industrial Classification (SIC) code, executive names/titles, public ownership, legal structure, import/export designators, and female/minority ownership.

*Directory of Wholesale Grocers.* Chain Store Guide. • Annual. $327.00. Online edition, $747.00. Profiles over 1,100 cooperatives, voluntaries, non-sponsoring wholesalers, cash and carry warehouses, and nearly 220 service merchandisers. Covers United States and Canada.

*Directory of Wholesale Printing & Office Supplies Sources.* Gordon Press Publishers. • Irregular. $260.95.

*Duplicating Machines & Supplies-Wholesalers Directory.* InfoGroup Inc. • Updated continuously; printed on request. Number of listings: 560. Entries include: Name, address, phone (including area code), size of advertisement, year first in "Yellow Pages," name or owner or manager, number of employees. Compiled from telephone company "Yellow Pages," nationwide.

*General Merchandise--Wholesale Directory.* Info-Group Inc. • Annual. Number of listings: 1,045. Entries include: Name, address, phone, size of advertisement, name of owner or manager, number of employees, year first in "Yellow Pages." Compiled from telephone company "Yellow Pages," nationwide.

*Grocery Headquarters: The Newspaper for the Food Industry.* Trend Publishing Inc. • Monthly. $80. Covers the sale and distribution of food products and other items sold in supermarkets and grocery stores. Edited mainly for retailers and wholesalers. Incorporates (Grocery Distribution).

*Illinois Services Directory.* Manufacturers' News Inc. • Annual. $209 Individuals Print (Hardcover); plus Shipping and Handling. Covers: Over 26,548 wholesalers, jobbers, contractors, retailers, services, and 76,898 executives in Illinois. Entries include: Company name, address, phone; names, titles, and functions of key personnel; year established, number of employees, office square footage, services,

Standard Industrial Classification (SIC) code, net worth, parent company and subsidiary company information, type of in-house computer system, email address, fax, web address.

*Juke Boxes Wholesalers Directory.* InfoGroup Inc. • Annual. Number of listings: 1,002. Entries include: Name, address, phone, size of advertisement, name of owner or manager, number of employees, year first in "Yellow Pages." Compiled from telephone company "Yellow Pages," nationwide.

*The Wholesaler--Directory of Manufacturers Representatives Issue.* TMB Publishing Inc. • Annual. $50 Individuals hardcopy or CD-ROM. Publication includes: 2,000 manufacturers' representatives handling plumbing, heating, piping, air conditioning, and refrigeration products. Entries include: Representative's name or firm name, address, phone, fax, territory, and lines carried.

*The Wholesaler--'The Wholesaling 100' Issue.* TMB Publishing Inc. • Annual. $50 Individuals print or CD-ROM. Publication includes: Ranks 100 leading wholesalers of plumbing, heating, air conditioning, refrigeration equipment, and industrial pipe, valves and fittings. Entries include: Company name, address, phone, fax, names and titles of key personnel, number of employees, business breakdown (percentage).

## E-BOOKS

*Encyclopedia of American Industries.* Cengage Learning Inc. • 2011. $807.00. 6th edition. Three volumes. Volume one is Manufacturing Industries and volume two is Service and Non-Manufacturing Industries. Provides the history, development, and recent status of approximately 1,000 industries. Includes statistical graphs, with industry and general indexes. Also available as eBook.

## INTERNET DATABASES

*Bureau of Economic Analysis.* U. S. Department of Commerce, Bureau of Economic Analysis. Phone: (202)606-9900; Fax: (202)606-5310; Email: webmaster@bea.doc.gov • URL: http://www.bea.doc.gov • Web site includes "News Release Information" covering national, regional, and international economic estimates from the BEA. Highlights of releases appear online the same day, complete text and tables appear the next day. "Recent News Releases" section provides titles for past nine months, with links. "BEA Data and Methodology" includes "Frequently Requested NIPA Data" (national income and product accounts, such as gross domestic product and personal income). Other statistics are available. Fees: Free.

*Business 2.0 Web Guide to the Best Business Links.* Business 2.0 Media Inc. Phone: (415)293-4800; Email: support@business2.com • URL: http://www.business2.com/webguide • Web site presents an extensive, searchable directory of links to "the best, most informative, and authoritative web pages." Twenty main categories cover business, finance, career, company information, people, and technology topics, with thousands of subtopics, all linking to Web sites recommended by experienced business researchers. Fees: Free.

*Fedstats.* Federal Interagency Council on Statistical Policy. Phone: (202)395-7254 • URL: http://www.fedstats.gov • Web site features an efficient search facility for full-text statistics produced by more than 100 federal agencies, including the Census Bureau, the Bureau of Economic Analysis, and the Bureau of Labor Statistics. Boolean searches can be made within one agency or for all agencies combined. Links are offered to international statistical bureaus, including the UN, IMF, OECD, UNESCO, Eurostat, and 20 individual countries. Fees: Free.

*FreeLunch.com.* Economy.com, Inc. Phone: (610)696-8700; Fax: (610)696-1678 • URL: http://www.freelunch.com • Web site provides free access to more than 200 million economic and financial

data series, covering industry, demographics, labor markets, prices, retail sales, government spending, trade, interest rates, housing starts, the stock market, etc. Data is available in either chart or table form. Searching is offered. Free, but registration required. Economy.com, Inc. also offers fee-based economic analysis at *The Dismal Scientist* site (www.dismal.com).

## ONLINE DATABASES

*American Business Directory.* InfoGroup Inc. • Provides brief online information on more than 10 million U. S. companies, including individual plants and branches. Entries typically include address, phone number, industry classification code, and contact name. Updating is quarterly. Inquire as to online cost and availability.

*Battery Product Businesses in the World.* Momentum Technologies L.L.C. • Contains directory listings for approximately 600 wholesale suppliers of batteries and related products from around the world. Includes business name, address, phone number, fax number, e-mail address, and web site address. Includes brief descriptions of product lines, services offered, and business type. Covers suppliers of deep cycle batteries, lithium ion batteries, nickel cadmium batteries, sealed lead acid batteries, and more. Offers information on battery supplies in industries such as renewable energy, electric vehicles, marine transportation, telecommunications, and portable computers. Provides keyword search functions.

## OTHER SOURCES

*Product Distribution Law Guide.* Wolters Kluwer Law & Business CCH. • $199.00. Looseleaf service. Annual updates available. Covers the legal aspects of various methods of product distribution, including franchising.

## PRICE SOURCES

*PPI Detailed Report.* Periodical covering business. Bureau of Labor Statistics, U.S. Department of Labor. U. S. Government Printing Office. • Monthly. $55 Individuals.

## STATISTICS SOURCES

*Manufacturing & Distribution USA.* Cengage Learning Inc. • Biennial. $631 Individuals three-volume set. 2012. 7th edition. eBook. Three volumes. Presents statistics and projections relating to economic activity in more than 600 business classifications.

*Survey of Current Business.* U. S. Government Printing Office. • Published by Bureau of Economic Analysis, U. S. Department of Commerce. Presents a wide variety of business and economic data.

*United States Census of Wholesale Trade.* Bureau of the Census, U.S. Department of Commerce. U. S. Government Printing Office. • Quinquennial.

## TRADE/PROFESSIONAL ASSOCIATIONS

National Association of Wholesaler-Distributors. 1325 G St. NW, Ste. 1000, Washington, DC 20005. Phone: (202)872-0885; Fax: (202)785-0586; Email: naw@naw.org • URL: http://www.naw.org • Formerly National Association of Wholesalers.

# WILLS

*See also* ESTATE PLANNING

## CD-ROM DATABASES

*Authority Tax and Estate Planning Library.* Matthew Bender and Company Inc. • Periodic revisions. Price on request. CD contains updated full text of *Bender's Payroll Tax Guide, Depreciation Handbook, Federal Income Taxation of Corporations, Tax Planning for Corporations, Modern Estate Planning, Planning for Large Estates, Murphy's Will Clauses, Tax & Estate Planning for the*

*Elderly*, and 12 other Matthew Bender publications. The Internal Revenue Code is also included.

## HANDBOOKS AND MANUALS

*Murphy's Will Clauses: Annotations and Forms with Tax Effects*. Matthew Bender and Company Inc. • Semiannual. $2,071 book. Five looseleaf volumes. Over 1,400 framed will and trust clauses.

## TRADE/PROFESSIONAL ASSOCIATIONS

American College of Trust and Estate Counsel. 901 15th St. NW, Ste. 525, Washington, DC 20005-2348. Phone: (202)684-8460; Fax: (202)684-8459; Email: info@actec.org • URL: http://www.actec.org • Represents attorneys specializing in probate law. Sends delegates to American Bar Association's Real Property, Probate, and Trust Law Section; maintains liaison with other organizations involved in probate law. Operates ACTEC Foundation, which makes available grants.

# WIND ENERGY

*See* COGENERATION OF ENERGY

# WINDOW COVERING INDUSTRY

*See also* INTERIOR DECORATION

## ABSTRACTS AND INDEXES

*Art Index*. EBSCO Publishing Inc. • Quarterly. Annual cumulations. Price varies. Subject and author index to periodicals in art, architecture, industrial design, city planning, photography, and various related topics.

## CD-ROM DATABASES

*Art Index*. EBSCO Publishing Inc. • Indexing for over 600 periodicals and 13,000 art dissertations.

## DIRECTORIES

*Draperies and Window Coverings: Directory and Buyer's Guide*. L.C. Clark Publishing Company Inc. • Annual. $15.00. Includes about 2,000 manufacturers and distributors of window coverings and related products.

*Draperies & Window Coverings--Directory & Buyer's Guide Issue: 2005*. L.C. Clark Publishing Company Inc. • Annual. Publication includes: List of about 2,000 manufacturers and distributors of window coverings and other products used in the window coverings and interior fashions industry. Entries include: Company name, address, phone, key executives, brand names carried.

*Window Fashions Magazine: Design and Education Magazine*. Grace McNamara Publishing, Inc. • Monthly. $39.00 per year. A directory of suppliers, manufacturers, and fabricators of vertical blinds, soft shades, curtains, draperies, and other window treatment items. Appears as a regular feature of *Window Fashions Magazine* and covers a different product category each month.

## FINANCIAL RATIOS

*Annual Statement Studies*. Risk Management Association. • Annual. Compiled from over 280,000 financial statements.

*Annual Statement Studies: Industry Default Probabilities and Cash Flow Measures*. Risk Management Association. • Annual. $405 Nonmembers. Serves as a companion volume to the original *Annual Statement Studies*. Gives probability of default estimates on a percentage scale for more than 450 industries. Includes changes in position year-by-year for eight financial statement line items and provides percentage measures of cash flow.

## ONLINE DATABASES

*Art Index Online*. H.W. Wilson Co. • Indexes a wide variety of art-related periodicals, 1984 to date.

Monthly updates. Inquire as to online cost and availability.

*Avery Architectural Periodicals Index*. Columbia University Avery Architectural and Fine Arts Library. • Indexes a wide range of periodicals related to architecture and design. Subjects include building design, building materials, interior design, housing, land use, and city planning. Time span: 1977 to date. *bul* URL: www.rlg.stanford.edu/cit-ave.html.

## PERIODICALS AND NEWSLETTERS

*Draperies and Window Coverings*. L.C. Clark Publishing Company Inc. • 13 times a year. $33.00 per year. Published for retailers, designers, manufacturers, and distributors of window coverings.

## RESEARCH CENTERS AND INSTITUTES

Interior Design Laboratory. Lambuth University, 101 Wilder Tower, Memphis, TN 38152-3520. Phone: 800-669-2679 • URL: http://www.memphis.edu/lambuth.

# WINDOW DISPLAYS

*See* DISPLAY OF MERCHANDISE

# WINDOWS (SOFTWARE)

*See also* COMPUTER SOFTWARE INDUSTRY

## ABSTRACTS AND INDEXES

*Computer and Information Systems Abstracts Journal: An Abstract Journal Pertaining to the Theory, Design, Fabrication and Application of Computer and Information Systems*. CSA. • Monthly. $1,750 per year.

*Computer Science Index*. EBSCO Publishing Inc. • Quarterly. $245 per year. Contains brief abstracts of book and periodical literature covering all phases of computing, including approximately 70 specific application areas.

*Internet and Personal Computing Abstracts (print edition)*. EBSCO Publishing Inc. • Quarterly. $269.00 per year, including cumulative index. Provides more than 10,000 abstracts annually from both trade and academic publications. Covers computer hardware, software, product reviews, Web topics, e-commerce, networks, corporate news, security, and related topics. Formerly *Microcomputer Abstracts*.

## HANDBOOKS AND MANUALS

*Windows NT Server Concise*. Jerry Dixon and J. Scott Reeves. New Riders Publishing. • Date not set. $19.99.

## INTERNET DATABASES

*InfoTech Trends*. Data Analysis Group. Phone: (925)462-1202; Fax: (925)462-1225; Email: support@infotechtrends.com • URL: http://www.infotechtrends.com • Web site provides both free and fee-based market research data on the information technology industry, including computers, peripherals, telecommunications, the Internet, software, CD-ROM/DVD, e-commerce, and workstations. Fees: Free for current (most recent year) data; more extensive information has various fee structures. Formerly *Computer Industry Forecasts*.

## ONLINE DATABASES

*Computer Database*. Cengage Learning Inc. • Provides one year of full-text online for 150 leading computer-related publications. Also includes 70,000 product specifications and brief profiles of 13,000 computer product vendors and manufacturers. Inquire as to prices and availability.

## PERIODICALS AND NEWSLETTERS

*Exploring Windows NT for Professionals*. Skillsoft Ireland Ltd. • Monthly. $139.00 per year. Newsletter on the Windows operating system for networks. Formerly *Exploring Windows NT*.

*MSDN Magazine*. UBM L.L.C. • Monthly. $25 U.S. 1-year subscription (online). Produced for professional software developers using Windows, MS-DOS, Visual Basic, and other Microsoft Corporation products. Incorporates *Microsoft Internet Developer*.

*Windows in Financial Services*. • Quarterly. $39.00 per year. Covers information technology applications and products for Microsoft Windows users in the financial sector.

# WINE INDUSTRY

*See also* DISTILLING INDUSTRY

## ALMANACS AND YEARBOOKS

*The U.S. Wine Market: Impact Databank Review and Forecast*. M. Shanken Communications Inc. • Annual. $845.00. Includes industry commentary and statistics.

## CD-ROM DATABASES

*OECD Statistical Compendium*. Organization for Economic Cooperation and Development. • Semiannual. $1,905.00 per year for 1 to 10 users. CD-ROM contains more than 730,000 monthly, quarterly, and annual time series for OECD countries, 1960 to date. Includes fully searchable data on agriculture, food, economic indicators, national accounts, employment, energy, finance, industry, technology, and foreign trade. Results can be displayed in various forms.

## DIRECTORIES

*Beverage Marketing Directory*. Beverage Marketing Corp. • Annual. $995 Individuals print. Covers: Over 25,500 beer wholesalers, wine and spirits wholesalers, soft drink bottlers and franchisors, breweries, wineries, distilleries, alcoholic beverage importers, bottled water companies; and trade associations, government agencies, micro breweries, juice, coffee, tea, milk companies, and others concerned with the beverage and bottling industries; coverage includes Canada. Entries include: Beverage and bottling company listings contain company name, address, phone, names of key executives, number of employees, brand names, and other information, including number of franchisees, number of delivery trucks, sales volume. Suppliers and related companies and organizations listings include similar but less detailed information.

*Major Food and Drink Companies of the World*. Cengage Learning Inc. • 12th edition. eBook. Published by Graham & Whiteside. Contains profiles and trade names for more than 9,200 important food and beverage companies in various countries. In addition to foods, includes both alcoholic and nonalcoholic drink products.

*Wines and Vines: Annual Directory/Buyer's Guide*. Wines & Vines. • Annual. $95.00. List of wineries and wine bottlers in the United States, Canada, and Mexico; also lists industry suppliers.

## FINANCIAL RATIOS

*Annual Statement Studies*. Risk Management Association. • Annual. Compiled from over 280,000 financial statements.

*Annual Statement Studies: Industry Default Probabilities and Cash Flow Measures*. Risk Management Association. • Annual. $405 Nonmembers. Serves as a companion volume to the original *Annual Statement Studies*. Gives probability of default estimates on a percentage scale for more than 450 industries. Includes changes in position year-by-year for eight financial statement line items and provides percentage measures of cash flow.

## INTERNET DATABASES

*Business 2.0 Web Guide to the Best Business Links.* Business 2.0 Media Inc. Phone: (415)293-4800; Email: support@business2.com • URL: http://www.business2.com/webguide • Web site presents an extensive, searchable directory of links to "the best, most informative, and authoritative web pages." Twenty main categories cover business, finance, career, company information, people, and technology topics, with thousands of subtopics, all linking to Web sites recommended by experienced business researchers. Fees: Free.

*Fedstats.* Federal Interagency Council on Statistical Policy. Phone: (202)395-7254 • URL: http://www.fedstats.gov • Web site features an efficient search facility for full-text statistics produced by more than 100 federal agencies, including the Census Bureau, the Bureau of Economic Analysis, and the Bureau of Labor Statistics. Boolean searches can be made within one agency or for all agencies combined. Links are offered to international statistical bureaus, including the UN, IMF, OECD, UNESCO, Eurostat, and 20 individual countries. Fees: Free.

*FreeLunch.com.* Economy.com, Inc. Phone: (610)696-8700; Fax: (610)696-1678 • URL: http://www.freelunch.com • Web site provides free access to more than 200 million economic and financial data series, covering industry, demographics, labor markets, prices, retail sales, government spending, trade, interest rates, housing starts, the stock market, etc. Data is available in either chart or table form. Searching is offered. Free, but registration required. Economy.com, Inc. also offers fee-based economic analysis at *The Dismal Scientist* site (www.dismal.com).

## OTHER SOURCES

*Liquor Control Law Reporter.* Wolters Kluwer Law & Business CCH. • Biweekly. Federal and state regulation and taxation of alcoholic beverages.

## PERIODICALS AND NEWSLETTERS

*Fancy Food and Culinary Products.* Talcott Communications Corp. • Monthly. $34.00 per year. Emphasizes new specialty food products and the business management aspects of the specialty food and confection industries. Includes special issues on wine, cheese, candy, "upscale" cookware, and gifts. Formerly (Fancy Foods).

*Impact: U.S. News and Research for the Wine, Spirits, and Beer Industries.* M. Shanken Communications Inc. • Semimonthly. $375.00 per year. Newsletter covering the marketing, economic, and financial aspects of alcoholic beverages.

*International Journal of Wine Business Research.* Emerald Group Publishing Ltd. • Daily. Journal dedicated to the academic field of wine business, particularly management and marketing. Includes applications of marketing principles to wine and spirit products, the place of viticulture in local economies, especially its relationship with tourism, case studies on wine brands, ethical issues in marketing of alcoholic beverages, structure of brand ownership, and marketing through retail outlets, hotel and catering outlets.

*Wine Business Monthly: The Industry's Leading Publication for Wineries and Growers.* New World Wine Communications Inc. • Monthly. $39 Individuals. Trade magazine for the wine industry.

*Wine Enthusiast.* • 13 times a year. $29.95 per year. Covers domestic and world wine. Formerly *Wine Times.*

## PRICE SOURCES

*Beverage Media.* Beverage Network. Beverage Media Group. • Monthly. $78 Individuals. Wholesale prices.

*Consumers Guide to Varietal Wines.* Wine Appreciation Guild. • Annual. $45.00.

## STATISTICS SOURCES

*Survey of Current Business.* U. S. Government Printing Office. • Published by Bureau of Economic Analysis, U. S. Department of Commerce. Presents a wide variety of business and economic data.

## TRADE/PROFESSIONAL ASSOCIATIONS

American Society for Enology and Viticulture. PO Box 1855, Davis, CA 95617-1855. Phone: (530)753-3142; Fax: (530)753-3318; Email: society@asev.org • URL: http://asev.org • Persons concerned with the management and technical aspects of the wine and grape industry including owners, technicians, academic personnel, and farm advisors. Promotes technical advancement in enology and viticulture through integrated research by science and industry; provides a medium for the free exchange of technical information and information on problems of interest to the wine and grape industries.

American Wine Society. PO Box 279, Englewood, OH 45322. Phone: 888-297-9070 or (937)529-7800; Fax: (937)529-7888; Email: executivedirector@americanwinesociety.org • URL: http://www.americanwinesociety.org • Represents amateur and professional winemakers, wine enthusiasts, wine merchants, and anyone who enjoys wine and wants to learn more about it. Seeks to further the knowledge, appreciation and enjoyment of wine. Sponsors educational programs. Conducts wine tastings and trips to vineyards and wineries.

International Organisation of Vine and Wine. 18 Rue d'Aguesseau, F-75008 Paris, France. Phone: 33 1 44948080; Fax: 33 1 42669063; Email: contact@oiv.int • URL: http://www.oiv.int • Representatives of governments of vine-growing consumers and countries. Addresses scientific, technical, economic, and legal issues concerning viticulture and vine-derived products such as wine, grape juice, table grapes, and raisins. Determines standards regarding vine products and advises member governments on accepted norms. Works to create international research programs and to encourage information exchange among scholars and research institutions. Conducts technological research with a view toward rationalizing the production process and reducing production costs; compiles statistics. Strives to develop a general viticultural policy based on the resources and specific needs of members. Cooperates with the Food and Agriculture Organization of the United Nations and other international groups. Offers courses on marketing and management of wine and spirits and on viticulture and enology in hot climates.

Sweet and Fortified Wine Association. PO Box 193, Applegate, CA 95703. Phone: (916)258-7115; Email: sweetandfortified@sbcglobal.net • URL: http://sweetandfortifiedwine.org • Aims to expand and develop the market for sweet and fortified wines. Provides a forum for industry partners and the general public to share ideas and information on sweet and fortified wines. Advocates for responsible consumption of alcoholic beverages.

# WIRE INDUSTRY

## CD-ROM DATABASES

*OECD Statistical Compendium.* Organization for Economic Cooperation and Development. • Semiannual. $1,905.00 per year for 1 to 10 users. CD-ROM contains more than 730,000 monthly, quarterly, and annual time series for OECD countries, 1960 to date. Includes fully searchable data on agriculture, food, economic indicators, national accounts, employment, energy, finance, industry, technology, and foreign trade. Results can be displayed in various forms.

## DIRECTORIES

*Directory of American Manufacturers & Exporters of Wire, Chain & Wire Products.* EXIM Infotek Private Ltd. • $5 Individuals. Covers: 20 American manufacturers and exporters of cables-mechanical, silver wire, steel wire rope, and wires. Entries include: Company name, postal address, city, country, phone, fax, e-mail and websites, contact person, designation, and product details.

*Directory of American Manufacturers & Exporters of Wires & Cables--Electrical.* EXIM Infotek Private Ltd. • Covers: 280 American manufacturers and exporters of assemblies coaxial cables, bonding and grounding cables, booster cables, cable accessories, cable assemblies, coaxial cable, electrical cables, electronic cables, fiber optic cables, triaxial cables, twisted pair cables, conduits electrical cables, copper cable, electric cables, electrical wire, high temperature wire and cables, high temperature wires, magnet insulated wires, public utility electrical cables, PVC coaxial cables, retractile cables, teflon cables, teflon insulated wires, high voltage wire, insulated wire, and wire-plastic coated. Entries include: Company name, postal address, telephone, fax, e-mail, website, contact person, designation, and product details.

*Directory of Asian Importers of Wires & Cables--Electrical.* EXIM Infotek Private Ltd. • Covers: 190 Asian importers of cables, cables and accessories, copper winding wires, copper wires, electric cables, electrical cable, electrical wires, enameled copper wires, instrumentation cables, power cables, power cords, speaker AV cable, thermocouple wire, and wiring accessories. Entries include: Company name, postal address, telephone, fax, e-mail, website, contact person, designation, and product details.

*Directory of Chinese Manufacturers & Exporters of Wire, Chain & Wire Products.* EXIM Infotek Private Ltd. • $10 Individuals. Covers: 90 Chinese manufacturers & exporters of anchors, barbed wire, brass wire mesh, chains, copper wires, galvanized iron wires, hexagonal wire mesh, hexagonal wire netting, iron wire, mesh products, metal wire mesh, metal wires, pet chains, roller chains, steel wire, welded wire mesh, wire, wire harness, wire mesh, wire netting, wire products, wire rack & accessories, wire rope, wire rope clips. Entries include: Company name, postal address, city, country, phone, fax, e-mail & websites, contact person, designation, products detail.

*Directory of European Importers of Wires & Cables--Electrical.* EXIM Infotek Private Ltd. • Covers: 170 European importers of wires and cables. Entries include: Company name, postal address, telephone, fax, e-mail, website, contact person, designation, and product details.

*Directory of Indian Importers of Wires & Cables--Electrical.* EXIM Infotek Private Ltd. • Covers: 40 Indian importers of cables, copper wires, power cords, thermocouple wire, and wires and cables. Entries include: Company name, postal address, telephone, fax, e-mail, website, contact person, designation, and product details.

*Directory of Japanese Manufacturers & Exporters of Wire, Chain & Wire Products.* EXIM Infotek Private Ltd. • $5 Individuals. Covers: 40 Japanese manufacturers and exporters of chain and chain block, chains, steel wire, wire, wire netting, and wire products. Entries include: Company name, postal address, city, country, phone, fax, e-mail and websites, contact person, designation, and product details.

*Directory of Japanese Manufacturers & Exporters of Wires & Cables--Electrical.* EXIM Infotek Private Ltd. • $200 Individuals. Covers: 50 Japanese manufacturers and exporters of arc welding machinery and equipment, electrodes, resistance welding machines, used welder, welding machinery, and welding rods. Entries include: Company name, postal address, telephone, fax, e-mail, website, contact person, designation, and product details.

*Directory of Middle East Importers of Wires & Cables--Electrical.* EXIM Infotek Private Ltd. • Covers: 180 Middle East importers of cable equipment, cables, copper cable and accessories, copper wire, electrical cables, electrical wires, and power cables. Entries include: Company name, postal address, telephone, fax, e-mail, website, contact person, designation, and product details.

*Directory of North American Importers of Wires & Cables--Electrical.* EXIM Infotek Private Ltd. • $200 Individuals. Covers: 60 American and Canadian importers for wires, cables, electrical cables, electrical wires, extension cords, and combination wires. Entries include: Company name, postal address, telephone, fax, e-mail, website, contact person, designation, and product details.

*Directory of SAARC Importers of Wire & Cables--Electrical.* EXIM Infotek Private Ltd. • Covers: 25 companies in member countries of the South Asian Association for Regional Cooperation (SAARC) that import armored cables, armored jelly filled cables, bare wires, cables and accessories, coaxial cables, copper winding wires, copper wires, enamel and cotton insulated winding wires, enameled copper wires, instrumentation cables, internal cables, non-armored SF cables, overhead cables, plastic coated wire products, power cables, PVC flexible flat cables, PVC insulated automobile cables and battery cables, and wiring accessories. Entries include: Company name, postal address, telephone, fax, e-mail, website, contact person, designation, and product details.

*Directory of South Korean Manufacturers & Exporters of Wire, Chain & Wire Products.* EXIM Infotek Private Ltd. • $15 Individuals. Covers: 140 South Korean manufacturers and exporters of chains/chain slings/grips-metal, chain-tire, ferrous wires, fine bare-copper wire, metal cables/cords/ropes, metal fencing and barbed wire, metal gauze/cloth/netting, wire goods-metal. Entries include: Company name, postal address, city, country, phone, fax, e-mail and websites, contact person, designation, and product details.

*Directory of South Korean Manufacturers & Exporters of Wires & Cables--Electrical.* EXIM Infotek Private Ltd. • $300 Individuals. Covers: 120 South Korean manufacturers and exporters of cable-battery, cable-control, cable-high tension, cables, electric wires/cables-non insulated, lead wires, power cable, power wires/cables-insulated, power-line cable and wire fittings, phone wires, wires and cables for electronics, and telecom wires and cables. Entries include: Company name, postal address, telephone, fax, e-mail, website, contact person, designation, and product details.

*Directory of Taiwanese Manufacturers & Exporters of Wire, Chain & Wire Products.* EXIM Infotek Private Ltd. • $20 Individuals. Covers: 260 Taiwanese manufacturers and exporters of chains, chains/chain slings/grips-metal, ferrous wires, fine bare-copper wire, galvanized steel wire rope, metal cables/cords/ropes, metal fencing and barbed wire, metal gauze/cloth/netting, stainless steel wire rope, steel wire-zinc coated strands, wire goods-metal, wire products, wire racks and accessories. Entries include: Company name, postal address, city, country, phone, fax, e-mail and websites, contact person, designation, and product details.

*Dun's Industrial Guide: The Metalworking Directory.* Dun & Bradstreet Inc. • Annual. Libraries, $485; commercial institutions, $795.00. Lease basis. Three volumes. Lists about 65,000 U. S. manufacturing plants using metal and suppliers of metalworking equipment and materials. Includes names and titles of key personnel. Products, purchases, and processes are indicated.

*Wire & Cable Technology Buyer's Guide.* Initial

Publications Inc. • Annual. $50. Lists 2,300 companies by over 1,200 product categories.

*Wire Journal International Reference Guide.* Wire Journal Inc. • Annual. $140 Nonmembers. Covers: Manufacturers and suppliers of steel and nonferrous rods, strip, wire, wire products, electrical wire and cable, fiber optics, and machinery and equipment to the industry (SIC 33). Entries include: Company name, address, phone, fax, e-mail and website addresses, year established, number of employees, names of executives, trade and brand names, product indices and geographical cross reference.

## FINANCIAL RATIOS

*Annual Statement Studies.* Risk Management Association. • Annual. Compiled from over 280,000 financial statements.

*Annual Statement Studies: Industry Default Probabilities and Cash Flow Measures.* Risk Management Association. • Annual. $405 Nonmembers. Serves as a companion volume to the original *Annual Statement Studies.* Gives probability of default estimates on a percentage scale for more than 450 industries. Includes changes in position year-by-year for eight financial statement line items and provides percentage measures of cash flow.

## INTERNET DATABASES

*Business 2.0 Web Guide to the Best Business Links.* Business 2.0 Media Inc. Phone: (415)293-4800; Email: support@business2.com • URL: http://www.business2.com/webguide • Web site presents an extensive, searchable directory of links to "the best, most informative, and authoritative web pages." Twenty main categories cover business, finance, career, company information, people, and technology topics, with thousands of subtopics, all linking to Web sites recommended by experienced business researchers. Fees: Free.

*Fedstats.* Federal Interagency Council on Statistical Policy. Phone: (202)395-7254 • URL: http://www.fedstats.gov • Web site features an efficient search facility for full-text statistics produced by more than 100 federal agencies, including the Census Bureau, the Bureau of Economic Analysis, and the Bureau of Labor Statistics. Boolean searches can be made within one agency or for all agencies combined. Links are offered to international statistical bureaus, including the UN, IMF, OECD, UNESCO, Eurostat, and 20 individual countries. Fees: Free.

*FreeLunch.com.* Economy.com, Inc. Phone: (610)696-8700; Fax: (610)696-1678 • URL: http://www.freelunch.com • Web site provides free access to more than 200 million economic and financial data series, covering industry, demographics, labor markets, prices, retail sales, government spending, trade, interest rates, housing starts, the stock market, etc. Data is available in either chart or table form. Searching is offered. Free, but registration required. Economy.com, Inc. also offers fee-based economic analysis at *The Dismal Scientist* site (www.dismal.com).

*Manufacturing Profiles.* U. S. Bureau of the Census. Phone: (301)763-4636 or (301)763-4100; Fax: (301)763-4794; Email: webmaster@census.gov • URL: http://www.census.gov/prod/www/abs/mfg-prof.html • The Census Bureau makes available free on PDF (Portable Document Format) an annual consolidation of the entire Current Industrial Report series, presenting "all the data compiled." Contains statistics on production, shipments, inventories, consumption, exports, imports, and orders for a wide variety of manufactured products.

## STATISTICS SOURCES

*Survey of Current Business.* U. S. Government Printing Office. • Published by Bureau of Economic Analysis, U. S. Department of Commerce. Presents a wide variety of business and economic data.

## TRADE/PROFESSIONAL ASSOCIATIONS

American Wire Producers Association. 7011 A Manchester Blvd., No. 178, Alexandria, VA 22310-3202. Phone: (703)299-4434; Fax: (703)299-4434; Email: info@awpa.org • URL: http://www.awpa.org • Represents manufacturers of steel wire and wire products; suppliers of wire rods, dies, machinery, and related equipment. Assures free and fair access to a global supply of wire rod and to encourage an adequate domestic supply.

# WIRING, ELECTRIC

*See* ELECTRICAL CONSTRUCTION INDUSTRY

# WOMEN ACCOUNTANTS

## ABSTRACTS AND INDEXES

*Accounting and Tax Index.* ProQuest L.L.C. • Quarterly. Indexes accounting, auditing, and taxation literature appearing in journals, books, pamphlets, conference proceedings, and newsletters.

## BIOGRAPHICAL SOURCES

*Who's Who of American Women.* Marquis Who's Who L.L.C. • Biennial. $305.00. Provides over 30,444 biographical profiles of important women, including individuals prominent in business, finance, and industry.

## INTERNET DATABASES

*Rutgers Accounting Web.* Rutgers University Accounting Research Center. Phone: (973)353-5172; Fax: (973)353-1283 • URL: http://www.rutgers.edu/accounting • RAW Web site provides extensive links to sources of national and international accounting information, such as the Big Six accounting firms, the Financial Accounting Standards Board (FASB), SEC filings (EDGAR), journals, publishers, software, the International Accounting Network, and "Internet's largest list of accounting firms in USA." Searching is offered. Fees: Free.

## TRADE/PROFESSIONAL ASSOCIATIONS

Accounting and Financial Women's Alliance. 1760 Old Meadow Rd., Ste. 500, McLean, VA 22102. Phone: 800-326-2163 or (703)506-3265; Fax: (703)506-3266; Email: aswa@aswa.org • URL: http://www.aswa.org • Professional society of women accountants, educators and others in the field of accounting dedicated to the achievement of personal, professional and economic potential. Assists women accountants in their careers and promotes development in the profession. Conducts educational and research programs.

American Woman's Society of Certified Public Accountants. 136 S Keowee St., Dayton, OH 45402. Phone: 800-297-2721 or (937)222-1872; Fax: (937)222-5794; Email: info@awscpa.org • URL: http://www.awscpa.org • Citizens who hold Certified Public Accountant certificates as well as those who have passed the CPA examination but do not have certificates. Works to improve the status of professional women and to make the business community aware of the professional capabilities of the woman CPA. Conducts semiannual statistical survey of members; offers specialized education and research programs.

# WOMEN ENGINEERS

## BIOGRAPHICAL SOURCES

*Who's Who of American Women.* Marquis Who's Who L.L.C. • Biennial. $305.00. Provides over 30,444 biographical profiles of important women, including individuals prominent in business, finance, and industry.

**PERIODICALS AND NEWSLETTERS**

*SWE.* Anne Perusek, editor. Society of Women Engineers. • Bimonthly. Members, $10.00 per year; non-members, $20.00 per year. Covers technical articles, continuing development, career guidance and recruitment and product advertising. Formerly *U.S. Woman Engineer.*

# WOMEN EXECUTIVES

*See also* ENTREPRENEURS AND INTRA-PRENEURS

**ABSTRACTS AND INDEXES**

*Women Studies Abstracts.* Springer ScienceBusiness Media LLC. • Quarterly. Covers significant research in women's studies.

**BIOGRAPHICAL SOURCES**

*Who's Who of American Women.* Marquis Who's Who L.L.C. • Biennial. $305.00. Provides over 30,444 biographical profiles of important women, including individuals prominent in business, finance, and industry.

**DIRECTORIES**

*American Women Managers and Administrators: A Selective Biographical Dictionary of Twentieth-Century Leaders in Business, Education, and Government.* Greenwood Electronic Media. • $105 Single issue. Covers 225 twentieth-century women who hold or have held administrative, managerial, or leadership positions in business, education, or government, including founders and presidents of colleges and companies, vice presidents of major corporations, and women who were first in their profession or position.

*Women Directors of the Top Corporate 1,000.* National Women's Economic Alliance Foundation. • Annual. $100. Covers: about 600 women serving on the boards of Fortune 1,000 corporations; compiled from surveys of Fortune 500 Industrial and Fortune 500 Service corporations and the Corporate Yellow Book. Entries include: Name, title, company name, address, corporate boards on which serves.

**INTERNET DATABASES**

*MBEMAG.* Minority Business Entrepreneur Magazine. Phone: (310)540-9398; Fax: (310)792-8263; Email: webmaster@mbemag.com • URL: http://www.mbemag.com • Web site's main feature is the "MBE Business Resources Directory." This provides complete mailing addresses, phone, fax, and Web site addresses (URL) for more than 40 organizations and government agencies having information or assistance for ethnic minority and women business owners. Some other links are "Current Events," "Calendar of Events," and "Business Opportunities." Updating is bimonthly. Fees: Free.

**PERIODICALS AND NEWSLETTERS**

*Minority Business Entrepreneur.* Minority Business Entrepreneur. • Bimonthly. $25 Individuals print amd digital. Reports on issues "critical to the growth and development of minority and women-owned firms." Provides information on relevant legislation and profiles successful women and minority entrepreneurs.

*Perspective.* Magna Publications Inc. • Description: Provides administrators with guidelines for keeping their schools out of court. Examines current trends in law related to higher education, as well as past and future legal issues affecting students, faculty, administrators and the public. Recurring features include columns titled Key Case Review, Follow-Up, Resources, Legislative Note, Outside the Courts, Cross-Examination, and Cases Noted.

*Self.* Conde Nast Publications. • Monthly. $13 One year subscription. Provides content, tools and community for modern women.

*Today's Insurance Professionals.* International Association of Insurance Professionals. • Quarterly. $15 Individuals. Provides advice on professional and personal development in the insurance business. Formerly *Today's Insurance Woman.*

*Women in Business.* Ogden/Weber Chamber of Commerce. • Quarterly.

**RESEARCH CENTERS AND INSTITUTES**

Baylor University - Center for Private Enterprise. PO Box 98003, Waco, TX 76798. Phone: (254)710-2263 or (254)710-6898; Fax: (254)710-1092; Email: kimberly_mencken@baylor.edu • URL: http://www. baylor.edu/business • Includes studies of entrepreneurship and women entrepreneurs.

Business and Professional Women's Foundation. 1718 M St. NW, No. 148, Washington, DC 20036. Phone: (202)293-1100; Fax: (202)861-0298; Email: foundation@bpwfoundation.org • URL: http:// bpwfoundation.org • Formerly National Federation of Business and Professional Women's Clubs.

Institute for Case Development and Research. Simmons College, Graduate School of Management, 300 The Fenway, Boston, MA 02115. Phone: (617)521-3840; Fax: (617)521-3880; Email: somadm@simmons.edu • URL: http://www. simmons.edu • Studies issues and problems confronting women in management.

Re:Gender. 11 Hanover Sq., New York, NY 10005-2843. Phone: (212)785-7335; Email: regender@ regender.org • URL: http://www.regender.org • Serves as a national network of organizations representing the academic community, policy makers, and others interested in women's issues. Works to bring institutional resources to bear on feminist research, policy analysis, and educational programs addressing legal, economic, and social inequities. Promotes collaborative research on issues affecting women; acts as clearinghouse. Houses the National Network of Women's Caucuses and Committees in the Disciplinary and Professional Associations.

**TRADE/PROFESSIONAL ASSOCIATIONS**

Business and Professional Women's Foundation. 1718 M St. NW, No. 148, Washington, DC 20036. Phone: (202)293-1100; Fax: (202)861-0298; Email: foundation@bpwfoundation.org • URL: http:// bpwfoundation.org • Formerly National Federation of Business and Professional Women's Clubs.

Canadian Association of Women Executives and Entrepreneurs. 401 Bay St., Ste. 1600, Toronto, ON, Canada M5K 2Y4. Phone: (416)756-0000; Fax: (416)756-0000; Email: contact@cawee.net • URL: http://www.cawee.net • Seeks to provide opportunities for women to empower other women in the development and advancement of their business and professional lives; which fosters financial independence, professional development and personal satisfaction.

Career Women's Forum. PO Box 1200, CH-1211 Geneva, Switzerland. Phone: 41 22 3183200; Fax: 41 22 3183300; Email: administration@cwf.ch • URL: http://www.cwf.ch • Represents executive business women active in the arts, business, and government in Switzerland. Provides a forum for business contacts.

Catalyst. 120 Wall St., 5th Fl., New York, NY 10005-3904. Phone: (212)514-7600; Fax: (212)514-8470; Email: info@catalyst.org • URL: http://www. catalyst.org • Works to advance women in Business and the professions. Serves as a source of information on women in business for past four decades. Helps companies and women maximize their potential. Holds current statistics, print media, and research materials on issues related to women in business.

City Women's Network. 7 Berghem Mews, Blythe Rd., London W14 0HN, United Kingdom. Phone: 44 20 3784592 • URL: http://www.citywomen.org • Senior executive and professional businesswomen.

Provides a forum for members to share common professional and social interests and experiences.

Committee of 200. 980 N Michigan Ave., Ste. 1575, Chicago, IL 60611. Phone: (312)255-0296; Fax: (312)255-0789; Email: info@c200.org • URL: http://www.c200.org • Represents women executives who are recognized as leaders in their industries (though originally intended to have a membership of 200 top-ranking businesswomen, the committee is no longer limited to 200). Encourages successful entrepreneurship by women and the active participation of women business owners and senior corporate executives in business, economic, social, and educational concerns. Seeks to strengthen the influence of women business leaders. Provides forum for exchange of ideas and enhancement of business opportunities for women.

Cosmetic Executive Women. 286 Madison Ave., 19th Fl., New York, NY 10017. Phone: (212)685-5955 or (646)929-8000; Fax: (212)685-3334 • URL: http://cew.org • Women in the cosmetic and allied industries. Unites women executives in the cosmetic field for industry awareness and business advancement. Promotes products, people, professional development and philanthropy.

Executive Women International. 3860 S 2300 E, Salt Lake City, UT 84109. Phone: (801)355-2800; Fax: (801)355-2852; Email: ewi@ewiconnect.com • URL: http://www.ewiconnect.com • Individuals holding key positions in business professions. Conducts networking educational and charitable programs.

The International Alliance for Women. 1101 Pennsylvania Ave. NW, 6th Fl., Washington, DC 20004. Phone: 888-712-5200 or (202)351-6839; Email: admin@tiaw.org • URL: http://www.tiaw.org • Local networks comprising 50,000 professional and executive women in 12 countries; individual businesswomen without a network affiliation are alliance associates. Promotes recognition of the achievements of women in business. Encourages placement of women in senior executive positions. Maintains high standards of professional competence among members. Facilitates communication on an international scale among professional women's networks and their members. Represents members' interests before policymaking business and government. Sponsors programs that support equal opportunity and enhance members' business and professional skills. Operates appointments and directors service. Maintains speakers' bureau.

National Association for Female Executives. 2 Park Ave., New York, NY 10016. • URL: http://www. nafe.com • Represents and supports professional women and women business owners; provides resources and services through education, networking and public advocacy to empower members to achieve career success and financial security.

National Association of Women Business Owners. 601 Pennsylvania Ave. NW, South Bldg., Ste. 900, Washington, DC 20004. Phone: 800-556-2926; Fax: (202)403-3788; Email: national@nawbo.org • URL: http://www.nawbo.org • Formerly Association of Women Business Owners.

Women Business Owners. 9594 1st Ave. NE, No. 274, Seattle, WA 98115-2012. Phone: (206)575-3232; Email: info@womenbusinessowners.org • URL: http://www.womenbusinessowners.org • Aims to empower, educate and enhance the lives of children and women business owners throughout the world. Provides programs and workshops on educating future entrepreneurs. Works to develop and encourage entrepreneurship, achievement and success in business.

# WOMEN IN THE WORK FORCE

*See also* EMPLOYMENT OF WOMEN

## ABSTRACTS AND INDEXES

*Social Sciences Citation Index.* Thomson Reuters Corp. • Weekly. Product is accessed via *Web of Science.*

*Social Sciences Index Retrospective: 1907-1983.* EBSCO Publishing Inc. • Indexing for 1,000,000 articles. Coverage includes international index and social sciences and humanities index.

*Sociological Abstracts.* ProQuest L.L.C. • Monthly. A compendium of non-evaluative abstracts covering the field of sociology and related disciplines.

## CD-ROM DATABASES

*Social Sciences Abstracts.* EBSCO Publishing Inc. • Provides indexing from 1983 and abstracting from 1994 of more than 750 periodicals covering economics, area studies, community health, public administration, public welfare, urban studies, and many other topics related to the social sciences.

*Social Sciences Citation Index.* Thomson Reuters Corp. • Weekly. Product is accessed via *Web of Science.*

## DIRECTORIES

*Albuquerque Women in Business Directory.* Duval Publications Inc. • Annual. Covers approximately 400 women business executives and owners in the Albuquerque, New Mexico area. Informative articles, government resources, related women's resources and organizations.

*The Business of Supplier Diversity: A Handbook of Essential Contacts and Information for Navigating the Industry.* Diversity Information Resources. • Annual. $129 Individuals. Covers: Business opportunity fairs, seminars, and workshops; National Supplier Development Council regional offices; Small Business Administration and Minority Business Development Administration offices; minority and women-owned business directories; and other resources for minority and women-owned businesses. Database includes: Summaries of legislation affecting minority businesses; glossary.

*Directory of Minority and Women Owned Businesses.* Louisiana Office of Minority and Women's Business Enterprise Department of Economic Development. • Quarterly. Contains information on minority and women-owned businesses.

*National Directory of Woman-Owned Business Firms.* Business Research Services Inc. • Annual. $295 Individuals paperback. Covers more than 28,000 entries with up to 17 points of data about each firm. Each business listing is arranged first by SIC code and business description, then alphabetically by state, city and company name within the SIC category.

## GENERAL WORKS

*Business Woman.* Business and Professional Women's Foundation. • Quarterly Periodic. $12/year. Features articles reflecting member's concerns including issues affecting working women.

## HANDBOOKS AND MANUALS

*Women and the Law.* Carol H. Lefcourt, editor. Thomson West. • Annual. $691.60 Individuals book - softbound. Covers such topics as employment discrimination, pay equity (comparable worth), sexual harassment in the workplace, property rights, and child custody issues.

## INTERNET DATABASES

*U.S. Census Bureau: The Official Statistics.* U. S. Bureau of the Census. Phone: (301)763-4636 or (301)763-4100; Fax: (301)763-4794; Email: webmaster@census.gov • URL: http://www.census.gov/prod/www/abs/mfg-prof.html • Web site is "Your Source for Social, Demographic, and Economic Information." Contains "Current U. S. Population Count," "Current Economic Indicators," and a wide variety of data under "Other Official Statistics." Keyword searching is provided. Fees: Free.

## ONLINE DATABASES

*Contemporary Women's Issues.* Cengage Learning Inc. • Provides full-text articles online from 150 periodicals and a wide variety of additional sources relating to economic, legal, social, political, education, health, and other women's issues. Time span is 1992 to date. Weekly updates. Inquire as to online cost and availability.

*Wilson Social Sciences Abstracts Online.* H.W. Wilson Co. • Provides online abstracting and indexing of more than 500 periodicals covering area studies, community health, public administration, public welfare, urban studies, and many other social science topics. Time period is 1994 to date for abstracts and 1983 to date for indexing, with updates weekly. Inquire as to online cost and availability.

## OTHER SOURCES

*Sex Discrimination and Sexual Harassment in the Work Place.* ALM Media Properties LLC. • $565. Considers both sides: the point of view of employers and the point of view of employees filing complaints. Coverage includes sexual harassment statutes, the Family Medical Leave Act, the Equal Pay Act, "glass ceiling" issues, pregnancy discrimination, childcare issues, reinstatement after a leave, and other legal matters. (Law Journal Press).

## PERIODICALS AND NEWSLETTERS

*Feminist Economics.* International Association for Feminist Economics. Taylor & Francis Ltd. • Three times a year. Individuals, $68.00 per year; institutions, $184.00 per year. Includes articles on issues relating to the employment and economic opportunities of women.

*Nine to Five Newsletter.* 9 to 5, National Association of Working Women. • 5/year. $25 Individuals. A newsletter dealing with the rights and concerns of women office workers.

*Perspective.* Magna Publications Inc. • Description: Provides administrators with guidelines for keeping their schools out of court. Examines current trends in law related to higher education, as well as past and future legal issues affecting students, faculty, administrators and the public. Recurring features include columns titled Key Case Review, Follow-Up, Resources, Legislative Note, Outside the Courts, Cross-Examination, and Cases Noted.

*Women in Business.* The ABWA Company Inc. • Bimonthly. Women's business magazine.

## RESEARCH CENTERS AND INSTITUTES

Carleton University - Centre for Research and Education on Women and Work. 702 Dunton Tower, Sprott School of Business, 1125 Colonel By Dr., Ottawa, ON, Canada K1S 5B6. Phone: (613)520-2600; Fax: (613)520-2652; Email: merridee. bujaki@carleton.ca • URL: http://sprott.carleton.co/research/research-centres/centre-for-research-and-education-on-women-and-work • Issues that women face in the workplace.

Consumer Research Center. The Conference Board. 845 3rd Ave., New York, NY 10022. Phone: (212)339-0232; Fax: (212)836-9754; Email: crc@conference-board.org • URL: http://www.conference-board.org/economics/crc.cfm • Conducts research on the consumer market, including elderly and working women segments.

Cooperative State Research, Education, and Extension Service - Small and Home-Based Business. 4435 Waterfront Ctr., 800 9th St. SW, Washington, DC 20250. Phone: (202)720-5997; Fax: (202)690-2975; Email: amclaren@csrees.usda.gov • URL: http://www.csrees.usda.gov/smallhomebasedbusiness.cfm • Women-owned and operated farms and ranches, rural entrepreneurship, small and home-based businesses.

## STATISTICS SOURCES

*Statistical Abstract of the United States.* U. S. Government Printing Office. • Annual. $44.00. Issued by the U. S. Bureau of the Census.

## TRADE/PROFESSIONAL ASSOCIATIONS

Airport Minority Advisory Council. 2001 Jefferson Davis Hwy., Ste. 500, Arlington, VA 22202. Phone: (703)414-2622; Fax: (703)414-2686; Email: amac. info@amac-org.com • URL: http://www.amac-org. com • Advocates for equal opportunity for minorities and women in airport contracting and employment.

Alpha Iota Sorority. 3219 SE 18th Ct., Des Moines, IA 50320-1901. Phone: (515)282-4896; Email: clmekus@aol.com • URL: http://www.alphaiota.org • Honorary sorority - business. Helps each member to become a better businesswoman through development of self-confidence, leadership and awareness of responsibility to herself and her community.

American Business Women's Association. 11050 Roe Ave., Ste. 200, Overland Park, KS 66211. Phone: 800-228-0007; Fax: (913)660-0101; Email: webmail@abwa.org • URL: http://www.abwa.org • Women in business, including women owning or operating their own businesses, women in professions and women employed in any level of government, education, or retailing, manufacturing and service companies. Provides opportunities for businesswomen to help themselves and others grow personally and professionally through leadership, education, networking support and national recognition. Offers leadership training, business skills training and business education; special membership options for retired businesswomen and the Company Connection for business owners, a resume service, credit card and programs, various travel and insurance benefits. Sponsors American Business Women's Day and National Convention and regional conferences held annually.

Arab International Women's Forum. Berkeley Square House, Berkeley Sq., London W1J 6BD, United Kingdom. Phone: 44 20 78877630; Fax: 44 20 78876001 • URL: http://www.aiwfonline.com/home.aspx • Promotes the role of women in the economy and society. Serves as a link between the Arab business and professional women and their counterparts in the international community.

Association des Femmes Chefs d'Entreprises du Cote d'Ivoire. BP 8232, Abidjan 08, Côte d'Ivoire. Phone: 225 3 327571; Email: fcem_ci@yahoo.fr • URL: http://www.fcem.org/en/pays-membres.html • Promotes women's entrepreneurial initiatives. Reinforces national associations of women business entrepreneurial potentials. Lobbies before the public and private institutions, policy makers and governments on issues that impede women's entrepreneurial potentials. Facilitates the development of business, partnership and trade. Fosters professional growth and business skills perfection. Encourages women to create enterprises.

Association des Femmes Chefs d'Entreprises du Maroc. Residence El Amri, Rue du 6 octubre, Quartie Racine, Casablanca, Morocco. Phone: 212 22 397593; Fax: 212 22 397736; Email: afem@afem.ma • URL: http://afem.ma • Promotes women's entrepreneurial initiatives. Reinforces national associations of women business entrepreneurial potentials. Lobbies before the public and private institutions, policy makers and governments on issues that impede women's entrepreneurial potentials. Facilitates the development of business, partnership and trade. Fosters professional growth and business skills perfection. Encourages women to create enterprises.

Association des Femmes d'Affaires et Chefs d'Entreprises du Benin. BP 1226, Cotonou, Benin. Phone: 229 331617; Fax: 229 332627; Email: hotelgl@leland.bj • URL: http://fcem.org/en/pays-membres/195-pays-membres/fiche-pays-details/afrique-membres/1523-republique-de-benin-afrique-membres.html • Promotes women's entrepreneurial initiatives. Reinforces national associations of women business entrepreneurial potentials. Lobbies before the public and private institutions, policy makers and governments on issues that impede women's entrepreneurial potentials. Facilitates the development of business, partnership and trade. Fosters professional growth and business skills perfection. Encourages women to create enterprises.

Association des Femmes d'Affaires et Chefs d'Entreprises du Gabon. B.P. 6023, Libreville, Gabon. Phone: 241 6 264216; Fax: 241 723883; Email: refegcham@yahoo.fr • URL: http://www.fcem.org/en/pays-membres.html • Promotes women's entrepreneurial initiatives. Reinforces national associations of women business entrepreneurial potentials. Lobbies before the public and private institutions, policy makers and governments on issues that impede women's entrepreneurial potentials. Facilitates the development of business, partnership and trade. Fosters professional growth and business skills perfection. Encourages women to create enterprises.

Association des Femmes Entrepreneurs Chefs d'Entreprises. Ave. Le Marinel N 9-11, Commune de la Gombe, Kinshasa, Republic of the Congo. Phone: 243 998911092; Fax: 243 3225667; Email: bismura2@yahoo.fr • URL: http://www.fcem.org/en/pays-membres.html • Promotes women's entrepreneurial initiatives. Reinforces national associations of women business entrepreneurial potentials. Lobbies before the public and private institutions, policy makers and governments on issues that impede women's entrepreneurial potentials. Facilitates the development of business, partnership and trade. Fosters professional growth and business skills perfection. Encourages women to create enterprises.

Association Mauricienne des Femmes Chefs d'Entreprise. Regency Sq., 1st Fl., 4 Conal and McIrvine St., Beau Bassin, Mauritius. Email: cheelichop@intnet.mu • URL: http://fcem.org/en/pays-membres/195-pays-membres/fiche-pays-details/afrique-membres/1517-ile-maurice-afrique-membres.html • Promotes women's entrepreneurial initiatives. Reinforces national associations of women business entrepreneurial potentials. Lobbies before the public and private institutions, policy makers and governments on issues that impede women's entrepreneurial potentials. Facilitates the development of business, partnership and trade. Fosters professional growth and business skills perfection. Encourages women to create enterprises.

Association of Business Women in Iceland. Kringlunni 7, IS-103 Reykjavik, Iceland. Email: fka@fka.is • URL: http://www.fka.is • Promotes women's entrepreneurial initiatives. Reinforces national associations of women business entrepreneurial potentials. Lobbies before the public and private institutions, policy makers and governments on issues that impede women's entrepreneurial potentials. Facilitates the development of business, partnership and trade. Fosters professional growth and business skills perfection. Encourages women to create enterprises.

Association of Business Women of Serbia. Volgina 15, 11060 Belgrade, Serbia. Phone: 38 11 2776801; Fax: 38 11 2776801; Email: upz.office@pupin.rs • URL: http://www.poslovnezene.org.rs/en • Promotes women's genuine business interests.

Establishes links with similar associations in Europe and worldwide. Trains women in starting and running a business.

Association of Slovenia Entrepreneurs. PO Box 40-95, 1000 Ljubljana, Slovenia. Phone: 386 1 5443678; Fax: 386 1 5443680; Email: marta.turk1@guest.arnes.si • URL: http://fcem.org • Promotes women's entrepreneurial initiatives. Lobbies before the public and private institutions, policy makers and governments on issues that impede women's entrepreneurial potentials. Facilitates the development of business, partnership and trade. Fosters professional growth and business skills perfection. Encourages women to create enterprises.

Association Senegalaise des Femmes Chefs d'Entreprise. B.P. 30081, Dakar, Senegal. Phone: 221 338241010; Fax: 221 8257246; Email: hadjadiordiop2000@yahoo.fr • URL: http://www.fcem.org/en/pays-membres.html • Promotes women's entrepreneurial initiatives. Lobbies before the public and private institutions, policy makers and governments on issues that impede women's entrepreneurial potentials. Facilitates the development of business, partnership and trade. Fosters professional growth and business skills perfection. Encourages women to create enterprises.

Association Women and Business in Russia. 8, Zaozernaya str., 196084 Saint Petersburg, Russia. Phone: 7 812 3162733; Fax: 7 812 7101191; Email: info@demetra.su • URL: http://www.fcem.org/en/pays-membres.html • Advances and supports businesswomen's interests in public, political and business circles of Russia. Helps develop women's business in Russia. Raises well-being and establishes a civilized, socially-responsible business in Russia.

Beta Pi Sigma Sorority. 256 Waterville St., San Francisco, CA 94124. Email: bpssi@betapisigmasorority.org • URL: http://betapisigmasorority.org • Business and professional sorority. Conducts civic, cultural, charitable, and educational projects. Cooperates with the Close Up Foundation on the Program for Older Americans. Offers tutoring services. Youth programs partnerships with schools, book donation programs (schools and libraries), and youth programs.

British Association of Women Entrepreneurs. 112 John Player Bldg., Stirling FK7 7RP, United Kingdom. Phone: 44 18 2725 5170; Email: deb@bawe-uk.org • URL: http://www.bawe-uk.org • Encourages the personal development of member entrepreneurs. Provides opportunities for members to expand their business through informal and formal networking. Represents and promotes British entrepreneurship worldwide.

Business Women's Association of Uzbekistan. Usman Yusupov St., 119, 100200 Tashkent, Uzbekistan. Phone: 998 71 2418861 or 998 71 2413453; Fax: 998 71 2443522; Email: bwa@ars.uz • URL: http://bwa.uzorg.net/about_eng.html • Seeks to improve the climate of mutual trust and business partnership. Supports women competitiveness in labor markets through retraining and raising skills. Creates institutional legal mechanisms for improving economic and social opportunities for women. Provides legal support to women entrepreneurs.

Businesswomen's Association. Oakhurst Bldg., W Wing, 2nd Fl., Rm. 2004, 11/13 St. Andrews Rd., Johannesburg 2193, South Africa. Phone: 27 11 484 4945; Email: admin@bwasa.co.za • URL: http://www.bwasa.co.za • Represents businesswomen in South Africa. Creates opportunities to advance the interests of women in business. Provides local and national forums where members can exchange ideas and be informed about current issues.

Canadian Federation of Business and Professional Women's Clubs. PO Box 62054, Orleans, ON, Canada K1C 7H8. URL: http://www.bpwcanada.com • Canadian women engaged in business, the

professions, or industry. Works to enhance the economic, social, and employment status of women. Encourages women to become active in government at every level. Strives to improve business service standards. Networks with related organizations to promote common concerns.

Catalyst. 120 Wall St., 5th Fl., New York, NY 10005-3904. Phone: (212)514-7600; Fax: (212)514-8470; Email: info@catalyst.org • URL: http://www.catalyst.org • Works to advance women in Business and the professions. Serves as a source of information on women in business for past four decades. Helps companies and women maximize their potential. Holds current statistics, print media, and research materials on issues related to women in business.

Chambre Nationale des Femmes Chefs d'Entreprise. 17, Rue Abderrahamen El Jaziri, 1002 Tunis, Tunisia. Phone: 216 71 860112; Fax: 216 71 862049; Email: cnfce.tunisie@fcem.ws • URL: http://www.fcem.org/en/pays-membres.html • Represents the interests of women entrepreneurs before national and international organizations and institutions. Reinforces the presence and representation of women within employer organizations and national chambers. Promotes women entrepreneurship. Promotes exchanges, relationships, and development of regional, national and international contacts aimed at reinforcing partnerships and access to new markets.

Chinese Women's Business Association. 11F, 157-1, Section 1, Xin-Shen South Rd., Taipei, Taiwan. Phone: 886 937 515276; Fax: 886 2 23821655; Email: taimay@ms16.hinet.net • URL: http://www.fcem.org/en/pays-membres.html • Promotes women's entrepreneurial initiatives. Lobbies before the public and private institutions, policy makers and governments on issues that impede women's entrepreneurial potentials. Facilitates the development of business, partnership and trade. Fosters professional growth and business skills perfection. Encourages women to create enterprises.

Committee of 200. 980 N Michigan Ave., Ste. 1575, Chicago, IL 60611. Phone: (312)255-0296; Fax: (312)255-0789; Email: info@c200.org • URL: http://www.c200.org • Represents women executives who are recognized as leaders in their industries (though originally intended to have a membership of 200 top-ranking businesswomen, the committee is no longer limited to 200). Encourages successful entrepreneurship by women and the active participation of women business owners and senior corporate executives in business, economic, social, and educational concerns. Seeks to strengthen the influence of women business leaders. Provides forum for exchange of ideas and enhancement of business opportunities for women.

Diversity Information Resources. 2105 Central Ave. NE, Minneapolis, MN 55418. Phone: (612)781-6819; Fax: (612)781-0109; Email: info@diversityinforesources.com • URL: http://www.diversityinforesources.com • Promotes businesses with minority, women, veteran, service-disabled veteran and HUBZone ownership. Compiles and publishes minority and women-owned business directories to acquaint major corporations and government purchasing agents with the products and services of minority and women-owned firms. Sponsors national supplier diversity seminars.

Emergency Management Professional Organization for Women's Enrichment. PO Box 10803, McLean, VA 22102-8803. Email: information@empower-women.com • URL: http://www.empower-women.com • Promotes the presence of women in the field of emergency management. Creates opportunities for women to empower themselves in the field of emergency management. Seeks to help women advance their careers through networking, mentoring and promoting educational opportunities in the field of emergency management.

Eta Phi Beta. 19983 Livernois Ave., Detroit, MI 48221-1299. Phone: (313)862-0600; Fax: (313)862-6245; Email: contact@etaphibetasorority.com • URL: http://www.etaphibetasorority.com • Professional sorority - business. Conducts national projects concerning retarded citizens and retarded children. Conducts leadership and career programs and seminars; sponsors competitions. Operates speakers' bureau; provides children's services; maintains charitable program.

European Professional Women's Network. 4, rue Galvani, F-75838 Paris, France. Phone: 33 9 70446262; Email: contact@europeanpwn.net • URL: http://www.europeanpwn.net • Promotes the sustainable and innovative professional career paths of women. Raises the visibility of European women in business.

European Women's Management Development Austria. Schmiedinger strasse 67, 5020 Salzburg, Austria. Email: austria@ewmd.org • URL: http://www.ewmd.org/chapter/104 • Aims to improve the quality of management with respect to people, children, age and the cultural diversity of Europe. Provides a forum for collecting and exchanging information about trends management development in Europe and worldwide. Promotes women in management. Facilitates communication among individuals involved in the development of new role models for better work-life-balance.

European Women's Management Development International Network. Geisbergweg 6c, 65205 Wiesbaden, Germany. • URL: http://www.ewmd.org • Strives to improve management by developing women's managerial skills, and raising the professional profile of women as managers. Disseminates and exchange knowledge and experience in establishing best practices for management development.

European Women's Management Development Switzerland. Stockerstrasse 56, 8002 Zurich, Switzerland. Email: switzerland@ewmd.org • URL: http://www.ewmd.org • Aims to improve the quality of management with respect to people, children, age and the cultural diversity of Europe. Provides a forum for collecting and exchanging information about trends management development in Europe and worldwide. Promotes women in management. Facilitates communication among individuals involved in the development of new role models for better work-life-balance.

EWMD ITALY: European Women's Management Development. c/o EWMD Brescia, via Papa Giovanni XXIII 74, Rezzato, I-25086 Brescia, Italy. Phone: 39 30 2793124; Email: italy@ewmd.org • URL: http://www.ewmd.org/chapter/106 • Aims to improve the quality of management with respect to people, children, age and the cultural diversity of Europe. Promotes the best practices for work-life-balance management. Provides a forum for collecting and exchanging information about trends management development in Europe and worldwide. Promotes women in management. Facilitates communication among individuals involved in the development of new role models for better work-life-balance.

Executive Women International. 3860 S 2300 E, Salt Lake City, UT 84109. Phone: (801)355-2800; Fax: (801)355-2852; Email: ewi@ewiconnect.com • URL: http://www.ewiconnect.com • Individuals holding key positions in business professions. Conducts networking educational and charitable programs.

Financial Women's Association of New York. 355 Lexington Ave., 15th Fl., New York, NY 10017. Phone: (212)297-2133; Fax: (212)370-9047 or (212)982-3008; Email: fwaoffice@fwa.org • URL: http://www.nywici.org/links/link_fwa.html • Persons of professional status in the field of finance

in the New York metropolitan area. Works to promote and maintain high professional standards in the financial and business communities; provide an opportunity for members to enhance one another's professional contacts; achieve recognition of the contribution of women to the financial and business communities; encourage other women to seek professional positions within the financial and business communities. Activities include educational trips to foreign countries; college internship program including foreign student exchange; high school mentorship program; Washington and international briefings; placement service for members. Maintains speakers' bureau.

Global Grassroots. 1950 Lafayette Rd., Ste. 200, Portsmouth, NH 03801-8663. Phone: (603)643-0400; Email: info@globalgrassroots.org • URL: http://www.globalgrassroots.org/index.htm • Works to empower, unite, and support relief of poor, distressed and underprivileged women worldwide. Benefits women by establishing a global network of leading entrepreneurs. Raises awareness of critical issues facing women worldwide, especially sexual and gender-based violence during conflict.

Groupement des Femmes d'Affaires de la Guinee. B.P. 3009, Conakry, Guinea. Phone: 224 453899; Fax: 224 453518; Email: cenafodgn@eti-bull.net • URL: http://www.fcem.org/en/pays-membres.html • Promotes women's entrepreneurial initiatives. Reinforces national associations of women business entrepreneurial potentials. Lobbies before the public and private institutions, policy makers and governments on issues that impede women's entrepreneurial potentials. Facilitates the development of business, partnership and trade. Fosters professional growth and business skills perfection. Encourages women to create enterprises.

Groupement des Femmes d'Affaires du Cameroun. BP 1940, Douala, Cameroon. Phone: 237 33401732; Fax: 237 33406533; Email: gfacnational@yahoo.fr • URL: http://fcem.org/en/pays-membres.html • Promotes women's entrepreneurial initiatives. Reinforces national associations of women business entrepreneurial potentials. Lobbies before the public and private institutions, policy makers and governments on issues that impede women's entrepreneurial potentials. Facilitates the development of business, partnership and trade. Fosters professional growth and business skills perfection. Encourages women to create enterprises.

Home-Based Working Moms. PO Box 1628, Spring, TX 77383-1628. Phone: (281)757-2207 • URL: http://www.hbwm.com • Individuals who work at home or would like to. Promotes working at home as an option for people in applicable positions; seeks to enhance the careers of members currently working at home. Serves as a forum for exchange of information among members. Makes available member matching service. Advocates for creation of more work-at-home opportunities by American businesses.

Hong Kong Women Professionals and Entrepreneurs Association. Kingswell Commercial Tower, 171-173 Lockhart Rd., Rm. B, 18 Fl., Hong Kong, Hong Kong, China. Phone: 852 28822555; Fax: 852 28824673; Email: info@hkwpea.org • URL: http://www.hkwpea.org • Works to create practical and innovative learning and business opportunities for members and for others. Promotes high professional standards. Reaches out and establishes relationships with counterparts in Mainland China and abroad.

The International Alliance for Women. 1101 Pennsylvania Ave. NW, 6th Fl., Washington, DC 20004. Phone: 888-712-5200 or (202)351-6839; Email: admin@tiaw.org • URL: http://www.tiaw.org • Local networks comprising 50,000 professional and executive women in 12 countries; individual businesswomen without a network affiliation are al-

liance associates. Promotes recognition of the achievements of women in business. Encourages placement of women in senior executive positions. Maintains high standards of professional competence among members. Facilitates communication on an international scale among professional women's networks and their members. Represents members' interests before policymaking business and government. Sponsors programs that support equal opportunity and enhance members' business and professional skills. Operates appointments and directors service. Maintains speakers' bureau.

International Association of Women in Family Enterprises. 1906 Vista Del Lago Dr., No. L-119, Valley Springs, CA 95252. Phone: (209)772-9200 or (209)772-2810; Fax: (209)772-2810; Email: info@iawife.com • URL: http://www.iawife.com • Aims to support women who are building and growing family businesses. Offers opportunities to help members become successful in family enterprises. Provides support, education and networking among members.

Iota Phi Lambda. 1015 15th St. NW, Ste. 1110, Washington, DC 20005. Phone: (202)462-4682; Email: iotahq@verizon.net • URL: http://iota1929.org • Business and professional civic sorority. Seeks to: develop leadership expertise among business and professional women; promote increased interest in business education among high school and college girls through planned programs and scholarships; encourage the development of personalities for all areas of leadership through provision of educational opportunities; establish and promote civic and social service activities for youth and adults. Conducts children's services and tutoring sessions. Maintains small library. Provides educational, tutorial, senior citizen, and health programs.

Korean Women Entrepreneurs Association. 7F, 733-24, Yeoksam-dong, Gangnam-Gu, Seoul, South Korea. Phone: 82 2 3690922; Fax: 82 2 3690950; Email: ceo@wbiz.or.kr • URL: http://www.womanbiz.or.kr • Represents Korean businesswomen and provides full-support for the growth and development of their businesses. Helps entrepreneurs gain confidence and improve their competitiveness through counseling and training. Implements government-commissioned projects.

Malta Association of Women in Business. TaL-Imriekeb, Ramla Rd., Naxxar NXR 08, Malta. Phone: 356 21 422009 or 356 21 334394; Email: info@mawb.eu • URL: http://www.mawb.eu • Encourages reciprocal support, exchange of ideas, sharing of experiences and business and economic opportunities among its members both nationally and internationally. Organizes seminars, workshops, social and informative evenings. Promotes an environment for women to grow and develop in their businesses and professions. Promotes the interests of its members in the pursuit of innovative and effective changes in business, economic, social and public policy.

Mothers' Home Business Network. PO Box 423, East Meadow, NY 11554. Phone: (516)997-7394; Fax: (516)997-0839; Email: momhomebiz@mhbn.com • URL: http://www.homeworkingmom.com • Mothers choosing to work at home so they can earn income, maintain careers, and remain the primary caretakers of their children. Offers advice and support services on how to begin a successful business at home; helps members communicate with others who have chosen the same career option. Provides information on home business products and services, including home furnishings, raw materials and office supplies, and publications. Consults with corporations and manufacturers on reaching the home-based market. Refers media to potential interviewees and writers specializing in home business topics.

National Association of Professional Asian

American Women. 304 Oak Knoll Terr., Rockville, MD 20850. Phone: (301)785-8585; Email: napaw@comcast.net • URL: http://www.napaw.org • Represents the professional interests of Asian-American women. Promotes continued personal and professional development; works to enhance career opportunities. Encourages greater visibility of Asian-American women in public decision-making. Conducts educational programs.

National Latina Business Women Association. 11664 National Blvd., Ste. 283, Los Angeles, CA 90064. Phone: 888-MY-NLBWA; Email: info@nlbwa.org • URL: http://nlbwa.org • Strives to promote, develop, and support the growth of Latina business owners and professionals. Seeks to create networking and mentoring opportunities for members.

Nine to Five: National Association of Working Women. 207 E Buffalo St., Ste.211, Milwaukee, WI 53202. Phone: 800-522-0925 or (414)274-0925; Fax: (414)272-2870; Email: 9to5@9to5.org • URL: http://www.feminist.com/9to5.htm • Members are women office workers. Strives for the improvement of office working conditions for women and the elimination of sex and race discrimination.

100 Women in Hedge Funds. 888C 8th Ave., No. 453, New York, NY 10019-8511. • URL: http://www.100womeninhedgefunds.org • Represents individuals who are professional women. Conducts educational programming, professional leverage initiatives and philanthropy. Provides fundraising and volunteer opportunities for members.

Pro Mujer. 253 W 35th St., 11th Fl., New York, NY 10001. Phone: (646)626-7000; Fax: (212)904-1038; Email: communications@promujer.org • URL: http://promujer.org • Establishes microfinance organizations that provide financial and human development services for women. Provides business training and healthcare support.

Professional Organization of Women in the Arts. 365 Bridge St., Ste. 7F, Brooklyn, NY 11201. Email: powarts@gmail.com • URL: http://www.powarts.org • Promotes the advancement of women in the visual arts industry. Aims to educate, empower and promote leadership among women employed in the visual arts. Serves as a medium for the communication and exchange of ideas between women in the visual arts industry.

WAM International: Women Advancing Microfinance. 402 Constitution Ave. NE, Washington, DC 20002. Phone: (202)547-4546; Email: wam.international.president@gmail.com • URL: http://waminternational.org • Promotes the advancement of women working in the microfinance industry. Seeks to extend economic opportunities to women globally and encourages active participation of women in management and governance roles.

Women Business Owners. 9594 1st Ave. NE, No. 274, Seattle, WA 98115-2012. Phone: (206)575-3232; Email: info@womenbusinessowners.org • URL: http://www.womenbusinessowners.org • Aims to empower, educate and enhance the lives of children and women business owners throughout the world. Provides programs and workshops on educating future entrepreneurs. Works to develop and encourage entrepreneurship, achievement and success in business.

Women Chiefs of Enterprises International. c/o Julie Ankers, President, Level 6 276 Pitt St., Sydney, NSW 2000, Australia. Phone: 61 2 92675220; Fax: 61 2 92674202 • URL: http://www.wcei.com.au • Represents women entrepreneurs in Australia. Encourages innovation in the development of entrepreneurial skills. Creates opportunities for business development.

Women Entrepreneurs of Canada. 720 Spadina Ave., Ste. 202, Toronto, ON, Canada M5S 2T9. Phone: 866-207-4439 or (416)921-5050; Fax: (416)929-5256; Email: wec@wec.ca • URL: http://www.wec.ca • Addresses the need of women entrepreneurs and supports their growth and development. Provides meaningful networking opportunities to connect with peers as well as the larger business community, government and the international business community. Builds entrepreneurship acumen and business leadership capacity.

Women in Housing and Finance. 400 N Washington St., Ste. 300, Alexandria, VA 22314. Phone: (703)683-4742; Fax: (703)683-0018; Email: whf@whfdc.org • URL: http://www.whfdc.org • Professionals employed in the fields of housing or finance. Provides women finance professionals with the opportunity for continued professional development through interaction with others with similar interests. Promotes educational development of women in housing and finance; provides members with services and benefits to help them attain higher levels of expertise. Sponsors social events for members; holds receptions for congressional and regulatory leaders; conducts monthly luncheon and programs featuring speakers from federal agencies, Congress and the private sector. Sponsors career development workshops. Activities are concentrated in the Washington, DC, area.

Women in Management. PO Box 6690, Elgin, IL 60121-6690. Email: wimfoxvalley@gmail.com • URL: http://www.wimonline.org • Supports network of women in professional and management positions that facilitate the exchange of experience and ideas. Promotes self-growth in management; provides speakers who are successful in management; sponsors workshops and special interest groups to discuss problems and share job experiences.

Women Organizing for Change in Agriculture and Natural Resource Management. 1775 K St. NW, Ste. 410, Washington, DC 20006. Phone: (202)331-9099; Fax: (202)331-9366 • URL: http://www.wocan.org • Builds leadership among women and men in agriculture and natural resource management towards gender equality. Seeks to empower women as leaders and agents in adapting to, mitigating and reducing the adverse effects of climate change. Creates global awareness campaigns on the impact of climate change in women. Conducts and publishes gender-specific climate change research.

Women's High Tech Coalition. c/o MaryClare Fitzgerald, Chief Executive Officer, Dutko Grayling, 100 M St. SE, No. 500, Washington, DC 20003. Phone: (202)479-7141 • URL: http://www.womenshightech.org • Provides resources and opportunities for professional women in the technology industry. Works to create an atmosphere that generates sincere discussions and access to industry leaders both in the private and public sector.

Young Women Social Entrepreneurs. 6006 Colton Blvd., Oakland, CA 94611. Phone: (415)378-4417; Email: sara@ywse.org • URL: http://www.ywse.org • Serves women, primarily ages 25-40, with socially conscious agenda who are founders and leaders within businesses, non-profits, and government organizations. Aims to promote young women entrepreneurs by providing training and development, access to resources, and networking opportunities.

# WOMEN LAWYERS

*See also* LAWYERS

## BIOGRAPHICAL SOURCES

*Who's Who in American Law.* Marquis Who's Who L.L.C. • Biennial. $345 Individuals. Contains over 23,000 concise biographies of American lawyers, judges, and others in the legal field.

*Who's Who of American Women.* Marquis Who's Who L.L.C. • Biennial. $305.00. Provides over 30,444 biographical profiles of important women, including individuals prominent in business, finance, and industry.

## PERIODICALS AND NEWSLETTERS

*National Association of Women Lawyers. President's Newsletter.* National Association of Women Lawyers. • Quarterly. Newsletter. Price on application.

## TRADE/PROFESSIONAL ASSOCIATIONS

National Association of Women Lawyers. American Bar Ctr. MS 21.1, 321 N Clark St., Chicago, IL 60654-4714. Phone: (312)988-6186; Fax: (312)988-5100; Email: nawl@nawl.org • URL: http://www.nawl.org • Membership is open to any person who is a member in good standing of the bar of any state or U.S. territory, any non-U.S. legal professional (attorney or judge), any prospective attorney currently attending law school, and any state or local bar or law school association with compatible objectives. Men are welcome and encouraged to join.

# WOMEN MANAGERS

*See* WOMEN EXECUTIVES

# WOMEN PHYSICIANS

## BIOGRAPHICAL SOURCES

*Who's Who of American Women.* Marquis Who's Who L.L.C. • Biennial. $305.00. Provides over 30,444 biographical profiles of important women, including individuals prominent in business, finance, and industry.

## ONLINE DATABASES

*Embase.* Elsevier. • Worldwide medical literature, 1974 to present. Weekly updates. Inquire as to online cost and availability.

## TRADE/PROFESSIONAL ASSOCIATIONS

American Medical Women's Association. 12100 Sunset Hills Rd., Ste. 130, Reston, VA 20190. Phone: 866-564-2483 or (703)234-4069; Fax: (703)435-4390; Email: info@amwa-doc.org • URL: http://www.amwa-doc.org • Women holding a MD or DO degree from approved medical colleges; women interns, residents, and medical students. Promotes women's health issues in medical education and public policy. Seeks to find solutions to problems common to women studying or practicing medicine, such as career advancement and the integration of professional and family responsibilities. Provides student members with educational loans and personal counseling. Sponsors continuing medical education programs.

# WOMEN'S APPAREL

*See also* CLOTHING INDUSTRY; FASHION INDUSTRY; MILLINERY INDUSTRY; UNDERWEAR INDUSTRY

## ABSTRACTS AND INDEXES

*Textile Technology Index™.* EBSCO Publishing Inc. • Monthly. $545 Individuals. Includes indexing and abstracts for more than 470 periodicals.

## CD-ROM DATABASES

*OECD Statistical Compendium.* Organization for Economic Cooperation and Development. • Semiannual. $1,905.00 per year for 1 to 10 users. CD-ROM contains more than 730,000 monthly, quarterly, and annual time series for OECD countries, 1960 to date. Includes fully searchable data on agriculture, food, economic indicators, national accounts, employment, energy, finance, industry, technology, and foreign trade. Results can be displayed in various forms.

## DIRECTORIES

*Directory of Apparel Specialty Stores.* Chain Store Guide. • Annual. $495 Individuals Directory. Covers 4,700 apparel and sporting goods specialty stores in the United States and Canada, operating more than 80,000 stores. Include company name, phone and fax numbers, company e-mail and web addresses and other information.

## FINANCIAL RATIOS

*Annual Statement Studies.* Risk Management Association. • Annual. Compiled from over 280,000 financial statements.

*Annual Statement Studies: Industry Default Probabilities and Cash Flow Measures.* Risk Management Association. • Annual. $405 Nonmembers. Serves as a companion volume to the original *Annual Statement Studies.* Gives probability of default estimates on a percentage scale for more than 450 industries. Includes changes in position year-by-year for eight financial statement line items and provides percentage measures of cash flow.

## HANDBOOKS AND MANUALS

*Women's Accessories Store.* Entrepreneur Press. • Looseleaf. $59.50. A practical guide to starting a women's clothing accessories shop. Covers profit potential, start-up costs, market size evaluation, owner's time required, site selection, lease negotiation, pricing, accounting, advertising, promotion, etc. (Start-Up Business Guide No. E1333.).

*Women's Apparel Shop.* Entrepreneur Press. • Looseleaf. $59.50. A practical guide to starting a women's clothing store. Covers profit potential, start-up costs, market size evaluation, owner's time required, site selection, lease negotiation, pricing, accounting, advertising, promotion, etc. (Start-Up Business Guide No. E1107.).

## INTERNET DATABASES

*Advance Monthly Retail Trade Report.* U. S. Census Bureau. Phone: 800-541-8345 or (301)457-4100 or (301)763-2713; Fax: (301)457-1296 or (301)457-3842; Email: naics@census.gov • URL: http://www.census.gov/epcd/www/naicstab.htm • Web pages provide monthly sales figures for a wide range of retail businesses. Advance, preliminary, and final statistics are provided for the latest month available in each case, with a previous-year comparison. Updates are monthly.

*Business 2.0 Web Guide to the Best Business Links.* Business 2.0 Media Inc. Phone: (415)293-4800; Email: support@business2.com • URL: http://www.business2.com/webguide • Web site presents an extensive, searchable directory of links to "the best, most informative, and authoritative web pages." Twenty main categories cover business, finance, career, company information, people, and technology topics, with thousands of subtopics, all linking to Web sites recommended by experienced business researchers. Fees: Free.

*Fedstats.* Federal Interagency Council on Statistical Policy. Phone: (202)395-7254 • URL: http://www.fedstats.gov • Web site features an efficient search facility for full-text statistics produced by more than 100 federal agencies, including the Census Bureau, the Bureau of Economic Analysis, and the Bureau of Labor Statistics. Boolean searches can be made within one agency or for all agencies combined. Links are offered to international statistical bureaus, including the UN, IMF, OECD, UNESCO, Eurostat, and 20 individual countries. Fees: Free.

*FreeLunch.com.* Economy.com, Inc. Phone: (610)696-8700; Fax: (610)696-1678 • URL: http://www.freelunch.com • Web site provides free access to more than 200 million economic and financial data series, covering industry, demographics, labor markets, prices, retail sales, government spending, trade, interest rates, housing starts, the stock market, etc. Data is available in either chart or table form. Searching is offered. Free, but registration required. Economy.com, Inc. also offers fee-based economic analysis at *The Dismal Scientist* site (www.dismal.com).

*Manufacturing Profiles.* U. S. Bureau of the Census. Phone: (301)763-4636 or (301)763-4100; Fax: (301)763-4794; Email: webmaster@census.gov • URL: http://www.census.gov/prod/www/abs/mfg-prof.html • The Census Bureau makes available free on PDF (Portable Document Format) an annual consolidation of the entire Current Industrial Report series, presenting "all the data compiled." Contains statistics on production, shipments, inventories, consumption, exports, imports, and orders for a wide variety of manufactured products.

## ONLINE DATABASES

*Textile Technology Index™.* EBSCO Publishing Inc. • Monthly. $545 Individuals. Includes indexing and abstracts for more than 470 periodicals.

*World Textiles.* Elsevier. • Provides abstracting and indexing from 1970 of worldwide textile literature (periodicals, books, pamphlets, and reports). Includes U. S., European, and British patent information. Updating is monthly. Inquire as to on-line cost and availability.

## PERIODICALS AND NEWSLETTERS

*Femme-Lines.* Earl Barron Publications Inc. • Bimonthly. $8.00 per year.

*Harper's Bazaar.* The Hearst Corp. • Monthly. Monthly. $18.00 per year.

*Tobe Report.* Tobe Associates Inc. • Monthly. Edited for fashion retailers. Provides detailed information and analysis relating to current trends in the women's, children's, and men's apparel and accessories markets.

## STATISTICS SOURCES

*Annual Benchmark Report for Retail Trade and Food Services..A Detailed Summary of Retail Sales, Purchases, Accounts Receivable, Inventories, and Food Service Sales.* U. S. Government Printing Office. • Annual. $13.00. Issued by the U.S. Census Bureau. Provides detailed annual and monthly retail statistics for the most recent 10 years. Includes data for various kinds of retail outlets, including automobiles, furniture, appliances, building supplies, grocery stores, drug stores, gasoline stations, clothing, sporting goods, department stores, and restaurants.

*Survey of Current Business.* U. S. Government Printing Office. • Published by Bureau of Economic Analysis, U. S. Department of Commerce. Presents a wide variety of business and economic data.

## TRADE/PROFESSIONAL ASSOCIATIONS

International Bridal Manufacturers Association. 118 W 20th St., 3rd Fl., New York, NY 10011-3627. Email: info@ibma.us • URL: http://ibma.us • Represents wedding apparel and accessory manufacturers. Promotes economic opportunities and fosters better relationships between manufacturers and retailers of bridal apparel. Coordinates and sets non-conflicting dates for bridal industry markets.

# WOMEN'S CLUBS

## PERIODICALS AND NEWSLETTERS

*GFWC Clubwoman: Magazine of the General Federation of Women's Club.* General Federation of Women's Clubs. • Bimonthly. $6 Individuals.

## RESEARCH CENTERS AND INSTITUTES

Business and Professional Women's Foundation. 1718 M St. NW, No. 148, Washington, DC 20036. Phone: (202)293-1100; Fax: (202)861-0298; Email: foundation@bpwfoundation.org • URL: http://bpwfoundation.org • Formerly National Federation of Business and Professional Women's Clubs.

## TRADE/PROFESSIONAL ASSOCIATIONS

Business and Professional Women's Foundation. 1718 M St. NW, No. 148, Washington, DC 20036. Phone: (202)293-1100; Fax: (202)861-0298; Email: foundation@bpwfoundation.org • URL: http://bpwfoundation.org • Formerly National Federation of Business and Professional Women's Clubs.

Canadian Federation of Business and Professional Women's Clubs. PO Box 62054, Orleans, ON, Canada K1C 7H8. • URL: http://www.bpwcanada.com • Canadian women engaged in business, the professions, or industry. Works to enhance the economic, social, and employment status of women. Encourages women to become active in government at every level. Strives to improve business service standards. Networks with related organizations to promote common concerns.

Central Association of Women Entrepreneurs. Kaisaniemenkatu 1 B a 74, FIN-00100 Helsinki, Finland. Phone: 358 40 5222252; Email: toimisto@yrittajanaiset.fi • URL: http://www.yrittajanaiset.fi • Women entrepreneurs in Finland. Promotes the participation of women in Finland's economic structure. Assists women in small business development.

Female Europeans of Medium and Small Enterprises. Rue Jacques de Lalaing 4, B-1040 Brussels, Belgium. Phone: 32 2 2850714; Fax: 32 2 2307861 • URL: http://www.fem-online.eu • Represents female co-entrepreneurs and entrepreneurs working in small and medium-sized businesses in Europe. Seeks to improve the cultural, legal, and social position of female co-entrepreneurs and self-employed women. Acts as the European point of contact dealing with all issues related to female co-entrepreneurs or self-employed women. Aims to achieve an exchange of knowledge and experience amongst women of all EU Member states and also other European countries. Encourages an entrepreneurial spirit amongst women.

National Council of Women of the United States. 777 United Nations Plz., New York, NY 10017. Phone: (212)697-1278; Fax: (212)972-0164; Email: info@ncw-us.org • URL: http://www.ncwus.org • Works for the education, participation and advancement of women in all areas of society. Affiliated with International Council of Women.

National Women's Network. c/o The Admin Center, 46 Beaumont Manor, Northumberland, Blyth NE24 4LP, United Kingdom. Phone: 44 1670 618628 or 44 7855 746777 • URL: http://national-womens-network.co.uk • Professional women in England. Seeks to enhance the status of women. Provides a forum for women to develop social and professional contacts.

Professional Women Controllers. PO Box 23924, Washington, DC 20024. Email: info@pwcinc.org • URL: http://www.pwcinc.org • Women controllers. Promotes the advancement of women within the financial industry. Represents members' interests; facilitates networking among women controllers; and makes available educational programs.

# WOOD FINISHING

*See* WOODWORKING INDUSTRIES

# WOODPULP INDUSTRY

*See also* PAPER INDUSTRY; TALL OIL INDUSTRY

## CD-ROM DATABASES

*OECD Statistical Compendium.* Organization for Economic Cooperation and Development. •

Semiannual. $1,905.00 per year for 1 to 10 users. CD-ROM contains more than 730,000 monthly, quarterly, and annual time series for OECD countries, 1960 to date. Includes fully searchable data on agriculture, food, economic indicators, national accounts, employment, energy, finance, industry, technology, and foreign trade. Results can be displayed in various forms.

## DIRECTORIES

*Directory of South American Importers of Machinery for Paper & Pulp Industry.* EXIM Infotek Private Ltd. • Covers: 40 South American importers of paper and pulp mill machinery and equipment and paper making machinery. Entries include: Company name, postal address, telephone, fax, e-mail, website, contact person, designation, and product details.

*International Pulp and Paper Directory.* UBM L.L.C. • Annual. $287.00. Lists over 6,000 pulp and papermills. International coverage.

*Lockwood-Post's Directory of the Pulp, Paper and Allied Trades.* Miller Freeman Inc. • Annual. $257 Individuals add shipping & handling regular ed. Covers about 1,000 U.S. and Canadian pulp and paper companies and their mills; 4,000 paper converters; 3,000 paper merchants; and industry associations. Formerly *Lockwood's Directory of the Paper and Allied Trades.*

## INTERNET DATABASES

*Business 2.0 Web Guide to the Best Business Links.* Business 2.0 Media Inc. Phone: (415)293-4800; Email: support@business2.com • URL: http://www.business2.com/webguide • Web site presents an extensive, searchable directory of links to "the best, most informative, and authoritative web pages." Twenty main categories cover business, finance, career, company information, people, and technology topics, with thousands of subtopics, all linking to Web sites recommended by experienced business researchers. Fees: Free.

*Fedstats.* Federal Interagency Council on Statistical Policy. Phone: (202)395-7254 • URL: http://www.fedstats.gov • Web site features an efficient search facility for full-text statistics produced by more than 100 federal agencies, including the Census Bureau, the Bureau of Economic Analysis, and the Bureau of Labor Statistics. Boolean searches can be made within one agency or for all agencies combined. Links are offered to international statistical bureaus, including the UN, IMF, OECD, UNESCO, Eurostat, and 20 individual countries. Fees: Free.

*FreeLunch.com.* Economy.com, Inc. Phone: (610)696-8700; Fax: (610)696-1678 • URL: http://www.freelunch.com • Web site provides free access to more than 200 million economic and financial data series, covering industry, demographics, labor markets, prices, retail sales, government spending, trade, interest rates, housing starts, the stock market, etc. Data is available in either chart or table form. Searching is offered. Free, but registration required. Economy.com, Inc. also offers fee-based economic analysis at *The Dismal Scientist* site (www.dismal.com).

## PERIODICALS AND NEWSLETTERS

*Pulp and Paper.* Paperloop. • 11 times a year. $135.00 per year.

*Pulp and Paper Canada.* Pulp and Paper Technical Association of Canada. Scott's Directories. • Bimonthly. Contains accurate, technical information and news to assist those involved in the management and operation of Canada's pulp and paper industry.

*Pulp and Paper International.* Paperloop. • Monthly. Contains latest business developments, operations techniques and technical innovations throughout the world.

*Solutions! The Official Publication of TAPPI and*

*PIMA.* Technical Association of the Pulp & Paper Industry. • Monthly. Membership. Formerly *TAPPI Journal.*

## PRICE SOURCES

*Official Board Markets: "The Yellow Sheet".* Mark Arzoumanian. Advanstar Communications. • Weekly. $160.00 per year. Covers the corrugated container, folding carton, rigid box and waste paper industries.

## STATISTICS SOURCES

*The Pulp and Paper Industry in OECD Member Countries.* Organization for Economic Cooperation and Development. Organisation for Economic Co-operation and Development Publications and Information Center. • Annual. $31.00. Presents annual data on production, consumption, capacity, utilization, and foreign trade. Covers 33 pulp and paper products in OECD countries. Text in English and French.

*Survey of Current Business.* U. S. Government Printing Office. • Published by Bureau of Economic Analysis, U. S. Department of Commerce. Presents a wide variety of business and economic data.

## TRADE/PROFESSIONAL ASSOCIATIONS

Forest Resources Association. 1901 Pennsylvania Ave. NW, Ste. 303, Washington, DC 20006. Phone: (202)296-3937; Fax: (202)296-0562; Email: dhawkinson@forestresources.org • URL: http://www.forestresources.org • Provides a forum to members of the forest resources community-foresters, loggers, landowners, and product manufacturers-where they can meet to solve problems and leverage opportunities within the wood fiber supply chain. Promotes sharing of information, facilitates networking, coordinates activism, serves as a change agent, structures problem-solving workshops, and provides education for members.

# WOODWORKING INDUSTRIES

*See also* CARPENTRY; FOREST PRODUCTS; FURNITURE INDUSTRY; VENEERS AND VENEERING

## DIRECTORIES

*Directory of American Manufacturers and Exporters of Woodworking Equipment and Tools.* EXIM Infotek Private Ltd. • Covers: 240 American manufacturers and exporters of automatic saws and circular, band sawing machine, band saw, band saw blades, belt conveyors, circular cold sawing machine, circular saw blades for wood, circular saw, compass saw, cut off saw, forestry equipment, high speed saw, lumber, machinery for woodworking industry, panel saw, plywood, reciprocating saw, re-saw, sabre saw, saw blades, saw mill, saw mill machinery, saws woodworking, chain saw and parts, portable saws, round hole saw, slitting and slotting saw, stackers, trimmers, wood machinery, and woodworking accessories. Entries include: Company name, postal address, telephone, fax, e-mail, website, contact person, designation, and product details.

*Directory of Australia and New Zealand Importers of Woodworking Equipment and Tools.* EXIM Infotek Private Ltd. • $150 Individuals. Covers: 30 Australian and New Zealand importers of band saw and blades, chain saw, circular saw, dimension saw, forestry equipment, hydraulic chain saw, new and reconditioned woodworking machine, saw blades, saw mill equipment, wood chipping machine, woodworking equipment, woodworking machine and accessories, and woodworking tools. Entries include: Company name, postal address, telephone, fax, e-mail, website, contact person, designation, and product details.

*Directory of British Importers of Woodenware & Wooden Products.* EXIM Infotek Private Ltd. • Covers: 30 British importers of baskets and basket ware, wooden millwork, and wooden products. Entries include: Company name, postal address, telephone, fax, e-mail, website, contact person, designation, and product details.

*Directory of Chinese Manufacturers & Exporters of Woodenware & Wooden Products.* EXIM Infotek Private Ltd. • $15 Individuals. Covers: 160 Chinese manufacturers and exporters of bamboo basketry, bamboo crafts, bamboo curtains, bamboo decorations, bamboo floorings, bamboo handicraft products, bamboo mats, bamboo products, bamboo tableware, baskets-various, cane and wicker products, carvings and marquetry-wooden, rattan products, wicker products, willow baskets, willow products, wood and wood articles, wood products, wooden baskets, wooden boxes, wooden crafts, wooden decorations, wooden floorings, wooden gifts, wooden handicraft products, wooden products, and woodenware. Entries include: Company name, postal address, city, country, phone, fax, e-mail and websites, contact person, designation, and product details.

*Directory of Chinese Manufacturers and Exporters of Woodworking Equipment and Tools.* EXIM Infotek Private Ltd. • Covers: 20 Chinese manufacturers and exporters of hacksaw blades, saw blades, saw cutting machinery, sawing machine, wood working machine, and wood working tools. Entries include: Company name, postal address, telephone, fax, e-mail, website, contact person, designation, and product details.

*Directory of European Importers of Woodworking Equipment & Tools.* EXIM Infotek Private Ltd. • Covers: 160 European importers of bamboo, rattan, wicker products, baskets and basket ware, caskets, desks, logs moldings, wooden millwork, oak strips, planks, raw wood, sculptures, wood panels, wood slabs, wooden handicrafts, wooden bedroom furniture, wooden materials, wooden products and woodenware. Entries include: Company name, postal address, telephone, fax, e-mail, website, contact person, designation, and product details.

*Directory of Japanese Importers of Woodenware & Wooden Products.* EXIM Infotek Private Ltd. • Covers: 270 Japanese importers of bamboo products, bamboo, rattan and wicker products, bamboo/rattan/wicker products, baskets, baskets and basket ware, chopsticks, folding fan, lacquer ware, rattan baskets, rattan products, softwood products, wood and wooden products, wood articles, wood products, wood pulp products, wooden articles, wooden decoration goods, wooden housing components, wooden interior goods, wooden kitchenware, wooden pallets, wooden products, wooden products, wooden tableware, wooden tray, woodenware, and woodworks. Entries include: Company name, postal address, telephone, fax, e-mail, website, contact person, and product details.

*Directory of Japanese Manufacturers and Exporters of Woodworking Equipment and Tools.* EXIM Infotek Private Ltd. • Covers: 20 Japanese manufacturers and exporters of band saw blades, band sawing machine, circle saw, plywood machinery, wood processing machinery, and wood working machine. Entries include: Company name, postal address, telephone, fax, e-mail, website, contact person, designation, and product details.

*Directory of Middle East Importers of Woodenware & Wood Products.* EXIM Infotek Private Ltd. • Covers: 40 Middle East importers of baskets and basket ware, wooden poles, wooden products, and wooden screws. Entries include: Company name, postal address, telephone, fax, e-mail, website, contact person, designation, and product details.

*Directory of South Korean Manufacturers & Exporters of Woodenware & Wood Products.* EXIM Infotek Private Ltd. • $5 Individuals. Covers: 40 South Korean manufacturers and exporters of cane and wicker products, carvings and marquetry-wooden, ladders-wooden, molding and frames-wooden, wooden cases/boxes, wooden decorative cases/boxes, wooden products for industrial use, and wooden products for non-industrial use. Entries include: Company name, postal address, city, country, phone, fax, e-mail and websites, contact person, designation, and product details.

*Directory of South Korean Manufacturers and Exporters of Woodworking Equipment and Tools.* EXIM Infotek Private Ltd. • $150 Individuals. Covers: 40 South Korean manufacturers and exporters of sawing and cutting tools, folding saw, tools for wood working machinery, wood boring and mortising machine, wood conditioning and surface treatment equipment, wood deforming machine, wood joining machine, wood milling and molding machine, wood sanding machine, wood sawing machine, wood turning lathes, wooden picture frame making machinery, and woodworking tools. Entries include: Company name, postal address, telephone, fax, e-mail, website, contact person, designation, and product details.

*Directory of Taiwanese Manufacturers and Exporters of Woodworking Equipment and Tools.* EXIM Infotek Private Ltd. • Covers: 290 Taiwanese manufacturers and exporters of ancillary equipment for wood working machine, multi-operational wood working machine, sawing and cutting tools, timber preparing machinery and equipment, tools for wood working machinery, wood boring and mortising machine, wood conditioning treatment equipment, wood deforming machine, wood joining machine, wood milling and molding machine, wood planning machine, wood sanding machine, wood sawing machine, wood turning lathes, portable wood working machine, wooden picture frame making machinery, woodworking machinery, and woodworking tools. Entries include: Company name, postal address, telephone, fax, e-mail, website, contact person, designation, and product details.

*FDM--The Source--Woodworking Industry Directory.* Reed Elsevier Group plc Reed Business Information. • Annual. $25. Publication includes: List of over 1,800 suppliers to secondary woodworking industry; coverage includes Canada. Entries include: Company name, address, phone, fax, product lines.

*House Furnishings Directory--Retail.* InfoGroup Inc. • Annual. Number of listings: 2,728. Entries include: Name, address, phone, size of advertisement, name of owner or manager, number of employees, year first in "Yellow Pages." Compiled from telephone company "Yellow Pages," nationwide.

*The International Directory of Importers - Woodworking Equipment and Tools Importers.* Interdata. • $200 Individuals print edition. Covers: 1,800 international firms importing woodworking equipment and tools. Entries include: Company name and address, contact person, email, number of employees, year established, phone and telefaxes, business activity, bank references, as well as a listing of woodworking equipment and tools currently being imported.

*Wood Digest-Showcase.* Cygnus Business Media Inc. • Monthly. Publication includes: List of suppliers of materials, machinery, tools, and services for woodworking, cabinetry, casegoods, and furniture manufacturing processes (SIC 24, 25, 37, and 39). Entries include: Company name, phone number, photograph of product, services.

## FINANCIAL RATIOS

*Annual Statement Studies.* Risk Management Association. • Annual. Compiled from over 280,000 financial statements.

*Annual Statement Studies: Industry Default Probabilities and Cash Flow Measures.* Risk Management Association. • Annual. $405 Nonmembers. Serves as a companion volume to the original *Annual Statement Studies.* Gives probability of default estimates on a percentage scale for more than 450 industries. Includes changes in position year-by-year for eight financial statement line items and provides percentage measures of cash flow.

## PERIODICALS AND NEWSLETTERS

*CWB Custom Woodworking Business: Environmental Studies.* Vance Publishing Corp. • Monthly. Magazine for professional custom woodworkers.

*FDM: For Builders of Cabinets, Fixtures, Furniture, Millwork Furniture Design a nd Manufacturing.* Chartwell Communications, Inc. • Monthly. Free to qualified personnel. Edited for furniture executives, production managers, and designers. Covers the manufacturing of household, office, and institutional furniture, store fixtures, and kitchen and bathroom cabinets.

*Forest Products Journal (FPJ).* Forest Products Society. • 8/year. $230 Members individuals:complimentary; Institutions, electronic. Peer-reviewed journal of wood science and technology.

*National Home Center News: News and Analysis for the Home Improvement, Building Material Industry.* Lebhar-Friedman Inc. • 22 times a year. $99.00 per year. Includes special feature issues on hardware and tools, building materials, millwork, electrical supplies, lighting, and kitchens.

## RESEARCH CENTERS AND INSTITUTES

Department of Forest Biomaterials. North Carolina State University, Campus Box 8005, Raleigh, NC 27695. Phone: (919)515-5807; Fax: (919)515-6302; Email: contactfb@ncsu.edu • URL: http://cnr.ncsu.edu • Studies the mechanical and engineering properties of wood, wood finishing, wood anatomy, wood chemistry, etc.

Purdue University - Wood Research Laboratory. Department of Forestry and Natural Resources, 175 Marsteller St., West Lafayette, IN 47907-2033. Phone: (765)494-3619; Fax: (765)496-1344; Email: ehaviar@purdue.edu • URL: http://ag.purdue.edu/fnr/Pages/labwoodresearch.aspx • Use of wood and wood-base materials in engineered structures, ranging from furniture through residential and industrial/commercial building components; wood processing of wood and wood-base materials into furniture and cabinetry; structural applications of wood-base composites; and use, re-use, and care of wood in historic preservation and restoration. Research includes cross-disciplinary projects with engineering disciplines in simulation, machine vision and CAD.

## STATISTICS SOURCES

*U.S. Industry and Trade Outlook.* U.S. Department of Commerce National Technical Information Service. • Annual. Produced by the International Trade Administration, U.S. Department of Commerce, in a "public-private" partnership with DRI/McGraw-Hill and Standard & Poor's. Provides basic data, outlook for the current year, and "Long-Term Prospects" (five-year projections) for a wide variety of products and services. Includes high technology industries. Formerly *U.S. Industrial Outlook.*

## TRADE/PROFESSIONAL ASSOCIATIONS

Architectural Woodwork Institute. 46179 Westlake Dr., Ste. 120, Potomac Falls, VA 20165. Phone: (571)323-3636; Fax: (571)323-3630; Email: info@awinet.org • URL: http://www.awinet.org • Manufacturers of architectural woodwork products (casework, fixtures, and paneling) and associated suppliers of equipment and materials. Works to: raise industry standards; research new and improved materials and methods; publish technical data helpful in the design and use of architectural woodwork. Conducts seminars and training course.

# WOOL AND WORSTED INDUSTRY

*See also* SHEEP INDUSTRY; TEXTILE INDUSTRY; YARN

## ABSTRACTS AND INDEXES

*Textile Technology Index™.* EBSCO Publishing Inc. • Monthly. $545 Individuals. Includes indexing and abstracts for more than 470 periodicals.

## ALMANACS AND YEARBOOKS

*CRB Commodity Yearbook.* Commodity Research Bureau. CRB. • Annual. $179 plus $10.00 shipping cost. The single most comprehensive source of commodity and futures market information available.

## CD-ROM DATABASES

*OECD Statistical Compendium.* Organization for Economic Cooperation and Development. • Semiannual. $1,905.00 per year for 1 to 10 users. CD-ROM contains more than 730,000 monthly, quarterly, and annual time series for OECD countries, 1960 to date. Includes fully searchable data on agriculture, food, economic indicators, national accounts, employment, energy, finance, industry, technology, and foreign trade. Results can be displayed in various forms.

## INTERNET DATABASES

*Business 2.0 Web Guide to the Best Business Links.* Business 2.0 Media Inc. Phone: (415)293-4800; Email: support@business2.com • URL: http://www.business2.com/webguide • Web site presents an extensive, searchable directory of links to "the best, most informative, and authoritative web pages." Twenty main categories cover business, finance, career, company information, people, and technology topics, with thousands of subtopics, all linking to Web sites recommended by experienced business researchers. Fees: Free.

*Fedstats.* Federal Interagency Council on Statistical Policy. Phone: (202)395-7254 • URL: http://www.fedstats.gov • Web site features an efficient search facility for full-text statistics produced by more than 100 federal agencies, including the Census Bureau, the Bureau of Economic Analysis, and the Bureau of Labor Statistics. Boolean searches can be made within one agency or for all agencies combined. Links are offered to international statistical bureaus, including the UN, IMF, OECD, UNESCO, Eurostat, and 20 individual countries. Fees: Free.

*FreeLunch.com.* Economy.com, Inc. Phone: (610)696-8700; Fax: (610)696-1678 • URL: http://www.freelunch.com • Web site provides free access to more than 200 million economic and financial data series, covering industry, demographics, labor markets, prices, retail sales, government spending, trade, interest rates, housing starts, the stock market, etc. Data is available in either chart or table form. Searching is offered. Free, but registration required. Economy.com, Inc. also offers fee-based economic analysis at *The Dismal Scientist* site (www.dismal.com).

*Manufacturing Profiles.* U. S. Bureau of the Census. Phone: (301)763-4636 or (301)763-4100; Fax: (301)763-4794; Email: webmaster@census.gov • URL: http://www.census.gov/prod/www/abs/mfg-prof.html • The Census Bureau makes available free on PDF (Portable Document Format) an annual consolidation of the entire Current Industrial Report series, presenting "all the data compiled." Contains statistics on production, shipments, inventories, consumption, exports, imports, and orders for a wide variety of manufactured products.

*USDA.* U.S. National Institute of Standards and

Technology. 100 Bureau Dr., Gaithersburg, MD 20899-1070. Phone: 800-877-8339 or (301)975-6478 or (202)720-2791; Fax: (301)975-8295; Email: inquiries@nist.gov • URL: http://www.nist.gov • The USDA home page has six sections: News and Information; What's New; About USDA; Agencies; Opportunities; Search and Help. Keyword searching is offered from the USDA home page and from various individual agency home pages. Agencies are the Economic Research Service, Agricultural Marketing Service, National Agricultural Statistics Service, National Agricultural Library, and about 12 others. Updating varies. Fees: Free.

## ONLINE DATABASES

*Textile Technology Index™*. EBSCO Publishing Inc. • Monthly. $545 Individuals. Includes indexing and abstracts for more than 470 periodicals.

*World Textiles*. Elsevier. • Provides abstracting and indexing from 1970 of worldwide textile literature (periodicals, books, pamphlets, and reports). Includes U. S., European, and British patent information. Updating is monthly. Inquire as to on-line cost and availability.

## PERIODICALS AND NEWSLETTERS

*Canadian Co-Operative Wool Growers Magazine*. Canadian Co-Operative Wool Growers. • Annual. $3 Nonmembers. Contains information and a mail order catalogue for livestock supplies, equestrian products and clothing.

*Journal of Natural Fibers*. The Haworth Press Inc. • Quarterly. $400.00 per year to libraries; $45.00 per year to individuals. Covers applications, technology, research, and world markets relating to fibers from silk, wool, cotton, flax, hemp, jute, etc. Previously *Natural Fibres*, published annually.

## STATISTICS SOURCES

*Agricultural Statistics*. U.S. Department of Agriculture National Agricultural Statistics Service. • Annual. $46 Individuals. Provides a wide variety of statistical data relating to agricultural production, supplies, consumption, prices/price-supports, foreign trade, costs, and returns, as well as farm labor, loans, income, and population. In many cases, historical data is shown annually for 10 years. In addition to farm data, includes detailed fishery statistics.

*Survey of Current Business*. U. S. Government Printing Office. • Published by Bureau of Economic Analysis, U. S. Department of Commerce. Presents a wide variety of business and economic data.

## TRADE/PROFESSIONAL ASSOCIATIONS

American Sheep Industry Association. 9785 Maroon Cir., Ste. 360, Englewood, CO 80112. Phone: (303)771-3500; Fax: (303)771-8200; Email: info@sheepusa.org • URL: http://www.sheepusa.org • Producers of sheep and wool. Goal is to advance the standards and profitability of the sheep industry. Conducts lobbying activities to promote legislation beneficial to the industry.

# WORD PROCESSING

*See also* COMPUTERS; DESKTOP PUBLISHING; MICROCOMPUTERS AND MINICOMPUTERS; OFFICE AUTOMATION; OFFICE EQUIPMENT AND SUPPLIES; OFFICE MANAGEMENT

## ABSTRACTS AND INDEXES

*Computer and Information Systems Abstracts Journal: An Abstract Journal Pertaining to the Theory, Design, Fabrication and Application of Computer and Information Systems*. CSA. • Monthly. $1,750 per year.

*Computer Science Index*. EBSCO Publishing Inc. • Quarterly. $245 per year. Contains brief abstracts of

book and periodical literature covering all phases of computing, including approximately 70 specific application areas.

*Internet and Personal Computing Abstracts (print edition)*. EBSCO Publishing Inc. • Quarterly. $269.00 per year, including cumulative index. Provides more than 10,000 abstracts annually from both trade and academic publications. Covers computer hardware, software, product reviews, Web topics, e-commerce, networks, corporate news, security, and related topics. Formerly *Microcomputer Abstracts*.

## HANDBOOKS AND MANUALS

*Secretarial/Word Processing Service*. Entrepreneur Press. • Looseleaf. $59.50. A practical guide to starting a secretarial and word processing business. Covers profit potential, start-up costs, market size evaluation, owner's time required, site selection, pricing, accounting, advertising, promotion, etc. (Start-Up Business Guide No. E1136.).

## ONLINE DATABASES

*Computer Database*. Cengage Learning Inc. • Provides one year of full-text online for 150 leading computer-related publications. Also includes 70,000 product specifications and brief profiles of 13,000 computer product vendors and manufacturers. Inquire as to prices and availability.

## PERIODICALS AND NEWSLETTERS

*In Command! A Series of Messages About Getting the Most From Your Word Processor*. Economics Press Inc. • Weekly. $146.00 per year. Quantity prices available. A newsletter for word processing operators.

*Inside Microsoft Word: Tips and Techniques for Microsoft Windows*. Skillsoft Ireland Ltd. • Monthly. $87.00 per year. Newsletter on word processing with Microsoft Word for Windows. Covers applications and problem-solving.

*Inside Wordperfect for Windows*. Skillsoft Ireland Ltd. • Monthly. $59.00 per year. Newsletter on word processing with Wordperfect software. Includes tips and techniques for both beginners and experts.

*The Page*. Skillsoft Ireland Ltd. • Description: Acts as a visual guide to McIntosh computer desktop publishing.

*Prompt*. Pasadena IBM User Group. • Monthly. Membership. Helps users of IBM compatibles understand their system.

# WORDS

*See* VOCABULARY

# WORK CLOTHES

*See* UNIFORMS

# WORK FORCE

*See* LABOR SUPPLY

# WORK MEASUREMENT

*See* TIME AND MOTION STUDY

# WORK SIMPLIFICATION

*See* TIME AND MOTION STUDY

# WORK STOPPAGES

*See* STRIKES AND LOCKOUTS

# WORK STUDY

*See* TIME AND MOTION STUDY

# WORKERS' COMPENSATION

## ABSTRACTS AND INDEXES

*Current Law Index*. Cengage Learning Inc. • $1,332 Individuals. Monthly. $1269.00 per year. Produced in cooperation with the American Association of Law Libraries. Indexes more than 900 law journals, legal newspapers, and specialty publications from the U.S., Canada, U.K., Ireland, Australia, and New Zealand.

*Index to Legal Periodicals and Books*. H.W. Wilson Co. • Monthly. $490.00 per year. Quarterly and annual cumulations.

*Insurance Periodicals Index*. Specials Libraries Association, Insurance and Employees Benefits Div. NILS Publishing Co. • Annual. $250.00. Compiled by the Insurance and Employee Benefits Div., Special Libraries Association. A yearly index of over 15,000 articles from about 35 insurance periodicals. Arrangement is by subject, with an index to authors.

## BIBLIOGRAPHIES

*Insurance and Employee Benefits Literature*. Special Libraries Association. • Bimonthly. $15.00 per year. Lists a wide variety of literature in all branches of the insurance industry. Includes annotations.

## CD-ROM DATABASES

*Authority Worker's Compensation Library*. Matthew Bender and Company Inc. • Periodic revisions. Price on request. CD-ROM contains updated full text of *Larson's Workmen's Compensation, Occupational Injuries and Illnesses*, and other Matthew Bender publications relating to worker's compensation laws.

## DIRECTORIES

*Understanding Workers Compensation: A Guide for Safety and Health Professionals*. Government Institutes. • $72 Individuals Paperback. Publication includes: Listing of state and provincial workers compensation administrators. Database includes: Sample forms, checklists, U.S. Chamber of Commerce analysis. Entries include: Name, address, phone. Principal content of publication is explanation of the Workers Compensation System.

## HANDBOOKS AND MANUALS

*Modern Workers Compensation*. Thomson West. • $1,137.81 Four volumes. Provides detailed coverage of workers' compensation law and procedure, including medical benefits, rehabilitation benefits, compensation costs, noncompensable injuries, etc.

*U.S. Master Employee Benefits Guide*. Wolters Kluwer Law & Business CCH. • Annual. $102.50 Individuals. Explains federal tax and labor laws relating to health care benefits, disability benefits, workers' compensation, employee assistance plans, etc.

## INTERNET DATABASES

*Lexis.com Research System*. Lexis-Nexis Group. Phone: 800-227-4908 or (937)865-6800; Fax: (937)865-6909; Email: webmaster@prod.lexisnexis.com • URL: http://www.nexis.com • Fee-based Web site offers extensive searching of a wide variety of legal sources. Additional features include Daily Opinion Service, lexis.com Bookstore, Career Center, CLE Center, Law Schools, and Practice Pages ("Pages specific to areas of specialty").

*National Center for Health Statistics: Monitoring the Nation's Health*. National Center for Health Statistics, Centers for Disease Control and Prevention. Phone: (301)458-4000; Email: nchsquery@cdc.gov • URL: http://www.cdc.gov/nchswww • Web site provides detailed data on diseases, vital statistics, and health care in the U. S. Includes a search facility and links to many other health-related Web sites. "Fastats A to Z" offers quick data on hundreds of topics from Accidents to Work-Loss Days, with links to Comprehensive Data and related sources. Frequent updates. Fees: Free.

## ONLINE DATABASES

*I.I.I. Data Base Search.* Insurance Information Institute. • Provides online citations and abstracts of insurance-related literature in magazines, newspapers, trade journals, and books. Emphasis is on property and casualty insurance issues, including highway safety, product safety, and environmental liability. Inquire as to online cost and availability.

## OTHER SOURCES

*BNA's Workers' Compensation Report.* Bloomberg BNA. • Biweekly. $604.00 per year. Looseleaf business and legal service.

## PERIODICALS AND NEWSLETTERS

*Business Insurance: News Magazine for Corporate Risk, Employee Benefit and Financial Executives.* Crain Communications Inc. • Weekly. $95.00 per year. Covers a wide variety of business insurance topics, including risk management, employee benefits, workers compensation, marine insurance, and casualty insurance.

*Human Resource Executive.* LRP Publications Library. • 16 times a year. $89.95 per year. Edited for directors of corporate human resource departments. Special issues emphasize training, benefits, retirement planning, recruitment, outplacement, workers' compensation, legal pitfalls, and oes emphasize training, benefits, retirement planning, recruitment, outplacement, workers' compensation, legal pitfalls, and other personnel topics.

*Risk and Insurance.* LRP Publications Library. • Monthly. Price on application. Topics include risk management, workers' compensation, reinsurance, employee benefits, and managed care.

*Workers' Compensation Law Bulletin.* Quinlan Publishing Co. • Description: Summarizes in layman's terms recent court cases deriving from the worker compensation law, with specific identification of cases and brief explanations of the court decisions.

*Workers' Compensation Monitor.* LRP Publications Library. • Description: Suggests ways to reduce workers' compensation costs and improve your return-to-work programs. Provides proven solutions your colleagues have implemented to resolve their challenges. Keeps readers up-to-date on the latest developments in national workers' compensation issues including benefits, insurance coverage, legislative reform and costs.

## RESEARCH CENTERS AND INSTITUTES

Brandeis University - Center for Youth and Communities. Heller Bldg., 3rd Fl., MS 035, 415 S St., Waltham, MA 02454. Phone: (781)736-4835 or (781)736-3729; Fax: (781)736-3773; Email: curnan@brandeis.edu • URL: http://cyc.brandeis.edu • Formerly Center for Human Resources.

W.E. Upjohn Institute for Employment Research. 300 S Westnedge Ave., Kalamazoo, MI 49007-4686. Phone: 888-227-8569 or (269)343-5541; Fax: (269)343-7310; Email: communications@upjohn.org • URL: http://www.upjohninstitute.org • Research fields include unemployment, unemployment insurance, worker's compensation, labor productivity, profit sharing, the labor market, economic development, earnings, training, and other areas related to employment.

## TRADE/PROFESSIONAL ASSOCIATIONS

UWC: Strategic Services on Unemployment and Workers' Compensation. 910 17th St. NW, Ste. 1070, Washington, DC 20006. Phone: (202)223-8902; Fax: (202)783-1616; Email: info@

uwcstrategy.org • URL: http://www.uwcstrategy.org • Works to serve the business community by promoting Unemployment Insurance (UI) and Workers' Compensation (WC) programs that provide fair benefits to workers at affordable cost to employers and the community.

# WORKING CLASS

*See* LABOR

# WORKMEN'S COMPENSATION

*See* WORKERS' COMPENSATION

# WORKSHOPS

*See* CONFERENCES, WORKSHOPS, AND SEMINARS

# WORLD BANKING

*See* INTERNATIONAL FINANCE

# WORLD LAW

*See* INTERNATIONAL LAW AND REGULATION

# WORLD TRADE

*See* FOREIGN TRADE

# WORLD WIDE WEB

*See* INTERNET

# WORSTED INDUSTRY

*See* WOOL AND WORSTED INDUSTRY

# WORTHLESS SECURITIES

*See* OBSOLETE SECURITIES

# WRITERS AND WRITING

*See also* REPORT WRITING; TECHNICAL WRITING

## BIOGRAPHICAL SOURCES

*Contemporary Authors.* Cengage Learning Inc. • $336 Individuals. Back volumes available. Provides biographical information on over 130,000 modern authors, including novelists, nonfiction writers, poets, playwrights, journalists, and scriptwriters.

*International Who's Who of Authors and Writers.* Taylor & Francis. • $490. Over 8,000 authors, writers, and poets, primarily American and British but including writers from nearly 40 countries in the English-speaking world.

## DIRECTORIES

*AWP Official Guide to Writing Programs.* Association of Writers and Writing Programs. • Biennial Annual. $28.45 Individuals including shipping and handling. Covers: About 300 graduate and 400 undergraduate programs in creative writing; approximately 250 writers' conferences, festivals, and

centers; coverage includes Canada and the United Kingdom. Entries include: Institution name, department name, contact name and address; web site, description of program, including degree or other credit offered; description of faculty, including titles of their publications; tuition fees and dates.

*Business and Legal Forms for Authors and Self-publishers.* Allworth Press. • $24.99 Single issue paperback. Publication includes: Contact information for volunteer lawyers for the arts. Principal content of publication is instruction and use of business and legal forms for authors and self-publishers.

*Editor and Publisher Syndicate Directory: Annual Directory of Syndicate Services.* Editor & Publisher Magazine. • Annual. $28 Individuals. Directory of several hundred syndicates serving newspapers in the United States and abroad with news, columns, features, comic strips, editorial cartoons, etc.

*Hollywood Creative Directory: Film Writers.* IFILMpro. • Annual. $85.00. Lists more than 8,000 screenwriters and their associated 35,000 film titles. Includes projects in development and unsold screenplays.

*International Literary Market Place: The Directory of the International Book Publishing Industry.* Information Today, Inc. • Annual. $299 Individuals softbound. Covers more than 180 countries. Listings include publishers, literary agents, major booksellers, book clubs, literary prizes, distributors, trade associations, etc. Formerly published by R. R. Bowker.

*Literary Market Place: The Directory of the American Book Publishing Industry.* Information Today, Inc. • Annual. $399 Individuals 2-volume set/softbound plus $25 shipping/handling. Listings include publishers, agents, ad agencies, associations, distributors, events, key executives, services, and suppliers (50 directory sections in all). Formerly published by R. R. Bowker.

*Short Story Writers.* Magill's Choice. • $217 Individuals 3 volumes. Covers: 102 short story writers of the 19th and 20th centuries. Entries include: Writer name, principal works of short fiction, other literary forms produced, notable career and technical achievements related to the short story form, brief biography, glossary.

*Working Press of the Nation.* R.R. Bowker L.L.C. • Annual. $530.00. $295.00 per volume. Three volumes: (1) *Newspaper Directory*; (2) *Magazine and Internal Publications Directory*; (3) *Radio and Television Directory*. Includes names of editors and other personnel.

*Writers' and Artists' Yearbook: A Directory for Writers, Artists, Playwrights, Writers for Film, Radio and Television, Photographers and Composers.* Midpoint Trade Books. • Annual. $25.00. A worldwide guide to markets for various kinds of writing and artwork. Published in England by A O C Black. Formerly *International Writers' and Artists' Yearbook.*

*Writers Directory.* InfoGroup Inc. • Updated continuously; printed on request. Number of listings: 2,400. Entries include: Name, address, phone, size of advertisement, name of owner or manager, number of employees, year first in "Yellow Pages." Compiled from telephone company "Yellow Pages," nationwide.

*Writer's Guide to Book Editors, Publishers, and Literary Agents, Who They Are, What They Want, and How to Win Them Over.* Prima Publishing Inc. • Annual. $27.95; with CD-ROM, $49.95. Directory for authors includes information on publishers' response times and pay rates.

*Writer's Market: Where & How to Sell What You Write.* North Light Books. • Annual. $19.79 Individuals paperback. Covers: Over 3,500 buyers of books, articles, short stories, plays, gags, verse, fillers, and other original written material. Includes book and periodical publishers, greeting card publishers, play producers and publishers, audiovisual material producers, syndicates, and contests and awards. Database includes: Interviews with editors and writers and advice on writing, freelancing, and marketing. Entries include: Name and address of buyer, phone, payment rates, editorial requirements, reporting time, how to break in.

## HANDBOOKS AND MANUALS

*Personnel Management: Communications.* Prentice Hall PTR. • Looseleaf. Periodic supplementation. Price on application. Includes how to write effectively and how to prepare employee publications.

## OTHER SOURCES

*Lindey on Entertainment, Publishing and the Arts.* Alexander Lindey, editor. Thomson West. • $1,582.86 Full Set. Provides basic forms, applicable law, and guidance.

## PERIODICALS AND NEWSLETTERS

*Copy Editor: Language News for the Publishing Profession.* McMurry Newsletters. • Bimonthly. Newsletter for professional copy editors and proofreaders. Includes such items as "Top Ten Resources for Copy Editors.".

*Publishers Weekly: The International News Magazine of Book Publishing.* Reed Elsevier Group plc Reed Business Information. • Weekly. $20.95 print and online; monthly. The international news magazine of book publishing.

*Quill: The Magazine for Journalists.* Society of Professional Journalists. • Bimonthly. $75 Individuals.

## TRADE/PROFESSIONAL ASSOCIATIONS

American Society of Business Publications Editors. 214 N Hale St., Wheaton, IL 60187. Phone: (603)510-4588; Fax: (603)510-4501; Email: info@asbpe.org • URL: http://www.asbpe.org.

American Society of Journalists and Authors. Times Square, 1501 Broadway, Ste. 403, New York, NY 10036. Phone: (212)997-0947; Fax: (212)937-2315 or (212)768-7414; Email: asjaoffice@asja.org • URL: http://www.asja.org • Represents freelance writers of nonfiction magazine articles and books. Seeks to elevate the professional and economic position of nonfiction writers, provide a forum for discussion of common problems among writers and editors, and promote a code of ethics for writers and

editors. Operates writer referral service for individuals, institutions, or companies seeking writers for special projects; sponsors Llewellyn Miller Fund to aid professional writers who no longer able to work due to age, disability, or extraordinary professional crisis.

Association for Business Communication. 181 Turner St. NW, Blacksburg, VA 24061. Phone: (540)231-8460 or (540)231-1939; Email: abcoffice@businesscommunication.org • URL: http://www.businesscommunication.org • College teachers of business communication; management consultants in business communications; training directors and correspondence supervisors of business firms, direct mail copywriters, public relations writers, and others interested in communication for business.

Association of Authors' Representatives. 676A 9th Ave., Ste. 312, New York, NY 10036. Phone: (212)840-5770; Email: administrator@aaronline.org • URL: http://www.aaronline.org • Literary and dramatic agents who market books, plays, and other literary and dramatic material.

Association of Writers and Writing Programs. George Mason University, 4400 University Dr., MSN 1E3, Fairfax, VA 22030-4444. Phone: (703)993-4301 or (703)933-4301; Fax: (703)993-4302 or (703)933-4302; Email: awp@awpwriter.org • URL: http://www.awpwriter.org • Supports writers and writing programs worldwide.

Authors Guild. 31 E 32nd St., 7th Fl., New York, NY 10016. Phone: (212)563-5904; Fax: (212)564-5363; Email: staff@authorsguild.org • URL: http://www.authorsguild.net/ • Professional book and magazine writers. Maintains legal staff to provide book and magazine contract reviews for members. Group health insurance available. Members of the guild are also members of the Authors League of America.

Editorial Freelancers Association. 71 W 23rd St., 4th Fl., New York, NY 10010-4102. Phone: 866-929-5439 or (212)929-5400; Fax: (212)929-5439; Email: office@the-efa.org • URL: http://www.the-efa.org • Represents persons who work full or part-time as freelance writers or editorial freelancers. Promotes professionalism and facilitates the exchange of information and support. Conducts professional training seminars; and offers job listings.

National Sportscasters and Sportswriters Association. PO Box 1545, Salisbury, NC 28145.

Phone: (704)633-4275; Fax: (704)633-2027 • URL: http://nssafame.com • Members are sportswriters and radio/TV sportscasters.

National Writers Association. 10940 S Parker Rd., No. 508, Parker, CO 80134. Phone: (303)841-0246; Fax: (303)841-2607; Email: natlwritersassn@hotmail.com • URL: http://www.nationalwriters.com • Professional full- or part-time freelance writers who specialize in business writing. Aims to serve as a marketplace whereby business editors can easily locate competent writing talent. Establishes communication among editors and writers.

# WRITING INSTRUMENTS

*See also* OFFICE EQUIPMENT AND SUPPLIES

## DIRECTORIES

*Directory of South Korean Manufacturers & Exporters of Stationery Articles & Education Supplies.* EXIM Infotek Private Ltd. • $250 Individuals. Covers: 70 South Korean manufacturers and exporters of drawing and mathematical instruments, filing systems, inks and artists colors, pencil cases, pens, pencils, rubber stamps and pads, staplers, stationeries, stationery and greeting cards, stationery articles, writing and drawing equipment. Entries include: Company name, postal address, telephone, fax, e-mail, website, contact person, designation, and product details.

## TRADE/PROFESSIONAL ASSOCIATIONS

International PEN - Writers in Prison Committee. Brownlow House, 50/51 High Holborn, London WC1V 6ER, United Kingdom. Phone: 44 20 74050338; Fax: 44 20 74050339; Email: info@pen-international.org • URL: http://www.pen-international.org • Serves as a key resource for the writing instruments industry. Provides leadership and direction for its members by staying at the forefront of trends, education, and technology in order to promote and procure the future of writing instrument development and distribution. Offers strategic analysis of manufacturer and retail marketing efforts.

# WRITING, TECHNICAL

*See* TECHNICAL WRITING

# X

## X-RAY EQUIPMENT INDUSTRY

*See also* HOSPITAL EQUIPMENT; MEDICAL TECHNOLOGY

### ABSTRACTS AND INDEXES

*Applied Science and Technology Index.* EBSCO Publishing Inc. • 11/year. Indexes a wide variety of English language technical, industrial, and engineering periodicals.

### CD-ROM DATABASES

*Applied Science and Technology Abstracts.* EBSCO Publishing Inc. • Citations for more than 700 prominent scientific, technical, engineering, and industrial periodicals.

### INTERNET DATABASES

*Manufacturing Profiles.* U. S. Bureau of the Census. Phone: (301)763-4636 or (301)763-4100; Fax: (301)763-4794; Email: webmaster@census.gov • URL: http://www.census.gov/prod/www/abs/mfg-prof.html • The Census Bureau makes available free on PDF (Portable Document Format) an annual consolidation of the entire Current Industrial Report series, presenting "all the data compiled." Contains statistics on production, shipments, inventories, consumption, exports, imports, and orders for a wide variety of manufactured products.

### ONLINE DATABASES

*Applied Science and Technology Index Online.* H.W. Wilson Co. • Provides online indexing of 500 major scientific, technical, industrial, and engineering periodicals. Time period is 1983 to date. Monthly updates. Inquire as to online cost and availability.

### PERIODICALS AND NEWSLETTERS

*Decisions in Imaging Economics: The Journal of Imaging Technology Management.* CurAnt Communications Inc. • Bimonthly. Controlled circulation. Edited for health care executives and radiologists concerned with the purchase and management of imaging technology.

*The Gray Sheet Reports: Medical Devices, Diagnostics and Instrumentation.* Elsevier Business Intelligence. • Weekly. Institutions, $1,172.00 per year. Newsletter. Provides industry and financial news, including a medical sector stock index. Monitors regulatory developments at the Center for Devices and Radiological Health of the U. S. Food and Drug Administration.

*Healthcare Purchasing News: A Magazine for Hospital Materials Management Central Service, Infection Control Practitioners.* Thomson Medical Economics. • Monthly. $72. Edited for personnel responsible for the purchase of medical, surgical, and hospital equipment and supplies. Features new purchasing techniques and new products. Includes news of the activities of two major purchasing associations, Health Care Material Management Society and International Association of Healthcare Central Service Materiel Management.

### RESEARCH CENTERS AND INSTITUTES

Mallinckrodt Institute of Radiology - Hyperthermia Service. Washington University Medical Center, 510 S Kingshighway Blvd., St. Louis, MO 63110. Phone: (314)362-8503; Fax: (314)362-8521 • URL: http://www.mir.wustl.edu • Maintains laboratories for research pertaining to various kinds of radiological equipment.

### TRADE/PROFESSIONAL ASSOCIATIONS

American College of Radiology. 1891 Preston White Dr., Reston, VA 20191. Phone: (703)648-8900; Email: info@acr.org • URL: http://www.acr.org • A professional society of physicians. Affiliated with International Society of Radiology.

Association for Healthcare Resource and Materials Management. 155 N Wacker Dr., Chicago, IL 60606. Phone: (312)422-3840; Fax: (312)422-4573; Email: ahrmm@aha.org • URL: http://www.ahrmm.org • Members are involved with the purchasing and distribution of supplies and equipment for hospitals and other healthcare establishments. Formerly American Society for Healthcare Materials Management.

Radiological Society of North America. 820 Jorie Blvd., Oak Brook, IL 60523-2251. Phone: 800-381-6660 or (630)571-2670; Fax: (630)571-7837; Email: mwatson@rsna.org • URL: http://www.rsna.org • Members are radiologists and scientists. Includes a Technical Exhibits Committee and a Scientific Exhibits Committee. Formerly Western Roentgen Society.

Radiology Business Management Association. 10300 Eaton Pl., Ste. 460, Fairfax, VA 22030. Phone: 888-224-7262 or (703)621-3355; Fax: (703)621-3356 • URL: http://www.rbma.org • Provides education, resources and solutions to manage the business of radiology. Offers an online course in radiology coding.

# Y

## YACHTS

*See* BOAT INDUSTRY

## YARN

*See also* COTTON INDUSTRY; SILK INDUSTRY; TEXTILE INDUSTRY; WEAVING; WOOL AND WORSTED INDUSTRY

### ABSTRACTS AND INDEXES

*Textile Technology Index*™. EBSCO Publishing Inc. • Monthly. $545 Individuals. Includes indexing and abstracts for more than 470 periodicals.

### CD-ROM DATABASES

*OECD Statistical Compendium*. Organization for Economic Cooperation and Development. • Semiannual. $1,905.00 per year for 1 to 10 users. CD-ROM contains more than 730,000 monthly, quarterly, and annual time series for OECD countries, 1960 to date. Includes fully searchable data on agriculture, food, economic indicators, national accounts, employment, energy, finance, industry, technology, and foreign trade. Results can be displayed in various forms.

### DIRECTORIES

*Directory of African Importers of Yarns and Threads*. EXIM Infotek Private Ltd. • $300 Individuals. Covers: 90 African importers of acrylic yarn, cotton yarn and thread, embroidery threads, polyester yarn, sewing threads, synthetic yarns and thread, and wool yarn. Entries include: Company name, postal address, telephone, fax, e-mail, website, contact person, designation, and product details.

*Directory of American Manufacturers & Exporters of Yarns & Threads*. EXIM Infotek Private Ltd. • $10 Individuals. Covers: 80 American manufacturers and exporters of bleaching and space dyeing yarns, carpet yarns, cotton yarns, synthetic yarns, textile yarn, woolen yarns, and yarns. Entries include: Company name, postal address, city, country, phone, fax, e-mail and websites, contact person, designation, and product details.

*Directory of Asian Importers of Yarns and Threads*. EXIM Infotek Private Ltd. • $950 Individuals. Covers: 580 Asian importers of 100% cotton yarn for weaving cotton, acetate filament yarn, acrylic yarn, acrylic yarn carded and dyed, carpet yarn, cotton yarn and thread, dupion silk yarn, fancy yarns, fibers and yarns, filament yarn, jute yarn, knitting yarn, linen yarn, man-made fiber, man-made yarn, metallic yarn and thread, nylon filament yarn, nylon thread, nylon yarn, polyester filament yarn,

polyester yarn, polypropylene yarn, raw silk yarn, rayon yarn, sewing threads, silk yarn and thread, spun silk yarn, stitching thread, synthetic yarn and thread, viscose filament yarn, viscose rayon filament yarn, viscose yarn, wool yarn, yarn twister, and yarn waste. Entries include: Company name, postal address, telephone, fax, e-mail, website, contact person, designation, and product details.

*Directory of Australia and New Zealand Importers of Yarns and Threads*. EXIM Infotek Private Ltd. • $150 Individuals. Covers: 25 Australian and New Zealand importers of cotton yarn, embroidery thread, filament yarn, industrial filament yarn, knitting yarn, metallic yarn and thread, polyster yarn, sewing threads, silk yarn and thread, synthetic yarn and thread, textile fibers, wool yarn, and worsted weaving yarn. Entries include: Company name, postal address, telephone, fax, e-mail, website, contact person, designation, and product details.

*Directory of British Importers of Yarns and Threads*. EXIM Infotek Private Ltd. • $150 Individuals. Covers: 20 British importers of yarn and thread, cotton yarn and thread, synthetic yarn and thread. Entries include: Company name, postal address, telephone, fax, e-mail, website, contact person, designation, and product details.

*Directory of Chinese Manufacturers & Exporters of Yarns & Threads*. EXIM Infotek Private Ltd. • $10 Individuals. Covers: 80 Chinese manufacturers and exporters of cashmere yarn, chenille yarn, cotton yarn, embroidery thread, knitting yarn, linen yarns, metallic yarns, polyester filaments, polyester thread, polyester yarn, sewing thread, thread, viscose filament yarns, yarn products, yarns, and yarns-blended. Entries include: Company name, postal address, city, country, phone, fax, e-mail and websites, contact person, designation, and product details.

*Directory of European Importers of Yarns and Threads*. EXIM Infotek Private Ltd. • $550 Individuals. Covers: 190 European importers of 100% cotton yarn, acrylic yarn, cotton sewing thread, cotton yarn and thread, embroidery thread, flax yarn, nylon filaments, polyester textured yarn, silk yarn and thread, synthetic elementary filament yarn, synthetic yarn and thread, textured yarn of polymers, twists, wool yarn, and yarn waste. Entries include: Company name, postal address, telephone, fax, e-mail, website, contact person, designation, and product details.

*Directory of Indian Importers of Yarns and Threads*. EXIM Infotek Private Ltd. • $400 Individuals. Covers: 90 Indian importers of cotton yarn, dupion silk yarn, fibers, yarns, filament yarn, man-made yarn, metallic yarn and thread, nylon yarn, polyester yarn, raw silk yarn, sewing threads, silk yarn and thread, synthetic yarn and thread, viscose yarn, wool yarn,

and yarn waste. Entries include: Company name, postal address, telephone, fax, e-mail, website, contact person, designation, and product details.

*Directory of Japanese Importers of Yarns and Threads*. EXIM Infotek Private Ltd. • $250 Individuals. Covers: 75 Japanese importers of yarns and thread, cotton yarn and thread, silk yarn and thread, synthetic yarn and thread, and yarn twister. Entries include: Company name, postal address, telephone, fax, e-mail, website, contact person, designation, and product details.

*Directory of Middle East Importers of Yarns and Threads*. EXIM Infotek Private Ltd. • $500 Individuals. Covers: 200 Middle East importers of acetate yarns, cotton yarn and thread, elastic yarn, metallic yarn and thread, nylon filament yarn, nylon yarn, polyester yarn, sewing thread, silk yarns, sisal yarns and ropes, synthetic yarn and thread, viscose yarns, and wool yarn. Entries include: Company name, postal address, telephone, fax, e-mail, website, contact person, designation, and product details.

*Directory of North American Importers of Yarns and Threads*. EXIM Infotek Private Ltd. • $300 Individuals. Covers: 100 North American importers of acrylic yarn, cotton yarn, embroidery thread, filament yarn, metallic yarn, polyester yarn, sewing thread, silk yarn and thread, synthetic yarn, thread, viscose, wool yarn, cotton, and silk. Entries include: Company name, postal address, telephone, fax, e-mail, website, contact person, designation, and product details.

*Directory of South American Importers of Yarns and Threads*. EXIM Infotek Private Ltd. • $250 Individuals. Covers: 100 South American importers of cotton yarn and thread, embroidery threads, metallic yarn and thread, nylon yarn for carpets, polyester yarn, sewing thread, synthetic yarns and thread, and wool yarn. Entries include: Company name, postal address, telephone, fax, e-mail, website, contact person, designation, and product details.

*Directory of South Korean Manufacturers & Exporters of Yarns & Threads*. EXIM Infotek Private Ltd. • $25 Individuals. Covers: 310 South Korean manufacturers and exporters of cotton yarn, dyeing and finishing for textile fiber/yarn, sewing and embroidery thread, textile fiber-manmade, yarn and twists-silk, yarn and twists-manmade fiber, yarns and twists-vegetable fibers, yarns and twists-wool/hair. Entries include: Company name, postal address, city, country, phone, fax, e-mail and websites, contact person, designation, and product details.

*Directory of Taiwanese Manufacturers & Exporters of Yarns & Threads*. EXIM Infotek Private Ltd. • $20 Individuals. Covers: 270 Taiwanese manufacturers and exporters of cotton yarn, dying and finishing for textile fiber/yarn, reflective filaments, sewing and embroidery thread, textile fiber-manmade, thread, yarn and twist-silk, yarn and twists-manmade fiber, yarns and twists-vegetable fibers, yarns and twists-wool/hair. Entries include: Company name, postal address, city, country, phone, fax, e-mail and websites, contact person, designation, and product details.

## FINANCIAL RATIOS

*Annual Statement Studies.* Risk Management Association. • Annual. Compiled from over 280,000 financial statements.

*Annual Statement Studies: Industry Default Probabilities and Cash Flow Measures.* Risk Management Association. • Annual. $405 Nonmembers. Serves as a companion volume to the original *Annual Statement Studies.* Gives probability of default estimates on a percentage scale for more than 450 industries. Includes changes in position year-by-year for eight financial statement line items and provides percentage measures of cash flow.

## INTERNET DATABASES

*Business 2.0 Web Guide to the Best Business Links.* Business 2.0 Media Inc. Phone: (415)293-4800; Email: support@business2.com • URL: http://www.business2.com/webguide • Web site presents an extensive, searchable directory of links to "the best, most informative, and authoritative web pages." Twenty main categories cover business, finance, career, company information, people, and technology topics, with thousands of subtopics, all linking to Web sites recommended by experienced business researchers. Fees: Free.

*Fedstats.* Federal Interagency Council on Statistical Policy. Phone: (202)395-7254 • URL: http://www.fedstats.gov • Web site features an efficient search facility for full-text statistics produced by more than 100 federal agencies, including the Census Bureau, the Bureau of Economic Analysis, and the Bureau of Labor Statistics. Boolean searches can be made within one agency or for all agencies combined. Links are offered to international statistical bureaus, including the UN, IMF, OECD, UNESCO, Eurostat, and 20 individual countries. Fees: Free.

*FreeLunch.com.* Economy.com, Inc. Phone: (610)696-8700; Fax: (610)696-1678 • URL: http://www.freelunch.com • Web site provides free access

to more than 200 million economic and financial data series, covering industry, demographics, labor markets, prices, retail sales, government spending, trade, interest rates, housing starts, the stock market, etc. Data is available in either chart or table form. Searching is offered. Free, but registration required. Economy.com, Inc. also offers fee-based economic analysis at *The Dismal Scientist* site (www.dismal.com).

*Manufacturing Profiles.* U. S. Bureau of the Census. Phone: (301)763-4636 or (301)763-4100; Fax: (301)763-4794; Email: webmaster@census.gov • URL: http://www.census.gov/prod/www/abs/mfg-prof.html • The Census Bureau makes available free on PDF (Portable Document Format) an annual consolidation of the entire Current Industrial Report series, presenting "all the data compiled." Contains statistics on production, shipments, inventories, consumption, exports, imports, and orders for a wide variety of manufactured products.

## ONLINE DATABASES

*Textile Technology Index™.* EBSCO Publishing Inc. • Monthly. $545 Individuals. Includes indexing and abstracts for more than 470 periodicals.

*World Textiles.* Elsevier. • Provides abstracting and indexing from 1970 of worldwide textile literature (periodicals, books, pamphlets, and reports). Includes U. S., European, and British patent information. Updating is monthly. Inquire as to online cost and availability.

## PERIODICALS AND NEWSLETTERS

*DNR: The Men's Fashion Retail Textile Authority.* Fairchild Publications. • Daily. $85.00 per year. Formerly *Daily News Record.*

*International Textile Bulletin: Yarn and Fabric Forming Edition.* ITS Publishing, International Textile Service. • Quarterly. $170.00 per year. Editions in Chinese, English, French, German, Italian and Spanish.

## STATISTICS SOURCES

*Survey of Current Business.* U. S. Government Printing Office. • Published by Bureau of Economic Analysis, U. S. Department of Commerce. Presents a wide variety of business and economic data.

## TRADE/PROFESSIONAL ASSOCIATIONS

American Yarn Spinners Association. 2500 Lowell Rd., Gastonia, NC 28053. Phone: (704)824-3522;

Fax: (704)824-0630 • URL: http://www.textileweb.com/BuyersGuide.mvc/CompanyDetail/ • Manufacturers of combed cotton sales yarn and carded yarns spun from cotton, wool, and/or synthetics. Provides full service to the sales yarn industry.

# YOUTH MARKET

*See also* CHILDREN'S APPAREL INDUSTRY

## ALMANACS AND YEARBOOKS

*Research Alert Yearbook: Vital Facts on Consumer Behavior and Attitudes.* EPM Communications Inc. • Annual. $349 Individuals Single user (PDF) or Print. Provides summaries of consumer market research from the newsletters *Research Alert, Youth Markets Alert,* and *Minority Markets Alert.* Includes tables, charts, graphs, and textual summaries for 41 subject categories. Sources include reports, studies, polls, and focus groups.

## PERIODICALS AND NEWSLETTERS

*Selling to Kids: News and Practical Advice on Successfully Marketing to Kids and Teens.* EPM Communications Inc. • Biweekly. $495 per year. Includes market research information, news items, and case studies.

*Youth Markets Alert.* EPM Communications Inc. • Description: Features information and research results related to young consumers from elementary school through high school.

## TRADE/PROFESSIONAL ASSOCIATIONS

Team Success. 5050 Laguna Blvd., Ste. 112-415, Elk Grove, CA 95758-4151. Phone: (916)629-4229; Email: admin@teamsuccessinc.com • URL: http://www.teamsuccessinc.org • Promotes the education and improvement of youth throughout the United States. Seeks to improve the social development, life skills, employability, social skills and entrepreneurship abilities of youth. Assists the community by providing business related workshops, mentoring and job assistance.

Youth Venture. 1700 N Moore St., Ste. 2000, Arlington, VA 22209. Phone: (703)527-8300; Fax: (703)527-8383; Email: yvinfo@youthventure.org • URL: http://www.youthventure.org • Works to empower young people to create and launch their own enterprises in order to take greater responsibility for their lives and communities.

# Z

## ZERO-BASE BUDGETING

*See* BUDGETING, BUSINESS

## ZERO DEFECTS

*See* QUALITY CONTROL

## ZINC INDUSTRY

*See also* METAL INDUSTRY; MINES AND
MINERAL RESOURCES

### ALMANACS AND YEARBOOKS

*CRB Commodity Yearbook*. Commodity Research
Bureau. CRB. • Annual. $179 plus $10.00 shipping
cost. The single most comprehensive source of commodity and futures market information available.

### CD-ROM DATABASES

*METADEX Materials Collection: Metals-Polymers-
Ceramics*. Cambridge Scientific Abstracts L.P. •
Quarterly. Provides CD-ROM citations to the
worldwide literature of materials science and
metallurgy. Corresponds to *Metals Abstracts, Alloys
Index, Steels Alert, Nonferrous Alert, Polymers/
Ceramics/Composites Alert*, and *Engineered Materi-
als Abstracts*. (Formerly produced by ASM
International.).

*OECD Statistical Compendium*. Organization for
Economic Cooperation and Development. •
Semiannual. $1,905.00 per year for 1 to 10 users.
CD-ROM contains more than 730,000 monthly,
quarterly, and annual time series for OECD
countries, 1960 to date. Includes fully searchable
data on agriculture, food, economic indicators,
national accounts, employment, energy, finance,
industry, technology, and foreign trade. Results can
be displayed in various forms.

### INTERNET DATABASES

*Business 2.0 Web Guide to the Best Business Links*.
Business 2.0 Media Inc. Phone: (415)293-4800;
Email: support@business2.com • URL: http://www.
business2.com/webguide • Web site presents an
extensive, searchable directory of links to "the best,
most informative, and authoritative web pages."
Twenty main categories cover business, finance,
career, company information, people, and technology topics, with thousands of subtopics, all linking
to Web sites recommended by experienced business
researchers. Fees: Free.

*Fedstats*. Federal Interagency Council on Statistical
Policy. Phone: (202)395-7254 • URL: http://www.
fedstats.gov • Web site features an efficient search

facility for full-text statistics produced by more than
100 federal agencies, including the Census Bureau,
the Bureau of Economic Analysis, and the Bureau of
Labor Statistics. Boolean searches can be made
within one agency or for all agencies combined.
Links are offered to international statistical bureaus,
including the UN, IMF, OECD, UNESCO, Eurostat,
and 20 individual countries. Fees: Free.

*FreeLunch.com*. Economy.com, Inc. Phone:
(610)696-8700; Fax: (610)696-1678 • URL: http://
www.freelunch.com • Web site provides free access
to more than 200 million economic and financial
data series, covering industry, demographics, labor
markets, prices, retail sales, government spending,
trade, interest rates, housing starts, the stock market,
etc. Data is available in either chart or table form.
Searching is offered. Free, but registration required.
Economy.com, Inc. also offers fee-based economic
analysis at *The Dismal Scientist* site (www.dismal.
com).

### PERIODICALS AND NEWSLETTERS

*The Mining Record*. Howell International
Enterprises. • Monthly. $85 Individuals second class
mail. Description: Discusses a myriad of issues
within the mining industry, particularly exploration,
development, production, and milling.

### PRICE SOURCES

*Platt's Metals Week*. Platts Global Energy. • Weekly.
$770 Individuals.

### STATISTICS SOURCES

*Non-Ferrous Metal Data Yearbook*. American
Bureau of Metal Statistics. • Annual. $405.00.
Provides worldwide data on approximately about
200 statistical tables covering many nonferrous
metals. Includes production, consumption,
inventories, exports, imports, and other data.

*Survey of Current Business*. U. S. Government Printing Office. • Published by Bureau of Economic
Analysis, U. S. Department of Commerce. Presents
a wide variety of business and economic data.

### TRADE/PROFESSIONAL ASSOCIATIONS

Non-Ferrous Metals Producers Committee. 2030 M
St. NW, Ste. 800, Washington, DC 20036. Phone:
(202)466-7720; Fax: (202)466-2710 • URL: http://
www.arcat.com/arcatcos/cos37/arc37679.cfm •
Represents domestic copper, lead, and zinc
producers. Promotes the interests of copper, lead,
and zinc mining and metal industries in the U.S.
with emphasis on tariffs, laws, regulations, and
government policies affecting international trade
and foreign imports.

## ZIP CODE

*See* POSTAL SERVICES

## ZONING

*See also* CITY PLANNING

### ABSTRACTS AND INDEXES

*Current Law Index*. Cengage Learning Inc. • $1,332
Individuals. Monthly. $1269.00 per year. Produced
in cooperation with the American Association of
Law Libraries. Indexes more than 900 law journals,
legal newspapers, and specialty publications from
the U.S., Canada, U.K., Ireland, Australia, and New
Zealand.

*Index to Legal Periodicals and Books*. H.W. Wilson
Co. • Monthly. $490.00 per year. Quarterly and an-
nual cumulations.

*PAIS International*. ProQuest L.L.C. • Monthly.
$850.00 per year; cumulations three times a year.
Provides topical citations to the worldwide literature
of public affairs, economics, demographics, sociol-
ogy, and trade. Text in English; indexed materials in
English, French, German, Italian, Portuguese and
Spanish.

### ALMANACS AND YEARBOOKS

*American Law Yearbook*. Cengage Learning Inc. •
$308 Individuals. Annual. $280.00. Serves as a
yearly supplement to *West's Encyclopedia of
American Lawa*. Describes new legal developments
in many subject areas.

### CD-ROM DATABASES

*Index to Legal Periodicals and Books*. EBSCO
Publishing Inc. • Contains indexing of more than
1,400 English language legal periodicals from 1981
to date and 2,500 books.

*PAIS International*. ProQuest L.L.C. • Monthly.
$1,995.00 per year. Contains over 650,000 citations
to the literature of contemporary social, political,
and economic issues.

### ENCYCLOPEDIAS AND DICTIONARIES

*West's Encyclopedia of American Law*. Cengage
Learning Inc. • 2004. eBook. Second edition. Covers a wide variety of legal topics for the general
reader. Inquire for pricing.

### HANDBOOKS AND MANUALS

*Zoning and Planning Deskbook, 2d*. Katherine
Kmiec Turner and Douglas W. Kmiec, authors. Thomson West. • Annual. $530.60 book - softbound;
full set. Emphasis is on legal issues. Examines the
latest developments in land use control, discussing
procedural and substantive considerations,
remedies, strategies, and state and federal litigation.

*Zoning and Planning Law Handbook*. Patricia
Salkin. Thomson West. • Annual. $601.30. As-
sembles the insights and guidance offered by the

country's leading authorities in zoning law, land use planning, and conservation.

## INTERNET DATABASES

*Lexis.com Research System.* Lexis-Nexis Group. Phone: 800-227-4908 or (937)865-6800; Fax: (937)865-6909; Email: webmaster@prod.lexis-nexis.com • URL: http://www.nexis.com • Fee-based Web site offers extensive searching of a wide variety of legal sources. Additional features include Daily Opinion Service, lexis.com Bookstore, Career Center, CLE Center, Law Schools, and Practice Pages ("Pages specific to areas of specialty").

## PERIODICALS AND NEWSLETTERS

*Planning and Zoning News.* Planning & Zoning Center Inc. • Monthly. $185 per year. Newsletter on planning and zoning issues in the United States.

## RESEARCH CENTERS AND INSTITUTES

Pennsylvania State University at Harrisburg - Institute of State and Regional Affairs - Pennsylvania State Data Center. 777 W Harrisburg Pike, Middletown, PA 17057-4898. Phone: (717)948-6336; Fax: (717)948-6754; Email: pasdc@psu.edu • URL: http://www.pasdc.hbg.psu.edu • Conducts research in environmental, general, and socioeconomic planning. Zoning is included.

# SOURCES CITED

*A/C Flyer: Best Read Resale Magazine Worldwide*. McGraw Hill Financial Inc., 1221 Avenue of the Americas New York, NY 10020-1095. Phone: (212)512-2000; Fax: (212)512-3840 • URL: http://www.mhfi.com • Monthly. Individuals $49.00 per year; students, $28.00 per year. Lists used airplanes for sale by dealers, brokers, and private owners. Provides news and trends relating to the aircraft resale industry. Special issues include "Product & Service Buyer's Guide" and "Dealer/Broker Directory.".

*A-V Online*. National Information Center for Educational Media, c/o Access Innovations, Inc., 4725 Indian School Rd. NE, Ste. 100 Albuquerque, NM 87198-8640. Phone: 800-926-8328 or (505)998-0800; Fax: (505)256-1080; Email: info-request@ nicem.com • URL: http://www.nicem.com • Provides online descriptions of non-print educational materials for all levels, kindergarten to graduate school. Includes all types of audio, film, and video media. Updated quarterly. Inquire as to online cost and availability.

*A-Z Credit Directory*. Legal & Commercial State Services Ltd., St. Mary's Naas, Ireland. • Annual. Covers: Over 30,000 credit records of companies and individuals in the Republic of Ireland. Entries include: Company or personal name and address.

*AAACE Adult Learning*. American Association for Adult and Continuing Education, 10111 Martin Luther King, Jr. Hwy., Ste. 200C Bowie, MD 20720. Phone: (301)459-6261; Fax: (301)459-6241; Email: office@aaace.org • URL: http://www.aaace.org • Quarterly. Included in membership; $216 Institutions print and online; $194 Institutions online; $212 Institutions print; $32 Individuals print; $58 Institutions single print issue; $10 Individuals single print issue.

*AACE International. Transactions of the Annual Meetings*. American Assoiciation of Cost Engineers. AACE International, 1265 Suncrest Towne Ctr Dr. Morgantown, WV 26505-1876. Phone: 800-858-2678 or (304)296-8444; Fax: (304)291-5728; Email: info@aacei.org • URL: http://www.aacei.org • Annual. Price varies. Contains texts of papers presented at AACE meetings.

*AACSB Newsline*. Association to Advance Collegiate Schools of Business, 77 S Harbour Island Blvd., Ste. 750 Tampa, FL 33602. Phone: (813)769-6500; Fax: (813)769-6559; Email: events@aacsb.edu • URL: http://www.aacsb.edu • Monthly. Description: Covers issues and events affecting management education, and Association projects and activities. Recurring features include notices of publications available and news of educational opportunities.

*AAID Business Bite*. American Academy of Implant Dentistry, 211 E Chicago Ave., Ste. 750 Chicago, IL 60611, Phone: 877-335-2243 or (312)335-1550; Fax: (312)335-9090; Email: info@aaid.com • URL: http://www.aaid.com/index.html • AAID's monthly electronic newsletter providing practical practice management information for those involved in implant dentistry.

*AAII Journal*. American Association of Individual Investors, 625 N Michigan Ave. Chicago, IL 60611. Phone: 800-428-2244 or (312)280-0170; Fax: (312)280-9883 or (312)280-1625; Email: members@aaii.com • URL: http://www.aaii.com • 10/year. $49 Individuals. Covers strategy and investment techniques.

**Aalborg University - Center for Labor Market Research**. Fibigerstraede 1 9220 Alborg, Denmark. Phone: 45 99409940; Fax: 45 98155346 • URL: http://www.dps.aau.dk/forskningsenheder/carma-english • Work organization, technology developments, cooperation and management styles, collective bargaining, wage and personnel policies in private enterprises and public institutions.

**Aalborg University - Department of Business and Management - Innovation, Knowledge and Economic Dynamics Research Group**. Fibigerstraede 11 DK-9220 Alborg, Denmark. Phone: 45 99408235; Email: ike-secr@business.

aau.dk • URL: http://www.ike.aau.dk • Economic, technical and institutional changes, especially economic evolutionary modeling, theory of the firm, national systems of innovation, international trade and competitiveness, and the interplay between economic and ecological issues.

**Aalborg University - Economic Research Group**. Department of Economics, Politics & Public Administration, Fibigerstraede 3 DK-9220 Alborg, Denmark. Phone: 45 96358200; Email: cbruun@socsci.auc.dk • URL: http://www.socsci.aau.dk/econ • Macroeconomics, econometrics, computable economics, agent-based computational economics, finance and history of economic thought.

**Aalto University - Center for Markets in Transition**. PO Box 21230 FIN-00076 Aalto, Finland. Phone: 358 9 403538149; Fax: 358 9 47038706; Email: riitta.kosonen@aalto.fi • URL: http://cemat.aalto.fi/en • Markets and economies in transition in Central and Eastern Europe. Research focuses on economic development in Northwest Russia, strategies of foreign enterprises in Russia and the Baltic States, post-socialist transformation on enterprise and industry level, business cultures and norms around the Baltic Sea, Russian raw materials as a business, and tourism development.

*AAMVA Bulletin*. American Association of Motor Vehicle Administrators, 4301 Wilson Blvd., Ste. 400 Arlington, VA 22203. Phone: (703)522-4200; Fax: (703)522-1905 • URL: http://www.aamva.org • Description: Provides news and legislative information for motor vehicle administrators. Recurring features include news of research, announcements, and legislative information.

*AAPEX Export Interest Directory: 2008*. • URL: http://www.oac-intl.org • Lists U.S. companies that are interested in overseas markets, and exhibited at AAPEX 2008.

*AAPOR Newsletter*. American Association for Public Opinion Research, 111 Deer Lake Rd., Ste. 100 Deerfield, IL 60015. Phone: (847)205-2651; Fax: (847)480-9282; Email: info@aapor.org • URL: http://www.aapor.org • Semiannual Quarterly. Description: Publishes news of the Association. Recurring features include a president's column, new member list, and personal notes.

**Aarhus University - School of Business and Social Sciences - Department of Business Communication - Center for Corporate Communication**. Fuglesangs Allè 4 DK-8210 Aarhus, Denmark. Phone: 45 89486268; Fax: 45 86150188 • URL: http://bcom.au.dk/research/academicareas/ccc • Business communications, including management communication, market communication, corporate communication, public relations, internal communication, business journalism, etc.

*AARP Bulletin*. AARP, 601 E St. NW Washington, DC 20049-0001. Phone: 888-687-2277 or (202)434-3525; Email: member@aarp.org • URL: http://www.aarp.org • Monthly. Description: Monitors issues and events affecting Americans aged 50 and over. Covers medical benefits and other services of interest. Recurring features include Association news, editorials, and columns titled As We See It, Bulletin Board, Washingtonwatch, Stateswatch, and Reader Forum.

*AATCC Review*. American Association of Textile Chemists and Colorists, 1 Davis Dr. Research Triangle Park, NC 27709-2215. Phone: (919)549-8141 or (919)549-3532; Fax: (919)549-8933; Email: orders@aatcc.org • URL: http://www.aatcc.org • Monthly. Included in membership; $650 Individuals print + online; $550 Individuals online only; $180 Individuals print only. Monthly magazine for professionals in the textile wet processing and dyestuff industries. Formerly Textile Chemist and Colorist and American Dyestuff Reporter.

*AAUW Outlook*. AAUW Legal Advocacy Fund, 1111 16th St. NW Washington, DC 20036. Phone: 800-326-2289 or (202)785-7700; Fax: (202)872-1425; Email: connect@aauw.org • URL: http://www.aauw.org/resources/by-tag/legal-advocacy •

3/year. Magazine covering women's concerns including current family, education and legislative issues. Formerly *Graduate Woman*.

*ABA Banking Journal*. American Bankers Association, Member Communications. Simmons-Boardman Books Inc., 1809 Capitol Ave. Omaha, NE 68102-4972. Phone: 800-228-9670 or (402)346-4300; Fax: (402)346-1783; Email: customer_service@transalert.com • URL: http://www.transalert.com • Monthly. Monthly. Free to qualified personnel.

*ABA/BNA Lawyer's Manual on Professional Conduct*. Bloomberg BNA, 3 Bethesda Metro Center, Ste. 250 Bethesda, MD 20814-5377. Phone: 800-372-1033 or (703)341-3000; Fax: (800)253-0332; Email: customercare@bna.com • URL: http://www.bna.com • Updated monthly. Available via print and web. Covers American Bar Association's model rules governing ethical practice of law.

*ABA Book Buyer's Handbook*. American Booksellers Association, 333 Westchester Ave., Ste. S202 White Plains, NY 10604. Phone: 800-637-0037 or (914)417-4013; Fax: (914)406-7500; Email: info@bookweb.org • URL: http://www.bookweb.org • Annual. Available electronically to members. Includes trade terms, discount informatio, return policies, and imprint listings.

*ABA Journal: The Lawyer's Magazine*. American Bar Association, 321 N Clark St. Chicago, IL 60654-7598. Phone: 800-285-2221 or (312)988-5000; Email: orders@abanet.org • URL: http://www.americanbar.org/aba.html • Monthly. $75 Individuals; $120 Institutions. Includes five regular sections: news affecting lawyers, practical applications of court decisions, pratice management advice, feature articles, and lifestyle stories.

*Abacus: A Journal of Accounting, Finance and Business Studies*. John Wiley & Sons Inc. Wiley-Blackwell, 9600 Garsington Rd. Oxford OX4 2DQ, United Kingdom. Phone: 44 1865 776868 or 44 186 5778054; Fax: 44 1865 714591 or 44 186 5471777; Email: customerservice@oxon.blackwellpublishing.com • URL: http://www.as.wiley.com/wileycda/brand/id-35.html • Quarterly. $597 Institutions Australia & New Zealand, print and online; $770 Institutions print and online; £539 Institutions print and online; €617 Institutions print and online; $1,056 Institutions, other countries print and online; $670 Institutions print or online; €536 Institutions print or online; £469 Institutions print or online; $917 Institutions, other countries print or online; $156 Individuals print and online. Journal covering academic and professional aspects of accounting, finance and business.

*ABC/Dienstverleners*. ABC Business Directories BV, Paasheuvelweg 40 NL-1105 BJ Amsterdam, Netherlands. Phone: 31 20 7154 340; Email: info@abc-d.nl • URL: http://www.abc-d.com • Quarterly. Database covers: 24,000 Dutch service companies, including accounting firms, law firms, car leasing firms, audiovisual consultants, transport companies, advertising agencies, hotels, and restaurants. Entries include: Company name, address, phone, fax, telex; executive names; capital; bank affiliation; year founded; number of employees; product information.

*ABC Netherlands*. ABC voor Handel en Industries C.V., Koningin Wilhelminalaan 16 NL-2000 AD Haarlem, Netherlands. Phone: 23 5533533; Fax: 23 5533501; Email: info@abc-d.nl • Quarterly. Database covers: 120,000 profiles of Dutch companies in all lines of business. Entries include: Company name, address, management, products, number of employees, sales, founding year, parent companies, subsidiaries, branches and offices abroad, export/import activities.

*ABC voor Handel en Industrie*. ABC voor Handel en Industries C.V., Koningin Wilhelminalaan 16 NL-2000 AD Haarlem, Netherlands. Phone: 23 5533533; Fax: 23 5533501; Email: info@abc-d.nl • Quarterly. Database covers: Approximately 120,000 profiles of Dutch manufacturers, importers, import agents and service providers and their products/services; also includes some 46,000 foreign houses' representatives in Holland. Entries include: Company name, address, phone, fax, telex; executive names; capital; bank affiliation; year founded; number of employees.

***ABD—Aviation Buyer's Directory***. Air Service Directory Inc., 116 Radio Circle Dr., Ste. 302 Mount Kisco, NY 10549. Phone: (914)242-8700; Fax: (914)242-5422; Email: abd@abdonline.com • URL: http://www.abdonline.com • Quarterly. Covers: aircraft, parts, and equipment manufacturers and dealers, and service firms in the aviation industry. Entries include: Company name, address, phone.

***ABI/INFORM***. ProQuest L.L.C., 789 E Eisenhower Pkwy. Ann Arbor, MI 48106-1346. Phone: 800-521-0600 or (734)761-4700; Fax: (734)662-4554; Email: info@proquest.com • URL: http://www.proquest.com • Monthly. Provides CD-ROM indexing and abstracting of worldwide business literature. Archival discs are available from 1971. Formerly *ABI/INFORM OnDisc*.

**Åbo Academy University - Laboratory of Industrial Management**. Biskopsgatan 8 FI-20500 Abo, Finland. Phone: 358 2 221531; Email: infowww@abo.fi • URL: http://www.abo.fi/student/en/Content/Document/document/9465 • How industrial companies operate now and in the future within different industries, especially what is offered, the organization of the companies and what capabilities are needed. There is a special focus on international industrial project-based business.

***Abrasive Engineering Society Conference Proceedings***. Abrasive Engineering Society, 144 Moore Rd. Butler, PA 16001. Phone: (724)282-6210; Fax: (724)234-2376; Email: aes@abrasiveengineering.com • URL: http://www.abrasiveengineering.com • Irregular. Price on application.

***The Absolute Sound: The High End Journal of Audio and Music***. Absolute Multimedia Inc., 4544 S Lamar Blvd. G300 Austin, TX 78745-1500. Phone: 888-475-5991 or (512)892-8682 or (512)479-4661; Fax: (512)328-7528; Email: info@avguide.com • URL: http://www.theabsolutesound.com • 10/year. $14.95 Individuals print; $12.95 Individuals online. Preeminent source of expert reviews, features, and commentary on high-performance audio and music.

***Abstract Bulletin of Paper Science and Technology***. Engineering Information Inc., 1 Castle Pt. Ter. Hoboken, NJ 07030-5996. Phone: 800-221-1044 • URL: http://www.elsevier.com • Monthly. Institutions, $1,874.00 per year. Worldwide coverage of the scientific and technical literature of interest to the pulp and paper industry.

**ACA International**. 4040 W 70th St. Minneapolis, MN 55435. Phone: (952)926-6547; Email: aca@acainternational.org • URL: http://www.acainternational.org • Formerly American Collectors Association.

***ACADEME***. American Association of University Professors, 1133 19th St. NW, Ste. 200 Washington, DC 20036. Phone: (202)737-5900; Fax: (202)737-5526; Email: aaup@aaup.org • URL: http://www.aaup.org • Bimonthly. Included in membership; $85 Nonmembers /year; individual; domestic; $78 Nonmembers /year; institution; domestic; $89 Nonmembers /year; individual; other countries; $83 Nonmembers /year; institution; other countries. Explores developments in higher education from the perspective of faculty members.

**Academia Sinica - Sun Yat-Sen Institute for Social Sciences and Philosophy**. Nankang Taipei 11529, Taiwan. Phone: 886 2 27821693; Fax: 886 2 27854160; Email: tpleung@ccvax.sinica.edu.tw • URL: http://www.sinica.edu.tw/as/intro/issp.html • Interdisciplinary studies on social sciences and humanities, including history and philosophy, sociology, political science, economics and jurisprudence.

***Academy of Accounting Historians—Membership Directory***. Academy of Accounting Historians, Case Western Reserve University, Weatherhead School of Management, 10900 Euclid Ave. Cleveland, OH 44106-7235. Fax: (216)368-2030; Email: weatherhead@case.edu • URL: http://www.aahhq.org • Annual. Covers: over 900 member individuals and organizations concerned with accounting and business history. Entries include: Member name, address, phone, and fax.

***Academy of International Business—Membership Directory***. Academy of International Business, Michigan State University, The Eli Broad College of Business, 645 N Shaw Ln., Rm. 7 East Lansing, MI 48824-1121. Phone: (517)432-1452; Fax: (517)432-1009; Email: aib@aib.msu.edu • URL: http://aib.msu.edu • Covers: About 3,068 members. Entries include: Name, address, phone, fax, Bitnet, discipline.

**Academy of International Business**. Michigan State University, The Eli Broad College of Business, 645 N Shaw Ln., Rm. 7 East Lansing, MI 48824-1121. Phone: (517)432-1452; Fax: (517)432-1009; Email: aib@aib.msu.edu • URL: http://aib.msu.edu • Consists primarily of university professors, doctoral students, researchers, writers, consultants, executives, and policy setters in the international business/trade research and education fields. Facilitates information exchange among people in academia, business, and government and encourages research activities that advance the knowledge of international business operations and increase the available body of teaching materials. Compiles an inventory of collegiate courses in international business, a survey of research projects, and statistics.

***Academy of Management Journal***. Academy of Management, PO Box 3020 Briarcliff Manor, NY 10510-8020. Phone: (914)923-2607; Fax: (914)923-2615; Email: membership@aom.org • URL: http://www.aom.org • Bimonthly. $180 /year for individuals and academic libraries (print only); $340 /year for individuals and academic libraries (print and electronic). Presents research papers on management-related topics.

***Academy of Management Perspectives***. Academy of Management, PO Box 3020 Briarcliff Manor, NY 10510-8020. Phone: (914)923-2607; Fax: (914)923-2615; Email: membership@aom.org • URL: http://www.aom.org • Quarterly. $130 /year for individuals in U.S. (print only); $245 /year for individuals in U.S. (print and electronic); $125 Individuals. Contains articles relating to the practical application of management principles and theory.

***Academy of Management Review***. Academy of Management, PO Box 3020 Briarcliff Manor, NY 10510-8020. Phone: (914)923-2607; Fax: (914)923-2615; Email: membership@aom.org • URL: http://www.aom.org • Quarterly. $350 Individuals print + online; $350 Other countries print + online. A scholarly journal concerned with the theory of management and organizations.

**Academy of Management**. PO Box 3020 Briarcliff Manor, NY 10510-8020. Phone: (914)923-2607; Fax: (914)923-2615; Email: membership@aom.org • URL: http://www.aom.org • Professors in accredited universities and colleges who teach management; selected business executives who have made significant written contributions to the literature in the field of management and organization. Offers placement service.

**Academy of Nutrition and Dietetics**. 120 S Riverside Plaza, Ste. 2000 Chicago, IL 60606-6995. Phone: 800-877-1600 or (312)899-0040; Email: knowledge@eatright.org • URL: http://www.eatright.org • Represents food and nutrition professionals. Promotes nutrition, health and well-being.

**Academy of Television Arts and Sciences**. 5220 Lankershim Blvd. North Hollywood, CA 91601. Phone: (818)754-2800 • URL: http://www.emmys.com • Professionals in the television and film industry. Aims to advance the arts and sciences of television through services to the industry in education, preservation of television programs, and information and community relations; to foster creative leadership in the television industry. Sponsors Television Academy Hall of Fame. Maintains library on television credits and historical material, the Television Academy Archives, and archives at UCLA of over 35,000 television programs. Offers internships to students. Holds luncheon and speakers series and meetings on problems of the various crafts.

***Access Business News***. NewsBank Inc., 5801 Pelican Bay Blvd., Ste. 600 Naples, FL 34108. Phone: 800-762-8182 or (802)875-2910; Fax: (239)263-3004; Email: sales@newsbank.com • URL: http://www.newsbank.com • Contains the full-text of current and archived editions of approximately 200 business and law journals, local and regional news weeklies, and other news sources across North America.

***Access Nippon: How to Succeed in Japan***. Hoover's Inc., 5800 Airport Blvd. Austin, TX 78752-4204. Phone: 866-443-3939 or (512)374-4500 or (866)281-5969; Fax: (512)374-4501; Email: salesteam@hoovers.com • URL: http://www.hoovers.com • Annual. $34.95 plus $3.50 shipping. Covers: Brief profiles of 498 companies and 493 of their affiliates in Japan. Database includes: Overview of major industries & trends; Japan business practices/regulations; listing of major trade shows to be held in Japan; business travel guide; information on hotels, transportation, emergency services, etc. Entries include: Company headquarters, address, phone, date established, capital maintained, number of employees, financial data, product/service.

***Access Reports: Freedom of Information***. Access Reports Inc., 1624 Dogwood Ln. Lynchburg, VA 24503. Phone: (434)384-5334; Fax: (434)384-8272; Email: hhammitt@accessreports.com • URL: http://www.accessreports.com • Semimonthly. $400 Individuals.

***Accessories Resources Directory***. Business Journals Inc., 50 Day St. Norwalk, CT 06854. Phone: (203)853-6015; Fax: (203)852-8175; Email: macb@busjour.com • URL: http://www.busjour.com • Annual. Covers: 1,600 manufacturers, importers, and sales representatives producing or handling belts, gloves, handbags, scarves, hosiery, jewelry, sunglasses, and umbrellas. Entries include: Company, name, address, phone, fax.

***Accident Analysis and Prevention***. Elsevier, Secondary Publishing Division, 650 Ave. of the Americas New York, NY 10011. Phone: 888-437-4636 or (212)633-3980; Fax: (212)633-3975; Email: t.reller@elsevier.com • URL: http://www.elsevier.com • Monthly. $461 Individuals print; $2,838 Institutions print; $2,837.60 Institutions online; access for 5 users. Provides wide coverage of the general areas relating to accidental injury and damage, including the pre-injury and immediate post-injury phases.

***Accident Prevention***. Flight Safety Foundation, 801 N Fairfax St., Ste. 400 Alexandria, VA 22314-1754. Phone: (703)739-6700; Fax: (703)739-6708; Email: setze@flightsafety.org • URL: http://flightsafety.org • Monthly. Description: Carries items of particular value to professional pilots: general air safety material and reports of dangerous situations, incidents, near misses by professional pilots, ground crew, or other persons involved.

***The Accountable Leader***. Cengage Learning Inc., 20 Channel Center St. Boston, MA 02210. Phone: 800-487-8488 or (617)289-7700; Fax: (617)289-7844; Email: investors@cengage.com • URL: http://www.cengage.com • 2010. eBook. Published by Kogan Page. Centered around three themes — leadership, accountability, and organizational structure — this book highlights how most leadership related problems arise from the ineffectiveness of organizational structures that lack accountable jobs.

***Accountant's Business Manual***. American Institute of Certified Public Accountants, 1211 Avenue of the Americas New York, NY 10036-8775. Phone: 888-777-7077 or (212)596-6200; Fax: (212)596-6213; Email: service@aicpa.org • URL: http://www.aicpa.org • $198.75. Looseleaf. Two volumes. Semiannual updates. Covers a wide variety of topics relating to financial and accounting management, including types of ownership, business planning, financing, cash management, valuation, retirement plans, estate planning, workers' compensation, unemployment insurance, social security, and employee benefits management.

***Accountants' Liability***. Practising Law Institute, 1177 Avenue of the Americas New York, NY 10036. Phone: 800-260-4754 or (212)824-5700; Fax: (212)824-5733; Email: info@pli.edu • URL: http://www.pli.edu • $335 free shipping. Covers all aspects of accountants' professional liability issues, including depositions and court cases.

**Accounting and Auditing Organization for Islamic Financial Institutions**. Yateem Center, Blk. 304, Al Muthana Rd. Manama, Bahrain. Phone: 973 17 244 496; Fax: 973 17 250 194 • URL: http://www.aaoifi.com • Represents central banks, Islamic financial institutions, and other participants from the international Islamic banking and finance industry. Aims to uphold the accounting and auditing standards of Islamic financial institutions. Provides its members the necessary resources needed to improve and maintain the quality of service of Islamic financial institutions.

***Accounting and Bookkeeping General Services Directory***. InfoGroup Inc., 5711 S 86th Cir. Omaha, NE 68127-4146. Phone: (402)593-4500 • URL: http://www.infogroup.com • Annual. Number of listings: 27,213. Entries include: Name, address, phone, size of advertisement, name of owner or manager, number of employees, year first in "Yellow Pages." Compiled from telephone company "Yellow Pages," nationwide.

***Accounting and Bookkeeping Systems (Wholesale) Directory***. InfoGroup Inc., 5711 S 86th Cir. Omaha, NE 68127-4146. Phone: (402)593-4500 • URL: http://www.infogroup.com • Annual. Number of listings: 547. Entries include: Name, address, phone, size of advertisement, name of owner or manager, number of employees, year first in "Yellow Pages." Compiled from telephone company "Yellow Pages," nationwide.

***Accounting and Business Research***. Routledge, 711 3rd Ave., 8th Fl. New York, NY 10017. Phone: 800-634-7064 or (212)216-7800; Fax: (212)564-7854 or (212)563-2269; Email: book.orders@tandf.co.uk • URL: http://www.routledge.com • 6/year. $137 Individuals print; $421 Institutions online; $468 Institutions print and online; $132 Individuals print. Publication for the banking, finance, and accounting industries.

**Accounting and Finance Benchmarking Consortium**. 4606 FM 1960 W, Ste. 250 Houston, TX 77069-9949. Phone: (281)440-5044 • URL: http://www.afbc.org • Accounting and finance managers of corporations with an interest in benchmarking. Promotes the use of benchmarking, wherein businesses compare their processes with those of their competitors, as a means of improving corporate efficiency and profitability. Facilitates exchange of information among members; conducts target operations, procurement, development, and maintenance studies; identifies model business practices.

***Accounting and Financial Planning for Law Firms***. ALM Media Properties LLC, 120 Broadway, 5th Fl. New York, NY 10271-1100. Phone: (212)457-9400; Fax: (646)417-7705; Email: customercare@alm.com • URL: http://www.alm.com • Monthly. $499 /year. Covers budgeting, liability issues, billing systems, benefits management, and other topics relating to law firm administration. (A Law Journal Newsletter, formerly published by Leader Publications).

**Accounting and Financial Women's Alliance**. 1760 Old Meadow Rd., Ste. 500 McLean, VA 22102. Phone: 800-326-2163 or (703)506-3265; Fax: (703)506-3266; Email: aswa@aswa.org • URL: http://www.aswa.org • Professional society of women accountants, educators and others in the field of accounting dedicated to the achievement of personal, professional and economic potential. Assists women accountants in their careers and promotes development in the profession. Conducts educational and research programs.

***Accounting and Tax Database***. ProQuest L.L.C., 789 E Eisenhower Pkwy. Ann Arbor, MI 48106-1346. Phone: 800-521-0600 or (734)761-4700; Fax: (734)662-4554; Email: info@proquest.com • URL: http://www.proquest.com • Provides indexing and abstracting of the literature of accounting, taxation, and financial management, 1971 to date. Updating is weekly. Especially covers accounting, auditing, banking, bankruptcy, employee compensation and benefits, cash management, financial planning, and credit. Inquire as to online cost and availability.

***Accounting and Tax Index***. ProQuest L.L.C., 789 E Eisenhower Pkwy. Ann Arbor, MI 48106-1346. Phone: 800-521-0600 or (734)761-4700; Fax: (734)662-4554; Email: info@proquest.com • URL: http://www.proquest.com • Quarterly. Indexes accounting, auditing, and taxation literature appearing in journals, books, pamphlets, conference proceedings, and newsletters.

***Accounting Articles***. Wolters Kluwer Law & Business CCH, 2700 Lake Cook Rd. Riverwoods, IL 60015. Phone: 888-224-7377 or (847)267-7000; Email: cust_serv@cch.com • URL: http://www.cchgroup.com • Monthly. $624. Covers accounting news.

**Accounting Research Program**. UCLA Anderson School of Management, 110 Westwood Plz. Los Angeles, CA 90095-1481. Phone: (310)206-8711; Fax: (310)825-3165 • URL: http://www.anderson.ucla.edu.

***Accounting Research Studies***. American Institute of Certified Public Accountants, 1211 Avenue of the Americas New York, NY 10036-8775. Phone: 888-777-7077 or (212)596-6200; Fax: (212)596-6213; Email: service@aicpa.org • URL: http://www.aicpa.org • Irregular.

***The Accounting Review***. American Accounting Association, 5717 Bessie Dr. Sarasota, FL 34233-2399. Phone: (941)921-7747; Fax: (941)923-4093; Email: info@aaahq.org • URL: http://aaahq.org • Bimonthly. $450 Individuals print. Accounting education, research, financial reporting, and book reviews.

***Accounting Technology: Turning Technology into Business Know How***. SourceMedia Inc., 1 State Street Plz., 27th Fl. New York, NY 10004. Phone: 800-221-1809 or (212)803-8200 or (212)803-8333; Fax: (212)843-9635 or (212)292-5216; Email: custserv@sourcemedia.com • URL: http://www.sourcemedia.com • 11 times a year. $61.00 per year. Provides advice and information on computers and software for the accounting profession. Formerly *Computers in Accounting*.

***Accounting Today: The Business Newspaper for the Tax & Accounting Community***. SourceMedia Inc., 1 State Street Plz., 27th Fl. New York, NY 10004. Phone: 800-221-1809 or (212)803-8200 or (212)803-8333; Fax: (212)843-9635 or (212)292-5216; Email: custserv@sourcemedia.com • URL: http://www.sourcemedia.com • Biweekly. $99.00 per year. Covers news affecting tax and accounting professionals.

***Accounts Receivable (Financing) Directory***. InfoGroup Inc., 5711 S 86th Cir. Omaha, NE 68127-4146. Phone: (402)593-4500 • URL: http://www.infogroup.com • Annual. Number of listings: 19,980. Entries include: Name, address, phone, size of advertisement, name of owner or manager, number of employees, year first in "Yellow Pages." Compiled from telephone company "Yellow Pages," nationwide.

***ACCRA Cost of Living Index***. Council for Community and Economic Research, 1700 N Moore St., Ste. 2225 Arlington, VA 22209. Phone: (703)522-4980; Fax: (480)393-5098 or (703)522-4985; Email: info@c2er.org • URL: http://www.c2er.org • Quarterly. $165 Individuals. Compares price levels for 280-310 U.S. cities.

***Accreditation Process Guide***. American Camping Association, 5000 State Rd. 67 N Martinsville, IN 46151-7902. Phone: 800-428-2267 or (765)342-8456; Fax: (765)342-2065 • URL: http://www.acacamps.org • Annual. Lists camp standards for camps undergoing on-site accreditation visits.

**Accrediting Council on Education in Journalism and Mass Communications**. Stauffer-Flint Hall, 1435 Jayhawk Blvd. Lawrence, KS 66045-7575. Phone: (785)864-3973 or (785)864-3986; Fax: (785)864-5225 • URL: http://www2.ku.edu/acejmc • Consists of journalism education associations and related industry groups. Encourages cooperation between the mass media and colleges and universities in education for journalism and accredits professional programs in schools and departments of journalism. Approved list currently includes 112 colleges and universities and one university outside the country.

***Accu-Data***. Accu-Weather Inc., 385 Science Park Rd. State College, PA 16803-2215. Phone: 888-438-9847 or (814)235-8770 or (814)237-0309; Fax: (215)244-5329 or (814)235-8609; Email: sales@accuweather.com • URL: http://www.accuweather.com • Provides detailed, current weather conditions and weather forecasts for many U. S. and foreign cities and regions. Updating is continuous. Inquire as to online cost and availability.

***ACGA: Partners in Philanthropy***. American Council on Gift Annuities, Phone: (317)269-6271; Fax: (317)269-6276; Email: acga@acga-web.org • URL: http://www.acga-web.org • Web site provides detailed information on gift annuities, including suggested charitable gift annuity rates for use by charities and their donors. Rates for immediate and deferred annuities are presented in the form of tables for ages 20 to 90 (and over), for both "Single Life" and "Two Lives - Joint and Survivor." Other items covered include the philosophy of gift annuities, state regulations, "What's New," and a search site. Fees: Free.

**ACI - Financial Markets Association**. 8, Rue du Mail F-75002 Paris, France. Phone: 33 1 42975115 • URL: http://www.aciforex.org • National financial markets associations representing individuals and firms. Seeks to advance the foreign exchange and related financial businesses. Represents members at the international level; facilitates communication and cooperation among financial markets professionals and firms; sponsors educational and career development programs.

***ACI Manual of Concrete Practice***. American Concrete Institute, 38800 Country Club Dr. Farmington Hills, MI 48331-3439. Phone: (248)848-3700; Fax: (248)848-3701; Email: ann.daugherty@acifoundation.org • URL: http://www.concrete.org • $846.50 Nonmembers Print (7 Volume Set); $508 Members Print (7 Volume Set); $681.50 Nonmembers CD; $409 Members CD. Contains all of the widely used ACI concrete and masonry code requirements, specifications, guides and reports.

***ACLI Life Insurers Fact Book***. American Council of Life Insurance, 101 Constitution Ave. NW Washington, DC 20001. Phone: (202)624-2000 • Annual. Free. Provides statistics and information on trends in the life insurance industry.

***ACM Computing Surveys: The Survey and Tutorial Journal of the ACM***. Association for Computing Machinery, 2 Penn Plz., Ste. 701 New York, NY 10121-0701. Phone: 800-342-6626 or (212)626-0500 or (212)869-7440; Fax: (212)944-1318; Email: acmhelp@acm.org • URL: http://www.acm.org • Quarterly. $26 Members; $160 Nonmembers; $21 Students.

***ACM Electronic Guide to Computing Literature: Bibliographic Listing, Author Index, Keyword Index, Category Index, Proper Noun Subject Index, Reviewer Index, Source Index***. Association for Computing Machinery, 2 Penn Plz., Ste. 701 New York, NY 10121-0701. Phone: 800-342-6626 or (212)626-0500 or (212)869-7440; Fax: (212)944-1318; Email: acmhelp@acm.org • URL: http://www.acm.org • Quarterly. Members, $175.00; non-members, $499.00 per year. A comprehensive guide to each year's computer literature (books, proceedings, journals, etc.), with an emphasis on technical material. Indexed by author, keyword, category, proper noun, reviewer, and source. Formerly *A C M Guide to Computing Literature*.

***ACM Transactions on Graphics***. Association for Computing Machinery, 2 Penn Plz., Ste. 701 New York, NY 10121-0701. Phone: 800-342-6626 or (212)626-0500 or (212)869-7440; Fax: (212)944-1318; Email: acmhelp@acm.org • URL: http://www.acm.org • Bimonthly. $41 Members; $170 Nonmembers; $36 Students.

***Acoustical Society of America Journal***. Acoustical Society of America. One Physics Ellipse, Two Huntington Quadrangle, Ste. 1NO1 College Park, MD 20740-3843. Phone: 800-344-6902 or (301)209-3100; Fax: (301)209-0843; Email: aip@aip.org • URL: http://www.aip.org • Monthly. Institutions, $1,325.00 per year. Includes print and online editions.

***Acoustics Abstracts***. Multi-Science Publishing Company Ltd., 5 Wates Way Brentwood CM15 9TB, United Kingdom. Phone: 44 1277224632; Fax: 44 1277223453; Email: info@multi-science.co.uk • URL: http://www.multi-science.co.uk • Monthly. $600.

***Acquisitions and Mergers: Negotiated and Contested Transactions***. Joy M. Bryan and Simone M. Lorne. Thomson West, 610 Opperman Dr. Eagan, MN 55123. Phone: 800-328-9352 or (651)687-7000 • $342 Individuals per month. Includes legal forms and documents. (Securities Law Series).

***Acquisitions Monthly***. Thomson Financial Inc., 195 Broadway New York, NY 10007-3100. Phone: (646)822-2000; Email: custserv@tfn.com • URL: http://www.thomsonreuters.com • Monthly. $790.00 per year. Published in London. Provides detailed information, commentary, and statistics on merger, acquisition, and buyout activity in Europe, the U.S., and Asia.

***Acronym Finder: The Web's Most Comprehensive Database of Acronyms, Abbreviations, and Initialisms***. Mountain Data Systems, Phone: (970)586-5556; Email: acronyms@mtnds.com • URL: http://www.acronymfinder.com • Web site provides more than 750,000 definitions. Searching offers a choice of "exact acronym," "acronym begins with," "acronym (wildcard)", or "reverse lookup (keywords)." Fees: Free.

***Acronyms, Initialisms, & Abbreviations Dictionary***. Cengage Learning Inc., 20 Channel Center St. Boston, MA 02210. Phone: 800-487-8488 or (617)289-7700; Fax: (617)289-7844; Email: investors@cengage.com • URL: http://www.cengage.com • Annual. $1474.00. Provides more than 780,000 definitions in all subject areas. eBook also available.

**ACT and Region Chamber of Commerce and Industry**. 12a Thesiger Ct. Canberra, ACT 2600, Australia. Phone: 61 2 62835200; Fax: 61 2 62822436; Email: chamber@actchamber.com.au • URL: http://www.actchamber.com.au • Represents businesses in the Australian Capital Territory of Australia.

**ACT Inc.** 500 ACT Dr. Iowa City, IA 52243-0168. Phone: (319)337-1000; Fax: (319)339-3020 • URL: http://www.act.org.

***ACTE Global Business Journal***. Association of Corporate Travel Executives, 510 King St., Ste. 220 Alexandria, VA 22314. Phone: (703)683-5322; Fax: (703)683-2720; Email: info@acte.org • URL: http://www.acte.org • Quarterly. Magazine covering corporate travel.

***Active Real Estate Lenders***. Todd Publications, PO Box 500 Millwood, NY 10546. Phone: 866-896-0916 or (914)373-4750; Fax: (914)373-4750; Email: toddpub@aol.com • URL: http://www.toddpublications.com • Biennial. $35. Covers: 2,500 banks, finance companies, mortgage lenders, real estate investment trusts, brokers, and other firms offering real estate investment money.

**Acton Institute for the Study of Religion and Liberty - Center for Academic Research**. 98 E Fulton St. Grand Rapids, MI 49503. Phone: 800-345-2286 or (616)454-3080; Fax: (616)454-9454; Email: info@acton.org • URL: http://www.acton.org/index/research • Generating new economic models synthesizing free market economic theory and the central tenets of Christian social thought, morality and the free market, welfare reform, poverty and development, and other methodological and moral considerations.

***The Actuary***. Society of Actuaries, 475 N Martingale Rd., Ste. 600 Schaumburg, IL 60173. Phone: (847)706-3500; Fax: (847)706-3599; Email: feedback@soa.org • URL: http://www.soa.org • Bimonthly. Description: Features information about actuaries practicing in life and health insurance, pensions, and investments in the U.S. and Canada. Recurring features include letters to the editor, news of research and education, a calendar of events, reports of meetings, notices of publications available, and puzzles.

***ADA Compliance Guide***. Thompson Publishing Group Inc., Government Information Services, Education Funding Research Council, 1725 K St. NW, Ste. 700 Washington, DC 20006. Phone: 800-677-3789 or (202)444-8741; Fax: (800)759-7179 or (202)296-1091; Email: service@thompson.com • URL: http://www.thompson.com • $499 print only. Provides detailed information for employers and others on complying with the Americans With Disabilities Act (ADA). Includes material on employment discrimination, transportation accessibility, accessibility in public accommodations, and state disability laws.

***ADA Compliance Manual for Employers***. Matthew Bender and Company Inc., 1275 Broadway Albany, NY 12204-2638. Phone: 800-424-4200 or (518)487-3000; Fax: (518)487-3573 or (800)424-4200; Email: customer.support@lexisnexis.com • URL: http://www.matthewbender.com • Looseleaf. $95.00. Periodic supplementation available. "Every business with more than 15 employees must comply with the Amricans with Disabilities Act." This guide provides practical advice on job requirements, accessibility, employee selection, reasonable accomodations, termination issues, and other matters.

***Adaptive Technologies and Business Integration: Social, Managerial, and Organizational Dimensions***. Cengage Learning Inc., 20 Channel Center St. Boston, MA 02210. Phone: 800-487-8488 or (617)289-7700; Fax: (617)289-7844; Email: investors@cengage.com • URL: http://www.cengage.com • 2007. eBook. Provides an authoritative review of both intra-organizational and inter-organizational aspects in business integration, including: managerial and organizational integration, social integration, and technology integration, along with the resources to accomplish this competitive advantage.

***ADB Business Opportunities***. Asian Development Bank, 6 ADB Ave., Mandaluyong Manila 0980, Philippines. Phone: 63 263 24444; Fax: 63 263 62444 • URL: http://www.adb.org • Monthly. Publication covering economic development.

***Addiction Research Foundation Journal: Addiction News for Professionals***. Addiction Research Foundation of Ontario, Subscription-Marketing Dept., 33 Russell St. Toronto, ON, Canada M5S 2S1. Phone: 800-661-1111 or (416)595-6059 • Six times a year. $19.00 per year. News and opinions from the drug and alcohol field around th world. Formerly *Alcoholism and Drug Addiction Research Foundation Journal*.

**Addiction Research Unit**. University at Buffalo, Dept. of Psychology Buffalo, NY 14260-4110. Phone: (716)887-2566; Fax: (716)887-2252; Email: connors@ria.org • URL: http://wings.buffalo.edu/aru.

***Addison County Business Directory & Community Profile***. Addison County Chamber of Commerce, 93 Court St. Middlebury, VT 05753. Phone: (802)388-7951; Fax: (802)388-8066; Email: info@addisoncounty.com • URL: http://www.addisoncounty.com • Description: Serves as a resource guide for businesses and individuals that are relocating to Addison County, Vermont, and surrounding areas. Covers: over 500 member businesses, and local government officials in Addison County, Vermont. Entries include: For businesses—Name, address, phone, business description, name and title of contact, fax, e-mail and URL addresses. For government officials—Name, business office address, phone, hours of operation.

***Addressing & Letter Service Directory***. InfoGroup Inc., 5711 S 86th Cir. Omaha, NE 68127-4146. Phone: (402)593-4500 • URL: http://www.infogroup.com • Annual. Number of listings: 8,077. Entries include: Name, address, phone, size of advertisement, name of owner or manager, number of employees, year first in "Yellow Pages." Compiled from telephone company "Yellow Pages," nationwide.

***ADFIAP Factbook***. Association of Development Financing Institutions in Asia and the Pacific, Skyland Plaza, 2nd Fl., Sen. Gil Puyat Ave. Makati 1200, Philippines. Phone: 63 2 8161672 or 63 2 8430932; Fax: 63 2 8176498 • URL: http://www.adfiap.org • 64. $10 postpaid. Covers: about 80 member institutions in Asia-Pacific whose main purpose is to provide capital for industrial development. Entries include: Institution name, address, phone.

***Adhesives Age Buyers Guide***. Chemical Week Associates, 2 Grand Central Tower, 140 E 45th St., 40th Fl. New York, NY 10017. Phone: 800-774-5733 or (212)884-9528 or (212)621-4900; Fax: (212)883-9514 or (212)884-9514; Email: webmaster@chemweek.com • URL: http://www.chemweek.com • Annual. Lists manufacturers and suppliers of raw materials, chemicals, equipment, and machinery for the adhesives industry.

***Adhesives Age***. Chemical Week Associates, 2 Grand Central Tower, 140 E 45th St., 40th Fl. New York, NY 10017. Phone: 800-774-5733 or (212)884-9528 or (212)621-4900; Fax: (212)883-9514 or (212)884-9514; Email: webmaster@chemweek.com • URL: http://www.chemweek.com • Monthly. $60 Individuals.

**Adjusters Directory.** InfoGroup Inc., 5711 S 86th Cir. Omaha, NE 68127-4146. Phone: (402)593-4500 • URL: http://www.infogroup.com • Annual. Number of listings: 5,785. Entries include: Name, address, phone, size of advertisement, name of owner or manager, number of employees, year first in "Yellow Pages." Compiled from telephone company "Yellow Pages," nationwide.

**Adjustment & Collection Services Directory.** InfoGroup Inc., 5711 S 86th Cir. Omaha, NE 68127-4146. Phone: (402)593-4500 • URL: http://www.infogroup.com • Annual. Number of listings: 7,138. Entries include: Name, address, phone, size of advertisement, name of owner or manager, number of employees, year first in "Yellow Pages." Compiled from telephone company "Yellow Pages," nationwide.

**Adjutants General Association of the United States.** 100 Minuteman Pkwy. Frankfort, KY 40601-6168. • URL: http://www.agaus.org • Adjutants General (National Guard) of the states and territories.

**Administration and Society.** Pine Forge Press, 2455 Teller Rd. Thousand Oaks, CA 91320-2234. Phone: 800-818-7243 or (805)499-4224 or (805)499-9774; Fax: (805)499-0871 or (805)583-2665; Email: sales@pfp.sagepub.com • URL: http://www.sagepub.com/sociologybooks • 9/year. $1,546 Institutions print; $1,420 Institutions e-access; $200 Individuals print; $189 Institutions single print issue; $29 Individuals single print issue. Scholarly journal concerned with public administration and the effects of bureaucracy.

**Administrative Assistant's Update.** MPL Communications Inc., 133 Richmond St. W, Ste. 700 Toronto, ON, Canada M5H 3M8. Phone: 800-804-8846 or (416)869-1177 or (416)869-2777; Fax: (416)869-0456 or (416)869-0616; Email: investors@mplcomm.com • URL: http://www.adviceforinvestors.com • Monthly. $189 Individuals Annual. Description: Offers useful news, information, and suggestions to administrative assistants. Features articles on aspects of secretarial work, including items on problem-solving, office automation, computerization, and grammar and vocabulary development.

**Administrative Law.** Matthew Bender and Company Inc., 1275 Broadway Albany, NY 12204-2638. Phone: 800-424-4200 or (518)487-3000; Fax: (518)487-3573 or (800)424-4200; Email: customer.support@lexisnexis.com • URL: http://www.matthewbender.com • Three times a year. $1,416.00. Six looseleaf volumes. Covers investigations, adjudications, hearings, licenses, judicial review, and so forth.

**Administrative Law Review.** American Bar Association, 321 N Clark St. Chicago, IL 60654-7598. Phone: 800-285-2221 or (312)988-5000; Email: orders@abanet.org • URL: http://www.americanbar.org/aba.html • Quarterly. $10 Single issue; $40 Nonmembers; $45 Out of country; included in membership dues; $35 /year for non-lawyers; $35 Members. Scholarly legal journal on developments in the field of administrative law.

**Administrative Radiology Journal: The Journal of Medical Imaging Business, Management & Administration.** Glendale Publishing Corp., 934 W Glenoaks Blvd., Ste. 1 Glendale, CA 91202-2755. Email: arjournal@aol.com • Monthly. $96 Individuals; $126 Canada and Mexico; $196 Other countries; $15 Single issue. Monthly Journal of Imaging Administration for Chief Imaging M.D.'s, Imaging Department Managers, Radiation Oncology Directors, and Healthcare Administrators.

**Administrative Science Quarterly.** Cornell University, Johnson Graduate School of Management, 114 East Ave. Ithaca, NY 14850. Phone: 800-847-2082 or (607)255-6418; Fax: (607)255-5117; Email: dean@johnson.cornell.edu • URL: http://www.johnson.cornell.edu • Quarterly. $299 Institutions combined (print & e-access); $293 Institutions print; $269 Institutions e-access; $99 Individuals combined (print & e-access); $81 Institutions single print issue; $32 Individuals single print issue.

**Ads to Icons.** Cengage Learning Inc., 20 Channel Center St. Boston, MA 02210. Phone: 800-487-8488 or (617)289-7700; Fax: (617)289-7844; Email: investors@cengage.com • URL: http://www.cengage.com • 2011. eBook. 2nd edition. Published by Kogan Page. Examines current and future trends in advertising. Through 50 international case studies of new and iconic advertising campaigns, author Paul Springer identifies why these campaigns were successful and analyzes their contribution to the continued development of advertising.

**Adult and Continuing Education Today.** Learning Resources Network, PO Box 9 River Falls, WI 54022. Phone: 800-678-5376 or (715)426-9777; Fax: (888)234-8633; Email: tammyp@lern.org • URL: http://www.lern.org • Biweekly. $95 Individuals.

**Adult Education Quarterly: A Journal of Research and Theory.** American Association for Adult and Continuing Education. Pine Forge Press, 2455 Teller Rd. Thousand Oaks, CA 91320-2234. Phone: 800-818-7243 or (805)499-4224 or (805)499-9774; Fax: (805)499-0871 or (805)583-2665; Email: sales@pfp.sagepub.com • URL: http://www.sagepub.com/sociologybooks • Quarterly. $445 Institutions combined (print & e-access); $401 Institutions e-access; $436 Institutions print; $105 Individuals print; $120 Institutions single print issue; $34 Individuals single print issue. Scholarly journal committed to advancing the understanding and practice of adult and continuing education.

**Advance-Decline Album.** Dow Theory Letters, Inc., PO Box 1759 La Jolla, CA 92038-1759. Phone: (858)454-0481; Email: staff@dowtheoryletters.com • URL: http://ww2.dowtheoryletters.com • Annual. Contains one page for each year since 1931. Includes charts of the New York Stock Exchange advance-decline ratio and the Dow Jones industrial average.

**Advance Monthly Retail Trade Report.** U. S. Census Bureau, Phone: 800-541-8345 or (301)457-4100 or (301)763-2713; Fax: (301)457-1296 or (301)457-3842; Email: naics@census.gov • URL: http://www.census.gov/epcd/www/naicstab.htm • Web pages provide monthly sales figures for a wide range of retail businesses. Advance, preliminary, and final statistics are provided for the latest month available in each case, with a previous-year comparison. Updates are monthly.

**Advance Payment Directory.** InfoGroup Inc., 5711 S 86th Cir. Omaha, NE 68127-4146. Phone: (402)593-4500 • URL: http://www.infogroup.com • Annual. Number of listings: 14,867. Entries include: Name, address, phone, size of advertisement, name of owner or manager, number of employees, year first in "Yellow Pages." Compiled from telephone company "Yellow Pages," nationwide.

**Advanced Battery Technology.** Seven Mountains Scientific Inc., 913 Tressler St. Boalsburg, PA 16827. Phone: (814)466-6559; Fax: (814)466-2777 • URL: http://www.7ms.com • Monthly. $165 Individuals. Provides technical and marketing information for the international battery industry.

**Advanced Coatings and Surface Technology.** Technical Insights, 605 Third Ave. New York, NY 10158-0012. Phone: 800-825-7550 or (212)850-8600; Fax: (212)850-8800; Email: insights@wiley.com • URL: http://www.wiley.com • Monthly. $650 Institutions. Newsletter on technical developments relating to industrial coatings.

**Advanced Composites Monthly.** Composite Market Reports Inc., 7670 Opportunity Rd., Ste. 250 San Diego, CA 92111. Phone: (619)560-1085; Fax: (619)560-0234; Email: customers@mplcomm.com • Description: Covers advanced composite materials processes and markets in the aerospace industry worldwide. "Prepared for engineering, program, and manufacturing management at primes and their subcontractors where aerospace components made of high-performance composite materials are designed, fabricated, or assembled." Discusses subcontract opportunities of interest to U.S., Canadian, and overseas aerospace companies. Recurring features include a calendar of events, reports of meetings, interviews, news of research, and application case histories.

**Advanced Imaging: Solutions for the Electronic Imaging Professional.** Cygnus Business Media, 3 Huntington Quadrangle, Ste. 301N Melville, NY 11747. Phone: 800-308-6397 or (631)845-2700; Fax: (631)845-2741 or (631)845-2798; Email: rich.reiff@cygnuspub.com • URL: http://www.cygnusb2b.com • Monthly. $60.00 per year Covers document-based imaging technologies, products, systems, and services. Coverage is also devoted to multimedia and electronic printing and publishing.

**Advanced Manufacturing Engineering Institute.** University of Hartford, College of Engineering, Technology, and Architecture, 200 Bloomfield Ave. West Hartford, CT 06117. Phone: 800-678-4844 or (860)768-4112; Fax: (860)768-5073; Email: shetty@mail.hartford.edu.

**Advanced Manufacturing Technology.** John Wiley & Sons Inc. Scientific, Technical, Medical, and Scholarly Div. (Wiley-Blackwell), 111 River St. Hoboken, NJ 07030-5774. Phone: (201)748-6000; Fax: (201)748-6088; Email: info@wiley.com • URL: http://www.wiley.com • Monthly. Publication includes: List of companies involved in developing advanced manufacturing technologies such as robotics, artificial intelligence in computers, ultrasonics, lasers, and waterjet cutters; also lists sources of information and education on high-technology. Entries include: Company or organization name, address, phone, name of contact; description of process, product, or service. Principal content is articles and analysis of advanced manufacturing technology.

**Advanced Manufacturing Technology: Monthly Report.** Technical Insights, 605 Third Ave. New York, NY 10158-0012. Phone: 800-825-7550 or (212)850-8600; Fax: (212)850-8800; Email: insights@wiley.com • URL: http://www.wiley.com • Monthly. $695 Institutions. Covers technological developments relating to robotics, computer graphics, automation, computer-integrated manufacturing, and machining.

**Advanced Materials and Processes.** ASM International, 9639 Kinsman Rd. Materials Park, OH 44073-0002. Phone: 800-336-5152 or (440)338-5151; Email: memberservicecenter@asminternational.org • URL: http://www.asminternational.org • Monthly. Members free; $325 Institutions. Incorporates *Metal Progress*.Technical information and reports on new developments in the technology of engineered materials and manufacturing processes.

**Advanced Networking Research Group.** Washington University, One Brookings Dr. St. Louis, MO 63130-4899. Phone: (314)935-5455; Fax: (314)935-7302; Email: jst@cs.wustl.edu • Research fields include the design of high speed internetworks and the design of host interfaces.

**Advances in Agronomy.** American Society for Agronomy, Inc. Elsevier, Secondary Publishing Division, 650 Ave. of the Americas New York, NY 10011. Phone: 888-437-4636 or (212)633-3980; Fax: (212)633-3975; Email: t.reller@

elsevier.com • URL: http://www.elseveier.com • Annual. $193. A leading reference and a first-rate source for the latest research in agronomy.

**Advances in Chemical Engineering.** Elsevier, Secondary Publishing Division, 650 Ave. of the Americas New York, NY 10011. Phone: 888-437-4636 or (212)633-3980; Fax: (212)633-3975; Email: t.reller@elsevier.com • URL: http://www.elseveier.com • $260 Individuals. Provides information on modeling of complex chemical systems. Multiple volumes available. Contact for pricing.

**Advances in Computers.** Elsevier, Secondary Publishing Division, 650 Ave. of the Americas New York, NY 10011. Phone: 888-437-4636 or (212)633-3980; Fax: (212)633-3975; Email: t.reller@elsevier.com • URL: http://www.elseveier.com • $182 Individuals. Coverage of innovations in computer hardware, software, theory, design, and applications. Contact for pricing.

**Advances in Cryogenic Engineering.** Cryogenic Engineering Conference, 1 Research Cir., K1-EP119 Niskayuna, NY 12309. Email: ammk@crd.ge.com • URL: http://tdserver1.fnal.gov/nicol/cec • Biennial. $235 /volume. Includes invited, unsolicited, and government-sponsored research papers in the research areas of superconductors and structural materials for cryogenic applications.

**Advances in Electronic Marketing.** Cengage Learning Inc., 20 Channel Center St. Boston, MA 02210. Phone: 800-487-8488 or (617)289-7700; Fax: (617)289-7844; Email: investors@cengage.com • URL: http://www.cengage.com • 2006. eBook. Published by Information Science Reference. Examines the challenges that organizations face today within three major themes: the global environment, the strategic/technological realm, and the buyer behavior of online consumers.

**Advances in Industrial and Labor Relations.** David Levin and Paul Gollan, editors. Elsevier, Secondary Publishing Division, 650 Ave. of the Americas New York, NY 10011. Phone: 888-437-4636 or (212)633-3980; Fax: (212)633-3975; Email: t.reller@elsevier.com • URL: http://www.elseveier.com • Multiple volumes. Prices vary.

**Advances in Investment Analysis and Portfolio Management.** Chung-Few Lee, editor. Elsevier, Secondary Publishing Division, 650 Ave. of the Americas New York, NY 10011. Phone: 888-437-4636 or (212)633-3980; Fax: (212)633-3975; Email: t.reller@elsevier.com • URL: http://www.elseveier.com • Focus on investment analysis and portfolio theory.

**Advances in Librarianship.** Elsevier, Secondary Publishing Division, 650 Ave. of the Americas New York, NY 10011. Phone: 888-437-4636 or (212)633-3980; Fax: (212)633-3975; Email: t.reller@elsevier.com • URL: http://www.elseveier.com • Irregular. Prices vary.

**Advances in Library Administration and Organization.** Delmus E. Williams and Janine Golden, editors. Emerald Group Publishing Ltd., Howard House, Wagon Ln. Bingley BD16 1WA, United Kingdom. Phone: 44 1274 777 700; Fax: 44 1274 785 201 • URL: http://www.emeraldinsight.com • Annual. Price varies per volume. 31 volumes.

**Advances in Polymer Technology.** Polymer Processing Institute. John Wiley & Sons Inc., 111 River St. Hoboken, NJ 07030-5774. Phone: 800-225-5945 or (201)748-6000; Fax: (201)748-6088; Email: info@wiley.com • URL: http://www.wiley.com • Quarterly. $950 Institutions; $998 Individuals online.

**Advances in Small Animal Medicine and Surgery.** Elsevier, Secondary Publishing Division, 650 Ave. of the Americas New York, NY 10011. Phone: 888-437-4636 or (212)633-3980; Fax: (212)633-3975; Email: t.reller@elsevier.com • URL: http://www.elseveier.com • Monthly. $458 Institutions, other countries print; $265 Other countries print; $90 Students print; $315 Institutions print; $160 Individuals print; $106 Students, other countries print. Contains abstracts from the field.

**Advances in the Astronautical Sciences.** American Astronautical Society. Univelt Inc., 740 Metcalf St., Ste. 13 & 15 San Diego, CA 92198. Phone: (760)746-4005; Fax: (760)746-3139; Email: 76121.1532@compuserve.com • URL: http://www.univelt.com • $215 Individuals; $140 Individuals CD-Rom only. Price varies. Volumes in this series cover the proceedings of various astronautical conferences and symposia.

**ADVERTISE.** Deutscher Sparkassenverlag GmbH, Am Wallgraben 115 70565 Stuttgart, Germany. Phone: 49 0711 7 82-0 or 711 7821790; Fax: 49 0711 7 82 16 35 or 711 7822158; Email: info@dsv-gruppe.de • URL: http://www.dsv-gruppe.de • Weekly. Database covers: Worldwide cooperative venture offers and requests, covering product import and export, technology transfer, joint ventures, and related ventures. Emphasis is on opportunities for small and medium-sized European companies. Entries include: Company name, address, phone; company profile; descriptors and codes for products and services; type of cooperation sought; dates of entry and validity.

**Advertiser & Agency Red Books Plus.** LexisNexis, 9443 Springboro Pke. Dayton, OH 45342. Phone: 800-227-4908 or (937)865-6800; Fax: (937)865-1211; Email: legalnotices@lexisnexis.com • URL: http://www.bender.com • Quarterly. $2,195 Individuals. CD-ROM. Covers 15,750 of the world's top advertisers, their products and what media they use, as well as 13,900 U.S. and international ad agencies and nearly

100,000 key executives worldwide in management, creative, and media positions. Entries include: For advertisers—Company name, job function/title, product/brand name, advertising expenditures by media. For personnel—Name and title.

***Advertiser and Agency Red Books Plus***. National Register Publishing Co., 300 Connell Dr., Ste. 2000 Berkeley Heights, NJ 07922. Phone: 800-473-7020; Fax: (908)673-1189; Email: nrpeditorial@marquiswhoswho.com • URL: http://www.nationalregisterpub.com • Quarterly. $1,295.00 per year. The CD-ROM version of *Standard Directory of Advertisers, Standard Directory of Advertising Agencies*, and *Standard Directory of International Advertisers and Agencies*.

***Advertiser's Yearbook***. Oekonomisk Literatur Norge A/S, PO Box 457 Sentrum N-0150 Oslo, Norway. Phone: 47 2242 0042; Fax: 47 2242 6089 • Annual. $780. Covers: Advertising agencies in Norway. Entries include: Company name, address, phone, fax, management/ad/text, list of customers, special services, number of employees, share capital, sales.

***Advertising Age—Agencies Ranked by Gross Income Issue***. Crain Communications Inc., 150 N Michigan Ave. Chicago, IL 60601-7553. Phone: 800-678-9595 or (312)649-5200 or (312)649-5411; Fax: (312)280-3150 or (312)280-3174; Email: info@crain.com • URL: http://www.crain.com • Annual. $25 Individuals PDF; $45 Individuals Excel; $3.50. Covers: More than 600 advertising agencies. Publication includes: Ranked lists of about 650 U.S advertising agencies, 1,600 foreign agencies, the world's Top 50 advertising organizations, top media services companies in the U.S. and worldwide, top U.S. healthcare agencies, and multicultural agencies, which reported billings and gross income, or whose billings and gross incomes were ascertained through research. Entries include: For agencies with gross income over three million dollars: agency name, rank for two years, billing, gross income, and number of employees.

***Advertising Age: National Expenditures in Newspapers***. Crain Communications Inc., 711 3rd Ave. New York, NY 10017. Phone: (212)210-0100; Email: info@crain.com • URL: http://www.crain.com • Annual.

***Advertising Age: The International Newspaper of Marketing***. Crain Communications Inc., 711 3rd Ave. New York, NY 10017. Phone: (212)210-0100; Email: info@crain.com • URL: http://www.crain.com • Weekly. $178.50 Individuals. Includes supplement *Creativity*.

***Advertising Agency***. Entrepreneur Press, 2445 McCabe Way, Ste. 400 Irvine, CA 92614-6244. Phone: 800-864-6864 or (949)261-2325 or (949)622-7131; Fax: (949)261-7729 or (949)261-0234; Email: press@entrepreneur.com • URL: http://www.entrepreneurpress.com • Looseleaf. $69.00. A practical guide to starting a small advertising agency. Covers profit potential, start-up costs, market size evaluation, pricing, accounting, advertising, promotion, etc. (Start-Up Business Guide No. E1223.).

***Advertising Age's Euromarketing***. Crain Communications Inc., 711 3rd Ave. New York, NY 10017. Phone: (212)210-0100; Email: info@crain.com • URL: http://www.crain.com • Weekly. $295 Individuals. Newsletter on European advertising and marketing.

***Advertising & Press Annual in Africa***. International Publications Service, 114 E 32nd St. New York, NY 10016. Phone: (212)685-9351 • Annual. Covers: African newspapers, magazines, radio and television stations, annuals, poster and transportation advertising and exhibits and shows; leading advertisers and professionals in the field in Africa; associations involved in a variety of fields of advertising and publicity in Africa.

***Advertising Companies Contact Lists***. Sheila Greco Associates L.L.C., 174 County Highway 67 Amsterdam, NY 12010. Phone: 888-400-8049 or (518)843-4611; Fax: (518)843-5498; Email: info@sheilagreco.com • URL: http://www.sheilagreco.com • $65. Consists of 3 individually-priced lists covering advertising companies in the U.S. Each list features details for one company and includes global headquarter name, address, phone, fax, U.S. headquarter phone number, URL, company description, ticker symbol, revenues reported, industry type, key executive names and titles. All lists downloadable via PDF format.

***Advertising Compliance Service Newsletter***. John Lichtenberger, 26 Hawthorn Dr. Roxbury, NJ 07876-2112. Phone: (973)252-7552; Fax: (973)252-7552; Email: lawpublish@aol.com • Bimonthly. $495.00 per year.

***Advertising Consultants Directory***. InfoGroup Inc., 5711 S 86th Cir. Omaha, NE 68127-4146. Phone: (402)593-4500 • URL: http://www.infogroup.com • Annual. Number of listings: 51,839. Entries include: Name, address, phone, size of advertisement, name of owner or manager, number of employees, year first in "Yellow Pages." Compiled from telephone company "Yellow Pages," nationwide.

***Advertising—Displays Directory***. InfoGroup Inc., 5711 S 86th Cir. Omaha, NE 68127-4146. Phone: (402)593-4500 • URL: http://www.infogroup.com • Annual. Number of listings: 4,029. Entries include: Name, address, phone, size of advertisement, name of owner or manager, number of employees, year first in "Yellow Pages." Compiled from telephone company "Yellow Pages," nationwide.

***Advertising Law Guide***. Wolters Kluwer Law & Business CCH, 2700 Lake Cook Rd. Riverwoods, IL 60015. Phone: 888-224-7377 or (847)267-7000; Email: cust_serv@cch.com • URL: http://www.cchgroup.com • Monthly. $2,115. Contains full-text reporting of state and federal laws as well as federal regulations.

**Advertising Media Credit Executives Association**. 24600 Detroit Rd., Ste. 100 Bay Village, OH 44140-0036. Email: amcea@tx.rr.com • URL: http://www.amcea.org • Credit executives for advertising media such as newspapers, magazines, radio, and television. Provides information for exchange of ideas on credit management methods and procedures; encourages study in advanced educational courses in fundamentals, such as business law, finance, banking, accounting, and economics.

***Advertising (Promotional) Directory***. InfoGroup Inc., 5711 S 86th Cir. Omaha, NE 68127-4146. Phone: (402)593-4500 • URL: http://www.infogroup.com • Annual. Number of listings: 6,226. Entries include: Name, address, phone, size of advertisement, name of owner or manager, number of employees, year first in "Yellow Pages." Compiled from telephone company "Yellow Pages," nationwide.

***Advertising (Signs) Directory***. InfoGroup Inc., 5711 S 86th Cir. Omaha, NE 68127-4146. Phone: (402)593-4500 • URL: http://www.infogroup.com • Annual. Number of listings: 28,945. Entries include: Name, address, phone, size of advertisement, name of owner or manager, number of employees, year first in "Yellow Pages." Compiled from telephone company "Yellow Pages," nationwide.

***Advice from the Presidents: The Student's Guide to Reaching the Top in Business and Politics***. Cengage Learning Inc., 20 Channel Center St. Boston, MA 02210. Phone: 800-487-8488 or (617)289-7700; Fax: (617)289-7844; Email: investors@cengage.com • URL: http://www.cengage.com • 2010. eBook. Author details 2 years of research examining the lives of nearly 200 presidential candidates to make up the advice offerec in this work.

***The ADWEEK Directory: The Directory of U.S. Advertising Agencies, Public Relations Firms and Media Buying Services***. ADWEEK Magazines, 770 Broadway, 7th Fl. New York, NY 10003-9595. Phone: 800-641-2030 or (212)493-4122 or (212)536-5336; Fax: (212)536-1416 or (646)654-5350; Email: erica.bartman@adweek.com • URL: http://www.adweek.com • Annual. $499 Individuals 1 Directory; $799 Individuals 2 directories. Covers: Over 23,000 personal listings and it has information on more than 5,900 full-service advertising agencies, public relations firms, media buying services, direct marketing and related organizations. Database includes: List of over 30,000 major accounts managed by agencies. Entries include: Agency name, address, phone, fax/e-mail, URL; names and titles of key personnel; major accounts; Ultimate parent company; headquarters location; major subsidiaries and other operating units; year founded; number of employees; fee income; billings; percentage of billings by medium. Individual listings for each agency branch.

***Adweek Magazines' Technology Marketing***. Nielsen Business Media Inc., 770 Broadway New York, NY 10003-9522. Phone: 866-890-8541 or (646)654-4500 or (646)654-5000; Fax: (646)654-5584 or (646)654-4500; Email: bmcomm@nielsen.com • URL: http://www.nielsenbusinessmedia.com • Monthly. $55.00 per year. Edited for marketing executives in high technology industries. Covers both advertising and marketing. Formerly *MC Technology Marketing Intelligence*.

***ADWEEK***. Nielsen Business Media Inc., 770 Broadway New York, NY 10003-9522. Phone: 866-890-8541 or (646)654-4500 or (646)654-5000; Fax: (646)654-5584 or (646)654-4500; Email: bmcomm@nielsen.com • URL: http://www.nielsenbusinessmedia.com • Weekly. $149 Individuals. Covers local, national, and international advertising news and trends. Includes critiques of advertising campaigns.

***AEDC Resource Directory***. American Economic Development Council, 1030 Higgins Rd., Ste. 301 Park Ridge, IL 60068. Phone: (847)692-9944; Fax: (847)696-2990 • URL: http://www.iedconline.org • Annual. Covers: Approximately 2,800 member industrial and economic development managers, including executive directors of chambers of commerce; federal, state, and regional industrial organizations; transportation agencies, utility companies, banks, and others who promote economic and industrial development. Entries include: Name, title, affiliation, address, phone, fax, email, and web, as well as practice speciality.

***Aerospace America Magazine***. American Institute of Aeronautics and Astronautics, 1801 Alexander Bell Dr., Ste. 500 Reston, VA 20191-4344. Phone: 800-639-2422 or (703)264-7500; Fax: (703)264-7551; Email: custserv@aiaa.org • URL: http://www.aiaa.org • Monthly. $200 Institutions non member, domestic; $163 Nonmembers in U.S. Covers aeronautics and space technology with special attention to aerospace defense, design, and electronics.

***Aerospace Consultants Directory***. InfoGroup Inc., 5711 S 86th Cir. Omaha, NE 68127-4146. Phone: (402)593-4500 • URL: http://www.infogroup.com • Annual. Number of listings: 10,653. Entries include: Name, address, phone, size of advertisement, name of owner or manager, number of employees, year first in "Yellow Pages." Compiled from telephone company "Yellow Pages," nationwide.

***Aerospace Daily***. McGraw Hill Financial Inc., 1221 Avenue of the Americas New York, NY 10020-1095. Phone: (212)512-2000; Fax: (212)512-3840 • URL: http://www.mhfi.com • Description: Reports on developments in the aerospace industry in the U.S. and overseas. Covers related political decisions. **Remarks:** Available in print, e-mail, and URL format.

***Aerospace Database***. American Institute of Aeronautics and Astronautics, 1801 Alexander Bell Dr., Ste. 500 Reston, VA 20191-4344. Phone: 800-639-2422 or (703)264-7500; Fax: (703)264-7551; Email: custserv@aiaa.org • URL: http://www.aiaa.org • Contains abstracts of literature covering all aspects of the aerospace and aircraft industry 1983 to date. Monthly updates. Inquire as to online cost and availability.

***Aerospace Engineering Magazine***. Society of Automotive Engineers, 400 Commonwealth Dr. Warrendale, PA 15096-0001. Phone: 877-606-7323 or (724)776-4841; Fax: (724)776-0790; Email: customerservice@sae.org • URL: http://www.sae.org • Monthly. $66.00 per year. Provides technical information that can be used in the design of new and improved aerospace systems.

***Aerospace Facts and Figures***. Aerospace Industries Association of America, 1250 I St. NW Washington, DC 20005. Phone: (202)371-8400 • Annual. $35 Individuals. Includes financial data for the aerospace industries.

***AF and PA Statistical Roundup***. American Forest and Paper Association, 1101 K St., NW, Ste. 700 Washington, DC 20005. Phone: (202)463-2700; Fax: (202)463-2785; Email: info@afandpa.org • URL: http://www.afandpa.org • Monthly. Members, $57.00 per year; non-members, $157.00 per year. Contains monthly statistical data for hardwood and softwood products. Formerly *NFPA Statistical Roundup*.

**AFCEA International**. 4400 Fair Lakes Ct. Fairfax, VA 22033. Phone: 800-336-4583 or (703)631-6100; Fax: (703)631-6169; Email: info@afcea.org • URL: http://www.afcea.org • Serves as a bridge between government requirements and industry capabilities. Represents top government, industry, and military professionals in the fields of communications, intelligence, information systems, imaging, and multi-media. Aims for the continuing education of its members and for peace through civil government effectiveness and military and industrial preparedness. Supports global security by providing an ethical environment encouraging a close cooperative relationship among civil government agencies, the military and industry.

**AFCOM**. 9100 Chester Towne Centre Rd. West Chester, OH 45069. Phone: (714)643-8110 or (714)997-7966; Fax: (714)997-9743; Email: membership@afcom.com • URL: http://www.afcom.com • Data center, networking and enterprise systems management professionals from medium and large scale mainframe, midrange and client/server data centers worldwide. Works to meet the professional needs of the enterprise system management community. Provides information and support through educational events, research and assistance hotlines, and surveys.

***AFE Newsline elsewhere***. Association for Facilities Engineering, 12801 Worldgate Dr., Ste. 500 Herndon, VA 20170. Phone: (571)203-7171; Fax: (571)766-2142; Email: info@afe.org • URL: http://www.afe.org • Bimonthly. Description: Internal newsletter of the association.

***Affirmative Action Compliance Manual for Federal Contractors***. Bloomberg BNA, 3 Bethesda Metro Center, Ste. 250 Bethesda, MD 20814-5377. Phone: 800-372-1033 or (703)341-3000; Fax: (800)253-0332; Email: customercare@bna.com • URL: http://www.bna.com • Monthly. 410. Resource guide for employers and attorneys so that they can more easily monitor and measure affirmative action requirements, implement policies, and quickly access other compliance information.

***Affirmative Action Register: The E E O Recruitment Publication***. INSIGHT Into Diversity, c/o Potomac Publishing, Inc., 225 Meramec Ave., Ste. 400 Saint Louis, MO 63105. Phone: 800-537-0655 or (314)863-2900 or (314)991-1335; Fax: (314)863-2905 or (314)997-1788; Email: info@aarjobs.com • URL: http://www.insightintodiversity.com/ • Monthly. free to qualified personnel; $15 Individuals. "The *Affirmative Action Register* is the only nationwide publication that provides for systematic distribution to mandated minorities, females, handicapped, veterans, and Native Americans." Each issue consists of recruitment advertisements placed by equal opportunity employers (institutions and companies).

***Affordable Housing Finance***. Alexander & Edwards Publishing, 220 Samsone St., 11th Fl. San Francisco, CA 94104. Phone: (415)546-7255; Fax: (415)249-1595; Email: ahf@housingfinance.com • URL: http://www.housingfinance.com • 10/year. $119 Individuals. Provides advice and information on obtaining financing for lower-cost housing. Covers both government and private sources.

**Afghan Peace and Democracy Act**. 220 St. 9, District 4, Taimani Kabul, Afghanistan. Email: info@afghanact.org • URL: http://www.alternatives.ca/en/about-us • Enhances the role of civil society organizations. Helps the NGOs in advocating peace and democracy in Afghanistan. Provides direct support and collaboration to Afghan NGOs and civil societies.

***Afghanistan Business Law Handbook***. International Business Publications, USA, PO Box 15343 Washington, DC 20003. Phone: (202)546-2103; Fax: (202)546-3275; Email: ibpusa@comcast.net • URL: http://ibpus.com • $99.95 Individuals hardcover; $99.95 Individuals CD-ROM; $99.95 Individuals E-book. Covers: Information on basic business legislation, laws and climate, export-import regulations, and contacts.

***Afghanistan Investment and Business Guide***. International Business Publications, USA, PO Box 15343 Washington, DC 20003. Phone: (202)546-2103; Fax: (202)546-3275; Email: ibpusa@comcast.net • URL: http://ibpus.com • Annual. $99.95 Individuals hardcover; $99.95 Individuals CD-ROM; $99.95 Individuals E-book. Covers: Strategic and business information, contacts, regulations and more.

**Afghanistan Microfinance Association**. House No 547 St. 3, Taimani Project, District 4 Kabul, Afghanistan. Phone: 93 799 308876; Email: info@ama.org.af • URL: http://www.ama.org.af • Promotes the microfinance sector of Afghanistan. Seeks to enhance the security measures between microfinance institutions (MFIs) and increase government support in terms of securing microfinance operations. Develops and delivers a number of training modules in local languages to ensure the best use of the training programs by employees of the microfinance sector.

**AFL-CIO - Building and Construction Trades Department**. 815 16th St., Ste. 600 Washington, DC 20006. Phone: (202)347-1461; Fax: (202)628-0724; Email: insulatorslocal78@aol.com • URL: http://www.bctd.org • Federation of labor unions in the construction industry including asbestos workers, bricklayers, masons, plasterers, carpenters, electrical workers, elevator constructors, operating engineers, granite cutters, hood carriers, common laborers, ironworkers, carpet, tile and stone workers, painters, decorators, paperhangers, plumbers, steamfitters, roofers, boilermakers, lathers, sheet metal workers, and other related trades. Maintains liaison with Center to Protect Workers Rights that provides independent research and support.

***AFP Exchange***. Association for Financial Professionals, 4520 E West Hwy., Ste. 750 Bethesda, MD 20814. Phone: (301)907-2862; Fax: (301)907-2864 • URL: http://www.afponline.org • Bimonthly. free for members; $90 for nonmembers. Treasury and finance newsletter.

***Africa-North America Business Register***. KWL Associates, PO Box 264, Sta. P Toronto, ON, Canada M5S 2S8. Fax: (416)532-5427; Email: kwl@pathcom.com • Annual. $70 postpaid. Covers: African, Canadian, and U.S. business organizations involved in import/export trade inquiries. Database includes: Trade statistics and demographic data; list of trade associations, chambers of commerce, foreign trade representatives, government agencies, calendar of trade events. Entries include: Company name, address, phone, names and titles of key personnel, product/service, banking references, subsidiaries, annual revenue.

***African Business***. IC Publications Ltd., 7 Coldbath Sq. London EC1R 4QL, United Kingdom. Phone: 44 20 78413210; Fax: 44 20 78413211 • URL: http://www.africasia.com • Monthly. £40 Individuals U.K.; £70 Two years U.K. Business publication.

**African Development Bank**. BP 1387, Rue Joseph Anoma Abidjan, Côte d'Ivoire. Phone: 225 20 20 44 44; Fax: 225 20 20 49 59; Email: afdb@afdb.org • URL: http://www.afdb.org • Representatives of national financial institutions. Seeks to further economic development of member states. Serves as a clearinghouse on national and regional economic development. Provides financial support and consulting services to development programs and agencies. Sponsors research and educational programs.

***African International Business Directory of Importers***. Coble International, 1420 Steeple Chase Dover, PA 17315. Phone: (717)467-1835 • URL: http://www.importexporthelp.com • $285 print or CD-ROM; $325 print and CD-ROM. Covers: 9,000 importers from 42 countries in Africa. Entries include: Name, address, phone, fax, primary contact person, list of products, e-mail addresses, and Web site.

***African Journal of Business and Economic Research***. Adonis & Abbey Publishers Ltd., PO Box 43418 London SE11 4XZ, United Kingdom. Phone: 44 845 3887248; Email: editor@adonis-abbey.com • URL: http://www.adonisandabbey.com • £200 Institutions print; £180 Institutions online; £100 Individuals print; £60 Individuals online. Peer-reviewed journal covering theoretical and empirical research of business and economy of Africa.

**African Private Equity and Venture Capital Association**. The Banking Hall, Cropthorne Ct., 26 Maide Vale London, United Kingdom. Phone: 44 20 3632 0408; Email: avca@avca-africa.org • URL: http://www.avcanet.com • Advances, develops and stimulates private equity and venture capital in Africa. Promotes high ethical standards of business conduct and professional competence in the private equity and venture capital industries.

***African Publishers Network Consultants Register***. Bellagio Publishing Network, PO Box 1369 Oxford OX4 4ZR, United Kingdom. Phone: 44 1865 250024; Fax: 44 1865 250024; Email: bellagio@bellagiopublishingnetwork.com • URL: http://www.bellagiopublishingnetwork.com • Covers: 66 publishing consultants in Africa with specializations in bookselling, children's books, copyright, design, distribution, electronic publishing, finance, editing, librarianship, management, marketing, printing, production, training, scholarly publishing, translation, and writing.

***African Review of Business and Technology***. Alain Charles Publishing Ltd., University House, 11-13 Lower Grosvenor Pl. London SW1W 0EX, United Kingdom. Phone: 44 20 78347676 • URL: http://www.alaincharles.com • Magazine covering technology and business information about Africa.

***African Telecommunications Directory***. Information Gatekeepers Inc., 1340 Soldiers Field Rd., Ste. 2 Boston, MA 02135. Phone: 800-323-1088 or (617)782-5033 or (617)232-3111; Fax: (617)782-5735 or (617)734-8562; Email: info@igigroup.com • URL: http://www.igigroup.com • $495 Individuals. Publication includes: Lists of service providers and equipment providers in 36 African countries in the fields of fiber optics, optical networks, WDM, ADSL, ATM, Internet, high-speed local area networks, wireless, and the emerging telecom markets.

***Afro-Brazilian Organization Directory***. Universal Publishers Inc., 23331 Water Cir. Boca Raton, FL 33486-8540. Fax: (561)750-6797 • URL: http://www.universal-publishers.com • Covers: Listings of Black entities and organizations in Brazil.

***Aftermarket Business***. Advanstar Communications, 545 Boylston St. Boston, MA 02116. Phone: 888-527-7008 or (617)267-6500; Fax: (617)267-6900; Email: info@advanstar.com • URL: http://www.advanstar.com • Monthly. $48 Individuals. Automobile aftermarket, including batteries.

***Ag Equipment Power***. Clintron Publishers, PO Box 30998 Spokane, WA 99223-3016. Phone: (509)458-3924 • URL: http://www.agpowermag.com • Monthly. $12 Individuals. Publication includes: Featuring news agricultural equipment and technology for growers in Washington, Idaho, and Oregon. List of about 750 manufacturers, distributors, dealers, and suppliers of new and used farm machinery and chemicals; coverage limited to Washington, Oregon, and Idaho. Entries include: Company name, address, product lines.

***Ag Executive***. Ag Executive Inc., 115 E Twyman St. Bushnell, IL 61422. Phone: (309)772-2168; Fax: (309)772-2167; Email: agexecutive@earthlink.net • URL: http://www.agexecutive.com • Description: Focuses on financial, personnel, and risk management issues for commercial agriculture. Covers business analysis and practical management ideas for improving profitability. Includes such topics as accounting, farm business organization, financing, economic forecasting, resource/risk control, and taxes.

***Ag Lender***. Doane Agricultural Services Co., 11701 Borman Dr., Ste. 300 Saint Louis, MO 63146-4193. Phone: 866-647-0918 or (314)569-2700; Email: doane@doane.com • URL: http://www.doane.com • Monthly. $139 Individuals.

***Ag Professional***. Doane Agricultural Services Co., 11701 Borman Dr., Ste. 300 Saint Louis, MO 63146-4193. Phone: 866-647-0918 or (314)569-2700; Email: doane@doane.com • URL: http://www.doane.com • 10/year. Published to meet the business needs of the retail fertilizer and agrichemical dealer industry. Formerly *Ag Retailer Magazine*.

***AGA Rate Service***. American Gas Association, 400 N Capitol St. NW Washington, DC 20001. Phone: (202)824-7000; Email: ggardner@aga.org • URL: http://www.aga.org • Semiannual. $175 Members; $300 Nonmembers. Looseleaf service.

***Ageline***. AARP, 601 E St. NW Washington, DC 20049-0001. Phone: 888-687-2277 or (202)434-3525; Email: member@aarp.org • URL: http://www.aarp.org • Provides indexing and abstracting of the literature of social gerontology, including consumer aspects, financial planning, employment, housing, health care services, mental health, social security, and retirement. Time period is 1978 to date. Inquire as to online cost and availability.

**Agency for Healthcare Research and Quality - Center for Financing, Access, and Cost Trends**. John M. Eisenberg Bldg., 540 Gaither Rd. Rockville, MD 20850. Phone: (301)427-1104; Fax: (301)427-1276; Email: joel.cohen@ahrq.hhs.gov • URL: http://www.ahrq.gov/about/cfact • Cost and financing of health care and access to health care services and related trends. Develops data sets to support policy and behavioral research and analyses.

**Agency for Healthcare Research and Quality - Center for Primary Care, Prevention, and Clinical Partnerships - Partnerships for Quality Program**. 540 Gaither Rd. Rockville, MD 20850. Phone: (301)427-1495; Fax: (301)427-1597; Email: charlotte.mullican@ahrq.hhs.gov • URL: http://www.ahrq.gov/about/cp3/cp3ptqual.htm • Improvement of health care services and their security, safety, outcomes, quality, effectiveness, and cost-effectiveness.

**Agency for Healthcare Research and Quality - Office of Communications and Knowledge Transfer**. 540 Gaither Rd. Rockville, MD 20850-6649. Phone: (301)427-1364; Fax: (301)427-1873; Email: howard.holland@ahrq.hhs.gov • URL: http://www.ahrq.gov/cpi/centers/ockt/index.html • Disseminates health services research and other initiatives to the health care industry, health care providers, consumers and patients, policy makers, research, and the media with particular emphasis on communicating agency initiatives in the ways each of these constituencies are most interested and are likely to lead to behavior change.

***Agency Sales: The Marketing Magazine for Manufacturers' Agencies and Their Principals***. Manufacturers' Agents National Association, 6321 W Dempster St., Ste. 110 Morton Grove, IL 60053. Phone: 877-626-2776 or (949)859-4040; Fax: (949)855-2973; Email: mana@manaonline.org • URL: http://www.manaonline.org • Monthly. $79 Individuals; $102 Other countries.

***Agent Systems in Electronic Business***. Cengage Learning Inc., 20 Channel Center St. Boston, MA 02210. Phone: 800-487-8488 or (617)289-7700; Fax: (617)289-7844; Email: investors@cengage.com • URL: http://www.cengage.com • 2008. eBook. Agent technologies are believed to be one of the most promising tools to conduct business via networks and the Web in an autonomous, intelligent, and efficient way. The ever-expanding application of business automation necessitates clarification of the methods and techniques of agent-based electronic business systems.

***AgExporter***. U. S. Government Printing Office, 732 N Capitol St. NW Washington, DC 20401. Phone: 866-512-1800 or (202)512-1800 or (866)512-1800; Fax: (202)512-2104 or (202)512-2250; Email: contactcenter@gpo.gov • URL: http://www.gpo.gov • Monthly. $44 Individuals. Issued by the Foreign Agricultural Service, U. S. Department of Agriculture. Edited for U. S. exporters of farm products. Provides practical information on exporting, including overseas trade opportunities.

***Aggregate Reserves of Depository Institutions and the Monetary Base***. U.S. Federal Reserve System Board of Governors Publications Services, 20th and Constitution Ave. NW Washington, DC 20551. Phone: (202)452-3244; Fax: (202)728-5886 • URL: http://www.federalreserve.gov • Weekly. $20 Individuals.

***AgProfessional***. Vance Publishing Corp., 400 Knightsbridge Pkwy. Lincolnshire, IL 60069-3613. Phone: 800-255-5113 or (847)634-2600; Fax: (847)634-4342 or (847)634-4379; Email: info@vancepublishing.com • URL: http://www.vancepublishing.com • Provides agronomic and business management solutions to retailers/distributors, professional farm managers and crop consultants, resulting in increased production and profitability in the food, fiber and energy markets.

***Agri-Business Update***. Kings County Farm Bureau, 870 Greenfield Ave. Hanford, CA 93230. Phone: (559)584-3557; Fax: (559)584-1614; Email: kcfb@kcfb.org • URL: http://www.kcfb.org • Monthly. Covers agricultural business information.

***Agri Marketing: The Magazine for Professionals Selling to the Farm Market***. Doane Agricultural Services Co., 11701 Borman Dr., Ste. 300 Saint Louis, MO 63146-4193. Phone: 866-647-0918 or (314)569-2700; Email: doane@doane.com • URL: http://www.doane.com • Monthly. $30 Individuals.

**Agribusiness Association of Australia**. 1 Torrdale Rd. Farrell Flat, SA 5416, Australia. Fax: 61 8 81278052; Email: agri@agribusiness.asn.au • URL: http://www.agribusiness.asn.au • Works to raise knowledge on issues affecting the development of an efficient and competitive agri-food value chain.

***Agribusiness Connections***. Agribusiness Association of Australia, 1 Torrdale Rd. Farrell Flat, SA 5416, Australia. Fax: 61 8 81278052; Email: agri@agribusiness.asn.au • URL: http://www.agribusiness.asn.au • Peer-reviewed journal dealing with resource management and economic issues in the food and fibre sectors.

**Agribusiness Council**. PO Box 5565 Washington, DC 20016-1165. Phone: (202)296-4563; Email: info@agribusinesscouncil.org • URL: http://agribusinesscouncil.org • Business organizations, universities and foundations, and individuals interested in stimulating and encouraging agribusiness in cooperation with the public sector, both domestic and international. Seeks to aid in relieving the problems of world food supply. Supports coordinated agribusiness in the developing nations by identifying opportunities for investment of U.S. private-sector technology management and financial resources. Advises agribusiness leaders about selected developing countries with good investment climates; brings potential investment opportunities to the attention of U.S. agribusiness firms; coordinates informal network of state agribusiness councils and grassroots organization; encourages companies to make investment feasibility studies in agribusiness; provides liaison and information exchange between agribusiness firms, governments, international organizations, universities, foundations, and other groups with the objective of identifying areas of cooperation and mutual interest; encourages projects geared to the conversion of subsistence farming to intensive, higher income agriculture in order to bring the world's rural populations, wherever feasible, into the market economy.

***Agribusiness Fieldman***. Agricultural Publishing Co., 4969 E Clinton Way, Ste. 104 Fresno, CA 93727-1558. Phone: 888-382-9772 or (559)252-7000 or (209)252-7000; Fax: (559)252-7387 or (209)252-7387; Email: publisher@westagpubco.com • Monthly. $19.95 per year.

***Agribusiness Worldwide***. Keller International Publishing L.L.C., 150 Great Neck Rd. Ste. 400 Great Neck, NY 11021-3309. Phone: (516)829-9210; Fax: (516)829-9722 or (516)829-9306; Email: tbeirne@kellerpubs.com • Bimonthly. $30 Individuals. Trade magazine for those involved in agriculture and livestock development in Asia, Africa, Latin America, and the Middle East. Subjects covered include agricultural production, financing, marketing, and handling.

***AGRICOLA on SilverPlatter***. Ovid Technologies Inc., 333 7th Ave., 20th Fl. New York, NY 10001-5004. Phone: 800-950-2035 or (646)674-6300; Fax: (646)674-6301 or (647)674-6301; Email: sales@ovid.com • URL: http://www.ovid.com • Updated monthly. Price varies. Produced by the National Agricultural Library. Provides over 4 million citations to the literature of agriculture, agricultural economics, animal sciences, entomology, fertilizer, food, forestry, nutrition, pesticides, plant science, water resources, and other topics.

***Agricola***. U.S. National Agricultural Library World List of Agricultural Serials, Abraham Lincoln Bldg., 10301

Baltimore Ave. Beltsville, MD 20705-2351. Phone: (301)504-6813 or (301)504-5755; Fax: (301)504-7473; Email: director@nal.usda.gov • URL: http://www.NALUSDA.gov • Covers worldwide agricultural literature. Over 3.3 million citations, 1970 to present, with monthly updates. Inquire as to online cost and availability.

***Agricultural and Environmental Biotechnology Abstracts***. Cambridge Scientific Abstracts L.P., 7200 Wisconsin Ave., Ste. 601 Bethesda, MD 20814. Phone: 800-843-7751 or (301)961-6700 or (301)961-6785; Fax: (301)961-6720 or (301)961-6708; Email: sales@proquest.com • URL: http://www.proquest.co.uk • Monthly. $345 Individuals; $365 Other countries. Scientific journal covering agricultural and environmental biotechnology. Formerly *Biotechnology Research Abstracts*.

***Agricultural and Mineral Commodities Year Book***. Routledge Reference, 2 Park Sq. Milton Park, Abingdon Oxford OX14 4RN, United Kingdom. Phone: 44 20 70176000; Fax: 44 20 70176699; Email: book.orders@tandf.co.uk • URL: http://www.routledge.com/ • $420 Individuals Hardback. Publication includes: List of international commodity organizations. Entries include: Name, address, phone, fax, e-mail, URL, publications, name of the chairperson, and description. Principal content of publication is a gathering of information about 40 commodities traded internationally, including barley, phosphates, soybeans, wool, zinc, lead, and natural gas.

**Agricultural Development Initiatives**. PO Box 50006 Nashville, TN 37205. Phone: (615)599-2015; Email: adi@onepost.net • URL: http://www.agri-develop.org • Aims to serve rural households by teaching them sustainable agriculture. Encourages enterprise development among local entrepreneurs toward the end goal of financial freedom. Facilitates the transfer of appropriate technology to local agricultural enterprises.

**Agricultural Economics Association of South Africa**. Private Bag x935 Pretoria 0001, South Africa. Phone: 27 12 3411115 • URL: http://www.aeasa.org.za • Represents the interests of agricultural economists. Promotes training, research and interest in agricultural economics. Fosters the applications of scientific principles of agricultural economics in solving agricultural and rural problems of Southern Africa.

**Agricultural Economics Society**. Holtwood, Red Lion St., Cropredy Banbury OX17 1PD, United Kingdom. Phone: 44 1295 750182 • URL: http://www.aes.ac.uk • Agricultural economists in the UK, students of agricultural economics, and interested individuals. Promotes the study and teaching of all disciplines relevant to agricultural economics. Areas of interest include agricultural industry; food and related industries; rural communities. Conducts studies in fields of economics, statistics, marketing, business management, politics, history, and sociology.

***Agricultural Engineering Abstracts***. CABI Publishing North America, 38 Chauncey St., Ste. 1002 Boston, MA 02111. Phone: 800-552-3083; Email: cabi-nao@cabi.org • URL: http://www.cabi.org • Bimonthly. Published in England by CABI Publishing.

***Agricultural Law***. Matthew Bender and Company Inc., 1275 Broadway Albany, NY 12204-2638. Phone: 800-424-4200 or (518)487-3000; Fax: (518)487-3573 or (800)424-4200; Email: customer.support@lexisnexis.com • URL: http://www.matthewbender.com • Semiannual. $2,501.00. 15 looseleaf volumes. Covers all aspects of state and federal law relating to farms, ranches and other agricultural interests. Includes five volumes dealing with agricultural estate, tax and business planning.

***Agricultural Letter***. Federal Reserve Bank of Chicago, 230 S LaSalle St. Chicago, IL 60604-1427. Phone: 888-372-2446 or (312)322-5322 or (312)322-5111; Fax: (312)322-5515 • URL: http://www.chicagofed.org • Quarterly. Looseleaf service.

***Agricultural Policy Monitoring and Evaluation***. Organization for Economic Cooperation and Development. Organisation for Economic Co-operation and Development Publications and Information Center, 2001 L St. NW, Ste. 650 Washington, DC 20036-4922. Phone: 800-456-6323 or (202)785-6323; Fax: (202)785-0350; Email: washington.contact@oecd.org • URL: http://www.oecd.org • Annual. Provides estimates of support to agriculture as well as chapters on agricultural policy developments.

***Agricultural Producers Directory***. InfoGroup Inc., 5711 S 86th Cir. Omaha, NE 68127-4146. Phone: (402)593-4500 • URL: http://www.infogroup.com • Annual. Number of listings: 22,572. Entries include: Name, address, phone, size of advertisement, name of owner or manager, number of employees, year first in "Yellow Pages." Compiled from telephone company "Yellow Pages," nationwide.

**Agricultural Research Service, Pacific West Area - Carl Hayden Bee Research Center - Honey Bee Research Unit**. 2000 E Allen Rd. Tucson, AZ 85719. Phone: (520)647-9107; Fax: (520)670-6493; Email: gloria.hoffman@ars.usda.gov • URL: http://www.ars.usda.gov/main/site_main.htm?modecode=53-42-03-00 • Biology of honey bees, including: biochemistry and physiology of bees to determine specific requirements for individual and colony growth, development, and reproduction; role of mites and microorganisms in the physiology of bees; behavior of bees, including modes of communication, structure and function of sensory receptors, and identification and roles of pheromones; pollination ecology and colony foraging dynamics of bees in crop ecosystems; development of computer simulated models; and remote sensing using radar, microwave frequencies, and other techniques to monitor the activities of bees.

**Agricultural Research Service, Southern Plains Area - Kika de la Garza Subtropical Agricultural Research Center**. USDA Agricultural Research Center, 2413 E Highway 83, Bldg. 200 Weslaco, TX 78596. Phone: (956)447-6301; Fax: (956)447-6345; Email: jquisenberry@welasco.ars.usda.gov • URL: http://www.ars.usda.gov.

***Agricultural Research***. U. S. Government Printing Office, 732 N Capitol St. NW Washington, DC 20401. Phone: 866-512-1800 or (202)512-1800 or (866)512-1800; Fax: (202)512-2104 or (202)512-2250; Email: contactcenter@gpo.gov • URL: http://www.gpo.gov • Monthly. $50 Individuals. Issued by the Agricultural Research Service of the U. S. Department of Agriculture. Presents results of research projects related to a wide variety of farm crops and products.

***Agricultural Statistics***. U.S. Department of Agriculture National Agricultural Statistics Service, 1400 Independence Ave. SW Washington, DC 20250. Phone: 800-727-9540; Email: nass@nass.usda.gov • URL: http://www.nass.usda.gov • Annual. $46 Individuals. Provides a wide variety of statistical data relating to agricultural production, supplies, consumption, prices/price-supports, foreign trade, costs, and returns, as well as farm labor, loans, income, and population. In many cases, historical data is shown annually for 10 years. In addition to farm data, includes detailed fishery statistics.

***Agriculture Fact Book***. U. S. Government Printing Office, 732 N Capitol St. NW Washington, DC 20401. Phone: 866-512-1800 or (202)512-1800 or (866)512-1800; Fax: (202)512-2104 or (202)512-2250; Email: contactcenter@gpo.gov • URL: http://www.gpo.gov • Annual. $26 Individuals. Issued by the Office of Communications, U. S. Department of Agriculture. Includes data on U. S. agriculture, farmers, food, nutrition, and rural America. Programs of the Department of Agriculture in six areas are described: rural economic development, foreign trade, nutrition, the environment, inspection, and education.

***Agrindex: International Information System for the Agricultural Sciences and Technology***. Food and Agriculture Organization of the United Nations. Bernan Press, PO Box 191 Blue Ridge Summit, PA 17214. Phone: 800-865-3457 or (301)459-7666; Fax: (301)459-6988; Email: customercare@bernan.com • URL: http://www.bernan.com • Monthly. $500.00 per year. Text in English, French, and Spanish.

***The Agrochemical Companies Fact File***. Hemming Information Services, 32 Vauxhall Bridge Rd. London SW1V 2SS, United Kingdom. Phone: 44 207 79736400 or 71 9736400; Fax: 44 207 72335056 or 71 2335057; Email: info@hgluk.com • URL: http://www.hgluk.com • $695; $1,460. Covers: 300 agrochemical manufacturers; formulators; biopesticide manufacturers, and agrochemical trading companies worldwide. Entries include: Details on key executives, financial data, operating locations, main markets, products, subsidiaries, joint ventures, and portfolios.

***Agronomists Directory***. InfoGroup Inc., 5711 S 86th Cir. Omaha, NE 68127-4146. Phone: (402)593-4500 • URL: http://www.infogroup.com • Annual. Number of listings: 1,029. Entries include: Name, address, phone, size of advertisement, name of owner or manager, number of employees, year first in "Yellow Pages." Compiled from telephone company "Yellow Pages," nationwide.

***Agronomy Journal: An International Journal***. American Society of Agronomy, 5585 Guilford Rd. Madison, WI 53711-5801. Phone: (608)273-8080 or (608)273-8085; Fax: (608)273-2021; Email: headquarters@sciencesocieties.org • URL: http://www.agronomy.org • Bimonthly. Members free; $216 Nonmembers.

***AGS Quarterly: Bulletin of the Association for Gravestone Studies***. Association for Gravestone Studies, 101 Munson St., Ste. 108 Greenfield, MA 01301. Phone: (413)772-0836; Email: info@gravestonestudies.org • URL: http://www.gravestonestudies.org • Quarterly. Description: Concerned with the study and preservation of national and international gravestones: folk art carvings, lettering, epitaphs, shapes, materials used, and symbolism. Recurring features include articles on conservation procedures, Association news, book reviews, news of research, and regional news.

***AHA Guide to the Health Care Field***. American Hospital Association. 155 N Wacker Dr. Chicago, IL 60606. Phone: 800-242-2626 or (312)422-3000; Fax: (312)422-4796; Email: kjackson@healthforumcom • URL: http://www.aha.org • Annual. $295.00. A directory of hospitals and health care systems.

***AHA Hospital Statistics***. American Hospital Association. Health Forum L.L.C., 155 N Wacker Dr., Ste. 400 Chicago, IL 60606. Phone: 800-821-2039 or (312)893-6800; Fax: (312)422-4500 • URL: http://www.healthforum.com • Annual. $370 Members book/CD; $700 Nonmembers book/CD. Provides detailed statistical data on the nation's hospitals, including revenues, expenses, utilization, and personnel. Formerly *Hospital Statistics*.

***AHA Integrated Delivery Network Directory: U.S. Health Care Systems, Networks, and Alliances***. American Hospital Association, 155 N Wacker Dr. Chicago, IL 60606. Phone: 800-424-4301 or (312)422-3000 or (312)422-2050; Fax: (312)422-4700 • URL: http://www.aha.org • Annual. $250.00. Provides information about a wide variety of U.S. health care groups and affiliations, including hospitals, nursing homes, rehabilitation centers, psychiatric facilities, home health care agencies, clinical laboratories, outpatient facilities, and diagnostic imaging centers. Includes names of more than 8,000 key executives.

***AHA News***. American Hospital Association. HealthForum, 155 N Wacker Dr., Ste. 400 Chicago, IL 60606. Phone: (312)893-6800; Fax: (312)422-4500; Email: hfcustsvc@healthforum.com • URL: http://www.healthforum.com • Description: Highlights major news affecting hospitals and the health care field. Reports on legislation and regulation, court cases, surveys, and federal programs. Carries information on individual hospitals and allied hospital associations.

**AHS International** . 217 N Washington St. Alexandria, VA 22314-2538. Phone: 855-247-4685 or (703)684-6777; Fax: (703)739-9279; Email: staff@vtol.org • URL: http://www.vtol.org • Represents aircraft designers, engineers, government personnel, operators, and industry executives in over 40 countries interested in V/STOL aircraft. (V/STOL stands for Vertical/Short Takeoff and Landing.) Conducts research and educational and technical meetings concerning professional training and updated information.

***AI Magazine***. American Association for Artificial Intelligence. Association for the Advancement of Artificial Intelligence, 2275 E Bayshore Rd., Ste. 160 Palo Alto, CA 94303. Phone: (650)328-3123; Fax: (650)321-4457; Email: info@aaai.org • URL: http://www.aaai.org/home.html • Quarterly. Information on artificial intelligence research and innovative applications of the science.

***The AI Week Directory***. R.R. Bowker L.L.C., 630 Central Ave New Providence, NJ 07974. Phone: 888-269-5372 or (908)286-1090; Email: info@bowker.com • URL: http://www.bowker.com • Irregular. $99. Covers: The US and international artificial intelligence community and related businesses. Entries include: Company name, size, and financial status; names of key personnel; products and services.

***AIAA Journal***. American Institute of Aeronautics and Astronautics, 1801 Alexander Bell Dr., Ste. 500 Reston, VA 20191-4344. Phone: 800-639-2422 or (703)264-7500; Fax: (703)264-7551; Email: custserv@aiaa.org • URL: http://www.aiaa.org • Monthly. $80 Members /year for members in the U.S.; print and online; $140 Members foreign; print and online; $2,360 Nonmembers domestic; print and online; $2,520 Nonmembers foreign; print and online; $2,230 Nonmembers domestic; print; $2,380 Nonmembers foreign; print; $2,050 Nonmembers online. Technical journal providing original archival research papers on new theoretical developments and/or experimental results in the fields of aeronautics and astronautics. For research-oriented readers.

***AIChe Journal***. Center for Chemical Process Safety, 3 Park Ave., 19th Fl. New York, NY 10016-5991. Phone: 800-242-4363 or (646)495-1370 or (646)495-1371; Fax: (646)495-1504 or (203)775-5177; Email: ccps@aiche.org • URL: http://www.aiche.org/ccps • Monthly. $105 Members; $950 Nonmembers. Devoted to research and technological developments in chemical engineering and allied fields. Available online.

***AICP Membership Directory***. Association of Independent Commercial Producers, 3 W 18th St., 5th Fl. New York, NY 10011. Phone: (212)929-3000; Fax: (212)929-3359; Email: info@aicp.com • URL: http://www.aicp.com • Free to members; $45 Nonmembers. Covers: General member companies that specialize in producing commercials on various media, including film, video, and computer, for advertisers and agencies. Associate member companies listed serve the industry, such as post-production and editorial houses, equipment and prop suppliers, casting agencies and others. AMP members are music production shops; press members are those in the press who cover the industry. Entries include: Company name, address, phone, fax, e-mail, URL, contact names, and names of people represented.

***AIDS and Public Policy Journal***. University Publishing Group Inc., 2 Public Sq., Ste. 206 Hagerstown, MD 21740. Phone: (240)420-0036; Fax: (240)718-7100; Email: orders@upgbooks.com • URL: http://www.upgbooks.com • Quarterly. Individuals, $59.00 per year; institutions, $115.00 per year.

***AIDS Literature and Law Review***. University Publishing Group Inc., 2 Public Sq., Ste. 206 Hagerstown, MD 21740. Phone: (240)420-0036; Fax: (240)718-7100; Email: orders@upgbooks.com • URL: http://www.upgbooks.com • Monthly. $225.00 per year. Contains abstracts of journal and newspaper articles. Formerly *AIDS Literature and News Review*.

***AIDS Litigation Reporter (Acquired Immune Deficiency Syndrome): The National Journal of Record of AIDS-Related Litigation***. Andrews Publications, 175 Strafford Ave., Bldg. 4, Suite 140 Wayne, PA 19087. Phone: 800-345-1101 or (610)225-0510 or (610)622-0510; Fax: (610)225-0501 or (610)622-0501; Email: customer@andrewspub.com • URL: http://www.andrewspub.com • Semimonthly. $951.00 per year. Newsletter. Provides reports on a wide variety of legal cases in which AIDS is a factor.

***AIDS Policy and Law: The Biweekly Newsletter on Legislation, Regulation, and Litigation Concerning AIDS***. LRP Publications Library, lrp.com Technology Contacts, 747 Dresher Rd., Ste. 500 Horsham, PA 19044. Phone: 800-341-7874 or

(215)784-0860 or (215)784-0910; Fax: (215)784-9639 or (215)784-0275; Email: techsup@lrp.com • URL: http://www.lrp.com • 11/year. Newsletter for personnel managers, lawyers, and others.

***AIDS Reference Guide: A Sourcebook for Planners and Decision Makers***. Frances Fernald, editor. • $448.00 Looseleaf Service. Two volumes. Includes twelve updates and twelve newsletters. Covers a wide range of AIDS topics, including "Employment Policies and Issues," "Legal Issues," "Financing Issues," "Impact on Healthcare Providers," "Global Issues," and "Legislative, Regulatory, and Governance Issues."

**AIDS United**. 1424 K St. NW, Ste. 200 Washington, DC 20005-2411. Phone: (202)408-4848; Fax: (202)408-1818 • URL: http://www.aidsunited.org • Serves as a representative in Washington, DC, of community-based AIDS service organizations. Advocates, at the federal level, for more effective AIDS policy, legislation, and funding. Works collaboratively with AIDS Action Foundation, a national public policy research organization.

***The AIER Chart Book***. AIER Research Staff. American Institute for Economic Research, 250 Division St. Great Barrington, MA 01230-1000. Phone: 888-528-1216; Fax: (413)528-0103; Email: info@aier.org • URL: http://www.aier.org • Annual. $4 Individuals. A compact compilation of long-range charts ("Purchasing Power of the Dollar," for example, goes back to 1780) covering various aspects of the U. S. economy. Includes inflation, interest rates, debt, gold, taxation, stock prices, etc. (Economic Education Bulletin.).

**AIESEC Alumni International**. Ave. de Tervuren 300 B-1150 Brussels, Belgium. Email: info@aiesec-alumni.org • URL: http://www.aiesec-alumni.org • Alumni of the International Association of Students in Economics and Management. Promotes excellence in the study and practice of economics. Facilitates exchange of information among members; sponsors social programs.

**AIESEC Bahrain**. BBIC Headquarters, Hidd Area Manama, Bahrain. Phone: 973 17358819; Email: info.bh@aiesec.net • URL: http://www.aiesec.org/bahrain • Represents students of economics or business and related fields presently studying at affiliated universities worldwide. Aims to develop internationally educated managers. Manages the international exchange of students on internships around the world. Conducts training of members in the management of international business operations.

**AIESEC Canada**. 161 Eglinton Ave. E, Ste. 402 Toronto, ON, Canada M4P 1J5. Phone: (416)368-1001; Fax: (416)368-4490; Email: info2010@aiesec.ca • URL: http://aiesec.ca • Develops students through international internship exchange. Serves as a platform for young people to discover their potential so as to have a positive impact in the society.

**AIESEC China**. c/o Zachary Law, VP Communication, Block E, Rm. 1108, 16th St., hongguancun, Haidian mansion, Haidian District Beijing, China. Phone: 86 10 82866532; Email: mainland.china@aiesec.net • URL: http://www.aiesec.cn • Provides leadership and work abroad opportunities. Organizes conferences and virtual tools to build networks. Contributes to the development of the communities with an overriding commitment to international co-operation and understanding. Facilitates international traineeship exchanges for its members and stakeholders.

**AIESEC Kenya**. PO Box 30197-00200 Nairobi, Kenya. Phone: 254 20 2608757; Email: info@aiesec.or.ke • URL: http://ke.aiesec.org • Enables students and recent graduate the opportunity to live and work in another country. Serves as a platform for young people to discover and develop their potential. Organizes conferences.

**AIESEC Pakistan**. 201 2nd Fl., Cotton Exchange, Bldg., II Chundrigarh Rd. Karachi, Pakistan. Phone: 92 21 35464958; Email: info@aiesec.pk • URL: http://www.aiesec.org/pakistan • Represents students of economics or business and related fields presently studying at affiliated universities worldwide. Aims to develop internationally educated managers. Manages the international exchange of students on internships around the world. Conducts training of members in the management of international business operations.

**AIESEC Qatar**. PO Box 24475 Doha, Qatar. Phone: (974)5542-6271; Email: qatar@aiesec.net • URL: http://www.aiesec.org/qatar • Represents students of economics or business and related fields presently studying at affiliated universities worldwide. Aims to develop internationally educated managers. Manages the international exchange of students on internships around the world. Conducts training of members in the management of international business operations.

**AIESEC United States**. 11 Hanover Sq., Ste. 1700 New York, NY 10005. Phone: (212)757-3774 • URL: http://aiesecus.org • Students of economics or business and related fields presently studying at affiliated universities worldwide. Aims to develop an internationally educated managers. Manages the international exchange of students on internships around the world. Conducts training of members in the management of international business operations.

***AIIM Buying Guide***. Association for Information and Image Management International Headquarters, 1100 Wayne Ave., Ste. 1100 Silver Spring, MD 20910. Phone: 800-477-2446 or (301)587-8202; Fax: (301)587-2711; Email: aiim@aiim.org • URL: http://www.aiim.org/ • Annual. $64. Publication includes: List of approximately 460 manufacturers, software developers, suppliers, service companies, consultants, and system integrators in the document management industry. Entries include: Company name, address, phone, product/service provided, product or sales contact, business description, number of employees. Organization was formerly called National Micrographics Association.

**AIM Global**. One Landmark N, 20399 Rte. 19, Ste. 203 Cranberry Township, PA 16066. Phone: (724)742-4473; Fax: (724)742-4476; Email: info@aim-na.org • URL: http://www.aimglobal.org • Serves as a trade association for the automatic identification data captures technology industry.

***Air and Waste Management Association Journal***. One Gateway Center, 3rd Fl. Pittsburgh, PA 15222. Phone: 800-270-3444 or (412)232-3444; Fax: (412)232-3450 • URL: http://www.awma.org • Monthly. Individuals, $150.00 per year; institutions, $329.00 per year: nonprofit institutions, $229.00 per year. Includes annual *Directory of Governmental Air Pollution Agencies*.

***Air Cargo News***. Air Cargo News, Inc., Borough Hall Station Portage, MI 49081. Phone: (718)651-3591 • Monthly. $39.95 per year.

***Air Cargo World: International Trends and Analysis***. 980 Canton St., Bldg. 1, Ste. D Roswell, GA 30075. Phone: (770)642-9170; Fax: (770)642-9982; Email: customerservice@bizmedia.com • URL: http://www.aircargoworld.com • Monthly. $58.00 per year. Provides news and information concerning air freight carriers, freight forwarding, and cargo operations at airports.

***Air Carrier Industry Scheduled Service Traffic Statistics***. U.S. Department of Transportation, 1200 New Jersey Ave. SE Washington, DC 20590. Phone: (855)368-4200; Fax: (202)366-6031; Email: DOTCFO@dot.gov • URL: http://www.dot.gov • Quarterly. Includes data for commuter airlines.

***Air Carrier Traffic Statistics Monthly***. U.S. Department of Transportation, 1200 New Jersey Ave. SE Washington, DC 20590. Phone: (855)368-4200; Fax: (202)366-6031; Email: DOTCFO@dot.gov • URL: http://www.dot.gov • Monthly. Provides passenger traffic data for large airlines.

**AIR Commercial Real Estate Association**. 500 N Brand Blvd., Ste. 900 Glendale, CA 91203-3315. Phone: 866-946-2472 or (213)687-8777; Fax: (213)687-8616; Email: membershipla@airea.com • URL: http://www.airea.com • Real estate men and women specializing in industrial and commercial properties; affiliate members are title companies, mortgage loan companies, public utilities, and developers. Membership concentrated in Southern California. Encourages high professional standards. Sponsors a course on industrial real estate, in cooperation with the University of California. Develops industrial multiple listing system and standard lease forms. Supports the Industrial Multiple, a clearinghouse for information on industrial listings. Maintains a computerized multiple listing system.

***Air Compressors Directory***. InfoGroup Inc., 5711 S 86th Cir. Omaha, NE 68127-4146. Phone: (402)593-4500 • URL: http://www.infogroup.com • Annual. Number of listings: 3,405. Entries include: Name, address, phone, size of advertisement, name of owner or manager, number of employees, year first in "Yellow Pages." Compiled from telephone company "Yellow Pages," nationwide.

***Air Conditioning & Heating & Refrigeration Equipment Directory***. InfoGroup Inc., 5711 S 86th Cir. Omaha, NE 68127-4146. Phone: (402)593-4500 • URL: http://www.infogroup.com • Annual. Number of listings: 689. Entries include: Name, address, phone, size of advertisement, name of owner or manager, number of employees, year first in "Yellow Pages." Compiled from telephone company "Yellow Pages," nationwide.

***Air Conditioning Contractors of America—Membership Directory***. Air Conditioning Contractors of America, 2800 Shirlington Rd., Ste. 300 Arlington, VA 22206. Phone: 888-290-2220 or (703)575-4477 or (703)824-8862; Fax: (703)575-4449 or (703)575-8651; Email: paul.stalknecht@acca.org • URL: http://www.acca.org • Annual. Covers: Member air conditioning and heating contractors, manufacturers, vocational technical schools. Entries include: Company name, address, phone, fax, names and titles of key personnel, description of fields, and types of work performed.

***Air Conditioning, Heating, and Refrigeration News: The HVACR Contractor's Weekly Newsmagazine***. BNP Media, 2401 W Big Beaver Rd., Ste. 700 Troy, MI 48084. Phone: 800-952-6643 or (248)362-3700 or (847)763-9534; Fax: (248)362-5103 or (248)362-0317; Email: privacy@bnpmedia.com • URL: http://www.bnpmedia.com • Weekly. $87.00 per year. Includes *Supplement*.

***Air Duct Cleaning Directory***. InfoGroup Inc., 5711 S 86th Cir. Omaha, NE 68127-4146. Phone: (402)593-4500 • URL: http://www.infogroup.com • Annual. Number of listings: 2,109. Entries include: Name, address, phone, size of advertisement, name of owner or manager, number of employees, year first in "Yellow Pages." Compiled from telephone company "Yellow Pages," nationwide.

**Air Force Association**. 1501 Lee Hwy. Arlington, VA 22209-1198. Phone: 800-727-3337 or (703)247-5800; Fax: (703)247-5853; Email: membership@afa.org • URL: http://www.afa.org • Promotes public understanding of aerospace power and the pivotal role it plays in the security of the nation.

***Air Force Journal of Logistics***. U. S. Government Printing Office, 732 N Capitol St. NW Washington, DC 20401. Phone: 866-512-1800 or (202)512-1800 or (866)512-1800; Fax: (202)512-2104 or (202)512-2250; Email: contactcenter@gpo.gov • URL: http://www.gpo.gov • Quarterly. $15.00 per year. Issued by the Air Force Logistics Management Center, Air Force Department, Defense Department. Presents research and information of interest to professional Air Force logisticians.

***Air Force Magazine***. Air Force Association, 1501 Lee Hwy. Arlington, VA 22209-1198. Phone: 800-727-3337 or (703)247-5800; Fax: (703)247-5853; Email: membership@afa.org • URL: http://www.afa.org • Monthly. Magazine for personnel of United States Air Force, government agencies, and aerospace industry.

**Air Force Sergeants Association**. 5211 Auth Rd. Suitland, MD 20746-4339. Phone: 800-638-0594 or (301)899-3500; Fax: (301)899-8136 • URL: http://www.hqafsa.org//AM/Template.cfm?Section=Home • Any enlisted man or woman, active or retired, in the Air Force, Air National Guard, Air Force Reserve, Army Air Corps, or Army Air Forces; women auxiliaries. Works to: promote, preserve, and uphold fair and equitable legislation as it pertains to the welfare of the airmen who served and are serving in the U.S.A.F.; maintain the highest professional standards and integrity among members; promote the interests of members, the U.S., and the rest of the "free world"; promote religious, educational, and recreational activities among members, in order to develop a better understanding and mutual respect. Sponsors educational seminars, Air Force training, JOBCAP, a job placement service, and programs for retired members. Provides congressional representation, insurance, and other services.

***Air Force Times***. Gannett Government Media Corp., 6883 Commercial Dr. Springfield, VA 22159-0500. Phone: 800-368-5718 or (703)750-7400 • URL: http://www.gannettgovernmentmedia.com • Weekly (Mon.). $55 Individuals print and online; $19.95 Individuals online only. Independent newspaper serving Air Force personnel worldwide.

***Air Freight Directory***. Air Cargo Inc., 1819 Bay Ridge Ave. Annapolis, MD 21403. Phone: (410)280-8911; Fax: (410)268-3154 • Bimonthly. $34.50 single copy; $84 yearly subscription. Publication includes: Directory of more than 500 motor carriers contracting with Air Cargo, Inc. for delivery and pick up of freight. Air Cargo is a ground service specialist organization jointly owned by 18 major air carriers. Entries include: Airport city and code, firm name, address, phone, and services offered. Principal content of publication is chart of service points and rates.

***Air Line Pilot; The Magazine of Professional Flight Deck Crews***. Air Line Pilots Association Engineering and Air Safety Resource Center, 535 Herndon Pkwy. Herndon, VA 20170. Phone: (703)689-2270; Fax: (703)689-4370 • URL: http://www.alpa.org • 10 times a year. $30.00 per year.

***Air Market News***. General Publications Inc., PO Box 480 Hatch, NM 87937-0480. Phone: (505)267-1030 • Bimonthly. Free to qualified personnel. Subject matter is news of aircraft products and services.

***Air Pollution Control***. Bloomberg BNA, 3 Bethesda Metro Center, Ste. 250 Bethesda, MD 20814-5377. Phone: 800-372-1033 or (703)341-3000; Fax: (800)253-0332; Email: customercare@bna.com • URL: http://www.bna.com • Biweekly. $798.00 per year. Newsletter.

***Air Quality Data***. U.S. Environmental Protection Agency, 1200 Pennsylvania Ave., Ariel Rios Bldg. Washington, DC 20460. Phone: 800-775-5037 or (202)272-0167 or (202)260-3682; Fax: (202)260-4997; Email: r3public@epa.gov • URL: http://www.epa.gov • Annual.

***Air Transport***. Airlines for America, 1301 Pennsylvania Ave. NW, Ste. 1100 Washington, DC 20004-7017. Phone: (202)626-4000; Email: a4a@airlines.org • URL: http://www.airlines.org • Annual. $20. Airline industry information.

**Air Transport Association of Canada**. 255 Albert St., Ste. 700 Ottawa, ON, Canada K1P 6A9. Phone: (613)233-7727; Fax: (613)230-8648; Email: atac@atac.ca • URL: http://www.atac.ca/web/en • Air transport companies. Promotes a business climate beneficial to members. Represents' members interests before government agencies. Conducts research and educational programs; compiles industry statistics.

***Air Transport World***. Intertec Publishing, 5 Penn Plz., 13th Fl. New York, NY 10001-1810. Phone: 800-795-5445 or (212)613-9700 or (212)204-4200; Fax: (212)613-9749 or (212)206-3622; Email: bethany.weaver@penton.com • URL: http://www.penton.com • Monthly. $89 Individuals print and online. Includes supplement *World Airline Reports*.

***Air University Library Index to Military Periodicals***. U.S. Air Force, Muir S. Fairchild Research Information Ctr., 600 Chennault Cir., Bldg. 1405 Maxwell AFB, AL 36112. Phone: (334)953-2888; Email: mstewart@max1.au.af.mil • URL: http://www.au.af.mil/au/aul/aul.htm • Quarterly. Annual cumulation.

***Aircraft Parts & Auxiliary Equipment NEC Directory***. InfoGroup Inc., 5711 S 86th Cir. Omaha, NE 68127-4146. Phone: (402)593-4500 • URL: http://www.infogroup.com • Annual. Number of listings: 1,412. Entries include: Name, address, phone, size of advertisement, name of owner or manager, number of employees, year first in "Yellow Pages." Compiled from telephone company "Yellow Pages," nationwide.

***Airfinance Annual***. Euromoney Institutional Investor P.L.C., 11

N Hill Colchester CO1 1DZ, United Kingdom. Phone: 44 1206 579591; Fax: 44 1206 560121; Email: yearbooks@ euromoneyplc.com • URL: http://www.euromoney-yearbooks.com • Annual. £295 Individuals; €350 Individuals; $450 Individuals. Covers: About 1,200 banks, finance houses, insurers, consultants, brokers, legal consultants, accountants, and leasing companies serving the aviation industry worldwide. Entries include: Company name, address, phone, e-mail, contact, key personnel, servicers provided, branch office names and locations.

*Airline Business*. Dagens Industri, Box 3177 S-103 63 Stockholm, Sweden. • Monthly. Publication covering the transportation industry.

*Airline Business: The Voice of Airline Managements*. Reed Aerospace, 333 N Fairfax St., Ste. 301 Alexandria, VA 22314. Phone: (703)836-7444; Fax: (703)836-7446 • URL: http://www.reedbusiness.com/about-us/locations • Monthly. $130.00 per year. Published in England by Reed Business Information. Covers management and financial topics for international airline executives.

*Airline Handbook*. Aerotravel Research, PO Box 3694 Cranston, RI 02910. Phone: (401)941-6140 • Annual. Covers: 2,000 commercial airlines (scheduled and chartered) serving over 200 nations and territories worldwide. Entries include: Airline name, address of main office, phone, telex, financial keys, number of employees, routes and destinations, aircraft fleets, passenger traffic totals, company history.

*Airman: Official Magazine of the U.S. Air Force*. U. S. Government Printing Office, 732 N Capitol St. NW Washington, DC 20401. Phone: 866-512-1800 or (202)512-1800 or (866)512-1800; Fax: (202)512-2104 or (202)512-2250; Email: contactcenter@gpo.gov • URL: http://www.gpo.gov • Monthly. $41.00 per year.

*Airport Activity Statistics of Certificated Route Air Carriers*. U. S. Department of Transportation. U. S. Government Printing Office, 732 N Capitol St. NW Washington, DC 20401. Phone: 866-512-1800 or (202)512-1800 or (866)512-1800; Fax: (202)512-2104 or (202)512-2250; Email: contactcenter@gpo.gov • URL: http://www.gpo.gov • Annual. $58 Individuals.

*Airport Business*. Cygnus Business Media Inc., 1233 Janesville Ave. Fort Atkinson, WI 53538. Phone: 800-547-7377; Email: info@cygnus.com • URL: http://www.cygnus.com • 10 times a year. $55.00 per year.

*Airport/Facility Directory*. U.S. National Ocean Service, SSMC4, Rm. 9149, 1305 East-West Hwy. Silver Spring, MD 20910. Phone: (301)713-3066; Email: nos.info@noaa.gov • URL: http://oceanservice.noaa.gov • Covers: Non-military airports in the continental United States; separate volumes cover the southeast, northeast, northwest, east central, north central, southwest, and south central states (including Puerto Rico and the Virgin Islands). Entries include: Airport name, location, weather service phone number, control center frequencies, and information concerning navigational and other aids and systems.

**Airport Minority Advisory Council**. 2001 Jefferson Davis Hwy., Ste. 500 Arlington, VA 22202. Phone: (703)414-2622; Fax: (703)414-2686; Email: amac.info@amac-org.com • URL: http://www.amac-org.com • Advocates for equal opportunity for minorities and women in airport contracting and employment.

*Airports: The Weekly for Airport Users, Managers, and Suppliers*. Aviation Week Business Intelligence Services, 1200 G St., N.W., Suite 200 Washington, DC 20005. Phone: 800-752-4959 or (202)383-2350; Fax: (202)383-2438 • URL: http://www.aviationnow.com/bis • Weekly. $649.00 per year. Newsletter. Covers news of worldwide airport development, financing, operations, marketing, bidding, improvements, and personnel.

**AISE Steel Technology**. Association for Iron and Steel Technology, 186 Thorn Hill Rd. Warrendale, PA 15086-7528. Phone: (724)814-3000; Fax: (724)814-3001; Email: memberservices@aist.org • URL: http://www.aist.org • Monthly. $165 U.S., Canada, and Mexico; $205 Other countries; $20 U.S., Canada, and Mexico single copy; $35 Other countries single copy.

*Al-Batinah Tourist Guide*. Oman Chamber of Commerce and Industry, PO Box 1400 Ruwi 112, Oman. Phone: 968 24763700 or 96 824 707674; Fax: 968 24708497 or 96 824 708497; Email: occi@chamberoman.com • URL: http://www.chamberoman.com • Provides information and data on tourist sites, locations, services, and facilities they offer in Batinah Region. Entries include: Names and addresses of travel and tourism organizations and companies.

*Alabama Business Directory*. InfoGroup Inc., 5711 S 86th Cir. Omaha, NE 68127-4146. Phone: (402)593-4500 • URL: http://www.infogroup.com • Annual. Covers: 184,277 businesses in Alabama. Entries include: Company name, address, phone, number of employees, name of owner or manager, sales volume. Compiled from telephone company "Yellow Pages," statewide. All states covered (see separate entries).

*Alabama Industrial Directory*. Alabama Development Office Alabama Center for Commerce, 401 Adams Ave. Montgomery, AL 36130-4106. Phone: 800-248-0033 or (334)242-0400; Fax: (334)353-1330; Email: idinfo@ado.state.al.us • URL: http://www.ado.state.al.us • Biennial. $75 Individuals print; $250 Individuals annual subscription. Covers: More than 6,000 industrial companies in Alabama.

Entries include: Company name, address, phone, fax number, e-mail and website addresses, NAICS code, name and title of principal executive, name and address of parent company, number of employees, product or service provided, Standard Industrial Classification (SIC) code, year established.

**Alabama Law Institute**. Law Center, Rm. 326 Tuscaloosa, AL 35486-0013. Phone: (205)348-7411; Fax: (205)348-8411 • URL: http://ali.state.al.us • Statutes of Alabama, including studies of existing laws with systematic revision of laws to be proposed to Alabama legislature. Conducts investigations into state tax structure, evidence, criminal law, business law, probate law, real property, and family law. Develops manuals for legislators, county commissioners, tax assessors and collectors, and other governmental offices.

*Alameda County Business Directory*. Rich's Business Directories Inc., 1820 Gateway Blvd., Ste. 170 San Mateo, CA 94404. Phone: 800-969-7424 or (650)362-1020; Fax: (650)350-4084; Email: info@richsdata.com • URL: http://www.hightechdirectories.com • $199 Individuals online; $450 Individuals database; $215 Individuals. Contains directory information for more than 3700 companies and 12,000 contacts in Alameda County, California.

*Alarm Systems Directory*. InfoGroup Inc., 5711 S 86th Cir. Omaha, NE 68127-4146. Phone: (402)593-4500 • URL: http://www.infogroup.com • Annual. Number of listings: 11,847. Entries include: Name, address, phone, size of advertisement, name of owner or manager, number of employees, year first in "Yellow Pages." Compiled from telephone company "Yellow Pages," nationwide.

*Alaska Business License Directory*. Alaska Department of Community and Economic Development, State Office Bldg., Box 110806 Juneau, AK 99811-0806. Phone: (907)465-2550; Fax: (907)465-2974; Email: license@dced.state.ak.us • Covers: Approx. 70,000 businesses licensed by the state of Alaska. Entries include: Company name, address, name of owner, license number, line of business.

*Alaska Industrial Directory*. Harris InfoSource, 2057 E Aurora Rd. Twinsburg, OH 44087-1999. Phone: 800-888-5900 or (330)425-9000 or (973)921-5500; Fax: (800)643-5997 or (877)252-3375; Email: customerservice@harrisinfo.com • URL: http://www.harrisinfo.com • Annual. $495 Individuals Online. Covers: 6,200 manufacturing companies in Alaska. Database includes: Statistical data, trade show calendar. Entries include: Company name, address, county, phone, fax, web site address (on CD-ROM only), number of employees, names and titles of key executives, plant size, year established, parent company, annual sales, import/export information, Standard Industrial Classification (SIC) code, and product description.

*Albany Business Review*. American City Business Journals, Inc., 120 W Morehead St. Charlotte, NC 28202. Phone: (704)973-1000; Fax: (704)973-1001; Email: americancity@bizjournals.com • URL: http://www.acbj.com • $86 Individuals print + online. Contains the full text of The Business Review, a local business tabloid covering news in the Albany, New York, area.

*Alberta & Saskatchewan Business*. Scott's Directories, 12 Concorde Pl., Ste. 800 Toronto, ON, Canada M3C 4J2. Phone: 800-668-2374 or (416)442-2122; Fax: (416)510-6870; Email: customercare@scottsdirectories.com • URL: http://www.scottsdirectories.com • Contains information on more than 41,000 individuals at more than 26,000 companies in the areas of Alberta and Saskatchewan, Canada.

*Alberta Business*. Alberta Business, 218 100 3rd St. E Regina, SK, Canada S7N 1Y7. • Monthly. Regional business magazine.

*Alberta Business Directory*. InfoGroup Inc., 5711 S 86th Cir. Omaha, NE 68127-4146. Phone: (402)593-4500 • URL: http://www.infogroup.com • Annual. Covers: 122,660 businesses in Alberta, Canada. Entries include: Company name, address, phone, number of employees, name of owner or manager, sales volume. Compiled from telephone company "Yellow Pages," statewide (see separate entry).

**Alberta Innovates Technology Futures**. 250 Karl Clark Rd. Edmonton, AB, Canada T6N 1E4. Phone: 800-661-2000 or (780)450-5111; Fax: (780)450-5333; Email: referral@albertainnovates.ca • URL: http://www.albertatechfutures.ca • Development and commercialization technologies that provide solutions to the petroleum, energy and environment, and bio and industrial sectors.

*Albuquerque Business First*. American City Business Journals, Inc., 120 W Morehead St. Charlotte, NC 28202. Phone: (704)973-1000; Fax: (704)973-1001; Email: americancity@bizjournals.com • URL: http://www.acbj.com • Weekly. $81 Individuals print and digital. Local business newspaper.

*Albuquerque Economic Development Business Directory*. Albuquerque Economic Development Inc., 851 University Blvd. SE, Ste. 203 Albuquerque, NM 87106. Phone: 800-451-2933 or (505)246-6200; Email: info@abq.org • URL: http://www.abq.org • Covers: Business resources in the Albuquerque, New Mexico, metropolitan area. Includes list of categories with links and a searchable database. Entries include: Name, address, phone, fax, URL, map link.

*Albuquerque Women in Business Directory*. Duval Publications Inc., PO Box 12955 Albuquerque, NM 87195. Phone: (505)247-9195; Fax: (505)842-5129 • Annual. Covers approximately 400 women business executives and owners in

the Albuquerque, New Mexico area. Informative articles, government resources, related women's resources and organizations.

*Alcohol Research and Health*. U. S. Government Printing Office, 732 N Capitol St. NW Washington, DC 20401. Phone: 866-512-1800 or (202)512-1800 or (866)512-1800; Fax: (202)512-2104 or (202)512-2250; Email: contactcenter@gpo.gov • URL: http://www.gpo.gov • Quarterly. $33.00 per year. Issued by the National Institute on Alcohol Abuse and Alcoholism. Presents alcohol-related research findings and descriptions of alcoholism prevention and treatment programs.

*Alcoholic Beverage Control: State Capitals*. Wakeman/Walworth Inc., PO Box 7376 Alexandria, VA 22307-7376. Phone: 800-876-2545 or (703)768-9600; Fax: (703)768-9690; Email: newsletters@statecapitals.com • URL: http://statecapitals.com/ • 50 times a year. $245.00 per year; print and online editions, $350.00 per year. Formerly *From the State Capitals: Alcoholic Beverage Control*.

*Alcoholism: Clinical and Experimental Research*. Research Society on Alcoholism. Lippincott Williams & Wilkins, 2 Commerce Sq., 2001 Market St. Philadelphia, PA 19103. Phone: 800-638-3030 or (301)223-2300; Email: ronna.ekhouse@wolterskluwer.com • URL: http://www.lww.com • Monthly. Individuals, $331.00 per year; institutions, $639.00 per year.

*Alcoholism Treatment Quarterly: The Practitioner's Quarterly for Individual, Group, and Family Therapy*. The Haworth Press Inc., 10 Alice St. Binghamton, NY 13904. Phone: 800-429-6784 or (607)722-5857; Fax: (607)771-0012 or (607)722-6362; Email: getinfo@haworthpress.com • URL: http://www.haworthpressinc.com/store/product.asp?sku=J014 • Quarterly. $535.00 per year. Edited for professionals working with alcoholics and their families. Formerly *Alcoholism Counseling and Treatment*.

**Alexandria Chamber of Commerce**. 801 N Fairfax St., Ste. 402 Alexandria, VA 22314. Phone: (703)549-1000; Fax: (703)549-1001; Email: info@alexchamber.com • URL: http://www.alexchamber.com • Promotes business and community development in Alexandria, VA.

*Algeria Business Directory*. Business Guide, PO Box 27669 Dubai, United Arab Emirates. Phone: 971 4 2651719; Fax: 971 4 2692151; Email: sales@africa-business.com • URL: http://www.africa-business.com • $150 download. Covers: 10,000 business listings including wholesalers, importers, retailers, business houses, and agents in Algeria.

*Algeria Industrial and Business Directory*. International Business Publications, USA, PO Box 15343 Washington, DC 20003. Phone: (202)546-2103; Fax: (202)546-3275; Email: ibpusa@comcast.net • URL: http://ibpus.com • Annual. $99.95 Individuals. Covers industrial, investment, and business contacts for conducting export-import and investment activity in the country.

*Algeria Investment and Business Guide*. International Business Publications, USA, PO Box 15343 Washington, DC 20003. Phone: (202)546-2103; Fax: (202)546-3275; Email: ibpusa@comcast.net • URL: http://ibpus.com • $99.95 Individuals hardcover; $99.95 Individuals CD-ROM; $99.95 Individuals E-book. Covers: Basic information on economy, export-import and investment climate, opportunities, industrial development, banking, and government. Entries include: Important business contacts and business travel.

*ALI-ABA Business Law Course Materials Journal*. ALI-ABA Continuing Professional Education, American Law Institute, 4025 Chestnut St. Philadelphia, PA 19104-3099. Phone: 800-CLE-NEWS or (215)243-1600; Fax: (215)243-1636 or (215)243-1664; Email: ddissinger@ali.org • URL: http://www.ali-cle.org • Bimonthly. $40 /year; $59 Individuals; $109 Two years; $50 Individuals online. Provides articles from ALI-ABA continuing education course books.

*Aligning & Wheel Service Directory*. InfoGroup Inc., 5711 S 86th Cir. Omaha, NE 68127-4146. Phone: (402)593-4500 • URL: http://www.infogroup.com • Annual. Number of listings: 11,406. Entries include: Name, address, phone, size of advertisement, name of owner or manager, number of employees, year first in "Yellow Pages." Compiled from telephone company "Yellow Pages," nationwide.

*All About Folsom Business*. Folsom Chamber of Commerce, 200 Wool St. Folsom, CA 95630. Phone: (916)985-2698; Fax: (916)985-4117 • URL: http://www.folsomchamber.com • Monthly. Contains updates on current and upcoming events and new members.

*All India Directory/Database of Automobile Components/Parts Manufacturers, Exporters, Dealers, Suppliers*. NIIR Project Consultancy Services, 106 - E, Kamla Nagar New Delhi 110007, India. Phone: 91 11 23843955; Fax: 91 11 23841561; Email: npcs.india@gmail.com • URL: http://www.niir.org • $250 Individuals CD-ROM; Rs 3,933 Individuals CD-ROM. Covers: 11,000 automobile components/parts manufacturers and exporters, dealers, suppliers in India. Entries include: Company name, addresses, pin, city, phone, mobile (wherever available), fax (wherever available), e-mail (wherever available), website (wherever available), products details.

*All India Manufacturers & Exporters of Herbal Products*. NIIR Project Consultancy Services, 106 - E, Kamla Nagar New Delhi 110007, India. Phone: 91 11 23843955; Fax: 91 11 23841561; Email: npcs.india@gmail.com • URL: http://

www.niir.org • Rs 2,023 Individuals CD-ROM; $200 Individuals CD-ROM. Covers: 2,500+ manufacturers and exporters of herbal products in India. Entries include: Name of company, address, city, phone (wherever available), fax (wherever available), e-mail (wherever available), activities (wherever available).

*All India Textile Exporters and Manufacturers*. NIIR Project Consultancy Services, 106 - E, Kamla Nagar New Delhi 110007, India. Phone: 91 11 23843955; Fax: 91 11 23841561; Email: npcs.india@gmail.com • URL: http://www.niir.org • $100 Individuals CD-ROM; $1,324 Individuals CD-ROM. Covers: 4,000 textile exporters and manufacturers in India. Entries include: Company name, contact person name, email (wherever available).

*All Ordinaries Index Companies Handbook*. Australian Stock Exchange Ltd. Exchange Centre, Level 7, 123 Eagle St. Brisbane, NSW 4000, Australia. Fax: 02 9227 0885; Email: info@asx.com.au • $29.95 plus $10.00 postage and handling. Covers: approximately 314 companies that comprise the Australian All Ordinaries Index as of September of the year issued, plus Health-Biotechnology and Telecommunications Index companies that are not included in the All Ordinaries Companies Index. Entries include: Company name, address, phone, names and titles of key personnel, key business summary, financial data, description of product/service, list of major shareholders, share price chart.

*All States Tax Guide*. Prentice Hall PTR, 1 Lake St. Upper Saddle River, NJ 07458. Phone: 800-227-1816 or (201)236-7676 or (201)236-7000; Fax: (800)445-6991 or (317)428-3343 • URL: http://phbusiness.prenhall.com • Looseleaf. Periodic supplementation. Price on application. One volume summary of taxes for all states.

*All States Tax Handbook*. Thomson RIA, 195 Broadway New York, NY 10007-3100. Phone: 800-431-9025 or (212)367-6300 or (212)807-2298; Fax: (212)367-6305 or (212)337-4207; Email: ttacommunications@riag.com • URL: http://www.ria.thomson.com • Annual. $89. Tax structures for fifty states.

*Alliance Credit Counseling*. 15720 John J. Delaney Dr., Ste. 575 Charlotte, NC 28277. Phone: 888-594-9554 or (704)341-1010; Fax: (704)540-5495; Email: service@knowdebt.org • URL: http://www.knowdebt.org • Provides help and hope through personalized education, counseling and support programs that seek to reduce and avoid the burdens of financial crisis, debt stress, bankruptcy and consequences. Provides empowerment to the public through charitable education programs of financial literacy, money management, credit management and debt reduction. Offers services of financial counseling, education and debt management.

**Alliance for American Manufacturing**. 711 D St. NW, 3rd Fl. Washington, DC 20004. Phone: 800-915-4609 or (202)393-3430; Email: info@aamfg.org • URL: http://www.americanmanufacturing.org • Seeks to strengthen manufacturing in the U.S. Provides research, public education, advocacy, strategic communications and coalition building around the issues that matter to America's manufacturing sector. Promotes policy solutions on priorities such as international trade, energy security, health care, retirement security, currency manipulation and other issues of mutual concern.

**Alliance for Nonprofit Management**. 12 Middlesex Rd. Chestnut Hill, MA 02467. Phone: 888-776-2434; Email: info@allianceonline.org • URL: http://www.allianceonline.org • Members are devoted to building the capacity of nonprofit organizations in order to increase their effectiveness.

**Alliance for Wellness ROI**. 390 Main St., Ste. 400 Worcester, MA 01608. Email: info@roiwellness.org • URL: http://www.roiwellness.org • Promotes corporate wellness programs by demonstrating, through an objective Return on Investment (ROI) measurement, that wellness programs are an investment rather than an expense to a company. Conducts research on corporate wellness programs as well as the costs and the Return on Investment by working with epidemiologists, actuaries, consultants, wellness experts, IT professionals and health management professionals.

**Alliance for Women in Media**. 1760 Old Meadow Rd., Ste. 500 McLean, VA 22102. Phone: (703)506-3290; Fax: (703)506-3266; Email: info@allwomeninmedia.org • URL: http://allwomeninmedia.org • Formerly known as the American Women in Radio and Television.

*Alliance of Area Business Publications—Membership Directory*. Alliance of Area Business Publications, 1970 E Grand Ave., Ste. 330 El Segundo, CA 90245. Phone: (310)364-0193; Fax: (310)364-0196; Email: info@bizpubs.org • URL: http://www.bizpubs.org • Annual. Covers over 70 local, state, and regional member business publications in the United States, Canada, Australia and Puerto Rico.

**Alliance of Merger and Acquisition Advisors**. 200 E Randolph St., 24th Fl. Chicago, IL 60601. Phone: 877-844-2535; Fax: (312)729-9800; Email: info@amaaonline.org • URL: http://www.amaaonline.com • Serves the educational and resource needs of mergers and acquisitions professionals. Helps members improve their level of knowledge to better market and deliver their advisory services. Maintains the highest recognized standards of professional excellence for corporate advisory and transaction services.

**Alliance of Supplier Diversity Professionals**. PO Box 782049 Orlando, FL 32878-2049. Phone: 877-405-6565; Email:

info@asdp.us • URL: http://www.asdp.us • Represents supplier diversity professionals throughout the United States. Offers education and professional development opportunities, certification for professionals within management, supplier diversity, procurement and similar career paths. Provides a forum for members to exchange information on all aspects of the supplier diversity profession.

*Alloys Index*. CSA, 7200 Wisconsin Ave. Bethesda, MD 20814. Phone: 800-843-7751 or (301)961-6700; Fax: (301)961-6720; Email: service@csa.com • URL: http://www.csa.com • Monthly. $775 print and online.

*Almanac of American Politics*. National Journal Group Inc., The Watergate, 600 New Hampshire Ave. NW Washington, DC 20037. Phone: 800-613-6701 or (202)739-8400; Fax: (202)833-8069; Email: service@nationaljournal.com • URL: http://www.nationaljournal.com • Biennial. $60.73 Individuals hardcover; $49.57 Individuals softcover. Biennial. Includes biographies of U.S. senators and representatives, with group ratings, key votes, and election results.

*Almanac of Famous People*. Cengage Learning Inc., 20 Channel Center St. Boston, MA 02210. Phone: 800-487-8488 or (617)289-7700; Fax: (617)289-7844; Email: investors@cengage.com • URL: http://www.cengage.com • $308 Individuals. 2011. $280.00. 10th edition. Contains about 30,000 short biographies, with bibliographic citations. Chronological, geographic, and occupational indexes. Formerly *Biography Almanac*.

*Almanac of the Canning, Freezing, Preserving Industries*. Food Institute, 10 Mountainview Rd., Ste. S125 Upper Saddle River, NJ 07458. Phone: (201)791-5570; Fax: (201)791-5222; Email: questions@foodinstitute.com • URL: http://www.foodinstitute.com • Annual. $110 Individuals Hard Copy mail delivery or pdf email from publisher. Contains U.S. food laws and regulations and detailed production statistics.

*Almanac of the Fifty States: Basic Data Profiles with Comparative Tables*. Information Publications Inc., 2995 Woodside Rd. Woodside, CA 94062-2446. Phone: 877-544-4635 or (650)568-6170 or (650)965-4449; Fax: (650)568-6150 or (650)965-3801; Email: info@informationpublications.com • URL: http://www.informationpublications.com/ • Annual. $65.00.

*Alpha Beta Gamma International*. 75 Grasslands Rd. Valhalla, NY 10595. Phone: (914)606-6877; Fax: (914)606-6481; Email: ceo@abg.org • URL: http://www.abg.org • Honor Society - Business. Students enrolled at accredited two-year community, technical, and junior colleges in North America; also initiates distinguished International business persons and academics as honorary members. Sponsors training sessions and cultural and college activities. Maintains speakers' bureau.

*Alpha Iota Delta*. University of Detroit Mercy, 4001 W McNichols Rd. Detroit, MI 48221. Phone: (313)993-1219; Fax: (313)993-1052; Email: ulfertgw@udmercy.edu • URL: http://www.alphaiotadelta.com • Serves as honor society for men and women in decision sciences and information systems.

*Alpha Iota Sorority*. 3219 SE 18th Ct. Des Moines, IA 50320-1901. Phone: (515)282-4896; Email: clmekus@aol.com • URL: http://www.alphaiota.org • Honorary sorority - business. Helps each member to become a better businesswoman through development of self-confidence, leadership and awareness of responsibility to herself and her community.

*Alpha Kappa Psi*. 7801 E 88th St. Indianapolis, IN 46256-1233. Phone: (317)872-1553; Fax: (317)872-1567; Email: mail@akpsi.org • URL: http://www.akpsi.org • Professional fraternity - business administration. Conducts educational and charitable programs. Focuses on leadership development.

*Alteration Contractors Directory*. InfoGroup Inc., 5711 S 86th Cir. Omaha, NE 68127-4146. Phone: (402)593-4500 • URL: http://www.infogroup.com • Annual. Number of listings: 22,248. Entries include: Name, address, phone, size of advertisement, name of owner or manager, number of employees, year first in "Yellow Pages." Compiled from telephone company "Yellow Pages," nationwide.

*Alternative Energy Directory & Handbook*. Grey House Publishing, 4919 Rte. 22 Amenia, NY 12501. Phone: 800-562-2139 or (518)789-8700; Fax: (518)789-0556; Email: books@greyhouse.com • URL: http://www.greyhouse.com • $165 Individuals softcover. Covers: Alternative energy sources including hydro, wind, solar, coal, natural gas and atomic energy sources. Includes information on associations, magazines, trade shows and vendors.

*Alternative Energy Retailer*. Zackin Publications Inc., PO Box 2180 Waterbury, CT 06722. Phone: 800-325-6745 or (203)262-4670; Fax: (203)262-4680; Email: info@zackin.com • URL: http://www.zackin.com • Monthly. $32.00 per year.

*Alternative Fuel Vehicle Businesses in the World*. Momentum Technologies L.L.C., PO Box 460813 Glendale, CO 80246. Phone: (303)229-4841; Fax: (408)705-2031 • URL: http://www.mtt.com • Contains detailed directory listings and contact information for dozens of businesses involved with alternative fuel vehicles in operation throughout the world. Includes business name, address, phone number, fax number, e-mail address, and web site address. Includes brief descriptions of product lines, services offered, and business type.

Covers manufacturers, wholesale and retail suppliers, system design businesses, system installers, nonprofit organizations, trade organizations, and more.

*Alternative Travel Directory: The Complete Guide to Traveling, Studying, and Living Overseas*. Transitions Abroad Publishing, 18 Hulst Rd. Amherst, MA 01002. Phone: 800-293-0373 or (413)256-3414; Fax: (413)256-0373; Email: senioreditor@transitionsabroad.com • URL: http://www.transitionsabroad.com • Annual. Covers: Over 2,000 sources of information on international employment, education, and specialty travel opportunities. Entries include: Source name, address, phone, description, cost dates.

*Aluminum Extrusion Press Directory*. Aluminum Association, 1525 Wilson Blvd., Ste. 600 Arlington, VA 22209. Phone: (703)358-2960; Email: info@aluminum.org • URL: http://www.aluminum.org • Irregular. $70 Members; $135 Nonmembers. Covers: Locations of 496 aluminum presses at 217 plants in 148 US companies; details on extruders, locations, press sizes, anodizing, painting and billet casting facilities. Entries include: Names of extruders and plant addresses.

*Aluminum Industry Abstracts: A Monthly Review of the World's Technical Literature on Aluminum*. Aluminum Association. 1525 Wilson Blvd. Arlington, VA 22209. Phone: (703)358-2960; Fax: (703)358-2961; Email: slarkin@aluminum.org • URL: http://www.aluminum.org • Monthly. $975.00 per year. Includes print and online editions. Formerly *World Aluminum Abstracts*.

*Aluminum Standards and Data*. Aluminum Association, 1525 Wilson Blvd., Ste. 600 Arlington, VA 22209. Phone: (703)358-2960; Email: info@aluminum.org • URL: http://www.aluminum.org • Biennial. $75 Members; $150 Nonmembers.

*Aluminum Statistical Review*. Aluminum Association, 1525 Wilson Blvd. Ste. 600 Arlington, VA 22209. Phone: (703)358-2960; Email: info@aluminum.org • URL: http://www.aluminum.org • Annual. $95 Members; $190 Nonmembers.

*AM/FM Broadcast Financial Data/TV Broadcast Financial Data*. U.S. Federal Communications Commission, 445 12th St. SW Washington, DC 20554. Phone: 888-225-5322 or (888)225-5322 or (202)418-0500; Fax: (202)418-0232 or (202)418-1440; Email: fccinfo@fcc.gov • URL: http://www.fcc.gov • Annual. Free.

*Amber Waves*. Economic Research Service Hazard Analysis and Critical Control Points, 1800 M St. NW, Rm. N2081 Washington, DC 20036-5831. Phone: (202)694-5454; Fax: (202)694-5688; Email: ollinger@ers.usda.gov • URL: http://www.ers.usda.gov/Data/haccpsurvey • Quarterly. Replaces *Agricultural Outlook; Food Review*; and *Rural America*. Provides research and analysis from the U.S. Department of Agriculture's Economic Research Service. Includes economic data on agriculture, food, trade, and environmental factors.

*AmCham Yearbook*. American Chamber of Commerce for Brazil - Sao Paulo, Rua Da Paz, 1431 CEP 04713-001 Sao Paulo, Brazil. Phone: 55 11 30116000; Fax: 55 11 51803777; Email: vasco@amcham.com.br • URL: http://www.amcham.com.br • Annual. $250 Individuals for associates; $750 Individuals not associates. Covers: More than 5,400 corporate members of the American Chamber of Commerce for Brazil.

*America at Work*. AFL-CIO, 815 16th St. NW Washington, DC 20006. • URL: http://www.aflcio.org • 11/year. Covers information on working in America. Formerly *AFL-CIO News*.

*American Academy of Optometry*. 2909 Fairgreen St. Orlando, FL 32803. Phone: 800-969-4226 or (321)710-3937; Fax: (407)893-9890; Email: aaoptom@aaoptom.org • URL: http://www.aaopt.org • Optometrists, educators and scientists interested in optometric education and standards of care in visual problems.

*American Accounts Payable Association*. 660 N Main Ave., Ste. 200 San Antonio, TX 78205-1217. Phone: (210)630-4373; Fax: (210)630-4410; Email: membership@americanap.org • URL: http://www.americanap.org • Seeks to uphold the standards of practice in the accounts payable profession. Fosters the professional development of members. Offers comprehensive educational programs for accounts payable professionals.

*American Advertising*. American Advertising Federation, 1101 Vermont Ave. NW, Ste. 500 Washington, DC 20005-6306. Phone: 800-999-2231 or (202)898-0089; Fax: (202)898-0159; Email: aaf@aaf.org • URL: http://www.aaf.org • Quarterly. Membership.

*American and Common Market Club Directory*. American and Common Market Club, 17, rue Emile Claus, bte. 3 B-1050 Brussels, Belgium. Phone: 32 2 6475801 • Annual. Entries include: name, address, phone, fax.

*American Apparel and Footwear Association*. 1601 N Kent St., Ste. 1200 Arlington, VA 22209. Phone: (703)524-1864; Fax: (703)522-6741; Email: mstorch@wewear.org • URL: http://www.wewear.org • Formerly National Knitwear Manufacturers Association.

*American Apparel Producers' Network—Directory for Sourcing Apparel*. American Apparel Producers' Network, PO Box 720693 Atlanta, GA 30358. Phone: (404)843-3171; Fax: (404)671-9456; Email: source@aapnetwork.net • URL: http://www.aapnetwork.net • Annual. Covers: Over 300 member contractors, manufacturers, and suppliers in the apparel industry. Entries include: Firm name, address, phone, names and titles of key personnel, apparel and services provided.

**American Armed Forces Mutual Aid Association**. 102 Sheridan Ave. Fort Myer, VA 22211-1110. Phone: 800-522-5221 or (703)707-4600; Fax: (888)210-4882; Email: info@aafmaa.com • URL: http://www.aafmaa.com • A mutual aid organization providing aid to families of deceased career Army and Air Force officers and noncommissioned officers.

**American Association for Justice**. 777 6th St. NW, Ste. 200 Washington, DC 20001. Phone: 800-424-2725 or (202)965-3500; Fax: (202)625-7084; Email: membership@justice.org • URL: http://www.justice.org/cps/rde/xchg/justice/hs.xsl/default.htm • Concerned with the behavioral aspects of litigation.

**American Association of Individual Investors**. 625 N Michigan Ave. Chicago, IL 60611. Phone: 800-428-2244 or (312)280-0170; Fax: (312)280-9883 or (312)280-1625; Email: members@aaii.com • URL: http://www.aaii.com • Individuals who make their own investment decisions. Assists individuals in becoming effective managers of their own assets through educational programs and research. Provides programs to help individuals develop an investment philosophy and decision-making process based on their objectives, capabilities and attitudes. Offers home-study curriculum on investment topics and a videotape course on investing fundamentals and mutual funds.

**American Association of Inside Sales Professionals**. 14530 Florissant Path Apple Valley, MN 55124. Phone: 800-604-7085; Email: info@aa-isp.org • URL: http://www.aa-isp.org • Serves as an authoritative resource to leaders and individual sales representatives. Aims to perfect the skills of inside sale professionals. Conducts leadership and career development trainings, member forums and networking, conferences, education and accreditation programs that will help advance the inside sales profession.

**American Association of Preferred Provider Organizations**. 222 S 1st St., Ste. 303 Louisville, KY 40202. Phone: 800-642-2515 or (502)403-1122; Fax: (502)403-1129 • URL: http://www.aappo.org • Formerly Association of Managed Healthcare Organizations.

**American Association of Professional Technical Analysts**. 10621 Big Canoe, 5516 Red Fox Dr. Big Canoe, GA 30143. Phone: 800-222-7636; Email: membership@aapta.com • URL: http://www.aapta.com • Aims to promote the use of technical analysis. Provides a forum for members to share ideas, information, research and analytical techniques. Encourages the highest professional ethics and competence among technical analysts.

***American Banker Full Text***. American Banker-Bond Buyer, Database Services, One State St. Plaza New York, NY 10004. Phone: 800-221-1809 or (212)967-7000; Fax: (212)843-9600 • Provides complete text online of the daily *American Banker*. Inquire as to cost and availability.

***American Banker: The Financial Services Daily***. SourceMedia Inc., 1 State Street Plz., 27th Fl. New York, NY 10004. Phone: 800-221-1809 or (212)803-8200 or (212)803-8333; Fax: (212)843-9635 or (212)292-5216; Email: custserv@sourcemedia.com • URL: http://www.sourcemedia.com • Daily. $895.00 per year. Provides news of banking, investment products, mortgages, credit unions, finance, bank technology, and legal developments.

***American Banker—Top World Banks by Deposits and Assets***. American Banker/Bond Buyer Inc., 1 State St. Plz. 27 Fl. New York, NY 10004. Phone: 800-221-1809 or (212)803-8200 or (212)967-7000; Fax: (212)843-9600 or (212)843-9613; Email: custserv@americanbanker.com • URL: http://www.americanbanker.com • Annual. $25. Publication includes: List of 500 largest banks in the world by assets with total deposits and deposit rank; also, the risk-based capital position of the 100 largest banking companies in the world as measured by total assets. Entries include: Bank name, headquarters, rankings by assets and amount of deposits and assets for two previous years.

***American Bankers Association Directory of Trust Banking***. Accuity Inc., 4709 W Golf Rd. Skokie, IL 60076. Phone: 800-321-3373 or (847)676-9600; Fax: (847)933-8101; Email: custserv@accuitysolutions.com • URL: http://www.accuitysolutions.com • Annual. $575 Individuals. Covers: Approximately 3,000 financial institutions in the U.S. that are involved in trust banking. Database includes: Number of accounts under management by type for the past year and three year compounded growth. Entries include: Name, address, phone, fax, key trust officials with title and functional responsibility, personal and employee benefit assets for the two most current years along with a three year compounded growth rate.

**American Bankers Association**. 1120 Connecticut Ave. NW Washington, DC 20036. Phone: 800-226-5377 or (202)663-5268; Fax: (202)828-5053; Email: custserv@aba.com • URL: http://www.aba.com • Members are principally commercial banks and trust companies; combined assets of members represent approximately 90% of the U.S. banking industry; approximately 94% of members are community banks with less than $500 million in assets. Seeks to enhance the role of commercial bankers as preeminent providers of financial services through communications, research, legal action, lobbying of federal legislative and regulatory bodies, and education and training programs. Serves as spokesperson for the banking industry; facilitates exchange of information among members. Maintains the American Institute of Banking, an industry-sponsored adult education program. Conducts educational and training programs for bank employees and officers through a wide range of banking schools and national conferences. Maintains liaison with federal bank regulators; lobbies Congress on issues affecting commercial banks; testifies before congressional committees; represents members in U.S. postal rate proceedings. Serves as secretariat of the International Monetary Conference and the Financial Institutions Committee for the American National Standards Institute. Files briefs and lawsuits in major court cases affecting the industry. Conducts teleconferences with state banking associations on such issues as regulatory compliance; works to build consensus and coordinate activities of leading bank and financial service trade groups. Provides services to members including: public advocacy; news media contact; insurance program providing directors and officers with liability coverage, financial institution bond, and trust errors and omissions coverage; research service operated through ABA Center for Banking Information; fingerprint set processing in conjunction with the Federal Bureau of Investigation; discounts on operational and income-producing projects through the Corporation for American Banking. Conducts conferences, forums, and workshops covering subjects such as small business, consumer credit, agricultural and community banking, trust management, bank operations, and automation. Sponsors ABA Educational Foundation and the Personal Economics Program, which educates schoolchildren and the community on banking, economics, and personal finance.

***American Bankruptcy Law Journal***. National Conference of Bankruptcy Judges, c/o Jeanne Sleeper, 954 La Mirada St. Laguna Beach, CA 92651-3751. Phone: (949)497-3673; Fax: (949)497-2523 • URL: http://www.ncbj.org • Quarterly. $45 Individuals /year for new lawyers (less than two years in practice); $75 Individuals /year for new and renewals; $85 Other countries. Peer-reviewed journal focusing on bankruptcy law and related subjects.

***American Bar Association—Directory: The Redbook***. American Bar Association, 321 N Clark St. Chicago, IL 60654-7598. Phone: 800-285-2221 or (312)988-5000; Email: orders@abanet.org • URL: http://www.americanbar.org/aba.html • Annual. $17.95 Individuals. Covers: Approximately 7,500 lawyers active in the affairs of the Association, including officers, members of Boards of Governors and House of Delegates, section officers and council members, committee leaders, headquarters staff, state and local bars, affiliated and other legal organizations. Entries include: Section, council, or other unit name; names, addresses, and phone numbers of officers or chairpersons and members.

***The American Beauty Industry Encyclopedia***. Cengage Learning Inc., 20 Channel Center St. Boston, MA 02210. Phone: 800-487-8488 or (617)289-7700; Fax: (617)289-7844; Email: investors@cengage.com • URL: http://www.cengage.com • 2011. eBook. Published by Greenwood Publishing Group. Focuses exclusively on the many aspects of the American beauty industry, covering both its diverse origins and its global reach.

***American Bee Journal***. Dadant and Sons Inc., 51 S 2nd St., Ste. 2 Hamilton, IL 62341-1397. Phone: 888-922-1293 or (217)847-3324; Fax: (217)847-3660; Email: dadant@dadant.com • URL: http://www.dadant.com • Monthly. $27.00 per year. Magazine for hobbyist and professional beekeepers.

***American Beekeeping Federation Newsletter***. American Beekeeping Federation, 3525 Piedmont Rd., Bldg. 5, Ste. 300 Atlanta, GA 30305. Phone: (404)760-2875; Fax: (404)240-0998; Email: info@abfnet.org • URL: http://www.abfnet.org • Bimonthly. $25.00 per year. Newsletter.

***American Behavioral Scientist***. Pine Forge Press, 2455 Teller Rd. Thousand Oaks, CA 91320-2234. Phone: 800-818-7243 or (805)499-4224 or (805)499-9774; Fax: (805)499-0871 or (805)583-2665; Email: sales@pfp.sagepub.com • URL: http://www.sagepub.com/sociologybooks • Fourteen per year. Institutions, $1,425.00 per year.

**American Benefits Council**. 1501 M St. NW, Ste. 600 Washington, DC 20005-1775. Phone: (202)289-6700; Fax: (202)289-4582; Email: info@abcstaff.org • URL: http://www.americanbenefitscouncil.org • Serves as national trade association for companies concerned about federal legislation and regulations affecting all aspects of the employee benefits system. Represents the entire spectrum of the private employee benefits community and sponsors or administers retirement and health plans covering more than one hundred million Americans.

**American Beverage Association**. 1101 16th St. NW Washington, DC 20036. Phone: (202)463-6732 or (202)463-6770; Fax: (202)659-5349; Email: info@ameribev.org • URL: http://www.ameribev.org • Active members are bottlers and distributors of soft drinks and franchise companies; associate members are suppliers of materials and services. Conducts government affairs activities on the national and state levels, discussion of industry problems, and general improvement of operating procedures. Conducts research on beverage laws.

**American Beverage Licensees**. 5101 River Rd., Ste. 108 Bethesda, MD 20816-1560. Phone: (301)656-1494; Fax: (301)656-7539; Email: info@ablusa.org • URL: http://www.ablusa.org • Federation of associations of alcohol beverage retailers.

***American Bicyclist***. Willow Publishing Co., 400 Skokie Blvd. Northbrook, IL 60062-2816. Phone: (847)291-1117; Fax: (847)559-4444 • Monthly. Free to qualified personnel; others, $35.00 per year. Trade journal edited for bicycle retailers and wholesalers. Includes product reviews.

***American Big Businesses Directory***. InfoGroup Inc., 5711 S 86th Cir. Omaha, NE 68127-4146. Phone: (402)593-4500 • URL: http://www.infogroup.com • Annual. $295; $595 both print & CD-ROM. Covers: 218,000 U.S. businesses with more than 100 employees, and 500,000 key executives and directors. CD-ROM version contains 160,000 top firms and 431,000 key executives. Entries include: Name, address, phone, names and titles of key personnel, number of employees, sales volume, Standard Industrial Classification (SIC) codes, subsidiaries and parent company names, stock exchanges on which traded.

***American Book Prices Current***. Bancroft-Parkman Inc., PO Box 1236 Washington, CT 06793-0236. Phone: (860)868-7408; Fax: (860)868-0080; Email: abpc@snet.net • URL: http://www.bookpricescurrent.com • Annual. $119.95 Individuals.

***American Book Publishing Record: Arranged by Dewey Decimal Classification and Indexed by Author, Title, and Subject***. R.R. Bowker L.L.C., 630 Central Ave New Providence, NJ 07974. Phone: 888-269-5372 or (908)286-1090; Email: info@bowker.com • URL: http://www.bowker.com • Monthly. $365 Individuals Annual. Offers access to the newest cataloging records from the Library of Congress.

***American Book Trade Directory (ABD)***. Information Today, Inc., 143 Old Marlton Pke. Medford, NJ 08055-8750. Phone: 800-300-9868 or (609)654-6266; Fax: (609)654-4309; Email: custserv@infotoday.com • URL: http://www.infotoday.com • Annual. $379.50 Individuals softbound; $341.55 first time standing order. Covers: Nearly 20,000 retail and antiquarian book dealers, plus 1,200 book and magazine wholesalers, distributors, and jobbers-in all 50 states and U.S. territories. Also included are sections of auctioneers of literary property, exporters/importers, booktrade associations, foreign language book dealers, book and literary appraisers, and rental library chains. Entries include: Bookstore name, address, phone, owner or manager, types and subjects of books stocked, specialty, sidelines, year established, SAN (Standard Address Number), number of volumes stocked, square footage.

***American Brewer: The Business of Beer***. American Brewer, PO Box 20268 Alexandria, VA 22320-1268. Phone: (703)312-7967 • $50 Individuals; $100 Out of country; $17.50 Single issue. Business magazine aimed primarily at small and medium-sized breweries in the U.S. and Canada.

***American Bureau of Shipping International Directory of Offices***. American Bureau Of Shipping Inc., 16855 Northchase Dr. Houston, TX 77060-6010. Phone: (281)877-5800 • URL: http://www.eagle.org • Annual. $520. ABS Employee and office listings.

**American Business Council of Pakistan**. F-30, Block-7, K.D.A., Scheme No. 5, Kehkashan, Clifton Karachi, Pakistan. Phone: 92 21 5877351 or 92 21 5877390; Fax: 92 21 5877391; Email: abcpak@cyber.net.pk • URL: http://www.abcpk.org.pk • Promotes private American business efforts in Pakistan and friendly relations between Americans and Pakistani nationals. Provides information on the business climate and development and trade issues in Pakistan.

***American Business Database***. Mailer's Software, 970 Calle Negocio San Clemente, CA 92673-6201. Phone: 800-443-8834 or (714)492-7000; Fax: (714)492-7086 • Covers: More than 1.2 million listings of all the companies and organizations in the U.S. that possess their own unique ZIP Plus 4 code. Entries include: Company name, phone, complete mailing address with ZIP Plus 4 and Carrier Route Codes; state and county FIPS Codes; Standard Industrial Classification (SIC) code.

***American Business Directory: Directory and Year Book of American Business in Ireland***. American Chamber of Commerce Ireland, 6 Wilton Pl. Dublin 2, Ireland. Phone: 353 1 6616201; Fax: 353 1 6616217; Email: info@amcham.ie • URL: http://www.amcham.ie • Annual. Contains lists of American owned, associated, and affiliated companies in the Republic of Ireland with company listings by name and type of business.

***American Business Directory for the USSR***. Amtorg Trading Corp., 15 W 36th St., 6th Fl. New York, NY 10018. Phone: (212)956-3010 • Publication consists of paid advertisements and business reply cards from U.S. companies wishing to do business with the U.S.S.R.

***American Business Directory***. InfoGroup Inc., 5711 S 86th Cir. Omaha, NE 68127-4146. Phone: (402)593-4500 • URL: http://www.infogroup.com • Provides brief online information on more than 10 million U. S. companies, including individual plants and branches. Entries typically include address, phone number, industry classification code, and contact name. Updating is quarterly. Inquire as to online cost and availability.

***American Business Directory***. ProQuest LLC, 2250 Perimeter Park Dr., Ste. 300 Morrisville, NC 27560. Phone: 800-334-2564 or (919)804-6400; Fax: (919)804-6410; Email: contact@dialog.com • URL: http://www.dialog.com • Quarterly. An electronic directory of more than 9 million

SOURCES CITED

businesses currently operating in the U.S. It is produced by InfoUSA, and lists companies with all available contact information and SIC (Standard Industrial Classification) codes, yellow pages information, trade and financial data, as well as corporate linkages on more than 10 million U.S. business establishments. Public companies, private companies, small businesses, government agencies, professionals, and schools are among the types of entities listed. Descriptions of brand names and franchises are included with many SIC codes. Contact information includes addresses, telephone numbers, employment data, key contact and title. Print sources, telephone interviews, and companies' annual reports are used in gathering the data in this database. Among the print sources are more than 5,000 yellow-page books.

*American Business in China*. Caravel Inc., 23545 Crenshaw Blvd., Ste. 101 E Torrance, CA 90505. Phone: (310)325-0100; Fax: (310)325-2583; Email: info@china4us.com • URL: http://www.china4us.com • Annual. $99 print edition. Publication includes: More than 1,000 U.S. firms with offices in China and Hong Kong, including Beijing, Shanghai, and Guangzhou. Database includes: Exporting to China; Marketing, Advertising and Exhibiting in China; China's major cites for foreign investments. Entries include: Company name, address, phone, fax; websites and e-mail addresses, name of contact for both U.S. Headquarters and China branch offices; and products or services provided.

*American Business Law Journal*. Academy of Legal Studies in Business, University of Florida, College of Business Administration Gainesville, FL 32611. Phone: (215)898-9369 or (814)865-6205 • URL: http://www.alsb.org • Quarterly. $681 Institutions print & online; $905 Institutions, other countries print & online; $592 Institutions print or online; £463 Institutions print & online; $786 Institutions, other countries print or online; £402 Institutions print or online; $769 Institutions print and online; $669 Institutions print, online; €665 Institutions print and online; £523 Institutions print and online; £455 Institutions print, online; €577 Institutions print, online; $1,023 Institutions, other countries print and online; $889 Institutions, other countries print, online. Journal focusing on a range of topics related to business law.

*American Business Leaders from Colonial Times to the Present*. ABC-Clio Inc., 130 Cremona Dr. Santa Barbara, CA 93117-5516. Phone: 800-368-6868 or (805)968-1911; Fax: (805)685-9685; Email: crussell@abc-clio.com • URL: http://www.abc-clio.com • $175 Individuals print. Covers: The last three centuries of visionary figures in American business.

*American Business Lists—Online*. InfoUSA, 5711 S 86th Cir. Omaha, NE 68127. Phone: 800-321-0869 or (402)593-4500; Fax: (402)593-4671; Email: help@infousa.com • URL: http://www.infousa.com • Allows subscribers to access three databases containing directory information: 1) U.S. Businesses—contains 10 million listings for U.S. businesses. 2) Canadian Business Listings—contains 1.1 million listings for Canadian businesses. 3) Residential Listings - U.S. The databases can be used as a source for new sales leads, market planning, direct mail lists, telemarketing, distribution analysis, and locating suppliers.

*American Business Women's Association*. 11050 Roe Ave., Ste. 200 Overland Park, KS 66211. Phone: 800-228-0007; Fax: (913)660-0101; Email: webmail@abwa.org • URL: http://www.abwa.org • Women in business, including women owning or operating their own businesses, women in professions and women employed in any level of government, education, or retailing, manufacturing and service companies. Provides opportunities for businesswomen to help themselves and others grow personally and professionally through leadership, education, networking support and national recognition. Offers leadership training, business skills training and business education; special membership options for retired businesswomen and the Company Connection for business owners, a resume service, credit card and programs, various travel and insurance benefits. Sponsors American Business Women's Day and National Convention and regional conferences held annually.

*American Businesspersons Association*. Hillsboro Executive Center North, 350 Fairway Dr., Ste. 107 Deerfield Beach, FL 33441-1834. Phone: 800-221-2168; Fax: (954)571-8582; Email: membership@assnservices.com • URL: http://www.aba-assn.com • Owners of businesses and individuals in executive, managerial, and sales capacities. Provides substantial discounts, affordable insurance, products and other special services to members.

*American Buyers: Demographics of Shopping*. Cengage Learning Inc., 20 Channel Center St. Boston, MA 02210. Phone: 800-487-8488 or (617)289-7700; Fax: (617)289-7844; Email: investors@cengage.com • URL: http://www.cengage.com • 2010. eBook. Published by New Strategist Publications. While most businesses have a feel for what is happening in their own establishment, this work lets them see the big picture beyond their walls or web site. Its weekly and quarterly data show you how many households buy certain products and services and how much buyers pay for them, all broken down by demographics.

*American Casino Guide*. Casino Vacations, PO Box 703 Dania, FL 33004. Phone: (954)989-2766 • URL: http://www.americancasinoguide.com/contact-us.html • Annual. $18.95 Individuals plus shipping charges; $12.95 Individuals discounted price. Covers: more than 700 casino/resorts, river-

boat casinos, and Indian casinos in the U.S. Database includes: Maps, photos. Entries include: Casino name, address, phone, toll-free number, room rates, dining information, games offered, features, web site addresses.

*American Cement Directory*. Bradley Pulverizer Co., 123 S Third St. Allentown, PA 18102-4909. Phone: (610)434-5191; Fax: (610)770-9400 • URL: http://www.bradleypulverizer.com • Annual. $90 U.S. and Canada Postpaid. Covers: Approximately 100 cement manufacturing companies in the United States, Canada, Mexico, Central and South America. Entries include: Company Name, address, phone, fax, names of principal executives, capacity, capitalization, brand names and process, plant locations.

*American Ceramic Society Bulletin*. American Ceramic Society, 600 N Cleveland Ave., Ste. 210 Westerville, OH 43082. Phone: 866-721-3322 or (240)646-7054; Fax: (204)396-5637; Email: customerservice@ceramics.org • URL: http://www.ceramics.org • 9/year. $95 U.S. and Canada nonmembers; $150 Other countries non-members. Contains items of interest to the ceramics community, and provides current information on R&D, technology, manufacturing, engineered ceramics, fuel cells, nanotechnology, glass, refractories, environmental concerns, whitewares, etc. Bulletin publishes "the Glass Researcher" as a quarterly feature section. The December issue of Bulletin includes ceramic Source, an annual buyer's guide.

*American Ceramic Society Journal*. American Ceramic Society, 600 N Cleveland Ave., Ste. 210 Westerville, OH 43082. Phone: 866-721-3322 or (240)646-7054; Fax: (204)396-5637; Email: customerservice@ceramics.org • URL: http://www.ceramics.org • Monthly. Members, $150.00 per year; non-members, $750.00 per year. Includes subscription to *Ceramic Bulletin and Abstracts*.

**American Ceramic Society**. 600 N Cleveland Ave., Ste. 210 Westerville, OH 43082. Phone: 866-721-3322 or (240)646-7054; Fax: (204)396-5637; Email: customerservice@ceramics.org • URL: http://www.ceramics.org • Formerly National Institute of Ceramic Engineers.

**American Chain of Warehouses**. 156 Flamingo Dr. Beecher, IL 60401. Phone: (708)946-9792; Fax: (708)946-9793; Email: bjurus@acwi.org • URL: http://www.acwi.org • Represents commercial warehouses. Provides national sales representation. Disseminates information.

**American Chamber of Commerce Executives**. 1330 Braddock Pl., Ste. 300 Alexandria, VA 22314. Phone: 888-577-9883 or (703)998-0072; Email: hero@acce.org • URL: http://www.acce.org • Professional society of chamber of commerce executives and staff members.

**American Chamber of Commerce in Lithuania**. Konstitucijos 7, 10th Fl. LT-09308 Vilnius, Lithuania. Phone: 370 5 2611181; Email: acc@iti.lt • URL: http://www.amcham.lt • American, international, and Lithuanian corporations; interested organizations and individuals. Promotes members' common business interests. Strives to improve business climate in Lithuania. Provides referral service for new members; consults on investment and business environment.

**American Chamber of Commerce in Moldova**. 45 B, Puskin St., 3rd Fl. MD-2005 Chisinau, Moldova. Phone: 373 22 211781; Fax: 373 22 211782; Email: info@amcham.md • URL: http://www.amcham.md • Open to all business leaders with a common interest in improving the business climate in Moldova and increasing foreign trade and investment with Moldova. Promotes American trade and investment in Moldova and works with the Moldovan government and business leaders to foster a more favorable business climate in Moldova for foreign trade and investment.

**American Chamber of Commerce in the Kyrgyz Republic**. Office No. 123, 191 Abdrakhmanov Str. 720011 Bishkek, Kyrgyzstan. Phone: 996 312 623389; Fax: 996 312 623406; Email: memberservices@amcham.kg • URL: http://www.amcham.kg • Represents foreign and local companies. Fosters a favorable business climate for local and foreign companies by promoting members' businesses and lobbying for their interests. Works on different areas such as corruption fighting, business services and attraction of foreign investment.

**American Chamber of Commerce to the European Union**. Ave. des Arts/Kunstlaan 53 B-1000 Brussels, Belgium. Phone: 32 2 5136892; Fax: 32 2 5137928; Email: info@amchameu.eu • URL: http://www.amchameu.eu • Works to represent the companies of American parentage committed to Europe towards the institutions and governments of the European Union. Helps improve the business and investment climate in Europe. Facilitates the resolution of EU - US issues that impact business and plays a role in creating better understanding of EU and US positions on business matters.

**American Chemical Society**. 1155 16th St. NW Washington, DC 20036. Phone: 800-227-5558 or (202)872-4600; Email: help@acs.org • URL: http://www.acs.org • Scientific and educational society of chemists and chemical engineers. Conducts: studies and surveys; special programs for disadvantaged persons; legislation monitoring, analysis, and reporting; courses for graduate chemists and chemical engineers; radio and television programming. Offers career guidance counseling; administers the Petroleum Research Fund and other grants and fellowship programs. Operates Employment Clearing Houses. Compiles statistics. Maintains speakers' bureau and 33 divisions.

**American Chemistry Council**. 700 2nd St. NE Washington, DC

20002. Phone: (202)249-7000; Fax: (202)249-6100 • URL: http://www.americanchemistry.com • Represents the leading companies engaged in the business of chemistry. Members apply the science of chemistry to make innovative products and services that make people's lives "better, healthier and safer." Improves environmental, health and safety performance through "Responsible Care"(R), common sense advocacy designed to address major public policy issues and health and environmental research and product testing.

*American City and County: Administration, Engineering and Operations in Relation to Local Government*. RentPath Inc., 3585 Engineering Dr., Ste. 100 Norcross, GA 30092-2831. Phone: 800-216-1423 or (678)421-3000 • URL: http://www.rentpath.com • Monthly. Free to qualified personnel. Edited for mayors, city managers, and other local officials. Emphasis is on equipment and basic services.

**American Civil Liberties Union**. 125 Broad St., 18th Fl. New York, NY 10004. Phone: (212)549-2500; Email: media@aclu.org • URL: http://www.aclu.org • Champions the rights set forth in the Bill of Rights of the U.S. Constitution: freedom of speech, press, assembly, and religion; due process of law and fair trial; equality before the law regardless of race, color, sexual orientation, national origin, political opinion, or religious belief. Conducts activities including litigation, advocacy, and public education. Sponsors litigation projects on topics such as women's rights, gay and lesbian rights, and children's rights.

*American Clean Car*. Crain Communications Inc., 150 N Michigan Ave. Chicago, IL 60601-7553. Phone: 800-678-9595 or (312)649-5200 or (312)649-5411; Fax: (312)280-3150 or (312)280-3174; Email: info@crain.com • URL: http://www.crain.com • Bimonthly. $135.00 per year. Provides articles on new products and management for the carwash industry.

**American Clinical Laboratory Association**. 1100 New York Ave. NW, Ste. 725 W Washington, DC 20005. Phone: (202)637-9466; Fax: (202)637-2050; Email: info@clinical-labs.org • URL: http://www.acla.com • Corporations, partnerships, or individuals owning or controlling one or more independent clinical laboratory facilities operating for a profit and licensed under the Clinical Laboratories Improvement Act of 1967 or the Clinical Laboratories Improvement Amendment of 1988, or accredited by the Medicare program. Promotes the development of uniformly high quality laboratory testing; eliminates the present inequalities in the standards applied to different segments of the clinical laboratory market; discourages the enactment of restrictive legislative or regulatory policies that may impede the free flow of commerce or operate to the detriment of the public. Examines federal and state health care and laboratory regulatory and legislative proposals and submits comments and opinions to the appropriate agencies or legislative bodies.

**American Coatings Association**. 1500 Rhode Island Ave. NW Washington, DC 20005. Phone: (202)462-6272; Fax: (202)462-8549 • URL: http://www.paint.org • Formerly National Paint and Coatings Association.

*American Coin-Op: The Magazine for Coin-Operated Laundry and Drycleaning Businessmen*. Crain Communications Inc., 150 N Michigan Ave. Chicago, IL 60601-7553. Phone: 800-678-9595 or (312)649-5200 or (312)649-5411; Fax: (312)280-3150 or (312)280-3174; Email: info@crain.com • URL: http://www.crain.com • Monthly. Free.

**American Coke and Coal Chemicals Institute**. 25 Massachusetts Ave. NW, Ste. 800 Washington, DC 20001. Phone: (202)452-7198; Fax: (202)463-6573; Email: information@accci.org • URL: http://www.accci.org • Producers of oven coke and coal chemicals; producers of metallurgical coal; tar distillers; producers of chemicals and suppliers to the industry.

**American College of Apothecaries**. 2830 Summer Oaks Dr. Bartlett, TN 38134. Phone: (901)383-8119; Fax: (901)473-8187; Email: info@acainfo.org • URL: http://acainfo.org • A professional society of pharmacists.

**American College of Counselors**. 273 Glossip Ave. Highlandville, MO 65669-8133. Phone: (417)885-7632 or (417)885-7632; Fax: (417)443-3002 • URL: http://acconline.us • Formerly National Alliance for Family Life.

**American College of Health Care Administrators**. 1321 Duke St., Ste. 400 Alexandria, VA 22314. Phone: (202)536-5120; Fax: (866)874-1585; Email: mgrachek@achca.org • URL: http://www.achca.org • Formerly American College of Nursing Home Administrators.

**American College of Healthcare Executives**. 1 N Franklin St., Ste. 1700 Chicago, IL 60606-3529. Phone: (312)424-2800 or (312)424-9400; Fax: (312)424-0023 or (312)424-9405; Email: contact@ache.org • URL: http://www.ache.org • Formerly American College of Hospital Administrators.

**American College of Medical Practice Executives**. 104 Inverness Terr. E Englewood, CO 80112-5306. Phone: 877-275-6462 or (303)799-1111; Fax: (303)643-4439; Email: acmpe@mgma.com • URL: http://www.mgma.com/about/default.aspx?id=242 • Formerly American College of Medical Group Administrators.

*American College of Occupational and Environmental Medicine-Membership Directory*. 25 Northwest Point Blvd., Ste. 700 Elk Grove Village, IL 60007-1030. Phone: (847)818-1800; Fax: (847)818-9266; Email: acoeminfo@acoem.org • Annual. $195.00. Lists 6,500 medical directories and plant physicians specializing in occupational medicine and surgery; coverage includes Canada and other foreign countries. Geographically arranged.

**American College of Radiology**. 1891 Preston White Dr. Reston, VA 20191. Phone: (703)648-8900; Email: info@acr.org • URL: http://www.acr.org • A professional society of physicians. Affiliated with International Society of Radiology.

**American College of Trial Lawyers**. 19900 MacArthur Blvd., Ste. 530 Irvine, CA 92612. Phone: (949)752-1801; Fax: (949)752-1674; Email: nationaloffice@actl.com • URL: http://www.actl.com • Maintains and improves the standards of trial practice, the administration of justice and the ethics of the profession. Brings together members of the profession who are qualified and who, by reason of probity and ability, will contribute to the accomplishments and good fellowship of the College.

**American College of Trust and Estate Counsel**. 901 15th St. NW, Ste. 525 Washington, DC 20005-2348. Phone: (202)684-8460; Fax: (202)684-8459; Email: info@actec.org • URL: http://www.actec.org • Represents attorneys specializing in probate law. Sends delegates to American Bar Association's Real Property, Probate, and Trust Law Section; maintains liaison with other organizations involved in probate law. Operates ACTEC Foundation, which makes available grants.

***American Companies: A Guide to Sources of Information***. CBD Research Ltd., PO Box 524 Beckenham BR3 5JS, United Kingdom. Phone: 44 20 86507745; Fax: 44 20 86500768; Email: cbd@cbdresearch.com • URL: http://www.cbdresearch.com • Biennial. £78 Individuals. Covers: Business information sources from over 50 countries in North, South, and Central America and the Caribbean. Entries include: For companies—company name, address, phone, fax, telex, year established, description, countries of specialization, branch offices, and languages spoken; for publications—title, publisher, address, telephone, fax, telex, year first published, frequency; latest edition, price, page count, description, company information, types of indexes, languages, and formats available.

***American Companies Directory***. NIIR Project Consultancy Services, 106 - E, Kamla Nagar New Delhi 110007, India. Phone: 91 11 23843955; Fax: 91 11 23841561; Email: npcs.india@gmail.com • URL: http://www.niir.org • Rs 3,371 Individuals CD-ROM; $200 Individuals CD-ROM. Covers: 1.5 million American companies. Entries include: Company name, email, phone, fax, email, websites and SIC code.

***American Companies' Hong Kong Agents and Distributors***. American Chamber of Commerce in Hong Kong, 1904 Bank of America Tower, 12 Harcourt Rd. Hong Kong, China. Phone: 86 852 25306900; Fax: 86 852 28101289; Email: amcham@amcham.org.hk • URL: http://www.amcham.org.hk • $500 Nonmembers; $350 Members; $65 Nonmembers; $45 Members. Covers: Over 1,000 U.S. companies represented by 120 agents and distributors from Hong Kong.

***American Companies in Brazil***. U.S. Chamber of Commerce, 1615 H St. NW Washington, DC 20062-2000. Phone: 800-638-6582 or (202)463-5500 or (202)659-6000; Fax: (202)463-3129; Email: foundation@uschamber.com • URL: http://www.uschambersmallbusinessnation.com • $75 plus $4.00 shipping. Covers: U.S. subsidiary and affiliate companies in Brazil. Entries include: Company name, address, phone.

**American Concrete Institute**. 38800 Country Club Dr. Farmington Hills, MI 48331-3439. Phone: (248)848-3700; Fax: (248)848-3701; Email: ann.daugherty@acifoundation.org • URL: http://www.concrete.org • Technical and educational society of engineers, architects, contractors, educators, and others interested in improving techniques of design construction and maintenance of concrete products and structures. Offers certification program.

**American Concrete Pavement Association**. 500 New Jersey Ave. NW, 7th Fl. Washington, DC 20001. Phone: (202)638-2272; Fax: (202)638-2688; Email: acpa@pavement.com • URL: http://www.pavement.com • Contractors, cement companies, equipment manufacturers, material service suppliers, ready mixed concrete producers, consultants, trucking companies/material haulers and others allied with the concrete pavement industry. Advocates the use of concrete pavement for highways, airports, streets, and roads.

**American Conference of Governmental Industrial Hygienists**. 1330 Kemper Meadow Dr. Cincinnati, OH 45240-4147. Phone: (513)742-2020 or (513)742-6163; Fax: (513)742-3355; Email: mail@acgih.org • URL: http://www.acgih.org • Members are government employees. Formerly National Conference of Governmental Industrial Hygients.

**American Consulting Engineers Council**. 1015 15th St. NW, 8th Fl. Washington, DC 20005-2605. Phone: (202)347-7474; Fax: (202)898-0068; Email: acec@acec.org • URL: http://www.acec.org • Represents consulting engineering firms engaged in private practice. Conducts programs concerned with public relations, business practices, governmental affairs, international practice and professional liability. Compiles statistics on office practices, insurance, employment, insurance clients served and services provided. Holds professional development seminars. Conducts educational programs; maintains speakers' bureau.

**American Council on Education**. 1 Dupont Cir. NW Washington, DC 20036. Phone: (202)939-9300 or (202)939-9420; Email: membership@ace.nche.edu • URL: http://www.acenet.edu • A council of colleges and universities, educational organizations, and affiliates. Represents accredited, degree-granting postsecondary institutions directly or through national and regional higher education associations; advocates on their behalf before congress, the federal government, and federal and state courts. Advances education and educational methods through comprehensive voluntary action on the part of American educational associations, organizations, and institutions. Serves as an advocate for adult education and nationally administers the GED high school equivalency exam. Provides college credit equivalency evaluations for courses taught outside the traditional campus classroom by corporations and the military. Maintains numerous commissions, committees, and councils.

**American Council for Capital Formation Center for Policy Research**. 1750 K St. NW, Ste. 400 Washington, DC 20006-2302. Phone: (202)293-5811; Fax: (202)785-8165; Email: info@accf.org • URL: http://www.accf.org/center.php • Economic growth through sound tax, regulatory, and environmental policies, including Individual Retirement Accounts, personal savings, corporate income taxes, consumption taxes, capital gains taxes, estate taxes, international competitiveness, climate policy, investment and economic growth.

**American Council for Capital Formation**. 1001 Connecticut Ave. NW, Ste. 620 Washington, DC 20036. Phone: (202)293-5811; Fax: (202)785-8165; Email: info@accf.org • URL: http://accf.org • Supports capital formation as a general concept. Formerly American Council on Capitol Gain and Estate Taxation.

**American Council of Life Insurers**. 101 Constitution Ave. NW, Ste. 700 Washington, DC 20001-2133. Phone: 877-674-4659 or (202)624-2000 or (202)624-2424; Email: webadmin@acli.com • URL: http://www.acli.com • Represents the interests of legal reserve life insurance companies in legislative, regulatory and judicial matters at the federal, state and municipal levels of government and at the NAIC. Member companies hold majority of the life insurance in force in the United States.

**American Council of State Savings Supervisors**. 1129 20th St. NW, 9th Fl. Washington, DC 20036. Phone: (202)728-5757 or (703)669-5440; Fax: (703)669-5441 • URL: http://www.acsss.org • Members are state savings and loan supervisors. Includes a Joint Committee on Examinations and Education.

**American Council on Consumer Awareness, Inc.** 1251 Kent St. St. Paul, MN 55117-4263. Phone: (651)489-2835; Fax: (651)489-5650; Email: bennerassociates@aol.com.

**American Council on Consumer Interests**. PO Box 2528 Tarpon Springs, FL 34688-2528. Phone: (727)493-2131 • URL: http://www.consumerinterests.org • Formerly Council on Consumer Information.

**American Counseling Association**. 5999 Stevenson Ave. Alexandria, VA 22304. Phone: 800-347-6647; Fax: (703)823-0252; Email: membership@counseling.org • URL: http://www.counseling.org • Counseling professionals in elementary and secondary schools, higher education, community agencies and organizations, rehabilitation programs, government, industry, business, private practice, career counseling, and mental health counseling. Conducts professional development institutes and provides liability insurance. Maintains Counseling and Human Development Foundation to fund counseling projects.

***American Craft—News Section***. American Craft Council, 1224 Marshall St. NE, Ste. 200 Minneapolis, MN 55413-1089. Phone: 800-836-3470 or (612)206-3100 or (612)206-3118; Fax: (612)355-2330; Email: council@craftcouncil.org • URL: http://www.craftcouncil.org • Bimonthly. $5 per issue; $40 per year. Publication includes: List of exhibitions, sales, workshops, seminars, conferences, and competitions for contemporary American craftspersons. Entries include: Event name, dates, location; name of gallery, museum, or sponsoring organization. For shows and sales—Whether juried, deadline for applications, fees, contact name and address, media accepted. For workshops, courses, conferences, etc.—Contact name and address, guest artist presiding, dates of events.

**American Culinary Federation**. 180 Center Place Way Saint Augustine, FL 32095. Phone: 800-624-9458; Fax: (904)825-4758; Email: acf@acfchefs.net • URL: http://www.acfchefs.org • Aims to promote the culinary profession and provide ongoing educational training and networking for members. Provides opportunities for competition, professional recognition, and access to educational forums with other culinary experts at local, regional, national, and international events. Operates the National Apprenticeship Program for Cooks and pastry cooks. Offers programs that address certification of the individual chef's skills, accreditation of culinary programs, apprenticeship of cooks and pastry cooks, professional development, and the fight against childhood hunger.

***American Demographics: Consumer Trends for Business Leaders***. Media Central, 470 Park Ave., S, 8th Fl. New York, NY 10016. Phone: 800-529-7502; Email: adedit@inside.com • URL: http://www.demographics.com • Monthly. $58.00 per year.

***American Dental Association Journal***. American Dental Association, 211 E Chicago Ave. Chicago, IL 60611-2678. Phone: 800-947-4746 or (312)440-2500; Fax: (312)440-3542; Email: berryj@ada.org • URL: http://www.ada.org • Monthly. Free to members; non-members, $173.00 per year; institutions, $205.00 per year.

**American Dental Association**. 211 E Chicago Ave. Chicago, IL 60611-2678. Phone: 800-947-4746 or (312)440-2500; Fax: (312)440-3542; Email: berryj@ada.org • URL: http://www.ada.org • Professional society of dentists. Encourages the improvement of the health of the public and promotes the art and science of dentistry in matters of legislation and regulations. Inspects and accredits dental schools and schools for dental hygienists, assistants, and laboratory technicians. Conducts research programs at ADA Foundation Research Institute. Produces dental health education material used in the U.S. Sponsors National Children's Dental Health Month and Give Kids a Smile Day. Compiles statistics on personnel, practice, and dental care needs and attitudes of patients with regard to dental health.

**American Design Drafting Association**. 105 E Main St. Newbern, TN 38059. Phone: (731)627-0802; Fax: (731)627-9321; Email: corporate@adda.org • URL: http://www.adda.org • Designers, drafters, drafting managers, chief drafters, supervisors, administrators, instructors, and students of design and drafting. Encourages a continued program of education for self-improvement and professionalism in design and drafting and computer-aided design/drafting. Informs members of effective techniques and materials used in drawings and other graphic presentations. Evaluates curriculum of educational institutions through certification program; sponsors drafter certification program.

**American Disabled for Attendant Program Today**. 1208 S Logan St. Denver, CO 80210. Phone: (303)733-9324 or (512)442-0252; Fax: (303)733-6211; Email: adapt@adapt.org • URL: http://www.adapt.org • Members are disabled individuals promoting wheelchair accessibility in all forms of public transportation.

***American Doctoral Dissertations***. Association of Research Libraries. ProQuest L.L.C., 789 E Eisenhower Pkwy. Ann Arbor, MI 48106-1346. Phone: 800-521-0600 or (734)761-4700; Fax: (734)662-4554; Email: info@proquest.com • URL: http://www.proquest.com • Annual. Price on application.

**American Driver and Traffic Safety Education Association**. Highway Safety Services, LLC, 1434 Trim Tree Rd. Indiana, PA 15701. Phone: 877-485-7172 or (724)801-8246; Fax: (724)349-5042; Email: office@adtsea.org • URL: http://www.adtsea.org • Professional organization of teachers and supervisors interested in improving driver and traffic safety education in colleges and secondary and elementary schools. Awards honorary memberships to retired persons distinguished in the field. Provides assistance to state departments of education, colleges and universities, state associations, and local school districts.

***American Drug Index***. Wolters Kluwer Health, 77 Westport Plz., Ste. 450 Saint Louis, MO 63146-3125. Phone: 800-223-0554 or (314)392-0000; Email: service@fandc.com • URL: http://www.factsandcomparisons.com • Annual. $99.95 Individuals. Lists over 20,000 drug entries in dictionary style.

***American Drycleaner***. Crain Communications Inc., 150 N Michigan Ave. Chicago, IL 60601-7553. Phone: 800-678-9595 or (312)649-5200 or (312)649-5411; Fax: (312)280-3150 or (312)280-3174; Email: info@crain.com • URL: http://www.crain.com • Monthly. Free.

**American Economic Association**. 2014 Broadway, Ste. 305 Nashville, TN 37203. Phone: (615)322-2595; Fax: (615)343-7590; Email: aeainfo@vanderbilt.edu • URL: http://www.aeaweb.org • Educators, business executives, government administrators, journalists, lawyers, and others interested in economics and its application to present-day problems. Encourages historical and statistical research into actual conditions of industrial life and provides a nonpartisan forum for economic discussion.

***American Economic Review***. American Economic Association, 2014 Broadway, Ste. 305 Nashville, TN 37203. Phone: (615)322-2595; Fax: (615)343-7590; Email: aeainfo@vanderbilt.edu • URL: http://www.aeaweb.org • Monthly. $455 Individuals print subscription to seven journals; $560 Individuals non-US, print subscription to seven journals; $910 Individuals print and online access to seven journals; $1,015 Individuals non-US, print and online access to seven journals; $735 Individuals online access to seven journals (US & non-US); $195 Institutions. Includes *Journal of Economic Literature* and *Journal of Economic Persepective*.

***American Editor***. American Society of News Editors, Missouri School of Journalism, 209 Reynolds Journalism Inst. Columbia, MO 65211. Phone: (573)884-2405 or (703)453-1133 • URL: http://www.asne.org • Nine times a year. $29.00 per year. Formerly *American Society of Newspaper Editors Bulletin*.

**American Egg Board**. 1460 Renaissance Dr., Ste. 301 Park Ridge, IL 60068. Phone: (847)296-7043; Fax: (847)296-7007; Email: aeb@aeb.org • URL: http://www.aeb.org • Board of American egg producers appointed by the Secretary of Agriculture. Offers advertising, educational, research, and promotional programs designed to increase consumption of eggs and egg products. Conducts consumer educators and food-service seminars, and food safety education programs.

***American Entomologist***. Entomological Society of America, 3

Park Pl., Ste. 307 Annapolis, MD 21401-3722. Phone: (301)731-4535 or (301)731-4541; Fax: (301)731-4538; Email: esa@entsoc.org • URL: http://www.entsoc.org • Quarterly. $122 Institutions agent; print; $181 Institutions print + online; $62 /year for nonmembers. A quarterly magazine publishing articles and information of general interest to entomologists. Formerly *Entomological Society of America Bulletin*.

**American Escrow Association**. 211 N Union St., Ste. 100 Alexandria, VA 22314. Phone: (703)519-1240; Email: hq@a-e-a.org • URL: http://www.a-e-a.org • Furthers the education and professionalism of the escrow industry. Enhances the education of escrow/settlement professionals. Increases the public knowledge and understanding of escrow and closing services. Coordinates legislative efforts throughout the United States.

**American Fair Credit Council**. 100 W Cypress Creek Rd., Ste. 700 Fort Lauderdale, FL 33309. Phone: 888-657-8272; Fax: (954)343-6960; Email: info@americanfaircreditcouncil.org • URL: http://www.americanfaircreditcouncil.org • Promotes good practice in the debt settlement industry. Protects the interests of consumer debtors. Advances the application of consumer protection, principals in marketing, sales, and fulfillment of debt settlement services.

**American Farm Bureau Federation**. 600 Maryland Ave. SW, Ste. 1000W Washington, DC 20024-2555. Phone: (202)406-3600 or (202)406-3614; Fax: (202)406-3602 or (202)406-3604; Email: fbnews@fb.org • URL: http://www.fb.org • Federation of 50 state farm bureaus and Puerto Rico, with membership on a family basis. Analyzes problems of members and formulates action to achieve educational improvement, economic opportunity, and social advancement. Maintains speakers' bureau; sponsors specialized education program.

**American Federation of Government Employees**. 80 F St. NW Washington, DC 20001. Phone: (202)737-8700 or (202)639-6435; Fax: (202)639-6490 or (202)639-6441; Email: comments@afge.org • URL: http://www.afge.org • Affiliated with AFL-CIO.

**American Federation of Mineralogical Societies**. PO Box 302 Glyndon, MD 21071-0302. Phone: (410)833-7926; Email: central_office@amfed.org • URL: http://www.amfed.org • Aims to further the earth sciences and the education of the public regarding earth sciences.

**American Federation of State, County and Municipal Employees**. 1625 L St. NW Washington, DC 20036-5687. Phone: (202)429-1000; Fax: (202)429-1293; Email: recruiting@afscme.org • URL: http://www.afscme.org • Represents service and health care workers in the public and private sectors. Organizes for social and economic justice in the workplace and through political action and legislative advocacy.

**American Feed Industry Association**. 2101 Wilson Blvd., Ste. 916 Arlington, VA 22201. Phone: (703)524-0810; Fax: (703)524-1921; Email: afia@afia.org • URL: http://www.afia.org/afia/home.aspx • Manufacturers of formula feed and pet food; suppliers to feed manufacturers; other trade related associations. Maintains Equipment Manufacturing Council.

**American Fiber Manufacturers Association**. 1530 Wilson Blvd., Ste. 690 Arlington, VA 22209-2418. Phone: (703)875-0432; Fax: (703)875-0907 • URL: http://www.fibersource.com/afma/afma.htm • Producers of manufactured fibers used in apparel, household goods, industrial materials, and other types of products. Represents the industry in educational, governmental, and foreign trade matters. Distributes a video depicting production and end uses of manufactured fibers.

**American Finance Association**. University of California, Haas School of Business Berkeley, CA 94720-1900. Phone: 800-835-6770 or (781)388-8599; Fax: (781)388-8232; Email: pyle@haas.berkeley.edu • URL: http://www.afajof.org • College and university professors of economics and finance, bankers, treasurers, analysts, financiers and others interested in financial problems; libraries and other institutions. Seeks to improve public understanding of financial problems and to provide for exchange of analytical ideas. Areas of special interest include: corporate finance, investments, banking and international and public finance.

**American Financial Services Association**. 919 18th St. NW, Ste. 300 Washington, DC 20006. Email: info@afsamail.org • URL: http://www.afsaonline.org • Represents companies whose business is primarily direct credit lending to consumers and/or the purchase of sales finance paper on consumer goods. Has members that have insurance and retail subsidiaries; some are themselves subsidiaries of highly diversified parent corporations. Encourages the business of financing individuals and families for necessary and useful purposes at reasonable charges, including interest; promotes consumer understanding of basic money management principles as well as constructive uses of consumer credit. Includes educational services such as films, textbooks and study units for the classroom and budgeting guides for individuals and families. Compiles statistical reports; offers seminars.

***American Firearms Industry***. National Association of Federally Licensed Firearms Dealers. AFI Communications Group, Inc., 1525 S. Andrew Ave., Ste. 214 Fort Lauderdale, FL 33316. Phone: (954)467-9994; Fax: (954)463-2501 • URL: http://www.amfire.com • Monthly. $35.00 per year.

**American Fisheries Society**. 5410 Grosvenor Ln. Bethesda, MD 20814. Phone: (301)897-8616; Fax: (301)897-8096; Email: main@fisheries.org • URL: http://fisheries.org • International scientific organization of fisheries and aquatic science professionals, including fish culturists, fish biologists, water quality scientists, fish health professionals, fish technologists, educators, limnologists, and oceanographers. Promotes the development of all branches of fishery science and practice, and the conservation, development, and wise utilization of fisheries, both recreational and commercial. Strengthens professional standards by certifying fisheries scientists, stressing professional ethics, and providing forums for the exchange of scientific and management information. Represents members through written and verbal testimony before legislative and administrative bodies concerning aquatic environmental issues. Maintains over 30 committees.

**American Foreign Service Association**. 2101 E St. NW Washington, DC 20037. Phone: 800-704-AFSA or (202)338-4045; Fax: (202)338-6820; Email: afsa@afsa.org • URL: http://www.afsa.org • Associate membership is open to individuals and international organizations and corporations interested in foreign affairs, international trade, and economic policy. Conducts international conferences and symposia; holds monthly speaker programs. Operates the Foreign Service Club; sponsors member insurance programs. Maintains Speakers' Bureau.

**American Forensic Association**. PO Box 256 River Falls, WI 54022. Phone: 800-228-5424 or (715)425-3198; Fax: (715)425-9533; Email: amforensicassoc@aol.com • URL: http://www.americanforensics.org • High school and college directors of forensics and debate coaches. Promotes debate and other speech activities. Sponsors annual collegiate National Individual Events Tournament and National Debate Tournament; sells debate ballots; makes studies of professional standards and debate budgets. Supports research grants.

**American Forest and Paper Association**. 1101 K St., NW, Ste. 700 Washington, DC 20005. Phone: (202)463-2700; Fax: (202)463-2785; Email: info@afandpa.org • URL: http://www.afandpa.org • National trade association of the forest, pulp, paper, paperboard and wood products industry. Represents approximately 400 member companies and related trade associations that grow, harvest, and process wood and wood fiber, manufacture pulp, paper and paperboard from both virgin and recycled fiber, and produce solid wood products.

**American Foundation for AIDS Research**. 120 Wall St., 13th Fl. New York, NY 10005-3908. Phone: (212)806-1600; Fax: (212)806-1601 • URL: http://www.amfar.org • Purpose is to raise funds to support AIDS research.

**American Foundry Society**. 1695 N Penny Ln. Schaumburg, IL 60173. Phone: 800-537-4237 or (847)824-0181; Fax: (847)824-2174 or (847)824-7848; Email: jcall@afsinc.org • URL: http://www.afsinc.org • Technical, trade and management association of foundrymen, patternmakers, technologists, and educators. Sponsors foundry training courses through the Cast Metals Institute on all subjects pertaining to the castings industry; conducts educational and instructional exhibits of foundry industry; sponsors 10 regional foundry conferences and 400 local foundry technical meetings. Maintains Technical Information Center providing literature searching and document retrieval service; and Metalcasting Abstract Service involving abstracts of the latest metal casting literature. Provides environmental services and testing; conducts research programs; compiles statistics, provides marketing information.

**American Frozen Food Institute**. 2000 Corporate Ridge, Ste. 1000 McLean, VA 22102. Phone: (703)821-0770; Fax: (703)821-1350; Email: info@affi.com • URL: http://www.affi.com • Frozen food processors and allied industry companies who work for the advancement of the frozen food industry. Seeks to improve consumer understanding and acceptance of frozen foods and to increase sales of frozen products through promotional and communications programs. Sponsors retail trade study, consumer and industry education on care and handling of frozen foods. Promotes a cooperative relationship between frozen food processors, suppliers and marketing associates. Represents the frozen food industry before federal, state and local governments. Conducts research to improve the quality of frozen food products.

***American Fruit Grower***. Meister Media, 37733 Euclid Ave. Willoughby, OH 44094-5992. Phone: 800-572-7740 or (440)942-2000; Fax: (440)975-3447; Email: info@meistermedia.com • URL: http://www.meistermedia.com • Monthly. $27.47 per year.

**American Fuel and Petrochemical Manufacturers**. 1667 K St. NW, Ste. 700 Washington, DC 20006. Phone: (202)457-0480; Fax: (202)457-0486; Email: info@afpm.org • URL: http://www.afpm.org • Formerly National Petrochemical and Refiners Association.

***American Funeral Director***. Kates-Boylston Publications, Inc., 3349 Rte. 138, Bldg. D, Ste. D Wall Township, NJ 07719. Phone: 800-500-4585 or (732)730-2584; Fax: (732)730-2515; Email: asullivan@katesboylston.com • URL: http://www.kates-boylston.com • Monthly. $59.00 per year.

***American Gas: The Monthly Magazine of the American Gas Association***. American Gas Association, 400 N Capitol St. NW Washington, DC 20001. Phone: (202)824-7000; Email: ggardner@aga.org • URL: http://www.aga.org • Monthly. $59 Nonmembers U.S. & Canada; $110 Nonmembers other countries; Free full and limited members. Magazine for gas distribution and transmission industry senior and mid-level executives focusing on business, legislative, regulatory, and technical issues.

**American Gas Association**. 400 N Capitol St. NW Washington, DC 20001. Phone: (202)824-7000; Email: ggardner@aga.org • URL: http://www.aga.org • Advocates for local natural gas utility companies; provides a broad range of programs and services for member natural gas pipelines, marketers, gatherers, international gas companies and industry associates.

**American Gear Manufacturers Association**. 1001 N Fairfax St., Ste. 500 Alexandria, VA 22314-1587. Phone: (703)684-0211; Fax: (703)684-0242; Email: foundation@agma.org • URL: http://www.agma.org • Represents manufacturers of gears, geared speed changers and related equipment; manufacturers of gear cutting and checking equipment; teachers of mechanical engineering and gearing. Conducts educational and research programs; compiles statistics and financial data. Develops technical standards for domestic and international industry.

**American Gem Society**. 8881 W Sahara Ave. Las Vegas, NV 89117. Phone: 866-805-6500 or (702)255-6500; Fax: (702)255-7420; Email: rbatson@ags.org • URL: http://www.americangemsociety.org • Represents 1,600 retail and manufacturer jewelry firms in North America dedicated to proven ethics, knowledge and consumer protection. Encourages members to pursue studies in gemology; confers titles of Registered Jeweler, Registered Supplier, Certified Gemologist, and Certified Gemologist Appraiser upon those taking recognized courses and passing extensive examinations. Sponsors national promotional programs. Conducts educational programs.

**American Gem Trade Association**. 3030 LBJ Fwy., Ste. 840 Dallas, TX 75234. Phone: 800-972-1162 or (214)742-4367; Fax: (214)742-7334; Email: webmaster@agta.org • URL: http://www.agta.org • Represents suppliers of natural colored gemstones; retail jewelers and jewelry manufacturers. Promotes natural colored gemstones; encourages high ethical standards among members and within the industry. Seeks to establish closer communication within the industry; works to protect consumers from fraud and to create a greater awareness of natural colored gemstones. Conducts seminars; maintains speakers' bureau.

**American Genetic Association**. c/o Anjanette Baker, Managing Editor, 2030 SE Marine Science Dr. Newport, OR 97365-5300. Phone: (541)867-0334; Email: agajoh@oregonstate.edu • URL: http://www.theaga.org • Represents biologists, zoologists, geneticists, botanists, and others engaged in basic and applied research in genetics. Explores transmission genetics of plants and animals.

**American Hardware Manufacturers Association**. The William P. Farrell Bldg., 801 N Plaza Dr. Schaumburg, IL 60173. Phone: (847)605-1025; Fax: (847)605-1030; Email: info@ahma.org • URL: http://www.ahma.org • Represents the hardware, home improvement, lawn and garden, paint and decorating, and related industries.

**American Hardwood Export Council**. 1825 Michael Faraday Dr. Reston, VA 20190. Phone: (703)435-2900; Fax: (703)435-2537; Email: msnow@ahec.org • URL: http://www.ahec.org • Represents exporting companies and hardwood trade associations that serve the hardwood lumber industry. Promotes the export of U.S. hardwood lumber worldwide.

***American Health Care Association: Provider***. American Health Care Association, 1201 L St. NW Washington, DC 20005. Phone: (202)842-4444; Fax: (202)842-3860 • URL: http://www.ahcancal.org/Pages/Default.aspx • Monthly. $48.00 per year. Formerly *American Health Care Association Journal*.

**American Health Care Association**. 1201 L St. NW Washington, DC 20005. Phone: (202)842-4444; Fax: (202)842-3860 • URL: http://www.ahcancal.org/Pages/Default.aspx • Federation of state associations of long-term health care facilities. Promotes standards for professionals in long-term health care delivery and quality care for patients and residents in a safe environment. Focuses on issues of availability, quality, affordability, and fair payment. Operates as liaison with governmental agencies, Congress, and professional associations. Compiles statistics.

**American Highway Users Alliance**. 1101 14th St. NW, Ste. 750 Washington, DC 20005. Phone: (202)857-1200; Fax: (202)857-1220; Email: info@highways.org • URL: http://www.highways.org • Broad-based consumers group for American motorists, truckers and businesses. Employs lobbying, media, communications and grassroots advocacy, promotes public policy that devotes highway use taxes to investments in safe and uncongested national highway systems.

**American Home Business Association**. 53 W 9000 S Sandy, UT 84070. Phone: 866-396-7773 or (801)273-2350; Fax: (866)396-7773 or (801)273-2399; Email: info@homebusinessworks.com • URL: http://www.homebusinessworks.com • Offers benefits and services dedicated to supporting the needs of home business, small business and entrepreneurs. Benefits include health-auto-home insurance, legal, low long distance and 800 numbers, business line of credit, merchant accounts, tax programs, office supply and travel discounts and more. Seeks to provide members access to the best traditional benefits and timely information that is critical to conduct a successful home, small or Internet business.

**American Home Furnishings Alliance**. 1912 Eastchester Dr., Ste. 100 High Point, NC 27265. Phone: (336)884-5000; Fax: (336)884-5303 • URL: http://www.ahfa.us • Furniture manufacturers seeking to provide a unified voice for the furniture industry and to aid in the development of industry personnel. Provides: market research data; industrial relations services; costs and operating statistics; transportation information; general management and information services. Compiles statistics; develops quarterly Econometric Forecast.

**American Hospital Association**. 155 N Wacker Dr. Chicago, IL 60606. Phone: 800-424-4301 or (312)422-3000 or (312)422-2050; Fax: (312)422-4700 • URL: http://www.aha.org • Represents health care provider organizations. Seeks to advance the health of individuals and communities. Leads, represents, and serves health care provider organizations that are accountable to the community and committed to health improvement.

***American Hospital Directory***. American Hospital Directory, Inc., 4350 Brownsboro Rd., Ste. 110 Louisville, KY 40207. Fax: (502)899-7738; Email: inbox@ahd.com • URL: http://www.ahd.com • $395 Individuals single user. Database covers: Comparative data on hospitals in the U.S. Entries include: Hospital name, address, phone, fax, characteristics, financial statistics, services, accreditation status, utilization statistics, hospital web page.

***American Housing Survey for the United States in (year)***. U. S. Government Printing Office, 732 N Capitol St. NW Washington, DC 20401. Phone: 866-512-1800 or (202)512-1800 or (866)512-1800; Fax: (202)512-2104 or (202)512-2250; Email: contactcenter@gpo.gov • URL: http://www.gpo.gov • Biennial. $51.00. Issued by the U. S. Census Bureau (www.census.gov). Covers both owner-occupied and renter-occupied housing. Includes data on such factors as condition of building, type of mortgage, utility costs, and housing occupied by minorities. (Current Housing Reports, H150.).

**American Humor Studies Association**. Averett University, 316 Frith Hall Danville, VA 24541. Phone: (434)791-7242 • URL: http://americanhumorstudiesassociation.wordpress.com • Academics, general readers, and professional humorists. Encourages the study and appreciation of American humor from interdisciplinary perspectives.

**American Immigration Lawyers Association**. 1331 G St. NW, Ste. 300 Washington, DC 20005-3142. Phone: (202)216-2400 or (202)507-7600; Fax: (202)783-7853; Email: executive@aila.org • URL: http://www.aila.org • Lawyers specializing in the field of immigration and nationality law. Fosters and promotes the administration of justice with particular reference to the immigration and nationality laws of the United States.

***American Incomes: Demographics of Who Has Money***. New Strategist Publications Inc., 120 W State St., 4th Fl. Ithaca, NY 14850. Phone: 800-848-0842 or (607)273-0913; Fax: (607)277-5009; Email: demographics@newstrategist.com • URL: http://www.newstrategist.com • $138 Individuals hardcover. Publication includes: List of telephone numbers for agencies involved in economic information gathering. Principal content of publication is household income, women's and discretionary income, and wealth and poverty.

**American Indian Business Leaders**. Gallagher Business Bldg., Ste. 366 Missoula, MT 59812. Phone: 877-245-2425; Fax: (406)243-2086 • URL: http://www.aibl.org • Provides a support system for American Indian students interested in learning the skills necessary to acquire a job, design their own business, raise capital, and network with successful American Indian business people. Provides career development opportunities for members as well as opportunities to develop strong work ethics and gain professional experience.

**American Indonesian Chamber of Commerce**. 317 Madison Ave., Ste. 1619 New York, NY 10017. Phone: (212)687-4505; Fax: (212)867-5844; Email: wayne@aiccusa.org • URL: http://www.aiccusa.org • Holds briefings on new trade policies in Indonesia and offers orientation workshops to company personnel traveling in Indonesia.

**American Industrial Hygiene Association**. 3141 Fairview Park Dr., Ste. 777 Falls Church, VA 22042. Phone: (703)849-8888; Fax: (703)207-3561; Email: infonet@aiha.org • URL: http://www.aiha.org • Professional society of industrial hygienists. Promotes the study and control of environmental factors affecting the health and well-being of workers. Sponsors continuing education courses in industrial hygiene, government affairs program, and public relations. Accredits laboratories. Maintains 40 technical committees and a foundation. Operates placement service. Conducts educational and research programs.

**American Institute for CPCU**. 720 Providence Rd., Ste. 100 Malvern, PA 19355-3433. Phone: 800-644-2101 or (610)644-2100; Fax: (610)640-9576 • URL: http://www.aicpcu.org • Determines qualifications for professional certification of insurance personnel; conducts examinations and awards designation of Chartered Property Casualty Underwriter (CPCU).

**American Institute for Economic Research**. 250 Division St. Great Barrington, MA 01230-1000. Phone: 888-528-1216; Fax: (413)528-0103; Email: info@aier.org • URL: http://www.aier.org • Through research and publications, provides "information on economic and financial subjects that is useful and completely independent of special interests." Sponsors a fellowship program for graduate study of economics at the institute and in absentia.

**American Institute for Medical and Biological Engineering**. 1701 K St. NW, Ste. 510 Washington, DC 20006. Phone: (202)496-9660; Email: info@aimbe.org • URL: http://www.aimbe.org • Represents individuals with an interest in medical and biological engineering. Fosters exchange of ideas and information among members; works to establish a clear identity for the field and improve public awareness of members' activities; serves as liaison between members and government agencies. Conducts educational programs; promotes public interest in science and science education.

**American Institute of Aeronautics and Astronautics**. 1801 Alexander Bell Dr., Ste. 500 Reston, VA 20191-4344. Phone: 800-639-2422 or (703)264-7500; Fax: (703)264-7551; Email: custserv@aiaa.org • URL: http://www.aiaa.org • Represents scientists and engineers in the field of aeronautics and astronautics. Facilitates interchange of technological information through publications and technical meetings in order to foster overall technical progress in the field and increase the professional competence of members. Operates Public Policy program to provide federal decision-makers with the technical information and policy guidance needed to make effective policy on aerospace issues. Public Policy program activities include congressional testimony, position papers, section public policy activities, and workshops. Offers placement assistance; compiles statistics; offers educational programs. Provides abstracting services through its AIAA Access.

**American Institute of Architects**. 1735 New York Ave. NW Washington, DC 20006-5209. Phone: 800-AIA-3837 or (202)626-7300; Fax: (202)626-7547; Email: infocentral@aia.org • URL: http://www.aia.org • Represents architects, licensed architects, graduate architects, not yet licensed and retired architects. Fosters professionalism and accountability among members through continuing education and training. Promotes design excellence by influencing change in the industry. Sponsors educational programs with schools of architecture, graduate students, and elementary and secondary schools. Advises on professional competitions. Supplies construction documents. Established the American Architectural Foundation. Sponsors Octagon Museum; operates bookstore; stages exhibitions; compiles statistics. Provides monthly news service on design and construction. Conducts professional development programs, research programs, charitable activities, and children's services.

**American Institute of Baking**. 1213 Bakers Way Manhattan, KS 66505-3999. Phone: 800-633-5137 or (785)537-4750; Fax: (785)537-1493; Email: info@aibonline.org • URL: http://www.aibonline.org • Nutrition, including effects of ingredients, processing, and baked products on physiological responses in humans; and cereal science, particularly applied technology. Contract research projects include performance characteristics of new and improved ingredients for the baking industry and product and process development utilizing laboratory and pilot bakeries.

**American Institute of Biological Sciences**. 1444 I St. NW, Ste. 200 Washington, DC 20005. Phone: 800-992-2427 or (202)628-1500; Fax: (202)628-1509 • URL: http://www.aibs.org.

**American Institute of Building Design**. 529 14th St. NW, Ste. 750 Washington, DC 20045. Phone: 800-366-2423; Fax: (866)204-0293 • URL: http://www.aibd.org • Represents professional building designers engaged in the professional practice of designing residential and light commercial buildings. Other membership categories include draftspersons, educators, and students. Corporate members are residential and light commercial building manufacturers. Keeps members informed of techniques and principles of building design; seeks to stimulate public interest in the aesthetic and practical efficiency of building design; engages in legislative activities and lobbying; provides consumer referral service. Aids in the development of better and continuing education. Local groups meet monthly.

**American Institute of Certified Public Accountants**. 1211 Avenue of the Americas New York, NY 10036-8775. Phone: 888-777-7077 or (212)596-6200; Fax: (212)596-6213; Email: service@aicpa.org • URL: http://www.aicpa.org • Professional society of accountants certified by the states and territories. Responsibilities include establishing auditing and reporting standards; influencing the development of financial accounting standards underlying the presentation of U.S. corporate financial statements; preparing and grading the national Uniform CPA Examination for the state licensing bodies. Conducts research and continuing education programs and oversight of practice. Maintains over 100 committees including Accounting Standards, Accounting and Review Services, AICPA Effective Legislation Political Action, Auditing Standards, Taxation, Consulting Services, Professional Ethics, Quality Review, Women and Family Issues, and Information Technology.

**American Institute of Constructors**. 700 N Fairfax St., Ste. 510 Alexandria, VA 22314. Phone: (703)683-4999; Fax: (571)527-3105; Email: info@professionalconstructor.org • URL: http://www.professionalconstructor.org • Professionals engaged in construction practice, education, and research. Serves as the certifying body for the professional constructor. Promotes the study and advances the practice of construction. Facilitates the exchange of information and ideas relating to construction.

**American Institute of Graphic Arts**. 164 5th Ave. New York, NY 10010-5901. Phone: (212)807-1990; Fax: (212)807-1799 • URL: http://www.aiga.org • Graphic designers, art directors, illustrators and packaging designers. Sponsors exhibits and projects in the public interest. Sponsors traveling exhibitions. Operates gallery. Maintains library of design books and periodicals; offers slide archives.

**American Institute of Marine Underwriters**. 14 Wall St., Ste. 820 New York, NY 10005-2101. Phone: (212)233-0550; Fax: (212)227-5102; Email: aimu@aimu.org • URL: http://www.aimu.org/contactus.html • Marine insurance companies authorized to conduct business in one or more states of the U.S. Services to members includes: referral information on legislative and regulatory questions; training and educational programs; analysis of international conventions and agreements affecting the business of marine insurance; access to offices of correspondents worldwide; development of forms and clauses to meet changing maritime requirements; information-gathering assistance. Sponsors educational programs.

**American Institute of Parliamentarians**. 550M Ritchie Hwy., No. 271 Severna Park, MD 21146. Phone: 888-664-0428; Fax: (410)544-4640; Email: aip@aipparl.org • URL: http://www.aipparl.org • Parliamentarians and others interested in parliamentary procedure. Promotes the preparation and use of parliamentary literature. Conducts certification program qualifying members in two classes: Certified Parliamentarian and Certified Professional Parliamentarian. Encourages teaching of and provides speakers on parliamentary procedure in universities, colleges, and high schools. Conducts research. Sponsors practicum (four-day seminars in different parts of the country; scholarships available). Offers correspondence courses.

**American Institute of Stress**. 9112 Camp Bowie West Blvd., No. 228 Fort Worth, TX 76116. Phone: (682)239-6823; Fax: (817)394-0593; Email: info@stress.org • URL: http://www.stress.org • Explores personal and social consequences of stress. Compiles research data on occupational stress and executive stress or "burn out."

**American Insurance Alliance**. PO Box 7105 Sterling Heights, MI 48311-7105. Phone: 855-242-4321; Email: cstonehill@allianceai.org • URL: http://www.americaninsurancealliance.com.

**American Insurance Association**. 2101 L St. NW, Ste. 400 Washington, DC 20037. Phone: (202)828-7100; Fax: (202)293-1219 • URL: http://www.aiadc.org/aiapub • Represents companies providing property and casualty insurance and suretyship. Monitors and reports on economic, political, and social trends; serves as a clearinghouse for ideas, advice, and technical information. Represents members' interests before state and federal legislative and regulatory bodies; coordinates members' litigation.

**American Intellectual Property Law Association**. 241 18th St. S, Ste. 700 Arlington, VA 22202. Phone: (703)415-0780; Fax: (703)415-0786; Email: aipla@aipla.org • URL: http://www.aipla.org/Pages/default.aspx • Voluntary bar association of lawyers practicing in the fields of patents, trademarks, copyrights, and trade secrets. Aids in the operation and improvement of U.S. patent, trademark, and copyright systems, including the laws by which they are governed and rules and regulations under which federal agencies administer those laws. Sponsors moot court and legal writing competitions.

**American International Automobile Dealers Association**. 500 Montgomery St., Ste. 800 Alexandria, VA 22314. Phone: 800-462-4232; Fax: (703)519-7810; Email: membership@aiada.org • URL: http://www.aiada.org • Trade association for America's international nameplate automobile dealerships and their employees who sell and service automobiles manufactured in the U.S. and abroad. Works to preserve a free market for international automobiles in the U.S. and is dedicated to increasing public awareness of the benefits the industry provides.

***American Iron and Steel Annual Statistical Report***. American Iron and Steel Institute, 25 Massachusetts Ave. NW, Ste. 800 Washington, DC 20001. Phone: (202)452-7100 • URL: http://www.steel.org • Annual. $100 Individuals.

**American Iron and Steel Institute**. 25 Massachusetts Ave. NW, Ste. 800 Washington, DC 20001. Phone: (202)452-7100 • URL: http://www.steel.org • Represents basic manufacturers in the steel industry. Operates steel mills, blast furnaces, finishing mills, and iron ore mines. Includes products such as pig iron, steel ingots, sheets, plates, bars, shapes, strips, tin plate, nails, pipe and tubes, railroad rails, wire products, and other basic forms of ferrous metals. Conducts extensive research programs on manufacturing technology, basic materials, environmental quality control, energy, and fuels consumption. Compiles statistics.

***American Journal of Business (AJB)***. Ball State University, 2000 W University Ave. Muncie, IN 47306. Phone: 800-382-8540 or (765)289-1241; Fax: (765)285-2374; Email: askus@bsu.edu • URL: http://cms.bsu.edu • Semiannual. $25 Individuals; $40 Institutions; $45 Two years; $75 Institutions two years; $60 Individuals three years; $110 Institutions three years. Journal informing business professionals about recent research developments and their practical implications.

**American Judges Association.** 300 Newport Ave. Williamsburg, VA 23185-4147. Phone: (757)259-1841; Fax: (757)259-1520; Email: aja@ncsc.dni.us • URL: http://aja.ncsc.dni.us • Seeks to improve the administration of justice at all levels of the courts.

**American Judicature Society.** Center Building, 2014 Broadway, Ste. 100 Nashville, TN 37203. Phone: 800-626-4089 or (615)873-4675; Fax: (615)873-4671 • URL: http://www.ajs.org • Lawyers, judges, law teachers, government officials, and citizens interested in the effective administration of justice. Conducts research; presents educational programs; offers a consultation service; sponsors and organizes citizens' conferences on judicial improvement. Coordinates the work of states in judicial discipline and removal through its Center for Judicial Conduct Organizations.

**American-Kuwaiti Alliance.** 2550 M St. NW Washington, DC 20037. Phone: (202)429-4999; Email: info@americankuwaitialliance.org • URL: http://ww.american-kuwaitialliance.com • Aims to expand and deepen the political, commercial and cultural ties between the U.S. and Kuwait. Fosters the existing U.S.-Kuwaiti relations by facilitating expanded political relationships and policies. Promotes increased trade and commerce, and creates opportunities for American and Kuwaiti citizens to exchange cultural experiences.

***American Land Planning Law.*** John Taylor and Norma Williams. Thomson West, 610 Opperman Dr. Eagan, MN 55123. Phone: 800-328-9352 or (651)687-7000 • $1,058 Individuals full set; $77 Individuals per month. Examines the changing priorities in zoning and land use practices, focusing on the relationship between private activity and governmental power, and analyzing over 15,000 cases from all 50 states.

**American Land Title Association.** 1828 L St. NW, Ste. 705 Washington, DC 20036-5104. Phone: 800-787-2582 or (202)296-3671; Fax: (202)223-5843 or (800)329-2582; Email: service@alta.org • URL: http://www.alta.org • Represents the abstracters, title insurance companies, and attorneys specializing in real property law.

**American Law Institute.** 4025 Chestnut St. Philadelphia, PA 19104-3081. Phone: (215)243-1600 or (215)243-1627; Fax: (215)243-1636; Email: ali@ali.org • URL: http://www.ali.org • Judges, law teachers, and lawyers. Promotes the clarification and simplification of the law and its better adaptation to social needs by continuing work on the Restatement of the Law, model and uniform codes, and model statutes. Conducts a program of continuing legal education jointly with the American Bar Association called "ALI-ABA."

***American Law of Mining.*** Rocky Mountain Mineral Law Institute. Matthew Bender and Company Inc., 1275 Broadway Albany, NY 12204-2638. Phone: 800-424-4200 or (518)487-3000; Fax: (518)487-3573 or (800)424-4200; Email: customer.support@lexisnexis.com • URL: http://www.matthewbender.com • $768.00. Six looseleaf volumes. Periodic supplementation.

***American Law Yearbook.*** Cengage Learning Inc., 20 Channel Center St. Boston, MA 02210. Phone: 800-487-8488 or (617)289-7700; Fax: (617)289-7844; Email: investors@cengage.com • URL: http://www.cengage.com • $308 Individuals. Annual. $280.00. Serves as a yearly supplement to *West's Encyclopedia of American Lawa.* Describes new legal developments in many subject areas.

***American Leather Chemists Association—Membership Directory.*** American Leather Chemists Association, 1314 50th St., Ste. 103 Lubbock, TX 79412-2940. Phone: (806)744-1798; Fax: (806)744-1785; Email: alca@leatherchemists.org • URL: http://www.leatherchemists.org • Annual. Covers: About 500 chemists, leather technologists, and educators concerned with the tanning and leather industry. Entries include: Personal name, address; company name, address, phone, fax.

**American Leather Chemists Association.** 1314 50th St., Ste. 103 Lubbock, TX 79412-2940. Phone: (806)744-1798; Fax: (806)744-1785; Email: alca@leatherchemists.org • URL: http://www.leatherchemists.org • Chemists, leather technologists, and educators concerned with the tanning and leather industry. Works to devise and perfect methods for the analysis and testing of leathers and materials used in leather manufacture. Promotes advancement of chemistry and other sciences, especially their application to problems confronting the leather industry.

**American Legal Finance Association.** 228 Park Ave. S. No. 23315 New York, NY 10003. Phone: (212)837-2911 • URL: http://www.americanlegalfin.com • Develops an awareness of the legal funding industry. Works to establish legal and regulatory frameworks to meet the needs and concerns of all parties interested in legal funding. Establishes and maintains ethical standards and fair business practices within the legal funding industry.

**American Legion.** 700 N Pennsylvania St. Indianapolis, IN 46206. Phone: 800-504-4098 or (317)630-1200; Fax: (317)630-1223; Email: acy@legion.org • URL: http://www.legion.org • Consists of honorably discharged wartime veterans of the U.S. armed forces. Provides a unified voice for veterans in Washington, DC. Offers free assistance with Veterans Administration claims and benefits. Sponsors American Legion baseball competition, national high school oratorical contest, and children's services; cosponsors National Education Week. Maintains museum.

**American Library Association - Gay, Lesbian, Bisexual and Transgendered Roundtable.** c/o American Library Association, 50 E Huron St. Chicago, IL 60611-2795. Phone: 800-545-2433 or (312)944-6780; Fax: (312)440-9374; Email: ala@ala.org • URL: http://www.ala.org/glbtrt/glbtrt • Promotes gay, lesbian, bisexual and transgendered professionals in the library industry.

***American Library Association Guide to Information Access.*** Library and Information Technology Association, 50 E Huron St. Chicago, IL 60611-2795. Phone: 800-545-2433; Fax: (312)280-3257; Email: lita@ala.org • URL: http://www.ala.org/lita • $18.95. Publication includes: List of reference sources for areas including business and finance, consumer information, education, jobs and careers, and science and technology. Principal content of publication is a guide to general research methods.

***American Library Directory (ALD).*** Information Today, Inc., 143 Old Marlton Pke. Medford, NJ 08055-8750. Phone: 800-300-9868 or (609)654-6266; Fax: (609)654-4309; Email: custserv@infotoday.com • URL: http://www.infotoday.com • Annual. American Library Directory, 2 vol. set, 59th edition (2006): $299.95. For site-licensing, call 1-888-269-5372, ext. 6726.; $369.50 Individuals hardbound; plus $25 shipping and handling; $332.55 Individuals first time standing order. Covers: Over 36,000 U.S. and Canadian academic, public, county, provincial, and regional libraries; library systems; medical, law, and other special libraries; and libraries for the blind and physically handicapped. Separate section lists over 350 library networks and consortia and 220 accredited and unaccredited library school programs. Entries include: For libraries—Name, supporting or affiliated institution or firm name, address, phone, fax, electronic mail address, Standard Address Number (SANs), names of librarian and department heads, income, collection size, special collections, computer hardware, automated functions, and type of catalog. For library systems—Name, location. For library schools—Name, address, phone, fax, electronic mail address, director, type of training and degrees, admission requirements, tuition, faculty size. For networks and consortia—Name, address, phone, names of affiliates, name of director, function.

***American Library Directory Online.*** Information Today, Inc., 143 Old Marlton Pke. Medford, NJ 08055-8750. Phone: 800-300-9868 or (609)654-6266; Fax: (609)654-4309; Email: custserv@infotoday.com • URL: http://www.infotoday.com • Provides information on more than 30,000 public, college, and special libraries in the U.S. and Canada, with annual updates. Includes library networks, consortia, organizations, and schools. Inquire as to online cost and availability.

**American Lighting Association.** 2050 N Stemmons Fwy., Unit 100 Dallas, TX 75207-3206. Phone: 800-605-4448 or (214)698-9898; Fax: (214)698-9899; Email: skelley@americanlightingassoc.com • URL: http://www.americanlightingassoc.com • Manufacturers, manufacturers' representatives, distributors, and retailers of residential lighting fixtures, portable lamps, component parts, accessories, and bulbs. Trains and certifies lighting consultants; conducts showroom sales seminars; disseminates marketing and merchandising information. Compiles statistics.

**American-Lithuanian Business Council.** 701 8th St., NW Ste. 500 Washington, DC 20001. Phone: (202)973-5975; Fax: (202)659-5249; Email: info@amlithbc.org • URL: http://www.amlithbc.org • Executive firms having significant actual or potential trade involvement with Lithuania, including coverage of policy issues related to Russia, Ukraine, Belarus, Turkey, Iran, the Caucasus and Central Asia. Provides a forum for discussing trade and investment issues and formulation of policy issues to promote and expand economic relations between the U.S. and Lithuania.

**American Logistics Association.** 1101 Vermont Ave. NW, Ste. 1002 Washington, DC 20005. Phone: (202)466-2520; Fax: (202)296-4419 • URL: http://www.ala-national.org • Promotes, protects and ensures the continued viability of the military resale (Commissary and Exchange Benefits) and Morale, Welfare and Recreations (MWR Benefits) industries. Acts as liaison between manufacturers and the Armed Forces' purchasing agencies. Promotes cooperation between the Congress, Defense Department and the industries which it conducts business.

**American Lumber Standard Committee.** PO Box 210 Germantown, MD 20875-0210. Phone: (301)972-1700; Fax: (301)540-8004; Email: alsc@alsc.org • URL: http://www.alsc.org • Members appointed by the Department of Commerce to represent producers, consumers, and specifiers of softwood lumber. Establishes and maintains standards for size, grade, and other matters; elects an independent board of review to approve softwood lumber grading rules and accredit agencies that audit treating plants and accredit agencies that audit pallet, box and crate manufacturers for international trade.

**American Management Association.** 1601 Broadway New York, NY 10019-7420. Phone: 877-566-9441 or (212)586-8100 or (518)891-5510; Fax: (212)903-8168 or (518)891-0368; Email: customerservice@amanet.org • URL: http://www.amanet.org • Provides educational forums worldwide where members and their colleagues learn superior, practical business skills and explore best practices of world-class organizations through interaction with each other and expert faculty practitioners. Maintains a publishing program providing tools individuals use to extend learning beyond the classroom in a process of life-long professional growth and development through education.

***American Manufacturers Directory.*** InfoGroup Inc., 5711 S 86th Cir. Omaha, NE 68127-4146. Phone: (402)593-4500 • URL: http://www.infogroup.com • Annual. $295; $595 both print & CD-ROM. Covers: more than 150,000 manufacturing companies with 20 or more employees. CD-ROM version lists all 531,000 U.S. manufacturers, in all employee size ranges. Entries include: Company name, address, phone, contact name, Standard Industrial Classification (SIC) codes, number of employees, sales volume code, credit rating scores.

**American Marketing Association.** 311 S Wacker Dr., Ste. 5800 Chicago, IL 60606. Phone: 800-AMA-1150 or (312)542-9000; Fax: (312)542-9001 • URL: http://www.marketingpower.com • Serves as a professional society of marketing and market research executives, sales and promotion managers, advertising specialists, academics, and others interested in marketing. Fosters research; sponsors seminars, conferences, and student marketing clubs; provides educational placement service and doctoral consortium.

**American Meat Institute.** 1150 Connecticut Ave. NW, 12th Fl. Washington, DC 20036. Phone: (202)587-4200; Fax: (202)587-4300 • URL: http://www.meatami.com • Represents the interests of packers and processors of beef, pork, lamb, veal, and turkey products and their suppliers throughout North America. Provides legislative, regulatory, and public relations services. Conducts scientific research. Offers marketing and technical assistance. Sponsors educational programs.

**American Medical Association.** AMA Plaza, 330 N Wabash Ave. Chicago, IL 60611. Phone: 800-621-8335 or (312)464-4430; Fax: (312)464-5226; Email: amalibrary@ama-assn.org • URL: http://www.ama-assn.org • Represents county medical societies and physicians. Disseminates scientific information to members and the public. Informs members on significant medical and health legislation on state and national levels and represents the profession before Congress and governmental agencies. Cooperates in setting standards for medical schools, hospitals, residency programs, and continuing medical education courses. Offers physician placement service and counseling on practice management problems. Operates library that lends material and provides specific medical information to physicians. Maintains Ad-hoc committees for such topics as health care planning and principles of medical ethics.

**American Medical Group Association.** 1 Prince St. Alexandria, VA 22314-3318. Phone: (703)838-0033; Fax: (703)548-1890; Email: dfisher@amga.org • URL: http://www.amga.org • Represents the interests of medical groups. Advocates for the medical groups and patients through innovation and information sharing, benchmarking, developing leadership, and improving patient care. Provides political advocacy, educational and networking programs and publications, benchmarking data services, and financial and operations assistance.

**American Medical Political Action Committee.** 25 Massachusetts Ave. NW, Ste. 600 Washington, DC 20001-7400. Phone: (202)789-7400 • URL: http://www.ampaconline.org • Represents physicians, their spouses, and others interested in political action and participation in public affairs. Seeks to further political knowledge of its members and to provide them with means for concerted political action.

**American Medical Rehabilitation Providers Association.** 1710 N St. NW Washington, DC 20036. Phone: 888-346-4624 or (202)223-1920; Fax: (202)223-1925 • URL: http://www.amrpa.org • Rehabilitation facilities in the U.S. and Canada; agencies operating established medical, residential and vocational rehabilitation facilities. Promotes expansion and improvement of rehabilitation services to disabled persons as provided in rehabilitation facilities. Represents the concerns of rehabilitation providers before Congress and government agencies. Is concerned with quality operation of rehabilitation centers and facilities. Conducts research and development programs in national rehabilitation policy. Sponsors seminars and provides specialized education programs.

**American Medical Women's Association.** 12100 Sunset Hills Rd., Ste. 130 Reston, VA 20190. Phone: 866-564-2483 or (703)234-4069; Fax: (703)435-4390; Email: info@amwa-doc.org • URL: http://www.amwa-doc.org • Women holding a MD or DO degree from approved medical colleges; women interns, residents, and medical students. Promotes women's health issues in medical education and public policy. Seeks to find solutions to problems common to women studying or practicing medicine, such as career advancement and the integration of professional and family responsibilities. Provides student members with educational loans and personal counseling. Sponsors continuing medical education programs.

***American Men & Women of Science (AMWS).*** Cengage Learning Inc., 20 Channel Center St. Boston, MA 02210. Phone: 800-487-8488 or (617)289-7700; Fax: (617)289-7844; Email: investors@cengage.com • URL: http://www.cengage.com • 2013. $1508.00. 31st edition. Over 135,000 scientists active in the physical, biological, mathematical, computer science and engineering fields in the United States and Canada.

**American Mental Health Counselors Association.** 801 N Fairfax St., Ste. 304 Alexandria, VA 22314. Phone: 800-326-2642 or (703)548-6002; Fax: (703)548-4775 • URL: http://www.amhca.org • Professional counselors employed in mental health services; students. Aims to: deliver quality mental health services to children, youth, adults, families, and organizations; improve the availability and quality of counseling services through licensure and certification, training standards, and consumer advocacy. Supports specialty and special interest networks. Fosters communication among members. A division of the American Counseling Association.

**American Meteorological Society**. 45 Beacon St. Boston, MA 02108-3693. Phone: (617)227-2425 or (617)227-2426; Fax: (617)742-8718; Email: amsinfo@ametsoc.org • URL: http://www.ametsoc.org • Professional meteorologists, oceanographers, and hydrologists; interested students and nonprofessionals. Develops and disseminates information on the atmospheric and related oceanic and hydrospheric sciences; seeks to advance professional applications. Activities include guidance service, scholarship programs, career information, certification of consulting meteorologists, and a seal of approval program to recognize competence in radio and television weathercasting. Issues statements of policy to assist public understanding on subjects such as weather modification, forecasting, tornadoes, hurricanes, flash floods, and meteorological satellites. Provides abstracting services. Prepares educational films, filmstrips, and slides for a new curriculum in meteorology at the ninth grade level. Issues monthly announcements of job openings for meteorologists.

**American Military Society**. PO Box 90740 Washington, DC 20090-0740. Phone: 800-379-6128; Fax: (301)583-8717 • URL: http://www.amsmilitary.org • Active or retired members of the armed services (Army, Navy, Air Force, Marine Corps, and Coast Guard), and civilians. Develops and supports activities which promote the general well-being of the members; upholds and defends the Constitution; supports national defense; and preserves the memories and traditions of the Armed Forces.

***American Motor Carrier Directory***. UBM Global Trade, 400 Windsor Corporate Pk., 50 Millstone Rd., Ste. 200 East Windsor, NJ 08520-1415. Phone: 800-221-5488 or (609)371-7700 or (609)371-7701; Fax: (609)371-7885 or (609)371-7883; Email: customerservice@cbizmedia.com • URL: http://www.cbizmedia.com • Annual. Publication includes: Lists of all licensed Less Than Truckload (LTL) general commodity carriers in the United States; includes specialized motor carriers and related services; includes refrigerated carriers, heavy haulers, bulk haulers, riggers, and specified commodity carriers; state and federal regulatory bodies governing the trucking industry; tariff publishing bureaus; freight claim councils; industry associations, etc. Entries include: For carriers and services—Company name, address of headquarters and terminals, phones, tariffs followed, names of executives, insurance, and equipment information, services or commodities handled. Principal content of publication is listing of direct point-to-point services of LTL general commodity carriers throughout the United States and to Canada and Mexico.

**American Motorcyclist Association**. 13515 Yarmouth Dr. Pickerington, OH 43147. Phone: 800-262-5646 or (614)856-1900; Fax: (614)856-1920 • URL: http://www.americanmotorcyclist.com • Represents motorcycle enthusiasts. Acts as a rulemaking body for motorcycle competition. Promotes highway safety. Maintains museum and hall of fame.

**American Moving and Storage Association**. 1611 Duke St. Alexandria, VA 22314-3406. Phone: 888-849-2672 or (703)683-7410; Fax: (703)683-7527 or (703)548-1845; Email: amconf@amconf.org • URL: http://www.promover.org • Members are household goods movers, storage companies, and trucking firms.

**American Mushroom Institute**. 1 Massachusetts Ave. NW, Ste. 800 Washington, DC 20001. Phone: (202)842-4344; Fax: (202)408-7763; Email: ami@mwmlaw.com • URL: http://www.americanmushroom.org • Mushroom growers, processors, suppliers, and researchers united to promote the growing and marketing of cultivated mushrooms. Aims to: increase cultivated mushroom consumption; develop better and more economical methods of growing and marketing mushrooms; collect and disseminate the latest statistics and other information; foster research programs beneficial to the industry; aid members with any problems. Supports a short course on mushroom science at Penn State University and an international congress on mushroom science.

**American National Metric Council**. 1625 Massachusetts Ave. NW Washington, DC 20036. Phone: (203)232-4545; Email: anmcmetric@pi-c.com • URL: http://lamar.colostate.edu/hillger/anmc.htm • Companies, organizations, and individuals interested in keeping up-to-date on all the latest information on the status of metric transition in the U.S. Aims to coordinate metric transition planning activities for all affected segments in the private sector of American society.

**American National Standards Institute** . 1899 L St. NW, 11th Fl. Washington, DC 20036-3807. Phone: (202)293-8020; Fax: (202)293-9287; Email: info@ansi.org • URL: http://www.ansi.org • Industrial firms, trade associations, technical societies, labor organizations, consumer organizations, and government agencies. Serves as clearinghouse for nationally coordinated voluntary standards for fields ranging from information technology to building construction. Gives status as American National Standards to standards developed by agreement from all groups concerned, in such areas as: definitions, terminology, symbols, and abbreviations; materials, performance characteristics, procedure, and methods of rating; methods of testing and analysis; size, weight, volume, and rating; practice, safety, health, and building construction. Provides information on foreign standards and represents United States interests in international standardization work.

**American Nuclear Insurers**. 95 Glastonbury Blvd., Ste. 300 Glastonbury, CT 06033-4412. Phone: (860)682-1301; Fax: (860)659-0002; Email: info@nuclearinsurance.com • URL: http://www.amnucins.com • Domestic property/casualty nuclear insurance companies. Strives to ensure safe and secure insurance capacity for customers. Audits financial performance of all member companies annually, ensures compliance with guidelines.

**American Nuclear Society**. 555 N Kensington Ave. La Grange Park, IL 60526. Phone: 800-323-3044 or (708)352-6611; Fax: (708)352-0499; Email: nuclear@ans.org • URL: http://www.ans.org • Physicists, chemists, educators, mathematicians, life scientists, engineers, metallurgists, managers, and administrators with professional experience in nuclear science or nuclear engineering. Works to advance science and engineering in the nuclear industry. Disseminates information; promotes research; conducts meetings devoted to scientific and technical papers; works with government agencies, educational institutions, and other organizations dealing with nuclear issues.

**American Numismatic Association**. 818 N Cascade Ave. Colorado Springs, CO 80903-3208. Phone: 800-367-9723 or (719)632-2646 or (719)482-9821; Fax: (719)634-4085; Email: ana@money.org • URL: http://www.money.org • Collectors of coins, medals, tokens, and paper money. Promotes the study, research, and publication of articles on coins, coinage, and history of money. Sponsors correspondence courses; conducts research. Maintains museum, archive, authentication service for coins, and hall of fame. Sponsors National Coin Week; operates speakers' bureau.

**American Numismatic Society**. 75 Varick St., 11th Fl. New York, NY 10013. Phone: (212)571-4470; Fax: (212)571-4479; Email: meadows@numismatics.org • URL: http://www.numismatics.org • Collectors and others interested in coins, medals, and related materials. Advances numismatic knowledge as it relates to history, art, archaeology, and economics by collecting coins, medals, tokens, decorations, and paper money. Maintains only museum devoted entirely to numismatics. Presents annual Graduate Fellowship in Numismatics. Sponsors Graduate Seminar in Numismatics, a nine-week individual study program for ten students.

**American Nurses Credentialing Center**. 8515 Georgia Ave., Ste. 400 Silver Spring, MD 20910-3492. Phone: 800-284-2378 • URL: http://www.nursecredentialing.org • Empowers nurses within their professional sphere of activity and contributes to better patient outcome. Provides Board Certification in the following nursing specialties: Acute Care Nurse Practitioner, Adult Health Clinical Nurse Specialist (formerly Med-Surg), Adult Nurse Practitioner, Adult Psychiatric and Mental Health Clinical Nurse Specialist, Adult Psychiatric and Mental Health Nurse Practitioner, Ambulatory Care Nurse, Cardiac Vascular Nurse, Nursing Case Management, Child/Adolescent Psychiatric and Mental Health Clinical Nurse Specialist, Diabetes Management, Family Nurse Practitioner, Family Psychiatric and Mental Health Nurse Practitioner, Gerontological Clinical Nurse Specialist, Gerontological Nursing, Gerontological Nurse Practitioner, Informatics Nurse, Medical-Surgical Nurse, Nurse Executive, Nursing Professional Development, Pain Management, Pediatric Clinical Nurse Specialist, Pediatric Nurse, Pediatric Nurse Practitioner, Psychiatric and Mental Health Nurse, Advanced Public/Community Health Nurse.

**American Occupational Therapy Association**. 4720 Montgomery Ln., Ste. 200 Bethesda, MD 20814-3449. Phone: 800-SAY-AOTA or (301)652-6611; Fax: (301)652-7711; Email: members@aota.org • URL: http://www.aota.org • Occupational therapists and occupational therapy assistants. Provides services to people whose lives have been disrupted by physical injury or illness, developmental problems, the aging process, or social or psychological difficulties. Occupational therapy focuses on the active involvement of the patient in specially designed therapeutic tasks and activities to improve function, performance capacity, and the ability to cope with demands of daily living.

**American Oil Chemists' Society**. 2710 S Boulder Urbana, IL 61803-7190. Phone: (217)359-2344; Fax: (217)351-8091; Email: general@aocs.org • URL: http://www.aocs.org • Chemists, biochemists, chemical engineers, research directors, plant personnel, and others in laboratories and chemical process industries concerned with animal, marine, and vegetable oils and fats, and their extraction, refining, safety, packaging, quality control, and use in consumer and industrial products such as foods, drugs, paints, waxes, lubricants, soaps, and cosmetics. Sponsors short courses; certifies referee chemists; distributes cooperative check samples; sells official reagents. Maintains 100 committees. Operates job placement service for members only.

**American Optometric Association - Contact Lens and Cornea Section**. 243 N Lindbergh Blvd., 1st Fl. Saint Louis, MO 63141-7881. Phone: 800-365-2219; Fax: (314)991-4101; Email: clcs@aoa.org • URL: http://www.aoa.org • Members are optometrists, students of optometry and paraoptometric assistants and technicians. Formerly American Optical Association.

**American Optometric Association**. 243 N Lindbergh Blvd., Fl. 1 Saint Louis, MO 63141-7881. Phone: 800-365-2219 or (314)991-4100; Fax: (314)991-4101; Email: ilamo@aoa.org • URL: http://www.aoa.org • Professional association of optometrists, students of optometry, and paraoptometric assistants and technicians. Purposes are: to improve the quality, availability, and accessibility of eye and vision care; to represent the optometric profession; to help members conduct their practices; to promote the highest standards of patient care. Monitors and promotes legislation concerning the scope of optometric practice, alternate health care delivery systems, health care cost containment, Medicare, and other issues relevant to eye/vision care. Supports the International Library, Archives and Museum of Optometry which includes references on ophthalmic and related sciences with emphasis on the history and socioeconomic aspects of optometry. Operates Vision U.S.A. program, which provides free eye care to the working poor, and the InfantSEE program, which provides free vision assessments for infants between six and twelve months of age. Conducts specialized education programs; operates placement service; compiles statistics. Maintains museum. Conducts Seal of Acceptance Program.

**American Orthotic and Prosthetic Association**. 330 John Carlyle St., Ste. 200 Alexandria, VA 22314. Phone: (571)431-0876; Fax: (571)431-0899; Email: info@aopanet.org • URL: http://www.aopanet.org • Represents more than 1,400 member companies that custom fit or manufacture componentry for patients with prostheses (artificial limbs) and orthoses (braces).

**American Payroll Association**. 660 N Main Ave., Ste. 100 San Antonio, TX 78205-1217. Phone: (210)226-4600 or (210)224-6406; Fax: (210)226-4027 or (210)224-6038; Email: APA@americanpayroll.org • URL: http://www.americanpayroll.org • Payroll employees. Works to increase members' skills and professionalism through education and mutual support. Represents the interest of members before legislative bodies. Conducts training courses. Operates speakers' bureau; conducts educational programs. Administers the certified payroll professional program of recognition.

***American Peanut Council—Membership Directory: Peanut Industry Directory***. American Peanut Council, 1500 King St., Ste. 301 Alexandria, VA 22314-2737. Phone: (703)838-9500; Email: info@peanutsusa.com • URL: http://www.peanutsusa.com • Annual. Covers: About 250 growers, shellers, processors, manufacturers, brokers, and allied businesses providing goods and services to the peanut industry. Entries include: Company name, address, phone, fax, telex, e-mail, names of principal executives, subsidiary and branch names and locations, products.

**American Peanut Council**. 1500 King St., Ste. 301 Alexandria, VA 22314-2737. Phone: (703)838-9500; Email: info@peanutsusa.com • URL: http://www.peanutsusa.com • Growers, shellers, brokers, processors, and manufacturers; allied businesses providing goods and services to the peanut industry. Encourages research to improve quality of peanuts.

**American Peanut Research and Education Society**. PO Box 15825 College Station, TX 77841. Phone: (979)845-8278 or (229)329-2949 • URL: http://www.apresinc.com • Federal, state, and private company employees involved in the peanut industry. Works to improve the welfare of all segments of the peanut industry. Provides for exchange of information, cooperative planning, and review of all phases of peanut research and extension being carried on by government agencies and private industry.

**American Pet Products Association**. 255 Glenville Rd. Greenwich, CT 06831. Phone: 800-452-1225 or (203)532-0000; Fax: (203)532-0551 • URL: http://www.americanpetproducts.org • U.S. Manufacturers and importers of pet products. Provides public relations program to promote pet ownership and pet care. Sponsors the association's annual National Pet Products Trade Show; publishes the National Pet Owner's Survey, the association's research study in the pet industry.

**American Petroleum Institute**. 1220 L St. NW Washington, DC 20005-4070. Phone: (202)682-8000 • URL: http://www.api.org • Corporations in the petroleum and allied industries, including producers, refiners, marketers, and transporters of crude oil, lubricating oil, gasoline and natural gas. Provides public policy development, advocacy, research, and technical services to enhance the ability of the petroleum industry to fulfill its mission: meeting the nation's energy needs; enhancing the environmental, health, and safety performance of the industry; conducting research to advance petroleum technology, equipment, and standards; Consensus policies and collective action on issues impacting its members; and works collaboratively with all industry oil and gas associations, and other organizations, to enhance industry unity and effectiveness in its advocacy. Also provides the opportunity for standards development, technical cooperation and other activities to improve the industry's competitiveness through sponsorship of self-supporting programs.

**American Philatelic Society**. 100 Match Factory Pl. Bellefonte, PA 16823. Phone: (814)933-3803; Fax: (814)933-6128; Email: webmaster@stamps.org • URL: http://www.stamps.

org • Collectors of postage and revenue stamps, first day covers, postal history, and related philatelic items. Helps members buy and sell stamps; operates expertise service; offers stamp insurance program; circulates slide programs. Maintains hall of fame; offers correspondence courses; accredits judges for philatelic competitions. Conducts philatelic seminars.

**American Planning Association**. 205 N Michigan Ave., Ste. 1200 Chicago, IL 60601. Phone: (312)431-9100; Fax: (312)786-6700; Email: customerservice@planning.org • URL: http://www.planning.org • Public and private planning agency officials, professional planners, planning educators, elected and appointed officials, and other persons involved in urban and rural development. Works to foster the best techniques and decisions for the planned development of communities and regions. Provides extensive professional services and publications to professionals and laypeople in planning and related fields; serves as a clearinghouse for information. Through Planning Advisory Service, a research and inquiry-answering service, provides, on an annual subscription basis, advice on specific inquiries and a series of research reports on planning, zoning, and environmental regulations. Supplies information on job openings and makes definitive studies on salaries and recruitment of professional planners. Conducts research; collaborates in joint projects with local, national, and international organizations.

*American Pomological Society Journal*. American Pomological Society, 102 Tysons Bldg. University Park, PA 16802. Phone: (814)863-6163; Fax: (814)863-6139; Email: aps@psu.edu • URL: http://americanpomological.org • Quarterly. $30 Individuals. Presents reports and general information on fruit varieties.

**American Poultry Association**. PO Box 306 Burgettstown, PA 15021-0306. Phone: (724)729-3459; Email: secretaryapa@comcast.net • URL: http://www.amerpoultryassn.com • Poultry industry. Strives to protect and promote the standard-bred poultry industry in all of its phases.

**American Professional Practice Association**. Association Member Service Center, Hillsboro Executive Center N, 550 Fairway Dr., Ste. 107 Deerfield Beach, FL 33441-1834. Phone: 800-221-2168; Fax: (954)571-8582; Email: membership@assnservices.com • URL: http://www.appa-assn.com • Provides physicians with economic benefits and financial services including the following: unsecured loan plans, mortgage loans, group insurance discounts, accounts receivable collections, office supplies, wealth protection and a vision and dental plan.

**American Public Gas Association**. 201 Massachusetts Ave. NE, Ste. C-4 Washington, DC 20002. Phone: 800-927-4204 or (202)464-2742; Fax: (202)464-0246 • URL: http://www.apga.org/ • Publicly owned gas systems; private corporations, persons or firms dealing with public gas systems are associate members. Promotes efficiency among public gas systems and protects the interests of the gas consumer. Provides information service on federal developments affecting natural gas; surveys municipal systems.

**American Public Human Services Association**. 1133 19th St. NW, Ste. 400 Washington, DC 20036. Phone: (202)682-0100; Fax: (202)289-6555; Email: pubs@aphsa.org • URL: http://www.aphsa.org • Public human service agencies, their professional staff members, and others interested in public human services. Works to develop, promote and implement human service policies that improve the health and well-being of families, children and adults.

**American Public Power Association**. 1875 Connecticut Ave. NW, Ste. 1200 Washington, DC 20009-5715. Phone: 800-515-2772 or (202)467-2900; Fax: (202)467-2910; Email: info@publicpower.org • URL: http://www.publicpower.org • Municipally owned electric utilities, public utility districts, state and county-owned electric systems, and rural cooperatives. Conducts research programs; compiles statistics; offers utility education courses; sponsors competitions.

**American Public Transportation Association**. 1666 K St. NW, Ste. 1100 Washington, DC 20006. Phone: (202)496-4800; Fax: (202)496-4324; Email: info@apta.com • URL: http://www.apta.com • Motor bus and rapid transit systems; organizations responsible for planning, designing, constructing, financing and operating transit systems; business organizations which supply products and services to transit, academic institutions and state associations and departments of transportation. Represents the public interest in improving transit. Encourages cooperation among its members, their employees, the general public and compliance with the letter and spirit of equal opportunity principles. Seeks to: collect information relative to public transit; assist in the training, education and professional development of all persons involved in public transit; and engage in activities which promote public transit. Provides a medium for exchange of experiences, discussion, and a comparative study of public transit affairs; Promotes research.

**American Public Works Association**. 1275 K St. NW, Ste. 750 Washington, DC 20005. Phone: 800-848-APWA or (202)408-9541; Fax: (202)408-9542; Email: apwa@apwa.net • URL: http://www.apwa.net • Chief administrators, commissioners, and directors of public works, city engineers, superintendents, and department heads of transportation, water, waste water, solid waste, equipment services, and buildings and grounds;

federal, provincial, and state administrators and engineers; consultants and educators; associate members are equipment manufacturers' representatives, utility company officials, and contractors; student members are engineering and public administration students interested in the theory and practice of the design, construction, maintenance, administration, and operation of public works facilities and services. Conducts historical research on public works subjects and demonstrates applicability of history to current public works problems and issues through Public Works Historical Society. Sponsors research and education foundations.

**American Railway Car Institute**. c/o Edward Whalen, Chairman, FreightCar America Inc., 2 N Riverside Plz., Ste. 1300 Chicago, IL 60606. Phone: (202)347-4664; Fax: (312)928-0890 • URL: http://rsiweb.org/about/rsi-committees/arci • Conducts research and standardization activities, particularly in freight car design and container standards. Provides for exchange of data on new devices used in freight cars. Compiles statistics on orders, deliveries, and backlogs of railroad cars with Association of American Railroads.

**American Railway Engineering and Maintenance of Way Association**. 10003 Derekwood Ln., Ste. 210 Lanham, MD 20706-4875. Phone: (301)459-3200; Fax: (301)459-8077 • URL: http://www.arema.org • Professional organization of railway and transit officials concerned with design, construction, and maintenance of bridges, buildings, water service facilities, communications and signals systems, and other railway structures; engineering professors, editors, and government and private timber specialists.

**American Real Estate and Urban Economics Association**. The Center for Real State Education and Research, 821 Academic Way, 223 RBB Tallahassee, FL 32306-1110. Phone: 866-273-8321 or (850)644-7898; Fax: (850)644-4077; Email: areuea@areuea.org • URL: http://www.areuea.org • Members are real estate teachers, researchers, economists, and others concerned with urban real estate and investment.

*American Reference Books Annual*. Bohdan S. Wynar, editor. Libraries Unlimited, 88 Post Rd. W Westport, CT 06881. Phone: 800-225-5800 or (203)226-3571; Fax: (203)222-1502 • Annual. $155 Individuals Hardcover. Provides librarians with insightful, critical reviews of all reference resources released in 2013 as well as some from 2012 and 2014.

**American Rehabilitation Counseling Association**. c/o Quiteya Walker, President-Elect, Albany State University, College of Education, 504 College Dr. Albany, GA 31705. Phone: (252)744-6297 or (229)430-4783; Fax: (229)430-4993 • URL: http://www.arcaweb.org • A division of the American Counseling Association. Rehabilitation counselors and interested professionals and students. Aims to improve the rehabilitation counseling profession and its services to individuals with disabilities. Promotes high standards in rehabilitation counseling, practice, research, and education. Encourages the exchange of information between rehabilitation professionals and consumer groups. Serves as liaison among members and public and private rehabilitation counselors across the country. Sponsors educational and training programs.

**American Renewal Foundation**. PO Box 930 Charlottesville, VA 22904. Email: info@americanrenewal.org • URL: http://www.americanrenewal.org/believe.html • Explores opportunities for renewal; seeks to provide a voice in the national conversation as well as the vision of the nation's founders, through research and promotion of Christian, ethical solutions to national and global issues. Broadcasts a daily radio news show, The World from Washington, and a weekly radio show for teens called SpeakOut. Runs the web newspaper, Page One Daily. Maintains a large student program; new members are always invited to apply. Provides internship opportunities.

**American Rental Association**. 1900 19th St. Moline, IL 61265-4179. Phone: 800-334-2177 or (309)764-2475; Fax: (309)764-1533 • URL: http://www.ararental.org • Firms engaged in the rental of event and party equipment, tools, machinery, and other products; includes independent, franchised, and chain store operators. Associates are suppliers of equipment, merchandise, and other items. Seeks to foster better business methods; promote study of economic trends in the rental industry.

**American Retirees Association**. PO Box 2333 Redlands, CA 92373-0781. Phone: (909)557-0107 or (505)856-2080; Fax: (909)335-2711; Email: contactara@rocketmail.com • URL: http://www.americanretirees.org • Active, reserve, and retired members of the uniformed military services of the United States. Seeks to address what the group feels are inequities in the Uniformed Services Former Spouses' Protection Act (USFSPA). Provides advisory services to military retirees and second families adversely affected by these laws; lobbies for amendments to the USFSPA.

**American Risk and Insurance Association**. 716 Providence Rd. Malvern, PA 19355-3402. Phone: (610)640-1997; Fax: (610)725-1007; Email: aria@theinstitutes.org • URL: http://www.aria.org • Promotes education and research in the science of risk and insurance.

**American Road and Transportation Builders Association**. 1219 28th St. NW Washington, DC 20007-3389. Phone: (202)289-4434; Fax: (202)289-4435; Email: general@artba.org • URL: http://www.artba.org • Promotes on-the-job training programs.

*American Salaries and Wages Survey*. Cengage Learning Inc., 20 Channel Center St. Boston, MA 02210. Phone: 800-487-8488 or (617)289-7700; Fax: (617)289-7844; Email: investors@cengage.com • URL: http://www.cengage.com • Annual. $342. Arranged alphabetically by occupational classifications. Provides salary data for different experience levels and in specific areas of the U.S. Includes cost of living data for metropolitan areas.

*American Salon's Green Book*. Advanstar Communications Inc., 2501 Colorado Ave., Ste. 280 Santa Monica, CA 90404. Phone: (310)857-7500; Fax: (310)857-7510; Email: info@advanstar.com • URL: http://www.advanstar.com • Annual. $225 Individuals. Covers: about 1,300 manufacturers of supplies and equipment for salons and spas; 130 manufacturers' representatives; 3,200 distributors; employment agencies, show management companies, and related trade organizations. Entries include: For manufacturers and agents—Company name, address, phone, names of principal executives, products available. For distributors—Company name, address, phone, branches, name of owner or president, number of sales representatives, trade association affiliation, Metropolitan Statistical Area (MSA) in which located. For representatives—Company name, address, phone, territory covered.

**American Scientific Glassblowers Society**. PO Box 453 Machias, NY 14101. Phone: (716)353-8062; Fax: (716)353-4259; Email: natl-office@asgs-glass.org • URL: http://www.asgs-glass.org • Glassblowers with more than 5 years' experience in making scientific glass apparatus (condensers, distillation apparatus, glass-to-metal seals and vacuum devices); junior members are glassblowers with less than 5 years' professional experience; associates are persons connected with the manufacture or use of glass or glassblowing equipment in scientific work. Seeks to gather and disseminate information concerning scientific glassblowing, apparatus, equipment and materials.

**American Seed Research Foundation**. 1701 Duke St., Ste. 275 Alexandria, VA 22314. Phone: (703)837-8140; Fax: (703)837-9365 • URL: http://www.seedresearch.org • Breeders, producers, and distributors of seeds. Seeks to advance seed technology by supporting research on seeds.

**American Seed Trade Association**. 1701 Duke St., Ste. 275 Alexandria, VA 22314-3415. Phone: 888-890-7333 or (703)837-8140; Fax: (703)837-9365; Email: info@amseed.org • URL: http://www.amseed.org • Breeders, growers, assemblers, conditioners, wholesalers, and retailers of grain, grass, vegetable, flower, and other seed for planting purposes.

**American Sheep Industry Association**. 9785 Maroon Cir., Ste. 360 Englewood, CO 80112. Phone: (303)771-3500; Fax: (303)771-8200; Email: info@sheepusa.org • URL: http://www.sheepusa.org • Producers of sheep and wool. Goal is to advance the standards and profitability of the sheep industry. Conducts lobbying activities to promote legislation beneficial to the industry.

*American Shoemaking Directory*. Shoe Trades Publishing Co. Research Services, 241 Senneville Rd. Senneville, QC, Canada H9X 3X5. Phone: (514)457-8787; Fax: (514)457-5832; Email: books@shoetrades.com • URL: http://www.shoetrades.com • Annual. $60 Individuals. Covers: Shoe manufacturers in the United States, Puerto Rico, and Canada. Entries include: Company name, address, phone, fax, names of executives, product information brand names. Also key personnel; Plant output, trade sold, and sales offices included.

*American Small Business Coalition—Membership Directory*. American Small Business Council, 1750 Tysons Blvd., Ste. 1500 McLean, VA 22102. Phone: (410)381-7378 • URL: http://www.theasbc.org • Quarterly. Covers individual professionals and companies doing business in support of government agency requirements.

**American Small Business Coalition**. 6700 Alexander Bell Dr., Ste. 200 Columbia, MD 21046. Phone: (410)381-7378; Email: sponsor@theasbc.org • URL: http://www.theasbc.org • Focuses on supporting the development of relationships, best practices and market intelligence for companies doing business in the government sector. Seeks to augment industry education and outreach efforts as a resource partner to agencies of the U.S. Government. Assists in the ongoing development and growth of member companies who support agency mission requirements through their direct and indirect provisioning of goods and services. Provides industry education, relationship development and strategy alignment assistance to member companies new to government contracting. Supports the success of government contractors designated "other than small business" who seek assistance with identifying viable small business partners in multiple industry domains.

**American Small Manufacturers Coalition**. PO Box 15289 Washington, DC 20003. Phone: (202)341-7066; Fax: (202)315-3906 • URL: http://www.smallmanufacturers.org • Strives to help small manufacturers to succeed. Improves the innovativeness and productivity of America's manufacturing community. Advocates for legislative and programmatic resources to allow small manufacturers to compete in the global marketplace.

**American Society for Clinical Laboratory Science**. 1861 International Dr., Ste. 200 McLean, VA 22102. Phone: (571)748-3770; Email: ascls@ascls.org • URL: http://www.ascls.org • Seeks to promote high standards in clincal laboratory methods. Formerly American Society for Medical Technology.

**American Society for Competitiveness**. 664 Pratt Dr., 304 Eberly, IUP Indiana, PA 15705. Phone: (724)357-5928; Fax: (724)357-7768; Email: office.asc2@gmail.com • URL: http://www.eberly.iup.edu/ASCWeb • Seeks to foster education and knowledge in subjects related to competitiveness by: facilitating exchange of information and ideas among educators, policy makers, and business people, and by encouraging and assisting research activities which advance knowledge of competitiveness practices and increase the available body of teaching and practice materials. Seeks to serve the needs of entrepreneurial scholars and intellectual managers. Specifically through its conferences and publications, intends to effectively serve the needs of academicians interested in the practical application of organizational theory and practicing managers interested in the intellectual development of the discipline.

**American Society for Enology and Viticulture**. PO Box 1855 Davis, CA 95617-1855. Phone: (530)753-3142; Fax: (530)753-3318; Email: society@asev.org • URL: http://asev.org • Persons concerned with the management and technical aspects of the wine and grape industry including owners, technicians, academic personnel, and farm advisors. Promotes technical advancement in enology and viticulture through integrated research by science and industry; provides a medium for the free exchange of technical information and information on problems of interest to the wine and grape industries.

**American Society for Indexing**. 1628 E Southern Ave., No. 9-223 Tempe, AZ 85282. Phone: (480)245-6750; Email: info@asindexing.org • URL: http://www.asindexing.org • Affiliated with the American Library Association, the American Society for Information Science, and other organizations.

**American Society for Information Science and Technology**. 8555 16th St., Ste. 850 Silver Spring, MD 20910. Phone: (301)495-0900; Fax: (301)495-0810; Email: asis@asis.org • URL: http://www.asis.org • Members are information managers, scientists, librarians, and others who are interested in the storage, retrieval, and use of information.

**American Society for Nutrition**. 9650 Rockville Pike Bethesda, MD 20814-3998. Phone: (301)634-7050 or (301)634-7110; Fax: (301)634-7892 or (301)634-7894; Email: info@nutrition.org • URL: http://www.nutrition.org • Affiliated with American Society for Clinical Nutrition. Formerly American Institute of Nutrition.

**American Society for Public Administration**. 1301 Pennsylvania Ave. NW, Ste. 700 Washington, DC 20004-1716. Phone: (202)393-7878; Fax: (202)638-4952; Email: info@aspanet.org • URL: http://www.aspanet.org/public • Promotes excellence in public service, including government, non-profit and private sectors, and academic community.

**American Society for Quality**. PO Box 3005 Milwaukee, WI 53201-3005. Phone: 800-248-1946 or (414)272-8575; Email: help@asq.org • URL: http://asq.org • Individuals and organizations dedicated to the ongoing development, advancement, and promotion of quality concepts, principles, and technologies. Through its Education Development Department, offers courses in quality engineering, reliability engineering, managing for quality, management of quality costs, quality audit-development and administration, management of the inspection function, probability and statistics for engineers and scientists, and product liability and prevention.

**American Society of Access Professionals**. 1444 I St. NW, Ste. 700 Washington, DC 20005. Phone: (202)712-9054; Fax: (202)216-9646; Email: asap@bostrom.com • URL: http://www.accesspro.org • Members are individuals concerned with safeguarding freedom of information, privacy, open meetings, and fair credit reporting laws.

**American Society of Agricultural Consultants**. N78 W 14573 Appleton Ave., Ste. 287 Menomonee Falls, WI 53051. Phone: (262)253-6902; Fax: (262)253-6903; Email: emerry@agconsultants.org • URL: http://www.agconsultants.org • Members are independent, full-time consultants in many specialty areas serving agribusiness interests throughout the world. Strives to maintain high standards of ethics and competence in the consulting field. Provides referral service to agribusiness interests seeking consultants having specific knowledge, experience, and expertise. Maintains liaison with governmental agencies utilizing consultants and with legislative and administrative acts affecting consultants.

**American Society of Agronomy**. 5585 Guilford Rd. Madison, WI 53711-5801. Phone: (608)273-8080 or (608)273-8085; Fax: (608)273-2021; Email: headquarters@sciencesocieties.org • URL: http://www.agronomy.org • Professional society of agronomists, plant breeders, physiologists, soil scientists, chemists, educators, technicians, and others concerned with crop production and soil management, and conditions affecting them. Sponsors fellowship program and student essay and speech contests. Provides placement service.

**American Society of Animal Science**. PO Box 7410 Champaign, IL 61826-7410. Phone: (217)356-9050 or (212)621-4623; Email: asas@asas.org • URL: http://www.asas.org • Professional organization for animal scientist designed to help members provide effective leadership through research, extension, teaching, and service for the animal industries.

**American Society of Appraisers**. 11107 Sunset Hills Rd., Ste. 310 Reston, VA 20190. Phone: 800-272-8258 or (703)478-2228; Fax: (703)742-8471; Email: asainfo@appraisers.org • URL: http://www.appraisers.org • Professional appraisal educator, testing, and accrediting society. Sponsors mandatory recertification program for all members. Offers a consumer information service to the public.

***American Society of Baking Proceedings***. American Society of Baking, 7809 N Chestnut Ave. Kansas City, MO 64119. Phone: 800-713-0462; Fax: (888)315-2612; Email: info@asbe.org • URL: http://www.asbe.org • Annual. Membership.

**American Society of Baking**. 7809 N Chestnut Ave. Kansas City, MO 64119. Phone: 800-713-0462; Fax: (888)315-2612; Email: info@asbe.org • URL: http://www.asbe.org • Professional organization of persons engaged in bakery production; chemists, production supervisors, engineers, technicians, and others from allied fields. Maintains information service and library references to baking and related subjects.

**American Society of Brewing Chemists**. 3340 Pilot Knob Rd. Saint Paul, MN 55121-2097. Phone: (651)454-7250; Fax: (651)454-0766; Email: asbc@scisoc.org • URL: http://www.asbcnet.org • Serves as professional organization of chemists in brewing and malting industries. Develops standard methods of analysis for raw materials, supplies, and products of brewing, malting, and related industries. Provides professional development resources to members through publications, continuing education courses.

**American Society of Business Publications Editors**. 214 N Hale St. Wheaton, IL 60187. Phone: (603)510-4588; Fax: (603)510-4501; Email: info@asbpe.org • URL: http://www.asbpe.org.

**American Society of Cataract and Refractive Surgery**. 4000 Legato Rd., Ste. 700 Fairfax, VA 22033. Phone: (703)591-2220; Fax: (703)591-0614 • URL: http://www.ascrs.org • Affiliated with American Medical Association and American Society Ophthalmic Administrators.

**American Society of Cinematographers**. 1782 N Orange Dr. Hollywood, CA 90078. Phone: 800-448-0145; Fax: (323)882-6391 • URL: http://www.theasc.com • Professional directors of photography in motion picture and television photography and others affiliated with cinematography.

***American Society of Civil Engineers: Transactions***. Architectural Engineering Institute of ASCE, 1801 Alexander Bell Dr. Reston, VA 20191-4400. Phone: 800-548-2723; Email: aei@asce.org • URL: http://www.asce.org/aei • $422 Nonmembers; $316.50 Members. Publication for civil engineers.

**American Society of Comparative Law**. 1420 N Charles St. Baltimore, MD 21201. Phone: (410)837-4689; Fax: (410)837-4560 • URL: http://www.comparativelaw.org • Members are law schools and law-related institutes. Promotes the comparative study of law and the understanding of foreign legal systems and private international law. Supports the American Journal of Comparative Law and other publications concerning comparative, foreign, and private international law; also co-sponsors conferences in these fields.

**American Society of Composers, Authors and Publishers**. 1900 Broadway New York, NY 10023. Phone: 800-952-7227 or (212)621-6000; Fax: (212)621-8453 • URL: http://www.ascap.com • Composers, lyricists, and publishers. Serves as a clearinghouse in the field of music performing rights. Grants licenses and distributes royalties for the public performance of the copyrighted musical works of its members by broadcasters, symphony orchestras, and other users.

**American Society of Cost Segregation Professionals**. 1101 Pennsylvania Ave. NW, 6th Fl. Washington, DC 20004. Phone: (203)671-7372; Fax: (203)745-0724; Email: info@ascsp.org • URL: http://www.ascsp.org • Seeks to address the growing need for credentials, educational programs, technical standards and a code of ethics for the cost segregation industry. Establishes a measurable standard by which cost segregation consultants will be evaluated. Develops benchmark technical standards for reporting that are aligned with the IRS Audit Techniques Guide for Cost Segregation.

**American Society of Criminology**. 1314 Kinnear Rd., Ste. 212 Columbus, OH 43212-1156. Phone: (614)292-9207; Fax: (614)292-6767; Email: asc@asc41.com • URL: http://www.asc41.com • Formerly Society for the Advancement of Criminology.

**American Society of Farm Managers and Rural Appraisers**. 950 S Cherry St., Ste. 508 Denver, CO 80246-2664. Phone: (303)758-3513; Fax: (303)758-0190; Email: info@asfmra.org • URL: http://www.asfmra.org • Professional farm managers, appraisers, lenders, consultants, educators and researchers in farm and ranch management and/or rural appraisal. Bestows registered ARA (Accredited Rural Appraiser), Accredited Agricultural Consultant (ACC), AFM (Accredited Farm Manager) and RPRA (Real Property Review Appraiser) designations. Operates management and appraisal schools, Internet course offerings. Maintains placement service.

**American Society of Gas Engineers**. PO Box 66 Artesia, CA 90702. Phone: (949)733-4304; Email: asgecge@aol.com • URL: http://www.asge-national.org • Serves as professional society of engineers in the field of gas appliances and equipment.

**American Society of Golf Course Architects**. 125 N Executive Dr., Ste. 302 Brookfield, WI 53005-6035. Phone: (262)786-5960; Fax: (262)786-5919; Email: info@asgca.org • URL: http://www.asgca.org • Members are professional designers and architects of golf courses.

**American Society of Health-System Pharmacists**. 7272 Wisconsin Ave. Bethesda, MD 20814. Phone: 866-279-0681 or (301)664-8700 or (301)657-3000; Fax: (301)657-1251; Email: custserv@ashp.org • URL: http://www.ashp.org • Affiliated with American Hospital Association and American Nurses Association.

**American Society of Heating, Refrigerating and Air-Conditioning Engineers**. 1791 Tullie Cir. NE Atlanta, GA 30329. Phone: 800-527-4723 or (404)636-8400; Fax: (404)321-5478; Email: ashrae@ashrae.org • URL: http://www.ashrae.org • Represents Technical society of heating, ventilating, refrigeration, and air-conditioning engineers. Sponsors numerous research programs in cooperation with universities, research laboratories, and government agencies on subjects such as human and animal environmental studies, effects of air-conditioning, quality of inside air, heat transfer, flow, and cooling processes. Conducts professional development seminars. Writes method of test standards and other standards addressing energy conservation in buildings, indoor air quality, and refrigerants. Publishes extensive literature and electronic products.

**American Society of Interior Designers**. 718 7th St. NW, 4th Fl. Washington, DC 20001. Phone: (202)546-3480; Fax: (202)546-3240; Email: membership@asid.org • URL: http://www.asid.org • Represents practicing professional interior designers, students and industry partners. ASID Educational Foundation sponsors scholarship competitions, finances educational research and awards special grants.

**American Society of International Law**. 2223 Massachusetts Ave. NW Washington, DC 20008. Phone: (202)939-6000; Fax: (202)797-7133 or (202)319-1670 • URL: http://www.asil.org • Scholars, practitioners, government officials, political scientists, and specialists in subjects. Such as human rights, law of the sea, disarmament and more. Provides access to insight and information on the world of international law.

**American Society of Inventors**. PO Box 354 Feasterville, PA 19053. Phone: (215)546-6601; Email: info@asoi.org • URL: http://asoi.org • Engineers, scientists, businessmen, and others who are interested in a cooperative effort to serve both the short- and long-term needs of the inventor and society. Works with government and industry to improve the environment for the inventor. Aims to encourage invention and innovation; help the independent inventor become self-sufficient. Establishes a networking system for inventors and businessmen to solve problems. Sponsors educational programs.

**American Society of Journalists and Authors**. Times Square, 1501 Broadway, Ste. 403 New York, NY 10036. Phone: (212)997-0947; Fax: (212)937-2315 or (212)768-7414; Email: asjaoffice@asja.org • URL: http://www.asja.org • Represents freelance writers of nonfiction magazine articles and books. Seeks to elevate the professional and economic position of nonfiction writers, provide a forum for discussion of common problems among writers and editors, and promote a code of ethics for writers and editors. Operates writer referral service for individuals, institutions, or companies seeking writers for special projects; sponsors Llewellyn Miller Fund to aid professional writers who no longer able to work due to age, disability, or extraordinary professional crisis.

**American Society of Landscape Architects**. 636 Eye St. NW Washington, DC 20001-3736. Phone: 888-999-2752 or (202)898-2444; Fax: (202)898-1185; Email: info@asla.org • URL: http://www.asla.org • Professional society of landscape architects. Promotes the advancement of education and skill in the art of landscape architecture as an instrument in service to the public welfare. Seeks to strengthen existing and proposed university programs in landscape architecture. Offers counsel to new and emerging programs; encourages state registration of landscape architects. Sponsors annual educational exhibit. Offers placement service; conducts specialized education and research.

**American Society of Magazine Editors**. c/o Nina Fortuna, Director, 757 3rd Ave., 11th Fl. New York, NY 10017-2194. Phone: (212)872-3700 or (212)872-3737; Fax: (212)906-0128 • URL: http://www.magazine.org/asme • Represents magazine editors. Sponsors annual editorial internship program for college juniors and the National Magazine Awards.

***American Society of Media Photographers—Membership Directory***. American Society of Media Photographers, 150 N 2nd St. Philadelphia, PA 19106-1912. Phone: (215)451-2767; Fax: (215)451-0880; Email: info@asmp.org • URL: http://www.asmp.org • Covers: 5,000 professional photographers for publications. Entries include: Name, address, phone, fax, e-mail address, specialty.

**American Society of Media Photographers** . 150 N 2nd St. Philadelphia, PA 19106-1912. Phone: (215)451-2767; Fax: (215)451-0880; Email: info@asmp.org • URL: http://www.asmp.org • Professional society of freelance photographers. Works to evolve trade practices for photographers in communications fields. Provides business information to photographers and their potential clients; promotes ethics and rights of members. Holds educational programs and seminars. Compiles statistics.

**American Society of Military Comptrollers**. 415 N Alfred St. Alexandria, VA 22314. Phone: 800-462-5637 or (703)549-0360; Fax: (703)549-3181 • URL: http://www.asmconline.

org • Civilians and military personnel who are now or who have been involved in the overall field of military comptrollership; other interested individuals. Conducts research programs. Compiles statistics; maintains speakers' bureau. Plans to establish library.

**American Society of Military Insignia Collectors**. 350 Whitestone Dr. Spring Branch, TX 78070-6046. • URL: http://www.asmic.org • Represents oldest military insignia collectors group in the U.S. Promotes the collection and preservation of U.S. and foreign military insignia. Disseminates information on the symbolism and historical significance of insignia. Assists veterans and individuals in search of insignia.

**American Society of Naval Engineers**. 1452 Duke St. Alexandria, VA 22314. Phone: (703)836-6727; Fax: (703)836-7491; Email: asnehq@navalengineers.org • URL: http://www.navalengineers.org • Professional civilian and Navy engineers interested in naval engineering including ordnance, navigation, aeronautics, propulsion, hull, electrical and electronic, naval architecture, ocean engineering, space systems, logistics, and related subjects.

**American Society of News Editors**. Missouri School of Journalism, 209 Reynolds Journalism Inst. Columbia, MO 65211. Phone: (573)884-2405 or (703)453-1133 • URL: http://www.asne.org • Consists of leaders of multimedia news organizations, deans and endowed chairs at accredited journalism schools. Focuses on open government and the First Amendment, journalism education, leadership and diversity.

**American Society of Notaries**. PO Box 5707 Tallahassee, FL 32314-5707. Phone: (850)671-5164; Fax: (850)671-5165 • URL: http://www.asnnotary.org • Notaries Public. Provides members with educational services and technical support. Promotes high ethical standards for notaries. Seeks to increase public awareness of the valuable contribution of notaries.

**American Society of Pension Professionals and Actuaries**. 4245 N Fairfax Dr., Ste. 750 Arlington, VA 22203. Phone: (703)516-9300; Fax: (703)516-9308; Email: customercare@asppa.org • URL: http://www.asppa.org • Members are involved in the pension and insurance aspects of employee benefits. Includes an Insurance and Risk Management Committee, and sponsors an annual 401(k) Workshop.

**American Society of Plumbing Engineers**. 6400 Shafer Ct., Ste. 350 Rosemont, IL 60018. Phone: (847)296-0002; Fax: (847)296-2963; Email: info@aspe.org • URL: http://aspe.org • Represents engineers and designers involved in the design and specification of plumbing systems; manufacturers, governmental officials, and contractors related to the industry may become members on a limited basis. Seeks to resolve professional problems in plumbing engineering; advocates greater cooperation among members and plumbing officials, contractors, laborers, and the public. Code committees examine regulatory codes pertaining to the industry and submit proposed revisions to code writing authorities to simplify, standardize, and modernize all codes. Sponsors American Society of Plumbing Engineers Research Foundation; operates certification program.

**American Society of Professional Estimators**. 2525 Perimeter Place Dr., Ste. 103 Nashville, TN 37214. Phone: 888-EST-MATE or (615)316-9200; Fax: (615)316-9800; Email: psmith@aspenational.org • URL: http://www.aspenational.org • Members are construction cost estimators and construction educators.

**American Society of Safety Engineers**. 1800 E Oakton St. Des Plaines, IL 60018. Phone: (847)699-2929; Fax: (847)768-3434; Email: customerservice@asse.org • URL: http://www.asse.org • Professional society of safety engineers, safety directors, and others concerned with accident prevention, environmental protection and safety and health programs. Sponsors National Safety Month and conducts research and educational programs. Develops/publishes ANSI safety-related standards and other technical literature. Compiles statistics; maintains job placement service.

**American Society of Sanitary Engineering**. 18927 Hickory Creek Dr., Ste. 220 Mokena, IL 60448. Phone: (708)995-3019; Fax: (708)479-6139 • URL: http://www.asse-plumbing.org • Plumbing officials, sanitary engineers, plumbers, plumbing contractors, building officials, architects, engineers, designing engineers, physicians, and others interested in health. Conducts research on plumbing and sanitation, and develops performance standards for components of the plumbing system. Sponsors disease research program and other studies of water-borne epidemics.

**American Society of Transportation and Logistics**. 8430 W Bryn Mawr Ave., Ste. 1000 Chicago, IL 60631. Phone: (773)355-4900; Fax: (773)355-4888; Email: info@astl.org • URL: http://www.astl.org • Persons engaged in transportation, traffic, logistics, or physical distribution management. Works to establish standards of knowledge, technical training, experience, conduct, and ethics, and to encourage high standards of education and technical training requisite for the proper performance of traffic, transportation, logistics, and physical distribution management. Conducts extensive educational programs.

*American Society of Women Accountants—Membership Directory*. Accounting and Financial Women's Alliance, 1760 Old Meadow Rd., Ste. 500 McLean, VA 22102. Phone: 800-326-2163 or (703)506-3265; Fax: (703)506-3266; Email: aswa@aswa.org • URL: http://www.aswa.org • Annual. Cov-

ers: Approximately 5,000 members in accounting and accounting-related fields. Entries include: Name, address, phone, fax, e-mail.

**American Soybean Association**. 12125 Woodcrest Executive Dr., Ste. 100 Saint Louis, MO 63141-5009. Phone: 800-688-7692 or (314)576-1770; Fax: (314)576-2786; Email: membership@soy.org • URL: http://soygrowers.com • Develops and implements policies to increase the profitability of its members and the entire soybean industry.

*American Speaker: Your Guide to Successful Speaking*. Briefings Publishing Group, 1101 King St., Ste. 110 Alexandria, VA 22314. Phone: 800-722-9221 or (703)518-2343; Fax: (703)684-2136 • Bimonthly. $399.00. Newsletter. Provides practical advice on public speaking.

**American Spice Trade Association**. 1101 17th St. NW, Ste. 700 Washington, DC 20036. Phone: (202)331-2460; Fax: (202)463-8998 • URL: http://www.astaspice.org • Works to foment the export of American spices. Promotes the interests of the American spice industry.

**American Sportscasters Association**. 225 Broadway, Ste. 2030 New York, NY 10007. Phone: (212)227-8080; Fax: (212)571-0556; Email: inquiry@americansportscastersonline.com • URL: http://www.americansportscastersonline.com • Radio and television sportscasters. Sponsors seminars, clinics, and symposia for aspiring announcers and sportscasters. Compiles statistics. Operates speakers' bureau, placement service, hall of fame, and biographical archives. Maintains American Sportscaster Hall of Fame Trust. Is currently implementing Hall of Fame Museum, Community Programs.

**American Staffing Association**. 277 S Washington St., Ste. 200 Alexandria, VA 22314-3675. Phone: (703)253-2020; Fax: (703)253-2053; Email: asa@americanstaffing.net • URL: http://www.americanstaffing.net/index.cfm • Promotes and represents the staffing industry through legal and legislative advocacy, public relations, education, and the establishment of high standards of ethical conduct.

**American Stamp Dealers Association**. PO Box 692 Leesport, PA 19533-0692. Phone: 800-369-8207; Email: asda@americanstampdealer.com • URL: http://www.asdaonline.com • Dealers and wholesalers of stamps, albums and other philatelic materials. Sponsors National Stamp Collecting Week in November.

**American Statistical Association**. 732 N Washington St. Alexandria, VA 22314-1943. Phone: 888-231-3473 or (703)684-1221; Fax: (703)684-2037; Email: asainfo@amstat.org • URL: http://www.amstat.org • Professional society of persons interested in the theory, methodology, and application of statistics to all fields of human endeavor.

*American Stock Exchange Guide*. Wolters Kluwer Law & Business CCH, 2700 Lake Cook Rd. Riverwoods, IL 60015. Phone: 888-224-7377 or (847)267-7000; Email: cust_serv@cch.com • URL: http://www.cchgroup.com • Annual. $896 Individuals print. Covers: About 1,275 member companies listed as traders with the American Stock Exchange, and exchange and floor officials. Entries include: Company name, address, date admitted, names of representatives.

*American Stock Exchange Weekly Bulletin*. Nasdaq-AMEX Market Group, 86 Trinity Place New York, NY 10006-1872. Phone: (212)306-1442 • Weekly. $20.00 per year. Looseleaf service.

**American Subcontractors Association**. 1004 Duke St. Alexandria, VA 22314. Phone: (703)684-3450; Fax: (703)836-3482; Email: asaoffice@asa-hq.com • URL: http://www.asaonline.com • Construction subcontractors of trades and specialties such as foundations, concrete, masonry, steel, mechanical, drywall, electrical, painting, plastering, roofing and acoustical. Formed to deal with issues common to subcontractors. Works with other segments of the construction industry in promoting ethical practices, beneficial legislation and education of construction subcontractors and suppliers. Manages the Foundation of the American Subcontractors Association (FASA).

*American Subsidiaries and Affiliates of French Firms*. French Embassy Trade Office, 810 Seventh Ave., 38th Fl. New York, NY 10019-5818. Phone: (212)307-8800; Fax: (212)315-1017 • URL: http://www.dree.org • $125. Covers: French firms and their American subsidiaries. Database includes: Address, telephone and fax of french parent company. Entries include: firm address, telephone and fax numbers, activity.

**American Sugar Alliance**. 2111 Wilson Blvd., Ste. 600 Arlington, VA 22201. Phone: (703)351-5055; Fax: (703)351-6698; Email: info@sugaralliance.org • URL: http://www.sugaralliance.org • Domestic producers, processors, and refiners of sugar beets, and sugarcane; labor organizations; allied organizations that supply goods and services to the domestic sweetener producing industry. Works to increase public awareness of the international economic and political factors influencing sweetener production; seeks increased support from consumers and the government for a U.S. sugar policy that is favorable to domestic sugar and sweetener producers; strives to maintain among domestic producers the ability to meet the sweetener needs of the U.S.

**American Sugar Cane League**. 206 E Bayou Rd. Thibodaux, LA 70301. Phone: (985)448-3707; Fax: (985)448-3722 • URL: http://www.amscl.org • Louisiana sugar cane growers and processors.

*American Supply Association Operating Performance Report*. American Supply Association, 1200 N Arlington Heights Rd.,

Ste. 150 Itasca, IL 60143. Phone: (630)467-0000; Fax: (630)467-0001; Email: info@asa.net • URL: http://www.asa.net • Annual. $399 Members; $799 Nonmembers. Report provides details on operating performance.

**American Supply Association**. 1200 N Arlington Heights Rd., Ste. 150 Itasca, IL 60143. Phone: (630)467-0000; Fax: (630)467-0001; Email: info@asa.net • URL: http://www.asa.net • Represents wholesale, distributors, and manufacturers of plumbing and heating, cooling, pipes, valves, and fittings. Compiles statistics on operating costs and makes occasional studies of compensation, fringe benefits, wages, and salaries. Conducts research studies and forecasting surveys. Offers group insurance. Maintains management institutes, home study courses under the ASA Education Foundation and Endowment program, provides technology and produces a CD-ROM and internet catalogue of manufacturers.

*American Tanker Rate Schedule*. Association of Ship Brokers and Agents U.S.A., 510 Sylvan Ave., Ste. 201 Englewood Cliffs, NJ 07632-3039. Phone: (201)569-2882; Fax: (201)569-9082; Email: asba@asba.org • URL: http://www.asba.org • Biennial Annual. $3,400 Two years; $1,500 Individuals. Contains tanker freight rates.

**American Technical Education Association**. Dunwoody College of Technology, 818 Dunwoody Blvd. Minneapolis, MN 55403. Phone: (612)381-3315; Email: info@ateaonline.org • URL: http://www.ateaonline.org • Dedicated to excellence in the quality of post-secondary technical education with emphasis on professional development.

**American Textile Machinery Association**. 201 Park Washington Ct. Falls Church, VA 22046. Phone: (703)538-1789; Email: info@atmanet.org • URL: http://www.atmanet.org • Manufacturers of capital equipment for textile manufacture and interested individuals from academia, industry, banking, transportation, insurance, engineering, textiles, and other industries.

*American Trade Schools Directory*. Croner Publications Inc., 10951 Sorrento Valley Rd., Ste. 1-D San Diego, CA 92121-1613. Phone: 800-441-4033 or (858)546-1894; Fax: (800)809-0334; Email: rosa@croner.com • $120 base and supplements; plus $9.95 shipping, payment with order. Covers: over 12,000 private and public trade, technical, and vocational schools. Entries include: School name, address, phone, contact person, year school founded, private or public, accrediting agencies, whether approved by state or Veterans Administration, home study courses offered.

**American Translators Association**. 225 Reinekers Ln., Ste. 590 Alexandria, VA 22314. Phone: (703)683-6100; Fax: (703)683-6122; Email: ata@atanet.org • URL: http://www.atanet.org • Fosters the professional development of translators and interpreters and promotes the translation and interpretation professions.

**American Trucking Associations**. 950 N Glebe Rd., Ste. 210 Arlington, VA 22203-4181. Phone: (703)838-1700; Email: media@trucking.org • URL: http://www.truckline.com • Motor carriers, suppliers, state trucking associations, and national conferences of trucking companies. Works to influence the decisions of federal, state, and local government bodies; promotes increased efficiency, productivity, and competitiveness in the trucking industries; sponsors American Trucking Associations Foundation. Provides quarterly financial and operating statistics service. Offers comprehensive accounting service for all sizes of carriers. Promotes highway and driver safety; supports highway research projects; and studies technical and regulatory problems of the trucking industry. Sponsors competitions; compiles statistics. Maintains numerous programs and services including: Management Information Systems Directory; Compensation Survey; Electronic Data Interchange Standards.

*American Trucking Trends*. American Trucking Associations. Trucking Information Services, Inc., 2200 Mill Rd. Alexandria, VA 22314-4677. Phone: 800-282-5463 or (703)838-1700; Fax: (703)684-5720; Email: ata-infocenter@trucking.org • URL: http://www.truckline.com • Annual. $95.00 for members, $200.00 for nonmembers.

*American Universities and Colleges*. American Council on Education USA. Walter de Gruyter Inc., 121 High St., 3rd Fl. Boston, MA 02110. Phone: (857)284-7073; Fax: (857)284-7358; Email: service@degruyter.com • URL: http://www.degruyter.com • Quadrennial. $249.50. Two volumes. Produced in collaboration with the American Council on Education. Provides full descriptions of more than 1,900 institutions of higher learning, including details of graduate and professional programs.

*American Vegetable Grower—Source Book*. Meister Media Worldwide, 37733 Euclid Ave. Willoughby, OH 44094-5992. Phone: 800-572-7740 or (440)942-2000; Fax: (440)975-3447; Email: info@meistermedia.com • URL: http://www.meistermedia.com • Annual. Publication includes: Lists of suppliers of agricultural chemicals and manufacturers and suppliers of other agricultural products, equipment, and services including packaging equipment, transportation services, direct marketing suppliers, plants and seeds, etc. Entries include: Company name, address, phone, fax, e-mail.

*American Veterinary Medical Association—Directory and Resource Manual: AVMA Membership Directory and Resource Manual*. American Veterinary Medical Association, 1931 N Meacham Rd., Ste. 100 Schaumburg, IL 60173-

4360. Phone: 800-248-2862 or (847)925-8070; Fax: (847)925-1329; Email: info@avma.org • URL: http://www.avma.org • Annual. $150 Nonmembers in USA and their territories; $175 Nonmembers other countries. Covers: AVMA members; code of ethics, AVMA bylaws. Database includes: Extensive list of veterinary medical and related associations, veterinary schools, related government agencies. Entries include: Name, spouse's name, address, email, phones and codes for practice activity, type of employer, institution granting degree, and year received.

**American Veterinary Medical Association**. 1931 N Meacham Rd., Ste. 100 Schaumburg, IL 60173-4360. Phone: 800-248-2862 or (847)925-8070; Fax: (847)925-1329; Email: info@avma.org • URL: http://www.avma.org • Professional society of veterinarians. Conducts educational and research programs. Provides placement service. Sponsors American Veterinary Medical Association Foundation and Educational Commission for Foreign Veterinary Graduates. Compiles statistics. Accredits veterinary medical education programs and veterinary technician education programs.

**American Water Resources Association**. PO Box 1626 Middleburg, VA 20118-1626. Phone: (540)687-8390; Fax: (540)687-8395; Email: info@awra.org • URL: http://www.awra.org • Engineers; natural, physical, and social scientists; other persons engaged in any aspect of the field of water resources; business concerns and other organizations; students in water resources. Includes members from 62 nations. Seeks to advance water resources research, planning, development, and management. Endeavors to collect and disseminate ideas and information relative to water resources science and technology via scientific journal, newsletter, conferences and symposia and published proceedings.

***American Water Works Association—Sourcebook***. American Water Works Association, 6666 W Quincy Ave. Denver, CO 80235-3098. Phone: 800-926-7337 or (303)794-7711; Fax: (303)347-0804 • URL: http://www.awwa.org • Annual. Covers: Member suppliers and distributors of water supply products and services, contractors for water supply projects, and engineering consultants. Entries include: Company name, address, names of executives, trade and brand names, products and services offered.

**American Water Works Association**. 6666 W Quincy Ave. Denver, CO 80235-3098. Phone: 800-926-7337 or (303)794-7711; Fax: (303)347-0804 • URL: http://www.awwa.org • Water utility managers, superintendents, engineers, chemists, bacteriologists, and other individuals interested in public water supply; municipal- and investor-owned water departments; boards of health; manufacturers of waterworks equipment; government officials and consultants interested in water supply. Develops standards and supports research programs in waterworks design, construction, operation, and management. Conducts in-service training schools and prepares manuals for waterworks personnel. Maintains hall of fame. Offers placement service via member newsletter; compiles statistics. Offers training; children's services; and information center on the water utilities industry, potable water, and water reuse.

**American Welding Society**. 8669 Doral Blvd., Ste. 130 Miami, FL 33166. Phone: 800-443-9353 or (305)443-9353; Fax: (305)443-7559; Email: info@aws.org • URL: http://www.aws.org • One of several sponsors of the Welding Research Council and the Materials Properties Council. Professional engineering society in the field of welding. Sponsors seminars. Maintains over 130 technical and handbook committees, 171 sections, educational committees, and task forces.

**American Wholesale Marketers Association**. 2750 Prosperity Ave., Ste. 530 Fairfax, VA 22031. Phone: 800-482-2962; Fax: (703)573-5738 • URL: http://www.awmanet.org • Represents the interests of distributors of convenience-related products. Its members include wholesalers, retailers, manufacturers, brokers and allied organizations from across the U.S. and abroad. Programs include strong legislative representation in Washington and a broad spectrum of targeted education, business and information services. Sponsors the country's largest show for candy and convenience related products in conjunction with its semi-annual convention.

***American Wholesalers and Distributors Directory***. Cengage Learning Inc., 20 Channel Center St. Boston, MA 02210. Phone: 800-487-8488 or (617)289-7700; Fax: (617)289-7844; Email: investors@cengage.com • URL: http://www.cengage.com • Annual. $450 Individuals print. Lists more than 27,000 national, regional, state, and local wholesalesrs.

**American Wind Energy Association**. 1501 M St. NW, Ste. 1000 Washington, DC 20005. Phone: (202)383-2500 or (202)383-2557; Fax: (202)383-2505; Email: windmail@awea.org • URL: http://www.awea.org • Wind energy equipment manufacturers; project developers and dealers; individuals from industry, government, and academia; interested others. Works to: advance the art and science of using energy from the wind for human purposes; encourage the use of wind turbines and wind power plants as alternatives to current energy systems that depend on depletable fuels; facilitate the widespread use of wind as a renewable, non-polluting energy source by fostering communication within the field of wind energy and between the technical community and the public. Provides federal and state legislators with information on wind as an energy source; offers consultation to federal, state, and local government and private industry. Promotes exportation of U.S. manufactured wind energy equipment.

**American Wine Society**. PO Box 279 Englewood, OH 45322. Phone: 888-297-9070 or (937)529-7800; Fax: (937)529-7888; Email: executivedirector@americanwinesociety.org • URL: http://www.americanwinesociety.org • Represents amateur and professional winemakers, wine enthusiasts, wine merchants, and anyone who enjoys wine and wants to learn more about it. Seeks to further the knowledge, appreciation and enjoyment of wine. Sponsors educational programs. Conducts wine tastings and trips to vineyards and wineries.

**American Wire Producers Association**. 7011 A Manchester Blvd., No. 178 Alexandria, VA 22310-3202. Phone: (703)299-4434; Fax: (703)299-4434; Email: info@awpa.org • URL: http://www.awpa.org • Represents manufacturers of steel wire and wire products; suppliers of wire rods, dies, machinery, and related equipment. Assures free and fair access to a global supply of wire rod and to encourage an adequate domestic supply.

**American Woman's Society of Certified Public Accountants**. 136 S Keowee St. Dayton, OH 45402. Phone: 800-297-2721 or (937)222-1872; Fax: (937)222-5794; Email: info@awscpa.org • URL: http://www.awscpa.org • Citizens who hold Certified Public Accountant certificates as well as those who have passed the CPA examination but do not have certificates. Works to improve the status of professional women and to make the business community aware of the professional capabilities of the woman CPA. Conducts semiannual statistical survey of members; offers specialized education and research programs.

***American Women Managers and Administrators: A Selective Biographical Dictionary of Twentieth-Century Leaders in Business, Education, and Government***. Greenwood Electronic Media, c/o ABC-CLIO, 130 Cremona Dr. Santa Barbara, CA 93117. Phone: 800-368-6868 or (805)968-1911; Fax: (866)270-3856; Email: customerservice@abc-clio.com • URL: http://www.abc-clio.com • $105 Single issue; £59.95 Single issue. Covers 225 twentieth-century women who hold or have held administrative, managerial, or leadership positions in business, education, or government, including founders and presidents of colleges and companies, vice presidents of major corporations, and women who were first in their profession or position.

**American Yarn Spinners Association**. 2500 Lowell Rd. Gastonia, NC 28053. Phone: (704)824-3522; Fax: (704)824-0630 • URL: http://www.textileweb.com/BuyersGuide.mvc/CompanyDetail/ • Manufacturers of combed cotton sales yarn and carded yarns spun from cotton, wool, and/or synthetics. Provides full service to the sales yarn industry.

***American Yearbook and Leadership Manual***. American Academy of Actuaries, 1850 M St. NW, Ste. 300 Washington, DC 20036. Phone: (202)223-8196; Fax: (202)872-1948 • URL: http://www.actuary.org • Annual. $15.00.

**Americans for the Arts**. 1000 Vermont Ave. NW, 6th Fl. Washington, DC 20005. Phone: (202)371-2830; Fax: (202)371-0424; Email: info@artsusa.org • URL: http://www.americansforthearts.org • Members are arts organizations and interested individuals. Conducts research and provides information and clearinghouse services relating to the visual arts.

***America's Best Midsized Companies***. Financial World Publishing, 4-9 Burgate Ln. Canterbury CT1 2XJ, United Kingdom. Phone: 44 0 1277 818688; Email: msmith@ifslearning.com • Annual. $1.95. Entries include: Company name, address, phone.

***America's Corporate Families***. Dun & Bradstreet Inc., 103 JFK Pkwy. Short Hills, NJ 07078. Phone: 800-526-0651 or (973)921-5500 or (973)921-5000; Fax: (866)560-7035 or (512)794-7670; Email: info@dnb.com • URL: http://www.dnb.com • Annual. Covers approximately 12,700 U.S. corporations. Ultimate companies must meet all of the following criteria for inclusion: two or more business locations, 250 or more employees at that location or in excess of $25 million in sales volume or a tangible net worth greater than $500,000, and controlling interest in one or more subsidiary company.

***America's Corporate Finance Directory***. LexisNexis, 9443 Springboro Pke. Dayton, OH 45342. Phone: 800-227-4908 or (937)865-6800; Fax: (937)865-1211; Email: legalnotices@lexisnexis.com • URL: http://www.bender.com • Annual. $1,399 Individuals print. Covers: Financial personnel and outside financial services relationships of 5,000 leading United States corporations and their wholly-owned United States subsidiaries. Entries include: Company name, address, phone, fax, telex, e-mail addresses, stock exchange information, earnings, total assets, size of pension/profit-sharing fund portfolio, number of employees, description of business, wholly-owned U.S. Subsidiaries of parent company; name and title of key executives; outside suppliers of financial services.

**America's Edge**. 1212 New York Ave. NW, Ste. 300 Washington, DC 20005-3988. Phone: (202)408-9284 • URL: http://www.americasedge.org • Encourages business leaders to support education policies and initiatives aimed at providing all Americans the skills and knowledge essential for success in a competitive global marketplace. Facilitates exchange of information on best practices in business advocacy and support for education reform. Supports legislative changes in public policy and programs that will help build a qualified workforce.

***America's International Trade: A Reference Handbook***. ABC-Clio Inc., 130 Cremona Dr. Santa Barbara, CA 93117-5516. Phone: 800-368-6868 or (805)968-1911; Fax: (805)685-9685; Email: crussell@abc-clio.com • URL: http://www.abc-clio.com • $45 Individuals print. Covers: The importance of international trade to the American economy and the influence it has on American businesses. Publication includes: List of organizations relevant to America and international trade, such as the World Bank. Entries include: Contact data. Principal content of publication is a discussion of international trade and the American economy and businesses and international trade agreement.

***The Americas Review: The Economic and Business Report***. Kogan Page, Limited, 120 Pentonville Rd. London N1 9JN, United Kingdom. Phone: 44 20 72780433 or (440)2072780433; Fax: 44 20 78376348 or (783)76348; Email: kpinfo@kogan-page.co.uk • URL: http://www.kogan-page.co.uk/ • £50 Individuals. Covers: about 200 United States manufacturers and remanufacturers; includes facts on suppliers, country profiles, business guides, and directories for areas of North, Central, and South America, and all the Caribbean states and South Atlantic. Entries include: Heads of States, currencies, official languages, capital city, population, GNP, inflation, oil revenues, exports/imports, country profile, information for international visitors, name, address, phone of hotels, chambers of commerce, airlines, banks, government ministries and industrial associations.

**Americas Society/Council of the Americas**. 680 Park Ave. New York, NY 10065. Phone: (212)249-8950; Fax: (212)249-5868; Email: inforequest@as-coa.org • URL: http://www.americas-society.org • Members are U. S. corporations with business interests in Latin America. Formerly Council of the Americas.

***America's Top Rated Cities: A Statistical Handbook***. Grey House Publishing, 4919 Rte. 22 Amenia, NY 12501. Phone: 800-562-2139 or (518)789-8700; Fax: (518)789-0556; Email: books@greyhouse.com • URL: http://www.greyhouse.com • Annual. $250.00. Four volumes. $75.00 per volume. Each volume covers major cities in a region of the U. S.: Eastern, Southern, Central, and Western. City statistics cover the "Business Environment" (finances, employment, taxes, utilities, etc.) and the "Living Environment" (cost of living, housing, education, health care, climate, etc.).

***America's Top-Rated Smaller Cities: A Statistical Handbook***. Grey House Publishing, 4919 Rte. 22 Amenia, NY 12501. Phone: 800-562-2139 or (518)789-8700; Fax: (518)789-0556; Email: books@greyhouse.com • URL: http://www.greyhouse.com • Biennial. $225 Individuals. Provides detailed profiles of 60 smaller U. S. cities ranging in population from 25,000 to 100,000. Includes data on cost of living, employment, income, taxes, climate, media, and many other factors.

***AMS Conference Proceedings***. American Meteorological Society, 45 Beacon St. Boston, MA 02108-3693. Phone: (617)227-2425 or (617)227-2426; Fax: (617)742-8718; Email: amsinfo@ametsoc.org • URL: http://www.ametsoc.org • Annual.

**Amusement Industry Manufacturers and Suppliers International**. 3026 S Orange Santa Ana, CA 92707. Phone: (714)425-5747; Fax: (714)276-9666; Email: info@aimsintl.org • URL: http://www.aimsintl.org • Represents manufacturers and suppliers of amusement riding devices and equipment used by amusement parks, carnivals, and traveling amusement companies. Exchanges information on safety, maintenance, state laws, transportation, and credit. Works to develop safety programs and codes at the federal and state levels; carries out public relations activities; and cooperates with the ASTM to develop voluntary standards for amusement rides and devices.

***Anaheim Business Advocate***. Anaheim Chamber of Commerce, 2400 E Katella Ave., Ste. 725 Anaheim, CA 92806. Phone: (714)758-0222; Fax: (714)758-0468; Email: info@anaheimchamber.org • URL: http://www.anaheimchamber.org • Monthly.

***Analyse Major Databases from European Sources***. Bureau van Dijk S.A., Ave. Louise, Louizalaan 250 B-1050 Brussels, Belgium. Phone: 32 2 6390606 or 32 2 639 06 06; Fax: 32 2 6488230 or 32 2 648 82 30; Email: brussels@bvdinfo.com • URL: http://www.bvdinfo.com • Annual. Covers: 150,000 of the top companies in Europe. Entries include: Company name, address, phone, fax, telex; date of incorporation.

***Analysis***. FT Analysis, Ibex House, 42/47 Minories London EC3 1DY, United Kingdom. Phone: 71 7020991; Fax: 71 7022067 • Daily. Database covers: all U.K. publicly quoted and Unlisted Securities Market (USM) companies. Database includes: Company name, address, phone, principal activities, names and titles of key personnel, business history, major holdings, capital structure, and share prices, key ratios, dividend data, balance sheets, and profit and loss summaries for the most recent five years. Also includes complete text of recent company announcements filed with the London Stock Exchange, complete text of more than 7,000 stockbroker research reports, and complete text of U.K. annual reports.

***Analyst's Handbook: Composite Corporate Per Share Data by Industry***. Standard & Poor's Financial Services L.L.C., 55 Water St. New York, NY 10041. Phone: 877-772-5436 or

(212)438-2000; Fax: (212)438-1000; Email: questions@standardandpoors.com • URL: http://www.standardandpoors.com • Annual. $795.00. Monthly updates.

***Andersen Horticultural Library's Source List of Plants and Seeds***. Andersen Horticultural Library, University of Minnesota Landscape, 3675 Arboretum Dr. Chaska, MN 55318. Phone: (952)443-1405; Email: hortlib@umn.edu • URL: http://www.arboretum.umn.edu/library.aspx • Irregular. $39.95 Individuals postpaid. Covers: More than 600 nurseries that offer over 70,000 different plants. Entries include: Company name, address, phone.

***Andorra Offshore Investment and Business Guide***. International Business Publications, USA, PO Box 15343 Washington, DC 20003. Phone: (202)546-2103; Fax: (202)546-3275; Email: ibpusa@comcast.net • URL: http://ibpus.com • $99.95 Individuals hardcover; $99.95 Individuals CD-ROM; $99.95 Individuals E-book. Covers: Information on conducting business and investment activity in the country with offshore status.

***Andrews' Professional Liability Litigation Reporter***. Andrews Publications, 175 Strafford Ave., Bldg. 4, Suite 140 Wayne, PA 19087. Phone: 800-345-1101 or (610)225-0510 or (610)622-0510; Fax: (610)225-0501 or (610)622-0501; Email: customer@andrewspub.com • URL: http://www.andrewspub.com • Monthly. $550.00 per year. Provides reports on lawsuits against attorneys, accountants, and investment professionals.

***Angel Capital: How to Raise Early-Stage Private Equity Financing***. John Wiley & Sons Inc., 111 River St. Hoboken, NJ 07030-5774. Phone: 800-225-5945 or (201)748-6000; Fax: (201)748-6088; Email: info@wiley.com • URL: http://www.wiley.com • $85 Individuals hardcover. Covers: How to find investors and take control of the private placement process; alternative capital resources.

***Angola Business Directory***. Business Guide, PO Box 27669 Dubai, United Arab Emirates. Phone: 971 4 2651719; Fax: 971 4 2692151; Email: sales@africa-business.com • URL: http://www.africa-business.com • $25 download. Covers: Over 7,300 business listings including wholesalers, importers, retailers, business houses, and agents in Angola.

***Angola Industrial and Business Directory***. International Business Publications, USA, PO Box 15343 Washington, DC 20003. Phone: (202)546-2103; Fax: (202)546-3275; Email: ibpusa@comcast.net • URL: http://ibpus.com • $99.95 Individuals hardcover; $99.95 Individuals CD-ROM; $99.95 Individuals E-book. Covers: Strategic and practical economic and business information. Entries include: Business contacts for conducting business activity in the country.

***Angola Investment and Business Guide***. International Business Publications, USA, PO Box 15343 Washington, DC 20003. Phone: (202)546-2103; Fax: (202)546-3275; Email: ibpusa@comcast.net • URL: http://ibpus.com • $99.95 Individuals hardcover; $99.95 Individuals CD-ROM; $99.95 Individuals E-book. Covers: Basic information on economy, export-import and investment climate, regulations, industrial development, banking, opportunities and government. Entries include: Business contacts and business travel.

***Animal Breeding Abstracts: A Monthly Abstract of World Literature***. CABI Publishing North America, 38 Chauncey St., Ste. 1002 Boston, MA 02111. Phone: 800-552-3083; Email: cabi-nao@cabi.org • URL: http://www.cabi.org • Monthly. $1,305.

***Ankara Chamber of Industry Export Catalogue***. Ankara Chamber of Industry, Ataturk Bulvari No. 193, Kavaklidere 06680 Ankara, Turkey. Phone: 312 4 17 12 00; Fax: 312 4 17 20 60 • Irregular. $5. Covers: Manufacturing and exporting companies associated with the Ankara Chamber of Industry. Entries include: Names, addresses, and products.

***Ann Arbor Area Chamber of Commerce—Business Directory***. Ann Arbor/Ypsilanti Regional Chamber, 115 W Huron St., 3rd Fl. Ann Arbor, MI 48104. Phone: (734)665-4433; Fax: (734)665-4191; Email: katie@a2ychamber.org • URL: http://www.annarborchamber.org • Covers: Member companies in Ann Arbor, Michigan. Entries include: Name of firm, address, phone, number of employees, line of business, names and titles of key personnel, products or services.

***Annotated Business Agreements***. Thomson Reuters Canada Ltd., 1 Corporate Plz., 2075 Kennedy Rd. Toronto, ON, Canada M1T 3V4. Phone: 800-387-5164 or (416)298-5141 or (416)609-3800; Fax: (416)298-5094 or (416)298-5082; Email: carswell.customerrelations@thomson.com • URL: http://www.carswell.com • Contains information on business agreement law in Canada. Includes precedents for the most common types of business organization agreements, such as shareholders' agreements, partnership agreements, and other related agreements.

***Annuaire Bureautique—Informatique***. Alphamedian Louis Johanet, 38 Bd. Henri Sellier F-92150 Suresnes, France. Phone: 1 47287070; Fax: 1 47287383; Email: erick.mounoury@alphamedian.fr • URL: http://www.alphamedian.fr/cadre_alphamedian.htm • Annual. Covers: manufacturers and suppliers of office machinery in France.

***Annuaire des Entreprises et Organismes d'Outre-Mer l'Afrique Noire Francophone***. Rene Moreux et Cie, 190, Blvd. Haussmann F-75008 Paris, France. Phone: 1 44959950 • Biennial. $715 payment must accompany order. Covers: about 10,000 national and multinational companies in or related to Benin, Burundi, Central African Empire, Chad, Congo, Gabon, Guinea, Ivory Coast, Malagasy Republic, Mali, Mauritania, Niger, Rwanda, Senegal, Togo, Cameroon, Upper Volta, Zaire, and the French overseas departments and territories. Includes banking and other financial institutions, chambers of commerce, government agencies, and associations. Entries include: Company name, address, capital, line of business, names and titles of key personnel, year established, products, branch offices, associated companies in France.

***Annuaire France Telexport***. Paris Chamber of Commerce and Industry, 27, Ave. de Friedland F-75382 Paris, France. Phone: 33 8 20012112; Email: cpdp@ccip.fr • URL: http://www.cci-paris-idf.fr • Annual. €210.35 Individuals includes tax; $179.40. Covers: Approximately 40,000 French companies involved in international trade. Entries include: Company name, address, phone, telex, names and titles of key personnel, number of employees, geographical area served, financial data, product/service, main business activity, date/type of incorporation, products imported/exported, countries of export/import.

***Annuaire National de Fournisseurs des Administrations Francaises***. Editions le Fil d'Ariane, 17 rue Cler F-75007 Paris, France. Phone: 33 1 44 11 22 05; Fax: 33 1 47 05 74 61 • Annual. Covers: Over 2,00 industrial firms and merchant and service companies which are the main suppliers to the French Civil Service. Entries include: Company name, address, phone, fax, telex number, data on clients.

***Annual Benchmark Report for Retail Trade and Food Services.A Detailed Summary of Retail Sales, Purchases, Accounts Receivable, Inventories, and Food Service Sales***. U. S. Government Printing Office, 732 N Capitol St. NW Washington, DC 20401. Phone: 866-512-1800 or (202)512-1800 or (866)512-1800; Fax: (202)512-2104 or (202)512-2250; Email: contactcenter@gpo.gov • URL: http://www.gpo.gov • Annual. $13.00. Issued by the U.S. Census Bureau. Provides detailed annual and monthly retail statistics for the most recent 10 years. Includes data for various kinds of retail outlets, including automobiles, furniture, appliances, building supplies, grocery stores, drug stores, gasoline stations, clothing, sporting goods, department stores, and restaurants.

***Annual Bulletin of Trade in Chemical Products***. Economic Commission for Europe. United Nations Publications, c/o National Book Network, 15200 NBN Way Blue Ridge Summit, PA 17214. Phone: 888-254-4286 or (212)963-7680 or (212)963-8302; Fax: (800)338-4550; Email: unpublications@nbnbooks.com • URL: http://www.unp.un.org • Annual. $47.00.

***Annual Business and Pleasure Guide***. Sebago Lakes Region Chamber of Commerce, 747 Roosevelt Trail Windham, ME 04062. Phone: (207)892-8265; Fax: (207)893-0110; Email: info@sebagolakeschamber.com • URL: http://www.sebagolakeschamber.com • Annual. Covers businesses in Windham and the Sebago Lake Region.

***The Annual Directory of the Information Industry Association***. Software and Information Industry Association, 1090 Vermont Ave. NW, 6th Fl. Washington, DC 20005-4095. Phone: (202)289-7442 or (202)789-4440; Fax: (202)289-7097 or (202)638-4403; Email: rcollier@siia.net • URL: http://www.siia.net • Annual. Members, $75.00; non-members, $125.00.

***Annual Energy Outlook, with Projections to (year)***. U. S. Government Printing Office, 732 N Capitol St. NW Washington, DC 20401. Phone: 866-512-1800 or (202)512-1800 or (866)512-1800; Fax: (202)512-2104 or (202)512-2250; Email: contactcenter@gpo.gov • URL: http://www.gpo.gov • Annual. $39.00. Issued by the Energy Information Administration, U. S. Department of Energy (www.eia.doe.gov). Contains detailed statistics and 20-year projections for electricity, oil, natural gas, coal, and renewable energy. Text provides extensive discussion of energy issues and "Market Trends.".

***Annual Energy Review***. U. S. Government Printing Office, 732 N Capitol St. NW Washington, DC 20401. Phone: 866-512-1800 or (202)512-1800 or (866)512-1800; Fax: (202)512-2104 or (202)512-2250; Email: contactcenter@gpo.gov • URL: http://www.gpo.gov • Annual. $59.00. Issued by the Energy Information Administration, Office of Energy Markets and End Use, U. S. Department of Energy. Presents long-term historical as well as recent data on production, consumption, stocks, imports, exports, and prices of the principal energy commodities in the U. S.

***The Annual Register: A Record of World Events***. ProQuest L.L.C., 789 E Eisenhower Pkwy. Ann Arbor, MI 48106-1346. Phone: 800-521-0600 or (734)761-4700; Fax: (734)662-4554; Email: info@proquest.com • URL: http://www.proquest.com • Annual. Contains yearly British and world events.

***Annual Register of Grant Support: A Directory of Funding Sources***. Information Today, Inc., 143 Old Marlton Pke. Medford, NJ 08055-8750. Phone: 800-300-9868 or (609)654-6266; Fax: (609)654-4309; Email: custserv@infotoday.com • URL: http://www.infotoday.com • Annual. $299 Individuals Softbound; $269.10 Individuals First-Time Standing Order. Contains information on more than 3,500 corporate, private, and public organizations that provide grants in 11 major subject areas, including 61 specific sub-categories.

***Annual Report of Postmaster General***. United States Postal Service, 475 W L'enfant Plz. SW Washington, DC 20260-0004. Phone: 800-275-8777 or (202)268-2500 or (202)268-2000; Fax: (202)268-4860 or (202)268-2304 • URL: http://www.usps.com • Annual.

***Annual Report of the Bank Commissioner of the State of Maryland***. Maryland Department of Labor, Licensing and Regulation, 500 N Calvert St., No. 401 Baltimore, MD 21202. Phone: (410)230-6001; Fax: (410)333-0853 or (410)767-2986; Email: dli@dllr.state.md.us • URL: http://www.dllr.state.md.us/ • Biennial. Covers: State-chartered banks and credit unions in Maryland. Entries include: Financial institution name, address, phone, fax, names and titles of key personnel, financial data.

***Annual Report of the Director***. Administrative Office of the United States Courts, 1 Columbus Cir. NE Washington, DC 20544. Phone: (202)502-2600 • URL: http://www.uscourts.gov/FederalCourts/UnderstandingtheFederalCourts/AdministrativeOffice.aspx • Annual.

***Annual Report of the Secretary of Defense***. U.S. Department of Defense - Office of the Secretary, c/o Chuck Hagel, Secretary, 1000 Defense Pentagon Washington, DC 20301. • URL: http://www.defense.gov/osd • Annual.

***Annual Report of the Secretary of Veterans Affairs***. U.S. Department of Veterans Affairs, Office of Public Affairs, 810 Vermont Ave., NW Washington, DC 20420. • URL: http://www.va.gov/ • Annual. Shows monies distributed and received by the Dept. of Veterans Affairs. Describes the activities of the Department during the fiscal year.

***The Annual Report on the Economic Status of the Profession***. American Association of University Professors, 1133 19th St. NW, Ste. 200 Washington, DC 20036. Phone: (202)737-5900; Fax: (202)737-5526; Email: aaup@aaup.org • URL: http://www.aaup.org • Special annual issue of *ACADEME*.

***Annual Review of Biophysics***. Annual Reviews, 4139 El Camino Way Palo Alto, CA 94306-4010. Phone: 800-523-8635 or (650)493-4400; Fax: (650)855-9815 or (650)424-0910; Email: service@annualreviews.org • URL: http://www.annualreviews.org • Annual. $99 Individuals online only; $255 Institutions online or print; $383 Institutions online and print.

***Annual Review of Entomology***. Annual Reviews, 4139 El Camino Way Palo Alto, CA 94306-4010. Phone: 800-523-8635 or (650)493-4400; Fax: (650)855-9815 or (650)424-0910; Email: service@annualreviews.org • URL: http://www.annualreviews.org • Annual. $99 Individuals; $255 Institutions online or print; $383 Institutions online and print.

***Annual Review of Environment and Resources***. Annual Reviews, 4139 El Camino Way Palo Alto, CA 94306-4010. Phone: 800-523-8635 or (650)493-4400; Fax: (650)855-9815 or (650)424-0910; Email: service@annualreviews.org • URL: http://www.annualreviews.org • Annual. $93 Individuals online only; $234 Institutions online or print; $351 Institutions online and print. Focuses on emerging scientific and policy issues at the interface of environment, resource management, and development.

***Annual Review of Medicine: Selected Topics in the Clinical Sciences***. Annual Reviews, 4139 El Camino Way Palo Alto, CA 94306-4010. Phone: 800-523-8635 or (650)493-4400; Fax: (650)855-9815 or (650)424-0910; Email: service@annualreviews.org • URL: http://www.annualreviews.org • Annual. $99 Individuals online only; $255 Institutions online or print; $383 Institutions online and print. Covers significant developments in various fields of Medicine.

***Annual Review of Nuclear and Particle Science***. Annual Reviews, 4139 El Camino Way Palo Alto, CA 94306-4010. Phone: 800-523-8635 or (650)493-4400; Fax: (650)855-9815 or (650)424-0910; Email: service@annualreviews.org • URL: http://www.annualreviews.org • Annual. $99 Individuals online only; $255 Institutions online or print; $383 Institutions online and print.

***Annual Review of Pharmacology and Toxicology***. Annual Reviews, 4139 El Camino Way Palo Alto, CA 94306-4010. Phone: 800-523-8635 or (650)493-4400; Fax: (650)855-9815 or (650)424-0910; Email: service@annualreviews.org • URL: http://www.annualreviews.org • Annual. $99 Individuals online only; $255 Institutions online or print; $383 Institutions online and print.

***Annual Review of Public Health***. Annual Reviews, 4139 El Camino Way Palo Alto, CA 94306-4010. Phone: 800-523-8635 or (650)493-4400; Fax: (650)855-9815 or (650)424-0910; Email: service@annualreviews.org • URL: http://www.annualreviews.org • Annual. $93 Individuals online only; $234 Institutions online or print; $351 Institutions online and print.

***Annual Review of the Chemical Industry***. United Nations Publications, c/o National Book Network, 15200 NBN Way Blue Ridge Summit, PA 17214. Phone: 888-254-4286 or (212)963-7680 or (212)963-8302; Fax: (800)338-4550; Email: unpublications@nbnbooks.com • URL: http://www.unp.un.org • Annual. $100.00.

***Annual Reviews in Control***. Elsevier, Secondary Publishing Division, 650 Ave. of the Americas New York, NY 10011. Phone: 888-437-4636 or (212)633-3980; Fax: (212)633-3975; Email: t.reller@elsevier.com • URL: http://www.elseveier.com • Annual. $807 Institutions print only.

***Annual Society for Information Science and Technology, Information and Business Div***. Martha E. Williams, editor. Information Today, Inc., 143 Old Marlton Pke. Medford, NJ 08055-8750. Phone: 800-300-9868 or (609)654-6266; Fax: (609)654-4309; Email: custserv@infotoday.com • URL:

http://www.infotoday.com • Annual. $79.95 Members; $99.95 Nonmembers. Published on behalf of the American Society for Information Science (ASIS). Covers trends in planning, basic techniques, applications, and the information profession in general.

***Annual Statement Studies: Industry Default Probabilities and Cash Flow Measures***. Risk Management Association, 1801 Market St., Ste. 300 Philadelphia, PA 19103-1613. Phone: (215)446-4000; Fax: (215)446-4101; Email: rmaar@rmahq.org • URL: http://www.rmahq.org • Annual. $405 Nonmembers. Serves as a companion volume to the original *Annual Statement Studies*. Gives probability of default estimates on a percentage scale for more than 450 industries. Includes changes in position year-by-year for eight financial statement line items and provides percentage measures of cash flow.

***Annual Statement Studies***. Risk Management Association, 1801 Market St., Ste. 300 Philadelphia, PA 19103-1613. Phone: (215)446-4000; Fax: (215)446-4101; Email: rmaar@rmahq.org • URL: http://www.rmahq.org • Annual. 425 Members; 725 Nonmembers. Compiled from over 280,000 financial statements.

***Annual Statistical Reports of Independent Telephone Companies***. Federal Communications Commission Wireless Telecommunications Bureau, 445 12th St. SW Washington, DC 20554. Phone: 877-480-3201; Fax: (866)418-0232; Email: fccinfo@fcc.gov • URL: http://wireless.fcc.gov • Annual.

***Annuity Market News***. SourceMedia Inc., 1 State Street Plz., 27th Fl. New York, NY 10004. Phone: 800-221-1809 or (212)803-8200 or (212)803-8333; Fax: (212)843-9635 or (212)292-5216; Email: custserv@sourcemedia.com • URL: http://www.sourcemedia.com • Monthly. $625.00 per year. Newsletter. Edited for investment and insurance professionals. Covers the marketing, management, and servicing of variable and fixed annuity products.

***ANR National Directory of Community Newspapers***. American Newspaper Representatives Inc., 2075 W Big Beaver Rd., Ste. 310 Troy, MI 48084. Phone: 800-550-7557 or (248)643-9910; Fax: (248)643-9914 or (248)643-0606; Email: info@anrinc.net • URL: http://www.anrinc.net • Annual. $125 Individuals; $75 Individuals CD-ROM. Covers more than 10,000 newspapers.

***ANSI Standards Action***. American National Standards Institute, 1899 L St. NW, 11th Fl. Washington, DC 20036-3807. Phone: (202)293-8020; Fax: (202)293-9287; Email: info@ansi.org • URL: http://www.ansi.org • Weekly. Description: Lists new and proposed American National Standards and draft international standards of the International Organization for Standardization (ISO), International Electrotechnical Commission (IEC), European Committee for Standardization (CEN), and European Committee for Electrotechnical Standardization (CENELEC). Lists proposed foreign government regulations from countries that signed the General Agreement on Tariffs and Trade (GATT) Standards Code. Provides listing for registration of organization names in the United States. **Remarks:** Subscription includes ANSI Reporter (see separate listing).

***Answering Bureaus Directory***. InfoGroup Inc., 5711 S 86th Cir. Omaha, NE 68127-4146. Phone: (402)593-4500 • URL: http://www.infogroup.com • Annual. Number of listings: 5,102. Entries include: Name, address, phone, size of advertisement, name of owner or manager, number of employees, year first in "Yellow Pages." Compiled from telephone company "Yellow Pages," nationwide.

***Antenna Industry Directory and Buyers Guide***. Webcom Communications Corp., 7355 E Orchard Rd., Ste. 100 Englewood, CO 80111. Phone: 800-803-9488 or (720)528-3770; Fax: (720)528-3771; Email: general@webcomcommunications.com • URL: http://www.webcomcommunications.com • $195 Individuals hardcopy; $225 Individuals PDF. Covers: Over 2,000 antenna designers, manufacturers, distributors, installers, suppliers, consultants, government agencies and information sources worldwide. Entries include: Company name, address, phone, fax, email, website address, executive names and titles, year founded, sales, company description, and antenna types offered.

***Antilles (Netherlands) Business Law Handbook***. International Business Publications, USA, PO Box 15343 Washington, DC 20003. Phone: (202)546-2103; Fax: (202)546-3275; Email: ibpusa@comcast.net • URL: http://ibpus.com • $99.95 Individuals hardcopy, E-book and CD-ROM. Covers: Basic information on business laws and legislations, export-import regulations, business climate and contacts.

**Antiquarian Booksellers Association of America**. 20 W 44th St., Ste. 507 New York, NY 10036-6604. Phone: (212)944-8291; Fax: (212)944-8293 • URL: http://www.abaa.org • Dealers and appraisers of fine, rare and out-of-print books, manuscripts, and related materials. Sponsors two annual regional international book fairs and four biennial regional international book fairs. Promotes ethical standards in the industry. Sponsors educational programs for members, librarians, archivists, and the public. Administers the Antiquarian Booksellers' Benevolent Fund.

***Antique Shop Guide—Central Edition***. Mayhill Publications Midcountry Media, 27 N Jefferson St. Knightstown, IN 46148. Phone: 800-876-5133 or (765)345-5133; Fax: (765)345-3398; Email: mthoe@midcountrymedia.com • URL: http://www.midcountrymedia.com • Annual. $6.25 Individuals. Covers: Antique shops in Illinois, Indiana, Iowa, Kentucky, Michigan, Minnesota, Missouri, Ohio, Tennessee, Wisconsin, western Pennsylvania, and West Virginia. Entries include: For antique shops—Shop name, address, map reference, specialty, whether reproductions are stocked, hours and seasons open, phone. Listings for other categories have similar detail.

***Antitrust and Trade Regulation Report***. Bloomberg BNA, 3 Bethesda Metro Center, Ste. 250 Bethesda, MD 20814-5377. Phone: 800-372-1033 or (703)341-3000; Fax: (800)253-0332; Email: customercare@bna.com • URL: http://www.bna.com • Weekly. $1,479.00 per year. Looseleaf service.

***Antitrust Basics***. ALM Media Properties LLC, 120 Broadway, 5th Fl. New York, NY 10271-1100. Phone: (212)457-9400; Fax: (646)417-7705; Email: customercare@alm.com • URL: http://www.alm.com • $535 /year. Discusses "business practices consistently upheld, as well as those consistently condemned." Covers a wide variety of antitrust legal topics. (Law Journal Press).

***Antitrust Counseling and Litigation Techniques***. Matthew Bender and Company Inc., 1275 Broadway Albany, NY 12204-2638. Phone: 800-424-4200 or (518)487-3000; Fax: (518)487-3573 or (800)424-4200; Email: customer.support@lexisnexis.com • URL: http://www.matthewbender.com • Annual. Guide to corporate antitrust counseling and successful antitrust litigation.

***Antitrust Division Manual***. U. S. Government Printing Office, 732 N Capitol St. NW Washington, DC 20401. Phone: 866-512-1800 or (202)512-1800 or (866)512-1800; Fax: (202)512-2104 or (202)512-2250; Email: contactcenter@gpo.gov • URL: http://www.gpo.gov • Looseleaf. $60.00. Includes basic manual, with supplementary material for an indeterminate period. Serves as a guide to the operating policies and procedures of the Antitrust Division of the U. S. Department of Justice (www.usdoj.gov). Covers suggested methods of conducting investigations and litigation.

***Antitrust-Intellectual Property Handbook***. Alan J. Weinschel. Glasser LegalWorks, 150 Clove Rd. Little Falls, NJ 07424. Phone: 800-308-1700 or (973)890-0008; Fax: (973)890-0042; Email: legalwks@aol.com • URL: http://www.glasserlegalworks.com • Looseleaf. $175.00. Periodic supplementation. Covers patent licensing, patent antitrust issues, innovation markets, intervention by government agencies, standard-setting activities, royalty arrangements, and related intellectual property/antitrust topics. Provides explanations, legal guidance, and historical background.

***Antitrust Law Handbook***. Thomson West, 610 Opperman Dr. Eagan, MN 55123. Phone: 800-328-9352 or (651)687-7000 • $699.30. Designed for practitioners and students.

***Antitrust Laws and Trade Regulation***. Matthew Bender and Company Inc., 1275 Broadway Albany, NY 12204-2638. Phone: 800-424-4200 or (518)487-3000; Fax: (518)487-3573 or (800)424-4200; Email: customer.support@lexisnexis.com • URL: http://www.matthewbender.com • $1,990.00. 11 looseleaf volumes. Periodic supplementation. Covers provisions and applications of the Sherman, Clayton, Robinson-Patman, and Federal Trade Commission Acts. Also covers state antitrust laws.

***Antitrust Laws and Trade Regulation: Desk Edition***. Matthew Bender and Company Inc., 1275 Broadway Albany, NY 12204-2638. Phone: 800-424-4200 or (518)487-3000; Fax: (518)487-3573 or (800)424-4200; Email: customer.support@lexisnexis.com • URL: http://www.matthewbender.com • $1,999 Print (2 Volumes); $1,817 E-book (2 Volumes). Includes the history and organization of the antitrust laws.

***Antitrust Litigation Reporter: The National Journal of Record on Antitrust Litigation***. Andrews Publications, 175 Strafford Ave., Bldg. 4, Suite 140 Wayne, PA 19087. Phone: 800-345-1101 or (610)225-0510 or (610)622-0510; Fax: (610)225-0501 or (610)622-0501; Email: customer@andrewspub.com • URL: http://www.andrewspub.com • Monthly. $775.00 per year. Newsletter. Provides reports on federal and state antitrust statutes.

**AOAC International**. 481 N Frederick Ave., Ste. 500 Gaithersburg, MD 20877-2417. Phone: 800-379-2622 or (301)924-7077; Fax: (301)924-7089; Email: aoac@aoac.org • URL: http://www.aoac.org • Government, academic, and industry analytical scientists who develop, test, and collaboratively study methods for analyzing fertilizers, foods, feeds, pesticides, drugs, cosmetics, and other products related to agriculture and public health. Offers short courses for analytical laboratory personnel in chemical and microbiological quality assurance, lab waste management, statistics, giving expert testimony, and technical writing.

**APA: The Engineered Wood Association**. 7011 S 19th St. Tacoma, WA 98466. Phone: (253)565-6600 or (253)620-7400; Fax: (253)565-7265; Email: help@apawood.org • URL: http://www.apawood.org • Manufacturers of structural panel products, oriented strand board and composites. Conducts trade promotion through advertising, publicity, merchandising, and field promotion. Maintains quality supervision in accordance with U.S. product standards, APA performance standards, and APA trademarking. Conducts research to improve products, applications, and manufacturing techniques. Sponsors Engineered Wood Research Foundation; compiles statistics.

***Apartment Building Income-Expense Analysis***. Institute of Real Estate Management, 430 N Michigan Ave. Chicago, IL 60611. Phone: 800-837-0706 or (312)329-6000; Fax: (800)338-4736; Email: custserv@irem.org • URL: http://www.irem.org • Annual.

**APEC - Automated Procedures for Engineering Consultants, Inc.** Talbott Tower, 141 N Ludlow St., Ste. 318 Dayton, OH 45402. Phone: (937)228-2602; Fax: (937)228-5652; Email: webmaster@hvacmall.com.

**APhA Academy of Pharmacy Practice and Management**. 2215 Constitution Ave. NW Washington, DC 20037. Phone: 800-237-APHA or (202)628-4410 or (202)429-7557; Fax: (202)783-2351; Email: infocenter@aphanet.org • URL: http://www.pharmacist.com/apha-appm • Pharmacists concerned with rendering professional services directly to the public, without regard for status of employment or environment of practice. Formerly Academy of Pharmacy Practice and Management.

**APICS** . 8430 W Bryn Mawr Ave., Ste. 1000 Chicago, IL 60631. Phone: 800-444-2742 or (773)867-1777; Fax: (773)639-3000; Email: service@apics.org • URL: http://www.apics.org • Members are professional resource managers.

***Apicultural Abstracts (AA)***. International Bee Research Association, Unit 6 Centre Ct., Main Ave. Rhondda Cynon Taf CF37 5YR, United Kingdom. Phone: 44 29 20372409; Email: mail@ibra.org.uk • URL: http://www.ibra.org.uk • Quarterly. $295. Up-to-date summary of world literature on bees and beekeeping.

**Appalachian Hardwood Manufacturers**. 816 Eastchester Dr. High Point, NC 27262. Phone: (336)885-8315; Fax: (336)886-8865; Email: office@appalachianwood.org • URL: http://www.appalachianwood.org • Promotes Appalachian hardwoods.

**Appalachian State University - Center for Economic Research and Policy Analysis**. Raley Hall, Rm. 3095, Walker College of Business Boone, NC 28608. Phone: (828)262-6081; Fax: (828)262-6105; Email: cherrytl@appstate.edu • URL: http://cerpa.appstate.edu • Economics and public policy, focusing on environment and energy, economic development, survey research and experimental methods.

**Apple Products Research and Education Council**. 1100 Johnson Ferry Rd., Ste. 300 Atlanta, GA 30342. Phone: (404)252-3663; Email: jpa@kellencompany.com • URL: http://www.appleproducts.org • Represents processors of apple products and suppliers to the industry. Conducts program to improve business conditions in the apple products industry and to enable the industry to serve the interests of consumers. Conducts research programs on the health benefits of apple products.

**Appliance Parts Distributors Association**. 3621 N Oakley Ave. Chicago, IL 60618. Phone: (773)230-9851; Fax: (888)308-1423 • URL: http://www.apda.com • Wholesale distributors of appliance parts, supplies and accessories. Promotes the sale of appliance parts through independent parts distributors.

***Applied Mechanics Reviews: An Assessment of World Literature in Engineering Sciences***. ASME International, 2 Park Ave. New York, NY 10016-5990. Phone: 800-843-2763 or (973)882-1170; Fax: (973)882-1717; Email: customercare@asme.org • URL: http://www.asme.org • Bimonthly. $129 print and online; $691 U.S. and Canada print and online.

***Applied Radiation and Isotopes***. Elsevier, Secondary Publishing Division, 650 Ave. of the Americas New York, NY 10011. Phone: 888-437-4636 or (212)633-3980; Fax: (212)633-3975; Email: t.reller@elsevier.com • URL: http://www.elseveier.com • Monthly. $374 Institutions. Journal presenting isotopic and radiation techniques, especially novel ones, and those capable of a wide application in industry and medicine.

***Applied Science & Business Periodicals Retrospective***. EBSCO Publishing Inc., 10 Estes St. Ipswich, MA 01938-2106. Phone: 800-653-2726 or (978)356-6500; Fax: (978)356-6565; Email: information@ebscohost.com • URL: http://www.ebscohost.com • Includes citations for more than 3 million articles detailing events, issues, and trends in business and industry.

***Applied Science and Technology Abstracts***. EBSCO Publishing Inc., 10 Estes St. Ipswich, MA 01938-2106. Phone: 800-653-2726 or (978)356-6500; Fax: (978)356-6565; Email: information@ebscohost.com • URL: http://www.ebscohost.com • Citations for more than 700 prominent scientific, technical, engineering, and industrial periodicals.

***Applied Science and Technology Index***. EBSCO Publishing Inc., 10 Estes St. Ipswich, MA 01938-2106. Phone: 800-653-2726 or (978)356-6500; Fax: (978)356-6565; Email: information@ebscohost.com • URL: http://www.ebscohost.com • 11/year. Indexes a wide variety of English language technical, industrial, and engineering periodicals.

***Applied Science and Technology Index Online***. H.W. Wilson Co., 950 University Ave. Bronx, NY 10452-4224. Phone: 800-367-6770 or (718)588-8400 or (718)558-8400; Fax: (718)590-1617 or (800)590-1617; Email: custserv@hwwilson.com • URL: http://www.hwwilson.com • Provides online indexing of 500 major scientific, technical, industrial, and engineering periodicals. Time period is 1983 to date. Monthly updates. Inquire as to online cost and availability.

***Applied Stochastic Models in Business and Industry***. John Wiley & Sons Inc., 111 River St. Hoboken, NJ 07030-5774. Phone: 800-225-5945 or (201)748-6000; Fax: (201)748-6088; Email:

info@wiley.com • URL: http://www.wiley.com • Bimonthly. €1,772 Institutions print only; $2,744 Institutions, other countries print only; £1,401 Institutions print only; €2,038 Institutions print with online; £1,611 Institutions print with online; $3,156 Institutions, other countries print with online. Journal covering applications and problem-solving techniques of applied probability and data analysis.

*Applying GAAP and GAAS*. Matthew Bender and Company Inc., 1275 Broadway Albany, NY 12204-2638. Phone: 800-424-4200 or (518)487-3000; Fax: (518)487-3573 or (800)424-4200; Email: customer.support@lexisnexis.com • URL: http://www.matthewbender.com • $898 Print; $756 E-book; $837 CD-ROM. In-depth explanations of generally accepted accounting principles (GAAP) and generally accepted auditing standards (GAAS).

**Appraisal Institute**. 200 W Madison St., Ste. 1500 Chicago, IL 60606. Phone: 888-756-4624 or (312)335-4401 or (312)335-4100; Fax: (312)335-4415; Email: aiservice@appraisalinstitute.org • URL: http://www.appraisalinstitute.org • General appraisers who hold the MAI designation, and residential members who hold the SRA designation. Enforces Code of Professional Ethics and Standards of Professional Appraisal Practice. Confers one general designation, the MAI, and one residential designation, the SRA. Provides training in valuation of residential and income properties, market analysis, and standards of professional appraisal practice. Sponsors courses in preparation for state certification and licensing; offers continuing education programs for designated members.

**Appraisers Association of America**. 212 W 35th St., 11th Fl. S New York, NY 10001. Phone: (212)889-5404; Fax: (212)889-5503; Email: referrals@appraisersassociation.org • URL: http://www.appraisersassociation.org • Professional society of appraisers of personal property such as: Americana; antiques; armor; art objects; bibelot; books; bronzes; china and porcelain; clocks and watches; coins; crystal and glass; curios; diamonds and jewelry; enamels; etchings; fine art; firearms; furniture; furs; graphic art; guns; household furnishings; ivories; leather goods; lighting fixtures; linens and lace; miniatures; music; musical instruments; oriental art; paintings; pewter; pianos; primitive art; prints; rugs; sculpture; Sheffield plate; silver and silverware; stamps; steins and tankards; taxes; and woodcarvings.

*Approved Drug Products, with Therapeutic Equivalence Evaluations*. U. S. Government Printing Office, 732 N Capitol St. NW Washington, DC 20401. Phone: 866-512-1800 or (202)512-1800 or (866)512-1800; Fax: (202)512-2104 or (202)512-2250; Email: contactcenter@gpo.gov • URL: http://www.gpo.gov • $273 U.S.; $382.20 Other countries. Issued by the Food and Drug Administration, U. S. Department of Health and Human Services. Lists prescription drugs that have been approved by the FDA. Includes therapeutic equivalents to aid in containment of health costs and to serve State drug selection laws.

**APQC**. 123 N Post Oak Ln. Houston, TX 77024. Phone: 800-776-9676 or (713)681-4020; Fax: (713)681-8578; Email: apqcinfo@apqc.org • URL: http://www.apqc.org • Resource for process and performance improvement. Helps organizations adapt to rapidly changing environments, build new and better ways to work, and succeed in a competitive marketplace. Focuses on productivity, knowledge management, benchmarking, and quality improvement initiatives. Works with member organizations to identify best practices, discover effective methods of improvement, broadly disseminate findings, and connect individuals with one another and the knowledge and tools they need to succeed. Serves approximately 500 organizations worldwide in all sectors of business, education, and government.

*Aqualine*. Cambridge Scientific Abstracts L.P., 7200 Wisconsin Ave., Ste. 601 Bethesda, MD 20814. Phone: 800-843-7751 or (301)961-6700 or (301)961-6785; Fax: (301)961-6720 or (301)961-6708; Email: sales@proquest.com • URL: http://www.proquest.co.uk • Provides online citations and abstracts to a wide variety of literature relating to the aquatic environment, including 400 journals, from 1960 to date. Updating is monthly. Inquire as to online cost and availability.

**Aquatic Research Interactive**. 1100 W Columbus Dr. East Chicago, IL 46312. Phone: (219)391-4138; Fax: (219)391-4168; Email: fishmail@arii.org

*Aquatic Sciences and Fisheries Abstracts: Aquatic Pollution and Environmental Quality*. Food and Agriculture Organization of the United Nations, CSA, 7200 Wisconsin Ave. Bethesda, MD 20814. Phone: 800-843-7751 or (301)961-6700; Fax: (301)961-6720; Email: service@csa.com • URL: http://www.csa.com • Bimonthly. Part three. Includes print and online editions.

*Arab-British Trade Directory*. Arab-British Chamber of Commerce, 43 Upper Grosvenor St. London W1K 2NJ, United Kingdom. Phone: 71 2354363; Fax: 71 2456688; Email: info@abcc.org.uk • URL: http://www.abcc.org.uk • £125; Free members; £4.50 additional copy; $6 Other countries additional copy. Covers: Over 5,000 UK and Arab companies from the manufacturing, trading, services, and financial sectors. Entries include: Contact details of companies from joint Arab-Foreign chambers around the world.

**Arab International Women's Forum**. Berkeley Square House, Berkeley Sq. London W1J 6BD, United Kingdom. Phone: 44 20 78877630; Fax: 44 20 78876001 • URL: http://www.

aiwfonline.com/home.aspx • Promotes the role of women in the economy and society. Serves as a link between the Arab business and professional women and their counterparts in the international community.

*Arabian Business*. The Information & Technology Publishing Company Ltd., PO Box 500024 Dubai, United Arab Emirates. Phone: 971 4 4443000; Fax: 971 4 4443030; Email: info@itp.com • URL: http://www.itp.com • Weekly. English-language business magazine for the Middle East.

*Arbitron Radio County Coverage*. Arbitron Inc., 9705 Patuxent Woods Dr. Columbia, MD 21046-1572. Phone: 800-543-7300 or (410)312-8000 or (212)887-1300; Fax: (212)887-1390 or (212)887-1401; Email: info@arbitron.com • URL: http://www.arbitron.com • Ratings of radio and TV stations plus audience measurement data, updated frequently. Inquire as to online cost and availability.

*Archery Business: The Voice of the Archery Industry*. Grand View Media Group Inc., 200 Croft St., Ste. 1 Birmingham, AL 35242. Phone: 888-431-2877 or (205)408-3797; Fax: (205)408-3797; Email: webmaster@grandviewmedia.com • URL: http://www.gvmg.com • Bimonthly. Trade magazine covering the business side of archery and bowhunting.

**Architectural Engineering Institute of ASCE**. 1801 Alexander Bell Dr. Reston, VA 20191-4400. Phone: 800-548-2723; Email: aei@asce.org • URL: http://www.asce.org/aei • Seeks to advance the state-of-the-art and state-of-the-practice of the building industry worldwide by facilitating effective and timely technology transfer. Provides a multidisciplinary forum for building industry professionals to examine technical, scientific and professional issues of common interest.

**Architectural Woodwork Institute**. 46179 Westlake Dr., Ste. 120 Potomac Falls, VA 20165. Phone: (571)323-3636; Fax: (571)323-3630; Email: info@awinet.org • URL: http://www.awinet.org • Manufacturers of architectural woodwork products (casework, fixtures, and paneling) and associated suppliers of equipment and materials. Works to: raise industry standards; research new and improved materials and methods; publish technical data helpful in the design and use of architectural woodwork. Conducts seminars and training course.

*Area Business Councils/Small Business Update*. Greater San Antonio Chamber of Commerce, 602 E Commerce St. San Antonio, TX 78205. Phone: (210)229-2100 or (210)229-2128; Fax: (210)229-1600; Email: infostore@sachamber.org • URL: http://sachamber.org • Weekly.

*Area Development Sites & Facility Planning—Industrial Development Directory of Canada Issue*. Halcyon Business Publications Inc., 400 Post Ave. Westbury, NY 11590-2289. Phone: 800-735-2732 or (516)338-0900; Fax: (516)338-0100; Email: areadev@area-development.com • URL: http://www.area-development.com • Annual. $25. Publication includes: List of industrial development organizations at provincial and municipal levels. Entries include: Name, address, phone, and name and title of contact.

*Argentina Business Forecast Report*. Telecommunications Insight, 85 Queen Victoria St. London EC4V 4AB, United Kingdom. Phone: 20 72 465100 or 44 20 7248 0468; Fax: 20 72 480467 or 44 20 7248 0467; Email: enquiries@telecomsinsight.com • URL: http://www.telecomsinsight.com • Quarterly. $1,195 Individuals Single User; $1,795 Individuals Up to 3 users. Business forecast report for Argentina.

*Argentina Company Handbook*. Hoover's Inc., 5800 Airport Blvd. Austin, TX 78752-4204. Phone: 866-443-3939 or (512)374-4500 or (866)281-5969; Fax: (512)374-4501; Email: salesteam@hoovers.com • URL: http://www.hoovers.com • Annual. $49.95. Covers: 32 of Argentina's major public companies. Database includes: Information on Argentina's economy, the securities market, the stock exchange, and the rules governing foreign investments in the Argentina capital markets. Entries include: Name, address, phone, fax, year established, stock ticker symbol, names and titles of key personnel, number of employees, number of stockholders, company history, financial data, names of major stockholders, affiliated companies.

*Argentina Government and Business Contacts Handbook*. International Business Publications, USA, PO Box 15343 Washington, DC 20003. Phone: (202)546-2103; Fax: (202)546-3275; Email: ibpusa@comcast.net • URL: http://ibpus.com • $99.95 Individuals hardcopy, E-book and CD-ROM. Covers: Strategic government and business information, export-import activity in the country, investment, business contacts and regulations.

*Argentina Industrial and Business Directory*. International Business Publications, USA, PO Box 15343 Washington, DC 20003. Phone: (202)546-2103; Fax: (202)546-3275; Email: ibpusa@comcast.net • URL: http://ibpus.com • Annual. $99.95 Individuals hardcover; $99.95 Individuals CD-ROM; $99.95 Individuals E-book. Covers: Detailed information on investment, export-import business opportunities, foreign economic assistance projects, government and business contacts.

**Argentina Israel Chamber of Commerce**. Phone: 54 11 43726273; Email: info@ccai.com.ar • URL: http://www.ccai.com.ar • Promotes trade between Argentina and Israel.

**Argentine-American Chamber of Commerce**. 150 E 58th St. New York, NY 10155. Phone: (212)698-2238; Fax: (212)698-1144; Email: info@argentinechamber.org • URL: http://www.argentinechamber.org • Promotes business and trade between

Argentina and the United States.

**Argentine Chamber of Limited Companies**. Libertad 1340, PB C1016ABB Buenos Aires, Argentina. Phone: 54 11 40107701; Email: camaradesociedades@camaradesociedades.com • URL: http://www.camaradesociedades.com • Represents members of Chamber of Limited Companies in Argentina.

**Argentine Chinese Chamber of Production, Industry and Commerce**. Viamonte 1145 7 A C1053ABW Buenos Aires, Argentina. Phone: 54 11 43726133; Fax: 54 11 43726133; Email: argenchina@ciudad.com.ar • URL: http://www.argenchina.org/_en_index.asp • Promotes business trade between Argentina and China.

**Argentine Fiscal Associations**. IFLYSIB Calle 59, 789, CC 565 B19 00BTE La Plata, Argentina. Phone: 54 221 4254904; Fax: 54 221 4257317; Email: afa@iflysib.unlp.edu.ar • URL: http://www2.ib.edu.ar/afa • Promotes the study and advancement of international and comparative law with regards to public finance, specifically international, comparative fiscal law and the financial and economic aspects of taxation.

**Argentine Industry Association**. Av. de Mayo 1147/57 C1085ABB Buenos Aires, Argentina. Phone: 54 11 41242300; Fax: 54 11 41242301; Email: uia@uia.org.ar • URL: http://www.uia.org.ar • Represents members of industrial union in Argentina.

**Argonne National Laboratory - Office of Technology Transfer**. 9700 S Cass Ave., Bldg. 201 Lemont, IL 60439-4832. Phone: 800-627-2596; Fax: (630)252-5230; Email: partners@anl.gov • URL: http://www.anl.gov/technology/technology-development-and-commercialization • Formerly Industrial Technology Development Center.

**Arizona State University - Center for Solid State Electronics Research**. PO Box 876206 Tempe, AZ 85287-6206. Phone: (480)965-3708; Fax: (480)965-8118; Email: trevor.thornton@asu.edu • URL: http://more.engineering.asu.edu/nanofab • Fabrication and modeling of nanostructures, heterostructures, molecular beam epitaxy, integrated optoelectronics, and silicon integrated circuits, bio-molecular electronics, bio-mems, nano-fluids, high-k dielectrics.

**Arizona State University - Sandra Day O'Connor College of Law - Center for Law, Science and Innovation**. Armstrong Hall, 1100 S McAllister Ave. Tempe, AZ 85287. Phone: (480)965-6181 • URL: http://www.law.asu.edu/lsi • Studies the development of legal frameworks for new technologies and advancing the use of science in legal decision making.

*Arkansas Business Directory*. InfoGroup Inc., 5711 S 86th Cir. Omaha, NE 68127-4146. Phone: (402)593-4500 • URL: http://www.infogroup.com • Annual. $450. Covers: 126,071 businesses in Arkansas. Entries include: Company name, address, phone, number of employees, name of owner or manager, sales volume. Compiled from telephone company "Yellow Pages," statewide. All states covered (see separate entries).

*Arkansas Export Directory*. Arkansas Economic Development Commission, 900 W Capitol Ave. Little Rock, AR 72201. Phone: 800-ARKANSAS or (501)682-1121 • URL: http://www.arkansasedc.com • Annual. Covers: Products produced by Arkansas firms who export or are seeking to develop export sales. Entries include: Company name, address, phone.

*Arkansas Manufacturing Directory*. Arkansas Industrial Development Foundation, Box 1784 Little Rock, AR 72203. Phone: (501)682-7354 • Annual. $75 pre-payment required. Covers: about 2,800 firms in Arkansas. Entries include: Company name, address, phone, names of principal executives, number of employees, list of products or services, Standard Industrial Classification (SIC) codes, whether company exports, name of parent company if firm is a subsidiary.

**ARMA International - The Association of Information Management Professionals**. 11880 College Blvd., Ste. 450 Overland Park, KS 66210. Phone: 800-422-2762 or (913)341-3808; Fax: (913)341-3742; Email: headquarters@armaintl.org • URL: http://www.arma.org • Formerly ARMA International-The Information Management Professionals.

**Armed Forces Hostess Association**. The Pentagon, Rm. 1E541, 6604 Army Pentagon Washington, DC 20310. Phone: (703)614-0350 or (703)614-0485; Fax: (703)697-5542 • URL: http://sswafha.hqda.pentagon.mil • Information office operated by volunteer wives of the armed forces. Assists in welcoming service families to the Washington, DC area; provides information on living conditions at all U.S. installations in the U.S. and overseas. Maintains information files on topics ranging from animal care and camps to universities and local vacation areas.

**Armed Forces Sports**. 2455 Reynolds Rd. San Antonio, TX 78234-7588. Phone: (210)466-1335 or (210)466-1336 • URL: http://armedforcessports.defense.gov • Persons serving as head of the morale and welfare activities of the U.S. Army, Navy, Marines, and Air Force. Encourages physical fitness in the armed forces through a policy of "sports for all"; has established uniform rules to govern all service sports within its jurisdiction. Conducts interservice sports championship competitions. Develops and encourages spectator interest sports for the individual services. Selects and sends military athletes and teams to national and international competitions; has representative on the Executive Board and House of

Delegates of the U.S. Olympic Committee, various U.S. sports governing bodies, and the International Military Sports Council. Compiles statistics.

***Armenia Export-Import and Business Directory***. International Business Publications, USA, PO Box 15343 Washington, DC 20003. Phone: (202)546-2103; Fax: (202)546-3275; Email: ibpusa@comcast.net • URL: http://ibpus.com • $99.95 Individuals. Covers strategic, economic, investment, export-import, and business opportunities and contact numbers.

***Armenia Government and Business Contacts Handbook***. International Business Publications, USA, PO Box 15343 Washington, DC 20003. Phone: (202)546-2103; Fax: (202)546-3275; Email: ibpusa@comcast.net • URL: http://ibpus.com • $99.95 Individuals hardcopy, E-book and CD-ROM. Covers: Strategic government and business information, export-import activity in the country, investment, business contacts and regulations.

***Armenia Industrial and Business Directory***. International Business Publications, USA, PO Box 15343 Washington, DC 20003. Phone: (202)546-2103; Fax: (202)546-3275; Email: ibpusa@comcast.net • URL: http://ibpus.com • Annual. $99.95 Individuals. Covers industrial, investment and business contacts for conducting export-import and investment activity in the country.

**Armenian American Chamber of Commerce**. 225 E Broadway, Ste. 313C Glendale, CA 91205. Phone: (818)247-0196; Fax: (818)247-7668; Email: aacc@armenianchamber.com • URL: http://www.armenianchamber.org • Aims to serve the needs of the business community in the United States and abroad. Assists its members, which consist of business persons, professionals and scholars in business development and networking. Advances the industrial, commercial, professional and public interests of the Armenian American community.

***Army AL&T: Professional Publication of the AL&T Community***. U. S. Government Printing Office, 732 N Capitol St. NW Washington, DC 20401. Phone: 866-512-1800 or (202)512-1800 or (866)512-1800; Fax: (202)512-2104 or (202)512-2250; Email: contactcenter@gpo.gov • URL: http://www.gpo.gov • Quarterly. $21 U.S.; $29.40 Other countries; $9 Single issue US; $12.60 Single issue Other countries. Produced by the U.S. Army Materiel Command (www.amc.army.mil). Reports on Army research, development, and acquisition. Formerly *Army RD&A*.

**Army Aviation Association of America**. 593 Main St. Monroe, CT 06468-2830. Phone: (203)268-2450; Email: aaaa@quad-a.org • URL: http://www.quad-a.org • Commissioned officers, warrant officers, and enlisted personnel serving in U.S. Army aviation assignments in the active U.S. Army, Army National Guard, and Army Reserve; Department of Army civilian personnel and industry representatives affiliated with army aviation. Fosters fellowship among military and civilian persons connected with army aviation, past or present; seeks to advance status, overall esprit, and general knowledge of professionals engaged in army aviation. Activities include locator and placement services, technical assistance, and biographical archives. Sponsors speakers' bureau; maintains hall of fame.

**Army Emergency Relief**. 200 Stovall St., Rm. 5S33 Alexandria, VA 22332-4005. Phone: 866-878-6378 or (703)428-0000; Fax: (703)325-7183; Email: aer@aerhq.org • URL: http://www.aerhq.org/dnn563 • A private organization whose primary purpose is to relieve distress of members of the Army (active and retired) and their dependents, and to provide assistance to needy spouses and orphans of deceased Army members; a secondary purpose is to make available educational assistance (scholarships) to unmarried dependent children of soldiers (active, retired, or deceased) who need such assistance to pursue undergraduate studies.

**Army Nurse Corps Association**. PO Box 39235 San Antonio, TX 78218-1235. Phone: (210)650-3534; Fax: (210)650-3494; Email: membership@e-anca.org • URL: http://e-anca.org • Army Nurse Corps officers from active, or retiree status or those serving honorably for shorter periods, or reserve duty. Provides educational and social opportunities for members; disseminates information to the public. Seeks to preserve history of the U.S. Army Nurse Corps.

**Arnold Air Society**. Executive Management Ctr., 10411 Courthouse Rd., Ste. E Spotsylvania, VA 22553. Phone: (540)710-5696; Fax: (540)710-5697; Email: emc@arnold-air.org • URL: http://www.arnold-air.org • Honorary professional fraternity within AFROTC. Organizes community service projects. Sponsors Silver Wings, a nonmilitary campus service organization.

**Art and Antique Dealers League of America**. Lennox Hill Sta. New York, NY 10021. Phone: (212)879-7558; Fax: (212)772-7197; Email: secretary@artantiquedealersleague.com • URL: http://www.artantiquedealersleague.com • Members are retailers and wholesalers of antiques and art objects.

**Art and Creative Materials Institute**. 99 Derby St., Ste. 200 Hingham, MA 02043-4216. Phone: (781)556-1044; Fax: (781)207-5550; Email: debbieg@acminet.org • URL: http://www.acminet.org • Members are manufacturers of school and professional art and craft materials.

***Art Business News***. Advanstar Communications Inc., 2501 Colorado Ave., Ste. 280 Santa Monica, CA 90404. Phone: (310)857-7500; Fax: (310)857-7510; Email: info@advanstar.com • URL: http://www.advanstar.com • Monthly. $55 Canada and Mexico; $85 Two years in Canada, and Mexico; $80 Out of country; $145 Two years international; $120 Canada and Mexico 3-years; $210 Canada and Mexico 3-years. Trade magazine covering art business news.

***Art Business Today***. Fine Art Trade Guild, 16-18 Empress Pl. London SW6 1TT, United Kingdom. Phone: 44 20 73816616; Fax: 44 20 73812596; Email: info@fineart.co.uk • URL: http://www.fineart.co.uk/ • 5/year. £29 Individuals; £35 Individuals Europe; £43 Elsewhere; £52 Two years; £61 Two years Europe; £73 Elsewhere. Trade magazine covering the art business in the UK.

***Art Calendar: The Business Magazine for Visual Artists***. Art Calendar, 1500 Park Center Dr. Orlando, FL 32835. Phone: (407)563-7000; Fax: (407)563-7099 • URL: http://www.artcalendar.com • Monthly. $37 Individuals; $59 Two years; $85 Other countries; $155 Other countries 2 years; $65 Canada; $115 Canada 2 years. Business magazine for visual artists.

**Art Dealers Association of America**. 205 Lexington Ave., Ste. 901 New York, NY 10016. Phone: (212)488-5550; Fax: (646)688-6809 • URL: http://www.artdealers.org • Art dealers united to promote the highest standards of connoisseurship, scholarship, and ethical practice within the profession and to increase public awareness of the role and responsibilities of reputable art dealers. Works with museums and scholars on activities and problems of mutual concern; cooperates with domestic and international government agencies on art matters and offers assistance and expertise to these agencies; advises on legislation and other governmental activity regarding the fine arts; seeks to identify and remove fake works of art from the marketplace. Appraises, for tax purposes only, works of art donated to nonprofit institutions.

***Art Directors Annual***. Art Directors Club. 106 W 29th St. New York, NY 10001. Phone: (212)643-1440; Fax: (212)643-4266; Email: info@adcglobal.org • URL: http://www.adcglobal.org • Annual. $70.00. Formerly *Annual of Advertising, Editorial and Television Art and Design with the Annual Copy Awards*.

**Art Directors Club**. 106 W 29th St. New York, NY 10001. Phone: (212)643-1440; Fax: (212)643-4266; Email: info@adcglobal.org • URL: http://www.adcglobal.org • Art directors of advertising magazines and agencies, visual information specialists, and graphic designers; associate members are artists, cinematographers, photographers, copywriters, educators, journalists, and critics. Promotes and stimulates interest in the practice of art direction. Sponsors Annual Exhibition of Advertising, Editorial and Television Art and Design; International Traveling Exhibition. Provides educational, professional, and entertainment programs; on-premise art exhibitions; portfolio review program. Conducts panels for students and faculty.

***Art Index***. EBSCO Publishing Inc., 10 Estes St. Ipswich, MA 01938-2106. Phone: 800-653-2726 or (978)356-6500; Fax: (978)356-6565; Email: information@ebscohost.com • URL: http://www.ebscohost.com • Indexing for over 600 periodicals and 13,000 art dissertations.

***Art Index***. EBSCO Publishing Inc., 10 Estes St. Ipswich, MA 01938-2106. Phone: 800-653-2726 or (978)356-6500; Fax: (978)356-6565; Email: information@ebscohost.com • URL: http://www.ebscohost.com • Quarterly. Annual cumulations. Price varies. Subject and author index to periodicals in art, architecture, industrial design, city planning, photography, and various related topics.

***Art Index Online***. H.W. Wilson Co., 950 University Ave. Bronx, NY 10452-4224. Phone: 800-367-6770 or (718)588-8400 or (718)558-8400; Fax: (718)590-1617 or (800)590-1617; Email: custserv@hwwilson.com • URL: http://www.hwwilson.com • Indexes a wide variety of art-related periodicals, 1984 to date. Monthly updates. Inquire as to online cost and availability.

***Art Marketing Sourcebook: Where to Sell Fine Art***. ArtNetwork, 10647 Red Dog Rd. Nevada City, CA 95959-8857. Phone: 800-383-0677 or (530)470-0862; Fax: (530)470-0256; Email: info@artmarketing.com • URL: http://www.artmarketing.com • Biennial. $23.95 plus 4 shipping. Covers: over 2,000 representatives, consultants, galleries, architects, interior designers, museums, and specialty markets. Entries include: Company name, address, phone, description of services, style represented, mediums, years in business, types of companies dealt with, geographical limitations, number of clients, requirements for viewing slides.

***Art Now Gallery Guides***. Louise Blouin Media Inc., 601 W 26th St., Ste. 410 New York, NY 10001. Phone: (212)447-9555; Email: generalinfo@artinfo.com • URL: http://www.blouinartinfo.com • Monthly. $35 Individuals; $77 Other countries. Covers: in 'Art Now Gallery Guide—International Edition' current exhibitions in over 1,800 museums and galleries. Separate regional editions cover metropolitan New York, Boston and New England, the Philadelphia area, the southeast, Chicago and the midwest, the southwest, California and the northwest, Latin America, and Europe. Listings are paid. Entries include: Gallery or museum name, address, phone, days and hours of operation, artist's name or name of the exhibit, medium, and dates of showing.

***Arts Management***. Alvin H. Reiss, 110 Riverside Dr., Ste. 4E New York, NY 10024. Phone: (212)579-2039 or (212)787-1194; Fax: (212)579-2049; Email: skipreiss@aol.com • Five times a year. $22.00 per year. National news service for those who finance, manage and communicate the arts.

**Arts SA**. GPO Box 2308 Adelaide, SA 5001, Australia. Phone: 61 8 84635444; Fax: 61 8 84635420; Email: artssa@sa.gov.au • URL: http://arts.sa.gov.au • Works to develop, facilitate and administer the Government's vision and strategy for the arts and cultural sector.

***ASA Artisan***. American Society of Artists, PO Box 1326 Palatine, IL 60078. Phone: (312)751-2500 or (847)991-4748; Email: asoaartists@aol.com • URL: http://www.americansocietyofartists.us • Quarterly. Publication includes: Lists of shows and competitions accepting fine art, art and craft work and other information for and about members. Entries include: Show or competition name, location, sponsor, name and address of contact, dates, requirements, supple exhibit info, etc. Principal content of publication is information for and about ASA members.

***ASA Today***. American Subcontractors Association, 1004 Duke St. Alexandria, VA 22314. Phone: (703)684-3450; Fax: (703)836-3482; Email: asaoffice@asa-hq.com • URL: http://www.asaonline.com • Weekly. Weekly. $40.00 per year.

**ASAE: The Center for Association Leadership**. 1575 I St. NW Washington, DC 20005-1103. Phone: 888-950-ASAE or (202)371-0940; Fax: (202)371-8315; Email: mbrshpsec@asaenet.org • URL: http://www.asaecenter.org • Professional society of paid executives of international, national, state, and local trade, professional, and philanthropic associations. Seeks to educate association executives on effective management, including: the proper objectives, functions, and activities of associations; the basic principles of association management; the legal aspects of association activity; policies relating to association management; efficient methods, procedures, and techniques of association management; the responsibilities and professional standards of association executives. Maintains information resource center. Conducts resume, guidance, and consultation services; compiles statistics in the form of reports, surveys, and studies; carries out research and education.

***Asbestos Litigation Reporter: The National Journal of Record of Asbestos Litigation***. Andrews Publications, 175 Strafford Ave., Bldg. 4, Suite 140 Wayne, PA 19087. Phone: 800-345-1101 or (610)225-0510 or (610)622-0510; Fax: (610)225-0501 or (610)622-0501; Email: customer@andrewspub.com • URL: http://www.andrewspub.com • Semimonthly. $995.00 per year. Provides reports on legal cases involving asbestos as a health hazard.

***ASFA Aquaculture Abstracts (Online)***. Cambridge Scientific Abstracts L.P., 7200 Wisconsin Ave., Ste. 601 Bethesda, MD 20814. Phone: 800-843-7751 or (301)961-6700 or (301)961-6785; Fax: (301)961-6720 or (301)961-6708; Email: sales@proquest.com • URL: http://www.proquest.co.uk • Indexing and abstracting of the literature of marine life, 1984 to present. Inquire as to online cost and availability.

***ASHRAE Transactions***. American Society of Heating, Refrigerating and Air-Conditioning Engineers, 1791 Tullie Cir. NE Atlanta, GA 30329. Phone: 800-527-4723 or (404)636-8400; Fax: (404)321-5478; Email: ashrae@ashrae.org • URL: http://www.ashrae.org • Semiannual. Members, $169.00 per year; non-members, $211.00 per year.

***Asia: A Directory and Sourcebook***. Euromonitor International Business Reference Div., 224 S Michigan Ave., Ste. 1500 Chicago, IL 60604. Phone: (312)922-1115; Fax: (312)922-1157; Email: insight@euromonitorintl.com • URL: http://www.euromonitor.com • Irregular. $430. Publication includes: Regional overview, major companies, information sources statistical datafile. Entries include: Name of organization, firm, or agency, address, statistical data, purpose or service.

**Asia Academy of Management**. Chinese University of Hong Kong, Faculty of Business Administration, Shatin, New Territories Hong Kong, Hong Kong, China. Fax: 852 2603 6840; Email: asia-aom@cuhk.edu.hk • URL: http://www.baf.cuhk.edu.hk/asia-aom • Seeks to advance management theory, research, and education relevant to Asia. Encourages members to contribute to global management scholarship.

***The Asia and Pacific Review: The Economic and Business Report***. Kogan Page, Limited, 120 Pentonville Rd. London N1 9JN, United Kingdom. Phone: 44 20 72780433 or (440) 2072780433; Fax: 44 20 78376348 or (783)76348; Email: kpinfo@kogan-page.co.uk • URL: http://www.kogan-page.co.uk/ • Covers: Key facts, indicators, country profile, business guide and directory for 60 countries in Asia and the Pacific. Database includes: Charts, tables and maps. Entries include: Heads of States, currencies, official languages, capital city, population, GNP, inflation, oil revenues, exports/imports, country profile, information for international visitors, name, address, phone of hotels, chambers of commerce, airlines, banks, government ministries and associations.

**Asia Catalyst**. 39 W 32nd St., Ste. 1602 New York, NY 10001. Phone: (212)967-2123; Email: info@asiacatalyst.org • URL: http://www.asiacatalyst.org • Provides support services to non-governmental organizations (NGOs). Facilitates capacity-building training in personnel and financial management. Conducts fundraising, advocacy, and media outreach activities. Fosters research on human rights issues that are of direct concern to NGOs.

***Asia Corporate Profile and National Finance***. Dataline Asia-Pacific Ltd., 3 Fl.Hollywood Centre, 223 Hollywood Rd. Hong Kong, China. Phone: 8155221; Fax: 8542794 • Annual.

$70. Covers: about 1,900 companies in Asia; includes list of the 500 largest companies. Entries include: Company name, address, phone, fax, telex, names and titles of key personnel, number of employees, financial data.

***Asia Pacific Autos Directory***. Business Monitor International Ltd., Senator House, 85 Queen Victoria St. London EC4V 4AB, United Kingdom. Phone: 44 20 72480468; Fax: 44 20 72480467; Email: enquiry@businessmonitor.com • URL: http://www.businessmonitor.com • $975 Individuals CD; €780 Individuals CD. Covers: 1,612 top autos executives on 519 leading automotive companies from China, Hong Kong, India, Indonesia, Malaysia, Pakistan, Philippines, Singapore, Taiwan, Thailand, and Vietnam. Entries include: Parent company head offices; full company name and address; telephone, fax, email, and website address; senior contact personnel; full description of company activity; company profile; nationality; and ownership status and parentage.

***Asia Pacific Business Review***. Routledge Journals Taylor & Francis Group, 270 Madison Ave. New York, NY 10016-0601. • URL: http://www.routledge.com • $147 Individuals print only; $598 Institutions online only; $683 Institutions print and online. Journal covering the origins of national economic success.

***Asia Pacific Food and Drink Directory***. Business Monitor International Ltd., Senator House, 85 Queen Victoria St. London EC4V 4AB, United Kingdom. Phone: 44 20 72480468; Fax: 44 20 72480467; Email: enquiry@businessmonitor.com • URL: http://www.businessmonitor.com • $895 Individuals CD. Covers: 2,022 top food and drink executives on 688 leading food and drink companies from Asia Pacific. Entries include: Company name and address; phone, fax, email and website address; senior contact personnel; full description of company activity; local company profile; nationality; and ownership status and parentage.

***Asia-Pacific International Business Directory of Importers***. Coble International, 1420 Steeple Chase Dover, PA 17315. Phone: (717)467-1835 • URL: http://www.importexporthelp.com • $455 print or CD-ROM; $500 print and CD-ROM. Covers: 32,000 importers from South Korea, Australia, Philippines, New Zealand, India, Vietnam, Sri Lanka, Japan, Kazakhstan, Malaysia, Pakistan, Singapore, Indonesia, Mauritius, South Pacific Islands, Mongolia, Hong Kong, Taiwan, Thailand, China, and Uzbekistan. Entries include: Name, address, phone, fax, primary contact person, list of products, e-mail addresses, and Web site.

***Asia Pacific Kompass on Disc***. Kompass USA, Inc., 121 Whitney Ave. New Haven, CT 06510. Phone: (877)566-7277 or (203)503-6789; Fax: (203)503-6780; Email: mail@kompass-usa.com • URL: http://www.kompass.com • Annual. CD-ROM provides information on more than 200,000 companies in Australia, China, Hong Kong, India, Korea, Malaysia, New Zealand, Philippines, Singapore, Thailand, and Taiwan. Classification system covers approximately 50,000 products and services.

**Asia Pacific Loan Market Association**. Jardine House, 32nd Fl., One Connaught Pl., Central Hong Kong, Hong Kong, China. Phone: 852 28263500 • URL: http://www.aplma.com • Promotes growth and liquidity in the primary and secondary loan markets. Facilitates the standardization of primary and secondary loan documentation. Develops standard trading, settlement and valuation procedures. Organizes educational and social functions for syndicated loan professionals. Acts as a liaison between major loan market players and regional regulators.

**Asia Pacific Network for Global Change Research**. East Bldg., 4th Fl., 1-5-2 Wakinohama Kaigan Dori, Chuo-ku Kobe, Hyogo 651 0073, Japan. Phone: 81 78 2308017; Fax: 81 78 2308018; Email: info@apn-gcr.org • URL: http://www.apn-gcr.org • Promotes, encourages and supports research activities on long-term global changes in climate, ocean and terrestrial systems, and on related physical, chemical, biological and socio-economic processes. Fosters global environmental change research in the Asia-Pacific region; increases developing country participation in research; strengthens interactions between the science community and policy makers. Cooperates closely with various scientific programmers and other networks.

***Asia Pacific Oil and Gas Directory***. Business Monitor International Ltd., Senator House, 85 Queen Victoria St. London EC4V 4AB, United Kingdom. Phone: 44 20 72480468; Fax: 44 20 72480467; Email: enquiry@businessmonitor.com • URL: http://www.businessmonitor.com • $895 Individuals. Covers: 1,329 top oil and gas executives on 445 leading oil and gas companies from Asia Pacific. Entries include: Company name and address; phone, fax, email and website address; senior contact personnel; full description of company activity; local company profile; nationality; and ownership status and parentage.

***Asia Pacific Pharmaceuticals and Healthcare Directory***. Business Monitor International Ltd., Senator House, 85 Queen Victoria St. London EC4V 4AB, United Kingdom. Phone: 44 20 72480468; Fax: 44 20 72480467; Email: enquiry@businessmonitor.com • URL: http://www.businessmonitor.com • $895 Individuals. Covers: 3,353 top pharmaceutical executives at 1,120 leading pharmaceutical companies from China, Hong Kong, India, Indonesia, Malaysia, the Philippines, Singapore, South Korea, Taiwan, Thailand and Vietnam. Entries include: Company name and address; phone, fax, email and website address; senior contact personnel; full description of company activity; local company profile; nationality; and ownership status and parentage.

***Asia Pacific Telecommunications Directory***. Business Monitor International Ltd., Senator House, 85 Queen Victoria St. London EC4V 4AB, United Kingdom. Phone: 44 20 72480468; Fax: 44 20 72480467; Email: enquiry@businessmonitor.com • URL: http://www.businessmonitor.com • $895 Individuals. Covers: 2,438 top telecommunications executives at 893 leading telecommunications companies from Asia Pacific. Entries include: company name and address; phone, fax, email and website address; senior contact personnel; full description of company activity; local company profile; nationality; and ownership status and parentage.

***Asian and Australasian Companies: A Guide to Sources of Information***. CBD Research Ltd., PO Box 524 Beckenham BR3 5JS, United Kingdom. Phone: 44 20 86507745; Fax: 44 20 86500768; Email: cbd@cbdresearch.com • URL: http://www.cbdresearch.com • $160 Individuals; £87 Individuals. Covers: Over 2,000 company information sources for the 69 countries in the Far East and Australasian organizations responsible for registering business enterprises; stock exchanges; credit reporting and business information services; publishers of business and finance publications. Entries include: Generally, company, agency, or organization name, address, phone, telex, date founded, type of company, method of selection. For publications—Title, English translation (if necessary), publisher name, address, phone, and telex; description of contents, date of publication or frequency, language, price, size.

**Asian Association of Management Organisations**. Rua de Xangai No. 175, Edif. ACM, 9 Andar Macau, Macao, China. Phone: 853 28323283; Fax: 853 28323267 • URL: http://www.aamo.net • Organization representing the national management organizations of Asian countries. Seeks to advance management practice; promotes continuing professional development of managers. Facilitates exchange of information among members; conducts research and educational programs.

***Asian Business & Management***. Palgrave Macmillan, Houndsmills Basingstoke RG21 6XS, United Kingdom. Phone: 44 1256 329242 or 44 01256 329242; Fax: 44 1256 479476 or (012)56 320109; Email: booksellers@palgrave.com • URL: http://www.palgrave.com • 5/year. £588 Institutions, other countries print; $1,092 Institutions print; £98 Other countries print and online; $182 Individuals print and online. Peer-reviewed journal covering the field of business and management.

***Asian Business Intelligence***. Asian Business Intelligence Ltd., PO Box 52-118 Taipei, Taiwan. Phone: 886 228754355; Fax: 886 228736602; Email: mmah@asianbis.com • Continuous. Covers information on market size, future growth, competitors, distribution channels, price points, and potential distributors.

***Asian Business League of San Francisco Membership Directory***. Asian Business League of San Francisco, PO Box 191345 San Francisco, CA 94119-1345. Phone: (415)670-9022; Email: info@ablsf.org • URL: http://www.ablsf.org • Includes contact information for both Asian-Pacific Americans and non-Asian Pacific Americans with an interest in expanding leadership skills.

***Asian Business League of San Francisco—Membership Directory***. Asian Business League of San Francisco, PO Box 191345 San Francisco, CA 94119-1345. Phone: (415)670-9022; Email: info@ablsf.org • URL: http://www.ablsf.org • Includes contact information of Asian-American members.

**Asian Business League of San Francisco**. PO Box 191345 San Francisco, CA 94119-1345. Phone: (415)670-9022; Email: info@ablsf.org • URL: http://www.ablsf.org • Seeks to promote and further the success of Asian Americans in business. Provides its members with seminars and opportunities to meet with other business leaders in the community, to participate in the advocacy to issues important to Asian Americans and to learn and share pertinent information about the current economic and business climate on both local and international level.

**Asian Clearing Union**. 47, 7th Negarestan Alley, Pasdaran Ave. Tehran, Iran. Phone: 98 21 2842076 or 98 21 2854509; Fax: 98 21 2847677; Email: acusecret@cbi.ir • URL: http://www.asianclearingunion.org • Central banks, monetary authorities, and treasuries of Asian countries. Works to economize on the use of exchange reserves; promotes shifting of national banking services to domestic banks; seeks to enhance economic, financial, and commercial cooperation among Asian nations. Provides short-term credit facilities.

***Asian Company Handbook***. Toyo Keizai Inc., 1-2-1 Nihonbashi Hongokucho, Chuo-ku Tokyo 103-8345, Japan. Phone: 81 3 32465551 or 3 32465580; Fax: 81 3 32790332 or 3 32424067; Email: info@toyokeizai.co.jp • URL: http://www.toyokeizai.co.jp/english • $65. Covers: Approximately 1,060 companies listed on the stock exchanges of Hong Kong, Indonesia, Malaysia, the Republic of Korea, Singapore, Taiwan, and Thailand. Entries include: Company name, address, phone, fax, geographical area served, financial data, subsidiary and branch names and locations, stock price information, description of product/service, stock price charts.

***Asian Company Profiles***. Asian Company Profiles Ltd., PO Box 12-118 Taipei, Taiwan. Phone: 886 2 2875 4355 or 886 2 875 4355; Fax: 886 2 2875 4360 or 886 2 875 4360; Email: sales@asiancredit.com • URL: http://www.asiancredit.com • Bimonthly. Database covers: over 500,000 Asian-based companies (including companies in China, Malaysia, Singapore, Indonesia, Korea, Hong Kong, Philippines, Thailand, Vietnam, Australia, New Zealand, Laos, Cambodia, Taiwan, and Papua New Guinea). Database includes: Company name, address, phone, fax, E-mail, products, Standard Industrial Classification (SIC) codes and Harmonized codes, year established, number of employees, issued capital, names and titles of key personnel, company type, subsidiaries and affiliates, organizational chart, factory description and size, product descriptions, related companies, financial data, importers' agencies, trade statistics. Expanded coverage to include companies of other Asian nations is planned.

***Asian Directory of Trade & Business Associations***. Asia Pacific Infoserv, GPO Box 2987 Sydney, NSW 2001, Australia. Phone: 61 2 4934 6290; Fax: 61 2 4934 3692; Email: aapi@aapi.com.au • URL: http://www.api-publishing.com • $245 Individuals book only; $245 Individuals CD only; $375 Individuals book and CD; $245 Individuals PDF only. Covers: Trade associations and service sectors in every Asia Pacific country. Entries include: Association name, address, telephone number, fax number, e-mail, year of establishment, President and General Secretary, number of members, memberships of international associations, and field of activity.

***Asian Finance Directory***. Mead Ventures Inc., Box 44952 Phoenix, AZ 85064. Phone: (602)234-0044 • $195. Covers: about 400 Asian financial companies, banks, securities firms, venture capitalists, and real estate financers in the United States. Entries include: Company name, address, phone, telex, fax, names and titles of key personnel, number of employees, geographical area served, financial data, local offices, subsidiaries or parent companies, description of services provided, and description of projects.

**Asian Financial Society**. 32 Broadway, Ste. 1701 New York, NY 10004-1610. Phone: (646)580-5066; Email: event@afstoday.org • URL: http://afstoday.org • Fosters business relationships and opportunities for growth for professionals in the Asian financial community.

**Asian Institute of Management Policy Center**. Eugenio Lopez Foundation Bldg., 3rd Fl., 123 Paseo de Roxas Makati City 1260, Philippines. Phone: 63 2 8924011; Fax: 63 2 4039498; Email: policycenter@aim.edu • URL: http://policy.aim.edu • Business competitiveness, especially involving globalization, technological advances, and economic opportunities.

**Asian Institute of Management**. Eugenio Lopez Foundation Bldg., Joseph R. McMicking Campus, 123 Paseo de Roxas Ave. Makati City 1229, Philippines. Phone: 63 2 8924011 or 63 2 8924023; Fax: 63 2 8672114 or 63 2 8179240; Email: enrollment@aim.edu • URL: http://www.aim.edu • Managers and business and management educators. Seeks to advance the theory and practice of business and organizational management. Sponsors research and educational programs.

**Asian Pacific American Librarians Association**. PO Box 677593 Orlando, FL 32867-7593. • URL: http://www.apalaweb.org • Librarians and information specialists of Asian Pacific descent working in the U.S.; interested persons. Provides a forum for discussing problems and concerns; supports and encourages library services to Asian Pacific communities; recruits and supports Asian Pacific Americans in the library and information science professions. Offers placement service; compiles statistics. Conducts fundraising for scholarships.

***Asian Review of Business and Technology***. Alain Charles Publishing Ltd., University House, 11-13 Lower Grosvenor Pl. London SW1W 0EX, United Kingdom. Phone: 44 20 78347676 • URL: http://www.alaincharles.com • Bimonthly. $78 Individuals. Magazine covering technology and business in Asia.

***Asia's 7,500 Largest Companies***. GAP Books, Dephna House, 24-26 Arcadia Ave. London N3 2JU, United Kingdom. Phone: 44 20 8349 7199 or 44 71 706 0919; Fax: 44 20 8349 7198 or 44 71 723 6854; Email: info@gapbooks.com • URL: http://www.gapbooks.com • Annual. $180. Covers: top 7,500 companies of Hong Kong, Indonesia, Japan, Korea, Malaysia, the Philippines, Singapore, Taiwan, Thailand, and China. Entries include: Company name, address, line of business, International SIC numbers, financial data including assets, turnover, and capital.

**ASIS International**. 1625 Prince St. Alexandria, VA 22314. Phone: (703)519-6200; Fax: (703)519-6299; Email: asis@asisonline.org • URL: http://www.asisonline.org/Pages/default.aspx • ASIS is the world's largest organization dedicated to security professionals. Presents seminars and exhibits and offers a variety of educational programs on security issues in a number of fields including communications.

**ASM International**. 9639 Kinsman Rd. Materials Park, OH 44073-0002. Phone: 800-336-5152 or (440)338-5151; Email: memberservicecenter@asminternational.org • URL: http://www.asminternational.org • Metallurgists, materials engineers, executives in materials producing and consuming industries; teachers and students. Disseminates technical information about the manufacture, use, and treatment of engineered materials. Offers in-plant, home study, and intensive courses through Materials Engineering Institute.

**ASME International**. 2 Park Ave. New York, NY 10016-5990. Phone: 800-843-2763 or (973)882-1170; Fax: (973)882-1717; Email: customercare@asme.org • URL: http://www.asme.org • Technical society of mechanical engineers and students. Conducts research; develops boiler, pressure vessel, and power test codes. Develops safety codes and standards for equipment. Conducts short course programs, and Identifying Research Needs Program. Maintains 19 research committees and 38 divisions.

*Asphalt Emulsion Manufacturers Association—Membership Directory*. Asphalt Emulsion Manufacturers Association, No. 3 Church Cir. Annapolis, MD 21401. Phone: (410)267-0023; Fax: (410)267-7546 • URL: http://www.aema.org • Biennial. Covers: About 100 member manufacturers and their plants and suppliers to the industry; international coverage. Entries include: Company name, address, phone, names and titles of representatives. Plant listings include address and phone.

**Asphalt Emulsion Manufacturers Association**. No. 3 Church Cir. Annapolis, MD 21401. Phone: (410)267-0023; Fax: (410)267-7546 • URL: http://www.aema.org • Seeks to foster advancement and improvement of the asphalt emulsion industry.

*Asphalt Institute*. 2696 Research Park Dr. Lexington, KY 40511-8480. Phone: (859)288-4960; Fax: (859)288-4999; Email: info@asphaltinstitute.org • URL: http://www.asphaltinstitute.org • Composed of petroleum asphalt/bitumen producers, manufacturers and affiliated businesses. Promotes the use, benefits, and quality performance of petroleum asphalt through environmental marketing, research, engineering, and technical development, and through the resolution of issues affecting the industry.

*Asphalt Pavement*. National Asphalt Pavement Association, 5100 Forbes Blvd. Lanham, MD 20706. Phone: 888-468-6499 or (301)731-4748; Fax: (301)731-4621; Email: napa@hotmix.org • URL: http://www.hotmix.org • Bimonthly. Free.

*Asphalt Paving Technologists*. Association of Asphalt Paving Technologists, 6776 Lake Dr., Ste. 215 Lino Lakes, MN 55014-1191. Phone: (651)293-9188; Fax: (651)293-9193; Email: aaptinfo@gmail.com • URL: http://www.asphalttechnology.org • Annual. $50 Members; $150 Nonmembers; $200. Covers: About 850 member engineers and chemists engaged in paving or related fields, such as paving materials and construction equipment; international coverage. Entries include: Name, affiliation, address, phone.

*Asphalt Recycling & Reclaiming Association—Membership Directory*. Asphalt Recycling and Reclaiming Association, 3 Church Cir. Annapolis, MD 21401-1933. Phone: (410)267-0023; Fax: (410)267-7546; Email: krissoff@arra.org • URL: http://www.arra.org • Annual. Covers: About 200 contractors, manufacturers, consulting engineers, and public works officials involved in asphalt reclaiming and recycling. Entries include: Name of company, address, phone; key personnel; type of organization or company; product line, or contact person.

**Asphalt Roofing Manufacturers Association**. 750 National Press Bldg., 529 14th St. NW Washington, DC 20045. Phone: (202)591-2450; Fax: (202)591-2445; Email: rhitchcock@kellencompany.com • URL: http://www.asphaltroofing.org • Manufacturers of asphalt shingles, rollgoods, built-up roofing systems (BUR) and modified bitumen roofing systems. Compiles statistics.

*Assecuranz Compass CD-ROM*. Kompass USA, Inc., 121 Whitney Ave. New Haven, CT 06510. Phone: (877)566-7277 or (203)503-6789; Fax: (203)503-6780; Email: mail@kompass-usa.com • URL: http://www.kompass.com • Provides detailed financial and other information on more than 21,000 insurance companies in 209 countries worldwide. Includes listings of 47,000 insurance company executives.

*Assembly Buyers Guide*. Reed Elsevier Group plc Reed Business Information, 360 Park Ave. S New York, NY 11010. Phone: (212)791-4208; Email: corporatecommunications@reedbusiness.com • URL: http://www.reedbusiness.com • Annual. $68.00. Lists manufacturers and suppliers of equipment relating to assembly automation, fasteners, adhesives, robotics, and power tools.

**Asset Based Finance Association**. 3rd Fl., 20 Hill Rise, Surrey Richmond TW10 6UA, United Kingdom. Phone: 44 20 8332 9955; Fax: 44 20 8332 2585 • URL: http://www.abfa.org.uk • Brokers, business agents, and factors in the United Kingdom. Promotes and protects members' interests in the fields of factoring and invoice discounting. Conducts educational and research programs. Maintains a code of conduct; fosters the advancement of knowledge and experience; awards diplomas to students. Disseminates information; compiles statistics.

*Assisted Living and Elder Care Directory*. InfoGroup Inc., 5711 S 86th Cir. Omaha, NE 68127-4146. Phone: (402)593-4500 • URL: http://www.infogroup.com • Annual. Number of listings: 14,305. Entries include: Name, address, phone, size of advertisement, name of owner or manager, number of employees, year first in "Yellow Pages." Compiled from telephone company "Yellow Pages," nationwide.

**Associacao Brasileira de Private Equity and Venture Capital**. Avenida Rio Branco, 123, Rm. 1505 20040-005 Rio de Janeiro, RJ, Brazil. Phone: 55 21 39702432 • URL: http://www.abvcap.com.br • Promotes and develops the private equity and venture capital industry in Brazil. Represents the interests of the Brazilian private equity and venture capital community.

**Associated Builders and Contractors**. 440 1st St. NW, Ste. 200 Washington, DC 20001. Email: gotquestions@abc.org • URL: http://www.abc.org • Construction contractors, subcontractors, suppliers and associates. Aims to foster and perpetuate the principles of rewarding construction workers and management on the basis of merit. Sponsors management education programs and craft training; also sponsors apprenticeship and skill training programs. Disseminates technological and labor relations information.

**Associated Chambers of Commerce and Industry of India**. Corporate Office, 5, Sardar Patel Marg, Chanakyapuri New Delhi 110 021, Delhi, India. Phone: 91 11 46550555; Fax: 91 11 23017008; Email: assocham@nic.in • URL: http://www.assocham.org • Corporations, chambers of commerce, and business and trade organizations. Promotes increased international trade involving India. Works to ensure a domestic political and business climate conducive to trade; gathers and disseminates economic information.

**Associated Collegiate Press**. University of Minnesota, 2221 University Ave. SE, Ste. 121 Minneapolis, MN 55414. Phone: (612)625-8335; Fax: (612)605-0072; Email: info@studentpress.org • URL: http://www.studentpress.org/acp • Conducts annual critique of newspapers and annual critique of magazines and yearbooks. Sponsors competitions.

**Associated Cooperage Industries of America**. 10001 Taylorsville Rd., Ste. 201 Louisville, KY 40299-3116. Phone: (502)261-2242; Fax: (502)261-9425; Email: acia@att.net • URL: http://www.acia.net • Serves as contact point for members; disseminates information about the wooden barrel, with emphasis on white oak; promotes the common interest of those in the industry.

**Associated Equipment Distributors** . 600 22nd St., Ste. 220 Oak Brook, IL 60523. Phone: 800-388-0650 or (630)574-0650; Fax: (630)574-0132; Email: info@aednet.org • URL: http://www.aednet.org • Represents distributors and manufacturers of agriculture, and construction, mining, logging, forestry, public works and road maintenance equipment in the U.S., Canada, and overseas. Includes activities such as industry information and statistics, educational programs on customer service, financial management, rental management, sales management, and service and parts management program for younger executives. Maintains Washington, DC office. Oversees AED Foundation which offers industry educational programs and career/vocational services. Offers group and business insurance to members; conducts ongoing industry relations program with construction equipment manufacturers and users.

**Associated General Contractors of America**. 2300 Wilson Blvd., Ste. 400 Arlington, VA 22201. Phone: 800-242-1767 or (703)548-3118 or (703)837-5319; Fax: (703)548-3119 or (703)837-5407; Email: info@agc.org • URL: http://www.agc.org • General construction contractors; subcontractors; industry suppliers; service firms. Provides market services through its divisions. Conducts special conferences and seminars designed specifically for construction firms. Compiles statistics on job accidents reported by member firms. Maintains 65 committees, including joint cooperative committees with other associations and liaison committees with federal agencies.

**Associated Locksmiths of America**. 3500 Easy St. Dallas, TX 75247. Phone: 800-532-2562 or (214)819-9733; Fax: (214)819-9736; Email: mary@aloa.org • URL: http://www.aloa.org • Retail locksmiths; associate members are manufacturers and distributors of locks, keys, safes, and burglar alarms. Aims to educate and provide current information to individuals in the physical security industry. Maintains information and referral services for members; offers insurance and bonding programs. Holds annual five-day technical training classes and 3-day technical exhibit. Maintains museum.

**Associated Press Managing Editors**. c/o Debra Adams Simmons, President, 1801 Superior Ave. Cleveland, OH 44114. Phone: (216)999-4737 • URL: http://www.apme.com • Represents managing editors or executives on the news or editorial staff of The Associated Press newspapers. Aims to: advance the journalism profession; examine the news and other services of the Associated Press in order to provide member newspapers with services that best suit their needs; provide a means of cooperation between the management and the editorial representatives of the members of the Associated Press. Maintains committees dealing with newspapers and news services.

**Associated Specialty Contractors**. 3 Bethesda Metro Ctr., Ste. 1100 Bethesda, MD 20814. Email: dgw@necanet.org • URL: http://www.assoc-spec-con.org • Works to promote efficient management and productivity. Coordinates the work of specialized branches of the industry in management information, research, public information, government relations and construction relations. Serves as a liaison among specialty trade associations in the areas of public relations, government relations, and with other organizations. Seeks to avoid unnecessary duplication of effort and expense or conflicting programs among affiliates. Identifies areas of interest and problems shared by members, and develops positions and approaches on such problems.

**Associated Surplus Dealers**. 6255 W Sunset Blvd., 19th Fl. Los Angeles, CA 90028. Phone: 800-421-4511 or (323)817-2200; Fax: (310)481-1900; Email: camille.candella@nielsen.com •

URL: http://www.asdonline.com • Represents surplus, general merchandise, and close-out dealers, manufacturers, manufacturers' representatives, and others. Promotes trade shows; provides liaison with government agencies; offers group life insurance coverage.

**Association des Femmes Chefs d'Entreprises du Cote d'Ivoire**. BP 8232 Abidjan 08, Côte d'Ivoire. Phone: 225 3 327571; Email: fcem_ci@yahoo.fr • URL: http://www.fcem.org/en/pays-membres.html • Promotes women's entrepreneurial initiatives. Reinforces national associations of women business entrepreneurial potentials. Lobbies before the public and private institutions, policy makers and governments on issues that impede women's entrepreneurial potentials. Facilitates the development of business, partnership and trade. Fosters professional growth and business skills perfection. Encourages women to create enterprises.

**Association des Femmes Chefs d'Entreprises du Maroc**. Residence El Amri, Rue du 6 octubre, Quartie Racine Casablanca, Morocco. Phone: 212 22 397593; Fax: 212 22 397736; Email: afem@afem.ma • URL: http://afem.ma • Promotes women's entrepreneurial initiatives. Reinforces national associations of women business entrepreneurial potentials. Lobbies before the public and private institutions, policy makers and governments on issues that impede women's entrepreneurial potentials. Facilitates the development of business, partnership and trade. Fosters professional growth and business skills perfection. Encourages women to create enterprises.

**Association des Femmes d'Affaires et Chefs d'Entreprises du Benin**. BP 1226 Cotonou, Benin. Phone: 229 331617; Fax: 229 332627; Email: hotelgl@leland.bj • URL: http://fcem.org/en/pays-membres/195-pays-membres/fiche-pays-details/afrique-membres/1523-republique-de-benin-afrique-membres.html • Promotes women's entrepreneurial initiatives. Reinforces national associations of women business entrepreneurial potentials. Lobbies before the public and private institutions, policy makers and governments on issues that impede women's entrepreneurial potentials. Facilitates the development of business, partnership and trade. Fosters professional growth and business skills perfection. Encourages women to create enterprises.

**Association des Femmes d'Affaires et Chefs d'Entreprises du Gabon**. B.P. 6023 Libreville, Gabon. Phone: 241 6 264216; Fax: 241 723883; Email: refegcham@yahoo.fr • URL: http://www.fcem.org/en/pays-membres.html • Promotes women's entrepreneurial initiatives. Reinforces national associations of women business entrepreneurial potentials. Lobbies before the public and private institutions, policy makers and governments on issues that impede women's entrepreneurial potentials. Facilitates the development of business, partnership and trade. Fosters professional growth and business skills perfection. Encourages women to create enterprises.

**Association des Femmes Entrepreneurs Chefs d'Entreprises**. Ave. Le Marinel N 9-11, Commune de la Gombe Kinshasa, Republic of the Congo. Phone: 243 998911092; Fax: 243 3225667; Email: bismura2@yahoo.fr • URL: http://www.fcem.org/en/pays-membres.html • Promotes women's entrepreneurial initiatives. Reinforces national associations of women business entrepreneurial potentials. Lobbies before the public and private institutions, policy makers and governments on issues that impede women's entrepreneurial potentials. Facilitates the development of business, partnership and trade. Fosters professional growth and business skills perfection. Encourages women to create enterprises.

**Association for Accounting Administration**. 136 S Keowee St. Dayton, OH 45402. Phone: (937)222-0030; Fax: (937)222-5794; Email: aaainfo@cpaadmin.org • URL: http://www.cpaadmin.org • Members are accounting and office systems executives.

**Association for Advanced Life Underwriting**. 11921 Freedom Dr., Ste. 1100 Reston, VA 20190. Phone: 888-275-0092 or (703)641-9400; Fax: (703)641-9885 • URL: http://www.aalu.org • Represents advanced life underwriters who specialize in the more complex fields of estate analysis, business insurance, pension planning, employee benefit plans, and other subjects related to the sale and service of large volumes of life insurance. Serves as conference of the National Association of Life Underwriters.

**Association for Better Insulation**. 3906 Auburn Hills Dr. Greensboro, NC 27407. Phone: (603)768-3984; Fax: (270)721-0022; Email: service@betterinsulation.com • Informs homeowners about better insulation choices to help them make educated decisions. Promotes a green and more sustainable growth in the insulation industry. Acts as a proponent of green building products, environment responsibility and long term savings of energy and resources in the building industry.

**Association for Business Communication**. 181 Turner St. NW Blacksburg, VA 24061. Phone: (540)231-8460 or (540)231-1939; Email: abcoffice@businesscommunication.org • URL: http://www.businesscommunication.org • College teachers of business communication; management consultants in business communications; training directors and correspondence supervisors of business firms, direct mail copywriters, public relations writers, and others interested in communication for business.

**Association for Business Simulation and Experiential Learning**. The Citadel, School of Business Administration,

171 Moultrie St. Charleston, SC 29409. Phone: (936)294-1975 or (530)898-6395 • URL: http://absel.org • Business professors and practitioners dedicated to the development and use of experiential teaching techniques, both computerized and noncomputerized, in business education. Assists potential users through informal dialogue with experienced members and through tutorial sessions at annual meetings.

**Association for Career and Technical Education**. 1410 King St. Alexandria, VA 22314. Phone: 800-826-9972; Fax: (703)683-7424; Email: acte@acteonline.org • URL: http://www.acteonline.org • Represents teachers, supervisors, administrators, and others interested in the development and improvement of vocational, Technical, and practical arts education. Areas of interest include: secondary, postsecondary, and adult vocational education; education for special population groups; cooperative education. Works with such government agencies as: Bureau of Apprenticeship in Department of Labor; Office of Vocational Rehabilitation in Department of Health and Human Services; Veterans Administration; Office of Vocational and Adult Education of the Department of Education. Maintains hall of fame.

**Association for Computational Linguistics**. 209 N Eighth St. Stroudsburg, PA 18360. Phone: (570)476-8006; Fax: (570)476-0860; Email: acl@aclweb.org • URL: http://www.aclweb.org • Individuals interested in computational linguistics. Deals with algorithms, models, and computer systems or components of systems for research on language, applications (translation, documentation, and lexicography), and scholarly investigation (stylistics and content analysis).

**Association for Computing Machinery** . 2 Penn Plz., Ste. 701 New York, NY 10121-0701. Phone: 800-342-6626 or (212)626-0500 or (212)869-7440; Fax: (212)944-1318; Email: acmhelp@acm.org • URL: http://www.acm.org • Includes many Special Interest Groups.

**Association for Continuing Higher Education**. OCCE Admin Bldg., Rm. 233, 1700 Asp Ave. Norman, OK 73072-6407. Phone: 800-807-2243 or (405)329-0249; Fax: (405)325-4888; Email: admin@acheinc.org • URL: http://www.acheinc.org • Institutional members are accredited colleges or universities that offer credit and non-credit continuing education; individual members are persons currently or formerly on the faculty or staff of a university continuing education division and those interested in supporting the association's work. Promotes high standards for professional excellence, stimulates faculty leadership in constructive support of continuing higher education programs, and cooperates with other groups and organizations in the achievement of these goals.

**Association for Corporate Growth - Toronto Chapter**. 720 Spadina Ave., Ste. 202 Toronto, ON, Canada M5S 2T9. Phone: (416)868-1881; Fax: (416)391-3633; Email: acgtoronto@acg.org • URL: http://www.acg.org/toronto • Professionals with a leadership role in strategic corporate growth. Seeks to facilitate the professional advancement of members, and the practice of corporate growth management. Fosters communication and cooperation among members; conducts continuing professional education programs.

**Association for Corporate Growth**. 125 S Wacker Dr., Ste. 3100 Chicago, IL 60606. Phone: 877-358-2220 • URL: http://www.acg.org • Aims to drive middle market growth. Represents 14,000 members who are investors, lenders, advisors and leaders of more than 20,000 middle-market companies. Provides networking, resources and research.

**Association for Education in Journalism and Mass Communication**. 234 Outlet Pointe Blvd., Ste. A Columbia, SC 29210-5667. Phone: (803)798-0271; Fax: (803)772-3509; Email: aejmchq@aol.com • URL: http://www.aejmc.org • Professional organization of college and university journalism and communication teachers. Works to improve methods and standards of teaching and stimulate research. Compiles statistics on enrollments and current developments in journalism education. Maintains a listing of journalism and communication teaching positions available and teaching positions wanted, revised bimonthly.

**Association for Educational Communications and Technology**. 320 W 8th St., Ste. 101 Bloomington, IN 47404. Phone: 877-677-2328 or (812)335-7675; Fax: (812)335-7678; Email: aect@aect.org • URL: http://www.aect.org/newsite • Instructional technology professionals. Provides leadership in educational communications and technology by linking professionals holding a common interest in the use of educational technology and its application of the learning process.

**Association for Enterprise Information**. 2111 Wilson Blvd., Ste. 400 Arlington, VA 22201. Phone: (703)247-9474 or (703)247-2597; Fax: (703)522-3192; Email: dchesebrough@afei.org • URL: http://www.afei.org/Pages/default.aspx • Strives to advance enterprise integration and electronic business practices for industries and governments.

**Association for Facilities Engineering**. 12801 Worldgate Dr., Ste. 500 Herndon, VA 20170. Phone: (571)203-7171; Fax: (571)766-2142; Email: info@afe.org • URL: http://www.afe.org • Professional society of plant engineers and facilities managers engaged in the management, engineering, maintenance and operation of industrial, institutional, and commercial facilities. Compiles statistics. Offers three

certification programs, Certified Plant Engineer (CPE), Certified Plant Maintenance Manager (CPMM), and Certified Plant Supervisor.

**Association for Financial Counseling and Planning Education**. 1940 Duke St., Ste. 200 Alexandria, VA 22314-3452. Phone: (703)684-4484; Fax: (703)684-4485 • URL: http://www.afcpe.org • Members are researchers, academics, financial counselors and financial planners.

**Association for Financial Markets in Europe**. St. Michael's House, 1 George Yard London EC3V 9DH, United Kingdom. Phone: 44 207 7439300; Fax: 44 207 7439301 • URL: http://www.afme.eu • Principal trade association in the UK for firms active in the investment banking and securities industry. Represents the interests of its members on all aspects of their business and promotes their views to the authorities in the UK, the European Union, and elsewhere.

**Association for Financial Professionals**. 4520 E West Hwy., Ste. 750 Bethesda, MD 20814. Phone: (301)907-2862; Fax: (301)907-2864 • URL: http://www.afponline.org • Seeks to establish a national forum for the exchange of concepts and techniques related to improving the management of treasury and the careers of professionals through research, education, publications and recognition of the treasury management profession through a certification program. Conducts educational programs. Operates career center.

**Association for Financial Technology**. 34 N High St. New Albany, OH 43054-8507. Phone: (614)895-1208; Fax: (614)895-3466; Email: aft@aftweb.com • URL: http://www.aftweb.com/aws/AFT/pt/sp/home_page • Concerned with bank computer technology.

**Association for Healthcare Foodservice**. 455 S Fourth St., Ste. 650 Louisville, KY 40202. Phone: 888-528-9552 or (502)574-9930 or (502)574-9934; Fax: (502)589-3602; Email: info@healthcarefoodservice.org • URL: http://www.healthcarefoodservice.org • Formerly American Society for Hospital Food Service Administrators.

**Association for Healthcare Resource and Materials Management**. 155 N Wacker Dr. Chicago, IL 60606. Phone: (312)422-3840; Fax: (312)422-4573; Email: ahrmm@aha.org • URL: http://www.ahrmm.org • Members are involved with the purchasing and distribution of supplies and equipment for hospitals and other healthcare establishments. Formerly American Society for Healthcare Materials Management.

**Association for Information and Image Management International**. 1100 Wayne Ave., Ste. 1100 Silver Spring, MD 20910. Phone: 800-477-2446 or (301)587-8202; Fax: (301)587-2711; Email: aiim@aiim.org • URL: http://www.aiim.org • Manufacturers, vendors and individual users of information and image management equipment, products and services. Holds special meetings for trade members and companies. Maintains speakers' bureau. Operates resource center. Compiles statistics.

**Association for Library Collections and Technical Services**. 50 E Huron St. Chicago, IL 60611. Phone: 800-545-2433 or (312)280-5037; Fax: (312)280-5033; Email: cwilt@ala.org • URL: http://www.ala.org/alcts • Offers well-integrated and forward-looking services to library and information specialists in acquisitions, cataloging, classification, preservation, and collection development and management. Offers extensive programming, regional educational events, and practical publications.

*Association for Linen Management Membership Directory*. Association for Linen Management, 2161 Lexington Rd., Ste. 2 Richmond, KY 40475. Phone: 800-669-0863 or (859)624-0177; Fax: (859)624-3580 • URL: http://www.almnet.org • Annual. $150.00. Lists managers of in-house laundries for institutions, hotels, schools, etc.

**Association for Linen Management**. 2161 Lexington Rd., Ste. 2 Richmond, KY 40475. Phone: 800-669-0863 or (859)624-0177; Fax: (859)624-3580 • URL: http://www.almnet.org • Formerly National Assoiciation of Institutional Laundry Managers.

**Association for Management Information in Financial Services**. 14247 Saffron Cir. Carmel, IN 46032. Phone: (317)815-5857; Email: ami2@amifs.org • URL: http://www.amifs.org • Members are financial institution employees interested in management accounting and cost analysis.

**Association for Project Management Hong Kong**. c/o Agee Leung, 35/F Central Plaza, 18 Harbour Rd. Wan Chai, Hong Kong, China. Phone: 852 51810371; Email: agee.leung@apm.org.uk • URL: http://www.apm.org.uk/group/apm-hong-kong-branch • Aims to establish project management as the recognized profession essential for managing beneficial change in every type of business. Provides career development to project and management professionals.

**Association for Project Management**. Ibis House, Regent Park, Summerleys Rd. Princes Risborough HP27 9LE, United Kingdom. Email: info@apm.org.uk • URL: http://www.apm.org.uk • Strives to develop and promote the professional disciplines of project and programme management for the public benefit.

**Association for Research in Business Education - Delta Pi Epsilon**. 1914 Association Dr. Reston, VA 20191-1596. Phone: (703)860-8300 or (703)620-4483 • URL: http://www.dpe.org • Professional society - men and women, business education.

**Association for Retail Environments**. 4651 Sheridan St., Ste.

470 Hollywood, FL 33021. Phone: (954)893-7300; Fax: (954)893-7500; Email: are@retailenvironments.org • URL: http://www.retailenvironments.org • Formerly National Association of Display Industries.

**Association for the Advancement of Medical Instrumentation**. 4301 N Fairfax Dr., Ste. 301 Arlington, VA 22203-1633. Phone: 800-332-2264 or (703)525-4890 or (240)646-7031; Fax: (703)276-0793 or (301)206-9789; Email: customerservice@aami.org • URL: http://www.aami.org • Members are engineers, technicians, physicians, manufacturers, and others with an interest in medical instrumentation.

**Association for the Development of International Exchange of Food and Agricultural Productions and Techniques**. 41 rue de Bourgogne F-75007 Paris, France. Phone: 33 1 44180888; Fax: 33 1 44180889; Email: adepta@adepta.com • URL: http://www.adepta.com • Individuals involved in agribusiness. Promotes partnerships and networks among skilled agribusiness professionals.

*Association for University Business and Economic Research— Membership Directory*. Association for University Business and Economic Research, c/o Terry Creeth, IBRC, 801 W. Michigan, BS 4015 Indianapolis, IN 46202-5151. Phone: (317)274-2204; Fax: (317)274-3312 • Annual. $10. Covers: member institutions in the United States and abroad with centers, bureaus, departments, etc., concerned with business and economic research. Entries include: Name of bureau, center, etc., sponsoring institution name, address, phone, names and titles of director and staff, publications and frequency.

**Association for Unmanned Vehicle Systems International**. 2700 S Quincy St., Ste. 400 Arlington, VA 22206. Phone: (703)845-9671; Fax: (703)845-9679; Email: info@auvsi.org • URL: http://www.auvsi.org • Concerned with the development of unmanned systems and robotics technologies.

**Association Mauricienne des Femmes Chefs d'Entreprise**. Regency Sq., 1st Fl., 4 Conal and McIrvine St. Beau Bassin, Mauritius. Email: cheelichop@intnet.mu • URL: http://fcem.org/en/pays-membres/195-pays-membres/fiche-pays-details/afrique-membres/1517-ile-maurice-afrique-membres.html • Promotes women's entrepreneurial initiatives. Reinforces national associations of women business entrepreneurial potentials. Lobbies before the public and private institutions, policy makers and governments on issues that impede women's entrepreneurial potentials. Facilitates the development of business, partnership and trade. Fosters professional growth and business skills perfection. Encourages women to create enterprises.

**Association of AE Business Leaders**. 948 Capp St. San Francisco, CA 94110-3911. Phone: (415)713-5379; Email: events@aebl.org • URL: http://www.aebl.org • Individuals responsible for any or all aspects of business management in a professional design firm. Aims to improve the effectiveness of professional design firms through the growth and development of business management skills. Seeks to: provide a forum for the exchange of ideas and information and discussion and resolution of common problems and issues; establish guidelines for approaches to common management concerns; initiate and maintain professional relationships among members; improve recognition and practice of management as a science in professional design firms; advance and improve reputable service to clients; offer a variety of comprehensive educational programs and opportunities. Maintains speakers' bureau and placement service. Holds seminars. Conducts surveys and research programs. Compiles statistics.

**Association of African American Financial Advisors**. PO Box 4853 Capitol Heights, MD 20791. Phone: (240)396-2530; Fax: (888)392-5702; Email: info@aaafainc.cm • URL: http://aaafainc.com • Seeks to develop and foster professional relationships among African American professionals working in the financial advisory industry. Provides assistance and nurturing for those families that seek to improve their opportunities for participating and prospering financially in an economically progressive society. Strives to create support networks for minority financial professionals. Provides a forum for further education, training and visibility of its members.

**Association of American Chambers of Commerce in Latin America**. 1615 H St. NW Washington, DC 20062-0001. Phone: (202)463-5460; Fax: (202)463-3126; Email: info@aaccla.org • URL: http://www.aaccla.org • Umbrella organization for American chambers of commerce in Latin America. Affiliated with U.S. Chamber of Commerce.

**Association of American Colleges and Universities**. 1818 R St. NW Washington, DC 20009. Phone: 800-297-3775 or (202)387-3760; Fax: (202)265-9532 • URL: http://www.aacu.org • Advances and strengthens liberal learning for all students, regardless of academic specialization or intended career. Functions as a catalyst and facilitator, forging links among presidents, administrators, and faculty members who are engaged in institutional and curricular planning. Aims to reinforce the collective commitment to liberal education at both the national and local levels and to help individual institutions keep the quality of student learning at the core of their work as they evolve to meet new economic and social challenges.

**Association of American Military Uniform Collectors**. PO Box 1876 Elyria, OH 44036. Phone: (440)365-5321; Email:

aamucfl@comcast.net • URL: http://naples.net/clubs/aamuc • Collectors of American military and naval uniforms (1776-present). Promotes interest in uniform preservation and heritage along with patriotic interest in the U.S. armed forces. Loans uniform displays by members to various groups, including Boy Scouts of America, Girl Scouts of the U.S.A., American Legion, and Veterans of Foreign Wars of the U.S.A. branches, public schools, libraries, and public exhibitions. Reviews the books on U.S. military uniforms.

**Association of American Pesticide Control Officials.** PO Box 466 Milford, DE 19963-0466. Phone: (302)422-8152; Fax: (302)422-2435; Email: info@aapco.org • URL: http://www.aapco.org • State agencies controlling the sale, use, and distribution of pesticides. Promotes uniform laws, regulations, and policies of enforcement.

***Association of American Plant Food Control Officials Official Publication.*** Services. University of Kentucky, Lexington, KY 40506. Phone: (859)257-9000 • URL: http://www.uky.edu • Annual. $60. Source of information for AAPFCO, its membership, Rules & Standards (including the model "Uniform State Fertilizer Bill" and other model bills), Uniform Policy Statements and Official Terms.

**Association of American Plant Food Control Officials.** PO Box 3160 College Station, TX 77841-3160. Phone: (573)882-0007; Fax: (979)845-1389 • URL: http://www.aapfco.org • Represents officials of state agencies concerned with enforcement of laws relating to control of sale and distribution of mixed fertilizer and fertilizer materials.

**Association of American Publishers.** 71 5th Ave., 2nd Fl. New York, NY 10003-3004. Phone: (212)255-0200; Fax: (212)255-7007; Email: info@publishers.org • URL: http://www.publishers.org • Represents the major commercial publishers in the United States as well as smaller and non-profit publishers, university presses and scholarly societies. Helps in the protection of intellectual property rights in all media. Promotes reading and literacy and the freedom to publish at home and abroad. Conducts seminars and workshops on various publishing topics including rights and permission, sales, and educational publishing. Compiles statistics.

**Association of American Railroads.** 425 3rd St. SW Washington, DC 20024. Phone: (202)639-2100 or (202)639-2345; Fax: (202)639-2558; Email: media@aari.org • URL: http://www.aar.org • Coordinating and research agency of the American freight railway industry. Fields of interest include railroad operation and maintenance, statistics, research, public relations, communications, signals, car exchange rules, safety, police and security matters, and testing and standards of railroad equipment. Operates Transportation Technology Center in Pueblo, CO and Railinc in Cary, NC.

**Association of American Seed Control Officials.** c/o Fawad Shah, Legislation and Labeling Committee Member, 801 Summit Crossing Pl., Ste. C Gastonia, NC 28054-2194. Phone: (704)810-8884; Fax: (704)852-4109 • URL: http://www.seedcontrol.org • Officials who administer U.S. federal and state, and Dominion of Canada seed laws. Promotes uniformity in seed laws, rules and regulations, and in the administration of laws relative to the sale and distribution of seeds; furthers the exchange of constructive ideas among administrators of seed laws; seeks to study and suggest improvements in proposed seed legislation; cooperates with administrators of state, federal, and Canadian seed laws; promotes a general appreciation of the benefits of seed control to farmers, seedsmen, and the public by encouraging the marketing and use of correctly labeled seed of high quality.

**Association of American Universities.** 1200 New York Ave. NW, Ste. 550 Washington, DC 20005. Phone: (202)408-7500; Fax: (202)408-8184 • URL: http://www.aau.edu • Executive heads of universities; membership is determined by appraisal of breadth and quality of a university's research and education efforts. Conducts activities to encourage cooperative consideration of major issues concerning research universities, and to enable members to communicate effectively with the federal government.

**Association of American University Presses.** 28 W 36th St., Ste. 602 New York, NY 10018. Phone: (212)989-1010; Fax: (212)989-0275 or (212)989-0975; Email: info@aaupnet.org • URL: http://www.aaupnet.org • Helps university presses do their work more economically, creatively, and effectively through its own activities in education-training, fundraising and development, statistical research and analysis, and community and institutional relations.

**Association of Appraiser Regulatory Officials.** c/o Larry Disney, President, 135 W Irvin St., Ste. 301 Richmond, KY 40475. Phone: (605)773-4608; Fax: (605)773-5369 • URL: http://www.aaro.net • Represents real estate appraiser licensing agencies in the United States and its territories. Seeks to improve the administration and enforcement of real estate appraisal laws. Provides education, research, communication and cooperation among appraiser regulatory officials.

**Association of Asphalt Paving Technologists.** 6776 Lake Dr., Ste. 215 Lino Lakes, MN 55014-1191. Phone: (651)293-9188; Fax: (651)293-9193; Email: aaptinfo@gmail.com • URL: http://www.asphalttechnology.org • Represents engineers and chemists engaged in asphalt paving or related fields such as materials and construction equipment.

**Association of Authors' Representatives.** 676A 9th Ave., Ste. 312 New York, NY 10036. Phone: (212)840-5770; Email: administrator@aaronline.org • URL: http://www.aaronline.org • Literary and dramatic agents who market books, plays, and other literary and dramatic material.

**Association of British Certification Bodies.** c/o Trevor Nash, Chief Executive, PO Box 836 Bedford MK45 9DR, United Kingdom. Phone: 44 1525 630679 • URL: http://www.abcb.org.uk • Independent accredited certification bodies who undertake impartial certification of quality and environmental management systems, products, and personnel. Aims to provide a forum for the discussion and formulation of policy on matters of common concern; to represent the collective interests of members and, where consistent with such interests, those of individual members, in appropriate quarters; and to adopt, if thought fit, a code of professional practice in certification matters.

**Association of Business Executives.** 5th Fl., CI Tower, St. George Sq., New Maiden, Surrey London KT3 4TE, United Kingdom. Phone: 44 20 83292930; Fax: 44 20 83292945; Email: info@abeuk.com • URL: http://www.abeuk.com • Student membership sitting examinations.

**Association of Business Process Management Professionals.** 1000 Westgate Dr., Ste. 252 Saint Paul, MN 55114. Phone: (651)288-3420; Fax: (651)290-2266; Email: president@abpmp.org • URL: http://www.abpmp.org • Fosters the advancement of business process management concepts and its practices. Seeks to develop a common body of knowledge in business process management. Provides educational and networking activities for the continuing education of its members and their professional colleagues.

**Association of Business Women in Iceland.** Kringlunni 7 IS-103 Reykjavik, Iceland. Email: fka@fka.is • URL: http://www.fka.is • Promotes women's entrepreneurial initiatives. Reinforces national associations of women business entrepreneurial potentials. Lobbies before the public and private institutions, policy makers and governments on issues that impede women's entrepreneurial potentials. Facilitates the development of business, partnership and trade. Fosters professional growth and business skills perfection. Encourages women to create enterprises.

**Association of Business Women of Serbia.** Volgina 15 11060 Belgrade, Serbia. Phone: 38 11 2776801; Fax: 38 11 2776801; Email: upz.office@pupin.rs • URL: http://www.poslovnezene.org.rs/en • Promotes women's genuine business interests. Establishes links with similar associations in Europe and worldwide. Trains women in starting and running a business.

**Association of Canadian Pension Management.** 1255 Bay St., Ste. 304 Toronto, ON, Canada M5R 2A9. Phone: (416)964-1260; Fax: (416)964-0567; Email: info@acpm.com • URL: http://www.acpm.com/aboutACPM.aspx • Works to improve the health and growth of the Canadian public and private retirement income systems. Advocates clarity, good governance and administration and balanced consideration of shareholder interests to federal and provincial legislators and regulators on behalf of the Canadian pension industry.

**Association of Career Management Consulting Firms International.** 204 E St., NE Washington, DC 20002. Phone: (202)547-6344; Fax: (202)547-6348; Email: acf@acfinternational.org • Firms providing displaced employees who are sponsored by their organization, with counsel and assistance in job searching and the techniques and practices of choosing a career.

**Association of Certified Adizes Practitioners International.** 1212 Mark Ave. Carpinteria, CA 93013. Phone: (805)565-2901; Fax: (805)565-0741; Email: paula@adizes.com • URL: http://www.adizes.com • Professional management consultants who are certified to practice the Adizes Method of management. (The Adizes method, devised by Dr. Ichak Adizes, is a comprehensive approach to creating and managing healthy change within a company.) Promotes organizational transformation (consulting) as a profession. Facilitates discussion of ideas and exchange of information among members. Conducts research and educational programs.

**Association of Certified Treasury Managers.** 52, Nagarjuna Hills Hyderabad 500 082, Telangana, India. Phone: 91 40 23435368 or 91 40 23435374; Fax: 91 40 23352521; Email: info@actmindia.org • URL: http://www.qfinance.com/information-sources/association-of-certified-treasury-managers-india • Develops and regulates the growth of the treasury management profession. Organizes seminars, workshops, and training programs in treasury management, foreign exchange management, risk management, and allied areas. Provides placement assistance to members and students.

***The Association of Chartered Certified Accountants—Directory of Business Advisers.*** Association of Chartered Certified Accountants, 29 Lincoln's Inn Fields London WC2A 3EE, United Kingdom. Phone: 44 20 70595000; Fax: 44 20 70595050; Email: info@accaglobal.com • URL: http://www.accaglobal.com • Annual. $20. Covers practicing accounting firms and individual accountants acting as non-executive directors.

**Association of Chinese Finance Professionals.** 240 Hazelwood Ave. San Francisco, CA 94127. Email: acfp_us@yahoo.com • URL: http://www.acfp.net • Promotes cooperation between U.S. and China in the fields of commercial and investment banking, asset management, insurance, corporate finance, financial planning and financial software. Provides a forum for finance professionals to exchange ideas and discuss experiences.

**Association of Cinema and Video Laboratories.** 1833 Centinela Ave. Santa Monica, CA 90404. Phone: (310)828-1098; Fax: (310)828-9737; Email: lab@ntaudio.com • URL: http://www.acvl.org • Motion picture film or video transfer laboratories; non-laboratory firms with allied interests. Provides a forum for the exchange of ideas in connection with the technical, administrative and managerial problems of the motion picture and video laboratory industry. Concerns include: government relations; public and industry relations; product specifications; improvement of technical practices and procedures; other areas of interest to film and video laboratories.

**Association of Clean Water Administrators.** 1221 Connecticut Ave. NW, 2nd Fl. Washington, DC 20036. Phone: (202)756-0600; Fax: (202)756-0605.

**Association of College and Research Libraries.** 50 E Huron St. Chicago, IL 60611. Phone: 800-545-2433 or (312)280-2523; Fax: (312)280-2520; Email: acrl@ala.org • URL: http://www.ala.org/acrl • A division of the American Library Association. Academic and research librarians seeking to improve the quality of service in academic libraries; promotes the professional and career development of academic and research librarians; represent the interests and support the programs of academic and research libraries. Operates placement services; sponsors specialized education and research grants and programs; gathers, compiles, and disseminates statistics. Establishes and adopts standards; maintains publishing program; offers professional development courses.

**Association of Consulting Chemists and Chemical Engineers.** PO Box 902 Murray Hill, NJ 07974-0902. Phone: (908)464-3182 or (973)729-6671; Fax: (908)464-3182 or (973)729-7088; Email: accce@chemconsult.org • URL: http://www.chemconsult.org • Serves the chemical and related industries through its expertise on a wide variety of technical and business knowledge. Provides experienced counseling for new members.

**Association of Corporate Treasurers of Southern Africa.** PO Box 5853 Cresta 2118, South Africa. Phone: 27 11 4821512; Fax: 27 11 4821996 • URL: http://www.actsa.org.za • Provides a forum for the promotion of the common interests of corporate treasurers in Southern Africa. Provides learning and networking opportunities for its members.

**Association of Corporate Treasurers Singapore.** Block 51, Telok Blangah Dr., No. 06-142 Singapore 100051, Singapore. • URL: http://www.act.org.sg • Provides a platform for the exchange of ideas and information relating to treasury. Enhances treasury management skills through training and education. Facilitates a platform for dialogue between the industry and the government. Promotes the growth of the treasury profession to help Singapore develop into a financial hub in the region.

**Association of Corporate Treasurers.** 51 Moorgate London EC2R 6BH, United Kingdom. Phone: 44 20 7847 2540; Fax: 44 20 7374 8744; Email: enquiries@treasurers.co.uk • URL: http://www.treasurers.org • Professional body supporting those working in treasury, risk and corporate finance in the international marketplace. Promotes the study and best practice of finance and treasury management; offers education and examination, conferences, publications and training for financial professionals.

**Association of Correctional Food Service Affiliates.** 210 N Glenoaks Blvd., Ste. C Burbank, CA 91502. Phone: (818)843-6608; Fax: (818)843-7423 • URL: http://www.acfsa.org • Food service professionals from federal, state and county correctional institutions and vendors that serve them. Works to advance skills and professionalism through education, information and networking.

**Association of Danish Business Economists.** PO Box 2043 1012 Copenhagen, Denmark. Phone: 45 33141446; Fax: 45 33141149; Email: info@c3.dk • URL: http://www.c3.dk • Business administration alumni of Danish schools and universities. Sponsors educational courses, seminars, and forums; conducts research programs. Operates placement service.

**Association of Defense Trial Attorneys.** 4135 Topsail Trail New Port Richey, FL 34652. Phone: (727)859-0350 • URL: http://www.adtalaw.com • Trial lawyers who have over five years' experience in the preparation and trial of insurance cases and the handling of insurance matters, and who possess the knowledge, skill, and facilities to provide insurance companies and self-insurers a legal service of the highest standard. Maintains current biographical data on each member.

**Association of Diesel Specialists.** 400 Admiral Blvd. Kansas City, MO 64106. Phone: 888-401-1616 or (816)285-0810; Fax: (847)770-4952; Email: info@diesel.org • URL: http://diesel.org • Corporations and technically oriented professionals engaged in the sale and service of fuel injection, governor, supercharger, and turbocharger systems, and interested in improving the technology and servicing of these systems. Provides members with technical information and business management support. Sponsors a Parts Finder Program that compiles a monthly listing of obsolescent or surplus parts for sale by ADS members in the United States and Canada. Offers an ADS Nationwide Warranty Program which allows members to cooperate with each other and provide warranty service for transient customers. Conducts semiannual "Tech-Cert" exams in cooperation with the National Institute for Automotive Service Excellence to certify diesel technicians.

**Association of Directory Publishers**. 116 Cass St. Traverse City, MI 49685. Phone: 800-267-9002; Fax: (231)486-2182; Email: hq@adp.org • URL: http://www.adp.org • Represents publishers of printed and electronic telephone, city, and special interest directories.

**Association of Divorce Financial Planners**. 514 Fourth St. East Northport, NY 11731-2342. Phone: 888-838-7773; Email: adfp@divorceandfinance.org • URL: http://www.divorceandfinance.org • Aims to create awareness of the benefits of divorce financial planning. Provides members with continuing education. Promotes communication, networking and peer review.

**Association of Edison Illuminating Companies**. 600 N 18th St. N Birmingham, AL 35203-2206. Phone: (205)257-2530; Fax: (205)257-2540; Email: aeicdir@bellsouth.net • URL: http://www.aeic.org • Represents the interests of investor-owned public utilities, generating and transmitting or distributing companies.

**Association of Energy Engineers**. 4025 Pleasantdale Rd., Ste. 420 Atlanta, GA 30340. Phone: (770)447-5083; Fax: (770)446-3969; Email: info@aeecenter.org • URL: http://www.aeecenter.org • Members are engineers and other professionals concerned with energy management and cogeneration.

**Association of Equipment Manufacturers**. 6737 W Washington St., Ste. 2400 Milwaukee, WI 53214-5647. Phone: 866-AEM-0442 or (414)272-0943; Fax: (414)272-1170; Email: aem@aem.org • URL: http://www.aem.org • Provides business development services on a global basis for companies that manufacture equipment, products and services used worldwide in the agricultural, construction, industrial, mining, forestry, and utility fields.

**Association of European Businesses**. Krasnoproletarskaya ul 16, Bldg. 3, entrance 8, 4th Fl. 127473 Moscow, Russia. Phone: 7 495 2342764; Fax: 7 495 2342807; Email: info@aebrus.ru • URL: http://www.aebrus.ru • Represents and promotes the interests of European companies conducting business in the Russian Federation.

**Association of Executive Search Consultants**. 425 5thAve., 4th Fl. New York, NY 10016. Phone: (212)398-9556; Email: info@bluesteps.com • URL: http://www.aesc.org/eweb/StartPage.aspx • Represents executive search consulting firms worldwide, establishes professional and ethical standards for its members, and serves to broaden public understanding of the executive search process. Specialized form of management consulting, conducted through an exclusive engagement with a client organization.

**Association of Family and Conciliation Courts**. 6525 Grand Teton Plz. Madison, WI 53719. Phone: (608)664-3750; Fax: (608)664-3751; Email: afcc@afccnet.org • URL: http://www.afccnet.org • Members are judges, attorneys, and family counselors. Promotes conciliation counseling as a complement to legal procedures.

**Association of Food Industries**. 3301 Rte. 66, Ste. 205, Bldg. C Neptune, NJ 07753. Phone: (732)922-3008; Fax: (732)922-3590; Email: info@afius.org • URL: http://www.afius.org • Food processors, importers, and import agents nationally; food brokers in the New York metropolitan market and overseas food exporters. Maintains arbitration tribunal, government relations, and information services.

**Association of Free Community Papers**. 7445 Morgan Rd., Ste. 203 Liverpool, NY 13090. Phone: 877-203-2327; Fax: (781)459-7770 • URL: http://www.afcp.org • Represents publishers of nearly 3,000 free circulation papers and shopping/advertising guides. Offers national classified advertising placement service and national marketing for industry recognition. Conducts charitable programs. Sponsors competitions and compiles industry statistics.

**Association of Fundraising Professionals**. 4300 Wilson Blvd., Ste. 300 Arlington, VA 22203. Phone: 800-666-3863 or (703)684-0410; Fax: (703)684-0540; Email: afp@afpnet.org • URL: http://www.afpnet.org • Formerly National Society of Fundraising Executives.

**Association of Ghana Industries**. Trade Fair Centre, 2nd Fl., Addison House Accra, Ghana. Phone: 233 21 779023 or 233 21 779024; Fax: 233 21 773143 or 233 21 763383; Email: agi@agighana.org • URL: http://www.agighana.org • Voluntary business association, providing policy advocacy and advisory services, market development/market clinic, industrial subcontracting, management training, business plan preparation, export market promotion, information gathering, analysis and dissemination, media planning and events management, and networking.

**Association of Golf Merchandisers**. PO Box 7247 Phoenix, AZ 85011-7247. Phone: (602)604-8250; Fax: (602)604-8251; Email: info@agmgolf.org • URL: http://www.agmgolf.org • Members are vendors of golf equipment and merchandise.

**Association of Governing Boards of Universities and Colleges**. 1133 20th St. NW, Ste. 300 Washington, DC 20036-3475. Phone: (202)296-8400; Fax: (202)223-7053; Email: membership@agb.org • URL: http://www.agb.org • Members are governing boards of public and private 2- and 4-year colleges and universities; constituents include regents, trustees, presidents, and other high-level administrators of colleges and universities. Addresses the problems and responsibilities of trusteeship in all sectors of higher education and the relationships of trustees and regents to the president, the faculty, and the student body. Operates Zwingle Resource Center; conducts the National Conference on Trusteeship. Conducts research programs and the Robert L. Gale Fund for the Study of Trusteeship.

**Association of Government Accountants**. 2208 Mt. Vernon Ave. Alexandria, VA 22301-1314. Phone: 800-AGA-7211 or (703)684-6931; Fax: (703)548-9367; Email: agamembers@agacgfm.org • URL: http://www.agacgfm.org • Members are employed by federal, state, county, and city government agencies. Includes accountants, auditors, budget officers, and other government finance administrators and officials.

**Association of Government Relations Professionals**. 2121 Eisenhower Ave., Ste. 110 Alexandria, VA 22314-2530. Phone: 888-712-1357 or (703)960-3011; Email: info@agrp.org • URL: http://grprofessionals.org • Registered lobbyists and other professionals interested in the lobbying profession.

**Association of Governmental Risk Pools**. 9 Cornell Rd. Latham, NY 12110. Phone: (518)389-2782; Email: info@agrip.org • URL: http://www.agrip.org • Works to promote risk pooling as a practical extension of a public entity's obligation to be a good steward of public funds. Aims to act as an advocate for the advancement of intergovernmental pooling as the most appropriate risk financing mechanism for most public entities. Seeks to provide meaningful and significant educational and professional support for the governing bodies and employees of intergovernmental risk pools.

**Association of Graduate Schools**. 1200 New York Ave. NW, Ste. 550 Washington, DC 20005. Phone: (202)408-7500; Fax: (202)408-8184 • Deans of graduate studies in the 61 universities comprising the Association of American Universities. Works to consider matters of common interest relating to graduate study and research.

**Association of Graduates of the United States Air Force Academy**. 3116 Academy Dr. USAF Academy, CO 80840-4475. Phone: (719)472-0300; Fax: (719)333-4194; Email: aog@aogusafa.org • URL: http://www.usafa.org • Graduates and friends of the U.S. Air Force Academy. Promotes interest in and dedication to the mission, ideals, objectives, activities, and history of the Academy; encourages young people to attend the Academy; encourages and supports fundraising for the Academy; fosters camaraderie among Academy graduates and U.S. armed forces officer corps; professional development of the armed forces officer corps. Sponsors annual class reunions/homecomings. Offers scholarships to graduates of the academy and their dependents; provides placement service. Operates charitable program, including humanitarian support for next-of-kin of academy graduates. Compiles statistics.

**Association of Home Appliance Manufacturers**. 1111 19th St. NW, Ste. 402 Washington, DC 20036. Phone: (202)872-5955; Fax: (202)872-9354; Email: info@aham.org • URL: http://www.aham.org • Companies manufacturing major and portable appliances; supplier members provide products and services to the appliance industry. Major areas of activity include: market research and reporting of industry statistics; development of standard methods for measuring appliance performance and certification of certain characteristics of room air conditioners, refrigerators, freezers, humidifiers, dehumidifiers, and room air cleaners; public relations and press relations. Represents the appliance industry before government at the federal, state, and local levels.

**Association of Independent Asset Managers in Liechtenstein**. PO Box 134 FL-9496 Balzers, Liechtenstein. Phone: 423 3882350; Fax: 423 3882359; Email: info@vuvl.li • URL: http://www.vuvl.li/CFDOCS/cmsout/admin/content.cfm?GroupID=141 • Aims to protect and promote the reputation of independent asset managers in Liechtenstein and abroad. Seeks to establish professional guidelines within the framework of the Asset Management Accounting. Facilitates exchange of information within the business community.

**Association of Industrial Metallizers, Coaters and Laminators**. 201 Springs St. Fort Mill, SC 29715. Phone: (803)948-9470; Fax: (803)948-9471; Email: aimcal@aimcal.org • URL: http://www.aimcal.org • Metallizers, coaters, and laminators; producers of metallized film and/or paper on continuous rolls; manufacturers of metallizing, coating, and laminating equipment; suppliers of plastic films, papers, and adhesives. The end uses of the product are films and papers, solar control films, reflective insulation, decorative films and papers, and packaging. Monitors related legislative activities; reports on current industry developments. Conducts technical seminars.

**Association of Information Technology Professionals**. 15000 Commerce Parkway, Ste. C Mount Laurel, NJ 08054. Phone: 800-224-9371; Fax: (856)439-0525; Email: aitp_hq@aitp.org • URL: http://www.aitp.org • Managerial personnel, staff, educators, and individuals interested in the management of information resources. Founder of the Certificate in Data Processing examination program, now administered by an intersociety organization. Maintains Legislative Communications Network. Professional education programs include EDP-oriented business and management principles self-study courses and a series of videotaped management development seminars. Sponsors student organizations around the country interested in information technology and encourages members to serve as counselors for the Scout computer merit badge. Conducts research projects, including a business information systems curriculum for two- and four-year colleges.

**Association of Insolvency and Restructuring Advisors**. 221 Stewart Ave., Ste. 207 Medford, OR 97501. Phone: (541)858-1665; Fax: (541)858-9187; Email: aira@aira.org • URL: http://www.aira.org • Certified and licensed public accountants, attorneys, examiners, trustees and receivers. Seeks to define and develop the accountant's role provided by the Bankruptcy Reform Act of 1978 and to improve accounting skills used in insolvency cases. Promotes the primary role of creditors in insolvency situations and the enforcement of ethical standards of practice. Seeks to develop judicial reporting standards for insolvency and provide technical, analytical and accounting skills necessary in insolvent situations. Works to educate others in the field of the role of the accountant in order to foster better working relationships. Provides information about legislative issues that affect members and testifies before legislative bodies. Offers technical referral service. Administers the Certified Insolvency and Restructuring Advisor (CIRA) program.

**Association of Internal Management Consultants**. 824 Caribbean Ct. Marco Island, FL 34145. Phone: (239)642-0580; Fax: (239)642-1119 • URL: http://www.aimc.org • Consists of internal management consultants. Seeks to develop and encourage the professional practice of internal management-consulting; establish high standards of professional performance; serve as a forum for the exchange of information and the sharing of professional methods and techniques; cooperate with commercial, educational, and governmental bodies on matters of common interest. Conducts educational seminars.

**Association of Latino Administrators and Superintendents**. PO Box 65204 Washington, DC 20035. Phone: (202)466-0808; Email: contact@alasedu.org • URL: http://www.alasedu.net • Represents the interests of Latino superintendents and administrators. Provides professional development programs to strengthen the skills of superintendents, principals and other administrators. Advocates for policies to ensure the quality of the public education system.

**Association of Learned and Professional Society Publishers**. 1-3 Ship St., Shoreham-by-Sea West Sussex BN43 5DH, United Kingdom. Phone: 44 1442 828928 or 44 190 3 871686; Fax: 44 190 3 871457; Email: audrey.mcculloch@alpsp.org • URL: http://www.alpsp.org.

**Association of Life Insurance Counsel**. 14350 Mundy Dr., Ste. 800, No. 258 Noblesville, IN 46060. Phone: (317)774-7500; Fax: (317)614-7147 • URL: http://www.alic.cc • Members are attorneys for life insurance companies.

**Association of Management Consulting Firms**. 370 Lexington Ave., Ste. 2209 New York, NY 10017. Phone: (212)262-3055; Fax: (212)262-3054; Email: info@amcf.org • URL: http://www.amcf.org • Members are management consultants.

**Association of MBAs**. 25 Hosier Ln. London EC1A 9LQ, United Kingdom. Phone: 44 20 72462686 or 44 20 72462691; Fax: 44 20 72462687; Email: info@mbaworld.com • URL: http://www.mbaworld.com • Consists of students and graduates of Association of MBAs-approved MBA programmes, business schools, companies and organizations who share the objectives of the Association and who wish to contribute towards them. Seeks to enhance quality in management and provide a unique network of contracts for members. Provides a range of services including a membership book, networking/educational events, career opportunities, accreditation of MBA programmes, salary research, administration of a preferential rate MBA loan scheme for students of accredited programmes and an MBA information service.

**Association of Microfinance Organizations of Tajikistan**. 14 Firuz St. 734003 Dushanbe, Tajikistan. Phone: 992 44 6005794; Fax: 992 44 6005793; Email: office@amfot.tj • URL: http://www.amfot.tj • Facilitates the development of the microfinance sector in Tajikistan. Serves as a forum for interrelation and network of microfinance organizations in Tajikistan. Provides professional services for training and consultations and assists in the introduction of national standards of microfinance activity.

**Association of Military Colleges and Schools of the United States**. 12332 Washington Brice Rd. Fairfax, VA 22033. Phone: (703)272-8406; Email: amcsus@cox.net • URL: http://www.amcsus.org • Comprises of military colleges and secondary schools.

**Association of Military Surgeons of the U.S.** 9320 Old Georgetown Rd. Bethesda, MD 20814-1653. Phone: 800-761-9320 or (301)897-8800; Fax: (301)530-5446; Email: amsus@amsus.org • URL: http://www.amsus.org • Physicians, dentists, veterinarians, nurses, pharmacists, dietitians, therapists, and others of commissioned rank (or grades E5 through E9) or equivalent in the Army, Navy, Air Force, Public Health Service, and Veterans Administration; Reserve and National Guard officers are also eligible for membership. Advances all phases of federal medicine and allied sciences related to federal health services. Provides group insurance.

**Association of Moroccan Professionals in America**. PO Box 77254 San Francisco, CA 94107. Fax: (801)996-6334; Email: jaridati@amp-usa.org • URL: http://www.amp-usa.org • Promotes networking opportunities among Moroccan professionals. Advances the social and professional development of Moroccan professionals. Encourages bilateral commercial exchanges between the U.S. and Morocco. Provides community service and education initiatives in Morocco.

**Association of National Advertisers**. 708 3rd Ave., 33rd Fl. New York, NY 10017. Phone: (212)697-5950; Fax: (212)687-7310 • URL: http://www.ana.net • Serves the needs of members by providing marketing and advertising industry leadership in traditional and e-marketing, legislative leadership, information resources, professional development and industry-wide networking. Maintains offices in New York City and Washington, DC.

**Association of NROTC Colleges and Universities**. University of Rochester, 575 Mt. Hope Ave. Rochester, NY 14620. Phone: (585)273-1765; Fax: (585)275-8531; Email: scott.verrenti@rochester.edu • URL: http://www.conferences.rochester.edu/NROTCconstitution.html • Representatives from colleges and universities that have Naval Reserve Officers Training Corps units on their campuses. Promotes NROTC training and coordinates the efforts of institutions offering this service.

**Association of Oil Pipe Lines**. 1808 Eye St. NW, Ste. 300 Washington, DC 20006. Phone: (202)408-7970; Fax: (202)280-1949 • URL: http://www.aopl.org • Oil pipeline companies, most of which are regulated common carriers. Assembles statistical and other data relating to the pipeline industry for presentation to congress, governmental departments, agencies and commissions, trade associations, and the public.

**Association of Performing Arts Presenters**. 1211 Connecticut Ave. NW, Ste. 200 Washington, DC 20036-2716. Phone: 888-820-2787 or (202)833-2787; Fax: (202)833-1543; Email: info@artspresenters.org • URL: http://www.apap365.org/Pages/APAP365.aspx • Arts organizations involved in presentation of the professional performing arts; artists and artist management companies. Explores the roles, responsibilities, and opportunities for presenters, artists' managers, and artists, in order "to enable and celebrate the rich and diverse presenting field in its service to the public." Administers Lila Wallace/Reader's Digest Arts Partners regranting program.

**Association of Pool and Spa Professionals**. 2111 Eisenhower Ave., Ste. 500 Alexandria, VA 22314. Phone: (703)838-0083; Fax: (703)549-0493; Email: memberservices@apsp.org • URL: http://www.apsp.org • Formerly National Spa and Pool Institute.

**Association of Private Sector Colleges and Universities**. 1101 Connecticut Ave. NW, Ste. 900 Washington, DC 20036. Phone: 866-711-8574 or (202)336-6700; Fax: (202)336-6828; Email: apscu@apscu.org • URL: http://www.career.org • Represents private post-secondary schools, institutes, colleges and universities that provide career-specific educational programs.

**Association of Productivity Specialists**. 521 5th Ave., Ste. 1700 New York, NY 10175. Email: inquire@apsworld.org • URL: http://www.apsworld.org • Firms and individuals engaged in the Productivity Specialist segment of the management consultant profession. Seeks to promote greater public knowledge of the productivity specialist profession (productivity specialists develop management systems to achieve business objectives in numerous areas, including production levels, quality performance, inventory costs, operating costs and manufacturing lead times); to improve professional capabilities of member firms by promoting educational and research and development programs; to cooperate with federal, state, and local government agencies on matters of interest to members; to help member firms improve, develop and review skills of their professional employees. Has established standards of ethics and competence for productivity specialists.

**Association of Professional Material Handling Consultants**. 8720 Red Oak Blvd., Ste. 201 Charlotte, NC 28217-3992. Phone: (704)676-1190; Fax: (704)676-1199; Email: jworoniecki@mhi.org • URL: http://www.mhi.org/apmhc • Professional and independent material handling consultants; individuals who perform similar functions within multi-plant corporations. Promotes the art and science of material handling; aims to elevate the profession of the material handling consultant and establishes codes of ethics, conduct and qualifications. Develops, maintains and enforces rigorous membership requirements and high standards of ethical professional practice which will make membership in the association a recognized mark of experience, stability, competence, reliability and character.

**Association of Proposal Management Professionals**. PO Box 77272 Washington, DC 20013-8272. Phone: (202)450-2549; Email: rick.harris@apmp.org • URL: http://www.apmp.org • Proposal managers, proposal planners, proposal writers, consultants, desktop publishers and marketing managers. Encourages unity and cooperation among industry professionals. Seeks to broaden member knowledge and skills through developmental, educational and social activities. Maintains speakers' bureau. Provides current information and developments in the field.

**Association of Public Television Stations**. 2100 Crystal Dr., Ste. 700 Arlington, VA 22202. Phone: (202)654-4200; Fax: (202)654-4236; Email: pbutler@apts.org • URL: http://www.apts.org • Public television licensees whose goal is to organize efforts of public television stations in areas of planning and research and in representation before the government. Maintains current information on the public

television system including such areas as licensee characteristics, financing and industry trends; makes projections on system growth and income. Monitors social, economic and demographic trends that have an impact on public television services. Prepares and disseminates general information about public television to policymaking agencies, the press, and the public.

**Association of Real Estate Funds**. 65 Kingsway London WC2B 6TD, United Kingdom. Phone: 44 20 72694677; Email: info@aref.org.uk • URL: http://www.aref.org.uk • Aims to raise awareness of Real Estate Funds and demonstrate the advantages of these funds as effective real estate investment vehicles. Represents its members' interests on legislative, regulatory and fiscal matters affecting the real estate industry.

**Association of Research Libraries**. 21 Dupont Cir. NW, Ste. 800 Washington, DC 20036-1543. Phone: (202)296-2296; Fax: (202)872-0884; Email: webmgr@arl.org • URL: http://www.arl.org • Aims to influence the changing environment of scholarly communication and the public policies that affect research libraries and the diverse communities they serve. Pursues this mission by advancing the goals of its member research libraries, providing leadership in public and information policy to the scholarly and higher education communities, fostering the exchange of ideas and expertise, facilitating the emergence of new roles for research libraries, and shaping a future environment that leverages its interests with those of allied organizations.

**Association of Residential Cleaning Services International**. c/o Ernie Hartong, 7870 Olentangy River Rd., Ste. 301 Columbus, OH 43235. Phone: (614)547-0887; Fax: (614)505-7136; Email: chris@arcsi.org • URL: http://www.arcsi.org • Represents residential cleaning service owners and professionals. Advances and improves the residential cleaning industry. Shares knowledge and information to ensure the growth and development of cleaning service businesses.

**Association of Retail Travel Agents**. 4320 N Miller Rd. Scottsdale, AZ 85251-3606. Phone: 866-369-8969 or (859)269-9739; Fax: (866)743-2087 • URL: http://www.arta.travel • Represents retail travel agents and agencies in North America. Promotes the interests of retail travel agents through representation on industry councils, testimony before Congress and participation government proceedings. Conducts joint marketing and educational programs; sponsors work-study program.

**Association of School Business Officials International**. 11401 N Shore Dr. Reston, VA 20190-4232. Phone: 866-682-2729 or (703)478-0405; Fax: (703)708-7060 or (703)478-0205; Email: asboreq@asbointl.org • URL: http://asbointl.org • School business managers; assistant superintendents in charge of business; supervisors of accounting; directors of transportation, maintenance, food service, data processing, and operations; office managers; school business officials, school board members, and others interested in school business management. Business associates are vendors providing products and/or services to schools. Promotes improvement and advancement of school business management. Provides a forum for the exchange of information and ideas among professionals; keeps legislative bodies, governmental agencies, and members of the educational community informed of key issues relating to the administration of educational facilities. Maintains professional registration program, insurance and continuing education program, certificate of excellence program in financial reporting and meritorious budget awards program. Maintains 17 committees.

**Association of Ship Brokers and Agents**. 510 Sylvan Ave., Ste. 201 Englewood Cliffs, NJ 07632. Phone: (201)569-2882; Fax: (201)569-9082; Email: asba@asba.org • URL: http://www.asba.org • Includes a Tanker Committee.

**Association of Slovenia Entrepreneurs**. PO Box 40-95 1000 Ljubljana, Slovenia. Phone: 386 1 5443678; Fax: 386 1 5443680; Email: marta.turk1@guest.arnes.si • URL: http://fcem.org • Promotes women's entrepreneurial initiatives. Lobbies before the public and private institutions, policy makers and governments on issues that impede women's entrepreneurial potentials. Facilitates the development of business, partnership and trade. Fosters professional growth and business skills perfection. Encourages women to create enterprises.

**Association of Small and Medium Enterprises**. 167 Jalan Bukit Merah, Tower 4, No.03-13 Singapore 150167, Singapore. Phone: 65 65130388; Fax: 65 65130399; Email: enquiries@edc-asme.sg • URL: http://www.asme.org.sg • Seeks to bring together entrepreneurs of various industries and service sectors for information exchange; promotes relationship between various national interest bodies; provides continuous business education and training; fosters entrepreneurship networking both locally and internationally; works toward the institutionalization of ASME as a business association network body.

**Association of Steel Distributors**. 401 N Michigan Ave., Ste. 2200 Chicago, IL 60611. Phone: (312)673-5793; Fax: (312)527-6705; Email: headquarters@steeldistributors.org • URL: http://www.steeldistributors.org • Represents wholesalers of steel and steel products. Provides the steel distribution industry a forum for ideas exchange and market information.

**Association of TeleServices International**. 222 S Westmonte Dr., Ste. 101 Altamonte Springs, FL 32714. Phone: 866-896-ATSI; Fax: (407)774-6440; Email: admin@atsi.org • URL:

http://www.atsi.org • An organization of telephone answering and voice message services.

*Association of Thai Industries—Industrial Directory*. Business Company Ltd., 972, Soi Saeng Cham, Rama IX Rd. Bangkok 10310, Thailand. Phone: 66 22471519; Fax: 66 224832579 • Biennial. $350; $20. Covers: 827 manufacturers, wholesalers, and distributors in Thailand. Entries include: Company name, address, phone, telex, and names of directors and officials.

**Association of the United States Army**. 2425 Wilson Blvd. Arlington, VA 22201. Phone: 800-336-4570 or (703)841-4300 • URL: http://www.ausa.org/Pages/default.aspx • Professional society of: active, retired, and reserve military personnel; West Point and Army ROTC cadets; civilians interested in national defense. Seeks to advance the security of the United States and consolidate the efforts of all who support the United States Army as an indispensable instrument of national security. Conducts industrial symposia for manufacturers of Army weapons and equipment, and those in the Department of the Army who plan, develop, test, and use weapons and equipment. Symposia subjects have included guided missiles, army aviation, electronics and communication, telemedicine, vehicles, and armor. Sponsors monthly PBS TV series, America's Army.

**Association of the Wall and Ceiling Industries International**. 513 W Broad St., Ste. 210 Falls Church, VA 22046. Phone: (703)538-1600; Fax: (703)534-8307 • URL: http://www.awci.org • Acoustical tile, drywall, demountable partitions, lathing and plastering, fireproofing, light-gauge steel framing, stucco and exterior insulation finish systems contractors, suppliers and manufacturers.

**Association of Theatrical Artists and Craftspeople**. 48 Fairway St. Bloomfield, NJ 07003-5515. Phone: (212)234-9001 • URL: http://www.atacbiz.com • Members are artists and craftspeople working in theatre, film, TV, and advertising. Areas of expertise include props, costumes, millinery, puppetry, display, and special effects.

**Association of Theatrical Press Agents and Managers**. Penn Plz., Ste. 1703, 225 W 34th St. New York, NY 10122. Phone: (212)719-3666; Fax: (212)302-1585; Email: info@atpam.com • URL: http://www.atpam.com • A labor union for theater managers and press agents. Affiliated with AFL-CIO.

**Association of Writers and Writing Programs**. George Mason University, 4400 University Dr., MSN 1E3 Fairfax, VA 22030-4444. Phone: (703)993-4301 or (703)933-4301; Fax: (703)993-4302 or (703)933-4302; Email: awp@awpwriter.org • URL: http://www.awpwriter.org • Supports writers and writing programs worldwide.

**Association Senegalaise des Femmes Chefs d'Entreprise**. B.P. 30081 Dakar, Senegal. Phone: 221 338241010; Fax: 221 8257246; Email: hadjadiordiop2000@yahoo.fr • URL: http://www.fcem.org/en/pays-membres.html • Promotes women's entrepreneurial initiatives. Lobbies before the public and private institutions, policy makers and governments on issues that impede women's entrepreneurial potentials. Facilitates the development of business, partnership and trade. Fosters professional growth and business skills perfection. Encourages women to create enterprises.

**Association to Advance Collegiate Schools of Business**. 77 S Harbour Island Blvd., Ste. 750 Tampa, FL 33602. Phone: (813)769-6500; Fax: (813)769-6559; Email: events@aacsb.edu • URL: http://www.aacsb.edu • Represents educational institutions, businesses, and other entities devoted to the advancement of management education. Works to advance quality management education worldwide through accreditation.

**Association Women and Business in Russia**. 8, Zaozernaya str. 196084 Saint Petersburg, Russia. Phone: 7 812 3162733; Fax: 7 812 7101191; Email: info@demetra.su • URL: http://www.fcem.org/en/pays-membres.html • Advances and supports businesswomen's interests in public, political and business circles of Russia. Helps develop women's business in Russia. Raises well-being and establishes a civilized, socially-responsible business in Russia.

**ASTD**. 1640 King St. Alexandria, VA 22314-2746. Phone: 800-628-2783 or (703)683-8100; Fax: (703)683-1523; Email: customercare@astd.org • URL: http://www.astd.org • Represents workplace learning and performance professionals.

*ASTM List of Publications*. ASTM International, 100 Barr Harbor Dr. West Conshohocken, PA 19428-2959. Phone: 877-909-2786 or (610)832-9500 or (610)832-9585; Fax: (610)832-9555; Email: service@astm.org • URL: http://www.astm.org • Annual.

*Aston Centre for e-Business Research Conference papers*. Aston University Aston Centre for e-Business Research, Aston Triangle, Aston Business School Birmingham B4 7ET, United Kingdom. Phone: 44 121 2043047; Email: a.j.broderick@aston.ac.uk • URL: http://www.abs.aston.ac.uk.

*Aston Centre for e-Business Research Journal articles*. Aston University Aston Centre for e-Business Research, Aston Triangle, Aston Business School Birmingham B4 7ET, United Kingdom. Phone: 44 121 2043047; Email: a.j.broderick@aston.ac.uk • URL: http://www.abs.aston.ac.uk.

*Aston Centre for e-Business Research Research reports*. Aston University Aston Centre for e-Business Research, Aston Triangle, Aston Business School Birmingham B4 7ET, United Kingdom. Phone: 44 121 2043047; Email: a.j.

broderick@aston.ac.uk • URL: http://www.abs.aston.ac.uk.

**Aston University - Economics and Strategy Group.** Aston Business School Birmingham B4 7ET, United Kingdom. Phone: 44 121 2043038; Email: l.woolley@aston.ac.uk • URL: http://www1.aston.ac.uk/aston-business-school/research/groups/esg • Strategic management, economics, innovation and entrepreneurship, and international business.

***ASTREE: L'Annuaire Commercial Electronique.*** Bureau van Dijk S.A., Ave. Louise, Louizalaan 250 B-1050 Brussels, Belgium. Phone: 32 2 6390606 or 32 2 639 06 06; Fax: 32 2 6488230 or 32 2 648 82 30; Email: brussels@bvdinfo.com • URL: http://www.bvdinfo.com • Quarterly. Database covers: Company reports on 800,000 French companies. Entries include: Company name, address, date of incorporation, company type, type of activity, managers, turnover, export, profit, shareholders' funds, debt, number of employees, shareholders, and subsidiaries.

***ASU.com.*** Airline Services Unlimited, 4340 Redwood Hwy., Ste. E356 San Rafael, CA 94903. Phone: 866-483-5056 or (415)898-9500; Fax: (415)373-0487; Email: subs@asu.com • URL: http://www.members.asu.com • Quarterly. $44.95 book plus 1 bonus issue and 16 months. Covers: Over 25,000 listings for airlines, lodgings, tours, car rental companies, and cruise lines, which allow travel discounts to airline employees worldwide. Entries include: Name, address, and phone of facility or service; description; regular price and type and amount of discount; credit cards accepted; validity dates; booking procedures; whether parents and retired airline employees are eligible.

***AT&T Easylink Services—Electronic Messaging Directory & Buyers Guide.*** AT&T National Toll-Free Directory, 295 N Maple Ave. Basking Ridge, NJ 07920-1002. Phone: 800-426-8686 or (908)221-2000; Fax: (908)221-1211 • URL: http://www.tollfree.att.net • Irregular. $30. Covers: about 200,000 AT&T customers with Easylink and Telex I/II numbers. Entries include: Company name, city, state, Telex I/II, or Easylink number and answerback.

***ATD Buyer's Guide.*** ASTD, 1640 King St. Alexandria, VA 22314-2746. Phone: 800-628-2783 or (703)683-8100; Fax: (703)683-1523; Email: customercare@astd.org • URL: http://www.astd.org • Annual. Database covers: Businesses and individual consultants offering products, services, and equipment for sale to persons in corporate training and human resource development. Entries include: Company name, contact information and name, profile, list of products and services.

***Athens Area Chamber of Commerce Membership Directory.*** Athens Area Chamber of Commerce, 246 W Hancock Ave. Athens, GA 30601. Phone: (706)549-6800; Fax: (706)549-5636; Email: info@athensga.com • URL: http://www.athenschamber.net • Lists member businesses in Athens, Georgia. Publication includes directory details for largest employers, retail centers, chamber member realtors and banks.

***Athletic Business—Professional Directory Section.*** Athletic Business Publications Inc., 4130 Lien Rd. Madison, WI 53704. Phone: 800-722-8764 or (608)249-0186; Fax: (608)249-1153; Email: editors@hardwoodfloorsmag.com • URL: http://www.athleticbusiness.com • Monthly. $8 per issue. Publication includes: List of architects, engineers, contractors, and consultants in athletic facility planning and construction; all listings are paid. Entries include: Company name, address, phone, fax and short description of company.

**Atkinson Center for a Sustainable Future.** Cornell University, 200 Rice Hall Ithaca, NY 14853-5601. Phone: (607)255-7535; Fax: (607)255-6714; Email: fjd3@cornell.edu • URL: http://hwww.sustainablefuture.cornell.edu • Advances multidisciplinary research and cultivates innovative collaborations to foster a sustainable future.

***Atlanta Business Chronicle's Book of Lists.*** Metro Atlanta Chamber of Commerce, 235 Andrew Young International Blvd. NW Atlanta, GA 30303-2718. Phone: (404)880-9000 • URL: http://www.metroatlantachamber.com • $49.95 Individuals. Lists companies in the Atlanta business community, including sections on business and industry, business services, commercial real estate, education and human resources, finance, general interests, healthcare, hospitality and travel, marketing, residential real estate and technology sections. Entries include name, address, phone, fax, facts and figures, and detailed information.

***Atlanta JobBank: The Job Hunter's Guide to Georgia.*** Adams Media Corp., 57 Littlefield St. Avon, MA 02322. Phone: 800-872-5627 or (508)427-7100; Fax: (508)427-6790 or (800)872-5628; Email: deskcopies@adamsmedia.com • URL: http://www.adamsmedia.com • $17.95 Individuals Paperback. Covers: 3,900 employers in the state of Georgia, including Albany, Columbus, Macon, and Savannah. Database includes: Information on the basics of job winning and writing resumes and cover letters; electronic job search information; 330 industry associations; 90 online career resources; 235 employment services. Entries include: Firm or organization name, address, local phone, toll-free phone, fax, description of organization, subsidiaries, other locations, recorded jobline, name and title of contact, typical titles for common positions, educational backgrounds desired, number of employees, benefits offered, training programs, internships, parent company, revenues, e-mail and URL address, projected number of hires.

***Atlanta Larger Employers.*** Metro Atlanta Chamber of Commerce, 235 Andrew Young International Blvd. NW Atlanta, GA 30303-2718. Phone: (404)880-9000 • URL: http://www.metroatlantachamber.com • Biennial. $5 plus $2 shipping. Covers: Approximately 600 companies in the metropolitan Atlanta, Georgia, area that employ 300 or more. Entries include: Company name, address, phone, Standard Industrial Classification (SIC) code.

***Atlantic Boating Almanac.*** Atlantic Boating Almanac, 3 Church Cir., Ste. 109 Annapolis, MD 21401. Phone: 800-481-6277; Fax: (800)487-6277; Email: editor@prostarpublications.com • URL: http://www.prostarpublications.com • Annual. $24.95 Individuals. Covers: Listings on coast piloting, electronics, GPS by Gordon West, first aid, weather, facilities and fuel docks. There are four separate regional editions: Florida & Bahamas; North & South Carolina and Georgia; Massachusetts, Rhode Island, Connecticut and Long Island; and Maine, New Hampshire & Massachusetts. Database includes: Tide and current tables; maps and fishing charts; navigation and star charts; first aid; US coast pilot.

***Atlantic Region Aviation Business Directory.*** Martin Charlton Communications Inc., 300-1914 Hamilton St. Regina, SK, Canada S4N 3N6. Phone: (306)584-1000; Fax: (306)352-4100; Email: marylynn@martincharlton.ca • URL: http://www.martincharlton.ca • Annual. $7.50. Covers companies involved in or serving the aviation industry in New Brunswick, Newfoundland, Nova Scotia, and Prince Edward Island, Canada.

***Atlas & Gazetteer Series.*** DeLorme, 2 DeLorme Dr. Yarmouth, ME 04096-6965. Phone: 800-561-5105 or (207)847-1165; Fax: (207)846-7051; Email: sales@delorme.com • URL: http://www.delorme.com • single (by State pricing varies); 649.95 boxed value sets. Consists of 50 volumes covering all areas of the U. S. Includes detailed maps, as well as descriptions of attractions, natural areas, and historic sites.

**Atmospheric Sciences Research Center - University of Albany, State University of New York.** 251 Fuller Rd. Albany, NY 12203. Phone: (518)437-8754 or (518)437-8705; Fax: (518)437-8758; Email: info@asrc.cestm.albany.edu • URL: http://www.asrc.cestm.albany.edu.

***ATTILA Business Database.*** Ost-West Direkt Werbegesellschaft mbH, Landwehrstrasse 17 D-80336 Munich, Germany. Phone: 89 598710; Fax: 89 557591 • Quarterly. Database covers: over 2.6 million companies in Bulgaria, Poland, the Czech Republic, Hungary, Lithuania, and the Slovak Republic. Database includes: Company name, address, phone, fax, legal status, ownership, foundation date/capital, registration court, governmental district, contact person, number of employees, products, line of business.

***Attorney's Dictionary of Patent Claims: Legal Materials and Practice Commentaries.*** Irwin M. Aisenberg. Matthew Bender and Company Inc., 1275 Broadway Albany, NY 12204-2638. Phone: 800-424-4200 or (518)487-3000; Fax: (518)487-3573 or (800)424-4200; Email: customer.support@lexisnexis.com • URL: http://www.matthewbender.com • $607.00. Three looseleaf volumes. Periodic supplementation. Operational guidance for bank officers, with analysis of statutory law and agency regulations.

***Attorneys' Textbook of Medicine.*** Matthew Bender and Company Inc., 1275 Broadway Albany, NY 12204-2638. Phone: 800-424-4200 or (518)487-3000; Fax: (518)487-3573 or (800)424-4200; Email: customer.support@lexisnexis.com • URL: http://www.matthewbender.com • Updated quarterly. 19 volumes. $5,476.00. Detailed information on injuries and diseases. Written specifically for attorneys.

**Auburn University - Alabama Agricultural Experiment Station - Department of Fisheries and Allied Aquacultures.** 203 Swingle Hall Auburn, AL 36849. Phone: (334)844-4786; Fax: (334)844-9208; Email: fish@auburn.edu • URL: http://www.ag.auburn.edu/fish • Aquaculture in fresh, brackish, and marine water; fisheries management in large and small impoundments, and rivers; aquatic plants management; nutrition and feeds; parasites and disease; limnology; water quality and management for aquaculture; international development for fisheries and aquaculture; aquatic ecology and environmental assessment; environmental education.

**Auburn University at Montgomery - Center for Business.** 7515 Halcyon Summit Dr., Ste. 305 Montgomery, AL 36117. Phone: (334)244-3700; Fax: (334)244-3718; Email: cforehand@cbed.aum.edu • URL: http://www.cbed.aum.edu • Economic impact studies, revenue forecasting, market research, equipment use and need analysis, management, and personnel research.

***Audio.*** Orion Research Corp., 14555 N Scottsdale Rd., Ste. 330 Scottsdale, AZ 85254. Phone: 800-844-0759 or (480)951-1114; Fax: (480)951-1117 or (800)375-1315 • Annual. $179 Individuals. Quotes retail and wholesale prices of used audio equipment. Original list prices and years of manufacture are also shown.

**Audit Bureau of Circulations.** 48 W Seegers Rd. Arlington Heights, IL 60005-3913. Phone: (224)366-6939 or (224)366-6500; Fax: (224)366-6949; Email: service@accessabc.com • URL: http://www.accessabc.com • Verifies newspaper and periodical circulation statements. Includes a Business Publications Industry Committee and a Magazine Directors Advisory Committee.

***Auditing Research Monographs.*** American Institute of Certified Public Accountants, 1211 Avenue of the Americas New York, NY 10036-8775. Phone: 888-777-7077 or (212)596-6200; Fax: (212)596-6213; Email: service@aicpa.org • URL: http://www.aicpa.org • Irregular. Price varies.

***Australia Business Directory.*** INFOT Inc., PO Box 2052 Rockville, MD 20847. Phone: 866-838-2619 • URL: http://www.infotusa.com • $64.60 Individuals. Covers: 96,347 companies, importers, and exporters from Australia. Entries include: Company name, email and website addresses, telephone and fax number, and business description.

***Australia Business Law Handbook.*** International Business Publications, USA, PO Box 15343 Washington, DC 20003. Phone: (202)546-2103; Fax: (202)546-3275; Email: ibpusa@comcast.net • URL: http://ibpus.com • $99.95 Individuals hardcopy, e-book, CD-ROM. Covers: Basic information on business laws and legislations, export-import regulations, business climate and contacts.

***Australia Government and Business Contacts Handbook.*** International Business Publications, USA, PO Box 15343 Washington, DC 20003. Phone: (202)546-2103; Fax: (202)546-3275; Email: ibpusa@comcast.net • URL: http://ibpus.com • $99.95 Individuals hardcopy, E-book and CD-ROM. Covers: Strategic government and business information, export-import activity in the country, investment, business contacts and regulations.

***Australia Industrial and Business Directory.*** International Business Publications, USA, PO Box 15343 Washington, DC 20003. Phone: (202)546-2103; Fax: (202)546-3275; Email: ibpusa@comcast.net • URL: http://ibpus.com • Annual. $99.95 Individuals hardcover; $99.95 Individuals CD-ROM; $99.95 Individuals E-book. Covers: Strategic industrial, investment, and business contacts for conducting export-import and investment activity in the country.

***Australia Investment and Business Guide.*** International Business Publications, USA, PO Box 15343 Washington, DC 20003. Phone: (202)546-2103; Fax: (202)546-3275; Email: ibpusa@comcast.net • URL: http://ibpus.com • $99.95 Individuals hardcover; $99.95 Individuals CD-ROM; $99.95 Individuals E-book. Covers: Basic information on economy and government, export-import activity and investment climate, regulations and industrial development, and banking. Entries include: Important business contacts and business travel.

**Australian Business in Europe.** c/o HWL Ebsworth Lawyers, 530 Collins St., Level 26 Melbourne, VIC VIC 3000, Australia. Phone: 61 3 86443616; Fax: 3 86154300 • URL: http://www.abie.com.au • Works to provide a forum for Australians working in Europe and for European business people associated with Australian industry and commerce.

***Australian Business News.*** NSW Business Chamber, 140 Arthur St., Level 15 Sydney, NSW 2060, Australia. Fax: 61 1 300655277 • URL: http://www.nswbusinesschamber.com.au • Bimonthly. A$7 for nonmembers; free for members.

**Australian Catholic University - Centre for Research into Ethics and Decision-Making in Organisations.** 24 Brunswick St., Locked Bag 4115 Fitzroy, VIC 3065, Australia. Phone: 61 3 99533270; Email: j.little@patrick.acu.edu.au • URL: http://www.acu.edu.au/research/Research_Centres_and_Flagships/credo • Values, policies, decision-making, and ethics in an organization.

***Australian Company Handbook.*** Hoover's Inc., 5800 Airport Blvd. Austin, TX 78752-4204. Phone: 866-443-3939 or (512)374-4500 or (866)281-5969; Fax: (512)374-4501; Email: salesteam@hoovers.com • URL: http://www.hoovers.com • $49.95. Covers: 300 Australian companies listed on the All Ordinaries Index and 300 other leading Australian companies not included on the index. Entries include: Company name, address, phone, fax, description.

***Australian Health and Medical Industry.*** APN News & Media Group Ltd. APN Business Information Group, Level 9, 468 St. Kilda Rd. Melbourne, VIC 3004, Australia. Phone: 61 3 88665290; Fax: 61 3 88665299; Email: info@apnbig.com.au • URL: http://www.australianexporters.net/companyID424.htm • Annual. Covers: Australian companies involved in the medical and health industry and interested in exporting their products and services.

***Australian Hospitality Directory.*** Associated Media Group, 385-389 Pacific Hwy., Ste. 5 Crows Nest, NSW 2065, Australia. Phone: 61 2 99553322; Fax: 61 2 99554006; Email: admin@amgroup.net.au • URL: http://www.hospitalitydirectory.com.au • Annual. Provides business information on transport, food service, entertainment, equipment and supplies, education and management, furniture, bedding, and lighting.

**Australian Industry Group.** Level 5, 51 Walker St. North Sydney, NSW 2060, Australia. Phone: 61 294665566; Fax: 61 294665599; Email: info@aigroup.asn.au • URL: http://www.aigroup.com.au • Promotes and develops the interests of industrial businesses.

**Australian Institute of Agricultural Science and Technology.** PO Box 576 Sydney, NSW 1585, Australia. Phone: 61 2 94318657; Fax: 61 2 94318677; Email: admin@aginstitute.com.au • URL: http://www.aginstitute.com.au • Provides expert services to its clients and the community, together with ways that these are enhanced through professional development, networking, and representation of the interests of agricultural industries.

**Australian Institute of Management.** 380 La Trobe St., Level 20 Melbourne, VIC 3000, Australia. Phone: 61 3 95348181; Fax: 61 3 95345050; Email: enquiry@aimvic.com.au • URL: http://www.aim.com.au • Promotes growth in management and leadership. Provides management training and consultancy services.

**Australian Institute of Project Management.** Level 9, 139 Macquarie St. Sydney, NSW 2000, Australia. Phone: 61 2 82888700; Fax: 61 2 82888711; Email: info@aipm.com.au • URL: http://www.aipm.com.au • Works to promote the progress of the profession of project management.

***Australian Key Business Directory.*** Dun & Bradstreet (Australia) Proprietary Ltd., 479 St. Kilda Rd. Melbourne, VIC 3004, Australia. Phone: 61 3 9828 3333 or 61 3 9828 3333; Fax: 61 3 9828 3300 or 61 3 9288 3300; Email: customerservice@dnb.com.au • URL: http://dnb.com.au • Covers: Leading companies in Australia whose annual sales are $10 million and who have 500 or more employees. Entries include: Company name, address, phone, fax, telex, number of employees, import/export designation, primary and secondary Standard Industrial Classification (SIC) codes, sales volume.

**Australian Marine Conservation Society.** 4/145 Melbourne St. Brisbane, QLD 4101, Australia. Phone: 61 7 38466777; Fax: 61 7 38466788; Email: amcs@amcs.org.au • URL: http://www.marineconservation.org.au • Aims to conserve the waterways, oceans and coasts of Australia by focusing on protecting the oceans from threats of pollution, habitat loss, unsustainable fisheries, coastal zone degradation and climate change. Acts as a resource on marine environmental issues for government agencies, politicians, media and the public.

**Australian National University - Research School of Social Sciences.** Canberra, ACT 0200, Australia. Phone: 61 2 252257; Fax: 61 2 250502; Email: adam.graycar@anu.edu.au • URL: http://rsss.anu.edu.au • Demography and sociology, economics, law, history, philosophy, political science, sociology, social and political theory, research evaluation and policy, immigration and multicultural studies.

***Australian Newsagent & Stationer Buyer's Guide.*** Thorpe-Bowker, 607 St Kilda Rd. Melbourne, VIC 3004, Australia. Phone: 61 3 8517 8333; Fax: 61 3 8517 8399; Email: yoursay@thorpe.com.au • URL: http://www.thorpe.com.au • Annual. $45. Covers: manufacturers and suppliers of office supplies in Australia; some foreign office supply manufacturers with their Australian agents; related organizations in Australia. Entries include: Manufacturer, supplier, agent, or organization name, address, phone.

**Australian Plants Society - South Australian Region.** PO Box 304 Unley, SA 5061, Australia. Email: president@australianplantssa.asn.au • URL: http://www.australianplantssa.asn.au • Encourages the cultivation and study of Australian plants. Promotes the establishment of gardens in all types of soil and climates for the preservation of Australian flora. Protects Australian plants and their habitats. Represents its members in government activity.

***Australian Public Companies Guide.*** Schwartz & Wilkinson Publishers PLC, 45 Flinders Ln. Melbourne, VIC 3000, Australia. Phone: 61 3 654 2800; Fax: 61 3 650 5261 • Annual. $395. Covers: 12,000 companies on the Australian Stock Exchange. Entries include: Company name, address, phone, telex, names of directors, financial data.

***Australian Scientific and Laboratory Exports.*** Peter Isaacson Publications, 45-50 Porter St. Prahraw, VIC 3181, Australia. Phone: 2 5434630 or 32 45 7777; Fax: 3 245 7840 • Annual. $80. Covers: Scientific and medical products and services available for export from Australia.

**Australian Venture Capital Association Limited.** Level 10, Kyle House, 27-31 Macquarie Pl. Sydney, NSW 2000, Australia. Phone: 61 2 82437000 or 61 2 82382600; Email: members@avcal.com.au • URL: http://www.avcal.com.au • Promotes the venture capital and private equity industry in Australia. Provides networking events for members, industry tools (non-disclosure agreement, valuation guidelines, Standard Industry Trust Deed and Standard VCLP), information for entrepreneurs seeking capital and employment database.

***Australia's Top 100.*** Australian Stock Exchange Ltd. Exchange Centre, Level 7, 123 Eagle St. Brisbane, NSW 4000, Australia. Fax: 02 9227 0885; Email: info@asx.com.au • Annual. $20 plus 10 dollars shipping. Covers: top 100 listed companies on the Australian Stock Exchange ranked by market capitalization. Entries include: Company name, address, phone, fax, telex, names and titles of key personnel, financial data, company history, description of products and activities.

***Austria Export-Import Trade and Business Directory.*** International Business Publications, USA, PO Box 15343 Washington, DC 20003. Phone: (202)546-2103; Fax: (202)546-3275; Email: ibpusa@comcast.net • URL: http://ibpus.com • $99.95 Individuals. Contains information on strategic economic, investment, export-import, and business opportunities and contact numbers.

***Austria in U.S.A.*** American Chamber of Commerce in Austria, Porzellangasse 39/7 A-1090 Vienna, Austria. Phone: 43 1 3195751; Fax: 43 1 3195151; Email: office@amcham.at • URL: http://www.amcham.at • Periodic. €150 Members; €190 Nonmembers; £150 Members CD-ROM; £190 Nonmembers CD-ROM. Covers: 550 Austrian companies with U.S. Subsidiaries, branch offices, associates, joint ventures, or representations in the U.S.; American representations and Austrian-American organizations in Austria, Austrian representations in the U.S., American Chambers of Commerce in Europe, and the representation of American states in Europe. Entries include: For companies—Name, address, phone; name, address, phone of U.S. Affiliated company; name of the Austrian company's general manager; a brief description of the U.S. Company; type of business and nature of relationship.

***Austria Industrial and Business Directory.*** International Business Publications, USA, PO Box 15343 Washington, DC 20003. Phone: (202)546-2103; Fax: (202)546-3275; Email: ibpusa@comcast.net • URL: http://ibpus.com • Annual. $99.95 Individuals hardcover; $99.95 Individuals; $99.95 Individuals. Covers: Detailed information on investment, export-import business opportunities, foreign economic assistance projects, government and business contacts.

***Austrian Commercial Directory.*** Jupiter Verlagsgesellschaft mbH, Robertgasse 2 A-1020 Vienna, Austria. Phone: 222 21422490; Fax: 222 2160720 • Annual. Covers: 120,000 Austrian industrial, trading, and service firms. Entries include: Company name, address, phone, fax, telex, products, names of owners, board members, directors, and other key personnel.

***Austrian Companies Database.*** Hoppenstedt Produktinformationen GmbH, Havelstrasse 9, Postfach 100139 D-64295 Darmstadt, Germany. Phone: 49 6151 1375444 or 49 6151 38 0; Fax: 49 6151 1375443 or 49 6151 380 360; Email: info@hoppenstedt.de • URL: http://www.hoppenstedt.com • Semiannual. €2,318. Database covers: 15,000 major companies (or those which bill at least 70 million annually and/or have at least 100 employees) and 55,000 business executives in Austria. Entries include: Name, address, phone, fax, management names, range of products or services, number of employees, revenue and equity.

**Austrian Trade Commission.** 120 W 45th St., 9th Fl. New York, NY 10036. Phone: (212)421-5250; Fax: (212)421-5251; Email: newyork@advantageaustria.org • Promotes U.S.-Austrian trade with particular emphasis on Austrian exports to the U.S.; identifies Austrian trade sources to meet U.S. commercial demand. Handles inquiries related to trade between the two nations and deals with issues such as customs duties, trade laws, and licensing. Compiles statistics. Sponsors trade exhibits.

***Authority Collier Bankruptcy Library.*** Matthew Bender and Company Inc., 1275 Broadway Albany, NY 12204-2638. Phone: 800-424-4200 or (518)487-3000; Fax: (518)487-3573 or (800)424-4200; Email: customer.support@lexisnexis.com • URL: http://www.matthewbender.com • Periodic revisions. Price on request. CD-ROM contains updated full text of *Collier on Bankruptcy* and 13 other Collier publications. Various aspects of bankruptcy are covered, including attorney compensation, proceedings, farm insolvencies, real estate failures, family law, taxation, and business workouts.

***Authority Computer and Telecommunications Law Library.*** Matthew Bender and Company Inc., 1275 Broadway Albany, NY 12204-2638. Phone: 800-424-4200 or (518)487-3000; Fax: (518)487-3573 or (800)424-4200; Email: customer.support@lexisnexis.com • URL: http://www.matthewbender.com • Quarterly. Price on request. Full text CD-ROM provides cases, analysis, sample agreements, and other information relating to computer law, telecommunications regulation (cable, broadcasting, satellite, Internet), international computer law, and computer contracts.

***Authority Health Care Law Library.*** Matthew Bender and Company Inc., 1275 Broadway Albany, NY 12204-2638. Phone: 800-424-4200 or (518)487-3000; Fax: (518)487-3573 or (800)424-4200; Email: customer.support@lexisnexis.com • URL: http://www.matthewbender.com • Periodic updates. Price on request. Full text CD-ROM provides legal information, case law, and analysis relating to health care facilities, health insurance, longterm care, Medigap, and Medicare.

***Authority Immigration Law Library.*** Matthew Bender and Company Inc., 1275 Broadway Albany, NY 12204-2638. Phone: 800-424-4200 or (518)487-3000; Fax: (518)487-3573 or (800)424-4200; Email: customer.support@lexisnexis.com • URL: http://www.matthewbender.com • Periodic revisions. Price on request. CD-ROM contains updated full text of *Immigration Case Reporter, Immigration Law and Procedure Treatise, INS Regulations*, and other immigration law publications issued by Matthew Bender.

***Authority Intellectual Property Library.*** Matthew Bender and Company Inc., 1275 Broadway Albany, NY 12204-2638. Phone: 800-424-4200 or (518)487-3000; Fax: (518)487-3573 or (800)424-4200; Email: customer.support@lexisnexis.com • URL: http://www.matthewbender.com • Quarterly. Price on request. CD-ROM contains updated full text of *Intellectual Property Counseling and Litigation, Computer Law, International Computer Law, Nimmer on Copyright, Milgrim on Trade Secrets, Patent Litigation, Patent Licensing Transactions, Trademark Protection and Practice*, and other Matthew Bender publications relating to the law of intellectual property.

***Authority on Administrative Law.*** Matthew Bender and Company Inc., 1275 Broadway Albany, NY 12204-2638. Phone: 800-424-4200 or (518)487-3000; Fax: (518)487-3573 or (800)424-4200; Email: customer.support@lexisnexis.com • URL: http://www.matthewbender.com • Periodic updates. Price on request. Full text CD-ROM provides detailed information on Federal administrative procedural law. Contains a large number of judicial, regulatory, and statutory references.

***Authority Tax and Estate Planning Library.*** Matthew Bender and Company Inc., 1275 Broadway Albany, NY 12204-2638. Phone: 800-424-4200 or (518)487-3000; Fax: (518)487-3573 or (800)424-4200; Email: customer.support@lexisnexis.com • URL: http://www.matthewbender.com • Periodic revisions. Price on request. CD contains updated full text of *Bender's Payroll Tax Guide, Depreciation Handbook, Federal Income Taxation of Corporations, Tax Planning for Corporations, Modern Estate Planning, Planning for Large Estates, Murphy's Will Clauses, Tax & Estate Planning for the Elderly*, and 12 other Matthew Bender publications. The Internal Revenue Code is also included.

***Authority Worker's Compensation Library.*** Matthew Bender and Company Inc., 1275 Broadway Albany, NY 12204-2638. Phone: 800-424-4200 or (518)487-3000; Fax: (518)487-3573 or (800)424-4200; Email: customer.support@lexisnexis.com • URL: http://www.matthewbender.com • Periodic revisions. Price on request. CD-ROM contains updated full text of *Larson's Workmen's Compensation, Occupational Injuries and Illnesses*, and other Matthew Bender publications relating to worker's compensation laws.

**Authors Guild.** 31 E 32nd St., 7th Fl. New York, NY 10016. Phone: (212)563-5904; Fax: (212)564-5363; Email: staff@authorsguild.org • URL: http://www.authorsguild.net/ • Professional book and magazine writers. Maintains legal staff to provide book and magazine contract reviews for members. Group health insurance available. Members of the guild are also members of the Authors League of America.

**Auto Suppliers Benchmarking Association.** 4606 FM 1960 W, Ste. 250 Houston, TX 77069-9949. Phone: (281)440-5044; Fax: (281)440-6677 • URL: http://www.asbabenchmarking.com • Automotive supplier firms with an interest in benchmarking. Promotes the use of benchmarking, wherein businesses compare their processes with those of their competitors, as a means of improving corporate efficiency and profitability. Facilitates exchange of information among members; conducts target operations, procurement, development, and maintenance studies; identifies model business practices.

***Automated Builder Annual Buyers' Guide.*** 2401 Grapevine Dr. Oxnard, CA 93036. Phone: 800-344-2537 or (805)351-5931; Fax: (805)351-5755; Email: info@automatedbuilder.com • URL: http://www.automatedbuilder.com • Annual. $12.00. Over 250 manufacturers and suppliers to the manufactured and pre-fabricated housing industry.

**Automated Imaging Association.** 900 Victors Way, Ste. 140 Ann Arbor, MI 48108. Phone: (734)994-6088; Email: dwhalls@robotics.org • URL: http://www.visiononline.org • Represents manufacturers of machine vision components and systems, users, system integrators, universities and non-profit research groups, and financial firms that track the machine vision industry. Promotes the use and understanding of image capture and analysis technology.

***Automated Sources of Information in the Department of Commerce.*** U.S. Department of Commerce National Technical Information Service, 5301 Shawnee Rd. Alexandria, VA 22312. Phone: 800-553-NTIS or (703)605-6050 or (703)605-6585; Email: info@ntis.gov • URL: http://www.ntis.gov • $25 plus $5 handling fee (PB88-132568AHT). Diskette. Covers: Agencies of the United States Department of Commerce that produce or support online databases, electronic bulletin boards, information centers, and publications. Database includes: Agency name, address, phone, name and title of contact, information system content, titles of principal publications.

**Automatic Fire Alarm Association.** 82 Mill St., Ste. 300 Gahanna, OH 43230. Phone: 844-438-2322 or (614)416-8076; Fax: (614)453-8744; Email: fire-alarm@afaa.org • URL: http://www.afaa.org • Represents automatic fire detection and fire alarm systems industry. Membership is made up of state and regional member associations, manufacturers, installing distributors, authorities having jurisdiction, and end users. Promotes Life Safety in America through involvement in the codes and standards making process and by providing training seminars on a national basis.

***Automatic Merchandiser—Blue Book Buyer's Guide Issue.*** Cygnus Business Media Inc., 1233 Janesville Ave. Fort Atkinson, WI 53538. Phone: 800-547-7377; Email: info@cygnus.com • URL: http://www.cygnus.com • Annual. Publication includes: Suppliers of products, services, and equipment to the merchandise vending, contract foodservice, and office coffee service industries. Entries include: Company name, address, phone, names of executives, trade and brand names, and products or services offered.

***Automatic Merchandising Machine Operation Directory.*** InfoGroup Inc., 5711 S 86th Cir. Omaha, NE 68127-4146. Phone: (402)593-4500 • URL: http://www.infogroup.com • Annual. Number of listings: 11,954. Entries include: Name, address, phone, size of advertisement, name of owner or manager, number of employees, year first in "Yellow Pages." Compiled from telephone company "Yellow Pages," nationwide.

***Automation.*** U. S. Government Printing Office, 732 N Capitol St. NW Washington, DC 20401. Phone: 866-512-1800 or (202)512-1800 or (866)512-1800; Fax: (202)512-2104 or (202)512-2250; Email: contactcenter@gpo.gov • URL: http://

www.gpo.gov • Annual. Free. Issued by the Superintendent of Documents. A list of government publications on automation, computers, and related topics. Formerly *Computers and Data Processing*. (Subject Bibliography No. 51.).

***Automobile Liability Insurance. 3d***. Irvin E. Schermer and William J. Schermer. Thomson West, 610 Opperman Dr. Eagan, MN 55123. Phone: 800-328-9352 or (651)687-7000 • Seminannual. $501.00. Four looseleaf volumes.

***Automobile Parts Used & Rebuilt Directory***. InfoGroup Inc., 5711 S 86th Cir. Omaha, NE 68127-4146. Phone: (402)593-4500 • URL: http://www.infogroup.com • Annual. Number of listings: 11,939. Entries include: Name, address, phone, size of advertisement, name of owner or manager, number of employees, year first in "Yellow Pages." Compiled from telephone company "Yellow Pages," nationwide.

***Automobile Racing Directory***. InfoGroup Inc., 5711 S 86th Cir. Omaha, NE 68127-4146. Phone: (402)593-4500 • URL: http://www.infogroup.com • Annual. Number of listings: 2,233. Entries include: Name, address, phone, size of advertisement, name of owner or manager, number of employees, year first in "Yellow Pages." Compiled from telephone company "Yellow Pages," nationwide.

***Automobile Telephones Directory***. InfoGroup Inc., 5711 S 86th Cir. Omaha, NE 68127-4146. Phone: (402)593-4500 • URL: http://www.infogroup.com • Annual. Number of listings: 16,202. Entries include: Name, address, phone, size of advertisement, name of owner or manager, number of employees, year first in "Yellow Pages." Compiled from telephone company "Yellow Pages," nationwide.

***Automobile Window Tinting Directory***. InfoGroup Inc., 5711 S 86th Cir. Omaha, NE 68127-4146. Phone: (402)593-4500 • URL: http://www.infogroup.com • Annual. Number of listings: 6,032. Entries include: Name, address, phone, size of advertisement, name of owner or manager, number of employees, year first in "Yellow Pages." Compiled from telephone company "Yellow Pages," nationwide.

**Automotive Engine Rebuilders Association**. 500 Coventry Ln., Ste. 180 Crystal Lake, IL 60014. Phone: 888-326-2372 or (815)526-7600; Fax: (815)526-7601; Email: info@aera.org • URL: http://www.aera.org • Wholesalers of automotive replacement parts and equipment with machine shop operations; associate members are suppliers of parts, equipment, tools and services to the rebuilder members. Acts as clearinghouse for automotive jobber machine shop information.

***Automotive Market Report***. Automotive Auction Publishing Inc., 607 Laurel Dr. Monroeville, PA 15146. Phone: (412)373-6383 • Biweekly. $130.00 Per Year. Current wholesale values of used vehicles.

***Automotive News Market Data Book***. Crain Communications Inc., 1155 Gratiot Ave. Detroit, MI 48207-2732. Phone: (313)446-6000; Email: info@crain.com • URL: http://www.crain.com • Semiannual. $19.95. Directory of automotive vendors and worldwide vehicle manufacturing. Formerly *Automotive News Almanac*.

***Automotive Parts: Industry Sector Profile***. Philippine-German Export Development Project Philippine Bureau of Export Trade Promotion, 6F Trade & Industry Bldg., 361 Sen. Gil Puyat Ave. Makati PH-1226, Philippines. Phone: 63 2 897 8199; Email: web@dti.dti.gov.ph • URL: http://www.dti.gov.ph • Publication includes: Companies exporting automotive parts from the Philippines. Entries include: Company name, address, phone, fax, name and title of contact, type of business, year established, subsidiary and branch names and locations, financial data, number of employees, government registrations, professional memberships, bank references, supply capability, export experience, business plan. Principal content of publication is an overview of the business environment and automotive parts industry in the Philippines.

**Automotive Service Association**. 8190 Precinct Line Rd., Ste. 100 Colleyville, TX 76034-7675. Phone: 800-272-7467 or (817)514-2900; Fax: (817)514-0770; Email: asainfo@asashop.org • URL: http://www.asashop.org • Automotive service businesses including body, paint, and trim shops, engine rebuilders, radiator shops, brake and wheel alignment services, transmission shops, tune-up services, and air conditioning services; associate members are manufacturers and wholesalers of automotive parts, and the trade press. Represents independent business owners and managers before private agencies and national and state legislative bodies. Promotes confidence between consumer and the automotive service industry, safety inspection of motor vehicles, and better highways.

**Automotive Trade Association Executives**. 8400 Westpark Dr. McLean, VA 22102. Phone: (703)821-7072; Fax: (703)556-8581 • URL: http://www.atae.info • Executives of state and local automotive dealer associations.

**Automotive Warehouse Distributors Association**. 7101 Wisconsin Ave., Ste. 1300 Bethesda, MD 20814-3415. Phone: (301)654-6664; Fax: (301)654-3299; Email: info@autocare.org • URL: http://www.autocare.org • Warehouse distributors of automotive parts and supplies; manufacturers of automotive parts and suppliers; jobbers, business services, major program groups.

***AV Market Place: The Complete Business Directory of Audio, Audio Visual, Computer Systems, Film, Video, and Programming, with Industry Yellow Pages***. Information Today, Inc., 143 Old Marlton Pke. Medford, NJ 08055-8750. Phone: 800-300-9868 or (609)654-6266; Fax: (609)654-4309; Email: custserv@infotoday.com • URL: http://www.infotoday.com • Annual. $279.50 Individuals list price; $251.55 Individuals first time standing order. Provides information on "more than 7,500 companies that create, apply, or distribute AV equipment and services for business, education, science, and government." Multimedia, virtual reality, presentation software, and interactive video are among the categories. Formerly published by R. R. Bowker.

***AV Presentation—Buyer's Guide***. Cygnus Business Media Inc., 1233 Janesville Ave. Fort Atkinson, WI 53538. Phone: 800-547-7377; Email: info@cygnus.com • URL: http://www.cygnus.com • Annual. $6. Covers: lists of film and slide laboratory services and manufacturers of media production and presentation equipment and audiovisual supplies. Entries include: Company name, address, product or service.

***Avery Architectural Periodicals Index***. Columbia University Avery Architectural and Fine Arts Library, 300 Avery, 1172 Amsterdam Ave., MC 0301 New York, NY 10027. Phone: (212)854-7309; Email: avery@libraries.cul.columbia.edu • URL: http://library.columbia.edu/indiv/avery.html • Indexes a wide range of periodicals related to architecture and design. Subjects include building design, building materials, interior design, housing, land use, and city planning. Time span: 1977 to date. *bul* URL: www-rlg.stanford.edu/cit-ave.html.

***Avery Index to Architectural Periodicals***. Columbia University, Avery Architectural Library. • Annual. $995.

**Aviation Development Council**. 141-07 20th Ave., Ste. 404 Whitestone, NY 11357. Phone: (718)746-0212; Fax: (718)746-1006; Email: root@aviationdevelopmentcouncil.org • URL: http://www.aviationdevelopmentcouncil.org • U.S. and foreign scheduled air carriers serving the New York-New Jersey metropolitan area; Port Authority of New York and New Jersey; Allied Pilots Association; and Air Line Pilots Association, International. Aims to explore, evaluate, and recommend to the proper authorities measures in various fields that will afford possible relief to people affected by noise of aircraft. Initiates public information on significant developments in the metropolitan area. Compiles runway analysis data on New York City area airports. Administers industry-funded outreach programs designed to encourage local purchasing; administers "crime and security watch" programs for JFK, LGA & EWR.

**Aviation Distributors and Manufacturers Association**. 100 N 20th St., Ste. 400 Philadelphia, PA 19103-1462. Phone: (215)320-3872; Fax: (215)564-2175; Email: adma@fernley.com • URL: http://www.adma.org • Wholesalers and manufacturers of general aviation aircraft parts, supplies and equipment. Strives to further the development of the aviation marketplace through the services and products produced and distributed by members.

***Aviation Law Reports***. Wolters Kluwer Law & Business CCH, 2700 Lake Cook Rd. Riverwoods, IL 60015. Phone: 888-224-7377 or (847)267-7000; Email: cust_serv@cch.com • URL: http://www.cchgroup.com • Semimonthly. Four looseleaf volumes covering aviation law.

***Aviation***. U. S. Government Printing Office, 732 N Capitol St. NW Washington, DC 20401. Phone: 866-512-1800 or (202)512-1800 or (866)512-1800; Fax: (202)512-2104 or (202)512-2250; Email: contactcenter@gpo.gov • URL: http://www.gpo.gov • Annual. Free. Lists government publications. (GPO Subject Bibliography Number 18).

**Avionics Maintenance Conference**. Aeronautical Radio, Inc., 2551 Riva Rd. Annapolis, MD 21401. Phone: (410)266-2008; Fax: (410)266-2047; Email: sbuckwal@arinc.com • URL: http://www.aviation-ia.com/amc • Avionics maintenance professionals from commercial airlines, airframe manufacturers, avionics suppliers, and government organizations. Seeks to improve safety and reliability and reduce the costs of operating and supporting avionics equipment. Contributes to reduce the growth of avionics maintenance costs per flight hour despite growth in avionics capital costs. Conducts projects such as: the establishment of a standard language source document for writing automatic test programs; definition of an economic alternative to costly dedicated automatic test systems provided by manufacturers; development of an industry standard for automated preparation of test software; specification of documentation standards for software-based avionics; coordination of technical training needs for maintenance; and development of voluntary standards for the avionics industry.

***AVMA Directory***. American Veterinary Medical Association, 1931 N Meacham Rd., Ste. 100 Schaumburg, IL 60173-4360. Phone: 800-248-2862 or (847)925-8070; Fax: (847)925-1329; Email: info@avma.org • URL: http://www.avma.org • Annual. $100.00. 62,500 veterinarians; not limited to AVMA members. Formerly *American Veterinary Medical Association Directory*.

**Awards and Recognition Association**. 8735 W Higgins Rd., Ste. 300 Chicago, IL 60631. Phone: 800-344-2148 or (847)375-4800; Fax: (847)375-6480 or (888)374-7257; Email: info@ara.org • URL: http://www.ara.org • Awards and recognition industry retailers and suppliers. Advances the business growth of recognition specialists.

***Awards Directory***. InfoGroup Inc., 5711 S 86th Cir. Omaha, NE 68127-4146. Phone: (402)593-4500 • URL: http://www.infogroup.com • Annual. Number of listings: 7,623. Entries include: Name, address, phone, size of advertisement, name of owner or manager, number of employees, year first in "Yellow Pages." Compiled from telephone company "Yellow Pages," nationwide.

***Awards, Honors & Prizes***. Cengage Learning Inc., 20 Channel Center St. Boston, MA 02210. Phone: 800-487-8488 or (617)289-7700; Fax: (617)289-7844; Email: investors@cengage.com • URL: http://www.cengage.com • 2014. $898.00. Two volumes. 35th edition. Comprises awards given in virtually every field. Domestic volume, $477.00. International volume, $520.00.

***Awards, Honors, and Prizes: An International Directory of Awards and Their Donors Recognizing Achievement in Advertising, Architecture, Arts and Humanities, Business and Finance***. Cengage Learning Inc., 20 Channel Center St. Boston, MA 02210. Phone: 800-487-8488 or (617)289-7700; Fax: (617)289-7844; Email: investors@cengage.com • URL: http://www.cengage.com • Annual. $898 Individuals set series (3 volumes). Volume 1 covers more than 21,6000 awards given by organizations in the U.S. and Canada, in recognition of achievement, and major competitive prizes, some fellowships are also described; Volume 2 contains approximately 12,500 international awards.

***AWP Official Guide to Writing Programs***. Association of Writers and Writing Programs, George Mason University, 4400 University Dr., MSN 1E3 Fairfax, VA 22030-4444. Phone: (703)993-4301 or (703)933-4301; Fax: (703)993-4302 or (703)933-4302; Email: awp@awpwriter.org • URL: http://www.awpwriter.org • Biennial Annual. Included in membership; $28.45 Individuals including shipping and handling. Covers: About 300 graduate and 400 undergraduate programs in creative writing; approximately 250 writers' conferences, festivals, and centers; coverage includes Canada and the United Kingdom. Entries include: Institution name, department name, contact name and address; web site, description of program, including degree or other credit offered; description of faculty, including titles of their publications; tuition fees and dates.

***Azerbaijan Export-Import Trade and Business Directory***. International Business Publications, USA, PO Box 15343 Washington, DC 20003. Phone: (202)546-2103; Fax: (202)546-3275; Email: ibpusa@comcast.net • URL: http://ibpus.com • $99.95 Individuals. Contains information on strategic economic, investment, export-import, and business opportunities and contact numbers.

***Azerbaijan Government and Business Contacts Handbook***. International Business Publications, USA, PO Box 15343 Washington, DC 20003. Phone: (202)546-2103; Fax: (202)546-3275; Email: ibpusa@comcast.net • URL: http://ibpus.com • $99.95 Individuals hardcopy, E-book and CD-ROM. Covers: Strategic government and business information, export-import activity in the country, investment, business contacts and regulations.

***Azerbaijan Industrial and Business Directory***. International Business Publications, USA, PO Box 15343 Washington, DC 20003. Phone: (202)546-2103; Fax: (202)546-3275; Email: ibpusa@comcast.net • URL: http://ibpus.com • Annual. $99.95 Individuals. Covers industrial, investment, and business contacts for conducting export-import and investment activity in the country.

***Azerbaijan Investment and Business Guide***. International Business Publications, USA, PO Box 15343 Washington, DC 20003. Phone: (202)546-2103; Fax: (202)546-3275; Email: ibpusa@comcast.net • URL: http://ibpus.com • $99.95 Individuals hardcover; $99.95 Individuals e-book; $99.95 Individuals CD-ROM. Covers: Strategic and practical information on economy, export-import and investment climate, regulations and industrial development, banking, and government. Entries include: Important business contacts and business travel.

***B to B: The Magazine for Marketing and E-Commerce Strategists***. Crain Communications Inc., 711 3rd Ave. New York, NY 10017. Phone: (212)210-0100; Email: info@crain.com • URL: http://www.crain.com • Monthly. $59.00 per year. Formerly *Advertising Age's Business Marketing*.

**Babson College - Arthur M. Blank Center for Entrepreneurship**. 231 Forest St. Wellesley Hills, MA 02481-6834. Phone: (781)233-5023; Fax: (781)239-4178; Email: jstrimaitis@babson.edu • URL: http://www.babson.edu/Academics/centers/blank-center/Pages/home.aspx • Sponsors annual Babson College Entrepreneurship Research Conference.

***Baby Shop: The Business Magazine for Independent Juvenile Product Retailers***. Spindle Publishing Company Inc., 2275 Swallow Hill Rd., Bldg. 800 Pittsburgh, PA 15220. Phone: (412)278-4900; Fax: (412)278-4906; Email: info@spindlepub.com • URL: http://www.spindlepub.com • Semiannual. Magazine providing relevant articles and resources that help maternity retailers better manage their stores.

***Bacon's International Directory—Western Europe***. Cision US Inc., 332 S Michigan Ave., Ste. 900 Chicago, IL 60604-4393. Phone: 866-639-5087; Email: info.us@cision.com • URL: http://us.cision.com • Annual. Covers: over 16,000 consumer, business, trade, and technical publications, and about 1,000 national and regional newspapers in 12 countries of western Europe. Entries include: Publication name, address, phone, telex, translation requirements for news releases, code indicating type of publicity in which interested (new products, trade literature, etc.), frequency, circulation.

***Bacon's Newspaper and Magazine Directories***. Cision US Inc., 332 S Michigan Ave., Ste. 900 Chicago, IL 60604-4393. Phone: 866-639-5087; Email: info.us@cision.com • URL: http://us.cision.com • Annual. $325.00 per year. Two volumes: Magazines and Newspapers. Covers print media in the United States and Canada. Formerly *Bacon's Publicity Checker*.

**Bahamas Agricultural and Industrial Corporation**. Levy Bldg., E Bay St. Nassau, Bahamas. Phone: (242)322-3740; Fax: (242)322-2123; Email: baic@bahamas.net.bs • URL: http://www.bahamas.gov.bs • Assists in the development of commerce and industry in the Bahamas and works to expand the economic opportunities available to Bahamians. Sponsors seminars; disseminates information.

***Bahamas Chamber of Commerce—Annual Chamber Directory***. Bahamas Chamber of Commerce, Shirley St., Collins Ave. Nassau, Bahamas. Phone: (242)322-2145; Fax: (242)322-4649 • URL: http://www.bahamasb2b.com/bahamaschamber • Annual. $8. Entries include: name, address, phone, fax.

***Bahamas Chamber of Commerce—Annual Membership Directory: Business Directory***. Bahamas Chamber of Commerce, Shirley St., Collins Ave. Nassau, Bahamas. Phone: (242)322-2145; Fax: (242)322-4649 • URL: http://www.bahamasb2b.com/bahamaschamber • Annual. $8 plus shipping. Covers about 500 member firms in construction, manufacturing, professional and business services, sales, tourism, and transportation.

**Bahrain British Business Forum**. PO Box 10051 Manama, Bahrain. Phone: 973 1781-3488; Fax: 973 1781-3489; Email: bbbforum@batelco.com.bh • URL: http://bbbforum.org • Seeks to complement and improve relations between the local British and Bahraini business communities. Demonstrates to the local business community the interest and commitment of British business in Bahrain. Acts as a forum for the exchange of information related to local business opportunities.

***Bahrain Golden Key Directory***. International Institute of Trade Relation Promotion, Trade Information Centre of Iran, No. 7, 3rd Fl., Abbasie Bazar, Ferdowsi Sq. Tehran, Iran. Phone: 98 21 88833900; Fax: 98 21 88820697; Email: order@irangoldenkey.com • URL: http://www.goldenkeydirectory.com/about.html • £100 Individuals. Covers: 4,879 companies in Bahrain. Entries include: Company name, address, telephone, fax, e-mail, products, services, Managing Director, and business activities.

***Bahrain Investment & Business Guide***. International Business Publications, USA, PO Box 15343 Washington, DC 20003. Phone: (202)546-2103; Fax: (202)546-3275; Email: ibpusa@comcast.net • URL: http://ibpus.com • $99.95 Individuals hardcover; $99.95 Individuals e-book; $99.95 Individuals CD-ROM. Covers: Major investment, strategic business opportunities and basic information on economy, export-import, industrial development, banking and government. Entries include: Business contacts and business travel.

**Bahrain Management Society**. PO Box 3268 Manama, Bahrain. Phone: 973 17827676; Fax: 973 17827678; Email: admin@bms.org.bh • URL: http://www.bms.org.bh • Promotes best practices and standards of professionalism in management. Fosters research pertaining to all aspects of management. Aims to strengthen ties with other related organizations for the purpose of developing a better understanding of all concepts in management.

**Bakery, Confectionery, Tobacco Workers and Grain Millers International Union**. 10401 Connecticut Ave. Kensington, MD 20895. Phone: (301)933-8600; Fax: (301)946-8452; Email: bctgmwebmaster@bctgm.org • URL: http://www.bctgm.org • Formerly Bakery, Confectionery and Tobacco Workers International Union.

***Bakery***. Entrepreneur Press, 2445 McCabe Way, Ste. 400 Irvine, CA 92614-6244. Phone: 800-864-6864 or (949)261-2325 or (949)622-7131; Fax: (949)261-7729 or (949)261-0234; Email: press@entrepreneur.com • URL: http://www.entrepreneurpress.com • Looseleaf. $59.50. A practical guide to starting a retail bakery. Covers profit potential, start-up costs, market size evaluation, owner's time required, site selection, lease negotiation, pricing, accounting, advertising, promotion, etc. (Start-Up Business Guide No. E1158.).

**Bakery Equipment Manufacturers and Allieds**. 10740 Nall Ave., Ste. 230 Overland Park, KS 66211. Phone: (913)338-1300; Fax: (913)338-1327; Email: info@bema.org • URL: http://www.bema.org.

**Baking Industry Sanitation Standards Committee**. PO Box 3999 Manhattan, KS 66505-3999. Phone: 866-342-4772 or (785)537-4750; Fax: (785)537-1493; Email: bissc@bissc.org • URL: http://www.bissc.org • Industry association representing 120 bakery equipment manufacturers. Seeks to establish standards of sanitation in bakery food processing equipment. Receives advisory assistance from national and international public health and food sanitation groups. Develops and publishes sanitation standards for the baking industry. Offers an equipment certification program for bakery equipment conforming to standards (annual).

***Baking/Snack Directory & Buyer's Guide***. Sosland Publishing Co., 4800 Main St., Ste. 100 Kansas City, MO 64112. Phone: (816)756-1000; Fax: (816)756-0494; Email: nwages@sosland.com • URL: http://www.sosland.com • Annual. $205 Individuals S&H for ea. additional copy is $2 reg., $16 prior. Covers: Wholesale bakers of bread, cake, cookies, crackers, pasta; manufacturers of snack foods, mixes, and frozen dough; licensors of proprietary brands; manufacturers of equipment and products and suppliers of services used in wholesale baking. For bakers—Company name, address, phone, principal headquarters and plant personnel, principal products, sales volume, production method, and number of employees. For manufacturers—Company name, address, phone, name and title of contact. Entries include: Company name, address, phone, executive name.

***Balance of Payments Statistics***. International Monetary Fund, 700 19th St. NW Washington, DC 20431. Phone: (202)623-7000 or (202)623-6220; Fax: (202)623-4661; Email: insinfo@imf.org • URL: http://www.imf.org/institute • Time series compiled by IMF, mid-1960's to present. Inquire as to online cost and availability.

***Balconies Directory***. InfoGroup Inc., 5711 S 86th Cir. Omaha, NE 68127-4146. Phone: (402)593-4500 • URL: http://www.infogroup.com • Annual. Number of listings: 2,199. Entries include: Name, address, phone, size of advertisement, name of owner or manager, number of employees, year first in "Yellow Pages." Compiled from telephone company "Yellow Pages," nationwide.

**Ball State University - Bureau of Business Research**. Whitinger Business Bldg., Rm. 149, 2000 W University Ave. Muncie, IN 47306. Phone: (765)285-5926; Fax: (765)285-8024; Email: mhicks@bsu.edu • URL: http://cms.bsu.edu/Academics/CentersandInstitutes/BBR.aspx • Business and economics, including special studies designed to contribute to policy research, economic development and growth of eastern/central Indiana. Compiles and disseminates current economic and business data.

***Balloons—Manned—Directory***. InfoGroup Inc., 5711 S 86th Cir. Omaha, NE 68127-4146. Phone: (402)593-4500 • URL: http://www.infogroup.com • Annual. Number of listings: 604. Entries include: Name, address, phone, size of advertisement, name of owner or manager, number of employees, year first in "Yellow Pages." Compiled from telephone company "Yellow Pages," nationwide.

***Baltia Kompass Business Disc***. Kompass USA, Inc., 121 Whitney Ave. New Haven, CT 06510. Phone: (877)566-7277 or (203)503-6789; Fax: (203)503-6780; Email: mail@kompass-usa.com • URL: http://www.kompass.com • Provides information on more than 22,000 companies in Estonia, Latvia, and Lithuania. Classification system covers approximately 50,000 products and services.

***Baltimore Business Journal***. American City Business Journal, 111 Market Place, Ste. 720 Baltimore, MD 21202. Phone: (410)576-1161; Fax: (410)752-3112 • URL: http://www.bizjournals.com/baltimore/ • Weekly. $88 Individuals print + online. Newspaper reporting Baltimore business news.

***Baltimore Business Journal—Book of Lists***. Baltimore Business Journal, 1 E Pratt St., Ste. 205 Baltimore, MD 21202. Phone: (410)576-1161; Fax: (410)752-3112; Email: baltimore@bizjournals.com • URL: http://www.baltimore.bizjournals.com/baltimore • $60 print only; $199.95 online only. Covers: Major companies, foundations, government officials, utilities, newspapers, radio and television stations, airlines, hospitals, financial institutions, shopping centers, resorts, and prominent individuals in the Baltimore, Maryland area. Entries include: Company, organization, or individual name, address, phone, name and title of contact.

***Bangladesh Government and Business Contacts Handbook***. International Business Publications, USA, PO Box 15343 Washington, DC 20003. Phone: (202)546-2103; Fax: (202)546-3275; Email: ibpusa@comcast.net • URL: http://ibpus.com • $99.95 Individuals hardcopy, E-book and CD-ROM. Covers: Strategic government and business information, export-import activity in the country, investment, business contacts and regulations.

***Bangladesh Industrial and Business Directory***. International Business Publications, USA, PO Box 15343 Washington, DC 20003. Phone: (202)546-2103; Fax: (202)546-3275; Email: ibpusa@comcast.net • URL: http://ibpus.com • Annual. $99.95 Individuals hardcover; $99.95 Individuals e-book; $99.95 Individuals CD-ROM. Covers: Strategic industrial, investment and business contacts for conducting export-import and investment activity in the country.

***Bangladesh Investment and Business Guide***. International Business Publications, USA, PO Box 15343 Washington, DC 20003. Phone: (202)546-2103; Fax: (202)546-3275; Email: ibpusa@comcast.net • URL: http://ibpus.com • $99.95 Individuals hardcover; $99.95 Individuals e-book; $99.95 Individuals CD-ROM. Covers: Practical and strategic information on economy, export-import activity, investment climate, regulations and industrial development, banking, and government. Entries include: Business contacts and business travel.

**Bank Administration Institute - Operations and Technology Commission**. 115 S LaSalle St., Ste. 3300 Chicago, IL 60603-3801. Phone: 800-224-9889 or (312)653-2464; Fax: (312)683-2373; Email: info@bai.org • URL: http://www.bai.org.

**Bank Administration Institute**. 115 S La Salle St., Ste. 3300 Chicago, IL 60603-3801. Phone: 800-375-5543; Fax: (312)683-2373; Email: info@bai.org • URL: http://www.bai.org • Works to improve the competitive position of banking companies through strategic research and educational offerings.

***Bank and Lender Litigation Reporter: The Nationwide Litigation Report of Failed National and State Banks and Savings and Loan Associations, including FDIC and FSLIC Complaints and Related Actions Among Shareholders, Officers, Directors, Ins***. Andrews Publications, 175 Strafford Ave., Bldg. 4, Suite 140 Wayne, PA 19087. Phone: 800-345-1101 or (610)225-0510 or (610)622-0510; Fax: (610)225-0501 or (610)622-0501; Email: customer@andrewspub.com • URL: http://www.andrewspub.com • Semimonthly. $875.00 per year. Newsletter. Provides summaries of significant litigation and regulatory agency complaints. Formerly *Lender Liability Litigation Reporter*.

***Bank and Quotation Record***. William B. Dana Co., P.O. Box 1839 Daytona Beach, FL 32115-1839. Phone: (386)252-0230; Fax: (904)252-6933 • Monthly. $130.00 per year.

***Bank CEO's Operating and Management Desk Reference***. SourceMedia Inc., 1 State Street Plz., 27th Fl. New York, NY 10004. Phone: 800-221-1809 or (212)803-8200 or (212)803-8333; Fax: (212)843-9635 or (212)292-5216; Email: custserv@sourcemedia.com • URL: http://www.sourcemedia.com • $395.00. Two looseleaf volumes. Periodic updates available. Provides up-to-date information and advice on all areas of bank management. (A Sheshunoff publication.).

***The Bank Directory***. Accuity Inc., 4709 W Golf Rd. Skokie, IL 60076. Phone: 800-321-3373 or (847)676-9600; Fax: (847)933-8101; Email: custserv@accuitysolutions.com • URL: http://www.accuitysolutions.com • Semiannual. $1,670 Individuals. Covers: In five volumes, about 11,000 banks and 50,000 branches of United States banks, and 60,000 foreign banks and branches engaged in foreign banking; Federal Reserve system and other United States government and state government banking agencies; 500 largest North American and International commercial banks; paper and automated clearinghouses. Volumes 1 and 2 contain North American listings; volumes 3 and 4, international listings (also cited as 'Thomson International Bank Directory; volume 5, Worldwide Correspondents Guide containing key correspondent data to facilitate funds transfer. Database includes: Bank operations information, asset ranking in state and country, bank routing numbers in numeric sequence, discontinued or changed bank names in geographical sequence. Entries include: For domestic banks—Bank name, address, phone, telex, cable, date established, routing number, charter type, bank holding company affiliation, memberships in Federal Reserve System and other banking organizations, principal officers by function performed, principal correspondent banks, and key financial data (deposits, etc.). For international banks—Bank name, address, phone, fax, telex, cable, SWIFT address, transit or sort codes within home country, ownership, financial data, names and titles of key personnel, branch locations. For branches—Bank name, address, phone, charter type, ownership and other details comparable to domestic bank listings.

***Bank Investment Consultant: Sales Strategies for the Financial Adviser***. SourceMedia Inc., 1 State Street Plz., 27th Fl. New York, NY 10004. Phone: 800-221-1809 or (212)803-8200 or (212)803-8333; Fax: (212)843-9635 or (212)292-5216; Email: custserv@sourcemedia.com • URL: http://www.sourcemedia.com • Monthly. Controlled circulation. Covers sales and marketing techniques for bank investment and asset management divisions. Formerly *Bank Investment Marketing*.

***Bank Loan Report***. IDD Enterprises L.P., Harborside Financial Ctr., 600 Plz. II, 4th Fl. Jersey City, NJ 07311. • Description: Discusses banking loans and transactions made by large corporations. Recurring features include a column titled Term Sheets.

***Banker News***. American Bankers Association, 1120 Connecticut Ave. NW Washington, DC 20036. Phone: 800-226-5377 or (202)663-5268; Fax: (202)828-5053; Email: custserv@aba.com • URL: http://www.aba.com • Biweekly. $48 Members; $96 Nonmembers.

***Bankers' Almanac***. Reed Business Information, Windsor Court, East Grinstead West Sussex RH19 1XA, United Kingdom. Phone: 44 1342 326972 • URL: http://www.reedbusiness.com/ • Semiannual. $1,170.00. Six volumes. Lists more than 27,000 financial institutions; international coverage. Formerly *Bankers' Almanac and Yearbook*.

**Bankers' Association for Finance and Trade**. 1120 Connecticut Ave. NW Washington, DC 20036. Phone: (202)663-7575; Fax: (202)663-5538; Email: info@baft-ifsa.com • URL: http://www.baft-ifsa.com • Formerly Bankers' Association for Foreign Trade.

***Banking Crimes: Fraud, Money Laundering & Embezzlement***. John K. Villa. Thomson West, 610 Opperman Dr. Eagan, MN 55123. Phone: 800-328-9352 or (651)687-7000 • $369.60 Full Set. Covers fraud and embezzlement.

***Banking Information Source***. ProQuest L.L.C., 789 E Eisenhower Pkwy. Ann Arbor, MI 48106-1346. Phone: 800-521-0600 or (734)761-4700; Fax: (734)662-4554; Email: info@proquest.com • URL: http://www.proquest.com • Provides indexing and abstracting of periodical and other literature from 1982 to date, with weekly updates. Covers the financial services industry: banks, savings institutions, investment houses, credit unions, insurance companies, and real estate organizations. Emphasis is on marketing and management. Inquire as to online cost and availability. (Formerly *FINIS: Financial Industry Information Service.*).

***Bankruptcy Law Fundamentals***. Thomson West, 610 Opperman Dr. Eagan, MN 55123. Phone: 800-328-9352 or (651)687-7000 • Annual. $412.30 Individuals book - softbound. Looseleaf service.

***Bankruptcy Law Reports***. Wolters Kluwer Law & Business CCH, 2700 Lake Cook Rd. Riverwoods, IL 60015. Phone: 888-224-7377 or (847)267-7000; Email: cust_serv@cch.com • URL: http://www.cchgroup.com • Biweekly. $1,150.00 per year. Three looseleaf volumes.

***The Bankruptcy Strategist***. Law Journal Newsletter, 105 Madison Ave. New York, NY 10016. Phone: 800-603-6571 or (212)313-9300; Fax: (212)481-8110; Email: lawcatalog@amlaw.com • URL: http://www.ljnonline.com • $510. Reports on substantive legal developments and successful strategy decisions by bankruptcy attorneys. Recurring features include a calendar of upcoming seminars.

***Bankruptcy Yearbook & Almanac***. New Generation Research Inc., 1212 Hancock St., Ste. LL-15 Quincy, MA 02169. Phone: 800-468-3810; Fax: (617)328-1419; Email: customersupport@bankruptcydata.com • URL: http://www.newgenerationresearch.com • Annual. $295. Contains updated information on US Bankruptcy Court data.

***BanxQuote Banking, Mortgage, and Finance Center***. BanxQuote, Inc., Phone: (914)722-1600; Fax: (914)722-6630; Email: info@banx.com • URL: http://www.banx.com • Daily. Web site quotes interest rates paid by banks around the country on various savings products, as well as rates paid by consumers for automobile loans, mortgages, credit cards, home equity loans, and personal loans. Also provided: stock quotes, indexes, stock options, futures trading data, economic indicators, and links to many other financial sites.

***Barbados Business Directory***. Barbados Chamber of Commerce and Industry, Braemar Ct., Deighton Road St. Saint Michael, Barbados. Phone: (246)434-4750; Fax: (246)228-2907 • URL: http://www.barbadoschamberofcommerce.com • Biennial. Serves as a concise business reference.

**Barbados Chamber of Commerce and Industry**. Braemar Ct., Deighton Road St. Saint Michael, Barbados. Phone: (246)434-4750; Fax: (246)228-2907 • URL: http://www.barbadoschamberofcommerce.com • Businesses, business and trade promotion organizations, and individuals with an interest in promoting trade and commerce in Barbados. Seeks to improve domestic business conditions and increase foreign trade. Facilitates communication among members; functions as liaison between members and government agencies and international business organizations. Gathers and disseminates business and trade information; compiles statistics. Administers Duty Free Scheme in Barbados.

***Barron's Guide to Graduate Business Schools***. Barron's Educational Series Inc., 250 Wireless Blvd. Hauppauge, NY 11788. Phone: 800-645-3476 or (631)434-3311; Fax: (631)434-3723; Email: barrons@barronseduc.com • URL: http://www.barronseduc.com • Biennial. Contains profiles of more than 600 business schools offering graduate business degrees in the U. S. and Canada. Includes advice on choosing a school.

***Barron's: The Dow Jones Business and Financial Weekly***. Dow Jones & Co., Inc., 1211 Avenue of the Americas New York, NY 10036. Phone: 800-369-5663; Email: service@dowjones.com • URL: http://new.dowjones.com • Weekly (Mon.). $100.94 Individuals; $26 Individuals digital; for the first 26 weeks. Business and finance magazine.

***Bartercard National Directory***. Bartercard International, 121 Scarborough St. Southport, QLD 4215, Australia. Email: info@au.bartercard.com • URL: http://www.au.bartercard.com • 3/year. Covers: 23,000 businesses in Australia and over 55,000 businesses around the world. Entries include: Detailed contact information.

***Baseball Batting Ranges Directory***. InfoGroup Inc., 5711 S 86th Cir. Omaha, NE 68127-4146. Phone: (402)593-4500 • URL: http://www.infogroup.com • Annual. Number of listings: 1,050. Entries include: Name, address, phone, size of advertisement, name of owner or manager, number of employees, year first in "Yellow Pages." Compiled from telephone company "Yellow Pages," nationwide.

***Basic Business Essentials: Concepts and Tools***. American CPE Inc., 826 Riviera Mansfield, TX 76063. Phone: 800-990-4273 or (817)477-0222; Fax: (817)473-4998; Email: director@americancpe.com • URL: http://www.americancpe.com • Contains detailed training information covering fundamental topics in business and business management.

***The Basic Business Library***. Greenwood Publishing Group Inc., 88 Post Rd. W Westport, CT 06881. Phone: (203)226-3571; Fax: (203)222-1502; Email: orders@greenwood.com • URL: http://www.greenwood.com • Lists current business resources and essays on topics in business librarianship.

***Basic Guide to Exporting***. Todd Publications, PO Box 500 Millwood, NY 10546. Phone: 866-896-0916 or (914)373-4750; Fax: (914)373-4750; Email: toddpub@aol.com • URL: http://www.toddpublications.com • Quadrennial. $20. Covers: Sources for aid in understanding foreign business practices, government regulations, taxes, and currency. Database includes: How to evaluate a product or service's overseas potential; how to make contacts and sell overseas; how to handle financing; and how to get paid.

**Basic Metals Processing Research Institute**. University of Pittsburgh, Swanson School of Engineering, 151 Benedum Hall Pittsburgh, PA 15261. Phone: (412)624-9800; Fax: (412)624-9808; Email: ssoeadm@pitt.edu • URL: http://www.engineering.pitt.edu/Research/Facilities/Basic_Metals_Processing_Research_Institute_(BAMPRI)/#.

***Batavia Business***. Batavia Chamber of Commerce, 106 W Wilson St. Batavia, IL 60510. Phone: (630)879-7134; Fax: (630)879-7215; Email: info@bataviachamber.org • URL: http://www.bataviachamber.org • Monthly. Contains information on businesses in Batavia.

**Battery Council International**. 401 N Michigan Ave., 24th Fl. Chicago, IL 60611-4227. Phone: (312)644-6610; Fax: (312)527-6640; Email: info@batterycouncil.org • URL: http://batterycouncil.org • Manufacturers, suppliers of materials and national distributors of lead-acid storage batteries. Recommends industry standards; compiles statistics.

***Battery Product Businesses in the World***. Momentum Technologies L.L.C., PO Box 460813 Glendale, CO 80246. Phone: (303)229-4841; Fax: (408)705-2031 • URL: http://www.mtt.com • Contains directory listings for approximately 600 wholesale suppliers of batteries and related products from around the world. Includes business name, address, phone number, fax number, e-mail address, and web site address. Includes brief descriptions of product lines, services offered, and business type. Covers suppliers of deep cycle batteries, lithium ion batteries, nickel cadmium batteries, sealed lead acid batteries, and more. Offers information on battery supplies in industries such as renewable energy, electric vehicles, marine transportation, telecommunications, and portable computers. Provides keyword search functions.

**Battery Recycling Association of North America**. 12505 N Main St., Ste. 212 Rancho Cucamonga, CA 91739. • URL: http://www.brana-online.org • Represents companies that handle, recycle, transport and manage portable power batteries. Seeks to establish guidance and training on the proper methods and regulations governing the safe handling of batteries. Fosters dialogue with battery handlers, recyclers, manufacturers and the regulatory community.

***The Bauer Group: Reporting On and Analyzing the Performance of U. S. Banks, Thrifts, and Credit Unions***. Bauer Financial Reports, Inc., Phone: 800-388-6686 or (305)445-9500; Fax: (305)445-6775 or (800)230-9569 • URL: http://www.bauerfinancial.com • Web site provides ratings (0 to 5 stars) of individual banks and credit unions, based on capital ratios and other financial criteria. Online searching for bank or credit union names is offered. Fees: Free.

***Bay Area Employer Directory***. James R. Albin, 431 Bridgeway Sausalito, CA 94965. Phone: (415)332-6438; Fax: (415)332-6468 • Annual. $99.95. Covers: over 2,000 employers in the San Francisco Bay Area each having 100 or more employees; includes both private and government employers. Entries include: Firm name, address, phone, year established, type of business or activity, number of employees, sales, names and titles of local chief executive and personnel manager.

**Baylor College of Medicine - Department of Molecular and Human Genetics**. Baylor Clinic, 6620 Main St., 12th Fl., Ste. 1225 Houston, TX 77030. Phone: (713)798-7820 or (713)798-3651; Fax: (713)798-6450 or (713)798-6521; Email: abeaudet@bcm.tmc.edu • URL: http://www.bcm.edu/genetics/index.cfm?PMID=10398.

**Baylor University - Center for Private Enterprise**. PO Box 98003 Waco, TX 76798. Phone: (254)710-2263 or (254)710-6898; Fax: (254)710-1092; Email: kimberly_mencken@baylor.edu • URL: http://www.baylor.edu/business • Includes studies of entrepreneurship and women entrepreneurs.

**BBB Wise Giving Council**. 3033 Wilson Blvd., Ste. 600 Arlington, VA 22201. Phone: (703)276-0100; Fax: (703)525-8277; Email: info@bbb.org • URL: http://www.bbb.org • Sets accountability standards and provides information for nonprofit organizations that solicit contributions from the public. Formerly National Charities Information Bureau.

***BC Business Magazine***. Canada Wide Magazines & Communications Ltd., 4180 Lougheed Hwy., 4th Fl. Burnaby, BC, Canada V5C 6A7. Phone: (604)299-7311; Fax: (604)299-9188; Email: cwm@canadawide.com • URL: http://www.canadawide.com • Monthly. $24.95 Individuals 12 issues; $39.95 Individuals 24 issues; $54.95 Individuals 36 issues. Magazine covering business for consumers in British Columbia.

**BC Innovation Council**. 1188 W Georgia St., 9th Fl. Vancouver, BC, Canada V6E 4A2. Phone: 800-665-7222 or (604)683-2724; Fax: (604)683-6567; Email: info@bcic.ca • URL: http://www.bcic.ca • Provides support and access to companies and institutions by using research results, development projects and programs to further enhance in creating innovations.

***BDO Stoy Hayward Guide to Venture & Buy-Out Capital***. BDO Stoy Hayward, 8 Baker St. London W1M 1DA, United Kingdom. Phone: 71 4865888; Fax: 71 4873686 • Annual. Covers: about 170 companies and agencies with funds available for new ventures. Entries include: Agency or company name, address, phone, description of services, financial data, funds available for venture and capital development.

**Bearing Specialists Association**. 800 Roosevelt Rd., Bldg. C, Ste. 312 Glen Ellyn, IL 60137. Phone: (630)858-3838; Fax: (630)790-3095; Email: info@bsahome.org • URL: http://www.bsahome.org • Distributors of anti-friction bearings. Promotes networking and knowledge sharing and promotes the sale of bearings through authorized distributors.

**Beauty and Barber Supply Institute**. 11811 N Tatum Blvd., No. 1085 Phoenix, AZ 85028-1625. Phone: 800-468-2274 or (602)404-1800; Fax: (602)404-8900; Email: denise@bbsi.org • URL: http://www.beautyweb.com/beauty_associations.htm#BBSI.

***Beauty Store Business***. Creative Age Publications Inc., 7628 Densmore Ave. Van Nuys, CA 91406-2042. Phone: 800-442-5667 or (818)782-7328; Fax: (818)782-7450 • URL: http://www.creativeage.com • Monthly. Business magazine for beauty industry professionals and beauty store owners.

***Bee Culture: The Magazine of American Beekeeping***. The A.I. Root Co., 623 W Liberty St. Medina, OH 44258-2225. Phone: 800-289-7668 or (330)725-6677; Fax: (330)725-5624; Email: contact@rootcandles.com • URL: http://www.rootcandles.com • Monthly. $25 Individuals; $47.50 Other countries; $99.50 Other countries airmail; $15 Individuals digital. Articles, reports and stories about beekeeping market. Latest industry news. Formerly *Gleanings in Bee Culture*.

***BEEF***. National Cattlemen's Beef Association, Phone: (303)694-0305; Fax: (303)694-2851; Email: cows@beef.org • URL: http://www.beef.org • Web site provides detailed information from the "Cattle and Beef Handbook," including "Beef Economics" (production, sales, consumption, retail value, foreign competition, etc.). Text of monthly newsletter is also available: "The Beef Brief-Issues & Trends in the Cattle Industry." Keyword searching is offered. Fees: Free.

**Beer Institute**. 122 C St., Ste. 350 Washington, DC 20001-2109. Phone: (202)737-2337; Fax: (202)737-7004; Email: info@beerinstitute.org • URL: http://www.beerinstitute.org • Brewers, importers, and suppliers to the industry. Committed to the development of public policy and to the values of civic duty and personal responsibility.

***Belarus Export-Import Trade and Business Directory***. International Business Publications, USA, PO Box 15343 Washington, DC 20003. Phone: (202)546-2103; Fax: (202)546-3275; Email: ibpusa@comcast.net • URL: http://ibpus.com • $99.95 Individuals. Contains information on strategic, economic, investment, export-import, and business opportunities and contact numbers.

***Belarus Industrial and Business Directory***. International Business Publications, USA, PO Box 15343 Washington, DC 20003. Phone: (202)546-2103; Fax: (202)546-3275; Email: ibpusa@comcast.net • URL: http://ibpus.com • Annual. $99.95 Individuals hardcover; $99.95 Individuals e-book; $99.95 Individuals CD-ROM. Covers: Strategic industrial, investment and business contacts for conducting export-import and investment activity in the country.

***Belfast Business Network***. Century Newspapers Ltd., 46-56 Boucher Crescent Belfast BT12 6OY, United Kingdom. • URL: http://directory.wan-ifra.org/companies/century-newspapers-ltd • $12.50. Covers: 13,500 business companies in Belfast. Entries include: Company name, address, phone, fax.

***Belgium Export-Import and Business Directory***. International Business Publications, USA, PO Box 15343 Washington, DC 20003. Phone: (202)546-2103; Fax: (202)546-3275; Email: ibpusa@comcast.net • URL: http://ibpus.com • $99.95 Individuals. Covers information on strategic, economic, investment, export-import, and business opportunities and contact numbers.

***Belgium Industrial and Business Directory***. International Business Publications, USA, PO Box 15343 Washington, DC 20003. Phone: (202)546-2103; Fax: (202)546-3275; Email: ibpusa@comcast.net • URL: http://ibpus.com • Annual. $99.95 Individuals hardcover; $99.95 Individuals e-book; $99.95 Individuals CD-ROM. Covers: Detailed information on investment, export-import business opportunities, foreign economic assistance projects, government and business contacts.

***Belgium-Luxembourg Chamber of Commerce in Hong Kong—Directory***. Belgium-Luxembourg Chamber of Commerce in Hong Kong, Kodak House II, 1st Fl., Unit 4, 321 Java Rd. Hong Kong, China. Phone: 852 31157709; Fax: 852 28663535; Email: info@blcchk.org • URL: http://www.blcchk.org • Covers: Member organizations involved in developing two-way trade between Belgium - Luxembourg and Hong Kong.

***Belize Investment & Business Guide***. International Business Publications, USA, PO Box 15343 Washington, DC 20003. Phone: (202)546-2103; Fax: (202)546-3275; Email: ibpusa@comcast.net • URL: http://ibpus.com • $99.95 Individuals hardcover; $99.95 Individuals e-book; $99.95 Individuals CD-ROM. Covers: Strategic business information, export-import activity in the state, regulations and industrial development, banking, government, and opportunities. Entries include: Guides for conducting investment and business contacts.

***Benedict on Admiralty***. Matthew Bender and Company Inc., 1275 Broadway Albany, NY 12204-2638. Phone: 800-424-4200 or (518)487-3000; Fax: (518)487-3573 or (800)424-4200; Email: customer.support@lexisnexis.com • URL: http://www.matthewbender.com • Three times a year. $3,138.00. 27 looseleaf volumes. Periodic supplementation. Covers American law of the sea and shipping.

***Benefits Survey***. Paul & Co., 814 N. Franklin St. Chicago, IL 60610. Phone: (312)337-0747; Fax: (312)337-5985; Email:

frontdesk@ipgbook.com • URL: http://www.ipgbook.com • Annual. $99.95. Published by the Society for Human Resource Management (www.shrm.org). Provides five-year data, with discussion, for 200 kinds of employee benefits.

*Benelux Kompass Business Disc*. Kompass USA, Inc., 121 Whitney Ave. New Haven, CT 06510. Phone: (877)566-7277 or (203)503-6789; Fax: (203)503-6780; Email: mail@kompass-usa.com • URL: http://www.kompass.com • Semiannual. CD-ROM provides information on more than 52,000 companies in Belgium, Netherlands, and Luxembourg. Classification system covers approximately 50,000 products and services.

*Benin Business Directory*. Business Guide, PO Box 27669 Dubai, United Arab Emirates. Phone: 971 4 2651719; Fax: 971 4 2692151; Email: sales@africa-business.com • URL: http://www.africa-business.com • $150 download. Covers: 4,400 business listings including wholesalers, importers, retailers, business houses, and agents in Benin.

*Bergano's Worldwide Register of Distributors*. Bergano Book Co., 38 Park Ln. Westport, CT 06880. Phone: (203)226-5780; Fax: (203)226-6720; Email: bergano@aol.com • Irregular. $125. Covers: Approximately 4,000 importing firms and distributors; international coverage. Entries include: Company name, address, phone, fax, name and title of contact, year established, number of employees, goods imported.

*Berkeley Business Law Journal*.

**Bermuda Business Development Agency**. Maxwell Roberts Bldg., 6th Fl., 1 Church St. Hamilton HM 11, Bermuda. Phone: (441)292-0632; Fax: (441)292-1797; Email: info@bermudabda.com • URL: http://bermudabda.com • Professionals and businesses. Promotes and supports high business standards among professionals in international business.

*Bermuda Business Directory*. Bermuda Directories Ltd., 13 Addendum Ln. Pembroke, Bermuda. Phone: 441295-6000; Fax: 441295-3445; Email: info@bermudadirectory.com • URL: http://www.bermudadirectory.com • Covers: Listings of businesses in Bermuda including insurance, banking and legal services, local events, sightseeing, shopping, dining, and restaurants. Entries include: Company name, contact information, and e-mail address.

**Bernard Baruch College of City University of New York - Center for the Study of Business and Government**. 1 Bernard Baruch Way New York, NY 10010-5518. Phone: (646)312-3540; Email: june.oneill@baruch.cuny.edu • URL: http://zicklin.baruch.cuny.edu/centers/csbg • Economic, social, and public policy issues, including regulation of banks and of capital markets, labor market patterns and the impact of government policies on them, differences and change in the incomes of demographic groups and regions with emphasis on New York and related government policies, urban problems and governmental solutions, particularly as related to New York City, and economic analysis of social issues, such as poverty, crime, and health.

**BEST Employers Association**. 2505 McCabe Way Irvine, CA 92614. Phone: 866-706-2225; Email: bestassoc@bestlife.com • URL: http://www.beassoc.org • Provides small independent businesses with managerial, economic, financial and sales information helpful for business improvement. Organizes and sponsors healthcare alliances for small employers. (The acronym BEST stands for Beneficial Employees Security Trust).

*Best of British*. Jordans Ltd., 21 St. Thomas St. Bristol BS1 6JS, United Kingdom. Phone: 44 117 923 0600; Fax: 44 117 923 0063; Email: customerservices@jordans.co.uk • URL: http://www.jordans.co.uk • Annual. $225 for four volume set; $95 pounds per volume. Covers: in four volumes, 20,000 leading companies in the United Kingdom; 5,000 per volume. Entries include: Company name, registered office address, chief executive, financial data for previous three years, business description.

*Best's Insurance Reports*. A.M. Best Company Inc., Ambest Rd. Oldwick, NJ 08858-7000. Phone: (908)439-2200; Fax: (908)439-3385; Email: customer_service@ambest.com • URL: http://www.ambest.com • Annual. 1,495. Covers life-health insurance covering about 1,750 companies, and property-casualty insurance covering over 3,200 companies. Includes subscription to both *Best's Review* and *Best's Insurance Management Reports*.

*Best's Insurance Reports: Property-Casualty*. A.M. Best Company Inc., Ambest Rd. Oldwick, NJ 08858-7000. Phone: (908)439-2200; Fax: (908)439-3385; Email: customer_service@ambest.com • URL: http://www.ambest.com • Annual. $750.00. Guide to over 3,200 major property/casualty companies.

*Best's Key Rating Guide*. A.M. Best Company Inc., Ambest Rd. Oldwick, NJ 08858-7000. Phone: (908)439-2200; Fax: (908)439-3385; Email: customer_service@ambest.com • URL: http://www.ambest.com • Annual. $200 Individuals regular service; $1,000 Individuals full service. Financial information and ratings on thousands of major property/casualty insurers.

*BestWeek: Insurance News and Analysis*. A.M. Best Company Inc., Ambest Rd. Oldwick, NJ 08858-7000. Phone: (908)439-2200; Fax: (908)439-3385; Email: customer_service@ambest.com • URL: http://www.ambest.com • Weekly. $495.00 per year. Newsletter. Focuses on key areas of the insurance industry.

**Beta Gamma Sigma Alumni**. PO Box 297-006 Brooklyn, NY

11229-7006. • URL: http://www.bgs-nyc.org • Alumni members of the collegiate national honor society Beta Gamma Sigma. Promotes excellence in business education, ethics, and scholastic achievement and recognition. Local New York chapter.

**Beta Gamma Sigma**. 125 Weldon Pkwy. Maryland Heights, MO 63043. Phone: 800-337-4677 or (314)432-5650; Fax: (314)432-7083; Email: bgshonors@betagammasigma.org • URL: http://www.betagammasigma.org • International honor society. For students in business and management at business programs accredited by AACSB International. Supports the advancement of business thought and practice to encourage lifelong learning.

**Beta Pi Sigma Sorority**. 256 Waterville St. San Francisco, CA 94124. Email: bpssi@betapisigmasorority.org • URL: http://betapisigmasorority.org • Business and professional sorority. Conducts civic, cultural, charitable, and educational projects. Cooperates with the Close Up Foundation on the Program for Older Americans. Offers tutoring services. Youth programs partnerships with schools, book donation programs (schools and libraries), and youth programs.

*Better Business Bureau—Directory & Consumer Guide*. Better Business Bureau of Metropolitan Toronto, 1 St. John's Rd., 5th Fl. Toronto, ON, Canada M6P 4C7. Phone: (416)766-5744; Fax: (416)766-1970 • Covers: about 7,000 member companies and over 500,000 homes in metropolitan Toronto, Ontario. Entries include: Company name, address, phone, products and services.

*Better Business Bureau of New Jersey Consumer Guide*. Better Business Bureau of New Jersey, 1262 Whitehorse-Hamilton Square Rd., Bldg. A, Ste. 202 Trenton, NJ 08690. Phone: (609)588-0808; Fax: (609)588-0546; Email: info@newjersey.bbb.org • URL: http://www.bbb.org/new-jersey • Annual.

**Better Business Bureau - Wise Giving Alliance**. 3033 Wilson Blvd., Ste. 600 Arlington, VA 22201. Phone: (703)276-0100; Fax: (703)525-8277; Email: info@bbb.org • URL: http://www.bbb.org • Supported by companies and local Better Business Bureaus operated autonomously in the United States and Puerto Rico, which are in turn supported by 270,000 local business members. Seeks to promote and foster the highest ethical relationship between businesses and the public through voluntary self-regulation, consumer and business education, and service excellence. Provides support to local Better Business Bureaus. Administers the advertising industry's self-regulatory program that monitors and investigates the truth and accuracy of national advertising claims; monitors and pre-screens advertising directed towards children. Develops information on national charitable organizations and whether they meet voluntary ethical standards for soliciting organizations. Provides information to help consumers and businesses make informed purchasing decisions and avoid costly scams and frauds; and settles consumer complaints through arbitration and other means. Operates BBB AUTO LINE, a national mediation and arbitration service providing an independent forum to resolve consumer complaints involving 32 participating auto manufacturers; Local Better Business Bureaus respond to more than 23 million requests for service annually, fielding 20 million pre-purchase inquiries and 3 million complaints.

**Better Government Association**. 223 W Jackson Blvd., Ste. 900 Chicago, IL 60606. Phone: (312)427-8330; Fax: (312)821-9038; Email: info@bettergov.org • URL: http://www.bettergov.org • Individuals and corporations concerned with major public policy questions and dedicated to promoting efficient use of tax dollars and high standards of public service. Encourages a responsive and economical government by improving government institutions' performance and maintaining high ethical standards among public officials. Uses official documents, on-the-record interviews, undercover operations, and sophisticated techniques of investigative reporting to uncover corruption. Works closely with national and local media to expose waste, inefficiency, and corruption and to educate the public on the inner workings of the government. Sponsors intern programs for students in law and investigative research.

*Better Roads—Annual Winter Maintenance Equipment & Materials Issue: Federal State County Township Road & Municipalities*. James Informational Media Inc., 2720 S River Rd. Des Plaines, IL 60018-5142. Phone: (847)391-9070; Fax: (847)391-9058; Email: kirk@jiminc.com • Annual. $95 Individuals per year prepaid. Publication includes: List of manufacturers of equipment and suppliers of materials and services for winter roads maintenance. Also features information on road agencies, construction/maintenance, and safety. Entries include: Company name, address.

**Better Vision Institute**. Vision Council of America, 225 Reinekers Ln., Ste. 700 Alexandria, VA 22314. Phone: (703)548-4560; Fax: (703)548-4580; Email: ezb@thevisioncouncil.org • URL: http://www.thevisioncouncil.org/bvi • Advisory council of the Vision Council of America. Carried out in consultation with a board of eye care professionals who inform the public of the need for more adequate vision care.

*Beverage Industry News*. BIN Publications, 171 Mayhew Way, Suite 202 Pleasant Hill, CA 94523-4348. Phone: (925)932-4999; Fax: (925)932-4966; Email: binmagqa.com • Monthly. $49 Individuals. Magazine for the alcoholic beverages retail

trade. Incorporates *Beverage Industry News Merchandiser*.

*Beverage Marketing Directory*. Beverage Marketing Corp., PO Box 126 Mingo Junction, OH 43938. Phone: 800-275-4630 or (740)598-4133; Fax: (740)598-3977; Email: consulting@beveragemarketing.com • URL: http://www.beveragemarketing.com • Annual. $995 Individuals print; $995 Individuals PDF. Covers: Over 25,500 beer wholesalers, wine and spirits wholesalers, soft drink bottlers and franchisors, breweries, wineries, distilleries, alcoholic beverage importers, bottled water companies; and trade associations, government agencies, micro breweries, juice, coffee, tea, milk companies, and others concerned with the beverage and bottling industries; coverage includes Canada. Entries include: Beverage and bottling company listings contain company name, address, phone, names of key executives, number of employees, brand names, and other information, including number of franchisees, number of delivery trucks, sales volume. Suppliers and related companies and organizations listings include similar but less detailed information.

*Beverage Media*. Beverage Network. Beverage Media Group, 152 Madison Ave., Ste. 600 New York, NY 10016. Phone: (212)571-3232 • URL: http://www.beveragemedia.com • Monthly. $78 Individuals. Wholesale prices.

**Beyster Institute**. 9500 Gilman Dr. Otterson Hall S, Fourth Fl. La Jolla, CA 92093-0553. Phone: (858)246-0654; Email: beysterinfo@rady.ucsd.edu • URL: http://beysterinstitute.ucsd.edu • Helps business leaders build successful companies worldwide through training, education and outreach. Serves entrepreneurs by teaching them how to be effective managers and showing them how employee ownership can be adapted to fit their individual companies.

*BIA's Radio Yearbook*. BIA/Kelsey, 15120 Enterprise Ct. Chantilly, VA 20151. Phone: 800-331-5086 or (703)818-2425; Email: info@bia.com • URL: http://www.biakelsey.com • Annual. $240 Individuals. U.S. Radio stations, radio equipment manufacturers, and related service providers and trade associations.

*BIA's Television Yearbook*. BIA/Kelsey, 15120 Enterprise Ct. Chantilly, VA 20151. Phone: 800-331-5086 or (703)818-2425; Email: info@bia.com • URL: http://www.biakelsey.com • Annual. $250 Individuals. U.S. Television markets and their inclusive stations, television equipment manufacturers, and related service providers and trade associations.

*Bibliographic Index: A Subject List of Bibliographies in English and Foreign Languages*. H.W. Wilson Co., 950 University Ave. Bronx, NY 10452-4224. Phone: 800-367-6770 or (718)588-8400 or (718)558-8400; Fax: (718)590-1617 or (800)590-1617; Email: custserv@hwwilson.com • URL: http://www.hwwilson.com • Three times a year. Third issues cumulates all three issues. Price varies.

**Bibliographical Society of America**. PO Box 1537, Lenox Hill Sta. New York, NY 10021. Phone: (212)452-2710; Fax: (212)452-2710; Email: bsa@bibsocamer.org • URL: http://www.bibsocamer.org • Scholars, collectors, librarians, rare book dealers, and others interested in books and descriptive bibliography. Promotes bibliographical research and issues bibliographical publications. Maintains Fellowship Program which supports bibliography inquiries and research in the history of publishing and book trades.

**Bibliographical Society of the University of Virginia**. PO Box 400152 Charlottesville, VA 22904. Phone: (434)924-7013; Fax: (434)924-1431; Email: bibsoc@virginia.edu • URL: http://www.bsuva.org.

*Bibliography: A Guide to Development Research Resources*. Bentz Whaley Flessner, 7251 Ohms Ln. Minneapolis, MN 55439. Phone: (952)921-0111; Fax: (952)921-0109; Email: bwf@bwf.com • URL: http://www.bwf.com • Annual. Covers: Online services, Internet sites, listservs, and other resources of interest to business prospectors. Entries include: Company name, address, phone, fax, e-mail, Web address, name and title of contact, biographical data, description of services/projects.

*Bibliography on the Project Manager and Project Oragnization*. Project Management Institute, 14 Campus Blvd. Newtown Square, PA 19073-3299. Phone: 855-746-4849 or (610)356-4600; Fax: (610)482-9971; Email: customercare@pmi.org • URL: http://www.pmi.org • $15.

**Bicycle Product Suppliers Association**. 740 34th St. Boulder, CO 80303. Phone: (303)442-2466; Fax: (303)552-2060 • URL: http://bpsa.org • Wholesalers of bicycles, bicycle parts, and accessories; vendor members are manufacturers and suppliers. Affiliate members supply services and products to bicycle retailers. Offers educational programs; compiles statistics and safety information.

*Big Business in Metro Detroit*. Detroit Regional Chamber, 1 Woodward Ave., Ste. 1900 Detroit, MI 48232-0840. Phone: 866-627-5463 or (313)964-4000; Fax: (313)964-0183; Email: members@detroitchamber.com • URL: http://www.detroitchamber.com • Covers: More than 1,500 businesses and agencies which represent the largest employers in Metro Detroit, Michigan. Entries include: Company name, address, phone, SIC code, fax, product description, e-mail, and website.

*bII BUSINESS*. British Institute of Innkeeping, Wessex House, 80 Park St., Surrey Camberley GU15 3PT, United Kingdom. Phone: 44 1276 684449; Email: join@bii.org • URL: http://www.bii.org/home • 10/year. Contains articles on licensing reform, smoking, qualifications and training.

***Billboard's International Buyer's Guide***. Nielsen Co., 770 Broadway New York, NY 10003-9595. Phone: 800-726-0600 or (646)654-4500 or (646)654-5000; Fax: (646)654-5001 or (212)940-7381; Email: crownpublicity@randomhouse.com • URL: http://www.nielsen.com • Annual. $135 $6.00 s/h. Covers: record companies; music publishers; record and tape wholesalers; services and supplies for the music-record-tape-video industry; record and tape dealer accessories, fixtures, and merchandising products; includes United States and over 65 other countries. Entries include: Company name, address, phone, names of principal executives, trade and brand names and/or list of products and services.

***BIN Number Directory of All Visa/Mastercard Issuing Banks***. Fraud and Theft Information Bureau, 9770 S Military Trl., Ste. 380 Boynton Beach, FL 33436. Phone: (561)737-8700; Fax: (561)737-5800; Email: sales@fraudandtheft.com • URL: http://www.fraudandtheft.com • Annual. $1,175 Individuals postpaid print edition; $5,075 Individuals on CD-ROM, postpaid. Covers: About 30,000 banks worldwide issuing Visa and Mastercard credit cards. Entries include: Name of issuing bank, bank identification number, address, phone. BIN numbers, the digits on credit cards that identify a credit card holder's issuing bank are also called prefix numbers and ISO numbers. Directory is used by merchants to prevent fraud by verifying that customer is actually the cardholder.

**Binational Tourism Alliance**. 143 Genesee St. Buffalo, NY 14203. Phone: 877-884-2736 or (716)856-6525; Fax: (716)856-6754; Email: arlene.white@btapartners.com • URL: http://www.btapartners.com • Promotes tourism products and services and supports tourism development in Canada and the United States. Seeks to improve business opportunities and growth potential of members. Provides industry research and information, training and professional development.

**Binding Industries Association International**. 200 Deer Run Rd. Sewickley, PA 15143. Phone: (317)347-2665; Fax: (317)347-2666; Email: printing@printing.org • URL: http://www.printing.org/bia • Formerly Binding Industries of America.

***Binley's Directory of NHS Estates & Facilities Management***. Beachwood House Publishing Ltd., 2-3 Commercial Way, Christy Close Basildon SS15 6EF, United Kingdom. Phone: 44 1268 495600; Fax: 44 1268 495601 • URL: http://www.binleys.com • Annual. £150 Individuals online version. Covers: 5,178 named personnel, located at 575 separate NHS sites. Entries include: Name, address, phone and fax numbers, email and website address.

***Binley's Directory of NHS Management***. Beachwood House Publishing Ltd., 2-3 Commercial Way, Christy Close Basildon SS15 6EF, United Kingdom. Phone: 44 1268 495600; Fax: 44 1268 495601 • URL: http://www.binleys.com • Annual. £250 Individuals online version; £225 Individuals. Covers: Over 30,649 named personnel working at NHS organizations throughout the U.K. from chief executives and medical directors to estates managers, IT managers, and suppliers and purchasing managers. Database includes: Maps. Entries include: Organization name, address, NHS code, phone and fax numbers, email and website address.

***BioCommerce Abstracts***. PharmaBooks, 1775 Broadway, Ste. 511 New York, NY 10019-1903. Phone: (212)262-8230; Fax: (212)262-8234; Email: subsreps@pharmabooks.com • Semimonthly. $996.00 per year. Quarterly cumulation. Includes CD-Rom. Emphasis is on commercial biotechnology.

***Biofuels Business***. Sosland Publishing Co., 4800 Main St., Ste. 100 Kansas City, MO 64112. Phone: (816)756-1000; Fax: (816)756-0494; Email: nwages@sosland.com • URL: http://www.sosland.com • Magazine covering the ethanol and biodiesel industries.

***Biographical Dictionary of American Business Leaders***. Greenwood Electronic Media, c/o ABC-CLIO, 130 Cremona Dr. Santa Barbara, CA 93117. Phone: 800-368-6868 or (805)968-1911; Fax: (866)270-3856; Email: customerservice@abc-clio.com • URL: http://www.abc-clio.com • $183.95 hardcover. Covers: In four volumes, over 1,100 American business people from early merchants and farmers through contemporary leaders. Entries include: Name, date and place of birth, summary of subject's business activities and historical significance, ethnic background, religion.

***Biography and Genealogy Master Index (BGMI)***. Cengage Learning Inc., 20 Channel Center St. Boston, MA 02210. Phone: 800-487-8488 or (617)289-7700; Fax: (617)289-7844; Email: investors@cengage.com • URL: http://www.cengage.com • $1,894 Individuals. Annual. $1,284.00. Two volumes. $642.00 per volume. Previous editions available. Provides coverage of contemporary and historcial figures. Also available online.

***Biography Index***. EBSCO Publishing Inc., 10 Estes St. Ipswich, MA 01938-2106. Phone: 800-653-2726 or (978)356-6500; Fax: (978)356-6565; Email: information@ebscohost.com • URL: http://www.ebscohost.com • Coverage from 1946 to present. Over 1 million article and book citations.

***Biography Index***. H.W. Wilson Co., 950 University Ave. Bronx, NY 10452-4224. Phone: 800-367-6770 or (718)588-8400 or (718)558-8400; Fax: (718)590-1617 or (800)590-1617; Email: custserv@hwwilson.com • URL: http://www.hwwilson.com • Quarterly. $280.00 per year. Annual and biennial cumulations.

***Biography Index Online***. H.W. Wilson Co., 950 University Ave. Bronx, NY 10452-4224. Phone: 800-367-6770 or (718)588-8400 or (718)558-8400; Fax: (718)590-1617 or (800)590-1617; Email: custserv@hwwilson.com • URL: http://www.hwwilson.com • An index to biographies appearing in periodicals, newspapers, current books, and other sources. Covers 1984 to date. Inquire as to online cost and availability.

**Biological and Agricultural Engineering**. Texas A & M University, 2117 TAMU, 201 Scoates Hall College Station, TX 77843-2117. Phone: (979)845-3931; Email: info@baen.tamu.edu • URL: http://baen.tamu.edu.

***Biological and Agricultural Index***. H.W. Wilson Co., 950 University Ave. Bronx, NY 10452-4224. Phone: 800-367-6770 or (718)588-8400 or (718)558-8400; Fax: (718)590-1617 or (800)590-1617; Email: custserv@hwwilson.com • URL: http://www.hwwilson.com • 11 times a year. Annual and quarterly cumulations. Price varies.

***Biological & Agricultural Index Plus***. EBSCO Publishing Inc., 10 Estes St. Ipswich, MA 01938-2106. Phone: 800-653-2726 or (978)356-6500; Fax: (978)356-6565; Email: information@ebscohost.com • URL: http://www.ebscohost.com • Full text of literature in biology and agriculture. Also includes podcasts, indexing and abstracts.

***Biological Sciences Database***. Cambridge Scientific Abstracts L.P., 7200 Wisconsin Ave., Ste. 601 Bethesda, MD 20814. Phone: 800-843-7751 or (301)961-6700 or (301)961-6785; Fax: (301)961-6720 or (301)961-6708; Email: sales@proquest.com • URL: http://www.proquest.co.uk • Includes online versions of *Biotechnology Research Abstracts*, *Entomology Abstracts*, *Genetics Abstracts*, and about 20 other abstract collections. Time period is 1978 to date, with monthly updates. Inquire as to online cost and availability.

***Biomass Energy System Businesses in the World***. Momentum Technologies L.L.C., PO Box 460813 Glendale, CO 80246. Phone: (303)229-4841; Fax: (408)705-2031 • URL: http://www.mtt.com • Contains directory listings for more than 500 biomass energy system businesses in operation throughout the world. Includes business name, address, phone number, fax number, e-mail address, and web site address. Provides brief descriptions of product lines, services offered, and business type. Includes information on manufacturers, component makers, wholesalers, retailers, system designers, system installers, architectural services, trade associations, and more. Searchable by location, business type, business name, and keyword.

***Biomass Industry Profile Directory***. DIANE Publishing Co., PO Box 617 Darby, PA 19023-0617. Phone: 800-782-3833 or (610)461-6200; Fax: (610)461-6130; Email: dianepublishing@gmail.com • URL: http://www.dianepublishing.net • $40 Individuals Paperback. Publication includes: Lists of all businesses and agencies involved in biomass energy in the Western United States.

**Biomedical Engineering Society**. 8201 Corporate Dr., Ste. 1125 Landover, MD 20785-2224. Phone: 877-871-2637 or (301)459-1999; Fax: (301)459-2444 • URL: http://www.bmes.org • Biomedical, chemical, electrical, civil, agricultural and mechanical engineers, physicians, managers, and university professors representing all fields of biomedical engineering; students and corporations. Encourages the development, dissemination, integration, and utilization of knowledge in biomedical engineering.

***Biometric Information Directory***. Grey House Publishing, 4919 Rte. 22 Amenia, NY 12501. Phone: 800-562-2139 or (518)789-8700; Fax: (518)789-0556; Email: books@greyhouse.com • URL: http://www.greyhouse.com • $225 Individuals softcover. Covers: 700+ manufacturers and service providers in the biometrics industry, including finger, voice, face, hand, signature, iris, vein and palm identification systems. Includes information resources such as organizations, trade & educational associations, publications, conferences, trade shows and expositions worldwide. Entries include: Name, address, phone, fax, email, website, key executives, company size and a detailed, indexed description of their product line.

***Biotech Business Week***. NewsRX, 2727 Paces Ferry Rd. SE, Ste. 2-440 Atlanta, GA 30339. Phone: 800-726-4550 or (770)507-7777 or (770)435-8286; Fax: (770)435-6800; Email: techsupport@newsrx.com • URL: http://www.newsrx.com • Weekly. $2,295 Other countries; $2,295 U.S. and Canada print; $2,525 U.S. and Canada print and online; $2,495 Other countries print; $2,755 Other countries print and online. Publication that provides news and information from pharmaceutical and biotechnology companies, with a focus on business trends and analysis.

***Biotechnology Abstracts on CD-ROM***. Thomson Derwent, Inc., 1725 Duke St., Suite 250 Alexandria, VA 22314. Phone: 800-337-9368 or (703)706-4220; Fax: (703)519-5838; Email: info@derwent.com • URL: http://www.derwent.com • Quarterly. Price on application. Provides CD-ROM indexing and abstracting of the world's biotechnology journal literature since 1982, including genetic engineering topics.

***Biotechnology and the Law***. Iver P. Cooper. Thomson West, 610 Opperman Dr. Eagan, MN 55123. Phone: 800-328-9352 or (651)687-7000 • Annual. $424.50. Three looseleaf volumes.

**Biotechnology Industry Organization**. 1201 Maryland Ave. SW, Ste. 900 Washington, DC 20024. Phone: (202)962-9200; Fax: (202)488-6301; Email: info@bio.org • URL: http://www.bio.org • Represents biotechnology companies, academic institutions, state biotechnology centers and related organizations in all 50 U.S. states and 33 other nations. Members are involved in the research and development of healthcare, agricultural, industrial and environmental biotechnology products.

***Birmingham and Solihull Business Guide and Directory***. Kemps Publishing Ltd., 11 The Swan Courtyard, Charles Edward Rd. Yardley B26 1BU, United Kingdom. Phone: 44 121 7654144 or (441)21 7654144; Fax: 44 121 7063491 or (441)21 7063491; Email: enquiries@kempspublishing.co.uk • URL: http://www.kempspublishing.co.uk • Annual. Covers: Chamber of Commerce listings in Birmingham and Solihull, Great Britain. Entries include: Name, address, phone, fax.

***Birmingham Area Industrial Directory***. Birmingham Regional Chamber of Commerce, 505 20th St. N, Ste. 200 Birmingham, AL 35203. Phone: (205)324-2100; Fax: (205)324-2560 • URL: http://birminghambusinessalliance.com • Biennial. $55 Members; $80 Public Price. Covers: about 2,800 manufacturing establishments in 21 counties of Alabama including maps. Features pinpointer county maps. Entries include: Company name, address, phone, name of principal executive, number of employees, product/service, SIC numbers.

***Birmingham Chamber of Commerce—Prospect List***. Birmingham Regional Chamber of Commerce, 505 20th St. N, Ste. 200 Birmingham, AL 35203. Phone: (205)324-2100; Fax: (205)324-2560 • URL: http://birminghambusinessalliance.com • Covers: 4,000 prospect companies for the Birmingham Chamber of Commerce. Entries include: Name, address, phone, fax.

**Biscuit and Cracker Manufacturers Association**. 6325 Woodside Ct., Ste. 125 Columbia, MD 21046. Phone: (443)545-1645; Fax: (410)290-8585 • URL: http://www.thebcma.org • Members are bakers of crackers and cookies. Formerly Biscuit Bakers Institute.

***BISNES Plus***. INFOTRADE N.V., Stationsstraat 30 bus 2 B-1702 Groot-Bijgaarden, Belgium. Phone: 32 2 4818283; Fax: 32 2 4818200; Email: infotrade@ift.be • Daily. Database covers: Financial and descriptive information on more than one million Belgian companies and private businesses. Entries include: Name, address, name and title of contact, commercial registration numbers, data and form of incorporation, bank accounts, association memberships, principal language, number of employees, names of management personnel, activities and products, trademarks, trading partners, financial statements for the most recent three years.

***Biz 2000: L&H Comprehensive Business Dictionary***. Gyldendals Red Dictionaries, Klareboderne 3 DK-1001 Copenhagen, Denmark. Phone: 45 3375 5600; Email: ordbog@gyldendal.dk • URL: http://ordbog.gyldendal.dk • Contains a detailed dictionary of business terms in Danish, English, and German. Available in four versions: Danish to English, English to Danish, Danish to German, and German to Danish.

***BizEd: The Leading Voice of Business Education***. Association to Advance Collegiate Schools of Business, 77 S Harbour Island Blvd., Ste. 750 Tampa, FL 33602. Phone: (813)769-6500; Fax: (813)769-6559; Email: events@aacsb.edu • URL: http://www.aacsb.edu • Bimonthly. $35 Individuals; $45 Canada; $55 Other countries. Magazine covering trends in business education.

***BizEkon News—Soviet Business Directory***. RIA Novosti Russian News & Information Agency, Zubovsky Blvd. 4 119021 Moscow, Russia. Phone: 7 495 645 6470 or 95 9325610; Fax: 7 495 637 4545 or 95 9326300; Email: sales@rian.ru • URL: http://www.en.rian.ru • Quarterly. Covers: over 2,500 companies in the Commonwealth of Independent States that have contracts abroad. Database includes: Company name, address, phone, fax, telex, names and titles of key personnel, banker, number of employees, production data, legal status, production program, list of products.

***Black Business Quarterly***. Cape Media, 28 Main Rd., Rondebosch Cape Town 7700, South Africa. Phone: 27 21 6817000; Fax: 27 21 6854445; Email: info@capemedia.co.za • URL: http://www.capemedia.co.za • Quarterly. Magazine featuring top black business leadership.

**Black Caucus of the American Library Association**. PO Box 1738 Hampton, VA 23669. Email: webmaster@bcala.org • URL: http://www.bcala.org • Black librarians; blacks interested in library services. Promotes librarianship; encourages active participation of blacks in library associations and boards and all levels of the profession. Monitors activities of the American Library Association with regard to its policies and programs and how they affect black librarians and library users. Reviews, analyzes, evaluates, and recommends to the ALA actions that influence the recruitment, development, advancement, and general working conditions of black librarians. Facilitates library services that meet the informational needs of black people including increased availability of materials related to social and economic concerns.

***Black Enterprise—Black Engineering Firms Issue***. Earl Graves Publishing Co., 130 5th Ave., 10th Fl. New York, NY 10011-4399. Phone: (212)242-8000; Email: benyc_ads@blackenterprise.com • URL: http://www.blackenterprise.com

• Irregular. $3.50. Covers: U.S. companies owned or controlled by African Americans. Entries include: Name, address, phone.

***Blackwell Encyclopedia of Management***. John Wiley & Sons Inc. Scientific, Technical, Medical, and Scholarly Div. (Wiley-Blackwell), 111 River St. Hoboken, NJ 07030-5774. Phone: (201)748-6000; Fax: (201)748-6088; Email: info@wiley.com • URL: http://www.wiley.com • 2010. eBook. 2nd edition. Published by John Wiley & Sons. Divided into 12 individual subject volumes and an index. Volumes provide clear, concise, expert definitions and explanations of the key concepts in each area.

***Blair Business Mirror***. Blair County Chamber of Commerce, 3900 Industrial Park Dr., Ste. 12 Altoona, PA 16602. Phone: (814)943-8151; Fax: (814)943-5239; Email: chamber@blairchamber.com • URL: http://www.blairchamber.com • Monthly. Features chamber news, stories of chamber members and notices of upcoming programs and events.

***Blinds-Venetian & Vertical- Retail Directory***. InfoGroup Inc., 5711 S 86th Cir. Omaha, NE 68127-4146. Phone: (402)593-4500 • URL: http://www.infogroup.com • Annual. Number of listings: 8,244. Entries include: Name, address, phone, size of advertisement, name of owner or manager, number of employees, year first in "Yellow Pages." Compiled from telephone company "Yellow Pages," nationwide.

***Bloomberg BusinessWeek***. Bloomberg L.P., 731 Lexington Ave. New York, NY 10022. Phone: (212)318-2000; Fax: (917)369-5000; Email: munis@bloomberg.com • URL: http://www.bloomberg.com • Contains the complete text (including images) of *Bloomberg BusinessWeek*, a business and industry news magazine. Covers finance, labor and production, corporate news and investment policies, and the effects of legislative and regulatory developments on commerce. Includes analyses of the economic outlook. Provides daily business briefings, market news, investing coverage, and other business information. Provides information on global business, technology, small business, investing, and electronic commerce. Offers reviews of hundreds of business books, including sample chapters. Provides data on the best business schools and provides coverage of work and career issues. Allows users to search back issues of the magazine.

***Blowing Rock Chamber of Commerce—Chamber Businesses***. Blowing Rock Chamber of Commerce, 132 Park Ave. Blowing Rock, NC 28605. Phone: 800-295-7851 or (828)295-7851 or (828)264-6126; Fax: (828)295-7651; Email: info@blowingrock.com • URL: http://www.blowingrock.com/chamber.php • Annual. Listing of businesses in Blowing Rock, North Carolina.

***BLR Job Descriptions Encyclopedia***. Business & Legal Resources, Inc., 141 Mill Rock Rd., E Old Saybrook, CT 06475. Phone: 800-454-0404 or (860)510-0100 or (800)727-5257; Fax: (860)510-7220 or (860)510-0100; Email: service@blr.com • URL: http://www.blr.com • $299 Individuals. $299.00. Two volumes. More than 700 prewritten job descriptions.

***Blue Book of Stock Reports***. MPL Communications Inc., 133 Richmond St. W, Ste. 700 Toronto, ON, Canada M5H 3M8. Phone: 800-804-8846 or (416)869-1177 or (416)869-2777; Fax: (416)869-0456 or (416)869-0616; Email: investors@mplcomm.com • URL: http://www.adviceforinvestors.com • Biweekly. $260.00 per year. Canadian Business Service reports on over 250 Canadian companies.

***Blue Book of the East—Asia, Africa, Middle East and Far East Directory***. Indian Export Trade Journal, 212 Arun Chambers, Tardeo Rd. Mumbai 400 034, India. • Biennial. $750; $125. Covers: Trade and industry in Asia, Africa, the Middle East and Far East.

**Blue Cross and Blue Shield Association**. 225 N Michigan Ave. Chicago, IL 60601. • URL: http://www.bcbs.com • Local Blue Cross and Blue Shield Plans in the U.S., and other licensees in Europe, Japan, and Jamaica. Aims to promote the betterment of public health and security; to secure the widest public acceptance of voluntary non-profit, prepayment of health services; to provide services to Blue Cross and Blue Shield Plans and licensees. Contracts with federal government as administrative agency for federal health programs; sponsors and conducts programs on health care and prepayment issues.

***Blue List of Current Municipal and Corporate Offerings***. Standard & Poor's Financial Services L.L.C., 55 Water St. New York, NY 10041. Phone: 877-772-5436 or (212)438-2000; Fax: (212)438-1000; Email: questions@standardandpoors.com • URL: http://www.standardandpoors.com • Daily. $940.00 per year. Compendium of municipal and corporate bond offers.

***Blue Ridge Business Journal***. Blue Ridge Business, PO Box 6982 Greenville, SC 29606-6982. • Monthly. $22 Individuals; $38 Two years; $1.50 Single issue. Tabloid covering business news about Henderson, Transylvania, and Buncombe counties.

***Blue Sky Law Reports***. Joseph C. Long. Wolters Kluwer Law & Business CCH, 2700 Lake Cook Rd. Riverwoods, IL 60015. Phone: 888-224-7377 or (847)267-7000; Email: cust_serv@cch.com • URL: http://www.cchgroup.com • Looseleaf service. $1,130.00 per year. Periodic supplementation. Semimonthly updates.

***Blue Sky Regulation***. Matthew Bender and Company Inc., 1275 Broadway Albany, NY 12204-2638. Phone: 800-424-4200 or (518)487-3000; Fax: (518)487-3573 or (800)424-4200; Email: customer.support@lexisnexis.com • URL: http://www.matthewbender.com • $2,448 per book. Four looseleaf volumes. Periodic supplementation. Covers state securities laws and regulations.

***BNA Fair Employment Practices***. Bloomberg BNA, 3 Bethesda Metro Center, Ste. 250 Bethesda, MD 20814-5377. Phone: 800-372-1033 or (703)341-3000; Fax: (800)253-0332; Email: customercare@bna.com • URL: http://www.bna.com • Biweekly. $938.00 per year. Looseleaf service.

***BNA Pension and Benefits Reporter***. Bloomberg BNA, 3 Bethesda Metro Center, Ste. 250 Bethesda, MD 20814-5377. Phone: 800-372-1033 or (703)341-3000; Fax: (800)253-0332; Email: customercare@bna.com • URL: http://www.bna.com • Weekly. $996.00 per year. Three looseleaf volumes. Legal developments affecting pensions. Formerly *BNA Pension Reporter*.

***BNA Policy and Practice Series***. Bloomberg BNA, 3 Bethesda Metro Center, Ste. 250 Bethesda, MD 20814-5377. Phone: 800-372-1033 or (703)341-3000; Fax: (800)253-0332; Email: customercare@bna.com • URL: http://www.bna.com • Weekly. $1,965.00 per year. Three looseleaf volumes. Includes personnel management, labor relations, fair employment practice, compensation, and wage-hour laws.

***BNA Policy and Practice Series: Wages and Hours***. Bloomberg BNA, 3 Bethesda Metro Center, Ste. 250 Bethesda, MD 20814-5377. Phone: 800-372-1033 or (703)341-3000; Fax: (800)253-0332; Email: customercare@bna.com • URL: http://www.bna.com • Weekly. $938.00 per year. Looseleaf service.

***BNA's Banking Report: Legal and Regulatory Developments in the Financial Services Industry***. Bloomberg BNA, 3 Bethesda Metro Center, Ste. 250 Bethesda, MD 20814-5377. Phone: 800-372-1033 or (703)341-3000; Fax: (800)253-0332; Email: customercare@bna.com • URL: http://www.bna.com • Weekly. $1,221.00 per year. Two looseleaf volumes. Emphasis on federal regulations.

***BNA's Workers' Compensation Report***. Bloomberg BNA, 3 Bethesda Metro Center, Ste. 250 Bethesda, MD 20814-5377. Phone: 800-372-1033 or (703)341-3000; Fax: (800)253-0332; Email: customercare@bna.com • URL: http://www.bna.com • Biweekly. $604.00 per year. Looseleaf business and legal service.

***Board of Immigration Appeals Interim Decisions***. U.S. Immigration and Naturalization Service. U. S. Government Printing Office, 732 N Capitol St. NW Washington, DC 20401. Phone: 866-512-1800 or (202)512-1800 or (866)512-1800; Fax: (202)512-2104 or (202)512-2250; Email: contactcenter@gpo.gov • URL: http://www.gpo.gov • Irregular.

**Board of Research**. Babson College, 204 Babson Babson Park, MA 02457-0310. Phone: (781)235-1200; Fax: (718)239-6416; Email: chern@babson.edu • URL: http://www.babson.edu/bor • Research areas include management, entrepreneurial characteristics, and multi-product inventory analysis.

***Boat and Motor Dealer: Business Solutions for the Boating Trade***. Preston Publications Inc., 6600 W Touhy Ave. Niles, IL 60714. Phone: 800-229-7569 or (847)647-2900 or (847)647-0611; Fax: (847)647-1155; Email: tpreston@prestonpub.com • URL: http://www.prestonpub.com • $75 Individuals; $125 Two years; $85 Other countries; $145 Other countries 2 years; $8.95 Single issue. Magazine for boat, motor, and accessory dealers.

***Boat Appraisers Directory***. InfoGroup Inc., 5711 S 86th Cir. Omaha, NE 68127-4146. Phone: (402)593-4500 • URL: http://www.infogroup.com • Annual. Number of listings: 17,331. Entries include: Name, address, phone, size of advertisement, name of owner or manager, number of employees, year first in "Yellow Pages." Compiled from telephone company "Yellow Pages," nationwide.

**Boat Owners Association of the United States**. 880 S Pickett St. Alexandria, VA 22304-4606. Phone: 800-395-2628; Email: mail@boatus.com • URL: http://www.boatus.com • Absorbed American Yachtmen's Association.

***Boating Business***. Formula Publications, 447 Speers Rd., Ste. 4 Oakville, ON, Canada L6K 3S7. Phone: (905)842-6591; Fax: (905)842-4432 • URL: http://www.metroland.com/Companies/100160/Formula_Media_Group • Bimonthly. Magazine for manufacturers, distributors, dealers, boatyards, and marinas serving the recreational marine industry.

**Bocconi University - Innocenzo Gasparini Institute for Economic Research**. Via Röntgen 1, 5th Fl. 20136 Milan, Italy. Phone: 39 2 58363300; Fax: 39 2 58363302; Email: igier@unibocconi.it • URL: http://www.igier.unibocconi.it • Economics, including open economy macroeconomics, financial markets, and politics and economic policy.

***Body Fashions/Intimate Apparel Buyer's Guide: BFIA Buyers Guide***. Advanstar Communications, 641 Lexington Ave., 8th Fl. New York, NY 10022. Phone: 800-346-0085 or (212)951-6600; Fax: (212)951-6793; Email: info@advanstar.com • URL: http://www.advanstar.com • Annual. Publication includes: List of suppliers and manufacturers within the intimate apparel and hosiery industry. Entries include: Company name, address, phone.

***Bodyshots - Business***. Digital Wisdom Inc., 300 Jeanette Dr. Tappahannock, VA 22560-3855. Phone: 800-800-8560 or (804)443-9000; Fax: (413)639-3999 or (804)443-3632; Email: contact@digiwis.com • URL: http://www.digiwis.com • Provides designers and desktop publishers with a comprehensive photographic stock collection of high-resolution images of people in a variety of everyday situations and activities.

**Bogazici University - Center for Economics and Econometrics**. Bebek TR-34342 Istanbul, Turkey. Phone: 90 212 3956505; Fax: 90 212 2872453; Email: ezran@boun.edu.tr • URL: http://www.cee.boun.edu.tr • Economic issues, electrical energy.

***Bolivia—American Chamber of Commerce—Membership Directory***. U.S. Chamber of Commerce, 1615 H St. NW Washington, DC 20062-2000. Phone: 800-638-6582 or (202)463-5500 or (202)659-6000; Fax: (202)463-3129; Email: foundation@uschamber.com • URL: http://www.uschambersmallbusinessnation.com • Annual. Covers: American and Bolivian companies and individuals interested in the development of trade within and between the two countries. Entries include: For firms—Company name, address, phone, fax, telex, cable address, names and titles of key personnel, line of business, subsidiary and branch names and locations, locations of plants or branch offices, product/service information. For individuals—Name, title, affiliation, address. Plus details on Bolivia's investment climate, economic indicators, new land reform laws, and trade agreement obligations.

***Bolivia Industrial and Business Directory***. International Business Publications, USA, PO Box 15343 Washington, DC 20003. Phone: (202)546-2103; Fax: (202)546-3275; Email: ibpusa@comcast.net • URL: http://ibpus.com • Annual. $99.95 Individuals hardcover; $99.95 Individuals e-book; $99.95 Individuals CD-ROM. Covers: Strategic industrial, investment and business contacts for conducting export-import and investment activity in the country.

***Bond's Franchise Guide***. Todd Publications, PO Box 500 Millwood, NY 10546. Phone: 866-896-0916 or (914)373-4750; Fax: (914)373-4750; Email: toddpub@aol.com • URL: http://www.toddpublications.com • Covers: 2,000 American and 500 Canadian franchisers divided into 54 business categories. Entries include: Company name, address, phone, fax, names and titles of key personnel for 1,500 franchise operations; for all entries: Company history, size, geographic distribution, financial requirements, staff, start-up assistance and training provided, ongoing royalty fees and franchiser services, and more.

***Bondtalk.com: Live Talk & Analysis on the Bond Market & the Economy***. Miller Tabak & Co., LLC, Phone: (212)370-0040; Email: acrescenzi@bondtalk.com • URL: http://www.bondtalk.com • Web site provides extensive, free data on the fixed income securities market, including individual bond prices, yields, interest rates, Federal Reserve information, charts, bond market news, and economic analysis. Also offered on a fee basis is "Bondtalkpro.com: The New and Enhanced Service for Market Professionals.".

***Book Auction Records***. RoweCom UK Ltd., Cannon House, Park Farm Rd. Folkestone CT19 5EE, United Kingdom. Phone: 44 1303 850101; Fax: (130)3 850440 • URL: http://www.dawson.co.uk • Annual. $150.00.

***Book Business***. North American Publishing Co., 1500 Spring Garden St., Ste. 1200 Philadelphia, PA 19130-4069. Phone: (215)238-5300; Email: customerservice@napco.com • URL: http://www.napco.com • Magazine publishing information about book production and manufacturing.

**Book Industry Study Group**. 145 W 45th St., Ste. 601 New York, NY 10036. Phone: (646)336-7141; Fax: (646)336-6214; Email: info@bisg.org • URL: http://www.bisg.org • Represents publishers, manufacturers, suppliers, wholesalers, retailers, librarians, and other engaged in the business of print and electronic media.

**Book Manufacturers' Institute**. Two Armand Beach Dr., Ste. 1B Palm Coast, FL 32137-2612. Phone: (386)986-4552; Fax: (386)986-4553; Email: info@bmibook.com • URL: http://www.bmibook.com • Represents the trade association for manufacturers of books.

***The Book of Lists***. Email: cox@ocbj.com • URL: http://www.ocbj.com • Annual. $125 Individuals Zip file download. Covers: Leading employers and private companies located in Orange County, California. Entries include: Company name, address, phone, names and titles of key personnel; product/service, financial data, number of employees.

***Book Review Digest: An Index to Reviews of Current Books***. H.W. Wilson Co., 950 University Ave. Bronx, NY 10452-4224. Phone: 800-367-6770 or (718)588-8400 or (718)558-8400; Fax: (718)590-1617 or (800)590-1617; Email: custserv@hwwilson.com • URL: http://www.hwwilson.com • 10 times a year. Quarterly and annual cumulation. Price varies.

***Book Review Index (BRI)***. Cengage Learning Inc., 20 Channel Center St. Boston, MA 02210. Phone: 800-487-8488 or (617)289-7700; Fax: (617)289-7844; Email: investors@cengage.com • URL: http://www.cengage.com • $591 paperback. Three-issue subscription. An index to reviews appearing in hundreds of periodicals. Back volumes available.

***Booklist***. Library and Information Technology Association, 50 E Huron St. Chicago, IL 60611-2795. Phone: 800-545-2433; Fax: (312)280-3257; Email: lita@ala.org • URL: http://www.ala.org/lita • Biweekly. $147.50 U.S. and Canada /year; $170 Other countries. Reviews library materials for school and public libraries. Incorporates *Reference Books Bulletin*.

***Bookman's Price Index***. Cengage Learning Inc., 20 Channel Center St. Boston, MA 02210. Phone: 800-487-8488 or (617)289-7700; Fax: (617)289-7844; Email: investors@cengage.com • URL: http://www.cengage.com • An index to rare and antiquarian books offered for sale in the catalogs of 100-200 book dealers in the U.S., Canada, and the British Isles. Approx. 15,000 tites listed per volume. 2013. Volumes 92-97. $686.00.

***Books in Print Online***. Bowker Electronic Publishing, 630 Central Ave. New Providence, NJ 07974. Phone: 888-269-5372 or (908)464-6800; Fax: (908)665-3528 • The online version of *Books in Print, Forthcoming Books, Paperbound Books in Print* and other Bowker bibliographic publications: lists the books of over 50,000 U.S. publishers. Includes books recently declared out-of-print. Updated monthly. Inquire as to online cost and availability.

***Books in Print***. R.R. Bowker L.L.C., 630 Central Ave New Providence, NJ 07974. Phone: 888-269-5372 or (908)286-1090; Email: info@bowker.com • URL: http://www.bowker.com • Combines the trusted and authoritative source of bibliographic information with powerful search, discovery and collection development tools designed specifically to streamline the book discovery and acquisition process.

***Books—Publishing & Printing Directory***. InfoGroup Inc., 5711 S 86th Cir. Omaha, NE 68127-4146. Phone: (402)593-4500 • URL: http://www.infogroup.com • Annual. Number of listings: 1,224. Entries include: Name, address, phone, size of advertisement, name of owner or manager, number of employees, year first in "Yellow Pages." Compiled from telephone company "Yellow Pages," nationwide.

***BookWeb***. American Booksellers Association, 333 Westchester Ave., Ste. S202 White Plains, NY 10604. Phone: 800-637-0037 or (914)417-4013; Fax: (914)406-7500; Email: info@bookweb.org • URL: http://www.bookweb.org • Web site provides descriptions of more than 4,500 independent bookstores, searchable by name, specialty, or zip code. Fees: Free.

***Border Business Review***. University of Texas at El Paso Institute for Policy and Economic Development, Kelly Hall, Rm. 414, 500 W University Ave. El Paso, TX 79968-0703. Phone: (915)747-7746; Fax: (915)747-7948; Email: iped@utep.edu • URL: http://iped.utep.edu • Quarterly.

***B.O.S.S.: A Supplier Directory for Doing Business in Canada***. International Press Publications Inc., 20-90 Nolan Ct. Markham, ON, Canada L3R 4L9. Phone: 800-679-2514; Fax: (905)946-9590; Email: sales@ippbooks.com • URL: http://www.ippbooks.com • Annual. $200. Canadian suppliers and products.

***Boston Business Journal***. American City Business Journals, 200 High St. Boston, MA 02110. Phone: (617)330-1000; Fax: (617)330-1016 • URL: http://www.amcity.com/boston • Weekly. $102 Individuals print and online; $179 Two years 108 issues; $234 Individuals 160 issues. Business newspaper specializing in local and regional business for upper management and CEO's of large and mid-sized businesses.

***Boston Business Journal—Book of Lists***. Boston Business Journal, 160 Federal St., 12th Fl. Boston, MA 02110-1700. Phone: (617)330-1000 • URL: http://www.bizjournals.com • Annual. $75 Institutions print; $199.95 Individuals electronic version. Covers 'Top 25' financial institutions, computer companies, law firms, insurance companies, advertising firms, architectural firms, and other companies and organizations in the Boston, Massachusetts area.

**Boston College - Center for Corporate Citizenship**. Carroll School of Management, 55 Lee Rd. Chestnut Hill, MA 02467-3942. Phone: (617)552-4545; Fax: (617)552-8499; Email: kv.smith@bc.edu • URL: http://www.bcccc.net • Areas of study include corporate images within local communities, corporate community relations, social vision, and philanthropy. Formerly Center for Corporate Community Relations.

**Boston College - Center on Wealth and Philanthropy**. 142 Beacon St. Chestnut Hill, MA 02467. Phone: (617)552-4070; Fax: (617)552-3903; Email: paul.schervish@bc.edu • URL: http://www.bc.edu/research/cwp • Spirituality, wealth, philanthropy and other aspects of cultural life in an age of affluence. Projects explore the association among philanthropy, income, and wealth; the organizational and moral determinants of giving and volunteering; and the implications for fundraising and philanthropy.

**Boston College - Institute for Scientific Research**. St. Clement's Hall, 400A, 140 Commonwealth Ave. Chestnut Hill, MA 02467. Phone: (617)552-8767; Fax: (617)552-4328; Email: patricia.doherty@bc.edu • URL: http://www.bc.edu/research/isr • Development and use of analysis tools to explain various physical phenomena in the areas of earth and space sciences, the environment, finance and economics.

***Boston JobBank: The Job Hunter's Guide to the Bay State***. Adams Media Corp., 57 Littlefield St. Avon, MA 02322. Phone: 800-872-5627 or (508)427-7100; Fax: (508)427-6790 or (800)872-5628; Email: deskcopies@adamsmedia.com • URL: http://www.adamsmedia.com • Annual. $17.95 Individuals Paperback. Covers: Over 7,000 employers in Massachusetts. Database includes: Information on the basics of job winning and writing resumes and cover letters; electronic job search information; 330 industry associations; 90 online career resources; 420 employment services. Entries include: Firm or organization name, address, local phone, toll-free phone, fax, e-mail, URL, recorded jobline, hours, names of management, name and title of contact, titles of common positions, entry-level positions, fringe benefits offered, stock exchange listing, description of organization, subsidiaries, location of headquarters, educational background desired, projected number of hires, training programs, internships, parent company, number of employees, revenues, other U.S. Locations, and international locations.

**Boston University - Center for Finance, Law and Policy**. 53 Bay State Rd., 1st Fl. Boston, MA 02215. Phone: 888-285-7003 or (617)353-3023; Fax: (617)353-2444; Email: ckhurley@bu.edu • URL: http://www.bu.edu/bucflp • Research fields include banking law, regulation of depository institutions, and deposit insurance.

**Boston University - Multimedia Communications Laboratory**. Department of Electrical & Computer Engineering, 8 Saint Mary's St. Boston, MA 02215. Phone: (617)353-9877; Fax: (617)353-6440; Email: tdcl@bu.edu • URL: http://hulk.bu.edu • Research areas include interactive multimedia applications.

***The Botanical Review: Interpreting Botanical Progress***. Society for Economic Botany. New York Botanical Garden Press, 2900 Southern Blvd. Bronx, NY 10458. Phone: (718)817-8700 or (718)817-8721; Fax: (718)562-6780 or (718)817-8842; Email: compost@nybg.org • URL: http://www.nybg.org • Quarterly. Individuals, $112.00 per year; institutions, $205.00 per year. Reviews articles in all fields of botany.

**Botanical Society of America**. 4475 Castleman Ave. Saint Louis, MO 63166. Phone: (314)577-9566; Fax: (314)577-9515; Email: bsa-manager@botany.org • URL: http://www.botany.org • Professional society of botanists and others interested in plant science. Conducts special research programs.

***Botswick Company Business Records***. Cengage Learning Inc., 20 Channel Center St. Boston, MA 02210. Phone: 800-487-8488 or (617)289-7700; Fax: (617)289-7844; Email: investors@cengage.com • URL: http://www.cengage.com.

***Bottin Entreprises***. Bottin S.A., 5 rue Alfred de Vingy F-75008 Paris, France. Phone: 1 47 48 7575; Fax: 1 4748 7550; Email: bettinwebmaster@bottin.fr • Annual. Database covers: about 100,000 French companies. Database includes: Company name, address, phone, telex, type of business, capital, legal incorporation, formal structure, branches or other locations, if any; some include names of directors, financial turnover (period specified), number of employees.

***Bottin Touristique du Quebec***. Quebec Dans Le Monde, 404-1001, Church Rd. Sainte-Foy, QC, Canada G1V 4N5. Phone: (418)659-5540; Fax: (418)659-4143; Email: info@quebecmonde.com • URL: http://www.quebecmonde.com • Annual. $51.95 Individuals. Covers: Approximately 800 business, cultural and recreational travel agencies and agents in Quebec. Entries include: Company name, address, phone, fax, agent name, address, phone, fax, activities.

***The Bottom Line: Managing Library Finances***. Emerald Group Publishing Inc., Brickyard Office Park, 84 Sherman St. Cambridge, MA 02140. Phone: (617)945-9130; Fax: (617)945-9136; Email: america@emeraldinsight.com • URL: http://www.emeraldinsight.com • Quarterly. $1,039.00 per year. Provides articles on the financial management of libraries: budgeting, funding, cost analysis, etc.

***Bottomline***. Hospitality Financial and Technology Professionals, 11709 Boulder Ln., Ste. 110 Austin, TX 78726. Phone: 800-646-4387 or (512)249-5333; Fax: (512)249-1533; Email: membership@hftp.org • URL: http://www.hftp.org • Bimonthly. Free to members, educational institutions and libraries; non-members, $50.00 per year. Contains articles on accounting, finance, information technology, and management for hotels, resorts, casinos, clubs, and other hospitality businesses.

***Boulder County Business Report (BCBR)***. Boulder County Business Report, 3180 Sterling Cir., Ste. 201 Boulder, CO 80301-2338. Phone: (303)440-4950 • URL: http://www.bcbr.com • Biweekly. $44.97 Individuals; $79.97 Two years; $114.97 Individuals 3 years. Local business newspaper.

***Bowdens International Directory***. Cision Canada Inc., 1100-150 Ferrand Dr. Toronto, ON, Canada M3C 3E5. Phone: 800-269-3367 or (416)750-2220; Fax: (416)750-2223; Email: info.ca@cision.com • URL: http://www.ca.cision.com • $275 Individuals per year (book). Covers daily and community newspapers, periodicals, radio and television broadcasting stations, and cable television systems; network television personnel, wire service offices, and other media in Canada.

***Bowker's Complete Video Directory on Disc***. Bowker Electronic Publishing, 630 Central Ave. New Providence, NJ 07974. Phone: 888-269-5372 or (908)464-6800; Fax: (908)665-3528 • Quarterly. $520.00 per year. An extensive CD-ROM directory of video tapes and laserdisks. Includes film reviews from *Variety*.

**Bowling Green State University - Department of Philosophy - Social Philosophy and Policy Center**. 225 Troup St. Bowling Green, OH 43403. Phone: (419)372-2536; Fax: (419)372-8738; Email: fmiller@bgsu.edu • URL: http://www.bgsu.edu/offices/sppc/ • Political philosophy and public policy, drawing upon disciplines of philosophy, history, political science, law, and economics.

***Boxoffice Magazine: The Business Magazine of The Global Motion Picture Industry***. Media Enterprises L.P., 155 S El Molino Ave, Ste. 100 Pasadena, CA 91101. Phone: (626)396-0250; Fax: (626)396-0248 • Monthly. $59.95 Individuals; $74.95 Canada; $135 Other countries. Trade magazine for the motion picture exhibition industry; including news of film distribution and exhibition, film reviews, and technical articles.

***Boxoffice: The Business Magazine of the Global Motion Picture Industry***. RLD Communication, 6640 Sunset Blvd., Ste. 100 Hollywood, CA 90028. Phone: (213)465-1186 • Monthly. $40.00 per year. Provides national and local news about theater management and operations, industry trends about film production and distribution.

**BPA Worldwide**. 100 Beard Sawmill Rd., 6th Fl. Shelton, CT 06484. Phone: (203)447-2800; Fax: (203)447-2900; Email: ghansen@bpaww.com • URL: http://www.bpaww.com • Verifies business and consumer periodical circulation statements. Includes a Circulation Managers Committee. Formerly Business Publications Audit of Circulation.

***BPIA Directory and Buyer's Guide***. Independent Office Products and Furniture Dealers Association, 3601 E Joppa Rd. Baltimore, MD 21234. Phone: (410)930-8100; Fax: (410)931-8111; Email: cbates@nopanet.org • URL: http://www.iopfda.org • Annual. $100 payment must accompany order. Covers: Approximately 3,000 manufacturers, wholesalers, retailers, and sales and marketing representatives in the office products industry. Entries include: Company name, address, phone, principal executives, number of employees, branch stores, and products or services.

**BPM-Focus**. 3640-B3 N Federal Hwy., No. 421 Lighthouse Point, FL 33064. Phone: (954)688-4922; Fax: (954)758-7219; Email: info@bpmfocus.org • URL: http://www.bpmfocus.org • Identifies and clarifies issues that are common to users of workflow, electronic commerce, knowledge management and those who are in the process of re-engineering their organizations.

***BPO, Call Center IT, Telecom, Computer Software & Hardware Companies Database, Directory of India***. NIIR Project Consultancy Services, 106 - E, Kamla Nagar New Delhi 110007, India. Phone: 91 11 23843955; Fax: 91 11 23841561; Email: npcs.india@gmail.com • URL: http://www.niir.org • Rs 2,809 Individuals CD-ROM; $200 Individuals CD-ROM. Covers: BPO, call center, telecom, computer software and hardware companies in India. Entries include: Name of companies, address, city, pin code, phone, fax, 2,250 e-mail, 2,350 website and contact person with designation.

***Braby's Durban Business Directory***. A.C. Braby (Pty) Ltd., 12 Caversham Rd. Pinetown 3610, South Africa. Email: support@brabys.co.za • URL: http://www.brabys.com • Covers: Businesses in Durban, South Africa. Entries include: Contact information and maps.

***Braby's Mpumalanga Business Directory***. A.C. Braby (Pty) Ltd., 12 Caversham Rd. Pinetown 3610, South Africa. Email: support@brabys.co.za • URL: http://www.brabys.com • Annual. $75. Covers: Businesses in South Africa's Lowveld region. Entries include: Contact information.

***Braby's Pretoria Business Directory***. A.C. Braby (Pty) Ltd., 12 Caversham Rd. Pinetown 3610, South Africa. Email: support@brabys.co.za • URL: http://www.brabys.com • Covers: Businesses in Pretoria, South Africa. Entries include: Contact information and maps.

***Braby's SADC Directory***. A.C. Braby (Pty) Ltd., 12 Caversham Rd. Pinetown 3610, South Africa. Email: support@brabys.co.za • URL: http://www.brabys.com • Annual. $420 2 volume set; $100 CDR; plus P&P. Covers: about 875,000 businesses in South Africa, Angola, Botswana, Lesotho, Malawi, Mauritius, Mozambique, Namibia, Swaziland, Tanzania, Zambia, Zimbabwe. Also includes foreign firms represented in South Africa and South African firms represented outside South Africa. Entries include: Company name, address, phone, telex, other details.

***Braby's Zambia Trade Directory***. A.C. Braby (Pty) Ltd., 12 Caversham Rd. Pinetown 3610, South Africa. Email: support@brabys.co.za • URL: http://www.brabys.com • Annual. $100. Covers: Businesses in Zambia. Database includes: Maps. Entries include: Contact information.

***Brake and Frontend: The Complete Undercar Service Magazine***. Babcox, 3550 Embassy Pkwy. Akron, OH 44333. Phone: (330)670-1234; Fax: (330)670-0874 • URL: http://www.babcox.com • Monthly. $64.00 per year.

***Brampton Business Times***. Metroland Media Group, 3125 Wolfedale Rd. Mississauga, ON, Canada L5C 1W1. Phone: (905)279-0440 or (905)281-5656; Fax: (905)279-7763 or (905)279-5103 • URL: http://www.metroland.com/ • Community business-to-business newspaper.

***Brandeis Law Journal***. University of Louisville Louis D. Brandeis School of Law. University of Louisville, 2301 S 3rd St. Louisville, KY 40292. Phone: 800-334-8635 or (502)852-5555 or (502)852-6396; Fax: (502)852-0862; Email: jenny.sawyer@louisville.edu • URL: http://www.louisville.edu • Quarterly. $30.00 per year.

**Brandeis University - Center for Youth and Communities**. Heller Bldg., 3rd Fl., MS 035, 415 S St. Waltham, MA 02454. Phone: (781)736-4835 or (781)736-3729; Fax: (781)736-3773; Email: curnan@brandeis.edu • URL: http://cyc.brandeis.edu • Formerly Center for Human Resources.

**Brandeis University - Council on Health Care Economics and Policy**. Schneider Institute for Health Policy, Heller School for Social Policy & Management, MS 035, 415 South St. Waltham, MA 02454-9110. Phone: (781)736-3940; Fax:

(781)736-3306; Email: doonan@brandeis.edu • URL: http://council.brandeis.edu • Critical issues generated by health system change and the economic impact of such changes.

**Brandeis University - Schneider Institutes for Health Policy**. Heller School for Social Policy & Management, MS 035, 415 S St. Waltham, MA 02454-9110. Phone: (781)736-3901; Fax: (781)736-3905; Email: wallack@brandeis.edu • URL: http://sihp.brandeis.edu • Health care, focusing on the intersection of health behavior and systems of care, including policy studies in the areas of financing organization, value of health services, quality, high cost and high risk populations, and technology.

*Branding Your Business*. Cengage Learning Inc., 20 Channel Center St. Boston, MA 02210. Phone: 800-487-8488 or (617)289-7700; Fax: (617)289-7844; Email: investors@cengage.com • URL: http://www.cengage.com • 2010. eBook. Details what a brand is and what it is not, how to conduct a 'DIY' brand audit and how to use marketing NLP and psychology principles to create a powerful brand.

*Brands and Their Companies (BTC)*. Cengage Learning Inc., 20 Channel Center St. Boston, MA 02210. Phone: 800-487-8488 or (617)289-7700; Fax: (617)289-7844; Email: investors@cengage.com • URL: http://www.cengage.com • Annual. 1,466. Coverage of more than 426,000 entries on trade names, trademarks, and brand names of consumer-oriented products and their 115,000 manufacturers, importers, marketers, or distributors. Formerly Trade Names Dictionary.

*Brandweek: The Newsweekly of Marketing Communications*. Nielsen Business Media Inc., 770 Broadway New York, NY 10003-9522. Phone: 866-890-8541 or (646)654-4500 or (646)654-5000; Fax: (646)654-5584 or (646)654-4500; Email: bmcomm@nielsen.com • URL: http://www.nielsenbusinessmedia.com • 46 times a year. $149.00 per year. Includes articles and case studies on mass marketing and mass media. Formerly *Adweek's Marketing Week*.

*Branson Business Journal*. Branson Business Journal, PO Box 1449 Forsyth, MO 65653. Phone: (417)546-2520; Fax: (417)546-6817 • $16.50 Individuals per year; $75 ASNG. Publication focusing on business issues.

*Brazil Business Directory*. INFOT Inc., PO Box 2052 Rockville, MD 20847. Phone: 866-838-2619 • URL: http://www.infotusa.com • Annual. $67.15 CD-ROM; additional $65 for MS Access format. Covers: 329,752 companies, from Brazil. Entries include: company name, email and website addresses, telephone and fax number, and business description.

*Brazil Business Forecast Report*. Telecommunications Insight, 85 Queen Victoria St. London EC4V 4AB, United Kingdom. Phone: 20 72 465100 or 44 20 7248 0468; Fax: 20 72 480467 or 44 20 7248 0467; Email: enquiries@telecomsinsight.com • URL: http://www.telecomsinsight.com • Quarterly. $1,195 Individuals Single user; $1,795 Individuals Up to 3 users. Business forecast report for Brazil.

*Brazil Business Law Handbook*. International Business Publications, USA, PO Box 15343 Washington, DC 20003. Phone: (202)546-2103; Fax: (202)546-3275; Email: ibpusa@comcast.net • URL: http://ibpus.com • Annual. $99.95 Individuals hardcover; $99.95 Individuals e-book; $99.95 Individuals CD-ROM. Covers: Information on basic business legislation, laws, business climate, and contacts.

*Brazil Company Handbook*. Hoover's Inc., 5800 Airport Blvd. Austin, TX 78752-4204. Phone: 866-443-3939 or (512)374-4500 or (866)281-5969; Fax: (512)374-4501; Email: salesteam@hoovers.com • URL: http://www.hoovers.com • Annual. $74.95 Individuals tradepaper. Covers: About 72 of Brazil's largest public companies. Database includes: Profile of Brazil's economy, international trade, and investment climate; data on stock exchanges. Entries include: Company name, address, phone, fax, year established, stock ticker symbol, names and titles of key personnel, number of employees, number of stockholders, bank references, auditor, company history, financial data, markets and competition, raw materials used and sources, names of major stockholders, affiliated companies.

*Brazil Dez Mil*. Dun & Bradstreet Inc., 103 JFK Pkwy. Short Hills, NJ 07078. Phone: 800-526-0651 or (973)921-5500 or (973)921-5000; Fax: (866)560-7035 or (512)794-7670; Email: info@dnb.com • URL: http://www.dnb.com • Biennial. Covers: 10,000 of the largest companies in Brazil. Entries include: Company name, address, phone, fax, telex, sales volume, Standard Industrial Classification (SIC) code, names and titles of key personnel, number of employees, import/export designation.

*Brazil Industrial and Business Directory*. International Business Publications, USA, PO Box 15343 Washington, DC 20003. Phone: (202)546-2103; Fax: (202)546-3275; Email: ibpusa@comcast.net • URL: http://ibpus.com • Annual. $99.95 Individuals hardcopy; $99.95 Individuals e-book; $99.95 Individuals CD-ROM. Covers: Strategic industrial, investment and business contacts for conducting export-import and investment activity in the country.

**Brazil Ministry of Planning - Brazilian Institute of Geography and Statistics**. Avda. Franklin Roosevelt 166/10 andar, Castelo 20021-120 Rio de Janeiro, RJ, Brazil. Phone: 55 21 21424501; Fax: 55 21 424933; Email: webmaster@ibge.gov.br • URL: http://www.ibge.gov.br • Main research activities include; periodical censuses and continuous surveys on prices, industrial, agricultural and services activities and the national accounts; population and household censuses and

yearly household surveys; systematic mapping of the Brazilian territory, geodesy and thematic studies on environment and natural resources.

**Brazil-U.S. Business Council**. 1615 H St. NW Washington, DC 20062. Phone: (202)463-5729; Email: brazilcouncil@uschamber.com • URL: http://www.brazilcouncil.org • Works to provide a high-level private sector forum for the business communities of both countries to engage in substantive dialogue on trade and investment issues and communicate private sector priorities to both governments.

**Brazilian-American Chamber of Commerce**. 509 Madison Ave., Ste. 304 New York, NY 10022. Phone: (212)751-4691; Fax: (212)751-7692 or (212)751-8929 • URL: http://www.brazilcham.com • Promotes trade between Brazil and the U.S.

*Brazilian-American Who's Who*. Brazilian-American Chamber of Commerce, 509 Madison Ave., Ste. 304 New York, NY 10022. Phone: (212)751-4691; Fax: (212)751-7692 or (212)751-8929 • URL: http://www.brazilcham.com • Irregular. $55. Covers: more than 1,300 firms, subsidiaries, and affiliates operating and/or having interests in both the United States and Brazil. Entries include: Company name, address, names and titles of key personnel.

**Brazilian Government Trade Bureau of the Consulate General of Brazil in New York**. 220 E 42nd St. New York, NY 10017-5806. Phone: (917)777-7777; Fax: (212)827-0225; Email: cg.novayork@itamaraty.gov.br • URL: http://novayork.itamaraty.gov.br/en-us • Commercial Office of the Brazil Consulate in New York. Offers online match between Brazilian exporters of goods and services and U.S. importers.

**Brazilian Trade Bureau of the Consulate General of Brazil in New York**. 220 E 42nd St., 26th Fl. New York, NY 10017-5806. Phone: (917)777-7777; Fax: (212)827-0225; Email: cg.novayork@itamaraty.gov.br • URL: http://novayork.itamaraty.gov.br/en-us • Offers assistance to American firms wishing to purchase Brazilian products, and promotes Brazilian firms and their exports. Formerly Brazilian Government Trade Bureau.

*Bremer Geschafts-Adressbuch*. Carl Ed. Schuenemann KG, Zweite Schlachtpforte 7 D-28195 Bremen, Germany. Phone: 49 421 369030; Fax: 49 421 3690339; Email: kontakt@schuenemann-verlag.de • URL: http://www.schuenemann-verlag.de • Annual. Covers: about 20,000 businesses in the state of Bremen, Germany. Entries include: Company name, address, phone.

**Bretton Woods Committee**. 1726 M St. NW, Ste. 200 Washington, DC 20036. Phone: (202)331-1616; Fax: (202)785-9423; Email: info@brettonwoods.org • URL: http://www.brettonwoods.org • Corporate CEOs, university administrators, former government officials, state governors, association and trade union executives, and bankers. Seeks to inform and educate the public regarding the activities of the World Bank, International Monetary Fund, and other Multinational Development Banks (MDB). Promotes U.S. participation in MDBs.

*Brewers Almanac*. Beer Institute, 122 C St., Ste. 350 Washington, DC 20001-2109. Phone: (202)737-2337; Fax: (202)737-7004; Email: info@beerinstitute.org • URL: http://www.beerinstitute.org • Annual. $170. Provides a wealth of information and statistics covering the beer industry.

**Brewers Association**. 1327 Spruce St. Boulder, CO 80302-5006. Phone: 888-822-6273 or (303)447-0816; Email: info@brewersassociation.org • URL: http://www.brewersassociation.org • Represents micro and regional brewers of beer. Aims to promote and protect American Craft Beer and American Craft Brewers and the community of brewing enthusiasts.

*Brewers Digest*. Siebel Publishing Co., Inc., P.O. Box 677 Thiensville, WI 53092. Phone: (312)463-3401 • Monthly. $25.00 per year. Covers all aspects of brewing. Annual *Buyers' Guide* and *Directory* available.

**Brewery and Soft Drink Conference**. 25 Louisiana Ave. NW Washington, DC 20001-2130. Phone: (202)624-6800; Fax: (202)624-8137; Email: brewery@teamster.org • URL: http://www.teamster.org/content/brewery-soft-drink-conference • Promotes the interests of brewery and soft drink workers in the United States and Canada.

*Brewing and Distilling International*. Brewery Traders Publications, Ltd., 52 Glenhouse Rd. Eltham SE19 1JQ, United Kingdom. Phone: 44 20 8859 4300; Fax: (885)9 5813; Email: bdilondon@dial.pipex.com • URL: http://www.bdinews.com • Monthly. $82.00 per year.

**Brick Industry Association**. 1850 Centennial Park Dr., Ste. 301 Reston, VA 20191. Phone: (703)620-0010; Fax: (703)620-3928; Email: brickinfo@bia.org • URL: http://www.gobrick.com • Manufacturers and distributors of clay brick. Promotes clay brick with the goal of increasing its market share.

*Brick Walkways & Patios Directory*. InfoGroup Inc., 5711 S 86th Cir. Omaha, NE 68127-4146. Phone: (402)593-4500 • URL: http://www.infogroup.com • Annual. Number of listings: 13,770. Entries include: Name, address, phone, size of advertisement, name of owner or manager, number of employees, year first in "Yellow Pages." Compiled from telephone company "Yellow Pages," nationwide.

*Bricker's International Directory: Long-Term University-Based Executive Programs*. Peterson's, 461 From Rd. Paramus, NJ 07652. Phone: 800-338-3282 or (609)896-1800 or (877)433-8277; Fax: (402)458-3042 or (609)896-4531; Email:

custsvc@petersons.com • URL: http://www.petersons.com • Annual. Covers: Several hundred residential management development programs at academic institutions in the United States and abroad. Criteria for listing include that program must be residential, at least one week in length, in English, not introductory in content, and with emphasis on "strategic" issues and functions covering a wide range of organizations. Entries include: Name of program; sponsoring institution; location, dates, and duration of program; tuition fees; curriculum content; modes of instruction; size of classes; information on participants; living accommodations; faculty; special features; official contact.

*Bridal Consultants Directory*. InfoGroup Inc., 5711 S 86th Cir. Omaha, NE 68127-4146. Phone: (402)593-4500 • URL: http://www.infogroup.com • Annual. Number of listings: 6,167. Entries include: Name, address, phone, size of advertisement, name of owner or manager, number of employees, year first in "Yellow Pages." Compiled from telephone company "Yellow Pages," nationwide.

**Bridal Show Producers International**. 2701 Del Paso Rd. 130-343 Sacramento, CA 95835. Fax: (800)573-6070 • URL: http://www.bspibridalshows.com • Represents and promotes the bridal show industry. Maintains and enhances the quality of bridal shows. Increases communications and integrity among exhibitors and producers. Fosters mutual support and camaraderie among members.

**British Association of Women Entrepreneurs**. 112 John Player Bldg. Stirling FK7 7RP, United Kingdom. Phone: 44 18 2725 5170; Email: deb@bawe-uk.org • URL: http://www.bawe-uk.org • Encourages the personal development of member entrepreneurs. Provides opportunities for members to expand their business through informal and formal networking. Represents and promotes British entrepreneurship worldwide.

*British Business in China Directory*. British Chamber of Commerce in Hong Kong, Emperor Group Ctre., Rm. 1201, 288 Hennessy Rd., Wan Chai Hong Kong, China. Phone: 852 28242211; Fax: 852 28241333 • URL: http://www.britcham.com • Annual. Provides full details of all British chamber members across Hong Kong, Macao and Guangdong.

*British Business Rankings*. Dun & Bradstreet Inc., 103 JFK Pkwy. Short Hills, NJ 07078. Phone: 800-526-0651 or (973)921-5500 or (973)921-5000; Fax: (866)560-7035 or (512)794-7670; Email: info@dnb.com • URL: http://www.dnb.com • Covers: 5,000 key British companies. Entries include: Company name, address, phone, telex, TWX, sales volume, number of employees, SIC codes.

**British Cheque Cashers Association**. Portal Business Ctr., Dallam Ct., Dallam Ln. Warrington WA2 7LT, United Kingdom. Phone: 44 1925 426090; Email: info@bcca.co.uk • URL: http://www.bcca.co.uk • Provides representation of its members' interests to government whether in London or Brussels - and its regulatory bodies. Also seeks to enhance understanding of the industry and to promote the interests of check cashers generally by helping to shape a climate of opinion which enables members to conduct their business profitably.

**British Council for Offices**. 78-79 Leadenhall St. London EC3A 3DH, United Kingdom. Phone: 44 20 7283 0125; Fax: 44 20 7626 1553; Email: mail@bco.org.uk • URL: http://www.bco.org.uk • Seeks to research, develop and communicate best practice in all aspects of the office sector. Provides a forum for the discussion and debate of issues affecting office sector. Advances understanding of effective office space.

**British Crop Protection Council**. c/o Chris Todd, Manager, 7 Omni Business Centre, Omega Park Alton GU34 2QD, United Kingdom. Phone: 44 1420 593 200 or 44 1420 593200; Fax: 44 1420 593 209 or 44 1420 593209; Email: md@bcpc.org • URL: http://www.bcpc.org • Promotes the knowledge and understanding of crop protection/production through conferences, publications, teaching resources for schools, training manuals, identifying R&D needs for policy makers.

*British Export Interactive Website*. Reed Business Information, Quadrant House, The Quadrant Surrey SM2 5AS, United Kingdom. Phone: 44 20 86523500 or 1 6618904; Fax: 44 20 86528932; Email: webmaster@rbi.co.uk • URL: http://www.reedbusiness.com • Database covers: 17,000 companies in the United Kingdom, as well as the products and services they actively export. Database includes: Full electronic commerce.

*British Firms in Germany*. British Chamber of Commerce in Germany, Heumarkt 14 D-50667 Cologne, Germany. Phone: 221 1234284; Fax: 221 231634 • $200. Covers: companies in the Federal Republic of Germany which are subsidiaries of or otherwise affiliated with United Kingdom firms. Entries include: German company name and address, name and address of British affiliate or owner, code indicating products.

**British Sociological Association**. Bailey Ste., Palatine House, Belmont Business Park Durham DH1 1TW, United Kingdom. Phone: 44 191 383 0839; Fax: 44 191 383 0782; Email: enquiries@britsoc.org.uk • URL: http://www.britsoc.co.uk • Individuals interested or employed in the fields of psychology, sociology, and other social sciences. Promotes the study of sociology and works to create a favorable climate for sociological research. Acts as a communication and information network.

**British Trade Office at Consulate-General**. 845 3rd Ave. New York, NY 10022. Phone: (212)745-0200; Fax: (212)745-0456 • URL: http://www.gov.uk/government/world/organisations/

british-consulate-general-new-york • British government office that promotes trade with the U.S.; assists British companies selling in the U.S.; aids American companies that wish to import goods from or invest in Britain.

**British Venture Capital Association**. 5th Fl. E, Chancery House, 53-64 Chancery Ln. London WC2A 1QS, United Kingdom. Phone: 44 20 74920400; Fax: 44 20 74201801; Email: bvca@bvca.co.uk • URL: http://www.bvca.co.uk • Venture capital, private equity, and professional firms connected with the venture capital industry. Represents virtually every major source of venture capital in the UK. Provides information about members to entrepreneurs and investors; represents members' views in discussions with Government and other bodies; provides a forum for the exchange of views among members; develops and maintains the highest standards of professional practice and provides training for members' employees.

***British Year Book of International Law***. Oxford University Press, 198 Madison Ave. New York, NY 10016. Phone: 866-445-8685 or (212)726-6000; Fax: (919)677-1303 or (212)726-6444; Email: oxfordonline@oup.com • URL: http://www.oup.com • Annual. $400. An essential work of reference for academics and practicing lawyers. It provides up-to-date information on important developments in modern international law.

***Broadband Technology: Newsletter on Technical Advances, Construction of New Systms and Rebuild of Existing Systems***. Paul Kagan Associates, Inc., 126 Clock Tower Pl. Carmel, CA 93923-8746. Phone: (831)624-1536; Fax: (831)625-3225; Email: info@kagan.com • URL: http://www.kagan.com • Monthly. $895.00 per year. Newsletter. Contains news of cable TV technical advances. Formerly (Cable TV Technology).

**Broadcast Education Association**. 1771 N St. NW Washington, DC 20036-2891. Phone: (202)429-5355 or (202)429-3935; Fax: (202)775-2981; Email: beamemberservices@nab.org • URL: http://www.beaweb.org • Universities and colleges; faculty and students; promotes improvement of curriculum and teaching methods, broadcasting research, television and radio production, and programming teaching on the college level.

***Broadcast Engineering—Equipment Reference Manual***. Penton, 9800 Metcalf Ave. Overland Park, KS 66212. Phone: 866-748-4926 or (913)341-1300; Fax: (913)967-1905 or (913)967-1898; Email: corporatecustomerservice@penton.com • URL: http://www.penton.com • Annual. Publication includes: List of more than 1,400 manufacturers and distributors of communications equipment for radio, television, and recording applications. Database includes: Specifications for major brands of professional broadcast hardware. Entries include: For manufacturers—Company name, address. For distributors and dealers—Company name, address, phone, product or service provided, geographic area covered.

***Broadcast Engineering: Journal of Broadcast Technology***. Penton, 9800 Metcalf Ave. Overland Park, KS 66212. Phone: 866-748-4926 or (913)341-1300; Fax: (913)967-1905 or (913)967-1898; Email: corporatecustomerservice@penton.com • URL: http://www.penton.com • 10 times a year. Free to qualified personnel; others, $65.00 per year. Technical magazine for the broadcast industry.

***Broadcast Investor: Newsletter on Radio-TV Station Finance***. Paul Kagan Associates, Inc., 126 Clock Tower Pl. Carmel, CA 93923-8746. Phone: (831)624-1536; Fax: (831)625-3225; Email: info@kagan.com • URL: http://www.kagan.com • Monthly. $925.00 per year. Newsletter for investors in publicly held radio and television broadcasting companies.

***Broadcasting and Cable***. NewBay Media, LLC, 28 E 28th St., 12th Fl. New York, NY 10016. Phone: (212)378-0400; Fax: (917)281-4704 or (212)378-4704 • URL: http://www.nbmedia.com • 51 times a year. $179.00 per year; includes print and online editions. Formerly *Broadcasting*.

**Broadsource**. 750 9th St. NW, Ste. 650 Washington, DC 20001-4793. Phone: 877-892-6273 or (202)349-2500; Fax: (202)349-2599 • URL: http://www.boardsource.org • Seeks to improve the effectiveness of nonprofit boards of trustees. Formerly National Center for Nonprofit Boards.

**Broadway League**. 729 7th Ave., 5th Fl. New York, NY 10019. Phone: (212)764-1122 or (212)703-0200; Fax: (212)944-2136; Email: league@broadway.org • URL: http://www.broadwayleague.com • Members are legitimate theater producers and owners and operators of legitimate theaters. Formerly League of American Theatres and Producers.

***Broker-Dealer Regulation***. David A. Lipton. Thomson West, 610 Opperman Dr. Eagan, MN 55123. Phone: 800-328-9352 or (651)687-7000 • Semiannual. $114 per month. Focuses on the basics of stockbroker license application procedure, registration, regulation, and responsibilities. (Securities Law Series).

***Broker: The Sales and Management Resource for Mortgage Originators***. SourceMedia Inc., 1 State Street Plz., 27th Fl. New York, NY 10004. Phone: 800-221-1809 or (212)803-8200 or (212)803-8333; Fax: (212)843-9635 or (212)292-5216; Email: custserv@sourcemedia.com • URL: http://www.sourcemedia.com • Bimonthly. $48.00 per year. Edited for mortgage brokers. Emphasis is on marketing, leads to new business, and profitability.

***Broker World***. Insurance Publications Inc., 9404 Reeds Rd. Overland Park, KS 66207-1010. Phone: 800-762-3387 or (913)383-9191; Fax: (913)383-1247 • URL: http://www.brokerworldmag.com • Bimonthly. $6.00 per year. Edited for independent insurance agents and brokers. Special feature issue topics include annuities, disability insurance, estate planning, and life insurance.

***Brokers***. IZUM Information Service, Presernova 17 2000 Maribor, Slovenia. Phone: 999386 2 2520331; Fax: 999386 2 2524334; Email: izum@izum.si • URL: http://www.izum.si • Quarterly. Database covers: Approximately 22 databases currently available on information providers and/or database producers in Slovenia. Part of the INFORS database. Entries include: Database name, acronym, date status, topic, language, number of records, update frequency, source of data, host, vendor, and producer.

***Brookers Sale and Purchase of a Business Precedents***. Thomson Reuters New Zealand Legal, Tax and Accounting Unit, Level 1, Guardian Trust House, 15 Willeston St. Wellington 6140, New Zealand. Phone: 64 4 499 8178; Fax: 64 4 499 8173; Email: service@thomsonreuters.co.nz • URL: http://www.thomsonreuters.co.nz • Contains a collection of documents and precedents needed to guide solicitors through the sale or purchase of a business in New Zealand.

**Brookings Institution - Center for Northeast Asian Policy Studies**. 1775 Massachusetts Ave. NW Washington, DC 20036. Phone: (202)797-6055; Fax: (202)797-2485; Email: communications@brookings.edu • URL: http://www.brookings.edu/cnaps.aspx • Security and architecture of Northeast Asia; U.S.-China strategic relations; the dynamics of relations across the Taiwan Strait; integrating China into the world economy and the international political system; Japan's structural rigidities; and U.S. foreign policy on the Korean peninsula.

**Brookings Institution - Center on Social Dynamics and Policy**. 1775 Massachusetts Ave. NW Washington, DC 20036. Phone: (202)797-6105; Fax: (202)797-6181; Email: csed@brookings.edu • URL: http://www.brookings.edu/about/centers/dynamics • Economic and social issues.

***Brookline Business Directory***. Brookline Chamber of Commerce, 251 Harvard St., Ste. 1 Brookline, MA 02446-3202. Phone: (617)739-1330; Fax: (617)739-1200; Email: info@brooklinechamber.com • URL: http://www.brooklinechamber.com • Covers: Approximately 700 businesses in Brookline, Massachusetts; 30 area restaurants; schools, neighborhood associations, and other community resources. Entries include: For businesses and institutions—Company or organization name, address, phone. For restaurants—Name, address, phone, hours of operation, type of cuisine, credit cards accepted, etc.

**Brown University - Center for Advanced Materials Research**. Box M Providence, RI 02912. Phone: (401)863-2859; Fax: (401)863-6701; Email: nitin_padture@brown.edu • URL: http://brown.edu/research/institute-molecular-nanoscale-innovation/research/center-advanced-materials-research • Fundamental and applied research in study of technologically important international materials issues of the 21st century embracing materials science, including studies of electronic and mechanical properties of semiconductor microstructures, fundamentals of plasticity and fracture, microscopic basis of glass formation, and physics and engineering of conductor/nonconductor interfaces. Collaborate with investigators from several universities.

**Brown University - A. Alfred Taubman Center for Public Policy and American Institutions**. 67 George St., Box 1977 Providence, RI 02912. Phone: (401)863-2201; Fax: (401)863-2452; Email: marion_orr@brown.edu • URL: http://www.brown.edu/academics/taubman-center • Urban issues, economic and urban development, elections, mass media, social and child welfare, comparative public policy, education policy, regulation, and federalism.

***Browning Database Review***. Browning Associates, 105 Browning Ave. Toronto, ON, Canada M4K 1W2. Phone: (416)465-9426 • Irregular. $50 payment with order; $60 billed. Covers: over 125 databases providing Canadian business information. Entries include: Database name and acronym, content, scope, time span, frequency of update, size, percentage of Canadian content, connect rates and requirements; name, address, and phone of producer and of the Canadian and/or United States distributor.

***Brunei Industrial and Business Directory***. International Business Publications, USA, PO Box 15343 Washington, DC 20003. Phone: (202)546-2103; Fax: (202)546-3275; Email: ibpusa@comcast.net • URL: http://ibpus.com • Annual. $99.95 Individuals. Covers industrial, investment and business contacts for conducting export-import and investment activity in the country.

***Brunei Yearbook***. Forward Media Sdn Bhd, Locked Bag No.2, MPC, Old Airport Rd. Bandar Seri Begawan BB3510, Brunei. Phone: 673 2 451468; Fax: 673 2 451460; Email: fmsb@yellowpages.com.sg • URL: http://www.bruneiyearbook.com • Information on Brunei companies, products and services. Entries include: Company name, address, phone and fax numbers, company's main business activities, names of top executives, e-mail and website addresses.

**Brunel University - Centre for Research in Rehabilitation**. Mary Seacole Bldg. 301D, School of Health Sciences & Social Care Uxbridge UB8 3PH, United Kingdom. Phone: 44 1895 274000; Fax: 44 1895 232806; Email: lorraine.desouza@brunel.ac.uk • URL: http://www.brunel.ac.uk/shssc/research/crr • Enabling people with disabilities to fulfill their potential for health and personal development. Current issues include: promotion of health research to build evidence based practice; development of research links between health care providers and academic researchers; evaluation of new and existing health technologies; and development of research that reflects clinical reality and that reduces the physical, psychological, and financial burden of care.

***BTA Membership Directory***. Business Technology Association, 12411 Wornall Rd., Ste. 200 Kansas City, MO 64145. Phone: 800-869-6688 or (816)941-3100; Fax: (816)941-4843 or (816)941-2829 • URL: http://www.bta.org • Annual. $125 for members; $995 for nonmembers. Publication includes: List of 3,000 retailers and 500 manufacturers of typewriters, calculators, word processors, computers, dictation equipment, copying machines, mailing equipment, network equipment, and other office machines. Entries include: Company name, address, phone, fax, e-mail, website, names of executives; dealer listings include codes showing products handled.

***BUC Used Boat Price Guide***. BUC International Corp., 1314 NE 17th Ct. Fort Lauderdale, FL 33305. Phone: 800-327-6929 or (954)565-6715; Fax: (954)561-3095; Email: info@buc.com • URL: http://www.buc.com • Semiannual. $172.95 Individuals. Current market price for about 3,500 manufacturers of outboard, inboard, outdrives, sailboats, houseboats, and custom boats as well as approximately 20 manufacturers of boat trailers. In three volumes—Volume 1 covers 1994-2003; volume 2 covers 1982-1993; volume 3 covers 1905-1981. Formerly *Older Boat Price Guide*.

***Budget and Economic Outlook: Fiscal Years (10-year period)***. U. S. Government Printing Office, 732 N Capitol St. NW Washington, DC 20401. Phone: 866-512-1800 or (202)512-1800 or (866)512-1800; Fax: (202)512-2104 or (202)512-2250; Email: contactcenter@gpo.gov • URL: http://www.gpo.gov • Annual. $27. Issued by the Congressional Budget Office (CBO). Reports on fiscal policy and provides baseline projections of federal budget for 10 years. Also offers "impartial analysis with no recommendations.".

***Buffalo Business First***. American City Business Journals, Inc., 120 W Morehead St. Charlotte, NC 28202. Phone: (704)973-1000; Fax: (704)973-1001; Email: americancity@bizjournals.com • URL: http://www.acbj.com • $96 Individuals print + online. Contains the full text of Buffalo Business First, a business tabloid covering Buffalo, New York.

***Builder: The Voice of America's Housing Industry***. Finance and Housing Policy Div. DoveTale Publishers, 1 Thomas Cir. NW Washington, DC 20005. Phone: 877-275-8647 or (202)339-0744 or (202)452-0800; Fax: (202)785-1974 or (202)339-0749; Email: hwmicustomerservice@hanleywood.com • URL: http://www.hwmarketintelligence.com • Monthly. $29.95 per year. Covers the home building and remodeling industry in general, including design, construction, and marketing.

**Builders Hardware Manufacturers Association**. 355 Lexington Ave., 15th Fl. New York, NY 10017. Phone: (212)297-2122; Fax: (212)370-9047; Email: bhma@kellencompany.com • URL: http://www.buildershardware.com • Manufacturers of builders' hardware, both contract and stock. Provides statistical services; maintains standardization program; sponsors certification programs for locks, latches, door closers and cabinet hardware. Maintains 12 product sections.

***Building & Loan Associations Directory***. InfoGroup Inc., 5711 S 86th Cir. Omaha, NE 68127-4146. Phone: (402)593-4500 • URL: http://www.infogroup.com • Annual. Number of listings: 11,966. Entries include: Name, address, phone, size of advertisement, name of owner or manager, number of employees, year first in "Yellow Pages." Compiled from telephone company "Yellow Pages," nationwide.

***Building Business & Apartment Management***. Home Builders Association of Southeastern Michigan, 2075 Walnut Lake Rd. West Bloomfield, MI 48323. Phone: (248)737-4477 • URL: http://www.builders.org • Monthly. $48 Individuals. Construction and apartment industry magazine.

***Building Construction Cost Data***. RSMeans, 700 Longwater Dr. Norwell, MA 02061. Phone: 800-334-3509; Fax: (800)632-6732 • URL: http://www.rsmeans.reedconstructiondata.com • Annual. $194.95 Individuals. Lists over 20,000 entries for estimating.

***Building Design and Construction: The Magazine for the Building Team***. Reed Elsevier Group plc Reed Business Information, 360 Park Ave. S New York, NY 11010. Phone: (212)791-4208; Email: corporatecommunications@reedbusiness.com • URL: http://www.reedbusiness.com • Monthly. $119.00 per year. For non-residential building owners, contractors, engineers and architects.

***Building Industry—Slovakia***. I.S.M.C. Information Systems and Marketing Contacts Ltd., Nam. Slobody 9, PO Box 47 81499 Bratislava, Slovakia. Phone: 421 7 265423783; Fax: 421 7 265422186; Email: ismc@ismc.sk • URL: http://www.ismc.sk • $65. Covers: Companies in the building industry in the Slovak Republic and their suppliers.

***Building Material Dealer***. National Lumber and Building Material Dealers Association, 2025 M St. NW, Ste. 800 Washington, DC 20036-3309. Phone: (202)367-1169; Fax: (202)367-2169; Email: info@dealer.org • URL: http://www.dealer.org • Monthly. $48.00 per year. Includes special feature issues on hand and power tools, lumber, roofing, kitchens, flooring, windows and doors, and insulation. Formerly *Builder Material Retailer*.

***Building Officials and Code Administrators International-Membership Directory***. 4051 W Flossmoor Rd. Country Club Hills, IL 60478. Phone: (708)799-7233; Fax: (708)799-4981; Email: boca@bocai.org • Annual. $16.00. Approximately 14,000 construction code officials, architects, engineers, trade associations, and manufacturers.

***Building Operating Management: The National Magazine for Commercial and Institutional Buildings Construction, Renovation, Facility Management***. Trade Press Media Group, 2100 W Florist Ave. Milwaukee, WI 53209. Phone: 800-727-7995 or (414)228-7701; Fax: (414)228-1134; Email: info@tradepress.com • URL: http://www.tradepress.com • Monthly. Free to qualified personnel.

**Building Owners and Managers Association International**. 1101 15th St. NW, Ste. 800 Washington, DC 20005-5021. Phone: 800-426-6292 or (202)408-2662; Fax: (202)326-6377; Email: info@boma.org • URL: http://www.boma.org • Formerly National Association of Building Owners and Managers.

**Building Security Council**. 1801 Alexander Bell Dr. Reston, VA 20191. Phone: (703)295-6314; Fax: (703)295-6415; Email: jschmid@burnsmcd.com • Aims to improve the security of state, municipal and privately owned buildings. Enhances public safety by promoting building security. Administers and maintains rating systems that enable building owners and operators to evaluate and improve the security of their facilities.

**Building Service Contractors Association International**. 330 N Wabash Ave., Ste. 2000 Chicago, IL 60611. Phone: 800-368-3414; Fax: (312)673-6735; Email: info@bscai.org • URL: http://www.bscai.org • Firms and corporations in 40 countries engaged in contracting building maintenance services including the provision of labor, purchasing materials and janitorial cleaning and maintenance of a building or its surroundings; associate members are manufacturers of cleaning supplies and equipment. Seeks to provide a unified voice for building service contractors and to promote increased recognition by government, property owners and the general business and professional public. Conducts continuing study and action, through committees and special task groups on areas such as public affairs, costs and ratios, uniform accounting, industrial relations and personnel, marketing and sales, contract improvement, research and planning, materials and supplies sources, group insurance, management training, statistics collection, safety and insurance costs. Has developed a certification program for building service executives and a registration program for building service managers.

**Building Stone Institute**. 5 Riverside Dr., Bldg. 2 Chestertown, NY 12817. Phone: 866-786-6313 or (518)803-4336; Fax: (518)803-6313 or (518)803-4338 • URL: http://www.buildingstoneinstitute.org • Represents natural stone quarriers, fabricators, installers, dealers, importers, expo and restorers. Serves as a clearinghouse of information for architects, contractors, and masons. Promotes the use of natural stone.

***Building Stone Magazine***. Building Stone Institute, 5 Riverside Dr., Bldg. 2 Chestertown, NY 12817. Phone: 866-786-6313 or (518)803-4336; Fax: (518)803-6313 or (518)803-4338 • URL: http://www.buildingstoneinstitute.org • Quarterly. $20 Individuals /year; $29 Other countries /year. Information on the natural stone industry.

***Building Supply Home Centers—Buyers Guide Issue***. Reed Elsevier Group plc Reed Business Information, 360 Park Ave. S New York, NY 11010. Phone: (212)791-4208; Email: corporatecommunications@reedbusiness.com • URL: http://www.reedbusiness.com • Annual. $30. Covers: U.S. manufacturers of building supply materials and products. Entries include: Company name and address, trade and brand names, list of products.

***Buildings: The Source for Facilities Decision-Makers***. Stamats Communications Inc., 615 5th St. SE Cedar Rapids, IA 52406-1888. Phone: 800-553-8878 or (319)364-6167; Fax: (319)365-5421; Email: info@stamats.com • URL: http://www.stamats.com • Monthly. $70.00 per year. Serves professional building ownership/management organizations.

***Bulgarian Trade Directory***. Bulgarian Chamber of Commerce and Industry, 9 Iskar St. BG-1058 Sofia, Bulgaria. Phone: 359 2 9872631 or 359 2 8117400; Fax: 359 2 9873209; Email: bcci@bcci.bg • URL: http://www.bcci.bg • Annual. Free; €35 Individuals EU member. Covers: 2,000 export/import companies and 120 economic committees and ministries in Bulgaria. Entries include: Name, address, phone, description of activities.

***Bulletin of American Mideast Business***. American Mideast Business Associates, 1137 S Green St. Tuckerton, NJ 08087-2428. Phone: (212)986-7229 • International business magazine.

***Bulletin of Bibliography***. Greenwood Publishing Group Inc., 88 Post Rd. W Westport, CT 06881. Phone: (203)226-3571; Fax: (203)222-1502; Email: orders@greenwood.com • URL: http://www.greenwood.com • Quarterly. $125.00 per year.

***Bulletin of Labour Statistics: Supplementing the Annual Data Presented in the Year Book of Labour Statistics***. International Labor Office. 1828 L St. NW Washington, DC 20036-5121. Phone: (202)653-7652; Fax: (202)653-7687; Email: washington@ilo.org • URL: http://www.ilo.org • Quarterly. $84.00 per year. Includes five Supplements. A supplement to *Yearbook of Labour Statistics*. Provides current labor and price index statistics for over 130 countries. Generally includes data for the most recent four years. Text in English, French and Spanish.

***Bulletin of the Atomic Scientists: The Magazine of Global Security News and Analysis***. Bulletin of the Atomic Scientists, 1155 E 60th St. Chicago, IL 60637. Phone: (772)702-6301 • URL: http://thebulletin.org • Bimonthly. $56.00 per year.

**Bulletin of the Atomic Scientists**. 1155 E 60th St. Chicago, IL 60637. Phone: (772)702-6301 • URL: http://thebulletin.org • Works to inform polic leaders and the public about risks to humanity from nuclear weapons, nuclear energy, climate change, and biotechnology.

***Bulletin on Narcotics***. United Nations Publications, c/o National Book Network, 15200 NBN Way Blue Ridge Summit, PA 17214. Phone: 888-254-4286 or (212)963-7680 or (212)963-8302; Fax: (800)338-4550; Email: unpublications@nbnbooks.com • URL: http://www.unp.un.org • Quarterly. $10.00 per issue. Editions in Chinese, French, Russian and Spanish.

***Bullinger's Postal and Shippers Guide for the United States and Canada***. Alber Leland Inc., 500 N Skinker Blvd. Saint Louis, MO 63130-4836. Phone: (314)725-5700; Email: pharig@alberland.com • Annual. $375.00. Approximately 260,000 communities in the United States and Canada.

***Bullion Advisory***. Moneypower, 1304 Edgewood Ave. Ann Arbor, MI 48103-5522. • Monthly. $36.00 per year. Specializes in gold, silver and platinum.

***Bullseye Ownership Report***. CDA/Equity Intelligence, 1455 Research Blvd. Rockville, MD 20850-3194. Phone: 800-232-6869 or (301)975-9600; Fax: (301)590-1389 • Weekly. $800. Covers: over 1,300 institutions that have filed statements of company ownership with the Securities and Exchange Commission, including 13D and 13G five-percent beneficial ownership, 14D-1 tender offers, 13(f) institutional common stock holdings, 13(f) institutional convertible holdings, U.S. investment company holdings, foreign investment company holdings. Entries include: Company name, value held, change in shares, going back five consecutive quarters, money center, turnover, investment style, type of institute, investment discretion, voting authority, filing date and percent of shares outstanding.

**Bunbury Chamber of Commerce and Industries**. 15 Stirling St. Bunbury, WA 6230, Australia. Phone: 61 97912292; Fax: 61 97916646; Email: ceo@bcci.asn.au • URL: http://www.bunburycci.com.au • Represents business and industry in the South West region of Western Australia.

***Burbank Business Journal***. Burbank Chamber of Commerce, 200 W Magnolia Blvd. Burbank, CA 91502-1724. Phone: (818)846-3111; Fax: (818)846-0109; Email: info@burbankchamber.org • URL: http://www.burbankchamber.org • Monthly. Contains a variety of articles about business, chamber members and the community at large.

***Bureau of Alcohol, Tobacco, and Firearms Quarterly Bulletin***. Bureau of Alcohol, Tobacco, and Firearms, U.S. Department of the Treasury. U. S. Government Printing Office, 732 N Capitol St. NW Washington, DC 20401. Phone: 866-512-1800 or (202)512-1800 or (866)512-1800; Fax: (202)512-2104 or (202)512-2250; Email: contactcenter@gpo.gov • URL: http://www.gpo.gov • Quarterly. $25.00 per year. Laws and regulations.

**Bureau of Economic Analysis - Office of Regional Economic Accounts**. 1441 L St. NW Washington, DC 20230. Phone: (202)606-9605 • URL: http://www.bea.gov/regional/index.htm • Analyses of regional (state and metropolitan) economic trends, developing new analysis methods and models, providing regional input-output multipliers, estimating gross state product by industry, publishing periodic regional economic analyses and projections, estimating state and county personal income (annual) and state personal income (quarterly), and estimating earnings and employment by industry for states and counties.

***Bureau of Economic Analysis***. U. S. Department of Commerce, Bureau of Economic Analysis, Phone: (202)606-9900; Fax: (202)606-5310; Email: webmaster@bea.doc.gov • URL: http://www.bea.doc.gov • Web site includes "News Release Information" covering national, regional, and international economic estimates from the BEA. Highlights of releases appear online the same day, complete text and tables appear the next day. "Recent News Releases" section provides titles for past nine months, with links. "BEA Data and Methodology" includes "Frequently Requested NIPA Data" (national income and product accounts, such as gross domestic product and personal income). Other statistics are available. Fees: Free.

**Bureau of International Labor Affairs - Office of International Economic Affairs - Foreign Economic Research Division**. 200 Constitution Ave. NW, Rm. S-5317 Washington, DC 20210. Phone: (202)693-4887; Fax: (202)693-4851 • URL: http://www.dol.gov/ilab/programs/oiea • Effects of international economic developments, including policies that affect international trade and investment on U.S. workers. Projects have included analysis of: multilateral trade negotiations; effects on U.S. workers of foreign investment and technology transfer by multinational corporations; compensation of earnings losses for workers who are displaced by trade; changing pattern of U.S. comparative advantage in trade; and effects of trade on employment opportunities, by industry and occupational categories.

***Burkina Faso Business Directory***. Business Guide, PO Box 27669 Dubai, United Arab Emirates. Phone: 971 4 2651719; Fax: 971 4 2692151; Email: sales@africa-business.com • URL: http://www.africa-business.com • $150 download. Covers: 3,600 business listings including wholesalers, importers, retailers, business houses, and agents in Burkina Faso.

***Burrelle's Media Directory: Broadcast Media***. BurrellesLuce, 75 E Northfield Rd. Livingston, NJ 07039. Phone: 800-631-1160 or (973)992-6600; Fax: (973)992-7675; Email: sross@burrelleluce.com • URL: http://www.burrellesluce.com • Annual. $550.00. Approximately 48,000 print and electronic media in North America. Provides detailed descriptions, including programming and key personnel.

***Burrelle's Media Directory: Magazines and Newsletters***. BurrellesLuce, 75 E Northfield Rd. Livingston, NJ 07039. Phone: 800-631-1160 or (973)992-6600; Fax: (973)992-7675; Email: sross@burrelleluce.com • URL: http://www.burrellesluce.com • Annual. $550.00. Provides detailed descriptions of more than 13,500 magazines and newsletters published in the U.S., Canada, and Mexico. Categories are professional, consumer, trade, and college. Semiannual *Updates*. Includes CD-ROM.

***Burrelle's Media Directory: Newspapers and Related Media***. BurrellesLuce, 75 E Northfield Rd. Livingston, NJ 07039. Phone: 800-631-1160 or (973)992-6600; Fax: (973)992-7675; Email: sross@burrelleluce.com • URL: http://www.burrellesluce.com • Annual. $550.00. *Daily Newspapers* volume lists more than 2,200 daily publications in the U. S., Canada, and Mexico. *Non-Daily Newspapers* volume lists more than 10,400 items published no more than three times a week. Provides detailed descriptions, including key personnel.

***Burrelle's New Jersey Media Directory***. BurrellesLuce, 75 E Northfield Rd. Livingston, NJ 07039. Phone: 800-631-1160 or (973)992-6600; Fax: (973)992-7675; Email: sross@burrelleluce.com • URL: http://www.burrellesluce.com • Annual. $60 plus $4.00 shipping. Covers: Over 1,200 New Jersey periodicals, newspapers, college publications, radio and television stations, and cable television systems. Also includes New York City and Philadelphia daily newspapers. Entries include: For publications—Title, publisher name, address, phone, names and titles of key personnel, frequency, circulation, geographical area covered, advertising and editorial deadlines. For others—Call letters and/or company name and address, names and titles of key personnel, markets covered.

***Burundi Business Directory***. Business Guide, PO Box 27669 Dubai, United Arab Emirates. Phone: 971 4 2651719; Fax: 971 4 2692151; Email: sales@africa-business.com • URL: http://www.africa-business.com • $150 download. Covers: 2,300 business listings including wholesalers, importers, retailers, and business houses in Burundi.

***Burundi Business Law Handbook***. International Business Publications, USA, PO Box 15343 Washington, DC 20003. Phone: (202)546-2103; Fax: (202)546-3275; Email: ibpusa@comcast.net • URL: http://ibpus.com • $99.95 Individuals hardcopy; $99.95 Individuals e-book; $99.95 Individuals CD-ROM. Covers: Information on basic business legislation, laws and climate, export-import regulations, and contacts.

***Busconi's Worldwide Importers Directory***. Small Business Publications, SBP Bldg., 4/45 Roop Nagar Delhi 110 007, India. • Irregular. $100; $25. Covers: Importers of Indian products, engineering goods, chemicals, pharmaceuticals, electronics, electrical goods, foodstuffs, handicrafts, jewelry, leather products, medicinal plants, spices, ready-made garments. Entries include: Contact details.

***Business Abstracts with Full Text***. EBSCO Publishing Inc., 10 Estes St. Ipswich, MA 01938-2106. Phone: 800-653-2726 or (978)356-6500; Fax: (978)356-6565; Email: information@ebscohost.com • URL: http://www.ebscohost.com • Includes full text articles from more than 460 business publications from 1982 to present. Indexing for nearly 880 publications.

***Business Agenda***. Top of Virginia Regional Chamber, 407 S Loudoun St. Winchester, VA 22601. Phone: (540)662-4118; Fax: (540)722-6365 • URL: http://www.regionalchamber.biz • Monthly.

***Business Air Today: The Premiere Source for Corporate Aviation Acquisitions***. Heartland Communications Group Inc., 1003 Central Ave., Ste. 1052 Fort Dodge, IA 50501. Phone: 800-247-2000 or (515)955-1600; Fax: (515)955-1668; Email: info@hlipublishing.com • URL: http://www.hlipublishing.com • Monthly. $19.95 Individuals. Source for corporate aircraft and services.

***Business Alabama***. PMT Publishing Company Inc., 2204 Lake Shore Dr., Ste. 120 Birmingham, AL 35209. Phone: (205)802-6363; Email: wsorrell@pmtpublishing.com • URL: http://www.pmtpublishing.com • Monthly. $22.95 Individuals; $32.95 Two years; $42.95 Individuals three years. Magazine for owners, managers, and presidents of companies covering issues and people in business in Alabama.

***Business***. Albany Area Chamber of Commerce - Georgia, 225 W Broad Ave. Albany, GA 31701-2566. Phone: 800-475-8700 or (229)434-8700; Fax: (229)434-8716; Email: chamber@albanyga.com • URL: http://albanyga.com • Bimonthly. free for members; $50/year for nonmembers. Contains chamber activities and items of interest to businesses.

**Business Alliance for Commerce in Hemp.** PO Box 1716 El Cerrito, CA 94530. Phone: (510)215-8326 • URL: http://www.equalrights4all.org/bach/BACHcore.html • Businesses, consumers, and other individuals and organizations with an interest in hemp and hemp products. Promotes "full and unrestricted restoration of hemp as a sustainable farm crop and industrial resource"; seeks to legalize therapeutic use of marijuana and regulate adult consumption. Conducts lobbying, community organization, and outreach activities supporting hemp producers and consumers; consulting services; disseminates information on the commercial and industrial uses of hemp and the therapeutic benefits of marijuana.

*Business Analyst.* University of Delhi, New Delhi, University Rd. New Delhi 110 007, India. Phone: 11 27667725; Fax: 11 27667126 • URL: http://www.du.ac.in/ • Semiannual. $300; $40 Other countries. Periodical focusing on business economics analysis.

*Business and Acquisition Newsletter.* Newsletters International, Inc., 2600 S. Gessner Rd. Houston, TX 77063. Phone: (713)783-0100 • Monthly. $300.00 per year. Information about firms that want to buy or sell companies, divisions, subsidiaries, product lines, patents, etc.

*Business and Commercial Aviation.* McGraw-Hill Aviation Week Group, Four International Dr. Rye Brook, NY 10573. Phone: 800-722-4726 or (914)939-0300; Fax: (914)939-1184; Email: customer.service@mcgraw-hill.com • URL: http://www.mcgraw-hill.com • Monthly. $52.00 per year. Supplement available: *Annual Planning Purchasing Handbook.*

**Business and Community Foundation.** 1D, 1st Fl., Shahpur Jat New Delhi 110049, Delhi, India. Phone: 91 11 3253-6392 • URL: http://www.bcfindia.org • Promotes awareness and practice of good corporate citizenship as a business operation; promotes businesses to become an integral part of the societal process whereby people have access and control over resources to make informed choices and decisions towards a more humane, compassionate and just society in India.

*Business & Company ASAP.* Cengage Learning Inc., 20 Channel Center St. Boston, MA 02210. Phone: 800-487-8488 or (617)289-7700; Fax: (617)289-7844; Email: investors@cengage.com • URL: http://www.cengage.com • Provides business and company information including 200,000 company directory listings, the complete text of PR Newswire releases for the preceding 30 days, and articles from leading business and industry publications. Includes more than 1300 indexed and 800 full-text periodical titles and over 200,000 combined directory listings, including the Graham & Whiteside international company directories.

*Business and Economic Forecasting Unit Annual reports.* Monash University Business and Economic Forecasting Unit, Menzies Bldg., Rm. 756E, Department of Econometrics & Business Statistics, Clayton Campus Clayton, VIC 3800, Australia. Phone: 61 3 99055141; Fax: 61 3 99055474; Email: rob.hyndman@monash.edu • URL: http://www.buseco.monash.edu.au/units/forecasting.

*Business and Economic Forecasting Unit Working papers.* Monash University Business and Economic Forecasting Unit, Menzies Bldg., Rm. 756E, Department of Econometrics & Business Statistics, Clayton Campus Clayton, VIC 3800, Australia. Phone: 61 3 99055141; Fax: 61 3 99055474; Email: rob.hyndman@monash.edu • URL: http://www.buseco.monash.edu.au/units/forecasting.

*Business and Economics Research Directory.* Routledge Reference, 2 Park Sq. Milton Park, Abingdon Oxford OX14 4RN, United Kingdom. Phone: 44 20 70176000; Fax: 44 20 70176699; Email: book.orders@tandf.co.uk • URL: http://www.routledge.com/ • £495 Individuals hardback. Covers: Approximately 1,500 institutes concerned with business and economics research worldwide. Entries include: Organization name, address, phone, fax, e-mail address, names and titles of key personnel, foundation date, description of activities, publications with frequencies.

*Business and Finance Division Bulletin.* Special Libraries Association, 331 S Patrick St. Alexandria, VA 22314-3501. Phone: (703)647-4900; Fax: (703)647-4901 • URL: http://www.sla.org • Quarterly. $12.00 per year.

*Business and Financial News Media.* Larriston Communications, 23 W 95th St. New York, NY 10025-6785. Phone: (212)864-0150 • Annual. $99 book; $149 disclersion. Covers: over 300 daily newspapers with at least 50,000 in circulation and a business or finance correspondent; television stations and all-news radio stations in the largest 40 markets; periodicals of general or business and finance interest; syndicated business and financial columnists and newswriters; news and wire services; and free-lance writers whose specialties include business and financial topics. Entries include: Outlet name, address, phone, names and titles of contacts who cover business, finance, or economic news; news services used; circulation or audience figures.

*Business & Industry™.* Cengage Learning Inc., 20 Channel Center St. Boston, MA 02210. Phone: 800-487-8488 or (617)289-7700; Fax: (617)289-7844; Email: investors@cengage.com • URL: http://www.cengage.com • A multi-industry business database with a strong global focus on company, product and industry information.

*Business & Industry—Who's Who in Purchasing Issue.* Business Magazine Inc., 65 School St., Ste. B Carlisle, IA 50047-

0580. Phone: (515)989-2099; Fax: (515)989-2098 • Annual. $5 postpaid. Contains rosters for 19 purchasing manager associations in Minnesota, Iowa, Nebraska, North and South Dakota, and Wisconsin.

*Business and Information Directory.* Buena Vista Area Chamber of Commerce, 343 Highway 24 S Buena Vista, CO 81211-2021. Phone: (719)395-6612; Email: buenavista@vtinet.com • URL: http://www.buenavistacolorado.org • Annual. Covers business in Buena Vista, CO.

**Business and Institutional Furniture Manufacturer's Association.** 678 Front Ave. NW, Ste. 150 Grand Rapids, MI 49504-5368. Phone: (616)285-3963; Fax: (616)285-3765 • URL: http://www.bifma.org • Organized group of furniture manufacturers and suppliers addressing issues of common concern to the contract furnishings industry. Works to develop, expand, and promote work environments that enhance the productivity and comfort of customers.

*Business & Legal CD-ROMs in Print.* Mecklermedia Corp., 475 Park Ave. S, 4th Fl. New York, NY 10016. Phone: (212)389-2000; Fax: (866)880-1429 or (212)725-4640; Email: info@webmediabrands.com • URL: http://www.webmediabrands.com • Annual. $55. Covers: Approximately 600 business and legal CD-ROMs. Entries include: Title, producer name, address, phone.

*Business and Legal Forms for Authors and Self-publishers.* Allworth Press, 307 W 36th St., 11th Fl. New York, NY 10018. Phone: (212)643-6816; Fax: (212)643-6819 • URL: http://www.allworth.com • $24.99 Single issue paperback. Publication includes: Contact information for volunteer lawyers for the arts. Principal content of publication is instruction and use of business and legal forms for authors and self-publishers.

*Business & Legal Reports (BLR).* Business & Legal Resources, Inc., 141 Mill Rock Rd., E Old Saybrook, CT 06475. Phone: 800-454-0404 or (860)510-0100 or (800)727-5257; Fax: (860)510-7220 or (860)510-0100; Email: service@blr.com • URL: http://www.blr.com • A multimedia publisher that specializes in reporting government regulatory developments to business and providing practical compliance advice.

*Business & Management Practices™.* Cengage Learning Inc., 20 Channel Center St. Boston, MA 02210. Phone: 800-487-8488 or (617)289-7700; Fax: (617)289-7844; Email: investors@cengage.com • URL: http://www.cengage.com • Focuses on the processes, methods, and strategies of managing a business. Includes information on business planning, decision making, and management issues.

*Business and Professional Communication Quarterly (BPCQ).* Association for Business Communication, 181 Turner St. NW Blacksburg, VA 24061. Phone: (540)231-8460 or (540)231-1939; Email: abcoffice@businesscommunication.org • URL: http://www.businesscommunication.org • Quarterly. Included in membership; $497 Institutions online only; $541 Institutions print only; $552 Institutions print and online. Features articles about teaching and writing course outlines. Description of training programs, problems, solutions, etc. Includes *Journal of Business Communication.*

*Business and Professional Directory.* Chamber of Commerce of the Bellmores, 2700 Pettit Ave. Bellmore, NY 11710. Phone: (516)679-1875; Fax: (516)409-0544; Email: info@bellmorechamber.com • URL: http://bellmorechamber.com • Annual. Journal containing listings of all current members of the Chamber of Commerce of The Bellmores area, NY.

*Business and Professional Organizations Directory.* Nashville Area Chamber of Commerce, 211 Commerce St., Ste. 100 Nashville, TN 37201-1806. Phone: (615)743-3000; Fax: (615)743-3002 • URL: http://www.nashvillechamber.com • $25 Members; $35 Nonmembers. Covers 300 business and professional organizations in 10-county Nashville Metropolitan area.

**Business and Professional Women Australia.** Level 1, 613 Centerbury Rd. Melbourne, VIC 3127, Australia. Phone: 61 3 98954487; Fax: 61 3 98980249; Email: bpwaust@bpw.com.au • URL: http://www.bpw.com.au • Provides a forum for businesswomen to establish personal and professional contacts. Seeks to improve the status of working women.

*Business and Professional Women.* Canadian Federation of Business and Professional Women's Clubs, PO Box 62054 Orleans, ON, Canada K1C 7H8. • URL: http://www.bpwcanada.com • Quarterly. C$4 for nonmembers.

**Business and Professional Women International.** PO Box 2042 Fitzroy, VIC 3065, Australia. Email: member.services@bpw-international.org • URL: http://www.bpw-international.org • Promotes the status of women worldwide. Seeks to uphold higher business and professional standards.

**Business and Professional Women the Netherlands.** PO Box 11069 NL-1001 GB Amsterdam, Netherlands. Phone: 31 681544025; Email: secretaris@bpwnl.org • URL: http://www.bpw-europe.org/countries?id=235 • Promotes equal opportunities for women in business, trade, and economic life. Upholds high standards for women in business and service professions. Encourages women and girls to acquire education, occupational training and advanced education.

**Business and Professional Women - UK.** 74, Fairfield Rise, Essex Billericay CM12 9NU, United Kingdom. Phone: 44 1277 623867; Email: hq@bpwuk.co.uk • URL: http://www.bpwuk.co.uk • Serves as networking and lobbying organization. Aims to enable business and professional women to achieve in their careers. Encourages women to take an active part in public life and decision making at all levels. Evaluates chang-

ing work patterns and press for development in education and training to meet them. Strives to ensure that the same opportunities and facilities are available to both men and women. Undertakes studies of problems common to business and professional women in Europe and worldwide.

**Business and Professional Women's Foundation.** 1718 M St. NW, No. 148 Washington, DC 20036. Phone: (202)293-1100; Fax: (202)861-0298; Email: foundation@bpwfoundation.org • URL: http://bpwfoundation.org • Formerly National Federation of Business and Professional Women's Clubs.

*Business and Society: A Journal of Interdisciplinary Exploration.* International Association for Business and Society Research Committee. Pine Forge Press, 2455 Teller Rd. Thousand Oaks, CA 91320-2234. Phone: 800-818-7243 or (805)499-4224 or (805)499-9774; Fax: (805)499-0871 or (805)583-2665; Email: sales@pfp.sagepub.com • URL: http://www.sagepub.com/sociologybooks • Quarterly. $402.00 per year.

*Business & Society.* Pine Forge Press, 2455 Teller Rd. Thousand Oaks, CA 91320-2234. Phone: 800-818-7243 or (805)499-4224 or (805)499-9774; Fax: (805)499-0871 or (805)583-2665; Email: sales@pfp.sagepub.com • URL: http://www.sagepub.com/sociologybooks • Bimonthly. $790 Institutions combined (print & e-access); $869 Institutions backfile lease, combined plus backfile; $711 Institutions e-access; $2,051 Institutions backfile, e-access (content through 1998); $774 Institutions print only; $138 Individuals print only; $142 Institutions single print; $30 Individuals single print. Peer-reviewed journal on business and society. Sponsored by the International Association for Business and Society.

*Business and Society Review: Journal of the Center for Business Ethics at Bentley College.* Blackwell Publishing Inc., 350 Main St. Malden, MA 02148. Phone: 800-216-2522 or (781)388-8200; Fax: (781)388-8210; Email: journaladsusa@bos.blackwellpublishing.com • URL: http://www.blackwellpublishing.com • Quarterly. Institutions, $359.00 per year. Includes online edition.

*Business and Technical Communication: An Annotated Guide to Sources, Skills, and Strategies.* Cengage Learning Inc., 20 Channel Center St. Boston, MA 02210. Phone: 800-487-8488 or (617)289-7700; Fax: (617)289-7844; Email: investors@cengage.com • URL: http://www.cengage.com • 2007. eBook. Includes research sources, an annotated bibliography of how-to information, and detailed indexes to identify the most relevant items in aiding business and technical communication.

*Business and Technology in China.* Cengage Learning Inc., 20 Channel Center St. Boston, MA 02210. Phone: 800-487-8488 or (617)289-7700; Fax: (617)289-7844; Email: investors@cengage.com • URL: http://www.cengage.com • 2011. eBook. Explores the inner workings of China's business world, highlighting the country's attempts to develop the scientific and technological base for a greener economic model.

*Business and the Environment: A Resource Guide.* Island Press-Center For Resource Economics, 1718 Connecticut Ave. Nw Ste. 300 Washington, DC 20009-1148. Phone: 800-621-2736 or (202)232-7933; Fax: (202)234-1328; Email: info@islandpress.org • URL: http://www.islandpress.org • Publication includes: List of approximately 185 business and environmental educators working to intergrate environmental issues into management research, education, and practices. Entries include: Name, address, phone, affiliation, publications, courses taught, research activity, education, employment.

*Business Applications and Computational Intelligence.* Cengage Learning Inc., 20 Channel Center St. Boston, MA 02210. Phone: 800-487-8488 or (617)289-7700; Fax: (617)289-7844; Email: investors@cengage.com • URL: http://www.cengage.com • 2005. eBook. Addresses the need for a compact overview of the diversity of applications in a number of business disciplines, and consists of chapters written by leading international researchers. Chapters cover most fields of business, including: marketing, data mining, e-commerce, production and operations, finance, decision-making, and general management.

**Business Architects Association.** 727 S Dearborn St., Ste. 710 Chicago, IL 60605-3826. Email: info@businessarchitects.org • URL: http://www.businessarchitectsassociation.org • Aims to promote and advance the business architecture profession through education, research, and application of methodologies. Provides educational and networking opportunities for the continuing education of members. Offers professional training and certification programs.

*Business Asia.* The Economist Intelligence Unit, 111 W 57th St. New York, NY 10019. Phone: 800-938-4685 or (212)554-0600; Fax: (212)586-1191 or (212)586-1182; Email: newyork@eiu.com • URL: http://www.economist.com • Provides news on political, economic, and legal developments throughout the region, including business and e-business news; regulatory changes; distribution, human resources, market-entry strategies and regulatory development issues; economic and political risk analysis; company case studies; business intelligence.

*Business Atlanta—Hotel and Meeting Services Guide Issue.* Primedia Business, 6151 Powers Ferry Rd. NW Atlanta, GA 30339. Phone: (770)955-2500 or (770)995-2500; Fax: (770)618-0204 • URL: http://www.primediabusiness.com • Annual. $6.50 postpaid. Covers over 150 hotels in and around the metropolitan Atlanta area, and nearly 200 Atlanta companies providing convention services.

***Business Automation Reference Service: Office Equipment.*** Alltech Publishing Co., 212 Cooper Center, North Park Dr. and Browning Rd. Pennsauken, NJ 08109. • Monthly. $100.00 per year. Looseleaf service.

***Business Beijing.*** Asia Systems Media Corp., CBD Pingguo Garden, Ste. 1905, S Bldg. 5-B, No.32, Baiziwan Rd. Beijing 100 022, China. Phone: 86 10 51661575; Fax: 86 10 59002947; Email: china@cbw.com • URL: http://www.cbw.com • Monthly. Chinese business magazine.

***Business Brokers Directory.*** InfoGroup Inc., 5711 S 86th Cir. Omaha, NE 68127-4146. Phone: (402)593-4500 • URL: http://www.infogroup.com • Annual. Number of listings: 3,487. Entries include: Name, address, phone (including area code), size of advertisement, year first in "Yellow Pages," name of owner or manager, number of employees. Compiled from telephone company "Yellow Pages," nationwide.

***Business Browser Asia Pacific.*** OneSource Information Services Inc., 300 Baker Ave. Concord, MA 01742-2131. Phone: 800-554-5501 or (978)318-4300; Fax: (978)318-4690; Email: Support@onesource.com • URL: http://www.onesource.com • Provides integrated industry information on thousands of public and private companies from countries in Asia and the Pacific Rim region.

***BUSINESS.*** BUSINESS Datenbanken GmbH, Kurfuersten-Anlage 6 D-69115 Heidelberg, Germany. Phone: 6221 166061; Fax: 6221 21536 • Monthly. Database covers: about 35,000 manufacturers, importers and exporters, research establishments, chambers of commerce, trade promotion agencies, banks and investment companies offering or seeking business opportunities worldwide. Database includes: Name of company, address, type of opportunity or business, product and country codes.

***Business Capital Sources.*** International Wealth Success, Inc., PO Box 186 Merrick, NY 11566-0186. Phone: 800-323-0548 or (516)766-5850; Fax: (516)766-5919 or (516)766-5619; Email: admin@iwsmoney.com • URL: http://www.iwsmoney.com • Annual. $20 Individuals. Covers: About 1,500 banks, insurance and mortgage companies, commercial finance, leasing, and venture capital firms that lend money for business investment. Entries include: Company or institution name, address, phone.

***Business Cards Tomorrow.*** BCT International Inc., 3000 NE 30th Pl., 5th Fl. Fort Lauderdale, FL 33306-1957. Phone: 800-627-9998 or (954)563-1224; Fax: (954)565-0742; Email: info@bctonline.net • URL: http://www.bct-net.com.

***Business.*** Chamber of Commerce and Industry of Tirana, Kavaja St., No. 6 Tirana, Albania. Phone: 355 45 800932; Email: info@cci.al • URL: http://www.cci.al • Monthly. Contains information on business and economics.

***Business China.*** The Economist Intelligence Unit, 111 W 57th St. New York, NY 10019. Phone: 800-938-4685 or (212)554-0600; Fax: (212)586-1191 or (212)586-1182; Email: newyork@eiu.com • URL: http://www.economist.com • Provides news on political, economic, and legal developments throughout the region, including business and e-business news; regulatory changes; distribution, human resources, market-entry strategies and regulatory development issues; company case studies; business intelligence.

***Business Commercial Aviation Planning & Purchasing Handbook.*** Aviation Week Group, 1200 G St.NW, Ste. 922 Washington, DC 20005-3814. Phone: 800-525-5003; Fax: (712)755-7423 or (888)385-1428; Email: feedback@aviationweek.com • URL: http://www.aviationweek.com • Monthly. Directory of airframe and avionics manufacturers, and suppliers of related products and services.

***Business Communications Made Simple.*** Butterworth-Heinemann, 225 Wildwood Ave. Woburn, MA 01801. Phone: 800-366-2665 or (781)904-2500; Fax: (800)568-5136; Email: custserv.bh@elsevier.com • URL: http://www.bh.com • Date not set. Price on application.

***Business Communications Review.*** Key3Media Group, Inc., 5700 Wilshire Blvd., Ste. 325 Los Angeles, CA 90036. Phone: (323)954-3000; Fax: (323)954-3010; Email: fknight@bcr.com • URL: http://www.bcr.com • Monthly. $45.00 per year. Edited for communications managers in large end-user companies and institutions. Includes special feature issues on intranets and network management.

***Business Computer Report.*** Lawrence Oakly, 5 Savage Ct. Bluffton, SC 29910-4430. Phone: (843)705-5591; Fax: (843)705-5592; Email: up415@aol.com • Monthly. $99 Individuals. Reviews business applications software and hardware for IBM and compatible computers.

***Business Confidence Report.*** Economic Policy Research Center, Makerere University, Plot 51 Pool Rd. Kampala, Uganda. Phone: 256 41 541023; Fax: 256 41 541022; Email: ssewanyana@eprc.or.ug • URL: http://www.eprc.or.ug • Annual.

***The Business Connection.*** Garner Chamber of Commerce, 401 Circle Dr. Garner, NC 27529. Phone: (919)772-6440; Fax: (919)772-6443; Email: info@garnerchamber.com • URL: http://www.garnerchamber.com • Monthly. Contains member and community news, information on upcoming Chamber and Town of Garner events and meetings.

***Business Consultants Directory.*** InfoGroup Inc., 5711 S 86th Cir. Omaha, NE 68127-4146. Phone: (402)593-4500 • URL: http://www.infogroup.com • Annual. Number of listings:

12,750 (U.S. edition); 1,667 (Canadian edition). Entries include: Company or individual name, address, and phone (including area code), size of advertisement, year first in "Yellow Pages," name of owner or manager, number of employees. Compiled from telephone company "Yellow Pages," nationwide.

***Business Consumer's Advisor.*** Buyers Laboratory L.L.C., 20 Railroad Ave. Hackensack, NJ 07601. Phone: (201)488-0404; Fax: (201)488-0461; Email: info@bertl.com • URL: http://www.buyerslab.com • Description: Focuses on office equipment and supplies, offering purchasing advice and exploring methods of increasing office productivity through appropriate management of the equipment and its operators. Offers readers a chance to share their experiences, evaluate products and equipment, and gives results of Buyers Laboratory's testing.

***Business Consumers's Network.*** Buyers Laboratory L.L.C., 20 Railroad Ave. Hackensack, NJ 07601. Phone: (201)488-0404; Fax: (201)488-0461; Email: info@bertl.com • URL: http://www.buyerslab.com • Monthly. $795.00 per year. Looseleaf service. Tests office equipment and issues reports. Formerly *Buyers Laboratory Report on Office Products.*

***Business Contacts in Finland.*** Larenco Oy, Kalevankatu 44 A 27 SF-00180 Helsinki, Finland. Phone: 0 90648292; Fax: 0 648250 • Annual. Covers: Approximately 200 Finnish companies interested in foreign trade. Entries include: Name, address, phone, fax, list of products exported/imported, geographical area served.

***Business Council of Australia.*** GPO Box 1472 Melbourne, VIC 3001, Australia. Phone: 61 3 86642664; Fax: 61 3 86642666 • URL: http://www.bca.com.au • Businesses and trade organizations. Promotes establishment of a national economic climate conducive to business growth. Represents members' interests before government agencies, trade organizations, and the public.

***Business Council of Fairfield County—Fairfield County Business Directory.*** Business Council of Fairfield County, 1 Landmark Sq., Ste. 300 Stamford, CT 06901-2679. Phone: (203)359-3220; Fax: (203)967-8294; Email: info@businessfairfield.com • URL: http://www.businessfairfield.com • Covers: Approximately 2,100 non-retail companies and service firms in Fairfield County, Connecticut. Entries include: Company name, address, phone, fax, names & titles of key employees, website, company description, number of employees, annual sales, Standard Industrial Classification (SIC) code code(s).

***Business Council of Papua New Guinea.*** PO Box 404 Konedobu, Papua New Guinea. Phone: 675 3200700; Fax: 675 3200701; Email: executive@bcpng.org.pg • URL: http://www.bcpng.org.pg • Represents the interests of the private sector to the government and public institutions. Promotes the importance and role of economic growth, freedom and enterprise. Fosters dialogue and debate between the public sector, the private sector and academia.

***Business Council.*** 1901 Pennsylvania Ave., NW Ste. 701 Washington, DC 20006. Phone: (202)298-7650; Fax: (202)785-0296 • URL: http://www.thebusinesscouncil.org • Represents business executives. Aims to serve the national interest, with the primary objectives of developing a constructive point of view on matters of public policy affecting the business interests of the country and by providing a medium for a better understanding of government problems by business. Members are former and present chief executive officers of corporations.

***Business Credit.*** National Association of Credit Management, 8840 Columbia 100 Pkwy. Columbia, MD 21045-2158. Phone: (410)740-5560; Fax: (410)740-5574; Email: nacm_national@nacm.org • URL: http://www.nacm.org • 9/year. $54 U.S.; $60 Canada; $65 Other countries. Formerly *Credit and Financial Management.* Covers business and trade credit as well as risk management.

***Business Crimes Bulletin.*** ALM Media Properties LLC, 120 Broadway, 5th Fl. New York, NY 10271-1100. Phone: (212)457-9400; Fax: (646)417-7705; Email: customercare@alm.com • URL: http://www.alm.com • Monthly. $510 per year. Provides news of the "multifaceted world of financial and white collar crime." Covers such items as foreign corrupt practices, mail fraud, money laundering, tax fraud, securities law violations, environmental crime, and antitrust violations. Includes developments in sentencing guidelines for white collar perpetrators. (A Law Journal Newsletter, formerly published by Leader Publications).

***Business Data Communications and Networking: A Research Perspective.*** Cengage Learning Inc., 20 Channel Center St. Boston, MA 02210. Phone: 800-487-8488 or (617)289-7700; Fax: (617)289-7844; Email: investors@cengage.com • URL: http://www.cengage.com.

***Business Database Finder.*** The Information Advisor, 3415 Dent Pl. NW Washington, DC 20007-2715. • Annual. $99. Covers: Business databases and online hosts. Database includes: Comparative charts/tables showing features and costs of databases. Entries include: Name of database, description of product/service.

***Business Day.*** BDFM Publishers Ltd., 4 Biermann Ave., Rosebank Johannesburg 2196, South Africa. • URL: http://www.bmie.co.za/ • Daily. R 1,700 Individuals. Business newspaper.

***Business Development News.*** World Teleport Association, 250 Park Ave., 7th Fl. New York, NY 10177. Phone: (212)825-

0218; Fax: (212)825-0075; Email: wta@worldteleport.org • URL: http://www.worldteleport.org • Bimonthly. Contains information on business opportunities in the teleport industry.

***Business Digest of Central Massachusetts.*** Business Digest of Central Massachusetts, 50 Franklin St. Worcester, MA 01608. • Bimonthly. $17 Individuals; $3 Single issue.

***Business Digest of Lehigh Valley.*** Business Digest of Lehigh Valley, 2449 Golf Rd. Philadelphia, PA 19131. Phone: (215)477-8620; Fax: (215)477-7054 • Monthly. Small business magazine (tabloid).

***Business Digest of Lower Fairfield County.*** Newfield Communications Inc., 495 Westport Ave. Norwalk, CT 06851. Phone: (203)661-5050 • Monthly. Regional business magazine.

***Business Directory for Americans Abroad.*** TeleDiplomacy Inc., PO Box 7615 Berkeley, CA 94707-0615. Email: info@stapleton-gray.com • URL: http://www.stapleton-gray.com • Database covers: Businesses and immigration, import, and export issues of interest to U.S. Citizens travelling abroad. Entries include: Contact information.

***Business Directory for Diplomats.*** TeleDiplomacy Inc., PO Box 7615 Berkeley, CA 94707-0615. Email: info@stapleton-gray.com • URL: http://www.stapleton-gray.com • Database covers: Businesses and immigration, import, and export issues of interest to diplomats in the Washington, DC, area. Entries include: Contact information.

***Business Directory for Educators.*** TeleDiplomacy Inc., PO Box 7615 Berkeley, CA 94707-0615. Email: info@stapleton-gray.com • URL: http://www.stapleton-gray.com • Database covers: Items of interest to educators on business trips abroad. Entries include: Contact information.

***Business Directory for Foreign Visitors.*** TeleDiplomacy Inc., PO Box 7615 Berkeley, CA 94707-0615. Email: info@stapleton-gray.com • URL: http://www.stapleton-gray.com • Database covers: Businesses and immigration, import, and export issues of interest to visitors to the United States. Entries include: Contact information.

***Business Directory of Hong Kong.*** Current Publications Ltd., 1503 Enterprise Bldg., 228-238 Queen's Rd. Central Hong Kong, China. Phone: 22 5434702; Fax: 22 8158396 • Annual. $180 surface mail postpaid; $200 airmail postpaid. Covers over 12,300 firms in Hong Kong, including manufacturers, exporters, importers, banks and financial firms, construction, transportation, service companies, professional firms and organizations, foreign government commissions and consulates in Hong Kong, and trade promotion organizations.

***Business Directory of Macedonia.*** Balkanika Publishing and Marketing Ltd., Blvd. Kuzman Josifovski Pitu No. 17, Lok. 16 1000 Skopje, Macedonia. Phone: 389 22462607; Fax: 389 22462607; Email: info@balkanika-publishing.com.uk • URL: http://www.balkanika-publishing.com.mk • Covers: Institutions and companies in the Republic of Macedonia. Entries include: Institution/company name, address, phone, fax, description, e-mail, and website.

***Business Directory of South India: Andhra Pradesh, Karnataka, Kerala, Tamil Nadu.*** NIIR Project Consultancy Services, 106 - E, Kamla Nagar New Delhi 110007, India. Phone: 91 11 23843955; Fax: 91 11 23841561; Email: npcs.india@gmail.com • URL: http://www.niir.org • Rs 3,933 Individuals CD-ROM; $200 Individuals CD-ROM. Covers: 31,000 South India companies. Entries include: Contact person, profile, address, city, pin. state, phone, fax, e-mail (wherever available) and website (wherever available).

***Business Directory of the Parry Sound Area.*** Parry Sound Area Chamber of Commerce, 70 Church St. Parry Sound, ON, Canada P2A 1Y9. Phone: 800-461-4261 or (705)746-4213; Email: info@parrysoundchamber.ca • URL: http://www.parrysoundchamber.ca • Covers businesses in Parry Sound, Ontario, Canada. Entries include contact details.

***Business Directory of United Kingdom.*** INFOT Inc., PO Box 2052 Rockville, MD 20847. Phone: 866-838-2619 • URL: http://www.infotusa.com • $51 CD-ROM. Covers: 67,281 companies from United Kingdom, importers, and exporters. Entries include: Email and website addresses, telephone and fax number, and business titles and descriptions.

***Business Documents: For Professional Buyers of Forms, Labels and Electronic Systems.*** Penton, 9800 Metcalf Ave. Overland Park, KS 66212. Phone: 866-748-4926 or (913)341-1300; Fax: (913)967-1905 or (913)967-1898; Email: corporatecustomerservice@penton.com • URL: http://www.penton.com • Quarterly. $24 Individuals.

***Business Dynamics in Information Technology.*** Cengage Learning Inc., 20 Channel Center St. Boston, MA 02210. Phone: 800-487-8488 or (617)289-7700; Fax: (617)289-7844; Email: investors@cengage.com • URL: http://www.cengage.com • 2007. eBook. Presents business-technology alignment processes, business-technology interaction processes, and business-technology decision processes, serving the purpose of helping the reader study information technology from a dynamic, rather than a static, perspective.

***Business Eastern Europe.*** The Economist Intelligence Unit, 111 W 57th St. New York, NY 10019. Phone: 800-938-4685 or (212)554-0600; Fax: (212)586-1191 or (212)586-1182; Email: newyork@eiu.com • URL: http://www.economist.com • Provides news on political, economic, and legal developments throughout the region, including business and e-business news; regulatory changes; distribution, human resources, market-entry strategies and regulatory development issues; economic and political risk analysis; company case studies; business intelligence.

***Business Eastern Europe***. Treasury & Risk, 475 Park Ave. S, 6th Fl. New York, NY 10016-6901. Phone: (212)557-7480; Fax: (212)557-7654 • URL: http://www.treasuryandrisk.com • Quarterly. $1,530 Individuals. Professional magazine covering business information in Eastern Europe.

***Business, Economics and Theory Collection***. Cengage Learning Inc., 20 Channel Center St. Boston, MA 02210. Phone: 800-487-8488 or (617)289-7700; Fax: (617)289-7844; Email: investors@cengage.com • URL: http://www.cengage.com • Contains the full-text of more than 7 million articles from 450 academic journals and magazines on all aspects of business and economics. Also offers feeds of videos from Forbes.com that contain business news coverage and interviews with CEOs and entrepreneurs.

***Business Economics: Designed to Serve the Needs of People Who Use Economics in Their Work***. National Association for Business Economics, 1920 L St. NW, Ste. 300 Washington, DC 20036. Phone: (202)463-6223; Fax: (202)463-6239; Email: nabe@nabe.com • URL: http://www.nabe.com • Quarterly. Quarterly. $85.00 per year. Features articles on applied economics.

***Business Economics—Membership Directory Issue***. National Association for Business Economics, 1920 L St. NW, Ste. 300 Washington, DC 20036. Phone: (202)463-6223; Fax: (202)463-6239; Email: nabe@nabe.com • URL: http://www.nabe.com • Annual. $125 electronic with membership; $150 printed. List of about 3,000 association members, including students.

***Business Edge***. Business Edge, Inc., 1260, 112 4th Ave. SW Calgary, AB, Canada T2P 0H3. Phone: (403)769-9359; Fax: (403)769-1810; Email: info@businessedge.ca • URL: http://www.businessedge.ca/news.cfm • Semimonthly. $96 Individuals; $154 Two years; $48 Canada; $72 Canada 2 years. Magazine covering Canada's local business scenes.

***Business Education Forum***. National Business Education Association, 1914 Association Dr. Reston, VA 20191-1596. Phone: (703)860-8300; Fax: (703)620-4483; Email: nbea@nbea.org • URL: http://www.nbea.org • Four times a year. Libraries, $70.00 per year. Includes *Yearbook* and *Keying In*, a newsletter.

***Business Education Forum—Professional Leadership Roster Issue***. National Business Education Association, 1914 Association Dr. Reston, VA 20191-1596. Phone: (703)860-8300; Fax: (703)620-4483; Email: nbea@nbea.org • URL: http://www.nbea.org • Quarterly. Publication includes: List of key personnel in business education, including officers of national, regional, and state associations and state and local supervisory personnel in business education. Entries include: Institution or association name, names of officers and board members, addresses, phone, and Internet address.

***Business Education Index***. Delta Pi Epsilon Inc., 1200 John Barrow Rd., Ste. 408 Little Rock, AR 72214. Phone: (501)219-1866; Email: dpe@ipa.net • URL: http://www.dpe.org • Annual. $25. Publication includes: List of selected periodicals and yearbooks which have published articles on business education in the previous year. Entries include: Publication acronym, full name, editor, address. Principal content of publication is an index of articles and authors.

**Business Educators Australasia**. Carringbush Business Ctre., 134-136 Cambridge St., Ste. 201, Level 2 Collingwood, VIC 3066, Australia. Phone: 61 3 94199622; Fax: 61 3 94191205 • URL: http://www.bea.asn.au • Promotes and represents business educators in Australasia.

**Business Ethics Forum**. 905 Main St. Houston, TX 77002-6408. Email: info@businessethicsforum.net • URL: http://businessethicsforum.net • Aims to develop partnerships among peer executives. Fosters philosophically sound and actionable frameworks for the ethical and effective management of organizations. Facilitates information exchange regarding research and activities in business ethics.

***Business Ethics Quarterly***. Philosophy Documentation Center, PO Box 7147 Charlottesville, VA 22906-7147. Phone: 800-444-2419 or (434)220-3300; Fax: (434)220-3301; Email: order@pdcnet.org • URL: http://www.pdcnet.org • Quarterly. $185 Institutions; $470 Institutions online; $590 Institutions print and online. Peer-reviewed scholarly journal covering business ethics studies.

***Business Ethics Survey***. Paul & Co., 814 N. Franklin St. Chicago, IL 60610. Phone: (312)337-0747; Fax: (312)337-5985; Email: frontdesk@ipgbook.com • URL: http://www.ipgbook.com • Annual. $99.95. Published by the Society for Human Resource Management (www.shrm.org). Provides benchmarks, with trends in business ethics data since 1997.

***Business Ethics: The Magazine of Corporate Responsibility***. Business Ethics, 55 W 39th St., Ste. 800 New York, NY 10018. Phone: (646)688-3620; Fax: (212)202-3561 • URL: http://www.business-ethics.com • Quarterly. Business newsletter.

***Business Europe: The Essential Guide to Who's Who and What's What in Europe***. Macmillan Publishers Ltd., The Macmillan Bldg., 4 Crinan St. London N1 9XW, United Kingdom. Phone: 44 020 7833 4000 or 44 20 78434000; Fax: 44 020 7843 4640 or 44 20 78434640 • URL: http://www.macmillan.co.uk • $14.99. Covers: Businesses in Europe, encompassing service industries, wholesale and retail trades, professions, and trade unions. Entries include: Name, address, phone.

***The Business Examiner***. Business Examiner Newspaper Group, PO Box 1575 Tacoma, WA 98401-1575. Phone: 800-540-8322 or (253)404-0891; Fax: (253)404-0892; Email: admin@businessexaminer.com • URL: http://www.businessexaminer.com • Biweekly. $50 Individuals; $82 Two years. Local business newspaper.

***Business Executive***. Advantage Canada Inc., 466 Speers Rd., Ste. 220 Oakville, ON, Canada L6K 3W9. Phone: (905)845-8300; Fax: (905)845-9086 • Monthly. $28 Canada plus GST; $44 Individuals; $44 Other countries. Business magazine for southern and southwestern Ontario, Canada.

***Business Facilities: The Location Advisor***. Group C Media Inc., 44 Apple St., Ste. 3 Tinton Falls, NJ 07724. Phone: 800-524-0337 or (732)842-7433; Fax: (732)758-6634; Email: lconnor@groupc.com • URL: http://www.facilitycity.com • Monthly. Free to qualified personnel; others, $30.00 per year. Facility planning and site selection.

***Business Finance***. Intertec Publishing, 5 Penn Plz., 13th Fl. New York, NY 10001-1810. Phone: 800-795-5445 or (212)613-9700 or (212)204-4200; Fax: (212)613-9749 or (212)206-3622; Email: bethany.weaver@penton.com • URL: http://www.penton.com • Quarterly. $39 Individuals; $59 Canada; $79 Other countries. Magazine reporting on key financial issues, strategies, trends and technologies, significant to senior finance executives.

***Business Finance***. Penton, 1166 Avenue of the Americas New York, NY 10036. Phone: (212)204-4200; Email: information@penton.com • URL: http://www.penton.com • Monthly. $59.00 per year. Covers trends in finance, technology, and economics for corporate financial executives.

***Business Finland***. Helsinki Media, Blue Book, Hoylaamotie 1 D FIN-00040 Helsinki, Finland. Phone: 358 9 1201 or 0 1205971; Fax: 358 9 1205599 or 0 1205999; Email: info@bluebook.fi • URL: http://www.sanoma.com/contact-us/sanoma-media-finland • Annual. Publication includes: Lists of 250 major exporters and the 50 largest business groups in Finland. Principal content of publication is information on Finnish business and economic issues. Entries include: Company or organization name, address, phone, name and title of contact, number of employees, financial data, description, Standard Industrial Classification (SIC) code.

***Business First of Buffalo: Western New York's Business Newspaper***. American City Business Journals, Inc., 120 W Morehead St. Charlotte, NC 28202. Phone: (704)973-1000; Fax: (704)973-1001; Email: americancity@bizjournals.com • URL: http://www.acbj.com • Weekly. $100 Individuals; $170 Two years; $216 Individuals 160 issues. Business Newspaper.

***Business Focus***. Bunbury Chamber of Commerce and Industries, 15 Stirling St. Bunbury, WA 6230, Australia. Phone: 61 97912292; Fax: 61 97916646; Email: ceo@bcci.asn.au • URL: http://www.bunburycci.com.au • Contains articles and reports about the Bunbury Chamber of Commerce and Industries organization's works and accomplishments.

**Business for Social Responsibility**. 88 Kearny St., 12th Fl. San Francisco, CA 94108. Phone: (415)984-3200; Fax: (415)984-3201; Email: connect@bsr.org • URL: http://www.bsr.org • Large, small, and medium-sized businesses. Promotes responsible business behavior and serves as a resource to companies striving to make ethical business decisions.

***Business Forms & Systems (Wholesale) Directory***. InfoGroup Inc., 5711 S 86th Cir. Omaha, NE 68127-4146. Phone: (402)593-4500 • URL: http://www.infogroup.com • Annual. Number of listings: 7,565. Entries include: Company name, address, phone (including area code), size of advertisement, year first in "Yellow Pages," name of owner or manager, number of employees. Compiled from telephone company "Yellow Pages," nationwide.

***Business Forms, Labels and Systems***. North American Publishing Co., 1500 Spring Garden St., Ste. 1200 Philadelphia, PA 19130-4069. Phone: (215)238-5300; Email: customerservice@napco.com • URL: http://www.napco.com • Semimonthly. $95.00 per year. Formerly *Business Forms and Systems*.

***Business Forms, Labels & Systems—Who's Who of Manufacturers and Suppliers***. North American Publishing Co., 1500 Spring Garden St., Ste. 1200 Philadelphia, PA 19130-4069. Phone: (215)238-5300; Email: customerservice@napco.com • URL: http://www.napco.com • Annual. Covers: More than 800 manufacturers of business forms, labels, and related products, and 500 suppliers of equipment and paper used to manufacture business forms. Entries include: Company name, address, phone, fax, toll-free number, company profile.

**Business Forms Management Association**. 1147 Fleetwood Ave. Madison, WI 53716-1417. Phone: 888-367-3078 or (402)216-0479; Fax: (937)885-5320; Email: bfma@bfma.org • URL: http://www.bfma.org • Persons engaged in forms management work, forms procedures analysis, forms design, or in education in this field; customer service firms selling, manufacturing, or servicing forms and supplies. Provides leadership and education to businesses in areas where the forms profession has demonstrated its special competence; promotes a broader function as a component of effective management; encourages, establishes, and maintains high standards of professional education, competence, and performance; provides a means for the sharing of information through study, programs, and research.

***Business Foundation Book: General Trade Index & Business Guide—Poland***. Business Foundation Company Ltd., Krucza 38-42 PL-00 512 Warsaw, Poland. Phone: 22 21 99 93; Fax: 22 21 97 61 • Annual. $90 plus $40.00 shipping. Covers: Approximately 3,500 Polish businesses and firms seeking foreign cooperation and trade with the West. Database includes: General information on Polish industry and trade, including the Polish economy, business and labor law, finance, taxation, import/export regulations, and laws pertaining to foreign investment and business. Entries include: Abbreviated trade names; firm name, address, phone, fax, telex; year established; name and title of contact and languages spoken; line of business; proposed fields of cooperation or goods sought; number of employees; financial data.

***Business Franchise Guide***. Wolters Kluwer Law & Business CCH, 2700 Lake Cook Rd. Riverwoods, IL 60015. Phone: 888-224-7377 or (847)267-7000; Email: cust_serv@cch.com • URL: http://www.cchgroup.com • Contains extensive legal and regulatory information related to all aspects of business franchising.

***Business Futures***. University of Stellenbosch Institute for Futures Research, PO Box 2010 Bellville 7535, South Africa. Phone: 27 21 9184144; Fax: 27 21 9184146; Email: andre@ifr.sun.ac.za • URL: http://www.ifr.sun.ac.za/Home • Annual.

***Business Gazette***. Post-Newsweek Media Inc., 9030 Comprint Ct. Gaithersburg, MD 20877. Phone: (301)948-3120 • URL: http://www.gazette.net • Weekly (Fri.). Community business newspaper.

***Business Guide Central—East Europe***. Overseas-Post-Organisation, Dr. Harnisch Verlags GmbH, Blumenstrabe 15 D-90402 Nuremberg, Germany. Phone: 49 911 20180; Fax: 49 911 2018100; Email: info@harnisch.com • URL: http://www.harnisch.com • Annual. $30. Publication includes: Businesses and organizations in the Baltic States, Bulgaria, Czech Republic, Hungary, Poland, Romania, Slovakia, Belarus, Moldova, Russia, and Ukraine. Entries include: Name, address, phone, telex. Principal content of publication is general business information for each country or region.

***Business guide***. National Institutes of Health Office of Administration Office of Acquisition Management and Policy, 6100 Executive Blvd., Rm. 6D01 Bethesda, MD 20892-7540. Phone: (301)496-4422; Fax: (301)402-2425; Email: colet@od.nih.gov • URL: http://oamp.od.nih.gov.

***Business Guide to Trinidad & Tobago***. American Chamber of Commerce of Trinidad and Tobago, 62 Maraval Rd., Newtown Port of Spain, Trinidad and Tobago. Phone: (868)622-0340 or (868)622-4466; Fax: (868)628-9428 • URL: http://www.amchamtt.com • Biennial. $50. Contains market entry information for foreign companies doing business in Trinidad and Tobago.

***Business Hellas***. Trade Publishing Resources, PO Box 1283 Randburg 2175, South Africa. Phone: 27 11 8862636; Fax: 27 11 8865424; Email: info@tradepublishing.co.za • URL: http://www.africaexports.co.za • Provides information on Greek companies covering all sectors of business and economy, manufacturing, and trade services.

***Business Herald***. K.G.P. Nayar, Herald House, Box 133 Trivandrum 695 001, India. • Monthly. $32.50; $10 Other countries. Journal on business management.

**Business-Higher Education Forum**. 2025 M St. NW, Ste. 800 Washington, DC 20036-2422. Phone: (202)367-1189; Fax: (202)367-2269; Email: info@bhef.com • URL: http://www.bhef.com • Board chairmen and chief executive officers of Fortune 500 corporations; presidents and chancellors of universities and colleges. Addresses issues of interest to American business and higher education institutions such as: tax incentives for university research; worker training and retraining; new links between industry and academia; innovative methods of corporate support for higher education. Seeks to expand public awareness of the concerns of business and academic leaders and to influence policymaking affecting those concerns; to enhance relationships between corporate America and institutions of higher learning. Provides interchange between the business and academic communities. Has recently completed several studies on competitiveness; believes that improving the ability of American industry and workers to compete is essential to all other economic and societal goals. Organizes special task forces for in-depth studies on special issues. Disseminates reports and recommendations to policymakers in the public and private sector.

***Business History Conference—Membership Directory***. Business History Conference, c/o Hagley Museum and Library, PO Box 3630 Wilmington, DE 19807-0630. Phone: (302)658-2400; Fax: (302)655-3188 • URL: http://www.thebhc.org • Quadrennial. $25. Lists 500 Business History Conference members.

**Business History Conference**. c/o Hagley Museum and Library, PO Box 3630 Wilmington, DE 19807-0630. Phone: (302)658-2400; Fax: (302)655-3188 • URL: http://www.thebhc.org • Business historians and economic historians (most are from the academic community but a number of business firms are represented through their corporate historians). Brings together persons who are active historians of American and international business, with interests ranging from writing biographies of businessmen and histories of firms to the application of economic theory to analysis of the evolution of American business.

**Business History**. Frank Cass Publishers, 5804 N.E. Hassalo St. Portland, OR 97213-3644. Phone: 800-944-6190; Fax: (503)280-8832; Email: cass@isbs.com • URL: http://www.frankcass.com • Quarterly. Institutions, $382.00 per year. Includes print and online editions.

**Business History Review**. Harvard Business School, Soldiers Field Rd. Boston, MA 02163. Phone: (617)495-1003 or (617)495-6128; Email: admissions@hbs.edu • URL: http://www.hbs.edu • Quarterly. $70 Individuals; $187 Institutions; $40 Students; $40 Members. A scholarly journal that seeks to publish articles with rigorous primary research that addresses major topics of debate, offers comparative perspectives, and contributes to the broadening of the subject.

**Business History Studies**. KK Roy Ltd., 55 Gariahat Rd. Calcutta 700 019, India. • Quarterly. $460; $114 Other countries. Journal on business and economics.

**Business I**. ITHAKA JSTOR, the Journal Storage Project, 301 E Liberty, Ste. 400 Ann Arbor, MI 48104-2262. Phone: 888-388-3574 or (734)887-7001; Email: support@jstor.org • URL: http://www.ithaka.org • Contains more than 2 million pages from 47 titles in the fields of economics and finance, accounting, labor relations, marketing, management, operations research, and risk assessment.

**Business II**. ITHAKA JSTOR, the Journal Storage Project, 301 E Liberty, Ste. 400 Ann Arbor, MI 48104-2262. Phone: 888-388-3574 or (734)887-7001; Email: support@jstor.org • URL: http://www.ithaka.org • Contains more than 1.3 million pages from 60 titles in the fields of international business as well as the intersections between economics and law, policy, and psychology.

**Business Immigration Law: Strategies for Employing Foreign Nationals**. ALM Media Properties LLC, 120 Broadway, 5th Fl. New York, NY 10271-1100. Phone: (212)457-9400; Fax: (646)417-7705; Email: customercare@alm.com • URL: http://www.alm.com • $540 per year. Provides step-by-step employment procedures relating to the law and regulations of the State Department, the Immigration and Naturalization Service, specific visa programs, and the Labor Department. Includes guidelines and samples of forms. (Law Journal Press).

**Business in Calgary**. Business in Calgary, 101 - 6th Ave. SW Calgary, AB, Canada T2P 3P4. Phone: 800-465-0322 or (403)264-3270; Fax: (403)264-3276; Email: info@businessincalgary.com • URL: http://www.businessincalgary.com • Bimonthly. $45 Individuals; $85 Other countries; $31.50 Canada. Trade magazine for monument and bronze makers, and the managers of cemeteries, crematoriums, and mausoleums.

**Business in Russia**. Business in Russia, B Polyanka 13, str. 1 109180 Moscow, Russia. Phone: 7 0952380711 • Monthly. $197. Journal covering business and economics.

**Business in the Arab World**. National United States-Arab Chamber of Commerce, 1023 15th St. NW, Ste. 400 Washington, DC 20005. Phone: (202)289-5920; Fax: (202)289-5938; Email: info@nusacc.org • URL: http://www.nusacc.org • $2 /profile; $1 /profile (7 or more). Contains series of business profiles with regulations, procedures, and contacts for each Arab country.

**Business in the Arts Award Brochures**. Business Committee for the Arts, 29-27 Queens Plz. N, 4th Fl. Long Island City, NY 11101. Phone: (718)482-9900; Fax: (718)482-9911; Email: epeck@bcainc.org • URL: http://www.bcainc.org • $4 plus shipping and handling. Presents highlights of theatre-support programs developed by businesses receiving the national Business in the Arts Awards.

**Business Incubators of North America**. National Business Incubation Association, 340 W State St., Unit 25 Athens, OH 45701-1565. Phone: (740)593-4331; Fax: (740)593-1996; Email: info@nbia.org • URL: http://www.nbia.org • Biennial. $10 Members; $395 Nonmembers. Covers: approximately 800 facilities that house small businesses in the beginning stage of development; coverage includes Canada and Mexico. Entries include: Facility name, address, phone, fax, e-mail; name and title of contact; type of incubator; year opened; sponsorship; square footage; number of clients; incubator sponsor information.

**Business India**. Business India Group of Publications, Wadia Bldg., 17/19 Dalal St. Mumbai 400 001, India. Phone: 91 0222674161 • Biweekly. Periodical covering business news.

**Business India Intelligence**. The Economist Intelligence Unit, 111 W 57th St. New York, NY 10019. Phone: 800-938-4685 or (212)554-0600; Fax: (212)586-1191 or (212)586-1182; Email: newyork@eiu.com • URL: http://www.economist.com • Provides news on political, economic, and legal developments throughout the region, including business and e-business news; regulatory changes; distribution, human resources, market-entry strategies and regulatory development issues; economic and political risk analysis; company case studies; business intelligence.

**Business-Industry Political Action Committee**. 888 16th St. NW, Ste. 305 Washington, DC 20006-4103. Phone: (202)833-1880; Fax: (202)833-2338; Email: info@bipac.org • URL: http://www.bipac.org • Works as independent, bipartisan organization that works to elect pro-business candidates to Congress; has group's Business Institute for Political Analysis that carries out extensive programs of political analysis, research, and communication on campaigns and elections, and fosters business participation in the political process.

**Business Industry Promotion Association of Pakistan**. 455 Shadman 1 Lahore, Pakistan. Phone: 92 42 7581288; Fax: 92 42 7581288; Email: bipap@brain.net.pk • Seeks to integrate the activities of professionals in the fields of trade, industry, manufacturing, exporting, engineering, investment, finance and general services. Facilitates cooperation and networking among business professionals.

**Business Information Alert: Sources, Strategies and Signposts for Information Professionals**. Alert Publications Inc., 47 W Division St., No. 385 Chicago, IL 60610-5277. Phone: (312)337-1362; Fax: (312)337-1388; Email: info@alertpub.com • URL: http://www.alertpub.com • 10 times per year. Libraries, $162.00 per year. Newsletter for business librarians and information specialists.

**Business Information Center Newsletter**. University of Richmond Business Information Center, Boatwright Memorial Library, 1st Fl., 28 Westhampton Way Richmond, VA 23173. Phone: (804)287-6400; Email: lmaxwell@richmond.edu • URL: http://is.richmond.edu/hardware-software/campus/business-info-center.html.

**Business Information Desk Reference: Where to Find Answers to Business Questions**. Macmillan Creative Services, 300 Pk. Ave. S, 9th Fl. New York, NY 10010-5354. Fax: (212)605-3068 • $20 paper; $90 library cloth binders. Covers: Approximately 1,000 print materials, online databases, federal agencies, private organizations and other information sources covering 24 business areas.

**Business Information Handbook**. David Mort. Cengage Learning Inc., 20 Channel Center St. Boston, MA 02210. Phone: 800-487-8488 or (617)289-7700; Fax: (617)289-7844; Email: investors@cengage.com • URL: http://www.cengage.com • 2005. Published by K.G. Saur. Serves as a general guide to the world of business information. Inquire as to price and availability.

**The Business Information Report**. Dun & Bradstreet Inc., 103 JFK Pkwy. Short Hills, NJ 07078. Phone: 800-526-0651 or (973)921-5500 or (973)921-5000; Fax: (866)560-7035 or (512)794-7670; Email: info@dnb.com • URL: http://www.dnb.com • Continuous. Database covers: More than 9 million public and private U.S. Companies. Database includes: Company name, address, history, financial and sales data, number of employees, selling terms, products/services.

**Business Information Sources**. Hoover's Inc., 5800 Airport Blvd. Austin, TX 78752-4204. Phone: 866-443-3939 or (512)374-4500 or (866)281-5969; Fax: (512)374-4501; Email: salesteam@hoovers.com • URL: http://www.hoovers.com • $39.95. Covers: Sources of business information, including books, periodicals, CD-ROMs, and online databases.

**Business Information Systems: Concepts, Methodologies, Tools and Applications**. Cengage Learning Inc., 20 Channel Center St. Boston, MA 02210. Phone: 800-487-8488 or (617)289-7700; Fax: (617)289-7844; Email: investors@cengage.com • URL: http://www.cengage.com • 2011. eBook. Offers a complete view of current business information systems within organizations and the advancements that technology has provided to the business community, including how technological advancements have revolutionized financial transactions, management infrastructure, and knowledge workers.

**Business Insider**. Cerritos Chamber of Commerce, 13259 E South St. Cerritos, CA 90703. Phone: (562)467-0800; Fax: (562)467-0840; Email: chamber@cerritos.org • URL: http://www.cerritos.org • Monthly.

**Business Insights: Essentials (BI:E)**. Cengage Learning Inc., 20 Channel Center St. Boston, MA 02210. Phone: 800-487-8488 or (617)289-7700; Fax: (617)289-7844; Email: investors@cengage.com • URL: http://www.cengage.com • Formerly Business & Company Resource Center. Contact for pricing. Contains in-depth, searchable information on U.S. and International businesses, industries, and products.

**Business Insights**. ProQuest LLC, 2250 Perimeter Park Dr., Ste. 300 Morrisville, NC 27560. Phone: 800-334-2564 or (919)804-6400; Fax: (919)804-6410; Email: contact@dialog.com • URL: http://www.dialog.com • Dtabase of market research reports based on primary research, data houses, consultancy and author research, and trade/industry associations, from Reuters Business Insight. The reports contain data on e-commerce, consumer goods, energy, financial services, healthcare, technology, and human resources. Users can analyze consumer and business-to-business purchasing attitudes in e-commerce, find advice on individual issues in niche healthcare markets and the technological revolution, and read interviews with oil, gas, electricity, and renewable energy industry executives, among other things.

**Business Insurance**. Crain Communications Inc., 1155 Gratiot Ave. Detroit, MI 48207-2732. Phone: (313)446-6000; Email: info@crain.com • URL: http://www.crain.com • Weekly. $799 Individuals data + print and digital; $149 Individuals print & digital; $125 Individuals digital edition. Contains the complete text of *Business Insurance*, a newspaper providing information on the purchase and administration of corporate insurance and self-insurance programs, including property and liability insurance, reinsurance, and employee benefit and risk management programs.

**Business Insurance-Directory of HMOs, POSs and PPOs**. Crain Communications Inc., 711 3rd Ave. New York, NY 10017. Phone: (212)210-0100; Email: info@crain.com • URL: http://www.crain.com • Annual. $149 per year. Provides detailed information on more than 600 managed care providers in the U. S., chiefly health maintenance organizations (HMOs) and preferred provider organizations (PPOs).

**Business Insurance: News Magazine for Corporate Risk, Employee Benefit and Financial Executives**. Crain Communications Inc., 711 3rd Ave. New York, NY 10017. Phone: (212)210-0100; Email: info@crain.com • URL: http://www.crain.com • Weekly. $95.00 per year. Covers a wide variety of business insurance topics, including risk management, employee benefits, workers compensation, marine insurance, and casualty insurance.

**Business InsuranceQuote.com**. Tornado Solutions, PO Box 965 Spanish Fork, UT 84660. • URL: http://www.insideinsurance.com • Offers helpful articles on topics such as adjuster claims, insurance processing, medical billing, processing software, life insurance school, and automobile fraud.

**Business, Investor & Government Relations Directory**. PIMS UK Ltd., PIMS House, Mildmay Ave. London N1 4RS, United Kingdom. Phone: 44 20 7354 7000; Fax: 44 20 7354 7053; Email: enquiries@pims.co.uk • URL: http://www.pims.co.uk • Quarterly. $60 per issue; $150 per year. Covers over 7,000 companies, organizations, and individuals involved in the financial industry in the United Kingdom, including financial press, securities analysts, stock exchanges, banks, insurance companies, related trade associations, and members of the British and European parliaments.

**Business Ireland**. Ashville Media Group, Longboat Quay, 57-59 Sir John Rogerson's Quay Dublin 2, Ireland. Phone: 353 1 4322200; Fax: 353 1 6727100; Email: info@ashville.com • URL: http://www.ashville.com • Quarterly. Magazine featuring business in Ireland.

**Business Ireland**. Dublin Chamber of Commerce, 7 Clare St. Dublin 2, Ireland. Phone: 353 1 6447200; Fax: 353 1 6447234; Email: info@dubchamber.ie • URL: http://www.dubchamber.ie • Quarterly. Covers all areas of interest for business within the Dublin region.

**Business Job Finder**. Ohio State University Department of Finance, Max M. Fisher College of Business, 700 Fisher Hall, 2100 Neil Ave. Columbus, OH 43210. Phone: (614)292-5026 • URL: http://www.fisher.osu.edu • Internet site containing information on jobs in the business sector, primarily in accounting, finance, and consulting. Links to many corporations who hire extensively in this area are included for those wishing to make contacts and/or mail out resumes. Detailed information on job search aids and employer profiles are provided with job areas broken down into subject.

**Business Journal**. American Chamber of Commerce of the Philippines, Corinthian Plz., 2nd Fl. Makati City 1229, Philippines. Phone: 63 8187911; Fax: 63 8113081; Email: amcham@amchamphilippines.com • URL: http://www.amchamphilippines.com • Monthly. Members free; 300 P additional copy; $220 overseas. Contains business updates, corporate information and current trends in the different industries within the Philippines.

**The Business Journal**. The Business Journal, 1315 Van Ness, Ste. 200 Fresno, CA 93721. Phone: (559)490-3400; Fax: (559)490-3531 • URL: http://www.thebusinessjournal.com • Weekly. $49 Individuals electronic; $69 Individuals print and electronic; $79 Individuals print; $99 Individuals public notices and national news, electronic; $109 Individuals public notices and national news, print. Journal covering business interests.

**The Business Journal: Monthly Business Magazine**. Lee Enterprises Inc., 201 N Harrison St. Davenport, IA 52801-1932. Phone: 888-406-6450 or (563)383-2100; Email: information@lee.net • URL: http://www.lee.net • Monthly. Local business editorial.

**Business Lanka**. Sri Lanka Export Development Board Trade Information Service, 115 Sir Chittampalam A Gardiner Mawatha Colombo 00300, Sri Lanka. • Quarterly. $320. Provides information on Sri Lankan exports and products for business people.

**Business Latin America: Weekly Report to Managers of Latin American Operations**. The Economist Intelligence Unit, 111 W 57th St. New York, NY 10019. Phone: 800-938-4685 or (212)554-0600; Fax: (212)586-1191 or (212)586-1182; Email: newyork@eiu.com • URL: http://www.economist.com • Weekly. $1,250.00 per year. Newsletter covering Latin American business trends, politics, regulations, exchange rates, economics, and finance. Provides statistical data on foreign debt, taxes, labor costs, gross domestic product (GDP), and inflation rates.

**Business Law Journal**.

**Business Law Monographs**. Matthew Bender and Company Inc., 1275 Broadway Albany, NY 12204-2638. Phone: 800-424-4200 or (518)487-3000; Fax: (518)487-3573 or (800)424-4200; Email: customer.support@lexisnexis.com • URL: http://www.matthewbender.com • Quarterly. $3,645 book; $3,314 e-book. Intended for in-house and outside corporate counsel. Each monograph concentrates on a particular subject.

**The Business Lawyer**. American Bar Association, 321 N Clark St. Chicago, IL 60654-7598. Phone: 800-285-2221 or (312)988-5000; Email: orders@abanet.org • URL: http://www.americanbar.org/aba.html • Quarterly. $65 Individuals; $75

Out of country; $20 Single issue. Law journal.

***Business Leader Profiles for Students***. Cengage Learning Inc., 20 Channel Center St. Boston, MA 02210. Phone: 800-487-8488 or (617)289-7700; Fax: (617)289-7844; Email: investors@cengage.com • URL: http://www.cengage.com • $193 Individuals. Focuses on an additional 100 new business leaders to those listed in volume 1 and 25 updated profles from the first volume. Biographical profiles range from 1,250 to 2,500 words in length.

***Business Ledger***. Ledger Publishing Co., 1260 Iroquois Ave., Ste. 200 Naperville, IL 60563. Phone: (630)428-8788; Email: info@thebusinessledger.com • URL: http://www.dhbusinessledger.com • $45 Individuals; $70 Two years. Regional business newspaper covering DuPage, Northwest Cook County and the Fox Valley.

***Business Leksikon***. ARCO & BK Service, Bragesvej 20 DK-8230 Aabyhoej, Denmark. Phone: 45 86 25 6655; Fax: 45 86 25 6663; Email: bk@arco.dk • URL: http://www.arco.dk • Contains a dictionary of approximately 5200 terms related to the import/export industry. Includes a directory of import and export specialists throughout Denmark.

***The Business Link***. Union County Chamber of Commerce, 903 Skyway Dr. Monroe, NC 28110. Phone: (704)289-4567; Fax: (704)282-0122; Email: info@unioncountycoc.com • URL: http://www.unioncountycoc.com • Monthly. Provides updates on Chamber and member activities and events.

***Business Litigation Database***. Trans Union Credit Information Co., 185 Osea Ave. Hauppauge, NY 11788. Phone: (516)582-2690; Fax: (516)582-2767 • Continuous. Database covers: 8 million court records on companies from New York and New Jersey, including suits, judgments, satisfactions, bankruptcies, forecloseures (for New Jersey only), and federal, state, and city tax liens. Entries include: Defendant name and address, plaintiff name and address, court of filing, filing date, docket number, dollar amount of action, type of action.

***Business Luxembourg***. International City Magazines S.A.R.L., 25, rue Philippe II L-2340 Luxembourg, Luxembourg. Phone: 352 4611221; Fax: 352 470056 • Business magazine.

***Business Marketing CD***. Herold Business Data GmbH, Guntramsdorfer Str. 105 A-2340 Modling, Austria. Phone: 43 2236 401 133; Fax: 43 2236 401 8; Email: kundendienst@herold.at • URL: http://www.herold.at/ • Contains information on 320,000 Austrian companies. The database is available on CD-ROM. It supports such marketing activities as mailings and customer identification.

***Business Matters***. Chapel Hill - Carrboro Chamber of Commerce, 104 S Estes Dr. Chapel Hill, NC 27515-2897. Phone: (919)967-7075; Fax: (919)968-6874; Email: info@carolinachamber.org • URL: http://www.carolinachamber.org • Bimonthly. Provides weekly events, government updates, and chamber news.

***Business Media Advertising Source®***. Kantar Media SRDS, 1700 Higgins Rd., 5th Fl. Des Plaines, IL 60018-5610. Phone: 800-851-7737 or (847)375-5000; Email: next@srds.com • URL: http://next.srds.com • Contains in-depth information on advertising opportunities in healthcare trade media throughout the world.

***Business Media Matters***. Association of Business Information & Media Companies, 675 3rd Ave., 7th Fl. New York, NY 10017-5704. Phone: (212)661-6360; Fax: (212)370-0736; Email: info@abmmail.com • URL: http://www.abmassociation.com • Monthly.

***Business Mexico***. American Chamber of Commerce of Mexico - Mexico City, Blas Pascal 205, 3.er piso, Col. Los Morales 11510 Mexico City, Mexico. Phone: 52 55 51413800; Fax: 52 55 51413835 or 52 55 51413836; Email: amchammx@amcham.org.mx • URL: http://www.amcham.com.mx/ • Monthly. $145 /year for nonmembers. Covers business, economic, and policy developments in Mexico. Includes statistics and research reports.

***Business Middle East***. The Economist Intelligence Unit, 111 W 57th St. New York, NY 10019. Phone: 800-938-4685 or (212)554-0600; Fax: (212)586-1191 or (212)586-1182; Email: newyork@eiu.com • URL: http://www.economist.com • Provides news on political, economic, and legal developments throughout the region, including business and e-business news; regulatory changes; distribution, human resources, market-entry strategies and regulatory development issues; economic and political risk analysis; company case studies; business intelligence.

**Business Modeling and Integration Domain Task Force**. Object Management Group, 109 Highland Ave. Needham, MA 02494. Phone: (781)444-0404; Fax: (781)444-0320; Email: info@omg.org • URL: http://bmi.omg.org • Aims to empower all companies, across all industries, to develop and operate business processes that span multiple applications and business partners, behind the firewall and over the Internet.

***Business Money***. Business Money Ltd., Bowden's Business Centre, Somerset Hambridge TA10 0BP, United Kingdom. Phone: 44 145 8253536; Fax: 44 145 8253538; Email: editor@business-money.com • URL: http://www.business-money.com • Monthly. £149 Individuals single copy print, online and app; £177 Other countries single copy print, online and app; £217 Individuals two copy print, online and app; £254 Other countries two copy print, online and app. Professional magazine covering finance, business banking, and related topics.

***Business Month***. Central Pennsylvania Publishing Co., 2536 Eastern Blvd., No. 507 York, PA 17402. Phone: (717)757-9781; Fax: (717)852-8003 • Monthly. $15; $2 Single issue; Free. Community newspaper.

***Business Month: The Magazine of Corporate Management***. Goldhirsh Group, 488 Madison Ave., 6th Fl. New York, NY 10022. Phone: (212)326-2600 • Monthly. Magazine for business executives.

***Business Monthly***. • Monthly. $9 Individuals. Local business newspaper.

***Business Monthly***. American Chamber of Commerce in Egypt, 33 Soliman Abaza St., Dokki-Giza Cairo 12311, Egypt. Phone: 20 2 33381050; Fax: 20 2 33381060 • URL: http://www.amcham.org.eg • Monthly.

**Business Network International - Suriname**. Verl Hoogestraat No. 1 Paramaribo, Suriname. Phone: 597 424354 • URL: http://www.bnisuriname.com • Seeks to increase business opportunities for members. Encourages members to share ideas, contacts and business referrals. Fosters and develops personal relationships with other qualified business professionals.

***Business News Alaska***. Petroleum Newspapers of Alaska L.L.C., PO Box 231647 Anchorage, AK 99523-1651. Phone: (907)522-9469; Fax: (907)522-9583; Email: publisher@petroleumnews.com • URL: http://www.petroleumnews.com.

***Business News***. American Chamber of Commerce of El Salvador, World Trade Center, Torre II Nivel 3, Local 308, 89 Av. Norte, Col. Escalon San Salvador, El Salvador. Phone: 503 22639494; Fax: 503 22639393; Email: amchamsal@amchamsal.com • URL: http://www.amchamsal.com • Quarterly. Informs, educates and promotes member businesses.

***Business News and Views***. Battle Ground Chamber of Commerce, 317 E Main St. Battle Ground, WA 98604-4501. Phone: (360)687-1510; Fax: (360)687-4505; Email: info@battlegroundchamber.org • URL: http://www.battlegroundchamber.org • Monthly.

***Business News, Business Agenda, Programs and Services***. Campbell County Chamber of Commerce, 314 S Gillette Ave. Gillette, WY 82716. Phone: (307)682-3673; Fax: (307)682-0538; Email: info@gillettechamber.com • URL: http://www.gillettechamber.com • Monthly.

***Business News***. MDExpress CEOExpress Co., 1 Broadway, 14th Fl. Boston, MA 02142. Phone: (617)482-1200; Fax: (617)225-4440 • URL: http://www.mdexpress.com • Business News provides links for business oriented news sources, such as the Wall Street Journal.

***Business News: North of Scotland***. North of Scotland Publications, 18-22 Market St. Aberdeen AB11 5PL, United Kingdom. Phone: 44 1224575671; Fax: 44 1224586700; Email: nosp@ajl.co.uk • Monthly. $15 Individuals. Business newspaper.

***Business News***. Pleasant Hill Chamber of Commerce, 91 Gregory Ln., Ste. 11 Pleasant Hill, CA 94523-4914. Phone: (925)687-0700; Fax: (925)676-7422; Email: chamberinfo@pleasanthillchamber.com • URL: http://www.pleasanthillchamber.com • Monthly. Includes issues about the business community and information about the chamber.

***The Business News: The Miami Valley's Business and Financial News Journal***. ACBJ Business Publications, 137 N Main St., Ste. 400 Dayton, OH 45402. Fax: (513)222-9967 • Weekly. $50 Individuals. Newsmagazine containing information for business owners and company leaders in the Dayton, OH area.

***Business NH Magazine***. Millyard Communication Inc., 670 N Commercial St., Ste. 110 Manchester, NH 03101. Phone: (603)626-6354; Fax: (603)626-6359; Email: edit@businessnhmagazine.com • Monthly. $53 Individuals cover price. Business Magazine.

***Business Notes***. Tallmadge Chamber of Commerce, 80 Community Rd. Tallmadge, OH 44278. Phone: (330)633-5417; Fax: (330)633-5415; Email: tallmadgechamber@onecommail.com • URL: http://www.tallmadgechamber.com • Monthly. Includes reports and other artcles concerning Tallmadge Chamber of Commerce.

**Business NZ**. Level 6, Lumley House, 3-11 Hunter St. Wellington 6011, New Zealand. Phone: 64 4 4966555; Fax: 64 4 4966550; Email: info@businessnz.org.nz • URL: http://www.businessnz.org.nz • Advocacy body working to maintain a favorable business climate and reasonable conditions of employment in New Zealand. Facilitates communication and cooperation among members.

***The Business of Entertainment***. Cengage Learning Inc., 20 Channel Center St. Boston, MA 02210. Phone: 800-487-8488 or (617)289-7700; Fax: (617)289-7844; Email: investors@cengage.com • URL: http://www.cengage.com • 2010. eBook. Covers movies popular music, and television. Includes information on the nuts and bolts of daily life in the industry, including the challenges of digitizing content, globalization, promoting stars and shows, protecting intellectual property, and developing talent.

***Business of Fashion: Designing, Manufacturing and Marketing***. Conde Nast Inc., 750 3rd Ave., 8th Fl. New York, NY 10017. Phone: 800-932-4724 or (212)630-4600 or (212)630-3880; Fax: (212)630-3868; Email: bill_andrulevich@condenast.com • URL: http://www.fairchildfashiongroup.com • $100 Individuals. Business guide covering United States textile, apparel, and home fashions companies.

***The Business of Food: Encyclopedia of the Food and Drink Industries***. Cengage Learning Inc., 20 Channel Center St. Boston, MA 02210. Phone: 800-487-8488 or (617)289-7700; Fax: (617)289-7844; Email: investors@cengage.com • URL: http://www.cengage.com • 2010. eBook. Takes readers as consumers behind the scenes of the food and drink industries. Covers topics from food companies and brands to the environment, health, science and technology, culture, finance, and more. The more than 150 essay entries also cover those issues that have been and continue to be of perennial importance. Historical context is emphasized and the focus is mainly on business in the United States.

***The Business of Herbs***. Northwind Publications, 439 Ponderosa Way Jemez Springs, NM 87025-8036. Phone: (505)829-3448; Fax: (505)829-3449 • Bimonthly. $24 Individuals; $4.75 Single issue. Trade journal for the herb and specialty horticulture industry. Covers growing and marketing of herbs, including medicinal, culinary, fragrant, and ornamental.

***The Business of Sports***. Cengage Learning Inc., 20 Channel Center St. Boston, MA 02210. Phone: 800-487-8488 or (617)289-7700; Fax: (617)289-7844; Email: investors@cengage.com • URL: http://www.cengage.com • 2010. eBook. Covers the spectrum of topics and issues relating to the management and promotion of organized sports.

***The Business of Supplier Diversity: A Handbook of Essential Contacts and Information for Navigating the Industry***. Diversity Information Resources, 2105 Central Ave. NE Minneapolis, MN 55418. Phone: (612)781-6819; Fax: (612)781-0109; Email: info@diversityinforesources.com • URL: http://www.diversityinforesources.com • Annual. $129 Individuals. Covers: Business opportunity fairs, seminars, and workshops; National Supplier Development Council regional offices; Small Business Administration and Minority Business Development Administration offices; minority and women-owned business directories; and other resources for minority and women-owned businesses. Database includes: Summaries of legislation affecting minority businesses; glossary.

***The Business of Swimming***. Institute of Sport and Recreation Management, Sir John Beckwith Center for Sport Loughborough LE11 3QF, United Kingdom. Phone: 44 15 09226474; Fax: 44 15 09226475; Email: info@isrm.co.uk • URL: http://www.isrm.co.uk • £125 for members; £135 for nonmembers. Features information on consumer perspective and behavior in swimming pools.

***Business/Offices Services Guide***. Business in Vancouver Media Group, 102 E 4th Ave. Vancouver, BC, Canada V5T 1G2. Phone: (604)688-2398; Fax: (604)688-1963; Email: subscribe@biv.com • URL: http://www.biv.com • List of office supply firms in British Columbia.

***Business Opportunities Bulletin***. Mauritius Chamber of Commerce and Industry, 3 Royal St. Port Louis, Mauritius. Phone: 230 2083301; Fax: 230 2080076; Email: secretariat@mcci.intnet.mu • URL: http://www.mcci.org • Monthly. Includes information on import and export products and industrial opportunities.

***Business Opportunities Journal***. Business Service Corp., 2185 Faraday Ave., Ste. 110 Carlsbad, CA 92008-7206. Fax: (619)263-1763; Email: boj@boj.com • URL: http://www.boj.com • Monthly. Newspaper covering businesses for sale.

***Business Organizations with Tax Planning***. Zolman Cavitch, editor. Matthew Bender and Company Inc., 1275 Broadway Albany, NY 12204-2638. Phone: 800-424-4200 or (518)487-3000; Fax: (518)487-3573 or (800)424-4200; Email: customer.support@lexisnexis.com • URL: http://www.matthewbender.com • Quarterly. $6,433 book; $5,849 e-book. Periodic supplementation. In-depth analytical coverage of corporation law and all relevant aspects of federal corporation taxation.

***Business-Oriented Enterprise Integration for Organizational Agility***. Cengage Learning Inc., 20 Channel Center St. Boston, MA 02210. Phone: 800-487-8488 or (617)289-7700; Fax: (617)289-7844; Email: investors@cengage.com • URL: http://www.cengage.com.

***Business Owner***. Business Technology Association, 12411 Wornall Rd., Ste. 200 Kansas City, MO 64145. Phone: 800-869-6688 or (816)941-3100; Fax: (816)941-4843 or (816)941-2829 • URL: http://www.bta.org • Bimonthly. Delivers valuable information containing ideas, advisories, case studies and reports provided for members.

***Business Panama***. American Chamber of Commerce and Industry of Panama, Ocean Business Plz., Ste. 1709, Ave. Aquilino de la Guardia & 47th St. Marbella, Panama. Phone: 507 3013881; Fax: 507 3013882; Email: executivedirector@panamcham.com • URL: http://www.panamcham.com • Monthly. Covers timely news items, interviews, and business-related developments both within Panama and in the Americas.

***Business Performance Management***. Intertec Publishing, 5 Penn Plz., 13th Fl. New York, NY 10001-1810. Phone: 800-795-5445 or (212)613-9700 or (212)204-4200; Fax: (212)613-9749 or (212)206-3622; Email: bethany.weaver@penton.com • URL: http://www.penton.com • Magazine for business managers. Covers organizing, automating, and analyzing of business methodologies and processes.

***Business Periodicals Index Retrospective***. EBSCO Publishing Inc., 10 Estes St. Ipswich, MA 01938-2106. Phone: 800-653-2726 or (978)356-6500; Fax: (978)356-6565; Email: information@ebscohost.com • URL: http://www.ebscohost.

com • 11/year. Quarterly and annual cumulations.

***Business Periodicals Index Retrospective™: 1913-1982***. EBSCO Publishing Inc., 10 Estes St. Ipswich, MA 01938-2106. Phone: 800-653-2726 or (978)356-6500; Fax: (978)356-6565; Email: information@ebscohost.com • URL: http://www.ebscohost.com • Contains citations to more than 2.5 million articles and book reviews in more than 1000 general business periodicals and trade journals.

***Business Phone Directory***. Quincy Valley Chamber of Commerce, 119 F St. SE Quincy, WA 98848-0668. Phone: (509)787-2140; Fax: (509)787-4500; Email: qvcc@quincyvalley.org • URL: http://www.quincyvalley.org • Annual.

***Business Plans Handbook***. Cengage Learning Inc., 20 Channel Center St. Boston, MA 02210. Phone: 800-487-8488 or (617)289-7700; Fax: (617)289-7844; Email: investors@cengage.com • URL: http://www.cengage.com • Annual. $243 Individuals. Contains examples of detailed plans for starting or developing various kinds of businesses. Categories within plans include statement of purpose, market description, personnel requirements, financial needs, etc.

**Business Products Credit Association**. 607 Westridge Dr. O Fallon, MO 63366-2439. Phone: 888-514-2722 or (360)612-9507 or (636)294-5775; Fax: (636)754-0567; Email: service@bpca.org • URL: http://www.bpca.org • Member-owned credit association serving businesses. Assists members in protecting their accounts receivable. Provides credit reporting services, collection service letters and business alert reports. Conducts educational programs; compiles statistics.

***Business Products Industry Report***. Independent Office Products and Furniture Dealers Association, 3601 E Joppa Rd. Baltimore, MD 21234. Phone: (410)930-8100; Fax: (410)931-8111; Email: cbates@nopanet.org • URL: http://www.iopfda.org • Semimonthly. Free members; $95 Nonmembers. Magazine serving the business products industry.

***Business-Professional Online Markets***. SIMBA Information Inc., 60 Long Ridge Rd., Ste. 300 Stamford, CT 06902. Phone: (203)325-8193; Fax: (203)325-8975 • URL: http://www.simbainformation.com • Annual. $1,995 print; $3,390 print (with online edition). Provides a review of current conditions in the online information industry. Profiles of major database producers and online services are included.

***Business Pulse***. Chamber of Commerce and Industry of Western Australia, 180 Hay St. East Perth, WA 6004, Australia. Phone: 61 8 93657555; Fax: 61 8 93657550; Email: info@cciwa.com • URL: http://www.cciwa.com • Monthly. Journal containing information about business, employee relations, and international trade.

***Business Pulse***. Council of EU Chambers of Commerce in India, Y.B. Chavan Ctre., 3rd Fl., General J. Bhosale Marg Mumbai 400 021, India. Phone: 91 22 2854563; Fax: 91 22 2854564; Email: contact@euindiachambers.com • URL: http://www.euindiachambers.com • Quarterly.

***Business Rankings Annual (BRA)***. Cengage Learning Inc., 20 Channel Center St. Boston, MA 02210. Phone: 800-487-8488 or (617)289-7700; Fax: (617)289-7844; Email: investors@cengage.com • URL: http://www.cengage.com • Annual. $584 Individuals; $97 Individuals includes a cumulative index; 2-vol. set: $390. A guide to lists and rankings appearing in major business publications. The top ten names are listed in each case.

***Business Referral***. Palm Springs Chamber of Commerce, 190 W Amado Rd. Palm Springs, CA 92262. Phone: (760)325-1577; Fax: (760)325-8549; Email: info@pschamber.org • URL: http://www.pschamber.org • Annual. Covers businesses in the Palm Springs, CA area.

***Business Report***. 10 Publishing, 10 Clement St. Birmingham B1 2SL, United Kingdom. Phone: 44 1212341387; Fax: 44 1212369888; Email: info@10publishing.co.uk • Monthly. $22.50 Individuals. Professional business newspaper.

***Business Reporter***. Atascadero Chamber of Commerce, 6904 El Camino Real Atascadero, CA 93422. Phone: (805)466-2044; Fax: (805)466-9218; Email: info@atascaderochamber.org • URL: http://www.atascaderochamber.org • 11/year.

***Business Research Handbook: Methods and Sources for Lawyers and Business Professionals***. Kathy E. Shimpock. Wolters Kluwer Law and Business, 76 9th Ave., 7th Fl. New York, NY 10011-4962. Phone: 800-234-1660 or (212)771-0600; Fax: (800)901-9075 or (301)644-3550 • URL: http://www.wolterskluwerlb.com • Semiannual. $859 Individuals Looseleaf. Provides detailed advice on how to find business information. Describes a wide variety of data sources, both private and government.

***Business Researchers Network***. Penny Hill Press, 25411 Paine St. Damascus, MD 20872. Phone: (301)253-0881; Fax: (301)253-0721; Email: service@pennyhill.com • URL: http://www.pennyhill.com • Monthly. $195 per year. Publication includes: Listing of sources of critical data and insights on foreign competition, political risks, and new export markets. Entries include: Name, address, phone, description of information available.

***Business Resource Directory***. Plano Chamber of Commerce, 1200 E 15th St. Plano, TX 75074. Phone: (972)424-7547; Fax: (972)422-5182; Email: info@planochamber.org • URL: http://www.planochamber.org • Annual. Contains directory of all members listed by alpha and category.

**Business Retention and Expansion International**. PO Box 3212 Bismarck, ND 58502-3212. Email: brei@brei.org • URL: http://www.brei.org • Promotes business retention and expansion as a fundamental strategy for economic sustainability and growth. Provides leadership resources, education and networking opportunities in business retention and expansion. Fosters communication and collaboration among members.

***Business Russia***. The Economist Intelligence Unit, 111 W 57th St. New York, NY 10019. Phone: 800-938-4685 or (212)554-0600; Fax: (212)586-1191 or (212)586-1182; Email: newyork@eiu.com • URL: http://www.economist.com • Provides news on political, economic, and legal developments throughout the region, including business and e-business news; regulatory changes; distribution, human resources, market-entry strategies and regulatory development issues; political and economic risk analysis; company case studies; business intelligence.

**Business SA**. 136 Greenhill Rd. Adelaide, SA 5061, Australia. Phone: 61 8 83000000; Fax: 61 8 83000001; Email: accoutsquery@business-sa.com • URL: http://business-sa.com • Represents businesses in South Australia; provides services to businesses and employers, including management of export transactions.

***Business Schools Directory***. InfoGroup Inc., 5711 S 86th Cir. Omaha, NE 68127-4146. Phone: (402)593-4500 • URL: http://www.infogroup.com • Annual. Number of listings: 5,329. Entries include: Name, address, phone, size of advertisement, name of owner or manager, number of employees, year first in "Yellow Pages." Compiled from telephone company "Yellow Pages," nationwide.

***Business Services Directory***. German American Chamber of Commerce, 75 Broad St., 21st Fl. New York, NY 10004. Phone: (212)974-8830; Fax: (212)974-8867; Email: info@gaccny.com • URL: http://www.gaccny.com • $10. Covers: Member firms which provide business, engineering, research, accounting, technical, marketing, and personnel management consulting services. Entries include: Company name, address, phone, fax, contact, number of employees, geographical location, foreign language capabilities, activities, history.

***Business Services***. S1 Corp., 705 Westech Dr. Norcross, GA 30092-3506. Phone: 888-457-2237 or (404)923-3500; Fax: (404)923-6727; Email: moreinfo@s1.com • URL: http://www.s1.com • Offers applications and solutions for customer education and support services.

***Business Standards***. BSI Business Information, 389 Chiswick High Rd. London W4 4AL, United Kingdom. Phone: 44 20 8996 9001; Fax: 44 20 8996 7001; Email: cservices@bsi-global.com • URL: http://www.bsi-global.com • Quarterly.

***Business Start-Ups: Smart Ideas for Your Small Business***. Entrepreneur Press, 2445 McCabe Way, Ste. 400 Irvine, CA 92614-6244. Phone: 800-864-6864 or (949)261-2325 or (949)622-7131; Fax: (949)261-7729 or (949)261-0234; Email: press@entrepreneur.com • URL: http://www.entrepreneurpress.com • Monthly. $14.97 per year. Provides advice for starting a small business. Includes business trends, new technology, E-commerce, and case histories ("real-life stories").

***Business Strategies***. Wolters Kluwer Law & Business CCH, 2700 Lake Cook Rd. Riverwoods, IL 60015. Phone: 888-224-7377 or (847)267-7000; Email: cust_serv@cch.com • URL: http://www.cchgroup.com • Semimonthly. $795.00 per year. Four looseleaf volumes. Semimonthly updates. Legal, tax, and accounting aspects of business planning and decision-making. Provides information on start-ups, forms of ownership (partnerships, corporations), failing businesses, reorganizations, acquisitions, and so forth. Includes *Business Strategies Bulletin*, a monthly newsletter.

***Business Suite***. S1 Corp., 705 Westech Dr. Norcross, GA 30092-3506. Phone: 888-457-2237 or (404)923-3500; Fax: (404)923-6727; Email: moreinfo@s1.com • URL: http://www.s1.com • Provides solutions for business interaction with small to medium-sized companies.

***Business Taxation Manual***. Business SA, 136 Greenhill Rd. Adelaide, SA 5061, Australia. Phone: 61 8 83000000; Fax: 61 8 83000001; Email: accoutsquery@business-sa.com • URL: http://business-sa.com • $418 Nonmembers. Contains information on taxation obligations for businesses.

***Business Taxpayer Information Publications***. U. S. Government Printing Office, 732 N Capitol St. NW Washington, DC 20401. Phone: 866-512-1800 or (202)512-1800 or (866)512-1800; Fax: (202)512-2104 or (202)512-2250; Email: contactcenter@gpo.gov • URL: http://www.gpo.gov • Annual. $66 U.S. Looseleaf; $92.40 Other countries Looseleaf. Two volumes, consisting of *Circular E, Employer's Tax Guide* and *Employer's Supplemental Tax Guide*. Issued by the Internal Revenue Service (http://www.irs.ustreas.gov). Includes a variety of business-related tax information, including withholding tables, tax calendars, self-employment issues, partnership matters, corporation topics, depreciation, and bankruptcy.

***Business Teacher Education Journal***. National Association for Business Teacher Education, 1914 Association Dr. Reston, VA 20191-1596. Phone: (703)860-8300; Fax: (703)620-4483; Email: nbea@nbea.org • URL: http://www.nabte.org • Annual. $20 Members; $40 Nonmembers. Provides information on business education including curriculum and instructional implications, internships, and technologies.

**Business Technology Association**. 12411 Wornall Rd., Ste. 200 Kansas City, MO 64145. Phone: 800-869-6688 or (816)941-3100; Fax: (816)941-4843 or (816)941-2829 • URL: http://www.bta.org • Dealers and resellers of office equipment and networking products and services. Offers 60 seminars on management, service, technology, and business systems. Conducts research, provides business-supporting services and benefits, including insurance, and legal counsel.

***The Business Times of Western Colorado***. The Business Times of Western Colorado, 609 N Ave., Ste. 2 Grand Junction, CO 81501. Phone: (970)424-5133 • URL: http://www.thebusinesstimes.com • Biweekly. $24.95 Individuals 26 issues. Newspaper covering local business.

***Business to Business***. Geneva Area Chamber of Commerce, 1 Franklin Sq., Ste. 201 Geneva, NY 14456. Phone: 877-543-6382 or (315)789-1776; Email: info@genevany.com • URL: http://www.genevany.com • Monthly. Includes information about Geneva business community.

***The Business to Business Marketer***. Business Marketing Association, 1833 Centre Point Cir., Ste. 123 Naperville, IL 60563. Phone: (630)544-5054; Fax: (630)544-5055; Email: info@marketing.org • URL: http://www.marketing.org • 10/year Quarterly. included in membership dues; $59 /year for nonmembers. Magazine reporting on marketing and communications including database marketing, telemarketing, international marketing, direct marketing, and high-tech marketing.

***Business Today***. Chapel Hill - Carrboro Chamber of Commerce, 104 S Estes Dr. Chapel Hill, NC 27515-2897. Phone: (919)967-7075; Fax: (919)968-6874; Email: info@carolinachamber.org • URL: http://www.carolinachamber.org • Monthly. Contains member profile, articles for small business and information about the community.

***Business Today Egypt***. Egypt Today, 3a Rd. 199, IBA Media Bldg., Degla, Maadi Cairo, Egypt. Phone: 20 2 27555000; Fax: 20 2 27555050; Email: editor@egypttoday.com • URL: http://www.egypttoday.com • £E 135 Individuals; $100 Individuals Europe, US and Canada; $120 Individuals Canada, Asia and Australasia. Business magazine covering business in Egypt.

***Business Today***. Living Media India Ltd., Trade Ctr., 2nd Fl. Kamla City,, S.B. Marg Lower Parel (W) Mumbai 400 013, India. Phone: 91 22 24983355 • URL: http://www.indiatoday.digitaltoday.in • Biweekly. Periodical covering business news.

***Business Today: Published for Students by Students***. Foundation for Student Communication, 48 University Pl. Princeton, NJ 08544. Phone: (609)258-1111; Fax: (609)258-1222; Email: info@businesstoday.org • URL: http://www.businesstoday.org • 3/year. $3 /issue (for libraries and career service offices). Provides articles on careers, university campuses, and opinions of students. Includes employment listings.

***Business Travel Almanac***. Pearson Education Inc., 299 Jefferson Rd. Parsippany, NJ 07054. Phone: 800-526-9907 or (973)739-8000; Fax: (800)393-3156; Email: mc.school@pearsonlearning.com • URL: http://www.pearsonlearning.com • $23.99 Individuals print; $19.19 Individuals Ebook. List of travel advice, reference material, directory information and city guides.

***Business Travel Magazine***. Eco N.V., Lammekensraamveld 6 bus 52 B-2000 Antwerp, Belgium. Phone: 32 32933176; Fax: 32 32933180 • URL: http://www.eco-nv.com/index.php?english • Monthly. Business travel magazine covering destinations, suppliers and lifestyle.

***Business Travel News: News and Ideas for Business Travel Management***. Nielsen Business Media Inc., 770 Broadway New York, NY 10003-9522. Phone: 866-890-8541 or (646)654-4500 or (646)654-5000; Fax: (646)654-5584 or (646)654-4500; Email: bmcomm@nielsen.com • URL: http://www.nielsenbusinessmedia.com • Monthly. $119.00 per year. Includes annual directory of travel sources. Formerly *Corporate Travel*.

***Business Travel News***. Nielsen Business Media Inc., 770 Broadway New York, NY 10003-9522. Phone: 866-890-8541 or (646)654-4500 or (646)654-5000; Fax: (646)654-5584 or (646)654-4500; Email: bmcomm@nielsen.com • URL: http://www.nielsenbusinessmedia.com • Weekly. Tabloid newspaper covering business travel.

***Business Travel Planner-North American Edition***. Northstar Travel Media L.L.C., 100 Lighting Way, 2nd Fl. Secaucus, NJ 07094. Phone: 800-742-7076 or (201)902-2000 or (201)902-1800; Fax: (201)902-2045 or (201)319-1947; Email: secausushelpdesk@ntmllc.com • URL: http://www.northstartravelmedia.com • Quarterly. $169 Individuals online; C$187.59 Individuals. Magazine covering business and leisure travel.

***Business Traveller***. BRT Reise Publishing GmbH, Schulstr. 34 D-80634 Munich, Germany. Phone: 49 891 679971; Fax: 49 891 679937 • Bimonthly. Consumer magazine covering business travel.

***Business Trends***. Quebecor Media Inc., 612, Rue Saint-Jacques Montreal, QC, Canada H3C 4M8. Phone: (514)597-2231 or (514)380-1999; Fax: (514)380-1999 • URL: http://www.quebecor.com • Monthly. $24 Individuals Canadian (GST included); $2 Single issue outside of our regular delivery area; $48 Individuals Canadian funds (surface mail only). Magazine featuring local business-related articles for the Sarnia, Ontario area in Canada.

***Business 2.0***. Time Inc., Time-Life Bldg., 1271 Ave. of the

Americas New York, NY 10020. Phone: 800-843-8463 or (212)522-1212; Fax: (212)522-0602; Email: information@timeinc.com • URL: http://www.time.com • General business magazine emphasizing ideas, insight, and innovation.

***Business 2.0 Web Guide to the Best Business Links***. Business 2.0 Media Inc., Phone: (415)293-4800; Email: support@business2.com • URL: http://www.business2.com/webguide • Web site presents an extensive, searchable directory of links to "the best, most informative, and authoritative web pages." Twenty main categories cover business, finance, career, company information, people, and technology topics, with thousands of subtopics, all linking to Web sites recommended by experienced business researchers. Fees: Free.

***Business U.K.*** NewsBank Inc., 5801 Pelican Bay Blvd., Ste. 600 Naples, FL 34108. Phone: 800-762-8182 or (802)875-2910; Fax: (239)263-3004; Email: sales@newsbank.com • URL: http://www.newsbank.com • Contains the full-text of business-related journals, magazines, newspapers, newsletters, wire services, trade publications, and other publications from the United Kingdom.

***Business Valuation Review***. American Society of Appraisers, 11107 Sunset Hills Rd., Ste. 310 Reston, VA 20190. Phone: 800-272-8258 or (703)478-2228; Fax: (703)742-8471; Email: asainfo@appraisers.org • URL: http://www.appraisers.org • Quarterly. $45 Members; $140 Nonmembers. Journal containing topics regarding professional practice of appraising various business interests.

***Business Valuations: Businesses, Securities, and Real Estate***. American CPE Inc., 826 Riviera Mansfield, TX 76063. Phone: 800-990-4273 or (817)477-0222; Fax: (817)473-4998; Email: director@americancpe.com • URL: http://www.americancpe.com • Contains detailed training information covering the valuation of businesses and other instruments and property related to businesses, including bonds, securities, preferred and common stock, and real estate.

***Business Venezuela***. Venezuelan-American Chamber of Commerce and Industry, PO Box 5181 Caracas 1010-A, Venezuela. Phone: 58 212 2630833; Fax: 58 212 2631829 • URL: http://www.venamcham.org • Features in-depth and objective analyses on the changes that are happening in the country's economic, trade and business environment.

***Business Ventures***. Business Service Corp., 569-F Division St. Port Orchard, WA 98366. Phone: (206)876-0204; Fax: (206)876-0795 • Monthly. Journal covering franchising, real estate, and investments. Also lists businesses for sale by owner.

***Business Voice***. New Jersey Business & Industry Association, 10 W Lafayette St. Trenton, NJ 08608-2002. Phone: (609)393-7707; Fax: (609)695-0442; Email: info@njbia.org • URL: http://www.njbia.org • Monthly. Updates legislation and member services.

**Business Volunteers Unlimited**. 1300 E 9th St., Ste. 1805 Cleveland, OH 44114-1509. Phone: (216)736-7711; Fax: (216)736-7710; Email: bvu@bvuvolunteers.org • URL: http://www.bvuvolunteers.org • Works to promote effective volunteerism and strong leadership. Provides consulting, education and volunteer referral services to nonprofit and businesses. Trains business executives for leadership roles on nonprofit boards.

***Business Web Strategy: Design, Alignment, and Application***. Cengage Learning Inc., 20 Channel Center St. Boston, MA 02210. Phone: 800-487-8488 or (617)289-7700; Fax: (617)289-7844; Email: investors@cengage.com • URL: http://www.cengage.com • 2009. eBook. Published by Information Science Reference. Addresses the gap in business Web strategy through a collection of concentrated managerial issues, gathering the latest theoretical frameworks, case studies, and research pertaining to maximizing the power of the Web.

***Business Week China***. Ministry of Foreign Economic Relations and Trade, Institute of International Trade. McGraw Hill Financial Inc., 1221 Avenue of the Americas New York, NY 10020-1095. Phone: (212)512-2000; Fax: (212)512-3840 • URL: http://www.mhfi.com • Bimonthly. Price on application. Edited for business and government officials in the People's Republic of China. Selected Chinese translation of *Business Week*.

***Business Week International: The World's Only International Newsweekly of Business***. McGraw Hill Financial Inc., 1221 Avenue of the Americas New York, NY 10020-1095. Phone: (212)512-2000; Fax: (212)512-3840 • URL: http://www.mhfi.com • Weekly. $95.00 per year.

***Business Week***. The McGraw-Hill Companies Inc., PO Box 182604 Columbus, OH 43272. Phone: 877-833-5524 or (212)512-2000 or (212)904-2000; Fax: (614)759-3749 or (212)512-3840; Email: webmaster@mcgraw-hill.com • URL: http://www.mcgraw-hill.com • Weekly. $5 Individuals 12 issues; $35 Individuals 50 issues; $9 Individuals print and online; $40 Individuals print and online. Magazine providing business news and intelligence for executives.

***Business Week***. McGraw Hill Financial Inc., 1221 Avenue of the Americas New York, NY 10020-1095. Phone: (212)512-2000; Fax: (212)512-3840 • URL: http://www.mhfi.com • Weekly. $45.97 per year. Last volume is a double issue.

***Business Week—1,000 Issue***. The McGraw-Hill Companies Inc., PO Box 182604 Columbus, OH 43272. Phone: 877-833-5524 or (212)512-2000 or (212)904-2000; Fax: (614)759-3749 or (212)512-3840; Email: webmaster@mcgraw-hill.com • URL: http://www.mcgraw-hill.com • Annual. List of 1,000 U.S. Corporations by market value in all business, industrial, and financial categories, with financial results from preceding year and extensive analytical text.

***Business Week Online***. McGraw-Hill, Phone: (212)512-2511; Fax: (684)842-6101 • URL: http://www.businessweek.com • Web site provides complete contents of current issue of *Business Week* plus "BW Daily" with additonal business news, financial market quotes, and corporate information from Standard & Poor's. Includes various features, such as "Banking Center" with mortgage and interest data, and "Interactive Computer Buying Guide." The "Business Week Archive" is fully searchable back to 1996.

***Business Week—Survey of Executive Compensation Issue***. The McGraw-Hill Companies Inc., PO Box 182604 Columbus, OH 43272. Phone: 877-833-5524 or (212)512-2000 or (212)904-2000; Fax: (614)759-3749 or (212)512-3840; Email: webmaster@mcgraw-hill.com • URL: http://www.mcgraw-hill.com • Weekly. $46.95 for 1 year. Publication includes: Executives in major industries of the United States and their compensation in salary, bonuses, stock options, stock appreciation rights. Entries include: Company name, sales, and return on equity; names and titles of chief executives, salary, and total of salary and bonus with percentage of change from prior year, long term compensation, one-year and three-year pay to performance analysis.

***Business West***. Hagen Marketing & Communication, PO Box 707 Custer, SD 57730. Phone: (605)673-4100; Fax: (605)673-4020 • Quarterly. $20 Individuals. Magazine featuring Pacific Rim business news for Californians.

***The Business Who's Who of Australia***. Dun & Bradstreet (Australia) Proprietary Ltd., 479 St. Kilda Rd. Melbourne, VIC 3004, Australia. Phone: 61 3 9828 3333 or 61 3 9828 3333; Fax: 61 3 9828 3300 or 61 3 9288 3300; Email: customerservice@dnb.com.au • URL: http://dnb.com.au • Daily (eve.). $2,292.95 Individuals 2004 volume 1, price includes GST; $4,833.95 2004 volume 2, price includes GST; $6,763.90 2004 volume 1 and 2, price includes GST. Covers: In two volumes, over 40,029 business and associations. Volume 1 covers larger companies; volume 2 covers medium-sized companies. Database includes: Industry statistics. Entries include: Company name, address, names and locations of branches and names of subsidiary and associated companies, names and titles of directors and key personnel, number of employees, capital, annual sales, firms represented, banking firm, products and services, trade names, brief description of activities.

***Business Who's Who of Australia (BWW)***. Dun and Bradstreet Marketing, 479 St. Kilda Rd. Melbourne, VIC 3004, Australia. Phone: 61 3 9828 3333; Fax: 61 3 9828 3300; Email: customerservice@dnb.com.au • URL: http://www.dnb.com.au • Provides information on more than 22,000 public and private companies located in Australia. It provides coverage of company activities, financial details, and key personnel, products, and services. BWW is available in print as a two-volume directory, on CD-ROM, and via the Internet.

***Business Wire***. Business Wire, 44 Montgomery St., 39th Fl. San Francisco, CA 94104-4812. Phone: 888-381-9473 or (415)986-4422; Fax: (415)788-5335; Email: info@businesswire.com • URL: http://www.businesswire.com • Contains more than 1.4 million records that make up the complete text of press releases from public and private companies and other organizations, such as hospitals and universities.

***Business Wise***. New Bern Area Chamber of Commerce, 316 S Front St. New Bern, NC 28560. Phone: (252)637-3111; Fax: (252)637-7541; Email: marketing@newbernchamber.com • URL: http://www.newbernchamber.com • Monthly. Magazine highlighting news and information about the New Bern Area and Havelock Chambers of Commerce.

***Business Woman***. Business and Professional Women's Foundation, 1718 M St. NW, No. 148 Washington, DC 20036. Phone: (202)293-1100; Fax: (202)861-0298; Email: foundation@bpwfoundation.org • URL: http://bpwfoundation.org • Quarterly Periodic. $12 /year; Free. Features articles reflecting member's concerns including issues affecting working women.

***Business Woman***. Business Women's Committee of Armenia, Banaki St. 10 Vanadzor, Armenia. Phone: 374 5743435 • Periodic. Armenian and Russian language newspaper covering women in business.

***Business Woman Magazine***. Business and Professional Women/U.S.A., 1620 Eye St. NW, Ste. 210 Washington, DC 20006. Phone: (202)293-1100; Fax: (202)861-0298; Email: memberservices@bpwusa.org • URL: http://www.bpwusa.org • Monthly. $30 Individuals; $35 Two years. Focuses on the activities and interests of working women.

**Business Women's Association of Uzbekistan**. Usman Yusupov St., 119 100200 Tashkent, Uzbekistan. Phone: 998 71 2418861 or 998 71 2413453; Fax: 998 71 2443522; Email: bwa@ars.uz • URL: http://bwa.uzorg.net/about_eng.html • Seeks to improve the climate of mutual trust and business partnership. Supports women competitiveness in labor markets through retraining and raising skills. Creates institutional legal mechanisms for improving economic and social opportunities for women. Provides legal support to women entrepreneurs.

***Business World***. ABP Pvt. Limited Publication, 6 Prafulla Sarkar St. Kolkata 700 001, India. Phone: 91 33 22345374; Fax: 91 33 22253241 • URL: http://www.abp.in • Weekly. Journal on business and economics.

***Business World***. BusinessWorld Publishing Corp., Raul L. Locsin Bldg. I Quezon City 1112, Philippines. Phone: 63 2 535 9901; Fax: 63 2 535 9926; Email: customercare@bworldonline.com • URL: http://www.bworldonline.com • Daily. Business and financial newspaper.

***Business: Your Partner in China Plus***. Computing Center of the Ministry of Foreign Trade and Economic Cooperation, 2 Dongchanganjie Beijing 100731, China. Phone: 86 10 65198114; Fax: 86 10 65198039; Email: moftec@moftec.gov.cn • $650. Database covers: Listings concerning China's foreign trade, including customs, commodity inspection agencies, insurance agencies, and banks. Database includes: International transport information, animal quarantine laws, and travel agencies.

***BusinessAnalystCrossing.com***. • Offers business analyst job listings. Includes entry level business analyst, technical and business analyst jobs.

***Businessdele***. Helsinki Media, Blue Book, Hoylaamotie 1 D FIN-00040 Helsinki, Finland. Phone: 358 9 1201 or 0 1205971; Fax: 358 9 1205599 or 0 1205999; Email: info@bluebook.fi • URL: http://www.sanoma.com/contact-us/sanoma-media-finland • Annual. Covers: Businesses, government offices, and public institutions in Finland. Entries include: Entity name, address, phone, telex number, cable address, product/service.

***BusinessLinks***. Pittsburgh Airport Area Chamber of Commerce, 850 Beaver Grade Rd. Moon Township, PA 15108. Phone: (412)264-6270; Fax: (412)264-1575; Email: info@paacc.com • URL: http://www.paacc.com • Monthly. Contains information and updates on the latest issues, newest members, upcoming events, sponsorship, and recognition opportunities.

***Businessman's Directory of the Republic of China***. Taiwan Enterprise Press Ltd., PO Box 73-4 Taipei, Taiwan. Phone: 2 8313648; Fax: 2 8313649 • Annual. $75 airmail postpaid. Covers: Taiwan manufacturers, exporters, importers, and services.

***The Businessman's Guide to Southern Africa***. Safto, PO Box 9039 Johannesburg 2000, South Africa. • Covers: Travel information for countries in South Africa, including, Botswana, Lesotho, Malawi, Mozambique, Namibia, South Africa, Swaziland, Zambia, and Zimbabwe. Entries include: Country name, climate, geography, industries and trade, finance, economy, excise and customs duties.

***BusinessWeek Guide to the Best Business Schools***. The McGraw-Hill Companies Inc., PO Box 182604 Columbus, OH 43272. Phone: 877-833-5524 or (212)512-2000 or (212)904-2000; Fax: (614)759-3749 or (212)512-3840; Email: webmaster@mcgraw-hill.com • URL: http://www.mcgraw-hill.com • Covers: The top 25 business schools and 25 runners-up, ranked by recent graduates and corporate recruiters. Entries include: School contact information; tips on GMAT prep courses; free application software.

**Businesswomen's Association**. Oakhurst Bldg., W Wing, 2nd Fl., Rm. 2004, 11/13 St. Andrews Rd. Johannesburg 2193, South Africa. Phone: 27 11 484 4945; Email: admin@bwasa.co.za • URL: http://www.bwasa.co.za • Represents businesswomen in South Africa. Creates opportunities to advance the interests of women in business. Provides local and national forums where members can exchange ideas and be informed about current issues.

***BusinessWorld's Top 500 & the Next 500 Corporations in the Philippines***. BusinessWorld Publishing Corp., Raul L. Locsin Bldg. I Quezon City 1112, Philippines. Phone: 63 2 535 9901; Fax: 63 2 535 9926; Email: customercare@bworldonline.com • URL: http://www.bworldonline.com • Annual. $300 postpaid. Covers 1,000 leading corporations in the Philippines selected on the basis of gross revenues.

***BUSRide***. Power Trade Media L.L.C., 4742 N 24th St., Ste. 340 Phoenix, AZ 85016. Phone: 800-541-2670 or (602)265-7600; Fax: (602)227-7588 • Monthly. $39 U.S.; $42 Canada; $75 Other countries; $39 Individuals; $64 Individuals; $69 Two years Canada; $98 Canada 3 years; $125 Two years other countries; $175 3 years. Magazine covering all aspects of transit and motorcoach industry.

***Butane-Propane News***. Butane-Propane News Inc., 338 E Foothill Blvd. Arcadia, CA 91066. Phone: 800-214-4386 or (626)357-2168; Fax: (626)303-2854; Email: npeal@bpnews.com • URL: http://www.bpnews.com • Monthly. Qualified personnel, $30.00 per year.

***Buyers Directory of the Former Soviet Union: Medical Equipment & Pharmaceutical Products***. Flegon Press, 37B New Cavendish St. London W1M 8JR, United Kingdom. Phone: 44 181 752 1296; Fax: 44 181 752 1296 • $55. Covers: Health authorities and other medical organizations of the former Soviet Union responsible for medical supplies in health-care institutions. Entries include: Name, address, phone.

***Buyer's Guide for Morocco***. Annuaire de l'Acheteur, Ain-Sebaa Casablanca, Morocco. • Free Morocco residents; $100 Out of country. Covers: Commercial, industrial and service companies in Morocco. Entries include: Company name, address, phone, product/service, trade name.

**Buying Influence**. 801 W 47th St., Ste. 110, Country Club Plz. Kansas City, MO 64112. Phone: (816)931-7896; Email: info@buyinginfluence.com • Seeks to help consumers harness their buying power so that corporations make more socially responsible business decisions. Conducts corporate reviews of publicly-traded companies. Provides a forum for online discussions of issues concerning consumers and businesses.

**Buyout Financing Sources/M & A Intermediaries.** SourceMedia Inc., 1 State Street Plz., 27th Fl. New York, NY 10004. Phone: 800-221-1809 or (212)803-8200 or (212)803-8333; Fax: (212)843-9635 or (212)292-5216; Email: custserv@ sourcemedia.com • URL: http://www.sourcemedia.com • Annual. $895.00. Provides the CD-ROM combination of *Directory of Buyout Financing Sources* and *Directory of M & A Intermediaries*. Contains information on more than 1,000 financing sources (banks, insurance companies, venture capital firms, etc.) and 850 intermediaries (corporate acquirers, valuation firms, lawyers, accountants, etc.). Also includes back issues of *Buyouts Newsletter* and *Mergers & Acquisitions Report.* Fully searchable.

**The Buyouts Directory of Mergers & Acquisition Intermediaries.** Securities Data Publishing, 395 Hudson, 3rd Fl., 40 W 57th St. New York, NY 10014. Phone: 888-605-3385 or (212)765-5311 or (212)333-9264; Fax: (646)822-3230 or (212)765-6123; Email: sdp@tfn.com • Annual. $195. Covers: 600 U.S. and Canadian business brokers, as well as other merger and acquisition intermediaries. Database includes: Five articles explaining the role of acquisition intermediaries. Entries include: Company name, address, phone, profiles of commercial, merchant and investment banks.

**Buyouts: The Newsletter for Management Buyouts, Leveraged Aquisitions, and Special Situations.** Thomson Financial Inc., 195 Broadway New York, NY 10007-3100. Phone: (646)822-2000; Email: custserv@tfn.com • URL: http://www. thomsonreuters.com • Biweekly. $1,595.00 per year. Newsletter. Covers news and trends for the buyout industry. Provides information on deal makers and current buyout activity.

**BVI Association of Compliance Officers.** Road Town Tortola, British Virgin Islands. • URL: http://www.bviaco.com • Promotes the role and importance of compliance in the British Virgin Islands. Encourages education, training and standards of practice within the BVI financial industry. Provides a forum for the exchange of ideas among members.

**BWFA National Business News Bulletin.** Brotherhood of Working Farriers Association, 14013 E Hwy. 136 La Fayette, GA 30728-5660. Phone: (706)397-8047; Fax: (706)397-8047; Email: farrierhdq@aol.com • URL: http://www.bwfa.net • Quarterly. Includes business news for trade, letters, and calendar of events.

**C E D: The Premier Magazine of Technology.** Reed Elsevier Group plc Reed Business Information, 360 Park Ave. S New York, NY 11010. Phone: (212)791-4208; Email: corporatecommunications@reedbusiness.com • URL: http:// www.reedbusiness.com • 10/year. Formerly *Communications Engineering and Design.*

**CA Magazine: Leading Figures in Business.** Institute of Chartered Accountants of Scotland, CA House, 21 Haymarket Yards Edinburgh EH12 5BH, United Kingdom. Phone: 44 131 3470100; Fax: 44 131 3470105; Email: enquiries@icas. org.uk • URL: http://icas.org.uk/default.aspx • Monthly. £45 Individuals; £65 Other countries; £20 Students; £30 Students, other countries. Professional journal covering business, finance, management and accountancy of the Institute of Chartered Accountants of Scotland.

**CA Search.** American Chemical Society Chemical Abstracts Service, 2540 Olentangy River Rd. Columbus, OH 43202. Phone: 800-848-6538 or (614)447-3600 or (614)441-3600; Fax: (614)447-3713 or (614)447-3751; Email: help@cas.org • URL: http://www.cas.org • Guide to chemical literature, 1967 to present. Inquire as to online cost and availability.

**CA Selects: Selenium and Tellurium Chemistry.** American Chemical Society. American Chemical Society Chemical Abstracts Service, 2540 Olentangy River Rd. Columbus, OH 43202. Phone: 800-848-6538 or (614)447-3600 or (614)441-3600; Fax: (614)447-3713 or (614)447-3751; Email: help@ cas.org • URL: http://www.cas.org • Semiweekly. Members, $92.00 per year; non-members, $305.00 per year. Looseleaf service. Incorporates *Selenium and Tellurium Abstracts.*

**CAB Abstracts.** CABI, Nosworthy Way, Oxfordshire Wallingford OX10 8DE, United Kingdom. Phone: 44 1491 832111; Fax: 44 1491 833508; Email: enquiries@cabi.org • URL: http:// www.cabi.org • Contains 46 specialized abstract collections covering over 10,000 journals and monographs in the areas of agriculture, horticulture, forest products, farm products, nutrition, dairy science, poultry, grains, animal health, entomology, etc. Time period is 1972 to date, with monthly updates. Inquire as to online cost and availability. *CAB Abstracts on CD-ROM* also available, with annual updating.

**Cabell's Directory of Publishing Opportunities in Economics and Finance.** Cabell Publishing Inc., PO Box 5428 Beaumont, TX 77726. Phone: 800-899-0575 or (409)898-0575; Fax: (409)866-9554; Email: publish@cabells.com • URL: http://www.cabells.com • Irregular. Covers: Over 860 scholarly periodicals in economics and finance. Entries include: Publication name, address, subject interests, editorial guidelines and style, submission procedures, audience and circulation of the publication, and reviewer acceptance rate data.

**Cabell's Directory of Publishing Opportunities in Management.** Cabell Publishing Inc., PO Box 5428 Beaumont, TX 77726.

Phone: 800-899-0575 or (409)898-0575; Fax: (409)866-9554; Email: publish@cabells.com • URL: http://www. cabells.com • Irregular. $244.95 Individuals. Covers: Over 1,180 scholarly periodicals in management. Entries include: Publication name, address, subject interests, editorial guidelines and style, submission procedures, audience and circulation of the publication, and reviewer acceptance rate data.

**Cable Television Directory.** InfoGroup Inc., 5711 S 86th Cir. Omaha, NE 68127-4146. Phone: (402)593-4500 • URL: http://www.infogroup.com • Annual. Number of listings: 9,002. Entries include: Name, address, phone, size of advertisement, name of owner or manager, number of employees, year first in "Yellow Pages." Compiled from telephone company "Yellow Pages," nationwide.

**Cable TV Facts.** Cabletelevision Advertising Bureau, 830 3rd Ave., 2nd Fl. New York, NY 10022. Phone: (212)508-1200; Fax: (212)832-3268; Email: chuckt@cabletvadbureau.com • URL: http://www.thecab.tv • Annual. $50 Members; $75 Nonmembers. Publication includes: List of ad-supported cable networks. Principal content of publication is discussion of the growth of the cable television industry, changes in viewership, marketing, and research trends. Covers demographic information, audience ratings, cable penetration, regional sports and news networks, major market interconnects.

**Cable TV Financial Databook.** SNL Kagan, 40 Ragsdale Dr., Ste. 250 Monterey, CA 93940. Phone: (831)624-1536; Fax: (831)641-0961 • URL: http://www.kagan.com • Annual. $595. Publication includes: Lists of 100 top multiple system cable TV operators, 100 top single cable TV systems, top publicly-owned cable TV equipment suppliers, financial institutions active in cable TV financing, venture capitalists in the field, and appraisers, brokers, and consultants, Telcos in cable, High-Speed access rollouts, digital cable. Entries include: For leading operators—Name, total subscribers, homes passed, homes under franchise, plant miles, names of key personnel; ranked in separate lists by total revenues. For equipment suppliers—Name, product supplied, operating statistics from annual report. For single systems—Name, address, total subscribers, name of general manager. Principal content of publication is financial and statistical data on cable television companies, securities, accounting, etc.

**Cable TV Investor: Newsletter on Investments in Cable TV Systems and Publicly Held Cable TV Stocks.** Paul Kagan Associates, Inc., 126 Clock Tower Pl. Carmel, CA 93923-8746. Phone: (831)624-1536; Fax: (831)625-3225; Email: info@ kagan.com • URL: http://www.kagan.com • Monthly. $995.00 per year.

**Cable TV Programming: Newsletter on Programs for Pay Cable TV and Analysis of Basic Cable Networks.** Paul Kagan Associates, Inc., 126 Clock Tower Pl. Carmel, CA 93923-8746. Phone: (831)624-1536; Fax: (831)625-3225; Email: info@ kagan.com • URL: http://www.kagan.com • Monthly. $895.00 per year.

**Cabletelevision Advertising Bureau.** 830 3rd Ave., 2nd Fl. New York, NY 10022. Phone: (212)508-1200; Fax: (212)832-3268; Email: chuckt@cabletvadbureau.com • URL: http:// www.thecab.tv • Ad-supported cable networks. Provides marketing and advertising support to members and promotes the use of cable by advertisers and ad agencies locally, regionally, and nationally.

**Cairns Chamber of Commerce.** Ste. M2a, Mezzanine Level, The Pier, Pier Point Rd. Cairns, QLD 4870, Australia. Phone: 61 7 40311838; Fax: 61 7 40310883; Email: info@cairnschamber. com.au • URL: http://www.cairnschamber.com.au • Represents business in the Cairns region. Provides statistical and business advice. Works to attract investment and business relocation to the area. Provides trade and export support.

**California Bioscience Directory.** San Diego Regional Chamber of Commerce, Emerald Plz., Ste. 1000, 402 W Broadway San Diego, CA 92101-3585. Phone: (619)544-1300 or (619)544-1382; Fax: (619)744-7400; Email: webinfo@sdchamber.org • URL: http://sdchamber.org • $345 Members. Covers: 1,700 California companies and over 6,000 key managers in biotechnology, biomedical, pharmaceutical, bioresearch, and medical device firms.

**California Business Register.** Harris InfoSource, 2057 E Aurora Rd. Twinsburg, OH 44087-1999. Phone: 800-888-5900 or (330)425-9000 or (973)921-5500; Fax: (800)643-5997 or (877)252-3375; Email: customerservice@harrisinfo.com • URL: http://www.harrisinfo.com • Annual. $355 Individuals print; $295 for the print directory; $995 for the database. Profiles 56,750 top manufacturers, wholesalers, high-tech, and software companies in the state and lists the names and titles of more than 135,000 CEOs, owners, and key executives. Ninety-two percent of the companies are privately held. The listings include company name and address; telephone, fax, and toll-free numbers; Web site email addresses; number of employees; annual sales; products and services; SIC codes; export/import indicators; and primary bank.

**California Farmer: The Business Magazine for Commercial Agriculture.** Farm Progress Companies Inc., 255 38th Ave., Ste. P Saint Charles, IL 60174-5410. Phone: 800-441-1410 or (630)690-5600; Fax: (630)462-2869 or (630)462-4656; Email: wvogt@farmprogress.com • URL: http://www. farmprogress.com • $23.95 Individuals. Three editions:

Northern, Southern and Central Valley.

**California Institute of Technology - Division of the Humanities and Social Sciences - Laboratory for Experimental Economics and Political Science.** 337 Baxter Hall, MC 228-77 Pasadena, CA 91125. Phone: (626)395-4209; Fax: (626)405-9841; Email: cplott@hss.caltech.edu • URL: http:// eeps.caltech.edu • Economic and political behavior research, including studies in pricing strategies, competitive bidding and computer-controlled payload management.

**California Institute of Technology - Office of Sponsored Research.** 1200 E California Blvd., MC 231-15 Pasadena, CA 91125. Phone: (626)395-6219 or (626)395-6073; Fax: (626)795-4571; Email: david.mayo@caltech.edu • URL: http://researchadministration.caltech.edu/osr • Responsible for administrative and financial aspects of extramurally sponsored research conducted by faculty members and graduate students of the Institute.

**California Institute of Technology.** Caltech 17-6, 1200 E California Blvd. Pasadena, CA 91125. Phone: 800-514-2665 or (626)395-6811 or (818)395-6811; Fax: (818)393-4218 or (626)395-5768; Email: feefback@jpl.nasa.gov • URL: http:// www.caltech.edu.

**California International Trade Register.** Harris InfoSource, 2057 E Aurora Rd. Twinsburg, OH 44087-1999. Phone: 800-888-5900 or (330)425-9000 or (973)921-5500; Fax: (800)643-5997 or (877)252-3375; Email: customerservice@harrisinfo. com • URL: http://www.harrisinfo.com • Annual. $155. Covers: 15,656 California international trade companies. Entries include: Company name, address, county, phone, fax, web site address (on CD-ROM only), number of employees, names and titles of key executives, plant size, year established, parent company, annual sales, import/export information, Standard Industrial Classification (SIC) code, and product description.

**California Job Journal.** California Job Journal, 3050 Fite Cir., Ste. 100 Sacramento, CA 95827-1818. Phone: 800-655-5627 or (916)925-0800; Fax: (916)366-3436; Email: cjj@ jobjournal.com • URL: http://www.jobjournal.com • Weekly. Covers: Employment issues and job openings in California from entry-level to executive positions. Database includes: Career guidance and job search advice. Entries include: Company name, address, phone, type of business, name and title of contact; comprehensive description of position and required skills/background, salary and/or benefits offered.

**California Management Review.** University of California at Berkeley, University of California Campus, 101 Sproul Hall Berkeley, CA 94720-5400. Phone: (510)642-6000 • URL: http://www.berkeley.edu • Quarterly. $122 Individuals print and online; $110 Students print and online.

**California Manufacturers Register: 2008 Edition.** San Francisco Chamber of Commerce, 235 Montgomery St., Ste. 760 San Francisco, CA 94104. Phone: (415)392-4520; Fax: (415)392-0485; Email: info@sfchamber.com • URL: http://www. sfchamber.com • Annual. $259 Nonmembers (with book and Read only CD-ROM); $233 Members (with book and Read only CD-ROM); $198 Members; $220 NON. Covers: 34,000 manufacturing firms which are members of the California Manufacturers Association. Entries include: Contact details.

**California State Polytechnic University, Pomona - Industrial Research Institute for Pacific Nations.** School of Business Administration, 3801 W Temple Ave. Pomona, CA 91768. Phone: (909)869-2350 or (909)869-2399; Fax: (909)869-6799; Email: hkjin@csupomona.edu • URL: http://www. csupomona.edu • Conducts research on the Pacific nations marketplace.

**Call Center.** UBM L.L.C., 240 W 35th St. New York, NY 10001. • URL: http://www.ubm.com • Monthly. Free to qualified personnel. Emphasis is on telemarketing, selling, and customer service. Includes articles on communication technology. Formerly *Call Center Solutions.*

**Call Sheet.** Nielsen Business Media Inc., 770 Broadway New York, NY 10003-9522. Phone: 866-890-8541 or (646)654-4500 or (646)654-5000; Fax: (646)654-5584 or (646)654-4500; Email: bmcomm@nielsen.com • URL: http://www. nielsenbusinessmedia.com • 10 times per year. $59.00. per year. Directory, production and casting guide, designed for actors and writers. Formerly *Ross Reports Television.*

**Callmann on Unfair Competition, Trademarks and Monopolies.** Louis Altman and Rudolf Callmann. Thomson West, 610 Opperman Dr. Eagan, MN 55123. Phone: 800-328-9352 or (651)687-7000 • Semiannual. $2,973; $342 per month. Covers various aspects of anti-competitive behavior.

**Camara de Comercio Argentino-Brasilena.** Montevideo 770-12 Piso 1019 Buenos Aires, Argentina. Phone: 54 11 48114503; Email: institucionales@cambras.org.ar • URL: http://www. cambras.org.ar • Represents business and commerce in Argentina.

**Camara de Comercio Argentino-Britanica en la Republica Argentina.** Av. Corrientes 457, Piso 10 C1043AAE Buenos Aires, Argentina. Phone: 54 11 43942762; Fax: 54 11 43263860; Email: info@ccab.com.ar • URL: http://www. ccab.com.ar • Promotes bilateral Trade and Investment between Argentina and UK.

**Camara de Comercio de la Republica de Cuba.** Calle 21 esq. a Calle A, No. 661, Vedado Havana, Cuba. Phone: 53 7 833-8040; Fax: 53 7 838-1324; Email: ccicuba@camara.com.cu • URL: http://www.camaracuba.cu • Represents trade, industry, finance, transport, insurance and all sectors of international businesses. Shapes policies and raises awareness of international business concerns. Fosters networking and cooperation among members.

**Camara de Comercio e Industria de Trenque Lauquen**. Bvard. Villegas 150 6400 Buenos Aires, Argentina. Phone: 54 2392412000 or 54 2392431672; Fax: 54 2392430414; Email: info@lacamaradetrenque.com.ar • URL: http://www. tlauquen.com.ar • Represents business in Argentina.

**Camara de Comercio Exterior de Rosario**. 1868 Cordoba St., 1st Fl. 2000 Rosario, Argentina. Phone: 54 341 4257147; Fax: 54 341 4257486; Email: ccer@commerce.com.ar • URL: http://www.commerce.com.ar • Promotes international trade for export and import businesses in the Rosario region of Argentina.

**Camara de Comercio Exterior de Salta**. Alvarado 51 4400 Salta, Argentina. Phone 54 387 4311003; Fax: 54 387 4225293 • URL: http://www.camcomexsalta.com.ar • Represents businesses in the Salta region of Argentina.

**Camara de Comercio, Industria Y Servicios de Carlos Casares**. Avda. San Martin 318 B6530 Carlos Casares, Argentina. Fax: 54 2395451022 • URL: http://www. camaracarloscasares.com.ar • Promotes business and industry in the Carlos Casares region of Argentina.

**Camara de Comercio Italiana de Rosario**. Cordoba 1868 2000 Rosario, Argentina. Phone: 54 341 4266789 or 54 341 4245691; Email: info@italrosario.com • URL: http://www. italrosario.com/ • Represent Italian business interests in Rosario, Argentina.

*Camara de Comercio Luso-Britanica Directory*. British-Portuguese Chamber of Commerce, Rua da Estrela, 8 P-1200-669 Lisbon, Portugal. Phone: 1 3961586; Fax: 1 3901513; Email: bpcc@mail.telepac.pt • Annual. Free to members; $30 Nonmembers. Covers: Portuguese and United Kingdom economic, financial, and trade matters. Entries include: Organization name, address, phone, fax.

**Camara de Comercio Sueco Argentina**. Carlos Pellegrini 833 Buenos Aires, Argentina. Phone: 54 11 43428867; Fax: 54 11 43428867; Email: info@ccsa.com.ar • URL: http://www. ccsa.com.ar • Represents businesses in Argentina.

**Camara de Industria y Comercio Argentino-Alemana**. Av. Corrientes 327 C1043AAD Buenos Aires, Argentina. Phone: 54 11 52194000; Fax: 54 11 52194001; Email: ahkargentina@ ahkargentina.com.ar • URL: http://www.ahkargentina.com. ar/ • Represents German business in Argentina and promotes international trade between Argentina and Germany.

**Camara de Industria y Comercio de Matanza**. Cal. Entre Rios 3026, San Justo 1754 Buenos Aires, Argentina. Phone: 54 11 46511830; Fax: 54 11 46511830; Email: info@cicm.com.ar • URL: http://www.cicm.com.ar • Represents business in Argentina.

**Camara Empresaria Parque Industrial de Pilar**. Ruta 8, km. 60, Parque Industrial Pilar, Calle Del Canal Nro. 1758 1629 Buenos Aires, Argentina. Phone 54 230 4491994 or 54 230 4491892; Email: info@cepip.org.ar • URL: http://www.cepip. org.ar • Represents businesses in Argentina.

**Camara Espanola de Comercio de la Republica Argentina**. 863 Av. Belgrano, Piso 7 C1092AAI Buenos Aires, Argentina. Phone: 54 11 43355000; Fax: 54 11 43355022; Email: recepcion.cecra@cecra.com.ar • URL: http://www.cecra. com.ar • Represents Spanish-Argentine businesses in Buenos Aires.

*Cambodia Business Law Handbook*. International Business Publications, USA, PO Box 15343 Washington, DC 20003. Phone: (202)546-2103; Fax: (202)546-3275; Email: ibpusa@ comcast.net • URL: http://ibpus.com • $99.95 Individuals hardcopy; $99.95 Individuals e-book; $99.95 Individuals CD-ROM. Covers: Information on basic business legislation, laws, business climate, export-import regulations, taxation, banking and contacts.

*Cambodia Investment & Business Guide*. International Business Publications, USA, PO Box 15343 Washington, DC 20003. Phone: (202)546-2103; Fax: (202)546-3275; Email: ibpusa@ comcast.net • URL: http://ibpus.com • $99.95 Individuals hardcopy; $99.95 Individuals e-book; $99.95 Individuals CD-ROM. Covers: Information on economy, business, export-import and investment climate, regulations and industrial development, banking, government, and opportunities. Entries include: Important business contacts and business travel.

*Camera*. Orion Research Corp., 14555 N Scottsdale Rd., Ste. 330 Scottsdale, AZ 85254. Phone: 800-844-0759 or (480)951-1114; Fax: (480)951-1117 or (800)375-1315 • Annual. $144 Individuals. Quotes retail and wholesale prices of used cameras and equipment. Original list prices and years of manufacture are also shown.

*Cameras Directory—Retail Companies*. InfoGroup Inc., 5711 S 86th Cir. Omaha, NE 68127-4146. Phone: (402)593-4500 • URL: http://www.infogroup.com • Annual. Number of listings: 5,303. Entries include: Name, address, phone, size of advertisement, name of owner or manager, number of employees, year first in "Yellow Pages." Compiled from telephone company "Yellow Pages," nationwide.

*Camerdata*. Camerdata S.A., Calle Alfonso XI, 3 E-28014 Madrid, Spain. Phone: 1 5212984; Fax: 1 5228873 • Monthly. Database covers: Approximately 2 million Spanish business firms. Database includes: Company name, address, number of employees, sector of activity.

*Cameroon Business Directory*. Business Guide, PO Box 27669 Dubai, United Arab Emirates. Phone: 971 4 2651719; Fax: 971 4 2692151; Email: sales@africa-business.com • URL: http://www.africa-business.com • $150 download. Covers: 4,300 business listings including wholesalers, importers, retailers, business houses, and agents in Cameroon.

*Cameroon Business Law Handbook*. International Business Publications, USA, PO Box 15343 Washington, DC 20003. Phone: (202)546-2103; Fax: (202)546-3275; Email: ibpusa@ comcast.net • URL: http://ibpus.com • $99.95 Individuals hardcopy; $99.95 Individuals e-book; $99.95 Individuals CD-ROM. Covers: Information on basic business legislation, laws and climate, export-import regulations, and contacts.

*Cameroon Industrial and Business Directory*. International Business Publications, USA, PO Box 15343 Washington, DC 20003. Phone: (202)546-2103; Fax: (202)546-3275; Email: ibpusa@comcast.net • URL: http://ibpus.com • $99.95 Individuals hardcover; $99.95 Individuals e-book; $99.95 Individuals CD-ROM. Covers: Strategic and practical economic and business information. Entries include: Business contacts for conducting business activity in the country.

**Campaign for Working Families**. PO Box 1222 Merrifield, VA 22116-1222. Phone: (703)671-8800; Email: info@cwfpac. com • URL: http://www.cwfpac.com • Represents the interests and values of America's traditional families in the political arena. Works on electing pro-family, pro-life and pro-free enterprise candidates to federal and state offices. Conducts extensive media campaigns and distribution of literature.

*Campground Management: Business Publication for Profitable Outdoor Recreation*. Woodall Publications Corp., 8073 Constitution Dr. Syracuse, IN 46567. Phone: 800-323-9076 or (847)362-6700; Email: esmith@affinity.com • URL: http:// www.woodalls.com • Monthly. $24.95 per year.

*Camping Magazine*. American Camping Association, 5000 State Rd. 67 N Martinsville, IN 46151-7902. Phone: 800-428-2267 or (765)342-8456; Fax: (765)342-2065 • URL: http://www. acacamps.org • Bimonthly. $29.95 per year. Contains recent trends and latest research in the camp industry.

**Can Manufacturers Institute**. 1730 Rhode Island Island Ave. NW, Ste. 1000 Washington, DC 20036. Phone: (202)232-4677; Fax: (202)232-5756 • URL: http://www.cancentral. com • Represents can makers and can industry suppliers. Aims to foster the prosperity of the industry and bring value to its members in a cost effective way.

**Canada-Arab Business Council**. 1 Rideau St., Ste. 700 Ottawa, ON, Canada K1N 8S7. Phone: (613)670-5853 • URL: http:// canada-arabbusiness.org • Canadian business organizations interested in Middle East markets. Promotes business and trade between Canada and the Arab world; serves as a business advisory body to governments in Canada on matters relating to Canadian trade with the region; promotes awareness of Canada's business and commercial capabilities; seeks to advance Canada to the Region; assists members in trade and investment activities in each country in the Middle East.

*Canada Business Database*. The Data Supplier, 9107 Wilshire Blvd., Ste. 450 Beverly Hills, CA 90210. Phone: 888-930-3282; Fax: (818)221-0295; Email: contactus@ thedatasupplier.com • URL: http://www.thedatasupplier.com • Contains contact information for more than 2.7 million companies in Canada. Includes business name, full contact information, and type of business.

*Canada Business Email Database*. The Data Supplier, 9107 Wilshire Blvd., Ste. 450 Beverly Hills, CA 90210. Phone: 888-930-3282; Fax: (818)221-0295; Email: contactus@ thedatasupplier.com • URL: http://www.thedatasupplier.com • Contains e-mail addresses for more than 360,000 business contacts in Canada. Also includes contact name, business name, address, telephone and fax numbers, and Web site.

**Canada-China Business Council**. 330 Bay St., Ste. 1501 Toronto, ON, Canada M5H 2S8. Phone: (416)954-3800; Fax: (416)954-3806; Email: ccbc@ccbc.com • URL: http://www. ccbc.com • Promotes trade and investment between Canada and the People's Republic of China; seeks to stimulate trade in goods and services, investment and technology transfer; strives to achieve stronger economic growth and a closer relationship between Canada and China; provides assistance to business; advocates for Canadian business on matters of Canada - China relations to the government and public; disseminates market information.

*Canada Golden Key Directory*. International Institute of Trade Relation Promotion, Trade Information Centre of Iran, No. 7, 3rd Fl., Abbasie Bazar, Ferdowsi Sq. Tehran, Iran. Phone: 98 21 88833900; Fax: 98 21 88820697; Email: order@ irangoldenkey.com • URL: http://www.goldenkeydirectory. com/about.html • £60 Individuals. Covers: 8,000 companies in Canada. Entries include: Company name, address, telephone, fax, e-mail, products, services, Managing Director, and business activities.

*Canada Government and Business Contacts Handbook*. International Business Publications, USA, PO Box 15343 Washington, DC 20003. Phone: (202)546-2103; Fax: (202)546-3275; Email: ibpusa@comcast.net • URL: http:// ibpus.com • $99.95 Individuals hardcopy, E-book and CD-ROM. Covers: Strategic government and business information, export-import activity in the country, investment, business contacts and regulations.

*Canada Greater Montreal Business CD-ROM*. Manufacturers'

News Inc., 1633 Central St. Evanston, IL 60201-1569. Phone: (847)864-7000; Fax: (847)332-1100 • URL: http://www. manufacturersnews.com • Contains detailed directory information on companies in and around Montreal, Quebec. Covers more than 22,100 companies and provides information on nearly 29,200 executives and key decision-makers.

*Canada Greater Vancouver Business CD-ROM*. Manufacturers' News Inc., 1633 Central St. Evanston, IL 60201-1569. Phone: (847)864-7000; Fax: (847)332-1100 • URL: http://www. manufacturersnews.com • Contains detailed directory information on more than 18,600 companies in and around Vancouver, British Columbia.

**Canada-India Business Council**. 1 St. Clair Ave. E, Ste. 302 Toronto, ON, Canada M4T 2V7. Phone: (416)214-5947; Fax: (416)214-9081; Email: info@canada-indiabusiness.ca • URL: http://canada-indiabusiness.ca • Canadian businesses trading with India. Promotes increased trade between Canada and India. Advocates for legislation conducive to trade; represents members before trade and industrial organizations and the public.

*Canada Industrial and Business Directory*. International Business Publications, USA, PO Box 15343 Washington, DC 20003. Phone: (202)546-2103; Fax: (202)546-3275; Email: ibpusa@comcast.net • URL: http://ibpus.com • Annual. $99.95 Individuals hardcopy; $99.95 Individuals e-book; $99.95 Individuals CD-ROM. Covers: Detailed information on investment, export-import business opportunities, foreign economic assistance projects, government and business contacts.

**Canada - Japan Society of British Columbia**. 15-555 W 12th Ave. Vancouver, BC, Canada V5Z 3X0. Phone: (604)708-3306; Fax: (604)921-8192 • URL: http://www. canadajapansociety.bc.ca • Promotes opportunities with Japan in British Columbia; seeks to provide a better understanding between the people of Canada and Japan.

**Canada-United States Business Association**. 2000 Town Center Ste. 1800 Southfield, MI 48075. Email: info@cusbaonline. com • URL: http://www.canadainternational.gc.ca/detroit/ commerce_can/ba-ab.aspx?lang=eng • Consists of supporters of business such as labor, banking, consulting, government, and academia. Promotes stronger business and trading lineages between the U.S. and Canada by providing a forum to exchange information and ideas and to build relationships. Conducts educational programs; maintains speakers' bureau, panels, and special events.

*Canada Year Book*. Statistics Canada, Publications Division, 150 Tunney's Pasture Driveway Ottawa, ON, Canada K1A OT6. Phone: 800-263-1136 or (613)951-8116; Fax: (613)951-0581 or (800)899-9734 • URL: http://www.statcan.ca • Annual. Available via HTML or PDF.

**Canada's Venture Capital and Private Equity Association**. 1201-372 Bay St. Toronto, ON, Canada M5H 2W9. Phone: (416)487-0519; Fax: (416)487-5899; Email: cvca@cvca.ca • URL: http://www.cvca.ca • Ventures and risks capital companies. Promotes economic growth through provision of capital to emerging businesses. Conducts research; facilitates exchange of information among members; represents the venture capital industry before government agencies, industrial and financial organizations, and the public.

*Canadian Aboriginal Business and Communities Directory: British Columbia*. Indiana Marketing, 135, Chef Aime-Romain Wendake, QC, Canada G0A 4V0. Phone: 866-333-2332 or (418)842-0230; Fax: (418)842-5950; Email: info@ indianamarketing.com • URL: http://indianamarketing.com • C$74.95 Individuals plus $12.95 for shipping and handling. Aboriginal companies and organizations in British Columbia, Canada.

**Canadian Agri-Marketing Association - Manitoba**. 3336 Portage Ave., Ste. 509 Winnipeg, MB, Canada R3K 2H9. Phone: (204)782-6618 or (204)837-2853; Email: camamb@ mymts.net • URL: http://www.cama.org/manitoba/ ManitobaHome.aspx • Represents and supports individuals involved in agricultural marketing.

**Canadian Agri-Marketing Association - Ontario**. c/o Mary Thornly, Executive Director, 22 Guyers Dr., RR 3 Port Elgin, ON, Canada N0H 2C7. Phone: (519)389-6552; Email: camaont@bmts.com • URL: http://www.cama.org/Ontario/ OntarioHome.aspx • Represents and supports individuals involved in agricultural marketing.

*Canadian Almanac and Directory*. Micromedia ProQuest, 20 Victoria St. Toronto, ON, Canada M5C 2N8. Phone: 800-387-2689 or (416)362-5211; Fax: (416)362-6161; Email: info@ micromedia.ca • URL: http://www.proquest.com • Annual. $269.00. Contains general information and statistical data relating to Canada and provides information on about 60,000 Canadian agencies, associations, institutions, museums, libraries, etc.

**Canadian-American Business Council**. 1900 K St. NW, Ste. 100 Washington, DC 20006. Phone: (202)496-7906; Fax: (202)496-7756; Email: info@cabc.co • URL: http://cabc.co • Individuals, corporations, institutions and organizations with an interest in trade between the United States and Canada. Promotes free trade. Gathers and disseminates information; maintains speakers' bureau.

**Canadian Association of Physicians for the Environment**. 130 Spadina Ave., Ste. 301 Toronto, ON, Canada M5V 2L4. Phone: (416)306-2273; Fax: (416)960-9392 • URL: http:// cape.ca • Physicians, allied health care practitioners, and citizens committed to a healthy and sustainable environment. Works to protect and promote human health by addressing issues of local and global environmental degradation. Provides information on children's health, greening health care, climate change, regulatory reform, and toxins.

**Canadian Association of Women Executives and Entrepreneurs.** 401 Bay St., Ste. 1600 Toronto, ON, Canada M5K 2Y4. Phone: (416)756-0000; Fax: (416)756-0000; Email: contact@cawee.net • URL: http://www.cawee.net • Seeks to provide opportunities for women to empower other women in the development and advancement of their business and professional lives; which fosters financial independence, professional development and personal satisfaction.

*Canadian Business and Current Affairs Fulltext.* Micromedia ProQuest, 20 Victoria St. Toronto, ON, Canada M5C 2N8. Phone: 800-387-2689 or (416)362-5211; Fax: (416)362-6161; Email: info@micromedia.ca • URL: http://www.proquest.com • Provides full-text of eight Canadian daily newspapers and more than 480 Canadian business magazines and trade journals. Indexing is 1982 to date, with selected full text from 1993. Updates are twice a month. Inquire as to on-line cost and availability.

*Canadian Business.* Canadian Business Media, 1 Mt. Pleasant Rd., 11th Fl. Toronto, ON, Canada M5Y 2Y5. Phone: 800-465-0700; Fax: (416)764-2000; Email: service@cbmedia.ca • URL: http://www.canadianbusiness.com • Biweekly. $20 per year. Edited for corporate managers and executives, this is a major periodical in Canada covering a variety of business, economic, and financial topics. Emphasis is on the top 500 Canadian corporations.

*Canadian Business Directory.* Infogroup Inc. infoUSA Inc., 1020 E 1st St. Papillion, NE 68046. Phone: 800-321-0869; Email: corporate.communications@infogroup.com • URL: http://www.infousa.com • Contains contact information for more than 1.2 million Canadian business establishments. Includes address, telephone number, employment data, key contact and title, primary Standard Industrial Classification (SIC) code, yellow pages and brand/trade name information, actual and estimated financial data, and corporate linkages.

*Canadian Business.* Rogers Communications Inc., 333 Bloor St. E, 10th Fl. Toronto, ON, Canada M4W 1G9. Phone: 888-764-3771 or (416)935-7777 or (416)764-2000; Fax: (416)935-3597 or (416)764-2098; Email: info@rogers.com • URL: http://www.rogers.com • Contains the full text of the Canadian publication, *Canadian Business* magazine.

**Canadian Capital Markets Association.** 85 Richmond St. W Toronto, ON, Canada M5H 2C9. Phone: (416)410-1050; Email: info@ccma-acmc.ca • URL: http://www.ccma-acmc.ca • Enhances the competitiveness of the Canadian capital markets through a forum of industry experts who provide leadership and direction to the investment community. Promotes straight-through processing strategies that reduce ongoing errors and processing costs. Addresses the massive changes occurring in global securities markets such as increased on and off exchange securities trading volumes and volatility due in part to the growth of on-line trading.

*Canadian Co-Operative Wool Growers Magazine.* Canadian Co-Operative Wool Growers, 142 Franktown Rd. Carleton Place, ON, Canada K7C 3P3. Phone: 800-488-2714 or (613)257-2714; Fax: (613)257-8896; Email: ccwghq@wool.ca • URL: http://www.wool.ca • Annual. Free members; $3 Nonmembers. Contains information and a mail order catalogue for livestock supplies, equestrian products and clothing.

**Canadian Council for Aboriginal Business.** 2 Berkeley St., Ste. 310 Toronto, ON, Canada M5A 4J5. Phone: (416)961-8663; Fax: (416)961-3995; Email: info@ccab.com • URL: http://www.ccab.com • Promotes the full participation of aboriginal people in the Canadian economy. Seeks to connect aboriginal and non-aboriginal people and companies with the opportunities required to achieve personal and business success. Develops and operates the Progressive Aboriginal Relations (PAR) benchmarking and hallmarking program. Administers the Canadian Aboriginal Business Hall of Fame.

**Canadian Council of Chief Executives.** 99 Bank St., Ste. 1001 Ottawa, ON, Canada K1P 6B9. Phone: (613)238-3727; Fax: (613)238-3247; Email: info@ceocouncil.ca • URL: http://www.ceocouncil.ca • Businesses and trade organizations. Promotes a healthy national economy. Conducts research; lobbies for legislation favorable to business; represents members' interests.

*Canadian Directory of Shopping Centres.* Rogers Publishing Ltd., 333 Bloor St. E, 7th Fl. Toronto, ON, Canada M4W 1G9. Phone: 888-764-3771 or (416)764-2000 or (416)764-1300; Fax: (416)764-7730 • URL: http://www.rogerspublishing.ca • Annual Periodic. $1,125 1-year online subscription plus 3-volume print set; $760 1-year online subscription; $795 print (full set). (Eastern Canada and Western Canada). Describes about 2,200 shopping centers and malls, including those under development.

*Canadian Federal Corporations and Directors.* Postmedia Network Inc., 365 Bloor St. E Toronto, ON, Canada M4W 3L4. Phone: 800-661-7678 or (416)383-2300 or (416)442-2121; Fax: (416)442-2968; Email: aodaliaison@postmedia.com • URL: http://www.postmedia.com • Monthly. Covers: About 400,000 federally incorporated Canadian companies.

Database includes: Company name, address, date incorporated, parent or subsidiary companies, financial data for two years, names and home addresses of directors.

**Canadian Federation of Business and Professional Women's Clubs.** PO Box 62054 Orleans, ON, Canada K1C 7H8. URL: http://www.bpwcanada.com • Canadian women engaged in business, the professions, or industry. Works to enhance the economic, social, and employment status of women. Encourages women to become active in government at every level. Strives to improve business service standards. Networks with related organizations to promote common concerns.

**Canadian Federation of Independent Business.** 401-4141 Yonge St. Toronto, ON, Canada M2P 2A6. Phone: 888-234-2232 or (416)222-8022; Fax: (416)222-6103; Email: cfib@cfib.ca • URL: http://www.cfib-fcei.ca/english/index.html • Independent businesses. Promotes economic well-being of members and seeks to maintain a healthy domestic business climate. Represents members' interests before government agencies, labor and industrial organizations, and the public.

**Canadian Finance and Leasing Association.** 15 Toronto St., Ste. 301 Toronto, ON, Canada M5C 2E3. Phone: 877-213-7373 or (416)860-1133; Fax: (416)860-1140; Email: info@cfla-acfl.ca • URL: http://www.cfla-acfl.ca • Providers of financing and rental and leasing services. Promotes adherence to high standards of ethics and practice by members; seeks to advance the financing, renting, and leasing industries. Represents members' commercial and regulatory interests; conducts promotional and advocacy campaigns.

*Canadian Financial Database.* Globe Interactive, 444 Front St. W Toronto, ON, Canada M5V 2S9. Phone: 800-387-5400 or (416)585-5222; Fax: (416)585-5102; Email: circulation@globeandmail.ca • URL: http://www.theglobeandmail.com • Database covers: about 500 of the leading Canadian corporations. Database includes: Company name, address, phone, names and titles of key personnel, financial data.

*Canadian Florist Greenhouse & Nursery: The National Horticultural Business Publication.* Horticulture Publications, 1090 Aerowood Dr., Unit 1 Mississauga, ON, Canada L4W 1Y5. Phone: (905)625-2730; Fax: (905)625-1355 • Monthly. $18; $24 U.S. and other countries. Magazine for commercial florists, greenhouse growers, nurseries, garden centers, interior landscapers, and craft and hobby retailers.

*Canadian Industrial Equipment News: Reader Service On New, Improved and Redesigned Industrial Equipment and Supplies.* Scott's Directories, 12 Concorde Pl., Ste. 800 Toronto, ON, Canada M3C 4J2. Phone: 800-668-2374 or (416)442-2122; Fax: (416)510-6870; Email: customercare@scottsdirectories.com • URL: http://www.scottsdirectories.com • Monthly. Formerly *Electrical Equipment News.*

**Canadian Institute of Certified Administrative Managers.** 15 Collier St., Lower Level Toronto, ON, Canada M4T 2T5. Phone: (705)725-8926; Fax: (705)725-8196; Email: office@cim.ca • URL: http://www.cicam.org • Certified administrative managers. Promotes excellence in the practice of administrative management. Facilitates communication and cooperation among members; makes available continuing professional development courses.

**Canadian Institute of Chartered Business Valuators.** 277 Wellington St. W, Ste. 710 Toronto, ON, Canada M5V 3H2. Phone: (416)977-1117; Fax: (416)977-7066; Email: admin@cicbv.ca • URL: http://www.cicbv.ca • Chartered business valuators. Promotes excellence in the practice of business valuation. Serves as a forum for the exchange of information among members; makes available continuing professional development programs for business valuators.

**Canadian Institute of Management.** Lower Level, 15 Collier St. Barrie, ON, Canada L4M 1G5. Phone: (705)725-8926; Fax: (705)725-8196; Email: office@cim.ca • URL: http://www.cim.ca • Management personnel. Seeks to advance the practice of business management; promotes continuing professional development of members. Serves as a clearinghouse on management and related topics; facilitates exchange of information among members; makes available educational and training programs.

**Canadian Institutes of Health Research - Institute of Health Services and Policy Research.** 3666 McTavish Montreal, QC, Canada H3A 1Y2. Phone: (514)398-5940; Email: info.ihspr@mcgill.ca • URL: http://www.cihr-irsc.gc.ca/e/13733.html • Supports research on problems confronting health care systems, policy-makers, and managers regarding effective health services and products.

**Canadian Management Centre.** 150 York St., 5th Fl. Toronto, ON, Canada M5H 3S5. Phone: 877-262-2519; Fax: (416)214-6047; Email: cmcinfo@cmcoutperform.com • URL: http://cmcoutperform.com • Managers of corporations and organizations. Promotes excellence in management. Conducts educational and training programs for management personnel.

**Canadian Manufacturers and Exporters.** 1 Nicholas St., Ste. 1500 Ottawa, ON, Canada K1N 7B7. Phone: (613)238-8888; Fax: (613)563-9218 • URL: http://www.cme-mec.ca • Formerly Alliance of Manufacturers and Exporters of Canada.

*Canadian National Business Directory.* Todd Publications, PO Box 500 Millwood, NY 10546. Phone: 866-896-0916 or (914)373-4750; Fax: (914)373-4750; Email: toddpub@aol.com • URL: http://www.toddpublications.com • $250. Cov-

ers: 200,000 businesses, including tradeshows, exhibitions, and meetings. Database includes: Glossary of Internet terms; list of products and services online. Entries include: Address and phone number.

**Canadian Netherlands Business and Professional Association.** 600 The East Mall Etobicoke, ON, Canada M9B 4B1. Phone: (647)478-8620; Fax: (647)478-8620; Email: info@cnbpa.ca • URL: http://www.cnbpa.ca • Business people and professionals in Canada and the Netherlands. Promotes increased trade and communication between Canada and the Netherlands. Serves as a forum for the exchange of information among members.

*Canadian News Facts: The Indexed Digest of Canadian Current Events.* MPL Communications Inc., 133 Richmond St. W, Ste. 700 Toronto, ON, Canada M5H 3M8. Phone: 800-804-8846 or (416)869-1177 or (416)869-2777; Fax: (416)869-0456 or (416)869-0616; Email: investors@mplcomm.com • URL: http://www.adviceforinvestors.com • Bimonthly. $280.00 per year. Monthly and quarterly indexes. A summary of current events in Canada.

**Canadian Payroll Association.** 250 Bloor St. E, Ste. 1600 Toronto, ON, Canada M4W 1E6. Phone: 800-387-4693 or (416)487-3380; Fax: (416)487-3384; Email: Membership@payroll.ca • URL: http://www.payroll.ca • Represents the payroll community in Canada; offers education programs, advocacy efforts, products and services to help members enhance and adapt payroll operations, meet new legislative requirements, address changing workplace needs and take advantage of emerging technologies.

*Canadian Resources and PennyMines Analyst: The Canadian Newsletter for Penny-Mines Investors Who Insist on Geological Value.* MPL Communications Inc., 133 Richmond St. W, Ste. 700 Toronto, ON, Canada M5H 3M8. Phone: 800-804-8846 or (416)869-1177 or (416)869-2777; Fax: (416)869-0456 or (416)869-0616; Email: investors@mplcomm.com • URL: http://www.adviceforinvestors.com • Weekly. $145.00 per year. Newsletter. Mainly on Canadian gold mine stocks. Formerly *Canadian PennyMines Analyst.*

**Canadian Western Agribition.** Canada Centre Bldg., 2nd Fl., Evraz Pl. Regina, SK, Canada S4P 3J8. Phone: (306)565-0565; Fax: (306)757-9963; Email: info@agribition.com • URL: http://www.agribition.com • Agribusinesses. Aims create and maintain an effective, hospitable and entertaining atmosphere to market Canadian agriculture products and expertise to the world. Promotes the expansion, development and interest in agriculture and encourages the breeding and improvement of livestock. Promotes interest in agriculture and stock raising, and particularly to organize, sponsor and host an annual agriculture show. Encourages competition within and among various breeds of livestock, and among producers of other agricultural products. Focuses attention on the outstanding qualities of various agricultural products and breeds of livestock and promote the sale of agricultural products and livestock. Seeks to promote the export of agricultural products, foster improved urban-rural relations within the agricultural industry, and provide a forum in which to channel educational information to the agricultural industry and to the public generally.

*Canadian Who's Who.* University of Toronto Press Inc., 10 St. Mary St., Ste. 700 Toronto, ON, Canada M4Y 2W8. Phone: 800-565-9523 or (416)978-2239 or (416)595-5100; Fax: (416)978-4738 or (416)596-5155; Email: info@utpress.utoronto.ca • URL: http://www.utpress.utoronto.ca • Annual. $185.00. Provides concise biographical information in English and French on 15,000 prominent Canadians.

*The Candy Dish.* National Candy Brokers and Salesmen's Association, 710 E Ogden Ave., Suite 600 Naperville, IL 60563-8603. Phone: (630)369-2406; Fax: (630)369-2488; Email: ncba@b-online.com • URL: http://www.candynet.com • Monthly. Price on application. Provides industry news and event information for candy brokers and distributors.

*Candy Industry: The Global Magazine of Chocolate and Confectionery.* BNP Media, 2401 W Big Beaver Rd., Ste. 700 Troy, MI 48084. Phone: 800-952-6643 or (248)362-3700 or (847)763-9534; Fax: (248)362-5103 or (248)362-0317; Email: privacy@bnpmedia.com • URL: http://www.bnpmedia.com • Monthly.

*CANOE: Canadian Online Explorer.* Canoe Limited Partnership, Phone: (416)947-2154; Fax: (416)947-2209 • URL: http://www.canoe.ca • Web site provides a wide variety of Canadian news and information, including business and financial data. Includes "Money," "Your Investment," "Technology," and "Stock Quotes." Allows keyword searching, with links to many other sites. Daily updating. Fees: Free.

*Canoes Directory.* InfoGroup Inc., 5711 S 86th Cir. Omaha, NE 68127-4146. Phone: (402)593-4500 • URL: http://www.infogroup.com • Annual. Number of listings: 1,783. Entries include: Name, address, phone, size of advertisement, name of owner or manager, number of employees, year first in "Yellow Pages." Compiled from telephone company "Yellow Pages," nationwide.

*CANSIM Time Series Database.* Statistics Canada, Statistical Reference Center, R. H. Coats Bldg., Holland Ave. Ottawa, ON, Canada K1A OT6. Phone: 800-263-1136 or (613)951-8116; Fax: (613)951-0581; Email: infostats@statcan.ca • URL: http://www.statcan.ca • Daily. CANSIM is the Canadian Socio-Economic Information Management System. Contains more than 700,000 statistical time series relating to

Canadian business, industry, trade, economics, finance, labor, health, welfare, and demographics. Time period is mainly 1946 to date, with daily updating. Inquire as to online cost and availability.

***Cape Business News***. Cape Business News, 30 Study St. Cape Town 7441, South Africa. Phone: 27 215 574061; Fax: 27 215 574707; Email: subs@cbn.co.za • URL: http://www.cbn.co.za • Monthly. R 172 Individuals print; R 290 Two years. Business newspaper.

***Cape of Good Hope Business Guide***. Cape Town Regional Chamber of Commerce and Industry, 19 Louis Gradner St. Cape Town 8001, South Africa. Phone: 27 21 4024300; Fax: 27 21 4024302; Email: info@capechamber.co.za • URL: http://www.capetownchamber.com • Annual. Contains business information.

***Cape Verde Business Law Handbook***. International Business Publications, USA, PO Box 15343 Washington, DC 20003. Phone: (202)546-2103; Fax: (202)546-3275; Email: ibpusa@comcast.net • URL: http://ibpus.com • $99.95 Individuals hardcopy, e-book, CD-ROM. Covers: Information on basic business legislation, laws and climate, export-import regulations, and contacts.

***Capital Changes Reports***. Wolters Kluwer Law & Business CCH, 2700 Lake Cook Rd. Riverwoods, IL 60015. Phone: 888-224-7377 or (847)267-7000; Email: cust_serv@cch.com • URL: http://www.cchgroup.com • Weekly. $1,395.00. Six looseleaf volumes. Arranged alphabetically by company. This service presents a chronological capital history that includes reorganizations, mergers and consolidations. Recent actions are found in Volume One - "New Matters.".

***Capital for Shipping***. Informa Publishing Group, BioTechniques, One Research Dr. Ste. 400A Westborough, MA 01581. Phone: (508)614-1414 or (800)493-4080; Fax: (508)616-2930 or (508)231-0856; Email: enquiries@informa.com • URL: http://www.informa.com • Annual. $128.00. Published in the UK by Lloyd's List (www.lloydslist.com). Consists of a "Financial Directory" and a "Legal Directory," listing international ship finance providers and international law firms specializing in shipping. Included with subscription to *Lloyd's Shipping Economist*.

***Car and Driver***. Hachette Filipacchi Media U.S., Inc., 1633 Broadway New York, NY 10019. Phone: 800-289-9464 or (212)767-6000; Fax: (212)767-5600 or (212)767-5615; Email: soundandvision@hfmus.com • URL: http://www.hfmmag.com • Monthly. $11.97 per year.

***Car Stereo***. Orion Research Corp., 14555 N Scottsdale Rd., Ste. 330 Scottsdale, AZ 85254. Phone: 800-844-0759 or (480)951-1114; Fax: (480)951-1117 or (800)375-1315 • Annual. $144 Individuals. Quotes retail and wholesale prices of used stereo sound equipment for automobiles. Original list prices and years of manufacture are also shown.

**Car Wash Owners and Suppliers Association**. 1822 South St. Racine, WI 53404. Phone: (262)639-2289; Fax: (262)639-4393 • Formerly Car Wash Manufacturers and Suppliers Association.

***Car Washing & Polishing Directory***. InfoGroup Inc., 5711 S 86th Cir. Omaha, NE 68127-4146. Phone: (402)593-4500 • URL: http://www.infogroup.com • Annual. Number of listings: 18,030. Entries include: Name, address, phone, size of advertisement, name of owner or manager, number of employees, year first in "Yellow Pages." Compiled from telephone company "Yellow Pages," nationwide.

***Card News: The Executive Report on the Transaction Card Marketplace***. Access Intelligence L.L.C., 4 Choke Cherry Rd., 2nd Fl. Rockville, MD 20850. Phone: 800-777-5006 or (301)354-2000 or (301)354-2101; Fax: (301)309-3847 or (801)365-2300; Email: info@accessintel.com • URL: http://www.accessintel.com/ • 25 times per year. $997.00 per year. Newsletter on transaction cards, debit and credit cards, automatic teller machines, etc.

***Card Security & Fraud Prevention Sourcebook***. Thomson Financial Inc., 195 Broadway New York, NY 10007-3100. Phone: (646)822-2000; Email: custserv@tfn.com • URL: http://www.thomsonreuters.com • Annual. $245 Individuals. Covers: Credit card, debit card, and internet security products and services. Entries include: Company name, product name, profile.

***Card Technology***. SourceMedia Inc., 1 State Street Plz., 27th Fl. New York, NY 10004. Phone: 800-221-1809 or (212)803-8200 or (212)803-8333; Fax: (212)843-9635 or (212)292-5216; Email: custserv@sourcemedia.com • URL: http://www.sourcemedia.com • Monthly. $79.00 per year. Covers advanced technology for credit, debit, and other cards. Topics include smart cards, optical recognition, and card design.

**Cardiff University - Julian Hodge Institute of Applied Macroeconomics**. Aberconway Bldg., Rm. E46 Cardiff CF10 3EU, United Kingdom. Phone: 44 29 20875728; Fax: 44 29 20874419; Email: minfordp@cardiff.ac.uk • URL: http://business.cardiff.ac.uk/julian-hodge-institute-applied-macroeconomics • Behavior of the United Kingdom's economy, as well as its relationship with other economies in Europe.

**Cardiff University - Welsh Economy Research Unit**. Aberconway Bldg., Cardiff Business School, Colum Dr. Cardiff CF10 3EU, United Kingdom. Phone: 44 29 20875089; Fax: 44 29 20874419; Email: mundaymc@cf.ac.uk • URL: http://business.cardiff.ac.uk/welsh-economy-research-unit • Economic issues in Wales.

***Cards—Baseball Directory***. InfoGroup Inc., 5711 S 86th Cir. Omaha, NE 68127-4146. Phone: (402)593-4500 • URL: http://www.infogroup.com • Annual. Number of listings: 4,538. Entries include: Name, address, phone, size of advertisement, name of owner or manager, number of employees, year first in "Yellow Pages." Compiled from telephone company "Yellow Pages," nationwide.

**CardTrak**. 99 Vandebilt Beach Rd., 2nd Fl. Naples, FL 34108. Phone: 800-344-7714; Email: media@cardtrak.com • URL: http://www.cardtrak.com • Promotes the "wise and careful" use of credit cards. A consumer organization.

***Career Development Quarterly***. National Career Development Association. American Counseling Association, 5999 Stevenson Ave. Alexandria, VA 22304. Phone: 800-347-6647; Fax: (703)823-0252; Email: membership@counseling.org • URL: http://www.counseling.org • Quarterly. $226 Institutions print or online; $272 Institutions print and online; Included in membership. Features articles on career counseling, individual and organizational career development, work and leisure, career education, career coaching, and career management.

***Career Information Center***. Glencoe Publishing Co., • Biennial. $778 Individuals. Organized into 13 occupational clusters (comprising 13 volumes and an index volume). Each volume includes a section listing accredited occupational educational and vocational institutions. A second section lists more than 700 occupational profiles and over 3,000 organizations with jobs in the field of work with which the volume is concerned. Database includes: Job summary chart; industry snapshots that summarize major developments; photographs; overview of the job market; job hunting information and tips. Entries include: For institutions—Name, address, programs and degrees offered. For organizations—Name, address.

**Career Women's Forum**. PO Box 1200 CH-1211 Geneva, Switzerland. Phone: 41 22 3183200; Fax: 41 22 3183300; Email: administration@cwf.ch • URL: http://www.cwf.ch • Represents executive business women active in the arts, business, and government in Switzerland. Provides a forum for business contacts.

***Career World***. Weekly Reader Corp., 200 1st Stamford Pl. Stamford, CT 06912. Phone: (203)705-3500; Fax: (203)705-1665 or (800)724-4911; Email: info@weeklyreader.com • URL: http://www.weeklyreader.com • Six times a year. $33. 95. per year. Up-to-the-minute, important career and vocational news for students in grades 7 thru 12.

***Careers and the MBA***. Bob Adams Inc., 260 Center St. Holbrook, MA 02343. Phone: 800-872-5627 or (617)767-8100; Fax: (617)767-0994 • $12.95. Publication includes: List of over 200 companies that employ people with Master of Business Administration degrees. Database includes: Feature articles, career biographies, company profiles and industry reports for major industries. Entries include: For companies—Name, address, phone, name of contact person or office, description of company, possible positions open, and when to contact about them. For recruiters—Name, address.

***Careers-In-Business***. Careers-In-Business, LLC, 4101 N.W. Urbandale Dr. Urbandale, IA 50322. Email: bizjobs09l@gmail.com • Careers-In-Business contains information on employment in the business sector, primarily in accounting, finance and consulting. Links to many corporations who hire extensively in this area are included for those wishing to make contacts and/or mail out resumes. Detailed information on job search aids and employer profiles provided. Links to many other career sites also available, as well as links to career-related books for sale through Amazon.

***Careers in Focus—Business***. InfoBase Holdings Inc., 132 W 31st., 17 Fl. New York, NY 10001-3406. Phone: (212)967-8800; Fax: (800)678-3633; Email: info@infobasepublishing.com • URL: http://www.ferguson.infobasepublishing.com • $35 Individuals hardcover. Covers: An overview of business, followed by a selection of jobs profiled in detail, including the nature of the job, earnings, prospects for employment, what kind of training and skills it requires, and sources for further information.

***Careers in Focus—Business Managers***. InfoBase Holdings Inc., 132 W 31st., 17 Fl. New York, NY 10001-3406. Phone: (212)967-8800; Fax: (800)678-3633; Email: info@infobasepublishing.com • URL: http://www.ferguson.infobasepublishing.com • $35 Individuals hardcover. Covers: An overview of business managers, followed by a selection of jobs profiled in detail, including the nature of the job, earnings, prospects for employment, what kind of training and skills it requires, and sources for further information. Database includes: Black and white photographs.

***Careers in Focus—Entrepreneurs***. InfoBase Holdings Inc., 132 W 31st., 17 Fl. New York, NY 10001-3406. Phone: (212)967-8800; Fax: (800)678-3633; Email: info@infobasepublishing.com • URL: http://www.ferguson.infobasepublishing.com • $35 Individuals hardcover. Covers: An overview of entrepreneurship, followed by a selection of jobs profiled in detail, including the nature of the job, earnings, prospects for employment, what kind of training and skills it requires, and sources for further information. Database includes: Black and white photographs.

**CARF International**. 6951 E Southpoint Rd. Tucson, AZ 85756-9407. Phone: 888-281-6531 or (520)325-1044; Fax: (520)318-1129; Email: feedback@carf.org • URL: http://www.carf.org • Formerly Commission on Accreditation of Rehabilitation.

***Cargo Facts: The Airfreight and Express Industry Newsletter of Record***. Air Cargo Management Group, 520 Pke. St., Ste. 1010 Seattle, WA 98101. Phone: (206)587-6537; Fax: (206)587-6540; Email: jedinger@cargofacts.com • Monthly. $445 per year. Provides analysis of developments in the air freight and express industry.

***Caribbean Basin Investment and Business Guide***. International Business Publications, USA, PO Box 15343 Washington, DC 20003. Phone: (202)546-2103; Fax: (202)546-3275; Email: ibpusa@comcast.net • URL: http://ibpus.com • $99.95 Individuals hardcopy, e-book, CD-ROM. Covers: Strategic and basic business information, export-import activity, regulations and industrial development, banking, government, and opportunities. Entries include: Important business contacts and business travel.

***Caribbean Business***. Casiano Communications Inc., 1700 Fernandez Juncos Ave. San Juan, PR 00909-2938. Phone: (787)728-3000; Fax: (787)268-1001 or (787)728-1001; Email: nationalsales@casiano.com • URL: http://www.casiano.com • Weekly. $35.99.

***Caribbean Countries Mineral Industry Handbook***. International Business Publications, USA, PO Box 15343 Washington, DC 20003. Phone: (202)546-2103; Fax: (202)546-3275; Email: ibpusa@comcast.net • URL: http://ibpus.com • $99.95 Individuals hardcopy, E-book and CD-ROM. Covers: strategic information and contacts on mining and mineral industry of the Caribbean countries.

***Caribbean Exporters: A Directory of Caribbean Exporters***. Caribbean Export Development Agency, PO Box 34B Saint Michael, Barbados. Phone: (246)436-0578; Fax: (246)436-9999; Email: info@carib-export.com • URL: http://www.carib-export.com • $50. Covers: Approximately 1,600 exporting companies in the Caribbean community. Database includes: General information about the Caribbean community; maps. Entries include: Company name, address, phone, fax, number of employees, product/service provided.

***The Caricom Exporter: A Comprehensive Buyers' Guide to Caribbean Products and Services***. Caribbean Imprint Directory Service, PO Box 117 Bradenton Beach, FL 34217. Phone: 800-227-4835 • Annual. $50. Covers: 1,600 listings of Caribbean products and services. Database includes: A separate listing of service companies, maps, and facts-at-a-glance for each country. Entries include: Exporter name, address, telephone number, fax number, telex number, name of contact, product brand name, banker name, plant location, size of firm.

**Carleton University - Centre for Research and Education on Women and Work**. 702 Dunton Tower, Sprott School of Business, 1125 Colonel By Dr. Ottawa, ON, Canada K1S 5B6. Phone: (613)520-2600; Fax: (613)520-2652; Email: merridee.bujaki@carleton.ca • URL: http://sprott.carleton.ca/research/research-centres/centre-for-research-and-education-on-women-and-work • Issues that women face in the workplace.

***Carlsbad Business Journal***. Carlsbad Chamber of Commerce, 5934 Priestly Dr. Carlsbad, CA 92008. Phone: (760)931-8400; Fax: (760)931-9153; Email: carlsbadchamber@carlsbad.org • URL: http://www.carlsbad.org • Monthly.

**Carnegie Mellon Research Institute-The Robotics Institute**. 5000 Forbes Ave. Pittsburgh, PA 15213. Phone: (412)268-3818; Fax: (412)268-6436; Email: robotics@ri.cmu.edu • URL: http://www.ri.cmu.edu • Multidisciplinary research activities include expert systems applications, minicomputer and microcomputer systems design, genetic engineering, and transportation systems analysis.

**Carnegie Mellon University - Center for Analytical Research in Technology**. 5000 Forbes Ave., Tepper School of Business Pittsburgh, PA 15213. Phone: (412)268-6903; Fax: (412)268-7357; Email: holgers@andrew.cmu.edu • URL: http://www.tepper.cmu.edu/faculty-research/research-centers/center-for-analyticalresearch-in-technology-cart/index.aspx • Business and technology.

**Carnegie Mellon University - College of Fine Arts - Studio for Creative Inquiry**. 5000 Forbes Ave., Rm.111 Pittsburgh, PA 15213-3890. Phone: (412)268-3451; Fax: (412)268-2829; Email: mmbm@andrew.cmu.edu • URL: http://studioforcreativeinquiry.org • Research areas include artificial intelligence, virtual reality, hypermedia, multimedia, and telecommunications, in relation to the arts.

**Carnegie Mellon University - Imaging Systems Laboratory**. 5320 Wean Hall, Robotics Department Pittsburgh, PA 15213. Phone: (412)268-5601 or (412)268-3824; Fax: (412)621-7068 or (412)683-3763; Email: rht@cs.cmu.edu • URL: http://www.cs.cmu.edu/afs/cs.cmu.edu/project/pcvision/www/ • Fields of research include computer vision and document interpretation.

**Carnegie Mellon University - Robotics Institute**. 5000 Forbes Ave. Pittsburgh, PA 15213-3890. Phone: (412)268-3818; Fax: (412)268-6436; Email: matt.mason@cs.cmu.edu • URL: http://www.ri.cmu.edu • Robotics and artificial intelligence as they relate to the fields of computer science, electrical engineering, mechanical engineering, and operations research. Areas of research and development include robotics in hazardous environments, robots for work in unstructured environments, robotics for the factory of the future, and basic robotic technologies.

***Carolina JobBank: The Job Hunter's Guide to North and South Carolina***. Adams Media Corp., 57 Littlefield St. Avon, MA 02322. Phone: 800-872-5627 or (508)427-7100; Fax: (508)427-6790 or (800)872-5628; Email: deskcopies@adamsmedia.com • URL: http://www.adamsmedia.com • $12.21 Individuals Paperback. Covers: 4,600 employers in North Carolina and South Carolina. Database includes: Information on the basics of getting a job and writing resumes and cover letters; regional employment outlook; 330 industry associations; 90 online career resources; 280 employment services. Entries include: Firm or organization name, address, local phone, toll-free phone, fax, e-mail, URL, recorded jobline, description of organization, subsidiaries, other locations, hours, names of management, name and title of contact, location of headquarters, typical titles for common positions, educational backgrounds desired, projected number of hires, company benefits, stock exchange listing, training programs and internships, parent company, number of employees, revenues.

***The Carpenter***. United Brotherhood of Carpenters and Joiners of America, 1212 Massachusetts Ave., NW Washington, DC 20005. Phone: (202)393-0580; Fax: (202)393-0580 • URL: http://www.carpenters.org • Bimonthly.

***Carpet and Rug Industry***. Rodman Publications, 70 Hilltop Rd. Ramsey, NJ 07446. Phone: (201)825-2552; Fax: (201)825-0553; Email: happi@rodpub.com • URL: http://www.happi.com • Monthly. $42.00 per year. Edited for manufacturers and distributors of carpets and rugs.

**Carpet and Rug Institute**. 100 S Hamilton St. Dalton, GA 30720. Phone: (706)278-3176; Fax: (706)278-8835; Email: snewberry@carpet-rug.org • URL: http://www.carpet-rug.org • Formerly Tufted Textile Manufacturers Association.

**Carpet Cushion Council**. 5103 Brandywine Dr. Eagleville, PA 19403. Phone: (484)687-5170; Fax: (610)885-5131; Email: info@carpetcushion.org • URL: http://www.carpetcushion.org • Works to promote the sale and use of separate carpet cushions; to act as public relations counsel for the industry; to maintain contact with various government agencies; to establish quality and performance standards. Compiles statistics; maintains speakers' bureau.

***Carpet Flooring Retail***. CMP Information Ltd., Ludgate House, 245 Blackfriars Rd. London SE1 9UY, United Kingdom. Phone: 44 207 9215000 or 44 20 7940 8500; Fax: (740)7 7102; Email: enquiries@cmpinformation.com • URL: http://www.cmpi.biz/home • Biweekly. $92.00 per year. Formerly *Carpet and Floorcoverings Review*.

***Carpinteria Valley Business***. Carpinteria Valley Chamber of Commerce, 1056-B Eugenia Pl. Carpinteria, CA 93013-2050. Phone: (805)684-5479; Email: info@carpinteriachamber.org • URL: http://www.carpinteriachamber.org • Monthly.

***Carrageenan/Seaweeds: Industry Sector Profile***. Philippine-German Export Development Project Philippine Bureau of Export Trade Promotion, 6F Trade & Industry Bldg., 361 Sen. Gil Puyat Ave. Makati PH-1226, Philippines. Phone: 63 2 897 8199; Email: web@dti.dti.gov.ph • URL: http://www.dti.gov.ph • Publication includes: Companies exporting seaweed from the Philippines. Entries include: Company name, address, phone, fax, name and title of contact, type of business, year established, subsidiary and branch names and locations, financial data, number of employees, government registrations, professional memberships, bank references, supply capability, export experience, business plan. Principal content of publication is an overview of the business environment and seaweed industry in the Philippines.

***Carroll's County Directory***. Caroll Publishing, 4701 Sangamore Rd., Ste. S-155 Bethesda, MD 20816. Phone: 800-336-4240 or (301)263-9800; Fax: (301)263-9801; Email: info@carrollpub.com • URL: http://www.carrollpub.com • Annual. $500 Individuals 2 issues per year. Covers over 51,000 officials in more than 3,000 counties; includes elected, appointed, and career office holders.

***Carroll's Defense Industry Charts***. Caroll Publishing, 4701 Sangamore Rd., Ste. S-155 Bethesda, MD 20816. Phone: 800-336-4240 or (301)263-9800; Fax: (301)263-9801; Email: info@carrollpub.com • URL: http://www.carrollpub.com • Quarterly. $2,100 Individuals. Provides 180 large, fold-out paper charts showing personnel relationships at more than 100 major U. S. defense contractors. Charts are also available online and on CD-ROM.

***Carroll's Federal & Federal Regional Directory***. Caroll Publishing, 4701 Sangamore Rd., Ste. S-155 Bethesda, MD 20816. Phone: 800-336-4240 or (301)263-9800; Fax: (301)263-9801; Email: info@carrollpub.com • URL: http://www.carrollpub.com • Semiannual. $500 Individuals. Lists more than 23,000 U. S. government officials throughout the country, including military installations.

***Carroll's Federal Directory***. Caroll Publishing, 4701 Sangamore Rd., Ste. S-155 Bethesda, MD 20816. Phone: 800-336-4240 or (301)263-9800; Fax: (301)263-9801; Email: info@carrollpub.com • URL: http://www.carrollpub.com • $550 Single issue 4 issues per year. Covers approximately 37,000 executive managers in federal government offices in Washington, DC, including executive, congressional and judicial branches; members of Congress and Congressional committees and staff.

***Carroll's Federal Organization Charts***. Caroll Publishing, 4701 Sangamore Rd., Ste. S-155 Bethesda, MD 20816. Phone: 800-336-4240 or (301)263-9800; Fax: (301)263-9801; Email: info@carrollpub.com • URL: http://www.carrollpub.com • 8/year. $1,650 Individuals. Provides 200 large, fold-out paper charts showing personnel relationships in 2,100 federal departments and agencies. Charts are also available online and on CD-ROM.

***Carroll's Federal Regional Directory***. Caroll Publishing, 4701 Sangamore Rd., Ste. S-155 Bethesda, MD 20816. Phone: 800-336-4240 or (301)263-9800; Fax: (301)263-9801; Email: info@carrollpub.com • URL: http://www.carrollpub.com • Annual. $500 Individuals. Covers: Over 32,000 officials in federal congressional, judicial, and executive branch departments and agencies outside the District of Columbia. Database includes: Regional maps showing states covered in each federal region and Federal Information Centers. Entries include: Organization or agency name; names, addresses, and phone numbers of key personnel.

***Carroll's Municipal/County Directory***. Caroll Publishing, 4701 Sangamore Rd., Ste. S-155 Bethesda, MD 20816. Phone: 800-336-4240 or (301)263-9800; Fax: (301)263-9801; Email: info@carrollpub.com • URL: http://www.carrollpub.com • Semiannual. $500 Individuals. Provides listings of about 90,000 city, town, and county officials in the U. S.

***Carroll's Municipal Directory***. Caroll Publishing, 4701 Sangamore Rd., Ste. S-155 Bethesda, MD 20816. Phone: 800-336-4240 or (301)263-9800; Fax: (301)263-9801; Email: info@carrollpub.com • URL: http://www.carrollpub.com • Annual. $500 Individuals. Covers: About 51,000 officials in more than 7,900 cities towns and villages: includes top elected council or elected board members. Entries include: Name, county name, locator phone, address, population; officials' names, titles, addresses, and phone numbers.

***Carroll's State Directory***. Caroll Publishing, 4701 Sangamore Rd., Ste. S-155 Bethesda, MD 20816. Phone: 800-336-4240 or (301)263-9800; Fax: (301)263-9801; Email: info@carrollpub.com • URL: http://www.carrollpub.com • Annual. $500 Individuals 3 issues per year. Covers: About 70,000 state government officials in all branches of government; officers, committees and members of state legislatures; managers of boards and authorities. Entries include: Name, address, phone, fax, title.

***Carroll's State Directory: CD-ROM Edition***. Caroll Publishing, 4701 Sangamore Rd., Ste. S-155 Bethesda, MD 20816. Phone: 800-336-4240 or (301)263-9800; Fax: (301)263-9801; Email: info@carrollpub.com • URL: http://www.carrollpub.com • Three times a year. $325.00 per year. Provides CD-ROM listings of about 43,000 state officials, plus the text of all state constitutions and biographies of all governors. Also available online.

***Carry Out Food Service Directory***. InfoGroup Inc., 5711 S 86th Cir. Omaha, NE 68127-4146. Phone: (402)593-4500 • URL: http://www.infogroup.com • Annual. Number of listings: 28,970. Entries include: Name, address, phone, size of advertisement, name of owner or manager, number of employees, year first in "Yellow Pages." Compiled from telephone company "Yellow Pages," nationwide.

***Carson City Area Chamber of Commerce—Membership Business Directory***. Carson City Area Chamber of Commerce, 1900 S Carson St., Ste. 200 Carson City, NV 89701. Phone: (775)882-1565; Fax: (775)882-4179; Email: director@carsoncitychamber.com • URL: http://www.carsoncitychamber.com • Covers: Approximately 850 community profile and business listing member businesses in the greater Carson City, Nevada area. Entries include: Company name, address, phone, name and title of contact, products and services.

**CARTHA**. 33 Buchanan Ct. Iowa City, IA 52246. Phone: (319)248-9625; Email: cartha.global@gmail.com • URL: http://www.cartha.org • Aims to strengthen academic-practitioner partnerships. Seeks to train, build and empower networks of professionals. Enhances the positive impact of technological and social innovations in the lives of individuals. Provides education, training and professional development programs.

***Cartography and Geographic Information Science***. American Congress on Surveying and Mapping, 5119 Pegasus Ct., Ste. Q Frederick, MD 21704. Phone: (240)439-4615 or (240)632-9716; Fax: (240)439-4952 or (240)632-1321; Email: curtis.sumner@acsm.net • URL: http://www.acsm.net • 5/year. $229 Institutions.

***Cary Chamber of Commerce Member Directory***. Cary Chamber of Commerce, 307 N Academy St. Cary, NC 27513. Phone: 800-919-2279 or (919)467-1016; Fax: (919)469-2375; Email: info@carychamber.com • URL: http://www.carychamber.com • Covers chamber member businesses employing more than 100 people. Entries include company name, address, phone, fax, website, headquarters location, description of business.

**Case Western Reserve University - Center for Health Care Research and Policy**. Rammelkamp Research & Education Bldg., R221, MetroHealth Medical Ctr., 2500 Metrohealth Dr. Cleveland, OH 44109-1998. Phone: (216)778-3901; Fax: (216)778-3945; Email: rdc@case.edu • URL: http://www.chrp.org • Health care and health policy.

**Case Western Reserve University - Elderly Care Research Center**. Mather Memorial Bldg., Rm. 231B, 10900 Euclid Ave. Cleveland, OH 44106-1712. Phone: (216)368-2704; Fax: (216)368-1078; Email: exk@case.edu • URL: http://www.case.edu/artsci/soci/ecrc • Aging, health, and mental health, including public policy issues, predictors of wellness and vulnerability, environmental and social influences on well-being of the elderly, cross-national and cross-cultural comparisons, and health and mental health outcomes of stress, coping, and adaptation.

***CaseBase: Case Studies in Global Business***. Cengage Learning Inc., 20 Channel Center St. Boston, MA 02210. Phone: 800-487-8488 or (617)289-7700; Fax: (617)289-7844; Email: investors@cengage.com • URL: http://www.cengage.com • Details business case studies; focused on worldwide emerging markets and industries. Available in print ($218) and eBook. Second volume published June 2012.

***Cases on Business and Management in the MENA Region: New Trends and Opportunities***. Cengage Learning Inc., 20 Channel Center St. Boston, MA 02210. Phone: 800-487-8488 or (617)289-7700; Fax: (617)289-7844; Email: investors@cengage.com • URL: http://www.cengage.com • 2012. eBook. Presents a blend of conceptual, theoretical and applied research in regard to the relationship between the Middle East and North Africa region and business and management.

***Cases on Information Technology Entrepreneurship***. Cengage Learning Inc., 20 Channel Center St. Boston, MA 02210. Phone: 800-487-8488 or (617)289-7700; Fax: (617)289-7844; Email: investors@cengage.com • URL: http://www.cengage.com • 2007. eBook. Published by Information Science Reference. Offers a look into how IT can be the structural foundation of an entrepreneurship, and describes specific examples of IT as the base of a start-up company — providing insight into the successes and failures of applying IT in innovative ways.

***Cash Box: The International Music-Record Weekly***. Cash Box Publishing Co., Inc., 51 E. Eighth St., Suite 155 New York, NY 10003-6494. Phone: (212)586-2640 • Weekly. $185.00 per year.

***Cash Registers and Supplies-Wholesale Directory***. InfoGroup Inc., 5711 S 86th Cir. Omaha, NE 68127-4146. Phone: (402)593-4500 • URL: http://www.infogroup.com • Annual. Number of listings: 2,539. Entries include: Name, address, phone (including area code), size of advertisement, year first in "Yellow Pages," name of owner or manager, number of employees. Compiled from telephone company "Yellow Pages," nationwide.

***Casino Chronicle: A Weekly Newsletter Focusing on the Gaming Industry***. Ben Borowsky, PO Box 740465 Boynton Beach, FL 33474-0465. Phone: (561)732-6117; Email: casinochronicle@aol.com • 48 times a year. $175.00 per year. Newsletter focusing on the Atlantic City gambling industry.

***Casino Gaming in the United States: A Research Guide***. The Scarecrow Press Inc., 4501 Forbes Blvd., Ste. 200 Lanham, MD 20706-4346. Phone: 800-462-6420 or (301)459-3366; Fax: (301)429-5748; Email: custserv@rowman.com • URL: http://www.scarecrowpress.com • $95 Individuals Hardback; £59.95 Individuals Hardback. Covers: Bibliography of nearly 900 books, articles, periodicals, Internet sites and government publications from 1985-94 on casino gambling. Also includes state gambling agencies, associations, Indian gaming locations, consultants, and public gaming companies. Entries include: For publications—Publication title, subject, author, web site address where applicable. For organizations—Name, address, phone.

***Casinos Directory***. InfoGroup Inc., 5711 S 86th Cir. Omaha, NE 68127-4146. Phone: (402)593-4500 • URL: http://www.infogroup.com • Annual. Number of listings: 1,792. Entries include: Name, address, phone, size of advertisement, name of owner or manager, number of employees, year first in "Yellow Pages." Compiled from telephone company "Yellow Pages," nationwide.

***Caspian Business News***. Caspian Business News, 219 Bashir Safaroglu St. AZ1000 Baku, Azerbaijan. Phone: 99 412 4933189; Fax: 99 412 4932478; Email: media@cbnmail.com • Weekly. Local business newspaper.

***CASSIS***. U.S. Patent and Trademark Office - Office of Electronic Information Products, United States Patent and Trademark Office, 401 Dulany St., Randolph Bldg. Alexandria, VA 22314. Phone: 800-786-9199 or (703)306-2600; Fax: (703)306-2737; Email: oeip@uspto.gov • URL: http://www.uspto.gov • CD-ROM products include *Trademarks ASSIGN* (assignment deeds, bimonthly), *Trademarks ASSIST* (search tools, single- disc), *Trademarks PENDING* (applications on file, bimonthly), *Trademarks REGISTERED* (active trademarks, 1884 to date).

**Casting Industry Suppliers Association**. 14175 W Indian School Rd., Ste. B4-504 Goodyear, AZ 85395. Phone: (623)547-0920; Fax: (623)536-1486; Email: info@cisa.org • URL: http://www.foundry-suppliers.com/media/media?id=130743410326823318 • Manufacturers of foundry equipment and supplies such as molding machinery, dust control equipment and systems, blast cleaning machines, tumbling equipment, and related products. Fosters better trade practices; serves as industry representative before the government and the public. Encourages member research into new processes and methods of foundry operation and disseminates reports of progress in these fields. Compiles monthly statistics on booked and billed sales.

***Casual Living—Casual Outdoor Furniture and Accessory Directory Issue***. Reed Elsevier Group plc Reed Business Information, 360 Park Ave. S New York, NY 10010. Phone: (212)791-4208; Email: corporatecommunications@reedbusiness.com • URL: http://www.reedbusiness.com • Annual. $22.99 Individuals; C$55.99 Canada; $55.99 Other countries; $138.99 Individuals air delivery; $10 Individuals single copy; $15 Other countries single copy other. Publication includes: List of manufacturers, manufacturers' representatives, and suppliers of outdoor furniture, wicker and rattan furniture, and backyard accessories, such as barbecue grills, picnic accessories, outdoor lighting, cushions and pads, patio umbrellas, vinyl refinishing and maintenance products. Entries include: Name of firm, address, phone, products.

***Casualty Actuarial Society Yearbook and Proceedings***. Casualty Actuarial Society, 4350 N Fairfax Dr., Ste. 250 Arlington, VA 22203. Phone: (703)276-3100; Fax: (703)276-3108; Email: office@casact.org • URL: http://www.casact.org • Annual. $40. Approximately 2,500 actuaries working in insurance other than life insurance.

**Casualty Actuarial Society**. 4350 N Fairfax Dr., Ste. 250 Arlington, VA 22203. Phone: (703)276-3100; Fax: (703)276-3108; Email: office@casact.org • URL: http://www.casact.org • Professional society of property/casualty actuaries. Seeks to advance the body of knowledge of actuarial science applied to property, casualty and similar risk exposures, to maintain qualification standards, promote high standards of conduct and competence, and increase awareness of actuarial science. Examinations required for membership.

***Casualty Insurance Claims: Coverage-Investigation-Law***. Pat Magarick and Ken Brownlee. Thomson West, 610 Opperman Dr. Eagan, MN 55123. Phone: 800-328-9352 or (651)687-7000 • $917 full set; $108 per month. Insurance claim and law information.

***Catalog Age***. PRIMEDIA Business Magazine and Media, 11 Riverbend Dr. S Stamford, CT 06907. Phone: 800-795-5445 or (203)358-9900; Fax: (203)358-5823 or (203)358-5811; Email: inquiries@primediabusiness.com • URL: http://www.primediabusiness.com • 13 times a year. Free to qualified personnel; others, $85.00 per year. Edited for catalog marketing and management personnel.

***Catalog of Asphalt Institute Publications***. Asphalt Institute, 2696 Research Park Dr. Lexington, KY 40511-8480. Phone: (859)288-4960; Fax: (859)288-4999; Email: info@asphaltinstitute.org • URL: http://www.asphaltinstitute.org • Annual. Free.

***Catalog of Copyright Entries***. U.S. Library of Congress, Copyright Office. U. S. Government Printing Office, 732 N Capitol St. NW Washington, DC 20401. Phone: 866-512-1800 or (202)512-1800 or (866)512-1800; Fax: (202)512-2104 or (202)512-2250; Email: contactcenter@gpo.gov • URL: http://www.gpo.gov • Frequency and prices vary.

***Catalog of Nonprofit Literature***. • Dates vary. Covers the literature of philanthropy, foundations, nonprofit organizations, fund-raising, and federal aid.

***Catalog of United States Government Publications***. U. S. Government Printing Office, 732 N Capitol St. NW Washington, DC 20401. Phone: 866-512-1800 or (202)512-1800 or (866)512-1800; Fax: (202)512-2104 or (202)512-2250; Email: contactcenter@gpo.gov • URL: http://www.gpo.gov • Updated daily.

***Cataloging Handbook H4/H8 Commercial and Government Entity***. Defense Logistics Service Center U.S. Defense Logistics Agency, 74 N Washington Battle Creek, MI 49017. Phone: (616)961-4000 • Bimonthly. $40 per year (S/N 008-007-80003-5). Covers: about 92,000 companies, primarily manufacturers, that produce or maintain design control for products cataloged by federal government agencies. Entries include: Company name, address, five-digit Federal Supply Code for Manufacturers, and letter code indicating active or inactive status or other attributes; some listings include previous company name, previous location, or other information.

***Catalogue & E-business***. Catalogue & e-business, 155 High St. Ilfracombe EX34 9EZ, United Kingdom. Phone: 44 1271 866112; Fax: 44 1271 866040; Email: info@catalog-biz.com • URL: http://www.catalog-biz.com • Monthly. £65 Individuals; £75 Other countries. Trade magazine covering catalog, mail order, and electronic commerce.

***Catalogue of Firms in Slovakia***. I.S.M.C. Information Systems and Marketing Contacts Ltd., Nam. Slobody 9, PO Box 47 81499 Bratislava, Slovakia. Phone: 421 7 265423783; Fax: 421 7 265422186; Email: ismc@ismc.sk • URL: http://www.ismc.sk • Annual. $65. Covers: Over 50,000 firms in Slovakia with a list of 50,000 goods. Entries include: Company contact information, economic data.

***Catalogue of Firms in the Czech Republic***. I.S.M.C. Information Systems and Marketing Contacts Ltd., Nam. Slobody 9, PO Box 47 81499 Bratislava, Slovakia. Phone: 421 7 265423783; Fax: 421 7 265422186; Email: ismc@ismc.sk • URL: http://www.ismc.sk • Annual. $84. Covers: Over 50,000 firms located in the Czech Republic, as well as a list of 30,000 goods. Entries include: Company contact information, economic data.

***Catalogue of Manufacturers and Exporters***. Durban Regional Chamber of Business, PO Box 1506 Durban 4000, South Africa. Phone: 27 31335 1000; Fax: 27 31332 1288 or (313)32 1288; Email: chamber@durbanchamber.co.za • URL: http://www.durbanchamber.co.za • Publication includes: Company listings of manufacturing members that do business with Africa in the following categories: basic metal, chemicals, clothing, food and beverages, furniture, hair care products, hardware, household, and investment, among others. Entries include: Company name, address, phone, fax. Principal content of publication is advertisements.

***Catalogue of Statistical Materials of Developing Countries***. Institute of Developing Economies/Ajia Keizai Kenkyusho, 3-2-2 Wakaba, Mihama-ku Chiba-shi 261-8545, Japan. Phone: 81-43-299-9536; Fax: 81-43-299-9726; Email: info@ide.go.jp • URL: http://www.ide.go.jp/English/Info/Inquiries • Semiannual. Price varies. Text in English and Japanese.

**Catalyst**. 120 Wall St., 5th Fl. New York, NY 10005-3904. Phone: (212)514-7600; Fax: (212)514-8470; Email: info@catalyst.org • URL: http://www.catalyst.org • Works to advance women in Business and the professions. Serves as a source of information on women in business for past four decades. Helps companies and women maximize their potential. Holds current statistics, print media, and research materials on issues related to women in business.

***Catawba County Chamber of Commerce—Membership Directory/Relocation Guide***. Catawba County Chamber of Commerce, 1055 Southgate Corporate Park SW Hickory, NC 28603. Phone: (828)328-6111; Fax: (828)328-1175 • URL: http://www.catawbachamber.org • Covers: Chamber members. Entries include: Contact details.

***Catering Industry Employee***. Hotel Employees and Restaurant Employees International Union, 901 K St. NW, Ste. 200 Washington, DC 20001. Phone: (202)393-4373; Fax: (202)965-2958 • URL: http://www.unitehere.org • Quarterly. $5.00.

**Catholic Library Association**. 205 W Monroe St., Ste. 314 Chicago, IL 60606-5061. Phone: 855-739-1776 or (312)739-1776; Fax: (312)739-1778; Email: sbaron@regent.edu • URL: http://www.cathla.org • Librarians, teachers, and booksellers concerned with Catholic libraries and their specialized problems and the writing, publishing, and distribution of Catholic literature. Members represent lay and clergy in both Catholic and non-Catholic institutions.

**Catholic University of Louvain - Center for Economic Studies**. Department of Economics, Naamsestraat 69 B-3000 Louvain, Belgium. Phone: 32 16 326725; Fax: 32 16 326796; Email: erik.buyst@kuleuven.be • URL: http://www.econ.kuleuven.be/research/CES/display.aspx?URL=main • Information, international, monetary, industrial, public, and developmental economics, econometrics, and game theory.

***Cats Boarding Directory***. InfoGroup Inc., 5711 S 86th Cir. Omaha, NE 68127-4146. Phone: (402)593-4500 • URL: http://www.infogroup.com • Annual. Number of listings: 9,391. Entries include: Name, address, phone, size of advertisement, name of owner or manager, number of employees, year first in "Yellow Pages." Compiled from telephone company "Yellow Pages," nationwide.

**Cattle Fever Tick Research Laboratory**. US Department of Agricultural Livestock Insects Laboratory, Rte. 3 Edinburg, TX 78539. Phone: (956)580-7268; Fax: (956)580-7261; Email: ronald.b.davey@aphis.udsa.gov • URL: http://www.aphis.usda.gov.

***Cattleman***. Texas and Southwestern Cattle Raisers Association, 1301 W 7th St. Fort Worth, TX 76102. Phone: 800-242-7820 or (817)332-7064 or (817)332-7155; Fax: (817)332-8523 or (817)332-5446 • URL: http://www.texascattleraisers.org • Monthly. $40 per year; $50 Other countries per year.

**Cayman Finance**. Fidelity Financial Ctre., 2nd Fl., 1 Gecko Link, West Bay Rd. Grand Cayman, Cayman Islands. Phone: (345)623-6725; Email: enquiries@caymanfinance.ky • URL: http://caymanfinances.com • Represents Cayman's financial services industry. Promotes the integrity and quality of financial services in the Cayman Islands. Offers the media and the financial services industry with information on issues that affect Cayman's financial services.

***Cayman Islands Business Law Handbook***. International Business Publications, USA, PO Box 15343 Washington, DC 20003. Phone: (202)546-2103; Fax: (202)546-3275; Email: ibpusa@comcast.net • URL: http://ibpus.com • $99.95 Individuals hardcopy, E-book and CD-ROM. Covers: Basic information on business laws and legislations, export-import regulations, business climate and contacts.

**Cayman Islands Directors Association**. George Town Grand Cayman, Cayman Islands. Phone: (345)945-0012; Fax: (345)947-7328 • URL: http://www.cida2008.com • Represents individuals who hold office as directors of one or more Cayman Islands registered companies. Promotes and safeguards the interests of directors of Cayman Islands registered companies. Maintains code of conduct and best practice among members to ensure corporate governance.

***CBA Marketplace***. Christian Booksellers Association. CBA Service Corp., 9240 Explorer Dr., Ste. 200 Colorado Springs, CO 80920. Phone: (719)265-9895 or (800)252-1950; Email: info@cbaonline.org • URL: http://www.cbaonline.org • Monthly. $49.95 per year. Edited for religious book stores. Formerly *Bookstore Journal*.

**CBA: The Association for Christian Retail**. 9240 Explorer Dr., Ste. 200 Colorado Springs, CO 80920. Phone: 800-252-1950 or (719)265-9895; Fax: (719)272-3508; Email: info@cbaonline.org • URL: http://www.cbaonline.org • Serves as trade association for retail stores selling Christian books, Bibles, gifts, and Sunday school and church supplies. Compiles statistics; conducts specialized education programs.

***CBER-LIED Report on Housing-Market Conditions; Southern Nevada Business Confidence Index***. University of Nevada, Las Vegas Center for Business and Economic Research, 4505 S Maryland Pky., Box 456002 Las Vegas, NV 89154-6002. Phone: (702)895-3191; Fax: (702)895-3606; Email: spa.brown@unlv.edu • URL: http://business.unlv.edu/cber • Quarterly.

***CBI European Business Handbook***. Kogan Page, Limited, 120 Pentonville Rd. London N1 9JN, United Kingdom. Phone: 44 20 72780433 or (440) 2072780433; Fax: 44 20 78376348 or (783)76348; Email: kpinfo@kogan-page.co.uk • URL: http://www.kogan-page.co.uk/ • $35. Publication includes: A business directory of 27 countries in Europe. Principal content of publication is an analysis of economic, business, and industrial prospects in Europe.

***CBMC Contact Quarterly: The Magazine for Business Today***. Christian Business Men's Committee of USA, PO Box 8009 Chattanooga, TN 37414-0009. Phone: 800-566-2262 or (423)698-4444; Fax: (423)629-4434; Email: info@cbmc.com • URL: http://www.cbmc.com • Quarterly. $12.95 Individuals; $22.95 Out of country; $3.50 Single issue. Trade magazine of the Christian Business Men's Committee of USA covering Christian business issues.

***CC News: The Business Newspaper for Call Center and Customer Care Professionals***. HME News, PO Box 998 Yarmouth, ME 04096. Phone: (207)846-0600; Fax: (207)846-0657 • Monthly. Free to qualified personnel; others, $60.00 per year. Includes news of call center technical developments.

***CCBC—Membership Directory***. Canada-China Business Council, 330 Bay St., Ste. 1501 Toronto, ON, Canada M5H 2S8. Phone: (416)954-3800; Fax: (416)954-3806; Email: ccbc@ccbc.com • URL: http://www.ccbc.com • Annual. Covers: 200 Canadian companies in China. Entries include: Company profile.

***CCH Analysis of Top Tax Issues***. Wolters Kluwer Law & Business CCH, 2700 Lake Cook Rd. Riverwoods, IL 60015. Phone: 888-224-7377 or (847)267-7000; Email: cust_serv@cch.com • URL: http://www.cchgroup.com • Annual. $49.00. Covers yearly tax changes affecting business and personal transactions, planning, and returns.

***CCH Essentials: An Internet Tax Research and Primary Source Library***. CCH, Inc., Phone: 800-248-3248 or (773)866-6000; Fax: (773)866-3608 or (800)224-8299; Email: cust_serv@cch.com • URL: http://tax.cch.com/essentials • Fee-based Web site provides full-text coverage of federal tax law and regulations, including rulings, procedures, tax court decisions, and IRS publications, announcements, notices, and penalties. Includes explanation, analysis, tax planning guides, and a daily tax news service. Searching is offered, including citation search.

***CCH Guide to Car, Travel, Entertainment, and Home Office Deductions***. Wolters Kluwer Law & Business CCH, 2700 Lake Cook Rd. Riverwoods, IL 60015. Phone: 888-224-7377 or (847)267-7000; Email: cust_serv@cch.com • URL: http://www.cchgroup.com • Annual. Explains how to claim maximum tax deductions for common business expenses. Includes automobile depreciation tables, lease value tables, worksheets, and examples of filled-in tax forms.

***CCN Business Information Database***. CCN Business Information Ltd., Abbey House, Abbeyfield Rd. Lenton NG7 2SW, United Kingdom. Phone: 602 863864; Fax: 602 863592 • Continuous. Database covers: Approximately 3 million companies in the U.K. Database includes: Company name, address, phone, registration number, date and legal form of incorporation, holding company, directors, auditor, number of employees, prinicpal activities, financial data.

***CD-MAIL: The address database for mailings***. Wer liefert was GmbH, Normannenweg 16-20 D-20537 Hamburg, Germany. Phone: 49 40 254400 or 49 40 254 400; Fax: 49 40 25440100 or 49 40 254 40 100; Email: info@wlw.de • URL: http://www.wlw.de • Semiannual. $1,200. Covers: Approximately 184,000 companies in Germany, Austria, Switzerland, Belgium, Luxembourg, and the Netherlands. Entries include: Name, address, phone, fax, names and titles of key personnel, description of product/service.

***CD-ROM EEKOD***. Promar Ltd., Langov Trg 4 HR-10000 Zagreb, Croatia. Phone: 385 1 4893333; Fax: 385 1 4893399; Email: kompass@promar.hr • URL: http://www4.kompass.com/kinl/index.php • Annual. $2,500. Covers: More than 246,500 company profiles in Eastern Europe, including Austria, Czech Republic, Croatia, Latvia, Lithuania, Hungary, Poland, Slovenia, Azerbaidjan, Slovakia, Belarus, Estonia, Romania, Moldavia, Russia, Ukraine, and Yugoslavia.

***CD-ROM Information Products: The Evaluative Guide***. Ashgate Publishing Co., 101 Cherry St., Ste. 420 Burlington, VT 05401-4405. Phone: 800-535-9544 or (802)865-7641; Fax: (802)865-7847; Email: info@ashgate.com • URL: http://www.ashgate.com • Quarterly. $110.00 per year. Provides detailed evaluations of new CD-ROM information products.

***CDC Vessel Sanitation Program (VSP): Charting a Healthier Course***. U. S. Centers for Disease Control and Prevention, Phone: (770)488-7070; Fax: (888)232-6789; Email: vsp@cdc.gov • URL: http://www.cdc.gov/nceh/vsp/ • Annual. Web site provides details of unannounced sanitation inspections of individual cruise ships arriving at U. S. ports. Includes detailed results of the most recent inspection of each ship and results of inspections taking place in years past. There are lists of "Ships Inspected Past 2 Months" and "Ships with Not Satisfactory Scores" (passing grade is 85). CDC standards cover drinking water, food, and general cleanliness. Online searching is possible by ship name, inspection date, and numerical scores. Fees: Free.

***CEC Communications***. Taylor & Francis, 711 3rd Ave., 8th Fl. New York, NY 10017. Phone: 800-634-7064 or (212)216-7800 or (212)216-6000; Fax: (212)563-2269 or (212)685-4540; Email: bookorders@dekker.com • URL: http://www.routledge.com/ • Monthly. $6,593 Institutions. Formerly *Chemical Engineering Communications*.

***CEE News Buyers' Guide***. Primedia Business Magazines and Media, 330 N Wabash Ave., Suite 2300 Chicago, IL 60611. Phone: 800-795-5445 or (312)595-1080 or (312)726-2802; Fax: (312)595-0295 or (312)726-2574; Email: subs@primediabusiness.com • URL: http://www.primediabusiness.com • Annual. $25.00. List of approximately 1,900 manufacturers of products used in the electrical construction industry; coverage includes Canada.

***Cement and Concrete Research***. Elsevier, Secondary Publishing Division, 650 Ave. of the Americas New York, NY 10011. Phone: 888-437-4636 or (212)633-3980; Fax: (212)633-3975; Email: t.reller@elsevier.com • URL: http://www.elseveier.com • Monthly. $3,893 Institutions; $516 Individuals. Covers information regarding on cement, cement composites, concrete and other allied materials that incorporate cement.

***Census of Construction: Subject Bibliography No. 157***. U. S. Government Printing Office, 732 N Capitol St. NW Washington, DC 20401. Phone: 866-512-1800 or (202)512-1800 or (866)512-1800; Fax: (202)512-2104 or (202)512-2250; Email: contactcenter@gpo.gov • URL: http://www.gpo.gov • Annual. Free. Lists government publications.

***Census of Governments: Subject Bibliography No. 156***. U. S. Government Printing Office, 732 N Capitol St. NW Washington, DC 20401. Phone: 866-512-1800 or (202)512-1800 or (866)512-1800; Fax: (202)512-2104 or (202)512-2250; Email: contactcenter@gpo.gov • URL: http://www.gpo.gov • Annual. Free. Lists government publications.

**Center for Advanced Phototonic and Electronic Materials**. State University of New York at Buffalo, Fronczak Hall, Rm. 227-229, N Campus Buffalo, NY 14260. Phone: (716)645-2422; Fax: (716)645-5964; Email: ub-capem@acsu.buffalo.edu • URL: http://www.grad.buffalo.edu • Does integrated optics research, including photonic circuitry.

**Center for Applied Thermodynamics Studies**. University of Idaho, Dept. of Mechanical Engineering, 875 Perimeter Dr., MS 0902 Moscow, ID 83844-0902. Phone: (208)885-6779; Fax: (208)885-9031 • URL: http://www.uidaho.edu/engr/me/research/centersandinstitutes.

**Center for Artificial Intelligence**. University of Pennsylvania, Computer and Information Science Dept., Moore School of Electrical Engineering, 200 S 33rd St. Philadelphia, PA 19104-6389. Phone: (215)898-3191; Fax: (215)898-0587 • URL: http://www.upenn.edu.

**Center for Auto Safety**. 1825 Connecticut Ave. NW, Ste. 330 Washington, DC 20009-5708. Phone: (202)328-7700 • URL: http://www.autosafety.org • Seeks to "reduce the human and economic losses wrought by the automobile and the auto industry." As an auto and highway safety advocate, the center monitors government agencies charged with regulation of the industry, supports safety standards, participates in the rule-making procedures of the National Highway Traffic Safety Administration and the Federal Highway Administration, and occasionally institutes legal action. Collects literature and statistics on automobile safety and analyzes developments in the field. Letters are being coded by auto make, 2nd model, year.

**Center for Automation and Robotics Research**. University of Rhode Island, Kirk Bldg. Kingston, RI 02881. Phone: (401)874-2514; Fax: (401)874-2355 • URL: http://mcise.uri.edu/datseris/robotics/index.htm.

**Center for Chemical Process Safety**. 3 Park Ave., 19th Fl. New York, NY 10016-5991. Phone: 800-242-4363 or (646)495-1370 or (646)495-1371; Fax: (646)495-1504 or (203)775-5177; Email: ccps@aiche.org • URL: http://www.aiche.org/ccps • Chemical and hydrocarbon manufacturers; engineering firms. Purpose is to study process safety issues in the chemical and hydrocarbon industries and publish and disseminate the results. Is concerned with safety in the manufacture, handling, and storage of toxic and reactive materials and those scientific and engineering practices that can prevent episodic events involving the release of potentially hazardous materials. Conducts research on hazard evaluation procedures, bulk storage and handling of toxic or reactive materials, plant operating procedures, safety training, and dispersion modeling. Seeks to enhance the personal, professional, and technical development of engineers in process plant safety.

**Center for Consumer Research**. University of Florida Gainesville, FL 32611-7150. Phone: (352)392-2397; Fax: (352)392-2086; Email: joel.cohen@cba.ufl.edu • URL: http://www.cba.ufl.edu/.

**Center for Creative Leadership** . 1 Leadership Pl. Greensboro, NC 27410-9427. Phone: (336)288-7210 or (336)545-2810; Fax: (336)282-3284; Email: info@ccl.org • URL: http://www.ccl.org • Promotes behavioral science research and leadership education.

**Center for Defense Information**. 1779 Massachusetts Ave. NW Washington, DC 20036-2109. Phone: (202)332-0600; Fax: (202)462-4559; Email: info@cdi.org • URL: http://www.cdi.org • Aims to strengthen security through international cooperation; reduced reliance on unilateral military power to resolve conflict; reduced reliance on nuclear weapons; a transformed and reformed military establishment; and prudent oversight of, and spending on, weapons programs. Seeks to contribute alternative views on security to promote wide-ranging discourse and debate. Educates the public and informs policy-makers about issues of security policy, strategy, operations, weapons systems and defense budgeting, and pursues creative solutions to the problems of today and tomorrow. Aims to improve understanding between the United States and key nations on security matters through new media initiatives that inform and educate opinion-makers, policy-makers and the general public. Accepts no government or defense industry funding, and does not hold organizational positions. Believes on the concept that the public and political leaders "can, and will, make wise choices on complex security matters when provided with facts, and practical alternatives."

**Center for Energy and Environmental Studies - Carnegie Mellon University Department of Engineering and Public Policy**. Baker Hall 128-A Pittsburgh, PA 15213. Phone: (412)268-5897; Fax: (412)268-1089; Email: rubin@cmu.edu.

**Center for Entrepreneurial Studies & Development Inc.** 1062 Maple Dr., Ste. 2 Morgantown, WV 26505. Phone: (304)293-5551; Fax: (304)293-6707; Email: info@cesd.wvu.edu • URL: http://www.cesd.wvu.edu • Inventory control systems included as a research field.

**Center for Exhibition Industry Research**. 12700 Park Central Dr., Ste. 308 Dallas, TX 75251. Phone: (972)687-9242; Fax: (972)692-6020; Email: info@ceir.org • URL: http://www.ceir.org • Promotes the trade show as a marketing device. Formerly Trade Show Bureau.

**Center for Financial Responsibility**. Texas Tech University Lubbock, TX 79409-11210. Phone: (806)742-5050; Fax: (806)742-5033 • URL: http://www.depts.ttu.edu/cfr • Research areas include financial preparation for retirement, financial education, determinants of financial satisfaction, risk tolerance, and the career preparation of retirement industry professionals.

**Center for Imaging Science**. Rochester Institute of Technology, 54 Lomb Memorial Dr. Rochester, NY 14623. Phone: (585)475-5994; Fax: (585)475-5988; Email: contactus@cis.rit.edu • URL: http://www.cis.rit.edu • Activities include research in color science and digital image processing.

***Center for International Business and Public Policy Articles***. Johns Hopkins University Center for International Business and Public Policy, Paul H. Nitze School of Advanced International Studies, 1717 Massachusetts Ave. NW, Ste. 704, Rm. 713 Washington, DC 20036. Phone: (202)663-7786; Fax: (202)663-7718; Email: leeds@jhu.edu • URL: http://www.sais-jhu.edu/faculty-and-scholarship/research-centers/center-international-business-and-public-policy.

**Center for International Policy**. 2000 M St. NW, Ste. 720 Washington, DC 20036-3327. Phone: (202)232-3317; Fax: (202)232-3440; Email: cip@ciponline.org • URL: http://www.ciponline.org • Research subjects include the International Monetary Fund, the World Bank, and other international financial institutions. Analyzes the impact of policies on social and economic conditions in developing countries.

**Center for International Private Enterprise - Albanian Center for Economic Research**. Perlat Rexhepi St., Bldg. No. 10, 6th Fl., Apt. 64 Tirana, Albania. Phone: 355 4 2225021; Fax: 355 4 2274603; Email: acer@icc-al.org • URL: http://www.acer.org.al • Economic issues, financial and banking systems, development of small and medium enterprises, improvement of local government services, and issues of corruption.

**Center for International Private Enterprise - Egypt Office**. Fayoum St., No. 1, Off Cleopatra St., Heliopolis, Fl. 8, Ste. 8003 Cairo 11341, Egypt. Phone: 20 2 4143282; Fax: 20 2 4143295; Email: rzoghbi@cipe-egypt.org • URL: http://www.cipe.org • Encourages the growth of voluntary business organizations and private enterprise systems, such as chambers of commerce, trade associations, employers' organizations, and business-oriented research groups, particularly in developing countries. Creates exchanges among business leaders and institutions to strengthen the international private enterprise system. Offers leadership training for association executives.

**Center for International Private Enterprise - Russia Office**. Office 318, 101 Prospekt Mira 129085 Moscow, Russia. Phone: 7 495 3802571; Fax: 7 495 3802572; Email: eurasia@cipe.org • URL: http://www.cipe-eurasia.org • Encourages the growth of voluntary business organizations and private enterprise systems, such as chambers of commerce, trade associations, employers' organizations, and business-oriented research groups, particularly in developing countries. Creates exchanges among business leaders and institutions · strengthen the international private enterprise system. O leadership training for association executives.

**Center for International Private Enterprise**. 1155 15th St. NW, Ste. 700 Washington, DC 20005. Phone: (202)721-9200; Fax: (202)721-9250; Email: info@cipe.org • URL: http://www.cipe.org • Members are people involved in small businesses.

**Center for Latin American Studies**. University of Chicago, Kelly Hall 117, 5848 S University Ave. Chicago, IL 60637. Phone: (773)702-8420; Fax: (773)702-1755; Email: clas@uchicago.edu • URL: http://clas.uchicago.edu • Includes economic inquiry on Latin America.

**Center for Management Effectiveness**. PO Box 1202 Pacific Palisades, CA 90272. Phone: (310)459-6052; Email: info@cmeinc.com • URL: http://www.cmeinc.org • Participants are directors of training and management development from industry, government, and nonprofit organizations. Conducts programs for management trainers on topics such as stress management, resolution of disagreements, risk-taking, problem solving, strategic decision-making and managing change.

**Center for Mathematical Studies in Economics and Management Science**. Northwestern University, 580 Leverone Hall, 2001 Sheridan Rd. Evanston, IL 60208-2014. Phone: (847)491-3527; Fax: (847)491-2530; Email: cms-ems@kellogg.northwestern.edu • URL: http://www.kellogg.northwestern.edu/research/math.

**Center for Media and Public Affairs**. 933 N Kenmore St., Ste. 405 Arlington, VA 22201. Phone: (571)319-0029; Fax: (571)319-0034; Email: mail@cmpa.com • URL: http://www.cmpa.com • Analyzes scientifically how the media treat social and political issues. Conducts surveys to determine media impact on public opinion. Performs rapid response media analyses, enabling the impact of media coverage to be determined as it occurs.

**Center for Migration Studies**. 27 Carmine St. New York, NY 10014-4423. Phone: (212)337-3080; Fax: (646)998-4625; Email: cms@cmsny.org • URL: http://cmsny.org • A nonprofit institute whose goal is to provide a forum for debate on international migration.

**Center for National Policy**. 1250 I St. NW, Ste. 500 Washington, DC 20005. Phone: (202)216-9723; Email: info@trumancnp.org • URL: http://cnponline.org • Promotes open discussion of the fundamentals of American public policy, including understanding of the substance of issues, determination of individual and common interests, and assessment of the attitudes, values and opinions of the public.

**Center for Pension and Retirement Research**. Miami University, Department of Economics, 109E Laws Hall Oxford, OH 45056. Phone: (513)529-2850; Fax: (513)529-3308; Email: swilliamson@eh.net • Research areas include pension economics, pension plans, and retirement decisions.

**Center for Quality and Productivity**. University of North Texas, College of Business Administration, 1155 Union Cir., No. 311160 Denton, TX 76203. Phone: (940)369-8476; Email: prybutok@unt.edu • URL: http://www.coba.unt.edu • Fields of research include the management of quality systems and statistical methodology.

**Center for Strategic and Budgetary Assessments**. 1667 K St. NW, Ste. 900 Washington, DC 20006. Phone: (202)331-7990 or (202)719-1341; Fax: (202)331-8019; Email: info@csbaonline.org • URL: http://www.csbaonline.org • Serves as nonpartisan independent research organization that analyzes military spending and national security policy issues. Provides timely, independent analyses of military budget and defense issues to the media, citizens' organizations, policy-makers, and advocacy groups. Conducts research and educational programs. Sponsors briefings and discussions on defense and military issues. Analyzes issues such as the impact of the defense budget on other national spending priorities, the American economy, and the federal deficit; the relationship between defense spending, national security, and the development of alternatives to present national security policies. Maintains internship program.

**Center for Studies in Creativity - State University of New York College at Buffalo**. 1300 Elmwood Ave. Buffa... Phone: (716)878-6223 or (716)878-4000; ... 4040; Email: createps@buffalostate.edu ... buffalostate.edu.

**Center for Study of Librarianship**. Ke... OH 44242-0001. Phone: (330)6... 7965; Email: dwicks@kent.edu ... edu.

**Center for Study of Res**... Washington, DC 200... (202)234-5176 • UR... research group.

**Center for the Stud**... Hall, 303 Un... man Reso... 4175; F... Resea... Me...

**Cent**...

...du • ...are and

...**ongress**. 1020 ...C 20010. Phone: ...11; Email: email@ www.thepresidency.org • ...Executive Branch on policy ...hing presidential leadership and ...congressional relations. Formerly ...ial Papers.

**Center for Urban and Regional Studies**. University of North Carolina at Chapel Hill, 108 Battle Ln. Chapel Hill, NC 27599-3410. Phone: (919)962-3074 or (919)962-3077; Fax: (919)962-2518; Email: brohe@unc.edu • URL: http://curs.unc.edu • Founded by the Institute for Research in Social Science of the University of North Carolina to facilitate research in urban and regional affairs. Center is concerned with: the investigation of underlying processes responsible for rapid growth and change in the urban scene; the study of problems and issues associated with these processes; the development of systems for the stimulation of urban processes so that policy and program alternatives for achieving local objectives can be tested and their implications studied before putting them into effect. Current research projects include: studies of urban and regional problems such as housing and community development; coastal zone management; flood hazard management; land use management; urban growth management; water source protection in urbanizing watersheds, brown fields' redevelopment, sustainable development and poverty and equity issues.

**Center for Women Policy Studies**. 1776 Massachusetts Ave. NW, Ste. 450 Washington, DC 20036. Phone: (202)872-1770; Fax: (202)296-8962; Email: cwps@centerwomenpolicy.org • URL: http://www.centerwomenpolicy.org • Conducts research on the policy issues that affect the legal, economic, educational, and social status of women, including sexual harassment in the workplace, and women and AIDS.

***Central Africa Business Directory***. A.C. Braby (Pty) Ltd., 12 Caversham Rd. Pinetown 3610, South Africa. Email: support@brabys.co.za • URL: http://www.brabys.com • Annual. $35; $120 payment must accompany order. Covers: Businesses in Botswana, Lesotho, Mauritius, Malawi, Mozambique, Reunion, Seychelles, South West Africa, Swaziland, Zambia, and Zimbabwe. Entries include: Company name, address, phone, type of business.

**Central and East European Management Development Association**. Presernova cesta 33 4260 Bled, Slovenia. Phone: 386 4 5792505 or 386 4 5792570; Email: info@ceeman.org • URL: http://www.ceeman.org • Specialists in business education and management personnel in commercial business, industry, professional, and technical fields from 42 countries. Seeks to improve the quality of management education throughout central and Eastern Europe. Provides a forum for discussion and exchange among individuals teaching, practicing, or studying management; provides IQA accreditation.

**Central Asian Foundation for Management Development**. Abai Ave., No. 52 480008 Almaty, Kazakhstan. Phone: 7 3272 423545; Fax: 7 3272 509228; Email: caman@iab.almaty.kz • URL: http://caman-kz.euro.ru • Aims to promote formation and development of business education in the region. Promotes management and management education development and improvement in the Central Asian region.

**Central Association of Agricultural Valuers**. Market Chambers, 35 Market Pl., Gloucestershire Coleford GL16 8AA, United Kingdom. Phone: 44 1594 832979; Fax: 44 1594 810701; Email: enquire@caav.org.uk • URL: http://www.caav.org.uk • Members are land agents, agricultural valuers and auctioneers which awards the qualification FAAV on examination. Publishes technical guidance and briefings. Engages with government and others in professional matters.

**Central Association of Women Entrepreneurs**. Kaisaniemenkatu 1 B a 74 FIN-00100 Helsinki, Finland. Phone: 358 40 5222252; Email: toimisto@yrittajanaiset.fi • URL: http://www.yrittajanaiset.fi • Women entrepreneurs in Finland. Promotes the participation of women in Finland's economic structure. Assists women in small business development.

***Central Banking: Policy, Markets, Supervision***. European Business Publications Inc., Box 891 Darien, CT 06820-9859. Phone: (203)656-2701 or (203)658-2701; Fax: (203)655-8332; Email: gale.customerservice@cengage.com • URL: http://www.curt.org/pdf/283.pdf • Quarterly. $260.00 per year, including annual *Central Banking Directory*. Published in England by Central Banking Publications. Reports and comments on the activities of central banks around the world. Also provides discussions of the International Monetary Fund (IMF), the Organization for Economic Cooperation and Development (OECD), the Bank for International Settlements (BIS), and the World Bank.

***...al Europe Profiled: Essential Facts on Society, Business, ... Politics in Central Europe***. Palgrave Macmillan, 175 5th ... New York, NY 10010. Phone: 800-221-7945 or ...9300 or (646)307-5151; Fax: (212)777-6359 or ...77; Email: customerservice@mpsvirginia.com • ...w.us.macmillan.com • $19.95 paperback. List ...hanges, trade and labor associations, top ...transport and communications, social ...l market share.

**Centre for Bu...tion**. 8150 Leesburg Pike, Ste. ... Phone: (703)242-4670; Fax: ...in@csaaintl.org • URL: ...ms, associations, and ...ed primarily in the ...larm businesses. ...tween sellers, ...ment of the



**...art-ment of Civil Engineering**. 35 St. George St. Toronto, ON, Canada M5S 1A4. Phone: (416)978-6813; Fax: (416)978-6813 • URL: http://www.civ.utoronto.ca.

**Centre for History and Economics**. King's College Cambridge CB2 1ST, United Kingdom. Phone: 44 1223 331197; Fax: 44 1223 331198 • URL: http://www.histecon.magd.cam.ac.uk • Encourages participation of economists and historians in continuing efforts to address issues of immediate and practical public importance, such as economic security, poverty and inequality, the integration of national economies, and political and economic nationalism.

**Centre for Interfirm Comparison**. Wintex House, 4 Easton Lane Business Park, Easton Ln., Hants Winchester SO23 7RQ, United Kingdom. Phone: 44 1962 844144; Fax: 44 1962 843180; Email: enquiries@cifc.co.uk • URL: http://www.cifc.co.uk • Provides expertise in performance measurement and financial control of companies and other organizations. Services include interfirm comparison; benchmarking; development of performance indicators; surveys, statistics and business information; and training in these topics.

**Centre for Women in Business**. Mt. Saint Vincent University, The Meadows, 2nd Fl., 166 Bedford Hwy. Halifax, NS, Canada B3M 2J6. Phone: 888-776-9022 or (902)457-6449; Fax: (902)443-4687; Email: cwb@msvu.ca • URL: http://www.centreforwomeninbusiness.ca/en/home/default.aspx • Represents women entrepreneurs in Canada.

**CEO Netweavers**. PO Box 700393 Dallas, TX 75370. Email: info@ceonetweavers.org • URL: http://www.ceonetweavers.org • Represents servant leader CEOs and their trusted professional service advisors. Promotes servant leadership and relationship building among members. Provides communication, brand building, education, community outreach and learning.

***The CEO Report***. UCG Holdings L.P., 11300 Rockville Pike, Suite 1100 Rockville, MD 20852-3030. Phone: 800-929-4824 or (301)816-8950 or (301)287-2700; Fax: (301)816-8945; Email: dhernan@ucg.com • URL: http://www.ucg.com • Description: Contains information for managers of credit unions.

***Ceramic Industries International***. Turret Group Ltd., 173 High St. Rickmansworth WD3 1AY, United Kingdom. Phone: 44 1923 692660; Email: initial.surname@turretgroup.com • URL: http://www.turretgroup.com • Bimonthly. $94.00. per year.

***Ceramic Industry: The Magazine for Refractories, Traditional and Advanced Ceramic Manufacturers***. BNP Media, 2401 W Big Beaver Rd., Ste. 700 Troy, MI 48084. Phone: 800-952-6643 or (248)362-3700 or (847)763-9534; Fax: (248)362-5103 or (248)362-0317; Email: privacy@bnpmedia.com • URL: http://www.bnpmedia.com • Monthly. Includes *Data Buyers Guide*, *Materials Handbook*, *Economic Forecast*, and *Giants in Ceramic*.

**Ceramic Tile Distributors Association**. 800 Roosevelt Rd., Bldg. C, Ste. 312 Glen Ellyn, IL 60137. Phone: (630)545-9415; Fax: (630)790-3095; Email: info@ctdahome.org • URL: http://www.ctdahome.org • Wholesale distributors and manufacturers of ceramic tile and related products. Promotes the increase of sales volumes in the ceramic tile industry through educational programs and networking. Promotes independent ceramic tile distributors and represents their interests. Provides technical information; compiles statistics. Sponsors competitions. Maintains insurance program for members and speakers' bureau.

***Ceramics Abstracts/World Ceramics Abstracts***. American Ceramic Society. Cambridge Scientific Abstracts L.P., 7200 Wisconsin Ave., Ste. 601 Bethesda, MD 20814. Phone: 800-843-7751 or (301)961-6700 or (301)961-6785; Fax: (301)961-6720 or (301)961-6708; Email: sales@proquest.com • URL: http://www.proquest.co.uk • Monthly. Provide international coverage of the ceramics industry.

***Ceramics Monthly***. American Ceramic Society, 600 N Cleveland Ave., Ste. 210 Westerville, OH 43082. Phone: 866-721-3322 or (240)646-7054; Fax: (204)396-5637; Email: customerservice@ceramics.org • URL: http://www.ceramics.org • $34.95 Individuals; $40 Canada; $60 Other countries; $59.95 Two years; $75 Canada two years; $99 Other countries two years. Consumer magazine containing ceramic art and craft. Features articles on ceramic artists, exhibitions, production processes, critical commentary, book and video reviews, clay and glaze recipes, and kiln designs.

**Cereal Crops Research Unit U.S. Department of Agricultural Research Service**. 502 N Walnut St. Madison, WI 53726. Phone: (608)262-0377; Fax: (608)890-0306; Email: cynthia.henson@ars.usda.gov • URL: http://www.ars.usda.gov.

**Cereal Disease Laboratory-U.S. Department of Agricultural Research Service**. University of Minnesota, 1551 Lindig St. Saint Paul, MN 55108. Phone: (612)624-4155; Fax: (612)649-5054; Email: shahryar.kianian@ars.usda.gov • URL: http://www.cdl.umn.edu.

***CFA Institute—Membership Directory***. CFA Institute, 560 Ray C. Hunt Dr. Charlottesville, VA 22903-2981. Phone: 800-247-8132 or (434)951-5499; Fax: (434)951-5262; Email: info@cfainstitute.org • URL: http://www.cfainstitute.org/pages/index.aspx • Annual. $150 per year; Included in membership. Covers: 38,000 security and financial analysts who are practicing investment analysis. Entries include: Name, firm affiliation and address, phone, fax, e-mail.

**CFA Institute**. 560 Ray C. Hunt Dr. Charlottesville, VA 22903-2981. Phone: 800-247-8132 or (434)951-5499; Fax: (434)951-5262; Email: info@cfainstitute.org • URL: http://www.cfainstitute.org/pages/index.aspx • Formerly Association for Investment Management and Research.

**CFDA Foundation** . 65 Bleecker St., 11 Fl. New York, NY 10012. Phone: (212)302-1821; Fax: (212)768-0515; Email: info@cfda.com • URL: http://www.cfda.com • Persons of "recognized ability, standing, and integrity, who are actively engaged in creative fashion design in the United States, in the fields of wearing apparel, fabrics, accessories, jewelry, or related products." (Membership is individual and does not extend to the firm or associates.) Seeks "to further the position of fashion design as a recognized branch of American art and culture, to advance its artistic and professional standards, to establish and maintain a code of ethics and practices of mutual benefit in professional, public, and trade relations, and to promote and improve public understanding and appreciation of the fashion arts through leadership in quality and taste."

***CFMA Building Profits***. Construction Financial Management Association, 100 Village Blvd., Ste. 200 Princeton, NJ 08540. Phone: 888-421-9996 or (609)452-8000; Fax: (609)452-0474; Email: sbinstock@cfma.org • URL: http://www.cfma.org • Bimonthly. Covers the financial side of the construction industry.

***CFO: The Magazine for Senior Financial Executives***. CFO Publishing Corp., 253 Summer St. Boston, MA 02210. Phone: (617)345-9700; Fax: (617)951-4090; Email: juliahomer@cfopub.com • URL: http://www.cfo.com • Monthly.

***Chad Business Directory***. Business Guide, PO Box 27669 Dubai, United Arab Emirates. Phone: 971 4 2651719; Fax: 971 4 2692151; Email: sales@africa-business.com • URL: http://www.africa-business.com • $150 download. Covers: 3,600 business listings including wholesalers, importers, retailers, business houses, and agents in Chad.

***Chain Drug Review: The Reporter for the Chain Drug Store Industry***. Racher Press Inc., 220 5th Ave. New York, NY 10001. Phone: (212)213-6000 or (646)763-8268; Fax: (212)213-6106; Email: info@racherpress.com • URL: http://www.massmarketretailers.com • $199 Institutions; $299 Other countries. Covers news and trends of concern to the chain drug store industry. Includes special articles on OTC (over-the-counter) drugs.

***Chain Store Age: The NewsMagazine for Retail Executives***. Lebhar-Friedman Inc., 425 Park Ave. New York, NY 10022. Phone: (212)756-5000 or (603)432-4077; Email: info@lf.com • URL: http://www.lf.com • 9/year. Formerly *Chain Store Age Executive with Shopping Center Age*.

***Challenge: The Magazine of Economic Affairs***. M.E. Sharpe Inc., 80 Business Park Dr. Armonk, NY 10504. Phone: 800-541-6563 or (914)273-1800; Fax: (914)273-2106; Email: info@mesharpe.com • URL: http://www.mesharpe.com • 6/year. $72 Individuals print only; $420 Institutions print and online. A nontechnical journal on current economic policy and economic trends.

***Chamber Business Monthly***. South Snohomish County Chamber of Commerce, 3815 196th St. SW, Ste. 136 Lynnwood, WA 98036. Phone: (425)774-0507; Fax: (425)774-4636; Email: info@s2c3.com • URL: http://www.s2c3.com • Monthly.

***Chamber Business Update***. Greenville - Pitt County Chamber of Commerce, 302 S Greene St. Greenville, NC 27834-1564. Phone: (252)752-4101; Fax: (252)752-5934 • URL: http://www.greenvillenc.org • Monthly.

***Chamber News: A Focus on Business***. East Providence Area Chamber of Commerce, 1011 Waterman Ave. East Providence, RI 02914-1314. Phone: (401)438-1212; Fax: (401)435-4581; Email: office@eastprovchamber.com • URL: http://www.eastprovchamber.com • Quarterly.

***Chamber of Commerce of Hawaii—Business Networking Directory***. Chamber of Commerce of Hawaii, 1132 Bishop St., Ste. 402 Honolulu, HI 96813. Phone: (808)545-4300; Fax: (808)545-4369 • URL: http://www.cochawaii.org • Covers: Approximately 2,000 member businesses in Hawaii; approximately 20 associate regional and ethnic chambers of commerce and affiliate organizations. Entries include: Firm name; address; phone; e-mail; website; name, and title of key contact.

***Chamber of Commerce of the Bellmores Business and Professional Directory***. Chamber of Commerce of the Bellmores, 2700 Pettit Ave. Bellmore, NY 11710. Phone: (516)679-1875; Fax: (516)409-0544; Email: info@bellmorechamber.com • URL: http://bellmorechamber.com • Covers: All current members.

***Chamber South Business Directory***. Image Factory, 6410 SW 80th St. Miami, FL 33143. Phone: (305)661-1621; Fax: (305)666-0580 • Covers: about 4,400 member businesses, organizations, and other community resources in South Dade County, Florida. Entries include: Company name, address, phone, contact name and fax.

**Chambre Nationale des Femmes Chefs d'Entreprise**. 17, Rue Abderrahamen El Jaziri 1002 Tunis, Tunisia. Phone: 216 71 860112; Fax: 216 71 862049; Email: cnfce.tunisie@fcem.ws • URL: http://www.fcem.org/en/pays-membres.html • Represents the interests of women entrepreneurs before national and international organizations and institutions. Reinforces the presence and representation of women within employer organizations and national chambers. Promotes women entrepreneurship. Promotes exchanges, relationships, and development of regional, national and international contacts aimed at reinforcing partnerships and access to new markets.

***Champion***. Carrefour Participacoes S.A., Rua George Eastman 213, Vila Tramontino 05690-000 Sao Paulo, Brazil. Phone: 55 11 3779 6000; Fax: 55 11 3777 6694 • URL: http://www.carrefour.com.br • 10 times a year. $25.00 per year.

***Change: The Magazine of Higher Learning***. American Association of Higher Education. Taylor & Francis Group Heldref Publications, 325 Chestnut St., Ste. 800 Philadelphia, PA 19106. Phone: 800-354-1420 or (215)625-8900; Email: customer.service@taylorandfrancis.com • URL: http://www.heldref.org • 6/year. $70 Individuals print and online; $257 Institutions print and online. Contains issues regarding the implications of educational programs, policies and practices.

**Chapman University - A. Gary Anderson Center for Economic Research**. 1 University Dr. Orange, CA 92866. Phone: (714)997-6693; Fax: (714)997-6601; Email: adibi@chapman.edu • URL: http://www.chapman.edu/research-and-institutions/anderson-center/index.aspx • Economics and business in the U.S. and California, as well as in Orange County, Los Angeles County, and the Inland Empire in California.

***Chapter 11 Update: Monitors All Major Developments in Today's Corporate Bankruptcies and Examines Pertinent Court Decisions Related to Chapter 11 Filings***. Andrews Publications, 175 Strafford Ave., Bldg. 4, Suite 140 Wayne, PA 19087. Phone: 800-345-1101 or (610)225-0510 or (610)622-0510; Fax: (610)225-0501 or (610)622-0501; Email: customer@andrewspub.com • URL: http://www.andrewspub.com • Semimonthly. $500.00 per year. Newsletter on corporate Chapter 11 bankruptcy filings.

***Characteristics of Apartments Completed (year)***. U.S. Department of Commerce U.S. Census Bureau, 4600 Silver Hill Rd. Washington, DC 20233. Phone: 800-923-8282 or (301)763-4636 or (301)763-3030; Fax: (301)457-4714 or (301)763-6239; Email: webmaster@census.gov • URL: http://www.census.gov/ • Annual. Covers privately financed, nonsubsidized apartments in buildings with five units or more.

***Charitable Business Magazine: Canada's Non-Profit Management Magazine***. Momentum Media Management, 4040 Creditview Rd., Unit 11 Mississauga, ON, Canada L5C 3Y8. Fax: (905)813-7117 • Bimonthly. $15; $30 U.S.; $2.50 Single issue. Magazine for Canadian executives, administrators, purchasing and operations personnel at charitable and non-profit organizations.

***Charitable Giving and Solicitation***. Thomson RIA, 195 Broadway New York, NY 10007-3100. Phone: 800-431-9025 or (212)367-6300 or (212)807-2298; Fax: (212)367-6305 or (212)337-4207; Email: ttacommunications@riag.com • URL: http://www.ria.thomson.com • $495.00 per year. Looseleaf service. Updates 13 times a year. Bulletin discusses federal tax rules pertaining to charitable contributions.

**Charles University - Institute of Economic Studies**. Opletalova 26 CZ-110 00 Prague, Czech Republic. Phone: 420 2 22112330; Fax: 420 2 22112304; Email: gregor@fsv.cuni.cz • URL: http://ies.fsv.cuni.cz/content/tree/index/lang/en • Economics, the economy, the history of economics, corporate finance, banking, and analysis of capital markets.

***Charleston Regional Business Journal***. SC Biz News, 389 Johnnie Dodds Blvd., Ste. 200 Mount Pleasant, SC 29464. Phone: (843)401-1094 • URL: http://www.scbiznews.com • Contains the full text of Charleston Regional Business Journal, a business tabloid covering the Charleston, South Carolina and surrounding region.

***Charleston Regional Business Journal***. Setcom Inc., 389 Johnnie Dodds Blvd., Ste. 200 Mount Pleasant, SC 29464. Phone: (843)849-3100; Fax: (843)849-3122 • URL: http://www.charlestonbusiness.com • Biweekly. $99 Individuals /year; $349 Individuals /year, premium subscription. Local business journal.

***Charlotte Business Journal***. American City Business Journals, Inc., 120 W Morehead St. Charlotte, NC 28202. Phone: (704)973-1000; Fax: (704)973-1001; Email: americancity@bizjournals.com • URL: http://www.acbj.com • Weekly. $92 Individuals print + online. Newspaper for the business community of Charlotte and the surrounding thirteen-county area.

***Chartcraft Monthly NYSE and ASE Chartbook***. Chartcraft Inc., 30 Church St. New Rochelle, NY 10801. Phone: (914)632-0422; Fax: (914)632-0335 • Monthly. $402.00 per year. Includes all common stocks on New York and American Stock Exchanges.

***Chartcraft Over-the-Counter Chartbook***. Chartcraft Inc., 30 Church St. New Rochelle, NY 10801. Phone: (914)632-0422; Fax: (914)632-0335 • Quarterly. $114.00 per year. Includes more than 1,000 unlisted stocks. Long term charts.

***Charter Boats Directory***. InfoGroup Inc., 5711 S 86th Cir. Omaha, NE 68127-4146. Phone: (402)593-4500 • URL: http://www.infogroup.com • Annual. Number of listings: 5,435. Entries include: Name, address, phone, size of advertisement, name of owner or manager, number of employees, year first in "Yellow Pages." Compiled from telephone company "Yellow Pages," nationwide.

**Chartered Alternative Investment Analyst Association**. 100 University Dr. Amherst, MA 01002-2357. Phone: (413)253-7373; Fax: (413)253-4494; Email: info@caia.org • URL: http://caia.org • Seeks to establish the Chartered Alternative Investment Analyst designation as the educational standard for the alternative investment industry. Advocates for high standards of professional conduct in the field of alternative investment analysis. Promotes professional development through continuous education. Facilitates communication among industry professionals.

**Chartered Management Institute**. 2 Savoy Ct., Strand London WC2R 0EZ, United Kingdom. Phone: 44 20 74970580; Fax: 44 20 74970463; Email: enquiries@managers.org.uk • URL: http://www.managers.org.uk • Promotes the development, exercise and recognition of professional management. Provides services in the areas of management development, management advice, management information and management networks.

***Chartered Property and Casualty Underwriters eJournal***. Society of Chartered Property and Casualty Underwriters, 720 Providence Rd. Malvern, PA 19355. Phone: 800-932-2728 or (610)251-2716 or (610)644-2100; Fax: (610)725-5969; Email: MemberResources@theinstitutes.org • URL: http://www.cpcusociety.org • Monthly. Published by the Chartered Property and Casualty Underwriters Society (CPCU). Edited for professional insurance underwriters and agents.

***The Cheap Investor: The Investor's Guide to Microcap and Turn Around Stocks Under $5 Per Share***. Mathews and Associates Inc., 3 Golf Ctr., Ste. 404 Hoffman Estates, IL 60169-4910. Phone: (847)697-5666; Fax: (847)697-5699 • URL: http://www.thecheapinvestor.com • Monthly. $697 per year. Gives three to six buy recommendations, updates on precious recommendations and investment tips on quality stock under $5.00.

***Cheese Importers Association of America Bulletin***. Cheese Importers Association of America, 204 E St. NE Washington, DC 20002. Phone: (202)547-0899; Fax: (202)547-6348; Email: info@theciaa.org • URL: http://www.theciaa.org • Irregular.

**Cheese Importers Association of America**. 204 E St. NE Washington, DC 20002. Phone: (202)547-0899; Fax: (202)547-6348; Email: info@theciaa.org • URL: http://www.theciaa.org • Represents importers, brokers, steamship lines, warehousemen, and firms interested in the importation of cheese.

***Cheese Market News***. Quarne Publishing L.L.C., P. O. Box 620244 Middleton, WI 53562-0244. Phone: (608)831-6002; Fax: (608)831-1004; Email: chmarknews@aol.com • URL: http://www.cheesemarketnews.com • Weekly. $135 print and online. Covers market trends, legislation, and new products.

***Cheese Market News: The Weekly Newspaper of the Nation's Cheese and Dairy-Deli Business***. Quarne Publishing L.L.C., P. O. Box 620244 Middleton, WI 53562-0244. Phone: (608)831-6002; Fax: (608)831-1004; Email: chmarknews@aol.com • URL: http://www.cheesemarketnews.com • Weekly (Fri.). $145 U.S. 2nd class; $200 Canada and Mexico first class, airmail; $330 Other countries airmail; $205 Two years 2nd class; $325 Canada and Mexico two years, 1st class; $525 Other countries two years; $8.50 Single issue. Newspaper (tabloid) covering the cheese manufacturing and marketing business.

***Cheese Reporter***. Dick Groves, editor. Cheese Reporter Publishing Company Inc., 2810 Crossroads Dr., Ste. 3000 Madison, WI 53718. Phone: (608)246-8430; Fax: (608)246-8431; Email: info@cheesereporter.com • URL: http://www.cheesereporter.com • Weekly. $140. Reports technology, production, sales, merchandising, promotion, research and general industry news of and pertaining to the manufacture and marketing of cheese.

***Chef***. Aktiebolaget Electrolux, S:t Goeransgatan 143 SE-105 45 Stockholm, Sweden. Phone: 46 08 738 60 00; Fax: 46 08 738 74 61 • URL: http://www.electrolux.com • Monthly. $24.00 per year. Edited for executive chefs, food and beverage directors, caterers, banquet and club managers, and others responsible for food buying and food service. Special coverage of regional foods is provided.

***Chelsea Area Chamber of Commerce Community Profile & Business Directory***. Chelsea Area Chamber of Commerce, 222 S Main St., Ste. B Chelsea, MI 48118-1291. Phone: (734)475-1145; Fax: (734)475-6102; Email: info@chelseamichamber.org • URL: http://www.chelseamichamber.org • Covers businesses in Chelsea, Michigan.

***Chemical Abstracts***. American Chemical Society Chemical Abstracts Service, 2540 Olentangy River Rd. Columbus, OH 43202. Phone: 800-848-6538 or (614)447-3600 or (614)441-3600; Fax: (614)447-3713 or (614)447-3751; Email: help@cas.org • URL: http://www.cas.org • Available via CAS' electronic products including SciFinder and STN.

***Chemical & Engineering News***. American Chemical Society, 1155 16th St. NW Washington, DC 20036. Phone: 800-227-5558 or (202)872-4600; Email: help@acs.org • URL: http://www.acs.org • Weekly Annual. Included in membership; $120 Nonmembers. Magazine on chemical and engineering news.

***Chemical Business***. Colour Publications Private Ltd., 126-A Dhurwadi, A.V. Nagwekar Marg, Prabhadevi Mumbai 400 025, India. Phone: 91 222 4306319; Fax: 91 222 04300601; Email: colorpub@vsnl.com • Weekly Monthly. Technical journal.

**Chemical Coaters Association International**. 5040 Old Taylor Mill Rd. Taylor Mill, KY 41015. Phone: (859)356-1030; Fax: (859)356-0908 • URL: http://www.ccaiweb.com • Industrial users of organic finishing systems; suppliers of chemicals, equipment, and paints. Works toward the improvement of decorative, functional, and performance standards of chemical coatings. Encourages members to continue improvements in application technology. Provides coating industry with representation to public authorities and government agencies. Sponsors research and educational programs to control environmental pollution. Maintains placement service. Provides speaker's bureau.

***Chemical Engineering***. Chemical Week Associates, 2 Grand Central Tower, 140 E 45th St., 40th Fl. New York, NY 10017. Phone: 800-774-5733 or (212)884-9528 or (212)621-4900; Fax: (212)883-9514 or (212)884-9514; Email: webmaster@chemweek.com • URL: http://www.chemweek.com • Monthly. $299.97 print or online. Includes annual *Chemical Engineering Buyers Guide*.

***Chemical Engineering Progress***. Center for Chemical Process Safety, 3 Park Ave., 19th Fl. New York, NY 10016-5991. Phone: 800-242-4363 or (646)495-1370 or (646)495-1371; Fax: (646)495-1504 or (203)775-5177; Email: ccps@aiche.org • URL: http://www.aiche.org/ccps • Monthly. $170 Nonmembers in North America; $295 Nonmembers international; $210 Nonmembers with online; in North America; $335 Nonmembers with online; international; Included in membership. Covers current advances and trends in the chemical process and related industries. Supplement available *AICh Extra*.

***Chemical Processing***. Putman Media Inc., 555 W Pierce Rd., Ste. 301 Itasca, IL 60143-2649. Phone: (630)467-1301 or (630)467-1300; Fax: (630)467-1120 or (630)467-1109; Email: controlroundup@putman.net • URL: http://www.putman.net • Monthly.

***Chemical Regulation Reporter: A Weekly Review of Activity Affecting Chemical Users and Manufacturers***. Bloomberg BNA, 3 Bethesda Metro Center, Ste. 250 Bethesda, MD 20814-5377. Phone: 800-372-1033 or (703)341-3000; Fax: (800)253-0332; Email: customercare@bna.com • URL: http://www.bna.com • Weekly. $2,226 per year. Looseleaf service.

**Chemical Sources Association**. 3301 Rte. 66, Ste. 205, Bldg. C Neptune, NJ 07753. Phone: (732)922-3008; Fax: (732)922-3590 • URL: http://www.chemicalsources.org • Representatives of flavor and fragrance manufacturers. Purpose is to find suppliers and manufacturers for rare or hard-to-obtain chemicals and essential oils used in the flavor and fragrance industry. Compiles statistics.

***Chemical Week***. Chemical Week Associates, 2 Grand Central Tower, 140 E 45th St., 40th Fl. New York, NY 10017. Phone: 800-774-5733 or (212)884-9528 or (212)621-4900; Fax: (212)883-9514 or (212)884-9514; Email: webmaster@chemweek.com • URL: http://www.chemweek.com • 49 times a year. $139.00 per year. Includes annual *Buyers' Guide*.

***Chemicals, Plastics & Rubber Yearbook***. George Warman Publications Ltd., 76, Porter House, Belmont Rd., Rondebosch Cape Town 8001, South Africa. Phone: 27 21 6892640; Fax: 27 21 6893408; Email: marinfo@iafrica.com • URL: http://www.gwarmanpublications.co.za • Biennial. $45; $41.33. Covers: Chemical, plastics and rubber products, manufacturers, associations, and colleges/universities in South Africa. Entries include: Company name, address, phone, brand name, specifications, statistics, services, suppliers of machinery and instrumentation.

***CHF Newsbriefs***. Global Communities, 8601 Georgia Ave., Ste. 800 Silver Spring, MD 20910. Phone: (301)587-4700; Fax: (301)587-7315 • URL: http://www.globalcommunities.org • Description: Seeks to "help families throughout the world by focusing on the development of communities, habitat, and finance.".

***Chicago Area Business Directory***. InfoGroup Inc., 5711 S 86th Cir. Omaha, NE 68127-4146. Phone: (402)593-4500 • URL: http://www.infogroup.com • Annual. $495. Number of listings: 314,000. Entries include: Company name, address, phone, number of employees, name of owner or manager, annual sales. Compiled from telephone company "Yellow Pages," statewide.

***Chicago Board of Trade: The World's Leading Futures Exchange***. Chicago Board of Trade, Phone: (312)535-3500; Fax: (312)341-3392; Email: comments@cbot.com • URL: http://www.cbot.com • Web site provides a wide variety of statistics, commentary, charts, and news relating to both agricultural and financial futures trading. For example, Web page "MarketPlex: Information MarketPlace to the World" offers prices & volume, contract specifications & margins, government reports, etc. Searching is available, with daily updates for current data. Fees: Mostly free (some specialized services are fee-based).

**Chicago Board Options Exchange Inc.** 400 S LaSalle St. Chicago, IL 60605. Phone: 877-843-2263 or (312)786-5600; Fax: (312)786-7409; Email: help@cboe.com • URL: http://www.cboe.com • Individuals, institutions and firms engaged in the buying and selling of various products including stock options, cash-settled index options, options on HOLDRs, options on Exchange Traded Funds and Structured Products.

***Chicago Business***. Chicago Business, 5801 S Ellis Ave. Chicago,

IL 60637-1404. • Semimonthly. $15 Individuals. Collegiate business school publication.

***Chicago JobBank: The Job Hunter's Guide to Metro Chicago***. Adams Media Corp., 57 Littlefield St. Avon, MA 02322. Phone: 800-872-5627 or (508)427-7100; Fax: (508)427-6790 or (800)872-5628; Email: deskcopies@adamsmedia.com • URL: http://www.adamsmedia.com • Annual. $17.95 Individuals Paperback; $9 Individuals sale price. Covers: About 5,500 major employers in northern and central Illinois including Aurora, Peoria, Rockford, and Springfield. Database includes: Information on the basics of job winning and writing resumes and cover letters; electronic job search information; 330 industry association; 90 online career resources, 480 employment services. Entries include: Firm or organization name, address, local phone, toll-free phone, fax, e-mail, URL, description of organization, hours, recorded jobline, subsidiaries, names of management, name and title of contact, names of management, headquarters locations, typical titles for entry-level and middle-level positions, educational backgrounds desired, company benefits, stock exchange listing, training programs, internships, parent company, number of employees, revenues, other U.S. Locations, international locations.

**Chicago Stock Exchange Inc.** 440 S LaSalle St. Chicago, IL 60605-1028. Phone: (312)663-2222; Fax: (312)663-2231; Email: info@chx.com • URL: http://www.chx.com • Brokers and dealers in local and national securities. Wholly-owned subsidiaries: Midwest Securities Trust Company; Midwest Clearing Corp.; Mortgage Backed Securities Clearing Corporation. Provides an auction market for purchase and sale of equity securities.

***Chief Executive Magazine***. Chief Executive Group, LLC, 1 Sound Shore Dr., Ste. 100 Greenwich, CT 06830. Phone: (203)930-2700; Fax: (203)930-2701; Email: contact@chiefexecutive.net • URL: http://chiefexecutive.net • Monthly. $99 per year.

***Chief Executive Officers Newsletter: For the Entrepreneurial Manager and the Pr ofessionals Who Advise Him***. Center for Entrepreneurial Management Inc., 180 Varick St. New York, NY 10014. Phone: (212)633-0060; Fax: (212)633-0063 • Monthly. $96.00 per year. Looseleaf service. Formerly *Entrepreneurial Manager's Newsletter*.

**Chief Executives Organization**. 7920 Norfolk Ave., Ste. 400 Bethesda, MD 20814-2507. Phone: (301)656-9220; Fax: (301)656-9221; Email: info@ceo.org • URL: http://www.ceo.org • Invited members of the Young Presidents' Organization who have reached the age of 49, the mandatory "retirement" age for YPO. (Young Presidents' Organization comprises presidents of corporations with gross annual revenue of at least one million dollars and a minimum of 50 employees, of nonindustrial corporations with revenue of two million dollars and 25 employees, or of banking corporations with average deposits of 15 million dollars and 25 employees. Each member must have been elected president of a corporation before reaching the age of 40.) Sponsors educational programs.

**Chief Officers of State Library Agencies**. 201 E Main St., Ste. 1405 Lexington, KY 40507. Phone: 800-800-1910 or (859)514-9151 or (859)244-8000; Fax: (859)514-9166 or (859)244-8001; Email: lsingler@amrms.com • URL: http://www.cosla.org • Supersedes American Legislator Association.

**Chief Warrant and Warrant Officers Association**. 200 V St. SW Washington, DC 20024-3321. Phone: 800-792-8447 or (202)554-7753; Fax: (202)484-0641; Email: cwoauscg@verizon.net • URL: http://www.cwoauscg.org • Individuals who currently hold or once held the rank of Warrant Officer or Chief Warrant Officer on the active, retired, and reserve rolls of the U.S. Coast Guard. Works to aid members in advancing their professional abilities. Seeks to enhance their value, loyalty, and devotion to the service; promotes its unity and morale through social association.

***Child Therapists Directory***. InfoGroup Inc., 5711 S 86th Cir. Omaha, NE 68127-4146. Phone: (402)593-4500 • URL: http://www.infogroup.com • Annual. Number of listings: 41,340. Entries include: Name, address, phone, size of advertisement, name of owner or manager, number of employees, year first in "Yellow Pages." Compiled from telephone company "Yellow Pages," nationwide.

***Children's Book Review Index***. Cengage Learning Inc., 20 Channel Center St. Boston, MA 02210. Phone: 800-487-8488 or (617)289-7700; Fax: (617)289-7844; Email: investors@cengage.com • URL: http://www.cengage.com • $308 Individuals. Annual. $280.00. Back volumes available. Contains more than 25,000 review citations on books for children through age 10.

***Chile Business Forecast Report***. Telecommunications Insight, 85 Queen Victoria St. London EC4V 4AB, United Kingdom. Phone: 20 72 465100 or 44 20 7248 0468; Fax: 20 72 480467 or 44 20 7248 0467; Email: enquiries@telecomsinsight.com • URL: http://www.telecomsinsight.com • Quarterly. $1,195 Individuals Single user; $1,795 Individuals Up to 3 users. Business forecast report for Chile.

***Chile Business Law Handbook***. International Business Publications, USA, PO Box 15343 Washington, DC 20003. Phone: (202)546-2103; Fax: (202)546-3275; Email: ibpusa@comcast.net • URL: http://ibpus.com • $99.95 Individuals hardcopy, E-book and CD-ROM. Covers: Basic information

on business laws and legislations, export-import regulations, business climate and contacts.

***Chile Industrial and Business Directory***. International Business Publications, USA, PO Box 15343 Washington, DC 20003. Phone: (202)546-2103; Fax: (202)546-3275; Email: ibpusa@comcast.net • URL: http://ibpus.com • Annual. $99.95 Individuals hardcopy, e-book, CD-ROM. Covers: Strategic industrial, investment and business contacts for conducting export-import and investment activity in the country.

***Chile Investment and Business Guide***. International Business Publications, USA, PO Box 15343 Washington, DC 20003. Phone: (202)546-2103; Fax: (202)546-3275; Email: ibpusa@comcast.net • URL: http://ibpus.com • $99.95 Individuals hardcopy, e-book, CD-ROM. Covers: Strategic information on economy, export-import, business and investment climate, regulations and industrial development, banking, and government. Entries include: Important business contacts and business travel.

***Chilton's Automotive Marketing: A Monthly Publication for the Retail Jobber and Distributor of Automotive Aftermarket***. Reed Elsevier Group plc Reed Business Information, 360 Park Ave. S New York, NY 11010. Phone: (212)791-4208; Email: corporatecommunications@reedbusiness.com • URL: http://www.reedbusiness.com • Monthly. Free to qualified personnel; others, $48.00 per year. Includes marketing of automobile batteries. Formerly *Automotive Aftermarket News*.

***Chilton's Distribution: The Transportation and Business Logistics Magazine***. Reed Elsevier Group plc Reed Business Information, 360 Park Ave. S New York, NY 11010. Phone: (212)791-4208; Email: corporatecommunications@reedbusiness.com • URL: http://www.reedbusiness.com • Monthly. $65.00 per year.

**China-Africa Business Council**. Shimao International Ctr., Building 1, Rm. 1805, Chaoyang District Beijing 100027, Beijing, China. Phone: 86 10 64169865 or 86 10 64166409; Fax: 86 10 64169811; Email: cabc@cabc.org.cn • URL: http://www.cabc.org.cn/enindex/index.jhtml • Promotes trade and cooperation between China and Africa. Provides business tools that are designed to strengthen business ties between the two countries. Provides members with opportunities to share experiences and strengthen their capacity to address challenges through trainings, symposiums, workshops and forums.

***China and Venture Capital & Private Equity Directory 500***. Zero2IPO, Rm. 1202/03, Tower A, Eagle Run Plz., No.26, Xiao Yun Rd., Chaoyang Dist. Beijing 100125, China. Phone: 86 10 84580476; Fax: 86 10 84580480; Email: research@zero2ipo.com.cn • URL: http://www.pedaily.cn • Annual. $455 Individuals. Covers: 600 institutions specializing in venture capital and private equity investment in China. Entries include: Company contact information, executive team, criteria for investment, cases of investment, and amount of capital under the management.

**China Association of Microfinance**. RDI of CASS, Rm. 1343, 5 Jianguomennei St. Beijing 100732, Hebei, China. Phone: 86 10 8519 6476 or 86 10 8519 5660; Fax: 86 10 8519 6476; Email: cam.net@163.com • URL: http://www.chinamfi.net • Represents and supports the microfinance industry. Promotes governmental support and strengthens international cooperation on microfinance. Raises funds for microfinance development and provides financial services to populations living with poverty and low income. Enhances the management capacity of microfinance institutions.

**China-Britain Business Council**. Portland House, 3rd Fl., Bressenden Pl. London SW1E 5BH, United Kingdom. Phone: 44 20 78022000; Fax: 44 20 78022029; Email: enquiries@cbbc.org • URL: http://www.cbbc.org • British companies doing business in China. Promotes British trade in China. Acts as a liaison between the British and Chinese governments and member companies.

***China-Britain Business Review***. China-Britain Business Council, Portland House, 3rd Fl., Bressenden Pl. London SW1E 5BH, United Kingdom. Phone: 44 20 78022000; Fax: 44 20 78022029; Email: enquiries@cbbc.org • URL: http://www.cbbc.org • Magazine featuring China-Britain trade and China economic news.

***China Business***. China Business Hong Kong, 103 No. 23 Bldg., Guanying Yuan Xiqu, Xicheng District Beijing 100035, China. Phone: 86 10 66561371; Fax: 86 10 66561412; Email: songty@chinabusiness-press.com • URL: http://www.chinabusiness-press.com • English-language business magazine containing information involving domestic foreign trade companies, industrial-trading companies, power-enlarged enterprises, international hotels and commercial centers.

**China Business Council for Sustainable Development**. A6 Huixin E St., Chaoyang District Beijing 100029, China. Phone: 86 10 69166788; Fax: 86 10 69196630; Email: info@cbcsd.org.cn • URL: http://www.cbcsd.org.cn • Provides a platform for exchange and cooperation among Chinese and foreign enterprises, government and social communities. Shares information, experiences and best practices in the field of sustainable development. Improves understanding and performance in environment health safety, corporate social responsibility and climate change.

***China Business Database***. The Data Supplier, 9107 Wilshire Blvd., Ste. 450 Beverly Hills, CA 90210. Phone: 888-930-

3282; Fax: (818)221-0295; Email: contactus@thedatasupplier.com • URL: http://www.thedatasupplier.com • Contains contact information for more than 500,000 manufacturers in China. Covers approximately 50,000 manufacturers in the automobile, motor, and machinery industry; 55,000 in the shoes, watch, bags, toys, and sports industry; 70,000 in the textiles, clothing, fabrics, garments, and fashion industry; 55,000 in the electrical, electronics, computers, and digital entertainment industry; 75,000 in the furniture, appliance, arts, jewelry, stationery, and crafts industry; and 90,000 in the chemicals, plastics, ceramics, metals, petroleum, and leather industry. Includes business name and full contact information.

***China Business Directory***. American Chamber of Commerce in Hong Kong, 1904 Bank of America Tower, 12 Harcourt Rd. Hong Kong, China. Phone: 86 852 25306900; Fax: 86 852 28101289; Email: amcham@amcham.org.hk • URL: http://www.amcham.org.hk • Periodic. HK$350 for nonmembers (local delivery); HK$245 for members (local delivery); $45 for nonmembers (overseas delivery); $32 for members (overseas delivery). Features China offices and contact of companies with regional headquarters in Hong Kong.

***China Business Directory***. China Business Information Center, 175 Linmore Dr. Fremont, CA 94539. Phone: (510)252-9888; Fax: (510)623-6955 • Annual. $239. More than 25,000 companies in the People's Republic of China, excluding Taiwan and Hong Kong, with assets over $1.5 million.

***China Business Forecast Report***. Telecommunications Insight, 85 Queen Victoria St. London EC4V 4AB, United Kingdom. Phone: 20 72 465100 or 44 20 7248 0468; Fax: 20 72 480467 or 44 20 7248 0467; Email: enquiries@telecomsinsight.com • URL: http://www.telecomsinsight.com • Quarterly. $1,195 Individuals single user; $1,795 Individuals Up to 3 users. Business forecast reports.

***China Business Guide***. American Chamber of Commerce in Hong Kong, 1904 Bank of America Tower, 12 Harcourt Rd. Hong Kong, China. Phone: 86 852 25306900; Fax: 86 852 28101289; Email: amcham@amcham.org.hk • URL: http://www.amcham.org.hk • $40 Individuals. Covers: Companies engaged in business and trade in China. Database includes: Statistics, charts.

***China Business Law Handbook***. International Business Publications, USA, PO Box 15343 Washington, DC 20003. Phone: (202)546-2103; Fax: (202)546-3275; Email: ibpusa@comcast.net • URL: http://ibpus.com • $99.95 Individuals hardcopy, e-book, CD-ROM. Covers: Information on basic business legislation, laws, business climate, foreign investments, export-import regulations, and contacts.

***China Business Review***. United States-China Business Council, 1818 N St. NW, Ste. 200 Washington, DC 20036-2406. Phone: (202)429-0340; Fax: (202)775-2476; Email: info@uschina.org • URL: http://www.uschina.org • Bimonthly. $99 per year. Covers trends and issues affecting U. S. investment and trade with China and Hong Kong.

***The China Commercial Relations Directory***. American Chamber of Commerce in Hong Kong, 1904 Bank of America Tower, 12 Harcourt Rd. Hong Kong, China. Phone: 86 852 25306900; Fax: 86 852 28101289; Email: amcham@amcham.org.hk • URL: http://www.amcham.org.hk • Biennial. $215 Nonmembers; $175 Members. Covers: Approximately 230 top China trade and service companies in Hong Kong; 115 companies in the PRC. Entries include: Addresses, names and titles of key personnel.

**China Entrepreneur Club**. Peking University Technology Park, Innovation Ctr., Rm. 501, No. 127-1 Zhongguancun N Ave., Haidan District Beijing 100080, Beijing, China. Phone: 86 10 62766066; Fax: 86 10 62768122; Email: international@daonong.com • URL: http://www.daonong.com/English • Promotes comprehensive social development and enhances the important role played by Chinese enterprises in the sustainable development of China and the world. Seeks to bring together visionary business leaders to advance common values, discover new drives for commercial spirit and guide businesses to the right path.

**China Environment Chamber of Commerce**. 4 Districts Anhuili, 15th China Minmetals Tower. Rm. 1315, Chaoyang District Beijing 100029, China. Phone: 86 10 84640865; Fax: 86 10 84649343; Email: cesia@cesia.org • URL: http://www.cecc-china.org • Aims to promote the sustainable development of China's environmental industry. Provides a platform for its members to share information and experience and discuss critical issues regarding environmental technology and policy.

***China Industrial and Business Directory***. International Business Publications, USA, PO Box 15343 Washington, DC 20003. Phone: (202)546-2103; Fax: (202)546-3275; Email: ibpusa@comcast.net • URL: http://ibpus.com • Annual. $99.95 Individuals. Covers industrial, investment and business contacts for conducting export-import and investment activity in the country.

***China Investment and Business Guide***. International Business Publications, USA, PO Box 15343 Washington, DC 20003. Phone: (202)546-2103; Fax: (202)546-3275; Email: ibpusa@comcast.net • URL: http://ibpus.com • $99.95 Individuals hardcopy, e-book, CD-ROM. Covers: Basic information on economy, export-import and investment climate, regulations, industrial development, opportunities, banking, and government. Entries include: Important business contacts and business travel.

***China Investment Atlas***. American Chamber of Commerce in Hong Kong, 1904 Bank of America Tower, 12 Harcourt Rd. Hong Kong, China. Phone: 86 852 25306900; Fax: 86 852 28101289; Email: amcham@amcham.org.hk • URL: http://www.amcham.org.hk • $622 Nonmembers; $79.95 Nonmembers; $544 Members; $69.95 Members. Covers: 600 of China's leading listed companies. Database includes: Charts.

***China Logistics Directory***. SinoMedia Ltd., 1408 Golden Bell Plz., 98 Huaihai Zhong Lu Shanghai 200021, China. Phone: 86 21 5187 9633; Fax: 86 21 5385 8953; Email: ads@chinaeconomicreview.com • URL: http://www.sinomedia.net • $80 Individuals book; $160 Individuals CD-ROM; $200 Individuals book and CD-ROM. Covers: 2,300 logistics companies operating in China across 12 industry sectors including airlines, airport, harbor & station operators, associations & consultants, construction companies, express forwarders, IT resources, land transportation, logistics equipment suppliers, logistics industrial parks, logistics services (custom brokers, air carriers and service companies), non-vessel operating common carriers, shipping companies, warehousing, third party logistics & supply chain solution. Entries include: English and Chinese names, address, headquarters location, phone and faxes, emails, key contact individuals, website.

***China Product Handbook***. Chis Info-Consultants Company Ltd., Rm. 605, Bldg. 6, Kang Le Cun, Nanxin Rd., Nanshan Shenzhen 518052, China. Fax: 755 6568829; Email: chis@mh.sz.col.com.cn • $300 Individuals. Covers: 20,000 famous enterprises in China, including machinery, electric, electronic, light, textile, chemical, and pharmaceutical industries. Entries include: Enterprise name, address, phone, fax, director, major products.

**China Productivity Center**. 2F, No. 79 Xintai 5th Rd., Section 1, Xizhi District Taipei 221, Taiwan. Phone: 886 2 2698-2989; Fax: 886 2 2698-2976; Email: service@cpc.org.tw • URL: http://www.cpc.org.tw.

***China Stock Directory***. China Economic Review, 1408 Golden Bell Plz., 98 Huaihai Rd. Shanghai 200021, China. Phone: 86 21 51879633 • URL: http://www.chinaeconomicreview.com • $75 Individuals. Covers: 1,800 mainland-listed companies on the Shanghai and Shenzhen markets. Publication includes: Information about a company history, business operations, share price range, shareholders, key executives, contact details, complete financials top shareholders, their share types and percentage stakes.

**China Venture Capital and Private Equity Association**. Office Tower E1, 21/F, Rm. 2109, 1 E Chang An Ave. Beijing 100738, Hebei, China. Phone: 86 10 85183584; Fax: 86 10 85150835 • URL: http://www.cvca.com.cn • Promotes the interests and the development of venture capital and private equity industry in the Greater China Region. Fosters understanding of the importance of venture capital and private equity to the vitality of the Greater China economy and global economies.

***China's Machine & Electric Enterprises and Products Database***. Computing Center of the Ministry of Foreign Trade and Economic Cooperation, 2 Dongchanganjie Beijing 100731, China. Phone: 86 10 65198114; Fax: 86 10 65198039; Email: moftec@moftec.gov.cn • $1,600. Database covers: 100,000 Chinese machine and electric companies. Entries include: Contact information, office hours, executives, bankers, number of employees, contact person, registered capital, sales, list of products.

***China's Manufacturers and Products Database***. Computing Center of the Ministry of Foreign Trade and Economic Cooperation, 2 Dongchanganjie Beijing 100731, China. Phone: 86 10 65198114; Fax: 86 10 65198039; Email: moftec@moftec.gov.cn • $3,600. Database covers: 50,000 manufacturers in China. Entries include: Contact information, office hours, executives, bankers, number of employees, contact person, registered capital, sales, list of products.

**Chinese Academy of Sciences - Institute of Quantitative and Technical Economics**. 5 Jian Guomen St. Beijing 100732, China. Phone: 86 10 65137561; Fax: 86 10 65125895; Email: iqte@iqte.cass.net.cn • URL: http://iqte1.cass.cn/english/home.htm • Quantitative and technical economics, specifically economic system analysis, economic modeling, mathematical economic theory, environment technical economics, resources technical economics, and technical economic theory and methods. Studies include: analysis and forecast of China's economic situation; theory, management, and implications of China's productivity and economic growth; analysis and quantitative study of mechanisms of stable growth of China's economy; China's economic fluctuation; evaluation of comprehensive efficiency of the CIMS project; human resource development; industrial development policies and economic growth; informalization and economic growth; development strategies of the Bohai economic circle; strategies of China's science and technology in the nineties.

***Chinese Business in America***. Caravel Inc., 23545 Crenshaw Blvd., Ste. 101 E Torrance, CA 90505. Phone: (310)325-0100; Fax: (310)325-2583; Email: info@china4us.com • URL: http://www.china4us.com • Annual. $88 Individuals. Publication includes: Approximately 2,900 major ethnic Chinese enterprises in the U.S. Entries include: Contact name, address, phone, fax, websites, products/services imported/exported. Principal content of publication is is a how-to on establishing a new business in the U. S; marketing and sourcing in the U.S.

**Chinese Finance Association**. Church Street Station New York, NY 10008. • URL: http://www.tcfaglobal.org • Promotes Chinese finance, business, economy, financial institutions and financial markets.

**Chinese Women's Business Association**. 11F, 157-1, Section 1, Xin-Shen South Rd. Taipei, Taiwan. Phone: 886 937 515276; Fax: 886 2 23821655; Email: taimay@ms16.hinet.net • URL: http://www.fcem.org/en/pays-membres.html • Promotes women's entrepreneurial initiatives. Lobbies before the public and private institutions, policy makers and governments on issues that impede women's entrepreneurial potentials. Facilitates the development of business, partnership and trade. Fosters professional growth and business skills perfection. Encourages women to create enterprises.

***Chisum on Patents***. Matthew Bender and Company Inc., 1275 Broadway Albany, NY 12204-2638. Phone: 800-424-4200 or (518)487-3000; Fax: (518)487-3573 or (800)424-4200; Email: customer.support@lexisnexis.com • URL: http://www.matthewbender.com • 5/year. $5,864. 16 looseleaf volumes. An analysis of patent law in the U. S. Includes bibliography and glossary.

***Choice Magazine: Current Reviews for Academic Libraries***. Association of College Research Libraries. Library and Information Technology Association, 50 E Huron St. Chicago, IL 60611-2795. Phone: 800-545-2433; Fax: (312)280-3257; Email: lita@ala.org • URL: http://www.ala.org/lita • Monthly. $415. A publication of the Association of College and Research Libraries. Contains book reviews, primarily for college and university libraries.

***Choosing the Right Business Entity***. American CPE Inc., 826 Riviera Mansfield, TX 76063. Phone: 800-990-4273 or (817)477-0222; Fax: (817)473-4998; Email: director@americancpe.com • URL: http://www.americancpe.com • Contains detailed training information covering methods and factors involved in selecting the most advantageous type of business entity for a new venture.

***Christian Business Men's Committee of U.S.A.—Contact Quarterly***. Christian Business Men's Connection, Osborne Center, 5746 Marlin Rd., Ste. 602 Chattanooga, TN 37411-5680. Phone: 800-566-2262 or (423)698-4444; Fax: (423)629-4434; Email: ltruax@cbmc.com • URL: http://www.cbmc.com • Quarterly. free for members; $12.95 /year for nonmembers.

**ChristianTrade Association International**. PO Box 62187 Colorado Springs, CO 80962-2187. Phone: (719)432-8428; Email: info@christiantrade.com • URL: http://www.ctaintl.org • Forms, develops and recognizes national organizations committed to the growth of the Christian trade. Encourages the industry to grow based on fairness, equally accessible markets, and a biblical model. Facilitates networking and sharing of ideas publishes directory. Designs and develops training programs leading to professional excellence for participants in the Christian trade.

***Chromatographia: An International Journal for Rapid Communication in Chromatography and Associated Techniques***. Elsevier, Secondary Publishing Division, 650 Ave. of the Americas New York, NY 10011. Phone: 888-437-4636 or (212)633-3980; Fax: (212)633-3975; Email: t.reller@elsevier.com • URL: http://www.elseveier.com • Text in English; summaries in English, French and German.

***Chronicle Occupational Briefs***. Chronicle Guidance Publications Inc., 66 Aurora St. Moravia, NY 13118-3569. Phone: 800-899-0454 or (315)497-0330; Fax: (315)497-0339; Email: CustomerService@ChronicleGuidance.com • URL: http://www.chronicleguidance.com • $5.50 e-mailed, single title; $6 print, single title; $3 e-mailed, 2-4 titles; $3.50 print, 2-4 titles; $2.25 e-mailed, 5-9 titles; $2.75 print, 5-9 titles; $1.80 e-mailed, 10 or more titles; $2 print. 10 or more titles. Approximately 600 pamphlets about various occupations.

***The Chronicle of Higher Education***. The Chronicle of Higher Education, 1255 23rd St. NW, Ste. 700 Washington, DC 20037. Phone: 800-728-2803 or (202)466-1000 or (202)466-1755; Fax: (202)452-1033; Email: editor@chronicle.com • URL: http://www.chronicle.com • Weekly. $89 Individuals; $151 Two years. Includes *Almanac*. Provides news, book reviews and job listings for college professors and administrators.

***Chronicle of Latin American Economic Affairs (online)***. Latin America Data Base, University of New Mexico, 801 Yale Blvd. NE Albuquerque, NM 87131. Phone: (505)277-2961; Fax: (505)277-5989; Email: info@ladb.unm.edu • URL: http://ladb.unm.edu • Contains the complete text online of the weekly newsletter, *Chronicle of Latin American Economic Affairs*. Provides news and analysis of trade and economic developments in Latin America, including Caribbean countries. Time period is 1986 to date, with weekly updates. Inquire as to online cost and availability.

***Chronicle of Philanthropy:The Newspaper of the Non-Profit World***. The Chronicle of Higher Education, 1255 23rd St. NW, Ste. 700 Washington, DC 20037. Phone: 800-728-2803 or (202)466-1000 or (202)466-1755; Fax: (202)452-1033; Email: editor@chronicle.com • URL: http://www.chronicle.com • Biweekly. $77 per year.

***Chugiak-Eagle River Business & Service Directory***. Chugiak-Eagle River Chamber of Commerce, 12001 Business Blvd., Ste. 108 Eagle River, AK 99577-0353. Phone: (907)694-4702; Fax: (907)694-1205; Email: info@cer.org • URL: http://www.cer.org.

**Chuo University - Institute of Business Research**. 742-1 Higashinakano, Hachioji-shi Tokyo 192-0393, Japan. Phone: 81 3 426743272; Fax: 81 3 426743278; Email: kigyoken@tamajs.chuo-u.ac.jp • URL: http://www2.chuo-u.ac.jp/ipcs/kigyoeng.htm • Management science, accounting, commerce, marketing, banking, and business economics. Institute also conducts comparative studies of businesses and corporations.

***Church Executive: The First Source of Information for Business Administrators of America's Largest Churches***. Power Trade Media L.L.C., 4742 N 24th St., Ste. 340 Phoenix, AZ 85016. Phone: 800-541-2670 or (602)265-7600; Fax: (602)227-7588 • Monthly. $39 Individuals; $64 Two years; $89 Individuals 3 years. Magazine for church leaders.

**CIES, The Food Business Forum**. 8455 Colesville Rd., Ste. 705 Silver Spring, MD 20910-3318. Phone: (301)563-3383; Fax: (301)563-3386; Email: washington@theconsumergoodsforum.com • URL: http://www.ciesnet.com • Membership in 44 countries includes: food industry chain store firms with combined outlets of over 100,000; associations; firms supplying articles and services to chain food stores. Fosters cooperation between chain store organizations and their suppliers. Serves as a liaison between members. Assists in the exchange of trainees among member firms. Conducts studies on methods, technical progress, and the growth rate of chain store organizations throughout the world.

**Cigar Association of America**. 1100 G St. NW, Ste. 1050 Washington, DC 20005-7405. Phone: (202)223-8204; Fax: (202)833-0379 • URL: http://www.cigarassociation.org.

***Cincinnati Business Courier***. American City Business Journals, Inc., 120 W Morehead St. Charlotte, NC 28202. Phone: (704)973-1000; Fax: (704)973-1001; Email: americancity@bizjournals.com • URL: http://www.acbj.com • Contains the full text of Cincinnati Business Courier, a business tabloid covering Cincinnati, Ohio.

***Cincinnati U.S.A. Business Connections Directory***. Greater Cincinnati Chamber of Commerce, 3 E 4th St. Cincinnati, OH 45202. Phone: (513)579-3100 or (513)579-3111; Fax: (513)579-3101; Email: info@cincinnatichamber.com • URL: http://www.cincinnatichamber.com • Annual.

***Cinemas Directory***. InfoGroup Inc., 5711 S 86th Cir. Omaha, NE 68127-4146. Phone: (402)593-4500 • URL: http://www.infogroup.com • Annual. Number of listings: 9,544. Entries include: Name, address, phone, size of advertisement, name of owner or manager, number of employees, year first in "Yellow Pages." Compiled from telephone company "Yellow Pages," nationwide.

***CINFOLINK Directory of Information Services and the Internet in China***. CINFOLINK Services, 10 Malta Ave., Ste. 301 Brampton, ON, Canada L6Y 4G6. Phone: (905)456-3801; Email: cinfo@ican.net • URL: http://www.woodmedia.com • Biennial. $20 U.S. plus airmail postage within North America $2.50; $25 Canada plus airmail postage within North America $3. Covers: nearly 400 electronic databases and information networks, approximately 225 related publication and information sources (including associations, research institutes of the Chinese Academy of Sciences, universities and colleges, and libraries), and 150 current Internet sources in China and Hong Kong. Entries include: For database services—Name, description, type of data, language, size, updating frequency, timespan; producer name and address; contact name, phone, fax; other formats, subject(s), status, price, etc. For publication sources—Name, address, phone, fax, titles produced, description.

***CIO and Corporate Strategic Management: Changing Role of CIO to CEO***. Cengage Learning Inc., 20 Channel Center St. Boston, MA 02210. Phone: 800-487-8488 or (617)289-7700; Fax: (617)289-7844; Email: investors@cengage.com • URL: http://www.cengage.com • Published by Information Science Reference. Provides analysis within theoretical frameworks and consulting recommendations, and starts with the demand side of CEO successions, specifically highlighting approaches in IT foundations, e-business development and IT sourcing decisions.

***CIO: The Magazine for Chief Information Officers***. CXO Media Inc., 492 Old Connecticut Path Framingham, MA 01701-4584. Phone: 888-434-5478 or (508)872-0080; Fax: (508)879-7784; Email: stozeski@idglist.com • URL: http://www.cio.com • Monthly. $129 per year. Edited for chief information officers. Includes a monthly "Web Business" section (incorporates the former *WebMaster* periodical) and a monthly "Enterprise" section for other company executives.

***Circulation Management***. Media Central, 470 Park Ave., S, 8th Fl. New York, NY 10016. Phone: 800-529-7502; Email: adedit@inside.com • URL: http://www.demographics.com • Monthly. $39.00 per year. Edited for circulation professionals in the magazine and newsletter publishing industry. Covers marketing, planning, promotion, management, budgeting, and related topics.

***CIS-States Companies***. COMMIT GmbH, Walstrasse 76-79 D-10179 Berlin, Germany. Phone: 30 2750004; Fax: 30

2793598 • Quarterly. Database covers: companies in the nations of the Commonwealth of Independent States. Database includes: Company name, address, legal status, products, number of employees.

*Citation: Current Legal Developments Relating to Medicine and Allied Professions*. American Medical Association, Health Law Div. Citation Publishing Corp., 3538 Willow Valley Rd. Long Grove, IL 60047. Phone: 800-626-5210 or (847)438-2020; Fax: (847)438-2299 • Semimonthly. $130.00 per year. Newsletter. Contains summaries of lawsuits affecting medical personnel or hospitals.

*Cities of the United States*. Cengage Learning Inc., 20 Channel Center St. Boston, MA 02210. Phone: 800-487-8488 or (617)289-7700; Fax: (617)289-7844; Email: investors@cengage.com • URL: http://www.cengage.com • $731 Individuals per volume. Four regional volumes. $218.00 per volume. Detailed information is provided on U.S. cities. Includes economic data, climate, geography, government, and history, with maps and photographs.

*Cities of the World*. Cengage Learning Inc., 20 Channel Center St. Boston, MA 02210. Phone: 800-487-8488 or (617)289-7700; Fax: (617)289-7844; Email: investors@cengage.com • URL: http://www.cengage.com • 2003. 6th edition. eBook. Detailed information is provided for more than 3,400 cities in 177 countries (excluding U.S.) Includes maps and photographs. Based in U.S. State Department reports. Available as eBook.

*Citizen Soldier*. 267 5th Ave., Ste. 901 New York, NY 10016. Phone: (212)679-2250 or (347)828-2281; Fax: (212)679-2252; Email: citizensoldier1@aol.com • URL: http://www.citizen-soldier.org • Individuals concerned with military-civilian relationships within American society. Aims to help Vietnam War veterans who may have been harmed by highly toxic herbicides (including Agent Orange) that were used in Vietnam between 1962 and 1970. Works with veterans who were exposed to low-level radiation at Nevada and South Pacific A-bomb test sites and Persian Gulf War veterans suffering from unexplained chronic ailments. Represents GIs on active duty who are victims of military racism and/or sexism. Assists GIs who have been prosecuted or otherwise punished due to positive results on drug residue urine tests that CS believes to have been inaccurate because of defective laboratory work. Seeks to protect the rights of soldiers testing positive for the AIDS antibody. Advocates for veterans suffering from Persian Gulf Syndrome. Promotes a public service campaign to inform service members of their legal rights regarding the military's HIV testing program. Works with high school and college youths to address concerns on military recruiting practices. Maintains speakers' bureau. Advises GIs who wish alternatives to service in current Iraqi War.

*Citizens for a Sound Economy*. 1250 H St. NW, Ste. 700 Washington, DC 20005-3908. Phone: 888-564-6273 or (202)783-3870 or (202)942-7649; Fax: (202)783-4687; Email: cse@cse.org • URL: http://www.cse.org • Absorbed Council for a Competitive Economy and Tax Foundation.

*Citrograph: Magazine of the Citrus Industry*. Agricultural Publishing Co., 4969 E Clinton Way, Ste. 104 Fresno, CA 93727-1558. Phone: 888-382-9772 or (559)252-7000 or (209)252-7000; Fax: (559)252-7387 or (209)252-7387; Email: publisher@westagpubco.com • Monthly. $19.95 per year. Gives produce growing tips.

*Citrus Industry Magazine*. Associated Publications Corp., 495 E Summerlin St. Bartow, FL 33830, Phone: (863)533-4114 • Monthly. $24 per year. Gives food growing tips.

*City & Country Club Life: The Social Magazine for South Florida*. Club Publications, Inc., 665 La Villa Dr. Miami, FL 33166. Phone: (305)887-1701; Fax: (305)885-1923 • Five times a year. Controlled circulation.

*City University of New York - Martin E. Segal Theatre Center*. 365 5th Ave. New York, NY 10016-4309. Phone: (212)817-1860; Fax: (212)817-1562; Email: mestc@gc.cuny.edu • URL: http://thesegalcenter.org • Theatre arts, including studies of theatre, dance, and film as independent and interrelated arts. Current projects focus on publishing journals on American, Slavic, Russian, Western European, and East European theatre, drama, and film; and translations of foreign plays into English.

*City Women's Network*. 7 Berghem Mews, Blythe Rd. London W14 0HN, United Kingdom. Phone: 44 20 3784592 • URL: http://www.citywomen.org • Senior executive and professional businesswomen. Provides a forum for members to share common professional and social interests and experiences.

*Civil Affairs Association*. 6689 Kodiak Dr. Fayetteville, NC 28304. Email: civilaffairs@civilaffairsassoc.org • URL: http://www.civilaffairsassoc.org • U.S. Army active and reserve officers and enlisted personnel serving in Army or Marine Corps civil affairs units or in civil affairs staff positions in major military headquarters, and international members. Advocates and promotes a strong U.S. military civil affairs capability.

*Civil Defense Agencies Directory*. InfoGroup Inc., 5711 S 86th Cir. Omaha, NE 68127-4146. Phone: (402)593-4500 • URL: http://www.infogroup.com • Annual. Number of listings: 1,516. Entries include: Name, address, phone, size of advertisement, name of owner or manager, number of employees, year first in "Yellow Pages." Compiled from telephone company "Yellow Pages," nationwide.

*Civil Engineering Database*. Architectural Engineering Institute of ASCE, 1801 Alexander Bell Dr. Reston, VA 20191-4400. Phone: 800-548-2723; Email: aei@asce.org • URL: http://www.asce.org/aei • Provides abstracts of the U. S. and international literature of civil engineering, 1975 to date. Inquire as to online cost and availability.

*Civil Engineering: Engineered Design and Construction*. Architectural Engineering Institute of ASCE, 1801 Alexander Bell Dr. Reston, VA 20191-4400. Phone: 800-548-2723; Email: aei@asce.org • URL: http://www.asce.org/aei • Monthly. $160.00 per year.

*Civil Rights Actions*. Matthew Bender and Company Inc., 1275 Broadway Albany, NY 12204-2638, Phone: 800-424-4200 or (518)487-3000; Fax: (518)487-3573 or (800)424-4200; Email: customer.support@lexisnexis.com • URL: http://www.matthewbender.com • $2,492 book; $2,265 e-book. Seven looseleaf volumes. Periodic supplementation. Contains legal analysis of civil rights activities.

*Civil Rights: State Capitals*. Wakeman/Walworth Inc., PO Box 7376 Alexandria, VA 22307-7376. Phone: 800-876-2545 or (703)768-9600; Fax: (703)768-9690; Email: newsletters@statecapitals.com • URL: http://statecapitals.com/ • 50 times a year. $245.00 per year; print and online editions, $350.00 per year. Newsletter. Includes coverage of state affirmative action programs. Formerly *From the State Capitals: Civil Rights*.

**Civil Service Employees Association**. 143 Washington Ave. Albany, NY 12210. Phone: 800-342-4146 or (518)257-1000 • URL: http://cseany.org • AFL-CIO. Represents state and local government employees from all public employee classifications. Negotiates work contracts; represents members in grievances; provides legal assistance for on-the-job problems; provides advice and assistance on federal, state, and local laws affecting public employees. Conducts research, training and education programs. Compiles statistics.

*CLA Business Directory*. Country Land and Business Association, 16 Belgrave Sq. London SW1X 8PQ, United Kingdom. Phone: 44 20 72350511; Fax: 44 20 72354696; Email: mail@cla.org.uk • URL: http://www.cla.org.uk • Covers: 250 business organizations, owners of land, and properties in rural England and Wales. Entries include: Company name, address, contact information, and e-mail.

*Claims*. • Monthly. $46.00 per year. Edited for insurance adjusters, risk managers, and claims professionals. Covers investigation, fraud, insurance law, and other claims-related topics.

*CLAIMS*. IFI/Plenum Data Corp., 3202 Kirkwood Hwy., Ste. 203 Wilmington, DE 19808-6154. Phone: 800-331-4955 or (302)633-7200; Fax: (302)998-0733; Email: info@ificlaims.com • Includes seven separate databases: *CLAIMS/Citation*, *CLAIMS/Compound Registry*, *CLAIMS/Comprehensive Data Base*, *CLAIMS/Reassignment & Reexamination*, *CLAIMS/Reference*, *CLAIMS/U.S. Patent Abstracts*, and *CLAIMS/Uniterm*. Provides extensive current and historical information on U.S. Patents. Inquire as to online cost and availability.

**Claremont McKenna College - Lowe Institute of Political Economy**. Bauer Ctr. 322, 500 E 9th St. Claremont, CA 91711-6400. Phone: (909)621-8012; Fax: (909)607-8008; Email: marc.weidenmier@cmc.edu • URL: http://www.claremontmckenna.edu/lowe • Research topics include NAFTA.

**Clark University - Institute for Economic Policy Studies**. Department of Economics, 950 Main St. Worcester, MA 01610-1477. Phone: (508)793-7227; Fax: (508)793-7708; Email: aott@iespolicy.org • URL: http://www.iespolicy.org • Economic issues and policy options to deal with them.

*Classified Business Directory of the State of Connecticut: Buyer's Blue Book*. Connecticut Directory Company Inc., 35 E 35th St., Apt. 5D New York, NY 10016-3820. • Annual. $66.95. Covers: manufacturers, banks, schools, service companies, distributors, wholesalers, restaurants, and hotels in Connecticut and surrounding states. All listings are paid. Entries include: Company, name, address, phone. No sales in Connecticut except to libraries.

*Classified Directory of Products & Services*. SMC Business Councils, George Westinghouse Research and Technology Ctr., 1382 Beulah Rd., Bldg. 801 Pittsburgh, PA 15235-5068. Phone: 800-553-3260 or (412)371-1500 • URL: http://www.smc.org • Biennial. Covers: over 5,000 small business concerns in central and western Pennsylvania. Entries include: Company name, address, phone, e-mail address, URL, contact name, description of products or services provided, Standard Industrial Classification (SIC) code.

**Clay Minerals Society**. 3635 Concorde Pkwy., Ste. 500 Chantilly, VA 20151-1110. Phone: (703)652-9960; Fax: (703)652-9951; Email: cms@clays.org • URL: http://www.clays.org • Professionals concerned with clay mineralogy and technology in industry, university research, and government. Includes students of mineralogy, geology, soil science, astronomy, physics, geochemistry, and engineering, and representatives of such firms as oil companies, instrument makers, and clay mining companies. Seeks to stimulate research and disseminate information relating to all aspects of clay science and technology. Provides a forum for exchange of information and ideas. Maintains quantities of Source and Special Clays at the Source Clays Repository.

*Clays and Clay Minerals*. Clay Minerals Society, 3635 Concorde Pkwy., Ste. 500 Chantilly, VA 20151-1110. Phone: (703)652-9960; Fax: (703)652-9951; Email: cms@clays.org • URL: http://www.clays.org • Bimonthly. $510 Institutions; $50 Students.

**Clean Technology and Sustainable Industries Organization**. 3925 W Braker Ln. Austin, TX 78759. Email: community@ct-si.org • URL: http://www.ct-si.org • Advances the commercialization and global adoption of clean technologies and sustainable industry practices. Promotes clean technology development. Establishes programs and advocacy for clean technologies and global integration of sustainable industry practices.

*Cleaning Business: Published Monthly for the Self-Employed Cleaning and Maintenance Professionals*. William R. Griffin, Publisher, P.O. Box 1273 Seattle, WA 98111-1273. Phone: (206)622-4241; Fax: (206)622-6876; Email: wgriffin@cleaningconsultants.com • URL: http://www.cleaningconsultants.com • Monthly. $20. Formerly *Service Business*.

*Cleaning-House and Office-Directory*. InfoGroup Inc., 5711 S 86th Cir. Omaha, NE 68127-4146. Phone: (402)593-4500 • URL: http://www.infogroup.com • Annual. Number of listings: 37,431. Entries include: Name, address, phone, size of advertisement, name of owner or manager, number of employees, year first in "Yellow Pages." Compiled from telephone company "Yellow Pages," nationwide.

**Clearpoint Financial Solutions**. 8000 Franklin Farms Dr. Richmond, VA 23229-5004. Phone: 877-422-9040; Fax: (804)526-8271; Email: customer.service@clearpointccs.org • URL: http://www.clearpointfinancialsolutions.org • Provides consumer credit counseling services to all consumers in need. Strives to increase financial literacy.

**Cleveland State University - Center for Public Management**. Urban Bldg., Rm. 120, 2121 Euclid Ave. Cleveland, OH 44115-2214. Phone: (216)687-9221; Email: k.e.obrien@csuohio.edu • URL: http://urban.csuohio.edu/publicmanagement • Finance and economics, Ohio's revenue and tax systems, economic development, and historic preservation (including tax credit support).

**Climate Action Network Australia**. Level 1, 1 Smail St. Ultimo, NSW 2007, Australia. Phone: 61 2 82021248 • URL: http://www.cana.net.au • Increases understanding and the causes of climate change. Encourages governments, businesses and individuals to undertake actions to reduce greenhouse gas emissions. Promotes energy efficiency, renewable energy and sustainable transport and protects the natural ecosystem of Australia.

**Climate Action Network Europe**. Rue d'Edimbourg 26 B-1050 Brussels, Belgium. Phone: 32 2 8944670; Email: info@climnet.org • URL: http://www.climnet.org • European nongovernmental organizations with an interest in global climate and climatic change. Advocates a commitment to a 20% decrease in carbon dioxide emissions by the industrialized countries of the world over the next ten years. Gathers and disseminates information on greenhouse gases and global warming; works to increase public awareness of the implications of global climatic change.

**Climate Group**. 145 W 58th St., Ste. 2a New York, NY 10019. Phone: (646)233-0550; Email: info@theclimategroup.org • URL: http://www.theclimategroup.org • Advances business and government leadership on climate change. Creates international effort to stop climate change. Works to accelerate international action on global warming. Promotes profitability and competitiveness among the government, business and non-profit sectors.

**Clinical and Laboratory Standards Institute**. 940 W Valley Rd., Ste. 2500 Wayne, PA 19087. Phone: 877-447-1888 or (610)688-0100; Fax: (610)688-0700; Email: customerservice@clsi.org • URL: http://www.clsi.org • Government agencies, professional societies, clinical laboratories, and industrial firms with interests in medical testing. Purposes are to promote the development of national and international standards for medical testing and to provide a consensus mechanism for defining and resolving problems that influence the quality and cost of healthcare work performed.

**Clinical Laboratory Management Association**. 330 N Wabash Ave., Ste. 2000 Chicago, IL 60611. Phone: (312)321-5111; Fax: (312)673-6927; Email: info@clma.org • URL: http://www.clma.org • Individuals holding managerial or supervisory positions with clinical laboratories; persons engaged in education of such individuals; manufacturers or distributors of equipment or services to clinical laboratories. Objectives are: to enhance management skills and promote more efficient and productive department operations; to further exchange of professional knowledge, new technology, and colleague experience; to encourage cooperation among those engaged in management or supervisory functions. Activities include: workshops, seminars, and expositions; dissemination of information about legislation and other topics.

*Clinical Leadership and Management Review*. Clinical Laboratory Management Association. Lippincott Williams & Wilkins, 2 Commerce Sq., 2001 Market St. Philadelphia, PA 19103. Phone: 800-638-3030 or (301)223-2300; Email: ronna.ekhouse@wolterskluwer.com • URL: http://www.lww.com • *Clinical Laboratory Management Review*.

**Clinical Research Institute of Montreal - Centre for Bioethics**. 110 Pine Ave. W Montreal, QC, Canada H2W 1R7. Phone: (514)987-5617; Fax: (514)987-5695; Email: david.roy@

ircm.qc.ca • URL: http://www.ircm.qc.ca/bioethique/ • Works to identify and resolve ethical issues in medical practice and research. Monitors legal and policy issues such as "do not resuscitate" protocols and human experimentation. Facilitates exchange of information among physicians, medical scientists, and other health professionals. Conducts research and educational programs.

***Clothes & Accessories (Women) Wholesale Directory***. InfoGroup Inc., 5711 S 86th Cir. Omaha, NE 68127-4146. Phone: (402)593-4500 • URL: http://www.infogroup.com • Annual. Number of listings: 4,468. Entries include: Name, address, phone, size of advertisement, name of owner or manager, number of employees, year first in "Yellow Pages." Compiled from telephone company "Yellow Pages," nationwide.

**Clothing Manufacturers Association of the U.S.A.** 730 Broadway, 10th Fl. New York, NY 10003. Phone: (212)529-0823; Fax: (212)529-1739 or (212)529-1443; Email: kaplancma730@hotmail.com.

***Club Business International***. Fitness Industry Association, Argent House, 103 Frimley Rd. Camberley GU15 2PP, United Kingdom. Phone: 44 1276676275; Fax: 44 127629776 • Monthly. Publication covering physical fitness.

***Club Business International (CBI)***. International Health, Racquet and Sportsclub Association, 70 Fargo St. Boston, MA 02210. Phone: 800-228-4772 or (617)951-0055; Fax: (617)951-0056; Email: info@ihrsa.org • URL: http://www.ihrsa.org • Monthly. $25 Members U.S.; $100 Members international. Features the quality and profitability of commercial health, racquet, and sports clubs.

***Club Business Quarterly***. Boys and Girls Clubs, 1710 N Second St. Wausau, WI 54403. Phone: (715)845-2582 • URL: http://www.bgclub.com • Quarterly.

***Club Director***. National Club Association, 1201 15th St. NW, Ste. 450 Washington, DC 20005. Phone: 800-625-6221 or (202)822-9822; Fax: (202)822-9808; Email: info@nationalclub.org • URL: http://www.nationalclub.org • Quarterly. Magazine for directors, owners and managers of private clubs.

***Club Industry's Fitness Business Pro***. Penton, 9800 Metcalf Ave. Overland Park, KS 66212. Phone: 866-748-4926 or (913)341-1300; Fax: (913)967-1905 or (913)967-1898; Email: corporatecustomerservice@penton.com • URL: http://www.penton.com • Monthly. Trade magazine covering trends and news for owners and operators of commercial health and fitness facilities.

***Club Management: The Resource for Successful Club Operations***. Club Managers Association of America. Finan Publishing, 533 Colebrook, Ste. A Saint Louis, MO 63119. Phone: (314)517-2466 or (314)961-6644; Fax: (314)961-4809; Email: pfinan@finan.com • URL: http://www.finan.com • Bimonthly. $21.95 per year.

**Club Managers Association of America**. 1733 King St. Alexandria, VA 22314. Phone: (703)739-9500; Fax: (703)739-0124 • URL: http://www.cmaa.org • Professional managers and assistant managers of private golf, yacht, athletic, city, country, luncheon, university, and military clubs. Encourages education and advancement of members and promotes efficient and successful club operations. Provides reprints of articles on club management. Supports courses in club management. Compiles statistics; maintains management referral service.

***CMAA Yearbook***. Club Managers Association of America, 1733 King St. Alexandria, VA 22314. Phone: (703)739-9500; Fax: (703)739-0124 • URL: http://www.cmaa.org • Annual. Membership directory.

***CNW Group***. CNW Group Ltd., WaterPark Pl., 20 Bay St., Ste. 1500 Toronto, ON, Canada M5J 2N8. Phone: 877-269-7890; Fax: (877)269-5044; Email: info@newswire.ca • URL: http://www.newswire.ca • Provides the complete online text of current press releases from more than 5,000 Canadian companies, institutions, and government agencies, including stock exchanges and the Ontario Securities Commission. Emphasis is on mining, petroleum, technology, and pharmaceuticals. Time span is 1996 to date, with daily updates. Inquire as to online cost and availability.

***Co-Engineering Applications and Adaptive Business Technologies in Practice: Enterprise Service Ontologies, Models, and Frameworks***. Cengage Learning Inc., 20 Channel Center St. Boston, MA 02210. Phone: 800-487-8488 or (617)289-7700; Fax: (617)289-7844; Email: investors@cengage.com • URL: http://www.cengage.com • 2009. eBook. Provides knowledge that forms the basis for successful co-engineering of the adaptive complex enterprise for services delivery.

***Co-op America's National Green Pages: A Directory of Products and Services for People and the Planet***. Green America, 1612 K St. NW, Ste. 600 Washington, DC 20006. Phone: 800-584-7336 or (202)872-5307 or (202)872-5330; Fax: (202)331-8166 or (202)822-8471; Email: info@coopamerica.org • URL: http://www.greenamerica.org • Annual. Covers: 3,000 businesses and nonprofit organizations in the U.S. that produce environmentally benign products such as non-toxic household products, plant based paints, cruelty free body care products, organic foods, and energy saving devices. Also companies that offer socially responsible financial services. Database includes: List of producers of home-based crafts businesses and Native American-made products. Entries include: Company or organization name, address, phone, product/service, e-mail and web addresses.

***Coal Industry***. Charles Kernot. American Educational Systems, 46 Purdy St. Harrison, NY 10528. Phone: 800-431-1579 or (914)835-0015; Fax: (914)835-0398 • $710.00. Looseleaf service. Periodic supplementation.

***Coal Information***. Organization for Economic Cooperation and Development, 2001 L St. NW, Ste. 650 Washington, DC 20036-4922. Phone: 800-456-6323 or (202)785-6323; Fax: (202)785-0350; Email: washington.contact@oecd.org • URL: http://www.oecd.org • Annual. €165. Presents comprehensive data from the International Energy Agency (IEA) on the world coal market, including supply, demand, production, trade, and prices. In addition to coal itself, provides country-specific data on coal-fired power stations and coal-related environmental issues.

***Coal Leader: Coal's National Newspaper***. Coal, Inc., P.O. Box 858 Richlands, VA 24641-0858. Phone: (276)964-6363; Fax: (276)964-6342; Email: coalleader@netscope.net • URL: http://www.coalleader.com • Monthly. $18.00 per year. Formerly *National Coal Leader*.

***Coal Preparation Directory & Handbook***. • Annual. $95 Individuals Softcover. Covers: Suppliers and manufacturers of coal preparation equipment and services in the U.S.

**Coalition Against Counterfeiting and Piracy**. US Chamber of Commerce, Global Intellectual Property Center, 1615 H St. NW Washington, DC 20062-0001. Phone: (202)463-5601; Fax: (202)463-3114; Email: gipc@uschamber.com • URL: http://www.theglobalipcenter.com/index.php/cacp • Aims to fight the threat of counterfeiting and piracy to the economy, jobs, consumer health and safety. Strives to increase understanding of the negative impact of counterfeiting and piracy. Seeks to find real solutions by working with government, industry, opinion leaders, the media and consumers.

**Coalition for Intellectual Property Rights**. 607 14th St. NW, Ste. 500 Washington, DC 20036. Phone: (202)466-6210; Fax: (202)466-6205; Email: amanda.lahan@cipr.org • URL: http://www.cipr.org • Aims to advance intellectual property rights in Russia, Ukraine and other states in the Commonwealth for Independent States (CIS) region. Works with government and businesses to improve IPR laws and enforcement regimes consistent with international standards. Seeks to provide support to members addressing company-specific IP issues in Russia, Ukraine, and other countries of the region.

***Coalition for Minority Business Development Resource Directory***. Indianapolis Chamber of Commerce, Bank One Tower, 111 Monument Cir., Ste. 1950 Indianapolis, IN 46204. Phone: (317)464-2200 or (317)464-2222; Fax: (317)464-2217; Email: chamber@indylink.com • URL: http://www.indychamber.com • Annual. $25 Nonmembers; $10 Members. Covers: Agencies and organizations in Indiana devoted to aiding minority-owned businesses and entrepreneurs. Entries include: Organization name, address, phone.

**Coalition of Asian American Business Organizations**. 255 Rex Blvd. Auburn Hills, MI 48326. Phone: (248)760-5125; Fax: (248)853-0606; Email: mming66@caabo.org • URL: http://www.caabo.org • Aims to promote cooperation and growth among Asian businesses. Serves as a collective voice for Asian American businesses and entrepreneurs. Educates and advocates on local, state, regional and national issues that impact Asian business organizations. Provides leadership training, mentorship and scholarship programs to members.

**Coalition of Higher Education Assistance Organizations**. 1101 Vermont Ave. NW, Ste. 400 Washington, DC 20005-3586. Phone: (202)289-3910 or (202)289-3903; Fax: (202)371-0197 • URL: http://www.coheao.com • Purpose is to support student loan programs and monitor regulations.

**Coalition of Labor Union Women**. 815 16th St. NW, 2nd Fl. S Washington, DC 20006. Phone: (202)508-6969 or (202)223-8360; Fax: (202)508-6968 or (202)776-0537; Email: ksee@cluw.org • URL: http://www.cluw.org • Aims to: unify all union women in order to determine common problems within unions and deal effectively with objectives; promote unionism and encourage unions to be more aggressive in their efforts to bring unorganized women under collective bargaining agreements; inform members about what can be done within the labor movement to achieve equal opportunity and correct discriminatory job situations; educate and inspire union brothers to help achieve affirmative action in the workplace. Seeks to encourage members through action programs of the coalition to become more active participants in the political and legislative processes of their unions, to seek election to public office or selection for governmental appointive office at local, county, state, and national levels, and to increase their participation in union policymaking. Conducts training programs and project on empowerment of union women. Maintains Coalition of Labor Union Women Center for Education and Research.

**Coalition to Insure Against Terrorism**. 1875 Eye St. NW, Ste. 600 Washington, DC 20006-5413. Phone: (202)739-9454; Email: info@insureagainstterrorism.org • URL: http://www.insureagainstterrorism.org • Represents organizations in the transportation, real estate, manufacturing, construction, entertainment and retail sectors. Seeks the passage of legislation that will enable the nation's insurers to provide holders with comprehensive terrorism coverage. Supports the passage of the Terrorism Risk Insurance Revision and Extension Act (TRIREA).

***The Coast Guard Reservist***. U.S. Department of Homeland Security U.S. Coast Guard, 2100 2nd St. SW Washington, DC 20593. Phone: 800-323-7233 or (202)372-2100 or (202)372-4411; Fax: (202)372-4960 • URL: http://www.uscg.mil • Monthly.

**Cocoa Merchants' Association of America**. 55 E 52nd St., 40th Flr. New York, NY 10055. Phone: (212)748-4193; Email: cmaa@cocoamerchants.com • URL: http://www.cocoamerchants.com • Dealers and importers of raw cocoa beans and cocoa products. Provides arbitration in contract disputes. Maintains speakers' bureau and a voluntary warehouse inspection program; conducts traffic and orientation seminars; compiles statistics.

***Coffee and Cocoa International***. DMG World Media Ltd., Queensway House, 2 Queensway Red Hill RH1 1QS, United Kingdom. Phone: 44 1737 855527; Fax: (173)7 855470 • Seven times a year. $124.00 per year.

***Coffee Intelligence***. Coffee Publications, P.O. Box 1315 Stamford, CT 06904. Phone: (203)969-2107; Fax: (203)327-5343 • Monthly. $95.00 per year. Provides trade information for the coffee industry.

***The Coffee Reporter***. National Coffee Association of U.S.A., 45 Broadway, Ste. 1140 New York, NY 10006. Phone: (212)766-4007; Fax: (212)766-5815; Email: info@ncausa.org • URL: http://www.ncausa.org • Weekly.

***Coffee Shops Directory***. InfoGroup Inc., 5711 S 86th Cir. Omaha, NE 68127-4146. Phone: (402)593-4500 • URL: http://www.infogroup.com • Annual. Number of listings: 7,515. Entries include: Name, address, phone, size of advertisement, name of owner or manager, number of employees, year first in "Yellow Pages." Compiled from telephone company "Yellow Pages," nationwide.

**Coffs Harbour Chamber of Commerce and Industry**. The Promenade, 321 Harbour Dr. Coffs Harbour, NSW 2450, Australia. Phone: 61 2 66514101; Fax: 61 2 66514081; Email: info@coffschamber.com.au • URL: http://www.coffschamber.com.au • Represents the local interests of small, medium sized, and multinational organizations throughout the Coffs Harbour region.

**Cognitive Science Society**. 10200 W 44th Ave., Ste. 304 Wheat Ridge, CO 80033-2840. Phone: (303)327-7547; Fax: (720)881-6101; Email: info@cognitivesciencesociety.org • URL: http://cognitivesciencesociety.org • Represents published PhD's; students and PhD's not actively publishing in the fields of psychology, artificial intelligence, and cognitive science. Promotes the dissemination of research in cognitive science and allied sciences. (Cognitive science is a branch of artificial intelligence that seeks to simulate human reasoning and associative powers on a computer, using specialized software).

**Coin Laundry Association**. 1 S 660 Midwest Rd., Ste. 205 Oakbrook Terrace, IL 60181. Phone: 800-570-5629 or (630)953-7920; Fax: (630)953-7925; Email: info@coinlaundry.org • URL: http://coinlaundry.org • Manufacturers of equipment or supplies used in self-service (coin-operated) laundry or dry cleaning establishments; distributors of equipment services and supplies; owners and operators of self-service laundry and/or dry cleaning stores. Compiles statistics.

***Coin Prices: Complete Guide to U.S. Coin Values***. Krause Publications Inc., 700 E State St. Iola, WI 54990-0001. Phone: 800-726-9966 or (715)445-2214 or (715)445-4612; Fax: (715)445-4087 • URL: http://www.krause.com • Bimonthly. $18.98 Individuals. Gives current values of U. S. coins.

***Coin World: World's 1 Publication for Coin Collectors***. • URL: http://www.coinworldonline.com • Weekly. $19.99 Individuals; $34.99 Canada; $127.97 Canada 52 issues; $49.97 Individuals 52 issues. Newspaper for coin collectors.

***Coin Yearbook***. British Royal Mint, Cheyenne, WY 82008-0031. Phone: 800-221-1215 • Annual. $15.95.

***Coinage***. Miller Magazines Inc., 290 Maple Ct., Ste. 232 Ventura, CA 93003. Phone: (805)644-3824; Fax: (805)644-3875; Email: coinage@aol.com • URL: http://www.millermags.com • Monthly. $18.95.

***Coins***. Krause Publications Inc., 700 E State St. Iola, WI 54990-0001. Phone: 800-726-9966 or (715)445-2214 or (715)445-4612; Fax: (715)445-4087 • URL: http://www.krause.com • Monthly. $56.98 per year.

***Cold Facts Newsletter***. Cryogenic Society of America, 218 Lake St. Oak Park, IL 60302-2609. Phone: (708)383-6220; Fax: (708)383-9337; Email: laurie@cryogenicsociety.org • URL: http://www.cryogenicsociety.org • 5/year. Description: Technical newsletter serving individuals interested in cryogenics and cryobiology.

***Collection Management: A Quarterly Journal Devoted to the Management of Library Collections***. The Haworth Press Inc., 10 Alice St. Binghamton, NY 13904. Phone: 800-429-6784 or (607)722-5857; Fax: (607)771-0012 or (607)722-6362; Email: getinfo@haworthpress.com • URL: http://www.haworthpressinc.com/store/product.asp?sku=J014 • Quarterly. $235.00 per year.

***Collections Agency Directory***. InfoGroup Inc., 5711 S 86th Cir. Omaha, NE 68127-4146. Phone: (402)593-4500 • URL: http://www.infogroup.com • Annual. Number of listings: 7,183. Entries include: Name, address, phone, size of advertisement, name of owner or manager, number of employees, year first in "Yellow Pages." Compiled from telephone company "Yellow Pages," nationwide.

***Collections and Credit Risk: The Authority for Commercial and Consumer Credit Professionals***. SourceMedia Inc., 1 State Street Plz., 27th Fl. New York, NY 10004. Phone: 800-221-1809 or (212)803-8200 or (212)803-8333; Fax: (212)843-9635 or (212)292-5216; Email: custserv@sourcemedia.com • URL: http://www.sourcemedia.com • Monthly. $95.00 per year. Contains articles on the technology and business management of credit and collection functions. Includes coverage of bad debts, bankruptcy, and credit risk management.

***Collector***. ACA International, 4040 W 70th St. Minneapolis, MN 55435. Phone: (952)926-6547; Email: aca@acainternational.org • URL: http://www.acainternational.org • Monthly. $70 Nonmembers per year; $35 Members. Provides news and education in the field of credit and collections.

***College and Research Libraries***. Association of College and Research Libraries, 50 E Huron St. Chicago, IL 60611. Phone: 800-545-2433 or (312)280-2523; Fax: (312)280-2520; Email: acrl@ala.org • URL: http://www.ala.org/acrl • Bimonthly. $53 Nonmembers 1 year; $58 Nonmembers Canada and PUAS countries; $63 Other countries non-members; $11 Single issue. Magazine reporting news, trends, and research of interest to academic library professionals.

***College and Undergraduate Libraries***. The Haworth Press Inc., 10 Alice St. Binghamton, NY 13904. Phone: 800-429-6784 or (607)722-5857; Fax: (607)771-0012 or (607)722-6362; Email: getinfo@haworthpress.com • URL: http://www.haworthpressinc.com/store/product.asp?sku=J014 • Semiannual. $105.00 per year. A practical journal dealing with everyday library problems.

***College and University***. American Association of Collegiate Registrars and Admissions Officers, One Dupont Cir. NW, Ste. 520 Washington, DC 20036-1148. Phone: (202)293-9161; Fax: (202)872-8857; Email: meetings@aacrao.org • URL: http://www.aacrao.org • Quarterly. Included in membership; $80 Individuals non-member; $140 Individuals non-member (2 years); $90 Individuals non-member; other Countries; $160 Individuals non-member (2 years); other Countries; $100 Libraries; $170 Libraries for 2 years; $120 Libraries other Countries; $190 Libraries other Countries (2 years). Addresses issues in higher education; looks at new procedures, policies, technology; reviews new publications.

***The College Blue Book***. Cengage Learning Inc., 20 Channel Center St. Boston, MA 02210. Phone: 800-487-8488 or (617)289-7700; Fax: (617)289-7844; Email: investors@cengage.com • URL: http://www.cengage.com • Annual. $572 Individuals. Published by Macmillan Reference USA. Provides detailed information on programs, degrees, and financial aid sources in the U.S. and Canada.

***College Board Review***. The College Board, 45 Columbus Ave. New York, NY 10023-6917. Phone: (212)713-8000; Email: aces@info.collegeboard.org • URL: http://www.collegeboard.org • 3/year. $30 /year; $55 /2 years; $80 /3 years. Connects students to success and opportunity in college.

**The College Board**. 45 Columbus Ave. New York, NY 10023-6917. Phone: (212)713-8000; Email: aces@info.collegeboard.org • URL: http://www.collegeboard.org • Represents the schools, colleges, universities, and other educational organizations that seek to connect members to success and opportunity. Serves students, parents, high schools, and colleges through major programs and services in college admission, guidance, assessment, financial aid, enrollment, and teaching and learning.

**College Media Association**. 2301 Vanderbilt Pl,, VU Sta. B 35166 Nashville, TN 37235. Phone: (415)338-3134 or (615)322-6610; Fax: (901)678-4798; Email: rsplbrgr@memphis.edu • URL: http://www.collegemedia.org • Formerly National Council of College Publications Advisers.

***College Media Review***. College Media Association, 2301 Vanderbilt Pl,, VU Sta. B 35166 Nashville, TN 37235. Phone: (415)338-3134 or (615)322-6610; Fax: (901)678-4798; Email: rsplbrgr@memphis.edu • URL: http://www.collegemedia.org • Quarterly Periodic. Included in membership; $15 /year. Contains aricles on advising collegiate media in print, broadcast and electronic forms.

**College of Performance Management**. 101 S Whiting St., Ste. 320 Alexandria, VA 22304. Phone: (703)370-7885; Fax: (703)370-1757 • URL: http://www.mycpm.org • Serves as a forum for the exchange of information on project management and performance measurement in business. Conducts educational programs.

**College of Tropical Agriculture and Human Resources**. University of Hawaii at Manoa, 2515 Campus Rd., Miller Hall 110 Honolulu, HI 96822. Phone: (808)956-8234; Fax: (808)956-9105; Email: gallom@ctahr.hawaii.edu • URL: http://www.ctahr.hawaii.edu • Concerned with the production and marketing of tropical food and ornamental plant products, including pineapples, bananas, coffee, and macadamia nuts.

***The College Store***. The College Store, 500 E Lorain St. Oberlin, OH 44074. Phone: 800-622-7498; Fax: (440)775-4769; Email: webteam@nacs.org • URL: http://www.nacs.org • Bimonthly. $66 Members; $78 Nonmembers. Books and college supplies magazine. Formerly *College Store Journal*.

***College Store Executive***. Executive Business Media Inc., 825 Old Country Rd. Westbury, NY 11590-0812. Phone: (516)334-3030; Fax: (516)334-3059 or (516)334-8958; Email: ebm-mail@ebmpubs.com • URL: http://www.ebmpubs.com • 10/year.

***College Teaching: International Quarterly Journal***. Helen Dwight Reid Educational Foundation. Taylor & Francis Group Heldref Publications, 325 Chestnut St., Ste. 800 Philadelphia, PA 19106. Phone: 800-354-1420 or (215)625-8900; Email: customer.service@taylorandfrancis.com • URL: http://www.heldref.org • Quarterly. $73 Individuals print and onlione; $220 Institutions print and onlione. Practical ideas, successful methods, and new programs for faculty development.

**Collision Industry Electronic Commerce Association**. 3149 Dundee Rd., No. 181 Northbrook, IL 60062-2402. Phone: (847)498-6945; Fax: (847)897-2094 • URL: http://cieca.com • Aims to facilitate electronic commerce within the collision industry. Works to provide a forum and methods to develop and maintain objective and uniform electronic commerce standards and guidelines. Encourages and supports open competition and free choice for the mutual benefit of all parties.

***Colombia Business Forecast Report***. Telecommunications Insight, 85 Queen Victoria St. London EC4V 4AB, United Kingdom. Phone: 20 72 465100 or 44 20 7248 0468; Fax: 20 72 480467 or 44 20 7248 0467; Email: enquiries@telecomsinsight.com • URL: http://www.telecomsinsight.com • Quarterly. $1,195 Individuals Single user; $1,795 Individuals Up to 3 users. Business forecast report for Colombia.

***Colombia Government and Business Contacts Handbook***. International Business Publications, USA, PO Box 15343 Washington, DC 20003. Phone: (202)546-2103; Fax: (202)546-3275; Email: ibpusa@comcast.net • URL: http://ibpus.com • $99.95 Individuals hardcopy, E-book and CD-ROM. Covers: Strategic government and business information, export-import activity in the country, investment, business contacts and regulations.

***Colombia Industrial and Business Directory***. International Business Publications, USA, PO Box 15343 Washington, DC 20003. Phone: (202)546-2103; Fax: (202)546-3275; Email: ibpusa@comcast.net • URL: http://ibpus.com • Annual. $99.95 Individuals. Covers industrial, investment and business contacts for conducting export-import and investment activity in the country.

***Colombia Investment and Business Guide***. International Business Publications, USA, PO Box 15343 Washington, DC 20003. Phone: (202)546-2103; Fax: (202)546-3275; Email: ibpusa@comcast.net • URL: http://ibpus.com • $99.95 Individuals hardcopy, e-book, CD-ROM. Covers: Information on economy, export-import and investment climate, regulations and industrial development, banking, and government. Entries include: Important business contacts and business travel.

**Colombian American Association**. 641 Lexington Ave., Ste. 1430 New York, NY 10022. Phone: (212)233-7776; Fax: (212)233-7779; Email: info@andean-us.com • URL: http://www.colombianamerican.org • Facilitates commerce and trade between the Republic of Colombia and the U.S. Fosters and advances cultural relations and goodwill between the two nations. Encourages sound investments in Colombia by Americans and in the U.S. by Colombians. Disseminates information in the U.S. concerning Colombia.

***Colombian Business Guide***. Asesorias Finanzas Ltda., Apartado 153000 Bogota, Colombia. Phone: 12 826157 • Annual. $30. Covers: Colombia businesses, foreign investment, import and export credit, main imports, export products, chambers of commerce, mining, livestock, and Colombian enterprise abroad.

***Colombian Exportable Offer***. The Export Promotion Fund, Proexpo, Centro Comercio Internacional, Calle 28, Numero 13A-15 Bogota, Colombia. Phone: 12 690777 • Covers: Manufacturers, distributors, and wholesalers in Colombia. Entries include: Contact information.

**Color Association of the United States**. 33 Whitehall St., Ste. M3 New York, NY 10004. Phone: (212)947-7774; Fax: (212)757-4557; Email: info@colorassociation.com • URL: http://www.colorassociation.com • Formerly The Textile Color Card Association of America.

**Color Marketing Group**. 1908 Mt. Vernon Ave. Alexandria, VA 22301. Phone: (703)329-8500 or (703)647-4729; Fax: (703)329-0155 or (703)535-3190; Email: sgriffis@colormarketing.org • URL: http://www.colormarketing.org • International group of professionals who forecast colors for consumer and contract markets. Examines color as it applies to the profitable marketing of products and services. Provides a forum for the exchange of ideas for all phases of color marketing, including styling, design, trends, merchandising, sales, education and research.

**Color Pigments Manufacturers Association**. 300 N Washington St., Ste. 105 Alexandria, VA 22314. Phone: (703)684-4044 or (202)465-4900; Fax: (202)465-4905 or (703)684-1795; Email: cpma@cpma.com • URL: http://www.pigments.org/cms/ • Manufacturers of inorganic and organic color pigments. Disseminates technical, regulatory, and legislative information on laboratory testing, toxicity, and subjects of general interest to manufacturers of pigments.

***Color Publishing***. PennWell Corp., Advanced Technology Div., 98 Spit Brook Rd. Nashua, NH 03062-5737. Phone: 800-225-0556 or (603)891-0123; Fax: (603)891-9294; Email: atd@pennwell.com • URL: http://www.pennwell.com • Bimonthly. $29.70 per year.

***Color Research and Application***. John Wiley & Sons Inc., 111 River St. Hoboken, NJ 07030-5774. Phone: 800-225-5945 or (201)748-6000; Fax: (201)748-6088; Email: info@wiley.com • URL: http://www.wiley.com • Bimonthly. $2,208 Institutions print and online. Covers reports on science, technology and application of color in business, art, design, education and industry.

***Colorado Investment and Business Guide***. International Business Publications, USA, PO Box 15343 Washington, DC 20003. Phone: (202)546-2103; Fax: (202)546-3275; Email: ibpusa@comcast.net • URL: http://ibpus.com • $99.95 Individuals hardcopy, e-book, CD-ROM. Covers: State economy, business, investment and export-import opportunities, government structure, mineral resources, technology, and government. Entries include: Political and business contacts.

**Colorado School of Mines - Mesoscopic Physics Laboratory**. Department of Physics, 1500 Illinois St. Golden, CO 80401. Phone: 800-446-9488 or (303)273-3850 or (303)273-3000; Fax: (303)273-3919 or (303)273-3244; Email: jscales@mines.edu • URL: http://mesoscopic.mines.edu/ • Mesoscopic phenomena, millimeter wave physics, quantum chaos, wave propagation in random media, rock physics.

***Colorado School of Mines Quarterly Review***. Colorado School of Mines Press, 1500 Illinois St. Golden, CO 80401-1887. Phone: (303)273-3595; Fax: (303)273-3199; Email: lpang@mines.edu • Quarterly. $65.00 per year.

***Colstrip Chamber of Commerce—Business Directory***. Colstrip Chamber of Commerce, PO Box 1100 Colstrip, MT 59323. Email: info@colstripchamber.com • URL: http://www.colstripchamber.com • Covers businesses in Colstrip, Montana.

**Coltrade: Colombian Government Trade Bureau**. 1901 L St. NW, Ste. 700 Washington, DC 20036. Phone: (202)887-9000; Fax: (202)223-0526; Email: coltrade@coltrade.org • URL: http://www.coltrade.org • Promotes Colombian exports to the U. S.

***Columbia Journalism Review***. Columbia University, Graduate School of Journalism, 2950 Broadway New York, NY 10027. Phone: (212)854-8608 • URL: http://www.journalism.columbia.edu • Bimonthly. Critical review of news media.

**Columbia Scholastic Press Association**. Columbia University, Mail Code 5711 New York, NY 10027-6902. Phone: (212)854-9400; Fax: (212)854-9401; Email: cspa@columbia.edu • URL: http://www.columbia.edu/cu/cspa • Newspapers, magazines, and yearbooks and online student media issued by schools from junior high school level through college and university, with the majority being from secondary schools. Works to promote student writing through the medium of the school publication. Improves publications in all phases. Offers critiques for each regular member. Compiles statistics. Provides consultation and referral services to student publications.

**Columbia University - Asia-Pacific Economic Cooperation Study Center**. 2M-9 Uris Hall, 3022 Broadway New York, NY 10027-7004. Phone: (212)854-3976; Fax: (212)851-9508; Email: aw2040@columbia.edu • URL: http://www7.gsb.columbia.edu/apec • Issues of economic importance for the Asia-Pacific region.

**Columbia University - Center for Advanced Information Management**. 650 W 168th St., Black Bldg. - 130 New York, NY 10032. Phone: (212)305-2944 or (212)305-5334; Fax: (212)305-0196 or (212)305-3302; Email: tomaselli@cat.columbia.edu • URL: http://www.cat.columbia.edu • Biomedical informatics, computer science, computational and systems biology, biomedical imaging.

**Columbia University - Center for the Study of Wealth and Inequality**. International Affairs Bldg., 420 W 118th St., MC 3355 New York, NY 10027. Phone: (212)854-4273; Fax: (212)854-8925; Email: ss50@columbia.edu • URL: http://iserp.columbia.edu/content/center-wealth-and-inequality • Income and wealth, along with exploring the dimensions of societal inequality in these household resources. The center's interests encompass issues of poverty, labor market behavior, public transfer programs and tax policy, in that each has a clear relevance to economic inequality, family resources, and to living standards.

**Columbia University - Center on Global Brand Leadership**. Uris Hall, Rm. 2M3, Columbia Business School, 3022 Broadway New York, NY 10027. Phone: (212)854-0659; Fax: (212)854-3762; Email: bschmitt@globalbrands.org • URL: http://www8.gsb.columbia.edu/globalbrands • Challenges of branding and innovation in a global economy.

**Columbia University - College of Physicians and Surgeons - Center for the Study of Society and Medicine**. 630 W 168th St. New York, NY 10032. Phone: (212)305-4186; Fax: (212)305-6416 • URL: http://www.societyandmedicine.columbia.edu • Issues that arise in clinical and research settings, including studies in bioethics and health policy, bioethics and medical decision-making, social policy, analyses of the social history of patienthood.

**Columbia University - Columbia Business School - Center for Excellence in Accounting and Security Analysis**. 608 Uris Hall, 3022 Broadway New York, NY 10027. Phone: (212)854-3832; Fax: (212)316-9219; Email: ceasa@gsb.columbia.edu • URL: http://www8.gsb.columbia.edu/ceasa • Financial reporting that reflects economic reality and investment advice that communicates sound valuations.

**Columbia University - Columbia Business School - Center on Japanese Economy and Business.** Uris Hall, Rm. 2M9, 3022 Broadway New York, NY 10027. Phone: (212)854-3976; Fax: (212)678-6958; Email: dew35@columbia.edu • URL: http://www8.gsb.columbia.edu/cjeb • Research areas include Pacific Basin trade policy.

**Columbia University - Columbia Business School - Columbia Institute for Tele-Information.** Uris Hall, 3022 Broadway New York, NY 10027. Phone: (212)854-4222; Fax: (212)854-1471; Email: noam@columbia.edu • URL: http://www8.gsb.columbia.edu/citi • Areas of research include private and public networking, the economics of networks, pricing of network access, and economics of technology adoption in the public network.

**Columbia University - Columbia Center for Excellence in E-Business.** Corporate & Foundation Relations, Columbia Business School, 33 W 60th St., 7th Fl. New York, NY 10023-7905. Phone: (212)854-3427; Fax: (212)678-0825; Email: ejj3@columbia.edu • URL: http://www4.gsb.columbia.edu/ecbiz • Business, information technology, and e-commerce.

***Columbus Business First.*** American City Business Journals, Inc., 120 W Morehead St. Charlotte, NC 28202. Phone: (704)973-1000; Fax: (704)973-1001; Email: americancity@bizjournals.com • URL: http://www.acbj.com • Contains the full text of Columbus Business First, a business tabloid covering Columbus, Ohio.

***Columbus Business Journal.*** Columbus Business Journal, 148 N High St. Gahanna, OH 43230. Phone: (614)476-1108 • Monthly. $12. Business tabloid.

***Commerce Business Daily (CBD).*** Chicago Metropolitan Agency for Planning, 233 S Wacker Dr., Ste. 800 Chicago, IL 60606. Phone: (312)454-0400; Fax: (312)454-0411; Email: info@cmap.illinois.gov • URL: http://www.cmap.illinois.gov • Daily. $324 per yr. for priority subscription; $275 per yr. for non-priority subscription; payment must accompany order. Covers all planned federal contracts and contract awards in excess of $25,000; coming sales of surplus government property; notices for federal prime contractors seeking subcontractors; foreign government contract announcements.

***Commerce Business Daily Desktop (CBD).*** Information Systems and Services Inc., 8601 Georgia Ave., Ste. 708 Silver Spring, MD 20910-3439. Phone: (301)588-3800; Fax: (301)588-3986; Email: info@issinet.com • URL: http://www.issinet.com • Software package that provides download and query access to the Commerce Business Daily database.

***Commerce Business Daily.*** U. S. Government Printing Office, 732 N Capitol St. NW Washington, DC 20401. Phone: 866-512-1800 or (202)512-1800 or (866)512-1800; Fax: (202)512-2104 or (202)512-2250; Email: contactcenter@gpo.gov • URL: http://www.gpo.gov • Daily. $275 Individuals. Publication listing U.S. and foreign government procurements and contract awards.

***Commerce Directory of Costa Rica.*** Mercadeo Profesional, S.A., 1502-1002 Paseo de los Estudiantes San Jose, Costa Rica. Phone: 506 22965715; Fax: 506 22324871; Email: ventas@meprosa.com • URL: http://www.directorioscostarica.com • Annual. Covers: Member businesses and non-members of Chamber of Commerce of Costa Rica.

***Commerce News: Reaching Edmonton's Entire Business Community.*** Edmonton Chamber of Commerce, No. 700 - 9990 Jasper Ave. Edmonton, AB, Canada T5J 1P7. Phone: (780)426-4620; Fax: (780)424-7946; Email: info@edmontonchamber.com • URL: http://www.edmontonchamber.com • Monthly. Commerce News. Magazine (tabloid) for Edmonton's business community.

***Commercial and Financial Chronicle.*** William B. Dana Co., P.O. Box 1839 Daytona Beach, FL 32115-1839. Phone: (386)252-0230; Fax: (904)252-6933 • Weekly. $140.00. per year.

***Commercial and Industrial Directory.*** Impresos Litograficos de Centro America, Urbana Santa Adela, Zone Centro de Gobierno San Salvador, El Salvador. Phone: 503 261516 • Annual. $15. Covers: Commercial and industrial manufacturers, wholesalers, and distributors in El Salvador. Entries include: Company name, address, phone, telex, names of directors, type of company.

***Commercial and Industrial Directory of Switzerland.*** Mosse Adress AG, Raeffelstrasse 25 CH-8045 Zurich, Switzerland. Phone: 41 1 4637700 • Annual. $901 Individuals. Covers: 300,000 industrial, trade, and export businesses and services in Switzerland. Entries include: Company name, address, phone.

***Commercial & Industrial Register of Southern Africa.*** A.C. Braby (Pty) Ltd., 12 Caversham Rd. Pinetown 3610, South Africa. Email: support@brabys.co.za • URL: http://www.brabys.com • Annual. $120 payment must accompany order. Covers: businesses in southern Africa. Database includes: Maps, list of PO Box renters. Entries include: Company name, address, phone.

***Commercial Bar Association Directory.*** Wiley Chancery, Baffins Ln. Chichester PO19 1UD, United Kingdom. Phone: 243 770108; Fax: 243 538972 • Annual. $25. Covers: Over 700 barristers in the U.K. specializing in corporate and commercial law; includes chamber and individual members. Entries include: Chamber name, address, phone, fax, principal fields of work; associated barristers, with name, date of birth, date of call, Queen's counsel, inn, academic and professional qualifications, pubications, languages spoken.

***Commercial Building: Tranforming Plans into Buildings.*** Stamats Communications Inc., 615 5th St. SE Cedar Rapids, IA 52406-1888. Phone: 800-553-8878 or (319)364-6167; Fax: (319)365-5421; Email: info@stamats.com • URL: http://www.stamats.com • Bimonthly. $48.00 per year. Edited for building contractors, engineers, and architects. Includes special features on new products, climate control, plumbing, and vertical transportation.

***Commercial Carrier Journal.*** Randall-Reilly Publishing Company L.L.C., 3200 Rice Mine Rd. NE Tuscaloosa, AL 35406. Phone: 800-633-5953; Fax: (205)345-0958 • URL: http://www.randallpub.com • Monthly.

**Commercial Development and Marketing Association.** Product Development and Management Association, 401 N Michigan Ave., Ste. 2200 Chicago, IL 60611. Phone: 800-232-5241 or (312)321-5145; Fax: (312)673-6885; Email: cdma@pdma.org • URL: http://www.pdma.org/p/cm/ld/fid=78 • Formerly Commercial Chemical Development Association.

**Commercial Finance Association.** 370 7th Ave., Ste. 1801 New York, NY 10001. Phone: (212)792-9390; Fax: (212)564-6053; Email: info@cfa.com • URL: http://www.cfa.com • Organizations engaged in asset-based financial services including commercial financing and factoring and lending money on a secured basis to small- and medium-sized business firms. Acts as a forum for information and consideration about ideas, opportunities and legislation concerning asset-based financial services. Seeks to improve the industry's legal and operational procedures. Offers job placement and reference services for members. Sponsors School for Field Examiners and other educational programs. Compiles statistics; conducts seminars and surveys; maintains speakers' bureau and 21 committees.

***Commercial Fisheries News.*** Compass Publications, Fisheries Division, PO Box 37 Stonington, ME 04681. Phone: 800-989-5253; Fax: (207)348-1059; Email: comfish@fish-news.com • URL: http://www.fish-news.com • Monthly. $21.95 print only; $25.95 print and online; $15.95 online only. Covers the commercial fishing industry in New England. Includes news of marine technology, boatbuilding, fish and lobster prices, business trends, government regulation, and other topics.

**Commercial Food Equipment Service Association.** PO Box 77139 Greensboro, NC 27417. Phone: (336)346-4700; Fax: (336)346-4745 • URL: http://www.cfesa.com • Represents firms that repair food preparation equipment used by restaurants, hotels, and institutions. Provides training and education for members and their employees.

**Commercial Law League of America.** 205 N Michigan Ave., Ste. 2212 Chicago, IL 60601. Phone: 800-978-2552 or (312)240-1400; Fax: (312)240-1408; Email: info@clla.org • URL: http://www.clla.org • Represents lawyers and other professionals engaged in bankruptcy and other commercial law areas; commercial collection agencies; law list publishers. Elevates the standards and improve the practice of commercial law. Promotes uniformity of legislation in matters affecting commercial law. Conducts educational programs on legal topics and issues of public interest at regional and national meetings. Maintains speakers' bureau and over 40 special and standing committees covering areas of commercial law including Bankruptcy and Uniform Commercial Code.

***Commercial Leasing Law and Strategy.*** ALM Media Properties LLC, 120 Broadway, 5th Fl. New York, NY 10271-1100. Phone: (212)457-9400; Fax: (646)417-7705; Email: customercare@alm.com • URL: http://www.alm.com • Monthly. $489 per year. Covers commercial real estate leasing developments relating to large retailers, tenant inducements, tax consequences, unbilled rent obligations, and other matters. (A Law Journal Newsletter, formerly published by Leader Publications).

***Commercial Review.*** Oregon Feed and Grain Association Inc., PO Box 163 Dundee, OR 97115-0163. Phone: (503)538-6659; Email: orfeedandgrainassn@gmail.com • URL: http://www.oregonfeed.org • Weekly. $35.00 per year.

***Commission European Union Bulletin.*** Commision of the European Communities. Bernan Associates, 4611 Assembly Dr., Ste. F Lanham, MD 20706-4843. Phone: 800-416-4385 or (301)459-2255 or (301)459-7666; Fax: (301)459-0056 or (800)865-3450; Email: query@bernan.com • URL: http://www.bernan.com • 11 times a year. $210.00 per year. Published by the Office of Official Publications of the European Communities. Covers all main events within the Union. Supplement available. Text in Danish, Dutch, English, French, German, Greek, Italian, Spanish, Portuguese. Formerly *Bulletin of the European Communities*.

**Committee for a Responsible Federal Budget.** 1899 L St. NW, Ste. 225 Washington, DC 20036. Phone: (202)596-3597; Fax: (202)986-3696; Email: crfb@crfb.org • URL: http://crfb.org • Members are corporations and others seeking to improve the federal budget process.

**Committee for Economic Development.** 2000 L St. NW, Ste. 700 Washington, DC 20036-4915. Phone: 800-676-7353 or (202)296-5860; Fax: (202)223-0776; Email: info@ced.org • URL: http://www.ced.org • Committee conducts research and formulates policy recommendations on national and international economic issues, including education and trade policy.

**Committee for the Economic Growth of Israel.** 100 Manpower Pl. Milwaukee, WI 53212. Phone: (414)906-6250; Fax: (414)906-7878 • URL: http://elmerwinter.com • Businessmen and women. Seeks to expand business relationships between Israel and the U.S. by promoting investment and joint venture opportunities for U.S. and Israeli companies. Promotes the exchange of technology, research and development, and products from Israel.

**Committee of 200.** 980 N Michigan Ave., Ste. 1575 Chicago, IL 60611. Phone: (312)255-0296; Fax: (312)255-0789; Email: info@c200.org • URL: http://www.c200.org • Represents women executives who are recognized as leaders in their industries (though originally intended to have a membership of 200 top-ranking businesswomen, the committee is no longer limited to 200). Encourages successful entrepreneurship by women and the active participation of women business owners and senior corporate executives in business, economic, social, and educational concerns. Seeks to strengthen the influence of women business leaders. Provides forum for exchange of ideas and enhancement of business opportunities for women.

***Commline.*** Numeridex Inc., 632 Wheeling Rd. Wheeling, IL 60090. Phone: 800-323-7737 or (847)541-8840; Fax: (847)541-8392; Email: sales@numeridex.com • URL: http://www.numeridex.com • Bimonthly. Free to qualified personnel; others, $20.00 per year. Emphasizes NC/CNC (numerically controlled and computer numerically controlled machinery).

***Commodity Market Review.*** Bernan Associates, 4611 Assembly Dr., Ste. F Lanham, MD 20706-4843. Phone: 800-416-4385 or (301)459-2255 or (301)459-7666; Fax: (301)459-0056 or (800)865-3450; Email: query@bernan.com • URL: http://www.bernan.com • Biennial. $45. Published by the Food and Agriculture Organization of the United Nations (FAO). Reviews the global outlook for over 20 specific commodities.

**Commodity Markets Council.** 1300 L St. NW, Ste. 1020 Washington, DC 20005. Phone: (202)842-0400 • URL: http://www.commoditymkts.org • Represents and supports grain exchanges, boards of trade, grain companies, milling and processing companies, transportation companies, futures commission merchants, and banks.

***Commodity Price Statistics.*** United Nations Publications, c/o National Book Network, 15200 NBN Way Blue Ridge Summit, PA 17214. Phone: 888-254-4286 or (212)963-7680 or (212)963-8302; Fax: (800)338-4550; Email: unpublications@nbnbooks.com • URL: http://www.unp.un.org • Database covers: Free-market prices and price indices for selected commodities that concern commodity-dependant countries. Price indices are provided for commodity groups (including food, tropical beverages, vegetable oilseeds and oils, agricultural raw materials, minerals, ores and metals), and for all groups in current dollars and SDRs.

***Commodity Trading Guide.*** Commodity Research Bureau, 209 W Jackson Blvd., Ste. 200 Chicago, IL 60606. Phone: 800-621-5271 or (312)554-8456; Fax: (312)939-4135; Email: info@crbtrader.com • URL: http://www.crbtrader.com • Annual. Serves as a concise "Almanac, Encyclopedia, Yearbook, and Calendar for the Futures Market." Includes many price charts, tables, government report dates, contract specifications, and price outlooks.

**Common Cause.** 1133 19th St. NW, 9th Fl. Washington, DC 20036-3612. Phone: (202)833-1200 or (202)736-5740; Fax: (202)659-3716; Email: causenet@commoncause.org • URL: http://www.commoncause.org • Nonpartisan citizens' lobby. Dedicated to fighting for open, honest, and accountable government at the national, state, and local levels. Gathers and disseminates information on the effects of money in politics; lobbies for political finance and other campaign reforms.

**Communicating for America.** 112 E Lincoln Ave. Fergus Falls, MN 56537. Phone: 800-432-3276 or (218)739-3241; Fax: (218)739-3832; Email: memberbenefits@cainc.org • URL: http://www.communicatingforamerica.org • Promotes the general health, well being and advancement of people in agriculture and agribusiness. Participates in federal and state issues that affect the quality of life in rural America and provides members with a variety of money-saving benefit programs. Conducts grants program, research on rural issues, and international exchange programs with an agricultural focus.

***Communication Abstracts: An International Information Service.*** Pine Forge Press, 2455 Teller Rd. Thousand Oaks, CA 91320-2234. Phone: 800-818-7243 or (805)499-4224 or (805)499-9774; Fax: (805)499-0871 or (805)583-2665; Email: sales@pfp.sagepub.com • URL: http://www.sagepub.com/sociologybooks • Bimonthly. Institutions, $1,150.00 per year. Provides broad coverage of the literature of communications, including broadcasting and advertising.

***Communication Booknotes Quarterly : Recent Titles in Telecommunications, Informaation, and Media.*** Lawrence Erlbaum Associates Inc., 10 Industrial Ave. Mahwah, NJ 07430-2262. Phone: 800-9BO-OKS9 or (201)258-2200; Fax: (201)236-0072; Email: orders@erlbaum.com • URL: http://www.leaonline.com • Quarterly. Contains descriptive reviews of new publications.

***Communication Briefings: A Monthly Idea Source for Decision Makers.*** Briefings Publishing Group, 1101 King St., Ste. 110 Alexandria, VA 22314. Phone: 800-722-9221 or (703)518-2343; Fax: (703)684-2136 • Monthly. $97. Presents useful ideas for communication, public relations, customer service, human resources, and employee training.

***Communication Research***. Pine Forge Press, 2455 Teller Rd. Thousand Oaks, CA 91320-2234. Phone: 800-818-7243 or (805)499-4224 or (805)499-9774; Fax: (805)499-0871 or (805)583-2665; Email: sales@pfp.sagepub.com • URL: http://www.sagepub.com/sociologybooks • Bimonthly. Contains articles that explore the processes, antecedents, and consequences of communication in a broad range of societal systems.

***Communication World: The Magazine for Communication Professionals***. International Association of Business Communicators, 601 Montgomery St., Ste. 1900 San Francisco, CA 94111. Phone: 800-776-4222 or (415)544-4700; Fax: (415)544-4747; Email: member_relations@iabc.com • URL: http://www.iabc.com • Emphasis is on public relations, media relations, corporate communication, and writing.

***Communication Yearbook***. International Communication Association, 1500 21st St. NW Washington, DC 20036. Phone: (202)955-1444; Fax: (202)955-1448; Email: icahdq@icahdq.org • URL: http://www.icahdq.org • Annual. Literature reviews and essays.

**Communications and Information Processing Group**. Rensselaer Polytechnic Institute, 7010 JEC, 110 Eighth St. Troy, NY 12180-3590. Phone: (518)276-6823; Fax: (518)276-6261; Email: modestin@ipl.rpi.edu • URL: http://www.ecse.rpi.edu • Includes Optical Signal Processing Laboratory and Speech Processing Laboratory.

***Communications Daily: The Authoritative News Service of Electronic Communications***. Warren Communications News Inc., 2115 Ward Ct. NW Washington, DC 20037. Phone: 800-771-9202 or (202)872-9200; Fax: (202)318-8350 or (202)293-3435 • URL: http://www.warren-news.com • Covers telecommunications, including the telephone industry, broadcasting, cable TV, satellites, data communications, and electronic publishing. Features corporate and industry news.

***Communications***. Master Brewers Association of the Americas, 3340 Pilot Knob Rd. Saint Paul, MN 55121. Phone: (651)454-7250; Fax: (651)454-0766; Email: mbaa@mbaa.com • URL: http://www.mbaa.com • Bimonthly. Membership.

**Communications Media Management Association**. 20423 State Rd. 7, Ste. F6-491 Boca Raton, FL 33498. Phone: (561)477-8100 • URL: http://cmma.org • Professional association of managers of communications media departments of business, education, or government. Aims to provide networking and educational opportunities for communications media managers that build peer professional relationships, facilitate leadership development, deepen managerial skills, expand technical knowledge, and develop skills in business strategy.

***Communications News***. Nelson Publishing Inc., 2500 Tamiami Trl. N Nokomis, FL 34275. Phone: (941)966-9521; Fax: (941)966-2590; Email: webteam@nelsonpub.com • URL: http://www.nelsonpub.com • Monthly.

***Communications News: Solutions for Today's Networking Decision Managers***. Nelson Publishing Inc., 2500 Tamiami Trl. N Nokomis, FL 34275. Phone: (941)966-9521; Fax: (941)966-2590; Email: webteam@nelsonpub.com • URL: http://www.nelsonpub.com • Monthly. Free to qualified personnel; others, $84.00 per year. Includes coverage of "Internetworking" and "Intrenetworking." Emphasis is on emerging telecommunications technologies.

***Communities: Journal of Cooperative Living***. Fellowship for Intentional Communities, RR 1 Box 156 W Rutledge, MO 63563-9720. Phone: (660)883-5545; Fax: (660)883-5545 • URL: http://www.ic.org • Quarterly. Contains information, issues, stories, and ideas about intentional communities in North America from urban co-ops to cohousing groups to ecovillages to rural communes.

***Community and Junior College Libraries: The Journal for Learning Resources Centers***. The Haworth Press Inc., 10 Alice St. Binghamton, NY 13904. Phone: 800-429-6784 or (607)722-5857; Fax: (607)771-0012 or (607)722-6362; Email: getinfo@haworthpress.com • URL: http://www.haworthpressinc.com/store/product.asp?sku=J014 • Quarterly. $85.00 per year.

**Community Associations Institute**. 6402 Arlington Blvd., Ste. 500 Falls Church, VA 22042. Phone: 888-224-4321 or (703)970-9220; Fax: (703)970-9558; Email: cai-info@caionline.org • URL: http://www.caionline.org • Condominium and homeowner associations, cooperatives, and association-governed planned communities of all sizes and architectural types; community or property managers and management firms; individual homeowners; community association managers and management firms; public officials; and lawyers, accountants, engineers, reserve specialists, builder/developers and other providers of professional services and products for CAs. Seeks to educate and represent America's 250,000 residential condominium, cooperative and homeowner associations and related professionals and service providers. Aims to foster vibrant, responsive, competent community associations that promote harmony, community and responsible leadership.

***The Community Bank President***. Siefer Consultants Inc., PO Box 1384 Storm Lake, IA 50588. Phone: (712)660-1026; Email: info@siefer.com • URL: http://www.siefer.com • Monthly. $329.00 per year.

**Community College Business Officers**. 3 Boar's Head Ln., Ste. B Charlottesville, VA 22903-4604. Phone: (434)293-2825; Fax: (434)245-8453; Email: info@ccbo.org • URL: http://www.ccbo.org • Represents business officers. Works to support business officers.

***Community College Journal***. American Association of Community Colleges, 1 Dupont Cir. NW, Ste. 410 Washington, DC 20036-1145. Phone: (202)728-0200; Fax: (202)833-2467; Email: aaccpub@pmds.com • URL: http://www.aacc.nche.edu • Bimonthly. $36 Members. Highlights field research, outstanding programs, college leaders, and membership activities. Formerly *Community, Technical and Junior College Journal*.

***Community College Review***. Dept. of Adult and Community College Education, North Carolina State University, College of Textiles, Campus Box 8301, 2401 Research Dr. Raleigh, NC 27695. Phone: (919)515-2011 or (919)515-6640; Fax: (919)515-3057; Email: undergrad_admissions@ncsu.edu • URL: http://www.tx.ncsu.edu • Quarterly. £54 Individuals print only. Contains articles on all aspects of community college administration, education, and policy.

***Community College Week: The Independent Voice Serving Community, Technical and Junior Colleges***. Cox, Matthews and Associates Inc., 10520 Warwick Ave., Ste. B8 Fairfax, VA 22030. Phone: (703)385-2980 or (703)385-2981; Fax: (703)385-1839 • URL: http://www.bibookreview.com • Biweekly. $52. Covers a wide variety of current topics relating to the administration and operation of community colleges.

**Community Development Bankers Association**. 1444 Eye St., Ste. 201 Washington, DC 20005. Phone: (202)689-8935; Email: info@cdbanks.org • URL: http://www.cdbanks.org • Represents the interests of the community development bank sector. Educates policy makers on how to deliver credit and financial services to low and moderate income communities.

***Community Development Digest: Semi-Monthly Report on Development, Planning, Infrastructure Financing***. Community Services Development, Inc. CD Publications, 2222 Sedwick Dr. Durham, NC 27713. Phone: 855-237-1396; Fax: (800)508-2592; Email: info@cdpublications.com • URL: http://www.cdpublications.com • $362 6 months, print and online; $624 12 months, print and online. Contains authoritative reports on the Community Development Block Grant program (CDBG).

**Community Development Society**. 17 S High St., Ste. 200 Columbus, OH 43215. Phone: (614)221-1900; Fax: (614)221-1989; Email: cds@assnoffices.com • URL: http://www.comm-dev.org • Professionals and practitioners in community development; international, national, state, and local groups interested in community development efforts. Provides a forum for exchange of ideas and experiences; disseminates information to the public; advocates excellence in community programs, scholarship, and research; promotes citizen participation as essential to effective community development. Sponsors educational programs.

**Community Financial Services Association**. 515 King St., Ste. 300 Alexandria, VA 22314. Phone: 888-572-9329; Fax: (703)684-1219; Email: info@cfsaa.com • URL: http://cfsaa.com • Works to promote laws and regulations that balance the interests of the payday advance industry with consumers. Supports and encourages responsible industry practices.

***Community Guide & Business Directory***. Southern Berkshire Chamber of Commerce, 362 Main St. Great Barrington, MA 01230. Phone: 800-269-4825 or (413)528-4284 or (413)528-1510; Fax: (413)528-2200; Email: info@southernberkshirechamber.com • URL: http://southernberkshirechamber.com • Contains directory of members and community guide/relocation informational publication.

**Community Managers International Association**. PO Box 848 Dana Point, CA 92629-0848. Phone: (949)940-9263; Email: cmiamanager@gmail.com • URL: http://www.cmiamanager.org • Aims to promote the community management profession. Provides an environment for the exchange of ideas among members. Collaborates with other national and state organizations. Sponsors seminars and workshops.

***Community Pharmacist: Meeting the Professional and Educational Needs of Today's Practitioner***. ELF Publications, Inc., 2600 S Parker Rd., Ste. 1-313 Aurora, CO 80014. Phone: 800-922-8513 or (303)755-1400; Fax: (303)313-2183; Email: jlane@elfpublications.com • URL: http://www.elfpublications.com • Bimonthly. $25.00 per year. Edited for retail pharmacists in various settings, whether independent or chain-operated. Covers both pharmaceutical and business topics.

***Compact D/SEC***. Thomson Reuters Corp., 3 Times Sq. New York, NY 10036. Phone: 800-336-4474 or (646)223-4000 or (646)822-2000; Email: general.info@thomsonreuters.com • URL: http://www.thomsonreuters.com • Monthly. Provides 200 financial data items for 12,000 U. S. publicly-held corporations filing reports with the Securities and Exchange Commission. Includes company profiles.

***Compact Disc Monaci***. Guida Monaci S.p.A., Via Salaria 1319 I-00138 Rome, Italy. Phone: 39 6 8887777; Fax: 39 6 8889996; Email: infoitaly@guidamonaci.it • URL: http://www.guidamonaci.it • Semiannual. Covers: 110,000 companies and agencies of the public and private sector in Italy, along with 200,000 business professionals. Entries include: For individuals—Name, address, position, qualifications.

***Compact Disc of the National Bank of Belgium***. Banque Nationale de Belgique S.A., Blvd. de Berlaimont 14 BE-1000 Brussels, Belgium. Phone: 32 2 221 21 11 or 32 2 2212111; Fax: 32 2 221 31 00 or 32 2 2213100; Email: info@nbb.be • URL: http://www.nbb.be • Quarterly. $284.94 CD-ROM. CD-ROM. Database covers: About 260,000 Belgian companies. Database includes: Company name, address, national number, financial data, activity, juridical form, and juridical situation.

***Companies in Greenland at Randburg***. Randburg.com, Sidumuli 15, IS-101 IS-101 Reykjavik, Iceland. Phone: 354 515 5689; Fax: 354 565 5588; Email: info@randburg.com • URL: http://www.randburg.com • Database covers: Companies in Greenland. Entries include: Company name, address, phone, fax, description.

***Company Handbook—Hong Kong***. Reference Press Inc., 6448 Hwy. 290 E, Ste. E-104 Austin, TX 78723. Phone: 800-486-8666 or (512)454-7778; Fax: (512)454-9401; Email: orders@hoovers.com • Semiannual. $44.95 per issue, plus $3.50 shipping. Covers: about 400 companies in Hong Kong; 200 are profiled in detail. Entries include: Company name, address, phone, fax, description, major shareholders and officers, financial data; detailed entries include financial data for previous five years, commentary on recent performance and trends, and share prices for the previous year. Published in Hong Kong by Corporate International Ltd.

***Company Handbook Spain: The Maxwell Espinosa Shareholders Directory***. S.p.A., Lagasca 27-1-E E-28001 Madrid, Spain. Phone: 349 1 5759350; Fax: 349 1 5759962; Email: 101363.1076@compuserve.com • Annual. $84.95 plus $3.50 shipping. Covers: 2,000 corporations in Spain. Entries include: Company name, address, phone, fax, names and titles of key personnel, major shareholders, line of business, sales for previous year and preceding four years, number of employees, names of advertising agency, attorneys, auditors, banks, and investment relations director.

***Company Information***. Bowker Ltd., Farringdon House, Wood St., 3rd Fl. East Grinstead RM19 1U2, United Kingdom. Phone: 44 1342310450; Fax: 44 1342310463; Email: sales@bowker.co.uk • Biennial. $199 plus $15.00 shipping. Covers: Sources of company information in the United Kingdom, including print, online, and CD-ROM data sources, and organizations.

***Company Intelligence***. Information Access Co. Gale Group Inc., 362 Lakeside Dr. Foster City, CA 94404. Phone: 800-227-8431 or (650)378-5000; Fax: (650)358-4759; Email: cemarketing@iacnet.com • Daily. Database covers: over 160,000 private and public U.S. companies, and 30,000 international companies. Database includes: Company name, address, phone, variant company name, description of business, Standard Industrial Classification (SIC) codes, year founded, special features, ultimate and immediate parent companies, number of employees, information sources, names and titles of key personnel, financial data; ten most recent citations about the company from articles in over 5,000 publications indexed by Information Access Company.

**Company of Military Historians**. PO Box 910 Rutland, MA 01543-0910. Phone: (508)845-9229; Email: cmhhq@aol.com • URL: http://www.military-historians.org • Represents professional society of military historians, museologists, artists, writers, journalists, military personnel, teachers, researchers, and other individuals interested in the history of American military units, organization, tactics, uniforms, arms, and equipment. Maintains museum.

***Company Profiles for Students***. Cengage Learning Inc., 20 Channel Center St. Boston, MA 02210. Phone: 800-487-8488 or (617)289-7700; Fax: (617)289-7844; Email: investors@cengage.com • URL: http://www.cengage.com • $338 print. Covers approximately 280 most studied companies. Entries include company logos, illustrations, ticker symbol, market share, etc.

***The Company Secretary's Handbook***. Cengage Learning Inc., 20 Channel Center St. Boston, MA 02210. Phone: 800-487-8488 or (617)289-7700; Fax: (617)289-7844; Email: investors@cengage.com • URL: http://www.cengage.com • Published by Kogan Page. A practical guide that will help newly appointed company secretaries do their job efficiently and comply with company law. Covers the formation of companies, corporate governance and day-to-day administration, keeping the statutory records, annual routines and dissolution. It also includes useful addresses and examples of all the necessary official documentation.

***Compensation and Benefits Review: The Journal of Total Compensation Strategies***. Pine Forge Press, 2455 Teller Rd. Thousand Oaks, CA 91320-2234. Phone: 800-818-7243 or (805)499-4224 or (805)499-9774; Fax: (805)499-0871 or (805)583-2665; Email: sales@pfp.sagepub.com • URL: http://www.sagepub.com/sociologybooks • Bimonthly. $565 Individuals print only; $685 Institutions print only. Contains a summary of the latest compensation and benefits surveys, reports, and legal and regulatory developments.

***Compensation and Benefits Update***. Thomson RIA, 195 Broadway New York, NY 10007-3100. Phone: 800-431-9025 or (212)367-6300 or (212)807-2298; Fax: (212)367-6305 or (212)337-4207; Email: ttacommunications@riag.com • URL:

http://www.ria.thomson.com • Monthly. $149.00 per year. Provides information on the latest ideas and developments in the field of employee benefits. In-depth exploration of popular benefits programs. Formerly *Benefits and Compensation Update*.

***Competitive Intelligence Guide***. Fuld & Co., Phone: (617)492-5900; Fax: (617)492-7108; Email: info@fuld.com • URL: http://www.fuld.com • Web site includes "Intelligence Index" (links to Internet sites), "Strategic Intelligence Organizer" (game-board format), "Intelligence Pyramid"(graphics), "Thoughtleaders" (expert commentary), "Intelligence System Evaluator" (interactive questionnaire), and "Reference Resource" (book excerpts from *New Competitor Intelligence* ). Fees: information provided by Web site is free, but Fuld & Co. offers fee-based research and consulting services.

**Competitive Telecommunications Association**. 1200 G St., NW, Ste. 350 Washington, DC 20005. Phone: 800-468-7022 or (202)296-6650; Fax: (202)296-7585; Email: rhaisman@comptel.org • URL: http://www.comptel.org • Formerly Association of Long Distance Telephone Companies.

**Competitiveness Review: An International Business Journal**. Emerald Group Publishing Ltd., Howard House, Wagon Ln. Bingley BD16 1WA, United Kingdom. Phone: 44 1274 777 700; Fax: 44 1274 785 201 • URL: http://www.emeraldinsight.com • Semiannual. Professional journal covering business and competitiveness worldwide.

***The Complete Guide to Buying a Business***. Nolo, 950 Parker St. Berkeley, CA 94710-2524. Phone: 800-728-3555 or (510)549-4660 or (510)549-1976; Fax: (800)645-0895 or (510)548-5902; Email: publicity@nolo.com • URL: http://www.nolo.com • Contains information and forms for purchasing a business in the United States.

***Complete Guide to Public Employment***. Development Concepts Inc., 9104 Manassas Dr., Ste. N Manassas Park, VA 20111-5211. Phone: 800-361-1055 or (703)361-7300; Fax: (703)335-9486; Email: query@impactpublications.com • URL: http://www.impactpublications.com • Triennial. $19.95 Individuals paper. Publication includes: List of federal, state, and local government agencies and departments, trade and professional associations, contracting and consulting firms, nonprofit organizations, foundations, research organizations, political support groups, and other organizations offering public service career opportunities. Entries include: Organization name, address, phone, name and title of contact. Complete title is "Complete Guide to Public Employment: Opportunities and Strategies with Federal, State, and Local Government;" Trade and Professional Associations; Contracting and Consulting Firms; Foundations; Research Organizations; and Political Support Groups.

***Complete Guide to Your Real Estate Closing: Answers to All Your Questions from Opening Escrow to Negotiating Fees to Signing Closing Papers***. Sandy Gadow. McGraw Hill Financial Inc., 1221 Avenue of the Americas New York, NY 10020-1095. Phone: (212)512-2000; Fax: (212)512-3840 • URL: http://www.mhfi.com • Date not set. $19.95. Includes sample forms and work sheets, with specific real estate closing information for all 50 states. (Teach Yourself Series).

***Complete Marquis Who's Who***. Marquis Who's Who, Reed Reference Publishing, 121 Chanlon Rd. New Providence, NJ 07974. Phone: 800-323-3288 or (908)665-6780; Fax: (908)665-3528 or (800)836-7766 • Frequency and price on application. Contains CD-ROM biographical profiles of over 800,000 notable individuals. Includes *Who's Who in America, Who Was Who in America*, and 14 regional and professonal directories.

***Complete Mental Health Directory***. Grey House Publishing, 4919 Rte. 22 Amenia, NY 12501. Phone: 800-562-2139 or (518)789-8700; Fax: (518)789-0556; Email: books@greyhouse.com • URL: http://www.greyhouse.com • $165 Individuals. Covers: mental health resources including government agencies, professional meetings and seminars, clinic and hospital management companies, and pharmaceutical companies and their mental health product lines.

***Compliance Reporter***. Institutional Investor Inc. Journals Group, 225 Park Ave. S New York, NY 10003. Phone: 800-437-9997 or (212)224-3570; Email: info@iijournals.com • URL: http://www.iijournals.com • Newsletter for investment dealers and others on complying with securities laws and regulations.

**Composite Materials Research Group**. University of Wyoming, Department of Mechanical Engineering, 1000 E University Ave. Laramie, WY 82071. Phone: (307)766-2122; Fax: (307)766-2695; Email: me.info@uwyo.edu • URL: http://www.uwyo.edu/mechanical/facilities/compositematerials.

***The Composites and Adhesives Newsletter***. T/C Press, P.O. Box 36006 Los Angeles, CA 90036-0006. Phone: (323)938-6923; Email: tcpress@msn.com • Quarterly. $190.00. Presents news of the composite materials and adhesives industries, with particular coverage of new products and applications.

**Composites Manufacturing Association**. 1 SME Dr. Dearborn, MI 48121. Phone: 800-733-4763 or (313)271-1500; Fax: (313)271-2861; Email: service@sme.org • URL: http://www.sme.org • Members are composites manufacturing professionals and students.

***Comprehensive Directory of Mexican Importers***. Todd Publications, PO Box 500 Millwood, NY 10546. Phone: 866-896-0916 or (914)373-4750; Fax: (914)373-4750; Email: toddpub@aol.com • URL: http://www.toddpublications.com • Biennial. $75. Covers: More than 2,700 Mexican importers.

***Compuserve Companion: Finding Newspapers and Magazines Online***. BiblioData, PO Box 61 Needham Heights, MA 02494. Phone: (781)444-1154 or (781)444-1144; Fax: (781)449-4584; Email: ina@bibliodata.com • URL: http://www.bibliodata.com • $29.95. Covers: More than 3,200 newspapers, newsletters, and magazines that are available for full text searching on CompuServe. Database includes: Introductory chapter of searching tips. Entries include: Publication name, dates of coverage, lag times, and appropriate "Go" commands.

***Compustat***. Standard and Poor's, 7400 S Alton Ct. Centennial, CO 80112. Phone: 800-525-8640; Fax: (303)721-4846 • URL: http://www.standardandpoors.com • Financial data on publicly held U.S. and some foreign corporations; data held for 20 years. Inquire as to online cost and availability.

***Computational Linguistics***. Association for Computational Linguistics. The MIT Press, 55 Hayward St. Cambridge, MA 02142-1493. Phone: 800-356-0343 or (617)253-5646 or (617)253-5641; Fax: (617)258-6779 or (617)253-6779; Email: ewfaran@mit.edu • URL: http://mitpress.mit.edu • Quarterly. Covers developments in research and applications of natural language processing.

***Computer Abstracts***. Emerald Group Publishing Inc., Brickyard Office Park, 84 Sherman St. Cambridge, MA 02140. Phone: (617)945-9130; Fax: (617)945-9136; Email: america@emeraldinsight.com • URL: http://www.emeraldinsight.com • Bimonthly. $4,739.

***Computer-Aided Engineering; Data Base Applications in Design and Manufacturing***. Penton Media Inc., 1300 E 9th St. Cleveland, OH 44114-1501. Phone: (216)696-7000; Fax: (216)696-1752; Email: information@penton.com • URL: http://penton.com • Quarterly. $55.00 per year.

**Computer and Communications Industry Association**. 900 17th St. NW, Ste. 1100 Washington, DC 20006. Phone: (202)783-0070; Fax: (202)783-0534; Email: info@ccianet.org • URL: http://www.ccianet.org • Formerly Computer Industry Association.

***Computer and Electronic Component Businesses in the World***. Momentum Technologies L.L.C., PO Box 460813 Glendale, CO 80246. Phone: (303)229-4841; Fax: (408)705-2031 • URL: http://www.mtt.com • Contains directory listings for more than 170 businesses throughout the world that manufacture or sell computer components and electronic parts. Includes business name, address, phone number, fax number, e-mail address, and web site address. Provides brief descriptions of product lines, services offered, and business type. Includes information on manufacturers, component makers, wholesalers, retailers, system designers, system installers, trade associations, and more. Searchable by location, business type, company name, and keyword.

***Computer and Information Systems Abstracts Journal: An Abstract Journal Pertaining to the Theory, Design, Fabrication and Application of Computer and Information Systems***. CSA, 7200 Wisconsin Ave. Bethesda, MD 20814. Phone: 800-843-7751 or (301)961-6700; Fax: (301)961-6720; Email: service@csa.com • URL: http://www.csa.com • Monthly. $1,750 per year.

***Computer Animation Proceedings***. Institute of Electrical and Electronic Engineers, 3 Park Ave., 17th Fl. New York, NY 10016-5997. Phone: 800-810-4333 or (212)705-8900 or (212)419-7900; Fax: (212)705-8999 or (212)752-4929; Email: conference-services@ieee.org • URL: http://www.ieee.org • Annual. $110.00.

***Computer Communication Review***. Association for Computing Machinery - Special Interest Group on Management of Data, 2 Penn Plz., Ste. 701 New York, NY 10121-0701. Phone: 800-342-6626 or (212)869-7440; Fax: (212)944-1315; Email: sigs@acm.org • URL: http://www.sigmod.org • Quarterly. Contains articles on topics within the SIG's field of interest.

***Computer Database***. Cengage Learning Inc., 20 Channel Center St. Boston, MA 02210. Phone: 800-487-8488 or (617)289-7700; Fax: (617)289-7844; Email: investors@cengage.com • URL: http://www.cengage.com • Provides one year of full-text online for 150 leading computer-related publications. Also includes 70,000 product specifications and brief profiles of 13,000 computer product vendors and manufacturers. Inquire as to prices and availability.

***Computer Economics Networking Strategies Report: Advising IT Decision Maker ractices and Current Trends***. Computer Economics Inc., 2082 Business Center Dr., Ste. 240 Irvine, CA 92612-1164. Phone: (949)831-8700; Fax: (949)442-7688; Email: info@computereconomics.com • URL: http://www.computereconomics.com • Monthly. $395.00 per year. Newsletter. Edited for information technology managers. Covers news and trends relating to a variety of corporate computer network and management information systems topics. Emphasis is on costs. Formerly *Intranet and Networking Strategies Report*.

***Computer Economics Report: The Financial Advisor of Data Processing Users***. Computer Economics Inc., 2082 Business Center Dr., Ste. 240 Irvine, CA 92612-1164. Phone: (949)831-8700; Fax: (949)442-7688; Email: info@computereconomics.com • URL: http://www.computereconomics.com • Monthly. $695. Newsletter on lease/purchase decisions, prices, discounts, residual value forecasts, personnel allocation, cost control, and other corporate computer topics. Edited for information technology (IT) executives.

***Computer Fraud and Security***. Elsevier, Secondary Publishing Division, 650 Ave. of the Americas New York, NY 10011. Phone: 888-437-4636 or (212)633-3980; Fax: (212)633-3975; Email: t.reller@elsevier.com • URL: http://www.elseveier.com • Monthly. Formerly *Computer Fraud and Security Bulletin*.

***Computer Graphics***. Special Interest Group on Computer Graphics. Association for Computing Machinery, 2 Penn Plz., Ste. 701 New York, NY 10121-0701. Phone: 800-342-6626 or (212)626-0500 or (212)869-7440; Fax: (212)944-1318; Email: acmhelp@acm.org • URL: http://www.acm.org • Quarterly. Members, $59.00 per year; non-members, $95.00 per year; students, $50.00 per year.

**Computer Graphics Laboratory**. New York Institute of Technology, Fine Arts Old Westbury, NY 11568. Phone: (516)686-7542; Fax: (516)686-7428; Email: pvoci@nyit.edu • URL: http://www.nyit.edu • Research areas include computer graphics, computer animation, and digital sound.

***Computer Graphics World***. PennWell Publishing Co., Advanced Technology Div., 98 Spit Brook Rd. Nashua, NH 03062-5737. Phone: 800-331-4463 or (603)891-0123; Email: atd@pennwell.com • URL: http://www.pennwell.com • Bimonthly. $68.

***Computer Industry Almanac***. Computer Industry Almanac Inc., PO Box 53 Arlington Heights, IL 60006. Phone: (847)758-3687; Fax: (847)758-3686; Email: cj@c-i-a.com • URL: http://www.c-i-a.com • Annual. $53 Individuals paperback; $63 Individuals hardcover. Covers: Over 3,000 firms involved in the computer industry in the U.S. Database includes: Lists of firms in various categories; industry overview; lists of trade shows, associations, publications, market research companies, high-tech PR companies. Entries include: Company Name, address, phone, fax, products, sales, number of employees, names and titles of key personnel, e-mail addresses, websites.

***Computer***. Institute of Electrical and Electronic Engineers, 3 Park Ave., 17th Fl. New York, NY 10016-5997. Phone: 800-810-4333 or (212)705-8900 or (212)419-7900; Fax: (212)705-8999 or (212)752-4929; Email: conference-services@ieee.org • URL: http://www.ieee.org • Monthly. Covers all aspects of computer science.

***Computer Languages, Systems and Structures***. Elsevier, Secondary Publishing Division, 650 Ave. of the Americas New York, NY 10011. Phone: 888-437-4636 or (212)633-3980; Fax: (212)633-3975; Email: t.reller@elsevier.com • URL: http://www.elseveier.com • Quarterly. Contains papers on all aspects of the design, implementation and use of programming languages, from theory to practice.

***Computer Law Reporter: A Monthly Journal of Computer Law and Practice, Intellectual Property, Copyright and Trademark Law***. Computer Law Reporter, 1601 Connecticut Ave. NW, No. 602 Washington, DC 20009. Phone: (202)462-5755; Fax: (202)328-2430; Email: orders@lawreporters.com • URL: http://www.lawreporters.com • Monthly. $3,475. Contains reports on legal developments affecting high technology industries.

***Computer Law Strategist***. ALM Media Properties LLC, 120 Broadway, 5th Fl. New York, NY 10271-1100. Phone: (212)457-9400; Fax: (646)417-7705; Email: customercare@alm.com • URL: http://www.alm.com • Monthly. $265.00 per year. Newsletter.

***Computer Letter: Business Issues in Technology***. Technologic Partners, 120 Wooster St. Fl. 6 New York, NY 10012. Phone: (212)343-1900; Fax: (212)343-1915; Email: info@technologicp.com • URL: http://www.venturewire.com • 40 times a year. $695.00 per year. Newsletter. Computer industry newsletter with emphasis on information for investors.

***Computer Music Journal***. The MIT Press, 55 Hayward St. Cambridge, MA 02142-1493. Phone: 800-356-0343 or (617)253-5646 or (617)253-5641; Fax: (617)258-6779 or (617)253-6779; Email: ewfaran@mit.edu • URL: http://mitpress.mit.edu • Quarterly. Covers digital soound and the musical applications of computers.

**Computer Network Center**. Purdue University at Indianapolis, 799 W Michigan St., ET 003 Indianapolis, IN 46202-5160. Phone: (317)274-0814; Fax: (317)274-4567; Email: cnchelp@iupui.edu • URL: http://et.engr.iupui.edu/sites/cnc/index.php.

***Computer Price Guide: The Blue Book of Used IBM Computer Prices***. Computer Economics Inc., 2082 Business Center Dr., Ste. 240 Irvine, CA 92612-1164. Phone: (949)831-8700; Fax: (949)442-7688; Email: info@computereconomics.com • URL: http://www.computereconomics.com • Quarterly. $140.00 per year. Provides average prices of used IBM computer equipment, including "complete lists of obsolete IBM equipment." Includes a newsletter on trends in the used computer market. Edited for dealers, leasing firms, and business computer buyers.

***Computer Science Index***. EBSCO Publishing Inc., 10 Estes St. Ipswich, MA 01938-2106. Phone: 800-653-2726 or (978)356-6500; Fax: (978)356-6565; Email: information@ebscohost.com • URL: http://www.ebscohost.com • Quarterly. $245 per year. Contains brief abstracts of book and periodical literature covering all phases of computing, including approximately 70 specific application areas.

***Computer Sciences: Macmillan Science Library***. Cengage Learning Inc., 20 Channel Center St. Boston, MA 02210. Phone: 800-487-8488 or (617)289-7700; Fax: (617)289-7844; Email:

investors@cengage.com • URL: http://www.cengage.com • $690 Individuals. 2013. $629.00. Presents a general and historical review of the impact of computers on modern society. Includes biographical information and multidisciplinary examples. Macmillan Reference USA imprint. eBook also available.

***Computer Shopper: The Computer Magazine for Direct Buyers***. Media Inc., 28 E. 28th St. New York, NY 10016-7930. Phone: 800-451-1032 or (212)503-3500; Fax: (212)503-4399; Email: info@ziffdavis.com • URL: http://www.ziffdavis.com • Nationwide marketplace for computer equipment.

***Computer Video***. IMAS Publishing Group, 5827 Columbia Pke. Ste. 310 Falls Church, VA 22041. Phone: 800-336-3045 or (703)998-7600; Fax: (703)998-2966; Email: adsales@imaspub.com • URL: http://www.imaspub.com • Bimonthly. $35.00 per year.

**Computer Vision Laboratory**. University of Arizona, Department of Electrical and Computer Engineering, 1230 E Speedway Blvd. Tucson, AZ 85721. Phone: (520)621-2434; Fax: (520)621-8076; Email: strickland@ece.arizona.edu • Research areas include computer vision and speech synthesis.

**Computerized Conferencing and Communications Center**. New Jersey Institute of Technology, University Heights Newark, NJ 07102-1982. Phone: (973)596-3000 • URL: http://www.njit.edu • Research areas include computer conferencing software and computer-mediated communication systems.

***Computers and Graphics: International Journal of Systems Applications in Computer Graphics***. Elsevier, Secondary Publishing Division, 650 Ave. of the Americas New York, NY 10011. Phone: 888-437-4636 or (212)633-3980; Fax: (212)633-3975; Email: t.reller@elsevier.com • URL: http://www.elseveier.com • 8/year. Contains information on research and applications of computer graphics (CG) techniques.

***Computers and Industrial Engineering: An International Journal***. Elsevier, Secondary Publishing Division, 650 Ave. of the Americas New York, NY 10011. Phone: 888-437-4636 or (212)633-3980; Fax: (212)633-3975; Email: t.reller@elsevier.com • URL: http://www.elseveier.com • Monthly. Contains original contributions to the development of new computerized methodologies for solving industrial engineering problems.

***Computers & Office Equipment Importers & Buyers Directory***. BD International, 11th Fl., Nan Sing Bldg., 727 Nathan Road, Kowloon Hong Kong, China. Fax: 852 3 5248941; Email: enq@bdi-hk.com • URL: http://www.leadxpress.com • $132 Individuals; 837 ¥ Individuals; $128 CD donwload version; 786 ¥ CD donwload version. Covers: 8,000 importers, buyers, wholesalers, and distributors of computers and office equipment. Entries include: Name, address, phone, fax, contact person, nature of business, website, and e-mail.

***Computers and Security: The International Source of Innovation for the Information Security and IT Audit Professional***. Computer Security. Elsevier, Secondary Publishing Division, 650 Ave. of the Americas New York, NY 10011. Phone: 888-437-4636 or (212)633-3980; Fax: (212)633-3975; Email: t.reller@elsevier.com • URL: http://www.elseveier.com • Eight times a year. Institutions, $760.00 per year.

***Computers-Dealers (Used) Directory***. InfoGroup Inc., 5711 S 86th Cir. Omaha, NE 68127-4146. Phone: (402)593-4500 • URL: http://www.infogroup.com • Annual. Number of listings: 2,336. Entries include: Name, address, phone, size of advertisement, name of owner or manager, number of employees, year first in "Yellow Pages." Compiled from telephone company "Yellow Pages," nationwide.

***Computers in Education Today***. Steven L. Mandell. Thomson West, 610 Opperman Dr. Eagan, MN 55123. Phone: 800-328-9352 or (651)687-7000 • $52.00. Date not set.

***Computers in Human Behavior***. Elsevier, Secondary Publishing Division, 650 Ave. of the Americas New York, NY 10011. Phone: 888-437-4636 or (212)633-3980; Fax: (212)633-3975; Email: t.reller@elsevier.com • URL: http://www.elseveier.com • Bimonthly. Qualified personnel, $242.00 per year; institutions, $1,100.00 per year.

***Computers in Libraries***. Information Today, Inc., 143 Old Marlton Pke. Medford, NJ 08055-8750. Phone: 800-300-9868 or (609)654-6266; Fax: (609)654-4309; Email: custserv@infotoday.com • URL: http://www.infotoday.com • Monthly. 10 times a year. $98.95 per year.

***Computers in the Schools: The Interdisciplinary Journal of Practice, Theory, and Applied Research***. The Haworth Press Inc., 10 Alice St. Binghamton, NY 13904. Phone: 800-429-6784 or (607)722-5857; Fax: (607)771-0012 or (607)722-6362; Email: getinfo@haworthpress.com • URL: http://www.haworthpressinc.com/store/product.asp?sku=J014 • Quarterly. $450.00 per year. Includes print and online editions.

***Computertalk: For Contemporary Pharmacy Management***. ComputerTalk Associates Inc., 492 Norristown Rd., Ste. 160 Blue Bell, PA 19422. Phone: (610)825-7686; Fax: (610)825-7641; Email: wal@computertalk.com • URL: http://www.computertalk.com • Bimonthly. $50.00 per year. Provides detailed advice and information on computer systems for pharmacies, including a buyers' guide issue.

***Computerworld: Newsweekly for Information Technology Leaders***. ComputerWorld Inc., 492 Old Connecticut Path Framingham, MA 01701-4649. Phone: 800-343-6474 or (508)879-0700; Fax: (508)875-3202 • URL: http://www.computerworld.com/ • Weekly. $190.00 per year.

***Computing Reviews***. Association for Computing Machinery, 2 Penn Plz., Ste. 701 New York, NY 10121-0701. Phone: 800-342-6626 or (212)626-0500 or (212)869-7440; Fax: (212)944-1318; Email: acmhelp@acm.org • URL: http://www.acm.org • Price varies. New reviews published daily.

**Computing Technology Industry Association**. 3500 Lacey Rd., Ste. 100 Downers Grove, IL 60515. Phone: (630)678-8300; Fax: (630)678-8384; Email: membership@comptia.org • URL: http://www.comptia.org • Trade association of more than 19,000 companies and professional IT members in the rapidly converging computing and communications market. Has members in more than 89 countries and provides a unified voice for the industry in the areas of e-commerce standards, vendor-neutral certification, service metrics, public policy and workforce development. Serves as information clearinghouse and resource for the industry; sponsors educational programs.

***Concrete International***. American Concrete Institute, 38800 Country Club Dr. Farmington Hills, MI 48331-3439. Phone: (248)848-3700; Fax: (248)848-3701; Email: ann.daugherty@acifoundation.org • URL: http://www.concrete.org • Monthly. $126.00 per year. Covers practical technology, industry news, and business management relating to the concrete construction industry.

***The Concrete Producer***. DoveTale Publishers, 1 Thomas Cir. NW Washington, DC 20005. Phone: 877-275-8647 or (202)339-0744 or (202)452-0800; Fax: (202)785-1974 or (202)339-0749; Email: hwmicustomerservice@hanleywood.com • URL: http://www.hwmarketintelligence.com • Monthly. $27 Individuals; $33 Canada; $93 Other countries; $43 Two years; $58 Canada 2 years; $162 Other countries 2 years. Covers the production and marketing of various concrete products, including precast and prestressed concrete. Formerly *Aberdeen's Concrete Trader*.

***Concrete Products***. Primedia Business Magazines and Media, 330 N Wabash Ave., Suite 2300 Chicago, IL 60611. Phone: 800-795-5445 or (312)595-1080 or (312)726-2802; Fax: (312)595-0295 or (312)726-2574; Email: subs@primediabusiness.com • URL: http://www.primediabusiness.com • Monthly. $61.00 per year. Free to qualified personnel; others, $61.00 per year.

***The Concrete Yearbook***. EMAP Construction Ltd., 151 Roseberry Ave. London W4 4PH, United Kingdom. Phone: 44 20 7505 6970; Fax: (750)5 6970 • URL: http://www.emapconstruct.co.uk • Annual. $100.00.

***CondoBusiness***. MediaEdge Inc., 5255 Yonge St., Ste. 1000 Toronto, ON, Canada M2N 6P4. Phone: 866-216-0860 or (416)512-8186; Fax: (416)512-8344; Email: kevinb@mediaedge.ca • URL: http://www.mediaedge.ca • Monthly. $55.00 per year. Covers condominum development and administration industries.

***Confectioner: The Magazine***. BNP Media, 2401 W Big Beaver Rd., Ste. 700 Troy, MI 48084. Phone: 800-952-6643 or (248)362-3700 or (847)763-9534; Fax: (248)362-5103 or (248)362-0317; Email: privacy@bnpmedia.com • URL: http://www.bnpmedia.com • Bimonthly. $70.17 per year. Covers a wide variety of topics relating to the distribution and retailing of candy and snacks.

**Confederation of Bolivian Private Entrepreneurs**. Calle Mendez Arcos No. 117, Plz. Espana La Paz, Bolivia. Phone: 591 2 2420999 or 591 2421254; Fax: 591 2 2421272; Email: cepb@cepb.org.bo • URL: http://www.cepb.org.bo • Represents the interests of the private entrepreneurs in Bolivia.

**Confederation of British Industry**. Cannon Pl., 103 New Oxford St. London EC4N 6HN, United Kingdom. Phone: 44 20 73797400; Fax: 44 20 73797200; Email: enquiries@cbi.org.uk • URL: http://www.cbi.org.uk • Works to ensure that the government understands the intentions, needs, and problems of British business.

**Confederation of Indian Industry - United Kingdom**. c/o Confederation of British Industry, Centre Point, 103 New Oxford St. London WC1A 1DU, United Kingdom. Phone: 44 20 78364121 or 44 20 73797400; Fax: 44 20 78361972 • URL: http://www.cii.in • Works to create and sustain an environment conducive to growth of the Indian industry. Links the industry and the government through advisory and consultative process. Serves as a reference point for the Indian industry and the international business community.

**Confederation of Indian Industry**. Secretary, 23-26 Institutional Area, Lodi Rd. New Delhi 110 003, Delhi, India. Phone: 91 011694298 or 91 11 24629997; Fax: 91 11 24626149; Email: info@cii.in • URL: http://cii.in • Industrial firms. Promotes advancement of Indian industry. Represents members' interests; gathers and disseminates information.

**Confederation of Norwegian Enterprise**. Naeringslivets Hus, Middelthuns gate 27, Majorstuen N-0303 Oslo, Norway. Phone: 47 23 088000; Fax: 47 23 088001 • URL: http://www.nho.no • Promotes the interests of Norwegian companies as regards to exports and internationalization. Provides information on EU matters relevant for the business community.

**Confederation of Swedish Enterprise**. Storgatan 19 S-114 82 Stockholm, Sweden. Phone: 46 8 55343000; Fax: 46 8 55343099 • URL: http://www.svensktnaringsliv.se • Represents the interests of Swedish manufacturers. Conducts lobbying activities.

**Confederation of Tanzania Industries**. NIC Investment House, 9th Fl., Samora Ave. Dar es Salaam, Tanzania. Phone: 255 22 2114954 or 255 22 2123802; Fax: 255 22 2115414; Email: cti@cti.co.tz • URL: http://www.cti.co.tz • Promotes the interests of the manufacturing sector and supporting industries in Tanzania. Ensures a conducive legal, financial and economic environment in which the industry can operate effectively.

***Confederation of Zimbabwe Industries: Register & Buyers Guide—Brand Names, Manufacturers, Products***. Thomson Publications, PO Box 1683 Harare, Zimbabwe. • Annual. $115 please inquire. Covers: Commercial enterprises and members of the Confederation of Zimbabwe Industries. Entries include: Company name, address, phone, member name, address.

**Conference Board - Europe**. Chaussee de la Hulpe 178, 6th Fl. B-1170 Brussels, Belgium. Phone: 32 2 675 5405; Email: brussels@conferenceboard.org • URL: http://www.conference-board.org • Promotes management and the marketplace to help businesses strengthen their performance and better serve society. Conducts research, makes forecasts, assesses trends, publishes information and analysis, and brings executives together for exchange of ideas.

**Conference Board of Canada**. 255 Smyth Rd. Ottawa, ON, Canada K1H 8M7. Phone: 866-711-2262 or (613)526-3280; Fax: (613)526-4857; Email: contactcboc@conferenceboard.ca • URL: http://www.conferenceboard.ca • Research areas include economics, finance, international business, and consumer buying intentions.

**Conference of Consulting Actuaries**. 3880 Salem Lake Dr., Ste. H Long Grove, IL 60047-5292. Phone: (847)719-6500; Email: conference@ccactuaries.org • URL: http://www.ccactuaries.org • Formerly Conference of Actuaries of Public Practice.

**Conference of State Bank Supervisors**. 1129 20th St. NW, 9th Fl. Washington, DC 20036. Phone: (202)296-2840; Fax: (202)296-1928 • URL: http://www.csbs.org/Pages/default.aspx • Members are state officials responsible for supervision of state-chartered banking institutions.

**Conference on Consumer Finance Law**. Oklahoma City University School of Law, 2501 N Blackwelder Ave. Oklahoma City, OK 73106. Phone: (405)208-5198 or (405)208-5363 • URL: http://www.ccflonline.org • Formerly Conference on Personal Finance Law.

***Conference Papers Index***. Cambridge Scientific Abstracts L.P., 7200 Wisconsin Ave., Ste. 601 Bethesda, MD 20814. Phone: 800-843-7751 or (301)961-6700 or (301)961-6785; Fax: (301)961-6720 or (301)961-6708; Email: sales@proquest.com • URL: http://www.proquest.co.uk • Bimonthly. Citations to scientific and technical papers presented at meetings, 1973 to present. Inquire as to online cost and availability.

***Congo Business Directory***. Business Guide, PO Box 27669 Dubai, United Arab Emirates. Phone: 971 4 2651719; Fax: 971 4 2692151; Email: sales@africa-business.com • URL: http://www.africa-business.com • $150 download. Covers: 1,600 business listings including wholesalers, importers, retailers, business houses, and agents in Congo.

***Congo Business Law Handbook***. International Business Publications, USA, PO Box 15343 Washington, DC 20003. Phone: (202)546-2103; Fax: (202)546-3275; Email: ibpusa@comcast.net • URL: http://ibpus.com • $99.95 Individuals hardcopy, e-book, CD-ROM. Covers: Information on basic business legislation, laws, business climate, export-import regulations, and contacts.

***Congress in Print: The Weekly Catalog of Congressional Documents***. U. S. Government Printing Office, 732 N Capitol St. NW Washington, DC 20401. Phone: 866-512-1800 or (202)512-1800 or (866)512-1800; Fax: (202)512-2104 or (202)512-2250; Email: contactcenter@gpo.gov • URL: http://www.gpo.gov • Newsletter.

**Congressional Budget Office - Macroeconomic Analysis Division**. Ford House Office Bldg., 4th Fl., 2nd & D Sts. SW Washington, DC 20515-6925. Phone: (202)226-2602; Fax: (202)226-2714 • URL: http://www.cbo.gov/about/our-organization-and-people#mad • U.S. economy, prepares projections of future economic conditions, and studies how that future could be affected by different economic developments or policies. The economic projections serve the Senate and House budget committees in developing concurrent resolutions on the budget and the entire Congress as it considers and passes the budget. Division's analyses focus on such issues as inflation, employment, production, incomes, international economic affairs, and credit as well as on the interaction of those issues with the federal budget. Although the Congressional Budget Office does not have its own large-scale econometric model, its forecasts are based on information from major econometric models and other forecasting services that are available commercially, along with the advice of a panel of advisors who represent a wide spectrum of economic views.

**Congressional Budget Office - Tax Analysis Division**. Ford House Office Bldg., 4th Fl., 2nd & D Sts. SW Washington, DC 20515-6925. Phone: (202)226-2602; Fax: (202)226-2714 • URL: http://www.cbo.gov/about/our-organization-and-people#tad • Responsible for estimating tax revenues, analyzing tax expenditures, and preparing tax-policy studies. Division analyzes the U.S. tax structure and changes to that structure, focusing on such issues as the effect of changing economic conditions on tax revenues, consumption taxes, and the distribution of tax burdens.

***Congressional Index***. Wolters Kluwer Law & Business CCH, 2700 Lake Cook Rd. Riverwoods, IL 60015. Phone: 888-224-7377 or (847)267-7000; Email: cust_serv@cch.com • URL: http://www.cchgroup.com • Index to action on Public Bills from introduction to final disposition. Subject, author, and bill number indexes.

***Congressional Investigations: Law and Practice***. John C. Grabow. Wolters Kluwer Law and Business, 76 9th Ave., 7th Fl. New York, NY 10011-4962. Phone: 800-234-1660 or (212)771-0600; Fax: (800)901-9075 or (301)644-3550 • URL: http://www.wolterskluwerlb.com • $95.00. Looseleaf service. Periodic supplementation.

***Congressional Monitor: Daily Listing of All Scheduled Congressional Committee Hearings with Witnesses***. Congressional Quarterly Inc., 2300 North St. NW, Ste. 800 Washington, DC 20037-1122. Phone: 866-427-7737 or (202)729-1900 or (202)729-1800; Fax: (800)380-3810 or (202)728-1863; Email: customerservice@cqpress.com • URL: http://www.cqpress.com • Daily. $1,349.00 per year. Weekly *Supplements*.

***Congressional Quarterly Almanac***. CQ Press, 2300 N St. NW, Ste. 800 Washington, DC 20037. Phone: 866-427-7737 or (202)729-1900; Email: customerservice@cqpress.com • URL: http://www.cqpress.com • Annual. $549 print. Offers exclusive insight into the forces that drove action on legislation.

***Congressional Record***. U.S. Congress. U. S. Government Printing Office, 732 N Capitol St. NW Washington, DC 20401. Phone: 866-512-1800 or (202)512-1800 or (866)512-1800; Fax: (202)512-2104 or (202)512-2250; Email: contactcenter@gpo.gov • URL: http://www.gpo.gov • Daily. Daily. Indexes give names, subjects, and history of bills. Texts of bills not included.

***Connecticut Investment and Business Guide***. International Business Publications, USA, PO Box 15343 Washington, DC 20003. Phone: (202)546-2103; Fax: (202)546-3275; Email: ibpusa@comcast.net • URL: http://ibpus.com • $99.95 Individuals. Covers: Strategic and business information, contacts, regulations and more.

**Connecticut Society of Certified Public Accountants Education and Research Foundation**. 845 Brook St., Bldg. 2 Rocky Hill, CT 06067-3405. Phone: 800-232-2232 or (860)258-4800; Fax: (860)258-4859; Email: artr@cs-cpa.org • URL: http://www.cs-cpa.org • Accounting.

***Consensus Forecasts: A Worldwide Survey***. Consensus Economics Inc., 53 Upper Brook St. London W1K 2LT, United Kingdom. Phone: 44 20 7491 3211; Fax: 44 20 7409 2331; Email: editors@consensuseconomics.com • URL: http://www.consensuseconomics.com • Monthly. Provides a survey of more than 200 "prominent"financial and economic forecasters, covering 20 major countries. Two-year forecasts for each country include future growth, inflation, interest rates, and exchange rates. Each issue contains analysis of business conditions in various countries.

***Consensus: National Futures and Financial Weekly***. Consensus Inc., PO Box 520526 Independence, MO 64052-0526. Phone: 800-383-1441 or (816)373-3700; Fax: (816)373-3701; Email: editor@consensus-inc.com • URL: http://www.consensus-inc.com/ • Weekly. $365.00 per year. Newspaper. Contains news, statistics, and special reports relating to agricultural, industrial, and financial futures markets. Features daily basis price charts, reprints of market advice, and "The Consensus Index of Bullish Market Opinion" (charts show percent bullish of advisors for various futures).

**The Conservation Campaign**. 10 Milk St., Ste. 810 Boston, MA 02108. Phone: (617)371-0526; Email: tcc@conservationcampaign.org • URL: http://www.conservationcampaign.org • Provides practical and operational support to local and statewide voter campaigns and legislative lobbying efforts. Strives to help towns, cities, counties, special districts and states create the funding they need to preserve and enhance their landscapes, whether it is wilderness and natural areas, urban parks and playgrounds or working forests and farmlands. Promotes grassroots movements to gain public funding for conservation funding.

**Consortium for Graduate Study in Management**. 229 Chesterfield Business Pkwy. Chesterfield, MO 63005. Phone: (636)681-5460 or (636)681-5553; Fax: (636)681-5499 • URL: http://www.cgsm.org • Works as an alliance of American business schools and some of the country's top corporations including University of California Berkeley, University of California Los Angeles, Carnegie Mellon University, Cornell University, Dartmouth College, Indiana University-Bloomington, University of Michigan-Ann Arbor, New York University, University of North Carolina at Chapel Hill, University of Rochester, University of Southern California, Emory University, The University of Texas at Austin, University of Virginia, Washington University in St. Louis, University of Wisconsin-Madison and Yale University. Bestows award merit-based, full-tuition fellowships for up to two consecutive years of fulltime graduate business education.

***Construction Consultants Directory***. InfoGroup Inc., 5711 S 86th Cir. Omaha, NE 68127-4146. Phone: (402)593-4500 • URL: http://www.infogroup.com • Annual. Number of listings: 734. Entries include: Name, address, phone, size of advertisement, name of owner or manager, number of employees, year first in "Yellow Pages." Compiled from telephone company "Yellow Pages," nationwide.

***Construction Equipment Distribution***. Associated Equipment Distributors, 600 22nd St., Ste. 220 Oak Brook, IL 60523. Phone: 800-388-0650 or (630)574-0650; Fax: (630)574-0132; Email: info@aednet.org • URL: http://www.aednet.org • Monthly. Members, $20.00 per year; non-members, $40.00 per year.

***Construction Equipment Operation and Maintenance***. Construction Publications Inc., 829-2nd Ave. SE Cedar Rapids, IA 52403. Phone: (319)366-1597; Fax: (319)362-8808 • Bimonthly. $12.00 per year. Information for users of construction equipment and industry news.

***Construction Executive: The Magazine for the Business of Construction***. Associated Builders and Contractors, 440 1st St. NW, Ste. 200 Washington, DC 20001. Email: gotquestions@abc.org • URL: http://www.abc.org • Monthly. $15 Members; $65 Nonmembers. Magazine for contractors and subcontractors. Includes articles on national and regional construction news, construction management, project case histories, new products, building design, and legislative and regulatory updates.

**Construction Financial Management Association**. 100 Village Blvd., Ste. 200 Princeton, NJ 08540. Phone: 888-421-9996 or (609)452-8000; Fax: (609)452-0474; Email: sbinstock@cfma.org • URL: http://www.cfma.org • Contractors, subcontractors, architects, real estate developers and engineers; associate members are equipment and material suppliers, accountants, lawyers, bankers and others involved with the financial management of the construction industry. Provides a forum for the exchange of ideas; coordinates educational programs dedicated to improving the professional standards of financial management in the construction industry. Offers expanded national programs, technical assistance and industry representation. Conducts research programs; maintains speakers' bureau and placement service; compiles statistics.

***Construction Industry Annual Financial Survey***. Construction Financial Management Association, 100 Village Blvd., Ste. 200 Princeton, NJ 08540. Phone: 888-421-9996 or (609)452-8000; Fax: (609)452-0474; Email: sbinstock@cfma.org • URL: http://www.cfma.org • Annual. $262. Contains key financial ratios for various kinds and sizes of construction contractors.

***Construction Law***. Matthew Bender and Company Inc., 1275 Broadway Albany, NY 12204-2638. Phone: 800-424-4200 or (518)487-3000; Fax: (518)487-3573 or (800)424-4200; Email: customer.support@lexisnexis.com • URL: http://www.matthewbender.com • $1,844. Eight volumes. Periodic supplementation available. Edited for lawyers who prepare construction contracts or engage in construction dispute litigation.

***Construction Law Digest***. Matthew Bender and Company Inc., 1275 Broadway Albany, NY 12204-2638. Phone: 800-424-4200 or (518)487-3000; Fax: (518)487-3573 or (800)424-4200; Email: customer.support@lexisnexis.com • URL: http://www.matthewbender.com • $852. Provides practical information on emerging legal trends, issues, and court decisions relevant to the construction industry.

**Construction Management Association of America**. 7926 Jones Branch Dr., Ste. 800 McLean, VA 22102. Phone: (703)356-2622; Fax: (703)356-6388; Email: info@cmaanet.org • URL: http://cmaanet.org • Promotes the growth and development of construction management as a professional service; encourages high professional standards. Conducts conferences and forums on construction management topics. Sponsors a professional certification program.

***Construction Specifier: For Commercial and Industrial Construction***. Construction Specifications Institute, 110 S Union St., Ste. 100 Alexandria, VA 22314-3351. Phone: 800-689-2900; Fax: (703)236-4600; Email: csi@csinet.org • URL: http://www.csinet.org • Monthly. Free to members; non-members, $36.00 per year; libraries, $30.00 per year. Technical aspects of the construction industry.

***Constructor: The Management Magazine of the Construction Industry***. Associated General Contractors of America. AGC Information, Inc., 333 John Carlye St., Suite 200 Alexandria, VA 22314-5745. Phone: (703)548-3118; Fax: (703)837-5405; Email: scott@agc.org • URL: http://www.agc.org • Monthly. Members, $15.00 per year; non-members, $250.00 per year. Includes *Directory*.

***Consultants & Consulting Organizations Directory (CCOD)***. Cengage Learning Inc., 20 Channel Center St. Boston, MA 02210. Phone: 800-487-8488 or (617)289-7700; Fax: (617)289-7844; Email: investors@cengage.com • URL: http://www.cengage.com • Annual. $1,455 Individuals paperback. 2014. 39th edition. Over 26,000 firms, individuals, and organizations active in consulting. eBook available.

**Consultants Association for the Natural Products Industry**. PO Box 4014 Clovis, CA 93613-4014. Phone: (559)325-7192; Email: info@cani-consultants.org • URL: http://www.cani-consultants.org • Works to enhance the growth and integrity of the natural products industry. Offers professional services to help manufacturers, distributors, retailers, and non-profit organizations thrive in the nutraceutical marketplace. Promotes education and ethical standards for the improvement of manufacturing, distribution, marketing and advertising to help the industry develop safe and beneficial products for the public.

***Consultants News: Independent Commentary on Management Consulting Since 1970***. Kennedy Information Inc., 1 Phoenix Mill Ln., 3rd Fl. Peterborough, NH 03458. Phone: 800-531-0007 or (603)924-1006; Fax: (603)924-4460 or (603)924-4034; Email: customerservice@kennedyinfo.com • URL: http://www.kennedyinfo.com • Monthly. $295.00 per year. Newsletter. News and ideas for management consultants.

***Consultants (Tax) Directory***. InfoGroup Inc., 5711 S 86th Cir. Omaha, NE 68127-4146. Phone: (402)593-4500 • URL: http://www.infogroup.com • Annual. Number of listings: 63,898. Entries include: Name, address, phone, size of advertisement, name of owner or manager, number of employees, year first in "Yellow Pages." Compiled from telephone company "Yellow Pages," nationwide.

***Consulting-Specifying Engineer***. Reed Elsevier Group plc Reed Business Information, 360 Park Ave. S New York, NY 11010. Phone: (212)791-4208; Email: corporatecommunications@reedbusiness.com • URL: http://www.reedbusiness.com • 13 times a year. $95.90 per year. Formerly *Consulting Engineer*.

**Consumer Bankers Association**. 1225 Eye St. NW, Ste. 550 Washington, DC 20005. Phone: (202)552-6382 or (202)552-6363; Fax: (703)528-1290; Email: jpike@cbanet.org • URL: http://www.cbanet.org • Federally insured deposit-taking institutions. Sponsors Graduate School of Retail Bank Management at the university of Virginia.

***Consumer Credit and Truth-in-Lending Compliance Report***. Thomson RIA, 195 Broadway New York, NY 10007-3100. Phone: 800-431-9025 or (212)367-6300 or (212)807-2298; Fax: (212)367-6305 or (212)337-4207; Email: ttacommunications@riag.com • URL: http://www.ria.thomson.com • Monthly. $183.75 per year. Newsletter. Focuses on the latest regulatory rulings and findings involving consumer lending and credit activity. Incorporates (Consumer Lending Report).

**Consumer Credit Industry Association**. 6300 Powers Ferry Rd., Ste. 600-286 Atlanta, GA 30339. Phone: (678)858-4001; Email: sjcipinko@cciaonline.com • URL: http://www.cciaonline.com • Insurance companies underwriting consumer credit insurance in areas of life insurance, accident and health insurance, and property insurance.

**Consumer Credit Trade Association**. The Wave, Ste. 4, 1 View Croft Rd. Shipley BD17 7DU, United Kingdom. Phone: 44 127 4714959; Fax: 44 845 2571199 • URL: http://www.ccta.co.uk • Credit grantors of many types who offer credit to consumers. Includes finance companies, retailers, some building societies, other lenders and suppliers of ancillary services. Represents to government, the media and EC authorities the interests of companies providing and operating credit, leasing and rental facilities. Offers a range of services to members including advice, courses and seminars, standard agreement forms, Short Guides on legislation, magazine and discussion groups and forums.

**Consumer Data Industry Association**. 1090 Vermont Ave. NW, Ste. 200 Washington, DC 20005-4905. Phone: (202)371-0910; Fax: (202)371-0134; Email: cdia@cdiaonline.org • URL: http://www.cdiaonline.org • Serves as international association of credit reporting and collection service offices. Maintains hall of fame and biographical archives; conducts specialized educational programs. Offers computerized services and compiles statistics.

**Consumer Electronics Association**. 1919 S Eads St. Arlington, VA 22202. Phone: 866-858-1555 or (703)907-7600 or (703)907-7650; Fax: (703)907-7675 or (630)953-8957; Email: info@ce.org • URL: http://www.ce.org • Manufacturers of consumer technology and electronics products. Strives to aid members in growth through connections, education, exposure, and by providing information. Hosts workshops and educational programs.

**Consumer Federation of America - Food Policy Institute**. 1620 I St. NW, Ste. 200 Washington, DC 20006. Phone: (202)387-6121 or (202)737-0766; Fax: (202)265-7989; Email: cfa@consumerfed.org • URL: http://www.consumerfed.org/food-and-agriculture • National food, health, and environmental policies, including food safety, sustainable agriculture, children's nutrition, and inner-city retail food access.

**Consumer Federation of America**. 1620 I St. NW, Ste. 200 Washington, DC 20006. Phone: (202)387-6121 or (202)737-0766; Email: cfa@consumerfed.org • URL: http://www.consumerfed.org • Members are national, regional, state, and local consumer groups. Absorbed Electric Consumers Information Committee.

***Consumer Health Complete***. EBSCO Publishing Inc., 10 Estes St. Ipswich, MA 01938-2106. Phone: 800-653-2726 or (978)356-6500; Fax: (978)356-6565; Email: information@ebscohost.com • URL: http://www.ebscohost.com • Full text of more than 250 health references, health diagrams, videos, pamphlets.

**Consumer Healthcare Products Association**. 900 19th St. NW, Ste. 700 Washington, DC 20006. Phone: (202)429-9260; Fax: (202)223-6835; Email: melville@chpa-info.org • URL: http://www.chpa-info.org • Marketers of nonprescription medicines and dietary supplements, which are packaged and available over-the-counter; associate members include suppliers, consultants, research and testing laboratories, advertising agencies and media. Obtains and disseminates business, legislative, regulatory and scientific information; conducts voluntary labeling review service to assist members in complying with laws and regulations.

***Consumer Product Safety Review***. U. S. Government Printing Office, 732 N Capitol St. NW Washington, DC 20401. Phone: 866-512-1800 or (202)512-1800 or (866)512-1800; Fax: (202)512-2104 or (202)512-2250; Email: contactcenter@gpo.gov • URL: http://www.gpo.gov • Quarterly. $18.00 per year. Issued by the U. S. Consumer Product Safety Commission.

***Consumer Reports***. Consumers Union of United States, 101 Truman Ave. Yonkers, NY 10703-1057. Phone: (914)378-2000 • URL: http://www.consumersunion.org • Monthly. $30 Individuals; $6.95 Individuals monthly. Magazine featuring analyses and investigative reporting of products. Includes *Annual Buying Guide*.

**Consumer Research Center**. The Conference Board, 845 3rd Ave. New York, NY 10022. Phone: (212)339-0232; Fax: (212)836-9754; Email: crc@conference-board.org • URL: http://www.conference-board.org/economics/crc.cfm • Conducts research on the consumer market, including elderly and working women segments.

***Consumer Spain***. Euromonitor International Business Reference Div., 224 S Michigan Ave., Ste. 1500 Chicago, IL 60604. Phone: (312)922-1115; Fax: (312)922-1157; Email: insight@euromonitorintl.com • URL: http://www.euromonitor.com • Irregular. $575. Publication includes: Lists of 100 Spanish companies and retailers. Database includes: List of sources of information on Spain. Entries include: Company name, address, phone, brand and product information, market shares, sales and profits. Principal content of publication is business briefings and analysis of Spain's consumer markets.

**Consumer Specialty Products Association**. 1667 K St. NW, Ste. 300 Washington, DC 20006. Phone: (202)872-8110; Fax: (202)223-2636 • URL: http://www.cspa.org • Formerly National Association Insecticide and Disinfectant Manufacturers.

***Consumer USA: 2010***. Euromonitor International Business Reference Div., 224 S Michigan Ave., Ste. 1500 Chicago, IL 60604. Phone: (312)922-1115; Fax: (312)922-1157; Email: insight@euromonitorintl.com • URL: http://www.euromonitor.com • Annual. $995 Individuals U.S.D. An analytical overview of the U.S. market. Provides historic and forecast volume and value sales statistics on over 330 consumer product sectors. Database includes: Company and brand share data.

**Consumers' Checkbook**. 1625 K St. NW, 8th Fl. Washington, DC 20006. Phone: 800-213-7283; Email: editors@checkbook.org • URL: http://www.checkbook.org • Evaluates local consumer services and retailers in Washington D.C. and San Francisco metropolitan areas.

**Consumers Education and Protective Association International**. 6048 Ogontz Ave. Philadelphia, PA 19141-1347. Phone: (215)424-1441; Fax: (215)424-8045.

***Consumers Guide to Varietal Wines***. Wine Appreciation Guild, 360 Swift Ave. San Francisco, CA 94080. Phone: 800-231-9463 or (650)866-3020; Fax: (650)866-3513; Email: info@wineappreciation.com • URL: http://www.wineappreciation.com • Annual. $45.00.

***Consumer's Research Magazine: Analyzing Consumer Issues***. Consumers' Research, 800 Maryland Ave. NE Washington, DC 20002. Phone: (202)546-1713; Email: crmag@aol.com • Monthly. $24.00 per year.

**Consumers Union of United States**. 101 Truman Ave. Yonkers, NY 10703-1057. Phone: (914)378-2000 • URL: http://www.consumersunion.org • Testing, rating, and reporting organization providing information on competing brands of appliances, automobiles, food products, and household equipment. Aims to provide consumers with information and advice on consumer goods and services; to give information and assistance on all financial matters affecting consumers; to initiate and to cooperate with individual and group efforts seeking to create, maintain, and enhance the quality of life for consumers. Regional offices represent consumer interests in the legislature, courts, and administrative agencies. Derives income from sale of its publication, *Consumer Reports*, and other publications. All subscribers may become members. Produces a syndicated radio program, Report to Consumers; a syndicated newspaper column, *From Consumer Reports*; and television series for cable television, Consumer Reports Presents.

**Consumers United for Rail Equity**. 1050 Thomas Jefferson St. NW, 7th Fl. Washington, DC 20007. Phone: (202)298-1959; Fax: (202)338-2416; Email: sch@vnf.com • URL: http://www.railcure.org • Coalition of railroad shippers that are captive to a single railroad for their transportation needs.

**Contact Lens Association of Ophthalmologists**. 4000 Legato Rd., Ste. 700 Fairfax, VA 22033-9937. Phone: 855-264-8818 or (703)788-5799; Fax: (703)434-3003; Email: eyes@clao.org • URL: http://www.clao.org • Affiliated with American Academy of Ophthalmology, American Medical Association and American National Standards Institute.

***Contact Lens Manufacturers Association—Member Directory***. Contact Lens Manufacturers Association, PO Box 29398 Lincoln, NE 68529. Phone: 800-344-9060 or (402)465-4122; Fax: (402)465-4187 • URL: http://www.clma.net • Annual. Number of listings: 130. Entries include: Company name, address, phone, name and title of contact.

**Contact Lens Manufacturers Association**. PO Box 29398 Lincoln, NE 68529. Phone: 800-344-9060 or (402)465-4122; Fax: (402)465-4187 • URL: http://www.clma.net • Represents contact lens laboratories, material, solution and equipment manufacturers in the United States and abroad. Aims to increase awareness and utilization of custom-manufactured contact lenses.

**Contact Lens Society of America**. 491A Carlisle Dr. Herndon, VA 20170. Phone: 800-296-9776 or (703)437-5100; Fax: (703)437-0727; Email: clsa@clsa.info • URL: http://www.clsa.info • Contact lens fitters; manufacturers of products associated with contact lenses. Aims to share knowledge of contact lens technology and to foster the growth and ability of the contact lens technician throughout the world. Conducts activities such as: developing improvements in instrumentation, fitting procedures, and manufacturing processes; providing a national public relations medium through which information is disseminated to governmental agencies, legislative bodies, and other professional groups. Provides Home Study Course of Contact Lens Fitters. Operates speakers' bureau.

***Contact Peru***. American Chamber of Commerce of Peru, Av. Victor Andres Belaunde 177, San Isidro Lima 27, Peru. Phone: 51 1 7058000; Fax: 51 1 7058026 • URL: http://www.amcham.org.pe • Quarterly. Covers: Member companies and American Chambers of Commerce in Latin America. Entries include: Company name, address, phone, telex.

***Contacts for Kuwaiti Contracting***. International Executive Reports, 717 D St. NW, Ste. 300 Washington, DC 20004-2807. Phone: (202)628-6900; Fax: (202)628-6618 • $195. Covers: business contacts in Kuwait, including Kuwaiti federal and state government agencies; U.S. Defense Reconstruction Assistance Office; Kuwaiti importers, agents, banks, airlines, and hotels; and U.S., British, and German firms actively doing business in Kuwait. Entries include: Name, address.

**Containerization and Intermodal Institute**. PO Box 836 West Caldwell, NJ 07006. Phone: (201)226-0160 or (973)226-0160; Fax: (201)364-1212; Email: info@containerization.org • URL: http://www.containerization.org • Formerly Containerization Institute.

***Contemporary Authors***. Cengage Learning Inc., 20 Channel Center St. Boston, MA 02210. Phone: 800-487-8488 or (617)289-7700; Fax: (617)289-7844; Email: investors@cengage.com • URL: http://www.cengage.com • Contact Gale Customer Service for pricing information.; $336 Individuals. Back volumes available. Provides biographical information on over 130,000 modern authors, including novelists, nonfiction writers, poets, playwrights, journalists, and scriptwriters.

***Contemporary Chief Information Officers: Management Experiences***. Cengage Learning Inc., 20 Channel Center St. Boston, MA 02210. Phone: 800-487-8488 or (617)289-7700; Fax: (617)289-7844; Email: investors@cengage.com • URL: http://www.cengage.com • 2007. eBook. Published by Information Science Reference. Explores the experiences of contemporary Chief Information Officers in the United States, Taiwan, and New Zealand, who agreed to participate and to be identified by name and company.

***Contemporary Drug Problems***. Federal Legal Publications, Inc., 157 Chambers St. New York, NY 10007. Phone: (212)619-4949; Email: flp@bestweb.com • Quarterly. Individuals, $30.00 per year; institutions, $36.00 per year.

***Contemporary Entrepreneurs***. Omnigraphics Inc., PO Box 31-1640 Detroit, MI 48231. Phone: (313)961-1340; Fax: (313)961-1383; Email: customerservice@omnigraphics.com • URL: http://www.omnigraphics.com • Irregular. $95. Covers: Approximately 74 companies often cited as successful and the entrepreneurs who founded them. Entries include: Entrepreneur's name, year of birth, marital status, number of children, type of venture; venture's address, phone, founding, incorporation, revenues, number of employees, original investment, net worth; text describing the history, growth, and vision of the company and entrepreneurial lessons.

***Contemporary Longterm Care***. Leisure Publications Inc., 4160 Wilshire Blvd. Los Angeles, CA 90010-3500. Phone: 800-222-7209 or (323)964-4800; Fax: (323)417-4840 or (323)964-4837; Email: sales@fitnessmgmt.com • URL: http://www.fitnessworld.com • Monthly. Free to qualified personnel. Edited for the long term health care industry, including retirement centers with life care, continuing care communities, and nursing homes.

***Contemporary Musicians***. Cengage Learning Inc., 20 Channel Center St. Boston, MA 02210. Phone: 800-487-8488 or (617)289-7700; Fax: (617)289-7844; Email: investors@cengage.com • URL: http://www.cengage.com • $188 Individuals. Annual. $171.00 per volume. 75 volumes. Provides biographical information on more than 3,600 musical figures in a variety of genres. Also available in eBook format. Contact for pricing.

***Contemporary Research in E-Branding***. Cengage Learning Inc., 20 Channel Center St. Boston, MA 02210. Phone: 800-487-8488 or (617)289-7700; Fax: (617)289-7844; Email: investors@cengage.com • URL: http://www.cengage.com • 2009. eBook. Published by Information Science Reference. Provides research on the emergent issue of the Internet as a central organizing platform for integrating marketing communications.

***Contemporary Theatre, Film & Television***. Cengage Learning Inc., 20 Channel Center St. Boston, MA 02210. Phone: 800-487-8488 or (617)289-7700; Fax: (617)289-7844; Email: investors@cengage.com • URL: http://www.cengage.com • $338 Individuals. 2012. $308.00 per volume. Previous volumes available. Provides detailed biographical and career information on more than 20,000 currently popular performers, directors, writers, producers, designers, managers, choreographers, technicians, composers, executives, dancers, and critics. eBook also available. Contact for pricing.

***Contemporary Women's Issues***. Cengage Learning Inc., 20 Channel Center St. Boston, MA 02210. Phone: 800-487-8488 or (617)289-7700; Fax: (617)289-7844; Email: investors@cengage.com • URL: http://www.cengage.com • Provides full-text articles online from 150 periodicals and a wide variety of additional sources relating to economic, legal, social, political, education, health, and other women's issues. Time span is 1992 to date. Weekly updates. Inquire as to online cost and availability.

***Contingencies: The Magazine of the Actuarial Profession***. American Academy of Actuaries, 1850 M St. NW, Ste. 300 Washington, DC 20036. Phone: (202)223-8196; Fax: (202)872-1948 • URL: http://www.actuary.org • Bimonthly. $24 Nonmembers. Provides non-technical articles on the actuarial aspects of insurance, employee benefits, and pensions.

***Contingent Workforce: Business and Legal Strategies***. ALM Media Properties LLC, 120 Broadway, 5th Fl. New York, NY 10271-1100. Phone: (212)457-9400; Fax: (646)417-7705; Email: customercare@alm.com • URL: http://www.alm.com • $550 print and online; $525 online and eBook. Covers the legal, employee benefit, and taxation aspects of alternative work arrangements (temporary employees, independent contractors, outsourcing). (Law Journal Press).

***Continuing Care News: Supporting the Transition into Post Hospital Care***. Stevenson Publishing Corp., 5151 Beltline Rd., 10th Fl. Dallas, TX 75254. Phone: (972)687-6700; Fax: (972)687-6769 • URL: http://www.stevenspublishing.com • Monthly. $99.00 per year. Topics include insurance, legal issues, health business news, ethics, and case management. Includes annual *Buyer's Guide*.

***Continuous Computing Technologies for Enhancing Business Continuity***. Cengage Learning Inc., 20 Channel Center St. Boston, MA 02210. Phone: 800-487-8488 or (617)289-7700; Fax: (617)289-7844; Email: investors@cengage.com • URL: http://www.cengage.com • 2009. eBook. Provides an explanation of business continuity, business continuity management, and continuous computing technologies. Covers topics such as clustering technologies, fault tolerance, and technologies for reducing downtime.

***Contra Costa County Business Directory***. Rich's Business Directories Inc., 1820 Gateway Blvd., Ste. 170 San Mateo, CA 94404. Phone: 800-969-7424 or (650)362-1020; Fax: (650)350-4084; Email: info@richsdata.com • URL: http://www.hightechdirectories.com • $199 Individuals online; $450 Individuals database. Entries include: Company name, address, phone, fax, year established, branch or headquarters, SIC code, and product type.

***Contract Management***. National Contract Management Association, 21740 Beaumeade Cir., Ste. 125 Ashburn, VA 20147. Phone: 800-344-8096 or (571)382-0082 or (703)448-9231; Fax: (703)448-0939; Email: wearelistening@ncmahq.org • URL: http://www.ncmahq.org • Monthly. $158 Individuals non-members; $178 Other countries international non-members. Trade magazine for contract management professionals.

**Contract Services Association of America**. 1000 Wilson Blvd., Ste. 1800 Arlington, VA 22209-3920. Phone: (703)243-2020; Fax: (703)243-3601; Email: info@csa-dc.org • URL: http://www.csa-dc.org • Formerly National Council of Technical Services Industries.

***Contract: The Business Magazine of Commercial and Institutional Interior Design, and Architecture, Planning and Construction***. Nielsen Business Media Inc., 770 Broadway New York, NY 10003-9522. Phone: 866-890-8541 or (646)654-4500 or (646)654-5000; Fax: (646)654-5584 or (646)654-4500; Email: bmcomm@nielsen.com • URL: http://www.nielsenbusinessmedia.com • Monthly. $94.00 per year. Firms engaged in specifying furniture and furnishings for commercial installations. Formerly *Contract Design*.

**Contractors Pump Bureau**. 6737 W Washington St., Ste. 2400 Milwaukee, WI 53214-5647. Phone: (414)272-0943; Fax: (414)272-1170; Email: aem@aem.org • URL: http://www.aem.org/Groups/Groups/Group.asp?G=22 • A bureau of the Association of Equipment Manufacturers. Manufacturers of pumping machinery and engines for the construction industry; suppliers to the manufacturers. Works toward the standardization of sizes and capacities of contractors' pumps.

***Control Engineering: Covering Control, Instrumentation and Automation Systems Worldwide***. Reed Elsevier Group plc Reed Business Information, 360 Park Ave. S New York, NY 11010. Phone: (212)791-4208; Email: corporatecommunications@reedbusiness.com • URL: http://www.reedbusiness.com • Monthly. $109.90 per year.

***Convalescent Homes Directory***. InfoGroup Inc., 5711 S 86th Cir. Omaha, NE 68127-4146. Phone: (402)593-4500 • URL: http://www.infogroup.com • Annual. Number of listings: 2,178. Entries include: Name, address, phone, size of advertisement, name of owner or manager, number of employees, year first in "Yellow Pages." Compiled from telephone company "Yellow Pages," nationwide.

**Convenience Caterers and Food Manufacturers Association.** 1205 Spartan Dr. Madison Heights, MI 48071. Phone: (248)982-5379; Email: ccfma@ymail.com • URL: http://www.mobilecaterers.com • Firms and corporations engaged in the mobile catering business and in any other business catering to industrial feeding by mobile equipment; associate members are suppliers and manufacturers. Deals with common intra-industry problems through exchange of ideas, advice on legal problems, and safety standards and licensing regulations.

***Convenience Distribution.*** American Wholesale Marketers Association, 2750 Prosperity Ave., Ste. 530 Fairfax, VA 22031. Phone: 800-482-2962; Fax: (703)573-5738 • URL: http://www.awmanet.org • Weekly. Members free; $36 Nonmembers print and online (U.S.); $66 Nonmembers print and online (outside the U.S.); $20 Nonmembers online only. *Distribution Channels.* Official magazine of the American Wholesale Marketers Association (AWMA), owned and published by AWMA.

***Convenience Store Decisions.*** Donohue-Meehan Publishing Co., Two Greenwood Square, Suite 410, 3331 Street Rd. Bensalem, PA 19020-2023. Phone: (215)245-4555; Fax: (215)245-4060 • Monthly. $60.00 per year. Edited for headquarters and regional management personnel of convenience store chains.

***Convenience Store News: The Information Source for the Industry.*** Nielsen Business Media Inc., 770 Broadway New York, NY 10003-9522. Phone: 866-890-8541 or (646)654-4500 or (646)654-5000; Fax: (646)654-5584 or (646)654-4500; Email: bmcomm@nielsen.com • URL: http://www.nielsenbusinessmedia.com • 15 times a year. Free to qualified personnel; others, $89.00 per year. Contains news of industry trends and merchandising techniques.

***Convergence: The Journal of Research Into New Media Technologies.*** Reed Elsevier Group plc Reed Business Information, 360 Park Ave. S New York, NY 11010. Phone: (212)791-4208; Email: corporatecommunications@reedbusiness.com • URL: http://www.reedbusiness.com • Monthly. Individuals, $40.00 per year; institutions, $160.00 per year. Covers the merging of communications technologies. Includes telecommunications networks, interactive TV, multimedia, wireless phone service, and electronic information services.

**Conveyor Equipment Manufacturers Association.** 5672 Strand Ct., Ste. 2 Naples, FL 34110. Phone: (239)514-3441; Fax: (239)514-3470 • URL: http://www.cemanet.org • Manufacturers and engineers of conveyors and conveying systems and portable and stationary machinery used in the transportation of raw materials and finished products in warehouses and on assembly line operations. Aims to standardize design, manufacture and application of conveying machinery and component parts.

**Cookie and Snack Bakers Association.** c/o Craig Parrish, Executive Director, 1128 Maple Dr. NW Cleveland, TN 37312. Phone: (423)280-8056; Email: csparrish@bellsouth.net • URL: http://www.casba.us • Members are bakers of snacks and cookies.

***Cooking for Profit.*** CP Publishing Inc., P.O. Box 267 Fond du Lac, WI 54936-0267. Phone: (920)923-3700; Fax: (920)923-6805; Email: comments@cookingforprofit.com • URL: http://www.cookingforprofit.com • Monthly. $25.00 per year. The challenge of operations management in the food service industry.

**Cookware Manufacturers Association.** PO Box 531335 Birmingham, AL 35253-1335. Phone: (205)592-0389; Fax: (205)599-5598 • URL: http://www.cookware.org • Represents manufacturers of cooking utensils and cooking accessories. Compiles statistics.

***Cooperative Housing Bulletin.*** National Association of Housing Cooperatives, 1444 I St. NW, Ste. 700 Washington, DC 20005-6542. Phone: (202)737-0797; Fax: (202)216-9646; Email: info@nahc.coop • URL: http://www.coophousing.org • Quarterly. $75 per year. Includes *Cooperative Housing Journal*.

**Cooperative Program in Metallurgy.** Pennsylvania State University, Dept. of Materials and Engineering, 124 Steidle Bldg. University Park, PA 16802. Phone: (814)865-3760; Fax: (814)865-2917; Email: rx7@psu.edu • URL: http://www.matse.psu.edu.

**Cooperative State Research, Education, and Extension Service - Small and Home-Based Business.** 4435 Waterfront Ctr., 800 9th St. SW Washington, DC 20250. Phone: (202)720-5997; Fax: (202)690-2975; Email: amclaren@csrees.usda.gov • URL: http://www.csrees.usda.gov/smallhomebasedbusiness.cfm • Women-owned and operated farms and ranches, rural entrepreneurship, small and home-based businesses.

**Coordinating Committee of Agriculture, Commercial, Industrial and Financial Associations.** Route 6, 9-21, Zone 4, Level 9 01004 Guatemala City, Guatemala. Phone: 502 2201-0000; Email: unice@cacif.org.gt • URL: http://www.cacif.org.gt.

***Copier.*** Orion Research Corp., 14555 N Scottsdale Rd., Ste. 330 Scottsdale, AZ 85254. Phone: 800-844-0759 or (480)951-1114; Fax: (480)951-1117 or (800)375-1315 • Annual. $39 Individuals. Quotes retail and wholesale prices of used office equipment. Original list prices and years of manufacture are also shown.

**Copper and Brass Fabricators Council.** 3050 K St. NW, Ste. 400 Washington, DC 20007-5108. Phone: (202)833-8575; Fax: (202)342-8451 • URL: http://www.cbfc.us • Formerly Copper and Brass Fabricators Foreign Trade Association.

**Copper and Brass Servicenter Association.** 6734 W 121st St. Overland Park, KS 66209. Phone: (913)396-0697; Fax: (913)345-1006; Email: cbsahq@copper-brass.org • URL: http://www.copper-brass.org • Represents wholesalers of copper and brass sheet, tubing, pipe, and related products; supplier members are copper mills, metal strip platters and re-rollers. Compiles statistics.

**Copper Development Association.** 260 Madison Ave. New York, NY 10016-2401. Phone: (212)251-7200; Fax: (212)251-7234; Email: questions@copperalliance.us • URL: http://www.copper.org • Represents U.S. and foreign copper mining, smelting and refining companies, U.S. fabricating companies such as brass and wire mills, foundries, and ingot makers. Seeks to expand the uses and applications and to broaden the markets of copper and copper products. Functions in groups or divisions corresponding to principal market areas such as transportation, building construction, electrical and electronic products, industrial machinery and equipment, and consumer and general products. Provides technical service to users of copper and copper alloy products. Has industrywide responsibility for market statistics and research. Maintains 10 field offices in the U.S.

***Copy Editor: Language News for the Publishing Profession.*** McMurry Newsletters, 1010 E. Missouri Ave. Phoenix, AZ 85014. Phone: 888-626-8779 or (602)395-5850 • URL: http://www.copyeditor.com • Bimonthly. Newsletter for professional copy editors and proofreaders. Includes such items as "Top Ten Resources for Copy Editors.".

***Copying & Duplicating Machine & Supplies Directory.*** InfoGroup Inc., 5711 S 86th Cir. Omaha, NE 68127-4146. Phone: (402)593-4500 • URL: http://www.infogroup.com • Annual. Number of listings: 10,350. Entries include: Name, address, phone (including area code), size of advertisement, year first in "Yellow Pages." Coding indicates brands carried, specialties, or franchises held. Franchise editions also available. Compiled from telephone company "Yellow Pages," nationwide.

***Copying & Duplicating Service Directory.*** InfoGroup Inc., 5711 S 86th Cir. Omaha, NE 68127-4146. Phone: (402)593-4500 • URL: http://www.infogroup.com • Annual. Number of listings: 20,946. Entries include: Company name, address, phone (including area code), size of advertisement, year first in "Yellow Pages," name of owner or manager, number of employees. Compiled from telephone company "Yellow Pages," nationwide.

***Copyright Bulletin: Quarterly Review.*** Bernan Associates, 4611 Assembly Dr., Ste. F Lanham, MD 20706-4843. Phone: 800-416-4385 or (301)459-2255 or (301)459-7666; Fax: (301)459-0056 or (800)865-3450; Email: query@bernan.com • URL: http://www.bernan.com • Quarterly. Available online only.

**Copyright Clearance Center.** 222 Rosewood Dr., No. 910 Danvers, MA 01923-4510. Phone: (978)750-8400; Fax: (508)741-2318 or (978)646-8600; Email: info@copyright.com • URL: http://www.copyright.com • Facilitates compliance with U.S. copyright law. Provides licensing systems for the reproduction and distribution of copyrighted materials in print and electronic formats throughout the world. Manages rights relating to over 1.75 million works and represents more than 9600 publishers and hundreds of thousands of authors and other creators, directly or through their representatives.

***Copyright Society of the United States of America Journal.*** Copyright Society of the U.S.A., 1 East 53rd St., 8th Fl. New York, NY 10022. • URL: http://www.csusa.org • Quarterly. Individuals, $125.00 per year; nonprofit organizations, $50.00 per year; corporations, $500.00 per year.

**Copyright Society of the U.S.A.** 1 East 53rd St., 8th Fl. New York, NY 10022. • URL: http://www.csusa.org • Lawyers and laymen; libraries, universities, publishers, and firms interested in the protection and study of rights in music, literature, art, motion pictures, and other forms of intellectual property. Promotes research in the field of copyright; encourages study of economic and technological aspects of copyright by those who deal with problems of communication, book publishing, motion picture production, and television and radio broadcasting. Seeks better understanding among students and scholars of copyright in foreign countries, to lay a foundation for development of international copyright. Co-sponsors (with New York University School of Law) the Walter J. Derenberg Copyright and Trademark Library, which includes foreign periodicals dealing with literary and artistic property and related fields. Sponsors symposia and lectures on copyright. Encourages study of copyright in U.S. law schools.

**Cordage Institute.** 994 Old Eagle School Rd., Ste. 1019 Wayne, PA 19087. Phone: (610)971-4854; Fax: (610)971-4859; Email: info@cordageinstitute.com • URL: http://www.ropecord.com • Represents manufacturers of natural and synthetic fiber cordage, in constructions, industry suppliers, consultants, and machinery manufacturers. Offers standard technical information and educational programs. Operates speakers' bureau. Compiles statistics.

***Cordele-Crisp Chamber of Commerce—Business Directory.*** Cordele-Crisp Chamber of Commerce, PO Box 158 Cordele, GA 31010. Phone: (229)273-1668; Fax: (229)273-5132; Email: info@cordelecrispga.com • URL: http://cordelecrispga.com • Annual. Covers businesses and firms in Crisp County.

***CORE Magazine.*** Congress of Racial Equality. CORE Publications, 817 Broadway, 3rd Fl. New York, NY 10003-4709. Phone: 800-439-2673 or (212)598-4000; Fax: (212)982-0184; Email: core@core-online.org • URL: http://www.core-online.org • Quarterly. $10.00 per year.

***Corn and Soybean Digest.*** American Soybean Association. Penton, 1166 Avenue of the Americas New York, NY 10036. Phone: (212)204-4200; Email: information@penton.com • URL: http://www.penton.com • Weekly. 11 times a year. $25.00 per year. Provides high acreage farmers who grow soy beans in rotation with other crops timely production, marketing and management information.

***Corn Annual.*** Corn Refiners Association, 1701 Pennsylvania Ave. NW, Ste. 950 Washington, DC 20006. Phone: (202)331-1634 or (202)534-3494; Fax: (202)331-2054; Email: comments@corn.org • URL: http://www.corn.org • Annual. Annual.

**Corn Refiners Association.** 1701 Pennsylvania Ave. NW, Ste. 950 Washington, DC 20006. Phone: (202)331-1634 or (202)534-3494; Fax: (202)331-2054; Email: comments@corn.org • URL: http://www.corn.org • Corn refining firms that manufacture corn starches, sugars, syrups, oils, feed and alcohol by wet process.

***The Cornell Hotel and Restaurant Administration Quarterly.*** Cornell University School of Hotel Administration. Pine Forge Press, 2455 Teller Rd. Thousand Oaks, CA 91320-2234. Phone: 800-818-7243 or (805)499-4224 or (805)499-9774; Fax: (805)499-0871 or (805)583-2665; Email: sales@pfp.sagepub.com • URL: http://www.sagepub.com/sociologybooks • Bimonthly. Individuals, $113.00 per year; institutions, $319.00 per year.

**Cornell University - Agricultural Experiment Station.** 240 Roberts Hall Ithaca, NY 14853-5905. Phone: (607)255-2552; Fax: (607)255-9499; Email: cuaes@cornell.edu • URL: http://www.cuaes.cornell.edu/cuaes.

**Cornell University - Cornell Cooperative Extension.** Kennedy Hall, Box 26 Ithaca, NY 14853. Phone: (607)255-0789 or (607)255-2237; Fax: (607)255-0788; Email: ck236@cornell.edu • URL: http://cce.cornell.edu/Pages/Default.aspx • Coordinates campus research with needs of residents of the State of New York. Activities focus on five broad areas, including children, youth and family well-being; community and economic vitality; environmental and natural resource enhancement; agricultural and food systems sustainability; and nutrition, health and safety.

**Cornell University - Program in International Studies in Planning.** 106 W Sibley Hall Ithaca, NY 14853-3901. Phone: (607)255-4331 or (607)255-4613; Fax: (607)255-1971; Email: wwg1@cornell.edu • URL: http://aap.cornell.edu/crp/programs/grad/internation-studies.cfm • Research activities are related to international urban and regional planning, with emphasis on developing areas.

**Cornell University - Toxic Chemicals Laboratory.** New York State College of Agriculture, Tower Rd. Ithaca, NY 14853-7401. Phone: (607)255-4538; Fax: (607)255-0599; Email: djl22@cornell.edu.

***Corporate Acquisitions.*** ARCH Group, 55 Main St. Tiburon, CA 94920. Phone: (415)435-2175; Fax: (415)435-6310; Email: nrca@archgroup.org • Description: Summaries of trends and analysis of transactions in corporate mergers and acquisitions. Recurring features include interviews, reports of meetings, book reviews, and companies listed for sale.

***Corporate Affiliations.*** LexisNexis, 9443 Springboro Pke. Dayton, OH 45342. Phone: 800-227-4908 or (937)865-6800; Fax: (937)865-1211; Email: legalnotices@lexisnexis.com • URL: http://www.bender.com • Annual. $2,395 8 volume set. Covers: Business and financial information on approximately 3,800 U.S. parent companies and 44,500 subsidiaries, divisions, and affiliates worldwide, as well as 140,000 key executives. Entries include: Sales, assets, liabilities, ownership percentage.

***Corporate Affiliations Plus.*** LexisNexis, 9443 Springboro Pke. Dayton, OH 45342. Phone: 800-227-4908 or (937)865-6800; Fax: (937)865-1211; Email: legalnotices@lexisnexis.com • URL: http://www.bender.com • Quarterly. $2,595 Individuals 12 month single-user license (database); $3,985 Individuals premium. CD-ROM. Covers corporate statistics and current financial information on over 30,000 domestic and foreign parent companies and their 145,000 subsidiaries, as well as 306,000 key executives. Entries include: Sales, assets, liabilities, ownership percentage.

***Corporate and Business Law Journal.*** National Centre for Corporate Law and Policy Research, Phone: 61 262015768; Fax: 61 262015764; Email: lawinfo@management.canberra.edu.au • Semiannual. $44 Individuals. Law periodical.

***Corporate Board Member: The Magazine for Directors of Public Companies.*** Board Member Inc., 5110 Maryland Way, Ste. 250 Brentwood, TN 37027. Phone: (615)309-3200; Fax: (615)371-0899; Email: boardmember@boardmember.com • URL: http://www.boardmember.com • Quarterly. $115.00 per year. Edited for board members of publicly traded corporations. Includes such topics as liability, executive compensation, mergers, corporate administration, and management succession.

***The Corporate Contributions Plan: From Strategy to Budget.*** The Conference Board, 845 3rd Ave. New York, NY 10022-6601. Phone: (212)759-0900 or (212)339-0345; Fax: (212)980-7014 or (212)836-9740; Email: membership@conferenceboard.org • URL: http://www.conference-board.org • Annual. Members, $30.00, non-members, $120.00.

***Corporate Control Alert; A Report on Current Changes for Corporate Control.*** ALM Media Properties LLC, 120 Broadway, 5th Fl. New York, NY 10271-1100. Phone: (212)457-9400; Fax: (646)417-7705; Email: customercare@alm.com • URL: http://www.alm.com • Monthly. $1,595 per year. A monthly mergers and acquisitions newsletter.

***Corporate Controller.*** Thomson RIA, 195 Broadway New York, NY 10007-3100. Phone: 800-431-9025 or (212)367-6300 or (212)807-2298; Fax: (212)367-6305 or (212)337-4207; Email: ttacommunications@riag.com • URL: http://www.ria.thomson.com • $420. Bimonthly.

***Corporate Counselor.*** ALM Media Properties LLC, 120 Broadway, 5th Fl. New York, NY 10271-1100. Phone: (212)457-9400; Fax: (646)417-7705; Email: customercare@alm.com • URL: http://www.alm.com • Monthly. $459 /year. Covers issues involved with managing the legal department of a corporation, including relations with outside counsel. (A Law Journal Newsletter, formerly published by Leader Publications).

***The Corporate Directory of U.S. Public Companies.*** Grey House Publishing, 4919 Rte. 22 Amenia, NY 12501. Phone: 800-562-2139 or (518)789-8700; Fax: (518)789-0556; Email: books@greyhouse.com • URL: http://www.greyhouse.com • Annual. Covers: More than 11,000 publicly held corporations traded on the New York or American exchanges, NASDAQ, or other over-the-counter markets. Includes foreign companies filing American Depositary Receipts. Database includes: List of acronyms and common terms. Entries include: Company name, address, phone, stock data, business description, primary and additional Standard Industrial Classification (SIC) code, major subsidiaries, officers, directors, owners, and financial data.

***Corporate Disasters: What Went Wrong and Why.*** Cengage Learning Inc., 20 Channel Center St. Boston, MA 02210. Phone: 800-487-8488 or (617)289-7700; Fax: (617)289-7844; Email: investors@cengage.com • URL: http://www.cengage.com • Covers corporate misdeeds and mistakes in business. Published June 2012. Available in print ($483) and eBook.

***Corporate EFT Report.*** Phillips International, Inc., 7811 Montrose Rd. Potomac, MD 20854. Phone: (301)340-2100; Email: information@phillips.com • URL: http://www.phillips.com • Biweekly. $695.00 per year. Newsletter on subject of electronic funds transfer.

***Corporate Finance Sourcebook: The Guide to Major Capital Investment Sources and Related Financial Services.*** LexisNexis, 9443 Springboro Pke. Dayton, OH 45342. Phone: 800-227-4908 or (937)865-6800; Fax: (937)865-1211; Email: legalnotices@lexisnexis.com • URL: http://www.bender.com • Annual. $695 Individuals list price; $556 Individuals. Covers: Securities research analysts; major private lenders; investment banking firms; commercial banks; United States-based foreign banks; commercial finance firms; leasing companies; foreign investment bankers in the United States; pension managers; banks that offer master trusts; cash managers; business insurance brokers; business real estate specialists; lists about 3,500 firms; 14,500 key financial experts. Entries include: All entries include firm name, address, phone, e-mail, and names and titles of officers, contacts, or specialists in corporate finance. Additional details are given as appropriate, including names of major clients, number of companies served, services, total assets, branch locations, years in business.

***Corporate Financing Week: The Newsweekly of Corporate Finance, Investment Banking and M and A.*** Institutional Investor Inc. Journals Group, 225 Park Ave. S New York, NY 10003. Phone: 800-437-9997 or (212)224-3570; Email: info@iijournals.com • URL: http://www.iijournals.com • Weekly. $2,550.00 per year. Includes print and online editions. Newsletter for corporate finance officers. Emphasis is on debt and equity financing, mergers, leveraged buyouts, investment banking, and venture capital.

***Corporate 500: Directory of Corporate Philanthropy.*** Public Management Institute, 358 Brannen St. San Francisco, CA 94107. Phone: (415)896-1900 • Annual. $375 plus $10.00 shipping. Covers: 554 major corporations with philanthropic programs. Entries include: Corporation name, corporate foundation name (if applicable), address, philanthropic interests and priorities, policy statement, contribution committee members, financial profile, activities eligible for funding, contact person, sample grants, application procedures, analysis of giving patterns.

***Corporate Giving Directory.*** Information Today, Inc., 143 Old Marlton Pke. Medford, NJ 08055-8750. Phone: 800-300-9868 or (609)654-6266; Fax: (609)654-4309; Email: custserv@infotoday.com • URL: http://www.infotoday.com • Annual. $699.50 Individuals softbound; plus $20 shipping and handling; $629.55 First-time standing order. Covers: Top 1,000 major corporation- and company-sponsored foundations and direct-giving programs. Database includes: Appendix to abridged entries of more than 2,000 additional funders. Entries include: Giving program's sponsoring company name, address, phone, fax, e-mail, website; names and biographies of living officers, and contact person; grants data, including types, average amounts, sample grants; application procedures; analysis of giving priorities; and information on the company, including products, Fortune rank, sales, ticker symbol/stock exchange information, operating locations, number of employees, information on employee-matching gifts (including restrictions and ratio), and nonmonetary support.

***Corporate Giving Yellow Pages: Guide to Corporate Giving Contacts.*** Taft Group, 27500 Drake Rd. Farmington Hills, MI 48331-3535. Phone: 800-877-4253 or (248)699-4253 or (248)699-GALE; Fax: (800)414-5043 or (248)699-8061; Email: gale.salesassistance@thomson.com • URL: http://www.gale.com/taft • $99. Covers: more than 3,500 corporate contact persons with information on corporate charitable giving. Entries include: Company name, address, phone, fax, name and title of contact, name of company foundation (if any).

***Corporate Growth.*** Princeton Research Institute, Western Management Center Scottsdale, AZ 85252-2702. Phone: (609)396-0305 • Monthly. $198.00 per year.

***The Corporate Handbook.*** Riddell Information Services Proprietary Ltd., 19 Havilah St. Chatsworth, NSW 2065, Australia. Phone: 2 3682100 or 02 9935700; Fax: 2 3682150 or 02 99352777 • Annual. $145. Covers: over 400 corporate service agencies, consultancies, and suppliers in Australia. Database includes: Articles on how to identify and select appropriate companies; overviews of industry categories. Entries include: Company name, address, phone, fax, names and titles of key personnel, qualifications and experience, description of services, recent clients and projects, fee structure information, financial data.

***Corporate Philanthropy in New England.*** Development and Technical Assistance Center Inc., 70 Audubon St. New Haven, CT 06510. Phone: 800-788-5598 or (203)772-1345; Fax: (203)777-1614 • Irregular. $80 Connecticut; $5 Maine; $5 Vermont; $16.95 Rhode Island. Corporations in New England that have gross sales of over $10 million or at least 200 employees and an office in the state and that have given grants or have other funding programs; separate editions available for Connecticut, Maine, New Hampshire, Rhode Island, and Vermont.

***Corporate Public Issues and Their Management: The Executive Systems Approach to Public Policy Formation.*** Issue Action Publications Inc., 207 Loudoun St. SE Leesburg, VA 20175. Phone: (703)777-8450; Fax: (703)777-8484; Email: info@issueactionpublications.com • URL: http://www.issueactionpublications.com • Monthly. $195. Covers the approach to public policy creation.

***Corporate Report Fact Book.*** City Media Inc., • URL: http://www.corpreport.com • Annual. $147. Covers: about 320 public corporations in the Ninth Federal Reserve District (Minnesota, North and South Dakota, Montana, upper Michigan, and northwestern Wisconsin) having stock actively traded; 1,550 privately owned companies with over 50 employees; 650 regional operations with over 50 employees, 115 non-profit corporations; 600 top executives in businesses of the upper Midwest. Entries include: For public companies—Company name, address, phone, fax; names of officers, directors, and major shareholders; profile, two-year balance sheet and five-year earnings history; recent events, recent four quarters results; number of employees, number of stockholders; general counsel, auditors; state and year of incorporation, transfer agent and registrar, subsidiaries, SIC codes. For private and nonprofit companies and regional operations—Name, address, phone, fax, names of principal executives; revenue (if provided), description of business, number of employees, corporate affiliations, year established. For top executives—Name, title, affiliation, office address and phone, date and place of birth; personal, education, and career data; awards, activities, memberships.

**Corporate Responsibility Association.** 123 S Broad St., Ste. 1930 Philadelphia, PA 19109. Phone: (215)606-9520; Fax: (267)800-2701 • URL: http://www.croassociation.org • Seeks to advance the corporate responsibility officers (CRO) community and its role within corporations. Strengthens the community of practice across all corporate responsibility disciplines. Establishes professional development and certification programs for corporate responsibility officers.

**Corporate Social Responsibility Association.** 155 E Boardwalk Dr., No. 544 Fort Collins, CO 80525. Phone: (303)944-4225; Fax: (303)496-0437; Email: jhall@csrassn.com • URL: http://csrassn.com • Promotes information gathering, networking and implementation of corporate social responsibility. Works to integrate ethical, social and environmental concerns in business. Supports best management practices in consolidating corporate social responsibility.

**Corporate Speech Pathology Network.** 10 Glenlake Pkwy., Ste. 130 Atlanta, GA 30328. Phone: (678)592-0052 • URL: http://www.corspan.org • Represents the interests of corporate speech pathologists and other individuals and corporations exploring speech training. Seeks to promote and improve speech in the business and corporate settings. Encourages members to share information and ideas.

**Corporate Voices for Working Families.** 1020 19th St. NW, Ste. 750 Washington, DC 20036. Phone: (202)467-8130; Fax: (202)467-8140; Email: dklein@corporatevioces.org • URL: http://www.cvworkingfamilies.org • Represents the private sector on public policy issues involving working families. Aims to improve the lives of working families and the competitiveness of American businesses. Facilitates research and provides solutions to legislators and businesses on issues important to America's working families.

**Corporation for Public Broadcasting.** 401 9th St. NW Washington, DC 20004. Phone: 800-272-2190 or (202)879-9600; Fax: (202)879-9699; Email: oigemail@cpb.org • URL: http://www.cpb.org • Promotes and finances the growth and development of noncommercial radio and television. Makes grants to local public television and radio stations, program producers, and program distribution networks; studies emerging technologies; works to provide adequate long-range financing from the U.S. government and other sources for public broadcasting. Supports children's services; compiles statistics; sponsors training programs.

***Correctional News.*** Emlen Publications, Inc., 1241 Andersen Dr., Ste. N San Rafael, FL 94901. Phone: 800-965-8876 or (415)460-6185; Fax: (415)460-6288; Email: info@emlen.com • URL: http://www.correctionalnews.com • Bimonthly. Free to qualified personnel. Only available online.

***Corrections Today.*** American Correctional Association, 206 N Washington St., Ste. 200 Alexandria, VA 22314. Phone: 800-222-5646 or (703)224-0000; Fax: (703)224-0179 • URL: http://www.aca.org • 6/year. $25 Individuals. Magazine covering corrections, law enforcement, and rehabilitation. Includes "Annual Architecture, Construction, and Design Issue" on prisons and other correctional facilities.

***Corridor Directory.*** Miller Freeman UK Ltd., Miller Freeman House, Sovereign Way Tonbridge TN9 1RW, United Kingdom. Phone: 44 1732 364422; Fax: 44 1732 377137; Email: pbutler@unmf.com • Database covers: More than 10,000 UK manufacturers, retailers, agents, wholesalers, service suppliers, and associations in the furniture and furnishings industry. Entries include: Company information.

***Corrosion Abstracts: Abstracts of the World's Literature on Corrosion and Corrosion Mitigation.*** National Association of Corrosion Engineers, CSA, 7200 Wisconsin Ave. Bethesda, MD 20814. Phone: 800-843-7751 or (301)961-6700; Fax: (301)961-6720; Email: service@csa.com • URL: http://www.csa.com • Monthly. $240 Individuals per year; $340 Institutions per year. Includes print and online editions. Provides abstracts of the worldwide literature of corrosion and corrosion control. Also available on CD-ROM.

***Corrosion: Journal of Science and Engineering.*** National Association of Corrosion Engineers. NACE International: The Corrosion Society, 1440 S Creek Dr. Houston, TX 77084-4906. Phone: 800-797-6223 or (281)228-6200 or (281)228-6223; Fax: (281)228-6300; Email: firstservice@nace.org • URL: http://www.nace.org • Monthly. Individuals, $160.00 per year; institutions, $290.00 per year. Covers corrosion control science, theory, engineering, and practice.

**Cosmetic Executive Women.** 286 Madison Ave., 19th Fl. New York, NY 10017. Phone: (212)685-5955 or (646)929-8000; Fax: (212)685-3334 • URL: http://cew.org • Women in the cosmetic and allied industries. Unites women executives in the cosmetic field for industry awareness and business advancement. Promotes products, people, professional development and philanthropy.

***Cosmetic World News: The International News Magazine of the Perfumery, Cosmetic s and Toiletries Industry.*** World News Publications, 130 Wigmore St. London W1H 0AT, United Kingdom. Fax: (171) 4875436 • Bimonthly. $192.00 per year.

***Cosmetics & Toiletries—Cosmetic Bench Reference.*** • Annual. $199 Individuals. Publication includes: List of cosmetic ingredient suppliers. Entries include: Supplier name, address, phone, fax, chemicals, trade names. Principal content of publication is data on cosmetic ingredients, with label names, trade names, functions, EINECS, INCI names, and CAS numbers.

***Cosmetics and Toiletries: The International Journal of Cosmetic Technology.*** Allured Business Media, 336 Gundersen Dr., Ste. A Carol Stream, IL 60188-2403. Phone: (630)653-2155; Fax: (630)653-2192; Email: customerservice@allured.com • URL: http://www.allured.com • $98 U.S.; $137 Canada; $189 Other countries.

***Cosmetology Schools Directory.*** InfoGroup Inc., 5711 S 86th Cir. Omaha, NE 68127-4146. Phone: (402)593-4500 • URL: http://www.infogroup.com • Annual. Number of listings: 2,069. Entries include: Name, address, phone, size of advertisement, name of owner or manager, number of employees, year first in "Yellow Pages." Compiled from telephone company "Yellow Pages," nationwide.

***Cost of Doing Business.*** Associated Equipment Distributors, 600 22nd St., Ste. 220 Oak Brook, IL 60523. Phone: 800-388-0650 or (630)574-0650; Fax: (630)574-0132; Email: info@aednet.org • URL: http://www.aednet.org • Annual. $595 Members non-participants; $1,095 Nonmembers non-participant; $225 for members; $375 for nonmembers. For construction equipment distributors covering business costs, sales, and financial data.

***Cost of Doing Business Report.*** American Rental Association, 1900 19th St. Moline, IL 61265-4179. Phone: 800-334-2177 or (309)764-2475; Fax: (309)764-1533 • URL: http://www.

ararental.org • $650 Nonmembers; $300 Members.

*Cost of Doing Business Survey*. National Sporting Goods Association, 1601 Feehanville Dr., Ste. 300 Mount Prospect, IL 60056. Phone: 800-815-5422; Fax: (847)391-9827; Email: info@nsga.org • URL: http://www.nsga.org • Biennial. Includes income statements, balance sheets, sales per employee, sales per square foot, inventory turnover, etc.

*Cost of Doing Business Survey*. Professional School Photographers Association International, 3000 Picture Pl. Jackson, MI 49201. Phone: 800-762-9287 or (517)788-8100; Fax: (517)788-8371; Email: m.bell@bellphoto.com • URL: http://www.pmai.org • Biennial. $99. Emphasis is on photographic retailing.

*Costa Rica Investment and Business Guide*. International Business Publications, USA, PO Box 15343 Washington, DC 20003. Phone: (202)546-2103; Fax: (202)546-3275; Email: ibpusa@comcast.net • URL: http://ibpus.com • $99.95 Individuals hardcopy, e-book, CD-ROM. Covers: Strategic and business information, business contacts, and business travel. Entries include: Basic information on economy, business, export-import and investment climate, opportunities, and regulations.

*The Costco Connection: A Lifestyle Magazine for Small Business*. BPA International, 270 Madison Ave. New York, NY 10016-0699. Phone: (212)779-3200; Fax: (212)725-1721 • Monthly. Magazine serving small businesses who are members of Costco Wholesale.

*Costume Jewelry: Industry Sector Profile*. Philippine-German Export Development Project Philippine Bureau of Export Trade Promotion, 6F Trade & Industry Bldg., 361 Sen. Gil Puyat Ave. Makati PH-1226, Philippines. Phone: 63 2 897 8199; Email: web@dti.dti.gov.ph • URL: http://www.dti. gov.ph Publication includes: Companies exporting costume jewelry from the Philippines. Entries include: Company name, address, phone, fax, name and title of contact, type of business, year established, subsidiary and branch names and locations, financial data, number of employees, government registrations, professional memberships, bank references, supply capability, export experience, business plan. Principal content of publication is an overview of the business environment and costume jewelry industry in the Philippines.

*Cote d'Ivoire Investment and Business Guide*. International Business Publications, USA, PO Box 15343 Washington, DC 20003. Phone: (202)546-2103; Fax: (202)546-3275; Email: ibpusa@comcast.net • URL: http://ibpus.com • $99.95 Individuals hardcopy, e-book, CD-ROM. Covers: Basic information on economy, export-import and investment climate, regulations and industrial development, banking, and government. Entries include: Important business contacts and business travel.

*Cotton Council International Buyers' Guide*. Cotton Council International, 1521 New Hampshire Ave. NW Washington, DC 20036. Phone: (202)745-7805; Fax: (202)483-4040; Email: cottonusa@cotton.org • URL: http://www.cottonusa. org • Covers: Exporters of U.S. raw cotton. Entries include: Company name, addresses of exporting companies, production and ginning seasons, and official U.S. cotton standards, packaging, and transportation data.

*Cotton Council International*. 1521 New Hampshire Ave. NW Washington, DC 20036. Phone: (202)745-7805; Fax: (202)483-4040; Email: cottonusa@cotton.org • URL: http:// www.cottonusa.org • Representatives of all segments of the U.S. cotton industry. Works as an international cotton sales promotion organization cooperating with cotton interests in foreign countries.

*Cotton Digest International*. Cotton Digest Co., Inc., P.O. Box 820768 Houston, TX 77282-0768. Phone: (713)977-1644; Fax: (713)977-8193; Email: cottonabb@aol.com • Monthly. $40; $60 Two years. Textiles and Cotton merchandising magazine. Exports & Imports-Domestic & foreign.

*Cotton Farming*. One Grower Publishing L.L.C., 5118 Park Ave., Ste. 111 Memphis, TN 38117. Phone: (901)767-4020; Fax: (901)767-4026 • URL: http://www.ricefarming.com • Monthly. $40 Individuals.

*Cotton Grower*. Meister Media Worldwide, 37733 Euclid Ave. Willoughby, OH 44094-5992. Phone: 800-572-7740 or (440)942-2000; Fax: (440)975-3447; Email: info@ meistermedia.com • URL: http://www.meistermedia.com • Monthly.

**Cotton Inc.** 6399 Weston Pkwy. Cary, NC 27513. Phone: (919)678-2220; Fax: (919)678-2230; Email: contact@ cottoninc.com • URL: http://www.cottoninc.com • Represents cotton producers for research and promotion.

*Cotton Price Statistics*. U.S. Department of Agriculture, 1400 Independence Ave. SW Washington, DC 20250. Phone: 800-336-3747 or (202)720-2791 or (202)720-9904; Fax: (202)690-2164 or (202)720-6050; Email: fsis.outreach@ usda.gov • URL: http://www.usda.gov • Annual.

**Council for Advancement and Support of Education**. 1307 New York Ave. NW, Ste. 1000 Washington, DC 20005-4701. Phone: 800-554-8536 or (202)328-2273 or (202)478-5673; Fax: (202)387-4973; Email: membersupportcenter@case.org • URL: http://www.case.org • Formerly American College Public Relations Association.

**Council for Aid to Education**. 215 Lexington Ave., 16th Fl. New York, NY 10016-6023. Phone: (212)661-5800; Fax: (212)661-9766; Email: vse@cae.org • URL: http://www.cae. org • Works to improve quality and productivity in higher education. Supports research and promotes policy reforms in higher education. Conducts the annual Voluntary Support of Education Survey and operates the Collegiate Learning Assessment program for undergraduate education in the United States.

**Council for Court Excellence**. 1111 14th St. NW, Ste. 500 Washington, DC 20005-5628. Phone: (202)785-5917; Email: info@courtexcellence.org • URL: http://www. courtexcellence.org • Lawyers, business leaders, and civic and judicial branch members. Aims to develop and advocate methods of improving the administration of justice in local and federal courts. Stimulates understanding and communication between citizens and the courts. Conducts educational workshops.

**Council for Ethical Leadership**. 1 College and Main Columbus, OH 43209. Phone: (614)236-7222 • URL: http://www. businessethics.org • Leaders in business, education, and the professions. Seeks to "strengthen the ethical fabric of business and economic life." Facilitates the development of international networks of businesspeople interested in economic ethics; sponsors educational programs and develops and distributes educational materials; advises and supports communities wishing to implement character educational programs; makes available consulting services.

**Council for Hospitality Management Education**. University of Bournemouth, Dorset House, Talbot Campus, Fern Barrow, Dorset Poole BH12 5BB, United Kingdom. • URL: http:// www.chme.co.uk • Universities and colleges which offer degree and/or HND courses in hospitality management. Represents member institutions' interests in the field of hospitality management education at HE level, EC, government, industry and professional levels. Promotes hospitality management education in general, as well as specialist levels, e.g. industrial placement, research, access to courses, etc.

**Council for Responsible Genetics**. 5 Upland Rd., Ste. 3 Cambridge, MA 02140-2717. Phone: (617)868-0870; Fax: (617)491-5344; Email: crg@gene-watch.org • URL: http:// www.councilforresponsiblegenetics.org • Concerned with the social implications of genetic technologies. Formerly Committee for Responsible Genetics.

**Council on Licensure, Enforcement and Regulation**. 403 Marquis Ave., Ste. 200 Lexington, KY 40502. Phone: (859)269-1289; Fax: (859)231-1943; Email: clear@clearhq. org • URL: http://www.clearhq.org • Members are state government occupational and professional licensing officials. Formerly National Clearinghouse on Licensure, Enforcement and Regulation.

**Council of American Survey Research Organizations**. 170 N Country Rd., Ste. 4 Port Jefferson, NY 11777. Phone: (631)928-6954; Fax: (631)928-6041; Email: casro@casro. org • URL: http://www.casro.org • Members are survey research companies. Various committees are concerned with standards, survey research quality, and technology.

**Council of Communication Management**. 65 Enterprise Aliso Viejo, CA 92656. Phone: 866-463-6226; Email: info@ thecommunicationexchange.org • URL: http://www. ccmconnection.com • Formerly Industrial Communication Council.

**Council of Graduate Schools**. 1 Dupont Cir. NW, Ste. 230 Washington, DC 20036. Phone: (202)223-3791; Fax: (202)331-7157; Email: general_inquiries@cgs.nche.edu • URL: http://www.cgsnet.org • Formerly Council of Graduate Schools in the United States.

**Council of Institutional Investors**. 888 17th St. NW, Ste. 500 Washington, DC 20006. Phone: (202)822-0800; Fax: (202)822-0801; Email: info@cii.org • URL: http://www.cii. org • Members are nonprofit organization pension plans and other nonprofit institutional investors.

**Council of Insurance Agents and Brokers**. 701 Pennsylvania Ave. NW, Ste. 750 Washington, DC 20004-2608. Phone: (202)783-4400; Fax: (202)783-4410; Email: ciab@ciab.com • URL: http://www.ciab.com • Represents the interests of the leading commercial property and casualty insurance agencies and brokerage firms in the U.S. and around the world.

**Council of State Administrators of Vocational Rehabilitation**. 1 Research Ct., Ste. 450 Rockville, MD 20850. Phone: (301)519-8023 • URL: http://www.rehabnetwork.org • Administrators of state vocational rehabilitation agencies. Serves as an advisory body to federal agencies and the public in the development of policies affecting rehabilitation of handicapped persons; acts as a forum for discussion on the provision of quality rehabilitation services. Compiles statistics.

**Council of Supplier Diversity Professionals**. PO Box 70226 Rochester, MI 48307. Email: info@ncsdp.com • URL: http:// www.ncsdp.com • Aims to assist in the growth and development of the supplier diversity profession. Provides a forum to share information, ideas and issues concerning supplier diversity. Offers career-development strategies for supplier diversity professionals.

**Council of Supply Chain Management Professionals**. 333 E Butterfield Rd., Ste. 140 Lombard, IL 60148. Phone: (630)574-0985; Fax: (630)574-0989; Email: membership@ cscmp.org • URL: http://www.cscmp.org • Business executives with a professional interest in logistics and physical distribution management; includes members from industrial concerns as well as consultants and educators. Aims to advance and promote the management science of integrating transportation, warehousing, material handling, protective packaging, inventory size and location, and other areas of customer service, to reduce overall costs of selling and marketing while improving competitive status. Conducts research. Compiles bibliography available on website regarding subjects related to logistics issues. Provides employment clearinghouse.

**Council on Employee Benefits**. 1501 M St. NW, Ste. 620 Washington, DC 20005. Phone: (202)861-6025; Fax: (202)861-6027 • URL: http://www.ceb.org • Formerly Council on Employee Benefits Plans.

**Council on Foundations**. 2121 Crystal Dr., Ste. 700 Arlington, VA 22202-3706. Phone: 800-673-9036 or (703)879-0600; Email: membership@cof.org • URL: http://www.cof.org • Formerly National Council on Community Foundations.

*Council on Hotel, Restaurant and Institutional Education— Member Directory and Resource Guide*. International Council on Hotel, Restaurant, and Institutional Education, 2810 N Parham Rd., Ste. 230 Richmond, VA 23294. Phone: (804)346-4800; Fax: (804)346-5009; Email: publications@ chrie.org • URL: http://www.chrie.org • Biennial. Covers: Over 2,000 educational programs and institutions in the hotel, restaurant, and tourism industries. Entries include: Name, address, phone, fax.

**Council on International Educational Exchange USA**. 300 Fore St. Portland, ME 04101. Phone: 800-407-8839 or (207)553-4000; Fax: (207)553-4299; Email: contact@ciee.org • URL: http://www.ciee.org • Members are educational institutions and agencies that promote and sponsor international education exchange. Formerly Council on Student Travel.

*Counseling and Values*. Association for Spiritual, Ethical and Religious Values in Counseling. American Counseling Association, 5999 Stevenson Ave. Alexandria, VA 22304. Phone: 800-347-6647; Fax: (703)823-0252; Email: membership@counseling.org • URL: http://www.counseling. org • Semiannual. $107 Nonmembers print or online; $123 Nonmembers institutional, print & online; $41 Individuals; $50 Institutions. Journal focusing on the role of values and religion in counseling and psychology.

*The Counseling Psychologist*. Pine Forge Press, 2455 Teller Rd. Thousand Oaks, CA 91320-2234. Phone: 800-818-7243 or (805)499-4224 or (805)499-9774; Fax: (805)499-0871 or (805)583-2665; Email: sales@pfp.sagepub.com • URL: http://www.sagepub.com/sociologybooks • 8/year. £1,194 Institutions print & e-access; £25 Individuals single print; £1,075 Institutions e-access; £1,313 Institutions e-access (all online content); £2,376 Institutions e-access (content through 1998). Journal for counseling psychologists. Published in association with the Division of Counseling Psychology of the American Psychological Association.

*Counseling Services: IACS Newsletter*. International Association of Counseling Services, 101 S Whiting St., Ste. 211 Alexandria, VA 22304-3416. Phone: (703)823-9840; Fax: (703)823-9843; Email: admin@iacsinc.org • URL: http:// www.iacsinc.org • Three times a year. Membership.

*Counselor: The Magazine for Addiction Professionals*. Health Communications, Inc., 3201 SW 15th St. Deerfield Beach, FL 33442. Phone: 800-441-5569 or (954)360-0909; Fax: (954)360-0034; Email: doreenh@hcibooks.com • URL: http://www.hcibooks.com • Bimonthly. $9.95 Individuals /year, online only; $25.95 Individuals /year, print and online; $14.95 Individuals /year, tablet and mobile. Covers both clinical and societal aspects of substance abuse.

**Counselors of Real Estate**. 430 N Michigan Ave. Chicago, IL 60611-4089. Phone: (312)329-8427 or (312)329-8429; Fax: (312)329-8881; Email: info@cre.org • URL: http://www.cre. org • Formerly American Society of Real Estate Counselors.

*Countertrade and Offset*. CTO Data Services, 1512 Valley Run Durham, NC 27707-3640. Phone: (703)383-5816; Fax: (703)383-5815 • Semimonthly. $1,194 /year. Intelligence on reciprocal international trade and unconventional trade finance. Covers developments and trends in the directory publishing industry, including publisher profiles, start-ups, corporate acquisitions, and business opportunities. Includes *Directory of Countertrade Services*. Formerly *Countertrade Outlook*.

*Countries of the World and Their Leaders Yearbook*. Cengage Learning Inc., 20 Channel Center St. Boston, MA 02210. Phone: 800-487-8488 or (617)289-7700; Fax: (617)289-7844; Email: investors@cengage.com • URL: http://www. cengage.com • Annual. $475 Individuals. 2012. eBook. Contact publisher for pricing. Based on U.S. State Department data covering nearly 200 countries.

*Country Finance*. The Economist Intelligence Unit, 111 W 57th St. New York, NY 10019. Phone: 800-938-4685 or (212)554-0600; Fax: (212)586-1191 or (212)586-1182; Email: newyork@eiu.com • URL: http://www.economist.com • Annual $425.00 per year. Discusses banking and financial conditions in each of 47 countries. Includes foreign exchange regulations, the currency outlook, sources of capital, financing techniques, and tax considerations.

*Country Report Services*. The PRS Group Inc., 5800 Heritage Landing Dr., Ste. E East Syracuse, NY 13057-9378. Phone: (315)431-0511; Fax: (315)431-0200; Email: custserv@ prsgroup.com • URL: http://www.prsgroup.com • Provides full text of reports describing the business risks and opportunities currently existing in more than 150 countries of the world. Contains a wide variety of statistics and forecasts relating to economics political and social conditions. Also includes demographics, tax, and currency information. Updated monthly. Inquire as to online cost and availability.

***County News***. National Association of Counties, 25 Massachusetts Ave. NW, Ste. 500 Washington, DC 20001. Phone: 888-407-6226 or (202)393-6226; Fax: (202)393-2630; Email: naco@naco.org • URL: http://www.naco.org • Semimonthly.

***Court Filings***. ProQuest LLC, 2250 Perimeter Park Dr., Ste. 300 Morrisville, NC 27560. Phone: 800-334-2564 or (919)804-6400; Fax: (919)804-6410; Email: contact@dialog.com • URL: http://www.dialog.com • The three main sections of Tax Analysts home page are "Tax News" (Today's Tax News, Feature of the Week, Tax Snapshots, Tax Calendar); "Products & Services" (Product Catalog, Press Releases); and "Public Interest" (Discussion Groups, Tax Clinic, Tax History Project). Fees: Free for coverage of current tax events; fee-based for comprehensive information. Daily updating.

***Court Review***. American Judges Association. National Center for State Courts, 300 Newport Ave. Williamsburg, VA 23185. Phone: 800-616-6164 or (757)259-1525 or (757)259-1826; Fax: (757)220-0449; Email: jcochet@ncsc.org • URL: http://www.ncsc.org • Quarterly. Journal for members of the American Judges Association.

***Covina Business***. Covina Chamber of Commerce, 935 W Badillo St., Ste. 100 Covina, CA 91722. Phone: (626)967-4191; Fax: (626)966-9660; Email: chamber@covina.org • URL: http://www.covina.org • 10/year.

***The CPA Journal***. New York State Society of Certified Public Accountants, 14 Wall St., 19th Fl. New York, NY 10005. Phone: 800-633-6320 or (212)719-8300; Fax: (212)719-3364; Email: jbarry@nysscpa.org • URL: http://www.nysscpa.org • Monthly. $150 Individuals U.S.; $30 Students 1 year; $170 Other countries 1 year; $179 Individuals 2 years, U.S.; $39 Students 2 years; $199 Other countries 2 years; $204 Individuals 3 years, U.S.; $234 Other countries 3 years. Provides analysis, perspective, and debate on the issues affecting the financial world.

***CPA Managing Partner Report: Management News for Accounting Executives***. Strafford Publications Inc., 590 Dutch Valley Rd. Atlanta, GA 30324-0729. Phone: 800-926-7926 or (404)881-1141; Fax: (404)881-0074; Email: custservice@staffordpub.com • URL: http://www.straffordpub.com • Monthly. $396.00 per year. Newsletter. Covers practice management and professional relationships.

***CPA Practice Advisor***. Cygnus Business Media, 110 N Bell St., Suite 300 Shawnee, OK 74801. Phone: 800-308-6397; Email: rich.reiff@cygnuspub.com • URL: http://www.cygnus.com • Provides articles and reviews relating to computer technology and software for accountants.

***CPA Technology and Internet Tax Advisor***. Wolters Kluwer Law and Business, 76 9th Ave., 7th Fl. New York, NY 10011-4962. Phone: 800-234-1660 or (212)771-0600; Fax: (800)901-9075 or (301)644-3550 • URL: http://www.wolterskluwerlb.com • Monthly. $261.00 per year. Newsletter. Describes hardware and software products and makes recommendations. Formerly *CPA Technology and Internet Advisor*.

**CPCU Society**. 720 Providence Rd. Malvern, PA 19355-0709. Phone: 800-932-2728; Fax: (610)251-2780; Email: membercenter@cpcusociety.org • URL: http://www.cpcusociety.org • Serves as a professional society of individuals who have passed national examinations of the American Institute for Chartered Property Casualty Underwriters, have 3 years of work experience, have agreed to be bound by a code of ethics, and have been awarded CPCU designation. Promotes education, research, social responsibility, and professionalism in the field. Holds seminars, symposia, and workshops.

***CPI Detailed Report: Consumer Price Index***. U. S. Government Printing Office, 732 N Capitol St. NW Washington, DC 20401. Phone: 866-512-1800 or (202)512-1800 or (866)512-1800; Fax: (202)512-2104 or (202)512-2250; Email: contactcenter@gpo.gov • URL: http://www.gpo.gov • Monthly. $45 Individuals. Cost of living data.

***CPI Digest: Key to World Literature Serving the Coatings, Plastics, Fibers, Adhesives, and Related Industries***. CPI Information Services, 2117 Cherokee Parkway Louisville, KY 40204. Phone: (502)456-6288; Fax: (502)454-4808; Email: cpidigest@mindspring.com • Monthly. $397.00 per year. Abstracts of business and technical articles for polymer-based, chemical process industries. Includes a monthly list of relevant U. S. patents. International coverage.

***CPI.Q***. Cengage Learning Inc., 20 Channel Center St. Boston, MA 02210. Phone: 800-487-8488 or (617)289-7700; Fax: (617)289-7844; Email: investors@cengage.com • URL: http://www.cengage.com • Electronic version of the *Canadian Periodical Index*. Provides citations from 1988 to date for English and French language periodicals. Indexing from 1980 to present. Inquire as to price and availability.

**Craft Retailers Association for Tomorrow**. PO Box 293 Islamorada, FL 33036. Phone: (305)664-3650; Fax: (305)664-0199; Email: info@craftonline.org • URL: http://www.craftonline.org • Represents a network of galleries, shops and artists. Supports and encourages creativity and artistic excellence in American craftspeople. Promotes awareness of American crafts through communication programs, education, networking and marketing.

***Craighead's International Business, Travel, and Relocation Guide to 84 Countries***. Cengage Learning Inc., 20 Channel Center St. Boston, MA 02210. Phone: 800-487-8488 or (617)289-7700; Fax: (617)289-7844; Email: investors@cengage.com • URL: http://www.cengage.com • $775 Individuals hardcover. Publication includes: List of Web sites for children's organizations, spousal employment, telephones/telecommunications, visa requirements, and more. Principal content of publication is detailed information on relocating or traveling to foreign countries.

***Crain's Chicago Business***. Crain Communications Inc., 150 N Michigan Ave. Chicago, IL 60601-7553. Phone: 800-678-9595 or (312)649-5200 or (312)649-5411; Fax: (312)280-3150 or (312)280-3174; Email: info@crain.com • URL: http://www.crain.com • Weekly. $99 Individuals print & online; $59.99 Individuals online. Newspaper covering news stories about various aspects of business and labor activity in the Chicago market.

***Crain's Detroit Business***. Crain Communications Inc., 1155 Gratiot Ave. Detroit, MI 48207-2732. Phone: (313)446-6000; Email: info@crain.com • URL: http://www.crain.com • Weekly (Mon.). $59 Individuals print edition; $36 Individuals online edition. Local business tabloid covering Wayne, Macomb, Oakland, Livingston, and Washtenaw counties.

***Crain's Small Business***. Crain Communications Inc., 150 N Michigan Ave. Chicago, IL 60601-7553. Phone: 800-678-9595 or (312)649-5200 or (312)649-5411; Fax: (312)280-3150 or (312)280-3174; Email: info@crain.com • URL: http://www.crain.com • Monthly. Tabloid covering topics of interest for companies with under 100 employees.

***Crawford's Directory of City Connections***. AP Information Services Ltd., c/o Wilmington Publishing & Information Ltd., 6-14 Underworld St. London N1 7JQ, United Kingdom. Phone: 44 20 75498708; Fax: 44 20 74908238; Email: info@apinfo.co.uk • URL: http://www.apinfo.co.uk • $325. Covers: Approximately 3,500 private and public sector companies in the U.K., as well as advisers to the financial sector, including stockholders, solicitors, auditors, and insurance advisers. Entries include: Name, address, phone, names and titles of key personnel.

***Crawley Business Guide and Directory***. Crawley Borough Council, Town Hall, The Boulevard, West Sussex Crawley RH10 1UZ, United Kingdom. Phone: 44 1293 438000; Fax: 44 1293 511803; Email: comments@crawley.gov.uk • URL: http://www.crawley.gov.uk • Covers businesses in Crawley, United Kingdom.

***CRB Commodity Index Report***. Commodity Research Bureau. 330 S Wells St., Ste. 612 Chicago, IL 60606. Phone: 800-621-5271 or (312)554-8456; Fax: (312)939-4135; Email: info@crbtrader.com • URL: http://www.crbtrader.com • $795.00 per year. Coverage of all Commodity Research Bureau indexes in tabular and graphical format.

***CRB Commodity Yearbook***. Commodity Research Bureau. CRB, 209 W Jackson Bureau Chicago, IL 60606-7110. Phone: 800-621-5271 or (312)554-8456; Email: info@crbtrader.com • URL: http://www.crbyearbook.com • Annual. $179 plus $10.00 shipping cost. The single most comprehensive source of commodity and futures market information available.

***CRB Futures Perspective: Agricultural Edition***. Commodity Research Bureau. 330 S Wells St., Suite 1112 Chicago, IL 60606. Phone: 800-621-5271 or (312)554-8456; Fax: (312)939-4135; Email: info@crbtrader.com • URL: http://www.crbtrader.com • Weekly. $230.00 per year. Service provides comprehensive price charts for more than 20 agricultural commodity futures, from cocoa to wheat (includes lumber). Also provides technical analysis of price movements and market commentary. Formerly part of *CRB Futures Chart Service*.

***CRB Futures Perspective: Financial Edition***. Commodity Research Bureau. 330 S Wells St., Suite 1112 Chicago, IL 60606. Phone: 800-621-5271 or (312)554-8456; Fax: (312)939-4135; Email: info@crbtrader.com • URL: http://www.crbtrader.com • Weekly. $275.00 per year. Service provides comprehensive price charts for more than 50 financial futures, from Australian Bills to Swiss Francs (includes precious metals and oil). Also provides technical analysis of price movements and market commentary. Formerly part of *CRB Futures Chart Service*.

***CRB Market Overview***. Commodity Research Bureau, Phone: 800-621-5271 or (312)554-8456; Fax: (312)939-4135; Email: info@crbtrader.com • URL: http://www.crbtrader.com/data/ • Web site provides free, detailed, current price quotes for about 100 futures contracts, covering Currencies, Energies, Financials, Grains, Meats, Metals, "Softs" (orange juice, coffee, etc.) and stock price indexes. Includes contract specifications and detailed prices of options on futures.

***Creating Excellence: Vermont's Journal for people in growing businesses***. New World Publishing Inc., PO Box 2048 South Burlington, VT 05407. Phone: (802)655-7200; Fax: (802)655-7214 • Bimonthly. $12. Magazine featuring successful Vermont business people and emphasizing personal development.

**The Creative Coalition**. 360 Park Ave. S, 11th Fl. New York, NY 10010-1717. Phone: (646)717-9908 • URL: http://thecreativecoalition.org • Actors, writers, directors and other arts and entertainment professionals. Aims to educate members about social and political issues, particularly in the areas of the First Amendment, arts advocacy and public education.

***Creativity***. Art Directon Book Company Inc., 456 Glenbrook Rd. Glenbrook, CT 06906. Phone: (203)353-1441; Fax: (203)353-1371 • Annual. $62.95.

**Credit Builders Alliance**. 1701 K St. NW, Ste. 1000 Washington, DC 20006. Phone: (202)730-9390; Fax: (202)350-9430; Email: info@creditbuildersalliance.org • URL: http://www.creditbuildersalliance.org • Represents the interests of community lenders including CDFIs, microenterprise and housing development organizations, asset building organizations and community credit unions. Provides assistance to low and moderate income individuals served by non-traditional financial and asset building institutions to build their credit and financial access. Raises awareness to open new credit building opportunities for low-income and underserved populations.

***Credit Card Management: The Magazine of Electronic Payments***. SourceMedia Inc., 1 State Street Plz., 27th Fl. New York, NY 10004. Phone: 800-221-1809 or (212)803-8200 or (212)803-8333; Fax: (212)843-9635 or (212)292-5216; Email: custserv@sourcemedia.com • URL: http://www.sourcemedia.com • Monthly. $98.00 per year. Edited for bankers and other managers of electronic payment systems.

***Credit Executive Letter***. American Financial Services Association, 919 18th St. NW, Ste. 300 Washington, DC 20006. Email: info@afsamail.org • URL: http://www.afsaonline.org • Monthly. Members, $12.00 per year; non-members, $22.00 per year.

**Credit Professionals International**. 10726 Manchester Rd., Ste. 210 Saint Louis, MO 63122. Phone: (314)821-9393; Fax: (314)821-7171; Email: creditpro@creditprofessionals.org • URL: http://www.creditprofessionals.org • Represents individuals employed in credit or collection departments of business firms or professional offices. Conducts educational program in credit work. Sponsors Career Club composed of members who have been involved in credit work for at least 25 years.

**Credit Research Foundation**. 1812 Baltimore Blvd., Ste. H Westminster, MD 21157. Phone: (443)821-3000; Fax: (443)821-3627 • URL: http://www.crfonline.org • Represents credit, financial, and working capital executives of manufacturing and banking concerns. Aims to create a better understanding of the impact of credit on the economy. Plans, supervises, and administers research and educational programs. Conducts surveys on economic conditions, trends, policies, practices, theory, systems, and methodology. Sponsors formal educational programs in credit and financial management. Maintains library on credit, collections, and management.

***Credit Risk Management***. Phillips International, Inc., 7811 Montrose Rd. Potomac, MD 20854. Phone: (301)340-2100; Email: information@phillips.com • URL: http://www.phillips.com • Biweekly. $695.00 per year. Newsletter on consumer credit, including delinquency aspects.

***The Credit Union Directory***. Accuity Inc., 4709 W Golf Rd. Skokie, IL 60076. Phone: 800-321-3373 or (847)676-9600; Fax: (847)933-8101; Email: custserv@accuitysolutions.com • URL: http://www.accuitysolutions.com • Semiannual. $600 Individuals. Covers: Approximately 12,000 credit unions and head offices and over 6,000 branches. Entries include: Institution name, address, phone, fax, routing and transit number, managing officer, financial data, charter number, year established, number of members, number of employees.

***Credit Union Executive Center***. Credit Union National Association, Inc., Communications Div. CUNA Publications, PO Box 431 Madison, WI 53705-0431. Phone: 800-356-8010 or (608)231-4000; Fax: (608)231-1869; Email: dorothy@cuna.org • URL: http://www.cuna.org • Formerly CU Executive Journal. Provides detailed information for credit union professionals.

**Credit Union Executives Society**. 5510 Research Park Dr. Madison, WI 53711-5377. Phone: 800-252-2664 or (608)271-2664; Fax: (608)271-2303; Email: cues@cues.org • URL: http://www.cues.org • Advances the professional development of credit union CEOs, senior management and directors. Serves as an international membership association dedicated to the professional development of credit union CEOs, senior management and directors.

***Credit Union Journal: The Nation's Leading Independent Credit Union Newsweekly***. SourceMedia Inc., 1 State Street Plz., 27th Fl. New York, NY 10004. Phone: 800-221-1809 or (212)803-8200 or (212)803-8333; Fax: (212)843-9635 or (212)292-5216; Email: custserv@sourcemedia.com • URL: http://www.sourcemedia.com • Weekly. $109.00 per year. Edited for credit union executives. Covers trends and developments in lending, insurance, investments, mortgages, check processing, relevant technology, and other topics.

***Credit Union Magazine***. Credit Union National Association, Inc. Credit Union National Association, 5710 Mineral Point Rd. Madison, WI 53705. Phone: 800-356-9655 or (202)638-5777; Fax: (202)638-7734 or (608)231-4333 • URL: http://www.cuna.org • Monthly. $71 Individuals; $127 Two years; $169 Individuals 3 years. News analysis and operational information for credit union management, staff, directors, and committee executives.

**Credit Union National Association**. 5710 Mineral Point Rd. Madison, WI 53705. Phone: 800-356-9655 or (202)638-5777; Fax: (202)638-7734 or (608)231-4333 • URL: http://www.cuna.org • Serves as trade association serving more than

90% of credit unions in the U.S. through their respective state leagues with a total membership of more than 77 million persons. (A credit union is a member-owned, nonprofit institution formed to encourage saving and to offer low interest loans to members, usually people working for the same employer, belonging to the same association, or living in the same community.) Promotes credit union membership, use of services, and organization of new credit unions. Seeks to perfect credit union laws; aids in the development of new credit union services, including new payment systems techniques; assists in the training of credit union officials and employees; compiles statistics, annually, by state. Offers charitable program.

***Credit Union Report***. Credit Union National Association, 5710 Mineral Point Rd. Madison, WI 53705. Phone: 800-356-9655 or (202)638-5777; Fax: (202)638-7734 or (608)231-4333 • URL: http://www.cuna.org • Semiannual. 15. Covers credit union leagues, associations, for each of the 50 states and the District of Columbia.

***CreditDisk 2.0***. Fitch, 121-141 Westbourne Terr. London W2 6JR, United Kingdom. Phone: 440 20 7479 0900; Fax: 440 20 7479 0600 • URL: http://www.fitch.com • Price and frequency on application. CD-ROM provides credit research and ratings on individual banks throughout the world, with Internet updating. Includes graphic displays of rating histories and financial ratios.

***Creditreform-Datenbank***. Verband der Vereine Creditreform e.V., Hellersbergstr. 12, Postfach 101553 D-41460 Neuss, Germany. Phone: 49 2131 109 0 or 49 2131 109 0; Fax: 49 2131 1098000 or 49 2131 109 8000; Email: creditrefom@verband.creditrefom.de • URL: http://www.creditreform.de • Daily. Database covers: Credit information on more than 3,100,000 million joint stock and individual trading companies in Austria and Germany. Entries include: Company name, address, legal form, dates of formation or reformation, capital, partners, number of employees, product line, financial indicators covering capital, obligations, annual income, property and equipment, warehouse stocks, loan payment record, liabilities, credit rating, biographical information on company principal officials.

***CreditWeek***. Standard & Poor's Financial Services L.L.C., 55 Water St. New York, NY 10041. Phone: 877-772-5436 or (212)438-2000; Fax: (212)438-1000; Email: questions@standardandpoors.com • URL: http://www.standardandpoors.com • Weekly. Price on application. Provides news and analysis of the municipal bond market, including information on new issues.

***Crescenta Valley Chamber of Commerce Business Directory***. Crescenta Valley Chamber of Commerce, 3131 Foothill Blvd., Ste. D La Crescenta, CA 91214. Phone: (818)248-4957; Fax: (818)248-9625; Email: info@crescentavalleychamber.org • URL: http://www.crescentavalleychamber.org • Covers: Member companies and organizations in La Crescenta, La Canada, Montrose, Sunland, and Tujunga, California. Entries include: Company or organization name, address, phone.

***Criminal Law Advocacy Reporter***. Matthew Bender and Company Inc., 1275 Broadway Albany, NY 12204-2638. Phone: 800-424-4200 or (518)487-3000; Fax: (518)487-3573 or (800)424-4200; Email: customer.support@lexisnexis.com • URL: http://www.matthewbender.com • Monthly. $447.00 per year. Newsletter. Analysis of the latest cases and trends in criminal law and procedure.

***Criminology: An Interdisciplinary Journal***. American Society of Criminology, 1314 Kinnear Rd., Ste. 212 Columbus, OH 43212-1156. Phone: (614)292-9207; Fax: (614)292-6767; Email: asc@asc41.com • URL: http://www.asc41.com • Quarterly. Included in membership; $348 Institutions print and online; $304 Institutions online only. Focus is on crime and deviant behavior.

***Crittenden Report: Real Estate Financing***. Crittenden Research Inc., 45 Leveroni Ct., Ste. 204 Novato, CA 94949. Phone: 800-421-3483 or (619)393-1814 or (415)382-2400; Fax: (619)923-3518 or (415)382-2476; Email: market@crittendenonline.com • URL: http://www.crittendenonline.com • Semimonthly. Newsletter on real estate lending and mortgages. Includes semiannual *Crittenden Directory of Real Estate Financing*.

***CRN: The Newsweekly for Builders of Technology Solutions***. CMP Worldwide Media Networks, 600 Community Dr. Manhasset, NY 11030. Phone: (516)562-5000 • URL: http://www.cmp.com • Monthly. Incorporates *Computer Reseller Sources and Macintosh News*. Formerly *Computer Retailer News*.

***Croatia Business Law Handbook***. International Business Publications, USA, PO Box 15343 Washington, DC 20003. Phone: (202)546-2103; Fax: (202)546-3275; Email: ibpusa@comcast.net • URL: http://ibpus.com • $99.95 Individuals hardcopy, e-book, CD-ROM. Covers: Basic information on business, export-import regulations, and contacts.

***Croatia Business Services Providers Leads***. Business Information Agency Inc. PlanetInform, 52 Tuscan Way, Ste. 202-181 Saint Augustine, VA 32092. Phone: (904)342-6124; Fax: (904)592-2632; Email: info@biasales.com • URL: http://www.biasales.com • Monthly. $50 Individuals mailing list; $106 Individuals sales list; $180 Individuals marketing list. Covers: Croatian companies and all sub-industries that provide various services to commercial businesses, establishments, and organizations, including consulting, advertising and marketing services, and facilities maintenance.

***Croatia Investment and Business Guide***. International Business Publications, USA, PO Box 15343 Washington, DC 20003. Phone: (202)546-2103; Fax: (202)546-3275; Email: ibpusa@comcast.net • URL: http://ibpus.com • $99.95 Individuals hardcopy, e-book, CD-ROM. Covers: Strategic business information, export-import activity, regulations and industrial development, banking, government, and opportunities. Entries include: Important business contacts and business travel.

***Croner's A-Z of Business Information Sources***. Wolters Kluwer Ltd., 145 London Rd. Kingston upon Thames KT2 6SR, United Kingdom. Phone: 44 020 8547 3333; Fax: 44 020 8547 2637; Email: info@croner.co.uk • URL: http://www.wolterskluwer.co.uk • Annual. $71.50 includes first year's updates & shipping. Covers: Organizations, publications, and other sources of business information in the United Kingdom from abrasives to zinc and the aerospace industry to wire products. Entries include: Name, address, phone, telex, contact name, brief description.

***Crop Science***. Crop Science Society of America, 5585 Guilford Rd. Madison, WI 53711-5801. Phone: (608)273-8080; Fax: (608)273-2021; Email: headquarters@sciencesocieties.org • URL: http://www.crops.org • Bimonthly. $50 Members print; $50 Members electronic; $60 Members print & electronic; $25 Members print; $25 Members electronic; $35 Individuals print & electronic; $50 Other countries members print, + 48 postage; $50 Other countries members, electronic, + 48 postage; $60 Other countries members print and electronic, + 48 postage. Agricultural science journal.

**CropLife America**. 1156 15th St. NW Washington, DC 20005. Phone: (202)296-1585; Fax: (202)463-0474 • URL: http://www.croplifeamerica.org • Fosters the interests of the general public and member companies by promoting innovative and environmentally sound manufacture, distribution and use of crop protection and production technologies for safe, high quality, affordable, abundant food, fiber and other crops.

**CropLife Australia**. AMP Bldg., Level 2, 1 Hobart Pl., Locked Bag 916 Canberra, ACT 2601, Australia. Phone: 61 2 62306399; Fax: 61 2 62306355 • URL: http://www.croplifeaustralia.org.au • Works for a fair, science-based regulatory system, encourages research and development.

***Croplife***. Meister Media, 37733 Euclid Ave. Willoughby, OH 44094-5992. Phone: 800-572-7740 or (440)942-2000; Fax: (440)975-3447; Email: info@meistermedia.com • URL: http://www.meistermedia.com • Monthly. $36.00 per year. Formerly *Farm Chemicals*.

***Cross-Reference Christian Business Directory***. Cross-Reference Christian Business Directory, PO Box 1601 Wooster, OH 44691. Phone: (330)317-8725; Email: info@cross-ref.com • URL: http://www.cross-ref.com • Annual. Covers christ-centered businesses.

***Cruise Travel***. World Publishing Co., 990 Grove St. Evanston, IL 60201. Phone: (847)491-6440; Fax: (847)491-0459; Email: cs@cruisetravelmag.com • URL: http://www.cruisetravelmag.com • Bimonthly. $38.95 /year.

***CryoGas International***. J.R. Campbell and Associates Inc., 5 Militia Dr. Lexington, MA 02421. Phone: (781)862-0624; Fax: (781)863-9411; Email: cgi@cryogas.com • URL: http://www.cryogas.com • 11/year. $75 /year (online); $150 U.S. /year (print); $200 Other countries /year (print); $200 U.S. /year (print and online); $250 Other countries /year (print and online). Reports on technology market development and new products for the industrial gases and cryogenic equipment industries. Formerly *Cryogenic Information Report*.

**Cryogenic Society of America**. 218 Lake St. Oak Park, IL 60302-2609. Phone: (708)383-6220; Fax: (708)383-9337; Email: laurie@cryogenicsociety.org • URL: http://www.cryogenicsociety.org • Seeks to encourage the dissemination of information on low temperature industrial technology. Formerly Helium Society.

***Cryogenics***. Elsevier, Secondary Publishing Division, 650 Ave. of the Americas New York, NY 10011. Phone: 888-437-4636 or (212)633-3980; Fax: (212)633-3975; Email: t.reller@elsevier.com • URL: http://www.elseveier.com • Monthly. $3,400 Institutions print or online. Journal of low temperature engineering.

***CSANews***. American Society of Agronomy, 5585 Guilford Rd. Madison, WI 53711-5801. Phone: (608)273-8080 or (608)273-8085; Fax: (608)273-2021; Email: headquarters@sciencesocieties.org • URL: http://www.agronomy.org • Monthly. Description: Publishes information on agronomy, crop science, soil science, and related topics. Provides news of the societies and members; reports of annual meetings; listings of publications; announcements of awards, retirements, and deaths; job listings; and a calendar of events.

***CSG State Directories I: State Elective Officials***. Chief Officers of State Library Agencies, 201 E Main St., Ste. 1405 Lexington, KY 40507. Phone: 800-800-1910 or (859)514-9151 or (859)244-8000; Fax: (859)514-9166 or (859)244-8001; Email: lsingler@amrms.com • URL: http://www.cosla.org • Annual. $65 Individuals. Covers: About 8,000 state legislators, elected state executive branch officials, and state supreme court judges. Database includes: Miscellaneous state facts and term limit information. Entries include: Name, title, address, district, party affiliation, fax and facts about each state-motto, flower, bird, nickname, capitol address, bill status phone, land area, population, D. C. Liaison, term limits, election and session dates.

***CSM***. CSM Marketing, Inc., 195 Smithtown Blvd. Nesconset, NY 11767-1849. • Monthly. $30.00 per year. Formerly *Catalog Showroom Merchandiser*.

***CSO: The Resource for Security Executives***. CXO Media Inc., 492 Old Connecticut Path Framingham, MA 01701-4584. Phone: 888-434-5478 or (508)872-0080; Fax: (508)879-7784; Email: stozeski@idglist.com • URL: http://www.cio.com • 10/year. $70 U.S. and Canada. Edited for corporate chief security officers (CSOs). Covers a wide variety of business security issues, including computer security, identity theft, spam, physical security, loss prevention, risk management, privacy, and investigations.

***CSP: The Magazine for C-Store People***. CSP Information Group, 1100 Jorie Blvd. Oak Brook, IL 60523. Phone: (630)574-5075; Fax: (630)574-5175 • URL: http://www.cspnet.com • Monthly. Emphasizes the influence of people (both store personnel and consumers) on the C-store industry.

***CSR Professional Services Directory***. Dunstan Publishing, Stodmarsh Enterprise Center, Stodmarsh Canterbury CT3 4BE, United Kingdom. Phone: 44 1227 720900; Fax: 44 2227 200334; Email: subscriptions@ethicalperformance.com • URL: http://www.ethicalperformance.com • $65 Individuals; €95 Individuals; $130 Individuals; £29.95 Single issue. Covers: 675 service providers including consultants, academic institutions, rating agencies, ethical auditors, training providers, and research organizations. Entries include: Contact information and services they provide.

**CTAM: Cable and Telecommunications Association for Marketing**. 120 Waterfront St., Ste. 200 Oxon Hill, MD 20745. Phone: (301)485-8900; Fax: (301)560-4964; Email: info@ctam.com • URL: http://www.ctam.com • Formerly CTAM, The Marketing Society for Cable and Telecommunications Industry.

**CTC Inc.** 100 CTC Dr. Johnstown, PA 15904-1935. Email: info@ctc.com • URL: http://www.ctc.com • Formerly Center for Hazardous Materials Research.

***CTC Reporter***. United Nations Conference on Trade and Development. United Nations, Department of Public Information, Grand Central Sta. New York, NY 10163-5850. Phone: (212)963-1516 or (212)963-4475; Fax: (212)963-1381 or (212)963-7055; Email: inquiries@un.org • URL: http://www.devbusiness.com • Semiannual. $20; $45 Individuals airmail postage 18; $75 Two years airmail postage 36; $20 Single issue. Reports on both governmental and non-governmental aspects of multinational corporations. Issued by the United Nations Centre on Transnational Corporations (UNCTC). Formerly *CTC Reporter*.

**CTIA - The Wireless Association**. 1400 16th St. NW, Ste. 600 Washington, DC 20036. Phone: (202)736-3200 or (202)785-0081; Fax: (202)785-0721 • URL: http://www.ctia.org • Individuals and organizations actively engaged in cellular radiotelephone communications, including: telephone companies and corporations providing radio communications; lay firms; engineering firms; consultants and manufacturers. (A cellular radiotelephone is a mobile communications device. An area is geographically divided into low frequency cells monitored by a computer that switches callers from one frequency to another as they move from cell to cell.) Objectives are to: promote, educate, and facilitate the professional interests, needs, and concerns of members with respect to the development and commercial applications of cellular technology; provide an opportunity for exchanging experience and concerns; broaden the understanding and importance of cellular communication technology. Conducts discussions, studies, and courses.

***Cuba Investment and Business Guide***. International Business Publications, USA, PO Box 15343 Washington, DC 20003. Phone: (202)546-2103; Fax: (202)546-3275; Email: ibpusa@comcast.net • URL: http://ibpus.com • $99.95 Individuals hardcopy, e-book, CD-ROM. Covers: Strategic and business information, contacts, regulations and more.

***CUIS***. UCG Holdings L.P., 11300 Rockville Pike, Suite 1100 Rockville, MD 20852-3030. Phone: 800-929-4824 or (301)816-8950 or (301)287-2700; Fax: (301)816-8945; Email: dhernan@ucg.com • URL: http://www.ucg.com • Biweekly. $277.00 per year. Newsletter. Supplement available *CUIS Special Report*.

***Culver City Business***. Culver City Chamber of Commerce, 6000 Sepulveda Blvd., Ste. 1260 Culver City, CA 90230. Phone: (310)287-3850; Fax: (310)390-0395 • URL: http://www.culvercitychamber.com • Monthly.

**CUMELA Nederland**. Postbus 1156 NL-3860 BD Nijkerk, Netherlands. Phone: 31 33 2474900; Fax: 31 33 2474901; Email: info@cumela.nl • URL: http://www.cumela.nl • Agricultural and rural contractors. Seeks to advance the interests of agribusinesses. Represents members' commercial and regulatory interests at the national level.

***Cumulative Index to Nursing and Allied Health Literature***. EBSCO Publishing Inc., 10 Estes St. Ipswich, MA 01938-2106. Phone: 800-653-2726 or (978)356-6500; Fax: (978)356-6565; Email: information@ebscohost.com • URL: http://www.ebscohost.com • Includes annual *Cumulation Index*.

***Cupertino Business***. Cupertino Chamber of Commerce, 20455 Silverado Ave. Cupertino, CA 95014. Phone: (408)252-7054; Fax: (408)252-0638; Email: info@cupertino-chamber.org •

URL: http://www.cupertino-chamber.org • Monthly. $1.25 /issue.

***Current Biography Illustrated***. EBSCO Publishing Inc., 10 Estes St. Ipswich, MA 01938-2106. Phone: 800-653-2726 or (978)356-6500; Fax: (978)356-6565; Email: information@ebscohost.com • URL: http://www.ebscohost.com • Offers the content of the printed monthly magazine *Current Biography*.

***Current Biotechnology Abstracts***. DECHEMA, c/o Neil Forsyth, Information Systems, Theodor-Heuss-Allee 25 D-60486 Frankfurt am Main, Germany. Phone: 49 69 7564 349 or 69 75640; Fax: (756)4 201 or 69 7564201 • URL: http://www.dechema.de • Monthly. $1,229.00 per year. Reports on the latest scientific, technical and commercial advances in the field of technology.

***Current Contents Connect***. Thomson Reuters Intellectual Property and Science, 3501 Market St. Philadelphia, PA 19104-3302. Phone: 800-336-4474 or (215)386-0100; Fax: (215)386-2911; Email: general.info@thomsonreuters.com • URL: http://ip-science.thomsonreuters.com • Provides online abstracts of articles listed in the tables of contents of about 7,500 journals. Coverage is very broad, including science, social science, life science, technology, engineering, industry, agriculture, the environment, economics, and arts and humanities. Time period is two years, with weekly updates. Inquire as to online cost and availability.

***Current Contents: Engineering, Computing and Technology***. Thomson Reuters Intellectual Property and Science, 3501 Market St. Philadelphia, PA 19104-3302. Phone: 800-336-4474 or (215)386-0100; Fax: (215)386-2911; Email: general.info@thomsonreuters.com • URL: http://ip-science.thomsonreuters.com • Weekly. $730 per year. Reproductions of contents pages of technical journals. Includes *Author Index*, *Address Directory*, *Current Book Contents*, and *Title Word Index*. Formerly *Current Contents: Engineering, Technology and Applied Sciences*.

***Current Contents: Social and Behavioral Sciences***. Thomson Reuters Intellectual Property and Science, 3501 Market St. Philadelphia, PA 19104-3302. Phone: 800-336-4474 or (215)386-0100; Fax: (215)386-2911; Email: general.info@thomsonreuters.com • URL: http://ip-science.thomsonreuters.com • Weekly. $730. Includes *Author Index*.

***Current Directory of International Chambers of Commerce and Industry***. Current Pacific Ltd., Northcote Aucklannd 0748, New Zealand. Phone: 64 9 4801388; Fax: 64 9 4801387; Email: info@cplnz.com • URL: http://www.cplnz.com • $150 Individuals. Covers: More than 4,000 international chambers of commerce and industry selected from major cities in more than 165 countries in territories in the world.

***Current Index to Journals in Education (CIJE)***. Oryx Press, 4041 N Central Ave., Ste. 700 Phoenix, AZ 85012. Phone: 800-279-6799 or (602)265-2651; Fax: (602)265-6250 or (800)279-4663; Email: info@oryxpress.com • URL: http://www.greenwood.com • Monthly. $245.00 per year. Semiannual cumulations, $475.00.

***Current Index to Statistics: Applications, Methods, and Theory***. American Statistical Association, 732 N Washington St. Alexandria, VA 22314-1943. Phone: 888-231-3473 or (703)684-1221; Fax: (703)684-2037; Email: asainfo@amstat.org • URL: http://www.amstat.org • Annual. An index to journal articles on statistical applications and methodology.

***Current Law Index***. Cengage Learning Inc., 20 Channel Center St. Boston, MA 02210. Phone: 800-487-8488 or (617)289-7700; Fax: (617)289-7844; Email: investors@cengage.com • URL: http://www.cengage.com • $1,332 Individuals. Monthly. $1269.00 per year. Produced in cooperation with the American Association of Law Libraries. Indexes more than 900 law journals, legal newspapers, and specialty publications from the U.S., Canada, U.K., Ireland, Australia, and New Zealand.

***Current Municipal Problems***. Thomson West, 610 Opperman Dr. Eagan, MN 55123. Phone: 800-328-9352 or (651)687-7000 • Full text journal articles on municipal law and administration. Indexing included.

***Current Publications in Legal and Related Fields***. American Association of Law Libraries. Fred B. Rothman and Co., 2350 N Forest Rd. Getzville, NY 14068-1296. Phone: 888-361-3255 or (303)979-5657; Fax: (303)979-0707 • URL: http://www.wshein.com • Looseleaf service. Annual cumulation.

**Curtin University of Technology - Communication Economics and Electronic Markets Research Centre**. Department of Economics Perth, WA 6845, Australia. Phone: 61 8 92662391; Fax: 61 8 92669460; Email: g.madden@curtin.edu.au • URL: http://business.curtin.edu.au/research/centres_institutions/research_centres/ceem • Communications economics and electronic markets, focusing on legal, sociological, technical and policy aspects of current debate.

***Custom Builder: The Business Magazine for Builders of Premier Homes***. Willows Publishing Group Inc., 38 Lafayette St. Yarmouth, ME 04096. Phone: (207)846-0970; Fax: (207)846-1561 • Bimonthly. $23; $4.50 Single issue. Magazine reporting on energy efficiency and quality home construction.

***Custom Tailor***. Custom Tailors and Designers Association of America, 42732 Ridgeway Dr. Broadlands, VA 20148. Phone: 888-248-2832 • URL: http://www.ctda.com • Three times a year. $50.00 per year. Controlled circulation.

**Custom Tailors and Designers Association**. 42732 Ridgeway Dr. Broadlands, VA 20148. Phone: 888-248-2832; Fax: (866)661-1240; Email: info@ctda.com • URL: http://www.ctda.com • Formerly Merchant Tailors and Designers Association of America.

***Customs Law and Administration: Statutes and Treaties***. Oceana Publications Inc., 75 Main St. Dobbs Ferry, NY 10522-1632. Phone: 800-831-0758 or (914)693-8100; Fax: (914)693-0402; Email: info@oceanalaw.com • URL: http://www.oceanalaw.com • $475.00. Five volumes. Looseleaf service. Periodic supplementation.

***Cutting Technology***. Penton Media Inc., 1300 E 9th St. Cleveland, OH 44114-1501. Phone: (216)696-7000; Fax: (216)696-1752; Email: information@penton.com • URL: http://penton.com • Seven times a year. Free to qualified personnel; others, $55.00 per year. Provides abstracts of the international literature of metal cutting and machining. Formerly *Cutting Tool-Machine Digest*.

***Cutting Tool Engineering***. CTE Publications Inc., 40 Skokie Blvd., Ste. 450 Northbrook, IL 60062. Phone: (847)498-9100; Fax: (847)559-4444; Email: info@ctemag.com • URL: http://www.ctemag.com • Monthly. $75 U.S. One year subscription (free to qualified subscribers within the U.S.); $125 Canada One year subscription; $125 Other countries One year subscription. Serves manufacturers involved in cutting and grinding metals and other materials.

***CWB Custom Woodworking Business: Environmental Studies***. Vance Publishing Corp., 400 Knightsbridge Pkwy. Lincolnshire, IL 60069-3613. Phone: 800-255-5113 or (847)634-2600; Fax: (847)634-4342 or (847)634-4379; Email: info@vancepublishing.com • URL: http://www.vancepublishing.com • Monthly. Magazine for professional custom woodworkers.

***Cyberlaw for Global E-business: Finance, Payment and Dispute Resolution***. Cengage Learning Inc., 20 Channel Center St. Boston, MA 02210. Phone: 800-487-8488 or (617)289-7700; Fax: (617)289-7844; Email: investors@cengage.com • URL: http://www.cengage.com • 2009. eBook. Examines cyberlaw discussions worldwide on topics such as cybercrime and risk management, comparative electronic trading systems of securities, digital currency regulation, jurisdiction and consumer protection in cross-border markets, and case law on international bank transfers.

***Cyberlaw: Intellectual Property in the Digital Millennium***. ALM Media Properties LLC, 120 Broadway, 5th Fl. New York, NY 10271-1100. Phone: (212)457-9400; Fax: (646)417-7705; Email: customercare@alm.com • URL: http://www.alm.com • $530 per year. A basic guide to copyright as applied to the Internet and other electronic sources. (Law Journal Press).

***Cyberstocks: An Investors Guide to Internet Companies***. Hoover's Inc., 5800 Airport Blvd. Austin, TX 78752-4204. Phone: 866-443-3939 or (512)374-4500 or (866)281-5969; Fax: (512)374-4501; Email: salesteam@hoovers.com • URL: http://www.hoovers.com • $24.95. Covers: Companies involved in the Internet industry. Entries include: Name, address, phone.

***Cycle Projections***. Foundation for the Study of Cycles Inc., 5300 Sequoia Rd., Ste. 104 Albuquerque, NM 87120. Phone: (505)796-5699; Email: admin@cycles.cc • URL: http://www.foundationforthestudyofcycles.org • Monthly. Includes trend projections for stocks, commodities, real estate, and the economy. Short, intermediate, and long-term cycles are covered.

***Cycle World***. Bonnier Corp., 460 N Orlando Ave., Ste. 200 Winter Park, FL 32789. Phone: (407)628-4802; Fax: (407)628-7061 • URL: http://www.bonniercorp.com • Monthly. $22 Individuals 2 years; $12 Individuals /year; $22 Canada; $31.93 Other countries. Magazine on street, dirt, dual-purpose, and all-terrain motorcylces. Covering tests, aftermarket products, parts and accessories, competition, personalities, travel, and nostalgia.

***Cyprus Business Law Handbook***. International Business Publications, USA, PO Box 15343 Washington, DC 20003. Phone: (202)546-2103; Fax: (202)546-3275; Email: ibpusa@comcast.net • URL: http://ibpus.com • $99.95 Individuals hardcopy, e-book, CD-ROM. Covers: Basic information on business, laws, export-import, regulations, and contacts.

**Czech Republic Academy of Sciences - Institute of State and Law**. Narodni 18 116 00 Prague, Czech Republic. Phone: 420 221 990711; Fax: 420 221 933056; Email: ilaw@ilaw.cas.cz • URL: http://www.ilaw.cas.cz • Theory of state and law; selected issues of constitutional law; legal ramifications of the transition to a market economy; legal issues in environmental protection; problems with international law, especially law in the European Community and harmonization with Czech law with these systems; and legal informatics.

***Czech Republic Business Services Providers Leads***. Business Information Agency Inc. PlanetInform, 52 Tuscan Way, Ste. 202-181 Saint Augustine, VA 32092. Phone: (904)342-6124; Fax: (904)592-2632; Email: info@biasales.com • URL: http://www.biasales.com • Monthly. $109 Individuals mailing list; $230 Individuals sales list; $390 Individuals marketing list. Covers Czech companies and all sub-industries that provide various services to commercial businesses, establishments, and organizations, including consulting, advertising and marketing services, and facilities maintenance.

***Czech Republic Government and Business Contacts Handbook: Trade, Investment & Business Development Contacts***. International Business Publications, USA, PO Box 15343 Washington, DC 20003. Phone: (202)546-2103; Fax: (202)546-3275; Email: ibpusa@comcast.net • URL: http://ibpus.com • Annual. $99.95 Individuals hardcopy, E-book and CD-ROM. Covers: Strategic government and business information, export-import activity in the country, investment, business contacts and regulations.

***D & B Business Locator***. Dun & Bradstreet Inc., 103 JFK Pkwy. Short Hills, NJ 07078. Phone: 800-526-0651 or (973)921-5500 or (973)921-5000; Fax: (866)560-7035 or (512)794-7670; Email: info@dnb.com • URL: http://www.dnb.com • Quarterly. $2,495.00 per year. CD-ROM provides concise information on more than 10 million U. S. companies or businesses. Includes data on number of employees.

***D & B Business Rankings***. Dun & Bradstreet Inc., 103 JFK Pkwy. Short Hills, NJ 07078. Phone: 800-526-0651 or (973)921-5500 or (973)921-5000; Fax: (866)560-7035 or (512)794-7670; Email: info@dnb.com • URL: http://www.dnb.com • Annual. Covers more than 25,000 leading U.S. public and private businesses.

***D & B Business Register: Edinburgh***. Dun & Bradstreet (UK) Ltd., Marlow International, Parkway, Marlow Buckinghamshire SL7 1AJ, United Kingdom. Phone: 44 1628 492000; Fax: 44 1628 492260; Email: customerhelp@dnb.com • URL: http://www.dnb.co.uk • Local businesses in Edinburgh, Scotland including commercial and manufacturing companies, public and social sector services, shops and retail outlets, pubs, restaurants, entertainment outlets, schools, and education facilities.

***D & B Business Register: London - Western Central, Eastern Central, East, North***. Dun & Bradstreet (UK) Ltd., Marlow International, Parkway, Marlow Buckinghamshire SL7 1AJ, United Kingdom. Phone: 44 1628 492000; Fax: 44 1628 492260; Email: customerhelp@dnb.com • URL: http://www.dnb.co.uk • £270 Individuals. Local businesses in Western Central, Eastern Central, East, and North London including commercial and manufacturing companies, public and social sector services, shops and retail outlets, pubs, restaurants, entertainment outlets, schools, and education facilities.

***D & B Business Register: North of Scotland***. Dun & Bradstreet (UK) Ltd., Marlow International, Parkway, Marlow Buckinghamshire SL7 1AJ, United Kingdom. Phone: 44 1628 492000; Fax: 44 1628 492260; Email: customerhelp@dnb.com • URL: http://www.dnb.co.uk • £270 Individuals. Local businesses in North of Scotland including commercial and manufacturing companies, public and social sector services, shops and retail outlets, pubs, restaurants, entertainment outlets, schools, and education facilities.

***D & B Business Register: South of Scotland***. Dun & Bradstreet (UK) Ltd., Marlow International, Parkway, Marlow Buckinghamshire SL7 1AJ, United Kingdom. Phone: 44 1628 492000; Fax: 44 1628 492260; Email: customerhelp@dnb.com • URL: http://www.dnb.co.uk • £270 Individuals. Local businesses in South of Scotland including commercial and manufacturing companies, public and social sector services, shops and retail outlets, pubs, restaurants, entertainment outlets, schools, and education facilities.

***D & B Directory of Service Companies***. Dun & Bradstreet Inc., 103 JFK Pkwy. Short Hills, NJ 07078. Phone: 800-526-0651 or (973)921-5500 or (973)921-5000; Fax: (866)560-7035 or (512)794-7670; Email: info@dnb.com • URL: http://www.dnb.com • Annual. Covers: 50,000 U.S. businesses in the service sector, private and public, including accounting, auditing and bookkeeping, advertising and public relations, architecture and engineering, consumer services, executive search, health, hospitality, management consulting, motion pictures, repair, research, social services, and law. Entries include: DUNS number, company name, address, phone, year started, state of incorporation, sales volume, number of employees, primary and secondary Standard Industrial Classification (SIC) codes, names and titles of key personnel, principal bank, stock exchange symbol, accounting firm, line of business, trade name.

***D & B-Dun's Market Identifiers***. Dun & Bradstreet Inc., 103 JFK Pkwy. Short Hills, NJ 07078. Phone: 800-526-0651 or (973)921-5500 or (973)921-5000; Fax: (866)560-7035 or (512)794-7670; Email: info@dnb.com • URL: http://www.dnb.com • Quarterly. Covers 7.5 million public and private companies with at least five employees or $1 million in sales.

***D & B Europa Directory***. Dun & Bradstreet Inc., 103 JFK Pkwy. Short Hills, NJ 07078. Phone: 800-526-0651 or (973)921-5500 or (973)921-5000; Fax: (866)560-7035 or (512)794-7670; Email: info@dnb.com • URL: http://www.dnb.com • Annual. $650 commercial; $545 public/academic libraries. Covers: more than 62,000 leading manufacturers, distributors, finance, and service companies in 20 European countries. Database includes: Ranking of top 5,000 companies based on sales and number of employees,top 500 banks based on assets, top companies by main business activity. Entries include: DUNS number, company name, address, phone, fax, year established, line of business, primary and secondary Standard Industrial Classification (SIC) codes, company number (may be the V.A.T. number needed for export sales invoices), import/export designation, bankers' details, percentage of annual sales which go to export.

***D & B Million Dollar Directory***. Dun & Bradstreet Inc., 103 JFK Pkwy. Short Hills, NJ 07078. Phone: 800-526-0651 or (973)921-5500 or (973)921-5000; Fax: (866)560-7035 or (512)794-7670; Email: info@dnb.com • URL: http://www.dnb.com • Annual. Covers 1,600,000 public and private businesses with either a net worth of $500,000 or more, 250 or more employees at that location, or $25,000,000 or more in sales volume; includes industrial corporations, utilities, transportation companies, bank and trust companies, stock brokers, mutual and stock insurance companies, wholesalers, retailers, and domestic subsidiaries of foreign corporations.

***D & B Million Dollar Directory—Top 50,000 Companies***. Dun & Bradstreet Inc., 103 JFK Pkwy. Short Hills, NJ 07078. Phone: 800-526-0651 or (973)921-5500 or (973)921-5000; Fax: (866)560-7035 or (512)794-7670; Email: info@dnb.com • URL: http://www.dnb.com • Annual. $500 commercially; $450 for public libraries (lease basis). 50,000 top corporations, utilities, transportation companies, bank and trust companies, stock brokers, mutual and stock insurance companies, wholesalers, retailers, and domestic subsidiaries of foreign corporations; business must have 250 or more employees at main location, or have at least $25 million in sales volume.

***D & O Advisor: Risk Management for Directors and Officers***. ALM Media Properties LLC, 120 Broadway, 5th Fl. New York, NY 10271-1100. Phone: (212)457-9400; Fax: (646)417-7705; Email: customercare@alm.com • URL: http://www.alm.com • Quarterly. $125.00 per year. Covers a wide range of legal topics of concern to corporate boards and key executives.

**DACOR**. 1801 F St. NW Washington, DC 20006. Phone: (202)682-0500; Fax: (202)842-3295; Email: dacor@dacorbacon.org • URL: http://dacorbacon.org • Formerly Retired Foreign Service Officers Association.

***Dafsaliens Database of Ownership Links—France***. Dafsaliens, 1 rue de l'Union 92843 Paris, France. Phone: 33 1 47524500; Fax: 33 1 47524540; Email: info@dafsaliens.fr • URL: http://www.dafsaliens.fr • Monthly. Covers: More than 120,000 companies worldwide. Entries include: Company names, registration number, form of incorporation, addresses, telephone, fax, description of business, shareholders subsidiaries and cross holdings, and financial data. CD-ROM includes historical data to trace changing structures and current and former directors and officers.

***The Daily Record: Business and Legal News of Maryland***. The Daily Record CPN, 11 E Saratoga St. Baltimore, MD 21202. Phone: (443)524-8100; Email: customerservice@thedolancompany.com • URL: http://thedailyrecord.com • Mon.-Sat. $269 Individuals print and online; $169 Individuals online. Daily Business Newspaper reporting news and features on business, real estate, technology, healthcare and law.

***Daily Report for Executives***. Bloomberg BNA, 3 Bethesda Metro Center, Ste. 250 Bethesda, MD 20814-5377. Phone: 800-372-1033 or (703)341-3000; Fax: (800)253-0332; Email: customercare@bna.com • URL: http://www.bna.com • Daily. Covers legal, regulatory, economic, and tax developments affecting corporations.

***Daily Tax Report***. Bloomberg BNA, 3 Bethesda Metro Center, Ste. 250 Bethesda, MD 20814-5377. Phone: 800-372-1033 or (703)341-3000; Fax: (800)253-0332; Email: customercare@bna.com • URL: http://www.bna.com • Daily. Monitors tax legislation, hearings, rulings, and court decisions.

***Daily Variety***. Variety Media Publications, 6 Bell Yard London WC2A 2JR, United Kingdom. Phone: 44 20 75205200; Fax: 44 20 75205237; Email: richard.woolley@variety.co.uk • URL: http://www.chb.com • Daily. $199 Individuals. Covers entire scope of the entertainment business on the East and West coast.

***Daily Weather Maps***. U.S. Department of Commerce, 1401 Constitution Ave. NW Washington, DC 20230. Phone: 800-782-8872 or (202)482-2000 or (202)482-6607; Email: TheSec@doc.gov • URL: http://www.commerce.gov • Weekly series.

***Dairy Foods***. BNP Media, 2401 W Big Beaver Rd., Ste. 700 Troy, MI 48084. Phone: 800-952-6643 or (248)362-3700 or (847)763-9534; Fax: (248)362-5103 or (248)362-0317; Email: privacy@bnpmedia.com • URL: http://www.bnpmedia.com • Monthly. Provides broad coverage of new developments in the dairy industry, including cheese and ice cream products.

**Dairy Management, Inc.** 10255 W Higgins Rd., Ste. 900 Rosemont, IL 60018-5616. Phone: 800-853-2479; Fax: (847)627-2077 • URL: http://www.dairy.org • Operates under the auspices of the United Dairy Industry Association. Milk producers, milk dealers, and manufacturers of butter, cheese, ice cream, dairy equipment, and supplies. Conducts programs of nutrition research and nutrition education in the use of milk and its products.

***Dairy Market Statistics***. U.S. Department of Agriculture - Agricultural Marketing Service, Rm. 3071-S, Ag Stop 0201, 1400 Independence Ave., SW Washington, DC 20250. Phone: (800)333-4636; Email: amsadministratoroffice@ams.usda.gov • URL: http://www.ams.usda.gov/AMSv1.0 • Annual.

***Dairy Science Abstracts***. CABI Publishing North America, 38 Chauncey St., Ste. 1002 Boston, MA 02111. Phone: 800-552-3083; Email: cabi-nao@cabi.org • URL: http://www.cabi.org • Monthly. Published in England by CABI Publishing.

***Dakhiliya Region Tourist Guide***. Oman Chamber of Commerce and Industry, PO Box 1400 Ruwi 112, Oman. Phone: 968 24763700 or 96 824 707674; Fax: 968 24708497 or 96 824 708497; Email: occi@chamberoman.com • URL: http://www.chamberoman.com • Provides information and data on tourist sites, locations, services in Dakhiliya Region. Entries include: Names and addresses of travel and tourism organizations and companies.

***Dakotas-Montana Medical Directory***. Jola Publications, 2933 N 2nd St. Minneapolis, MN 55411. Phone: 866-565-2782 or (612)529-5001; Fax: (612)521-2289 or (612)605-4645; Email: medical@jolapub.com • URL: http://www.jolapub.com • Biennial. $25 Individuals. Covers: Approximately 5,000 doctors, hospitals, clinics, nursing homes, and other selected health care providers in North Dakota, South Dakota, and Montana. Entries include: Doctor or facility name, address, phone.

**Dalhousie University - Schulich School of Law - Health Law Institute**. 6061 University Ave. Halifax, NS, Canada B3H 4R2. Phone: (902)494-6881; Fax: (902)494-6879; Email: hli@dal.ca • URL: http://www.dal.ca/faculty/law/hli.html • Health law and policy.

***Dallas Business Journal***. American City Business Journals, Inc., 120 W Morehead St. Charlotte, NC 28202. Phone: (704)973-1000; Fax: (704)973-1001; Email: americancity@bizjournals.com • URL: http://www.acbj.com • Weekly. $95 Individuals print + online. Metro business journal.

***Dallas/Ft. Worth JobBank: The Job Hunter's Guide to the Dallas-Fort Worth Metroplex***. Adams Media Corp., 57 Littlefield St. Avon, MA 02322. Phone: 800-872-5627 or (508)427-7100; Fax: (508)427-6790 or (800)872-5628; Email: deskcopies@adamsmedia.com • URL: http://www.adamsmedia.com • Annual. $9 Individuals Paperback. Covers: 4,000 employers in the Dallas/Ft. Worth, Texas, area including Abilene, Amarillo, Arlington, Garland, Irving, Lubbock, Plano. Database includes: Information on the basics of getting a job and writing resumes and cover letters; electronic job search information. Entries include: Firm or organization name, address, local phone, toll-free phone, fax, e-mail, URL, recorded jobline, hours, description of organization, subsidiaries, names of management, name and title of contact, location of headquarters, typical titles for common positions, educational backgrounds desired, company benefits, stock exchange listing, training programs, internships, parent company, number of employees, revenues, projected number of hires.

***Dalton Carpet Journal***. The Daily Citizen News, 308 S Thornton Ave. Dalton, GA 30720. Phone: (404)278-1011 • Monthly. $12.00. Covers the international tufted carpet market.

***Dalton's Baltimore/Washington Metropolitan Directory of Business/Industry***. Dalton Directory, 24 N Bryn Mawr Ave., Ste. 278 Bryn Mawr, PA 19010. Phone: 800-221-1050 or (518)583-4545; Fax: (518)583-4545; Email: info@daltondirectory.com • URL: http://www.daltondirectory.com • Covers: over 8,500 companies in the Baltimore and Washington, D.C. metropolitan area, including manufacturers, law firms, hospitals, hotels, schools and colleges, accounting firms, etc. Entries include: Company name, address, phone, fax, names and titles of key personnel, number of employees, Standard Industrial Classification (SIC) code, product/service.

***Dana Point Official Visitors Guide & Business Directory***. Dana Point Chamber of Commerce, 24681 La Plaza, Ste. 115 Dana Point, CA 92629. Phone: (949)496-1555; Email: chamber@danapointchamber.com • URL: http://www.danapointchamber.com • Covers businesses in Dana Point, California.

***Dance Magazine College Guide***. Dance Magazine Inc., 333 7th Ave., 11th Fl. New York, NY 10001. Phone: 800-331-1750 or (646)459-4800; Fax: (646)459-4900; Email: dancemag@dancemagazine.com • URL: http://www.dancemagazine.com • Annual. $46.95 Individuals. Covers: Approximately 600 college-level dance programs. Entries include: College name, address, phone, and name of contact for dance department; degrees offered; degree requirements; facilities; special programs; admission requirements; tuition and fees; financial aid available. Also includes articles on issues in dance education.

**The Darla Moore School of Business - Division of Research**. University of South Carolina at Columbia, 1705 College St. Columbia, SC 29208. Phone: (803)777-2510; Fax: (803)777-2510; Email: steel@moore.sc.edu • URL: http://www.mooreschool.sc.edu.

**Darling Marine Center**. University of Maine, 193 Clarks Cove Rd. Walpole, ME 04573. Phone: (207)563-3146; Fax: (207)563-3119; Email: darling@maine.edu • URL: http://www.dmc.maine.edu • Formerly Ira C. Darling Center for Research, Teaching, and Service.

**Dartmouth College - Geisel School of Medicine - Dartmouth Institute for Health Policy and Clinical Practice**. 35 Centerra Pky. Lebanon, NH 03766. Phone: (603)653-0800; Fax: (603)653-0820; Email: the.dartmouth.institute@dartmouth.edu • URL: http://tdi.dartmouth.edu • Evaluative clinical science and health care delivery, including medical care epidemiology, health policy, health behavior, efficacy of medical procedures, quality of medical and surgical care, distribution of health care resources, medical interventions and consequences for patients, care at the end of life, distribution of health care resources across hospital market areas, geriatric health, and sociology of medical organizations.

**Dartmouth College - Glassmeyer/McNamee Center for Digital Strategies**. 100 Tuck Hall Hanover, NH 03755-9000. Phone: (603)646-0899; Fax: (603)646-0900; Email: digital.strategies@dartmouth.edu • URL: http://digitalstrategies.tuck.dartmouth.edu • Impact of information technologies on the ability of businesses to integrate and collaborate with customers and supply chain partners.

***Das Grosse Einkaufs 1x1 der Deutschen Wirtschaft: Band 3: Deutsche Wirtschafts-Standorte***. Deutscher Adressbuch-Verlag fur Wirtschaft und Verkehr GmbH, Arheilger Weg 17 D-64380 Rossdorf, Germany. Phone: 49 61 54 69 95 00; Fax: 49 61 54 6 99 54 90; Email: businessdeutschland@t online.de • Annual. $200 prepaid. Covers: federal and state govermental agencies of the Federal Republic of Germany; approximately 220,000 German industrial, retail, wholesale, and service companies; national and regional trade organizations. Database includes: List of place names with former names and geographical location; maps. Entries include: Agency, organization, or company name, address, phone; headquarters office location for branch companies.

***DASH: Directors and Shareholdings***. Bureau van Dijk S.A., Ave. Louise, Louizalaan 250 B-1050 Brussels, Belgium. Phone: 32 2 6390606 or 32 2 639 06 06; Fax: 32 2 6488230 or 32 2 648 82 30; Email: brussels@bvdinfo.com • URL: http://www.bvdinfo.com • Database covers: One million limited companies and two million directors combined with details on individual and corporate shareholders in the United Kingdom. Entries include: Company name, address, phone, fax, activity, employee range, legal form, status, capital, turnover, holding companies and corporate shareholders; director name, date of birth, address, marital status, nationality, occupation, qualification, appointment date.

***Data Sources for Business and Market Analysis***. Hoover's Inc., 5800 Airport Blvd. Austin, TX 78752-4204. Phone: 866-443-3939 or (512)374-4500 or (866)281-5969; Fax: (512)374-4501; Email: salesteam@hoovers.com • URL: http://www.hoovers.com • $54.95. Covers: Sources of business information from providers including the federal government, regional and local governments, foreign sources, universities, research centers, and professional and trade associations.

***Data, Where It Is and How to Get It: Directory of Business, Environment and Energy Data Sources***. Coleman/Morse, 1190 river Bay Rd. Annapolis, MD 21401. Phone: (410)757-3197 • $24.95. Covers: Over 2,500 sources of information produced by the U.S. government on business, environmental and energy activities; includes experts, federal departments and agencies, data centers, and user groups. Entries include: Data sources for agriculture, banking and finance, international trade, demographics, employment, prices, income, and rural development.

***Database, Directory of MNCs Companies in India***. NIIR Project Consultancy Services, 106 - E, Kamla Nagar New Delhi 110007, India. Phone: 91 11 23843955; Fax: 91 11 23841561; Email: npcs.india@gmail.com • URL: http://www.niir.org • Rs 1,124 Individuals CD-ROM; $100 U.S. CD-ROM. Covers: Multinational companies in India. Entries include: Name, address, country of origin, phone, fax, e-mail, website, CEO name.

***Database Marketer***. SIMBA Information Inc., 60 Long Ridge Rd., Ste. 300 Stamford, CT 06902. Phone: (203)325-8193; Fax: (203)325-8975 • URL: http://www.simbainformation.com • Monthly. $329.00 per year.

***Database of the Central Archives for Finnish Business Records***. Central Archives for Finnish Business Records, Tutkijantie 7 FIN-50100 Mikkeli, Finland. Phone: 358 15 321 340; Fax: 358 15 366 340; Email: e-mail@elka.fi • URL: http://www.elka.fi • Contains information about materials held at the Central Archives for Finnish Business Records, at various public institutes, and in the libraries of about 200 companies. Includes documents, drawings, photographs, and maps.

***Database of World Wide General Traders***. NIIR Project Consultancy Services, 106 - E, Kamla Nagar New Delhi 110007, India. Phone: 91 11 23843955; Fax: 91 11 23841561; Email: npcs.india@gmail.com • URL: http://www.niir.org • $200 Individuals CD-ROM; Rs 2,809 Individuals CD-ROM. Covers: Worldwide general traders (exporters and importers). Entries include: Company name, postal address, city, state, pin code, phone, fax and email (2,100,000+).

***Datalink Regional Business Directory***. Datatech Communications Inc., 3301-R Coors Rd. NW Albuquerque, NM 87120. Phone: 877-859-4409 • Covers: More than 180,000 companies in New York, Vermont, New Hampshire, Maine, Massachusetts, Rhode Island, Maryland, Connecticut, and New Jersey. Entries include: Company name, address, phone, fax, 800 numbers, URL, e-mail.

***Datapro on CD-ROM: Communications Analyst***. Gartner Inc., 56 Top Gallant Rd. Stamford, CT 06904-7747. Phone: (203)964-0096; Fax: (203)316-6488 or (203)324-7901; Email: info@gartner.com • URL: http://www.gartner.com • Monthly. Price on application. Provides detailed information on products and services for communications systems, including local area networks and voice systems.

***Datapro on CD-ROM: Computer Systems Analyst***. Gartner Inc., 56 Top Gallant Rd. Stamford, CT 06904-7747. Phone: (203)964-0096; Fax: (203)316-6488 or (203)324-7901; Email: info@gartner.com • URL: http://www.gartner.com • Monthly. Price on application. Includes detailed information on specific computer hardware and software products, such as peripherals, security systems, document imaging systems, and UNIX-related products.

***Datapro on CD-ROM: Computer Systems Hardware and Software***. Gartner Inc., 56 Top Gallant Rd. Stamford, CT 06904-7747. Phone: (203)964-0096; Fax: (203)316-6488 or (203)324-7901; Email: info@gartner.com • URL: http://www.gartner.com • Monthly. Price on application. CD-ROM provides product specifications, product reports, user surveys, and market forecasts for a wide range of computer hardware and software.

***Datapro Reports***. Datapro Information Services Group, 600 Delran Pkwy. Delran, NJ 08075. Phone: 800-328-2776 or (856)764-0100; Fax: (856)764-2814; Email: tom.mccall@gartner.com • URL: http://www.gartner.com • Monthly. $495 minimum cost per year, depending on service; $11,500 maximum cost per year, depending on service. Datapro produces sixty information services covering products, vendors, markets, and technologies in large systems, microcomputers, telecommunications, data communications, word processing, software, office automation systems, copiers and duplicators, information security systems, retail automation equipment, banking automation equipment, personal computer communications, communications alternatives, and electronic publishing systems. Reports generally include descriptions and analyses of each equipment model offered by each manufacturer in the field, comparison charts, and lists of suppliers, associations, consultants, etc., with addresses and phone numbers. Individual descriptions include a summary and detailed reports on technical characteristics and operation. Reports are on looseleaf pages.

***Datapro Software Finder***. Gartner Inc., 56 Top Gallant Rd. Stamford, CT 06904-7747. Phone: (203)964-0096; Fax: (203)316-6488 or (203)324-7901; Email: info@gartner.com • URL: http://www.gartner.com • Quarterly. $1,770.00 per year. CD-ROM provides detailed information on more than 18,000 software products for a wide variety of computers, personal to mainframe. Covers software for 130 types of business, finance, and industry. (Editions limited to either microcomputer or mainframe software are available at $995.00 per year.).

***Datatech Communications Business Directory***. Datatech Communications Inc., 3301-R Coors Rd. NW Albuquerque, NM 87120. Phone: 877-859-4409 • Covers: More than 160,000 companies throughout the U.S. Entries include: Company name, address, phone, fax, 800 numbers, URL, e-mail.

***Dayton Business Journal***. American City Business Journals, Inc., 120 W Morehead St. Charlotte, NC 28202. Phone: (704)973-1000; Fax: (704)973-1001; Email: americancity@bizjournals.com • URL: http://www.acbj.com • Contains the full text of Dayton Business Journal, a business tabloid covering Dayton, Ohio.

**De La Salle University - Ramon V. del Rosario College of Business - Center for Business and Economics Research and Development**. 2401 Taft Ave. Manila 1004, Philippines. Phone: 63 2 3030869; Fax: 63 2 5219094; Email: cbedean@dlsu.edu.ph • URL: http://www.dlsu.edu.ph/research/centers/cberd/default.asp • Business education, entrepreneurship, and administrative policy.

***DealBase II: An Electronic Database of Acquisition Opportunities***. Business Publications Inc., 9605 Scranton Rd., Ste. 840 San Diego, CA 92121. • Monthly. $425 per year. Diskette. Database covers: Over 675 of middle market companies, currently available for acquisition, with annual revenues between 3 and 75 million dollars. Database includes: Company name, location, description, revenues, profitability, purchase price, industry, contact information, merger/acquisition data.

***Dealer Progress: How Smart Agribusiness is Growing***. The Fertilizer Institute, 425 3rd St. SW, Ste. 950 Washington, DC 20024. Phone: (202)962-0490; Fax: (202)962-0577 • URL: http://www.tfi.org • Bimonthly. Free to qualified personnel; others, $40.00 per year. Published in association with the Fertilizer Institute. Includes information on fertilizers and agricultural chemicals, including farm pesticides. Formerly *Progress*.

***Dealernews: The Voice of Powersports Retailers***. Advanstar Communications, 545 Boylston St. Boston, MA 02116. Phone: 888-527-7008 or (617)267-6500; Fax: (617)267-6900; Email: info@advanstar.com • URL: http://www.advanstar.com • News concerning the power sports motor vehicle industry.

***Dealerscope: Product and Strategy for Consumer Technology Retailing***. North American Publishing Co., 1500 Spring Garden St., Ste. 1200 Philadelphia, PA 19130-4069. Phone: (215)238-5300; Email: customerservice@napco.com • URL: http://www.napco.com • Monthly. $79 /year; Free to qualified personnel. Formerly *Dealerscope Consumer Electronics Marketplace*. Provides product information and valuable strategy for consumer technology retailers.

***Dearborn Business Journal***. Dearborn Chamber of Commerce, 22100 Michigan Ave. Dearborn, MI 48124. Phone: (313)584-6100; Fax: (313)584-9818; Email: info@dearbornchamber.org • URL: http://www.dearbornchamber.org • Monthly. Magazine containing news about Dearborn businesses and information about Dearborn Chamber of Commerce events and activities.

***The Debt Finance Landscape for U.S. Farming and Farm Businesses***. U.S. Department of Agriculture Economic Research Service, 355 E St. SW Washington, DC 20024-3221. Phone: (202)694-5500 or (202)694-5000; Email: InfoCenter@ers.usda.gov • URL: http://www.ers.usda.gov • Annual.

**Debtors Anonymous**. PO Box 920888 Needham, MA 02492-0009. Phone: 800-421-2383 or (781)453-2743; Fax: (781)453-2745; Email: office@debtorsanonymous.org • URL: http://www.debtorsanonymous.org • Fellowship of men and women who share their experience, strength, and hope with each other that they may solve their common problem of compulsive debiting. Adapts the Twelve Steps and Twelve Traditions of Alcoholics Anonymous World Services for compulsive debtors. Establishes and coordinates self help support groups for people seeking to live without incurring unsecured debt. Helps members develop workable plans for long-term financial and lifestyle goals.

***Decatur Business Association—Membership Directory***. Decatur Business Association, PO Box 2208 Decatur, GA 30031. Phone: (404)371-8386; Fax: (404)371-1593; Email: info@decaturdba.com • URL: http://www.decaturdba.com • Covers businesses, professionals, financial institutions, art groups, associated agencies and organizations, and private individuals engaged in doing business in Decatur.

***Decatur Chamber of Commerce Business Directory***. Greater Decatur Chamber of Commerce, 101 S Main St., Ste. 102 Decatur, IL 62523-1048. Phone: (217)422-2200 • URL: http://www.decaturchamber.com • Covers chamber members. Entries include name, address, phone.

**Decision Sciences Institute**. C.T. Bauer College of Business, 334 Melchor Hall, Ste. 325 Houston, TX 77204-6021. Phone: (713)743-4815; Fax: (713)743-8984; Email: info@decisionsciences.org • URL: http://www.decisionsciences.org • Businesspersons and members of business school faculties. Maintains placement service.

***Decisions in Imaging Economics: The Journal of Imaging Technology Management***. CurAnt Communications Inc., 6701 Ctr. Dr. W, Ste. 450 Los Angeles, CA 90045. Phone: (310)642-4400 or (310)306-2206; Fax: (310)641-4444 • Bimonthly. Controlled circulation. Edited for health care executives and radiologists concerned with the purchase and management of imaging technology.

**Decorative Plumbing and Hardware Association**. 7508 Wisconsin Ave., 4th Fl. Bethesda, MD 20814-3561. Phone: (301)657-3642; Fax: (301)907-9326; Email: info@dpha.net • URL: http://www.dpha.net • Advances the business and professional development of independent dealers, manufacturers, representatives and others involved in the decorative plumbing and hardware industry. Offers educational programs to train staff, create career paths and provide recognition.

***Decorators Directory***. InfoGroup Inc., 5711 S 86th Cir. Omaha, NE 68127-4146. Phone: (402)593-4500 • URL: http://www.infogroup.com • Annual. Number of listings: 33,751. Entries include: Name, address, phone, size of advertisement, name of owner or manager, number of employees, year first in "Yellow Pages." Compiled from telephone company "Yellow Pages," nationwide.

**Deep Draft Lubricant Association**. c/o Shawn Konrad, Director, Belle Chasse Marine Transportation, 5813 Citrus Blvd. Harahan, LA 70123-5810. Phone: (504)837-3125; Email: information@ddla.org • URL: http://www.ddla.org • Promotes the interests of persons and firms engaged in the delivery of petroleum lubricants to deep draft vessels in the waters of the United States. Strives to create awareness of the individual operators, their suppliers and the industry of operational efficiencies and environmental regulations. Works to develop and improve performance standards and business methods.

***Defence & Public Service Helicopter***. Shephard Press Ltd., 111 High St. Burnham SL1 7JZ, United Kingdom. Phone: 44 1628 664334; Fax: (162)8 664075; Email: publishing@shephard.co.uk • URL: http://www.shephard.co.uk • Bimonthly. $130.00 per year. Provides international coverage of both the public service (police, emergency, etc.) and military helicopter industries and markets. Includes technical, piloting, and safety topics. Formerly *Defence Helicopter*.

***Defending Pesticides in Litigation***. David Whitacre and Shane Anderson. Thomson West, 610 Opperman Dr. Eagan, MN 55123. Phone: 800-328-9352 or (651)687-7000 • Annual. $1,155 book-softbound; $808.50 discounted price for subscription orders; $96 monthly. Discusses liability and other legal issues related to the manufacture and use of pesticides. Includes a guide to FIFRA (Federal Insecticide, Fungicide, and Rodenticide Act). (Environmental Law Series).

**Defense Advisory Committee on Women in the Services**. 4000 Defense Pentagon, Rm. 5A734 Washington, DC 20301-4000. Phone: (703)697-2122; Email: osd.pentagon.ousd-p-r.mbx.dacowits@mail.mil • URL: http://dacowits.defense.gov • Civilians appointed by Secretary of Defense to provide recommendations to optimize utilization and quality of life for women in U.S. armed forces. Assists the Department of Defense by advising on specified matters relating to the recruitment and retention, treatment, employment, integration, and well-being of highly qualified professional women in the Services. Advises on family issues related to the recruitment and retention of a highly qualified professional military.

***Defense and Security***. U. S. Government Printing Office, 732 N Capitol St. NW Washington, DC 20401. Phone: 866-512-1800 or (202)512-1800 or (866)512-1800; Fax: (202)512-2104 or (202)512-2250; Email: contactcenter@gpo.gov • URL: http://www.gpo.gov • Annual. Free. Issued by the Superintendent of Documents. A list of government publications on defense and related topics. Formerly *Defense Supply and Logistics*. (Subject Bibliography No. 153.).

***Defense Counsel Journal***. International Association of Defense Counsel, 303 W Madison St., Ste. 925 Chicago, IL 60606. Phone: (312)368-1494; Fax: (312)368-1854; Email: info@iadclaw.org • URL: http://www.iadclaw.org • Quarterly. $87 Individuals. Scholarly and practical articles dealing with defense of civil cases, particularly those involving insurance.

**Defense Credit Union Council**. 601 Pennsylvania Ave. NW, South Bldg., Ste. 600 Washington, DC 20004-2601. Phone: (202)638-3950; Fax: (202)638-3410; Email: admin@dcuc.org • URL: http://www.dcuc.org • Credit unions serving Department of Defense military and civilian personnel. Aims to assist credit unions serving DOD personnel with problems peculiar to military installations and personnel, and to maintain close liaison with DOD.

***Defense Daily Network: The Business Source for Aerospace and Defense***. Access Intelligence L.L.C., 4 Choke Cherry Rd., 2nd Fl. Rockville, MD 20850. Phone: 800-777-5006 or (301)354-2000 or (301)354-2101; Fax: (301)309-3847 or (801)365-2300; Email: info@accessintel.com • URL: http://www.accessintel.com/ • Daily. Covers the global defense industry.

***Defense Electronics***. RentPath Inc., 3585 Engineering Dr., Ste. 100 Norcross, GA 30092-2831. Phone: 800-216-1423 or (678)421-3000 • URL: http://www.rentpath.com • Monthly.

**Defense Research Institute**. 55 W Monroe St., Ste. 2000 Chicago, IL 60603-5121. Phone: (312)795-1101; Fax: (312)795-0749 • URL: http://www.dri.org • Lawyers, claims people, adjusters, insurance companies, trade associations, corporations, and "target" defendants in civil litigation, such as doctors, pharmacists, engineers, manufacturers, and other professional and skilled personnel. Seeks to increase the knowledge and improve the skills of defense lawyers and to improve the adversary system of justice. Maintains research facilities, including files of speeches, briefs, and names of expert witnesses in various fields. Maintains Expert Witness Index.

***Defense Systems Review and Military Communications***. Cosgriff-Martin Publishing Group, Inc., 2595 Solano Ave. Napa, CA 94558. Phone: (707)257-8480 • Monthly. $35.00 per year.

***Defense Transportation Journal***. National Defense Transportation Association, 50 S Pickett St., Ste. 220 Alexandria, VA 22304-7296. Phone: (703)751-5011; Fax: (703)823-8761 • URL: http://www.ndtahq.com • Bimonthly. $35 in U.S.; Included in membership; $45 overseas. Bimonthly. Free to members.

***Definitive Directory of Competitive Telecommunications Service Providers***. Advanstar Communications Inc., 7500 Old Oak Blvd. Cleveland, OH 44130. Phone: 800-225-4569 or (440)243-8100 or (216)826-2839; Fax: (440)891-2727; Email: info@advanstar.com • URL: http://www.advanstar.com • Annual. $275 Nonmembers plus $6 shipping; $233.75 Members plus $6 shipping. Covers: Hundreds of new and existing competitive telecommunications service providers. Entries include: Name, address, phone, fax, statistical data, company profiles, market research on revenues, services, operating territories.

***Delaware Agricultural Trade Directory***. Delaware Department of Agriculture, 2320 S DuPont Hwy. Dover, DE 19901. Phone: 800-232-8685 or (302)698-4500 or (302)698-4554; Fax: (302)697-6287 or (302)697-4749; Email: edwin.kee@state.de.us • URL: http://dda.delaware.gov • Irregular. Covers: about 300 producers, processors, and distributors of agricultural products in Delaware; includes exporters. Entries include: Company name, address, phone, type of product or service, quantity, variety, other information.

***Delaware Directory of Commerce and Industry***. Delaware State Chamber of Commerce Inc., 1201 N Orange St., Ste. 200 Wilmington, DE 19899-0671. Phone: 800-292-9507 or (302)655-7221 or (302)576-6560; Fax: (302)654-0691; Email: info@dscc.com • URL: http://www.dscc.com • Periodic Annual. $50 Members per additional copy for members; $100 Nonmembers. Covers: About 5,000 manufacturers, retailers, wholesalers, and service establishments. Entries include: Name, address, phone, name, address, phone, name and title of contact, list of products or services.

**Delhi Management Association**. India Habitat Ctre., Core 6A, 1st Fl., Lodi Rd. New Delhi 110 003, Delhi, India. Phone: 91 11 24649552; Fax: 91 11 24649553; Email: dmadelhi@sify.com • URL: http://www.dmadelhi.org • Unites to participate in an exciting venture of institution-building, evolving a unique equation of synergy within the India Habitat Centre complex. Shares common concern for habitat.

***Deli News***. Delicatessen Council of Southern California, Inc. Pacific Rim Publishing Co., P.O. Box 4533 Huntington Beach, CA 92605-4533. Phone: (714)375-3904; Fax: (714)375-3906 • Monthly. $25.00 per year. Includes product news and comment related to cheeses, lunch meats, packaged fresh meats, kosher foods, gourmet-specialty items, and bakery products.

***The Delmarva Farmer: The Agribusiness Newspaper of the Mid-***

*Atlantic Region*. American Farm Publications Inc., PO Box 2026 Easton, MD 21601. Phone: 800-634-5021 or (410)822-3965; Fax: (410)822-5068 • URL: http://www.americanfarm.com • Biweekly. $31 Individuals /year; $56 Two years; $69 Individuals three years. Newspaper (tabloid) featuring news of interest to agricultural concerns in Maryland, Delaware, Virginia, New Jersey, and Pennsylvania.

***Delphion Research***. Thomson Delphion, Phone: 800-411-4811 or (630)799-0600; Fax: (630)799-0688; Email: support@delphion.com • URL: http://www.delphion.com • Fee-based Web site provides more than 40 million records of full-text patent information from the U. S. Patent and Trademark Office and from about 70 foreign countries. Corporate and individual subscriptions are available.

**Delta Mu Delta Honor Society**. 9217 Broadway Ave. Brookfield, IL 60513-1251. Phone: 866-789-7067 or (708)485-8494; Fax: (708)221-6183; Email: dmd@dmd-ntl.org • URL: http://deltamudelta.org • Serves as honor society for business administration.

**Delta Sigma Pi**. 330 S Campus Ave. Oxford, OH 45056-2405. Phone: (513)523-1907; Fax: (513)523-7292; Email: centraloffice@dspnet.org • URL: http://www.dspnet.org • Professional fraternity - commerce and business administration. Operates Delta Sigma Pi Leadership Foundation. Maintains museum; sponsors competitions; offers computerized services; compiles statistics. Provides educational and career assistance.

**Demeter Biodynamic Trade Association**. PO Box 264 Talmage, CA 95481-0264. Email: info@demeterbta.com • URL: http://www.demeterbta.com • Represents Demeter Certified Biodynamic farms, vineyards, wineries, dairies, food processors, traders and distributors. Aims to further interest and education in Demeter Certified Biodynamic farming. Strives to promote Demeter Certified Biodynamic products in the marketplace. Supports and advocates for the protection of the Demeter certification marks.

**Democracy International**. 7600 Wisconsin Ave., Ste. 1010 Bethesda, MD 20814-5302. Phone: (301)961-1660; Fax: (301)961-6605; Email: info@democracyinternational.com • URL: http://www.democracyinternational.com • Seeks to build a movement of individuals dedicated to practical action on behalf of common commitments to human rights and pluralistic democracy including freedom of speech and press, religious liberty, free political parties, and the right to contest elections. Works to develop political and economic self-determination of citizens allowing them to control their resources, choose their social systems, and end discrimination. Aims to: revive democracy where it has been destroyed; encourage and sustain democrats trying to bring democracy to dictatorships. Calls upon democracies to: increase help for democratic leaders and politicians in the Third World; provide economic sustenance to relieve human suffering; strengthen democracy where it exists. Provides a forum for democrats to express solidarity and to help each other; encourages membership in an effort to build an international force of people working to make the cause of democracy an enduring ideal. Publicizes the efforts of democratic movements in dictatorships; attempts to increase the amount of uncensored information to closed societies.

***Demography***. Population Association of America, 8630 Fenton St., Ste. 722 Silver Spring, MD 20910-3812. Phone: (301)565-6710; Fax: (301)565-7850; Email: lmbrown@popassoc.org • URL: http://www.populationassociation.org • Quarterly. $295 Institutions incl. free access or e-only; $354 Individuals plus Enhanced Access. Scientific journal covering demographic research, including social sciences, geography, history, biology, statistics, business epidemiology and public health.

***Denmark Business Services Providers Leads***. Business Information Agency Inc. PlanetInform, 52 Tuscan Way, Ste. 202-181 Saint Augustine, VA 32092. Phone: (904)342-6124; Fax: (904)592-2632; Email: info@biasales.com • URL: http://www.biasales.com • Monthly. $211 Individuals mailing list; $444 Individuals sales list; $752 Individuals marketing list. Covers Danish companies and all sub-industries that provide various services to commercial businesses, establishments, and organizations, including consulting, advertising and marketing services, and facilities maintenance.

***Denmark Industrial and Business Directory***. International Business Publications, USA, PO Box 15343 Washington, DC 20003. Phone: (202)546-2103; Fax: (202)546-3275; Email: ibpusa@comcast.net • URL: http://ibpus.com • Annual. $99.95 Individuals hardcopy, e-book, CD-ROM. Covers: Detailed information on investment, export-import business opportunities, foreign economic assistance projects, government and business contacts.

***Denmark Investment and Business Guide***. International Business Publications, USA, PO Box 15343 Washington, DC 20003. Phone: (202)546-2103; Fax: (202)546-3275; Email: ibpusa@comcast.net • URL: http://ibpus.com • $99.95 Individuals hardcopy, e-book, CD-ROM. Covers: Basic information on economy, export-import and investment climate, regulations and industrial development, banking, and government. Entries include: Important business contacts and business travel.

***Denmark's 10,000 Largest Companies***. William Snyder Publishing Associates, Five Mile Dr. Oxford OX2 8HT, United Kingdom. Phone: 44 1865 513186; Fax: 44 1865 311015; Email: snyderpub@aol.com • Annual. $175 plus 30 pounds shipping. Covers: 10,000 "leading" (by turnover) companies in Denmark. Database includes: Table of companies ranked by common currency listing sales figures, percentage growth indicators, profitability, capital structure, number of employees, year established. Entries include: In an index—Company name, address, phone, turnover, profit, number of employees.

***Dennis Business Directory and Visitor Guide***. Dennis Chamber of Commerce, 242 Swan River Rd. South Dennis, MA 02660. Phone: 800-243-9920 or (508)398-3568; Fax: (508)760-5212; Email: dennisec@gis.net • Publication includes: List of about 250 member businesses in the Dennis, Massachusetts, area; list of 40 area accessories. Entries include: For businesses—Company name, address, phone. For accommodations—Hotel or inn name, address, phone, number of rooms, credit cards accepted, price range, operating season, whether handicapped access and other facilities are available. Principal content of publication is suggested routes for touring the area, descriptions of nearby attractions, etc.

***Dental Economics***. PennWell Publishing Co., 1421 S Sheridan Rd. Tulsa, OK 74112. Phone: 800-331-4463 or (918)835-3161 or (508)347-9324; Fax: (918)831-9555; Email: headquarter@pennwell.ocm • URL: http://www.pennwell.com • Monthly. $132 Individuals; $179 Canada and Mexico; $248 Other countries; $211 Two years; $312 Canada and Mexico; $428 Other countries two years; $65 online. Magazine featuring business-related articles for dentists.

***Dental Lab Products***. MEDEC Dental Communications, 2 Northfield Plz., Ste. 300 Northfield, IL 60093-1219. Phone: 800-323-3337 or (847)441-3700; Fax: (847)441-3702 • URL: http://www.dprworld.com/ • Bimonthly. $35.00 per year. Edited for dental laboratory managers. Covers new products and technical developments.

***Dental Practice and Finance***. MEDEC Dental Communications, 2 Northfield Plz., Ste. 300 Northfield, IL 60093-1219. Phone: 800-323-3337 or (847)441-3700; Fax: (847)441-3702 • URL: http://www.dprworld.com/ • Bimonthly. $55.00 per year. Covers practice management and financial topics for dentists. Includes investment advice.

***Dental Products Report Europe***. MEDEC Dental Communications, 2 Northfield Plz., Ste. 300 Northfield, IL 60093-1219. Phone: 800-323-3337 or (847)441-3700; Fax: (847)441-3702 • URL: http://www.dprworld.com/ • Seven times a year. $40.00 per year. Covers new dental products for the Europea market.

***Dental Products Report: Trends in Dentistry***. MEDEC Dental Communications, 2 Northfield Plz., Ste. 300 Northfield, IL 60093-1219. Phone: 800-323-3337 or (847)441-3700; Fax: (847)441-3702 • URL: http://www.dprworld.com/ • 11 times a year. $120.00 per year. Provides information on new dental products, technology, and trends in dentistry.

**Dental Trade Alliance**. 4350 N Fairfax Dr., Ste. 220 Arlington, VA 22203-1673. Phone: (703)379-7755; Fax: (703)931-9429 • URL: http://www.dentaltradealliance.org • Represents dental manufacturers, dental dealers, dental laboratories, dental market service providers and dental publications.

***Denton's Directories***. Denton's Directories Ltd., Edward St. Westbury BA13 8DR, United Kingdom. Phone: 44 1373 822224; Fax: 44 1373 825522 • Annual. $11. Covers: Local businesses and community services in various British towns; separate volumes cover Bath, Calne/Lyneham, Chippenham/Corsham, Cirencester, Devizes, Keynsham/Saltford, Malmesbury/Tetbury, Marlborough/Hungerford, Melksham, Shaftesbury/Gillingham/Mere, Sherborne/Milborne Port, Trowbridge/Bradford on Avon, Warminster, Westbury, Bridport, Dorchester, Wootton, and Bassett. Entries include: Company name, address, phone.

***Denver Business Journal***. American City Business Journals, 1700 Broadway, Ste. 515 Denver, CO 80290. Phone: (303)837-3500; Fax: (303)837-3535 • URL: http://www.amcity.com/denver • Weekly. $100 Individuals print and digital. Local business newspaper.

***Denver Business***. Tall Oaks Publishing Inc., PO Box 621669 Littleton, CO 80162-1669. • Monthly. $24 Individuals. Consumer business magazine serving metropolitan Denver.

***Denver JobBank: The Job Hunter's Guide to Colorado***. Adams Media Corp., 57 Littlefield St. Avon, MA 02322. Phone: 800-872-5627 or (508)427-7100; Fax: (508)427-6790 or (800)872-5628; Email: deskcopies@adamsmedia.com • URL: http://www.adamsmedia.com • $17.95 Individuals 4 used & new. Covers: 3,500 employers in Denver and the rest of Colorado including Aurora, Boulder, Colorado Springs, Lakewood. Database includes: Information on the basics of job winning and writing resumes and cover letters; searching for a job online; regional employment outlook; 330 industry associations; 90 online career resources; 150 employment services. Entries include: Firm or organization name, address, local phone, toll-free phone, fax, e-mail, URL, description of organization, subsidiaries, other locations, hours, recorded jobline, names of management, name and title of contact, headquarters location, projected number of hires; listings may also include typical titles for common positions, educational backgrounds desired, company benefits, stock exchange listing, training programs, internships, parent company, number of employees, revenues.

***Denver Merchandise Mart Directory***. Denver Merchandise Mart, 451 E 58th Ave., Ste. 4270 Denver, CO 80216-8470. Phone: 800-289-6278 or (303)292-6278 or (303)368-0040; Fax: (303)297-8473 or (303)368-0070; Email: info@denvermart.com • URL: http://www.denvermart.com • Annual. Covers: About 4,000 manufacturers, importers, and wholesale distributors of men's, women's, and children's clothing, western apparel, shoes, gifts, gourmet items, bath accessories, jewelry, resort merchandise, and home furnishings who are represented in the Denver Merchandise Mart. Entries include: Firm name, mart address; alphabetical listings include phone.

**Department of Electrical and Microelectronic Engineering**. Rochester Institute of Technology, Kate Gleason College of Engineering, 77 Lomb Memorial Dr. Rochester, NY 14623. Phone: (585)475-2165; Fax: (585)475-5845; Email: eme@rit.edu • URL: http://www.rit.edu/kgcoe/eme • Facilities include digital computer organization/microcomputer laboratory.

**Department of Finance Canada - Economic and Fiscal Policy Branch - Economic Studies and Policy Analysis Division - Structural Analysis Section**. East Tower, 19th Fl., 140 O'Connor St. Ottawa, ON, Canada K1A 0G5. Phone: (613)992-1573; Fax: (613)943-0938; Email: finpub@fin.gc.ca • URL: http://www.fin.gc.ca/branches-directions/efp-eng.asp#EconomicStudiesandPolicyAnalysisDivision • Economics and policy, focusing on labor economics, public finance, income distribution and educational issues.

**Department of Forest Biomaterials**. North Carolina State University, Campus Box 8005 Raleigh, NC 27695. Phone: (919)515-5807; Fax: (919)515-6302; Email: contactfb@ncsu.edu • URL: http://cnr.ncsu.edu • Studies the mechanical and engineering properties of wood, wood finishing, wood anatomy, wood chemistry, etc.

**Department of Ophthalmology**. Icahn School of Medicine at Mount Sinai, 1 Gustave L. Levy Pl., Box 1183 New York, NY 10029. Phone: (212)241-0939; Fax: (212)987-1799 • URL: http://icahn.mssm.edu/departments-and-institutes/ophthalmology.

**Department of Science and Technology - Philippine Textile Research Institute**. General Santos Ave., Bicutan Taguig City, Philippines. Phone: 63 2 8371325; Fax: 63 2 8371325; Email: carlos@dost.gov.ph • URL: http://www.ptri.dost.gov.ph • Applied research and development on textiles focusing on judicious utilization of fibrous materials and auxiliaries from indigenous resources, improving and/or inventing textile machinery, processes, and production methods for the Philippine textile, garment and allied industry. Areas of study include indigenous fibers, natural dyes, sericulture, processes, tool and machine development.

***Department of Trade and Industry—The Single Market: Guide to Sources of Advice***. Department of Trade and Industry, Response Center, 1 Victoria St. London SW1H 0ET, United Kingdom. Phone: 44 20 72155000 or 071 215 7877; Fax: 44 20 72150105; Email: dti.enquiries@dti.gsi.gov.uk • URL: http://www.dti.gov.uk • Covers: Organizations providing information on business and trade in the European Community, including representative organizations, research and technology organizations, chambers of commerce, public sector advisers, and language advisers. Entries include: For representative organizations and research and technology organizations—Name, address, phone, name and title of contact, sectors covered, restrictions on service, type of information offered, European links. For others—Name, address, phone, type of information offered.

***Der Runde Herold***. Herold Business Data GmbH, Guntramsdorfer Str. 105 A-2340 Modling, Austria. Phone: 43 2236 401 133; Fax: 43 2236 401 8; Email: kundendienst@herold.at • URL: http://www.herold.at/ • Annual. Database covers: Approximately 225,000 Austrian companies. Entries include: Company name, address, phone, type of business, region, and postal code. For the 10,000 largest companies, includes turnover figures, number of employees, and key personnel.

***Derivatives***. Imagine Software Inc., 233 Broadway, 17th Fl. New York, NY 10279. Phone: (212)317-7600; Fax: (212)317-7601 • URL: http://www.derivatives.com • Web site mainly promotes proprietary software for the use of derivatives in risk management, but also provides free access to articles on a variety of derivatives-related topics.

***Derwent Biotechnology Abstracts***. Derwent Information Ltd., 14 Great Queen St. London WC2B 5DF, United Kingdom. Phone: 44 20 7344 2800; Fax: 44 20 7344 2900 • Provides indexing and abstracting of the world's biotechnology journal literature since 1982, including genetic engineering topics. Monthly updates. Inquire as to online cost and availability.

***Derwent Crop Protection File***. Derwent Information Ltd., 14 Great Queen St. London WC2B 5DF, United Kingdom. Phone: 44 20 7344 2800; Fax: 44 20 7344 2900 • Provides citations to the international journal literature of agricultural chemicals and pesticides from 1968 to date, with updating eight times per year. Formerly *PESTDOC*. Inquire as to online cost and availability.

***Derwent Drug File***. Derwent Information Ltd., 14 Great Queen St. London WC2B 5DF, United Kingdom. Phone: 44 20 7344 2800; Fax: 44 20 7344 2900 • Provides indexing and abstracting of the world's pharmaceutical journal literature since 1964, with weekly updates. Formerly *RINGDOC*. Inquire as to online cost and availability.

***Derwent U. S. Patents***. Derwent Patent Agency, 1725 Duke St., Ste. 250 Alexandria, VA 22314. Phone: 800-336-5010 or (703)706-4220; Fax: (703)519-5829; Email: custserv@

derwentus.com • URL: http://science.thomsonreuters.com/ • Provides citations and abstracts for more then one million U. S. patents issued since 1971. Weekly updates. Inquire as to online cost and availability.

***Derwent Veterinary Drug File***. Derwent Information Ltd., 14 Great Queen St. London WC2B 5DF, United Kingdom. Phone: 44 20 7344 2800; Fax: 44 20 7344 2900 • Provides indexing and abstracting of the world's veterinary drug literature since 1968, with monthly updates. Formerly *VETDOC*. Inquire as to online cost and availability.

***Derwent World Patents Index***. Derwent Patent Agency, 1725 Duke St., Ste. 250 Alexandria, VA 22314. Phone: 800-336-5010 or (703)706-4220; Fax: (703)519-5829; Email: custserv@derwentus.com • URL: http://science.thomsonreuters.com/ • Contains abstracts of more than 20 million patent documents from many countries. Time span varies. Weekly updates. Inquire as to online cost and availability.

***Design Cost Data***. DC & D Technologies Inc., PO Box 948 Valrico, FL 33595-0948. Phone: 800-533-5680 or (813)662-6830; Fax: (813)662-6793; Email: info@dcd.com • URL: http://www.dcd.com • Bimonthly. $149 U.S. /year plus online access to archive; $174.80 Canada and Mexico /year plus online access to archive. Provides a preliminary cost estimating system for architects, contractors, builders, and developers, utilizing historical data. Includes case studies of actual costs. Formerly *Design Cost and Data*.

**Design Management Institute**. 38 Chauncy St., Ste. 800 Boston, MA 02111. Phone: (617)338-6380 • URL: http://www.dmi.org • In-house design groups and consultant design firms; individuals involved in the management of designers with in-house corporate design groups or consultant design firms. Aims to share management techniques as applied to design groups, and to facilitate better understanding by business management of the role design can play in achieving business goals. Design disciplines included are: architecture, advertising, communications, exhibit design, graphics, interior design, packaging and product design. Develops and distributes design management education materials. Sponsors seminars for design professionals. Identifies critical areas of design management study; conducts surveys and research on corporate design management. Maintains design management archive. Operates Center for Research, Center for Education, and Center for Design and Management Resources.

***Design Management Journal***. Design Management Institute, 38 Chauncy St., Ste. 800 Boston, MA 02111. Phone: (617)338-6380 • URL: http://www.dmi.org • 3/year. included in membership dues; $29 Nonmembers Print. Covers the management of product-related design. Dedicated to the highest standards of research, scholarship, and education.

***Desktop Publishing Directory***. InfoGroup Inc., 5711 S 86th Cir. Omaha, NE 68127-4146. Phone: (402)593-4500 • URL: http://www.infogroup.com • Annual. Number of listings: 5,952. Entries include: Name, address, phone, size of advertisement, name of owner or manager, number of employees, year first in "Yellow Pages." Compiled from telephone company "Yellow Pages," nationwide.

***Desktop Video Communications***. BCR Enterprises, Inc,, 999 Oakmont Plz. Dr., Ste. 100 Westmont, IL 60559-1381. Phone: 800-227-1234 or (630)986-1432; Fax: (630)323-5324; Email: info@bcr.com • URL: http://www.bcr.com/ • Bimonthly. Free per year. Covers multimedia technologies, with emphasis on video conferencing and the "virtual office."

***DETC News***. Distance Education and Training Council, 1601 18th St. NW, Ste. 2 Washington, DC 20009. Phone: (202)234-5100; Fax: (202)332-1386; Email: info@detc.org • URL: http://www.detc.org • Semiannual. Description: Discusses issues pertaining to distance study education and reports activities of the Council. Recurring features include news of research, book reviews, news of members, and a calendar of events.

***Detwiler's Directory of Health and Medical Resources***. S.M. Detwiler and Associates, PO Box 15308 Fort Wayne, IN 46885. Phone: (219)749-6534; Fax: (219)493-6717 • Biennial. $195.00. Lists a wide range of healthcare information resources, including more than 2,000 corporations, associations, government agencies, publishers, licensure organizations, market research firms, foundations, and institutes, as well as 6,000 publications. Indexed by type of information, publication, acronym, and 600 subject categories.

***Develop Your Marketing Skills***. Cengage Learning Inc., 20 Channel Center St. Boston, MA 02210. Phone: 800-487-8488 or (617)289-7700; Fax: (617)289-7844; Email: investors@cengage.com • URL: http://www.cengage.com • 2010. eBook. Published by Kogan Page. S user-friendly guide appropriate for business people for whom implementation is the key issue. It outlines the key concepts and principles which govern the subject of marketing, such as product management, market research, communications, market coverage, creating a marketing plan and pricing perspectives. It also gives key insights into how theories and tools work in actual business scenarios, shows you how to improve customer satisfaction and highlights contemporary issues, such as sustainability.

***Developing Business in Eastern Europe***. Intervisual Advertising Ltd., 20 Dering St. London W1R 0LR, United Kingdom. Phone: 71 6296696; Fax: 71 7535496; Email: interviz@dial.pipex.com • Monthly. Covers: Eastern European industries. Entries include: Company name, address, phone, fax, geographical area served, subsidiary and branch names and locations, description of product/services provided.

***Development Business***. United Nations, Department of Public Information, Grand Central Sta. New York, NY 10163-5850. Phone: (212)963-1516 or (212)963-4475; Fax: (212)963-1381 or (212)963-7055; Email: inquiries@un.org • URL: http://www.devbusiness.com • Semimonthly. $550 Individuals online; $590 Individuals print; $795 Individuals online + paper copies; $295 Individuals paper copy once a month. Provides leads on contract opportunities worldwide for engineering firms and multinational corporations. Text in English, French, Portuguese, and Spanish.

***The Development Directory: A Guide to the International Development Community in the U.S. and Canada***. Omnigraphics Inc., PO Box 31-1640 Detroit, MI 48231. Phone: (313)961-1340; Fax: (313)961-1383; Email: customerservice@omnigraphics.com • URL: http://www.omnigraphics.com • Irregular. $110. Covers: over 1,000 organizations and individuals involved in economic and social development worldwide. Entries include: For organizations—Name, address, phone, fax, telex, size of community, statement of purpose, geographical areas of interest or activity, names and titles of key personnel, publications, financial data. For individuals—Name, position or title, address, phone, affiliation, degrees, publications, experience, subjects, geographic areas, background comments.

***Development***. National Association of Industrial and Office Properties, 2201 Cooperative Way, Ste. 300 Herndon, VA 20171-3034. Phone: (703)904-7100; Fax: (703)904-7942 • URL: http://www.naiop.org • Quarterly. $35 /year. Focuses on issues, trends and new ideas affecting the commercial and industrial real estate development industry.

***Development of the Industrial U.S. Reference Library***. Cengage Learning Inc., 20 Channel Center St. Boston, MA 02210. Phone: 800-487-8488 or (617)289-7700; Fax: (617)289-7844; Email: investors@cengage.com • URL: http://www.cengage.com • 2005. $236. 4 volumes. Traces the influence of the British Industrial Revolution on America and other nations and discusses such potent forces as advances in transportation and communication, inventions that transformed manufacturing and agriculture, the growth of trade and much more. eBook available. Contact for pricing.

***DFISA Reporter***. Dairy and Food Industries Supply Association, Inc., 6245 Executive Blvd. Rockville, MD 20852-3906. Phone: (301)984-1444; Fax: (301)881-7832 • Monthly. Free. Provides industry and association news to manufacturers of equipment products and services to the dairy and food industry.

***Di Yiddishe Heim/Jewish Home***. Chabad Lubavitch, Lubavich World Headquarters, 770 Eastern Pkwy. Brooklyn, NY 11213. Phone: (718)774-4000 or (718)493-1537; Fax: (718)774-2718 or (718)756-2919; Email: info@lubavitch.com • URL: http://www.lubavitch.com • Text in English and Yiddishe.

***Dial-A-Fax Business Directory: World's Largest Resources of Fax Services***. Dial-A-Fax Directories Corp., 930 Fox Pavilion Jenkintown, PA 19046. Phone: (215)887-5700; Fax: (215)887-7076; Email: berylwolk@aol.com • $289 plus 4.95 postage. Database covers: Approximately 1,400,000 companies in the United States. Entries include: Name, city, state, phone, fax, Standard Industrial Classification (SIC) code.

***DIALOG Business Connection***. The Dialog Corp., 2440 W El Camino Real Mount View, CA 94040. Phone: 800-862-4599 or (415)254-7000; Fax: (415)254-7070 • Continuous. Database covers: 10,000,000 private and public companies in the United States; over 1,000,000 companies in Canada and Europe. Database includes: Company name, address, phone, corporate affiliations, key officers, names of directors, products or services, revenue, sales volume, market share, financial information, number of employees, merger activities, new equipment or facility purchases. This online service provides access to 25 databases already available on DIALOG as individual files, including "D&B—Dun's Market Identifiers," "D&B—Dun's Financial Records," "Disclosure," "Media General Databank," and "BusinessWire." The database provides the ability to conduct corporate intelligence, financial screening, and sales prospecting; to locate information on products and markets; to gain access to the latest news; and to set up an electronic clipping service.

**Diamond Council of America**. 3212 W End Ave., Ste. 400 Nashville, TN 37203. Phone: 877-283-5669 or (615)385-5301; Fax: (615)385-4955 • URL: http://www.diamondcouncil.org • Retail jewelry firms and suppliers of gemstones. Firms operating approximately 4900 retail jewelry stores; associated manufacturers and importers. Offers courses in "gemology" and "diamontology" to employees of member firms; bestows titles of Certified Diamontologist and Guild Gemologist upon those completing courses and examinations. Supplies members with advertising and educational materials, sales tools, displays, ad copy, radio and television scripts, and merchandise plans.

**Diamond Dealers Club**. 580 5th Ave., 10th Fl. New York, NY 10036. Phone: (212)790-3600; Fax: (212)869-5164 • URL: http://www.nyddc.com • Seeks to foster the interests of the diamond industry, promote equitable trade principles, eliminate abuses and unfair trade practices, disseminate accurate and reliable information concerning the industry, establish uniform business ethics, and cooperate with other persons and organizations for the advancement of the trade. Maintains active trading floor for all categories of wholesale diamonds and offers all members arbitration tribunals for dispute settlement. Operates charitable program.

***Diamond Manufacturers & Importers Association of America Yearbook***. 580 Fifth Ave., Ste. 2000 New York, NY 10036. Phone: (212)202-7525; Email: info@dmia.net • URL: http://www.dmia.net • Annual.

***Diamond World Review***. World Federation of Diamond Bourses. International Diamond Publications, Ltd., Diamond Towers, 3A Jabotinsky Rd. 52131 Ramat Gon, Israel. Phone: (972) 3 7512165 or (972) 3 751 2165; Fax: (972) 3 5752201 or (972) 3 575 2201 • Bimonthly. $78.00 per year. Text in English.

***Diamond's Japan Business Directory***. Diamond Lead Company Ltd., Minato-ku West Shinbashi 1-1-3, Sakurada Bldg. 5F Tokyo 105-0003, Japan. Phone: 81 3 55111071; Fax: 81 3 55111531 • URL: http://www.diamond-lead.co.jp • Annual. €964.40 Single issue approximative price. Covers more than 2,000 leading Japanese firms in all lines of business; business-related government agencies and organizations.

***Dictating Machines & Supplies Wholesale Directory***. InfoGroup Inc., 5711 S 86th Cir. Omaha, NE 68127-4146. Phone: (402)593-4500 • URL: http://www.infogroup.com • Updated continuously; printed on request. Number of listings: 585. Entries include: Name, address, phone, size of advertisement, name of owner or manager, number of employees, year first in "Yellow Pages." Compiled from telephone company "Yellow Pages," nationwide.

***Dictionary of Commercial, Financial and Legal Terms in Two Languages***. Adler's Foreign Books Inc., 915 Foster St. Evanston, IL 60201-3199. Phone: 800-433-9229 or (847)864-0664; Fax: (847)864-0804; Email: info@afb-adlers.com • URL: http://www.adlersforeignbooks.com • Two volumes. Vol. A, $179.50; vol. B $179.50. Text in English and German.

***Dictionary of International Trade***. Reference Press Inc., 6448 Hwy. 290 E, Ste. E-104 Austin, TX 78723. Phone: 800-486-8666 or (512)454-7778; Fax: (512)454-9401; Email: orders@hoovers.com • $16.45. Covers: More than 4,000 entries concerning international trade, including 200 trade groups, 750 acronyms and abbreviations, 180 country codes, 300 city codes, currencies for 200 countries, and a source guide for 125 publications. Database includes: Regional maps of the world. Entries include: For trade groups—name, address, phone, fax.

***Dictionary of 1040 Deductions***. Matthew Bender and Company Inc., 1275 Broadway Albany, NY 12204-2638. Phone: 800-424-4200 or (518)487-3000; Fax: (518)487-3573 or (800)424-4200; Email: customer.support@lexisnexis.com • URL: http://www.matthewbender.com • Annual. $131.00. Organized by schedule and supported by thousands of citations. Designed to quickly answer all questions about deductions.

***Die Casting Engineer***. North American Die Casting Association, 3250 N Arlington Heights Rd., Ste. 101 Arlington Heights, IL 60004. Phone: (847)279-0001; Fax: (847)279-0002; Email: nadca@diecasting.org • URL: http://www.diecasting.org • Bimonthly. $60 U.S., Canada, and Mexico; $120 U.S., Canada, and Mexico two years; $270 Other countries two years; $135 Other countries. Bimonthly. Included with membership.

***Diesel & Gas Turbine Worldwide***. Diesel and Gas Turbine Publications, 20855 Watertown Rd., Ste. 220 Waukesha, WI 53186. Phone: (262)754-4100; Fax: (262)754-4175; Email: news@dieselpub.com • URL: http://dieselpub.com • 10/year. $85. Covers engine room products and technologies in the power generation field.

**Dietary Managers Association**. 406 Surrey Woods Dr. Saint Charles, IL 60174. Phone: 800-323-1908; Fax: (630)587-6308 • URL: http://www.anfponline.org • Dietary managers united to maintain a high level of competency and quality in dietary departments through continuing education. Provides educational programs and placement service.

***Different Thinking***. Cengage Learning Inc., 20 Channel Center St. Boston, MA 02210. Phone: 800-487-8488 or (617)289-7700; Fax: (617)289-7844; Email: investors@cengage.com • URL: http://www.cengage.com • 2009. eBook. Published by Kogan Page. Presents practical tools and strategies your company can use to help you drastically increase productivity and earning power. The authors show you how you can question your strategies, create new markets, give your products a radical makeover, and invent innovative new price and profit models to give you a competitive advantage over your rivals.

**Digital Image Analysis Laboratory**. University of Arizona, Dept. of Electrical and Computer Engineering, 1230 E Speedway Blvd. Tucson, AZ 85721. Phone: (520)621-4554; Fax: (520)621-8076; Email: dial@ece.arizona.edu • URL: http://www.ece.arizona.edu • Research fields include image processing, computer vision, and artificial intelligence.

***Digital Imaging: The Magazine for the Imaging Professional***. Cygnus Business Media Inc., 1233 Janesville Ave. Fort Atkinson, WI 53538. Phone: 800-547-7377; Email: info@cygnus.com • URL: http://www.cygnus.com • Bimonthly. $24.95 per year. Edited for business and professional users of electronic publishing products and services. Topics covered include document imaging, CD-ROM publishing, digital video, and multimedia services. Formerly *Micro Publishing News*.

***Digital Information Network***. Buyers Laboratory L.L.C., 20 Railroad Ave. Hackensack, NJ 07601. Phone: (201)488-0404; Fax: (201)488-0461; Email: info@bertl.com • URL: http://www.buyerslab.com • Monthly. $725.00 per year. Newsletter. Information on the copier industry, including test reports on individual machines.

**Digital Screenmedia Association**. 13100 Eastpoint Park Blvd. Louisville, KY 40223. Phone: (502)489-3915 or (502)241-7545; Fax: (502)241-2795 • URL: http://www.digitalscreenmedia.org • Promotes the interests and serves the needs of companies engaged in the self-service and kiosk industry. Encourages its members to exercise effective and ethical business practices. Fosters the growth and health of the self-service and kiosk industry.

***Diplomatic Bookshelf and Review***. Arthur H. Thrower, Ltd., 44-46 S. Ealing Rd. London W5, United Kingdom. • Monthly. $4.00 per year.

***Diplomatic History***. Society for Historians of American Foreign Relations. Oxford University Press, Journals, 2001 Evans Rd. Cary, NC 27513. Phone: 800-852-7323 or (919)677-0977; Fax: (919)677-1714; Email: jnlorders@oup-usa.org • URL: http://www.oup-osa.org • 5/year. $548 Institutions print & online; €433 Institutions print & online; £289 Institutions print or online; $449 Institutions online; €356 Institutions online; £236 Institutions online; $503 Institutions print; €397 Institutions print; £265 Institutions print. The official journal of Society for Historians of American Foreign Relations (SHAFR).

***Diplomatic Observer***. Institute for International Sociological Research, 50858 Weiner Weg Six Cologne, Germany. • Monthly. $16.50 per year.

***Diplomatic World Bulletin and Delegates World Bulletin: Dedicated to Serving the United Nations and the International Community***. Diplomatic World Bulletin Publications, Inc., 307 E. 44th St., Suite A New York, NY 10017. Phone: (212)747-9500 • Biweekly. $45.00 per year.

***Direct***. Intertec Publishing, 5 Penn Plz., 13th Fl. New York, NY 10001-1810. Phone: 800-795-5445 or (212)613-9700 or (212)204-4200; Fax: (212)613-9749 or (212)206-3622; Email: bethany.weaver@penton.com • URL: http://www.penton.com • Provides analysis on direct marketing issues.

***Direct Mail Service***. Information Resource Group, 35200 Dequindre Rd. Sterling Heights, MI 48310. Phone: (810)978-3000 • Continuous. $150 per thousand names. Company maintains a database of about 1,200,000 Information Technology (IT) and corporate professionals at 200,000 companies throughout the United States and Canada; with more than 400 functional job titles to choose from. Database includes: Company name, address, names and titles of key personnel, number of employees, geographical area served, financial data, Standard Industrial Classification (SIC) code, type of hardware system and software utilized.

**Direct Marketing Association**. 1120 Ave. of the Americas New York, NY 10036-6700. Phone: (212)768-7277; Fax: (212)302-6714; Email: info@the-dma.org • URL: http://www.thedma.org • A division of the Direct Marketing Association. Members include publishers and circulation directors.

***Direct Marketing News***. Haymarket Media Group Ltd., 174 Hammersmith Rd. London W6 7JP, United Kingdom. Phone: 44 20 8267 5000; Email: info@haymarket.com • URL: http://www.haymarket.com • Monthly. $148 U.S. /year; $198 Canada /year; $228 Other countries /year. Includes special feature issues on catalog marketing, telephone marketing, database marketing, and fundraising. Includes monthly supplements, *DM News International*, *DRTV News*, and *TeleServices*.

***Direct Marketing: Using Direct Response Advertising to Enhance Marketing Database***. Hoke Communications Inc., 224 7th St., Ste. B1 Garden City, NY 11530-5777. Phone: 800-229-6700 or (516)746-6700; Fax: (516)294-8141; Email: 71410.2423@compuserve.com • URL: http://www.directmarketingmag.com/ • Monthly. $65.00 per year. Direct marketing to consumers and business.

***Direct Selling Association World Federation News***. Direct Selling Association. World Federation of Direct Selling Associations, 1667 K St. NW, Ste. 1100 Washington, DC 20006. Phone: (202)452-8866; Fax: (202)452-9010; Email: info@wfdsa.org • URL: http://www.wfdsa.org • Quarterly.

**Direct Selling Association**. 1667 K St. NW, Ste. 1100 Washington, DC 20006-1660. Phone: (202)452-8866; Fax: (202)452-9010; Email: info@dsa.org • URL: http://www.dsa.org • Manufacturers and distributors selling consumer products through person-to-person sales, by appointment, and through home-party plans. Products include food, gifts, house wares, dietary supplements, cosmetics, apparel, jewelry, decorative accessories, reference books, and telecommunications products and services. Offers specialized education; conducts research programs; compiles statistics. Maintains hall of fame. Sponsors Direct Selling Education Foundation.

***Direction: For the Moving and Storage Industry***. American Moving and Storage Association, 1611 Duke St. Alexandria, VA 22314-3406. Phone: 888-849-2672 or (703)683-7410; Fax: (703)683-7527 or (703)548-1845; Email: amconf@amconf.org • URL: http://www.promover.org • Monthly. $35.00 per year. Newsletter on developments affecting the household goods movingindustry. Formerly American Mover.

***Direction of Trade Statistics (DOT)***. International Monetary Fund. International Monetary Fund - Data and Statistics Department, 700 19th St. NW Washington, DC 20431. Phone: (202)623-7000; Fax: (202)623-4661; Email: publicaffairs@imf.org • URL: http://www.imf.org/external/data.htm • Quarterly. Individuals, $128.00 per year; libraries, $89.00 per year. Includes *Yearbook*.

***The Director***. National Funeral Directors Association. National Funeral Directors Association, 13625 Bishops Dr. Brookfield, WI 53005-6607. Phone: 800-228-6332 or (262)789-1880; Fax: (262)789-6977; Email: nfda@nfda.org • URL: http://www.nfda.org • Monthly. Offers in-depth features on the trends, expert analysis of legislative and regulatory developments, and thought-provoking opinions by industry leaders.

***Directories in Print***. Cengage Learning Inc., 20 Channel Center St. Boston, MA 02210. Phone: 800-487-8488 or (617)289-7700; Fax: (617)289-7844; Email: investors@cengage.com • URL: http://www.cengage.com • Annual. $1,009 Individuals. Provides profiles of more than 17,000 directories published worldwide. eBook also available.

***Directors and Officers Liability: Prevention, Insurance, and Indemnification***. ALM Media Properties LLC, 120 Broadway, 5th Fl. New York, NY 10271-1100. Phone: (212)457-9400; Fax: (646)417-7705; Email: customercare@alm.com • URL: http://www.alm.com • $530 per year. Covers the legal risks faced by corporate directors and officers. (Law Journal Press).

**Directors Guild of America**. 7920 Sunset Blvd. Los Angeles, CA 90046. Phone: 800-421-4173 or (310)289-2000; Email: dgawebsupport@dga.org • URL: http://www.dga.org • Negogiates agreements for members.

***Directory, Database of Small & Medium Enterprise (SMEs) in India***. NIIR Project Consultancy Services, 106 - E, Kamla Nagar New Delhi 110007, India. Phone: 91 11 23843955; Fax: 91 11 23841561; Email: npcs.india@gmail.com • URL: http://www.niir.org • Rs 5,955 Individuals CD-ROM; $250 Individuals CD-ROM. Covers: 250,000+ small & medium enterprises (SME's) in India. Entries include: Name, full postal address, postal code, phone, contact person, company name, address, city, pin code, fax, e-mail, website, products details.

***Directory for Setting Up Enterprises in Japan***. • URL: http://www.jetro.go.jp • Covers: Approximately 700 companies in Japan that offer market research, direct investment planning, and incorporation and other professional services. Entries include: Name, address, phone, fax, profile, services offered, and contact persons/divisions.

***Directory of Affiliates & Offices of Japanese Firms in USA & Canada***. Want Publishing Co., Graybar Bldg. - Grand Central, 420 Lexington Ave., Ste. 300 New York, NY 10170. Phone: (212)687-3774; Fax: (212)687-3779; Email: editor@nationscourts.com • URL: http://www.wantpublishing.com • Irregular. $190. Covers: over 6,000 Japanese-affiliated or owned firms in the U.S. and Canada.

***Directory of African Importers of Construction Machinery and Equipment***. EXIM Infotek Private Ltd., 604 Vishwa Deep, District Centre, Janakpuri New Delhi 110058, India. Phone: 91 11 25544793; Fax: 91 11 25544793; Email: info@eximinfo.org • URL: http://www.eximinfo.com • Covers: 120 African importers of caterpillar, concrete mixers, construction and building equipment, construction machinery, earthmoving equipment, excavating equipment, mixers and pavers, stone crusher, and street maintenance equipment. Entries include: Company name, postal address, telephone, fax, e-mail, website, contact person, designation, and product details.

***Directory of African Importers of Dyes, Colors, and Pigments***. EXIM Infotek Private Ltd., 604 Vishwa Deep, District Centre, Janakpuri New Delhi 110058, India. Phone: 91 11 25544793; Fax: 91 11 25544793; Email: info@eximinfo.org • URL: http://www.eximinfo.com • $250 Individuals; $10 Individuals. Covers: 90 African importers of textiles chemical, dye, colors, pigments, intermediates, dyestuff, and printing ink. Entries include: Company name, postal address, telephone, fax, e-mail, website, contact person, designation, and product details.

***Directory of African Importers of Energy and Power Equipment***. EXIM Infotek Private Ltd., 604 Vishwa Deep, District Centre, Janakpuri New Delhi 110058, India. Phone: 91 11 25544793; Fax: 91 11 25544793; Email: info@eximinfo.org • URL: http://www.eximinfo.com • $150 Individuals; $5 Individuals. Covers: 30 African importers of power transmission equipment and supplies, solar energy equipment, solar panels, solar water heaters, and wind energy equipment. Entries include: Company name, postal address, telephone, fax, e-mail, website, contact person, designation, and product details.

***Directory of African Importers of Environment Protection and Pollution Control Equipment***. EXIM Infotek Private Ltd., 604 Vishwa Deep, District Centre, Janakpuri New Delhi 110058, India. Phone: 91 11 25544793; Fax: 91 11 25544793; Email: info@eximinfo.org • URL: http://www.eximinfo.com • $200 Individuals; $10 Individuals. Covers: 40 African importers of pollution control equipment, wastewater treatment, water treatment, and purifying equipment. Entries include: Company name, postal address, telephone, fax, e-mail, website, contact person, designation, and product details.

***Directory of African Importers of Fibre Products***. EXIM Infotek Private Ltd., 604 Vishwa Deep, District Centre, Janakpuri New Delhi 110058, India. Phone: 91 11 25544793; Fax: 91 11 25544793; Email: info@eximinfo.org • URL: http://www.eximinfo.com • $150 Individuals; $5 Individuals. Covers: 35 African importers of fiberglass cloth and products, fiberglass resins, fiber products, and synthetic fiber. Entries include: Company name, postal address, telephone, fax, e-mail, website, contact person, designation, and product details.

***Directory of African Importers of Fire Fighting Equipment & Supplies***. EXIM Infotek Private Ltd., 604 Vishwa Deep, District Centre, Janakpuri New Delhi 110058, India. Phone: 91 11 25544793; Fax: 91 11 25544793; Email: info@eximinfo.org • URL: http://www.eximinfo.com • Covers: 35 African importers of fire fighting equipment. Entries include: Company name, postal address, telephone, fax, e-mail, website, contact person, designation, and product details.

***Directory of African Importers of Fodder and Animal Foodstuffs***. EXIM Infotek Private Ltd., 604 Vishwa Deep, District Centre, Janakpuri New Delhi 110058, India. Phone: 91 11 25544793; Fax: 91 11 25544793; Email: info@eximinfo.org • URL: http://www.eximinfo.com • $250 Individuals; $10 Individuals. Covers: 70 African importers of animal foodstuff additives, animal foodstuff, feed additives, fodder, cereals, livestock breeding supplies, and oats. Entries include: Company name, postal address, telephone, fax, e-mail, website, contact person, designation, and product details.

***Directory of African Importers of Food Additives and Aromatics***. EXIM Infotek Private Ltd., 604 Vishwa Deep, District Centre, Janakpuri New Delhi 110058, India. Phone: 91 11 25544793; Fax: 91 11 25544793; Email: info@eximinfo.org • URL: http://www.eximinfo.com • $150 Individuals; $5 Individuals. Covers: 40 African importers of aromatic chemicals, bakery and pastry ingredients, food additives, food colors, food colouring, fragrances, flavors, and yeast. Entries include: Company name, postal address, telephone, fax, e-mail, website, contact person, designation, and product details.

***Directory of African Importers of Handkerchives, Scarves and Neckwears***. EXIM Infotek Private Ltd., 604 Vishwa Deep, District Centre, Janakpuri New Delhi 110058, India. Phone: 91 11 25544793; Fax: 91 11 25544793; Email: info@eximinfo.org • URL: http://www.eximinfo.com • $150 Individuals; $5 Individuals. Covers: 20 African importers of handkerchieves, scarves, neckwear, and neckties.

***Directory of African Importers of Laboratory & Scientific Instruments & Supplies***. EXIM Infotek Private Ltd., 604 Vishwa Deep, District Centre, Janakpuri New Delhi 110058, India. Phone: 91 11 25544793; Fax: 91 11 25544793; Email: info@eximinfo.org • URL: http://www.eximinfo.com • Covers: 250 African importers of binoculars, microscopes, telescopes, laboratory and scientific glass, laboratory and scientific instruments, laboratory chemicals, laboratory equipment, laboratory glassware, laboratory reagents, magnifiers, scientific equipment, and testing equipment. Entries include: Company name, postal address, telephone, fax, e-mail, website, contact person, designation, and product details.

***Directory of African Importers of Lumber, Timber, Plywood and Hardboards***. EXIM Infotek Private Ltd., 604 Vishwa Deep, District Centre, Janakpuri New Delhi 110058, India. Phone: 91 11 25544793; Fax: 91 11 25544793; Email: info@eximinfo.org • URL: http://www.eximinfo.com • $300 Individuals; $10 Individuals. Covers: 70 African importers of doors and windows, formica sheets, gypsum board and sheetrock, hardboard and particle board, laminates (wood), hardwood lumber, softwood lumber, timber, plywood, medium-density fiberboard, millwork (wooden), veneer, special decorative plywood, poles, pilings and logs, sawn timber, saw and saw blades, and wood. Entries include: Company name, postal address, telephone, fax, e-mail, website, contact person, designation, and product details.

***Directory of African Importers of Machinery for Paper & Pulp Industry***. EXIM Infotek Private Ltd., 604 Vishwa Deep, District Centre, Janakpuri New Delhi 110058, India. Phone: 91 11 25544793; Fax: 91 11 25544793; Email: info@eximinfo.org • URL: http://www.eximinfo.com • Covers: 20 African importers of envelope making machinery, exercise book making machinery, paper making machinery and toilet paper making machines. Entries include: Company name, postal address, telephone, fax, e-mail, website, contact person, designation, and product details.

***Directory of African Importers of Material Handling Equipment & Supplies***. EXIM Infotek Private Ltd., 604 Vishwa Deep, District Centre, Janakpuri New Delhi 110058, India. Phone: 91 11 25544793; Fax: 91 11 25544793; Email: info@eximinfo.org • URL: http://www.eximinfo.com • $250 Individuals; $10 Individuals. Covers: 60 African importers of conveyors, cranes and hoists, elevators and lifts, forklifts, lifting machinery and equipment, liquid handling equipment, loading and unloading equipment, material handling systems for garment industries, and monorail materials handling equipment. Entries include: Company name, postal address, telephone, fax, e-mail, website, contact person, designation, and product details.

***Directory of African Importers of Motors and Motor Parts—Electric***. EXIM Infotek Private Ltd., 604 Vishwa Deep, District Centre, Janakpuri New Delhi 110058, India. Phone: 91 11 25544793; Fax: 91 11 25544793; Email: info@eximinfo.org • URL: http://www.eximinfo.com • $250 Individuals; $10 Individuals. Covers: 50 African importers of AC and DC motors, electric motors and spares, motor equipment, and motor parts. Entries include: Company name, postal address, telephone, fax, e-mail, website, contact person, designation, and product details.

***Directory of African Importers of Photographic Equipment and Supplies***. EXIM Infotek Private Ltd., 604 Vishwa Deep, District Centre, Janakpuri New Delhi 110058, India. Phone: 91 11 25544793; Fax: 91 11 25544793; Email: info@eximinfo.org • URL: http://www.eximinfo.com • $300 Individuals; $10 Individuals. Covers: 95 African importers of cameras and videos, lens and accessories, photographic chemicals, motion picture and theater equipment, digital camera, microfilm and blueprint equipment, photographic equipment and supplies, photographic goods, photographic materials and hardware, photographic processing supplies, and video cameras. Entries include: Company name, postal address, telephone, fax, e-mail, website, contact person, designation, and product details.

***Directory of African Importers of Plastic Scrap and Raw Materials***. EXIM Infotek Private Ltd., 604 Vishwa Deep, District Centre, Janakpuri New Delhi 110058, India. Phone: 91 11 25544793; Fax: 91 11 25544793; Email: info@eximinfo.org • URL: http://www.eximinfo.com • $300 Individuals; $10 Individuals. Covers: 90 African importers of plastic raw materials, plastic scrap and waste, polyethylene raw materials, PVC compounds, low-density polyethylene (LDPE) raw material, PF raw materials, molding powder, polester chips raw materials, PP/PVC/PE raw materials, PVC resins raw materials, and plasticizers. Entries include: Company name, postal address, telephone, fax, e-mail, website, contact person, designation, and product details.

***Directory of African Importers of Sewing Machines and Parts***. EXIM Infotek Private Ltd., 604 Vishwa Deep, District Centre, Janakpuri New Delhi 110058, India. Phone: 91 11 25544793; Fax: 91 11 25544793; Email: info@eximinfo.org • URL: http://www.eximinfo.com • $250 Individuals; $10 Individuals. Covers: 80 African importers of embroidery machine, garment industry machinery and equipment, industrial sewing machine and parts, and pleating machine. Entries include: Company name, postal address, telephone, fax, e-mail, website, contact person, designation, and product details.

***Directory of African Importers of Sporting Goods***. EXIM Infotek Private Ltd., 604 Vishwa Deep, District Centre, Janakpuri New Delhi 110058, India. Phone: 91 11 25544793; Fax: 91 11 25544793; Email: info@eximinfo.org • URL: http://www.eximinfo.com • $350 Individuals; $15 Individuals. Covers: 125 African importers of diving equipment, golf equipment and supplies, scuba and diving equipment and supply, sports equipment, sporting goods and toys, tennis and badminton equipment and supplies, and watersports equipment. Entries include: Company name, postal address, telephone, fax, e-mail, website, contact person, designation, and product details.

***Directory of African Importers of Telephone Instruments and Accessories***. EXIM Infotek Private Ltd., 604 Vishwa Deep, District Centre, Janakpuri New Delhi 110058, India. Phone: 91 11 25544793; Fax: 91 11 25544793; Email: info@eximinfo.org • URL: http://www.eximinfo.com • $400 Individuals; $15 Individuals. Covers: 120 African Importers of mobile phone, cordless telephone, fax machine, GSM cellular handset, GSM mobile phone, headphone, mobile accessories, telefax equipment, telephone equipment, and telephone systems. Entries include: Company name, postal address, telephone, fax, e-mail, website, contact person, designation, and product details.

***Directory of African Importers of Yarns and Threads***. EXIM Infotek Private Ltd., 604 Vishwa Deep, District Centre, Janakpuri New Delhi 110058, India. Phone: 91 11 25544793; Fax: 91 11 25544793; Email: info@eximinfo.org • URL: http://www.eximinfo.com • $300 Individuals; $10 Individuals. Covers: 90 African importers of acrylic yarn, cotton yarn and thread, embroidery threads, polyester yarn, sewing threads, synthetic yarns and thread, and wool yarn. Entries include: Company name, postal address, telephone, fax, e-mail, website, contact person, designation, and product details.

***Directory of American Agribusiness***. Agricultural Resources & Communications Inc., 4210 Wam-Teau Dr. Wamego, KS 66547. Phone: 800-404-7940 or (785)456-9705; Fax: (785)456-1654; Email: chris@agresources.com • URL: http://www.agresources.com • $64.95. Covers: Over 7,200 leading companies in agricultural chemicals, implements, seed, grain, feed, food processing, animal health and services, including public relations and consulting in 27 different types of agribusinesses in the U.S. Entries include: Company name, address, phone, fax, type of business, key company contacts.

***Directory of American Business in Hong Kong***. GTE Directories Ltd., 25/F China Resources Bldg., 26 Harbour Rd., Hong Kong Wanchai, China. Phone: 8278668; Fax: 827 8322 • $20. Covers: American companies, their agents, and distributors in Hong Kong; US State and Port of Authority representatives in Hong Kong; products and service of the American Consulate General in Hong Kong.

***Directory of American Business in South China***. American Chamber of Commerce in Hong Kong, 1904 Bank of America Tower, 12 Harcourt Rd. Hong Kong, China. Phone: 86 852 25306900; Fax: 86 852 28101289; Email: amcham@amcham.org.hk • URL: http://www.amcham.org.hk • Covers: Over 900 American companies that have regional headquarters or representative offices in Hong Kong.

***Directory of American Companies Operating in Mexico***. American Chamber of Commerce of Mexico - Mexico City, Blas Pascal 205, 3.er piso, Col. Los Morales 11510 Mexico City, Mexico. Phone: 52 55 51413800; Fax: 52 55 51413835 or 52 55 51413836; Email: amchammx@amcham.org.mx • URL: http://www.amcham.com.mx/ • Biennial. Covers: over 2,500 United States commercial and investment companies with operations in Mexico, and the 2,500 Mexican companies that represent them in Mexico. Entries include: For United States companies—Name, address, phone, fax, contact person, products, names of Mexican firm with which associated, type of affiliation. For Mexican companies—Name, address, phone, fax, contact person, products, sales, name of United States company.

***Directory of American Companies Overseas***. Overseas Employment Services, 1255 Laird, Ste. 208 Mount Royal, QC, Canada H3P 2T1. Phone: (514)739-1108; Fax: (514)739-0795 • Annual. $15. Covers: Approximately 250 American companies that have branch plants or offices outside the U.S. Entries include: Company name, address, geographical area served, and product/service.

***Directory of American Manufacturers & Exporters of Adhesive, Glues & Sealants***. EXIM Infotek Private Ltd., 604 Vishwa Deep, District Centre, Janakpuri New Delhi 110058, India. Phone: 91 11 25544793; Fax: 91 11 25544793; Email: info@eximinfo.org • URL: http://www.eximinfo.com • $30 Individuals. Covers: 390 American manufacturers and exporters of adhesive applicators, adhesive chemicals, adhesive fastening systems, adhesive paper rolls, adhesive products, adhesives, adhesives for duct insulation, adhesives for leather and rubber, adhesives-bonding, adhesives-bushing, adhesives-canvas, adhesives-ceramic, adhesives-concrete, adhesives-cyanocrylates, adhesives-electrical, adhesives-electrically conductive, adhesives-epoxy, adhesives-gasket, adhesives-gasoline resistant, adhesives-glass block, adhesives-graphite, adhesives-grinding and polishing wheel, adhesives-heat seal, adhesives-hot melt, adhesives-latex, adhesives-leather, adhesives-linoleum, adhesives-metal, adhesives-oil resistant, adhesives-paper, adhesives-patching and repair, adhesives-plastic, adhesives-pressure sensitive products, adhesives-raw materials, adhesives-resin, adhesives-structural laminating, adhesives-textile bonding, adhesives-therosetting and thermoplastic, adhesives-ultra violet curing, adhesives-urethane, adhesives-vinyl, adhesives-water resistant, adhesives-waterproofing, adhesives-wood and plywood, aerosol, animal glue, carpet and ceramic flooring, carton sealing adhesives, cyanoacrylates, cyanocrylate adhesives, epoxy, epoxy adhesives, epoxy solvent, eva and polyamide based adhesives for product assembly, floor covering installation adhesives, flooring adhesives, fluid applied roofing, glue, glue-bookbinders, glue-casein, heat seal adhesives, high temp adhesives, hot melt adhesives, industry adhesives, packaging adhesive, polishing wheel and belt inorganic adhesives, polyurethane adhesives, potting compounds, precision torque strength sealing, sealants, structural adhesives, stuffing box sealant, threadlocking and retaining anaerobic, tire sealants, white glue, wire self adhesive backed clips, and woodworking adhesive. Entries include: Company name, postal address, city, country, telephone, fax, e-mail and websites, contact person, designation, and product details.

***Directory of American Manufacturers & Exporters of Agro Chemicals***. EXIM Infotek Private Ltd., 604 Vishwa Deep, District Centre, Janakpuri New Delhi 110058, India. Phone: 91 11 25544793; Fax: 91 11 25544793; Email: info@eximinfo.org • URL: http://www.eximinfo.com • $10 Individuals. Covers: 50 American manufacturers and exporters of agricultural chemicals, agricultural deodorants for swine and manure, biochemicals, fungicides, insecticides, pesticides, and phosphatic chemicals. Entries include: Company name, postal address, city, country, phone, fax, e-mail and websites, contact person, designation, and product details.

***Directory of American Manufacturers & Exporters of Automobiles & Vehicles***. EXIM Infotek Private Ltd., 604 Vishwa Deep, District Centre, Janakpuri New Delhi 110058, India. Phone: 91 11 25544793; Fax: 91 11 25544793; Email: info@eximinfo.org • URL: http://www.eximinfo.com • $20 Individuals. Covers: 200 American manufacturers and exporters of armored vehicles, articulated dump vehicles, automobiles, fire trucks, heavy duty trucks, heavy trucks, industrial trucks, military truck bodies and utility trailers, military trucks, platform trucks, roll off containers, tilt trucks, trailers and tank trucks, truck beds, truck bodies, trucks-commercial, truck frame beam punch lines, truck mounted equipment, truck wheel covers and accessories, and trucks. Entries include: Company name, postal address, city, country, phone, fax, e-mail and websites, contact person, designation, and product details.

***Directory of American Manufacturers & Exporters of Automotive Service & Repair Equipment***. EXIM Infotek Private Ltd., 604 Vishwa Deep, District Centre, Janakpuri New Delhi 110058, India. Phone: 91 11 25544793; Fax: 91 11 25544793; Email: info@eximinfo.org • URL: http://www.eximinfo.com • $5 Individuals. Covers: 40 American manufacturers and exporters of analyzers-engine, auto test equipment, automotive analyzers, automotive hand tools, automotive tools, small engine maintenance instruments, and specialty heavy transmission rebuilding hand tools. Entries include: Company name, postal address, city, country, phone, fax, e-mail and websites, contact person, designation, and products detail.

***Directory of American Manufacturers & Exporters of Autoparts & Accessories***. EXIM Infotek Private Ltd., 604 Vishwa Deep, District Centre, Janakpuri New Delhi 110058, India. Phone: 91 11 25544793; Fax: 91 11 25544793; Email: info@eximinfo.org • URL: http://www.eximinfo.com • $50 Individuals. Covers: 850 American manufacturers and exporters of air fitting and tubing brakes, alternators, asbestos gaskets, assemblies, automatic transmission parts, automotive accessories, automotive axle components, automotive cable, automotive components, automotive composite transmission filters, automotive exhaust systems, automotive gaskets, automotive ignition wire sets, automotive mirrors, automotive parts, automotive parts and accessories, automotive parts and supplies, automotive parts-clutch plates, automotive parts-mufflers, automotive parts-spark plugs, automotive parts-starters and alternators, automotive relays, automotive replacement bushings, automotive replacement parts, automotive service tools, automotive spare parts and assemblies, automotive steering components, automotive transmission and friction parts, automotive transmission components, axle scale systems, axles, brake, brake drum, brake pads, brake shoes, camshafts, car care products, cargo truck, cars and light trucks superchargers, clutches, couplings, custom wheels, disc brakes for cars, felt gaskets, fifth wheels, flat gaskets, fork lift truck attachments, fuel filters, fuel system components, gasket materials, gaskets, gaskets and sealing for the automotive industry, heavy duty truck and trailer parts, horns, hubs, hydraulic equipment, hydraulic tailgates and inserts, industrial gaskets, light truck and van accessories, mobile home tires and wheels, molded gaskets, molded rubber gaskets, non-asbestos gaskets, non-metallic gasket material, plastic gaskets, powder metal products, radiators, replacement parts, replacement parts and accessories, seat belts, seat covers, shock absorbers, silicone gaskets, suspension/chassis components, Teflon encapsuled gaskets, Teflon gaskets, top gaskets, transmission, transmission and parts, transmission components, truck and automotive parts, truck clutches, truck dump bodies, truck equipment, truck parts, truck parts and equipment, truck parts and suppliers, truck replacement parts, truck tool boxes and rubber mats, truck wheel lifts, v bowl rings, vehicular lighting equipment, viton gaskets, wheels, and windshields. Entries include: Company name, postal address, city, country, telephone, fax, e-mail and websites, contact person, designation, and product details.

***Directory of American Manufacturers & Exporters of Batteries & Accumulators***. EXIM Infotek Private Ltd., 604 Vishwa Deep, District Centre, Janakpuri New Delhi 110058, India. Phone: 91 11 25544793; Fax: 91 11 25544793; Email: info@eximinfo.org • URL: http://www.eximinfo.com • $20 Individuals. Covers: 200 American manufacturers and exporters of aircraft batteries, automotive batteries, batteries, batteries-deep cycle, batteries-dry cell, batteries-electric storage, batteries-lead acid, batteries-lithium, batteries-military specifications, batteries-nickel cadmium, batteries-sealed lead acid, batteries-solar, batteries-storage, batteries-wet and sealed, battery cables, battery chargers, battery packs and chargers, battery testers, commercial and industrial batteries, marine batteries, primary batteries, rechargeable batteries, and truck batteries. Entries include: Company name, postal address, city, country, phone, fax, e-mail and websites, contact person, designation, and product details.

***Directory of American Manufacturers & Exporters of Bearings***. EXIM Infotek Private Ltd., 604 Vishwa Deep, District Centre, Janakpuri New Delhi 110058, India. Phone: 91 11 25544793; Fax: 91 11 25544793; Email: info@eximinfo.org • URL: http://www.eximinfo.com • $20 Individuals. Covers: 280 American manufacturers and exporters of air bearings, antifriction bearings, automotive bearings, ball bearings, bearingsmetal, bearing pads, bearing parts-ball and roller, bearings-jewel, bearings, bearings-acid and corrosion resistant, bearings-air, bearings-aircraft, bearings-instrument, bearings-non metallic, bearings-self lubricating, bearings-sleeve, bearings-thrust, bronze bearings, carbide bearings, carbon-graphite bearings, conveyor bearings, cylindrical bearings, engine bearings, linear bearings, linear motion bearings, magnetic bearings, miniature bearings, needle bearings, pillow block bearings, precision ball bearings, radial ball bearings, roller bearings, self aligning bearings, semi-precise bearings, slide bearings, specialty bearings, spherical bearings, stainless steel bearings, tapered roller bearings, water lubricated bearings. Entries include: Company name, postal address, city, country, telephone, fax, e-mail and websites, contact person, designation, and product details.

***Directory of American Manufacturers & Exporters of Beauty Supplies, Cosmetics, Perfumes & Toiletries***. EXIM Infotek Private Ltd., 604 Vishwa Deep, District Centre, Janakpuri New Delhi 110058, India. Phone: 91 11 25544793; Fax: 91 11 25544793; Email: info@eximinfo.org • URL: http://www.eximinfo.com • $20 Individuals. Covers: 200 American manufacturers and exporters of aloe vera products, bath products, beauty care products, beauty creams, blackhead removers, body lotions, cosmetic bags, cosmetic brushes, cosmetic chemicals, cosmetic pencils, cosmetic plastic containers, cosmetics, cosmetics raw materials, eyeliners, face make-up, facial sponges, hair conditioners, hair gels, Halloween accessories, health care, herbal products, lip glosses, lip care products, lipstick, mascara, mouthwash, nail care products, nail polish, oral hygiene products, perfumes, personal care products, scalp conditioners, shampoos, skin care creams and lotions, skin care products, sun care products, toiletries, and toothpaste. Entries include: Company name, postal address, city, country, phone, fax, e-mail and websites, contact person, designation, and product details.

***Directory of American Manufacturers and Exporters of Boiler and Boiler Parts***. EXIM Infotek Private Ltd., 604 Vishwa Deep, District Centre, Janakpuri New Delhi 110058, India. Phone: 91 11 25544793; Fax: 91 11 25544793; Email: info@eximinfo.org • URL: http://www.eximinfo.com • Covers: 100 American manufacturers and exporters of boilers, gas boilers, oil boilers, hot water boilers, packaged steam and hot water boilers, steam and hot water boilers. Entries include: Company name, postal address, telephone, fax, e-mail, website, contact person, designation, and product details.

***Directory of American Manufacturers & Exporters of Chemicals & Allied Products***. EXIM Infotek Private Ltd., 604 Vishwa Deep, District Centre, Janakpuri New Delhi 110058, India. Phone: 91 11 25544793; Fax: 91 11 25544793; Email: info@eximinfo.org • URL: http://www.eximinfo.com • $40 Individuals. Covers: 680 American manufacturers and exporters of aerosol chemicals, aircraft cleaning chemicals, allied accessories, analytical chemicals, automotive chemicals, boiler chemicals, chemicals for x-ray processing, chemical intermediates, chemical raw materials, chemical sprayers, chemicals, chemicals for laboratory, chlorine chemicals, construction chemicals, dry chemicals, electronic chemicals, electroplating chemicals, fertilizer chemicals, fine chemicals, germicides, household chemicals, hydrogen peroxide, industrial chemicals, inorganic chemicals, laboratory chemicals, leather chemicals, liquid chemicals, lubricant chemicals, magnesium chloride, metal working chemicals, natural chemicals, organic chemicals, paint chemicals, paper chemicals, pharmaceutical and cosmetic industry chemicals, pharmaceutical chemicals, plastic chemicals, polymer chemicals, polyurethane foam chemicals, reagent chemicals, resins, rubber chemicals, sodium bisulfite chemicals, sodium silico fluoride, solvent chemicals, specialty chemicals, specialty cleaning chemicals, starches, textile chemicals, water softeners, water treatment, water treatment chemicals, and zinc dies casting. Entries include: company name, postal address, city, country, telephone, fax, e-mail and websites, contact person, designation, and product details.

***Directory of American Manufacturers & Exporters of Confectionery & Bakery Products***. EXIM Infotek Private Ltd., 604 Vishwa Deep, District Centre, Janakpuri New Delhi 110058, India. Phone: 91 11 25544793; Fax: 91 11 25544793; Email: info@eximinfo.org • URL: http://www.eximinfo.com • $10 Individuals. Covers: 90 American manufacturers & exporters of baked foods, boxed chocolates, bubble gum, buttercrunch, candy, cheesecake & carrot cake, chewing gum base, chocolate coatings, chocolates, confectionery items, cookies, fruit snacks & fruit rolls, fudge making, hard candy, ingredients & chocolate products, jelly beans, marshmallows, peanuts. Entries include: Company name, postal address, city, country, phone, fax, e-mail & websites, contact person, designation, products detail.

***Directory of American Manufacturers & Exporters of Dyes, Colours, Pigments & Intermediates***. EXIM Infotek Private Ltd., 604 Vishwa Deep, District Centre, Janakpuri New Delhi 110058, India. Phone: 91 11 25544793; Fax: 91 11 25544793; Email: info@eximinfo.org • URL: http://www.eximinfo.com • $20 Individuals. Covers: 200 American manufacturers and exporters of color concentrates, colors and pigments, colors and pigments-dispersions and flushes, concentrates-colors and pigments, dies, dispersions, dye and pigment intermediates, dyes, dyes and dyestuffs, flushed color and presscakes, intermediates, leather dyes, organic and inorganic dyes, organic and inorganic pigments, organic pigments for printing inks, pigment dispersions, pigment preparations, pigments, pigments and colors-brick, pigments and colors-ceramic and glass, pigments and colors-dry and dispersed, pigments and colors-paint, pigments and colors-rubber, plastic dyes, plastic industry colorants and additives, rust remover, textile dyestuffs, and water colors. Entries include: Company name, postal address, city, country, phone, fax, e-mail and websites, contact person, designation, and product details.

***Directory of American Manufacturers & Exporters of Electronic Equipment***. EXIM Infotek Private Ltd., 604 Vishwa Deep, District Centre, Janakpuri New Delhi 110058, India. Phone: 91 11 25544793; Fax: 91 11 25544793; Email: info@eximinfo.org • URL: http://www.eximinfo.com • $250 Individuals. Covers: 90 American manufacturers and exporters of semiconductor materials, semiconductor processing equipment, and semiconductors. Entries include: Company name, postal address, telephone, fax, e-mail, website, contact person, designation, and product details.

***Directory of American Manufacturers and Exporters of Energy and Power Equipment***. EXIM Infotek Private Ltd., 604 Vishwa Deep, District Centre, Janakpuri New Delhi 110058, India. Phone: 91 11 25544793; Fax: 91 11 25544793; Email: info@eximinfo.org • URL: http://www.eximinfo.com • $200 Individuals; $10 Individuals. Covers: 50 American manufacturers and exporters of solar control film, power systems and components, battery-free solar equipment, solar battery charge regulators, solar control equipment, solar electric (photovoltaics), solar energy equipment, solar modules, solar panels, and solar photovoltics. Entries include: Company name, postal address, telephone, fax, e-mail, website, contact person, designation, and product details.

***Directory of American Manufacturers & Exporters of Engines & Engine Parts***. EXIM Infotek Private Ltd., 604 Vishwa Deep, District Centre, Janakpuri New Delhi 110058, India. Phone: 91 11 25544793; Fax: 91 11 25544793; Email: info@eximinfo.org • URL: http://www.eximinfo.com • $20 Individuals. Covers: 240 American manufacturers and exporters of auto engines, automobile engines, automotive and truck engines, automotive engines, boiler and air conditioning towers and engines, car engines, crankshafts, cylinders, cylinder sleeves, diesel engine parts, diesel engine parts and accessories, diesel engines, engines, engine aircraft modifications, engine parts, engine treatments, engines-gasoline, exhaust system parts, gasoline and diesel engines, gasoline engines, heavy duty diesel engines, industrial diesel engines, injectors, internal combustion engines, natural gas engines, piston automotive and light truck applications, piston pins, piston rings, piston-compressors, piston-engines, pistons, replacement parts for heavy duty diesel engines, steam engines, stern drive and inboard engines, timing components, truck engines, and turbine engines. Entries include: Company name, postal address, city, country, telephone, fax, e-mail and websites, contact person, designation, and product details.

***Directory of American Manufacturers and Exporters of Environment and Pollution Control Equipment***. EXIM Infotek Private Ltd., 604 Vishwa Deep, District Centre, Janakpuri New Delhi 110058, India. Phone: 91 11 25544793; Fax: 91 11 25544793; Email: info@eximinfo.org • URL: http://www.eximinfo.com • $650 Individuals; $25 Individuals. Covers: 340 American manufacturers and exporters of air filtration and cleaning equipment, environmental control and monitoring equipment, environmental products, gas absorbers, lease environmental instrument systems, oil and water separators, oil boom accessories, pollution control equipment and systems, pollution sampling equipment, portable water treatment plants, reverse osmosis, distillation water purifying equipment, waste heat recovery equipment, water pollution control equipment, water treatment equipment, water treatment for PH reduction utilizing carbon dioxide, water treatment plants and engineering services, and water treatment including ozone technology. Entries include: Company name, postal address, telephone, fax, e-mail, website, contact person, designation, and product details.

***Directory of American Manufacturers & Exporters of Essential Oils***. EXIM Infotek Private Ltd., 604 Vishwa Deep, District Centre, Janakpuri New Delhi 110058, India. Phone: 91 11 25544793; Fax: 91 11 25544793; Email: info@eximinfo.org • URL: http://www.eximinfo.com • $10 Individuals. Covers: 90 American manufacturers & exporters of essential oil of peppermint & spearmint, essential oils, fragrance, massage oils. Entries include: Company name, postal address, city, country, phone, fax, e-mail & websites, contact person, designation, products detail.

***Directory of American Manufacturers & Exporters of Filters & Strainers—Industrial***. EXIM Infotek Private Ltd., 604 Vishwa Deep, District Centre, Janakpuri New Delhi 110058, India. Phone: 91 11 25544793; Fax: 91 11 25544793; Email: info@eximinfo.org • URL: http://www.eximinfo.com • $30 Individuals. Covers: 400 American manufacturers and exporters of air filters, ceramic and iodine portable camping filters, cloth filters, compressed-air filters, cooling towers water filter systems, counter-top and under counter filters, filter media, filter pads, filter paper, filter systems and pumps, filters, fire restoration, interference filters, media filters, sand filters and replacement filter elements, screens, water filters for commercial, consumer water filters for home, business and restaurant, water filtration equipment, water filters, water filtration and purification conditioning, water filtration and purification equipment, water filtration and purification ultraviolet, water filtration equipment, water filtration treatment, water filtration and purification equipment, water purification and treatment systems, and water purifiers. Entries include: Company name, postal address, city, country, telephone, fax, e-mail and websites, contact person, designation, and product details.

***Directory of American Manufacturers & Exporters of Fire Fighting Equipment & Supplies***. EXIM Infotek Private Ltd., 604 Vishwa Deep, District Centre, Janakpuri New Delhi 110058, India. Phone: 91 11 25544793; Fax: 91 11 25544793; Email: info@eximinfo.org • URL: http://www.eximinfo.com • Covers: 250 American manufacturers and exporters of air-flame, fire alarms, detectors and holder releases, fire doors, fireproof, electric valves, electronic burglary equipment, fire alarm control equipment, extinguishers and cabinets, fire apparatus, residential fire alarm, fire fighting clothing, fire fighting equipment and supplies, gloves, pumps, nozzles, reels, adapters, fire protective coatings, fire rescue blankets, fire retardant products for fabrics, paper, wood and paint, fire sprinklers, fire suppression equipment, industrial foam fire, retardant coatings and mastics, life safety systems, pumpers, rated and non-rated doors, single and double jacket, smoke detectors, smoke vents, sprinkler systems, water tankers, wireless commercial and residential burglar alarm.

***Directory of American Manufacturers & Exporters of Food Additives & Aromatic Chemicals***. EXIM Infotek Private Ltd., 604 Vishwa Deep, District Centre, Janakpuri New Delhi 110058, India. Phone: 91 11 25544793; Fax: 91 11 25544793; Email: info@eximinfo.org • URL: http://www.eximinfo.com • $5 Individuals. Covers: 20 American manufacturers and exporters of aroma chemicals and chemicals for food and beverage. Entries include: Company name, postal address, city, country, phone, fax, e-mail and websites, contact person, designation, and product details.

***Directory of American Manufacturers & Exporters of Furniture—All Types***. EXIM Infotek Private Ltd., 604 Vishwa Deep, District Centre, Janakpuri New Delhi 110058, India. Phone: 91 11 25544793; Fax: 91 11 25544793; Email: info@eximinfo.org • URL: http://www.eximinfo.com • $25 Individuals. Covers: 330 American manufacturers and exporters of bed frames, bed liners, bedroom furniture, bookcases, chairs, church furniture, commercial furniture, computer furniture, computer tables, custom upholstered wood furniture, decorative furniture, dining room furniture, dining tables, edge-glued furniture panels, fine home theater furniture, finished furniture, folding chairs, folding tables, furniture, furniture and supplies, furniture parts, garden furniture, hardwood furniture, hotel furniture, institution furniture, metal furniture, motel furniture, occasional furniture, occasional tables, office furniture and accessories, outdoor furniture, residential furniture, restaurant furniture, safes, school furniture, steel furniture, steel shelving, unfinished wood furniture, upholstered furniture, vault doors, wood library furniture, wrought iron furniture. Entries include: Company name, postal address, city, country, telephone, fax, e-mail and websites, contact person, designation, and product details.

***Directory of American Manufacturers & Exporters of Gears & Gears Boxes***. EXIM Infotek Private Ltd., 604 Vishwa Deep, District Centre, Janakpuri New Delhi 110058, India. Phone: 91 11 25544793; Fax: 91 11 25544793; Email: info@eximinfo.org • URL: http://www.eximinfo.com • $15 Individuals. Covers: 150 American manufacturers and exporters of custom gears, gear boxes, gears, gears-bevel, gears-helical, gears-helical and worm, gears-instruments, gears-master, gears-miter, gears-pinions, gears-plastic, gears-precision, gears-racks, gears-speed reducers, gears-spiral bevel, gears-splines, gears-sprocket, gears-spur, gears-straight and spiral bevel, gears-worms, and zerol and hypoid gears. Entries include: Company name, postal address, city, country, phone, fax, e-mail and websites, contact person, designation, and product details.

***Directory of American Manufacturers & Exporters of Giftware & Novelties***. EXIM Infotek Private Ltd., 604 Vishwa Deep, District Centre, Janakpuri New Delhi 110058, India. Phone: 91 11 25544793; Fax: 91 11 25544793; Email: info@eximinfo.org • URL: http://www.eximinfo.com • $10 Individuals. Covers: 50 American manufacturers and exporters of ceramic mugs with logos, gift items, gift wrap, novelties, silverplate halloware and giftware cutlery. Entries include: Company name, postal address, city, country, phone, fax, e-mail and websites, contact person, designation, and product details.

***Directory of American Manufacturers & Exporters of Gold & Silvery Jewelry***. EXIM Infotek Private Ltd., 604 Vishwa Deep, District Centre, Janakpuri New Delhi 110058, India. Phone: 91 11 25544793; Fax: 91 11 25544793; Email: info@eximinfo.org • URL: http://www.eximinfo.com • $5 Individuals. Covers: 20 American manufacturers and exporters of gold, gold jewelry, silver, and silver jewelry. Entries include: Company name, postal address, city, country, phone, fax, e-mail and websites, contact person, designation, and product details.

***Directory of American Manufacturers & Exporters of Handtools***. EXIM Infotek Private Ltd., 604 Vishwa Deep, District Centre, Janakpuri New Delhi 110058, India. Phone: 91 11 25544793; Fax: 91 11 25544793; Email: info@eximinfo.org • URL: http://www.eximinfo.com • $30 Individuals. Covers: 400 American manufacturers and exporters of copper and aluminum press sleeve swagers, cutting tools, diamond saw blades, fixtures tools, flange spreaders, grinder tools, grooving and proofing tools, hacksaw, hand tools-electric and air, hand tools-files, hand tools-hammers, hand tools-modeling, hand tools-pillers, hand tools-power, hand tools, hand tools-shovels, hand tools-utica, hand tools-wrenches, high speed steel, hydraulic maintenance tools, jewelry, landscaping tools, miniature tools, non-sparking safety tools, nut splitters, pneumatic tools, pocket knives, power tool accessories, precision miniature tools, precision tools, reamers, rivet setting machines, safety tools, screwdrivers, serrated blades, sheet metal hand tools, sledges, pry bars and railroad track tools, socket sets, special tools-custom, special tools, tool holders, tooling, tools, torque tools, torque wrenches, tube tools, wire tools, and wrenches. Entries include: Company name, postal address, city, country, telephone, fax, e-mail and websites, contact person, designation, and product details.

*Directory of American Manufacturers & Exporters of Hardwares—All Types*. EXIM Infotek Private Ltd., 604 Vishwa Deep, District Centre, Janakpuri New Delhi 110058, India. Phone: 91 11 25544793; Fax: 91 11 25544793; Email: info@eximinfo.org • URL: http://www.eximinfo.com • $15 Individuals. Covers: 170 American manufacturers and exporters of builders' hardware, cabinet hardware, cabinet locks, door hardware, door hardware locks, door locks, electrical hardware, electronic hardware, furniture hardware, granite blocks and panels, hardware, hinges, industrial hardware, luggage hardware, metal and plastic adjustable hand levers, padlocks, panels, patch panels, structural and decorative panels, and wall panels. Entries include: Company name, postal address, city, country, phone, fax, e-mail and websites, contact person, designation, and product details.

*Directory of American Manufacturers & Exporters of Home Furnishing Materials*. EXIM Infotek Private Ltd., 604 Vishwa Deep, District Centre, Janakpuri New Delhi 110058, India. Phone: 91 11 25544793; Fax: 91 11 25544793; Email: info@eximinfo.org • URL: http://www.eximinfo.com • $5 Individuals. Covers: 40 American manufacturers and exporters of bedspreads and sleeping bags, cleaners, cushion grips, doors, earring cushions and accessories, home furnishings, pillows, table cloths, vacuum cleaners, and wooden bedroom. Entries include: Company name, postal address, city, country, phone, fax, e-mail and websites, contact person, designation, and product details.

*Directory of American Manufacturers & Exporters of Houseware, Kitchenware & Tableware*. EXIM Infotek Private Ltd., 604 Vishwa Deep, District Centre, Janakpuri New Delhi 110058, India. Phone: 91 11 25544793; Fax: 91 11 25544793; Email: info@eximinfo.org • URL: http://www.eximinfo.com • $10 Individuals. Covers: 90 American manufacturers & exporters of brooms, cleaning materials, coasters, cutlery, dinnerware, flatware cutlery, gas stoves, holloware cutlery, household brooms, household cutlery, housewares, kitchen cutlery, knife sets, knives, plastic cups, plastic cutlery, plastic disposable cutlery, professional cutlery, scissors & knives, stainless steel cutlery, stainless steel flatware cutlery. Entries include: Company name, postal address, city, country, phone, fax, e-mail & websites, contact person, designation, products detail.

*Directory of American Manufacturers & Exporters of Imitation & Fashion Jewellery*. EXIM Infotek Private Ltd., 604 Vishwa Deep, District Centre, Janakpuri New Delhi 110058, India. Phone: 91 11 25544793; Fax: 91 11 25544793; Email: info@eximinfo.org • URL: http://www.eximinfo.com • $10 Individuals. Covers: 80 American manufacturers and exporters of bracelets, costume jewelry, custom jewelry, diamond cabbing and polishing equipment, earrings, fashion jewelry, hair pins, jewelry casting investments, jewelry chains, jewelry findings, jewelry tools, and necklaces. Entries include: Company name, postal address, city, country, phone, fax, e-mail and websites, contact person, designation, and product details.

*Directory of American Manufacturers & Exporters of Lighting Fixtures, Lamps & Accessories*. EXIM Infotek Private Ltd., 604 Vishwa Deep, District Centre, Janakpuri New Delhi 110058, India. Phone: 91 11 25544793; Fax: 91 11 25544793; Email: info@eximinfo.org • URL: http://www.eximinfo.com • $25 Individuals. Covers: 320 American manufacturers and exporters of architectural lighting/dimming equipment, ballasts and fixture lamps, black light lamps, emergency lighting equipment, fixtures, fixtures-lamps, flash lamps, flashlights, floor lamps, fluorescent fixtures and supplies, fluorescent lamp ballasts, fluorescent lighting fixtures, fluorescent tubes, fuel lamps, H.I.D. lamps, halogen lamps, hand lamps, high intensity lamps, incandescent lamps, indoor/outdoor lighting equipment, lamp parts, lamp shades, lamp sockets, lamps, lamps-electric, lamps-fluorescent, lamps-germicidal, light bulbs, lights for nightclubs and discotheques, lighting control equipment for theatrical, lighting equipment and supplies, lighting fixture glassware, lighting fixtures, lighting systems, low voltage lighting, portable lamps, searchlights, solar lighting, solar rail and bus waiting station lights, solar-electric lighting, store display fixtures, table lamps. Entries include: Company name, postal address, city, country, telephone, fax, e-mail and websites, contact person, designation, and product details.

*Directory of American Manufacturers & Exporters of Machinery for Chemicals & Pharma Industry*. EXIM Infotek Private Ltd., 604 Vishwa Deep, District Centre, Janakpuri New Delhi 110058, India. Phone: 91 11 25544793; Fax: 91 11 25544793; Email: info@eximinfo.org • URL: http://www.eximinfo.com • $10 Individuals. Covers: 60 American manufacturers and exporters of chemical process equipment, petroleum chemical processing equipment. Entries include: Company name, postal address, city, country, phone, fax, e-mail and websites, contact person, designation, and product details.

*Directory of American Manufacturers & Exporters of Machinery for Rubber Industry*. EXIM Infotek Private Ltd., 604 Vishwa Deep, District Centre, Janakpuri New Delhi 110058, India. Phone: 91 11 25544793; Fax: 91 11 25544793; Email: info@eximinfo.org • URL: http://www.eximinfo.com • Covers: 25 American manufacturers and exporters of machinery for rubber, tire retreading equipment and supplies, tire spreaders, and inspection machines. Entries include: Company name, postal address, telephone, fax, e-mail, website, contact person, designation, and product details.

*Directory of American Manufacturers & Exporters of Machinery for Textile & Knitting Industry*. EXIM Infotek Private Ltd., 604 Vishwa Deep, District Centre, Janakpuri New Delhi 110058, India. Phone: 91 11 25544793; Fax: 91 11 25544793; Email: info@eximinfo.org • URL: http://www.eximinfo.com • $10 Individuals. Covers: 110 American manufacturers & exporters of dyeing machinery, knitting & braiding machinery, man-made fiber toe cutters, textile & printing machinery, textile machinery, weaving machinery. Entries include: Company name, postal address, city, country, phone, fax, e-mail & websites, contact person, designation, products detail.

*Directory of American Manufacturers & Exporters of Marine & Boating Equipment & Supplies*. EXIM Infotek Private Ltd., 604 Vishwa Deep, District Centre, Janakpuri New Delhi 110058, India. Phone: 91 11 25544793; Fax: 91 11 25544793; Email: info@eximinfo.org • URL: http://www.eximinfo.com • $25 Individuals. Covers: 330 American manufacturers and exporters of aluminum work boats, anchors, boat engines, boat ladders and accessories, boat windshields, boats, buoy and open link chains, capstans, diesel and electric, environmental samplers and equipment, fiberglass boats and houseboats, floodlights, junction boxes, keel coolers, marine accessories, marine barges, marine coatings, marine diesel engines, marine electronics, marine engines, marine engines-gasoline, marine equipment and spare parts, marine equipment and supplies, marine furniture, marine hardware, marine instruments, marine parts, marine portlights, marine propellers, marine propulsion units, marine pumps, marine safety equipment, marine suppliers and repair, marine windows, marine-engines, nautical instruments, nautical products, navigation equipment, navigation instruments, navigation systems, oceanographic instruments, outboard motors, plumbing fittings, power supplies, propellers, rollers, satcom systems, shipboard wire and cables, spot lights, starters, steering components, surface air supply dive systems, tachometers, tug boats, water makers and radios, water samplers and plankton nets, windlasses, wire ropes. Entries include: Company name, postal address, city, country, telephone, fax, e-mail and websites, contact person, designation, and product details.

*Directory of American Manufacturers & Exporters of Material Handling Equipment*. EXIM Infotek Private Ltd., 604 Vishwa Deep, District Centre, Janakpuri New Delhi 110058, India. Phone: 91 11 25544793; Fax: 91 11 25544793; Email: info@eximinfo.org • URL: http://www.eximinfo.com • $850 Individuals; $35 Individuals. Covers: 480 American manufacturers and exporters of airport baggage handling equipment, bag openers, bulk bag loading and unloading equipment, bulk handling systems, bulk materials handling equipment, carts, chain and cable conveyors, conveyor chains, conveyor bands, conveyor systems, cranes, endless conveyor belts, forklift trucks, hand trucks, hoists, hydraulic cranes, lift trucks, liquid handling products, lumber materials handling equipment, material handling booms, mining and construction equipment, non-powered materials handling equipment, pallet racks, platforms, pneumatic conveying systems, restraint equipment, turntables, weigh belt feeders, winches, and hoists.

*Directory of American Manufacturers & Exporters of Minerals*. EXIM Infotek Private Ltd., 604 Vishwa Deep, District Centre, Janakpuri New Delhi 110058, India. Phone: 91 11 25544793; Fax: 91 11 25544793; Email: info@eximinfo.org • URL: http://www.eximinfo.com • $10 Individuals. Covers: 70 American manufacturers and exporters of calcium carbonate, carbonate magnesium, crushed lime, dolomitic quicklime, high calcium lime, hydrated lime, lime and limestone, magnesia chemicals, magnesium, mica, minerals, oxide magnesium, pulverized lime, quartz, stearate magnesium, and talc. Entries include: Company name, postal address, city, country, phone, fax, e-mail and websites, contact person, designation, and product details.

*Directory of American Manufacturers and Exporters of Motors and Motor Parts—Electric*. EXIM Infotek Private Ltd., 604 Vishwa Deep, District Centre, Janakpuri New Delhi 110058, India. Phone: 91 11 25544793; Fax: 91 11 25544793; Email: info@eximinfo.org • URL: http://www.eximinfo.com • Covers: 230 American manufacturers and exporters of AC and DC motors, brushless motors, air motors, electric motors, fractional horsepower motors, gear motors, hydraulic motor, integral horsepower motors, miniature motors, permanent magnet motors, servo motor, springs motors, stepping motors, stepper motors, sub-fractional horsepower motors, and submersible motors. Entries include: Company name, postal address, telephone, fax, e-mail, website, contact person, designation, and product details.

*Directory of American Manufacturers & Exporters of Nuts, Bolts, Screws & Fasteners*. EXIM Infotek Private Ltd., 604 Vishwa Deep, District Centre, Janakpuri New Delhi 110058, India. Phone: 91 11 25544793; Fax: 91 11 25544793; Email: info@eximinfo.org • URL: http://www.eximinfo.com • $20 Individuals. Covers: 260 American manufacturers & exporters of belt fasteners, bolts, captive screws, clevis pins, electronic & electrical enclosure closing systems, fasteners, fasteners for electronics & aerospace, fasteners-aluminum steel, fasteners-automotive, fasteners-industrial, fasteners-military specialties, fasteners-nylon, fasteners-plastic, fasteners-specialty, fasteners-spring steel, fasteners-stainless steel, fasteners-textiles, hand adjusting & fastening components, hex head bolts, marine snap fasteners, metric fasteners, military snap fasteners, nuts, nuts & bolts, pins, plastic fasteners, plastic snap fasteners, precision fasteners for military & commercial aircraft, quarter-turn fasteners, rivets, screws, self-locking nuts, special threaded & non-threaded fasteners, staples, threaded inserts & related high-tech fasteners. Entries include: Company name, postal address, city, country, telephone, fax, e-mail & websites, contact person, designation, products detail.

*Directory of American Manufacturers & Exporters of Paints, Varnishes & Allied Products*. EXIM Infotek Private Ltd., 604 Vishwa Deep, District Centre, Janakpuri New Delhi 110058, India. Phone: 91 11 25544793; Fax: 91 11 25544793; Email: info@eximinfo.org • URL: http://www.eximinfo.com • $30 Individuals. Covers: 450 American manufacturers and exporters of abrasion resistant coatings, agricultural/horticultural foliar applied coatings, anodizing, anti-slip paints and coatings, buffing compound applicators, chartek intumescant epoxy for structural steel, coatings, coatings and coating materials, coatings-abrasion resistant, coatings-anti- graffiti, coatings-anti-skid, coatings-asphalt, coatings-ceramic, coatings-corrosion resistant, coatings-floor, coatings-heat resistant, coatings-metal, coatings-metallic, coatings-pipeline, coatings-ultraviolet, corrosion resistant, corrosion resistant coatings, custom coatings, decorative coatings, easels, electrically conductive coatings, encapsulating resins, epoxy coatings, flexible bright metallic coatings for auto wheels, trims, high performance coatings, industrial coatings, lacquers coatings, military specification coatings, optical coatings, paint brushes, paints, paper coatings, permanent protective coatings, pipe coatings, plastic coatings, polyester coatings, polyester resins and coatings, polyurethane coatings, primers coatings, refractory coatings, self locking coating for screws and studs, solvents, urethane coatings, waterproof, waterproofing coatings, wear and corrosion resistant, and wood coatings. Entries include: Company name, postal address, city, country, telephone, fax, e-mail and websites, contact person, designation, and product details.

*Directory of American Manufacturers & Exporters of Paper & Paper Products*. EXIM Infotek Private Ltd., 604 Vishwa Deep, District Centre, Janakpuri New Delhi 110058, India. Phone: 91 11 25544793; Fax: 91 11 25544793; Email: info@eximinfo.org • URL: http://www.eximinfo.com • $5 Individuals. Covers: 40 American manufacturers and exporters of bags-paper lined, carbon papers, collect and process paper for recycling, computer paper products, fax paper, paper, and white paper recycling. Entries include: Company name, postal address, city, country, phone, fax, e-mail and websites, contact person, designation, and product details.

*Directory of American Manufacturers & Exporters of Petroleum Products*. EXIM Infotek Private Ltd., 604 Vishwa Deep, District Centre, Janakpuri New Delhi 110058, India. Phone: 91 11 25544793; Fax: 91 11 25544793; Email: info@eximinfo.org • URL: http://www.eximinfo.com • $10 Individuals. Covers: 120 American manufacturers & exporters of additives for engines, brake & transmission fluid, gas, gear lubricants, hydraulic oils, industrial oil, lubricants, lubricating oil & greases, oils-cutting & drawing, oils-hardening, tempering & quenching, petroleum & chemical industry, synthetic oil, water soluble oils. Entries include: Company name, postal address, city, country, phone, fax, e-mail & websites, contact person, designation, products detail.

*Directory of American Manufacturers & Exporters of Pharmaceutical Products*. EXIM Infotek Private Ltd., 604 Vishwa Deep, District Centre, Janakpuri New Delhi 110058, India. Phone: 91 11 25544793; Fax: 91 11 25544793; Email: info@eximinfo.org • URL: http://www.eximinfo.com • $5 Individuals. Covers: 30 American manufacturers and exporters of animal health products, dental medicaments, dental pharmaceuticals, generic pharmaceuticals, nuclear medicine, pharmaceuticals. Entries include: Company name, postal address, city, country, phone, fax, e-mail and websites, contact person, designation, and product details.

*Directory of American Manufacturers and Exporters of Restaurant, Hotel and Catering Equipment and Supplies*. EXIM Infotek Private Ltd., 604 Vishwa Deep, District Centre, Janakpuri New Delhi 110058, India. Phone: 91 11 25544793; Fax: 91 11 25544793; Email: info@eximinfo.org • URL: http://www.eximinfo.com • Covers: 120 American manufacturers and exporters of beverage dispensers and equipment for hotels and restaurants. Entries include: Company name, postal address, telephone, fax, e-mail, website, contact person, designation, and product details.

*Directory of American Manufacturers & Exporters of Seeds & Bulbs—Flowers & Vegetables*. EXIM Infotek Private Ltd., 604 Vishwa Deep, District Centre, Janakpuri New Delhi 110058, India. Phone: 91 11 25544793; Fax: 91 11 25544793;

Email: info@eximinfo.org • URL: http://www.eximinfo.com • $10 Individuals. Covers: 80 American manufacturers and exporters of agricultural vegetable seeds, alfalfa seeds, cotton seeds, edible seeds, field seeds, flower seeds, forage seeds, grass seeds, hybrid sunflower seeds, livestock forage, rice seeds, seeds, sorghum seeds, soybeans seeds, sunflower seeds, turf seeds, vegetable seeds, and wheat seeds. Entries include: Company name, postal address, city, country, phone, fax, e-mail and websites, contact person, designation, and product details.

***Directory of American Manufacturers & Exporters of Soap, Detergent & Cleaning Supplies***. EXIM Infotek Private Ltd., 604 Vishwa Deep, District Centre, Janakpuri New Delhi 110058, India. Phone: 91 11 25544793; Fax: 91 11 25544793; Email: info@eximinfo.com • URL: http://www.eximinfo.com • $5 Individuals. Covers: 40 American manufacturers and exporters of carpet cleaning chemicals, cleaning chemicals, detergents, and detergents-chemicals. Entries include: Company name, postal address, city, country, phone, fax, e-mail and websites, contact person, designation, and product details.

***Directory of American Manufacturers & Exporters of Stationery Articles & Education Supplies***. EXIM Infotek Private Ltd., 604 Vishwa Deep, District Centre, Janakpuri New Delhi 110058, India. Phone: 91 11 25544793; Fax: 91 11 25544793; Email: info@eximinfo.org • URL: http://www.eximinfo.com • $15 Individuals; $400 Individuals. Covers: 180 American manufacturers and exporters of address books, air brush colors, appointment books, ball pens, ball point pens, artists' brush, card and passport cases, clip boards, desk pads and accessories, desk pens, desk sets, desk top accessories, envelopes, felt tip, files, filing folders, fluorescent, hobby brushes, ink, letter openers, markers, nibs, organizers, paper clips, parker pens, pencils, lead and mechanical pencils, non-mechanical pencils, steel pens, refills, rulers, scrapbooks, stationery products, stationery specialties, stationery supplies, stencil, and writing instruments. Entries include: Company name, postal address, telephone, fax, e-mail, website, contact person, designation, and product details.

***Directory of American Manufacturers & Exporters of Tobacco & Tobacco Products***. EXIM Infotek Private Ltd., 604 Vishwa Deep, District Centre, Janakpuri New Delhi 110058, India. Phone: 91 11 25544793; Fax: 91 11 25544793; Email: info@eximinfo.org • URL: http://www.eximinfo.com • Covers: 20 American manufacturers and exporters of cigarettes. Entries include: Company name, postal address, telephone, fax, e-mail, website, contact person, designation, and product details.

***Directory of American Manufacturers & Exporters of Toys & Games***. EXIM Infotek Private Ltd., 604 Vishwa Deep, District Centre, Janakpuri New Delhi 110058, India. Phone: 91 11 25544793; Fax: 91 11 25544793; Email: info@eximinfo.org • URL: http://www.eximinfo.com • $15 Individuals. Covers: 170 American manufacturers and exporters of arts and craft kits, baby cribs, balloons, carnival toys, children's toys, coin operated games, dolls, educational toys, games, infant toys, inflatable, joke novelties, juvenile furniture, kite reels, magic tricks, outdoor games, outdoor toys, pedal cars, plastic playing cards, plastic toys, playing cards and children's games, plush toys, pools, preschool toys, puzzles, ride-on toys, slot machines, sports memorabilia, stuffed toys, toy parts-plastic, toys, toys and games, and video games. Entries include: Company name, postal address, city, country, phone, fax, e-mail and websites, contact person, designation, and product details.

***Directory of American Manufacturers & Exporters of Tractors, Parts & Accessories***. EXIM Infotek Private Ltd., 604 Vishwa Deep, District Centre, Janakpuri New Delhi 110058, India. Phone: 91 11 25544793; Fax: 91 11 25544793; Email: info@eximinfo.org • URL: http://www.eximinfo.com • $5 Individuals. Covers: 25 American manufacturers and exporters of agricultural tractors and spare parts, farm tractors, tractor parts, and tractors. Entries include: Company name, postal address, city, country, phone, fax, e-mail and websites, contact person, designation, and product details.

***Directory of American Manufacturers & Exporters of Tyres & Tubes***. EXIM Infotek Private Ltd., 604 Vishwa Deep, District Centre, Janakpuri New Delhi 110058, India. Phone: 91 11 25544793; Fax: 91 11 25544793; Email: info@eximinfo.org • URL: http://www.eximinfo.com • $10 Individuals. Covers: 70 American manufacturers and exporters of tire repair materials, tires, tires and tubes, and tires for trucks and heavy equipment. Entries include: Company name, postal address, city, country, phone, fax, e-mail and websites, contact person, designation, and product details.

***Directory of American Manufacturers & Exporters of Waste Disposal & Recycling Equipment***. EXIM Infotek Private Ltd., 604 Vishwa Deep, District Centre, Janakpuri New Delhi 110058, India. Phone: 91 11 25544793; Fax: 91 11 25544793; Email: info@eximinfo.org • URL: http://www.eximinfo.com • Covers: 340 American manufacturers and exporters of advanced wash recycling systems, balers and recycling equipment, baling presses, compactors, decontamination waste disposable systems, garbage disposers, glass and can crushers, hazardous materials, hazardous waste disposal system, food waste disposers, indoor and outdoor steel and fiberglass receptacles, modern gas chlorinators, recycled wood and paper waste and fiber materials, recycling center equipment, aluminum can densors and flattener, sewage treatment systems, shredders, solid waste disposable systems, stump and wood waste disposable equipment, tire shredders, trash compactors, waste handling equipment, wastewater reclamation equipment, wastewater treatment systems, and wood waste recycling equipment.

***Directory of American Manufacturers & Exporters of Wax & Wax Products***. EXIM Infotek Private Ltd., 604 Vishwa Deep, District Centre, Janakpuri New Delhi 110058, India. Phone: 91 11 25544793; Fax: 91 11 25544793; Email: info@eximinfo.org • URL: http://www.eximinfo.com • $10 Individuals. Covers: 100 American manufacturers and exporters of car waxes, dental waxes, floor finishes wax, microcrystalline waxes, synthetic waxes, wax, waxes and polishes, wax floors. Entries include: Company name, postal address, city, country, phone, fax, e-mail and websites, contact person, designation, products detail.

***Directory of American Manufacturers & Exporters of Wire, Chain & Wire Products***. EXIM Infotek Private Ltd., 604 Vishwa Deep, District Centre, Janakpuri New Delhi 110058, India. Phone: 91 11 25544793; Fax: 91 11 25544793; Email: info@eximinfo.org • URL: http://www.eximinfo.com • $5 Individuals. Covers: 20 American manufacturers and exporters of cables-mechanical, silver wire, steel wire rope, and wires. Entries include: Company name, postal address, city, country, phone, fax, e-mail and websites, contact person, designation, and product details.

***Directory of American Manufacturers & Exporters of Wires & Cables—Electrical***. EXIM Infotek Private Ltd., 604 Vishwa Deep, District Centre, Janakpuri New Delhi 110058, India. Phone: 91 11 25544793; Fax: 91 11 25544793; Email: info@eximinfo.org • URL: http://www.eximinfo.com • Covers: 280 American manufacturers and exporters of assemblies coaxial cables, bonding and grounding cables, booster cables, cable accessories, cable assemblies, coaxial cable, electrical cables, electronic cables, fiber optic cables, triaxial cables, twisted pair cables, conduits electrical cables, copper cable, electric cables, electrical wire, high temperature wire and cables, high temperature wires, magnet insulated wires, public utility electrical cables, PVC coaxial cables, retractile cables, teflon cables, teflon insulated wires, high voltage wire, insulated wire, and wire-plastic coated. Entries include: Company name, postal address, telephone, fax, e-mail, website, contact person, designation, and product details.

***Directory of American Manufacturers and Exporters of Woodworking Equipment and Tools***. EXIM Infotek Private Ltd., 604 Vishwa Deep, District Centre, Janakpuri New Delhi 110058, India. Phone: 91 11 25544793; Fax: 91 11 25544793; Email: info@eximinfo.org • URL: http://www.eximinfo.com • Covers: 240 American manufacturers and exporters of automatic saws and circular, band sawing machine, band saw, band saw blades, belt conveyors, circular cold sawing machine, circular saw blades for wood, circular saw, compass saw, cut off saw, forestry equipment, high speed saw, lumber, machinery for woodworking industry, panel saw, plywood, reciprocating saw, resaw, sabre saw, saw blades, saw mill, saw mill machinery, saws woodworking, chain saw and parts, portable saws, round hole saw, slitting and slotting saw, stackers, trimmers, wood machinery, and woodworking accessories. Entries include: Company name, postal address, telephone, fax, e-mail, website, contact person, designation, and product details.

***Directory of American Manufacturers & Exporters of Yarns & Threads***. EXIM Infotek Private Ltd., 604 Vishwa Deep, District Centre, Janakpuri New Delhi 110058, India. Phone: 91 11 25544793; Fax: 91 11 25544793; Email: info@eximinfo.org • URL: http://www.eximinfo.com • $10 Individuals. Covers: 80 American manufacturers and exporters of bleaching and space dyeing yarns, carpet yarns, cotton yarns, synthetic yarns, textile yarn, woolen yarns, and yarns. Entries include: Company name, postal address, city, country, phone, fax, e-mail and websites, contact person, designation, and product details.

***Directory of American Manufacturers & Exporters of Zippers, Garment & Shoe Accessories***. EXIM Infotek Private Ltd., 604 Vishwa Deep, District Centre, Janakpuri New Delhi 110058, India. Phone: 91 11 25544793; Fax: 91 11 25544793; Email: info@eximinfo.org • URL: http://www.eximinfo.com • $5 Individuals. Covers: 40 American manufacturers and exporters of bar code labels, belts-buckles, buckles, buttons, metal snap fasteners, metal zippers, nylon molded zippers, and zippers. Entries include: Company name, postal address, city, country, phone, fax, e-mail and websites, contact person, designation, and product details.

***Directory of American Scholars***. Cengage Learning Inc., 20 Channel Center St. Boston, MA 02210. Phone: 800-487-8488 or (617)289-7700; Fax: (617)289-7844; Email: investors@cengage.com • URL: http://www.cengage.com • $928. Volumes one to volume five, $212.00; volume six, $72.00. Provides biographical information and publication history for more than 24,000 scholars in the humanities.

***Directory of Apparel Specialty Stores***. Chain Store Guide, 10117 Princess Palm Dr. Tampa, FL 33610. Phone: 800-927-9292 or (813)627-6800; Fax: (813)627-6888 or (813)627-6883; Email: info@csgis.com • URL: http://www.chainstoreguide.com • Annual. $495 Individuals Directory; $545 Individuals online lite; $1,150 Individuals online pro; $1,450 Individuals online pro plus. Covers 4,700 apparel and sporting goods specialty stores in the United States and Canada, operating more than 80,000 stores. Include company name, phone and fax numbers, company e-mail and web addresses and other information.

***Directory of Argentine Exporters and Importers***. Telmo G. Mirat, PO Box 1493 1000 Buenos Aires, Argentina. Phone: 5412427912; Fax: 5412427912 • Annual. $100 postpaid. Covers: 3,250 manufacturers, importers, and exporters in Argentina, and companies and organizations providing products and services to international traders. Entries include: Organization name, address, phone, telex, fax, description of product/service, and Brussels tariff number.

***Directory of Arizona Exporters***. Arizona Commerce Authority, 333 N Central Ave., Ste. 1900 Phoenix, AZ 85004. Phone: (602)845-1200; Fax: (602)845-1201; Email: NicoleM@azcommerce.com • URL: http://www.azcommerce.com • Annual. Covers: Arizona enterprises currently involved in international trade. Entries include: Company name, address, phone, fax, e-mail, names of principal executive, and international marketing contact, number of employees, products or services, date established, current or planned export regions.

***Directory of Asian Importers of Audio Visual Training Equipment and Projectors***. EXIM Infotek Private Ltd., 604 Vishwa Deep, District Centre, Janakpuri New Delhi 110058, India. Phone: 91 11 25544793; Fax: 91 11 25544793; Email: info@eximinfo.org • URL: http://www.eximinfo.com • $300 Individuals; $10 Individuals. Covers: 60 Asian importers of audio, audio visual equipment, audio visual training equipment, LCD projector, projectors, project equipment, slides, and slide projectors. Entries include: Company name, postal address, telephone, fax, e-mail, website, contact person, designation, and product details.

***Directory of Asian Importers of Biological Products***. EXIM Infotek Private Ltd., 604 Vishwa Deep, District Centre, Janakpuri New Delhi 110058, India. Phone: 91 11 25544793; Fax: 91 11 25544793; Email: info@eximinfo.org • URL: http://www.eximinfo.com • $250 Individuals; $10 Individuals. Covers: 20 Asian importers of biological products and molecular biology. Entries include: Company name, postal address, telephone, fax, e-mail, website, contact person, designation, and product details.

***Directory of Asian Importers of Boiler and Boiler Parts***. EXIM Infotek Private Ltd., 604 Vishwa Deep, District Centre, Janakpuri New Delhi 110058, India. Phone: 91 11 25544793; Fax: 91 11 25544793; Email: info@eximinfo.org • URL: http://www.eximinfo.com • Covers: 120 Asian importers of boiler machinery, boilers, boilers and parts, boiler fittings, gas boiler, hot water boilers, and steam boilers. Entries include: Company name, postal address, telephone, fax, e-mail, website, contact person, designation, and product details.

***Directory of Asian Importers of Calendars, Greeting, Prints and Lithographs***. EXIM Infotek Private Ltd., 604 Vishwa Deep, District Centre, Janakpuri New Delhi 110058, India. Phone: 91 11 25544793; Fax: 91 11 25544793; Email: info@eximinfo.org • URL: http://www.eximinfo.com • $300 Individuals; $10 Individuals. Covers: 105 Asian importers of calendars, greeting cards, postcards, diaries, posters, prints, lithographs, etching, serigraphs, original painting, smart cards, vinyl flooring, visiting cards, and wedding cards. Entries include: Company name, postal address, telephone, fax, e-mail, website, contact person, designation, and product details.

***Directory of Asian Importers of Dyes, Colors, and Pigments***. EXIM Infotek Private Ltd., 604 Vishwa Deep, District Centre, Janakpuri New Delhi 110058, India. Phone: 91 11 25544793; Fax: 91 11 25544793; Email: info@eximinfo.org • URL: http://www.eximinfo.com • $950 Individuals; $40 Individuals. Covers: 580 Asian importers of acrylic color, activated carbon, auxiliaries, candle additives, dye and scent, chemical for textile, chemical intermediates, dye for leather industry, dye for textile industry, colors and pigments, dyestuff, dyestuff intermediates, fluorescent pigments, ink, leather chemicals, phthalic anhydride, resin for printing ink, synthetic organic dyestuff, textile auxiliaries, textile chemicals, textile dye, and washing chemicals. Entries include: Company name, postal address, telephone, fax, e-mail, website, contact person, designation, and product details.

***Directory of Asian Importers of Energy and Power Equipment***. EXIM Infotek Private Ltd., 604 Vishwa Deep, District Centre, Janakpuri New Delhi 110058, India. Phone: 91 11 25544793; Fax: 91 11 25544793; Email: info@eximinfo.org • URL: http://www.eximinfo.com • Covers: 130 Asian importers of high voltage equipment and component, nuclear equipment and materials, power equipment, power generation projects, power plants, power transmission component, power transmission equipment and supplies, power transmission products, solar cells, solar charge controller and modules, solar energy equipment, wind energy equipment, and transmission and allied equipment. Entries include: Company name, postal address, telephone, fax, e-mail, website, contact person, designation, and product details.

***Directory of Asian Importers of Environment Protection and Pollution Control Equipment***. EXIM Infotek Private Ltd., 604 Vishwa Deep, District Centre, Janakpuri New Delhi 110058, India. Phone: 91 11 25544793; Fax: 91 11 25544793; Email: info@eximinfo.org • URL: http://www.eximinfo.com

• Covers: 230 Asian importers of air cleaner, dust collectors, dust extractor systems, environment equipment, environment protection equipment, environmental monitoring equipment, environmentally conserving or improving products, noise control equipment, ozone generators, pollution control equipment, sewage treatment, water purification equipment, water treatment, water treatment equipment, water treatment plants, and purifying equipment. Entries include: Company name, postal address, telephone, fax, e-mail, website, contact person, designation, and product details.

***Directory of Asian Importers of Fibre Products***. EXIM Infotek Private Ltd., 604 Vishwa Deep, District Centre, Janakpuri New Delhi 110058, India. Phone: 91 11 25544793; Fax: 91 11 25544793; Email: info@eximinfo.org • URL: http://www.eximinfo.com • $500 Individuals; $20 Individuals. Covers: 190 Asian importers of acrylic fiber, carbon fiber, fiberglass materials, fiber waste, fiberglass, fiberglass cloth, fiberglass products and cloth, fiber products, fiber materials, fiberglass chopped strands, fiberglass products, high-density fiberboard, natural fiber, optic fiber, polyester fiber, polyester staple fiber, polynosic staple fiber, synthetic fiber, viscose fiber, viscose rayon staple fiber, and vulcanized fiber. Entries include: Company name, postal address, telephone, fax, e-mail, website, contact person, designation, and product details.

***Directory of Asian Importers of Fire Fighting Equipment & Supplies***. EXIM Infotek Private Ltd., 604 Vishwa Deep, District Centre, Janakpuri New Delhi 110058, India. Phone: 91 11 25544793; Fax: 91 11 25544793; Email: info@eximinfo.org • URL: http://www.eximinfo.com • $500 Individuals; $20 Individuals. Covers: 250 Asian importers of automatic fire alarm systems, CO2 gas and extinguishers, fire alarm and detection systems, fire alarm equipment, fire alarm panels, fire blankets, fire detection products, fire fighting equipment, fire fighting supplies, fire hose reel, hydrant and sprinkler systems, fire hose systems, fire hydrants, fire panels, fire protective clothing, fire resistant products, fire sensors and components, fire suppression systems, firefighting vehicles and accessories, flame detectors, optical smoke detector, security and fire fighting equipment, smoke detection systems, and smoke detectors. Entries include: Company name, postal address, telephone, fax, e-mail, website, contact person, designation, and product details.

***Directory of Asian Importers of Fodder and Animal Foodstuffs***. EXIM Infotek Private Ltd., 604 Vishwa Deep, District Centre, Janakpuri New Delhi 110058, India. Phone: 91 11 25544793; Fax: 91 11 25544793; Email: info@eximinfo.org • URL: http://www.eximinfo.com • $450 Individuals; $20 Individuals. Covers: 210 Asian importers of alfalfa, alfalfa hay cubes, animal and foodstuff aditives, animal feeds, feed additives, animal food, cottonseed meal, feeder calves, fodder, cereals, and livestock breeding supplies, livestock products, and whey. Entries include: Company name, postal address, telephone, fax, e-mail, website, contact person, designation, and product details.

***Directory of Asian Importers of Food Additives and Aromatics***. EXIM Infotek Private Ltd., 604 Vishwa Deep, District Centre, Janakpuri New Delhi 110058, India. Phone: 91 11 25544793; Fax: 91 11 25544793; Email: info@eximinfo.org • URL: http://www.eximinfo.com • $750 Individuals; $30 Individuals. Covers: 410 Asian importers of agar, agar-agar, aromatic chemicals, chemical for food, essence, flavor and fragrance chemicals, flavoring materials, flavoring essence, food additives, food colors, food flavors, food ingredients, food raw materials, fragrances, fruit powder, natural coloring matters, oleoresin, raw material for flavors, raw materials for food colors, tapioca starch, vanillin (pollar BR), whey powder, xylitol, and yeasts. Entries include: Company name, postal address, telephone, fax, e-mail, website, contact person, designation, and product details.

***Directory of Asian Importers of Handkerchives, Scarves and Neckwears***. EXIM Infotek Private Ltd., 604 Vishwa Deep, District Centre, Janakpuri New Delhi 110058, India. Phone: 91 11 25544793; Fax: 91 11 25544793; Email: info@eximinfo.org • URL: http://www.eximinfo.com • $350 Individuals; $15 Individuals. Covers: 130 Asian importers of clothing accessories, ties, scarves, corsage, handkerchieves, neckwear, mufflers, necktie, pashmina shawls, silk neckties, silk scarves, and stoles. Entries include: Company name, postal address, telephone, fax, e-mail, website, contact person, designation, and product details.

***Directory of Asian Importers of Heaters and Heating Equipment***. EXIM Infotek Private Ltd., 604 Vishwa Deep, District Centre, Janakpuri New Delhi 110058, India. Phone: 91 11 25544793; Fax: 91 11 25544793; Email: info@eximinfo.org • URL: http://www.eximinfo.com • Covers: 120 Asian importers of electric heaters for industry, heat detectors, heat exchangers, heaters, heating and ventilation equipment, heating elements and spare parts, heating equipment, solar energy heating products, solar water systems, thermic fluid heaters, waste heat recovery systems, and water heaters. Entries include: Company name, postal address, telephone, fax, e-mail, website, contact person, designation, and product details.

***Directory of Asian Importers of Honey and Syrup***. EXIM Infotek Private Ltd., 604 Vishwa Deep, District Centre, Janakpuri New Delhi 110058, India. Phone: 91 11 25544793; Fax: 91 11 25544793; Email: info@eximinfo.org • URL: http://www.eximinfo.com • $150 Individuals; $5 Individuals. Covers: 35 Asian importers of honey, syrups, and honey products. Entries include: Company name, postal address, telephone, fax, e-mail, website, contact person, designation, and product details.

***Directory of Asian Importers of Juices and Soft Drinks***. EXIM Infotek Private Ltd., 604 Vishwa Deep, District Centre, Janakpuri New Delhi 110058, India. Phone: 91 11 25544793; Fax: 91 11 25544793; Email: info@eximinfo.org • URL: http://www.eximinfo.com • $750 Individuals; $30 Individuals. Covers: 410 Asian importers of beverages, concentrated juices, pure water, drinks and cakes, energy drinks, fruit and vegetable concentrates, fruit and vegetable juices, fruit drinks, fruit flavored drinks, fruit pulp, fruit syrups, lychee juice concentrate, malted food drinks, mango-purees, mineral water, non-alcoholic beverages, orange juice, pine pulp, puree, and softdrinks. Entries include: Company name, postal address, telephone, fax, e-mail, website, contact person, designation, and product details.

***Directory of Asian Importers of Laboratory & Scientific Instruments and Supplies***. EXIM Infotek Private Ltd., 604 Vishwa Deep, District Centre, Janakpuri New Delhi 110058, India. Phone: 91 11 25544793; Fax: 91 11 25544793; Email: info@eximinfo.org • URL: http://www.eximinfo.com • $1,400 Individuals; $55 Individuals. Covers: 620 Asian importers of analysis equipment, analytical instruments, anatomical models, binoculars, microscopes, telescopes, biotechnology instruments, borosilicate glass tubing, educational scientific equipment, electrical test equipment, glass tubular vial and ampoules, gyrocompass, laboratory equipment, laboratory and scientific glass, laboratory supplies, laboratory glassware, laboratory instruments, laboratory reagents, non-contact infrared thermometers, non-destructive testing equipment, radiology equipment, scientific instruments, testing and measuring equipment, testing instruments, testing machines, thermometers, and barometers. Entries include: Company name, postal address, telephone, fax, e-mail, website, contact person, designation, and product details.

***Directory of Asian Importers of Machinery for Rubber Industry***. EXIM Infotek Private Ltd., 604 Vishwa Deep, District Centre, Janakpuri New Delhi 110058, India. Phone: 91 11 25544793; Fax: 91 11 25544793; Email: info@eximinfo.org • URL: http://www.eximinfo.com • Covers: 30 Asian importers of rubber industry equipment and supplies and rubber processing machinery. Entries include: Company name, postal address, telephone, fax, e-mail, website, contact person, designation, and product details.

***Directory of Asian Importers of Material Handling Equipment & Supplies***. EXIM Infotek Private Ltd., 604 Vishwa Deep, District Centre, Janakpuri New Delhi 110058, India. Phone: 91 11 25544793; Fax: 91 11 25544793; Email: info@eximinfo.org • URL: http://www.eximinfo.com • Covers: 300 Asian importers of aerial lifts and platforms, backhoe loaders, chain hoist, conveying machine, conveyor systems, crane equipment, hoists, crawler crane, electric hoist, elevator lifts, elevators, escalators, forklift parts and accessories, hand pallet truck, hoisting blocks chipping machine and spares, liebherr tower cranes, liquid handling equipment, loaders, loading and unloading equipment, materials handling containers and equipment materials handling and lifting system, mobile cranes, monorail materials handling equipment, pallet truck, pulley, roller chain, used conveyor belts, used excavators, used forklift, wheel loaders, and winch. Entries include: Company name, postal address, telephone, fax, e-mail, website, contact person, designation, and product details.

***Directory of Asian Importers of Military & Police Equipment & Supplies***. EXIM Infotek Private Ltd., 604 Vishwa Deep, District Centre, Janakpuri New Delhi 110058, India. Phone: 91 11 25544793; Fax: 91 11 25544793; Email: info@eximinfo.org • URL: http://www.eximinfo.com • $250 Individuals; $10 Individuals. Covers: 70 Asian importers of ammunition, military clothing, military electronic equipment, military equipment and supplies, military surplus goods, police equipment, surplus military equipment and supplies, and traffic control systems. Entries include: Company name, postal address, telephone, fax, e-mail, website, contact person, designation, and product details.

***Directory of Asian Importers of Minerals***. EXIM Infotek Private Ltd., 604 Vishwa Deep, District Centre, Janakpuri New Delhi 110058, India. Phone: 91 11 25544793; Fax: 91 11 25544793; Email: info@eximinfo.org • URL: http://www.eximinfo.com • $800 Individuals; $30 Individuals. Covers: 370 Asian importers of acid phosphoric mineral, bauxite, borax, carbon and graphite products, copper mineral, crucibles made of alumina or quartz, faucets, ferrites, flourspar, fossils, graphite, gypsum, industrial minerals, iron ore, iron oxide, lead, limestone, magnesium oxide, manganese ore, metals and minerals, mica, mineral oil, mineral products and raw materials, mineral raw materials, ores, phosphoric acid, rare earth minerals, rare metal minerals, rare metals, rock phosphate, silica sand, soil, sulfur, zinc, zircon sand, zirconic, and zirconium sand. Entries include: Company name, postal address, telephone, fax, e-mail, website, contact person, designation, and product details.

***Directory of Asian Importers of Motors and Motor Parts—Electric***. EXIM Infotek Private Ltd., 604 Vishwa Deep, District Centre, Janakpuri New Delhi 110058, India. Phone: 91 11 25544793; Fax: 91 11 25544793; Email: info@eximinfo.org • URL: http://www.eximinfo.com • Covers: 150 Asian importers of DC motors, Eddy current variable speed motors, electric motor control, electric motors, geared motors, induction motors, motor equipment and parts, motor graders, motor parts and accessories, motor starters, pump and motor accessories, servo motors and controllers. Entries include: Company name, postal address, telephone, fax, e-mail, website, contact person, designation, and product details.

***Directory of Asian Importers of Photographic Equipment and Supplies***. EXIM Infotek Private Ltd., 604 Vishwa Deep, District Centre, Janakpuri New Delhi 110058, India. Phone: 91 11 25544793; Fax: 91 11 25544793; Email: info@eximinfo.org • URL: http://www.eximinfo.com • $500 Individuals; $20 Individuals. Covers: 170 Asian importers of cameras, lens and accessories, photographic chemicals, motion picture and theater equipment, colored film, black and white film, digital camera, plate and photographic papers, graphic films, microfilm and blueprint equipment, motion picture films, photo film, photo finishing equipment, photo finishing paper and chemicals, photographic equipment, photographic goods, photographic materials, photographic paper, and tripod. Entries include: Company name, postal address, telephone, fax, e-mail, website, contact person, designation, and product details.

***Directory of Asian Importers of Refrigeration Equipment and Supplies***. EXIM Infotek Private Ltd., 604 Vishwa Deep, District Centre, Janakpuri New Delhi 110058, India. Phone: 91 11 25544793; Fax: 91 11 25544793; Email: info@eximinfo.org • URL: http://www.eximinfo.com • $400 Individuals; $15 Individuals. Covers: 180 Asian importers of air cooled water chillers, centrifugal chillers, chest freezers, cold rooms, cooling towers, deep freezers, freezers, ice cream display, refrigeration and air conditioning equipment, refrigeration parts and supplies, refrigeration spare parts, refrigeration and air conditioning servicing accessories, commercial refrigeration, and industrial refrigeration. Entries include: Company name, postal address, telephone, fax, e-mail, website, contact person, designation, and product details.

***Directory of Asian Importers of Restaurant, Hotel and Catering Equipment***. EXIM Infotek Private Ltd., 604 Vishwa Deep, District Centre, Janakpuri New Delhi 110058, India. Phone: 91 11 25544793; Fax: 91 11 25544793; Email: info@eximinfo.org • URL: http://www.eximinfo.com • $250 Individuals; $10 Individuals. Covers: 70 Asian importers of catering equipment, catering supplies, commercial kitchen equipment, cooking equipment (patio and outdoors), food service equipment, food waste disposer, hotel and restaurant equipment, hotel amenity goods, hotel equipment and supplies, microwave equipment and component, hotel and catering service requisites. Entries include: Company name, postal address, telephone, fax, e-mail, website, contact person, designation, and product details.

***Directory of Asian Importers of Sewing Machines and Parts***. EXIM Infotek Private Ltd., 604 Vishwa Deep, District Centre, Janakpuri New Delhi 110058, India. Phone: 91 11 25544793; Fax: 91 11 25544793; Email: info@eximinfo.org • URL: http://www.eximinfo.com • $450 Individuals; $20 Individuals. Covers: 125 Asian importers of embroidery machinery, garment industry equipment and accessories, household sewing machine, industrial sewing machine, industrial sewing machine parts, new and reconditioned sewing machine, sewing machine and spare parts, sewing machine repairs, domestic sewing machine, sewing needles, stitch machine, and used embroidery machine. Entries include: Company name, postal address, telephone, fax, e-mail, website, contact person, designation, and product details.

***Directory of Asian Importers of Sporting Goods***. EXIM Infotek Private Ltd., 604 Vishwa Deep, District Centre, Janakpuri New Delhi 110058, India. Phone: 91 11 25544793; Fax: 91 11 25544793; Email: info@eximinfo.org • URL: http://www.eximinfo.com • $1,050 Individuals; $40 Individuals. Covers: 460 Asian importers of badminton, badminton rackets, baseball and golf caps, baseball supplies, basketball, billiard game table and equipment, billiard pool equipment, bowling equipment and supplies, cricket and hockey goods, firearms, football tools, golf accessories, golf ball, golf carts, golf club and bags, hobby and do-it-yourself articles, leisure and sports goods, playground equipment, equipment for sauna, spa, and swimming pool, shuttlecocks, ski equipment and supplies, snow sports goods, sports bags, sports wear, sports gloves, stadium equipment, table tennis equipment and accessories, tennis equipment and supplies, tennis rackets, volley balls, water sports equipment and supplies, windsurfing and surfing products.

***Directory of Asian Importers of Telephone Instruments and Accessories***. EXIM Infotek Private Ltd., 604 Vishwa Deep, District Centre, Janakpuri New Delhi 110058, India. Phone: 91 11 25544793; Fax: 91 11 25544793; Email: info@eximinfo.org • URL: http://www.eximinfo.com • $600 Individuals; $25 Individuals. Covers: 300 Asian importers of caller ID telephone instruments, CDMA phone, cellular phone accessories and parts, cordless telephone, EPABX systems, GSM mobile phone, handphone accessories, headphone, intercom systems, microphone, microwave components, PABX and intercom equipment, pager alphanumberic, pagers, beepers, telefax equipment, telephone accessories, telephone answering equipment, telephone electronic components, telephone (cables), and used cellular phone. Entries include: Company name, postal address, telephone, fax, e-mail, website, contact person, designation, and product details.

***Directory of Asian Importers of Waste Disposal & Recycling Equipment***. EXIM Infotek Private Ltd., 604 Vishwa Deep, District Centre, Janakpuri New Delhi 110058, India. Phone: 91 11 25544793; Fax: 91 11 25544793; Email: info@eximinfo.org • URL: http://www.eximinfo.com • $300 Individuals; $10 Individuals. Covers: 100 Asian importers of compactors, garbage disposals and compactors, incinerators, incubators, sand and recycles use, sewage systems, syringe and needle destroyers, waste disposal equipment, waste management, waste recycling equipment, waste water treatment equipment, and water treatment systems. Entries include: Company name, postal address, telephone, fax, e-mail, website, contact person, designation, and product details.

***Directory of Asian Importers of Wax & Wax Products***. EXIM Infotek Private Ltd., 604 Vishwa Deep, District Centre, Janakpuri New Delhi 110058, India. Phone: 91 11 25544793; Fax: 91 11 25544793; Email: info@eximinfo.org • URL: http://www.eximinfo.com • Covers: 90 Asian importers of micro waxes, normal paraffin, paraffin waxes, polishes and creams, and slack waxes. Entries include: Company name, postal address, telephone, fax, e-mail, website, contact person, designation, and product details.

***Directory of Asian Importers of Wires & Cables—Electrical***. EXIM Infotek Private Ltd., 604 Vishwa Deep, District Centre, Janakpuri New Delhi 110058, India. Phone: 91 11 25544793; Fax: 91 11 25544793; Email: info@eximinfo.org • URL: http://www.eximinfo.com • Covers: 190 Asian importers of cables, cables and accessories, copper winding wires, copper wires, electric cables, electrical cable, electrical wires, enameled copper wires, instrumentation cables, power cables, power cords, speaker AV cable, thermocouple wire, and wiring accessories. Entries include: Company name, postal address, telephone, fax, e-mail, website, contact person, designation, and product details.

***Directory of Asian Importers of Yarns and Threads***. EXIM Infotek Private Ltd., 604 Vishwa Deep, District Centre, Janakpuri New Delhi 110058, India. Phone: 91 11 25544793; Fax: 91 11 25544793; Email: info@eximinfo.org • URL: http://www.eximinfo.com • $950 Individuals; $40 Individuals. Covers: 580 Asian importers of 100% cotton yarn for weaving cotton, acetate filament yarn, acrylic yarn, acrylic yarn carded and dyed, carpet yarn, cotton yarn and thread, dupion silk yarn, fancy yarns, fibers and yarns, filament yarn, jute yarn, knitting yarn, linen yarn, man-made fiber, man-made yarn, metallic yarn and thread, nylon filament yarn, nylon thread, nylon yarn, polyester filament yarn, polyester yarn, polypropylene yarn, raw silk yarn, rayon yarn, sewing threads, silk yarn and thread, spun silk yarn, stitching thread, synthetic yarn and thread, viscose filament yarn, viscose rayon filament yarn, viscose yarn, wool yarn, yarn twister, and yarn waste. Entries include: Company name, postal address, telephone, fax, e-mail, website, contact person, designation, and product details.

***Directory of Australia and New Zealand Importers of Alcoholic Beverages, Wines***. EXIM Infotek Private Ltd., 604 Vishwa Deep, District Centre, Janakpuri New Delhi 110058, India. Phone: 91 11 25544793; Fax: 91 11 25544793; Email: info@eximinfo.org • URL: http://www.eximinfo.com • $250 Individuals; $10 Individuals. Covers: 70 Australian and New Zealand importers of alcohol, alcoholic beverages, beer, ale, champagne, Corona beer, distilled spirits, French wine, gin, grape wine, liquors, malt beer, rum, sparkling wine, vodka, and whisky. Entries include: Company name, postal address, telephone, fax, e-mail, website, contact person, designation, and product details.

***Directory of Australia and New Zealand Importers of Calendars***. EXIM Infotek Private Ltd., 604 Vishwa Deep, District Centre, Janakpuri New Delhi 110058, India. Phone: 91 11 25544793; Fax: 91 11 25544793; Email: info@eximinfo.org • URL: http://www.eximinfo.com • $150 Individuals; $5 Individuals. Covers: 20 Australian and New Zealand importers of calendars, greeting cards, postcards, cards, morals, posters, prints, lithographs and etching. Entries include: Company name, postal address, telephone, fax, e-mail, website, contact person, designation, and product details.

***Directory of Australia and New Zealand Importers of Carpets, Durries, Floor Coverings***. EXIM Infotek Private Ltd., 604 Vishwa Deep, District Centre, Janakpuri New Delhi 110058, India. Phone: 91 11 25544793; Fax: 91 11 25544793; Email: info@eximinfo.org • URL: http://www.eximinfo.com • $150 Individuals; $5 Individuals. Covers: 30 Australian and New Zealand importers of carpets, rugs, designer rugs, floor coverings, hand knotted rugs, hand tufted rugs, handloomed wool rugs, handmade carpets, handmade woollen rugs, linoleum (vinyl), mats (grass, rattan, bamboo, cotton), and rubber floor coverings. Entries include: Company name, postal address, telephone, fax, e-mail, website, contact person, designation, and product details.

***Directory of Australia and New Zealand Importers of Computer Hardware, Peripherals***. EXIM Infotek Private Ltd., 604 Vishwa Deep, District Centre, Janakpuri New Delhi 110058,

India. Phone: 91 11 25544793; Fax: 91 11 25544793; Email: info@eximinfo.org • URL: http://www.eximinfo.com • $250 Individuals; $10 Individuals. Covers: 75 Australian and New Zealand importers of compact disc, compressor parts, computer and computer accessories, computer components, computer consumables, computer driven routing systems, computer equipment and supplies, computer hardware, computer keyboards, computer networking hardware, computer parts, computer peripherals, printers, Dell P3 notebooks, dot matrix printers, DVR capture cards, graphic cards, imaging products, ink jet cartridges, ink jet printers, ink jet refill, laptop, laser printers, memories, modems-fax and data, monitors, motherboard, mouse pads, netservers, network equipment, and printing devices. Entries include: Company name, postal address, telephone, fax, e-mail, website, contact person, designation, and product details.

***Directory of Australia and New Zealand Importers of Computer Software***. EXIM Infotek Private Ltd., 604 Vishwa Deep, District Centre, Janakpuri New Delhi 110058, India. Phone: 91 11 25544793; Fax: 91 11 25544793; Email: info@eximinfo.org • URL: http://www.eximinfo.com • $150 Individuals; $5 Individuals. Covers: 30 Australian and New Zealand importers of architech design software, business software, computer software, geographic information systems technologies, LAN/network hardware and software, mapping software, and software for garment industry. Entries include: Company name, postal address, telephone, fax, e-mail, website, contact person, designation, and product details.

***Directory of Australia and New Zealand Importers of Construction Machinery and Equipment***. EXIM Infotek Private Ltd., 604 Vishwa Deep, District Centre, Janakpuri New Delhi 110058, India. Phone: 91 11 25544793; Fax: 91 11 25544793; Email: info@eximinfo.org • URL: http://www.eximinfo.com • $150 Individuals; $5 Individuals. Covers: 25 Australian and New Zealand importers of bulldozers, concrete machinery, concrete paving plant, concrete product plant, construction and building equipment, construction machinery, earthmoving equipment and machinery, excavating equipment, excavator parts, hot mix asphalt plant, hydraulic brake parts, parts for excavators and dozers, road construction machinery, scale model and construction kit, street maintenance equipment, and used construction equipment. Entries include: Company name, postal address, telephone, fax, e-mail, website, contact person, designation, and product details.

***Directory of Australia and New Zealand Importers of Energy and Power Equipment***. EXIM Infotek Private Ltd., 604 Vishwa Deep, District Centre, Janakpuri New Delhi 110058, India. Phone: 91 11 25544793; Fax: 91 11 25544793; Email: info@eximinfo.org • URL: http://www.eximinfo.com • $150 Individuals; $5 Individuals. Covers: 20 Australian and New Zealand importers of energy conservation products, industrial power system, industrial transmission products, power transmission equipment supplies, power transmission products, solar cells, solar charge controller and modules, solar energy equipment, solar pool heating, transmission and allied equipment. Entries include: Company name, postal address, telephone, fax, e-mail, website, contact person, designation, and product details.

***Directory of Australia and New Zealand Importers of Fibre and Fibre Products***. EXIM Infotek Private Ltd., 604 Vishwa Deep, District Centre, Janakpuri New Delhi 110058, India. Phone: 91 11 25544793; Fax: 91 11 25544793; Email: info@eximinfo.org • URL: http://www.eximinfo.com • $150 Individuals; $5 Individuals. Covers: 20 Australian and New Zealand importers of acrylic fibers, fiber glass grating, fiber optic cables, fiber glass, fiber glass products and cloth, fiber glass chopped strands, fiber glass products, microfibers, PU fiber glass, staple fibers, synthetic fibers, and viscose fiber. Entries include: Company name, postal address, telephone, fax, e-mail, website, contact person, designation, and product details.

***Directory of Australia & New Zealand Importers of Fire Fighting Equipment & Supplies***. EXIM Infotek Private Ltd., 604 Vishwa Deep, District Centre, Janakpuri New Delhi 110058, India. Phone: 91 11 25544793; Fax: 91 11 25544793; Email: info@eximinfo.org • URL: http://www.eximinfo.com • $150 Individuals; $5 Individuals. Covers: 20 Australian and New Zealand importers of CO2 gas and extinguishers, electrical fire stopping and protection systems, fire alarm, fire detection for smoke, flame, heat, and gas, fire detection products, fire extinguishers, fire fighting equipment, fire fighting supplies, fire hoses, fire panels, fire proofing chemicals, fire protection equipment, fire rescue equipment, firefighting powders and foams, paramedic and trauma products, fire rescue tools, flame detection instruments, flame protection products, monitors (foam/water), and pressure protection products. Entries include: Company name, postal address, telephone, fax, e-mail, website, contact person, designation, and product details.

***Directory of Australia and New Zealand Importers of Food Additives and Aromatic Chemicals***. EXIM Infotek Private Ltd., 604 Vishwa Deep, District Centre, Janakpuri New Delhi 110058, India. Phone: 91 11 25544793; Fax: 91 11 25544793; Email: info@eximinfo.org • URL: http://www.eximinfo.com • $150 Individuals; $5 Individuals. Covers: 30 Australian and New Zealand importers of bakery raw materials, baking improvers, carbohydrates derivatives, citrates, essence, flavor and fragrance chemicals, flavors, flower essences, food addi-

tives, food colors, food chemicals, food colors, food ingredients, fragrances, industrial food flavors, and industrial food ingredients. Entries include: Company name, postal address, telephone, fax, e-mail, website, contact person, designation, and product details.

***Directory of Australia and New Zealand Importers of Gold and Silver Jewellery***. EXIM Infotek Private Ltd., 604 Vishwa Deep, District Centre, Janakpuri New Delhi 110058, India. Phone: 91 11 25544793; Fax: 91 11 25544793; Email: info@eximinfo.org • URL: http://www.eximinfo.com • $150 Individuals; $5 Individuals. Covers: 20 Australian and New Zealand importers of bracelet, gold, silver jewelry, gold and silver leaf mirrors, jewelry parts and components. Entries include: Company name, postal address, telephone, fax, e-mail, website, contact person, designation, and product details.

***Directory of Australia & New Zealand Importers of Herbs & Herbal Medicine Products***. EXIM Infotek Private Ltd., 604 Vishwa Deep, District Centre, Janakpuri New Delhi 110058, India. Phone: 91 11 25544793; Fax: 91 11 25544793; Email: info@eximinfo.org • URL: http://www.eximinfo.com • $150 Individuals; $5 Individuals. Covers: 20 Australian and New Zealand importers of Chinese herbal products, Chinese herbs, Chinese medicines, herb extracts, herb seeds, herbal cosmetics, herbal extracts, herbal medicine, herbal powders, herbal products, herbal remedies, herbal tea, herbs, legumes, medicinal herb and botanicals, natural and herbal medicines, natural cosmetic ingredients, and natural health. Entries include: Company name, postal address, telephone, fax, e-mail, website, contact person, designation, and product details.

***Directory of Australia and New Zealand Importers of Lumber, Timber, Plywood and Hardwood***. EXIM Infotek Private Ltd., 604 Vishwa Deep, District Centre, Janakpuri New Delhi 110058, India. Phone: 91 11 25544793; Fax: 91 11 25544793; Email: info@eximinfo.org • URL: http://www.eximinfo.com • $150 Individuals; $5 Individuals. Covers: 40 Australian and New Zealand importers of board, construction plywood, decorative plywood, doors and windows, hardboard and particleboard, hardwood flooring, floor tiles, laminates, hardwood lumber, softwood lumber, marine plywood, medium-density fiberboards, millwork (wooden), plywood, veneer, poles, pilings and logs, sawn lumber, teak, timber, timber products, timberland products, and wood. Entries include: Company name, postal address, telephone, fax, e-mail, website, contact person, designation, and product details.

***Directory of Australia & New Zealand Importers of Material Handling Equipment***. EXIM Infotek Private Ltd., 604 Vishwa Deep, District Centre, Janakpuri New Delhi 110058, India. Phone: 91 11 25544793; Fax: 91 11 25544793; Email: info@eximinfo.org • URL: http://www.eximinfo.com • $150 Individuals; $5 Individuals. Covers: 35 Australian and New Zealand importers of chain hoist, chip conveyer, conveyor products, conveyor systems, crane equipment, cranes and hoists, electric hoist, elevators lifts, escalators, forklifts, forklift parts and accessories, forklift trucks, freight and shipping containers, grain handling equipment, hand trolleys, industrial brake equipment, lifting equipment, liquid handling equipment, loaders, loading and unloading equipment, materials handling equipment and hardware, monorail materials handling equipment, pulley, and winches. Entries include: Company name, postal address, telephone, fax, e-mail, website, contact person, designation, and product details.

***Directory of Australia & New Zealand Importers of Paper & Paper Products***. EXIM Infotek Private Ltd., 604 Vishwa Deep, District Centre, Janakpuri New Delhi 110058, India. Phone: 91 11 25544793; Fax: 91 11 25544793; Email: info@eximinfo.org • URL: http://www.eximinfo.com • $150 Individuals; $5 Individuals. Covers: 30 Australian and New Zealand importers of cardboard vases, coated paper, colored copy paper, construction paper in rolls, graphic papers, greaseproof paper, kraft paper, label papers, newsprint paper, paper products, paper bags, paper cups and plates, paper napkins, paper waste, photocopy paper, printing paper, recycled paper, rice paper, specialty papers, tissue paper products, and toilet paper rolls. Entries include: Company name, postal address, telephone, fax, e-mail, website, contact person, designation, and product details.

***Directory of Australia and New Zealand Importers of Photographic Equipment***. EXIM Infotek Private Ltd., 604 Vishwa Deep, District Centre, Janakpuri New Delhi 110058, India. Phone: 91 11 25544793; Fax: 91 11 25544793; Email: info@eximinfo.org • URL: http://www.eximinfo.com • $150 Individuals; $5 Individuals. Covers: 20 Australian and New Zealand importers of camera bags and cases, camera lenses, photographic chemicals, motion picture and theater equipment, digital camera, film, plate and photographic papers, infrared cameras, infrared camera accessories, photo film, photo process equipment, photographic equipment and supplies. Entries include: Company name, postal address, telephone, fax, e-mail, website, contact person, designation, and product details.

***Directory of Australia and New Zealand Importers of Plastic Scrap and Raw Materials***. EXIM Infotek Private Ltd., 604 Vishwa Deep, District Centre, Janakpuri New Delhi 110058, India. Phone: 91 11 25544793; Fax: 91 11 25544793; Email: info@eximinfo.org • URL: http://www.eximinfo.com • $5

Individuals. Covers: 20 Australian and New Zealand importers of fiberglass resins, high-density polyethylene (HDPE), HMS scrap, industrial polyurethane, nylon resin, plastic raw materials, plastic scrap and waste, poly propylene, polyethylene resin, polymers, polyurethane chemicals, polyurethane form, polyurethane products, and polypropylene raw materials. Entries include: Company name, postal address, telephone, fax, e-mail, website, contact person, designation, and product details.

***Directory of Australia & New Zealand Importers of Sporting Goods***. EXIM Infotek Private Ltd., 604 Vishwa Deep, District Centre, Janakpuri New Delhi 110058, India. Phone: 91 11 25544793; Fax: 91 11 25544793; Email: info@eximinfo.org • URL: http://www.eximinfo.com • $300 Individuals; $10 Individuals. Covers: 95 Australian and New Zealand importers of adventure sporting goods, baseball supplies, basketball equipment, beach accessories, firearms, footballs, golf ball, golf carts, golf course accessories, golf equipment, golf tools, handballs, hobby and do-it-yourself articles, judo accessories, motorcycle boots, mountaineering equipment and supplies, net balls, rugby balls, skates and accessories, ski equipment, ski gloves, ski sports goods, snow sports goods, snowboards, soccer balls, sports bags, sports gloves, sports water equipment, string for rackets, surfing products, volley balls, water sports equipment and supplies, wind surfing accessories and equipment, winter sports equipment and goods.

***Directory of Australia and New Zealand Importers of Telephone Instruments and Accessories***. EXIM Infotek Private Ltd., 604 Vishwa Deep, District Centre, Janakpuri New Delhi 110058, India. Phone: 91 11 25544793; Fax: 91 11 25544793; Email: info@eximinfo.org • URL: http://www.eximinfo.com • $150 Individuals; $5 Individuals. Covers: 20 Australian and New Zealand importers of cellular phone accessories and parts, cellular phone camera lens, EPABX systems, GSM phones, handphone accessories, intercom systems, microphones, microwave components, pagers, beepers, telephone headsets, telephone systems, and used mobile phones. Entries include: Company name, postal address, telephone, fax, e-mail, website, contact person, designation, and product details.

***Directory of Australia and New Zealand Importers of Woodworking Equipment and Tools***. EXIM Infotek Private Ltd., 604 Vishwa Deep, District Centre, Janakpuri New Delhi 110058, India. Phone: 91 11 25544793; Fax: 91 11 25544793; Email: info@eximinfo.org • URL: http://www.eximinfo.com • $150 Individuals; $5 Individuals. Covers: 30 Australian and New Zealand importers of band saw and blades, chain saw, circular saw, dimension saw, forestry equipment, hydraulic chain saw, new and reconditioned woodworking machine, saw blades, saw mill equipment, wood chipping machine, woodworking equipment, woodworking machine and accessories, and woodworking tools. Entries include: Company name, postal address, telephone, fax, e-mail, website, contact person, designation, and product details.

***Directory of Australia and New Zealand Importers of Yarns and Threads***. EXIM Infotek Private Ltd., 604 Vishwa Deep, District Centre, Janakpuri New Delhi 110058, India. Phone: 91 11 25544793; Fax: 91 11 25544793; Email: info@eximinfo.org • URL: http://www.eximinfo.com • $150 Individuals; $5 Individuals. Covers: 25 Australian and New Zealand importers of cotton yarn, embroidery thread, filament yarn, industrial filament yarn, knitting yarn, metallic yarn and thread, polyster yarn, sewing threads, silk yarn and thread, synthetic yarn and thread, textile fibers, wool yarn, and worsted weaving yarn. Entries include: Company name, postal address, telephone, fax, e-mail, website, contact person, designation, and product details.

***Directory of Automated Criminal Justice Information Systems***. U.S. Bureau of Justice Statistics, 810 7th St. NW Washington, DC 20531. Phone: (202)307-0765; Email: askbjs@usdoj.gov • URL: http://www.ojp.usdoj.gov/bjs • $60. Covers: Over 1,870 computerized information systems serving over 700 police, courts, state and local government judicial and correctional agencies. Entries include: Description of system or agency; acronym; type of system; functions; hardware and software configuration; function names, addresses, and phone numbers of agency contact.

***Directory of Belgian Importers of American Products***. American Chamber of Commerce in Belgium, rue du Trone 60, Troonstraat B-1050 Brussels, Belgium. Phone: 32 2 5136770; Fax: 32 2 5133590; Email: gchamber@amcham.be • URL: http://www.amcham.be • Annual. $125. Covers: 1,000 Belgian importers and distributors and 3,000 U.S. exporters of U.S. products in Belgium. Entries include: Company name, address, phone, fax, executives, products.

***Directory of Belgian Research Centers with Libraries or Documentation Services***. National Center for Scientific & Technical Documentation Royal Library, Blvd. de l'Empereur 4 B-1000 Brussels, Belgium. • Annual. $1,000. Covers: 1,090 research centers, including universities and companies, in Belgium. Entries include: Center name, address, phone, databases, uses of information.

***Directory of Belgium Importers of Computer Hardware and Peripherals***. EXIM Infotek Private Ltd., 604 Vishwa Deep, District Centre, Janakpuri New Delhi 110058, India. Phone: 91 11 25544793; Fax: 91 11 25544793; Email: info@eximinfo.org • URL: http://www.eximinfo.com • $300 Individuals; $10 Individuals. Covers: 110 Belgium importers of computer equipment and supplies, computer peripherals, computer supplies, computers and components, LAN/network hardware and software, and laser printers. Entries include: Company name, postal address, telephone, fax, e-mail, website, contact person, designation, and product details.

***Directory of Belgium Importers of Computer Software***. EXIM Infotek Private Ltd., 604 Vishwa Deep, District Centre, Janakpuri New Delhi 110058, India. Phone: 91 11 25544793; Fax: 91 11 25544793; Email: info@eximinfo.org • URL: http://www.eximinfo.com • $150 Individuals; $5 Individuals. Covers: 35 Belgium importers of computer software. Entries include: Company name, postal address, telephone, fax, e-mail, website, contact person, designation, and product details.

***Directory of Belgium Importers of Construction Machinery and Equipment***. EXIM Infotek Private Ltd., 604 Vishwa Deep, District Centre, Janakpuri New Delhi 110058, India. Phone: 91 11 25544793; Fax: 91 11 25544793; Email: info@eximinfo.org • URL: http://www.eximinfo.com • Covers: 30 Belgium importers of construction, building equipment and parts, earthmoving equipment, excavating equipment, industrial and construction vehicles, scale model and construction kit, and street maintenance equipment. Entries include: Company name, postal address, telephone, fax, e-mail, website, contact person, designation, and product details.

***Directory of Belgium Importers of Laboratory & Scientific Instruments & Supplies***. EXIM Infotek Private Ltd., 604 Vishwa Deep, District Centre, Janakpuri New Delhi 110058, India. Phone: 91 11 25544793; Fax: 91 11 25544793; Email: info@eximinfo.org • URL: http://www.eximinfo.com • $250 Individuals; $10 Individuals. Covers: 50 Belgium importers of binoculars, microscopes, telescopes, scientific and laboratory instrument, and testing equipment. Entries include: Company name, postal address, telephone, fax, e-mail, website, contact person, designation, and product details.

***Directory of Belgium Importers of Lumber, Timber, Plywood and Hardboards***. EXIM Infotek Private Ltd., 604 Vishwa Deep, District Centre, Janakpuri New Delhi 110058, India. Phone: 91 11 25544793; Fax: 91 11 25544793; Email: info@eximinfo.org • URL: http://www.eximinfo.com • $150 Individuals; $5 Individuals. Covers: 25 Belgium importers of doors, windows, hardwood flooring, floor tiles, hardwood lumber, softwood lumber, plywood, veneer, poles, wood, pilings and logs. Entries include: Company name, postal address, telephone, fax, e-mail, website, contact person, designation, and product details.

***Directory of Belgium Importers of Materials Handling Equipment***. EXIM Infotek Private Ltd., 604 Vishwa Deep, District Centre, Janakpuri New Delhi 110058, India. Phone: 91 11 25544793; Fax: 91 11 25544793; Email: info@eximinfo.org • URL: http://www.eximinfo.com • $150 Individuals; $5 Individuals. Covers: 35 companies in Belgium that import conveyors, cranes and hoisting equipment, fork lifts, liquid handling equipment, loading and unloading equipment, materials handling equipment and parts, winches, and pulleys. Entries include: Company name, postal address, telephone, fax, e-mail, website, contact person, designation, and product details.

***Directory of Blue Chip Companies***. InfoGroup Inc., 5711 S 86th Cir. Omaha, NE 68127-4146. Phone: (402)593-4500 • URL: http://www.infogroup.com • Entries include: Company name, address, phone, name and title of chief executive, Standard Industrial Classification (SIC) codes, code indicating annual sales and number of employees.

***Directory of British Footwear Exporters***. British Footwear Association, 3 Burystead Pl. Wellingborough NN8 1AH, United Kingdom. Phone: 44 1933 229005; Fax: 44 1933 225009; Email: info@britishfootwearassociation.co.uk • URL: http://www.britishfootwearassociation.co.uk • Biennial. Covers: Manufacturers of footwear who export products. Entries include: Company name, address, phone, telex, trade name.

***Directory of British Importers of Alcoholic Beverages and Wines***. EXIM Infotek Private Ltd., 604 Vishwa Deep, District Centre, Janakpuri New Delhi 110058, India. Phone: 91 11 25544793; Fax: 91 11 25544793; Email: info@eximinfo.org • URL: http://www.eximinfo.com • $250 Individuals; $10 Individuals. Covers: 60 British importers of alcohol, beer, ale, beverages, champagne, distilled spirits, spirits, whisky, wine, and alcoholic beverages. Entries include: Company name, postal address, telephone, fax, e-mail, website, contact person, designation, and product details.

***Directory of British Importers of Carpets, Durries and Floor Coverings***. EXIM Infotek Private Ltd., 604 Vishwa Deep, District Centre, Janakpuri New Delhi 110058, India. Phone: 91 11 25544793; Fax: 91 11 25544793; Email: info@eximinfo.org • URL: http://www.eximinfo.com • $200 Individuals; $10 Individuals. Covers: 25 British importers of carpets, rugs, oriental carpets, oriental rugs, and vinyl floorings. Entries include: Company name, postal address, telephone, fax, e-mail, website, contact person, designation, and product details.

***Directory of British Importers of Computer Hardwares and Peripherals***. EXIM Infotek Private Ltd., 604 Vishwa Deep, District Centre, Janakpuri New Delhi 110058, India. Phone: 91 11 25544793; Fax: 91 11 25544793; Email: info@eximinfo.org • URL: http://www.eximinfo.com • $300 Individuals; $10 Individuals. Covers: 95 British importers of computer equipment and supplies, computer hardware, computer monitors, computer parts, computer peripherals, computer supplies, computers, computer components, inkjet cartridges, LAN/network hardware and software, and laser printers. Entries include: Company name, postal address, telephone, fax, e-mail, website, contact person, designation, and product details.

***Directory of British Importers of Construction Machinery and Equipment***. EXIM Infotek Private Ltd., 604 Vishwa Deep, District Centre, Janakpuri New Delhi 110058, India. Phone: 91 11 25544793; Fax: 91 11 25544793; Email: info@eximinfo.org • URL: http://www.eximinfo.com • $150 Individuals; $5 Individuals. Covers: 30 British importers of construction, building equipment and parts, excavating equipment, scale model and construction kit. Entries include: Company name, postal address, telephone, fax, e-mail, website, contact person, designation, and product details.

***Directory of British Importers of Environmental Protection and Pollution Control Equipment***. EXIM Infotek Private Ltd., 604 Vishwa Deep, District Centre, Janakpuri New Delhi 110058, India. Phone: 91 11 25544793; Fax: 91 11 25544793; Email: info@eximinfo.org • URL: http://www.eximinfo.com • $150 Individuals; $5 Individuals. Covers: 40 British importers of environmental protection equipment, pollution control equipment, water treatment, and purifying equipment. Entries include: Company name, postal address, telephone, fax, e-mail, website, contact person, designation, and product details.

***Directory of British Importers of Juices and Soft Drinks***. EXIM Infotek Private Ltd., 604 Vishwa Deep, District Centre, Janakpuri New Delhi 110058, India. Phone: 91 11 25544793; Fax: 91 11 25544793; Email: info@eximinfo.org • URL: http://www.eximinfo.com • $200 Individuals; $10 Individuals. Covers: 45 British importers of coca-cola, fruit and vegetable juices, mineral water, non-alcoholic beverages, and soft drinks. Entries include: Company name, postal address, telephone, fax, e-mail, website, contact person, designation, and product details.

***Directory of British Importers of Laboratory & Scientific Instruments & Supplies***. EXIM Infotek Private Ltd., 604 Vishwa Deep, District Centre, Janakpuri New Delhi 110058, India. Phone: 91 11 25544793; Fax: 91 11 25544793; Email: info@eximinfo.org • URL: http://www.eximinfo.com • $300 Individuals; $10 Individuals. Covers: 120 British importers of binoculars, microscopes, telescopes, laboratory and scientific glass, scientific and laboratory instrument, and testing equipment. Entries include: Company name, postal address, telephone, fax, e-mail, website, contact person, designation, and product details.

***Directory of British Importers of Lumber, Timber, Plywood and Hardboards***. EXIM Infotek Private Ltd., 604 Vishwa Deep, District Centre, Janakpuri New Delhi 110058, India. Phone: 91 11 25544793; Fax: 91 11 25544793; Email: info@eximinfo.org • URL: http://www.eximinfo.com • $250 Individuals; $10 Individuals. Covers: 80 British importers of doors, windows, hardboard, particleboard, hardwood flooring, floor tiles, wood laminates, lumber, timber, plywood, hardwood lumber, softwood lumber, plywood, veneer, poles, pilings and logs. Entries include: Company name, postal address, telephone, fax, e-mail, website, contact person, designation, and product details.

***Directory of British Importers of Material Handling Equipment***. EXIM Infotek Private Ltd., 604 Vishwa Deep, District Centre, Janakpuri New Delhi 110058, India. Phone: 91 11 25544793; Fax: 91 11 25544793; Email: info@eximinfo.org • URL: http://www.eximinfo.com • $200 Individuals; $10 Individuals. Covers: 45 British importers of conveyors, cranes and hoisting equipment, elevators lifts, forklifts, liquid handling equipment, loading and unloading equipment, materials handling equipment and parts, monorail materials handling equipment, winches, and pulleys. Entries include: Company name, postal address, telephone, fax, e-mail, website, contact person, designation, and product details.

***Directory of British Importers of Restaurant, Hotel and Catering Equipment***. EXIM Infotek Private Ltd., 604 Vishwa Deep, District Centre, Janakpuri New Delhi 110058, India. Phone: 91 11 25544793; Fax: 91 11 25544793; Email: info@eximinfo.org • URL: http://www.eximinfo.com • Covers: 25 British importers of catering equipment and supplies, cooking equipment (patio and outdoors), microwave equipment and component, restaurant and hotel equipment. Entries include: Company name, postal address, telephone, fax, e-mail, website, contact person, designation, and product details.

***Directory of British Importers of Woodenware & Wooden Products***. EXIM Infotek Private Ltd., 604 Vishwa Deep, District Centre, Janakpuri New Delhi 110058, India. Phone: 91 11 25544793; Fax: 91 11 25544793; Email: info@eximinfo.org • URL: http://www.eximinfo.com • Covers: 30 British importers of baskets and basket ware, wooden millwork, and wooden products. Entries include: Company name, postal address, telephone, fax, e-mail, website, contact person, designation, and product details.

***Directory of British Importers of Yarns and Threads***. EXIM Infotek Private Ltd., 604 Vishwa Deep, District Centre, Janakpuri New Delhi 110058, India. Phone: 91 11 25544793; Fax: 91 11 25544793; Email: info@eximinfo.org • URL: http://

www.eximinfo.com • $150 Individuals; $5 Individuals. Covers: 20 British importers of yarn and thread, cotton yarn and thread, synthetic yarn and thread. Entries include: Company name, postal address, telephone, fax, e-mail, website, contact person, designation, and product details.

**The Directory of Business Information Resources.** Grey House Publishing, 4919 Rte. 22 Amenia, NY 12501. Phone: 800-562-2139 or (518)789-8700; Fax: (518)789-0556; Email: books@greyhouse.com • URL: http://www.greyhouse.com • Annual. $195 Libraries Softcover; $495 Individuals Softcover. Provides contact names as well as editorial and advertising personnel, phone and fax numbers, description, frequency, pricing information, industry's associations, newsletters, magazines, trade shows, directories, databases and industry websites of 21,000 businesses.

**Directory of Business Information.** John Wiley and Sons Inc. Technical Insights, 111 River St. Hoboken, NJ 07030-5774. Phone: 800-825-7550 or (201)748-6000; Fax: (201)748-6088; Email: subinfo@wiley.com • URL: http://www.wiley.com • $290 Individuals. Covers: Over 10,000 sources of business information, including publications, associations, companies, government offices, and libraries.

**Directory of Business Opportunities.** Todd Publications, PO Box 500 Millwood, NY 10546. Phone: 866-896-0916 or (914)373-4750; Fax: (914)373-4750; Email: toddpub@aol.com • URL: http://www.toddpublications.com • Annual. $15. Covers: Hundreds of business opportunities, new products, franchises, dealerships and investment opportunities, including import/export deals and wholesale merchandising. Entries include: Contact name, address, phone.

**The Directory of Business to Business Catalogs.** Grey House Publishing, 4919 Rte. 22 Amenia, NY 12501. Phone: 800-562-2139 or (518)789-8700; Fax: (518)789-0556; Email: books@greyhouse.com • URL: http://www.greyhouse.com • Annual. $450 Libraries softcover; $250 Individuals print. More than 5,000 suppliers of business products, including computers, laboratory supplies, office products, office design, marketing resources, safety equipment, landscaping firms, maintenance supplies, building construction, and others.

**Directory of Business/Trade/Professional Associations, Chambers of Commerce and Industrial Development Authorities.** West Virginia Chamber of Commerce, 1624 Kanawha Blvd. E Charleston, WV 25311. Phone: (304)342-1115; Fax: (304)342-1130; Email: forjobs@wvchamber.com • URL: http://www.wvchamber.com • Biennial. $5 Individuals. Covers: About 50 chambers of commerce, 95 chamber and association executives, 50 trade associations, and about 50 development authority offices. Entries include: For chambers, associations, and development offices—Name, address, phone, names and titles of key officials. For chamber and association executives—Name, address, phone, name of affiliated chamber or association, title.

**Directory of Buyout Financing Sources.** Buyout Publications, Inc., • URL: http://www.ventureeconomics.com/vec/publications.html#dbfs_b • Annual. $445 plus $9.00 shipping. Covers: over 1,000 sources of acquisition financing, including banks, asset-based lenders, small business investment companies, insurance companies, and venture capital firms. Entries include: Company name, address, phone, E-mail, URL, names and titles of key personnel, financial data, type of company and size requirements, underwriting criteria, equity requirements, post-closing role, information required, response time, sample transactions. Also promoted under title 'Financing Sourcebook for Buyouts & Acquisitions.'.

**Directory of California Agricultural Exporters.** • URL: http://www.databasepublishing.com • Biennial. $50. Covers: Approximately 1,600 California companies in the growing, processing, and trading of food and fiber products in the worldwide market. Entries include: Company name, address, phone, fax, E-mail/web address, name and title of contact, number of employees, year established, products grown, processed, or traded, names and titles of key personnel, type of company.

**Directory of California Technology Companies.** San Francisco Chamber of Commerce, 235 Montgomery St., Ste. 760 San Francisco, CA 94104. Phone: (415)392-4520; Fax: (415)392-0485; Email: info@sfchamber.com • URL: http://www.sfchamber.com • $161 Members; $179 Nonmembers; $206 Members (with book and read-only CD Rom); $229 Nonmembers (with book and read-only CD Rom). Covers: 12,000 California-based technology manufacturers, wholesalers, and software and service companies working in fields such as research and development, aerospace, software, biotech, aerospace and others. Entries include: Contact details.

**Directory of California Wholesalers and Service Companies.** Harris InfoSource, 2057 E Aurora Rd. Twinsburg, OH 44087-1999. Phone: 800-888-5900 or (330)425-9000 or (973)921-5500; Fax: (800)643-5997 or (877)252-3375; Email: customerservice@harrisinfo.com • URL: http://www.harrisinfo.com • Annual. $210 Individuals hardcover. Covers: Approximately 225,200 wholesalers, distributors, and other service firms in California. Includes key executives. Database includes: Statistical data, trade show calendar. Entries include: Company name, address, parent name/location, telephone, fax and 800 numbers, web site address (on CD-ROM only), number of employees, year established, annual revenue, plant size, business description, Standard Industrial Classification (SIC) code, executive names/titles, public

ownership, legal structure, import/export designators, and female/minority ownership.

**Directory of Canadian Companies Overseas.** Overseas Employment Services, 1255 Laird, Ste. 208 Mount Royal, QC, Canada H3P 2T1. Phone: (514)739-1108; Fax: (514)739-0795 • Annual. $15 postpaid. Covers: about 250 Canadian companies and professional firms with branch plants or offices outside of Canada and the U.S. Entries include: Company name, address, geographical area served, product/service.

**Directory of Canadian Information Sources.** Browning Associates, • Covers: approximately 1,500 directories, market surveys, trade guides, association publications, and special periodical issues that are sources of Canadian information. Entries include: Publication title, publisher name, address, phone, frequency, price, scope of coverage, description of contents and arrangement, whether advertising is accepted, other details.

**Directory of Caribbean Importers.** Caribbean Export Development Agency, PO Box 34B Saint Michael, Barbados. Phone: (246)436-0578; Fax: (246)436-9999; Email: info@carib-export.com • URL: http://www.carib-export.com • $15. Covers: Companies importing goods in the Carribean business community. Database includes: Profiles of sixteen Caribbean countries. Entries include: Name, address, phone, products imported.

**Directory of Catholic Charities USA Directories.** Catholic Charities USA, 2050 Ballenger Ave., Ste. 400 Alexandria, VA 22314. Phone: 800-919-9338 or (703)549-1390 or (703)236-6228; Fax: (703)549-1656; Email: info@catholiccharitiesusa.org • URL: http://www.catholiccharitiesusa.org • Annual. $25 Individuals. Covers: Nearly 1,200 Catholic community and social service agencies. Listings include diocesan agencies, state Catholic conferences. Entries include: Organization name, address, name and title of director, phone, fax.

**Directory of Central Atlantic States Manufacturers.** George D. Hall Company Inc., 50 Franklin St., 4th Fl. Boston, MA 02110-1306. Phone: 800-446-1215 or (617)523-3745; Fax: (617)523-4862 • Biennial. $83 plus $4.90 shipping (1994 edition). Covers: about 18,000 companies in Maryland, Delaware, Virginia, West Virginia, North Carolina, and South Carolina. Entries include: Company name, address, phone, name of principal executive, number of employees, products or services, Standard Industrial Classification (SIC) code.

**Directory of CEOs.** IBCON S.A., Gutenberg 224, Col. Anzures 11590 Mexico, Mexico. Phone: 52 55 52554577; Email: ibcon@ibcon.com.mx • URL: http://www.ibcon.com.mx • Irregular. $458 Individuals. Covers: 14,640 companies incorporated in Mexico City. Entries include: Name and position of top executive, company name, address, phone, fax, industry code.

**Directory of Certified Business Counselors.** Institute of Certified Business Counselors, 18831 Willamette Dr. West Linn, OR 97068. Phone: 877-844-2535 • URL: http://www.i-cbc.org • Irregular. Covers: 160 member counselors, brokers, and attorneys qualified to act as advisors for persons with business problems. Entries include: Name, address, phone, business specialty.

**Directory of Certified Local, Small, and Disadvantaged Business Enterprises.** District of Columbia Local Business Opportunity Commission, 441 4th St. NW, 9th Fl. N Washington, DC 20001. Phone: (202)724-1385; Fax: (202)724-3786 • Annual. Covers about 700 suppliers of professional, commercial, and industrial products and services, and construction services, all firms in which minority ownership and control has been certified by the District of Columbia Local Business Opportunity Commission in accordance with D.C. Law I-95.

**Directory of Chartered Accountants in Business.** Institute of Chartered Accountants in Australia, 33 Erskine St. Sydney, NSW 2001, Australia. Phone: 61 2 9290 1344; Fax: 61 2 9262 1512; Email: service@charteredaccountants.com.au • URL: http://www.charteredaccountants.com.au • Annual. $35. Covers business members in Australia and overseas.

**Directory of China Address—China Enterprises and Institutes Volume.** Xinhua Publishing House, Xuanwumen Xi Dajie Beijing 100803, China. Phone: 1 3073897 or 86 010 6307 1114; Fax: 3073880 or 86 010 6307 5134; Email: english@xinhuanet.com • URL: http://www.xinhuanet.com • $160. Covers: More than 80,000 enterprises and institutes in over 300 cities, districts, and countries of China. Entries include: Contact information, business scope, products.

**Directory of Chinese and Foreign Industrial and Commercial Enterprises Special Issue on Chemicals and Petroleum.** Xinhua Publishing House, Xuanwumen Xi Dajie Beijing 100803, China. Phone: 1 3073897 or 86 010 6307 1114; Fax: 3073880 or 86 010 6307 5134; Email: english@xinhuanet.com • URL: http://www.xinhuanet.com • $30. Covers: industrial and commercial petroleum and chemical companies worldwide. Database includes: Statistics on China's chemical export. Entries include: Company name, address, phone, telex, names and titles of key personnel, registered capital, export data, and description.

**Directory of Chinese and Foreign Management and Sales Personnel.** Standards Press of China, St. 16 Sanlihe Beijie Fuwai, Beijie Fuwai Beijing 100045, China. Phone: 86 10 68571142; Fax: 86 10 68517910 • Biennial. $30. Covers: 8,700 companies, organizations, and individuals in business,

industry, and other professionals. Entries include: Name, address, phone, telex, name and title of contact, names and titles of key personnel, geographical area covered, description of activities.

**Directory of Chinese Importers of Chemicals & Allied Products.** EXIM Infotek Private Ltd., 604 Vishwa Deep, District Centre, Janakpuri New Delhi 110058, India. Phone: 91 11 25544793; Fax: 91 11 25544793; Email: info@eximinfo.org • URL: http://www.eximinfo.com • Covers: 900 Chinese importers of acetic anhydride, acetone, acids, chemical and allied products, chemical products, chemical raw materials, glycerin, industrial chemicals, liquid chemicals, molybdenum concentrate, naphthalene, organic chemicals, oxalic acid, plastic chemicals, potassium hydroxide, reagents, resins and gums, specialty chemicals, tetra ethyl lead, and toluene. Entries include: Company name, postal address, telephone, fax, e-mail, website, contact person, designation, and product details.

**Directory of Chinese Importers of Fibre Products.** EXIM Infotek Private Ltd., 604 Vishwa Deep, District Centre, Janakpuri New Delhi 110058, India. Phone: 91 11 25544793; Fax: 91 11 25544793; Email: info@eximinfo.org • URL: http://www.eximinfo.com • $150 Individuals; $5 Individuals. Covers: 20 Chinese importers of fibers, high-density fiberboard, optic fibers, polyester staple fibers, and synthetic fibers. Entries include: Company name, postal address, telephone, fax, e-mail, website, contact person, designation, and product details.

**Directory of Chinese Importers of Leather, Hides, Skins & Furs.** EXIM Infotek Private Ltd., 604 Vishwa Deep, District Centre, Janakpuri New Delhi 110058, India. Phone: 91 11 25544793; Fax: 91 11 25544793; Email: info@eximinfo.org • URL: http://www.eximinfo.com • Covers: 30 Chinese importers of cow leathers, hides, skins and fur, leather, mink and fox tails, pig skins, scrap sheep, and fox skin. Entries include: Company name, postal address, telephone, fax, e-mail, website, contact person, designation, and product details.

**Directory of Chinese Importers of Lumber, Timber, Plywood and Hardboards.** EXIM Infotek Private Ltd., 604 Vishwa Deep, District Centre, Janakpuri New Delhi 110058, India. Phone: 91 11 25544793; Fax: 91 11 25544793; Email: info@eximinfo.org • URL: http://www.eximinfo.com • $150 Individuals; $5 Individuals. Covers: 30 Chinese importers of beechwood lumber, hardwood lumber, softwood lumber, plywood, veneer, poles, pilings and logs, sawn timber, and wood. Entries include: Company name, postal address, telephone, fax, e-mail, website, contact person, designation, and product details.

**Directory of Chinese Importers of Minerals.** EXIM Infotek Private Ltd., 604 Vishwa Deep, District Centre, Janakpuri New Delhi 110058, India. Phone: 91 11 25544793; Fax: 91 11 25544793; Email: info@eximinfo.org • URL: http://www.eximinfo.com • $150 Individuals; $5 Individuals. Covers: 25 Chinese importers of copper mineral, iron ore, iron oxide, metals, and minerals. Entries include: Company name, postal address, telephone, fax, e-mail, website, contact person, designation, and product details.

**Directory of Chinese Importers of Packaging Materials & Supplies.** EXIM Infotek Private Ltd., 604 Vishwa Deep, District Centre, Janakpuri New Delhi 110058, India. Phone: 91 11 25544793; Fax: 91 11 25544793; Email: info@eximinfo.org • URL: http://www.eximinfo.com • Covers: 35 Chinese importers of bopp film, cardboard, packaging materials, and wrapping paper. Entries include: Company name, postal address, telephone, fax, e-mail, website, contact person, designation, and product details.

**Directory of Chinese Importers of Paper & Paper Products.** EXIM Infotek Private Ltd., 604 Vishwa Deep, District Centre, Janakpuri New Delhi 110058, India. Phone: 91 11 25544793; Fax: 91 11 25544793; Email: info@eximinfo.org • URL: http://www.eximinfo.com • $150 Individuals; $5 Individuals. Covers: 40 Chinese importers of newsprint, paper, wood pulp, paper products, paper waste, printing paper, pulp, and specialty paper. Entries include: Company name, postal address, telephone, fax, e-mail, website, contact person, designation, and product details.

**Directory of Chinese Importers of Plastic Scrap and Raw Materials.** EXIM Infotek Private Ltd., 604 Vishwa Deep, District Centre, Janakpuri New Delhi 110058, India. Phone: 91 11 25544793; Fax: 91 11 25544793; Email: info@eximinfo.org • URL: http://www.eximinfo.com • $200 Individuals; $10 Individuals. Covers: 60 Chinese importers of ABS scrap, high-density polyethylene (HDPE), pet bottle scrap in flakes and PVC waste, plastic raw materials, plastic resins, plastic scrap and waste, plastic additives, and polypropylene. Entries include: Company name, postal address, telephone, fax, e-mail, website, contact person, designation, and product details.

**Directory of Chinese Manufacturers & Exporters of Adhesive, Glues, Sealants.** EXIM Infotek Private Ltd., 604 Vishwa Deep, District Centre, Janakpuri New Delhi 110058, India. Phone: 91 11 25544793; Fax: 91 11 25544793; Email: info@eximinfo.org • URL: http://www.eximinfo.com • $10 Individuals. Covers: 50 Chinese manufacturers and exporters of adhesive products, adhesives, bone glue, epoxy resins, glue, glue products, hot melt adhesives, polyurethane adhesive, and sealing materials. Entries include: Company name, postal address, city, country, phone, fax, e-mail and websites, contact person, designation, and product details.

**Directory of Chinese Manufacturers & Exporters of Agro Chemicals, Fertilizers, Pesticides, Insecticides.** EXIM Infotek Private Ltd., 604 Vishwa Deep, District Centre, Janakpuri New Delhi 110058, India. Phone: 91 11 25544793; Fax: 91 11 25544793; Email: info@eximinfo.org • URL: http://www.eximinfo.com • $20 Individuals. Covers: 210 Chinese manufacturers and exporters of agricultural chemical products, agricultural chemicals, agrochemicals, biochemical products, biological pesticides, bio-pesticides, chemical fertilizers, farm chemicals, fertilizers, herbicides, insecticide, nitrogen fertilizer, pesticide intermediates, pesticides, and phosphate fertilizers. Entries include: Company name, postal address, city, country, phone, fax, e-mail and websites, contact person, designation, and product details.

**Directory of Chinese Manufacturers & Exporters of Agro Commodities.** EXIM Infotek Private Ltd., 604 Vishwa Deep, District Centre, Janakpuri New Delhi 110058, India. Phone: 91 11 25544793; Fax: 91 11 25544793; Email: info@eximinfo.org • URL: http://www.eximinfo.com • $10 Individuals. Covers: 80 Chinese manufacturers and exporters of agricultural products, beans, broad beans, buckwheat, farm products, grains, maize, rice, soy beans, sugar, and wheats. Entries include: Company name, postal address, city, country, phone, fax, e-mail and websites, contact person, designation, and product details.

**Directory of Chinese Manufacturers and Exporters of Alcoholic Beverages, Wines.** EXIM Infotek Private Ltd., 604 Vishwa Deep, District Centre, Janakpuri New Delhi 110058, India. Phone: 91 11 25544793; Fax: 91 11 25544793; Email: info@eximinfo.org • URL: http://www.eximinfo.com • $200 Individuals; $10 Individuals. Covers: 60 Chinese manufacturers and exporters of beer, beverages, dry red wine, fruit wine, grape wine, and liquor. Entries include: Company name, postal address, telephone, fax, e-mail, website, contact person, designation, and product details.

**Directory of Chinese Manufacturers & Exporters of Autoparts and Accessories.** EXIM Infotek Private Ltd., 604 Vishwa Deep, District Centre, Janakpuri New Delhi 110058, India. Phone: 91 11 25544793; Fax: 91 11 25544793; Email: info@eximinfo.org • URL: http://www.eximinfo.com • $20 Individuals. Covers: 190 Chinese manufacturers and exporters of auto accessories, auto fittings, auto lamps, auto parts, auto safety glass, automobile accessories, automobile electric appliances, automobile glass, automobile halogen lamps, automobile lights, automobile locks, automobile parts, automobile spare parts, automobile switches, automobile wipers, automotive glass, automotive parts, brake drums and hubs, brake shoes, brakes, car accessories, car audio devices, car parts, car speakers, clutch covers, clutch discs, gaskets, indicator lights, motor vehicle accessories, plastic autoparts, radiators, sealing products, shock absorbers, spare parts, transmission equipment, vehicle accessories, vehicle fittings, vehicle parts, and wheels. Entries include: Company name, postal address, city, country, phone, fax, e-mail and websites, contact person, designation, and product details.

**Directory of Chinese Manufacturers & Exporters of Batteries & Accumulators.** EXIM Infotek Private Ltd., 604 Vishwa Deep, District Centre, Janakpuri New Delhi 110058, India. Phone: 91 11 25544793; Fax: 91 11 25544793; Email: info@eximinfo.org • URL: http://www.eximinfo.com • $10 Individuals. Covers: 110 Chinese manufacturers and exporters of accumulator cells, batteries, batteries for ups, batteries-rechargeable, batteries-storage, battery chargers, batteries for vehicles, dry batteries, lead acid batteries. Entries include: Company name, postal address, city, country, phone, fax, e-mail and websites, contact person, designation, products detail.

**Directory of Chinese Manufacturers & Exporters of Bearings.** EXIM Infotek Private Ltd., 604 Vishwa Deep, District Centre, Janakpuri New Delhi 110058, India. Phone: 91 11 25544793; Fax: 91 11 25544793; Email: info@eximinfo.org • URL: http://www.eximinfo.com • $10 Individuals. Covers: 60 Chinese manufacturers and exporters of ball bearings, bearings, needles and rollers, cylindrical roller bearings, engine bearings, needle bearings, needle roller bearings, roller bearings, sliding bearings, spherical roller bearings, steel balls, and tapered roller bearings. Entries include: Company name, postal address, city, country, phone, fax, e-mail and websites, contact person, designation, and product details.

**Directory of Chinese Manufacturers & Exporters of Beauty Supplies, Cosmetics, Perfumes, Toiletries.** EXIM Infotek Private Ltd., 604 Vishwa Deep, District Centre, Janakpuri New Delhi 110058, India. Phone: 91 11 25544793; Fax: 91 11 25544793; Email: info@eximinfo.org • URL: http://www.eximinfo.com • $10 Individuals. Covers: 80 Chinese manufacturers and exporters of bathing products, beauty products, brushes-cosmetics, cosmetic accessories, cosmetic brushes, cosmetics, eyebrow pencils, eyeshadow pencil, fragrances, hair brushes, lipstick, manicure sets, perfume, perfume bottles, perfumes, shampoo, skin care products, talcum, and talcum powder. Entries include: Company name, postal address, city, country, phone, fax, e-mail and websites, contact person, designation, and product details.

**Directory of Chinese Manufacturers & Exporters of Bicycles, Parts & Accessories.** EXIM Infotek Private Ltd., 604 Vishwa

Deep, District Centre, Janakpuri New Delhi 110058, India. Phone: 91 11 25544793; Fax: 91 11 25544793; Email: info@eximinfo.org • URL: http://www.eximinfo.com • $5 Individuals. Covers: 25 Chinese manufacturers and exporters of bicycle frames, bicycle lamps, bicycle parts, bicycles, electric bicycles, and sprockets. Entries include: Company name, postal address, city, country, phone, fax, e-mail and websites, contact person, designation, and product details.

**Directory of Chinese Manufacturers & Exporters of Candles & Candle Products.** EXIM Infotek Private Ltd., 604 Vishwa Deep, District Centre, Janakpuri New Delhi 110058, India. Phone: 91 11 25544793; Fax: 91 11 25544793; Email: info@eximinfo.org • URL: http://www.eximinfo.com • $5 Individuals. Covers: 35 Chinese manufacturers and exporters of candle holders, candle lamps, candles, craft candles. Entries include: Company name, postal address, city, country, phone, fax, e-mail and websites, contact person, designation, and product details.

**Directory of Chinese Manufacturers & Exporters of Carpets, Durries, Floor Coverings.** EXIM Infotek Private Ltd., 604 Vishwa Deep, District Centre, Janakpuri New Delhi 110058, India. Phone: 91 11 25544793; Fax: 91 11 25544793; Email: info@eximinfo.org • URL: http://www.eximinfo.com • $10 Individuals. Covers: 50 Chinese manufacturers and exporters of carpets, PVC floor tiles, PVC tiles, rugs, silk carpets, and woolen carpets. Entries include: Company name, postal address, city, country, phone, fax, e-mail and websites, contact person, designation, and product details.

**Directory of Chinese Manufacturers & Exporters of Castings and Forgings.** EXIM Infotek Private Ltd., 604 Vishwa Deep, District Centre, Janakpuri New Delhi 110058, India. Phone: 91 11 25544793; Fax: 91 11 25544793; Email: info@eximinfo.org • URL: http://www.eximinfo.com • $15 Individuals. Covers: 130 Chinese manufacturers and exporters of cast iron, cast iron fittings, cast iron pipes, cast iron products, cast steel products, casting, casting-iron, castings, die casting mould, die castings, forging, forging parts, grey cast iron, iron casting, manhole covers, nodular cast iron, precision castings, steel castings. Entries include: Company name, postal address, city, country, phone, fax, e-mail & websites, contact person, designation, products detail.

**Directory of Chinese Manufacturers & Exporters of Chemicals & Allied Products.** EXIM Infotek Private Ltd., 604 Vishwa Deep, District Centre, Janakpuri New Delhi 110058, India. Phone: 91 11 25544793; Fax: 91 11 25544793; Email: info@eximinfo.org • URL: http://www.eximinfo.com • $50 Individuals. Covers: 900 Chinese manufacturers & exporters of acids, acrylic acid, activated carbon, activated carbon fiber, activated carbon products, alkali, allyl chloride, ammonia, ammonium bicarbonate, ammonium carbonate, ammonium chloride, ammonium hydrogen carbonate, ammonium nitrate, ammonium paratungstate, ammonium persulphate, ammonium phosphate, ammonium sulphate, ammonium thiocyanate, antimony potassium tartrate, antioxidants, barium carbonate, barium hydroxide, barium nitrate, barium salts, barium sulfates, benzene, benzoic acid, benzotriazole, benzotri-fluoride, boric acid, calcium carbide, calcium chloride, calcium citrate, calcium hydroxide, calcium nitrite, calcium superphosphate, carbon additives, carbon black, carbon block, catalysts, caustic soda, chemical & allied products, chemical additives, chemical assistants, chemical fiber, chemical industrial materials, chemical industrial products, chemical materials, chemical products, chemical raw materials & products, chemical reagent, chemicals, chemicals for cosmetics/perfumery/detergent/soaps, chemicals for textiles, chemistry reagents, chlorinated polyethylene, chlorine, chlorine alkali, chlorine dioxide, chlorine-liquefied, chondroitin sulfate, chromic acid, citric acid, coatings, dicalcium phosphate, dicyandiamide, dsd acid, fine chemical products, fine chemicals, formic acid, hydrochloric acid, hydrofluoric acid, hydrogen peroxide, industrial chemicals, inorganic acids & anhydrides, inorganic chemicals, inorganic products, l-cysteic acid, liquid chemicals, methanol, molybdenum chemical products, mono ammonium phosphate, naphthenic acid, natural resins & pithces, nitrate, nitric acid, nitrobenzene, nitrofurazone, nitromethane, organic chemical material, organic chemicals, organic products, organo pophasphorus, oxalic acid, paper making chemicals, petrochemical products, p-fluoro benzaldehyde, phosphate chemicals, potassium, potassium bicarbonate, potassium carbonate, potassium chloride, potassium hydroxide, potassium nitrate, potassium permaganate, potassium persulfate, potassium sulfate, raw material for chemicals, raw material for cosmetic, refined chemical products, sebacic acid, silicon, soda, soda ash, sodium acetate, sodium alginate, sodium bicarbonate, sodium bromate, sodium carnllite, sodium chlorate, sodium citrate, sodium cyanide, sodium fluoride, sodium hydrosulfite, sodium hydroxide, sodium magnesium chlorophyllin, sodium nitrate, sodium silicate, sodium sulphate, sodium tartrate, sodium thiocyanate, stearic acids, sulfuric acid, sulphur, sulphur black, sulphuric acids, synthetic ammonia, synthetic chemicals, tannic acid, tartaric acid, water treatment chemicals, zirconium chemicals. Entries include: Company name, postal address, city, country, telephone, fax, e-mail & websites, contact person, designation, products detail.

**Directory of Chinese Manufacturers & Exporters of Confectionery and Bakery Products.** EXIM Infotek Private

Ltd., 604 Vishwa Deep, District Centre, Janakpuri New Delhi 110058, India. Phone: 91 11 25544793; Fax: 91 11 25544793; Email: info@eximinfo.org • URL: http://www.eximinfo.com • $5 Individuals. Covers: 20 Chinese manufacturers and exporters of biscuits/crackers, cakes and pastries, candy, fried peanuts, instant noodles, and vinegar. Entries include: Company name, postal address, city, country, phone, fax, e-mail and websites, contact person, designation, and product details.

**Directory of Chinese Manufacturers and Exporters of Construction Machinery and Equipment.** EXIM Infotek Private Ltd., 604 Vishwa Deep, District Centre, Janakpuri New Delhi 110058, India. Phone: 91 11 25544793; Fax: 91 11 25544793; Email: info@eximinfo.org • URL: http://www.eximinfo.com • $150 Individuals; $5 Individuals. Covers: 30 Chinese manufacturers and exporters of building machinery, construction equipment, construction machinery, crusher, dust collectors, and mixers. Entries include: Company name, postal address, telephone, fax, e-mail, website, contact person, designation, and product details.

**Directory of Chinese Manufacturers & Exporters of Cotton, Silk, Wool Raw and Waste.** EXIM Infotek Private Ltd., 604 Vishwa Deep, District Centre, Janakpuri New Delhi 110058, India. Phone: 91 11 25544793; Fax: 91 11 25544793; Email: info@eximinfo.org • URL: http://www.eximinfo.com • $10 Individuals. Covers: 50 Chinese manufacturers and exporters of cotton, cotton products, cotton pulp, goat's wool, mulberry silk, wool, wool and wool products. Entries include: Company name, postal address, city, country, phone, fax, e-mail and websites, contact person, designation, and product details.

**Directory of Chinese Manufacturers & Exporters of Dyes, Colors, Pigments, Intermediates.** EXIM Infotek Private Ltd., 604 Vishwa Deep, District Centre, Janakpuri New Delhi 110058, India. Phone: 91 11 25544793; Fax: 91 11 25544793; Email: info@eximinfo.org • URL: http://www.eximinfo.com • $25 Individuals. Covers: 290 Chinese manufacturers and exporters of acid dyestuffs, auxiliaries, auxiliary materials, cationic dyestuff, chemical dyes, chemical intermediates, disperse dyes, dye intermediates, dyeing materials, dyes, dyes intermediates, dyes-red base, dyestuff, dyes-vet, fluorescent brightener series, fluorescent pigment products, fluorescent whitening, inorganic pigments, intermediate for dyestuffs, intermediates, intermediates-various, iron oxide pigments, iron oxide yellow, organic intermediates, organic pigments, pigment intermediates, pigments, pigments-natural, plastic dyes, reactive dyes, vat dyes. Entries include: Company name, postal address, city, country, phone, fax, e-mail and websites, contact person, designation, and product details.

**Directory of Chinese Manufacturers & Exporters of Electronic Equipment & Supplies.** EXIM Infotek Private Ltd., 604 Vishwa Deep, District Centre, Janakpuri New Delhi 110058, India. Phone: 91 11 25544793; Fax: 91 11 25544793; Email: info@eximinfo.org • URL: http://www.eximinfo.com • Covers: 90 Chinese manufacturers and exporters of electronic devices, electronic equipment, electronic instrument, oscilloscope, and television transmission equipment. Entries include: Company name, postal address, telephone, fax, e-mail, website, contact person, designation, and product details.

**Directory of Chinese Manufacturers & Exporters of Engines & Engine Parts.** EXIM Infotek Private Ltd., 604 Vishwa Deep, District Centre, Janakpuri New Delhi 110058, India. Phone: 91 11 25544793; Fax: 91 11 25544793; Email: info@eximinfo.org • URL: http://www.eximinfo.com • $5 Individuals. Covers: 35 Chinese manufacturers and exporters of diesel engines, engine beds-ordinary, engine parts and accessories, engines, inlet valves, piston rings, pistons, spark plugs. Entries include: Company name, postal address, city, country, phone, fax, e-mail and websites, contact person, designation, and product details.

**Directory of Chinese Manufacturers & Exporters of Fire Fighting Equipment & Supplies.** EXIM Infotek Private Ltd., 604 Vishwa Deep, District Centre, Janakpuri New Delhi 110058, India. Phone: 91 11 25544793; Fax: 91 11 25544793; Email: info@eximinfo.org • URL: http://www.eximinfo.com • Covers: 20 Chinese manufacturers and exporters of fire alarm systems, fire extinguishing systems, fire fighting equipment, fire proof materials, fire protection equipment, fireclay bricks, and flame retardant. Entries include: Company name, postal address, telephone, fax, e-mail, website, contact person, designation, and product details.

**Directory of Chinese Manufacturers & Exporters of Flowers, Plants & Trees, Seeds & Bulbs.** EXIM Infotek Private Ltd., 604 Vishwa Deep, District Centre, Janakpuri New Delhi 110058, India. Phone: 91 11 25544793; Fax: 91 11 25544793; Email: info@eximinfo.org • URL: http://www.eximinfo.com • $5 Individuals. Covers: 35 Chinese manufacturers and exporters of artificial flowers, artificial plants, asparagus, flower plants, flowers-cut, flowers-dried, flowers-manmade, flowers-various, lotus roots, ornamental plants, plants, plants-natural, potpourri, roses. Entries include: Company name, postal address, city, country, phone, fax, e-mail and websites, contact person, designation, and product details.

**Directory of Chinese Manufacturers & Exporters of Food Additives & Aromatic Chemicals.** EXIM Infotek Private Ltd., 604 Vishwa Deep, District Centre, Janakpuri New Delhi 110058, India. Phone: 91 11 25544793; Fax: 91 11 25544793; Email:

info@eximinfo.org • URL: http://www.eximinfo.com • $5 Individuals. Covers: 40 Chinese manufacturers and exporters of essence, flavors, food additives, food flavor, food ingredients, and yeast. Entries include: Company name, postal address, city, country, phone, fax, e-mail and websites, contact person, designation, and product details.

***Directory of Chinese Manufacturers & Exporters of Fruits & Vegetables***. EXIM Infotek Private Ltd., 604 Vishwa Deep, District Centre, Janakpuri New Delhi 110058, India. Phone: 91 11 25544793; Fax: 91 11 25544793; Email: info@eximinfo.org • URL: http://www.eximinfo.com • $15 Individuals. Covers: 150 Chinese manufacturers and exporters of apples, bamboo shoots, canned fruits, canned mushrooms, canned pineapples, carrots, cherries, dehydrated vegetables, dried carrots, dried mushrooms, dried vegetables, frozen bamboo shoots, frozen carrots, frozen fruits, frozen vegetables, fruit, garlic, garlic sprouts, ginger, grapes, green beans, vermicelli, green vegetables, lychee, mushrooms, mushrooms and fungi, onion slices, onions, onions-Chinese, oranges, pea pods, salted vegetables, strawberries, vegetable products, vegetables, and vegetables-canned. Entries include: Company name, postal address, city, country, phone, fax, e-mail and websites, contact person, designation, and product details.

***Directory of Chinese Manufacturers & Exporters of Furniture—All Types***. EXIM Infotek Private Ltd., 604 Vishwa Deep, District Centre, Janakpuri New Delhi 110058, India. Phone: 91 11 25544793; Fax: 91 11 25544793; Email: info@eximinfo.org • URL: http://www.eximinfo.com • $15 Individuals. Covers: 170 Chinese manufacturers and exporters of aluminum chairs, bamboo furniture, beach chairs, beds, benches, cabinets, chairs, Chinese antique furniture, coffee tables, dinner tables, foldable chairs, furniture-domestic, furniture-garden, furniture-hotel/restaurant/bar, furniture-kitchen, furniture-office, furniture, furniture-antique, furniture-outdoor, metal furniture, plastic chairs, plastic tables, racks and fittings, sofas, steel furniture, steel tube furniture, tables, wood furniture, and wooden furniture. Entries include: Company name, postal address, city, country, phone, fax, e-mail and websites, contact person, designation, and product details.

***Directory of Chinese Manufacturers & Exporters of Garden Tools, Equipment & Supplies***. EXIM Infotek Private Ltd., 604 Vishwa Deep, District Centre, Janakpuri New Delhi 110058, India. Phone: 91 11 25544793; Fax: 91 11 25544793; Email: info@eximinfo.org • URL: http://www.eximinfo.com • $5 Individuals. Covers: 20 Chinese manufacturers and exporters of garden decorations, garden products, garden tools, and garden tools-all kinds. Entries include: Company name, postal address, city, country, phone, fax, e-mail and websites, contact person, designation, and product details.

***Directory of Chinese Manufacturers & Exporters of Giftwares & Novelties***. EXIM Infotek Private Ltd., 604 Vishwa Deep, District Centre, Janakpuri New Delhi 110058, India. Phone: 91 11 25544793; Fax: 91 11 25544793; Email: info@eximinfo.org • URL: http://www.eximinfo.com • $10 Individuals. Covers: 90 Chinese manufacturers & exporters of Christmas articles, Christmas gifts, gifts, giftware, key chain, novelty, photo frames, picture frames, plastic photo frames, premiums, promotional items, souvenirs. Entries include: Company name, postal address, city, country, phone, fax, e-mail & websites, contact person, designation, products detail.

***Directory of Chinese Manufacturers & Exporters of Glassware, Chinaware, Ceramicware & Porcelainware***. EXIM Infotek Private Ltd., 604 Vishwa Deep, District Centre, Janakpuri New Delhi 110058, India. Phone: 91 11 25544793; Fax: 91 11 25544793; Email: info@eximinfo.org • URL: http://www.eximinfo.com • $10 Individuals. Covers: 100 Chinese manufacturers and exporters of artistic porcelain, ashtrays, ceramic pots, ceramic tea sets, ceramics household, Chinaware, daily use porcelain, glass art decoration, glass candle holders, glass chimneys, glass vases, glassware, porcelain and ceramic products-commercial/industrial, porcelain dolls, porcelains, porcelainware, pottery, white porcelainware. Entries include: Company name, postal address, city, country, phone, fax, e-mail and websites, contact person, designation, products detail.

***Directory of Chinese Manufacturers & Exporters of Handicrafts & Decorative Items***. EXIM Infotek Private Ltd., 604 Vishwa Deep, District Centre, Janakpuri New Delhi 110058, India. Phone: 91 11 25544793; Fax: 91 11 25544793; Email: info@eximinfo.org • URL: http://www.eximinfo.com • $25 Individuals. Covers: 310 Chinese manufacturers and exporters of antiques, arts and crafts, art decoration, artware, building decoration materials, carvings, Christmas decorations, Christmas items, Christmas tree ornaments, Christmas tree sets, crafts, craft clocks, craft products, craft works, decoration items, decorative products, figurines, folk crafts, Halloween decorations, handicrafts, hanging decorations, hanging objects, hanging pictures, metal crafts, oil paintings, sculptures, tombstones, tourist articles, vases. Entries include: Company name, postal address, city, country, phone, fax, e-mail and websites, contact person, designation, and product details.

***Directory of Chinese Manufacturers & Exporters of Handkerchieves, Scarves & Neckwear***. EXIM Infotek Private Ltd., 604 Vishwa Deep, District Centre, Janakpuri New Delhi 110058, India. Phone: 91 11 25544793; Fax: 91 11 25544793; Email: info@eximinfo.org • URL: http://www.eximinfo.com • $10 Individuals. Covers: 60 Chinese manufacturers and exporters of bows and ties, cashmere scarves, neckties/scarves, scarves, shawls, silk ties, textile accessories, and ties. Entries include: Company name, postal address, city, country, phone, fax, e-mail and websites, contact person, designation, and product details.

***Directory of Chinese Manufacturers & Exporters of Handtools***. EXIM Infotek Private Ltd., 604 Vishwa Deep, District Centre, Janakpuri New Delhi 110058, India. Phone: 91 11 25544793; Fax: 91 11 25544793; Email: info@eximinfo.org • URL: http://www.eximinfo.com • $10 Individuals. Covers: 70 Chinese manufacturers and exporters of air tools, electric power tools, hammers, hand tools, hardware tools, pliers/clamps and similar tools, screwdrivers, tool cabinets, tool cases, and tools. Entries include: Company name, postal address, city, country, phone, fax, e-mail and websites, contact person, designation, and product details.

***Directory of Chinese Manufacturers & Exporters of Hardwares—All Types***. EXIM Infotek Private Ltd., 604 Vishwa Deep, District Centre, Janakpuri New Delhi 110058, India. Phone: 91 11 25544793; Fax: 91 11 25544793; Email: info@eximinfo.org • URL: http://www.eximinfo.com • $20 Individuals. Covers: 200 Chinese manufacturers and exporters of abrasive materials, abrasive paper, abrasives products, brackets, brass locks, clamps, clips, decorations-indoor, door closers, door locks, fittings, flanges, hardware, hardware fittings, hardware minerals, hardware products, hardware tools, hinges, locks, locksets, pad locks, panels, and pins. Entries include: Company name, postal address, city, country, phone, fax, e-mail and websites, contact person, designation, and product details.

***Directory of Chinese Manufacturers & Exporters of Hats & Headwears***. EXIM Infotek Private Ltd., 604 Vishwa Deep, District Centre, Janakpuri New Delhi 110058, India. Phone: 91 11 25544793; Fax: 91 11 25544793; Email: info@eximinfo.org • URL: http://www.eximinfo.com • $10 Individuals. Covers: 70 Chinese manufacturers and exporters of baseball caps, caps, hats, headwear, knitted hats, sports caps, and straw hats. Entries include: Company name, postal address, city, country, phone, fax, e-mail and websites, contact person, designation, and product details.

***Directory of Chinese Manufacturers & Exporters of Heaters & Heating Equipment***. EXIM Infotek Private Ltd., 604 Vishwa Deep, District Centre, Janakpuri New Delhi 110058, India. Phone: 91 11 25544793; Fax: 91 11 25544793; Email: info@eximinfo.org • URL: http://www.eximinfo.com • Covers: 30 Chinese manufacturers and exporters of electric water heaters, electrical heaters, heat exchangers, heaters, plate heat exchanger, solar energy water heaters, solar water heaters, and water heaters. Entries include: Company name, postal address, telephone, fax, e-mail, website, contact person, designation, and product details.

***Directory of Chinese Manufacturers & Exporters of Herbs & Herbal Medicine Products***. EXIM Infotek Private Ltd., 604 Vishwa Deep, District Centre, Janakpuri New Delhi 110058, India. Phone: 91 11 25544793; Fax: 91 11 25544793; Email: info@eximinfo.org • URL: http://www.eximinfo.com • $10 Individuals. Covers: 110 Chinese manufacturers & exporters of biological medicine, botanical extracts, burdock, Chinese herbs, Chinese medicine, Chinese medicine-traditional, ginseng, herbal extracts, herbal medicines, herbs, natural plant extracts. Entries include: Company name, postal address, city, country, phone, fax, e-mail & websites, contact person, designation, products detail.

***Directory of Chinese Manufacturers & Exporters of Home Furnishing Materials***. EXIM Infotek Private Ltd., 604 Vishwa Deep, District Centre, Janakpuri New Delhi 110058, India. Phone: 91 11 25544793; Fax: 91 11 25544793; Email: info@eximinfo.org • URL: http://www.eximinfo.com • $15 Individuals. Covers: 170 Chinese manufacturers and exporters of baby quilts, bath towels, beach towels, bed cloths, bed covers, bed sheets, bedding products, bedroom articles, blankets, curtains, cushion covers, cushions, doormats, down quilts, face towels, home decorations, home textiles, household textiles, kitchen towels, linen clothing, mats, mattresses, cushions and pillows, pillowcases, pillows, PVC table cloths, quilt cases, quilts, sanitary towels and baby napkins, shower curtains, silk towels, sleeping bags, table cloths, textiles-household, towels-jacquard bath, towels-plain bath, towels, and woolen blankets. Entries include: Company name, postal address, city, country, phone, fax, e-mail and websites, contact person, designation, and product details.

***Directory of Chinese Manufacturers & Exporters of Houseware, Kitchenware & Tableware***. EXIM Infotek Private Ltd., 604 Vishwa Deep, District Centre, Janakpuri New Delhi 110058, India. Phone: 91 11 25544793; Fax: 91 11 25544793; Email: info@eximinfo.org • URL: http://www.eximinfo.com • $20 Individuals. Covers: 210 Chinese manufacturers and exporters of aluminum utensils, beer mugs, bottle openers, bowls, brooms and brushes for domestic use, brushes, choppers, chopsticks, coffee and tea sets, coffee mugs, coffee pots, combs, cooking utensils, cookwares, cups, cutlery, daily use goods, dinnerware, electric mosquito killer series, flasks, gas lighters, gas stoves, hangers, household goods, household plastic products, household utensils, housewares, ice cream spoons, kitchen articles-metal, kitchen products, kitchen tools, kitchen utensils, kitchenware, knives-metal, mugs, plastic household goods, plastic products for daily use, pressure cookers, scissors, stainless steel cookware sets, stainless steel kitchenware, stainless steel knives, stainless steel tableware, stainless steel utensils, tableware, trays, utensils, and vacuum flasks. Entries include: Company name, postal address, city, country, telephone, fax, e-mail and websites, contact person, designation, and product details.

***Directory of Chinese Manufacturers & Exporters of Imitation & Fashion Jewelry***. EXIM Infotek Private Ltd., 604 Vishwa Deep, District Centre, Janakpuri New Delhi 110058, India. Phone: 91 11 25544793; Fax: 91 11 25544793; Email: info@eximinfo.org • URL: http://www.eximinfo.com • $10 Individuals. Covers: 70 Chinese manufacturers and exporters of bangles, beads, bracelets, brooches, buckles, costume accessories, costume jewelry, costumes, earrings, fashion accessories, glass beads, glass ornaments, hair accessories, hair clips, hair pins, imitation jewelry, jewelry, jewelry boxes, necklaces, ornament chains, ornaments, pendants, and synthetic diamonds. Entries include: Company name, postal address, city, country, phone, fax, e-mail and websites, contact person, designation, and product details.

***Directory of Chinese Manufacturers & Exporters of Laces, Ribbons & Embroidery Products***. EXIM Infotek Private Ltd., 604 Vishwa Deep, District Centre, Janakpuri New Delhi 110058, India. Phone: 91 11 25544793; Fax: 91 11 25544793; Email: info@eximinfo.org • URL: http://www.eximinfo.com • $10 Individuals. Covers: 50 Chinese manufacturers & exporters of badges, embroidery-all types, embroideries, embroidery products, garlands, laces, ribbons. Entries include: Company name, postal address, city, country, phone, fax, e-mail & websites, contact person, designation, products detail.

***Directory of Chinese Manufacturers & Exporters of Leather Products***. EXIM Infotek Private Ltd., 604 Vishwa Deep, District Centre, Janakpuri New Delhi 110058, India. Phone: 91 11 25544793; Fax: 91 11 25544793; Email: info@eximinfo.org • URL: http://www.eximinfo.com • $15 Individuals. Covers: 170 Chinese manufacturers and exporters of artificial leather products, bags, fashion bags, fur clothing & products, fur products, hand bags, leather articles, leather bags, leather belts, leather cases, leather clothing, leather garments, leather goods, leather jackets, leather products, leather purses, leather waist belts, purses, sheep and lamb skin leather products, and wallets. Entries include: Company name, postal address, city, country, phone, fax, e-mail and website, contact person, designation, and product details.

***Directory of Chinese Manufacturers & Exporters of Lighting Fixtures, Lamps & Accessories***. EXIM Infotek Private Ltd., 604 Vishwa Deep, District Centre, Janakpuri New Delhi 110058, India. Phone: 91 11 25544793; Fax: 91 11 25544793; Email: info@eximinfo.org • URL: http://www.eximinfo.com • $20 Individuals. Covers: 190 Chinese manufacturers and exporters of bulbs, ceramic lamps, Christmas lights, compact fluorescent lamps, decorative lights, electric bulbs, electric lamps, electric lighting, emergency lighting, energy saving lamps, energy saving tubes, flashlights, floodlights, floor lamps, fluorescent lamps, garden lamps, glass lighting products, halogen lamps, lampholders, lamps, lanterns, lighting, lighting appliances, lighting electric appliances, lighting equipment, lighting fixtures, lighting products, metal halide lamps and ballast, neon lamps, rope lights, solar lights, solar powered lights, solar warning lights, spotlights, table lamps, and tungsten lamps. Entries include: Company name, postal address, city, country, phone, fax, e-mail and websites, contact person, designation, and product details.

***Directory of Chinese Manufacturers & Exporters of Machinery for Chemical & Pharmaceutical Industry***. EXIM Infotek Private Ltd., 604 Vishwa Deep, District Centre, Janakpuri New Delhi 110058, India. Phone: 91 11 25544793; Fax: 91 11 25544793; Email: info@eximinfo.org • URL: http://www.eximinfo.com • $5 Individuals. Covers: 40 Chinese manufacturers and exporters of auxiliary equipments, chemical equipment, chemical industrial equipment, chemical industries machinery, chemical machinery, chemical process equipment, essence/perfume production plant equipment, pharmaceutical machinery, pharmacy equipments, and pharmacy machinery. Entries include: Company name, postal address, city, country, phone, fax, e-mail and websites, contact person, designation, and product details.

***Directory of Chinese Manufacturers & Exporters of Machinery for Textile & Knitting Industry***. EXIM Infotek Private Ltd., 604 Vishwa Deep, District Centre, Janakpuri New Delhi 110058, India. Phone: 91 11 25544793; Fax: 91 11 25544793; Email: info@eximinfo.org • URL: http://www.eximinfo.com • $5 Individuals. Covers: 40 Chinese manufacturers and exporters of arrow-shaft looms, drying machines, knitting machines, textile machinery, and textile machinery parts. Entries include: Company name, postal address, city, country, phone, fax, e-mail and websites, contact person, designation, and product details.

***Directory of Chinese Manufacturers & Exporters of Material Handling Equipment***. EXIM Infotek Private Ltd., 604 Vishwa Deep, District Centre, Janakpuri New Delhi 110058, India. Phone: 91 11 25544793; Fax: 91 11 25544793; Email: info@eximinfo.org • URL: http://www.eximinfo.com • $150 Individuals; $5 Individuals. Covers: 40 Chinese manufacturers and exporters of conveyors, cranes, electric hoist, elevators, escalators, forklift trucks, hand trucks, handling tools, hoisting machine, lifting equipment, lifts, materials handling equipment, pallets, containers, and pulleys. Entries include: Company name, postal address, telephone, fax, e-mail, website, contact person, designation, and product details.

***Directory of Chinese Manufacturers & Exporters of Meat & Meat Products***. EXIM Infotek Private Ltd., 604 Vishwa Deep, District Centre, Janakpuri New Delhi 110058, India. Phone: 91 11 25544793; Fax: 91 11 25544793; Email: info@eximinfo.org • URL: http://www.eximinfo.com • $5 Individuals. Covers: 30 Chinese manufacturers and exporters of chicken meat, crabs and crabmeat, frozen beef, lean meat products, meat, meat and meat products, pork meat, walnut meat. Entries include: Company name, postal address, city, country, phone, fax, e-mail and websites, contact person, designation, and product details.

***Directory of Chinese Manufacturers & Exporters of Minerals***. EXIM Infotek Private Ltd., 604 Vishwa Deep, District Centre, Janakpuri New Delhi 110058, India. Phone: 91 11 25544793; Fax: 91 11 25544793; Email: info@eximinfo.org • URL: http://www.eximinfo.com • $15 Individuals. Covers: 170 Chinese manufacturers and exporters of alumina products, carbon graphite, dolomite, faucet, feldspar, graphite, graphite-natural, iron oxide red, magnesium sulphate, mica and mecanite products, mineral products, minerals, natural quartz powder, non-metallic minerals, phosphate, phosphoric acid, phosphorous acid, phosphorous yellow, phosphorus products, quartz, rare earths, rare metals, and sulphate. Entries include: Company name, postal address, city, country, phone, fax, e-mail and websites, contact person, designation, and product details.

***Directory of Chinese Manufacturers & Exporters of Motorcycles, Parts & Accessories***. EXIM Infotek Private Ltd., 604 Vishwa Deep, District Centre, Janakpuri New Delhi 110058, India. Phone: 91 11 25544793; Fax: 91 11 25544793; Email: info@eximinfo.org • URL: http://www.eximinfo.com • $10 Individuals. Covers: 50 Chinese manufacturers and exporters of bikes, motor bike accessories, motorcycle bulbs, motorcycle fittings, motorcycle locks, motorcycle parts, motorcycle starting motors, motorcycles, and scooters. Entries include: Company name, postal address, city, country, phone, fax, e-mail and websites, contact person, designation, and product details.

***Directory of Chinese Manufacturers and Exporters of Motors and Motor Parts—Electric***. EXIM Infotek Private Ltd., 604 Vishwa Deep, District Centre, Janakpuri New Delhi 110058, India. Phone: 91 11 25544793; Fax: 91 11 25544793; Email: info@eximinfo.org • URL: http://www.eximinfo.com • $200 Individuals; $10 Individuals. Covers: 50 Chinese manufacturers and exporters of DC motors, electric motors, induction motors, motorcycle parts and accessories, AC motors, and sewing machine motors. Entries include: Company name, postal address, telephone, fax, e-mail, website, contact person, designation, and product details.

***Directory of Chinese Manufacturers & Exporters of Nuts & Dried Fruits***. EXIM Infotek Private Ltd., 604 Vishwa Deep, District Centre, Janakpuri New Delhi 110058, India. Phone: 91 11 25544793; Fax: 91 11 25544793; Email: info@eximinfo.org • URL: http://www.eximinfo.com • $5 Individuals. Covers: 30 Chinese manufacturers and exporters of chestnuts, dried fruits, dry fruits, nuts-dried, peanut kernels, walnuts. Entries include: Company name, postal address, city, country, phone, fax, e-mail and websites, contact person, designation, and product details.

***Directory of Chinese Manufacturers & Exporters of Nuts, Bolts, Screws & Fasteners***. EXIM Infotek Private Ltd., 604 Vishwa Deep, District Centre, Janakpuri New Delhi 110058, India. Phone: 91 11 25544793; Fax: 91 11 25544793; Email: info@eximinfo.org • URL: http://www.eximinfo.com • $5 Individuals. Covers: 40 Chinese manufacturers and exporters of bolts, chestnut kernels, fasteners, nuts and bolts, rivets, screws, slide fasteners, and washers. Entries include: Company name, postal address, city, country, phone, fax, e-mail and websites, contact person, designation, and product details.

***Directory of Chinese Manufacturers & Exporters of Oil & Fats—Cooking & Vegetable***. EXIM Infotek Private Ltd., 604 Vishwa Deep, District Centre, Janakpuri New Delhi 110058, India. Phone: 91 11 25544793; Fax: 91 11 25544793; Email: info@eximinfo.org • URL: http://www.eximinfo.com • $5 Individuals. Covers: 30 Chinese manufacturers and exporters of cooking oil, edible oil, oils and fats-edible, peanut oil, pine oils, rapeseed, soybean oil, vegetable oil. Entries include: Company name, postal address, city, country, phone, fax, e-mail and websites, contact person, designation, and product details.

***Directory of Chinese Manufacturers & Exporters of Paints, Varnishes & Allied Products***. EXIM Infotek Private Ltd., 604 Vishwa Deep, District Centre, Janakpuri New Delhi 110058, India. Phone: 91 11 25544793; Fax: 91 11 25544793; Email: info@eximinfo.org • URL: http://www.eximinfo.com • $10 Individuals. Covers: 70 Chinese manufacturers and exporters of absorbent resin, coating materials, coating raw materials, coating-automobiles, coating-fire proof, coating-water proof, lacquer, latex paints, paint, paint brushes, paint mixers, paint rollers, paints, polyester paints, polyurethane resins, powder coatings, and wall paints. Entries include: Company name, postal address, city, country, phone, fax, e-mail and websites, contact person, designation, and product details.

***Directory of Chinese Manufacturers & Exporters of Paper & Paper Products***. EXIM Infotek Private Ltd., 604 Vishwa Deep, District Centre, Janakpuri New Delhi 110058, India. Phone: 91 11 25544793; Fax: 91 11 25544793; Email: info@eximinfo.org • URL: http://www.eximinfo.com • $10 Individuals. Covers: 60 Chinese manufacturers and exporters of cardboard, disposable paper products, craft paper tapes, napkins, paper, paper products, paper pulp, paperboard, and tissue papers. Entries include: Company name, postal address, city, country, phone, fax, e-mail and websites, contact person, designation, and product details.

***Directory of Chinese Manufacturers & Exporters of Petroleum Products***. EXIM Infotek Private Ltd., 604 Vishwa Deep, District Centre, Janakpuri New Delhi 110058, India. Phone: 91 11 25544793; Fax: 91 11 25544793; Email: info@eximinfo.org • URL: http://www.eximinfo.com • $10 Individuals. Covers: 50 Chinese manufacturers and exporters of coal tar, fuel, lubricating oil, natural gases, petrochemicals, petroleum chemicals, and petroleum products. Entries include: Company name, postal address, city, country, phone, fax, e-mail and websites, contact person, designation, and product details.

***Directory of Chinese Manufacturers & Exporters of Pharmaceutical Products***. EXIM Infotek Private Ltd., 604 Vishwa Deep, District Centre, Janakpuri New Delhi 110058, India. Phone: 91 11 25544793; Fax: 91 11 25544793; Email: info@eximinfo.org • URL: http://www.eximinfo.com • $25 Individuals. Covers: 330 Chinese manufacturers and exporters of antibiotics, biopharmaceuticals, bulk drugs, capsules, drugs, eye drops, intermediate for medicines, medicaments, medicines, medicines for animals, paracetamol, pharmaceutical materials, pharmaceutical products, pharmaceuticals, veterinary medicines. Entries include: Company name, postal address, city, country, phone, fax, e-mail and websites, contact person, designation, and product details.

***Directory of Chinese Manufacturers & Exporters of Pharmaceutical Raw Materials***. EXIM Infotek Private Ltd., 604 Vishwa Deep, District Centre, Janakpuri New Delhi 110058, India. Phone: 91 11 25544793; Fax: 91 11 25544793; Email: info@eximinfo.org • URL: http://www.eximinfo.com • $10 Individuals. Covers: 80 Chinese manufacturers and exporters of amino-acid, enzymes, medicine industrial chemicals, pharmaceutical chemicals, pharmaceutical intermediates, pharmaceutical raw material, raw material for medicines, and vitamins/hormones and organ extracts. Entries include: Company name, postal address, city, country, phone, fax, e-mail and websites, contact person, designation, and product details.

***Directory of Chinese Manufacturers & Exporters of Readymade Garments***. EXIM Infotek Private Ltd., 604 Vishwa Deep, District Centre, Janakpuri New Delhi 110058, India. Phone: 91 11 25544793; Fax: 91 11 25544793; Email: info@eximinfo.org • URL: http://www.eximinfo.com • $40 Individuals. Covers: 580 Chinese manufacturers and exporters of apparel, aprons, baby clothing, blouses, boxer shorts, cardigans, cashmere sweaters, casual and leisurewear, children's wear, clothing, coats, cotton garments, cotton knitwear, cotton shirts, cotton t-shirts, cowboy leisure clothes, denimwears, down garments, dress, fashionable garments, fashionable ladies garments, garments, handkerchiefs, handmade clothings, hosiery, jackets, jeans, jogging suits, kimono dresses, knitted children's tights, knitted garments, knitted goods, knitting garments, knitting products, knitwear, knitwear-children, ladies fashionable garments, ladies wear, men's suits, night wears, nylon garments, outerwears, overcoats, pajamas, pants, plastic clothes, polo t-shirts, readymade garments for men/boys, shirts, shorts, silk garments, silk knitted garments, silk knitted products, skirts, sleepwears, sleeveless garments, sportswear, suits, surgical gowns, sweaters, swim and beach wear, textile clothings, tracksuits, trousers, t-shirts, uniforms, winter wears, woolen garments, woolen sweaters, working clothes, workwear, woven and knitted garments, woven and knitted shirts, and woven garments. Entries include: Company name, postal address, city, country, telephone, fax, e-mail and websites, contact person, designation, and product details.

***Directory of Chinese Manufacturers & Exporters of Seafood & Fish***. EXIM Infotek Private Ltd., 604 Vishwa Deep, District Centre, Janakpuri New Delhi 110058, India. Phone: 91 11 25544793; Fax: 91 11 25544793; Email: info@eximinfo.org • URL: http://www.eximinfo.com • $10 Individuals. Covers: 50 Chinese manufacturers and exporters of Alaska pollack fillets, asparagus-frozen, canned asparagus, fish, fish fillets, frozen cooked crawfish, frozen fillets, frozen fish, frozen octopus, frozen seafood products, marine products, scallops, seafood, seaweed, shrimps and prawns. Entries include: Company name, postal address, city, country, phone, fax, e-mail and websites, contact person, designation, and product details.

***Directory of Chinese Manufacturers & Exporters of Shoes & Footwears***. EXIM Infotek Private Ltd., 604 Vishwa Deep, District Centre, Janakpuri New Delhi 110058, India. Phone: 91 11 25544793; Fax: 91 11 25544793; Email: info@eximinfo.org • URL: http://www.eximinfo.com • $20 Individuals. Covers: 260 Chinese manufacturers and exporters of baby shoes, boots-rubber, boots, canvas shoes, casual shoes, children's shoes, footwear, jogging shoes, ladies leather shoes, leather shoes, plastic sandals, plastic slippers, up shoes, rubber boots, rubber shoes, sandals, school shoes, shoes, slippers, snow boots. Entries include: Company name, postal address, city, country, phone, fax, e-mail and websites, contact person, designation, and product details.

***Directory of Chinese Manufacturers & Exporters of Soap, Detergent & Cleaning Supplies***. EXIM Infotek Private Ltd., 604 Vishwa Deep, District Centre, Janakpuri New Delhi 110058, India. Phone: 91 11 25544793; Fax: 91 11 25544793; Email: info@eximinfo.org • URL: http://www.eximinfo.com • $5 Individuals. Covers: 25 Chinese manufacturers and exporters of cleaning products, detergent liquid, detergent powder, detergents, soap, synthetic detergent. Entries include: Company name, postal address, city, country, phone, fax, e-mail and websites, contact person, designation, and product details.

***Directory of Chinese Manufacturers & Exporters of Spices, Seasonings & Flavorings***. EXIM Infotek Private Ltd., 604 Vishwa Deep, District Centre, Janakpuri New Delhi 110058, India. Phone: 91 11 25544793; Fax: 91 11 25544793; Email: info@eximinfo.org • URL: http://www.eximinfo.com • $5 Individuals. Covers: 30 Chinese manufacturers and exporters of chili, dried chili, dried ginger, garlic powder, pepper, salt, seasonings, spices. Entries include: Company name, postal address, city, country, phone, fax, e-mail and websites, contact person, designation, and product details.

***Directory of Chinese Manufacturers & Exporters of Sporting Goods***. EXIM Infotek Private Ltd., 604 Vishwa Deep, District Centre, Janakpuri New Delhi 110058, India. Phone: 91 11 25544793; Fax: 91 11 25544793; Email: info@eximinfo.org • URL: http://www.eximinfo.com • Covers: 170 Chinese manufacturers and exporters of athletic sports equipment, badminton rackets, basket balls, bowling equipment, camping goods, fishing accessories, fishing nets, fishing tackle, football, golf accessories, golf carts and vans, golf goods, gymnasium and exercise equipment, handball, leisure goods, mountaineering products, outdoor products, ruck sack, shuttle cock, skate scooters, sporting goods, sports bags, sports equipment, sports goods, sports shoes, sports suits, sportswear, tennis rackets, and volleyball. Entries include: Company name, postal address, telephone, fax, e-mail, website, contact person, designation, and product details.

***Directory of Chinese Manufacturers & Exporters of Tea & Coffee***. EXIM Infotek Private Ltd., 604 Vishwa Deep, District Centre, Janakpuri New Delhi 110058, India. Phone: 91 11 25544793; Fax: 91 11 25544793; Email: info@eximinfo.org • URL: http://www.eximinfo.com • $10 Individuals. Covers: 50 Chinese manufacturers and exporters of black tea, Chinese tea, coffee, green tea, jasmine tea, oolong tea, and organic tea. Entries include: Company name, postal address, city, country, phone, fax, e-mail and websites, contact person, designation, and product details.

***Directory of Chinese Manufacturers & Exporters of Textiles & Fabrics***. EXIM Infotek Private Ltd., 604 Vishwa Deep, District Centre, Janakpuri New Delhi 110058, India. Phone: 91 11 25544793; Fax: 91 11 25544793; Email: info@eximinfo.org • URL: http://www.eximinfo.com • $30 Individuals. Covers: 380 Chinese manufacturers and exporters of acrylic fabric, cloth, cotton fabrics, cotton textiles, dyed fabrics, fabrics-blended, fabrics-grey, fabrics, fabrics for industrial use, fabrics-denim, fabrics-silk, garment fabrics, industrial cloths, jacquard fabrics, knitted fabrics, linens, nonwoven fabrics, polyester cloth, polyester fabrics, printed fabrics, pure silk, rayon products, silk, silk products, silk velvet, spinning fabrics, synthetic textiles, textile fabrics, textile materials, textile products, textile raw material and products, textiles, textiles accessories, tricot fabrics, woolen fabric garments, woolen fabrics, worsted fabrics, and woven fabrics. Entries include: Company name, postal address, city, country, phone, fax, e-mail and websites, contact person, designation, and product details.

***Directory of Chinese Manufacturers & Exporters of Toys & Games***. EXIM Infotek Private Ltd., 604 Vishwa Deep, District Centre, Janakpuri New Delhi 110058, India. Phone: 91 11 25544793; Fax: 91 11 25544793; Email: info@eximinfo.org • URL: http://www.eximinfo.com • $20 Individuals. Covers: 240 Chinese manufacturers and exporters of baby care products, baby carriages, baby products, baby strollers, babyware, chess sets, child bicycles, children's toys, children's vehicles, cloth toys, craft toys, dolls, electric toys, electrical toys (a/c), electronic toys, firecrackers, fireworks, games, masks, plastic toys, playing cards, plush toys, porcelain toys, remote control toys, rubber toys, stuffed toys, toy fireworks, toy guns, toys, toy parts, toys-intelligent-adults, waterguns, wooden puzzles, and wooden toys. Entries include: Company name, postal address, city, country, phone, fax, e-mail and websites, contact person, designation, and product details.

***Directory of Chinese Manufacturers & Exporters of Travel & Luggage Accessories***. EXIM Infotek Private Ltd., 604 Vishwa Deep, District Centre, Janakpuri New Delhi 110058, India. Phone: 91 11 25544793; Fax: 91 11 25544793; Email: info@eximinfo.org • URL: http://www.eximinfo.com • $10 Individuals. Covers: 60 Chinese manufacturers and exporters of briefcases, hardside luggage, leather briefcases, luggage carts, luggage, suitcases, suitcase accessories, travel bags, and travel goods. Entries include: Company name, postal address, city, country, phone, fax, e-mail and websites, contact person, designation, and product details.

***Directory of Chinese Manufacturers & Exporters of Tyres & Tubes***. EXIM Infotek Private Ltd., 604 Vishwa Deep, District Centre, Janakpuri New Delhi 110058, India. Phone: 91 11 25544793; Fax: 91 11 25544793; Email: info@eximinfo.org • URL: http://www.eximinfo.com • $10 Individuals. Covers: 60 Chinese manufacturers and exporters of automobile tires and tubes, inner tubes for tires, rubber tires and tubes, tires and tubes, tires for truck, vehicle tires and inner tubes. Entries include: Company name, postal address, city, country, phone, fax, e-mail and websites, contact person, designation, and product details.

***Directory of Chinese Manufacturers & Exporters of Undergarments***. EXIM Infotek Private Ltd., 604 Vishwa Deep, District Centre, Janakpuri New Delhi 110058, India. Phone: 91 11 25544793; Fax: 91 11 25544793; Email: info@eximinfo.org • URL: http://www.eximinfo.com • $10 Individuals. Covers: 50 Chinese manufacturers and exporters of briefs, socks, sport socks, stockings, underwear, and underwear-ladies. Entries include: Company name, postal address, city, country, phone, fax, e-mail and websites, contact person, designation, and product details.

***Directory of Chinese Manufacturers & Exporters of Watches & Clocks***. EXIM Infotek Private Ltd., 604 Vishwa Deep, District Centre, Janakpuri New Delhi 110058, India. Phone: 91 11 25544793; Fax: 91 11 25544793; Email: info@eximinfo.org • URL: http://www.eximinfo.com • $10 Individuals. Covers: 50 Chinese manufacturers and exporters of alarm clocks, clocks, electronic quartz clocks, electronic watches, quartz clock LCD clocks, quartz clocks, quartz watches, table clocks, wall clock, and watches. Entries include: Company name, postal address, city, country, phone, fax, e-mail and websites, contact person, designation, and product details.

***Directory of Chinese Manufacturers & Exporters of Wire, Chain & Wire Products***. EXIM Infotek Private Ltd., 604 Vishwa Deep, District Centre, Janakpuri New Delhi 110058, India. Phone: 91 11 25544793; Fax: 91 11 25544793; Email: info@eximinfo.org • URL: http://www.eximinfo.com • $10 Individuals. Covers: 90 Chinese manufacturers & exporters of anchors, barbed wire, brass wire mesh, chains, copper wires, galvanized iron wires, hexagonal wire mesh, hexagonal wire netting, iron wire, mesh products, metal wire mesh, metal wires, pet chains, roller chains, steel wire, welded wire mesh, wire, wire harness, wire mesh, wire netting, wire products, wire rack & accessories, wire rope, wire rope clips. Entries include: Company name, postal address, city, country, phone, fax, e-mail & websites, contact person, designation, products detail.

***Directory of Chinese Manufacturers & Exporters of Wooden-ware & Wooden Products***. EXIM Infotek Private Ltd., 604 Vishwa Deep, District Centre, Janakpuri New Delhi 110058, India. Phone: 91 11 25544793; Fax: 91 11 25544793; Email: info@eximinfo.org • URL: http://www.eximinfo.com • $15 Individuals. Covers: 160 Chinese manufacturers and exporters of bamboo basketry, bamboo crafts, bamboo curtains, bamboo decorations, bamboo floorings, bamboo handicraft products, bamboo mats, bamboo products, bamboo tableware, baskets-various, cane and wicker products, carvings and marquetry-wooden, rattan products, wicker products, willow baskets, willow products, wood and wood articles, wood products, wooden baskets, wooden boxes, wooden crafts, wooden decorations, wooden floorings, wooden gifts, wooden handicraft products, wooden products, and woodenware. Entries include: Company name, postal address, city, country, phone, fax, e-mail and websites, contact person, designation, and product details.

***Directory of Chinese Manufacturers and Exporters of Woodworking Equipment and Tools***. EXIM Infotek Private Ltd., 604 Vishwa Deep, District Centre, Janakpuri New Delhi 110058, India. Phone: 91 11 25544793; Fax: 91 11 25544793; Email: info@eximinfo.org • URL: http://www.eximinfo.com • Covers: 20 Chinese manufacturers and exporters of hacksaw blades, saw blades, saw cutting machinery, sawing machine, wood working machine, and wood working tools. Entries include: Company name, postal address, telephone, fax, e-mail, website, contact person, designation, and product details.

***Directory of Chinese Manufacturers & Exporters of Yarns & Threads***. EXIM Infotek Private Ltd., 604 Vishwa Deep, District Centre, Janakpuri New Delhi 110058, India. Phone: 91 11 25544793; Fax: 91 11 25544793; Email: info@eximinfo.org • URL: http://www.eximinfo.com • $10 Individuals. Covers: 80 Chinese manufacturers and exporters of cashmere yarn, chenille yarn, cotton yarn, embroidery thread, knitting yarn, linen yarns, metallic yarns, polyester filaments, polyester thread, polyester yarn, sewing thread, thread, viscose filament yarns, yarn products, yarns, and yarns-blended. Entries include: Company name, postal address, city, country, phone, fax, e-mail and websites, contact person, designation, and product details.

***Directory of Chinese Manufacturers & Exporters of Zipper, Garment & Shoe Accessories***. EXIM Infotek Private Ltd., 604 Vishwa Deep, District Centre, Janakpuri New Delhi 110058, India. Phone: 91 11 25544793; Fax: 91 11 25544793; Email: info@eximinfo.org • URL: http://www.eximinfo.com • $10 Individuals. Covers: 80 Chinese manufacturers and exporters of apparel accessories, belt buckles, buttons, buttons-resin, clothing accessories, fashion garment accessories, garment accessories, hooks, lining cloths, metal buckles, metal zippers, needles, plastic zipper, sewing kits, sewing needles, tailoring accessories, zipper products, and zippers. Entries include: Company name, postal address, city, country, phone, fax, e-mail and websites, contact person, designation, and product details.

***Directory of Colorado Manufacturers—Information, Science, & Technology***. University of Colorado at Boulder Leeds School of Business Business Research Division, 995 Regent Dr., UCB 419 Boulder, CO 80309-0420. Phone: (303)492-3307; Fax: (303)492-3620; Email: brdinfo@colorado.edu • URL: http://leeds.colorado.edu/brd#overview • $25 clearance price. Covers: More than 1,600 Colorado manufacturers in the information, science and technology fields. Entries include: Plant address, mailing address, telephone number, e-mail, Web address, names and titles of key personnel, NAICS code numbers, number of employees, branch and subsidiary details, area of distribution.

***Directory of Colorado Manufacturers***. University of Colorado at Boulder Leeds School of Business Business Research Division, 995 Regent Dr., UCB 419 Boulder, CO 80309-0420. Phone: (303)492-3307; Fax: (303)492-3620; Email: brdinfo@colorado.edu • URL: http://leeds.colorado.edu/brd#overview • $100 Individuals book; plus tax; $125 Individuals CD; plus tax; $150 Individuals book and CD package; plus tax. Covers: 6,000 manufacturing firms in Colorado. Entries include: Company name, mailing address, plant address, phone, Standard Metropolitan Statistical Area (SMSA), names and titles of executives, date founded, distribution area, approximate employment, products or services.

***Directory of Companies, Board Members and Directors***. Dicodi S.A., C/Villanueva 35 E-28001 Madrid, Spain. Phone: 34 1 577 72 16; Fax: 34 1 577 92 00 • Annual. Covers: 25,000 companies and 80,000 board members in Spain. Entries include: Company name, address, phone, director names.

***Directory of Companies by Quarters***. IBCON S.A., Gutenberg 224, Col. Anzures 11590 Mexico, Mexico. Phone: 52 55 52554577; Email: ibcon@ibcon.com.mx • URL: http://www.ibcon.com.mx • Irregular. $473 Individuals. Covers: 14,041 companies incorporated in Mexico City. Entries include: Company name, address, phone, fax; industry code; Producing, Distributing, or Servicing initials, name and position of the top executive.

***Directory of Companies***. IBCON S.A., Gutenberg 224, Col. Anzures 11590 Mexico, Mexico. Phone: 52 55 52554577; Email: ibcon@ibcon.com.mx • URL: http://www.ibcon.com.mx • Irregular. $473 Individuals. Covers: 14,640 companies that are SA corporations located in Mexico City. Entries include: Company name, address, phone, fax, industry code, Producing, Distributing, Servicing initials, name and position of the top executive.

***Directory of Computer and Point-of-Sale Systems for Office Products and Furniture Dealers***. Independent Office Products and Furniture Dealers Association, 3601 E Joppa Rd. Baltimore, MD 21234. Phone: (410)930-8100; Fax: (410)931-8111; Email: cbates@nopanet.org • URL: http://www.iopfda.org • Irregular. $60. Covers: Approximately 45 manufacturers and distributors of computer, point-of-sale, and contract furniture systems for the office products industry. Entries include: Company name, address, phone, description of product or service.

***Directory of Consulting Offices in Arab Countries***. Arab Industrial Development and Metrology Organization League of Arab States, Tahrir Sq. Cairo, Egypt. Phone: 2 750511; Fax: 2 740331 • Irregular.

***Directory of Contract Staffing Firms***. C.E. Publications Inc., PO Box 3006 Bothell, WA 98041-3006. Phone: (425)806-5200; Fax: (425)806-5585; Email: staff@cjhunter.com • URL: http://www.cjhunter.com • Annual. Covers: Nearly 1,300 contract firms actively engaged in the employment of engineering, IT/IS, and technical personnel for 'temporary' contract assignments throughout the world. Entries include: Company name, address, phone, name of contact, email, web address.

***Directory of Cordoba Exporters***. Imagen S.A., Antonio del Viso 687 5001 Cordoba, Argentina. Phone: 54 51 730 578 • Covers: Products exported from Cordoba. Entries include: Product name, company name.

***Directory of Corporate and Foundation Givers***. Taft Group, 27500 Drake Rd. Farmington Hills, MI 48331-3535. Phone: 800-877-4253 or (248)699-4253 or (248)699-GALE; Fax: (800)414-5043 or (248)699-8061; Email: gale.salesassistance@thomson.com • URL: http://www.gale.com/taft • $270. Covers: 8,000 private foundations, corporate foundations, and companies that give money to nonprofit organizations. Entries include: Foundation name, sponsoring company name, address, phone, fax, e-mail, URL, contact name; financial summary, including assets and amounts given for up to previous three years; Employer Identification Number; summary of contributions, including typical recipients, grant types, nonmonetary support types, geographic distribution; names and titles of key personnel; application procedures; grants summary including total grants, highest grant, typical grant range, and list of recent grants, giving amounts and names of recipients.

***Directory of Corporate and Foundation Grants***. Taft Group, 27500 Drake Rd. Farmington Hills, MI 48331-3535. Phone: 800-877-4253 or (248)699-4253 or (248)699-GALE; Fax: (800)414-5043 or (248)699-8061; Email: gale.salesassistance@thomson.com • URL: http://www.gale.com/taft • $155. Covers: in two sections; Section 1 lists over 95,000 grants and their recipients. Section 2 lists over 5,500 corporate and foundation grantmakers. Entries include: Section 1—Recipient category, location, name of recipient, amount of grant, grant description, name of corporate or foundation grantmaker. Section 2—Foundation/company name, location, grants data, alpha record of grants.

***Directory of Corporate Name Changes***. The Scarecrow Press Inc., 4501 Forbes Blvd., Ste. 200 Lanham, MD 20706-4346. Phone: 800-462-6420 or (301)459-3366; Fax: (301)429-5748; Email: custserv@rowman.com • URL: http://www.scarecrowpress.com • $104 Individuals Hardback; £65 Individuals Hardback. Lists names by which corporations have been known, including original and current names. Entries include: Name, preceding and succeeding names, year changed, original name (if the name listed isn't the original).

***Directory of Corporations and Corporate Officers***. DAFSA, 25 rue Leblanc F-75010 Paris, France. Phone: 33 14604060; Fax: 33 140605151 • Annual. Covers: 13,000 corporation board members and 1,200 companies on the stock exchange in France. Entries include: For members—Name, address, positions held, responsibilities. For companies—Company name, address, phone, line of business, executives, shareholders, subsidiaries, financial data.

***Directory of Credit Card Merchant Processors: The Directory of Credit Card & Ecommerce Sources for Small Business***. PM Financial Services, PO Box 1406 Hoboken, NJ 07030. Phone: (201)714-4953; Fax: (201)944-4734 • Annual. $10. Credit card merchant processors in the United States.

***Directory of Danish Importers of Computer Hardwares and Peripherals***. EXIM Infotek Private Ltd., 604 Vishwa Deep, District Centre, Janakpuri New Delhi 110058, India. Phone: 91 11 25544793; Fax: 91 11 25544793; Email: info@eximinfo.org • URL: http://www.eximinfo.com • $250 Individuals; $10 Individuals. Covers: 70 Danish importers of computer equipment and supplies, computer peripherals, computer supplies, computer components, LAN/network hardware and software. Entries include: Company name, postal address, telephone, fax, e-mail, website, contact person, designation, and product details.

***Directory of Danish Importers of Construction Machinery and Equipment***. EXIM Infotek Private Ltd., 604 Vishwa Deep, District Centre, Janakpuri New Delhi 110058, India. Phone: 91 11 25544793; Fax: 91 11 25544793; Email: info@eximinfo.org • URL: http://www.eximinfo.com • $150 Individuals; $5 Individuals. Covers: 20 Danish importers of construction, building equipment and parts, industrial and construction vehicles, and snow removal equipment. Entries include: Company name, postal address, telephone, fax, e-mail, website, contact person, designation, and product details.

***Directory of Danish Importers of Office Equipment & Supplies***. EXIM Infotek Private Ltd., 604 Vishwa Deep, District Centre, Janakpuri New Delhi 110058, India. Phone: 91 11 25544793; Fax: 91 11 25544793; Email: info@eximinfo.org • URL: http://www.eximinfo.com • $10 Individuals; $200 Individuals. Covers: 50 Danish importers of accounting and bookkeeping equipment, addressing and mailing equipment, banking equipment and supplies, calculators, cash registers, copying machines and supplies, fax and duplicating papers, office equipment and supplies, office machines, time recorders and timers, and typewriters. Entries include: Company name, postal address, telephone, fax, e-mail, website, contact person, designation, and product details.

***Directory of Development Research and Training Institutes in Africa***. Organisation for Economic Co-operation and Development Washington Center, 1776 I St. NW, Ste. 450 Washington, DC 20006. Phone: 800-456-6323 or (202)785-6323; Fax: (202)315-2508; Email: washington.contact@oecd.org • URL: http://www.oecd.org/washington • Irregular. $40. Covers: Nearly 500 organizations engaged in research and training in the fields of economic and social development in Africa. Entries include: Name of organization, address, phone, telex, cable address, name of director, number of professional staff, year established, research and training activities, other activities, periodicals, library facilities, computer facilities, and conference facilities.

***Directory of Development Research and Training Institutes in Europe***. OECD Publishing, 2, rue Andre Pascal F-75775 Paris, France. Phone: 33 1 45248200; Fax: 33 1 45248500; Email: news.contact@oecd.org • URL: http://www.oecd.org • Irregular. €50 Individuals; $70 Individuals; £45 Individuals; Y6,500 Individuals; $900 Individuals. Covers: Approximately 540 organizations and institutes in Europe engaged in research and training in the fields of development policy, international relations, foreign aid, industry, rural development, social change, environmental protection, and other economic and social issues. Entries include: Institution name, address, phone, fax, telex, cable address, name of director, number of professional staff, year established, research and training activities, other activities, periodicals, library facilities, computer facilities, and conference facilities.

***Directory of Development Research and Training Institutes in***

***Latin America***. OECD Publishing, 2, rue Andre Pascal F-75775 Paris, France. Phone: 33 1 45248200; Fax: 33 1 45248500; Email: news.contact@oecd.org • URL: http://www.oecd.org • Irregular. $27. Covers: 122 Latin American organizations in 19 countries of South and Central America engaged in research and training in the fields of economic and social development. Entries include: Name of institution, address, phone, telex, cable address, name of director, number of professional staff, year established, research and training activities, other activities, periodicals, library facilities, computer facilities, and conference facilities.

***Directory of Directors***. Financial Post Datagroup, 333 King St., E. Toronto, ON, Canada M5A 4N2. Phone: 800-661-7678 or (416)350-6500 or (416)350-6300; Fax: (416)350-6501 or (416)350-6601; Email: fpdg@fpdata.finpost.com • URL: http://www.financialpost.com • Annual. $175.00. Provides brief biographical information on 16,000 directors and key officers of Canadian companies who are also Canadian residents.

***Directory of Directors***. Reed Business Information, Quadrant House, The Quadrant Surrey SM2 5AS, United Kingdom. Phone: 44 20 86523500 or 1 6618904; Fax: 44 20 86528932; Email: webmaster@rbi.co.uk • URL: http://www.reedbusiness.com • Annual. $275 plus 7.50 pounds shipping; 15 pounds overseas. Covers: Approximately 50,000 directors of the top 15,000 public and private corporations in the United Kingdom. Entries include: Name, address, phone, fax, title and/or profession, list of companies of which a director, code indicating business interest.

***Directory of East European Businesses***. Mercury Books Gold Arrow Publications Ltd., 862 Garratt Ln. London SW17 0NB, United Kingdom. Phone: 81 6823858; Fax: 81 6823859 • $74.95 plus $3.50 shipping. Covers: 2,000 leading manufacturing and engineering companies in Albania, Bulgaria, the Commonwealth of Independent States, eastern Germany, Hungary, Poland, Romania, and Czechoslovakia and Yugoslavia (prior to their separations). Entries include: Company name, address, phone, fax, telex, name and title of contact, line of business, sales, profits.

***Directory of EC Industry Information Sources***. Macmillan Publishers Ltd. Nature Publishing Group, 75 Varick St., 9th Fl. New York, NY 10013-1917. Phone: 888-331-6288 or (212)726-9200; Fax: (212)696-9006; Email: institutions@natureny.com • URL: http://www.nature.com • $105 plus $6.00 postage. Covers: Organizations and individuals in the European Communities responsible for specific industrial information, including finding business partners, business start-ups, lobbying, electronic information services, and statistics.

***Directory of Economic Development Organizations in Oregon***. Council for Economic Development in Oregon, 10200 SW Nimbus, No. G-3 Tigard, OR 97223. Phone: (503)620-1142; Fax: (503)624-0641 • Irregular. $25. Covers: public and private organizations concerned with economic development in Oregon; includes federal, state, and local governmental agencies. Entries include: Organization or agency name, address, phone, name and title of contact, geographic territory covered.

***The Directory of EU Information Sources: The Red Book***. Euroconfidentiel S. A., Rue de Rixensart 18 B-1332 Genval, Belgium. Phone: 32 02 652 02 84 or 32 2 6520284; Fax: (653) 01 80 or (653)0180; Email: nigel.hunt@skynet.be • URL: http://www.euroconfidential.com • Annual. $230.00. Lists publications, associations, consultants, law firms, diplomats, jounalists, and other sources of information about Europe and the European Union.

***Directory of European Importers of Biological Products***. EXIM Infotek Private Ltd., 604 Vishwa Deep, District Centre, Janakpuri New Delhi 110058, India. Phone: 91 11 25544793; Fax: 91 11 25544793; Email: info@eximinfo.org • URL: http://www.eximinfo.com • $15 Individuals. Covers: 50 European importers of biological products. Entries include: Company name, postal address, telephone, fax, e-mail, website, contact person, designation, and product details.

***Directory of European Importers of Energy and Power Equipment***. EXIM Infotek Private Ltd., 604 Vishwa Deep, District Centre, Janakpuri New Delhi 110058, India. Phone: 91 11 25544793; Fax: 91 11 25544793; Email: info@eximinfo.org • URL: http://www.eximinfo.com • Covers: 180 European importers of alternative energy equipment, energy saving equipment, nuclear equipment and materials, power transmission component, power transmission equipment and supplies, power transmission equipment, solar energy equipment, and wind energy equipment. Entries include: Company name, postal address, telephone, fax, e-mail, website, contact person, designation, and product details.

***Directory of European Importers of Fodder & Animal Foodstuffs***. EXIM Infotek Private Ltd., 604 Vishwa Deep, District Centre, Janakpuri New Delhi 110058, India. Phone: 91 11 25544793; Fax: 91 11 25544793; Email: info@eximinfo.org • URL: http://www.eximinfo.com • $20 Individuals. Covers: 270 European importers of animal food meals, animal foodstuff additives, feed additives, fodder, livestock breeding supplies, and oats. Entries include: Company name, postal address, telephone, fax, e-mail, website, contact person, designation, and product details.

***Directory of European Importers of Gears & Boxes***. EXIM Infotek Private Ltd., 604 Vishwa Deep, District Centre, Janakpuri New Delhi 110058, India. Phone: 91 11 25544793; Fax: 91 11 25544793; Email: info@eximinfo.org • URL: http://www.eximinfo.com • $10 Individuals. Covers: 90 European importers of gears and boxes. Entries include: Company name, postal address, telephone, fax, e-mail, website, contact person, designation, and product details.

***Directory of European Importers of Heaters and Heating Equipment***. EXIM Infotek Private Ltd., 604 Vishwa Deep, District Centre, Janakpuri New Delhi 110058, India. Phone: 91 11 25544793; Fax: 91 11 25544793; Email: info@eximinfo.org • URL: http://www.eximinfo.com • Covers: 270 European importers of air heaters, copper tubes for central heating, heat exchangers, heating equipment, heating household application of iron and steel (non-electric), heating systems, and water heaters. Entries include: Company name, postal address, telephone, fax, e-mail, website, contact person, designation, and product details.

***Directory of European Importers of Hoses & Fittings***. EXIM Infotek Private Ltd., 604 Vishwa Deep, District Centre, Janakpuri New Delhi 110058, India. Phone: 91 11 25544793; Fax: 91 11 25544793; Email: info@eximinfo.org • URL: http://www.eximinfo.com • Covers: 40 European importers of hoses, hose fittings, and adaptors. Entries include: Company name, postal address, telephone, fax, e-mail, website, contact person, designation, and product details.

***Directory of European Importers of Laboratory & Scientific Instruments & Supplies***. EXIM Infotek Private Ltd., 604 Vishwa Deep, District Centre, Janakpuri New Delhi 110058, India. Phone: 91 11 25544793; Fax: 91 11 25544793; Email: info@eximinfo.org • URL: http://www.eximinfo.com • Covers: 1,300 European importers of binoculars, microscopes, telescopes, evaporators, laboratory and scientific glass, laboratory diagnostic equipment and supplies, laboratory instruments, reagents for laboratories, scientific instrument, and testing equipment. Entries include: Company name, postal address, telephone, fax, e-mail, website, contact person, designation, and product details.

***Directory of European Importers of Lumber, Timber, Plywood and Hardboards***. EXIM Infotek Private Ltd., 604 Vishwa Deep, District Centre, Janakpuri New Delhi 110058, India. Phone: 91 11 25544793; Fax: 91 11 25544793; Email: info@eximinfo.org • URL: http://www.eximinfo.com • $950 Individuals; $40 Individuals. Covers: 580 European importers of coniferous raw wood, doors and windows, glued timber, gypsum board and sheetrock, hardboard and particleboard, hardwood flooring and tiles, hardwood lumber, hardwood, laminates, wood laminates, lumber goods, timber and plywood, softwood lumber, oak flooring, oak sheets, parquet, particle boards, pinewood, planed wood, plywood and veneer, poles, pilings and logs, round logs, sawdust, softwood, solid wood, teak and mahogany wood, teak logs, veneering wood, wood particle slabs, wood sawn, and wooden moldings. Entries include: Company name, postal address, telephone, fax, e-mail, website, contact person, designation, and product details.

***Directory of European Importers of Machinery for Glass and Ceramic Industry***. EXIM Infotek Private Ltd., 604 Vishwa Deep, District Centre, Janakpuri New Delhi 110058, India. Phone: 91 11 25544793; Fax: 91 11 25544793; Email: info@eximinfo.org • URL: http://www.eximinfo.com • $150 Individuals; $5 Individuals. Covers: 20 European importers of ceramic industry equipment and supplies, glass making machinery and equipment. Entries include: Company name, postal address, telephone, fax, e-mail, website, contact person, designation, and product details.

***Directory of European Importers of Machinery for Rubber Industry***. EXIM Infotek Private Ltd., 604 Vishwa Deep, District Centre, Janakpuri New Delhi 110058, India. Phone: 91 11 25544793; Fax: 91 11 25544793; Email: info@eximinfo.org • URL: http://www.eximinfo.com • Covers: 35 European importers of industrial equipment tires and rubber industry equipment and supplies. Entries include: Company name, postal address, telephone, fax, e-mail, website, contact person, designation, and product details.

***Directory of European Importers of Material Handling Equipment & Supplies***. EXIM Infotek Private Ltd., 604 Vishwa Deep, District Centre, Janakpuri New Delhi 110058, India. Phone: 91 11 25544793; Fax: 91 11 25544793; Email: info@eximinfo.org • URL: http://www.eximinfo.com • Covers: 450 European importers of conveyors, cranes and hoisting equipment, elevating work platforms, elevators lifts, elevators, lifts and escalators, forklifts, handling equipment, lifting and hoisting tools, lifting equipment, liquid handling equipment, loading and unloading equipment, material handling systems for garment industries, monorail materials handling equipment, winches, and pulleys. Entries include: Company name, postal address, telephone, fax, e-mail, website, contact person, designation, and product details.

***Directory of European Importers of Motors and Motor Parts—Electric***. EXIM Infotek Private Ltd., 604 Vishwa Deep, District Centre, Janakpuri New Delhi 110058, India. Phone: 91 11 25544793; Fax: 91 11 25544793; Email: info@eximinfo.org • URL: http://www.eximinfo.com • Covers: 160 European importers of electric motor, gas fuel equipment for motor vehicle, and motor equipment and parts. Entries include: Company name, postal address, telephone, fax, e-mail, website, contact person, designation, and product details.

***Directory of European Importers of Paper & Paper Products***. EXIM Infotek Private Ltd., 604 Vishwa Deep, District Centre, Janakpuri New Delhi 110058, India. Phone: 91 11 25544793; Fax: 91 11 25544793; Email: info@eximinfo.org • URL: http://www.eximinfo.com • Covers: 480 European importers of coated paper, envelopes, handmade paper and products, newsprint, office goods of paper and cardboard, office papers, paper and paper products, wood pulp, paper bags, paper cups and plates, paper waste, photographic paper, printing paper, sanitary and toilet paper goods, sanitary napkins, specialty papers, sugarcane paper, tissue paper, and wrapping articles. Entries include: Company name, postal address, telephone, fax, e-mail, website, contact person, designation, and product details.

***Directory of European Importers of Photographic Equipment and Supplies***. EXIM Infotek Private Ltd., 604 Vishwa Deep, District Centre, Janakpuri New Delhi 110058, India. Phone: 91 11 25544793; Fax: 91 11 25544793; Email: info@eximinfo.org • URL: http://www.eximinfo.com • $600 Individuals; $25 Individuals. Covers: 300 European importers of cameras, lens and accessories, photographic chemicals, motion picture and theater equipment, digital still camera, film, plates and photographic papers, microfilm and blueprint equipment, motion picture films, photo films, photo processing and developing equipment, photocameras, photographic chemicals and papers, photographic equipment and supplies, photographic films for offset reproduction, photographic processing equipment, and thermographic camera. Entries include: Company name, postal address, telephone, fax, e-mail, website, contact person, designation, and product details.

***Directory of European Importers of Plastic Scrap and Raw Materials***. EXIM Infotek Private Ltd., 604 Vishwa Deep, District Centre, Janakpuri New Delhi 110058, India. Phone: 91 11 25544793; Fax: 91 11 25544793; Email: info@eximinfo.org • URL: http://www.eximinfo.com • $550 Individuals; $20 Individuals. Covers: 260 European importers of acrylic polymers, fiberglass resins, low-density polyethylene (LDPE), pet scrap and waste, plastic granules, plastic raw materials, plastic scrap and waste, polymer and plastic raw materials, polymers for textile and plastic, polypropylene, polyvinyl chloride, polypropylene raw material, ABS/PC and pet raw materials, HDPE and pet raw materials, PVC raw materials, and reagents. Entries include: Company name, postal address, telephone, fax, e-mail, website, contact person, designation, and product details.

***Directory of European Importers of Sewing Machines & Parts***. EXIM Infotek Private Ltd., 604 Vishwa Deep, District Centre, Janakpuri New Delhi 110058, India. Phone: 91 11 25544793; Fax: 91 11 25544793; Email: info@eximinfo.org • URL: http://www.eximinfo.com • $10 Individuals. Covers: 60 European importers of industrial sewing machines and parts, knitting equipment parts and articles, knitting machine needles, and sewing machine needles. Entries include: Company name, postal address, telephone, fax, e-mail, website, contact person, designation, and product details.

***Directory of European Importers of Soap, Detergent and Cleaning Supplies***. EXIM Infotek Private Ltd., 604 Vishwa Deep, District Centre, Janakpuri New Delhi 110058, India. Phone: 91 11 25544793; Fax: 91 11 25544793; Email: info@eximinfo.org • URL: http://www.eximinfo.com • $400 Individuals; $15 Individuals. Covers: 170 European importers of cleaning products, cleaning supplies, soap, detergents, household cleaning products, preparations for soap, and bleach. Entries include: Company name, postal address, telephone, fax, e-mail, website, contact person, designation, and product details.

***Directory of European Importers of Sporting Goods***. EXIM Infotek Private Ltd., 604 Vishwa Deep, District Centre, Janakpuri New Delhi 110058, India. Phone: 91 11 25544793; Fax: 91 11 25544793; Email: info@eximinfo.org • URL: http://www.eximinfo.com • $1,350 Individuals; $55 Individuals. Covers: 610 European importers of balls, baseball supplies, billiard pool equipment and supplies, bowling equipment and supplies, climbing equipment and supplies, footwear, golf equipment and supplies, hiking accessories, uniforms and accessories, mountaineering equipment and supplies, playground equipment, scuba and diving equipment and supply, ski equipment and supplies, ski bindings, snow sports goods, snowmobiles and accessories, soccer training ball, sporting goods and toys, sporting guns and rifles, sports bags, sports gloves, sports inventory, stadium equipment, surfboards, tennis and badminton equipment and supplies, water ski equipment and supplies, water sports equipment and supplies, windsurfing accessories, windsurfing equipment and supplies, and wintersports goods.

***Directory of European Importers of Telephone Instruments and Accessories***. EXIM Infotek Private Ltd., 604 Vishwa Deep, District Centre, Janakpuri New Delhi 110058, India. Phone: 91 11 25544793; Fax: 91 11 25544793; Email: info@eximinfo.org • URL: http://www.eximinfo.com • $600 Individuals; $25 Individuals. Covers: 320 European importers of cellular phone, mobile phone accessories, faces for mobile phone, GSM cellular phone, microphone, headphone, wireless phone, Nokia phone, pagers, beepers, telefax equipment, telephone answering equipment, telephone housing, telephonic switching apparatus, wires and cables. Entries include: Company name, postal address, telephone, fax, e-mail, website, contact person, designation, and product details.

***Directory of European Importers of Vending and Coin Operated Machines***. EXIM Infotek Private Ltd., 604 Vishwa Deep, District Centre, Janakpuri New Delhi 110058, India. Phone: 91 11 25544793; Fax: 91 11 25544793; Email: info@eximinfo.org • URL: http://www.eximinfo.com • $200 Individuals; $10 Individuals. Covers: 60 European importers of vending and coin operated machine. Entries include: Company name, postal address, telephone, fax, e-mail, website, contact person, designation, and product details.

***Directory of European Importers of Wax & Wax Products***. EXIM Infotek Private Ltd., 604 Vishwa Deep, District Centre, Janakpuri New Delhi 110058, India. Phone: 91 11 25544793; Fax: 91 11 25544793; Email: info@eximinfo.org • URL: http://www.eximinfo.com • Covers: 50 European importers of paraffin, paraffin waxes, polishes and creams. Entries include: Company name, postal address, telephone, fax, e-mail, website, contact person, designation, and product details.

***Directory of European Importers of Welding Equipment and Supplies***. EXIM Infotek Private Ltd., 604 Vishwa Deep, District Centre, Janakpuri New Delhi 110058, India. Phone: 91 11 25544793; Fax: 91 11 25544793; Email: info@eximinfo.org • URL: http://www.eximinfo.com • $350 Individuals; $15 Individuals. Covers: 130 European importers of arc welding equipment, electrodes, soldering equipment, welding equipment, and welding supplies. Entries include: Company name, postal address, telephone, fax, e-mail, website, contact person, designation, and product details.

***Directory of European Importers of Wires & Cables—Electrical***. EXIM Infotek Private Ltd., 604 Vishwa Deep, District Centre, Janakpuri New Delhi 110058, India. Phone: 91 11 25544793; Fax: 91 11 25544793; Email: info@eximinfo.org • URL: http://www.eximinfo.com • Covers: 170 European importers of wires and cables. Entries include: Company name, postal address, telephone, fax, e-mail, website, contact person, designation, and product details.

***Directory of European Importers of Woodworking Equipment & Tools***. EXIM Infotek Private Ltd., 604 Vishwa Deep, District Centre, Janakpuri New Delhi 110058, India. Phone: 91 11 25544793; Fax: 91 11 25544793; Email: info@eximinfo.org • URL: http://www.eximinfo.com • Covers: 160 European importers of bamboo, rattan, wicker products, baskets and basket ware, caskets, desks, logs moldings, wooden millwork, oak strips, planks, raw wood, sculptures, wood panels, wood slabs, wooden handicrafts, wooden bedroom furniture, wooden materials, wooden products and woodenware. Entries include: Company name, postal address, telephone, fax, e-mail, website, contact person, designation, and product details.

***Directory of European Importers of Yarns and Threads***. EXIM Infotek Private Ltd., 604 Vishwa Deep, District Centre, Janakpuri New Delhi 110058, India. Phone: 91 11 25544793; Fax: 91 11 25544793; Email: info@eximinfo.org • URL: http://www.eximinfo.com • $550 Individuals; $20 Individuals. Covers: 190 European importers of 100% cotton yarn, acrylic yarn, cotton sewing thread, cotton yarn and thread, embroidery thread, flax yarn, nylon filaments, polyester textured yarn, silk yarn and thread, synthetic elementary filament yarn, synthetic yarn and thread, textured yarn of polymers, twists, wool yarn, and yarn waste. Entries include: Company name, postal address, telephone, fax, e-mail, website, contact person, designation, and product details.

***Directory of European Information Brokers and Consultants***. Information Marketmakers Ltd., 12 City Business Centre, Lower Rd. London SE16 2XB, United Kingdom. Phone: 71 2523108; Fax: 71 2321455 • Annual. $59. Covers: information systems brokers and consultants in Europe. Entries include: Company name, address, phone, name and title of contact, names and titles of key personnel, subject expertise, and description of products and services.

***Directory of Exporting Industrialists***. Istanbul Chamber of Industry, Mesrutiyet cad. 118 Tepebasi 80050 Istanbul, Turkey. Phone: 1 2522900; Fax: 1 2454937 • Annual. $8 Restricted circulation. Covers: Approximately 700 exporting industrialist members of the Istanbul Chamber of Industry. Entries include: Company name, address, phone, telex number; Standard Industrial Classification (SIC) code; export amounts; description of products/services offered.

***Directory of Festivals, Schools and Workshops***. Chamber Music America, 243 5th Ave. New York, NY 10016. Phone: (212)242-2022; Fax: (646)430-5667 or (212)242-7955; Email: mlioi@chamber-music.org • URL: http://www.chamber-music.org • Annual. Covers: over 150 chamber music workshops and schools for students, young professionals, and adult amateurs; international listings. Entries include: Name, location or address, description of program and participants sought, procedure for auditions, type of accommodations and recreational facilities, dates, age requirements, and fees as of spring 2000.

***Directory of Fisheries of the Former Soviet Union***. Flegon Press, 37B New Cavendish St. London W1M 8JR, United Kingdom. Phone: 44 181 752 1296; Fax: 44 181 752 1296 • $100. Covers: Fisheries of the former USSR, including production associations, research and design institutes, nautical and fishery schools, shipyards, fishing gear factories, netting mills, fish processing and breeding plants, fish farms, and retail fish vendors among others. Entries include: Name, address, phone, telex, managing personnel.

***Directory of Florida Industries***. Florida Chamber of Commerce, PO Box 11309 Tallahassee, FL 32302-3309. Phone: (850)521-1200; Email: info@flchamber.com • URL: http://www.flchamber.com • Annual. Covers: About 15,300 manufacturing, mining, and processing concerns with 4 or more employees. Entries include: Company name, address, phone, names of principal executives, number of employees, products or services, Standard Industrial Classification (SIC) numbers, whether firm imports or exports.

***Directory of Foreign Buyers, Importers of Food and Agro Based Products***. NIIR Project Consultancy Services, 106 - E, Kamla Nagar New Delhi 110007, India. Phone: 91 11 23843955; Fax: 91 11 23841561; Email: npcs.india@gmail.com • URL: http://www.niir.org • Rs 1,686 Individuals CD-ROM; $100 Individuals CD-ROM. Covers: 1,000 buyers/importers of food and agro-based products, processed food, additives and ingredients. Entries include: Company name, full postal address, phone, fax, email (wherever available), website address (wherever available).

***Directory of Foreign Firms Operating in the United States***. Uniworld Business Publications Inc., 6 Seward Ave. Beverly, MA 01915. Phone: (978)927-0219; Email: info@uniworldbp.com • URL: http://www.uniworldbp.com • Biennial. $350 Individuals hardcover plus s&h. Covers: Approximately 4,900 firms in 86 countries that own or have substantial investments in about 18,250 U.S. Companies. Entries include: Company name, address, phone, fax, name of chief executive officer, number of employees, annual sales, web address, product or service; affiliated U.S. company name, address, phone, fax, name of chief executive, number of employees, product or service, percent foreign-owned. Separate country editions are also available.

***Directory of Foreign Investors That Invest in U.S.A. Property and Real Estate***. Communication Network International Inc., 3918 Ave. T Brooklyn, NY 11234-5028. Phone: (718)339-6245; Fax: (718)998-5915 • Biennial. $650. Covers: more than 3,500 investors. Entries include: Personal name, address; United States representative name, address, phone; approximate dollar amount of U.S. investments.

***Directory of Foreign Manufacturers in the United States***. Georgia State University Business Press, College of Business Administration, University Plz. Atlanta, GA 30303-3093. Phone: (404)651-4253; Fax: (404)651-4256 • Biennial. $195 payment must accompany orders from individuals. Covers: over 7,300 United States manufacturing, mining, and petroleum companies, and the over 6,800 firms abroad that own them. Entries include: Company name, address, phone, fax, products or services, Standard Industrial Classification (SIC) codes, parent company name and address.

***Directory of French Importers of Advertising and Display Articles and Supplies***. EXIM Infotek Private Ltd., 604 Vishwa Deep, District Centre, Janakpuri New Delhi 110058, India. Phone: 91 11 25544793; Fax: 91 11 25544793; Email: info@eximinfo.org • URL: http://www.eximinfo.com • $150 Individuals; $5 Individuals. Covers: 35 French importers of advertising articles, displays, flags, banners, and signs. Entries include: Company name, postal address, telephone, fax, e-mail, website, contact person, designation, and product details.

***Directory of French Importers of Computer Hardwares and Peripherals***. EXIM Infotek Private Ltd., 604 Vishwa Deep, District Centre, Janakpuri New Delhi 110058, India. Phone: 91 11 25544793; Fax: 91 11 25544793; Email: info@eximinfo.org • URL: http://www.eximinfo.com • $400 Individuals; $15 Individuals. Covers: 150 French importers of computer equipment and supplies, computer peripherals, computer components, LAN/network hardware and software, and laser printers. Entries include: Company name, postal address, telephone, fax, e-mail, website, contact person, designation, and product details.

***Directory of French Importers of Computer Softwares***. EXIM Infotek Private Ltd., 604 Vishwa Deep, District Centre, Janakpuri New Delhi 110058, India. Phone: 91 11 25544793; Fax: 91 11 25544793; Email: info@eximinfo.org • URL: http://www.eximinfo.com • $150 Individuals; $5 Individuals. Covers: 40 French importers of computer software. Entries include: Company name, postal address, telephone, fax, e-mail, website, contact person, designation, and product details.

***Directory of French Importers of Construction Machinery and Equipment***. EXIM Infotek Private Ltd., 604 Vishwa Deep, District Centre, Janakpuri New Delhi 110058, India. Phone: 91 11 25544793; Fax: 91 11 25544793; Email: info@eximinfo.org • URL: http://www.eximinfo.com • $150 Individuals; $5 Individuals. Covers: 40 French importers of construction, building equipment and parts, excavating equipment, industrial and construction vehicles, scale model and construction kit, and street maintenance equipment. Entries include: Company name, postal address, telephone, fax, e-mail, website, contact person, designation, and product details.

***Directory of French Importers of Environmental and Pollution Control Equipment***. EXIM Infotek Private Ltd., 604 Vishwa Deep, District Centre, Janakpuri New Delhi 110058, India. Phone: 91 11 25544793; Fax: 91 11 25544793; Email: info@eximinfo.org • URL: http://www.eximinfo.com • Covers: 30 French importers of environmental protection equipment, pollution control equipment, water treatment, and purifying equipment. Entries include: Company name, postal address, telephone, fax, e-mail, website, contact person, designation, and product details.

***Directory of French Importers of Juices and Soft Drinks***. EXIM Infotek Private Ltd., 604 Vishwa Deep, District Centre, Janakpuri New Delhi 110058, India. Phone: 91 11 25544793; Fax: 91 11 25544793; Email: info@eximinfo.org • URL: http://www.eximinfo.com • $150 Individuals; $5 Individuals. Covers: 20 French importers of fruit and vegetable juices, mineral water, non-alcoholic beverages, and soft drinks. Entries include: Company name, postal address, telephone, fax, e-mail, website, contact person, designation, and product details.

***Directory of French Importers of Laboratory & Scientific Instruments & Supplies***. EXIM Infotek Private Ltd., 604 Vishwa Deep, District Centre, Janakpuri New Delhi 110058, India. Phone: 91 11 25544793; Fax: 91 11 25544793; Email: info@eximinfo.org • URL: http://www.eximinfo.com • Covers: 110 French importers of binoculars, microscopes, binoculars, telescopes, scientific and laboratory instruments, and testing equipment. Entries include: Company name, postal address, telephone, fax, e-mail, website, contact person, designation, and product details.

***Directory of French Importers of Lumber, Timber, Plywood and Hardboards***. EXIM Infotek Private Ltd., 604 Vishwa Deep, District Centre, Janakpuri New Delhi 110058, India. Phone: 91 11 25544793; Fax: 91 11 25544793; Email: info@eximinfo.org • URL: http://www.eximinfo.com • $200 Individuals; $10 Individuals. Covers: 60 French importers of doors, windows, hardboard and particleboard, hardwood flooring, floor tiles, wood laminates, lumber goods, lumber, timber, plywood, hardwood lumber, softwood lumber, plywood, veneer, poles, wood, pilings and logs. Entries include: Company name, postal address, telephone, fax, e-mail, website, contact person, designation, and product details.

***Directory of French Importers of Material Handling Equipment***. EXIM Infotek Private Ltd., 604 Vishwa Deep, District Centre, Janakpuri New Delhi 110058, India. Phone: 91 11 25544793; Fax: 91 11 25544793; Email: info@eximinfo.org • URL: http://www.eximinfo.com • $250 Individuals; $10 Individuals. Covers: 70 French importers of conveyors, cranes and hoisting equipment, elevators lifts, forklifts, liquid handling equipment, loading and unloading equipment, materials handling equipment and parts, winches, and pulleys. Entries include: Company name, postal address, telephone, fax, e-mail, website, contact person, designation, and product details.

***Directory of French Importers of Photographic Equipment and Supplies***. EXIM Infotek Private Ltd., 604 Vishwa Deep, District Centre, Janakpuri New Delhi 110058, India. Phone: 91 11 25544793; Fax: 91 11 25544793; Email: info@eximinfo.org • URL: http://www.eximinfo.com • $150 Individuals; $5 Individuals. Covers: 25 French importers of cameras, lenses and accessories, photographic chemicals motion picture and theater equipment, film, plate photographic papers, microfilm and blueprint equipment, photo processing and developing equipment, photographic equipment and supplies. Entries include: Company name, postal address, telephone, fax, e-mail, website, contact person, designation, and product details.

***Directory of French Importers of Plastics Scrap and Raw Materials***. EXIM Infotek Private Ltd., 604 Vishwa Deep, District Centre, Janakpuri New Delhi 110058, India. Phone: 91 11 25544793; Fax: 91 11 25544793; Email: info@eximinfo.org • URL: http://www.eximinfo.com • $150 Individuals; $5 Individuals. Covers: 20 French importers of plastic raw materials and reagents. Entries include: Company name, postal address, telephone, fax, e-mail, website, contact person, designation, and product details.

***Directory of French Importers of Refrigeration Equipment and Supplies***. EXIM Infotek Private Ltd., 604 Vishwa Deep, District Centre, Janakpuri New Delhi 110058, India. Phone: 91 11 25544793; Fax: 91 11 25544793; Email: info@eximinfo.org • URL: http://www.eximinfo.com • Covers: 20 French importers of freezers, refrigerators, and refrigeration equipment. Entries include: Company name, postal address, telephone, fax, e-mail, website, contact person, designation, and product details.

***Directory of French Importers of Soap, Detergents and Cleaning Supplies***. EXIM Infotek Private Ltd., 604 Vishwa Deep, District Centre, Janakpuri New Delhi 110058, India. Phone: 91 11 25544793; Fax: 91 11 25544793; Email: info@eximinfo.org • URL: http://www.eximinfo.com • $150 Individuals; $5 Individuals. Covers: 25 French importers of cleaning supplies, soap, and detergent. Entries include: Company name, postal address, telephone, fax, e-mail, website, contact person, designation, and product details.

***Directory of French Importers of Sporting Goods***. EXIM Infotek Private Ltd., 604 Vishwa Deep, District Centre, Janakpuri New Delhi 110058, India. Phone: 91 11 25544793; Fax: 91 11 25544793; Email: info@eximinfo.org • URL: http://www.eximinfo.com • $250 Individuals; $10 Individuals. Covers: 80 French importers of firearms, golf equipment and supplies, playground equipment, scuba and diving equipment and supply, ski equipment and supplies, sporting goods and toys, sporting goods, tennis and badminton equipment and supplies, water sports equipment and supplies. Entries include: Company name, postal address, telephone, fax, e-mail, website, contact person, designation, and product details.

**Directory of Fund Raising and Nonprofit Management Consultants**. Taft Group, 27500 Drake Rd. Farmington Hills, MI 48331-3535. Phone: 800-877-4253 or (248)699-4253 or (248)699-GALE; Fax: (800)414-5043 or (248)699-8061; Email: gale.salesassistance@thomson.com • URL: http://www.gale.com/taft • $49. Covers: 1,500 consultants and training organizations for nonprofit groups. Entries include: Organization name, address, phone, fax, year founded, publications and videos, partners or executives, description of service.

**Directory of German Importers of Alcoholic Beverages and Wines**. EXIM Infotek Private Ltd., 604 Vishwa Deep, District Centre, Janakpuri New Delhi 110058, India. Phone: 91 11 25544793; Fax: 91 11 25544793; Email: info@eximinfo.org • URL: http://www.eximinfo.com • Covers: 50 German importers of alcoholic beverages, beer, ale, distilled spirits, rum, whisky, wine, and alcoholic beverages. Entries include: Company name, postal address, telephone, fax, e-mail, website, contact person, designation, and product details.

**Directory of German Importers of Carpets, Durries and Floor Coverings**. EXIM Infotek Private Ltd., 604 Vishwa Deep, District Centre, Janakpuri New Delhi 110058, India. Phone: 91 11 25544793; Fax: 91 11 25544793; Email: info@eximinfo.org • URL: http://www.eximinfo.com • $200 Individuals; $10 Individuals. Covers: 20 German importers of carpets, rugs, coir mats, coir mattings, floor coverings, and oriental rugs. Entries include: Company name, postal address, telephone, fax, e-mail, website, contact person, designation, and product details.

**Directory of German Importers of Computer Hardwares and Peripherals**. EXIM Infotek Private Ltd., 604 Vishwa Deep, District Centre, Janakpuri New Delhi 110058, India. Phone: 91 11 25544793; Fax: 91 11 25544793; Email: info@eximinfo.org • URL: http://www.eximinfo.com • $250 Individuals; $10 Individuals. Covers: 70 German importers of CD-ROM, computer equipment and supplies, computer peripherals, computer components, LAN/network hardware and software, toner, and cartridges. Entries include: Company name, postal address, telephone, fax, e-mail, website, contact person, designation, and product details.

**Directory of German Importers of Computer Softwares**. EXIM Infotek Private Ltd., 604 Vishwa Deep, District Centre, Janakpuri New Delhi 110058, India. Phone: 91 11 25544793; Fax: 91 11 25544793; Email: info@eximinfo.org • URL: http://www.eximinfo.com • $150 Individuals; $5 Individuals. Covers: 30 German importers of CAD software and computer software. Entries include: Company name, postal address, telephone, fax, e-mail, website, contact person, designation, and product details.

**Directory of German Importers of Laboratory & Scientific Instruments & Supplies**. EXIM Infotek Private Ltd., 604 Vishwa Deep, District Centre, Janakpuri New Delhi 110058, India. Phone: 91 11 25544793; Fax: 91 11 25544793; Email: info@eximinfo.org • URL: http://www.eximinfo.com • $250 Individuals; $10 Individuals. Covers: 50 German importers of binoculars, microscopes, telescopes, scientific and laboratory instrument, and testing equipment. Entries include: Company name, postal address, telephone, fax, e-mail, website, contact person, designation, and product details.

**Directory of German Importers of Lumber, Timber, Plywood and Hardboards**. EXIM Infotek Private Ltd., 604 Vishwa Deep, District Centre, Janakpuri New Delhi 110058, India. Phone: 91 11 25544793; Fax: 91 11 25544793; Email: info@eximinfo.org • URL: http://www.eximinfo.com • $250 Individuals; $10 Individuals. Covers: 60 German importers of doors, windows, glued timber, hardboard, particleboard, hardwood flooring, floor tiles, laminates, wood laminates, lumber, timber, plywood, hardwood lumber, softwood lumber, parquet, pine wood, planed wood, veneer, poles, pilings and logs, round logs, softwood, solid wood, wood, and wooden moldings. Entries include: Company name, postal address, telephone, fax, e-mail, website, contact person, designation, and product details.

**Directory of German Importers of Photographic Equipment and Supplies**. EXIM Infotek Private Ltd., 604 Vishwa Deep, District Centre, Janakpuri New Delhi 110058, India. Phone: 91 11 25544793; Fax: 91 11 25544793; Email: info@eximinfo.org • URL: http://www.eximinfo.com • $150 Individuals; $5 Individuals. Covers: 25 German importers of cameras, lens and accessories, motion picture and theater equipment, film, plate and photographic papers, photographic equipment and supplies. Entries include: Company name, postal address, telephone, fax, e-mail, website, contact person, designation, and product details.

**Directory of German Importers of Sporting Goods**. EXIM Infotek Private Ltd., 604 Vishwa Deep, District Centre, Janakpuri New Delhi 110058, India. Phone: 91 11 25544793; Fax: 91 11 25544793; Email: info@eximinfo.org • URL: http://www.eximinfo.com • Covers: 40 German importers of golf equipment and supplies, mountaineering equipment and supplies, scuba and diving equipment and supply, ski equipment and supplies, sporting goods and toys, sporting goods, tennis

and badminton equipment and supplies, water ski equipment and supplies, and water sports equipment and supplies. Entries include: Company name, postal address, telephone, fax, e-mail, website, contact person, designation, and product details.

**Directory of German Importers of Telephone Instruments and Accessories**. EXIM Infotek Private Ltd., 604 Vishwa Deep, District Centre, Janakpuri New Delhi 110058, India. Phone: 91 11 25544793; Fax: 91 11 25544793; Email: info@eximinfo.org • URL: http://www.eximinfo.com • $200 Individuals; $10 Individuals. Covers: 40 German importers of mobile phone, cellular phone accessories, microphone, Nokia phone, telefax equipment, and telephone answering equipment. Entries include: Company name, postal address, telephone, fax, e-mail, website, contact person, designation, and product details.

**Directory of Global eCommerce Companies**. Nandini Institute of Chemical Industries, M 60/1 IV Cross St., Besant Nagar Chennai 600 090, India. Phone: 91 44 24961346; Fax: 91 44 24916037; Email: info@nandinichemical.com • URL: http://www.nandinichemical.com • $50. Covers: List of names and addresses of eCommerce companies.

**Directory of High Volume Independent Restaurants**. Chain Store Guide, 10117 Princess Palm Dr. Tampa, FL 33610. Phone: 800-927-9292 or (813)627-6800; Fax: (813)627-6888 or (813)627-6883; Email: info@csgis.com • URL: http://www.chainstoreguide.com • Annual. $1,375 Individuals online pro plus; $1,075 Individuals online pro; $445 Individuals online lite. Approximately 4,200 independently owned restaurants with annual sales of at least $1 million.

**Directory of Hong Kong Traders**. Hong Kong Productivity Council, HKPC Bldg., 78 Tat Chee Ave. Hong Kong, China. Phone: 852 27885678; Fax: 852 27885900 • URL: http://www.hkpc.org • $380 pick up at HKPC Office; $430 delivery by courier within Hong Kong; $85 airmail to countries in southeast Asia; $90 airmail to countries outside southeast Asia. Covers: major traders in Hong Kong, over 8,000 products, and 7,000 brand names. Entries include: Companies—name, address, phone, fax, number of employees, sales turnover, major products, and brand names.

**Directory of ICT Companies in Mauritius**. National Computer Board, Stratton Ct., 7th Fl., La Poudriere St. Port Louis 0511, Mauritius. Phone: 230 2105520; Fax: 230 2124240; Email: contact@ncb.mu • URL: http://www.operators.ict.mu • Annual. Covers: 300 companies operating in the ICT sector in Mauritius in a wide range of activities including software development, call centre, BPO, web-enabled activities, training, hardware assembly and sales, networking and other support services. Entries include: Company name, address, phone, fax, e-mail, website, directors, contact person, number of employees, company profile, competencies, export markets, products, and services.

**Directory of Importers**. IBCON S.A., Gutenberg 224, Col. Anzures 11590 Mexico, Mexico. Phone: 52 55 52554577; Email: ibcon@ibcon.com.mx • URL: http://www.ibcon.com.mx • Irregular. $488 Individuals. 2,284 Mexican companies importing at least $1,000,000 a year, for their own supplies or commercial distribution with executive in charge of imports.

**Directory of Incorporated (Registered) Companies in Nigeria**. ICIC Ltd., Directory House, 6 Taoridi St., POB 7536, Surulere Lagos, Nigeria. • Biennial. $50; $100. Covers: Companies from 1912 to present in Nigeria. Entries include: Company name, address.

**Directory of Indian Importers of Computer Softwares**. EXIM Infotek Private Ltd., 604 Vishwa Deep, District Centre, Janakpuri New Delhi 110058, India. Phone: 91 11 25544793; Fax: 91 11 25544793; Email: info@eximinfo.org • URL: http://www.eximinfo.com • $150 Individuals; $5 Individuals. Covers: 30 Indian importers of computer software and LAN/network hardware. Entries include: Company name, postal address, telephone, fax, e-mail, website, contact person, designation, and product details.

**Directory of Indian Importers of Construction Machinery and Equipment**. EXIM Infotek Private Ltd., 604 Vishwa Deep, District Centre, Janakpuri New Delhi 110058, India. Phone: 91 11 25544793; Fax: 91 11 25544793; Email: info@eximinfo.org • URL: http://www.eximinfo.com • $200 Individuals; $10 Individuals. Covers: 50 Indian importers of construction and building equipment, construction machinery, earthmoving spare parts, excavating equipment, spare parts for earthmoving machinery, and spare parts for heavy construction machine. Entries include: Company name, postal address, telephone, fax, e-mail, website, contact person, designation, and product details.

**Directory of Indian Importers of Dyes, Colors, and Pigments**. EXIM Infotek Private Ltd., 604 Vishwa Deep, District Centre, Janakpuri New Delhi 110058, India. Phone: 91 11 25544793; Fax: 91 11 25544793; Email: info@eximinfo.org • URL: http://www.eximinfo.com • $350 Individuals; $15 Individuals. Covers: 80 Indian importers of activated carbon, dye, dye intermediates, colors, pigments, dyestuff, ink, and leather chemicals. Entries include: Company name, postal address, telephone, fax, e-mail, website, contact person, designation, and product details.

**Directory of Indian Importers of Fibre Products**. EXIM Infotek Private Ltd., 604 Vishwa Deep, District Centre, Janakpuri New Delhi 110058, India. Phone: 91 11 25544793; Fax: 91

11 25544793; Email: info@eximinfo.org • URL: http://www.eximinfo.com • $200 Individuals; $10 Individuals. Covers: 45 Indian importers of acrylic fiber, fiber waste, fiberglass, fiberglass cloth, fiberglass products, staple fiber, and synthetic fiber. Entries include: Company name, postal address, telephone, fax, e-mail, website, contact person, designation, and product details.

**Directory of Indian Importers of Fire Fighting Equipment & Supplies**. EXIM Infotek Private Ltd., 604 Vishwa Deep, District Centre, Janakpuri New Delhi 110058, India. Phone: 91 11 25544793; Fax: 91 11 25544793; Email: info@eximinfo.org • URL: http://www.eximinfo.com • Covers: 20 Indian importers of fire alarm panels, fire alarm systems, fire detection systems, fire extinguishers, fire fighting equipment, and fire hydrants. Entries include: Company name, postal address, telephone, fax, e-mail, website, contact person, designation, and product details.

**Directory of Indian Importers of Food Additives and Aromatics**. EXIM Infotek Private Ltd., 604 Vishwa Deep, District Centre, Janakpuri New Delhi 110058, India. Phone: 91 11 25544793; Fax: 91 11 25544793; Email: info@eximinfo.org • URL: http://www.eximinfo.com • $5 Individuals; $150 Individuals. Covers: 40 Indian importers of aroma chemicals, flavors, food additives, food colors, fragrances, and vanillin (pollar Br). Entries include: Company name, postal address, telephone, fax, e-mail, website, contact person, designation, and product details.

**Directory of Indian Importers of Heaters and Heating Equipment**. EXIM Infotek Private Ltd., 604 Vishwa Deep, District Centre, Janakpuri New Delhi 110058, India. Phone: 91 11 25544793; Fax: 91 11 25544793; Email: info@eximinfo.org • URL: http://www.eximinfo.com • Covers: 20 Indian importers of heat exchangers, heaters, and heating equipment. Entries include: Company name, postal address, telephone, fax, e-mail, website, contact person, designation, and product details.

**Directory of Indian Importers of Herbs & Herbal Medicine Products**. EXIM Infotek Private Ltd., 604 Vishwa Deep, District Centre, Janakpuri New Delhi 110058, India. Phone: 91 11 25544793; Fax: 91 11 25544793; Email: info@eximinfo.org • URL: http://www.eximinfo.com • $200 Individuals; $10 Individuals. Covers: 30 Indian importers of herbs, legumes, medicinal herbs, and botanicals. Entries include: Company name, postal address, telephone, fax, e-mail, website, contact person, designation, and product details.

**Directory of Indian Importers of Laboratory & Scientific Instruments & Supplies**. EXIM Infotek Private Ltd., 604 Vishwa Deep, District Centre, Janakpuri New Delhi 110058, India. Phone: 91 11 25544793; Fax: 91 11 25544793; Email: info@eximinfo.org • URL: http://www.eximinfo.com • $300 Individuals; $10 Individuals. Covers: 120 Indian importers of binoculars, microscope, telescopes, borosilicate glass tubing, educational scientific equipment, laboratory equipment, laboratory glassware, laboratory instruments, scientific instruments, testing and measuring equipment, testing instruments, thermometers, and barometers. Entries include: Company name, postal address, telephone, fax, e-mail, website, contact person, designation, and product details.

**Directory of Indian Importers of Lumber, Timber, Plywood and Hardboards**. EXIM Infotek Private Ltd., 604 Vishwa Deep, District Centre, Janakpuri New Delhi 110058, India. Phone: 91 11 25544793; Fax: 91 11 25544793; Email: info@eximinfo.org • URL: http://www.eximinfo.com • $250 Individuals; $10 Individuals. Covers: 80 Indian importers of gypsum board, hard boards, wood laminates, logs, hardwood lumber, softwood lumber, particle boards, plywood, veneer, poles, pilings and logs, sheetrock, spruce logs, teak wood, timber, timber logs, veneer sheets, and wood. Entries include: Company name, postal address, telephone, fax, e-mail, website, contact person, designation, and product details.

**Directory of Indian Importers of Material Handling Equipment & Supplies**. EXIM Infotek Private Ltd., 604 Vishwa Deep, District Centre, Janakpuri New Delhi 110058, India. Phone: 91 11 25544793; Fax: 91 11 25544793; Email: info@eximinfo.org • URL: http://www.eximinfo.com • $150 Individuals; $5 Individuals. Covers: 20 Indian importers of loading equipment, unloading equipment, and materials handling equipment. Entries include: Company name, postal address, telephone, fax, e-mail, website, contact person, designation, and product details.

**Directory of Indian Importers of Minerals**. EXIM Infotek Private Ltd., 604 Vishwa Deep, District Centre, Janakpuri New Delhi 110058, India. Phone: 91 11 25544793; Fax: 91 11 25544793; Email: info@eximinfo.org • URL: http://www.eximinfo.com • Covers: 80 Indian Importers of borax, graphite, iron ore, lead, mica, mineral oil, minerals, ores, sulfur, zinc, and zirconium sand. Entries include: Company name, postal address, telephone, fax, e-mail, website, contact person, designation, and product details.

**Directory of Indian Importers of Paper & Paper Products**. EXIM Infotek Private Ltd., 604 Vishwa Deep, District Centre, Janakpuri New Delhi 110058, India. Phone: 91 11 25544793; Fax: 91 11 25544793; Email: info@eximinfo.org • URL: http://www.eximinfo.com • $450 Individuals; $20 Individuals. Covers: 200 Indian importers of absorbent tissue, art paper, base paper, coated paper, decorative paper, kraft paper, newsprints paper, paper and paper boards, paper products, wood pulp, paper bags, paper waste, printing paper, sanitary and toilet paper goods, sanitary napkins, specialty paper, thermal paper reels for fax, and tissue paper. Entries include: Company name, postal address, telephone, fax, e-mail, website, contact person, designation, and product details.

***Directory of Indian Importers of Plastic Scrap and Raw Materials***. EXIM Infotek Private Ltd., 604 Vishwa Deep, District Centre, Janakpuri New Delhi 110058, India. Phone: 91 11 25544793; Fax: 91 11 25544793; Email: info@eximinfo.org • URL: http://www.eximinfo.com • $600 Individuals; $25 Individuals. Covers: 200 Indian importers of ABS scrap, acrylamide, butyl acrylate, granules, HD, high-density polyethylene (HDPE), HDPE granules, HMS scrap, low-density polyethylene (LDPE), LDPE granules, linear low-density polyethylene (LLDPE), master batches, plastic granules, plastic raw materials, plastic scrap and waste, polycarbonate, polypropylene, polymers, polypropylene scraps, polypropylene granules, polyurethane chemicals, polyurethane resin, polyvinyl alcohol, polytetrafluoroethylene (PTFE) products, PVC compound, PVC resin, raw materials, and styrene monomer. Entries include: Company name, postal address, telephone, fax, e-mail, website, contact person, designation, and product details.

***Directory of Indian Importers of Wax & Wax Products***. EXIM Infotek Private Ltd., 604 Vishwa Deep, District Centre, Janakpuri New Delhi 110058, India. Phone: 91 11 25544793; Fax: 91 11 25544793; Email: info@eximinfo.org • URL: http://www.eximinfo.com • Covers: 30 Indian importers of micro waxes, paraffin waxes, polishes and creams, and slack waxes. Entries include: Company name, postal address, telephone, fax, e-mail, website, contact person, designation, and product details.

***Directory of Indian Importers of Wires & Cables—Electrical***. EXIM Infotek Private Ltd., 604 Vishwa Deep, District Centre, Janakpuri New Delhi 110058, India. Phone: 91 11 25544793; Fax: 91 11 25544793; Email: info@eximinfo.org • URL: http://www.eximinfo.com • Covers: 40 Indian importers of cables, copper wires, power cords, thermocouple wire, and wires and cables. Entries include: Company name, postal address, telephone, fax, e-mail, website, contact person, designation, and product details.

***Directory of Indian Importers of Yarns and Threads***. EXIM Infotek Private Ltd., 604 Vishwa Deep, District Centre, Janakpuri New Delhi 110058, India. Phone: 91 11 25544793; Fax: 91 11 25544793; Email: info@eximinfo.org • URL: http://www.eximinfo.com • $400 Individuals; $15 Individuals. Covers: 90 Indian importers of cotton yarn, dupion silk yarn, fibers, yarns, filament yarn, man-made yarn, metallic yarn and thread, nylon yarn, polyester yarn, raw silk yarn, sewing threads, silk yarn and thread, synthetic yarn and thread, viscose yarn, wool yarn, and yarn waste. Entries include: Company name, postal address, telephone, fax, e-mail, website, contact person, designation, and product details.

***Directory of Industrial Suppliers***. Hong Kong Productivity Council, HKPC Bldg., 78 Tat Chee Ave. Hong Kong, China. Phone: 852 27885678; Fax: 852 27885900 • URL: http://www.hkpc.org • Annual. $280 pick up at HKPC Office; $310 delivery by courier within Hong Kong; $75 airmail to countries in Southeast Asia; $80 airmail to countries outside Southeast Asia. Covers: Over 3,000 industrial suppliers in Hong Kong as well as their operations in Mainland China. Entries include: Name, address, phone, fax, e-mail, URL, number of employees, turnover, and products/brand names.

***Directory of International Benefits***. AP Information Services Ltd., c/o Wilmington Publishing & Information Ltd., 6-14 Underworld St. London N1 7JQ, United Kingdom. Phone: 44 20 75498708; Fax: 44 20 74908238; Email: info@apinfo.co.uk • URL: http://www.apinfo.co.uk • Irregular. $78.50 bpd. Publication includes: List of private organizations worldwide providing information on international employee benefits, including actuarial benefits, insurance companies and associations, benefit consultants, publishing companies, property managers, and accounting, communication, and legal firms. Database includes: Statistics on education, working population, economics, business, and benefit surveys. Entries include: Company name, address, phone, contact person, fax, telex, parent and subsidiary companies.

***Directory of International Buyers***. Auto Care Association, 7101 Wisconsin Ave., Ste. 1300 Bethesda, MD 20814-3415. Phone: (301)654-6664; Fax: (301)654-3299; Email: info@autocare.org • URL: http://www.autocare.org • Annual. $70. Covers: 650 foreign firms that attended the association's annual show. Entries include: Company name, address, name and title of contact, type of buyer.

***Directory of International Chambers of Commerce in the World***. EXIM Infotek Private Ltd., 604 Vishwa Deep, District Centre, Janakpuri New Delhi 110058, India. Phone: 91 11 25544793; Fax: 91 11 25544793; Email: info@eximinfo.org • URL: http://www.eximinfo.com • $55 Individuals. Covers: 1,000 international chambers of commerce. Entries include: Company name, postal address, telephone, fax, e-mail, website, contact person, designation, and product details.

***Directory of International Corporate Giving in America and Abroad***. Taft Group, 27500 Drake Rd. Farmington Hills, MI 48331-3535. Phone: 800-877-4253 or (248)699-4253 or (248)699-GALE; Fax: (800)414-5043 or (248)699-8061; Email: gale.salesassistance@thomson.com • URL: http://

www.gale.com/taft • $215. Covers: 443 foreign-owned companies that support nonprofit organizations in the U.S., and 170 U.S. companies that support organizations overseas. Entries include: Corporation name, foundation name; name, title, and phone of contact; location of U.S. headquarters, number of employees, total foundation assets, name and address of overseas parent company; summary of grant support, including amounts given, geographical area and types of activities preferred, and recently funded programs.

***Directory of International Sources of Business Information***. Pearson Education Ltd., Edinburgh Gate Harlow CM20 2JE, United Kingdom. Phone: 44 01279 623 623; Fax: 44 0870 850 5255 • URL: http://www.pearsoned.co.uk • Annual. $85. Covers: Sources of business information worldwide, including business information brokers, Euro-Info centers, banks, stockbrokers, associations, embassies and councils, market research organizations, economic and statistical organizations, publishers, publications, online databases, and United Kingdom packet switching exchanges. Entries include: For business information brokers and Euro-Info centers—Name, address, phone, fax, host and databases accessed, subject areas covered, languages spoken, description of services offered. For banks, stockbrokers, associations, embassies and councils, market research organizations, economic and statistical organizations, and publications—Name, address, phone. For online databases—Name, address, phone, host. For United Kingdom packet switching exchanges—Phone. For publishers—Name, address, phone, fax, telex.

***Directory of International Trade & Industrial Association in the World***. EXIM Infotek Private Ltd., 604 Vishwa Deep, District Centre, Janakpuri New Delhi 110058, India. Phone: 91 11 25544793; Fax: 91 11 25544793; Email: info@eximinfo.org • URL: http://www.eximinfo.com • Covers: 2,150 international trade and industrial associations. Entries include: Company name, postal address, telephone, fax, e-mail, website, contact person, designation, and product details.

***Directory of Japanese-Affiliated Companies in the USA and Canada***. • URL: http://www.jetro.go.jp • Covers: Over 5,000 Japanese-affiliated companies operating in the United States or Canada. Entries include: Name, address, phone, fax, year of establishment, capital, annual sales, managing directors, and main products/services.

***Directory of Japanese-Affiliated Companies in USA & Canada***. Database S.L., c/o Taylor & Francis Inc., 325 Chesnut St. Philadelphia, PA 19106. Phone: 800-821-8312 or (215)625-8900; Fax: (215)625-2940; Email: info@taylorandfrancis.com • Biennial. $260. Covers: Approximately 8,200 Japanese-affiliated companies operating in North America. Entries include: Company name, address, phone, status, type of business, product/service, names and titles of key personnel, Japanese parent company.

***Directory of Japanese Giving***. Corporate Citizen, 23501 NE Redmond Fall City Rd. Redmond, WA 98053-8377. Phone: (206)329-0422; Fax: (206)325-1382 • $190. Covers: Approximately 190 Japanese firms that participate in philanthropic activities in the U.S. Entries include: Company; name, address, phone; telex, names and titles of key personnel; description of policies, programs, and foundations; history of giving and volunteer activities in the U.S.; U.S. nonprofit organizations funded, geographical area served.

***Directory of Japanese Importers of Alcoholic Beverages and Wines***. EXIM Infotek Private Ltd., 604 Vishwa Deep, District Centre, Janakpuri New Delhi 110058, India. Phone: 91 11 25544793; Fax: 91 11 25544793; Email: info@eximinfo.org • URL: http://www.eximinfo.com • $500 Individuals; $20 Individuals. Covers: 250 Japanese importers of alcoholic beverages, barley malt, beer and ale, bourbon, brandy, distilled spirits, hard liquor, soft liquor, whisky, wine, and alcoholic beverages. Entries include: Company name, postal address, telephone, fax, e-mail, website, contact person, designation, and product details.

***Directory of Japanese Importers of Camping and Backpacking Equipments and Supplies***. EXIM Infotek Private Ltd., 604 Vishwa Deep, District Centre, Janakpuri New Delhi 110058, India. Phone: 91 11 25544793; Fax: 91 11 25544793; Email: info@eximinfo.org • URL: http://www.eximinfo.com • $150 Individuals; $5 Individuals. Covers: 40 Japanese importers of camping and backpacking equipment, camping goods, mountaineering equipment, and outdoor goods. Entries include: Company name, postal address, telephone, fax, e-mail, website, contact person, designation, and product details.

***Directory of Japanese Importers of Carpets, Durries, Rugs and Floor Coverings***. EXIM Infotek Private Ltd., 604 Vishwa Deep, District Centre, Janakpuri New Delhi 110058, India. Phone: 91 11 25544793; Fax: 91 11 25544793; Email: info@eximinfo.org • URL: http://www.eximinfo.com • $250 Individuals; $10 Individuals. Covers: 80 Japanese importers of carpets, rugs, floor coverings, flooring goods, and mats. Entries include: Company name, postal address, telephone, fax, e-mail, website, contact person, designation, and product details.

***Directory of Japanese Importers of Computer Hardwares and Peripherals***. EXIM Infotek Private Ltd., 604 Vishwa Deep, District Centre, Janakpuri New Delhi 110058, India. Phone: 91 11 25544793; Fax: 91 11 25544793; Email: info@eximinfo.org • URL: http://www.eximinfo.com • $350

Individuals; $15 Individuals. Covers: 125 Japanese importers of bar coding equipment, compact disc, computers, computer accessories, computer components, computer equipment and supplies, computer hardware, computer peripherals, computer supplies, printers, information processing equipment and peripherals, ink jet printers, laser printers, LCD monitor, monitors, personal computers, and scanners. Entries include: Company name, postal address, telephone, fax, e-mail, website, contact person, designation, and product details.

***Directory of Japanese Importers of Computer Softwares***. EXIM Infotek Private Ltd., 604 Vishwa Deep, District Centre, Janakpuri New Delhi 110058, India. Phone: 91 11 25544793; Fax: 91 11 25544793; Email: info@eximinfo.org • URL: http://www.eximinfo.com • $200 Individuals; $10 Individuals. Covers: 55 Japanese importers of computer software and internet technology. Entries include: Company name, postal address, telephone, fax, e-mail, website, contact person, designation, and product details.

***Directory of Japanese Importers of Construction Machinery and Equipment***. EXIM Infotek Private Ltd., 604 Vishwa Deep, District Centre, Janakpuri New Delhi 110058, India. Phone: 91 11 25544793; Fax: 91 11 25544793; Email: info@eximinfo.org • URL: http://www.eximinfo.com • $250 Individuals; $10 Individuals. Covers: 80 Japanese importers of construction and building equipment, construction machinery, mixers and pavers, road rollers, scale model and construction kit, shovels, street maintenance equipment, and used construction equipment. Entries include: Company name, postal address, telephone, fax, e-mail, website, contact person, designation, and product details.

***Directory of Japanese Importers of Dyes, Colors, Pigments and Intermediates***. EXIM Infotek Private Ltd., 604 Vishwa Deep, District Centre, Janakpuri New Delhi 110058, India. Phone: 91 11 25544793; Fax: 91 11 25544793; Email: info@eximinfo.org • URL: http://www.eximinfo.com • $300 Individuals; $10 Individuals. Covers: 100 Japanese importers of activated carbon, chemical intermediates, dyes, colors, pigments, dyestuff, dyestuff intermediates, ink, pigment colors and metallic, and printing ink. Entries include: Company name, postal address, telephone, fax, e-mail, website, contact person, designation, and product details.

***Directory of Japanese Importers of Environment and Pollution Control Equipment***. EXIM Infotek Private Ltd., 604 Vishwa Deep, District Centre, Janakpuri New Delhi 110058, India. Phone: 91 11 25544793; Fax: 91 11 25544793; Email: info@eximinfo.org • URL: http://www.eximinfo.com • $200 Individuals; $10 Individuals. Covers: 45 Japanese importers of dust collectors, environmental equipment, environmental protection equipment, environmentally conserving or improving products, noise control equipment, pollution control equipment, water purification equipment, water treatment, water treatment equipment, and purifying equipment. Entries include: Company name, postal address, telephone, fax, e-mail, website, contact person, designation, and product details.

***Directory of Japanese Importers of Fibre and Fibre Products***. EXIM Infotek Private Ltd., 604 Vishwa Deep, District Centre, Janakpuri New Delhi 110058, India. Phone: 91 11 25544793; Fax: 91 11 25544793; Email: info@eximinfo.org • URL: http://www.eximinfo.com • $200 Individuals; $10 Individuals. Covers: 40 Japanese importers of fiber glass cloth, fiber products, glass fibers, natural fiber, and synthetic fiber. Entries include: Company name, postal address, telephone, fax, e-mail, website, contact person, designation, and product details.

***Directory of Japanese Importers of Fishing & Hunting Equipment & Supplies***. EXIM Infotek Private Ltd., 604 Vishwa Deep, District Centre, Janakpuri New Delhi 110058, India. Phone: 91 11 25544793; Fax: 91 11 25544793; Email: info@eximinfo.org • URL: http://www.eximinfo.com • Covers: 35 Japanese importers of fishing and hunting equipment, fishing supplies, fishing nets and floats, and fishing tackles. Entries include: Company name, postal address, telephone, fax, e-mail, website, contact person, designation, and product details.

***Directory of Japanese Importers of Fodder and Animal Foodstuffs***. EXIM Infotek Private Ltd., 604 Vishwa Deep, District Centre, Janakpuri New Delhi 110058, India. Phone: 91 11 25544793; Fax: 91 11 25544793; Email: info@eximinfo.org • URL: http://www.eximinfo.com • $200 Individuals; $10 Individuals. Covers: Japanese importers of animal foodstuff, food additives, feeder calves, fodder, cereals, and livestock products. Entries include: Company name, postal address, telephone, fax, e-mail, website, contact person, designation, and product details.

***Directory of Japanese Importers of Food Additives and Aromatic Chemicals***. EXIM Infotek Private Ltd., 604 Vishwa Deep, District Centre, Janakpuri New Delhi 110058, India. Phone: 91 11 25544793; Fax: 91 11 25544793; Email: info@eximinfo.org • URL: http://www.eximinfo.com • $350 Individuals; $15 Individuals. Covers: 145 Japanese importers of agar-agar, aromatic chemicals, essence, food additives, food colors, food flavors, food ingredients, fragrances, natural coloring matters, raw materials for food colors, and yeasts. Entries include: Company name, postal address, telephone, fax, e-mail, website, contact person, designation, and product details.

***Directory of Japanese Importers of Handkerchieves, Scarves***

***and Neckwears***. EXIM Infotek Private Ltd., 604 Vishwa Deep, District Centre, Janakpuri New Delhi 110058, India. Phone: 91 11 25544793; Fax: 91 11 25544793; Email: info@eximinfo.org • URL: http://www.eximinfo.com • $250 Individuals; $10 Individuals. Covers: 90 Japanese importers of clothing accessories, ties, scarves, handkerchieves, neckwear, mufflers, and silk neckties. Entries include: Company name, postal address, telephone, fax, e-mail, website, contact person, designation, and product details.

***Directory of Japanese Importers of Heaters and Heating Equipment***. EXIM Infotek Private Ltd., 604 Vishwa Deep, District Centre, Janakpuri New Delhi 110058, India. Phone: 91 11 25544793; Fax: 91 11 25544793; Email: info@eximinfo.org • URL: http://www.eximinfo.com • Covers: 35 Japanese importers of heat exchangers, heaters, and heating equipment. Entries include: Company name, postal address, telephone, fax, e-mail, website, contact person, designation, and product details.

***Directory of Japanese Importers of Juices and Soft Drinks***. EXIM Infotek Private Ltd., 604 Vishwa Deep, District Centre, Janakpuri New Delhi 110058, India. Phone: 91 11 25544793; Fax: 91 11 25544793; Email: info@eximinfo.org • URL: http://www.eximinfo.com • $400 Individuals; $15 Individuals. Covers: 180 Japanese importers of beverages, concentrated fruit juices, vegetable juices, fruit puree, mineral water, non-alcoholic beverages, and soft drinks. Entries include: Company name, postal address, telephone, fax, e-mail, website, contact person, designation, and product details.

***Directory of Japanese Importers of Laboratory & Scientific Instruments & Supplies***. EXIM Infotek Private Ltd., 604 Vishwa Deep, District Centre, Janakpuri New Delhi 110058, India. Phone: 91 11 25544793; Fax: 91 11 25544793; Email: info@eximinfo.org • URL: http://www.eximinfo.com • $450 Individuals; $20 Individuals. Covers: 200 Japanese importers of analytical instruments, binoculars, microscopes, telescopes, laboratory and scientific glass, laboratory instruments, laboratory reagents, scientific and laboratory equipment, scientific instruments, testing and measuring equipment, testing instruments, testing machines, thermometers, and barometers. Entries include: Company name, postal address, telephone, fax, e-mail, website, contact person, designation, and product details.

***Directory of Japanese Importers of Lumber, Timber, Plywood and Hardboards***. EXIM Infotek Private Ltd., 604 Vishwa Deep, District Centre, Janakpuri New Delhi 110058, India. Phone: 91 11 25544793; Fax: 91 11 25544793; Email: info@eximinfo.org • URL: http://www.eximinfo.com • $650 Individuals; $25 Individuals. Covers: 340 Japanese importers of bamboo shoots, bamboo and rattan (raw), doors and door frames, windows, gypsum board, hardboard, particleboard, hardwood flooring, floor tiles, hardwood products, laminated lumber, wood laminates, logs, lumber, hardwood lumber, softwood lumber, timber, plywood, medicament plywood, millwork (wooden), veneer, poles, pilings and logs, rattans, sandalwood, sawn goods, sawn timber, sheetrock, teak wood, timber, wood, wood housing products, woodchips, and wooden doors. Entries include: Company name, postal address, telephone, fax, e-mail, website, contact person, designation, and product details.

***Directory of Japanese Importers of Material Handling Equipment***. EXIM Infotek Private Ltd., 604 Vishwa Deep, District Centre, Janakpuri New Delhi 110058, India. Phone: 91 11 25544793; Fax: 91 11 25544793; Email: info@eximinfo.org • URL: http://www.eximinfo.com • $150 Individuals; $5 Individuals. Covers: 40 Japanese importers of conveying machine, conveyors, cranes and hoists, elevators lifts, elevators, lifts and escalators, forklifts, loading and unloading equipment, materials handling equipment and parts. Entries include: Company name, postal address, telephone, fax, e-mail, website, contact person, designation, and product details.

***Directory of Japanese Importers of Minerals***. EXIM Infotek Private Ltd., 604 Vishwa Deep, District Centre, Janakpuri New Delhi 110058, India. Phone: 91 11 25544793; Fax: 91 11 25544793; Email: info@eximinfo.org • URL: http://www.eximinfo.com • Covers: 150 Japanese importers of carbon and graphite products, crucibles made of alumina or quartz, graphite, gypsum, iron ore, limestone, manganese ore, mica, mineral oil, mineral products and raw materials, minerals, ores, rare metal minerals, silica sand, soil, sulfur, and zinc. Entries include: Company name, postal address, telephone, fax, e-mail, website, contact person, designation, and product details.

***Directory of Japanese Importers of Paper & Paper Products***. EXIM Infotek Private Ltd., 604 Vishwa Deep, District Centre, Janakpuri New Delhi 110058, India. Phone: 91 11 25544793; Fax: 91 11 25544793; Email: info@eximinfo.org • URL: http://www.eximinfo.com • Covers: 120 Japanese importers of base paper for coatings, corrugated paper, foreign paper, kraft paper, paper and paper boards, paper products, wood pulp, paper bags, paper boards, paper lantern, paper napkins, paper pulp products article, paperboards, printing paper, pulp, screen paper, special paper, specialty paper, tissue paper, and waste paper. Entries include: Company name, postal address, telephone, fax, e-mail, website, contact person, designation, and product details.

***Directory of Japanese Importers of Plastic Scrap and Raw Materials***. EXIM Infotek Private Ltd., 604 Vishwa Deep, District Centre, Janakpuri New Delhi 110058, India. Phone: 91 11 25544793; Fax: 91 11 25544793; Email: info@eximinfo.org • URL: http://www.eximinfo.com • $200 Individuals; $10 Individuals. Covers: 30 Japanese importers of plastic raw materials, plastic resins, plasticizers, plastics, and plastic additives. Entries include: Company name, postal address, telephone, fax, e-mail, website, contact person, designation, and product details.

***Directory of Japanese Importers of Soap, Detergents and Cleaning Supplies***. EXIM Infotek Private Ltd., 604 Vishwa Deep, District Centre, Janakpuri New Delhi 110058, India. Phone: 91 11 25544793; Fax: 91 11 25544793; Email: info@eximinfo.org • URL: http://www.eximinfo.com • $200 Individuals; $10 Individuals. Covers: 60 Japanese importers of cleaning supplies, detergent, soap chip, soap, toiletry and bathroom preparations. Entries include: Company name, postal address, telephone, fax, e-mail, website, contact person, designation, and product details.

***Directory of Japanese Importers of Woodenware & Wooden Products***. EXIM Infotek Private Ltd., 604 Vishwa Deep, District Centre, Janakpuri New Delhi 110058, India. Phone: 91 11 25544793; Fax: 91 11 25544793; Email: info@eximinfo.org • URL: http://www.eximinfo.com • Covers: 270 Japanese importers of bamboo products, bamboo, rattan and wicker products, bamboo/rattan/wicker products, baskets, baskets and basket ware, chopsticks, folding fan, lacquer ware, rattan baskets, rattan products, softwood products, wood and wooden products, wood articles, wood products, wood pulp products, wooden articles, wooden decoration goods, wooden housing components, wooden interior goods, wooden kitchenware, wooden pallets, wooden products, wooden products, wooden tableware, wooden tray, woodenware, and woodworks. Entries include: Company name, postal address, telephone, fax, e-mail, website, contact person, designation, and product details.

***Directory of Japanese Importers of Yarns and Threads***. EXIM Infotek Private Ltd., 604 Vishwa Deep, District Centre, Janakpuri New Delhi 110058, India. Phone: 91 11 25544793; Fax: 91 11 25544793; Email: info@eximinfo.org • URL: http://www.eximinfo.com • $250 Individuals; $10 Individuals. Covers: 75 Japanese importers of yarns and thread, cotton yarn and thread, silk yarn and thread, synthetic yarn and thread, and yarn twister. Entries include: Company name, postal address, telephone, fax, e-mail, website, contact person, designation, and product details.

***Directory of Japanese Manufacturers & Exporters of Adhesive, Glues & Sealants***. EXIM Infotek Private Ltd., 604 Vishwa Deep, District Centre, Janakpuri New Delhi 110058, India. Phone: 91 11 25544793; Fax: 91 11 25544793; Email: info@eximinfo.org • URL: http://www.eximinfo.com • $5 Individuals. Covers: 20 Japanese manufacturers & exporters of adhesives, epoxy resins, glue, plastic adhesives. Entries include: Company name, postal address, city, country, phone, fax, e-mail & websites, contact person, designation, products detail.

***Directory of Japanese Manufacturers and Exporters of Alcoholic Beverages and Wines***. EXIM Infotek Private Ltd., 604 Vishwa Deep, District Centre, Janakpuri New Delhi 110058, India. Phone: 91 11 25544793; Fax: 91 11 25544793; Email: info@eximinfo.org • URL: http://www.eximinfo.com • Covers: 30 Japanese manufacturers and exporters of beer, beverages, liquor, sake plum wine, and wine. Entries include: Company name, postal address, telephone, fax, e-mail, website, contact person, designation, and product details.

***Directory of Japanese Manufacturers & Exporters of Automobiles & Vehicles***. EXIM Infotek Private Ltd., 604 Vishwa Deep, District Centre, Janakpuri New Delhi 110058, India. Phone: 91 11 25544793; Fax: 91 11 25544793; Email: info@eximinfo.org • URL: http://www.eximinfo.com • $65 Individuals. Covers: 1,570 Japanese manufacturers and exporters of automobiles, buses, cars, motor vehicles, reconditioned cars, trailers, transport equipment, used buses, used cargo trucks, used cars, used commercial vehicles, used mini buses, used motor vehicles, used passenger cars, used trucks, used vans, used vehicles, used vehicles and spare parts, used wagons, vehicles, and wagons for hotel and restaurants. Entries include: Company name, postal address, city, country, phone, fax, e-mail and websites, contact person, designation, and product details.

***Directory of Japanese Manufacturers & Exporters of Automotive Service & Repair Equipment***. EXIM Infotek Private Ltd., 604 Vishwa Deep, District Centre, Janakpuri New Delhi 110058, India. Phone: 91 11 25544793; Fax: 91 11 25544793; Email: info@eximinfo.org • URL: http://www.eximinfo.com • $10 Individuals. Covers: 60 Japanese manufacturers and exporters of automotive emission analysis systems, automotive service equipment, car care tools, grinding wheels, lubricants, and lubricating equipments. Entries include: Company name, postal address, city, country, phone, fax, e-mail and websites, contact person, designation, and product details.

***Directory of Japanese Manufacturers & Exporters of Autoparts & Accessories***. EXIM Infotek Private Ltd., 604 Vishwa Deep, District Centre, Janakpuri New Delhi 110058, India. Phone: 91 11 25544793; Fax: 91 11 25544793; Email: info@eximinfo.org • URL: http://www.eximinfo.com • $35 Individuals. Covers: 530 Japanese manufacturers and exporters of accelerator pedals, clutch pedals, alternators, auto accessories, auto doors, automobile parts and equipment, automobile switches, automotive interior products, automotive lamp accessories, automotive lighting supplies, head lamps, horns, ignition coils, joints-universal, light alloy wheels, motor vehicle parts and supplies, radiators, rear-view mirrors, sealed beam units, seat adjusters, signal and indicator lamps, spare parts, steering columns, steering gears, steering wheels, transmission equipment, transmission parts, truck and bus accessories, truck parts and supplies, used auto parts, used automobile engine and body parts, used automobile parts and accessories, used car parts, used light trucks parts, used motor spare parts, used rims, used spare parts, wheels, window regulators, wiper motors, and wiring harnesses. Entries include: Company name, postal address, city, country, telephone, fax, e-mail and websites, contact person, designation, and product details.

***Directory of Japanese Manufacturers & Exporters of Batteries & Accumulators***. EXIM Infotek Private Ltd., 604 Vishwa Deep, District Centre, Janakpuri New Delhi 110058, India. Phone: 91 11 25544793; Fax: 91 11 25544793; Email: info@eximinfo.org • URL: http://www.eximinfo.com • $5 Individuals. Covers: 20 Japanese manufacturers and exporters of batteries and accumulators, batteries, and battery chargers. Entries include: Company name, postal address, city, country, phone, fax, e-mail and websites, contact person, designation, and product details.

***Directory of Japanese Manufacturers & Exporters of Bearings***. EXIM Infotek Private Ltd., 604 Vishwa Deep, District Centre, Janakpuri New Delhi 110058, India. Phone: 91 11 25544793; Fax: 91 11 25544793; Email: info@eximinfo.org • URL: http://www.eximinfo.com • $10 Individuals. Covers: 60 Japanese manufacturers and exporters of ball bearings, ball screws, balls for bearings, bearing parts, bearing units, bearings, bushings, clutch release bearings, cylindrical roller bearings, engine bearings, linear motion rolling guide units and bearings, needle roller bearings, roller bearings, rollers for bearings, slide bearing and processing materials, spherical roller bearings, and tapered roller bearings. Entries include: Company name, postal address, city, country, phone, fax, e-mail and websites, contact person, designation, and product details.

***Directory of Japanese Manufacturers & Exporters of Beauty Supplies, Cosmetics, Perfumes & Toiletries***. EXIM Infotek Private Ltd., 604 Vishwa Deep, District Centre, Janakpuri New Delhi 110058, India. Phone: 91 11 25544793; Fax: 91 11 25544793; Email: info@eximinfo.org • URL: http://www.eximinfo.com • $10 Individuals. Covers: 120 Japanese manufacturers & exporters of air fresheners, cosmetics, fragrances, hand sprayers, perfumes. Entries include: Company name, postal address, city, country, phone, fax, e-mail & websites, contact person, designation, products detail.

***Directory of Japanese Manufacturers & Exporters of Confectionery & Bakery Products***. EXIM Infotek Private Ltd., 604 Vishwa Deep, District Centre, Janakpuri New Delhi 110058, India. Phone: 91 11 25544793; Fax: 91 11 25544793; Email: info@eximinfo.org • URL: http://www.eximinfo.com • $5 Individuals. Covers: 20 Japanese manufacturers and exporters of biscuits/crackers, confectionery, and vinegar. Entries include: Company name, postal address, city, country, phone, fax, e-mail and websites, contact person, designation, and product details.

***Directory of Japanese Manufacturers and Exporters of Construction Machinery and Equipment***. EXIM Infotek Private Ltd., 604 Vishwa Deep, District Centre, Janakpuri New Delhi 110058, India. Phone: 91 11 25544793; Fax: 91 11 25544793; Email: info@eximinfo.org • URL: http://www.eximinfo.com • $1,000 Individuals; $40 Individuals. Covers: 610 Japanese manufacturers and exporters of building machinery, bulldozers (new and used), construction equipment and spare parts, crushers, dust collectors, excavators (new and used), land machinery, mixers and pavers, used concrete mixer trucks, used cranes, used crawler cranes, used crawler dump, used crawler loader, used dump trucks, used earthmoving equipment, used heavy equipment, used hydraulic excavators and truck cranes, used loaders, used mechanical truck cranes, used mini-excavators, used mixer truck, used motor grader, used road rollers, used rough terrain cranes, used tire shovels, used truck crane, used vibratory road rollers, and used wheel loaders. Entries include: Company name, postal address, telephone, fax, e-mail, website, contact person, designation, and product details.

***Directory of Japanese Manufacturers & Exporters of Cotton, Silk, Wool Raw & Waste***. EXIM Infotek Private Ltd., 604 Vishwa Deep, District Centre, Janakpuri New Delhi 110058, India. Phone: 91 11 25544793; Fax: 91 11 25544793; Email: info@eximinfo.org • URL: http://www.eximinfo.com • $5 Individuals. Covers: 20 Japanese manufacturers and exporters of cotton, cotton products, felt, wool and wool products. Entries include: Company name, postal address, city, country, phone, fax, e-mail and websites, contact person, designation, and product details.

***Directory of Japanese Manufacturers & Exporters of Dyes, Colours, Pigments & Intermediates***. EXIM Infotek Private Ltd., 604 Vishwa Deep, District Centre, Janakpuri New Delhi 110058, India. Phone: 91 11 25544793; Fax: 91 11 25544793; Email: info@eximinfo.org • URL: http://www.eximinfo.com

• $5 Individuals. Covers: 30 Japanese manufacturers and exporters of dyes, inks, pigments. Entries include: Company name, postal address, city, country, phone, fax, e-mail and websites, contact person, designation, and product details.

***Directory of Japanese Manufacturers & Exporters of Electronic Equipment & Supplies***. EXIM Infotek Private Ltd., 604 Vishwa Deep, District Centre, Janakpuri New Delhi 110058, India. Phone: 91 11 25544793; Fax: 91 11 25544793; Email: info@eximinfo.org • URL: http://www.eximinfo.com • Covers: 20 Japanese manufacturers and exporters of electronic devices, electronic equipment, electronic instrument, and semiconductor equipment. Entries include: Company name, postal address, telephone, fax, e-mail, website, contact person, designation, and product details.

***Directory of Japanese Manufacturers & Exporters of Engines & Engine Parts***. EXIM Infotek Private Ltd., 604 Vishwa Deep, District Centre, Janakpuri New Delhi 110058, India. Phone: 91 11 25544793; Fax: 91 11 25544793; Email: info@eximinfo.org • URL: http://www.eximinfo.com • $15 Individuals. Covers: 130 Japanese manufacturers and exporters of diesel engines, diesel engine parts, electric equipment for diesel engines, engine parts and accessories, engine valves, engines, internal combustion engines, oil seals, parts for internal combustion engines, piston pin bushings, pistons, plugs, spark plugs, used car engines, used diesel engines, used engines and body parts, used gasoline engines, and used truck engines. Entries include: Company name, postal address, city, country, phone, fax, e-mail and websites, contact person, designation, and product details.

***Directory of Japanese Manufacturers and Exporters of Environment and Pollution Control Equipment***. EXIM Infotek Private Ltd., 604 Vishwa Deep, District Centre, Janakpuri New Delhi 110058, India. Phone: 91 11 25544793; Fax: 91 11 25544793; Email: info@eximinfo.org • URL: http://www.eximinfo.com • Covers: 20 Japanese manufacturers and exporters of air pollution systems, environmental equipment, evaporators, ion exchange equipment, and pollution control equipment. Entries include: Company name, postal address, telephone, fax, e-mail, website, contact person, designation, and product details.

***Directory of Japanese Manufacturers & Exporters of Food Additives & Aromatic Chemicals***. EXIM Infotek Private Ltd., 604 Vishwa Deep, District Centre, Janakpuri New Delhi 110058, India. Phone: 91 11 25544793; Fax: 91 11 25544793; Email: info@eximinfo.org • URL: http://www.eximinfo.com • $5 Individuals. Covers: 30 Japanese manufacturers and exporters of aromatic chemicals, dairy farming products, food additives, food flavoring. Entries include: Company name, postal address, city, country, phone, fax, e-mail and websites, contact person, designation, and product details.

***Directory of Japanese Manufacturers & Exporters of Furniture—All Types***. EXIM Infotek Private Ltd., 604 Vishwa Deep, District Centre, Janakpuri New Delhi 110058, India. Phone: 91 11 25544793; Fax: 91 11 25544793; Email: info@eximinfo.org • URL: http://www.eximinfo.com • $5 Individuals. Covers: 20 Japanese manufacturers and exporters of furniture, safes and strong boxes, showcases, steel furniture, upholstered furniture, and wooden furniture. Entries include: Company name, postal address, city, country, phone, fax, e-mail and websites, contact person, designation, and product details.

***Directory of Japanese Manufacturers & Exporters of Gemstones & Diamonds***. EXIM Infotek Private Ltd., 604 Vishwa Deep, District Centre, Janakpuri New Delhi 110058, India. Phone: 91 11 25544793; Fax: 91 11 25544793; Email: info@eximinfo.org • URL: http://www.eximinfo.com • $5 Individuals. Covers: 30 Japanese manufacturers and exporters of crystal, cultured pearls, diamonds, natural pearls, precious stones. Entries include: Company name, postal address, city, country, phone, fax, e-mail and websites, contact person, designation, and product details.

***Directory of Japanese Manufacturers & Exporters of Giftware & Novelties***. EXIM Infotek Private Ltd., 604 Vishwa Deep, District Centre, Janakpuri New Delhi 110058, India. Phone: 91 11 25544793; Fax: 91 11 25544793; Email: info@eximinfo.org • URL: http://www.eximinfo.com • $5 Individuals. Covers: 30 Japanese manufacturers and exporters of gift items, gifts, giftware, souvenirs, trophies/ceremonial plates. Entries include: Company name, postal address, city, country, phone, fax, e-mail and websites, contact person, designation, and product details.

***Directory of Japanese Manufacturers & Exporters of Handicrafts & Decorative Items***. EXIM Infotek Private Ltd., 604 Vishwa Deep, District Centre, Janakpuri New Delhi 110058, India. Phone: 91 11 25544793; Fax: 91 11 25544793; Email: info@eximinfo.org • URL: http://www.eximinfo.com • $5 Individuals. Covers: 20 Japanese manufacturers and exporters of art and crafts, art handicrafts, Christmas decorations, Christmas goods, folk crafts, handicrafts, and vases. Entries include: Company name, postal address, city, country, phone, fax, e-mail and websites, contact person, designation, and product details.

***Directory of Japanese Manufacturers & Exporters of Handtools***. EXIM Infotek Private Ltd., 604 Vishwa Deep, District Centre, Janakpuri New Delhi 110058, India. Phone: 91 11 25544793; Fax: 91 11 25544793; Email: info@eximinfo.org • URL: http://www.eximinfo.com • $10 Individuals. Covers: 60 Japanese manufacturers and export-

ers of air tools, hand tools, tools, and turning tools. Entries include: Company name, postal address, city, country, phone, fax, e-mail and websites, contact person, designation, and product details.

***Directory of Japanese Manufacturers & Exporters of Hardwares—All Types***. EXIM Infotek Private Ltd., 604 Vishwa Deep, District Centre, Janakpuri New Delhi 110058, India. Phone: 91 11 25544793; Fax: 91 11 25544793; Email: info@eximinfo.org • URL: http://www.eximinfo.com • $5 Individuals. Covers: 40 Japanese manufacturers and exporters of builders' hardware, casters, door handles, door locks, door operators, fittings, pins, and springs. Entries include: Company name, postal address, city, country, phone, fax, e-mail and websites, contact person, designation, and product details.

***Directory of Japanese Manufacturers & Exporters of Herbs & Herbal Medicine Products***. EXIM Infotek Private Ltd., 604 Vishwa Deep, District Centre, Janakpuri New Delhi 110058, India. Phone: 91 11 25544793; Fax: 91 11 25544793; Email: info@eximinfo.org • URL: http://www.eximinfo.com • $5 Individuals. Covers: 20 Japanese manufacturers and exporters of agricultural medicines, and herbal medicines. Entries include: Company name, postal address, city, country, phone, fax, e-mail and websites, contact person, designation, and product details.

***Directory of Japanese Manufacturers & Exporters of Home Furnishing Materials***. EXIM Infotek Private Ltd., 604 Vishwa Deep, District Centre, Janakpuri New Delhi 110058, India. Phone: 91 11 25544793; Fax: 91 11 25544793; Email: info@eximinfo.org • URL: http://www.eximinfo.com • $5 Individuals. Covers: 20 Japanese manufacturers and exporters of curtains, interior goods for housing, venetian blinds, and wallpaper. Entries include: Company name, postal address, city, country, phone, fax, e-mail and websites, contact person, designation, and product details.

***Directory of Japanese Manufacturers & Exporters of Houseware, Kitchenware & Tableware***. EXIM Infotek Private Ltd., 604 Vishwa Deep, District Centre, Janakpuri New Delhi 110058, India. Phone: 91 11 25544793; Fax: 91 11 25544793; Email: info@eximinfo.org • URL: http://www.eximinfo.com • $10 Individuals. Covers: 110 Japanese manufacturers & exporters of combs, cutlery, daily use goods, gas utensils, home accessories, housing components for various system equipment, kitchen utensils, kitchenware, knives, scissors, tableware. Entries include: Company name, postal address, city, country, phone, fax, e-mail & websites, contact person, designation, products detail.

***Directory of Japanese Manufacturers & Exporters of Imitation & Fashion Jewellery***. EXIM Infotek Private Ltd., 604 Vishwa Deep, District Centre, Janakpuri New Delhi 110058, India. Phone: 91 11 25544793; Fax: 91 11 25544793; Email: info@eximinfo.org • URL: http://www.eximinfo.com • $5 Individuals. Covers: 30 Japanese manufacturers and exporters of costume accessories, fancy goods, hair accessories, imitation jewelry, imitation pearls, personal accessories, personal ornaments. Entries include: Company name, postal address, city, country, phone, fax, e-mail and websites, contact person, designation, and product details.

***Directory of Japanese Manufacturers & Exporters of Leather, Hides, Skins & Furs***. EXIM Infotek Private Ltd., 604 Vishwa Deep, District Centre, Janakpuri New Delhi 110058, India. Phone: 91 11 25544793; Fax: 91 11 25544793; Email: info@eximinfo.org • URL: http://www.eximinfo.com • $5 Individuals. Covers: 20 Japanese manufacturers and exporters of artificial fur, leather, rabbit fur and skin, raw hide leather, raw hide skins (fresh, salted), raw skins, and synthetic leather. Entries include: Company name, postal address, city, country, phone, fax, e-mail and websites, contact person, designation, and product details.

***Directory of Japanese Manufacturers & Exporters of Leather Products***. EXIM Infotek Private Ltd., 604 Vishwa Deep, District Centre, Janakpuri New Delhi 110058, India. Phone: 91 11 25544793; Fax: 91 11 25544793; Email: info@eximinfo.org • URL: http://www.eximinfo.com • $5 Individuals. Covers: 20 Japanese manufacturers and exporters of bags, hand bags, leather goods, and leather products. Entries include: Company name, postal address, city, country, phone, fax, e-mail and websites, contact person, designation, and product details.

***Directory of Japanese Manufacturers & Exporters of Lighting Fixtures, Lamps & Accessories***. EXIM Infotek Private Ltd., 604 Vishwa Deep, District Centre, Janakpuri New Delhi 110058, India. Phone: 91 11 25544793; Fax: 91 11 25544793; Email: info@eximinfo.org • URL: http://www.eximinfo.com • $5 Individuals. Covers: 30 Japanese manufacturers and exporters of fog lamps, halogen lamps, incandescent lamps, lamps, lighting fixtures-glass, lighting fixtures, lighting fixtures and parts, mercury lamps. Entries include: Company name, postal address, city, country, phone, fax, e-mail and websites, contact person, designation, and product details.

***Directory of Japanese Manufacturers & Exporters of Machinery for Chemicals & Pharma Industry***. EXIM Infotek Private Ltd., 604 Vishwa Deep, District Centre, Janakpuri New Delhi 110058, India. Phone: 91 11 25544793; Fax: 91 11 25544793; Email: info@eximinfo.org • URL: http://www.eximinfo.com • $5 Individuals. Covers: 20 Japanese manufacturers and exporters of chemical equipment, chemical industrial equipment, chemical industries machinery, chemical machinery,

chemical plant equipment, and pharmaceutical plant equipment. Entries include: Company name, postal address, city, country, phone, fax, e-mail and websites, contact person, designation, and product details.

***Directory of Japanese Manufacturers & Exporters of Machinery for Textile & Knitting Industry***. EXIM Infotek Private Ltd., 604 Vishwa Deep, District Centre, Janakpuri New Delhi 110058, India. Phone: 91 11 25544793; Fax: 91 11 25544793; Email: info@eximinfo.org • URL: http://www.eximinfo.com • $5 Individuals. Covers: 20 Japanese manufacturers and exporters of dyeing machines, knitting machines, knitting needles, spindle machines, textile machinery, and textile machinery parts. Entries include: Company name, postal address, city, country, phone, fax, e-mail and websites, contact person, designation, and product details.

***Directory of Japanese Manufacturers & Exporters of Marine & Boating Equipment & Supplies***. EXIM Infotek Private Ltd., 604 Vishwa Deep, District Centre, Janakpuri New Delhi 110058, India. Phone: 91 11 25544793; Fax: 91 11 25544793; Email: info@eximinfo.org • URL: http://www.eximinfo.com • $10 Individuals. Covers: 70 Japanese manufacturers and exporters of boat accessories, boats, fishing boat, marine engine spare parts, marine equipment and supplies, marine radios, naval stores products, ships, and used marine engines. Entries include: Company name, postal address, city, country, phone, fax, e-mail and websites, contact person, designation, and product details.

***Directory of Japanese Manufacturers & Exporters of Material Handling Equipment***. EXIM Infotek Private Ltd., 604 Vishwa Deep, District Centre, Janakpuri New Delhi 110058, India. Phone: 91 11 25544793; Fax: 91 11 25544793; Email: info@eximinfo.org • URL: http://www.eximinfo.com • $250 Individuals; $10 Individuals. Covers: 80 Japanese manufacturers and exporters of conveying machines, conveyors, cranes, escalators, forklifts, hand trolleys, hand trucks, materials handling equipment, used forklift trucks, and warehousing equipment. Entries include: Company name, postal address, telephone, fax, e-mail, website, contact person, designation, and product details.

***Directory of Japanese Manufacturers & Exporters of Meat Products***. EXIM Infotek Private Ltd., 604 Vishwa Deep, District Centre, Janakpuri New Delhi 110058, India. Phone: 91 11 25544793; Fax: 91 11 25544793; Email: info@eximinfo.org • URL: http://www.eximinfo.com • $5 Individuals. Covers: 20 Japanese manufacturers and exporters of fresh and frozen meat, meat, salmon, and salmon products. Entries include: Company name, postal address, city, country, phone, fax, e-mail and websites, contact person, designation, and product details.

***Directory of Japanese Manufacturers & Exporters of Minerals***. EXIM Infotek Private Ltd., 604 Vishwa Deep, District Centre, Janakpuri New Delhi 110058, India. Phone: 91 11 25544793; Fax: 91 11 25544793; Email: info@eximinfo.org • URL: http://www.eximinfo.com • $5 Individuals. Covers: 20 Japanese manufacturers and exporters of graphite, limestones, mineral products, phosphate, and rare metals. Entries include: Company name, postal address, city, country, phone, fax, e-mail and websites, contact person, designation, and product details.

***Directory of Japanese Manufacturers & Exporters of Motorcycles, Parts & Accessories***. EXIM Infotek Private Ltd., 604 Vishwa Deep, District Centre, Janakpuri New Delhi 110058, India. Phone: 91 11 25544793; Fax: 91 11 25544793; Email: info@eximinfo.org • URL: http://www.eximinfo.com • $20 Individuals. Covers: 280 Japanese manufacturers and exporters of motorcycle parts, motorcycles, motorcycles and accessories, used motorcycles and parts, used scooters. Entries include: Company name, postal address, city, country, phone, fax, e-mail and websites, contact person, designation, and product details.

***Directory of Japanese Manufacturers and Exporters of Motors and Motor Parts—Electric***. EXIM Infotek Private Ltd., 604 Vishwa Deep, District Centre, Janakpuri New Delhi 110058, India. Phone: 91 11 25544793; Fax: 91 11 25544793; Email: info@eximinfo.org • URL: http://www.eximinfo.com • Covers: 20 Japanese manufacturers and exporters of DC motors, electric motors, motorcycle parts and accessories, starter motors, and stepping motors. Entries include: Company name, postal address, telephone, fax, e-mail, website, contact person, designation, and product details.

***Directory of Japanese Manufacturers & Exporters of Nuts, Bolts, Screws & Fasteners***. EXIM Infotek Private Ltd., 604 Vishwa Deep, District Centre, Janakpuri New Delhi 110058, India. Phone: 91 11 25544793; Fax: 91 11 25544793; Email: info@eximinfo.org • URL: http://www.eximinfo.com • $5 Individuals. Covers: 20 Japanese manufacturers and exporters of bifurcated rivets, bolts and nuts, bolts, fasteners, hexagon socket button head cap screws, hexagon socket cap screws, hexagon socket flat cap screws, hexagon socket set screws, industrial fasteners, rivets, screws, socket cap screws, tubular rivets, washers, and wood screws. Entries include: Company name, postal address, city, country, phone, fax, e-mail and websites, contact person, designation, and product details.

***Directory of Japanese Manufacturers & Exporters of Paints, Varnishes & Allied Products***. EXIM Infotek Private Ltd., 604 Vishwa Deep, District Centre, Janakpuri New Delhi 110058, India. Phone: 91 11 25544793; Fax: 91 11 25544793; Email:

info@eximinfo.org • URL: http://www.eximinfo.com • $5 Individuals. Covers: 20 Japanese manufacturers and exporters of paint, paints, polyurethane resin coatings, powder coatings, and synthetic resins for paint. Entries include: Company name, postal address, city, country, phone, fax, e-mail and websites, contact person, designation, and product details.

***Directory of Japanese Manufacturers & Exporters of Paper & Paper Products***. EXIM Infotek Private Ltd., 604 Vishwa Deep, District Centre, Janakpuri New Delhi 110058, India. Phone: 91 11 25544793; Fax: 91 11 25544793; Email: info@eximinfo.org • URL: http://www.eximinfo.com • $10 Individuals. Covers: 50 Japanese manufacturers and exporters of copying paper, corrugated paper and board, decorative laminating paper, foreign paper, craft paper, paper, paper cups, paper napkins, paper pulp products articles, paperboard, plain paper for copying machines, printing paper, pulp, screen paper, sensitized paper for blue printing machines, special paper, stencil paper, thermal paper, and wood pulp. Entries include: Company name, postal address, city, country, phone, fax, e-mail and websites, contact person, designation, and product details.

***Directory of Japanese Manufacturers & Exporters of Petroleum Products***. EXIM Infotek Private Ltd., 604 Vishwa Deep, District Centre, Janakpuri New Delhi 110058, India. Phone: 91 11 25544793; Fax: 91 11 25544793; Email: info@eximinfo.org • URL: http://www.eximinfo.com • $5 Individuals. Covers: 20 Japanese manufacturers and exporters of fuel, mineral oils and greases, petrochemical industries, petroleum hydrocarbon resins, petroleum products, and petroleum utensils. Entries include: Company name, postal address, city, country, phone, fax, e-mail and websites, contact person, designation, and product details.

***Directory of Japanese Manufacturers & Exporters of Pharmaceutical Products***. EXIM Infotek Private Ltd., 604 Vishwa Deep, District Centre, Janakpuri New Delhi 110058, India. Phone: 91 11 25544793; Fax: 91 11 25544793; Email: info@eximinfo.org • URL: http://www.eximinfo.com • $10 Individuals. Covers: 120 Japanese manufacturers & exporters of hygienic-pharmaceutical goods, medicaments, medicines, pharmaceutical materials, pharmaceuticals. Entries include: Company name, postal address, city, country, phone, fax, e-mail & websites, contact person, designation, products detail.

***Directory of Japanese Manufacturers & Exporters of Readymade Garments***. EXIM Infotek Private Ltd., 604 Vishwa Deep, District Centre, Janakpuri New Delhi 110058, India. Phone: 91 11 25544793; Fax: 91 11 25544793; Email: info@eximinfo.org • URL: http://www.eximinfo.com • $10 Individuals. Covers: 50 Japanese manufacturers and exporters of baby clothing, blouses, garments, mufflers, pajamas, regulators, scarfs, shirts, sweaters, and used clothing. Entries include: Company name, postal address, city, country, phone, fax, e-mail and websites, contact person, designation, and product details.

***Directory of Japanese Manufacturers and Exporters of Refrigeration Equipment and Supplies***. EXIM Infotek Private Ltd., 604 Vishwa Deep, District Centre, Janakpuri New Delhi 110058, India. Phone: 91 11 25544793; Fax: 91 11 25544793; Email: info@eximinfo.org • URL: http://www.eximinfo.com • Covers: 20 Japanese manufacturers and exporters of fluorocarbon refrigerants, refrigeration equipment, and used refrigerators. Entries include: Company name, postal address, telephone, fax, e-mail, website, contact person, designation, and product details.

***Directory of Japanese Manufacturers & Exporters of Spices, Seasoning & Flavourings***. EXIM Infotek Private Ltd., 604 Vishwa Deep, District Centre, Janakpuri New Delhi 110058, India. Phone: 91 11 25544793; Fax: 91 11 25544793; Email: info@eximinfo.org • URL: http://www.eximinfo.com • $5 Individuals. Covers: 20 Japanese manufacturers and exporters of seasonings. Entries include: Company name, postal address, city, country, phone, fax, e-mail and websites, contact person, designation, and product details.

***Directory of Japanese Manufacturers & Exporters of Sporting Goods***. EXIM Infotek Private Ltd., 604 Vishwa Deep, District Centre, Janakpuri New Delhi 110058, India. Phone: 91 11 25544793; Fax: 91 11 25544793; Email: info@eximinfo.org • URL: http://www.eximinfo.com • Covers: 30 Japanese manufacturers and exporters of fishing nets, fishing nets and floats, golf bags, leisure goods, ski carrier and roof racks, sporting goods, sports goods, sports shoes, and sportswear. Entries include: Company name, postal address, telephone, fax, e-mail, website, contact person, designation, and product details.

***Directory of Japanese Manufacturers & Exporters of Textile & Fabrics***. EXIM Infotek Private Ltd., 604 Vishwa Deep, District Centre, Janakpuri New Delhi 110058, India. Phone: 91 11 25544793; Fax: 91 11 25544793; Email: info@eximinfo.org • URL: http://www.eximinfo.com • $10 Individuals. Covers: 80 Japanese manufacturers and exporters of chenille, clothing and textile products, cords and tassels, core fabrics, dyed fabrics, fabrics, knitted fabrics, net and tulle, non woven fabrics, PTFE coated glass fiber fabrics, silk, silk products, textile and its articles, textile piece goods, textile products, textiles, and woven fabrics. Entries include: Company name, postal address, city, country, phone, fax, e-mail and websites, contact person, designation, and product details.

***Directory of Japanese Manufacturers & Exporters of Toys & Games***. EXIM Infotek Private Ltd., 604 Vishwa Deep, District Centre, Janakpuri New Delhi 110058, India. Phone: 91 11 25544793; Fax: 91 11 25544793; Email: info@eximinfo.org • URL: http://www.eximinfo.com • $10 Individuals. Covers: 80 Japanese manufacturers and exporters of baby chairs, battery operated toys, board games, cloth toys, dolls, educational toys, electronic toys, games, general toys, hobbies, hobby crafts, inflatable vinyl toys, jigsaw puzzles, metal and plastic toys, plastic toys, pre-school toys, puzzles, radio controlled cars, ride on toys, shadow masks, stuffed toys, stuffed animals, toys, trading cards, vehicles for children, and wooden toys. Entries include: Company name, postal address, city, country, phone, fax, e-mail and websites, contact person, designation, and product details.

***Directory of Japanese Manufacturers & Exporters of Tractors, Parts & Accessories***. EXIM Infotek Private Ltd., 604 Vishwa Deep, District Centre, Janakpuri New Delhi 110058, India. Phone: 91 11 25544793; Fax: 91 11 25544793; Email: info@eximinfo.org • URL: http://www.eximinfo.com • $5 Individuals. Covers: 30 Japanese manufacturers and exporters of used agricultural tractor, used farm tractors, used tractors. Entries include: Company name, postal address, city, country, phone, fax, e-mail and websites, contact person, designation, and product details.

***Directory of Japanese Manufacturers & Exporters of Tyres & Tubes***. EXIM Infotek Private Ltd., 604 Vishwa Deep, District Centre, Janakpuri New Delhi 110058, India. Phone: 91 11 25544793; Fax: 91 11 25544793; Email: info@eximinfo.org • URL: http://www.eximinfo.com • $10 Individuals. Covers: 70 Japanese manufacturers and exporters of automobile tires and tubes, rubber tires and tubes, tires, tires and tubes, tires-used, used truck tires, and used tires. Entries include: Company name, postal address, city, country, phone, fax, e-mail and websites, contact person, designation, and product details.

***Directory of Japanese Manufacturers & Exporters of Watches & Clocks***. EXIM Infotek Private Ltd., 604 Vishwa Deep, District Centre, Janakpuri New Delhi 110058, India. Phone: 91 11 25544793; Fax: 91 11 25544793; Email: info@eximinfo.org • URL: http://www.eximinfo.com • $5 Individuals. Covers: 20 Japanese manufacturers and exporters of clocks, watch bands and straps, and watches. Entries include: Company name, postal address, city, country, phone, fax, e-mail and websites, contact person, designation, and product details.

***Directory of Japanese Manufacturers & Exporters of Wire, Chain & Wire Products***. EXIM Infotek Private Ltd., 604 Vishwa Deep, District Centre, Janakpuri New Delhi 110058, India. Phone: 91 11 25544793; Fax: 91 11 25544793; Email: info@eximinfo.org • URL: http://www.eximinfo.com • $5 Individuals. Covers: 40 Japanese manufacturers and exporters of chain and chain block, chains, steel wire, wire, wire netting, and wire products. Entries include: Company name, postal address, city, country, phone, fax, e-mail and websites, contact person, designation, and product details.

***Directory of Japanese Manufacturers & Exporters of Wires & Cables—Electrical***. EXIM Infotek Private Ltd., 604 Vishwa Deep, District Centre, Janakpuri New Delhi 110058, India. Phone: 91 11 25544793; Fax: 91 11 25544793; Email: info@eximinfo.org • URL: http://www.eximinfo.com • $200 Individuals; $10 Individuals. Covers: 50 Japanese manufacturers and exporters of arc welding machinery and equipment, electrodes, resistance welding machines, used welder, welding machinery, and welding rods. Entries include: Company name, postal address, telephone, fax, e-mail, website, contact person, designation, and product details.

***Directory of Japanese Manufacturers and Exporters of Woodworking Equipment and Tools***. EXIM Infotek Private Ltd., 604 Vishwa Deep, District Centre, Janakpuri New Delhi 110058, India. Phone: 91 11 25544793; Fax: 91 11 25544793; Email: info@eximinfo.org • URL: http://www.eximinfo.com • Covers: 20 Japanese manufacturers and exporters of band saw blades, band sawing machine, circle saw, plywood machinery, wood processing machinery, and wood working machine. Entries include: Company name, postal address, telephone, fax, e-mail, website, contact person, designation, and product details.

***Directory of Kansas Manufacturers and Products***. Kansas Department of Commerce & Housing, • Biennial. $50. Covers: Approximately 2,500 manufacturers in Kansas. Entries include: Company name, address, phone, fax, name of principal executive, products or services, codes for number of employees.

***Directory of Linkage Industries***. Hong Kong Productivity Council, HKPC Bldg., 78 Tat Chee Ave. Hong Kong, China. Phone: 852 27885678; Fax: 852 27885900 • URL: http://www.hkpc.org • Annual. $220 pick up at HKPC Office; $250 delivery by courier within Hong Kong; $50 airmail to countries in Southeast Asia; $55 airmail to countries outside Southeast Asia. Covers: Major jobshops and suppliers in the metal industry in Hong Kong as well as their operations in Mainland China including mold and tool making, surface finishing, industrial machinery repair and maintenance, and hot and cold working and metal machinery.

***Directory of Listed Plumbing Products***. International Association of Plumbing and Mechanical Officials, 4755 E Philadelphia St. Ontario, CA 91761. Phone: (909)472-4100; Fax: (909)472-4150; Email: iapmo@iapmo.org • URL: http://www.iapmo.org • Bimonthly. $118 Members per year. Covers: About 1,500 manufacturers of approximately 10,000 plumbing products and appliances. Entries include: Manufacturer name, address, product name, model number, product description.

***Directory of Louisiana Manufacturers***. Dun & Bradstreet Inc., 103 JFK Pkwy. Short Hills, NJ 07078. Phone: 800-526-0651 or (973)921-5500 or (973)921-5000; Fax: (866)560-7035 or (512)794-7670; Email: info@dnb.com • URL: http://www.dnb.com • Annual. Covers: Over 6,500 manufacturing companies in Louisiana. Database includes: Statistical data, trade show calendar. Entries include: Company name, address, county, phone, fax, number of employees, names and titles of key executives, plant size, year established, parent company, annual sales, import and export information, Standard Industrial Classification (SIC) code, and product description.

***Directory of Major Manufacturers of T&D Equipment***. NRG Expert, 8 Quarry Rd. London SW18 2QJ, United Kingdom. Phone: 44 20 84326378; Fax: 44 20 83287117; Email: info@absenergyresearch.com • URL: http://www.absenergyresearch.com • Covers: More than 1,500 international manufacturers of equipment used in the power sector, including switchgear, HV transformers, insulated cables, uninsulated lines, insulators, bushings, and fittings. Entries include: Company name, address, telephone and fax numbers.

***Directory of Manufacturers of Pressure-Sensitive Tape, Label Stock, and Other Coated Products***. Satas & Associates, 99 Shenandoah Rd. Warwick, RI 02886. Phone: (401)884-9572; Fax: (401)884-7620 • $99. Covers: 92 manufacturers of specialized coated tapes and labeling products. Entries include: Company name, address, phone, product/service.

***Directory of Mexican Corporations***. IBCON S.A., Gutenberg 224, Col. Anzures 11590 Mexico, Mexico. Phone: 52 55 52554577; Email: ibcon@ibcon.com.mx • URL: http://www.ibcon.com.mx • Irregular. $488 Individuals. 1,621 Mexican corporations selling at least $10,000,000 a year.

***Directory of Middle East Importers of Boiler and Boiler Parts***. EXIM Infotek Private Ltd., 604 Vishwa Deep, District Centre, Janakpuri New Delhi 110058, India. Phone: 91 11 25544793; Fax: 91 11 25544793; Email: info@eximinfo.org • URL: http://www.eximinfo.com • $200 Individuals; $10 Individuals. Covers: 50 Middle East importers of boilers and parts, oil/gas/electric boilers, and pressure vessels. Entries include: Company name, postal address, telephone, fax, e-mail, website, contact person, designation, and product details.

***Directory of Middle East Importers of Calendars, Greeting, Prints and Lithographs***. EXIM Infotek Private Ltd., 604 Vishwa Deep, District Centre, Janakpuri New Delhi 110058, India. Phone: 91 11 25544793; Fax: 91 11 25544793; Email: info@eximinfo.org • URL: http://www.eximinfo.com • $200 Individuals; $10 Individuals. Covers: 55 Middle East importers of calendars, greeting cards, postcards, Christmas cards, greeting cards, morals, pictures, etchings, posters, prints, and lithographs. Entries include: Company name, postal address, telephone, fax, e-mail, website, contact person, designation, and product details.

***Directory of Middle East Importers of Dyes, Colors, and Pigments***. EXIM Infotek Private Ltd., 604 Vishwa Deep, District Centre, Janakpuri New Delhi 110058, India. Phone: 91 11 25544793; Fax: 91 11 25544793; Email: info@eximinfo.org • URL: http://www.eximinfo.com • $250 Individuals; $10 Individuals. Covers: 80 Middle East importers of carbon black, dyes, colors, pigments, and dyestuff. Entries include: Company name, postal address, telephone, fax, e-mail, website, contact person, designation, and product details.

***Directory of Middle East Importers of Energy and Power Equipment***. EXIM Infotek Private Ltd., 604 Vishwa Deep, District Centre, Janakpuri New Delhi 110058, India. Phone: 91 11 25544793; Fax: 91 11 25544793; Email: info@eximinfo.org • URL: http://www.eximinfo.com • $300 Individuals; $10 Individuals. Covers: 100 Middle East importers of alternative energy equipment, nuclear equipment and material, power generation equipment, power transmission equipment and supplies, solar energy equipment, wind energy equipment, and transmission and allied equipment. Entries include: Company name, postal address, telephone, fax, e-mail, website, contact person, designation, and product details.

***Directory of Middle East Importers of Environment Protection and Pollution Control Equipment***. EXIM Infotek Private Ltd., 604 Vishwa Deep, District Centre, Janakpuri New Delhi 110058, India. Phone: 91 11 25544793; Fax: 91 11 25544793; Email: info@eximinfo.org • URL: http://www.eximinfo.com • Covers: 200 Middle East importers of environmental protection equipment, garbage disposals and compactors, pollution control equipment, water purification equipment, and water treatment equipment. Entries include: Company name, postal address, telephone, fax, e-mail, website, contact person, designation, and product details.

***Directory of Middle East Importers of Fibre and Fibre Products***. EXIM Infotek Private Ltd., 604 Vishwa Deep, District Centre, Janakpuri New Delhi 110058, India. Phone: 91 11

25544793; Fax: 91 11 25544793; Email: info@eximinfo.org • URL: http://www.eximinfo.com • $300 Individuals; $10 Individuals. Covers: 100 Middle East importers of acrylic fibers, fiber optic equipment, fiber glass, fiber glass cloth and products, fiber products, glass fibers, polyester fibers, polyester staple fibers, synthetic fibers, and viscose fibers. Entries include: Company name, postal address, telephone, fax, e-mail, website, contact person, designation, and product details.

***Directory of Middle East Importers of Fire Fighting Equipment & Supplies.*** EXIM Infotek Private Ltd., 604 Vishwa Deep, District Centre, Janakpuri New Delhi 110058, India. Phone: 91 11 25544793; Fax: 91 11 25544793; Email: info@eximinfo.org • URL: http://www.eximinfo.com • Covers: 200 Middle East importers of fire alarm equipment and fire fighting equipment. Entries include: Company name, postal address, telephone, fax, e-mail, website, contact person, designation, and product details.

***Directory of Middle East Importers of Fodder and Animal Foodstuffs.*** EXIM Infotek Private Ltd., 604 Vishwa Deep, District Centre, Janakpuri New Delhi 110058, India. Phone: 91 11 25544793; Fax: 91 11 25544793; Email: info@eximinfo.org • URL: http://www.eximinfo.com • $400 Individuals; $15 Individuals. Covers: 170 Middle East importers of animal and poultry fodder, animal feeds, animal feed additives, animal feed ingredients, animal food, animal foodstuff additives, fodder, cereals, and livestock breeding supplies. Entries include: Company name, postal address, telephone, fax, e-mail, website, contact person, designation, and product details.

***Directory of Middle East Importers of Food Additives and Aromatics.*** EXIM Infotek Private Ltd., 604 Vishwa Deep, District Centre, Janakpuri New Delhi 110058, India. Phone: 91 11 25544793; Fax: 91 11 25544793; Email: info@eximinfo.org • URL: http://www.eximinfo.com • $250 Individuals; $10 Individuals. Covers: 90 Middle East importers of additives, aromatic chemicals, artificial sweeteners, food additives, food colors, food chemicals, margarine, and yeast. Entries include: Company name, postal address, telephone, fax, e-mail, website, contact person, designation, and product details.

***Directory of Middle East Importers of Handkerchives, Scarves and Neckwears.*** EXIM Infotek Private Ltd., 604 Vishwa Deep, District Centre, Janakpuri New Delhi 110058, India. Phone: 91 11 25544793; Fax: 91 11 25544793; Email: info@eximinfo.org • URL: http://www.eximinfo.com • $150 Individuals; $5 Individuals. Covers: 20 Middle East importers of handkerchieves, scarves, and neckwear.

***Directory of Middle East Importers of Heaters and Heating Equipment.*** EXIM Infotek Private Ltd., 604 Vishwa Deep, District Centre, Janakpuri New Delhi 110058, India. Phone: 91 11 25544793; Fax: 91 11 25544793; Email: info@eximinfo.org • URL: http://www.eximinfo.com • Covers: 130 Middle East importers of central heating plants and equipment, heat exchangers, and heaters. Entries include: Company name, postal address, telephone, fax, e-mail, website, contact person, designation, and product details.

***Directory of Middle East Importers of Herbs & Herbal Medicine Products.*** EXIM Infotek Private Ltd., 604 Vishwa Deep, District Centre, Janakpuri New Delhi 110058, India. Phone: 91 11 25544793; Fax: 91 11 25544793; Email: info@eximinfo.org • URL: http://www.eximinfo.com • Covers: 20 Middle East importers of medicinal herbs and botanicals. Entries include: Company name, postal address, telephone, fax, e-mail, website, contact person, designation, and product details.

***Directory of Middle East Importers of Honey and Syrup.*** EXIM Infotek Private Ltd., 604 Vishwa Deep, District Centre, Janakpuri New Delhi 110058, India. Phone: 91 11 25544793; Fax: 91 11 25544793; Email: info@eximinfo.org • URL: http://www.eximinfo.com • $150 Individuals; $5 Individuals. Covers: 20 Middle East importers of honey and syrups. Entries include: Company name, postal address, telephone, fax, e-mail, website, contact person, designation, and product details.

***Directory of Middle East Importers of Laboratory & Scientific Instruments & Supplies.*** EXIM Infotek Private Ltd., 604 Vishwa Deep, District Centre, Janakpuri New Delhi 110058, India. Phone: 91 11 25544793; Fax: 91 11 25544793; Email: info@eximinfo.org • URL: http://www.eximinfo.com • Covers: 510 Middle East importers of analysis equipment, binoculars, microscopes, telescopes, laboratory and scientific glass ware, laboratory and scientific instruments, laboratory equipment, material testing equipment, microscopes, scientific and laboratory instruments, scientific equipment, scientific instruments, soil testing equipment, and testing equipment. Entries include: Company name, postal address, telephone, fax, e-mail, website, contact person, designation, and product details.

***Directory of Middle East Importers of Lumber, Timber, Plywood and Hardboards.*** EXIM Infotek Private Ltd., 604 Vishwa Deep, District Centre, Janakpuri New Delhi 110058, India. Phone: 91 11 25544793; Fax: 91 11 25544793; Email: info@eximinfo.org • URL: http://www.eximinfo.com • $500 Individuals; $20 Individuals. Covers: 260 Middle East importers of blockboard and hardboard, doors and windows, formica, gypsum boards, hardboard and particle board, hardwood flooring and floor tiles, laminates, hardwood lumber, softwood lumber, timber, plywood, medium-density fiberboard, millwork (wooden), veneer, poles, pilings and logs, and sawdust. Entries include: Company name, postal address, telephone, fax, e-mail, website, contact person, designation, and product details.

***Directory of Middle East Importers of Machinery for Glass and Ceramic Industry.*** EXIM Infotek Private Ltd., 604 Vishwa Deep, District Centre, Janakpuri New Delhi 110058, India. Phone: 91 11 25544793; Fax: 91 11 25544793; Email: info@eximinfo.org • URL: http://www.eximinfo.com • $150 Individuals; $5 Individuals. Covers: 20 Middle East importers of ceramic industry equipment, ceramic industry supplies, glass making machinery and equipment. Entries include: Company name, postal address, telephone, fax, e-mail, website, contact person, designation, and product details.

***Directory of Middle East Importers of Machinery for Paper & Pulp Industry.*** EXIM Infotek Private Ltd., 604 Vishwa Deep, District Centre, Janakpuri New Delhi 110058, India. Phone: 91 11 25544793; Fax: 91 11 25544793; Email: info@eximinfo.org • URL: http://www.eximinfo.com • Covers: 30 Middle East importers of paper bag manufacturing machinery and paper making machinery. Entries include: Company name, postal address, telephone, fax, e-mail, website, contact person, designation, and product details.

***Directory of Middle East Importers of Material Handling Equipment & Supplies.*** EXIM Infotek Private Ltd., 604 Vishwa Deep, District Centre, Janakpuri New Delhi 110058, India. Phone: 91 11 25544793; Fax: 91 11 25544793; Email: info@eximinfo.org • URL: http://www.eximinfo.com • Covers: 320 Middle East importers of conveying equipment and supplies, conveyors, crane overload indicators, cranes and hoists, elevators and lifts, escalators, forklifts, electric and hydraulic lifts, liquid handling equipment, loading and unloading equipment, materials handling systems for garment industries, monorail materials handling equipment, road construction handling equipment, winches, and pulleys. Entries include: Company name, postal address, telephone, fax, e-mail, website, contact person, designation, and product details.

***Directory of Middle East Importers of Military & Police Equipment & Supplies.*** EXIM Infotek Private Ltd., 604 Vishwa Deep, District Centre, Janakpuri New Delhi 110058, India. Phone: 91 11 25544793; Fax: 91 11 25544793; Email: info@eximinfo.org • URL: http://www.eximinfo.com • $200 Individuals; $10 Individuals. Covers: 45 Middle East importers of ammunition, military electronic equipment, military equipment and supplies, police equipment, surplus military equipment and supplies, traffic control systems and equipment. Entries include: Company name, postal address, telephone, fax, e-mail, website, contact person, designation, and product details.

***Directory of Middle East Importers of Minerals.*** EXIM Infotek Private Ltd., 604 Vishwa Deep, District Centre, Janakpuri New Delhi 110058, India. Phone: 91 11 25544793; Fax: 91 11 25544793; Email: info@eximinfo.org • URL: http://www.eximinfo.com • $250 Individuals; $10 Individuals. Covers: 60 Middle East importers of aluminum alloy ingot, clay, lead, mica, minerals, ores, titanium dioxide, zinc, zinc concentrate, zinc ingot, and zinc ingueat. Entries include: Company name, postal address, telephone, fax, e-mail, website, contact person, designation, and product details.

***Directory of Middle East Importers of Motors and Motor Parts—Electric.*** EXIM Infotek Private Ltd., 604 Vishwa Deep, District Centre, Janakpuri New Delhi 110058, India. Phone: 91 11 25544793; Fax: 91 11 25544793; Email: info@eximinfo.org • URL: http://www.eximinfo.com • Covers: 170 Middle East importers of electric motors, motor equipment and parts, motor oil, and outboard motor. Entries include: Company name, postal address, telephone, fax, e-mail, website, contact person, designation, and product details.

***Directory of Middle East Importers of Photographic Equipment and Supplies.*** EXIM Infotek Private Ltd., 604 Vishwa Deep, District Centre, Janakpuri New Delhi 110058, India. Phone: 91 11 25544793; Fax: 91 11 25544793; Email: info@eximinfo.org • URL: http://www.eximinfo.com • $350 Individuals; $15 Individuals. Covers: 130 Middle East importers of cameras, lens and accessories, photographic chemicals, motion picture and theater equipment, cinematographic equipment and accessories, film, microfilm and blueprint equipment, motion picture film, photo processing and developing equipment, photographic apparatus and accessories, and photographic equipment. Entries include: Company name, postal address, telephone, fax, e-mail, website, contact person, designation, and product details.

***Directory of Middle East Importers of Plastic Scrap and Raw Materials.*** EXIM Infotek Private Ltd., 604 Vishwa Deep, District Centre, Janakpuri New Delhi 110058, India. Phone: 91 11 25544793; Fax: 91 11 25544793; Email: info@eximinfo.org • URL: http://www.eximinfo.com • $450 Individuals; $20 Individuals. Covers: 180 Middle East importers of fiberglass resins, high-density polyethylene (HDPE), LDPE scrap, phenol formaldehyde resin, plastic materials, plastic raw materials, plastic scrap and waste, polyester powder, polymer, polypropylene, PVC (granule), and waste plastic. Entries include: Company name, postal address, telephone, fax, e-mail, website, contact person, designation, and product details.

***Directory of Middle East Importers of Restaurant, Hotel and Catering Equipment.*** EXIM Infotek Private Ltd., 604 Vishwa Deep, District Centre, Janakpuri New Delhi 110058, India. Phone: 91 11 25544793; Fax: 91 11 25544793; Email: info@eximinfo.org • URL: http://www.eximinfo.com • Covers: 160 Middle East importers of catering equipment, cooking ranges and oven, restaurant and hotel equipment. Entries include: Company name, postal address, telephone, fax, e-mail, website, contact person, designation, and product details.

***Directory of Middle East Importers of Sewing Machines and Parts.*** EXIM Infotek Private Ltd., 604 Vishwa Deep, District Centre, Janakpuri New Delhi 110058, India. Phone: 91 11 25544793; Fax: 91 11 25544793; Email: info@eximinfo.org • URL: http://www.eximinfo.com • $250 Individuals; $10 Individuals. Covers: 70 Middle East importers of embroidery machinery, garment industry equipment, industrial sewing machine and parts, new and used industrial sewing machine and spare parts, and domestic sewing machine. Entries include: Company name, postal address, telephone, fax, e-mail, website, contact person, designation, and product details.

***Directory of Middle East Importers of Soap, Detergent and Cleaning Supplies.*** EXIM Infotek Private Ltd., 604 Vishwa Deep, District Centre, Janakpuri New Delhi 110058, India. Phone: 91 11 25544793; Fax: 91 11 25544793; Email: info@eximinfo.org • URL: http://www.eximinfo.com • $450 Individuals. Covers: 180 Middle East importers of cleaning supplies, soap, detergent, disinfectant products, polishes and cleansing materials, and bleach. Entries include: Company name, postal address, telephone, fax, e-mail, website, contact person, designation, and product details.

***Directory of Middle East Importers of Sporting Goods.*** EXIM Infotek Private Ltd., 604 Vishwa Deep, District Centre, Janakpuri New Delhi 110058, India. Phone: 91 11 25544793; Fax: 91 11 25544793; Email: info@eximinfo.org • URL: http://www.eximinfo.com • Covers: 280 Middle East importers of billiard, pool equipment and supplies, bowling equipment and supplies, diving equipment, firearms, golf equipment and supplies, hiking accessories, mountain climbing equipment, playground equipment, ski boots, skiing accessories, sporting goods and toys, sporting goods, sporting guns and cartridges, sports goods, stadium equipment, tennis and badminton equipment and supplies, turf maintenance equipment, water ski equipment and supplies, water sports equipment and supplies, and windsurfing goods. Entries include: Company name, postal address, telephone, fax, e-mail, website, contact person, designation, and product details.

***Directory of Middle East Importers of Telephone Instruments and Accessories.*** EXIM Infotek Private Ltd., 604 Vishwa Deep, District Centre, Janakpuri New Delhi 110058, India. Phone: 91 11 25544793; Fax: 91 11 25544793; Email: info@eximinfo.org • URL: http://www.eximinfo.com • $350 Individuals; $15 Individuals. Covers: 110 Middle East importers of mobile phone, microphone, mobile accessories, pagers, beepers, telefax equipment, telephone control unit, and telephone index. Entries include: Company name, postal address, telephone, fax, e-mail, website, contact person, designation, and product details.

***Directory of Middle East Importers of Waste Disposal & Recycling Equipment.*** EXIM Infotek Private Ltd., 604 Vishwa Deep, District Centre, Janakpuri New Delhi 110058, India. Phone: 91 11 25544793; Fax: 91 11 25544793; Email: info@eximinfo.org • URL: http://www.eximinfo.com • Covers: 55 Middle East importers of sewage equipment, waste disposal equipment, and waste recycling equipment. Entries include: Company name, postal address, telephone, fax, e-mail, website, contact person, designation, and product details.

***Directory of Middle East Importers of Wax & Wax Products.*** EXIM Infotek Private Ltd., 604 Vishwa Deep, District Centre, Janakpuri New Delhi 110058, India. Phone: 91 11 25544793; Fax: 91 11 25544793; Email: info@eximinfo.org • URL: http://www.eximinfo.com • Covers: 40 Middle East importers of paraffin, paraffin waxes, polishes and creams. Entries include: Company name, postal address, telephone, fax, e-mail, website, contact person, designation, and product details.

***Directory of Middle East Importers of Welding Equipment and Supplies.*** EXIM Infotek Private Ltd., 604 Vishwa Deep, District Centre, Janakpuri New Delhi 110058, India. Phone: 91 11 25544793; Fax: 91 11 25544793; Email: info@eximinfo.org • URL: http://www.eximinfo.com • $350 Individuals; $15 Individuals. Covers: 140 Middle East importers of electrodes, soldering equipment, soldering supplies, welding equipment, welding products, and welding supplies. Entries include: Company name, postal address, telephone, fax, e-mail, website, contact person, designation, and product details.

***Directory of Middle East Importers of Wires & Cables—Electrical.*** EXIM Infotek Private Ltd., 604 Vishwa Deep, District Centre, Janakpuri New Delhi 110058, India. Phone: 91 11 25544793; Fax: 91 11 25544793; Email: info@eximinfo.org • URL: http://www.eximinfo.com • Covers: 180 Middle East importers of cable equipment, cables, copper cable and accessories, copper wire, electrical cables, electrical wires, and power cables. Entries include: Company name, postal address, telephone, fax, e-mail, website, contact person, designation, and product details.

***Directory of Middle East Importers of Woodenware & Wood***

***Products***. EXIM Infotek Private Ltd., 604 Vishwa Deep, District Centre, Janakpuri New Delhi 110058, India. Phone: 91 11 25544793; Fax: 91 11 25544793; Email: info@eximinfo.org • URL: http://www.eximinfo.com • Covers: 40 Middle East importers of baskets and basket ware, wooden poles, wooden products, and wooden screws. Entries include: Company name, postal address, telephone, fax, e-mail, website, contact person, designation, and product details.

***Directory of Middle East Importers of Yarns and Threads***. EXIM Infotek Private Ltd., 604 Vishwa Deep, District Centre, Janakpuri New Delhi 110058, India. Phone: 91 11 25544793; Fax: 91 11 25544793; Email: info@eximinfo.org • URL: http://www.eximinfo.com • $500 Individuals; $20 Individuals. Covers: 200 Middle East importers of acetate yarns, cotton yarn and thread, elastic yarn, metallic yarn and thread, nylon filament yarn, nylon yarn, polyester yarn, sewing thread, silk yarns, sisal yarns and ropes, synthetic yarn and thread, viscose yarns, and wool yarn. Entries include: Company name, postal address, telephone, fax, e-mail, website, contact person, designation, and product details.

***Directory of Minority & Women-Owned Businesses***. Business Service Div. Birmingham Area Chamber of Commerce, 505 N 20th St. Birmingham, AL 35203. Phone: (205)324-2100; Fax: (205)324-2560 • URL: http://www.birminghamchamber.com • Covers: Approximately 1,200 businesses in Birmingham, Alabama, that are owned by women or minorities. Entries include: Company name, address, phone, name and title of contact, Standard Industrial Classification (SIC) code.

***Directory of Minority and Women Owned Businesses***. Louisiana Office of Minority and Women's Business Enterprise Department of Economic Development, PO Box 94185 Baton Rouge, LA 70804-9185. Phone: 800-450-8115; Fax: (225)342-3000 • URL: http://www.lded.state.la.us • Quarterly. Contains information on minority and women-owned businesses.

***Directory of Multinationals***. Macmillan Publishers Ltd. Nature Publishing Group, 75 Varick St., 9th Fl. New York, NY 10013-1917. Phone: 888-331-6288 or (212)726-9200; Fax: (212)696-9006; Email: institutions@natureny.com • URL: http://www.nature.com • Irregular. $595 plus s/h. Approximately 450 multinational corporations with sales of $1 billion during 1996 and significant foreign investments.

***Directory of North American Importers of Calendars, Greeting, Prints and Lithographs***. EXIM Infotek Private Ltd., 604 Vishwa Deep, District Centre, Janakpuri New Delhi 110058, India. Phone: 91 11 25544793; Fax: 91 11 25544793; Email: info@eximinfo.org • URL: http://www.eximinfo.com • $300 Individuals; $10 Individuals. Covers: 110 North American importers of art prints, cards, calendars, greeting cards, postcards, pictures, posters, prints, lithograph and etching, printing and graphic arts. Entries include: Company name, postal address, telephone, fax, e-mail, website, contact person, designation, and product details.

***Directory of North American Importers of Camping and Backpacking Equipment and Supplies***. EXIM Infotek Private Ltd., 604 Vishwa Deep, District Centre, Janakpuri New Delhi 110058, India. Phone: 91 11 25544793; Fax: 91 11 25544793; Email: info@eximinfo.org • URL: http://www.eximinfo.com • $300 Individuals; $10 Individuals. Covers: 100 North American importers of awnings, backpack, backsacks, backpacking equipment and supplies, camping equipment, outdoor recreational equipment and tents. Entries include: Company name, postal address, telephone, fax, e-mail, website, contact person, designation, and product details.

***Directory of North American Importers of Dyes, Colors, and Pigments***. EXIM Infotek Private Ltd., 604 Vishwa Deep, District Centre, Janakpuri New Delhi 110058, India. Phone: 91 11 25544793; Fax: 91 11 25544793; Email: info@eximinfo.org • URL: http://www.eximinfo.com • $250 Individuals; $10 Individuals. Covers: 50 North American importers of chemical intermediates, dyes, colors, pigments, and dyestuff. Entries include: Company name, postal address, telephone, fax, e-mail, website, contact person, designation, and product details.

***Directory of North American Importers of Energy and Power Equipment***. EXIM Infotek Private Ltd., 604 Vishwa Deep, District Centre, Janakpuri New Delhi 110058, India. Phone: 91 11 25544793; Fax: 91 11 25544793; Email: info@eximinfo.org • URL: http://www.eximinfo.com • Covers: 100 North American importers of alternative energy equipment, power supply system, power transmission component, power transmission equipment and supplies, solar cell products, solar energy equipment, and wind energy equipment. Entries include: Company name, postal address, telephone, fax, e-mail, website, contact person, designation, and product details.

***Directory of North American Importers of Environment Protection and Pollution Control Equipment***. EXIM Infotek Private Ltd., 604 Vishwa Deep, District Centre, Janakpuri New Delhi 110058, India. Phone: 91 11 25544793; Fax: 91 11 25544793; Email: info@eximinfo.org • URL: http://www.eximinfo.com • $200 Individuals; $10 Individuals. Covers: 50 North American importers of environmental protection equipment, pollution control equipment, water purification equipment, water treatment, and purifying equipment. Entries include: Company name, postal address, telephone, fax, e-mail, website, contact person, designation, and product details.

***Directory of North American Importers of Fodder and Animal Foodstuffs***. EXIM Infotek Private Ltd., 604 Vishwa Deep, District Centre, Janakpuri New Delhi 110058, India. Phone: 91 11 25544793; Fax: 91 11 25544793; Email: info@eximinfo.org • URL: http://www.eximinfo.com • $150 Individuals; $5 Individuals. Covers: 40 North American importers of animal feed, animal food, animal foodstuff additives, animal foodstuff, feed additives, fodder, cereals, and livestock breeding supplies. Entries include: Company name, postal address, telephone, fax, e-mail, website, contact person, designation, and product details.

***Directory of North American Importers of Food Additives and Aromatics***. EXIM Infotek Private Ltd., 604 Vishwa Deep, District Centre, Janakpuri New Delhi 110058, India. Phone: 91 11 25544793; Fax: 91 11 25544793; Email: info@eximinfo.org • URL: http://www.eximinfo.com • $250 Individuals; $10 Individuals. Covers: 80 North American importers of aromatic chemicals, aromatics, baking ingredients, citric acid, flavor ingredients, flavoring extracts, food additives, food colors, food ingredients, food preparations, fragrances, preservatives, and starches. Entries include: Company name, postal address, telephone, fax, e-mail, website, contact person, designation, and product details.

***Directory of North American Importers of Handkerchives, Scarves and Neckwears***. EXIM Infotek Private Ltd., 604 Vishwa Deep, District Centre, Janakpuri New Delhi 110058, India. Phone: 91 11 25544793; Fax: 91 11 25544793; Email: info@eximinfo.org • URL: http://www.eximinfo.com • $250 Individuals; $10 Individuals. Covers: 60 North American importers of bows, handkerchieves, scarves, neckwear, mufflers, napkins, neckties, pashmina shawls, silk scarves, and wool shawls. Entries include: Company name, postal address, telephone, fax, e-mail, website, contact person, designation, and product details.

***Directory of North American Importers of Heaters and Heating Equipment***. EXIM Infotek Private Ltd., 604 Vishwa Deep, District Centre, Janakpuri New Delhi 110058, India. Phone: 91 11 25544793; Fax: 91 11 25544793; Email: info@eximinfo.org • URL: http://www.eximinfo.com • $300 Individuals; $10 Individuals. Covers: 120 North American importers of heat exchangers, heating and ventilation equipment, and heating elements. Entries include: Company name, postal address, telephone, fax, e-mail, website, contact person, designation, and product details.

***Directory of North American Importers of Herbs & Herbal Medicine Products***. EXIM Infotek Private Ltd., 604 Vishwa Deep, District Centre, Janakpuri New Delhi 110058, India. Phone: 91 11 25544793; Fax: 91 11 25544793; Email: info@eximinfo.org • URL: http://www.eximinfo.com • $300 Individuals; $10 Individuals. Covers: 60 North American importers of ayurvedic medicines, ayurvedic products, botanicals, bulk herbs, Chinese herbs, crude botanical drugs, ginseng, herb products, herb seeds, herbal cosmetics, herbal extracts, herbal products, herbal tea, herbicides, herbs, medicinal herbs, and botanical. Entries include: Company name, postal address, telephone, fax, e-mail, website, contact person, designation, and product details.

***Directory of North American Importers of Honey and Syrup***. EXIM Infotek Private Ltd., 604 Vishwa Deep, District Centre, Janakpuri New Delhi 110058, India. Phone: 91 11 25544793; Fax: 91 11 25544793; Email: info@eximinfo.org • URL: http://www.eximinfo.com • $150 Individuals; $5 Individuals. Covers: 25 North American importers of cinnamon honey, honey, and syrup. Entries include: Company name, postal address, telephone, fax, e-mail, website, contact person, designation, and product details.

***Directory of North American Importers of Laboratory & Scientific Instruments and Supplies***. EXIM Infotek Private Ltd., 604 Vishwa Deep, District Centre, Janakpuri New Delhi 110058, India. Phone: 91 11 25544793; Fax: 91 11 25544793; Email: info@eximinfo.org • URL: http://www.eximinfo.com • Covers: 150 North American importers of binoculars, microscope, telescopes, laboratory equipment, laboratory and scientific glass, laboratory apparatus, magnifiers, microscope accessories, microscopes, scientific instruments, soil testing equipment, and testing equipment. Entries include: Company name, postal address, telephone, fax, e-mail, website, contact person, designation, and product details.

***Directory of North American Importers of Lumber, Timber, Plywood and Hardboards***. EXIM Infotek Private Ltd., 604 Vishwa Deep, District Centre, Janakpuri New Delhi 110058, India. Phone: 91 11 25544793; Fax: 91 11 25544793; Email: info@eximinfo.org • URL: http://www.eximinfo.com • $700 Individuals; $30 Individuals. Covers: 350 North American importers of bamboo and rattan raw, doors, windows, exotic wood, forestry products, gypsum board and sheetrock, hardboard, particleboard, hardwood, hardwood flooring, hardwood floor tiles, lumber, laminates (wood), lumber (hardwood), lumber (softwood), lumber products, lumber timber and plywood, mahogany, millwork (wooden), oak vanities, plywood, veneer, poles, pilings and logs, rattan, teakwood, timber, tropical hardwood, and wicker. Entries include: Company name, postal address, telephone, fax, e-mail, website, contact person, designation, and product details.

***Directory of North American Importers of Material Handling Equipment & Supplies***. EXIM Infotek Private Ltd., 604 Vishwa Deep, District Centre, Janakpuri New Delhi 110058, India. Phone: 91 11 25544793; Fax: 91 11 25544793; Email: info@eximinfo.org • URL: http://www.eximinfo.com • Covers: 120 North American importers of cargo handling equipment, conveyors, cranes and hoists, elevators and lifts, forklift parts, liquid handling equipment and supplies, loading and unloading equipment, materials handling equipment and parts, and winches. Entries include: Company name, postal address, telephone, fax, e-mail, website, contact person, designation, and product details.

***Directory of North American Importers of Minerals***. EXIM Infotek Private Ltd., 604 Vishwa Deep, District Centre, Janakpuri New Delhi 110058, India. Phone: 91 11 25544793; Fax: 91 11 25544793; Email: info@eximinfo.org • URL: http://www.eximinfo.com • $200 Individuals; $10 Individuals. Covers: 50 North American importers of alabaster, clay, graphite, industrial minerals, limestone, magnesium, mica, minerals, and ores. Entries include: Company name, postal address, telephone, fax, e-mail, website, contact person, designation, and product details.

***Directory of North American Importers of Oil Seeds***. EXIM Infotek Private Ltd., 604 Vishwa Deep, District Centre, Janakpuri New Delhi 110058, India. Phone: 91 11 25544793; Fax: 91 11 25544793; Email: info@eximinfo.org • URL: http://www.eximinfo.com • Covers: 30 North American importers of mustard, oil seeds, peanut, sesame seeds, soybeans, and sunflower seeds. Entries include: Company name, postal address, telephone, fax, e-mail, website, contact person, designation, and product details.

***Directory of North American Importers of Paper & Paper Products***. EXIM Infotek Private Ltd., 604 Vishwa Deep, District Centre, Janakpuri New Delhi 110058, India. Phone: 91 11 25544793; Fax: 91 11 25544793; Email: info@eximinfo.org • URL: http://www.eximinfo.com • Covers: 210 North American importers of copier paper, decorative paper, fax and duplicating paper, gift wrap, gold foil paper, handmade paper, handmade paper materials, kraft paper, newsprint, paper and paper products, wood pulp, paper bags, paper cups, paper goods, paper napkins, paper plates, paper waste, printing paper, recycled paper, sanitary and toilet paper goods, specialty paper, and tissue paper. Entries include: Company name, postal address, telephone, fax, e-mail, website, contact person, designation, and product details.

***Directory of North American Importers of Photographic Equipment and Supplies***. EXIM Infotek Private Ltd., 604 Vishwa Deep, District Centre, Janakpuri New Delhi 110058, India. Phone: 91 11 25544793; Fax: 91 11 25544793; Email: info@eximinfo.org • URL: http://www.eximinfo.com • $300 Individuals; $10 Individuals. Covers: 130 North American importers of camera film, cameras, lens and accessories, motion picture and theater equipment, digital camera, disposable flash camera, film, plates and photographic papers, graphic art supplies, graphic arts equipment, microfilm equipment, motion picture film, photographic equipment and supplies, photographic goods, photographic papers, photographic products, professional motion picture equipment, and slide projectors. Entries include: Company name, postal address, telephone, fax, e-mail, website, contact person, designation, and product details.

***Directory of North American Importers of Plastic Scrap and Raw Materials***. EXIM Infotek Private Ltd., 604 Vishwa Deep, District Centre, Janakpuri New Delhi 110058, India. Phone: 91 11 25544793; Fax: 91 11 25544793; Email: info@eximinfo.org • URL: http://www.eximinfo.com • $250 Individuals; $10 Individuals. Covers: 80 North American importers of high-density polyethylene (HDPE), low-density polyethylene (LDPE), phenolic, plastic raw materials, plastic resins, plastic scrap and waste, polyester, polyvinyl alcohol, and polypropylene (PP). Entries include: Company name, postal address, telephone, fax, e-mail, website, contact person, designation, and product details.

***Directory of North American Importers of Refrigeration Equipment and Supplies***. EXIM Infotek Private Ltd., 604 Vishwa Deep, District Centre, Janakpuri New Delhi 110058, India. Phone: 91 11 25544793; Fax: 91 11 25544793; Email: info@eximinfo.org • URL: http://www.eximinfo.com • $300 Individuals; $10 Individuals. Covers: 110 North American importers of freezer, refrigeration and air conditioning equipment, and refrigerator parts. Entries include: Company name, postal address, telephone, fax, e-mail, website, contact person, designation, and product details.

***Directory of North American Importers of Restaurant, Hotel and Catering Equipment***. EXIM Infotek Private Ltd., 604 Vishwa Deep, District Centre, Janakpuri New Delhi 110058, India. Phone: 91 11 25544793; Fax: 91 11 25544793; Email: info@eximinfo.org • URL: http://www.eximinfo.com • $250 Individuals; $10 Individuals. Covers: 80 North American importers of bar supplies, barbecue, catering equipment and supplies, cooking equipment (patio and outdoors), cooking range and oven, food service components, painted serving trays, restaurant equipment, restaurant supplies, hotel equipment and supplies, tray and chafing dishes, wine baskets and racks. Entries include: Company name, postal address, telephone, fax, e-mail, website, contact person, designation, and product details.

***Directory of North American Importers of Sewing Machines and Parts***. EXIM Infotek Private Ltd., 604 Vishwa Deep, District

Centre, Janakpuri New Delhi 110058, India. Phone: 91 11 25544793; Fax: 91 11 25544793; Email: info@eximinfo.org • URL: http://www.eximinfo.com • $250 Individuals; $10 Individuals. Covers: 60 North American importers of embroidery machinery, industrial sewing machine and parts, sewing machine and sewing accessories, domestic sewing machine, and sewing machine needles. Entries include: Company name, postal address, telephone, fax, e-mail, website, contact person, designation, and product details.

***Directory of North American Importers of Soap, Detergent and Cleaning Supplies***. EXIM Infotek Private Ltd., 604 Vishwa Deep, District Centre, Janakpuri New Delhi 110058, India. Phone: 91 11 25544793; Fax: 91 11 25544793; Email: info@eximinfo.org • URL: http://www.eximinfo.com • $350 Individuals; $15 Individuals. Covers: 140 North American importers of antiseptics, disinfectant soap, cleaning supplies, detergent, shampoo, toilet and bathroom preparations. Entries include: Company name, postal address, telephone, fax, e-mail, website, contact person, designation, and product details.

***Directory of North American Importers of Sporting Goods***. EXIM Infotek Private Ltd., 604 Vishwa Deep, District Centre, Janakpuri New Delhi 110058, India. Phone: 91 11 25544793; Fax: 91 11 25544793; Email: info@eximinfo.org • URL: http://www.eximinfo.com • Covers: 440 North American importers of baseball caps, baseball supplies, billiard, pool equipment and supplies, climbing equipment, climbing gear, exercise equipment, firearms, golf ball, golf caps, golf cart accessories, golf course accessories and tools, golf equipment and supplies, martial arts supplies, medals, mountain climbing equipment, playground equipment, polo seats, scuba and diving equipment, skateboards and accessories, ski equipment and supplies, snowboard, soccer balls, soccer equipment, soccer games, sport bags, sporting goods, toys, sports bags, sports footwear, tennis and badminton equipment, trekking wear, water ski equipment and supplies, water sports equipment and supplies, and windsurfing accessories.

***Directory of North American Importers of Telephone Instruments and Accessories***. EXIM Infotek Private Ltd., 604 Vishwa Deep, District Centre, Janakpuri New Delhi 110058, India. Phone: 91 11 25544793; Fax: 91 11 25544793; Email: info@eximinfo.org • URL: http://www.eximinfo.com • $300 Individuals; $10 Individuals. Covers: 100 North American importers of beepers, cellular accessories, cellular mobile phone, cellular phone, cordless telephone, GSM phones, headphone, microphone, Nokia phone, pagers, telephone accessories, telephone answering equipment, telephone equipment, and used cellphone. Entries include: Company name, postal address, telephone, fax, e-mail, website, contact person, designation, and product details.

***Directory of North American Importers of Wires & Cables—Electrical***. EXIM Infotek Private Ltd., 604 Vishwa Deep, District Centre, Janakpuri New Delhi 110058, India. Phone: 91 11 25544793; Fax: 91 11 25544793; Email: info@eximinfo.org • URL: http://www.eximinfo.com • $200 Individuals; $10 Individuals. Covers: 60 American and Canadian importers for wires, cables, electrical cables, electrical wires, extension cords, and combination wires. Entries include: Company name, postal address, telephone, fax, e-mail, website, contact person, designation, and product details.

***Directory of North American Importers of Yarns and Threads***. EXIM Infotek Private Ltd., 604 Vishwa Deep, District Centre, Janakpuri New Delhi 110058, India. Phone: 91 11 25544793; Fax: 91 11 25544793; Email: info@eximinfo.org • URL: http://www.eximinfo.com • $300 Individuals; $10 Individuals. Covers: 100 North American importers of acrylic yarn, cotton yarn, embroidery thread, filament yarn, metallic yarn, polyester yarn, sewing thread, silk yarn and thread, synthetic yarn, thread, viscose, wool yarn, cotton, and silk. Entries include: Company name, postal address, telephone, fax, e-mail, website, contact person, designation, and product details.

***Directory of North Carolina Manufacturing Firms: Federal ID 56-1611-847***. Harris InfoSource, 2057 E Aurora Rd. Twinsburg, OH 44087-1999. Phone: 800-888-5900 or (330)425-9000 or (973)921-5500; Fax: (800)643-5997 or (877)252-3375; Email: customerservice@harrisinfo.com • URL: http://www.harrisinfo.com • Annual. $70 payment must accompany order. Covers: Approximately 7,200 manufacturers in North Carolina. Entries include: Company name, address, names and titles of principal executives, names and address of parent company, geographical area served, Standard Industrial Classification (SIC) code, product/service provided, number of employees, year established.

***Directory of Packaging and Allied Industries***. NIIR Project Consultancy Services, 106 - E, Kamla Nagar New Delhi 110007, India. Phone: 91 11 23843955; Fax: 91 11 23841561; Email: npcs.india@gmail.com • URL: http://www.niir.org • Rs 1,686 Individuals; $100 Individuals. Covers: 1,000 companies/industries (manufacturers and suppliers) of packaging industries, packaging raw material, packaging machineries in India. Entries include: Company name, full postal address, phone, fax, email (wherever available), website address (wherever available).

***Directory of Physician Groups and Networks***. Dorland Healthcare Information, 1500 Walnut St., Ste. 1000 Philadelphia, PA 19102. Phone: 855-225-5341; Fax: (301)287-2535; Email: chi@healthcare-info.com • URL: http://www.dorlandhealth.com • Annual. $495.00. Available only online. Approximately 8,000 independent practice associations (IPAs), physician hospital organizations (PHOs), management service organizations (MSOs), physician practice management companies (PPMCs), and group practices having 20 or more physicians.

***Directory of Plastics Industry***. Hong Kong Productivity Council, HKPC Bldg., 78 Tat Chee Ave. Hong Kong, China. Phone: 852 27885678; Fax: 852 27885900 • URL: http://www.hkpc.org • Annual. $300 pick up at HKPC office; $330 delivery by courier within Hong Kong; $80 airmail to countries in southeast Asia; $85 airmail to countries outside of southeast Asia. Covers: Over 3,000 companies from plastic manufacturers in Hong Kong as well as their operations in mainland China. Entries include: Name, address, phone, fax, e-mail, URL, number of employees, turnover, and products/name brands.

***Directory of Printing and Allied Industries***. NIIR Project Consultancy Services, 106 - E, Kamla Nagar New Delhi 110007, India. Phone: 91 11 23843955; Fax: 91 11 23841561; Email: npcs.india@gmail.com • URL: http://www.niir.org • Rs 1,686 Individuals CD-ROM; $100 Individuals CD-ROM. Covers: 1,000 companies/industries (manufacturers and suppliers), printing inks, printing machineries, printing raw material in India. Entries include: Company name, full postal address, phone, fax, email (wherever available), website address (wherever available).

***Directory of Private Sector Services to Cities***. Texas Municipal League, 1821 Rutherford Ln., Ste. 400 Austin, TX 78754. Phone: 800-537-6655 or (512)231-7400; Fax: (512)231-7490 or (512)231-7495; Email: tmli@tml.org • URL: http://www.tml.org • Annual. $10. Covers: about 300 firms providing services to city governments in Texas, including attorneys, accountants, architects, auditors, construction managers, engineers, inspectors, real estate appraisers and counselors, and water resource and supply companies. Entries include: Firm name, address, phone, name and title of contact, services, geographical area served.

***Directory of Public Companies in Canada***. Micromedia ProQuest, 20 Victoria St. Toronto, ON, Canada M5C 2N8. Phone: 800-387-2689 or (416)362-5211; Fax: (416)362-6161; Email: info@micromedia.ca • URL: http://www.proquest.com • Irregular. $125. Covers: over 3,500 public companies in Canada. Database includes: Citations of recent newspaper articles in a Corporate News Index. Entries include: Company name, address, phone, fax, names and titles of key personnel, date and location of incorporation, ticker symbols, auditor, financial data, history.

***Directory of Real Estate Development & Related Education Programs***. Urban Land Institute, 1025 Thomas Jefferson St. NW, Ste. 500 W Washington, DC 20007. Phone: 800-321-5011 or (202)624-7000; Fax: (202)624-7140; Email: customerservice@uli.org • URL: http://www.uli.org • Biennial. $24.95 Individuals paperback; C$27.95 Individuals paperback. Covers: over 60 real estate development education programs currently being offered at colleges and universities. Entries include: College or university name, address, list of faculty members, curriculum, tuition, length of program, degrees offered, financial aid information, job placement services, international programs, e-mail addresses.

***Directory of Registered Belgian Entrepreneurs and Companies***. Cite Administrative de l'Etat, Tour Finances, Blvd. du Jardin Botanique 52 Box 32 B-1010 Brussels, Belgium. Phone: 212702246; Fax: 212702277 • Annual. Covers: Companies in Belgium. Entries include: Company name, address, phone, registration number, line of business, number of employees, business code.

***Directory of Retail Chains in Canada***. Rogers Publishing Ltd., 333 Bloor St. E, 7th Fl. Toronto, ON, Canada M4W 1G9. Phone: 888-764-3771 or (416)764-2000 or (416)764-1300; Fax: (416)764-7730 • URL: http://www.rogerspublishing.ca • Annual Monthly. $1,399 print and online; $869 online; 879 Dh print. Provides detailed information on approximately 2,500 retail chains of all sizes in Canada.

***Directory of Rhode Island Manufacturers***. Rhode Island Economic Development Corporation, 315 Iron Horse Way, Ste. 101 Providence, RI 02908. Phone: 800-250-7384 or (401)278-9100 or (401)222-2601; Fax: (401)273-8270 or (401)222-2102; Email: info@riedc.com • URL: http://www.commerceri.com • Annual. Covers: 2800 manufacturers in Rhode Island. Entries include: Company name, address, phone, product/service, name and title of contact, number of employees, parent company, and estimated sales.

***Directory of SAARC Importers of Construction Machinery and Equipment***. EXIM Infotek Private Ltd., 604 Vishwa Deep, District Centre, Janakpuri New Delhi 110058, India. Phone: 91 11 25544793; Fax: 91 11 25544793; Email: info@eximinfo.org • URL: http://www.eximinfo.com • $300 Individuals; $10 Individuals. Covers: 80 companies in member countries of the South Asian Association for Regional Cooperation (SAARC) that import asphalt mixing plants, asphalt paving equipment, bulldozers, chip spreaders, road sweepers, concrete breakers, chipping hammer, concrete machinery and mixer, concrete production equipment, construction equipment and spare parts, dumpers, earthmoving equipment, excavating equipment, heavy construction machinery, hoists for construction, hydraulic concrete mixer, mixers and pavers, plate compactors, prime movers, rammers, road rollers, used construction machinery, used hydraulic truck mounted cranes, vibrators, and vibrating and pneumatic rollers. Entries include: Company name, postal address, telephone, fax, e-mail, website, contact person, designation, and product details.

***Directory of SAARC Importers of Dyes, Colors, Pigments and Intermediates***. EXIM Infotek Private Ltd., 604 Vishwa Deep, District Centre, Janakpuri New Delhi 110058, India. Phone: 91 11 25544793; Fax: 91 11 25544793; Email: info@eximinfo.org • URL: http://www.eximinfo.com • $350 Individuals; $15 Individuals. Covers: 80 SAARC countries importers of acrylic color, activated carbon, auxiliaries, chemical for pashmina, dye intermediates, dye, colors, pigments, dyestuff, fabric colors, ink, leather chemicals, leather dyestuff and chemicals, phthalic anhydride, pigment emulsions, printing ink, textile auxiliaries, textile chemicals, textile dye, textile binder, and washing chemicals. Entries include: Company name, postal address, telephone, fax, e-mail, website, contact person, designation, and product details.

***Directory of SAARC Importers of Environment Protection and Pollution Control Equipment***. EXIM Infotek Private Ltd., 604 Vishwa Deep, District Centre, Janakpuri New Delhi 110058, India. Phone: 91 11 25544793; Fax: 91 11 25544793; Email: info@eximinfo.org • URL: http://www.eximinfo.com • Covers: 20 companies in member countries of the South Asian Association for Regional Cooperation (SAARC) that import carbon dioxide and kitchen hood flooring systems, deionizers, environmental control equipment, environmental noise monitor, pollution control equipment, sewage cleaning equipment, sewage treatment, water purification equipment, water treatment equipment and plants. Entries include: Company name, postal address, telephone, fax, e-mail, website, contact person, designation, and product details.

***Directory of SAARC Importers of Fibre and Fibre Products***. EXIM Infotek Private Ltd., 604 Vishwa Deep, District Centre, Janakpuri New Delhi 110058, India. Phone: 91 11 25544793; Fax: 91 11 25544793; Email: info@eximinfo.org • URL: http://www.eximinfo.com • $150 Individuals; $5 Individuals. Covers: 20 SAARC Countries importers of acrylic fiber, carbon fiber, fiber glass materials, fiber glass products and cloth, fiber rods and sheets, Mexican fiber, mineral fiber board, natural fiber, palmyra fiber, polyester fiber, polyester staple fiber, staple fiber, synthetic fiber, viscose fiber, and vulcanized fiber. Entries include: Company name, postal address, telephone, fax, e-mail, website, contact person, designation, and product details.

***Directory of SAARC Importers of Fire Fighting Equipment & Supplies***. EXIM Infotek Private Ltd., 604 Vishwa Deep, District Centre, Janakpuri New Delhi 110058, India. Phone: 91 11 25544793; Fax: 91 11 25544793; Email: info@eximinfo.org • URL: http://www.eximinfo.com • Covers: 40 companies in member countries of the South Asian Association for Regional Cooperation (SAARC) that import fire and safety instruments, fire alarm systems, fire clothing and equipment, fire demonstration and training, fire detection and alarm systems, fire detection products, fire doors and panic hardware, fire extinguishers, fire fighting equipment, fire hose reel, hydrant and sprinkler systems, fire hose systems, fire rated shutters, fire resistant products, fire trucks and sewerage equipment, fire vehicles and accessories, firefighting uniforms, helmet, emblems, badges, tarpaulins, foam extinguishers, and smoke detection systems. Entries include: Company name, postal address, telephone, fax, e-mail, website, contact person, designation, and product details.

***Directory of SAARC Importers of Hardwares—All Types***. EXIM Infotek Private Ltd., 604 Vishwa Deep, District Centre, Janakpuri New Delhi 110058, India. Phone: 91 11 25544793; Fax: 91 11 25544793; Email: info@eximinfo.org • URL: http://www.eximinfo.com • Covers: 90 companies in member countries of the South Asian Association for Regional Cooperation (SAARC) that import abrasives, anchors, blades, brass ball knob, brass collars, knobs for brass beds, brass fittings, brass hardware, builder's hardware, cabinet hardware, castor wheel, ceiling fittings, coated abrasives, curtain fittings, curtain rails, door accessories, door closers, door fittings, door handles, door locks, emery paper, furniture hardware and parts, general hardware, hardware merchants, hinges, hooded ball casters, hooks, lipped channel, cylinder lock, locks for homes and hotels, magnet catches, nails, overhead sliding door systems, pantry cupboards fittings, railings, roller doors, roller shutter spring, sand paper, spring, flat washers, taper lock bushes, tug pins, twin wheel casters, vibrator roller, water sand paper, zigzag, and engineering tools.

***Directory of SAARC Importers of Lumber, Timber, Plywood and Hardboards***. EXIM Infotek Private Ltd., 604 Vishwa Deep, District Centre, Janakpuri New Delhi 110058, India. Phone: 91 11 25544793; Fax: 91 11 25544793; Email: info@eximinfo.org • URL: http://www.eximinfo.com • $200 Individuals; $10 Individuals. Covers: 60 SAARC countries importers of artificial timber, bio-fold doors, windows, board, ebonite rods and sheets, false ceiling board, formica, gypsum board, hard boards, particleboard, laminated boards, laminated wooden boards, doors, windows, laminated decorative-sheets, laminates, hardwood lumber, softwood lumber, medium-density fiberboards, particle boards, plywood, veneer, doors, plywood sheets, sawn goods, sliding doors, straw boards, swing door, teak wood, timber, timber products, white boards, window shutters, window type, and wood. Entries include: Company name, postal address, telephone, fax, e-mail, website, contact person, designation, and product details.

***Directory of SAARC Importers of Material Handling Equipment.*** EXIM Infotek Private Ltd., 604 Vishwa Deep, District Centre, Janakpuri New Delhi 110058, India. Phone: 91 11 25544793; Fax: 91 11 25544793; Email: info@eximinfo.org • URL: http://www.eximinfo.com • Covers: 45 companies in member countries of the South Asian Association for Regional Cooperation (SAARC) that import backhoe loaders, cargo hooks, cement factory chains, chain for conveyors, container handling equipment, conveyors, crane lorries, cranes and hoists, crawler crane, electric chain block, elevators lifts, escalators, forklift parts and accessories, hand pallet truck, hoisting blocks chipping machine and spares, electrical and manual hoists, hydraulic excavators, loaders, loading and unloading equipment, materials handling containers and equipment, material handling systems, material lifting system, mobile cranes, mop carts, pallet truck, pulley, roller and accumulating conveyors, rough terrain crane, and wheel loaders. Entries include: Company name, postal address, telephone, fax, e-mail, website, contact person, designation, and product details.

***Directory of SAARC Importers of Minerals.*** EXIM Infotek Private Ltd., 604 Vishwa Deep, District Centre, Janakpuri New Delhi 110058, India. Phone: 91 11 25544793; Fax: 91 11 25544793; Email: info@eximinfo.org • URL: http://www.eximinfo.com • Covers: 20 companies in member countries of the South Asian Association for Regional Cooperation (SAARC) that import borax, faucets, graphite, gypsum, lead, magnesium oxide, manganese ore, mica, mineral products, rock phosphate, silica base, soil, sulfur, and zinc. Entries include: Company name, postal address, telephone, fax, e-mail, website, contact person, designation, and product details.

***Directory of SAARC Importers of Motors and Motor Parts—Electric.*** EXIM Infotek Private Ltd., 604 Vishwa Deep, District Centre, Janakpuri New Delhi 110058, India. Phone: 91 11 25544793; Fax: 91 11 25544793; Email: info@eximinfo.org • URL: http://www.eximinfo.com • $200 Individuals; $10 Individuals. Covers: 40 companies in member countries of the South Asian Association for Regional Cooperation (SAARC) that import agitators and geared motors, Eddy current variable speed motors, electric motor control, flange mounted motors, geared and variable speed geared motors, speed controllers, induction motors, motorboard, motor graders, motor parts and accessories, motor starters, single wiper motor, swing motors, variable speed motors, and vertical deep tubewell motor. Entries include: Company name, postal address, telephone, fax, e-mail, website, contact person, designation, and product details.

***Directory of SAARC Importers of Plastic Scrap and Raw Materials.*** EXIM Infotek Private Ltd., 604 Vishwa Deep, District Centre, Janakpuri New Delhi 110058, India. Phone: 91 11 25544793; Fax: 91 11 25544793; Email: info@eximinfo.org • URL: http://www.eximinfo.com • $300 Individuals; $10 Individuals. Covers: 95 SAARC Countries importers of ABS scrap, acrylic thickener, granules, high-density polyethylene (HDPE), HDPE film grade granules, low-density polyethylene (LDPE), linear low density polythylene (LLDPE), pet resin, plastic granules, plastic molding compounds, plastic raw materials and semi-finished products, plastic scrap and waste, polycarbonate, polyethylene granules, polypropylene and waste, polyvinyl alcohol, PP and PE resins for rope making, PP granules, PVC compound, PVC resin, PVC scrap, raw materials for polyurethane form, raw materials for printed laminate, soft PVC scrap, and transparent PVC scrap. Entries include: Company name, postal address, telephone, fax, e-mail, website, contact person, designation, and product details.

***Directory of SAARC Importers of Sewing Machines and Parts.*** EXIM Infotek Private Ltd., 604 Vishwa Deep, District Centre, Janakpuri New Delhi 110058, India. Phone: 91 11 25544793; Fax: 91 11 25544793; Email: info@eximinfo.org • URL: http://www.eximinfo.com • $200 Individuals; $10 Individuals. Covers: 55 SAARC countries importers of buttonholer and button covering machine, compact fusing press M/C, embroidery machinery, garment industry equipment and accessories, household sewing machine and parts, sewing machine equipment, sewing machine repairs, domestic and industrial sewing machine, sewing needles, stitch machine, thread trimmers, used embroidery machine, and used schiffli embroidery. Entries include: Company name, postal address, telephone, fax, e-mail, website, contact person, designation, and product details.

***Directory of SAARC Importers of Sporting Goods.*** EXIM Infotek Private Ltd., 604 Vishwa Deep, District Centre, Janakpuri New Delhi 110058, India. Phone: 91 11 25544793; Fax: 91 11 25544793; Email: info@eximinfo.org • URL: http://www.eximinfo.com • Covers: 50 companies in member countries of the South Asian Association for Regional Cooperation (SAARC) that import cricket and hockey goods, rafting equipment, equipment for sauna, spa, swimming pool, shuttlecocks, sporting goods, sports gloves, swimming accessories, tennis and badminton equipment and supplies, tennis balls, and trekking equipment. Entries include: Company name, postal address, telephone, fax, e-mail, website, contact person, designation, and product details.

***Directory of SAARC Importers of Telephone Instruments and Accessories.*** EXIM Infotek Private Ltd., 604 Vishwa Deep, District Centre, Janakpuri New Delhi 110058, India. Phone: 91 11 25544793; Fax: 91 11 25544793; Email: info@eximinfo.org • URL: http://www.eximinfo.com • $200 Individuals; $10 Individuals. Covers: 55 SAARC Countries importers of cellular phone accessories and parts, cordless telephone, digital telephone systems, EPABX systems, headphone, intercom systems, PABX and intercom equipment, pagers, beepers, telecommunication products, telefax equipment, telephone accessories, telephone answering equipment, telephone (cables), used auto phone set, and VHF/SSB radio telephone. Entries include: Company name, postal address, telephone, fax, e-mail, website, contact person, designation, and product details.

***Directory of SAARC Importers of Welding Equipments and Supplies.*** EXIM Infotek Private Ltd., 604 Vishwa Deep, District Centre, Janakpuri New Delhi 110058, India. Phone: 91 11 25544793; Fax: 91 11 25544793; Email: info@eximinfo.org • URL: http://www.eximinfo.com • $150 Individuals; $5 Individuals. Covers: 30 SAARC Countries importers of crush electrodes, ferrosillicon and graphite electrodes, M.S. welding rods, soldering and earthing materials, welding equipment, welding electrodes, welding gases, welding generators, welding machine and materials, welding products, welding rods, and welding supplies. Entries include: Company name, postal address, telephone, fax, e-mail, website, contact person, designation, and product details.

***Directory of SAARC Importers of Wire & Cables—Electrical.*** EXIM Infotek Private Ltd., 604 Vishwa Deep, District Centre, Janakpuri New Delhi 110058, India. Phone: 91 11 25544793; Fax: 91 11 25544793; Email: info@eximinfo.org • URL: http://www.eximinfo.com • Covers: 25 companies in member countries of the South Asian Association for Regional Cooperation (SAARC) that import armored cables, armored jelly filled cables, bare wires, cables and accessories, coaxial cables, copper winding wires, copper wires, enamel and cotton insulated winding wires, enameled copper wires, instrumentation cables, internal cables, non-armored SF cables, overhead cables, plastic coated wire products, power cables, PVC flexible flat cables, PVC insulated automobile cables and battery cables, and wiring accessories. Entries include: Company name, postal address, telephone, fax, e-mail, website, contact person, designation, and product details.

***Directory of SAARC Importers of Zipper and Garment Accessories.*** EXIM Infotek Private Ltd., 604 Vishwa Deep, District Centre, Janakpuri New Delhi 110058, India. Phone: 91 11 25544793; Fax: 91 11 25544793; Email: info@eximinfo.org • URL: http://www.eximinfo.com • $250 Individuals; $10 Individuals. Covers: 90 SAARC Countries importers of badges and crests, buckles, buttons, eyelets, fusing multiflexible, garment accessories, labels (textile), ladies garment accessories, leather hardware, needles, sewing notions/zippers/buttons, shirt clips, stitching needles, and zipper. Entries include: Company name, postal address, telephone, fax, e-mail, website, contact person, designation, and product details.

***Directory of St. Petersburg Free-Zone Region.*** Flegon Press, 37B New Cavendish St. London W1M 8JR, United Kingdom. Phone: 44 181 752 1296; Fax: 44 181 752 1296 • $75 postpaid. Covers: import-export enterprises in St. Petersburg (formerly Leningrad) and surrounding areas in Russia. Entries include: Enterprise name, address, phone, telex, names and titles of key personnel.

***Directory of Scottish Grant Making Trusts.*** Scottish Council for Voluntary Organisations, Mansfield Traquair Ctre., 15 Mansfield Pl. Edinburgh EH3 6BB, United Kingdom. Phone: 44 131 4748000 or 44 131 5563882; Fax: 44 131 5560279; Email: enquiries@scvo.org.uk • URL: http://www.scvo.org.uk • Irregular. $9.50 Members; $12.50 Nonmembers. Number of listings: 524. Entries include: Company name, address, phone, grant name and subject, requirements, recipients.

***Directory of Service Companies.*** Dun & Bradstreet Inc., 103 JFK Pkwy. Short Hills, NJ 07078. Phone: 800-526-0651 or (973)921-5500 or (973)921-5000; Fax: (866)560-7035 or (512)794-7670; Email: info@dnb.com • URL: http://www.dnb.com • Annual. Covers: Management consulting services; executive search services; public relations, engineering, and architectural services; business services; accounting, auditing, and bookkeeping services; consumer services; health services; legal services; social services; research services; repair services; and hospitality, motion picture, amusement, and recreation services.

***Directory of Service, Industrial and Foreign Trading Companies in Egypt.*** International Trade Consulting Co., 22 El Gaber St., Auberge-Giza Cairo, Egypt. • $45; $89. Covers: Companies in Egypt. Entries include: Company name, address, phone.

***Directory of Services to Exporters.*** IBCON S.A., Gutenberg 224, Col. Anzures 11590 Mexico, Mexico. Phone: 52 55 52554577; Email: ibcon@ibcon.com.mx • URL: http://www.ibcon.com.mx • Irregular. $283 Individuals. Covers: 654 companies, associations and government agencies, located in Mexico City, that offer a variety of services needed by exporters.

***Directory of South American Importers of Calendars, Greeting, Prints and Lithographs.*** EXIM Infotek Private Ltd., 604 Vishwa Deep, District Centre, Janakpuri New Delhi 110058, India. Phone: 91 11 25544793; Fax: 91 11 25544793; Email: info@eximinfo.org • URL: http://www.eximinfo.com • $150 Individuals; $5 Individuals. Covers: 30 South American importers of calendars, greeting cards, postcards, prints, lithographs, and etchings. Entries include: Company name, postal address, telephone, fax, e-mail, website, contact person, designation, and product details.

***Directory of South American Importers of Construction Machinery and Equipment.*** EXIM Infotek Private Ltd., 604 Vishwa Deep, District Centre, Janakpuri New Delhi 110058, India. Phone: 91 11 25544793; Fax: 91 11 25544793; Email: info@eximinfo.org • URL: http://www.eximinfo.com • $550 Individuals; $20 Individuals. Covers: 260 South American importers of building and construction materials, concrete production equipment, construction and building equipment, construction machinery, excavating equipment, mixers and pavers, new parquet machinery, scale models and construction kit, street maintenance equipment, and used construction equipment. Entries include: Company name, postal address, telephone, fax, e-mail, website, contact person, designation, and product details.

***Directory of South American Importers of Dyes, Colors, and Pigments.*** EXIM Infotek Private Ltd., 604 Vishwa Deep, District Centre, Janakpuri New Delhi 110058, India. Phone: 91 11 25544793; Fax: 91 11 25544793; Email: info@eximinfo.org • URL: http://www.eximinfo.com • $300 Individuals; $10 Individuals. Covers: 100 South American importers of dye, colors, pigments, and food colors. Entries include: Company name, postal address, telephone, fax, e-mail, website, contact person, designation, and product details.

***Directory of South American Importers of Energy and Power Equipment.*** EXIM Infotek Private Ltd., 604 Vishwa Deep, District Centre, Janakpuri New Delhi 110058, India. Phone: 91 11 25544793; Fax: 91 11 25544793; Email: info@eximinfo.org • URL: http://www.eximinfo.com • $250 Individuals; $10 Individuals. Covers: 70 South American importers of power transmission equipment and supplies, solar energy equipment, wind energy equipment, transmission and allied equipment. Entries include: Company name, postal address, telephone, fax, e-mail, website, contact person, designation, and product details.

***Directory of South American Importers of Environment Protection and Pollution Control Equipment.*** EXIM Infotek Private Ltd., 604 Vishwa Deep, District Centre, Janakpuri New Delhi 110058, India. Phone: 91 11 25544793; Fax: 91 11 25544793; Email: info@eximinfo.org • URL: http://www.eximinfo.com • $200 Individuals; $10 Individuals. Covers: 80 South American importers of environmental protection equipment, pollution control equipment, water treatment, and purifying equipment. Entries include: Company name, postal address, telephone, fax, e-mail, website, contact person, designation, and product details.

***Directory of South American Importers of Fibre and Fibre Products.*** EXIM Infotek Private Ltd., 604 Vishwa Deep, District Centre, Janakpuri New Delhi 110058, India. Phone: 91 11 25544793; Fax: 91 11 25544793; Email: info@eximinfo.org • URL: http://www.eximinfo.com • $200 Individuals; $10 Individuals. Covers: 30 South American importers of fiberboard products, fiber glass cloth and products, fiber products, glass fiber, and synthetic fiber. Entries include: Company name, postal address, telephone, fax, e-mail, website, contact person, designation, and product details.

***Directory of South American Importers of Fire Fighting Equipment.*** EXIM Infotek Private Ltd., 604 Vishwa Deep, District Centre, Janakpuri New Delhi 110058, India. Phone: 91 11 25544793; Fax: 91 11 25544793; Email: info@eximinfo.org • URL: http://www.eximinfo.com • Covers: 40 South American importers of fire fighting equipment. Entries include: Company name, postal address, telephone, fax, e-mail, website, contact person, designation, and product details.

***Directory of South American Importers of Fodder and Animal Foodstuffs.*** EXIM Infotek Private Ltd., 604 Vishwa Deep, District Centre, Janakpuri New Delhi 110058, India. Phone: 91 11 25544793; Fax: 91 11 25544793; Email: info@eximinfo.org • URL: http://www.eximinfo.com • $300 Individuals; $10 Individuals. Covers: 140 South American importers of animal food, animal foodstuff additives, fodder, livestock breeding supplies, oats, and sorghum. Entries include: Company name, postal address, telephone, fax, e-mail, website, contact person, designation, and product details.

***Directory of South American Importers of Furnaces and Ovens—Industrial.*** EXIM Infotek Private Ltd., 604 Vishwa Deep, District Centre, Janakpuri New Delhi 110058, India. Phone: 91 11 25544793; Fax: 91 11 25544793; Email: info@eximinfo.org • URL: http://www.eximinfo.com • $150 Individuals; $5 Individuals. Covers: 20 South American importers of industrial furnaces and oven. Entries include: Company name, postal address, telephone, fax, e-mail, website, contact person, designation, and product details.

***Directory of South American Importers of Hardwares—All Types***. EXIM Infotek Private Ltd., 604 Vishwa Deep, District Centre, Janakpuri New Delhi 110058, India. Phone: 91 11 25544793; Fax: 91 11 25544793; Email: info@eximinfo.org • URL: http://www.eximinfo.com • $35 Individuals; $850 Individuals. Covers: 500 South American importers of abrasives, builders hardware, casters, furniture hardware and parts, and locks. Entries include: Company name, postal address, telephone, fax, e-mail, website, contact person, designation, and product details.

***Directory of South American Importers of Heaters and Heating Equipment***. EXIM Infotek Private Ltd., 604 Vishwa Deep, District Centre, Janakpuri New Delhi 110058, India. Phone: 91 11 25544793; Fax: 91 11 25544793; Email: info@eximinfo.org • URL: http://www.eximinfo.com • Covers: 50 South American importers of heat exchangers and heating equipment. Entries include: Company name, postal address, telephone, fax, e-mail, website, contact person, designation, and product details.

***Directory of South American Importers of Laboratory & Scientific Instruments & Supplies***. EXIM Infotek Private Ltd., 604 Vishwa Deep, District Centre, Janakpuri New Delhi 110058, India. Phone: 91 11 25544793; Fax: 91 11 25544793; Email: info@eximinfo.org • URL: http://www.eximinfo.com • Covers: 480 South American importers of binoculars, microscopes, telescopes, laboratory and scientific instruments, laboratory articles and equipment, laboratory glassware, laboratory products, and testing equipment. Entries include: Company name, postal address, telephone, fax, e-mail, website, contact person, designation, and product details.

***Directory of South American Importers of Lumber, Timber, Plywood and Hardboards***. EXIM Infotek Private Ltd., 604 Vishwa Deep, District Centre, Janakpuri New Delhi 110058, India. Phone: 91 11 25544793; Fax: 91 11 25544793; Email: info@eximinfo.org • URL: http://www.eximinfo.com • $400 Individuals; $15 Individuals. Covers: 200 South American importers of doors and windows, gypsum boards, hardboard and particle board, hardwood flooring and floor tiles, laminates (wood), hardwood lumber, softwood lumber, timber, plywood, millwork (wooden), veneer, poles, pilings and logs. Entries include: Company name, postal address, telephone, fax, e-mail, website, contact person, designation, and product details.

***Directory of South American Importers of Machinery for Paper & Pulp Industry***. EXIM Infotek Private Ltd., 604 Vishwa Deep, District Centre, Janakpuri New Delhi 110058, India. Phone: 91 11 25544793; Fax: 91 11 25544793; Email: info@eximinfo.org • URL: http://www.eximinfo.com • Covers: 40 South American importers of paper and pulp mill machinery and equipment and paper making machinery. Entries include: Company name, postal address, telephone, fax, e-mail, website, contact person, designation, and product details.

***Directory of South American Importers of Material Handling Equipment & Supplies***. EXIM Infotek Private Ltd., 604 Vishwa Deep, District Centre, Janakpuri New Delhi 110058, India. Phone: 91 11 25544793; Fax: 91 11 25544793; Email: info@eximinfo.org • URL: http://www.eximinfo.com • Covers: 140 South American importers of conveyors, cranes and hoists, elevator parts, elevators and lifts, escalators, forklifts, loading and unloading equipment, materials handling equipment and parts, monorail material handling equipment, winches, and pulleys. Entries include: Company name, postal address, telephone, fax, e-mail, website, contact person, designation, and product details.

***Directory of South American Importers of Motors and Motor Parts—Electric***. EXIM Infotek Private Ltd., 604 Vishwa Deep, District Centre, Janakpuri New Delhi 110058, India. Phone: 91 11 25544793; Fax: 91 11 25544793; Email: info@eximinfo.org • URL: http://www.eximinfo.com • $250 Individuals; $10 Individuals. Covers: 80 South American importers of electric motors, motor equipment, and motor parts. Entries include: Company name, postal address, telephone, fax, e-mail, website, contact person, designation, and product details.

***Directory of South American Importers of Petroleum Products***. EXIM Infotek Private Ltd., 604 Vishwa Deep, District Centre, Janakpuri New Delhi 110058, India. Phone: 91 11 25544793; Fax: 91 11 25544793; Email: info@eximinfo.org • URL: http://www.eximinfo.com • $350 Individuals; $15 Individuals. Covers: 120 South American importers of crude oil, fuel products, hydraulic fluid, lubricants, oil, grease and petroleum products, propane gas, and specialty lubricants. Entries include: Company name, postal address, telephone, fax, e-mail, website, contact person, designation, and product details.

***Directory of South American Importers of Photographic Equipment and Supplies***. EXIM Infotek Private Ltd., 604 Vishwa Deep, District Centre, Janakpuri New Delhi 110058, India. Phone: 91 11 25544793; Fax: 91 11 25544793; Email: info@eximinfo.org • URL: http://www.eximinfo.com • $350 Individuals; $15 Individuals. Covers: 130 South American importers of cameras, lens and accessories, cinema, motion picture equipment, theater equipment and supplies, film, plates and photographic papers, microfilm and blueprint equipment, photographic equipment and supplies, and photographic processing equipment. Entries include: Company name, postal address, telephone, fax, e-mail, website, contact person, designation, and product details.

***Directory of South American Importers of Plastic Scrap and Raw Materials***. EXIM Infotek Private Ltd., 604 Vishwa Deep, District Centre, Janakpuri New Delhi 110058, India. Phone: 91 11 25544793; Fax: 91 11 25544793; Email: info@eximinfo.org • URL: http://www.eximinfo.com • $300 Individuals; $10 Individuals. Covers: 110 South American importers of pet resins, plastic raw materials, plastic scrap and waste, polyester resins, and PVC compounds. Entries include: Company name, postal address, telephone, fax, e-mail, website, contact person, designation, and product details.

***Directory of South American Importers of Restaurant, Hotel and Catering Equipment***. EXIM Infotek Private Ltd., 604 Vishwa Deep, District Centre, Janakpuri New Delhi 110058, India. Phone: 91 11 25544793; Fax: 91 11 25544793; Email: info@eximinfo.org • URL: http://www.eximinfo.com • Covers: 100 South American importers of catering equipment, cooking equipment (patio and outdoors), cooking range and oven, fast food equipment, restaurant and hotel equipment. Entries include: Company name, postal address, telephone, fax, e-mail, website, contact person, designation, and product details.

***Directory of South American Importers of Sewing Machines and Parts***. EXIM Infotek Private Ltd., 604 Vishwa Deep, District Centre, Janakpuri New Delhi 110058, India. Phone: 91 11 25544793; Fax: 91 11 25544793; Email: info@eximinfo.org • URL: http://www.eximinfo.com • $350 Individuals; $15 Individuals. Covers: 110 South American importers of garment industry equipment, sewing machine and parts (domestic and industrial), and sewing machine needles. Entries include: Company name, postal address, telephone, fax, e-mail, website, contact person, designation, and product details.

***Directory of South American Importers of Sporting Goods***. EXIM Infotek Private Ltd., 604 Vishwa Deep, District Centre, Janakpuri New Delhi 110058, India. Phone: 91 11 25544793; Fax: 91 11 25544793; Email: info@eximinfo.org • URL: http://www.eximinfo.com • Covers: 140 South American importers of bowling equipment and supplies, fire arms, golf equipment and supplies, hiking accessories, mountaineering equipment and supplies, play ground equipment, riding accessories, skating equipment, ski boots, skiing accessories, sporting goods and toys, sporting goods, tennis and badminton equipment and supplies, and water sports equipment and supplies. Entries include: Company name, postal address, telephone, fax, e-mail, website, contact person, designation, and product details.

***Directory of South American Importers of Telephone Instruments and Accessories***. EXIM Infotek Private Ltd., 604 Vishwa Deep, District Centre, Janakpuri New Delhi 110058, India. Phone: 91 11 25544793; Fax: 91 11 25544793; Email: info@eximinfo.org • URL: http://www.eximinfo.com • $300 Individuals; $10 Individuals. Covers: 110 South American importers of mobile phone, mobile phone accessories, microphone, headphone, pagers, telecommunication equipment, telefax equipment, and telephone equipment. Entries include: Company name, postal address, telephone, fax, e-mail, website, contact person, designation, and product details.

***Directory of South American Importers of Vending and Coin Operated Machines***. EXIM Infotek Private Ltd., 604 Vishwa Deep, District Centre, Janakpuri New Delhi 110058, India. Phone: 91 11 25544793; Fax: 91 11 25544793; Email: info@eximinfo.org • URL: http://www.eximinfo.com • $150 Individuals; $5 Individuals. Covers: 20 South American importers of vending and coin operated machinery. Entries include: Company name, postal address, telephone, fax, e-mail, website, contact person, designation, and product details.

***Directory of South American Importers of Waste Disposal & Recycling Equipment***. EXIM Infotek Private Ltd., 604 Vishwa Deep, District Centre, Janakpuri New Delhi 110058, India. Phone: 91 11 25544793; Fax: 91 11 25544793; Email: info@eximinfo.org • URL: http://www.eximinfo.com • Covers: 40 South American importers of garbage disposals and compactors, waste disposal equipment, and waste recycling equipment. Entries include: Company name, postal address, telephone, fax, e-mail, website, contact person, designation, and product details.

***Directory of South American Importers of Wax & Wax Products***. EXIM Infotek Private Ltd., 604 Vishwa Deep, District Centre, Janakpuri New Delhi 110058, India. Phone: 91 11 25544793; Fax: 91 11 25544793; Email: info@eximinfo.org • URL: http://www.eximinfo.com • Covers: 20 South American importers of paraffin waxes, polishes and creams. Entries include: Company name, postal address, telephone, fax, e-mail, website, contact person, designation, and product details.

***Directory of South American Importers of Yarns and Threads***. EXIM Infotek Private Ltd., 604 Vishwa Deep, District Centre, Janakpuri New Delhi 110058, India. Phone: 91 11 25544793; Fax: 91 11 25544793; Email: info@eximinfo.org • URL: http://www.eximinfo.com • $250 Individuals; $10 Individuals. Covers: 100 South American importers of cotton yarn and thread, embroidery threads, metallic yarn and thread, nylon yarn for carpets, polyester yarn, sewing thread, synthetic yarns and thread, and wool yarn. Entries include: Company name, postal address, telephone, fax, e-mail, website, contact person, designation, and product details.

***Directory of South Korean Manufacturers & Exporters of Adhesive, Glues & Sealants***. EXIM Infotek Private Ltd., 604 Vishwa Deep, District Centre, Janakpuri New Delhi 110058, India. Phone: 91 11 25544793; Fax: 91 11 25544793; Email: info@eximinfo.org • URL: http://www.eximinfo.com • $5 Individuals. Covers: 30 South Korean manufacturers and exporters of processed rubber-solution and adhesives, synthetic adhesives. Entries include: Company name, postal address, city, country, phone, fax, e-mail and websites, contact person, designation, and product details.

***Directory of South Korean Manufacturers & Exporters of Agro Chemicals***. EXIM Infotek Private Ltd., 604 Vishwa Deep, District Centre, Janakpuri New Delhi 110058, India. Phone: 91 11 25544793; Fax: 91 11 25544793; Email: info@eximinfo.org • URL: http://www.eximinfo.com • $5 Individuals. Covers: 20 South Korean manufacturers and exporters of fertilizers, fungicides/insecticides/bactericides, and herbicides/plant growth control substances. Entries include: Company name, postal address, city, country, phone, fax, e-mail and websites, contact person, designation, and product details.

***Directory of South Korean Manufacturers and Exporters of Alcoholic Beverages and Wines***. EXIM Infotek Private Ltd., 604 Vishwa Deep, District Centre, Janakpuri New Delhi 110058, India. Phone: 91 11 25544793; Fax: 91 11 25544793; Email: info@eximinfo.org • URL: http://www.eximinfo.com • Covers: 20 South Korean manufacturers and exporters of alcoholic spirits, beer, fermented cider, grape wine, whisky, bourbon, and wine (non-grape). Entries include: Company name, postal address, telephone, fax, e-mail, website, contact person, designation, and product details.

***Directory of South Korean Manufacturers & Exporters of Automobiles & Vehicles***. EXIM Infotek Private Ltd., 604 Vishwa Deep, District Centre, Janakpuri New Delhi 110058, India. Phone: 91 11 25544793; Fax: 91 11 25544793; Email: info@eximinfo.org • URL: http://www.eximinfo.com • $5 Individuals. Covers: 20 South Korean manufacturers and exporters of automobile body builders, automobiles, buses and trucks, buses, cars, tractors/trucks/trailers-industrial, truck and lorry trailers, trucks/lorries, used cars, used trucks, used vehicles, and vehicles-special purpose. Entries include: Company name, postal address, city, country, phone, fax, e-mail and websites, contact person, designation, and product details.

***Directory of South Korean Manufacturers & Exporters of Automotive Service & Repair Equipment***. EXIM Infotek Private Ltd., 604 Vishwa Deep, District Centre, Janakpuri New Delhi 110058, India. Phone: 91 11 25544793; Fax: 91 11 25544793; Email: info@eximinfo.org • URL: http://www.eximinfo.com • $5 Individuals. Covers: 30 South Korean manufacturers and exporters of grills-radiator, mechanical lubrication tools, motor vehicle testing equipment, vehicle service and repair equipment. Entries include: Company name, postal address, city, country, phone, fax, e-mail and websites, contact person, designation, and product details.

***Directory of South Korean Manufacturers & Exporters of Autoparts & Accessories***. EXIM Infotek Private Ltd., 604 Vishwa Deep, District Centre, Janakpuri New Delhi 110058, India. Phone: 91 11 25544793; Fax: 91 11 25544793; Email: info@eximinfo.org • URL: http://www.eximinfo.com • $30 Individuals. Covers: 400 South Korean manufacturers and exporters of alternators, auto parts, auto spare parts, automobiles relay, automotive accessories, automotive lighting equipment, automotive plastic parts, axles-rear, axles-front (beam/drive), airbags, bars-automotive, brake systems, bulbs-auto, bumpers-plastic, cables-speed meter, caps-wheel, car rear view systems, clutch systems, couplings and clutches, cylinder head gaskets, disc brakes, hardware for motorcars, head lamps, horns-automotive, hydraulic shock absorbers, industrial trailer/truck parts/accessories, joints-universal, liners and pads-brake, motor vehicle accessories, motor vehicle body components and spare parts, motor vehicle transmission parts, radiators, rods-connecting, seats-automotive, shafts-axle, shafts-cam, shafts-crank, signal and indicator lamps, spare parts, springs/shock absorbers, steering and suspension parts, steering wheels, suspension parts, transmission parts, used auto parts, vehicle brake parts, vehicle control instruments and panels, vehicle electrical and electronic equipment, wheels and wheel rims, window regulators, wiper arms, and yokes-automotive. Entries include: Company name, postal address, city, country, telephone, fax, e-mail and websites, contact person, designation, and product details.

***Directory of South Korean Manufacturers & Exporters of Batteries & Accumulators***. EXIM Infotek Private Ltd., 604 Vishwa Deep, District Centre, Janakpuri New Delhi 110058, India. Phone: 91 11 25544793; Fax: 91 11 25544793; Email: info@eximinfo.org • URL: http://www.eximinfo.com • $10 Individuals. Covers: 90 South Korean manufacturers & exporters of automotive batteries, batteries & accumulators, battery, ups & battery chargers. Entries include: Company name, postal address, city, country, phone, fax, e-mail & websites, contact person, designation, products detail.

***Directory of South Korean Manufacturers & Exporters of Bearings***. EXIM Infotek Private Ltd., 604 Vishwa Deep, District Centre, Janakpuri New Delhi 110058, India. Phone: 91 11 25544793; Fax: 91 11 25544793; Email: info@

eximinfo.org • URL: http://www.eximinfo.com • $10 Individuals. Covers: 50 South Korean manufacturers and exporters of bearing and bushing-metal, bearings-ball, needle and roller, cap-bearings, clutch release bearings, plain bearings, plumber and pillow blocks/bushing, and roller bearings. Entries include: Company name, postal address, city, country, phone, fax, e-mail and websites, contact person, designation, and product details.

***Directory of South Korean Manufacturers & Exporters of Beauty Supplies, Cosmetics, Perfumes & Toiletries***. EXIM Infotek Private Ltd., 604 Vishwa Deep, District Centre, Janakpuri New Delhi 110058, India. Phone: 91 11 25544793; Fax: 91 11 25544793; Email: info@eximinfo.org • URL: http://www.eximinfo.com • $5 Individuals. Covers: 40 South Korean manufacturers and exporters of air fresheners, cosmetic brushes, cosmetic/hair/skin and dental products, cosmetics, hair brushes, hair combs, hand mirrors, manicure sets, nail clippers, and perfume. Entries include: Company name, postal address, city, country, phone, fax, e-mail and websites, contact person, designation, and product details.

***Directory of South Korean Manufacturers & Exporters of Bicycles, Parts & Accessories***. EXIM Infotek Private Ltd., 604 Vishwa Deep, District Centre, Janakpuri New Delhi 110058, India. Phone: 91 11 25544793; Fax: 91 11 25544793; Email: info@eximinfo.org • URL: http://www.eximinfo.com • $5 Individuals. Covers: 30 South Korean manufacturers and exporters of bicycle parts and accessories, bicycles and exercisers, flywheels. Entries include: Company name, postal address, city, country, phone, fax, e-mail and websites, contact person, designation, and product details.

***Directory of South Korean Manufacturers and Exporters of Boiler and Boiler Parts***. EXIM Infotek Private Ltd., 604 Vishwa Deep, District Centre, Janakpuri New Delhi 110058, India. Phone: 91 11 25544793; Fax: 91 11 25544793; Email: info@eximinfo.org • URL: http://www.eximinfo.com • Covers: 20 South Korean manufacturers and exporters of boilers and accessories, industrial steam boilers and accessories. Entries include: Company name, postal address, telephone, fax, e-mail, website, contact person, designation, and product details.

***Directory of South Korean Manufacturers & Exporters of Castings & Forgings***. EXIM Infotek Private Ltd., 604 Vishwa Deep, District Centre, Janakpuri New Delhi 110058, India. Phone: 91 11 25544793; Fax: 91 11 25544793; Email: info@eximinfo.org • URL: http://www.eximinfo.com • $10 Individuals. Covers: 80 South Korean manufacturers and exporters of casting, casting-aluminum and zinc, forging, iron castings, and steel castings. Entries include: Company name, postal address, city, country, phone, fax, e-mail and websites, contact person, designation, and product details.

***Directory of South Korean Manufacturers & Exporters of Chemicals & Allied Products***. EXIM Infotek Private Ltd., 604 Vishwa Deep, District Centre, Janakpuri New Delhi 110058, India. Phone: 91 11 25544793; Fax: 91 11 25544793; Email: info@eximinfo.org • URL: http://www.eximinfo.com • $25 Individuals. Covers: 350 South Korean manufacturers and exporters of acid coolers, alcohols and epoxides, amines, artificial resins, barium/boron/bromine/hydrogen compounds, base materials for non-metallic elements, calcium-strontium and thallium compounds, carbohydrates/proteins and enzymes, carbon based materials and products, catalysts, chemicals for basic metal industries, chemicals for building materials, chemicals for cosmetics/perfumery/detergent/soaps, chemicals for electrical/electronic industries, chemicals for laboratory and microbiology, chemicals for leather and fur tanning extract, chemicals for lubricants and waxes, chemicals for metal surface treatment, chemicals for metal welding/soldering fluxes, chemicals for paint/lacquer/varnish, chemicals for paper making/printing/photography, chemicals for plastic/rubber/ceramic, chemicals for unspecified uses, chemicals for water treatment, chemotherapeutic agents, compressed and liquefied gases/chemicals for refrigeration, detergents/cleansers and bleaching agents, disinfections and indoor deodorants, esters/acetates/ethyls and methyls, explosives, hydrocarbons and halcarbons, inorganic acids and anhydrides, inorganic alkalis-hydroxides, miscellaneous organic chemicals, natural resins and pitches, organic acids and anhydrides, phosphorus/sulphur/carbon/silicon and cassium compounds, polyphenols/ethers/aldehydes/ketones, potassium and ammonium compounds, pyrotechnic products, soaps/fatty-acid based detergents, sodium compounds. Entries include: Company name, postal address, city, country, telephone, fax, e-mail and websites, contact person, designation, and product details.

***Directory of South Korean Manufacturers & Exporters of Confectionery & Bakery Products***. EXIM Infotek Private Ltd., 604 Vishwa Deep, District Centre, Janakpuri New Delhi 110058, India. Phone: 91 11 25544793; Fax: 91 11 25544793; Email: info@eximinfo.org • URL: http://www.eximinfo.com • $10 Individuals. Covers: 80 South Korean manufacturers and exporters of biscuits/crackers, bread/cakes and pastry, noodles-instant, soups and extracts, sugar confectionery, and vinegar and sauce. Entries include: Company name, postal address, city, country, phone, fax, e-mail and websites, contact person, designation, and product details.

***Directory of South Korean Manufacturers and Exporters of Construction Machinery and Equipment***. EXIM Infotek Private Ltd., 604 Vishwa Deep, District Centre, Janakpuri New Delhi 110058, India. Phone: 91 11 25544793; Fax: 91 11 25544793; Email: info@eximinfo.org • URL: http://www.eximinfo.com • $250 Individuals; $10 Individuals. Covers: 90 South Korean manufacturers and exporters of asphalt mixing plant, bridge and tunnel construction machinery, building machinery, cement production plant, cement and plaster making plant, clay tile and brick production plant, concrete elements production plant, concrete making machinery, construction equipment, cranes and construction platforms, earthmoving and road making machinery, harbor and canal construction machinery, heavy mechanical handling equipment, road maintenance machinery, road rollers, scaffoldings and ladders, used construction equipment, and used cranes. Entries include: Company name, postal address, telephone, fax, e-mail, website, contact person, designation, and product details.

***Directory of South Korean Manufacturers & Exporters of Cotton, Silk, Wool Raw & Waste***. EXIM Infotek Private Ltd., 604 Vishwa Deep, District Centre, Janakpuri New Delhi 110058, India. Phone: 91 11 25544793; Fax: 91 11 25544793; Email: info@eximinfo.org • URL: http://www.eximinfo.com • $5 Individuals. Covers: 40 South Korean manufacturers and exporters of raw cotton and vegetable textile fiber, raw wool and other animal fibers, silkworms and silkworm cocoons. Entries include: Company name, postal address, city, country, phone, fax, e-mail and websites, contact person, designation, and product details.

***Directory of South Korean Manufacturers & Exporters of Dairy Products***. EXIM Infotek Private Ltd., 604 Vishwa Deep, District Centre, Janakpuri New Delhi 110058, India. Phone: 91 11 25544793; Fax: 91 11 25544793; Email: info@eximinfo.org • URL: http://www.eximinfo.com • $5 Individuals. Covers: 20 South Korean manufacturers and exporters of goat and sheep cheese, ice cream and sorbet, milk and milk products, and milk-condensed/dried. Entries include: Company name, postal address, city, country, phone, fax, e-mail and websites, contact person, designation, and product details.

***Directory of South Korean Manufacturers & Exporters of Dyes, Colours, Pigments & Intermediates***. EXIM Infotek Private Ltd., 604 Vishwa Deep, District Centre, Janakpuri New Delhi 110058, India. Phone: 91 11 25544793; Fax: 91 11 25544793; Email: info@eximinfo.org • URL: http://www.eximinfo.com • $10 Individuals. Covers: 90 South Korean manufacturers & exporters of chemicals for textiles, colorants for leather/rubber/plastic & cosmetics, dyes-synthetic, pigments-natural, pigments-synthetic, textile coatings. Entries include: Company name, postal address, city, country, phone, fax, e-mail & websites, contact person, designation, products detail.

***Directory of South Korean Manufacturers and Exporters of Energy and Power Equipment***. EXIM Infotek Private Ltd., 604 Vishwa Deep, District Centre, Janakpuri New Delhi 110058, India. Phone: 91 11 25544793; Fax: 91 11 25544793; Email: info@eximinfo.org • URL: http://www.eximinfo.com • Covers: 30 South Korean manufacturers and exporters of nuclear engineering plants, nuclear protection and detection instruments, power distribution equipment for various uses, power relays, and solar energy equipment. Entries include: Company name, postal address, telephone, fax, e-mail, website, contact person, designation, and product details.

***Directory of South Korean Manufacturers & Exporters of Engines & Engine Parts***. EXIM Infotek Private Ltd., 604 Vishwa Deep, District Centre, Janakpuri New Delhi 110058, India. Phone: 91 11 25544793; Fax: 91 11 25544793; Email: info@eximinfo.org • URL: http://www.eximinfo.com • $15 Individuals. Covers: 140 South Korean manufacturers and exporters of engine components/spare parts, engine parts and accessories, gaskets-various, internal combustion engines, pin-pistons, piston engines, piston brakes, used engines. Entries include: Company name, postal address, city, country, phone, fax, e-mail and websites, contact person, designation and product details.

***Directory of South Korean Manufacturers and Exporters of Environment and Pollution Control Equipment***. EXIM Infotek Private Ltd., 604 Vishwa Deep, District Centre, Janakpuri New Delhi 110058, India. Phone: 91 11 25544793; Fax: 91 11 25544793; Email: info@eximinfo.org • URL: http://www.eximinfo.com • $200 Individuals; $10 Individuals. Covers: 60 South Korean manufacturers and exporters of air pollution control equipment, air cleaner, noise pollution control equipment, water and sewage treatment plant. Entries include: Company name, postal address, telephone, fax, e-mail, website, contact person, designation, and product details.

***Directory of South Korean Manufacturers & Exporters of Filters & Strainers—Industrial***. EXIM Infotek Private Ltd., 604 Vishwa Deep, District Centre, Janakpuri New Delhi 110058, India. Phone: 91 11 25544793; Fax: 91 11 25544793; Email: info@eximinfo.org • URL: http://www.eximinfo.com • $10 Individuals. Covers: 50 South Korean manufacturers and exporters of bolting and filter cloths/gauzes, filters, filters and strainers for processing industries, filters and strainers-metal, line filters, and water and waste water filters. Entries include: Company name, postal address, city, country, phone, fax, e-mail and websites, contact person, designation, and product details.

***Directory of South Korean Manufacturers & Exporters of Fire Fighting Equipment & Supplies***. EXIM Infotek Private Ltd., 604 Vishwa Deep, District Centre, Janakpuri New Delhi 110058, India. Phone: 91 11 25544793; Fax: 91 11 25544793; Email: info@eximinfo.org • URL: http://www.eximinfo.com • Covers: 30 South Korean manufacturers and exporters of fire fighting equipment. Entries include: Company name, postal address, telephone, fax, e-mail, website, contact person, designation, and product details.

***Directory of South Korean Manufacturers & Exporters of Furniture—All Types***. EXIM Infotek Private Ltd., 604 Vishwa Deep, District Centre, Janakpuri New Delhi 110058, India. Phone: 91 11 25544793; Fax: 91 11 25544793; Email: info@eximinfo.org • URL: http://www.eximinfo.com • $15 Individuals. Covers: 140 South Korean manufacturers and exporters of arm-rockers, furniture and fittings for shops/stores, furniture for manufactured products, furniture/racking-industrial/lab, furniture-children, furniture-domestic, furniture-garden, furniture-hospital, furniture-hotel/restaurant/bar, furniture-kitchen, furniture-office, furniture-public places, furniture-school, furniture-ships, furniture-upholstered, knockdown furniture, metal cabinets, small furniture articles. Entries include: Company name, postal address, city, country, phone, fax, e-mail and websites, contact person, designation and product details.

***Directory of South Korean Manufacturers & Exporters of Gears & Gears Boxes***. EXIM Infotek Private Ltd., 604 Vishwa Deep, District Centre, Janakpuri New Delhi 110058, India. Phone: 91 11 25544793; Fax: 91 11 25544793; Email: info@eximinfo.org • URL: http://www.eximinfo.com • $5 Individuals. Covers: 20 South Korean manufacturers and exporters of gear boxes and gears. Entries include: Company name, postal address, city, country, phone, fax, e-mail and websites, contact person, designation, and product details.

***Directory of South Korean Manufacturers & Exporters of Gemstones & Diamonds***. EXIM Infotek Private Ltd., 604 Vishwa Deep, District Centre, Janakpuri New Delhi 110058, India. Phone: 91 11 25544793; Fax: 91 11 25544793; Email: info@eximinfo.org • URL: http://www.eximinfo.com • $5 Individuals. Covers: 20 South Korean manufacturers and exporters of colored precious stones-polished, diamond-polished, diamonds-rough, ivory/coral/pearl articles, and rough colored precious stones. Entries include: Company name, postal address, city, country, phone, fax, e-mail and websites, contact person, designation, and product details.

***Directory of South Korean Manufacturers & Exporters of Giftware & Novelties***. EXIM Infotek Private Ltd., 604 Vishwa Deep, District Centre, Janakpuri New Delhi 110058, India. Phone: 91 11 25544793; Fax: 91 11 25544793; Email: info@eximinfo.org • URL: http://www.eximinfo.com • $5 Individuals. Covers: 40 South Korean manufacturers and exporters of albums and files, coins/medals/decorations and badges, key holders, medals, photo albums, photo frames, promotional giftware, and trophies/ceremonial plates. Entries include: Company name, postal address, city, country, phone, fax, e-mail and websites, contact person, designation, and product details.

***Directory of South Korean Manufacturers & Exporters of Glass, China, Ceramic & Porcelainware***. EXIM Infotek Private Ltd., 604 Vishwa Deep, District Centre, Janakpuri New Delhi 110058, India. Phone: 91 11 25544793; Fax: 91 11 25544793; Email: info@eximinfo.org • URL: http://www.eximinfo.com • $150 Individuals; $5 Individuals. Covers: 40 South Korean manufacturers and exporters of glass tableware, glassware, handmade glassware, porcelain and ceramic products, pottery, Chinaware, and shaped glass products. Entries include: Company name, postal address, telephone, fax, e-mail, website, contact person, designation, and product details.

***Directory of South Korean Manufacturers & Exporters of Handtools***. EXIM Infotek Private Ltd., 604 Vishwa Deep, District Centre, Janakpuri New Delhi 110058, India. Phone: 91 11 25544793; Fax: 91 11 25544793; Email: info@eximinfo.org • URL: http://www.eximinfo.com • $10 Individuals. Covers: 70 South Korean manufacturers and exporters of box-tool, builders tools, carbide tools, chisels/taps/dies and similar tools, electric and electro-magnetic tools, hammers/mallets and similar tools, metal hand and diamond tools, pliers/clamps and similar tools, roofers and decorators tools, and screwdrivers/wrenches. Entries include: Company name, postal address, city, country, phone, fax, e-mail and websites, contact person, designation, and product details.

***Directory of South Korean Manufacturers & Exporters of Hardwares—All Types***. EXIM Infotek Private Ltd., 604 Vishwa Deep, District Centre, Janakpuri New Delhi 110058, India. Phone: 91 11 25544793; Fax: 91 11 25544793; Email: info@eximinfo.org • URL: http://www.eximinfo.com • $15 Individuals. Covers: 160 South Korean manufacturers and exporters of abrasive coated products, abrasive paper, brackets, clips, frame-doors (channel), haberdashery metalware, hinge-doors/trunks/hoods, ironmongery and hardware, ironmongery and hardware for furniture, locksmith articles, metal fittings, metal smallwares for various uses, nails/tacks/spikes/staples-metal, paint brushes and rollers, pins, and springs-various types. Entries include: Company name, postal address, city, country, phone, fax, e-mail and websites, contact person, designation, and product details.

***Directory of South Korean Manufacturers & Exporters of Health Care Products & Foods***. EXIM Infotek Private Ltd.,

604 Vishwa Deep, District Centre, Janakpuri New Delhi 110058, India. Phone: 91 11 25544793; Fax: 91 11 25544793; Email: info@eximinfo.org • URL: http://www.eximinfo.com • Covers: 20 South Korean manufacturers and exporters of health and diet products. Entries include: Company name, postal address, telephone, fax, e-mail, website, contact person, designation, and product details.

*Directory of South Korean Manufacturers & Exporters of Heaters & Heating Equipment.* EXIM Infotek Private Ltd., 604 Vishwa Deep, District Centre, Janakpuri New Delhi 110058, India. Phone: 91 11 25544793; Fax: 91 11 25544793; Email: info@eximinfo.org • URL: http://www.eximinfo.com • $350 Individuals; $15 Individuals. Covers: 130 South Korean manufacturers and exporters of air and gas heaters, central heating equipment, central heating systems, driers, drying plants, electric heating equipment, heat exchangers, heaters, and heating machine. Entries include: Company name, postal address, telephone, fax, e-mail, website, contact person, designation, and product details.

*Directory of South Korean Manufacturers & Exporters of Herbs & Herbal Medicine Products.* EXIM Infotek Private Ltd., 604 Vishwa Deep, District Centre, Janakpuri New Delhi 110058, India. Phone: 91 11 25544793; Fax: 91 11 25544793; Email: info@eximinfo.org • URL: http://www.eximinfo.com • $5 Individuals. Covers: 30 South Korean manufacturers and exporters of Chinese medical preparations, herb plants, herbal medicines. Entries include: Company name, postal address, city, country, phone, fax, e-mail and websites, contact person, designation, and product details.

*Directory of South Korean Manufacturers & Exporters of Home Furnishing Materials.* EXIM Infotek Private Ltd., 604 Vishwa Deep, District Centre, Janakpuri New Delhi 110058, India. Phone: 91 11 25544793; Fax: 91 11 25544793; Email: info@eximinfo.org • URL: http://www.eximinfo.com • $10 Individuals. Covers: 50 South Korean manufacturers and exporters of blankets, household linen and soft furnishings, mattresses, cushions and pillows, sanitary towels and baby napkins, and tapestries. Entries include: Company name, postal address, city, country, phone, fax, e-mail and websites, contact person, designation, and product details.

*Directory of South Korean Manufacturers & Exporters of Imitation & Fashion Jewellery.* EXIM Infotek Private Ltd., 604 Vishwa Deep, District Centre, Janakpuri New Delhi 110058, India. Phone: 91 11 25544793; Fax: 91 11 25544793; Email: info@eximinfo.org • URL: http://www.eximinfo.com • $15 Individuals. Covers: 150 South Korean manufacturers and exporters of bracelets, buckles, ladies belts, costume jewelry, cuff links, custom jewelry, earrings, fashion goods, fashion jewelry, hair bands, hair ornaments, hair pins, imitation jewelry, jewelry, necklaces, synthetic diamonds, synthetic jewels for watches, and tie pins. Entries include: Company name, postal address, city, country, phone, fax, e-mail and websites, contact person, designation, and product details.

*Directory of South Korean Manufacturers & Exporters of Laces, Ribbons & Embroidery Products.* EXIM Infotek Private Ltd., 604 Vishwa Deep, District Centre, Janakpuri New Delhi 110058, India. Phone: 91 11 25544793; Fax: 91 11 25544793; Email: info@eximinfo.org • URL: http://www.eximinfo.com • $10 Individuals. Covers: 50 South Korean manufacturers and exporters of badges, embroidery-all types, embroidery/lace mending services, embroidery-hand made, lace, lace-machine made, ribbons, ribbons and tapes for industrial use, ribbons and tapes-non industrial, and trimmings/cordings/braids and fringes. Entries include: Company name, postal address, city, country, phone, fax, e-mail and websites, contact person, designation, and product details.

*Directory of South Korean Manufacturers & Exporters of Leather, Hides, Skins & Furs.* EXIM Infotek Private Ltd., 604 Vishwa Deep, District Centre, Janakpuri New Delhi 110058, India. Phone: 91 11 25544793; Fax: 91 11 25544793; Email: info@eximinfo.org • URL: http://www.eximinfo.com • $10 Individuals. Covers: 110 South Korean manufacturers & exporters of leather- reconstituted, leather-processed, PVC leathercloth, sheep & goat skins, sheep & lamb skins, skins, hides & leather, swine skins/leather. Entries include: Company name, postal address, city, country, phone, fax, e-mail & websites, contact person, designation, products detail.

*Directory of South Korean Manufacturers & Exporters of Leather Products.* EXIM Infotek Private Ltd., 604 Vishwa Deep, District Centre, Janakpuri New Delhi 110058, India. Phone: 91 11 25544793; Fax: 91 11 25544793; Email: info@eximinfo.org • URL: http://www.eximinfo.com • $15 Individuals. Covers: 130 South Korean manufacturers and exporters of bags, cases and covers of leather, fancy leather goods, fur clothing and products, leather airbags/sportbags, leather clothing, leather goods for industrial use and leather waist belts. Entries include: Company name, postal address, city, country, phone, fax, e-mail and websites, contact person, designation, and product details.

*Directory of South Korean Manufacturers & Exporters of Lighting Fixtures, Lamps & Accessories.* EXIM Infotek Private Ltd., 604 Vishwa Deep, District Centre, Janakpuri New Delhi 110058, India. Phone: 91 11 25544793; Fax: 91 11 25544793; Email: info@eximinfo.org • URL: http://www.eximinfo.com • $10 Individuals. Covers: 90 South Korean manufacturers & exporters of aluminum flashlights, bulbs-halogen, discharge & special purpose lamps, electric lamp components, filament lamps-all types, fluorescent lamps, halogen lamps, indoor electric lighting equipment, lamp accessories & parts, lamp-combination, lamps, lamp various, lighting appliances-non electric, lighting equipment-outdoor, matches, pilot lamps, portable electric lamps & accessories, sub-miniature lamps. Entries include: Company name, postal address, city, country, phone, fax, e-mail & websites, contact person, designation, products detail.

*Directory of South Korean Manufacturers & Exporters of Machinery for Chemicals & Pharma Industry.* EXIM Infotek Private Ltd., 604 Vishwa Deep, District Centre, Janakpuri New Delhi 110058, India. Phone: 91 11 25544793; Fax: 91 11 25544793; Email: info@eximinfo.org • URL: http://www.eximinfo.com • $10 Individuals. Covers: 60 South Korean manufacturers and exporters of crushers/pulverizers for chemical industries, dryers/evaporators/crystallizers for chemical industries, electrochemical and electrolytic plant equipment, electroplating plant machinery, glycerine production plant machinery, heaters/boilers/distillers for chemical industries, organic chemical production plant equipment, paint/varnish/enamel/ink production plant equipment, pharmaceutical/cosmetic production plant equipment, reactors for chemical industry, screeners/mixers/centrifuges for chemical industry, and technical gas production plant equipment. Entries include: Company name, postal address, city, country, phone, fax, e-mail and websites, contact person, designation, and product details.

*Directory of South Korean Manufacturers & Exporters of Machinery for Leather & Shoe Industry.* EXIM Infotek Private Ltd., 604 Vishwa Deep, District Centre, Janakpuri New Delhi 110058, India. Phone: 91 11 25544793; Fax: 91 11 25544793; Email: info@eximinfo.org • URL: http://www.eximinfo.com • $5 Individuals. Covers: 20 South Korean manufacturers and exporters of boot and shoe making machinery/equipment, leather working and saddlery making equipment. Entries include: Company name, postal address, city, country, phone, fax, e-mail and websites, contact person, designation, and product details.

*Directory of South Korean Manufacturers & Exporters of Machinery for Paper & Pulp Industry.* EXIM Infotek Private Ltd., 604 Vishwa Deep, District Centre, Janakpuri New Delhi 110058, India. Phone: 91 11 25544793; Fax: 91 11 25544793; Email: info@eximinfo.org • URL: http://www.eximinfo.com • $5 Individuals. Covers: 30 South Korean manufacturers and exporters of cardboard finishing/forming/cutting machinery/equipment, cardboard making machinery/equipment, paper finishing/converting machinery/equipment, paper making plant equipment, pulp and cellulose production plant equipment. Entries include: Company name, postal address, city, country, phone, fax, e-mail and websites, contact person, designation, and product details.

*Directory of South Korean Manufacturers & Exporters of Machinery for Textile and Knitting Industry.* EXIM Infotek Private Ltd., 604 Vishwa Deep, District Centre, Janakpuri New Delhi 110058, India. Phone: 91 11 25544793; Fax: 91 11 25544793; Email: info@eximinfo.org • URL: http://www.eximinfo.com • $15 Individuals. Covers: 150 South Korean manufacturers and exporters of beam brakes and discs for textile machinery, belts/hoses/webbing-textile, bobbins for textile industry, carpet and tapestry looms, cotton preparation machinery and equipment, felt and non-woven fabric making machinery, knitting machinery and attachments, lace and net making machinery, manmade fiber production and processing plants, ribbon and trim making machinery, silk and schappe preparation machinery and equipment, sleeves and strips for spinning mills, textile dyeing and boiling machinery/equipment, textile finishing machinery and equipment, textile machinery, textile machinery parts, textile printing machinery and equipment, textile printings, textile spinning and twisting machinery, textile washing/mercerizing machinery and equipment, textile waste processing, textile waste processing machinery and equipment, textile weaving machinery parts/accessories, textile weaving machinery/looms, textile winding and reeling machinery, weaving machines, yarn preparation machinery/equipment, and yarn tensioners. Entries include: Company name, postal address, city, country, telephone, fax, e-mail and websites, contact person, designation, and product details.

*Directory of South Korean Manufacturers & Exporters of Marine & Boating Equipment & Supplies.* EXIM Infotek Private Ltd., 604 Vishwa Deep, District Centre, Janakpuri New Delhi 110058, India. Phone: 91 11 25544793; Fax: 91 11 25544793; Email: info@eximinfo.org • URL: http://www.eximinfo.com • $5 Individuals. Covers: 40 South Korean manufacturers and exporters of boat parts and accessories, coastal vessels, control and navigational instruments-ship, equipment/signals for ships/boats, marine propulsion units, radar and navigation systems/equipment-marine, yacht and pleasure craft. Entries include: Company name, postal address, city, country, phone, fax, e-mail and websites, contact person, designation, and product details.

*Directory of South Korean Manufacturers & Exporters of Material Handling Equipment.* EXIM Infotek Private Ltd., 604 Vishwa Deep, District Centre, Janakpuri New Delhi 110058, India. Phone: 91 11 25544793; Fax: 91 11 25544793; Email: info@eximinfo.org • URL: http://www.eximinfo.com • $400 Individuals; $15 Individuals. Covers: 170 South Korean manufacturers and exporters of automated handling and storage equipment, barrows, trolleys, carts, conveyors and elevators, cranes, hoists, winches, forklift trucks, handling equipment parts and accessories, ice crushers, lifts, mobile cranes, overhead conveyors, pallets and containers, pneumatic handling equipment, pulleys, and cable wheels. Entries include: Company name, postal address, telephone, fax, e-mail, website, contact person, designation, and product details.

*Directory of South Korean Manufacturers & Exporters of Meat & Meat Products.* EXIM Infotek Private Ltd., 604 Vishwa Deep, District Centre, Janakpuri New Delhi 110058, India. Phone: 91 11 25544793; Fax: 91 11 25544793; Email: info@eximinfo.org • URL: http://www.eximinfo.com • $5 Individuals. Covers: 20 South Korean manufacturers and exporters of meat and game-processed/preserved, meat and meat products, meat-dried, and sausage casings. Entries include: Company name, postal address, city, country, phone, fax, e-mail and websites, contact person, designation, and product details.

*Directory of South Korean Manufacturers & Exporters of Minerals.* EXIM Infotek Private Ltd., 604 Vishwa Deep, District Centre, Janakpuri New Delhi 110058, India. Phone: 91 11 25544793; Fax: 91 11 25544793; Email: info@eximinfo.org • URL: http://www.eximinfo.com • $10 Individuals. Covers: 70 South Korean manufacturers and exporters of clays, graphite and clay bonded graphite products, graphite-natural, gypsum and anhydrite, gypsum/plaster and lime, gypsum/plaster and stucco products, limestones, magnesium minerals, mica and mecanite products, quartz and silica electro thermic products, quartzite of crystal, silicon minerals, slate products, and steatite and pyrophillite. Entries include: Company name, postal address, city, country, phone, fax, e-mail and websites, contact person, designation, and product details.

*Directory of South Korean Manufacturers and Exporters of Motors and Motor Parts—Electric.* EXIM Infotek Private Ltd., 604 Vishwa Deep, District Centre, Janakpuri New Delhi 110058, India. Phone: 91 11 25544793; Fax: 91 11 25544793; Email: info@eximinfo.org • URL: http://www.eximinfo.com • $250 Individuals; $10 Individuals. Covers: 70 South Korean manufacturers and exporters of motorcycles and mopeds. Entries include: Company name, postal address, telephone, fax, e-mail, website, contact person, designation, and product details.

*Directory of South Korean Manufacturers & Exporters of Nuts, Bolts, Screws & Fasteners.* EXIM Infotek Private Ltd., 604 Vishwa Deep, District Centre, Janakpuri New Delhi 110058, India. Phone: 91 11 25544793; Fax: 91 11 25544793; Email: info@eximinfo.org • URL: http://www.eximinfo.com • $10 Individuals. Covers: 50 South Korean manufacturers and exporters of bolts and nuts, nails, fasteners-metal, metal nuts/bolts/washers, metal rivets, metal screws/bolts/nuts, and screws-metal. Entries include: Company name, postal address, city, country, phone, fax, e-mail and websites, contact person, designation, and product details.

*Directory of South Korean Manufacturers & Exporters of Oil & Fats—Cooking & Vegetable.* EXIM Infotek Private Ltd., 604 Vishwa Deep, District Centre, Janakpuri New Delhi 110058, India. Phone: 91 11 25544793; Fax: 91 11 25544793; Email: info@eximinfo.org • URL: http://www.eximinfo.com • $5 Individuals. Covers: 20 South Korean manufacturers and exporters of oils and fats-edible. Entries include: Company name, postal address, city, country, phone, fax, e-mail and websites, contact person, designation, and product details.

*Directory of South Korean Manufacturers & Exporters of Paints, Varnishes & Allied Products.* EXIM Infotek Private Ltd., 604 Vishwa Deep, District Centre, Janakpuri New Delhi 110058, India. Phone: 91 11 25544793; Fax: 91 11 25544793; Email: info@eximinfo.org • URL: http://www.eximinfo.com • $5 Individuals. Covers: 40 South Korean manufacturers and exporters of anti-corrosion products, lacquers and paints-primers, varnishes and stains-distempers, and vitreous colors/enamels and glazes. Entries include: Company name, postal address, city, country, phone, fax, e-mail and websites, contact person, designation, and product details.

*Directory of South Korean Manufacturers & Exporters of Paper & Paper Products.* EXIM Infotek Private Ltd., 604 Vishwa Deep, District Centre, Janakpuri New Delhi 110058, India. Phone: 91 11 25544793; Fax: 91 11 25544793; Email: info@eximinfo.org • URL: http://www.eximinfo.com • $20 Individuals. Covers: 280 South Korean manufacturers and exporters of base and backing paper, cardboard, cardboard/corrugated-packaging, coated and laminated paper/board, corrugated paper and board, paper and cardboard tubes, paper and paper rolls for technical use, paper and paper rolls printed for writing/technical, paper article-diecut/embossed, paper packaging/bags and sacks, photographic paper/board/film, printing and drawing paper/board, pulp mechanical and chemicals, reinforced cardboard and vulcanized fiber products, reinforced cardboard products, tissue paper and cellulose wadding, wallpaper and paper backed wallcoverings, wrapping/crepe paper. Entries include: Company name, postal address, city, country, phone, fax, e-mail and websites, contact person, designation, and product details.

*Directory of South Korean Manufacturers & Exporters of Petroleum Products.* EXIM Infotek Private Ltd., 604 Vishwa Deep, District Centre, Janakpuri New Delhi 110058, India. Phone: 91 11 25544793; Fax: 91 11 25544793; Email: info@

eximinfo.org • URL: http://www.eximinfo.com • $10 Individuals. Covers: 60 South Korean manufacturers and exporters of mineral oils and greases, natural oils and greases for technical use, petroleum products/fuels and lubricants, solvents-petroleum based, tar and bituminous products, tar and resin distillation products. Entries include: Company name, postal address, city, country, phone, fax, e-mail and websites, contact person, designation, and product details.

***Directory of South Korean Manufacturers & Exporters of Pharmaceutical Products***. EXIM Infotek Private Ltd., 604 Vishwa Deep, District Centre, Janakpuri New Delhi 110058, India. Phone: 91 11 25544793; Fax: 91 11 25544793; Email: info@eximinfo.org • URL: http://www.eximinfo.com • $10 Individuals. Covers: 120 South Korean manufacturers & exporters of antibiotics, microencapsulated pharmaceuticals, ophthalmic preparations, pharmaceutical preparations for cardio-vascular, pharmaceutical preparations, veterinary preparations-general, vitamin preparations. Entries include: Company name, postal address, city, country, phone, fax, e-mail & websites, contact person, designation, products detail.

***Directory of South Korean Manufacturers & Exporters of Pharmaceutical Raw Materials***. EXIM Infotek Private Ltd., 604 Vishwa Deep, District Centre, Janakpuri New Delhi 110058, India. Phone: 91 11 25544793; Fax: 91 11 25544793; Email: info@eximinfo.org • URL: http://www.eximinfo.com • $5 Individuals. Covers: 20 South Korean manufacturers and exporters of gelatins for pharmaceuticals, hypodermoclysis and phleboclysis solutions, pharmaceutical base and suppository compounds, vitamins/hormones and organ extracts. Entries include: Company name, postal address, city, country, phone, fax, e-mail and websites, contact person, designation, and product details.

***Directory of South Korean Manufacturers & Exporters of Plastics & Plastic Products***. EXIM Infotek Private Ltd., 604 Vishwa Deep, District Centre, Janakpuri New Delhi 110058, India. Phone: 91 11 25544793; Fax: 91 11 25544793; Email: info@eximinfo.org • URL: http://www.eximinfo.com • $600 Individuals; $25 Individuals. Covers: 300 South Korean manufacturers and exporters of doors, windows, skylights, glass fiber reinforced plastic products, haberdasher articles, laminating roll film, offlets drain channels, plastic articles for shops, plastic films, plastic injection molding products, plastic laminated sheets, plastic products for agricultural industry, building industry, chemical industry, pharmaceutical industry, cosmetic industry, electrical and electronics industry, mechanical engineering industry, optical and photographic industry, surgical and orthopedic use, textile industry, food and beverage industry; plastic semi-finished products-bars/rods/shapes, plastic semi-finished products-plates/sheets/film/tape, plastic-injection molding, polyester film, and sponges.

***Directory of South Korean Manufacturers & Exporters of Readymade Garments***. EXIM Infotek Private Ltd., 604 Vishwa Deep, District Centre, Janakpuri New Delhi 110058, India. Phone: 91 11 25544793; Fax: 91 11 25544793; Email: info@eximinfo.org • URL: http://www.eximinfo.com • $30 Individuals. Covers: 400 South Korean manufacturers and exporters of casual and leisurewear, clothing and accessories-rubber, garments, handkerchiefs, hosiery, knitwear, ladies blouses, mufflers, protective work clothing, readymade for infants, readymade for ladies/girls, readymade garment for men/boy, scarves, shirts-all types, sundries, swim and beach wear, uniforms and professional clothing, and waterproof garments. Entries include: Company name, postal address, city, country, phone, fax, e-mail and websites, contact person, designation, and product details.

***Directory of South Korean Manufacturers & Exporters of Safety & Security Equipment & Supplies***. EXIM Infotek Private Ltd., 604 Vishwa Deep, District Centre, Janakpuri New Delhi 110058, India. Phone: 91 11 25544793; Fax: 91 11 25544793; Email: info@eximinfo.org • URL: http://www.eximinfo.com • Covers: 40 South Korean manufacturers and exporters of alarms, intruder detection systems, protection and life saving equipment, signaling and alarm equipment, video doorphones, and video security systems. Entries include: Company name, postal address, telephone, fax, e-mail, website, contact person, designation, and product details.

***Directory of South Korean Manufacturers & Exporters of Sea Food & Fish***. EXIM Infotek Private Ltd., 604 Vishwa Deep, District Centre, Janakpuri New Delhi 110058, India. Phone: 91 11 25544793; Fax: 91 11 25544793; Email: info@eximinfo.org • URL: http://www.eximinfo.com • $400 Individuals; $15 Individuals. Covers: 160 South Korean manufacturers and exporters of crustaceans, fish and shelfish by-products, fish roes, fish (canned/bottled), fish, processed fish, saltwater fish, frozen sea food products, marine algae and plankton, mollusks, shelfish and seaweed (canned/bottled), shrimps and prawns. Entries include: Company name, postal address, telephone, fax, e-mail, website, contact person, designation, and product details.

***Directory of South Korean Manufacturers & Exporters of Shoes & Footwears***. EXIM Infotek Private Ltd., 604 Vishwa Deep, District Centre, Janakpuri New Delhi 110058, India. Phone: 91 11 25544793; Fax: 91 11 25544793; Email: info@eximinfo.org • URL: http://www.eximinfo.com • $10 Individuals. Covers: 90 South Korean manufacturers & exporters of boots-rubber, footwear soles/components, footwear-industrial/protective, footwear-sports, footwear-standard. Entries include: Company name, postal address, city, country, phone, fax, e-mail & websites, contact person, designation, products detail.

***Directory of South Korean Manufacturers & Exporters of Sporting Goods***. EXIM Infotek Private Ltd., 604 Vishwa Deep, District Centre, Janakpuri New Delhi 110058, India. Phone: 91 11 25544793; Fax: 91 11 25544793; Email: info@eximinfo.org • URL: http://www.eximinfo.com • $250 Individuals; $10 Individuals. Covers: 90 South Korean manufacturers and exporters of ball sports equipment, billiard table sets/cues, camping equipment, fishing tackle, golf carts and van, golf club and badminton shafts, gymnasium and exercise equipment, sports equipment, winter and mountaineering sports equipment. Entries include: Company name, postal address, telephone, fax, e-mail, website, contact person, designation, and product details.

***Directory of South Korean Manufacturers & Exporters of Stationery Articles & Education Supplies***. EXIM Infotek Private Ltd., 604 Vishwa Deep, District Centre, Janakpuri New Delhi 110058, India. Phone: 91 11 25544793; Fax: 91 11 25544793; Email: info@eximinfo.org • URL: http://www.eximinfo.com • $250 Individuals; $10 Individuals. Covers: 70 South Korean manufacturers and exporters of drawing and mathematical instruments, filing systems, inks and artists colors, pencil cases, pens, pencils, rubber stamps and pads, staplers, stationeries, stationery and greeting cards, stationery articles, writing and drawing equipment. Entries include: Company name, postal address, telephone, fax, e-mail, website, contact person, designation, and product details.

***Directory of South Korean Manufacturers & Exporters of Textile & Fabrics***. EXIM Infotek Private Ltd., 604 Vishwa Deep, District Centre, Janakpuri New Delhi 110058, India. Phone: 91 11 25544793; Fax: 91 11 25544793; Email: info@eximinfo.org • URL: http://www.eximinfo.com • $30 Individuals. Covers: 390 South Korean manufacturers and exporters of dyeing and finishing for fabrics and textile goods, fabric-cotton for furnishing, fabrics for industrial use, fabrics-cotton, fabrics-hemp/jute/paper, fabric-silk, fabrics-knitted, fabrics-linen, fabrics-manmade fiber, fabrics-non woven, felts/felted fabrics, net and tulle, textiles, velvet items, wadding and flock textile for industrial use, and woolen fabrics. Entries include: Company name, postal address, city, country, phone, fax, e-mail and websites, contact person, designation, and product details.

***Directory of South Korean Manufacturers & Exporters of Toys & Games***. EXIM Infotek Private Ltd., 604 Vishwa Deep, District Centre, Janakpuri New Delhi 110058, India. Phone: 91 11 25544793; Fax: 91 11 25544793; Email: info@eximinfo.org • URL: http://www.eximinfo.com • $10 Individuals. Covers: 90 South Korean manufacturers & exporters of animal toys, dolls & puppets, model aircrafts, musical articles & toys, party & educational games, plush toys, stuffed toys, toys & games-electric/electronic, toys & games-mechanical, toys & games-plastic, toys & games-rubber, toys & games-wooden. Entries include: Company name, postal address, city, country, phone, fax, e-mail & websites, contact person, designation, products detail.

***Directory of South Korean Manufacturers & Exporters of Travel & Luggage Accessories***. EXIM Infotek Private Ltd., 604 Vishwa Deep, District Centre, Janakpuri New Delhi 110058, India. Phone: 91 11 25544793; Fax: 91 11 25544793; Email: info@eximinfo.org • URL: http://www.eximinfo.com • $10 Individuals. Covers: 70 South Korean manufacturers and exporters of leather travel goods/handbags, umbrellas and walking sticks. Entries include: Company name, postal address, city, country, phone, fax, e-mail and websites, contact person, designation, and product details.

***Directory of South Korean Manufacturers & Exporters of Tyres & Tubes***. EXIM Infotek Private Ltd., 604 Vishwa Deep, District Centre, Janakpuri New Delhi 110058, India. Phone: 91 11 25544793; Fax: 91 11 25544793; Email: info@eximinfo.org • URL: http://www.eximinfo.com • $5 Individuals. Covers: 20 South Korean manufacturers and exporters of tires-remolded, vehicle tires and inner tubes. Entries include: Company name, postal address, city, country, phone, fax, e-mail and websites, contact person, designation, and product details.

***Directory of South Korean Manufacturers & Exporters of Undergarments***. EXIM Infotek Private Ltd., 604 Vishwa Deep, District Centre, Janakpuri New Delhi 110058, India. Phone: 91 11 25544793; Fax: 91 11 25544793; Email: info@eximinfo.org • URL: http://www.eximinfo.com • $10 Individuals. Covers: 60 South Korean manufacturers and exporters of lingerie/corsetry, nightwear, underwear, and stockings. Entries include: Company name, postal address, city, country, phone, fax, e-mail and websites, contact person, designation, and product details.

***Directory of South Korean Manufacturers & Exporters of Ventilation Equipment***. EXIM Infotek Private Ltd., 604 Vishwa Deep, District Centre, Janakpuri New Delhi 110058, India. Phone: 91 11 25544793; Fax: 91 11 25544793; Email: info@eximinfo.org • URL: http://www.eximinfo.com • $250 Individuals; $10 Individuals. Covers: 80 South Korean manufacturers and exporters of blowers and ventilators, dust and fume collectors, fans and blowers. Entries include: Company name, postal address, telephone, fax, e-mail, website, contact person, designation, and product details.

***Directory of South Korean Manufacturers & Exporters of Watches & Clocks***. EXIM Infotek Private Ltd., 604 Vishwa Deep, District Centre, Janakpuri New Delhi 110058, India. Phone: 91 11 25544793; Fax: 91 11 25544793; Email: info@eximinfo.org • URL: http://www.eximinfo.com • $10 Individuals. Covers: 60 South Korean manufacturers and exporters of clocks and clock parts, timing mechanisms, watch bracelets/straps, watch/clock and instrument parts, watch/clock and instrument springs, watches, wrist and pocket watches. Entries include: Company name, postal address, city, country, phone, fax, e-mail and websites, contact person, designation, and product details.

***Directory of South Korean Manufacturers & Exporters of Wire, Chain & Wire Products***. EXIM Infotek Private Ltd., 604 Vishwa Deep, District Centre, Janakpuri New Delhi 110058, India. Phone: 91 11 25544793; Fax: 91 11 25544793; Email: info@eximinfo.org • URL: http://www.eximinfo.com • $15 Individuals. Covers: 140 South Korean manufacturers and exporters of chains/chain slings/grips-metal, chain-tire, ferrous wires, fine bare-copper wire, metal cables/cords/ropes, metal fencing and barbed wire, metal gauze/cloth/netting, wire goods-metal. Entries include: Company name, postal address, city, country, phone, fax, e-mail and websites, contact person, designation, and product details.

***Directory of South Korean Manufacturers & Exporters of Wires & Cables—Electrical***. EXIM Infotek Private Ltd., 604 Vishwa Deep, District Centre, Janakpuri New Delhi 110058, India. Phone: 91 11 25544793; Fax: 91 11 25544793; Email: info@eximinfo.org • URL: http://www.eximinfo.com • $300 Individuals; $10 Individuals. Covers: 120 South Korean manufacturers and exporters of cable-battery, cable-control, cable-high tension, cables, electric wires/cables-non insulated, lead wires, power cable, power wires/cables-insulated, powerline cable and wire fittings, phone wires, wires and cables for electronics, and telecom wires and cables. Entries include: Company name, postal address, telephone, fax, e-mail, website, contact person, designation, and product details.

***Directory of South Korean Manufacturers & Exporters of Woodenware & Wood Products***. EXIM Infotek Private Ltd., 604 Vishwa Deep, District Centre, Janakpuri New Delhi 110058, India. Phone: 91 11 25544793; Fax: 91 11 25544793; Email: info@eximinfo.org • URL: http://www.eximinfo.com • $5 Individuals. Covers: 40 South Korean manufacturers and exporters of cane and wicker products, carvings and marquetry-wooden, ladders-wooden, molding and frames-wooden, wooden cases/boxes, wooden decorative cases/boxes, wooden products for industrial use, and wooden products for non-industrial use. Entries include: Company name, postal address, city, country, phone, fax, e-mail and websites, contact person, designation, and product details.

***Directory of South Korean Manufacturers and Exporters of Woodworking Equipment and Tools***. EXIM Infotek Private Ltd., 604 Vishwa Deep, District Centre, Janakpuri New Delhi 110058, India. Phone: 91 11 25544793; Fax: 91 11 25544793; Email: info@eximinfo.org • URL: http://www.eximinfo.com • $150 Individuals; $5 Individuals. Covers: 40 South Korean manufacturers and exporters of sawing and cutting tools, folding saw, tools for wood working machinery, wood boring and mortising machine, wood conditioning and surface treatment equipment, wood deforming machine, wood joining machine, wood milling and molding machine, wood sanding machine, wood sawing machine, wood turning lathes, wooden picture frame making machinery, and woodworking tools. Entries include: Company name, postal address, telephone, fax, e-mail, website, contact person, designation, and product details.

***Directory of South Korean Manufacturers & Exporters of Yarns & Threads***. EXIM Infotek Private Ltd., 604 Vishwa Deep, District Centre, Janakpuri New Delhi 110058, India. Phone: 91 11 25544793; Fax: 91 11 25544793; Email: info@eximinfo.org • URL: http://www.eximinfo.com • $25 Individuals. Covers: 310 South Korean manufacturers and exporters of cotton yarn, dyeing and finishing for textile fiber/yarn, sewing and embroidery thread, textile fiber-manmade, yarn and twists-silk, yarn and twists-manmade fiber, yarns and twists-vegetable fibers, yarns and twists-wool/hair. Entries include: Company name, postal address, city, country, phone, fax, e-mail and websites, contact person, designation, and product details.

***Directory of Special Libraries and Information Centers***. Cengage Learning Inc., 20 Channel Center St. Boston, MA 02210. Phone: 800-487-8488 or (617)289-7700; Fax: (617)289-7844; Email: investors@cengage.com • URL: http://www.cengage.com • Annual. $966 Individuals. 2010. 38th edition. eBook. Provides detailed contact and descriptive information on subject-specific resource collections maintained by government agencies, businesses, publishers, educational and nonprofit organizations, and associations worldwide.

***Directory of SRCC Certified Collectors and Solar Water Heating Systems Ratings***. Solar Rating and Certification Corporation, 400 High Point Dr., Ste. 400 Cocoa, FL 32926. Phone: (321)213-6037; Fax: (321)821-0910; Email: srcc@solar-rating.org • URL: http://www.solar-rating.org • Irregular. Covers: Nearly 20 manufacturers of solar collectors and water heaters certified by the organization. Entries include: Company name, address, system model and description, including technical specifications, thermal performance ratings, etc., for one or more systems.

*Directory of State Level Enterprises in China*. Han Ying Shan Research Inc., PO Box 71006 Wuhan 430071, China. Phone: 27 812804; Fax: 27 711242 • Irregular. $165. Covers: 1,064 "first or second grade enterprises" in China. Entries include: Company name, address, phone, telex, name and title of contact, number of employees, geographical area served, financial data, names and titles of key personnel, description of product/service.

*Directory of Taiwanese Manufacturers & Exporters of Adhesive, Glues & Sealants*. EXIM Infotek Private Ltd., 604 Vishwa Deep, District Centre, Janakpuri New Delhi 110058, India. Phone: 91 11 25544793; Fax: 91 11 25544793; Email: info@ eximinfo.org • URL: http://www.eximinfo.com • $20 Individuals. Covers: 190 Taiwanese manufacturers and exporters of adhesives-instant settings, adhesive packing materials, glue, processed rubber-solution and adhesives, and synthetic adhesives. Entries include: Company name, postal address, city, country, phone, fax, e-mail and websites, contact person, designation, and product details.

*Directory of Taiwanese Manufacturers & Exporters of Agro Chemicals*. EXIM Infotek Private Ltd., 604 Vishwa Deep, District Centre, Janakpuri New Delhi 110058, India. Phone: 91 11 25544793; Fax: 91 11 25544793; Email: info@ eximinfo.org • URL: http://www.eximinfo.com • $10 Individuals. Covers: 50 Taiwanese manufacturers and exporters of agrochemicals, fertilizers, fungicides/insecticides/ bactericides destroyers, and herbicides/plant growth control substances. Entries include: Company name, postal address, city, country, phone, fax, e-mail and websites, contact person, designation, and product details.

*Directory of Taiwanese Manufacturers & Exporters of Automobiles & Vehicles*. EXIM Infotek Private Ltd., 604 Vishwa Deep, District Centre, Janakpuri New Delhi 110058, India. Phone: 91 11 25544793; Fax: 91 11 25544793; Email: info@eximinfo.org • URL: http://www.eximinfo.com • $5 Individuals. Covers: 40 Taiwanese manufacturers and exporters of automobile body builders, tractors/trucks/trailers-industrial, truck and lorry trailers, trucks/lorries, and vehicles-special purpose. Entries include: Company name, postal address, city, country, phone, fax, e-mail and websites, contact person, designation, and product details.

*Directory of Taiwanese Manufacturers & Exporters of Automotive Service & Repair Equipment*. EXIM Infotek Private Ltd., 604 Vishwa Deep, District Centre, Janakpuri New Delhi 110058, India. Phone: 91 11 25544793; Fax: 91 11 25544793; Email: info@eximinfo.org • URL: http://www.eximinfo.com • $10 Individuals. Covers: 70 Taiwanese manufacturers and exporters of garage jacks, mechanical lubrication tools, motor vehicle testing equipment, vehicle service and repair equipment. Entries include: Company name, postal address, city, country, phone, fax, e-mail and websites, contact person, designation, and product details.

*Directory of Taiwanese Manufacturers & Exporters of Autoparts & Accessories*. EXIM Infotek Private Ltd., 604 Vishwa Deep, District Centre, Janakpuri New Delhi 110058, India. Phone: 91 11 25544793; Fax: 91 11 25544793; Email: info@ eximinfo.org • URL: http://www.eximinfo.com • $50 Individuals. Covers: 890 Taiwanese manufacturers & exporters of auto accessories, auto electrical parts, auto lamps, auto parts, auto parts & accessories, auto spare parts, automobile parts, automotive lighting equipment, automotive parts, automotive plastic parts, brake shoes, brass silencers, car alarm systems, car mats, couplings, couplings & clutches, hardware for motorcars, head lamps, hose clamps, hydraulic shock absorbers, industrial trailer/truck parts/accessories, locking devices for cars, motor vehicle accessories, motor vehicle body components & spare parts, motor vehicle transmission parts, socket hoses for trucks, springs/shock absorbers, steering & suspension parts, truck parts, v belts, vehicle brake parts, vehicle control instruments & panels, vehicle electrical & electronic equipment, vehicle ventilation/ heating & air conditioning systems, wheels & wheel rims, windshield wiper blades. Entries include: Company name, postal address, city, country, telephone, fax, e-mail & websites, contact person, designation, products detail.

*Directory of Taiwanese Manufacturers & Exporters of Batteries & Accumulators*. EXIM Infotek Private Ltd., 604 Vishwa Deep, District Centre, Janakpuri New Delhi 110058, India. Phone: 91 11 25544793; Fax: 91 11 25544793; Email: info@ eximinfo.org • URL: http://www.eximinfo.com • $25 Individuals. Covers: 290 Taiwanese manufacturers and exporters of batteries and accumulators, batteries for ups, battery back-up sirens, mobility small scooter (battery operated), ups and battery chargers. Entries include: Company name, postal address, city, country, phone, fax, e-mail and websites, contact person, designation, and product details.

*Directory of Taiwanese Manufacturers & Exporters of Bearings*. EXIM Infotek Private Ltd., 604 Vishwa Deep, District Centre, Janakpuri New Delhi 110058, India. Phone: 91 11 25544793; Fax: 91 11 25544793; Email: info@eximinfo.org • URL: http://www.eximinfo.com • $10 Individuals. Covers: 110 Taiwanese manufacturers and exporters of balls, bearings-ball, needle and roller, plain bearings, plumber and pillow blocks/bushing. Entries include: Company name, postal address, city, country, phone, fax, e-mail and websites, contact person, designation, products detail.

*Directory of Taiwanese Manufacturers & Exporters of Beauty Supplies, Cosmetics, Perfumes & Toiletries*. EXIM Infotek Private Ltd., 604 Vishwa Deep, District Centre, Janakpuri New Delhi 110058, India. Phone: 91 11 25544793; Fax: 91 11 25544793; Email: info@eximinfo.org • URL: http://www. eximinfo.com • $15 Individuals. Covers: 140 Taiwanese manufacturers and exporters of air fresheners, body glitter gel, cosmetic accessories, cosmetic brushes, cosmetic/hair/ skin and dental products, cosmetics, cosmetics accessories, eye liner, eye pencil, eyebrow needles, eyebrow pencils, eyelash stick, eyelash wave lotion kit, eyelets, eyeshadow pencil, face foundation, fragrance bottles, hair brushes, hair combs, hair steamers, lip pens, lipstick, lipstick cases, lipstick containers, make-up kits, mascara, nail polish, perfume, perfume atomizers, perfume bottles, perfumes, shampoo. Entries include: Company name, postal address, city, country, phone, fax, e-mail and websites, contact person, designation and product details.

*Directory of Taiwanese Manufacturers & Exporters of Bicycles, Parts & Accessories*. EXIM Infotek Private Ltd., 604 Vishwa Deep, District Centre, Janakpuri New Delhi 110058, India. Phone: 91 11 25544793; Fax: 91 11 25544793; Email: info@ eximinfo.org • URL: http://www.eximinfo.com • $45 Individuals. Covers: 770 Taiwanese manufacturers and exporters of bicycle accessories, bicycle parts and accessories, bicycles and exercisers, and electric powered wheelchairs. Entries include: Company name, postal address, city, country, phone, fax, e-mail and websites, contact person, designation, and product details.

*Directory of Taiwanese Manufacturers & Exporters of Carpets, Durries, Rugs & Floor Coverings*. EXIM Infotek Private Ltd., 604 Vishwa Deep, District Centre, Janakpuri New Delhi 110058, India. Phone: 91 11 25544793; Fax: 91 11 25544793; Email: info@eximinfo.org • URL: http://www.eximinfo.com • $5 Individuals. Covers: 20 Taiwanese manufacturers and exporters of carpets and rugs. Entries include: Company name, postal address, city, country, phone, fax, e-mail and websites, contact person, designation, and product details.

*Directory of Taiwanese Manufacturers & Exporters of Castings & Forgings*. EXIM Infotek Private Ltd., 604 Vishwa Deep, District Centre, Janakpuri New Delhi 110058, India. Phone: 91 11 25544793; Fax: 91 11 25544793; Email: info@ eximinfo.org • URL: http://www.eximinfo.com • $15 Individuals. Covers: 170 Taiwanese manufacturers and exporters of casting, iron castings, and steel castings. Entries include: Company name, postal address, city, country, phone, fax, e-mail and websites, contact person, designation, and product details.

*Directory of Taiwanese Manufacturers & Exporters of Chemicals & Allied Products*. EXIM Infotek Private Ltd., 604 Vishwa Deep, District Centre, Janakpuri New Delhi 110058, India. Phone: 91 11 25544793; Fax: 91 11 25544793; Email: info@eximinfo.org • URL: http://www.eximinfo.com • $30 Individuals. Covers: 380 Taiwanese manufacturers and exporters of alcohols and epoxides, amines, artificial resins, barium/boron/bromine/hydrogen compounds, calcium-strontium and thallium compounds, carbohydrates/proteins and enzymes, carbon based materials and products, chemicals, chemicals for basic metal industries, chemicals for building materials, chemicals for cosmetics/perfumery/ detergent/soaps, chemicals for electrical/electronic industries, chemicals for laboratory and microbiology, chemicals for leather and fur tanning extract, chemicals for lubricants and waxes, chemicals for metal welding/soldering fluxes, chemicals for mining/oil extraction, chemicals for paint/ lacquer/varnish, chemicals for paper making/printing/ photography, chemicals for plastic/rubber/ceramic, chemicals for unspecified uses, chemicals for water treatment, chemotherapeutic agents, compact & conventional detergent powder, compressed and liquefied gases/chem for refrigeration, detergents/cleansers and bleaching agents, dish wash detergent, disinfections and indoor deodorants, esters/ acetates/ethyls and methyls, explosives, hydrocarbons and halcarbons, inorganic acids and anhydrides, inorganic alkalis-hydroxides, liquid bleaching agent, misc. organic chemicals, natural resins and pitches, organic acids and anhydrides, phosphorus/sulphur/carbon/silicon and cassium compounds, polyphenols/ethers/aldehydes/ketones, potash vats, potassium and ammonium compounds, soaps/fatty-acid based detergents, and sodium compounds. Entries include: Company name, postal address, city, country, telephone, fax, e-mail and websites, contact person, designation, and product details.

*Directory of Taiwanese Manufacturers & Exporters of Confectionery & Bakery Products*. EXIM Infotek Private Ltd., 604 Vishwa Deep, District Centre, Janakpuri New Delhi 110058, India. Phone: 91 11 25544793; Fax: 91 11 25544793; Email: info@eximinfo.org • URL: http://www.eximinfo.com • $10 Individuals. Covers: 80 Taiwanese manufacturers and exporters of biscuits/crackers, bread/cakes and pastry, fruit-candied, instant porridge, noodles-instant, soups and extracts, sugar confectionery, vinegar and sauce. Entries include: Company name, postal address, city, country, phone, fax, e-mail and websites, contact person, designation, and product details.

*Directory of Taiwanese Manufacturers and Exporters of Construction Machinery and Equipment*. EXIM Infotek Private Ltd., 604 Vishwa Deep, District Centre, Janakpuri

New Delhi 110058, India. Phone: 91 11 25544793; Fax: 91 11 25544793; Email: info@eximinfo.org • URL: http://www. eximinfo.com • $350 Individuals; $15 Individuals. Covers: 150 Taiwanese manufacturers and exporters of bridge and tunnel construction machinery, building machinery and equipment, cement production plant, cement and plaster making plant, clay tile and brick production plant, concrete elements production plant, concrete making machinery, cranes and construction platform, crushing machinery, earthmoving and road making machinery, harbor and canal construction machinery, heavy mechanical handling equipment, mixers, railway track construction machinery, road rollers, scaffoldings and ladders. Entries include: Company name, postal address, telephone, fax, e-mail, website, contact person, designation, and product details.

*Directory of Taiwanese Manufacturers & Exporters of Cotton, Silk, Wool Raw & Waste*. EXIM Infotek Private Ltd., 604 Vishwa Deep, District Centre, Janakpuri New Delhi 110058, India. Phone: 91 11 25544793; Fax: 91 11 25544793; Email: info@eximinfo.org • URL: http://www.eximinfo.com • $5 Individuals. Covers: 20 Taiwanese manufacturers and exporters of raw cotton and vegetable textile fiber, raw wool and other animal fibers. Entries include: Company name, postal address, city, country, phone, fax, e-mail and websites, contact person, designation, and product details.

*Directory of Taiwanese Manufacturers & Exporters of Dyes, Colours, Pigments & Intermediates*. EXIM Infotek Private Ltd., 604 Vishwa Deep, District Centre, Janakpuri New Delhi 110058, India. Phone: 91 11 25544793; Fax: 91 11 25544793; Email: info@eximinfo.org • URL: http://www.eximinfo.com • $10 Individuals. Covers: 90 Taiwanese manufacturers & exporters of chemicals for textiles, colorants for leather/ rubber/plastic & cosmetics, dyes, dyes-synthetic, pigments-natural, pigments-synthetic, textile coatings. Entries include: Company name, postal address, city, country, phone, fax, e-mail & websites, contact person, designation, products detail.

*Directory of Taiwanese Manufacturers and Exporters of Energy and Power Equipment*. EXIM Infotek Private Ltd., 604 Vishwa Deep, District Centre, Janakpuri New Delhi 110058, India. Phone: 91 11 25544793; Fax: 91 11 25544793; Email: info@eximinfo.org • URL: http://www.eximinfo.com • $250 Individuals; $10 Individuals. Covers: 80 Taiwanese manufacturers and exporters of fuel and elements for nuclear energy industry, nuclear engineering plants, nuclear protection and detection instruments, nuclear reactors, power distribution equipment for various uses, and solar energy equipment. Entries include: Company name, postal address, telephone, fax, e-mail, website, contact person, designation, and product details.

*Directory of Taiwanese Manufacturers & Exporters of Engines & Engine Parts*. EXIM Infotek Private Ltd., 604 Vishwa Deep, District Centre, Janakpuri New Delhi 110058, India. Phone: 91 11 25544793; Fax: 91 11 25544793; Email: info@ eximinfo.org • URL: http://www.eximinfo.com • $15 Individuals. Covers: 130 Taiwanese manufacturers and exporters of engine components/spare parts, internal combustion engines, oil seals, pistons and plugs. Entries include: Company name, postal address, city, country, phone, fax, e-mail and websites, contact person, designation and product details.

*Directory of Taiwanese Manufacturers and Exporters of Environment and Pollution Control Equipment*. EXIM Infotek Private Ltd., 604 Vishwa Deep, District Centre, Janakpuri New Delhi 110058, India. Phone: 91 11 25544793; Fax: 91 11 25544793; Email: info@eximinfo.org • URL: http:// www.eximinfo.com • $400 Individuals; $15 Individuals. Covers: 160 Taiwanese manufacturers and exporters of air pollution control equipment, noise pollution control equipment, water and sewage treatment plant. Entries include: Company name, postal address, telephone, fax, e-mail, website, contact person, designation, and product details.

*Directory of Taiwanese Manufacturers & Exporters of Filters & Strainers—Industrial*. EXIM Infotek Private Ltd., 604 Vishwa Deep, District Centre, Janakpuri New Delhi 110058, India. Phone: 91 11 25544793; Fax: 91 11 25544793; Email: info@eximinfo.org • URL: http://www.eximinfo.com • $10 Individuals. Covers: 80 Taiwanese manufacturers and exporters of bolting and filter cloths/gauzes, filters and strainers for processing industries, filters and strainers-metal, glue for air filters, and water and waste water filters. Entries include: Company name, postal address, city, country, phone, fax, e-mail and websites, contact person, designation, products detail.

*Directory of Taiwanese Manufacturers & Exporters of Fire Fighting Equipment & Supplies*. EXIM Infotek Private Ltd., 604 Vishwa Deep, District Centre, Janakpuri New Delhi 110058, India. Phone: 91 11 25544793; Fax: 91 11 25544793; Email: info@eximinfo.org • URL: http://www.eximinfo.com • Covers: 30 Taiwanese manufacturers and exporters of fire extinguishing systems and fire fighting equipment. Entries include: Company name, postal address, telephone, fax, e-mail, website, contact person, designation, and product details.

*Directory of Taiwanese Manufacturers & Exporters of Fishing & Hunting Equipment & Supplies*. EXIM Infotek Private Ltd., 604 Vishwa Deep, District Centre, Janakpuri New Delhi 110058, India. Phone: 91 11 25544793; Fax: 91 11 25544793;

Email: info@eximinfo.org • URL: http://www.eximinfo.com • $250 Individuals; $10 Individuals. Covers: 70 Taiwanese manufacturers and exporters of fish farming equipment, fishing lure, knotted nets, and nettings. Entries include: Company name, postal address, telephone, fax, e-mail, website, contact person, designation, and product details.

***Directory of Taiwanese Manufacturers & Exporters of Food Additives & Aromatic Chemicals***. EXIM Infotek Private Ltd., 604 Vishwa Deep, District Centre, Janakpuri New Delhi 110058, India. Phone: 91 11 25544793; Fax: 91 11 25544793; Email: info@eximinfo.org • URL: http://www.eximinfo.com • $5 Individuals. Covers: 40 Taiwanese manufacturers and exporters of aromo compounds, chemicals for food and beverages, colorants for food and beverages, and natural additives for the food and beverages. Entries include: Company name, postal address, city, country, phone, fax, e-mail and websites, contact person, designation, and product details.

***Directory of Taiwanese Manufacturers & Exporters of Furniture—All Types***. EXIM Infotek Private Ltd., 604 Vishwa Deep, District Centre, Janakpuri New Delhi 110058, India. Phone: 91 11 25544793; Fax: 91 11 25544793; Email: info@eximinfo.org • URL: http://www.eximinfo.com • $40 Individuals. Covers: 690 Taiwanese manufacturers and exporters of bamboo furniture, chairs, flexible shelving systems, furniture and fittings for shops/stores, furniture fittings, furniture for manufactured products, furniture/racking-industrial/lab, furniture-cane and wicker, furniture-children, furniture-domestic, furniture-garden, furniture-hospital, furniture-hotel/restaurant/bar, furniture-institutional, furniture-kitchen, furniture-office, furniture-public places, furniture-school, furniture-upholstered, knockdown furniture, leisure folding chairs, metal cabinets, small furniture articles, store fixtures, walking cane chairs, and wooden furniture. Entries include: Company name, postal address, city, country, phone, fax, e-mail and websites, contact person, designation, and product details.

***Directory of Taiwanese Manufacturers & Exporters of Garden Tools, Equipment & Supplies***. EXIM Infotek Private Ltd., 604 Vishwa Deep, District Centre, Janakpuri New Delhi 110058, India. Phone: 91 11 25544793; Fax: 91 11 25544793; Email: info@eximinfo.org • URL: http://www.eximinfo.com • $10 Individuals. Covers: 70 Taiwanese manufacturers and exporters of garden irrigation accessories, garden tools, and garden tools-all kinds. Entries include: Company name, postal address, city, country, phone, fax, e-mail and websites, contact person, designation, and product details.

***Directory of Taiwanese Manufacturers & Exporters of Gears & Gears Boxes***. EXIM Infotek Private Ltd., 604 Vishwa Deep, District Centre, Janakpuri New Delhi 110058, India. Phone: 91 11 25544793; Fax: 91 11 25544793; Email: info@eximinfo.org • URL: http://www.eximinfo.com • $10 Individuals. Covers: 70 Taiwanese manufacturers and exporters of gears, worm gear reducers.

***Directory of Taiwanese Manufacturers & Exporters of Giftware & Novelties***. EXIM Infotek Private Ltd., 604 Vishwa Deep, District Centre, Janakpuri New Delhi 110058, India. Phone: 91 11 25544793; Fax: 91 11 25544793; Email: info@eximinfo.org • URL: http://www.eximinfo.com • $20 Individuals. Covers: 250 Taiwanese manufacturers and exporters of albums and files, ceramic faucet accessories, coins/medals/decorations and badges, enamel badges, gift articles, gift sets, gifts, key chains, key holders, kitchen utensils, medals, novelty glasses, photo frames, promotional giftware, religious festive seasonal gifts, solid brass quick release key chains, souvenirs, trophies/ceremonial plates. Entries include: Company name, postal address, city, country, phone, fax, e-mail and websites, contact person, designation, and product details.

***Directory of Taiwanese Manufacturers & Exporters of Handicrafts & Decorative Items***. EXIM Infotek Private Ltd., 604 Vishwa Deep, District Centre, Janakpuri New Delhi 110058, India. Phone: 91 11 25544793; Fax: 91 11 25544793; Email: info@eximinfo.org • URL: http://www.eximinfo.com • $10 Individuals. Covers: 120 Taiwanese manufacturers and exporters of bronze/copper/brass and wrought iron artistic goods, candle holders, Christmas tree ornaments, Christmas tree sets, fancy metal boxes, festival articles and decorations, handicrafts, religious articles-Buddhist/Hindu, religious articles-Christian, religious articles-Jewish. Entries include: Company name, postal address, city, country, phone, fax, e-mail and websites, contact person, designation, products detail.

***Directory of Taiwanese Manufacturers & Exporters of Handkerchieves, Scarves & Neckwares***. EXIM Infotek Private Ltd., 604 Vishwa Deep, District Centre, Janakpuri New Delhi 110058, India. Phone: 91 11 25544793; Fax: 91 11 25544793; Email: info@eximinfo.org • URL: http://www.eximinfo.com • $5 Individuals. Covers: 20 Taiwanese manufacturers & exporters of neckties/scarves. Entries include: Company name, postal address, city, country, phone, fax, e-mail & websites, contact person, designation, products detail.

***Directory of Taiwanese Manufacturers & Exporters of Handtools***. EXIM Infotek Private Ltd., 604 Vishwa Deep, District Centre, Janakpuri New Delhi 110058, India. Phone: 91 11 25544793; Fax: 91 11 25544793; Email: info@eximinfo.org • URL: http://www.eximinfo.com • $35 Individuals. Covers: 510 Taiwanese manufacturers and exporters of builders tools, carbide tools, chisels/taps/dies and similar tools, electric and electro-magnetic tools, files/rasps and similar tools, hammers/mallets and similar tools, hand tools, handy scaler, metal hand and diamond tools, multipurpose tools, pliers/clamps and similar tools, roofers and decorators tools, screwdrivers/wrenches, tagging guns, tool cases, and tools for powerline maintenance. Entries include: Company name, postal address, city, country, phone, fax, e-mail and websites, contact person, designation, and product details.

***Directory of Taiwanese Manufacturers & Exporters of Hardwares—All Types***. EXIM Infotek Private Ltd., 604 Vishwa Deep, District Centre, Janakpuri New Delhi 110058, India. Phone: 91 11 25544793; Fax: 91 11 25544793; Email: info@eximinfo.org • URL: http://www.eximinfo.com • $40 Individuals. Covers: 650 Taiwanese manufacturers and exporters of abrasive coated products, abrasive media, blind rivets, brass hardware, brass knobs and pulls, brass padlocks, builders' hardware, building hardware, cabinet hardware, cam locks, casters, ceramic cabinet hardware, door edge guards, door fittings, door handles, door hardware, door knob/lever handles, door locks, d-rings, furniture hardware, furniture lock sets, haberdashery metalware, home hardwares, ironmongery and hardware, ironmongery and hardware for furniture, key lock switches, locking handles, locks, locks for luggage and bags, locksmith articles, luggage hardware and accessories, metal fittings, metal smallwares for various uses, nails/tacks/spikes/staples-metal, pad locks, paint brushes and rollers, pins, plastic foot studs, plastic handles w/loops, roller strips, screen door hardware, sliders, springs, and stainless steel hardware. Entries include: Company name, postal address, city, country, telephone, fax, e-mail and websites, contact person, designation, and product details.

***Directory of Taiwanese Manufacturers & Exporters of Hats & Headwears***. EXIM Infotek Private Ltd., 604 Vishwa Deep, District Centre, Janakpuri New Delhi 110058, India. Phone: 91 11 25544793; Fax: 91 11 25544793; Email: info@eximinfo.org • URL: http://www.eximinfo.com • $10 Individuals. Covers: 120 Taiwanese manufacturers and exporters of caps, hats, hats and headwear, shower caps. Entries include: Company name, postal address, city, country, phone, fax, e-mail and websites, contact person, designation, products detail.

***Directory of Taiwanese Manufacturers & Exporters of Heaters & Heating Equipment***. EXIM Infotek Private Ltd., 604 Vishwa Deep, District Centre, Janakpuri New Delhi 110058, India. Phone: 91 11 25544793; Fax: 91 11 25544793; Email: info@eximinfo.org • URL: http://www.eximinfo.com • $450 Individuals; $20 Individuals. Covers: 200 Taiwanese manufacturers and exporters of central heating systems, driers, drying plants, electric heating equipment, heat exchanger, heating elements and accessories, heating machine, high frequency induction heating machine, and water heaters. Entries include: Company name, postal address, telephone, fax, e-mail, website, contact person, designation, and product details.

***Directory of Taiwanese Manufacturers & Exporters of Herbs & Herbal Medicine Products***. EXIM Infotek Private Ltd., 604 Vishwa Deep, District Centre, Janakpuri New Delhi 110058, India. Phone: 91 11 25544793; Fax: 91 11 25544793; Email: info@eximinfo.org • URL: http://www.eximinfo.com • $15 Individuals. Covers: 160 Taiwanese manufacturers and exporters of Chinese medical preparations, and herbal medicines. Entries include: Company name, postal address, city, country, phone, fax, e-mail and websites, contact person, designation, and product details.

***Directory of Taiwanese Manufacturers & Exporters of Home Furnishing Materials***. EXIM Infotek Private Ltd., 604 Vishwa Deep, District Centre, Janakpuri New Delhi 110058, India. Phone: 91 11 25544793; Fax: 91 11 25544793; Email: info@eximinfo.org • URL: http://www.eximinfo.com • $15 Individuals. Covers: 140 Taiwanese manufacturers and exporters of bathroom mats, crochet lace table cloths, curtains, curtain blinds, door curtains, household linens and soft furnishings, mattresses, cushions and pillows, sanitary towels and baby napkins, shower curtain cloths, table cloths, table lamps, vertical blinds, vinyl placemats, vinyl table cloths, and window curtains. Entries include: Company name, postal address, city, country, phone, fax, e-mail and websites, contact person, designation, and product details.

***Directory of Taiwanese Manufacturers & Exporters of Houseware, Kitchenware & Tableware***. EXIM Infotek Private Ltd., 604 Vishwa Deep, District Centre, Janakpuri New Delhi 110058, India. Phone: 91 11 25544793; Fax: 91 11 25544793; Email: info@eximinfo.org • URL: http://www.eximinfo.com • $30 Individuals. Covers: 470 Taiwanese manufacturers and exporters of baskets-plastic, brooms and brushes for domestic use, cloth hangers-plastic, cutlery, decorative plastic articles, domestic articles-metal, fashion acrylic houseware, gold-plated/silverplated and pewterware, hangers, household cutlery-metal, household plastic products, kitchen articles/tableware-plastic, kitchen articles-metal, knife, knives-metal, plastic houseware, scissors, and scissors for cloth or paper cutting. Entries include: Company name, postal address, city, country, phone, fax, e-mail and websites, contact person, designation, and product details.

***Directory of Taiwanese Manufacturers & Exporters of Imitation & Fashion Jewellery***. EXIM Infotek Private Ltd., 604 Vishwa Deep, District Centre, Janakpuri New Delhi 110058, India. Phone: 91 11 25544793; Fax: 91 11 25544793; Email: info@eximinfo.org • URL: http://www.eximinfo.com • $10 Individuals. Covers: 90 Taiwanese manufacturers & exporters of bracelets, buckles, costume jewelry, cuff links, earrings, fashion goods, fashion metal accessories, hair bands, hair clips, hair ornaments, imitation jewelry, jewelry, necklaces, synthetic jewels for watches, theatrical masks for arts, craft & festivals, tie pins. Entries include: Company name, postal address, city, country, phone, fax, e-mail & websites, contact person, designation, products detail.

***Directory of Taiwanese Manufacturers & Exporters of Jute, Hemp, Sisal, Burlap & Its Products***. EXIM Infotek Private Ltd., 604 Vishwa Deep, District Centre, Janakpuri New Delhi 110058, India. Phone: 91 11 25544793; Fax: 91 11 25544793; Email: info@eximinfo.org • URL: http://www.eximinfo.com • $10 Individuals. Covers: 60 Taiwanese manufacturers and exporters of canvas and duck, canvas and duck products. Entries include: Company name, postal address, city, country, phone, fax, e-mail and websites, contact person, designation, and product details.

***Directory of Taiwanese Manufacturers & Exporters of Laces, Ribbons & Embroidery Products***. EXIM Infotek Private Ltd., 604 Vishwa Deep, District Centre, Janakpuri New Delhi 110058, India. Phone: 91 11 25544793; Fax: 91 11 25544793; Email: info@eximinfo.org • URL: http://www.eximinfo.com • $15 Individuals. Covers: 180 Taiwanese manufacturers and exporters of badges, decorative trim, embroidery-all types, embroidered emblems, embroideries, embroidery, embroidery emblems, embroidery-hand made, flower tapes, lace and embroidery, lace-hand made, lace-machine made, ribbons, ribbons and tapes for industrial use, ribbons and tapes-non industrial, trimmings/cordings/braids and fringes, and woven ribbon. Entries include: Company name, postal address, city, country, phone, fax, e-mail and websites, contact person, designation, and product details.

***Directory of Taiwanese Manufacturers & Exporters of Leather, Hides, Skins & Furs***. EXIM Infotek Private Ltd., 604 Vishwa Deep, District Centre, Janakpuri New Delhi 110058, India. Phone: 91 11 25544793; Fax: 91 11 25544793; Email: info@eximinfo.org • URL: http://www.eximinfo.com • $20 Individuals. Covers: 190 Taiwanese manufacturers and exporters of leather-reconstituted, leather-processed, PVC leathercloth, PVC sponge leather, sheep and goat skins, sheep and lamb skins, skins, hides and leather, and swine skins/leather. Entries include: Company name, postal address, city, country, phone, fax, e-mail and websites, contact person, designation, and product details.

***Directory of Taiwanese Manufacturers & Exporters of Leather Products***. EXIM Infotek Private Ltd., 604 Vishwa Deep, District Centre, Janakpuri New Delhi 110058, India. Phone: 91 11 25544793; Fax: 91 11 25544793; Email: info@eximinfo.org • URL: http://www.eximinfo.com • $20 Individuals. Covers: 280 Taiwanese manufacturers and exporters of bags, cases and covers of leather, fancy leather goods, fur clothing and products, leather airbags/sportbags, leather clothing, leather goods for industrial use, leather purses, leather waist belts. Entries include: Company name, postal address, city, country, phone, fax, e-mail and websites, contact person, designation, and product details.

***Directory of Taiwanese Manufacturers & Exporters of Lighting Fixtures, Lamps & Accessories***. EXIM Infotek Private Ltd., 604 Vishwa Deep, District Centre, Janakpuri New Delhi 110058, India. Phone: 91 11 25544793; Fax: 91 11 25544793; Email: info@eximinfo.org • URL: http://www.eximinfo.com • $30 Individuals. Covers: 450 Taiwanese manufacturers and exporters of bulbs, decoration bulbs, discharge and special purpose lamps, electric lamp components, filament lamps-all types, flash light, fluorescent lamps, fog lamps, halogen lamps, indoor electric lighting equipment, laser lights, lighting equipment-outdoor, miniature lamps, portable electric lamps and accessories, and turning lamps. Entries include: Company name, postal address, city, country, phone, fax, e-mail and websites, contact person, designation, and product details.

***Directory of Taiwanese Manufacturers & Exporters of Machinery for Chemicals & Pharma Industry***. EXIM Infotek Private Ltd., 604 Vishwa Deep, District Centre, Janakpuri New Delhi 110058, India. Phone: 91 11 25544793; Fax: 91 11 25544793; Email: info@eximinfo.org • URL: http://www.eximinfo.com • $25 Individuals. Covers: 290 Taiwanese manufacturers and exporters of crushers/pulverizers for chemical industries, dryers/evaporators/crystallizers for chemical industries, electrochemical and electrolytic plant equipment, electroplating plant machinery, essence/perfume production plant equipment, explosive/match production plant equipment, fertilizer production plant equipment, glue/gelatin making plant equipment, heaters/boilers/distillers for chemical industries, inorganic chemical production plant equipment, organic chemical production plant equipment, paint/varnish/enamel/ink production plant equipment, pharmaceutical/cosmetic production plant equipment, reactors for chemical industry, screeners/mixers/centrifuges for chemical industry, soap making equipment, technical gas production plant equipment. Entries include: Company name, postal address, city, country, phone, fax, e-mail and websites, contact person, designation, and product details.

***Directory of Taiwanese Manufacturers & Exporters of***

*Machinery for Leather & Shoe Industry*. EXIM Infotek Private Ltd., 604 Vishwa Deep, District Centre, Janakpuri New Delhi 110058, India. Phone: 91 11 25544793; Fax: 91 11 25544793; Email: info@eximinfo.org • URL: http://www.eximinfo.com • $10 Individuals. Covers: 100 Taiwanese manufacturers and exporters of boot and shoe making machinery/equipment, leather working and saddlery making/equipment, shoe industry equipment, tannery machinery and equipment. Entries include: Company name, postal address, city, country, phone, fax, e-mail and websites, contact person, designation, products detail.

*Directory of Taiwanese Manufacturers & Exporters of Machinery for Paper & Pulp Industry*. EXIM Infotek Private Ltd., 604 Vishwa Deep, District Centre, Janakpuri New Delhi 110058, India. Phone: 91 11 25544793; Fax: 91 11 25544793; Email: info@eximinfo.org • URL: http://www.eximinfo.com • $10 Individuals. Covers: 120 Taiwanese manufacturers and exporters of cardboard finishing/forming/cutting machinery/equipment, cardboard making machinery/equipment, paper finishing/converting machinery/equipment, paper making plant equipment, pulp and cellulose production plant equipment. Entries include: Company name, postal address, city, country, phone, fax, e-mail and websites, contact person, designation, products detail.

*Directory of Taiwanese Manufacturers & Exporters of Machinery for Rubber Industry*. EXIM Infotek Private Ltd., 604 Vishwa Deep, District Centre, Janakpuri New Delhi 110058, India. Phone: 91 11 25544793; Fax: 91 11 25544793; Email: info@eximinfo.org • URL: http://www.eximinfo.com • $250 Individuals; $10 Individuals. Covers: 80 Taiwanese manufacturers and exporters of bicycle tire building machine, raw rubber processing and vulcanizing machine and equipment, rubber injection molding machine, rubber products, and tire making machinery. Entries include: Company name, postal address, telephone, fax, e-mail, website, contact person, designation, and product details.

*Directory of Taiwanese Manufacturers & Exporters of Machinery for Textile & Knitting Industry*. EXIM Infotek Private Ltd., 604 Vishwa Deep, District Centre, Janakpuri New Delhi 110058, India. Phone: 91 11 25544793; Fax: 91 11 25544793; Email: info@eximinfo.org • URL: http://www.eximinfo.com • $30 Individuals. Covers: 400 Taiwanese manufacturers and exporters of automatic mini thread winders, beam brakes and discs for textile machinery, belts/hoses/webbing-textile, bobbins for textile industry, carpet and tapestry looms, cone type automatic cross cone winders, cordage/rope/twine and braid production machinery, cotton preparation machinery and equipment, cotton wool and surgical dressing making machinery/equipment, felt and non woven fabric making machinery, hemp/flex fiber preparation machinery and equipment, knitting machinery and attachments, lace and net making machinery, manmade fiber production and processing plants, mattress and upholstery making machinery/equipment, parts for textile machinery, ribbon and trimming making machinery, sleeves and strips for spinning mills, textile calendaring machinery and equipment, textile cleaning spray guns, textile coating machinery and equipment, textile dyeing and boiling machinery/equipment, textile finishing machinery and equipment, textile printing machinery and equipment, textile printings, textile spinning and twisting machinery, textile spinning/twisting/winding/reeling machine parts, textile steaming/conditioning/folding/shearing machinery, textile washing/mercerizing machinery and equipment, textile waste processing machinery and equipment, textile weaving machinery parts/accessories, textile weaving machinery/looms, textile winding and reeling machinery, thread and high speed drum winders, universal type multipurpose combiner and thread winders, washing machines for textile industry, weaving machinery for metal thread, wool carding and combing machinery and equipment, yarn preparation machinery/equipment, and yarn tensioners. Entries include: Company name, postal address, city, country, telephone, fax, e-mail and websites, contact person, designation, and product details.

*Directory of Taiwanese Manufacturers & Exporters of Marine & Boating Equipment & Supplies*. EXIM Infotek Private Ltd., 604 Vishwa Deep, District Centre, Janakpuri New Delhi 110058, India. Phone: 91 11 25544793; Fax: 91 11 25544793; Email: info@eximinfo.org • URL: http://www.eximinfo.com • $10 Individuals. Covers: 120 Taiwanese manufacturers and exporters of boat parts and accessories, coastal vessels, control and navigational instruments-ship, equipment/signals for ships/boats, marine propulsion units, radar and navigation systems/equipment-marine, submersible vessels and equipment, yacht and pleasure craft. Entries include: Company name, postal address, city, country, phone, fax, e-mail and websites, contact person, designation, products detail.

*Directory of Taiwanese Manufacturers & Exporters of Material Handling Equipment*. EXIM Infotek Private Ltd., 604 Vishwa Deep, District Centre, Janakpuri New Delhi 110058, India. Phone: 91 11 25544793; Fax: 91 11 25544793; Email: info@eximinfo.org • URL: http://www.eximinfo.com • $750 Individuals; $30 Individuals. Covers: 400 Taiwanese manufacturers and exporters of automated handling storage equipment, barrows, trolleys, carts, conveyors, elevators, cranes, hoists, winches, forklift trucks, handling equipment parts and accessories, hydraulic dump hoists, lifts, elevators, mobile cranes, overhead conveyors, pallets and containers, pneumatic handling equipment, pulleys, and cable wheels. Entries include: Company name, postal address, telephone, fax, e-mail, website, contact person, designation, and product details.

*Directory of Taiwanese Manufacturers & Exporters of Meat & Meat Products*. EXIM Infotek Private Ltd., 604 Vishwa Deep, District Centre, Janakpuri New Delhi 110058, India. Phone: 91 11 25544793; Fax: 91 11 25544793; Email: info@eximinfo.org • URL: http://www.eximinfo.com • $5 Individuals. Covers: 30 Taiwanese manufacturers and exporters of meat and game-processed/preserved, meat and meat products, meat-dried. Entries include: Company name, postal address, city, country, phone, fax, e-mail and websites, contact person, designation, and product details.

*Directory of Taiwanese Manufacturers & Exporters of Minerals*. EXIM Infotek Private Ltd., 604 Vishwa Deep, District Centre, Janakpuri New Delhi 110058, India. Phone: 91 11 25544793; Fax: 91 11 25544793; Email: info@eximinfo.org • URL: http://www.eximinfo.com • $5 Individuals. Covers: 30 Taiwanese manufacturers and exporters of clays, gypsum/plaster and stucco products, limestones, magnesium minerals, mica and mecanite products, quartz and silica electro thermic products, quartzite of crystal, silicon minerals, slate products. Entries include: Company name, postal address, city, country, phone, fax, e-mail and websites, contact person, designation, and product details.

*Directory of Taiwanese Manufacturers & Exporters of Motorcycles, Parts & Accessories*. EXIM Infotek Private Ltd., 604 Vishwa Deep, District Centre, Janakpuri New Delhi 110058, India. Phone: 91 11 25544793; Fax: 91 11 25544793; Email: info@eximinfo.org • URL: http://www.eximinfo.com • $10 Individuals. Covers: 50 Taiwanese manufacturers and exporters of motorcycle mirrors, motorcycle parts, motorcycles and mopeds. Entries include: Company name, postal address, city, country, phone, fax, e-mail and websites, contact person, designation, and product details.

*Directory of Taiwanese Manufacturers and Exporters of Motors and Motor Parts—Electric*. EXIM Infotek Private Ltd., 604 Vishwa Deep, District Centre, Janakpuri New Delhi 110058, India. Phone: 91 11 25544793; Fax: 91 11 25544793; Email: info@eximinfo.org • URL: http://www.eximinfo.com • $650 Individuals; $25 Individuals. Covers: 340 Taiwanese manufacturers and exporters of electric motors below 1hp, electric motors over 1hp, explosion proof motors, motorcycle parts and accessories. Entries include: Company name, postal address, telephone, fax, e-mail, website, contact person, designation, and product details.

*Directory of Taiwanese Manufacturers & Exporters of Nuts, Bolts, Screws & Fasteners*. EXIM Infotek Private Ltd., 604 Vishwa Deep, District Centre, Janakpuri New Delhi 110058, India. Phone: 91 11 25544793; Fax: 91 11 25544793; Email: info@eximinfo.org • URL: http://www.eximinfo.com • $20 Individuals. Covers: 260 Taiwanese manufacturers and exporters of bolts and nuts, bolts, fasteners, fasteners-metal, metal nuts/bolts/washers, metal rivets, metal screws/bolts/nuts, rivet nuts, rivets, screws, screws-metal, self-drilling screws, special screws and nuts, washers. Entries include: Company name, postal address, city, country, phone, fax, e-mail and websites, contact person, designation, and product details.

*Directory of Taiwanese Manufacturers & Exporters of Oil & Fats—Cooking & Vegetable*. EXIM Infotek Private Ltd., 604 Vishwa Deep, District Centre, Janakpuri New Delhi 110058, India. Phone: 91 11 25544793; Fax: 91 11 25544793; Email: info@eximinfo.org • URL: http://www.eximinfo.com • $5 Individuals. Covers: 20 South Korean manufacturers and exporters of oils and fats-edible. Entries include: Company name, postal address, city, country, phone, fax, e-mail and websites, contact person, designation, and product details.

*Directory of Taiwanese Manufacturers & Exporters of Paints, Varnishes & Allied Products*. EXIM Infotek Private Ltd., 604 Vishwa Deep, District Centre, Janakpuri New Delhi 110058, India. Phone: 91 11 25544793; Fax: 91 11 25544793; Email: info@eximinfo.org • URL: http://www.eximinfo.com • $10 Individuals. Covers: 60 Taiwanese manufacturers and exporters of anti-corrosion products, lacquers and paints-primers, mastics/putties and sealing compounds, varnishes and stains-distempers, and vitreous colors/enamels and glazes. Entries include: Company name, postal address, city, country, phone, fax, e-mail and websites, contact person, designation, and product details.

*Directory of Taiwanese Manufacturers & Exporters of Paper & Paper Products*. EXIM Infotek Private Ltd., 604 Vishwa Deep, District Centre, Janakpuri New Delhi 110058, India. Phone: 91 11 25544793; Fax: 91 11 25544793; Email: info@eximinfo.org • URL: http://www.eximinfo.com • $20 Individuals. Covers: 240 Taiwanese manufacturers and exporters of base and backing paper, cardboard, cardboard articles-diecut/embossed, cardboard/corrugated-packaging, coated and laminated paper/board, corrugated paper and board, heat transfer printing paper, paper and cardboard tubes, paper and paper rolls for technical use, paper and paper rolls printed for writing/technical, paper articles-diecut/embossed, paper packaging/bags and sacks, printing and drawing paper/board, pulp mechanical and chemicals, recycled paper pulp, reinforced cardboard products, tissue paper and cellulose wadding, wallpaper and paper backed wallcoverings, and wrapping/crepe paper. Entries include: Company name,

postal address, city, country, phone, fax, e-mail and websites, contact person, designation, and product details.

*Directory of Taiwanese Manufacturers & Exporters of Petroleum Products*. EXIM Infotek Private Ltd., 604 Vishwa Deep, District Centre, Janakpuri New Delhi 110058, India. Phone: 91 11 25544793; Fax: 91 11 25544793; Email: info@eximinfo.org • URL: http://www.eximinfo.com • $10 Individuals. Covers: 50 Taiwanese manufacturers and exporters of mineral oils and greases, natural gases, natural oils and greases for technical use, petroleum products/fuels and lubricants, tar and bituminous products, and tar and resin distillation products. Entries include: Company name, postal address, city, country, phone, fax, e-mail and websites, contact person, designation, products detail.

*Directory of Taiwanese Manufacturers & Exporters of Pharmaceutical Products*. EXIM Infotek Private Ltd., 604 Vishwa Deep, District Centre, Janakpuri New Delhi 110058, India. Phone: 91 11 25544793; Fax: 91 11 25544793; Email: info@eximinfo.org • URL: http://www.eximinfo.com • $20 Individuals. Covers: 250 Taiwanese manufacturers and exporters of antibiotics, microencapsulated pharmaceuticals, ophthalmic preparations, pharmaceutical preparations for cardio-vascular, pharmaceutical preparations, veterinary preparations-general, vitamin preparations. Entries include: Company name, postal address, city, country, phone, fax, e-mail and websites, contact person, designation, and product details.

*Directory of Taiwanese Manufacturers & Exporters of Pharmaceutical Raw Materials*. EXIM Infotek Private Ltd., 604 Vishwa Deep, District Centre, Janakpuri New Delhi 110058, India. Phone: 91 11 25544793; Fax: 91 11 25544793; Email: info@eximinfo.org • URL: http://www.eximinfo.com • $20 Individuals. Covers: 190 Taiwanese manufacturers and exporters of gelatins for pharmaceuticals, hypodermoclysis and phleboclysis solution, pharmaceutical base and suppository compounds, vitamins/hormones and organ extracts. Entries include: Company name, postal address, city, country, phone, fax, e-mail and websites, contact person, designation, and product details.

*Directory of Taiwanese Manufacturers & Exporters of Railway Equipment & Supplies*. EXIM Infotek Private Ltd., 604 Vishwa Deep, District Centre, Janakpuri New Delhi 110058, India. Phone: 91 11 25544793; Fax: 91 11 25544793; Email: info@eximinfo.org • URL: http://www.eximinfo.com • $5 Individuals. Covers: 20 Taiwanese manufacturers and exporters of locomotives/railcars and tramcars, railway equipments, railways and tram carriage/wagons. Entries include: Company name, postal address, city, country, phone, fax, e-mail and websites, contact person, designation, and product details.

*Directory of Taiwanese Manufacturers & Exporters of Ready-made Garments*. EXIM Infotek Private Ltd., 604 Vishwa Deep, District Centre, Janakpuri New Delhi 110058, India. Phone: 91 11 25544793; Fax: 91 11 25544793; Email: info@eximinfo.org • URL: http://www.eximinfo.com • $45 Individuals. Covers: 710 Taiwanese manufacturers and exporters of casual and leisurewear, clothing and accessories-rubber, dressing gowns, hosiery, knitwear, ladies blouses, protective work clothing, readymade for infants, readymade for ladies/girls, readymade for men/boys, reflective jackets, shirts-all types, swim and beach wear, uniforms and professional clothing, and waterproof garments. Entries include: Company name, postal address, city, country, phone, fax, e-mail and websites, contact person, designation, and product details.

*Directory of Taiwanese Manufacturers and Exporters of Restaurant, Hotel and Catering Equipment*. EXIM Infotek Private Ltd., 604 Vishwa Deep, District Centre, Janakpuri New Delhi 110058, India. Phone: 91 11 25544793; Fax: 91 11 25544793; Email: info@eximinfo.org • URL: http://www.eximinfo.com • $150 Individuals; $5 Individuals. Covers: 30 Taiwanese manufacturers and exporters of catering machinery and equipment. Entries include: Company name, postal address, telephone, fax, e-mail, website, contact person, designation, and product details.

*Directory of Taiwanese Manufacturers & Exporters of Shoes & Footwears*. EXIM Infotek Private Ltd., 604 Vishwa Deep, District Centre, Janakpuri New Delhi 110058, India. Phone: 91 11 25544793; Fax: 91 11 25544793; Email: info@eximinfo.org • URL: http://www.eximinfo.com • $30 Individuals. Covers: 430 Taiwanese manufacturers and exporters of baby shoes, footwear soles/components, footwear-industrial/protective, footwear-sports, footwear-standard, footwear-wooden, shoes, and shoes materials. Entries include: Company name, postal address, city, country, phone, fax, e-mail and websites, contact person, designation, and product details.

*Directory of Taiwanese Manufacturers & Exporters of Sporting Goods*. EXIM Infotek Private Ltd., 604 Vishwa Deep, District Centre, Janakpuri New Delhi 110058, India. Phone: 91 11 25544793; Fax: 91 11 25544793; Email: info@eximinfo.org • URL: http://www.eximinfo.com • $1,200 Individuals; $50 Individuals. Covers: 830 Taiwanese manufacturers and exporters of athletic sports equipment, ball sports equipment, billiard equipment, billiard table sets and cues, camping equipment, camping goods, fishing tackle, golf carts and vans, golf club and badminton shafts, golf putter, gymnasium and exercise equipment, martial arts, sports equipment, water sports equipment, and winter and mountaineering sports equipment. Entries include: Company name, postal address, telephone, fax, e-mail, website, contact person, designation, and product details.

***Directory of Taiwanese Manufacturers & Exporters of Tea & Coffee***. EXIM Infotek Private Ltd., 604 Vishwa Deep, District Centre, Janakpuri New Delhi 110058, India. Phone: 91 11 25544793; Fax: 91 11 25544793; Email: info@eximinfo.org • URL: http://www.eximinfo.com • $5 Individuals. Covers: 20 Taiwanese manufacturers and exporters of Chinese tea, cocoa and chocolate products, coffee and coffee substitutes. Entries include: Company name, postal address, city, country, phone, fax, e-mail and websites, contact person, designation, and product details.

***Directory of Taiwanese Manufacturers & Exporters of Textile & Fabrics***. EXIM Infotek Private Ltd., 604 Vishwa Deep, District Centre, Janakpuri New Delhi 110058, India. Phone: 91 11 25544793; Fax: 91 11 25544793; Email: info@eximinfo.org • URL: http://www.eximinfo.com • $30 Individuals. Covers: 410 Taiwanese manufacturers and exporters of clothing and textile products, cotton fabrics, dyeing and finishing for fabrics and textile goods, fabric-cotton for furnishing, fabrics, fabrics for industrial use, fabrics-cotton, fabrics-hemp/jute/paper, fabric-silk, fabrics-knitted, fabrics-linen, fabrics-manmade fiber, fabrics-non woven, felts/felted fabrics, garment fabrics, knitted fabrics, knitted fabrics-pile/plush, net and tulle, non woven fabrics, polyester cloth, reflective fabrics, textiles, wadding and flock textiles for industrial use, and woolen fabrics. Entries include: Company name, postal address, city, country, phone, fax, e-mail and websites, contact person, designation, and product details.

***Directory of Taiwanese Manufacturers & Exporters of Toys & Games***. EXIM Infotek Private Ltd., 604 Vishwa Deep, District Centre, Janakpuri New Delhi 110058, India. Phone: 91 11 25544793; Fax: 91 11 25544793; Email: info@eximinfo.org • URL: http://www.eximinfo.com • $40 Individuals. Covers: 670 Taiwanese manufacturers and exporters of aircraft models, baby buggies, baby carriages, baby music potties, baby prams and cycles, baby tricycles and bicycles, baby walkers, cots, cradles and prams, dart game sets, dolls and puppets, educational toys, jumping balls, model aircrafts, music planes, musical articles and toys, party and educational games, plastic sporting games, puzzles/jigsaw puzzles, stuffed toys, talking planes, toys, toys and games-electric/electronic, toys and games-mechanical, toys and games-plastic, toys and games-rubber, toys and games-wooden, and video game machines. Entries include: Company name, postal address, city, country, phone, fax, e-mail and websites, contact person, designation, and product details.

***Directory of Taiwanese Manufacturers & Exporters of Travel & Luggage Accessories***. EXIM Infotek Private Ltd., 604 Vishwa Deep, District Centre, Janakpuri New Delhi 110058, India. Phone: 91 11 25544793; Fax: 91 11 25544793; Email: info@eximinfo.org • URL: http://www.eximinfo.com • $30 Individuals. Covers: 370 Taiwanese manufacturers and exporters of all kinds of umbrellas, leather travel goods/handbags, luggage carts, travel bags, umbrellas and walking sticks. Entries include: Company name, postal address, city, country, phone, fax, e-mail and websites, contact person, designation, and product details.

***Directory of Taiwanese Manufacturers & Exporters of Tyres & Tubes***. EXIM Infotek Private Ltd., 604 Vishwa Deep, District Centre, Janakpuri New Delhi 110058, India. Phone: 91 11 25544793; Fax: 91 11 25544793; Email: info@eximinfo.org • URL: http://www.eximinfo.com • $10 Individuals. Covers: 110 Taiwanese manufacturers & exporters of tire repair materials, tires, tires-remolded, vehicle tires & inner tubes. Entries include: Company name, postal address, city, country, phone, fax, e-mail & websites, contact person, designation, products detail.

***Directory of Taiwanese Manufacturers & Exporters of Undergarments***. EXIM Infotek Private Ltd., 604 Vishwa Deep, District Centre, Janakpuri New Delhi 110058, India. Phone: 91 11 25544793; Fax: 91 11 25544793; Email: info@eximinfo.org • URL: http://www.eximinfo.com • $10 Individuals. Covers: 50 Taiwanese manufacturers and exporters of brassieres/panties, lingerie/corsetry and nightwear, pantyhose, socks, underwear-men, and underwear-stockings. Entries include: Company name, postal address, city, country, phone, fax, e-mail and websites, contact person, designation, and product details.

***Directory of Taiwanese Manufacturers and Exporters of Waste Disposal and Recycling Equipment***. EXIM Infotek Private Ltd., 604 Vishwa Deep, District Centre, Janakpuri New Delhi 110058, India. Phone: 91 11 25544793; Fax: 91 11 25544793; Email: info@eximinfo.org • URL: http://www.eximinfo.com • $250 Individuals; $10 Individuals. Covers: 70 Taiwanese manufacturers and exporters of domestic refuse and waste incinerators. Entries include: Company name, postal address, telephone, fax, e-mail, website, contact person, designation, and product details.

***Directory of Taiwanese Manufacturers & Exporters of Watches & Clocks***. EXIM Infotek Private Ltd., 604 Vishwa Deep, District Centre, Janakpuri New Delhi 110058, India. Phone: 91 11 25544793; Fax: 91 11 25544793; Email: info@eximinfo.org • URL: http://www.eximinfo.com • $20 Individuals. Covers: 220 Taiwanese manufacturers and exporters of blank movements for quartz watches, clocks, clocks and clock parts, meters-time interval, table clocks, timing mechanisms, watch bracelets/straps, watch/clock and instrument parts, watch/clock and instrument springs, watches, wrist and pocket watches. Entries include: Company name, postal address, city, country, phone, fax, e-mail and websites, contact person, designation, product details.

***Directory of Taiwanese Manufacturers & Exporters of Wire, Chain & Wire Products***. EXIM Infotek Private Ltd., 604 Vishwa Deep, District Centre, Janakpuri New Delhi 110058, India. Phone: 91 11 25544793; Fax: 91 11 25544793; Email: info@eximinfo.org • URL: http://www.eximinfo.com • $20 Individuals. Covers: 260 Taiwanese manufacturers and exporters of chains, chains/chain slings/grips-metal, ferrous wires, fine bare-copper wire, galvanized steel wire rope, metal cables/cords/ropes, metal fencing and barbed wire, metal gauze/cloth/netting, stainless steel wire rope, steel wire-zinc coated strands, wire goods-metal, wire products, wire racks and accessories. Entries include: Company name, postal address, city, country, phone, fax, e-mail and websites, contact person, designation, and product details.

***Directory of Taiwanese Manufacturers and Exporters of Woodworking Equipment and Tools***. EXIM Infotek Private Ltd., 604 Vishwa Deep, District Centre, Janakpuri New Delhi 110058, India. Phone: 91 11 25544793; Fax: 91 11 25544793; Email: info@eximinfo.org • URL: http://www.eximinfo.com • Covers: 290 Taiwanese manufacturers and exporters of ancillary equipment for wood working machine, multi-operational wood working machine, sawing and cutting tools, timber preparing machinery and equipment, tools for wood working machinery, wood boring and mortising machine, wood conditioning treatment equipment, wood deforming machine, wood joining machine, wood milling and molding machine, wood planning machine, wood sanding machine, wood sawing machine, wood turning lathes, portable wood working machine, wooden picture frame making machinery, woodworking machinery, and woodworking tools. Entries include: Company name, postal address, telephone, fax, e-mail, website, contact person, designation, and product details.

***Directory of Taiwanese Manufacturers & Exporters of Yarns & Threads***. EXIM Infotek Private Ltd., 604 Vishwa Deep, District Centre, Janakpuri New Delhi 110058, India. Phone: 91 11 25544793; Fax: 91 11 25544793; Email: info@eximinfo.org • URL: http://www.eximinfo.com • $20 Individuals. Covers: 270 Taiwanese manufacturers and exporters of cotton yarn, dying and finishing for textile fiber/yarn, reflective filaments, sewing and embroidery thread, textile fiber-manmade, thread, yarn and twist-silk, yarn and twists-manmade fiber, yarns and twists-vegetable fibers, yarns and twists-wool/hair. Entries include: Company name, postal address, city, country, phone, fax, e-mail and websites, contact person, designation, and product details.

***Directory of Taiwanese Manufacturers & Exporters of Zippers, Garment & Shoe Accessories***. EXIM Infotek Private Ltd., 604 Vishwa Deep, District Centre, Janakpuri New Delhi 110058, India. Phone: 91 11 25544793; Fax: 91 11 25544793; Email: info@eximinfo.org • URL: http://www.eximinfo.com • $15 Individuals. Covers: 140 Taiwanese manufacturers and exporters of apparel accessories, belt buckles, buttons, elastic band accessories, elastic braid, elastic cords, elastic ribbons, elastic yarn and fabrics, eyelets, garment accessories, hooks, loop fasteners, metal buttons, patches, plastic buckles, sewing kits, sewing notions, shoe buckles, woven labels, zipper products, and zippers. Entries include: Company name, postal address, city, country, phone, fax, e-mail and websites, contact person, designation, and product details.

***Directory of Taiwan's Leading Exporters***. China Economic News Service, 555 Chunghsiao E Rd., Sec. 4 Taipei 110, Taiwan. Phone: 886 2 2642 2629; Fax: 886 2 2642 7422; Email: news@cens.com • URL: http://www.cens.com • Annual. $90. Covers: 6,000 suppliers of machinery, toys, giftware, stationery, jewelry, sporting goods, leather goods, footwear, bicycles, automobiles, hardware, building materials, electronics, computers, textiles, furniture, and lighting.

***Directory of Texas Manufacturers***. University of Texas at Austin IC2 Institute Bureau of Business Research, 2815 San Gabriel St. Austin, TX 78705. Phone: (512)475-8900; Fax: (512)475-8903; Email: bkellison@ic2.utexas.edu • URL: http://ic2.utexas.edu/bbr • Annual. $139; $399 includes CD-Rom. Covers: more than 17,000 manufacturers in Texas and Texarkana, Arkansas; includes Standard Industrial Classification (SIC) manufacturing codes, products. Entries include: Company name, address, phone, toll-free number, fax number, geographical territory covered, form of company organization, number of employees, products, sales volume, SIC code. Updated monthly by "Texas Industrial Expansion" (see separate entry).

***Directory of the Coal Industry of the Former Soviet Union***. Flegon Press, 37B New Cavendish St. London W1M 8JR, United Kingdom. Phone: 44 181 752 1296; Fax: 44 181 752 1296 • $150. Covers: Over 450 coal mines and companies associated with the industry of the former Soviet Union, including collieries, machinery manufacturing, equipment repair, and associations. Database includes: Full coal specifications and import requests. Entries include: Company national, telex, and names of managing personnel.

***Directory of the Russian Far East***. Flegon Press, 37B New Cavendish St. London W1M 8JR, United Kingdom. Phone: 44 181 752 1296; Fax: 44 181 752 1296 • Irregular. $99. Covers: Industry in the Far East of Russia. Entries include: Company name and location, manager name, phone, telex, number of employees, products, and import/export details.

***Directory of Top Computer Executives***. Applied Computer Research Inc., PO Box 41730 Phoenix, AZ 85080. Phone: 800-234-2227; Email: alan@acrhq.com • URL: http://www.itmarketintelligence.com • Semiannual. $345 Individuals single volume, per issue; $520 U.S. and Canada single volume, per year; $620 Individuals two-volume set, per issue; $930 U.S. and Canada two-volume set, per year; $925 Individuals three-volume set, per issue; $1,390 U.S. and Canada three-volume set, per year. Covers: In three volumes, over 65,000 U.S. and Canadian executives with major information technology or communications responsibilities in over 35,500 U.S. and Canadian companies. Database includes: Listings of manufacturer and model numbers of systems that are installed at each company. Entries include: Company name, address, phone, subsidiary and/or division names, major systems installed, names and titles of top information system executives, number of IT employees, number of PCs, and web address.

***The Directory of Toronto Recruiters***. Continental Records Company Ltd., 2665 Thomas St., Ste. 37 Mississauga, ON, Canada L5M 6G4. Phone: 800-494-6129 or (905)813-9544; Fax: (905)812-4993; Email: conrecs@gocontinental.com • URL: http://www.gocontinental.com • Annual. $49.95 Individuals plus express post shipping cost and GST. Covers: More than 1,200 recruiting firms in the Toronto, Canada area. Entries include: Firm name, address, phone, fax, e-mail, URL, name and title of contact, and industry and professional specialties.

***Directory of Trade and Professional Associations in the European Union - The Blue Book***. Euroconfidentiel S. A., Rue de Rixensart 18 B-1332 Genval, Belgium. Phone: 32 02 652 02 84 or 32 2 6520284; Fax: (653) 01 80 or (653)0180; Email: nigel.hunt@skynet.be • URL: http://www.euroconfidential.com • Annual. $160.00. Includes more than 9,000 EU-related associations.

***Directory of Training Programmes***. Gower Publishing Australia Proprietary Ltd., 100 Harris St. Pyrmont, NSW 2009, Australia. Phone: 2 5522366 • Annual. $275 postpaid. Covers: Approximately 700 organizations and other institutions in Australia that provide management training programs. Entries include: Organization name, address, phone, fax, name and title of contact, geographical area served, description of programs offered.

***Directory of Training***. Training Information Network Ltd., 51 High St., Jubilee House, The Oaks Ruislip HA4 7LF, United Kingdom. Phone: 895622112; Fax: 895621582 • Annual. $170 Set; $60 Dir. of Multi-Media Training; $70 other volumes, each. A three-volume set: "Directory of Computer Training" lists 5,000 computer courses from over 500 training companies; "Directory of Management Training" describes more than 5,000 management and supervisory courses; and "Directory of Multi-Media Training" lists 2,000 computer-based, interactive video, self-study, and other training packages; coverage includes the United Kingdom. Database includes: Lists of consultants, training venues, training associations, and sources of training advice; glossaries. Entries include: Company or institute name, address, phone, contact name, company profile; title, cost, duration, frequency, and location of each course offered.

***Directory of Trust Banking***. Thomson Financial Publishing, 4709 W Golf Rd. Skokie, IL 60076-1253. Phone: 800-800321-3373 or (847)676-9600 or (708)676-9600; Fax: (708)933-8101 or (847)933-8101; Email: support@bankinfo.com • URL: http://www.tfp.com • Annual. $344.00. Contains profiles of bank affiliated trust companies, independent trust companies, trust investment advisors, and trust fund managers. Provides contact information for professional personnel at more than 3,000 banking and other financial institutions.

***Directory of 20 South Korean Manufacturers & Exporters of Jute, Hemp, Sisal, Burlap & Its Products***. EXIM Infotek Private Ltd., 604 Vishwa Deep, District Centre, Janakpuri New Delhi 110058, India. Phone: 91 11 25544793; Fax: 91 11 25544793; Email: info@eximinfo.org • URL: http://www.eximinfo.com • $5 Individuals. Covers: 20 South Korean manufacturers and exporters of canvas and duck, canvas and duck products. Entries include: Company name, postal address, city, country, phone, fax, e-mail and websites, contact person, designation, and product details.

***Directory of 2,500 Active Real-Estate Lenders***. International Wealth Success Inc., 24 Canterbury Rd. Rockville Centre, NY 11570-1310. Phone: 800-323-0548 or (516)766-5850; Fax: (516)766-5919; Email: admin@iwsmoney.com • URL: http://www.iwsmoney.com • Annual. $25 Individuals. Covers: About 2,500 financial institutions that actively lend money for real estate investments and purchases. Entries include: Company name, address.

***Directory of U. S. Labor Organizations***. BNA, Inc., 1231 25th St., NW Washington, DC 20037. Phone: 800-372-1033; Email: customercare@bna.com • URL: http://www.bna.com • $180

Individuals softcover. More than 150 national unions and professional and state employees associations engaged in labor representation.

***Directory of UK Exporters***. Hemming Information Services, 32 Vauxhall Bridge Rd. London SW1V 2SS, United Kingdom. Phone: 44 207 79736400 or 71 9736400; Fax: 44 207 72335056 or 71 2335057; Email: info@hgluk.com • URL: http://www.hgluk.com • $275 plus $9.00 shipping. Covers: 10,500 manufacturing exporters. Entries include: Named export contact, products, countries of destination, tonnage shipped and turnover.

***Directory of U.S. Agricultural Cooperative Exporters: SR21***. U.S. Department of Agriculture, 1400 Independence Ave. SW Washington, DC 20250. Phone: 800-336-3747 or (202)720-2791 or (202)720-9904; Fax: (202)690-2164 or (202)720-6050; Email: fsis.outreach@usda.gov • URL: http://www.usda.gov • Covers: 102 U.S. agricultural cooperatives that export or have the capability of exporting commodities to foreign countries. Entries include: Cooperative name, address, phone, name and title of contact, commodities available, communications numbers.

***Directory of U.S. Companies Doing Business in Central and Eastern Europe and the Commonwealth of Independent States***. Wetherby International Co., PO Box 5393 Arlington, VA 22205. Phone: (703)241-0586; Fax: (703)941-1516 • Quarterly. $25 postpaid. Covers: over 500 U.S. firms with operations in the Commonwealth of Independent States and Central and Eastern Europe; sources of assistance for U.S. business at the Commerce Department. Entries include: Company or agency name, address, phone, type of activity.

***Directory of United States Importers/Directory of United States Exporters***. Piers Publishing Group, 33 Washington St., 13th Fl. Newark, NJ 08865. Phone: 877-203-5277 or (973)848-1341; Fax: (973)848-7133; Email: customersvs@joc.com • URL: http://www.joc.com • Annual. $675.00. Two volumes. $475.00 per volume. Approximately 55,000 firms with import and export interests; export and import managers, agents, and merchants in the United States; World ports; consulates and embassies. Formerly *United States Importers and Exporters Directories*.

***Directory of U.S. Importers***. Journal of Commerce Group, 2 Penn Pl. E Newark, NJ 07105-2257. Phone: (973)776-8660; Email: joc@halldata.com • URL: http://www.joc.com • Annual. $2,750 Master Edition CD; $995 Reference Edition CD; $475 U.S Importers w/FREE Electronic Index; $675 U.S. Importers/Exporters Set w/FREE Electronic Ind; $450. Covers: 32,000 importers in the United States. Database includes: Lists of world ports and international banks; trade commissions, consulates, embassies, and foreign trade zones; guide to operations of the U.S. Customs Service and company name. Entries include: Company name, address, phone, fax, names and titles of key personnel, SIC code, commodities imported, import country, U.S. port of entry, tonnage and volume indicators.

***Directory of U.S. Meat Suppliers***. United States Meat Export Federation, 1855 Blake St., Ste. 200 Denver, CO 80202. Phone: (303)623-6328; Fax: (303)623-0297; Email: migoe@usmef.org • URL: http://www.usmef.org • Annual. Covers: U.S. packers, processors, purveyors, and exporters of red meat and red meat products. Directory is included with payment of membership dues.

***Directory of Vendors***. IBCON S.A., Gutenberg 224, Col. Anzures 11590 Mexico, Mexico. Phone: 52 55 52554577; Email: ibcon@ibcon.com.mx • URL: http://www.ibcon.com.mx • Irregular. $473 Individuals. Covers: 14,640 companies that are SA corporations located in Mexico City. Entries include: Company name, address, phone, fax, industry code, Producing, Distributing, Servicing initials, name and position of the top executive.

***Directory of Venture Capital and Private Equity Firms***. Grey House Publishing, 4919 Rte. 22 Amenia, NY 12501. Phone: 800-562-2139 or (518)789-8700; Fax: (518)789-0556; Email: books@greyhouse.com • URL: http://www.greyhouse.com • $750 Individuals; $395 Libraries; $395 Individuals. Covers: 2,300 domestic and international venture capital and private equity firms. Entries include: Firm name, address, phone, fax, e-mail, URL, description of services, names and titles of key personnel.

***Directory of Venture Capital: 2nd Edition***. John Wiley & Sons Inc., 111 River St. Hoboken, NJ 07030-5774. Phone: 800-225-5945 or (201)748-6000; Fax: (201)748-6088; Email: info@wiley.com • URL: http://www.wiley.com • $59.95 Individuals paperback. Covers: More than 600 actively investing venture capital firms and funding sources. Database includes: Samples of standard agreements and contracts. Entries include: Company name, address, phone, types of investments, geographic preference.

***Directory of Washington, DC Chief Executive Officers***. Labor Market Information and Research Division District of Columbia Department of Employment Services, 4058 Minnesota Ave., NE Washington, DC 20019. Phone: (202)671-1633 or (202)724-7000; Fax: (202)673-6993; Email: does@dc.gov • URL: http://does.dc.gov • Annual. Covers: 200 large nongovernmental companies in the District of Columbia, selected on the basis of number of employees. Entries include: Company name, name of chief executive officer, address and the telephone numbers.

***Directory of Websites for International Jobs***. Development Concepts Inc., 9104 Manassas Dr., Ste. N Manassas Park, VA 20111-5211. Phone: 800-361-1055 or (703)361-7300; Fax: (703)335-9486; Email: query@impactpublications.com • URL: http://www.impactpublications.com • $19.95 Individuals. Covers: 1,400 websites.

***Directory of White & Yellow Goods Manufacturers in India***. Steel Guru, Major & Minor Exims Pvt. Ltd., 704B, Millennium Plz., Sushant Lok I Gurgaon 122002, India. Phone: 91 9871 193457; Email: info@steelguru.com • URL: http://www.steelguru.com • $250 Individuals additional fee for delivery of CD or printed form. Covers: 56 white and yellow goods manufacturers in India. Entries include: Company name, address, telephone number, mobile number, fax number, and e-mail address.

***Directory of Wholesale Grocers***. Chain Store Guide, 10117 Princess Palm Dr. Tampa, FL 33610. Phone: 800-927-9292 or (813)627-6800; Fax: (813)627-6888 or (813)627-6883; Email: info@csgis.com • URL: http://www.chainstoreguide.com • Annual. $327.00. Online edition, $747.00. Profiles over 1,100 cooperatives, voluntaries, non-sponsoring wholesalers, cash and carry warehouses, and nearly 220 service merchandisers. Covers United States and Canada.

***Directory of Wholesale Printing & Office Supplies Sources***. Gordon Press Publishers, PO Box 459., Bowling Green Sta. New York, NY 10004. Phone: (212)969-8419 or (718)624-8419 • Irregular. $260.95.

***The Directory of World Industrial & Commercial Organizations: China, Mainland Volume***. Economic Management Publishing House, 8 Hongyuan Hutong, Xinjiekou Hutong Beijing 100035, China. • $195. Covers: About 4,000 major import and export businesses in mainland China. Database includes: An introduction to China's economic situation, trade control, regulation, investment policy, exchange control, banking services, insurance, China's Coastal Open Areas, major economic management organizations, major chambers of commerce. Entries include: Company name, address, phone, fax, scope of business.

***Directory of World Trade Center & Trade Points***. EXIM Infotek Private Ltd., 604 Vishwa Deep, District Centre, Janakpuri New Delhi 110058, India. Phone: 91 11 25544793; Fax: 91 11 25544793; Email: info@eximinfo.org • URL: http://www.eximinfo.com • Covers: 280 World Trade Centers and trade points. Entries include: Company name, postal address, telephone, fax, e-mail, website, contact person, designation, and product details.

***Directory of Worldwide Export-Import Promotion Center***. EXIM Infotek Private Ltd., 604 Vishwa Deep, District Centre, Janakpuri New Delhi 110058, India. Phone: 91 11 25544793; Fax: 91 11 25544793; Email: info@eximinfo.org • URL: http://www.eximinfo.com • Covers: 550 export and import promotion centers worldwide. Entries include: Company name, postal address, telephone, fax, e-mail, website, contact person, designation, and product details.

***Dirigeants and Cadres***. Editus S.A.R.L., Rue Michel Rodange 28 L-2340 Luxembourg, Luxembourg. Phone: 496051 • Annual. Covers: 4,500 executives in the commerce trade and industry in Luxembourg. Entries include: Names and addresses.

**Disability Rights Center**. 24 Stone St., Ste. 204 Augusta, ME 04330. Phone: 800-452-1948 or (207)626-2774; Fax: (207)621-1419; Email: advocate@drcme.org • URL: http://www.drcme.org • Represents public interest research group committed on educating society about the disability rights movement. Aims to inform the public, political activists, consumer activists, advocates, and students on the disability movement. Seeks to involve as many disabled citizens as possible in processes that directly affect their lives, to work closely with other disability-related, consumer-based advocacy groups, and to educate the public in the legitimate demands and needs of the disabled. Compiles statistics.

***Disclosure SEC Database***. Disclosure Inc., 15 Court Sq., Ste. 8 Boston, MA 02108. Phone: 800-945-3647 or (617)742-5179; Fax: (617)718-2300 • URL: http://www.thomson.com/solutions/financial • Weekly. Database covers: Approximately 11,000 public companies that have at least 500 shareholders of one class of stock and a minimum of five million dollars in assets, and have filed a 10K, 20F, or Registration Statement with the Securities and Exchange Commission within the preceding 18 months. Database includes: Company name, address, phone, names and titles of key personnel and directors, state in which incorporated; Standard Industrial Classification (SIC) code; Fortune, Forbes, CUSIP, DUNS numbers; auditors, subsidiaries; annual and quarterly balance sheets and income statements; five-year financial summary; sources and uses of funds, price/earnings data, stock transfer agent, text of management discussion and President's letter, and other information. Institutional holdings, 5% ownership holdings, and ownership by insiders for 5,000 companies are reported in "Disclosure/Spectrum Ownership," updated quarterly; detailed data list of specific institutions and individuals, their relationship to the company, their holdings, and their most recent trades. Full text of documents available in print and on microfiche.

***Discount Store News - Top Chains***. Lebhar-Friedman Inc., 425 Park Ave. New York, NY 10022. Phone: (212)756-5000 or (603)432-4077; Email: info@lf.com • URL: http://www.lf.com • Annual. $79.00.

***Dispute Resolution Journal***. American Arbitration Association, 1633 Broadway, 10th Fl. New York, NY 10019. Phone: 800-778-7879 or (212)716-5800; Email: websitemail@adr.org • URL: http://www.adr.org • Quarterly. included in membership dues; $55 /year for nonmembers. Professional journal covering topics on dispute resolution. Formerly *Arbitration Journal*.

***Dissertation Abstracts International***. ProQuest L.L.C., 789 E Eisenhower Pkwy. Ann Arbor, MI 48106-1346. Phone: 800-521-0600 or (734)761-4700; Fax: (734)662-4554; Email: info@proquest.com • URL: http://www.proquest.com • Monthly.

***Dissertation Abstracts Online***. ProQuest L.L.C., 789 E Eisenhower Pkwy. Ann Arbor, MI 48106-1346. Phone: 800-521-0600 or (734)761-4700; Fax: (734)662-4554; Email: info@proquest.com • URL: http://www.proquest.com • Citations to all dissertations accepted for doctoral degrees by accredited U.S. educational institutions, 1861 to date. Includes British theses, 1988 to date. Inquire as to online cost and availability.

**Distance Education and Training Council**. 1601 18th St. NW, Ste. 2 Washington, DC 20009. Phone: (202)234-5100; Fax: (202)332-1386; Email: info@detc.org • URL: http://www.detc.org • Formerly National Home Study Council.

**Distilled Spirits Council of the United States**. 1250 Eye St. NW, Ste. 400 Washington, DC 20005. Phone: (202)628-3544; Fax: (202)682-8888 • URL: http://www.discus.org • Serves as national trade association of producers and marketers of distilled spirits sold in the U.S. Provides statistical and legal data for industry and the public and serves as public information source; conducts educational programs.

***Distribution Business***. UK Transport Press Ltd., 3rd Fl., Simpson House, 6 Cherry Orchard Rd. Croydon CR0 6BA, United Kingdom. Phone: 44 20 86807474; Fax: 44 20 86499747; Email: bernardsteel@uktpl.com • URL: http://www.applegate.co.uk • Monthly. $75 Individuals; $85 Individuals Europe; $95 Elsewhere; $10 Single issue. Business to business magazine covering logistics and distribution.

**Diversity Information Resources**. 2105 Central Ave. NE Minneapolis, MN 55418. Phone: (612)781-6819; Fax: (612)781-0109; Email: info@diversityinforesources.com • URL: http://www.diversityinforesources.com • Promotes businesses with minority, women, veteran, service-disabled veteran and HUBZone ownership. Compiles and publishes minority and women-owned business directories to acquaint major corporations and government purchasing agents with the products and services of minority and women-owned firms. Sponsors national supplier diversity seminars.

***Divorce, Separation, and the Distribution of Property***. ALM Media Properties LLC, 120 Broadway, 5th Fl. New York, NY 10271-1100. Phone: (212)457-9400; Fax: (646)417-7705; Email: customercare@alm.com • URL: http://www.alm.com • $540 per year. Covers such thorny divorce settlement issues as earning power, stock options, pensions, repayment of student loans, tort claims, closely held businesses, premarital agreement enforcement, and alimony awards. (Law Journal Press).

***Djibouti Business Directory***. Business Guide, PO Box 27669 Dubai, United Arab Emirates. Phone: 971 4 2651719; Fax: 971 4 2692151; Email: sales@africa-business.com • URL: http://www.africa-business.com • $150 Individuals Soft copy. Covers: 1,500 business listings including wholesalers, importers, retailers, business houses, and agents in Djibouti.

***DM Review: The Premier Publication for Business Intelligence and Analytics***. SourceMedia Inc., 1 State Street Plz., 27th Fl. New York, NY 10004. Phone: 800-221-1809 or (212)803-8200 or (212)803-8333; Fax: (212)843-9635 or (212)292-5216; Email: custserv@sourcemedia.com • URL: http://www.sourcemedia.com • Monthly. $49.00 per year. Edited for corporate executives and information technology personnel. Covers data management, business intelligence, data warehousing, systems management, data integration, knowledge management, data mining, and related topics.

**DMA Nonprofit Federation**. 1615 L St. NW, Ste. 1100 Washington, DC 20036. Phone: (202)861-2427; Fax: (202)628-4383; Email: aosgood@the-dma.org • URL: http://www.nonprofitfederation.org • Trade and lobbying group for non-profit organizations that use direct and online marketing to raise funds and communicate with members. Sponsors professional development conferences and seminars, lobbies on state and federal legislation, regulation, and standards related to direct marketing and related issues. Provides information about and participants in litigation affecting non-profits. Promotes the overall welfare of non-profits. Represents health care charities, social service agencies, religious groups, colleges and universities and fraternal organizations.

***DMA Politically Direct***. Direct Marketing Association, 1120 Ave. of the Americas New York, NY 10036-6700. Phone: (212)768-7277; Fax: (212)302-6714; Email: info@the-dma.org • URL: http://www.thedma.org • Quarterly. Available in print and digital to members.

***DMA's Who's Who in Hong Kong Trading Industries***. Asian Market Information & Analysis Centre, 1802, Eastern Harbour Ctr., 28 Hoi Chak St., Quarry Bay Hong Kong, China. Phone: 852 21041958; Fax: 852 21277581; Email: prime@asia-lists.com • URL: http://www.asia-lists.com • Covers: 1,500 companies in Hong Kong's trading industries. Entries include: Company name, website; contact address, phone, fax, and e-mail; contact person, job title, and e-mail address.

***DNR: The Men's Fashion Retail Textile Authority***. Fairchild

Publications, 750 Third Ave. New York, NY 10017. Phone: 800-360-1700 or (212)630-4600 or (212)630-4000; Fax: (212)630-3675 or (212)630-4015; Email: hillary_kribben@condenast.com • URL: http://www.fairchildmediakit.com • Daily. $85.00 per year. Formerly *Daily News Record*.

**DOCHAS, The Irish Association of Non-Governmental Development Organisations**. 1-2 Baggot Ct., Lower Baggot St. Dublin 2, Dublin, Ireland. Phone: 353 1 4053801; Fax: 353 1 4053802 • URL: http://www.dochas.ie • Brings together 38 Irish NGDO involved in development and relief overseas and/or in the provision of development education. Aims to provide a forum for consultation and cooperation between its members and acts as the Irish Assembly of Development and Relief Organisations in relation to the CONCORD - a European Confederation for relief and development.

***Dr. Dobb's Journal: Software Tools for the Professional Programmer***. UBM L.L.C., 600 Community Dr. Manhasset, NY 11030. Phone: (516)562-5000 or (512)562-5000; Fax: (212)378-2160 or (516)562-5036; Email: cmp@cmp.com • URL: http://www.cmp.com • Monthly. $34.95 per year. A technical publication covering software development, languages, operating systems, and applications.

***DOCUMENT***. RB Publishing Co., 2901 International Ln. Madison, WI 53704. Phone: (608)241-8777 • URL: http://www.rbpub.com/ME2/Default.asp • Monthly Quarterly. Covers document management tools.

***Documents to the People (DttP)***. Government Documents Round Table. Library and Information Technology Association, 50 E Huron St. Chicago, IL 60611-2795. Phone: 800-545-2433; Fax: (312)280-3257; Email: lita@ala.org • URL: http://www.ala.org/lita • Quarterly. Official publication of the Government Documents Round Table (GODORT) of the American Library Association (ALA). DttP features articles on local, state, national, and international government information, government activities, and documents the professional activities of GODORT.

***DOE This Month***. U. S. Government Printing Office, 732 N Capitol St. NW Washington, DC 20401. Phone: 866-512-1800 or (202)512-1800 or (866)512-1800; Fax: (202)512-2104 or (202)512-2250; Email: contactcenter@gpo.gov • URL: http://www.gpo.gov • Monthly. $22 per year. Describes the U.S. Department of Energy's research and development activities and DOE publications. Includes information on nuclear energy, renewable energy sources, and synthetic fuels.

***Doing Business in Beijing***. China Knowledge Press, 13B Zhao Feng World Trade Bldg., 369 Jiangsu Rd., Chang Ning District Shanghai 200050, China. Phone: 86 21 52379039; Fax: 86 21 52375156; Email: shanghai@chinaknowledge.com • URL: http://www.chinaknowledge.com • $49.95 Individuals. Covers: Information on Beijing's vital economic statistics, trends, business opportunities, and many more. Entries include: Contact information of government departments, embassies, courier services, executive search firms, and banks.

***Doing Business in Emerging Europe***. Palgrave Macmillan, Houndsmills Basingstoke RG21 6XS, United Kingdom. Phone: 44 1256 329242 or 44 01256 329242; Fax: 44 1256 479476 or (012)56 320109; Email: booksellers@palgrave.com • URL: http://www.palgrave.com • £110 Individuals Hardback. Publication includes: Additional details about conducting business in each country featured. Entries include: Name, address, phone, fax, and URL. Principal content of publication is practical information about doing business in twelve countries in eastern Europe: Belarus, Croatia, the Czech Republic, Estonia, Hungary, Latvia, Lithuania, Poland, Slovakia, Slovenia, Turkey, and Ukraine.

***Doing Business in Europe***. Wolters Kluwer Law & Business CCH, 2700 Lake Cook Rd. Riverwoods, IL 60015. Phone: 888-224-7377 or (847)267-7000; Email: cust_serv@cch.com • URL: http://www.cchgroup.com • Biweekly. $970 Individuals. Loose leaf series on international trade.

***Doing Business in Hong Kong: Your Guide to Establishing an Office***. American Chamber of Commerce in Hong Kong, 1904 Bank of America Tower, 12 Harcourt Rd. Hong Kong, China. Phone: 86 852 25306900; Fax: 86 852 28101289; Email: amcham@amcham.org.hk • URL: http://www.amcham.org.hk • Annual. $180 Nonmembers; $23 Nonmembers; $120 Members; $16 Members. Provides an overview of the various factors to consider when establishing a business in Hong Kong.

***Doing Business in Memphis: A Directory of Business and Industry***. Doing Business in Memphis, 1779 Kirby Pkwy., Ste. 128 Germantown, TN 38138-0631. Phone: (901)590-0050; Fax: (901)590-0100; Email: chamber@indylink.com • URL: http://www.memphisbusiness.com • Biennial. $199.95 plus $18.50 tax and $6 shipping; $149.95 1998 edition; $149.95 1999 edition; $159.95 2000-2001 edition; $159.95 2001-2002 edition; $169.95 2003 edition; $169.95 2004 edition. Over 10,000 Memphis, Tennessee companies and, 25,000 contact names.

***Doing Business in Memphis***. Doing Business in Memphis, 1779 Kirby Pkwy., Ste. 128 Germantown, TN 38138-0631. Phone: (901)590-0050; Fax: (901)590-0100; Email: chamber@indylink.com • URL: http://www.memphisbusiness.com • Covers: Over 10,000 Memphis, Tennessee companies and, 25,000 contact names. Entries include: Company name, ad-

dress, phone, fax, toll-free number, Standard Industrial Classification (SIC) code, names and titles of key personnel, number of employees, descriptions of product/service, product/service provided, e-mail addresses, website, square footage.

***Doing Business in Shanghai***. China Knowledge Press, 13B Zhao Feng World Trade Bldg., 369 Jiangsu Rd., Chang Ning District Shanghai 200050, China. Phone: 86 21 52379039; Fax: 86 21 52375156; Email: shanghai@chinaknowledge.com • URL: http://www.chinaknowledge.com • $49.95 Individuals. Covers: Information on Shanghai's vital economic statistics, trends, business opportunities, and many more. Entries include: Contact information of service-related organizations and government bodies, trade fairs, history, geography, and political system.

***Doing Business in Today's Hong Kong***. American Chamber of Commerce in Hong Kong, 1904 Bank of America Tower, 12 Harcourt Rd. Hong Kong, China. Phone: 86 852 25306900; Fax: 86 852 28101289; Email: amcham@amcham.org.hk • URL: http://www.amcham.org.hk • Publication includes: In an appendix lists of business organizations in Hong Kong, including quality and standards organizations, government agencies, chambers of commerce, and industry-specific associations. Entries include: Organization name, address, phone, fax, telex. Principal content of publication is information on investment, business, sales and manufacturing trade, real estate, and the electronics industry in Hong Kong.

***Doing Business in Washington Country***. Portland General Electric Co., • $20 plus $3.00 shipping. Covers government agencies, schools and universities, utilities, economic development organizations, financing sources, parks and recreation, social services, arts and cultural agencies, business services, waste disposal and recycling services, and other agencies and organizations in Washington County, Oregon.

***Doing Business with China***. Kogan Page US, 525 S 4th St. Philadelphia, PA 19147. Phone: 800-961-2026 or (215)928-9112; Fax: (215)928-9113; Email: info@koganpage.com • URL: http://www.kogan-page.com • Publication includes: List of helpful business contacts in China. Entries include: Name, address, phone, fax. Principal content of publication is extensive general and business information about China.

***Doing Business with Korea***. Korea Chamber of Commerce and Industry, 39, Sejong-daero, Jung-gu Seoul 100-743, South Korea. Phone: 82 2 60503114; Fax: 82 2 60503400 • URL: http://www.korcham.net • Semiannual. Contains information on Korea's export and import status.

***Doing Business with the Department of Energy: Directory***. U.S. Department of Energy, 1000 Independence Ave. SW Washington, DC 20585. Phone: (202)586-5000; Fax: (202)586-4403; Email: The.Secretary@hq.doe.gov • URL: http://energy.gov • Irregular. Covers regional offices and field organizations of the Energy Department, and major contractors for the department.

***Dominica Investment and Business Guide***. International Business Publications, USA, PO Box 15343 Washington, DC 20003. Phone: (202)546-2103; Fax: (202)546-3275; Email: ibpusa@comcast.net • URL: http://ibpus.com • $99.95 Individuals hardcopy, e-book, CD-ROM. Covers: Strategic information on economy, business, export-import and investment climate, regulations and industrial development, banking, government, and opportunities. Entries include: Important business contacts and business travel.

***Dominican Republic—American Chamber of Commerce—Membership Directory***. U.S. Chamber of Commerce, 1615 H St. NW Washington, DC 20062-2000. Phone: 800-638-6582 or (202)463-5500 or (202)659-6000; Fax: (202)463-3129; Email: foundation@uschamber.com • URL: http://www.uschambersmallbusinessnation.com • Covers: American and Dominican Republic companies and individuals interested in the development of trade within and between the two countries. Entries include: For firms—Company name, address, phone, fax, telex, cable address, names and titles of key personnel, line of business, subsidiary and branch names and locations, locations of plants or branch offices, product/service information. For individuals—Name, title, affiliation, address.

***Dominican Republic Industrial and Business Directory***. International Business Publications, USA, PO Box 15343 Washington, DC 20003. Phone: (202)546-2103; Fax: (202)546-3275; Email: ibpusa@comcast.net • URL: http://ibpus.com • Annual. $99.95 Individuals hardcopy, e-book, CD-ROM. Covers: Strategic industrial, investment and business contacts for conducting export-import and investment activity in the country. Contains strategic practical economic and business information.

**Door and Access Systems Manufacturers Association International**. 1300 Sumner Ave. Cleveland, OH 44115-2851. Phone: (216)241-7333; Fax: (216)241-0105; Email: dasma@dasma.com • URL: http://www.dasma.com • Members are manufacturers of "upward-acting" garage doors and related products, both residential and commercial.

**Door and Hardware Institute**. 14150 Newbrook Dr., Ste. 200 Chantilly, VA 20151-2223. Phone: (703)222-2010; Fax: (703)222-2410; Email: membership@dhi.org • URL: http://www.dhi.org • Commercial distributors, manufacturers and specifiers involved in doors and builders' hardware (locks, door hardware, latches, hinges, and electrified products). Works with architects, contractors, and building owners.

Conducts management and technical courses and membership-related surveys. Offers certification program for the Architectural Openings Industry (AHC, CDC).

***Door and Window Retailing***. Jervis and Associates, 11300 US Highway 1.Suite 400 North Palm Beach, FL 33408. Phone: (908)850-8100; Fax: (908)850-6464 • Bimonthly. $15.00 per year. Edited for door and window retailers. Formerly *Door and Window Business*.

***Doors & Hardware***. Door and Hardware Institute, 14150 Newbrook Dr., Ste. 200 Chantilly, VA 20151-2223. Phone: (703)222-2010; Fax: (703)222-2410; Email: membership@dhi.org • URL: http://www.dhi.org • Monthly. $75 Life member; $100 U.S., Canada, and Mexico; $175 Other countries. Covers the architectural openings industry.

***Dorland's Directory of Health Plans***. Dorland Healthcare Information, 1500 Walnut St., Ste. 1000 Philadelphia, PA 19102. Phone: 855-225-5341; Fax: (301)287-2535; Email: chi@healthcare-info.com • URL: http://www.dorlandhealth.com • Annual. $195.00. Published in association with the American Association of Health Plans (www.aahp.org). Lists more than 2,400 health plans, including Health Maintenance Organizations (HMOs), Preferred Provider Organizations (PPOs), and Point of Service plans (POS). Includes the names of about 9,000 health plan executives.

***Dorland's Medical Directory***. Access Intelligence L.L.C., 4 Choke Cherry Rd., 2nd Fl. Rockville, MD 20850. Phone: 800-777-5006 or (301)354-2000 or (301)354-2101; Fax: (301)309-3847 or (801)365-2300; Email: info@accessintel.com • URL: http://www.accessintel.com/ • Annual. $69.95 Individuals plus $3.95 shipping. Covers: Nearly 15,000 physicians in Eastern Pennsylvania and Southern New Jersey, Northern Delaware. Also includes group practices, hospitals, healthcare facilities, and medical organizations. Entries include: For physicians—Name, office and home addresses and phone, fax numbers, email addresses, medical school attended and year graduated, medical specialties, certifications, hospital affiliations. For hospitals—Name, address, names and specialties of staff members.

***The Dow Jones Guide to the World Stock Market***. Reference Press Inc., 6448 Hwy. 290 E, Ste. E-104 Austin, TX 78723. Phone: 800-486-8666 or (512)454-7778; Fax: (512)454-9401; Email: orders@hoovers.com • Annual. $39.95. Covers: 2,600 companies in 20 countries that form the Dow Jones World Stock Index. Database includes: A ranking of the companies listed by country, market value, industry, and other factors. Entries include: Company name, address, phone, description, main lines of business, history, sales, earnings, dividends, and financial performance.

***Dow Jones News Service***. Dow Jones and Co., Inc., 4300 N Rte. 1 Monmouth Junction, NJ 08852. • URL: http://new.dowjones.com • Full text and edited news stories and articles on business affairs. Inquire as to online cost and availability.

***Dow Theory Forecasts***. Horizon Publishing Co., 7412 Calumet Ave. Hammond, IN 46324-2622. Phone: 800-233-5922; Fax: (219)931-6487; Email: custserv@horizonpublishing.com • URL: http://www.horizonpublishing.com • Weekly. Provides information and advice on blue chip and income stocks.

***Dow Theory Letters***. Dow Theory Letters, Inc., PO Box 1759 La Jolla, CA 92038-1759. Phone: (858)454-0481; Email: staff@dowtheoryletters.com • URL: http://ww2.dowtheoryletters.com • Triweekly. $300 /year. Newsletter on stock market trends, investing, and economic conditions.

***DownBeat***. Maher Publications Inc., 102 N Haven Rd. Elmhurst, IL 60126. Phone: 800-554-7470 or (630)941-2030; Fax: (630)941-3210; Email: editor@downbeat.com • URL: http://www.downbeat.com • Monthly. $32.99 print or print and online; $26.99 online. Information on contemporary music.

***Downey Business***. Downey Chamber of Commerce, 11131 Brookshire Ave. Downey, CA 90241-3860. Phone: (562)923-2191; Fax: (562)869-0461; Email: info@downeychamber.com • URL: http://www.downeychamber.com • Monthly. Features updates on chamber activities, future events and business community news.

***Downstate Illinois Business Directory***. InfoGroup Inc., 5711 S 86th Cir. Omaha, NE 68127-4146. Phone: (402)593-4500 • URL: http://www.infogroup.com • Annual. $415. Number of listings: 188,000. Entries include: Company name, address, phone (including area code). Compiled from telephone company "Yellow Pages," statewide.

***Downtown Idea Exchange: Essential Information for Downtown Research and Development Center***. Downtown Research and Development Center. Alexander Communications Group Inc., 28 W 25th St., 8th Fl. New York, NY 10010. Phone: 800-232-4317 or (212)228-0246; Fax: (212)228-0376; Email: info@alexcommgrp.com • URL: http://www.alexcommgrp.com • Monthly. $227 Individuals. Newsletter for those concerned with central business districts. Provides news and other information on planning, development, parking, mass transit, traffic, funding, and other topics.

***Draperies and Window Coverings***. L.C. Clark Publishing Company Inc., 840 US Hwy. 1, Ste. 330 North Palm Beach, FL 33408-3874. Phone: 800-537-4271 or (561)627-3393; Fax: (561)694-6578 or (561)627-1447; Email: jmoody@lcclark.com • URL: http://www.dwconline.com/ • 13 times a year. $33.00 per year. Published for retailers, designers, manufacturers, and distributors of window coverings.

***Draperies and Window Coverings: Directory and Buyer's Guide***. L.C. Clark Publishing Company Inc., 840 US Hwy. 1, Ste.

330 North Palm Beach, FL 33408-3874. Phone: 800-537-4271 or (561)627-3393; Fax: (561)694-6578 or (561)627-1447; Email: jmoody@lcclark.com • URL: http://www.dwconline.com/ • Annual. $15.00. Includes about 2,000 manufacturers and distributors of window coverings and related products.

***Draperies & Window Coverings—Directory & Buyer's Guide Issue: 2005***. L.C. Clark Publishing Company Inc., 840 US Hwy. 1, Ste. 330 North Palm Beach, FL 33408-3874. Phone: 800-537-4271 or (561)627-3393; Fax: (561)694-6578 or (561)627-1447; Email: jmoody@lcclark.com • URL: http://www.dwconline.com/ • Annual. Publication includes: List of about 2,000 manufacturers and distributors of window coverings and other products used in the window coverings and interior fashions industry. Entries include: Company name, address, phone, key executives, brand names carried.

***DRIP Investor: Your Guide to Buying Stocks Without a Broker***. Horizon Publishing Co., 7412 Calumet Ave. Hammond, IN 46324-2622. Phone: 800-233-5922; Fax: (219)931-6487; Email: custserv@horizonpublishing.com • URL: http://www.horizonpublishing.com • Monthly. $89.00 per year. Newsletter covering the dividend reinvestment plans (DRIPs) of various publicly-owned corporations. Includes model portfolios and *Directory of Dividend Reinvestment Plans*.

***Drop Shipping Source Directory of Major Consumer Product Lines***. Consolidated Marketing Services, Inc., PO Box 7838 New York, NY 10150. Phone: (212)688-8797; Email: nschneel@drop-shipping-news.com • URL: http://www.drop-shipping-news.com • Irregular. $15.00. Lists over 700 firms of a wide variety of consumer products that can be drop shipped.

***Drug and Alcohol Abuse Education***. Editorial Resources Inc., PO Box 21129 Washington, DC 20009. • Monthly. $84.00 per year. Newsletter covering education, prevention, and treatment relating to abuse of drugs and alcohol.

***Drug Benefit Trends: For Pharmacy Managers and Managed HealthCare Professionals***. Cliggott Publishing Co., 330 Boston Post Rd. Darien, CT 06820. Phone: (203)662-6400; Email: editor@scp.com • Monthly. Individuals, $95.00 per year; libraries, $120.00 per year; students, $40.00 per year. Covers the business of managed care drug benefits.

**Drug, Chemical and Associated Technologies Association**. One Washington Blvd., Ste. 7 Robbinsville, NJ 08691-3162. Phone: 800-640-3228 or (609)448-1000; Fax: (609)448-1944 • URL: http://www.dcat.org • Formerly Drug, Chemical and Allied Trades Section of the New York Board of Trade.

***Drug Development Research***. John Wiley & Sons Inc., 111 River St. Hoboken, NJ 07030-5774. Phone: 800-225-5945 or (201)748-6000; Fax: (201)748-6088; Email: info@wiley.com • URL: http://www.wiley.com • Monthly. $8,040 U.S., Canada, and Mexico Online only - institution; $9,246 Institutions print and online; $8,040 Institutions print only; $9,358 Institutions print and online - Canada and Mexico; $8,152 Institutions print only - Canada and Mexico; £4,102 Institutions Online only; £4,819 Institutions Print and Online; £4,188 Institutions Print only.

***Drug Facts and Comparisons***. Wolters Kluwer Health, 77 Westport Plz., Ste. 450 Saint Louis, MO 63146-3125. Phone: 800-223-0554 or (314)392-0000; Email: service@fandc.com • URL: http://www.factsandcomparisons.com • $565 Individuals Loose-leaf. Provides detailed information on more than 20,000 prescription drugs and 6000 over-the-counter products. Arrangement is according to 13 therapeutic categories. Includes charts and tables.

**Drug Information Association**. 800 Enterprise Rd., Ste. 200 Horsham, PA 19044-3595. Phone: (215)442-6100; Fax: (215)442-6199; Email: dia@diahome.org • URL: http://www.diahome.org • Provides neutral, global forum promoting exchange of information critical to professional performance and achievement in the discovery, development, regulation, surveillance, or marketing of pharmaceuticals or related products.

***Drug Information Fulltext (DIF)***. American Society of Health-System Pharmacists, 7272 Wisconsin Ave. Bethesda, MD 20814. Phone: 866-279-0681 or (301)664-8700 or (301)657-3000; Fax: (301)657-1251; Email: custserv@ashp.org • URL: http://www.ashp.org • Provides full text monographs from the *American Hospital Formulary Service* and the *Handbook On Injectable Drugs*. Inquire as to online cost and availability.

***Drug Interaction Facts***. Wolters Kluwer Health, 77 Westport Plz., Ste. 450 Saint Louis, MO 63146-3125. Phone: 800-223-0554 or (314)392-0000; Email: service@fandc.com • URL: http://www.factsandcomparisons.com • Contains data on the interactions of some 20,000 prescription drugs. Interactions are rated according to magnitude and likelihood of effects, from one (most severe) to five (least severe). Includes drug/drug and drug/food interactions.

***Drug Store News Continuing Education Quarterly***. Lebhar-Friedman Inc., 425 Park Ave. New York, NY 10022. Phone: (212)756-5000 or (603)432-4077; Email: info@lf.com • URL: http://www.lf.com • Quarterly. $59.95 per year. Formerly *Drug Store News Chain Pharmacy*.

***Drug Store News***. Lebhar-Friedman Inc., 425 Park Ave. New York, NY 10022. Phone: (212)756-5000 or (603)432-4077; Email: info@lf.com • URL: http://www.lf.com • Biweekly. Free to qualified personnel; others, $99.00 per year.

***Drug Topics***. Thomson Medical Economics, 5 Paragon Dr. Montvale, NJ 07645-1742. Phone: 800-526-4870 or (201)358-7200; Fax: (201)573-8999 or (201)722-2680; Email: customer.service@medec.com • URL: http://www.medec.com • Monthly. Edited for retail pharmacists, hospital pharmacists, pharmacy chain store executives, wholesalers, buyers, and others concerned with drug dispensing and drug store management. Provides information on new products, including personal care items and cosmetics.

***Drugs, Alcohol & Tobacco: Learning About Addictive Behavior***. Edited by Rosalyn Carson-Dewitt, M.D. Cengage Learning Inc., 20 Channel Center St. Boston, MA 02210. Phone: 800-487-8488 or (617)289-7700; Fax: (617)289-7844; Email: investors@cengage.com • URL: http://www.cengage.com • $512. Three volumes. Contains 200 articles on various aspects of addiction. Includes color illustrations, a glossary, and comprehensive indexing. Macmillan Reference USA imprint. eBook also available. Inquire for pricing.

***Dry Cleaners Directory***. InfoGroup Inc., 5711 S 86th Cir. Omaha, NE 68127-4146. Phone: (402)593-4500 • URL: http://www.infogroup.com • Annual. Number of listings: 50,053. Entries include: Name, address, phone, size of advertisement, name of owner or manager, number of employees, year first in "Yellow Pages." Compiled from telephone company "Yellow Pages," nationwide.

***Drycleaners News***. Zackin Publications Inc., PO Box 2180 Waterbury, CT 06722. Phone: 800-325-6745 or (203)262-4670; Fax: (203)262-4680; Email: info@zackin.com • URL: http://www.zackin.com • Monthly. $36.00.

***Duarte Business***. Duarte Chamber of Commerce, 1634 3rd St. Duarte, CA 91009. Phone: (626)357-3333; Fax: (626)357-3645 • URL: http://www.duartechamber.com • Biennial.

***Dubai Business Law Handbook***. International Business Publications, USA, PO Box 15343 Washington, DC 20003. Phone: (202)546-2103; Fax: (202)546-3275; Email: ibpusa@comcast.net • URL: http://ibpus.com • $99.95 Individuals hardcopy, e-book, CD-ROM. Covers: Basic information on business, laws, export-import, business climate, regulations, and contacts.

***Dubai Industrial and Business Directory***. International Business Publications, USA, PO Box 15343 Washington, DC 20003. Phone: (202)546-2103; Fax: (202)546-3275; Email: ibpusa@comcast.net • URL: http://ibpus.com • $99.95 Individuals hardcopy, e-book, CD-ROM. Covers: Strategic investment and business contacts for conducting export-import activity in the country. Entries include: Strategic economic and business information.

***Dubai Investment and Business Guide***. International Business Publications, USA, PO Box 15343 Washington, DC 20003. Phone: (202)546-2103; Fax: (202)546-3275; Email: ibpusa@comcast.net • URL: http://ibpus.com • Annual. $99.95 Individuals hardcopy, e-book, CD-ROM. Covers: Detailed information on investment, business opportunities, foreign economic assistance projects, government and business contacts and more. An ultimate guide for starting and conducting a successful business in the country.

***Dublin Business***. Dublin Chamber of Commerce, 7 Clare St. Dublin 2, Ireland. Phone: 353 1 6447200; Fax: 353 1 6447234; Email: info@dubchamber.ie • URL: http://www.dubchamber.ie • Quarterly.

**Dublin City Business Association**. 21 Dawson St. Dublin 2, Dublin, Ireland. Phone: 353 1 6622995; Email: info@dcba.ie • URL: http://www.dcba.ie • Retail Federation in the city of Dublin. Promotes a sustainable city centre that is attractive to live, work, visit, and shop in.

**Ductile Iron Pipe Research Association**. 1322 Riverhaven Pl. Birmingham, AL 35244-2560. Phone: (205)402-8700; Email: info@dipra.org • URL: http://www.dipra.org • Provides engineering information about cast iron and ductile iron pipe to utility and construction engineers.

**Duke University - David M. Rubenstein Rare Book and Manuscript Library - John W. Hartman Center for Sales, Advertising and Marketing History**. PO Box 90185 Durham, NC 27708-0185. Phone: (919)660-5827; Fax: (919)660-5934; Email: hartman-center@duke.edu • URL: http://library.duke.edu/rubenstein/hartman • Concerned with the study of the roles of sales, advertising, and marketing in society.

**Duke University - Sanford School of Public Policy - Center for Health Policy and Inequalities Research**. 310 Trent Dr. Durham, NC 27705. Phone: (919)613-5430; Fax: (919)613-5466 • URL: http://chpir.org • Quantitative analysis of clinical policies, decision analysis, Bayesian statistics, health economics, disease prevention, cancer and cancer detection, stroke prevention and management, and technology assessment, including evaluation of reimbursement policies for medical procedures, hospital and health care policies, and Health Maintenance Organization (HMO) medical policies.

***Dun & Bradstreet Germany***. Dun & Bradstreet Inc., 103 JFK Pkwy. Short Hills, NJ 07078. Phone: 800-526-0651 or (973)921-5500 or (973)921-5000; Fax: (866)560-7035 or (512)794-7670; Email: info@dnb.com • URL: http://www.dnb.com • €70 Individuals. Database covers: Over 160 million companies in Germany. Database includes: Company name, address, phone, names and titles of key personnel, number of employees, turnover, financial data, SIC code.

***Dun & Bradstreet Guide to Hong Kong Businesses***. Dun & Bradstreet Inc., 103 JFK Pkwy. Short Hills, NJ 07078. Phone: 800-526-0651 or (973)921-5500 or (973)921-5000; Fax: (866)560-7035 or (512)794-7670; Email: info@dnb.com • URL: http://www.dnb.com • Annual. $380. Covers 20,000 companies in Hong Kong, including foreign-owned companies operating in Hong Kong.

***Dun & Bradstreet Italy***. CRIBIS D & B Ltd., Via dei Valtorta 48 I-20127 Milan, Italy. Phone: 39 2 284551; Fax: 39 2 2845501; Email: direzionegenerale@cribisdnb.com • URL: http://www.cribis.com • Database covers: Approximately 473,000 companies in Italy. Database includes: Company name, address, names and titles of key personnel, number of employees, turnover, financial data, line of business, SIC code.

***Dun & Bradstreet Reference Book of American Businesses***. Dun & Bradstreet Inc., 103 JFK Pkwy. Short Hills, NJ 07078. Phone: 800-526-0651 or (973)921-5500 or (973)921-5000; Fax: (866)560-7035 or (512)794-7670; Email: info@dnb.com • URL: http://www.dnb.com • Covers: more than 3 million large and small, public and private U.S. companies. Entries include: Company name and phone, branch offices, D&B credit rating, Standard Industrial Classification (SIC) code, new business and rating change indicators, year established, finansial data.

***Dun & Bradstreet Regional Business Directories***. Dun & Bradstreet Inc., 103 JFK Pkwy. Short Hills, NJ 07078. Phone: 800-526-0651 or (973)921-5500 or (973)921-5000; Fax: (866)560-7035 or (512)794-7670; Email: info@dnb.com • URL: http://www.dnb.com • Annual. Covers: Top 20,000 businesses in one of 54 metropolitan areas in the U.S. Entries include: Company name, address, phone, trade name, Dun & Bradstreet D-U-N-S number, line of business, Standard Industrial Classification (SIC) code, sales volume names and titles of key personnel, number of employees, number of employees at location, parent company, year established, stock exchange symbol, indication of public or private ownership.

***Dun & Bradstreet State Sales Guide***. Dun & Bradstreet Inc., 103 JFK Pkwy. Short Hills, NJ 07078. Phone: 800-526-0651 or (973)921-5500 or (973)921-5000; Fax: (866)560-7035 or (512)794-7670; Email: info@dnb.com • URL: http://www.dnb.com • Quarterly. $69 Available only to Dun & Bradstreet Credit Services customers. Covers: all businesses in each state that are included in Dun & Bradstreet's national "Reference Book of American Business." A separate "State Sales Guide" is published for each state and the District of Columbia. Entries include: Company name, phone, D&B credit rating, branches, primary Standard Industrial Classification (SIC) code, year established; indicators note new businesses and those with ratings changes.

***Dun & Bradstreet Swiss Company Information***. Dun & Bradstreet AG, In der Luberzen 1 8902 Urdorf, Switzerland. Phone: 41 1 7356464 or 1 2956111; Fax: 1 2425307 or 41 1 735 61 61; Email: info.ch@dnb.com • URL: http://dbswitzerland.dnb.com • Monthly. Database covers: more than 180,000 businesses in Switzerland and Liechtenstein. Database includes: Company name, address, phone, headquarter and subsidiary, name and title of contact, year founded, SIC code, business activities, number of employees, senior executive name, sales volume, accounting and banking firm, DUNS number.

***Dun & Bradstreet 25,000 Series Directory***. Dun & Bradstreet Inc., 103 JFK Pkwy. Short Hills, NJ 07078. Phone: 800-526-0651 or (973)921-5500 or (973)921-5000; Fax: (866)560-7035 or (512)794-7670; Email: info@dnb.com • URL: http://www.dnb.com • Annual. $250 per volume. Covers: In three separate volumes, top 25,000 businesses, based on number of employees, for the Asia Pacific, Latin America, and Western Europe. Entries include: Company name, address, phone, fax, telex, Dun & Bradstreet D-U-N-S number, Standard Industrial Classification (SIC) code, name of CEO, number of employees, import/export designation, ownership date.

***Dun & Bradstreet United States***. Dun & Bradstreet Canada Ltd., 6750 Century Ave., Ste. 305 Mississauga, ON, Canada L5N 0B7. Phone: 800-463-6362; Fax: (800)668-7800 or (905)688-7800; Email: customercarecan@dnb.com • URL: http://www.dnb.ca • Quarterly. Database covers: 1.1 million U.S. businesses with 10 or more employees. Database includes: Company name, address, phone, chief executive officer, type of business, DUNS number, company status, subsidiary, manufacturing activity, language preference, geographic code, SIC codes, year current control of company established, date record was updated, number of employees at listed location, number of employees total, total sales volume for listed location.

**Dundalk Institute of Technology - Centre for Entrepreneurship Research**. Dublin Rd. Dundalk, Louth, Ireland. Phone: 353 42 9370200; Fax: 353 42 9370201; Email: info@dkit.ie • URL: http://ww2.dkit.ie/research/research_centres/cer • Entrepreneurship, on a regional, national, and international basis.

***Dundsdata***. Dun & Bradstreet France S.A., 345 Ave. Georges Clemenceau, tour Defense Bergere F-92000 Nanterre, France. Phone: 14135 1700 or 8 25805802; Fax: 14135 1777 or 33 1 41 35 17 77 • URL: http://dbfrance.dnb.com • Database covers: more than 9 million European businesses, with emphasis on France. Database includes: Company name, address, product trade name, capital, net value, financial data, affiliates and subsidiaries, principal directors.

***Dun's Asia Pacific Key Business Enterprises***. Dun & Bradstreet Inc., 103 JFK Pkwy. Short Hills, NJ 07078. Phone: 800-526-

0651 or (973)921-5500 or (973)921-5000; Fax: (866)560-7035 or (512)794-7670; Email: info@dnb.com • URL: http://www.dnb.com • Annual. Covers 30,000 leading companies in 14 Pacific Rim countries whose annual sales are $10 million and who have 500 or more employees.

***Dun's Business Update***. Dun & Bradstreet Inc., 103 JFK Pkwy. Short Hills, NJ 07078. Phone: 800-526-0651 or (973)921-5500 or (973)921-5000; Fax: (866)560-7035 or (512)794-7670; Email: info@dnb.com • URL: http://www.dnb.com • Biweekly. Database covers: more than 600,000 business establishments in the U.S. Database includes: Company name, address, phone, line of business, chief executive officer, number of employees, corporation affiliation, company status, sales.

***Dun's Electronic Business Directory***. Dun & Bradstreet Inc., 103 JFK Pkwy. Short Hills, NJ 07078. Phone: 800-526-0651 or (973)921-5500 or (973)921-5000; Fax: (866)560-7035 or (512)794-7670; Email: info@dnb.com • URL: http://www.dnb.com • Quarterly. Database covers: about 9 million U.S. financial services, professionals, hospitals and other medical facilities, wholesalers, retailers, construction firms, business services, government agencies, manufacturers, agriculture and mining companies, transportation firms, and utilities. Database includes: For businesses—Name, address, phone, county, Standard Industrial Classification (SIC) code, description of business, population of city, number of employees, type of advertising in yellow pages, whether a company, a corporation, or an individual.

***Dun's 15,000 Largest Companies—Belgium***. Dun & Bradstreet Inc., 103 JFK Pkwy. Short Hills, NJ 07078. Phone: 800-526-0651 or (973)921-5500 or (973)921-5000; Fax: (866)560-7035 or (512)794-7670; Email: info@dnb.com • URL: http://www.dnb.com • Covers: 15,000 industrial, trading, banking, insurance, and service companies in Belgium. Entries include: Company name, address, phone, fax, telex, equity capital, number of employees, primary and secondary Standard Industrial Classification (SIC) codes, profit/loss ratios, export percentages.

***Dun's 15,000 Largest Companies—Portugal***. Dun & Bradstreet Inc., 103 JFK Pkwy. Short Hills, NJ 07078. Phone: 800-526-0651 or (973)921-5500 or (973)921-5000; Fax: (866)560-7035 or (512)794-7670; Email: info@dnb.com • URL: http://www.dnb.com • Covers: 15,000 industrial, trading, banking, insurance, and service companies in Portugal. Entries include: Company name, address, phone, fax, telex, equity capital, number of employees, primary and secondary Standard Industrial Classification (SIC) codes, profit/loss ratios, export percentages.

***Dun's 15,000 Largest Companies—Spain***. Dun & Bradstreet Inc., 103 JFK Pkwy. Short Hills, NJ 07078. Phone: 800-526-0651 or (973)921-5500 or (973)921-5000; Fax: (866)560-7035 or (512)794-7670; Email: info@dnb.com • URL: http://www.dnb.com • Covers: 15,000 industrial, trading, banking, insurance, and service companies in Spain. Entries include: Company name, address, phone, fax, telex, equity capital, number of employees, primary and secondary Standard Industrial Classification (SIC) codes, profit/loss ratios, export percentages.

***Dun's 50,000—Spain's Largest Companies***. Dun & Bradstreet Inc., 103 JFK Pkwy. Short Hills, NJ 07078. Phone: 800-526-0651 or (973)921-5500 or (973)921-5000; Fax: (866)560-7035 or (512)794-7670; Email: info@dnb.com • URL: http://www.dnb.com • Annual. £438. Covers: 50,000 of the largest marketing companies in Spain. Entries include: Company name, address, operation information, key marketing information, key financial information.

***Dun's Financial Reference Plus***. Dun & Bradstreet Inc., 103 JFK Pkwy. Short Hills, NJ 07078. Phone: 800-526-0651 or (973)921-5500 or (973)921-5000; Fax: (866)560-7035 or (512)794-7670; Email: info@dnb.com • URL: http://www.dnb.com • $5,275 3 years; $6,180 4 years; $6,900 5 years; $7,395 6 years. Database covers: over 1,500,000 public and private U.S. companies. Database includes: For all companies—Company name, address, phone, D-U-N-S company number, Standard Industrial Classification (SIC) code, year established, number of employees, name of principal and owners, executive profiles, business activities, subsidiary and branch names and locations. For 750,000 businesses—Up to three-year detailed spreadsheet analysis of financial statements, including 14 key performance ratios, and balance sheet, income statement, and other financial data.

***Dun's Guide to Israel***. Dun & Bradstreet Inc., 103 JFK Pkwy. Short Hills, NJ 07078. Phone: 800-526-0651 or (973)921-5500 or (973)921-5000; Fax: (866)560-7035 or (512)794-7670; Email: info@dnb.com • URL: http://www.dnb.com • Covers: over 10,000 leading companies in Israel. Entries include: Company name, address, phone, fax, product exported, names and titles of key personnel, Standard Industrial Classification (SIC) code, number of employees, sales volume.

***Dun's Industrial Guide: The Metalworking Directory***. Dun & Bradstreet Inc., 103 JFK Pkwy. Short Hills, NJ 07078. Phone: 800-526-0651 or (973)921-5500 or (973)921-5000; Fax: (866)560-7035 or (512)794-7670; Email: info@dnb.com • URL: http://www.dnb.com • Annual. Libraries, $485; commercial institutions, $795.00. Lease basis. Three volumes. Lists about 65,000 U. S. manufacturing plants using metal and suppliers of metalworking equipment and materials.

Includes names and titles of key personnel. Products, purchases, and processes are indicated.

***Dun's Key Decision-Makers in Hong Kong***. Dun & Bradstreet Inc., 103 JFK Pkwy. Short Hills, NJ 07078. Phone: 800-526-0651 or (973)921-5500 or (973)921-5000; Fax: (866)560-7035 or (512)794-7670; Email: info@dnb.com • URL: http://www.dnb.com • Quarterly. HK$3,850 Individuals. Covers: 10,000 directors and senior executives from leading businesses in Hong Kong. Entries include: D&B D-U-N-S number, company name, address, phone, fax, descriptive line of business, SIC codes, presence in People's Republic of China, number of employees, multiple executive names and titles, year started.

***Dun's Regional Business Directory***. Dun & Bradstreet Inc., 103 JFK Pkwy. Short Hills, NJ 07078. Phone: 800-526-0651 or (973)921-5500 or (973)921-5000; Fax: (866)560-7035 or (512)794-7670; Email: info@dnb.com • URL: http://www.dnb.com • Annual. $495 commercial; $410 public academic libraries. Covers: in regional three-volume sets, approximately 20,000 companies employing 10 or more persons in each of 52 metropolitan areas. Database includes: Marketing advice. Entries include: DUNS number, company name, address, phone, number of employees, parent company, year established, primary and secondary Standard Industrial Classification (SIC) codes, names and titles of key personnel, sales volume, number of employees, stock exchange symbol.

***Dun's Regional Directory of Service Companies—Canada***. Dun & Bradstreet Inc., 103 JFK Pkwy. Short Hills, NJ 07078. Phone: 800-526-0651 or (973)921-5500 or (973)921-5000; Fax: (866)560-7035 or (512)794-7670; Email: info@dnb.com • URL: http://www.dnb.com • Covers: more than 10,000 service enterprises in Canada with eight or more employees and from Standard Industrial Classification (SIC) codes 07, 47, 60-80, and 82-89. Entries include: Company name, address, phone, SIC codes, parent company, number of employees, names and titles of key personnel, DUNS number.

***Dunsmarketing***. Dun & Bradstreet France S.A., 345 Ave. Georges Clemenceau, tour Defense Bergere F-92000 Nanterre, France. Phone: 14135 1700 or 8 25805802; Fax: 14135 1777 or 33 1 41 35 17 77 • URL: http://dbfrance.dnb.com • Database covers: over 240,000 French companies with more than 10 employees or annual turnover exceeding 10 million French Francs. Database includes: Company name, address, phone, year founded, executive officer name and title, number of employees, sector of activity, SIC code, business and import/export volume, affiliate and subsidiary companies, financial data.

***DunsPrint Worldwide***. Dun & Bradstreet Inc., 103 JFK Pkwy. Short Hills, NJ 07078. Phone: 800-526-0651 or (973)921-5500 or (973)921-5000; Fax: (866)560-7035 or (512)794-7670; Email: info@dnb.com • URL: http://www.dnb.com • Continuous. Database covers: Approximately 16 million companies worldwide. Database includes: Company name, address, phone, legal structure, products and services, SIC code, number of employees, branch offices, officer name, parent and subsidiary companies, company history, operation summary, legal suits against company, financial data, stock issues, projected sales, payment history, DUNS number.

***DunsScope***. Dun & Bradstreet France S.A., 345 Ave. Georges Clemenceau, tour Defense Bergere F-92000 Nanterre, France. Phone: 14135 1700 or 8 25805802; Fax: 14135 1777 or 33 1 41 35 17 77 • URL: http://dbfrance.dnb.com • Daily. Database covers: Approximately 2 million French businesses and 18 million businesses in other countries. Database includes: Company name, address, phone, legal structure, products/services, SIC code, number of employees, officer name and title, parent and subsidiary companies, branch offices, company history, operations summary, legal suits against company, financial data, stock issues and mergers, dividends, review of payment history, credit rating, company's bank.

***Duplicating Machines & Supplies-Wholesalers Directory***. InfoGroup Inc., 5711 S 86th Cir. Omaha, NE 68127-4146. Phone: (402)593-4500 • URL: http://www.infogroup.com • Updated continuously; printed on request. Number of listings: 560. Entries include: Name, address, phone (including area code), size of advertisement, year first in "Yellow Pages," name or owner or manager, number of employees. Compiled from telephone company "Yellow Pages," nationwide.

***Duquesne Business Law Journal***.

***Durban Regional Chamber of Business—Directory***. Durban Regional Chamber of Business, PO Box 1506 Durban 4000, South Africa. Phone: 27 31335 1000; Fax: 27 31332 1288 or (313)32 1288; Email: chamber@durbanchamber.co.za • URL: http://www.durbanchamber.co.za • Covers: about 7,500 businesses in the Durban, South Africa area; welfare organizations in Natal and businesses outside Natal (associate members). Entries include: Company name, address, phone, telex, fax, products or services.

***Durham Business Directory & Consumers' Guide***. Lloyd Local Directory Div. Lloyd Publications of Canada, 66 Falby Ct., Ste. 1603 Ajax, ON, Canada L1S 3L2. Phone: (416)619-0421 • Annual. $40. Covers: 12,000 businesses, professions, services, institutions, and government office within the Durham region of Ontario. Entries include: Company name, address, phone, subsidiary and branch names and locations, product/service.

***Durham Business Times***. Metroland Media Group, 3125

Wolfedale Rd. Mississauga, ON, Canada L5C 1W1. Phone: (905)279-0440 or (905)281-5656; Fax: (905)279-7763 or (905)279-5103 • URL: http://www.metroland.com/ • Community newspaper covering issues affecting Durham businesses.

**Dutch Association of Corporate Treasurers**. PO Box 279 1400 AG Bussum, Netherlands. Phone: 31 35 6954101; Fax: 31 35 6945045 • URL: http://www.dact.nl • Represents the Dutch treasury community. Promotes the development of treasury in The Netherlands.

***Dutch Chamber of Commerce—Business Directory***. Dutch Chamber of Commerce, 57/F Cheung Kong Center, Ste. 5702, 2 Queen's Rd. Central Hong Kong, China. Phone: 852 28152801; Fax: 852 28 152173 • URL: http://www.dutchchamber.hk • Annual. Covers: 480 individual members representing 180 companies in Hong Kong and mainland China.

**Dutch Corporate Finance Association**. Koopvaardijweg 2 4906 CV Oosterhout, Netherlands. Email: secretariaat@dcfa.nl • URL: http://www.dcfa.nl • Represents the interests of financial professionals. Facilitates sharing of knowledge and information among members. Creates a platform for managers within the financial sector.

***DV Buyer's Guide***. UBM L.L.C., 600 Community Dr. Manhasset, NY 11030. Phone: (516)562-5000 or (512)562-5000; Fax: (212)378-2160 or (516)562-5036; Email: cmp@cmp.com • URL: http://www.cmp.com • Annual. $10.00. A directory of professional video products, including digital cameras, monitors, editing systems, and software.

***DV Magazine***. UBM L.L.C., 240 W 35th St. New York, NY 10001. • URL: http://www.ubm.com • Monthly. 29.97. Edited for producers and creators of digital media. Includes topics relating to video, audio, animation, multimedia, interactive design, and special effects. Covers both hardware and software, with product reviews. Formerly *Digital Video Magazine*.

***DVD Replication Directory***. Corbell Publishing Co., 4640 Admiralty Way, Ste. 500 Marina Del Rey, CA 90292-6636. Phone: (310)581-6515; Email: info@corbell.com • URL: http://www.corbell.com • Annual. $457 Individuals plus 40 shipping. Covers: Over 100 video duplicators in the U.S. and Canada. Database includes: Statistics. Entries include: Name, address, phone, fax, url, e-mail address, names and titles of key personnel, financial data, types of accounts, geographical area served, number of employees, formats duplicated, other services offered.

***DVM: The Newsmagazine of Veterinary Medicine***. Advanstar Communications, Healthcare Group, 2501 Colorado Ave., Ste. 280 Santa Monica, CA 90404. Phone: (310)857-7500; Fax: (310)857-7510 • URL: http://www.advanstar.com/healthcare • Monthly. $39.00 per year. Includes new drugs and new products.

***Dynamic Business***. SMC Business Councils, George Westinghouse Research and Technology Ctr., 1382 Beulah Rd., Bldg. 801 Pittsburgh, PA 15235-5068. Phone: 800-553-3260 or (412)371-1500 • URL: http://www.smc.org • Bimonthly.

***E-Business Innovation and Process Management***. Cengage Learning Inc., 20 Channel Center St. Boston, MA 02210. Phone: 800-487-8488 or (617)289-7700; Fax: (617)289-7844; Email: investors@cengage.com • URL: http://www.cengage.com • 2007. eBook. Provides researchers and practitioners with information on recent advances and developments in emerging e-business models and technologies. This book covers a variety of topics, such as e-business models, e-business strategies, online consumer behavior, e-business process modeling and practices, electronic communication adoption and service provider strategies, privacy policies, and implementation issues.

***E-Business Institute Reports***. University of Wisconsin—Madison E-Business Institute, 4101 Mechanical Engineering Bldg., 1513 University Ave. Madison, WI 53706-1572. Phone: (608)262-0861; Fax: (608)262-8454; Email: raj.veeramani@uwebc.wisc.edu • URL: http://www.uwebc.org/uwebi.

***E-Business, Internet, and Online Transactions***. Michael L. Taviss and others. Glasser LegalWorks, 150 Clove Rd. Little Falls, NJ 07424. Phone: 800-308-1700 or (973)890-0008; Fax: (973)890-0042; Email: legalwks@aol.com • URL: http://www.glasserlegalworks.com • Looseleaf. $225.00, including CD-ROM version. Periodic Supplementation. Covers the legal aspects of online content, marketing, advertising, domain names, software licensing, and other Internet issues. Includes many sample forms. (Emerging Growth Companies Series.).

• ***E-Business Models, Services and Communications***. Cengage Learning Inc., 20 Channel Center St. Boston, MA 02210. Phone: 800-487-8488 or (617)289-7700; Fax: (617)289-7844; Email: investors@cengage.com • URL: http://www.cengage.com • 2008. eBook. Provides researchers and practitioners with valuable information on recent advances and developments in emerging e-business models and technologies.

***E-Business Process Management: Technologies and Solutions***. Cengage Learning Inc., 20 Channel Center St. Boston, MA 02210. Phone: 800-487-8488 or (617)289-7700; Fax: (617)289-7844; Email: investors@cengage.com • URL: http://www.cengage.com • 2007. eBook. Explores supply chain management by providing examples of integrated framework for global SCM, novel ways of improving flexibility, responsiveness and competitiveness via strategic IT alliances among channel members in a supply chain network, and techniques that might facilitate improved strategic decision-making in a SCM environment.

***E-Commerce and Internet Law: Treatise with Forms***. Ian C. Ballon. Glasser LegalWorks, 150 Clove Rd. Little Falls, NJ 07424. Phone: 800-308-1700 or (973)890-0008; Fax: (973)890-0042; Email: legalwks@aol.com • URL: http://www.glasserlegalworks.com • $1,479 Individuals Binder/Looseleaf (Full Set); $90 Individuals Monthly pricing. Periodic supplementation. Analyzes Internet legalities, including litigious matters relating to downloading, streaming, music, video, content aggregation, domain names, chatrooms, and search engines. Includes forms, contracts, checklists, sample pleadings, and an extensive glossary.

***E-Commerce Law and Strategy***. ALM Media Properties LLC, 120 Broadway, 5th Fl. New York, NY 10271-1100. Phone: (212)457-9400; Fax: (646)417-7705; Email: customercare@alm.com • URL: http://www.alm.com • Monthly. $505 print and online; $485 online only. Covers electronic commerce contracts, licensing, copyright, fraud, taxation, etc. (A Law Journal Newsletter, formerly published by Leader Publications).

***E-Commerce Tax Alert***. Wolters Kluwer Law & Business CCH, 2700 Lake Cook Rd. Riverwoods, IL 60015. Phone: 888-224-7377 or (847)267-7000; Email: cust_serv@cch.com • URL: http://www.cchgroup.com • Description: Print and online newsletter covering e-commerce taxation issues, including compliance and sourcing, e-cash implications, the Internet tax debate, and other topics.

***E-Logistics and E-Supply Chain Management: Applications for Evolving Business***. Cengage Learning Inc., 20 Channel Center St. Boston, MA 02210. Phone: 800-487-8488 or (617)289-7700; Fax: (617)289-7844; Email: investors@cengage.com • URL: http://www.cengage.com • 2013. eBook. Explores the creation of integrated supply chains, the developments of virtual business, and the processes of re-engineering for business development.

***E Magazine: The Environmental***. Earth Action Network, Inc., 28 Knight St. Norwalk, CT 06851. Phone: (203)854-5559; Fax: (203)866-0602; Email: info@emagazine.com • URL: http://www.emagazine.com • Bimonthly. $20.00 per year. A popular, consumer magazine providing news, information, and commentary on a wide range of environmental issues.

***E-Marketing in Developed and Developing Countries: Emerging Practices***. Cengage Learning Inc., 20 Channel Center St. Boston, MA 02210. Phone: 800-487-8488 or (617)289-7700; Fax: (617)289-7844; Email: investors@cengage.com • URL: http://www.cengage.com • 2013. eBook. Highlights the strategies and applications used in both developed and developing countries; proving to be beneficial for entrepreneurs, policy makers, researchers, and students wishing to expand their comprehensive knowledge in this field.

***E-Supply Chain Technologies and Management***. Cengage Learning Inc., 20 Channel Center St. Boston, MA 02210. Phone: 800-487-8488 or (617)289-7700; Fax: (617)289-7844; Email: investors@cengage.com • URL: http://www.cengage.com • 2007. eBook. Explores concepts, models, and IT infrastructures of the e-supply chain, and develops a broad understanding of issues pertaining to the use of emerging technologies and their impact on supply chain flexibility and management.

***E: The Environmental Magazine (online)***. Earth Action Network, 1536 Crest Dr. Los Angeles, CA 90035. Email: eanla@aol.com • URL: http://www.emagazine.com/view/?289&printview • Bimonthly. $24.95 Individuals; $34.95 Two years; $34.95 Canada; $64.95 Other countries. Web site provides full-text articles from *E: The Environmental Magazine* for a period of about two years. Searching is provided. Alphabetical and subject links are shown for a wide variety of environmental Web sites. Fees: Free.

***Earnshaw's Infants, Girls and Boys Wear Review - Children's Wear Directory***. Earnshaw Publications Inc., 225 W 34th St. New York, NY 10122. Phone: (212)629-3249; Fax: (212)629-3249 • URL: http://www.earnshaws.com • Annual. Controlled circulation.

***Earth Almanac: An Annual Geophysical Review of the State of the Planet***. Natalie Goldstein. Greenwood Publishing Group Inc., 88 Post Rd. W Westport, CT 06881. Phone: (203)226-3571; Fax: (203)222-1502; Email: orders@greenwood.com • URL: http://www.greenwood.com • $91.95. Provides background information, statistics, and a summary of major events relating to the atmosphere, oceans, land, and fresh water.

***Earth and Mineral Sciences***. College of Earth and Mineral Sciences. Pennsylvania State University, 201 Old Main University Park, PA 16802. Phone: (814)865-4700 • URL: http://www.psu.edu • Semiannual. Free. Current research in material science, mineral engineering, geosciences, meteorology, geography and mineral economics.

***East European Business Handbook***. Euromonitor International Business Reference Div., 224 S Michigan Ave., Ste. 1500 Chicago, IL 60604. Phone: (312)922-1115; Fax: (312)922-1157; Email: insight@euromonitorintl.com • URL: http://www.euromonitor.com • $190. Publication includes: List of sources of information on doing business in eastern Europe. Principal content of publication is a guide in identifying market opportunities in eastern Europe.

***East European Business Information***. Headland Press, One Henry Smith's Ter. Headland TS24 0PD, United Kingdom. Phone: 1429231902; Fax: 1429861403 • Annual. $99. Covers: Organizations providing commercial and industrial information in Eastern Europe, including information on joint ventures, banking, legislation, and marketing. Entries include: Name, address, phone.

***East European Kompass on Disc***. Kompass USA, Inc., 121 Whitney Ave. New Haven, CT 06510. Phone: (877)566-7277 or (203)503-6789; Fax: (203)503-6780; Email: mail@kompass-usa.com • URL: http://www.kompass.com • Provides information on more than 294,000 companies in Austria, Azerbaijan, Belarus, Croatia, Czech Republic, Estonia, Hungary, Latvia, Lithuania, Moldova, Poland, Romania, Russia, Slovakia, Slovenia, Ukraine, and Yugoslavia. Classification system covers approximately 50,000 products and services.

***East Midlands Chambers of Commerce Business Directory***. Kemps Publishing Ltd., 11 The Swan Courtyard, Charles Edward Rd. Yardley B26 1BU, United Kingdom. Phone: 44 121 7654144 or (441)21 7654144; Fax: 44 121 7063491 or (441)21 7063491; Email: enquiries@kempspublishing.co.uk • URL: http://www.kempspublishing.co.uk • Annual. Covers: Chamber of Commerce listings in East Midlands, Great Britain. Entries include: Name, address, phone, fax.

**East Tennessee State University - Tennessee Small Business Development Center**. College of Business & Technology, 2109 W Market St. Johnson City, TN 37604. Phone: (423)439-8505; Fax: (423)439-8506; Email: bjustice@mail.tsbdc.org • URL: http://www.tsbdc.org • Small business assistance in the areas of business plans and strategies, financial forecasts, feasibility studies, financial statement analysis, credit establishment and collection policies, inventory control analysis, marketing plans, accounting and record-keeping systems, licenses, permits, tax authorities, organizational structure, management succession, professional development, and buying and selling.

***The East-West Business Directory***. Duncan Publishing, • Irregular. $65 plus $3.50 shipping. Covers: Approximately 863 companies that have central and eastern European capital participation, located in over 20 European and North American countries, Australia, and Japan. Database includes: Lists (with addrs.) of official Eastern bloc trade missions and commercial, shipping, banking, airline, and tourist offices in the OECD countries, and an overview of investment activities of Soviet and eastern European state ent. Entries include: Company name, address, phone, telex, name and title of principal executive, number of employees, financial information, ownership structure, statistical data, products or services.

**East-West Center**. 1601 E West Rd. Honolulu, HI 96848-1601. Phone: (808)944-7111; Fax: (808)944-7376 • URL: http://www.eastwestcenter.org • Established by congress as a national education and research organization to promote US-Asia-Pacific relations and understanding through cooperative study, training and research. Assists in "building an Asia Pacific community in which the United States is a natural, valued and leading partner." Provides awards annually to scholars, researchers, graduate students, and professionals in business and government. Holds seminars and workshops in conjunction with long-term research projects and research grants. Education and dialogue programs seek to prepare Americans for an era in which the Asia-Pacific region is vastly more important to the United States.

**Eastern and Southern Africa Management Institute**. PO Box 3030 Arusha, Tanzania. Phone: 255 27 2508384 or 255 27 2508385; Fax: 255 27 2508285; Email: esamihq@esamihq.ac.tz • URL: http://www.esami-africa.org • Management personnel and vocational training programs. Seeks to advance the practice of business and organizational administration. Facilitates exchange of information among members; makes available educational and training programs.

***Eastern Europe: A Directory and Sourcebook***. Euromonitor International Business Reference Div., 224 S Michigan Ave., Ste. 1500 Chicago, IL 60604. Phone: (312)922-1115; Fax: (312)922-1157; Email: insight@euromonitorintl.com • URL: http://www.euromonitor.com • $440. Publication includes: Lists of publishers of private research, journals and newsletters, online databases, consultants, and abstracts and indexes providing information on eastern Europe. Database includes: Economic and demographic data, analysis of business practices, markets, investment opportunities, and rankings.

**Eastern Finance Association**. PO Box 244023 Montgomery, AL 36124-4023. Phone: (850)644-4220; Fax: (850)644-4225; Email: membershipservices@blackwellpublishers.co.uk • URL: http://etnpconferences.net/efa • College and university professors and financial officers; libraries. Provides a meeting place for persons interested in any aspect of finance, including financial management, investments, and banking. Sponsors research competitions.

***EBN Benefits Sourcebook***. SourceMedia Inc., 1 State Street Plz., 27th Fl. New York, NY 10004. Phone: 800-221-1809 or (212)803-8200 or (212)803-8333; Fax: (212)843-9635 or (212)292-5216; Email: custserv@sourcemedia.com • URL: http://www.sourcemedia.com • Annual. $36.95. Lists vendors of products and services for the employee benefits industry. Includes industry trends and statistics.

***EBRI Pension Investment Report***. Employee Benefit Research Institute, 1100 13th St. NW, Ste. 878 Washington, DC 20005-4051. Phone: (202)659-0670 or (202)775-6348; Fax: (202)775-6312; Email: info@ebri.org • URL: http://www.ebri.org • Periodic Quarterly. included in membership dues; $500 /issue for nonmembers. Irregular. Membership.

***EBSCO Information Services***. EBSCO Publishing Inc., 10 Estes St. Ipswich, MA 01938-2106. Phone: 800-653-2726 or (978)356-6500; Fax: (978)356-6565; Email: information@ebscohost.com • URL: http://www.ebscohost.com • Fee-based Web site providing Internet access to a wide variety of databases, including business-related material. Full text is available for many periodical titles, with daily updates. Fees: Apply.

***Ebusiness Forum: Global Business Intelligence for the Digital Age***. Economist Intelligence Unit (EIU), Economist Group, Phone: 800-938-4685 or (212)554-0600; Fax: (212)586-0248; Email: newyork@eiu.com • URL: http://www.ebusinessforum.com • Web site provides information relating to multinational business, with an emphasis on activities in specific countries. Includes rankings of countries for "e-business readiness," additional data on the political, economic, and business environment in 180 nations ("Doing Business in" and "Today's News Analysis.") Fees: Free, but registration is required for access to all content. Daily updates.

***eBusiness***. KANA Software Inc., 840 W California Ave., Ste. 100 Sunnyvale, CA 94086. Phone: 800-737-738 or (650)614-8300; Fax: (408)736-7613; Email: info@kana.com • URL: http://www.kana.com • A Web-based framework for enabling and managing personalized interactions, collaborations, and transactions with customers, partners or employees.

***EC-EDI Solution Provider Directory***. Vantage Point & Associates Inc., 17 Acerdon Cres., Ste. 201 Toronto, ON, Canada M3A 1P4. Phone: 877-463-2334; Fax: (858)248-8053; Email: info@vantagepoint.ca • URL: http://www.vantagepoint.ca • Covers: 300 EC/EDI vendors serving business to business (B2B) and healthcare industries.

***EC&M's Electrical Products Yearbook***. Penton, 9800 Metcalf Ave. Overland Park, KS 66212. Phone: 866-748-4926 or (913)341-1300; Fax: (913)967-1905 or (913)967-1898; Email: corporatecustomerservice@penton.com • URL: http://www.penton.com • Annual. $10.00.

***ECN Literature News***. Reed Elsevier Group plc Reed Business Information, 360 Park Ave. S New York, NY 11010. Phone: (212)791-4208; Email: corporatecommunications@reedbusiness.com • URL: http://www.reedbusiness.com • Bimonthly. Price on application.

***The Eco-antique and Retro Guide: Supporting Local Businesses—Promoting Source Reduction and Energy Conservation—Helping Our Communities***. Ariela Press, 4134 N Vancouver, Ste. 301A Portland, OR 97217. Phone: (503)284-2908; Fax: (503)284-2645; Email: ariela@teleport.com • Free available in local shops; $1 from publisher. Covers Oregon stores and other organizations that recycle, recondition, or resell, and/or promote the use of recycled materials.

***Ecology***. Ecological Society of America, 1990 M St. NW, Ste. 700 Washington, DC 20036. Phone: (202)833-8773; Fax: (202)833-8775; Email: esahq@esa.org • URL: http://www.esa.org • Monthly. $470.00 per year. All forms of life in relation to environment.

***Ecology Law Quarterly***. University of California Boalt Hall School of Law, 215 Boalt Hall Berkeley, CA 94720-7200. Phone: (510)643-1741 or (510)642-1741; Email: bblj@law.berkeley.edu • URL: http://www.law.berkeley.edu • Quarterly. $35 Individuals; $60 Institutions. Journal covering ecology and law.

***eComp: The Most Powerful Executive Compensation Online Research Tool***. AON Consulting Inc., Phone: (212)441-2047; Fax: (212)441-1944; Email: sales@ecomp-online.com • URL: http://www.ecomponline.com • Web site provides free access to executive compensation data by company name or industry. Gives names and titles of top executives for each company, with the following information for each corporate officer: salary, bonus, long-term incentive plan data (LTIP), options granted, options expiration date, dollar value of options, and detailed options exercisable data. More extensive, customized data is available on a fee basis.

***EconLit***. Ovid Technologies Inc., 333 7th Ave., 20th Fl. New York, NY 10001-5004. Phone: 800-950-2035 or (646)674-6300; Fax: (646)674-6301 or (647)674-6301; Email: sales@ovid.com • URL: http://www.ovid.com • Updated monthly. Lists journal articles, book reviews, disserations of economic literature. Over 1,400 journals covered.

**Econometric Society**. New York University, Department of Economics, 19 W 4th St., 6th Fl. New York, NY 10012. Phone: (212)998-3820; Fax: (212)995-4487; Email: sashi@econometricsociety.org • URL: http://www.econometricsociety.org • Economists, statisticians, and mathematicians. Promotes studies that are directed towards unification of the theoretical and empirical approaches to economic problems and advancement of economic theory in its relation to statistics and mathematics.

***Econometric Theory***. Cambridge University Press Journals Dept., 40 W. 20th St. New York, NY 10011-4221. Phone: 800-221-4512 or (212)924-3900; Fax: (212)691-3239; Email: information@cup.org • URL: http://www.cup.org •

Bimonthly. Individuals, $152.00 per year; institutions, $440.00 per year. Devoted to the advancement of theoretical research in econometrics.

***Econometrica***. Blackwell Publishing Inc., 350 Main St. Malden, MA 02148. Phone: 800-216-2522 or (781)388-8200; Fax: (781)388-8210; Email: journaladsusa@bos.blackwellpublishing.com • URL: http://www.blackwellpublishing.com • $586 Institutions Online only; $746 Institutions Print and Online; £373 Institutions Online only; £480 Institutions Print and Online; €458 Institutions Online only; €586 Institutions Print and Online. Bimonthly. Includes print and online editions. Published in England by Basil Blackwell Ltd.

***Economic and business reports***. University of Nebraska—Lincoln Bureau of Business Research, 347 College of Business Administration Bldg. Lincoln, NE 68588-0406. Phone: 800-742-7511 or (402)472-3318 or (402)472-2334; Fax: (402)472-9700 or (402)472-3878; Email: ethompson2@unl.edu • URL: http://www.bbr.unl.edu • Monthly.

***Economic and Social Progress in Latin America***. Inter-American Development Bank, 1300 New York Ave. NW Washington, DC 20577. Phone: (202)623-1000; Fax: (202)623-3096; Email: reference@iadb.org • URL: http://www.iadb.org • Monthly. $24.95 per year. Covers developments in Latin America affecting business and trade. Text in Spanish.

***Economic and Social Survey of Asia and the Pacific***. United Nations Publications, c/o National Book Network, 15200 NBN Way Blue Ridge Summit, PA 17214. Phone: 888-254-4286 or (212)963-7680 or (212)963-8302; Fax: (800)338-4550; Email: unpublications@nbnbooks.com • URL: http://www.unp.un.org • Annual. $85 print; $42.50 pdf. Emphasis is on trends in economic policy and economic development strategies.

***Economic Botany: Devoted to Applied Botany and Plant Utilization***. Society for Economic Botany. New York Botanical Garden Press, 2900 Southern Blvd. Bronx, NY 10458. Phone: (718)817-8700 or (718)817-8721; Fax: (718)562-6780 or (718)817-8842; Email: compost@nybg.org • URL: http://www.nybg.org • Quarterly. $115 Individuals Electronic only version with E-access to back issues through 1997; $115 Individuals Print only + $28.00 (shipping); $196 Institutions Electronic and print version with E-access to back issues through 1997; $196 Institutions Print only + $28.00 (shipping). Original research and review articles on the uses of plants.

***Economic Development Administration—Annual Report***. U.S. Economic Development Administration, U.S. Department of Commerce, 1401 Constitution Ave. NW, Ste. 71014 Washington, DC 20230. Phone: (202)482-2000 • URL: http://www.eda.gov • Annual. Covers: Recipients of grants, grant supplements, and loan guarantees from the Economic Development Administration under the Public Works and Economic Development Act of 1965. Projects funded include public works, business development, research, planning, and disaster recovery. Entries include: Recipient name, location, date of obligation, funds received by type of assistance, type of project, identification number.

***Economic Development and Cultural Change***. The University of Chicago Press, Journals Div., 1427 E 60th St. Chicago, IL 60637. Phone: 877-705-1878 or (773)702-7700; Email: subscriptions@press.uchicago.edu • URL: http://www.press.uchicago.edu/journals.html • Quarterly. $77 Individuals Print and electronic; $68 Individuals Electronic version only; $70 Individuals Print Only; $39 Students Electronic version only. Examines the economic and social forces that affect development and the impact of development on culture.

***Economic Development Monitor***. Whitaker Newsletters Inc., 313 S Ave. Fanwood, NJ 07023-0192. Phone: 800-359-6049 • Biweekly. $247.00 per year. Newsletter. Covers the news of U. S. economic and industrial development, including legislation, regulation, planning, and financing.

***Economic Development Quarterly: The Journal of American Revitalization***. Pine Forge Press, 2455 Teller Rd. Thousand Oaks, CA 91320-2234. Phone: 800-818-7243 or (805)499-4224 or (805)499-9774; Fax: (805)499-0871 or (805)583-2665; Email: sales@pfp.sagepub.com • URL: http://www.sagepub.com/sociologybooks • Quarterly. $877 Institutions Print & E-access; $965 Institutions Backfile Lease, Combined Plus Backfile (Current Volume Print & All Online Content); $789 Institutions E-access; $877 Institutions Backfile Lease, E-access Plus Backfile (All Online Content); $805 Institutions Backfile Purchase, E-access (Content through 1998); $859 Institutions Print Only; $147 Individuals Print Only. Bridges the gap between academics, policymakers, and practitioners and links the various economic development communities.

***Economic Development Review***. International Economic Development Council, 734 15th St. NW, Ste. 900 Washington, DC 20005. Phone: (202)223-7800; Fax: (202)223-4745 • URL: http://www.iedconline.org • Quarterly. $50.00 per year.

***Economic Geology and the Bulletin of the Society of Economic Geologists***. Society of Economic Geologist. Economic Geology Publishing Company Inc., 7811 Shaffer Pkwy. Littleton, CO 80127. Phone: (720)981-7882; Fax: (720)981-7874; Email: seg@segweb.org • URL: http://www.segweb.org • Irregular. Individuals, $75.00 per year; institutions, $145.00 per year.

***Economic Guide—Tunisia***. Information Economique Africaine, 16, St. of Rome 1015 Tunis, Tunisia. Phone: 216 71 347 441; Fax: 216 71 353 172; Email: iea@planet.tn • Biennial. $50. Covers: Industrial, commercial and agricultural entities in Tunisia. Entries include: Company name, address, phone.

**Economic History Association**. University of Arizona, Dept. of Economics, McClelland Hall, 401GG Tucson, AZ 85721-0108. Phone: (520)621-4421; Fax: (520)621-8450 • URL: http://eh.net/eha • Represents scholars, teachers and students of economic history.

**Economic Justice Institute**. University of Wisconsin Law School, 975 Bascom Mall Madison, WI 53706-1399. Phone: (608)262-2240 • URL: http://law.wisc.edu/eji • Provides advocate services for consumers and low-income families through education, research, training and representation. Aims to educate and empower consumers by providing services and information.

***Economic Justice Report: Global Issues of Economic Justice***. Ecumenical Coalition for Economic Justice, 77 Charles St. W, Ste. 402 Toronto, ON, Canada M5S 1K5. Phone: (416)921-4615 or (416)462-1613; Fax: (416)922-1419 or (416)463-5569; Email: ecej@accessv.com • URL: http://www.ecej.org • Quarterly. Individuals, $30.00 per year; institutions, $40.00 per year. Reports on economic fairness in foreign trade. Formerly *Gatt-Fly Report*.

***Economic Outlook Statistics***. Organization for Economic Cooperation and Development, 2001 L St. NW, Ste. 650 Washington, DC 20036-4922. Phone: 800-456-6323 or (202)785-6323 or (202)822-3865; Fax: (202)785-0350; Email: washington.contact@oecd.org • URL: http://www.oecd.org • Includes country and global forecasts of over 170 economic and business variables. Actual data is shown for two years, with forecasts up to ten years.

***Economic Perspectives***. Federal Reserve Bank of Chicago, 230 S LaSalle St. Chicago, IL 60604-1427. Phone: 888-372-2446 or (312)322-5322 or (312)322-5111; Fax: (312)322-5515 • URL: http://www.chicagofed.org • Quarterly. Contains in-depth articles reporting on the Bank's economic research.

**Economic Research Service - Canada Division**. 1800 M St. NW Washington, DC 20036. Phone: 800-999-6779 or (202)694-5227; Email: jwainio@ers.usda.gov • URL: http://www.ers.usda.gov/Briefing/canada/ • Canadian agricultural supply, consumption, and trade, including Canadian policies related to agriculture.

**Economic Research Service - Cattle and Beef**. 355 E St. SW Washington, DC 20024-3221. Phone: 800-999-6779 or (202)694-5183; Email: kmathews@ers.usda.gov • URL: http://ers.usda.gov/topics/animal-products/cattle-beef.aspx#.U5Eq73I2aDg • Market analysis and research on the U.S. cattle and beef sectors, including domestic supply and utilization, live cattle and retail beef prices, and international trade.

**Economic Research Service - Information Services Division**. 1400 Independence Ave. SW Washington, DC 20250. Phone: (202)694-5100; Fax: (202)245-4781; Email: rbianchi@ers.usda.gov • URL: http://www.ers.usda.gov/contact-us/management-directory.aspx#ISD • Manages and directs agency-wide information technology, communications, and administrative activities in support of the economic research and analysis mission of ERS.

***Economic Survey of Europe***. United Nations Economic Commission for Europe, Palais des Nations CH-1211 Geneva, Switzerland. Phone: 41 22 9174444; Fax: 41 22 9170505; Email: info.ece@unece.org • URL: http://www.unece.org • Semiannual. Provides yearly analysis and review of the European economy, including Eastern Europe and the USSR. Text in English.

***Economic Survey of Latin America and the Caribbean***. United Nations Publications, c/o National Book Network, 15200 NBN Way Blue Ridge Summit, PA 17214. Phone: 888-254-4286 or (212)963-7680 or (212)963-8302; Fax: (800)338-4550; Email: unpublications@nbnbooks.com • URL: http://www.unp.un.org • Annual. $25. Includes reports on economic trends in 20 Latin American countries.

***Economic World Directory of Japanese Companies in the U.S.A.*** Economic Salon Ltd., 60 E 42nd St. New York, NY 10165. Phone: (212)986-1588; Fax: (212)557-7541 • Biennial. $300. Covers: about 850 companies in the United States that are subsidiaries, divisions, etc., of Japanese parent firms. Entries include: United States company name, address, phone; branch facilities, addresses, and phone numbers; financial data, type of business, names of executives, number of Japanese and United States employees, history, current company information, and similar but less extensive data on parent company.

**Economics, Business and Enterprise Association**. Adur Business Ctre., Little High St. Shoreham-by-Sea BN43 5EG, United Kingdom. Phone: 44 1273 467542; Email: office@ebea.org.uk • URL: http://www.ebea.org.uk/home • Teachers of economics, business studies and related subjects in schools and colleges. Represents teachers of economics, business studies and related subjects in schools and colleges throughout the UK and provides its members with the professional support they need in the classroom. Aims to encourage and promote the teaching and study of economics and related subjects within a broadly based curriculum.

**Economiesuisse**. Verband der Schweizer Unternehmen, Hegibachstrasse 47 CH-8032 Zurich, Switzerland. Phone: 41 44 4213535; Fax: 41 44 4213434; Email: info@economiesuisse.ch • URL: http://www.economiesuisse.ch • Aims to preserve entrepreneurial freedom for all businesses, to continuously improve Switzerland's global competitiveness in manufacturing, services, and research, and to promote sustained growth as a prerequisite for a high level of employment in Switzerland. Creates an optimal economic environment for Swiss business.

***The Economist***. The Economist Intelligence Unit, 111 W 57th St. New York, NY 10019. Phone: 800-938-4685 or (212)554-0600; Fax: (212)586-1191 or (212)586-1182; Email: newyork@eiu.com • URL: http://www.economist.com • 190 ₱ Individuals Print and Digital per week; 2,880 ₱ Individuals 12 weeks; 11,400 ₱ Individuals 1 year; 167.65 ₱ Students Print and Digital per week; 4,577 ₱ Students 6 months; 8,550 ₱ Students 1 year.

***EContent: Digital Content Strategies and Resources***. Online Inc., 213 Danbury Rd. Wilton, CT 06897-4007. Phone: 800-248-8466 or (203)761-1466; Fax: (203)761-1444; Email: dbmag@onlineinc.com • URL: http://www.infotoday.com • Monthly. $110.00 per year. Emphasis is on the business management and financial aspects of the digital content industry. (Formerly published by Online, Inc.).

**ECRI: Emergency Care Research Institute**. 5200 Butler Pike Plymouth Meeting, PA 19462-1298. Phone: (610)825-6000; Fax: (610)834-1275; Email: info@ecri.org • URL: http://www.ecri.org • Major research area is health care technology.

***Ecuador Business Law Handbook***. International Business Publications, USA, PO Box 15343 Washington, DC 20003. Phone: (202)546-2103; Fax: (202)546-3275; Email: ibpusa@comcast.net • URL: http://ibpus.com • $99.95 Individuals hardcopy, e-book, CD-ROM. Covers: Business laws and climate, export-import regulations, investment, tax, and contacts.

***Ecuador Investment and Business Guide***. International Business Publications, USA, PO Box 15343 Washington, DC 20003. Phone: (202)546-2103; Fax: (202)546-3275; Email: ibpusa@comcast.net • URL: http://ibpus.com • $99.95 Individuals hardcopy, e-book, CD-ROM. Covers: Strategic information on economy, business, export-import and investment climate, regulations and industrial development, banking, government, and opportunities. Entries include: Important business contacts and business travel.

**Edexcel International**. 190 High Holborn London WC1V 7BH, United Kingdom. Phone: 44 1204 770696; Email: internationaleo@pearson.com • URL: http://www.edexcel.com/international/europe • Approves academic and work-related programmes of study including GNVQs, NVQs and GCSEs, A levels and A/S levels throughout England, Wales and Northern Ireland, and overseas and awards qualifications to students who successfully complete these and HND programmes.

***EdgarPlus: SEC Basic Filings***. Thomson Reuters Markets, 22 Thomson Pl. Boston, MA 02210-1212. Phone: 888-989-8373 or (617)856-2000; Fax: (617)330-1986; Email: moves@thomsonreuters.com • URL: http://www.thomsonreuters.com • Online service provides full text of about 60,000 documents that have been filed with the U.S. Securities and Exchange Commission, 1987 to date, with daily updates. Filings include 6-K, 8-K, 10-K, 10-C, 10-Q, 20-F, and proxy statements. Inquire as to online cost and availability.

**Edison Electric Institute**. 701 Pennsylvania Ave. NW Washington, DC 20004-2696. Phone: 800-334-5453 or (202)508-5000; Fax: (800)525-5562; Email: eblume@eei.org • URL: http://www.eei.org/Pages/default.aspx • Shareholder-owned electric utility companies operating in the U.S.; international affiliates and associates worldwide.

***Editor & Publisher International Yearbook: Encyclopedia of the Newspaper Industry***. Editor and Publisher Company Inc., 17782 Cowan St, Ste. C Irvine, CA 92614-6042. Phone: (949)660-6150; Fax: (949)660-6172 • URL: http://www.editorandpublisher.com • Annual. $150.00. Daily and Sunday newspapers in the United States and Canada.

***Editor & Publisher Journalism Awards and Fellowship Directory***. Editor and Publisher Company Inc., 17782 Cowan St, Ste. C Irvine, CA 92614-6042. Phone: (949)660-6150; Fax: (949)660-6172 • URL: http://www.editorandpublisher.com • Annual. Over 500 cash prizes scholarships, fellowships, and grants available to journalists and students for work on special subjects or in specific fields.

***Editor & Publisher Market Guide***. Editor and Publisher Company Inc., 17782 Cowan St, Ste. C Irvine, CA 92614-6042. Phone: (949)660-6150; Fax: (949)660-6172 • URL: http://www.editorandpublisher.com • Annual. $150 Individuals. Market data for more than 1,600 cities and 3,096 counties.

***Editor and Publisher Syndicate Directory: Annual Directory of Syndicate Services***. Editor & Publisher Magazine, 17782 Cowan, Ste. A Irvine, CA 92614. Phone: (949)660-6150; Fax: (949)660-6172 or (949)660-6150 • URL: http://www.editorandpublisher.com • Annual. $28 Individuals. Directory of several hundred syndicates serving newspapers in the United States and abroad with news, columns, features, comic strips, editorial cartoons, etc.

***Editor and Publisher - The Newsmagazine of the Fourth Estate Since 1894***. Editor & Publisher Magazine, 17782 Cowan, Ste. A Irvine, CA 92614. Phone: (949)660-6150; Fax: (949)660-6172 or (949)660-6150 • URL: http://www.editorandpublisher.com • Weekly. $79 Individuals Total Access - Print and Digital; $49 Individuals Digital Access. Trade journal of the newspaper industry.

**Editorial Freelancers Association**. 71 W 23rd St., 4th Fl. New York, NY 10010-4102. Phone: 866-929-5439 or (212)929-5400; Fax: (212)929-5439; Email: office@the-efa.org • URL: http://www.the-efa.org • Represents persons who work full or part-time as freelance writers or editorial freelancers. Promotes professionalism and facilitates the exchange of information and support. Conducts professional training seminars; and offers job listings.

***Edmonds Chamber of Commerce Preferred Business Directory***. Greater Edmonds Chamber of Commerce, 121 5th Ave. N Edmonds, WA 98020. Phone: (425)670-1496 or (425)776-6711; Fax: (425)712-1808; Email: chamberofcommerce@edmondswa.com • URL: http://www.edmondswa.com • Annual. Covers member businesses in Edmonds, Washington. Entries include contact details.

***Edmonton and Homersham Commerce & Industry: Report on Business***. Edmonton and Homersham Commerce & Industry, 11802 124th St., Ste. 215 Edmonton, AB, Canada T5L 0M3. Fax: (403)453-2553 • Monthly. $5. Business newspaper.

***Edmund's New Cars***. Edmund Publications Corp., 2401 Colorado Blvd., Suite 250 Santa Monica, CA 90404. Phone: (310)309-6300; Fax: (310)309-6400 • URL: http://www.edmunds.com • Quarterly. $39.96 Individuals; $26.80 Libraries. Wholesale and retail prices for all American and import models and accessories. Includes federal crash reports, leasing facts, and accident report forms. Formerly *Edmund's New Car Prices*.

***Edmund's Used Cars and Trucks, Prices and Ratings***. Edmund Publications Corp., 2401 Colorado Blvd., Suite 250 Santa Monica, CA 90404. Phone: (310)309-6300; Fax: (310)309-6400 • URL: http://www.edmunds.com • Quarterly. $39.96 Individuals; $26.80 Libraries. Lists American and foreign used car prices for the past 10 years.

***EDP Weekly: The Leading Weekly Computer News Summary***. Computer Age and EDP News Services, 1150 Connecticut Ave., NW, Ste. 900 Washington, DC 20036. Phone: (202)862-4375; Fax: (202)659-3493; Email: millin@erols.com • URL: http://www.millinpubs.com • Weekly. $495.00 per year. Newsletter. Summarizes news from all areas of the computer and microcomputer industries.

***Education Business***. Public Sector Publishing Ltd., 226 High Rd. Loughton IG10 1ET, United Kingdom. Phone: 44 20 85320055; Fax: 44 20 85320066; Email: info@psi-media.co.uk • URL: http://www.psi-media.co.uk • Bimonthly. Magazine featuring administrative and commercial issues affecting education.

***Education Index***. H.W. Wilson Co., 950 University Ave. Bronx, NY 10452-4224. Phone: 800-367-6770 or (718)588-8400 or (718)558-8400; Fax: (718)590-1617 or (800)590-1617; Email: custserv@hwwilson.com • URL: http://www.hwwilson.com • 10 times a year. Quarterly and annual cumulations. Price varies.

***Education Index Online***. H.W. Wilson Co., 950 University Ave. Bronx, NY 10452-4224. Phone: 800-367-6770 or (718)588-8400 or (718)558-8400; Fax: (718)590-1617 or (800)590-1617; Email: custserv@hwwilson.com • URL: http://www.hwwilson.com • Indexes a wide variety of periodicals related to schools, colleges, and education, 1984 to date. Monthly updates. Inquire as to online cost and availability.

***Education Index Retrospective: 1929-1983***. EBSCO Publishing Inc., 10 Estes St. Ipswich, MA 01938-2106. Phone: 800-653-2726 or (978)356-6500; Fax: (978)356-6565; Email: information@ebscohost.com • URL: http://www.ebscohost.com • Provides indexing of education-related literature from 1983 to date.

***Education Technology News: Insiders Guide to Multimedia in the K-12 Classroom***. Business Publishers Inc., PO Box 17592 Baltimore, MD 21297-1592. Phone: 800-223-8720; Fax: (800)508-2592; Email: custserv@bpinews.com • URL: http://www.bpinews.com • Biweekly. $357.00 per year. Looseleaf service. Formerly *Education Computer News*.

***Education Week: American Education's Newspaper of Record***. Editorial Projects in Education, 6935 Arlington Rd., Ste. 100 Bethesda, MD 20814. Phone: 800-346-1834 or (301)280-3100; Fax: (301)280-3200; Email: library@epe.org • URL: http://www.edweek.org/ew/index.html • $39 Individuals 20 printed and online access; $29 Individuals 6 months online access. 43 times a year.

***Educational Administration Abstracts***. Pine Forge Press, 2455 Teller Rd. Thousand Oaks, CA 91320-2234. Phone: 800-818-7243 or (805)499-4224 or (805)499-9774; Fax: (805)499-0871 or (805)583-2665; Email: sales@pfp.sagepub.com • URL: http://www.sagepub.com/sociologybooks • Quarterly. $722 Institutions.

***Educational Administration Quarterly***. University Council for Educational Administratiotion. Pine Forge Press, 2455 Teller Rd. Thousand Oaks, CA 91320-2234. Phone: 800-818-7243 or (805)499-4224 or (805)499-9774; Fax: (805)499-0871 or (805)583-2665; Email: sales@pfp.sagepub.com • URL: http://www.sagepub.com/sociologybooks • 5/year. $956 Institutions Print & E-access; $1,052 Institutions Backfile Lease, Combined Plus Backfile (Current Volume Print & All Online Content); $860 Institutions E-access; $956 Institutions Backfile Lease, E-access Plus Backfile (All Online Content); $2,485 Institutions Backfile Purchase, E-access (Content through 1998); $937 Institutions Print Only; $166 Individuals Print Only. Publishes prominent empirical and conceptual articles focused on timely and critical leadership and policy issues of educational organizations.

***Educational and Psychological Measurement: Devoted to the Development and Application of Measures of Individual Differences***. Pine Forge Press, 2455 Teller Rd. Thousand Oaks, CA 91320-2234. Phone: 800-818-7243 or (805)499-4224 or (805)499-9774; Fax: (805)499-0871 or (805)583-2665; Email: sales@pfp.sagepub.com • URL: http://www.sagepub.com/sociologybooks • Bimonthly. $1,235 Institutions Print & E-access; $1,359 Institutions Backfile Lease, Combined Plus Backfile (Current Volume Print & All Online Content); $1,112 Institutions E-access; $1,236 Institutions Backfile Lease, E-access Plus Backfile (All Online Content); $5,482 Institutions Backfile Purchase, E-access (Content through 1998); $1,210 Institutions Print Only; $204 Individuals Print Only; $222 Institutions Single print issue; $44 Individuals Single print issue. Offers the most current theoretical and applied papers in the measurement field.

***Educational Dealer—Buyers' Guide Issue***. Fahy-Williams Publishing Inc., 171 Reed St. Geneva, NY 14456. Phone: 800-344-0559 or (315)789-0458; Fax: (315)789-4263; Email: kfahy@fwpi.com • URL: http://www.fwpi.com • Annual. Publication includes: List of approximately 2,000 suppliers of educational materials and equipment. Entries include: Company name, address, phone, products or services.

***Educational Marketer: The Educational Publishing Industry's Voice of Authority Since 1968***. SIMBA Information Inc., 60 Long Ridge Rd., Ste. 300 Stamford, CT 06902. Phone: (203)325-8193; Fax: (203)325-8975 • URL: http://www.simbainformation.com • Biweekly. $695 Individuals Online download; $4,865 Individuals Departmental License (up to 10 users in one office); $11,815 Individuals Global License (unlimited users); $1,250 Individuals Online download - 2 years; $1,770 Individuals Online download - 3 years; $100 Single issue. Edited for suppliers of educational materials to schools and colleges at all levels. Covers print and electronic publishing, software, audiovisual items, and multimedia. Includes corporate news and educational statistics.

***Educational Media and Technology Yearbook***. Libraries Unlimited, 88 Post Rd. W Westport, CT 06881. Phone: 800-225-5800 or (203)226-3571; Fax: (203)222-1502 • Annual. $80 print.

***Educational Technology Research and Development***. Association for Educational Communications and Technology, 320 W 8th St., Ste. 101 Bloomington, IN 47404. Phone: 877-677-2328 or (812)335-7675; Fax: (812)335-7678; Email: aect@aect.org • URL: http://www.aect.org/newsite • Bimonthly. Focuses entirely on research and development in educational technology.

***Educational Technology: The Magazine for Managers of Change in Education***. Educational Technology Publications, Inc., 700 Palisade Ave. Englewood Cliffs, NJ 07632-0564. Phone: 800-952-2665 or (201)871-4007; Fax: (201)871-4009; Email: edtecpubs@aol.com • URL: http://asianvu.com/bookstoread/etp • Bimonthly. $139.00 per year.

**Educational Testing Service**. 225 Phillips Blvd. Ewing, NJ 08628. Phone: (609)921-9000; Fax: (609)734-5410 • URL: http://www.ets.org • Educational measurement and research organization, founded by merger of the testing activities of American Council on Education, Carnegie Foundation for the Advancement of Teaching, and The College Board. Provides tests and related services for schools, colleges, governmental agencies, and the professions; offers advisory services in the sound application of measurement techniques and materials; conducts educational, psychological, and measurement research. Offers a summer program in educational testing for scholars and educators from other countries, continuing education programs, and measurement, evaluation, and other instructional activities.

***Educators' Guide to Corporate Support***. Information Interface Institute, 1330 Rte. 206 N Skillman, NJ 08558. Fax: (609)497-1259 • $375 per year. Covers: Approximately 450 corporations, 300 associations, 200 government agencies, and 100 foundations that provide support to educational concerns. Entries include: Sponsoring organization name, address, phone, programs and teaching aids, contact person, geographic preferences for funding, program preferences, and grade levels supported.

***Educators Guide to Free Guidance Materials***. Educators Progress Service Inc., 214 Center St. Randolph, WI 53956-1408. Phone: 888-951-4469 or (920)326-3126; Fax: (920)326-3127; Email: questions@freeteachingaids.com • URL: http://www.freeteachingaids.com • Annual. $37.95 Individuals. Lists free-loan films, filmstrips, audiotapes, videotapes and free printed materials on guidance.

***Educators Resource Directory***. Grey House Publishing, 4919 Rte. 22 Amenia, NY 12501. Phone: 800-562-2139 or (518)789-8700; Fax: (518)789-0556; Email: books@greyhouse.com • URL: http://www.greyhouse.com • Annual. $145 Individuals softcover. Covers: Publishing opportunities, state by state information on enrollment, funding and grant resources, associations and conferences, teaching jobs abroad all geared toward elementary and secondary school professionals. Also covers online databases, textbook publishers, school suppliers, plus state and federal agencies. Entries include: Contact name, address, phone, fax, description, publications. A unique compilation of over 6,500 educational resources and over 130 tables and charts of education statistics and rankings.

***EE Product News***. Penton Media Inc., 1300 E 9th St. Cleveland, OH 44114-1501. Phone: (216)696-7000; Fax: (216)696-1752; Email: information@penton.com • URL: http://penton.com • Monthly. Free to qualified personnel; others, $60.00 per year.

***EEKOD—East European Kompass on Disc***. Kompass Deutschland Verlags- und Vertriebsgesellschaft, mbH, Heinrich-von-Stephan Strasse 8b D-79100 Freiburg, Germany. Phone: 49 761 137630; Fax: 49 761 1376399; Email: mail@kompass.info.de • URL: http://www.de.kompass.com • €1,789.52 Individuals includes print, data export, and 1 update. Covers: Approximately 464,498 East European company profiles, including Austria, Azerbaidjan, Belarus, Boznia-Herzegovina, Bulgaria, Croatia, Czech Republic, Estonia, Hungary, Latvia, Lithuania, Moldavia, Poland, Romania, Russia, Slovakia, Slovenia, Ukraina, and Yugoslavia.

**EF Foundation for Foreign Study**. 1 Education St. Cambridge, MA 02141. Phone: 800-447-4273; Fax: (617)619-1401; Email: exchangeyear@ef.com • URL: http://www.effoundation.org • Seeks to further international understanding through cultural and academic exchange. Sponsors academic homestay programs, such as High School Year in Europe. Formerly EF Educational Foundation for Foreign Study.

***Effective Clinical Practice***. American College of Physicians, 190 N Independance Mall W Philadelphia, PA 19106-1572. Phone: 800-523-1546 or (215)351-2400 or (215)351-2600; Email: sweinberger@acponline.org • URL: http://www.acponline.org • Bimonthly. Individuals, $54.00 per year; institutions, $70.00 per year. Formerly *HMO Practice*.

***Effective Web Presence Solutions for Small Businesses: Strategies for Successful Implementation***. Cengage Learning Inc., 20 Channel Center St. Boston, MA 02210. Phone: 800-487-8488 or (617)289-7700; Fax: (617)289-7844; Email: investors@cengage.com • URL: http://www.cengage.com • 2009. eBook. Provides small businesses with a holistic approach to implementing their Web presence through identification of Web site content that matches their business strategy.

***Egg Industry: Covering Egg Production, Processing and Marketing***. Watt Publishing, 122 S Wesley Ave. Mount Morris, IL 61054-1497. Phone: (815)734-4171 • Monthly. Free to qualified personnel; others, $36.00 per year. Newsletter. Formerly *Poultry Tribune*.

***Egypt Business Directory***. Business Guide, PO Box 27669 Dubai, United Arab Emirates. Phone: 971 4 2651719; Fax: 971 4 2692151; Email: sales@africa-business.com • URL: http://www.africa-business.com • $150 Individuals Soft copy. Covers: 65,000 business listings including wholesalers, importers, retailers, business houses, and agents in Egypt.

***Egypt Business Forecast Report***. Telecommunications Insight, 85 Queen Victoria St. London EC4V 4AB, United Kingdom. Phone: 20 72 465100 or 44 20 7248 0468; Fax: 20 72 480467 or 44 20 7248 0467; Email: enquiries@telecomsinsight.com • URL: http://www.telecomsinsight.com • Quarterly. $1,195 Individuals Single user; $1,795 Individuals Up to 3 users. Business forecast report for Egypt.

***Egypt Business Law Handbook***. International Business Publications, USA, PO Box 15343 Washington, DC 20003. Phone: (202)546-2103; Fax: (202)546-3275; Email: ibpusa@comcast.net • URL: http://ibpus.com • $99.95 Individuals hardcopy, e-book, CD-ROM. Covers: Information on basic business legislation, property rights, laws, business climate, export-import regulations, taxation, banking and contacts.

***Egypt Golden Key Directory***. International Institute of Trade Relation Promotion, Trade Information Centre of Iran, No. 7, 3rd Fl., Abbasie Bazar, Ferdowsi Sq. Tehran, Iran. Phone: 98 21 88833900; Fax: 98 21 88820697; Email: order@irangoldenkey.com • URL: http://www.goldenkeydirectory.com/about.html • £100 Individuals. Covers: 51,901 companies in Egypt. Entries include: Company name, address, telephone, fax, products, services, managing director, and business activities.

***Egypt Industrial and Business Directory***. International Business Publications, USA, PO Box 15343 Washington, DC 20003. Phone: (202)546-2103; Fax: (202)546-3275; Email: ibpusa@comcast.net • URL: http://ibpus.com • Annual. $99.95 Individuals paperback, e-book, CD-ROM. Covers: Strategic industrial, investment and business contacts for conducting export-import and investment activity in the country.

***Egypt Investment and Business Guide***. International Business Publications, USA, PO Box 15343 Washington, DC 20003. Phone: (202)546-2103; Fax: (202)546-3275; Email: ibpusa@comcast.net • URL: http://ibpus.com • $99.95 Individuals hardcover, e-book, CD-ROM. Covers: Strategic and business information, contacts, regulations and more.

***EHS Today***. Penton Media Inc., 1300 E 9th St. Cleveland, OH 44114-1501. Phone: (216)696-7000; Fax: (216)696-1752; Email: information@penton.com • URL: http://penton.com • Monthly. $55.00 per year. Industrial safety and security management.

***EIA Publications Index/EIA Trade Directory***. Electronic Industries Alliance, 2500 Wilson Blvd. Arlington, VA 22201. Phone: (703)907-7500 or (703)907-8021; Fax: (703)907-7514 or (703)907-7501; Email: rwillis@ecaus.org • URL: http://www.ecaus.org/eia/site/index.html • Annual. Free.

***850 Key Decision Makers of Listed Companies in Hong Kong***. Asian Market Information & Analysis Centre, 1802, Eastern

Harbour Ctr., 28 Hoi Chak St., Quarry Bay Hong Kong, China. Phone: 852 21041958; Fax: 852 21277581; Email: prime@asia-lists.com • URL: http://www.asia-lists.com • Covers: 850 businesses with over 50 employees in Hong Kong. Entries include: Company name, Website, contact address, phone, fax, e-mail, contact person, and job title.

***EIU: Business Newsletters***. The Economist Intelligence Unit Ltd., 26 Red Lion Sq. London WC1R 4HQ, United Kingdom. Phone: 44 020 7576 8181; Fax: 44 020 7576 8476; Email: emea@eiu.com • URL: http://www.eiu.com • Offers access to a variety of business journals in electronic form. Coverage extends from January 2001 to the present, and the database is updated weekly with new records. The journals covered include: CFO magazine, The Economist, The Journal of Commerce, and Roll Call, among others. The publications covered in this database offer international coverage of business issues, news, and information, and government activities in the U.S. and U.K. Subject areas include the arts, banking and capital markets, economic trends, politics, science, technology, transportation, international political issues, environmental issues, government, investment, and privatization.

***El Salvador—American Chamber of Commerce—Membership Directory***. U.S. Chamber of Commerce, 1615 H St. NW Washington, DC 20062-2000. Phone: 800-638-6582 or (202)463-5500 or (202)659-6000; Fax: (202)463-3129; Email: foundation@uschamber.com • URL: http://www.uschambersmallbusinessnation.com • Annual. $100 Nonmembers for investment. Covers: Companies in the U.S. and El Salvador and individuals interested in the development of trade, labor law, investment regulations, economic trends, and foreign policy within and between the two countries. Entries include: For firms—Company, name, address, phone, fax, telex, cable address, names and titles of key personnel, line of business, subsidiary and branch names and locations, locations of plants or branch offices, product/service information. For individuals—Name, title, affiliation, address.

***El Salvador Investment and Business Guide***. International Business Publications, USA, PO Box 15343 Washington, DC 20003. Phone: (202)546-2103; Fax: (202)546-3275; Email: ibpusa@comcast.net • URL: http://ibpus.com • $99.95 Individuals hardcover, e-book, CD-ROM. Covers: Basic information on economy, export-import and investment climate, regulations and industrial development, banking, and government. Entries include: Important business contacts and business travel.

***Electrial Construction and Maintenance***. Penton, 9800 Metcalf Ave. Overland Park, KS 66212. Phone: 866-748-4926 or (913)341-1300; Fax: (913)967-1905 or (913)967-1898; Email: corporatecustomerservice@penton.com • URL: http://www.penton.com • Monthly. Free to qualified personnel; individuals, $30.00 per year; libraries, $25.00 per year.

***Electric Appliances Major Repair & Parts Directory***. InfoGroup Inc., 5711 S 86th Cir. Omaha, NE 68127-4146. Phone: (402)593-4500 • URL: http://www.infogroup.com • Annual. Number of listings: 13,612. Entries include: Name, address, phone, size of advertisement, name of owner or manager, number of employees, year first in "Yellow Pages." Compiled from telephone company "Yellow Pages," nationwide.

***Electric Perspectives***. Edison Electric Institute, 701 Pennsylvania Ave. NW Washington, DC 20004-2696. Phone: 800-334-5453 or (202)508-5000; Fax: (800)525-5562; Email: eblume@eei.org • URL: http://www.eei.org/Pages/default.aspx • Bimonthly. $100 Nonmembers; Free to management-level employees at EEI. Covers business, financial, and operational aspects of the investor-owned electric utility industry. Edited for utility executives and managers.

**Electric Power Supply Association**. 1401 New York Ave. NW, Ste. 1230 Washington, DC 20005-2110. Phone: (202)628-8200; Fax: (202)628-8260 • URL: http://www.epsa.org • Represents competitive power suppliers, including generators and power marketers. Provides reliable, competitively priced electricity from environmentally responsible facilities serving global power markets. Seeks to bring the benefits of competition to all power customers.

***Electric Utility Week: The Electric Utility Industry Newsletter***. Platts Global Energy, 2 Penn Plz., 25th Fl. New York, NY 10121-2298. Phone: 800-752-8878 or (212)904-3070 or (212)904-2977; Fax: (212)904-3070 or (212)904-4209; Email: support@platts.com • URL: http://www.platts.com • Weekly. $1,625.00 per year. Newsletter. Formerly *Electric Week*.

***Electrical Apparatus: Electromechanical Bench Reference Supplement***. Barks Publications Inc., 500 N Michigan Ave., Ste. 901 Chicago, IL 60611-4104. Phone: 800-288-7493 or (312)321-9440; Fax: (312)321-1288; Email: info@barks.com • URL: http://www.barks.com • Monthly. $45 U.S. /year; $95 Other countries /year. Included in subscription to Electric Apparatus Magazine. Lists 3,000 manufacturers and distributors of electrical and electronic products. Formerly *Electrical Apparatus Magazine. Electromechanical Bench Reference Book*.

***Electrical Construction Materials Directory***. Underwriters Laboratories Inc., 333 Pfingsten Rd. Northbrook, IL 60062-2096. Phone: 877-854-3577 or (847)664-3035; Fax: (847)664-6243; Email: cec@us.ul.com • URL: http://www.ul.com/global/eng/pages/ • Annual. $22 Individuals. Lists construction materials manufacturers authorized to use UL label.

***Electrical Contractor***. National Electrical Contractors Association, 3 Bethesda Metro Ctr., Ste. 1100 Bethesda, MD 20814. Phone: (301)657-3110; Fax: (301)215-4500 • URL: http://www.necanet.org • Monthly. Serves the field of electrical construction, including inside, line work, lighting, maintenance, control, electrical work, voice/data systems, security, fire and life safety, fiber optics, home and building automation systems, integrated building systems applications and others applicable to the field.

**Electrical Equipment Representatives Association**. 638 W 39th St. Kansas City, MO 64111. Phone: (816)561-5323; Fax: (816)561-1249; Email: info@eera.org • URL: http://www.eera.org • Represents sales agents for manufacturers of electrical equipment used by utilities, industrial firms and the government.

**Electrical Generating Systems Association**. 1650 S Dixie Hwy., Ste. 400 Boca Raton, FL 33432-7462. Phone: (561)750-5575; Fax: (561)395-8557; Email: e-mail@egsa.org • URL: http://www.egsa.org • Manufacturers, distributor/dealers, and manufacturers' representatives of devices used to generate electrical power through the use of an internal combustion engine or a gas turbine coupled to a generator. Conducts training programs and publishes material on On-Site Power Generation.

***Electrical Wholesaling***. Penton, 9800 Metcalf Ave. Overland Park, KS 66212. Phone: 866-748-4926 or (913)341-1300; Fax: (913)967-1905 or (913)967-1898; Email: corporatecustomerservice@penton.com • URL: http://www.penton.com • Monthly. $20.00 per year.

***Electrical World T and D Magazine***. Platts Global Energy, 2 Penn Plz., 25th Fl. New York, NY 10121-2298. Phone: 800-752-8878 or (212)904-3070 or (212)904-2977; Fax: (212)904-3070 or (212)904-4209; Email: support@platts.com • URL: http://www.platts.com • Monthly. Free to qualified personnel. Formerly *Electrical World*.

**Electrochemical Analysis and Diagnostic Laboratory**. Argonne National Laboratory, 9700 S Cass Ave. Lemont, IL 60439-4803. Phone: (630)252-2000; Fax: (630)252-4176; Email: bloom@cmt.anl.gov • URL: http://www.anl.gov.

***Electronic Business: Concepts, Methodologies, Tools, and Applications***. Cengage Learning Inc., 20 Channel Center St. Boston, MA 02210. Phone: 800-487-8488 or (617)289-7700; Fax: (617)289-7844; Email: investors@cengage.com • URL: http://www.cengage.com • 2009. eBook. Contains articles in topic areas such as e-commerce technologies, online marketing, social networking, and virtual business communities.

***Electronic Business: The Management Magazine for the Electronics Industry***. Reed Elsevier Group plc Reed Business Information, 360 Park Ave. S New York, NY 11010. Phone: (212)791-4208; Email: corporatecommunications@reedbusiness.com • URL: http://www.reedbusiness.com • Monthly. $100.99 per year. For the non-technical manager and executive in the electronics industry. Offers news, trends, figures and forecasts. Formerly *Electronic Business Today*.

***Electronic Commerce World***. SourceMedia Inc., 1 State Street Plz., 27th Fl. New York, NY 10004. Phone: 800-221-1809 or (212)803-8200 or (212)803-8333; Fax: (212)843-9635 or (212)292-5216; Email: custserv@sourcemedia.com • URL: http://www.sourcemedia.com • Monthly. $45.00 per year. Provides practical information on the application of electronic commerce technology. Also covers such items as taxation of e-business, cash management, copyright, and legal issues.

**Electronic Components Industry Association**. 1111 Alderman Dr., Ste. 400 Alpharetta, GA 30005. Phone: (678)393-9990; Fax: (678)393-9998 • URL: http://www.eciaonline.org • Represents authorized distributors and manufacturers of electronic components. Conducts research. Compiles statistical reports and surveys.

***Electronic Design***. Penton Media Inc., 1300 E 9th St. Cleveland, OH 44114-1501. Phone: (216)696-7000; Fax: (216)696-1752; Email: information@penton.com • URL: http://penton.com • Biweekly. Free to qualified personnel; others, $100.00 per year. Provides technical information for U.S. design engineers and managers.

***Electronic Engineering Times: The Industry Newspaper for Engineers and Technical Management***. UBM L.L.C., 240 W 35th St. New York, NY 10001. • URL: http://www.ubm.com • Weekly. Free to qualified personnel; others, $319.00 per year.

***Electronic Equipment & Supplies—Retail Directory***. InfoGroup Inc., 5711 S 86th Cir. Omaha, NE 68127-4146. Phone: (402)593-4500 • URL: http://www.infogroup.com • Annual. Number of listings: 13,108. Entries include: Name, address, phone, size of advertisement, name of owner or manager, number of employees, year first in "Yellow Pages." Compiled from telephone company "Yellow Pages," nationwide.

**Electronic Frontier Foundation**. 815 Eddy St. San Francisco, CA 94109. Phone: (415)436-9333; Fax: (415)436-9993; Email: info@eff.org • URL: http://www.eff.org • Promotes the creation of legal and structural approaches to help ease the assimilation of new technologies by society. Seeks to: help policymakers develop a better understanding of issues underlying telecommunications; increase public understanding of the opportunities and challenges posed by computing and telecommunications fields. Fosters awareness of civil liberties issues arising from the advancements in new computer-based communications media and supports litigation to preserve, protect, and extend First Amendment rights in computing and telecommunications technology. Maintains speakers' bureau; conducts educational programs. Encourages and supports the development of tools to endow non-technical users with access to computer-based telecommunications.

**Electronic Funds Transfer Association**. 4000 Legato Rd., Ste. 1100 Fairfax, VA 22033. Phone: (571)318-5556; Fax: (571)318-5557; Email: dennisambach@efta.org • URL: http://www.efta.org • Financial institutions, credit card companies, ATM owners, networks and processors, hardware and software manufacturers and e-commerce companies dedicated to the advancement of electronic payment systems and commerce.

**Electronic Industry Citizenship Coalition**. 1155 15th St. NW, Ste. 500 Washington, DC 20005. Email: info@eicc.info • URL: http://www.eicc.info • Represents global ICT companies and their suppliers. Aims to promote a common code of conduct for the electronics, information and communications technology (ICT) industry. Works to improve environmental and worker conditions.

***The Electronic Industry Sector in Switzerland***. AT Zeitschriftenverlag, • Covers: Computer and electronics companies and products in Switzerland and Liechtenstein. Entries include: Company name, address, phone, product description.

***Electronic Information Report: Empowering Industry Decision Makers Since 1979***. SIMBA Information Inc., 60 Long Ridge Rd., Ste. 300 Stamford, CT 06902. Phone: (203)325-8193; Fax: (203)325-8975 • URL: http://www.simbainformation.com • 46 times a year. $649.00 per year. Newsletter. Provides business and financial news and trends for online services, electronic publishing, storage media, multimedia, and voice services. Includes information on relevant IPOs (initial public offerings) and mergers. Formerly *Electronic Information Week*.

***Electronic Learning***. Scholastic Inc., 557 Broadway New York, NY 10012. Phone: (212)343-6100 or (212)343-6166; Email: custserv@scholastic.com • URL: http://www.scholastic.com • Eight times a year. $19.95 per year. Includes classroom applications for computers. For teachers of grades K-12.

***Electronic Messaging News: Strategies, Applications, and Standards***. Access Intelligence L.L.C., 4 Choke Cherry Rd., 2nd Fl. Rockville, MD 20850. Phone: 800-777-5006 or (301)354-2000 or (301)354-2101; Fax: (301)309-3847 or (801)365-2300; Email: info@accessintel.com • URL: http://www.accessintel.com/ • Biweekly. $597.00 per year. Newsletter.

***Electronic Musician***. Primedia Business Magazines and Media, 6400 Hollis St., Ste. 12 Emeryville, CA 94608. Phone: 800-795-5445 or (510)653-3307; Fax: (510)653-5142; Email: subs@primediabusiness.com • URL: http://www.primediabusiness.com • Monthly. $23.97 per year.

***Electronic News***. Reed Elsevier Group plc Reed Business Information, 360 Park Ave. S New York, NY 11010. Phone: (212)791-4208; Email: corporatecommunications@reedbusiness.com • URL: http://www.reedbusiness.com • 51 times a year. $119.00 per year. Serves the electronic OEM industry.

***Electronic Products: The Engineer's Magazine of Product Technology***. Hearst Business Communications, UTP Div., 645 Stewart Ave. Garden City, NY 11530. Phone: 800-289-8696 or (516)227-1300; Fax: (516)227-1444; Email: lens@electronicproducts.com • URL: http://www.hearstcorp.com • Monthly. $65.00 per year.

***Electronic Publishing: For the Business Leaders Who Buy Technology***. PennWell Corp., Advanced Technology Div., 98 Spit Brook Rd. Nashua, NH 03062-5737. Phone: 800-225-0556 or (603)891-0123; Fax: (603)891-9294; Email: atd@pennwell.com • URL: http://www.pennwell.com • Monthly. Free to qualified personnel; others, $55.00$ per year. Edited for digital publishing professionals. New products are featured.

**Electronic Security Association**. 6333 N State Hwy. 161, Ste. 350 Irving, TX 75038-2228. Phone: 888-447-1689 or (972)807-6800 or (214)260-5970; Fax: (972)807-6883 or (214)260-5979; Email: staff@alarm.org • URL: http://www.esaweb.org • Formerly National Burglar and Fire Alarm Association.

***Electronic Servicing & Technology: The How-To Magazine of Electronics***. CQ Communications, 25 Newbridge Rd. Hicksville, NY 11801. Phone: 800-853-9797 or (516)681-2922; Fax: (516)681-2926; Email: cq@cq-amateur-radio.com • URL: http://www.cq-amateur-radio.com • Monthly. Free to qualified personnel; others, $26.95 per year. Provides how-to technical information to technicians who service consumer electronics equipment.

***Electronics and Communications Abstracts Journal: Comprehensive Coverage of Essential Scientific Literature***. CSA, 7200 Wisconsin Ave. Bethesda, MD 20814. Phone: 800-843-7751 or (301)961-6700; Fax: (301)961-6720; Email: service@csa.com • URL: http://www.csa.com • Monthly. $1,665.00 per year. Includes print and online editions.

***Electronics: Industry Sector Profile***. Philippine-German Export Development Project Philippine Bureau of Export Trade Promotion, 6F Trade & Industry Bldg., 361 Sen. Gil Puyat Ave. Makati PH-1226, Philippines. Phone: 63 2 897 8199;

Email: web@dti.dti.gov.ph • URL: http://www.dti.gov.ph • Publication includes: Companies exporting electronics from the Philippines. Entries include: Company name, address, phone, fax, name and title of contact, type of business, year established, subsidiary and branch names and locations, financial data, number of employees, government registrations, professional memberships, bank references, supply capability, export experience, business plan. Principal content of publication is an overview of the business environment and electronics industry in the Philippines.

**Electronics Representatives Association.** 309 W Washington St., Ste. 500 Chicago, IL 60606. Phone: (312)419-1432 or (312)559-3050; Fax: (312)419-1660; Email: info@era.org • URL: http://www.era.org • Professional field sales organizations selling components and materials; computer, instrumentation and data communications products; audiovisual, security, land/mobile communications and commercial sound components and consumer products to the electronics industry. Sponsors insurance programs and educational conference for members.

**Electronics TakeBack Coalition.** 4200 Park Blvd. No. 228 Oakland, CA 94602-1312. Phone: (510)614-0110; Email: info@etakeback.org • URL: http://www.electronicstakeback.com • Promotes green design and responsible recycling in the electronics industry. Aims to protect the health and well being of electronics users, workers, and the communities where electronics are produced and discarded. Encourages electronics manufacturers to offer programs to take back and recycle old electronics.

*Elevator World.* Elevator World, 356 Morgan Ave. Mobile, AL 36606-1737. Phone: 800-730-5093 or (251)479-4514; Fax: (251)479-7043; Email: sales@elevator-world.com • URL: http://www.elevator-world.com • Monthly. $75 U.S. Print - 1 year; $125 Other countries Print - 1 year; $25 Individuals Digital version - 1 year. Publishes latest news, newest innovations, imperative safety issues, current code requirements, events coverage and accessibility, legal and maintenance issues.

*Elsevier Manufacturing and Processing Data Base Directory.* Reed Elsevier Group plc Reed Business Information, 360 Park Ave. S New York, NY 11010. Phone: (212)791-4208; Email: corporatecommunications@reedbusiness.com • URL: http://www.reedbusiness.com • Annual. $599. Covers: the manufacturing/processing industry. Entries include: Individual name and title and/or function, company or facility name, address, phone, Standard Industrial Classification (SIC) code, number of employees.

*EM: A&WMA's Environmental Solutions That Make Good Business Sense.* Air and Waste Management Association, 1 Gateway Ctr., 3rd Fl., 420 Fort Duquesne Blvd. Pittsburgh, PA 15222-1435. Phone: 800-270-3444 or (412)232-3444; Fax: (412)232-3450; Email: info@awma.org • URL: http://www.awma.org • Monthly. Institutions, $299.00 per year; nonprofit and government agencies, $199.00 per year. Newsletter. Provides news of regulations, legislation, and technology relating to the environment, recycling, and waste control. Formerly *Environmental Manager.*

*EMB: Embroidery/Monogram Business.* EMB, 1717 Main St., Ste. 3300 Dallas, TX 75201. Phone: 800-527-0207; Fax: (214)290-9982 • Monthly. Trade magazine for the embroidery industry.

*Embase.* Elsevier, Secondary Publishing Division, 650 Ave. of the Americas New York, NY 10011. Phone: 888-437-4636 or (212)633-3980; Fax: (212)633-3975; Email: t.reller@elsevier.com • URL: http://www.elseveier.com • Worldwide medical literature, 1974 to present. Weekly updates. Inquire as to online cost and availability.

*EMECA Review of Business.* European Major Exhibition Centres Association, c/o Ms. Barbara Weizsacker,Secretary General, Rue de l'Amazone 2 1050 Brussels, Belgium. Phone: 32 2 5357250; Email: info@emeca.eu • URL: http://www.emeca.eu • Annual.

*eMedia: The Digital Studio Magazine.* Online Inc., 213 Danbury Rd. Wilton, CT 06897-4007. Phone: 800-248-8466 or (203)761-1466; Fax: (203)761-1444; Email: dbmag@onlineinc.com • URL: http://www.infotoday.com • Monthly. $98.00 per year. Covers video production equipment, digital video editing, electronic publishing, digital content streaming, encoding, and other topics related to digital content creation and multimedia. (Formerly published by Online, Inc.).

**Emergency Management Professional Organization for Women's Enrichment.** PO Box 10803 McLean, VA 22102-8803. Email: information@empower-women.com • URL: http://www.empower-women.com • Promotes the presence of women in the field of emergency management. Creates opportunities for women to empower themselves in the field of emergency management. Seeks to help women advance their careers through networking, mentoring and promoting educational opportunities in the field of emergency management.

*Emergent Strategies for E-Business Processes, Services and Implications: Advancing Corporate Frameworks.* Cengage Learning Inc., 20 Channel Center St. Boston, MA 02210. Phone: 800-487-8488 or (617)289-7700; Fax: (617)289-7844; Email: investors@cengage.com • URL: http://www.cengage.com • A collection of original, in-depth, and innovative research articles on e-business concepts, models,

processes, services, and applications.

*Emerging Europe Autos Directory.* Business Monitor International Ltd., Senator House, 85 Queen Victoria St. London EC4V 4AB, United Kingdom. Phone: 44 20 72480468; Fax: 44 20 72480467; Email: enquiry@businessmonitor.com • URL: http://www.businessmonitor.com • $895 Individuals. Covers: 1,275 top autos executives on 443 leading automotive companies from Bosnia-Herzegovina, Bulgaria, Croatia, the Czech Republic, Estonia. Hungary, Latvia, Lithuania, Macedonia, Poland, Romania, Russia, Serbia, Slovakia, Slovenia and the Ukraine. Entries include: parent company head offices, full company name, address, phone and fax numbers, email and website address, senior contact personnel, company description and profile, nationality, and ownership status.

*Emerging Europe Food and Drink Directory.* Business Monitor International Ltd., Senator House, 85 Queen Victoria St. London EC4V 4AB, United Kingdom. Phone: 44 20 72480468; Fax: 44 20 72480467; Email: enquiry@businessmonitor.com • URL: http://www.businessmonitor.com • $895 Individuals. Covers: 1,577 top food and drink executives on 559 leading food and drink companies from Emerging Europe. Entries include: parent company head offices, full company name, address, phone and fax numbers, email and website address, senior contact personnel, company description and profile, nationality, and ownership status.

*Emerging Europe Oil and Gas Directory.* Business Monitor International Ltd., Senator House, 85 Queen Victoria St. London EC4V 4AB, United Kingdom. Phone: 44 20 72480468; Fax: 44 20 72480467; Email: enquiry@businessmonitor.com • URL: http://www.businessmonitor.com • $895 Individuals. Covers: 698 top oil and gas executives on 234 leading oil and gas companies from Emerging Europe. Entries include: Parent company head offices, full company name, address, phone and fax numbers, email and website address, senior oil and gas contact personnel, company description and profile, nationality, and ownership status.

*Emerging Europe Pharmaceuticals and Healthcare Directory.* Business Monitor International Ltd., Senator House, 85 Queen Victoria St. London EC4V 4AB, United Kingdom. Phone: 44 20 72480468; Fax: 44 20 72480467; Email: enquiry@businessmonitor.com • URL: http://www.businessmonitor.com • $895 Individuals. Covers: 2,212 top pharmaceutical executives at 794 leading pharmaceutical companies from Bosnia, Bulgaria, Croatia, the Czech Republic, Estonia, Hungary, Latvia, Lithuania, Macedonia, Poland, Romania, Russia, Serbia, Slovakia, Slovenia and the Ukraine. Entries include: Parent company head offices, full company name, address, phone and fax numbers, email and website address, senior contact personnel, company description and profile, nationality, and ownership status.

*Emerging Europe Telecommunications Directory.* Business Monitor International Ltd., Senator House, 85 Queen Victoria St. London EC4V 4AB, United Kingdom. Phone: 44 20 72480468; Fax: 44 20 72480467; Email: enquiry@businessmonitor.com • URL: http://www.businessmonitor.com • $895 Individuals. Covers: 1,333 top telecommunications executives at 445 leading telecommunications companies from Emerging Europe. Entries include: parent company head offices, full company name, address, phone and fax numbers, email and website address, senior contact personnel, company description and profile, nationality, and ownership status.

*Emerging Growth.* Navellier and Associates Inc., 1 E Liberty St., 3rd Fl., Ste. 504 Reno, NV 89501-2100. Phone: 800-887-8671 or (775)785-2300; Fax: (775)562-8212; Email: info@navellier.com • URL: http://www.navellier.com • Monthly. $275.00 per year. Newsletter. Provides specific stock selection and model portfolio advice (conservative, moderately aggressive, and aggressive) based on quantitative analysis and modern portfolio theory.

*Emerging Markets Debt Report.* SourceMedia Inc., 1 State Street Plz., 27th Fl. New York, NY 10004. Phone: 800-221-1809 or (212)803-8200 or (212)803-8333; Fax: (212)843-9635 or (212)292-5216; Email: custserv@sourcemedia.com • URL: http://www.sourcemedia.com • Weekly. $895.00 per year. Newsletter. Provides information on new and prospective sovereign and corporate bond issues from developing countries. Includes an emerging market bond index and pricing data.

*Emerging Markets Finance & Trade.* M.E. Sharpe Inc., 80 Business Park Dr. Armonk, NY 10504. Phone: 800-541-6563 or (914)273-1800; Fax: (914)273-2106; Email: info@mesharpe.com • URL: http://www.mesharpe.com • Bimonthly. $1,421 Institutions per year, print and online; $149 Individuals per year, print and online. Provides research papers on developing markets in Europe, Asia, Latin America, the Middle East, and Africa.

*Emerging Markets Quarterly.* Institutional Investor Inc. Journals Group, 225 Park Ave. S New York, NY 10003. Phone: 800-437-9997 or (212)224-3570; Email: info@iijournals.com • URL: http://www.iijournals.com • Quarterly. Price on application. Newsletter on financial markets in developing areas, such as Africa, Latin America, Southeast Asia, and

Eastern Europe. Topics include institutional investment opportunities and regulatory matters. Formerly *Emerging Markets Weekly.*

*Emerging Trends in Securities Law.* Thomson West, 610 Opperman Dr. Eagan, MN 55123. Phone: 800-328-9352 or (651)687-7000 • Annual. $536.90. Presents a detailed chronicle of events and analysis of evolving trends. (Securities Law Handbook Series).

*Emerson's Directory of Leading U.S. Accounting Firms.* Emerson Co., 12342 Northup Way Bellevue, WA 98005-1915. Phone: (206)869-0655 or (425)869-0655; Fax: (425)869-0746; Email: emerson@emersoncompany.com • URL: http://www.emersoncompany.com • Biennial. $195.00. Provides information on 500 major CPA firms.

**EMILY's List.** 1800 M St. NW, Ste. 375-N Washington, DC 20036. Phone: 800-683-6459 or (202)326-1400; Fax: (202)326-1415; Email: enquiries@emilyslist.org.uk • URL: http://emilyslist.org • Political network for Democratic women. Seeks to raise campaign funds for the election of pro-choice Democratic women to political office.

*EMMA: Easy Mailing and Marketing Applications.* Bureau van Dijk S.A., Ave. Louise, Louizalaan 250 B-1050 Brussels, Belgium. Phone: 32 2 6390606 or 32 2 639 06 06; Fax: 32 2 6488230 or 32 2 648 82 30; Email: brussels@bvdinfo.com • URL: http://www.bvdinfo.com • Quarterly. Database covers: More than 1,000,000 companies in the United Kingdom. Entries include: Company name, address, date of incorporation, company type, activity, directors, holding companies, turnover, net assets, pre-tax profit, number of employees.

*Employee Benefit News: The News Magazine for Employee Benefit Management.* SourceMedia Inc., 1 State Street Plz., 27th Fl. New York, NY 10004. Phone: 800-221-1809 or (212)803-8200 or (212)803-8333; Fax: (212)843-9635 or (212)292-5216; Email: custserv@sourcemedia.com • URL: http://www.sourcemedia.com • Monthly. $94.00 per year. Edited for human relations directors and other managers of employee benefits.

*Employee Benefit Plan Review.* Charles D. Spencer and Associates, Inc., 250 S. Wacker Dr., Suite 600 Chicago, IL 60606-5834. Phone: (312)993-7900; Fax: (312)993-7910; Email: editor@spencernet.com • URL: http://www.spencernet.com • $395 Individuals. Monthly. Provides a review of recent events affecting the administration of employee benefit programs.

*Employee Benefits Infosource.* International Foundation of Employee Benefit Plans, 18700 W Bluemound Rd. Brookfield, WI 53045. Phone: 888-334-3327 or (262)786-6700 or (262)786-6710; Email: membership@ifebp.org • URL: http://www.ifebp.org • Provides citations and abstracts to the literature of employee benefits, 1986 to present. Monthly updates. Inquire as to online cost and availability.

*Employee Benefits Journal.* International Foundation of Employee Benefit Plans, 18700 W Bluemound Rd. Brookfield, WI 53045. Phone: 888-334-3327 or (262)786-6700 or (262)786-6710; Email: membership@ifebp.org • URL: http://www.ifebp.org • Quarterly. $80.00 per year. Selected articles on timely and important benefit subjects.

*Employee Benefits Law: ERISA and Beyond.* ALM Media Properties LLC, 120 Broadway, 5th Fl. New York, NY 10271-1100. Phone: (212)457-9400; Fax: (646)417-7705; Email: customercare@alm.com • URL: http://www.alm.com • $710 two volumes. Explains the rules and regulations put forth by the Employee Retirement Income Security Act. Three federal agencies are involved: the Internal Revenue Service, the Labor Department, and the Pension Benefit Guaranty Corporation. (Law Journal Press).

**Employee Morale and Recreation Association.** PO Box 10517 Rockville, MD 20849. • URL: http://employeemorale.org • Corporations and governmental agencies that sponsor recreation, fitness, and service programs for their employees; associate members are manufacturers and suppliers in the employee recreation market and distributors of consumer products and services. Serves as an information resource network for members nationwide. Implements and maintains a diverse range of employee services; believes that employee services, as practical solutions to work/life issues, are essential to sound business management. Conducts programs that improves relations between employees and management, increases overall productivity, boosts morale, and reduces absenteeism and turnover.

*Employee Policy for the Private and Public Sector: State Capitals.* Wakeman/Walworth Inc., PO Box 7376 Alexandria, VA 22307-7376. Phone: 800-876-2545 or (703)768-9600; Fax: (703)768-9690; Email: newsletters@statecapitals.com • URL: http://statecapitals.com/ • Weekly. $245.00 per year; print and online editions, $350.00 per year. Newsletter. Formerly *From the State Capitals: Employee Policy for the Private and Public Sector.*

*Employee Services Management: The Journal of Employee Services Recreation, Heal th and Education.* Employee Services Management, 2211 York Rd., Ste. 207 Oak Brook, IL 60523-2371. Phone: (630)368-1280; Fax: (630)368-1286; Email: esmahq@esmassh.org • URL: http://www.esmassn.org • Bimonthly. Free to members; non-members, $52.00 per year.

*Employer Directory for the United States.* James R. Albin, 431 Bridgeway Sausalito, CA 94965. Phone: (415)332-6438; Fax: (415)332-6468 • Annual. $99.95. Covers: Approximately 2,000 corporations in the U.S. with more than 500 employees, including all Double Fortune and Forbes 500 companies. Entries include: Company name, address, phone, fax, telex, names and titles of key personnel, number of employees, financial data, description.

**Employers Council on Flexible Compensation.** 1444 I St. NW, Ste. 700 Washington, DC 20005-2210. Phone: (202)659-4300; Fax: (202)216-9646 • URL: http://www.ecfc.org • Promotes flexible or "cafeteria" plans for employee compensation and benefits.

**Employers Group.** 4000 Continental Blvd., Ste. 300 El Segundo, CA 90245. Phone: 800-748-8484 or (213)765-3989; Fax: (213)742-0301; Email: serviceone@employersgroup.com • URL: http://www.employersgroup.com • Provides human resources management services including wage, salary, and benefit surveys; personnel practices surveys; management counseling; management education programs; litigation surveillance; government relations; and research library service. Provides customized human resources services including employee opinion surveys and employee communications programs through its subsidiary, The Employers Group Service Corp. Offers unemployment insurance services, workers' compensation programs, and in-house management training programs. Conducts research and educational programs; maintains speakers' bureau.

**Employment Forms and Policies.** Matthew Bender and Company Inc., 1275 Broadway Albany, NY 12204-2638. Phone: 800-424-4200 or (518)487-3000; Fax: (518)487-3573 or (800)424-4200; Email: customer.support@lexisnexis.com • URL: http://www.matthewbender.com • $150 print and e-book. Periodic supplementation available. Contains more than 300 forms, policies, and checklists for use by small or medium-sized businesses. Covers such topics as employee selection, payroll issues, benefits, performance appraisal, dress codes, and employee termination.

**Employment Law Strategist.** Law Journal Newsletter, 105 Madison Ave. New York, NY 10016. Phone: 800-603-6571 or (212)313-9300; Fax: (212)481-8110; Email: lawcatalog@amlaw.com • URL: http://www.ljnonline.com • $439 per year. Covers employment law topics, including immigration laws, repetitive stress claims, workplace violence, liability of actions of intoxicated employees, record keeping, liability for fetal injury, independent contractor, and employee issues. Monthly. 229 individuals electronic edition. Description: Reports on legal strategy and substantive developments in the area of matrimonial law, including such topics as tax considerations, custody, visitation, division of property, and valuation. Recurring features include litigation roundup and a legislative update.

**EMPRESAS.** Brazilian Institute for Information in Science and Technology, SAS Q. 5, Lot 6, Block H 70070-912 Brasilia, DF, Brazil. Phone: 55 61 32176145 or 55 61 32176144; Fax: 55 61 32176490; Email: webmaster@ibict.br • URL: http://www.ibict.br • Monthly. Database covers: companies that sell publicly available software programs. Entries include: Name of firm, address, phone, telex, products and services.

**EMTA.** 360 Madison Ave., 17th Fl. New York, NY 10017. Phone: (646)289-5410 or (646)289-5414; Fax: (646)289-5429; Email: sortiz@emta.org • URL: http://www.emta.org • Promotes orderly trading markets for emerging market instruments. Formerly Emerging Markets Traders Association.

**Emulsion Polymers Institute.** Lehigh University, Iacocca Hall, Rm. D-325, 111 Research Dr. Bethlehem, PA 18015. Phone: (610)758-3602; Fax: (610)758-5880; Email: eric.daniels@lehigh.edu • URL: http://www.lehigh.edu/inemuls/epi/ • Includes latex paint research.

**Enactus Canada.** 920 Yonge St., Ste. 800 Toronto, ON, Canada M4W 3C7. Phone: 800-766-8169 or (416)304-1566; Fax: (416)864-0514 • URL: http://www.enactus.ca • Young people, business owners, or engaged in entrepreneurial activities. Promotes growth and development of members' business interests. Provides support and services to businesses owned by young people; encourages communication and mutual support among collegiate entrepreneurs.

**Encyclopedia of Aging.** David J. Ekerdt, editor. Cengage Learning Inc., 20 Channel Center St. Boston, MA 02210. Phone: 800-487-8488 or (617)289-7700; Fax: (617)289-7844; Email: investors@cengage.com • URL: http://www.cengage.com • $770. Includes articles relating to the financial aspects of aging, such as housing, long-term care insurance, pensions, social security, individual retirement accounts, savings, and retirement planning. eBook also available. Inquire for pricing.

**Encyclopedia of American Business.** Cengage Learning Inc., 20 Channel Center St. Boston, MA 02210. Phone: 800-487-8488 or (617)289-7700; Fax: (617)289-7844; Email: investors@cengage.com • URL: http://www.cengage.com • 2013. eBook. 2 volumes. 800 essays. A guide to the nuts and bolts of business jargon. Difficult ideas are explained in straightforward language to help non-specialists, students, and general readers understand the complex and sometimes confusing concepts and terms that are used in business. Five general areas of business are covered: accounting, banking, finance, marketing, and management.

**Encyclopedia of American Industries.** Cengage Learning Inc., 20 Channel Center St. Boston, MA 02210. Phone: 800-487-8488 or (617)289-7700; Fax: (617)289-7844; Email: investors@cengage.com • URL: http://www.cengage.com • 2011. $807. 00. 6th edition. Three volumes. Volume one is Manufacturing

Industries and volume two is Service and Non-Manufacturing Industries. Provides the history, development, and recent status of approximately 1,000 industries. Includes statistical graphs, with industry and general indexes. Also available as eBook.

**Encyclopedia of Associations: International Organizations.** Cengage Learning Inc., 20 Channel Center St. Boston, MA 02210. Phone: 800-487-8488 or (617)289-7700; Fax: (617)289-7844; Email: investors@cengage.com • URL: http://www.cengage.com • Annual. $1,144 Individuals. 2010. eBook. Covers multinational and national membership organizations worldwide. Contact for pricing.

**Encyclopedia of Associations: National Organizations of the U.S.** Cengage Learning Inc., 20 Channel Center St. Boston, MA 02210. Phone: 800-487-8488 or (617)289-7700; Fax: (617)289-7844; Email: investors@cengage.com • URL: http://www.cengage.com • Annual. $778 Individuals. Provides detailed information on nonprofit American membership organizations of national scope. eBook also available.

**Encyclopedia of Associations: Regional, State and Local Organizations.** Cengage Learning Inc., 20 Channel Center St. Boston, MA 02210. Phone: 800-487-8488 or (617)289-7700; Fax: (617)289-7844; Email: investors@cengage.com • URL: http://www.cengage.com • 2013. $278. 5 volumes. Covers more than 100,000 U.S. nonprofit membership organizations with interstate, state, intrastate, city or local scope and interest, including trade and professional associations, social welfare and public affairs organizations and religious, sports, and hobby groups with voluntary members.eBook also available.

**Encyclopedia of Business and Finance.** Cengage Learning Inc., 20 Channel Center St. Boston, MA 02210. Phone: 800-487-8488 or (617)289-7700; Fax: (617)289-7844; Email: investors@cengage.com • URL: http://www.cengage.com • 2014. $485. 3rd edition. Two volumes. Published by Macmillan Reference USA. Contains articles on accounting, business administration, banking, finance, management information systems, and marketing.

**Encyclopedia of Business Ethics and Society.** Cengage Learning Inc., 20 Channel Center St. Boston, MA 02210. Phone: 800-487-8488 or (617)289-7700; Fax: (617)289-7844; Email: investors@cengage.com • URL: http://www.cengage.com • 2007. eBook. 5 volumes. Spans the relationships among business, ethics, and society by including more than 800 entries that feature broad coverage of corporate social responsibility, the obligation of companies to various stakeholder groups, the contribution of business to society and culture, and the relationship between organizations and the quality of the environment.

**Encyclopedia of Business Information Sources.** Cengage Learning Inc., 20 Channel Center St. Boston, MA 02210. Phone: 800-487-8488 or (617)289-7700; Fax: (617)289-7844; Email: investors@cengage.com • URL: http://www.cengage.com • Annual. $626 Individuals. Contains bibliographic information on more than 35,000 live, print, and electronic sources of information covering more than 1,100 subjects of interest to business personnel. Includes abstracts and indexes, almanacs and yearbooks, bibliographies, online databases, research centers and institutes, and more. Available as eBook.

**Encyclopedia of Chinese-Foreign Joint Ventures, Contractual Joint Ventures, Foreign-Funded Enterprises.** Jinghua Publishing House, 1 Dingfu, Xicheng District Beijing 10030, China. • $300. Covers: Approximately 30,000 Chinese-foreign joint ventures, contractual joint ventures, and foreign-funded enterprises. Database includes: An introduction to China's laws, regulations, and rules related to Chinese-foreign joint ventures, contractual joint ventures, and foreign-funded enterprises. Entries include: Contact information.

**Encyclopedia of Communication and Information.** Cengage Learning Inc., 20 Channel Center St. Boston, MA 02210. Phone: 800-487-8488 or (617)289-7700; Fax: (617)289-7844; Email: investors@cengage.com • URL: http://www.cengage.com • 2003. eBook. Published by Macmillan Reference USA. Provides an overview of universal modes of communication. Inquire about price and availability.

**Encyclopedia of Computer Science and Technology.** Taylor & Francis Online, 270 Madison Ave. New York, NY 10016. Phone: 800-228-1160 or (212)696-9000 or (212)216-7800; Fax: (212)685-4540 or (212)563-2269; Email: support@tandfonline.com • URL: http://www.tandfonline.com/ • Dates vary. 45 volumes. $8,775.00. $195.00 per volume. Contains scholarly articles written by computer experts. Includes bibliographies.

**Encyclopedia of Crime and Justice.** Cengage Learning Inc., 20 Channel Center St. Boston, MA 02210. Phone: 800-487-8488 or (617)289-7700; Fax: (617)289-7844; Email: investors@cengage.com • URL: http://www.cengage.com • 2001. $737. 2nd edition. 4 volumes. Published by Macmillan Reference USA. Contains extensive information on a wide variety of topics pertaining to crime, criminology, social issues, and the courts. Also available as eBook.

**Encyclopedia of Drugs, Alcohol, and Addictive Behavior.** Cengage Learning Inc., 20 Channel Center St. Boston, MA 02210. Phone: 800-487-8488 or (617)289-7700; Fax: (617)289-7844; Email: investors@cengage.com • URL: http://www.cengage.com • $820 Individuals. 2009. 3rd Edition. eBook. Published by Macmillan Reference USA.

Covers the social, economic, political, and medical aspects of addiction. Inquire for price and availability.

**Encyclopedia of E-Commerce, E-Government and Mobile Commerce.** Cengage Learning Inc., 20 Channel Center St. Boston, MA 02210. Phone: 800-487-8488 or (617)289-7700; Fax: (617)289-7844; Email: investors@cengage.com • URL: http://www.cengage.com • 2 volumes. Includes contributions highlighting current concepts, trends, challenges, applications, and dot.com experiences in the field of e-commerce, e-government, and mobile commerce.

**Encyclopedia of E-Leadership, Counseling and Training.** Cengage Learning Inc., 20 Channel Center St. Boston, MA 02210. Phone: 800-487-8488 or (617)289-7700; Fax: (617)289-7844; Email: investors@cengage.com • URL: http://www.cengage.com • Offers an in-depth description of key terms and concepts related to different themes, issues, and trends in educational leadership, counseling, and technology integration in modern universities and organizations worldwide.

**Encyclopedia of Emerging Industries.** Cengage Learning Inc., 20 Channel Center St. Boston, MA 02210. Phone: 800-487-8488 or (617)289-7700; Fax: (617)289-7844; Email: investors@cengage.com • URL: http://www.cengage.com • $546 6th edition. Provides detailed information on 140 "newly flourishing" industries. Includes historical background, organizational structure, significant individuals, current conditions, major companies, work force, technology trends, research developments, and other industry facts.

**Encyclopedia of Emerging Markets.** Cengage Learning Inc., 20 Channel Center St. Boston, MA 02210. Phone: 800-487-8488 or (617)289-7700; Fax: (617)289-7844; Email: investors@cengage.com • URL: http://www.cengage.com • Covers emerging markets and industry profiles in 33 nations worldwide. Available in print ($549) and eBook. Published June 2013.

**Encyclopedia of Environmental Science and Engineering.** CRC Press, c/o Taylor & Francis Group, LLC, 6000 Broken Sound Pkwy., NW Boca Raton, FL 33487-2713. Phone: 800-272-7737; Fax: (800)374-3401; Email: ncarter@taylorandfrancis.com • URL: http://www.crcpress.com • $900.00. Two volumes. Covers 89 entries on a variety of environmental topics.

**Encyclopedia of Food and Culture.** Cengage Learning Inc., 20 Channel Center St. Boston, MA 02210. Phone: 800-487-8488 or (617)289-7700; Fax: (617)289-7844; Email: investors@cengage.com • URL: http://www.cengage.com • 2003. $657. 00. Three volumes. Contains 600 articles covering various aspects of food and its place in society, from agronomy to zucchini. Includes illustrations and a detailed index. eBook also available, updated in 2004.

**Encyclopedia of Global Brands.** Cengage Learning Inc., 20 Channel Center St. Boston, MA 02210. Phone: 800-487-8488 or (617)289-7700; Fax: (617)289-7844; Email: investors@cengage.com • URL: http://www.cengage.com • 2013. $735. 2 volumes. Contains 270 entries, written in case-study style, that highlight details including how a product originated and was first marketed, how it developed commercially and how it fares today compared with its competitors and its own history. eBook available. Contact for pricing.

**Encyclopedia of Governmental Advisory Organizations.** Cengage Learning Inc., 20 Channel Center St. Boston, MA 02210. Phone: 800-487-8488 or (617)289-7700; Fax: (617)289-7844; Email: investors@cengage.com • URL: http://www.cengage.com • Annual. $1,178 Individuals print. Contains more than 7,300 entries describing activities and personnel. Complete contact information.

**Encyclopedia of Library and Information Science.** CRC Press, c/o Taylor & Francis Group, LLC, 6000 Broken Sound Pkwy., NW Boca Raton, FL 33487-2713. Phone: 800-272-7737; Fax: (800)374-3401; Email: ncarter@taylorandfrancis.com • URL: http://www.crcpress.com • Available in print or as an online subscription.

**Encyclopedia of Major Marketing Strategies.** Cengage Learning Inc., 20 Channel Center St. Boston, MA 02210. Phone: 800-487-8488 or (617)289-7700; Fax: (617)289-7844; Email: investors@cengage.com • URL: http://www.cengage.com • $500 Individuals. Covers 100 major marketing strategies for some of the top global and emerging brands from 2011-2012.

**Encyclopedia of Management (EoM).** Cengage Learning Inc., 20 Channel Center St. Boston, MA 02210. Phone: 800-487-8488 or (617)289-7700; Fax: (617)289-7844; Email: investors@cengage.com • URL: http://www.cengage.com • $434 Individuals. 2012. 7th Edition. Contains 316 essays on business management topics. eBook available. Inquire for pricing.

**Encyclopedia of Microcomputers.** Allen Kent and James G. Williams, editors. Taylor & Francis Online, 270 Madison Ave. New York, NY 10016. Phone: 800-228-1160 or (212)696-9000 or (212)216-7800; Fax: (212)685-4540 or (212)563-2269; Email: support@tandfonline.com • URL: http://www.tandfonline.com/ • 27 volumes. $5,265.00. $195.00 per volume. Dates vary. Contains scholarly articles written by microcomputer experts. Includes bibliographies.

**Encyclopedia of Networked and Virtual Organizations.** Cengage Learning Inc., 20 Channel Center St. Boston, MA 02210. Phone: 800-487-8488 or (617)289-7700; Fax: (617)289-7844; Email: investors@cengage.com • URL: http://www.cengage.com • Documents 249 of the most relevant contributions authored by over 400 of the world's leading experts to the introduction of networked, dynamic, agile, and virtual organizational models; definitions; taxonomies; opportunities; and reference models and architectures.

***Encyclopedia of Population***. Cengage Learning Inc., 20 Channel Center St. Boston, MA 02210. Phone: 800-487-8488 or (617)289-7700; Fax: (617)289-7844; Email: investors@cengage.com • URL: http://www.cengage.com • 2003. $443.00. Two volumes. Published by Macmillan Reference USA. Formerly *Macmillan's International Encyclopedia of Population*. Covers a broad range of topics in demography and neighboring disciplines. Emphasis is on developments in population research during the past 20 years. eBook also available.

***Encyclopedia of Products & Industries - Manufacturing (EPIM)***. Cengage Learning Inc., 20 Channel Center St. Boston, MA 02210. Phone: 800-487-8488 or (617)289-7700; Fax: (617)289-7844; Email: investors@cengage.com • URL: http://www.cengage.com • $978 Individuals. 2007. 2 volumes. Designed to assist college students who need to research products and the relationships between products and their industries. Includes tables, charts, and statistics. eBook available. Inquire for pricing.

***Encyclopedia of Small Business***. Cengage Learning Inc., 20 Channel Center St. Boston, MA 02210. Phone: 800-487-8488 or (617)289-7700; Fax: (617)289-7844; Email: investors@cengage.com • URL: http://www.cengage.com • $763 Individuals. 2010. $696.00. 4th edition. Two volumes. Contains about 600 informative entries on a wide variety of topics affecting small business. Arrangement is alphabetical. eBook also available. Inquire for pricing.

***Encyclopedia of the Great Depression***. Cengage Learning Inc., 20 Channel Center St. Boston, MA 02210. Phone: 800-487-8488 or (617)289-7700; Fax: (617)289-7844; Email: investors@cengage.com • URL: http://www.cengage.com • $465 Individuals. Covers about two decades of U.S. economic history, from the farm crisis of the mid-1920s, through the gradual recovery of the 1930s, to the beginning of World War II. (Macmillan Reference USA imprint). eBook also available.

***Encyclopedia of White-Collar & Corporate Crime***. Cengage Learning Inc., 20 Channel Center St. Boston, MA 02210. Phone: 800-487-8488 or (617)289-7700; Fax: (617)289-7844; Email: investors@cengage.com • URL: http://www.cengage.com • 2 volumes. More than 500 entries. This work gathers history, definitions, examples, investigation, prosecution, assessments, challenges, and projections into one definitive reference work on the topic.

***Energy & Fuels***. American Chemical Society, 1155 16th St. NW Washington, DC 20036. Phone: 800-227-5558 or (202)872-4600; Email: help@acs.org • URL: http://www.acs.org • Bimonthly. $1,537 Institutions; $1,603 Institutions, other countries. An interdisciplinary technical journal covering non-nuclear energy sources: petroleum, gas, synthetic fuels, etc.

***Energy Compass***. Energy Intelligence Group, 5 E 37th St., 5th Fl. New York, NY 10016-2807. Phone: (212)532-1112; Fax: (212)532-4479; Email: customerservice@energyintel.com • URL: http://www.energyintel.com • Description: Focuses on worldwide geopolitical developments and their impact on the oil industry. Also includes marketing and trading information, political risk assessment, and current events and trends. **Remarks:** Available via fax, e-mail, or online.

***Energy Magazine***. Business Communications Co., Inc., 70 New Canaan Ave. Norwalk, CT 06850. Phone: (203)853-4266; Email: info@bccresearch.com • URL: http://www.ien.com • Quarterly. Quarterly. $395.00 per year.

***Energy Prices and Taxes***. International Energy Agency. Organisation for Economic Co-operation and Development Publications and Information Center, 2001 L St. NW, Ste. 650 Washington, DC 20036-4922. Phone: 800-456-6323 or (202)785-6323; Fax: (202)785-0350; Email: washington.contact@oecd.org • URL: http://www.oecd.org • Quarterly. $385 Individuals. Compiled by the International Energy Agency. Provides data on prices and taxation of petroleum products, natural gas, coal, and electricity. Diskette edition, $800.00. (Published in Paris).

***Energy Sources: Recovery, Utilization, and Environmental Effects***. Taylor & Francis Ltd., 2 Park Sq., Milton Park Abingdon OX14 4RN, United Kingdom. Phone: 44 22 70176000 or 44 20 70176000; Fax: 44 22 70176699 or (701)76336; Email: info@e-elgar.co.uk • URL: http://www.taylorandfrancisgroup.com • Monthly. Individuals, $498.00 per year; institutions, $1,325.00 per year.

**Energy Storage Council**. 3963 Flora Pl., 2nd Fl. Saint Louis, MO 63110. Phone: (314)495-4545; Email: info@energystoragecouncil.org • URL: http://www.energystoragecouncil.org • Promotes research, development and deployment of storage technologies within the energy storage industry. Raises awareness of the importance of storage for the future of America's electricity supply and energy security. Develops policies on key legislative and regulatory issues affecting the energy storage industry.

***Energy User News: Energy Technology Buyers Guide***. BNP Media, 2401 W Big Beaver Rd., Ste. 700 Troy, MI 48084. Phone: 800-952-6643 or (248)362-3700 or (847)763-9534; Fax: (248)362-5103 or (248)362-0317; Email: privacy@bnpmedia.com • URL: http://www.bnpmedia.com • Annual. $10.00. List of about 400 manufacturers, manufacturers' representatives, dealers, and distributors of energy management equipment. *Annual Review* and *Forecast* issue.

***Engineered Materials Abstracts***. Cambridge Information Group, 7200 Wisconsin Ave., Ste. 601 Bethesda, MD 20814. Phone: 800-526-9537 or (301)961-6700; Fax: (301)961-6790 or (301)961-6720; Email: info@cambridgeinformationgroup.com • URL: http://www.cambridgeinformationgroup.com • Monthly. $995.00 per year. Provides citations to the technical and engineering literature of plastic, ceramic, and composite materials.

***Engineered Materials Abstracts (online)***. Cambridge Scientific Abstracts L.P., 7200 Wisconsin Ave., Ste. 601 Bethesda, MD 20814. Phone: 800-843-7751 or (301)961-6700 or (301)961-6785; Fax: (301)961-6720 or (301)961-6708; Email: sales@proquest.com • URL: http://www.proquest.co.uk • Provides online citations to the technical and engineering literature of plastic, ceramic, and composite materials. Time period is 1986 to date, with monthly updates. (Formerly produced by ASM International.) Inquire as to online cost and availability.

**Engineered Wood Technology Association**. APA - The Engineered Wood Association, 7011 S 19th St. Tacoma, WA 98466-5333. Phone: (253)620-7237 or (253)565-6600; Fax: (253)565-7265 • URL: http://www.apawood.org/ewrf_level_b.cfm?content=srv_sup_about • Represents manufacturers of construction and industrial panels and related products; associate members. Sponsors research programs on improvement in panel production processes and techniques.

***Engineering and Mining Journal Annual Buyers' Guide***. Primedia Business Magazines and Media, 330 N Wabash Ave., Suite 2300 Chicago, IL 60611. Phone: 800-795-5445 or (312)595-1080 or (312)726-2802; Fax: (312)595-0295 or (312)726-2574; Email: subs@primediabusiness.com • URL: http://www.primediabusiness.com • Annual. Free to qualified subscribers; others, $69.00. List of manufacturers and suppliers of mining equipment; international coverage. Formerly *Engineering and Mining Journal Buying Directory*.

**Engineering Dean's Office**. University of California at Berkeley, 320 McLaughlin Hall Berkeley, CA 94720-1700. Phone: (510)642-5771; Fax: (510)642-9178; Email: sastry@coe.berkeley.edu • URL: http://www.coe.berkeley.edu • Research fields include civil, electrical, industrial, mechanical, and other types of engineering.

***Engineering Design Graphics Journal***. American Society for Engineering Education, 1818 N St. NW, Ste. 600 Washington, DC 20036-2479. Phone: (202)331-3500 or (202)331-3511; Fax: (202)265-8504; Email: board@asee.org • URL: http://www.asee.org • Three times a year. Free to members; Nonmembers, $24.00 per year. Concerned with engineering graphics, computer graphics, geometric modeling, computer-aided drafting, etc.

**Engineering Experiment Station**. Purdue University, 701 W Stadium Ave., Ste. 3000 West Lafayette, IN 47907. Phone: (765)494-5345; Fax: (765)494-9321; Email: dean.of.engineering@purdue.edu • URL: http://www.ecn.purdue.edu • Research fields include chemical, civil, electrical, industrial, mechanical, and other types of engineering.

***Engineering Index Annual***. Elsevier Engineering Information, 360 Park Ave. S New York, NY 10010-1710. Phone: (212)989-5800; Fax: (212)633-3990; Email: sales.inquiry@elsevier.com • URL: http://www.elsevier.com • Annual. $7,720 Individuals for all countries except Europe, JPN and IRN; ¥991,100 Individuals; 7,070 Rl Individuals European countries included. Publication includes: Authors and publishers of engineering literature worldwide. Entries include: Author Biographical data and Company name. Principal content of publication is bibliographic citations and abstracts.

***Engineering Index Monthly: Abstracting and Indexing Services Covering Sources ofthe World's Engineering Literature***. Engineering Information Inc., 1 Castle Pt. Ter. Hoboken, NJ 07030-5996. Phone: 800-221-1044 • URL: http://www.elsevier.com • Monthly. Institutions, $5,279.00 per year. Provides indexing and abstracting of the world's engineering and technical literature.

**Enlisted Association of National Guard of the United States**. 3133 Mt. Vernon Ave. Alexandria, VA 22305-2640. Phone: 800-234-3264 or (703)519-3846; Fax: (703)519-3849; Email: eangus@eangus.org • URL: http://www.eangus.org • Active and retired members of the U.S. National Guard. Conducts educational, legislative and charitable programs.

***ENR: Connecting the Industry Worldwide***. McGraw Hill Financial Inc., 1221 Avenue of the Americas New York, NY 10020-1095. Phone: (212)512-2000; Fax: (212)512-3840 • URL: http://www.mhfi.com • Weekly. $74.00 per year.

***ENR Top 400 Construction Contractors***. McGraw Hill Financial Inc., 1221 Avenue of the Americas New York, NY 10020-1095. Phone: (212)512-2000; Fax: (212)512-3840 • URL: http://www.mhfi.com • Annual. Lists 400 United States contractors receiving largest dollar volume of contracts in preceding calendar year.

***ENR-Top International Design Firms***. McGraw Hill Financial Inc., 1221 Avenue of the Americas New York, NY 10020-1095. Phone: (212)512-2000; Fax: (212)512-3840 • URL: http://www.mhfi.com • Annual. $49.95 Individuals. Lists 200 firms. Includes U.S. firms. Formerly *Engineering News Record - Top International Design Firms*.

***Enterprise Business Modeling, Optimization Techniques, and Flexible Information Systems***. Cengage Learning Inc., 20 Channel Center St. Boston, MA 02210. Phone: 800-487-8488 or (617)289-7700; Fax: (617)289-7844; Email: investors@cengage.com • URL: http://www.cengage.com • 2013. eBook. Provides research on the intersections of business modeling, information systems, and optimization techniques. These various business models and structuring methods are proposed to provide ideas, methods, and points of view for managers, practitioners, entrepreneurs, and researchers on how to improve business processes.

***Enterprise Development and Microfinance Journal***. Practical Action, The Schumacher Centre, Rugby Bourton-on-Dunsmore CV23 9QZ, United Kingdom. Phone: 44 1926 634400; Fax: 44 1926 634401; Email: practicalaction@practicalaction.org.uk • URL: http://www.practicalaction.org • Quarterly. £52 Individuals UK, Europe, print; €78 Individuals print; £52 Other countries print; $104 Other countries print. Journal covering small enterprise development.

***Enterprise: Greater Portland Business Directory***. Tower Publishing Co., 588 Saco Rd. Standish, ME 04084. Phone: 800-969-8693 or (207)642-5400; Fax: (207)642-5463 or 800-264-3870; Email: info@towerpub.com • URL: http://www.towerpub.com • Annual. $47.50. Covers: more than 7,000 companies in the Portland, Maine metropolitan area. Entries include: Company name, address, phone, fax, names and titles of contact and key personnel, number of employees, product or service, year established.

***Enterprise Information Systems for Business Integration in SMEs: Technological, Organizational, and Social Dimensions***. Cengage Learning Inc., 20 Channel Center St. Boston, MA 02210. Phone: 800-487-8488 or (617)289-7700; Fax: (617)289-7844; Email: investors@cengage.com • URL: http://www.cengage.com • 2010. eBook. Covers the main issues, challenges, opportunities, and trends related to the impact of IT on every part of organizational and inter-organizational environments.

**EnterpriseWorks - Senegal**. BP 10251 Dakar, Senegal. Phone: 221 8254523; Email: ewws@sentoo.sn • URL: http://www.angelfire.com/yt2/EnterpriseWorks/english.htm • Works to fight poverty in the developing world through business development programs that allow small agricultural producers and other entrepreneurs to increase productivity and incomes. Pursues sustainable business opportunities. Creates jobs that benefit families, communities and regions.

***Entertainment Design: The Art and Technology of Show Business***. Primedia Business Magazines, 32 W. 18th St. New York, NY 10011-4612. Phone: 800-827-0315 or (212)229-2965; Fax: (212)229-2084 • URL: http://www.primediabusiness.com • Monthly. $34.97 per year. Contains material on performing arts management, staging, scenery, costuming, etc. Supersedes *TCI - Theatre Crafts International*.

***Entertainment Law and Finance***. ALM Media Properties LLC, 120 Broadway, 5th Fl. New York, NY 10271-1100. Phone: (212)457-9400; Fax: (646)417-7705; Email: customercare@alm.com • URL: http://www.alm.com • Monthly. $485 print and online. Covers contracts, royalties, litigation, copyright, taxation, etc., for the music industry, motion pictures, broadcasting, publishing, video, and related media. (A Law Journal Newsletter, formerly published by Leader Publications.).

***Entertainment Sourcebook: An Insider's Guide on Where to Find Everything***. Applause Theatre & Cinema Books, 19 W 21st St., Ste. 201 New York, NY 10010. Phone: 800-637-2852 or (212)575-9265; Fax: (212)575-9270 or (212)721-2856; Email: info@applausepub.com • URL: http://www.applausepub.com • Annual. $45.00. Compiled by the Association of Theatrical Artists and Craftspeople (www.entertainmentsourcebook.com/ATAC.htm). Lists more than 5,000 sources of theatrical and entertainment supplies and services, such as props, costumes, publicity agencies, scenic shops, amusement park equipment, audio/video products, balloons, wigs, make-up, magic supplies, etc.

***Entomological Society of America Annals: Devoted to the Interest of Classical Entomology***. Entomological Society of America, 3 Park Pl., Ste. 307 Annapolis, MD 21401-3722. Phone: (301)731-4535 or (301)731-4541; Fax: (301)731-4538; Email: esa@entsoc.org • URL: http://www.entsoc.org • Bimonthly. $384 Institutions Print or Online only - back issue; $480 Individuals Print and Online; $188 Nonmembers Print or Online only - back issue; $236 Nonmembers Print and Online. Contains manuscripts that integrate different areas of insect biology, and address issues that are likely to be of broad relevance to entomologists.

***Entomology Abstracts***. CSA, 7200 Wisconsin Ave. Bethesda, MD 20814. Phone: 800-843-7751 or (301)961-6700; Fax: (301)961-6720; Email: service@csa.com • URL: http://www.csa.com • Monthly. 11 times a year. $1,570.00 per year. Includes print and online editions.

***Entrepreneur: The Small Business Authority***. Entrepreneur Press, 2445 McCabe Way, Ste. 400 Irvine, CA 92614-6244. Phone: 800-864-6864 or (949)261-2325 or (949)622-7131; Fax: (949)261-7729 or (949)261-0234; Email: press@entrepreneur.com • URL: http://www.entrepreneurpress.com • Monthly. $19.97 per year. Contains advice for small business owners and prospective owners. Includes numerous franchise advertisements.

***Entrepreneurial Business Law Journal***.

***Entrepreneur's Annual Franchise 500 Issue***. Entrepreneur Press,

2445 McCabe Way, Ste. 400 Irvine, CA 92614-6244. Phone: 800-864-6864 or (949)261-2325 or (949)622-7131; Fax: (949)261-7729 or (949)261-0234; Email: press@entrepreneur.com • URL: http://www.entrepreneurpress.com • Annual. Provides a ranking of 500 "top franchise opportunities," based on a combination of financial strength, growth rate, size, stability, number of years in business, litigation history, and other factors. Includes 17 major business categories, further divided into about 140 very specific groups (22 kinds of fast food, for example).

**Entrepreneurs Association of Slovakia**. Cukrova 14 813 39 Bratislava, Slovakia. Phone: 421 2 59324344 or 421 2 59324343; Fax: 421 2 59324350; Email: zps@zps.sk • URL: http://www.zps.sk • Aims to contribute towards the development of modern and developed market economy; to protect entrepreneur status of business rights and free market restrictions, and to prevent political and economic measures leading to decline of equal market business background.

**Entrepreneurs' Organization - Pakistan Chapter**. 121 Ferozepur Rd. Lahore, Pakistan. Phone: 92 42 35058218; Email: tm.admin@eolahore.org • URL: http://eoaccess.eonetwork.org/lahore/Pages/default.aspx • Represents the interests of entrepreneurs who wish to learn and grow from each other. Provides opportunities for members to connect through forums and one-on-one interactions with fellow entrepreneurs. Provides venues which will allow members to meet and learn from influential members of the community.

**Entrepreneurs' Organization**. 500 Montgomery St., Ste. 700 Alexandria, VA 22314. Phone: (703)519-6700; Fax: (703)519-1864; Email: info@eonetwork.org • URL: http://www.eonetwork.org • Entrepreneurs under the age of 50 who have either founded, co-founded, are a controlling shareholder of, or own a firm with annual gross revenues exceeding $1,000,000 (membership is by invitation only). Engages leading entrepreneurs to learn and grow. Serves as a focal point for networking and development of members through small group learning sessions, regular local chapter social and learning events, and global conference-based education programs.

***Entrepreneur's Showcase: Market Research for Small Businesses and the Woman Entrepreneur's Guide to Financing a Business***. Cengage Learning Inc., 20 Channel Center St. Boston, MA 02210. Phone: 800-487-8488 or (617)289-7700; Fax: (617)289-7844; Email: investors@cengage.com • URL: http://www.cengage.com • 2006. eBook. Published by Know-!Books Press. Provides information on multiple aspects of entrepreneurship, focusing on market research for small business as well as on more gender-specific topics involved in starting a business.

***The Entrepreneur's Sourcebook***. Todd Publications, PO Box 500 Millwood, NY 10546. Phone: 866-896-0916 or (914)373-4750; Fax: (914)373-4750; Email: toddpub@aol.com • URL: http://www.toddpublications.com • $25. Covers: 7,000 organizations, publications, companies, and consultants that provide advice to entrepreneurs and small business owners. Database includes: List of more than 500 books, videos, CDs, and audiocassettes. Entries include: Name, address, phone, fax.

***Entrepreneurship and Innovations in E-Business: An Integrative Perspective***. Cengage Learning Inc., 20 Channel Center St. Boston, MA 02210. Phone: 800-487-8488 or (617)289-7700; Fax: (617)289-7844; Email: investors@cengage.com • URL: http://www.cengage.com • 2006. eBook. Published by Information Science Reference. Develops and explores theoretical constructs and the working concepts of e-entrepreneurship and e-innovation through comprehensive and collective studies conducted by a number of researchers and practitioners with e-business and management expertise.

**The Entrepreneurship Institute**. 3700 Corporate Dr., Ste. 145 Columbus, OH 43231. Phone: (614)895-1153 • URL: http://www.tei.net • Provides encouragement and assistance to entrepreneurs who operate companies with revenue in excess of $1 million. Unites financial, legal, and community resources to help foster the success of companies. Promotes sharing of information and interaction between members. Operates President's forums and projects which are designed to improve communication between businesses, develop one-to-one business relationships between small and mid-size businesses and local resources, provide networking, and stimulate the growth of existing companies.

***Entrepreneurship: Theory and Practice***. Blackwell Publishing Inc., 350 Main St. Malden, MA 02148. Phone: 800-216-2522 or (781)388-8200; Fax: (781)388-8210; Email: journaladsusa@bos.blackwellpublishing.com • URL: http://www.blackwellpublishing.com • Bimonthly. $590 Institutions Online or Print only; $680 Institutions Print and Online; $139 Individuals Print and Online; $111 Members Print and Online.

***Environment Abstracts Annual: A Guide to the Key Environmental Literature of the Year***. University Publications of America, 4501 Forbes Blvd., Ste. 200 Lanham, MD 20706. Phone: 800-462-6420 or (301)459-3366; Fax: (301)429-5748; Email: pqsales@proquest.com • URL: https://rowman.com/Imprint/UPA • Annual. $495.00. A yearly cumulation of *Environment Abstracts*.

***Environment Abstracts on CD-ROM***. University Publications of America, 4501 Forbes Blvd., Ste. 200 Lanham, MD 20706. Phone: 800-462-6420 or (301)459-3366; Fax: (301)429-5748; Email: pqsales@proquest.com • URL: https://rowman.com/Imprint/UPA • Quarterly. $1,295.00 per year. Contains the following CD-ROM databases: *Environment Abstracts, Energy Abstracts*, and *Acid Rain Abstracts*. Length of coverage varies.

***Environment Abstracts***. University Publications of America, 4501 Forbes Blvd., Ste. 200 Lanham, MD 20706. Phone: 800-462-6420 or (301)459-3366; Fax: (301)429-5748; Email: pqsales@proquest.com • URL: https://rowman.com/Imprint/UPA • Monthly. Price varies. Provides multidisciplinary coverage of the world's environmental literature. Incorporates *Acid Rain Abstracts*.

***Environment Advisor***. J.J. Keller and Associates Inc., 3003 W Breezewood Ln. Neehah, WI 54956-9611. Phone: (877)564-2333; Fax: (800)727-7516 • URL: http://www.jjkeller.com • Monthly. $90.00 per year. Newsletter. Formerly *Hazardous Substances Advisor*.

***Environment: Where Science and Policy Meet***. Scientists' Institute for Public Information. Taylor & Francis Group Heldref Publications, 325 Chestnut St., Ste. 800 Philadelphia, PA 19106. Phone: 800-354-1420 or (215)625-8900; Email: customer.service@taylorandfrancis.com • URL: http://www.heldref.org • 10 times a year. Individuals, $48.00 per year; institutions, $98.00 per year.

***Environmental Business Journal***. Environmental Business International Inc., 4452 Park Blvd., Ste. 306 San Diego, CA 92116. Phone: (619)295-7685; Fax: (619)295-5743; Email: ebi@ebiusa.com • URL: http://www.ebiusa.com • Contains the complete text of *Environmental Business Journal*, a monthly newsletter covering business-related information on the environmental industry.

***Environmental Business Journal: Strategic Information for a Changing Industry***. Environmental Business International Inc., 4452 Park Blvd., Ste. 306 San Diego, CA 92116. Phone: (619)295-7685; Fax: (619)295-5743; Email: ebi@ebiusa.com • URL: http://www.ebiusa.com • Monthly. $250 Single issue; $995 Individuals; $1,250 Institutions up to 5 readers - online; $1,500 Institutions up to 10 readers - online. Includes both industrial and financial information relating to individual companies and to the environmental industry in general. Covers air pollution, wat es, U. S. Department of Health and Human Services. Provides conference, workshop, and symposium proceedings, as well as extensive reviews of environmental prospects.

***Environmental Encyclopedia***. Cengage Learning Inc., 20 Channel Center St. Boston, MA 02210. Phone: 800-487-8488 or (617)289-7700; Fax: (617)289-7844; Email: investors@cengage.com • URL: http://www.cengage.com • $327 Individuals. 2011. $298.00. 4th edition. Provides over 1,300 articles on all aspects of the environment. Written in non-technical style. eBook also available. Inquire for pricing.

**Environmental Engineering Center**. Michigan Technological University, 1400 Townsend Dr. Houghton, MI 49931. Phone: (906)487-2025; Fax: (906)487-3167; Email: biology@mtu.edu • URL: http://www.bio.mtu.edu/research • Applies biotechnological research to waste management and resource recovery.

**Environmental Entrepreneurs**. Natural Resources Defense Council, 40 W 20th St. New York, NY 10011. Phone: (212)727-2700 or (212)727-4437; Fax: (212)727-1773; Email: yli@nrdc.org • URL: http://www.e2.org • Represents business people who believe in protecting the environment while building economic prosperity. Serves as a champion on the economic side of good environmental policy by taking an economically sound approach to environmental issues. Focuses on environmental policies that drive economic growth in a healthy direction.

***Environmental Epidemiology and Toxicology***. Macmillan Publishers Ltd. Nature Publishing Group, 75 Varick St., 9th Fl. New York, NY 10013-1917. Phone: 888-331-6288 or (212)726-9200; Fax: (212)696-9006; Email: institutions@natureny.com • URL: http://www.nature.com • Quarterly. Individuals, $365.00 per year; institutions, $430.00 per year. *Formerly Environmental Epidemiology and Toxicology*.

***Environmental Guide to the Internet***. Government Institutes, 4501 Forbes Bvld., Ste. 200 Lanham, MD 20706. Phone: 800-462-6420 or (301)459-3366; Fax: (301)429-5748; Email: orders@rowman.com • URL: http://rowman.com • $83 Individuals Paperback; £51.95 Individuals Paperback. Covers: 1,200 resources covering the environment on the Internet, including organizations, products, and resources, including discussion groups, electronic journals, newsgroups, and discussion groups. Entries include: Name, online address, description, e-mail address.

**Environmental Industries Commission**. Alliance House, 12 Caxton St. London SW1H 0QL, United Kingdom. Phone: 44 207 2224148 or 44 207 6549942; Email: info@eic-uk.co.uk • URL: http://www.eic-uk.co.uk • Provides environmental technology equipment and services suppliers with a strong and effective voice to influence the debate on the future of the industry among policy makers in Westminster, Whitehall and Brussels. Promotes constructive cooperation between the regulated, the regulators and the UK's environmental technology suppliers.

***Environmental Law Reporter (ELR)***. Environmental Law Institute, 2000 L St. NW, Ste. 620 Washington, DC 20036. Phone: (202)939-3800; Fax: (202)939-3868; Email: cruden@eli.org • URL: http://www.eli.org • Monthly. $1,995 Individuals /year. Provides full text online of *Environmental Law Reporter*, covering administrative materials, news, pending legislation, statutes, bibliography, etc. Time periods vary. Inquire as to online cost and availability.

***Environmental Management Information Systems Report***. Donley Technology, 220 Garfield Ave. Colonial Beach, VA 22443-2316. Phone: (804)224-9427; Fax: (804)224-7958 • URL: http://www.donleytech.com • $389 Individuals single; $699 Individuals multiple; $999 Individuals company-wide license. Covers: 26 software systems that manage environmental data, including inventory and waste tracking, air pollution tracking, report and label generation, mapping, and help with emergency response. Entries include: Company name, address, phone, hardware and software requirements, description of system, cost.

***Environmental Regulation: State Capitals***. Wakeman/Walworth Inc., PO Box 7376 Alexandria, VA 22307-7376. Phone: 800-876-2545 or (703)768-9600; Fax: (703)768-9690; Email: newsletters@statecapitals.com • URL: http://statecapitals.com/ • 50 times a year. $245.00 per year; print and online editions, $350.00 per year. Newsletter. Formerly *From the State Capitals: Environmental Regulation*.

***Environmental Toxicology: An International Journal***. John Wiley and Sons, Inc., Journals Div., 111 River St. Hoboken, NJ 07030. Phone: 800-526-5368 or (201)748-6000; Fax: (201)748-6088; Email: consumers@wiley.com • URL: http://www.wiley.com • Publishes in the areas of toxicity and toxicology of environmental pollutants in air, dust, sediment, soil and water, and natural toxins in the environment.

***EPRI Journal***. Electric Power Research Institute, 3420 Hillview Ave. Palo Alto, CA 94304. Phone: 800-313-3774 or (650)855-2121 or (650)855-2000; Fax: (650)846-7306 or (650)855-8588; Email: askepri@epri.com • URL: http://www.epri.com • Bimonthly. Free to members; non-members, $29.00 per year.

***The Equal Employer***. Y. S. Publications, Inc., P.O. Box 2172 Silver Springs, MD 20902-2172. Phone: (301)649-1231 • Biweekly. $245.00 per year. Newsletter on fair employment practices.

***Equatorial Guinea Business Law Handbook***. International Business Publications, USA, PO Box 15343 Washington, DC 20003. Phone: (202)546-2103; Fax: (202)546-3275; Email: ibpusa@comcast.net • URL: http://ibpus.com • $99.95 Individuals hardcopy, e-book, CD-ROM. Covers: Basic information on business, laws, export-import, business climate, regulations, and contacts.

***Equipment Leasing and Finance***. Equipment Leasing and Finance Association, 1825 K St. NW, Ste. 900 Washington, DC 20006. Phone: (202)238-3400; Fax: (202)238-3401 • URL: http://www.elfaonline.org • 10 times a year. $100.00 per year. Edited for equipment leasing companies. Covers management, funding, marketing, etc.

***Equipment Leasing Newsletter***. ALM Media Properties LLC, 120 Broadway, 5th Fl. New York, NY 10271-1100. Phone: (212)457-9400; Fax: (646)417-7705; Email: customercare@alm.com • URL: http://www.alm.com • Monthly. $549 per year. Covers a wide range of legal topics relating to the leasing of business and industrial equipment, including taxation, insurance, dealing with banks, lease securitization, and letter of credit issues. (A Law Journal Newsletter, formerly published by Leader Publications).

***Equipment Today***. Cygnus Business Media Inc., 1233 Janesville Ave. Fort Atkinson, WI 53538. Phone: 800-547-7377; Email: info@cygnus.com • URL: http://www.cygnus.com • Monthly. $65 Individuals. Includes annual *Product* issue.

***Equities: Investment News of Promising Public Companies***. Equities Magazine LLC, PO Box 130 H Scarsdale, NY 10583. Phone: (914)726-6702; Fax: (914)723-0176; Email: equitymag@aol.com • URL: http://www.equitiesmagazine.com • Bimonthly. $21.00 per year. Formerly *OTC Review*.

**Erasmus University of Rotterdam - Erasmus Institute for Philosophy and Economics**. EIPE Office, Rm. H5-23, Faculty of Philosophy 3000 DR Rotterdam, Netherlands. Phone: 31 10 4088967; Fax: 31 10 4089030; Email: vromen@fwb.eur.nl • URL: http://www.eur.nl/fw/english/eipe • Philosophy and methodology of economics.

***Ergonomics: An International Journal of Research and Practice in Human Factors and Ergonomics***. Taylor & Francis Ltd., 2 Park Sq., Milton Park Abingdon OX14 4RN, United Kingdom. Phone: 44 22 70176000 or 44 20 70176000; Fax: 44 22 70176699 or (701)76336; Email: info@e-elgar.co.uk • URL: http://www.taylorandfrancisgroup.com • Monthly. Research journal for human factors and ergonomics industry.

***ERIC SilverPlatter***. U.S. Department of Education Institute of Education Sciences Education Resources Information Center, c/o Computer Sciences Corp., 655 15th St. NW, Ste. 500 Washington, DC 20005. Phone: 800-LET-ERIC or (781)769-2599; Fax: (781)769-8763 • URL: http://www.eric.ed.gov • Opinion papers, evaluations, speeches.

***ERIC***. U.S. Department of Education Institute of Education Sciences Educational Resources Information Center, 555 New Jersey Ave. NW Washington, DC 20208. Phone: 800-538-3742; Email: ocio@ed.gov • URL: http://eric.ed.gov • Funded by the U.S. Department of Education, Institute of Education Sciences (formerly Office of Educational Research and Improvement). Provides access to more than one million online records covering education-related journal and report literature, 1966 to date. Updating is monthly. Inquire as to online cost and availability.

***ERISA Top 25,000 Companies: The Red Book of Pension Funds, National Edition***. Dun & Bradstreet Inc., 103 JFK Pkwy. Short Hills, NJ 07078. Phone: 800-526-0651 or (973)921-5500 or (973)921-5000; Fax: (866)560-7035 or (512)794-7670; Email: info@dnb.com • URL: http://www.dnb.com • Annual. Covers: 25,000 companies with the largest combined sum of the assets in their pension plans. Entries include: Company name, address, phone, number of employees, total net plan assets, number and type of plans, names and titles of key personnel.

***Eritrea Business Law Handbook***. International Business Publications, USA, PO Box 15343 Washington, DC 20003. Phone: (202)546-2103; Fax: (202)546-3275; Email: ibpusa@comcast.net • URL: http://ibpus.com • $99.95 Individuals hardcopy, E-book and CD-ROM. Covers: Basic business laws and legislations, export-import regulations, business climate and contacts.

***Eritrea Investment and Business Guide***. International Business Publications, USA, PO Box 15343 Washington, DC 20003. Phone: (202)546-2103; Fax: (202)546-3275; Email: ibpusa@comcast.net • URL: http://ibpus.com • $99.95 Individuals hardcopy, e-book, CD-ROM. Covers: Strategic business information, export-import activity, regulations and industrial development, banking, government, and opportunities. Entries include: Guides for conducting investment and business contacts.

***ESOP Report***. ESOP Association, 1726 M St. NW, Ste. 501 Washington, DC 20036. Phone: 866-366-3832 or (202)293-2971; Fax: (202)293-7568; Email: esop@esopassociation.org • URL: http://www.esopassociation.org • Monthly. Contains latest regulatory and case law updates, Capitol Hill briefings, technical and managerial advice from ESOP professionals, tips on winning ESOP companies and employee owners plus Association news to keep you in the loop.

***Espicom Business Intelligence Country Healthcare (MDST)***. ProQuest LLC, 2250 Perimeter Park Dr., Ste. 300 Morrisville, NC 27560. Phone: 800-334-2564 or (919)804-6400; Fax: (919)804-6410; Email: contact@dialog.com • URL: http://www.dialog.com • An electronic database with reports profiling health care systems in various countries. The database provides data on medical equipment, health care, and hospital services in 77 countries worldwide.

***Espresso and Espresso Bars Directory***. InfoGroup Inc., 5711 S 86th Cir. Omaha, NE 68127-4146. Phone: (402)593-4500 • URL: http://www.infogroup.com • Annual. Number of listings: 1,696. Entries include: Name, address, phone, size of advertisement, name of owner or manager, number of employees, year first in "Yellow Pages." Compiled from telephone company "Yellow Pages," nationwide.

***Essential Business Guide***. National Federation of Meat and Food Traders, 1 Belgrove Tunbridge Wells TN1 1YW, United Kingdom. Phone: 44 1892 541412; Fax: 44 1892 535462; Email: info@nfmft.co.uk • URL: http://www.nfmft.co.uk • £20 /copy for nonmembers; included in membership dues.

***Essential Managers: Ethical Business***. Cengage Learning Inc., 20 Channel Center St. Boston, MA 02210. Phone: 800-487-8488 or (617)289-7700; Fax: (617)289-7844; Email: investors@cengage.com • URL: http://www.cengage.com • 2010. eBook. Published by Dorling Kindersley US. Goal of this book is to teach you how to improve your bottom line and employee morale while listening to your conscience.

***Essentials of Federal Income Taxation for Individuals and Business***. Wolters Kluwer Law & Business CCH, 2700 Lake Cook Rd. Riverwoods, IL 60015. Phone: 888-224-7377 or (847)267-7000; Email: cust_serv@cch.com • URL: http://www.cchgroup.com • Annual. $165. Covers basic tax planning and tax reduction strategies as affected by tax law changes and IRS interpretations. Includes sample filled-in forms.

***Essex Business Directory***. Burrows Publishing Ltd., 106 Stafford Rd. Wallington SM6 9AY, United Kingdom. Phone: 44 20 87733000; Email: generalservices@burrows.co.uk • URL: http://www.burrows.co.uk • Covers: Over 10,000 businesses in Essex. Entries include: Name, address, phone, fax, e-mail, website, key organization contact, year of establishment, size of company, turnover, and a brief description of company activity.

***ESSOR***. Union Francaise d'Annuaires Professionnels, 13 Ave. Roger-Hennequin, BP 36 Quaint-Quentin-en-Yvelines F-78192 Trappes, France. Phone: 1 30138200; Fax: 1 30138211; Email: info@enor-contacts.tm.fr • Annual. Covers: more than 200,000 French companies involved in industry and services. Entries include: Company name, address, phone, fax, telex, names and titles of key personnel, line of business, number of employees, registered capital, sales, product descriptions, legal and administrative information.

***Estate Planner's Alert***. Thomson RIA, 195 Broadway New York, NY 10007-3100. Phone: 800-431-9025 or (212)367-6300 or (212)807-2298; Fax: (212)367-6305 or (212)337-4207; Email: ttacommunications@riag.com • URL: http://www.ria.thomson.com • Monthly. $290 Individuals Print; $350 Individuals Online. Covers the tax aspects of personal finance, including home ownership, investments, insurance, retirement planning, and charitable giving. Formerly *Estate and Financial Planners Alert*.

***Estate Planning***. ALM Media Properties LLC, 120 Broadway, 5th Fl. New York, NY 10271-1100. Phone: (212)457-9400; Fax: (646)417-7705; Email: customercare@alm.com • URL: http://www.alm.com • $670 two volumes. Covers all legal aspects of estate planning, including wills, trusts, taxation, gifts, charitable contributions, family business considerations, and insurance. Includes forms and checklists. (Law Journal Press).

***Estate Planning Journal***. Thomson RIA, 195 Broadway New York, NY 10007-3100. Phone: 800-431-9025 or (212)367-6300 or (212)807-2298; Fax: (212)367-6305 or (212)337-4207; Email: ttacommunications@riag.com • URL: http://www.ria.thomson.com • Monthly. $525 Individuals Print; $575 Individuals Online; $755 Individuals Print and Online. Contains a variety of practical ideas and analysis of recent developments in each issue.

***Estonia Business Law Handbook***. International Business Publications, USA, PO Box 15343 Washington, DC 20003. Phone: (202)546-2103; Fax: (202)546-3275; Email: ibpusa@comcast.net • URL: http://ibpus.com • $99.95 Individuals hardcopy, e-book, CD-ROM. Covers: Basic information on business, laws, export-import, investment, tax, regulations, and contacts.

***Estonia Government and Business Contacts Handbook***. International Business Publications, USA, PO Box 15343 Washington, DC 20003. Phone: (202)546-2103; Fax: (202)546-3275; Email: ibpusa@comcast.net • URL: http://ibpus.com • $99.95 Individuals hardcopy, E-book and CD-ROM. Covers: Strategic government and business information, export-import activity in the country, investment, business contacts and regulations.

***Estonia Industrial and Business Directory***. International Business Publications, USA, PO Box 15343 Washington, DC 20003. Phone: (202)546-2103; Fax: (202)546-3275; Email: ibpusa@comcast.net • URL: http://ibpus.com • Annual. $99.95 Individuals paperback, e-book, CD-ROM. Covers: Strategic industrial, investment and business contacts for conducting export-import and investment activity in the country. Contains strategic practical economic and business information.

**Estonian Business Association**. Sadama 5/7 EE-10111 Tallinn, Estonia. Email: esea@esea.ee • URL: http://www.esea.ee • Fosters active business community in the country. Develops cooperation with foreign business associations. Keeps its members updated through local and international seminars and workshops. Meets with state authorities to advance the organization's interests.

**Eta Phi Beta**. 19983 Livernois Ave. Detroit, MI 48221-1299. Phone: (313)862-0600; Fax: (313)862-6245; Email: contact@etaphibetasorority.com • URL: http://www.etaphibetasorority.com • Professional sorority - business. Conducts national projects concerning retarded citizens and retarded children. Conducts leadership and career programs and seminars; sponsors competitions. Operates speakers' bureau; provides children's services; maintains charitable program.

***ETF Connect***. Nuveen Investments, Phone: 800-257-8787 • URL: http://www.etfconnect.com • Free Web site makes available extensive, searchable information on individual closed-end investment funds, preferred share funds, and exchange-traded index funds. Information on a particular fund is available by name or as part of a classification (high yield, investment grade, municipal, emerging markets, global equity, etc.). Fund charts are available for various time periods, as is data concerning premiums or discounts, dividends, annualized total return, credit quality, "Top 10 Holdings," and so forth.

***Ethical Issues in E-Business: Models and Frameworks***. Cengage Learning Inc., 20 Channel Center St. Boston, MA 02210. Phone: 800-487-8488 or (617)289-7700; Fax: (617)289-7844; Email: investors@cengage.com • URL: http://www.cengage.com • 2012. eBook. Published by IGI Global. Offers a diverse and global perspective concerning the ethical consequences of e-business transactions, e-commerce applications, and technological advancements in secure online use.

**Ethics and Compliance Officer Association**. 411 Waverley Oaks Rd., Ste. 324 Waltham, MA 02452-8420. Phone: (781)647-9333; Fax: (781)647-9399; Email: membership@theecoa.org • URL: http://www.theecoa.org • Managers of ethics, compliance, and business conduct programs. Offers educational business ethics and compliance programs; conducts national research; and provides free job-listing service.

**Ethics Resource Center**. 2345 Crystal Dr., Ste. 201 Arlington, VA 22202-4807. Phone: 800-777-1285 or (703)647-2185; Fax: (703)647-2180; Email: ethics@ethics.org • URL: http://www.ethics.org • Seeks to serve as a catalyst to improve the ethical practices of individuals and organizations from the classroom to the boardroom. Fulfills its mission through three distinct areas of expertise: as a leader in the fields of organizational/business ethics consulting; as a provider and facilitator of character education programs; and as an ethics information clearinghouse.

***Ethiopia Business Directory***. Business Guide, PO Box 27669 Dubai, United Arab Emirates. Phone: 971 4 2651719; Fax: 971 4 2692151; Email: sales@africa-business.com • URL: http://www.africa-business.com • $150 Individuals Soft copy. Covers: 9,000 business listings including wholesalers, importers, retailers, business houses, and agents in Ethiopia.

***The EU Institutions' Register***. Routledge Reference, 2 Park Sq. Milton Park, Abingdon Oxford OX14 4RN, United Kingdom. Phone: 44 20 70176000; Fax: 44 20 70176699; Email: book.orders@tandf.co.uk • URL: http://www.routledge.com/ • £305 Individuals hardback. Covers: Over 5,900 key personnel in each of the major institutions, including: European Commission, European Parliament, Economic and Social Committee, Council of the European Union, Court of Justice, European Investment Bank, Court of Auditors, Committee of Regions and EU Agencies. Entries include: Contact information.

***Euroguide Yearbook of the Institutions of the European Union***. Bernan Associates, 4611 Assembly Dr., Ste. F Lanham, MD 20706-4843. Phone: 800-416-4385 or (301)459-2255 or (301)459-7666; Fax: (301)459-0056 or (800)865-3450; Email: query@bernan.com • URL: http://www.bernan.com • Annual. $440. Published by Editions Delta. Information on public and private institutions in the European Union contributing to European integration.

***The Euromoney Syndicated Lending Handbook***. Euromoney Institutional Investor P.L.C., 11 N Hill Colchester CO1 1DZ, United Kingdom. Phone: 44 1206 579591; Fax: 44 1206 560121; Email: yearbooks@euromoneyplc.com • URL: http://www.euromoney-yearbooks.com • Annual. £115 Individuals; $195 Individuals; €170 Individuals. Covers: Contact details for 307 relevant personnel in banks, law firms, rating agencies, and associations involved in syndicated lending worldwide. Entries include: Company name, address, phone, fax, e-mail address, Web site, telex number, and names and titles of key personnel.

***Euromoney: The Monthly Journal of International Money and Capital Markets***. American Educational Systems, PO Box 236 New York, NY 10024-0246. Phone: 800-431-1579; Email: aesbooks@aol.com • Monthly. $490.00 per year. Includes print and online editions. Supplement available *Guide to World Equity Markets*.

***Europa—Key European Enterprises***. AP Information Services Ltd., c/o Wilmington Publishing & Information Ltd., 6-14 Underworld St. London N1 7JQ, United Kingdom. Phone: 44 20 75498708; Fax: 44 20 74908238; Email: info@apinfo.co.uk • URL: http://www.apinfo.co.uk • $600 Individuals. Covers: Over 50,000 leading European companies. Entries include: Statistical profiles and geographical information.

***Europa 2000: The American Business Report on Europe***. Wolfe Publishing, Inc., South Nashua Station Nashua, NH 03060-9883. Phone: 800-882-3876 or (603)888-0338; Fax: (603)888-5816 • Monthly. $119.00 per year. Newsletter on consumer and industrial marketing in a unified European Economic Community. Includes classified business opportunity advertisements and a listing by country of forthcoming major trade shows in Europe.

***The Europa World of Learning***. Routledge, 711 3rd Ave., 8th Fl. New York, NY 10017. Phone: 800-634-7064 or (212)216-7800; Fax: (212)564-7854 or (212)563-2269; Email: book.orders@tandf.co.uk • URL: http://www.routledge.com • Annual. $1,500 Individuals hardback. Covers about 33,000 colleges, libraries, museums, learned societies, academies, and research institutions throughout the world. Edited by Europa Publications.

***Europe and Eurasia Business Committee Dispatch***. Bulgarian-U.S. Business Council, Bulgarian-American Chamber of Commerce, 1427 N Wilcox Ave. Hollywood, CA 90028-8123. Phone: (323)962-2414; Fax: (323)962-2010 • URL: http://www.bcci.bg • Monthly. Provides current information on regulations, legislation and specific industries for Central/Eastern Europe, New Independent States, Turkey and Iran.

***Europe and Eurasia Business Committee Dispatch***. Hungarian-U.S. Business Council, Chamber of Commerce of the US, 1615 H St. NW Washington, DC 20062-2000. Phone: 800-638-6582 or (202)659-6000; Fax: (202)463-3173; Email: mbrsvcs@uschamber.com • URL: http://www.uschamber.org • Weekly. included in membership dues; $350 /year for nonmembers. Provides information on regulations, legislation and specific industries for Central/Eastern Europe, New Independent States, Turkey and Iran.

***Europe Business Review***. First Charlton Communications Proprietary Ltd., Level 1, 56 Berry St., 56 Berry St. North Sydney, NSW 2060, Australia. Phone: 61 2 94550272; Email: peter@charlton.com.au • URL: http://www.charlton.com.au • Quarterly. General business publication.

***European Access***. European Commission-United Kingdom Offices. Chadwyck-Healey Inc., 300 N Zeeb Rd. Ann Arbor, MI 48103-1553. Phone: 800-521-0600 or (734)761-4700; Email: info@proquest.com • URL: http://www.chadwyck.com • Bimonthly. $195.00 per year. Published in England. A journal providing general coverage of developments and trends within the European Community.

**European Aluminum Foil Association**. Am Bonneshof 5 40474 Dusseldorf, Germany. Phone: 49 211 4796150; Fax: 49 211 4796408; Email: enquiries@alufoil.org • URL: http://www.alufoil.org • Represents the European aluminum foil industry.

***The European Association for Business Research***. European Association for Business Research, Planning, and Development in the Chemical Industry, Ave. van Nieuwenhuvse 6 B-1435 Mont-Saint-Guibert, Belgium. Phone: 32 10 650975; Fax: 32

10 659706; Email: info@ecmsa.org • Annual. Includes memebers of the European Association for Business Research.

**European Association for Personnel Management.** c/o Chartered Institute of Personnel and Development, 151 The Broadway, Wimbledon London SW19 1JQ, United Kingdom. Phone: 44 20 86126200; Fax: 44 20 86126201 • URL: http://www.eapm.org • Represents national personnel management associations. Seeks to maintain professional standards of personnel management and act as representative for personnel management associations in Europe. Disseminates information.

**European Association of Consultants to and about Not-For-Profit Organisations.** Sarphatistraat 370 B22 NL-1018 GW Amsterdam, Netherlands. Phone: 49 30 4053 6845; Fax: 49 30 4053 6846; Email: info@euconsult.org • URL: http://www.euconsult.org • Provides international forum for consultants to the not-for-profit sector. Encourages and stimulates ethical and professional behavior and collaboration. Develops the technical and business skills of members.

**European Association of Craft, Small and Medium-Sized Enterprises.** Rue Jacques de Lalaingstraat 4 B-1040 Brussels, Belgium. Phone: 32 2 230 75 99; Fax: 32 2 2 230 78 61; Email: info@ueapme.com • URL: http://www.ueapme.com • Represents the interests, at the European level, of crafts, trades and SMEs in the European Union and countries applying for accession to the European Union.

***European Business Air News.*** Stansted News Ltd., 134 S St. Bishop's Stortford CM23 3BQ, United Kingdom. Phone: 44 127 9714502 • URL: http://www.stanstednews.com • Professional publication for business aircraft owners and operators in Europe.

**European Business and Innovation Centre Network.** Ave. de Tervueren 168 B-1150 Brussels, Belgium. Phone: 32 2 772 89 00; Fax: 32 2 772 9574; Email: info@ebn.eu • URL: http://www.ebn.be • Promotes business innovation and the entrepreneurial spirit in Europe.

**European Business Angel Network.** Rue de la Science 14B B-1040 Brussels, Belgium. Phone: 32 2 626 20 60; Fax: 32 2 626 20 69; Email: info@eban.org • URL: http://www.eban.org • Encourages exchange of experience among business angels networks. Promotes recognition of business angels networks. Works to create and develop a positive environment for business angels' activities.

***European Business Association—Membership Directory.*** European Business Association, 1 A Andriyvsky Uzviz 04070 Kiev, Ukraine. Phone: 380 44 4960601; Fax: 380 44 4960602; Email: office@eba.com.ua • URL: http://www.eba.com.ua • Annual. Features profiles of member businesses. Entries include: Company contact information.

**European Business Ethics Network.** c/o Mario Silar, Secretary, C/Elizmendi 31, Bajo B, Sarriguren 31621 Navarra, Spain. Email: secretariat@eben-net.org • URL: http://www.eben-net.org • Supports research centers in Europe researching business ethics issues.

**European Business History Association.** Gessellschaft fur Unternehmensgeschichte e.V., Sophienstr. 44 D-60487 Frankfurt am Main, Germany. Phone: 49 69 97203314; Fax: 49 69 97203357 • URL: http://www.ebha.org • Promotes research on all aspects of European business and management history.

***European Business Information Sourcebook.*** Headland Press, One Henry Smith's Ter. Headland TS24 0PD, United Kingdom. Phone: 1429231902; Fax: 1429861403 • Annual. $139. Covers: Sources of European business information, including databanks, online services, market research firms, sources of official statistics, business research services, libraries, directories, magazines, and newspapers. Entries include: Name, address, phone, fax.

***European Business Journal.*** Whurr Publisher Ltd., 19B Compton Ter. London NI 2UN, United Kingdom. Phone: 44 20 7359 5979; Fax: 44 20 7226 5290; Email: info@whurr.co.uk • URL: http://www.whurr.co.uk/ • Quarterly. $195 Individuals; €310 Individuals; $350 Individuals. International business publication.

***European Business Register (EBR).*** Patent- och Registreringsverket PRV InterPat, PO Box 5055 SE-102 42 Stockholm, Sweden. Phone: 46 8 782 25 00 or 46 8 782 2500; Fax: 46 8 666 02 86 or 46 8 666 0286; Email: prv.patent@prv.se • URL: http://www.prv.se • Provides online access to official company information from several European countries. The database contains company directory details, board of directors listings, company profiles, and other information.

***European Business Top 1000.*** European Business Press Group N.V., • Annual. $398. Covers: About 1,500 companies in 19 European countries ranked according to financial success; approximately 4,000 company executives. Database includes: Private corporations, government and union controlled enterprises, non-European multinational companies consolidated at the European level, mergers, acquisitions. Entries include: Company name, address, phone, fax, names and titles of key personnel, gross and net profit, number of employees, depreciation, equity, cash flow, affiliations.

**European Confederation of Junior Enterprises.** Rue Potagere 119 B-1210 Brussels, Belgium. Phone: 32 2 4201752; Email: mail@jadenet.org • URL: http://www.jadenet.org • Represents young entrepreneurs in Europe; provides training and assistance to set up new organizations, including legal and contact information.

***European Cooler Company Directory.*** Zenith International Ltd., 7 Kingsmead Sq. Bath BA1 2AB, United Kingdom. Phone: 44 1225 327900 or 1225 327 900; Fax: 44 1225 327901 or 1225 327 901; Email: info@zenithinternational.com • URL: http://www.zenithinternational.com • $823 Individuals hard copy; $1,306 Individuals PDF. Covers: active cooler distributors in the markets of West and East Europe. Entries include: company name, address, telephone number, fax number, website, email, company ownership, number of employees, subsidiaries, company activities, and names and job titles of senior management.

***European Development Directory.*** Euromonitor International Business Reference Div., 224 S Michigan Ave., Ste. 1500 Chicago, IL 60604. Phone: (312)922-1115; Fax: (312)922-1157; Email: insight@euromonitorintl.com • URL: http://www.euromonitor.com • Irregular. $335. Covers: over 700 government agencies, banks, and other organizations in Europe that administer business development grants and related financial aid. Database includes: List of available grants and funding opportunities, with contact information. Entries include: Organization or agency name, address, phone, fax, names and titles of key personnel, description.

***European Directory of Business Information Libraries.*** Euromonitor International Business Reference Div., 224 S Michigan Ave., Ste. 1500 Chicago, IL 60604. Phone: (312)922-1115; Fax: (312)922-1157; Email: insight@euromonitorintl.com • URL: http://www.euromonitor.com • Irregular. $650; $700 Individuals plus 60 for delivery; $575 Individuals printed book plus PDF download; $475 Individuals printed book or PDF download. Covers: More than 2,000 European business libraries and services. Entries include: location, accessibility, fees, stock, and subject area.

***European Directory of Financial Information Sources.*** Euromonitor International Business Reference Div., 224 S Michigan Ave., Ste. 1500 Chicago, IL 60604. Phone: (312)922-1115; Fax: (312)922-1157; Email: insight@euromonitorintl.com • URL: http://www.euromonitor.com • $160. Covers: Sources of financial information for companies in Europe, including official sources and publications, libraries, information services, banks and other financial institutions, accountancy firms and tax advisors, stockbrokers, stock exchanges, databases, indexes, abstracts, banking journals, and European business contacts. Entries include: Name, address, phone, fax, year founded.

***European Directory of Management Consultants.*** AP Information Services Ltd., c/o Wilmington Publishing & Information Ltd., 6-14 Underworld St. London N1 7JQ, United Kingdom. Phone: 44 20 75498708; Fax: 44 20 74908238; Email: info@apinfo.co.uk • URL: http://www.apinfo.co.uk • Biennial. $130. Covers: Approximately 3,500 management consultancy firms in varying areas of activity and industry in Europe. Entries include: Company name, address, phone, fax, managing director, principal consultants, business contacts, year established, number of consulting staff, financial data, geographical area served, languages, locations of branch offices, description of activities, industry area expertise, major clients, professional memberships.

***European Drinks Marketing Directory.*** Euromonitor International Business Reference Div., 224 S Michigan Ave., Ste. 1500 Chicago, IL 60604. Phone: (312)922-1115; Fax: (312)922-1157; Email: insight@euromonitorintl.com • URL: http://www.euromonitor.com • Irregular Biennial. $215; $475 Individuals printed edition; £325 Individuals; €375 Individuals. Covers: The European drinks industry, including marketing, retailers, wholesalers, leading companies, market trends, and industry details. Entries include: Name, address, phone, fax, telex.

**European Facility Management Network.** PO Box 5135 NL-1410 AC Naarden, Netherlands. Phone: 31 35 6942785; Email: eurofm@eurofm.org • URL: http://www.eurofm.org • Promotes knowledge in facility management in Europe and its application in practice, education and research.

**European Federation of Financial Analysts Societies.** c/o Claudia Stinnes, Secretary, Mainzer Landstrasse 47a DE-60329 Frankfurt, Germany. Phone: 49 69 264848300; Fax: 49 69 264848335; Email: info@effas.com • URL: http://effas.net • Associations and individuals active in the area of financial analysis. Objectives are to provide investors with accurate and comprehensive data on financial matters and to develop a general methodology of financial analysis based on approaches utilized in different European countries.

**European Federation of Management Consultancies Associations.** Kunstlaan Ave. des Arts 3-5 B-1210 Brussels, Belgium. Phone: 32 2 2500650 or 32 2 2500651; Email: feaco@feaco.org • URL: http://www.feaco.org • European associations of national management consultancy associations. Purposes are to: promote and develop the profession of management consultancy; foster high standards of professional practice and ethics; mediate the exchange of information and experience among member associations and companies and individuals within member associations; establish relations with other organizations interested in management practice. Upholds professional Guidelines for Business Ethics; studies, promotes, and protects the professional interests of members. Maintains liaison with other management consultancy organizations.

***European Federation of Management Consultants Associations—European Directory: European Directory of Management Consultants.*** European Federation of Management Consultants Associations, 145 Rue Royale B-1000 Brussels, Belgium. Phone: 2223 0413; Fax: 2223 0674; Email: feaco@feaco.org • Covers: 22 associations plus members. Entries include: Name, address, phone, fax; activities; date established; number of consultants.

**European Finance Association.** Pl. de Brouckere Plein 31 B-1000 Brussels, Belgium. Phone: 32 2 2266660 or 32 2 2266665; Fax: 32 2 5121929; Email: kannel@eiasm.be • URL: http://www.efa-online.org/r/default.asp?iId=ILGLJ • Academics and practitioners interested in financial management and theory and application. Fosters dissemination and exchange of information; provides forum for presentation of research results in the areas of company finance, investment, financial markets, and banking.

**European Financial Management and Marketing Association.** 8, rue Bayen F-75017 Paris, France. Phone: 33 1 47425272; Fax: 33 1 47425676; Email: info@efma.com • URL: http://www.efma.com • European financial organizations in 17 countries. Goals are to: establish communication among individuals working with European financial organizations and supporting the concept of marketing; encourage innovation in the field; foster initiation of financial marketing research projects; represent the interests of European financial marketing. Sponsors seminars and professional training sessions. Maintains documentation center. Compiles data on credit card systems.

**European Foundation for Management Development.** Rue Gachard 88 1050 Brussels, Belgium. Phone: 32 2 6290810; Fax: 32 2 6290811 • URL: http://www.efmd.org • Corporations, educational institutions, employers associations, management consultants, and individuals in 45 countries with an interest in management development, training, and education. Seeks to identify, research, and address leading management development issues. Fosters development of professional competence of those responsible for management development within companies and educational institutions; promotes education, development, and research in the field through working groups, seminars and conferences. Strives to organize effective interaction among all those involved in the management development process.

***European International Business Academy—Membership Directory.*** European International Business Academy, c/o EIASM, Hotel Metropole, 2nd Fl., Pl. de Brouckere Plein, 31 B-1000 Brussels, Belgium. Phone: 32 2 2266660; Fax: 32 2 5121929 • URL: http://www.eiba-online.org • Covers: 300 individuals involved in international business.

**European International Business Academy.** c/o EIASM, Hotel Metropole, 2nd Fl., Pl. de Brouckere Plein, 31 B-1000 Brussels, Belgium. Phone: 32 2 2266660; Fax: 32 2 5121929 • URL: http://www.eiba-online.org • Individuals and associations involved in international business. Encourages exchange of ideas; fosters communication among members; serves as an information clearinghouse for those interested in education and research of international business.

***European Kompass on Disc.*** Kompass USA, Inc., 121 Whitney Ave. New Haven, CT 06510. Phone: (877)566-7277 or (203)503-6789; Fax: (203)503-6780; Email: mail@kompass-usa.com • URL: http://www.kompass.com • Provides information on more than 350,000 companies in Belgium, Denmark, France, Germany, Ireland, Italy, Luxembourg, Netherlands, Norway, Spain, Sweden, and UK. Classification system covers approximately 50,000 products and services.

***European Legal Business.*** Legalese Ltd., Kensington Sq. House, 12-14 Ansdell St. London W8 5BN, United Kingdom. Phone: 44 20 73969292; Fax: 44 20 73969303 • URL: http://www.legalease.co.uk • Bimonthly. $195 Individuals; $351 Two years. Journal covering the European legal market.

**European Lime Association.** c/o IMA-Europe, Rue des Deux Eglises 26 B-1000 Brussels, Belgium. Phone: 32 2 2104410; Fax: 32 2 2104429; Email: info@eula.be • URL: http://www.eula.eu • Maintains a close relationship with the European Institutions, and the International and European Trade Associations. Represents the lime industry's views on issues, policies and strategies being developed in various areas such as industry competitiveness, environmental protection, energy consumption and climate change. Promotes lime acknowledgement in regulatory and scientific authorities.

***European Management Journal.*** Elsevier, Secondary Publishing Division, 650 Ave. of the Americas New York, NY 10011. Phone: 888-437-4636 or (212)633-3980; Fax: (212)633-3975; Email: t.reller@elsevier.com • URL: http://www.elseveier.com • Bimonthly. $1,162 Individuals Print. Covers a wide variety of topics, including management problems of the European Single Market.

***The European Market for High Voltage Switchgear.*** ABS Publications, 75 Updown Hill Windlesham GU20 6DS, United Kingdom. Phone: 276 474828; Fax: 272 471796 • $800. Covers: European manufacturers of high voltage switchgear (greater than 1kV). Entries include: Utility statistics, company profiles, trade production and market data for both supply and demand.

**European Marketing Academy.** Pl. de Brouckere Plein, 31 B-1000 Brussels, Belgium. Phone: 32 2 2266660; Fax: 32 2 5121929; Email: emac@eiasm.be • URL: http://www.emac-online.org/r/default.asp?iId=FLFDIE • Persons involved or interested in teaching or research in the field of marketing. Serves as forum for exchange of information concerning marketing; fosters improved dissemination of information; promotes international exchange in the field of marketing.

***European Marketing Data and Statistics***. Cengage Learning Inc., 20 Channel Center St. Boston, MA 02210. Phone: 800-487-8488 or (617)289-7700; Fax: (617)289-7844; Email: investors@cengage.com • URL: http://www.cengage.com • 2013. $475.00. Published by Euromonitor International. Presents essential marketing data, including demographics and consumer expenditure patterns for 44 European countries. Also available as eBook.

***European Markets: A Guide to Company and Industry Information Sources***. MarketResearch.com, 11200 Rockville Pke., Ste. 504 Rockville, MD 20852. Phone: 800-298-5699 or (240)747-3093; Fax: (240)747-3004; Email: customerservice@marketresearch.com • URL: http://www.marketresearch.com • Irregular. $335. Covers: sources worldwide of information on European companies. Entries include: Source name, contact name, address, phone, fax, telex.

**European Money and Finance Forum**. c/o Oesterreichische Nationalbank, Otto Wagner-Platz 3 A-1090 Vienna, Austria. Phone: 43 1 404207206; Fax: 43 1 404207298; Email: suerf@oenb.at • URL: http://www.suerf.org • Represents academics, bank economists, and interested individuals in 37 countries. Develops contacts among members in order to discuss monetary and financial questions. Sponsors research in monetary, economic, and financial areas. Aims to create an active network between professional economists, financial practitioners, central bankers and academics for the analysis and mutual understanding of monetary and financial issues. Sponsors conferences, seminars, workshops and lectures. Publishes study volumes each year.

**European Operations Management Association**. c/o EIASM, Pl. de Brouckere Plein 31 B-1000 Brussels, Belgium. Phone: 32 2 2266660; Fax: 32 2 5121929; Email: euroma@eiasm.be • URL: http://www.euroma-online.org • Advances operations management in both manufacturing and service through research, education and practice.

**European Organisation for the Exploitation of Meteorological Satellites** . Eumetsat-Allee 1 D-64295 Darmstadt, Germany. Phone: 49 6151 8077; Fax: 49 6151 807555; Email: press@eumetsat.int • URL: http://www.eumetsat.int • Seeks to establish and maintain the long-term continuity of European systems of operational meteorological satellites. Contributes to a global meteorological satellite observing system coordinated with other space-faring nations, for operational meteorology and the monitoring of climate change. Sponsors students attending the International Space University.

**European Organisation of Supreme Audit Institutions**. c/o Ramon Alvarez de Miranda, Secretary General, Fuencarral 81 28004 Madrid, Spain. Phone: 34 91 446 04 66; Fax: 34 91 593 38 94; Email: eurosai@tcu.es • URL: http://www.eurosai.org • Promotes professional and technical understanding of audit and public finance; works to secure unification of terminology in the field of audit of public finance.

**European Professional Women's Network**. 4, rue Galvani F-75838 Paris, France. Phone: 33 9 70446262; Email: contact@europeanpwn.net • URL: http://www.europeanpwn.net • Promotes the sustainable and innovative professional career paths of women. Raises the visibility of European women in business.

***European Regional Incentives***. Bowker-Saur, Maypole House, Maypole Rd. East Grinstead RH19 1HV, United Kingdom. Phone: 44 1342 330100; Fax: 44 1342 330198; Email: customer.services@bowker-saur.co.uk • Annual. $85. Directory and review of regional grants and other aid available for industrial and business expansion or relocation from European Community member state governments and Sweden. Entries include: Program title, organization name, address, phone, name and title of contact, description of program, type of incentives (grant, loan, tax concession, etc.), application procedure, selection procedure, eligibility requirements, legislative authority, maximum and average awards.

**European Round Table of Industrialists**. Karabiniersplein, Pl. de Carabiniers 18a B-1030 Brussels, Belgium. Phone: 32 2 5343100; Fax: 32 2 5347348; Email: contact@ert.eu • URL: http://www.ert.eu • Chief executive officers of large manufacturing companies headquartered in 16 European countries. Promotes an improved business climate in Europe in an attempt to expand Europe's international as well as domestic technical and industrial market. Encourages entrepreneurial initiatives.

***European Sources of Scientific and Technical Information***. Cartermill International, Maple House, 149 Tottenham Ct. Rd. London W1P 9LL, United Kingdom. Phone: 44 171 896 2424; Fax: 44 171 896 2449; Email: lizg@pearson-pro.com • Irregular. $225. Covers: over 1,500 patents and standards offices, national offices of information, and organizations active in scientific fields in Europe, including former Soviet bloc nations. Provides English-language version of foreign terminology. Entries include: Organization name, address, phone, fax, e-mail and website addresses, year founded, name of contact, parent company, subject(s) covered, publications, library facilities, and information, consulting, and training services.

***European System for Security and Cooperation Handbook***. International Business Publications, USA, PO Box 15343 Washington, DC 20003. Phone: (202)546-2103; Fax: (202)546-3275; Email: ibpusa@comcast.net • URL: http://ibpus.com • $99.95 Individuals hardcover, e-book, CD-ROM. Covers: U.S. security strategic materials and contacts.

***European Union Encyclopedia and Directory***. Routledge Reference, 2 Park Sq. Milton Park, Abingdon Oxford OX14 4RN, United Kingdom. Phone: 44 20 70176000; Fax: 44 20 70176699; Email: book.orders@tandf.co.uk • URL: http://www.routledge.com/ • Semiannual. £450 Individuals Hardback. Published by Europa. Provides directory information for major European Union organizations, with detailed descriptions of various groups or concepts in an "Encyclopedia" section. A statistics section contains a wide variety of data related to business, industry, and economics. Formerly *European Communities Encyclopedia and Directory*.

***European Union—Food and Drinks Directory***. Trade Publishing Resources, PO Box 1283 Randburg 2175, South Africa. Phone: 27 11 8862636; Fax: 27 11 8865424; Email: info@tradepublishing.co.za • URL: http://www.africaexports.co.za • Covers: 100,000 brand names, 29,000 executives, and 16,000 companies engaged in importing, wholesaling, and retailing of food and drinks.

**European Union of National Associations of Water Suppliers and Waste Water Services**. Rue du Luxembourg 47-51 B-1050 Brussels, Belgium. Phone: 32 2 7064080; Fax: 32 2 7064081 • URL: http://eureau.org • Represents water suppliers and waste water operators united to defend their common interests. Assesses and monitors water supply problems; reviews and discusses prospective legislation affecting the industry. Recommends practical and legislative solutions to problems with respect to differing technologies, climates, and geographical and economic situations in member states. Collaborates with other technical associations.

***European Valves for Control, Isolation and Safety***. Roles & Associates Ltd., PO Box 25 Sunbury-on-Thames TW16 5QB, United Kingdom. Phone: 208 7830088; Fax: 208 7830088; Email: roles@easynet.co.uk • Irregular. $96. Covers: suppliers of valves, actuators, auxiliary equipment, piping and connectors in Europe. Entries include: Company name, address, phone, descriptions of services, products provided.

***European Venture Capital Association—Yearbook***. KPMG L.L.P. (U.K.), 8 Salisbury Sq. London EC4Y 8BB, United Kingdom. Phone: 44 20 7311 1000 or 71 2368000; Fax: 44 20 7311 3311 • URL: http://www.kpmg.com/UK • Annual. Covers: about 175 member companies that provide venture capital funding and services; 10 national venture capital associations in Europe. Database includes: Report and statistics on the venture capital industry in Europe. Entries include: For companies—Name, address, phone, telex, name of chief executive, type of firm, minimum and preferred investment amounts, type of financing, industry and geographical preferences, contact names. For associations—Name, address, phone, telex, contact name.

**European Women's Management Development Austria**. Schmiedinger strasse 67 5020 Salzburg, Austria. Email: austria@ewmd.org • URL: http://www.ewmd.org/chapter/104 • Aims to improve the quality of management with respect to people, children, age and the cultural diversity of Europe. Provides a forum for collecting and exchanging information about trends management development in Europe and worldwide. Promotes women in management. Facilitates communication among individuals involved in the development of new role models for better work-life-balance.

**European Women's Management Development International Network**. Geisbergweg 6c 65205 Wiesbaden, Germany. • URL: http://www.ewmd.org • Strives to improve management by developing women's managerial skills, and raising the professional profile of women as managers. Disseminates and exchange knowledge and experience in establishing best practices for management development.

**European Women's Management Development Switzerland**. Stockerstrasse 56 8002 Zurich, Switzerland. Email: switzerland@ewmd.org • URL: http://www.ewmd.org • Aims to improve the quality of management with respect to people, children, age and the cultural diversity of Europe. Provides a forum for collecting and exchanging information about trends management development in Europe and worldwide. Promotes women in management. Facilitates communication among individuals involved in the development of new role models for better work-life-balance.

***Europe's 15,000 Largest Companies***. GAP Books, Dephna House, 24-26 Arcadia Ave. London N3 2JU, United Kingdom. Phone: 44 20 8349 7199 or 44 71 706 0919; Fax: 44 20 8349 7198 or 44 71 723 6854; Email: info@gapbooks.com • URL: http://www.gapbooks.com • Annual. £415 Individuals hardcover. Covers: 8,000 leading industrial companies, 2,500 trading companies, 350 banks, 350 transportation firms, 200 insurance firms, 100 hotels and restaurants, 150 advertising agencies; and 250 other firms; also includes ranked lists (without extensive data) of 125 largest money losers, 500 most profitable firms, 250 most profitable firms using profits as percentage of sales. Entries include: Company name, headquarters, contact, International Standard Industrial Classification (ISIC) code, sales, rank, number of employees and shareholders, profit, sales per employee, and other operating ratios. Headings are in English, German, and French.

***Europe's Major and Medium Sized Companies Directory***. Euromonitor International Business Reference Div., 224 S Michigan Ave., Ste. 1500 Chicago, IL 60604. Phone: (312)922-1115; Fax: (312)922-1157; Email: insight@euromonitorintl.com • URL: http://www.euromonitor.com • Irregular. $990. Covers: 12,000 companies headquartered in eastern and western Europe. Database includes: Ranked lists of companies. Entries include: Company name, address, phone, fax, telex, type of company, ownership, major subsidiaries, names and titles of key personnel, products, outlets, number of employees, sales, recent company developments.

***Europe's Medium Sized Companies Directory***. Euromonitor International Business Reference Div., 224 S Michigan Ave., Ste. 1500 Chicago, IL 60604. Phone: (312)922-1115; Fax: (312)922-1157; Email: insight@euromonitorintl.com • URL: http://www.euromonitor.com • $550 Individuals. Covers: More than 4,000 medium-sized companies in Europe. Entries include: Company name, address, phone, fax, contact experts.

***Europe's Top 1,000 Food & Drink Companies***. Datamonitor, Charles House, 108-110 Finchley Rd. London NW3 5JJ, United Kingdom. Phone: 44 20 7675 7000; Fax: 44 20 7675 7500; Email: euroinfo@datamonitor.com • $995. Covers: 1,000 leading food and drink companies in Europe. Entries include: Company name, address, phone, telex, names and titles of key personnel, number of employees; financial data, product/service, Standard Industrial Classification (SIC) code, production locations.

***Europe's Top Quoted Companies: A Comparative Directory from Seventeen European Stock Exchanges***. Kogan Page, Limited, 120 Pentonville Rd. London N1 9JN, United Kingdom. Phone: 44 20 72780433 or (440) 2072780433; Fax: 44 20 78376348 or (783)76348; Email: kpinfo@kogan-page.co.uk • URL: http://www.kogan-page.co.uk/ • Annual. $325.00. Provides detailed, 5-year financial data on 850 major European companies that are publicly traded. Includes company addresses.

***Euroretailnet***. Corporate Intelligence Group, 48 Bedford Sq. London WC1B 3DP, United Kingdom. Phone: 44 2078143814; Fax: 44 2076969006; Email: sales@cior.com • Database covers: Approximately 3,000 retailers in 17 European countries, including U.S. and Japanese companies doing business in Europe. Entries include: Company name, address, phone, fax, names and titles of key personnel, geographical area served; number of employees, financial data, subsidiary and branch names and locations; description; promotional activity; distribution system; information technology utilized.

***Eurostat Regional Yearbook***. Bernan Associates, 4611 Assembly Dr., Ste. F Lanham, MD 20706-4843. Phone: 800-416-4385 or (301)459-2255 or (301)459-7666; Fax: (301)459-0056 or (800)865-3450; Email: query@bernan.com • URL: http://www.bernan.com • Annual. $50.00. Published by the Commission of European Communities. Provides data on the social and economic situation in specific European areas. Includes population, employment, migration, industry, living standards, etc.

***Everett Business Journal***. The Wenatchee Business Journal Inc., 304 S Mission St. Wenatchee, WA 98801. Phone: (509)663-6730; Fax: (509)663-4599 • URL: http://www.ncwbusiness.com • Monthly. Publication covering local business issues.

***Everyday Finance: Economics, Personal Money Management, and Entrepreneurship***. Cengage Learning Inc., 20 Channel Center St. Boston, MA 02210. Phone: 800-487-8488 or (617)289-7700; Fax: (617)289-7844; Email: investors@cengage.com • URL: http://www.cengage.com • $258 Individuals. 2008. 2 volumes. Contains 300 topical entries that are organized into 3 units: How the Economy Works; Personal Finance: Buying, Borrowing, Saving, and Insuring; and The World of Business. eBook available. Inquire for pricing.

***Evolution of Modern Business Series***. Cengage Learning Inc., 20 Channel Center St. Boston, MA 02210. Phone: 800-487-8488 or (617)289-7700; Fax: (617)289-7844; Email: investors@cengage.com • URL: http://www.cengage.com • Contains in-depth surveys on business trends and waves of industrial progress. Offers a critical look at the practices and evolution of the business world. Series includes: Curtiss-Wright, History of Black Business in America, Incorporating Women, and The Invisible Fuel: A History of Natural Gas in America. Volumes available individually.

**Ewing Marion Kauffman Foundation**. 4801 Rockhill Rd. Kansas City, MO 64110. Phone: (816)932-1000; Email: contact@kauffman.org • URL: http://www.kauffman.org • Works to accelerate entrepreneurship in America.

**EWMD ITALY: European Women's Management Development**. c/o EWMD Brescia, via Papa Giovanni XXIII 74, Rezzato I-25086 Brescia, Italy. Phone: 39 30 2793124; Email: italy@ewmd.org • URL: http://www.ewmd.org/chapter/106 • Aims to improve the quality of management with respect to people, children, age and the cultural diversity of Europe. Promotes the best practices for work-life-balance management. Provides a forum for collecting and exchanging information about trends management development in Europe and worldwide. Promotes women in management. Facilitates communication among individuals involved in the development of new role models for better work-life-balance.

***Excerpta Medica: Biophysics, Bioengineering, and Medical***

***Instrumentation***. Elsevier, Secondary Publishing Division, 650 Ave. of the Americas New York, NY 10011. Phone: 888-437-4636 or (212)633-3980; Fax: (212)633-3975; Email: t.reller@elsevier.com • URL: http://www.elseveier.com • $7,353 Institutions print journal. 16 times a year. Institutions, $2,859 per year. Section 27 of *Excerpta Medica*.

***Excerpta Medica: Drug Dependence, Alcohol Abuse, and Alcoholism***. Elsevier, Secondary Publishing Division, 650 Ave. of the Americas New York, NY 10011. Phone: 888-437-4636 or (212)633-3980; Fax: (212)633-3975; Email: t.reller@elsevier.com • URL: http://www.elseveier.com • Bimonthly. 1,398. Section 40 of *Excerpta Medica*.

***Excerpta Medica: Environmental Health and Pollution Control***. Elsevier, Secondary Publishing Division, 650 Ave. of the Americas New York, NY 10011. Phone: 888-437-4636 or (212)633-3980; Fax: (212)633-3975; Email: t.reller@elsevier.com • URL: http://www.elseveier.com • 16 times a year. Institutions, $3,246.00 per year. Section 46 of *Excerpta Medica*. Covers air, water, and land pollution and noise control.

***Excerpta Medica: Health Policy, Economics and Management***. Elsevier, Secondary Publishing Division, 650 Ave. of the Americas New York, NY 10011. Phone: 888-437-4636 or (212)633-3980; Fax: (212)633-3975; Email: t.reller@elsevier.com • URL: http://www.elseveier.com • Bimonthly. 336 qualified personnel; 1,719 institutions. Section 36 of *Excerpta Medica*.

***Excerpta Medica: Human Genetics***. Elsevier, Secondary Publishing Division, 650 Ave. of the Americas New York, NY 10011. Phone: 888-437-4636 or (212)633-3980; Fax: (212)633-3975; Email: t.reller@elsevier.com • URL: http://www.elseveier.com • Semimonthly. 409 qualified personnel; 4,140 institutions. Section 22 of *Excerpta Medica*.

***Excerpta Medica: Occupational Health and Industrial Medicine***. Elsevier, Secondary Publishing Division, 650 Ave. of the Americas New York, NY 10011. Phone: 888-437-4636 or (212)633-3980; Fax: (212)633-3975; Email: t.reller@elsevier.com • URL: http://www.elseveier.com • Monthly. 2,375 institutions. Section 35 of *Excerpta Medica*.

***Exchange and Commissary News***. Executive Business Media Inc., 825 Old Country Rd. Westbury, NY 11590-0812. Phone: (516)334-3030; Fax: (516)334-3059 or (516)334-8958; Email: ebm-mail@ebmpubs.com • URL: http://www.ebmpubs.com • Monthly. $95.00 per year.

***Executive Compensation***. ALM Media Properties LLC, 120 Broadway, 5th Fl. New York, NY 10271-1100. Phone: (212)457-9400; Fax: (646)417-7705; Email: customercare@alm.com • URL: http://www.alm.com • $570. Covers many topics relating to the legal aspects of executive compensation, including taxation, securities law, payments in stock, fringe benefits, employment agreements, and severance arrangements. (Law Journal Press).

***Executive Compensation for Emerging Companies***. Daniel Niehans and Shawn E. Lampron. Glasser LegalWorks, 150 Clove Rd. Little Falls, NJ 07424. Phone: 800-308-1700 or (973)890-0008; Fax: (973)890-0042; Email: legalwks@aol.com • URL: http://www.glasserlegalworks.com • $599 Individuals Binder/Looseleaf (Full set); $44 Individuals Monthly pricing. Periodic Supplementation. Covers various aspects of executive compensation, with emphasis on stock option plans and stock ownership. Includes many annotated legal forms. (Emerging Growth Companies Series.).

**Executive Education**. University of Wisconsin-Madison, School of Business, 601 University Ave. Madison, WI 53706-1035. Phone: 800-292-8964 or (608)441-7357; Fax: (608)441-7133; Email: info@exed.wisc.edu • URL: http://exed.wisc.edu.

***Executive Excellence: The Newsletter of Personal Development, Managerial Effectiveness, and Organizational Productivity***. Kenneth M. Shelton, editor. Executive Excellence Publishing, 1806 North 1120 West Provo, UT 84604. Phone: 877-250-1983 or (801)375-4060; Fax: (801)377-5960; Email: info@eep.com • URL: http://www.eep.store.merchandizer.com • Monthly. $129.00 per year. Newsletter.

***Executive Guide to Specialists in Industrial and Office Real Estate***. Society of Industrial and Office Realtors, 1201 New York Ave. NW, Ste. 350 Washington, DC 20005-6126. Phone: (202)449-8200; Fax: (202)216-9325; Email: membership@sior.com • URL: http://www.sior.com • Annual. Lists approximately 5,000 corporate real estate specialists.

**Executive Leadership Council**. 1001 N Fairfax St., Ste. 300 Alexandria, VA 22314. Phone: (703)706-5200; Email: elcinfo@elcinfo.com • URL: http://www.elcinfo.com • Provides senior African-American corporate executives with a network and leadership forum that adds perspective and direction to the achievement of excellence in business, economic and public policies for the African-American community and its corporations, and the community at large. Conducts educational and research programs.

***Executive Search Books***. Kennedy Information Inc., 1 Phoenix Mill Ln., 3rd Fl. Peterborough, NH 03458. Phone: 800-531-0007 or (603)924-1006; Fax: (603)924-4460 or (603)924-4034; Email: customerservice@kennedyinfo.com • URL: http://www.kennedyinfo.com • Annual. Free. Contains descriptions of selected books from various publishers on executive recruitment.

***Executive Stock Options and Stock Appreciation Rights***. ALM Media Properties LLC, 120 Broadway, 5th Fl. New York, NY 10271-1100. Phone: (212)457-9400; Fax: (646)417-7705; Email: customercare@alm.com • URL: http://www.alm.com • $525. Coverage includes non-qualified stock options and incentive stock options. Contains sample forms and documents. (Law Journal Press).

***Executive Update***. Personal Care Product Council, 1620 L St. NW, Ste. 1200 Washington, DC 20036. Phone: (202)331-1770; Fax: (202)331-1969; Email: membership@personalcarecouncil.org • URL: http://www.personalcarecouncil.org • Monthly newsletter for members.

**Executive Women International**. 3860 S 2300 E Salt Lake City, UT 84109. Phone: (801)355-2800; Fax: (801)355-2852; Email: ewi@ewiconnect.com • URL: http://www.ewiconnect.com • Individuals holding key positions in business professions. Conducts networking educational and charitable programs.

**Executives Association of Great Britain**. The Limes, High Rd., Orsett London RM16 3ER, United Kingdom. Phone: 44 1375 893414 • URL: http://www.eagb.co.uk • Executives of businesses in the United Kingdom. Provides a forum for the exchange of information between members.

**Executives Without Borders**. 281 Summer St., 5th Fl. Boston, MA 02210. Phone: 800-790-6134; Email: contactus@execwb.org • URL: http://www.executiveswithoutborders.org • Encourages businessmen and businesswomen to use their leadership positions to foster the growth of business in developing countries. Provides humanitarian aid to alleviate the effects of natural and economic disasters. Promotes cooperation and works with research institutions to find sustainable business solutions.

***Exhibit Builder***. Exhibit Builder, PO Box 4144 Woodland Hills, CA 91364. Phone: 800-356-4451 or (818)225-0100; Fax: (818)225-0138; Email: jillb@exhibitbuilder.net • URL: http://www.exhibitbuilder.net • Seven timees a year. $40.00 per year. For designers and builders of trade show exhibits.

***Exhibitor: Best Practices in Trade Shows and Events***. Exhibitor Publications Inc., 206 S Broadway, Ste. 745 Rochester, MN 55904-6565. Phone: 888-235-6155 or (507)289-6556; Fax: (507)289-5253 • URL: http://www.exhibitoronline.com • Annual. $18 /year; print or online. Covers about 200 manufacturers of trade show exhibit equipment. Formerly *Buyer's Guide to Trade Show Displays*.

***Expansion Management—Atlas/Guide Issue: The Resource Manual for Companies on the Move***. Intertec Publishing, 5 Penn Plz., 13th Fl. New York, NY 10001-1810. Phone: 800-795-5445 or (212)613-9700 or (212)204-4200; Fax: (212)613-9749 or (212)206-3622; Email: bethany.weaver@penton.com • URL: http://www.penton.com • Annual. $10 for just Atlas issue; $40 for full subscription (12 issues). Publication includes: List of companies and agencies providing assistance to expanding or relocating businesses, including state and city departments of commerce, public and private economic development agencies, financial institutions, consultants, utility companies, and other professionals. Entries include: Company name, address, phone, fax, name and title of contact.

***Expansion Management: Growth Strategies for Companies on the Move***. Penton Media Inc., Industry Div., 1300 E 9th St. Cleveland, OH 44114. Phone: (216)696-7000; Fax: (216)696-1752; Email: information@penton.com • URL: http://www.penton.com • Monthly. Free to qualified personnel; others, $40.00 per year. Subject matter is concerned with expansion and relocation of industrial facilities.

***Expatriate's Guide to Savings & Investments***. Public Relations Consultants Association, 17-23 Willow Pl., 1st Fl. London SW1P 1JH, United Kingdom. Phone: 44 20 72336026; Fax: 44 20 78284797 • URL: http://www.prca.org.uk • Biennial. $20. Covers: Over 400 investment funds and their management companies situated outside of the United Kingdom. Entries include: Name, address, phone, fax, names and titles of key personnel, procedures, policy, financial data.

**Expediting Management Association**. c/o Patricia Murphy, Executive Administrator, 534 Bridlecreek Green SW Calgary, AB, Canada T2Y 3P2. Phone: (403)201-6401; Fax: (403)201-6402 • URL: http://www.expedite.org • Expediting managers; associate members are organizations, firms, and other individuals involved in the profession. (Expeditors work to ensure the efficient delivery of goods and services within or between businesses.) Promotes high professional and ethical standards in expediting. Conducts training programs, seminars, and workshops. Certifies expediting managers and associates; offers courses. Conducts on-site programs for corporations and groups.

***The Expert Marketplace***. Dun & Bradstreet Inc., 103 JFK Pkwy. Short Hills, NJ 07078. Phone: 800-526-0651 or (973)921-5500 or (973)921-5000; Fax: (866)560-7035 or (512)794-7670; Email: info@dnb.com • URL: http://www.dnb.com • Database covers: More than 200,000 business consulting firms, business case studies and business improvement articles. Entries include: Consulting firm name, address, phone, fax, services, areas of expertise, executive name and title, staff, e-mail address, client list.

***Explorations in Economic History***. Elsevier, Secondary Publishing Division, 650 Ave. of the Americas New York, NY 10011. Phone: 888-437-4636 or (212)633-3980; Fax: (212)633-3975; Email: t.reller@elsevier.com • URL: http://www.elseveier.com • Quarterly. Individuals, $214.00 per year; institutions, $439.00 per year.

***Exploring Windows NT for Professionals***. Skillsoft Ireland Ltd., 500 Canal View Rochester, NY 14623. Phone: 800-434-3466 or (585)240-7500; Fax: (585)240-7760 or (585)292-4392; Email: info@elementk.com • URL: http://www.skillsoft.com • Monthly. $139.00 per year. Newsletter on the Windows operating system for networks. Formerly *Exploring Windows NT*.

***Export and Import Directory of Peru***. Association of Peruvian Exporters, Av. Javier Prado Este 2875 Lima, Peru. Phone: 51 1 6183333 • URL: http://www.adexperu.org.pe • Annual. $60; $60. Covers: Exporters, importers, and export service firms in Peru.

***Export—Buyers Guide Issue***. Johnston International Publishing Corp., 25 NW Point Blvd., Ste. 800 Elk Grove Village, IL 60007. Phone: (708)427-2089 or (708)296-0770; Fax: (708)427-2013 or (708)296-3403 • Annual. $10. Publication includes: About 250 manufacturers and exporters of hardware, air conditioning and refrigeration equipment, garden supplies, sporting goods, automotive accessories, and building products. Limited to advertisers. Entries include: Company name, address, phone, telex, names of contacts.

***Export Denmark***. Kongeriget Danmarks Handels-Kalender, Gl. Klausdalsbrovej 482, Hjortespring DK-2730 Herlev, Denmark. Phone: 45 70202023; Fax: 45 70202065; Email: info@export-denmark.dk • URL: http://www.export-denmark.dk • Annual. Covers: 10,000 exporters in Denmark. Entries include: Company name, address, phone, telex number, products, trade names.

***Export/Import Markets: Puerto Rico Edition***. Direct Marketing & Media Group Inc., Little Tower Bldg., 1473 Calle Wilson San Juan, PR 00907. Phone: (787)268-1111; Fax: (787)268-7044 • $30. Covers: about 1,000 firms located in Puerto Rico and engaged in exporting, importing, and supplying services to international trade (including steamship lines and agents, banks, rental firms, freight forwarders, and custom house brokers). Entries include: For steamship lines and agents—Firm name, address, phone, fax, telex, name of firms represented. For others—Company name, address, phone, fax, telex, names and titles of key personnel, number of employees, product/service.

***Export-Import News: International Business and Economics Fortnightly***. India - International News Service, 12 India Exchange Pl. Calcutta 700 001, India. • Biweekly. $500; $100 Other countries. Periodical covering international business news.

***Export Mail-Order***. Todd Publications, PO Box 500 Millwood, NY 10546. Phone: 866-896-0916 or (914)373-4750; Fax: (914)373-4750; Email: toddpub@aol.com • URL: http://www.toddpublications.com • Biennial. $20. Covers: Suppliers, overseas firms seeking exports, firms serving as export management companies, and other information to aid in choosing products to export.

***Export Today: The Global Business and Technology Magazine***. Trade Communications Inc., 733 15th St. NW, Ste. 1100 Washington, DC 20005. Fax: (202)783-5966 • Monthly. $49.00 per year. Edited for corporate executives to provide practical information on international business and exporting.

***Exporter Directory***. People Publishing Ltd., PO Box 7070, Wellesley St. Auckland 4040, New Zealand. Phone: 64 9 3666879; Fax: 64 9 3666838 • URL: http://www.peoplepublishing.co.nz • Annual. Covers: 2,000 export companies in New Zealand seeking overseas contacts and clients.

***Extel Handbook of Market Leaders***. Extel Financial Ltd., Fitzroy House,13-17 Epworth St., 13-17 Epworth St. London EC2A 4DL, United Kingdom. Phone: 44 71 2513333; Fax: 44 71 2512725 • Semiannual. $90; $115. Covers: Major quoted companies. Entries include: Adress, phone, name of chairman, financial data.

***Eye and Contact Lens: Science and Clinical Practices***. University of Texas, Dept. of Ophthalmology. Lippincott Williams & Wilkins, 2 Commerce Sq., 2001 Market St. Philadelphia, PA 19103. Phone: 800-638-3030 or (301)223-2300; Email: ronna.ekhouse@wolterskluwer.com • URL: http://www.lww.com • 6/year. $237 Individuals; $359 Institutions. Formerly *The CLAO Journal*.

***Eyecare Business: The Magazine for Progressive Dispensing***. Boucher Communications, Inc., 1300 Virginia Dr. Fort Washington, PA 19034. Phone: (215)643-8000; Fax: (215)643-8099 • URL: http://www.boucher1.com • Monthly. Individuals, $75.00 per year. Covers the business side of optometry and optical retailing. Each issue features "Frames and Fashion.".

***Eyeglasses Directory***. InfoGroup Inc., 5711 S 86th Cir. Omaha, NE 68127-4146. Phone: (402)593-4500 • URL: http://www.infogroup.com • Annual. Number of listings: 18,811. Entries include: Name, address, phone, size of advertisement, name of owner or manager, number of employees, year first in "Yellow Pages." Compiled from telephone company "Yellow Pages," nationwide.

***F & S Index: Europe***. Cengage Learning Inc., 20 Channel Center St. Boston, MA 02210. Phone: 800-487-8488 or (617)289-7700; Fax: (617)289-7844; Email: investors@cengage.com • URL: http://www.cengage.com • Monthly. $2,532.00 per year, including quarterly and annual cumulations. Provides annotated citations to marketing, business, financial, and industrial literature. Coverage of European business activity includes trade journals, financial magazines, business newspapers, and special reports. Formerly Predicasts F & S Index: Europe.

***F & S Index: International.*** Cengage Learning Inc., 20 Channel Center St. Boston, MA 02210. Phone: 800-487-8488 or (617)289-7700; Fax: (617)289-7844; Email: investors@cengage.com • URL: http://www.cengage.com • $2,659 Individuals. Monthly. $2,532.00 per year, including quarterly and annual cumulations. Provides annotated citations to marketing, business, financial, and industrial literature. Coverage of international business activity includes trade journals, financial magazines, business newspapers, and special reports. Areas included are Asia, Latin America, Africa, the Middle East, Oceania, and Canada.

***F & S Index: United States.*** Cengage Learning Inc., 20 Channel Center St. Boston, MA 02210. Phone: 800-487-8488 or (617)289-7700; Fax: (617)289-7844; Email: investors@cengage.com • URL: http://www.cengage.com • $2,659 Individuals. Monthly. $2,532.00 per year, including quarterly and annual cumulations. Provides annotated citations to marketing, business, financial, and industrial literature. Coverage of U.S. business activity includes trade journals, financial magazines, business newspapers, and special reports.

***F-D-C Reports.*** Elsevier Business Intelligence, 5635 Fishers Ln., Ste. 6000 Rockville, MD 20852. Phone: 800-332-2181 or (240)221-4500 or (800)332-2181; Fax: (240)221-4400 or (301)656-3094; Email: fdc.customer.service@fdcreports.com • URL: http://www.elsevierbi.com • An online version of "The Gray Sheet" (medical devices), "The Pink Sheet" (pharmaceuticals), "The Rose Sheet" (cosmetics), "The Blue Sheet" (biomedical), and "The Tan Sheet" (nonprescription). Contains full-text information on legal, technical, corporate, financial, and marketing developments from 1987 to date, with weekly updates. Inquire as to online cost and availability.

***FAA Aviation News.*** Federal Aviation Administration. U. S. Government Printing Office, 732 N Capitol St. NW Washington, DC 20401. Phone: 866-512-1800 or (202)512-1800 or (866)512-1800; Fax: (202)512-2104 or (202)512-2250; Email: contactcenter@gpo.gov • URL: http://www.gpo.gov • Bimonthly. $28.00. per year. Designed to help airmen become safer pilots. Includes updates on major rule changes and proposals.

***Facial Skin Care Directory.*** InfoGroup Inc., 5711 S 86th Cir. Omaha, NE 68127-4146. Phone: (402)593-4500 • URL: http://www.infogroup.com • Annual. Number of listings: 11,460. Entries include: Name, address, phone, size of advertisement, name of owner or manager, number of employees, year first in "Yellow Pages." Compiled from telephone company "Yellow Pages," nationwide.

***Facilities Design & Management—Directory Issue.*** Bpi Communications Inc., 1515 Broad Way New York, NY 10036. Phone: (646)654-4420 or (212)536-1471; Fax: (646)654-4420 or (212)536-5318; Email: bmcomm@meetingnews.com • URL: http://www.vnubusinessmedia.com/ • $10. Publication includes: List of about 2,000 suppliers of office furnishings, equipment, services; professional associations. Entries include: For suppliers—Company name, address, phone, products or services. For associations—Name, address.

***Facilities Design & Management—Directory of Consultants & Service Firms Issue.*** Bpi Communications Inc., 1515 Broad Way New York, NY 10036. Phone: (646)654-4420 or (212)536-1471; Fax: (646)654-4420 or (212)536-5318; Email: bmcomm@meetingnews.com • URL: http://www.vnubusinessmedia.com/ • Annual. $7. Publication includes: Listing of firms offering products, services, and consulting services to facilities designers and managers.

**Facility Management Association of Australia.** 313 La Trobe St., Level 6 Melbourne, VIC 3000, Australia. Phone: 61 3 86416666; Fax: 61 3 86416600; Email: info@fma.com.au • URL: http://www.fma.com.au/cms • Promotes the facility management profession in Australia.

***Facility Manager.*** International Association of Venue Managers, 635 Fritz Dr., Ste. 100 Coppell, TX 75019-4442. Phone: 800-935-4226 or (972)906-7441; Fax: (972)906-7418; Email: vicki.hawarden@iavm.org • URL: http://www.iavm.org • Quarterly. Free to members; non-members, $55.00 per year.

***Factiva.*** Dow Jones Reuters Business Interactive, LLC, Phone: 800-369-7466 or (609)452-1511; Fax: (609)520-5770; Email: solutions@factiva.com • URL: http://www.factiva.com • Fee-based Web site provides "global news and business information through Web sites and content integration solutions." Includes Dow Jones and Reuters newswires, The Wall Street Journal, and more than 7,000 other sources of current news, historical articles, market research reports, and investment analysis. Content includes 96 major U. S. newspapers, 900 non-English sources, trade publications, media transcripts, country profiles, news photos, etc.

***Facts-on-File World News Digest With Index.*** InfoBase Holdings Inc., 132 W 31st., 17 Fl. New York, NY 10001-3406. Phone: (212)967-8800; Fax: (800)678-3633; Email: info@infobasepublishing.com • URL: http://www.ferguson.infobasepublishing.com • Weekly. $725.00 per year. Looseleaf service.

***Fair Employment Compliance: A Confidential Letter to Management.*** Management Resources, Inc., 380 Ocean Rd., Unit 2 Portsmouth, NH 03801-6051. • Semimonthly. $245.00 per year. Newsletter.

***Fair Oaks Business Directory.*** Fair Oaks Chamber of Commerce, 10014 Fair Oaks Blvd. Fair Oaks, CA 95628. Phone: (916)967-2903; Email: info@fairoakschamber.com • URL: http://www.fairoakschamber.com • Annual.

***Fairfax County Business Database.*** Fairfax County Economic Development Authority, 8300 Boone Blvd., Ste. 450 Vienna, VA 22182-2633. Phone: (703)790-0600; Fax: (703)893-1269; Email: info@thepartnership.org • URL: http://www.fairfaxcountyeda.org • Description: Database cover approximately 7,000 Fairfax County-located businesses, including high-tech firms, financial and legal firms, retail, and personal services. Government agencies are not included. Entries include: Company name, address, phone, fax, e-mail (if available), name and title of contact; number of employees, occupied space in square feet, and geographical submarket of county. Formerly available in print edition; latest edition 1990.

***Fairplay World Shipping Directory.*** Fairplay Publications Ltd., Lombard House, 3 Princess Way Redhill RH1 1UP, United Kingdom. Phone: 44 1737 379000; Fax: 44 1737 379001; Email: sales@fairplay.co.uk • URL: http://www.fairplay.co.uk • Daily. Covers: More than 76,000 companies worldwide engaged in some aspect of shipping, including over 10,000 ship-owners with fleets totaling over 45,000 vessels, shipbuilders and repairers, marine insurance shipping finance, protection and indemnity associations, marine equipment suppliers, and towing, salvage, and dredging; also lists marine organizations, shipbrokers, and consulting engineers and surveyors. Entries include: Company name, address, phone, fax, e-mail, URL, names of directors and executives, brief description of business; listings may also include associated and subsidiary companies and financial data.

***CampdenFB.*** Campden Publishing Ltd., 1 St. John's Sq. London EC1M 4PN, United Kingdom. Phone: 44 20 72140500; Fax: 44 20 72140501; Email: enquiries@campden.com • URL: http://www.campden.com • Quarterly. $415; €312; £210. Magazine featuring home-based family businesses.

***Family Advocate.*** American Bar Association - Family Law Section, 321 N Clark St. Chicago, IL 60654. Phone: (312)988-5145 or (312)988-5613; Fax: (312)988-6800; Email: familylaw@americanbar.org • URL: http://www.americanbar.org/groups/family_law.html • Quarterly. Members $39.50; non-members, $44.50 per year. Practical advice for attorneys practicing family law.

***Family Almanac.*** National Association of Retail Druggists. Creative Publishing, 722 E Hwy. 38, No. 108 Hartford, SD 57033. Phone: 800-423-7158 or (605)528-3919; Email: info@creativepublishingsv.com • URL: http://www.creativepublishingsv.com • Annual. $4. Formerly *NARD Almanac and Health Guide*.

***Family Business Advisor.*** Family Enterprise Publishers, 1220-B Kennestone Cir. Marietta, GA 30061. Phone: 800-551-0633 or (770)421-0110 or (770)425-6673; Fax: (770)425-1776; Email: info@efamilybusiness.com • Monthly. Covers business management, family relations, and asset protection. Addresses succession planning, estate planning, conflict management, compensation, family meetings, strategic planning, and board composition. Recurring features include news of research.

***Family Business Magazine.*** Canadian Association of Family Enterprise, 465 Morden Rd., Ste. 112 Oakville, ON, Canada L6K 3W6. Phone: 866-849-0099 or (905)337-8375; Fax: (905)337-0572 • URL: http://www.cafecanada.ca • Quarterly.

***Family Clothing Stores Directory.*** InfoGroup Inc., 5711 S 86th Cir. Omaha, NE 68127-4146. Phone: (402)593-4500 • URL: http://www.infogroup.com • Annual. Number of listings: 22,853. Entries include: Name, address, phone, size of advertisement, name of owner or manager, number of employees, year first in "Yellow Pages." Compiled from telephone company "Yellow Pages," nationwide.

***Family Court Review: An Interdisciplinary Journal.*** Association of Family and Conciliation Courts. Pine Forge Press, 2455 Teller Rd. Thousand Oaks, CA 91320-2234. Phone: 800-818-7243 or (805)499-4224 or (805)499-9774; Fax: (805)499-0871 or (805)583-2665; Email: sales@pfp.sagepub.com • URL: http://www.sagepub.com/sociologybooks • Quarterly. Institutions, $456.00 per year.

***Family Economics and Nutrition Review.*** U. S. Government Printing Office, 732 N Capitol St. NW Washington, DC 20401. Phone: 866-512-1800 or (202)512-1800 or (866)512-1800; Fax: (202)512-2104 or (202)512-2250; Email: contactcenter@gpo.gov • URL: http://www.gpo.gov • Semiannual. $13.00 per year. Issued by the Consumer and Food Economics Institute, U. S. Department of Agriculture. Provides articles on consumer expenditures and budgeting for food, clothing, housing, energy, education, etc.

**Family Federation of Finland.** PO Box 849 FIN-00101 Helsinki, Finland. Phone: 358 9 228050 or 358 9 22805101; Fax: 358 9 6121211 • URL: http://www.vaestoliitto.fi • Organizations concerned with the state of the family in Finland. Works for a social climate favorable to families, children, and demographic balance. Initiates reform legislation and strives to guide social planning, housing policy, and social services to meet the needs of families with children. Offers family and genetic counseling, infertility treatment, and child care and family planning services. Conducts occupational training courses, medical research programs and conferences. Participates in cooperative development projects and does advocacy work among decision-makers on global population issues and sexual and reproductive health and rights.

***Family Law Quarterly.*** American Bar Association - Family Law Section, 321 N Clark St. Chicago, IL 60654. Phone: (312)988-5145 or (312)988-5613; Fax: (312)988-6800; Email: familylaw@americanbar.org • URL: http://www.americanbar.org/groups/family_law.html • Quarterly. Free to members; non-members, $49.95 per year.

***Family Relations: State Capitals.*** Wakeman/Walworth Inc., PO Box 7376 Alexandria, VA 22307-7376. Phone: 800-876-2545 or (703)768-9600; Fax: (703)768-9690; Email: newsletters@statecapitals.com • URL: http://statecapitals.com/ • 50 times a year. $245.00 per year; print and online editions, $350.00 per year. Newsletter. Formerly *From the State Capitals: Family Relations*.

***Family Studies Abstracts.*** EBSCO Publishing Inc., 10 Estes St. Ipswich, MA 01938-2106. Phone: 800-653-2726 or (978)356-6500; Fax: (978)356-6565; Email: information@ebscohost.com • URL: http://www.ebscohost.com • Subject coverage includes divorce, family therapy, and marriage.

***Family Tree.*** Dun & Bradstreet Inc., 103 JFK Pkwy. Short Hills, NJ 07078. Phone: 800-526-0651 or (973)921-5500 or (973)921-5000; Fax: (866)560-7035 or (512)794-7670; Email: info@dnb.com • URL: http://www.dnb.com • Continuous. Database covers: About 200,000 corporations and their subsidiaries and branch companies. Database includes: Company name, address, phone, corporate standing (whether parent or holding company, subsidiary, or other), Standard Industrial Classification (SIC) code, names and titles of key personnel, sales volume, financial information, Dun & Bradstreet rating.

***Fancy Food and Culinary Products.*** Talcott Communications Corp., 704 N Wells St., 2nd Fl. Chicago, IL 60654. Phone: 800-229-1967 or (312)849-2220; Fax: (312)849-2174 • URL: http://www.talcott.com/index.htm • Monthly. $34.00 per year. Emphasizes new specialty food products and the business management aspects of the specialty food and confection industries. Includes special issues on wine, cheese, candy, "upscale" cookware, and gifts. Formerly (Fancy Foods).

***Far Eastern Economic Review.*** Dow Jones International Marketing Service, 420 Lexington Ave. New York, NY 10170. Phone: 800-568-7625 or (212)808-6615; Fax: (212)808-6652 • Weekly. $205.00 per year (air mail). Published in Hong Kong by Review Publishing Co., a Dow Jones subsidiary (GPO Box 160, Hong Kong). Covers Asian business, economics, politics, and international relations. Includes reports on individual countries and companies, business trends, and stock price quotations.

***Farm & Country: The Farm Business Resource.*** Agricultural Publishing Company Ltd., 1 Yonge St., Ste. 1504 Toronto, ON, Canada M5E 1E5. Phone: 800-463-3211 or (416)364-5324; Fax: (416)364-5857; Email: agpub@inforamp.net • $26 Individuals; $54 U.S. and other countries; $99 Foreign. Agricultural business magazine.

***Farm Equipment.*** Cygnus Business Media Inc., 1233 Janesville Ave. Fort Atkinson, WI 53538. Phone: 800-547-7377; Email: info@cygnus.com • URL: http://www.cygnus.com • Seven times a year. $48.00 per year. Includes annual *Product* issue.

**Farm Financial Standards Council.** c/o Carroll Merry, N78 W14573 Appleton Ave., No. 287 Menomonee Falls, WI 53051. Phone: (262)253-6902; Fax: (262)253-6903 • URL: http://www.ffsc.org • Aims to create and promote uniformity and integrity in financial reporting and analysis for agricultural producers. Strives to be recognized as the definitive resource of financial guidelines to benefit agricultural producers.

***Farm Industry News.*** Primedia Business Magazines and Media, 7900 International Dr., Ste. 300 Minneapolis, MN 55425. Phone: 800-795-5445 or (925)851-9329 or (952)851-9329; Fax: (925)851-4601 or (952)851-4601; Email: subs@primediabusiness.com • URL: http://www.primediabusiness.com • Monthly. $25.00 per year. Includes new products for farm use.

***Farm Journal: The Magazine of American Agriculture.*** Farm Journal Corp., 1818 Market St., 31st Fl. Philadelphia, PA 19103-3654. Phone: 800-523-1537 or (215)557-8900; Fax: (215)568-3989; Email: fjletters@farmjournal.com • URL: http://www.agweb.com • Monthly. $25 Individuals. Agricultural news magazine for people who own or operate farms or ranches.

***Farmer's Digest.*** Heartland Communications Group Inc., 1003 Central Ave., Ste. 1052 Fort Dodge, IA 50501. Phone: 800-247-2000 or (515)955-1600; Fax: (515)955-1668; Email: info@hlipublishing.com • URL: http://www.hlipublishing.com • 10 times a year. $17.95 per year. Current information on all phases of agriculture.

***Fashion Calendar.*** Ruth Finley, 153 E 87th St. New York, NY 10128. Phone: (212)289-0420; Email: info@fashioncalendar.com • URL: http://www.fashioncalendar.net • Biweekly. $550 Individuals print and online; $495 Individuals online; $150 Single issue 2 days subscription. Covers: Events of interest to the fashion industry, including private and public fashion openings, and important events in other fields which are scheduled for principal fashion cities; coverage is heavily New York City, but major cities worldwide are also covered. Entries include: For openings—Event name, date, address, phone. For other events—Event name, date, time, location, phone.

***Fashion Supply Chain Management: Industry and Business Analysis***. Cengage Learning Inc., 20 Channel Center St. Boston, MA 02210. Phone: 800-487-8488 or (617)289-7700; Fax: (617)289-7844; Email: investors@cengage.com • URL: http://www.cengage.com • 2012. eBook. Published by IGI Global. Covers quantitative research on Fashion Supply Chain Management (FSCM) and exploratory studies on emerging supply chain management issues in the fashion industry.

***Fast Company: How Smart Business Works***. Fast Company, Inc., 7 World Trade Ctr. New York, NY 10007-2195. Phone: 800-542-6029 or (212)389-5300; Fax: (212)389-5496 • URL: http://www.fastcompany.com • Monthly. $12.00 per year. Covers business management, with emphasis on creativity, leadership, innovation, career advancement, teamwork, the global economy, and the "new workplace.".

***Fastener Technology International Buyers' Guide***. Initial Publications Inc., 3869 Darrow Rd., Ste. 109 Stow, OH 44224. Phone: (330)686-9544; Fax: (330)686-9563; Email: mcnulty@fastenertech.com • URL: http://www.fastenertech.com • Annual. $50 Individuals print; Free online. Lists over 1,800 international manufacturers and distributors of fasteners and precision-formed parts.

***Fastener Technology International***. Initial Publications Inc., 3869 Darrow Rd., Ste. 109 Stow, OH 44224. Phone: (330)686-9544; Fax: (330)686-9563; Email: mcnulty@fastenertech.com • URL: http://www.fastenertech.com • Bimonthly. $40.00 per year.

***Faulkner & Gray's European Business Directory***. Thomson Financial Inc., 195 Broadway New York, NY 10007-3100. Phone: (646)822-2000; Email: custserv@tfn.com • URL: http://www.thomsonreuters.com • Annual. $295. Covers: over 2,000 attorneys, accountants, consultants, search firms, translators, shippers, commercial and investment banks, and industry leaders in Europe and the U.S. interested in or presently doing business in Europe. Database includes: Profiles of 40 countries. Entries include: Company or personal name, address, phone, telex, name and title of contact, subsidiary and branch names and locations, description of service.

***The Fax Banque***. InterCom Projects Ltd., 407 Lincoln Rd., Ste. 4-L Miami, FL 33139. Phone: (305)538-3884; Fax: (305)538-3884 • Quarterly. Diskette. Covers: Over 16,000 businesses in Central America and Miami, Florida. Entries include: Company name, address, phone, fax, description of commercial activity.

***FAX Magazine***. Technical Data Publishing Corp., 195A State, Route 33 Hartfield, VA 23071. Phone: (201)770-2633 • Quarterly. Price on application.

***FBI Law Enforcement Bulletin***. U. S. Government Printing Office, 732 N Capitol St. NW Washington, DC 20401. Phone: 866-512-1800 or (202)512-1800 or (866)512-1800; Fax: (202)512-2104 or (202)512-2250; Email: contactcenter@gpo.gov • URL: http://www.gpo.gov • Monthly. $36.00 per year. Issued by Federal Bureau of Investigation, U. S. Department of Justice. Contains articles on a wide variety of law enforcement and crime topics, including computer-related crime.

***FCC Record***. U. S. Government Printing Office, 732 N Capitol St. NW Washington, DC 20401. Phone: 866-512-1800 or (202)512-1800 or (866)512-1800; Fax: (202)512-2104 or (202)512-2250; Email: contactcenter@gpo.gov • URL: http://www.gpo.gov • Semimonthly. $813 U.S. 1 year; $1,138.20 Other countries 1 year; $65 Single issue US; $50 U.S. Supplements; $91 Single issue Other countries; $70 Other countries Supplements. Produced by the Federal Communications Commission (www.fcc.gov). An inclusive compilation of decisions, reports, public notices, and other documents of the FCC.

***FCC Report: An Exclusive Report on Domestic and International Telecommunications Policy and Regulation***. Warren Communications News Inc., 2115 Ward Ct. NW Washington, DC 20037. Phone: 800-771-9202 or (202)872-9200; Fax: (202)318-8350 or (202)293-3435 • URL: http://www.warren-news.com • 26 times a year. $670.00 per year. Newsletter concerned principally with Federal Communications Commission reglations and policy.

***FCCIA Directory***. Union des Chambers de Commerce et d'Industrie Francaises a l'Etranger, 46 Ave. de la Grande Armee, CS 50071 F-75858 Paris, France. Phone: 33 1 40693760; Fax: 33 1 40693783; Email: direction@uccife.org • URL: http://www.uccife.org • $45 Individuals available in French version only. Covers: 107 Chambers of Commerce and industry in Europe, Africa, Middle East, North America, South America, Asia, and Oceania. Entries include: Contact information and name of staff in 77 countries.

***FCIB International Bulletin***. cment. FCIB-NACM Corp., 8840 Columbia 100 Pkwy. Columbia, MD 21045-2158. Phone: 888-256-3242 or (410)423-1840; Fax: (410)740-5574; Email: fcib_info@fcibglobal.com • URL: http://www.fcibglobal.com • Quarterly. Membership.

***FDA Consumer***. U. S. Government Printing Office, 732 N Capitol St. NW Washington, DC 20401. Phone: 866-512-1800 or (202)512-1800 or (866)512-1800; Fax: (202)512-2104 or (202)512-2250; Email: contactcenter@gpo.gov • URL: http://www.gpo.gov • Bimonthly. $14.00 per year. Issued by the U. S. Food and Drug Administration. Provides consumer information about FDA regulations and product safety.

***FDM: For Builders of Cabinets, Fixtures, Furniture, Millwork Furniture Design a nd Manufacturing***. Chartwell Communications, Inc., 380 E. Northwest Highway Des Plaines, IL 60016. Phone: (847)390-6700; Fax: (847)299-7100 • URL: http://www.fdmmag.com • Monthly. Free to qualified personnel. Edited for furniture executives, production managers, and designers. Covers the manufacturing of household, office, and institutional furniture, store fixtures, and kitchen and bathroom cabinets.

***FDM—The Source—Woodworking Industry Directory***. Reed Elsevier Group plc Reed Business Information, 360 Park Ave. S New York, NY 11010. Phone: (212)791-4208; Email: corporatecommunications@reedbusiness.com • URL: http://www.reedbusiness.com • Annual. $25. Publication includes: List of over 1,800 suppliers to secondary woodworking industry; coverage includes Canada. Entries include: Company name, address, phone, fax, product lines.

***FED in Print: Economics and Banking Topics***. Federal Reserve Bank of Philadelphia, 10 Independence Mall Philadelphia, PA 19106-1521. Phone: (215)574-6000; Fax: (215)574-2512; Email: consumerhelp@federalreserve.gov • URL: http://www.phil.frb.org • Semiannual. Free. Business and banking topics.

***Federal Assistance Monitor: Semi-Monthly Report on Federal and Private Grant Opportunities***. Community Development Services. CD Publications, 8204 Fenton St. Silver Spring, MD 20910. Phone: 800-666-6380 or (301)588-6380; Fax: (301)588-6385; Email: info@cdpublications.com • URL: http://www.cdpublications.com • Semimonthly. $339.00 per year; with online edition, $379.00 per year. Newsletter. Provides news of federal grant and loan programs for social, economic, and community purposes. Monitors grant announcements, funding, and availability. Formerly *Federal Research Report*.

***Federal Aviation Regulations***. U. S. Government Printing Office, 732 N Capitol St. NW Washington, DC 20401. Phone: 866-512-1800 or (202)512-1800 or (866)512-1800; Fax: (202)512-2104 or (202)512-2250; Email: contactcenter@gpo.gov • URL: http://www.gpo.gov • Annual. Free. Lists government publications. GPO Subject Bibliography Number 12.

***Federal Career Opportunities***. Federal Research Service Inc., 7505 Pleasant Way Annadale, VA 22003-4568. Phone: 800-822-5627; Email: info@fedjobs.com • URL: http://www.fedjobs.com • Biweekly. $195 Individuals 26 issues, 1 year; $7.95 Individuals single issue; $92 Individuals 6 months, 12 issues. Covers: More than 3,000 current federal job vacancies in the United States and overseas; includes permanent, part-time, and temporary positions. Entries include: Position title, location, series and grade, job requirements, special forms, announcement number, closing date, application address.

***Federal Computer Week: The Newspaper for the Government Systems Community***. FCW Government Technology Group, 3141 Fairview Pk. Dr., Ste. 777 Falls Church, VA 22042. Phone: (703)876-5100 • URL: http://www.fcw.com/ • 41 times a year. $95.00 per year.

***Federal Employee News Digest***. Federal Employee News Digest, Inc., 1850 Centennial Park Dr., Suite 520 Reston, VA 20191. Phone: 800-989-3363 or (703)648-9551; Fax: (703)648-0265 • URL: http://www.fedforce.com • Weekly. $59.00 per year. Provides essential information for federal employees.

***Federal Employees Almanac***. 1105 Media Inc., 8609 Westwood Center Dr., Ste. 500 Vienna, VA 22182. Phone: 800-989-3363 or (703)648-9551; Fax: (703)648-0265 • URL: http://www.federaldaily.com • Annual. $20.95 print. Comprehensive guide for federal employees.

**Federal Employment Services - Institute of Employment Research**. Regensburger Strasse 104 D-90478 Nuremberg, Germany. Phone: 49 911 1790; Fax: 49 911 1793258; Email: joachim.moeller@iab.de • URL: http://www.iab.de • Situations and trends in the employment market, in general and in relation to various occupations, vocational training opportunities, and economic sectors. Activities include research (in-house and through contracts with other institutions); theoretical and methodological studies; surveys; advisory services in matters of employment policy; and promotion of activities in the field of labor market statistics in the areas of medium and long-term projections related to employment and the labor market; short-term labor market analysis; working-time studies; sociological research; occupational and qualification studies; research in technology and business economics; and work in analytical statistics, econometrics, and regional and international labor market research.

***Federal Grants and Contracts Weekly: Funding Opportunities in Research, Training and Services***. Wolters Kluwer Law and Business, 76 9th Ave., 7th Fl. New York, NY 10011-4962. Phone: 800-234-1660 or (212)771-0600; Fax: (800)901-9075 or (301)644-3550 • URL: http://www.wolterskluwerlb.com • 50 times a year. $450.00 per year. Newsletter.

**Federal Highway Administration - Office of Transportation Policy Studies**. 1200 New Jersey Ave. SE, 8th Fl. Washington, DC 20590. Phone: (202)366-9232; Fax: (202)366-3297; Email: mary.tischer@dot.gov • URL: http://www.fhwa.dot.gov/policy/otps • Formulation of highway policy and legislative initiatives. Principal areas of research interest are highway use, performance, and requirements and the relationship of these factors to commercial highway transport; truck sizes and weights; cost allocations; transportation user charge substructures, taxing policies and subsidy issues, and the effects of these issues upon various public and private groups; and the economic characteristics of specific industries (as necessary for the formulation of highway program policy).

***Federal Human Resources Week: News, Strategies and Best Practices for the HR Professional***. LRP Publications Library, lrp.com Technology Contacts, 747 Dresher Rd., Ste. 500 Horsham, PA 19044. Phone: 800-341-7874 or (215)784-0860 or (215)784-0910; Fax: (215)784-9639 or (215)784-0275; Email: techsup@lrp.com • URL: http://www.lrp.com • 48 times a year. $350.00 per year. Newsletter. Covers federal personnel issues, including legislation, benefits, budgets, and downsizing.

***Federal Jobs Digest***. Federal Jobs Digest, 326 Main St. Emmaus, PA 18049. Phone: 800-824-5000 • URL: http://www.jobsfed.com • $20 Individuals 3 months; $40 Individuals 6 months; $80 Individuals /year; $155 Two years. Covers: Over 10,000 specific job openings in the federal government in each issue. Vacancies from over 300 Federal Agencies are covered. Entries include: Position name, title, General Schedule (GS) grade, and Wage Grade (WG), closing date for applications, announcement number, application address, phone, and name of contact.

***The Federal Manager***. Federal Managers Association, 1641 Prince St. Alexandria, VA 22314-2818. Phone: (703)683-8700; Fax: (703)683-8707; Email: info@fedmanagers.org • URL: http://www.fedmanagers.org • Quarterly. Covers management and legislative issues in the government that affect federal managers. Formerly *Federal Managers Quarterly*.

***Federal Regional Yellow Book: Who's Who in the Federal Government's Departments, Agencies, Military Installations, and Service Academies Outside of Washington, DC***. Leadership Directories Inc., 104 5th Ave. New York, NY 10011-6901. Phone: (212)627-4140; Fax: (212)645-0931; Email: info@leadershipdirectories.com • URL: http://www.leadershipdirectories.com • Semiannual. $465 Individuals annual. Lists over 35,000 federal officials and support staff at 8,000 regional offices.

***Federal Register***. Office of the Federal Register. U. S. Government Printing Office, 732 N Capitol St. NW Washington, DC 20401. Phone: 866-512-1800 or (202)512-1800 or (866)512-1800; Fax: (202)512-2104 or (202)512-2250; Email: contactcenter@gpo.gov • URL: http://www.gpo.gov • Daily except Saturday and Sunday. $764.00 per year. Publishes regulations and legal notices issued by federal agencies, including executive orders and presidential proclamations. Issued by the National Archives and Records Administration (www.nara.gov).

***Federal Research in Progress (FEDRIP)***. National Technical Information Service Office of Product Management, 5285 Port Royal Rd. Springfield, VA 22161. Phone: (703)605-6515; Email: info@ntis.gov • URL: http://www.ntis.gov/products/database.aspx • Monthly. $450 single user subscription; $625 1 network; $950 2-5 networks; $1,400 6-10 networks. Database covers: more than 150,000 federally-funded research projects currently in progress in the physical sciences, engineering, health, agriculture, and life sciences areas. Database includes: Project title, starting date, principal investigator, performing and sponsoring organization, detailed abstract, description of the research, objective, and findings (when available).

***Federal Reserve Bank of Atlanta: Economic Review***. Federal Reserve Bank of Atlanta, 1000 Peachtree St. NE Atlanta, GA 30309-4470. Phone: (404)498-8500 • URL: http://www.frbatlanta.org • Quarterly. Free.

***Federal Reserve Bank of Dallas: Southwest Ecomomy Economic Review***. Federal Reserve Bank of Dallas, 2200 N Pearl St. Dallas, TX 75201-2216. Phone: 800-333-4460 or (214)922-6000 or (214)922-5254; Fax: (214)922-6500 or (214)922-5268; Email: info@dallasfed.org • URL: http://www.dallasfed.org • Quarterly. Economic banking review.

***Federal Reserve Bank of Kansas City***. Federal Reserve Bank of Kansas City, 1 Memorial Dr. Kansas City, MO 64108-4604. Phone: 800-333-1010 or (816)881-2000; Fax: (816)881-2846 or (816)881-2569 • URL: http://www.kc.frb.org • Quarterly. Free.

***Federal Reserve Bank of Minneapolis: Quarterly Review***. Federal Reserve Bank of Minneapolis, Research Department, 90 Hennepin Ave. Minneapolis, MN 55401. Phone: (612)204-5000 • URL: http://www.minneapolisfed.org/research/economic_research • Quarterly. Free.

***Federal Reserve Bank of New York: Economic Policy Review***. Federal Reserve Bank of New York, Public Information Office, 33 Liberty St. New York, NY 10045-0001. Phone: (212)720-5000; Email: general.info@ny.frb.org • URL: http://www.newyorkfed.org • Quarterly. Free.

***Federal Reserve Bank of Philadelphia: Business Review***. Federal Reserve Bank of Philadelphia, Research Dept., 10 Independence Mall Philadelphia, PA 19106-1574. Phone: (215)574-6000; Fax: (215)574-3847 • URL: http://www.phil.frb.org • Quarterly. Free. Contains articles on current topics in economics, finance, and banking.

***Federal Reserve Bank of Richmond: Economic Quarterly***. Federal Reserve Bank of Richmond - Research Department,

701 E Byrd St. Richmond, VA 23219-3921. Phone: (804)697-8000; Fax: (804)697-8287 • URL: http://www.richmondfed.org/research • Quarterly. Free. Formerly *Federal Reserve Bank of Richmond: Economic Review*.

***Federal Reserve Bank of Saint Louis: Review***. Federal Reserve Bank of Saint Louis, 1 Federal Reserve Bank Plz., Broadway and Locust St. Saint Louis, MO 63101. Phone: 800-333-0810 or (314)444-8444 • URL: http://www.stlouisfed.org • Quarterly. Bimonthly. Free.

***Federal Reserve Bank of San Francisco Economic Letter***. Federal Reserve Bank of San Francisco. Economic Letter, PO Box 7702 San Francisco, CA 94105. Phone: 888-339-3506 or (415)974-2000; Fax: (415)974-3341 • URL: http://www.frbsf.org/economic-research/publications/economic-letter • 38 times a year. Free. Formerly *Federal Reserve Bank of San Francisco: Weekly Letter*.

***Federal Reserve Bank of San Francisco: Economic Review***. Federal Reserve Bank of San Francisco, 101 Market St. San Francisco, CA 94105. Phone: 800-227-4133 or (415)974-2000 • URL: http://www.frbsf.org • Annual. Free.

**Federal Reserve Board - Division of International Finance - Advanced Foreign Economies Section**. 20th St. & Constitution Ave. NW Washington, DC 20551. Phone: (202)452-2865; Email: paul.wood@frb.gov • URL: http://www.federalreserve.gov/econresdata/ifafe-staff.htm • Economic developments and policies in major industrial countries that affect international payments, foreign exchange markets, and U.S. economic activity and policy. Research focuses on open-economy macroeconomic issues.

***Federal Reserve Board Publications and Education Resources***. Board of Governors of the Federal Reserve System, Phone: (202)452-3000; Fax: (202)452-3819 • URL: http://www.federalreserve.gov/publications.htm • Web site provides access to statistics, surveys, and research from the Federal Reserve Board. *Federal Reserve Bulletin* articles are available as abstracts or full text (PDF) currently or from six-year archives. The link "Statistics: Releases and Historical Data" offers daily, weekly, monthly, quarterly, and annual data in great detail for interest rates, foreign exchange, consumer credit, money stock measures, industrial production indexes, bank reserves, and other items. Historical tabulations are available for various time periods. Free.

***Federal Reserve Board Publications***. U.S. Board of Governors of the Federal Reserve System, 20th St. and Constitution Ave. NW Washington, DC 20551. Phone: 800-827-3340 or (202)452-6400 • URL: http://www.federalreserve.gov • Semiannual. Free.

***Federal Staff Directory: With Biographical Information on Executive Staff Personnel***. CQ Press, 2300 N St. NW, Ste. 800 Washington, DC 20037. Phone: 866-427-7737 or (202)729-1900; Email: customerservice@cqpress.com • URL: http://www.cqpress.com • Three times a year. $259.00 per year. Single copies, $149.00. Lists 35,000 staff members of federal departments and agencies, with biographies of 3,200 key executives. Includes keyword and name indexes.

***Federal-State Court Directory***. Leadership Directories Inc., 104 5th Ave. New York, NY 10011-6901. Phone: (212)627-4140; Fax: (212)645-0931; Email: info@leadershipdirectories.com • URL: http://www.leadershipdirectories.com • Annual. $20 Individuals plus s&h; $120 Individuals print paperback. Covers: All federal court judges and clerks of court, and United States attorneys and magistrates, judges; state supreme court chief justices and state court administrators; Supreme Court Chief Justices of Canada and other nations. Database includes: Organization charts for state court systems. Entries include: Judge, clerk, probation office, or magistrate's name, address, phone.

***Federal Tax Products***. U. S. Government Printing Office, 732 N Capitol St. NW Washington, DC 20401. Phone: 866-512-1800 or (202)512-1800 or (866)512-1800; Fax: (202)512-2104 or (202)512-2250; Email: contactcenter@gpo.gov • URL: http://www.gpo.gov • Annual. $27.00. CD-ROM issued by the Internal Revenue Service (www.irs.treas.gov/forms_pubs/). Provides current tax forms, instructions, and publications. Also includes older tax forms beginning with 1991.

***Federal Taxation of Income, Estates and Gifts***. Warren, Gorham & Lamont/RIA, 395 Hudson St. New York, NY 10014. Phone: 800-950-1216 or (212)367-6300; Fax: (914)749-5042; Email: customer_services@riag.com • URL: http://www.riahome.com • 3/year. $1,950 print; $1,640 online. Five looseleaf volumes. Updates three times a year. Covers aspects of income taxation of individuals, corporations, partnerships, estates, and gifts. Clear analysis to exact answers to tax questions.

***Federal Taxation of Insurance Companies***. Dennis P. Van Mieghem and others. Prentice Hall PTR, 1 Lake St. Upper Saddle River, NJ 07458. Phone: 800-227-1816 or (201)236-7676 or (201)236-7000; Fax: (800)445-6991 or (317)428-3343 • URL: http://phbusiness.prenhall.com • $447.00 per year. Looseleaf service. Biweekly updates.

***Federal Taxation of Oil and Gas Transactions***. Matthew Bender and Company Inc., 1275 Broadway Albany, NY 12204-2638. Phone: 800-424-4200 or (518)487-3000; Fax: (518)487-3573 or (800)424-4200; Email: customer.support@lexisnexis.com • URL: http://www.matthewbender.com • $771 book; $701 e-book. Covers the depletion deduction; tax treament of costs incurred in drilling; oil and gas partnerships; equipment depreciation, and more.

***Federal Taxes Affecting Real Estate***. Matthew Bender and Company Inc., 1275 Broadway Albany, NY 12204-2638. Phone: 800-424-4200 or (518)487-3000; Fax: (518)487-3573 or (800)424-4200; Email: customer.support@lexisnexis.com • URL: http://www.matthewbender.com • Semiannual. $573 book; $487 e-book. Explains and illustrates the most important federal tax principles applying to daily real estate transactions.

***Federal Taxes and the Private Club***. PKF International, 534 Broadhollow Rd. Melville, NY 11747. Phone: (631)756-5555; Fax: (631)756-5120 • URL: http://www.pkf.com • Annual. $25.00. Provides a summary of tax issues affecting private clubs.

***Federal Taxes Citator***. MacMillan Publishing Co., 200 Old Tappan Rd. Old Tappan, NJ 07675. Phone: 800-223-2336 • $550.00 per year. Two looseleaf volumes. Monthly supplements.

***Federal Taxes: Internal Memoranda of the IRS***. Prentice Hall PTR, 1 Lake St. Upper Saddle River, NJ 07458. Phone: 800-227-1816 or (201)236-7676 or (201)236-7000; Fax: (800)445-6991 or (317)428-3343 • URL: http://phbusiness.prenhall.com • Looseleaf. Periodic supplementation. Price on application.

***Federal Times***. Gannett Government Media Corp., 6883 Commercial Dr. Springfield, VA 22159-0500. Phone: 800-368-5718 or (703)750-7400 • URL: http://www.gannettgovernmentmedia.com • Weekly (Mon.). Federal bureaucracy; technology in government.

**Federal Trade Commission - Bureau of Economics**. 600 Pennsylvania Ave. NW Washington, DC 20580. Phone: (202)326-3419; Fax: (202)326-2380; Email: mgaynor@ftc.gov • URL: http://www.ftc.gov/about-ftc/bureaus-offices/bureau-economics • Economics of antitrust, consumer protection, and regulation.

**Federal University of Mines Gerais - Center for Regional Development and Planning**. Av. Antonio Carlos, 6627 31270-901 Belo Horizonte, MT, Brazil. Phone: 55 31 34097100; Fax: 55 31 34097203 • URL: http://web.face.ufmg.br/cedeplar/site/ • Regional economics, especially the intersection of economics and demography with other disciplines, particularly health and the environment.

**Federal University of Santa Catarina - Socio-Economic Center**. Campus Universitário - Trinidade 88040-900 Florianópolis, SC, Brazil. Phone: 55 48 33319560; Fax: 55 48 33319585; Email: rcalves@cse.ufsc.br • URL: http://www.cse.ufsc.br/ • Social and economic issues, including the effectiveness of economic policies designed to direct social change.

***Federal Withholding Tax Tables***. Wolters Kluwer Law & Business CCH, 2700 Lake Cook Rd. Riverwoods, IL 60015. Phone: 888-224-7377 or (847)267-7000; Email: cust_serv@cch.com • URL: http://www.cchgroup.com • Annual. $18.00.

**Federation of Euro-Asian Stock Exchanges**. Borsa Istanbul Bldg., Emirgan TR-34467 Istanbul, Turkey. Phone: 90 212 298 2160; Fax: 90 212 298 2209; Email: secretariat@feas.org • URL: http://www.feas.org • Committed to a fair, efficient and transparent market environment. Works to eliminate trade barriers, and to promote development of the Euro-Asian stock markets. Provides cross listing and trading opportunities for securities issued within member countries.

**Federation of European Private Port Operators**. Ave. des Arts 3-4-5 B-1210 Brussels, Belgium. Phone: 32 2 7367552; Fax: 32 2 7323149; Email: info@feport.be • URL: http://www.feport.be • European Private port operators. Represents members' interests.

**Federation of European Risk Management Associations**. Ave. de Tervuren, 237 B-12 B-1150 Brussels, Belgium. Phone: 32 2 7619432; Fax: 32 2 7718720; Email: info@ferma.eu • URL: http://www.ferma.eu • Exists to widen and raise the culture of Risk Management throughout Europe to its members and to the risk management and insurance community.

**Federation of Industries Products Systems and Services for Construction**. Via Brenta, 13 I-00198 Rome, Italy. Phone: 39 6 8555203; Fax: 39 6 8559860; Email: finco@fincoweb.org • URL: http://www.fincoweb.org • Promotes the products systems and services used by the construction industries.

**Federation of Thai Industries**. Queen Sirikit National Convention Centre, 4th Fl., Zone C, 60th Rachadapisek Rd., Klongtoey Bangkok 10110, Thailand. Phone: 66 2 3451000; Fax: 66 2 3451296; Email: information@off.fti.or.th • URL: http://www.fti.or.th • Represents the industrial enterprises in Thailand. Seeks to identify and solve problems and issues arising in the conduct of industrial enterprises.

***Fedstats***. Federal Interagency Council on Statistical Policy, Phone: (202)395-7254 • URL: http://www.fedstats.gov • Web site features an efficient search facility for full-text statistics produced by more than 100 federal agencies, including the Census Bureau, the Bureau of Economic Analysis, and the Bureau of Labor Statistics. Boolean searches can be made within one agency or for all agencies combined. Links are offered to international statistical bureaus, including the UN, IMF, OECD, UNESCO, Eurostat, and 20 individual countries. Fees: Free.

***FedWorld: A Program of the United States Department of Commerce***. National Technical Information Service, Phone: 800-553-NTIS or (703)605-6000; Fax: (703)605-6900; Email: webmaster@fedworld.gov • URL: http://www.fedworld.gov • Web site offers "a comprehensive central access point for searching, locating, ordering, and acquiring government and business information." Emphasis is on searching the Web pages, databases, and government reports of a wide variety of federal agencies. Fees: Free.

***Fee Income Growth Strategies***. Siefer Consultants Inc., PO Box 1384 Storm Lake, IA 50588. Phone: (712)660-1026; Email: info@siefer.com • URL: http://www.siefer.com • Description: Discusses the role of fees and service charges for money orders, cashier's checks, nonsufficient funds, loans, automatic teller machine cards, and other ancillary services in the profitability of financial institutions.

***Feed Additive Compendium***. Miller Publishing Co., 5810 W 78th St., Ste. 200 Bloomington, MN 55439. Phone: (952)930-4344 or (952)931-0211; Fax: (952)938-1832; Email: tlundeen@feedstuffs.com • URL: http://www.feedstuffs.com • Annual. $260 U.S. and Canada; $275 Other countries. Covers the use of drugs as additives to livestock and poultry feed.

***Feed and Feeding Digest***. National Grain and Feed Association, 1250 I St. NW, Ste. 1003 Washington, DC 20005. Phone: (202)289-0873; Fax: (202)289-5388; Email: ngfa@ngfa.org • URL: http://www.ngfa.org • Monthly. Membership.

***Feed Bulletin***. Jacobsen Publishing Co., 1123 W Washington Blvd. Chicago, IL 60607. Phone: (312)726-6600; Fax: (312)733-2561; Email: info@thejacobsen.com • URL: http://www.thejacobsen.com • Daily. $750.00 per year.

***Feedstuffs***. Miller Publishing Co., 5810 W 78th St., Ste. 200 Bloomington, MN 55439. Phone: (952)930-4344 or (952)931-0211; Fax: (952)938-1832; Email: tlundeen@feedstuffs.com • URL: http://www.feedstuffs.com • Weekly. $144 Individuals; $230 Two years; $150 Canada; $235 Individuals Europe and Mid East; airmail; $280 Other countries Japan, Far E./Aus. airmail; $210 Individuals Mexico/Central/South America; $196 Individuals print & internet version; $334 Two years print & internet version; $202 Canada print & internet version; $344 Canada print & internet version, 2 years.

**Female Europeans of Medium and Small Enterprises**. Rue Jacques de Lalaing 4 B-1040 Brussels, Belgium. Phone: 32 2 2850714; Fax: 32 2 2307861 • URL: http://www.femonline.eu • Represents female co-entrepreneurs and entrepreneurs working in small and medium-sized businesses in Europe. Seeks to improve the cultural, legal, and social position of female co-entrepreneurs and self-employed women. Acts as the European point of contact dealing with all issues related to female co-entrepreneurs or self-employed women. Aims to achieve an exchange of knowledge and experience amongst women of all EU Member states and also other European countries. Encourages an entrepreneurial spirit amongst women.

***Feminist Economics***. International Association for Feminist Economics. Taylor & Francis Ltd., 2 Park Sq., Milton Park Abingdon OX14 4RN, United Kingdom. Phone: 44 22 70176000 or 44 20 70176000; Fax: 44 22 70176699 or (701)76336; Email: info@e-elgar.co.uk • URL: http://www.taylorandfrancisgroup.com • Three times a year. Individuals, $68.00 per year; institutions, $184.00 per year. Includes articles on issues relating to the employment and economic opportunities of women.

***Femme-Lines***. Earl Barron Publications Inc., 225 E 36 St. New York, NY 10016. Phone: (212)683-6593 • Bimonthly. $8.00 per year.

***Ferrara on Insider Trading and The Wall***. Ralph C. Ferrara. ALM Media Properties LLC, 120 Broadway, 5th Fl. New York, NY 10271-1100. Phone: (212)457-9400; Fax: (646)417-7705; Email: customercare@alm.com • URL: http://www.alm.com • $540. Demonstrates how firms can use "Chinese Walls" and other devices to control the dissemination of material, nonpublic information by employees. Includes "suggested guidelines for deterring insider trading by employees." (Law Journal Press).

**FHI 360 - National Institute for Work and Learning**. 1825 Connecticut Ave. NW Washington, DC 20009. Phone: (202)884-8184; Fax: (202)884-8422; Email: icharner@fhi360.org • URL: http://www.niwl.org • Research areas include adult education, training, unemployment insurance, and career development.

**Fiber and Electro Optics Research Center**. Virginia Polytechnic Institute and State University, Dept. of Electrical Engineering, 106 Plantation Rd. Blacksburg, VA 24061. Phone: (540)231-7203; Fax: (540)231-4561; Email: roclaus@vt.edu • URL: http://www.unirel.vt.edu/history/extension_outreach_research/technology_development_centers.html.

***Fiber Optics and Communications***. Information Gatekeepers Inc., 1340 Soldiers Field Rd., Ste. 2 Boston, MA 02135. Phone: 800-323-1088 or (617)782-5033 or (617)232-3111; Fax: (617)782-5735 or (617)734-8562; Email: info@igigroup.com • URL: http://www.igigroup.com • Monthly. $695.00. Emphasis on the use of fiber optics in telecommunications.

***Fiber Optics News***. Access Intelligence L.L.C., 4 Choke Cherry Rd., 2nd Fl. Rockville, MD 20850. Phone: 800-777-5006 or (301)354-2000 or (301)354-2101; Fax: (301)309-3847 or (801)365-2300; Email: info@accessintel.com • URL: http://

www.accessintel.com/ • Weekly. $797.00 per year. Newsletter.

***Fiber Optics Yellow Pages: The International Optical Networks/ Fiberoptics Yellow Pages***. Information Gatekeepers Inc., 1340 Soldiers Field Rd., Ste. 2 Boston, MA 02135. Phone: 800-323-1088 or (617)782-5033 or (617)232-3111; Fax: (617)782-5735 or (617)734-8562; Email: info@igigroup.com • URL: http://www.igigroup.com • Annual. $89.95 print. Includes manufacturers of fiber optics products. Provides a glossary and a discussion of current uses of fiber optics. Formerly *Fiber Optics Yellow Pages*.

***Fiber Organon: Featuring Manufactured Fibers***. Fiber Economics Bureau, 1530 Wilson Blvd., Ste. 690 Arlington, VA 22209. Phone: (703)875-0676; Fax: (703)875-0675; Email: ddezan@afma.org • URL: http://www.fibereconomics.com • Monthly. $300.00 per year. Summarizes "confidential producer information on the U.S. manufactured fiber market." Provides detailed statistics on production, shipments, exports, and capacity. Special issues cover worldwide data and specific end use products. (Fiber Economics Bureau is a subsidiary of the American Fiber Manufacturers Association.).

***Fiberoptic Product News***. Reed Elsevier Group plc Reed Business Information, 360 Park Ave. S New York, NY 11010. Phone: (212)791-4208; Email: corporatecommunications@reedbusiness.com • URL: http://www.reedbusiness.com • Monthly. $167.75 per year. Includes annual *Directory* and five *European editions*. Provides general coverage of the fiber optics industry, for both producers and users.

**Fibrous Materials Research Center**. Drexel University, Dept. of Materials Engineering, 3141 Chestnut St. Philadelphia, PA 19104. Phone: (215)895-2323; Fax: (215)895-6760; Email: materials@coe.drexel.edu • URL: http://www.materials.drexel.edu • Research fields include computer-aided design of nonwoven fabrics and design curves for industrial fibers.

***Fiduciary Tax Guide***. Wolters Kluwer Law & Business CCH, 2700 Lake Cook Rd. Riverwoods, IL 60015. Phone: 888-224-7377 or (847)267-7000; Email: cust_serv@cch.com • URL: http://www.cchgroup.com • Monthly. $478.00 per year. Looseleaf service. Covers federal income taxation of estates, trusts, and beneficiaries. Provides information on gift and generation- skipping taxation.

***Field Crop Abstracts***. CABI Publishing North America, 38 Chauncey St., Ste. 1002 Boston, MA 02111. Phone: 800-552-3083; Email: cabi-nao@cabi.org • URL: http://www.cabi.org • Monthly. Published in England by CABI Publishing, formerly Commonwealth Agricultural Bureaux.

***Field Trade Directory of Peru***. Field Servicio de Informaciones del Peru, Coronel Incian 135-OF 601, Miraflores Lima, Peru. • Annual. $65. Covers: 7,000 Peruvian importers, factories, exporters, wholesalers, retailers, and more than 1,000 business activities. Database includes: Information on hotels, restaurants, and general information on selling, buying, and information sources in Peru. Entries include: Name, address, phone, cable, telex, manager name.

***FII Annual Guide to Stocks***. Financial Information Inc., 30 Montgomery St. Jersey City, NJ 07302. Phone: (201)332-5400 • Annual. $2,250. Two volumes. Formerly *Financial Stock Guide Service: Directory of Active Stocks*.

**Fiji Commerce and Employers Federation**. PO Box 575 Suva, Fiji. Phone: 679 679 3313188; Fax: 679 679 3302183; Email: employer@fcef.com.fj • URL: http://www.fcef.com.fj • Employers. Seeks to create and maintain a domestic political and social climate conducive to business. Represents members' interests before government agencies, labor and industrial organizations, and the public; gathers and disseminates information.

***Film and Video Finder***. National Information Center for Educational Media. Plexus Publishing Inc., 143 Old Marlton Pke. Medford, NJ 08055-8750. Phone: 800-300-9868 or (609)654-6500; Fax: (609)654-4309; Email: info@plexuspublishing.com • URL: http://www.plexuspublishing.com • Biennial. Contains 675,000 listings of film and video educational, technical and vocational children's programs and literary materials.

***Film Journal International***. Nielsen Business Media Inc., 770 Broadway New York, NY 10003-9522. Phone: 866-890-8541 or (646)654-4500 or (646)654-5000; Fax: (646)654-5584 or (646)654-4500; Email: bmcomm@nielsen.com • URL: http://www.nielsenbusinessmedia.com • Monthly. $65.00 per year. Formerly *Film Journal*.

***Film Quarterly: Quarterly of Film, Radio and Television***. University of California Press - Journals and Digital Publishing Division, Journals Fulfillment Dept., Ste. 400, 155 Grand Ave. Oakland, CA 94612-3758. Phone: (510)883-8232; Fax: (510)836-8910; Email: customerservice@ucpress.edu • URL: http://ucpressjournals.com • Quarterly. 102 Institutions. Review of radio, tv, and fim.

***Films and Audiovisual Information***. U. S. Government Printing Office, 732 N Capitol St. NW Washington, DC 20401. Phone: 866-512-1800 or (202)512-1800 or (866)512-1800; Fax: (202)512-2104 or (202)512-2250; Email: contactcenter@gpo.gov • URL: http://www.gpo.gov • Annual. Free. Issued by the Superintendent of Documents. A list of government publications on motion picture and audiovisual topics. Formerly *Motion Pictures, Films and Audiovisual Information*. (Subject Bibliography No. 73.).

***Films and Videos on Photography***. A and C Black Publishers Ltd., 50 Bedford Sq. London WC1B 3DP, United Kingdom. Phone: 44 020 7631 5600 or 44 20 7631 5600; Fax: 44 020 7631 5800 or 44 20 7631 5800; Email: customerservices@acblack.com • URL: http://www.acblack.com • $15 Individuals. Covers: Films and videos dealing with photography. Entries include: Title, length, whether in color or black-and-white, format, release date, country in which produced, language, name of director, names of producing agency and distributors, synopsis, series note, review citations, and awards; distributors' name and address given in a separate list.

***Filtration News***. Eagle Publications Inc., 2 Eastport Plz. Dr. Ste. 100 Collinsville, IL 62234-6109. Phone: (618)345-5400; Fax: (618)345-5474; Email: info@hometownphonebook.com • URL: http://www.hometownphonebook.com • Bimonthly. Controlled circulation. Emphasis is on new filtration products for industrial use.

***Finance and Accounting for Nonfinancial Managers***. American Management Association Extension Institute, 1601 Broadway New York, NY 10019. Phone: 800-262-9699 or (518)586-8100; Fax: (518)903-8168 • $19.95. Looseleaf. Self-study course. Emphasis is on practical explanations, examples, and problem solving. Quizzes and a case study are included.

***Finance and Development***. International Monetary Fund, Publication Services, 700 19th St. NW Washington, DC 20431. Phone: (202)623-7430; Fax: (202)623-7201; Email: publications@imf.org • URL: http://www.imf.org • Quarterly. Free.

**Finance and Leasing Association**. Imperial House, 2nd Fl., 15-19 Kingsway London WC2B 6UN, United Kingdom. Phone: 44 20 78366511; Fax: 44 20 74209600; Email: info@fla.org.uk • URL: http://www.financeleasingassociation.co.uk • Trade association representing the UK asset, consumer, and motor finance sectors. Provides high-level representation and lobbying at both national and EU levels, supported by technical information and industry statistics. Complies with the association's code of conduct, which is supported by their conciliation and arbitration schemes. Provides a focus and forum for the industry, and has a high level of member involvement in its many working groups. Organizes conferences, workshops, and training courses.

**Finance Project**. 1150 18th St. NW, Ste. 325 Washington, DC 20036-3856. Phone: (202)628-4200; Fax: (202)628-1293; Email: info@financeproject.org • URL: http://www.financeproject.org • Develops and disseminates information, knowledge, tools, technical assistance for improved policies, programs, financing strategies that will benefit children, families and communities.

**Finance Sector Union of Australia**. 341 Queen St. Melbourne, VIC 3000, Australia. Fax: 61 39 1300366378 or 61 39 1300307943; Email: fsuinfo@fsunion.org.au • URL: http://www.fsunion.org.au • Employees of private and public sector financial services companies. Works to enhance members' welfare and conditions of employment. Conducts union organization training and insurance industry research.

***Financial Accounting Series***. Financial Accounting Standards Board, PO Box 5116 Norwalk, CT 06856-5116. Phone: 800-748-0659 or (203)847-0700; Fax: (203)849-9714; Email: director@fasb.org • URL: http://www.fasb.org • Monthly. Price on application.

***Financial Analysts Journal***. CFA Institute, 560 Ray C. Hunt Dr. Charlottesville, VA 22903-2981. Phone: 800-247-8132 or (434)951-5499; Fax: (434)951-5262; Email: info@cfainstitute.org • URL: http://www.cfainstitute.org/pages/index.aspx • Bimonthly. $50 Members print and online; $100 Individuals print and online; $395 Institutions print and online. Contains important topics related to the investment industry.

***Financial and Estate Planning: Analysis, Strategies and Checklists***. Wolters Kluwer Law & Business CCH, 2700 Lake Cook Rd. Riverwoods, IL 60015. Phone: 888-224-7377 or (847)267-7000; Email: cust_serv@cch.com • URL: http://www.cchgroup.com • 4 looseleaf volumes. Price on application. services.

**Financial and Security Products Association**. 1024 Mebane Oaks Rd., No. 273 Mebane, NC 27302. Phone: 800-843-6082 or (919)648-0664; Fax: (919)648-0670 • URL: http://fspa1.com • Formerly National Independent Bank Equipment and Systems Association.

***Financial Annual Registrars Service***. Extel Financial Ltd., Fitzroy House,13-17 Epworth St., 13-17 Epworth St. London EC2A 4DL, United Kingdom. Phone: 44 71 2513333; Fax: 44 71 2512725 • Annual. $110. Covers: United Kingdom companies listed on one of the UK stock exchanges. Entries include: Company name, registrar's name, address, phone, fax, telex, types of stocks and shares, nominal value.

***Financial Concepts and Tools for Business Management***. American CPE Inc., 826 Riviera Mansfield, TX 76063. Phone: 800-990-4273 or (817)477-0222; Fax: (817)473-4998; Email: director@americancpe.com • URL: http://www.americancpe.com • Contains detailed training information covering basic financial concepts and their use in business management settings.

***Financial Counseling and Planning (JFCP)***. Association for Financial Counseling and Planning Education, 1940 Duke St., Ste. 200 Alexandria, VA 22314-3452. Phone: (703)684-4484; Fax: (703)684-4485 • URL: http://www.afcpe.org • Semiannual. Disseminates scholarly research relating to financial planning and counseling.

***Financial Executive***. Financial Executives International, 1250 Headquarters Plz., West Tower, 7th Fl. Morristown, NJ 07960. Phone: 877-359-1070 or (973)765-1000; Fax: (973)765-1018; Email: membership@financialexecutives.org • URL: http://www.financialexecutives.org • Monthly. $69 Individuals; $115 Two years; $79 Other countries; $129 Two years international; $39 Individuals online. Magazine covering corporate financial management for senior executives of major corporations. Published for corporate financial officers and managers.

**Financial Executives International**. 1250 Headquarters Plz., West Tower, 7th Fl. Morristown, NJ 07960. Phone: 877-359-1070 or (973)765-1000; Fax: (973)765-1018; Email: membership@financialexecutives.org • URL: http://www.financialexecutives.org • Professional organization of corporate financial executives performing duties of chief financial officer, controller, treasurer, or vice-president-finance. Sponsors research activities through its affiliated Financial Executives Research Foundation. Maintains offices in Toronto, Canada, and Washington, DC.

**Financial Executives Research Foundation**. Financial Executives International, 1250 Headquarters Plz., West Tower, 7th Fl. Morristown, NJ 07960. Phone: (973)765-1000; Fax: (973)765-1018; Email: mhollein@financialexecutives.org • URL: http://www.financialexecutives.org • Publishes research in business management, with emphasis on corporate financial management issues. Maintains inquiry services.

***Financial Flows and the Developing Countries***. World Bank Group, 1818 H St. NW Washington, DC 20433. Phone: 800-831-0463 or (202)473-1000; Fax: (202)477-6391; Email: books@worldbank.org • URL: http://www.worldbank.org • Quarterly. $150.00 per year. Concerned mainly with debt, capital markets, and foreign direct investment. Includes statistical tables.

***Financial History: Chronicling the History of America's Capital Markets***. Museum of American Finance, 48 Wall St. New York, NY 10005. Phone: (212)908-4110; Fax: (212)908-4601 • URL: http://www.moaf.org/index • Quarterly. Membership. Contains articles on early stock and bond markets and trading in the U. S., with photographs and other illustrations. Current trading in rare and unusual, obsolete stock and bond certificates is featured. Formerly *Friends of Financial History*.

**Financial Industry Regulatory Authority**. 1735 K St. Washington, DC 20006. Phone: (301)590-6500; Fax: (202)293-6260; Email: francine.lee@finra.org • URL: http://www.finra.org • Formerly National Association of Securities Dealers.

**Financial Institutions and Markets Research Center**. c/o Ravi Jagannathan, Director, Kellogg School of Management, Northwestern University, 2001 Sheridan Rd., Jacobs Ctr., Rm. 4213 Evanston, IL 60208. Phone: (847)491-8338; Fax: (847)491-5719 • URL: http://www.kellogg.northwestern.edu/research/fimrc/index.htm • Does research in the management and public regulation of financial institutions. A unit of the J. L. Kellogg Graduate School of Management.

***Financial Institutions***. U. S. Government Printing Office, 732 N Capitol St. NW Washington, DC 20401. Phone: 866-512-1800 or (202)512-1800 or (866)512-1800; Fax: (202)512-2104 or (202)512-2250; Email: contactcenter@gpo.gov • URL: http://www.gpo.gov • Annual. Free. Lists government publications. Formerly *Banks and Banking*. GPO Subject Bibliography No. 128.

***Financial Management Association: Membership/Professional Directory***. Financial Management Association, College of Business Administration 3331, University of South Florida, 4202 E Fowler Ave., BSN 3331 Tampa, FL 33620-5500. Phone: (813)974-2084; Fax: (813)974-3318; Email: fma@coba.usf.edu • URL: http://www.fma.org • Annual. Lists 4,800 corporate financial officers and professors of financial management.

***Financial Management (FM)***. Financial Management Association International, University of South Florida, College of Business Administration, 4202 E Fowler Ave., BSN 3331 Tampa, FL 33620-5500. Phone: (813)974-2084; Fax: (813)974-3318; Email: fma@coba.usf.edu • URL: http://www.fma.org • Quarterly. $392 Institutions for Americas, online only; $450 Institutions for Americas, print + online; £218 Institutions for UK, online only; £251 Institutions for UK, print + online; €276 Institutions for non euro zone, online only; €317 Institutions for non euro zone, print + online; €276 Institutions for Euro zones, online only; €317 Institutions for Euro zones, print + online. Covers theory and practice of financial planning, international finance, investment banking, and portfolio management. Includes *Financial Practice* and *Education and Contemporary Finance Digest*.

**Financial Managers Society**. 1 N La Salle St., Ste. 3100 Chicago, IL 60602-4003. Phone: 800-275-4367 or (312)578-1300; Fax: (312)578-1308; Email: info@fmsinc.org • URL: http://www.fmsinc.org • Works for the needs of finance and accounting professionals from banks, thrifts and credit unions. Offers career-enhancing education, specialized publications, national leadership opportunities and worldwide connections with other industry professionals.

**Financial Markets Association of Pakistan**. Treasury Management Group, National Bank of Pakistan, NBP Head Office, 1st Flr.,, I.I. Chundrigar Rd. Karachi 74000, Pakistan. Phone: 92 21 143738; Fax: 92 21 1439440 • URL: http://www.fma.com.pk • Represents the interest of financial markets. Aims to promote educational, professional, ethical and social interests of the financial markets and the banking industry. Provides training and development support and conducts survey studies and research of the various fields of financial markets.

**Financial Markets Association**. 333 2nd St. NE, No. 104 Washington, DC 20002. Phone: (202)544-6327; Email: dpfma@starpower.net • URL: http://www.fmaweb.org • Accountants, brokers, retail and investment bankers. Dedicated to meeting the needs of the financial industry for capital markets, fiduciary services, data processing, banking, asset/liability management, broker/dealer activities and investment advisory services. Offers educational seminars.

***Financial Markets, Institutions, and Instruments***. New York University, Salomon Center. Blackwell Publishing Inc., 350 Main St. Malden, MA 02148. Phone: 800-216-2522 or (781)388-8200; Fax: (781)388-8210; Email: journaladsusa@bos.blackwellpublishing.com • URL: http://www.blackwellpublishing.com • Five times a year. Institutions, $338.00 per year. Includes online edition. Edited to "bridge the gap between the academic and professional finance communities." Special fifth issue each year provides surveys of developments in four areas: money and banking, derivative securities, corporate finance, and fixed-income securities.

***Financial Planning and Financial Planning Ideas***. Prentice Hall PTR, 1 Lake St. Upper Saddle River, NJ 07458. Phone: 800-227-1816 or (201)236-7676 or (201)236-7000; Fax: (800)445-6991 or (317)428-3343 • URL: http://phbusiness.prenhall.com • Two looseleaf volumes. Periodic supplementation. Price on application.

**Financial Planning Association**. 7535 E Hampden Ave., Ste. 600 Denver, CO 80231. Phone: 800-322-4237 or (303)759-4900; Fax: (303)759-0749; Email: webfeedback@fpanet.org • URL: http://www.plannersearch.org/Pages/home.aspx • Works to support the financial planning process in order to help people achieve their goals and dreams. Believes that everyone needs objective advice to make smart financial decisions and that when seeking the advice of a financial planner, the planner should be a CFP professional.

***Financial Planning: The Magazine for Financial Service Professionals***. SourceMedia Inc., 1 State Street Plz., 27th Fl. New York, NY 10004. Phone: 800-221-1809 or (212)803-8200 or (212)803-8333; Fax: (212)843-9635 or (212)292-5216; Email: custserv@sourcemedia.com • URL: http://www.sourcemedia.com • Monthly. $79.00 per year. Edited for independent financial planners and insurance agents. Covers retirement planning, estate planning, tax planning, and insurance, including long-term healthcare considerations. Special features include a Retirement Planning Issue, Mutual Fund Performance Survey, and Variable Life and Annuity Survey.

***The Financial Post: Canadian's Business Voice***. Financial Post Datagroup, 333 King St., E. Toronto, ON, Canada M5A 4N2. Phone: 800-661-7678 or (416)350-6500 or (416)350-6300; Fax: (416)350-6501 or (416)350-6601; Email: fpdg@fpdata.finpost.com • URL: http://www.financialpost.com • Daily. $200.00 per year. Provides Canadian business, economic, financial, and investment news. Features extensive price quotes from all major Canadian markets: stocks, bonds, mutual funds, commodities, and currencies. Supplement available: *Financial Post 500*. Includes annual supplement.

***Financial Post Corporate Surveys***. Financial Post DataGroup, 1450 Don Mills Rd., Ste. 300 Don Mills, ON, Canada M3B 3R5. Phone: (416)383-2516; Fax: (416)386-2696 • URL: http://www.nationalpost.com • Database covers: 6,300 Canadian public companies and 19,000 defunct companies. Includes financial and operational information, key events, and key executives.

***The Financial Post***. National Post Online, Phone: 800-805-1184 or (244)383-2300; Fax: (416)383-2443 • URL: http://www.nationalpost.com/financialpost/ • Provides a broad range of Canadian business news online, with daily updates. Includes news, opinion, and special reports, as well as "Investing," "Money Rates," "Market Watch," and "Daily Mutual Funds." Allows advanced searching (Boolean operators), with links to various other sites. Fees: Free.

**Financial Publishers Association**. 15430 Endeavor Dr. Jupiter, FL 33478-6402. Phone: (561)515-8555; Fax: (561)282-4509; Email: support@financialpublishers.org • URL: http://www.financialpublishers.org • Aims to enhance the financial publishing industry's reputation for excellence. Shares knowledge of business best practices to help members. Provides financial information to guide investors.

***Financial Report of the United States Government***. U. S. Government Printing Office, 732 N Capitol St. NW Washington, DC 20401. Phone: 866-512-1800 or (202)512-1800 or (866)512-1800; Fax: (202)512-2104 or (202)512-2250; Email: contactcenter@gpo.gov • URL: http://www.gpo.gov • Annual. $21.00. Issued by the U. S. Treasury Department (www.treas.gov). Presents information about the financial condition and operations of the federal government. Program accounting systems of various government agencies provide data for the report.

***Financial Review of Alien Insurers***. National Association of Insurance Commissioners, 1100 Walnut St., Ste. 1500 Kansas City, MO 64106-2277. Phone: (816)842-3600; Fax: (816)783-8175 • URL: http://www.naic.org • Annual. $275 per year, including updates; payment with order. Covers: alien insurance companies operating in the United States market. Entries include: Company name, address, balance sheet, operating statement, financial statement with notes, and names of auditors; description of trust account with location, valuation, and expiration date.

***Financial Sentinel: Your Beacon to the World of Investing***. Gulf Atlantic Publish, Inc., 1947 Lee Rd. Winter Park, FL 32789-1834. Phone: (407)628-5700; Fax: (407)628-0807 • Monthly. $29.95 per year. Provides "The only complete listing of all OTC Bulletin Board stocks traded, with all issues listed on the Nasdaq SmallCap Market, the Toronto, and Vancouver Stock Exchanges." Also includes investment advice and recommendations of small capitalization stocks.

**Financial Services Round Table**. 1001 Pennsylvania Ave. NW, Ste. 500 S Washington, DC 20004. Phone: (202)289-4322; Fax: (202)628-2507; Email: info@fsroundtable.org • URL: http://fsroundtable.org • Companies registered with the Federal Reserve Board under the Bank Holding Company Act of 1956.

***Financial Times Business Reports: Technology***. The Economist, 25 St. James's St. London SW1A 1HG, United Kingdom. Phone: 44 20 7830 7000; Fax: 44 20 7839 2968; Email: letters@economist.com • URL: http://www.economistgroup.com • A database containing the full text of articles appearing in selected Financial Times newsletters covering developments in the business aspects of new technology, especially in the computer and telecommunications industries. It is commercially available online.

***Financial Times Currency Forecaster: Consensus Forecasts of the Worldwide Currency and Economic Outlook***. Briefings Publishing Group, 1101 King St., Ste. 110 Alexandria, VA 22314. Phone: 800-722-9221 or (703)518-2343; Fax: (703)684-2136 • Monthly. $695.00 per year. Newsletter. Provides forecasts of foreign currency exchange rates and economic conditions. Supplement available: *Mid-Month Global Financial Report*.

***Financial Times (London)***. The Financial Times, Inc., 1330 Ave. of the Americas New York, NY 10019. Phone: 800-628-8088 or (212)641-6544; Fax: (212)641-6515; Email: uscirculation@ft.com • URL: http://www.ft.com • Daily, except Sunday. $572.88 per year. An international business and financial newspaper, featuring news from London, Paris, Frankfurt, New York, and Tokyo. Includes worldwide stock and bond market data, commodity market data, and monetary/currency exchange information.

***Financial Times: Where Information Becomes Intelligence***. FT Group, Phone: (800)628-8088 • URL: http://www.ft.com • Web site provides extensive data and information relating to international business and finance, with daily updates. Includes Markets Today, Company News, Economic Indicators, Equities, Currencies, Capital Markets, Euro Prices, etc. Fees: Free (registration required).

**Financial Women's Association of New York**. 355 Lexington Ave., 15th Fl. New York, NY 10017. Phone: (212)297-2133; Fax: (212)370-9047 or (212)982-3008; Email: fwaoffice@fwa.org • URL: http://www.nywici.org/links/link_fwa.html • Persons of professional status in the field of finance in the New York metropolitan area. Works to promote and maintain high professional standards in the financial and business communities; provide an opportunity for members to enhance one another's professional contacts; achieve recognition of the contribution of women to the financial and business communities; encourage other women to seek professional positions within the financial and business communities. Activities include educational trips to foreign countries; college internship program including foreign student exchange; high school mentorship program; Washington and international briefings; placement service for members. Maintains speakers' bureau.

***Financial Yellow Book: Who's Who at the Leading U. S. Financial Institutions***. Leadership Directories Inc., 104 5th Ave. New York, NY 10011-6901. Phone: (212)627-4140; Fax: (212)645-0931; Email: info@leadershipdirectories.com • URL: http://www.leadershipdirectories.com • Semiannual. $465. Gives the names and titles of over 28,000 key executives in financial institutions. Includes the areas of banking, investment, money management, and insurance. Five indexes are provided: institution, executive name, geographic by state, financial service segment, and parent company.

***Financing Manufacturing Efficiency and Growth: A Manufacturer's Guide to State & Federal Resources***. Northeast-Midwest Institute, 50 F St. NW, Ste. 950 Washington, DC 20001. Phone: (202)464-4014 or (202)544-5200; Fax: (202)544-0043; Email: info@nemw.org • URL: http://www.nemw.org • Triennial. $36. Covers: federal and state government programs in business development, finance, targeted development, infrastructure, cooperative research and technology centers, trade, training, tax incentive, and similar activities. Entries include: For federal agencies—Agency or unit name, address, description of program with objectives, funding, eligible applicants, eligible activities, requirements, funding cycle, and examples of past recipients. For state agencies—Agency name, address, phone, description of program, requirements, case studies.

***Financing Opportunities for New Hampshire-Based Businesses***. Office of Economic Initiatives, 1000 Elm St., 12th Fl. Manchester, NH 03101. Phone: (603)644-1119 or (603)862-0710; Fax: (603)647-4410 or (603)862-0701; Email: ahj@christa.unit.edu • Covers: sources of financial assistance for businesses in New Hampshire, including federal, state, and local government agencies, nonprofit organizations, and venture capital firms. Entries include: Name, address, phone, description of activities.

***Find a Business***. Switchboard Inc., 120 Flanders Rd. Westborough, MA 01581. Phone: (508)898-1122; Fax: (508)870-2000 • URL: http://www.switchboard.com • Offers a solution to find business information on merchants with a web presence. Switchboard provides web generated leads to businesses providing services and technologies which utilize the Internet to facilitate commerce.

***Find A Christian Business***. Initiate Media Ltd., PO Box 47212 Auckland 1144, New Zealand. Email: advertise@initiatemedia.net • URL: http://www.initiatemedia.net • Annual. $29.95 Individuals. Covers: Service providers and businesses owned and managed by Christians in New Zealand.

***FindContractors.com***. Associated Builders and Contractors, Inc. 4250 N Fairfax Dr., 9th Fl. Arlington, VA 22203. Phone: (703)812-2000; Fax: (703)812-8203; Email: info@abc.org • URL: http://www.abc.org • Online member directory.

***Findex: The Worldwide Directory of Market Research Reports, Studies, and Surveys***. MarketResearch.com, 11200 Rockville Pke., Ste. 504 Rockville, MD 20852. Phone: 800-298-5699 or (240)747-3093; Fax: (240)747-3004; Email: customerservice@marketresearch.com • URL: http://www.marketresearch.com • Annual. Provides brief annotations of market research reports and related publications from about 1,000 publishers, arranged by topic. Back of book includes Report Titles by Publisher, Publishers/Distributors Directory, Subject Index, Geography Index, and Company Index. (Formerly published by Cambridge Information Group.).

***FindLaw: Internet Legal Resources***. FindLaw, 610 Opperman Dr. Eagan, MN 55123. Phone: 800-455-4565 or (408)524-4799 or (650)940-4300; Fax: (800)392-6206 or (408)524-4798; Email: findlawexperience@thomsonreuters.com • URL: http://www.findlaw.com • Web site provides a wide variety of information and links relating to laws, law schools, professional development, lawyers, the U. S. Supreme Court, consultants (experts), law reviews, legal news, etc. Online searching is provided. Fees: Free.

***The Finger Lakes Business Almanac: Your Window into Finger Lakes Businesses and Their Concerns***. OnPoint Publishing, 2 S St., Ste. 204 Auburn, NY 13021. Fax: (315)258-8148 • Biweekly. $38.75 local annual. Tabloid containing news about business and the economy in the northeast Finger Lakes.

***Finishers' Management***. Publication Management Inc., 4350 Di-Paolo Ctr. Glenview, IL 60025. Phone: (847)699-1706; Fax: (847)699-1703 • 10 times a year. $35.00 per year.

***Finland Government and Business Contacts Handbook***. International Business Publications, USA, PO Box 15343 Washington, DC 20003. Phone: (202)546-2103; Fax: (202)546-3275; Email: ibpusa@comcast.net • URL: http://ibpus.com • $99.95 Individuals. Covers: Strategic government and business information, export-import activity in the country, investment, business contacts and regulations.

***Finnish Export Companies***. FINPRO, PO Box 358 FIN-00181 Helsinki, Finland. Phone: 358 2046951 or 358 9 204 6951; Fax: 358 9 204 695200 or 358 204 200; Email: info@finpro.fi • URL: http://www.finpro.fi/en-US/Finpro/ • Database covers: over 2,500 Finnish export companies. Database includes: Company name, address, names and titles of key personnel, products.

***Finnish Trade***. Federation of Finnish Trade and Commerce, Mannerheimintie 76A FIN-00250 Helsinki, Finland. Phone: 358 9 431560; Fax: 358 9 43156302; Email: @kaupankl.fi • Annual. Covers: Member firms of the Federation of Finnish Commerce and Trade. Entries include: Company name, address, phone, fax, telex.

***Fire and Casualty Insurance Law Reports***. Wolters Kluwer Law & Business CCH, 2700 Lake Cook Rd. Riverwoods, IL 60015. Phone: 888-224-7377 or (847)267-7000; Email: cust_serv@cch.com • URL: http://www.cchgroup.com • $870.00 per year. Looseleaf service. Semimonthly updates.

***Fire and Materials: An International Journal***. John Wiley and Sons, Inc., Journals Div., 111 River St. Hoboken, NJ 07030. Phone: 800-526-5368 or (201)748-6000; Fax: (201)748-6088; Email: consumers@wiley.com • URL: http://www.wiley.com • 8/year. Bimonthly. Individuals, $1,215.00 per year; institutions, $1,620.00 per year. Published in England by John Wiley & Sons Ltd. Provides international coverage of subject matter.

***Fire, Casualty and Surety Bulletin***. • Monthly. $420.00 per year. Five looseleaf volumes.

***Fire Chief: Administration, Training, Operations***. Primedia Business Magazines and Media, 330 N Wabash Ave., Suite 2300 Chicago, IL 60611. Phone: 800-795-5445 or (312)595-1080 or (312)726-2802; Fax: (312)595-0295 or (312)726-2574; Email: subs@primediabusiness.com • URL: http://www.primediabusiness.com • Monthly. $54.00 per year.

***Fire Engineering: The Journal of Fire Suppression and Protection***. PennWell Corp., Industrial Div., 1421 S Sheridan Rd. Tulsa, OK 74112. Phone: 800-331-4463 or (918)835-

3161; Email: bid@pennwell.com • URL: http://www.pennwell.com • Monthly. $19.95 per year.

***Fire International: The Journal of the World's Fire Protection Services***. DMG World Media Ltd., Queensway House, 2 Queensway Red Hill RH1 1QS, United Kingdom. Phone: 44 1737 855527; Fax: (173)7 855470 • 10 times a year. $158.00 per year. Text in English. Summaries in French, German and Spanish.

***Fire Technology: An International Journal of Fire Protection Research and Engineering***. National Fire Protection Association, 1 Batterymarch Park Quincy, MA 02169-7471. Phone: 800-344-3555 or (617)770-3000; Fax: (617)770-0700; Email: library@nfpa.org • URL: http://www.nfpa.org • Quarterly. $199.00 per year.

***Firms Headquartered in Kansas***. Kansas Department of Commerce - Office of Minority and Women Business Development, 1000 SW Jackson St., Ste. 100 Topeka, KS 66612-1354. Phone: (785)296-3425; Fax: (785)296-3490 • URL: http://ks-kdoc.civicplus.com/index.aspx?NID=231 • Annual. $5. Covers: 400 firms headquartered in Kansas. Entries include: For companies—Name, address, phone, principal officials, sales, number of employees, products.

***First Alaskans: A Statewide Magazine of Business and Culture***. Alaska Newspapers Inc., 301 Calista Ct., Ste. B Anchorage, AK 99518. Phone: 800-770-9830 or (907)272-9830; Fax: (907)272-9512 • URL: http://www.alaskanewspapers.com • Quarterly. $16 Individuals. Consumer magazine covering business and culture in Alaska.

***First Call Consensus Earnings Estimates***. Thomson Financial Inc., 195 Broadway New York, NY 10007-3100. Phone: (646)822-2000; Email: custserv@tfn.com • URL: http://www.thomsonreuters.com • Online service provides corporate earnings estimates for more than 2,500 U. S. companies, based on data from leading brokerage firms. Weekly updates. Inquire as to online cost and availability.

***First-Level Leadership: Supervising in the New Organization***. American Management Association Extension Institute, 1601 Broadway New York, NY 10019. Phone: 800-262-9699 or (518)586-8100; Fax: (518)903-8168 • Looseleaf. $139.00. Self-study course. Emphasis is on practical explanations, examples, and problem solving. Quizzes and a case study are included.

***First-Line Supervision***. American Management Association Extension Institute, 1601 Broadway New York, NY 10019. Phone: 800-262-9699 or (518)586-8100; Fax: (518)903-8168 • Looseleaf. $139.00. Self-study course. Focuses on the day-to-day concerns of the first line supervisor. A self-study course.

**FIRST Union**. 120 Church St., Onehunga Auckland 1643, New Zealand. Phone: 64 9 6228355 or 64 9 6228351; Fax: 64 9 6228353; Email: contact@firstunion.org.nz • URL: http://www.firstunion.org.nz • Organizing union for workers in the financial services industry. Seeks to obtain optimal conditions of employment for members. Represents members in negotiations with employers.

***FirstGov: Your First Click to the U. S. Government***. General Services Administration, Phone: 800-333-4636 or (202)501-0705; Email: public.affairs@gsa.gov • URL: http://www.gsa.gov • Free Web site provides extensive links to federal agencies covering a wide variety of topics, such as agriculture, business, consumer safety, education, the environment, government jobs, grants, health, social security, statistics sources, taxes, technology, travel, and world affairs. Also provides links to federal forms, including IRS tax forms. Searching is offered, both keyword and advanced.

***Fish (Tropical) Dealers Directory***. InfoGroup Inc., 5711 S 86th Cir. Omaha, NE 68127-4146. Phone: (402)593-4500 • URL: http://www.infogroup.com • Annual. Number of listings: 2,236. Entries include: Name, address, phone, size of advertisement, name of owner or manager, number of employees, year first in "Yellow Pages." Compiled from telephone company "Yellow Pages," nationwide.

***Fisheries***. American Fisheries Society, 5410 Grosvenor Ln. Bethesda, MD 20814. Phone: (301)897-8616; Fax: (301)897-8096; Email: main@fisheries.org • URL: http://fisheries.org • Monthly. $1,530 Institutions American Fisheries Society Pack (online only); $486 Institutions Fisheries Infobase Online Pack (online only); $508 Institutions Fisheries Infobase (online only); $1,791 Institutions American Fisheries Society Pack (print and online). Covers the management of fisheries and aquatic resources, including related technology.

***Fishermen's News***. Fishermen's News, Inc., 2201 W Commodore Way Seattle, WA 98199. Phone: (206)284-8285; Fax: (206)284-0391; Email: info@fishermansnews.com • URL: http://www.fishermensnews.com • Monthly. $15.00 per year.

***Fitch Insights***. Fitch Investors Service, Inc., One State Street Plaza New York, NY 10004. Phone: 800-753-4824 or (212)908-0500; Fax: (212)480-4435 • Biweekly. $1,040.00 per year. Includes bond rating actions and explanation of actions. Provides commentary and Fitch's view of the financial markets.

***Fitch Ratings Delivery Service***. Fitch, 121-141 Westbourne Terr. London W2 6JR, United Kingdom. Phone: 440 20 7479 0900; Fax: 440 20 7479 0600 • URL: http://www.fitch.com • Daily. Provides online delivery of Fitch financial ratings in three sectors: "Corporate Finance" (corporate bonds, insurance companies), "Structured Finance" (asset-backed securities), and "U.S. Public Finance" (municipal bonds).

***Fitness Centers Directory***. InfoGroup Inc., 5711 S 86th Cir. Omaha, NE 68127-4146. Phone: (402)593-4500 • URL: http://www.infogroup.com • Annual. Number of listings: 17,012. Entries include: Name, address, phone, size of advertisement, name of owner or manager, number of employees, year first in "Yellow Pages." Compiled from telephone company "Yellow Pages," nationwide.

***Fitness Management***. Leisure Publications Inc., 4160 Wilshire Blvd. Los Angeles, CA 90010-3500. Phone: 800-222-7209 or (323)964-4800; Fax: (323)417-4840 or (323)964-4837; Email: sales@fitnessmgmt.com • URL: http://www.fitnessworld.com • Monthly. $24.00 per year. Published for owners and managers of physical fitness centers, both commercial and corporate.

***Fitness Management Products and Services Source Guide***. Leisure Publications Inc., 4160 Wilshire Blvd. Los Angeles, CA 90010-3500. Phone: 800-222-7209 or (323)964-4800; Fax: (323)417-4840 or (323)964-4837; Email: sales@fitnessmgmt.com • URL: http://www.fitnessworld.com • Annual. $24.00. A directory of more than 1,250 fitness equipment manufacturers and suppliers of services. Includes a glossary of terms related to the fitness industry and employee wellness programs.

***500 Contractors Receiving the Largest Dollar Volume of Prime Contract Awards for RDT&E***. U.S. Department of Defense, 1400 Defense Pentagon Washington, DC 20301-1400. Phone: (703)571-3343 or (703)545-6700 • URL: http://www.defense.gov • Annual. Covers the 500 largest contractors (including business, nonprofit organizations, foreign contractors, and government agencies) that received the largest dollar volume of prime contract awards over $25,000 for military research, development, test, and evaluation projects.

***The 5,000 Largest French Companies***. Le Nouvel Economiste, 33 Rue de la Tremmoille F-75008 Paris, France. Phone: 33 140747800; Fax: 33 1402259473 • Annual. Covers: 5,000 leading companies in France. Entries include: Company name, address, phone.

***Flavour and Fragrance Journal***. John Wiley and Sons, Inc., Journals Div., 111 River St. Hoboken, NJ 07030. Phone: 800-526-5368 or (201)748-6000; Fax: (201)748-6088; Email: consumers@wiley.com • URL: http://www.wiley.com • Bimonthly. Individuals, $890.00 per year; institutions, $1,185.00 per year.

***Fleet Owner***. Primedia Business Magazines and Media, 11 River Bend Dr., S Stamford, CT 06907. Phone: 800-795-5445 or (203)358-9900 or (203)358-4159; Fax: (203)358-5811 or (203)358-5812; Email: kjoyce@primediabusiness.com • Monthly. $45.00 per year.

***Fleet Owner Specs and Buyers' Directory***. Primedia Business Magazines and Media, 11 River Bend Dr., S Stamford, CT 06907. Phone: 800-795-5445 or (203)358-9900 or (203)358-4159; Fax: (203)358-5811 or (203)358-5812; Email: kjoyce@primediabusiness.com • Annual. $5.00. Lists of manufacturers of equipment and materials used in the operation, management, and maintenance of truck and bus fleets.

***Fletcher Corporation Forms Annotated***. Thomson West, 610 Opperman Dr. Eagan, MN 55123. Phone: 800-328-9352 or (651)687-7000 • Annual. $5,220 hardbound (full set); $327 monthly. Cover all aspects of corporate law.

***Flight International***. Reed Business Information Ltd., Quadrant House, The Quadrant, Surrey Sutton SM2 5AS, United Kingdom. Phone: 44 20 8652 3500; Fax: 44 20 8652 8932; Email: rbi.subscriptions@qss-uk.com • URL: http://www.reedbusiness.com.uk • Weekly. $140.00 per year. Technical aerospace coverage.

**Flight Mechanics Laboratory**. Texas A & M University, 701 HR Bright Bldg. College Station, TX 77843-3141. Phone: (979)862-1749; Fax: (979)845-6051; Email: saric@tamu.edu • URL: http://flight.tamu.edu.

***Floor Covering News***. RO-EL Productions Inc., 550 W Old Country Rd., Ste. 204 Hicksville, NY 11801. Phone: (516)932-7860; Fax: (516)932-7639; Email: info@fcnews.net • URL: http://www.fcnews.net • Biweekly. $25 Individuals; $40 Two years; $200 Other countries via air; $100 Other countries surface; $50 Canada. Magazine featuring articles of interest to floor covering retailers, distributors, and manufacturers.

***Floor Covering Weekly: The Business Newspaper of the Floor Covering Industry***. FCW, 50 Charles Lindbergh Blvd., Ste. 100 Uniondale, NY 11553. Phone: (516)229-3600; Fax: (516)227-1342; Email: smontero@hearst.com • URL: http://www.floorcoveringweekly.com • 32 times a year. $61.00 per year.

***Florafacts***. Florafax International, Inc., P.O. Box 45745 Tulsa, OK 74145. Phone: (918)622-8415 • Monthly. $15.00 per year.

***Floral Retailing Magazine: We Build Floral Business***. Vance Publishing Corp., 400 Knightsbridge Pkwy. Lincolnshire, IL 60069-3613. Phone: 800-255-5113 or (847)634-2600; Fax: (847)634-4342 or (847)634-4379; Email: info@vancepublishing.com • URL: http://www.vancepublishing.com • Monthly. $35 Individuals; $50 Out of country; $80 airmail. Magazine for managers and buyers in the high volume retail floral industry.

***Florida Business***. Business Journal Publishing Co., 1720 Euclid Ave., No. 300 Cleveland, OH 44115-2106. Phone: (813)289-0100; Fax: (813)289-0520 • Monthly. $36 Institutions; $3 Single issue. Regional business journal.

***Florida Industries Guide***. Industries Guides Inc., 303 E Altamonte Dr. Altamonte Springs, FL 32716. Phone: (407)834-8181 • Biennial. $95. Number of listings: 10,000. Entries include: Company name, address, phone, name of contact, products or services, number of employees, sic codes, fax and 800 numbers.

***Florida JobBank: The Job Hunter's Guide to the Sunshine State***. Adams Media Corp., 57 Littlefield St. Avon, MA 02322. Phone: 800-872-5627 or (508)427-7100; Fax: (508)427-6790 or (800)872-5628; Email: deskcopies@adamsmedia.com • URL: http://www.adamsmedia.com • $17.95 Individuals payment with order; $9 Individuals sale price. Covers: 5,500 employers in Florida including Fort Lauderdale, Jacksonville, Miami, Orlando, Tampa. Database includes: Information on the basics of job winning and writing resumes and cover letters; electronic job search information; 330 industry associations; 90 online career resources; 285 employment services. Entries include: Firm or organization name, address, local phone, toll-free phone, fax, e-mail addresses, web addresses, description of organization, subsidiaries, hours, recorded jobline, name and title of contact, headquarters location, typical titles for common positions, educational backgrounds desired, number of projected hires, company benefits, stock exchange listing, training programs, internships, parent company, number of employees, revenues, other U.S. Locations, international locations.

**Florida State University - Department of Art Education - Center for Arts Administration Program**. 1033 William Johnston Bldg. Tallahassee, FL 32306. Phone: (850)644-5473 or (850)644-2158; Fax: (850)644-5067 • URL: http://arted.fsu.edu/Programs/Arts-Administration-Change-your-World • Serves as an administrative and resource base for the development of research, service, and education in arts administration. Provides psychological, social, business, governance, and art related information to private and public arts agencies. Administers research capabilities at the University in arts, business, and public administration.

***Florida Trend—Directory of Public Companies Issue***. Trend Book Div., 490 1st Ave. S, 8th Fl. Saint Petersburg, FL 33701. Phone: 800-829-9103 or (727)821-5800; Fax: (727)822-5083; Email: lkeever@fltrend.com • URL: http://www.floridatrend.com • Annual. $3.95. Publication includes: List of 250 publicly owned companies headquartered in Florida. Entries include: Name, address, phone, name of chief executive, financial keys, product or service.

***Florida's Gold Coast Business & Employer's Directory: Palm Beach, Ft. Lauderdale, Miami***. Silver Reede Services, 15909 75th Ave. N Palm Beach Gardens, FL 33418-7413. Phone: (305)775-5194 • Covers: Approximately 1,000 manufacturers, banks, hospitals, retailers, resorts, real estate development firms, and other corporate organizations employing 20 or more people in the metropolitan Palm Beach, Ft. Lauderdale, and Miami, Florida areas. Entries include: Company or organization name, address, phone, name and title of contact, number of employees, description of products, services, or projects, and Standard Industrial Classification (SIC) code (where appropriate).

***Florida's Gulf Coast Business and Employers Directory: Tampa, Clearwater, St. Petersburg***. Silver Reede Services, 15909 75th Ave. N Palm Beach Gardens, FL 33418-7413. Phone: (305)775-5194 • Covers: manufacturers, banks, hospitals, retailers, resorts, real estate development firms, and other corporate organizations employing 20 or more people, in the Tampa/Clearwater/St. Petersburg, Florida area. Entries include: Company or organization name, address, phone, name and title of contact, number of employees, description of products, services, or projects, Standard Industrial Classification (SIC) code (where appropriate).

***Florist-Buyers Directory***. FTD Association, 33031 Schoolcraft Rd. Livonia, MI 48150-1618. Phone: 888-419-1515; Fax: (734)466-8979 or (734)466-8978; Email: info@ftdassociation.org • Annual. $7.00. Lists 1,200 suppliers in floral industry.

***Florists' Review***. Florist's Review Enterprises Inc., PO Box 4368 Topeka, KS 66604. Phone: 800-367-4708 or (785)266-0888; Fax: (785)266-0333; Email: mail@floristsreview.com • URL: http://www.floristsreview.com/main/contactus.html • Monthly. $42.00 per year.

***Flour Milling and Baking Abstracts***. CCFAA Technology Ltd., Station Rd. Chipping Campden GL55 6LD, United Kingdom. Phone: 44 1386 842000; Fax: 44 1386 842100; Email: information@campdenbri.co.uk • URL: http://www.campdenbri.co.uk • Bimonthly. Members, $275.00 per year; non-members, $325.00 per year. Includes print and online editions.

***Flowers &: The Beautiful Magazine About the Business of Flowers***. Teleflora, 11444 W Olympic Blvd. Los Angeles, CA 90064. Phone: 800-321-2665 or (310)966-3517 • URL: http://www.teleflora.com • Monthly. $38.95 per year.

***Fluid Abstracts: Civil Engineering***. Elsevier, Secondary Publishing Division, 650 Ave. of the Americas New York, NY 10011. Phone: 888-437-4636 or (212)633-3980; Fax: (212)633-3975; Email: t.reller@elsevier.com • URL: http://www.elseveier.com • Monthly. $3,804 Institutions print. Monthly. Institutions, $1,709.00 per year. Includes annual cumulation. Includes the literature of coastal structures. Published in England by Elsevier Science Publishing Ltd. Formerly *Civil*

*Engineering Hydraulics Abstracts.*

***Fluid Abstracts: Process Engineering***. Elsevier, Secondary Publishing Division, 650 Ave. of the Americas New York, NY 10011. Phone: 888-437-4636 or (212)633-3980; Fax: (212)633-3975; Email: t.reller@elsevier.com • URL: http://www.elseveier.com • Monthly. Institutions, $1,709.00 per year. Includes annual cumulation. Formerly *Pumps and Other Fluids Machinery: Abstracts.*

***Fluid Power Handbook and Directory***. Penton Media Inc., 1300 E 9th St. Cleveland, OH 44114-1501. Phone: (216)696-7000; Fax: (216)696-1752; Email: information@penton.com • URL: http://penton.com • Biennial. Over 1,500 manufacturers and 3,000 distributors of fluid power products in the United States and Canada.

**Fluid Power Laboratory**. Ohio State University, Mechanical Engineering Department, 206 W 19th Ave. Columbus, OH 43210. Phone: (614)292-2289; Fax: (614)292-3163 • URL: http://mae.osu.edu.

***FLUIDEX***. Elsevier, Secondary Publishing Division, 650 Ave. of the Americas New York, NY 10011. Phone: 888-437-4636 or (212)633-3980; Fax: (212)633-3975; Email: t.reller@elsevier.com • URL: http://www.elseveier.com • Produced in the Netherlands by Elsevier Science B.V. Provides indexing and abstracting of the international literature of fluid engineering and technology, 1973 to date, with monthly updates. Also known as *Fluid Engineering Abstracts*. Inquire as to online cost and availability.

***Flying***. Bonnier Corp., 460 N Orlando Ave., Ste. 200 Winter Park, FL 32789. Phone: (407)628-4802; Fax: (407)628-7061 • URL: http://www.bonniercorp.com • Monthly. $14 Individuals print; $22 Two years print; $29 Canada print; $44 Other countries print. General aviation magazine. Includes three *Special Issues*. Price on application.

***Flying Safety***. U.S. Air Force. U. S. Government Printing Office, 732 N Capitol St. NW Washington, DC 20401. Phone: 866-512-1800 or (202)512-1800 or (866)512-1800; Fax: (202)512-2104 or (202)512-2250; Email: contactcenter@gpo.gov • URL: http://www.gpo.gov • Monthly. $50.00 per year. Published in the interest of safer flying. Articles cover many fields of flight, aircraft engineering, training and safety measures in the air and on the ground.

***FMI Annual Financial Review***. Food Marketing Institute, 2345 Crystal Dr., Ste. 800 Arlington, VA 22202. Phone: (202)452-8444; Fax: (202)429-4519 • URL: http://www.fmi.org • Annual. $150 Members; $350 Nonmembers. Provides financial data on the supermarket industry.

***Focus on Business Education***. STBED, 28 Norlands Cres. Chislehurst BR7 5RN, United Kingdom. Phone: 44 2084023569; Email: editor@stbe.clara.co.uk • $39 Individuals. Publication covering business education.

***Focus: On the Center for Research Libraries***. Center for Research Libraries, 6050 S Kenwood Ave. Chicago, IL 60637-2804. Phone: 800-621-6044 or (773)955-4545; Fax: (773)955-4339 • URL: http://www.crl.edu • Bimonthly. Free. Newsletter. Provides news of Center activites.

***Folio: The New Dynamics of Magazine Publishing***. Penton, 9800 Metcalf Ave. Overland Park, KS 66212. Phone: 866-748-4926 or (913)341-1300; Fax: (913)967-1905 or (913)967-1898; Email: corporatecustomerservice@penton.com • URL: http://www.penton.com • Monthly. $96.00 per year.

***The Fono Directory***. CMP Information Ltd., Ludgate House, 245 Blackfriars Rd. London SE1 9UY, United Kingdom. Phone: 44 207 9215000 or 44 20 7940 8500; Fax: (740)7 7102; Email: enquiries@cmpinformation.com • URL: http://www.cmpi.biz/home • $66; $99. Covers: Radio, record labels, television stations, artist management, and retail organizations in Europe including the United Kingdom and Ireland for those interested in the music industry. Entries include: Name, address, phone, fax.

***Food Additives and Contaminants: Analysis, Surveillance, Evaluation, Control***. Taylor & Francis Ltd., 2 Park Sq., Milton Park Abingdon OX14 4RN, United Kingdom. Phone: 44 22 70176000 or 44 20 70176000; Fax: 44 22 70176699 or (701)76336; Email: info@e-elgar.co.uk • URL: http://www.taylorandfrancisgroup.com • Monthly. Institutions $2,038.00 per year.

***Food Business Mergers and Acquisitions***. American Institute of Food Distribution, Inc. Information and Research Center, 1 Broadway Plz., 2nd Fl. Elmwood Park, NJ 07407. Phone: (201)791-5570; Fax: (201)791-5222; Email: food1@foodinstitute.com • URL: http://www.foodinstitute.com • Annual. $295 Individuals book & CD-ROM; $395 Individuals PDF only. Gives names, locations, and industry categories of all companies involved in food business mergers during the previous year.

***Food Business Mergers & Acquisitions***. Food Institute, 10 Mountainview Rd., Ste. S125 Upper Saddle River, NJ 07458. Phone: (201)791-5570; Fax: (201)791-5222; Email: questions@foodinstitute.com • URL: http://www.foodinstitute.com • Annual. $295 Individuals print version and disk; $295 Individuals PDF version. Covers: Companies involved in food industry company mergers or take-overs, including import-export, banking, and advertising firms. Database includes: Ratings and financial information for selected firms from Moody's Investors Service. Entries include: Acquiring company name, location; acquired company name, location, products, number of units or stores.

***Food Chemicals News Directory***. Food Chemical News. CRC Press, c/o Taylor & Francis Group, LLC, 6000 Broken Sound Pkwy., NW Boca Raton, FL 33487-2713. Phone: 800-272-7737; Fax: (800)374-3401; Email: ncarter@taylorandfrancis.com • URL: http://www.crcpress.com • Semiannual. $497.00. Over 2,000 subsidiaries belonging to nearly 250 corporate parents plus an additional 3,000 independent processors. Formerly *Hereld's 1,500.*

***Food Distribution Magazine***. Phoenix Media Network Inc., 5400 Broken Sound Blvd. NW, Ste. 400 Boca Raton, FL 33487-3521. Phone: (561)994-1118 or (813)443-2723; Fax: (561)368-9125 • Monthly. $49.00 per year. Edited for marketers and buyers of domestic and imported, specialty or gourmet food products, including ethnic foods, seasonings, and bakery items.

**Food Industries Center**. Ohio State University, 110 Parker Food Science & Technology Bldg., 2015 Fyffe Rd. Columbus, OH 43210. Phone: (614)292-6281; Fax: (614)292-0218; Email: fst@osu.edu • URL: http://www.fst.ohio-state.edu.

***Food Industry Newsletter: All the Food News That Matters***. Newsletters Inc., P.O. Box 342730 Bethesda, MD 20827-2730. Phone: (301)469-8507; Fax: (301)469-7271; Email: foodltr@aol.com • 26 times a year. $245.00 per year. Newsletter. A summary of key industry news for food executives.

***Food Industry—Slovakia***. I.S.M.C. Information Systems and Marketing Contacts Ltd., Nam. Slobody 9, PO Box 47 81499 Bratislava, Slovakia. Phone: 421 7 265423783; Fax: 421 7 265422186; Email: ismc@ismc.sk • URL: http://www.ismc.sk • $65. Covers: Companies in the food industry in Slovakia, including suppliers of technologies for food processing and packaging.

***The Food Institute Report***. Food Institute, 10 Mountainview Rd., Ste. S125 Upper Saddle River, NJ 07458. Phone: (201)791-5570; Fax: (201)791-5222; Email: questions@foodinstitute.com • URL: http://www.foodinstitute.com • Description: Reports on developments in the food industry, including new products, the food service industry, mergers and acquisitions, current legislation and regulations, judicial decisions, and financial and marketing information.

**Food Institute**. 10 Mountainview Rd., Ste. S125 Upper Saddle River, NJ 07458. Phone: (201)791-5570; Fax: (201)791-5222; Email: questions@foodinstitute.com • URL: http://www.foodinstitute.com • Growers, food processors, importers, exporters, brokers, wholesalers, supermarket chains, independent retailers, food industry suppliers, food service distributors, advertising and banking executives, and government officials. Strives to provide food industry-related information to its members.

***Food Law Reports***. Wolters Kluwer Law & Business CCH, 2700 Lake Cook Rd. Riverwoods, IL 60015. Phone: 888-224-7377 or (847)267-7000; Email: cust_serv@cch.com • URL: http://www.cchgroup.com • Weekly. $1,459.00 per year. Six looseleaf volumes. Covers regulation of adulteration, packaging, labeling, and additives. Formerly *Food Drug Cosmetic Law Reports.*

***Food Management: Ideas for Colleges, Healthcare, Schools, and Business Dining***. Penton Media Inc., 1300 E 9th St. Cleveland, OH 44114-1501. Phone: (216)696-7000; Fax: (216)696-1752; Email: information@penton.com • URL: http://penton.com • Monthly. Free to qualified personel; others.

***Food Manufacturing***. Advantage Business Media L.L.C., 100 Enterprise Dr., Ste. 600 Rockaway, NJ 07866-0912. Phone: (973)920-7000; Email: advantagecommunications@advantagemedia.com • URL: http://www.advantagebusinessmedia.com • 9/year. Free to members; $54 Individuals; $63 Canada; $108 Other countries; $45 Individuals digital. Edited for food processing operations managers and food engineering managers. Includes end-of-year *Food Products and Equipment Literature Review.*

***Food Processing Guide and Directory***. Putman Media Inc., 555 W Pierce Rd., Ste. 301 Itasca, IL 60143-2649. Phone: (630)467-1301 or (630)467-1300; Fax: (630)467-1120 or (630)467-1109; Email: controlroundup@putman.net • URL: http://www.putman.net • Annual. $90. Lists over 5,390 food ingredient and equipment manufacturers.

***Food Processing Newsletter***. Putman Media Inc., 555 W Pierce Rd., Ste. 301 Itasca, IL 60143-2649. Phone: (630)467-1301 or (630)467-1300; Fax: (630)467-1120 or (630)467-1109; Email: controlroundup@putman.net • URL: http://www.putman.net • Weekly. $100 Individuals. Covers food processing industry news and trends.

***Food Processing***. Putman Media Inc., 555 W Pierce Rd., Ste. 301 Itasca, IL 60143-2649. Phone: (630)467-1301 or (630)467-1300; Fax: (630)467-1120 or (630)467-1109; Email: controlroundup@putman.net • URL: http://www.putman.net • Monthly. Free to qualified subscribers; $89 others. Edited for executive and operating personnel in the food processing industry.

***Food Production-Management: Monthly Publication of the Canning, Glass-Packing, As eptic, and Frozen Food Industry***. CTI Publications Inc., 2 Oakway Rd. Timonium, MD 21093-4247. Phone: (410)308-2080; Fax: (410)308-2079; Email: sales@ctipubs.com • Monthly. $35.00 per year.

***Food Retailing Industry Speaks***. Food Marketing Institute, 2345 Crystal Dr., Ste. 800 Arlington, VA 22202. Phone: (202)452-8444; Fax: (202)429-4519 • URL: http://www.fmi.org • Annual. Members, $150; non-members, $350. Provides data on overall food industry marketing performance, including retail distribution and store operations.

***Food Science and Technology Abstracts (online)***. IFIS North American Desk, National Food Laboratory, 6363 Clark Ave. Dublin, CA 94568. Phone: 800-336-3782 or (925)828-1440; Fax: (925)833-8795 • URL: http://www.ifis.org • Produced by International Food Information Service. Provides about 500,000 online citations, with abstracts, to the international literature of food science, technology, commodities, engineering, and processing. Approximately 2,000 periodicals are covered. Time period is 1969 to date, with monthly updates. Inquire as to online cost and availability.

***Food Science and Technology Abstracts***. Ovid Technologies Inc., 333 7th Ave., 20th Fl. New York, NY 10001-5004. Phone: 800-950-2035 or (646)674-6300; Fax: (646)674-6301 or (647)674-6301; Email: sales@ovid.com • URL: http://www.ovid.com • Monthly. $1,780.00 per year. Provides worldwide coverage of the literature of food technology and food production.

***Food Technology***. Institute of Food Technologists, 525 W Van Buren St., Ste. 1000 Chicago, IL 60607. Phone: 800-438-3663 or (312)782-8424; Fax: (312)782-8348; Email: info@ift.org • URL: http://www.ift.org • Monthly. $190 U.S. and Canada. Articles cover food product development, food ingredients, production, packaging, research, and regulation.

***Food Trade News***. Best-Met Publishing Company Inc., 5537 Twin Knolls Rd., Ste. 438 Columbia, MD 21045. Phone: (410)730-5013; Fax: (410)740-4680; Email: office@best-met.com • URL: http://www.best-met.com • Monthly. Reports on the retail food industry in Pennsylvania, Delaware, southern New Jersey and northern Maryland.

***Foods Adlibra: Key to the World's Food Literature***. General Mills, Inc. Foods Adlibra Publications, 9000 Plymouth Ave., N. Minneapolis, MN 55427. Phone: (612)540-4759; Fax: (612)540-3166 • Semimonthly. $240.00 per year. Provides journal citations and abstracts to the literature of food technology and packaging.

***Foodservice and Hospitality Magazine: Canada's Hospitality Business Magazine***. Kostuch Publications Ltd., 23 Lesmil Rd., Ste. 101 Toronto, ON, Canada M3B 3P6. Phone: (416)447-0888; Fax: (416)447-5333 • URL: http://www.foodserviceworld.com • Monthly. $55 Canada; $100 Individuals U.S.; $80 Other countries. Magazine for restaurant and hotel operators.

***Foodservice Consultants Society International—Membership Directory***. Foodservice Consultants Society International, PO Box 4961 Louisville, KY 40204-0961. Phone: (502)379-4122; Email: info@fcsi.org • URL: http://www.fcsi.org • Annual. $450. About 950 food service consultants.

***Foodservice Equipment and Supplies Product Source Guide***. Reed Elsevier Group plc Reed Business Information, 360 Park Ave. S New York, NY 11010. Phone: (212)791-4208; Email: corporatecommunications@reedbusiness.com • URL: http://www.reedbusiness.com • Annual. $35.00. Nearly 1,700 manufacturers of food service equipment and supplies. Formerly *Foodservice Equipment Buyer's Guide and Product Directory.*

***Foodservice Equipment and Supplies***. Reed Elsevier Group plc Reed Business Information, 360 Park Ave. S New York, NY 11010. Phone: (212)791-4208; Email: corporatecommunications@reedbusiness.com • URL: http://www.reedbusiness.com • $106.90 Individuals.

***Footwear News***. Fairchild Publications, 750 Third Ave. New York, NY 10017. Phone: 800-360-1700 or (212)630-4600 or (212)630-4000; Fax: (212)630-3675 or (212)630-4015; Email: hillary_kribben@condenast.com • URL: http://www.fairchildmediakit.com • Weekly. $72 Individuals; $59 domestic retailer.

***For Your Information***. Western New York Library Resources Council, 4455 Genesee St. Buffalo, NY 14225-0400. Phone: (716)633-0705; Fax: (716)633-1736; Email: gstaines@wnylrc.org • URL: http://www.wnylrc.org • Bimonthly. Free.

***Forbes—Chief Executive Compensation Survey Issue***. Forbes Inc., 60 5th Ave. New York, NY 10011-8868. Phone: 800-295-0893 or (212)366-8900; Email: service@forbes.net • URL: http://www.forbes.com • Annual. $4.95. Publication includes: List of 800 firms. Entries include: (In tabular form) Company name, name of chief executive officer, age, rank, compensation in salary and bonus, other remuneration, stock gains, total remuneration, years with company, years as chief executive, place of birth, educational and business background.

***Forbes***. Forbes Inc., 60 5th Ave. New York, NY 10011-8868. Phone: 800-295-0893 or (212)366-8900; Email: service@forbes.net • URL: http://www.forbes.com • Biweekly. $29.99 Individuals; $22.25 Canada. Magazine reporting on industry, business and finance management.

***Forbes—The Forbes International 500 Issue***. Forbes Inc., 60 5th Ave. New York, NY 10011-8868. Phone: 800-295-0893 or (212)366-8900; Email: service@forbes.net • URL: http://www.forbes.com • Annual. Publication includes: 500 largest foreign corporations, 50 largest corporations in the world. Entries include: For foreign companies—Company name, revenue, net income, assets, market value of common stock, location of corporate headquarters, number of employees.

***Forecasts and Strategies***. Access Intelligence L.L.C., 4 Choke Cherry Rd., 2nd Fl. Rockville, MD 20850. Phone: 800-777-5006 or (301)354-2000 or (301)354-2101; Fax: (301)309-

3847 or (801)365-2300; Email: info@accessintel.com • URL: http://www.accessintel.com/ • Monthly. $99.00 per year. Covers inflation, taxes and government controls.

***Foreign Companies in Asia Yearbook***. Business Monitor International Ltd., Senator House, 85 Queen Victoria St. London EC4V 4AB, United Kingdom. Phone: 44 20 72480468; Fax: 44 20 72480467; Email: enquiry@businessmonitor.com • URL: http://www.businessmonitor.com • $5,445 Individuals 40% discount; €3,860 Individuals 40% discount; $9,240 CD and print; €6,600 CD and print. Covers: 49,270 senior executive contacts on 16,775 foreign company subsidiaries across 32 industry sectors in Asia. Entries include: full company name, address, phone and fax numbers, email and web addresses, and key contact names and titles.

***Foreign Consular Offices in the United States***. U.S. Department of State. U. S. Government Printing Office, 732 N Capitol St. NW Washington, DC 20401. Phone: 866-512-1800 or (202)512-1800 or (866)512-1800; Fax: (202)512-2104 or (202)512-2250; Email: contactcenter@gpo.gov • URL: http://www.gpo.gov • $7.99. Lists foreign consular offices in the U.S.

***Foreign Direct Investment Database***. United Nations Conference on Trade and Development, DC2-1120, United Nations New York, NY 10017. Phone: (212)963-0027; Email: unctadny1@un.org • URL: http://www.unctad.org • $80 Individuals. Database covers: Statistics on foreign direct investment for 196 countries. The FDI database presents aggregate inflows, outflows, inward stocks and outward stocks of foreign direct investment.

***Foreign Exchange Letter***. Institutional Investor Inc. Journals Group, 225 Park Ave. S New York, NY 10003. Phone: 800-437-9997 or (212)224-3570; Email: info@iijournals.com • URL: http://www.iijournals.com • Biweekly. $1,625.00 per year. Newsletter. Provides information on foreign exchange rates, trends, and opportunities. Edited for banks, multinational corporations, currency traders, and others concerned with money rates.

***Foreign Exchange Rates***. U.S. Federal Reserve System Board of Governors Publications Services, 20th and Constitution Ave. NW Washington, DC 20551. Phone: (202)452-3244; Fax: (202)728-5886 • URL: http://www.federalreserve.gov • $20 weekly; $5 monthly.

***Foreign Labor Trends***. U. S. Government Printing Office, 732 N Capitol St. NW Washington, DC 20401. Phone: 866-512-1800 or (202)512-1800 or (866)512-1800; Fax: (202)512-2104 or (202)512-2250; Email: contactcenter@gpo.gov • URL: http://www.gpo.gov • Irregular (50 to 60 issues per year, each on an individual country). $95.00 per year. Prepared by various American Embassies. Issued by the Bureau of International Labor Affairs, U. S. Department of Labor. Covers labor developments in important foreign countries, including trends in wages, working conditions, labor supply, employment, and unemployment.

***Foreign Representatives in the U. S. Yellow Book: Who's Who in the U. S. Offices of Foreign Corporations, Foreign Nations, the Foreign Press, and Intergovernmental Organizations***. Leadership Directories Inc., 104 5th Ave. New York, NY 10011-6901. Phone: (212)627-4140; Fax: (212)645-0931; Email: info@leadershipdirectories.com • URL: http://www.leadershipdirectories.com • Semiannual. $465 per year. Lists executives located in the U. S. for 1,200 foreign companies, 300 foreign banks and other financial institutions, 175 embassies and consulates, and 375 foreign press outlets. Includes five indexes.

***Foreign Service Journal***. American Foreign Service Association, 2101 E St. NW Washington, DC 20037. Phone: 800-704-AFSA or (202)338-4045; Fax: (202)338-6820; Email: afsa@afsa.org • URL: http://www.afsa.org • Monthly. $50 Individuals; $30 Students. Written for United States foreign service members.

***Foreign Subsidiaries in Michigan***. Global Business Development, 300 N Washington Sq. Lansing, MI 48913. Phone: 888-522-0103 or (517)373-9808; Fax: (217)789-5410 • Irregular. Covers: over 930 Michigan subsidiaries of companies from outside the U.S. Entries include: Subsidiary company name, address; parent company name, address; product/service, type of establishment in Michigan.

***Foreign Tax and Trade Briefs***. Matthew Bender and Company Inc., 1275 Broadway Albany, NY 12204-2638. Phone: 800-424-4200 or (518)487-3000; Fax: (518)487-3573 or (800)424-4200; Email: customer.support@lexisnexis.com • URL: http://www.matthewbender.com • Quarterly. $1,054 book; $958 e-book. The latest tax and trade information for over 100 foreign countries.

***Forensic Accounting and Financial Fraud***. American Management Association Extension Institute, 1601 Broadway New York, NY 10019. Phone: 800-262-9699 or (518)586-8100; Fax: (518)903-8168 • Looseleaf. $159.00. Self-study course. Emphasis is on practical explanations, examples, and problem solving. Quizzes and a case study are included.

***Forest Products Abstracts***. CABI Publishing North America, 38 Chauncey St., Ste. 1002 Boston, MA 02111. Phone: 800-552-3083; Email: cabi-nao@cabi.org • URL: http://www.cabi.org • Weekly updates.

***Forest Products Journal (FPJ)***. Forest Products Society, 15 Technology Pkwy. S, Ste. 115 Peachtree Corners, GA 30092-8201. Phone: 855-475-0291 or (770)209-7294 • URL: http://

www.forestprod.org • 8/year. $230 Members individuals:complimentary; Institutions, electronic; $100 Members electronic and print; $380 Institutions electronic and print; $155 Nonmembers electronic; $330 Institutions electronic; $330 Nonmembers electronic and print; $400 Institutions electronic and print. Peer-reviewed journal of wood science and technology.

**Forest Resources Association**. 1901 Pennsylvania Ave. NW, Ste. 303 Washington, DC 20006. Phone: (202)296-3937; Fax: (202)296-0562; Email: dhawkinson@forestresources.org • URL: http://www.forestresources.org • Provides a forum to members of the forest resources community-foresters, loggers, landowners, and product manufacturers-where they can meet to solve problems and leverage opportunities within the wood fiber supply chain. Promotes sharing of information, facilitates networking, coordinates activism, serves as a change agent, structures problem-solving workshops, and provides education for members.

***Forestry Abstracts: Compiled from World Literature***. CABI Publishing North America, 38 Chauncey St., Ste. 1002 Boston, MA 02111. Phone: 800-552-3083; Email: cabi-nao@cabi.org • URL: http://www.cabi.org • Monthly. Institutions, $1,435.00 per year. Print and online edition, $1,460.00 per year. Published in England by CABI Publishing. Provides worldwide coverage of the literature.

**Forius Business Credit Resources**. 8441 Wayzata Blvd., Ste. 270 Golden Valley, MN 55426. Phone: 800-279-6226 or (763)253-4300 • URL: http://www.forius.com • Represents credit executives and owners of distribution and manufacturing companies. Promotes mutually beneficial ideas on credit techniques and methods. Provides a forum for the exchange of credit information.

***Formation and Financing of Emerging Companies***. Daniel E. O'Connor and others. Glasser LegalWorks, 150 Clove Rd. Little Falls, NJ 07424. Phone: 800-308-1700 or (973)890-0008; Fax: (973)890-0042; Email: legalwks@aol.com • URL: http://www.glasserlegalworks.com • $499 Individuals Binder/Looseleaf (Full set); $44 Individuals Monthly pricing. Periodic Supplementation. Covers incorporation, bylaws, indemnification, intellectual property, financing sources, venture capital, due diligence, bridge loans, investor rights, compliance, and other legal issues associated with company formation. (Emerging Growth Companies Series.)

***Forms and Agreements for Architects, Engineers and Contractors***. Albert Dib. Thomson West, 610 Opperman Dr. Eagan, MN 55123. Phone: 800-328-9352 or (651)687-7000 • $2,687.25 full set; $271 monthly. Three times a year. Five looseleaf volume. Covers evaluation of construction documents and alternative clauses. Includes pleadings for litigation and resolving of claims. (Real Property Law Series).

***Forms of Business Agreements and Resolutions-Annotated, Tax Tested***. Prentice Hall PTR, 1 Lake St. Upper Saddle River, NJ 07458. Phone: 800-227-1816 or (201)236-7676 or (201)236-7000; Fax: (800)445-6991 or (317)428-3343 • URL: http://phbusiness.prenhall.com • Three looseleaf volumes. Periodic supplementation. Price on application.

***Fort Bend Business Journal***. Carter Publications Inc., 869 Dulles Ave., Ste. C Stafford, TX 77477. Phone: (281)499-5600; Fax: (281)499-5002; Email: starnews@fortbendstar.com • URL: http://www.fortbendstar.com • Monthly. $35 Individuals. Journal highlighting business in the Fort Bend community.

**Fort Lewis College - Office of Business and Economic Research**. 1000 Rim Dr. Durango, CO 81301. Phone: (970)247-7296; Fax: (970)247-7205; Email: sonora_t@fortlewis.edu • URL: http://www.fortlewis.edu/ober/Home.aspx • Economics and local economic conditions.

***Forthcoming Books***. R.R. Bowker L.L.C., 630 Central Ave New Providence, NJ 07974. Phone: 888-269-5372 or (908)286-1090; Email: info@bowker.com • URL: http://www.bowker.com • Quarterly. $299.95 per year; $375 Individuals Annual. Reference database listing forthcoming publications and new issues, editions, or volumes of previously published books or serials. Supplement to *Books in Print*.

***Fortune—Deals of the Year Issue***. Time Inc., Time-Life Bldg., 1271 Ave. of the Americas New York, NY 10020. Phone: 800-843-8463 or (212)522-1212; Fax: (212)522-0602; Email: information@timeinc.com • URL: http://www.time.com • $5. Publication includes: 50 largest United States corporate financial transactions, including mergers, acquisitions, leveraged buyouts, and debt and equity offerings. Entries include: Companies involved, value (value and percent of book value), date and type of transaction, type of industry, financial intermediary, fee charged.

***Fortune Directory***. Fortune Directories, Time Inc., Time & Life Bldg., Rockefeller Ctr. New York, NY 10020. Phone: (212)586-1212 • Annual. $25 payment with order. Covers: combined, in a fall reprint, 500 largest United States industrial corporations (published in an April issue each year) and the Service 500 (published in a June issue). The Service 500 comprises 100-company rankings of each of the largest diversified service, and commercial banking companies, and 50-company rankings each of the largest, diversified financial, savings institutions, life insurance, retailing, transportation, and utility companies. Database includes: Various other rankings by different measures. Entries include: Company name, address, headquarters city, sales, assets, net income, market value, comparative earnings per share for ten years, names and titles of key personnel, phone, and various

other statistical and financial information.

***Fortune Directory of United States Corporations***. Time Inc., Time-Life Bldg., 1271 Ave. of the Americas New York, NY 10020. Phone: 800-843-8463 or (212)522-1212; Fax: (212)522-0602; Email: information@timeinc.com • URL: http://www.time.com • Annual. $25. Publication includes: The top 500 firms in the U.S. Entries include: Company name, address, headquarters address, financial data.

***Fortune India: Indian Magazine for Business, Finance and Investment***. Fortune Publications Private Ltd., 98 Mody St., Karachiwala Bldg., Fort Mumbai 400 001, India. Phone: 91 0222671009; Fax: 91 0222642553 • Biweekly. Rs 555 Individuals; Rs 25 Single issue; Rs 3,000 For 10 years. Trade publication on premier business, finance and investment.

***Fortune Magazine***. Time Inc., Business Information Group, 1271 Ave. of the Americas New York, NY 10020. Phone: 800-621-8000 or (212)522-1212; Fax: (212)522-0970 • URL: http://www.fortune.com • Biweekly. $19.99 all access. Edited for top executives and upper-level managers.

***Foundation Directory***. Foundation Center, 79 5th Ave./16th St. New York, NY 10003-3076. Phone: 800-424-9836 or (212)620-4230; Fax: (212)807-3677; Email: communications@foundationcenter.org • URL: http://foundationcenter.org • Annual. $215 Individuals main; $125 Individuals supplement; $179.95 Individuals for online professional directory access per month; $1,295 Individuals for online professional directory access per year; $195 Individuals for single user, online basic dir. access per year; $19.95 Individuals for single user, onl. basic dir. access per month; $149.95 Individuals for online platinum directory access per month; $995 Individuals for online platinum directory access per year; $29.95 Individuals for online plus directory access per month; $595 Individuals for online premium directory access per year. Over 10,000 of the largest foundations in the United States, all having $1.3 million or more in assets or awarding $400,000 or more in grants in a recent year.

***Foundation Directory Online***. Foundation Center, 79 5th Ave./16th St. New York, NY 10003-3076. Phone: 800-424-9836 or (212)620-4230; Fax: (212)807-3677; Email: communications@foundationcenter.org • URL: http://foundationcenter.org • Formerly *Foundation Grants Index*. Five plan levels with monthly, annual, and two-year subscription options.

**Foundation for Student Communication**. 48 University Pl. Princeton, NJ 08544. Phone: (609)258-1111; Fax: (609)258-1222; Email: info@businesstoday.org • URL: http://www.businesstoday.org • Student subscribers and conference participants who desire to promote communication among students and businesspersons. Sponsors student/business forums.

***Foundation Grants to Individuals***. Foundation Center, 79 5th Ave./16th St. New York, NY 10003-3076. Phone: 800-424-9836 or (212)620-4230; Fax: (212)807-3677; Email: communications@foundationcenter.org • URL: http://foundationcenter.org • Annual. $99.95 Individuals. Nearly 10,000 foundations that make grants to individuals. Subscriptions available in one-, three-, six-month, and yearly rates.

**Foundation News & Commentary**. Council on Foundations, 2121 Crystal Dr., Ste. 700 Arlington, VA 22202-3706. Phone: 800-673-9036 or (703)879-0600; Email: membership@cof.org • URL: http://www.cof.org • Bimonthly. Bimonthly. $48.00 per year. Formerly *Foundation News*.

***Foundation Reporter: Comprehensive Profiles and Giving Analyses of America's Major Private Foundations***. Taft Group, 27500 Drake Rd. Farmington Hills, MI 48331-3535. Phone: 800-877-4253 or (248)699-4253 or (248)699-GALE; Fax: (800)414-5043 or (248)699-8061; Email: gale.salesassistance@thomson.com • URL: http://www.gale.com/taft • Annual. $490.00. Provides detailed information on major U. S. foundations. Eight indexes (location, grant type, recipient type, personnel, etc.).

***Foundations of the 1990s: A Directory of Newly Established Foundations***. • URL: http://www.fdncenter.org • $150 plus shipping cost. Covers: Over 9,000 independent, community, and corporate foundations incorporated since 1989. Entries include: Foundation name, address, phone, name and title of contact, names of trustees and officers, application procedures, financial data, grantmaking interests and giving limitations, and grant descriptions.

***Foundry Directory and Register of Forges***. Metal Bulletin Inc., 1250 Broadway, 26th Fl. New York, NY 10001-7781. Phone: 800-638-2525 or (212)213-6202 or (800)638-2525; Fax: (212)213-1870 or (212)213-6619; Email: sales@metbul.com • URL: http://www.metalbulletin.com • Biennial. $165.00. Foundries and forges in the United Kingdom and Europe; suppliers of foundry and forging equipment, raw materials and services.

***Foundry Management and Technology***. Penton Media Inc., 1300 E 9th St. Cleveland, OH 44114-1501. Phone: (216)696-7000; Fax: (216)696-1752; Email: information@penton.com • URL: http://penton.com • Monthly. Free to qualified subscribers; $50 others. Coverage includes nonferrous casting technology and production.

***401(k) Handbook***. Thompson Publishing Group Inc., Government Information Services, Education Funding Research Council, 1725 K St. NW, Ste. 700 Washington, DC 20006. Phone: 800-677-3789 or (202)444-8741; Fax: (800)759-7179 or (202)296-1091; Email: service@thompson.com • URL: http://www.thompson.com • Two looseleaf volumes. $387.00 per year, including monthly updates and newsletters. Provides detailed information on 401(k) retirement plan design, administration, employee communication, rollovers, federal regulations, plan loans, investment vehicles, and related topics. Includes a glossary.

***FP500 Database***. International Press Publications Inc., 20-90 Nolan Ct. Markham, ON, Canada L3R 4L9. Phone: 800-679-2514; Fax: (905)946-9590; Email: sales@ippbooks.com • URL: http://www.ippbooks.com • $139 Individuals for subscribers of National Post; $169 Individuals. Publication includes: Company contact information, revenue, assets, net income, return on investment capital and officer information. Principal content of publication is 1,000 Canadian corporations, including Canada's top 500 private and public companies plus 300 additional corporations.

***Fragrance and Olfactory Dictionary***. Fragrance Foundation, 621 2nd Ave., 2nd Fl. New York, NY 10016. Phone: (212)725-2755; Fax: (646)786-3260; Email: info@fragrance.org • URL: http://www.fragrance.org • Irregular. $5 for members; $7 for nonmembers. Principal content of publication definitions of fragrance and olfactory terms.

***France Business Database***. The Data Supplier, 9107 Wilshire Blvd., Ste. 450 Beverly Hills, CA 90210. Phone: 888-930-3282; Fax: (818)221-0295; Email: contactus@thedatasupplier.com • URL: http://www.thedatasupplier.com • Contains contact information for more than 136,000 companies in France. Includes business name, full contact information, e-mail addresses, and Web site.

***France Business Directory, Database***. NIIR Project Consultancy Services, 106 - E, Kamla Nagar New Delhi 110007, India. Phone: 91 11 23843955; Fax: 91 11 23841561; Email: npcs.india@gmail.com • URL: http://www.niir.org • $100 Individuals CD-ROM; Rs 2,248 Individuals CD-ROM. Covers: 40,000 categorized listings of French business companies. Entries include: Company name, phone, fax, email, website address, details of business/services provided.

***France Environment***. Editions Louis Johanet, 30, Rue Ren Boulanger 75010 Paris, France. Phone: 33 147287070; Fax: 33 147287383; Email: info@editions-johanet.com • Annual. Covers: 8,000 office machinery and supply manufacturers, wholesalers, and distributors in France. Entries include: Company name, address, phone, telex number.

***France Government and Business Contacts Handbook***. International Business Publications, USA, PO Box 15343 Washington, DC 20003. Phone: (202)546-2103; Fax: (202)546-3275; Email: ibpusa@comcast.net • URL: http://ibpus.com • $99.95 Individuals. Covers: Strategic government and business information, export-import activity in the country, investment, business contacts and regulations.

***France Industrial and Business Directory***. International Business Publications, USA, PO Box 15343 Washington, DC 20003. Phone: (202)546-2103; Fax: (202)546-3275; Email: ibpusa@comcast.net • URL: http://ibpus.com • Annual. $99.95 Individuals hardcopy, e-book, CD-ROM. Covers: Detailed information on investment, export-import business opportunities, foreign economic assistance projects, government and business contacts.

***France Investment and Business Guide***. International Business Publications, USA, PO Box 15343 Washington, DC 20003. Phone: (202)546-2103; Fax: (202)546-3275; Email: ibpusa@comcast.net • URL: http://ibpus.com • $99.95 Individuals hardcover, e-book, CD-ROM. Covers: Basic information on economy, export-import activity and investment climate, regulations and industrial development, banking, and government. Entries include: Important business contacts and business travel.

***France 30,000***. Dun & Bradstreet France S.A., 345 Ave. Georges Clemenceau, tour Defense Bergere F-92000 Nanterre, France. Phone: 14135 1700 or 8 25805802; Fax: 14135 1777 or 33 1 41 35 17 77 • URL: http://dbfrance.dnb.com • Annual. Covers: 30,000 companies in France. Entries include: Company name, address, phone, date founded, number of employees, key personnel, capital, turnover, affiliations.

***Franchise Opportunities Guide***. International Franchise Association, 1501 K St. NW, Ste. 350 Washington, DC 20005. Phone: 800-543-1038 or (202)628-8000; Fax: (202)628-0812; Email: ifa@franchise.org • URL: http://www.franchise.org • Semiannual. $12 Members per year; plus $10.00 for shipping and handling; $20 Nonmembers per year; plus $10.00 for shipping and handling. More than 600 companies which offer franchises.

***Franchising Business and Law Alert***. ALM Media Properties LLC, 120 Broadway, 5th Fl. New York, NY 10271-1100. Phone: (212)457-9400; Fax: (646)417-7705; Email: customercare@alm.com • URL: http://www.alm.com • Monthly. $469 per year. Provides news of legal developments affecting both franchisors and franchisees. (A Law Journal Newsletter, formerly published by Leader Publications).

***Franchising: Realities and Remedies***. Harold Brown. ALM Media Properties LLC, 120 Broadway, 5th Fl. New York, NY 10271-1100. Phone: (212)457-9400; Fax: (646)417-7705; Email: customercare@alm.com • URL: http://www.alm.com • $399. Revised edition.

***Franchising World***. International Franchise Association, 1501 K St. NW, Ste. 350 Washington, DC 20005. Phone: 800-543-1038 or (202)628-8000; Fax: (202)628-0812; Email: ifa@franchise.org • URL: http://www.franchise.org • Monthly. $50 Individuals. Trade magazine covering topics of interest to franchise company executives and the business world. Formerly *Franchising Opportunities*.

**Franco-Argentina Chamber of Commerce and Industry**. Av. Libertador 498, 17e etage C1001AAO Buenos Aires, Argentina. Phone: 54 11 43101000; Fax: 54 11 43101021; Email: ccifa@ccifa.com.ar • URL: http://www.ccifa.com.ar • Promotes business and trade between Argentine and French companies.

***Frasers Canadian Trade Directory***. Rogers Publishing Ltd., 333 Bloor St. E, 7th Fl. Toronto, ON, Canada M4W 1G9. Phone: 888-764-3771 or (416)764-2000 or (416)764-1300; Fax: (416)764-7730 • URL: http://www.rogerspublishing.ca • Annual. $220 Individuals print/CDR combo; includes s&h; PST and GST extra; $195 Individuals print; includes s&h; PST and GST are extra; $195 Individuals CD-ROM; includes s&h; PST and GST are extra. Covers: over 42,000 manufacturers and distributors and over 14,000 foreign companies with Canadian representatives. Entries include: Company name, address. Products are included for manufacturers; name and address of Canadian representative is included for foreign firms.

**Free Congress Foundation**. 901 N Washington, Ste. 206 Alexandria, VA 22314-1535. Email: contact@freecongress.org • URL: http://www.freecongress.org • Brings messages of traditional values, conservative government, and institutional reform to America through publications and TV programs on America's Voice network. Includes projects such as: Judicial Selection Monitoring Project, "Taking Back Our Constitution" seminar services and the Center for Technology Policy's privacy papers.

***Free Help from Uncle Sam to Start Your Own Business***. Puma Publishing Co., 1670 Coral Dr. Santa Maria, CA 93454. Phone: 800-255-5730 or (805)925-3216; Fax: (805)925-2656; Email: publications@pumapublishing.com • URL: http://www.pumapublishing.com • Irregular. $15.95 plus $3.00 shipping. Covers: over 100 federal programs that provide loans, services, and information to businesses. Entries include: Program name, agency name, address, phone, name of contact.

***Free Insurance Advice***. InsWeb, Inc., 2868 Prospect Park Dr., Ste. 650 Rancho Cordova, CA 95670. Phone: (916)853-3300; Fax: (916)853-3300; Email: customercare@insweb.com • URL: http://www.insweb.com • Web site offers a wide variety of advice and information on automobile, life, health, and "other" insurance. Includes glossaries of insurance terms, Standard & Poor's ratings of individual insurance companies, and "Financial Needs Estimators." Searching is available. Fees: Free.

***Free Money from the Federal Government for Small Businesses and Entrepreneurs***. John Wiley and Sons Inc. Technical Insights, 111 River St. Hoboken, NJ 07030-5774. Phone: 800-825-7550 or (201)748-6000; Fax: (201)748-6088; Email: subinfo@wiley.com • URL: http://www.wiley.com • $18.95 Individuals. Covers: Approximately 1,500 grants and funding programs from 52 government agencies. Database includes: Bibliography. Entries include: Program name, description, contact information.

***Free State Directory***. A.C. Braby (Pty) Ltd., 12 Caversham Rd. Pinetown 3610, South Africa. Email: support@brabys.co.za • URL: http://www.brabys.com • Annual. R 100. Covers: businesses in Free State province of South Africa. Entries include: Company name, address, phone, fax, descriptive text.

**Free University of Berlin - Institute for East-European Studies**. Garystr. 55 14195 Berlin, Germany. Phone: 49 30 83854058; Fax: 49 30 83856419; Email: institutsrat@oei.fu-berlin.de • URL: http://www.oei.fu-berlin.de/en/index.html • Eastern, central, and southern Europe, including studies in Slavic languages and literatures, economics, law, history, geography, political sciences, sociology, education, arts, cultural studies, and Balkan studies.

**Free University of Brussels - Institute for European Studies**. Ave. F.D. Roosevelt 39, CP 172 B-1050 Brussels, Belgium. Phone: 32 2 6503079; Fax: 32 2 6503069; Email: iee@admin.ulb.ac.be • URL: http://www.iee-ulb.eu • European studies, including law, economics, politics.

**FreedomWorks**. 400 N Capitol St. NW, Ste. 765 Washington, DC 20001. Phone: 888-564-6273 or (202)783-3870; Fax: (202)942-7649 • URL: http://www.freedomworks.org • Devoted to ensuring that government actions foster growth, economic well being and individual responsibility. Sponsors an internship program, introducing its participants to the Washington policy world, giving them a broader base of knowledge about the organization and its inner operations.

***FreeLunch.com***. Economy.com, Inc., Phone: (610)696-8700; Fax: (610)696-1678 • URL: http://www.freelunch.com • Web site provides free access to more than 200 million economic and financial data series, covering industry, demographics, labor markets, prices, retail sales, government spending, trade, interest rates, housing starts, the stock market, etc. Data is available in either chart or table form. Searching is offered. Free, but registration required. Economy.com, Inc. also offers fee-based economic analysis at *The Dismal Scientist* site (www.dismal.com).

***Fremont Business Review***. Fremont Chamber of Commerce, 39488 Stevenson Place, Ste. 100 Fremont, CA 94539-3085. Phone: (510)795-2244; Fax: (510)795-2240; Email: fmtcc@fremontbusiness.com • URL: http://www.fremontbusiness.com • Monthly. Included in membership; 135 /year. Includes promotional articles and meeting information.

***Fremont Chamber of Commerce—Community Profile and Business Directory***. Fremont Chamber of Commerce, 39488 Stevenson Place, Ste. 100 Fremont, CA 94539-3085. Phone: (510)795-2244; Fax: (510)795-2240; Email: fmtcc@fremontbusiness.com • URL: http://www.fremontbusiness.com • Annual. Covers: Listing of member businesses. Entries include: name, address, phone, fax.

**French Bruneian Business Association**. Kompleks Jalan Sultan, Rm. 301-306, 3rd Fl., Jalan Sultan Bandar Seri Begawan BS8811, Brunei. Phone: 673 2240924 or 673 2220960; Fax: 673 2243373 • URL: http://www.fbbabrunei.com • Brings together people actively involved in trade and commerce between France and Brunei Darussalam. Provides a mutual forum for French and Bruneian business partners. Disseminates economic information to members on matters of interest. Develops business opportunities between Brunei Darussalam and France.

***French Companies and their Partners Abroad***. DAFSA, 25 rue Leblanc F-75010 Paris, France. Phone: 33 14604060; Fax: 33 140605151 • Annual. Covers: 80,000 French companies in France and abroad. Entries include: Company name, address, phone, ownership connections, subsidiaries, ownership percentages.

***French Companies Full Financials***. RENCOM S&W, 4, quai Jean Moulin F-69282 Lyon, France. Phone: 78 286690; Fax: 78 273500 • Monthly. Database covers: Over 100,000 French companies in various sectors of industry and commerce. Entries include: Name, address, phone, senior management personnel, legal status, year founded, line of business, products, financial information.

***French Company Handbook***. International Herald Tribune, 6 Bis, rue des Graviers F-92521 Neuilly, France. Phone: 33 141 439361 or 33 0141439396; Fax: 33 0141439393 • URL: http://www.global.nytimes.com • Annual. $50. Covers: 120 major French companies included in the SBF 120 Index, plus other important bond issuers. Entries include: Company name, address, phone, fax, telex, names of principal officials, description of business, background, sales breakdown, major known shareholders and percentages of stock held, subsidiaries and holdings (with brief details on each), international activities, key recent developments, investments, and financial data for five years.

**French Society of Agricultural Economics**. 19 Av. du Maine F-75732 Paris, France. Phone: 33 1 45498840; Fax: 33 1 45498841; Email: sfer.asso@orange.fr • URL: http://www.sfer.asso.fr • Educators, social scientists, civil servants, and other interested persons. Promotes research and instruction in the economic, political, and social applications of agriculture and rural space. Acts as a forum for the exchange of ideas and information. Conducts colloquia.

***Frequent Flyer: For Business People Who Must Travel***. Official Airline Guides, 3025 Highland Pkwy., Ste. 200 Downers Grove, IL 60515-5561. Phone: 800-342-5624 or (630)515-5300; Fax: (630)515-5301; Email: contactus@oag.com • URL: http://www.oag.com • Monthly. $89.00 per year to individuals. Also known as *OAG Frequent Flyer*. Edited for business travelers. Contains news of frequent flyer programs, airport developments, airline services, and business travel trends. Available only with *OAG Flight Guide*.

***Fresh Produce Journal***. Lockwood Press, Ltd., 430-438 Market Towers, 1 Nine Elms Ln. London SW8 5NN, United Kingdom. Phone: 44 20 7622 6677 or 44 20 75010300; Fax: (772)0 2047 or 44 20 77202047; Email: info@fpj.co.uk • URL: http://www.freshinfo.com • Weekly (Fri.). £125 Individuals; £148 Other countries. Trade magazine for the fresh produce industry. Formerly *Fruit Trades Journal*.

**Friedrich Ebert Foundation - Latin American Social Sciences Research Institute**. Av. República 500 y Diego de Almagro, Edif. Pucará, 4to. Piso, Of. 404, Casilla 17-03-367 Quito, Ecuador. Phone: 593 2 2562103; Fax: 593 2 2504337; Email: info@fes.ec • URL: http://www.fes-ecuador.org • Conducts investigations around political, social and economic problems in Latin America.

**Friends of the Earth - Australia**. PO Box 222 Melbourne, VIC 3065, Australia. Phone: 61 3 94198700; Fax: 61 3 94162081; Email: foe@foe.org.au • URL: http://www.foe.org.au • Serves as national organization working on environmental issues within a social framework. Works for national campaigns on climate justice, environment and population, uranium, indigenous land rights, multinationals. Local groups active on local, national, and international issues.

**Friends of the Earth - Costa Rica**. PO Box 12423-1000 San Jose 1000, Costa Rica. Phone: 506 2233 3925; Fax: 506 2223 3925 • URL: http://www.coecoceiba.org • Member of the organization, Friends of the Earth International. Promotes conservation of the earth's natural resources. Supports campaigns on climate change, ecological debt, forests, gender issues, genetically modified organisms, sustainable societies, and wetlands.

**Friends of the Earth - England, Wales, and Northern Ireland**. 26-28 Underwood St. London N1 7JQ, United Kingdom. Phone: 44 20 74901555 or 44 1714901555; Fax: 44 20 74900881 or 44 1714900881; Email: info@foe.co.uk • URL: http://www.foe.co.uk • Operates as an environmental pressure group, campaigning on a wide range of issues including climate change corporate accountability, resource use, transport, energy, waste, habitats, forests, and sustainable development. Exists to protect and improve the environment, now and for the future, through changing political policies and business practices, empowering individuals and communities to take personal and political action, and stimulating wide and intelligent public debate on sustainability issues.

**Friends of the Earth - Haiti**. Delmas 65, Rue Durandis, No. 2 Port-au-Prince, Haiti. Phone: 509 2137973 or 509 4019684; Fax: 509 2210172 • URL: http://www.haitisurvie.org • Member of the organization, Friends of the Earth International. Promotes conservation of the earth's natural resources, including toxic wastes, desertification, ozone, and trade. Haiti Survie has many activities: climate change campaign, the organization works on reforestation program and plant tree at the community level.

**Friends of the Earth - Indonesia**. Jl. Tegal Parang Utara No. 14 12790 Jakarta, Indonesia. Phone: 62 21 79193363; Fax: 62 21 7941673; Email: informasi@walhi.or.id • URL: http://www.walhi.or.id • Members of the organization, Friends of the Earth International. Promotes conservation of the earth's natural resources, indigenous rights, marginalization of communities, pollution, climate change, and biodiversity conservation.

**Friends of the Earth - Ireland**. 9 Upper Mount St. Dublin 2, Dublin, Ireland. Phone: 353 1 6394652; Email: info@foe.ie • URL: http://www.foe.ie • Works to increase public awareness of environmental problems. Conducts media and educational campaigns on topics such as air pollution, toxic waste issues, alternative energy, and climate change. Maintains an information service.

**Friends of the Earth - Mauritius/Maudesco**. PO Box 1124 Port Louis, Mauritius. Phone: 230 4672565; Fax: 230 4248500; Email: maudesco@intnet.mu • URL: http://www.foei.org/member-groups/africa/mauritius • Member of the organization, Friends of the Earth International. Promotes conservation of the earth's natural resources. Main areas of focus are sustainable tourism, protection of the ocean/coral reefs, climate changes, solar energy, organic farming, and compost from household wastes; committed to raising awareness and capacity building.

*Fringe Benefits Tax Guide*. Wolters Kluwer Law & Business CCH, 2700 Lake Cook Rd. Riverwoods, IL 60015. Phone: 888-224-7377 or (847)267-7000; Email: cust_serv@cch.com • URL: http://www.cchgroup.com • Monthly. $539.00. Looseleaf service.

*FRM Weekly*. Hoke Communications Inc., 224 7th St., Ste. B1 Garden City, NY 11530-5777. Phone: 800-229-6700 or (516)746-6700; Fax: (516)294-8141; Email: 71410.2423@compuserve.com • URL: http://www.directmarketingmag.com/ • Weekly. $115.00 per year.

*The Froehlich-Kent Encyclopedia of Telecommunications*. Fritz E. Froehlich and Allen Kent, editors. Taylor & Francis Online, 270 Madison Ave. New York, NY 10016. Phone: 800-228-1160 or (212)696-9000 or (212)216-7800; Fax: (212)685-4540 or (212)563-2269; Email: support@tandfonline.com • URL: http://www.tandfonline.com/ • 18 volumes. $3,510.00. $195.00 per volume. Dates vary. Contains scholarly articles written by telecommunications experts. Includes bibliographies.

*Front Row Advisor: Business and First Class Air Travel and the Alluring World of Free Upgrades*. Diversified Specialties Inc., 10 Airline Ave. Belmont, NC 28012-3854. Phone: 800-634-5630 or (704)825-3671; Fax: (704)825-4538 • URL: http://www.diversifiedspecialtiespt.com/ • Bimonthly. $145.00 per year. Newsletter. Contains information on opportunities provided by airlines to upgrade coach seats to business class, including frequent flyer upgrades.

*Frontier West/Great Plains & Mountain Region Campground Guide*. Woodall Publications Corp., 2575 Vista Del Mar Dr. Ventura, CA 93001-3920. Email: info@woodallpub.com • URL: http://www.woodalls.com • Annual. $4.95 Individuals discounted price. Covers: Campground site listings for Colorado, Montana, Nebraska, North Dakota, South Dakota, Utah, and Wyoming. Entries include: Site name, address, phone, facility description, driving directions, camping fees, attractions and seasonal events. It also includes, new for 2004, "Discover Outdoor RV Adventures" and Woodall's Guide to Seasonal Sites.

*Frontline Solutions Buyer's Guide*. Advanstar Communications, Bridgegate Pavilion, Chester Business Pk., Wrexham Rd. Chester CH4 9QH, United Kingdom. Phone: 44 1244 629300; Fax: 44 1244 678008; Email: info@advanstar.com • URL: http://www.advanstar.com • Annual. $34.95 plus $3.50 shipping. Publication includes: List of manufacturers, suppliers, consultants, value added resellers, and dealers/distributors of automatic identification and data capture software, technology, equipment, and products for bar code, biometric identification, electronic data interchange, machine vision, magnetic stripe, optical character recognition, radio frequency data communications, radio frequency identification, smart cards, and voice data entry; also includes related organizations, and sources for industry standards. Entries include: Company name, address, phone, e-mail, web address, products or services.

*FTC Freedom of Information Log*. Washington Regulatory Reporting Associates, 21 Forrest St. Basye, VA 22810. Email: info@ftcwatch.com • URL: http://www.ftcwatch.com •

Weekly. $451 Individuals. Newsletter listing Freedom of Information Act requests that have been submitted to the Federal Trade Commission.

*Fuel and Energy Abstracts: A Summary of World Literature on All Scientific, Technical, Commercial and Environmental Aspects of Fuel and Energy*. Elsevier, Secondary Publishing Division, 650 Ave. of the Americas New York, NY 10011. Phone: 888-437-4636 or (212)633-3980; Fax: (212)633-3975; Email: t.reller@elsevier.com • URL: http://www.elseveier.com • Bimonthly. $3,287 Institutions.

*Fuel Oil News: Source Book*. Fuel Oil News, 1030 W Higgins Rd., Ste. 230 Park Ridge, IL 60068. Phone: (847)720-5600; Fax: (847)720-5610; Email: lbaron@aip.com • URL: http://www.fueloilnews.com • Annual. $28.00. Provides fuel (heating) oil industry data.

*Fuel: Science and Technology of Fuel and Energy*. Elsevier, Secondary Publishing Division, 650 Ave. of the Americas New York, NY 10011. Phone: 888-437-4636 or (212)633-3980; Fax: (212)633-3975; Email: t.reller@elsevier.com • URL: http://www.elseveier.com • $98 Qualified personnel; $4,811 Institutions.

*Fulbright Scholar Program Grants for U.S. Faculty and Professionals*. Council for International Exchange of Scholars, Institute of International Education, 1400 K St. NW, Ste. 700 Washington, DC 20005. Phone: (202)686-4000; Fax: (202)686-4029; Email: scholars@iie.org • URL: http://www.cies.org • Annual. Lists about 800 grants available for postdoctoral university lecturing and advanced research by American citizens in more than 140 countries.

**Fullblood Simmental Fleckvieh Federation**. PO Box 321 Cisco, TX 76437. Phone: 855-353-2584; Fax: (855)638-2582; Email: info@fleckvieh.com • URL: http://www.fleckvieh.com • Aims to develop and promote Fullblood Simmental and Fullblood Fleckvieh cattle. Seeks to educate beef producers on the economic traits of Fullblood Simmental and Fullblood Fleckvieh cattle. Strives to promote the use of Fullblood Simmental and Fullblood Fleckvieh beef cattle genetics and to preserve and market the breeds in North America and worldwide to both purebred and commercial beef producers.

*Fund Action*. Institutional Investor Inc. Journals Group, 225 Park Ave. S New York, NY 10003. Phone: 800-437-9997 or (212)224-3570; Email: info@iijournals.com • URL: http://www.iijournals.com • Weekly. $2,475.00 per year. Newsletter. Includes print and online editions. Edited for mutual fund executives. Covers competition among funds, aggregate statistics, new products, regulations, service providers, and other subjects of interest to fund managers.

*Fund Governance: Legal Duties of Investment Company Directors*. ALM Media Properties LLC, 120 Broadway, 5th Fl. New York, NY 10271-1100. Phone: (212)457-9400; Fax: (646)417-7705; Email: customercare@alm.com • URL: http://www.alm.com • $580 print and online + ebook; $545 ebook and online. Covers the legal obligations of directors of mutual funds and closed-end funds. (Law Journal Press).

*FUND ME! Sources*. IGW Canada Inc., 4500 16th Ave. NW, Ste. 300 Calgary, AB, Canada T3B 0M6. Phone: (403)247-9506; Fax: (403)247-9915; Email: ask_us@igw.ca • Quarterly. $495. CD-ROM, diskette. Database covers: over 2,000 programs, grants, and subsidies for research and business available in Canada from a variety of sources, including government agencies and departments, private foundations, international associations, banks, and venture capital companies. Entries include: Program title, sponsoring organization name, address, phone, areas of interest, program criteria and description, funding amount and type.

*FundAlarm*. Roy Weitz, Phone: (818)345-7516; Fax: (818)776-1562 • URL: http://www.fundalarm.com • Web site subtitle: "Know when to hold'em, know when to fold'em, know when to walk away, know when to run." Provides lists of underperforming mutual funds ("3-ALARM Funds") and severely underperforming funds ("Most Alarming 3-ALARM Funds"). Performance is based on various benchmarks. Site also provides mutual fund news, recent manager changes, and basic data for each of about 2,100 funds. Monthly updates. Fees: Free.

*Fundamentals of Human Resources*. American Management Association Extension Institute, 1601 Broadway New York, NY 10019. Phone: 800-262-9699 or (518)586-8100; Fax: (518)903-8168 • Looseleaf. $139.00. Self-study course on a wide range of personnel topics. Emphasis is on practical explanations, examples, and problem solving. Quizzes and a case study are included.

*FUNDED!*. IGW Canada Inc., 4500 16th Ave. NW, Ste. 300 Calgary, AB, Canada T3B 0M6. Phone: (403)247-9506; Fax: (403)247-9915; Email: ask_us@igw.ca • CD-ROM. Database covers: over 500 researchers, companies, and projects that have been awarded funds by public sector agencies and selected private sector organizations.

*Funworld*. International Association of Amusement Parks and Attractions, 1448 Duke St. Alexandria, VA 22314. Phone: (703)836-4800; Fax: (703)836-4801; Email: iaapa@iaapa.org • URL: http://www.iaapa.org • Monthly 11/year. $70 Members; $90 Nonmembers. Analysis and statistics of the international amusement park industry. Text in English; sections in French, German, Japanese and Spanish.

*Fur Business-Retail Directory*. InfoGroup Inc., 5711 S 86th Cir. Omaha, NE 68127-4146. Phone: (402)593-4500 • URL: http://www.infogroup.com • Updated continuously; printed

on request. Covers fur businesses.

*Fur World: The Newsmagazine of Fur and Better Outerware*. Creative Marketing Plus, Inc., 19 W 21st St., Ste. 403 New York, NY 10010. Phone: (212)727-1210; Fax: (212)727-1218 or (212)620-0122; Email: info@cmponline.com • URL: http://www.cmponline.com • Semimonthly. $50.00 per year. Edited for fur retailers, ranchers, pelt dealers, and manufacturers. Provides news and statistics relating to the retail and wholesale fur business.

*Furniture Today: The Weekly Business Newspaper of the Furniture Industry*. Reed Elsevier Group plc Reed Business Information, 360 Park Ave. S New York, NY 11010. Phone: (212)791-4208; Email: corporatecommunications@reedbusiness.com • URL: http://www.reedbusiness.com • $119 U.S.; $249.99 Other countries. Furniture retailing and manufacturing magazine (tabloid).

*Furniture-Today: The Weekly Business Newspaper of the Furniture Industry*. Reed Elsevier Group plc Reed Business Information, 360 Park Ave. S New York, NY 11010. Phone: (212)791-4208; Email: corporatecommunications@reedbusiness.com • URL: http://www.reedbusiness.com • Weekly. $169.97 U.S. and Canada; $10 Single issue.

*Furniture World*. Towse Publishing Co., 1333A N Ave. New Rochelle, NY 10804. Phone: 877-235-3095 or (914)235-3095; Fax: (914)235-3278; Email: russ@furninfo.com • URL: http://www.furninfo.com • Monthly. $19.00 per year. Formerly *Furniture World and Furniture Buyer and Decorator*.

*Futons Directory*. InfoGroup Inc., 5711 S 86th Cir. Omaha, NE 68127-4146. Phone: (402)593-4500 • URL: http://www.infogroup.com • Annual. Number of listings: 1,793. Entries include: Name, address, phone, size of advertisement, name of owner or manager, number of employees, year first in "Yellow Pages." Compiled from telephone company "Yellow Pages," nationwide.

**Future Business Leaders of America - Phi Beta Lambda**. 1912 Association Dr. Reston, VA 20191-1591. Phone: 800-325-2946; Fax: (866)500-5610; Email: general@fbla.org • URL: http://www.fbla-pbl.org • Maintains 4 divisions: Future Business Leaders of America for high school students preparing for business and related careers; Phi Beta Lambda for post-secondary and college men and women enrolled in business or teacher education programs; Professional Division for business persons FBLA - parents and teachers; Middle Level for students in junior high schools. Sponsors educational program and National Student Award program based on national competition for members.

*Future Survey Annual: A Guide to the Recent Literature of Trends, Forecasts, and Policy Proposals*. World Future Society, 7910 Woodmont Ave., Ste. 450 Bethesda, MD 20814. Phone: 800-989-8274 or (301)656-8274; Fax: (301)951-0394; Email: info@wfs.org • URL: http://www.wfs.org • Annual. $35.00.

*Futures and OTC World*. Russell R. Wasendorf, P.O. Box 849 Cedar Falls, IA 50613. Phone: (319)268-0441; Fax: (319)277-0880 • Weekly. $435.00 per year. Newsletter. Futures market information. Includes Daily Hotline Information to update advice. Formerly *Futures and Options Factors*.

*Futures Magazine SourceBook: The Most Complete List of Exchanges, Companies, Regulators, Organizations, etc., Offering Products and Services to the Futures and Options Industry*. Futures Magazine Inc., 250 S. Wacker Dr. Suite 1150 Chicago, IL 60606. Phone: 800-972-9316 or (312)977-0999 or (312)846-4600; Fax: (312)977-1042 or (312)846-4638; Email: gszala@futuresmag.com • URL: http://www.futuresmag.com • Annual. $19.50. Provides information on commodity futures brokers, trading method services, publications, and other items of interest to futures traders and money managers.

*Futures Market Service*. Commodity Research Bureau, 209 W Jackson Blvd., Ste. 200 Chicago, IL 60606. Phone: 800-621-5271 or (312)554-8456; Fax: (312)939-4135; Email: info@crbtrader.com • URL: http://www.crbtrader.com • Weekly. $155 Individuals.

*Futures: News, Analysis, and Strategies for Futures, Options, and Derivatives Traders*. Futures Magazine Inc., 250 S. Wacker Dr. Suite 1150 Chicago, IL 60606. Phone: 800-972-9316 or (312)977-0999 or (312)846-4600; Fax: (312)977-1042 or (312)846-4638; Email: gszala@futuresmag.com • URL: http://www.futuresmag.com • Monthly. $39 Individuals. Edited for institutional money managers and traders, brokers, risk managers, and individual investors or speculators. Includes special feature issues on interest rates, technical indicators, currencies, charts, precious metals, hedge funds, and derivatives. Supplements available.

*Futures Online*. Futures Magazine Inc., Phone: (312)846-4600; Fax: (312)846-4638 • URL: http://www.futuresmag.com • Web site presents updates of *Futures* magazine and links to other futures-related sites.

*Futures Research Quarterly*. World Future Society, 7910 Woodmont Ave., Ste. 450 Bethesda, MD 20814. Phone: 800-989-8274 or (301)656-8274; Fax: (301)951-0394; Email: info@wfs.org • URL: http://www.wfs.org • Quarterly. Members, $77.00 per year; others, $99.00 per year.

*Futures; The Journal of Forecasting, Planning and Policy*. Elsevier, Secondary Publishing Division, 650 Ave. of the Americas New York, NY 10011. Phone: 888-437-4636 or (212)633-3980; Fax: (212)633-3975; Email: t.reller@

elsevier.com • URL: http://www.elseveier.com • 10/year. $1,618 Institutions.

***The Futurist: A Journal of Forecasts, Trends, and Ideas About the Future***. World Future Society, 7910 Woodmont Ave., Ste. 450 Bethesda, MD 20814. Phone: 800-989-8274 or (301)656-8274; Fax: (301)951-0394; Email: info@wfs.org • URL: http://www.wfs.org • Bimonthly. $89 Institutions; $79 Individuals.

***The Futurist***. World Future Society, 7910 Woodmont Ave., Ste. 450 Bethesda, MD 20814. Phone: 800-989-8274 or (301)656-8274; Fax: (301)951-0394; Email: info@wfs.org • URL: http://www.wfs.org • $89 Institutions libraries. Monthly. Individuals, $98.00 per year; libraries, $145.00 per year.

***GAAP Guide***. Aspen Publishers, Inc., 7201 McKinney Cir. Frederick, MD 21704. Phone: 800-234-1660 or (301)698-7100 or (301)417-7500; Fax: (800)901-9075 or (301)695-7931; Email: customerservice@aspenpublisher.com • URL: http://www.aspenpublishers.com • Annual. $364. Also available in eBook format. Provides information on understanding GAAP literature in clear language.

***GAAS Guide***. Larry P. Bailey. Aspen Publishers, Inc., 7201 McKinney Cir. Frederick, MD 21704. Phone: 800-234-1660 or (301)698-7100 or (301)417-7500; Fax: (800)901-9075 or (301)695-7931; Email: customerservice@aspenpublisher.com • URL: http://www.aspenpublishers.com • Annual. $235. Describes standards, practices, and procedures.

***Gabon Business Law Handbook***. International Business Publications, USA, PO Box 15343 Washington, DC 20003. Phone: (202)546-2103; Fax: (202)546-3275; Email: ibpusa@comcast.net • URL: http://ibpus.com • $99.95 Individuals hardcopy, E-book and CD-ROM. Covers: Basic business laws and legislations, export-import regulations, business climate and contacts.

***Gale Business Insights: Global***. Cengage Learning Inc., 20 Channel Center St. Boston, MA 02210. Phone: 800-487-8488 or (617)289-7700; Fax: (617)289-7844; Email: investors@cengage.com • URL: http://www.cengage.com • Contains broad yet detailed coverage of international business. Includes case studies, full-text articles, and data sets coupled with authoritative references and tools for analysis. Features topic overviews, interactive rankings and statistics, company histories and market share data, global industry research reports, hundreds of economic and business indicators, case studies, and full-text articles from academic journals, business periodicals, newswires, and other media outlets.

***Gale Business Insights Handbook Of***. Cengage Learning Inc., 20 Channel Center St. Boston, MA 02210. Phone: 800-487-8488 or (617)289-7700; Fax: (617)289-7844; Email: investors@cengage.com • URL: http://www.cengage.com • $627 Individuals. Examines the questions "What is social media marketing" and "How can it be used in my business?".

***Gale BusinessForms***. Cengage Learning Inc., 20 Channel Center St. Boston, MA 02210. Phone: 800-487-8488 or (617)289-7700; Fax: (617)289-7844; Email: investors@cengage.com • URL: http://www.cengage.com • Contains professionally drafted state-specific documents and forms for businesses. Covers dozens of topics, including arbitration, bills of sale, collections, confidentiality and nondisclosure, distributorships, guaranty, liens, limited liability companies, power of attorney, and technology.

***Gale Digital Archives***. Cengage Learning Inc., 20 Channel Center St. Boston, MA 02210. Phone: 800-487-8488 or (617)289-7700; Fax: (617)289-7844; Email: investors@cengage.com • URL: http://www.cengage.com • Provides ownership of archival content from Gale proprietary data, including the following databases: *Associations Unlimited, Biography and Genealogy Master Index, Biography Resource Center, Contemporary Authors, Dictionary of Literary Biography, History Resource Center, Literature Resource Center, The Times Digital Archive*, the *Times Literary Supplement Centenary Digital Archive*, and *Ward's Business Directory*.

***Gale Directory Library***. Cengage Learning Inc., 20 Channel Center St. Boston, MA 02210. Phone: 800-487-8488 or (617)289-7700; Fax: (617)289-7844; Email: investors@cengage.com • URL: http://www.cengage.com • Contains the full-text of more than 40 directories published by Gale. Offers search and export features. Customizable. Contact for pricing.

***Gale Directory of Databases (GDD)***. Cengage Learning Inc., 20 Channel Center St. Boston, MA 02210. Phone: 800-487-8488 or (617)289-7700; Fax: (617)289-7844; Email: investors@cengage.com • URL: http://www.cengage.com • Semiannual. $723 Individuals in 6 volumes. Offers comprehensive coverage of the electronic database industry with profiles for more than 15,000 databases and more than 3,000 producers, online services, and vendors.

***Gale Directory of Early Stage Investment***. Cengage Learning Inc., 20 Channel Center St. Boston, MA 02210. Phone: 800-487-8488 or (617)289-7700; Fax: (617)289-7844; Email: investors@cengage.com • URL: http://www.cengage.com • $606 print only. Covers several types of early stage investors including: venture capitalists, business incubators, angel investors and angel groups, corporate investment divisions, crowd-funding and co-operative groups.

***Gale Directory of Publications and Broadcast Media (GDPBM)***. Cengage Learning Inc., 20 Channel Center St. Boston, MA 02210. Phone: 800-487-8488 or (617)289-7700; Fax: (617)289-7844; Email: investors@cengage.com • URL: http://www.cengage.com • Annual. $1,362 Individuals. Covers approximately 57,000 publications and broadcasting stations, including newspapers, magazines, journals, radio stations, television stations, radio/television/cable networks, syndicates and cable systems in the U.S. and Canada. Newsletters and directories are excluded.

***Gale E-Commerce Sourcebook***. Cengage Learning Inc., 20 Channel Center St. Boston, MA 02210. Phone: 800-487-8488 or (617)289-7700; Fax: (617)289-7844; Email: investors@cengage.com • URL: http://www.cengage.com • $532 Individuals hardcover. Covers over 4,700 organizations, associations, and agencies related to e-commerce such as Web site designers, government regulatory agencies, publications, and trade shows. Also covers 250 leading e-commerce companies worldwide.

***Gale Encyclopedia of E-Commerce***. Cengage Learning Inc., 20 Channel Center St. Boston, MA 02210. Phone: 800-487-8488 or (617)289-7700; Fax: (617)289-7844; Email: investors@cengage.com • URL: http://www.cengage.com • $507 Individuals print. Contains about 470 entries covering Web site development, e-commerce financing, advertising, marketing, legal issues, and other topics related to doing business through the Internet. Includes a bibliography.

***Gale Encyclopedia of Psychology***. Cengage Learning Inc., 20 Channel Center St. Boston, MA 02210. Phone: 800-487-8488 or (617)289-7700; Fax: (617)289-7844; Email: investors@cengage.com • URL: http://www.cengage.com • 2000. $267.00. Second edition. Includes bibliographies arranged by topic and a glossary. More than 650 topics are covered.

***Gale Encyclopedia of U.S. Economic History***. Cengage Learning Inc., 20 Channel Center St. Boston, MA 02210. Phone: 800-487-8488 or (617)289-7700; Fax: (617)289-7844; Email: investors@cengage.com • URL: http://www.cengage.com • 2003. eBook. Contains about 1,000 alphabetically arranged entries. Includes industry profiles, biographies, social issue profiles, geographic profiles, and chronological tables. Inquire as to price and availability.

***Gale Group PharmaBiomed Business Journals***. Cengage Learning Inc., 20 Channel Center St. Boston, MA 02210. Phone: 800-487-8488 or (617)289-7700; Fax: (617)289-7844; Email: investors@cengage.com • URL: http://www.cengage.com • Contains international coverage of full-text articles from trade journals on pharmaceuticals, biotechnology, and healthcare, including information on methods and techniques, business practices, new products, companies, markets, market share, research and development, regulations, and applied technologies in these fields.

***GAMA International Journal***. GAMA International, 2901 Telestar Ct., Ste. 140 Falls Church, VA 22042-1205. Phone: 800-345-2687; Fax: (571)499-4302 • URL: http://www.gamaweb.com • Bimonthly. $30 for members (in addition to annual dues); $150 for nonmembers; $175 for international subscriptions; Included in membership. Contains practical articles on the management of life insurance agencies.

***Gambia Business Law Handbook***. International Business Publications, USA, PO Box 15343 Washington, DC 20003. Phone: (202)546-2103; Fax: (202)546-3275; Email: ibpusa@comcast.net • URL: http://ibpus.com • $99.95 Individuals hardcover, e-book, CD-ROM. Covers: Information on basic business legislation, laws and climate, export-import regulations, and contacts.

***Gardena Valley Business Directory***. Gardena Valley Chamber of Commerce, 1204 W Gardena Blvd., Ste. E Gardena, CA 90247. Phone: (310)532-9905; Fax: (310)329-7307; Email: info@gardenachamber.org • URL: http://www.gardenachamber.com • Covers: About 500 member industrial, commercial, and service firms in the Gardena, California area. Entries include: Company name, address, phone, line of business, contact name.

***Gardena Valley Chamber of Commerce Business Directory***. Gardena Valley Chamber of Commerce, 1204 W Gardena Blvd., Ste. E Gardena, CA 90247. Phone: (310)532-9905; Fax: (310)329-7307; Email: info@gardenachamber.org • URL: http://www.gardenachamber.com • Annual.

***Gardeners Directory***. InfoGroup Inc., 5711 S 86th Cir. Omaha, NE 68127-4146. Phone: (402)593-4500 • URL: http://www.infogroup.com • Annual. Number of listings: 33,994. Entries include: Name, address, phone, size of advertisement, name of owner or manager, number of employees, year first in "Yellow Pages." Compiled from telephone company "Yellow Pages," nationwide.

***Gas Business***. Society of British Gas Industries, Warwick Rd. Kenilworth CV8 1TH, United Kingdom. Phone: 44 1926 513777; Fax: 44 1926 511923; Email: mail@eua.org.uk • URL: http://www.eua.org.uk • Quarterly. Publication covering gases.

***Gas Digest: The Magazine of Gas Operations***. T-P Graphics, 5731 Arboles Dr. Houston, TX 77035. Phone: (713)723-6736 • Quarterly. Free. Articles and data relating to operations and management phases of natural gas operations.

***Gas Turbine World***. Pequot Publishing Inc., PO Box 447 Southport, CT 06490. Phone: (203)259-1812 or (203)259-1112; Fax: (203)255-3313; Email: orders@gasturbineworld.com • URL: http://www.gtwbooks.com • Bimonthly. $130 Individuals.

***Gas Utility Manager***. James Informational Media Inc., 2720 S River Rd. Des Plaines, IL 60018-5142. Phone: (847)391-9070; Fax: (847)391-9058; Email: kirk@jiminc.com • Monthly. $95 Free to qualified subscribers USA; $95 Other countries. Trade magazine covering the natural gas market for industry professionals. Formerly *Gas Utility and Pipeline Industries*.

**Gases and Welding and Distributors Association**. 8669 Doral Blvd., Ste. 130 Doral, FL 33166. Phone: 877-382-6440; Fax: (305)442-7451; Email: gawda@gawda.org • URL: http://www.gawda.org • Formerly National Welding Supply Assoication.

***The Gases and Welding Distributor***. Penton Media Inc., 1300 E 9th St. Cleveland, OH 44114-1501. Phone: (216)696-7000; Fax: (216)696-1752; Email: information@penton.com • URL: http://penton.com • Bimonthly. Free to qualified personnel; others, $55.00 per year. Formerly *Welding Distributor*.

***Gateway to the European Union***. European Union, Email: pressoffice@eurostat.cec.be • URL: http://www.europa.eu.int • Web site provides access to a wide variety of EU information, including statistics (Eurostat), news, policies, publications, key issues, and official exchange rates for the euro. Includes links to the European Central Bank, the European Investment Bank, and other institutions. Fees: Free.

***GATEWAYS***. IZUM Information Service, Presernova 17 2000 Maribor, Slovenia. Phone: 999386 2 2520331; Fax: 999386 2 2524334; Email: izum@izum.si • URL: http://www.izum.si • Monthly. Database covers: 10 databases currently available online on records on the Internet and other networks providers in Slovenia. Entries include: Database name, acronym, date status, topic, language, number of records, update frequency, source of data, host, vendor, and producer.

***Gauteng Business Directory***. Intratex Holdings, 12 Caversham Rd. Pinetown 3610, South Africa. Phone: 27 31 7174000; Fax: (717)4001; Email: webmaster@brabys.com • Covers: Businesses in the Rand/Pretoria area. Entries include: Company name, address, phone.

***GDL Alert***. Thomson RIA, 195 Broadway New York, NY 10007-3100. Phone: 800-431-9025 or (212)367-6300 or (212)807-2298; Fax: (212)367-6305 or (212)337-4207; Email: ttacommunications@riag.com • URL: http://www.ria.thomson.com • Monthly. $110.98 per year. Newsletter. Covers current legal developments of interest to employers. Formerly *Disabilities in the Workplace Alert*.

***Gear Technology: The Journal of Gear Manufacturing***. Randall Publishing Inc., 1425 Lunt Ave. Elk Grove Village, IL 60007. Phone: (847)437-6604; Fax: (847)437-6618; Email: publisher@geartechnology.com • URL: http://www.geartechnology.com • Bimonthly. $45 Individuals. Edited for manufacturers, engineers, and designers of gears.

**Geelong Chamber of Commerce**. 10 Moorabool St. Geelong, VIC 3220, Australia. Phone: 61 3 52222234; Fax: 61 3 52222235 • URL: http://www.geelongchamber.com.au • Represents businesses in Geelong and the Surfcoast region of Australia.

***Gems & Gemology: The Quarterly Journal of GIA***. Gemological Institute of America, The Robert Mouawad Campus, 5345 Armada Dr. Carlsbad, CA 92008. Phone: 800-421-7250 or (760)603-4000 or (760)603-4031; Fax: (760)603-4080; Email: admissions@gia.edu • URL: http://www.gia.edu • Quarterly. $79.99 Individuals print only. Peer-reviewed scientific journal covering gemology and related issues: diamonds, colored stones, treatments, synthetics, identification techniques, gem instruments, innovative jewelry and lapidary arts.

***General Aviation News***. Flyer Media Inc., 11120 Gravelly Lake Dr. SW, Ste. 7 Lakewood, WA 98439-0099. Phone: 800-426-8538 or (253)471-9888; Fax: (253)471-9911 • Semimonthly. $29.95 Individuals 1 year; $49.95 Individuals 2 years. General aviation newspaper (tabloid) for aircraft pilots and owners.

***General BusinessFile ASAP***. Cengage Learning Inc., 20 Channel Center St. Boston, MA 02210. Phone: 800-487-8488 or (617)289-7700; Fax: (617)289-7844; Email: investors@cengage.com • URL: http://www.cengage.com • A fully international database designed to provide users with access to 200,000 company profiles; more than 50,000 full-text Investext reports; late-breaking news and event coverage on companies, industries, products, and executives; and the latest in business theory, economics, and favored practices.

***General Merchandise—Wholesale Directory***. InfoGroup Inc., 5711 S 86th Cir. Omaha, NE 68127-4146. Phone: (402)593-4500 • URL: http://www.infogroup.com • Annual. Number of listings: 1,045. Entries include: Name, address, phone, size of advertisement, name of owner or manager, number of employees, year first in "Yellow Pages." Compiled from telephone company "Yellow Pages," nationwide.

**General Robotics, Automation, Sensing & Perception**. University of Pennsylvania, GRASP Laboratory, Levine Hall, 4th Fl., 3330 Walnut St. Philadelphia, PA 19104-6228. Phone: (215)898-5814; Fax: (215)573-2048; Email: betsy@central.cis.upenn.edu • URL: http://www.cis.upenn.edu/grasp/.

***General Trade Index & Business Guide***. Business Foundation Company Ltd., Krucza 38-42 PL-00 512 Warsaw, Poland. Phone: 22 21 99 93; Fax: 22 21 97 61 • Annual. $135. Publication includes: More than 3,500 public and private Polish companies seeking foreign joint ventures or foreign trade opportunities. Entries include: Company name, address, phone. Principal content of publication is information on doing business and living in Poland.

***Generic Line***. Scitec Services Inc., PO Box 261641 Columbus, OH 43226-1641. Phone: (614)433-0648; Fax: (614)433-0432 • Description: Focuses on the pharmaceutical industry, emphasizing generic products. Discusses regulatory, legislative, technical, and business developments of interest to generic and small pharmaceutical manufacturers. Recurring features include reports on current research and actions of pharmaceutical companies.

***Genetic Engineering and Biotechnology Firms Worldwide Directory***. Mega-Type Publishing, 701 Sayre Dr. Princeton, NJ 08542-4602. Phone: 800-962-7004 or (609)683-0660; Fax: (609)275-8011 • Annual. $299.00. About 6,000 firms, including major firms with biotechnology divisions as well as small independent firms.

***Genetic Engineering News: The Information Source of the Biotechnology Industry***. Mary Ann Liebert, Inc., 140 Huguenot St., 3rd Fl. New Rochelle, NY 10801. Phone: (914)740-2100; Fax: (914)740-2101; Email: info@liebertpub.com • URL: http://www.liebertpub.com • $666 Individuals. Newsletter. Business and financial coverage.

***Genetic Technology News***. John Wiley & Sons Inc., 111 River St. Hoboken, NJ 07030-5774. Phone: 800-225-5945 or (201)748-6000; Fax: (201)748-6088; Email: info@wiley.com • URL: http://www.wiley.com • Description: Informs corporate development and research managers of advances in genetic engineering with applications in medical, agricultural, chemical, food, and other businesses. Covers areas such as recombinant DNA, monoclonal antibodies, and interferon. Recurring features include news of research, company reports, a calendar of events, and supplements titled Market Forecasts, Patent Update, and Strategic Partners. **Remarks:** Also available as part of Biotechnology Information Package, which includes Industrial Bioprocessing (see separate listings).

***Genetics Abstracts***. CSA, 7200 Wisconsin Ave. Bethesda, MD 20814. Phone: 800-843-7751 or (301)961-6700; Fax: (301)961-6720; Email: service@csa.com • URL: http://www.csa.com • Monthly. $1,595.00 per year. Includes print and online editions.

**Geode Resource, Conservation, and Development**. 308 N 3rd St. Burlington, IA 52601. Phone: (319)752-6395; Fax: (319)752-0106 • URL: http://geodercd.org • Provides rural development services in natural resources in such areas as water quality, crop diversification, grant writing, community facilities or services, and planning resource economic development projects for an administration cost.

***Geographical Abstracts: Human and Physical Geography***. Elsevier, Secondary Publishing Division, 650 Ave. of the Americas New York, NY 10011. Phone: 888-437-4636 or (212)633-3980; Fax: (212)633-3975; Email: t.reller@elsevier.com • URL: http://www.elseveier.com • Monthly. Institutions, $4,213.00 per year. *Human Geography*, $1,822.00 per year. Annual cumulation. *Physical Geography*, $2,391.00 per year. Annual cumulation.

***George D. Hall's Directory of New England Manufacturers***. George D. Hall Company Inc., 50 Franklin St., 4th Fl. Boston, MA 02110-1306. Phone: 800-446-1215 or (617)523-3745; Fax: (617)523-4862 • $128 plus $4.95 shipping. Covers: about 21,000 manufacturers in Connecticut, Maine, Massachusetts, New Hampshire, Rhode Island, and Vermont. Entries include: For manufacturers—company name, address, phone, names of principal executives, Standard Industrial Classification (SIC) code, product/service, number of employees, whether firm exports or imports. For banks—Name, address, phone, names of principal executives, service, number of employees.

**George Mason University - James M. Buchanan Center for Political Economy**. MSN 1D3 Fairfax, VA 22030. Phone: (703)993-2330; Fax: (703)993-2323; Email: tcowen@gmu.edu • URL: http://www.gmu.edu/jbc • Interrelationship of politics, law, and the economy.

**George Mason University - Interdisciplinary Center for Economic Science**. 3330 Washington Blvd. Arlington, VA 22201. Phone: (703)993-4856; Fax: (703)993-4851; Email: dhouser@gmu.edu • URL: http://ices.gmu.edu • Behavioral and neuro-economics, economic systems design, and experimental economics.

**George Mason University - Law and Economics Center**. School of Law, Hazel Hall, Ste. 440, 3301 Fairfax Dr. Arlington, VA 22201. Phone: (703)993-8040; Fax: (703)993-8181 or (703)993-8088; Email: hnbutler@gmu.edu • URL: http://www.masonlec.org • Research fields include product liability law.

***The George Washington International Law Review***. George Washington University Law School, 2000 H St. NW Washington, DC 20052. Phone: (202)994-6261 or (202)994-1010; Fax: (202)994-8980; Email: www@law.gwu.edu • URL: http://www.law.gwu.edu • Quarterly. $42 domestic; $47 foreign. Articles dealing with a variety of topics within the area of private international comparative law and economics.

**George Washington University - Center for International Science and Technology Policy**. Elliott School of International Affairs, 1957 E St. NW, Ste. 403 Washington, DC 20052. Phone: (202)994-7292; Fax: (202)994-1639; Email: space1@gwu.edu • URL: http://www.gwu.edu/cistp • Research areas include technology transfer.

**George Washington University - Center for Latin American Issues**. Duques Hall, Ste. 450, 2201 G St. NW Washington, DC 20052. Phone: (202)994-5205; Fax: (202)994-5225; Email: clai@gwu.edu • URL: http://www.gwu.edu/clai • U.S.-Latin American relations, focusing on strengthening business-government relations throughout the region, resolving differences, identifying areas for expanded relations, and managing economic and business issues.

***Georgia Business and Economic Conditions***. University of Georgia Selig Center for Economic Growth, c/o Dr. Jeffrey M. Humphreys, Director, 110 E Clayton St. Athens, GA 30602. Phone: (706)542-4085; Email: jhumphre@uga.edu • URL: http://www.terry.uga.edu/about/centers-institutes/selig • Bimonthly Quarterly.

***Georgia Business Directory***. InfoGroup Inc., 5711 S 86th Cir. Omaha, NE 68127-4146. Phone: (402)593-4500 • URL: http://www.infogroup.com • Annual. $520 both print & CD-ROM. Covers: 346,843 businesses in Georgia. Entries include: Company name, address, phone, number of employees, name of owner or manager, sales volume. Compiled from telephone company "Yellow Pages," statewide. All states covered (see separate entries).

***Georgia Industries Guide***. Industries Guides Inc., 303 E Altamonte Dr. Altamonte Springs, FL 32716. Phone: (407)834-8181 • $95. Covers: Approximately 9,000 manufacturers in Georgia. Entries include: Company name, address, phone.

**Georgia Institute of Technology - Tennenbaum Institute**. Centergy Bldg., Ste. 600, 75 5th St. NW Atlanta, GA 30338. Phone: (404)385-6013; Fax: (404)385-6127; Email: ron.johnson@gatech.edu • URL: http://www.ti.gatech.edu • Fundamental changes of private and public sector enterprises.

***Georgia Manufacturing Directory***. Georgia Chamber of Commerce, 270 Peachtree St. NW, Ste. 2200 Atlanta, GA 30303-1240. Phone: 800-241-2286 or (404)233-2264 or (404)223-2467; Fax: (404)233-2290; Email: communications@gachamber.com • URL: http://www.gachamber.com • Annual. $99.95 book; payment must accompany order; $199.95 CD-ROM or diskette; payment must accompany order; $249.95 book and CD-ROM; payment must accompany order. Covers: about 9,400 firms manufacturing products within Standard Industrial Classification (SIC) codes 20-39. Entries include: Company name, address, phone, names of principal executives, number of men and women employees, products or services, 4-digit SIC numbers, date established, market served, e-mail and web addresses.

***Georgia Republic Business and Industrial Directory***. International Business Publications, USA, PO Box 15343 Washington, DC 20003. Phone: (202)546-2103; Fax: (202)546-3275; Email: ibpusa@comcast.net • URL: http://ibpus.com • Annual. $99.95 Individuals hardcover, e-book, CD-ROM. Covers: Strategic industrial, investment and business contacts for conducting export-import and investment activity in the country.

***Georgia (Republic) Business Law Handbook***. International Business Publications, USA, PO Box 15343 Washington, DC 20003. Phone: (202)546-2103; Fax: (202)546-3275; Email: ibpusa@comcast.net • URL: http://ibpus.com • $99.95 Individuals hardcover, e-book, CD-ROM. Covers: Information on basic business legislation, laws, business climate, foreign investments, export-import regulations, and contacts.

**Georgia State University - Andrew Young School of Policy Studies - Georgia Health Policy Center**. 14 Marietta St. NW, Ste. 221 Atlanta, GA 30303-2813. Phone: (404)413-0314; Fax: (404)413-0316; Email: ghpc@gsu.edu • URL: http://ghpc.gsu.edu • Health care policy in order to improve health care delivery systems in Georgia, focusing on children's health, end of life and long-term care improvement, and networks for rural health.

**Georgia State University - Center for Mature Consumer Studies**. J. Mack Robinson College of Business, 35 Broad St. NW Atlanta, GA 30303. Phone: (404)413-7670 or (404)413-7650; Fax: (404)413-7699; Email: gmoschis@gsu.edu • URL: http://marketing.robinson.gsu.edu/research-centers-roundtables/cmcs • Serves as an information resource, assisting in strategy development for reaching the mature consumer market.

**Georgia State University - Center for Risk Management and Insurance Research**. PO Box 4036 Atlanta, GA 30302-4036. Phone: (404)413-7515 or (404)413-7500; Fax: (404)413-7516 or (404)413-7499; Email: rwklein@gsu.edu • URL: http://rmictr.gsu.edu • Insurance, finance, and economics. Provides technical materials and policy research in the areas of health care financing, international issues, law and regulation, corporate finance, retirement financing, risk, risk management, insurance, finance, economics. Research focuses on risk management and insurance including insurance markets, catastrophe risk, financial instruments, social insurance, health care financing, retirement, law, public policy, and regulation.

**Georgia State University - Center for the Study of Regulated Industry**. Department of Finance, Robinson College of Business Atlanta, GA 30302-3989. Phone: (404)413-7310; Fax: (404)413-7312; Email: profmorin@msn.com • URL: http://robinson.gsu.edu/faculty/csri.html • Energy consumption and the regulation of public utilities.

**Georgia State University - Economic Forecasting Center**. PO Box 3988 Atlanta, GA 30302-3988. Phone: (404)413-7260; Fax: (404)413-7264; Email: rdhawan@gsu.edu • URL: http://efc.robinson.gsu.edu • Concerned with national and regional economic analysis and forecasting.

**Geosynthetics Materials Association**. c/o Industrial Fabrics Association International, 1801 County Rd. B W Roseville, MN 55113-4061. Phone: 800-225-4324 or (651)222-2508; Fax: (651)631-9334; Email: generalinfo@ifai.com • URL: http://www.ifai.com/groups/gma • Represents members of the geosynthetics industry including manufacturers, testing firms and service companies. Aims to promote the acceptance and use of geosynthetic materials in a variety of applications. Provides resources and offers networking opportunities among members.

***Geothermal Energy System Businesses in the World***. Momentum Technologies L.L.C., PO Box 460813 Glendale, CO 80246. Phone: (303)229-4841; Fax: (408)705-2031 • URL: http://www.mtt.com • Contains directory listings for more than 490 geothermal energy system businesses and related companies throughout the world. Includes business name, address, phone number, fax number, e-mail address, and web site address. Provides brief descriptions of product lines, services offered, and business type. Includes information on manufacturers, component makers, wholesalers, retailers, system designers, architectural services, system installers, trade associations, and more. Searchable by location, business type, company name, and keyword.

***Geothermics: International Journal of Geothermal Research and Its Applications***. Elsevier, Secondary Publishing Division, 650 Ave. of the Americas New York, NY 10011. Phone: 888-437-4636 or (212)633-3980; Fax: (212)633-3975; Email: t.reller@elsevier.com • URL: http://www.elseveier.com • Bimonthly. $1,807 Institutions. Covers theory, exploration, development, and utilization of geothermal energy. Text and summaries in English and French.

***Geriatric Care Directory***. InfoGroup Inc., 5711 S 86th Cir. Omaha, NE 68127-4146. Phone: (402)593-4500 • URL: http://www.infogroup.com • Annual. Number of listings: 5,059. Entries include: Name, address, phone, size of advertisement, name of owner or manager, number of employees, year first in "Yellow Pages." Compiled from telephone company "Yellow Pages," nationwide.

***Geriatric Care***. Eymann Publications Inc., 1490 Huntington Cir. Reno, NV 89505. Phone: (775)358-1554; Fax: (775)358-1476; Email: eymann@care4elders.com • URL: http://www.wackywhiddles.com • Monthly. $87.50 Individuals.

***German Business CD-ROM***. Datamedia GmbH, Dieselstrasse 5 D-50996 Cologne, Germany. Phone: 2234 40040; Fax: 2234 400438 • Description: CD-ROM. Database covers: approximately 1.8 businesses in Germany. Entries include: Company name, address, phone, fax, classification information.

**German Business Council Qatar**. PO Box 24481 Doha, Qatar. Phone: 974 44 311152; Fax: 974 44 311154; Email: gbcq@ahkqatar.com • URL: http://www.gbcqatar.com • Aims to promote, cultivate and assist business relations between Germany and Qatar, as well as other international business communities, by forming a platform where business representatives of both nations can meet and exchange views and ideas.

***German Business Scope***. Representative of German Industry and Trade, 1776 I St. NW, Ste. 1000 Washington, DC 20006. Phone: (202)659-4777; Fax: (202)659-4779; Email: info@rgit-usa.com • URL: http://www.rgit-usa.com • A biweekly online publication which describes politico-economic developments in Germany (and the European Union) from the perspective of German industry.

***German Canadian Business and Trade Directory***. German Canadian and Trade Publication, Queen St., E Toronto, ON, Canada M4E 1G3. Phone: (416)465-9957; Fax: (416)465-8169; Email: directory@germancanadian.com • URL: http://www.germancanadian.com • Covers: Companies in all business sectors. Entries include: Multinational corporations, public institutions, professional associations, and importer/exporter.

***German Chamber of Commerce in China—Membership Directory***. German Industry & Commerce Company Ltd., Landmark Tower 2, Unit 0830, 8 N Dongsanhuan Rd., Chaoyang District Beijing 100004, China. Phone: 86 10 65396633; Fax: 86 10 65396689; Email: info@bj.china.ahk.de • URL: http://www.china.ahk.de • 1,200 ¥ Nonmembers; 600 ¥ Members. Number of listings: 1,800. Entries include: Company name, address, e-mail, phone, and fax numbers.

**German-Chinese Business Association**. Unter Sachsenhausen 10-26 D-50667 Cologne, Germany. Phone: 49 221 120370; Fax: 49 221 120417; Email: info@dcw-ev.de • URL: http://www.dcw-ev.de • Promotes mutual co-operation in the economic sphere, particularly between medium-sized Chinese and German companies. Supports intensive exchange of thoughts and experiences between all institutions and companies interested in doing business in China. Organizes information seminars on a regular basis in various cities.

**German Foods North America**. 719 6th St. NW Washington, DC 20001. Phone: 800-881-6419; Email: info@germanfoods.org • URL: http://germanfoods.org • Promotes imported German foods, beverages, and agricultural products in the U.S. and Canada through advertising, public relations programs, and promotional campaigns with supermarket chains and individual retailers. Acts as a liaison between U.S. and

Canadian importers and German manufacturers and exporters. Provides assistance to German manufacturers and their importers and distributors in complying with U.S. regulations.

**German Industry UK**. Ymwlch Isaf, Gwynedd Criccieth LL52 0PW, United Kingdom. Phone: 44 1766 523113; Email: info@gi-uk.co.uk • URL: http://www.gi-uk.co.uk • Works to provide forum for the discussion and exchange of experience and views on subjects relating to industry, economy and politics. Provides sales opportunities for members.

**German Private Equity and Venture Capital Association**. Residenz Deutschen Theater, Reinhardtstrasse 27c D-10117 Berlin, Germany. Phone: 49 30 3069820; Fax: 49 30 30698220; Email: bvk@bvkap.de • URL: http://www.bvkap.de • Represents the venture capital and private equity companies in Germany. Aims to create a favorable environment for the industry through publications and cooperation with other institutions.

***Germany Business Database***. The Data Supplier, 9107 Wilshire Blvd., Ste. 450 Beverly Hills, CA 90210. Phone: 888-930-3282; Fax: (818)221-0295; Email: contactus@thedatasupplier.com • URL: http://www.thedatasupplier.com • Contains contact information for more than 136,000 companies in Germany. Includes business name, full contact information, e-mail addresses, Web site, and contacts.

***Germany Government and Business Contacts Handbook***. International Business Publications, USA, PO Box 15343 Washington, DC 20003. Phone: (202)546-2103; Fax: (202)546-3275; Email: ibpusa@comcast.net • URL: http://ibpus.com • $99.95 Individuals. Covers: Strategic government and business information, export-import activity in the country, investment, business contacts and regulations.

***Germany Industrial and Business Directory***. International Business Publications, USA, PO Box 15343 Washington, DC 20003. Phone: (202)546-2103; Fax: (202)546-3275; Email: ibpusa@comcast.net • URL: http://ibpus.com • Annual. $99.95 Individuals hardcover, e-book, CD-ROM. Covers: Strategic industrial, investment and business contacts for conducting export-import and investment activity in the country.

***Germany's Top 300***. Frankfurter Allgemeine Zeitung GmbH, Hellerhofstr. 2-4 D-60327 Frankfurt, Germany. Phone: 49 69 7591 2180; Fax: 49 69 7577 9113; Email: vertrieb@faz.de • URL: http://www.faz.net • Annual. $595. Covers: Germany's top 300 corporations, banks, and insurance companies; corporations are ranked based on their turnover; banks are ranked according to business volume; insurance companies are ranked according to premium income. Entries include: Company name, address, phone, fax ranking, products and activities, Standard Industrial Classification (SIC) codes, names of key management personnel, number of employees, turnover, pre-tax profit, net profit, cash flow, assets, investments, cash reserves, shareholders, investor relations, dividend, and high/low share price.

***Getting Cash Out of Your Business***. American CPE Inc., 826 Riviera Mansfield, TX 76063. Phone: 800-990-4273 or (817)477-0222; Fax: (817)473-4998; Email: director@americancpe.com • URL: http://www.americancpe.com • Contains detailed training information covering methods of minimizing tax burdens and maximizing owner benefits and opportunities to draw cash from businesses.

***Gevers International Consultants***. Gevers International Consultants, 91 Rue de Taillepied CH-1095 Lutry Lausanne, Switzerland. • Annual. $75 Individuals. Covers: 10,000 consulting firms, including accountants, property consultants, lawyers, management consultants, and tax consultants in 124 countries. Entries include: Company name, address, phone, telex number, description, associate firms, language, clients, countries covered.

***GFWC Clubwoman: Magazine of the General Federation of Women's Club***. General Federation of Women's Clubs, 1734 N St. NW Washington, DC 20036-2990. Phone: 800-443-4392 or (202)347-3168; Fax: (202)835-0246; Email: gfwc@gfwc.org • URL: http://www.gfwc.org • Bimonthly. $6 Individuals.

**Ghent University - Center for Russian International Socio-political and Economic Studies**. Tweekerkenstraat 2 9000 Ghent, Belgium. Phone: 32 9 2643487; Fax: 32 9 2643599; Email: koen.schoors@ugent.be • URL: http://www.ceriseonline.be • Problems of economic transition in former Soviet republics.

***Gibaud Directory—Industrial, Commercial and Trade Enterprises***. Annuaire Gibaud, Bel Abord F-44880 Sautron, France. Phone: 40 634333 • Annual. Covers: 27,000 industrial, commercial and trade enterprises in France. Entries include: Company name, address, phone, name and title of contact, year established, number of employees, subsidiaries, manager name, product/service.

**Gibraltar Association of Compliance Officers**. PO Box 1493 Gibraltar, Gibraltar. Phone: 350 200 74518; Email: info@gaco.gi • URL: http://www.gaco.gi • Represents and protects the interests of compliance officers. Seeks to promote the exchange of views and the professional development of officers engaged in the performance of a compliance function within the Gibraltar Finance Centre.

***Gids bij de Officiele Prijscourant van de Amsterdamse Effectenbeurs***. Uitgeverij J. H. de Bussy B.V., Postbus 162 NL-1000 AD Amsterdam, Netherlands. Phone: 20 6606464; Fax: 20 6952076 • Annual. $195. Covers: companies listed on the Amsterdam Stock Exchange. Database includes: Information on shares, bonds, warrants, etc. Entries include: Company name, address, financial data.

**Gift and Home Trade Association**. 2550 Sandy Plains Rd. Ste. 225 Marietta, GA 30066. Phone: 877-600-4872; Email: info@giftandhome.org • URL: http://www.giftandhome.org • Aims to ensure the viability of the gift and home industry. Promotes business practices and professional development. Establishes standards and ethical guidelines.

**Gift Sales Manager Association**. 14710 Quaker Bottom Rd. Sparks, MD 21152. Phone: (410)472-3593; Email: ldcolson@comcast.net • URL: http://www.giftsalesmanagers.org • Represents the interests of sales managers in the gift and home decor industry. Works to improve company operations and increase sales. Serves as a forum to exchange information and ideas among members.

***Gifts and Decorative Accessories: The International Business Magazine of Gifts, Tabletop, Gourmet, Home Accessories, Greeting Card and Social Stationery***. Reed Elsevier Group plc Reed Business Information, 360 Park Ave. S New York, NY 11010. Phone: (212)791-4208; Email: corporatecommunications@reedbusiness.com • URL: http://www.reedbusiness.com • Monthly. $53.95 per year. Includes *Annual Directory*.

***Gifts & Tablewares—Directory Issue***. Scott's Directories, 12 Concorde Pl., Ste. 800 Toronto, ON, Canada M3C 4J2. Phone: 800-668-2374 or (416)442-2122; Fax: (416)510-6870; Email: customercare@scottsdirectories.com • URL: http://www.scottsdirectories.com • Annual. C$46.95 Individuals; $52.95 Individuals; $57.95 Other countries. Publication includes: List of approximately 1,000 manufacturers and suppliers of gift, home decor, stationery, and tableware items in Canada. Database includes: Calendar of Canadian, American, European, and Asian trade shows. Entries include: Company name, address, phone, fax, name, address, and phone of branches and showrooms; description of products and services; email and web sites.

***Gifts and Tablewares***. Scott's Directories, 12 Concorde Pl., Ste. 800 Toronto, ON, Canada M3C 4J2. Phone: 800-668-2374 or (416)442-2122; Fax: (416)510-6870; Email: customercare@scottsdirectories.com • URL: http://www.scottsdirectories.com • Seven times a year. $47.95 per year. Includes annual *Trade Directory*.

***Giftware News: The International Magazine for Gifts, China and Glass, Stationery and Home Accessories***. Talcott Communications Corp., 704 N Wells St., 2nd Fl. Chicago, IL 60654. Phone: 800-229-1967 or (312)849-2220; Fax: (312)849-2174 • URL: http://www.talcott.com/index.htm • Monthly.

***Giftwares—Manufacturers Directory***. InfoGroup Inc., 5711 S 86th Cir. Omaha, NE 68127-4146. Phone: (402)593-4500 • URL: http://www.infogroup.com • Annual. Number of listings: 1,180. Entries include: Name, address, phone, size of advertisement, name of owner or manager, number of employees, year first in "Yellow Pages." Compiled from telephone company "Yellow Pages," nationwide.

***Gilson Trademark Protection and Practice***. Jerome Gilson. Matthew Bender and Company Inc., 1275 Broadway Albany, NY 12204-2638. Phone: 800-424-4200 or (518)487-3000; Fax: (518)487-3573 or (800)424-4200; Email: customer.support@lexisnexis.com • URL: http://www.matthewbender.com • 3/year. $2,579 Individuals Book; $2,344 Individuals Electronic version. Periodic supplementation. Covers U.S. trademark practice.

***Giving USA Update***. American Association of Fund-Raising Counsel. AAFRC Trust for Philanthropy, 10293 N Meridian St., Ste. 175 Indianapolis, IN 46290. Phone: 800-462-2372 or (317)816-1613 or (317)816-1633; Fax: (317)816-1633; Email: info@aafrc.org • URL: http://www.aafrc.org • Quarterly. $110 Individuals. Legal, economic and social essays on philanthropy.

***Glass Digest: Trade Magazine Serving the Flat Glass, Architectural Metal an d Allied Products Industry***. Dialysis Inc., 18 Penthouse E 41st St. New York, NY 10017. Phone: (212)376-7722; Fax: (212)376-7723; Email: ashleepub@aol.com • URL: http://www.ashlee.com • Monthly. $40.00 per year.

***Glass Magazine***. National Glass Association, 1945 Old Gallows Rd., Ste. 750 Vienna, VA 22182. Phone: 866-342-5642 or (703)442-4890; Fax: (703)442-0630 or (703)827-0557; Email: pjames@glass.org • URL: http://www.glass.org • 11/year. Free to qualified subscribers; $34.95 Individuals; $49.95 Canada; $79.95 U.S. and Canada.

***Glasses Directory—Sun & Ski***. InfoGroup Inc., 5711 S 86th Cir. Omaha, NE 68127-4146. Phone: (402)593-4500 • URL: http://www.infogroup.com • Annual. Number of listings: 3,278. Entries include: Name, address, phone, size of advertisement, name of owner or manager, number of employees, year first in "Yellow Pages." Compiled from telephone company "Yellow Pages," nationwide.

***Glasses Directory—Wholesale***. InfoGroup Inc., 5711 S 86th Cir. Omaha, NE 68127-4146. Phone: (402)593-4500 • URL: http://www.infogroup.com • Annual. Number of listings: 2,221. Entries include: Name, address, phone, size of advertisement, name of owner or manager, number of employees, year first in "Yellow Pages." Compiled from telephone company "Yellow Pages," nationwide.

***Glassware (Collectible) Directory***. InfoGroup Inc., 5711 S 86th Cir. Omaha, NE 68127-4146. Phone: (402)593-4500 • URL: http://www.infogroup.com • Annual. Number of listings: 12,366. Entries include: Name, address, phone, size of advertisement, name of owner or manager, number of employees, year first in "Yellow Pages." Compiled from telephone company "Yellow Pages," nationwide.

**Global Automakers**. 1050 K St. NW, Ste. 650 Washington, DC 20001. Phone: (202)650-5555; Email: info@globalautomakers.org • URL: http://www.globalautomakers.org • Formerly known as the Association of International Automobile Manufacturers.

**Global Automotive Management Council**. 5305 Plymouth Rd. Ann Arbor, MI 48105. Phone: (734)997-9249; Fax: (734)997-9443; Email: info@gamcinc.com • URL: http://gamcinc.com • Represents senior executives from the global automotive industry. Promotes the globalization of automotive industries through meetings, seminars and educational forums. Provides educational and networking opportunities for senior executives.

***Global Business and Economics Review***. Inderscience Enterprises Limited, World Trade Center Bldg. II, 29, Rte. de Pre-Bois, Case Postale 896 CH-1215 Geneva, Switzerland. Phone: 41 1234 240515; Fax: 41 22 7910885 • URL: http://www.inderscience.com/ • €520 Individuals print or online; €706 Individuals print and online. Peer-reviewed journal focusing on the discussion and analysis of advanced concepts, initial treatments, and fundamental research in all fields of business and economics.

***Global Business and Finance Review***. Global Business and Finance Review, 8600 University Blvd. Evansville, IN 47712-3596. Phone: (812)464-8600; Fax: (812)465-1044 • URL: http://www.usi.edu • Semiannual. $50 Individuals; $125 Institutions; $20 Individuals overseas postage fee. The GBFR is a referred journal specializing in global business and finance.

***Global Business and Industrial Directories Publishers Directory***. International Business Publications, USA, PO Box 15343 Washington, DC 20003. Phone: (202)546-2103; Fax: (202)546-3275; Email: ibpusa@comcast.net • URL: http://ibpus.com • $99.95 Individuals. Covers: Largest business and industrial directories publishers worldwide.

***Global Business and Organizational Excellence***. Society of Competitive Intelligence Professionals. John Wiley and Sons, Inc., Journals Div., 111 River St. Hoboken, NJ 07030. Phone: 800-526-5368 or (201)748-6000; Fax: (201)748-6088; Email: consumers@wiley.com • URL: http://www.wiley.com • Bimonthly. $931 U.S., Canada, and Mexico print only,other countries; $1,118 Institutions print with online; $931 U.S., Canada, and Mexico institutional (print); $967 Institutions, other countries print. Journal covering best practices and trends that organizations use to excel. Formerly *Competitive Intelligence Review*.

***Global Business Associations***. International Business Publications, USA, PO Box 15343 Washington, DC 20003. Phone: (202)546-2103; Fax: (202)546-3275; Email: ibpusa@comcast.net • URL: http://ibpus.com • Covers: Approximately 1,000 largest business associations in over 100 countries.

***Global Business: Concepts***. Cengage Learning Inc., 20 Channel Center St. Boston, MA 02210. Phone: 800-487-8488 or (617)289-7700; Fax: (617)289-7844; Email: investors@cengage.com • URL: http://www.cengage.com • 2013. eBook. Published by IGI Global. Examines critical issues and emerging trends in global business, with topics ranging from managing new information technology in global business operations to ethics and communication strategies.

***Global Business Contacts Directory***. International Business Publications, USA, PO Box 15343 Washington, DC 20003. Phone: (202)546-2103; Fax: (202)546-3275; Email: ibpusa@comcast.net • URL: http://ibpus.com • $99.95 Individuals. Covers: Major business and government contacts in over 100 countries.

***Global Business Directory***. INFOT Inc., PO Box 2052 Rockville, MD 20847. Phone: 866-838-2619 • URL: http://www.infotusa.com • $51.85 CD-ROM; $229.50 additional fee for MS access format. Covers: 801,813 major global companies, businesses and services, suppliers, manufacturers, buyers, agents, importers, exporters, and organizations by industry. Entries include: Email and website addresses, telephone and fax number, and business titles and descriptions.

***Global Business Jet: The News Magazine For Intercontinental Business Jet Owners***. Stansted News Ltd., 134 S St. Bishop's Stortford CM23 3BQ, United Kingdom. Phone: 44 127 9714502 • URL: http://www.stanstednews.com • Monthly. Professional magazine for owners and operators of long-range business jets worldwide.

***Global Business Law Review***.

***Global Central Banks Directory***. International Business Publications, USA, PO Box 15343 Washington, DC 20003. Phone: (202)546-2103; Fax: (202)546-3275; Email: ibpusa@comcast.net • URL: http://ibpus.com • $99.95 Individuals paperback. Covers: Central banks for over 150 countries.

***Global Chambers of Commerce Directory***. International Business Publications, USA, PO Box 15343 Washington, DC 20003. Phone: (202)546-2103; Fax: (202)546-3275; Email: ibpusa@comcast.net • URL: http://ibpus.com • $99.95 Individuals paperback. Covers: Approximately 3,000 U.S. Local chambers of commerce interested in international trade.

**Global Cosmetic Industry: The Business Magazine for the Global Beauty Industry**. Allured Business Media, 336 Gundersen Dr., Ste. A Carol Stream, IL 60188-2403. Phone: (630)653-2155; Fax: (630)653-2192; Email: customerservice@allured.com • URL: http://www.allured.com • Monthly. Free to qualified subscribers all countries - Digital; Free to qualified subscribers US - print; 45 Other countries print only. Trade publication covering the cosmetics industry worldwide.

**The Global Directory of Financial Information Vendors**. QSU Publishing, PO Box 546436 Surfside, FL 33154. Phone: 866-225-3122; Fax: (703)359-8462; Email: news@qsuonline.com • URL: http://www.qsuonline.com • $95. Covers: Online financial services vendors and their operating systems. Database includes: Geographic market information and principal applications.

**Global Economic, Financial, and Development Organizations Directory**. International Business Publications, USA, PO Box 15343 Washington, DC 20003. Phone: (202)546-2103; Fax: (202)546-3275; Email: ibpusa@comcast.net • URL: http://ibpus.com • $99.95 Individuals paperback. Covers: International economic development agencies and organizations in over 100 countries.

**Global Electronic Business Research: Opportunities and Directions**. Cengage Learning Inc., 20 Channel Center St. Boston, MA 02210. Phone: 800-487-8488 or (617)289-7700; Fax: (617)289-7844; Email: investors@cengage.com • URL: http://www.cengage.com • 2006. eBook. Published by Information Science Reference. Encourages researchers and professionals interested in SMEs (small to medium-sized enterprises) and e-commerce to address the next phase in this field. This book points to some of the impending issues concerning e-commerce in SMEs, and highlights the need to do something in order to bridge the existing divide between the two. Global Electronic Business Research raises the importance of addressing the e-commerce phenomenon in SMEs at a global level.

**Global Foreign Trade Barriers to U.S. Products and Services Exports Handbook**. International Business Publications, USA, PO Box 15343 Washington, DC 20003. Phone: (202)546-2103; Fax: (202)546-3275; Email: ibpusa@comcast.net • URL: http://ibpus.com • $99.95 Individuals paperback. Covers: Foreign trade barriers to the U.S. Products and services exports to various countries.

**Global Grassroots**. 1950 Lafayette Rd., Ste. 200 Portsmouth, NH 03801-8663. Phone: (603)643-0400; Email: info@globalgrassroots.org • URL: http://www.globalgrassroots.org/index.htm • Works to empower, unite, and support relief of poor, distressed and underprivileged women worldwide. Benefits women by establishing a global network of leading entrepreneurs. Raises awareness of critical issues facing women worldwide, especially sexual and gender-based violence during conflict.

**Global Health Directory**. Global Health Council, 66 Canal Center Plz., Ste. 310 Alexandria, VA 22314. Phone: (703)717-5200; Fax: (703)717-5215; Email: membership@globalhealth.org • URL: http://www.globalhealth.org • Irregular. Covers: Over 500 private voluntary organizations, universities, civic groups, professional associations, and other groups involved with global health. Entries include: Organization name, address, e-mail, website, contact name, number of employees, mission, services, regions served, publications, internships available, and volunteer information.

**Global Information Society: Operating Information Systems in a Dynamic Global Business Environment**. Cengage Learning Inc., 20 Channel Center St. Boston, MA 02210. Phone: 800-487-8488 or (617)289-7700; Fax: (617)289-7844; Email: investors@cengage.com • URL: http://www.cengage.com • 2006. eBook. Published by Information Science Reference. Addresses the importance of information technology management and issues in operating information systems in the global dynamic business environment. This title offers a collection of new ideas, latest technology applications and experiences in global information systems development and operations.

**Global Investment Funds Directory**. International Business Publications, USA, PO Box 15343 Washington, DC 20003. Phone: (202)546-2103; Fax: (202)546-3275; Email: ibpusa@comcast.net • URL: http://ibpus.com • $99.95 Individuals paperback. Covers: Major investment funds interested in international ventures.

**Global Money Management**. Wolters Kluwer Law and Business, 76 9th Ave., 7th Fl. New York, NY 10011-4962. Phone: 800-234-1660 or (212)771-0600; Fax: (800)901-9075 or (301)644-3550 • URL: http://www.wolterskluwerlb.com • Description: Reports on international fund management, including investment strategies; pension fund searches; hires for consultants, managers, and custodians; performance measurement; developing markets, and significant personnel changes.

**Global Offshore Business and Investment Contacts Handbook**. International Business Publications, USA, PO Box 15343 Washington, DC 20003. Phone: (202)546-2103; Fax: (202)546-3275; Email: ibpusa@comcast.net • URL: http://ibpus.com • Annual. $99.95. Covers: Business and investment contacts in 33 offshore countries and territories. Entries include: Contact details.

**Global Offshore Business Laws and Regulations Handbook**. International Business Publications, USA, PO Box 15343 Washington, DC 20003. Phone: (202)546-2103; Fax: (202)546-3275; Email: ibpusa@comcast.net • URL: http://ibpus.com • Annual. $99.95. Covers: Business laws and regulations for conducting business in 33 offshore countries and territories.

**Global Offshore Investment and Business Guide**. International Business Publications, USA, PO Box 15343 Washington, DC 20003. Phone: (202)546-2103; Fax: (202)546-3275; Email: ibpusa@comcast.net • URL: http://ibpus.com • $99.95 Individuals paperback. Comprehensive guide for conducting offshore business.

**Global Offshore Tax Guide**. International Business Publications, USA, PO Box 15343 Washington, DC 20003. Phone: (202)546-2103; Fax: (202)546-3275; Email: ibpusa@comcast.net • URL: http://ibpus.com • Annual. $99.95. Covers: Tax regulations guidelines for 33 offshore countries and territories.

**Global Pere Investors Directory**. PEI London, Sycamore House, Sycamore St. London EC1Y 0SG, United Kingdom. Phone: 44 20 75665444; Email: fran.h@peimedia.com • URL: http://www.peimedia.com • $1,195 Individuals. Covers: 1,200 institutions investing in unlisted real estate funds. Entries include: Contact information.

**Global Power Report: An Exclusive Biweekly Covering the Cogeneration and Small Power Market**. Platts Global Energy, 2 Penn Plz., 25th Fl. New York, NY 10121-2298. Phone: 800-752-8878 or (212)904-3070 or (212)904-2977; Fax: (212)904-3070 or (212)904-4209; Email: support@platts.com • URL: http://www.platts.com • Biweekly. $1,165.00 per year. Newsletter. Covers industry trends, new projects, new contracts, rate changes, and regulations, with emphasis on the Federal Energy Regulatory Commission (FERC). Formerly *Cogeneration Report*.

**Global Salary Survey Report**. Association to Advance Collegiate Schools of Business, 77 S Harbour Island Blvd., Ste. 750 Tampa, FL 33602. Phone: (813)769-6500; Fax: (813)769-6559; Email: events@aacsb.edu • URL: http://www.aacsb.edu • Annual. Reports aggregate salary data of business school administrators and faculty. Text in English and Spanish.

**Global Seed Guide: World Reference Source for the Commercial Seed Industry**. Ball Publishing, 335 N River St. Batavia, IL 60510. Phone: (630)208-9080; Fax: (630)208-9350; Email: sbruhn@seedtradenews.com • URL: http://www.seedtradenews.com • Annual. $40.00. Includes company listings, type of business, type of seed, research centers, industry data, events calendar, and associations.

**Global Sourcing Council**. 750 Third Ave., 11th Fl. New York, NY 10017. Phone: (631)398-3366; Email: sanjaysrr@gmail.com • URL: http://www.gscouncil.org • Supports people and organizations with an interest in the social and economic effects of sourcing. Serves as a forum for the discussion of the social and economic impacts of global sourcing. Provides opportunities for professional networking and business development. Addresses issues relevant to any company involved in global business operations.

**Global Tax Guide Handbook**. International Business Publications, USA, PO Box 15343 Washington, DC 20003. Phone: (202)546-2103; Fax: (202)546-3275; Email: ibpusa@comcast.net • URL: http://ibpus.com • $149. Basic tax guide for over 80 countries.

**Global Top 1,000 Bakery Companies**. Datamonitor, Charles House, 108-110 Finchley Rd. London NW3 5JJ, United Kingdom. Phone: 44 20 7675 7000; Fax: 44 20 7675 7500; Email: euroinfo@datamonitor.com • $995. Covers: 1,000 leading international bakery companies. Entries include: Company name, address, phone, telex, names and titles of key personnel, number of employees; financial data, product/service, Standard Industrial Classification (SIC) code, production locations.

**Global Top 1,000 Canned Food Companies**. Datamonitor, Charles House, 108-110 Finchley Rd. London NW3 5JJ, United Kingdom. Phone: 44 20 7675 7000; Fax: 44 20 7675 7500; Email: euroinfo@datamonitor.com • $995. Covers: 1,000 leading international canned food companies. Entries include: Company name, address, phone, telex, names and titles of key personnel, number of employees; financial data, product/service, Standard Industrial Classification (SIC) code, production locations.

**Global Top 1,000 Confectionery Companies**. Datamonitor, Charles House, 108-110 Finchley Rd. London NW3 5JJ, United Kingdom. Phone: 44 20 7675 7000; Fax: 44 20 7675 7500; Email: euroinfo@datamonitor.com • $995. Covers: 1,000 leading international confectionery companies. Entries include: Company name, address, phone, telex, names and titles of key personnel, number of employees; financial data, product/service, Standard Industrial Classification (SIC) code, production locations.

**Global Top 1,000 Dairy Companies**. Datamonitor, Charles House, 108-110 Finchley Rd. London NW3 5JJ, United Kingdom. Phone: 44 20 7675 7000; Fax: 44 20 7675 7500; Email: euroinfo@datamonitor.com • $995. Covers: 1,000 leading international dairy companies. Entries include: Company name, address, phone, telex, names and titles of key person-

nel, number of employees; financial data, product/service, Standard Industrial Classification (SIC) code, production locations.

**Global Top 1,000 Frozen Food Companies**. Datamonitor, Charles House, 108-110 Finchley Rd. London NW3 5JJ, United Kingdom. Phone: 44 20 7675 7000; Fax: 44 20 7675 7500; Email: euroinfo@datamonitor.com • $995. Covers: 1,000 leading international frozen food companies. Entries include: Company name, address, phone, telex, names and titles of key personnel, number of employees; financial data, product/service, Standard Industrial Classification (SIC) code, production locations.

**Global Top 1,000 Ready Meals Companies**. Datamonitor, Charles House, 108-110 Finchley Rd. London NW3 5JJ, United Kingdom. Phone: 44 20 7675 7000; Fax: 44 20 7675 7500; Email: euroinfo@datamonitor.com • $995. Covers: 1,000 leading international companies that provide ready meals. Entries include: Company name, address, phone, telex, names and titles of key personnel, number of employees; financial data, product/service, Standard Industrial Classification (SIC) code, production locations.

**Global Trade & Business Show Directory**. International Business Publications, USA, PO Box 15343 Washington, DC 20003. Phone: (202)546-2103; Fax: (202)546-3275; Email: ibpusa@comcast.net • URL: http://ibpus.com • $99.95 Individuals paperback. Covers: Approximately 1,000 largest trade, business, and professional shows and exhibitions in the U.S. and other countries.

**Global Trade Atlas**. Global Trade Information Services Inc., 2218 Devine St. Columbia, SC 29205-2426. Phone: 800-982-4847 or (803)765-1860; Fax: (803)799-5589; Email: info3@gtis.com • URL: http://www.gtis.com • Subscription fees are tailored. Provides government statistics on trade between the U. S. and each of more than 80 countries. Includes import-export data, trade balances, product information, market share, price data, etc.

**Global Trade Leads**. INFOT Inc., PO Box 2052 Rockville, MD 20847. Phone: 866-838-2619 • URL: http://www.infotusa.com • $114.75 CD-ROM; additional $150 for MS Access format. Covers: More than 493,448 suppliers & buyers active in major online market places. Entries include: Email and website addresses, telephone and fax number, and business titles and descriptions.

**Global Trade Review Directory**. Exporta Publishing & Events Ltd., 3-C Hillgate Pl. London SW12 9ER, United Kingdom. Phone: 44 208 6739666; Fax: 44 208 6738662; Email: info@exportagroup.com • URL: http://www.gtreview.com • Annual. Free subscribers; £125 Individuals non-subscribers. Covers: 450 service providers to global trade, commodity, and export finance markets. Entries include: Company contact information.

**Global U.S. Economic Assistance Guide**. International Business Publications, USA, PO Box 15343 Washington, DC 20003. Phone: (202)546-2103; Fax: (202)546-3275; Email: ibpusa@comcast.net • URL: http://ibpus.com • $99.95. Covers: Information on U.S. economic assistance worldwide.

**Global World Trade Centers Directory**. International Business Publications, USA, PO Box 15343 Washington, DC 20003. Phone: (202)546-2103; Fax: (202)546-3275; Email: ibpusa@comcast.net • URL: http://ibpus.com • $99.95 Individuals paperback. Covers: World Trade Centers located in over 100 countries.

**The Globe and Mail Report on Business: Canada Company Handbook**. Globe Interactive, 444 Front St. W Toronto, ON, Canada M5V 2S9. Phone: 800-387-5400 or (416)585-5222; Fax: (416)585-5102; Email: circulation@globeandmail.ca • URL: http://www.theglobeandmail.com • Annual. $49.95. Covers: over 400 Canadian companies. Entries include: Company name, address, phone, line of business, names and titles of key personnel, financial data including balance sheets, stock ratios and prices, and debts, rankings by profit, revenues, and assets, description of activities, stock exchange symbols.

**Globe and Mail Report on Business**. Globe and Mail Publishing, 444 Front St. W Toronto, ON, Canada M5V 2S9. Phone: (416)585-5250; Fax: (416)585-5249 • Daily. Controlled circulation. Provides general coverage of business activity in Canada, with emphasis on the economy, foreign trade, technology, and personal finance.

**Globeandmail.com:**. Bell Globemedia Publishing, Inc., Phone: 800-268-9128 or (416)585-5000; Fax: (416)585-5249 • URL: http://www.globeandmail.ca • Web site provides access to selected sections of *The Globe and Mail*. Includes current news, national issues, career information, "Report on Business," and other topics. Keyword searching is offered for "a seven-day archive of the portion of the *Globe and Mail* that we publish online." Daily updates. Fees: free.

**Glues Directory—Wholesalers**. InfoGroup Inc., 5711 S 86th Cir. Omaha, NE 68127-4146. Phone: (402)593-4500 • URL: http://www.infogroup.com • Annual. Number of listings: 916. Entries include: Name, address, phone, size of advertisement, name of owner or manager, number of employees, year first in "Yellow Pages." Compiled from telephone company "Yellow Pages," nationwide.

**Goff's Business Travellers' Guide**. Adprint, • Annual. $1.95. Covers: about 200 hotels in the United Kingdom. Entries include: Hotel name, address, phone, telex, fax, location, proximity of major city and airport, description of facilities, rates, whether credit cards are accepted, restaurants, symbols for amenities.

***Going Private***. ALM Media Properties LLC, 120 Broadway, 5th Fl. New York, NY 10271-1100. Phone: (212)457-9400; Fax: (646)417-7705; Email: customercare@alm.com • URL: http://www.alm.com • $560 print + online + ebook; $535 print + ebook. Discusses the legal ramifications of a publicly-owned company "going private" by way of a sale, leveraged buyout, reverse stock split, or merger. (Law Journal Press).

***Going Public and the Public Corporation***. Harold S. Bloomenthal and Samuel Wolff. Thomson West, 610 Opperman Dr. Eagan, MN 55123. Phone: 800-328-9352 or (651)687-7000 • Semiannual. $1,827.75 full set; $194 monthly. Includes legal forms and documents. (Securities Law Series).

***Gold Book of Venture Capital Firms***. Todd Publications, PO Box 500 Millwood, NY 10546. Phone: 866-896-0916 or (914)373-4750; Fax: (914)373-4750; Email: toddpub@aol.com • URL: http://www.toddpublications.com • $75. Covers: 869 venture capital firms in 37 specialties. Database includes: Introduction on working with venture capital firms. Entries include: Firm name, names and titles of key personnel, specialty, preferred stage of financing.

***Gold Newsletter***. Jefferson Financial Inc., 2400 Jefferson Hwy., Ste. 600 Jefferson, LA 70121. Phone: 800-877-8847 or (504)837-3033; Fax: (504)837-4885; Email: info@accessintel.com • URL: http://www.jeffersoncompanies.com • Description: Reports on the relationship between gold and the economic system. Covers news of the "world gold markets, other precious metals markets, monetary reform, international economics, inflation, deflation, future of gold prices," and related economic and political matters. Remarks: Also available via e-mail.

***Golden States Financial Directory***. Accuity Inc., 4709 W Golf Rd. Skokie, IL 60076. Phone: 800-321-3373 or (847)676-9600; Fax: (847)933-8101; Email: custserv@accuitysolutions.com • URL: http://www.accuitysolutions.com • Semiannual. $540 Individuals. Holding companies, head offices and branches of all commercial banks, savings and loans, and credit unions with assets over $5 million in Alaska, Arizona, California, Colorado, Hawaii, Idaho, Montana, New Mexico, Oregon, Utah, Washington, and Wyoming.

***Goldsmiths' Kress Library of Economic Literature: A Consolidated Guide to the Microfilm Collection, 1976-1983***. Primary Source Microfilm, 12 Lunar Dr. Woodbridge,, CT 06525-2398. Phone: 800-444-0799 or (203)397-2600; Fax: (203)397-3892; Email: sales@gale.com • URL: http://www.psmedia.com • $1,200.00. Four volumes. Individual volumes, $300.00. An estimated 60,000 titles on 1,500 reels of microfilm (or fiche).

***Golf Cars & Carts Dealers***. InfoGroup Inc., 5711 S 86th Cir. Omaha, NE 68127-4146. Phone: (402)593-4500 • URL: http://www.infogroup.com • Annual. Number of listings: 1,507. Entries include: Name, address, phone, size of advertisement, name of owner or manager, number of employees, year first in "Yellow Pages." Compiled from telephone company "Yellow Pages," nationwide.

***Golf Course Directory***. National Golf Foundation, 1150 S US Hwy. 1, Ste. 401 Jupiter, FL 33477. Phone: 888-275-4643 or (561)744-6006; Fax: (561)744-6107; Email: general@ngf.org • URL: http://www.ngf.org • Annual. $199. Lists about 15,000 public and private golf facilities, with information as to size, number of holes, year opened, and practice ranges.

***Golf Course Management***. Golf Course Superintendents Association of America, 1421 Research Park Dr. Lawrence, KS 66049-3859. Phone: 800-472-7878 or (785)841-2240; Fax: (785)832-3643; Email: mbrhelp@gcsaa.org • URL: http://www.gcsaa.org • Monthly. $60 Individuals; $110 Canada and Mexico. Contains articles on golf course maintenance, equipment, landscaping, renovation, and management.

***Golf Course News: The Newspaper for the Golf Course Industry***. HME News, PO Box 998 Yarmouth, ME 04096. Phone: (207)846-0600; Fax: (207)846-0657 • Monthly. $60.00 per year. Edited for golf course superintendents, managers, architects, and developers.

***Golf Digest: How to Play, What to Play, Where to Play***. Golf Digest, 20 Westport Rd. Wilton, CT 06897. Phone: 800-962-5513 or (203)761-5100; Fax: (203)761-5131 or (203)761-5129; Email: bret.hopman@golfdigest.com • Monthly. $14.97 Individuals. A high circulation consumer magazine for golfers. Editions available in various languages. Supplement available *Golf Digest Woman*.

***Golf Magazine Buyers' Guide***. Times4 Media Inc., Two Park Ave. New York, NY 10016-5601. Phone: 800-227-2224 or (212)779-5000; Fax: (212)779-5522 • URL: http://www.golfmagazine.com • Annual. $10 per year. Price on application. Lists golf club manufacturers, with description of products and prices.

***Golf Magazine***. Time Inc., Time-Life Bldg., 1271 Ave. of the Americas New York, NY 10020. Phone: 800-843-8463 or (212)522-1212; Fax: (212)522-0602; Email: information@timeinc.com • URL: http://www.time.com • Monthly. $19.95 Individuals. Popular consumer magazine for golfers.

***Golf World Business***. Golf Digest, 20 Westport Rd. Wilton, CT 06897. Phone: 800-962-5513 or (203)761-5100; Fax: (203)761-5131 or (203)761-5129; Email: bret.hopman@golfdigest.com • 9/year. $72 Individuals. Edited for retailers of golf equipment. Formerly *Golf Shop Operations*.

***Golfdom***. Elsevier, Secondary Publishing Division, 650 Ave. of the Americas New York, NY 10011. Phone: 888-437-4636 or (212)633-3980; Fax: (212)633-3975; Email: t.reller@elsevier.com • URL: http://www.elseveier.com • Monthly. $30.00 per year. Covers marketing, financing, insurance, human resources, maintenance, environmental factors, and other aspects of golf course management. *Formerly Golf Business*.

***Golfweek: America's Golf Newspaper***. Golfweek, 1500 Park Ctr. Dr. Orlando, FL 32835. Phone: 800-830-5182 or (407)563-7000; Fax: (407)563-7077 or (407)563-7076; Email: golfweek@wrightsreprints.com • URL: http://www.golfweek.com • Weekly. $34.95 Individuals U.S, print; $59.95 Canada; $139.95 Other countries. Includes biweekly supplement, *Golfweek's Strictly Business*, covering business and marketing for the golfing industry.

***Golob's Environmental Business Report***. World Information Systems, PO Box 038535, Harvard Sq. Sta. Cambridge, MA 02238. Phone: (617)491-5100; Fax: (617)492-3312; Email: info@golob.com • Description: Provides news and analysis on environmental business, hazardous materials, waste management, and pollution prevention and control. Covers regulations, legislation and court decisions, new technology, contract opportunities and awards, and conferences.

***Good Fruit Grower***. Fruit Commission, 105 S 18th St., Ste. 217 Yakima, WA 98901. Phone: (509)575-2315; Fax: (509)469-9476 • URL: http://www.goodfruit.com • $35 Individuals; $55 Canada; $100 Other countries.

***Goods and Services—Firm Directory***. International Bureau for Information and Telecommunications, Leningradsky Ave. 80/2, p/b 44 125190 Moscow, Russia. Phone: 95 1588080; Fax: 95 1585665; Email: ieit@mbt.ru • Annual. $17. Covers: 5,000 leading and active companies in the Moscow region and their products and services. Entries include: Company name, address, phone, products or services provided.

***Gourmet News: The Business Newspaper for the Gourmet Industry***. HME News, PO Box 998 Yarmouth, ME 04096. Phone: (207)846-0600; Fax: (207)846-0657 • Monthly. $60.00 per year. Provides news of the gourmet food industry, including specialty food stores, upscale cookware shops, and gift shops.

***Gourmet Retailer***. Nielsen Business Media Inc., 770 Broadway New York, NY 10003-9522. Phone: 866-890-8541 or (646)654-4500 or (646)654-5000; Fax: (646)654-5584 or (646)654-4500; Email: bmcomm@nielsen.com • URL: http://www.nielsenbusinessmedia.com • Monthly. Free to qualified personnel; others, $75.00 per year. Covers upscale food and housewares, including confectionery items, bakery operations, and coffee.

***Governing: The States and Localities***. 1100 Connecticut Ave. NW, Ste. 1300 Washington, DC 20036. Phone: 888-955-4688 or (202)862-8802; Fax: (202)862-0032; Email: mailbox@governing.com • URL: http://www.governing.com • Monthly. $39.95 per year. Edited for state and local government officials. Covers finance, office management, computers, telecommunications, environmental concerns, etc.

***Government Affairs Yellow Book: Who's Who in Government Affairs***. Leadership Directories Inc., 104 5th Ave. New York, NY 10011-6901. Phone: (212)627-4140; Fax: (212)645-0931; Email: info@leadershipdirectories.com • URL: http://www.leadershipdirectories.com • Semiannual. $465 per year. Includes in-house lobbyists of corporations and organizations, Political Action Committees (PACs), congressional liaisons, and independent lobbying firms.

***Government Assistance Almanac: The Guide to Federal, Domestic, Financial and Other Programs Covering Grants, Loans, Insurance, Personal Payments and Benefits***. Omnigraphics Inc., PO Box 31-1640 Detroit, MI 48231. Phone: (313)961-1340; Fax: (313)961-1383; Email: customerservice@omnigraphics.com • URL: http://www.omnigraphics.com • Annual. $275 print; $250 online. Gives users updated information on all available federal domestic assistance programs. These programs represent nearly $2 trillion worth of federal assistance earmarked for distribution to consumers, children, parents, veterans, senior citizens, students, businesses, civic groups, state and local agencies, and others.

***Government Business***. Public Sector Publishing Ltd., 226 High Rd. Loughton IG10 1ET, United Kingdom. Phone: 44 20 85320055; Fax: 44 20 85320066; Email: info@psi-media.co.uk • URL: http://www.psi-media.co.uk • Bimonthly. Magazine featuring news and case studies that explain the commercial issues affecting local and central government.

***Government Computer News: The Newspaper Serving Computer Users Throughout the Federal Government***. Business Information, Inc., 8601 Georgia Ave., Ste. 300 Silver Spring, MD 20910. Phone: 800-417-0258 or (301)650-2129; Fax: (301)350-2111; Email: ttemin@gcn.com • URL: http://www.gcn.com.

***Government Contract Litigation Reporter: Covers Defense Procurement Fraud Litigation As Well as False Claims Acts (Qui Tam) Litigation***. Andrews Publications, 175 Strafford Ave., Bldg. 4, Suite 140 Wayne, PA 19087. Phone: 800-345-1101 or (610)225-0510 or (610)622-0510; Fax: (610)225-0501 or (610)622-0501; Email: customer@andrewspub.com • URL: http://www.andrewspub.com • Semimonthly. $875.00 per year. Newsletter. Provides reports on defense procurement fraud lawsuits.

***Government Contractor***. West DC Editorial, 901 15th St., NW, Ste. 200 Washington, DC 20005. Phone: (202)842-7570; Fax: (202)842-7565; Email: west.customer.service@cengage.com • URL: http://www.west.thomson.com • Weekly. $1,700 Individuals.

***Government Contracts: Law, Administration and Procedure***. Matthew Bender and Company Inc., 1275 Broadway Albany, NY 12204-2638. Phone: 800-424-4200 or (518)487-3000; Fax: (518)487-3573 or (800)424-4200; Email: customer.support@lexisnexis.com • URL: http://www.matthewbender.com • Quarterly. $3,165. Coverage of important aspects of government contracts.

***Government Contracts Reports***. Wolters Kluwer Law & Business CCH, 2700 Lake Cook Rd. Riverwoods, IL 60015. Phone: 888-224-7377 or (847)267-7000; Email: cust_serv@cch.com • URL: http://www.cchgroup.com • Weekly. $2,600.00 per year. 10 looseleaf volumes. Laws and regulations affecting government contracts.

***Government Discrimination: Equal Protection Law and Litigation***. James A. Kushner. Thomson West, 610 Opperman Dr. Eagan, MN 55123. Phone: 800-328-9352 or (651)687-7000 • Semiannual. $708.75 full set; $79 monthly. Covers discrimination in employment, housing, and other areas by local, state, and federal offices or agencies. (Civil Rights Series).

***Government Employee Relations Report***. Bloomberg BNA, 3 Bethesda Metro Center, Ste. 250 Bethesda, MD 20814-5377. Phone: 800-372-1033 or (703)341-3000; Fax: (800)253-0332; Email: customercare@bna.com • URL: http://www.bna.com • Weekly. $1,144.00 per year. Three looseleaf volumes. Concerned with labor relations in the public sector.

***Government Executive: Federal Government's Business Magazine***. National Journal Group Inc., The Watergate, 600 New Hampshire Ave. NW Washington, DC 20037. Phone: 800-613-6701 or (202)739-8400; Fax: (202)833-8069; Email: service@nationaljournal.com • URL: http://www.nationaljournal.com • Monthly. $48 Individuals. Includes management of computerized information systems in the federal government.

***Government Finance Review***. Government Finance Officers Association of United States and Canada, 203 N LaSalle St., Ste. 2700 Chicago, IL 60601-1210. Phone: (312)977-9700; Fax: (312)977-4806; Email: inquiry@gfoa.org • URL: http://www.gfoa.org • Bimonthly. $35 Individuals.

**Government Investment Officers Association**. 10655 Park Run Dr., Ste. 120 Las Vegas, NV 89144. Phone: (702)255-3224; Fax: (702)575-6670; Email: mday@gioa.us • URL: http://www.gioa.us • Provides education and training to government investment officers to assist them in their responsibilities. Promotes educational and professional development among investment officers in state and local governments. Seeks to instill higher levels of investment management skills, ethics and efficiency. Interacts with the public investment community and other public investment officers so that members will have the opportunity to gain the skills, knowledge and contacts that will greatly aid them in discharging their duties.

***Government Periodicals Index***. ProQuest L.L.C., 789 E Eisenhower Pkwy. Ann Arbor, MI 48106-1346. Phone: 800-521-0600 or (734)761-4700; Fax: (734)662-4554; Email: info@proquest.com • URL: http://www.proquest.com • An index to approximately 180 periodicals issued by various agencies of the federal government.

***Government Phone Book USA: Your Comprehensive Guide to Federal, State, County, and Local Government Offices in the United States***. Omnigraphics Inc., PO Box 31-1640 Detroit, MI 48231. Phone: (313)961-1340; Fax: (313)961-1383; Email: customerservice@omnigraphics.com • URL: http://www.omnigraphics.com • Annual. $265.00. Contains more than 270,000 listings of federal, state, county, and local government offices and personnel, including legislatures. Formerly *Government Directory of Addresses and Phone Numbers*.

***Government Primecontracts Monthly***. Government Data Publications Inc., 2300 M St. NW Washington, DC 20037. Phone: 800-275-4688 or (202)416-1761 or (718)627-0819; Fax: (718)998-5960; Email: gdp@govdata.com • URL: http://www.govdata.com • Monthly. $96.00 per year.

***Government Product News—Buyers Guide for Office Equipment Issue***. Intertec Publishing, 5 Penn Plz., 13th Fl. New York, NY 10001-1810. Phone: 800-795-5445 or (212)613-9700 or (212)204-4200; Fax: (212)613-9749 or (212)206-3622; Email: bethany.weaver@penton.com • URL: http://www.penton.com • Annual. $5. Publication includes: List of over 1,000 manufacturers of office equipment. Entries include: Company name, address, phone, name and title of contact.

***Government Product News***. Penton Media Inc., 1300 E 9th St. Cleveland, OH 44114-1501. Phone: (216)696-7000; Fax: (216)696-1752; Email: information@penton.com • URL: http://penton.com.

***Government Publications News***. Bernan Associates, 4611 Assembly Dr., Ste. F Lanham, MD 20706-4843. Phone: 800-416-4385 or (301)459-2255 or (301)459-7666; Fax: (301)459-0056 or (800)865-3450; Email: query@bernan.com • URL: http://www.bernan.com • Monthly. Free. Controlled circulation newsletter providing information on recent publications from the U. S. Government Printing Office and selected international agencies.

***Government Standard***. American Federation of Government

Employees, 80 F St. NW Washington, DC 20001. Phone: (202)737-8700 or (202)639-6435; Fax: (202)639-6490 or (202)639-6441; Email: comments@afge.org • URL: http://www.afge.org • Bimonthly.

***Government Technology: Solutions for State and Local Government in the Information Age.*** e.Republic Inc., 100 Blue Ravine Rd. Folsom, CA 95630. Fax: (916)932-1470; Email: info@erepublic.com • URL: http://www.erepublic.com • Monthly.

***Government Union Review and Public Policy Digest.*** Public Service Research Foundation, 320 D Maple Ave. E Vienna, VA 22180. Phone: (703)242-3575; Fax: (703)242-3579; Email: info@psrf.org • URL: http://www.psrf.org • Quarterly.

***Gown—Rental and Sales Directory.*** InfoGroup Inc., 5711 S 86th Cir. Omaha, NE 68127-4146. Phone: (402)593-4500 • URL: http://www.infogroup.com • Annual. Number of listings: 8,328. Entries include: Name, address, phone, size of advertisement, name of owner or manager, number of employees, year first in "Yellow Pages." Compiled from telephone company "Yellow Pages," nationwide.

***GPO Access.*** U. S. Government Printing Office Sales Program, Bibliographic Systems Branch, Phone: (888)293-6498 or (202)512-1530; Fax: (202)512-1262; Email: gpoaccess@gpo.gov • URL: http://www.access.gpo.gov • Web site provides searching of the GPO's Sales Product Catalog (SPC), also known as Publications Reference File (PRF). Covers all "Government information products currently offered for sale by the Superintendent of Documents." There are also specialized search pages for individual databases, such as the *Code of Federal Regulations*, the *Federal Register*, and *Commerce Business Daily*. Updated daily. Fees: Free.

***GQ: Gentleman's Quarterly for Men.*** Conde Nast Publications, 4 Times Sq. New York, NY 10036-6518. Phone: 800-289-9330 or (212)286-2860 or (212)286-3700; Fax: (212)286-6763 or (212)286-7093; Email: contact@condenast.com • URL: http://www.condenast.com • Monthly. $15 Individuals.

***GRA Reporter.*** Governmental Research Association, c/o Center for Governmental Research, 1 S Washington St., Ste. 400 Rochester, NY 14614. Phone: (205)870-2482 or (205)726-2482; Fax: (205)726-2900 • URL: http://www.graonline.org • Quarterly. included in membership dues; $50 /year for nonmembers. Description: Provides a research bibliography and news of members and their organizations. Recurring features include news of research, reports of meetings, and notices of publications available.

***Graduate Assistantship Directory in Computing.*** Association for Computing Machinery, 2 Penn Plz., Ste. 701 New York, NY 10121-0701. Phone: 800-342-6626 or (212)626-0500 or (212)869-7440; Fax: (212)944-1318; Email: acmhelp@acm.org • URL: http://www.acm.org • Database covers: Fellowships and assistantships in the computer sciences offered at U.S. and Canadian educational institutions. Entries include: Institution name, address, name and title of contact, degrees offered, area of expertise, financial aid offered, stipend amount, department facilities (hardware and software), school enrollment, required exams, admission deadlines.

**Graduate Management Admission Council.** 11921 Freedom Dr., Ste. 300 Reston, VA 20190. Phone: 866-505-6559 or (703)668-9600; Fax: (703)668-9601; Email: customercare@gmac.com • URL: http://www.gmac.com • Graduate schools of management and business administration. Works to establish criteria for use in admission to graduate management programs. Provides professional development for academic administrators and seminars for admissions officers. Maintains Graduate Management Admission Search Service, a program that provides institutions with the names of qualified students with desirable characteristics. Employs Educational Testing Service to develop and administer the Graduate Management Admission Test. Conducts research on student selection issues and political and social issues related to graduate management education.

**Graduate Management Association of Australia.** PO Box 6328 Melbourne, VIC 8008, Australia. Phone: 61 3 95363109; Fax: 61 3 95253656; Email: service@gmaa.com.au • URL: http://www.gmaa.asn.au • Promotes the standing graduate schools and postgraduate management. Enhances the value of graduate management qualifications. Contributes to the development of Australia and its managerial resources. Provides a forum for the interaction of members and students from various management schools. Pursues the regular exchange of ideas and knowledge between members and leaders in industry and management education.

***Grand Junction Area Chamber of Commerce—Business Directory.*** Grand Junction Area Chamber of Commerce, 360 Grand Ave. Grand Junction, CO 81501. Phone: 800-352-5286 or (970)242-3214; Fax: (970)242-3694 • URL: http://www.gjchamber.org/index.asp • Covers businesses in Grand Junction, Colorado.

**Grand Valley State University - Michigan Small Business and Technology Development Center.** 1020-L William Seidman Center, 50 Front Ave. SW Grand Rapids, MI 49504. Phone: (616)331-7480; Fax: (616)331-7485; Email: sbtdchq@gvsu.edu • URL: http://misbtdc.org • Manufacturing, financing, and international business information (particularly the export process) for small businesses. Resources for the export process includes determining and detailing international feasibility, foreign market entry plans, and responding to international inquiries. Foreign market information includes business etiquette and negotiating, country demographics, detailed tax information, financing sources, industry specific information, intellectual property rights, market contracts, rules and regulations, specific market information, and tariff reduction schedules.

***Grants for Libraries & Information Services.*** • Available only as a downloadable file. Single use version $39.95; library use version $$99.95. Foundations and organizations which have awarded grants made the preceding year for public, academic, research, special, and school libraries; for archives and information centers; for consumer information; and for philanthropy information centers.

***Grant's Interest Rate Observer.*** Grant's Financial Publishing Inc., 2 Wall St., Ste. 603 New York, NY 10005. Phone: (212)809-7994; Fax: (212)809-8492; Email: subscriptions@grantspub.com • URL: http://www.grantspub.com • Biweekly. $1,025 Individuals. Newsletter containing detailed analysis of money-related topics, including interest rate trends, global credit markets, fixed-income investments, bank loan policies, and international money markets.

***GrantSelect.*** Schoolhouse Partners L.L.C., Kurz Purdue Technology Ctr., 1281 Win Hintschel Blvd. West Lafayette, IN 47906. Phone: (765)237-3390; Fax: (765)594-4302; Email: info@schoolhousepartners.net • URL: http://www.schoolhousepartners.net • Online service provides detailed descriptions of more than 10,000 grants offered by government and organizations in the U. S. Includes grants in a wide variety of subject fields. Contains current information with daily updates. Inquire as to online cost and availability.

***Grantsmanship Center Magazine.*** The Grantsmanship Center, 350 S Bixel St., Ste. 110 Los Angeles, CA 90017. Phone: 800-421-9512 or (213)482-9860; Fax: (213)482-9863; Email: info@tgci.com • URL: http://www.tgci.com • Quarterly. Irregular. Free to qualified personnel. Contains a variety of concise articles on grant-related topics, such as program planning, proposal writing, fundraising, non-cash gifts, federal project grants, benchmarking, taxation, etc.

***Granville Market Letter.*** Joseph Granville, editor. PO Box 413006 Kansas City, MO 64141. Phone: 800-876-5388; Email: info@granvilleletter.com • 46 times a year. $250.00 per year.

***Graphic Arts Monthly: The Magazine of the Printing Industry.*** Reed Elsevier Group plc Reed Business Information, 360 Park Ave. S New York, NY 11010. Phone: (212)791-4208; Email: corporatecommunications@reedbusiness.com • URL: http://www.reedbusiness.com • Monthly. Free to qualified personnel; others, $142.99 per year.

***Graphic Design: U.S.A.*** Kaye Publishing Corp., 1556 3rd Ave., Ste. 405 New York, NY 10128. Phone: (212)534-5500 or (212)534-5003; Fax: (212)534-4415 • Monthly. $60.00.

***Graphis Design Annual.*** Graphis Inc., 307 5th Ave., 10th Fl. New York, NY 10016. Phone: (212)532-9387; Fax: (212)213-3229; Email: help@graphis.com • URL: http://www.graphis.com • Annual. $120 Hardcover. Text in English, French, and German.

***Graphis: International Journal of Visual Communication.*** Graphis Inc., 307 5th Ave., 10th Fl. New York, NY 10016. Phone: (212)532-9387; Fax: (212)213-3229; Email: help@graphis.com • URL: http://www.graphis.com • Bimonthly. $90.00 per year. Text in English, French and German.

***Gravel Directory—Wholesalers.*** InfoGroup Inc., 5711 S 86th Cir. Omaha, NE 68127-4146. Phone: (402)593-4500 • URL: http://www.infogroup.com • Annual. Number of listings: 12,943. Entries include: Name, address, phone, size of advertisement, name of owner or manager, number of employees, year first in "Yellow Pages." Compiled from telephone company "Yellow Pages," nationwide.

***The Gray Sheet Reports: Medical Devices, Diagnostics and Instrumentation.*** Elsevier Business Intelligence, 5635 Fishers Ln., Ste. 6000 Rockville, MD 20852. Phone: 800-332-2181 or (240)221-4500 or (800)332-2181; Fax: (240)221-4400 or (301)656-3094; Email: fdc.customer.service@fdcreports.com • URL: http://www.elsevierbi.com • Weekly. Institutions, $1,172.00 per year. Newsletter. Provides industry and financial news, including a medical sector stock index. Monitors regulatory developments at the Center for Devices and Radiological Health of the U. S. Food and Drug Administration.

***Great American Trials - Trials from 1637-2001.*** Cengage Learning Inc., 20 Channel Center St. Boston, MA 02210. Phone: 800-487-8488 or (617)289-7700; Fax: (617)289-7844; Email: investors@cengage.com • URL: http://www.cengage.com • 2001. $286.00. Second edition. Two volumes. Contains discussions and details of momentous American trials from 1637 to 2001.

***Great Big Book of Business Lists.*** Entrepreneur Press, 2445 McCabe Way, Ste. 400 Irvine, CA 92614-6244. Phone: 800-864-6864 or (949)261-2325 or (949)622-7131; Fax: (949)261-7729 or (949)261-0234; Email: press@entrepreneur.com • URL: http://www.entrepreneurpress.com • $34.95 Individuals paperback. Covers: Approximately 10,000 listings of business information. Entries include: Business' contact information.

***Great Depression and New Deal Reference Library.*** Cengage Learning Inc., 20 Channel Center St. Boston, MA 02210. Phone: 800-487-8488 or (617)289-7700; Fax: (617)289-7844; Email: investors@cengage.com • URL: http://www.cengage.com • 2003. $236.00. Four volumes. Published by UXL. Includes Great Depression and New Deal: Almanac; Great Depression and New Deal: Biographies and Great Depression and New Deal: Primary Sources. Also available as eBook.

***Greater Bowie Chamber of Commerce—Business Directory.*** Greater Bowie Chamber of Commerce, 2614 Kenhill Dr., Ste. 117 Bowie, MD 20715. Phone: (301)262-0920; Fax: (301)262-0921; Email: info@bowiechamber.org • URL: http://www.bowiechamber.org • Annual. Covers businesses in Greater Bowie, Maryland.

***Greater Calgary & Edmonton Business.*** Scott's Directories, 12 Concorde Pl., Ste. 800 Toronto, ON, Canada M3C 4J2. Phone: 800-668-2374 or (416)442-2122; Fax: (416)510-6870; Email: customercare@scottsdirectories.com • URL: http://www.scottsdirectories.com • Annual. $209 Individuals CD-ROM, pinpointer; $459 Individuals CD-ROM, profiler; $899 Individuals CD-ROM, prospector; $459 Individuals online, profiler; $899 Individuals online, prospector. Covers: 15,400+ manufacturers, manufacturers' sales offices, wholesalers, wholesale agents, and distributors operating in Greater Calgary and Edmonton along with 28,900+ business contact names. Entries include: Company name, address, phone, fax, names and titles of key personnel, number of employees, parent companies, SIC, product, year established.

***Greater Cincinnati Chamber of Commerce—Cincinnati USA Business Connections Directory.*** Greater Cincinnati Chamber of Commerce, 3 E 4th St. Cincinnati, OH 45202. Phone: (513)579-3100 or (513)579-3111; Fax: (513)579-3101; Email: info@cincinnatichamber.com • URL: http://www.cincinnatichamber.com • Covers: Over 5,000 member firms in the Greater Cincinnati area (Hamilton, Clermont, Butler, Brown, and Warren counties in Ohio; Boone, Campbell, Grant, Gallatin, Pendleton, and Kenton counties in Kentucky; Dearborn and Ohio counties in Indiana). Entries include: Company name, address, phone, market area, names and titles of principal executives, number of employees, product/service, Standard Industrial Classification (SIC) code, date established, whether firm imports or exports, branches, parent company, annual sales, whether publicly or privately held.

***Greater Dover Chamber of Commerce Business Directory.*** Greater Dover Chamber of Commerce, 550 Central Ave. Dover, NH 03820. Phone: (603)742-2218; Fax: (603)749-6317; Email: info@dovernh.org • URL: http://www.dovernh.org • Covers: Member businesses in New Hampshire. Entries include: Company name, address, phone, name of contact, category of product or service.

***Greater Hartford Business Review.*** Middlesex Magazine & Business Review, 615 Main St. Cromwell, CT 06416. Phone: (203)635-1819; Fax: (203)632-7203; Email: ctbizmag@suet.net • Monthly. Business journal.

***Greater Hermiston Chamber of Commerce—Member Business Directory.*** Greater Hermiston Chamber of Commerce, 415 S Highway 395 Hermiston, OR 97838. Phone: (541)567-6151; Fax: (541)564-9109 • URL: http://www.hermistonchamber.com • Covers businesses in Hermiston, Oregon.

***Greater Kendall Business Association—Member Directory.*** Greater Kendall Business Association, 14221 SW 120th St., Ste. 120 Miami, FL 33186. Phone: (305)386-4030; Email: info@westkendallbusiness.com • URL: http://www.westkendallbusiness.com • Lists business members in Miami, Florida.

***Greater Madison Area Christian Business Directory.*** Red Letter Publishing, PO Box 272682 Fort Collins, CO 80527. Phone: 800-445-5614; Fax: (970)267-9669; Email: info@redletter.com • URL: http://www.christianbusinessdirectoryonline.com • Covers: Businesses, churches, organizations, and schools in Madison, Wisconsin. Entries include: Company or organization name, address, e-mail, website, contact person, and hours of operation.

***Greater Montreal Business.*** Scott's Directories, 12 Concorde Pl., Ste. 800 Toronto, ON, Canada M3C 4J2. Phone: 800-668-2374 or (416)442-2122; Fax: (416)510-6870; Email: customercare@scottsdirectories.com • URL: http://www.scottsdirectories.com • Contains information on more than 40,000 individuals at more than 21,000 companies in greater Montreal, Quebec, Canada.

***Greater Omaha Area Christian Business Directory.*** Red Letter Publishing, PO Box 272682 Fort Collins, CO 80527. Phone: 800-445-5614; Fax: (970)267-9669; Email: info@redletter.com • URL: http://www.christianbusinessdirectoryonline.com • Businesses, churches, organizations, and schools in Greater Omaha Area.

***Greater Phoenix Chamber Membership List—Home-Based Businesses.*** Greater Phoenix Chamber of Commerce, 201 N Central Ave., 27th Fl. Phoenix, AZ 85004-2715. Phone: (602)495-2195; Fax: (602)495-8913; Email: info@phoenixchamber.com • URL: http://www.phoenixchamber.com • $295 Members; $500 Nonmembers. Covers: 67 home-based businesses in the greater Phoenix, Arizona area. Entries include: Contact details.

***Greater San Diego Chamber of Commerce Business Referral Directory.*** San Diego Regional Chamber of Commerce, Emerald Plz., Ste. 1000, 402 W Broadway San Diego, CA 92101-3585. Phone: (619)544-1300 or (619)544-1382; Fax: (619)744-7400; Email: webinfo@sdchamber.org • URL: http://sdchamber.org • Covers: Approximately 4,500 member businesses in San Diego, California. Entries include: Company name, address, phone, name and title of contact, products or services.

**Greater Seattle & Eastside Christian Business Directory**. Red Letter Publishing, PO Box 272682 Fort Collins, CO 80527. Phone: 800-445-5614; Fax: (970)267-9669; Email: info@redletter.com • URL: http://www.christianbusinessdirectoryonline.com • Businesses, churches, organizations, and schools in Greater Seattle and Eastside, Washington.

**Greater Topeka Christian Business Directory**. Red Letter Publishing, PO Box 272682 Fort Collins, CO 80527. Phone: 800-445-5614; Fax: (970)267-9669; Email: info@redletter.com • URL: http://www.christianbusinessdirectoryonline.com • Businesses, churches, organizations, and schools in Greater Topeka, Kansas.

**Greater Toronto & Golden Horseshoe Business**. Scott's Directories, 12 Concorde Pl., Ste. 800 Toronto, ON, Canada M3C 4J2. Phone: 800-668-2374 or (416)442-2122; Fax: (416)510-6870; Email: customercare@scottsdirectories.com • URL: http://www.scottsdirectories.com • Contains information on more than 84,000 individuals at more than 50,000 companies in greater Toronto and the Golden Horseshoe area of Ontario, Canada.

**Greater Tucson Christian Business Directory**. Red Letter Publishing, PO Box 272682 Fort Collins, CO 80527. Phone: 800-445-5614; Fax: (970)267-9669; Email: info@redletter.com • URL: http://www.christianbusinessdirectoryonline.com • Businesses, churches, organizations, and schools in Greater Tucson, Arizona.

**Greater Vancouver Business**. Scott's Directories, 12 Concorde Pl., Ste. 800 Toronto, ON, Canada M3C 4J2. Phone: 800-668-2374 or (416)442-2122; Fax: (416)510-6870; Email: customercare@scottsdirectories.com • URL: http://www.scottsdirectories.com • Annual. $299 Individuals CD-ROM, pinpointer; $599 Individuals CD-ROM, profiler; $1,199 Individuals CD-ROM, prospector; $499 online, profiler; $999 online, prospector. Covers: 17,900+ manufacturers, manufacturers' sales offices, wholesalers, wholesale agents, and distributors operating in Vancouver, Port Coquitlam, Surrey, North Vancouver, Langley, Burnaby, Maple Ridge, Victoria and capital region along with 28,200+ business contact names. Entries include: Company name, address, phone, fax, names and titles of key personnel, number of employees, parent companies, SIC, product, year established.

**The Greater Washington Board of Trade—Membership Directory**. Greater Washington Board of Trade, 1725 I St. NW, Ste. 200 Washington, DC 20006. Phone: (202)857-5900; Fax: (202)223-2648; Email: info@bot.org • URL: http://www.bot.org • Annual. $150; Free online access. Covers: Over 900 member firms in the greater Washington, DC, metropolitan area. Entries include: Organization name, address, phone, name of key executive, type of organization, Standard Industrial Classification (SIC) code.

**Greater Windham Chamber of Commerce—Annual Business and Pleasure Guide**. Sebago Lakes Region Chamber of Commerce, 747 Roosevelt Trail Windham, ME 04062. Phone: (207)892-8265; Fax: (207)893-0110; Email: info@sebagolakeschamber.com • URL: http://www.sebagolakeschamber.com • Annual. Covers: Attractions for business or pleasure in Windham, Maine.

**Greece Business Law Handbook**. International Business Publications, USA, PO Box 15343 Washington, DC 20003. Phone: (202)546-2103; Fax: (202)546-3275; Email: ibpusa@comcast.net • URL: http://ibpus.com • $99.95 Individuals hardcover, e-book, CD-ROM. Covers: Information on business laws and climate, investment, tax, export-import regulations, and contacts.

**Greece Industrial and Business Directory**. International Business Publications, USA, PO Box 15343 Washington, DC 20003. Phone: (202)546-2103; Fax: (202)546-3275; Email: ibpusa@comcast.net • URL: http://ibpus.com • Annual. $99.95 Individuals hardcopy, e-book, CD-ROM. Covers: Strategic industrial, investment and business contacts for conducting export-import and investment activity in the country. Contains strategic, practical economic and business information.

**Greek Exporters**. European P.L.C., Farantaton 34 11527 Athens, Greece. Phone: 30 210 7481581; Fax: 30 210 7797271 • URL: http://www.greekexporters.gr/publ.asp • Provides specific proposals of co-operation between Greek companies and their counterparts within the Eastern European, Balkans and N.I.S. countries. Covers: Greek export companies in Eastern Europe, Balkans, and N.I.S.

**Greek Financial Directory**. ICAP AE, 2 Eleftheriou Venizelou Ave. 176 76 Kallithea, Greece. Phone: 30 210 7200000; Fax: 30 210 7220815; Email: icap@icap.gr • URL: http://www.icap.gr • Annual. Covers: Over 20,000 companies operating in Greece; volume 1 includes manufacturing firms; volume 2 includes trading firms (representatives, importers, distributors, and exporters); foreign firms represented in Greece, and tradenames; volume 3 includes service rendering firms and firms related to the tourism industry; volume 4 includes alphabetical index of all listed firms; volume 5 includes statistics on Greek firms. Entries include: Company name, address, phone, fax, telex, year established, names and titles of key personnel, line of business, products/services, trademarks, number of employees, foreign firms represented,

financial data for two prior years.

**Green Book**. Independent Bankers Association of Texas, 1700 Rio Grande St., No. 100 Austin, TX 78701-1683. Phone: 800-749-4228 or (512)474-6889; Fax: (512)322-9004 • URL: http://www.ibat.org • Covers: Banks and loan institutions in Texas.

**Green Business**. Annex Publishing & Printing Inc., PO Box 530, 105 Donly Drive St. Simcoe, ON, Canada N3Y 4N5. Phone: 800-265-2827 or (519)429-3966; Fax: (519)429-3094 or (519)429-3112; Email: mfredericks@annexweb.com • URL: http://www.annexweb.com • Bimonthly. Magazine focusing on issues related to corporate sustainable development, including energy, environmental management, and emissions trading.

**Green Channel Business**. Indo-American Chamber of Commerce, Vulcan Insurance Bldg., 1-C, Veer Nariman Rd., Churchgate Mumbai 400 020, India. Phone: 91 22 22821413 or 91 22 22836340; Fax: 91 22 22046141; Email: ho@iaccindia.com • URL: http://www.iaccindia.com • Monthly.

**Green Data Centers and Internet Business**. Information Gatekeepers Inc., 1340 Soldiers Field Rd., Ste. 2 Boston, MA 02135. Phone: 800-323-1088 or (617)782-5033 or (617)232-3111; Fax: (617)782-5735 or (617)734-8562; Email: info@igigroup.com • URL: http://www.igigroup.com • Monthly. $695 U.S. and Canada print; $745 Elsewhere print; $695 Individuals PDF - 1 user; $2,500 Individuals PDF - 2 to 10 users; $4,000 Individuals PDF - 11 to 20 users. Provides marketing and technology information on new developments in the internet telephone industry on a worldwide basis.

**Green Industry Pros**. Cygnus Business Media Inc., 1233 Janesville Ave. Fort Atkinson, WI 53538. Phone: 800-547-7377; Email: info@cygnus.com • URL: http://www.cygnus.com • Irregular. Nine times a year. Includes retailers and distributors of lawn and garden power equipment, lawn and plant care products, patio furniture, etc. Arranged by type of product. Includes a *Product* issue.

**Green Markets**. Pike and Fischer Inc., 8505 Fenton St., Ste. 208 Silver Spring, MD 20910-4499. Phone: 800-255-8131 or (301)562-1530; Fax: (301)562-1521; Email: pike@pf.com • URL: http://www.pf.com • Weekly. $915.00 per year. Newsletter including prices for potash and other agricultural chemicals.

**Green Partners**. • URL: http://www.greenpartnersllc.com • Represents the interests of businesses that are committed to protect the environment. Promotes environmentally an "green" concept to the business sectors. Educates businesses on ways to be environmentally friendly through classes, on-site inspections and mentorship.

**The Green Sheet**. Elsevier Business Intelligence, 5635 Fishers Ln., Ste. 6000 Rockville, MD 20852. Phone: 800-332-2181 or (240)221-4500 or (800)332-2181; Fax: (240)221-4400 or (301)656-3094; Email: fdc.customer.service@fdcreports.com • URL: http://www.elsevierbi.com • Weekly. $109.00 per year. Newsletter for retailers and wholesalers of pharmaceutical products. Includes pricing developments and new drug announcements.

**Green Technologies and Business Practices: An IT Approach**. Cengage Learning Inc., 20 Channel Center St. Boston, MA 02210. Phone: 800-487-8488 or (617)289-7700; Fax: (617)289-7844; Email: investors@cengage.com • URL: http://www.cengage.com • 2012. eBook. Published by IGI Global. An international platform that brings together academics, researchers, lecturers, policy makers, practitioners, and persons in decision-making positions from all backgrounds who ultimately share new theories, research findings and case studies, together enhancing understanding and collaboration of green issues in business and the role of information technologies and also analyze recent developments in theory and practice.

**GreenBook**. New York American Marketing Association, 116 E 27th St., 6th Fl. New York, NY 10016. Phone: (212)687-3280; Email: info@nyama.org • URL: http://www.nyama.org • Annual. Contains information on companies offering focus group facilities, including recruiting, moderating, and transcription services.

**GreenBook Worldwide Directory of Marketing Research Companies and Services**. New York AMA - Green Book, 116 E 27th St., 6th Fl. New York, NY 10016. Phone: (212)849-2752 • URL: http://www.greenbook.org • Annual. Contains information in 300 categories on more than 2,500 market research companies, consultants, field services, computer services, survey research companies, etc. Indexed by specialty, industry, company, computer program, and personnel. Available online. Formerly *Greenbook Worldwide International Directory of Marketing Research Companies and Services*.

**Greenhouse Grower**. Meister Media, 37733 Euclid Ave. Willoughby, OH 44094-5992. Phone: 800-572-7740 or (440)942-2000; Fax: (440)975-3447; Email: info@meistermedia.com • URL: http://www.meistermedia.com • $37.45 Individuals. Concerned with all crops grown under glass or plastic.

**Greenpeace Australia Pacific**. 33 Mountain St., Level 2, Ultimo Sydney, NSW 2007, Australia. Phone: 61 2 92816100; Fax: 61 2 92800380; Email: support.au@greenpeace.org • URL: http://www.greenpeace.org/australia • Campaigns to ensure a just, peaceful, sustainable environment for future generations. Works to end the nuclear threat by global nuclear disarmament and closure of the nuclear industry, replacing with non-

radioactive alternatives; save the oceans by bringing end to overfishing, pirate fishing and commercial whaling; eliminate toxics; stop climate change by phasing out fossil fuels (oil, coal, gas) and replace with renewable energy, such as wind and solar power; save the forests.

**Greenpeace Sweden**. Rosenlundsgatan 29B, PO Box 151 64104 65 Stockholm, Sweden. Phone: 46 8 7027070; Fax: 46 8 6949013; Email: info.se@greenpeace.org • URL: http://www.greenpeace.org/sweden • Regional branch of Greenpeace. Uses nonviolent, creative confrontation to expose global environmental problems and their causes. Researches solutions and alternatives to help provide a path for a green and peaceful future. Aims to ensure the ability of the earth to nurture life in all its diversity. Organizes public campaigns for the protection of oceans and ancient forest, for the phasing-out of fossil fuels and the promotion of renewable energies in order to stop climate change for the elimination of toxic chemicals against the release of genetically modified organisms into nature for nuclear disarmament and an end to nuclear contamination.

**Greenpeace UK**. Canonbury Villas London N1 2PN, United Kingdom. Phone: 44 20 78658100; Fax: 44 20 78658200 • URL: http://www.greenpeace.org.uk • Individuals interested in environmental protection and peace issues. Greenpeace campaigns on global issues such as climate change, forests, oceans, toxic pollution, nuclear, genetic engineering and peace.

**Greenville Business Magazine (GBM)**. Integrated Media Publishing, 303 Haywood Rd. Greenville, SC 29607. Phone: (864)271-1105; Fax: (864)271-1165 • URL: http://www.greenvillemagazine.com • Monthly. $23.95 Individuals; $35.95 Two years. Magazine featuring Greenville businesses and communities.

**Grey House Directory of Special Issues: A Guide to Business Magazines**. Grey House Publishing, 4919 Rte. 22 Amenia, NY 12501. Phone: 800-562-2139 or (518)789-8700; Fax: (518)789-0556; Email: books@greyhouse.com • URL: http://www.greyhouse.com • $175 Softcover; $345 Online Database, with free directory. Covers: 4,000 business magazines with special issues as well as industry-specific magazines targeting researchers. Entries include: Publisher name, address, phone, fax, e-mail, brief description of content or audience.

**The Grey House Performing Arts Directory**. Grey House Publishing, 4919 Rte. 22 Amenia, NY 12501. Phone: 800-562-2139 or (518)789-8700; Fax: (518)789-0556; Email: books@greyhouse.com • URL: http://www.greyhouse.com • Annual. $250 Individuals Softcover. Covers: More than 8,500 dance companies, instrumental music programs, opera companies, choral groups, theatre companies, performing arts series, and performing arts facilities. Database includes: Information resources section covering hundreds of performing arts associations, publications, and Web sites. Entries include: Mailing address, telephone and fax numbers, e-mail addresses, Web sites, mission statement, key management contacts, and facility information such as capacity, season, and attendance.

**Grills—Gas & Electric—Parts Directory**. InfoGroup Inc., 5711 S 86th Cir. Omaha, NE 68127-4146. Phone: (402)593-4500 • URL: http://www.infogroup.com • Annual. Number of listings: 2,171. Entries include: Name, address, phone, size of advertisement, name of owner or manager, number of employees, year first in "Yellow Pages." Compiled from telephone company "Yellow Pages," nationwide.

**Grinding and Abrasive Magazine**. Abrasive Magazine, Inc., PO Box 11 Byron Center, MI 49315. Phone: (616)530-2220; Fax: (616)530-6466; Email: abrasivesmagazine@attbi.com • URL: http://www.abrasivesmagazine.com • Eight times a year. $27.00 per year. Formerly *Abrasive Magazine*.

**Grits and Grinds**. Saint-Gobain Abrasives Inc., 1 New Bond St. Worcester, MA 01615-0008. Phone: 800-243-0028 or (508)795-5000; Fax: (508)795-5741 or (508)795-2220; Email: sgnhamericainfo@saint-gobain.com • URL: http://www.saint-gobain-northamerica.com • Quarterly. Free.

**Grocery Headquarters: The Newspaper for the Food Industry**. Trend Publishing Inc., 625 N Michigan Ave., Ste. 1100 Chicago, IL 60611-3118. Phone: 800-278-7363 or (312)654-2300 or (312)932-1158; Fax: (312)654-2323 • URL: http://www.trendpublishing.com/ • Monthly. $80. Covers the sale and distribution of food products and other items sold in supermarkets and grocery stores. Edited mainly for retailers and wholesalers. Incorporates (Grocery Distribution).

**Grocery Manufacturers Association**. 1350 I St. NW Washington, DC 20005. Phone: (202)639-5900; Fax: (202)639-5932; Email: info@gmaonline.org • URL: http://www.gmaonline.org • Absorbed Association of Sales and Marketing Companies.

**Grooming Directory—Pets**. InfoGroup Inc., 5711 S 86th Cir. Omaha, NE 68127-4146. Phone: (402)593-4500 • URL: http://www.infogroup.com • Annual. Number of listings: 21,803. Entries include: Name, address, phone, size of advertisement, name of owner or manager, number of employees, year first in "Yellow Pages." Compiled from telephone company "Yellow Pages," nationwide.

**Grossman on Circulation**. Gordon W. Grossman, Penton, 9800 Metcalf Ave. Overland Park, KS 66212. Phone: 866-748-4926 or (913)341-1300; Fax: (913)967-1905 or (913)967-1898; Email: corporatecustomerservice@penton.com • URL: http://www.penton.com • Annual. $99.95. Covers magazine circulation management and marketing, with emphasis on circulaton incentives, such as free-issue offers, sweepstakes, premiums, "freemiums," and professional courtesy offers. Includes examples of promotions used by consumer and trade publications.

***Ground Water***. National Ground Water Association. National Ground Water Association, 601 Dempsey Rd. Westerville, OH 43081. Phone: 800-551-7379 or (614)898-7791; Fax: (614)898-7786; Email: ngwa@ngwa.org • URL: http://www.ngwa.org • Bimonthly. $19 Members; $260 Nonmembers.

***Group Practice Journal***. American Medical Group Association, 1 Prince St. Alexandria, VA 22314-3318. Phone: (703)838-0033; Fax: (703)548-1890; Email: dfisher@amga.org • URL: http://www.amga.org • 10/year. $75 Institutions.

**Group Underwriters Association of America**. c/o Roland Birkner, Co-Chairperson, 233 S Wacker Dr., Ste. 2000 Chicago, IL 60606. Phone: (312)288-7206; Email: roland.birkner@willis.com • URL: http://www.guaa.com • Promotes the study, analysis, and discussion pertaining to all matters of mutual interest in underwriting group products. Seeks to uphold the standards of practices within the group insurance industry. Provides its members the opportunities for professional development, networking and information gathering.

**Groupement des Femmes d'Affaires de la Guinee**. B.P. 3009 Conakry, Guinea. Phone: 224 453899; Fax: 224 453518; Email: cenafodgn@eti-bull.net • URL: http://www.fcem.org/en/pays-membres.html • Promotes women's entrepreneurial initiatives. Reinforces national associations of women business entrepreneurial potentials. Lobbies before the public and private institutions, policy makers and governments on issues that impede women's entrepreneurial potentials. Facilitates the development of business, partnership and trade. Fosters professional growth and business skills perfection. Encourages women to create enterprises.

**Groupement des Femmes d'Affaires du Cameroun**. BP 1940 Douala, Cameroon. Phone: 237 33401732; Fax: 237 33406533; Email: gfacnational@yahoo.fr • URL: http://fcem.org/en/pays-membres.html • Promotes women's entrepreneurial initiatives. Reinforces national associations of women business entrepreneurial potentials. Lobbies before the public and private institutions, policy makers and governments on issues that impede women's entrepreneurial potentials. Facilitates the development of business, partnership and trade. Fosters professional growth and business skills perfection. Encourages women to create enterprises.

***The Grower: Profitable Business Strategies for Fruit and Vegetable Growers***. Vance Publishing Corp., 400 Knightsbridge Pkwy. Lincolnshire, IL 60069-3613. Phone: 800-255-5113 or (847)634-2600; Fax: (847)634-4342 or (847)634-4379; Email: info@vancepublishing.com • URL: http://www.vancepublishing.com • Monthly. $45 Individuals; $65 Canada; $150 Other countries; Free to qualified subscribers. Magazine providing management information for the commercial fruit and vegetable producer with emphasis on management, industry trends, effective marketing, chemicals, and legislative and regulatory environments.

***The Growing Business Handbook***. Cengage Learning Inc., 20 Channel Center St. Boston, MA 02210. Phone: 800-487-8488 or (617)289-7700; Fax: (617)289-7844; Email: investors@cengage.com • URL: http://www.cengage.com • 2010. eBook. 12th edition. Published by Kogan Page. Focuses on key issues such as funding, innovation, customer service, business technology and international expansion. Includes case studies from top companies.

***Growth Companies Register***. Financial Publishing Ltd., Marlen House,31/37 Cursitor St., 31/37 Cursitor St. London EC4A 1LT, United Kingdom. Phone: 44 1 430 0208 • Annual. $175. Covers: Private companies in Britain with profits of 50,000 or more. Entries include: Financial data, company profile, name of company directors, SIC codes, addresses.

***Growth Fund Guide: The Investor's Guide to Dynamic Growth Funds***. Growth Fund Research Inc., 409 Kansas City St. Rapid City, SD 57701. Phone: 800-621-8322 or (605)341-1971 • Monthly. $99.00 per year. Newsletter. Covers no-load growth mutual funds.

***Growth Stock Outlook***. Charles Allmon, editor. Growth Stock Outlook Inc., 4405 E W Hwy., Ste. 305 Bethesda, MD 20814. Phone: 800-742-5476 or (301)654-5205; Fax: (301)986-0722 • Description: Provides data on stock earnings, sales, price-earnings ratios, dividends, book values, returns on shareholder equity, and institutional holdings. Recommends specific companies for long-term investment. Recurring features include a stock selection guide, and a $10,000 supervised portfolio. **Remarks:** Subscription includes the supplements Junior Growth Stocks, New Issue Digest, and (see separate listings); also includes access to a telephone hotline.

***GSA Business***. GSA Business, 1204-B E Washington St. Greenville, SC 29601. Phone: (864)235-5677; Email: gsanews@scbiznews.com • URL: http://www.gsabusiness.com • Biweekly. $49.95 Individuals /year; $84.95 Two years; $119.95 for three years. Local business newspaper.

***The Guardian Guide to the UK's Top Companies***. Hoover's Inc., 5800 Airport Blvd. Austin, TX 78752-4204. Phone: 866-443-3939 or (512)374-4500 or (866)281-5969; Fax: (512)374-4501; Email: salesteam@hoovers.com • URL: http://www.hoovers.com • Annual. $49.95. Covers: 150 top British business companies. Database includes: Five years of detailed financial data. Entries include: Company name, address, phone, top officers and directors, information on board compensation, major subsidiaries; information on donations, history, policies and outlook for the future.

***Guelph Business Directory***. City of Guelph Guelph Economic Development, City Hall, 2nd Fl., 1 Carden St. Guelph, ON, Canada N1H 3A1. Phone: (519)837-5600; Fax: (519)837-5636; Email: bizinfo@guelph.ca • URL: http://www.guelph.ca/business.cfm • $30 Individuals print version; $50 Individuals CD version. Covers 1,100 businesses in the city of Guelph.

***Guia Senior***. Guia Senior, Bartolome Mitre 1232 C1036AAX Buenos Aires, Argentina. Phone: 54 11 52352245; Email: info@guiasenior.com • URL: http://www.guiasenior.com • Covers: Argentina's national government, provincial government, diplomatic corps, foreign diplomatic corps, armed forces, political groups, banks, saving banks, loan companies, stocks, investment, credit companies, financial associations, insurance companies, stock exchange, and advertising agencies.

***The Guide: A Practical Handbook of Marketing Research Sources in the United Kingdom and Western Europe***. Key Note Publications Ltd., Harlequin Hse., 5th Fl. Teddington TW11 8EE, United Kingdom. Phone: 44 845 5040452 or 845 504 0452; Fax: 44 845 5040453 or 845 504 0453; Email: sales@keynote.co.uk • URL: http://www.keynote.co.uk • $165. Covers: Sources of marketing research in the United Kingdom and Western Europe, including business information sources, market research sources, advertising organizations, periodicals, newspapers, magazines, official statistical sources, online databases, and libraries. Entries include: For databases—Database name, host, producer, contents, frequency of updates. For others—Name, address, phone, fax, description.

***Guide to American Directories***. Todd Publications, PO Box 635 Nyack, NY 10960. Phone: 800-747-1056 or (914)358-6213 or (845)358-6213; Fax: (914)358-1059 or (845)358-6213 • Biennial. $125.00. Provides more than 11,000 listings with descriptions, prices, etc.

***Guide to Arts Administration Training and Research***. Americans for the Arts, 1000 Vermont Ave. NW, 6th Fl. Washington, DC 20005. Phone: (202)371-2830; Fax: (202)371-0424; Email: info@artsusa.org • URL: http://www.americansforthearts.org • Triennial. $12.95. Lists 33 institutions.

***Guide to Banks and Thrifts: A Quarterly Compilation of Financial Institutions Ratings and Analysis***. Weiss Research Inc., 15430 Endeavour Dr. Jupiter, FL 33478-6402. Phone: 800-291-8545 or (561)627-3300; Fax: (561)625-6685; Email: wr@weissinc.com • URL: http://www.weissinc.com • Quarterly. $438.00 per year. Emphasis is on rating of financial safety and relative risk. Includes annual summary.

***Guide to Business and Real Estate Loan Sources***. International Wealth Success, Inc., PO Box 186 Merrick, NY 11566-0186. Phone: 800-323-0548 or (516)766-5850; Fax: (516)766-5919 or (516)766-5619; Email: admin@iwsmoney.com • URL: http://www.iwsmoney.com • Annual. $25 Individuals. Covers: Several hundred financial institutions that lend money for real estate investment. Entries include: Institution name, address, phone.

***Guide to Business Information on Central and Eastern Europe***. Taylor & Francis Ltd., 2 Park Sq., Milton Park Abingdon OX14 4RN, United Kingdom. Phone: 44 22 70176000 or 44 20 70176000; Fax: 44 22 70176699 or (701)76336; Email: info@e-elgar.co.uk • URL: http://www.taylorandfrancisgroup.com • $98.95 Individuals Paperback. Covers: Twelve countries of Central and Eastern Europe. Entries include: Country overview; current developments; company name, address, phone, fax; names and titles of key personnel; industries and services; legislation; and organizations.

***Guide to Business Information on Russia, the NIS, and the Baltic States***. Taylor & Francis Ltd., 2 Park Sq., Milton Park Abingdon OX14 4RN, United Kingdom. Phone: 44 22 70176000 or 44 20 70176000; Fax: 44 22 70176699 or (701)76336; Email: info@e-elgar.co.uk • URL: http://www.taylorandfrancisgroup.com • $104.95 Individuals Paperback. Covers: Fifteen countries of Russia, the NIS, and the Baltic States. Entries include: Current developments; company name, address, phone, fax; industries and services; legislation; and organizations.

***Guide to Centres of International Document Delivery***. International Federation of Library Associations and Institutions - Offices for UAP and International Lending, Prins Willem-Alexanderhof 5 2595 BE The Hague, Netherlands. Phone: 31 70 3140884; Fax: 31 70 3834827; Email: ifla@ifla.org • URL: http://www.ifla.org • $20. Covers: Centers of copying and document delivery, including some commercial suppliers, in nearly 190 countries. Entries include: details of major collections and union catalogues; postal address, phone, fax and e-mail address; types of forms accepted; charges; method of payment; restrictions.

***A Guide to China's New and High-Tech Development Zone Enterprises***. Social Sciences Documentation Publishing House, 5 Jianguomennai Dajie Beijing 100732, China. • $75. Covers: 5,000 high-tech enterprises in China. Entries include: Contact information, administrative person, revenues, fixed assets, number of employees, product names.

***A Guide to College Programs in Hospitality, Tourism, & Culinary Arts***. International Council on Hotel, Restaurant, and Institutional Education, 2810 N Parham Rd., Ste. 230 Richmond, VA 23294. Phone: (804)346-4800; Fax: (804)346-5009; Email: publications@chrie.org • URL: http://www.chrie.org • Biennial. Covers: About 500 secondary and technical institutes, colleges, and universities; international coverage. Entries include: School name, address, areas of study, degrees offered, name and title of contact, program description, financial aid information, tuition and fees, admission and graduation requirements.

***Guide to Computer Law***. Wolters Kluwer Law & Business CCH, 2700 Lake Cook Rd. Riverwoods, IL 60015. Phone: 888-224-7377 or (847)267-7000; Email: cust_serv@cch.com • URL: http://www.cchgroup.com • Monthly. Computer and internet law.

***Guide to Credit Cards on the Internet***. Thomson Financial Inc., 195 Broadway New York, NY 10007-3100. Phone: (646)822-2000; Email: custserv@tfn.com • URL: http://www.thomsonreuters.com • Annual. $235 Individuals. Covers: Credit card issuers and credit card related web sites. Entries include: Product/service name, web site address.

***Guide to Doing Business in Egypt***. American Chamber of Commerce in Egypt, 33 Soliman Abaza St., Dokki-Giza Cairo 12311, Egypt. Phone: 20 2 33381050; Fax: 20 2 33381060 • URL: http://www.amcham.org.eg.

***Guide to East European Business Education***. Imec Publishing, Sint-Pietersnieuwstraat 41 9000 Ghent, Belgium. • URL: http://www.imec.be • Covers: Institutions offering business education in Eastern Europe. Entries include: Name, address, phone, year founded, organizations represented, funding sources, main areas of activity, type of students, faculty information.

***Guide to Employment Sources in the Library and Information Professions***. Library and Information Technology Association, 50 E Huron St. Chicago, IL 60611-2795. Phone: 800-545-2433; Fax: (312)280-3257; Email: lita@ala.org • URL: http://www.ala.org/lita • Annual. Associations and agencies offering library placement services.

***Guide to EU Information Sources on the Internet***. Euroconfidentiel S. A., Rue de Rixensart 18 B-1332 Genval, Belgium. Phone: 32 02 652 02 84 or 32 2 6520284; Fax: (653) 01 80 or (653)0180; Email: nigel.hunt@skynet.be • URL: http://www.euroconfidential.com • Annual. $210.00. Contains descriptions of more than 1,700 Web sites providing information relating to the European Union and European commerce and industry. Includes a quarterly e-mail newsletter with new sites and address changes.

***Guide to Federal Funding for Governments and Nonprofits***. Thompson Publishing Group Inc., Customer Service Center Tampa, FL 26185. Phone: 800-677-3789; Fax: (202)739-9657; Email: service@thompson.com • URL: http://www.thompson.com • Updated continuously; printed on request. $399. Contains detailed descriptions of federal grant programs in economic development, housing, transportation, social services, science, etc.

***The Guide to Graduate Environmental Programs***. Island Press-Center For Resource Economics, 1718 Connecticut Ave. Nw Ste. 300 Washington, DC 20009-1148. Phone: 800-621-2736 or (202)232-7933; Fax: (202)234-1328; Email: info@islandpress.org • URL: http://www.islandpress.org • $19.99 Individuals. Covers: Graduate study facilities and 160 programs in the environmental sciences in the U.S. Entries include: Facility name, address, phone, program name, profile, Number of students and faculty in the program, requirements for master's and doctoral degrees, faculty/advisee ratio, e-mail contact and Web site address, special program features, auxiliary services.

***Guide to Grants for Business***. Associated Management Services Ltd., 93 Windsor Rd. Swindon SN3 1LG, United Kingdom. Phone: 1793 480374; Fax: 1793 617026; Email: romada@globalnet.co.uk • Annual. $39.50. Covers: Sources of grants in the European Community and the United Kingdom, including national and local government sources, job centers, environmental organizations, energy efficiency organizations, and loan guarantee schemes. Entries include: For national and local government sources—Name, address, phone, fax, name and title of contact. For others—Name, address, phone, fax, name and title of contact, benefits, amount available, description.

***Guide to HMOs and Health Insurers: A Quarterly Compilation of Health Insurance Company Ratings and Analysis***. Weiss Research Inc., 15430 Endeavour Dr. Jupiter, FL 33478-6402. Phone: 800-291-8545 or (561)627-3300; Fax: (561)625-6685; Email: wr@weissinc.com • URL: http://www.weissinc.com • Quarterly. $499. Emphasis is on rating of financial safety and relative risk. Includes annual summary.

***Guide to Life, Health, and Annuity Insurers: A Quarterly Compilation of Insurance Company Ratings and Analysis***. Weiss Research Inc., 15430 Endeavour Dr. Jupiter, FL 33478-6402. Phone: 800-291-8545 or (561)627-3300; Fax: (561)625-6685; Email: wr@weissinc.com • URL: http://www.weissinc.com • Quarterly. $499. Emphasis is on rating of financial safety and relative risk. Includes annual summary.

***Guide to Montana's Economic Development and Community Development Programs***. Economic Development Div. Montana Department of Commerce, 1424 9th Ave. Helena, MT 59620. Phone: (406)444-3814; Fax: (406)444-1872 • Covers: 28 state and local government agencies that offer economic development programs. Entries include: Program name, sponsoring agency name, address, phone.

***Guide to Products and Services of Small Chemical Businesses.*** Division of Small Chemical Businesses, American Chemical Society (ACS) Columbus, OH 43214-0373. Phone: (614)268-2976 • Includes information for small chemical businesses.

***Guide to Property and Casualty Insurers: A Quarterly Compilation of Insurance Company Ratings and Analysis.*** Weiss Research Inc., 15430 Endeavour Dr. Jupiter, FL 33478-6402. Phone: 800-291-8545 or (561)627-3300; Fax: (561)625-6685; Email: wr@weissinc.com • URL: http://www.weissinc.com • Quarterly. $499. Emphasis is on rating of financial safety and relative risk. Includes annual summary.

***Guide to Shipbuilding, Repair, and Maintenance.*** Informa Marine and Transport, 69-77 Paul St. London EC2A 4LQ, United Kingdom. Phone: 44 20 7553 1000; Fax: (755)3 1105 • URL: http://www.informaritime.com • Annual. Price on application. Provides worldwide coverage of shipbuilding, repair, and maintenance facilities and marine equipment suppliers for the maritime industry. Included with subscription to *Lloyd's Ship Manager*.

***Guide to State Government Services for Business in Alabama.*** Alabama Development Office Alabama Center for Commerce, 401 Adams Ave. Montgomery, AL 36130-4106. Phone: 800-248-0033 or (334)242-0400; Fax: (334)353-1330; Email: idinfo@ado.state.al.us • URL: http://www.ado.state.al.us • Quarterly. Covers: Alabama state government agencies and other public and private entities that provide economic development and other business and technical assistance in Alabama, including training, research, information, and other services.

***Guide to Stock Mutual Funds: A Quarterly Compilation of Mutual Fund Ratings and Analysis Covering Equity and Balanced Funds.*** Weiss Research Inc., 15430 Endeavour Dr. Jupiter, FL 33478-6402. Phone: 800-291-8545 or (561)627-3300; Fax: (561)625-6685; Email: wr@weissinc.com • URL: http://www.weissinc.com • Quarterly. $438.00 per year. Emphasis is on rating of financial safety and relative risk. Includes annual summary.

***Guide to the Canadian Financial Services Industry.*** Globe Interactive, 444 Front St. W Toronto, ON, Canada M5V 2S9. Phone: 800-387-5400 or (416)585-5222; Fax: (416)585-5102; Email: circulation@globeandmail.ca • URL: http://www.theglobeandmail.com • Annual. $349.99. Covers: over 800 financial service companies operating in Canada. Database includes: Executive listings with biographical information; lists of government agencies which deal with the financial services industry, industry associations, and top accounting firms in Canada. Entries include: Company name, address, phone, company officers and directors, regional offices, total assets, revenue, net income, number of branches, number of employees, Canadian Standard Industrial Classification.

***Guide to the Port of New York-New Jersey.*** Port Authority of New York and New Jersey, 225 Park Ave. S, 101th Fl. New York, NY 10003-1604. Phone: (212)435-7000; Fax: (212)436-7390 • URL: http://www.panynj.gov • Annual. Covers: commercial shipping facilities at the port areas of New York and New Jersey: about 20 freight terminals; Port Authority offices and U.S. government departments; 80 international trade, maritime, and transportation associations; 385 companies providing trucking and freight hauling services; 90 warehouse facilities; 500 international freight forwarders, custom house brokers, and firms that combine the services of forwarder and broker; 55 airlines providing freight services from John F. Kennedy International Airport, LaGuardia Airport, and Newark International Airport; 75 steamship lines, steamship line agents, terminal operators and steve dores; 1,230 companies providing maritime services, e.g. international banking, marine insurance, contracting, brokering, and engineering; 180 suppliers of marine equipment; and 85 inland (i.e. interstate) freight services. Database includes: Glossary of shipping terms, customs acronyms, list of related books, reports, and periodicals; shipping information hotlines, truck routes to harbors, customs documents, hazardous materials identification symbols, and others. Entries include: For terminals—Terminal name, address, phone, owner name, terminal operator, description of facilities and services, routes of access. For Port Authority offices—Office name; names, titles, addresses, and phones of key personnel. For government departments—Department name, address, phone; name, address, phone, and name of key official for each branch office or division. For associations—Name, address, phone, brief history, description of projects and services. For trucking and freight companies—Name, address, phone, name and title of contact, geographical area served. For warehouse facilities—Company name, address, phone, telex, fax, cable address, storage capacity, description of facilities and services, including export packaging and automobile processing capabilities. For freight forwarders and custom house brokers—Company name, address, phone, telex, fax, cable address, name and title of chief officer. For air cargo services—Airline name, New York address; name, title, and phone of sales contact; address and phone of cargo operations at each airport; specialized services, cargo space available. For steamship services—Company name; name, address, phone of New York/New Jersey port area agent; types of service offered, countries served, name and location of

terminal at which cargo is loaded. For others—Company name, address, phone.

***Guide to UK Company Giving.*** The Directory of Social Change, 24 Stephenson Way London NW1 2DP, United Kingdom. Phone: 20 73914800 or 44 20 73914800; Fax: 20 73914808 or 44 20 7391 4808; Email: training@dsc.org.uk • URL: http://www.dsc.org.uk • Biennial. $75 Individuals. Covers: Over 600 largest corporate donors in the United Kingdom. Entries include: Company name, address, phone, name and title of contact, financial data, including donation figures (additional information given for companies donating in excess of 500 million Ls per year).

***Guide to U.S. Foundations, Their Trustees, Officers, and Donors.*** Foundation Center, 79 5th Ave./16th St. New York, NY 10003-3076. Phone: 800-424-9836 or (212)620-4230; Fax: (212)807-3677; Email: communications@foundationcenter.org • URL: http://foundationcenter.org • Annual. $650 U.S. Directory set; $395 Individuals single. Covers: over 74,000 currently active grantmaking foundations in the United States, including community and operating foundations, based on information returns to the Internal Revenue Service. Database includes: Bibliography of state and local directories of grantmaking foundations. Entries include: Foundation name, address, phone, name of principal contact, assets, amount of grants made, donor information, gifts received during most recent period reported; giving limitations, key officials, codes identifying coverage in other Foundation Center publications.

***Guide to U.S. Government Publications.*** Cengage Learning Inc., 20 Channel Center St. Boston, MA 02210. Phone: 800-487-8488 or (617)289-7700; Fax: (617)289-7844; Email: investors@cengage.com • URL: http://www.cengage.com • Annual. $662.00. Catalogs "important series, periodicals, and reference tools" published annually by the federal government. Includes references to annual reports of various agencies.

***Guinea-Bissau Business Law Handbook.*** International Business Publications, USA, PO Box 15343 Washington, DC 20003. Phone: (202)546-2103; Fax: (202)546-3275; Email: ibpusa@comcast.net • URL: http://ibpus.com • $99.95 Individuals hardcopy, E-book and CD-ROM. Covers: Basic business laws and legislations, export-import regulations, business climate and contacts.

***Guinea Business Law Handbook.*** International Business Publications, USA, PO Box 15343 Washington, DC 20003. Phone: (202)546-2103; Fax: (202)546-3275; Email: ibpusa@comcast.net • URL: http://ibpus.com • $99.95 Individuals hardcopy, e-book, CD-ROM. Covers: Basic information on business laws and legislations, export-import regulations, business climate and contacts.

***Guitars and Musical Instruments.*** Orion Research Corp., 14555 N Scottsdale Rd., Ste. 330 Scottsdale, AZ 85254. Phone: 800-844-0759 or (480)951-1114; Fax: (480)951-1117 or (800)375-1315 • Annual. $179 Individuals. List of manufacturers of guitars and musical instruments. Original list prices and years of manufacture are also shown.

***Gulf Business Development Handbook.*** National United States-Arab Chamber of Commerce, 1023 15th St. NW, Ste. 400 Washington, DC 20005. Phone: (202)289-5920; Fax: (202)289-5938; Email: info@nusacc.org • URL: http://www.nusacc.org • $5 for members; $7.50 for nonmembers. Includes public and private trade resources.

***Gulf Business.*** Motivate Publishing, Al Wahaibi Bldg., Al Garhoud Bridge Rd., Deira Dubai, United Arab Emirates. Phone: 971 428 24060; Fax: 971 428 20428; Email: motivate@motivate.ae • URL: http://www.motivatepublishing.com • Monthly. 15 Dh Individuals. Consumer magazine covering business in the Middle East and worldwide.

***Gulf Coast Industrial Atlas/Directory.*** Industrial Info Resources Inc., 2277 Plaza Dr., Ste. 300 Sugar Land, TX 77479-1271. Phone: 800-762-3361 or (713)783-5147; Fax: (713)266-9306; Email: industrialmanufacturing@industrialinfo.com • URL: http://www.industrialinfo.com • Continuous. Covers: about 2,400 heavy industrial plants (including refineries, steel mills, power plants, pulp and paper mills, terminals, docks, storage saltdomes, gas processing plants, chemical plants) and 4,800 management contacts in Florida, Alabama, Mississippi, Louisiana, and Texas. Database includes: Wall maps from Laredo, Texas to St. Marks, Florida. Entries include: For plants—Company or plant name, mailing address, street address, phone, fax, names of plant manager and purchasing agent. For engineering and service companies—Name, address, phone, fax, line of business, description of company.

***Guns and Ammo.*** PRIMEDIA Inc., 350 Fifth Ave., 59th Fl. New York, NY 10118. Phone: (212)601-1960 or (212)745-0100; Fax: (516)222-2357 or (212)745-0121; Email: information@primedia.com • URL: http://www.primediany.com • Monthly. $14.97 per year.

***Guns Magazine: Finest in the Firearms Field.*** Publishers Development Corp., 12345 World Trade Dr. San Diego, CA 92128. Fax: (858)605-0247; Email: subs@shootingindustry.com • URL: http://www.shootingindustry.com • Monthly. $24.95 U.S.; $59.95 Other countries. Firearms information on current shooting products and trends.

***Guyana Business Law Handbook.*** International Business Publications, USA, PO Box 15343 Washington, DC 20003. Phone: (202)546-2103; Fax: (202)546-3275; Email: ibpusa@comcast.net • URL: http://ibpus.com • $99.95 Individuals

hardcopy, E-book and CD-ROM. Covers: Basic information on business laws and legislations, export-import regulations, business climate and contacts.

***Hair Removing Services Directory.*** InfoGroup Inc., 5711 S 86th Cir. Omaha, NE 68127-4146. Phone: (402)593-4500 • URL: http://www.infogroup.com • Annual. Number of listings: 4,169. Entries include: Name, address, phone, size of advertisement, name of owner or manager, number of employees, year first in "Yellow Pages." Compiled from telephone company "Yellow Pages," nationwide.

***Hairdressers' Journal International.*** Reed Business Information Ltd., Quadrant House, The Quadrant, Surrey Sutton SM2 5AS, United Kingdom. Phone: 44 20 8652 3500; Fax: 44 20 8652 8932; Email: rbi.subscriptions@qss-uk.com • URL: http://www.reedbusiness.com.uk • Weekly. Contains latest styling techniques and fashions, product features, a celebrity style feature and the latest hairdressing industry news.

***Hairstyling Services Directory.*** InfoGroup Inc., 5711 S 86th Cir. Omaha, NE 68127-4146. Phone: (402)593-4500 • URL: http://www.infogroup.com • Annual. Number of listings: 230,354. Entries include: Name, address, phone, size of advertisement, name of owner or manager, number of employees, year first in "Yellow Pages." Compiled from telephone company "Yellow Pages," nationwide.

***The Halton Business Journal.*** The Halton Business Journal, 1492 Wallace Rd. Oakville, ON, Canada L6L 2Y2. Phone: (416)847-1404 • Monthly. $24; $30 Out of area. Regional business magazine.

***Hampshire Business Directory.*** Hampshire County Council, The Castle Winchester SO23 8UJ, United Kingdom. Phone: 44 1962 841841; Email: info@hants.gov.uk • URL: http://www.hants.gov.uk • Covers 6,000 Hampshire-based companies and business contacts within and outside Hampshire County.

***Handbook of Internet Stocks.*** Mergent Inc., 60 Madison Ave., Fl. 6 New York, NY 10010. Phone: 888-411-0893 or (212)413-7700; Fax: (212)413-7670; Email: shirley.petersen@mergent.com • URL: http://www.mergent.com • Annual. $19.95. Contains detailed financial information on more than 200 Internet-related corporations, including e-commerce firms and telecommunications hardware manufacturers. Lists and rankings are provided.

***Handbook of NASDAQ Stocks.*** Mergent Inc., 580 Kingsley Park Dr. Fort Mill, SC 29715. Phone: 800-937-1398 or (704)527-2700 or (704)559-7601; Fax: (704)559-6837 or (704)559-6960; Email: customerservice@mergent.com • URL: http://www.mergent.com • Quarterly. $105 Individuals. Covers: Over 600 corporations whose stocks are among the most actively traded in dollar volume on the Nasdaq market. Entries include: Company name, address, phone, names and titles of key personnel, product/service, number of employees, detailed financial data, analysis of stock performance and trends, trading volume, per share earnings and yields, and other stock performance evaluations.

***Handbook of Ontologies for Business Interaction.*** Cengage Learning Inc., 20 Channel Center St. Boston, MA 02210. Phone: 800-487-8488 or (617)289-7700; Fax: (617)289-7844; Email: investors@cengage.com • URL: http://www.cengage.com • 2008. eBook. Published by Information Science Reference. Documents high-quality research addressing ontological issues that are relevant to the modeling of enterprises and information systems in general and business processes in particular covering both static and dynamic aspects of structural concepts.

***Handbook of Research in Mobile Business: Technical, Methodological, and Social Perspectives.*** Cengage Learning Inc., 20 Channel Center St. Boston, MA 02210. Phone: 800-487-8488 or (617)289-7700; Fax: (617)289-7844; Email: investors@cengage.com • URL: http://www.cengage.com • 2011. eBook. 2 volumes. 2nd edition. Published by Information Science Reference. Provides research and scientific findings in the constantly expanding field of mobile business. 63 chapters.

***Handbook of Research on Business Social Networking: Organizational, Managerial, and Technological Dimensions.*** Cengage Learning Inc., 20 Channel Center St. Boston, MA 02210. Phone: 800-487-8488 or (617)289-7700; Fax: (617)289-7844; Email: investors@cengage.com • URL: http://www.cengage.com • 2012. eBook. Published by IGI Global. Investigates the beginning of social networks and provides perspectives on how they can enhance business, covering discussions on the main issues, challenges, opportunities, and trends related to the range of new developments and applications in business social networking.

***Handbook of Research on E-Business Standards and Protocols: Documents, Data and Advanced Web Technologies.*** Cengage Learning Inc., 20 Channel Center St. Boston, MA 02210. Phone: 800-487-8488 or (617)289-7700; Fax: (617)289-7844; Email: investors@cengage.com • URL: http://www.cengage.com • 2012. eBook. Published by IGI Global. Contains an overview of new achievements in the field of e-business standards and protocols, offers in-depth analysis of and research on the development and deployment of cutting-edge applications, and provides insight into future trends.

***Handbook of Research on Serious Games as Educational, Business and Research Tools.*** Cengage Learning Inc., 20 Channel Center St. Boston, MA 02210. Phone: 800-487-8488 or (617)289-7700; Fax: (617)289-7844; Email: investors@

cengage.com • URL: http://www.cengage.com • 2012. eBook. Published by IGI Global. Collects research on the most recent technological developments in all fields of knowledge or disciplines of computer games development, including planning, design, development, marketing, business management, users and behavior.

*Handbook of Research on Virtual Workplaces and the New Nature of Business Practices.* Cengage Learning Inc., 20 Channel Center St. Boston, MA 02210. Phone: 800-487-8488 or (617)289-7700; Fax: (617)289-7844; Email: investors@cengage.com • URL: http://www.cengage.com • 2008. eBook. Published by Information Science Reference. Compiles authoritative research from 51 scholars from 17 countries, covering the issues surrounding the influx of information technology to the office environment, from choice and effective use of technologies to necessary participants in the virtual workplace.

*Handbook of Rupee Companies.* Colombo Brokers Association, c/o Professional Assignments and Secretarial Services(Pvt) Ltd., 15 1/A, Maitland Crescent Colombo 7, Sri Lanka. Phone: 94 11 2429100 • URL: http://www.colombostockbrokers.com • Annual. $30; $3. Covers: Companies registered in Sri Lanka and quoted on the share market.

*Handbook of World Stock and Commodity Exchanges.* Blackwell Publishing Inc., 350 Main St. Malden, MA 02148. Phone: 800-216-2522 or (781)388-8200; Fax: (781)388-8210; Email: journaladsusa@bos.blackwellpublishing.com • URL: http://www.blackwellpublishing.com • Annual. $265.00. Provides detailed information on over 200 stock and commodity exchanges in more than 50 countries.

*Handheld Computing: The Number One Guide to Handheld Devices.* Mobile Media Group, 1670 South Amphlett Blvd., Ste. 105 San Mateo, CA 94402. Phone: 888-406-4048 or (650)378-8522 or (650)378-8522; Fax: (650)378-8513; Email: editor@hhcmag.com • URL: http://www.hhcmag.com • 9/year. Covers handheld devices for consumers, including PDAs, cell phones, digital cameras, MP3 players, tablet PCs, accessories, and software. Includes product reviews.

*Handicraft Supplies Directory.* InfoGroup Inc., 5711 S 86th Cir. Omaha, NE 68127-4146. Phone: (402)593-4500 • URL: http://www.infogroup.com • Annual. Number of listings: 9,320. Entries include: Name, address, phone, size of advertisement, name of owner or manager, number of employees, year first in "Yellow Pages." Compiled from telephone company "Yellow Pages," nationwide.

*Hanover Association of Business and Chamber of Commerce— Business Directory.* Hanover Association of Business and Chamber of Commerce, 9097 Atlee Station Rd., Ste. 117 Mechanicsville, VA 23116. Phone: (804)798-8130; Fax: (804)798-0014; Email: habcc@habcc.com • URL: http://www.habcc.com • Annual. List of businesses in Hanover. Also provides information for companies and families moving to Hanover county and the town of Ashland.

*Hard at Work.* Professional Training Associates Inc., 46 S Linden St., Ste. C Duquesne, PA 15110-1091. Phone: (412)460-0266; Fax: (412)460-0269 • URL: http://www.ptainc.com • Monthly. $89.00 per year. Newsletter on common personnel problems of supervisors and office managers. Formerly *Practical Supervision.*

*Hardware Age.* Reed Elsevier Group plc Reed Business Information, 360 Park Ave. S New York, NY 11010. Phone: (212)791-4208; Email: corporatecommunications@reedbusiness.com • URL: http://www.reedbusiness.com • Monthly. $75.00 per year.

*Hardware Retailing: Serving Hardware, Home Center, Building Material Retailers.* North American Retail Hardware Association, 6325 Digital Way, Ste. 300 Indianapolis, IN 46278-1787. Phone: 800-772-4424 or (317)275-9400 or (317)290-0338; Fax: (317)275-9403 or (317)328-4354; Email: hwegeng@nrha.org • URL: http://www.nrha.org • Monthly. $8 Individuals; $2 Single issue. Trade magazine for hardware retailers selling do-it-yourself products. Formerly *DIY Retailing.*

**Hardwood Federation.** 1111 19th St. NW, Ste. 800 Washington, DC 20036. Phone: (202)463-2452; Fax: (202)463-4702 • URL: http://www.hardwoodfederation.wildapricot.org • Represents organizations engaged in the manufacturing, wholesaling or distribution of North American hardwood lumber, veneer, plywood, flooring and related products. Seeks to promote and represent the common business interests of and improve business conditions among members of the hardwood industry. Strives to maintain a healthy business environment for family businesses and small companies in the hardwood community.

*Hardwood Floors.* National Wood Flooring Association. Athletic Business Publications Inc., 4130 Lien Rd. Madison, WI 53704. Phone: 800-722-8764 or (608)249-0186; Fax: (608)249-1153; Email: editors@hardwoodfloorsmag.com • URL: http://www.athleticbusiness.com • Bimonthly. Covers the marketing and installation of hardwood flooring. Published for contractors and retailers.

*Hardwood Manufacturers Association Buyers Guide.* Hardwood Manufacturers Association, 665 Rodi Rd., Ste. 305 Pittsburgh, PA 15235. Phone: (412)244-0440; Fax: (412)244-9090; Email: info@hardwood.org • URL: http://www.hmamembers.org • provides details on members and products.

*Harley Hahn's Internet Yellow Pages.* Harley Hahn. Harley Hahn, 2600 10th St., 6th Fl. Berkeley, CA 94710. Phone: 800-227-0900; Email: pbg. ecommerce_custserv@mcgraw-hill.com • URL: http://www.harley.com • Annual. Lists World Wide Web sites in more than 193 categories.

*Harper's Bazaar.* The Hearst Corp., 300 W 57th St. New York, NY 10019. Phone: (212)649-2000; Fax: (212)765-2639; Email: corpcommunications@hearst.com • URL: http://www.hearst.com • Monthly. Monthly. $18.00 per year.

*Harris County Business Guide.* Business Extension Bureau Inc., 4802 Travis Houston, TX 77002. Phone: 800-969-5568 or (713)528-5568; Fax: (713)528-1648 • URL: http://bebtexas.com • Biennial. $150 Individuals Hardcopies; $60 Individuals online; 1 mo subscript.; $135 Individuals online; 3 mo subscript.; $420 Individuals online; 1 yr subscript. (incl. 2,000 free records). Covers: 70,000 industrial, service, retail, wholesale, and professional firms in Harris County, Texas. Database includes: List of 110,000 top executives, includes phone numbers. Entries include: Company name, mailing and street addresses, phone, names and titles of key personnel, number of employees, product or service, years in business, URLs for about 40 percent of companies.

*Harris Manufacturers Directory 2000: National Edition.* Harris InfoSource, 2057 E Aurora Rd. Twinsburg, OH 44087-1999. Phone: 800-888-5900 or (330)425-9000 or (973)921-5500; Fax: (800)643-5997 or (877)252-3375; Email: customerservice@harrisinfo.com • URL: http://www.harrisinfo.com • Annual. $565.00. Two volumes. Provides statistical and descriptive information for about 47,062 U.S. industrial firms having 100 or more employees.

*Harris Minnesota Directory of Manufacturers.* Dun & Bradstreet Inc., 103 JFK Pkwy. Short Hills, NJ 07078. Phone: 800-526-0651 or (973)921-5500 or (973)921-5000; Fax: (866)560-7035 or (512)794-7670; Email: info@dnb.com • URL: http://www.dnb.com • Annual. Covers: over 11,500 manufacturers in Minnesota. Entries include: Company name, address, key executives, annual sales, phone, fax, toll-free number, number of employees, date established, Standard Industrial Classification (SIC) codes, list of products, international trade, and plant square footage.

*Hart's E and P.* Hart Energy, 1616 S Voss Rd., Ste. 1000 Houston, TX 77057-2627. Phone: 800-874-2544 or (713)260-6400 or (713)993-9320; Fax: (713)840-8585; Email: custserv@hartenergy.com • URL: http://www.hartenergy.com • Monthly. Edited for "decision makers" in petroleum exploration and production. Emphasis is on technology. Formerly *Petroleum Engineer International.*

*Hart's Oil and Gas Finance Sourcebook.* Hart Energy, 1616 S Voss Rd., Ste. 1000 Houston, TX 77057-2627. Phone: 800-874-2544 or (713)260-6400 or (713)993-9320; Fax: (713)840-8585; Email: custserv@hartenergy.com • URL: http://www.hartenergy.com • Annual. $495 Individuals. Covers: More than 3,500 oil and gas companies in eight categories: drilling risk capital, reserve purchasers, downstream risk capital, financial institutions, and intermediaries. Entries include: Company name, address, phone, fax, telex, e-mail address, website, names and titles of key personnel, geographic and operating preferences, deal criteria, total assets, recent deal history, number of wells owned and/or participating in, total annual production figures, primary contact for proposals, proposal turn around time.

*Harvard Business Review.* Harvard Business Review Press, 60 Harvard Way Boston, MA 02163. Phone: 800-795-5200 or (617)783-7400; Email: custserv@hbsp.harvard.edu • URL: http://hbr.org/books • Monthly. $89 U.S.; $99 U.S. all access; $109 Canada; $119 Canada all access. Magazine for business executives.

*Harvard Business Review.* Harvard University, Graduate School of Business Administration. Harvard Business School Publishing, 300 N Beacon St. Watertown, MA 02472. Phone: 800-988-0886 or (617)783-7500 or (617)783-7400; Fax: (617)783-7555 or (617)783-7556; Email: corpcustserv@hbsp.harvard.edu • URL: http://www.hbr.org • 10/year.

*Harvard Business School Guide to Careers in Management Consulting.* Harvard Business Review Press, 60 Harvard Way Boston, MA 02163. Phone: 800-795-5200 or (617)783-7400; Email: custserv@hbsp.harvard.edu • URL: http://hbr.org/books • $10.83 Individuals. Publication includes: Well-known consulting firms, a mailing list of recruiting contacts, and a selective bibliography of relevant books and directories compiled by the Harvard Business School.

*Harvard Law Review.* Harvard Law Review, Gannett House, 1511 Massachusetts Ave. Cambridge, MA 02138. Phone: (617)495-7889; Fax: (617)495-5053 • URL: http://www.harvardlawreview.org • 8/year. $60 Individuals; $200 Individuals.

**Harvard Law School International Tax Program.** Harvard Law School, 1563 Massachusetts Ave., 1563 Massachusetts Ave. Cambridge, MA 02138. Phone: (617)495-3100 or (617)495-4406; Fax: (617)495-1110; Email: sfs@law.harvard.edu • URL: http://www.law.harvard.edu/programs/index.html • Studies the worldwide problems of taxation, including tax law and tax administration.

**Harvard Legislative Research Bureau.** Harvard University, Harvard Law School, 1541 Massachusetts Ave. Cambridge, MA 02138. Phone: (617)495-4400; Fax: (617)495-1110; Email: pgowder@law.harvard.edu • Concerned with federal and state legislation in all fields.

*Harvard Management Communication Letter.* Harvard Business School Publishing, 300 N Beacon St. Watertown, MA 02472. Phone: 800-988-0886 or (617)783-7500 or (617)783-7400; Fax: (617)783-7555 or (617)783-7556; Email: corpcustserv@hbsp.harvard.edu • URL: http://www.hbr.org • Description: Provides information and techniques for managers on effective communication.

*Harvard Management Update.* Harvard Business School Publishing, 300 N Beacon St. Watertown, MA 02472. Phone: 800-988-0886 or (617)783-7500 or (617)783-7400; Fax: (617)783-7555 or (617)783-7556; Email: corpcustserv@hbsp.harvard.edu • URL: http://www.hbr.org • Description: Provides information on current management techniques and trends.

**Harvard University - Center for Population and Development Studies.** 9 Bow St. Cambridge, MA 02138. Phone: (617)495-2021; Fax: (617)495-5418; Email: lberkman@hsph.harvard.edu • URL: http://www.hsph.harvard.edu/population-development • Demography, human ecology, and economic, social, and environmental determinants and consequences of population changes in developing countries, including studies of public health aspects of fertility and the balance between populations and their resources, theories of population dynamics and their implications for public policy, political and ethical aspects of population, and the effect of nutrition and exercise on female reproduction.

**Harvard University - John F. Kennedy School of Government - Mossavar-Rahmani Center for Business and Government.** Weil Hall, 79 John F. Kennedy St. Cambridge, MA 02138. Phone: (617)495-1110; Fax: (617)495-5821; Email: mrcbg@hks.harvard.edu • URL: http://www.hks.harvard.edu/centers/mrcbg • Governmental regulations, focusing on energy and environmental industries, Asia programs, international trade, corporate social responsibility and collaborative governance.

*Hastings Business Law Journal.* University of California Hastings College of the Law, 200 McAllister St. San Francisco, CA 94102. Phone: (415)565-4623 or (415)565-4600; Fax: (415)581-8946 or (415)565-4809; Email: admiss@uchastings.edu • URL: http://www.uchastings.edu.

*Hatboro Online Business Directory.* Greater Hatboro Chamber of Commerce, Red Barn Mall, Ste. 6, 120 S York Rd. Hatboro, PA 19040. Phone: (215)956-9540; Fax: (215)956-9635; Email: office@hatborochamber.org • URL: http://hatborochamber.org • $170 /year for members; $340 /year for nonmembers. Highlights participating businesses and services in the Greater Hatboro area.

*Havre de Grace Chamber of Commerce Directory and Business Guide.* Havre de Grace Chamber of Commerce, 450 Pennington Ave. Havre de Grace, MD 21078. Phone: (410)939-3303; Fax: (410)939-3490 • URL: http://www.hdgchamber.com • Annual. Covers: List of members and information on the area's history.

*Hawaii Business Abroad.* Hawaii Department of Business, Economic Development, and Tourism Research and Economic Analysis Division, No. 1 Capitol District Bldg., 250 S Hotel St. Honolulu, HI 96813. Phone: (808)586-2355 • URL: http://dbedt.hawaii.gov/economic • Irregular. Covers: approximately 400 Hawaiian firms that export, import, maintain overseas offices, or have business activities in foreign countries. Entries include: Company name, address, phone, fax, telex, name of contact, cable address, line of business, year established, number of employees, locations of overseas offices, description of overseas activities, parent company name and address (if any), names of countries with which business is done.

**Hawaii Department of Business, Economic Development, and Tourism - Research and Economic Analysis Division.** No. 1 Capitol District Bldg., 250 S Hotel St. Honolulu, HI 96813. Phone: (808)586-2355 • URL: http://dbedt.hawaii.gov/economic • Business, economic development, tourism.

*Hawaii Industrial Directory.* Harris InfoSource, 2057 E Aurora Rd. Twinsburg, OH 44087-1999. Phone: 800-888-5900 or (330)425-9000 or (973)921-5500; Fax: (800)643-5997 or (877)252-3375; Email: customerservice@harrisinfo.com • URL: http://www.harrisinfo.com • Annual. $495 Individuals Online. Covers: 9,400 manufacturing companies in Hawaii. Entries include: Company name, address, phone, fax, web site address (on CD-ROM only), toll-free, names and titles of key personnel, number of employees, geographical area served, financial data, descriptions of product/service, Standard Industrial Classification (SIC) code, year established, annual revenues, plant size, legal structure, export/import information.

*Hazardous Materials Newsletter.* John R. Cashman, Silver Cir. Barre, VT 05641. Phone: (802)479-2307 • Description: Focuses on response to and control of hazardous materials emergencies, particularly appropriate tools, equipment, materials, methods, procedures, strategies, and lessons learned. Addresses leak, fire, and spill control for incident commanders and experienced responders, including incident causes, prevention, and remedial actions; decisionmaking; scene management; control and containment; response teams; and product identification and hazards. Recurring features include incident reports, a calendar of events, description of public safety agency/commercial/industrial response team operations, coverage of research sources and resources, networking ideas, and chemical and biological agents.

**Hazardous Substance Management Research Center**. New Jersey Institute of Technology, University Heights Newark, NJ 07102-1982. Phone: (973)596-3233; Fax: (973)642-7170; Email: watts@admin.njit.edu • URL: http://ycees.njit.edu/ycees/about_ycees.

***Hazardous Substances Data Bank***. SilverPlatter Information Inc., 100 River Ridge Dr. Norwood, MA 02062. Phone: 800-343-0064 or (781)769-2599; Fax: (781)769-8763; Email: sales@ovid.com • URL: http://www.silverplatter.com • Provides CD-ROM information on hazardous substances, including 140,000 chemicals in the *Registry of Toxic Effects of Chemical Substances* and 60,000 materials covered by the *Toxic Substances Control Act Initial Inventory*.

***Hazardous Waste Consultant Directory of Commercial Hazardous Waste Management Facilities***. Elsevier, Secondary Publishing Division, 650 Ave. of the Americas New York, NY 10011. Phone: 888-437-4636 or (212)633-3980; Fax: (212)633-3975; Email: t.reller@elsevier.com • URL: http://www.elseveier.com • Annual. $115.00. List of 170 facilities that process, store, and dispose of hazardous waste materials.

***Hazardous Waste Consultant***. Elsevier, Secondary Publishing Division, 650 Ave. of the Americas New York, NY 10011. Phone: 888-437-4636 or (212)633-3980; Fax: (212)633-3975; Email: t.reller@elsevier.com • URL: http://www.elseveier.com • Seven times a year. $798.00 per year. Discusses the technical, regulatory and legal aspects of the hazardous waste industry.

***Hazardous Waste Litigation Reporter: The National Journal of Record of Hazardous Waste-Related Litigation***. Andrews Publications, 175 Strafford Ave., Bldg. 4, Suite 140 Wayne, PA 19087. Phone: 800-345-1101 or (610)225-0510 or (610)622-0510; Fax: (610)225-0501 or (610)622-0501; Email: customer@andrewspub.com • URL: http://www.andrewspub.com • Semimonthly. $875.00 per year. Newsletter. Reports on hazardous waste legal cases.

***Hazardous Waste/Superfund Week***. Business Publishers Inc., PO Box 17592 Baltimore, MD 21297-1592. Phone: 800-223-8720; Fax: (800)508-2592; Email: custserv@bpinews.com • URL: http://www.bpinews.com • Description: Examines issues and developments in the hazardous waste management industry. Covers legislative and regulatory actions, technology research and development, disposal site controversies, Superfund contracting, and other news of interest. Recurring features include columns titled Slants & Trends, Business and Technology News, Grants and Contracts, calendar, Around the States, Market News, and Industrial Waste Focus.

***The HCEA Directory of Healthcare Meetings and Conventions***. Healthcare Convention and Exhibitors Association, 1100 Johnson Ferry Rd., Ste. 300 Atlanta, GA 30342. Phone: (404)252-3663; Fax: (404)252-0774; Email: hcea@kellencompany.com • URL: http://www.hcea.org • Annual. $345 Nonmembers; $69 Members additional copies. Lists more than 6,000 health care meetings, most of which have an exhibit program. Formerly *Handbook-A Directory of Health Care Meetings and Conventions*.

***Headquarters USA: A Directory of Contact Information for Headquarters and Other Central Offices of Major Businesses and Organizations Nationwide***. Omnigraphics Inc., PO Box 31-1640 Detroit, MI 48231. Phone: (313)961-1340; Fax: (313)961-1383; Email: customerservice@omnigraphics.com • URL: http://www.omnigraphics.com • $195 Individuals Hardcover - Web price; $216 Individuals List price. Two volumes. Volume one is alphabetical by name of business or organization. Volume two is classified by subject. Includes more than 112,000 businesses, organizations, agencies, institutions, and "high-profile" individuals. Listings include addresses, telephone numbers, fax numbers, and toll-free numbers and Web addresses where available. Formerly *Business Phone Book USA*.

***Headquarters USA***. Omnigraphics Inc., PO Box 31-1640 Detroit, MI 48231. Phone: (313)961-1340; Fax: (313)961-1383; Email: customerservice@omnigraphics.com • URL: http://www.omnigraphics.com • Annual. $210 Individuals web price; $231 Individuals list price. Covers: Approximately 110,000 U.S. Businesses, federal, state, and local government offices, banks, colleges and universities, associations, labor unions, political organizations, newspapers, magazines, TV and radio stations, foundations, postal and shipping services, hospitals, office equipment suppliers, airlines, hotels and motels, profiles of top cities, accountants, law firms, computer firms, foreign corporations, overseas trade contacts, and other professional services. Also covers Internet access providers; Internet mailing lists, publications, and sources; freenets. Personal names now included. Entries include: Company, organization, agency, or firm name, address, phone, fax, website addresses as available, and toll-free phone.

***Health & Beauty Aids—Retail Directory***. InfoGroup Inc., 5711 S 86th Cir. Omaha, NE 68127-4146. Phone: (402)593-4500 • URL: http://www.infogroup.com • Annual. Number of listings: 18,716. Entries include: Name, address, phone, size of advertisement, name of owner or manager, number of employees, year first in "Yellow Pages." Compiled from telephone company "Yellow Pages," nationwide.

***Health and Safety Science Abstracts***. Institute of Safety and Systems Management. Cambridge Information Group, 7200 Wisconsin Ave., Ste. 601 Bethesda, MD 20814. Phone: 800-526-9537 or (301)961-6700; Fax: (301)961-6790 or (301)961-6720; Email: info@cambridgeinformationgroup.com • URL: http://www.cambridgeinformationgroup.com • Monthly. Provides coverage of world literature on general safety, environmental and ecological safety, industrial hygiene and occupational safety, transportation safety, aviation and aerospace safety, and medical safety. Formerly *Safety Science Abstracts Journal*.

***Health and Vital Statistics***. U. S. Government Printing Office, 732 N Capitol St. NW Washington, DC 20401. Phone: 866-512-1800 or (202)512-1800 or (866)512-1800; Fax: (202)512-2104 or (202)512-2250; Email: contactcenter@gpo.gov • URL: http://www.gpo.gov • Annual. Free. Lists government publications. (GPO Subject Bibliography Number 121).

***Health Business***. Public Sector Publishing Ltd., 226 High Rd. Loughton IG10 1ET, United Kingdom. Phone: 44 20 85320055; Fax: 44 20 85320066; Email: info@psi-media.co.uk • URL: http://www.psi-media.co.uk • Monthly. Magazine featuring news and case studies that explain the administrative and commercial issues affecting healthcare and hospital management.

***Health Care Benefits Law***. ALM Media Properties LLC, 120 Broadway, 5th Fl. New York, NY 10271-1100. Phone: (212)457-9400; Fax: (646)417-7705; Email: customercare@alm.com • URL: http://www.alm.com • $565. Covers the legal compliance aspects of employer health care plans. Includes checklists and sample forms. (Law Journal Press).

***Health Care Financing Review***. U. S. Government Printing Office, 732 N Capitol St. NW Washington, DC 20401. Phone: 866-512-1800 or (202)512-1800 or (866)512-1800; Fax: (202)512-2104 or (202)512-2250; Email: contactcenter@gpo.gov • URL: http://www.gpo.gov • Quarterly. $48 Individuals; $67.20 Other countries; $23 Single issue; $32.20 Other countries single copy. Issued by the Health Care Financing Administration, U. S. Department of Health and Human Services. Presents articles by professionals in the areas of health care costs and financing.

***Health Care Fraud and Abuse Newsletter***. ALM Media Properties LLC, 120 Broadway, 5th Fl. New York, NY 10271-1100. Phone: (212)457-9400; Fax: (646)417-7705; Email: customercare@alm.com • URL: http://www.alm.com • Monthly. $195.00 per year. Newsletter. Provides legal news relating mainly to fraudulent or excessive medical billing practices. Covers both civil and criminal proceedings. (A Law Journal Newsletter, formerly published by Leader Publications).

***Health Care Strategic Management: The Newsletter for Hospital Strategies***. The Business Word, 11211 E Arapahoe Rd., Ste. 101 Centennial, CO 80112-3851. Phone: 800-328-3211 or (303)290-8500; Fax: (303)290-9025; Email: thebusinessword@yahoo.com • URL: http://www.businessword.com • Monthly. $284.00 per year. Planning, marketing and resource allocation.

***Health Data Management***. SourceMedia Inc., 1 State Street Plz., 27th Fl. New York, NY 10004. Phone: 800-221-1809 or (212)803-8200 or (212)803-8333; Fax: (212)843-9635 or (212)292-5216; Email: custserv@sourcemedia.com • URL: http://www.sourcemedia.com • Monthly. $98.00 per year. Covers the management and automation of clinical data and health care insurance claims. Provides news and analysis of various aspects of health care information technology for administrators of hospitals, clinics, and managed care plans.

***Health Devices Alerts: A Summary of Reported Problems, Hazards, Recalls, and Updates***. ECRI Institute, 5200 Butler Pke. Plymouth Meeting, PA 19462-1298. Phone: (610)825-6000; Fax: (610)834-1275; Email: info@ecri.org • URL: http://www.ecri.org • Weekly. $3,649.40 per year. Looseleaf service. Contains reviews of health equipment problems. Includes *Health Devices Alerts Action Items, Health Devices Alerts Abstracts, Health Devices Alerts FDA Data, Health Devices Alerts Implants, Health Devices Alerts Hazards Bulletin*.

***Health Devices Journals***. ECRI Institute, 5200 Butler Pke. Plymouth Meeting, PA 19462-1298. Phone: (610)825-6000; Fax: (610)834-1275; Email: info@ecri.org • URL: http://www.ecri.org • Monthly. $285 each.

***Health Facilities Management***. American Hospital Association. Health Forum L.L.C., 155 N Wacker Dr., Ste. 400 Chicago, IL 60606. Phone: 800-821-2039 or (312)893-6800; Fax: (312)422-4500 • URL: http://www.healthforum.com • Covers building maintenance and engineering for hospitals and nursing homes.

***Health Food Business Magazine***. Target Publishing Ltd., The Old Dairy, Hudsons Farm, Fieldgate Ln. Ugley Green CM22 6HJ, United Kingdom. Phone: 44 12 79816300; Fax: 44 12 79816496; Email: info@targetpublishing.com • URL: http://www.targetpublishing.com/ • Monthly. £54 Individuals United Kingdom only. Trade magazine for the health food retail industry.

***Health Forum Journal: Leadership Strategies for Healthcare Executives***. Healthcare Forum, One N. Franklin St., 29th Fl. Chicago, IL 60606. Phone: (415)436-4300; Fax: (415)356-9300 • URL: http://www.healthonline.com • Bimonthly. $65.00 per year.

***Health Grants and Contracts Weekly: Selected Federal Project Opportunities***. Wolters Kluwer Law and Business, 76 9th Ave., 7th Fl. New York, NY 10011-4962. Phone: 800-234-1660 or (212)771-0600; Fax: (800)901-9075 or (301)644-3550 • URL: http://www.wolterskluwerlb.com • 50 times a year. $459.00 per year. Newsletter. Lists new health-related federal contracts and grants.

***Health Groups in Washington: A Directory***. National Health Council, 1730 M St. NW, Ste. 500 Washington, DC 20036-4561. Phone: (202)785-3910; Fax: (202)785-5923 • URL: http://www.nationalhealthcouncil.org • Biennial. $40 Members; $60 Nonmembers. Covers: Over 900 professional, voluntary, consumer, insurance, union, business, and academic organizations with some impact on the development of federal health policies. Entries include: Name of organization, address, phone, e-mail address, website address, names of Washington representatives.

***Health Industry Today: The Market Letter for Health Care Industry Vendors***. The Business Word, 11211 E Arapahoe Rd., Ste. 101 Centennial, CO 80112-3851. Phone: 800-328-3211 or (303)290-8500; Fax: (303)290-9025; Email: thebusinessword@yahoo.com • URL: http://www.businessword.com • Monthly. $360.00 per year; online edition, $420.00 per year.

***Health Information for International Travel***. U.S. Dept. of Health and Human Services - Centers for Disease Control and Prefabricated, Epidemiology Program Office, MS C-08, 1600 Clifton Rd., NE Atlanta, GA 30333. Phone: 800-232-4636 • URL: http://www.cdc.gov/nchs • Annual. $38. Produced by the Centers for Disease Control and Prevention (CDC). Primarily edited for "healthcare providers who administer pre- and post-travel counseling and care." Also serves as a reference for airlines, cruise lines, and the travel industry in general. Covers such items as injuries during travel, motion sickness, disabilities, vaccines, insect repellents, and travel with children. Sometimes known as "The Yellow Book.".

***Health Insurance Underwriter***. National Association of Health Underwriters, 1212 New York Ave. NW, Ste. 1100 Washington, DC 20005. Phone: (202)552-5060; Fax: (202)747-6820; Email: info@nahu.org • URL: http://www.nahu.org • Monthly. Includes special feature issues on long-term care insurance, disability insurance, managed health care, and insurance office management.

***The Health Letter***. Sidney M. Wolfe, editor. North America Syndicate, PO Box 90190 Collingswood, NJ 08108. Phone: 800-443-8199 or (609)869-3464; Fax: (202)785-3584; Email: custserv@bpinews.com • Description: Addresses health topics, with discussion of cause and effect, practical counsel, and information on normal variations. Carries news of research, briefings from current medical literature, and highlights of conferences and other events.

***Health Maintenance Organization (HMO) Directory and Market Report***. FIRSTMARK Inc., 25 Vintinner Rd. Campton, NH 03223. Phone: 800-729-2600 or (603)726-4800; Fax: (603)726-4840; Email: info@firstmark.com • URL: http://www.firstmark.com • Annual. $630.00. Three looseleaf volumes. Contains information relating to over 700 HMOs. Relevant market data is also provided.

***Health Management Technology***. Nelson Publishing Inc., 2500 Tamiami Trl. N Nokomis, FL 34275. Phone: (941)966-9521; Fax: (941)966-2590; Email: webteam@nelsonpub.com • URL: http://www.nelsonpub.com • Monthly. $38.00 per year. Formerly *Computers in Healthcare*.

***Health Marketing Quarterly***. The Haworth Press Inc., 10 Alice St. Binghamton, NY 13904. Phone: 800-429-6784 or (607)722-5857; Fax: (607)771-0012 or (607)722-6362; Email: getinfo@haworthpress.com • URL: http://www.haworthpressinc.com/store/product.asp?sku=J014 • Quarterly. $580.00 per year.

***Health News Daily***. Elsevier Business Intelligence, 5635 Fishers Ln., Ste. 6000 Rockville, MD 20852. Phone: 800-332-2181 or (240)221-4500 or (800)332-2181; Fax: (240)221-4400 or (301)656-3094; Email: fdc.customer.service@fdcreports.com • URL: http://www.elsevierbi.com • Description: Tracks developments in health care policy, legislation and regulation, insurance, pharmaceuticals, delivery, manufacturing, technology and treatment, funding, and research.

***Health Policy and Biomedical Research: The Blue Sheet***. Elsevier Business Intelligence, 5635 Fishers Ln., Ste. 6000 Rockville, MD 20852. Phone: 800-332-2181 or (240)221-4500 or (800)332-2181; Fax: (240)221-4400 or (301)656-3094; Email: fdc.customer.service@fdcreports.com • URL: http://www.elsevierbi.com • 51 times a year. $716.00 per year. Newsletter. Emphasis is on news of medical research agencies and institutions, especially the National Institutes of Health (NIH).

**Health Policy Institute**. 1200 Pressler St. Houston, TX 77025. Phone: (713)500-9494; Fax: (713)500-9493; Email: Stephen.H.Linder@uth.tmc.edu • URL: http://sph.uth.edu/research/centers/ihp.

***Health Products Business Purchasing Guide***. Cygnus Business Media, 3 Huntington Quadrangle, Ste. 301N Melville, NY 11747. Phone: 800-308-6397 or (631)845-2700; Fax: (631)845-2741 or (631)845-2798; Email: rich.reiff@cygnuspub.com • URL: http://www.cygnusb2b.com • Annual. $10.00. Listing of manufacturers, importers, exclusive distributors, brokers, and wholesalers of health food products, publishers of health food related books and magazines, and associations interested in the health foods industry. Formerly *Health Foods Business Purchasing Guide*.

***Health Products Business: The Business Publication of the Natural Foods In dustry***. Cygnus Business Media, 3

SOURCES CITED

Huntington Quadrangle, Ste. 301N Melville, NY 11747. Phone: 800-308-6397 or (631)845-2700; Fax: (631)845-2741 or (631)845-2798; Email: rich.reiff@cygnuspub.com • URL: http://www.cygnusb2b.com • Monthly. $60.00 per year.

**Healthcare Distribution Management Association**. 901 N Glebe Rd., Ste. 1000 Arlington, VA 22203. Phone: (703)787-0000; Fax: (703)812-5282 • URL: http://www.healthcaredistribution.org • Wholesalers and manufacturers of drug and health care products and industry service providers. Seeks to secure safe and effective distribution of healthcare products, create and exchange industry knowledge affecting the future of distribution management, and influence standards and business processes that produce efficient health care commerce. Compiles statistics; sponsors research and specialized education programs.

***Healthcare Distributor: The Industry's Multi-Market Information Resource***. ELF Publications Inc., 5285 W Louisiana Ave. Lakewood, CO 80232-5976. Phone: 800-922-8513 or (303)975-0075; Email: elfpub@qwest.net • URL: http://www.elfpublications.com • Bimonthly. Formerly *Wholesale Drugs Magazine*.

***Healthcare Executive***. American College of Healthcare Executives, 1 N Franklin St., Ste. 1700 Chicago, IL 60606-3529. Phone: (312)424-2800 or (312)424-9400; Fax: (312)424-0023 or (312)424-9405; Email: contact@ache.org • URL: http://www.ache.org • Bimonthly. $110 Individuals in the U.S. Focuses on critical management issues in the healthcare industry.

**Healthcare Financial Management Association**. 3 Westbrook Corporate Ctr., Ste. 600 Westchester, IL 60154. Phone: 800-252-4362 or (708)531-9600; Fax: (708)531-0032; Email: memberservices@hfma.org • URL: http://www.hfma.org • Financial management professionals employed by hospitals and long-term care facilities, public accounting and consulting firms, insurance companies, medical groups, managed care organizations, government agencies, and other organizations. Conducts conferences, including annual conference in late June and audio teleconferences. Publishes books on healthcare financial issues. A Fellowship in Healthcare Financial Management (FHFMA) as well as the Certified Healthcare Professional (CHFP) in Finance and Accounting, Financial Management of Physician Practices, Managed Care, and Patient Financial Services are offered.

***Healthcare Financial Management***. Healthcare Financial Management Association, 1825 K St. NW, Ste. 900 Washington, DC 20006. Phone: 800-252-HFMA or (202)296-2920; Fax: (202)238-3456 • URL: http://www.hfma.org • Monthly. $260 Individuals; $150 Institutions.

***Healthcare Marketing Report***. HMR Publication Group, 3180 Presidential Dr., Ste. K Atlanta, GA 30340. Phone: (770)457-6106; Fax: (770)457-4606; Email: info@hmrpublicationsgroup.com • URL: http://www.hmrpublicationsgroup.com/index.html • $235 U.S.; $275 Other countries. Contains the latest news on winning market strategies, concepts and trends in the healthcare industry.

***Healthcare Products Today Magazine***. Health Industry Distribution Association. Communication Publications & Resources, 2807 N Parham Rd., Ste. 200 Richmond, VA 23294. Phone: 800-780-4066; Email: customerservice@briefings.com • URL: http://www.briefingsmediagroup.com • 10 times a year. $49.95 per year. Formerly *Medical Product Sales*.

***Healthcare Purchasing News: A Magazine for Hospital Materials Management Central Service, Infection Control Practitioners***. Thomson Medical Economics, 5 Paragon Dr. Montvale, NJ 07645-1742. Phone: 800-526-4870 or (201)358-7200; Fax: (201)573-8999 or (201)722-2680; Email: customer.service@medec.com • URL: http://www.medec.com • Monthly. $72; $110 Canada; $130 Other countries. Edited for personnel responsible for the purchase of medical, surgical, and hospital equipment and supplies. Features new purchasing techniques and new products. Includes news of the activities of two major purchasing associations, Health Care Material Management Society and International Association of Healthcare Central Service Materiel Management.

***Healthcare QuickDisc***. American Hospital Association, 155 N Wacker Dr. Chicago, IL 60606. Phone: 800-424-4301 or (312)422-3000 or (312)422-2050; Fax: (312)422-4700 • URL: http://www.aha.org • Corresponds to the printed *AHA Guide*, with additional material and extensive search capabilities (400 data fields). Provides detailed information on 6,000 hospitals and hospital systems, including utilization data.

***Healthcare Risk Management***. AHC Media, 950 E Paces Ferry Rd. NE Atlanta, GA 30326. Phone: 800-688-2421 or (404)262-5476; Fax: (404)262-5560; Email: editorial_questions@ahcmedia.com • URL: http://www.ahcmedia.com • Description: Analyzes specific legal cases and trends relevant to healthcare liability. Discusses malpractice, liability for patients, staff and visitor injury, injury prevention, biomedical engineering, and medical staff credentials. Also covers high-risk areas of hospitals, hospital-owned home health and physician practices, accreditation, Medicare reimbursement, physician liability, medical records, and claims management. Recurring features include interviews, statistics, news of research, guest columns, legal briefs, and commentaries.

***HealthLeaders-InterStudy***. One Vantage Way, Ste. B-300 Nashville, TN 37228. Phone: 999-203-0675 or (615)385-4979 or (615)385-4979; Fax: (615)385-4979; Email: sales@hl-isy.com • URL: http://www.hl-isy.com • Bimonthly. Provides broad coverage of finance, marketing, management, and technology for executives in the health care industry. Includes "Roundtable" discussions of particular health care issues. Formerly *Healthcare Business*.

***Healthplan: The Magazine of Trends, Insights, and Best Practices***. American Association of Health Plans, 601 Pennsylvania Ave., NW, S Bldg., Ste. 500 Washington, DC 20004. Phone: (202)778-3200; Fax: (202)331-7487; Email: ahip@ahip.org • URL: http://www.aahp.org • Bimonthly. $60 Individuals; $88 Other countries. Trade magazine covering news and analysis of managed health care for HMO and PPO executives.

***Heartland Real Estate Business***. France Publications Inc., 3500 Piedmont Rd., Ste. 415 Atlanta, GA 30305. Phone: (404)832-8262; Fax: (404)832-8260; Email: jerry@francepublications.com • URL: http://www.francepublications.com/contact.html • Monthly. $65 Individuals; $112 Two years. Magazine that covers the latest news, developments and trends in commercial real estate in the Midwest.

***Heating Equipment—Manufacturers Directory***. InfoGroup Inc., 5711 S 86th Cir. Omaha, NE 68127-4146. Phone: (402)593-4500 • URL: http://www.infogroup.com • Annual. Number of listings: 1,419. Entries include: Name, address, phone, size of advertisement, name of owner or manager, number of employees, year first in "Yellow Pages." Compiled from telephone company "Yellow Pages," nationwide.

***Heating/Piping/Air Conditioning Engineering: The Magazine of Mechanical Systems Engineering***. Penton Media Inc., 1300 E 9th St. Cleveland, OH 44114-1501. Phone: (216)696-7000; Fax: (216)696-1752; Email: information@penton.com • URL: http://penton.com • Monthly. Covers design, specification, installation, operation, and maintenance for systems in industrial, commercial, and institutional buildings. Formerly (Heating, Piping and Air Conditioning).

***Heating, Ventilation and Air Conditioning Businesses in the World***. Momentum Technologies L.L.C., PO Box 460813 Glendale, CO 80246. Phone: (303)229-4841; Fax: (408)705-2031 • URL: http://www.mtt.com • Contains detailed directory listings and contact information for heating, ventilation, and air conditioning (HVAC) businesses in operation throughout the world. Includes business name, address, phone number, fax number, e-mail address, and web site address. Provides keyword search functions.

***Heavy Duty Trucking—Council of Fleet Specialists Equipment Buyer's Guide & Services Directory***. Newport Communications Div. HIC Corp., 38 Executive Park, Ste. 300 Irvine, CA 92614. Phone: (949)261-1636; Fax: (949)261-2904 • URL: http://www.newportcommunicationsgroup.com • Annual. $45 included in subscription; free to equipment and maintenance managers. Covers: 500 Council of Fleet Specialists member manufacturers and wholesalers specializing in heavy-duty truck parts and repairs. Entries include: Company name, address, phone, names of executives, parts or services manufactured or available; wholesaler listings also show area served. A special section of 'Heavy Duty Trucking' magazine prepared by the Council of Fleet Specialists, 315 Delaware, Kansas City, MO 64105 (816-421-2600).

***Heavy Duty Trucking: The Business Magazine of Trucking***. H.I.C. Corp., 38 Executive Pk., Ste. 300 Irvine, CA 92614-6755. Phone: (949)261-1636 • Monthly.

***HedgeWorld Annual Compendium: The Hedge Fund Industry's Definitive Reference Guide***. HedgeWorld, 3 Times Sq., 17th Fl. New York, NY 10036. Phone: (646)223-4431; Fax: (646)223-4470; Email: custserv@hedgeworld.com • URL: http://www.hedgeworld.com • Annual. $499.00. Contains profiles of 500 domestic and offshore hedge funds with more than $50 million in assets under management. Includes articles on "The Basics of Investing in Hedge Funds," "Beyond the Basics," and other information.

***HedgeWorld Service Provider League Tables & Analyses***. HedgeWorld, 3 Times Sq., 17th Fl. New York, NY 10036. Phone: (646)223-4431; Fax: (646)223-4470; Email: custserv@hedgeworld.com • URL: http://www.hedgeworld.com • Annual. $595.00. Provides quantitative and qualitative information on firms providing services to hedge funds: accountants/auditors, administrators, custodians, legal counsel, and prime brokers. Detailed categories cover banks, clearing services, consultants, derivatives business, investment companies, wealth management services, etc.

***Helicopter News***. Access Intelligence L.L.C., 4 Choke Cherry Rd., 2nd Fl. Rockville, MD 20850. Phone: 800-777-5006 or (301)354-2000 or (301)354-2101; Fax: (301)309-3847 or (801)365-2300; Email: info@accessintel.com • URL: http://www.accessintel.com/ • Description: Reports to company executives, military leaders, and ancillary industries on the state of the helicopter industry. Tracks buying and selling information, news of contracts, and new programs. Also concerned with related issues, including EMS (Emergency Mission Support) and insurance. Recurring features include interviews and news of technology and new products. **Remarks:** Also available online and via e-mail.

**HELIO International**. 31-33 rue de la Colonie 75013 Paris, France. Phone: 33 1 45802607; Email: helio@helio-international.org • URL: http://www.helio-international.org • Aims to identify, assess, measure and publicize the contribution of energy systems and policies to sustainable and equitable development. Provides independent input to the design and implementation of ecodevelopment, energy and climate projects. Designs analytical tools and promotes the creation and integration of citizen in the energy decision-making process.

***Herb Quarterly***. EGW Publishing Co., 1041 Shary Circle Concord, CA 94518. Phone: (925)671-9852; Fax: (925)671-0692; Email: herbquart@aol.com • URL: http://www.herbquarterly.com • Quarterly. A magazine for herb enthusiasts covering all aspects of herb uses.

***Herbarist***. Herb Society of America, 9019 Kirtland Chardon Rd. Kirtland, OH 44094. Phone: (440)256-0514; Fax: (440)256-0541; Email: herbs@herbsociety.org • URL: http://www.herbsociety.org • Annual. $12.50 Members; $15 Nonmembers. Journal of The Herb Society of America.

**HERTY Advanced Materials Development Center**. 110 Brampton Rd. Savannah, GA 31408. Phone: (912)963-2600; Fax: (912)963-2614; Email: info@herty.com • URL: http://www.herty.com.

***HFN (Home Furnishing News): The Newsweekly of Home Products Retailing***. Fairchild Publications, 750 Third Ave. New York, NY 10017. Phone: 800-360-1700 or (212)630-4600 or (212)630-4000; Fax: (212)630-3675 or (212)630-4015; Email: hillary_kribben@condenast.com • URL: http://www.fairchildmediakit.com • Formerly *HFD-Home Furnishing Daily*.

**High Council for Private Enterprise**. Las Colinas, Calle Alta, Casa N 12, Detras De Gasolinera Puma Managua, Nicaragua. Phone: 505 2276-3333 or 505 2276-2708; Fax: 505 2276-1666; Email: relacionespublicas@cosep.org.ni • URL: http://www.cosep.org.ni • Promotes the establishment of the democracy in terms of economic, political and social aspects of Nicaragua through programs and actions.

***High Performance Business Strategy***. Cengage Learning Inc., 20 Channel Center St. Boston, MA 02210. Phone: 800-487-8488 or (617)289-7700; Fax: (617)289-7844; Email: investors@cengage.com • URL: http://www.cengage.com • 2009. eBook. Published by Kogan Page. Designed to help senior management analyse the weak points in a business and focus HR on transforming problem areas by maximizing staff and business performance.

***High Performance Review: Definitive Magazine for Audiophiles and Music Lovers***. High Performance Review Publishing, 296 Amherst Dr. Murfreesboro, TN 37128-6233. Phone: (615)893-9788; Fax: (615)893-9717 • Quarterly. $15.00 per year.

***High-Tech Materials Alert: Advanced Materials: Their Uses and Manufacture***. Technical Insights, 605 Third Ave. New York, NY 10158-0012. Phone: 800-825-7550 or (212)850-8600; Fax: (212)850-8800; Email: insights@wiley.com • URL: http://www.wiley.com • Monthly. Institutions, $695.00 per year. Newsletter on technical developments relating to high-performance materials, including metals and ceramics. Includes market forecasts.

***High-Tech Materials Alert***. John Wiley & Sons Inc. Scientific, Technical, Medical, and Scholarly Div. (Wiley-Blackwell), 111 River St. Hoboken, NJ 07030-5774. Phone: (201)748-6000; Fax: (201)748-6088; Email: info@wiley.com • URL: http://www.wiley.com • Monthly. Publication includes: List of manufacturers and suppliers of high performance alloys, metals, ceramics, plastics, graphite, and other materials. Entries include: Company name, address, phone. Principal content is articles and analyses of new materials for industrial processes.

***High Technology Business***. Infotechnology Publishing Corp., 9990 Lee Hwy., No. 301 Fairfax, VA 22030-1720. Phone: (703)359-6100 • Monthly. $60 Individuals; $5 Single issue. Magazine containing information on current trends and developments in the full range of high technology industries. Material is directed toward business people in the high technology field.

***High Yield Report***. American Banker/Bond Buyer Inc., 1 State St. Plz. 27 Fl. New York, NY 10004. Phone: 800-221-1809 or (212)803-8200 or (212)967-7000; Fax: (212)843-9600 or (212)843-9613; Email: custserv@americanbanker.com • URL: http://www.americanbanker.com • Description: Examines markets for high-yield corporate bonds, work-outs, bankruptcies, and secondary markets for distressed securities. Contains pricing information for primary and secondary markets and analysis of the high-yield sector. Reports on developments affecting the senior and subordinated debt of companies in bankruptcy or working their way out of debt, detailing proposed financial restructurings. Tracks regulatory decisions affecting trade of distressed debt and funds purchased and sold. **Remarks:** Incorporates the former Distressed Debt Report.

***Higher Education and National Affairs***. American Council on Education, 1 Dupont Cir. NW Washington, DC 20036. Phone: (202)939-9300 or (202)939-9420; Email: membership@ace.nche.edu • URL: http://www.acenet.edu • Biweekly.

***Highlights and Documents***. Tax Analysts, 400 S Maple Ave., Ste. 400 Falls Church, VA 22046. Phone: 800-955-2444 or (703)533-4400; Fax: (703)533-4444; Email: cservice@tax.org • URL: http://www.tax.org • Daily. $2,599.95 Individuals. Provides daily coverage of IRS, congressional, judicial, state, and international tax developments. Includes abstracts and citations for "all tax documents released within the previous 24 to 48 hours." Annual compilation available *Highlights and Documents on Microfiche*.

***Highway Financing and Construction: State Capitals***. Wakeman/Walworth Inc., PO Box 7376 Alexandria, VA 22307-7376. Phone: 800-876-2545 or (703)768-9600; Fax: (703)768-9690; Email: newsletters@statecapitals.com • URL: http://statecapitals.com/ • 50 times a year. $345.00 per year.; print and online editions, $490.00 per year. Newsletter. Formerly *From the State Capitals: Highway Financing and Construction*.

***Highway Safety Literature***. National Highway Traffic Safety Administration, 1200 New Jersey Ave. SE, West Bldg. Washington, DC 20590. Phone: 888-327-4236 or (202)366-9550 • URL: http://www.nhtsa.gov • Annual. $80.00.

***Highways***. Good Sam club. Affinity Group Inc., T L Enterprises, 2575 Vista Del Mar Dr. Ventura, CA 93001. Phone: 800-825-6861 or (805)667-4100; Fax: (805)667-4484 or (805)667-4379; Email: info@trailerlife.com • URL: http://www.rv.net • 11 times a year. Membership. Five regional editions. Formerly *Good Sam's Hi-Way Herald*.

**Hillsdale College - Center for Constructive Alternatives/ National Leadership Institute**. 33 E College St. Hillsdale, MI 49242. Phone: (517)437-7341; Fax: (517)437-3923; Email: cca@hillsdale.edu • URL: http://www.hillsdale.edu • Political theory, public policy, culture.

***Hindu Business Line***. Kasturi & Sons Ltd., Kasturi Buildings, 859 & 860 Anna Salai Chennai 600 002, India. Phone: 91 44 28589060; Fax: 91 44 28545703 • URL: http://www.hinduonnet.com/ • Daily. Rs 1,496 Individuals all days; Rs 1,857 Individuals by post; Rs 208 Individuals any specific day; Rs 260 Individuals by post. Newspaper covering business, economics, banks and banking.

***HireDiversity.com***. Hispanic Business Inc., 5385 Hollister Ave., Ste. 204 Santa Barbara, CA 93111. Phone: 800-806-4268 or (805)964-4554; Fax: (805)964-5539; Email: hd@hirediversity.com • URL: http://www.HispanicBusiness.com • Database covers: Over 95,000 resumes of multicultural professionals and recent college graduates who are seeking employment with Fortune 500 companies; job listings with a large variety of companies. Entries include: Name, address, phone, employment history, salary requirements, level of management experience, education, geographical preference, and language.

***Hispanic American Periodicals Index***. University of California, Los Angeles. Latin American Studies Center Publications, 10347 Bunche Hall Los Angeles, CA 90095. Phone: (310)825-0810; Email: bvalk@ucla.edu • Daily. $425. Annual. Indexes about 250 periodicals that regularly include material on Latin America. Supplement available.

***Hispanic Media & Market Source***. Kantar Media SRDS, 1700 Higgins Rd., 5th Fl. Des Plaines, IL 60018-5610. Phone: 800-851-7737 or (847)375-5000; Email: next@srds.com • URL: http://next.srds.com • Quarterly. $445 per year. Provides detailed information on the following Hispanic advertising media in the U.S.: TV, radio, newspapers, magazines, direct mail, outdoor, and special events.

***Historical Dictionary of Aid and Development Organizations***. The Scarecrow Press Inc., 4501 Forbes Blvd., Ste. 200 Lanham, MD 20706-4346. Phone: 800-462-6420 or (301)459-3366; Fax: (301)429-5748; Email: custserv@rowman.com • URL: http://www.scarecrowpress.com • $55 Individuals Hardback; £34.95 Individuals Hardback. Covers: Major organizations involved in the post-WWII economic development.

***Historical Encyclopedia of American Business***. Cengage Learning Inc., 20 Channel Center St. Boston, MA 02210. Phone: 800-487-8488 or (617)289-7700; Fax: (617)289-7844; Email: investors@cengage.com • URL: http://www.cengage.com • 2009. eBook. Published by Salem Press. Long overviews on different sectors of the economy, such as agriculture and banking; individual industries such as advertising and electronics; and general topics such as business cycles, labor strikes and outsourcing. There are also overviews on broad legal topics such as antitrust legislation, bankruptcy laws and patent laws.

***History of Rocketry and Astronautics***. American Astronautical Society. Univelt Inc., 740 Metcalf St., Ste. 13 & 15 San Diego, CA 92198. Phone: (760)746-4005; Fax: (760)746-3139; Email: 76121.1532@compuserve.com • URL: http://www.univelt.com • $95. Various volumes and prices. Covers the history of rocketry and astronautics since 1880. Prices vary. (AAS History Series).

***HME News***. HME News, PO Box 998 Yarmouth, ME 04096. Phone: (207)846-0600; Fax: (207)846-0657 • Monthly. Covers the home medical equipment business for dealers and manufacturers. Provides information on a wide variety of home health care supplies and equipment.

***HME News: The Business Newspaper for Home Medical Equipment Providers***. HME News, PO Box 998 Yarmouth, ME 04096. Phone: (207)846-0600; Fax: (207)846-0657 • Monthly. Business newspaper for home medical equipment providers. Editorial coverage focuses on industry news, mergers and acquisitions, governmental and regulatory impact on the HME industry, as well as product reviews and industry trend coverage.

***Hobart Business Directory***. Hobart Chamber of Commerce, 1001 Lillian St. Hobart, IN 46342. Phone: (219)942-5774; Fax: (219)942-4928; Email: info@hobartchamber.com • URL: http://www.hobartchamber.com • Covers: More than 450 businesses and professionals in Hobart, Indiana; 65 clubs and organizations; schools and day care centers, local government officials and boards, churches, etc. Entries include: Company, institution, or organization name, address, phone, name of contact; government boards also include meeting days and times or office hours.

***Hog Farm Management: Journal of the Nation's Pork Business***. Miller Publishing Co., 5810 W 78th St., Ste. 200 Bloomington, MN 55439. Phone: (952)930-4344 or (952)931-0211; Fax: (952)938-1832; Email: tlundeen@feedstuffs.com • URL: http://www.feedstuffs.com • Monthly. Magazine serving hog producers.

***Holden's Annual Directory 1811***. S&N British Data Archive Ltd., West Wing, Manor Farm Salisbury SP3 5AF, United Kingdom. Phone: 44 1722 716121; Fax: 44 1722 716160 • URL: http://www.genealogysupplies.com • £16.95 Individuals. Database covers: Professions, trades, and residents in London and other towns in Great Britain. Entries include: Name and address.

***Hollis Sponsorship & Donations Yearbook***. Hobsons PLC, IDT House, 44 Featherstone St. London EC1Y 8RN, United Kingdom. Phone: 44 020 7250 6600; Email: enquiries@hobsons.co.uk • URL: http://www.hobsons.com • Annual. £145 Individuals; £105 Individuals for charities. Covers: Companies in the United Kingdom offering commercial sponsorships and donations to arts, charity, educational, media, and sports organizations; organizations looking for sponsorships and donations; sponsorship consultants; providers of services such as speakers, caterers, lawyers, insurance, and suppliers of promotional merchandise. Over 3,000 companies and organizations are listed. Entries include: Company or organization name, address, phone, fax, name and title of contact; sponsors list projects sponsored, sponsorship budget and date set, preferred areas of support, total donations; organizations seeking sponsors list projects needing aid, amount of funding required, benefits to the sponsoring company; consultants list number of employees, main interests.

***Hollywood Creative Directory: Below-the-Line Talent***. IFILMpro, 1024 N Orange Dr. Hollywood, CA 90038. Phone: 800-815-0503 or (323)308-3490; Fax: (323)308-3493 or (323)468-7689; Email: hcd@ifilm.com • URL: http://www.ifilmpro.com • Annual. $80.00. Lists more than 6,000 cinematographers, production designers, costume designers, film editors, set decorators, and art directors and their associated 15,000 film titles.

***Hollywood Creative Directory: Film Writers***. IFILMpro, 1024 N Orange Dr. Hollywood, CA 90038. Phone: 800-815-0503 or (323)308-3490; Fax: (323)308-3493 or (323)468-7689; Email: hcd@ifilm.com • URL: http://www.ifilmpro.com • Annual. $85.00. Lists more than 8,000 screenwriters and their associated 35,000 film titles. Includes projects in development and unsold screenplays.

***Hollywood Creative Directory: The Phone Book to Hollywood***. IFILM Publishing, 1024 N Orange Dr. Hollywood, CA 90038. Phone: 800-815-0503 or (323)308-3400 or (323)308-3490; Fax: (310)471-4969 or (323)308-3493; Email: advertising@ifilm.com • URL: http://www.ifilm.com/ • Semiannual. $149.95 per year. Three issues per year. Single issue, $59.95. Lists about 9,900 talent agents, personal managers, and casting directors.

***Hollywood Financial Directory***. Hollywood Creative Directory, 5055 Wilshire Blvd. Los Angeles, CA 90036-4396. Phone: 800-815-0503 or (323)525-2369; Fax: (323)525-2398; Email: hcdcustomerservice@hcdonline.com • URL: http://www.hcdonline.com • Annual. $49.50. Covers: Over 600 entertainment-related companies and their corporate, financial, legal, and business affairs staff. Entries include: Name, address, phone, names and titles of key personnel, subsidiary and branch names and locations, description, company type.

***The Hollywood Reporter***. 5700 Wilshire Blvd. Los Angeles, CA 90036. Phone: 866-525-2150 or (323)525-2150; Fax: (323)525-2377; Email: mailbox@hollywoodreporter.com • URL: http://www.hollywoodreporter.com • Daily. $199.00 per year. Covers the latest news in film, TV, cable, multimedia, music, and theatre. Includes box office grosses and entertainment industry financial data.

***Holo-Pack Holo-Print Guidebook and Business Directory: 2nd Edition***. Smithers Pira, Cleeve Rd. Leatherhead KT22 7RU, United Kingdom. Phone: 44 1372 802000; Fax: 44 1372 802079 • URL: http://www.smitherspira.com/Home.aspx • $47.50 Individuals. Covers: Organizations around the world which supply holograms or holographic products and services.

***Home Banking Report***. Jupitermedia Corp., 23 Old Kings Hwy. S Darien, CT 06820. Phone: 800-488-4345 or (203)662-2800; Fax: (203)655-4686; Email: ameckler@jupitermedia.com • URL: http://www.webmediabrands.com • Annual. $695.00. Market research report. Covers banking from home by phone or online, with projections of growth in future years.

**Home-Based Working Moms**. PO Box 1628 Spring, TX 77383-1628. Phone: (281)757-2207 • URL: http://www.hbwm.com • Individuals who work at home or would like to. Promotes working at home as an option for people in applicable positions; seeks to enhance the careers of members currently working at home. Serves as a forum for exchange of information among members. Makes available member matching service. Advocates for creation of more work-at-home opportunities by American businesses.

***The Home Business Report***. The Kerner Group Inc., 1319 Howard Ln. Palmer, PA 18045-2153. • Provides information on how to operate a home-based business or work from home. Features real life success stories, how-to articles on marketing, and strategies to keep focused on goals. Recurring features include letters to the editor, interviews, news of research, job listings, book reviews, and notices of publications available.

***Home Decorating Services Directory***. InfoGroup Inc., 5711 S 86th Cir. Omaha, NE 68127-4146. Phone: (402)593-4500 • URL: http://www.infogroup.com • Annual. Number of listings: 33,751. Entries include: Name, address, phone, size of advertisement, name of owner or manager, number of employees, year first in "Yellow Pages." Compiled from telephone company "Yellow Pages," nationwide.

***Home Design and Planning Service Directory***. InfoGroup Inc., 5711 S 86th Cir. Omaha, NE 68127-4146. Phone: (402)593-4500 • URL: http://www.infogroup.com • Annual. Number of listings: 3,518. Entries include: Name, address, phone, size of advertisement, name of owner or manager, number of employees, year first in "Yellow Pages." Compiled from telephone company "Yellow Pages," nationwide.

***Home Furnishings Business***. North American Publishing Co., 1500 Spring Garden St., Ste. 1200 Philadelphia, PA 19130-4069. Phone: (215)238-5300; Email: customerservice@napco.com • URL: http://www.napco.com • Magazine publishing articles in the field of furniture retail.

***Home Health Agencies Report and Directory***. SMG Marketing Group Inc., 875 N Michigan Ave., Ste. 3100 Chicago, IL 60611. Phone: 800-678-3026 or (312)642-3026; Fax: (312)642-9729 • URL: http://www.smg.com/ • Annual. $575.00. Lists over 13,000 home healthcare agencies and corporations. Includes a market analysis and growth projections.

***Home Health Care Dealer-Provider***. CurAnt Communications Inc., 6701 Ctr. Dr. W, Ste. 450 Los Angeles, CA 90045. Phone: (310)642-4400 or (310)306-2206; Fax: (310)641-4444 • Bimonthly. Free. For home care dealer and home care pharmacies. Formerly *Home Health Care Dealer - Supplier*.

***Home Health Care Services Quarterly: The Journal of Community Care***. The Haworth Press Inc., 10 Alice St. Binghamton, NY 13904. Phone: 800-429-6784 or (607)722-5857; Fax: (607)771-0012 or (607)722-6362; Email: getinfo@haworthpress.com • URL: http://www.haworthpressinc.com/store/product.asp?sku=J014 • Quarterly. $535.00 per year. An academic and practical journal focusing on the marketing and administration of home care.

***Home Health Line: The Home Care Industry's National Independent Newsletter***. 2 Washingtonian Center, 9737 Washingtonian Blvd., Ste. 100 Gaithersburg, MD 20878. Phone: (855)225-5341; Fax: (301)287-2535 • URL: http://www.homehealthline.com • 48 times per year. $527.00 per year. Newsletter on legislation and regulations affecting the home health care industry, with an emphasis on federal funding and Medicare programs.

***Home Health Products***. Stevens Publishing Corp., 5151 Belt Line Rd., 10th Fl. Dallas, TX 75240. Phone: (972)687-6700; Fax: (972)687-6769 or (972)687-6799 • URL: http://www.pollutiononline.com/storefronts/stevenspub.html • 10 times a year. $99.00 per year. Covers new medical equipment products for the home care industry.

***Home Healthcare Nurse: The Journal for the Home Care and Hospice Professional***. The Home Healthcare Nurses Association. Lippincott Williams & Wilkins, 2 Commerce Sq., 2001 Market St. Philadelphia, PA 19103. Phone: 800-638-3030 or (301)223-2300; Email: ronna.ekhouse@wolterskluwer.com • URL: http://www.lww.com • $49.99 Individuals; $421 Institutions; $177 Other countries; $594 Institutions, other countries; $44 Individuals in-training; $80 Canada and Mexico; $441 Institutions, Canada and Mexico. For professional nurses in the home health care field.

***Home Improvements Directory***. InfoGroup Inc., 5711 S 86th Cir. Omaha, NE 68127-4146. Phone: (402)593-4500 • URL: http://www.infogroup.com • Annual. Number of listings: 43,179. Entries include: Name, address, phone, size of advertisement, name of owner or manager, number of employees, year first in "Yellow Pages." Compiled from telephone company "Yellow Pages," nationwide.

***Home Lighting and Accessories***. Doctorow Communications, Inc., 1011 Clifton Ave. Clifton, NJ 07013. Phone: (973)779-1600; Fax: (973)779-3242 • Monthly. Trade magazine of the residential lighting industry for retailers, distributors, designers, architects, specifiers, manufacturers and all lighting professionals.

***Home Lighting and Accessories Suppliers Directory***. Doctorow Publishing, 180 Phillips Rd., Ste. 1B New York, NY 10956. Phone: (973)779-1600; Fax: (845)708-5166; Email: info@homelighting.com • URL: http://www.homelighting.com • Semiannual. $6.00 per issue. Lists almost 1,000 suppliers of residential lighting fixtures and accessories.

***Home Office Connections: A Monthly Journal of News, Ideas, Opportunities, and Savings for Those Who Work at Home***. Home Office Association of America, PO Box 51 East Meadow, NY 11554. Phone: 800-809-4622 or (516)997-

7394; Fax: (516)997-0839; Email: hoaa@aol.com • Monthly. Free to members; non-members, $49.00 per year.

***HomeCare Magazine: For Business Leaders in Home Medical Equipment***. Cahaba Media Group, 1900 28th Ave. S Birmingham, AL 35209. Phone: (205)212-9402 • URL: http://www.cahabamedia.com/ • Monthly. Free in US; $135 Canada; $150 Two years Canada; $250 Other countries; $250 Two years other countries. Magazine serving home medical equipment suppliers, including independent and chain centers specializing in home care, pharmacies or chain drug stores with home care products, and joint-ventured hospital home health care businesses. Contains industry news and new product launches and marketing strategies.

***Homecare Magazine: The Business Magazine of the Home Health Industry***. RentPath Inc., 3585 Engineering Dr., Ste. 100 Norcross, GA 30092-2831. Phone: 800-216-1423 or (678)421-3000 • URL: http://www.rentpath.com • Monthly. Edited for dealers and suppliers of home medical equipment, including pharmacies and chain stores. Includes information on new products.

***Homecare News***. National Association for Home Care, 228 Seventh St. SE Washington, DC 20003. Phone: (202)547-7424; Fax: (202)547-3540; Email: pr@nahc.org • URL: http://www.nahc.org • Description: Reports on National Association for Home Care news plus home care industry developments for the entire industry.

***Homeland Security and Defense: Weekly Intelligence for the Global Homeland Security and Defense Community***. Aviation Week Business Intelligence Services, 1200 G St., N.W., Suite 200 Washington, DC 20005. Phone: 800-752-4959 or (202)383-2350; Fax: (202)383-2438 • URL: http://www.aviationnow.com/bis • Weekly. $595.00 per year. Newsletter. Emphasis is on airline and airport programs (federal, state, and local). Also covers counterterrorism, protection of military units, Department of Homeland Security activities, industrial security, communications equipment, and other topics related to homeland security.

***Homemade Money: How to Select, Start, Manage, Market and Multiply the Profits of a Business at Home***. Rowman and Littlefield Publishers Inc., 4501 Forbes Blvd., Ste. 200 Lanham, MD 20706. Phone: 800-462-6420 or (301)459-3366; Fax: (301)429-5748; Email: customercare@rowman.com • URL: http://www.rowmanlittlefield.com • $24.95 Individuals book 1 and 2. Provides information on beginning and developing a home-based business.

***HomeOffice: The Homebased Office Authority***. Entrepreneur Press, 2445 McCabe Way, Ste. 400 Irvine, CA 92614-6244. Phone: 800-864-6864 or (949)261-2325 or (949)622-7131; Fax: (949)261-7729 or (949)261-0234; Email: press@entrepreneur.com • URL: http://www.entrepreneurpress.com • Bimonthly. $11.97 per year. Contains advice for operating a business in the home.

***Homes for the Aged Directory***. InfoGroup Inc., 5711 S 86th Cir. Omaha, NE 68127-4146. Phone: (402)593-4500 • URL: http://www.infogroup.com • Annual. Number of listings: 5,059. Entries include: Name, address, phone, size of advertisement, name of owner or manager, number of employees, year first in "Yellow Pages." Compiled from telephone company "Yellow Pages," nationwide.

***Homes—Nursing—Directory***. InfoGroup Inc., 5711 S 86th Cir. Omaha, NE 68127-4146. Phone: (402)593-4500 • URL: http://www.infogroup.com • Annual. Number of listings: 22,509. Entries include: Name, address, phone, size of advertisement, name of owner or manager, number of employees, year first in "Yellow Pages." Compiled from telephone company "Yellow Pages," nationwide.

**Honduran Private Enterprise Council**. apdo. 3240 Tegucigalpa, Honduras. Phone: 504 2 2353336; Fax: 504 2 2353345 • URL: http://www.cohep.com/l • Acts in the defense of the principles and indoctrinates of the free company. Works for the enterprise development, economic and social growth of Honduras.

***Hong Kong Classified Business Telephone Directory***. Hong Kong Telephone Company Ltd., 39/F Hong Kong Telecom Twr., Taikoo Pl., 979 Kings Rd., Quarry Bay Hong Kong, China. Phone: 852 25288942 • Covers: Company listings for Hong Kong businesses.

***Hong Kong Commercial/Industrial Guide***. GTE Directories Ltd., 25/F China Resources Bldg., 26 Harbour Rd., Hong Kong Wanchai, China. Phone: 8278668; Fax: 827 8322 • $30. Covers: over 200,000 suppliers of 2,000 products and services in Hong Kong; banks, importers and exporters. Entries include: Company name, address, phone, telex, fax.

***Hong Kong for the Business Visitor***. Hong Kong Trade Development Council, Hong Kong Convention and Exhibition Centre, 1 Expo Dr., Wanchai Hong Kong, China. Phone: 852 1830668; Fax: 852 28240249; Email: hktdc@hktdc.org • URL: http://www.hktdc.com/en-buyer • Annual. Journal of travel, tourism, business and economics.

**Hong Kong General Chamber of Commerce**. 22nd Fl., United Ctr., 95 Queensway Hong Kong, Hong Kong, China. Phone: 852 52 99229 or 852 28231236; Fax: 852 5279843; Email: chamber@chamber.org.hk • URL: http://www.chamber.org.hk/en/index.aspx • Businesses and industries that operates in Hong Kong. Seeks to protect and develop a trading climate conducive to members' interests; promotes investment in Hong Kong businesses. Facilitates international trade by: issuing certificates of origin for goods produced in Hong Kong; disseminating information about business, trade, and industrial opportunities in Hong Kong. Represents members' interests before government bodies; acts as a forum for exchange of information among members; informs members about proposed legislation of interest to the business community. Facilitates meetings between members and business visitors.

***Hong Kong Importer Directory***. Biz Focus Company Ltd., 124 Soi Grand Village, Ladprao Rd., Wangthonglang Bangkok 10310, Thailand. Phone: 66 2 5395726; Fax: 66 2 5395726; Email: support@importerdata.com • URL: http://www.importerdata.com • $240 Individuals. Covers: 4,972 importers with various product categories. Entries include: Company name, contact person, contact address, telephone number, fax number, e-mail, URL, and import products.

***Hong Kong Importers List***. INFOT Inc., PO Box 2052 Rockville, MD 20847. Phone: 866-838-2619 • URL: http://www.infotusa.com • $80.75 CD-ROM; additional $119 for MS Access format. Covers: 15,826 selected importers and buyers from Hong Kong and P.R. China. Entries include: Company name, contact person, physical addresses, email and website addresses, telephone and fax number, and business description.

**Hong Kong Management Association**. W Haking Management Development Ctre., 14th Fl. Fairmont House, 8 Cotton Tree Dr., Central Hong Kong, Hong Kong, China. Phone: 852 25266516; Fax: 852 28684387; Email: hkma@hkma.org.hk • URL: http://www.hkma.org.hk • Business managers and administrators. Promotes efficient and successful business management. Conducts management education and training courses.

**Hong Kong Polytechnic University - Research Center for Construction and Real Estate Economics**. Department of Bldg. & Real Estate, Hung Hom, Kowloon Hong Kong, China. Phone: 86 852 27665821; Fax: 86 852 27645131; Email: bskwwong@polyu.edu.uk • URL: http://www.bre.polyu.edu.hk/rccree/index.htm • Construction and real estate economics.

**Hong Kong Productivity Council**. HKPC Bldg., 78 Tat Chee Ave. Hong Kong, Hong Kong, China. Phone: 852 27885678; Fax: 852 27885900 • URL: http://www.hkpc.org • Representatives of management, labor, academia, the professions, and government agencies. Promotes productivity excellence through the provision of integrated support across the value chain of Hong Kong firms. Defines productivity as "the effective use of innovation and resources to increase the value-added content of products and services." Provides services in four major areas: manufacturing technologies, management systems, information technologies, and environmental technologies.

***Hong Kong Public Companies***. Data Base Asia Ltd., Arion Commercial Centre, Two Queen's Rd. W Hong Kong, China. • Irregular. $700; $116. Covers: Investing in 245 local and 15 overseas companies of the Hong Kong Stock Exchange. Entries include: Company name, details, history, balance sheet.

**Hong Kong Venture Capital and Private Equity Association**. Rm. 2001, Wilson House, 19 - 27 Wyndham St., Central Hong Kong, Hong Kong, China. Phone: 852 21677518; Fax: 852 21677530 ; Email: hkvca@hkvca.com.hk • URL: http://web.hkvca.com.hk/en • Promotes and protects the interests of the venture capital industry in Hong Kong. Educates enterprises about venture capital/private equity as a partner in creating value in the business. Seeks to improve the investment environment in Hong Kong and in the People's Republic of China.

***Hong Kong Week***. Dow Jones & Co., Inc., 1211 Avenue of the Americas New York, NY 10036. Phone: 800-369-5663; Email: service@dowjones.com • URL: http://new.dowjones.com • Weekly. $260.00 per year (air mail). A guide to investing in Hong Kong and China. Provides stock prices, market analysis, and commentary. Edited and published in Hong Kong by the *Asian Wall Street Journal*.

**Hong Kong Women Professionals and Entrepreneurs Association**. Kingswell Commercial Tower, 171-173 Lockhart Rd., Rm. B, 18 Fl. Hong Kong, Hong Kong, China. Phone: 852 28822555; Fax: 852 28824673; Email: info@hkwpea.org • URL: http://www.hkwpea.org • Works to create practical and innovative learning and business opportunities for members and for others. Promotes high professional standards. Reaches out and establishes relationships with counterparts in Mainland China and abroad.

***Hoover's Company Capsules on CD-ROM***. Hoover's Inc., 5800 Airport Blvd. Austin, TX 78752-4204. Phone: 866-443-3939 or (512)374-4500 or (866)281-5969; Fax: (512)374-4501; Email: salesteam@hoovers.com • URL: http://www.hoovers.com • Quarterly. $399.95. CD-ROM contains information on approximately 11,000 U.S. companies and over 30,000 CEOs and CFOs. Database includes: Built-in mailing label capability. Entries include: Company name, address, phone, fax, operations overview, web site address, CEO, CFO, sales, employment size, ticker symbol, stock exchange, industry, fiscal year end.

***Hoover's Company Profiles on CD-ROM***. Hoover's Inc., 5800 Airport Blvd. Austin, TX 78752-4204. Phone: 866-443-3939 or (512)374-4500 or (866)281-5969; Fax: (512)374-4501; Email: salesteam@hoovers.com • URL: http://www.hoovers.com • Quarterly. $324.95 per year. CD-ROM. Contains over 1,200 in-depth company profiles and approximately 200 detailed industry profiles of U.S., international, and private companies. Database includes: 200 industry profiles from the U.S. Department of Commerce. Entries include: Operations, strategies, histories, products and brand names, officers, competitors, locations, and financial informtion.

***Hoover's Guide to the Top New York Companies***. Hoover's Inc., 5800 Airport Blvd. Austin, TX 78752-4204. Phone: 866-443-3939 or (512)374-4500 or (866)281-5969; Fax: (512)374-4501; Email: salesteam@hoovers.com • URL: http://www.hoovers.com • Annual. $24.95 plus $3.50 shipping. Covers: 1,390 leading public and private companies located in New York City. Entries include: Company name, address, phone, fax, web sites, names and titles of key personnel, industry, stock symbols, sales, number of employees.

***Hoover's Guide to the Top Texas Companies: The Ultimate Guide to Texas***. Hoover's Inc., 5800 Airport Blvd. Austin, TX 78752-4204. Phone: 866-443-3939 or (512)374-4500 or (866)281-5969; Fax: (512)374-4501; Email: salesteam@hoovers.com • URL: http://www.hoovers.com • Biennial. $24.95 plus $3.50 shipping. Covers: 850 private and public companies in Texas. The 55 largest companies; another 70 selected firms are described in detail. Database includes: Lists of the top 500 companies ranked by sales and the 50 fastest-growing companies; overview of the Texas economy and business environment. Entries include: For the 30 largest firms—Company name, address, phone, fax, overview of operations and strategies, history, financial data for previous 10 years, names and titles of key personnel, products/services/brand names. For selected firms—Company name, address, phone, fax, names and titles of key personnel, line of business, stock symbols, sales, number of employees. Less detail is given for the remaining firms.

***Hoover's Handbook of American Business***. Dun & Bradstreet Inc. Hoover's Inc., 5800 Airport Blvd. Austin, TX 78752. Phone: 866-739-8839 or (512)374-4500; Fax: (512)374-4051 or (512)374-4501; Email: orders@hoovers.com • URL: http://www.hoovers.com • Annual. $245 Individuals hardcover. Provides detailed profiles of more than 750 large public and private companies, including history, executives, brand names, key competitors, and up to 10 years of financial data. Includes indexes by industry, location, executive name, company name, and brand name.

***Hoover's Handbook of Emerging Companies***. Dun & Bradstreet Inc. Hoover's Inc., 5800 Airport Blvd. Austin, TX 78752. Phone: 866-739-8839 or (512)374-4500; Fax: (512)374-4051 or (512)374-4501; Email: orders@hoovers.com • URL: http://www.hoovers.com • Annual. $213. Contains detailed profiles of 600 rapidly growing corporations. Includes indexes by industry, location, executive name, company name, and brand name.

***Hoover's Handbook of Private Companies***. Dun & Bradstreet Inc. Hoover's Inc., 5800 Airport Blvd. Austin, TX 78752. Phone: 866-739-8839 or (512)374-4500; Fax: (512)374-4051 or (512)374-4501; Email: orders@hoovers.com • URL: http://www.hoovers.com • Annual. $245. Contains profiles of 900 private companies and organizations. Includes indexes by industry, location, executive name, and product.

***Hoover's Handbook of Private Companies: Profiles of Major U.S. Private Enterprises***. Hoover's Inc., 5800 Airport Blvd. Austin, TX 78752-4204. Phone: 866-443-3939 or (512)374-4500 or (866)281-5969; Fax: (512)374-4501; Email: salesteam@hoovers.com • URL: http://www.hoovers.com • Annual. $215 Individuals hardcover. Covers: 900 privately held companies and other enterprises; 250 firms are covered in detail. Entries include: Company name, address, phone, fax, brief overview of operations, products, competitors, names and titles of key personnel, sales, number of employees; detailed entries add in-depth profile of operations and strategies, financial data for preceding 10 years.

***Hoover's Handbook of World Business***. Dun & Bradstreet Inc. Hoover's Inc., 5800 Airport Blvd. Austin, TX 78752. Phone: 866-739-8839 or (512)374-4500; Fax: (512)374-4051 or (512)374-4501; Email: orders@hoovers.com • URL: http://www.hoovers.com • Annual. $225 Individuals Hardcover. Covers: Hundreds of companies headquartered outside the U.S., including many with substantial activity in the U.S.; global enterprises, businesses that dominate their respective industries, and representative companies from all major industries. Entries include: Company name, overview, history, exchange and stock symbols, fiscal year-end date, names and titles of key personnel, name of auditors, number of employees, headquarters address, phone, fax, description of where the company does business, specific products/services/brand names produced, key competitors, 10 years of key financial data.

***Hoover's Masterlist of Latin American Companies***. Hoover's Inc., 5800 Airport Blvd. Austin, TX 78752-4204. Phone: 866-443-3939 or (512)374-4500 or (866)281-5969; Fax: (512)374-4501; Email: salesteam@hoovers.com • URL: http://www.hoovers.com • $79.95 Book. Covers: 2,500 profiles of the largest public and private companies in Latin America. Database includes: All financial information converted to U.S. dollars. Entries include: Headquarters, address, phone, fax, key officers, industry description, sales figures, employment data.

***Hoover's Masterlist of Major Asian Companies***. Hoover's Inc., 5800 Airport Blvd. Austin, TX 78752-4204. Phone: 866-443-

3939 or (512)374-4500 or (866)281-5969; Fax: (512)374-4501; Email: salesteam@hoovers.com • URL: http://www.hoovers.com • $79.95. Covers: More than 3,000 companies in 10 Asian countries. Entries include: Name, address, phone, fax, names and titles of key personnel, financial data, employment data, description of industry.

***Hoover's Masterlist of Major European Companies***. Hoover's Inc., 5800 Airport Blvd. Austin, TX 78752-4204. Phone: 866-443-3939 or (512)374-4500 or (866)281-5969; Fax: (512)374-4501; Email: salesteam@hoovers.com • URL: http://www.hoovers.com • $79.95 Book. Covers: 2,500 profiles of the largest public and private companies in Western Europe, including Greece and Turkey, plus all companies on the major European stock indexes. Database includes: All financial information converted to U.S. dollars. Entries include: Headquarters, address, phone, fax, key officers, industry description, sales figures, employment data.

***Hoover's MasterList of Major U.S. Companies***. Hoover's Inc., 5800 Airport Blvd. Austin, TX 78752-4204. Phone: 866-443-3939 or (512)374-4500 or (866)281-5969; Fax: (512)374-4501; Email: salesteam@hoovers.com • URL: http://www.hoovers.com • $320 Individuals hardcover. Covers: Over 10,000 of the largest public and private companies in the U.S. Entries include: Company name, address, phone, fax, web site addresses, names and titles of key personnel, company overview, stock symbols, net income, market value, sales and employment data, fiscal year end.

***Hoover's Online***. Hoover's Inc., 5800 Airport Blvd. Austin, TX 78752-4204. Phone: 866-443-3939 or (512)374-4500 or (866)281-5969; Fax: (512)374-4501; Email: salesteam@hoovers.com • URL: http://www.hoovers.com • Web site provides stock quotes, lists of companies, and a variety of business information at no charge. In-depth company profiles are available.

***Horse Riding & Rentals Directory***. InfoGroup Inc., 5711 S 86th Cir. Omaha, NE 68127-4146. Phone: (402)593-4500 • URL: http://www.infogroup.com • Annual. Number of listings: 6968. Entries include: Name, address, phone, size of advertisement, name of owner or manager, number of employees, year first in "Yellow Pages." Compiled from telephone company "Yellow Pages," nationwide.

***Horseman and Fair World: Devoted to the Trotting and Pacing Horse***. Horseman Publishing Co., Insite Communications, P.O. Box 8480 Lexington, KY 40533-8480. Phone: (606)276-4026; Fax: (606)277-8100 • URL: http://www.harnessracing.com • $50.

***Horticultural Science Abstracts***. CABI Publishing North America, 38 Chauncey St., Ste. 1002 Boston, MA 02111. Phone: 800-552-3083; Email: cabi-nao@cabi.org • URL: http://www.cabi.org • Updated weekly online; also available in print, delivered monthly.

***Horticulture: Gardening at its Best***. Krause Publications Inc., 700 E State St. Iola, WI 54990-0001. Phone: 800-726-9966 or (715)445-2214 or (715)445-4612; Fax: (715)445-4087 • URL: http://www.krause.com • Bimonthly. $19.95 per year.

**Hosiery Association**. 7421 Carmel Executive Park Dr., Ste. 200 Charlotte, NC 28226. Phone: (704)365-0913; Fax: (704)362-2056; Email: thainfo@hosieryassociation.com • URL: http://www.hosieryassociation.com • Hosiery manufacturers and suppliers. Develops standards for hosiery measurement. Sponsors annual "Celebrate Hosiery" to educate consumers on hosiery varieties. Conducts field visitations for assistance in technical areas. Compiles statistics; conducts research programs. Operates Group Purchasing Program.

***Hosiery News***. Hosiery Association, 7421 Carmel Executive Park Dr., Ste. 200 Charlotte, NC 28226. Phone: (704)365-0913; Fax: (704)362-2056; Email: thainfo@hosieryassociation.com • URL: http://www.hosieryassociation.com • Monthly. Hosiery-related news including new offerings for retail, industry changes, legislative updates of hosiery-impacting laws, foreign trade and statistical information.

***Hospital Home Health: The Monthly Updates for Executives and Health Care Professionals***. AHC Media, 950 E Paces Ferry Rd. NE Atlanta, GA 30326. Phone: 800-688-2421 or (404)262-5476; Fax: (404)262-5560; Email: editorial_questions@ahcmedia.com • URL: http://www.ahcmedia.com • Monthly. $399.00 per year. Newsletter for hospital-based home health agencies.

***Hospital Liability***. ALM Media Properties LLC, 120 Broadway, 5th Fl. New York, NY 10271-1100. Phone: (212)457-9400; Fax: (646)417-7705; Email: customercare@alm.com • URL: http://www.alm.com • $550. Written for attorneys representing either hospitals or patients of hospitals. Covers a wide variety of legal topics relating to hospital/physician malpractice, including the expansion of HMO liability. (Law Journal Press).

***Hospital Pharmacist Report***. Thomson Medical Economics, 5 Paragon Dr. Montvale, NJ 07645-1742. Phone: 800-526-4870 or (201)358-7200; Fax: (201)573-8999 or (201)722-2680; Email: customer.service@medec.com • URL: http://www.medec.com • Monthly. $39.00 per year. Covers both business and clinical topics for hospital pharmacists.

**Hospitality Financial and Technology Professionals**. 11709 Boulder Ln., Ste. 110 Austin, TX 78726. Phone: 800-646-4387 or (512)249-5333; Fax: (512)249-1533; Email: membership@hftp.org • URL: http://www.hftp.org • Accountants, financial officers and MIS managers in 50 countries working in hotels, resorts, casinos, restaurants, and clubs. Develops uniform system of accounts. Conducts education, training, and certification programs; offers placement service; maintains hall of fame.

***Hospitality Technology: Guiding High-Growth Businesses to Best-Choice IT Solutions***. Edgell Communications Inc., 4 Middlebury Blvd., Ste. 1 Randolph, NJ 07869-1121. Fax: (973)252-9020 • URL: http://www.edgellcommunications.com • 10/year. Covers information technology, computer communications, and software for foodservice and lodging enterprises.

***Hospitals Directory***. InfoGroup Inc., 5711 S 86th Cir. Omaha, NE 68127-4146. Phone: (402)593-4500 • URL: http://www.infogroup.com • Annual. Number of listings: 13,914. Entries include: Name, address, phone, size of advertisement, name of owner or manager, number of employees, year first in "Yellow Pages." Compiled from telephone company "Yellow Pages," nationwide.

***Hospodarsky Almanach***. CompAlmanach spol S.R.O., Jezkova 1 13000 Prague, Czech Republic. Phone: 420 2 272773; Fax: 420 2 279356; Email: compalm@cmicron.Felle.cvnt.cz • Annual. $110. Covers: Approximately 20,000 Czech companies in commerce, industry, service, and trading. Entries include: Company name, address, phone, fax, founding date, capital, name of general manager, board, owner, turnover rate, number in trade register, languages for correspondence, banking-relations, number of employees, countries of import, countries of export, branches, mechanical equipment, production lines.

***Hotel & Restaurant: The Accommodation, Food and Beverage Business Magazine for Southern Africa***. Ramsay, Son & Parker Ltd., Uitvlught 3 Howard Dr., Howard Pl. Pinelands 7405, South Africa. Phone: 27 21 5303100; Fax: 27 21 5313333; Email: email@ramsaymedia.co.za • URL: http://www.rsp.co.za • Monthly. $168 Individuals; $17 Single issue. Trade magazine for the hospitality industry in South Africa.

***Hotel and Travel Index: The World Wide Hotel Directory***. Northstar Travel Media L.L.C., 100 Lighting Way, 2nd Fl. Secaucus, NJ 07094. Phone: 800-742-7076 or (201)902-2000 or (201)902-1800; Fax: (201)902-2045 or (201)319-1947; Email: secaushelpdesk@ntmllc.com • URL: http://www.northstartravelmedia.com • Quarterly. $185 per year; $60 Single issue. Contains concise information on more than 41,000 hotels in the U. S. and around the world. Includes 400 maps showing location of hotels and airports.

***Hotel Business***. ICD Publications, 45 Research Way, Ste. 106 East Setauket, NY 11733. Phone: (631)246-9300; Fax: (631)246-9496; Email: info@hotelbusiness.com • URL: http://www.homeworldbusiness.com • Biweekly. $260 Individuals domestic; $315 Canada and Mexico; $695 Other countries; $395 Individuals digital. Trade magazine covering the hotel industry.

***Hotel Directory and Travel Guide***. Radius, the Global Travel Co., 4330 East-West W Hwy., Ste. 1100 Bethesda, MD 20814-4408. Phone: (301)718-9500; Fax: (301)718-4290; Email: information@radiustravel.com • URL: http://www.raduistravel.com • $1,475 U.S. 1/8 page; $2,875 U.S. 1/4 page; $4,250 U.S. 1/2 page; $7,150 U.S. full page black & white; $7,925 U.S. adjacent lack cover; $8,150 U.S. adjacent front cover; $9,050 U.S. black & white inserts; $11,775 U.S. full page coupon 2-color,2- sided; $12,350 U.S. 4-color text inserts; $16,125 U.S. insert back cover. Covers: nearly 9,000 hotels in 135 countries offering 'preferred rates'; international coverage. Entries include: Hotel name, address, phone, regular rate for single room, preferred rate for single and double rooms, facilities, amenities, city and county travel information, and maps.

***Hotel Management***. Advanstar Communications, 545 Boylston St. Boston, MA 02116. Phone: 888-527-7008 or (617)267-6500; Fax: (617)267-6900; Email: info@advanstar.com • URL: http://www.advanstar.com.

**Hotel Technology Next Generation**. 650 E Algonquin Rd., Ste. 207 Schaumburg, IL 60173. Phone: (847)303-5560; Email: info@htng.org • URL: http://www.htng.org • Promotes collaboration and partnership among hoteliers and technology providers. Serves as the voice of the global hotel community and facilitates the development of technology models for the hospitality industry. Works to increase the effectiveness and efficiency of hotels and creates a healthy ecosystem of technology suppliers.

***Hotels: The Magazine of the Worldwide Hotel Industry***. International Hotel Association. Reed Elsevier Group plc Reed Business Information, 360 Park Ave. S New York, NY 11010. Phone: (212)791-4208; Email: corporatecommunications@reedbusiness.com • URL: http://www.reedbusiness.com • Contains critical information on all aspects of the worldwide hotel industry including design, food & beverage, finance, development marketing and technology.

***Hourly Precipitation Data***. U.S. National Climatic Data Center, Federal Bldg., 151 Patton Ave. Asheville, NC 28801-5001. Phone: (828)271-4800; Fax: (828)271-4010; Email: ncdc.orders@noaa.gov • URL: http://www.ncdc.noaa.gov • Monthly. Published separately for 41 states.

***House Furnishings Directory—Retail***. InfoGroup Inc., 5711 S 86th Cir. Omaha, NE 68127-4146. Phone: (402)593-4500 • URL: http://www.infogroup.com • Annual. Number of listings: 2,728. Entries include: Name, address, phone, size of advertisement, name of owner or manager, number of employees, year first in "Yellow Pages." Compiled from telephone company "Yellow Pages," nationwide.

***Houseboats Directory—Rentals***. InfoGroup Inc., 5711 S 86th Cir. Omaha, NE 68127-4146. Phone: (402)593-4500 • URL: http://www.infogroup.com • Annual. Number of listings: 5274. Entries include: Name, address, phone, size of advertisement, name of owner or manager, number of employees, year first in "Yellow Pages." Compiled from telephone company "Yellow Pages," nationwide.

***Household and Personal Products Industry Buyers Guide***. Rodman Publications, 70 Hilltop Rd. Ramsey, NJ 07446. Phone: (201)825-2552; Fax: (201)825-0553; Email: happi@rodpub.com • URL: http://www.happi.com • Annual. Lists of suppliers to manufacturers of cosmetics, toiletries, soaps, detergents, and related household and personal products.

***Household and Personal Products Industry Contract Manufacturing/Private Label Directory***. Rodman Publications, 70 Hilltop Rd. Ramsey, NJ 07446. Phone: (201)825-2552; Fax: (201)825-0553; Email: happi@rodpub.com • URL: http://www.happi.com • Annual. Provides information for about 450 companies offering private label or contract packaged household and personal care products, such as detergents, cosmetics, polishes, insecticides, and various aerosol items.

***Household and Personal Products Industry: The Magazine for the Detergent, Soap, Cosmetic and Toiletry, Wax, Polish and Aerosol Industries***. Rodman Publications, 70 Hilltop Rd. Ramsey, NJ 07446. Phone: (201)825-2552; Fax: (201)825-0553; Email: happi@rodpub.com • URL: http://www.happi.com • Monthly. Covers marketing, packaging, production, technical innovations, private label developments, and aerosol packaging for soap, detergents, cosmetics, insecticides, and a variety of other household products.

***Household Appliances (Major) Directory—Dealers***. InfoGroup Inc., 5711 S 86th Cir. Omaha, NE 68127-4146. Phone: (402)593-4500 • URL: http://www.infogroup.com • Annual. Number of listings: 21,271. Entries include: Name, address, phone, size of advertisement, name of owner or manager, number of employees, year first in "Yellow Pages." Compiled from telephone company "Yellow Pages," nationwide.

***Housing Affairs Letter: The Weekly Washington Report on Housing***. Community Development Services, Inc. CD Publications, 8204 Fenton St. Silver Spring, MD 20910. Phone: 800-666-6380 or (301)588-6380; Fax: (301)588-6385; Email: info@cdpublications.com • URL: http://www.cdpublications.com • Weekly. $624 print and online, 12 months. Covers mortgage activity news, including forecasts of mortgage rates.

***Housing and Commercial Real Estate News Roundup***. Urban Land Institute, 1025 Thomas Jefferson St. NW, Ste. 500 W Washington, DC 20007. Phone: 800-321-5011 or (202)624-7000; Fax: (202)624-7140; Email: customerservice@uli.org • URL: http://www.uli.org • Description: Summarizes current developments in land use, real estate development, and related areas.

***Housing Discrimination: Law and Litigation***. Robert G. Schwemm. Thomson West, 610 Opperman Dr. Eagan, MN 55123. Phone: 800-328-9352 or (651)687-7000 • Annual. $593 full set; $47 monthly. Covers provisions of the Fair Housing Act and related topics.

***Housing the Elderly Report***. Community Development Services, Inc. CD Publications, 8204 Fenton St. Silver Spring, MD 20910. Phone: 800-666-6380 or (301)588-6380; Fax: (301)588-6385; Email: info@cdpublications.com • URL: http://www.cdpublications.com • Monthly. $249.00 per year. Newsletter. Edited for retirement communities, apartment projects, and nursing homes. Covers news relative to business and property management issues.

***Houston International Business Directory***. Houston Chamber of Commerce, 1200 Smith Ste. 700 Houston, TX 77002. Phone: (713)844-3600 or (713)644-7070; Fax: (713)844-0200 or (713)644-7377; Email: ghp@houston.org • URL: http://www.houston.org • Annual. $20 Individuals MBS; $40 Individuals NON. Covers: More than 3,300 U.S. and foreign companies involved in international business activities in Houston, Texas. Entries include: Company name, address, phone, principal executives, type of business, imports/exports.

***Houston JobBank: The Job Hunter's Guide to Houston***. Adams Media Corp., 57 Littlefield St. Avon, MA 02322. Phone: 800-872-5627 or (508)427-7100; Fax: (508)427-6790 or (800)872-5628; Email: deskcopies@adamsmedia.com • URL: http://www.adamsmedia.com • Annual. $17.95 Individuals 3 used & new. Covers: Over 4,000 employers in Houston, Texas and the surrounding areas including Bayton, Beaumont, Galveston, Pasadena. Database includes: Information on the basics of job winning and writing resumes and cover letters; electronic job search information; 330 industry associations; 90 online career resources; 145 employment services. Entries include: Firm or organization name, address, local phone, toll-free phone, fax, recorded jobline, e-mail, URL, hours, name and title of contact; description of organization; headquarters location, subsidiaries, operations at the facility, names of management, typical titles for common positions, educational backgrounds desired, number of projected hires, fringe benefits offered, stock exchange listing, training programs, internships, parent company, number of employees, revenues, other U.S. locations, international locations.

***Houston 1000 Corporate Directory.*** • $115 Members plus $3.00 shipping and handling; $155 Nonmembers plus $3.00 shipping and handling. Covers: 7,000 major businesses in the Houston area. Entries include: Company name, address, phone, fax, type of business, names and titles of key officers and personnel, number of employees.

***How Products Are Made.*** Cengage Learning Inc., 20 Channel Center St. Boston, MA 02210. Phone: 800-487-8488 or (617)289-7700; Fax: (617)289-7844; Email: investors@cengage.com • URL: http://www.cengage.com • $211 Individuals. 2007. Volume 7. $192. Provides easy-to-read, step-by-step descriptions of how approximately 100 different products are manufactured. eBook also available.

***How to Find Business Intelligence in Washington.*** MarketResearch.com, 11200 Rockville Pke., Ste. 504 Rockville, MD 20852. Phone: 800-298-5699 or (240)747-3093; Fax: (240)747-3004; Email: customerservice@marketresearch.com • URL: http://www.marketresearch.com • $295 payment with order; $301 billed. Covers: over 500 government libraries, archives, offices, agencies, statistical centers, and other sources of publications, market studies, statistical summaries, and census data. Entries include: Office, agency, or organization name, address, phone, description of information, price (if any).

***How to Find Information about Companies.*** MarketResearch.com, 11200 Rockville Pke., Ste. 504 Rockville, MD 20852. Phone: 800-298-5699 or (240)747-3093; Fax: (240)747-3004; Email: customerservice@marketresearch.com • URL: http://www.marketresearch.com • Annual. $395 per volume; $885 entire set. Covers: in Part 1, over 9,000 sources of corporate intelligence, including federal, state, and local repositories of company filings, individual industry experts, published sources, databases, CD-ROM products, and corporate research services. Entries include: Source name, address, phone, contact name, description. Parts 2 and 3 provide guidelines for company research.

***How to Find Information about Private Companies.*** MarketResearch.com, 11200 Rockville Pke., Ste. 504 Rockville, MD 20852. Phone: 800-298-5699 or (240)747-3093; Fax: (240)747-3004; Email: customerservice@marketresearch.com • URL: http://www.marketresearch.com • Irregular. $59. Covers: Organizations, publications, and individuals that collect information on private companies. Database includes: Corporate research tips. Entries include: Name, address, phone.

***How to Manage Conflict in the Organization.*** American Management Association Extension Institute, 1601 Broadway New York, NY 10019. Phone: 800-262-9699 or (518)586-8100; Fax: (518)903-8168 • Looseleaf. $139.00. Self-study course. Emphasis is on practical explanations, examples, and problem solving. Quizzes and a case study are included.

***How to Market Your Business.*** • 2009. eBook. Published by Kogan Page. Covers market research, advertising, promotion, selling techniques, product launches, and use of the internet - everything you need to ensure your product reaches your market successfully.

***How to Organize and Run a Small Business.*** American CPE Inc., 826 Riviera Mansfield, TX 76063. Phone: 800-990-4273 or (817)477-0222; Fax: (817)473-4998; Email: director@americancpe.com • URL: http://www.americancpe.com • Contains detailed training information covering the basics of creating, organizing, and running a small business.

***How to Plan and Manage Warehouse Operations.*** American Management Association Extension Institute, 1601 Broadway New York, NY 10019. Phone: 800-262-9699 or (518)586-8100; Fax: (518)903-8168 • Looseleaf. $159.00. Self-study course. Emphasis is on practical explanations, examples, and problem solving. Quizzes and a case study are included.

***How to Prepare a Business Plan.*** Cengage Learning Inc., 20 Channel Center St. Boston, MA 02210. Phone: 800-487-8488 or (617)289-7700; Fax: (617)289-7844; Email: investors@cengage.com • URL: http://www.cengage.com • 2009. eBook. 5th edition. Published by Kogan Page. Offers advice on writing a business plan, producing cash flow forecasts, planning the borrowing and expanding the business.

***How to Start a Business in Alabama.*** Entrepreneur Press, 2445 McCabe Way, Ste. 400 Irvine, CA 92614-6244. Phone: 800-864-6864 or (949)261-2325 or (949)622-7131; Fax: (949)261-7729 or (949)261-0234; Email: press@entrepreneur.com • URL: http://www.entrepreneurpress.com • $24.95 Individuals paperback. Entries include: Detailed information on mailing addresses, Internet addresses, and telephone numbers of federal, state, local and private agencies.

***How to Start a Business in Alaska.*** Entrepreneur Press, 2445 McCabe Way, Ste. 400 Irvine, CA 92614-6244. Phone: 800-864-6864 or (949)261-2325 or (949)622-7131; Fax: (949)261-7729 or (949)261-0234; Email: press@entrepreneur.com • URL: http://www.entrepreneurpress.com • Annual. $24.95 Individuals paperback. Entries include: Detailed information on mailing addresses, Internet addresses, and telephone numbers of federal, state, local and private agencies.

***How to Start a Business in Arkansas.*** Entrepreneur Press, 2445 McCabe Way, Ste. 400 Irvine, CA 92614-6244. Phone: 800-864-6864 or (949)261-2325 or (949)622-7131; Fax: (949)261-7729 or (949)261-0234; Email: press@entrepreneur.com • URL: http://www.entrepreneurpress.com • Annual. $24.95 Individuals paperback. Entries include: Detailed information on mailing addresses, Internet addresses, and telephone numbers of federal, state, local and private agencies.

***How to Start a Business in Delaware.*** Entrepreneur Press, 2445 McCabe Way, Ste. 400 Irvine, CA 92614-6244. Phone: 800-864-6864 or (949)261-2325 or (949)622-7131; Fax: (949)261-7729 or (949)261-0234; Email: press@entrepreneur.com • URL: http://www.entrepreneurpress.com • Annual. $24.95 Individuals paperback. Entries include: Detailed information on mailing addresses, Internet addresses, and telephone numbers of federal, state, local and private agencies.

***How to Start a Business in District of Columbia.*** Entrepreneur Press, 2445 McCabe Way, Ste. 400 Irvine, CA 92614-6244. Phone: 800-864-6864 or (949)261-2325 or (949)622-7131; Fax: (949)261-7729 or (949)261-0234; Email: press@entrepreneur.com • URL: http://www.entrepreneurpress.com • Annual. $24.95 Individuals paperback. Entries include: Detailed information on mailing addresses, Internet addresses, and telephone numbers of federal, state, local and private agencies.

***How to Start a Business in Idaho.*** Entrepreneur Press, 2445 McCabe Way, Ste. 400 Irvine, CA 92614-6244. Phone: 800-864-6864 or (949)261-2325 or (949)622-7131; Fax: (949)261-7729 or (949)261-0234; Email: press@entrepreneur.com • URL: http://www.entrepreneurpress.com • Annual. $24.95 Individuals paperback. Entries include: Detailed information on mailing addresses, Internet addresses, and telephone numbers of federal, state, local and private agencies.

***How to Start a Business in Iowa.*** Entrepreneur Press, 2445 McCabe Way, Ste. 400 Irvine, CA 92614-6244. Phone: 800-864-6864 or (949)261-2325 or (949)622-7131; Fax: (949)261-7729 or (949)261-0234; Email: press@entrepreneur.com • URL: http://www.entrepreneurpress.com • $24.95 Individuals paperback. Entries include: Detailed information on mailing addresses, Internet addresses, and telephone numbers of federal, state, local and private agencies.

***How to Start a Business in Kansas.*** Entrepreneur Press, 2445 McCabe Way, Ste. 400 Irvine, CA 92614-6244. Phone: 800-864-6864 or (949)261-2325 or (949)622-7131; Fax: (949)261-7729 or (949)261-0234; Email: press@entrepreneur.com • URL: http://www.entrepreneurpress.com • Annual. $24.95 Individuals paperback. Entries include: Detailed information on mailing addresses, Internet addresses, and telephone numbers of federal, state, local and private agencies.

***How to Start a Business in Kentucky.*** Entrepreneur Press, 2445 McCabe Way, Ste. 400 Irvine, CA 92614-6244. Phone: 800-864-6864 or (949)261-2325 or (949)622-7131; Fax: (949)261-7729 or (949)261-0234; Email: press@entrepreneur.com • URL: http://www.entrepreneurpress.com • Annual. $24.95 Individuals paperback. Entries include: Detailed information on mailing addresses, Internet addresses, and telephone numbers of federal, state, local and private agencies.

***How to Start a Business in Louisiana.*** Entrepreneur Press, 2445 McCabe Way, Ste. 400 Irvine, CA 92614-6244. Phone: 800-864-6864 or (949)261-2325 or (949)622-7131; Fax: (949)261-7729 or (949)261-0234; Email: press@entrepreneur.com • URL: http://www.entrepreneurpress.com • Annual. $24.95 Individuals paperback. Entries include: Detailed information on mailing addresses, Internet addresses, and telephone numbers of federal, state, local and private agencies.

***How to Start a Business in Maine.*** Entrepreneur Press, 2445 McCabe Way, Ste. 400 Irvine, CA 92614-6244. Phone: 800-864-6864 or (949)261-2325 or (949)622-7131; Fax: (949)261-7729 or (949)261-0234; Email: press@entrepreneur.com • URL: http://www.entrepreneurpress.com • Annual. $24.95 Individuals paperback. Entries include: Detailed information on mailing addresses, Internet addresses, and telephone numbers of federal, state, local and private agencies.

***How to Start a Business in Mississippi.*** Entrepreneur Press, 2445 McCabe Way, Ste. 400 Irvine, CA 92614-6244. Phone: 800-864-6864 or (949)261-2325 or (949)622-7131; Fax: (949)261-7729 or (949)261-0234; Email: press@entrepreneur.com • URL: http://www.entrepreneurpress.com • Annual. $24.95 Individuals paperback. Entries include: Detailed information on mailing addresses, Internet addresses, and telephone numbers of federal, state, local and private agencies.

***How to Start a Business in Montana.*** Entrepreneur Press, 2445 McCabe Way, Ste. 400 Irvine, CA 92614-6244. Phone: 800-864-6864 or (949)261-2325 or (949)622-7131; Fax: (949)261-7729 or (949)261-0234; Email: press@entrepreneur.com • URL: http://www.entrepreneurpress.com • $24.95 Individuals paperback. Entries include: Detailed information on mailing addresses, Internet addresses, and telephone numbers of federal, state, local and private agencies.

***How to Start a Business in Nebraska.*** Entrepreneur Press, 2445 McCabe Way, Ste. 400 Irvine, CA 92614-6244. Phone: 800-864-6864 or (949)261-2325 or (949)622-7131; Fax: (949)261-7729 or (949)261-0234; Email: press@entrepreneur.com • URL: http://www.entrepreneurpress.com • Annual. $24.95 Individuals paperback. Entries include: Detailed information on mailing addresses, Internet addresses, and telephone numbers of federal, state, local and private agencies.

***How to Start a Business in Nevada.*** Entrepreneur Press, 2445 McCabe Way, Ste. 400 Irvine, CA 92614-6244. Phone: 800-864-6864 or (949)261-2325 or (949)622-7131; Fax: (949)261-7729 or (949)261-0234; Email: press@entrepreneur.com • URL: http://www.entrepreneurpress.com • Annual. $24.95 Individuals paperback. Entries include: Detailed information on mailing addresses, Internet addresses, and telephone numbers of federal, state, local and private agencies.

***How to Start a Business in New Mexico.*** Entrepreneur Press, 2445 McCabe Way, Ste. 400 Irvine, CA 92614-6244. Phone: 800-864-6864 or (949)261-2325 or (949)622-7131; Fax: (949)261-7729 or (949)261-0234; Email: press@entrepreneur.com • URL: http://www.entrepreneurpress.com • Annual. $24.95 Individuals paperback. Entries include: Detailed information on mailing addresses, Internet addresses, and telephone numbers of federal, state, local and private agencies.

***How to Start a Business in New York City.*** Entrepreneur Press, 2445 McCabe Way, Ste. 400 Irvine, CA 92614-6244. Phone: 800-864-6864 or (949)261-2325 or (949)622-7131; Fax: (949)261-7729 or (949)261-0234; Email: press@entrepreneur.com • URL: http://www.entrepreneurpress.com • Annual. $24.95 Individuals paperback. Entries include: Detailed information on mailing addresses, Internet addresses, and telephone numbers of federal, state, local and private agencies.

***How to Start a Business in North Dakota.*** Entrepreneur Press, 2445 McCabe Way, Ste. 400 Irvine, CA 92614-6244. Phone: 800-864-6864 or (949)261-2325 or (949)622-7131; Fax: (949)261-7729 or (949)261-0234; Email: press@entrepreneur.com • URL: http://www.entrepreneurpress.com • $24.95 Individuals paperback. Entries include: Detailed information on mailing addresses, Internet addresses, and telephone numbers of federal, state, local and private agencies.

***How to Start a Business in Oklahoma.*** Entrepreneur Press, 2445 McCabe Way, Ste. 400 Irvine, CA 92614-6244. Phone: 800-864-6864 or (949)261-2325 or (949)622-7131; Fax: (949)261-7729 or (949)261-0234; Email: press@entrepreneur.com • URL: http://www.entrepreneurpress.com • Annual. $24.95 Individuals paperback. Entries include: Detailed information on mailing addresses, Internet addresses, and telephone numbers of federal, state, local and private agencies.

***How to Start a Business in Rhode Island.*** Entrepreneur Press, 2445 McCabe Way, Ste. 400 Irvine, CA 92614-6244. Phone: 800-864-6864 or (949)261-2325 or (949)622-7131; Fax: (949)261-7729 or (949)261-0234; Email: press@entrepreneur.com • URL: http://www.entrepreneurpress.com • Annual. $24.95 Individuals paperback. Entries include: Detailed information on mailing addresses, Internet addresses, and telephone numbers of federal, state, local and private agencies.

***How to Start a Business in South Dakota.*** Entrepreneur Press, 2445 McCabe Way, Ste. 400 Irvine, CA 92614-6244. Phone: 800-864-6864 or (949)261-2325 or (949)622-7131; Fax: (949)261-7729 or (949)261-0234; Email: press@entrepreneur.com • URL: http://www.entrepreneurpress.com • Annual. $24.95 Individuals paperback. Entries include: Detailed information on mailing addresses, Internet addresses, and telephone numbers of federal, state, local and private agencies.

***How to Start a Business in Utah.*** Entrepreneur Press, 2445 McCabe Way, Ste. 400 Irvine, CA 92614-6244. Phone: 800-864-6864 or (949)261-2325 or (949)622-7131; Fax: (949)261-7729 or (949)261-0234; Email: press@entrepreneur.com • URL: http://www.entrepreneurpress.com • Annual. $24.95 Individuals paperback. Entries include: Detailed information on mailing addresses, Internet addresses, and telephone numbers of federal, state, local and private agencies.

***How to Start a Business in Vermont.*** Entrepreneur Press, 2445 McCabe Way, Ste. 400 Irvine, CA 92614-6244. Phone: 800-864-6864 or (949)261-2325 or (949)622-7131; Fax: (949)261-7729 or (949)261-0234; Email: press@entrepreneur.com • URL: http://www.entrepreneurpress.com • Annual. $24.95 Individuals paperback. Entries include: Detailed information on mailing addresses, Internet addresses, and telephone numbers of federal, state, local and private agencies.

***How to Start a Business in West Virginia.*** Entrepreneur Press, 2445 McCabe Way, Ste. 400 Irvine, CA 92614-6244. Phone: 800-864-6864 or (949)261-2325 or (949)622-7131; Fax: (949)261-7729 or (949)261-0234; Email: press@entrepreneur.com • URL: http://www.entrepreneurpress.com • Annual. $24.95 Individuals paperback. Entries include: Detailed information on mailing addresses, Internet addresses, and telephone numbers of federal, state, local and private agencies.

***How to Start a Business in Wyoming.*** Entrepreneur Press, 2445 McCabe Way, Ste. 400 Irvine, CA 92614-6244. Phone: 800-864-6864 or (949)261-2325 or (949)622-7131; Fax: (949)261-7729 or (949)261-0234; Email: press@entrepreneur.com • URL: http://www.entrepreneurpress.com • Annual. $24.95 Individuals paperback. Entries include: Detailed information on mailing addresses, Internet addresses, and telephone numbers of federal, state, local and private agencies.

***How to Start, Run, and Stay in Business: The Nuts-and-Bolts***

***Guide to Turning Your Business Dream into a Reality***. John Wiley & Sons Inc., 111 River St. Hoboken, NJ 07030-5774. Phone: 800-225-5945 or (201)748-6000; Fax: (201)748-6088; Email: info@wiley.com • URL: http://www.wiley.com • $20 Individuals paperback. Covers: Every aspect of starting and running a business.

***How to Value and Sell Your Business***. Cengage Learning Inc., 20 Channel Center St. Boston, MA 02210. Phone: 800-487-8488 or (617)289-7700; Fax: (617)289-7844; Email: investors@cengage.com • URL: http://www.cengage.com • 2009. eBook. Published by Kogan Page. Provides in-depth commentary and advice on the valuation and sale of a small- to medium-sized business, developing an exit strategy, tax and legal issues, marketing your business, managing the sale process, etc, in order to ensure maximum profit.

***How to Write a Business Plan***. American Management Association Extension Institute, 1601 Broadway New York, NY 10019. Phone: 800-262-9699 or (518)586-8100; Fax: (518)903-8168 • Looseleaf. $159.00. Self-study course. Emphasis is on practical explanations, examples, and problem solving. Quizzes and a case study are included.

***Howick, Lidgetton, Merrivale, Mpophomeni Directory***. A.C. Braby (Pty) Ltd., 12 Caversham Rd. Pinetown 3610, South Africa. Email: support@brabys.co.za • URL: http://www.brabys.com • Annual. Covers: Businesses in Howick, Lidgetton, Merrivale, and Mpophomeni. Database includes: Maps. Entries include: Company name, address, phone, and descriptive text.

***HPAC Engineering Info-Dex***. Penton Media Inc., 1300 E 9th St. Cleveland, OH 44114-1501. Phone: (216)696-7000; Fax: (216)696-1752; Email: information@penton.com • URL: http://penton.com • Annual. $30. Industry directory of products, manufacturers, and trade names and a composite of catalog data for mechanical systems engineering professionals.

***HPAC Techlit Selector***. Penton Media Inc., 1300 E 9th St. Cleveland, OH 44114-1501. Phone: (216)696-7000; Fax: (216)696-1752; Email: information@penton.com • URL: http://penton.com • Semiannual. Free to qualified personnel. Manufacturers' catalogs and technical literature.

***HQ: Good Design is Good Business***. McGraw-Hill Inc., 4747 E Elliot Rd., No. 29-339 Phoenix, AZ 85044. • URL: http://www.southwest.construction.com • Quarterly. Design magazine for C-level executives, building owners and developers, and design and construction professionals.

***HR Briefing***. Wolters Kluwer Law and Business, 76 9th Ave., 7th Fl. New York, NY 10011-4962. Phone: 800-234-1660 or (212)771-0600; Fax: (800)901-9075 or (301)644-3550 • URL: http://www.wolterskluwerlb.com • Monthly. $249.00 per year. Newsletter. Provides HR professionals and other business people with concise, up-to-date information on employment practices and trends, with an emphasis on compliance with federal employment laws.

***HR Magazine (Human Resources): Strategies and Solutions for Human Resource Professionals***. Society for Human Resource Management, 1800 Duke St. Alexandria, VA 22314. Phone: 800-253-7476 or (703)548-3440 or (703)548-6999; Fax: (703)535-6490 or (703)548-6490; Email: shrm@shrm.org • URL: http://www.shrm.org • Monthly. $70; $90 Canada; $125 Other countries. Formerly *Personnel Administrator*.

**HR People and Strategy**. 1800 Duke St. Alexandria, VA 22314. Phone: 888-602-3270; Fax: (703)535-6490; Email: info@hrps.org • URL: http://www.hrps.org • Human resource planning professionals representing 160 corporations and 3,000 individual members, including strategic human resources planning and development specialists, staffing analysts, business planners, line managers, and others who function as business partners in the application of strategic human resource management practices. Seeks to increase the impact of human resource planning and management on business and organizational performance. Sponsors program of professional development in human resource planning concepts, techniques, and practices. Offers networking opportunities.

**HR Policy Association**. 1100 13th St. NW, Ste. 850 Washington, DC 20005. Phone: (202)789-8670; Fax: (202)789-0064; Email: info@hrpolicy.org • URL: http://www.hrpolicy.org • Senior human resource executives of Fortune 500 companies. Conducts research and publishes findings on matters relating to federal human resources policy and its application and effects. Maintains task forces to study pending employment issues; conducts seminars, and offers a suite of labor relations and HR effectiveness training courses.

***HR Strategy for the High Performing Business***. Cengage Learning Inc., 20 Channel Center St. Boston, MA 02210. Phone: 800-487-8488 or (617)289-7700; Fax: (617)289-7844; Email: investors@cengage.com • URL: http://www.cengage.com • 2009. eBook. Published by Kogan Page. Designed to help senior management analyze the weak points in their business and focus HR on transforming problem areas by maximizing staff and business performance.

***HRfocus: The Hands-On Tool for Human Resources Professionals***. American Management Association. IOMA Inc., 3 Park Ave., 30th Fl. New York, NY 10016. Phone: 800-313-8650 or (212)244-0360; Fax: (212)564-0465 or (212)903-8168; Email: subserve@ioma.com • URL: http://www.ioma.com • Monthly. Covers "all aspects of HR management," including corporate culture, the impact of technology, recruiting strategies, and training. Formerly *Personnel*.

**Hrvatsko Udruženje Menadžera I Poduzetnik**. Ban Josip Jelacic Square 15 / II. HR-10000 Zagreb, Croatia. Phone: 385 1 4838709; Fax: 385 1 4811787 • URL: http://www.croma.hr • Works to foster professional management practices in Croatian business and industry. Offers educational programs and business related information.

***Hudson Valley Business Journal***. The Hudson Valley Business Journal, 86 E Main St. Wappingers Falls, NY 12590. Phone: (845)298-6236; Fax: (845)298-6238; Email: hvbjmail@aol.com • URL: http://www.hvbizjournal.com • Semiweekly. $20 Individuals. Business and financial newspaper.

***Huenefeld Report: For Managers and Planners in Modest-Sized Book Publishing Houses***. John Huenefeld, editor. The Huenefeld Company Inc., 41 North Rd., Ste. 201 Bedford, MA 01730-0665. Phone: 800-333-7716 or (781)275-1070; Fax: (781)275-1713 • Biweekly. $88.00 per year.

***Hulbert Financial Digest***. Hulbert Financial Digest, 5051-B Backlick Rd. Annandale, VA 22003-6045. Phone: 888-485-2378 or (703)750-9060 • Monthly. Description: Provides performance ratings on more than 400 portfolios recommended by more than 145 financial newsletters, calculated on the basis of model portfolios constructed according to each newsletter's advice. Includes a timing scoreboard, analysis of newsletter performance, list of mutual funds most frequently recommended for sale or purchase, a stock market sentiment index, and a question and answer section.

***Human Communication Research***. International Communication Association. Oxford University Press, Journals, 2001 Evans Rd. Cary, NC 27513. Phone: 800-852-7323 or (919)677-0977; Fax: (919)677-1714; Email: jnlorders@oup-usa.org • URL: http://www.oup-osa.org • A scholarly journal of interpersonal communication.

***Human Factors and Aviation Medicine***. Flight Safety Foundation, 801 N Fairfax St., Ste. 400 Alexandria, VA 22314-1754. Phone: (703)739-6700; Fax: (703)739-6708; Email: setze@flightsafety.org • URL: http://flightsafety.org • Bimonthly. $120 Members; $240 Nonmembers. Contains information important to the training and performance of all aviation professionals.

***Human Factors and Ergonomics in Manufacturing & Service Industries***. John Wiley and Sons, Inc., Journals Div., 111 River St. Hoboken, NJ 07030. Phone: 800-526-5368 or (201)748-6000; Fax: (201)748-6088; Email: consumers@wiley.com • URL: http://www.wiley.com • Bimonthly. Published in England by John Wiley and Sons Ltd. Formerly *International Journal of Human Factors in Manufacturing*.

**Human Power, Biochemechanics, and Robotics Laboratory**. Cornell University, Dept. of Theoretical and Applied Mechanics, 306 Kimball Hall Ithaca, NY 14853-1503. Phone: (607)255-7108; Fax: (607)255-2011; Email: ruina@cornell.edu • URL: http://ruina.tam.cornell.edu/ • Conducts research relating to human muscle-powered machines, such as bicycles and rowers.

***Human Relations: Towards the Integration of Social Sciences***. Tavistock Institute of Human Relations. Pine Forge Press, 2455 Teller Rd. Thousand Oaks, CA 91320-2234. Phone: 800-818-7243 or (805)499-4224 or (805)499-9774; Fax: (805)499-0871 or (805)583-2665; Email: sales@pfp.sagepub.com • URL: http://www.sagepub.com/sociologybooks • Monthly. $163 Individuals print only; $2,468 Institutions print only. Contains high quality research papers of social relationships at work and organizational forms, practices and processes that affect the nature, structure and conditions of work and work organizations.

***Human Resource Executive***. LRP Publications Library, lrp.com Technology Contacts, 747 Dresher Rd., Ste. 500 Horsham, PA 19044. Phone: 800-341-7874 or (215)784-0860 or (215)784-0910; Fax: (215)784-9639 or (215)784-0275; Email: techsup@lrp.com • URL: http://www.lrp.com • 16 times a year. $89.95 per year. Edited for directors of corporate human resource departments. Special issues emphasize training, benefits, retirement planning, recruitment, outplacement, workers' compensation, legal pitfalls, and oes emphasize training, benefits, retirement planning, recruitment, outplacement, workers' compensation, legal pitfalls, and other personnel topics.

***Human Resources Management Whole***. Wolters Kluwer Law & Business CCH, 2700 Lake Cook Rd. Riverwoods, IL 60015. Phone: 888-224-7377 or (847)267-7000; Email: cust_serv@cch.com • URL: http://www.cchgroup.com • Nine looseleaf volumes. $1,572 per year. Includes monthly updates. Components are *Ideas and Trends Newsletter, Employment Relations, Compensation, Equal Employment Opportunity, Personnel Practices/Communications* and *OSHA Compliance*. Components are available separately.

***Human Rights Organizations and Periodicals Directory***. Meiklejohn Civil Liberties Institute, PO Box 673 Berkeley, CA 94701-0673. Phone: (510)848-0599 or (510)642-3781; Fax: (510)642-7589; Email: mcli@mcli.org • URL: http://mcli.org • Quadrennial Biennial. $150 Individuals per year; $200 Institutions per year. Over 1,200 United States organiations and periodicals dedicated to improving human rights.

***Humanities Index***. H.W. Wilson Co., 950 University Ave. Bronx, NY 10452-4224. Phone: 800-367-6770 or (718)588-8400 or (718)558-8400; Fax: (718)590-1617 or (800)590-1617; Email: custserv@hwwilson.com • URL: http://www.hwwilson.com • Quarterly. Annual cumulation. Price varies.

**Humboldt University of Berlin - Center for Applied Statistics and Economics**. Spandauer Str. 1 10178 Berlin, Germany. Phone: 49 30 20935630; Fax: 49 30 20935649; Email: stat@wiwi.hu-berlin.de • URL: http://www.case.hu-berlin.de • Statistics and economics.

**Hungarian Academy of Sciences - Centre for Economic and Regional Studies - Institute of Economics**. Budaörsi út. 45 H-1112 Budapest, Hungary. Phone: 36 1 3092652; Fax: 36 1 3193136; Email: kti.titkarsag@krtk.mta.hu • URL: http://www.econ.core.hu • Economics and applied research on transition to market economy.

**Hungarian Academy of Sciences - Institute of Cognitive Neuroscience and Psychology**. PO Box 398 H-1394 Budapest, Hungary. Phone: 36 1 2396726; Fax: 36 1 2396727; Email: info@mtapi.hu • URL: http://www.mtapi.hu • Elementary cognitive psychology, cognitive psychophysiology, social information processing, and organization of personal and social identity.

***Hungarian Companies***. S2UV Rt. Computing and Management Services, Sauglo u. 9-15 M-1145 Budapest, Hungary. Phone: 361163 4074; Fax: 361183 2770 • Continuous. Database covers: Approximately 30,000 companies in Hungary. Database includes: Company name, address, phone, management, official tax and company registration numbers, industry activity codes, year founded, number of employees.

**Hungarian Venture Capital and Private Equity Association**. 11 Pauler St. H-1013 Budapest, Hungary. Phone: 36 1 4750924; Email: hvca@hvca.hu • URL: http://www.hvca.hu • Promotes the interests and the development of the venture capital and private equity industry in Hungary. Creates a set of professional and ethical standards for member companies. Provides a regular forum for the exchange of ideas among members.

***Hungary Business Forecast Report***. Telecommunications Insight, 85 Queen Victoria St. London EC4V 4AB, United Kingdom. Phone: 20 72 465100 or 44 20 7248 0468; Fax: 20 72 480467 or 44 20 7248 0467; Email: enquiries@telecomsinsight.com • URL: http://www.telecomsinsight.com • Quarterly. $1,195 Individuals Single user; $1,795 Individuals Up to 3 users. Business forecast report for Hungary.

***Hungary Government and Business Contacts Handbook: Trade, Investment & Business Development Contacts***. International Business Publications, USA, PO Box 15343 Washington, DC 20003. Phone: (202)546-2103; Fax: (202)546-3275; Email: ibpusa@comcast.net • URL: http://ibpus.com • $99.95 Individuals hardcopy. Covers: Strategic government and business information, export-import activity in the country, investment, business contacts and regulations.

***Hungary Investment and Business Guide***. International Business Publications, USA, PO Box 15343 Washington, DC 20003. Phone: (202)546-2103; Fax: (202)546-3275; Email: ibpusa@comcast.net • URL: http://ibpus.com • $99.95 Individuals hardcopy, e-book, CD-ROM. Covers: Strategic and business information, contacts, regulations, etc. Entries include: Business contacts and business travel.

***Hybrid Electric Vehicle Businesses in the World***. Momentum Technologies L.L.C., PO Box 460813 Glendale, CO 80246. Phone: (303)229-4841; Fax: (408)705-2031 • URL: http://www.mtt.com • Contains directory listings and contact information for more than 60 businesses involved with hybrid electric vehicles and related automotive areas throughout the world. Includes business name, address, phone number, fax number, e-mail address, and web site address. Includes brief descriptions of product lines, services offered, and business type. Covers businesses concerned with vehicles with hybrid power systems, such as electric power and traditional gasoline fuel. Includes manufacturers, component makers, wholesalers, retailers, component installers, and more. Searchable by location, business type, company name, and keyword.

***Hydraulics and Pneumatics: The Magazine of Fluid Power and Motion Control Systems***. Penton Media Inc., 1300 E 9th St. Cleveland, OH 44114-1501. Phone: (216)696-7000; Fax: (216)696-1752; Email: information@penton.com • URL: http://penton.com.

***Hydro Energy Businesses in the World***. Momentum Technologies L.L.C., PO Box 460813 Glendale, CO 80246. Phone: (303)229-4841; Fax: (408)705-2031 • URL: http://www.mtt.com • Contains detailed directory listings and contact information for dozens of hydro energy businesses in operation throughout the world. Includes business name, address, phone and fax numbers, and online contact addresses. Includes brief descriptions of product lines, services offered, and business type. Covers businesses providing large hydro energy systems (more than 50 KW) and smaller hydro energy systems (less than 50 KW); large and small hydro energy system components; and large and small hydroelectric turbines. Provides keyword search functions.

***Hydro Review: A Magazine Covering the North American Hydroelectric Industry***. PennWell Hydro Group, 410 Archibald St. Kansas City, MO 64111. Phone: (816)931-1311; Fax: (816)931-2015; Email: info@hcipub.com • URL: http://www.hcipub.com/ • Covers hydroelectric power generation in North America. Supplement available *Industry Directory*.

***Hydro Review Worldwide***. PennWell Publishing Co., 1421 S Sheridan Rd. Tulsa, OK 74112. Phone: 800-331-4463 or

SOURCES CITED

(918)835-3161 or (508)347-9324; Fax: (918)831-9555; Email: headquarter@pennwell.ocm • URL: http://www. pennwell.com • Bimonthly. Provides network for sharing information regarding practical, technical and expertise on hydroelectric power.

*Hydrocarbon Processing*. Gulf Publishing Co., 2 Greenway Plz., Ste. 1020 Houston, TX 77046-0208. Phone: 800-231-6275 or (713)529-4301 or (713)525-4626; Fax: (713)520-4433; Email: customerservices@gulfpub.com • URL: http://www. gulfpub.com • $239 Individuals. Contains practical analysis and insight into the latest technological advances in the refining, petrochemical and natural gas/LNG industries.

*Hypertension*. American Heart Association. • Individuals, $256.00 per year; institutions, $401.00 per year.

*I Love Pasta*. National Pasta Association, Phone: (202)637-5888; Fax: (202)223-9741; Email: npa@ilovepasta.org • URL: http://www.ilovepasta.org • Web site provides a wide variety of information about pasta and the pasta industry. Includes 300 pasta recipes, pasta FAQs, and nutritional data. Industry statistics can be displayed, including data on imports, production, and per capita use in various countries. Extensive durum wheat data is provided.

*IAA National & World News*. International Advertising Association, 747 3rd Ave., 2nd Fl. New York, NY 10017. Phone: (646)722-2612; Fax: (646)722-2501; Email: iaa@iaaglobal. org • URL: http://www.iaaglobal.org • Description: Supplies information on Association policies and activities. Includes reviews of publications and reports from the 62 chapters worldwide.

*IAFE Membership Directory*. International Association of Fairs and Expositions, 3043 E Cairo St. Springfield, MO 65802. Phone: 800-516-0313 or (417)862-5771; Fax: (417)862-0156; Email: iafe@fairsandexpos.com • URL: http://www. fairsandexpos.com • Annual. Included in membership; $125 Nonmembers. Lists member agricultural fairs in the United States and Canada. Formerly *International Association of Fairs and Expositions Directory*.

*IAL Directory of European Industrial and Business Market Reports*. IAL Consultants, 14 Buckingham Palace Rd. London SW1W 0QP, United Kingdom. Phone: 071 828 5036 • Irregular. $250 postpaid. Covers: publishers and producers of market reports, statistical summaries, and other data; includes government and non-government organizations, libraries, press, and international sources in Europe, including the socialist states of Eastern Europe. Entries include: Publisher name and address, title and subject of report, language, number of pages, price.

*IBIMA Business Review (IBIMABR)*. IBIMA Publishing, 34 E Germantown Pke., No. 327 Norristown, PA 19401. Email: contact@ibimapublishing.com • URL: http://www. ibimapublishing.com • Peer-reviewed journal publishing case studies for business organizations.

*IBM Journal of Research and Development*. International Business Machines Corp., 1 New Orchard Rd. Armonk, NY 10504-1722. Phone: 800-426-4968 or (914)499-1900 • URL: http://www.ibm.com • Bimonthly. Contains work of authors in the science, technology and engineering of information systems.

*IC Master (Integrated circuits): The Electronics Industry's Leading Source of ICInformation*. IC Master, Uniondale, NY 11553-4709. Phone: (516)227-1300; Fax: (516)227-1453; Email: feedback@icmaster.com • URL: http://www. icmaster.com • Annual. $195.00. Semiannual supplements. Product information on 120,000 commercially available integrated circuits.

*The ICAO Journal*. International Civil Aviation Organization, 999 University St. Montreal, QC, Canada H3C 5H7. Phone: (514)954-8219 or (514)954-8022; Fax: (514)954-6077; Email: icaohq@icao.int • URL: http://www.icao.int • Bimonthly. $10 Single issue. Contains concise account of the activities of the International Civil Aviation Organization and features additional information of interest to Contracting States and the international aeronautical world.

*ICC UK Company Directory*. ICC Information Ltd., Marlow International Marlow SL7 1AJ, United Kingdom. Phone: 44 16 28492260 or 1628 492 260; Fax: 44 16 28492000; Email: ukenquiries@dnb.com • URL: http://www.myicc.co.uk • Weekly. Database covers: approximately 3.83 million registered companies in England, Wales, Scotland, and Northern Ireland. Contains a record for each company included on the Index of Companies maintained by the official Companies Registration office in the UK. Also incorporates companies that have been dissolved since 1968.

*ICC UK Company Financial Database*. Dun & Bradstreet U.K. ICC Information, Marlow International Pky., Marlow Buckinghamshire SL7 1AJ, United Kingdom. Phone: 44 1628 492000; Email: customerhelp@dnb.co.uk • URL: http:// www.dnb.co.uk • Weekly. Database covers: Comprehensive analysis on 2.2 million companies with limited liability in the UK—large, medium, and small, quoted and non-quoted, public and private, from all sectors on industry and commerce. Provides data for all types of company research, providing extended profit and loss accounts and balance sheet information, new cash flow items, together with new auditors' qualification reference data, comprehensive business ratios, industrial comparisons, growth rates, and an improved credit rating system. Access to complete database of U.K. Directors with over 5 million directorships covered exact im-

ages of alt company accounts and annual returns.

*Ice Cream Reporter: The Newsletter for Ice Cream Executives*. MarketResearch.com, 11200 Rockville Pke., Ste. 504 Rockville, MD 20852. Phone: 800-298-5699 or (240)747-3093; Fax: (240)747-3004; Email: customerservice@ marketresearch.com • URL: http://www.marketresearch.com • Monthly. $395.00 per year. Covers new products, mergers, research, packaging, etc.

*Iceland Business*. Iceland Review, Borgartuni 23-105 IS-105 Reykjavik, Iceland. Phone: 354 512 7575; Fax: 354 561 8646; Email: icelandreview@icelandreview.com • URL: http:// www.icelandreview.com • Magazine covering business in Iceland.

*ICMA Newsletter*. International City/County Management Association, 777 N Capitol St. NE, Ste. 500 Washington, DC 20002-4201. Phone: (202)289-4262; Fax: (202)962-3500; Email: customerservices@icma.org • URL: http://icma.org/ en/icma/home • Description: Discusses local government, professional management, and federal regulation. Publishes news of Association activities. Recurring features include news of members; reports of publications, educational workshops, positions open in public management; and two main supplements titled Nuts & Bolts and ICMA University.

*ICS Cleaning Specialist*. BNP Media, 2401 W Big Beaver Rd., Ste. 700 Troy, MI 48084. Phone: 800-952-6643 or (248)362-3700 or (847)763-9534; Fax: (248)362-5103 or (248)362-0317; Email: privacy@bnpmedia.com • URL: http://www. bnpmedia.com • Monthly. Free to qualified personnel. Written for floor covering installers and cleaners. Formerly *Installation and Cleaning Specialist*.

*ICS Cleaning Specialists Annual Trade Directory and Buying Guide*. Specialist Publications Inc., 22801 Ventura Blvd., Ste. 115 Woodland Hills, CA 91364. Phone: 800-835-4398 or (818)224-8035; Fax: (818)224-8042; Email: ics@bnp.com • URL: http://www.bnpmedia.com • Annual. $35. Lists about 6,000 manufacturers and distributors of floor covering installation and cleaning equipment. Formerly *Installation and Cleaning Specialists Trade Directory and Buying Guide*.

*ICTA Travel Management Text Series*. Institute of Certified Travel Agents, 945 Concord St. Framingham, MA 01701. Phone: 800-542-4282 or (781)237-0280; Fax: (781)237-3860; Email: info@thetravelinstitue.com • URL: http:// thetravelinstitute.com • Four volumes. Volume one, *Business Management for Travel Agents*; volume two, *Personnel Management for Travel Agents*; volume three, *Marketing for Travel Agents*; volume four, *Domestic Leisure and International Tourism*.

*Idaho Manufacturers Directory and Industrial Database*. Manufacturers' News Inc., 1633 Central St. Evanston, IL 60201-1569. Phone: (847)864-7000; Fax: (847)332-1100 • URL: http://www.manufacturersnews.com • Annual. $89 Individuals print; $333 Individuals database (EZ select full); $196 Individuals database (EZ select with 20 plus employees); $116 Individuals database (EZ select basic). Covers: 2,560 manufacturers in Idaho. Entries include: Company name, address, phone, names and titles of key personnel, year established, number of employees, plant square footage, services, Standard Industry Classification (SIC) code, parent and subsidiary company information, type of in-house computer system, URL, e-mail address.

**Idaho National Laboratory - Energy Policy Institute**. Boise State University, 1910 University Dr. Boise, ID 83725-1014. Phone: (208)426-4845; Fax: (208)426-1830; Email: davidsolan@boisestate.edu • URL: http://epi.boisestate.edu • Energy issues important to the western U.S., including the relationships between energy and water with climate change, population and economic growth, and environmental impacts.

*Idea Source Guide; A Monthly Report to Executives in Advertising, Merchandising and Sales Promotion*. Bramlee, Inc., c/o Fred Davis Devon, PA 19333. • Monthly. $150.00 per year. Lists new premiums and novelty products.

*Ideas Unlimited: For Editors*. OmniPrint Inc., 9700 Philadelphia Ct. Lanham, MD 20706-4405. Phone: 800-774-6809 or (301)731-7000; Fax: (301)731-7001; Email: info@omniprint. net • URL: http://www.omniprint.net/ • Monthly. $195.00 per year. Includes CD-Rom. Contains fillers for company newsletters: articles, cartoons, jokes, seasonal items, etc.

**IdeasAmerica**. PO Box 210863 Auburn Hills, MI 48321. Phone: (248)961-2674; Fax: (248)253-9252; Email: ia@ideas-america.org • URL: http://www.ideas-america.org • Represents finance, commerce, industry, and government professionals. Dedicated to the worth, contributions, and benefits of employee suggestion systems and other employee involvement processes. Supports communication between employees and employer for the purpose of exchanging ideas.

**I.E. Canada**. PO Box 189 Sta. Don Mills, ON, Canada M3C 2S2. Phone: (416)595-5333; Fax: (416)595-8226; Email: info@ iecanada.com • URL: http://www.iecanada.com • Individuals and firms with an interest in Canada's international trade. Promotes increased participation by Canada in the global economy; seeks to maintain a business climate conducive to increased international trade. Represents members' interests before government agencies; prepares model trade programs, regulations, and policies. Provides advice and assistance to members; serves as a clearinghouse on international trade.

*ie: The Business of International Events*. International Festivals and Events Association, 2603 Eastover Terr. Boise, ID 83706. Phone: (208)433-0950; Fax: (208)433-9812; Email: nia@

ifea.com • URL: http://www.ifea.com/joomla1_5/index.php • Quarterly. included in membership dues; $50 for nonmembers; $25 additional subscription for members. Includes industry updates, trends and issues.

*IEEE Communications Magazine*. IEEE - Communications Society, 3 Park Ave., 17th Fl. New York, NY 10016-5902. Phone: 800-678-4333 or (212)705-8900; Fax: (212)705-8999; Email: customer-service@ieee.org • URL: http://www. comsoc.org • Monthly. Covers all areas of communications such as lightwave telecommunications, high-speed data communications, personal communications systems (PCS), ISDN, and more.

*IEEE Computer Graphics and Applications*. Institute of Electrical and Electronics Engineers, 2001 L St. NW, Ste. 700 Washington, DC 20036. Phone: (732)465-5821 or (202)785-0017; Fax: (732)981-1769; Email: contactcenter@ieee.org • URL: http://www.ieee.org • Bimonthly. $39 print only; $29.95 digital edition only. Covers a variety of topics catering to both computer graphics practitioners and researchers.

*IEEE Industry Applications Magazine*. IEEE - Communications Society, 3 Park Ave., 17th Fl. New York, NY 10016-5902. Phone: 800-678-4333 or (212)705-8900; Fax: (212)705-8999; Email: customer-service@ieee.org • URL: http://www. comsoc.org • Bimonthly. Covers new industrial applications of power conversion, drives, lighting, and control. Emphasis is on the petroleum, chemical, rubber, plastics, textile, and mining industries.

*IEEE Membership Directory*. IEEE - Communications Society, 3 Park Ave., 17th Fl. New York, NY 10016-5902. Phone: 800-678-4333 or (212)705-8900; Fax: (212)705-8999; Email: customer-service@ieee.org • URL: http://www.comsoc.org • Annual.

*IEEE Micro*. IEEE - Communications Society, 3 Park Ave., 17th Fl. New York, NY 10016-5902. Phone: 800-678-4333 or (212)705-8900; Fax: (212)705-8999; Email: customer-service@ieee.org • URL: http://www.comsoc.org • Bimonthly. Contains high-quality technical articles from designers, systems integrators, and users discussing the design, performance, or application of microcomputer and microprocessor systems.

*IEEE Multimedia Magazine*. Institute of Electrical and Electronic Engineers, 3 Park Ave., 17th Fl. New York, NY 10016-5997. Phone: 800-810-4333 or (212)705-8900 or (212)419-7900; Fax: (212)705-8999 or (212)752-4929; Email: conference-services@ieee.org • URL: http://www.ieee.org • Quarterly. $39 print only; $29.95 digital edtion only. Provides a wide variety of technical information relating to multimedia systems and applications. Articles cover research, advanced applications, working systems, and theory.

*IEEE Proceedings-Circuits, Devices and Systems*. IEEE - Communications Society, 3 Park Ave., 17th Fl. New York, NY 10016-5902. Phone: 800-678-4333 or (212)705-8900; Fax: (212)705-8999; Email: customer-service@ieee.org • URL: http://www.comsoc.org • Bimonthly. Covers all aspects of circuit theory, design, and implementation.

*IEEE Products and Publications Bulletin*. IEEE - Communications Society, 3 Park Ave., 17th Fl. New York, NY 10016-5902. Phone: 800-678-4333 or (212)705-8900; Fax: (212)705-8999; Email: customer-service@ieee.org • URL: http://www.comsoc.org • Quarterly. Free. Provides information on all IEEE journals, proceedings, and other publications. Formerly *IEEE Publications Bulletin*.

*IEEE Pulse*. IEEE - Communications Society, 3 Park Ave., 17th Fl. New York, NY 10016-5902. Phone: 800-678-4333 or (212)705-8900; Fax: (212)705-8999; Email: customer-service@ieee.org • URL: http://www.comsoc.org • Bimonthly. Published for biomedical engineers.

*IEEE Security & Privacy*. IEEE - Computer Society, 2001 L St. NW, Ste. 700 Washington, DC 20036-4928. Phone: 800-272-6657 or (202)371-0101 or (714)821-8380; Fax: (202)728-9614 or (714)821-4010; Email: help@computer.org • URL: http://www.computer.org • Bimonthly. Included in membership; $19.95 Nonmembers online. Emphasis is on computer and netwoek security for large systems.

*IEEE Software*. Institute of Electrical and Electronic Engineers, 3 Park Ave., 17th Fl. New York, NY 10016-5997. Phone: 800-810-4333 or (212)705-8900 or (212)419-7900; Fax: (212)705-8999 or (212)752-4929; Email: conference-services@ieee.org • URL: http://www.ieee.org • Bimonthly. Covers software engineering, technology, and development. Affiliated with the Institute of Electrical and Electronics Engineers.

*IEEE Spectrum*. IEEE - Communications Society, 3 Park Ave., 17th Fl. New York, NY 10016-5902. Phone: 800-678-4333 or (212)705-8900; Fax: (212)705-8999; Email: customer-service@ieee.org • URL: http://www.comsoc.org • Monthly. $19.95 U.S. and Canada print only or digital only; $29.95 U.S. and Canada print + digital; $39.95 Other countries print only; $19.95 Other countries digital only; $49.95 Other countries print + digital. Magazine for the scientific and engineering professional. Provides information on developments and trends in engineering, physics, mathematics, chemistry, medicine/biology, and the nuclear sciences.

*IEEE Transactions on Communications*. IEEE - Communications Society, 3 Park Ave., 17th Fl. New York, NY 10016-5902. Phone: 800-678-4333 or (212)705-8900; Fax: (212)705-8999; Email: customer-service@ieee.org • URL: http://www.comsoc.org • Monthly. $108 print only; $45 online only; $108 print and online.

***IEEE Transactions on Visualization and Computer Graphics***. IEEE - Communications Society, 3 Park Ave., 17th Fl. New York, NY 10016-5902. Phone: 800-678-4333 or (212)705-8900; Fax: (212)705-8999; Email: customer-service@ieee.org • URL: http://www.comsoc.org • Monthly. Contains research on subjects related to computer graphics and visualization techniques, systems, software, hardware, and user interface issues.

***IEG's Sponsorship Report: The International Newsletter of Event Sponsorship and Lifestyle Marketing***. IEG LLC, 350 N. Orleans St., Ste. 1200 Chicago, IL 60654. Phone: (312)944-1727; Email: ieg@sponsorship.com • URL: http://www.sponsorship.com • $499 multi-user subscription; $299 single-user subscription. Newsletter reporting on corporate sponsorship of special events: sports, music, festivals, and the arts. Edited for event producers, directors, and marketing personnel.

***IFAP Newsletter***. International Federation of Agricultural Producers, 60, rue St.-Lazare 75009 Paris, France. Phone: 33 1 45260553; Fax: 33 1 48747212; Email: ifap@ifap.org • URL: http://www.ifap.org • Bimonthly. Price on application.

***iGaming Business Directory***. Casino City Press, 95 Wells Ave. Newton, MA 02459. Phone: 800-490-1715 or (617)332-2850; Fax: (617)964-2280; Email: sales@casinocitypress.com • URL: http://www.casinocitypress.com • Annual. $449.95 Book and CD Package (Standard License); $299.95 Book (Standard License); $424.95 CD (Standard License); $749.95 Book and Multi-User CD (Organization-Wide License); $699.95 Multi-User CD (Organization-Wide License). Includes 2,500 iGaming sites, 679 site owners, 5,700 iGaming portal sites, site rankings, software manufacturers, and 400 affiliate programs.

***IIEPassport: Academic Year Abroad***. Institute of International Education, IIE New York City, 809 United Nations Plz. New York, NY 10017-3503. Phone: (212)883-8200 or (212)984-5412; Fax: (212)984-5452; Email: membership@iie.org • URL: http://www.iie.org • Annual. $54.95 Individuals. Covers: Almost 6,000 undergraduate and graduate study-abroad programs conducted worldwide during the academic year by United States and foreign colleges and universities and other organizations in 80 countries. Entries include: Program name, sponsoring institution, contact person, address, phone, e-mail, website, pertinent dates, orientation, subjects offered, credits, housing, scholarships, language of instruction, related travel, teaching methods, tuition and other costs, prerequisites, work-study or internship opportunities, etc. Not to be confused with 'Academic Year and Summer Programs Abroad,' described separately.

***I.I.I. Data Base Search***. Insurance Information Institute, 110 William St. New York, NY 10038. Phone: (212)346-5500; Email: members@iii.org • URL: http://www.iii.org • Provides online citations and abstracts of insurance-related literature in magazines, newspapers, trade journals, and books. Emphasis is on property and casualty insurance issues, including highway safety, product safety, and environmental liability. Inquire as to online cost and availability.

***Illinois Industries Guide***. Industries Guides Inc., 303 E Altamonte Dr. Altamonte Springs, FL 32716. Phone: (407)834-8181 • $95. Covers: Approximately 20,000 manufacturers in Illinois. Entries include: Company name, address, phone.

***Illinois Manufacturers Directory***. Manufacturers' News Inc., 1633 Central St. Evanston, IL 60201-1569. Phone: (847)864-7000; Fax: (847)332-1100 • URL: http://www.manufacturersnews.com • Annual. $211 Individuals print; plus shipping and handling; $815 Individuals Full Version - All Employees (12 months online database); $612 Individuals Full Version - 20+ Employees (12 months online database); $285 Individuals Basic Version - All Employees (12 months online database). Covers: 19,423 manufacturers and 61,317 executives in Illinois. Entries include: Company name, address, phone, titles and functions of key personnel, year established, number of employees, plant square footage, services, Standard Industrial Classification (SIC) code, parent and subsidiary company information, type of in-house computer system, fax, web address, e-mail address.

***Illinois Services Directory***. Manufacturers' News Inc., 1633 Central St. Evanston, IL 60201-1569. Phone: (847)864-7000; Fax: (847)332-1100 • URL: http://www.manufacturersnews.com • Annual. $209 Individuals Print (Hardcover); plus Shipping and Handling; $920 Individuals Full Version - All Employees (12 months online database); $710 Individuals Full Version - 20+ Employees (12 months online database); $322 Individuals Basic Version - All Employees (12 months online database). Covers: Over 26,548 wholesalers, jobbers, contractors, retailers, services, and 76,898 executives in Illinois. Entries include: Company name, address, phone; names, titles, and functions of key personnel; year established, number of employees, office square footage, services, Standard Industrial Classification (SIC) code, net worth, parent company and subsidiary company information, type of in-house computer system, email address, fax, web address.

***IMAGES***. IMAGE Society, PO Box 6221 Chandler, AZ 85246-6221. Email: image@image-society.org • URL: http://image-society.org • Semiannual. $25. Newsletter Provides news of virtual reality developments and the IMAGE Society.

***Imaging Abstracts***. Royal Photographic Society of Great Britain, Imaging Science and Technology Group. Elsevier, Secondary Publishing Division, 650 Ave. of the Americas New York, NY 10011. Phone: 888-437-4636 or (212)633-3980; Fax: (212)633-3975; Email: t.reller@elsevier.com • URL: http://www.elseveier.com • Bimonthly. $860.00 per year. Formerly *Photographic Abstracts*.

**Imaging and Computer Vision Center**. Drexel University, 3141 Chestnut St. Philadelphia, PA 19104. Phone: (215)895-2215; Fax: (215)895-4983; Email: icvc-support@cbis.ece.drexel.edu • URL: http://www.biomed.drexel.edu • Fields of research include computer vision, robot vision, and expert systems.

***Imaging Business: The Voice of the Document Imaging Channel***. Access Intelligence L.L.C., 4 Choke Cherry Rd., 2nd Fl. Rockville, MD 20850. Phone: 800-777-5006 or (301)354-2000 or (301)354-2101; Fax: (301)309-3847 or (801)365-2300; Email: info@accessintel.com • URL: http://www.accessintel.com/ • Monthly. Free to qualified personnel. Edited for resellers of document imaging equipment.

***Imaging KM: Creating and Managing the Knowledge-Based Enterprise***. Knowledge Management World, 22 Bayview St., 2nd Fl. Camden, ME 04843. Phone: (207)236-8524; Fax: (207)236-6452; Email: hugh_mckellar@kmworld.com • URL: http://www.kmworld.com • 10 times a year. Free to qualified personnel; others, $48.00 per year. Covers automated and networked document image handling.

***Imaging Supplies Annual***. Forrester Research Inc., 60 Acorn Park Dr. Cambridge, MA 02140. Phone: (617)613-6000; Email: customercenter@forrester.com • URL: http://www.forrester.com • Annual. $125. Publication includes: List of over 300 service companies, suppliers and manufacturers of products such as ribbons, ink jet ink, toner, photo conductors, technology-specific papers and print elements for computer printers, typewriters, copiers, and other office equipment. Entries include: Company name, address, phone, fax, telex, name and title of contact, products, services, coding to indicate distribution method. Principal content of publication is articles about the imaging supplies industry.

***IMF Survey***. International Monetary Fund, 700 19th St. NW Washington, DC 20431. Phone: (202)623-7000 or (202)623-6220; Fax: (202)623-4661; Email: insinfo@imf.org • URL: http://www.imf.org/institute • Description: Timely news on topics of general interest in the fields of international finance, country economics, trade, and commodities. Contains information on the IMF's activities, including press releases, major management speeches, and lending activity data rates.

***Immigration Law and Business***. Sam Bernsen. Thomson West, 610 Opperman Dr. Eagan, MN 55123. Phone: 800-328-9352 or (651)687-7000 • $552 full set; $43 monthly. Three times a year. Three looseleaf volumes. Covers labor certification, temporary workers, applications, petitions, etc.

***Immigration Law and Crimes***. Dan Kesselbrenner and Lory D. Rosenberg. Thomson West, 610 Opperman Dr. Eagan, MN 55123. Phone: 800-328-9352 or (651)687-7000 • $319.50 book; $59 monthly. Semiannual. Looseleaf service. Covers legal representation of the foreign-born criminal defendant.

***Immigration Law and Defense***. National Lawyers Guild. Thomson West, 610 Opperman Dr. Eagan, MN 55123. Phone: 800-328-9352 or (651)687-7000 • $536 book-softbound; $79 monthly. Semiannual. Two looseleaf volumes. Covers legal defense of immigrants and aliens.

***Immigration Law and Procedure***. Matthew Bender and Company Inc., 1275 Broadway Albany, NY 12204-2638. Phone: 800-424-4200 or (518)487-3000; Fax: (518)487-3573 or (800)424-4200; Email: customer.support@lexisnexis.com • URL: http://www.matthewbender.com • $3,446. 21 looseleaf volumes. Periodic supplementation.

***Immigration Law Report***. Austin T. Fragomen and Steven C. Bell. Thomson West, 610 Opperman Dr. Eagan, MN 55123. Phone: 800-328-9352 or (651)687-7000 • Description: Reports on U.S. immigration and nationality laws. Presents arguments that can be used in preparing Immigration and Naturalization Service (INS) cases and federal court cases. Carries analysis of material not readily available, such as internal INS policy statements and unpublished cases. Recurring features include reviews of recent decisions and regulations.

***Impact of Electronic Publishing: The Future for Libraries and Publishers***. David J. Brown. Cengage Learning Inc., 20 Channel Center St. Boston, MA 02210. Phone: 800-487-8488 or (617)289-7700; Fax: (617)289-7844; Email: investors@cengage.com • URL: http://www.cengage.com • 2009. Published by K.G. Saur. Explains how libraries and publishers navigate significant expansion in electronic publishing. Inquire for pricing.

***Impact: U.S. News and Research for the Wine, Spirits, and Beer Industries***. M. Shanken Communications Inc., 387 Park Ave. S New York, NY 10016. Phone: 800-227-1617 or (212)684-4224; Fax: (212)481-1540 or (212)481-0721; Email: mmorgenstern@mshanken.com • URL: http://www.mshanken.com • Semimonthly. $375.00 per year. Newsletter covering the marketing, economic, and financial aspects of alcoholic beverages.

***Implement and Tractor: The Business Magazine of the Farm and Industrial Equipment Industry***. Agra USA, 2302 W 1st St. Cedar Falls, IA 50613-1879. Phone: (319)277-3599; Fax: (319)277-3783 • URL: http://www.agra-net.com/ • Bimonthly. $35.00 per year. Includes annuals *Product File* and *Red Book*.

***Importcar: The Complete Import Service Magazine***. Babcox Publications Inc., 3550 Embassy Pkwy. Akron, OH 44333-8318. Phone: (330)670-1234; Fax: (330)670-0874; Email: info@babcox.com • URL: http://www.babcox.com • Monthly. News on imported cars. Includes *Automotive Aftermarket Training Guide*. Formerly *Importcar and Truck*.

***Importing for the Small Business: The Daily Telegraph Guide***. Kogan Page, Limited, 120 Pentonville Rd. London N1 9JN, United Kingdom. Phone: 44 20 72780433 or (440) 2072780433; Fax: 44 20 78376348 or (783)76348; Email: kpinfo@kogan-page.co.uk • URL: http://www.kogan-page.co.uk/ • Irregular. $8.99. Publication includes: List of organizations able to help small businesses in the United Kingdom. Entries include: Organization name, address. Principal contents are articles on ordering, transport, payment, customs, and related aspects of importing for small businesses.

***Imports and Exports of the Republic of China and Taiwan***. Taiwan External Trade Development Council, 333 Keelung Rd., Sec. 1, 5th-7th Fl. Taipei 11012, Taiwan. Phone: 886 2 27255200; Fax: 886 2 27576652; Email: taitra@taitra.org.tw • URL: http://www.taitra.org.tw • Annual. $150. Covers import commodities whose import value exceeds $200,000 (U.S. funds) annually.

***In Business: Dane County's Business Magazine***. Business Information L.L.C., 611 N Sherman Ave. Madison, WI 53704. Phone: (608)246-3599 • Monthly. $28 Individuals; $2.95 Single issue. Local business magazine.

***In Business for Business***. Bethlehem Chamber of Commerce, 318 Delaware Ave., Ste. 11 Delmar, NY 12054-1911. Phone: (518)439-0512; Fax: (518)475-0910; Email: info@bethlehemchamber.com • URL: http://www.bethlehemchamber.com • Monthly.

***In Business for Yourself***. Nashville Area Chamber of Commerce, 211 Commerce St., Ste. 100 Nashville, TN 37201-1806. Phone: (615)743-3000; Fax: (615)743-3002 • URL: http://www.nashvillechamber.com • List of businesses located in Nashville, TN.

***In Business: The Magazine for Environmental Entrepreneuring***. The JG Press Inc., 419 State Ave. Emmaus, PA 18049. Phone: (610)967-4135; Fax: (610)967-1345; Email: biocycle@jgpress.com • URL: http://www.biocycle.net • Bimonthly. $33.00 per year. Magazine for environmental entrepreneuring.

***In Car Business***. Vehicle Security News Ltd., Hazel Grove Cheshire SK7 6FR, United Kingdom. Phone: 44 1625261137; Fax: 44 1625261028 • Semimonthly. $21 Individuals; $31 Individuals Europe; $41 Individuals U.S.; $3.50 Single issue. Professional magazine covering automobile audio and security.

***In Command! A Series of Messages About Getting the Most From Your Word Processor***. Economics Press Inc., 12 Daniel Rd. Fairfield, NJ 07004-2565. Phone: 800-526-2554 or (973)227-1224; Fax: (973)227-9742 • Weekly. $146.00 per year. Quantity prices available. A newsletter for word processing operators.

***In Focus***. Lighthouse International, 111 E 59th St. New York, NY 10022-1202. Phone: 800-829-0500 or (212)821-9200; Fax: (212)821-9707; Email: info@lighthouse.org • URL: http://www.lighthouse.org • Description: Reaches visually handicapped children through stories, poems, and drawings contributed by young readers. Covers subjects of interest to youngsters, especially those related to their experiences and hopes for the future. Also includes puzzles, contests, and items of interest to parents and educators, such as new book and symposium announcements.

***In-Plant Graphics***. North American Publishing Co., 1500 Spring Garden St., Ste. 1200 Philadelphia, PA 19130-4069. Phone: (215)238-5300; Email: customerservice@napco.com • URL: http://www.napco.com • Contains articles, news, and features from the print magazine, *In-Plant Graphics*. Provides information on the in-plant printing industry, covering more than 24,000 in-house reproduction departments for companies, manufacturers, government organizations, and universities in the United States. Covers topics such as publishing, pre-press, printing, binding, and mailing. Includes editorials, salary surveys, company financial information, coverage of industry happenings, and more. Includes an article archive. Provides online searchable access to the magazine's annual *Buyers' and Specifiers' Guide*, with contact information and descriptions of printers, suppliers, and manufacturers throughout the United States. Also includes searchable access to a listing of used printing equipment.

***In-Plant Printer Buyer's Guide***. Innes Publishing Co., 28100 N Ashley Cir. Libertyville, IL 60048. Phone: 800-247-3306 or (847)816-7900; Fax: (847)247-8855 • URL: http://www.innespub.com • Annual. $10.00. Manufacturers of equipment for the in-plant and grahic arts industry. Formerly *In-Plant Printer and Electronic Publisher Buyer's Guide*.

***In-Plant Printer: The In-Plant Management Magazine***. Innes Publishing Co., 28100 N Ashley Cir. Libertyville, IL 60048. Phone: 800-247-3306 or (847)816-7900; Fax: (847)247-8855 • URL: http://www.innespub.com • Bimonthly. $75.00 per year. Formerly *In-Plant Printer and Electronic Publisher*.

***InBusiness***. American Chamber of Commerce in Romania, Union International Ctr., 4th Fl., 11 Ion Campineanu St. 010031 Bucharest, Romania. Phone: 40 21 3124834 or 40 21 3158694;

Fax: 40 21 3124851; Email: amcham@amcham.ro • URL: http://www.amcham.ro • Quarterly. Contains articles of interest to the U.S. and foreign business community in Romania.

***Incentive: Managing and Marketing Through Motivation***. Nielsen Business Media Inc., 770 Broadway New York, NY 10003-9522. Phone: 866-890-8541 or (646)654-4500 or (646)654-5000; Fax: (646)654-5584 or (646)654-4500; Email: bmcomm@nielsen.com • URL: http://www.nielsenbusinessmedia.com • Monthly. $59.00 per year.

***Income and Fees of Accountants in Public Practice***. National Society of Accountants, 1010 N Fairfax St. Alexandria, VA 22314. Phone: 800-966-6679 or (703)549-6400; Fax: (703)549-2984; Email: members@nsacct.org • URL: http://www.nsacct.org • Contains info on fees charged for tax and accounting services by geography. Members, $49.00; non-members, $125.00.

***Income Opportunities.Com: The Original Small Business - Home Office Magazine***. Newline, 2448 E. 81st St., 5300 City Plex Tower Tulsa, OK 74137-4207. Phone: (918)491-6100; Fax: (918)491-9424 • URL: http://www.eincomeopportunities.com • Monthly. $31.95 per year.

***Income Tax Service Directory***. InfoGroup Inc., 5711 S 86th Cir. Omaha, NE 68127-4146. Phone: (402)593-4500 • URL: http://www.infogroup.com • Annual. Number of listings: 63,898. Entries include: Name, address, phone, size of advertisement, name of owner or manager, number of employees, year first in "Yellow Pages." Compiled from telephone company "Yellow Pages," nationwide.

***Incorporate Your Business***. Nolo, 950 Parker St. Berkeley, CA 94710-2524. Phone: 800-728-3555 or (510)549-4660 or (510)549-1976; Fax: (800)645-0895 or (510)548-5902; Email: publicity@nolo.com • URL: http://www.nolo.com • Contains information on establishing a corporation in each state.

***Inc.: The Magazine for Growing Companies***. INC., 38 Commercial Warf Boston, MA 02110. Phone: (617)248-8000; Fax: (617)248-8090; Email: editors@inc.com • URL: http://www.inc.com • 10/year. $10 U.S. /year for two subscription; $32 Canada /year for two subscription; $40 Other countries /year for two subscription. Edited for small office and home businesses with one to 25 employees. Covers management, office technology, and lifestyle. Incorporates *Self-Employed Professional*.

***Independent Agent***. Independent Insurance Agents & Brokers of America Inc. 127 S Peyton St. Alexandria, VA 22314. Phone: 800-221-7917 or (703)683-4422; Fax: (703)683-7556; Email: info@iiaba.org • URL: http://www.iamagazine.com • Monthly. $24.00 per year.

***Independent Energy: The Power Industry's Business Magazine***. PennWell Corp., Industrial Div., 1421 S Sheridan Rd. Tulsa, OK 74112. Phone: 800-331-4463 or (918)835-3161; Email: bid@pennwell.com • URL: http://www.pennwell.com • 10 times a year. $127.00 per year. Covers non-utility electric power plants (cogeneration) and other alternative sources of electric energy.

**Independent Office Products and Furniture Dealers Association**. 3601 E Joppa Rd. Baltimore, MD 21234. Phone: (410)930-8100; Fax: (410)931-8111; Email: cbates@nopanet.org • URL: http://www.iopfda.org • Formerly Office Furniture Dealers Alliance.

***Independent Publisher: Leading the World of Book Selling in New Directions***. Jenkins Group Inc., 1129 Woodmere Ave., Ste. B Traverse City, MI 49686. Phone: 800-706-4636 or (231)933-0445; Fax: (231)933-0448; Email: publish@jenkinsgroupinc.com • URL: http://www.jenkinsgroupinc.com • Bimonthly. Free. Covers business, finance, production, marketing, and other management topics for small publishers, including college presses. Emphasis is on book publishing.

***Independent School***. National Association of Independent Schools, 1129 20th St. NW, Ste. 800 Washington, DC 20036-3425. Phone: (202)973-9700; Fax: (888)316-3862 or (202)973-9790; Email: info@nais.org • URL: http://www.nais.org • 3/year. $54 Nonmembers; $32 Members; $52 Members Canada and Mexico; $72 Nonmembers Canada and Mexico; $60 Members Outside North America; $84 Nonmembers Outside North America. An open forum for exchange of information about elementary and secondary education in general, and independent education in particular.

***Index and Directory of Industry Standards***. IHS Energy Group, 321 Inverness Dr. S Englewood, CO 80112-5895. Phone: 800-525-7052 or (303)790-0600 or (303)736-3001; Fax: (303)736-3150; Email: sales@ihsenergy.com • URL: http://www.ihsenergy.com • Annual. $395.00 Seven volumes. Covers approximately 20,000 international and 35,000 U.S. industrial standards as well as 362 industrial organizations.

***Index Medicus***. U.S. National Library of Medicine. U. S. Government Printing Office, 732 N Capitol St. NW Washington, DC 20401. Phone: 866-512-1800 or (202)512-1800 or (866)512-1800; Fax: (202)512-2104 or (202)512-2250; Email: contactcenter@gpo.gov • URL: http://www.gpo.gov • Monthly. $522 Individuals; $652.50 Other countries; $83 Single issue; $103.75 Single issue other countries. Bibliographic listing of references to current articles from approximately 3,000 of the world's biomedical journals.

***Index of Majors***. College Board Publications, 45 Columbus Ave. New York, NY 10023-6992. Phone: 800-323-7155 or (212)713-8000; Fax: (212)713-8143 • URL: http://www.collegeboard.com • Annual. $22.95.

***Index to AV Producers and Distributors***. National Information Center for Educational Media. Plexus Publishing Inc., 143 Old Marlton Pke. Medford, NJ 08055-8750. Phone: 800-300-9868 or (609)654-6500; Fax: (609)654-4309; Email: info@plexuspublishing.com • URL: http://www.plexuspublishing.com • Biennial. $89.00. A directory listing about 23,300 producers and distributors of all types of audiovisual educational materials.

***Index to Current Urban Documents***. Greenwood Publishing Group Inc., 88 Post Rd. W Westport, CT 06881. Phone: (203)226-3571; Fax: (203)222-1502; Email: orders@greenwood.com • URL: http://www.greenwood.com • Quarterly. $500.00 per year. Includes annual *Cumulation*.

***Index to Federal Tax Articles***. Thomson RIA, 195 Broadway New York, NY 10007-3100. Phone: 800-431-9025 or (212)367-6300 or (212)807-2298; Fax: (212)367-6305 or (212)337-4207; Email: ttacommunications@riag.com • URL: http://www.ria.thomson.com • Quarterly. $1,565. Bibliographic listing of every significant article on federal income, estate and gift taxation since 1913. Lists over 36,000 articles.

***Index to Foreign Legal Periodicals***. American Association of Law Libraries. University of California Press - Journals and Digital Publishing Division, Journals Fulfillment Dept., Ste. 400, 155 Grand Ave. Oakland, CA 94612-3758. Phone: (510)883-8232; Fax: (510)836-8910; Email: customerservice@ucpress.edu • URL: http://ucpressjournals.com • Quarterly. $725.00 per year. Annual cumulation.

***Index to Legal Periodicals and Books***. EBSCO Publishing Inc., 10 Estes St. Ipswich, MA 01938-2106. Phone: 800-653-2726 or (978)356-6500; Fax: (978)356-6565; Email: information@ebscohost.com • URL: http://www.ebscohost.com • Contains indexing of more than 1,400 English language legal periodicals from 1981 to date and 2,500 books.

***Index to Legal Periodicals and Books***. H.W. Wilson Co., 950 University Ave. Bronx, NY 10452-4224. Phone: 800-367-6770 or (718)588-8400 or (718)558-8400; Fax: (718)590-1617 or (800)590-1617; Email: custserv@hwwilson.com • URL: http://www.hwwilson.com • Monthly. $490.00 per year. Quarterly and annual cumulations.

***Index to Marquis Who's Who Publications***. Marquis Who's Who L.L.C., 300 Connell Dr., Ste. 2000 Berkeley Heights, NJ 07922. Phone: 800-473-7020 or (908)673-1000 or (908)673-1010; Fax: (908)673-1179; Email: customerservice@marquiswhoswho.com • URL: http://www.marquiswhoswho.com • Annual. $159. A combined index to current editions of most Marquis Who's Who publications. Contains over 320,000 entries.

***Index to Proceedings of the Economic and Social Council***. United Nations Publications, c/o National Book Network, 15200 NBN Way Blue Ridge Summit, PA 17214. Phone: 888-254-4286 or (212)963-7680 or (212)963-8302; Fax: (800)338-4550; Email: unpublications@nbnbooks.com • URL: http://www.unp.un.org • Irregular.

***Index Veterinarius: Comprehensive Monthly Subject and Author Index to the World's Veterinary Literature. Availabe in Print and on the Internet***. CABI Publishing North America, 38 Chauncey St., Ste. 1002 Boston, MA 02111. Phone: 800-552-3083; Email: cabi-nao@cabi.org • URL: http://www.cabi.org • Monthly. Institutions, $1,660.00 per year. Annual cumulation. Includes single site internet access. Published in England by CABI Publishing. Provides worldwide coverage of the literature.

***Indexer Locator***. American Society for Indexing, 1628 E Southern Ave., No. 9-223 Tempe, AZ 85282. Phone: (480)245-6750; Email: info@asindexing.org • URL: http://www.asindexing.org • Annual. Lists over 200 free-lance indexers in the U. S. and their subject specialties. Formerly *Register of Indexers*.

***The Indexer: The International Journal of Indexing***. American Society for Indexing, 1628 E Southern Ave., No. 9-223 Tempe, AZ 85282. Phone: (480)245-6750; Email: info@asindexing.org • URL: http://www.asindexing.org • Semiannual. Free to members; non-members, $65.00 per year. Devoted specifically to all aspects of indexing.

***India Business Database***. The Data Supplier, 9107 Wilshire Blvd., Ste. 450 Beverly Hills, CA 90210. Phone: 888-930-3282; Fax: (818)221-0295; Email: contactus@thedatasupplier.com • URL: http://www.thedatasupplier.com • Contains contact information for more than 256,000 manufacturers in India. Includes business name, full contact information, e-mail addresses, and Web site.

***India Business Law Handbook***. International Business Publications, USA, PO Box 15343 Washington, DC 20003. Phone: (202)546-2103; Fax: (202)546-3275; Email: ibpusa@comcast.net • URL: http://ibpus.com • $99.95 Individuals hardcopy, e-book, CD-ROM. Covers: Information on basic business legislation, laws and climate, export-import regulations, and contacts.

***India Government and Business Contacts Handbook***. International Business Publications, USA, PO Box 15343 Washington, DC 20003. Phone: (202)546-2103; Fax: (202)546-3275; Email: ibpusa@comcast.net • URL: http://ibpus.com • $99.95 Individuals hardcopy, e-book, CD-ROM. Covers: Strategic government and business information, export-import activity in the country, investment, business contacts and regulations.

***India Investment and Business Guide***. International Business Publications, USA, PO Box 15343 Washington, DC 20003. Phone: (202)546-2103; Fax: (202)546-3275; Email: ibpusa@comcast.net • URL: http://ibpus.com • $99.95 Individuals hardcopy, e-book, CD-ROM. Covers: Strategic and business information, contacts, regulations and more.

**Indian Council of Social Science Research - Center for Economic and Social Studies**. Begumpet Hyderabad 500 016, Andhra Pradesh, India. Phone: 91 40 23402789; Fax: 91 40 23406808; Email: manoj@cess.ac.in • URL: http://www.cess.ac.in/cesshome/cessmain.asp • Rural development and poverty; agriculture and food security; irrigation and water management; public finance; demography; health; the environment.

***The Indian Export Directory***. Indian Export Trade Journal, 212 Arun Chambers, Tardeo Rd. Mumbai 400 034, India. • Annual. $120; $40. Covers: Indian manufacturers, exporters, importers, foreign firms interested in trade with India, world chambers of commerce, trade associations, and products. Entries include: Company name, address, phone, telex, cable.

***Indian Export Yearbook***. M/S Sales Overseas, Green Park D-20 New Delhi 110 016, India. Phone: 91 11 666279; Fax: 91 11 6862206 • Annual. $80. Covers: Importers, exporters, manufacturers, Indian agents, foreign trade statistics, Indian economy, events, government trade offices, export firms, information for tourists; exporters and importers trading with SAARC countries (Bangladesh, Bhutan, Maldives, Nepal, Pakistan, and Sri Lanka). Entries include: Contact information.

***Indian Exporters Directory, Database***. NIIR Project Consultancy Services, 106 - E, Kamla Nagar New Delhi 110007, India. Phone: 91 11 23843955; Fax: 91 11 23841561; Email: npcs.india@gmail.com • URL: http://www.niir.org • Rs 2,809 Individuals CD-ROM; $200 U.S. CD-ROM. Covers: 43,000+ Indian exporters. Entries include: Company name, contact person name and designation, full postal address, phone, fax, email (wherever available), website address (wherever available), activity.

***Indian Handicrafts Directory: Exporters & Manufacturers***. NIIR Project Consultancy Services, 106 - E, Kamla Nagar New Delhi 110007, India. Phone: 91 11 23843955; Fax: 91 11 23841561; Email: npcs.india@gmail.com • URL: http://www.niir.org • Rs 2,529 Individuals CD-ROM; $200 Individuals CD-ROM. Covers: 1,850+ exporters and manufacturers of handicrafts in India. Entries include: Company name, full address, city, state, pin code, phone, fax, e-mail (wherever available), website (wherever available), product, contact person.

***Indian Importers Directory, Database***. NIIR Project Consultancy Services, 106 - E, Kamla Nagar New Delhi 110007, India. Phone: 91 11 23843955; Fax: 91 11 23841561; Email: npcs.india@gmail.com • URL: http://www.niir.org • Rs 2,809 Individuals CD-ROM; $150 Individuals CD-ROM. Covers: 20,000+ Indian importers. Entries include: Company name, contact person name and designation, full postal address, phone, fax, email (wherever available), website address (wherever available), activity.

***Indian Industrial & Business Register: All India Industrial & Commercial Directory***. NIIR Project Consultancy Services, 106 - E, Kamla Nagar New Delhi 110007, India. Phone: 91 11 23843955; Fax: 91 11 23841561; Email: npcs.india@gmail.com • URL: http://www.niir.org • Rs 2,500 Individuals CD-ROM; $350 Individuals CD-ROM. Covers: Indian industrial and business register. Entries include: Addresses, product details, e-mail, websites, phone and fax nos.

***Indian Management: Business and Management***. Vinod Shanbhag. All Indian Management Association, Management House, 14 Institutional Area, Lodi Rd. New Delhi 110 003, India. Phone: 91 11 617354; Fax: 91 11 4626689 • Monthly. $112; $30 Other countries. Management publication.

**Indian Society of Agricultural Economics**. C-104, 1st Fl., Sadguru Complex -1, Gen. A. K. Vaidya Marg, Goregaon E Mumbai 400 063, Maharashtra, India. Phone: 91 22 28493723; Fax: 91 22 28493724; Email: isae@bom7.vsnl.net.in • URL: http://www.isaeindia.org • Agricultural economists in India. Seeks to further the study of the social and economic problems of agriculture and rural areas and promotes technical competence for teaching and research in agricultural economics and related fields.

**Indian Venture Capital Association**. C-7, Pashchimi Marg, Vasant Vihar New Delhi 110 057, Delhi, India. Phone: 91 11 46160389; Email: aakriti@indiavca.org • URL: http://www.indiavca.org • Facilitates the growth of venture capital and private equity activities in India. Encourages and assists in the creation of more venture capital and private equity funds in India. Works to increase the skills of India's entrepreneurs.

***Indiana All-Business Database***. Harris InfoSource, 2057 E Aurora Rd. Twinsburg, OH 44087-1999. Phone: 800-888-5900 or (330)425-9000 or (973)921-5500; Fax: (800)643-5997 or (877)252-3375; Email: customerservice@harrisinfo.com • URL: http://www.harrisinfo.com • Database covers: 21,000 manufacturing and service companies throughout Indiana.

***Indiana Chamber of Commerce—Business Directory & Resource Guide***. Indiana Chamber of Commerce, 115 W Washington St., Ste. 850 S Indianapolis, IN 46204-3420. Phone: 800-804-6854 or (317)264-3110; Fax: (317)264-6855; Email: kbrinegar@indianachamber.com • URL: http://www.indianachamber.com • Covers: Approximately 5,000 member businesses; state agencies and institutions that offer business assistance services in Indiana. Entries include: For agencies and institutions—Name, address, phone, description of services. For businesses—Business name, address, phone, name and title of contact, products or services.

**Indiana Financial Institutions Directory.** Indiana Bankers Association, 6925 Parkdale Pl. Indianapolis, IN 46254-4673. Phone: (317)387-9380; Fax: (317)387-9374 • URL: http://www.indianabankers.org • $35 Members; $60 Nonmembers. Covers: State and federal agencies associated with the financial institutions industry. Entries include: Name, address, phone, officers and directors of every Indiana bank, savings and loan and credit union, plus listings of officers, directors, total assets, deposits, correspondent banks, counties and population.

**Indiana State University - Center for Research and Management Services.** School of Business Terre Haute, IN 47809. Phone: (812)237-6311; Fax: (812)237-8720; Email: Bev. Bitzegaio@indstate.edu • URL: http://cms.indstate.edu.

**Indiana University - School of Public Health - Department of Applied Health Science.** 1025 E 7th St., Ste. 111 Bloomington, IN 47405. Phone: (812)855-1561 • URL: http://www.publichealth.indiana.edu/departments/applied-health-science/index.shtml • Health behavior, quantitative and qualitative evaluation of instructional materials, and human behavior and attitudes relating to safety and driver education, including studies on industrial safety, health and safety practices in industry and recreational settings, childhood accident prevention and injury control, nutrition, family life, and human development.

*Individual Retirement Plans Guide.* Wolters Kluwer Law & Business CCH, 2700 Lake Cook Rd. Riverwoods, IL 60015. Phone: 888-224-7377 or (847)267-7000; Email: cust_serv@cch.com • URL: http://www.cchgroup.com • $540.00 per year. Looseleaf service. Monthly updates. Covers IRA plans (Individual Retirement Accounts), SEP plans (Simplified Employee Pensions), and Keogh plans (self-employed retirement accounts).

*Indo-German Business Directory.* Indo-German Chamber of Commerce, Maker Tower E, 1st Fl., Cuffe Parade Mumbai 400 005, India. Phone: 91 22 66652121; Fax: 91 22 66652120; Email: bombay@indo-german.com • URL: http://indien.ahk.de • Rs 1,500 for nonmembers; Rs 800 for members. Includes profiles of more than 6500 members of the Indo-German Chamber of Commerce.

*Indo-US Business.* Indo-American Chamber of Commerce, Vulcan Insurance Bldg., 1-C, Veer Nariman Rd., Churchgate Mumbai 400 020, India. Phone: 91 22 22821413 or 91 22 22836340; Fax: 91 22 22046141; Email: ho@iaccindia.com • URL: http://www.iaccindia.com • Monthly.

*Indonesia Business Database.* The Data Supplier, 9107 Wilshire Blvd., Ste. 450 Beverly Hills, CA 90210. Phone: 888-930-3282; Fax: (818)221-0295; Email: contactus@thedatasupplier.com • URL: http://www.thedatasupplier.com • Contains contact information for more than 230,537 companies in Indonesia. Includes business name, full contact information, e-mail addresses, Web site.

*Indonesia Business Forecast Report.* Telecommunications Insight, 85 Queen Victoria St. London EC4V 4AB, United Kingdom. Phone: 20 72 465100 or 44 20 7248 0468; Fax: 20 72 480467 or 44 20 7248 0467; Email: enquiries@telecomsinsight.com • URL: http://www.telecomsinsight.com • Quarterly. $1,195 Individuals Single user; $1,795 Individuals Up to 3 users. Business forecasting reports for Indonesia.

*Indonesia Business Weekly.* PT. Jurnalindo Aksara Grafika, Wisma Bisnis Indonesia Lt. 5 & 6, Slipi, Jl. Let. Jend. S Parman Kav 12 11480 Jakarta, Indonesia. Phone: 62 215304016; Fax: 62 215305866 • URL: http://www.bisnis.com • Weekly. Business magazine.

*Indonesia Industrial and Business Directory.* International Business Publications, USA, PO Box 15343 Washington, DC 20003. Phone: (202)546-2103; Fax: (202)546-3275; Email: ibpusa@comcast.net • URL: http://ibpus.com • $99.95 Individuals hardcopy, e-book, CD-ROM. Covers: Strategic investment, industrial and business contacts for conducting investment and export-import activity in the country.

*Indonesia Yellow Pages Business Directory.* Faust Information GmbH, Werstener Dorfstr. 17 D-40591 Dusseldorf, Germany. Phone: 49 211 976 9922; Fax: 49 211 976 9923; Email: order@faust-information.com • URL: http://www.faust-information.com • Contains comprehensive business and directory information on companies in Indonesia. Includes information on more than 470,000 companies in 3000 industries and classifications. Provides data such as company name, mailing address, phone and fax numbers, e-mail address, web site address, names of contact persons, and more. Where available, includes information on product lines, services offered, and number of employees, plus financial data, brand names, company location, company background, and more. Includes keyword search functions. Allows export of data for use in spreadsheets, mailing programs, and other applications.

*Indonesian Business Directory.* PT Sumber Daya Multimedia, Wisma Kosgoro, 7th Fl., Jl. M. Husni Thamrin No. 53 10350 Jakarta, Indonesia. Phone: 21 314 0578; Fax: 21 314 3034; Email: sdm@rad.net.id • $30. Database covers: 94,000 Indonesian importers, exporters, and other businesses. Entries include: Contact information, industry, and description of products and services.

*Indoor Comfort Marketing.* Industry Publications Inc., 3621 Hill Rd. Parsippany, NJ 07054. Phone: (973)331-9545 or (973)331-9545610; Fax: (973)331-9547 or (973)331-9537; Email: info@spraytechnology.com • URL: http://www.spraytechnology.com • Monthly. $30.00 per year. Formerly *Fueloil and Oil Heat with Air Conditioning.*

**The Indus Entrepreneurs Dubai.** Bldg. No. 1, DIC First Steps, Dubai Internet City Dubai, United Arab Emirates. Phone: 971 4 3913517; Fax: 971 4 3918665; Email: tiedubai@tiedubai.org • URL: http://tiedubai.org • Works to foster and promote the spirit of entrepreneurship in Dubai. Provides a strong and innovative platform for young start-ups and aspiring entrepreneurs. Provides guidance and support through mentoring and networking.

*Industrial and Corporate Services Directory.* Durham Region Economic Development and Tourism Department, 605 Rossland Rd., E Whitby, ON, Canada L1N 6A3. Phone: 800-706-9857 or (905)668-4113; Fax: (905)666-6228; Email: tourism@region.durham.on.ca • URL: http://www.durhambusiness.ca • Covers: Lists of industrial and corporate businesses located in Durham region.

*Industrial & Engineering Chemistry Research.* American Chemical Society, 1155 16th St. NW Washington, DC 20036. Phone: 800-227-5558 or (202)872-4600; Email: help@acs.org • URL: http://www.acs.org • Semimonthly. $2,388 Institutions; $2,949 Institutions, other countries; $90 Members /year for online subscription. Magazine on industrial and engineering chemistry. Formerly *Industrial and Engineering Chemistry Product Research and Development.*

*Industrial and Labor Relations Review.* Cornell University ILR School, 216 Ives Hall Ithaca, NY 14853-3901. Phone: 866-470-1922 or (607)255-2222 or (607)255-1522; Fax: (607)255-8016; Email: ILRCustomerService@cornell.edu • URL: http://www.ilr.cornell.edu • Quarterly. Individuals, $32.00 per year; institutions, $52.00 per year; students, $16.00 per year.

*Industrial & Service Contacts in Ex-Soviet Union Area Republics.* MZM Publications Publishing Promotion Co., PO Box 465 PL 81-705 Sopot, Poland. Phone: 58 55027306; Fax: 58 5513706; Email: mzmpublications@wp.pl • Irregular. Entries include: Company name, address, phone, telex.

*Industrial & Technology-Based Firms Directory.* Charleston Metro Chamber of Commerce, 4500 Leeds Ave., Ste. 100 North Charleston, SC 29405. Phone: (843)577-2510; Fax: (843)723-4853; Email: mail@charlestonchamber.org • URL: http://www.charlestonchamber.net • $150 Members; $300 Nonmembers. Covers: 1,500 plus manufacturing, distribution, and technology-based firms operating in the tri-county area. Technology-based firms included are not only from certain manufacturing sectors but also from the information technology, engineering, biotech, research and development, and other sciences sectors. Entries include: Company name, address, county, phone, web site if known, NAICS code, number of local employees, primary products or services, year established locally, and names of the top officer on site, human resource representative and purchasing agent where applicable.

**Industrial Asset Management Council.** 6625 The Corners Pkwy., Ste. 200 Peachtree Corners, GA 30092-3334. Phone: (770)325-3461; Fax: (770)263-8825; Email: info@iamc.org • URL: http://www.iamc.org • Represents the interests of industrial asset management and corporate real estate executives. Provides educational resources and networking opportunities for the leaders of the manufacturing and industrial asset management industry. Implements the best strategies for success in corporate operations.

**Industrial Auctioneers Association.** 3213 Ayr Ln. Dresher, PA 19025. Phone: 800-805-8359 or (215)366-5450; Fax: (215)657-1964; Email: info@industrialauctioneers.org • URL: http://www.industrialauctioneers.org • Represents industrial machinery and equipment auctioneers. Promotes the use of auction sales in idle industrial equipment. Maintains ethical and professional standards among member auctioneers.

*Industrial/Commercial Directory of Peru.* Confederacion Nacional de Comerciantes, 210 Avenida Abancay Lima, Peru. • Annual. $50. Covers: Industrial and commercial firms in Peru. Entries include: Name, address, phone, telex, products, services.

*Industrial Diamond Review.* De Beers Industrial Diamond Div., Charters, Sunninghill Ascot SL5 9PX, United Kingdom. Phone: 44 1344 623456; Fax: (134)4 638236 • Quarterly. Free to qualified personnel. Incorporating *Industrial Diamond Abstracts.*

*Industrial Directory of Colombia Guide.* Legis Ltda., Avenida Eldorado Ste. 81-10 Bogota, Colombia. Phone: 57 14100628; Fax: 57 1410028 • Annual. $18. Covers: Manufacturers, distributors, and services in Colombia. Entries include: Name, address, phone, telex.

*Industrial Directory of Israel.* Dun & Bradstreet Israel Ltd., 53 Derech Hashalom St. 61253 Tel Aviv, Israel. Phone: 972 3 7330 330; Fax: 972 3 7330 340; Email: custser@dbisrael.co.il • URL: http://www.dbisrael.co.il • Irregular. $48. Covers: Local industries in Israel. Entries include: Address, telephone, annual sales, names and titles of key personnel, products, exports.

*Industrial Distribution: For Industrial Distributors and Their Sales Personnel.* Reed Elsevier Group plc Reed Business Information, 360 Park Ave. S New York, NY 11010. Phone: (212)791-4208; Email: corporatecommunications@reedbusiness.com • URL: http://www.reedbusiness.com • Monthly. $109.90 per year.

**Industrial Energy Consumers of America.** 1155 15th St. NW, Ste. 500 Washington, DC 20005. Phone: (202)223-1661 or (202)223-1420; Fax: (202)530-0659; Email: pcicio@ieca-us.org • URL: http://www.ieca-us.com • Promotes the interests of manufacturing companies and enhances their ability to compete in domestic and world markets. Supports policy development, identification and monitoring of issues and developing and implementing action plans pertaining to energy efficiency and environmental progress. Provides a forum to address state, national and international energy related issues, meet with policy makers and advocate sound policy.

*Industrial Equipment News.* Thomas Publishing Company L.L.C., 5 Penn Plz. New York, NY 10001. Phone: (212)695-0500; Fax: (212)290-7362; Email: contact@thomaspublishing.com • URL: http://www.thomaspublishing.com • Monthly. Contains new product information for manufacturing industries.

*Industrial Fabrics Association International Membership Directory.* Industrial Fabrics Association International, 1801 County Rd. B W Roseville, MN 55113-4061. Phone: 800-225-4324 or (651)222-2508; Fax: (651)631-9334; Email: generalinfo@ifai.com • URL: http://www.ifai.com.

*Industrial Hygiene News Buyer's Guide.* Rimbach Publishing Inc., 8650 Babcock Blvd. Pittsburgh, PA 15237. Phone: 800-245-3182 or (412)364-5366; Fax: (800)245-3182; Email: info@rimbach.com • URL: http://www.rimbach.com • Annual. Lists about 1,000 manufacturers and suppliers of products, equipment, and services to the occupational health, industrial hygiene, and high-tech safety industry.

*Industrial Hygiene News.* Rimbach Publishing Inc., 8650 Babcock Blvd. Pittsburgh, PA 15237. Phone: 800-245-3182 or (412)364-5366; Fax: (800)245-3182; Email: info@rimbach.com • URL: http://www.rimbach.com • Seven times a year. Free to qualified personnel.

*Industrial Laser Solutions Buyer's Guide.* PennWell Corp., Advanced Technology Div., 98 Spit Brook Rd. Nashua, NH 03062-5737. Phone: 800-225-0556 or (603)891-0123; Fax: (603)891-9294; Email: atd@pennwell.com • URL: http://www.pennwell.com • Annual. Lists industrial laser suppliers by category and geographic location. (Included with subscription to *Industrial Laser Solutions.*).

*Industrial Laser Solutions for Manufacturing.* PennWell Corp., Advanced Technology Div., 98 Spit Brook Rd. Nashua, NH 03062-5737. Phone: 800-225-0556 or (603)891-0123; Fax: (603)891-9294; Email: atd@pennwell.com • URL: http://www.pennwell.com • Monthly. $300.00 per year. Covers industrial laser technology, especially machine tool applications.

*Industrial Launderer.* Uniform and Textile Service Association, 1501 Lee Hwy., Ste. 304 Arlington, VA 22209. Phone: 800-486-6745 or (703)247-2600 or (703)247-2601; Fax: (703)841-4750; Email: info@utsa.com • URL: http://www.utsa.com • Monthly. $100.00 per year.

*Industrial Maintenance and Plant Operation.* Reed Elsevier Group plc Reed Business Information, 360 Park Ave. S New York, NY 11010. Phone: (212)791-4208; Email: corporatecommunications@reedbusiness.com • URL: http://www.reedbusiness.com • Monthly. $95.99 per year.

*Industrial Market Location.* Market Location Ltd., 1 Warwick St. Leamington Spa CV32 5LW, United Kingdom. Phone: 44 1926 450388 or 926 450388; Fax: 44 1926 430590 or 926 450592; Email: info@marketlocation.com • URL: http://www.marketlocation.com • Database covers: about 150,000 manufacturing and distribution firms and commercial businesses in the United Kingdom. Database includes: Company name, address, phone, names and titles of key personnel, number of employees, description of product/service, Standard Industrial Classification (SIC) code.

*Industrial Marketing Management: The International Journal of Marketing for Industrial and High-Tech Firms.* Elsevier, Secondary Publishing Division, 650 Ave. of the Americas New York, NY 10011. Phone: 888-437-4636 or (212)633-3980; Fax: (212)633-3975; Email: t.reller@elsevier.com • URL: http://www.elseveier.com • $1,751 Institutions. Eight times a year. Qualified personnel, $127.00 per year; institutions, $816.00 per year.

*Industrial Paint and Powder Buyer's Guide.* Business News Publishing, 1050 IL Route 83, Ste. 200 Bensenville, IL 60106. Phone: (248)244-6474 • Annual. Free to qualified personnel; others, $15.00. List of about 2,000 manufacturers of finishing and formulating products. Formerly *Industrial Finishing Buyer's Guide.*

*Industrial Paint and Powder: Coatings Manufacturing and Application.* Reed Elsevier Group plc Reed Business Information, 360 Park Ave. S New York, NY 11010. Phone: (212)791-4208; Email: corporatecommunications@reedbusiness.com • URL: http://www.reedbusiness.com • Monthly. $72.90 per year. Supplement available, *Annual Buyer's Guide.* Formerly *Industrial Finishing.*

*Industrial Purchasing Agent.* Publications for Industry, 21 Russell Woods Rd. Great Neck, NY 11021. Phone: (516)487-0990; Fax: (516)487-0809 • Description: Covers new product releases pertaining to the industrial manufacturing industry.

Recurring features include by-line spreads, news of research, and new literature releases.

***Industrial Relations: A Journal of Economy and Society***. University of California at Berkeley. Blackwell Publishing Inc., 350 Main St. Malden, MA 02148. Phone: 800-216-2522 or (781)388-8200; Fax: (781)388-8210; Email: journaladsusa@bos.blackwellpublishing.com • URL: http://www.blackwellpublishing.com • 5/year. Bimonthly. Institutions, $862.00 per year. Includes online edition.

**Industrial Relations Research Institute**. University of Wisconsin-Madison, c Madison, WI 53706. Phone: (608)262-1300; Fax: (608)265-4591; Email: irri@mhub.facstaff.wisc.edu • URL: http://www.wisc.edu.

***Industrial Revolution Reference Library***. Cengage Learning Inc., 20 Channel Center St. Boston, MA 02210. Phone: 800-487-8488 or (617)289-7700; Fax: (617)289-7844; Email: investors@cengage.com • URL: http://www.cengage.com • 2003. $247. Three volumes. Individual volumes are available. Includes *Industrial Revolution: Almanac; Industrial Revolution: Biographies* and *Industrial Revolution: Primary Sources*. (UXL imprint).

***Industrial Safety and Hygiene News: News of Safety, Health and Hygiene, Environmental, Fire, Security and Emergency Protection Equipment***. BNP Media, 2401 W Big Beaver Rd., Ste. 700 Troy, MI 48084. Phone: 800-952-6643 or (248)362-3700 or (847)763-9534; Fax: (248)362-5103 or (248)362-0317; Email: privacy@bnpmedia.com • URL: http://www.bnpmedia.com • Monthly. Free to qualified personnel; others, $120.00 per year.

**Industrial Society**. Av. Andres Bello 2777, Piso 3, Las Condes Santiago, Chile. Phone: 56 2 3913100; Fax: 56 2 3913200; Email: sofofa@sofofa.cl • URL: http://web.sofofa.cl • Represents the views and interests of Chilean industry and business. Promotes the advancement and expansion of the private sector.

**Industrialists' Association of Panama**. Apartado 0819-05411 Panama City, Panama. Phone: 507 230-0169; Email: sip@cableonda.net • URL: http://www.industriales.org.

***Industridata: AA Enterprises***. Mercametrica Ediciones S.A., Av. Universidad 1621, Fl. 3, Col. Property of Guadalupe Chimalistac 01050 Mexico City, Mexico. Phone: 52 55 56616293; Fax: 52 55 56623308; Email: mercametrica@mercametrica.com • URL: http://www.mercametrica.com • Annual. $550 Individuals. Covers: Over 1,700 industrial, commercial, and services companies in Mexico with 251 to 500 employees. Includes banks and insurance companies. Companion volume of 'Industridata: AAA Enterprises' (see separate entry). Information from both titles is listed by postal code in 'Industridata by Zip Codes.' Entries include: Company name, location, phone, fax, telex, days and hours of operation, main products and brands, number of employees, sales, installed capacity and output for previous four years, government and foreign ownership, year established, names and titles of key personnel.

***L'Industrie Luxenbourgeoise***. Federation Des Industries Luxembourgeois, 7, rue Alcide de Gaspari, Kirchberg L-1013 Luxembourg, Luxembourg. Phone: 352 43 53 66 1; Fax: 352 43 23 28; Email: fedil@fedil.lu • URL: http://www.fedil.lu • Annual. Covers: Approximately 320 of Luxembourg's industries. Entries include: Company name, address, phone, telex number, names and titles of key personnel, number of employees, financial data, description of services and products provided.

***Industries in Transition; A Newsletter Written for Growth Directed Management and Business Planners***. Business Communications Co., Inc., 70 New Canaan Ave. Norwalk, CT 06850. Phone: (203)853-4266; Email: info@bccresearch.com • URL: http://www.ien.com • Monthly. $375.00 per year. Newsletter. Formerly *Growth Industry News*.

***Industry Business***. Upper Sandusky Area Chamber of Commerce, 108 E Wyandot Ave. Upper Sandusky, OH 43351. Phone: (419)294-3349; Email: uppersanduskychamber@gmail.com • URL: http://www.uppersanduskychamber.com • Periodic.

**Industry Council for Emergency Response Technologies**. PO Box 42563 Washington, DC 20015-2604. Phone: (240)398-3065; Email: george.rice@theindustrycouncil.org • URL: http://www.theindustrycouncil.org • Represents the emergency communications industry in the development of emergency technology infrastructure and policy for the good of public safety and the public it serves. Conducts scientifically credible and objective research to support innovation in the 9-1-1 industry for the benefit of the public. Brings together industry leaders in order to maximize the value of research and development investment.

***Industry Insider***. Thomson Financial, PO Box 95512 Chicago, IL 60694. Phone: 800-607-4463 or (312)288-6400 • URL: http://www.tfsd.com • Contains full-text online industry research reports from more than 200 leading trade associations, covering 50 specific industries. Reports include extensive statistics and market research data. Inquire as to online cost and availability.

***Industry—New and Expanding***. Alabama Development Office Alabama Center for Commerce, 401 Adams Ave. Montgomery, AL 36130-4106. Phone: 800-248-0033 or (334)242-0400; Fax: (334)353-1330; Email: idinfo@ado.state.al.us • URL: http://www.ado.state.al.us • Annual. Covers: List of industrial companies announcing plans to locate or expand facilities in Alabama. Entries include: Company name, location, products or services, amount of capital investment, number of jobs created.

***Industry Norms and Key Business Ratios***. Dun & Bradstreet Inc., 103 JFK Pkwy. Short Hills, NJ 07078. Phone: 800-526-0651 or (973)921-5500 or (973)921-5000; Fax: (866)560-7035 or (512)794-7670; Email: info@dnb.com • URL: http://www.dnb.com • Annual. Five volumes. Covers over 800 kinds of businesses, arranged by Standard Industrial Classification number. More detailed editions covering longer periods of time are also available.

***IndustryWeek: The Management Resource***. Penton Media Inc., 1300 E 9th St. Cleveland, OH 44114-1501. Phone: (216)696-7000; Fax: (216)696-1752; Email: information@penton.com • URL: http://penton.com • Monthly. Edited for industrial and business managers. Covers organizational and technological developments affecting industrial management.

**INFARMA - Employers' Union of Innovative Pharmaceutical Companies**. Pulawska 17 St. PL-02-515 Warsaw, Poland. Phone: 48 22 8528230; Fax: 48 22 8528231; Email: biuro@infarma.pl • URL: http://www.infarma.pl • Foreign-based pharmaceutical manufacturing companies maintaining operations in Poland. Promotes creation of a business climate favorable to members. Represents members' interests before government agencies and trade organizations; conducts educational and charitable programs.

***Influence: Clients' Guide to the Business of Lobbying***. ALM Media Properties LLC, 120 Broadway, 5th Fl. New York, NY 10271-1100. Phone: (212)457-9400; Fax: (646)417-7705; Email: customercare@alm.com • URL: http://www.alm.com • Monthly. $349.00 per year. Newsletter. Provides influence-related news about "lobby shops," companies, associations, and the government. Covers grass-roots campaigns, public relations strategies, new client signings, and fresh registrations. Edited for government relations personnel, public affairs professionals, and lawyers. (Legal Times).

***Info Franchise Newsletter***. Info Press Inc., 728 Ctr. St. Lewiston, NY 14092. Phone: 888-806-2665 or (716)754-4669; Fax: (905)688-7728 • URL: http://www.infonews.com • Description: Covers business format franchising in the U.S., Canada, and overseas; reports on trends, legislation and litigation, and on developments in the franchising business scene. Recurring features include lists of new franchisors, including descriptions, contact addresses and telephone numbers for each; and address changes of franchisor headquarters. Spotlights upcoming seminars, conferences and business opportunity shows.

***InfoAlert: Your Expert Guide to Online Business Information***. Economics Press Inc., 12 Daniel Rd. Fairfield, NJ 07004-2565. Phone: 800-526-2554 or (973)227-1224; Fax: (973)227-9742 • Monthly. $129.00 per year. Newsletter. Provides information on recommended World Wide Web sites in various business, marketing, industrial, and financial areas.

***The Infomation Management Journal: The Journal for the Information Management Professionals***. A R M A International, 13725 W 109th St., Ste. 101 Lenexa, KS 66215. Phone: 800-442-2762 or (913)341-3808; Fax: (913)341-3742 • URL: http://www.arma.org • Quarterly. Free to members; non-members, $95.00 per year; institutions and libraries, $53.00 per year. Formerly *Records Management Quarterly*.

***Inform: International News on Fats, Oils, and Related Materials***. American Oil Chemists Society. AOCS Press, 2211 W Bradley Ave. Champaign, IL 61821-1827. Phone: (217)359-2344; Fax: (217)351-8091; Email: general@aocs.org • URL: http://www.aocs.org • Monthly. Individuals, $120.00 per year; institutions, $360.00 per year. Covers a wide range of technical and business topics relating to the processing and utilization of edible oils, essential oils, and oilseeds.

***Inform Katalog Business Directory***. Inform Katalog Spol. S.R.O., Sumvaska 31 61254 Brno, Czech Republic. Phone: 420 5 41211428; Fax: 420 5 41213658; Email: inform@brn.pvtnet.cz • Annual. Covers: Approved contacts for 60,000 Czech companies. Entries include: Business contact information.

***Inform Katalog Export Import***. Inform Katalog Spol. S.R.O., Sumvaska 31 61254 Brno, Czech Republic. Phone: 420 5 41211428; Fax: 420 5 41213658; Email: inform@brn.pvtnet.cz • Annual. Covers: More than 4,000 of the leading Czech exporters and importers classified by commodities.

***Inform Katalog***. Inform Katalog Spol. S.R.O., Sumvaska 31 61254 Brno, Czech Republic. Phone: 420 5 41211428; Fax: 420 5 41213658; Email: inform@brn.pvtnet.cz • Annual. $190. Covers: Approximately 20,000 Czech companies. Entries include: Business information.

***Inform Katalog Slovakia***. Inform Katalog Slovakia Ltd., Cukrova 14 813 39 Bratislava, Slovakia. Phone: 421 7 367451; Fax: 421 7 367451 • Annual. $88. Covers: 6,000 companies in Slovakia. Entries include: Detailed business information.

***InForm***. Victor O. Schinnerer and Company Inc., 2 Wisconsin Cir. Chevy Chase, MD 20815-7003. Phone: (301)961-9800; Fax: (301)951-5444; Email: vos.info@schinnerer.com • URL: http://www.schinnerer.com • Description: Reports national and state developments affecting architects and engineers.

***Inform Slovenskych Podnikov***. Inform Katalog Slovakia Ltd., Cukrova 14 813 39 Bratislava, Slovakia. Phone: 421 7 367451; Fax: 421 7 367451 • Annual. $26. Covers: 15,000 business contacts at Slovakian companies classified in detail by area of activity.

***The Information Advisor: Tips and Techniques for Smart Information Users***. MarketResearch.com, 11200 Rockville Pke., Ste. 504 Rockville, MD 20852. Phone: 800-298-5699 or (240)747-3093; Fax: (240)747-3004; Email: customerservice@marketresearch.com • URL: http://www.marketresearch.com • Monthly. $159.00 per year. Newsletter. Evaluates and discusses online, CD-ROM, and published sources of business, financial, and market research information.

***The Information Advisor's Guide to Internet Research***. Information Today, Inc., 143 Old Marlton Pke. Medford, NJ 08055-8750. Phone: 800-300-9868 or (609)654-6266; Fax: (609)654-4309; Email: custserv@infotoday.com • URL: http://www.infotoday.com • 10/year. $199.95 U.S. One year subscription. Evaluates free and low-cost websites.

***Information and Image Management: The State of the Industry***. Association for Information and Image Management International, 1100 Wayne Ave., Ste. 1100 Silver Spring, MD 20910. Phone: 800-477-2446 or (301)587-8202; Fax: (301)587-2711; Email: aiim@aiim.org • URL: http://www.aiim.org • Annual. $130.00. Market data with five-year forecasts. Covers electronic imaging, micrographics supplies and equipment, software, and records management services.

***Information and Management; International Journal of Information Systems Applications***. Elsevier, Secondary Publishing Division, 650 Ave. of the Americas New York, NY 10011. Phone: 888-437-4636 or (212)633-3980; Fax: (212)633-3975; Email: t.reller@elsevier.com • URL: http://www.elseveier.com • Eight times a year. Institutions, $646.00 per year.

***Information Broker***. Helen P. Burwell, editor. Burwell Enterprises Inc., 5619 Plumtree Dr. Dallas, TX 75252-4928. Phone: (972)733-1951 or (972)732-0160; Fax: (972)733-1951 • Description: Covers companies that offer fee-based information services and issues related to "the business" of information brokering.

***Information Communication Technology Standardization for E-Business Sectors: Integrating Supply and Demand Factors***. Cengage Learning Inc., 20 Channel Center St. Boston, MA 02210. Phone: 800-487-8488 or (617)289-7700; Fax: (617)289-7844; Email: investors@cengage.com • URL: http://www.cengage.com • Published by Information Science Reference. Explores aspects affecting the nature, relevance, and quality of standards, and the impact they have on businesses.

***Information Executive: A Monthly Publication for DPMA and the Information Systems Profession***. Association of Information Technology Professionals, 15000 Commerce Parkway, Ste. C Mount Laurel, NJ 08054. Phone: 800-224-9371; Fax: (856)439-0525; Email: aitp_hq@aitp.org • URL: http://www.aitp.org • Monthly. $45.00 per year. Articles reporting developmental and technical aspects of EDP services, supplies, equipment, accessories and related contemporary trends and issues. Formerly *Inside DPMA*.

***The Information Freeway Report: Free Business and Government Information Via Modem***. Washington Researchers Ltd., 1655 N Fort Myer Dr., Ste. 800 Arlington, VA 22209. Phone: (703)312-2863; Fax: (703)527-4586; Email: research@researchers.com • URL: http://www.washingtonresearchers.com • Monthly. $160.00 per year. Newsletter. Provides news of business and government databases that are available free of charge through the Internet or directly. Emphasis is on federal government databases and electronic bulletin boards (Fedworld).

***Information Hotline***. Science Associates/International Inc., 6 Hastings Rd. Marlboro, NJ 07746-1313. Phone: 800-721-1080 or (908)536-7673; Fax: (908)536-7673 • Monthly. $150; $175 Other countries. Description: "The oldest, most respected, continuously published newsletter." Devoted to objective coverage of trends, policy, analysis, and opinion in the information field.

***Information Industry Directory***. Cengage Learning Inc., 20 Channel Center St. Boston, MA 02210. Phone: 800-487-8488 or (617)289-7700; Fax: (617)289-7844; Email: investors@cengage.com • URL: http://www.cengage.com • Annual. $1,160 Individuals. Provides information on companies that produce and provide electronic systems, services and products.

***Information Management Report: An International Newsletter for Information Professionals and Librarians***. R.R. Bowker L.L.C., 630 Central Ave New Providence, NJ 07974. Phone: 888-269-5372 or (908)286-1090; Email: info@bowker.com • URL: http://www.bowker.com • Monthly. $505.00 per year; includes print and online editions. Incorporates *Outlook on Research Libraries*.

***Information Outlook: The Monthly Magazine of the Special Libraries Association***. Special Libraries Association, 331 S Patrick St. Alexandria, VA 22314-3501. Phone: (703)647-4900; Fax: (703)647-4901 • URL: http://www.sla.org • Monthly. $65.00 per year. Topics include information technology, the Internet, copyright, research techniques, library management, and professional development. Replaces *Special Libraries* and *SpeciaList*.

***Information Please Business Almanac and Desk Reference***. Information Please L.L.C., 501 Boylston St., Ste. 900 Boston, MA 02116-3725. Phone: (617)832-0300 • URL: http://www.infoplease.com • Annual. $21.95.

***Information Processing and Management: An International***

***Journal***. Elsevier, Secondary Publishing Division, 650 Ave. of the Americas New York, NY 10011. Phone: 888-437-4636 or (212)633-3980; Fax: (212)633-3975; Email: t.reller@elsevier.com • URL: http://www.elseveier.com • $327 Individuals; $2,611 Institutions. Bimonthly. Qualified personnel, $301.00 per year; institutions, $1,196.00 per year. Text in English, French, German and Italian.

***The Information Report***. Washington Researchers Ltd., 1655 N Fort Myer Dr., Ste. 800 Arlington, VA 22209. Phone: (703)312-2863; Fax: (703)527-4586; Email: research@researchers.com • URL: http://www.washingtonresearchers.com • Description: Contains 40-140 items in each issue identifying little-known sources of information. Lists and describes directories, special libraries, booklets, seminars, studies, and other research sources available on markets, competition, federal regulation, and economic conditions. Covers government as well as corporate sources, trade, and professional organizations.

***Information Retrieval and Library Automation***. Lomond Publications, 7101 Woodville Rd. Mount Airy, MD 21771-7931. Phone: 800-443-6299 or (301)829-8222 or (301)694-0123; Fax: (301)694-5151; Email: lomondpubs@prodigy.net • URL: http://www.lomondpubs.com • Monthly. $75.00 per year. Summarizes research events and literature worldwide.

***Information Science Abstracts***. American Society for Information Science. Information Today, Inc., 143 Old Marlton Pke. Medford, NJ 08055-8750. Phone: 800-300-9868 or (609)654-6266; Fax: (609)654-4309; Email: custserv@infotoday.com • URL: http://www.infotoday.com • Nine times a year. $725.00 per year.

***Information Sciences; An International Journal***. Elsevier, Secondary Publishing Division, 650 Ave. of the Americas New York, NY 10011. Phone: 888-437-4636 or (212)633-3980; Fax: (212)633-3975; Email: t.reller@elsevier.com • URL: http://www.elseveier.com • $161 Individuals; $6,614 Institutions. 36 times a year. Individuals, $106.00 per year; institutions, $3,557.00 per year. Three sections, A: Informatics and Computer Science, B: Intelligent Systems, C: Applications.

***Information Services and Use: An International Journal***. IOS Press, Inc., 5795-G Burke Centre Pkwy. Burke, VA 22015. Phone: (703)323-5554; Fax: (703)323-3668 or (703)323-3368; Email: iosbooks@iospress.com • URL: http://www.iospress.nl • Quarterly. €105 Individuals online only; $140 Individuals online only. An information and information technology oriented publication with a wide scope of subject matters.

***The Information Society: An International Journal***. Taylor & Francis Ltd., 2 Park Sq., Milton Park Abingdon OX14 4RN, United Kingdom. Phone: 44 22 70176000 or 44 20 70176000; Fax: 44 22 70176699 or (701)76336; Email: info@e-elgar.co.uk • URL: http://www.taylorandfrancisgroup.com • 5/year. $209 Individuals. Five times a year. Individuals, $105.00 per year; institutions, $285.00 per year.

***Information Standards Quarterly***. National Information Standards Organization, 3600 Clipper Mill Rd., Ste. 302 Baltimore, MD 21211. Phone: (301)654-2512; Fax: (410)685-5278; Email: hreid@copyright.com • URL: http://www.niso.org • Quarterly. $130 Individuals /year; $165 Other countries /year; $36 Single issue. Newsletter. Reports on activities of the National Information Standards Organization.

***Information Strategy: The Executive's Journal***. Auerbach Publications, 345 Park Ave., S New York, NY 10017-1707. Phone: (212)286-1010; Fax: (212)297-9176 or (212)297-9716; Email: orders@crcpress.com • URL: http://www.auerbach-publications.com • Quarterly. $195.00 per year.

***Information Systems Management***. Auerbach Publications, 345 Park Ave., S New York, NY 10017-1707. Phone: (212)286-1010; Fax: (212)297-9176 or (212)297-9716; Email: orders@crcpress.com • URL: http://www.auerbach-publications.com • Quarterly. $175 Individuals. Journal provides expert guidance in the innovative management of information systems resources. Formerly *Journal of Information Systems Management*.

***Information Systems Security***. Auerbach Publications, 345 Park Ave., S New York, NY 10017-1707. Phone: (212)286-1010; Fax: (212)297-9176 or (212)297-9716; Email: orders@crcpress.com • URL: http://www.auerbach-publications.com • Quarterly. $175 Individuals. Journal provides standards, guidelines, and techniques for creating more secure, less vulnerable information systems. Formerly *Journal of Information Systems Security*.

***Information Systems; Data Bases: Their Creation, Management and Utilization***. Elsevier, Secondary Publishing Division, 650 Ave. of the Americas New York, NY 10011. Phone: 888-437-4636 or (212)633-3980; Fax: (212)633-3975; Email: t.reller@elsevier.com • URL: http://www.elseveier.com • $250 Individuals; $2,582 Institutions. Eight times a year. Institutions, $1,554.00 per year.

**Information Technology Alliance**. 23940 N 73rd Pl. Scottsdale, AZ 85255. Phone: (480)515-2003; Fax: (602)294-2399 • URL: http://www.italliance.com • Represents mid-market technology professionals, consultants, and product/service providers in North America. Aims to create a community where members share information and build relationships that improve the way they do business with their clients. Protects the quality of the profession and promotes public welfare.

***Information Technology Outlook***. Organisation for Economic Co-operation and Development Publications and Information Center, 2001 L St. NW, Ste. 650 Washington, DC 20036-4922. Phone: 800-456-6323 or (202)785-6323; Fax: (202)785-0350; Email: washington.contact@oecd.org • URL: http://www.oecd.org • Biennial. A review of recent developments in international markets for computer hardware, software, and services. Also examines current legal provisions for information systems security and privacy in OECD countries.

**Information Technology Services Marketing Association**. 91 Hartwell Ave. Lexington, MA 02421-3137. Phone: (781)862-8500; Fax: (781)674-1366; Email: info@itsma.com • URL: http://www.itsma.com • Supports marketing executives who market and sell technology-related services and solutions. Provides research, consulting and training to the world's leading technology, communications, and professional services providers. Facilitates peer sharing and networking opportunities among members.

***Information Times***. Software and Information Industry Association, 1090 Vermont Ave. NW, 6th Fl. Washington, DC 20005-4095. Phone: (202)289-7442 or (202)789-4440; Fax: (202)289-7097 or (202)638-4403; Email: rcollier@siia.net • URL: http://www.siia.net • Monthly. Membership. Formerly *Friday Memo*.

***Information Today: The Newspaper for Users and Producers of Electronic Information Services***. Information Today, Inc., 143 Old Marlton Pke. Medford, NJ 08055-8750. Phone: 800-300-9868 or (609)654-6266; Fax: (609)654-4309; Email: custserv@infotoday.com • URL: http://www.infotoday.com • 11 times a year. $68.95 per year.

***Information Week: Business Innovation Powered by Technology***. UBM L.L.C., 240 W 35th St. New York, NY 10001. • URL: http://www.ubm.com • Weekly. $199.00 per year. The magazine for information systems management.

***InfoTech Trends***. Data Analysis Group, Phone: (925)462-1202; Fax: (925)462-1225; Email: support@infotechtrends.com • URL: http://www.infotechtrends.com • Web site provides both free and fee-based market research data on the information technology industry, including computers, peripherals, telecommunications, the Internet, software, CD-ROM/DVD, e-commerce, and workstations. Fees: Free for current (most recent year) data; more extensive information has various fee structures. Formerly *Computer Industry Forecasts*.

***Infotel—The Electronic Directory of Companies from Romania***. Chamber of Commerce and Industry of Romania, Bd. Octavian Goga nr. 2, Sector 3 R-030982 Bucharest, Romania. Phone: 40 21 3190114 or 40 21 3190118; Email: ccir@ccir.ro • URL: http://www.ccir.ro • Covers: More than 500,00 Romanian companies. Entries include: Company name, headquarters address, telephone and fax number, registration, statistical and fiscal codes, profile, equity, shareholders, number of employees, gross profit.

***INFOTRADE Belgian Company Financial Data***. INFOTRADE N.V., Stationsstraat 30 bus 2 B-1702 Groot-Bijgaarden, Belgium. Phone: 32 2 4818283; Fax: 32 2 4818200; Email: infotrade@ift.be • Daily. Database covers: More than 1,000,000 descriptive and financial profiles of Belgian companies and private businesses. Entries include: Company name, address, name and title of contact; commercial registration numbers; date and form of incorporation; bank accounts; association memberships; principal language; number of employees; names of management personnel; activities and products; trademarks; trading partners; financial statements for the most recent three years.

***InfoWorld: Defining Technology for Business***. InfoWorld Publishing, 155 Bovet Rd., Suite 800 San Mateo, CA 94402. Phone: 800-227-8365 or (650)572-7341; Fax: (650)312-0584 • URL: http://www.infoworld.com • Weekly. $195.00 per year. For personal computing professionals.

***Ingram's: Kansas City's Business Magazine***. Show-Me Publishing Inc., 306 E. 12th St., Ste. 1014 Kansas City, MO 64106. Phone: (816)842-9994; Fax: (816)474-1111; Email: subscriptions@ingramsonline.com • URL: http://www.ingramsonline.com • Monthly. $44.95 Individuals; $69.95 Two years; $99.95 Individuals three years. Business and lifestyle magazine covering Lawrence, Topeka, Overland Park, KS, and Kansas City and St. Joseph, MO.

***INIS Newsletter***. International Atomic Energy Agency, Division of Publications, PO Box 100 W-1400 Vienna, Austria. Phone: 43 1 26000; Fax: 43 1 26007; Email: official.mail@iaea.org • URL: http://www-naweb.iaea.org/NAHU/index.html • Irregular. Free. Newsletter of the International Nuclear Information System (INIS).

***Initial Public Offerings***. Glasser LegalWorks, 150 Clove Rd. Little Falls, NJ 07424. Phone: 800-308-1700 or (973)890-0008; Fax: (973)890-0042; Email: legalwks@aol.com • URL: http://www.glasserlegalworks.com • Looseleaf. $225.00, including CD-ROM version. Periodic Supplementation. Includes explanations of legal procedures for IPOs, with annotated forms. (Emerging Growth Companies Series.).

***Initiative Europe***. ICC Online Services Div. ICC Information Group Ltd., Field House, 72 Oldfield Rd. Hampton TW12 2HQ, United Kingdom. Phone: 81 7831122; Fax: 81 7830049 • Monthly. Covers: Small- and medium-sized businesses in Europe seeking international joint venture, partnership, and licensing agreements.

**INJAZ Bahrain**. Manama Ctr. Entrance 3, 4th Fl., office 606/607, Government Rd. Manama, Bahrain. Phone: 973 17225050; Fax: 973 17225052; Email: websmaster@injazbh.org • URL: http://injazbh.org • Aims to educate and inspire young people to value enterprise, business and economics to improve the quality of their lives. Teaches economics, entrepreneurship and financial literacy, focusing on the importance of market-driven economies. Encourages students to apply lessons into action, and learn the value of contributing to their communities.

***Injury Facts***. National Safety Council, 1121 Spring Lake Dr. Itasca, IL 60143-3201. Phone: 800-621-7615 or (630)285-1121; Fax: (630)285-1315; Email: info@nsc.org • URL: http://www.nsc.org • Annual. $109.85 Nonmembers; $104.40 10-49 yr. of age; $99 50 and above.

***Inland River Guide***. Waterways Journal Inc., 319 N 4th St., Ste. 650 Saint Louis, MO 63102. Phone: (314)241-7354; Fax: (314)241-4207 • URL: http://www.waterwaysjournal.net • Annual. $73. Covers barge and towing companies operating on Mississippi River System, Warrior-Tom Bigbee System, and Gulf Intracoastal Waterwa: all inland and Gulf Coast shipyards; public and private terminals on waterway:: contracting and dredging firms; government agencies dealing with waterways.

***Innovation Masters: History's Best Examples of Business Transformation***. Cengage Learning Inc., 20 Channel Center St. Boston, MA 02210. Phone: 800-487-8488 or (617)289-7700; Fax: (617)289-7844; Email: investors@cengage.com • URL: http://www.cengage.com • $483 print only. Covers the best examples of successful businesses and/or business people that have incorporated or developed a new product, service or technology that help to reinvent or revolutionize their business and/or industry.

**Innovation Norway - United States**. 655 3rd Ave., Ste. 1810 New York, NY 10017-9111. Phone: (212)885-9700 or (212)421-9210; Fax: (212)885-9710 or (212)838-0374; Email: newyork@innovationnorway.no • URL: http://www.innovasjonnorge.no/Kontorer-i-utlandet/usa-newyork/ • U.S. branch of the Export Council of Norway. Assists Norwegian companies in marketing their goods and services in the U.S. Provides information to Norwegian exporters on U.S. markets, tariffs and statistics, trade constraints, and distribution channels. Establishes contacts with U.S. authorities, marketing and manufacturing firms, local lawyers, accountants, banks, patent offices, advertising and public relations agencies, consultants, and credit and debt collection agencies. Aids in establishing Norwegian subsidiaries in the U.S.

***Innovations in Education and Training International***. Association for Education and Training Technology. Routledge, 711 3rd Ave., 8th Fl. New York, NY 10017. Phone: 800-634-7064 or (212)216-7800; Fax: (212)564-7854 or (212)563-2269; Email: book.orders@tandf.co.uk • URL: http://www.routledge.com • Quarterly. Individuals, $81.00 per year; libraries and other institutions, $290.00 per year. Provides up-to-date coverage of educational and training technologies. Formerly *Educational and Training Technology International*.

***Innovative Publisher: Publishing Strategies for New Markets***. Emmelle Publishing Co., Inc., 370 Seventh Ave., Suite 905 New York, NY 10001. Phone: (212)714-1881; Fax: (212)714-1488 • Biweekly. $69.00 per year. Provides articles and news on electronic publishing (CD-ROM or online) and desktop publishing.

***Inquiry: The Journal of Health Care Organization, Provision, and Financing***. Blue Cross and Blue Shield Association of the Rochester Area, PO Box 25399 Rochester, NY 14625. Phone: (716)264-9122; Fax: (716)264-9122 • URL: http://www.inquiryjournal.org • $118 Individuals print and web /year; $203 Institutions print and web /year. Quarterly. Individuals, $53.00 per year; institutions, $75.00 per year.

***Inside Business***. Great Lakes Publishing Co., 1422 Euclid Ave., No. 730 Cleveland, OH 44115. Phone: (216)771-2833; Fax: (216)781-6318; Email: webmaster@glpublishing.com • URL: http://www.glpublishing.com • Monthly. Publication covering general business issues.

***Inside Chips Ventures: The Global Report with Executive Perspective***. HTE Research Inc., 2493 Erie Terr. Bellingham, WA 98229. Phone: (360)676-2260; Fax: (360)350-3472 or (360)676-2265; Email: szirom@insidechips.com • URL: http://www.hteresearch.com • Monthly. $595.00 per year. Tracks the activities of semiconductor firms worldwide. Formerly *Semiconductor Industry and Business Survey Newsletter*.

***Inside Flyer***. 1930 Frequent Flyer Point Colorado Springs, CO 80915. Phone: 800-767-8896 • URL: http://www.insideflyer.com • Monthly. $36.00 per year. Newsletter. Provides information relating to frequent flyer awards and air travel.

***Inside Japanese Support***. Taft Group, 27500 Drake Rd. Farmington Hills, MI 48331-3535. Phone: 800-877-4253 or (248)699-4253 or (248)699-GALE; Fax: (800)414-5043 or (248)699-8061; Email: gale.salesassistance@thomson.com • URL: http://www.gale.com/taft • Annual. $199. Covers: 340 U.S. subsidiaries of Japanese firms and 40 Japan-based foundations awarding grants in the United States. Entries include: Company name, address, phone, name and title of contact, application information, program descriptions, recent grants, U.S. operating locations; Japanese parent company name, address, and financial information. Graphs and essay entitled "The Current Status of Japanese Foundations" comprise Section 1; directory information is in Section 2.

***Inside Microsoft Word: Tips and Techniques for Microsoft Windows***. Skillsoft Ireland Ltd., 500 Canal View Rochester, NY 14623. Phone: 800-434-3466 or (585)240-7500; Fax: (585)240-7760 or (585)292-4392; Email: info@elementk. com • URL: http://www.skillsoft.com • Monthly. $87.00 per year. Newsletter on word processing with Microsoft Word for Windows. Covers applications and problem-solving.

***Inside Negotiations***. EFR Corp., P.O. Box 15236 Colorado Spring, FL 80935-5236. • Monthly. $98.00 per year. Newsletter. Labor negotiations.

***Inside R and D: A Weekly Report on Technical Innovation***. Technical Insights, 605 Third Ave. New York, NY 10158-0012. Phone: 800-825-7550 or (212)850-8600; Fax: (212)850-8800; Email: insights@wiley.com • URL: http:// www.wiley.com • Weekly. Institutions, $840.00 per year. Concentrates on new and significant developments. Formerly *Technology Transfer Week*.

***Inside the Indian Business Mind: A Tactical Guide for Managers***. Cengage Learning Inc., 20 Channel Center St. Boston, MA 02210. Phone: 800-487-8488 or (617)289-7700; Fax: (617)289-7844; Email: investors@cengage.com • URL: http://www.cengage.com • Published by Praeger. This title can help Western business people enter the Indian market, make the best use of Indian labor and manufacturing facilities, and create and develop successful, long-term business relationships.

***Inside Tucson Business***. Territorial Newspapers, 3280 E Hemisphere Loop, Ste. 180 Tucson, AZ 85706. Phone: (520)294-1200; Fax: (520)294-4040 or (520)295-4076 • URL: http://www.azbiz.com • Weekly. $50 Individuals; $85 Two years. Newspaper featuring business news.

***Inside U.S. Business: A Concise Encyclopedia of Leading Industries***. QSU Publishing, PO Box 546436 Surfside, FL 33154. Phone: 866-225-3122; Fax: (703)359-8462; Email: news@qsuonline.com • URL: http://www.qsuonline.com • Irregular. $65. List of largest companies and leading firms in major industries in the U.S.

***Inside Wordperfect for Windows***. Skillsoft Ireland Ltd., 500 Canal View Rochester, NY 14623. Phone: 800-434-3466 or (585)240-7500; Fax: (585)240-7760 or (585)292-4392; Email: info@elementk.com • URL: http://www.skillsoft.com • Monthly. $59.00 per year. Newsletter on word processing with Wordperfect software. Includes tips and techniques for both beginners and experts.

***Insider—The Business Magazine of North London***. Atom Publishing Ltd., 45/47 Clerkenwell Green London EC1R 0EB, United Kingdom. Phone: 20 7490 5595; Fax: 20 7490 4957; Email: info@atompublishing.co.uk • URL: http://www. atompublishing.co.uk • Quarterly. $2 Single issue. Trade magazine covering local business news and issues.

***Insiders' Chronicle***. American Banker Newsletters, Email: insiderwatch@cda.com • URL: http://www.thomsoninvest. net • Covers: publicly held companies in whose securities there has been significant buying or selling by executive officers, directors, and those who hold 10% or more of its shares. Database includes: Market news, quotations, and statistics. Entries include: Company name, name and title of person involved, number of shares held, number of shares bought or sold, price per share, date of transaction.

**Insight Center for Community Economic Development**. 2201 Broadway, Ste. 815 Oakland, CA 94612-3024. Phone: (510)251-2600; Fax: (510)251-0600; Email: info@ insightcced.org • URL: http://insightcced.org • Aims to build economic health in vulnerable communities. Develops and promotes innovative solutions that help people and communities become, and remain, economically secure. Collaborates with foundations, nonprofits, educational institutions, government and businesses to develop, strengthen and promote programs and public policy that: lead to good jobs, strengthen early care and education systems, and enable people and communities to build financial and educational assets.

***InSite 2***. Intelligence Data/Thomson Financial, Phone: 800-654-0393 or (617)856-1890; Fax: (617)737-3182; Email: intelligence.data@tfn.com • URL: http://www.insite2.gale. com/ • Fee-based Web site consolidates information in a "Base Pack" consisting of Business InSite, Market InSite, and Company InSite. Optional databases are Consumer InSite, Health and Wellness InSite, Newsletter InSite, and Computer InSite. Includes fulltext content from more than 2,500 trade publications, journals, newsletters, newspapers, analyst reports, and other sources. Continuous updating. Formerly produced by The Gale Group.

**Insol International**. 6 - 7 Queen St., 5th Fl. London EC4N 1SP, United Kingdom. Phone: 44 20 79296679 or 44 20 72483333; Fax: 44 20 79296678 or 44 20 72483384 • URL: http://www. insol.org • Organizations representing 7,300 insolvency practitioners from 62 countries worldwide. Seeks international professional recognition of insolvency practitioners. Works to improve communication and cooperation among members; facilitates the exchange of information; establishes working committees to examine international issues of insolvency practice. Is developing a bibliographic database of insolvency publications.

***Insolvency Law & Practice***. LexisNexis Butterworths Tolley, Tolley House, Two Addiscombe Rd., Croyden Surrey CR9 5AF, United Kingdom. Phone: 44 2086 622000; Fax: (208)6 622012; Email: customer.services@lexisnexis.co.uk • URL:

http://www.tolley.co.uk • Bimonthly. $181.00 per year. United Kingdom emphasis.

***Inspec Direct***. Institution of Engineering and Technology, Michael Faraday House, Six Hills Way Stevenage SG1 2AY, United Kingdom. Phone: 44 1438 313311; Fax: 44 1438 765526; Email: postmaster@theiet.org • URL: http://www.theiet.org • Monthly. $2,400 per year. Section C of *Science Abstracts*.

**INSPEC**. Institution of Electrical Engineers, London WC2R 0BL, United Kingdom. Phone: 44 20 72401871 or 44 20 72407735; Email: postmaster@iee.org.uk • URL: http://www.iee.org.uk • Provides online citations, with abstracts, to the world literature of electrical engineering, electronics, optoelectronics, telecommunications, industrial controls, instrumentation, computer technology, information technology, and physics. Coverage includes more than 4,000 technical and scientific journals from 1969 to date, with weekly updating. (INSPEC is Information Services in Physics, Electronics, and Computing.) Inquire as to online cost and availability.

**Institute for Advanced Studies - Health Economics and Health Policy**. Department of Economics & Finance, Stumpergasse 56 A-1060 Vienna, Austria. Phone: 43 1 59991127; Fax: 43 1 59991555; Email: thomas.czypionka@ihs.ac.at • URL: http:// www.ihs.ac.at/vienna/ • Health economics and policy.

**Institute for Alternative Futures**. 100 N Pitt St., Ste. 307 Alexandria, VA 22314-3134. Phone: (703)684-5880; Fax: (703)684-0640; Email: futurist@altfutures.org • URL: http:// www.altfutures.org • Conducts studies in the future of communications, health care, bioengineering, the legal system, etc.

**Institute for Case Development and Research**. Simmons College, Graduate School of Management, 300 The Fenway Boston, MA 02115. Phone: (617)521-3840; Fax: (617)521-3880; Email: somadm@simmons.edu • URL: http://www. simmons.edu • Studies issues and problems confronting women in management.

**Institute for Economic Analysis**. c/o John S. Atlee, President/ Director, 360 Mt. Auburn St., Ste. 001 Cambridge, MA 02138. Email: info@iea-macro-economics.org • URL: http:// iea-macro-economics.org • Seeks to develop tools for macroeconomic analysis and policy that can maintain stable full employment growth, low inflation, low interest rates and equitable distribution of income and wealth. Integrates GDP and financial accounts for more systematic coordination of monetary and fiscal policy. Focuses on federal monetary policy, federal budget deficit/surplus, social security, consumer credit, and world economic recovery.

**Institute for Operations Research and the Management Sciences**. 5521 Research Park Dr., Ste. 200 Catonsville, MD 21228. Phone: 800-446-3676 or (443)757-3500; Fax: (443)757-3515; Email: informs@informs.org • URL: http:// www.informs.org • International scientific society dedicated to improving operational processes, decision-making and management through the application of methods from science and mathematics. Represents operations researchers, management scientists and those working in related fields within engineering and the information, decision, mathematical and social sciences.

**Institute for Research on Labor, Employment, and the Economy**. 506 E Liberty St., 3rd Fl. Ann Arbor, MI 48104-2210. Phone: (734)998-6201; Fax: (734)998-6202 • URL: http://www.irlee.umich.edu.

**Institute for Supply Management**. 2055 E Centennial Cir. Tempe, AZ 85284-1898. Phone: 800-888-6276 or (480)752-6276; Fax: (480)752-7890; Email: custsvc@ism.ws • URL: http://www.ism.ws • Represents industrial, commercial and utility firms; educational institutions and government agencies. Disseminates information on procurement. Works to develop more efficient supply management methods. Conducts program for certification as a supply manager. Cosponsors executive purchasing management institutes at Michigan State University and Arizona State University. Provides in-company training. Maintains speakers' bureau and reference service.

**Institute for Telecommunications Studies**. School of Telecommunication, 9 S College St. Athens, OH 45701. Phone: (740)593-4866; Fax: (740)593-9184; Email: don.flournoy@ ohio.edu • URL: http://www.mediaschool.ohiou.edu • International telecommunications, social impact of mass communication, economic and management aspects of cable, wireless, satellite, broadcast and Internet industries, emerging telecommunication technologies, computer applications, multimedia TV, and training.

**Institute for Turnaround**. Juxon House, 2nd Fl., 100 St. Paul's Churchyard London EC4M 8BU, United Kingdom. Phone: 44 20 3102 7710; Fax: 44 20 3102 7301; Email: info@ instituteforturnaround.com • URL: http://www. instituteforturnaround.com • Raises the profile of turnaround professionals and its culture. Encourages intervention into underperforming businesses. Promotes turnaround knowledge among business community. Encourages high standards of ethics, behavior and quality of turnaround practitioners.

**Institute of Administrative Management**. Halesfield 7, Coppice House Telford TF7 4NA, United Kingdom. Phone: 44 20 70912600 or 44 20 70912606; Fax: 44 20 70917340; Email: info@instam.org • URL: http://www.instam.org • Seeks to promote and develop, for the public benefit, the science of administrative management in all branches; encourage the attainment of professional academic qualifications. Provides

the latest techniques and developments in the field of administrative management via conferences, seminars, meetings and publications.

***Institute of Business Appraisers—Directory***. Institute of Business Appraisers, 5217 S State St., Ste. 400 Salt Lake City, UT 84107. Phone: 800-299-4130; Fax: (866)353-5406; Email: hqiba@go-iba.org • URL: http://www.go-iba.org • $20 Members; $20 Nonmembers. Listing of members and certified business appraisers.

***Institute of Business Appraisers—Newsletter***. Institute of Business Appraisers, 5217 S State St., Ste. 400 Salt Lake City, UT 84107. Phone: 800-299-4130; Fax: (866)353-5406; Email: hqiba@go-iba.org • URL: http://www.go-iba.org • Quarterly. Covers association and industry news.

**Institute of Certified Professional Managers**. James Madison University, MSC 5504 Harrisonburg, VA 22807. Phone: (540)568-3247; Email: info@icm.biz • URL: http://icpm.biz • Seeks to raise competency and professionalism in the field of management through training and certification of individuals, management chapters, and corporate groups. Sets performance standards for managers worldwide, offers services in the areas of management education, academic assessment, and certification.

**Institute of Commercial Management**. ICM House, Castleman Way, Hampshire Ringwood BH24 3BA, United Kingdom. Phone: 44 1202 490555; Email: info@icm.education • URL: http://icm.education • Serves as a UK Examining and Awarding body for business and management students. Seeks to provide a range of high quality global education, training, and consulting services which raise performance standards for business and enhances the professional status of individuals. Offers a number of certified programs to meet special training needs.

**Institute of Consumer Financial Education**. PO Box 34070 San Diego, CA 92163-4070. Phone: (619)239-1401; Fax: (619)923-3284; Email: info@icfe.info • URL: http://www. financial-education-icfe.org • Aims to encourage Americans to improve spending, saving, investing, insuring, and financial planning habits to lessen their dependence on Social Security, welfare, or other individuals. Provides financial education courses to junior high and high school. Maintains a resource section of videos, books and home study courses in personal finance.

**Institute of Credit Management**. Station Rd., The Water Mill, Leicestershire South Luffenham LE15 8NB, United Kingdom. Phone: 44 1780 722900 or 44 1780 722912; Fax: 44 1780 721333; Email: info@icm.org.uk • URL: http:// www.icm.org.uk • Individuals working in credit management and its ancillary services. Serves as the central reference point in the UK on all matters relating to credit management. Raises professional standards through the provision of examinations, seminars, conferences and publications. Courses are offered at local colleges, by the Rapid Results Correspondence College and by distance learning.

**Institute of Cultural Affairs**. 4750 N Sheridan Rd. Chicago, IL 60640. Phone: (773)769-6363; Fax: (773)944-1582; Email: chicago@ica-usa.org • URL: http://www.ica-usa.org • U.S. branch of the Institute of Cultural Affairs International. Global research, training, and demonstration group concerned with the human factor in world development. Activities are based on the belief that effective human development must be initiated on the local level. Major training and demonstration programs include community development and facilitation services and training programs in 35 nations.

**Institute of Directors - England**. 116 Pall Mall London SW1Y 5ED, United Kingdom. Phone: 44 20 77668866; Fax: 44 20 77668833; Email: enquiries@iod.com • URL: http://www. iod.com/Home • Represents company directors and other people holding a similar position in industry, commerce, the professions or government organizations. Aims to advance company directors' interests and foster free enterprise. Includes services to members: branch network, professional development activities and conferences, information and advisory services. Provides meeting rooms and restaurant facilities to its members.

**Institute of Directors in Ireland**. Europa House, Harcourt St. Dublin 2, Dublin, Ireland. Phone: 353 1 4110010; Fax: 353 1 4110090; Email: info@iodireland.ie • URL: http://www. iodireland.ie • Provides a forum for the exchange of ideas and information, encourages members to improve the standards and performance as directors and represents the views of business leaders to government and other associations. Supports the provision of a wealth-creating environment in Ireland.

**Institute of Directors - Zimbabwe**. 1 Grantchester Close, Northwood, Mt. Pleasant Harare, Zimbabwe. Phone: 263 4 301866 or 263 4 301136 • URL: http://www.iodzim.com • Individuals employed as directors either in a managerial or administrative capacity or as a non-executive director by corporations in Zimbabwe. Promotes the interests of domestic businesses; works to develop management techniques particularly suited to local needs. Facilitates communication among members. Conducts research and educational programs.

**The Institute of Financial Operations**. 940 N Fern Creek Ave. Orlando, FL 32803. Phone: 877-885-4277 or (407)351-3322; Fax: (407)895-5031; Email: inquire@financialops.org • URL: http://www.tawpi.org • Members are companies that use or supply various recognition technologies equipment. Formerly The Association for Work Process Improvement.

**Institute of Financial Planning**. 1 Redcliff St. Bristol BS1 6NP, United Kingdom. Phone: 44 117 9452470; Fax: 44 117 9292214; Email: enquiries@financialplanning.org.uk • URL: http://www.financialplanning.org.uk • Consists of IFAs, accountants, solicitors, bankers and tax-consultants. Provides holistic financial planning objectively to members of the public and to companies. Seeks to promote the profession and practice of financial planning, increase public awareness of the need for financial planning and ensure high professional and ethical standards amongst its members. Shares knowledge and skills with other professionals for the benefit of mutual clients. Confers certified financial planner license to qualified individuals. Affiliated to Certified Financial Planner Board of Standards.

**Institute of Food Science**. Cornell University, 114 Stocking Hall Ithaca, NY 14853-7201. Phone: (607)255-7900; Fax: (607)254-4868; Email: ddm2@cornell.edu • URL: http://www.nysaes.cornell.edu/cifs • Research areas include the chemistry and processing of food commodities, food processing engineering, food packaging, and nutrition.

**Institute of Leadership and Management**. Stowe House, Netherstowe Lichfield WS13 6TJ, United Kingdom. Phone: 44 1543 266886 or 44 1543 266867; Fax: 44 1543 266811 or 44 1543 266893; Email: customer@i-l-m.com • URL: http://www.i-l-m.com • Fellows, Members and Associates - Corporate grades; Affiliates and Students Non-corporate grades. Aims to encourage and develop the science and practice of management and gain recognition of management as a profession.

**Institute of Management Accountants, Cost Management Group**. 10 Paragon Dr., Ste. 1 Montvale, NJ 07645-1718. Phone: 800-638-4427 or (201)573-9000; Fax: (201)474-1600; Email: ima@imanet.org • URL: http://www.imanet.org • A group within the Institute of Management Accountants. Seeks to improve the quality of corporate cost management systems. Educates business professionals about decision-making and productivity improvement. Provides a means of exchanging opinions and experiences about cost management systems. Conducts surveys; compiles statistics.

**Institute of Management Consultants and Advisers**. 19 Elgin Rd. Dublin 4, Dublin, Ireland. Phone: 353 1 6349636; Fax: 353 1 2815330; Email: info@imca.ie • URL: http://www.imca.ie • Aims to advance the management consultancy profession in Ireland. Provides Code of Professional Conduct to ensure that the members render the highest standards of performance and service.

*Institute of Management Consultants—Management Consultants Resource Guide*. Institute of Management Consultants USA, 2025 M St. NW, Ste. 800 Washington, DC 20036. Phone: (202)367-1261; Fax: (202)367-2134; Email: huchler@verizon.net • URL: http://www.imcusa.org • Database covers: 2,800 individuals who practice management consulting as individuals or members of firms worldwide. Database includes: Name, firm, address, phone; fax; email; website; areas of competence for certified management consultants.

**Institute of Management Consultants USA**. 2025 M St. NW, Ste. 800 Washington, DC 20036. Phone: (202)367-1261; Fax: (202)367-2134; Email: huchler@verizon.net • URL: http://www.imcusa.org • Individual management consultants who work privately or in consulting firms. Sets standards of professionalism and ethics for the management consulting profession.

**Institute of Management Consultants**. 45 Glenferrie Rd., Ste. 999 Melbourne, VIC 3144, Australia. Phone: 800-800719 • URL: http://www.imc.org.au • Represents management consultants in Australia.

**Institute of Management Services**. Brooke House, 24 Dam St., Staffordshire Lichfield WS13 6AA, United Kingdom. Phone: 44 1543 266909; Fax: 44 1543 257848; Email: admin@ims-stowe.fsnet.co.uk • URL: http://www.ims-productivity.com • Represents industry, commerce and the public sector including armed services and police. Serves as professional, qualifying body whose main activities are to provide qualifications and education and to disseminate knowledge in the field of management services. Investigates, advises and carries out solutions to management and organizational problems.

*Institute of Mathematical Statistics Bulletin*. Institute of Mathematical Statistics, PO Box 22718 Beachwood, OH 44122. Phone: 877-55-4674 or (216)295-2340 or (301)634-7029; Fax: (216)295-5661; Email: ims@imstat.org • URL: http://www.imstat.org • Bimonthly. $82 /year for institutions. Contains meeting programs, calendar of events, faculty recruitment advertising, book reviews, and abstracts of printed papers.

**Institute of Medicine - Board on Global Health**. Keck Ctr., 500 5th St. NW Washington, DC 20001. Phone: (202)334-2427; Fax: (202)334-3861; Email: pkelley@nas.edu • URL: http://www.iom.edu/About-IOM/Leadership-Staff/Boards/Board-on-Global-Health.aspx • Health of populations worldwide, including developing country health issues, enhancing the U.S. role in global health, and addressing health issues that have implications for U.S. health policy.

**Institute of Medicine - Board on Health Sciences Policy**. Keck Ctr., 500 5th St. NW Washington, DC 20001. Phone:

(202)334-1888; Fax: (202)334-1329; Email: apope@nas.edu • URL: http://www.iom.edu/About-IOM/Leadership-Staff/Boards/Board-on-Health-Sciences-Policy.aspx • Issues affecting the science base underlying health and health care.

**Institute of Personnel Management of Zimbabwe**. Union Ave. Harare, Zimbabwe. Phone: 263 4755241 or 263 4 755241; Fax: 263 4721454 or 263 4 755244; Email: ipmz@ecoweb.co.zw • URL: http://www.ipmz.org.zw • Works as a professional association of personnel workers in Zimbabwe. Promotes the profession of personnel training labor human resource management. Works to improve commercial and industrial productivity through people management.

**Institute of Public Utilities**. Michigan State University, Owen Graduate Hall, 735 E Shaw Ln., Rm. W157 East Lansing, MI 48825-1109. Phone: (517)355-1876; Fax: (517)355-1854; Email: ipu@msu.edu • URL: http://www.ipu.msu.edu • Represents the interests of privately and publicly owned utility companies in energy, telecommunications and water. Facilitates research and discussion of problems currently faced by public utility industry. Conducts educational programs in conjunction with National Association of Regulatory Utility Commissioners. Holds periodic seminars and special training programs.

**Institute of Textile Technology**. College of Textiles, Box 8301, N Carolina State University, 2401 Research Dr. Raleigh, NC 27695-8301. Phone: (919)513-7583; Fax: (888)348-3512; Email: wgoneal@itt.edu • URL: http://www.itt.edu • Textile materials, processes, and technology, with an emphasis on processing, instrumentation, statistical quality control, and testing of raw materials and finished products. Special attention given to yarn manufacture, carding, finishing operations, operations research applications, computer applications to manufacturing, techniques for evaluation of fiber quality, chemical treatment of raw materials, mechanical blending of fibers, environmental and energy conservation, methods of improving fabric finishes, applications of statistical methods, simulation, expert systems, processing, and interrelation of production, costs, and quality in yarn and fabric manufacture.

*Institutional Buyers of Energy Stocks*. bigdough.com Inc., 4833 Rugby Ave. Bethesda, MD 20814-3035. Phone: 800-254-1005 or (301)760-2500 or (301)657-4271; Fax: (301)654-5797 or (301)215-7104 • URL: http://www.bigdough.com • Annual. $645.00. Provides detailed profiles 555 institutional buyers of petroleum-related and other energy stocks. Includes names of financial analysts and portfolio managers.

*Institutional Buyers of REIT Securities*. bigdough.com Inc., 4833 Rugby Ave. Bethesda, MD 20814-3035. Phone: 800-254-1005 or (301)760-2500 or (301)657-4271; Fax: (301)654-5797 or (301)215-7104 • URL: http://www.bigdough.com • Semiannual. $995.00 per year. Provides detailed profiles of about 500 institutional buyers of REIT securities. Includes names of financial analysts and portfolio managers.

*Institutional Buyers of Small-Cap Stocks*. bigdough.com Inc., 4833 Rugby Ave. Bethesda, MD 20814-3035. Phone: 800-254-1005 or (301)760-2500 or (301)657-4271; Fax: (301)654-5797 or (301)215-7104 • URL: http://www.bigdough.com • Annual. $295.00. Provides detailed profiles of more than 837 institutional buyers of small capitalization stocks. Includes names of financial analysts and portfolio managers.

*Institutional Investor International Edition: The Magazine for International Finance and Investment*. Institutional Investor Inc. Journals Group, 225 Park Ave. S New York, NY 10003. Phone: 800-437-9997 or (212)224-3570; Email: info@iijournals.com • URL: http://www.iijournals.com • Monthly. $475.00 per year. Covers the international aspects of professional investing and finance. Emphasis is on Europe, the Far East, and Latin America.

*Institutional Investor: The Premier of Professional Magazine Finance*. Institutional Investor Inc. Journals Group, 225 Park Ave. S New York, NY 10003. Phone: 800-437-9997 or (212)224-3570; Email: info@iijournals.com • URL: http://www.iijournals.com • Monthly. $445.00 per year. Includes print and online editions. Edited for portfolio managers and other investment professionals. Special feature issues include "Country Credit Ratings," "Fixed Income Trading Ranking," "All-America Research Team," and "Global Banking Ranking.".

**Instructional Technology Center**. University of Delaware, College of Education, 305 Willard Hall Newark, DE 19716. Phone: (302)831-2394; Fax: (302)831-4110; Email: fth@udel.edu • URL: http://www.udel.edu.

*Instrumentalist: A Magazine for School and College Band and Orchestra Directors, Professional Instrumentalist, Teacher-Training Specialists in Instrumental Music Education and Instrumental Teachers*. Instrumentalist Co., 200 Northfield Rd. Northfield, IL 60093. Phone: 888-446-6888 or (847)446-5000; Fax: (847)446-6263; Email: advertising@theinstrumentalist.com • URL: http://www.instrumentalistmagazine.com • Monthly. $21 Individuals. Professional journal for school band and orchestra directors and teachers of instruments in those ensembles.

*Instrumentalist—Directory of Summer Music Camps, Clinics, and Workshops Issue*. Instrumentalist Co., 200 Northfield Rd. Northfield, IL 60093. Phone: 888-446-6888 or (847)446-5000; Fax: (847)446-6263; Email: advertising@theinstrumentalist.com • URL: http://www.instrumentalistmagazine.com • Annual. Publication includes:

List of nearly 250 summer music camps, clinics, and workshops in the United States; limited Canadian and foreign coverage. Entries include: Camp name, location, name of director, opening and closing dates, tuition fees, courses offered.

*Instrumentation and Automation News: Instruments, Controls, Manufacturing Software, Electronic and Mechanical Components*. Reed Elsevier Group plc Reed Business Information, 360 Park Ave. S New York, NY 11010. Phone: (212)791-4208; Email: corporatecommunications@reedbusiness.com • URL: http://www.reedbusiness.com • Monthly. $61.90 per year.

*Insulation Outlook: Business Solutions for Expanding or Relocating Companies*. National Insulation Association, 12100 Sunset Hills Rd., Ste. 330 Reston, VA 20190. Phone: (703)464-6422; Fax: (703)464-5896 • URL: http://www.insulation.org • $98.00 per year. Covers site selection and related topics.

*Insurance Advocate*. Emanuel Levy, editor. Shea-Haarmann Cos., P.O. Box 9001 Mount Vernon, NY 10552-9001. Phone: (914)699-2020; Fax: (914)664-1503; Email: insuranceadvocate@cinn.com • URL: http://www.cinn.com • Biweekly. Weekly. $59.00 per year. News and features on all aspects of insurance business for industry professionals.

*Insurance Almanac: Who, What, When and Where in Insurance*. Criterion Publishing Co., 244 N Main St. New City, NY 10956. Phone: 800-526-4700 or (845)634-2720; Fax: (845)634-2989; Email: jgcrothers@criterionpub.com • URL: http://www.criterioninsurancedirectory.com • Annual. $195. Lists insurance agencies and brokerage firms; U.S. and Canadian insurance companies, adjusters, appraisers, auditors, investigators, insurance officials and insurance organizations.

*Insurance and Employee Benefits Literature*. Special Libraries Association, 331 S Patrick St. Alexandria, VA 22314-3501. Phone: (703)647-4900; Fax: (703)647-4901 • URL: http://www.sla.org • Bimonthly. $15.00 per year. Lists a wide variety of literature in all branches of the insurance industry. Includes annotations.

*Insurance and Technology*. UBM L.L.C., 600 Community Dr. Manhasset, NY 11030. Phone: (516)562-5000 or (512)562-5000; Fax: (212)378-2160 or (516)562-5036; Email: cmp@cmp.com • URL: http://www.cmp.com • Monthly. $65.00 per year. Covers information technology and systems management as applied to the operation of life, health, casualty, and property insurance companies.

*Insurance Companies' Directory List of Mortgage Directors*. Communication Network International Inc., 3918 Ave. T Brooklyn, NY 11234-5028. Phone: (718)339-6245; Fax: (718)998-5915 • Irregular. $350. Covers: 170 mortgage officers of major insurance companies that make real estate mortgages and related investments. Entries include: Company name, address, phone, name and title of mortgage officer.

*Insurance Coverage Law Bulletin*. ALM Media Properties LLC, 120 Broadway, 5th Fl. New York, NY 10271-1100. Phone: (212)457-9400; Fax: (646)417-7705; Email: customercare@alm.com • URL: http://www.alm.com • Monthly. $510. Provides news of property insurance claims management and coverage disputes. Edited for both legal and non-legal insurance professionals. (A Law Journal Newsletter, formerly published by Leader Publications).

*Insurance Finance and Investment*. Institutional Investor Inc. Journals Group, 225 Park Ave. S New York, NY 10003. Phone: 800-437-9997 or (212)224-3570; Email: info@iijournals.com • URL: http://www.iijournals.com • Biweekly. $1,960.00 per year. Newsletter. Edited for insurance company investment managers.

*Insurance Forum: For the Unfettered Exchange of Ideas About Insurance*. Joseph M. Belth, editor. Insurance Forum Inc., PO Box 245 Ellettsville, IN 47429-0245. Phone: 888-876-9590 or (812)876-6502 • Monthly. $90.00 per year. Newsletter. Provides analysis of the insurance business, including occasional special issues showing the ratings of about 1,600 life-health insurance companies, as determined by four major rating services: Duff & Phelps Credit Rating Co., Moody's Investors Service, Standard & Poor's Corp., and Weiss Research, Inc.

**Insurance Institute for Highway Safety, Status Report**. Insurance Institute for Highway Safety, 1005 N Glebe Rd., Ste. 800 Arlington, VA 22201. Phone: (703)247-1500; Fax: (703)247-1588 • URL: http://www.iihs.org • 10 times a year. Free.

**Insurance Institute for Highway Safety**. 1005 N Glebe Rd., Ste. 800 Arlington, VA 22201. Phone: (703)247-1500; Fax: (703)247-1588 • URL: http://www.iihs.org • Studies highway safety, including seat belt use, air bags, property damage, vehicle recalls, and the role of alcohol and drugs.

*Insurance Marketing: The Ins and Outs of Recruiting and Retaining More Agents*. Agent Media Corp., 1255 Cleveland St., Suite 300 Clearwater, FL 33755. Phone: 800-933-9449 or (727)446-1100; Fax: (727)446-1166 • Bimonthly. Controlled circulation. Provides practical advice for insurance companies on how to hire and keep sales personnel.

*Insurance Marketplace: The Agents and Brokers Guide to Non-Standard and Special ty Lines, Aviation, Marine and International Insurance*. The Rough Notes Company Inc., 11690 Technology Dr. Carmel, IN 46032-5600. Phone: 800-428-4384 or (317)582-1600; Fax: (317)816-1000 or (800)321-1909; Email: rnc@roughnotes.com • URL: http://

www.roughnotes.com • Annual. Lists specialty, excess, and surplus insurance lines.

***Insurance Networking: Strategies and Solutions for Electronic Commerce***. SourceMedia Inc., 1 State Street Plz., 27th Fl. New York, NY 10004. Phone: 800-221-1809 or (212)803-8200 or (212)803-8333; Fax: (212)843-9635 or (212)292-5216; Email: custserv@sourcemedia.com • URL: http://www.sourcemedia.com • 10 times a year. Price on application. Covers information technology for the insurance industry, with emphasis on computer communications and the Internet.

***Insurance Periodicals Index***. Specials Libraries Association, Insurance and Employees Benefits Div. NILS Publishing Co., 21625 Prairie St. Chatsworth, CA 91311. Phone: 800-423-5910 • URL: http://library-dialog.com • Annual. $250.00. Compiled by the Insurance and Employee Benefits Div., Special Libraries Association. A yearly index of over 15,000 articles from about 35 insurance periodicals. Arrangement is by subject, with an index to authors.

***Insurance Regulation: State Capitals***. Wakeman/Walworth Inc., PO Box 7376 Alexandria, VA 22307-7376. Phone: 800-876-2545 or (703)768-9600; Fax: (703)768-9690; Email: newsletters@statecapitals.com • URL: http://statecapitals.com/ • 50 times a year. $245.00 per year; print and online editions, $350.00 per year. Formerly *From the State Capitals: Insurance Regulation*.

***InsuranceWeek***. I.W. Publications, Inc., 2033 6th Ave., Ste. 917 Seattle, WA 98121-2568. Phone: 800-638-6190 or (206)624-6965; Fax: (206)624-5021 • Weekly. $30.00 per year.

***IntdustryWeek***. 1300 E 9th St. Cleveland, OH 44114. Phone: 800-632-5537 or (216)696-7000; Fax: (203)559-2910; Email: iwinfoindianaustryweek.com • URL: http://www.iw.com • Resource for manufacturing operations knowledge.

***INTECH: The International Journal of Instrumentation and Control***. ISA Services Inc., 67 Alexander Dr. Research Triangle Park, NC 27709. Phone: (919)549-8411; Fax: (919)549-8288 • URL: http://www.isa.org • Monthly. $72.00 per year.

***Integrated Circuits International: An International Bulletin for Suppliers and Users of Integrated Circuits***. Elsevier, Secondary Publishing Division, 650 Ave. of the Americas New York, NY 10011. Phone: 888-437-4636 or (212)633-3980; Fax: (212)633-3975; Email: t.reller@elsevier.com • URL: http://www.elseveier.com • Monthly. $541.00 per year. For suppliers and users of integrated circuits.

***Intellectual Property and Antitrust Law***. William C. Holmes. Thomson West, 610 Opperman Dr. Eagan, MN 55123. Phone: 800-328-9352 or (651)687-7000 • Semiannual. $1,347 full set; $107 monthly. Includes patent, trademark, and copyright practices.

***Intellectual Property Law: Commercial, Creative, and Industrial Property***. ALM Media Properties LLC, 120 Broadway, 5th Fl. New York, NY 10271-1100. Phone: (212)457-9400; Fax: (646)417-7705; Email: customercare@alm.com • URL: http://www.alm.com • $1,025 two volumes. Covers the legal aspects of patents, trade secrets, copyright, technology protection, software protection, databases, etc. Also "compares the basic principles of U.S. law with those of Asian and European law." (Law Journal Press).

***Intellectual Property Newsletter***. L L Professional Publishing, 69-77 Paul St. London EC2A 4LQ, United Kingdom. Phone: 44 207 5531000; Fax: (207) 5531593 • Monthly. $261.00 per year.

***Intellectual Property Primary Law Sourcebook***. Matthew Bender and Company Inc., 1275 Broadway Albany, NY 12204-2638. Phone: 800-424-4200 or (518)487-3000; Fax: (518)487-3573 or (800)424-4200; Email: customer.support@lexisnexis.com • URL: http://www.matthewbender.com • $175 print only; $175 e-book. Provides federal copyright, patent, and trademark statutes, as well as the Leahy-Smith America Invents Act.

***Intellectual Property Strategist***. ALM Media Properties LLC, 120 Broadway, 5th Fl. New York, NY 10271-1100. Phone: (212)457-9400; Fax: (646)417-7705; Email: customercare@alm.com • URL: http://www.alm.com • Monthly. $505 print and online. Covers "business and litigation tactics" in the field of intellectual property law, including international issues. (A Law Journal Newsletter, formerly published by Leader Publications).

***Intellectual Property Today***. 381 W Northwest Hwy. Palantine, IL 60067. Phone: 800-232-8078 or (847)705-7194; Fax: (847)705-7112; Email: ddean@iptoday.com • URL: http://www.iptoday.com • Monthly. $96.00 per year. Covers legal developments in copyright, patents, trademarks, and licensing. Emphasizes the effect of new technology on intellectual property. Formerly *Law Works*.

***Intellectual Property World Directory***. World Bureau L.L.C., 1058 Thomas Jefferson St. NW, Ste. 250 Washington, DC 20007. Phone: (202)333-1010; Fax: (202)333-1011; Email: info@worldbureau.com • URL: http://www.worldbureau.com • Annual. Covers: Patent, trademark, and copyright agencies and officials in over 100 countries. Entries include: Name, address, phone, fax, and e-mail address of officials responsible for intellectual property issues. Also includes statistics, reports, full cabinets, embassies, and organizational charts.

***Intelligence Data***. Thomson Financial, Phone: 800-654-0393; Fax: (617)824-2477 • URL: http://www.intelligencedata.com

• Fee-based Web site provides a wide variety of information relating to competitive intelligence, strategic planning, business development, mergers, acquisitions, sales, and marketing. "Intelliscope" feature offers searching of other Thomson units, such as Investext, MarkIntel, InSite 2, and Industry Insider. Weekly updating.

***Intelligence Digest: A Review of World Affairs; International Political, Economic and Strategic Intelligence***. Jane's Information Group, Inc., 110 N Royal St., Ste. 200 Alexandria, VA 22314-1651. Phone: 800-836-0297 or (703)683-3700; Fax: (703)836-0029 or (703)863-0029; Email: info.us@janes.con • URL: http://www.janes.com • Weekly. $240.00 per year. Provides political, strategic and economic information. Gives warnings on political trends and current affairs. Published in England.

***Intelligent Systems Report***. Lionheart Publishing Inc., 506 Roswell St., Ste. 220 Marietta, GA 30060. Phone: 888-303-5639 or (770)431-0867; Fax: (770)432-6969; Email: lpi@lionhrtpub.com • URL: http://www.lionhrtpub.com • Monthly. $299.00 per year. Newsletter. Formed by merger of *Neural Network News* and *AI Week*.

***Inter-American Tropical Tuna Commission Annual Report***. William H. Bayliff, editor. Inter-American Tropical Tuna Commission, 8901 La Jolla Shores Dr. La Jolla, CA 92037-1509. Phone: (858)546-7100; Fax: (858)546-7133; Email: info@iattc.org • URL: http://www.iattc.org • Annual. Summary of scientific research carried on during the year. Includes financial statements. Text in English and Spanish.

***Inter-American Tropical Tuna Commission Bulletin***. Inter-American Tropical Tuna Commission, 8901 La Jolla Shores Dr. La Jolla, CA 92037-1509. Phone: (858)546-7100; Fax: (858)546-7133; Email: info@iattc.org • URL: http://www.iattc.org • Irregular. Price varies. Description of results of scientific studies. Text in English and Spanish.

***Inter-Corporate Ownership***. Industrial Organization and Finance Div. Statistics Canada, Phone: (613)951-2604; Fax: (613)951-0319 • Biennial. $350 plus shipping charges for outside country. Covers: 72,000 Canadian corporations with ownership links to one or more other corporations. Entries include: Parent corporation and subsidiaries, site of control, Canadian domicile, Standard Industrial Classification (SIC) code, etc.

***Inter Region***. Editus S.A.R.L., Rue Michel Rodange 28 L-2340 Luxembourg, Luxembourg. Phone: 496051 • Annual. Covers: the top 15,000 companies in the European area of Saar-Lor-Lux including: south Belgium, Saarland, Trier, Grand Duchy of Luxembourg and French region Lorraine. Entries include: Company name, address, phone, fax, number of employees, financial data, names and titles of key personnel and line of business, trademarks.

***Inter-University Seminar on Armed Forces and Society***. Loyola University Chicago, Dept. of Political Science, 1032 W Sheridan Rd. Chicago, IL 60660. Phone: (773)508-2930; Fax: (773)508-2929 • URL: http://www.iusafs.org • Individuals from both public and private life in the academic, military, and government fields who are primarily researchers. Promotes the study of armed forces and society; provides a focal point for the exchange of information on the subject; stimulates research in the field on a cross-national basis. Compiles statistics; recommends a scholar to conduct seminars and give lectures.

***InterActive Consumers***. MarketResearch.com, 11200 Rockville Pke., Ste. 504 Rockville, MD 20852. Phone: 800-298-5699 or (240)747-3093; Fax: (240)747-3004; Email: customerservice@marketresearch.com • URL: http://www.marketresearch.com • Monthly. $395.00 per year. Newsletter. Covers the emerging markets for digital content, products, and services. Includes market information on telecommuting, online services, the Internet, online investing, and other areas of electronic commerce.

***Interactive Content: Consumer Media Strategies Monthly***. Jupitermedia Corp., 23 Old Kings Hwy. S Darien, CT 06820. Phone: 800-488-4345 or (203)662-2800; Fax: (203)655-4686; Email: ameckler@jupitermedia.com • URL: http://www.webmediabrands.com • Monthly. $675.00 per year; with online edition, $775.00 per year. Newsletter. Covers the broad field of providing content (information, news, entertainment) for the Internet/World Wide Web.

***Interactive Home: Consumer Technology Monthly***. Jupiter Communications, 627 Broadway, 2nd Fl. New York, NY 10012-2612. Phone: 800-488-4345 or (212)780-6060 or (917)534-6900; Fax: (212)780-6075 or (917)534-6800 • Monthly. $625.00 per year; with online edition, $725.00 per year. Newsletter on devices to bring the Internet into the average American home. Covers TV set-top boxes, game devices, telephones with display screens, handheld computer communication devices, the usual PCs, etc.

***Interactive Marketing and P R News: News and Practical Advice on Using Interactive Advertising and Marketing to Sell Your Products***. Access Intelligence L.L.C., 4 Choke Cherry Rd., 2nd Fl. Rockville, MD 20850. Phone: 800-777-5006 or (301)354-2000 or (301)354-2101; Fax: (301)309-3847 or (801)365-2300; Email: info@accessintel.com • URL: http://www.accessintel.com/ • Biweekly. $495.00 per year. Newsletter. Provides information and guidance on merchandising via CD-ROM ("multimedia catalogs"), the Internet, and interactive TV. Topics include "cybermoney," addresses for e-mail marketing, "virtual malls," and other

interactive subjects. Formerly *Interactive Marketing News*.

***Interactive Oceanography Division***. University of California, San Diego, Scripps Institution of Oceanography, 8650 Discovery Way La Jolla, CA 92093. Phone: (858)534-2068; Fax: (858)534-6500 • URL: http://www.iod.ucsd.edu • Formerly Marine Life Research Group.

***Interactive TV Investor Buyer's Guide and Directory***. Paul Kagan Associates, Inc., 126 Clock Tower Pl. Carmel, CA 93923-8746. Phone: (831)624-1536; Fax: (831)625-3225; Email: info@kagan.com • URL: http://www.kagan.com • Annual. Price on application. (A special issue of the periodical *Convergence*.).

***Interactive TV Investor***. Paul Kagan Associates, Inc., 126 Clock Tower Pl. Carmel, CA 93923-8746. Phone: (831)624-1536; Fax: (831)625-3225; Email: info@kagan.com • URL: http://www.kagan.com • Semimonthly. $895.00. Provides current information on interactive-TV applications and technical developments. Includes forecasts. Formerly *Interactive Television*.

***Interactive Update***. Alexander & Associates, 38 E 32nd St., 12th Fl. New York, NY 10016-7911. Phone: (212)684-2333; Fax: (212)684-0291; Email: aainfo@alexassoc.com • Description: Provides information on the interactive entertainment industry, focusing on software.

***Intercompany Relations on Charts***. Hoppenstedt Produktinformationen GmbH, Havelstrasse 9, Postfach 100139 D-64295 Darmstadt, Germany. Phone: 49 6151 1375444 or 49 6151 38 0; Fax: 49 6151 1375443 or 49 6151 380 360; Email: info@hoppenstedt.de • URL: http://www.hoppenstedt.com • Shows in chart form the economic and financial relations between 700 parent companies from all over the world and their 90,000 subsidiaries.

***Interest Rate Service***. World Reports Ltd., 280 Madison Ave., Ste. 280 New York, NY 10016-0802. Phone: (212)679-0095; Fax: (212)679-1094 • 10 times a year. $950.00 per year.

***Intergovernmental Relations***. U. S. Government Printing Office, 732 N Capitol St. NW Washington, DC 20401. Phone: 866-512-1800 or (202)512-1800 or (866)512-1800; Fax: (202)512-2104 or (202)512-2250; Email: contactcenter@gpo.gov • URL: http://www.gpo.gov • Annual. Free. Lists government publications. (Subject Bibliography 211.).

**Interim Management Association**. Dorset House, 1st Fl., 27-45 Stamford St. London SE1 9NT, United Kingdom. • URL: http://www.interimmanagement.uk.com • Recruitment consultancies specializing in interim managers for industry and commerce at senior level.

***Interior Design Buyers Guide***. Reed Elsevier Group plc Reed Business Information, 360 Park Ave. S New York, NY 11010. Phone: (212)791-4208; Email: corporatecommunications@reedbusiness.com • URL: http://www.reedbusiness.com • Annual. $16.95. Included with subscription to *Interior Design*.

**Interior Design Laboratory**. Lambuth University, 101 Wilder Tower Memphis, TN 38152-3520. Phone: 800-669-2679 • URL: http://www.memphis.edu/lambuth.

***Interior Design***. Reed Elsevier Group plc Reed Business Information, 360 Park Ave. S New York, NY 11010. Phone: (212)791-4208; Email: corporatecommunications@reedbusiness.com • URL: http://www.reedbusiness.com • Monthly. $64.95 per year. For the professional designed, provides information on trends and new products.

***Interiors and Sources***. L.C. Clark Publishing Company Inc., 840 US Hwy. 1, Ste. 330 North Palm Beach, FL 33408-3874. Phone: 800-537-4271 or (561)627-3393; Fax: (561)694-6578 or (561)627-1447; Email: jmoody@lcclark.com • URL: http://www.dwconline.com/ • Bimonthly. $27.00 per year. Promotes professionalism for interior designers and design firms. Includes special features on office systems, work stations, and office furniture.

***Internal Auditing Alert***. Warren, Gorham & Lamont Inc., 117 E Stevens Ave. Valhalla, NY 10595-1254. Phone: 800-950-1216 or (914)749-5000; Fax: (914)741-2412; Email: research@researchers.com • URL: http://tax.thomsonreuters.com/products/brands/checkpoint/ria-wgl • Description: Presents unique coverage that includes reviews and explanations of current Institute of Internal Auditors releases, appraisals of new audit techniques, and highlights of successful audit management practices.

***Internal Auditor***. Institute of Internal Auditors, 247 Maitland Ave. Altamonte Springs, FL 32701-4201. Phone: (407)937-1111; Fax: (407)937-1101; Email: customerrelations@theiia.org • URL: http://na.theiia.org • Bimonthly. $75 U.S. and Canada print and online; $135 U.S. and Canada two years, print and online; $99 Other countries print and online; $183 Other countries two years, print and online; $60 online. Internal auditing.

***Internal Revenue Bulletin***. Thomson RIA, 195 Broadway New York, NY 10007-3100. Phone: 800-431-9025 or (212)367-6300 or (212)807-2298; Fax: (212)367-6305 or (212)337-4207; Email: ttacommunications@riag.com • URL: http://www.ria.thomson.com • Weekly. Description: Presents new treasury and IRS releases in full official text. Contains rulings and decisions, releases on treaties, tax legislation, administrative and procedural releases, disbarment and suspensions.

***Internal Revenue Cumulative Bulletin***. U. S. Government Printing Office, 732 N Capitol St. NW Washington, DC 20401. Phone: 866-512-1800 or (202)512-1800 or (866)512-1800; Fax: (202)512-2104 or (202)512-2250; Email:

contactcenter@gpo.gov • URL: http://www.gpo.gov • Semiannual. Issued by the Internal Revenue Service. Cumulates all items of a "permanent nature" appearing in the weekly *Internal Revenue Bulletin*.

***Internal Revenue Manual: Audit and Administration***. Wolters Kluwer Law & Business CCH, 2700 Lake Cook Rd. Riverwoods, IL 60015. Phone: 888-224-7377 or (847)267-7000; Email: cust_serv@cch.com • URL: http://www.cchgroup.com • Irregular. $1,254.00. Six looseleaf volumes. Reproduces IRS tax administration provisions and procedures.

***Internal Revenue Service IRS.gov***. Internal Revenue Service, Phone: 800-829-1040 or (202)622-5000; Fax: (202)622-5844 • URL: http://www.irs.gov • Web site provides a wide variety of tax information, including IRS forms and publications. Searching is available. Fees: Free.

***International Abstracts in Operations Research***. International Federation of Operational Research Societies. Palgrave Macmillan, Houndsmills Basingstoke RG21 6XS, United Kingdom. Phone: 44 1256 329242 or 44 01256 329242; Fax: 44 1256 479476 or (012)56 320109; Email: booksellers@palgrave.com • URL: http://www.palgrave.com • Bimonthly. Institutions, $980.00 per year. Includes print and online editions.

**International Academy of Management**. 21 Pearson Ave. 08034 Barcelona, Spain. Phone: 34 93 2534200; Email: epy@iese.edu • URL: http://theiam.ws • Leaders in management from 32 countries who have been elected fellows of the IAM in recognition for their contributions to the field. Seeks to: provide a body to safeguard the objectivity and precision of management and the disciplined integration of new/progressive managerial trends; stimulate intellectual interests in management.

***International Academy of Trial Lawyers Roster***. International Academy of Trial Lawyers, 5841 Cedar Lake Rd., Ste. 204 Minneapolis, MN 55416-5657. Phone: 866-823-2443 or (952)546-2364; Fax: (952)545-6073; Email: iatl@llmsi.com • URL: http://www.iatl.net • Biennial. Free. More than 2,400 trial lawyers board certified in civil and criminal trial advocacy; members of the board.

**International Action Center**. Solidarity Ctr., 147 W 24th St., 2nd Fl. New York, NY 10011. Phone: (212)633-6646; Fax: (212)633-2889; Email: iacenter@iacenter.org • URL: http://www.iacenter.org • Opposes U.S. militarism. Organizes opposition to U.S. intervention abroad and to racism and political repression at home. Sponsors educational activities and research.

***International Advertising Association Membership Directory***. International Advertising Association, 747 3rd Ave., 2nd Fl. New York, NY 10017. Phone: (646)722-2612; Fax: (646)722-2501; Email: iaa@iaaglobal.org • URL: http://www.iaaglobal.org • Annual. Membership. Available only online. Over 3,600 advertisers, advertising agencies, media, and other firms involved in advertising.

***International Aerospace Abstracts***. American Institute of Aeronautics and Astronautics, Inc. CSA, 1801 Alexander Bell Dr., Ste. 500 Reston, VA 20191. Phone: 800-639-2422 or (703)264-7500; Fax: (703)264-7551; Email: custserv@aiaa.org • URL: http://www.aiaa.org • 11 times a year. $2,260.00 per year. Includes print and online editions.

**International Air Filtration Certifiers Association**. c/o Michael Alleman, 129 S Gallatin Liberty, MO 64068. Phone: 888-679-1904; Fax: (816)792-8105 • URL: http://www.iafca.com • Promotes professionalism in the biological safety cabinet industry. Establishes and maintains certification program for biological safety cabinet certifiers. Provides information and guidance to legislative and regulatory agencies with regard to laws and standards affecting the industry.

**The International Alliance for Women**. 1101 Pennsylvania Ave. NW, 6th Fl. Washington, DC 20004. Phone: 888-712-5200 or (202)351-6839; Email: admin@tiaw.org • URL: http://www.tiaw.org • Local networks comprising 50,000 professional and executive women in 12 countries; individual businesswomen without a network affiliation are alliance associates. Promotes recognition of the achievements of women in business. Encourages placement of women in senior executive positions. Maintains high standards of professional competence among members. Facilitates communication on an international scale among professional women's networks and their members. Represents members' interests before policymaking business and government. Sponsors programs that support equal opportunity and enhance members' business and professional skills. Operates appointments and directors service. Maintains speakers' bureau.

**International Amusement and Leisure Defense Association**. PO Box 4563 Louisville, KY 40204. Phone: (502)473-0956; Fax: (502)473-7352; Email: info@ialda.org • URL: http://www.ialda.org • Promotes and protects the interests of the amusement and leisure industries. Encourages members to exchange information, share experiences and develop litigation strategies regarding the amusement and leisure industry. Serves as a clearinghouse for speakers and authors on industry-specific topics.

***International and Comparative Law Quarterly (ICLQ)***. British Institute of International and Comparative Law, Charles Clore House, 17 Russell Sq. London WC1B 5JP, United Kingdom. Phone: 44 20 78625151; Fax: 44 44 78625152; Email: info@biicl.org • URL: http://www.biicl.org • Quarterly. £197 Nonmembers print & online; $394 Nonmembers print & online; Free to members; £184 Individuals print only; $367 Individuals print only; free for members; £262 Institutions online and print; $525 Institutions online and print; £231 Institutions online only; $464 Institutions online only. Journal offering coverage of comparative law as well as public and private international law.

**International Association for Business and Society**. IABS Philosophy Dr. Center Charlottesville, VA 22906-7147. Phone: 800-444-2419 or (434)220-3300; Fax: (434)220-3301 • URL: http://www.iabs.net • Seeks to provide an international forum for discussion and scholarship regarding social, business and public policy issues.

**International Association for Chinese Management Research**. Kogod School of Business, 4400 Massachusetts Ave. NW Washington, DC 20016. Phone: (316)978-6788; Fax: (316)978-3349; Email: iacmrus@gmail.com • URL: http://www.iacmr.org • Promotes scholarly studies of organization and management of firms in the Chinese context. Fosters the development of management research capabilities in and on China. Facilitates international collaboration between management researchers from around the globe.

**International Association for Urban Climate**. School of Geography, Planning and Environment Policy, Newman Bldg., Belfield Dublin 4, Dublin, Ireland. Phone: 353 1 7168229; Email: gerald.mills@ucd.ie • URL: http://www.urban-climate.org • Represents professionals in the fields of climatology and meteorology. Promotes and facilitates the study of urban climate, urban ecosystems and urban air quality.

**International Association for Worksite Health Promotion**. c/o Heather Turner, Program Officer, 401 W Michigan St. Indianapolis, IN 46202. Phone: (317)637-9200; Email: iawhp@acsm.org • URL: http://www.acsm-iawhp.org • Members are physical fitness professionals hired by major corporations to conduct health and fitness programs. Formerly Association for Fitness in Business.

**International Association of Administrative Professionals**. 10502 N Ambassador Dr., Ste. 100 Kansas City, MO 64153. Phone: (816)891-6600; Fax: (816)891-9118; Email: jay.donohue@iaap-hq.org • URL: http://www.iaap-hq.org • Formerly Professional Secretaries International.

***International Association of Amusement Parks and Attractions International Directory and Buyers' Guide***. International Association of Amusement Parks and Attractions, 1448 Duke St. Alexandria, VA 22314. Phone: (703)836-4800; Fax: (703)836-4801; Email: iaapa@iaapa.org • URL: http://www.iaapa.org • Annual. Over 1,800 member amusement parks, attractions and industry suppliers.

***International Association of Assessing Officers Membership Directory***. International Association of Assessing Officers, 314 W 10th St. Kansas City, MO 64105-1616. Phone: 800-616-4226 or (816)701-8100; Fax: (816)701-8149; Email: info@iaao.org • URL: http://www.iaao.org • Annual. Lists about 8,500 state and local officials concerned with valuation of property tax.

**International Association of CFOs and Corporate Treasurers China**. c/o Mr. Francis Ho, CLP Holdings, Group Treasury Dept., 147 Argyle St., Mongkok, Kowloon Hong Kong, China. • URL: http://www.iacctchina.com • Promotes the development of professional corporate treasury practice in China. Fosters exchange and sharing among a network of corporate treasurers and CFOs in both mainland Chinese. Supports financial reforms in China by developing a platform for dialogue between members and financial regulators.

**International Association of Directional Drilling**. 525 Sam Houston Pkwy. E, Ste. 525 Houston, TX 77060. Phone: (281)931-8811 or (281)288-6484; Email: dallen@iadd-intl.org • URL: http://www.iadd-intl.org • Represents the interests of the directional drilling industry. Encourages members to share ideas and develop safety and performance standards. Fosters collaboration among operators, directional drilling vendors and suppliers.

***International Association of Financial Crimes Investigators: Membership Directory***. International Association of Financial Crimes Investigators, 1020 Suncast Ln., Ste. 102 El Dorado Hills, CA 95762. Phone: (916)939-5000 • URL: http://www.iafci.org • Annual. About 3,500 firms and individuals engaged in investigation of fraudulent use of credit cards. Formerly *International Association of Credit Card Investigators-Membership Directory*.

**International Association of Financial Executives Institutes**. 1003 Pasong Tamo Tower, 10th Fl., 2210 Don Chino Roces Ave. Makati City 1231, Philippines. Phone: 63 2 7280315 • URL: http://www.iafei.org • Seeks to build and improve mutual understanding internationally among financial executives through the exchange of financial information, experience, and ideas. Provides a basis for international cooperation among financial executives towards making financial systems and regulations more uniform, compatible, and harmonious worldwide. Promotes ethical considerations in the practice of financial management throughout the world.

***International Association of Food Industry Suppliers Reporter***. International Association on Food Industry Suppliers, 1451 Dolley Madison Blvd. McLean, VA 22101-3850. Phone: (703)761-2600; Fax: (703)761-4334; Email: info@iafis.org • Monthly. Free.

**International Association of Insurance Professionals**. 8023 E 63rd Pl., Ste. 540 Tulsa, OK 74133. Phone: 800-766-6249 or (918)294-3700; Fax: (918)294-3711 • URL: http://naiw.site-ym.com • Formerly Nationl Assoiciation of Insurance Women.

**International Association of Merger and Acquisition Professionals**. 6000 Cattleridge Dr., Ste. 300 Sarasota, FL 34232. Phone: (941)378-5500; Email: info@imap.com • URL: http://www.imap.com • Firms with experience in the merger/acquisition field that meet the association's criteria of professional background and financial ability (primarily specialists in selling, buying, and merging medium-sized businesses with sales in the range of 1 to 100 million dollars); allied members include individuals and firms that provide auxiliary services for the completion of merger/acquisition transactions. Purposes are: promotion of the science of merger/acquisition consultancy; encouragement of educational and training material in the field; enhancement of the image and professional standing of industry specialists; expeditious but confidential distribution of business information on available merger or acquisition prospects.

**International Association of Operative Millers**. 12351 W 96th Terr., Ste. 100 Lenexa, KS 66215. Phone: (913)338-3377; Fax: (913)338-3553; Email: info@iaom.info • URL: http://www.iaom.info • Represents operation managers, plant managers, superintendents, grinders, bolters, engineers, and others engaged in the production of flour, feeds and cereal products through processing of wheat, corn, oats, rice, seeds, and spices.

**International Association of Registered Financial Consultants**. Financial Planning Bldg., 2507 N Verity Pkwy. Middletown, OH 45042-0506. Phone: 800-532-9060; Fax: (513)424-5752; Email: info@iarfc.org • URL: http://www.iarfc.org • Financial professionals gathered to foster public confidence in the financial planning profession. Helps financial consultants exchange planning techniques. Offers educational programs and professional certifications.

**International Association of Women in Family Enterprises**. 1906 Vista Del Lago Dr., No. L-119 Valley Springs, CA 95252. Phone: (209)772-9200 or (209)772-2810; Fax: (209)772-2810; Email: info@iawife.com • URL: http://www.iawife.com • Aims to support women who are building and growing family businesses. Offers opportunities to help members become successful in family enterprises. Provides support, education and networking among members.

**International Band and Orchestra Products Association**. 262 W. 38th St., Room 1506 New York, NY 10018-5815. Phone: (212)302-0801; Fax: (212)302-0783; Email: assnhdqs@earthlink.net.

***International Bank Credit Analyst***. BCA Publications Ltd., 1002 Sherbrooke St., W., 16th Fl. Montreal, QC, Canada H3A 3L6. Phone: (514)499-9706; Fax: (514)499-9709 • Monthly. $795.00 per year. "A monthly forecast and analysis of currency movements, interest rates, and stock market developments in the principal countries, based on a continuous appraisal of money and credit trends worldwide." Includes many charts and graphs providing international coverage of money, credit, and securities.

***International Bibliography of Studies on Alcohol***. Sarah S. Jordy, compiler. Rutgers Center of Alcohol Studies Publications, 607 Alison Rd. Piscataway, NJ 08854-8001. Phone: (732)445-2190; Fax: (732)445-3500 • URL: http://alcoholstudies.rutgers.edu • $200.00. Three volumes. Volume one, *References*, 1901-1950; volume two, *Indexes*, 1901-1980; volume three, *References* and *Indexes*, 1951-1960.

**International Board of Certification of Safety Managers**. 173 Tucker Rd., Ste. 202 Helena, AL 35080. Phone: (205)664-8412; Fax: (205)663-9541; Email: info@ibfcsm.org • URL: http://www.ibfcsm.org • Evaluates qualifications of product safety managers. Formerly International Product Safety Management Certification Board.

**International Bridal Manufacturers Association**. 118 W 20th St., 3rd Fl. New York, NY 10011-3627. Email: info@ibma.us • URL: http://ibma.us • Represents wedding apparel and accessory manufacturers. Promotes economic opportunities and fosters better relationships between manufacturers and retailers of bridal apparel. Coordinates and sets non-conflicting dates for bridal industry markets.

***International Broadcast Engineer***. DMG World Media Ltd., Queensway House, 2 Queensway Red Hill RH1 1QS, United Kingdom. Phone: 44 1737 855527; Fax: (173)7 855470 • Eight times a year. $119.00 per year.

**International Brotherhood of Boilermakers**. 753 State Ave., Ste. 570 Kansas City, KS 66101. Phone: (913)371-2640 or (913)342-2100; Fax: (913)281-8101 or (913)281-8104; Email: ipjones@boilermakers.org • URL: http://www.boilermakers.org • Affiliated with International Brotherhood of Boilermakers, Iron Ship Builders, Blacksmiths, Forgers and Helpers.

***International Business: Your Passport to the Global Marketplace***. American International Publishing, 500 Mamaroneck Ave., Ste. 314 Harrison, NY 10528-1600. Phone: (914)381-7700; Fax: (914)381-2521 • Monthly. $48 Individuals; $24 Students; $5 Single issue. Magazine for senior managers of U.S. Based mid-market multi-national companies seeking to gor internationally through export/import, joint ventures, acquisitions or relocation/expansion.

***International Business & Economics Research Journal (IBER)***. The Clute Institute for Academic Research, 6901 S Pierce St.,

Ste. 239 Littleton, CO 80128. Phone: (303)904-4750; Fax: (303)259-2420; Email: staff@cluteinstitute.com • URL: http://www.cluteinstitute.com • Monthly. $495 Institutions. Applied business research magazine.

***International Business and Trade Directories***. Grey House Publishing, 4919 Rte. 22 Amenia, NY 12501. Phone: 800-562-2139 or (518)789-8700; Fax: (518)789-0556; Email: books@greyhouse.com • URL: http://www.greyhouse.com • $225 Individuals softcover. Covers: Approximately 8,000 directories concerned with international business and trade. Entries include: Directory title, publisher name, address, phone, fax, description of directory, ISBN, size, price, frequency, editor, U.S. Distributor.

**International Business Chamber Cambodia**. Phnom Penh Tower, 12th Fl., Monivong Blvd., No. 445 Phnom Penh, Cambodia. Phone: 855 23 964455; Email: info@ibccambodia.com • URL: http://www.ibccambodia.com • Provides leadership in creating a forum for international and local businesses and business associations that have an interest in Cambodia to work together in a spirit of friendship and cooperation for mutual benefit.

***International Business***. Chamber of Commerce and Industry Queensland, Phone: 61 1 300731988 • A$55.45. Contains guidelines to become a successful international business.

***International Business Handbook***. Chamber of Commerce and Industry Queensland, Phone: 61 1 300731988.

***International Business in South Africa***. Investor Responsibility Research Center Institute, 40 Wall St., 28th Fl. New York, NY 10005. Phone: (646)512-5807 • URL: http://www.irrcinstitute.org • Annual. $500. Covers: about 600 non-U.S. companies with business links to South Africa. Database includes: Lists of companies that do business in South Africa but do not own any assets there; companies with "non equity" links to South Africa. Entries include: Name and address of parent company, line of business, names and locations of South African subsidiaries, number of employees, policies. Companies based in the United States are listed in "U.S. Business in South Africa" (see separate entry). Updated monthly for "South Africa Review Service" subscribers.

***International Business Information on the Web: Searcher Magazine's Guide to Sites and Strategies for Global Business Research***. Information Today, Inc., 143 Old Marlton Pke. Medford, NJ 08055-8750. Phone: 800-300-9868 or (609)654-6266; Fax: (609)654-4309; Email: custserv@infotoday.com • URL: http://www.infotoday.com • $29.95. Lists directories, search engines, banks, financial institutions, news sources, government contacts, chambers of commerce, and other country-specific information. Covers: Approximately 1,000 Web sites related to international business research including general business sites in the United States and worldwide. Publication includes: URLs. Entries include: Information regarding each site.

***International Business Lawyers Index/Industrial Property/Chambers of Commerce***. Datapress Ltd., PO Box 150 CH-2027 Genevia, Switzerland. • Biennial. $35. Covers: 10,000 business lawyers, 10,000 chambers of commerce and industry, 2,000 official industrial property agencies, and 110 state property agencies for 140 countries. Entries include: Name, address, phone, telex numbers.

***International Business Opportunities Database***. NIIR Project Consultancy Services, 106 - E, Kamla Nagar New Delhi 110007, India. Phone: 91 11 23843955; Fax: 91 11 23841561; Email: npcs.india@gmail.com • URL: http://www.niir.org • Rs 2,809 Individuals CD-ROM; $100 Individuals CD-ROM. Covers: 180,000+ global importers, exporters, agents, representatives, business opportunity seekers, various trade opportunities. Entries include: Company name, address, phone and fax, email, and websites.

***International Business Planning: Law and Taxation***. William P. Streng and Jeswald W. Salacuse. Matthew Bender and Company Inc., 1275 Broadway Albany, NY 12204-2638. Phone: 800-424-4200 or (518)487-3000; Fax: (518)487-3573 or (800)424-4200; Email: customer.support@lexisnexis.com • URL: http://www.matthewbender.com • $475 book; $495 e-book. Three looseleaf volumes. Periodic supplementation.

***International Business Practices Guide***. University of Missouri, St. Louis, Thomas Jefferson Library, 1 University Blvd. Saint Louis, MO 63121-4400. Phone: (314)516-5060 or (314)516-5000; Fax: (314)516-5853 • URL: http://www.umsl.edu.

***International Business Quick Reference Guide***. U.S. Chamber of Commerce, 1615 H St. NW Washington, DC 20062-2000. Phone: 800-638-6582 or (202)463-5500 or (202)659-6000; Fax: (202)463-3129; Email: foundation@uschamber.com • URL: http://www.uschambersmallbusinessnation.com • $25 Members; $35 Nonmembers. Covers: American Chambers of Commerce abroad, foreign chambers of commerce in the U.S., embassies, overseas assistance, Commerce Departments and contacts. Chamber, department or embassy name, address, phone, contact name, title.

***International Business Review***. Elsevier, Secondary Publishing Division, 650 Ave. of the Americas New York, NY 10011. Phone: 888-437-4636 or (212)633-3980; Fax: (212)633-3975; Email: t.reller@elsevier.com • URL: http://www.elsevier.com • $1,692 Institutions print. Journal describing the latest developments and advances in knowledge and practice of international business.

***International Capital Markets and Securities Regulation***. Harold S. Bloomenthal. Thomson West, 610 Opperman Dr. Eagan, MN 55123. Phone: 800-328-9352 or (651)687-7000 • $3,876 full set; $323 monthly. Nine looseleaf volumes. Periodic supplementation. Securities regulation in industrialized nations. (Securities Law Series).

***International Centre for Settlement of Investment Disputes - Annual Report***. International Centre for Settlement of Investment Disputes, 1818 H St. NW Washington, DC 20433. Phone: (202)458-1534; Fax: (202)522-2615; Email: icsidsecretariat@worldbank.org • URL: http://icsid.worldbank.org/ICSID/Index.jsp • Annual. Contains an overview of the activities during the past ICSID fiscal year.

**International Christian Union of Business Executives**. c/o Pierre Lecocq, President, 15-25 Blvd. de l'Amiral Bruix F-75016 Paris, France. Phone: 33 1 56022121; Fax: 33 1 4526 • URL: http://www.uniapac.org • National Christian employers' associations in 29 countries. Works to promote Christian ethics and sound economic policies in both business and social sectors. Serves as liaison between members and Christian associations with common goals. Conducts biennial symposium.

**International Coatings and Formulation Institute**. University of Southern Mississippi, School of Polymers and High Performance Materials Hattiesburg, MS 39406-0037. Phone: (601)266-4781; Fax: (601)266-5880; Email: shelby.f.thames@usm.edu • URL: http://www.psrc.usm.edu/icfi.

***International Code Council Membership directory***. International Code Council, 500 New Jersey Ave. NW, 6th Fl. Washington, DC 20001-2070. Phone: 888-422-7233 or (202)370-1800; Fax: (202)783-2348; Email: carecenter@iccsafe.org • URL: http://www.iccsafe.org • Annual. Price on application.

***International Code Council, Uniform Building Code***. International Conference of Building Officials, 5360 Workman Mill Rd. Whittier, CA 90601. Phone: 800-423-6587 or (562)699-0543 or (562)669-0541; Fax: (562)695-4694 or (562)699-9721 • URL: http://www.icbo.org • Triennial. Two volumes. Members, $144.55; non-members, $180.70. (International Conference of Building Officials. Uniform Building Code).

**International Code Council**. 500 New Jersey Ave. NW, 6th Fl. Washington, DC 20001-2070. Phone: 888-422-7233 or (202)370-1800; Fax: (202)783-2348; Email: carecenter@iccsafe.org • URL: http://www.iccsafe.org • Formerly Building Officials Conference of America.

***International Coffee Organization***. 22 Berners St. London W1T 3DD, United Kingdom. Phone: 44 207 5808591; Fax: (207) 5806129; Email: info@ico.org • URL: http://www.ico.org.

***International Communications and Business Database on CD-ROM***. Jaeger and Waldmann, Postfach 111454 D-64229 Darmstadt, Germany. Phone: 6151 3302 0; Fax: 6151 3302 50; Email: jwemail@aol.com • Annual. $440. Covers: Extensive list of companies located in approximately 220 countries. Entries include: Company name, address, phone; products and services; various data.

***International Construction Directory***. Dataguide Inc., PO Box 796307 Dallas, TX 75379. Phone: (214)931-1160; Fax: (214)712-3927 • Irregular. Covers: Approximately 3,550 companies engaged in the construction of buildings, roads, public works, and industrial plants; international coverage. Database includes: Rankings of top 1,000 companies by revenue and by number of employees. Entries include: Company name, address, phone, fax, mailing address, telex, principal officers, number of employees, financial data, business activity, year established, stock exchange listing.

**International Contact Center Benchmarking Consortium**. The Benchmarking Network, 4606 FM 1960 W, Ste. 250 Houston, TX 77069-9949. Phone: (281)440-5044; Fax: (281)440-6677; Email: info@iccbc.org • URL: http://www.iccbc.org • Corporations that manage call centers. Promotes the use of benchmarking, wherein businesses compare their processes with those of their competitors, as a means of improving corporate efficiency and profitability. Facilitates exchange of information among members; conducts target operations, procurement, development, and maintenance studies; identifies model business practices.

***International Contact Lens Clinic***. Elsevier, Secondary Publishing Division, 650 Ave. of the Americas New York, NY 10011. Phone: 888-437-4636 or (212)633-3980; Fax: (212)633-3975; Email: t.reller@elsevier.com • URL: http://www.elsevier.com • Bimonthly. Individuals, $139.00 per year; institutions, $272.00 per year.

***International Corporate Yellow Book***. Leadership Directories Inc., 104 5th Ave. New York, NY 10011-6901. Phone: (212)627-4140; Fax: (212)645-0931; Email: info@leadershipdirectories.com • URL: http://www.leadershipdirectories.com • Semiannual. $170 per year. Covers: leading corporations outside of the United States. Entries include: Company name, address, phone, fax, telex, description of activities, assets or revenue, names and titles of key personnel, names and affiliations of board members; name, address, phone, fax and names and titles of key personnel for subsidiaries.

***International Country Risk Guide***. The PRS Group Inc., 5800 Heritage Landing Dr., Ste. E East Syracuse, NY 13057-9378. Phone: (315)431-0511; Fax: (315)431-0200; Email: custserv@prsgroup.com • URL: http://www.prsgroup.com • Monthly. $5,701 online/print/cd-rom subscription. Provides detailed analysis of a group of countries, covering financial risks, political trends, and economic developments. More than 140 countries are covered during the course of a year, with specific business risk point ratings assigned.

***International Currency Review***. World Reports Ltd., 280 Madison Ave., Ste. 280 New York, NY 10016-0802. Phone: (212)679-0095; Fax: (212)679-1094 • Quarterly. $475.00 per year.

***International Dallas***. Dallas Regional Chamber, 500 N Akard St., Ste. 2600 Dallas, TX 75201. Phone: (214)746-6600; Email: information@dallaschamber.org • URL: http://www.dallaschamber.org • Annual. $20 Members; $40 Nonmembers plus tax where applicable & $3.00 shipping. Covers: Listings of over 1,500 international businesses in the Dallas/Ft. Worth area, including importers, exporters, foreign-owned companies, plus trade statistics and a guide to exporting. Entries include: Company name, address, phone, fax; description; product codes; local executives; parent company.

**International Data Corp.** 5 Speen St., Ste. 1 Framingham, MA 01701-4674. Phone: 800-343-4935 or (508)872-8200; Fax: (508)935-4015 or (508)935-4271; Email: idcinfo@idc.com • URL: http://www.idc.com • Private research firm specializing in market research related to computers, multimedia, and telecommunications.

***International Development Statistics***. Organization for Economic Cooperation and Development, 2001 L St. NW, Ste. 650 Washington, DC 20036-4922. Phone: 800-456-6323 or (202)785-6323; Fax: (202)785-0350; Email: washington.contact@oecd.org • URL: http://www.oecd.org • Annual. $71.00. Issued by the OECD Development Assistance Committee. CD-ROM contains data on aid to more than 180 recipient countries, including amount, origin, type, and recipients' external debt.

***International Directory for Selling Military Products and Services***. DIANE Publishing Co., PO Box 617 Darby, PA 19023-0617. Phone: 800-782-3833 or (610)461-6200; Fax: (610)461-6130; Email: dianepublishing@gmail.com • URL: http://www.dianepublishing.net • $50 Individuals Paperback. Covers: Procurement policies and procedures for 13 European countries plus Australia, Canada, Egypt and Israel. Entries include: Points of contact, getting started, access to technical documents, procurement methods, types of contracts, contract provisions, pre-award surveys, classified information, restrictions on foreign competition, contract administration.

***International Directory of Business Information Sources and Services***. Routledge Reference, 2 Park Sq. Milton Park, Abingdon Oxford OX14 4RN, United Kingdom. Phone: 44 20 70176000; Fax: 44 20 70176699; Email: book.orders@tandf.co.uk • URL: http://www.routledge.com/ • $240. Covers: over 4,500 chambers of commerce, government agencies, foreign trade promotion agencies, associations, research organizations, business libraries, and other sources of business information in 50 countries. Entries include: Agency name, address, phone, fax, names and titles of key personnel, name and title of contact, description.

***International Directory of Commercial Vehicles***. Vogt-Schild AG, Druck & Verlag, Zuchwilerstrasse 21 CH-4501 Solothum, Switzerland. • Annual. $40. Covers: Manufacturers of light commercial vehicles, municipal vehicles, trucks, small buses, all-wheel drive vehicles, special vehicles, body and trailer manufacturing, and accessories worldwide. Entries include: Manufacturer name, address, phone, technical data.

***International Directory of Company Histories***. St. James Press, PO Box 9187 Farmington Hills, MI 48333-9187. Phone: 800-877-4253 or (248)699-4253; Fax: (248)699-8035; Email: gale.galeord@cengage.com • URL: http://www.gale.cengage.com/stjames • $343 Individuals. Multi-volume work that covers histories of companies that are a leading influence in a particular industry or geographic location. eBook available. Contact for pricing.

***International Directory of Corporate Affiliations: Public and Private Companies***. LexisNexis, 9443 Springboro Pke. Dayton, OH 45342. Phone: 800-227-4908 or (937)865-6800; Fax: (937)865-1211; Email: legalnotices@lexisnexis.com • URL: http://www.bender.com • $540. Covers: Approximately 1,500 U.S. and approximately 1,600 non-U.S. parent companies and their approximately 30,000 subsidiaries. Entries include: Name, address, phone, description of activities.

***International Directory of Corporate Art Collections***. International Art Alliance, Phone: (514)935-1228; Fax: (212)819-0394; Email: info@artnewsonline.com • URL: http://www.internationalartalliance.org • $115. Contains information on about 1,300 corporate art collections maintained or sponsored in the U. S., Canada, Europe, and Japan.

***International Directory of Corporate Philanthropy***. Taylor & Francis Group, 325 Chestnut St. Philadelphia, PA 19106. Phone: 800-248-4724 or (215)625-8900; Fax: (215)625-2940; Email: info@taylorandfrancis.com • URL: http://www.taylorandfrancis.com • Annual. $250.00. Published by Europa Publications (www.europapublications.com). Contains profiles of about 1,000 corporate foundations and "coordinating organizations" in various countries of the world. Provides details of charitable activities and philanthropic expenditures.

***International Directory of Importers—Africa***. Croner Publications Inc., 10951 Sorrento Valley Rd., Ste. 1-D San Diego, CA 92121-1613. Phone: 800-441-4033 or (858)546-1894;

Fax: (800)809-0334; Email: rosa@croner.com • Irregular. $225. Covers: 10,000 importers in 40 countries in Africa. Entries include: Company name, address, phone.

***The International Directory of Importers - Africa***. Interdata, 1741 Kekamek Dr. Poulsbo, WA 98370. Phone: 800-818-0140 or (360)779-1511; Fax: (360)697-4696 • $250 By mail print; $285 Individuals print- airmail; $285 Individuals CD-ROM; $325 Individuals print & CD-ROM. Covers: 9,000 firms importing in 44 African countries a broad variety of products from abrasives to zippers. Entries include: Company name and address, contact person, email, number of employees, year established, phone and telefaxes, business activity, bank references, as well as a detailed listing of products imported.

***The International Directory of Importers - Agricultural Machinery & Implements Importers***. Interdata, 1741 Kekamek Dr. Poulsbo, WA 98370. Phone: 800-818-0140 or (360)779-1511; Fax: (360)697-4696 • $220 Individuals print; $220 Individuals CD-ROM; $270 Individuals print & CD-ROM. Covers: 2,300 international firms importing agricultural equipment. Entries include: Company name and address, contact person, email, number of employees, year established, phone and telefaxes, business activity, bank references, as well as a listing of agricultural machinery & implements currently being imported.

***The International Directory of Importers—Aircraft and Aviation Equipment and Accessories Importers***. Interdata, 1741 Kekamek Dr. Poulsbo, WA 98370. Phone: 800-818-0140 or (360)779-1511; Fax: (360)697-4696 • $200 Individuals print; $200 Individuals CD-ROM; $250 Individuals print & CD-ROM. Covers: 500 international firms importing aircraft and aviation equipment and accessories. Entries include: Company name and address, contact person, email, number of employees, year established, phone and telefaxes, business activity, bank references, as well as listing of aircraft equipment currently being imported.

***The International Directory of Importers - Apparel & Clothing Importers***. Interdata, 1741 Kekamek Dr. Poulsbo, WA 98370. Phone: 800-818-0140 or (360)779-1511; Fax: (360)697-4696 • $320 Individuals print; $320 Individuals CD-ROM; $370 Individuals print & CD-ROM. Covers: 5,600 international firms importing apparel and clothing. Entries include: Company name and address, contact person, email, number of employees, year established, phone and telefaxes, business activity, bank references, as well as a listing of apparel and clothing currently being imported.

***International Directory of Importers—Asia/Pacific***. Croner Publications Inc., 10951 Sorrento Valley Rd., Ste. 1-D San Diego, CA 92121-1613. Phone: 800-441-4033 or (858)546-1894; Fax: (800)809-0334; Email: rosa@croner.com • Irregular. $350. Covers: 30,000 importers in Australia, Hong Kong, Indonesia, Japan, Malaysia, New Zealand, Pakistan, Philippines, Singapore, South Korea, Sri Lanka, Taiwan, and Thailand. Entries include: Company name, address, phone.

***The International Directory of Importers - Asia/Pacific***. Interdata, 1741 Kekamek Dr. Poulsbo, WA 98370. Phone: 800-818-0140 or (360)779-1511; Fax: (360)697-4696 • $385 U.S. print edition; $455 U.S. print edition- airmail; $455 U.S. CD-ROM edition; $500 U.S. print & CD-ROM version. Covers: 32,000 firms importing in 22 Asian countries a broad variety of products from abrasives to zippers. Entries include: Company name and address, contact person, email, number of employees, year established, phone and telefaxes, business activity, bank references, as well as a detailed listing of products imported.

***The International Directory of Importers—Automotive Equipment, Parts & Accessories Importers***. Interdata, 1741 Kekamek Dr. Poulsbo, WA 98370. Phone: 800-818-0140 or (360)779-1511; Fax: (360)697-4696 • $320 Individuals print edition; $320 Individuals CD-ROM; $370 Individuals both print and CD-ROM version. Covers: 6,400 international firms importing automotive equipment, parts & accessories. Entries include: Company name and address, contact person, email, number of employees, year established, phone and telefaxes, business activity, bank references, as well as a listing of automotive equipment, parts & accessories currently being imported.

***The International Directory of Importers - Beauty Supplies, Cosmetic and Toiletries Importers***. Interdata, 1741 Kekamek Dr. Poulsbo, WA 98370. Phone: 800-818-0140 or (360)779-1511; Fax: (360)697-4696 • $295 Individuals print; $295 Individuals CD-ROM; $345 Individuals print & CD-ROM. Covers: 4,100 international firms importing beauty supplies, cosmetics and toiletries. Entries include: Company name and address, contact person, email, number of employees, year established, phone and telefaxes, business activity, bank references, as well as a listing of beauty supplies, cosmetics and toiletries currently being imported.

***The International Directory of Importers—Bicycles, Mopeds and Motorcycles Importers***. Interdata, 1741 Kekamek Dr. Poulsbo, WA 98370. Phone: 800-818-0140 or (360)779-1511; Fax: (360)697-4696 • $200 Individuals print; $200 Individuals CD-ROM; $250 Individuals print & CD-ROM. Covers: 800 international firms importing bicycles, mopeds and motorcycles. Entries include: Company name and address, contact person, email, number of employees, year established, phone and telefaxes, business activity, bank references, as well as a listing of bicycles, mopeds and motorcycles currently being imported.

***The International Directory of Importers—Building and Construction Materials and Supplies Importers***. Interdata, 1741 Kekamek Dr. Poulsbo, WA 98370. Phone: 800-818-0140 or (360)779-1511; Fax: (360)697-4696 • $320 Individuals print; $320 Individuals CD-ROM; $370 Individuals print & CD-ROM. Covers: 6,400 international firms importing building, construction materials and supplies. Entries include: Company name and address, contact person, email, number of employees, year established, phone and telefaxes, business activity, bank references, as well as a listing of building, construction materials and supplies currently being imported.

***The International Directory of Importers—Chemicals and Allied Products Importers***. Interdata, 1741 Kekamek Dr. Poulsbo, WA 98370. Phone: 800-818-0140 or (360)779-1511; Fax: (360)697-4696 • Annual. $320 Individuals print; $320 Individuals CD-ROM; $370 Individuals print & CD-ROM. Covers: 6,200 international firms importing chemicals and allied products. Entries include: Company name and address, contact person, email, number of employees, year established, phone and telefaxes, business activity, bank references, as well as a listing of chemicals and allied products currently being imported.

***The International Directory of Importers—Communications Equipment Importers***. Interdata, 1741 Kekamek Dr. Poulsbo, WA 98370. Phone: 800-818-0140 or (360)779-1511; Fax: (360)697-4696 • $295 Individuals print; $345 Individuals print & CD-ROM; $295 Individuals CD-ROM version. Covers: 4,000 international firms importing communications equipment. Entries include: Company name and address, contact person, email, number of employees, year established, phone and telefaxes, business activity, bank references, as well as a listing of communications equipment currently being imported.

***The International Directory of Importers—Computers and Data Processing Equipment Importers***. Interdata, 1741 Kekamek Dr. Poulsbo, WA 98370. Phone: 800-818-0140 or (360)779-1511; Fax: (360)697-4696 • $320 Individuals print; $320 Individuals CD-ROM; $370 Individuals print & CD-ROM. Covers: 7,100 international firms importing computers and data processing equipment. Entries include: Company name and address, contact person, email, number of employees, year established, phone and telefaxes, business activity, bank references, as well as a listing of computers and data processing equipment currently being imported.

***The International Directory of Importers—Construction and Building Equipment Importers***. Interdata, 1741 Kekamek Dr. Poulsbo, WA 98370. Phone: 800-818-0140 or (360)779-1511; Fax: (360)697-4696 • $260 Individuals print; $260 Individuals CD-ROM; $310 Individuals print & CD-ROM. Covers: 3,100 international firms importing construction and building equipment. Entries include: Company name and address, contact person, email, number of employees, year established, phone and telefaxes, business activity, bank references, as well as a listing of construction and building equipment currently being imported.

***The International Directory of Importers - Consumer Electronics, Audio/Video, TV's and CD's Importers***. Interdata, 1741 Kekamek Dr. Poulsbo, WA 98370. Phone: 800-818-0140 or (360)779-1511; Fax: (360)697-4696 • $295 Individuals printed edition; $295 Individuals CD-ROM; $345 Individuals both printed and CD-ROM version. Covers: 4,000 international firms importing consumer electronics, audio/video, TV's and CD's. Entries include: Company name and address, contact person, email, number of employees, year established, phone and telefaxes, business activity, bank references, as well as a listing of consumer electronics, audio/video, TV's and CD's currently being imported.

***The International Directory of Importers—Control Equipment and Switches Importers***. Interdata, 1741 Kekamek Dr. Poulsbo, WA 98370. Phone: 800-818-0140 or (360)779-1511; Fax: (360)697-4696 • $200 Individuals print; $200 Individuals CD-ROM; $250 Individuals print & CD-ROM. Covers: 1,400 international firms importing control equipment and switches. Entries include: Company name and address, contact person, email, number of employees, year established, phone and telefaxes, business activity, bank references, as well as a listing of control equipment and switches currently being imported.

***The International Directory of Importers—Drugs and Pharmaceuticals Importers***. Interdata, 1741 Kekamek Dr. Poulsbo, WA 98370. Phone: 800-818-0140 or (360)779-1511; Fax: (360)697-4696 • Annual. $260 Individuals print; $260 Individuals CD-ROM; $310 Individuals print & CD-ROM. Covers: 2,900 international firms importing drugs and pharmaceuticals. Entries include: Company name and address, contact person, email, number of employees, year established, phone and telefaxes, business activity, bank references, as well as a listing of drugs and pharmaceuticals currently being imported.

***The International Directory of Importers—Electrical Equipment and Supplies Importers***. Interdata, 1741 Kekamek Dr. Poulsbo, WA 98370. Phone: 800-818-0140 or (360)779-1511; Fax: (360)697-4696 • $295 Individuals print edition; $295 Individuals CD-ROM; $345 Individuals both CD-ROM and print. Covers: 4,900 international firms importing electrical equipment and supplies. Entries include: Company name and address, contact person, email, number of employees, year established, phone and telefaxes, business activity, bank references, as well as a listing of electrical equipment and supplies currently being imported.

***The International Directory of Importers—Electronic and Computer Components and Parts Importers***. Interdata, 1741 Kekamek Dr. Poulsbo, WA 98370. Phone: 800-818-0140 or (360)779-1511; Fax: (360)697-4696 • $320 Individuals print; $320 Individuals CD-ROM; $370 Institutions, other countries print & CD-ROM. Covers: 7,000 international firms importing electronic and computer components and parts. Entries include: Company name and address, contact person, email, number of employees, year established, phone and telefaxes, business activity, bank references, as well as a listing of electronic and computer components and parts currently being imported.

***The International Directory of Importers—Environmental Protection Equipment Importers***. Interdata, 1741 Kekamek Dr. Poulsbo, WA 98370. Phone: 800-818-0140 or (360)779-1511; Fax: (360)697-4696 • $200 Individuals print; $200 Individuals CD-ROM; $250 Individuals print & CD-ROM. Covers: 1,100 international firms importing environmental protection equipment. Entries include: Company name and address, contact person, email, number of employees, year established, phone and telefaxes, business activity, bank references, as well as a listing of environmental protection equipment currently being imported.

***International Directory of Importers—Europe***. Croner Publications Inc., 10951 Sorrento Valley Rd., Ste. 1-D San Diego, CA 92121-1613. Phone: 800-441-4033 or (858)546-1894; Fax: (800)809-0334; Email: rosa@croner.com • Irregular. $450. Covers: 54,000 importers in Austria, Belgium, Denmark, France, Holland, Italy, Norway, Spain, Sweden, Switzerland, United Kingdom, and West Germany. Entries include: Company name, address, phone.

***The International Directory of Importers - Europe***. Interdata, 1741 Kekamek Dr. Poulsbo, WA 98370. Phone: 800-818-0140 or (360)779-1511; Fax: (360)697-4696 • $485 Individuals regular mail; $585 Individuals print- airmail; $585 Individuals CD-ROM; $650 Individuals print & CD-ROM. Covers: 54,000 firms importing in 35 European countries a broad variety of products from abrasives to zippers. Entries include: Company name and address, contact person, email, number of employees, year established, phone and telefaxes, business activity, bank references, as well as a detailed listing of products imported.

***The International Directory of Importers - Floor Coverings, Carpets and Rugs Importers***. Interdata, 1741 Kekamek Dr. Poulsbo, WA 98370. Phone: 800-818-0140 or (360)779-1511; Fax: (360)697-4696 • $200 Individuals print; $200 Individuals CD-ROM; $250 Individuals print & CD-ROM. Covers: 1,000 international firms importing floor coverings, carpets and rugs. Entries include: Company name and address, contact person, email, number of employees, year established, phone and telefaxes, business activity, bank references, as well as a listing of floor coverings, carpets and rugs currently being imported.

***The International Directory of Importers - Food & Beverage Importers***. Interdata, 1741 Kekamek Dr. Poulsbo, WA 98370. Phone: 800-818-0140 or (360)779-1511; Fax: (360)697-4696 • $320 Individuals print; $320 Individuals CD-ROM; $370 Individuals print & CD-ROM. Covers: 7,300 international firms importing food and beverage. Entries include: Company name and address, contact person, email, number of employees, year established, phone and telefaxes, business activity, bank references, as well as a listing of food and beverage currently being imported.

***The International Directory of Importers - Furniture and Home Furnishings Importers***. Interdata, 1741 Kekamek Dr. Poulsbo, WA 98370. Phone: 800-818-0140 or (360)779-1511; Fax: (360)697-4696 • $320 Individuals print; $320 Individuals CD-ROM; $370 Individuals print & CD-ROM. Covers: 5,100 international firms importing furniture and home furnishings. Entries include: Company name and address, contact person, email, number of employees, year established, phone and telefaxes, business activity, bank references, as well as a listing of furniture and home furnishings currently being imported.

***The International Directory of Importers - Garden, Lawn and Patio Equipment and Supplies Importers***. Interdata, 1741 Kekamek Dr. Poulsbo, WA 98370. Phone: 800-818-0140 or (360)779-1511; Fax: (360)697-4696 • $295 Individuals print edition; $295 Individuals CD-ROM version; $345 Individuals both print and CD-ROM version. Covers: 3,800 international firms importing garden, lawn, patio equipment and supplies. Entries include: Company name and address, contact person, email, number of employees, year established, phone and telefaxes, business activity, bank references, as well as a listing of garden, lawn, patio equipment and supplies currently being imported.

***The International Directory of Importers - Hand Tools and Power Tools Importers***. Interdata, 1741 Kekamek Dr. Poulsbo, WA 98370. Phone: 800-818-0140 or (360)779-1511; Fax: (360)697-4696 • $260 Individuals print; $260 Individuals CD-ROM; $310 Individuals print & CD-ROM. Covers: 3,000 international firms importing hand tools and power tools. Entries include: Company name and address, contact person, email, number of employees, year established, phone and telefaxes, business activity, bank references, as well as a listing of hand tools and power tools currently being imported.

*The International Directory of Importers - Household and Kitchen Appliances Importers*. Interdata, 1741 Kekamek Dr. Poulsbo, WA 98370. Phone: 800-818-0140 or (360)779-1511; Fax: (360)697-4696 • $220 Individuals print; $220 Individuals CD-ROM; $270 Individuals print & CD-ROM. Covers: 2,300 international firms importing household and kitchen appliances. Entries include: Company name and address, contact person, email, number of employees, year established, phone and telefaxes, business activity, bank references, as well as a listing of household and kitchen appliances currently being imported.

*The International Directory of Importers - Housewares and Home Accessories Importers*. Interdata, 1741 Kekamek Dr. Poulsbo, WA 98370. Phone: 800-818-0140 or (360)779-1511; Fax: (360)697-4696 • $320 Individuals print; $320 Individuals CD-ROM; $370 Individuals print & CD-ROM. Covers: 6,200 international firms importing housewares and home accessories. Entries include: Company name and address, contact person, email, number of employees, year established, phone and telefaxes, business activity, bank references, as well as a listing of housewares and home accessories currently being imported.

*The International Directory of Importers - Jewelry and Costume Jewelry Importers*. Interdata, 1741 Kekamek Dr. Poulsbo, WA 98370. Phone: 800-818-0140 or (360)779-1511; Fax: (360)697-4696 • $220 Individuals print; $220 Individuals CD-ROM; $270 Individuals print & CD-ROM. Covers: 2,100 international firms importing jewelry and costume jewelry. Entries include: Company name and address, contact person, email, number of employees, year established, phone and telefaxes, business activity, bank references, as well as a listing of jewelry and costume jewelry currently being imported.

*The International Directory of Importers - Kitchenware, Tableware and Glassware Importers*. Interdata, 1741 Kekamek Dr. Poulsbo, WA 98370. Phone: 800-818-0140 or (360)779-1511; Fax: (360)697-4696 • $220 Individuals print; $220 Individuals CD-ROM; $270 Individuals print & CD-ROM. Covers: 3,000 international firms importing kitchenware, tableware and glassware. Entries include: Company name and address, contact person, email, number of employees, year established, phone and telefaxes, business activity, bank references, as well as a listing of kitchenware, tableware and glassware currently being imported.

*The International Directory of Importers - Leather Goods, Footwear and Travel Accessories Importers*. Interdata, 1741 Kekamek Dr. Poulsbo, WA 98370. Phone: 800-818-0140 or (360)779-1511; Fax: (360)697-4696 • $260 Individuals print edition; $260 Individuals CD-ROM version; $310 Individuals both print and CD-ROM version. Covers: 3,200 international firms importing leather goods, footwear and travel accessories. Entries include: Company name and address, contact person, email, number of employees, year established, phone and telefaxes, business activity, bank references, as well as a listing of leather goods, footwear and travel accessories currently being imported.

*The International Directory of Importers - Lighting Equipment, Lamps and Accessories Importers*. Interdata, 1741 Kekamek Dr. Poulsbo, WA 98370. Phone: 800-818-0140 or (360)779-1511; Fax: (360)697-4696 • Annual. $220 Individuals print; $220 Individuals CD-ROM; $270 Individuals print & CD-ROM. Covers: 2,500 international firms importing lighting equipment, lamps and accessories. Entries include: Company name and address, contact person, email, number of employees, year established, phone and telefaxes, business activity, bank references, as well as a listing of lighting equipment, lamps and accessories currently being imported.

*The International Directory of Importers—Machine Tools and Accessories Importers*. Interdata, 1741 Kekamek Dr. Poulsbo, WA 98370. Phone: 800-818-0140 or (360)779-1511; Fax: (360)697-4696 • $220 Individuals print; $220 Individuals CD-ROM; $270 Individuals print & CD-ROM. Covers: 1,900 international firms importing machine tools and accessories. Entries include: Company name and address, contact person, email, number of employees, year established, phone and telefaxes, business activity, bank references, as well as a listing of machine tools and accessories currently being imported.

*The International Directory of Importers - Marine & Boating Equipment Supplies Importers*. Interdata, 1741 Kekamek Dr. Poulsbo, WA 98370. Phone: 800-818-0140 or (360)779-1511; Fax: (360)697-4696 • $260 Individuals print; $260 Individuals CD-ROM; $310 Individuals print & CD-ROM. Covers: 3,100 international firms importing marine & boating equipment and supplies. Entries include: Company name and address, contact person, email, number of employees, year established, phone and telefaxes, business activity, bank references, as well as a listing of marine & boating equipment and supplies currently being imported.

*The International Directory of Importers - Measuring Equipment and Scales Importers*. Interdata, 1741 Kekamek Dr. Poulsbo, WA 98370. Phone: 800-818-0140 or (360)779-1511; Fax: (360)697-4696 • $220 Individuals print version; $220 Individuals CD-ROM; $270 Individuals both print and CD-ROM version. Covers: 1,900 international firms importing measuring equipment and scales. Entries include: Company name and address, contact person, email, number

of employees, year established, phone and telefaxes, business activity, bank references, as well as a listing of measuring equipment and scales currently being imported.

*The International Directory of Importers - Medical, Hospital and Surgical Equipment and Supplies Importers*. Interdata, 1741 Kekamek Dr. Poulsbo, WA 98370. Phone: 800-818-0140 or (360)779-1511; Fax: (360)697-4696 • $295 Individuals print; $295 Individuals CD-ROM; $345 Individuals print & CD-ROM. Covers: 4,400 international firms importing medical, hospital and surgical equipment and supplies. Entries include: Company name and address, contact person, email, number of employees, year established, phone and telefaxes, business activity, bank references, as well as a listing of medical, hospital and surgical equipment and supplies currently being imported.

*International Directory of Importers—Medical, Hospital, and Surgical Equipment and Supplies*. International Directory of Importers, 1741 Kekamek NW Poulsbo, WA 98370. Phone: 800-818-0140 or (360)779-1511; Fax: (360)697-4696; Email: helpdesk@export-leads.com • URL: http://www.export-leads. com • Annual. $295 Individuals print; $295 Individuals CD-ROM; $345 Individuals print and CD-ROM. Covers: 5,000 worldwide manufacturers, importers, and firms trading in medical, hospital, and surgical equipment and supplies. Entries include: Company name, address, phone, fax, email address when available, importing manager, year established.

*International Directory of Importers—Middle East*. Croner Publications Inc., 10951 Sorrento Valley Rd., Ste. 1-D San Diego, CA 92121-1613. Phone: 800-441-4033 or (858)546-1894; Fax: (800)809-0334; Email: rosa@croner.com • Irregular. $225. Covers: 14,000 importers in Bahrain, Egypt, Iran, Iraq, Israel, Jordan, Kuwait, Lebanon, Oman, Qatar, Saudi Arabia, Syria, United Arab Emirates, and North/South Yemen. Entries include: Company name, address, phone.

*The International Directory of Importers - Middle East*. Interdata, 1741 Kekamek Dr. Poulsbo, WA 98370. Phone: 800-818-0140 or (360)779-1511; Fax: (360)697-4696 • $250 Individuals print; $285 Individuals print, airmail; $285 Individuals CD-ROM; $325 Individuals print & CD-ROM. Covers: 13,000 firms importing in 14 Middle East countries a broad variety of products from abrasives to zippers. Entries include: Company name and address, contact person, email, number of employees, year established, phone and telefaxes, business activity, bank references, as well as a detailed listing of products imported.

*International Directory of Importers—North America*. Croner Publications Inc., 10951 Sorrento Valley Rd., Ste. 1-D San Diego, CA 92121-1613. Phone: 800-441-4033 or (858)546-1894; Fax: (800)809-0334; Email: rosa@croner.com • Irregular. $225. Covers: 20,000 importers in the United States and Canada. Entries include: Company name, address, phone.

*The International Directory of Importers - North America*. Interdata, 1741 Kekamek Dr. Poulsbo, WA 98370. Phone: 800-818-0140 or (360)779-1511; Fax: (360)697-4696 • $250 Individuals print; $285 Individuals print, airmail; $285 Individuals CD-ROM; $325 Individuals print & CD-ROM. Covers: 19,000 firms importing in North America a broad variety of products from abrasives to zippers. Entries include: Company name and address, contact person, email, number of employees, year established, phone and telefaxes, business activity, bank references, as well as a detailed listing of products imported.

*The International Directory of Importers - Office Equipment, Stationery and Supplies Importers*. Interdata, 1741 Kekamek Dr. Poulsbo, WA 98370. Phone: 800-818-0140 or (360)779-1511; Fax: (360)697-4696 • Annual. $320 Individuals print; $320 Individuals CD-ROM; $370 Individuals print & CD-ROM. Covers: 7,100 international firms importing office equipment, stationery and supplies. Entries include: Company name and address, contact person, email, number of employees, year established, phone and telefaxes, business activity, bank references, as well as a listing of office equipment, stationery and supplies currently being imported.

*The International Directory of Importers - Optical Goods & Instruments Importers*. Interdata, 1741 Kekamek Dr. Poulsbo, WA 98370. Phone: 800-818-0140 or (360)779-1511; Fax: (360)697-4696 • $220 Individuals print; $220 Individuals CD-ROM; $270 Individuals print & CD-ROM. Covers: 2,100 international firms importing optical goods and instruments. Entries include: Company name and address, contact person, email, number of employees, year established, phone and telefaxes, business activity, bank references, as well as a listing of optical goods and instruments currently being imported.

*The International Directory of Importers - Paper, Paper Goods and Stationery Products Importers*. Interdata, 1741 Kekamek Dr. Poulsbo, WA 98370. Phone: 800-818-0140 or (360)779-1511; Fax: (360)697-4696 • $295 Individuals print version; $295 Individuals CD-ROM version; $345 Individuals both print and CD-ROM version. Covers: 4,400 international firms importing paper, paper goods and stationery products. Entries include: Company name and address, contact person, email, number of employees, year established, phone and telefaxes, business activity, bank references, as well as a listing of paper, paper goods and stationery products currently being imported.

*The International Directory of Importers—Photographic Equipment and Supplies Importers*. Interdata, 1741 Kekamek Dr.

Poulsbo, WA 98370. Phone: 800-818-0140 or (360)779-1511; Fax: (360)697-4696 • $200 Individuals print version; $200 Individuals CD-ROM version; $250 Individuals both print and CD-ROM version. Covers: 1,700 international firms importing photographic equipment and supplies. Entries include: Company name and address, contact person, email, number of employees, year established, phone and telefaxes, business activity, bank references, as well as a listing of photographic equipment and supplies currently being imported.

*The International Directory of Importers—Plastics & Plastic Products Importers*. Interdata, 1741 Kekamek Dr. Poulsbo, WA 98370. Phone: 800-818-0140 or (360)779-1511; Fax: (360)697-4696 • $295 Individuals print; $295 Individuals CD-ROM; $345 Individuals print & CD-ROM. Covers: 4,400 international firms importing plastics and plastic products. Entries include: Company name and address, contact person, email, number of employees, year established, phone and telefaxes, business activity, bank references, as well as a listing of plastics and plastic products currently being imported.

*The International Directory of Importers—Plumbing, Sanitary Ware, Pipes & Fittings Importers*. Interdata, 1741 Kekamek Dr. Poulsbo, WA 98370. Phone: 800-818-0140 or (360)779-1511; Fax: (360)697-4696 • $260 Individuals print; $260 Individuals CD-ROM; $310 Individuals print & CD-ROM. Covers: 3,700 international firms importing plumbing, sanitary ware, pipes and fittings. Entries include: Company name and address, contact person, email, number of employees, year established, phone and telefaxes, business activity, bank references, as well as a listing of plumbing, sanitary ware, pipes and fittings currently being imported.

*The International Directory of Importers—Printing and Graphic Arts Equipment and Supplies Importers*. Interdata, 1741 Kekamek Dr. Poulsbo, WA 98370. Phone: 800-818-0140 or (360)779-1511; Fax: (360)697-4696 • $220 Individuals print; $220 Individuals CD-ROM; $270 Individuals print & CD-ROM. Covers: 2,500 international firms importing printing and graphic arts equipment and supplies. Entries include: Company name and address, contact person, email, number of employees, year established, phone and telefaxes, business activity, bank references, as well as a listing of printing and graphic arts equipment and supplies currently being imported.

*The International Directory of Importers—Pumps & Compressors Importers*. Interdata, 1741 Kekamek Dr. Poulsbo, WA 98370. Phone: 800-818-0140 or (360)779-1511; Fax: (360)697-4696 • $220 Individuals print; $220 Individuals CD-ROM; $270 Individuals print & CD-ROM. Covers: 2,200 international firms importing pumps and compressors. Entries include: Company name and address, contact person, email, number of employees, year established, phone and telefaxes, business activity, bank references, as well as a listing of pumps and compressors currently being imported.

*The International Directory of Importers - Refrigeration, Ventilation and Heating Equipment Importers*. Interdata, 1741 Kekamek Dr. Poulsbo, WA 98370. Phone: 800-818-0140 or (360)779-1511; Fax: (360)697-4696 • $260 Individuals print; $260 Individuals CD-ROM; $310 Individuals print & CD-ROM. Covers: 3,300 international firms importing refrigeration, ventilation and heating equipment. Entries include: Company name and address, contact person, email, number of employees, year established, phone and telefaxes, business activity, bank references, as well as a listing of refrigeration, ventilation and heating equipment currently being imported.

*The International Directory of Importers—Safety, Security and Fire Fighting Equipment Importers*. Interdata, 1741 Kekamek Dr. Poulsbo, WA 98370. Phone: 800-818-0140 or (360)779-1511; Fax: (360)697-4696 • $260 Individuals print edition; $260 Individuals CD-ROM; $310 Individuals both print and CD-ROM version. Covers: 3,300 international firms importing safety, security and fire fighting equipment. Entries include: Company name and address, contact person, email, number of employees, year established, phone and telefaxes, business activity, bank references, as well as a listing of safety, security and fire fighting equipment currently being imported.

*The International Directory of Importers—Screws, Nuts, Bolts and Fasteners Importers*. Interdata, 1741 Kekamek Dr. Poulsbo, WA 98370. Phone: 800-818-0140 or (360)779-1511; Fax: (360)697-4696 • $200 Individuals print; $200 Individuals CD-ROM; $250 Individuals print & CD-ROM. Covers: 900 international firms importing screws, nuts, bolts and fasteners. Entries include: Company name and address, contact person, email, number of employees, year established, phone and telefaxes, business activity, bank references, as well as a listing of screws, nuts, bolts and fasteners currently being imported.

*The International Directory of Importers - South America*. Interdata, 1741 Kekamek Dr. Poulsbo, WA 98370. Phone: 800-818-0140 or (360)779-1511; Fax: (360)697-4696 • $250 Individuals print edition; $285 Individuals print edition-airmail; $285 Individuals CD-ROM edition; $325 Individuals print & CD-ROM. Covers: 23,000 firms importing in 27 South American countries a broad variety of products from abrasives to zippers. Entries include: Company name and address, contact person, e-mail address, number of employees, year established, phone and telefaxes, business activity, bank references, as well as a detailed listing of products imported.

***The International Directory of Importers—Sporting Goods and Toys Importers***. Interdata, 1741 Kekamek Dr. Poulsbo, WA 98370. Phone: 800-818-0140 or (360)779-1511; Fax: (360)697-4696 • Annual. $295 Individuals print; $295 Individuals CD-ROM; $345 Individuals print & CD-ROM. Covers: 4,700 international firms importing sporting goods and toys. Entries include: Company name and address, contact person, email, number of employees, year established, phone and telefaxes, business activity, bank references, as well as a listing of sporting goods and toys currently being imported.

***The International Directory of Importers—Textiles & Fabrics Importers***. Interdata, 1741 Kekamek Dr. Poulsbo, WA 98370. Phone: 800-818-0140 or (360)779-1511; Fax: (360)697-4696 • $260 Individuals print; $260 Individuals CD-ROM; $310 Individuals print & CD-ROM. Covers: 3,600 international firms importing textiles and fabrics. Entries include: Company name and address, contact person, email, number of employees, year established, phone and telefaxes, business activity, bank references, as well as a listing of textiles and fabrics currently being imported.

***The International Directory of Importers—Tires and Tubes Importers: Auto, Cycle, Truck***. Interdata, 1741 Kekamek Dr. Poulsbo, WA 98370. Phone: 800-818-0140 or (360)779-1511; Fax: (360)697-4696 • $200 Individuals print; $200 Individuals CD-ROM; $250 Individuals print & CD-ROM. Covers: 1,300 international firms importing tires and tubes (auto/cycle/truck). Entries include: Company name and address, contact person, email, number of employees, year established, phone and telefaxes, business activity, bank references, as well as a listing of tires and tubes (auto/cycle/truck) currently being imported.

***The International Directory of Importers - Watches and Clocks Importers***. Interdata, 1741 Kekamek Dr. Poulsbo, WA 98370. Phone: 800-818-0140 or (360)779-1511; Fax: (360)697-4696 • $200 Individuals print; $200 Individuals CD-ROM; $250 Individuals print & CD-ROM. Covers: 1,000 international firms importing watches and clocks. Entries include: Company name and address, contact person, email, number of employees, year established, phone and telefaxes, business activity, bank references, as well as a listing of watches and clocks currently being imported.

***International Directory of Importers—Welding and Soldering Equipment Importers***. Interdata, 1741 Kekamek Dr. Poulsbo, WA 98370. Phone: 800-818-0140 or (360)779-1511; Fax: (360)697-4696 • Annual. $200 Individuals print; $200 Individuals CD-ROM; $250 Individuals print & CD-ROM. Covers: 700 international firms importing welding and soldering equipment. Entries include: Company name and address, contact person, email, number of employees, year established, phone and telefaxes, business activity, bank references, as well as a listing of welding and soldering equipment currently being imported.

***The International Directory of Importers - Woodworking Equipment and Tools Importers***. Interdata, 1741 Kekamek Dr. Poulsbo, WA 98370. Phone: 800-818-0140 or (360)779-1511; Fax: (360)697-4696 • $200 Individuals print edition; $200 Individuals CD-ROM; $250 Individuals print & CD-ROM. Covers: 1,800 international firms importing woodworking equipment and tools. Entries include: Company name and address, contact person, email, number of employees, year established, phone and telefaxes, business activity, bank references, as well as a listing of woodworking equipment and tools currently being imported.

***International Directory of Little Magazines and Small Presses***. Dustbooks, PO Box 100 Paradise, CA 95967. Phone: (530)877-6110; Fax: (530)877-0222; Email: info@dustbooks.com • URL: http://www.dustbooks.com • Annual. $65 Individuals CD-ROM (3 directories); $49.95 Individuals online; $30 Individuals CD-ROM. Over 4,000 small, independent magazines, presses, and papers.

***International Directory of Marketing Information Sources***. Euromonitor International Business Reference Div., 224 S Michigan Ave., Ste. 1500 Chicago, IL 60604. Phone: (312)922-1115; Fax: (312)922-1157; Email: insight@euromonitorintl.com • URL: http://www.euromonitor.com • Irregular. $650; $155. Covers: Marketing sources in major non-European industrialized countries. Entries include: Over 6,000 contacts, services, and publications.

***International Directory of Refrigerated Warehouses and Distribution Centers***. Global Cold Chain Alliance, 1500 King St., Ste. 201 Alexandria, VA 22314-2730. Phone: (703)373-4300; Fax: (703)373-4301; Email: email@gcca.org • URL: http://www.gcca.org • Continuous. Lists locations/services of 1,000 public refrigerated warehouses in 30 countries. Formerly *International Directory of Public Refrigerated Warehouses*.

***International Directory of the Nonwoven Fabrics Industry***. INDA, Association of the Nonwoven Fabrics Industry, 1100 Crescent Green, Ste. 115 Cary, NC 27518. Phone: (919)233-1210; Fax: (919)233-1282; Email: info@inda.org • URL: http://www.inda.org • $100 Nonmembers. Lists more than 2,200 manufacturers of nonwoven fabrics and suppliers of raw material and equipment.

***International Door & Operator Industry***. International Door Association, PO Box 246 West Milton, OH 45383. Phone: 800-355-4432 or (937)698-8042; Fax: (937)698-6153; Email: info@longmgt.com • URL: http://www.doors.org • Bimonthly. Edited for garage door and opener dealers.

**International Downtown Association**. 1025 Thomas Jefferson St. NW, Ste. 500W Washington, DC 20007. Phone: (202)393-6801; Fax: (202)393-6869; Email: question@ida-downtown.org • URL: http://www.ida-downtown.org • Represents vital and livable urban centers. Works to build partnerships that anchor the well-being of towns, cities and regions throughout the world.

***International Drug Report***. International Narcotic Enforcement Officers Association, 112 State St., Ste. 1200 Albany, NY 12207. Phone: (518)463-6232; Fax: (518)463-6232 or (518)432-3378; Email: ineoa@iopener.net • URL: http://www.ineoa.org • Description: Discusses current trends in narcotic abuse and enforcement, legal decisions concerning drug abuse, and related subjects. Carries news articles, scientific reports, statistics, and agency information. Recurring features include book reviews, notices of meetings, and news from U.S. Customs and the Drug Enforcement Administration.

***International Dyer***. World Textile Publications Ltd., Perkins House, One Longlands St., c/o Keith Higgenbottom Bradford BD1 2TP, United Kingdom. Phone: 44 1274 378800; Fax: (127)4 378811; Email: info@worldtextile.com • URL: http://www.worldtextile.com • Monthly. $90.00 per year.

**International Economic Alliance**. 1 Mifflin Pl., Ste. 400 Cambridge, MA 02138-4946. Phone: (617)418-1981; Fax: (617)812-0499 • URL: http://www.iealliance.org • Aims to further global trade, economic development and advance business relations. Brings together the world's key players and decision-makers (business and government leaders, investors and leading intellectuals) for practical, open, bipartisan and solution-oriented exchange of ideas. Serves as a source of knowledge, facilitator of relationships, and catalyst for new business opportunities.

**International Economic Development Council**. 734 15th St. NW, Ste. 900 Washington, DC 20005. Phone: (202)223-7800; Fax: (202)223-4745 • URL: http://www.iedconline.org • Works to help economic development professionals improve the quality of life in their communities. Represents all levels of government, academia, and private industry; provides a broad range of member services including research, advisory services, conferences, professional certification, professional development, publications, legislative tracking and more.

***International Economic Scoreboard***. The Conference Board, 845 3rd Ave. New York, NY 10022-6601. Phone: (212)759-0900 or (212)339-0345; Fax: (212)980-7014 or (212)836-9740; Email: membership@conferenceboard.org • URL: http://www.conference-board.org • Description: Provides current data on the business outlook in 11 major industrial countries: Australia, Canada, France, West Germany, Italy, Japan, Korea, New Zealand, Taiwan, the United Kingdom, and the U.S. **Remarks:** A source for additional information on this indicator system and its uses is available at the Center for International Business Cycle Research, Columbia University Business School.

***International Employment Hotline***. Carlyle Corp., PO Box 6729 Charlottesville, VA 22906-6729. Phone: 800-291-4618 or (434)985-6444 or (434)985-4924; Fax: (434)985-6828; Email: ieo@mindspring.com • URL: http://www.jobspublichealth.com • Monthly. $69 Individuals per 1 year; $21 Individuals per 3 months; $39 Individuals per 6 months; $129 Individuals per 2 years. Description: Covers the latest developments in the international job market. Summarizes hiring cycles of major employers. Lists current overseas job openings by job title, description, employer contact, and address. Recurring features include editorials and news of research.

**International Energy Credit Association**. 1500 Commerce Pkwy., Ste. C Mount Laurel, NJ 08054. Phone: (856)380-6854; Fax: (856)439-0525 • URL: http://www.ieca.net • Credit executives of petroleum and energy related companies and vendors to the field. Conducts educational seminars.

**International Executive Service Corps**. 1900 M St. NW, Ste. 500 Washington, DC 20036. Phone: (202)589-2600; Fax: (202)326-0289; Email: iesc@iesc.org • URL: http://www.iesc.org • Provides technical and managerial assistance to enterprises, organizations and government bodies in emerging democracies and developing countries. Focuses on the knowledge, skill and experience of its 12,000 industry experts. Maintains a network of experts that includes high-level professionals drawn from nearly every area of private enterprise, government and non-governmental organizations; Geekcorps division includes experts in communications and information technology and is committed to closing the digital divide.

**International Factoring Association**. 6627 Bay Laurel Pl., Ste. C Avila Beach, CA 93424-0039. Phone: 800-563-1895; Fax: (805)773-0021; Email: info@factoring.org • URL: http://www.factoring.org • Represents the interests of the factoring industry. Assists the factoring community by providing information, training, purchasing power and resources. Provides opportunities for members to discuss issues and concerns in the industry.

**International Farm Management Association**. c/o Tony King, Honorary Secretary, 38 West End Cambridge CB22 4LX, United Kingdom. Phone: 44 1223 832527; Email: honsecretary@ifmaonline.org • URL: http://www.ifmaonline.org • Farmers, extension workers, academics, resource use planners, and managers in 68 countries concerned with the planning, production, and marketing in agriculture. Furthers the knowledge and understanding of farm business management and fosters the exchange of ideas and information about farm management theory and practice worldwide.

**International Fertilizer Development Center**. PO Box 2040 Muscle Shoals, AL 35662. Phone: (205)386-2874 or (256)381-6600; Fax: (256)381-7408; Email: general@ifdc.org • URL: http://www.ifdc.org • Conducts research relating to all aspects of fertilizer production, marketing, and use. Supported by the United Nations, the World Bank, and other international agencies.

***International Fiber Journal***. International Media Group Inc., 7421 Carmel Executive Pk. Dr., No. 105 Charlotte, NC 28226. Phone: (704)544-1969; Fax: (704)544-6559; Email: ifj@ifj.com • URL: http://www.fiberjournal.com • $125 print delivery; $95 e-mail delivery. Bimonthly. Covers manmade fiber technology and manufacturing.

***International Financial Law Review***. American Educational Systems, PO Box 236 New York, NY 10024-0246. Phone: 800-431-1579; Email: aesbooks@aol.com • Monthly. $750.00 per year. Includes print and online editions.

***International Foodservice Manufacturers Association: Membership Directory***. International Foodservice Manufacturers Association, 2 Prudential Plz., 180 N Stetson Ave., Ste. 4400 Chicago, IL 60601. Phone: (312)540-4400; Email: ifma@ifmaworld.com • URL: http://www.ifmaworld.com • Annual. Manufacturers of processed foods equipment and supplies for schools, hospitals, hotels, restaurants, and institutions and related services in the foodservice industry.

**International Foundation for Art Research**. 500 5th Ave., Ste. 935 New York, NY 10110. Phone: (212)391-6234; Fax: (212)391-8794 • URL: http://www.ifar.org • Research fields are art theft and the authenticity of art objects. Maintains an information archive on stolen art and operates an authentication service.

***International Freighting Weekly: Sea, Air, Rail, Road***. Informa UK Ltd., Mortimer House, 37-41 Mortimer St. London W1T 3JH, United Kingdom. Phone: 44 207 017 4994 or 44 20 7017 5537; Fax: 44 20 7017 4947; Email: marketing.enquiries@informa.com • URL: http://www.informatandm.com • Weekly. $289.00 per year. Looseleaf service.

**International Function Point Users Group**. 191 Clarksville Rd. Princeton Junction, NJ 08550. Phone: (609)799-4900; Fax: (609)799-7032; Email: ifpug@ifpug.org • URL: http://www.ifpug.org • Works to increase the "effectiveness of its members' information technology environments through the applications of function point analysis and other software measurement techniques."

***International Gaming and Wagering Business***. Gem Communications, 5857 Randolph Blvd. San Antonio, TX 78233. Phone: (210)590-4800; Fax: (210)590-8789; Email: sales@gemcomm.net • URL: http://www.gemcomm.net • Monthly. $113.00 per year.

**International Housewares Association**. 6400 Shafer Ct., Ste. 650 Rosemont, IL 60018. Phone: (847)292-4200; Fax: (847)292-4211 • URL: http://www.housewares.org • Manufacturers and distributors of housewares and small appliances. Conducts annual market research survey of the housewares industry. Manages the international housewares show.

**International Imaging Industry Association**. 2001 L St., NW Ste. 700 Washington, DC 20036-4928. Phone: 800-272-6657 or (202)371-0101; Fax: (202)728-9614; Email: help@computer.org • URL: http://www.ieee.org • Develops and promotes the adoption of open industry standards, addressing environmental issues and providing a voice for the industry that will benefit all users. Promotes environment, health and safety concerns; works with various government agencies including the EPA, TSA, and WTO to ensure the best interests of the imaging industry are represented.

***International Intertrade Index of New Imported Products***. International Intertrade Index, Federal Sq. Newark, NJ 07101. Phone: (973)686-2382; Fax: (973)622-1740 • Monthly. $45 per year. Covers: manufacturers of new products that are announced at foreign trade fairs and available to United States importers. Entries include: Company name, address, description of new products, and prices. Subscription includes "Foreign Trade Fairs" newsletter.

**International Janitorial Cleaning Services Association**. 2011 Oak St. Wyandotte, MI 48192. Phone: (734)252-6189; Email: info@ijcsa.com • URL: http://www.ijcsanetwork.com • Represents the interests of the janitorial industry. Promotes professionalism and ethics in the janitorial and cleaning services field. Provides training and education for cleaning professionals.

***International Journal for Vitamin and Nutrition Research***. Hogrefe & Huber Publishers, P.O. 2487 Kirkland, WA 98083. Phone: 800-228-3749 or (425)820-1500; Fax: (425)823-8324; Email: verlag@hanshuber.com • URL: http://www.hhpub.com/journals • Quarterly. $202.00 per year.

***International Journal of Adhesion and Adhesives***. Elsevier, Secondary Publishing Division, 650 Ave. of the Americas New York, NY 10011. Phone: 888-437-4636 or (212)633-3980; Fax: (212)633-3975; Email: t.reller@elsevier.com • URL: http://www.elsevier.com • $1,858.40 Institutions; $267 Individuals. Six times a year. Published in England.

***International Journal of Advertising: The Quarterly Review of***

***Marketing Communications***. Advertising Association. NTC Publications Ltd., Farm Rd., Henley-on-Thames Oxon RG9 1EJ, United Kingdom. Phone: 44 1491 411000; Fax: (149)1 571188; Email: ijoa@ntc.co.uk • URL: http://www.warc.com • Quarterly. $490 standard subscription; $975 premium subscription with enhanced online access. Advertising journal.

***International Journal of Bank Marketing***. Emerald Group Publishing Inc., Brickyard Office Park, 84 Sherman St. Cambridge, MA 02140. Phone: (617)945-9130; Fax: (617)945-9136; Email: america@emeraldinsight.com • URL: http://www.emeraldinsight.com • Seven times a year. $12,519.00 per year.

***International Journal of Business and Systems Research (IJBSR)***. Inderscience Publishers, PO Box 735 Olney MK46 5WB, United Kingdom. Fax: 44 12 34240515; Email: editor@inderscience.com • URL: http://www.inderscience.com • €494 Individuals print or online only for 1 user; €840 Individuals online only for 2-3 users; €672 Individuals print and online; €1,230 Individuals online only for 4-5 users; €1,600 Individuals online only for 6-7 users; €1,950 Individuals online only for 8-9 users; €2,275 Individuals online only for 10-14 users; €2,580 Individuals online only for 15-19 users; €3,020 Individuals online only for 20 users. Journal covering advances in business & systems research.

***International Journal of Business Communication (IJBC)***. Association for Business Communication, 181 Turner St. NW Blacksburg, VA 24061. Phone: (540)231-8460 or (540)231-1939; Email: abcoffice@businesscommunication.org • URL: http://www.businesscommunication.org • Quarterly. Included in membership; $497 Institutions online only; $541 Institutions print only; $552 Institutions print and online; $528 Institutions print and e-access; $475 Institutions e-access; $517 Institutions print. Journal focusing on professional business communication.

***International Journal of Business Communication***. Association for Business Communication, 181 Turner St. NW Blacksburg, VA 24061. Phone: (540)231-8460 or (540)231-1939; Email: abcoffice@businesscommunication.org • URL: http://www.businesscommunication.org • Quarterly. Includes empirical and theoretically conceptual research results in business communication.

***International Journal of Business Continuity and Risk Management (IJBCRM)***. Inderscience Enterprises Limited, World Trade Center Bldg. II, 29, Rte. de Pre-Bois, Case Postale 896 CH-1215 Geneva, Switzerland. Phone: 41 1234 240515; Fax: 41 22 7910885 • URL: http://www.inderscience.com/ • Quarterly. €520 Individuals print; €706 Individuals print and online. Peer-reviewed journal covering risk management and business continuity.

***International Journal of Business Process Integration & Management (IJBPIM)***. Inderscience Publishers, PO Box 735 Olney MK46 5WB, United Kingdom. Fax: 44 12 34240515; Email: editor@inderscience.com • URL: http://www.inderscience.com • €494 Individuals print or online only for 1 user; €840 Individuals online only for 2-3 users; €672 Individuals print and online; €1,230 Individuals online only for 4-5 users; €1,600 Individuals online only for 6-7 users; €1,950 Individuals online only for 8-9 users; €2,275 Individuals online only for 10-14 users; €2,580 Individuals online only for 15-19 users; €3,020 Individuals online only for 20 users. Journal covering the emerging business process modeling, simulation, integration and management using emerging technologies.

***International Journal of Climatology***. Royal Meteorological Society. John Wiley and Sons, Inc., Journals Div., 111 River St. Hoboken, NJ 07030. Phone: 800-526-5368 or (201)748-6000; Fax: (201)748-6088; Email: consumers@wiley.com • URL: http://www.wiley.com • 15 times a year. $1,065.00 per year; institutions, $2,135.00 per year. Published in England by John Wiley and Sons Ltd.

***International Journal of Communication Systems***. John Wiley and Sons, Inc., Journals Div., 111 River St. Hoboken, NJ 07030. Phone: 800-526-5368 or (201)748-6000; Fax: (201)748-6088; Email: consumers@wiley.com • URL: http://www.wiley.com • Monthly. $3,378 Institutions. Published in England by John Wiley and Sons Ltd. Formerly *International Journal of Digital and Analog Communication Systems*.

***International Journal of Disaster Recovery and Business Continuity***. Science and Engineering Research Support Society, Man-Je Bldg., Rm. 402, 449-8, Ojung-Dong, Daedoek-Gu Daejon 306-791, South Korea. Phone: 82 42 6242265; Fax: 82 42 6242205 • URL: http://www.sersc.org • Annual. Peer-reviewed journal focusing on research related to disaster recovery and business continuity technology and applications.

***International Journal of Economics and Business Modeling***. Bioinfo Publications, 49/F-72, Vighnahar Complex, Sector-12, Kharghar Mumbai 410210, India. Phone: 91 22 27743967; Fax: 91 22 27743967; Email: editor@bioinfo.in • URL: http://www.bioinfo.in/index.php • Peer-reviewed journal publishing information in areas of business modeling, management and applied research.

***International Journal of Energy Research***. John Wiley and Sons, Inc., Journals Div., 111 River St. Hoboken, NJ 07030. Phone: 800-526-5368 or (201)748-6000; Fax: (201)748-6088; Email: consumers@wiley.com • URL: http://www.wiley.com • 15 times a year. Individuals, $2,685.00 per year; institutions, $3,500.00 per year. Published in England by John Wiley & Sons Ltd.

***International Journal of Environmental Science and Technology***. Kluwer Academic Publishers, 233 Spring St., Fl. 7 New York, NY 10013-1522. Phone: (212)460-1500; Fax: (212)460-1575 • URL: http://www.springerlink.com/home/main.mpx • Refereed research journal which aims to promote the theory and practice of environmental science and technology, innovation, engineering and management.

***International Journal of Health Planning and Management***. John Wiley and Sons, Inc., Journals Div., 111 River St. Hoboken, NJ 07030. Phone: 800-526-5368 or (201)748-6000; Fax: (201)748-6088; Email: consumers@wiley.com • URL: http://www.wiley.com • Quarterly. Individuals, $960.00 per year; institutions, $1,280.00 per year. Published in England by John Wiley and Sons Ltd.

***International Journal of Indian Culture and Business Management (IJICBM)***. Inderscience Publishers, PO Box 735 Olney MK46 5WB, United Kingdom. Fax: 44 12 34240515; Email: editor@inderscience.com • URL: http://www.inderscience.com • 8/year. €735 Individuals print or online only for 1 user; €1,240 Individuals online only for 2-3 users; €1,025 Individuals print and online; €1,815 Individuals online only for 4-5 users; €2,360 Individuals online only for 6-7 users; €2,870 Individuals online only for 8-9 users; €3,350 Individuals online only for 10-14 users; €3,800 Individuals online only for 15-19 users; €4,440 Individuals online only for 20 users. Journal covering field of new developments in Indian culture and their implications on business.

***International Journal of Intelligent Systems***. John Wiley and Sons, Inc., Journals Div., 111 River St. Hoboken, NJ 07030. Phone: 800-526-5368 or (201)748-6000; Fax: (201)748-6088; Email: consumers@wiley.com • URL: http://www.wiley.com • Monthly. $1,925.00 per year; with online edition, $2,022.00 per year.

***International Journal of Machine Tools and Manufacture: Design, Research and Application***. Elsevier, Secondary Publishing Division, 650 Ave. of the Americas New York, NY 10011. Phone: 888-437-4636 or (212)633-3980; Fax: (212)633-3975; Email: t.reller@elsevier.com • URL: http://www.elseveier.com • $4,493 Institutions. 15 times a year.

***International Journal of Mechanical Sciences***. Elsevier, Secondary Publishing Division, 650 Ave. of the Americas New York, NY 10011. Phone: 888-437-4636 or (212)633-3980; Fax: (212)633-3975; Email: t.reller@elsevier.com • URL: http://www.elseveier.com • $4,702 Institutions. Monthly. Qualified personnel, $228.00 per year.

***International Journal of Powder Metallurgy***. American Powder Metallurgy Institute. APMI International, 105 College Rd. E Princeton, NJ 08540-6992. Phone: (609)452-7700; Fax: (609)987-8523; Email: apmi@mpif.org • URL: http://www.mpif.org • Quarterly. Individuals, $85.00 per year; institutions, $180.00 per year.

***International Journal of Refrigeration***. Elsevier, Secondary Publishing Division, 650 Ave. of the Americas New York, NY 10011. Phone: 888-437-4636 or (212)633-3980; Fax: (212)633-3975; Email: t.reller@elsevier.com • URL: http://www.elseveier.com • Monthly. $2,048 Institutions. Qualified personnel, $99.00 per year. Text in English and French.

***International Journal of Robotics Research***. Pine Forge Press, 2455 Teller Rd. Thousand Oaks, CA 91320-2234. Phone: 800-818-7243 or (805)499-4224 or (805)499-9774; Fax: (805)499-0871 or (805)583-2665; Email: sales@pfp.sagepub.com • URL: http://www.sagepub.com/sociologybooks • $2,494 Institutions print and e-access; $2,425 Institutions e-access; $2,444 Institutions print; $236 Individuals print; $192 Institutions single print issue; $22 Individuals single print issue. Offers incisive and thought-provoking original research papers and articles, perceptive reviews, and lively editorials on ground-breaking trends issues, technical developments, and theories in robotics by the outstanding scholars and practitioners in the field.

***International Journal of Strategic Business Alliances (IJSBA)***. Inderscience Enterprises Limited, World Trade Center Bldg. II, 29, Rte. de Pre-Bois, Case Postale 896 CH-1215 Geneva, Switzerland. Phone: 41 1234 240515; Fax: 41 22 7910885 • URL: http://www.inderscience.com/ • Quarterly. €520 Individuals print; €706 Individuals print and online. Peer-reviewed journal covering strategic alliances in businesses.

***International Journal of Wine Business Research***. Emerald Group Publishing Ltd., Howard House, Wagon Ln. Bingley BD16 1WA, United Kingdom. Phone: 44 1274 777 700; Fax: 44 1274 785 201 • URL: http://www.emeraldinsight.com • Daily. Journal dedicated to the academic field of wine business, particularly management and marketing. Includes applications of marketing principles to wine and spirit products, the place of viticulture in local economies, especially its relationship with tourism, case studies on wine brands, ethical issues in marketing of alcoholic beverages, structure of brand ownership, and marketing through retail outlets, hotel and catering outlets.

***International Journal: The News and Views Paper for the Hobbyist***. Levine Publications, Box 9090 Trenton, NJ 08650. • Quarterly. $52.50.

***International Labour Review***. International Labour Office. ILO Publications Center, Nine Jay Gould Ct. Waldorf, MD 20602. Phone: (301)638-3152; Fax: (301)843-0159; Email: ilo@ilo.org • URL: http://www.ilo.org • $431 Institutions; $123 Individuals. Bimonthly. $80.00. Editions in English, French and Spanish.

***The International Lawyer***. American Bar Association, International Law and Practice Section. 740 15th St. NW Washington, DC 20005. Phone: 800-285-2221 or (202)662-1000; Fax: (202)662-1669; Email: price@staff.abanet.org • URL: http://www.abanet.org • Quarterly. Free to members; non-members, $60.00 per year.

***International Legal Materials***. American Society of International Law, 2223 Massachusetts Ave. NW Washington, DC 20008. Phone: (202)939-6000; Fax: (202)797-7133 or (202)319-1670 • URL: http://www.asil.org • Bimonthly. $190.00 per year.

***International Literary Market Place: The Directory of the International Book Publishing Industry***. Information Today, Inc., 143 Old Marlton Pke. Medford, NJ 08055-8750. Phone: 800-300-9868 or (609)654-6266; Fax: (609)654-4309; Email: custserv@infotoday.com • URL: http://www.infotoday.com • Annual. $299 Individuals softbound; $269.10 Individuals first time standing order. Covers more than 180 countries. Listings include publishers, literary agents, major booksellers, book clubs, literary prizes, distributors, trade associations, etc. Formerly published by R. R. Bowker.

***International M & A Review***. Euromoney Institutional Investor P.L.C., 11 N Hill Colchester CO1 1DZ, United Kingdom. Phone: 44 1206 579591; Fax: 44 1206 560121; Email: yearbooks@euromoneyplc.com • URL: http://www.euromoney-yearbooks.com • $375 Individuals; £245 Individuals; €295 Individuals; €295 Individuals E-book. Covers: Merger and acquisition advising companies in Europe and U.S. Database includes: Country profiles and reviews of mergers and acquisitions by industry. Entries include: Name, address, phone, fax, names and titles of key personnel, year founded, description of business activities.

**International Maritime Industries Forum**. c/o The Baltic Exchange, 38 St. Mary Axe London EC3A 8BH, United Kingdom. Phone: 44 20 79296429; Fax: 44 20 79296430; Email: info@imif.org • URL: http://www.imif.org • Shipowners and builders, shipbreakers, oil companies, insurance companies, classification societies, and bankers in 25 countries. Seeks to: maintain a healthy commercial and financial climate for all sectors of shipping, including ownership, operation, construction, and international trade; encourage discussions of mutual interest; foster change and stimulate action to benefit the maritime industry. Strives to upgrade the standards of ships, port state control and to establish shipbreaking plants in the Third World to promote its large market for rerolled and recycled ship scrap.

***International Market Alert***. UCG Holdings L.P., 11300 Rockville Pike, Suite 1100 Rockville, MD 20852-3030. Phone: 800-929-4824 or (301)816-8950 or (301)287-2700; Fax: (301)816-8945; Email: dhernan@ucg.com • URL: http://www.ucg.com • Description: Provides a fax service covering financial markets, world economy developments, foreign exchange, and U.S. interest rates.

***International Marketing Data and Statistics***. Cengage Learning Inc., 20 Channel Center St. Boston, MA 02210. Phone: 800-487-8488 or (617)289-7700; Fax: (617)289-7844; Email: investors@cengage.com • URL: http://www.cengage.com • 2013. $475.00. Published by Euromonitor International. Contains statistics on population, economic factors, energy, consumer expenditures, prices, and other items affecting marketing in 160 non-European countries of the world. Also available as eBook.

***International Materials Review***. ASM International, 9639 Kinsman Rd. Materials Park, OH 44073-0002. Phone: 800-336-5152 or (440)338-5151; Email: memberservicecenter@asminternational.org • URL: http://www.asminternational.org • $1,801 Nonmembers online; $2,043 Nonmembers online and print; $746 Members online; $808 Members online and print. Bimonthly. Provides technical and research coverage of metals, alloys, and advanced materials. Formerly *International Metals Review*.

***International Media Guide: Business-Professional: Asia/Pacific, Middle East, Africa***. Kantar Media SRDS, 1700 Higgins Rd., 5th Fl. Des Plaines, IL 60018-5610. Phone: 800-851-7737 or (847)375-5000; Email: next@srds.com • URL: http://next.srds.com • $553 Individuals online; 1 year; $1,825 Institutions online; 1 year; 5 users. Provides information on 3,800 trade publications "from Africa to the Pacific Rim," including advertising rates and circulation data.

***International Media Guide Business-Professional Publications: Europe***. Kantar Media SRDS, 1700 Higgins Rd., 5th Fl. Des Plaines, IL 60018-5610. Phone: 800-851-7737 or (847)375-5000; Email: next@srds.com • URL: http://next.srds.com • $553 Individuals online; 1 year; $1,825 Institutions online; 1 year; 5 users. Describes 8,800 trade journals from Eastern and Western Europe, with advertising rates and circulation data.

***International Media Guide: Business/Professional Publications: The Americas***. Kantar Media SRDS, 1700 Higgins Rd., 5th Fl. Des Plaines, IL 60018-5610. Phone: 800-851-7737 or (847)375-5000; Email: next@srds.com • URL: http://next.srds.com • $553 Individuals online; 1 year; $1,825 Institutions online; 1 year; 5 users. Describes over 4,400 trade publications from North, South, and Central America, with advertising rates and circulation data.

***International Media Guide: Newspapers Worldwide***. Kantar Media SRDS, 1700 Higgins Rd., 5th Fl. Des Plaines, IL

60018-5610. Phone: 800-851-7737 or (847)375-5000; Email: next@srds.com • URL: http://next.srds.com • $553 Individuals online; 1 year; $1,825 Institutions online; 1 year; 5 users. Covers over 3,400 papers in every major city in the world.

***International Migration Review: A Quarterly Studying Sociological, Demographic, Economic, Historical, and Legislative Aspects of Human Migration Movements and Ethnic Group Relations***. Center for Migration Studies, 27 Carmine St. New York, NY 10014-4423. Phone: (212)337-3080; Fax: (646)998-4625; Email: cms@cmsny.org • URL: http://cmsny.org • Quarterly. Individuals, $39.00 per year; institutions, $80.00 per year.

***International Monetary Fund Staff Papers***. International Monetary Fund, Publication Services, 700 19th St. NW Washington, DC 20431. Phone: (202)623-7430; Fax: (202)623-7201; Email: publications@imf.org • URL: http://www.imf.org • Quarterly. Individuals, $56.00 per year; students, $28.00 per year. Contains studies by IMF staff members on balance of payments, foreign exchange, fiscal policy, and related topics. Formerly *International Monetary Fund Staff Papers*.

***International Motion Picture Almanac: Reference Tool of the Film Industry***. Quigley Publishing Co., 64 Wintergreen Ln. Groton, MA 01450. Phone: 800-231-8239 or (978)448-0272 or (860)228-0247; Fax: (860)228-0157 or (978)448-9325; Email: quigleypub@quigleypublishing.com • URL: http://www.quigleypublishing.com • Annual. $275 print; $200 online (one year subscription). Reference covering the motion picture industry.

**International Network of Alternative Financial Institution**. Mermoz, 11 rue MZ - 157 Dakar, Senegal. Email: claudeabsa@yahoo.fr • URL: http://www.mixmarket.org/networks/inafi • Seeks to advance microfinance programs for the poor by increasing the quality of service and performance of microfinancial institutions through counselling, research, and publications.

***International New Product Newsletter***. International New Product Newsletter, Box 1146 Marblehead, MA 01945. Phone: (508)741-0224; Fax: (508)741-0224 • Monthly. $25 per issue; $175 per year. Description: Provides "advance news of new products and processes, primarily from sources outside the U.S." Emphasizes new products which can cut costs and improve efficiency. Recurring features include the column Special Licensing Opportunities which lists new products and processes that are available for manufacture under license, or are for sale or import.

***International Oil News***. William F. Bland Co., 709 Turmeric Ln. Durham, NC 27713. Phone: (919)544-1717; Fax: (919)544-1999; Email: mbs@PetroChemical-News.com • URL: http://www.petrochemical-news.com • Description: Covers "timely and significant developments in the international oil business, including exploration, production, transportation, refining, and marketing.".

**International Ombudsman Association**. 111 Deer Lake Rd., Ste. 100 Deerfield, IL 60015. Phone: (847)509-7991; Fax: (847)480-9282; Email: info@ombudsassociation.org • URL: http://www.ombudsassociation.org/home.aspx • Individuals actively engaged in the practice of organizational ombudsmanry, as designated neutrals. Works to enhance the quality and value of the ombudsman function by: establishing and communicating appropriate standards of excellence for the profession; developing and disseminating ethical guidelines for organizational ombudspeople; training new and experienced ombuds practitioners in complaint handling skills and principles of effective practice; communicating the latest developments of the profession; and fostering appropriate forums to share common interests and strengthen skills.

**International Organisation of Vine and Wine**. 18 Rue d'Aguesseau F-75008 Paris, France. Phone: 33 1 44948080; Fax: 33 1 42669063; Email: contact@oiv.int • URL: http://www.oiv.int • Representatives of governments of vine-growing consumers and countries. Addresses scientific, technical, economic, and legal issues concerning viticulture and vine-derived products such as wine, grape juice, table grapes, and raisins. Determines standards regarding vine products and advises member governments on accepted norms. Works to create international research programs and to encourage information exchange among scholars and research institutions. Conducts technological research with a view toward rationalizing the production process and reducing production costs; compiles statistics. Strives to develop a general viticultural policy based on the resources and specific needs of members. Cooperates with the Food and Agriculture Organization of the United Nations and other international groups. Offers courses on marketing and management of wine and spirits and on viticulture and enology in hot climates.

**International PEN - Writers in Prison Committee**. Brownlow House, 50/51 High Holborn London WC1V 6ER, United Kingdom. Phone: 44 20 74050338; Fax: 44 20 74050339; Email: info@pen-international.org • URL: http://www.pen-international.org • Serves as a key resource for the writing instruments industry. Provides leadership and direction for its members by staying at the forefront of trends, education, and technology in order to promote and procure the future of writing instrument development and distribution. Offers strategic analysis of manufacturer and retail marketing efforts.

**International Petroleum Industry Environmental Conservation Association**. 209-215 Blackfriars Rd., 5th Fl. London SE1 8NL, United Kingdom. Phone: 44 20 76332388; Fax: 44 20 76332389; Email: info@ipieca.org • URL: http://www.ipieca.org • Represents 52% of worldwide oil and gas production drawn from 26 private and state-owned companies as well as 12 national, regional, international associations. Represents both upstream and downstream of the oil and gas industry on key global environmental issues, including oil spill preparedness and response, global climate change, health, fuel quality, biodiversity and social responsibility.

***International Pharmaceutical Abstracts: Key to the World's Literature of Pharmacy***. American Society of Health-System Pharmacists, 7272 Wisconsin Ave. Bethesda, MD 20814. Phone: 866-279-0681 or (301)664-8700 or (301)657-3000; Fax: (301)657-1251; Email: custserv@ashp.org • URL: http://www.ashp.org • Semimonthly. $565.50 per year.

***International Pharmaceutical Abstracts***. Ovid Technologies Inc., 333 7th Ave., 20th Fl. New York, NY 10001-5004. Phone: 800-950-2035 or (646)674-6300; Fax: (646)674-6301 or (647)674-6301; Email: sales@ovid.com • URL: http://www.ovid.com • Quarterly. International pharmaceutical literature from 1970 to date.

**International Photovoltaic Equipment Association**. PO Box 771507 Orlando, FL 32877. Phone: (407)856-9100; Email: ekus@ipvea.com • URL: http://www.ipvea.org • Represents manufacturers and suppliers of photovoltaic (PV) fabrication equipment and related raw materials used in PV ingot, wafer, cell and panel manufacturing. Fosters the development of the photovoltaic equipment manufacturing industry. Provides members with a forum for information, discussion and exchange of ideas to develop business opportunities and strategic partnerships.

**International Plant Nutrition Institute**. 3500 Parkway Ln., Ste. 550 Norcross, GA 30092-2844. Phone: (770)447-0335; Fax: (770)448-0439; Email: info@ipni.net • URL: http://www.ipni.net • Formerly Potash and Phosphate Institute.

***International Plastics Directory***. Verlag fur Internationale Wirtschaftsliteratur Ltd., Box 28 CH-8047 Zurich, Switzerland. Phone: 1 4926130 or 41 1 492 61 30; Fax: 41 1 401 05 45; Email: Angela.Wall@was.rep.admin.ch • 64. $600. Covers: Plastics producers and processors worldwide. Entries include: Company name, address, phone, description, production line, trademarks, number of machines, associated companies.

**International Premium Cigar and Pipe Retailers**. No. 4 Bradley Park Ct., Ste. 2-H Columbus, GA 31904-3637. Phone: (706)494-1143; Fax: (706)494-1893; Email: info@ipcpr.org • URL: http://www.ipcpr.org • Formerly Retail Tobacco Dealers of America.

***International Private Label Directory***. E.W. Williams Publications Co., 2125 Center Ave., Ste. 305 Fort Lee, NJ 07024-5898. Phone: (201)592-7007 or (201)532-9290; Fax: (201)592-7171 or (201)779-8345; Email: philpl@ewwpi.com • URL: http://www.williamspublications.com • Annual. Provides information on over 2,000 suppliers of a wide variety of private label and generic products: food, over-the-counter health products, personal care items, and general merchandise.

**International Project Management Association**. PO Box 7905 1008 AC Amsterdam, Netherlands. Phone: 31 33 2473430; Fax: 31 33 2460470; Email: info@ipma.ch • URL: http://www.ipma.ch • National project management associations in 43 countries. Liaises the international exchange of project management information and promotes the advancement of project management methods, systems, and practical application techniques. Encourages the development of and cooperates with national organizations with common interests; provides for individual participation in countries without national societies.

***International Pulp and Paper Directory***. UBM L.L.C., 600 Community Dr. Manhasset, NY 11030. Phone: (516)562-5000 or (512)562-5000; Fax: (212)378-2160 or (516)562-5036; Email: cmp@cmp.com • URL: http://www.cmp.com • Annual. $287.00. Lists over 6,000 pulp and papermills. International coverage.

***International Radio and Television Society Newsletter***. International Radio and Television Society Foundation, 1697 Broadway, 10th Fl. New York, NY 10019. Phone: (212)867-6650 • URL: http://irtsfoundation.org • Quarterly.

***International Railway Journal: The First International Railway and Rapid Transit Journal***. Simmons-Boardman Publishing Corp., 345 Hudson St., 12th Fl. New York, NY 10014. Phone: 800-895-4389 or (212)620-7200; Fax: (212)633-1165; Email: tjudge@rtands.com • URL: http://www.simmonsboardman.com • Monthly. $72.00 per year. Formerly *International Railway Journal and Rapid Transit Review*. Text in English; summaries in French, German and Spanish.

***International Rehabilitation Review***. Rehabilitation International, 25 E 21st St., 4th Fl. New York, NY 10010. Phone: (212)420-1500; Fax: (212)505-0871; Email: ri@riglobal.org • URL: http://rehab-international.org • Triennial. $45 Individuals print. Description: Contains news and articles on international, national, and local developments in the fields of disability prevention and rehabilitation. Provides regular coverage of United Nations agencies, discusses the elimination of architectural and attitudinal barriers to disabled persons, and examines new trends in service delivery. Recurring features include news of research, book reviews, and a calendar of events.

***International Review for Business Education***. International Society for Business Education, 6302 Mineral Point Rd., No. 100 Madison, WI 53705. Email: secretary@siec-isbe.org • URL: http://www.siec-isbe.org • Semiannual. $36.00 per year. Text in English, French, German, Italian, and Spanish.

***International Review of Applied Economics***. Routledge, 711 3rd Ave., 8th Fl. New York, NY 10017. Phone: 800-634-7064 or (212)216-7800; Fax: (212)564-7854 or (212)563-2269; Email: book.orders@tandf.co.uk • URL: http://www.routledge.com • Quarterly. Individuals, $310.00 per year; institutions, $1,007.00 per year.

***International Review of Industrial and Organizational Psychology***. John Wiley and Sons, Inc., Journals Div., 111 River St. Hoboken, NJ 07030. Phone: 800-526-5368 or (201)748-6000; Fax: (201)748-6088; Email: consumers@wiley.com • URL: http://www.wiley.com • Annual. $154.95. Published in England by John Wiley and Sons Ltd. Contains comprehensive, state-of-the-art overview of topic areas which cover the entire spectrum of industrial and organizational psychology, including job design, work motivation, stress and new and emergent areas.

***International Satellite Directory: A Complete Guide to the Satellite Communications Industry***. SatNews Publishers, 14788 Wolfgang Rd. Truckee, CA 96161. Phone: (707)939-9306; Fax: (707)939-9235; Email: orders@satnews.com • URL: http://www.satnews.com • Annual. $495 plus shipping and handling. Lists over 25,000 satellite operators, common carriers, earth stations, manufacturers, associations, etc.

**International Society for Business Education**. 21 Russell Rd. Wellesley, MA 02482. Phone: (781)237-3035; Email: msherry@massasoit.mass.edu • URL: http://www.isbeusa.org • Educators involved in business education; heads of in-company training institutions; firms; schools and universities at various levels. Aims to promote the international exchange of ideas and experiences in business education and to further the education of teachers in business fields. Organizes courses in economic and business education. New members must join National Business Education Association before joining ISBE.

**International Society of Financiers**. 64 Brookside Dr. Hendersonville, NC 28792. Phone: (828)393-8908; Fax: (828)393-8919; Email: insofin@gmail.com • URL: http://www.insofin.com • Membership in more than 25 countries includes: real estate, minerals, commodities, and import-export brokers; corporate, industrial, and private lenders; and other financial professionals. Provides information and referrals on major domestic and international financial projects and transactions, and fosters integrity and professionalism among members.

***International Society of Weighing and Measurement Membership Directory and Product Guide***. International Society of Weighing and Measurement, 13017 Wisteria Dr., No. 341 Germantown, MD 20874. Phone: 866-285-3512 or (240)753-4397; Email: scalesales@aol.com • URL: http://www.iswm.org • Annual.

***International Spectrum: The Businessperson's Computer Magazine***. IDBMA Inc., 10675 Treena St., Ste. 103 San Diego, CA 92131. Phone: 800-767-SHOW or (619)578-3152; Fax: (619)271-1032 • Bimonthly. $40 Individuals; $7 Single issue. News magazine for the computer industry focusing on the PICK/UNIX/DOS-based computer operating environment.

***International Stocks Database Directory***. Vision Information Inc., PO Box 3503 New York, NY 10008. Phone: (212)840-6557; Fax: (510)472-6763 • Monthly. Database covers: publicly traded companies listed on various stock exchanges globally. Database includes: Company name; contact data; exchanges on which traded; financial, business, and news information.

***International Tax Agreements***. United Nations Publications, c/o National Book Network, 15200 NBN Way Blue Ridge Summit, PA 17214. Phone: 888-254-4286 or (212)963-7680 or (212)963-8302; Fax: (800)338-4550; Email: unpublications@nbnbooks.com • URL: http://www.unp.un.org • Irregular. Price varies. Looseleaf.

***International Tax Journal***. Wolters Kluwer Law and Business, 76 9th Ave., 7th Fl. New York, NY 10011-4962. Phone: 800-234-1660 or (212)771-0600; Fax: (800)901-9075 or (301)644-3550 • URL: http://www.wolterskluwerlb.com • Quarterly. $297.00 per year. Articles, columns and tax notes pertaining to the international tax market.

***International Tax Planning Manual-Corporations***. Wolters Kluwer Law & Business CCH, 2700 Lake Cook Rd. Riverwoods, IL 60015. Phone: 888-224-7377 or (847)267-7000; Email: cust_serv@cch.com • URL: http://www.cchgroup.com • Two looseleaf volumes. Periodic supplementation. Price on application. Tax strategies for doing business in 42 major countries.

***International Tax Report: Maximizing Tax Opportunities Worldwide***. Informa Group PLC, Suffolk House, Church Field Rd. Sudbury C010 2YA, United Kingdom. Phone: 44 1787 378607; Fax: (178)7 881147 • URL: http://www.monitorpress.com • Monthly. $1,100.00 per year.

**International Technology Law Association**. 401 Edgewater Pl., Ste. 600 Wakefield, MA 01880. Phone: (781)876-8877; Fax: (781)224-1239; Email: office@itechlaw.org • URL: http://www.itechlaw.org • Lawyers, law students, and others interested in legal problems related to computer-communications technology. Aids in: contracting for computer-communications goods and services; perfecting and protecting proprietary rights chiefly in software; and taxing computer-communications goods, services, and transactions, and liability for acquisition and use of computer-communications goods and services. Provides specialized educational programs; and offers limited placement service. Holds Annual Computer Law Update.

***International Textile & Apparel Association—Membership Directory***. International Textile and Apparel Association, PO Box 70687 Knoxville, TN 37938-0687. Phone: (865)992-1535; Email: executivedirector@itaaonline.org • URL: http://www.itaaonline.org • Irregular. Covers: About 1,000 college professors of clothing and textile studies. Entries include: Name, address, phone, academic credentials.

***International Textile Bulletin: Dyeing-Printing-Finishing Edition***. ITS Publishing, International Textile Service, Univer-Haus, Kesslerstrasse 9 CH-8952 Schlieren, Switzerland. Phone: 41 1 7384800; Fax: (738)4830 or (738)4832; Email: its@its-publishing.com • URL: http://www.its-publishing.com • Quarterly. $170.00 per year. Editions in Chinese, English, French, German, Italian and Spanish.

***International Textile Bulletin: Nonwovens and Industrial Textiles Edition***. ITS Publishing, International Textile Service, Univer-Haus, Kesslerstrasse 9 CH-8952 Schlieren, Switzerland. Phone: 41 1 7384800; Fax: (738)4830 or (738)4832; Email: its@its-publishing.com • URL: http://www.its-publishing.com • Quarterly. $170.00 per year. Editions in Chinese, English, French, German, Italian and Spanish.

***International Textile Bulletin: Yarn and Fabric Forming Edition***. ITS Publishing, International Textile Service, Univer-Haus, Kesslerstrasse 9 CH-8952 Schlieren, Switzerland. Phone: 41 1 7384800; Fax: (738)4830 or (738)4832; Email: its@its-publishing.com • URL: http://www.its-publishing.com • Quarterly. $170.00 per year. Editions in Chinese, English, French, German, Italian and Spanish.

***International Textiles: Information and Inspiration***. Textile Institute. Benjamin Dent & Company Ltd., 33 Bedford Pl. London WC1B 5JX, United Kingdom. Phone: 71 6372211 or 44 20 7637 2211; Fax: (763)7 2248 • 10 times a year. $220.00 per year. Text in English, French and German; supplement in Japanese.

**International Theatre Studies Center**. University of Kansas, 339 Murphy Hall, 1530 Naismith Dr., Rm. 356 Lawrence, KS 66045. Phone: (785)864-3511.

***International Titanium Association Buyers Guide***. International Titanium Association, 11674 Huron St., Ste. 100 Northglenn, CO 80234. Phone: (303)404-2221; Fax: (303)404-9111; Email: ita@titanium.org • URL: http://www.titanium.org • Annual.

***International Trade Alert***. American Association of Exporters and Importers, 1200 G St.,NW, Ste. 800 Washington, NY 20005. Phone: (212)983-7008; Fax: (212)983-6430; Email: aaei5ie@aol.com • Weekly. Description: Reports on trade issues as they affect importers and exporters. Contains news of actions by Customs, the Federal Drug Administration (FDA), and the Department of Commerce, CITA, CPSC, FTC, and the USDA, as well as other federal agencies and departments; and the status of regulations on imported/exported products. Also contains information on legislative activity affecting importers and exporters.

***International Trade and Investment Letter: Trends in U.S Policies, Trade Finance and Trading Operations***. International Business Affairs Corp., 5523 Brige Dr Bethesda, MD 20817. Phone: (301)907-8647; Fax: (301)907-8650 • Monthly. $240.00 per year. Newsletter.

***International Trade Directory for Dayton, Ohio***. Dayton Area Chamber of Commerce, 22 E 5th St., Chamber Plz. Dayton, OH 45402-2400. Phone: (937)226-1444; Fax: (937)226-8254; Email: info@dacc.org • URL: http://www.daytonchamber.org • Biennial. $25 Members; $50 Nonmembers. Covers: International firms importing and exporting in Dayton. Entries include: Company name, address, phone.

***International Trade Directory***. Indian Export Trade Journal, 212 Arun Chambers, Tardeo Rd. Mumbai 400 034, India. • Biennial. $50; $30. Covers: Importers, exporters, shipping, clearing agents, banks, and chambers of commerce in 150 countries. Entries include: Contact information.

***International Trade Directory of Contacts/Sources/Services***. Hilary House Publishers Inc., 4001 N Ocean Blvd., No. 1101 Boca Raton, FL 33431. Phone: (561)750-7822 • Biennial. $120 plus $5.00 shipping. Covers: more than 14,800 U.S. organizations and key executives in 26 international business categories. Entries include: Company or personal name, address, phone, name and title of contact, service provided.

***International Trade Reporter Export Reference Manual***. Bloomberg BNA, 3 Bethesda Metro Center, Ste. 250 Bethesda, MD 20814-5377. Phone: 800-372-1033 or (703)341-3000; Fax: (800)253-0332; Email: customercare@bna.com • URL: http://www.bna.com • Biweekly. $874.00 per year. Looseleaf service.

***International Warehouse Logistics Association—Roster of Members***. International Warehouse Logistics Association, 2800 S River Rd., Ste. 260 Des Plaines, IL 60018-6003. Phone: 800-525-0165 or (847)813-4699; Fax: (847)813-0115; Email: email@iwla.com • URL: http://www.iwla.com • Annual. Covers: 550 warehouses, general storage facilities and distribution centers for non-refrigerated products in the US, Canada, Panama, Mexico, Venezuela, Puerto Rico, Dominican Republic and Costa Rica.

***International Wealth Success Newsletter: The Monthly Newsletter of Worldwide Wealth Opportunities***. Tyler G. Hicks, editor. International Wealth Success, Inc., PO Box 186 Merrick, NY 11566-0186. Phone: 800-323-0548 or (516)766-5850; Fax: (516)766-5919 or (516)766-5619; Email: admin@iwsmoney.com • URL: http://www.iwsmoney.com • Monthly. $24.00 per year. Newsletter. Provides information on a variety of small business topics, including financing, mail order, foreign opportunities, licensing, and franchises.

***International Who's Who of Authors and Writers***. Taylor & Francis, 711 3rd Ave., 8th Fl. New York, NY 10017. Phone: 800-634-7064 or (212)216-7800 or (212)216-6000; Fax: (212)563-2269 or (212)685-4540; Email: bookorders@dekker.com • URL: http://www.routledge.com/ • $490. Over 8,000 authors, writers, and poets, primarily American and British but including writers from nearly 40 countries in the English-speaking world.

***International Who's Who***. Taylor & Francis Group, 325 Chestnut St. Philadelphia, PA 19106. Phone: 800-248-4724 or (215)625-8900; Fax: (215)625-2940; Email: info@taylorandfrancis.com • URL: http://www.taylorandfrancis.com • Annual. £490.00. Includes print and online editions. Published by Europa Publications (www.europapublications.com). Contains brief biographical information on important people in many different countries.

***Internet Access Providers: An International Resource Direcctory***. Mecklermedia Corp., 475 Park Ave. S, 4th Fl. New York, NY 10016. Phone: (212)389-2000; Fax: (866)880-1429 or (212)725-4640; Email: info@webmediabrands.com • URL: http://www.webmediabrands.com • $30. Covers: 150 private companies, electronic bulletin board systems, and regional networks that offer dial-in access to the Internet. Entries include: Description.

***Internet and Electronic Commerce Strategies: Using Technology to Improve Your Bottom Line***. Computer Economics Inc., 2082 Business Center Dr., Ste. 240 Irvine, CA 92612-1164. Phone: (949)831-8700; Fax: (949)442-7688; Email: info@computereconomics.com • URL: http://www.computereconomics.com • Monthly. Price on application. Newsletter on management strategies for making money from the Internet. Compares online marketing with traditional marketing.

***Internet and Personal Computing Abstracts (print edition)***. EBSCO Publishing Inc., 10 Estes St. Ipswich, MA 01938-2106. Phone: 800-653-2726 or (978)356-6500; Fax: (978)356-6565; Email: information@ebscohost.com • URL: http://www.ebscohost.com • Quarterly. $269.00 per year, including cumulative index. Provides more than 10,000 abstracts annually from both trade and academic publications. Covers computer hardware, software, product reviews, Web topics, e-commerce, networks, corporate news, security, and related topics. Formerly *Microcomputer Abstracts*.

***The Internet Blue Pages: The Guide to Federal Government Web Sites***. Information Today, Inc., 143 Old Marlton Pke. Medford, NJ 08055-8750. Phone: 800-300-9868 or (609)654-6266; Fax: (609)654-4309; Email: custserv@infotoday.com • URL: http://www.infotoday.com • Annual. $34.95. Provides information on more than 1,800 Web sites used by various agencies of the federal government. Includes indexes to agencies and topics. Links to all Web sites listed are available at www.fedweb.com. (CyberAge Books.).

***Internet Business Report: Software, Tools and Platforms***. Jupitermedia Corp., 23 Old Kings Hwy. S Darien, CT 06820. Phone: 800-488-4345 or (203)662-2800; Fax: (203)655-4686; Email: ameckler@jupitermedia.com • URL: http://www.webmediabrands.com • Semimonthly. $695.00 per year; with electronic software, $795.00 per year. Newsletter. Covers Internet advertising, fee collection, and attempts in general to make the Internet/World Wide Web profitable. Includes news of how businesses are using the Internet for sales promotion and public relations.

***Internet Connection: Your Guide to Government Resources***. Glasser LegalWorks, 150 Clove Rd. Little Falls, NJ 07424. Phone: 800-308-1700 or (973)890-0008; Fax: (973)890-0042; Email: legalwks@aol.com • URL: http://www.glasserlegalworks.com • 10 times a year. $89.00 per year. Newsletter (print) devoted to finding free or low-cost U. S. Government information on the Internet. Provides detailed descriptions of government Web sites.

***Internet Industry Magazine***. Jonas Publishing, 101 W. 23rd St., Suite 2286 New York, NY 10011. Phone: (212)977-3800; Fax: (212)977-4545 • URL: http://www.internetindustry.com • Semiannual. Price on application. Lists products and services for Internet service providers. Includes Internet-related articles and interviews.

***Internet Law and Strategy***. ALM Media Properties LLC, 120 Broadway, 5th Fl. New York, NY 10271-1100. Phone: (212)457-9400; Fax: (646)417-7705; Email: customercare@alm.com • URL: http://www.alm.com • Monthly. $459 per year. Primarily concerned with doing legal research online. Contains reviews of the best Web sites for lawyers. (A Law Journal Newsletter, formerly published by Leader Publications.).

***Internet Marketing and Technology Report: Advising Marketing, Sales, and Corporate Executives on Online Opportunities***. Computer Economics Inc., 2082 Business Center Dr., Ste. 240 Irvine, CA 92612-1164. Phone: (949)831-8700; Fax: (949)442-7688; Email: info@computereconomics.com • URL: http://www.computereconomics.com • Monthly. $387.00 per year. Newsletter. Covers strategic marketing, sales, advertising, public relations, and corporate communications, all in relation to the Internet. Includes information on "cutting-edge technology" for the Internet.

***Internet Marketing Report: News and Advice to Help Companies Harness the Power of the Internet to Achieve Business Objectives***. American Future Systems Inc., 370 Technology Dr. Malvern, PA 19355-1315. Phone: 800-220-5000 or (610)695-8600; Fax: (610)647-8089; Email: customer_service@pbp.com • URL: http://www.pbp.com • Semimonthly. $299.00 per year. Newsletter. Covers Internet marketing strategy, site traffic, success stories, technology, cost control, and other Web site advertising and marketing topics.

***Internet Payments Report***. Jupitermedia Corp., 23 Old Kings Hwy. S Darien, CT 06820. Phone: 800-488-4345 or (203)662-2800; Fax: (203)655-4686; Email: ameckler@jupitermedia.com • URL: http://www.webmediabrands.com • Annual. $1,095.00. Market research report. Provides data, comment, and forecasts on the collection of electronic payments ("e-money") for goods and services offered through the Internet.

***Internet Reference Services Quarterly: A Journal of Innovative Information Practice, Technologies, and Resources***. The Haworth Press Inc., 10 Alice St. Binghamton, NY 13904. Phone: 800-429-6784 or (607)722-5857; Fax: (607)771-0012 or (607)722-6362; Email: getinfo@haworthpress.com • URL: http://www.haworthpressinc.com/store/product.asp?sku=J014 • Quarterly. $110.00 per year. Covers both theoretical research and practical applications.

***Internet Resources and Services for International Business: A Global Guide***. Greenwood Electronic Media, c/o ABC-CLIO, 130 Cremona Dr. Santa Barbara, CA 93117. Phone: 800-368-6868 or (805)968-1911; Fax: (866)270-3856; Email: customerservice@abc-clio.com • URL: http://www.abc-clio.com • $82.95 Single issue Paperback. Covers: More than 2,500 business-related Web sites, most of which are government and university sites, international. Entries include: Web site, content.

***Internet Resources and Services for International Marketing and Advertising: A Global Guide***. Greenwood Electronic Media, c/o ABC-CLIO, 130 Cremona Dr. Santa Barbara, CA 93117. Phone: 800-368-6868 or (805)968-1911; Fax: (866)270-3856; Email: customerservice@abc-clio.com • URL: http://www.abc-clio.com • $75 Individuals hardcover; £47 Individuals hardcover; €59 Individuals hardcover; A$81 Individuals hardcover. Covers: Over 2,000 Web sites with information pertaining to marketing and advertising in more than 150 countries.

***Internet Retailer: E-Business Strategies***. Thomson Financial Inc., 195 Broadway New York, NY 10007-3100. Phone: (646)822-2000; Email: custserv@tfn.com • URL: http://www.thomsonreuters.com • 10 times a year. $98.00 per year. Trade journal on the selling of retail merchandise through the Internet. Provides information on pricing, payment systems, order management, fraud, digital imaging, advertising, Web trends, and other topics.

***Internet Service Providers Directory (ISP)***. InfoGroup Inc., 5711 S 86th Cir. Omaha, NE 68127-4146. Phone: (402)593-4500 • URL: http://www.infogroup.com • Annual. Number of listings: 27,032. Entries include: Name, address, phone, size of advertisement, name of owner or manager, number of employees, year first in "Yellow Pages." Compiled from telephone company "Yellow Pages," nationwide.

***Internet Ships Register***. IHS Global Ltd. Lloyd's Register—Fairplay Ltd., Lombard House, 3 Princess Way, Surrey Redhill RH1 1UP, United Kingdom. Phone: 44 1737 379000; Fax: 44 1737 379001; Email: marketing@ihs.com • URL: http://www.ihs.com • £695 Individuals single user; $1,350 Individuals single user; €1,020 Individuals single user; £1,210 Individuals company account; $2,350 Individuals company account; €1,780 Individuals company account. Database covers: Over 180,000 shipowners, operators, managers, and builders. Entries include: Name, address, phone. Database also includes details on over 83,000 commercial vessels with photographs. Fixture information also available at an additional cost.

***Internet.com: The E-Business and Internet Technology Network***. Jupitermedia, Phone: (203)226-6967; Fax: (203)454-5840; Email: info@internet.com • URL: http://www.internet.com • Web site provides a wide variety of information relating to Internet commerce, search engines, news, Web design, servers, browsers, Java, service providers, advertising, marketing, etc. Online searching is offered. Fees: Free. (Formerly produced by Mecklermedia Corp.).

***Interservice***. American Logistics Association, 1101 Vermont Ave. NW, Ste. 1002 Washington, DC 20005. Phone: (202)466-2520; Fax: (202)296-4419 • URL: http://www.ala-national.org • Quarterly. $20.00 per year. Official Journal of the American Logistics Association.

***Interstate Tax Insights***. Interstate Tax Corporation, 85 E Ave., Ste.

110 Norwalk, CT 06851. Phone: (203)854-0704; Fax: (203)853-9510; Email: info@interstatetaxcorp.com • URL: http://www.interstatetaxcorp.com • Monthly. $100 for 6 issues. In-depth analyses, tax savings ideas, and updates for state tax practitioners.

***IntraNets: Enterprise Strategies and Solutions***. Information Today, Inc., 143 Old Marlton Pke. Medford, NJ 08055-8750. Phone: 800-300-9868 or (609)654-6266; Fax: (609)654-4309; Email: custserv@infotoday.com • URL: http://www.infotoday.com • $199.50 U.S.; $223 Canada and Mexico; $240 Other countries. Bimonthly. Newsletter on the use of Internet technology for local library networks.

***An Introduction to the Advertising Business***. Japan Advertising Agencies Association, Dentsu Ginza Bldg., 7-4-17 Ginza, Chuo-Ku Tokyo 104-0061, Japan. Phone: 81 3 55680876; Fax: 81 3 55680889; Email: info@jaaa.ne.jp • URL: http://www.jaaa.ne.jp • Biennial. Contains advertising information for employees newly recruited to member companies.

***Introduction to the Kuwaiti Economy and Major Business Laws and Regulations***. Kuwait Chamber of Commerce and Industry, PO Box 775 Safat 13008, Kuwait. Phone: 965 180 5580 or 965 224 23666; Fax: 965 224 04110; Email: bc@kcci.org.kw • URL: http://www.kuwaitchamber.org.kw.

***InvesTech Market Analyst: Technical and Monetary Investment Analysis***. Investech Research, 2472 Birch Glen Dr. Whitefish, MT 59937-3349. Phone: 800-955-8500 or (406)862-7777; Fax: (406)862-7707; Email: investech@investech.com • URL: http://www.investech.com • Every three weeks. $190.00 per year. Newsletter. Provides interpretation of monetary statistics and Federal Reserve actions, especially as related to technical analysis of stock market price trends.

***InvesTech Mutual Fund Advisor: Professional Portfolio Allocation***. Investech Research, 2472 Birch Glen Dr. Whitefish, MT 59937-3349. Phone: 800-955-8500 or (406)862-7777; Fax: (406)862-7707; Email: investech@investech.com • URL: http://www.investech.com • Every three weeks. $190.00 per year. Newsletter. Contains model portfolio for mutual fund investing.

***InvesText***. Thomson Financial, PO Box 95512 Chicago, IL 60694. Phone: 800-607-4463 or (312)288-6400 • URL: http://www.tfsd.com • Monthly. Contains full text on CD-ROM of investment research reports from about 630 sources, including leading brokers and investment bankers. Reports are available on both U. S. and international publicly traded corporations. Separate industry reports cover more than 50 industries. Time span is 1982 to date.

***InvesText***. Thomson Financial, PO Box 95512 Chicago, IL 60694. Phone: 800-607-4463 or (312)288-6400 • URL: http://www.tfsd.com • Provides full text online of investment research reports from more than 600 sources, including leading brokers and investment bankers. Reports are available on approximately 60,000 U. S. and international corporations. Separate industry reports cover 54 industries. Time span is 1982 to date, with daily updates. Inquire as to online cost and availability.

***Investing in Radio Market Report***. BIA/Kelsey, 15120 Enterprise Ct. Chantilly, VA 20151. Phone: 800-331-5086 or (703)818-2425; Email: info@bia.com • URL: http://www.biakelsey.com • Quarterly. $1,475 Individuals. Covers: U.S. Radio industry markets and inclusive stations. Database includes: Market data, including revenues, demographics, and economic indicators. Entries include: For stations—Call letters, technical attributes, format, estimated revenues, owner, last acquisition date and price, ratings for eight books.

***Investing, Licensing, and Trading***. The Economist Intelligence Unit, 111 W 57th St. New York, NY 10019. Phone: 800-938-4685 or (212)554-0600; Fax: (212)586-1191 or (212)586-1182; Email: newyork@eiu.com • URL: http://www.economist.com • Semiannual. $345.00 per year for each country. Key laws, rules, and licensing provisions are explained for each of 60 countries. Information is provided on political conditions, markets, price policies, foreign exchange practices, labor, and export-import.

***Investment Blue Book***. Securities Investigations Inc., 2626 Rte. 212 Woodstock, NY 12498. Phone: (845)679-2300; Fax: (845)679-2301; Email: ober@stuartober.com • URL: http://www.duediligencefirm.com • Irregular. $145. Covers: 6,000 brokers and dealers in tax shelter plans; 2,000 sponsors of tax shelter product and suppliers of services to the industry. Entries include: Company name, address, phone, toll-free, phone, fax, name of contact.

**Investment Company Institute**. 1401 H St. NW, Ste. 1200 Washington, DC 20005. Phone: (202)326-5800 or (202)371-5413; Fax: (202)326-5986; Email: chris@ici.org • URL: http://www.ici.org • Formerly American Association of Minority Enterprise Small Business Investment Companies.

***Investment Company Yearbook***. Thomson Financial Inc., 195 Broadway New York, NY 10007-3100. Phone: (646)822-2000; Email: custserv@tfn.com • URL: http://www.thomsonreuters.com • Annual. $310.00. Provides an "entire history of recent events in the mutual funds industry," with emphasis on changes during the past year. About 100 pages are devoted to general information and advice for fund investors. Includes 600 full-page profiles of popular mutual funds, with brief descriptions of 10,000 others, plus 7,000 variable annuities and 500 closed-end funds. Contains a glossary of technical terms, a Web site index, and an overall book index. Also known as *Wiesenberger Investment Companies Yearbook*.

***Investment Counsel Association of America—Directory of Member Firms***. Investment Adviser Association, 1050 17th St. NW, Ste. 725 Washington, DC 20036-5514. Phone: (202)293-4222; Fax: (202)293-4223; Email: info@investmentadviser.org • URL: http://www.investmentadviser.org • Annual. Covers: over 300 member investment counseling firms. Entries include: Name and address of firm; contact, number of clients, assets under management, staff, type of account, minimum account and fee.

***Investment Dealers' Digest***. SourceMedia Inc., 1 State Street Plz., 27th Fl. New York, NY 10004. Phone: 800-221-1809 or (212)803-8200 or (212)803-8333; Fax: (212)843-9635 or (212)292-5216; Email: custserv@sourcemedia.com • URL: http://www.sourcemedia.com • Weekly. $750.00 per year. Covers financial news, trends, new products, people, private placements, new issues of securities, and other aspects of the investment business. Includes feature stories.

**Investment Education Institute**. 711 W 13 Mile Rd., Ste. 900 Madison Heights, MI 48071. Phone: 877-275-6242 or (248)583-6242 or (248)654-3047; Fax: (248)583-4880; Email: service@betterinvesting.org • URL: http://www.better-investing.org • Affiliated with the National Association of Investors Corporation and conducted through various business schools. Seeks to enlarge the scope and quality of investment education, especially through investment clubs. Has held conferences for educators, financial institutions, financial writers, and corporate shareholder relations executives to gain information and to stimulate activity in these groups. Representatives from 50 investment club councils have taken a series of special courses to improve their teaching skills. Individuals and corporations have contributed funds to establish the program.

***Investment Guide (IG)***. American Investment Services Inc., POB 1000 Great Barrington, MA 01230. Phone: 888-528-1216 or (413)528-1216; Fax: (413)528-0008; Email: aaei5ie@aol.com • URL: http://www.americaninvestment.com • Monthly. $59 printed version; $49 PDF format. Description: Contains analyses of stock market activity and strategies for investment. Recurring features include market statistics, Dow high-yield stock investing.

***Investment Management Mandate Pipeline***. SourceMedia Inc., 1 State Street Plz., 27th Fl. New York, NY 10004. Phone: 800-221-1809 or (212)803-8200 or (212)803-8333; Fax: (212)843-9635 or (212)292-5216; Email: custserv@sourcemedia.com • URL: http://www.sourcemedia.com • Weekly. $1,295.00 per year. Newsletter. Edited for money managers and other investment professionals. Covers personnel news, investment strategies, and industry trends.

***Investment News: The Weekly Newspaper for Financial Advisers***. Crain Communications Inc., 711 3rd Ave. New York, NY 10017. Phone: (212)210-0100; Email: info@crain.com • URL: http://www.crain.com • Weekly. $29.00 per year. Edited for both personal and institutional investment advisers, planners, and managers.

***Investment Opportunities in China: Chemical Industry***. Pasha Publications, PO Box 9188 Arlington, VA 22219-0188. Phone: 800-424-2908 or (703)528-1244; Fax: (703)528-3742 • $255. Covers: Approximately 530 Chinese projects in the chemical industry seeking international offshore capital investments. Entries include: Project name, address, phone, cable number; name and title of contact; financial data; description of project.

***The Investment Reporter***. MPL Communications Inc., 133 Richmond St. W, Ste. 700 Toronto, ON, Canada M5H 3M8. Phone: 800-804-8846 or (416)869-1177 or (416)869-2777; Fax: (416)869-0456 or (416)869-0616; Email: investors@mplcomm.com • URL: http://www.adviceforinvestors.com • Description: Profiles specific companies and market trends and developments, making recommendations to assist in formulating investment strategies. Includes short articles offering advice on investment decisions.

***Investor Relations Business***. SourceMedia Inc., 1 State Street Plz., 27th Fl. New York, NY 10004. Phone: 800-221-1809 or (212)803-8200 or (212)803-8333; Fax: (212)843-9635 or (212)292-5216; Email: custserv@sourcemedia.com • URL: http://www.sourcemedia.com • Semimonthly. $495.00 per year. Covers the issues affecting stockholder relations, corporate public relations, and institutional investor relations.

***Investor's Business Daily***. Investor's Business Daily, Inc., 12655 Beatrice St. Los Angeles, CA 90066. Email: ibdnews@investors.com • URL: http://www.investors.com • Daily. $329 Individuals print; $259 Individuals online; $389 Individuals print and online. Business and financial newspaper.

***The Investor's Guide to Closed-End Funds***. Thomas J. Herzfeld Advisors Inc., 119 Washington Ave., Ste. 504 Miami Beach, FL 33139. Phone: 800-854-3863 or (305)271-1900; Fax: (305)270-1040; Email: herzfeld@bellsouth.net • URL: http://www.herzfeld.com • Monthly. $475.00 per year. Looseleaf service. Provides detailed information on closed-end investment funds, including charts and recommendations.

***Investors Intelligence***. Michael Burke, editor. Chartcraft Inc., 30 Church St. New Rochelle, NY 10801. Phone: (914)632-0422; Fax: (914)632-0335 • Description: Serves as a "comprehensive and authoritative Stock Market Advisory Service dedicated to bringing the investor facts, original projections, and a cross section of the recommendations of other leading Services.".

***IOMA Business Directory***. Institute of Management & Administration Inc., 1 Washington Pk., Ste. 1300 Newark, NJ 07102-3130. Phone: 800-401-5937 or (973)718-4700; Fax: (973)622-0595 • URL: http://www.ioma.com • Covers: Business Web sites. Entries include: Web links.

***IOMA's Report on Defined Contribution Plan Investing***. Institute of Management and Administration, 29 W. 35th St., 5th Fl. New York, NY 10001-2299. Phone: (212)244-0360; Fax: (212)564-0465; Email: subserve@ioma.com • URL: http://www.ioma.com • Semimonthly. $1,189.90 per year. Newsletter. Edited for 401(k) and other defined contribution retirement plan managers, sponsors, and service providers. Reports on such items as investment manager performance, guaranteed investment contract (GIC) yields, and asset allocation trends.

***IOMA's Report on Managing 401(k) Plans***. Institute of Management and Administration, 29 W. 35th St., 5th Fl. New York, NY 10001-2299. Phone: (212)244-0360; Fax: (212)564-0465; Email: subserve@ioma.com • URL: http://www.ioma.com • Monthly. $521 print and online. Newsletter for retirement plan managers.

**Iota Phi Lambda**. 1015 15th St. NW, Ste. 1110 Washington, DC 20005. Phone: (202)462-4682; Email: iotahq@verizon.net • URL: http://iota1929.org • Business and professional civic sorority. Seeks to: develop leadership expertise among business and professional women; promote increased interest in business education among high school and college girls through planned programs and scholarships; encourage the development of personalities for all areas of leadership through provision of educational opportunities; establish and promote civic and social service activities for youth and adults. Conducts children's services and tutoring sessions. Maintains small library. Provides educational, tutorial, senior citizen, and health programs.

**Iowa State University of Science and Technology - Center for Industrial Research and Service**. 2272 Howe Hall, Ste. 2620 Ames, IA 50011-2272. Phone: (515)294-3420; Fax: (515)294-4925; Email: rcox@iastate.edu • URL: http://www.ciras.iastate.edu • Problem areas of business, manufacturing, technology transfer, productivity, new product design, manufacturing processes, marketing, and related topics. Acts as a problem-handling facility and a clearinghouse for efforts to help Iowa's industry grow through studies highlighting not only production and management problems but also markets and profit potential of possible new developments.

***IP Almanac***. ALM Media Properties LLC, 120 Broadway, 5th Fl. New York, NY 10271-1100. Phone: (212)457-9400; Fax: (646)417-7705; Email: customercare@alm.com • URL: http://www.alm.com • Annual. $20.00. Provides a digest of the year's most important developments in the area of intellectual property. Also included with subscription to *IP Law and Business*.

***IP Law and Business***. ALM Media Properties LLC, 120 Broadway, 5th Fl. New York, NY 10271-1100. Phone: (212)457-9400; Fax: (646)417-7705; Email: customercare@alm.com • URL: http://www.alm.com • Monthly. $125.00 per year. Covers intellectual property litigation and business issues. Includes annual *IP Almanac*.

***IPA Magazine***. Involvement and Participation Association, 2nd Fl., West Wing, Somerset House, Strand London WC2R 1LA, United Kingdom. Phone: 44 20 77591000; Fax: 44 20 77591001; Email: involve@ipa-involve.com • URL: http://www.ipa-involve.com • Quarterly. $66 outside the United Kingdom; $66 outside the United Kingdom; £66 /year outside UK. Magazine covering human development. Formerly *Involvement of Participation*.

***IPOfn***. IPO Financial Network, Phone: (973)379-5100; Fax: (973)379-1696; Email: info@ipofinancial.com • URL: http://www.ipofinancial.com • Web site provides free information on initial public offerings: "Pricing Recap" (price performance), "Calendar Update" (weekly listing of new offerings), "Company Roster" (Web sites), "Stock Brokers" (IPO dealers), and "Brokerage Firms" (underwriters). Fees: Basic data is free. Extensive analysis and recommendations are available through fee-based telephone, fax, and database services. Daily updates.

**IQNet Association - International Certification Network**. Bollwerk 31 CH-3000 Bern, Switzerland. Phone: 41 31 3102440; Fax: 41 31 3102449; Email: headoffice@iqnet.ch • URL: http://www.iqnet-certification.com • National management systems certification bodies. Seeks to advance the practice of corporate and organizational management and business excellence. Evaluates management systems and bestows certification upon qualified organizations; serves as a clearinghouse on management systems.

***The IRA Reporter***. Universal Pensions Inc., 431 Golf Course Rd. N Brainerd, MN 56401. Phone: 800-346-3860 or (218)829-4781 or (218)825-0552; Fax: (218)825-5011 or (218)825-5010; Email: upi@upi-net.com • Monthly. $115.00 per year. Newsletter. Edited for financial planners. Provides information on the rules and regulations of individual retirement accounts (IRAs).

***Iran Business Database***. Faust Information GmbH, Werstener Dorfstr. 17 D-40591 Dusseldorf, Germany. Phone: 49 211 976 9922; Fax: 49 211 976 9923; Email: order@faust-information.com • URL: http://www.faust-information.com •

$539 Individuals CD-ROM. Covers 30,000 companies in Iran.

***Iran Business Forecast Report***. Telecommunications Insight, 85 Queen Victoria St. London EC4V 4AB, United Kingdom. Phone: 20 72 465100 or 44 20 7248 0468; Fax: 20 72 480467 or 44 20 7248 0467; Email: enquiries@telecomsinsight.com • URL: http://www.telecomsinsight.com • Quarterly. $1,195 Individuals Single user; $1,795 Individuals up to 3 users. Business forecast report for Iran.

***Iran Business Law Handbook***. International Business Publications, USA, PO Box 15343 Washington, DC 20003. Phone: (202)546-2103; Fax: (202)546-3275; Email: ibpusa@comcast.net • URL: http://ibpus.com • $99.95 Individuals hardcover, e-book, CD-ROM. Covers: Information on basic business legislation, laws, business climate, export-import regulations and contacts.

***Iran Golden Key Directory***. International Institute of Trade Relation Promotion, Trade Information Centre of Iran, No. 7, 3rd Fl., Abbasie Bazar, Ferdowsi Sq. Tehran, Iran. Phone: 98 21 88833900; Fax: 98 21 88820697; Email: order@irangoldenkey.com • URL: http://www.goldenkeydirectory.com/about.html • £100 Individuals CD version. Covers: 19,000 companies in Iran. Entries include: Company name, telephone, fax, e-mail, Managing Director, date established, number of employees, and business date.

***Iran Industrial and Business Directory***. International Business Publications, USA, PO Box 15343 Washington, DC 20003. Phone: (202)546-2103; Fax: (202)546-3275; Email: ibpusa@comcast.net • URL: http://ibpus.com • Annual. $99.95 Individuals hardcopy, e-book, CD-ROM. Covers: Strategic industrial, investment and business contacts for conducting export-import and investment activity in the country.

***Iran Investment and Business Guide***. International Business Publications, USA, PO Box 15343 Washington, DC 20003. Phone: (202)546-2103; Fax: (202)546-3275; Email: ibpusa@comcast.net • URL: http://ibpus.com • $99.95 Individuals hardcopy, e-book, CD-ROM. Covers: Basic information on economy, export-import and investment climate, regulations and industrial development, banking, and government. Entries include: Business contacts and business travel.

**Iran Management Consultant Association**. Unit 3, No. 70, Mahdinejad Alley, 4th St. Tehran, Iran. Phone: 98 21 88246929 or 98 21 88248548; Fax: 98 21 88246929 or 98 21 88248548; Email: info@imca.ir • URL: http://en.imca.ir • Aims to protect the legal rights and interests of management consultants in Iran. Provides the means of propagating management culture to increase productivity, economic and social sustainable development.

**Iran National Union of Agro Products**. No. 94, Keyvan Alley, Kashani St. Urmia, Iran. Phone: 98 441 3451988 or 98 441 3455780; Fax: 98 441 3455606; Email: shakor_a@iranazarfruit.com • URL: http://www.iranazarfruit.com • Represents the interests of exporters of agricultural products. Aims to create coordination in the export of fruits and vegetables and the promotion of export products. Assists members by providing facilities and marketing services for their agricultural products.

**Iran-Netherlands Business Council**. No. 254 Taleghani Ave. Tehran, Iran. Phone: 98 21 88346736; Fax: 98 21 88346736; Email: info@inbc.ir • URL: http://www.inbc.ir/pages/default.aspx?lan=en • Promotes investment, trade, and political and cultural cooperation between Iran and Netherlands. Fosters business to business relationships between entrepreneurs of Iran and Netherlands.

**Iranian Institute of Project and Process Management**. Jalale-Ale-Ahmad 87 Tehran, Iran. Phone: 98 21 8826 8881; Fax: 98 21 8826 8881; Email: info@ippma.ir • Works to promote project management.

***Iraq Business Law Handbook***. International Business Publications, USA, PO Box 15343 Washington, DC 20003. Phone: (202)546-2103; Fax: (202)546-3275; Email: ibpusa@comcast.net • URL: http://ibpus.com • $99.95 Individuals hardcopy, e-book, CD-ROM. Covers: Information on basic business legislation, laws and climate, export-import regulations, and contacts.

***Iraq Industrial and Business Directory***. International Business Publications, USA, PO Box 15343 Washington, DC 20003. Phone: (202)546-2103; Fax: (202)546-3275; Email: ibpusa@comcast.net • URL: http://ibpus.com • Annual. $99.95 Individuals hardcopy, e-book, CD-ROM. Covers: Strategic industrial, investment and business contacts for conducting export-import and investment activity in the country. Contains strategic practical economic and business information.

**Iraqi Businessmen Union**. Kahramana Sq. Baghdad, Iraq. Phone: 964 1 7193887; Email: info@ibmu-iq.org • URL: http://www.ibmu-iq.org • Aims to strengthen the relationship between businessmen in Iraq, Arab and international countries. Enhances capabilities of Iraqi businessmen through contribution and participation in conferences and symposiums. Encourages businessmen and supports them to establish development projects in Pakistan.

***IRE Journal***. Investigative Reporters and Editors, Missouri School of Journalism, 141 Neff Annex Columbia, MO 65211. Phone: (573)882-2042 or (573)882-2772; Fax: (573)882-5431 or (573)884-5544; Email: info@ire.org • URL: http://www.ire.org • Quarterly. Members free; $70 Nonmembers. Contains practical information relating to investigative journalism.

**Ireland China Association**. 28 Merrion Sq. Dublin 2, Dublin, Ireland. Phone: 353 1 6424178; Fax: 353 1 6612315; Email: info@irelandchina.org • URL: http://www.irelandchina.org • Aims to bring together Irish and Chinese businesspeople for the purpose of exploring business opportunities and making contracts. Promotes greater economic ties and increases trade and commerce between Ireland and China. Furthers the cultural links and greater knowledge of both countries.

***Ireland Government and Business Contacts Handbook***. International Business Publications, USA, PO Box 15343 Washington, DC 20003. Phone: (202)546-2103; Fax: (202)546-3275; Email: ibpusa@comcast.net • URL: http://ibpus.com • $99.95 Individuals hardcopy, e-book, CD-ROM. Covers: Strategic government and business information, export-import activity in the country, investment, business contacts and regulations.

***Ireland Industrial and Business Directory***. International Business Publications, USA, PO Box 15343 Washington, DC 20003. Phone: (202)546-2103; Fax: (202)546-3275; Email: ibpusa@comcast.net • URL: http://ibpus.com • Annual. $99.95 Individuals hardcover, e-book, CD-ROM. Covers: Strategic industrial, investment and business contacts for conducting export-import and investment activity in the country. Contains strategic practical economic and business information.

**Ireland Japan Association**. 28 Merrion Sq. Dublin 2, Dublin, Ireland. Phone: 353 1 6424178; Email: info@ija.ie • URL: http://www.ija.ie • Aims to enhance and develop relations between Ireland and Japan. Promotes economic and business ties and increases trade and commerce between Ireland and Japan. Fosters mutual understanding between the peoples of both countries. Creates a forum for Irish and Japanese people to interact in both business and social environments.

**Irish Agriculture and Food Development Authority - Rural Economy Research Centre**. Teagasc Athenry 4, Galway, Ireland. Phone: 353 59 9170200; Fax: 353 59 9182097; Email: cathal.odonoghue@teagasc.ie • URL: http://www.agresearch.teagasc.ie/rerc • Agricultural economics, production economics, agricultural policy, and rural development.

**Irish Business and Employers' Confederation**. Confederation House, 84-86 Lower Baggot St. Dublin IRL-2, Dublin, Ireland. Phone: 353 1 6051500; Fax: 353 1 6381500; Email: info@ibec.ie • URL: http://www.ibec.ie • Firms: industrial, commercial, and public sector firms that manufacture products or provide services. Promotes the growth and development of Irish industry and commercial activity. Advises the government and represents interests of industry on relevant legislative issues. Maintains the Irish Business Bureau in conjunction with Irish Business and Employers Confederation and the Chambers of Commerce of Ireland. Develops public awareness of the role of industry in national development through press, radio, television, and public meetings. Monitors technological developments; compiles statistics; provides advice and assistance to members; maintains speakers' bureau.

**Irish Institute of Training and Development**. Millennium Business Park, 4 Sycamore House Naas, Kildare, Ireland. Phone: 353 45 881166; Fax: 353 45 881192; Email: info@iitd.com • URL: http://www.iitd.ie • Individuals working in human resource development in Ireland. Fosters communication among members. Conducts educational programs.

**Irish Management Institute**. Sandyford Rd. Dublin 16, Dublin, Ireland. Phone: 353 1 2955147 or 353 1 2078513; Email: programmeadvisors@imi.ie • URL: http://www.imi.ie • Works with individuals and organisations to improve the practice of management in Ireland.

***Iron and Steel International Directory***. DMG World Media, Northcliffe House, 2 Derry St. London W8 5TT, United Kingdom. Phone: 44 20 79386000; Fax: 44 20 31806550; Email: info@gastech.co.uk • URL: http://www.dmgworldmedia.com • Annual. $48; $54 over seas; $86. Covers: Plant and equipment manufacturers in the steel industry, worldwide. Entries include: Company name, address, phone, fax, product/service provided.

***IRRA Newsletter***. Labor and Employment Relations Association, University of Illinois at Urbana-Champaign, 121 Labor & Employment Relations Bldg., 504 E Armory Ave. Champaign, IL 61820. Phone: (217)333-0072; Fax: (217)265-5130; Email: leraoffice@illinois.edu • URL: http://www.leraweb.org • Description: Presents news of meetings, elections, and programs of this Association of business, labor, and government leaders interested in researching labor and management relationships.

***Irrigation and Drainage Abstracts***. CABI Publishing North America, 38 Chauncey St., Ste. 1002 Boston, MA 02111. Phone: 800-552-3083; Email: cabi-nao@cabi.org • URL: http://www.cabi.org • Bimonthly. Published in England by CABI Publishing. Provides worldwide coverage of the literature.

***Irrigation Association Membership Directory and Industry Buyers' Guide***. Irrigation Association, 6540 Arlington Blvd. Falls Church, VA 22042-6638. Phone: (703)536-7080; Fax: (703)536-7019; Email: info@irrigation.org • URL: http://www.irrigation.org • Annual. Free to members; nonmembers, $25.00. Includes manufacturing, distribution, contracting, consultation, research and educational information.

***IRS Publications***. Wolters Kluwer Law & Business CCH, 2700 Lake Cook Rd. Riverwoods, IL 60015. Phone: 888-224-7377 or (847)267-7000; Email: cust_serv@cch.com • URL: http://www.cchgroup.com • Irregular. $352.00. Three looseleaf volumes. Periodic supplementation. Photographic reproductions of current Internal Revenue Service tax publications intended for public use.

***Irwin Business and Investment Almanac***. QSU Publishing, PO Box 546436 Surfside, FL 33154. Phone: 866-225-3122; Fax: (703)359-8462; Email: news@qsuonline.com • URL: http://www.qsuonline.com • Annual. $75. Publication includes: Lists of online databases and their producers; executive search firms, accounting firms, and advertising agencies. Principal content of publication is review of significant business and finance events and statistical data for the year covered. Database includes: Major and group stock market averages, reviews of major futures markets and charts for futures-traded commodities, expanded coverage of foreign business and investment activity.

***ISA Directory of Automation***. The International Society of Automation, 67 Alexander Dr. Research Triangle Park, NC 27709. Phone: (919)549-8411; Fax: (919)549-8288; Email: info@isa.org • URL: http://www.isa.org • Over 2,400 manufacturers of control and instrumentation equipment, over 1,000 manufacturers' representatives, and several hundred service companies; coverage includes Canada.

***ISA Transactions***. ISA-The Instrumentation, Systems and Automation Society. American Institute of Physics, 1 Physics Ellipse College Park, MD 20740-3843. Phone: 800-874-6383 or (301)209-3100; Fax: (516)576-2604; Email: aipinfo@aip.org • URL: http://www.aip.org • Quarterly. $310.00 per year.

***Isle of Man: General Information Factfile***. Commercial Development Div. The Treasury Isle of Man Government, Government Offices Douglas, United Kingdom. Phone: 624685755; Fax: 624 685747 • Annual. Covers: financial institutions, insurance companies, real estate agencies, legal and accounting firms, shipowners, manufacturer, and other service trades on the Isle of Man; government service agencies. Database includes: Summaries of economic activity and opportunity; government policies regarding trade and industry; information on education and social issues. Entries include: Company or agency name, address, phone; shipowners and stockbrokers also include telex and fax numbers; financial institutions and real estate agencies include names of contact or other key personnel; banks and insurance companies include branch office and subsidiary names, addresses, and phone numbers.

***ISO Management Systems***. American National Standards Institute, 1899 L St. NW, 11th Fl. Washington, DC 20036-3807. Phone: (202)293-8020; Fax: (202)293-9287; Email: info@ansi.org • URL: http://www.ansi.org • Bimonthly. Price on application. Newsletter on quality standards. Published by the International Organization for Standardization (ISO). Text in English. Formerly *ISO 9000 and ISO 14000 News*.

***ISP Business | IPTB***. Information Gatekeepers Inc., 1340 Soldiers Field Rd., Ste. 2 Boston, MA 02135. Phone: 800-323-1088 or (617)782-5033 or (617)232-3111; Fax: (617)782-5735 or (617)734-8562; Email: info@igigroup.com • URL: http://www.igigroup.com • Monthly. $695 U.S. and Canada print; $745 Elsewhere print; $695 Individuals PDF - 1 user; $2,500 Individuals PDF - 2 to 10 users; $4,000 Individuals PDF - 11 to 20 users. Covers news of the business aspects of Internet service providers worldwide. Includes information on finances, marketing, mergers and acquisitions, joint ventures, technologies, customer billing and service, new products, and international developments.

**Israel Advanced Technologies Industries**. PO Box 12591 46733 Herzliya, Israel. Phone: 972 73 7136313; Fax: 972 73 7136314; Email: orit@iati.co.il • URL: http://www.iati.co.il • Promotes the development of the venture capital industry in Israel. Supports and enhances the growth of Israeli high-technology industries. Secures special conditions and privileges for members from service organizations in Israel and abroad.

***Israel Agro and Biotechnology Industry Export-Import Directory***. International Business Publications, USA, PO Box 15343 Washington, DC 20003. Phone: (202)546-2103; Fax: (202)546-3275; Email: ibpusa@comcast.net • URL: http://ibpus.com • Annual. $99.95 Individuals hardcover, e-book, CD-ROM. Covers: Information on strategic economic, investment, export-import, and business opportunities. Contains important export-import, government, and business contacts. Ultimate directory for conducting export-import operations in the country.

***Israel Business & Government Directory***. Jerusalem Marketing Group, PO Box 23859 91237 Jerusalem, Israel. Phone: 50 266 598; Fax: 2 625 0946; Email: jmg@netvision.net.il • Semiannual. $39. Covers: over 750 persons active in national government, local municipalities, foreign embassies and consulates, political parties, government companies, and major business organizations and associations in Israel. Entries include: Organization or company name, address, phone, fax, name and title of contact, names and titles of key personnel, number of employees, financial data.

***Israel Business Law Handbook***. International Business Publications, USA, PO Box 15343 Washington, DC 20003. Phone:

(202)546-2103; Fax: (202)546-3275; Email: ibpusa@comcast.net • URL: http://ibpus.com • $99.95 Individuals hardcover, e-book, CD-ROM. Covers: Information on basic business legislation, laws, business climate, export-import regulations, and contacts.

***Israel Business Services Providers Leads***. Business Information Agency Inc. PlanetInform, 52 Tuscan Way, Ste. 202-181 Saint Augustine, VA 32092. Phone: (904)342-6124; Fax: (904)592-2632; Email: info@biasales.com • URL: http:// www.biasales.com • Monthly. $98 Individuals mailing list; $207 Individuals sales list; $350 Individuals marketing list. Covers Israeli companies and all sub-industries that provide services to commercial businesses, establishments, and organizations, including consulting, advertising and marketing services, and facilities maintenance.

***Israel Diamond and Precious Stones***. International Diamond Publications, Ltd., Diamond Towers, 3A Jabotinsky Rd. 52131 Ramat Gon, Israel. Phone: (972) 3 7512165 or (972) 3 751 2165; Fax: (972) 3 5752201 or (972) 3 575 2201 • Bimonthly. $78.00 per year. Text in English. Formerly *Israel Diamonds*.

***Israel IT and Telecommunication Industry Export-Import Directory***. International Business Publications, USA, PO Box 15343 Washington, DC 20003. Phone: (202)546-2103; Fax: (202)546-3275; Email: ibpusa@comcast.net • URL: http:// ibpus.com • Annual. $99.95 Individuals hardcover, e-book, CD-ROM. Covers: Major investment, export-import and other strategic business opportunities, contacts, and basic information for conducting business in the country.

***ISSA Today***. International Sanitary Supply Association, 7373 N Lincoln Ave. Lincolnwood, IL 60712-1799. Phone: 800-225-4772 or (847)982-0800; Fax: (847)982-1012; Email: info@issa.com • URL: http://www.issa.com • Bimonthly. $20; C$30; €25. Covers industry trends, certifications, and technologies to ever-changing legislation, business advice, and how-to applications.

***Issaquah! Chamber Business News***. Greater Issaquah Chamber of Commerce, 155 NW Gilman Blvd. Issaquah, WA 98027. Phone: (425)392-7024; Fax: (425)392-8101 • URL: http:// www.issaquahchamber.com • Monthly.

***ISWM News***. International Society of Weighing and Measurement, 13017 Wisteria Dr., No. 341 Germantown, MD 20874. Phone: 866-285-3512 or (240)753-4397; Email: scalesales@aol.com • URL: http://www.iswm.org • Description: Contains calendar of events, new product information, industry updates, technical articles, and association news.

***ISWorld Net Faculty Directory***. MIS Research Center, University of Minnesota, Carlson School of Management, 321 19th Ave. S, Ste. 3-365 Minneapolis, MN 55455-0438. Phone: (612)624-0862 or (612)625-0862; Fax: (612)626-1600; Email: misrc@umn.edu • URL: http://www.misrc.umn.edu/ • Database covers: college-level teachers of subjects related to management information systems and technology. Database includes: Faculty name, school, address, office phone, research and teaching areas, highest degree.

***IT Companies Database***. NIIR Project Consultancy Services, 106 - E, Kamla Nagar New Delhi 110007, India. Phone: 91 11 23843955; Fax: 91 11 23841561; Email: npcs.india@gmail.com • URL: http://www.niir.org • Rs 1,124 Individuals CD-ROM; $100 Individuals CD-ROM. Covers: 5,000+ contacts of IT companies in India. Entries include: Company name, address, phone, fax, e-mail and website, contact person and product details.

***IT Cost Management Strategies: The Planning Assistant for IT Directors***. Computer Economics Inc., 2082 Business Center Dr., Ste. 240 Irvine, CA 92612-1164. Phone: (949)831-8700; Fax: (949)442-7688; Email: info@computereconomics.com • URL: http://www.computereconomics.com • Monthly. $495.00 per year. Newsletter for information technology professionals. Covers data processing costs, budgeting, financial management, and related topics.

**I.T. Financial Management Association**. PO Box 30188 Santa Barbara, CA 93130. Phone: (805)687-7390; Fax: (805)687-7382; Email: info@itfma.com • URL: http://www.itfma.com • Individuals and corporations interested in the financial management of information technology (IT) organizations. Works for the education and improvement of members and the industry. Offers certification in IT financial management. Conducts peer studies, in-house seminars, and chargeback system reviews. Operates educational programs.

***IT Legal Guide***. VNU Business Publications Ltd., VNU House, 32-34 Broadwick St. London W1A 2HG, United Kingdom. Phone: 44 20 7316 9000 or 44 20 73169000; Fax: 44 20 7316 9440 or 44 20 73169440; Email: feedback@vnunet.com • Annual. $45 plus 4 postage. Covers: More than 400 manufacturers, distributors, and consultants in the United Kingdom specializing with information on 300 technology products and services for the legal profession. Database includes: List of pertinent information sources. Entries include: Name, address, phone, fax, description of products/ services.

***The IT Locator***. Information Resource Group, • Monthly. Covers: computer installations in the following states: Connecticut, the District of Columbia, Georgia, Illinois, Maryland, Massachusetts, Michigan, Missouri, Minnesota, New Jersey, New York, Ohio, Pennsylvania, Texas, Wisconsin, Colorado, Florida, North Carolina, South Carolina, Iowa, Indiana, Kansas, Tennessee, California, Arizona, Washington, and Oregon; separate edition available on a lease basis for each region. Entries include: Company name, address, phone, names and titles of key personnel in data processing and management information systems, hardware systems and software utilized.

***ITALI***. SEAT, SS 148 Pontina, KM 29,100 I-00040 Rome, Italy. Phone: 6 910981; Fax: 6 9105111 • Monthly. Database covers: Over 260,000 Italian companies in all lines of business.

**Italian American Alliance for Business and Technology**. 535 Griswold, Ste. 1844 Detroit, MI 48226. Phone: (248)227-6143; Email: info@iaabt.org • URL: http://iaabt.org • Serves the needs of Italian industrial companies wanting to do business in the United States and U.S. industrial companies seeking to do business in Italy. Promotes the technological, scientific, research and development, design and manufacturing capabilities of member companies. Fosters business opportunities and facilitates exchange of ideas among its members.

**Italian Business Council Qatar**. PO Box 22058 Doha, Qatar. Email: ibcqatar@gmail.com • URL: http://www.itachamqatar.org • Aims to promote economical, commercial and cultural relations between Italy and Qatar. Assists Italian companies in Qatar to establish relationships with Qatari representatives in the private sector through events, meetings and seminars.

**Italian Confederation of Retailers, Commerce, Tourism and Service**. Via Nazionale, 60 I-00184 Rome, Italy. Phone: 39 6 47251; Fax: 39 6 4746886; Email: confes@confesercenti.it • URL: http://www.confesercenti.it • Small and mid-sized enterprises in the commercial, tourist, and service sectors in Italy. Represents and promotes the retailing, tourism, service and other commercial industries.

**Italian Private Equity and Venture Capital Association**. Via Pietro Mascagni n. 7 I-20122 Milan, Italy. Phone: 39 2 7607531; Fax: 39 2 76398044; Email: info@aifi.it • URL: http://www.aifi.it • Lobbies in the legislative and institutional process. Organizes symposia and seminars, educational programs and supports research activities.

***Italy Business Database***. The Data Supplier, 9107 Wilshire Blvd., Ste. 450 Beverly Hills, CA 90210. Phone: 888-930-3282; Fax: (818)221-0295; Email: contactus@thedatasupplier.com • URL: http://www.thedatasupplier.com • Contains contact information for more than 80,000 companies in Italy. Includes business name, full contact information, e-mail addresses, Web site, and contacts.

***Italy Business Directory (ITBD)***. INFOT Inc., PO Box 2052 Rockville, MD 20847. Phone: 866-838-2619 • URL: http:// www.infotusa.com • $55.25 CD-ROM. Covers: 80,063 major industries from Italy and related regions. Entries include: Contact person, physical addresses, email and website addresses, telephone and fax number, and business description.

***Italy Business Law Handbook***. International Business Publications, USA, PO Box 15343 Washington, DC 20003. Phone: (202)546-2103; Fax: (202)546-3275; Email: ibpusa@comcast.net • URL: http://ibpus.com • $99.95 Individuals hardcover, e-book, CD-ROM. Covers: Information on basic business legislation, laws and climate, export-import regulations, and contacts.

***Italy Business Services Providers Leads***. Business Information Agency Inc. PlanetInform, 52 Tuscan Way, Ste. 202-181 Saint Augustine, VA 32092. Phone: (904)342-6124; Fax: (904)592-2632; Email: info@biasales.com • URL: http:// www.biasales.com • Monthly. $181 Individuals mailing list; $381 Individuals sales list; $645 Individuals marketing list. Covers Italian companies and all sub-industries that provide various services to commercial businesses, establishments, and organizations, including consulting, advertising and marketing services, and facilities maintenance.

***Italy Industrial and Business Directory***. International Business Publications, USA, PO Box 15343 Washington, DC 20003. Phone: (202)546-2103; Fax: (202)546-3275; Email: ibpusa@comcast.net • URL: http://ibpus.com • Annual. $99.95 Individuals hardcover, e-book, CD-ROM. Covers: Strategic industrial, investment and business contacts for conducting export-import and investment activity in the country. Contains strategic, practical economic and business information.

***Italy Investment and Business Guide***. International Business Publications, USA, PO Box 15343 Washington, DC 20003. Phone: (202)546-2103; Fax: (202)546-3275; Email: ibpusa@comcast.net • URL: http://ibpus.com • $99.95 Individuals hardcopy, e-book, CD-ROM. Covers: Basic information on economy, export-import and investment climate, regulations and industrial development, banking, and government. Entries include: Business contacts and business travel.

***ITE Journal***. Institute of Transportation Engineers, 1627 Eye St. NW, Ste. 600 Washington, DC 20006. Phone: (202)289-0222 or (202)785-0060; Fax: (202)289-7722 or (202)785-0609; Email: ite_staff@ite.org • URL: http://www.ite.org • Monthly. $75 U.S., Canada, and Mexico; $110 Other countries; $170 U.S., Canada, and Mexico 3 years; $275 Other countries 3 years; $5 Single issue back issue. Technical magazine focusing on the plan, design, and operation of surface transportation systems. Formerly *Transportation Engineering*.

***Item Processing Report***. Access Intelligence L.L.C., 4 Choke Cherry Rd., 2nd Fl. Rockville, MD 20850. Phone: 800-777-5006 or (301)354-2000 or (301)354-2101; Fax: (301)309-3847 or (801)365-2300; Email: info@accessintel.com • URL: http://www.accessintel.com/ • Description: Monitors developments in the processing of remittances and checks, including image processing, optical character recognition, check truncation, hardware, and software. **Remarks:** Absorbed The Powell Report, 1992.

***It's Your Business***. Marlborough Regional Chamber of Commerce, 11 Florence St. Marlborough, MA 01752-2822. Phone: (508)485-7746; Fax: (508)481-1819; Email: marlcham@marlboroughchamber.org • URL: http://www.marlboroughchamber.org • Monthly. Contains latest information and events of Marlborough Regional Chamber of Commerce.

***IVCI Directory of Domestic and International Venture Groups***. International Venture Capital Institute Inc. Baxter Associates Inc., 49 E Ave. Norwalk, CT 06851-3919. • Annual. $9.95 per issue. Covers: over 200 venture capital clubs; international coverage. Entries include: Organization name, address, phone, name and title of contact.

***IVCI Directory of Venture Capital Seed and Early-Stage Funds***. International Venture Capital Institute Inc. Baxter Associates Inc., 49 E Ave. Norwalk, CT 06851-3919. • Covers: Over 225 venture capital firms which do seed and/or early-stage joint ventures. Entries include: Contact information.

***J W Business International: International Business Communications Directory***. Telex-Verlag Jaeger + Waldmann GmbH, Birkenweg 8-10 D-64295 Darmstadt, Germany. Phone: 6151 33020; Fax: 6151 330250; Email: jwemail@aol.com • Annual. $210. Covers: Approximately 2,000,000 companies on fax and telex worldwide in all trades and industries classified by products and services within 43 main groups. Entries include: Company name, address, fax and telex numbers; subsidiary and branch names and locations.

***J W CD-ROM Fax Directory***. Telex-Verlag Jaeger + Waldmann GmbH, Birkenweg 8-10 D-64295 Darmstadt, Germany. Phone: 6151 33020; Fax: 6151 330250; Email: jwemail@aol.com • Annual. $690. Covers: Nearly 95,000 Canadian businesses and other institutions and organizations owning fax machines. Also includes some listings for North and South America, Asia, Africa, and Australia. Entries include: Company or organization name, address, phone, fax, telex, and information on product/service, J+W trade codes.

***J W Communications CD International and J W Business CD International***. Telex-Verlag Jaeger + Waldmann GmbH, Birkenweg 8-10 D-64295 Darmstadt, Germany. Phone: 6151 33020; Fax: 6151 330250; Email: jwemail@aol.com • Annual. $440. Covers: Six million companies worldwide. Entries include: Company name and address, communications data, and products and services code. Country database includes dialing codes, products and services, and trade classification in four languages.

***Jacksonville Business Journal***. The Business Journals, 120 W. Morehead St., Ste. 400 Charlotte, NC 28202. Phone: (704)973-1000; Fax: (704)973-1001; Email: info@bizjournals.com • URL: http://www.bizjournals.com/ • $92 Individuals print and online. Local business news coverage.

***JAMA: Journal of the American Medical Association***. American Medical Association, AMA Plaza, 330 N Wabash Ave. Chicago, IL 60611. Phone: 800-621-8335 or (312)464-4430; Fax: (312)464-5226; Email: amalibrary@ama-assn.org • URL: http://www.ama-assn.org • Weekly. $111 Individuals print and online; member; $185 Individuals print and online; nonmember; $125 Individuals online only; $185 Institutions print and online; $125 Institutions online only; $114 Students print and online; $45 Students online. Scientific general medical journal.

***Jamaica Hills Association—Business Directory***. Jamaica Hills Association, PO Box 300392 Jamaica Plain, MA 02130. Email: advocate@jamaicahills.org • URL: http://jamaicahills.org • Covers entrepreneurs, businesses, and artists in Jamaica Plain, Massachusetts.

**Jamaica Manufacturers' Association**. 85a Duke St. Kingston, Jamaica. Phone: (876)922-8880 or (876)922-8869; Fax: (876)922-9205; Email: jma@cwjamaica.com • URL: http:// www.jma.com.jm • Promotes the development of the manufacturing sector and increase its contribution to the socio-economic welfare of the country by creating jobs and improving the standard of living for all.

**James Madison University - Health Communication Institute**. School of Communication Studies Harrisonburg, VA 22807. Phone: (540)568-3586; Email: gabbaras@jmu.edu • URL: http://www.jmu.edu/healthcom/index.shtml • Health communication.

***Jane's Air Traffic Control***. IHS Global Ltd. IHS Jane's: Defense & Security Intelligence & Analysis, 321 Inverness Dr. S Englewood, CO 80112. Phone: 800-447-2273 or (703)683-3700; Fax: (703)836-0297 or (800)836-0297; Email: info.us@janes.com • URL: http://www.ihs.com • Annual. $495.00. International coverage of equipment and supplies for both civil and military airports. Formerly *Jane's Airport and ATC Equipment*.

***Jane's Airport Review: The Global Airport Business Magazine***. Jane's Information Group, Inc., 110 N Royal St., Ste. 200 Alexandria, VA 22314-1651. Phone: 800-836-0297 or (703)683-3700; Fax: (703)836-0029 or (703)863-0029; Email: info.us@janes.con • URL: http://www.janes.com • 10 times a year. $190.00 per year. CD-Rom edition, $775.00 per year. Edited for airport managers. Covers all aspects of airport operations.

***Jane's All the World's Aircraft***. Jane's Information Group, Inc., 110 N Royal St., Ste. 200 Alexandria, VA 22314-1651. Phone: 800-836-0297 or (703)683-3700; Fax: (703)836-0029 or (703)863-0029; Email: info.us@janes.con • URL: http://www.janes.com • Annual. $630.00; CD-ROM edition, $1,455.00; online edition, $1,566.00; microfiche edition, $3,075.00. Lists civil and military aircraft, helicopters, airships, and aero engines.

***Jane's Police and Homeland Security Equipment***. IHS Global Ltd. IHS Jane's: Defense & Security Intelligence & Analysis, 321 Inverness Dr. S Englewood, CO 80112. Phone: 800-447-2273 or (703)683-3700; Fax: (703)836-0297 or (800)836-0297; Email: info.us@janes.com • URL: http://www.ihs.com • Provides information on sources of more than 2,000 items of law enforcement equipment. Covers traffic control, riot control, communications, personal protection, surveillance, and other equipment categories. Includes detailed product descriptions.

***Jane's Road Traffic Management and ITS***. Jane's Information Group, Inc., 110 N Royal St., Ste. 200 Alexandria, VA 22314-1651. Phone: 800-836-0297 or (703)683-3700; Fax: (703)836-0029 or (703)863-0029; Email: info.us@janes.con • URL: http://www.janes.com • Annual. $470.00. A directory of traffic control equipment and services. Includes detailed product descriptions.

**Japan Association of Corporate Executives**. 1-4-6, Marunouchi, Chiyoda-ku Tokyo 100-0005, Japan. Phone: 81 3 32111271 or 81 3 32840220; Fax: 81 3 32132946 or 81 3 32123774; Email: kdcontact1207@doyukai.or.jp • URL: http://www.doyukai.or.jp • Businesspersons in Japan. Formulates social, economic, policy proposals through research and discussion among members.

**Japan Auto Parts Industries Association**. Jidosha Buhin Kaikan, 5th Fl., 1-16-15 Takanawa, Minato-ku Tokyo, Tokyo 108-0074, Japan. Phone: 81 3 34454211; Fax: 81 3 34475372; Email: info@japia.or.jp • URL: http://www.japia.or.jp • Manufacturers of automotive parts and components; suppliers to the automotive parts industry. Seeks to improve the business climate for members. Facilitates exchange of information among members and between members and related international organizations and overseas manufacturing concerns. Gathers technical and economic data of interest to members.

***Japan Business Directory, Database***. NIIR Project Consultancy Services, 106 - E, Kamla Nagar New Delhi 110007, India. Phone: 91 11 23843955; Fax: 91 11 23841561; Email: npcs.india@gmail.com • URL: http://www.niir.org • $100 Individuals CD-ROM; Rs 2,248 Individuals CD-ROM. Covers: 12,800 categorized listings of Japanese business companies. Entries include: Company name, phone, fax, email, website address, details of business/services provided.

**Japan Business Incubation Association**. Shiba-Koen, Minato-ku 3-5-8 Kikai Tokyo 105 0011, Japan. Phone: 81 50 36021751; Email: reception@jbia.jp • URL: http://jbia.jp • Promotes new business creation in local communities and encourages the exchange of information among major international organizations. Conducts studies and makes proposals on new business creation and implements training programs for incubation managers. Provides consulting support, implementation, and policy proposals related to business incubation.

***Japan Camera Trade News: Monthly Information on Photographic Products, Optical Instruments and Accessories***. K. Eda, editor. Genyosha Publications Inc., 2-15-1 Shibuya, Mail box SP-466, Shibuya-Ku Tokyo 150-8944, Japan. Phone: 81 337 230539; Email: info@genyosha.co.jp • URL: http://www.genyosha.com • Monthly. $130.00 per year. Information on the photographic industry worldwide. Text in English.

***Japan Company Handbook***. Toyo Keizai Inc., 1-2-1 Nihonbashi Hongokucho, Chuo-ku Tokyo 103-8345, Japan. Phone: 81 3 32465551 or 3 32465580; Fax: 81 3 32790332 or 3 32424067; Email: info@toyokeizai.co.jp • URL: http://www.toyokeizai.co.jp/english • Quarterly. $148 per issue; airmail postpaid; ¥37,600 4 quarter editions; $528 4 quarter editions; airmail postpaid; $492 Out of country airmail postpaid; ¥9,600 latest edition. Covers: In two sections: over 3,700 Japanese corporations listed on the 'First Section' of Tokyo, Osaka, and Nagoya stock exchanges, listed in one volume; about 900 firms, smaller in capital but 'considered promising' and listed on the 'Second Section,' are given in a separate volume titled 'Japan Company Handbook—Second Section'; 800 over-the counter companies; and nearly 80 local market companies. Entries include: Company name, address, phone, fax, telex, description, outlook, year established, fiscal year, overseas offices, president, references, capital, other financial data, stock exchanges on which listed, underwriters, number of employees, names of major stockholders and percentage of Japanese and foreign ownership, principal products, and export ratio.

***Japan Electronics Buyers' Guide***. Dempa Publications Inc., 1-11-15 Higashi Gotanda, Shinagawa-Ku Tokyo 141-8715, Japan. Phone: 81 334 456111; Fax: 81 334 447515 • URL: http://www.dempa.net • Annual. $220. Covers: manufacturers of electronic equipment and components in Japan, and import-export firms and agents dealing in those products. Entries include: For manufacturers and traders—Company name, address, phone, fax, branches, names and titles of president and key sales executives, establishment, capital, sales, number of employees, products, trade names, percentage of sales in export, main factory. For agents—Company name, address, phone, companies represented.

***Japan Government and Business Contacts Handbook***. International Business Publications, USA, PO Box 15343 Washington, DC 20003. Phone: (202)546-2103; Fax: (202)546-3275; Email: ibpusa@comcast.net • URL: http://ibpus.com • $99.95 Individuals hardcopy, e-book, CD-ROM. Covers: Strategic government and business information, export-import activity in the country, investment, business contacts and regulations.

***J@pan Inc Magazine: Business Technology People***. Japan Incorporated Communications K.K., Minami-Aoyama 1st Bldg., 10th Fl., 7-8-1 Minami Aoyama, Minato-Ku Tokyo 107-0062, Japan. Phone: 81 334 992099 or 81 334 992 099; Fax: 81 334 993109; Email: info@japaninc.com • URL: http://www.japaninc.com • Monthly. English language magazine covering business and technology in Japan for professionals worldwide.

***Japan Industrial and Business Directory***. International Business Publications, USA, PO Box 15343 Washington, DC 20003. Phone: (202)546-2103; Fax: (202)546-3275; Email: ibpusa@comcast.net • URL: http://ibpus.com • $99.95 Individuals hardcopy, e-book, CD-ROM. Covers: Customs, trade regulations and procedures.

***Japan Investment and Business Guide***. International Business Publications, USA, PO Box 15343 Washington, DC 20003. Phone: (202)546-2103; Fax: (202)546-3275; Email: ibpusa@comcast.net • URL: http://ibpus.com • $99.95 Individuals hardcopy, e-book, CD-ROM. Covers: Strategic information on economy, business, export-import and investment climate, regulations and industrial development, banking, government, and opportunities. Entries include: Important business contacts and business travel.

**Japan Machinery Center for Trade and Investment**. Kikai Shinkou Kaikan, 4th Fl., 3-8-5, Shiba Koen, Minato Tokyo, Tokyo 105-0011, Japan. Phone: 81 3 34319507; Fax: 81 3 34366455 • URL: http://www.jmcti.org • Exporters of machinery. Seeks to establish and maintain a domestic and international business climate beneficial to the exportation of machinery. Represents members' interests; gathers and disseminates information.

**Japan Management Association**. Convention Div., 3-1-22 Shibakoen, Minato-ku Tokyo 105-8522, Japan. Phone: 81 3 34346211 or 81 334 341246; Fax: 81 3 34341087 or 81 334 340269; Email: global@jma.or.jp • URL: http://www.jma.or.jp • Japanese corporations and individuals. Management education organization working to develop and conduct public business education and training programs including seminars, conferences, symposia, and overseas study tours. Makes available correspondence courses, audiovisual and computer-assisted instruction programs, in-company training programs, and cruise seminars. Conducts research and disseminates information on topics including white-collar productivity in Japan, creativity development in business and industry, and globally oriented management reform. Maintains liaison with similar organizations worldwide. Organizes conferences and exhibitions for trade associations. Maintains 14 interdisciplinary divisions and 13 supporting departments. Provides management consulting service; operates speakers' bureau.

**Japan Paper Exporters' Association**. Kami Parupu Bldg., 3-9-11, Ginza, Chuo-ku Tokyo, Tokyo 104-8139, Japan. Phone: 81 3 32484831; Fax: 81 3 32484834; Email: info@jpeta.or.jp • URL: http://www.jpeta.or.jp • Exporters of paper and related products. Seeks to establish and maintain a domestic and international business climate beneficial to the paper trade. Represents members' interests; gathers and disseminates information.

**Japan Paper Importers' Association**. Kami Papuru Bldg., 3-9-11, Ginza, Chuo-ku Tokyo, Tokyo 104-8139, Japan. Phone: 81 3 32484831; Fax: 81 3 32484834 • URL: http://www.jpeta.or.jp • Importers of paper and related products. Seeks to establish and maintain a domestic and international business climate beneficial to the paper trade. Represents members' interests; gathers and disseminates information.

**Japan Securities Dealers' Association**. 1-5-8, Kayaba-cho Nihonbashi Chuo, Tokyo 103-0025, Japan. Phone: 81 3 3667-8537; Email: international@wan.jsda.or.jp • URL: http://www.jsda.or.jp/en • Represents securities companies and registered financial institutions. Aims to protect investors by ensuring fair and smooth trading in securities and other transactions by members of the association. Promotes the implementation of policy measures for the revitalization of the Japanese securities markets in order to contribute to the growth and development of the Japanese economy.

***The Japan Times***. 5-4, Shibaura 4-chome Tokyo 108-8071, Japan. Phone: 03 3453 5312; Email: overseas@japantimes.co.jp • Weekly. $120.00 per year. Provides news and commentary on Japan's economy, trade policies, and Japanese life in general. Regular features include "Business Briefs," "Market Reports," "Lifestyle," and "Issue Analysis." Supplement available *The Japan Times Weekly*. Text in English.

***Japan-U.S. Business Report***. Japan Economic Institute, 1000 Connecticut Ave. NW, Ste. 211 Washington, DC 20036. Phone: (202)296-5633; Fax: (202)296-8333; Email: jei@jei.org • Monthly. $185 /year; $185 Individuals North America; $195 Other countries. Provides updates on major sales and investment developments among U.S. and Japanese firms; arranged by industry groupings.

***Japanese-Affiliated Companies in U.S.A. and Canada***. Japan External Trade Organization, 1221 McKinney St., Ste. 4141 Houston, TX 77010. Phone: (713)759-9595; Fax: (713)759-9210; Email: info@jetro.org • URL: http://www.jetro.org • Biennial. Covers: 9,870 Japanese firms, restaurants, and various information sources. Database includes: Area maps. Entries include: Company name, address, phone, fax, line of business, parent company, executive officers, year established.

***Japanese Business in Britain***. Culver Financial Surveys, 12 Orchard St. Saint Albans AL3 4HL, United Kingdom. • Annual. $100 2000 edition. Covers: Approximately 550 Japanese-owned, United Kingdom-registered limited companies. Entries include: Company name, address, names and titles of key personnel, number of employees, financial data, subsidiary and branch names and locations, description, ownership information, sales and profits data.

***Japanese Companies in the UK***. Jordans Ltd., 21 St. Thomas St. Bristol BS1 6JS, United Kingdom. Phone: 44 117 923 0600; Fax: 44 117 923 0063; Email: customerservices@jordans.co.uk • URL: http://www.jordans.co.uk • Annual. $195. Covers: Top 180 Japanese companies in the United Kingdom. Entries include: Company name, address, phone, contact name, description of business.

***Japanese Company Factfinder: Teikoku Databank***. Teikoku Databank America, Inc., 780 Third Ave., 22nd Fl. New York, NY 10017. Phone: (212)421-9805; Fax: (212)421-9806; Email: info@teikoku.com • URL: http://www.teikoku.com • Monthly. $60 Individuals per connect hour + US$ 5.60/record; $2,000 Individuals CD-ROM (Annual). CD-ROM provides detailed financial and descriptive information on more than 186,000 Japanese companies doing business overseas.

***Japanese Investment in U.S. and Canadian Real Estate Directory***. Mead Ventures Inc., Box 44952 Phoenix, AZ 85064. Phone: (602)234-0044 • Annual. $295. Covers: about 550 Japanese investors, brokers, lenders, consultants, and developers in the United States and Canada; and about 275 companies in Japan. Entries include: Company name, address, phone, fax, telex, name and title of contact, geographical area served, services provided and description of projects and services.

***Japanese Overseas Investments***. Toyo Keizai Inc., 1-2-1 Nihonbashi Hongokucho, Chuo-ku Tokyo 103-8345, Japan. Phone: 81 3 32465551 or 3 32465580; Fax: 81 3 32790332 or 3 32424067; Email: info@toyokeizai.co.jp • URL: http://www.toyokeizai.co.jp/english • $550. Covers: over 13,000 Japanese affiliate and subsidiary companies operating in over 100 countries. Entries include: Company name, address, phone, capital and business lines, product/service.

**Japanese Society of Certified Pension Actuaries**. Mita NN Bldg., B1F, 4-1-23 Shiba, Minato-ku Tokyo, Tokyo 108-0014, Japan. Phone: 81 3 54420208; Fax: 81 3 54420700 • URL: http://www.jscpa.or.jp/english • Maintains and upholds standards of practice for certified pension actuaries.

***JASA***. American Statistical Association, 732 N Washington St. Alexandria, VA 22314-1943. Phone: 888-231-3473 or (703)684-1221; Fax: (703)684-2037; Email: asainfo@amstat.org • URL: http://www.amstat.org • Quarterly. $652 Individuals. Statistics information.

***Java Developer's Journal***. SYS-CON Media Inc., 135 Chestnut Ridge Rd. Montvale, NJ 07645. Phone: (201)802-3000 • URL: http://www.sys-con.com • Monthly. $69.99 per year. Provides technical information for Java professionals.

***Java Pro***. Fawcette Technical Publications, 2600 S El Camino Real, Ste. 300 San Mateo, CA 94403-2332. Phone: 800-848-5523 or (650)378-7100; Fax: (650)570-6307; Email: customerservice@fawcette.com • URL: http://www.fawcette.com • Monthly. $29.95 per year. Contains technical articles for Java developers.

***Jax Fax Travel Marketing Magazine: The Official Leisure Travel Booking Magazine***. Jet Airtransport Exchange Inc., 52 W Main St. Milford, CT 06460-3310. Phone: 800-952-9329 or (203)301-0255; Fax: (203)301-0250; Email: editor@jaxfax.com • URL: http://www.jaxfaxmagazine.com • Monthly. $15.00 per year. Trade magazine for travel agents.

***JCT: Journal of Coatings Technology***. American Coatings Association, 1500 Rhode Island Ave. NW Washington, DC 20005. Phone: (202)462-6272; Fax: (202)462-8549 • URL: http://www.paint.org • 6/year. A forum for the exchange of research, experience, knowledge and ideas among those with a professional interest in the science, technology and manufacture of functional, protective and decorative coatings including paints, inks and related coatings and their raw materials, and similar topics.

**JEDEC**. 3103 N 10th St., Ste. 240-S Arlington, VA 22201-2107. Phone: (703)907-7515 • URL: http://www.jedec.org • Affiliated with Electronic Industries Alliance. Formerly Joint Electron Device Engineering Council.

***Jet and PropJet Business Aircraft Directory***. Avcom International Inc., 312 E Murdock St. Wichita, KS 67214-3605. Phone: (316)262-1493; Fax: (316)262-5333 • Annual. $26.95. Owners of business jet and turboprop aircraft. Worldwide coverage. Formerly *Propjet*.

***Jewelers' Circular/Keystone-Jewelers' Directory***. Reed Elsevier

Group plc Reed Business Information, 360 Park Ave. S New York, NY 11010. Phone: (212)791-4208; Email: corporatecommunications@reedbusiness.com • URL: http://www.reedbusiness.com • About 8,500 manufacturers, importers and wholesale jewelers providing merchandise and supplies to the jewelry retailing industry; and related trade organizations. Included with subscription to *Jewelers' Circular Keystone.*

*Jewelers' Circular Keystone (JCK).* Reed Elsevier Group plc Reed Business Information, 360 Park Ave. S New York, NY 11010. Phone: (212)791-4208; Email: corporatecommunications@reedbusiness.com • URL: http://www.reedbusiness.com • Monthly. $90.00 per year.

*Jewelers Directory—Supplies.* InfoGroup Inc., 5711 S 86th Cir. Omaha, NE 68127-4146. Phone: (402)593-4500 • URL: http://www.infogroup.com • Annual. Number of listings: 594. Entries include: Name, address, phone, size of advertisement, name of owner or manager, number of employees, year first in "Yellow Pages." Compiled from telephone company "Yellow Pages," nationwide.

*Jewelers' Security Alliance.* 6 E 45th St. New York, NY 10017. Phone: 800-537-0067; Fax: (212)808-9168; Email: jsa2@jewelerssecurity.org • URL: http://www.jewelerssecurity.org • Formerly Jewelers Security Alliance of U.S.

*Jewelers Vigilance Committee.* 25 W 45th St., Ste. 1406 New York, NY 10036. Phone: (212)997-2002; Fax: (212)997-9148 • URL: http://www.jvclegal.org • Represents manufacturers, importers, wholesalers, and retailers. Combats deceptive trade practices and misleading advertising. Aims to develop and maintain high trade standards. Provides advice on markings and assists in prosecution of violations of marking, advertising, and related jewelry industry laws.

*Jewelry Business Directory.* Hong Kong Jewelry Manufacturers Association, Unit G, 2nd Fl., Phase 2, Kaiser Estate, 51 Man Yue St., Hunghom, Kowloon Hong Kong, China. Phone: 852 27663002; Fax: 852 23623647; Email: enquiry@jewelry.org.hk • URL: http://www.jewelry.org.hk/jma/html/index.jsp • Annual. Contains more than 400 company listings, including all major Hong Kong jewelry manufacturers and related business.

*Jewelry Information Center.* 120 Broadway, Ste. 2820 New York, NY 10271. Phone: 800-223-0673 or (646)658-0246; Fax: (646)658-0256; Email: info@jic.org • URL: http://www.jic.org • Represents retailers, wholesalers, and manufacturers of fine jewelry products. Conducts industry-wide promotional and educational programs; sponsors marketing seminars and consumer-oriented programs on radio, television, and print media.

*Jiu Jitsu Instruction Directory.* InfoGroup Inc., 5711 S 86th Cir. Omaha, NE 68127-4146. Phone: (402)593-4500 • URL: http://www.infogroup.com • Annual. Number of listings: 5,198. Entries include: Name, address, phone, size of advertisement, name of owner or manager, number of employees, year first in "Yellow Pages." Compiled from telephone company "Yellow Pages," nationwide.

*Job & Career Books.* Kennedy Information Inc., 1 Phoenix Mill Ln., 3rd Fl. Peterborough, NH 03458. Phone: 800-531-0007 or (603)924-1006; Fax: (603)924-4460 or (603)924-4034; Email: customerservice@kennedyinfo.com • URL: http://www.kennedyinfo.com • Annual. Free. Contains descriptions of selected books from various publishers on job searching and choice of career.

*Job Hunter's Sourcebook.* Cengage Learning Inc., 20 Channel Center St. Boston, MA 02210. Phone: 800-487-8488 or (617)289-7700; Fax: (617)289-7844; Email: investors@cengage.com • URL: http://www.cengage.com • $243 Individuals. 2012. $231.00. 12th edition. Covers over 200 professions and occupations.

*Job Safety and Health Quarterly.* U. S. Government Printing Office, 732 N Capitol St. NW Washington, DC 20401. Phone: 866-512-1800 or (202)512-1800 or (866)512-1800; Fax: (202)512-2104 or (202)512-2250; Email: contactcenter@gpo.gov • URL: http://www.gpo.gov • Quarterly. $17.00 per year. Issued by the Occupational Safety and Health Administration (OSHA), U. S. Department of Labor. Contains articles on employee safety and health, with information on current OSHA activities.

*The Job-Seeker's Guide to On-line Resources.* Kennedy Information Inc., 1 Phoenix Mill Ln., 3rd Fl. Peterborough, NH 03458. Phone: 800-531-0007 or (603)924-1006; Fax: (603)924-4460 or (603)924-4034; Email: customerservice@kennedyinfo.com • URL: http://www.kennedyinfo.com • $14.95 plus $4 shipping. Covers: Approximately 140 candidate databases, job-posting services, and related resources with introductory text containing tips for novices. Entries include: On-line name, address, phone, fax; e-mail address, description.

*Job Seeker's Guide to 1000 Top Employers.* Visible Ink Press, 43311 Joy Rd., Ste. 414 Canton, MI 48187-2075. Phone: (734)667-3211; Fax: (734)667-4311 • URL: http://www.visibleinkpress.com • $22.95. Covers: 1,000 large or prominent private and public companies in the U.S. Entries include: Company name, address, phone, fax, year founded, type of company, stock exchanges on which traded, stock symbol, description, locations of operating units, subsidiaries and affiliated companies, corporate officers, financial data, number of employees, human resources contact, job application procedures.

*Job Training & Vocational Rehabilitation Services Directory.* InfoGroup Inc., 5711 S 86th Cir. Omaha, NE 68127-4146. Phone: (402)593-4500 • URL: http://www.infogroup.com • Annual. Number of listings: 1,605. Entries include: Name, address, phone, size of advertisement, name of owner or manager, number of employees, year first in "Yellow Pages." Compiled from telephone company "Yellow Pages," nationwide.

*Jobson's Yearbook of Public Companies.* Dun & Bradstreet (Australia) Proprietary Ltd., 479 St. Kilda Rd. Melbourne, VIC 3004, Australia. Phone: 61 3 9828 3333 or 61 3 9828 3333; Fax: 61 3 9828 3300 or 61 3 9288 3300; Email: customerservice@dnb.com.au • URL: http://dnb.com.au • Daily (eve.). $520 Individuals. Database covers: All companies (about 1,400) listed on the Industrial Boards of the Australian and New Zealand stock exchanges; includes mining and petroleum industries. Database includes: Information on money market companies, trust companies, and stockbrokers, ranking of top 100 companies by revenue and profit. Entries include: Company name, address, phone, fax; DUNS number; subsidiaries; associated companies; names and titles of key personnel; branch office locations; share register; home exchange subsidiaries; voting rights; auditors; bankers; solicitors; financial data; major shareholder; history; operations, and ACN number.

*JOC Shipping Digest: For Export and Transportation Executives.* Shipper Group, 33 Washington St., 13th Fl. Newark, NJ 07102. Phone: 800-223-0243; Fax: (973)848-7045; Email: customerservice@joc.com • URL: http://www.shippingdigest.com • Weekly.

*The John Liner Letter.* Standard Publishing Corp., 155 Federal St., 13th Fl. Boston, MA 02110. Phone: 800-682-5759 or (617)457-0600; Fax: (617)457-0608; Email: customerservice@spcpub.com • URL: http://www.spcpub.com • $245 /year; $317 /year, print and online. Description: Provides risk management and technical insurance advice for business firms, such as broadening coverage, cutting costs, and anticipating special insurance problems.

**Johns Hopkins University - Johns Hopkins Berman Institute of Bioethics.** Deering Hall, 1809 Ashland Ave. Baltimore, MD 21205. Phone: (410)614-5550; Email: bioethics@jhu.edu • URL: http://www.bioethicsinstitute.org • Moral and policy issues in biomedical science, health care, and health policy, and the development of thoughtful solutions for the benefit of society.

**Johns Hopkins University Bloomberg School of Public Health - Center for Health Services and Outcomes Research.** Hampton House, 6th Fl., Department of Health Policy & Management, 624 N Broadway Baltimore, MD 21205-1901. Phone: (410)955-6567; Fax: (410)955-0470; Email: awu@jhsph.edu • URL: http://www.jhsph.edu/research/centers-and-institutes/health-services-outcomes-research/index.html • Health services, including determinants of health outcomes; the impacts of alternative health care systems on cost and quality; effective strategies for health promotion and disease prevention; and methods of meeting the needs of high risk populations such as the poor, elderly, mentally ill, disabled, and children.

**Johns Hopkins University - Johns Hopkins Bloomberg School of Public Health - Department of Population, Family and Reproductive Health - Women's and Children's Health Policy Center.** 615 N Wolfe St. Baltimore, MD 21205. Phone: (410)502-5450; Fax: (410)502-5831; Email: cminkovi@jhsph.edu • URL: http://www.jhsph.edu/research/centers-and-institutes/womens-and-childrens-health-policy-center • Health system reforms impacting the health of women, children, and adolescents.

*Johnson Matthey Technology Review.* Johnson Matthey PLC, 5th Fl., 25 Farringdon St. London EC4A 4AB, United Kingdom. Phone: 44 020 7269 8400; Fax: 44 020 7269 8433; Email: jmpr@matthey.com • URL: http://www.matthey.com • Quarterly. Covers research on the science and technology of the platinum group metals and developments in their application in industry.

**Joint Industry Board of the Electrical Industry.** 158-11 Harry Van Arsdale Jr. Ave. Flushing, NY 11365. Phone: (718)591-2000; Fax: (718)380-7741 • URL: http://www.jibei.org • Concerned with labor-management relations of electrical contractors.

**Joint Institute for Advancement of Flight Sciences.** 725 23rd St. NW, 227 Hunting Ave. Washington, DC 20052. Phone: (202)994-6080; Fax: (202)994-3394; Email: jiafs@seas.gwu.edu • Conducts research in aeronautics, astronautics, and acoustics (flight-produced noise).

*Joint Venture Directory of the New Independent States.* Triumph Books Inc., 814 N Franklin St. Chicago, IL 60610. Phone: 800-888-4741 or (312)337-0747; Fax: (312)280-5470 or (312)337-5985; Email: orders@ipgbook.com • URL: http://www.triumphbooks.com • $295 payment must accompany order. Covers: about 2,650 firms in the Commonwealth of Independent States that are joint ventures between CIS companies and foreign firms. Entries include: Company name, address, phone, fax, telex, name and title of contact, product or service, names of domestic and foreign partners, capitalization, number of employees, date registered, objectives.

*Joint Venture Partner Search Directory.* Michigan Department of Agriculture, PO Box 30017 Lansing, MI 48909. Phone: 800-292-3939 or (616)925-3270; Fax: (616)925-3272; Email: mda-info@michigan.gov • Irregular. $15. Covers: more than 200 Michigan companies interested in forming international partnerships. Entries include: Company name, address, phone, Standard Industrial Classification (SIC) code, annual sales (if available), number of employees, geographical areas in which interested in conducting business.

*Joint Ventures.* Glasser LegalWorks, 150 Clove Rd. Little Falls, NJ 07424. Phone: 800-308-1700 or (973)890-0008; Fax: (973)890-0042; Email: legalwks@aol.com • URL: http://www.glasserlegalworks.com • Looseleaf. $225.00, including CD-ROM version. Periodic Supplementation. Includes explanations of legal procedures for joint ventures, with annotated forms. (Emerging Growth Companies Series.).

*JOM: The Member Journal of the Minerals, Metals and Materials Society.* The Minerals, Metals, and Materials Society, 184 Thorn Hill Rd. Warrendale, PA 15086-7514. Phone: 800-759-4867 or (724)776-9000; Fax: (724)776-3770; Email: webmaster@tms.org • URL: http://www.tms.org/TMSHome.aspx • Four times a year. Membership. A scholarly journal covering all phases of metals and metallurgy.

*Jones NCTI.* 9697 E Mineral Ave. Centennial, CO 80112. Phone: 866-575-7206 or (303)797-9393; Fax: (303)797-9394; Email: info@jonesncti.com • URL: http://www.jonesncti.com.

*Jordan Business Law Handbook.* International Business Publications, USA, PO Box 15343 Washington, DC 20003. Phone: (202)546-2103; Fax: (202)546-3275; Email: ibpusa@comcast.net • URL: http://ibpus.com • $99.95 Individuals hardcopy, E-book and CD-ROM. Covers: Basic business laws and legislations, export-import regulations, business climate and contacts.

*Jordan Golden Key Directory.* International Institute of Trade Relation Promotion, Trade Information Centre of Iran, No. 7, 3rd Fl., Abbasie Bazar, Ferdowsi Sq. Tehran, Iran. Phone: 98 21 88833900; Fax: 98 21 88820697; Email: order@irangoldenkey.com • URL: http://www.goldenkeydirectory.com/about.html • £100 Individuals. Covers: 29,424 companies in Jordan. Entries include: Company name, address, telephone, fax, products, services, Managing Director, and business activities.

**Jordan Information Bureau.** 3504 International Dr. NW Washington, DC 20008. Phone: (202)966-2664 or (202)265-1606; Fax: (202)966-3110; Email: hkjembassydc@jordanembassyus.org • URL: http://www.jordanembassyus.org • Provides cultural, economic, and travel information on Jordan.

*Journal of Academic and Business Ethics (JABE).* Academic and Business Research Institute, PO Box 350997 Jacksonville, FL 32235-0997. Email: editorial.staff@aabri.com • URL: http://www.aabri.com • Journal containing information on the ethical issues of business and education.

*The Journal of Academic Librarianship: Articles, Features, and Book Reviews for the Academic Library Professional.* Elsevier, Secondary Publishing Division, 650 Ave. of the Americas New York, NY 10011. Phone: 888-437-4636 or (212)633-3980; Fax: (212)633-3975; Email: t.reller@elsevier.com • URL: http://www.elseveier.com • $472 Institutions. Bimonthly. Qualified personnel.

*Journal of Accountancy.* American Institute of Certified Public Accountants, 1211 Avenue of the Americas New York, NY 10036-8775. Phone: 888-777-7077 or (212)596-6200; Fax: (212)596-6213; Email: service@aicpa.org • URL: http://www.aicpa.org • Monthly. $75 Individuals; $60 Members. Accounting journal.

*Journal of Accounting, Auditing and Finance.* New York University Vincent C. Ross Institute of Accounting Research. Greenwood Publishing Group Inc., 88 Post Rd. W Westport, CT 06881. Phone: (203)226-3571; Fax: (203)222-1502; Email: orders@greenwood.com • URL: http://www.greenwood.com • Quarterly. Individuals, $70.00 per year; institutions, $165.00 per year.

*Journal of Accounting Research.* Institute of Professional Accounting. Blackwell Publishing Inc., 350 Main St. Malden, MA 02148. Phone: 800-216-2522 or (781)388-8200; Fax: (781)388-8210; Email: journaladsusa@bos.blackwellpublishing.com • URL: http://www.blackwellpublishing.com • Five times a year. Institutions, $425.00 per year. Includes online edition. Annual *Supplement* available. Accepts for review unpublished research in the fields of empirical and experimental accounting.

*Journal of Adhesion.* Taylor & Francis Ltd., 2 Park Sq., Milton Park Abingdon OX14 4RN, United Kingdom. Phone: 44 22 70176000 or 44 20 70176000; Fax: 44 22 70176699 or (701)76336; Email: info@e-elgar.co.uk • URL: http://www.taylorandfrancisgroup.com • Monthly. $3,193 Individuals. Three volumes. Individuals, $1,575.00 per year; institutions, $3,056.00 per year; corporations, $6,760.00 per year.

*Journal of Advanced Materials.* Society for the Advancement of Material and Process Engineering, 1161 Park View Dr., Ste. 200 Covina, CA 91724-3759. Phone: 800-562-7360 or (626)331-0616; Fax: (626)332-8929; Email: sampe@sampe.org • URL: http://www.sampe.org • Quarterly. Individuals, $60.00 per year; institutions, $150.00 per year. Contains technical and research articles. Formerly *SAMPE Quarterly.*

*Journal of Advertising.* M.E. Sharpe Inc., 80 Business Park Dr. Armonk, NY 10504. Phone: 800-541-6563 or (914)273-1800; Fax: (914)273-2106; Email: info@mesharpe.com •

URL: http://www.mesharpe.com • Quarterly. $90 per year. An academic journal devoted to advertising theory and research.

***Journal of Advertising Research***. Advertising Research Foundation, 432 Park Ave. S, 6th Fl. New York, NY 10016-8013. Phone: (212)751-5656; Fax: (212)319-5265; Email: info@thearf.org • URL: http://www.thearf.org • Quarterly. $365 Individuals standard subscription; $730 Individuals with enhanced online. Journal of advertising, marketing, and media research.

***Journal of African Research in Business and Technology (JARBT)***. IBIMA Publishing, 34 E Germantown Pke., No. 327 Norristown, PA 19401. Email: contact@ibimapublishing.com • URL: http://www.ibimapublishing.com • Peer-reviewed journal covering business and technology research in Africa.

***Journal of Aging and Social Policy: A Journal Devoted to Aging and Social Policy***. The Haworth Press Inc., 10 Alice St. Binghamton, NY 13904. Phone: 800-429-6784 or (607)722-5857; Fax: (607)771-0012 or (607)722-6362; Email: getinfo@haworthpress.com • URL: http://www.haworthpressinc.com/store/product.asp?sku=J014 • Quarterly. $415.00 per year.

***Journal of Agribusiness in Developing and Emerging Economies***. Emerald Group Publishing Ltd., Howard House, Wagon Ln. Bingley BD16 1WA, United Kingdom. Phone: 44 1274 777 700; Fax: 44 1274 785 201 • URL: http://www.emeraldinsight.com • Peer-reviewed journal publishing information on agriculture and food chains and their implications for economic and societal development and public policy in Asia, Africa, Latin America and Eastern Europe.

***Journal of Agricultural and Food Information***. The Haworth Press Inc., 10 Alice St. Binghamton, NY 13904. Phone: 800-429-6784 or (607)722-5857; Fax: (607)771-0012 or (607)722-6362; Email: getinfo@haworthpress.com • URL: http://www.haworthpressinc.com/store/product.asp?sku=J014 • Quarterly. Institutions, $95.00 per year. A journal for librarians and others concerned with the acquisition of information on food and agriculture.

***Journal of Alcohol and Drug Education***. American Alcohol and Drug Information Foundation, PO Box 10212 Lansing, MI 48901-0212. Phone: (517)484-1770; Fax: (517)487-2474; Email: jadejournal@earthlink.net • URL: http://www.jadejournal.org/ • Three times a year. $45.00 per year.

***Journal of Animal Science***. American Society of Animal Science, PO Box 7410 Champaign, IL 61826-7410. Phone: (217)356-9050 or (212)621-4623; Email: asas@asas.org • URL: http://www.asas.org • Monthly. $135 Members U.S. online; $135 Canada and Mexico members online; $235 Members U.S. print + online; $235 Canada and Mexico members print + online; $260 Other countries members print + online; $685 Institutions U.S. print + online; $685 Canada and Mexico print + online; $710 Other countries print + online; $185 /year for individuals in North America; $210 /year for individuals outside North America; $450 /year for institutions online. Professional journal covering animal science.

***Journal of Apicultural Research***. International Bee Research Association, Unit 6 Centre Ct., Main Ave. Rhondda Cynon Taf CF37 5YR, United Kingdom. Phone: 44 29 20372409; Email: mail@ibra.org.uk • URL: http://www.ibra.org.uk • Quarterly. £90 Individuals /year; £278 Institutions /year. Publishes original research articles, original theoretical papers, notes, comments and authoritative reviews on scientific aspects of the biology, ecology, natural history, conservation and culture of all types of bees.

***Journal of Applied Behavioral Science***. Pine Forge Press, 2455 Teller Rd. Thousand Oaks, CA 91320-2234. Phone: 800-818-7243 or (805)499-4224 or (805)499-9774; Fax: (805)499-0871 or (805)583-2665; Email: sales@pfp.sagepub.com • URL: http://www.sagepub.com/sociologybooks • $943 Institutions print and e-access; $849 Institutions e-access; $924 Institutions print; $146 Individuals print; $254 Institutions single print issue; $47 Individuals single print issue. Quarterly. Includes print and online editions.

***Journal of Applied Communication Research***. National Communication Association, 1765 N St. NW Washington, DC 20036. Phone: (202)464-4622 or (202)467-4868; Fax: (202)464-4600 or (202)872-1331; Email: nkidd@natcom.org • URL: http://www.natcom.org • Quarterly. $110.00 per year.

***Journal of Applied Econometrics***. John Wiley and Sons, Inc., Journals Div., 111 River St. Hoboken, NJ 07030. Phone: 800-526-5368 or (201)748-6000; Fax: (201)748-6088; Email: consumers@wiley.com • URL: http://www.wiley.com • 7/year. Individuals, $85.00 per year; institutions, $1,050.00 per year.

***Journal of Applied Mechanics***. ASME International, 2 Park Ave. New York, NY 10016-5990. Phone: 800-843-2763 or (973)882-1170; Fax: (973)882-1717; Email: customercare@asme.org • URL: http://www.asme.org • $129 Members; $791 Nonmembers. Bimonthly.Subscription includes online edition.

***Journal of Applied Meteorology and Climatology***. American Meteorological Society, 45 Beacon St. Boston, MA 02108-3693. Phone: (617)227-2425 or (617)227-2426; Fax: (617)742-8718; Email: amsinfo@ametsoc.org • URL: http://www.ametsoc.org • Monthly. $1,110 Members corporation and institution; online and print; $454 Members corporation and institution; online only; $1,480 Nonmembers online and print; $605 Nonmembers online only. Peer-reviewed journal exploring the applications of the atmospheric sciences to operational and practical goals.

***Journal of Applied Polymer Science***. John Wiley and Sons, Inc., Journals Div., 111 River St. Hoboken, NJ 07030. Phone: 800-526-5368 or (201)748-6000; Fax: (201)748-6088; Email: consumers@wiley.com • URL: http://www.wiley.com • Semimonthly. $14,495.00 per year; with online edition, $15,220.00, four volumes.

***Journal of Applied Research for Business Instruction***. Association for Research in Business Education - Delta Pi Epsilon, 1914 Association Dr. Reston, VA 20191-1596. Phone: (703)860-8300 or (703)620-4483 • URL: http://www.dpe.org • Quarterly. $15 /year; $5 /single issue. Includes research articles to improve instruction in all business disciplines.

***Journal of Aquatic Food Product Technology: An International Journal Devoted to Foods from Marine and Inland Waters of the World***. The Haworth Press Inc., 10 Alice St. Binghamton, NY 13904. Phone: 800-429-6784 or (607)722-5857; Fax: (607)771-0012 or (607)722-6362; Email: getinfo@haworthpress.com • URL: http://www.haworthpressinc.com/store/product.asp?sku=J014 • Quarterly. $375.00 per year.

***Journal of Architectural Education***. Association of Collegiate Schools of Architecture. The MIT Press, 55 Hayward St. Cambridge, MA 02142-1493. Phone: 800-356-0343 or (617)253-5646 or (617)253-5641; Fax: (617)258-6779 or (617)253-6779; Email: ewfaran@mit.edu • URL: http://mitpress.mit.edu • Quarterly. Free to members; nonmembers, $50.00. Articles on architectural education, theory and practice.

***Journal of Arts Management, Law, and Society***. Helen Dwight Reid Educational Foundation. • Quarterly. $108 Individuals print only; $109 Individuals print and online; $280 Institutions print only; $320 Institutions print and online. Addresses current and ongoing issues in arts policy, management, law and governance from a range of philosophical and national perspectives encompassing diverse disciplinary viewpoints. Formerly *Journal of Arts Management and Law*.

***Journal of Asia-Pacific Business***. The Haworth Press Inc., 10 Alice St. Binghamton, NY 13904. Phone: 800-429-6784 or (607)722-5857; Fax: (607)771-0012 or (607)722-6362; Email: getinfo@haworthpress.com • URL: http://www.haworthpressinc.com/store/product.asp?sku=J014 • Quarterly. $225.00 per year. Includes print and online editions. An academic and practical journal concerned with marketing, finance, and other aspects of doing business in Asia.

***Journal of Asia-Pacific Business***. Routledge Journals Taylor & Francis Group, 270 Madison Ave. New York, NY 10016-0601. • URL: http://www.routledge.com • Quarterly. $405 Institutions online only; $147 Individuals online only; $463 Institutions print + online; $162 Individuals print + online. Journal featuring managerially oriented as well as academic articles centered on the Asia-Pacific region.

***Journal of Asian Business***. Southeast Asia Business Program. University of Michigan, 500 S State St. Ann Arbor, MI 48109. Phone: (734)764-1817; Email: info@umich.edu • URL: http://www.umich.edu • 3/year. An international academic journal covering business in all parts of Asia.

***Journal of Astronautical Sciences***. American Astronautical Society, 6352 Rolling Mill Pl., Ste. 102 Springfield, VA 22152-2370. Phone: (703)866-0020; Fax: (703)866-3526; Email: aas@astronautical.org • URL: http://astronautical.org • Quarterly. free to AAS members; $189 Institutions 1-year subscription. An archival publication devoted to the sciences and technology of astronautics.

***Journal of Bank Cost and Management Accounting***. Association for Management Information in Financial Services, 14247 Saffron Cir. Carmel, IN 46032. Phone: (317)815-5857; Email: ami2@amifs.org • URL: http://www.amifs.org • 3/year.

***Journal of Behavioral Health Services and Research***. Association of Behaviorial Healthcare Management. Lippincott Williams & Wilkins, 2 Commerce Sq., 2001 Market St. Philadelphia, PA 19103. Phone: 800-638-3030 or (301)223-2300; Email: ronna.ekhouse@wolterskluwer.com • URL: http://www.lww.com • Quarterly. Individuals, $81.95 per year; institutions, $231.95 per year. Pertains to the financing and organization of behavioral health services. Formerly *Journal of Mental Health Administration*.

***Journal of Behavioral Studies in Business (JBSB)***. Academic and Business Research Institute, PO Box 350997 Jacksonville, FL 32235-0997. Email: editorial.staff@aabri.com • URL: http://www.aabri.com • Journal containing manuscripts of behavioral studies in business related disciplines.

***Journal of Biotechnology***. Elsevier, Secondary Publishing Division, 650 Ave. of the Americas New York, NY 10011. Phone: 888-437-4636 or (212)633-3980; Fax: (212)633-3975; Email: t.reller@elsevier.com • URL: http://www.elseveier.com • 5,897 Institutions print. Provides a medium for the rapid publication of both full-length articles and short communications on novel and innovative aspects of biotechnology.

***Journal of Broadcasting and Electronic Media***. Broadcast Education Association, 1771 N St. NW Washington, DC 20036-2891. Phone: (202)429-5355 or (202)429-3935; Fax: (202)775-2981; Email: beamemberservices@nab.org • URL: http://www.beaweb.org • Quarterly. Included in membership; $40 Nonmembers /year in U.S.; $25 Students /year at member schools; $50 Nonmembers /year outside U.S. Scholarly articles about developments, trends and research.

***Journal of Business and Economic Statistics***. American Statistical Association, 732 N Washington St. Alexandria, VA 22314-1943. Phone: 888-231-3473 or (703)684-1221; Fax: (703)684-2037; Email: asainfo@amstat.org • URL: http://www.amstat.org • Quarterly. $62 for members; $10 for student members; $145 for nonmembers; $170 print and online. Emphasis is on statistical measurement and applications for business and economics.

***Journal of Business and Finance Librarianship***. The Haworth Press Inc., 10 Alice St. Binghamton, NY 13904. Phone: 800-429-6784 or (607)722-5857; Fax: (607)771-0012 or (607)722-6362; Email: getinfo@haworthpress.com • URL: http://www.haworthpressinc.com/store/product.asp?sku=J014 • Quarterly. $165.00 per year.

***Journal of Business and Psychology***. Business Psychology Research Institute. Springer ScienceBusiness Media LLC, 233 Spring St. New York, NY 10013-1578. Phone: (212)460-1500 or (732)445-2280; Fax: (212)460-1575; Email: trans@transactionpub.com • URL: http://www.springer.com • Quarterly. €948 Institutions print or online; €1,138 Institutions print & enchanced access; $614 Institutions print; $736.80 Institutions print and online; $548 Institutions. An international outlet publishing high quality research designed to advance organizational science and practice.

***Journal of Business Case Studies (JBCS)***. The Clute Institute for Academic Research, 6901 S Pierce St., Ste. 239 Littleton, CO 80128. Phone: (303)904-4750; Fax: (303)259-2420; Email: staff@cluteinstitute.com • URL: http://www.cluteinstitute.com • Monthly. $495 Institutions. Journal containing case studies for use in business and economics courses.

***Journal of Business Ethics Education***. Dienas Zurnali, Mukusalas str. 15, Midlothian LV-1004 Riga, Latvia. Phone: 371 6 7273311; Fax: 371 6 7292701; Email: pasts@dienaszurnali.lv • URL: http://www.dienaszurnali.lv • $490 Institutions library - hard copy; $495 Institutions library - hard copy & e-access; €375 Institutions library - hard copy; €385 Institutions library - hard copy & e-access; £300 Institutions library - hard copy; £320 Institutions library - hard copy & e-access. Journal assisting educators by providing conceptual tools managers needed to make choices those are ethically responsible and culturally sensitive as well as technically sound.

***Journal of Business Ethics***. European Business Ethics Network, c/o Mario Silar, Secretary, C/Elizmendi 31, Bajo B, Sarriguren 31621 Navarra, Spain. Email: secretariat@eben-net.org • URL: http://www.eben-net.org • Annual.

***Journal of Business Logistics***. Council of Supply Chain Management Professionals, 333 E Butterfield Rd., Ste. 140 Lombard, IL 60148. Phone: (630)574-0985; Fax: (630)574-0989; Email: membership@cscmp.org • URL: http://www.cscmp.org • Quarterly. $88 Individuals print + online; $300 Institutions print + online; Members free complimentary access to the digital journal. Provides a forum for the dissemination of thoughts, research, and practices within the logistics and supply chain arenas. Features articles in subject areas which have significant current impact on thought and practice in logistics and supply chain management.

***Journal of Business Process Oriented Software Engineering***. IBIMA Publishing, 34 E Germantown Pke., No. 327 Norristown, PA 19401. Email: contact@ibimapublishing.com • URL: http://www.ibimapublishing.com • Peer-reviewed journal covering the area of business software engineering.

***Journal of Business Strategies***. Gibson D. Lewis Center for Business and Economic Research, Sam Houston State University, College of Business Administration Huntsville, TX 77341. Phone: (936)294-1284; Fax: (936)294-1982 • URL: http://www.shsu.edu/centers/cbed • Semiannual. $45 Individuals domestic; $80 Individuals international; $80 Institutions domestic; $120 Institutions international; $25 Individuals back issue. Periodical covering issues in business.

***Journal of Business Strategy***. Emerald Group Publishing Ltd., Howard House, Wagon Ln. Bingley BD16 1WA, United Kingdom. Phone: 44 1274 777 700; Fax: 44 1274 785 201 • URL: http://www.emeraldinsight.com • Bimonthly. Business magazine.

***Journal of Business Strategy***. SourceMedia Inc., 1 State Street Plz., 27th Fl. New York, NY 10004. Phone: 800-221-1809 or (212)803-8200 or (212)803-8333; Fax: (212)843-9635 or (212)292-5216; Email: custserv@sourcemedia.com • URL: http://www.sourcemedia.com • Bimonthly. $98.00 per year. Covers managememt planning techniques and corporate strategy for senior executives.

***The Journal of Business***. The University of Chicago Press, Journals Div., 1427 E 60th St. Chicago, IL 60637. Phone: 877-705-1878 or (773)702-7700; Email: subscriptions@press.uchicago.edu • URL: http://www.press.uchicago.edu/journals.html • Quarterly. Individuals, $31.00 per year; institutions, $125.00 per year; students, $25.00 per year.

***The Journal of Business Valuation***. Thomson Reuters Canada Ltd., 1 Corporate Plz., 2075 Kennedy Rd. Toronto, ON, Canada M1T 3V4. Phone: 800-387-5164 or (416)298-5141 or (416)609-3800; Fax: (416)298-5094 or (416)298-5082; Email: carswell.customerrelations@thomson.com • URL: http://www.carswell.com • Annual. C$85 Individuals; $52.52 Individuals. Journal including papers presented at the Business Valuation Conference in Canada.

***Journal of Case Research in Business and Economics (JCRBE)***.

Academic and Business Research Institute, PO Box 350997 Jacksonville, FL 32235-0997. Email: editorial.staff@aabri.com • URL: http://www.aabri.com • Journal containing case studies on business related issues.

***Journal of Computer Security***. Sushil Jajodia and Jonathan K. Millen, editors. IOS Press, Inc., 5795-G Burke Centre Pkwy. Burke, VA 22015. Phone: (703)323-5554; Fax: (703)323-3668 or (703)323-3368; Email: iosbooks@iospress.com • URL: http://www.iospress.nl • Bimonthly. $1,330 Institutions. Contains research and development results of lasting significance in the theory, design, implementation, analysis, and application of secure computer systems.

***Journal of Crop Improvement***. The Haworth Press Inc., 10 Alice St. Binghamton, NY 13904. Phone: 800-429-6784 or (607)722-5857; Fax: (607)771-0012 or (607)722-6362; Email: getinfo@haworthpress.com • URL: http://www.haworthpressinc.com/store/product.asp?sku=J014 • 6/year. $377 Individuals online; $455 Individuals print & online; $1,336 Institutions online; $1,527 Institutions print & online. Topics include plant biotechnology, plant genetics, crop productivity, quality, safety, pest control, and environmental concerns. Formerly *Journal of Crop Production*.

***Journal of Current Laser Abstracts***. PennWell Corp., Advanced Technology Div., 98 Spit Brook Rd. Nashua, NH 03062-5737. Phone: 800-225-0556 or (603)891-0123; Fax: (603)891-9294; Email: atd@pennwell.com • URL: http://www.pennwell.com • Monthly. $465 Individuals; $485 Out of country. Covers the world's literature of lasers: industrial, medical, and military. Subscription includes annual subject and author index.

***Journal of Derivatives (JOD)***. Institutional Investor Inc. Journals Group, 225 Park Ave. S New York, NY 10003. Phone: 800-437-9997 or (212)224-3570; Email: info@iijournals.com • URL: http://www.iijournals.com • Quarterly. $780 /year plus online access to the complete archive of articles. Includes analysis of theoretical models.

***Journal of Dietary Supplements***. The Haworth Press Inc., 10 Alice St. Binghamton, NY 13904. Phone: 800-429-6784 or (607)722-5857; Fax: (607)771-0012 or (607)722-6362; Email: getinfo@haworthpress.com • URL: http://www.haworthpressinc.com/store/product.asp?sku=J014 • Quarterly. $175.00 per year to libraries; $50.00 per year to individuals. Edited with a view to both academic research and industry concerns. Sections are dedicated to health professionals, educators, and dieticians. Includes book reviews and short reviews of research appearing elsewhere. Formerly *Journal of Nutraceuticals, Functional & Medical Foods*.

***Journal of East-West Business***. Routledge Journals Taylor & Francis Group, 270 Madison Ave. New York, NY 10016-0601. • URL: http://www.routledge.com • Quarterly. $530 Institutions online only; $152 Individuals online only; $606 Institutions print + online; $168 Individuals print + online. Journal dealing with contemporary and emerging topics of business studies, strategies, development, and practice relating to Eastern Europe and Asia.

***Journal of Economic Perspectives***. American Economic Association, 2014 Broadway, Ste. 305 Nashville, TN 37203. Phone: (615)322-2595; Fax: (615)343-7590; Email: aeainfo@vanderbilt.edu • URL: http://www.aeaweb.org • Quarterly. Quarterly. Membership. Emphasis is on the economic analysis of public policy issues.

***Journal of Education for Business***. Routledge, 711 3rd Ave., 8th Fl. New York, NY 10017. Phone: 800-634-7064 or (212)216-7800; Fax: (212)564-7854 or (212)563-2269; Email: book.orders@tandf.co.uk • URL: http://www.routledge.com • 8/year. $227 Institutions online only; $98 Individuals print and online; $259 Institutions print and online. Journal for business teachers, featuring business fundamentals, career and distributive education, consumer economics, management and trends in communications, information systems, and knowledge systems for business.

***Journal of Electronic Resources in Medical Libraries***. The Haworth Press Inc., 10 Alice St. Binghamton, NY 13904. Phone: 800-429-6784 or (607)722-5857; Fax: (607)771-0012 or (607)722-6362; Email: getinfo@haworthpress.com • URL: http://www.haworthpressinc.com/store/product.asp?sku=J014 • Quarterly. $240.00 per year to libraries; $75.00 per year to individuals.

***Journal of Energy Engineering: The International Journal***. Architectural Engineering Institute of ASCE, 1801 Alexander Bell Dr. Reston, VA 20191-4400. Phone: 800-548-2723; Email: aei@asce.org • URL: http://www.asce.org/aei • Quarterly. $350 Individuals Online only; $449 Individuals Print only; $566 Individuals Print and Online; $88 Members Online only; $127 Members Print only; $157 Members Print and Online. Contains reports on the development of scientific and engineering knowledge in the planning, management, and generation of electrical power.

***Journal of Enterprise Business Intelligence Systems***. IBIMA Publishing, 34 E Germantown Pke., No. 327 Norristown, PA 19401. Email: contact@ibimapublishing.com • URL: http://www.ibimapublishing.com • Peer-reviewed journal featuring the latest research and practices in enterprise business intelligence systems.

***A Journal of Ethnicity in Substance Abuse***. The Haworth Press Inc., 10 Alice St. Binghamton, NY 13904. Phone: 800-429-6784 or (607)722-5857; Fax: (607)771-0012 or (607)722-6362; Email: getinfo@haworthpress.com • URL: http://www.haworthpressinc.com/store/product.asp?sku=J014 • Quarterly. $380.00 per year. Includes print and online editions. Edited for researchers and practitioners. Covers various areas of susbstance abuse, including alcoholism. Formerly *Drugs and Society*.

***Journal of EU Research in Business***. IBIMA Publishing, 34 E Germantown Pke., No. 327 Norristown, PA 19401. Email: contact@ibimapublishing.com • URL: http://www.ibimapublishing.com • Peer-reviewed journal publishing information on research management and new ideas regarding the economics in Europe.

***Journal of Family Business Management***. Emerald Group Publishing Ltd., Howard House, Wagon Ln. Bingley BD16 1WA, United Kingdom. Phone: 44 1274 777 700; Fax: 44 1274 785 201 • URL: http://www.emeraldinsight.com • Peer-reviewed journal publishing research on all aspects of family business management.

***Journal of Government Financial Management***. Association of Government Accountants, 2208 Mt. Vernon Ave. Alexandria, VA 22301-1314. Phone: 800-AGA-7211 or (703)684-6931; Fax: (703)548-9367; Email: agamembers@agacgfm.org • URL: http://www.agacgfm.org • Quarterly. $95 Individuals; $115 Other countries. *Government Accountants Journal*.

***Journal of Innovation and Business Best Practices (JIBBP)***. IBIMA Publishing, 34 E Germantown Pke., No. 327 Norristown, PA 19401. Email: contact@ibimapublishing.com • URL: http://www.ibimapublishing.com • Peer-reviewed journal focusing on business innovation and best practices.

***Journal of Integrated Business Decisions***. IBIMA Publishing, 34 E Germantown Pke., No. 327 Norristown, PA 19401. Email: contact@ibimapublishing.com • URL: http://www.ibimapublishing.com • Peer-reviewed journal publishing research in business decision-making practices.

***Journal of International Business and Cultural Studies (JIBCS)***. Academic and Business Research Institute, PO Box 350997 Jacksonville, FL 32235-0997. Email: editorial.staff@aabri.com • URL: http://www.aabri.com • Journal containing manuscripts related to international business and cultural relations issues.

***Journal of International Business Studies (JIBS)***. Academy of International Business, Michigan State University, The Eli Broad College of Business, 645 N Shaw Ln., Rm. 7 East Lansing, MI 48824-1121. Phone: (517)432-1452; Fax: (517)432-1009; Email: aib@aib.msu.edu • URL: http://aib.msu.edu • 9/year. $498 Institutions in U.S. (print only); $212 Individuals in U.S. (print and online); £310 Institutions Other Countries (print only); £133 Individuals Other Countries (print and online); Included in membership. Publishes academic papers of significant interest that contribute to the theoretical basis of business and management studies.

***Journal of International Business Studies***. Journal of International Business Studies, 3240 Prospect St. NW Washington, DC 20007. Phone: (202)944-3755; Fax: (202)944-3762; Email: jibs@msb.edu • URL: http://www.palgrave-journals.com/jibs/index.html • Bimonthly. £133 Institutions print and online, Europe; $498 Institutions print only, U.S.; £310 Institutions rest of world. Scholarly business journal, covering topics from e-commerce to foreign markets.

***Journal of Internet and e-Business Studies***. IBIMA Publishing, 34 E Germantown Pke., No. 327 Norristown, PA 19401. Email: contact@ibimapublishing.com • URL: http://www.ibimapublishing.com • Peer-reviewed journal publishing research, analyses, case studies and reviews relating to internet and electronic business.

***Journal of Internet Commerce***. Taylor & Francis Ltd., 2 Park Sq., Milton Park Abingdon OX14 4RN, United Kingdom. Phone: 44 22 70176000 or 44 20 70176000; Fax: 44 22 70176699 or (701)76336; Email: info@e-elgar.co.uk • URL: http://www.taylorandfrancisgroup.com • Quarterly. $115 Individuals print and online; $578 Institutions print and online. Presents scholarly articles on marketing and other aspects of electronic commerce.

***Journal of Library and Information Services in Distance Learning***. The Haworth Press Inc., 10 Alice St. Binghamton, NY 13904. Phone: 800-429-6784 or (607)722-5857; Fax: (607)771-0012 or (607)722-6362; Email: getinfo@haworthpress.com • URL: http://www.haworthpressinc.com/store/product.asp?sku=J014 • Quarterly. $150.00 per year to libraries; $48.00 per year to individuals.

***Journal of Media Business Studies***. Joenkoeping International Business School, Media Management and Transformation Centre, Jonkoping International Business School, Jonkoping University SE-551 11 Jonkoping, Sweden. • URL: http://www.jombs.com • Quarterly. 535 kr Individuals; €60 Individuals; $65 Individuals; 1,735 kr Institutions; €195 Institutions; $225 Institutions. Peer-reviewed journal devoted to research on business aspects of media including strategic, organizational, financial, marketing, and entrepreneurial issues and practices.

***Journal of Natural Fibers***. The Haworth Press Inc., 10 Alice St. Binghamton, NY 13904. Phone: 800-429-6784 or (607)722-5857; Fax: (607)771-0012 or (607)722-6362; Email: getinfo@haworthpress.com • URL: http://www.haworthpressinc.com/store/product.asp?sku=J014 • Quarterly. $400.00 per year to libraries; $45.00 per year to individuals. Covers applications, technology, research, and world markets relating to fibers from silk, wool, cotton, flax, hemp, jute, etc. Previously *Natural Fibres*, published annually.

***Journal of Nature-Inspired Business Computing***. IBIMA Publishing, 34 E Germantown Pke., No. 327 Norristown, PA 19401. Email: contact@ibimapublishing.com • URL: http://www.ibimapublishing.com • Peer-reviewed journal focusing on nature-inspired computing for businesses.

***Journal of New Seeds: Innovations in Production, Biotechnology, Quality, and Marketing***. The Haworth Press Inc., 10 Alice St. Binghamton, NY 13904. Phone: 800-429-6784 or (607)722-5857; Fax: (607)771-0012 or (607)722-6362; Email: getinfo@haworthpress.com • URL: http://www.haworthpressinc.com/store/product.asp?sku=J014 • Quarterly. $240.00 per year to libraries; $65.00 per year to individuals. Covers research and development for a new generation of seeds having a high degree of quality and productivity. Topics relating to global seed production include marketing, economics, and intellectual property rights.

***Journal of Offshore Technology***. Institute of Marine Engineering, Science and Technology, Aldgate House, 33 Aldgate High St. London EC3N 1EN, United Kingdom. Phone: 44 20 73822694 or 44 20 73822600; Fax: 44 20 73822670; Email: info@imarest.org • URL: http://www.imarest.org • Bimonthly. Free to members; non-members, £52.00 per year. Covers the latest technological developments and trends for senior offshore engineers.

***Journal of Personal Selling and Sales Management (JPSSM)***. M.E. Sharpe Inc., 80 Business Park Dr. Armonk, NY 10504. Phone: 800-541-6563 or (914)273-1800; Fax: (914)273-2106; Email: info@mesharpe.com • URL: http://www.mesharpe.com • Quarterly. $84 Individuals; $430 Institutions print and online; $99 Other countries print; $462 Institutions, other countries print and online. An academic journal containing peer-reviewed articles. Includes "Selling and Sales Management Abstracts" (summaries of relevant articles appearing in various publications).

***Journal of Planning Literature***. Ohio State University, Dept. of City and Regional Planning. Pine Forge Press, 2455 Teller Rd. Thousand Oaks, CA 91320-2234. Phone: 800-818-7243 or (805)499-4224 or (805)499-9774; Fax: (805)499-0871 or (805)583-2665; Email: sales@pfp.sagepub.com • URL: http://www.sagepub.com/sociologybooks • Quarterly. $1,380 Institutions Print and E-access; $1,518 Institutions with Back files (online and print); $1,242 Institutions e-access; $1,380 Institutions with Back files (all online content); $1,352 Institutions print only; $161 Individuals print only; $372 Institutions single issue, print; $52 Individuals single issue, print. Provides reviews and abstracts of city and regional planning lierature.

***Journal of Poverty: Innovations on Social, Political, and Economic Inequalities***. The Haworth Press Inc., 10 Alice St. Binghamton, NY 13904. Phone: 800-429-6784 or (607)722-5857; Fax: (607)771-0012 or (607)722-6362; Email: getinfo@haworthpress.com • URL: http://www.haworthpressinc.com/store/product.asp?sku=J014 • Quarterly. $180.00 per year to libraries; $50.00 per year to individuals. Covers the social, emotional, and economic consequences of public assistance. Topics include welfare policy, immigrants' rights, hiring practices, managed healthcare, child support, disabilities, food programs, and affirmative action. (See also www.journalofpoverty.org).

***Journal of Quality Assurance in Hospitality and Tourism: Improvements in Marketing, Management, and Development***. The Haworth Press Inc., 10 Alice St. Binghamton, NY 13904. Phone: 800-429-6784 or (607)722-5857; Fax: (607)771-0012 or (607)722-6362; Email: getinfo@haworthpress.com • URL: http://www.haworthpressinc.com/store/product.asp?sku=J014 • Quarterly. $240.00 per year to libraries; $50.00 per year to individuals. Includes research papers, case studies, abstracts of dissertations, book reviews, conference reviews, and Web site reviews.

***The Journal of Research Administration***. Society of Research Administrators International, 500 N Washington St., Ste. 300 Falls Church, VA 22046. Phone: (703)741-0140; Fax: (703)741-0142; Email: info@srainternational.org • URL: http://www.srainternational.org • Publishes articles dedicated to the education and the professional development of research administrators. Also serves to provide articles covering the changing research environment worldwide, and to highlight quality and innovation in research administration. Quarterly. Members, $35.00 per year; non-members, $45.00 per year. Formerly *SRA Journal*.

***Journal of System Safety***. System Safety Society, PO Box 70 Unionville, VA 22567-0070. Phone: (540)854-8630; Email: syssafe@ns.gemlink.com • URL: http://www.system-safety.org • Bimonthly. included in membership dues; $100 for nonmembers (in U.S. Canada and International). Contains technical information, industry reports, expert opinions, book reviews and conference previews. Formerly *Hazard Prevention*.

***Journal of Taxation of Global Transactions***. Wolters Kluwer Law & Business CCH, 2700 Lake Cook Rd. Riverwoods, IL 60015. Phone: 888-224-7377 or (847)267-7000; Email: cust_serv@cch.com • URL: http://www.cchgroup.com • Quarterly. $215.00 per year. Covers tax laws affecting international business activity.

***Journal of the Academy of Nutrition and Dietetics***. Academy of

Nutrition and Dietetics. Elsevier, Secondary Publishing Division, 650 Ave. of the Americas New York, NY 10011. Phone: 888-437-4636 or (212)633-3980; Fax: (212)633-3975; Email: t.reller@elsevier.com • URL: http://www.elseveier.com • Monthly. Individuals, $208.00 per year; institutions, $288.00 per year.

***Journal of the American Medical Association—Physician Service Opportunities Overseas Section***. American Medical Association, AMA Plaza, 330 N Wabash Ave. Chicago, IL 60611. Phone: 800-621-8335 or (312)464-4430; Fax: (312)464-5226; Email: amalibrary@ama-assn.org • URL: http://www.ama-assn.org • Irregular. Publication includes: List of more than 60 organizations that provide assignments overseas for physicians from the United States. Entries include: Organization name, address, phone, contact person, countries served, and medical specialties sought.

***Journal of Translational Business Institution Management***. IBIMA Publishing, 34 E Germantown Pke., No. 327 Norristown, PA 19401. Email: contact@ibimapublishing.com • URL: http://www.ibimapublishing.com • Peer-reviewed journal covering the management of transnational business institutions.

***Journal of Website Promotion: Innovations in Internet Business Research, Theory, and Practice***. The Haworth Press Inc., 10 Alice St. Binghamton, NY 13904. Phone: 800-429-6784 or (607)722-5857; Fax: (607)771-0012 or (607)722-6362; Email: getinfo@haworthpress.com • URL: http://www.haworthpressinc.com/store/product.asp?sku=J014 • Semiannual. $250.00 per year to libraries; $45.00 per year to individuals. Presents a scholarly view of such items as spam, banner ads, pop-ups, click rates, and the use of search engines for advertising.

***Journal of Workplace Behavior Health***. The Haworth Press Inc., 10 Alice St. Binghamton, NY 13904. Phone: 800-429-6784 or (607)722-5857; Fax: (607)771-0012 or (607)722-6362; Email: getinfo@haworthpress.com • URL: http://www.haworthpressinc.com/store/product.asp?sku=J014 • Quarterly. $160 Individuals print + online; $1,031 Institutions print + online; $141 Individuals online only; $152 Individuals print + online; $859 Institutions online only; $982 Institutions print + online. An academic and practical journal focusing on employee alcoholism and mental health problems. Formerly *Labor-Management Alcoholism Journal*.

***Journal Suisse d'Horlogerie et de Bijouterie Internationale***. Editions Scriptar S.A., 25 Chemin du Creux-de-Corsy CH-1093 41 La Conversion-Lausanne 1093, Switzerland. Phone: 41 21 7960096; Fax: (791)4084; Email: info@jsh.ch • URL: http://www.jsh.ch • Six times a year. $95.00. Text in English, French and German. Formery J S H- Journal Suisse d'Horlogerie e de Bijouterie Internationale.

***Journalism & Mass Communication Directory***. Association for Education in Journalism and Mass Communication, 234 Outlet Pointe Blvd., Ste. A Columbia, SC 29210-5667. Phone: (803)798-0271; Fax: (803)772-3509; Email: aejmchq@aol.com • URL: http://www.aejmc.org • Annual. Lists more than 400 schools and departments of journalism and mass communication.

***The Journalist's Road to Success***. Dow Jones & Co., PO Box 300 Princeton, NJ 08543. Phone: 800— or (609)520-4000 or (609)452-2820; Fax: (609)520-5804 or (609)520-7315; Email: djnf@dowjones.com • URL: http://www.dowjones.com • $2 per copy. Lists more than 400 colleges and universities offering journalism/mass communications; general journalism career information; section of minority scholarships and special training programs; section on fellowships for continuing education. Formerly *Journalism Career and Scholarship Guide*.

**Judge Advocates Association**. PO Box 30380 Alexandria, VA 22310-8380. • URL: http://jaa.org • Active, reserve, retired and former Judge Advocates of the Army, Navy, Air Force, Marine Corps, Coast Guard and practitioners of military and veterans law. Assists in the development of military law and an efficient military and veterans legal and judicial system.

***Judicial Staff Directory: With Biographical Information on Judges and Key Court Staff***. CQ Press, 2300 N St. NW, Ste. 800 Washington, DC 20037. Phone: 866-427-7737 or (202)729-1900; Email: customerservice@cqpress.com • URL: http://www.cqpress.com • Semiannual. $450.00. $225.00 per volume. Lists 33,500 federal court personnel, including 1,900 federal judges and their staffs, including biographies of judges and key executives. Includes maps of court jurisdictions.

***Judicial Yellow Book: Who's Who in Federal and State Courts***. Leadership Directories Inc., 104 5th Ave. New York, NY 10011-6901. Phone: (212)627-4140; Fax: (212)645-0931; Email: info@leadershipdirectories.com • URL: http://www.leadershipdirectories.com • Semiannual. $465 /year. Lists more than 3,200 judges and staffs in various federal courts and 1,200 judges and staffs in state courts. Includes biographical profiles of judges.

***Juke Boxes Wholesalers Directory***. InfoGroup Inc., 5711 S 86th Cir. Omaha, NE 68127-4146. Phone: (402)593-4500 • URL: http://www.infogroup.com • Annual. Number of listings: 1,002. Entries include: Name, address, phone, size of advertisement, name of owner or manager, number of employees, year first in "Yellow Pages." Compiled from telephone company "Yellow Pages," nationwide.

***Jumbo Rate News***. BauerFinancial Inc., 2655 LeJeune Rd. Coral Gables, FL 33134-5832. Phone: 800-388-6686 or (305)445-9500; Fax: (800)230-9569; Email: customerservice@bauerfinancial.com • URL: http://www.bauerfinancial.com • Description: Reports on high-yielding, insured Jumbo CD (Certificate of Deposit) rates nationwide. Analyzes each institution by current credit-worthiness, and lists current assets and capital ratios. Provides phone numbers, contacts, methods of computation, and information on how interest is paid. Also contains financial news, insights, and commentary of interest to Jumbo CD investors. Recurring features include editorials and news of interest.

**JumpStart Coalition for Personal Financial Literacy**. 919 18th St. NW, Ste. 300 Washington, DC 20006. Phone: 888-45-EDUCATE; Fax: (202)223-0321 • URL: http://www.jumpstartcoalition.org • Aims to improve the financial literacy of kindergarten through college-age youth. Seeks to prepare youth for life-long, successful financial decision-making. Provides advocacy, research, standards, and educational resources.

**Junior Achievement China**. Bldg. 5, Ste. 201, Unit 5, Julong Garden, 68 Xinzhongjie, Dongcheng District Beijing 100027, Hebei, China. Phone: 86 10 65515235; Fax: 86 10 65527850; Email: beijing@jachina.org • URL: http://www.jachina.org • Educates young people to value free enterprise, business and economics. Serves as a catalyst for character, creativity and leadership development of young people. Implements principle-centered, interactive business and economic education programs.

**Junior Achievement Ireland**. 8 Longford Pl., Monkstown Dublin, Dublin, Ireland. Phone: 353 1 2366644; Fax: 353 1 2803758; Email: info@jai.ie • URL: http://www.juniorachievement.ie • Aims to build a bridge between classroom and workplace. Provides young people the opportunity to participate in educational programs. Recruits persons who are qualified to teach students about business.

**Junior Achievement of Canada**. 1 Eva Rd., Ste. 218 Toronto, ON, Canada M9C 4Z5. Phone: 800-265-0699 or (416)622-4602; Fax: (416)622-6861 • URL: http://jacan.org • Works to help young Canadians discover leadership, entrepreneurial and workforce readiness skills to achieve highest potential as citizens for the global community.

**Junior Achievement Russia**. Leninsky Prospekt, 113/1 Park Pl., 3rd Fl., Ste. B-301 117 198 Moscow, Russia. Phone: 7 95 9565810; Fax: 7 95 9565246; Email: ja-russia@inbox.ru • URL: http://www.ja-russia.ru • Promotes the growth and development of business and economic educational programs for youth. Establishes partnerships between business and educational communities.

**Junior Achievement Tajikistan**. 169, Lenina St., Sughd 735700 Khujand, Tajikistan. Phone: 992 927777917; Email: ja-tajikistan@mail.ru • URL: http://www.ja-ap.org • Aims to educate and inspire young people to value free enterprise and understand the mechanisms of market economy. Facilitates innovative teaching methods of business and economics. Fosters a spirit of entrepreneurship among young people.

**Junior Achievement**. 1 Education Way Colorado Springs, CO 80906. Phone: (719)540-8000; Fax: (719)540-6299; Email: newmedia@ja.org • URL: http://www.juniorachievement.org/web/ja-usa/home • Aims to educate students in grades K-12 about entrepreneurship, work readiness, and financial literacy through experiential, hands-on programs. Helps prepare young people for the "real world" by showing them how to generate wealth and effectively manage it, how to create jobs which make their communities more robust, and how to apply entrepreneurial thinking to the workplace. Encourages students to apply lessons into action, and learn the value of contributing to their communities.

**Jute Carpet Backing Council and Burlap and Jute Association**. Dayton National Sales Office and Plant, 322 Davis Ave. Dayton, OH 45403. Phone: 800-543-3400 or (937)258-8000; Fax: (937)258-0029 • Affiliated with Burlap and Jute Association. Formerly Jute Carpet Backing Council.

***Juvenile Joys—Toys and Games of the Philippines***. Philippine-German Export Development Project Philippine Bureau of Export Trade Promotion, 6F Trade & Industry Bldg., 361 Sen. Gil Puyat Ave. Makati PH-1226, Philippines. Phone: 63 2 897 8199; Email: web@dti.dti.gov.ph • URL: http://www.dti.gov.ph • $350. Publication includes: List of almost 60 manufacturers and exporters of toys in the Philippines; also lists 25 overseas trade posts. Entries include: Company name, address, phone, telex, name and title of contact. Principal content of publication is a catalog of toys exported from the Philippines.

***Kansas City Business Journal***. American City Business Journal, 1100 Main St., Ste. 210 Kansas City, MO 64105-5123. Phone: (816)421-5900; Fax: (816)472-4010; Email: kansascity@bizjournals.com • URL: http://www.bizjournals.com/kansascity • Weekly Weekly (Fri.). $50 Individuals print and digital - 52 weeks; $4.99 Single issue PDF. Local business newspaper.

***Kansas Directory of Manufacturers and Products***. Wichita Eagle, 825 E Douglas Wichita, KS 67201-0820. Phone: 800-825-6397 or (316)268-6000 or (316)268-6344; Email: circserv@wichitaeagle.com • URL: http://www.kansas.com • Biennial. $50. Covers: Approximately 2,400 manufacturers in Kansas; includes Standard Industrial Classification (SIC) code 02, 07, 13, 14, 20, 22-39, and 49. Entries include: Company name, address, phone, telex, names and titles of key personnel, number of employees, description of products, Standard Industrial Classification (SIC) code.

***Kansas International Trade Resource Directory***. Kansas Department of Commerce - Office of Minority and Women Business Development, 1000 SW Jackson St., Ste. 100 Topeka, KS 66612-1354. Phone: (785)296-3425; Fax: (785)296-3490 • URL: http://ks-kdoc.civicplus.com/index.aspx?NID=231 • Annual. Covers: Agencies and organizations in Kansas that provide international trade information. Entries include: Agency or organization name, address, phone, telex, name and title of contact, description of services.

***Kansas Manufacturers Register***. Harris InfoSource, 2057 E Aurora Rd. Twinsburg, OH 44087-1999. Phone: 800-888-5900 or (330)425-9000 or (973)921-5500; Fax: (800)643-5997 or (877)252-3375; Email: customerservice@harrisinfo.com • URL: http://www.harrisinfo.com • Annual. $145 Individuals All-Businesses Price. Covers: Over 4,900 manufacturers in Kansas. Entries include: Company name, address, phone, fax, toll-free numbers, names and titles of key personnel, number of employees, annual sales, square feet, Standard Industrial Classification (SIC) codes, products produced, year established, foreign trade, and headquarters information.

***Kansas Manufacturing Firms in Export***. Kansas Department of Commerce - Office of Minority and Women Business Development, 1000 SW Jackson St., Ste. 100 Topeka, KS 66612-1354. Phone: (785)296-3425; Fax: (785)296-3490 • URL: http://ks-kdoc.civicplus.com/index.aspx?NID=231 • Biennial. Covers: nearly 1,000 Kansas companies in major groups 20 through 39 of the Standard Industrial Classification (SIC). Entries include: Company name, address, phone, name of principal executive, parent or subsidiary company, number of employees, products or services.

**Kansas State University - Community Health Institute**. 1 Natatorium Manhattan, KS 66506-0700. Phone: (785)532-7750; Email: dadx@ksu.edu • URL: http://www.k-state.edu/media/webzine/institute/communityhealth.html • Healthy and sustainable communities, healthy eating and physical activity, and quality of life.

***Katy Business Association—Directory***. Katy Business Association, PO Box 1399 Katy, TX 77492. Phone: (281)691-5564; Email: katybusinessassociation@yahoo.com • URL: http://www.katybusinessassociation.org • List of businesses in Katy, Texas.

***Kawana Waters Chamber of Commerce and Industry—Business Directory***. Kawana Waters Chamber of Commerce and Industry Inc., PO Box 36 Buddina, QLD 4575, Australia. Phone: 61 7 54139217; Fax: 61 7 54139299; Email: chamber@kawanabiz.com.au • URL: http://www.kawanabiz.com.au • Annual. Covers businesses in Kawana, Queensland, Australia.

***Kazakhstan Business Law Handbook***. International Business Publications, USA, PO Box 15343 Washington, DC 20003. Phone: (202)546-2103; Fax: (202)546-3275; Email: ibpusa@comcast.net • URL: http://ibpus.com • $99.95 Individuals hardcopy, E-book and CD-ROM. Covers: Basic information on business laws and legislations, export-import regulations, business climate and contacts.

***Kazakhstan Government and Business Contacts Handbook***. International Business Publications, USA, PO Box 15343 Washington, DC 20003. Phone: (202)546-2103; Fax: (202)546-3275; Email: ibpusa@comcast.net • URL: http://ibpus.com • $99.95 Individuals hardcopy, e-book, CD-ROM. Covers: Strategic government and business information, export-import activity in the country, investment, business contacts and regulations.

***Kazakhstan Health Care Directory***. Flegon Press, 37B New Cavendish St. London W1M 8JR, United Kingdom. Phone: 44 181 752 1296; Fax: 44 181 752 1296 • $100. Covers: Health care organizations, schools, provides, trade unions, and departments of health in the republic of Kazakhstan of the former Soviet Union. Entries include: Name, address, phone, fax, contact person.

***Kazakhstan Trade Directory***. Flegon Press, 37B New Cavendish St. London W1M 8JR, United Kingdom. Phone: 44 181 752 1296; Fax: 44 181 752 1296 • $200 Complete set; $150 Part I; $100 Part II. Covers: Business contacts from all industrial branches and government offices, including Agriculture, Fisheries, Health Care, Science and Tourism, in Kazakhstan, the richest republic of the former Soviet Union. Database includes: Over 1,000 trade propositions and requests for partnerships. Entries include: For contacts—name, address, phone; for producers—name, address, phone, fax, telex, directors' name, output/import needs, requests for partnership.

***Kearsarge Area Chamber of Commerce—Business Directory***. Kearsarge Area Chamber of Commerce, PO Box 301 Warner, NH 03278. • URL: http://www.kearsargechamber.org • Covers businesses in Kearsarge Area, New Hampshire.

***Kelly's Industrial Directory Book***. Reed Business Information, Quadrant House, The Quadrant Surrey SM2 5AS, United Kingdom. Phone: 44 20 86523500 or 1 6618904; Fax: 44 20 86528932; Email: webmaster@rbi.co.uk • URL: http://www.reedbusiness.com • Annual. Directory of over 94,600 U.K. industrial companies.

***Kelly's Industrial Directory—CD***. Reed Business Information, Quadrant House, The Quadrant Surrey SM2 5AS, United Kingdom. Phone: 44 20 86523500 or 1 6618904; Fax: 44 20

86528932; Email: webmaster@rbi.co.uk • URL: http://www.reedbusiness.com • Annual. Database of UK industrial companies. Database covers: 200,000 companies under 17,000 headings.

***Kelly's Post Office—London Business Directory***. Reed Business Information, Quadrant House, The Quadrant Surrey SM2 5AS, United Kingdom. Phone: 44 20 86523500 or 1 6618904; Fax: 44 20 86528932; Email: webmaster@rbi.co.uk • URL: http://www.reedbusiness.com • Covers: 96,000 London businesses, 70,000 streets with postal district name, 21,000 buildings, local and regional government offices and officials, public bodies and societies, and professional firms. Entries include: Company name, address, phone, government official name, position, title.

***Kentucky Business and Economic Outlook Newsletter***. University of Kentucky Center for Business and Economic Research, 335-BA Gatton College of Business & Economics Lexington, KY 40506-0034. Phone: (859)257-7675; Fax: (859)257-7671; Email: cber@uky.edu • URL: http://cber.uky.edu • Quarterly. Contains forecasts for the Kentucky economy as well as other business and economic issues.

***Kentucky Directory of Manufacturers***. Kentucky Cabinet for Economic Development, Old Capital Annex, 300 W Broadway Frankfort, KY 40601. Phone: 800-626-2930 or (502)564-7140 or (502)564-4886; Fax: (502)564-0023 • URL: http://www.thinkkentucky.com • Annual. $87. Covers: Approximately 5,900 manufacturing firms in Kentucky. Entries include: Company name, address, phone, names of principal executives, number of employees, products or services, date established, parent company (with name and address).

***Kenya Business Directory***. Business Guide, PO Box 27669 Dubai, United Arab Emirates. Phone: 971 4 2651719; Fax: 971 4 2692151; Email: sales@africa-business.com • URL: http://www.africa-business.com • $250 Individuals Soft copy. Covers: 48,000 business listings including wholesalers, importers, retailers, business houses, and agents in Kenya.

***Kenya Business Law Handbook***. International Business Publications, USA, PO Box 15343 Washington, DC 20003. Phone: (202)546-2103; Fax: (202)546-3275; Email: ibpusa@comcast.net • URL: http://ibpus.com • $99.95 Individuals hardcopy, e-book, CD-ROM. Covers: Information on basic business legislation, laws and climate, export-import regulations, and contacts.

***Kenya Industrial and Business Directory***. International Business Publications, USA, PO Box 15343 Washington, DC 20003. Phone: (202)546-2103; Fax: (202)546-3275; Email: ibpusa@comcast.net • URL: http://ibpus.com • Annual. $99.95 Individuals hardcopy, e-book, CD-ROM. Covers: Strategic industrial, investment and business contacts for conducting export-import and investment activity in the country. Contains strategic practical economic and business information.

**Kenya Institute of Management**. PO Box 43706 Nairobi, Kenya. Phone: 254 20 2445600 or 254 20 2445555; Email: kim@kim.ac.ke • URL: http://www.kim.ac.ke • Individuals and businesses in Kenya. Works to increase and disseminate information on the science of management; stimulates interest in effective management; formulates standards for professional conduct, experience, and training; encourages education in the principles and practices of management by establishing and promoting training courses, scholarships, and grants; conducts examinations and awards certificates and diplomas; provides facilities for research into management problems; organizes management seminars for professional training and small business creation.

**Kenya Medical Research Institute - Center for Geographic Medicine Research-Coast**. PO Box 54840-00200 Nairobi, Kenya. Phone: 254 2 2722541; Fax: 254 2 2720030; Email: director@kemri.org • URL: http://www.kemri.org/index.php/cgmr-c • Malaria and other parasitic diseases, HIV/AIDS/STI, health systems, maternal/child health, and reproductive health.

**Kenya Medical Research Institute - Center for Public Health Research**. PO Box 20752 – 00202 Nairobi, Kenya. Phone: 254 20 2725017; Fax: 254 20 2720030; Email: ykombe@kemri-nuitm.or.ke • URL: http://www.kemri.org/index.php/cphr • Health systems, applied human nutrition, child health, and population and behavioral studies.

***Kenya Telecom Industry Investment Guide***. International Business Publications, USA, PO Box 15343 Washington, DC 20003. Phone: (202)546-2103; Fax: (202)546-3275; Email: ibpusa@comcast.net • URL: http://ibpus.com • $99.95 Individuals hardcopy, e-book, CD-ROM. Covers: Kenya Telecom Industry. Entries include: Investment opportunities, regulations, and contacts.

***Key Abstracts: Advanced Materials***. Institution of Engineering and Technology, Michael Faraday House, Six Hills Way Stevenage SG1 2AY, United Kingdom. Phone: 44 1438 313311; Fax: 44 1438 765526; Email: postmaster@theiet.org • URL: http://www.theiet.org • $790 per year. Provides international coverage of journal and proceedings literature, including publications on ceramics and composite materials.

***Key Abstracts: Artificial Intelligence***. The Insititution of Engineering and Technology, 379 Thornall St. Edison, NJ 08837. Phone: 888-438-2517 or (732)321-5575; Fax: (732)321-5702; Email: inspec@inspecinc.com • URL: http://www.theiet.org/publishing/inspec • Monthly. $250.00 per year. Provides international coverage of journal and proceedings literature, including material on expert systems and knowledge engineering. Published in England by the Institution of Electrical Engineers (IEE).

***Key Abstracts: Business Automation***. Institution of Engineering and Technology, Michael Faraday House, Six Hills Way Stevenage SG1 2AY, United Kingdom. Phone: 44 1438 313311; Fax: 44 1438 765526; Email: postmaster@theiet.org • URL: http://www.theiet.org • Monthly. £662; $1,138. Provides international coverage of journal and proceedings literature.

***Key Abstracts: Computer Communications and Storage***. Institution of Engineering and Technology, Michael Faraday House, Six Hills Way Stevenage SG1 2AY, United Kingdom. Phone: 44 1438 313311; Fax: 44 1438 765526; Email: postmaster@theiet.org • URL: http://www.theiet.org • Monthly. £662; $1,138. Provides international coverage of journal and proceedings literature, including material on optical disks and networks.

***Key Abstracts: Computing in Electronics and Power***. Institution of Engineering and Technology, Michael Faraday House, Six Hills Way Stevenage SG1 2AY, United Kingdom. Phone: 44 1438 313311; Fax: 44 1438 765526; Email: postmaster@theiet.org • URL: http://www.theiet.org • Bimonthly. £662; $1,138. Provides international coverage of journal and proceedings literature.

***Key Abstracts: Electronic Circuits***. Institution of Engineering and Technology, Michael Faraday House, Six Hills Way Stevenage SG1 2AY, United Kingdom. Phone: 44 1438 313311; Fax: 44 1438 765526; Email: postmaster@theiet.org • URL: http://www.theiet.org • Monthly. £662; $1,138. Provides international coverage of journal and proceedings literature.

***Key Abstracts: Electronic Instrumentation***. The Insititution of Engineering and Technology, 379 Thornall St. Edison, NJ 08837. Phone: 888-438-2517 or (732)321-5575; Fax: (732)321-5702; Email: inspec@inspecinc.com • URL: http://www.theiet.org/publishing/inspec • Monthly. £662; $1,138. Provides international coverage of journal and proceedings literature. Published in England by the Institution of Electrical Engineers (IEE).

***Key Abstracts: Factory Automation***. Institution of Engineering and Technology, Michael Faraday House, Six Hills Way Stevenage SG1 2AY, United Kingdom. Phone: 44 1438 313311; Fax: 44 1438 765526; Email: postmaster@theiet.org • URL: http://www.theiet.org • Monthly. £662; $1,138. Provides international coverage of journal and proceedings literature, including publications on CAD/CAM, materials handling, robotics, and factory management.

***Key Abstracts: High Temperature Superconductors***. Institution of Engineering and Technology, Michael Faraday House, Six Hills Way Stevenage SG1 2AY, United Kingdom. Phone: 44 1438 313311; Fax: 44 1438 765526; Email: postmaster@theiet.org • URL: http://www.theiet.org • Monthly. £662; $1,138. Approximately 250 summaries on superconductors.

***Key Abstracts: Machine Vision***. Institution of Engineering and Technology, Michael Faraday House, Six Hills Way Stevenage SG1 2AY, United Kingdom. Phone: 44 1438 313311; Fax: 44 1438 765526; Email: postmaster@theiet.org • URL: http://www.theiet.org • Monthly. £662; $1,138. Provides international coverage of journal and proceedings literature on optical noncontact sensing.

***Key Abstracts: Microwave Technology***. Institution of Engineering and Technology, Michael Faraday House, Six Hills Way Stevenage SG1 2AY, United Kingdom. Phone: 44 1438 313311; Fax: 44 1438 765526; Email: postmaster@theiet.org • URL: http://www.theiet.org • Monthly. £662; $1,138. Provides international coverage of journal and proceedings literature.

***Key Abstracts: Optoelectronics***. Institution of Engineering and Technology, Michael Faraday House, Six Hills Way Stevenage SG1 2AY, United Kingdom. Phone: 44 1438 313311; Fax: 44 1438 765526; Email: postmaster@theiet.org • URL: http://www.theiet.org • Monthly. £662; $1,138. Provides international coverage of journal and proceedings literature relating to fiber optics, lasers, and optoelectronics in general.

***Key Abstracts: Power Systems and Applications***. Institution of Engineering and Technology, Michael Faraday House, Six Hills Way Stevenage SG1 2AY, United Kingdom. Phone: 44 1438 313311; Fax: 44 1438 765526; Email: postmaster@theiet.org • URL: http://www.theiet.org • Monthly. £662; $1,138. Provides international coverage of journal and proceedings literature, including publications on electric power apparatus and machines.

***Key Abstracts: Robotics and Control***. Institution of Engineering and Technology, Michael Faraday House, Six Hills Way Stevenage SG1 2AY, United Kingdom. Phone: 44 1438 313311; Fax: 44 1438 765526; Email: postmaster@theiet.org • URL: http://www.theiet.org • Monthly. £662; $1,138. Provides international coverage of journal and proceedings literature.

***Key Abstracts: Semiconductor Devices***. Institution of Engineering and Technology, Michael Faraday House, Six Hills Way Stevenage SG1 2AY, United Kingdom. Phone: 44 1438 313311; Fax: 44 1438 765526; Email: postmaster@theiet.org • URL: http://www.theiet.org • Monthly. £662; $1,138. Provides international coverage of journal and proceedings literature.

***Key Abstracts: Software Engineering***. Institution of Engineering and Technology, Michael Faraday House, Six Hills Way Stevenage SG1 2AY, United Kingdom. Phone: 44 1438 313311; Fax: 44 1438 765526; Email: postmaster@theiet.org • URL: http://www.theiet.org • Monthly. £662; $1,138. Provides international coverage of journal and proceedings literature.

***Key Abstracts: Telecommunications***. The Insititution of Engineering and Technology, 379 Thornall St. Edison, NJ 08837. Phone: 888-438-2517 or (732)321-5575; Fax: (732)321-5702; Email: inspec@inspecinc.com • URL: http://www.theiet.org/publishing/inspec • Monthly. £662; $1,138. Provides international coverage of journal and proceedings literature. Published in England by the Institution of Electrical Engineers (IEE).

***Key British Enterprises Financial Performance***. Dun & Bradstreet Inc., 103 JFK Pkwy. Short Hills, NJ 07078. Phone: 800-526-0651 or (973)921-5500 or (973)921-5000; Fax: (866)560-7035 or (512)794-7670; Email: info@dnb.com • URL: http://www.dnb.com • Monthly. Database covers: Approximately 50,000 of the largest companies in the United Kingdom. Database includes: Company name, address, director name, parent company, product trade name, annual and export sales, number of employees, export markets, trade description, trade awards, Companies Registration Office number, pre-tax profit, net worth, total assets, current assets, current liabilities, working capital, long-term debt, return on capital, profit margin, current ratio, profit per employee, U.S. and U.K. SIC code.

***Key Business Directory—Latin America***. Dun & Bradstreet Inc., 103 JFK Pkwy. Short Hills, NJ 07078. Phone: 800-526-0651 or (973)921-5500 or (973)921-5000; Fax: (866)560-7035 or (512)794-7670; Email: info@dnb.com • URL: http://www.dnb.com • Covers: Leading companies in Latin America whose annual sales are $10 million and who have 500 or more employees. Entries include: Company name, address, phone, fax, telex, number of employees, import/export designation, primary and secondary Standard Industrial Classification (SIC) codes, sales volume.

***Key Business Directory of Indonesia/Thailand***. Dun & Bradstreet Inc., 103 JFK Pkwy. Short Hills, NJ 07078. Phone: 800-526-0651 or (973)921-5500 or (973)921-5000; Fax: (866)560-7035 or (512)794-7670; Email: info@dnb.com • URL: http://www.dnb.com • Covers: Approximately 1,500 public and private companies in Indonesia and Thailand; Indonesian companies listed have an annual turnover of over 10 billion Rupiah and more than 50 employees; Thai companies listed have an annual turnover of over 150 Baht and more than 50 employees.

***Key Business Directory of Malaysia***. Dun & Bradstreet Inc., 103 JFK Pkwy. Short Hills, NJ 07078. Phone: 800-526-0651 or (973)921-5500 or (973)921-5000; Fax: (866)560-7035 or (512)794-7670; Email: info@dnb.com • URL: http://www.dnb.com • Covers: 1,500 public and private companies in Malaysia, each with an annual turnover of $18 million and over 50 employees.

***Key Business Directory of Singapore***. Dun & Bradstreet Inc., 103 JFK Pkwy. Short Hills, NJ 07078. Phone: 800-526-0651 or (973)921-5500 or (973)921-5000; Fax: (866)560-7035 or (512)794-7670; Email: info@dnb.com • URL: http://www.dnb.com • Covers: leading companies in Singapore. Database includes: Directory of company directors. Entries include: Company name, address, phone, fax, line of business, sales volume, industry designation, names and titles of key personnel, year established, number of employees, import/export designation, accountants and bankers.

***Keyboard: The World's Leading Music Technology Magazine***. United Entertainment Media, 460 Pk. Ave. S, 9th Fl. New York, NY 10016. Phone: (212)378-0400; Fax: (212)378-2160; Email: keyboard@uemedia.com • URL: http://www.mesquared.com/brmscn.htm • Monthly. $25.95 per year. Emphasis is on recording systems, keyboard technique, and computer-assisted music (MIDI) systems.

***Keynotes***. USA Section/International College of Dentists, c/o Carol I. Turner, Registrar, 610 Professional Dr., Ste. 201 Gaithersburg, MD 20879. Phone: (301)251-8861 or (605)583-2546; Fax: (240)499-8975; Email: office@usa-icd.org • URL: http://www.usa-icd.org • Description: Contains news of the activities and projects of the organization, which provides networking and educational opportunities for professionals in the dental field. Recurring features include a calendar of events, reports of meetings, news of educational opportunities, and a column titled the History Corner.

***Keywords***. SPSS Inc., 233 S Wacker Dr., 11th Fl. Chicago, IL 60606-6306. Phone: 800-543-2185 or (312)651-3000 or (800)543-2185; Fax: (312)651-3668 or (312)329-3668; Email: pr@spss.com • URL: http://www.spss.com • Monthly. $40 Individuals non-members. Description: Intended for users of SPSS, Inc. computer software. Offers advice and technical information on using SPSS products and carries data on new products. Recurring features include training schedules and publications ordering information.

**Kingdom Chamber of Commerce**. 383 Kings Hwy. N, Ste. 201 Cherry Hill, NJ 08034. Phone: (856)414-0818; Fax: (856)414-6140; Email: partnerservices@kingdomchamberofcommerce.org • URL: http://www.kingdomchamberofcommerce.org • Christians who own and operate their own businesses; other Christian professionals. Seeks to: identify members in the Christian community;

encourage fellowship and cooperation among members, ministries, and other organizations.

***The Kiplinger Agriculture Letter***. Kiplinger Washington Editors Inc., 1100 13th St. NW, Ste. 750 Washington, DC 20005. Phone: 800-544-0155 or (202)887-6400; Fax: (202)223-8990 or (202)331-8637; Email: sub.services@kiplinger.com • URL: http://www.kiplinger.com • Description: Publishes information on actions and proposals by the administration, U.S. Department of Agriculture, and Congress affecting all aspects of agriculture. Includes analysis and forecasts on a broad range of issues affecting the farm/food industry, government production and price support programs, commodity production and consumption data, food marketing and processing, consumer trends, taxes, farm credit, and financial matters.

***The Kiplinger Letter***. Kiplinger Washington Editors Inc., 1100 13th St. NW, Ste. 750 Washington, DC 20005. Phone: 800-544-0155 or (202)887-6400; Fax: (202)223-8990 or (202)331-8637; Email: sub.services@kiplinger.com • URL: http://www.kiplinger.com • Description: Provides information on current events and future outlook in business, economics, legislation, politics, finance, labor, and other topics of interest to business professionals.

***The Kiplinger Tax Letter***. Kiplinger Washington Editors Inc., 1100 13th St. NW, Ste. 750 Washington, DC 20005. Phone: 800-544-0155 or (202)887-6400; Fax: (202)223-8990 or (202)331-8637; Email: sub.services@kiplinger.com • URL: http://www.kiplinger.com • Description: Reports new tax regulations, changes, decisions, and pending legislation. Includes coverage of the House Ways and Means and Senate Committees, federal monetary and fiscal policy, securities, finance, and social security.

***Kiplinger's Retirement Report***. Kiplinger Washington Editors Inc., 1100 13th St. NW, Ste. 750 Washington, DC 20005. Phone: 800-544-0155 or (202)887-6400; Fax: (202)223-8990 or (202)331-8637; Email: sub.services@kiplinger.com • URL: http://www.kiplinger.com • $39.95 /year. Description: Offers information for the retired and soon-to-be-retired. Discusses such topics as money management, estate planning, health, travel and what's going on in Washington DC.

***Kitchen and Bath Business Buyers' Guide***. CMP Books, 460 Park Ave. S, 9th Fl. New York, NY 10016. Phone: 800-950-1314 or (212)615-2247; Email: kitchen@billcom.com • URL: http://www.kitchen-bath.com • Guide to kitchen and bath products, supplies and services. Formerly *Kitchen and Bath Business and Buyers' Guide/Almanac*.

***Kitchen Cabinet Manufacturers Association Income & Expense Report***. Kitchen Cabinet Manufacturers Association, 1899 Preston White Dr. Reston, VA 20191-5435. Phone: (703)264-1690; Fax: (703)620-6530 • URL: http://www.kcma.org • Annual. Covers 40 key operating ratios that measure company performance.

**Kitchen Cabinet Manufacturers Association**. 1899 Preston White Dr. Reston, VA 20191-5435. Phone: (703)264-1690; Fax: (703)620-6530 • URL: http://www.kcma.org • Serves as a national trade association representing cabinet and countertop manufacturers and suppliers to the industry. Promotes the cabinet manufacturing industry, develops standards for the industry, administers a testing and certification program, conducts education programs and meetings, provides management information and industry data, and engages in activities on behalf of members on legislative and regulatory issues.

***Kitchen Cabinets & Equipment Directory—Household***. InfoGroup Inc., 5711 S 86th Cir. Omaha, NE 68127-4146. Phone: (402)593-4500 • URL: http://www.infogroup.com • Annual. Number of listings: 17,583. Entries include: Name, address, phone, size of advertisement, name of owner or manager, number of employees, year first in "Yellow Pages." Compiled from telephone company "Yellow Pages," natyonwide.

***KMWorld Buyer's Guide***. Knowledge Asset Media Inc., 18 Bayview St. Camden, ME 04843. Phone: 800-248-0588 or (207)236-8524; Fax: (207)236-6452 • URL: http://www.kmworld.com • Semiannual. $2,395 (Basic Corporate Profile Package) One Issue — Spring 2014 Edition PLUS 6 Months Online; $4,100 (Basic Corporate Profile Package) Two Issues — Spring 2014 and Fall 2014 Editions PLUS 12 Months Online; 3,195 (Complete Corporate/Product Profile Package) One Issue — Spring 2014 Edition PLUS 6 Months Online; 5,450 (Complete Corporate/Product Profile Package) Two Issues — Spring 2014 and Fall 2014 Editions PLUS 12 Months Online. Controlled circulation as part of *KMWorld*. Contains corporate and product profiles related to various aspects of knowledge management and information systems. (Knowledge Asset Media is a an affiliate of Information Today, Inc.).

***Knowledge Ecology in Global Business: Managing Intellectual Capital***. Cengage Learning Inc., 20 Channel Center St. Boston, MA 02210. Phone: 800-487-8488 or (617)289-7700; Fax: (617)289-7844; Email: investors@cengage.com • URL: http://www.cengage.com • Published by Information Science Reference. Provides ideas on how intellectual capital through emerging technologies can support business performance. Covers topics such as competitive strategy, human resource management, and organizational learning.

***Knowledge Management Strategies for Business Development***. Cengage Learning Inc., 20 Channel Center St. Boston, MA 02210. Phone: 800-487-8488 or (617)289-7700; Fax: (617)289-7844; Email: investors@cengage.com • URL: http://www.cengage.com • Published by IGI Global. Addresses the relevance of knowledge management strategies for the advancement of organizations worldwide. Supplies business practitioners, academicians, and researchers with comprehensive tools to systematically guide through a process that focuses on data gathering, analysis, and decision making.

***Kompass***. AffarsData, News Line Group, Ynglingagatan 2 S-113 47 Stockholm, Sweden. Phone: 46 8 5175 7734 or 8 7365919; Fax: 46 8 736 5555 or 8 7231390; Email: information.se@bisnode.com • URL: http://www.ad.se • Quarterly. Database covers: Approximately 400,000 manufacturers and distributors of approximately 70,000 products and services in Sweden, Norway, Denmark, Germany, United Kingdom, Switzerland, Netherlands, Belgium, Luxemberg, France, Spain, Italy, and Finland. Database includes: Company name, address, phone, products and services, turnover, share capital, year of establishment, export areas, and managing director.

***Kompass Agribusiness, Food, and Beverage***. APN News & Media Group Ltd. APN Business Information Group, Level 9, 468 St. Kilda Rd. Melbourne, VIC 3004, Australia. Phone: 61 3 88665290; Fax: 61 3 88665299; Email: info@apnbig.com.au • URL: http://www.australianexporters.net/companyID424.htm • Annual. $85. Covers: Agricultural food and beverage companies and their products and services.

***Kompass Asia/Pacific***. Kompass International Management Corp., Rutistrasse 38 CH-8044 Zurich, Switzerland. Phone: 1 8203495; Fax: 1 8203653 • Annual. Database covers: over 260,000 Asian and Pacific companies in Japan, Korea, Hong Kong, Taiwan, China, Singapore, Malaysia, Thailand, Indonesia, Philippines, Brunei/Darussalem, India, Australia, and New Zealand. Database includes: Company name, address, phone, names and titles of key personnel, foreign trade status, number of employees, languages spoken, business descriptions, industry and product listings.

***Kompass-Benelux***. Kompass Belgium Products, Vorstlaan 100 Blvd. du Souverain B-1170 Brussels, Belgium. Phone: 32 2 3459070; Fax: 32 2 3473340; Email: info@kompass.be • URL: http://www.be.kompass.com • Database covers: 50,000 companies in the Benelux countries, which includes Belgium, the Netherlands, and Luxembourg. Entries include: Company name, address, product list, directors and management, turnover, number of employees.

***Kompass (Branchenauszuge)—Chemische Industrie***. Kompass Deutschland Verlags- und Vertriebsgesellschaft, mbH, Heinrich-von-Stephan Strasse 8b D-79100 Freiburg, Germany. Phone: 49 761 137630; Fax: 49 761 1376399; Email: mail@kompass.info.de • URL: http://www.de.kompass.com • Annual. $98. Covers: Chemical industry profiles and products in Germany for purchasers and marketers.

***Kompass Canada***. Micromedia ProQuest, 20 Victoria St. Toronto, ON, Canada M5C 2N8. Phone: 800-387-2689 or (416)362-5211; Fax: (416)362-6161; Email: info@micromedia.ca • URL: http://www.proquest.com • Irregular. $399 plus 9.95 shipping. Covers: Approximately 30,000 Canadian companies. Entries include: Company name, address, phone, fax, senior executives, statement of activities, financial information, number of employees, parent and affiliated companies, date established.

***Kompass CD-ROM Editions***. Kompass USA, Inc., 121 Whitney Ave. New Haven, CT 06510. Phone: (877)566-7277 or (203)503-6789; Fax: (203)503-6780; Email: mail@kompass-usa.com • URL: http://www.kompass.com • Semiannual or annual. Prices vary. CD-ROM versions of Kompass international trade directories are available for each of 36 major countries and nine world regions. Searching is provided for 50,000 product/service items and for many company details.

***Kompass Concord CD-ROM***. Kompass USA, Inc., 121 Whitney Ave. New Haven, CT 06510. Phone: (877)566-7277 or (203)503-6789; Fax: (203)503-6780; Email: mail@kompass-usa.com • URL: http://www.kompass.com • Provides information on more than 105,000 companies in 17 rapidly developing East European countries: Armenia, Azerbaijan, Belarus, Bulgaria, Czech Republic, Estonia, Hungary, Kazakhstan, Kyrgyzstan, Latvia, Lithuania, Moldova, Poland, Romania, Russia, Ukraine, and Uzbekistan. Classification system covers approximately 50,000 products and services.

***Kompass Croatia Direct***. Promar Ltd., Langov Trg 4 HR-10000 Zagreb, Croatia. Phone: 385 1 4893333; Fax: 385 1 4893399; Email: kompass@promar.hr • URL: http://www4.kompass.com/kinl/index.php • Annual. $100. Covers: 19,000 companies in Croatia. Entries include: Company name and address, directors and management, turnover, trade marks, employment, complete product list according to Kompass classification.

***Kompass Croatia—Register***. Promar Ltd., Langov Trg 4 HR-10000 Zagreb, Croatia. Phone: 385 1 4893333; Fax: 385 1 4893399; Email: kompass@promar.hr • URL: http://www4.kompass.com/kinl/index.php • Annual. $1,700. Covers: More than 19,000 Croatian companies with a complete product list of 58,000 products and services classified according to Kompass. Entries include: Company name and address, directors and management, turnover rate, employment.

***Kompass Deutschland: Jahrbuch der Deutschen Wirtschaft***. Kompass Deutschland Verlags- und Vertriebsgesellschaft, mbH, Heinrich-von-Stephan Strasse 8b D-79100 Freiburg, Germany. Phone: 49 761 137630; Fax: 49 761 1376399; Email: mail@kompass.info.de • URL: http://www.de.kompass.com • Annual. Covers: Major German manufacturers, distributors, and service companies linked to 40,000 products and services. Database includes: Glossary. Entries include: Company name, address, phone, telex, names and titles of key personnel, bank, key to product and service listings, year established, symbols indicating whether company is a manufacturer, wholesaler, or agent, and whether it imports and exports, turnover, number of employees, shareholders; reference to dot-chart index.

***Kompass—Diamonds***. Kompass Belgium Products, Vorstlaan 100 Blvd. du Souverain B-1170 Brussels, Belgium. Phone: 32 2 3459070; Fax: 32 2 3473340; Email: info@kompass.be • URL: http://www.be.kompass.com • Annual. Covers: All Belgian diamond cutters/merchants.

***Kompass Finance***. Kompass France, 66, Quai du Marechal Joffre FR-92415 Courbevoie, France. Phone: 33 1 43343434; Fax: 33 1 41165118 • URL: http://www.fr.kompass.com • Annual. $1,650. Database covers: Financial information for approximately 50,000 French industrial and commercial firms. Database includes: Company name, address, phone, products and services; financial data and alliances.

***Kompass International***. Kompass France, 66, Quai du Marechal Joffre FR-92415 Courbevoie, France. Phone: 33 1 43343434; Fax: 33 1 41165118 • URL: http://www.fr.kompass.com • Annual. Covers: Over 1,500,000 commercial and industrial firms worldwide; over 500,000 prominent business and industry professionals in 64 countries.

***Kompass***. Kompass Deutschland Verlags- und Vertriebsgesellschaft, mbH, Heinrich-von-Stephan Strasse 8b D-79100 Freiburg, Germany. Phone: 49 761 137630; Fax: 49 761 1376399; Email: mail@kompass.info.de • URL: http://www.de.kompass.com • Annual. $88. Covers: German products and companies specializing in coal extraction, ore mining, quarries, cement industry, glass and ceramics.

***Kompass New Zealand***. Reg Birchfield, Wellesley St. Auckland, New Zealand. Phone: 9 6308940; Fax: 9 6301046 • Annual. $350 plus GST. Covers: 12,000 organizations classified by the products and services they offer. Entries include: Company name, address, phone, fax, contact person, key personnel, directors, number of employees, turnover, paid capital, banks, date established, description of activity, products and services classification, brand names, export markets.

***Kompass Philippines***. Croner Publications Inc., 10951 Sorrento Valley Rd., Ste. 1-D San Diego, CA 92121-1613. Phone: 800-441-4033 or (858)546-1894; Fax: (800)809-0334; Email: rosa@croner.com • Annual. $225. Covers: 5,000 companies and 15,000 products in 400 categories of industry and commerce in the Philippines.

***Kompass Poland***. EUROSTART Sp. z o.o., ul. Nagorskiego 3 60-408 Poznan, Poland. Phone: 48 61475264 or 61475264; Fax: 48 61475448 or 61475448 • Semiannual. Database covers: 25,000 Polish companies. Entries include: Company name, address, name and title of contact; general manager's name; rate of turnover; employment information; details of products and services offered.

***Kompass Professionnel Chimie—Plastiques***. Kompass France, 66, Quai du Marechal Joffre FR-92415 Courbevoie, France. Phone: 33 1 43343434; Fax: 33 1 41165118 • URL: http://www.fr.kompass.com • Annual. Covers: French chemical industry companies. Entries include: Company name, activity, products, services, decision makers and their functions, key figures.

***Kompass Register United Kingdom***. Reed Business Information, Quadrant House, The Quadrant Surrey SM2 5AS, United Kingdom. Phone: 44 20 86523500 or 1 6618904; Fax: 44 20 86528932; Email: webmaster@rbi.co.uk • URL: http://www.reedbusiness.com • Annual. Covers: In 3 volumes, information on over 45,000 industrial and commercial companies in UK. Financial data. Entries include: Company name, address, phone, fax, product, trade name.

***Kompass Sweden***. Kompass Sverige AB Ett foretag inom Bonnier Affarsinformation, Luntmakargatan 34, Box 3347 103-67 Stockholm, Sweden. Phone: 46 8 41200600; Fax: 46 8 41200619; Email: info@kompass.se • URL: http://se.kompass.com • Annual. $289. Covers: 12,000 industrial and commercial firms, including wholesalers, manufacturers, importers/exporters, and distributors, in Sweden. Entries include: Company name, address, phone, line of business, product/service.

***Kontaks Philippines***. Massmark Philippines Publishers, PO Box 3333 Manila 1073, Philippines. Phone: 63 2 805 0955; Fax: 63 2 833 921 • Biennial. $950; $70. Covers: Members of Chambers of Commerce, including those in industry, manufacturing, exporting, importing, distributing, dealers, wholesalers, retailers, trade entities, banking investments, finance, real estate, housing, tourism, health industries, and consumer groups.

***KOOPERACJA***. EUROSTART Sp. z o.o., ul. Nagorskiego 3 60-408 Poznan, Poland. Phone: 48 61475264 or 61475264; Fax: 48 61475448 or 61475448 • Semiannual. Database covers: small and medium-sized businesses in Poland. Database includes: Company name, address, phone, line of business, products.

***Korea Business Directory, Database***. NIIR Project Consultancy

Services, 106 - E, Kamla Nagar New Delhi 110007, India. Phone: 91 11 23843955; Fax: 91 11 23841561; Email: npcs.india@gmail.com • URL: http://www.niir.org • Rs 2,248 Individuals CD-ROM; $100 Individuals CD-ROM. Covers: 85,000 categorized listings of Korean business companies. Entries include: Company name, phone, fax, email, website address, details of business/services provided.

**Korea Employers Federation**. KEF Bldg., 276-1 Daehung-dong Mapo-ku Seoul 121-726, South Korea. Phone: 82 2 32707310 or 82 2 32707324; Fax: 82 2 32707431 • URL: http://eng.kef.or.kr • Represents bus owners and operators. Seeks to establish and maintain a domestic political, labor, and social climate conducive to business. Represents members' interests; conducts lobbying activities; gathers and disseminates economic information.

**Republic of Korea Ministry of Health and Welfare - Korea Institute for Health and Social Affairs**. Jinhungro 235, Bulgwang-dong, Eunpyeonggu Seoul 122-705, South Korea. Phone: 82 2 3808000; Fax: 82 2 3522181; Email: master@kihasa.re.kr • URL: http://www.kihasa.re.kr/html/jsp/english/main.jsp • National health, social welfare, and population. Also provides information and guidelines for the formulation of government policy in these fields. Health Policy, Social Insurance, Social Welfare, Population and Family, and Survey and Statistics. Also provides information and guidelines for the formulation of government policy in these fields.

***Korea North Business Law Handbook***. International Business Publications, USA, PO Box 15343 Washington, DC 20003. Phone: (202)546-2103; Fax: (202)546-3275; Email: ibpusa@comcast.net • URL: http://ibpus.com • $99.95 Individuals hardcopy, e-book, CD-ROM. Covers: Information on basic business legislation, laws, business climate, and contacts.

***Korea South Business Law Handbook***. International Business Publications, USA, PO Box 15343 Washington, DC 20003. Phone: (202)546-2103; Fax: (202)546-3275; Email: ibpusa@comcast.net • URL: http://ibpus.com • $99.95 Individuals hardcopy, e-book, CD-ROM. Covers: Information on basic business legislation, laws and climate, export-import regulations, and contacts.

***Korea South Government and Business Contacts Handbook: Trade, Investment & Business Development Contacts***. International Business Publications, USA, PO Box 15343 Washington, DC 20003. Phone: (202)546-2103; Fax: (202)546-3275; Email: ibpusa@comcast.net • URL: http://ibpus.com • $99.95 Individuals hardcopy. Covers: Strategic government and business information, export-import activity in the country, investment, business contacts and regulations.

**Korean American Society of Entrepreneurs**. 2882 Sand Hill Rd., Ste. 100 Menlo Park, CA 94025. Email: ben@kase.org • URL: http://www.kase.org • Brings together entrepreneurs, engineers, corporate executives, venture capitalists, and other professionals with roots or interests in Korea. Fosters and supports network of Korean Americans interested in starting or playing key roles in companies in the United States. Facilitates the professional development, networking, and mentoring of its members. Provides information on all areas related to its members' interests.

***Korean Importers Association Directory***. Korean Importers Association, KOIMA Bldg., 76, Sapyeong-daero, Seocho-gu Seoul, South Korea. Phone: 82 2 7921581; Email: koima@koima.or.kr • URL: http://www.import.or.kr • Annual. 10,000 &won;; $12. Covers: 3,600 Korean companies. Entries include: Company name, address, phone, telex, name of official, items traded, suppliers.

**Korean Standards Association**. Korean Technology Ctr., 701-7, Yeoksam-Dong, Gangnam-Gu Seoul 135-513, South Korea. Phone: 82 2 60094513; Fax: 82 2 69194006; Email: ksaicd@ksa.or.kr • URL: http://www.ksa.or.kr/eng • Provides industrial research and survey, education and training on quality and standardization; serves as the national KS certification body; promotes globalization of local enterprises.

***Korean Trade Directory***. Korean Foreign Trade Association, 511, Yeongdong-daero, Gangnam-gu Seoul 135-729, South Korea. Phone: 82 2 15665114; Email: kitainfo@kita.net • URL: http://www.kita.org • Annual. Covers: Exporters, importers, commodities, and foreign firms established in Korea, including airline offices, marine insurance companies, shipping firms, and trade associations. Database includes: Details on trade and investment laws and regulations. Entries include: Company name, address, phone, telex, names and titles of key personnel.

**Korean Women Entrepreneurs Association**. 7F, 733-24, Yeoksam-dong, Gangnam-Gu Seoul, South Korea. Phone: 82 2 3690922; Fax: 82 2 3690950; Email: ceo@wbiz.or.kr • URL: http://www.womanbiz.or.kr • Represents Korean businesswomen and provides full-support for the growth and development of their businesses. Helps entrepreneurs gain confidence and improve their competitiveness through counseling and training. Implements government-commissioned projects.

***Kosher Directory :Directory of Kosher Products and Services***. Orthodox Union, 11 Broadway New York, NY 10004. Phone: (212)563-4000 or (202)513-6484; Fax: (212)564-9058; Email: info@ou.org • URL: http://www.ou.org • Over 10,000 consumer, institutional and industrial products and services produced under the rabbinical supervision of the Union.

***Kovels' on Antiques and Collectibles: The Newsletter for Dealers, Collectors, and Investors***. Antiques Inc., 49 Richmondville Ave. Westport, CT 06880. Phone: 800-829-9158 or (216)752-2252 • URL: http://www.kovel.com • Monthly. $27 Individuals; $49 Two years.

***Kraks Industrial and Commercial Directory of Denmark***. Kraks Forlag A.S., Virumgaardsvej 21 DK-2830 Virum, Denmark. Phone: 45 45956500 or 45 4595 6500; Fax: 45 45956565 or 45 4595 6565; Email: krak@krak.dk • URL: http://www.krak.dk/ • Annual. $2,765. Covers: 73,400 industrial and commercial firms in Denmark; 94,000 companies in the Register of Limited Liability Companies, the Insurance Register, and Trade Register in Denmark; public authorities, institutions, libraries, churches, hospitals, museums, schools, universities, and societies in Denmark. Entries include: Organization name, address, phone, product/service (where applicable).

**Kurata Thermodynamics Laboratory**. University of Kansas, Dept. of Chemical and Petroleum Engineering, 2330 Crowell Dr. Lawrence, KS 66047. Phone: (785)864-4965 • URL: http://www2.ku.edu/build/cgi-bin/kurata-thermodynamics-laboratories • Investigates the behavior of various materials over a wide range of temperatures.

***Kuwait Business Guides Series III: Contacts for Kuwaiti Contracting***. International Executive Reports, 717 D St. NW, Ste. 300 Washington, DC 20004-2807. Phone: (202)628-6900; Fax: (202)628-6618 • $145 payment must accompany order. Covers: contact names and addresses at the Kuwaiti Task Force; U.S. Army Corps of Engineers, Kuwaiti ministries, local merchants, government offices, banks and financial institutions; local offices of foreign companies and the Kuwait Petroleum Corporation.

***Kuwait Business Law Handbook***. International Business Publications, USA, PO Box 15343 Washington, DC 20003. Phone: (202)546-2103; Fax: (202)546-3275; Email: ibpusa@comcast.net • URL: http://ibpus.com • $99.95 Individuals hardcopy, e-book, CD-ROM. Covers: Information on basic business legislation, laws, business climate, export-import regulations, and contacts.

***Kuwait Golden Key Directory***. International Institute of Trade Relation Promotion, Trade Information Centre of Iran, No. 7, 3rd Fl., Abbasie Bazar, Ferdowsi Sq. Tehran, Iran. Phone: 98 21 88833900; Fax: 98 21 88820697; Email: order@irangoldenkey.com • URL: http://www.goldenkeydirectory.com/about.html • £100 Individuals. Covers: 22,064 companies in Kuwait. Entries include: Company name, address, telephone, fax, e-mail, products, services, Managing Director, and business activities.

***Kwazulu/Natal Business Register***. Intratex Holdings, 12 Caversham Rd. Pinetown 3610, South Africa. Phone: 27 31 7174000; Fax: (717)4001; Email: webmaster@brabys.com • Covers: businesses in the Kwazulu/Natal area. Entries include: Company name, address, phone.

***Kyle Area Chamber of Commerce Business Directory and Guidebook***. Kyle Area Chamber of Commerce and Visitors' Bureau, 401 Center St. Kyle, TX 78640-0900. Phone: (512)268-4220; Email: info@kylechamber.org • URL: http://www.kylechamber.org • Biennial. Covers businesses in the city of Kyle.

***Kyrgyzstan Business Law Handbook***. International Business Publications, USA, PO Box 15343 Washington, DC 20003. Phone: (202)546-2103; Fax: (202)546-3275; Email: ibpusa@comcast.net • URL: http://ibpus.com • $99.95 Individuals hardcopy, e-book, CD-ROM. Covers: Business climate and legislation, laws, export-import regulations affecting business and contacts.

***Kyrgyzstan Government and Business Contacts Handbook***. International Business Publications, USA, PO Box 15343 Washington, DC 20003. Phone: (202)546-2103; Fax: (202)546-3275; Email: ibpusa@comcast.net • URL: http://ibpus.com • $99.95 Individuals hardcopy, e-book, CD-ROM. Covers: Strategic government and business information, export-import activity in the country, investment, business contacts and regulations.

***Kyrgyzstan Industrial and Business Directory***. International Business Publications, USA, PO Box 15343 Washington, DC 20003. Phone: (202)546-2103; Fax: (202)546-3275; Email: ibpusa@comcast.net • URL: http://ibpus.com • Annual. $99.95 Individuals hardcopy, e-book, CD-ROM. Covers: Strategic industrial, investment and business contacts for conducting export-import and investment activity in the country.

***L D A: Lighting Equipment Accessories Directory***. Illuminating Engineering Society of North America, 120 Wall St., 17th Fl. New York, NY 10005-4001. Phone: (212)248-5000; Fax: (212)248-5017 or (212)248-5018; Email: ies@ies.org • URL: http://www.iesna.org • Annual. $48 U.S. /year; $72 Other countries /year; Included in membership. Lists over 800 manufacturers of lighting fixtures, controls, components, mounting devices, maintenance equipment, etc.

***Labels Directory***. InfoGroup Inc., 5711 S 86th Cir. Omaha, NE 68127-4146. Phone: (402)593-4500 • URL: http://www.infogroup.com • Updated continuously; printed on request. Number of listings: 1,730. Entries include: Name, address, phone, size of advertisement, name of owner or manager, number of employees, year first in "Yellow Pages." Compiled from telephone company "Yellow Pages," nationwide.

***Labels—Paper Directory***. InfoGroup Inc., 5711 S 86th Cir. Omaha, NE 68127-4146. Phone: (402)593-4500 • URL: http://www.infogroup.com • Annual. Number of listings: 1,366. Entries include: Name, address, phone, size of advertisement, name of owner or manager, number of employees, year first in "Yellow Pages." Compiled from telephone company "Yellow Pages," nationwide.

***Labor Arbitration Awards***. Wolters Kluwer Law & Business CCH, 2700 Lake Cook Rd. Riverwoods, IL 60015. Phone: 888-224-7377 or (847)267-7000; Email: cust_serv@cch.com • URL: http://www.cchgroup.com • Weekly. $1,239.00 per year. Looseleaf service.

***Labor Rates for the Construction Industry***. RSMeans, 700 Longwater Dr. Norwell, MA 02061. Phone: 800-334-3509; Fax: (800)632-6732 • URL: http://www.rsmeans.reedconstructiondata.com • Annual. $424.95 Individuals.

***Labor Relations Bulletin***. Aspen Publishers Inc., 125 Eugene O'Neill Dr., Ste. 103 New London, CT 06320. Phone: 800-876-9105 or (860)442-4365; Fax: (860)437-3150; Email: customer.service@aspenpubl.com • URL: http://www.aspenpublishers.com • Description: Provides information and insight to management and labor officials to help them avoid or resolve conflicts. Recurring features include reports on current developments in labor law and relations, discipline and grievance cases based on actual arbitration, a question and answer column on labor and employment relations, and a column titled Reflections of an Arbitrator, offering the insight and experience of prominent national arbitrators.

***Labor Relations Reporter***. Bloomberg BNA, 3 Bethesda Metro Center, Ste. 250 Bethesda, MD 20814-5377. Phone: 800-372-1033 or (703)341-3000; Fax: (800)253-0332; Email: customercare@bna.com • URL: http://www.bna.com • Weekly. $4,998.00 per year. Looseleaf service.

***Labor Relations***. Wolters Kluwer Law & Business CCH, 2700 Lake Cook Rd. Riverwoods, IL 60015. Phone: 888-224-7377 or (847)267-7000; Email: cust_serv@cch.com • URL: http://www.cchgroup.com • $2,589.00 per year. Seven looseleaf volumes. Weekly updates. Covers labor relations, wages and hours, state labor laws, and employment practices. Supplement available, *Labor Law Reports*. Summary Newsletter.

**Laboratory of Electronics**. Rockefeller University, 1230 York Ave. New York, NY 10065. Phone: (212)327-8000; Fax: (212)327-7613; Email: ros@rockvax.rockefeller.edu • URL: http://www.rockefeller.edu • Studies the application of computer engineering and electronics to biomedicine.

***Labuan Offshore Investment & Business Guide***. International Business Publications, USA, PO Box 15343 Washington, DC 20003. Phone: (202)546-2103; Fax: (202)546-3275; Email: ibpusa@comcast.net • URL: http://ibpus.com • $99.95 Individuals hardcopy, e-book, CD-ROM. Covers: Basic information on economy, export-import and investment climate, regulations and industrial development, banking, and government. Entries include: Important business contacts and business travel.

***Lacrosse Equipment & Suppliers Directory***. InfoGroup Inc., 5711 S 86th Cir. Omaha, NE 68127-4146. Phone: (402)593-4500 • URL: http://www.infogroup.com • Annual. Number of listings: 22,706. Entries include: Name, address, phone, size of advertisement, name of owner or manager, number of employees, year first in "Yellow Pages." Compiled from telephone company "Yellow Pages," nationwide.

**Ladies Professional Golf Association**. 100 International Golf Dr. Daytona Beach, FL 32124-1092. Phone: (386)274-6200; Fax: (386)274-1099; Email: feedback@lpga.com • URL: http://www.lpga.com • Represents and promotes women golfers, teachers and competitors. Compiles statistics on tournaments, money winnings, and scoring.

***Lafayette Business Digest***. Kapp Crowell Communications, Box 587 Lafayette, IN 47902. Phone: (765)471-1518; Fax: (765)471-4789; Email: lbd@lbd.lafayette.in.us • Weekly. $43.50 Individuals. Newspaper covering local business.

**Lahore University of Management Sciences - Center for Management and Economic Research**. Scholarship of Arts & Sciences, Department of Economics Lahore 54792, Pakistan. Phone: 92 42 5722670; Fax: 92 42 5722591; Email: burki@lums.edu.pk • URL: http://www.lums.edu.pk/ • Management and economic issues facing Pakistan and the region.

***Land Use and Environment Law Review***. Thomson West, 610 Opperman Dr. Eagan, MN 55123. Phone: 800-328-9352 or (651)687-7000 • Annual. $1,392. Features property rights and economic allocation of natural resources.

***Land Use Law Report***. Business Publishers Inc., 2222 Sedwick Dr. Durham, NC 27713. Phone: 800-223-8720 or (301)587-6300; Fax: (800)508-2592 or (301)587-4530; Email: custserv@bpinews.com • URL: http://www.bpinews.com • Monthly. $297 Individuals online; $397 Individuals print and online. Description: Provides up-to-date information on court decisions, legislation, and regulations that impact today's most pressing land-use policy, planning, and legal issues. Readers receive in-depth coverage on zoning and planning policies, regulatory takings, undesirable land uses, environmental legislation, and much more. **Remarks:** Also available via e-mail.

***Landscape Maintenance News***. Landscape Information Services, 6401 Yellowstone Casper, WY 82602. Phone: (307)265-7801 • Description: Provides landscape service companies with information to help them manage their services; covers changes and events in the industry. Covers image, customer service, advertising and marketing, estimating, mowing, poweraking, fertilization, weed control, maintenance, and miscellaneous services. Discusses trade shows, products and services, associations, and franchise opportunities. Recurring features include news of research, news of educational opportunities, book reviews, and notices of publications available.

***Laos Business Law Handbook***. International Business Publications, USA, PO Box 15343 Washington, DC 20003. Phone: (202)546-2103; Fax: (202)546-3275; Email: ibpusa@comcast.net • URL: http://ibpus.com • $99.95 Individuals hardcopy, e-book, CD-ROM. Covers: Information on basic business legislation, laws and climate, export-import regulations, and contacts.

***LaPorte Business Resource Guide***. Greater La Porte Chamber of Commerce, 803 Washington St. La Porte, IN 46352-0486. Phone: (219)362-3178; Fax: (219)324-7349; Email: info@lpchamber.com • URL: http://www.lpchamber.com • Annual. Covers businesses, professional firms, and individuals in La Porte, IN.

***Laptop Magazine***. Bedford Communications Inc., 1410 Broadway, 21st Fl. New York, NY 10018. Phone: (212)807-8220 or (212)703-5800; Fax: (212)807-1098 or (212)703-5801; Email: webeditor@bedfordmags.com • URL: http://www.bedfordcommunications.com • Monthly. Consumer magazine containing articles and product reviews for notebook/laptop computers, handheld computers, tablet devices, cell phones, digital cameras, and other consumer electronic products.

***Laptop: Mobile Solutions for Business & Life***. Bedford Communications Inc., 1410 Broadway, 21st Fl. New York, NY 10018. Phone: (212)807-8220 or (212)703-5800; Fax: (212)807-1098 or (212)703-5801; Email: webeditor@bedfordmags.com • URL: http://www.bedfordcommunications.com • Magazine covering the innovation of advance technology.

***Large Employers of Metro St. Louis***. St. Louis Regional Chamber & Growth Association, 1 Metropolitan Sq., Ste. 1300 Saint Louis, MO 63102. Phone: (314)321-5555 or (314)231-5555; Fax: (314)206-3222 or (314)206-3244; Email: inforcga@stlrcga.org • URL: http://www.stlrcga.org • Biennial. $50. Covers: 700 business firms employing 200 persons or more in the City of St. Louis, six Missouri counties (Franklin, Jefferson, Lincoln, St. Charles, St. Louis, and Warren), and five Illinois counties (Clinton, Jersey, Madison, Monroe, and St. Clair); includes companies that are not members of the association. Entries include: Company name, address, phone, fax, names of principal executives, Standard Industrial Classification (SIC) code, type of business, year established, number of employees, product or service.

***Large Equipment Sales Report***. Dental Trade Alliance, 4350 N Fairfax Dr., Ste. 220 Arlington, VA 22203-1673. Phone: (703)379-7755; Fax: (703)931-9429 • URL: http://www.dentaltradealliance.org • Monthly Quarterly. $7,680 Individuals Monthly; $6,000 Individuals Quarterly. Monthly and quarterly reports and heavy equipment sales.

***The Largest Companies in Norway***. Okonomisk literatur Norge A.S., Langkai 1, Havnelageret N-0104 Oslo, Norway. Phone: 47 22474900; Fax: 47 22474901; Email: post@ekolit.no • Annual. $1,300. Covers: 10,000 of the largest industrial companies, trading companies, banks, shipping companies, insurance companies, hotels, restaurants, travel agencies, advertising agencies, insurance companies, and consultant companies in Norway. Entries include: Company name, address, phone, telex number.

***Largest Employers Directory***. Greater San Antonio Chamber of Commerce, 602 E Commerce St. San Antonio, TX 78205. Phone: (210)229-2100 or (210)229-2128; Fax: (210)229-1600; Email: infostore@sachamber.org • URL: http://sachamber.org • Annual. $75 Nonmembers CD/email; $20 Members CD/email; $75 Nonmembers by category, CD/email (MS Excel file); $20 Members by category, CD/email (MS Excel file); $75 Nonmembers PDF of Avery 5160 Labels; $20 Members PDF of Avery 5160 Labels. Covers: About 1,700 manufacturing and nonmanufacturing firms in the San Antonio metropolitan statistical area; manufacturing firms each have at least 25 employees, nonmanufacturing firms have at least 50 employees. Entries include: Company name, address, phone; names and titles of key personnel, number of employees, year established, description of service, marketing area, and Standard Industrial Classification (SIC) code.

***Las Colinas Business News***. Dallas-Fort Worth Suburban Newspapers Inc., 508 Young St. Dallas, TX 75202. Fax: (214)977-7047 • URL: http://www.subscribe.dallasnews.com • Weekly (Wed.). Community newspaper.

***Las Vegas Chamber of Commerce—Business Directory***. Las Vegas Metro Chamber of Commerce, 8363 W Sunset Rd., Ste. 250 Las Vegas, NV 89119. Phone: (702)641-5822 or (702)735-1616; Fax: (702)735-0406 • URL: http://www.lvchamber.com • Covers: Businesses in Las Vegas, Nevada, who are chamber members. Entries include: Company name, address, phone, contact name.

***Las Vegas Christian Business Directory***. Red Letter Publishing, PO Box 272682 Fort Collins, CO 80527. Phone: 800-445-5614; Fax: (970)267-9669; Email: info@redletter.com • URL: http://www.christianbusinessdirectoryonline.com • Businesses, churches, organizations, and schools in Las Vegas, Nevada.

***LaSalle Bank Guide: Major Publicly Held Corporations and Financial Institutions Headquartered in Illinois***. Scholl Corporate Guides, PO Box 560 Deerfield, IL 60015. Phone: (847)945-1891; Fax: (847)945-1897; Email: info@schollcorporateguides.com • URL: http://www.schollcorporateguides.com • Annual. $29.95 Single issue. Covers: Approximately 232 major publicly held corporations and financial institutions headquartered in Illinois. Database includes: List of companies ranked by revenue and assets; (NAICS) code listings; list of changes from previous edition. Entries include: Company name, headquarters location and phone, brief description of product lines and organizational structure, names of outside directors, names and titles of key personnel; consolidated balance sheet in abbreviated form, consolidated income statement; number of employees, date of annual meeting, stockholder information.

**Laser Institute of America**. 13501 Ingenuity Dr., Ste. 128 Orlando, FL 32826. Phone: 800-345-2737 or (407)380-1553; Fax: (407)380-5588 • URL: http://www.lia.org • Formerly Laser Industry Association.

***The Last Word***. American Consulting Engineers Council, 1015 15th St. NW, 8th Fl. Washington, DC 20005-2605. Phone: (202)347-7474; Fax: (202)898-0068; Email: acec@acec.org • URL: http://www.acec.org • Description: Contains summaries of Council activities and legislative actions of interest to consulting engineers.

***Latin America and Caribbean Autos Directory***. Business Monitor International Ltd., Senator House, 85 Queen Victoria St. London EC4V 4AB, United Kingdom. Phone: 44 20 72480468; Fax: 44 20 72480467; Email: enquiry@businessmonitor.com • URL: http://www.businessmonitor.com • $975 Individuals CD; €780 Individuals CD. Covers: 1,145 top autos executives on 374 leading automotive companies from Argentina, Brazil, Chile, Colombia, Mexico, Peru, Venezuela, Anguilla, Antigua & Barbuda, Aruba, the Bahamas, Barbados, Bermuda, British Virgin Islands, Cayman Islands, Cuba, Dominica, Dominican Rep, French Guiana, Grenada, Guadeloupe, Guyana, Haiti, Jamaica, Martinique, Montserrat, Netherland Antilles, Puerto Rico, St Kitts, St Lucia, St Vincent, Suriname, Trinidad & Tobago, Turks & Caicos and US Virgin Islands. Entries include: parent company head offices, full company name, address, phone and fax numbers, email and website address, senior contact personnel, company description and profile, nationality, and ownership status.

***Latin America and Caribbean Food and Drink Directory***. Business Monitor International Ltd., Senator House, 85 Queen Victoria St. London EC4V 4AB, United Kingdom. Phone: 44 20 72480468; Fax: 44 20 72480467; Email: enquiry@businessmonitor.com • URL: http://www.businessmonitor.com • $975 Individuals CD; €780 Individuals CD. Covers: 1,642 top food and drink executives on 550 leading food and drink companies from Latin America and Caribbean. Entries include: parent company head offices, full company name, address, phone and fax numbers, email and website address, senior contact personnel, company description and profile, nationality, and ownership status.

***Latin America & Caribbean Oil and Gas Directory***. Business Monitor International Ltd., Senator House, 85 Queen Victoria St. London EC4V 4AB, United Kingdom. Phone: 44 20 72480468; Fax: 44 20 72480467; Email: enquiry@businessmonitor.com • URL: http://www.businessmonitor.com • $995 Individuals CD; €780 Individuals CD. Covers: 828 top oil and gas executives on 309 leading oil and gas companies from Latin America. Entries include: parent company head offices, full company name, address, phone and fax numbers, email and website address, senior contact personnel, company description and profile, nationality, and ownership status.

***Latin America and Caribbean Pharmaceuticals and Healthcare Directory***. Business Monitor International Ltd., Senator House, 85 Queen Victoria St. London EC4V 4AB, United Kingdom. Phone: 44 20 72480468; Fax: 44 20 72480467; Email: enquiry@businessmonitor.com • URL: http://www.businessmonitor.com • $995 Individuals CD; €780 Individuals CD. Covers: 1,908 top pharmaceutical executives at 598 leading pharmaceutical companies from Argentina, Brazil, Chile, Colombia, Mexico, Peru, Venezuela and the Caribbean. Entries include: parent company head offices, full company name, address, phone and fax numbers, email and website address, senior contact personnel, company description and profile, nationality, and ownership status.

***Latin America and Caribbean Telecommunications Directory***. Business Monitor International Ltd., Senator House, 85 Queen Victoria St. London EC4V 4AB, United Kingdom. Phone: 44 20 72480468; Fax: 44 20 72480467; Email: enquiry@businessmonitor.com • URL: http://www.businessmonitor.com • $995 Individuals CD; €780 Individuals CD. Covers: 2,506 top telecommunications executives at 808 leading telecommunications companies from Latin America and Caribbean. Entries include: parent company head offices, full company name, address, phone and fax numbers, email and website address, senior contact personnel, company description and profile, nationality, and ownership status.

**Latin America Trade Coalition**. 1615 H St. NW Washington, DC 20062. Phone: (202)463-5485; Fax: (202)463-3126; Email: americas@uschamber.com • URL: http://www.uschamber.com • Represents U.S. companies, farmers and business organizations. Aims to secure congressional approval of the U.S.-Colombia Trade Promotion Agreement and the U.S.-Panama Trade Promotion Agreement.

**Latin American and Caribbean Center-Intercultural Dance and Music Institute**. Florida International University, 11200 SW 8th St. Miami, FL 33199. Phone: (305)348-2894; Fax: (305)348-3593; Email: lacc@fiu.edu • URL: http://www.lacc.fiu.edu • Research fields include economic development and trade.

***Latin American Environmental Directory***. Business Publishers Inc., PO Box 17592 Baltimore, MD 21297-1592. Phone: 800-223-8720; Fax: (800)508-2592; Email: custserv@bpinews.com • URL: http://www.bpinews.com • Annual. $179. Covers: Associations, corporations, embassies, consulates, legal specialists, U.S. registered foreign agents, and research centers located in Latin America involved in the environmental community. Entries include: Organization name, address, phone, fax, telex, key officers, SIC codes.

***Latin American Import-Export Directory***. International Trade Council, PO Box 73 San Jose 1007, Costa Rica. • Annual. Covers: 24,500 importing and exporting companies in Argentina, Bolivia, Brazil, Chile, Panama, Paraguay, Peru, Uruguay, Venezuela, Colombia, Costa Rica, Ecuador, El Salvador, Guatemala, Honduras, Mexico, Nicaragua, and the Dominican Republic; lists top companies in Latin American markets.

***Latin American Law and Business Report***. Prentice Hall Press, 240 Frisch Ct. Paramus, NJ 07652. Phone: (212)366-2000 • URL: http://www.us.penguingroup.com • Monthly. $345 Individuals. Journal covering current business and legal developments and practices in Latin America.

***Latin American Markets: A Guide to Company and Information Sources***. MarketResearch.com, 11200 Rockville Pke., Ste. 504 Rockville, MD 20852. Phone: 800-298-5699 or (240)747-3093; Fax: (240)747-3004; Email: customerservice@marketresearch.com • URL: http://www.marketresearch.com • Irregular. $335. Covers: sources of information on businesses in Central America, South America, and the Caribbean. Entries include: Source name, address, phone, fax, names and titles of key personnel.

***Latin American Product Guide***. Todd Publications, PO Box 500 Millwood, NY 10546. Phone: 866-896-0916 or (914)373-4750; Fax: (914)373-4750; Email: toddpub@aol.com • URL: http://www.toddpublications.com • $125. Covers: Over 10,000 exporters from 18 Latin American countries.

**Latin American Venture Capital Association**. 589 8th Ave., 18th Fl. New York, NY 10018. Phone: (646)315-6735; Fax: (646)349-1047; Email: info@lavca.org • URL: http://www.lavca.org • Promotes the growth of the private equity and venture capital industry in Latin America and the Caribbean. Advocates on behalf of the industry by disseminating information to the media, promoting the region to investors and supporting efforts to improve the regulatory framework. Conducts research on industry trends, performance and policy environment. Develops model documents, industry guides and standards.

***Latin Business Association Business Journal***. Latin Business Association, 120 S San Pedro St., Ste. 530 Los Angeles, CA 90012. Phone: (213)628-8510; Fax: (213)628-8519 • URL: http://www.lbausa.com • Weekly. $129.95 Individuals 52 issues; $219.95 Two years 104 issues. Journal providing comprehensive data and statistics on top-ranked Los Angeles companies across all industries.

***Latin Business Association Business Newsletter***. Latin Business Association, 120 S San Pedro St., Ste. 530 Los Angeles, CA 90012. Phone: (213)628-8510; Fax: (213)628-8519 • URL: http://www.lbausa.com • Monthly.

**Latin Business Association**. 120 S San Pedro St., Ste. 530 Los Angeles, CA 90012. Phone: (213)628-8510; Fax: (213)628-8519 • URL: http://www.lbausa.com • Latino business owners and corporations. Assists Latino business owners to develop their businesses.

***Latin Fund Management***. SourceMedia Inc., 1 State Street Plz., 27th Fl. New York, NY 10004. Phone: 800-221-1809 or (212)803-8200 or (212)803-8333; Fax: (212)843-9635 or (212)292-5216; Email: custserv@sourcemedia.com • URL: http://www.sourcemedia.com • Monthly. $495.00 per year. Newsletter (also available online at www.latinfund.net). Provides news and analysis of Latin American mutual funds, pension funds, and annuities.

***Latino-Hispanic Historical Collection***. EBSCO Publishing Inc., 10 Estes St. Ipswich, MA 01938-2106. Phone: 800-653-2726 or (978)356-6500; Fax: (978)356-6565; Email: information@ebscohost.com • URL: http://www.ebscohost.com • 60,000 historical articles, complete texts, political and religious pamphlets. Available in two series.

***Latvia Business Services Providers Leads***. Business Information Agency Inc. PlanetInform, 52 Tuscan Way, Ste. 202-181 Saint Augustine, VA 32092. Phone: (904)342-6124; Fax: (904)592-2632; Email: info@biasales.com • URL: http://www.biasales.com • Monthly. $67 Individuals mailing list; $142 Individuals sales list; $240 Individuals marketing list. Covers Latvian companies and all sub-industries that provide various services to commercial businesses, establishments, and organizations, including consulting, advertising and marketing services, and facilities maintenance.

***Latvia Industrial and Business Directory***. International Business Publications, USA, PO Box 15343 Washington, DC 20003.

Phone: (202)546-2103; Fax: (202)546-3275; Email: ibpusa@comcast.net • URL: http://ibpus.com • Annual. $99.95 Individuals hardcopy, e-book, CD-ROM. Covers: Strategic industrial, investment and business contacts for conducting export-import and investment activity in the country.

***Latvia Investment and Business Guide***. International Business Publications, USA, PO Box 15343 Washington, DC 20003. Phone: (202)546-2103; Fax: (202)546-3275; Email: ibpusa@comcast.net • URL: http://ibpus.com • $99.95 Individuals hardcopy, e-book, CD-ROM. Covers: Basic information on economy, export-import and investment climate, regulations and industrial development, banking, and government. Entries include: Business contacts and business travel.

**Latvian Venture Capital and Private Equity Association**. Skolas St. 25-1 LV-1010 Riga, Latvia. Phone: 371 6 29477979 or 371 6 29265627; Email: info@lvca.lv • URL: http://www.lvca.lv • Promotes the development of the venture capital sector in Latvia. Informs businessmen and the society about venture capital financing possibilities. Promotes the exchange of information among members.

***LAW and ORDER Magazine***. Hendon Publishing Co., 130 Waukegan Rd. Deerfield, IL 60015-5652. Phone: 800-843-9764 or (847)444-3300; Fax: (847)444-3333; Email: info@hendonpub.com • URL: http://www.hendonpub.com • Lists manufacturers, dealers, and distributors of equipment and services for police departments.

***Law Enforcement Technology Directory***. Cygnus Business Media Inc., 1233 Janesville Ave. Fort Atkinson, WI 53538. Phone: 800-547-7377; Email: info@cygnus.com • URL: http://www.cygnus.com • Annual. $60.00 per year. $6.00 per issue; a directory of products, equipment, services, and technology for police professionals. Includes weapons, uniforms, communications equipment, and software.

***Law Firm Inc.*** ALM Media Properties LLC, 120 Broadway, 5th Fl. New York, NY 10271-1100. Phone: (212)457-9400; Fax: (646)417-7705; Email: customercare@alm.com • URL: http://www.alm.com • Quarterly. $49.95 per year. Covers human resources, insurance, financing, marketing, compensation, recruitment, etc., as related to law firm management.

***Law Firm Partnership and Benefits Report***. ALM Media Properties LLC, 120 Broadway, 5th Fl. New York, NY 10271-1100. Phone: (212)457-9400; Fax: (646)417-7705; Email: customercare@alm.com • URL: http://www.alm.com • Monthly. $499 per year. Covers personnel issues for law firms, including compensation, partnership agreements, malpractice, employment discrimination, training, health insurance, pension plans, and other matters relating to human resources management. (A Law Journal Newsletter, formerly published by Leader Publications).

***Law Firms Yellow Book: Who's Who in the Management of the Leading U. S. Law Firms***. Leadership Directories Inc., 104 5th Ave. New York, NY 10011-6901. Phone: (212)627-4140; Fax: (212)645-0931; Email: info@leadershipdirectories.com • URL: http://www.leadershipdirectories.com • Semiannual. $465. Provides detailed information on more than 700 major U. S. law firms. Includes domestic offices, foreign offices, subsidiaries, and affiliates. There are seven indexes: geographic, subject specialty, management, administrative, law school attended, personnel, and law firm.

***The Law of Distressed Real Estate: Foreclosure, Workouts, and Procedures***. Thomson West, 610 Opperman Dr. Eagan, MN 55123. Phone: 800-328-9352 or (651)687-7000 • $1,934.25 full set; $161 monthly. Five looseleaf volumes. Periodic supplementation. (Real Property LawSeries).

***The Law of Juries***. Nancy Gertner and Judith Mizner. Glasser LegalWorks, 150 Clove Rd. Little Falls, NJ 07424. Phone: 800-308-1700 or (973)890-0008; Fax: (973)890-0042; Email: legalwks@aol.com • URL: http://www.glasserlegalworks.com • Looseleaf. $124.00. Periodic supplementation. Topics include voir dire & juror selection, peremptory challenges, trial location (venue), jury structure, jury deliberation, and jury conduct or misconduct.

***The Law of Liability Insurance***. Matthew Bender and Company Inc., 1275 Broadway Albany, NY 12204-2638. Phone: 800-424-4200 or (518)487-3000; Fax: (518)487-3573 or (800)424-4200; Email: customer.support@lexisnexis.com • URL: http://www.matthewbender.com • $395. Five looseleaf volumes. Periodic supplementation. Explains the terms and phases essential for a general understanding of liability insurance, and discusses injuries to both persons and property.

***Law of Professional and Amateur Sports***. Thomson West, 610 Opperman Dr. Eagan, MN 55123. Phone: 800-328-9352 or (651)687-7000 • Annual. $624 full set; $66 monthly. Covers agent-player agreements, collective bargaining, negotiation of player contracts, taxation, and other topics.

***Law of the Sea: A Select Bibliography***. United Nations Publications, c/o National Book Network, 15200 NBN Way Blue Ridge Summit, PA 17214. Phone: 888-254-4286 or (212)963-7680 or (212)963-8302; Fax: (800)338-4550; Email: unpublications@nbnbooks.com • URL: http://www.unp.un.org • Annual. $17.00. Includes 23 subject categories.

***Law of the Sea Bulletin***. United Nations Publications, c/o National Book Network, 15200 NBN Way Blue Ridge Summit, PA 17214. Phone: 888-254-4286 or (212)963-7680 or (212)963-8302; Fax: (800)338-4550; Email: unpublications@nbnbooks.com • URL: http://www.unp.un.org • Three times per year.

***Law Technology News: Products, Systems, and Services for Legal Professionals***. ALM Media Properties LLC, 120 Broadway, 5th Fl. New York, NY 10271-1100. Phone: (212)457-9400; Fax: (646)417-7705; Email: customercare@alm.com • URL: http://www.alm.com • Monthly. 115 Dh. Features descriptions of new technology products and services of interest to the legal profession.

***Law.com: First in Legal News and Information***. ALM Media Properties Inc., Phone: 800-888-8300 or (212)779-9200; Fax: (212)481-8110 • URL: http://www.law.com • Web site provides free, law-related, current news (National News Sites and Regional News Sites). Free searching of martindale.com lawyer locator is offered, including lawyer ratings. Fee-based premium services for the legal profession are also available.

**Lawn Institute**. 2 E Main St. East Dundee, IL 60118. Phone: 800-405-8873 or (847)649-5555; Fax: (847)649-5678; Email: info@thelawninstitue.org • URL: http://www.thelawninstitute.org • Producers of lawn seed and lawn products. Seeks to help bridge the gap between professional research and an increasingly sophisticated consumer. Promotes better lawns through use of quality materials, research, and education.

**Lawrence Berkeley National Laboratory - Environment, Health and Safety Division - Safety Advisory Committee**. 1 Cyclotron Rd., MS 90R1140 Berkeley, CA 94720-8128. Phone: (510)486-7653; Fax: (510)486-7488; Email: paseidl@lbl.gov • URL: http://www.lbl.gov/ehs/sac/ • Development and implementation of environment, safety, and health policy, guidelines, codes, and regulatory interpretation of the Lawrence Berkeley National Laboratory.

***Lawrence's Anderson on the Uniform Commercial Code***. Lary Lawrence. Thomson West, 610 Opperman Dr. Eagan, MN 55123. Phone: 800-328-9352 or (651)687-7000 • $4,807 Individuals Book - Hardbound - Full Set; $317 Individuals Monthly pricing. Provides article-by-article analysis of the UCC.

**Lawyer-Pilots Bar Association**. PO Box 1510 Edgewater, MD 21037. Phone: (410)571-1750; Fax: (410)571-1780; Email: lpba@comcast.net • URL: http://www.lpba.org • Lawyers who are licensed pilots and engaged in the practice of aviation law or interested in aviation. Is concerned with law, safety, and general aviation.

***The Lawyer's Almanac; An Encyclopedia of Information about Law, Lawyers, and the Profession***. Aspen Law, 7201 McKinney Cir. Frederick, MD 21701. Phone: 800-234-1660 • Annual. $144.00. List of the 250 largest law firms.

***Lawyer's Register International by Specialties and Fields of Law Including a Directory of Corporate Counsel***. Lawyer's Register Publishing Co., 4555 Renaissance Pkwy., Ste. 101 Cleveland, OH 44128. Phone: 800-477-6345 or (216)591-1492; Fax: (216)591-0265; Email: info@lawyersregister.com • URL: http://www.lawyersregister.com • Annual. $359 Individuals. Referral source for law firms.

**LCD TV Association**. 16055 SW Walker Rd., Ste. 264 Beaverton, OR 97006-4942. Phone: (215)206-6506; Email: membership@lcdtvassociation.org • URL: http://www.lcdtvassociation.org • Aims to help the LCD TV supply chain and retail channel as well as the end customer. Creates and promotes new features and functions for the industry. Provides methods to improve members' products and services.

**Leadership Conference on Civil and Human Rights**. 1629 K St. NW, 10th Fl. Washington, DC 20006-1602. Phone: (202)466-3311; Fax: (202)466-3434 • URL: http://www.civilrights.org • Formerly Civil Rights Mobilization.

***Leading Employers of the New Hampshire & Southern Maine Seacoast***. Greater Portsmouth Chamber of Commerce, PO Box 239 Portsmouth, NH 03802-0239. Phone: (603)610-5510; Fax: (603)436-5118; Email: chambermaster@portsmouthchamber.org • URL: http://www.portsmouthchamber.org • Biennial. $10. Covers: Approximately 200 companies in the Portsmouth, New Hampshire area (including part of southern Maine) that employ over 25 people. Entries include: Company name, address, phone, name and title of contact, number of employees, products or services provided.

**League of Revolutionaries for a New America**. PO Box 477113 Chicago, IL 60647. Phone: (773)486-0028; Email: info@lrna.org • URL: http://www.lrna.org • Works toward a vision of a cooperative world where the full potential of all can contribute to the good of everyone.

**League of Women Voters Education Fund**. 1730 M St. NW, Ste. 1000 Washington, DC 20036-4508. Phone: (202)429-1965; Fax: (202)429-0854 • URL: http://www.lwv.org/education-fund • Research fields include federal deficit issues.

***Lean Manufacturing Advisor: Techniques and Technologies Supporting Lean Manufacturing and TPM***. Productivity Inc., 375 Bridgeport Ave., 3rd Fl. Shelton, CT 06484-6220. Phone: 800-966-5423 or (203)225-0451; Fax: (203)225-0771 • URL: http://www.productivityinc.com • Monthly. $167.00 per year. Formerly Productivity.

***Leasing Sourcebook: The Directory of the U. S. Capital Equipment Leasing Industry***. Bibliotechnology Systems and Publishing Co., PO Box 657 Lincoln, MA 01773-0657. Phone: (781)259-0524; Fax: (781)259-9861; Email: bibliotech@leasingsourcebook.com • URL: http://www.leasingsourcebook.com • Every 12-18 months. $135.00. Lists approximately 5,200 capital equipment leasing companies.

***Leather Goods Directory—Wholesalers***. InfoGroup Inc., 5711 S 86th Cir. Omaha, NE 68127-4146. Phone: (402)593-4500 • URL: http://www.infogroup.com • Annual. Number of listings: 690. Entries include: Name, address, phone, size of advertisement, name of owner or manager, number of employees, year first in "Yellow Pages." Compiled from telephone company "Yellow Pages," nationwide.

**Leather Industries of America**. 3050 K St. NW, Ste. 400 Washington, DC 20007. Phone: (202)342-8497; Fax: (202)342-8583; Email: info@leatherusa.com • URL: http://www.leatherusa.com • Formerly Tanners' Council of America.

**Leather Research Laboratory**. University of Cincinnati, 5997 Center Hill Ave. Cincinnati, OH 45224. Phone: (513)242-6300; Fax: (513)242-9797; Email: donmezk@uc.edu • URL: http://www.leatherusa.org • Automotive, upholstery, garment, apparel and chamois leather testing (physical, chemical, and toxicity).

***Lebanese Industrial and Commercial Directory***. Publitec Publications, Gedeon House, 139-141 John Kennedy St. Beirut, Lebanon. Phone: 961 1 495401; Fax: 961 1 493330; Email: publitecpublications@hotmail.com • URL: http://www.whoswhointhearabworld.info • Annual. $120. Covers: Industrial and commercial companies in Lebanon. Entries include: Contact information.

***Lebanon Golden Key Directory***. International Institute of Trade Relation Promotion, Trade Information Centre of Iran, No. 7, 3rd Fl., Abbasie Bazar, Ferdowsi Sq. Tehran, Iran. Phone: 98 21 88833900; Fax: 98 21 88820697; Email: order@irangoldenkey.com • URL: http://www.goldenkeydirectory.com/about.html • £100 Individuals. Covers: 14,209 companies in Lebanon. Entries include: Company name, address, telephone, fax, products, services, Managing Director, and business activities.

**Ledernes Hovedeorganisation**. Vermlandsgade 65 DK-2300 Copenhagen, Denmark. Phone: 45 32833283; Email: lederne@lederne.dk • URL: http://www.lederne.dk • Business managers and executives. Represents members' interests before government agencies, industry associations, and the public. Manages unemployment insurance fund for members; makes available legal services; conducts continuing professional training programs.

***Legal Business***. Legalese Ltd., Kensington Sq. House, 12-14 Ansdell St. London W8 5BN, United Kingdom. Phone: 44 20 73969292; Fax: 44 20 73969303 • URL: http://www.legalease.co.uk • 10/year. £495 Individuals. Journal covering commercial law in Europe.

***Legal Environments of Business***. American CPE Inc., 826 Riviera Mansfield, TX 76063. Phone: 800-990-4273 or (817)477-0222; Fax: (817)473-4998; Email: director@americancpe.com • URL: http://www.americancpe.com • Contains detailed training information covering legal structures and environments in which businesses operate in the United States.

**Legal Momentum**. 5 Hanover Sq., Ste. 1502 New York, NY 10004. Phone: (212)925-6635; Email: info@legalmomentum.org • URL: http://www.legalmomentum.org • Formerly NOW Legal Defense and Education Fund.

***Legal Research and Law Library Management***. ALM Media Properties LLC, 120 Broadway, 5th Fl. New York, NY 10271-1100. Phone: (212)457-9400; Fax: (646)417-7705; Email: customercare@alm.com • URL: http://www.alm.com • $565. Covers the planning and operation of libraries for law firms, including personnel selection and selection of books, periodicals, online services, microforms, and other materials. (Law Journal Press).

***Legal Times: Law and Lobbying in the Nation's Capital***. ALM Media Properties LLC, 120 Broadway, 5th Fl. New York, NY 10271-1100. Phone: (212)457-9400; Fax: (646)417-7705; Email: customercare@alm.com • URL: http://www.alm.com • Weekly. $318.00 per year. Published in Washington, DC. Provides news relating to lawyers and the federal government. Special features cover a variety of topics relating to law firm administration.

***LegalTrac***. Cengage Learning Inc., 20 Channel Center St. Boston, MA 02210. Phone: 800-487-8488 or (617)289-7700; Fax: (617)289-7844; Email: investors@cengage.com • URL: http://www.cengage.com • Online database. Provides indexing for approximately 875 titles of periodical literature relating to legal matters from 1980 to date. Corresponds to online *Legal Resource Index*. Inquire as to price and availability.

**Lehigh University - Martindale Center for the Study of Private Enterprise**. 621 Taylor St., Ste. 350 Bethlehem, PA 18015. Phone: (610)758-4771; Fax: (610)758-6549; Email: jral@lehigh.edu • URL: http://martindale.cc.lehigh.edu • Business and economics, including financial condition and future of public pension plans, labor markets, investment opportunities in Eastern Europe and Latin America, microfinance trends, health economics and U.S.-Canadian free trade.

**Lehigh University - Small Business Development Center**. 125 Goodman Dr. Bethlehem, PA 18015. Phone: (610)758-3980; Fax: (610)758-5205; Email: insbdc@lehigh.edu • URL: http://www.lehigh.edu/insbdc/index.html • Problems faced by small businesses, the impact of the general economy on the formation and operation of small business, and characteristics on entrepreneurs.

***Lehigh Valley Business Digest: The Newspaper in Business FOR Business***. Business Digest Inc., PO Box 324 Bala Cynwyd, PA 19004-0324. Phone: 800-527-6900 or (215)821-8350; Fax: (215)434-6776 • Monthly. $25; $40 Two years. Tabloid devoted to small- and medium-sized businesses in Lehigh Valley.

***Lehigh Valley Metro Business Directory***. Dalton Directory, 24 N Bryn Mawr Ave., Ste. 278 Bryn Mawr, PA 19010. Phone: 800-221-1050 or (518)583-4545; Fax: (518)583-4545; Email: info@daltondirectory.com • URL: http://www.daltondirectory.com • Covers: Approximately 5,000 companies in the Pennsylvania counties of Lehigh, Berks, Lancaster, and Northampton; includes manufacturers, banks, law firms, hospitals, schools and colleges, hotels, etc. Entries include: Company name, address, phone, fax, telex, names and titles of key personnel, number of employees, Standard Industrial Classification (SIC) code, product/service.

***Leisure, Recreation and Tourism Abstracts***. CABI Publishing North America, 38 Chauncey St., Ste. 1002 Boston, MA 02111. Phone: 800-552-3083; Email: cabi-nao@cabi.org • URL: http://www.cabi.org • Quarterly. Members, $280.00 per year; Institutions, $610.00 per year. Includes single site internet access. Provides coverage of the worldwide literature of travel, recreation, sports, and the hospitality industry.

***Lender Liability Law Report***. Thomson RIA, 195 Broadway New York, NY 10007-3100. Phone: 800-431-9025 or (212)367-6300 or (212)807-2298; Fax: (212)367-6305 or (212)337-4207; Email: ttacommunications@riag.com • URL: http://www.ria.thomson.com • Description: Discusses the impact of relevant cases and legislation on lenders and spotlights legal landmines which lenders may encounter. Recurring features include summaries of recent cases and avoidance techniques.

***Leonard's Annual Price Index of Art Auctions***. Auction Index Inc., 30 Valentine Pk. Newton, MA 02465-2940. Phone: (617)964-2876; Fax: (617)969-9912 • Annual. $245.00. List major auction houses.

***LERA Membership Directory***. Labor and Employment Relations Associations, 119 Labor and Employment Relations Bldg., 504 E Armory Ave. Champaign, IL 61820. Phone: (217)333-0072; Fax: (217)265-5130 • URL: http://www.leraweb.org • Quadrennial. $10 print only. About 3,200 business people, union leaders, government officials, lawyers, arbitrators, academics, consultants, and others interested in labor relations.

***Les Nouvelles***. Licensing Executives Society, 1800 Diagonal Rd., Ste. 280 Alexandria, VA 22314-2840. Email: info@les.org • URL: http://www.lesi.org • Quarterly. Description: Concerned with technological licensing and related subjects. Covers technology, patents, trademarks, and licensing "know-how" world-wide.

***Les Pages Pro***. Bureau van Dijk S.A., Ave. Louise, Louizalaan 250 B-1050 Brussels, Belgium. Phone: 32 2 6390606 or 32 2 639 06 06; Fax: 32 2 6488230 or 32 2 648 82 30; Email: brussels@bvdinfo.com • URL: http://www.bvdinfo.com • Annual. Database covers: Business to business directory of France Telecom with more than 300,000 subscribers. Entries include: Name, SIRET identification number, telephone number, type of number, full address, activity, employee range.

***Lesotho Business Directory***. A.C. Braby (Pty) Ltd., 12 Caversham Rd. Pinetown 3610, South Africa. Email: support@brabys.co.za • URL: http://www.brabys.com • Annual. Covers industrial, commercial, and service firms; trade unions; employers' organizations; societies and institutions in Lesotho.

**Lesotho Council of Non-Governmental Organizations**. Private Bag A445 Maseru 100, Lesotho. Phone: 266 223 17205 or 266 223 25798; Fax: 266 223 10412; Email: admin@lcn.org.ls • URL: http://www.lcn.org.ls • Promotes sustainable management of natural resources, socioeconomic development and social justice in Lesotho. Offers and provides support to the NGO community. Stimulates, promotes and builds capacity within Lesotho NGOs.

***The Levy Institute Forecast***. Forecasting Center Jerome Levy Economics Institute, Blithewood, Bard College Annandale on Hudson, NY 12504-5000. Phone: (845)758-7700 or (845)758-7711; Fax: (845)758-1149; Email: info@levy.org • URL: http://www.levy.org • Description: Provides analyses and forecasts of U.S. business conditions. Reports on production, sales, inflation, corporate profits, and interest rates.

***Lewiston Chamber Business Directory***. Lewiston Chamber of Commerce, 111 Main St., Ste. 120 Lewiston, ID 83501. Phone: 800-473-3543 or (208)743-3531; Fax: (208)743-2176; Email: info@lewistonchamber.org • URL: http://www.lewistonchamber.org • Covers: About 600 manufacturing and service companies in the Lewiston area. Entries include: Name, address, phone, fax, contact person.

***Lexis.com Research System***. Lexis-Nexis Group, Phone: 800-227-4908 or (937)865-6800; Fax: (937)865-6909; Email: webmaster@prod.lexis-nexis.com • URL: http://www.nexis.com • Fee-based Web site offers extensive searching of a wide variety of legal sources. Additional features include Daily Opinion Service, lexis.com Bookstore, Career Center, CLE Center, Law Schools, and Practice Pages ("Pages specific to areas of specialty").

***LGBT Friendly Directory***. VCS Gay Pride Rockland, 77 S Main St. New City, NY 10956. Phone: (845)634-5729; Email: gpr@vcs-inc.org • URL: http://www.gayprideroekland.org • Covers: Businesses, services, and community organizations. Entries include: Company name, address, contact information, e-mail, and website.

***Library Administrator's Digest***. The Foundation for Baltimore County Public Library Inc., 320 York Rd. Towson, MD 21204-5179. Phone: (410)887-6100; Fax: (410)887-6103; Email: bcpl@bcpl.info • Description: Designed to keep library administrators abreast of new ideas and developments, particularly in the public library field. Recurring features include editorials and letters to the editor.

***The Library and Book Trade Almanac***. Information Today, Inc., 143 Old Marlton Pke. Medford, NJ 08055-8750. Phone: 800-300-9868 or (609)654-6266; Fax: (609)654-4309; Email: custserv@infotoday.com • URL: http://www.infotoday.com • $209 Individuals Hardbound. Reviews key trends and events and provides basic statistical information. Includes financial averages: library expenditures, salaries, and book prices. Contains lists of "best books, literary prizes, winners, and bestsellers." Formerly published by R. R. Bowker.

**Library and Information Technology Association**. 50 E Huron St. Chicago, IL 60611-2795. Phone: 800-545-2433; Fax: (312)280-3257; Email: lita@ala.org • URL: http://www.ala.org/lita • Affiliated with the American Library Association. Formerly Information Science and Automation Division of ALA.

**Library Binding Council**. 4440 PGA Blvd., Ste. 600 Palm Beach Gardens, FL 33410. Phone: 800-837-7321 or (561)745-6821 • URL: http://www.lbibinders.org • Firms and certified library binders doing library binding in accordance with LBI Standard for Library Binding, including rebinding of worn volumes, prebinding of new volumes, initial hardcover binding of periodicals, and other binding principally for libraries and schools; associate members are suppliers and manufacturers of library binding materials and equipment. Certifies qualified binding companies after examination of work and investigation of experience, insurance for protection of customers' property, and examination of bank and library references. Conducts research on materials used in library binding. Conducts statistical surveys of unit production, operating statement data, and wage data.

***Library Journal: Reference: Print, CD-ROM, Online (year)***. Reed Elsevier Group plc Reed Business Information, 360 Park Ave. S New York, NY 11010. Phone: (212)791-4208; Email: corporatecommunications@reedbusiness.com • URL: http://www.reedbusiness.com • Annual. Issued in November as a supplement to *Library Journal*. Lists new and updated reference material, including general and trade print titles, directories, annuals, CD-ROM titles, and online sources. Includes material from more than 200 publishers, arranged by company name, with an index by subject.

***Library Journal Sourcebook: The Reference For Library Products & Services***. Reed Elsevier Group plc Reed Business Information, 360 Park Ave. S New York, NY 11010. Phone: (212)791-4208; Email: corporatecommunications@reedbusiness.com • URL: http://www.reedbusiness.com • Annual. Publication includes: List of over 600 suppliers of products and services used by libraries from abstracting to word processing equipment. Entries include: Company name, address, phone, list of products or services. Complete listings for more than 100 architectural firms; Disaster planning for librarians.

**Library Leadership and Management Association**. 50 E Huron St. Chicago, IL 60611-2729. Phone: 800-545-2433; Fax: (312)280-2169; Email: llama@ala.org • URL: http://www.ala.org/llama/ • Affiliated with American Library Association. Formerly Library Administration Division of ALA.

***Library Literature and Information Science Index***. H.W. Wilson Co., 950 University Ave. Bronx, NY 10452-4224. Phone: 800-367-6770 or (718)588-8400 or (718)558-8400; Fax: (718)590-1617 or (800)590-1617; Email: custserv@hwwilson.com • URL: http://www.hwwilson.com • Quarterly. Annual cumulation. Price varies.

***Library Resource Guide: A Catalog of Services and Suppliers for the Library Community***. Information Today, Inc., 143 Old Marlton Pke. Medford, NJ 08055-8750. Phone: 800-300-9868 or (609)654-6266; Fax: (609)654-4309; Email: custserv@infotoday.com • URL: http://www.infotoday.com • Annual. Free to libraries. An advertising directory listing several hundred manufacturers or distributors of library supplies, services, and equipment in such areas as audiovisual, automation, bar codes, binding, furniture, microfilm, shelving, and storage. Some book dealers, document delivery services, online services, and publishers are also included (www.libraryresource.com). Formerly published by R. R. Bowker.

***Library Technology Reports: Expert Guides to Library Systems and Services***. Library and Information Technology Association, 50 E Huron St. Chicago, IL 60611-2795. Phone: 800-545-2433; Fax: (312)280-3257; Email: lita@ala.org • URL: http://www.ala.org/lita • Bimonthly. $315.00 per year. Looseleaf service.

***Libya Business Directory***. Business Guide, PO Box 27669 Dubai, United Arab Emirates. Phone: 971 4 2651719; Fax: 971 4 2692151; Email: sales@africa-business.com • URL: http://www.africa-business.com • $150 Individuals Soft copy. Covers: 1,800 business listings including wholesalers, importers, retailers, business houses, and agents in Libya.

**Licensing Executives Society**. 1800 Diagonal Rd., Ste. 280 Alexandria, VA 22314-2840. Email: info@les.org • URL: http://www.lesi.org • U.S. and foreign businessmen, scientists, engineers, and lawyers having direct responsibility for the transfer of technology. Maintains placement service.

***The Licensing Letter (TLL)***. EPM Communications Inc., 19 W 21 St., Ste. 303 New York, NY 10010. Phone: 888-852-9467 or (212)941-0099; Fax: (212)941-1622; Email: info@epmcom.com • URL: http://www.epmcom.com • Description: Concerned with all aspects of licensed merchandising, "the business of associating someone's name, likeness or creation with someone else&'s product or service, for a consideration." Recurring features include statistics, research, events, mechanics, available properties, and identification of licensors, licensing agents, and licensees.

***Licensing of Intellectual Property***. ALM Media Properties LLC, 120 Broadway, 5th Fl. New York, NY 10271-1100. Phone: (212)457-9400; Fax: (646)417-7705; Email: customercare@alm.com • URL: http://www.alm.com • $680. Includes such licensing topics as royalties, infringement, antitrust, trade secrets, and patent agreements. Examples of licensing agreements and sample forms (on CD-ROM) are included. (Law Journal Press).

**LICU**. 1 Credit Union Plz., 24 McKinley Ave. Endicott, NY 13760. Phone: 800-434-1776 or (607)754-7900; Fax: (607)754-9772 • Member credit unions in the U.S. and Canada. Provides a network for information sharing. Compiles statistics.

***Lieber on Pensions***. William M. Lieber. Wolters Kluwer Law and Business, 76 9th Ave., 7th Fl. New York, NY 10011-4962. Phone: 800-234-1660 or (212)771-0600; Fax: (800)901-9075 or (301)644-3550 • URL: http://www.wolterskluwerlb.com • $595.00. Five volumes. Looseleaf service. Periodic supplementation. Organizes, describes, and analyzes ERISA and IRS pension rules. Topical arrangement.

***Liechtenstein Industrial and Business Directory***. International Business Publications, USA, PO Box 15343 Washington, DC 20003. Phone: (202)546-2103; Fax: (202)546-3275; Email: ibpusa@comcast.net • URL: http://ibpus.com • Annual. $99.95 Individuals hardcover, e-book, CD-ROM. Covers: Strategic industrial, investment and business contacts for conducting export-import and investment activity in the country.

***Life, Health, and Accident Insurance Law Reports***. Wolters Kluwer Law & Business CCH, 2700 Lake Cook Rd. Riverwoods, IL 60015. Phone: 888-224-7377 or (847)267-7000; Email: cust_serv@cch.com • URL: http://www.cchgroup.com • $835.00 per year. Looseleaf service. Monthly updates.

***Light & Medium Truck: The Business Magazine for Light & Medium Truck Operators***. TT Publishing, 2200 Mill Rd. Alexandria, VA 22314. Email: tteditor@trucking.org • Monthly. Magazine for users of pick-up and delivery trucks.

***Lighting Businesses in the World***. Momentum Technologies L.L.C., PO Box 460813 Glendale, CO 80246. Phone: (303)229-4841; Fax: (408)705-2031 • URL: http://www.mtt.com • Contains directory listings for hundreds of lighting businesses and related companies in operation throughout the world. Includes business name, address, phone number, fax number, e-mail address, and web site address. Provides brief descriptions of product lines, services offered, and business type. Includes information on manufacturers, component makers, wholesalers, retailers, system designers, system installers, architectural services, trade associations, and more. Covers businesses involved in fluorescent lighting, LED lighting, natural daylighting, tubular skylights, energy efficient lighting, and more. Provides keyword search functions.

***Lightwave Buyers Guide***. PennWell Corp., Advanced Technology Div., 98 Spit Brook Rd. Nashua, NH 03062-5737. Phone: 800-225-0556 or (603)891-0123; Fax: (603)891-9294; Email: atd@pennwell.com • URL: http://www.pennwell.com • Lists manufacturers and distributors of fiberoptic systems and components.

**LIMRA International**. 300 Day Hill Rd. Windsor, CT 06095. Phone: 800-235-4672 or (860)285-7789; Fax: (860)285-7792; Email: customer.service@limra.com • URL: http://www.limra.com • Life insurance and financial services companies. Conducts market, consumer, economic, financial, and human resources research; monitors industry distribution systems and product and service developments. Provides executive and field management development schools and seminars. Offers human resource development consulting services, including needs analysis and program design, evaluation, and implementation.

***The Lincoln Business Journal***. Midlands Business Journal Publications, 1324 S 119th St. Omaha, NE 68144. Phone: (402)330-1760; Fax: (402)758-9315 • URL: http://www.mbj.com • Semimonthly. $53.50 Individuals; $96.30 Two years; $139.10 Individuals 3 years. Business publication covering regional business and government issues in Lincoln, Nebraska.

***Lincoln Christian Business Directory***. Red Letter Publishing, PO Box 272682 Fort Collins, CO 80527. Phone: 800-445-5614; Fax: (970)267-9669; Email: info@redletter.com • URL: http://www.christianbusinessdirectoryonline.com • Businesses, churches, organizations, and schools in Lincoln, Nebraska.

***Lindey on Entertainment, Publishing and the Arts***. Alexander Lindey, editor. Thomson West, 610 Opperman Dr. Eagan, MN 55123. Phone: 800-328-9352 or (651)687-7000 • $1,582.86 Full Set. Provides basic forms, applicable law, and guidance.

**Lingnan University - Institute of Humanities and Social Sciences - Center for Public Policy Studies**. Tuen Mun Hong

Kong, China. Phone: 86 852 26167182; Fax: 86 852 25910690; Email: lsho@ln.edu.hk • URL: http://www.ln.edu.hk/cpps • Labor, human capital investment, and industrial policy; urban, health and environmental policy; and socio-economic justice and collective behavior.

***Liquid Filtration Newsletter***. The McIlvaine Co., 191 Waukegan Rd., Ste. 208 Northfield, IL 60093-2743. Phone: (847)784-0012; Fax: (847)784-0061; Email: editor@mcilvainecompany.com • URL: http://www.mcilvainecompany.com • Description: Focuses on the liquid filtration industry, providing information on technical developments and reports on individual companies in the field. Recurring features include a calendar of events and a column titled New & Different.

***Liquor Control Law Reporter***. Wolters Kluwer Law & Business CCH, 2700 Lake Cook Rd. Riverwoods, IL 60015. Phone: 888-224-7377 or (847)267-7000; Email: cust_serv@cch.com • URL: http://www.cchgroup.com • Biweekly. Federal and state regulation and taxation of alcoholic beverages.

***LISA: Library and Information Science Abstracts***. R.R. Bowker L.L.C., 630 Central Ave New Providence, NJ 07974. Phone: 888-269-5372 or (908)286-1090; Email: info@bowker.com • URL: http://www.bowker.com • 13 times a year. $1,055.00 per year; includes print and online editions.

***LISA Plus***. Cambridge Scientific Abstracts L.P., 7200 Wisconsin Ave., Ste. 601 Bethesda, MD 20814. Phone: 800-843-7751 or (301)961-6700 or (301)961-6785; Fax: (301)961-6720 or (301)961-6708; Email: sales@proquest.com • URL: http://www.proquest.co.uk • Quarterly. $2,000 per year. CD-ROM version of Library Information and Science Abstracts, providing abstracting and indexing of the world's library and information science literature, 1969 to date. Contains more than 180,000 citations.

***List of Certificated Pilot Schools***. Federal Aviation Administration. U. S. Government Printing Office, 732 N Capitol St. NW Washington, DC 20401. Phone: 866-512-1800 or (202)512-1800 or (866)512-1800; Fax: (202)512-2104 or (202)512-2250; Email: contactcenter@gpo.gov • URL: http://www.gpo.gov • Lists FAA-approved ground and flight schools and the pilot training courses each school offers.

***List of Shipowners, Managers, and Managing Agents***. Lloyd's Register of Shipping, Metrostar Plaza, 190 Middlesex Turnpike Iselin, NJ 08830. Phone: (732)404-9468 or (305)262-4070; Fax: (732)404-1946 • URL: http://www.fairplay.co.uk • Annual. $350.00, including 10 updates per year. Published in the UK by Lloyd's Register-Fairplay Ltd. Lists 40,000 shipowners, managers, and agents worldwide. Cross-referenced with *Lloyd's Register of Ships*.

***Listed Companies in Finland***. Kansallis-Osake-Pankki Sijoitustutkimus/Investment Research, C 7C48 FIN-00012 Helsinki, Finland. Phone: 0 1633760; Fax: 0 1633172 • Annual. $545. Covers: all Finnish companys listed on the Helsinki Stock Exchange. Database includes: Charts and tables summarizing developments such as income statements, balance sheet, financial ratios, and per-share ratios. Entries include: Company name, address, phone, year established, line of business, subsidiary and branch names and locations, names and titles of key personnel, number of shareholders, financial data.

***Literary Market Place: The Directory of the American Book Publishing Industry***. Information Today, Inc., 143 Old Marlton Pke. Medford, NJ 08055-8750. Phone: 800-300-9868 or (609)654-6266; Fax: (609)654-4309; Email: custserv@infotoday.com • URL: http://www.infotoday.com • Annual. $399 Individuals 2-volume set/softbound plus $25 shipping/handling. Listings include publishers, agents, ad agencies, associations, distributors, events, key executives, services, and suppliers (50 directory sections in all). Formerly published by R. R. Bowker.

***Literature Review***. Water Environment Federation, 601 Wythe St. Alexandria, VA 22314-1994. Phone: 800-666-0206; Fax: (703)684-2492; Email: inquiry@wef.org • URL: http://www.wef.org • Annual. Provides a review of published books and articles on water quality topics from the previous year.

***Lithuania Business Services Providers Leads***. Business Information Agency Inc. PlanetInform, 52 Tuscan Way, Ste. 202-181 Saint Augustine, VA 32092. Phone: (904)342-6124; Fax: (904)592-2632; Email: info@biasales.com • URL: http://www.biasales.com • Monthly. $67 Individuals mailing list; $142 Individuals sales list; $240 Individuals marketing list. Covers Lithuanian companies and all sub-industries that provide various services to commercial businesses, establishments, and organizations, including consulting, advertising and marketing services, and facilities maintenance.

***Lithuania Industrial and Business Directory***. International Business Publications, USA, PO Box 15343 Washington, DC 20003. Phone: (202)546-2103; Fax: (202)546-3275; Email: ibpusa@comcast.net • URL: http://ibpus.com • Annual. $99.95 Individuals hardcover, e-book, CD-ROM. Covers: Strategic industrial, investment and business contacts for conducting export-import and investment activity in the country.

***Lithuanian Companies***. Litauisches Informationsinstitut, Kalvariju 3 232659 Vilnius, Lithuania. Phone: 122 752284; Fax: 122 353017 • Quarterly. Database covers: companies in Lithuania. Database includes: Company name, address, legal status, products, number of employees.

***The Little Green Book—Business Directory for the Polish Community***. AdMark Graphics Inc., 135 Plymouth St. Brooklyn, NY 11219. Phone: (718)625-3465 • Annual. Covers: over 3,000 businesses of interest to the Polish communities of New York, New Jersey, Connecticut, Pennsylvania, and Massachusetts. Entries include: Company name, address, phone, subsidiary and branch names and locations, description of product/service.

***Little River News: The Oldest Business Institution in Little River County***. Little River News, 45 E Commerce Ashdown, AR 71822. Phone: (870)898-3462; Fax: (870)898-6213 • URL: http://www.littlerivernews.net/ • Weekly (Thurs.). $35 Individuals in Ashdown, Foreman, Wilton, Ogden, Horatio, Ben, Lomond, De Queen and Lockesburg; $40 Individuals in Mineral Springs, Nashville, Saratoga, Columbus and Washington; $52 Out of state. Newspaper with Democratic orientation.

***Livestock and Grain Market News Branch Weekly Summary***. U.S. Dept of Agriculture. Livestock and Grain Market News Branch, 1427 S. Pioneer Way Moses Lake, WA 98837. Phone: (509)675-3611 • URL: http://www.ams.usda.gov • Weekly. $85.00 per year. Formerly *Grain and Feed Weekly Summary and Statistics*.

**Livestock Marketing Association**. 10510 NW Ambassador Dr. Kansas City, MO 64153. Phone: 800-821-2048 • URL: http://www.lmaweb.com • Livestock marketing businesses and livestock dealers. Sponsors annual World Livestock Auctioneer Championships. Offers management and promotional services.

***Lloyd's Marine Equipment Buyers' Guide***. Informa Group PLC, Informa House, 30-32 Mortimer St. London W1W 7RE, United Kingdom. Phone: 44 020 7017 5000 or 44 207 0175000; Fax: 44 020 7017 4286; Email: headoffice@informa.com • URL: http://www.informa.com • Annual. $270.00. Published in the UK by Lloyd's List (www.lloydslist.com). Lists more than 6,000 companies worldwide supplying over 2,000 types of marine products and services, including offshore equipment.

***Lloyd's Maritime Atlas***. Informa P.L.C. Informa Sports Group, Gubelstr. 11 CH-6300 Zug, Switzerland. Phone: 41 41 444 1344 or 44 20 70175000; Email: info@informasportsgroup.com • URL: http://www.informa.com • Biennial. $119.00. Contains more than 70 pages of world, ocean, regional, and port maps in color. Provides additional information for the planning of world shipping routes, including data on distances, port facilities, recurring weather hazards at sea, international load line zones, and sailing times.

***Lloyd's Maritime Directory***. Informa P.L.C. Informa Sports Group, Gubelstr. 11 CH-6300 Zug, Switzerland. Phone: 41 41 444 1344 or 44 20 70175000; Email: info@informasportsgroup.com • URL: http://www.informa.com • Annual. Covers: Over 40,000 shipowners, managers, and operators with 75,000 vessels. Also includes Marine consultants; towing, salvage, solicitors, P&I clubs; ship building and repair firms; general maritime organizations, banking and finance and more. Entries include: Firm name, address, phone, fax, e-mail, Internet; branch offices; names of principal executives; agents; parent and associated companies; and, for shipowners and lines, detailed information on ships owned, type, or capacity, etc. The former second volume of 'International Shipping and Shipbuilding Directory' is now published separately with the title 'Lloyd's List Marine Equipment Buyers' Guide' (see separate entry).

***Lobbyists Directory***. InfoGroup Inc., 5711 S 86th Cir. Omaha, NE 68127-4146. Phone: (402)593-4500 • URL: http://www.infogroup.com • Annual. Number of listings: 1,107. Entries include: Name, address, phone, size of advertisement, name of owner or manager, number of employees, year first in "Yellow Pages." Compiled from telephone company "Yellow Pages," nationwide.

***Locaguide: Locaguide du BTP et de la Manutention***. Societe technique d'Editions pour l'Entreprise, Bord de Seine, 202 quai de Clichy F-92110 Clichy, France. Phone: 01 47561723; Fax: 01 47561432; Email: chandefr@club-internet.fr • Annual. €23. Covers: 1,000 French companies. Entries include: Company name, address, phone, fax, telex, names and titles of key personnel, product/service provided.

***Local Government Law***. Chester J. Antieau. Matthew Bender and Company Inc., 1275 Broadway Albany, NY 12204-2638. Phone: 800-424-4200 or (518)487-3000; Fax: (518)487-3573 or (800)424-4200; Email: customer.support@lexisnexis.com • URL: http://www.matthewbender.com • $2,619 Print; $2,381 E-book. States the principle of law for all types of local governments, and backs those principles with case citations from all jurisdictions. Examines the laws and their impact in three primary cases.

**Local Initiatives Support Corporation**. 501 7th Ave. New York, NY 10018-5903. Phone: (212)455-9800; Fax: (212)682-5929; Email: info@lisc.org • URL: http://www.lisc.org • Seeks to help independent community-based organizations in deteriorated areas to improve local, physical, and economic conditions while strengthening their own management and financial capabilities. Matches funds contributed by local corporations and foundations with those provided by national donors and investors; offers loans and grants to local organizations and projects. Administers national community development loan programs in cooperation with major financial institutions.

***Lockwood-Post's Directory of the Pulp, Paper and Allied Trades***. Miller Freeman Inc., 600 Harrison St. San Francisco, CA 94107. Phone: (415)905-2200; Fax: (415)905-2232 or (415)356-3480; Email: kgates@mfi.com • URL: http://www.telehealthmag.com • Annual. $257 Individuals add shipping & handling regular ed; $217 Individuals traveler's ed. Covers almost 1,000 U.S. and Canadian pulp and paper companies and their mills; 4,000 paper converters; 3,000 paper merchants; and industry associations. Formerly *Lockwood's Directory of the Paper and Allied Trades*.

***Lodging, Restaurant and Tourism Index***. Distance Learning Service. Purdue University - Consumer and Family Sciences Library, 504 W State St. West Lafayette, IN 47907-1002. Phone: (765)494-2900; Email: libinfo@purdue.edu • URL: http://www.lib.purdue.edu • Quarterly. $265.00 per year. Provides subject indexing to 52 periodicals related to the hospitality industry. Annual bound cumulations are available. Formerly *Lodging and Restaurant Index*.

***Logos of America's Fastest Growing Corporations***. Hoover's Inc., 5800 Airport Blvd. Austin, TX 78752-4204. Phone: 866-443-3939 or (512)374-4500 or (866)281-5969; Fax: (512)374-4501; Email: salesteam@hoovers.com • URL: http://www.hoovers.com • $39.95. Covers: Over 500 logotypes, trademarks, and symbols from growing U.S. companies.

***Logos of America's Largest Corporations***. Hoover's Inc., 5800 Airport Blvd. Austin, TX 78752-4204. Phone: 866-443-3939 or (512)374-4500 or (866)281-5969; Fax: (512)374-4501; Email: salesteam@hoovers.com • URL: http://www.hoovers.com • $39.95. Covers: Over 500 logotypes, trademarks, and symbols of U.S. companies.

***Logos of Major World Corporations***. Hoover's Inc., 5800 Airport Blvd. Austin, TX 78752-4204. Phone: 866-443-3939 or (512)374-4500 or (866)281-5969; Fax: (512)374-4501; Email: salesteam@hoovers.com • URL: http://www.hoovers.com • $39.95. Covers: Over 500 logotypes, trademarks, and symbols of international companies.

**LOMA**. 2300 Windy Ridge Pkwy., Ste. 600 Atlanta, GA 30339-8443. Phone: (770)951-1770 or (770)984-3720; Fax: (770)984-6422; Email: askloma@loma.org • URL: http://www.loma.org • Life and health insurance companies and financial services in the U.S. and Canada; and overseas in 45 countries; affiliate members are firms that provide professional support to member companies. Provides research, information, training, and educational activities in areas of operations and systems, human resources, financial planning and employee development. Administers FLMI Insurance Education Program, which awards FLMI (Fellow, Life Management Institute) designation to those who complete the ten-examination program.

***London Black Business and Professionals Directory***. Smart Choice Communications Inc., 4026 Meadowbrook Dr., Unit 133 London, ON, Canada N6L 1C8. Phone: (519)652-5599; Fax: (519)652-0339; Email: info@smartchoicecommunications.ca • Professionals, businesses, and community entities serving and working with the black community.

***London Business School: A SourceGuide to European Company Information***. Cengage Learning Inc., 20 Channel Center St. Boston, MA 02210. Phone: 800-487-8488 or (617)289-7700; Fax: (617)289-7844; Email: investors@cengage.com • URL: http://www.cengage.com • $108. Over 1,000 business information resources in 18 European countries, including trade councils, government agencies, directories, databases, newspapers, newsletters, and other media.

**London Metropolitan University - Faculty of Social Sciences and Humanities - Centre for Primary Health and Social Care**. 166-220 Holloway Rd. London N7 8DB, United Kingdom. Phone: 44 20 71335005; Fax: 44 20 71335203; Email: r.gevorgyan@londonmet.ac.uk • URL: http://www.londonmet.ac.uk/faculties/faculty-of-social-sciences-and-humanities/research/centre-for-primary-health-and-social-care • Health in its social, political and economic context, promoting wellbeing and challenging barriers to social exclusion.

**London School of Economics and Political Science - Business History Unit**. Houghton St. London WC2A 2AE, United Kingdom. Phone: 44 20 79557073; Email: t.r.gourvish@lse.ac.uk • URL: http://www.lse.ac.uk/economicHistory/BHU/Home.aspx • Business history, focusing on economic, social and political issues.

**London School of Economics and Political Science - Centre for Economic Performance**. Houghton St. London WC2A 2AE, United Kingdom. Phone: 44 20 79557673; Fax: 44 20 74040612; Email: j.vanreenen@lse.ac.uk • URL: http://cep.lse.ac.uk • Economic performance at the level of the company, the nation and the global economy, focusing on links between globalization, technology and institutions, particularly the labor market, education, technology and growth.

**London School of Economics and Political Science - Centre for Philosophy of Natural and Social Science**. Lakatos Bldg., Houghton St. London WC2A 2AE, United Kingdom. Phone: 44 207 9557573; Fax: 44 207 9556869; Email: philcent@lse.ac.uk • URL: http://www.lse.ac.uk/CPNSS/Home.aspx • Philosophy of natural and social science; Darwinism and the human sciences; causation; foundations of physics; economics and human values; and measuring voting power.

**London School of Economics and Political Science - Centre for Research into Economics and Finance in Southern Africa**. Rm. G409, 20 Kingsway, Houghton St. London WC2A 2AE, United Kingdom. Phone: 44 20 79557505; Email: j.leape@lse.ac.uk • URL: http://www.lse.ac.uk/researchAndExpertise/units/CREFSA/home.aspx • Private capital flows in Southern Africa; financial regulation and the development of financial systems in Southern Africa; prospects for regional trade and monetary integration in the SADC.

**London School of Economics and Political Science - Department of International Relations - International Trade Policy Unit**. Clement House, Rm. CLM 613, Houghton St. London WC2A 2AE, United Kingdom. Phone: 44 20 79557696; Fax: 44 20 79557980; Email: itpu@lse.ac.uk • URL: http://www.lse.ac.uk/internationalRelations/centresandunits/ITPU/ITPUhome.aspx • Policies and business implications of trade agreements at the multilateral, regional, and national levels.

**London School of Economics and Political Science - European Institute - Hellenic Observatory**. Houghton St. London WC2A 2AE, United Kingdom. Phone: 44 20 79556066; Fax: 44 20 79556497; Email: k.featherstone@lse.ac.uk • URL: http://www.lse.ac.uk/europeanInstitute/research/hellenicObservatory/home.aspx • Contemporary politics, economics and society of Greece and Cyprus.

**London School of Economics and Political Science - Health and Social Care Research Centre**. Cowdray House, Houghton St. London WC2A 2AE, United Kingdom. Phone: 44 20 79556840; Fax: 44 20 79556803; Email: e.a.mossialos@lse.ac.uk • URL: http://www.lse.ac.uk/LSEHealthAndSocialCare/Home.aspx • Health policy, including comparative health policy; health care financing and equity; international mental health policy and practice; health policy relating to pharmaceutical industries; health economics, including economic evaluation in health care; pharmaceutical economics; healthcare technology; economics of mental health and the hospital sector; health care workforce issues; social care, focusing on long-term care finance; health and social care integration; community care for the elderly; adulthood economic outcomes of childhood problems; and healthy living centers.

***Long Distance Telephone Services Directory***. InfoGroup Inc., 5711 S 86th Cir. Omaha, NE 68127-4146. Phone: (402)593-4500 • URL: http://www.infogroup.com • Annual. Number of listings: 2,403. Entries include: Name, address, phone, size of advertisement, name of owner or manager, number of employees, year first in "Yellow Pages." Compiled from telephone company "Yellow Pages," nationwide.

***Looking Fit Buyers Guide***. Virgo Publishing L.L.C., 3300 N Central Ave. Ste. 300 Phoenix, AZ 85012-2501. Phone: (480)990-1101; Fax: (480)990-0819 or (602)567-6852; Email: mikes@vpico.com • URL: http://www.vpico.com • Lists suppliers of products and equipment for the tanning industry.

***Los Angeles Business Journal—Book of Lists***. LABJ Inc., 5700 Wilshire Blvd. Los Angeles, CA 90036. Phone: (323)549-5225; Fax: (323)549-5255 • URL: http://www.labusinessjournal.com • Annual. $395. Covers: major companies, foundations, government officials, utilities, newspapers, radio and television stations, airlines, hospitals, financial institutions, shopping centers, resorts, and prominent individuals in Los Angeles County, California. Incorporates information in "Los Angeles Business Journal—Consultants Directory," now discontinued.

***The Los Angeles Business Journal***. The Los Angeles Business Journal, 5700 Wilshire, No. 170 Los Angeles, CA 90036. Phone: (213)549-5225; Fax: (213)549-5255 • URL: http://www.labusinessjournal.com • Weekly (Mon.). $129.95 Individuals; $219.95 Two years. Newspaper (tabloid) covering local business news, business trends, executive profiles, and information for the Los Angeles area executive.

***Los Angeles JobBank: The Job Hunter's Guide to Southern California***. Adams Media Corp., 57 Littlefield St. Avon, MA 02322. Phone: 800-872-5627 or (508)427-7100; Fax: (508)427-6790 or (800)872-5628; Email: deskcopies@adamsmedia.com • URL: http://www.adamsmedia.com • Annual. $16.95 Individuals Paperback. Covers: Over 7,900 southern California employers including Orange, Riverside, San Bernardino, San Diego, Santa Barbara and Ventura counties. Database includes: Information on the basics of job winning and writing resumes and cover letters; electronic job search information; 330 industry associations; 90 online career resources; 515 employment services. Entries include: Firm or organization name, address, local phone, toll-free phone, fax, e-mail, URL, recorded jobline, hours, subsidiaries, other locations, names of management, name and title of contact, description of organization, number of employees, headquarters location, typical titles for common positions, educational backgrounds desired, fringe benefits offered, stock exchange listing, training programs, internships, parent company, number of employees, revenues, corporate headquarters, and number of projected hires. Projected hires.

***Louisiana Business Directory***. InfoGroup Inc., 5711 S 86th Cir. Omaha, NE 68127-4146. Phone: (402)593-4500 • URL: http://www.infogroup.com • Annual. $795 for both print & CD-ROM. Covers: 184,886 businesses in Louisiana. Entries include: Company name, address, phone, number of employees, standard industrial classification (sic) code, line of business, name of owner or manager, sales volume, credit ratings. Compiled from telephone company 'Yellow Pages,' statewide. All states covered independently (see separate entries).

**Louisiana State University - Public Administration Institute**. Business Education Complex, Rm. 2000 Baton Rouge, LA 70803. Phone: (225)578-6743; Fax: (225)578-9078; Email: pai@lsu.edu • URL: http://business.lsu.edu/Public-Administration-Institute/Pages/About.aspx • Public administration, including studies on health policy, minority health care, economics and taxes, state and local governments, and public finance.

***Louisville Business First: The Weekly Business Newspaper of Greater Louisville***. American City Business Journals, Inc., 120 W Morehead St. Charlotte, NC 28202. Phone: (704)973-1000; Fax: (704)973-1001; Email: americancity@bizjournals.com • URL: http://www.acbj.com • Weekly. $80 Individuals; $135 Two years. Weekly Business Newspaper.

***The Low Priced Stock Survey***. Horizon Publishing Co., 7412 Calumet Ave. Hammond, IN 46324-2622. Phone: 800-233-5922; Fax: (219)931-6487; Email: custserv@horizonpublishing.com • URL: http://www.horizonpublishing.com • Weekly. Description: Reviews and analyzes stocks offered at a price of $20 or less. Analysis is divided into sections: Emerging Growth Opportunities, The Fundamentalist, Bargain Spotlight, Stock of the Month, and Master List Highlights. Includes weekly closes of the Dow Jones Industrials and NASDAQ, and statistics.

***Low Rate and No Fee Credit Card List***. Bankcard Holders of America, 333 Maple Ave. E, No. 2005 Vienna, VA 22180-4717. Phone: (703)481-1110; Email: current@credit-report-bureaus-credit-reporting-agency-agencies.com • Quarterly. $4.00 per copy. Lists about 50 banks offering relatively low interest rates and/or no annual fee for credit card accounts. Formerly *Low Interest Rate*.

***Low-Slope Roofing Materials Guide***. National Roofing Contractors Association, 10255 W Higgins Rd., Ste. 600 Rosemont, IL 60018-5607. Phone: (847)299-9070; Fax: (847)299-1183 • URL: http://www.nrca.net • Covers: Approximately 250 manufacturers and suppliers of low-slope roof membrane, metal roof panels, cements and coatings, insulation board, and roof fastener products for commercial, industrial, and institutional purposes. Entries include: Company name, location, phone, name and title of contact, description of products, warranty information.

**Lower Coastal Plain Research Station/Cunningham Research Station**. c/o Phillip Winslow, Manager, North Carolina Dept. of Agricultural and Consumer Services, 200 Cunningham Rd. Kinston, NC 28501-1700. Phone: (252)527-3579; Fax: (252)527-2036; Email: lowercoastal.resst@ncmail.net • URL: http://www.ncagr.com.

**Loyola University Chicago - Neiswanger Institute for Bioethics**. Bldg. 120, Rm. 292, Stritch School of Medicine, 2160 S 1st Ave. Maywood, IL 60153. Phone: (708)327-9219; Fax: (708)327-9208; Email: mkuczew@lumc.edu • URL: http://hsd.luc.edu/bioethics • Bioethics and health policy.

**Ludwig von Mises Institute for Austrian Economics**. 518 W Magnolia Ave. Auburn, AL 36832. Phone: (334)321-2100; Fax: (334)321-2119; Email: contact@mises.org • URL: http://www.mises.org.

***Lumbermens Red Book: Reference Book of the Lumbermens Credit Association***. Lumbermens Credit Association Inc., 20 N Wacker Dr., Ste. 1800 Chicago, IL 60606-2905. Phone: (954)771-2100 or (312)553-0943; Fax: (312)553-2149 • Semiannual $2,140.00 per year. Weekly supplements. Lists approximately 39,000 United States firms in the lumber and woodworking industries, with credit ratings. Available online.

**Lund University - School of Economics and Management - Center for Economic Demography**. Box 7083 SE-220 07 Lund, Sweden. Phone: 46 2220000 • URL: http://www.ed.lu.se • Population and economy.

***Lundberg Letter***. Lundberg Survey Inc., PO Box 6002 Camarillo, CA 93011. Phone: (805)383-2400; Fax: (805)383-2424; Email: lsi@lundbergsurvey.com • URL: http://www.lundbergsurvey.com • Description: Provides statistics and analysis of U.S. oil marketing primary data. Includes an in-depth single-subject profile of a development in the petroleum market in each issue. Discusses such topics as retail/wholesale pricing, market shares, and station characteristics nationwide and regionally.

***Luxembourg Business Journal***. Luxembourg American Chamber of Commerce, 17 Beekman Pl. New York, NY 10022. Phone: (212)888-6701; Fax: (212)935-5896; Email: info@luxembourgbusiness.org • URL: http://luxembourgbusiness.org • Contains organization's activities, member news and developments in the economic relations between the Grand Duchy and North America.

***Luxembourg Business Law Handbook***. International Business Publications, USA, PO Box 15343 Washington, DC 20003. Phone: (202)546-2103; Fax: (202)546-3275; Email: ibpusa@comcast.net • URL: http://ibpus.com • $99.95 Individuals hardcopy, e-book, CD-ROM. Covers: Information on basic business legislation, laws and regulations affecting business and foreign investments, property rights, taxation and banking.

***Luxembourg Industrial and Business Directory***. International Business Publications, USA, PO Box 15343 Washington, DC 20003. Phone: (202)546-2103; Fax: (202)546-3275; Email: ibpusa@comcast.net • URL: http://ibpus.com • Annual. $99.95 Individuals paperback, e-book, CD-ROM. Covers: Strategic industrial, investment and business contacts for conducting export-import and investment activity in the country. Contains strategic, practical economic and business information.

***The Lynch Municipal Bond Advisory***. James F. Lynch., editor. The Lynch Municipal Bond Advisory, PO Box 25114 Sante Fe, NM 87504. Phone: (505)984-9199; Fax: (505)984-0269 • Monthly. Description: Addresses the municipal bond market.

**Maastricht University - Limburg Institute of Financial Economics**. PO Box 616 NL-6200 Maastricht, Netherlands. Phone: 31 43 3883838; Fax: 31 43 3884875; Email: p.schotman@berfin.unimaas.nl • URL: http://www.maastrichtuniversity.nl/web/faculties/sbe/theme/researchportal/aboutgsbe/partnerinstitutes/sbeinstitutes.htm • Financial economics, especially exchange rates, microstructure, real estate and corporate bonds. Other research interests include pension funds, term structure modeling, overreaction in stock markets, tail estimation, corporate governance, financial fragility and mortgage pricing.

***Macao Government and Business Contacts Handbook***. International Business Publications, USA, PO Box 15343 Washington, DC 20003. Phone: (202)546-2103; Fax: (202)546-3275; Email: ibpusa@comcast.net • URL: http://ibpus.com • $99.95 Individuals hardcopy, e-book, CD-ROM. Covers: Strategic government and business information, export-import activity in the country, investment, business contacts and regulations.

***Machine Tool Reference Guide***. Machinery Dealers National Association, 315 S Patrick St. Alexandria, VA 22314-3501. Phone: 800-872-7807 or (703)836-9300; Fax: (703)836-9303; Email: office@mdna.org • URL: http://www.mdna.org • $29.95 Individuals CD-ROM; $59.95 Nonmembers CD-ROM. Covers: Nearly 1,000 metalworking machine tool manufacturers; international coverage. Database includes: Information on mergers and sources of parts. Entries include: Company name, address, phone, fax, product/service provided.

**Machine Vision Association of the Society of Manufacturing Engineers**. 1 SME Dr. Dearborn, MI 48128. Phone: 800-733-4763 or (313)425-3000; Fax: (313)425-3400; Email: service@sme.org • URL: http://www.sme.org • Members are professional engineers, managers, and students. Promotes the effective use of machine vision (optical sensing of actual scenes for use in machine control).

***Machinery Buyers' Guide: The Annual Directory of Engineering and Products Services***. Findlay Publications Ltd., Franks Hall, Horton Kirby Horton Kirby DA4 9LL, United Kingdom. Phone: 44 1322 860000; Fax: (132)2 289577; Email: enquiries@findlay.co.uk • Annual. About 6,000 firms offering machine tool, engineering products, machinery, industrial equipment and services worldwide.

**Machinery Dealers National Association**. 315 S Patrick St. Alexandria, VA 22314-3501. Phone: 800-872-7807 or (703)836-9300; Fax: (703)836-9303; Email: office@mdna.org • URL: http://www.mdna.org • Dealers in used, rebuilt, and reconditioned industrial machinery.

**Mack Center for Technological Innovation**. University of Pennsylvania, 1050 Steinberg Hall-Dietrich Hall, 3620 Locust Walk Philadelphia, PA 19104. Phone: (215)898-2104; Fax: (215)573-2129; Email: mackcenter@wharton.upenn.edu • URL: http://www.mackcenter.wharton.upenn.edu • Conducts research related to international business. Formerly Huntsman Center for Global Competition and Innovation.

***Macmillan Directory of Multinationals***. Palgrave Macmillan, Houndsmills Basingstoke RG21 6XS, United Kingdom. Phone: 44 1256 329242 or 44 01256 329242; Fax: 44 1256 479476 or (012)56 320109; Email: booksellers@palgrave.com • URL: http://www.palgrave.com • Biennial. $295 plus 9 for shipping. Covers over 400 multinational industrial companies with consolidated sales of over $1 billion.

***Macmillan Encyclopedia of Energy***. Cengage Learning Inc., 20 Channel Center St. Boston, MA 02210. Phone: 800-487-8488 or (617)289-7700; Fax: (617)289-7844; Email: investors@cengage.com • URL: http://www.cengage.com • 2003. eBook. Published by Macmillan Reference USA. Covers the business, technology, and history of a wide variety of energy sources. Inquire as to price and availability.

**Macquarie University - Center for Japanese Economic Studies**. Faculty of Business & Economics Sydney, NSW 2109, Australia. Phone: 61 2 98507444; Fax: 61 2 98508586; Email: cfreedma@efs.mq.edu.au • URL: http://www.econ.mq.edu.au/about_economics/centre_for_japanese_economic_studies • Economics, including theoretical and applied macroeconomics and microeconomics, econometrics, economic history, cultural economics, economies in transition, and Japanese economics and finance.

***MacRae's Blue Book***. MacRae's Blue Book, 2085 Hurontario St., Ste. 208 Mississauga, ON, Canada L5A 4G1. Phone: 877-463-6284 or (905)290-1818; Fax: (905)290-1760 or (905)361-0140; Email: customerservice@macraesbluebook.com • URL: http://www.macraesbluebook.com • Annual. Covers: about 50,000 manufacturing firms. Entries include: Company name, address, products or services, phone, email and URL addresses.

***Macroeconomics and Company Planning***. Continuing Professional Education Div. American Institute of Certified Public

Accountants, 1211 Avenue of the Americas New York, NY 10036-8775. Phone: 888-777-7077 or (212)596-6200; Fax: (212)596-6213; Email: service@aicpa.org • URL: http://www.aicpa.org • Looseleaf. Self-study course.

*Madagascar Business Directory*. Business Guide, PO Box 27669 Dubai, United Arab Emirates. Phone: 971 4 2651719; Fax: 971 4 2692151; Email: sales@africa-business.com • URL: http://www.africa-business.com • $150 Individuals Soft copy. Covers: 14,000 business listings including wholesalers, importers, retailers, business houses, and agents in Madagascar.

*Maddux Business Report: The Business of Tampa Bay*. Maddux Publishing L.C., PO Box 202 Saint Petersburg, FL 33731. Phone: 800-226-4394 or (727)823-4394; Fax: (727)821-1645; Email: nhowe@maddux.com • URL: http://www.maddux.com • Monthly. $35 Individuals online; $19.45 Single issue. Magazine on business and real estate activities in the seven-county Tampa Bay region.

*Made in Greece*. Trade Publishing Resources, PO Box 1283 Randburg 2175, South Africa. Phone: 27 11 8862636; Fax: 27 11 8865424; Email: info@tradepublishing.co.za • URL: http://www.africaexports.co.za • Covers: Greek companies engaged in establishing trade and business relations in 155 countries.

*Made in Malta*. Malta External Trade Corp., PO Box 8 San Gwann SGN01, Malta. Phone: 356 21446186; Fax: 356 21496687; Email: info@metco.net • Annual. Covers: Over 850 manufacturing companies and service providers in Malta. Entries include: Company name, address, phone, fax, name and title of contact, number of employees, product/services, company logo.

*The Magazine for Electronic Publishing Professionals*. Publish Media, 462 Boston St. Topsfield, MA 01983-1232. Phone: (978)887-7900; Fax: (978)887-6117; Email: edit@publish.com • URL: http://www.publish.com • Monthly. $39.90 per year. Edited for professional publishers, graphic designers, and industry service providers. Covers new products and emerging technologies for the electronic publishing industry.

*Magicians Directory*. InfoGroup Inc., 5711 S 86th Cir. Omaha, NE 68127-4146. Phone: (402)593-4500 • URL: http://www.infogroup.com • Annual. Number of listings: 1,133. Entries include: Name, address, phone, size of advertisement, name of owner or manager, number of employees, year first in "Yellow Pages." Compiled from telephone company "Yellow Pages," nationwide.

*Magill's Cinema Annual*. Cengage Learning Inc., 20 Channel Center St. Boston, MA 02210. Phone: 800-487-8488 or (617)289-7700; Fax: (617)289-7844; Email: investors@cengage.com • URL: http://www.cengage.com • $228 Individuals. Annual. $208.00. Provides reviews and facts for new films released each year in the United States. Typically covers about 300 movies, with nine indexes to title, director, screenwriter, actor, music, etc. Includes awards, obituaries, and "up-and- coming" performers of the year.

**Mahidol University - ASEAN Institute for Health Development**. Salaya, Phutthamonthon Nakhon Pathom 73170, Thailand. Phone: 66 2 4419040; Fax: 66 2 4419044; Email: directad@mahidol.ac.th • URL: http://www.aihd.mahidol.ac.th/new/en • Primary health care and quality of life networks in the ASEAN (Association of South East Asian Nations) region.

**Mailing and Fulfillment Service Association**. 1800 Diagonal Rd., Ste. 320 Alexandria, VA 22314-2806. Phone: (703)836-9200; Fax: (703)548-8204; Email: mfsa-mail@mfsanet.org • URL: http://www.mfsanet.org • Formerly Mail Advertising Service Association International.

*Main Line Chamber of Commerce—Membership Directory and Business Resource Guide*. Main Line Chamber of Commerce, 175 Strafford Ave., Ste. 130 Wayne, PA 19087-3331. Phone: (610)687-6232; Fax: (610)687-8085 • URL: http://www.mlcc.org • Annual. $10 Members; $25 Nonmembers plus 3.50 shipping and handling. Covers bsinesses in Chester, Delaware, and Montgomery counties, PA.

*Main Street Practitioner*. National Society of Accountants, 1010 N Fairfax St. Alexandria, VA 22314. Phone: 800-966-6679 or (703)549-6400; Fax: (703)549-2984; Email: members@nsacct.org • URL: http://www.nsacct.org • Bimonthly. For accounting and tax practitioners.

*The Maine Business and Professional Directory*. Tower Publishing Co., 588 Saco Rd. Standish, ME 04084. Phone: 800-969-8693 or (207)642-5400; Fax: (207)642-5463 or 800-264-3870; Email: info@towerpub.com • URL: http://www.towerpub.com • Annual. $115 Individuals; $165 Individuals CD-Rom. 42,588 Maine professional and industrial firms.

**Maine Lobstermen's Association**. 203 Lafayette Ctr. Kennebunk, ME 04043. Phone: (207)967-4555; Fax: (866)407-3770; Email: info@mainelobstermen.org • URL: http://www.mainelobstermen.org • Licensed lobstermen and supporting business. Gives Maine's lobstermen a voice and influence at the highest levels of government.

*Maine Manufacturers Register and Industrial Database*. Manufacturers' News Inc., 1633 Central St. Evanston, IL 60201-1569. Phone: (847)864-7000; Fax: (847)332-1100 • URL: http://www.manufacturersnews.com • Annual. $92 Individuals print; $340 Individuals database (EZ select full); $201 Individuals database (EZ select with 20 plus employees); $119 Individuals database (EZ basic). Covers: 2,683 manufacturers in Maine. Entries include: Company

name, address, phone, names and titles of key personnel, year established, number of employees, plant square footage, services, Standard Industry Classification (SIC) code, parent and subsidiary company information, type of in-house computer system, URL, e-mail address.

*Maine Manufacturing Directory*. Tower Publishing Co., 588 Saco Rd. Standish, ME 04084. Phone: 800-969-8693 or (207)642-5400; Fax: (207)642-5463 or 800-264-3870; Email: info@towerpub.com • URL: http://www.towerpub.com • Annual. $55 Individuals. Covers: Approximately 1,584 manufacturers and processors in Maine. Entries include: Company name, address, phone, fax, toll-free phone, e-mail and web addresses, names and titles of principal officers, number of employees, product or service, Standard Industrial Classification (SIC) code, parent company (if applicable), sales revenue, import/export data.

*Maintenance Supplies Buyers' Guide*. Cygnus Business Media Inc., 1233 Janesville Ave. Fort Atkinson, WI 53538. Phone: 800-547-7377; Email: info@cygnus.com • URL: http://www.cygnus.com • Approximately 1,000 manufacturers and associations for commercial, industrial, and institutional janitorial supplies; international coverage. Formerly *Maintenance Supplies Annual*.

*Maize Abstracts*. CABI Publishing North America, 38 Chauncey St., Ste. 1002 Boston, MA 02111. Phone: 800-552-3083; Email: cabi-nao@cabi.org • URL: http://www.cabi.org • Bimonthly. $840.00 per year. Published in England by CABI Publishing. Provides worldwide coverage of the literature.

*Major and Medium-Sized Companies in the Czech Republic*. Hoppenstedt Produktinformationen GmbH, Havelstrasse 9, Postfach 100139 D-64295 Darmstadt, Germany. Phone: 49 6151 1375444 or 49 6151 38 0; Fax: 49 6151 1375443 or 49 6151 380 360; Email: info@hoppenstedt.de • URL: http://www.hoppenstedt.com • Annual. €195. Covers: over 18,000 companies in the Czech Republic. Entries include: Name, address, phone, fax, management, production or services, number of employees, turnover (revenue), and capital.

*Major Chemical and Petrochemical Companies of the World*. Cengage Learning Inc., 20 Channel Center St. Boston, MA 02210. Phone: 800-487-8488 or (617)289-7700; Fax: (617)289-7844; Email: investors@cengage.com • URL: http://www.cengage.com • Annual. $1,460 Individuals. 2008. 12th edition. eBook. Published by Graham & Whiteside. Contains profiles of more than 8,500 important chemical and petrochemical companies in various countries. Subject areas include general chemicals, specialty chemicals, agricultural chemicals, petrochemicals, industrial gases, and fertilizers.

*The Major Companies Guide: The Charitable and Community Support of the UK's Leading Companies*. The Directory of Social Change, 24 Stephenson Way London NW1 2DP, United Kingdom. Phone: 20 73914800 or 44 20 73914800; Fax: 20 73914808 or 44 20 7391 4808; Email: training@dsc.org.uk • URL: http://www.dsc.org.uk • Biennial. $16.95. Covers: about 400 companies in the United Kingdom with 160 millions Ls in cash donations and 100 millions Ls in community contributions. Entries include: Company name, address, phone, names and titles of key personnel, financial data, amount of donations annually, donation policy and practice, number of employees, employee involvement, branch office or subsidiary names, descriptions of product/service, type of business, community support programs.

*Major Companies in China*. Hoppenstedt Produktinformationen GmbH, Havelstrasse 9, Postfach 100139 D-64295 Darmstadt, Germany. Phone: 49 6151 1375444 or 49 6151 38 0; Fax: 49 6151 1375443 or 49 6151 380 360; Email: info@hoppenstedt.de • URL: http://www.hoppenstedt.com • $520. Covers: 10,000 major companies in China. Entries include: Name, address, phone, fax, range of products or services, import and export, revenue, number of employees, and joint ventures.

*Major Companies in Southeast Asia*. Euromonitor International Business Reference Div., 224 S Michigan Ave., Ste. 1500 Chicago, IL 60604. Phone: (312)922-1115; Fax: (312)922-1157; Email: insight@euromonitorintl.com • URL: http://www.euromonitor.com • $550 Individuals; $550. Covers: Nearly 2,000 companies in Brunei, Hong Kong, Indonesia, Malaysia, the Philippines, Singapore, South Korea, Taiwan, and Thailand. Entries include: Company name, address, phone, fax, type of business, ownership, subsidiaries, key personnel, products and brands, main operations, outlets and trading names, number of employees, turnover, pre-tax profit, sales, background information.

*Major Companies in the Netherlands*. Netherlands-British Chamber of Commerce, 8 Northumberland Ave. London WC2N 5DY, United Kingdom. Phone: 44 3333 440799; Email: info@nbcc.co.uk • URL: http://www.nbcc.co.uk/ • Biennial. $10. Covers: Businesses in the Netherlands. Entries include: Company name, address, phone, telex, directors.

*Major Companies of Africa South of the Sahara*. Cengage Learning Inc., 20 Channel Center St. Boston, MA 02210. Phone: 800-487-8488 or (617)289-7700; Fax: (617)289-7844; Email: investors@cengage.com • URL: http://www.cengage.com • Annual. $980 Individuals. More than 2,150 major companies in South Africa are covered, plus 4,250 businesses in non-Arab countries south of the Sahara.

*Major Companies of Europe*. Cengage Learning Inc., 20 Channel Center St. Boston, MA 02210. Phone: 800-487-8488 or (617)289-7700; Fax: (617)289-7844; Email: investors@

cengage.com • URL: http://www.cengage.com • Annual. £550 Individuals for volume 1; £550 Individuals for volume 2; £550 Individuals for volume 3; £550 Individuals for volume 4; £550 Individuals for volume 5; £550 Individuals for volume 6; £550 Institutions for volume 7; $2,980 set; US $1,975.00. Published by Graham & Whiteside. Approximately 44,640 major companies and key executives in European countries in all lines of business.

*Major Companies of Latin America and the Caribbean*. Cengage Learning Inc., 20 Channel Center St. Boston, MA 02210. Phone: 800-487-8488 or (617)289-7700; Fax: (617)289-7844; Email: investors@cengage.com • URL: http://www.cengage.com • $1,275. Includes more than 8,650 major companies in Latin America and more than 1,100 leading Caribbean firms.

*Major Companies of Slovakia*. I.S.M.C. Information Systems and Marketing Contacts Ltd., Nam. Slobody 9, PO Box 47 81499 Bratislava, Slovakia. Phone: 421 7 265423783; Fax: 421 7 265422186; Email: ismc@ismc.sk • URL: http://www.ismc.sk • Annual. $164. Covers: The most important companies in the Slovak Republic. Entries include: Detailed business information and data.

*Major Companies of the Arab World*. Cengage Learning Inc., 20 Channel Center St. Boston, MA 02210. Phone: 800-487-8488 or (617)289-7700; Fax: (617)289-7844; Email: investors@cengage.com • URL: http://www.cengage.com • Annual. $1,480 Individuals. Published by Graham & Whiteside Ltd. Coverage of the world's largest companies in the Arab world. Includes names of senior executives, contact information, and financial information.

*Major Companies of Turkey Directory*. Poyraz Publications A.S., Halaskargazi Cad 309, Sisli TR-80260 Istanbul, Turkey. Phone: 1 148 87 20 • Annual. $50. Covers: 2,500 companies, products, and industries in Turkey. Entries include: Company name, address, phone, telex, names and titles of key personnel, products, and trade names.

*Major Companies on CD-ROM*. Graham & Whiteside, Cengage Learning, Cheriton House, North Way Andover Hampshire SP10 5BE, United Kingdom. Phone: 44 1264 332424; Fax: 44 1264 342763; Email: emea.enquiries@cengage.com • URL: http://www.gale.cengage.co.uk/graham—whiteside.aspx • $7,845 Individuals individual countries sold separately; inquire for. Database covers: 55,000 companies outside North America, including Europe, the Far East and Australia, Middle East, Africa, Latin America, Central Europe, Eastern Europe, the CIS, and Southwest Asia. Entries include: Company name, address, phone, fax, number of employees, sales, assets, profits, date established, SIC codes, parent and subsidiary companies, name and title of contact.

*Major Employers in Metropolitan Chicago*. Chicagoland Chamber of Commerce, The Wrigley Building, 410 N Michigan Ave., Ste. 900 Chicago, IL 60611. Phone: (312)494-6700; Fax: (312)861-0660; Email: info@chicagolandchamber.org • URL: http://www.chicagolandchamber.org/wdk_cc • Biennial. $55. Covers: over 2,000 firms employing at least 250 employees in their Chicago area plants and offices; also listed are subsidiaries, affiliates, and divisions. Entries include: Company name, address, phone, names of major officers; line of business and Standard Industrial Classification (SIC) code; coding to indicate number of employees and whether manufacturer or non-manufacturer.

*Major Energy Companies of the World*. Cengage Learning Inc., 20 Channel Center St. Boston, MA 02210. Phone: 800-487-8488 or (617)289-7700; Fax: (617)289-7844; Email: investors@cengage.com • URL: http://www.cengage.com • Annual. $1,460 Individuals. 2008. 12th edition. eBook. Published by Graham & Whiteside. Contains detailed information on more than 4,850 important energy companies in various countries. Industries include electricity generation, coal, natural gas, nuclear energy, petroleum, fuel distribution, and equipment for energy production.

*Major Financial Institutions of the World*. Cengage Learning Inc., 20 Channel Center St. Boston, MA 02210. Phone: 800-487-8488 or (617)289-7700; Fax: (617)289-7844; Email: investors@cengage.com • URL: http://www.cengage.com • $1,460 Individuals. 2012. 16th edition. eBook. Published by Graham & Whiteside. Contains detailed information on more than 10,000 important financial institutions in various countries. Includes banks, investment companies, and insurance companies.

*Major Firms in Czech Republic*. I.S.M.C. Information Systems and Marketing Contacts Ltd., Nam. Slobody 9, PO Box 47 81499 Bratislava, Slovakia. Phone: 421 7 265423783; Fax: 421 7 265422186; Email: ismc@ismc.sk • URL: http://www.ismc.sk • Annual. $164. Covers: Significant business firms in Czech Republic. Entries include: Detailed business information.

*Major Food & Drink Companies of the World*. Cengage Learning Inc., 20 Channel Center St. Boston, MA 02210. Phone: 800-487-8488 or (617)289-7700; Fax: (617)289-7844; Email: investors@cengage.com • URL: http://www.cengage.com • Annual. $1,460 Individuals. 2008. 12th edition. eBook. Published by Graham & Whiteside Ltd. Contains directory information on more than 9,200 of the leading food, alcoholic, and non-alcoholic drink companies worldwide.

*Major Food and Drink Companies of the World*. Cengage Learning Inc., 20 Channel Center St. Boston, MA 02210. Phone:

800-487-8488 or (617)289-7700; Fax: (617)289-7844; Email: investors@cengage.com • URL: http://www.cengage.com • 12th edition. eBook. Published by Graham & Whiteside. Contains profiles and trade names for more than 9,200 important food and beverage companies in various countries. In addition to foods, includes both alcoholic and nonalcoholic drink products.

***Major French Companies***. DAFSA, 25 rue Leblanc F-75010 Paris, France. Phone: 33 14604060; Fax: 33 140605151 • Annual. Covers: Companies with shares traded on the stock exchange in France. Entries include: Company name, address, phone, officers, directors, executives, banking information, financial institutions, broker-trading.

***Major Information Technology Companies of the World***. Cengage Learning Inc., 20 Channel Center St. Boston, MA 02210. Phone: 800-487-8488 or (617)289-7700; Fax: (617)289-7844; Email: investors@cengage.com • URL: http://www.cengage.com • Annual. $1,460 Individuals. 2008. 11th edition. eBook. Published by Graham & Whiteside. Contains profiles of more than 8,250 leading information technology companies in various countries.

***Major Market Share Companies***. Euromonitor International Business Reference Div., 224 S Michigan Ave., Ste. 1500 Chicago, IL 60604. Phone: (312)922-1115; Fax: (312)922-1157; Email: insight@euromonitorintl.com • URL: http://www.euromonitor.com • $1,295 Individuals hard copy mail delivery. Covers: List of top national and regional companies in the Americas, Asia-Pacific, Europe, and South Africa across 15 consumer sectors. Entries include: Company name, address, phone; company share; leading brands; and merger and acquisition information.

***Major Pharmaceutical & Biotechnology Companies of the World***. Cengage Learning Inc., 20 Channel Center St. Boston, MA 02210. Phone: 800-487-8488 or (617)289-7700; Fax: (617)289-7844; Email: investors@cengage.com • URL: http://www.cengage.com • Contains directory information on more than 4070 of the world's largest pharmaceutical companies, providing essential business profiles of the international leaders in the industry.

***Major Telecommunications Companies of Europe***. Graham & Whiteside, Cengage Learning, Cheriton House, North Way Andover Hampshire SP10 5BE, United Kingdom. Phone: 44 1264 332424; Fax: 44 1264 342763; Email: emea.enquiries@cengage.com • URL: http://www.gale.cengage.co.uk/graham—whiteside.aspx • Annual. $245 softback; $440 softback. Covers: Over 1,500 telecommunications companies in Austria, Belgium, Bulgaria, Croatia, Cyprus, Czech Republic, Denmark, Eire, Estonian Republic, Finland, France, Germany, Greece, Hungary, Israel, Italy, Latvian Republic, Lithuanian Republic, Luxembourg, Netherlands, Norway, Poland, Portugal, Romania, Slovakia, Slovenia, Spain, Sweden, Switzerland, and the United Kingdom involved in the telecommunications industry, including telecommunications companies, equipment suppliers, and Internet companies. Entries include: Company name, address, phone and names and titles of key personnel.

***Major Telecommunications Companies of the Far East & Australasia***. Graham & Whiteside, Cengage Learning, Cheriton House, North Way Andover Hampshire SP10 5BE, United Kingdom. Phone: 44 1264 332424; Fax: 44 1264 342763; Email: emea.enquiries@cengage.com • URL: http://www.gale.cengage.co.uk/graham—whiteside.aspx • Annual. $245 softback; $440 softback. Covers: Over 1,000 telecommunications companies in Australia, Brunei, Cambodia, China, Hong Kong, Indonesia, Japan, Laos, Malaysia, New Zealand, Philippines, Singapore, South Korea, Taiwan, Thailand, and Vietnam involved in the telecommunications industry, including telecommunications companies, equipment suppliers, and Internet companies. Entries include: Company name, address, phone and names and titles of key personnel.

***Major Telecommunications Companies of the World***. Cengage Learning Inc., 20 Channel Center St. Boston, MA 02210. Phone: 800-487-8488 or (617)289-7700; Fax: (617)289-7844; Email: investors@cengage.com • URL: http://www.cengage.com • Annual. $1,360 Individuals. Published by Graham & Whiteside. Contains detailed information and trade names for more than 5,950 important telecommunications companies in various countries.

***Malaysia Builders Directory***. Marshall Cavendish Business Information Private Ltd., Times Centre, 1 New Industrial Rd. Singapore 536196, Singapore. Phone: 65 6213 9300 or 65 6213 9288; Fax: 65 6285 0161 or 65 6284 4733; Email: bizinfo@sg.marshallcavendish.com • URL: http://www.timesdirectories.com • S$40 Individuals local, foreign and other countries; S$20 Individuals CD-ROM. Covers: building contractors & consultants, architects, engineers, property developers, quantity surveyors, and construction equipment and suppliers. Entries include: contact information, brand names, products and services, certified companies, trade associations and professional bodies.

***Malaysia Business Forecast Report***. Telecommunications Insight, 85 Queen Victoria St. London EC4V 4AB, United Kingdom. Phone: 20 72 465100 or 44 20 7248 0468; Fax: 20 72 480467 or 44 20 7248 0467; Email: enquiries@telecomsinsight.com • URL: http://www.telecomsinsight.com • Quarterly. $1,195 Individuals Single user; $1,795 Individuals Up to 3 users. Business forecast reports for Malaysia.

***Malaysia Business Law Handbook***. International Business Publications, USA, PO Box 15343 Washington, DC 20003. Phone: (202)546-2103; Fax: (202)546-3275; Email: ibpusa@comcast.net • URL: http://ibpus.com • $99.95 Individuals hardcopy, e-book, CD-ROM. Covers: Information on basic business legislation, laws, business climate, export-import regulations, and contacts.

***Malaysia Exporters of Halal Products and Services Directory***. Malaysia External Trade Development Corp., Jalan Khidmat Usaha, Off Jalan Duta 50480 Kuala Lumpur, Malaysia. Phone: 91 603 62077077; Fax: 91 603 62037037; Email: info@matrade.gov.my • URL: http://www.matrade.gov.my • Covers: 200 exporters of halal products including food and beverages, palm oil products, herbal, cosmetics, and dietary supplements.

***Malaysia Exports***. Malaysia External Trade Development Corp., Jalan Khidmat Usaha, Off Jalan Duta 50480 Kuala Lumpur, Malaysia. Phone: 91 603 62077077; Fax: 91 603 62037037; Email: info@matrade.gov.my • URL: http://www.matrade.gov.my • $60 Individuals. Includes manufacturers of a wide range of products in 31 categories that cover the agricultural & food sectors; electrical & electronics; building & construction materials; furniture; automotive components; and other sectors. Covers: 8,000 exporting companies from both manufacturing and exporting sectors.

***Malaysia Government and Business Contacts Handbook***. International Business Publications, USA, PO Box 15343 Washington, DC 20003. Phone: (202)546-2103; Fax: (202)546-3275; Email: ibpusa@comcast.net • URL: http://ibpus.com • $99.95 Individuals hardcopy, e-book, CD-ROM. Covers: Strategic government and business information, export-import activity in the country, investment, business contacts and regulations.

***Malaysia Industrial and Business Directory***. International Business Publications, USA, PO Box 15343 Washington, DC 20003. Phone: (202)546-2103; Fax: (202)546-3275; Email: ibpusa@comcast.net • URL: http://ibpus.com • $99.95 Individuals hardcopy, e-book, CD-ROM. Covers: Customs, trade regulations and procedures.

***Malaysia Logistics Directory (MLD)***. Marshall Cavendish Business Information Private Ltd., Times Centre, 1 New Industrial Rd. Singapore 536196, Singapore. Phone: 65 6213 9300 or 65 6213 9288; Fax: 65 6285 0161 or 65 6284 4733; Email: bizinfo@sg.marshallcavendish.com • URL: http://www.timesdirectories.com • $30 Individuals local, foreign and other countries. Covers: information and contacts on Malaysian logistics industry, freight forwarders, transport companies, airlines and other cargo related supporting industries.

***Malaysia Printing and Supporting Industries Directory (MPSID)***. Marshall Cavendish Business Information Private Ltd., Times Centre, 1 New Industrial Rd. Singapore 536196, Singapore. Phone: 65 6213 9300 or 65 6213 9288; Fax: 65 6285 0161 or 65 6284 4733; Email: bizinfo@sg.marshallcavendish.com • URL: http://www.timesdirectories.com • $30 Individuals local, foreign and other countries. Covers: information on the printing industry of Malaysia. Entries include: corporate profiles, contact details on printing and publishing companies, equipment, supplies and accessories.

**Malaysia South-South Association**. Bangunan AmBank Group, 17th Fl., Jaalan Raja Chulan 50200 Kuala Lumpur, Malaysia. Phone: 60 3 20783788; Fax: 60 3 20728411; Email: mail@massa.net.my • URL: http://www.massa.net.my • Promotes and enhances knowledge and understanding of economic, trade and investment policies and conditions of South-South countries. Acts as an informal liaison body between the private sector and the government in the promotion of trade and investment. Provides a forum for the dissemination of ideas and for the discussion of trade, economy and culture. Enhances trade and investment relations and fosters friendship and cooperation in South-South countries.

**Malaysian Business Council of Cambodia**. No. 87, 294 St., Boeng Keng Kong 1 Phnom Penh, Cambodia. Phone: 855 23 216176; Fax: 855 23 726101; Email: mbcc.secretariat@gmail.com • URL: http://mbccambodia.org • Fosters strong business ties between Malaysia and Cambodia. Encourages the development of Malaysian investment in Cambodia. Provides a forum for meetings, discussions and interaction between the Malaysian business community and governmental personnel in Cambodia.

**Malaysian Employers' Federation**. PO Box 11026 50732 Kuala Lumpur, Malaysia. Phone: 60 3 79557778; Fax: 60 3 79556808; Email: mef-hq@mef.org.my • URL: http://www.mef.org.my/public/default.aspx • Employers (3470) and employers' associations (10). Seeks to ensure a domestic political, business, and labor climate conducive to economic growth. Works to safeguard the rights and interests of Malaysian employers. Represents members in negotiations with labor organizations, at the Industrial Court, Labour Court, and conciliation proceedings; provides consultancy and advisory services to members; gathers and disseminates information; conducts lobbying activities. Sponsors human resources and industrial relations training programs; conducts surveys on salaries and compensation packages.

***Malaysian German Business***. Malaysian-German Chamber of Commerce and Industry, Menara AMBank, Ste. 47.01, Level 47, 8 Jalan Yap Kwan Seng 50450 Kuala Lumpur, Malaysia. Phone: 60 3 92351800; Fax: 60 3 20721198; Email: info@malaysia.ahk.de • URL: http://www.malaysia.ahk.de • Annual. RM150 Individuals; Ar60 Other countries. Covers: Listings of Malaysian-German business members. Entries include: Members' contact information and activities.

***Malaysian-Thai Chamber of Commerce—Handbook and Directory***. Malaysian-Thai Chamber of Commerce, 3601 Q Houses Lumpini Bldg., 36th Fl., S Sathorn Rd., Tungmahamek, Sathorn Bangkok, Thailand. Phone: 66 26777393; Fax: 66 26777394; Email: admin@mtcc.or.th • URL: http://www.mtcc.or.th • Covers: Malaysian and Thai member companies and individuals.

**Malaysian Venture Capital and Private Equity Association**. 54-3, Jalan 27/70A, Desa Sri Hartamas 50480 Kuala Lumpur, Malaysia. Phone: 60 3 23006550; Fax: 60 3 62062484; Email: info@mvca.org.my • URL: http://www.mvca.org.my • Promotes, develops and maintains the venture capital industry in Malaysia as a source of equity financing for the start-up or development of small and medium-sized enterprises. Encourages the promotion, research, and analysis of venture capital in Malaysia and other countries. Serves as a forum for the exchange of views among members. Represents the members to all governmental institutions or public authorities.

**Malcolm Wiener Center for Social Policy**. Harvard University, John F. Kennedy School of Government, 79 John F. Kennedy St. Cambridge, MA 02138. Phone: (617)495-1100; Fax: (617)496-9053; Email: mwcenter@harvaard.edu • URL: http://www.hks.harvard.edu • Does multidisciplinary research on health care access and financing.

***Mali Business Directory***. Business Guide, PO Box 27669 Dubai, United Arab Emirates. Phone: 971 4 2651719; Fax: 971 4 2692151; Email: sales@africa-business.com • URL: http://www.africa-business.com • $150 Individuals. Covers: 2,000 business listings including wholesalers, importers, retailers, business houses, and agents in Mali.

***Malibu Business and Community Directory***. Malibu Chamber of Commerce, 23805 Stuart Ranch Rd., Ste. 105 Malibu, CA 90265-4897. Phone: (310)456-9025; Fax: (310)456-0195; Email: info@malibu.org • URL: http://www.malibu.org • Covers businesses and communities in Malibu, California.

**Mallinckrodt Institute of Radiology - Hyperthermia Service**. Washington University Medical Center, 510 S Kingshighway Blvd. St. Louis, MO 63110. Phone: (314)362-8503; Fax: (314)362-8521 • URL: http://www.mir.wustl.edu • Maintains laboratories for research pertaining to various kinds of radiological equipment.

**Malta Association of Women in Business**. TaL-Imriekeb, Ramla Rd. Naxxar NXR 08, Malta. Phone: 356 21 422009 or 356 21 334394; Email: info@mawb.eu • URL: http://www.mawb.eu • Encourages reciprocal support, exchange of ideas, sharing of experiences and business and economic opportunities among its members both nationally and internationally. Organizes seminars, workshops, social and informative evenings. Promotes an environment for women to grow and develop in their businesses and professions. Promotes the interests of its members in the pursuit of innovative and effective changes in business, economic, social and public policy.

***Malta Export-Import, Economic, Financial, Trade and Industrial Development Handbook***. International Business Publications, USA, PO Box 15343 Washington, DC 20003. Phone: (202)546-2103; Fax: (202)546-3275; Email: ibpusa@comcast.net • URL: http://ibpus.com • $99.95. Covers: Government programs and plans for economic, industrial, and business development in Malta.

***Malta Trade Directory***. Malta Chamber of Commerce, Enterprise and Industry, Exchange Buildings, Republic St. Valletta VLT 1117, Malta. Phone: 356 21 233873; Fax: 356 21 245223; Email: info@maltachamber.org.mt • URL: http://www.maltachamber.org.mt • Annual. $10. Covers: Business and professional organizations, drydock facilities, tourist offices, government offices and agencies, and other businesses in Malta; overseas chambers of commerce. Database includes: Economic and trade statistics. Entries include: Company, agency, or organization name, address, phone, name and title of contact, products or services provided.

***Management Advisory Services Guideline Series***. American Institute of Certified Public Accountants, 1211 Avenue of the Americas New York, NY 10036-8775. Phone: 888-777-7077 or (212)596-6200; Fax: (212)596-6213; Email: service@aicpa.org • URL: http://www.aicpa.org • Irregular. Price varies.

**Management Consultancies Association**. 36-38 Cornhill, 5th Fl. London EC3V 3NG, United Kingdom. Phone: 44 20 76457950; Fax: 44 20 76457951; Email: info@mca.org.uk • URL: http://www.mca.org.uk • Enhances the consultancy management profession. Furthers the collective objectives and interests of its members. Acts as a focal point for individuals wishing to seek advice on management consultancy. Serves as a forum for members to discuss matters of current interest and future policy.

***Management Consultancy***. Jordans Ltd., 21 St. Thomas St. Bristol BS1 6JS, United Kingdom. Phone: 44 117 923 0600; Fax: 44 117 923 0063; Email: customerservices@jordans.co.uk • URL: http://www.jordans.co.uk • $50 plus 5 pounds shipping. Covers: management consultants in the United Kingdom. Database includes: Industry market profiles. Entries include: Company name, address, phone, name of chief executive, financial data for previous three years, corporate ownership, shareholder data, and business description.

***Management Consultant Books***. Kennedy Information Inc., 1 Phoenix Mill Ln., 3rd Fl. Peterborough, NH 03458. Phone: 800-531-0007 or (603)924-1006; Fax: (603)924-4460 or (603)924-4034; Email: customerservice@kennedyinfo.com • URL: http://www.kennedyinfo.com • Annual. Free. Contains descriptions of selected books from various publishers on management consulting.

***Management Consultants Directory***. InfoGroup Inc., 5711 S 86th Cir. Omaha, NE 68127-4146. Phone: (402)593-4500 • URL: http://www.infogroup.com • Annual. Number of listings: 51,839. Entries include: Name, address, phone, size of advertisement, name of owner or manager, number of employees, year first in "Yellow Pages." Compiled from telephone company "Yellow Pages," nationwide.

***Management Consulting: A Complete Guide to the Industry, 2nd Edition***. John Wiley & Sons Inc., 111 River St. Hoboken, NJ 07030-5774. Phone: 800-225-5945 or (201)748-6000; Fax: (201)748-6088; Email: info@wiley.com • URL: http://www.wiley.com • $60 Individuals hardcover. Covers: Top fifty consulting firms in the nation; complete game plan for novice management consultants trying to break into the business along with expert guidelines for veterans looking to expand their services.

***Management for Strategic Business Ideas***. Society of Management Accountants of Canada, 25 York St., Ste. 1100 Toronto, ON, Canada M5J 2V5. Phone: (416)977-7741; Fax: (416)977-6079; Email: info@cmaontario.org • URL: http://www.cma-canada.org/index.cfm/ci_id/1633/la_id/1.htm • 10 times a year. $60.00 per year. Text in English and French.

***Management OHS and E***. Stevens Publishing Corp., 5151 Belt Line Rd., 10th Fl. Dallas, TX 75240. Phone: (972)687-6700; Fax: (972)687-6769 or (972)687-6799 • URL: http://www.pollutiononline.com/storefronts/stevenspub.html • Monthly. Free to qualified personnel; others, $150.00 per year. Includes news, interviews, feature articles, legal developments, and reviews of literature. Includes *Buyer's Guide*.

***Management Professionals Association—Directory of MPA Members***. Management Professionals Association, 25 Krishna St., T Nagar Madras 600017, India. Phone: 44 4340677; Fax: 44 4341514 • Annual. Covers: 26,000 members worldwide. Entries include: Company name, member name and title, address, phone, biographical information.

***Management Services and Technical Assistance: Small Business Resource***. Metro Atlanta Chamber of Commerce, 235 Andrew Young International Blvd. NW Atlanta, GA 30303-2718. Phone: (404)880-9000 • URL: http://www.metroatlantachamber.com • $8. Covers: Resources available to small businesses in the metropolitan Atlanta area. Entries include: Organization name, address, phone, description.

***Management Training Buyer's Guide***. Training Information Network Ltd., 51 High St., Jubilee House, The Oaks Ruislip HA4 7LF, United Kingdom. Phone: 895622112; Fax: 895621582 • Annual. $25. Covers: Over 600 suppliers of management training courses, consultancy, videos, films, packages, and training aids throughout the United Kingdom. Entries include: Company name, address, phone, fax, name and title of contact, number of employees, geographical area served, branch office or subsidiary names and addresses, description.

***Manager's Handbook: Everything You Need to Know about How Business and Management Work***. Pearson Learning Group, 145 S Mount Zion Rd. Lebanon, IN 46052. Phone: 800-526-9907; Fax: (800)393-3156; Email: info@pearsonlearning.com • URL: http://www.k12pearson.com • $24.95. Publication includes: Business directory representing key areas of management in Canada and the United States. Principal content of publication is reference guide for new and experienced managers.

***Managing Business Risk***. Cengage Learning Inc., 20 Channel Center St. Boston, MA 02210. Phone: 800-487-8488 or (617)289-7700; Fax: (617)289-7844; Email: investors@cengage.com • URL: http://www.cengage.com • 2009. eBook. Published by Kogan Page. A guide that can help in identifying potential areas of risk within a business. Examines the five key areas of risk you need to consider in today's complex and competitive business market. Drawing on expert advice from leading risk consultants, lawyers and regulatory authorities, it shows you how to protect your business against a rising tide of business risks.

***Managing Financial Risk with Forwards, Futures, Options, and Swaps***. American Management Association Extension Institute, 1601 Broadway New York, NY 10019. Phone: 800-262-9699 or (518)586-8100; Fax: (518)903-8168 • Looseleaf. $159.00. Self-study course. Emphasis is on practical explanations, examples, and problem solving. Quizzes and a case study are included.

***Managing Housing Letter***. Community Development Services, Inc. CD Publications, 8204 Fenton St. Silver Spring, MD 20910. Phone: 800-666-6380 or (301)588-6380; Fax: (301)588-6385; Email: info@cdpublications.com • URL: http://www.cdpublications.com • Description: Provides news and advice for owners and managers of rental housing—public, private, and subsidized—including news from Washington and practical management tips. Recurring features include news of research.

**Mananga Management Centre**. PO Box 5100 Mbabane, Swaziland. Email: info@mananga.sz • URL: http://www.mananga.sz • Development organizations and individuals with an interest in development issues. Promotes more effective management of development projects. Sponsors training courses for development administrators; initiates programs in areas including agricultural development, women's rights, rural development, environmental protection, water supply and sanitation, and vocational education.

**Manpower Education Institute**. 1835 Charles Ave. Lancaster, SC 29720-1512. Phone: (718)548-4200; Email: info@meipublishing.com • URL: http://www.manpower-education.org • Individuals from the fields of business, labor, and education who develop educational film series for the U.S. labor force. Series includes: Ready or Not (pre-retirement planning), Your Future Is Now (high school equivalency programs), Read Your Way Up (reading skills improvement), Out of Work (for the unemployed), If You Don't Come In Sunday, Don't Come In Monday (history of the American labor movement), Plug Us In (to assist workers reentering the labor market), and Where Do I Fit In (new worker orientation).

***Mansfield Stock Chart Service***. R.W. Mansfield Co., 2973 Kennedy Blvd. Jersey City, NJ 07306-3884. Phone: 877-626-7353 or (201)795-0629 or (201)795-0630; Fax: (201)795-5476 • Weekly. Price varies. Newsletter. Covers New York Stock Exchange, American Stock Exchange, OTC exchange, international stocks and industry groups. Partial subscriptions available.

***Manual of Credit and Commercial Laws***. National Association of Credit Management. National Association of Credit Management, 8840 Columbia 100 Pkwy. Columbia, MD 21045-2158. Phone: (410)740-5560; Fax: (410)740-5574; Email: nacm_national@nacm.org • URL: http://www.nacm.org • Annual. $69.95 Individuals. Provides information for credit professionals. Formerly *Credit Manual of Commercial Laws*.

***Manual of Oil and Gas Terms***. Matthew Bender and Company Inc., 1275 Broadway Albany, NY 12204-2638. Phone: 800-424-4200 or (518)487-3000; Fax: (518)487-3573 or (800)424-4200; Email: customer.support@lexisnexis.com • URL: http://www.matthewbender.com • $148.00. 15th edition. Defines technical, legal, and tax terms relating to the oil and gas industry.

***Manufactured Fiber Fact Book***. Fiber Economics Bureau, 1530 Wilson Blvd., Ste. 690 Arlington, VA 22209. Phone: (703)875-0676; Fax: (703)875-0675; Email: ddezan@afma.org • URL: http://www.fibereconomics.com • Biennial. $10.00. Provides a general review of the history and development of the synthetic fiber industry. (Fiber Economics Bureau is a subsidiary of the American Fiber Manufacturers Association.).

***Manufactured Fiber Review***. Fiber Economics Bureau, 1530 Wilson Blvd., Ste. 690 Arlington, VA 22209. Phone: (703)875-0676; Fax: (703)875-0675; Email: ddezan@afma.org • URL: http://www.fibereconomics.com • Monthly. $350 Individuals. Provides a "quick-release four-page monthly review of the latest U.S. data on manufactured fiber." Coverage includes production, shipments, exports, and utilization rates. (Fiber Economics Bureau is a subsidiary of the American Fiber Manufacturers Association.).

***Manufactured Homes Manufacturers Directory***. InfoGroup Inc., 5711 S 86th Cir. Omaha, NE 68127-4146. Phone: (402)593-4500 • URL: http://www.infogroup.com • Annual. Number of listings: 2,002. Entries include: Name, address, phone, size of advertisement, name of owner or manager, number of employees, year first in "Yellow Pages." Compiled from telephone company "Yellow Pages," nationwide.

**Manufactured Housing Institute**. 1655 N Fort Myer Dr., Ste. 104 Arlington, VA 22209-3108. Phone: (703)558-0400; Fax: (703)558-0401 • URL: http://www.manufacturedhousing.org • Manufacturers of manufactured homes; suppliers of equipment, components, furnishings and services, financial services companies, state association organizations, retailers and community owners. Promotes sales of manufactured homes through programs and services in six key areas: government relations, technical activities, financing, public relations, site development and community operations. Conducts research and educational programs; provides statistics.

***Manufacturer Importers/Exporters***. Tower Publishing Co., 588 Saco Rd. Standish, ME 04084. Phone: 800-969-8693 or (207)642-5400; Fax: (207)642-5463 or 800-264-3870; Email: info@towerpub.com • URL: http://www.towerpub.com • $225. Covers: 5,034 manufacturing companies in Maine, Massachusetts, New Hampshire and Vermont which import or export products outside the U.S. Entries include: Company name, address, phone, fax, contact name and title, e-mail, URL, SIC code, type of office, countries to which the company exports.

**Manufacturers' Agents Association for the Foodservice Industry**. 1199 Euclid Ave. Atlanta, GA 30307. Phone: (404)214-9474; Fax: (404)522-0132; Email: info@mafsi.org • URL: http://www.mafsi.org • Members are independent manufacturers' representatives who sell food service equipment and supplies. Formerly Marketing Agents for Food Service Industry.

***Manufacturers' Agents National Association - Directory of Manufacturers' Sales Agencies***. Manufacturers' Agents National Association, 6321 W Dempster St., Ste. 110 Morton Grove, IL 60053. Phone: 877-626-2776 or (949)859-4040; Fax: (949)855-2973; Email: mana@manaonline.org • URL: http://www.manaonline.org • Lists over 4,000 independent agents and firms. Price includes one year subscription to Agency Sales Magazines. Formerly *Manufacturers' Agents National Association-Directory of Members*.

**Manufacturers' Agents National Association**. 6321 W Dempster St., Ste. 110 Morton Grove, IL 60053. Phone: 877-626-2776 or (949)859-4040; Fax: (949)855-2973; Email: mana@manaonline.org • URL: http://www.manaonline.org • Manufacturers' agents in all fields representing two or more manufacturers on a commission basis; associate members are manufacturers and others interested in improving the agent-principal relationship. Maintains code of ethics and rules of business and professional conduct; issues model standard form of agreement.

**Manufacturers Alliance for Productivity and Innovation**. 1600 Wilson Blvd., 11th Fl. Arlington, VA 22209-2594. Phone: (703)841-9000; Fax: (703)841-9514 • URL: http://www.mapi.net • Manufacturing and related business service companies. Membership concentrated in the following sectors: aerospace; automotive; scientific instruments; electronics; computers and telecommunication equipment; high technology; chemicals/pharmaceuticals; oil and oil-related equipment; electrical equipment farm, construction, food, material handling and other machinery; primary and fabricated metals. Provides member services through councils and research programs. Produces a variety of research, including economic, policy and benchmark work to assist members in their planning, compliance and process improvement efforts.

**Manufacturers Standardization Society**. 127 Park St. NE Vienna, VA 22180. Phone: (703)281-6613; Fax: (703)281-6671; Email: info@mss-hq.com • URL: http://www.mss-hq.com • Members are valve and fitting companies. Publishes standards and specifications.

***Manufacturers' Tax Alert***. Wolters Kluwer Law & Business CCH, 2700 Lake Cook Rd. Riverwoods, IL 60015. Phone: 888-224-7377 or (847)267-7000; Email: cust_serv@cch.com • URL: http://www.cchgroup.com • Monthly $297.00 per year. Newsletter. Covers the major tax issues affecting manufacturing companies. Includes current developments in various kind of federal, state, and international taxes: sales, use, franchise, property, and corporate income.

***Manufacturing & Distribution USA***. Cengage Learning Inc., 20 Channel Center St. Boston, MA 02210. Phone: 800-487-8488 or (617)289-7700; Fax: (617)289-7844; Email: investors@cengage.com • URL: http://www.cengage.com • Biennial. $631 Individuals three-volume set. 2012. 7th edition. eBook. Three volumes. Presents statistics and projections relating to economic activity in more than 600 business classifications.

**Manufacturing Jewelers and Suppliers of America**. 57 John L. Dietsch Sq. Attleboro Falls, MA 02763. Phone: 800-444-6572 or (401)274-3840 or (508)316-2132; Fax: (401)274-0265 or (508)316-1429; Email: info@mjsa.org • URL: http://www.mjsa.org • Formerly Manufacturing Jewelers and Silversmiths of America.

***Manufacturing Jewelers Buyers' Guide***. Manufacturing Jewelers and Suppliers of America, 57 John L. Dietsch Sq. Attleboro Falls, MA 02763. Phone: 800-444-6572 or (401)274-3840 or (508)316-2132; Fax: (401)274-0265 or (508)316-1429; Email: info@mjsa.org • URL: http://www.mjsa.org • $35 for nonmembers; Included in membership. Lists manufacturers and suppliers and has cross-reference by products listed.

***Manufacturing Profiles***. U. S. Bureau of the Census, Phone: (301)763-4636 or (301)763-4100; Fax: (301)763-4794; Email: webmaster@census.gov • URL: http://www.census.gov/prod/www/abs/mfg-prof.html • The Census Bureau makes available free on PDF (Portable Document Format) an annual consolidation of the entire Current Industrial Report series, presenting "all the data compiled." Contains statistics on production, shipments, inventories, consumption, exports, imports, and orders for a wide variety of manufactured products.

***Manufacturing Systems: Buyers Guide***. Reed Elsevier Group plc Reed Business Information, 360 Park Ave. S New York, NY 11010. Phone: (212)791-4208; Email: corporatecommunications@reedbusiness.com • URL: http://www.reedbusiness.com • Annual. Price on application. Contains information on companies manufacturing or supplying materials handling systems, CAD/CAM systems, specialized software for manufacturing, programmable controllers, machine vision systems, and automatic identification systems.

***Maps On File***. InfoBase Holdings Inc., 132 W 31st., 17 Fl. New York, NY 10001-3406. Phone: (212)967-8800; Fax: (800)678-3633; Email: info@infobasepublishing.com • URL: http://www.ferguson.infobasepublishing.com • Annual. $75 2012 Update. Up to 500 reproducable maps.

**Marble Institute of America**. 28901 Clemens Rd., Ste. 100 Cleveland, OH 44145-1166. Phone: (440)250-9222; Fax: (440)250-9223; Email: miainfo@marble-institute.com • URL: http://www.marble-institute.com • Quarriers, exporters, fabricators, importers, wholesalers, finishers, suppliers and installing contractors of dimension stone for interior and exterior application; persons involved in the refinishing and restoration of dimension stone. Promotes the uses of dimension stone to architects, engineers, designers and other specifying authorities. Sponsors visual aid projects; works with ASTM in developing standard specifications for the use of dimension stone in construction. Compiles statistics. Distributes consumer information. Publishes technical guidelines, advisories and manuals.

*Marconi's International Register*. Telegraphic Cable & Radio Registrations Inc., 280 Broadway New York, NY 10007-1868. Phone: (914)632-1392 • Annual. $150 payment with order. Covers: 45,000 firms worldwide which do business internationally. Entries include: Company name, address, phone, fax, e-mail and URL addresses, brief description of business or legal specialty, names of officers and partners.

*The Mardek Guide to the UK's Top Food & Drink Suppliers*. William Reed Publishing Ltd., Broadfield Pk. Crawley RH11 9RT, United Kingdom. Phone: 44 1293 613400; Email: customer.service@william-reed.co.uk • URL: http://www.william-reed.co.uk • Annual. $295. Covers: 260 leading companies and over 100 major subsidiaries of food and drink manufacturers in the United Kingdom. Entries include: Corporate structure, company activities, personnel, products, brands, new product launches, turnover/pre-tax profit—up to the last three year, mergers, acquisitions and disposals.

*Marine Business Journal: The Voice of the Marine Industries*. Marine Business Journal Inc., 330 N Andrews Ave. Fort Lauderdale, FL 33301. Phone: (954)522-5515; Fax: (954)522-2260; Email: mbj@marinebusinessjournal.com • URL: http://www.marinebusinessjournal.com/ • Bimonthly. $30 Other countries. Trade magazine.

**Marine Corps Association**. 715 Broadway St. Quantico, VA 22134. Phone: 800-336-0291 or (703)640-6161; Fax: (703)640-0823 • URL: http://www.mca-marines.org • Represents active duty, reserve, retired, Fleet Reserve, honorably discharged Marines, and members of other services who have served with Marine Corps units. Disseminates information about the military arts and sciences to members; assists members' professional advancement; fosters the spirit and works to preserve the traditions of the United States Marine Corps. Maintains discount book service and group insurance plan for members. Association founded by members of the Second Provisional Marine Brigade at Guantanamo Bay, Cuba.

**Marine Corps Aviation Association**. 715 Broadway St. Quantico, VA 22134. Phone: 800-280-3001 or (703)630-1903; Fax: (703)630-2713; Email: mcaa@flymcaa.org • URL: http://www.flymcaa.org • Members and former members of U.S. Marine aviation units and others with an interest in Marine Corps aviation; aerospace corporations. Aims to: perpetuate camaraderie in marine aviation; foster and encourage professional excellence and recognize important achievements in marine aviation. Conducts charitable programs.

**Marine Corps Reserve Association**. 8626 Lee Hwy., Ste. 205 Fairfax, VA 22031-2135. Phone: (703)289-1204; Email: usmcra1926@gmail.com • URL: http://www.usmcra.org • Marines who have served on active duty in peace or war. Seeks to: advance the professional skills of marines; represent and assist individual members; promote the interests of the U.S. Marine Corps in order to advance the welfare and preserve the security of the United States. Maintains speakers' bureau and placement service.

**Marine Technology Society**. 1100 H St. NW, Ste. LL100 Washington, DC 20005. Phone: (202)717-8705; Fax: (202)347-4302; Email: membership@mtsociety.org • URL: http://www.mtsociety.org • Scientists, engineers, educators, and others with professional interest in the marine sciences or related fields; includes institutional and corporate members. Disseminates marine scientific and technical information, including institutional, environmental, physical, and biological aspects; fosters a deeper understanding of the world's seas and attendant technologies. Maintains 13 sections and 29 professional committees. Conducts tutorials.

*Maritime IT & Electronics*. Institute of Marine Engineering, Science and Technology, Aldgate House, 33 Aldgate High St. London EC3N 1EN, United Kingdom. Phone: 44 20 73822694 or 44 20 73822600; Fax: 44 20 73822670; Email: info@imarest.org • URL: http://www.imarest.org • Bimonthly. £58.00 per year. Covers modern electronic technology as applied to all areas of the maritime industry. Includes navigation systems, communications, control systems, monitoring, diagnostics, and software.

**Maritime Law Association of the U.S.** c/o Robert B. Parrish, President, 501 W Bay St. Jacksonville, FL 32202-4428. Phone: (904)421-8436; Fax: (904)421-8437 • URL: http://www.mlaus.org • Lawyers and others interested in maritime law. Provides advisers to government and industry officials. Maintains microfiche collection.

*Market: Asia Pacific*. Edimax, 3350 Scott Blvd., Bldg.15 Santa Clara, CA 95054. Phone: (408)496-1105; Fax: (408)980-1530; Email: sales@edimax.com • URL: http://www.edimax.com • Description: Concerned with demographics, lifestyles, and business opportunities in the Asia Pacific region. Profiles a particular city or country in each issue, providing consumer market trends, surveys results, and articles on direct marketing and marketing management.

*Market: Europe*. Edimax, 3350 Scott Blvd., Bldg.15 Santa Clara, CA 95054. Phone: (408)496-1105; Fax: (408)980-1530; Email: sales@edimax.com • URL: http://www.edimax.com • Description: Profiles European consumers and provides ideas

for marketing strategies. Reports on European conferences and summarizes articles from international periodicals. Recurring features include analyses of specific countries and cities.

*Market: Latin America*. The PRS Group Inc., 5800 Heritage Landing Dr., Ste. E East Syracuse, NY 13057-9378. Phone: (315)431-0511; Fax: (315)431-0200; Email: custserv@prsgroup.com • URL: http://www.prsgroup.com • Monthly. $397.00 per year ($198.00 to academic institutions). Newsletter. Provides market trend information and demographic data for Latin American countries. Includes sales trend projections for various products and services, with consumer household buying patterns and industrial expenditures. Formerly published by Market Newsletters.

*Market Research Monitor*. Euromonitor International Inc., 60-61 Britton St. London EC1M 5UX, United Kingdom. Phone: 44 0 20 7251 8024 or 44 20 7251 8024; Fax: 44 0 20 7608 3149 or 44 20 7608 3149; Email: info@euromonitor.com • URL: http://www.euromonitor.com • Contains full-text reports online from *Market Research Europe, Market Research Great Britain, Market Research International, and Retail Monitor International*. Time period is 1995 to date, with monthly updates. Inquire as to online cost and availability.

*Market Research Reports*. MarketResearch.com, 11200 Rockville Pke., Ste. 504 Rockville, MD 20852. Phone: 800-298-5699 or (240)747-3093; Fax: (240)747-3004; Email: customerservice@marketresearch.com • URL: http://www.marketresearch.com • Provides online full text of market research reports produced by FIND/SVP, Packaged Facts, Specialists in Business Information and others. Contains market data for a wide variety of industries, products, and services, including market size, forecasts, trends, structure, and opportunities. Inquire as to online cost and availability.

*Market Share Reporter (MSR)*. Cengage Learning Inc., 20 Channel Center St. Boston, MA 02210. Phone: 800-487-8488 or (617)289-7700; Fax: (617)289-7844; Email: investors@cengage.com • URL: http://www.cengage.com • $777 Individuals. 2013. $740.00. Published by Gale. Provides consumer market share data for leading companies. Also available as eBook.

*Marketing Address Data*. Herold Business Data GmbH, Guntramsdorfer Str. 105 A-2340 Modling, Austria. Phone: 43 2236 401 133; Fax: 43 2236 401 8; Email: kundendienst@herold.at • URL: http://www.herold.at/ • Annual. Database covers: More than 246,000 businesses in Austria. Entries include: Company name, address, phone, fax, line of business.

**Marketing Agencies Association Worldwide**. 60 Peachcroft Dr. Bernardsville, NJ 07924. Phone: (908)428-4300; Fax: (908)766-1277; Email: simon.mahoney@maaw.org • URL: http://www.maaw.org • Represents the interests of CEOs, presidents, managing directors and principals of top marketing services agencies. Provides opportunity for marketing professionals to meet with peers, raise company profile on both a national and a global platform, and influence the future of industry. Fosters networking through conferences.

*Marketing Business*. Chartered Institute of Marketing, Moor Hall, Cookham Maidenhead SL6 9QH, United Kingdom. Phone: 44 1628 427120; Fax: 44 1628 427158 • URL: http://www.cim.co.uk/Home.aspx • Monthly. free for members and students in Europe; £35 for nonmembers and non-students in Europe. Provides information about the new technologies and marketing techniques that are being faced by today's marketers.

*Marketing Economics Key Plants: Guide to Industrial Purchasing Power*. Marketing Economics Institute Ltd., 186-26 Avon Rd. Jamaica, NY 11432. • Biennial. $136 national edition; $22 for each regional edition; postpaid, payment with order. Covers: more than 40,000 key manufacturing plants with 100 or more employees (SIC 2011-3999); there are also editions for New England, Middle Atlantic, East North Central, West North Central, South Atlantic, East South Central, West South Central, and Mountain/Pacific regions. Entries include: Company name, address, number of employees, phone, SIC numbers.

**Marketing EDGE**. 1120 Ave. of the Americas, 13th Fl. New York, NY 10036-6700. Phone: (212)768-7277; Fax: (212)790-1561; Email: admin@marketingedge.org • URL: http://www.marketingedge.org • Represents individuals, firms, and organizations interested in furthering college-level education in direct marketing. Functions as the collegiate arm of the direct marketing profession. Sponsors a summer internship, programs for students and professors, and campaign competition for students. Provides educational materials and course outlines to faculty members; arranges for speakers for college classes and clubs. Co-sponsors academic research competitions. Maintains hall of fame.

*Marketing for Dummies*. John Wiley & Sons Inc., 111 River St. Hoboken, NJ 07030-5774. Phone: 800-225-5945 or (201)748-6000; Fax: (201)748-6088; Email: info@wiley.com • URL: http://www.wiley.com • $24.95 Individuals paperback. Publication includes: Marketing web sites, marketing consultants, trade associations, market researchers, and other experts. Entries include: Individual or company name, address, phone number, web site address (where applicable). Principal content of publication is articles on marketing strategies.

*The Marketing Guide to Ireland*. Dun & Bradstreet International,

Holbrook House, Holles St., P O Box 455A, Holles St. Dublin 2, Ireland. Phone: 353 676 4239; Fax: 353 678 9301 • Annual. Covers: 4,000 Irish businesses, including 3,000 in the Republic of Ireland and 1,000 in Northern Ireland. Our new section contains exporters and importers. Entries include: Company name, address, phone, fax, name and title of up to 8 contacts, number of employees, line of business, sales turnover, parent company, importer/exporter indicator, year established.

*The Marketing Managers Yearbook*. AP Information Services Ltd., c/o Wilmington Publishing & Information Ltd., 6-14 Underworld St. London N1 7JQ, United Kingdom. Phone: 44 20 75498708; Fax: 44 20 74908238; Email: info@apinfo.co.uk • URL: http://www.apinfo.co.uk • Annual. £229 Single issue. Covers: Approximately 10,500 private and public sector companies in the U.K., as well as 6,000 companies providing marketing related products and services, including advertising agencies, public relations firms, consultancies, research experts, hospitality industry companies, media outlets, software producers, professional associations, and other organizations. Database includes: Articles written by marketing professionals; statistical tables; list of forthcoming exhibitions. Entries include: For major companies—Name, address, phone, fax, names and titles of key personnel, number of employees, number of sales employees, line of business, brand/product names, parent company, Standard Industrial Classification (SIC) codes. For service companies—Name, address, phone, fax, year established, name and title of contact, names and titles of key personnel, fields of specialization, number of employees, associated firms, major clients, subsidiary and branch names and locations.

**Marketing Research Association**. 1156 15th St. NW, Ste. 302 Washington, DC 20005. Phone: 888-512-1050 or (202)800-2545; Fax: (888)512-1050; Email: membership@marketingresearch.org • URL: http://www.marketingresearch.org • Companies and individuals involved in any area of opinion and marketing research, such as data collection, research, or as an end-user.

*Marketing Surveys Index*. Marketing Answers Ltd., Viscount House, River Ln., Saltney Chester CH4 8RH, United Kingdom. Phone: 244 681186; Fax: 244 681457; Email: marketinganswer@compuserve.com • $380 per year. Covers: about 8,000 recently-published market research and business reports from around the world. Entries include: Report title; publisher name, address, phone, fax, e-mail and contact name; countries covered by report, publication date, number of pages, price, description of report.

*Marketing the Law Firm*. ALM Media Properties LLC, 120 Broadway, 5th Fl. New York, NY 10271-1100. Phone: (212)457-9400; Fax: (646)417-7705; Email: customercare@alm.com • URL: http://www.alm.com • Monthly. $475. Focuses on actions that lawyers can take to find more clients and do more business. (A Law Journal Newsletter, formerly published by Leader Publications under the title *Marketing for Lawyers*).

*Marketing the Law Firm: Business Development Techniques*. ALM Media Properties LLC, 120 Broadway, 5th Fl. New York, NY 10271-1100. Phone: (212)457-9400; Fax: (646)417-7705; Email: customercare@alm.com • URL: http://www.alm.com • Looseleaf. $510.00. Updated as needed. Covers client surveys, brochures, direct mail, Web sites, seminars, newsletters, proposals, trade shows, and other marketing avenues for both large and small law firms. (Law Journal Press).

*Marketing to the Emerging Minorities*. EPM Communications Inc., 19 W 21 St., Ste. 303 New York, NY 10010. Phone: 888-852-9467 or (212)941-0099; Fax: (212)941-1622; Email: info@epmcom.com • URL: http://www.epmcom.com • Monthly. $295 /year. Newsletter on market research relating to African American, Asian American, and U. S. Hispanic populations.

*MarketPlace*. Dun and Bradstreet Sales and Marketing Solutions, 460 Totten Pond Rd. Waltham, MA 02451-1991. Phone: 800-590-0065 or (781)672-9200; Fax: (781)672-9290; Email: custersupport@imarketinc.com • URL: http://www.dnb.com • Quarterly. $850 list price. Database covers: Over 11 million U.S. businesses. Database includes: four quarterly updates of databases and software along with 1000 meter credits. Entries include: Company name, address, phone, name and title of contact, type of business, annual sales, number of employees, year founded, type of site, ownership, Standard Industrial Classification (SIC) code, DUNS number, latitude/longitude, firmographic and industry specific data.

*Marketplace Magazine: Northeast Wisconsin's Business Magazine*. Marketplace Magazine, 2075 S Washburn St. Oshkosh, WI 54904-8946. Phone: (920)252-8276; Fax: (920)235-1833 • URL: http://www.marketplacemagazine.com • Semimonthly. $48; $4.95 Institutions; $4.95 Single issue. Business magazine (tabloid).

*The Markets Directory*. The Markets Directory, 320 E 42 St., Ste. 2018 New York, NY 10017. Phone: (212)490-1212; Email: jimroxton@marketsdirectory.com • Annual. Database covers: Over 7,000 service organizations implementing marketing research projects for marketing professionals in the U.S. and around the world. Entries include: Company name, address, phone, fax, contact name, line of business, facilities.

*Marking Products and Equipment Buyer's Guide*. Marking

Devices Publishing Co., 136 W Vallette St., Ste. 6 Elmhurst, IL 60126. Phone: (630)832-5200 • URL: http://www.markingdevices.com • Annual. Included in subscription to *Marking Industry Magazine*.

***MarkIntel***. Thomson Financial, PO Box 95512 Chicago, IL 60694. Phone: 800-607-4463 or (312)288-6400 • URL: http://www.tfsd.com • Provides the current full text online of more than 50,000 market research reports covering 54 industries, from 85 leading research firms worldwide. Reports include extensive forecasts and market analysis. Inquire as to online cost and availability.

***MARKUS: Marketinguntersuchungen***. Bureau van Dijk S.A., Ave. Louise, Louizalaan 250 B-1050 Brussels, Belgium. Phone: 32 2 6390606 or 32 2 639 06 06; Fax: 32 2 6488230 or 32 2 648 82 30; Email: brussels@bvdinfo.com • URL: http://www.bvdinfo.com • Quarterly. Database covers: More than 900,000 German and Austrian companies. Entries include: Company name, address, date of incorporation, company type, register number, managers, shareholders, banks, WZ activity codes, trade description, number of employees, turnover, shareholders' funds.

**Marquette University - Center for Intelligent Systems, Controls, and Signal Processing**. College of Engineering, 1515 W Wisconsin Ave. Milwaukee, WI 53233. Phone: (414)288-3501; Fax: (414)288-5579; Email: ron.brown@marquette.edu • URL: http://www.marquette.edu • Intelligent controls, control systems, optimization, identification, time series modeling, multiple time-scale systems, digital signal processing, digital filtering, speech processing.

**Marquette University - Center for Mass Media Research**. 1250 W Wisconsin Ave. Milwaukee, WI 53233. Phone: (414)288-6787 or (414)288-3453; Fax: (414)288-3099; Email: robert.griffin@marquette.edu • URL: http://news.marquette.edu/experts/center-for-mass-media-research • Conducts social scientific research into the roles, processes, uses, and effects of mass communication among individuals and in society. Applies social science communication theory and research to the investigation and solution of social problems, especially those involving environment, energy, health risks, science, and technology.

**Marquette University - Law School - National Sports Law Institute**. 1215 W Michigan St. Milwaukee, WI 53233. Phone: (414)288-5816; Fax: (414)288-5818; Email: paul.anderson@marquette.edu • URL: http://law.marquette.edu/national-sports-law-institute/welcome • Promotes ethical practices in amateur and professional sports activities.

***Marriage & Family Counselors Directory***. InfoGroup Inc., 5711 S 86th Cir. Omaha, NE 68127-4146. Phone: (402)593-4500 • URL: http://www.infogroup.com • Annual. Number of listings: 55,129. Entries include: Name, address, phone, size of advertisement, name of owner or manager, number of employees, year first in "Yellow Pages." Compiled from telephone company "Yellow Pages," nationwide.

***Martindale-Hubbell Bar Register of Preeminent Lawyers***. LexisNexis Martindale-Hubbell, 121 Chanlon Rd. New Providence, NJ 07974. Phone: 800-526-4902 or (908)771-7777; Fax: (908)771-8704; Email: info@martindale.com • URL: http://www.martindale.com • Annual. $195 Individuals. Lists over 9,700 &"outstanding members of the bar" in general practice and in 28 specific fields. Covers the U. S. and Canada.

***Martindale-Hubbell International Dispute Resolution Directory: A Unique Guide to International ADR Professionals and Procedures***. LexisNexis Martindale-Hubbell, 121 Chanlon Rd. New Providence, NJ 07974. Phone: 800-526-4902 or (908)771-7777; Fax: (908)771-8704; Email: info@martindale.com • URL: http://www.martindale.com • Annual. $250 Individuals; Free. Covers: Service providers in over 90 countries of international arbitration and dispute resolution at both international levels and within the individual's national jurisdiction; Professionals and their credentials. Database covers: Judges, attorneys, law firms, and other neutral experts that specialize in alternative dispute resolution. Database includes: Information on the processes of dispute resolution and the rules which govern it. Entries include: Contact information.

***Martindale.com***. LexisNexis Martindale-Hubbell, 121 Chanlon Rd. New Providence, NJ 07974. Phone: 800-526-4902 or (908)771-7777; Fax: (908)771-8704; Email: info@martindale.com • URL: http://www.martindale.com • Database of more than 1 million lawyers and law firms.

**Mason Contractors Association of America**. 1481 Merchant Dr. Algonquin, IL 60102. Phone: 800-536-2225 or (224)678-9709; Fax: (224)678-9714 • URL: http://www.masoncontractors.org • Masonry construction firms. Conducts specialized education and research programs. Compiles statistics.

***Masonry Buyer's Guide***. Mason Contractors Association of America, 1481 Merchant Dr. Algonquin, IL 60102. Phone: 800-536-2225 or (224)678-9709; Fax: (224)678-9714 • URL: http://www.masoncontractors.org • Lists manufacturers or suppliers of products and services related to masonry construction.

***Masonry Design West***. Pleasanton Publishing Co., 6284 Wade Court Pleasanton, CA 95688. Phone: (415)846-5623; Fax: (415)846-1753 • Bimonthly. Price on application.

***Mass Customization Information Systems in Business***. Cengage Learning Inc., 20 Channel Center St. Boston, MA 02210. Phone: 800-487-8488 or (617)289-7700; Fax: (617)289-7844; Email: investors@cengage.com • URL: http://www.cengage.com • 2007. eBook. Published by Information Science Reference. Describes original, innovative works on IT systems for mass customization, and provides a multitude of solutions, tools, concepts and successful realizations of IT systems for mass customization.

***Mass Merchandisers & Off-Price Apparel Buyers***. Communication Publications & Resources, 2807 N Parham Rd., Ste. 200 Richmond, VA 23294. Phone: 800-780-4066; Email: customerservice@briefings.com • URL: http://www.briefingsmediagroup.com • Annual. $329 Individuals directory price; $659 Individuals directory/CD combo price. Covers: 7,900 buyers and 3,400 companies in mass merchandise and off-price apparel industry. Entries include: Company name, address, phone, fax, e-mail, URL, names and titles of key personnel, geographical area served, branch office or subsidiary names and addresses, products and/or services provided, sales volume, parent company name.

***Mass Storage News: Opportunities and Trends in Data Storage and Retrieval***. Jameson Publishing, 5340 Fryling Rd., Ste. 300 Erie, PA 16510. Phone: (814)897-9000; Fax: (814)899-5580 or (814)899-5583; Email: corrypub@corrypub.com • URL: http://www.jamesonpublishing.com • Biweekly. $597.00 per year. Newsletter. Provides descriptions of products and systems using optical storage. Formerly *Optical Memory News*.

***Mass Transit: Better Transit Through Better Management***. Cygnus Business Media Inc., 1233 Janesville Ave. Fort Atkinson, WI 53538. Phone: 800-547-7377; Email: info@cygnus.com • URL: http://www.cygnus.com • Bimonthly. 48.00 per year.

***Mass Transit: Consultants***. Cygnus Business Media Inc., 1233 Janesville Ave. Fort Atkinson, WI 53538. Phone: 800-547-7377; Email: info@cygnus.com • URL: http://www.cygnus.com • Annual. $64.00. Listings for over 300 urban transportation architects, designers, engineers, planners, consultants and other specialists serving the urban transportation industry.

***Mass Transit: Supplier's Guide***. Cygnus Business Media Inc., 1233 Janesville Ave. Fort Atkinson, WI 53538. Phone: 800-547-7377; Email: info@cygnus.com • URL: http://www.cygnus.com • Directory of over 800 manufacturers and distributors serving the urban transportation industry.

***The Massachusetts Business and Professional Directory***. Tower Publishing Co., 588 Saco Rd. Standish, ME 04084. Phone: 800-969-8693 or (207)642-5400; Fax: (207)642-5463 or 800-264-3870; Email: info@towerpub.com • URL: http://www.towerpub.com • Annual. $125 Individuals softcover; $165 Individuals CD-ROM. 25,000 Massachusetts professional and industrial firms with 20 or more employees.

**Massachusetts General Hospital - Institute for Health Policy**. 50 Staniford St., 9th Fl., Ste. 901 Boston, MA 02114. Phone: (617)724-4744; Fax: (617)724-4738; Email: info@instituteforhealthpolicy.org • URL: http://www.instituteforhealthpolicy.org • Health policy and health systems.

**Massachusetts Institute of Technology - Center for Transportation and Logistics**. 77 Massachusetts Ave., E40-276 Cambridge, MA 02139. Phone: (617)253-5320; Fax: (617)253-4560; Email: sheffi@mit.edu • URL: http://ctl.mit.edu • Transportation and logistics, with emphasis on problem-oriented, interdisciplinary, and multi-model studies, including studies on innovative urban transportation systems, transport technology innovations, railroad systems operations, trucking, energy policies, regional transportation planning and programming, highway location and design, flight transportation, ocean shipping, transportation systems analysis, logistics, supply chain management, logistics organizations, shipper/carrier relationships and logistics information technology.

**Massachusetts Institute of Technology - Computer Science and Artificial Intelligence Laboratory**. The Stata Ctr., Bldg. 32, 32 Vassar St. Cambridge, MA 02139. Phone: (617)253-5851; Fax: (617)258-8682; Email: rus@csail.mit.edu • URL: http://www.csail.mit.edu • Research is in four areas: Intelligent Systems; Parallel Systems; Systems, Languages, and Networks; and Theory. Emphasis is on the application of online computing.

**Massachusetts Institute of Technology - Department of Urban Studies and Planning - Community Innovators Lab**. Department of Urban Studies and Planning, Bldg./Rm. 9-419, 77 Massachusetts Ave. Cambridge, MA 02139. Phone: (617)253-3216; Fax: (617)258-6515; Email: colab-info@mit.edu • URL: http://web.mit.edu/colab • Provides opportunity for minority community activists and local governmental officials (10 to 12 per year) to spend a year of reflection, study, and research at the Massachusetts Institute of Technology. The Program is being redesigned to capture the potential of new information technologies for poor communities and communities of color.

**Massachusetts Institute of Technology - Kavli Institute for Astrophysics and Space Research**. 77 Massachusetts Ave., 37-241 Cambridge, MA 02139. Phone: (617)253-7501; Fax: (617)253-3111; Email: jhewitt@mit.edu • URL: http://space.mit.edu • Space sciences, including theoretical astrophysics. Experimental studies include X-ray astronomy, gravitational waves, interplanetary plasmas, optical and infrared astronomy, very-long-baseline interferometry, synthetic aperture radar, human/machine system interaction, response of human systems to zero-gravity environment, and space environmental studies.

**Massachusetts Institute of Technology - Laboratory for Information and Decision Systems**. 77 Massachusetts Ave., Rm. 32-D608 Cambridge, MA 02139. Phone: (617)253-2142; Fax: (617)253-3578; Email: willsky@mit.edu • URL: http://lids.mit.edu • Research areas include data communication networks and fiber optic networks.

**Massachusetts Institute of Technology - Laboratory for Manufacturing and Productivity**. 77 Massachusetts Ave., Rm. 35-231 Cambridge, MA 02139. Phone: (617)253-1759 or (617)452-2395; Email: jchun@mit.edu • URL: http://web.mit.edu/lmp • Photovoltaics, nano manufacturing development such as micro-fluidic devices, environmentally-benign manufacturing, axiomatic design theory, precision motion control, discrete die forming, precision machine design, droplet-based manufacturing, semiconductor manufacturing processes, design and operation of manufacturing systems, data and model integration, rapid autonomous machining, and three-dimensional printing.

**Massachusetts Institute of Technology - Laboratory for Nuclear Science**. Bldg. 26-505, 77 Massachusetts Ave. Cambridge, MA 02139. Phone: (617)253-2395; Email: milner@mit.edu • URL: http://web.mit.edu/lns • High energy, medium energy, relativistic heavy-ion, and neutrino physics, elementary particle and nuclear theory, plus applications of nuclear techniques.

**Massachusetts Institute of Technology - Laser Biomedical Research Center**. GR Harrison Spectroscopy Laboratory, 6-205, 77 Massachusetts Ave. Cambridge, MA 02139. Phone: (617)253-8418 or (617)253-7700; Fax: (617)253-4513; Email: rrdasari@mit.edu • URL: http://web.mit.edu/spectroscopy/facilities/lbrc.html • Concerned with the medical use of lasers.

**Massachusetts Institute of Technology - Lincoln Laboratory**. 244 Wood St. Lexington, MA 02420-9108. Phone: (781)981-5500; Fax: (781)981-7086; Email: llnews@ll.mit.edu • URL: http://www.ll.mit.edu • Multidisciplinary off-campus research unit. Research fields include solid state devices.

**Massachusetts Institute of Technology - Materials Processing Center**. 77 Massachusetts Ave. Cambridge, MA 02139-4301. Phone: (617)253-5179; Fax: (617)258-6900; Email: cthomp@mit.edu • URL: http://mpc-web.mit.edu • Conducts processing, engineering, and economic research in ferrous and nonferrous metals, ceramics, polymers, photonic materials, superconductors, welding, composite materials, and other materials.

**Massachusetts Institute of Technology - The Media Laboratory**. Bldg. E15, 77 Massachusetts Ave. Cambridge, MA 02139-4307. Phone: (617)253-5960; Fax: (617)258-6264; Email: walter@media.mit.edu • URL: http://www.media.mit.edu • Research areas include electronic publishing, spatial imaging, human-machine interface, computer vision, and advanced television.

**Massachusetts Institute of Technology - Office of Sponsored Programs**. Bldg. E19-750, 77 Massachusetts Ave. Cambridge, MA 02139. Phone: (617)324-9022; Fax: (617)253-4734; Email: mchristy@mit.edu • URL: http://osp.mit.edu • Administers sponsored research program of the Institute, negotiating research contracts, taking care of business and contractual obligations, and serving as liaison with research sponsors.

**Massachusetts Institute of Technology - Research Laboratory of Electronics**. 77 Massachusetts Ave., Rm. 36-413 Cambridge, MA 02139-4307. Phone: (617)253-2519; Fax: (617)253-1301; Email: hq@rle.mit.edu • URL: http://www.rle.mit.edu/ • Research areas include heat transfer and cryogenics.

**Massachusetts Institute of Technology - Sloan School of Management - Center for Information Systems Research**. Bldg. NE25, 7th Fl., 5 Cambridge Ctr. Cambridge, MA 02142. Phone: (617)253-2348; Fax: (617)253-4424; Email: cisr@mit.edu • URL: http://cisr.mit.edu • Defining, researching, and reporting on significant issues in the management of information technology, including the managerial use of computers and computer-based information, the management of the information systems (I/S) function, and the business value of information technology on organizations. Disseminates significant research findings to the information systems user community.

***Massachusetts Manufacturers Register and Industrial Database***. Manufacturers' News Inc., 1633 Central St. Evanston, IL 60201-1569. Phone: (847)864-7000; Fax: (847)332-1100 • URL: http://www.manufacturersnews.com • Annual. $141 Individuals print; $605 Individuals database (EZ select full); $443 Individuals database (EZ select with 20 plus employees); $212 Individuals database (EZ select basic). Covers: 9,577 manufacturers in Massachusetts. Entries include: Company name, address, phone, names and titles of key personnel, year established, number of employees, plant square footage, services, Standard Industry Classification (SIC) code, parent and subsidiary company information, type of in-house computer system, URL, e-mail address.

***Massachusetts Service Directory***. George D. Hall Company Inc., 50 Franklin St., 4th Fl. Boston, MA 02110-1306. Phone: 800-446-1215 or (617)523-3745; Fax: (617)523-4862 • $69 plus $4.95 shipping. Covers: over 12,700 non-manufacturing companies with five or more employees. Entries include:

Company name, address, phone, names of key executives, number of employees, product or service, Standard Industrial Classification (SIC) code.

***Massage: A Career at Your Fingertips***. Enterprise Publishing, 3 Londonderry Ln. Somers, NY 10589. Phone: (914)248-0325; Email: martash@cloud9.net • URL: http://www.careeratyourfingertips.com • Triennial. $25.95 Individuals. Publication includes: Approximately 1,000 organizations involved in the massage industry, including schools, associations, massage equipment suppliers, bodywork organizations, and massage marketing companies in the United States. Entries include: For schools—Name, address, phone, hours of training required, number of in-class hours required, cost, financial aid availability, subjects covered, unique aspects of school or curriculum. For others—Name, address, phone, description of products/services offered. Principal content of publication is information on becoming a successful massage therapist.

**Massey University - Centre for Public Policy Evaluation**. Private Bag Palmerston North, New Zealand. Phone: 64 6 3505799; Fax: 64 6 3505660; Email: k.s.birks@massey.ac.nz • URL: http://tur-www1.massey.ac.nz/wwcppe • Public policy and economics in the areas of education, health, law, gender issues and aspects of the policymaking process.

**Massey University - Dispute Resolution Centre**. College of Business, Private Bag 11222 Palmerston North, New Zealand. Phone: 64 6 3505799; Fax: 64 6 3505809; Email: dispute@massey.ac.nz • URL: http://www.massey.ac.nz/massey/learning/colleges/college-business/international-students/specialisation/dispute-resolution.cfm • Negotiation, mediation, and arbitration.

**Massey University - New Zealand Centre for Small and Medium Enterprise Research**. Private Box 756 Wellington, New Zealand. Phone: 64 4 8015799; Fax: 64 4 8020290; Email: d.deakins@massey.ac.nz • URL: http://www.massey.ac.nz/massey/learning/departments/centres-research/new-zealand-centre-for-sme-research/nzsmerc.cfm • Micro-enterprises, small enterprises, and medium enterprises.

**Master Brewers Association of the Americas**. 3340 Pilot Knob Rd. Saint Paul, MN 55121. Phone: (651)454-7250; Fax: (651)454-0766; Email: mbaa@mbaa.com • URL: http://www.mbaa.com • Formerly Master Brewers Association of America.

***MASTER: Marketing Strategy and Efficient Research***. Bureau van Dijk S.A., Ave. Louise, Louizalaan 250 B-1050 Brussels, Belgium. Phone: 32 2 6390606 or 32 2 639 06 06; Fax: 32 2 6488230 or 32 2 648 82 30; Email: brussels@bvdinfo.com • URL: http://www.bvdinfo.com • Quarterly. Database covers: More than 700,000 companies and business entities in Belgium. Entries include: Company name, address, date of incorporation, company type, activity, management, turnover, shareholders' funds, profit, debt, number of employees.

**Material Handling Equipment Distributors Association**. 201 US Hwy. 45 Vernon Hills, IL 60061-2398. Phone: (847)680-3500; Fax: (847)362-6989; Email: connect@mheda.org • URL: http://www.mheda.org • Distributors and manufacturers of material handling equipment. Aims to improve the proficiency of independent material handling distributors.

**Material Handling Industry**. 8720 Red Oak Blvd., Ste. 201 Charlotte, NC 28217-3996. Phone: 800-345-1815 or (704)676-1190; Fax: (704)676-1199; Email: jnofsinger@mhia.org • URL: http://www.mhia.org • Formerly Material Handling Industry.

***Material Handling Management: Educating Industry on Product Handling, Flow Strategies, and Automation Technology***. Penton Media Inc., 1300 E 9th St. Cleveland, OH 44114-1501. Phone: (216)696-7000; Fax: (216)696-1752; Email: information@penton.com • URL: http://penton.com • 13 times a year. Free to qualified personnel; others, $50.00 per year. Formerly *Material Handling Engineering*.

***Materials Business File™ (MBF)***. ProQuest LLC CSA, 789 E Eisenhower Pky. Ann Arbor, MI 48103. Phone: (734)761-4700; Fax: (734)997-4222; Email: info@proquest.com • URL: http://www.csa.com • Contains more than 896,000 citations, with abstracts, to worldwide literature on technical and commercial aspects of iron and steel, nonferrous metals, and relevant nonmetallic materials such as polymers, ceramics, and composites. Sources include more than 2000 technical journals, trade magazines, newspapers, news briefs, books, conference proceedings, and announcements worldwide.

***Materials Evaluation***. American Society for Nondestructive Testing, 1711 Arlingate Ln. Columbus, OH 43228. Phone: 800-222-2768 or (614)274-6003 or (509)210-2331; Fax: (614)274-6899; Email: wholliday@asnt.org • URL: http://www.asnt.org • Monthly. $135 Individuals; $245 Other countries; $105 /year. Provides up-to-date information about NDT applications and technical articles addressing nondestructive testing applications.

**Materials Handling Industry of America**. 8720 Red Oak Blvd., Ste. 201 Charlotte, NC 28217-3996. Phone: (704)676-1190; Fax: (704)676-1199 • URL: http://www.mhi.org • Formerly Materials Handling and Management Society.

***Materials Performance: Articles on Corrosion Science and Engineering Solutions for Corrosion Problems***. National Association of Corrosion Engineers. NACE International: The Corrosion Society, 1440 S Creek Dr. Houston, TX 77084-4906. Phone: 800-797-6223 or (281)228-6200 or (281)228-6223; Fax: (281)228-6300; Email: firstservice@nace.org • URL: http://www.nace.org • Monthly. Members included in membership dues; $115 Nonmembers 1-year subscription; $205 Individuals 1-year subscription. Covers the protection and performance of materials in corrosive environments. Includes information on new materials and industrial coatings.

***Materials Research Centres: A World Directory of Organizations and Programmes in Materials Science***. Specialist Journals, 345 Park Ave., S New York, NY 10010-1707. Phone: (212)726-9333; Fax: (212)696-0052; Email: sjsupport@nature.com • URL: http://www.nature.com • Biennial. $445.00. Profiles of research centers in 75 countries. Materials include plastics, metals, fibers, etc.

**Materials Research Society**. 506 Keystone Dr. Warrendale, PA 15086-7573. Phone: (724)779-3003 or (724)779-3004; Fax: (724)779-8313; Email: info@mrs.org • URL: http://www.mrs.org • Represents the interests of materials researchers from academia, industry, and government that promotes communication for the advancement of interdisciplinary materials research to improve the quality of life. Fosters interaction among researchers working on different classes of inorganic and organic materials and to promote interdisciplinary basic research on materials. Provides forum for industry, government, and university cooperation; conducts technical conferences, tutorial lectures. Maintains speakers' bureau.

***Materials Science Citation Index***. Thomson Reuters Intellectual Property & Science, 3 Times Sq. New York, NY 10036. Phone: 800-336-4474 or (646)223-4000; Fax: (215)386-2911 • URL: http://ip-science.thomsonreuters.com • Contains citations and abstracts, providing international coverage of materials science journals.

***Mathematical Finance: An International Journal of Mathematics, Statistics, and Financial Economics***. Blackwell Publishing Inc., 350 Main St. Malden, MA 02148. Phone: 800-216-2522 or (781)388-8200; Fax: (781)388-8210; Email: journaladsusa@bos.blackwellpublishing.com • URL: http://www.blackwellpublishing.com • Quarterly. $1,453 Institutions print only; $1,453 Institutions online only; $1,670 Institutions print and online; $202 Individuals print and online. Covers the use of sophisticated mathematical tools in financial research and practice.

***Mathematics and Computer Education***. George M. Miller, editor. MATYC Journal, Inc., P.O. Box 158 Old Bethpage, NY 11084-0158. Phone: (516)822-5475 • URL: http://www.macejournal.org • Quarterly. $36 U.S.; $46 Canada and Mexico; $76 Other countries; $135 U.S.; $165 Canada and Mexico; $180 Other countries. Articles for high school and college teachers.

***MathSciNet***. American Mathematical Society, 201 Charles St. Providence, RI 02904-2294. Phone: 800-321-4267 or (401)455-4000 or (401)455-4105; Fax: (401)331-3842; Email: cust-serv@ams.org • URL: http://www.ams.org • Electronic resource with citations, abstracts, and reviews to the literature of mathematics, statistics, and computer science, 1940 to date.

***Matrimonial Strategist***. ALM Media Properties LLC, 120 Broadway, 5th Fl. New York, NY 10271-1100. Phone: (212)457-9400; Fax: (646)417-7705; Email: customercare@alm.com • URL: http://www.alm.com • Monthly. $429 print and online; $409 online only. Newsletter on legal strategy and matrimonial law.

***Matthews Business News***. Matthews Chamber of Commerce, 210 Matthews Station St. Matthews, NC 28105. Phone: (704)847-3649; Fax: (704)847-3364; Email: info@matthewschamber.com • URL: http://www.matthewschamber.com • Monthly.

***Mauritius Industrial and Business Directory***. International Business Publications, USA, PO Box 15343 Washington, DC 20003. Phone: (202)546-2103; Fax: (202)546-3275; Email: ibpusa@comcast.net • URL: http://ibpus.com • Annual. $99.95 Individuals hardcopy, e-book, CD-ROM. Covers: Strategic industrial, investment and business contacts for conducting export-import and investment activity in the country.

**Max Planck Society for the Advancement of Science - Max Planck Institute of Economics**. Kahlaische Strasse 10 D-07745 Jena, Germany. Phone: 49 3641 6865; Fax: 49 3641 686990; Email: witt@econ.mpg.de • URL: http://www.mpiew-jena.mpg.de • Changing economic systems and the forces behind those changes.

***Maximizing Law Firm Profitability: Hiring, Training, and Developing Productive Lawyers***. ALM Media Properties LLC, 120 Broadway, 5th Fl. New York, NY 10271-1100. Phone: (212)457-9400; Fax: (646)417-7705; Email: customercare@alm.com • URL: http://www.alm.com • $590 print + online + ebook; $560 ebook + online. Covers subjects on how to enhance your skills as a lawyer and to develop the potential of your associates.

***Maximum PC***. Imagine Media, Inc., 150 N. Hill Dr. Brisbane, CA 94005. Phone: (415)468-4684; Fax: (415)468-4686; Email: webmaster@imaginemedia.com • URL: http://www.imaginemedia.com • Quarterly. $29.95 per year. Provides articles and reviews relating to multimedia hardware and software. Each issue includes a CD-ROM sampler (emphasis is on games). Formed by the merger of Home PC and Boot.

**Mayo Biomedical Imaging Resource**. Mayo Clinic, 200 First St. SW Rochester, MN 55905. Phone: (507)284-2511; Fax: (507)284-0161; Email: rar@mayo.edu • URL: http://www.mayoclinic.org • Develops three-dimensional medical imaging systems and software.

***Mayors of America's Principal Cities***. United States Conference of Mayors, 1620 Eye St. NW Washington, DC 20006-4005. Phone: (202)293-7330; Fax: (202)293-2352; Email: info@usmayors.org • URL: http://www.usmayors.org • Semiannual. About 1,000 mayors of cities with populations of 30,000 or more.

***MBA Track's Directory of Employers on Diskette***. Hoover's Inc., 5800 Airport Blvd. Austin, TX 78752-4204. Phone: 866-443-3939 or (512)374-4500 or (866)281-5969; Fax: (512)374-4501; Email: salesteam@hoovers.com • URL: http://www.hoovers.com • $99.95. Database covers: 2,500 companies employing the greatest number of MBAs in the U.S. Entries include: Company name, address, phone, fax, human resources director, industry type.

***MBAA Technical Quarterly***. Master Brewers Association of the Americas, 3340 Pilot Knob Rd. Saint Paul, MN 55121. Phone: (651)454-7250; Fax: (651)454-0766; Email: mbaa@mbaa.com • URL: http://www.mbaa.com • Quarterly. $60 for nonmembers in the brewing industry; $181 Nonmembers and institutions; $193 Elsewhere non-members & institutions. Technical brewing magazine.

***MBDA: Minority Business Development Agency***. U. S. Department of Commerce, Phone: 800-786-9199 or (703)308-4357; Fax: (703)305-7786; Email: help@mbda.gov • URL: http://www.uspto.gov • Web site provides links to a wide variety of advice and information for minority businesses. Main headings are Access to Markets, Access to Capital, Management & Technical Assistance, and Education & Training. An MBDA Resource Locator helps to locate sources of assistance in specific cities. Fees: Free. (Additional "business contracting and assistance tools" are offered to those who register with the site.).

***MBEMAG***. Minority Business Entrepreneur Magazine, Phone: (310)540-9398; Fax: (310)792-8263; Email: webmaster@mbemag.com • URL: http://www.mbemag.com • Web site's main feature is the "MBE Business Resources Directory." This provides complete mailing addresses, phone, fax, and Web site addresses (URL) for more than 40 organizations and government agencies having information or assistance for ethnic minority and women business owners. Some other links are "Current Events," "Calendar of Events," and "Business Opportunities." Updating is bimonthly. Fees: Free.

***MBI: The National Report on Minority, Women-Owned and Disadvantaged Business***. Community Development Services, Inc. CD Publications, 8204 Fenton St. Silver Spring, MD 20910. Phone: 800-666-6380 or (301)588-6380; Fax: (301)588-6385; Email: info@cdpublications.com • URL: http://www.cdpublications.com • Semimonthly. $379.00 per year. Newsletter. Provides news of affirmative action, government contracts, minority business employment, and education/training for minorities in business. Formerly *Minorities in Business*.

***McCutcheon's Functional Materials Volumes 2***. Manufacturing Confectioner Publishing Corp., 175 Rock Rd. Glen Rock, NJ 07452-1747. Phone: (201)652-2655; Fax: (201)652-3419; Email: mcinfo@gomc.com • URL: http://www.gomc.com • Edited for product development, quality control and research and development chemists.

***McCutcheon's Volume 1: Emulsifiers and Detergents***. Manufacturing Confectioner Publishing Corp., 175 Rock Rd. Glen Rock, NJ 07452-1747. Phone: (201)652-2655; Fax: (201)652-3419; Email: mcinfo@gomc.com • URL: http://www.gomc.com • Two volumes. International coverage.

**McGill Centre for Intelligent Machines**. McGill University, McConnell Engineering Bldg., Rm. 410, 3480 University St. Montreal, QC, Canada H3A 2A7. Phone: (514)398-6319; Fax: (514)398-7348; Email: cim@cim.mcgill.ca • URL: http://www.cim.mcgill.ca.

***McGraw-Hill Yearbook of Science and Technology***. McGraw Hill Financial Inc., 1221 Avenue of the Americas New York, NY 10020-1095. Phone: (212)512-2000; Fax: (212)512-3840 • URL: http://www.mhfi.com • Annual. $145.00.

***McGraw-Hill's Biotechnology Newswatch***. McGraw Hill Financial Inc., 1221 Avenue of the Americas New York, NY 10020-1095. Phone: (212)512-2000; Fax: (212)512-3840 • URL: http://www.mhfi.com • Semimonthly. Price on application. Newsletter.

***McKnight's Long Term Care News***. Thomson Medical Economics, 5 Paragon Dr. Montvale, NJ 07645-1742. Phone: 800-526-4870 or (201)358-7200; Fax: (201)573-8999 or (201)722-2680; Email: customer.service@medec.com • URL: http://www.medec.com • Monthly. Edited for retirement housing directors and nursing home administrators.

**McMaster University - Centre for Health Economics and Policy Analysis**. CRL Bldg., No. 282, 1280 Main St. W Hamilton, ON, Canada L8S 4K1. Phone: (905)525-9140; Fax: (905)546-5211; Email: chepa@mcmaster.ca • URL: http://www.chepa.org • Health economics and health policy analysis, including organization, funding, and delivery of health care; the evaluation of health care programs and technologies; the measurement of health at the individual and population level; the determinants of population health; and the processes of health policy making.

**McMaster University - McMaster Experimental Economics Laboratory**. Department of Economics, 1280 Main St. W

Hamilton, ON, Canada L8S 4M4. Phone: (905)525-9140; Fax: (905)521-8232; Email: mestelma@mcmaster.ca • URL: http://socserv.mcmaster.ca/econ/mceel/ • Economics.

**McMaster University - Research Institute for Quantitative Studies in Economics and Population.** Kenneth Taylor Hall, Rm. 426, 1280 Main St. W Hamilton, ON, Canada L8S 4M4. Phone: (905)525-9140; Fax: (905)521-8232; Email: qsep@mcmaster.ca • URL: http://socserv.mcmaster.ca/qsep • Broad-based studies in quantitative economics, demography, and related social science areas.

***Meadow's Greater New York Business.*** Meadow Publications Inc., 100 Clearbrook Rd. Elmsford, NY 10523-1116. • Quarterly. Magazine covering a variety of business topics concerning New York and suburban New York businesses.

***Means Construction Cost Indexes.*** RSMeans, 700 Longwater Dr. Norwell, MA 02061. Phone: 800-334-3509; Fax: (800)632-6732 • URL: http://www.rsmeans.reedconstructiondata.com • Quarterly. $362 Individuals.

***Means Facilities Construction Cost Data.*** RSMeans, 700 Longwater Dr. Norwell, MA 02061. Phone: 800-334-3509; Fax: (800)632-6732 • URL: http://www.rsmeans.reedconstructiondata.com • Annual. $496.95 Individuals. Provides costs for use in building estimating.

***Means Interior Cost Data.*** RSMeans, 700 Longwater Dr. Norwell, MA 02061. Phone: 800-334-3509; Fax: (800)632-6732 • URL: http://www.rsmeans.reedconstructiondata.com • Annual. $207.95 Individuals.

***Means Repair and Remodeling Cost Data.*** RSMeans, 700 Longwater Dr. Norwell, MA 02061. Phone: 800-334-3509; Fax: (800)632-6732 • URL: http://www.rsmeans.reedconstructiondata.com • Annual. $163.95 Individuals.

***Means Residential Cost Data.*** RSMeans, 700 Longwater Dr. Norwell, MA 02061. Phone: 800-334-3509; Fax: (800)632-6732 • URL: http://www.rsmeans.reedconstructiondata.com • Annual. $139.95 Individuals.

***Measurement and Evaluation in Counseling and Development.*** Association for Measurement and Evaluation in Counseling. American Counseling Association, 5999 Stevenson Ave. Alexandria, VA 22304. Phone: 800-347-6647; Fax: (703)823-0252; Email: membership@counseling.org • URL: http://www.counseling.org • Quarterly. Free to members; non-members, $60.00 per year.

***Measurements and Control.*** Measurements and Data Corp., 2165 Main St. Sarasota, FL 34237. Phone: (941)366-1153; Fax: (941)366-5743 • Bimonthly. $24.00 per year. Supplement available: ***M & C:*** *Measurement and Control News.*

***Meat and Poultry: The Business Journal of the Meat and Poultry Industry.*** Sosland Publishing Co., 4800 Main St., Ste. 100 Kansas City, MO 64112. Phone: (816)756-1000; Fax: (816)756-0494; Email: nwages@sosland.com • URL: http://www.sosland.com • Monthly. free to qualified subscribers; $85 Out of country print (digital access is free).

***Meat Business Magazine.*** Record Printing, 109 W Washington St. Millstadt, IL 62260. Phone: (618)476-9587; Fax: (618)476-9588 • URL: http://www.recordprinting.biz • Monthly. $20. Monthly publication for small to medium meat processors.

***Meat, Poultry and Egg Inspection Directory.*** U.S. Department of Agriculture. U.S. Department of Agriculture, 1400 Independence Ave. SW Washington, DC 20250. Phone: 800-336-3747 or (202)720-2791 or (202)720-9904; Fax: (202)690-2164 or (202)720-6050; Email: fsis.outreach@usda.gov • URL: http://www.usda.gov • Monthly. Lists companies that produce meat, poultry and egg products.

***Meat Processing-Buyer's Guide-North American Edition.*** Watt Publishing, 122 S Wesley Ave. Mount Morris, IL 61054-1497. Phone: (815)734-4171 • Annual. $12.00. In-depth statistical review of the meat, poultry, and seafood industries with graphs and tables; governmental phonebook; listing of meat associations, list of suppliers to the industry; list of equipment, services, and supplies, list of meat processors and their respective products.

***Meat Processing: North American Edition.*** Watt Publishing, 122 S Wesley Ave. Mount Morris, IL 61054-1497. Phone: (815)734-4171 • Monthly. $54.00 per year.

***Mechanical Engineering Abstracts.*** Cambridge Scientific Abstracts L.P., 7200 Wisconsin Ave., Ste. 601 Bethesda, MD 20814. Phone: 800-843-7751 or (301)961-6700 or (301)961-6785; Fax: (301)961-6720 or (301)961-6708; Email: sales@proquest.com • URL: http://www.proquest.co.uk • Quarterly. $1,620 Individuals print + web edition (includes shipping); $1,215 Individuals web edition. Database covering international literature on mechanical engineering, engineering management, and production engineering, including specific and theoretical applications. Formerly *ISMEC - Mechanical Engineering Abstracts.*

***Mechanical Engineering.*** ASME International, 2 Park Ave. New York, NY 10016-5990. Phone: 800-843-2763 or (973)882-1170; Fax: (973)882-1717; Email: customercare@asme.org • URL: http://www.asme.org • Monthly. $25 Members /year; $144 Nonmembers /year. The official monthly publication of the ASME.

**Mechanical Power Transmission Association.** 5672 Strand Ct., Ste. 2 Naples, FL 34110. Phone: (239)514-3441; Fax: (239)514-3470; Email: bob@mpta.org • URL: http://www.mpta.org • Manufacturers of multiple V-belt drive sheaves and elastomeric couplings for mechanical power transmission machinery.

***Mechanism and Machine Theory.*** Elsevier, Secondary Publishing Division, 650 Ave. of the Americas New York, NY 10011. Phone: 888-437-4636 or (212)633-3980; Fax: (212)633-3975; Email: t.reller@elsevier.com • URL: http://www.elseveier.com • Monthly. $4,537 Institutions /year; $149 Individuals. Provides a medium of communication between engineers and scientists engaged in research and development within the fields of knowledge embraced by IFToMM, the International Federation for the Promotion of Mechanism and Machine Science.

***Med Ad News.*** Engel Publishing Partners, 828 A Newton-Yardley Rd. Newton, PA 18940. Phone: (215)867-0044; Fax: (215)867-0053 • URL: http://www.engelpub.com • Monthly. $225.00 per year. Covers the field of pharmaceutical advertising and marketing.

***Medesthetics: Business Education for Medical Practitioners.*** Creative Age Publications Inc., 7628 Densmore Ave. Van Nuys, CA 91406-2042. Phone: 800-442-5667 or (818)782-7328; Fax: (818)782-7450 • URL: http://www.creativeage.com • Bimonthly. Trade magazine for medical practitioners.

***Media and Methods: Educational Products, Technologies and Programs for Schools and Universities.*** American Society of Educators, 1429 Walnut St. Philadelphia, PA 19102. Phone: 800-555-5657 or (215)563-6005; Fax: (215)587-9706; Email: michelesok@aol.com • 5/year. $35 /year. Dedicated to reporting on the latest advancements in the field of education.

***Media and the Law.*** SIMBA Information Inc., 60 Long Ridge Rd., Ste. 300 Stamford, CT 06902. Phone: (203)325-8193; Fax: (203)325-8975 • URL: http://www.simbainformation.com • Semimonthly. $327.00 per year. Newsletter.

***Media Communications Association International Membership Directory.*** Media Communications Association - International, 2810 Crossroads Dr., Ste. 3800 Madison, WI 53705-0135. Phone: 888-899-6224; Fax: (888)862-8150; Email: info@mca-i.org • URL: http://www.mca-i.org.

***Media Device Report.*** Jon Peddie Associates, 100 Shoreline Hwy., Bldg. A, 2nd Fl. Mill Valley, CA 94941. • Description: Covers media and electronic devices and companies, as well as business information for those devices and companies. Recurring features include a company profile, editorial articles, technology briefs, IPO's, stocks, and stock indices.

**Media Financial Management Association.** 550 W Frontage Rd., Ste. 3600 Northfield, IL 60093. Phone: (847)716-7000; Fax: (847)716-7004; Email: info@mediafinance.org • URL: http://www.mediafinance.org • Members are accountants and other financial personnel in the radio and television broadcasting industries. Formerly Broadcast Financial Management Association.

***Media Industry Newsletter.*** Access Intelligence L.L.C., 4 Choke Cherry Rd., 2nd Fl. Rockville, MD 20850. Phone: 800-777-5006 or (301)354-2000 or (301)354-2101; Fax: (301)309-3847 or (801)365-2300; Email: info@accessintel.com • URL: http://www.accessintel.com/ • Description: Covers the media industry, including advertising, marketing, publishing, radio, and television. Recurring features include weekly box scores of advertising pages in major magazines, salaries of top executives, earnings reports, and news of people in the industry.

***Media Rates & Data.*** Media-Daten AG, Klausstrasse 33 CH-8034 Zurich, Switzerland. Phone: 41 1 694125 • Biennial. Covers: National and international newspapers, journals, trade press and local Swiss newsletters, radio and television. Entries include: Publications name, address, phone, rates, schedules.

**Media Rating Council.** 420 Lexington Ave., Ste. 343 New York, NY 10170. Phone: (212)972-0300; Fax: (212)972-2786; Email: staff@mediaratingcouncil.org • URL: http://www.mediaratingcouncil.org • Broadcast and cable trade associations, media owners, advertising agencies, cable networks, and national networks including National Association of Broadcasters, Television Bureau of Advertising, Radio Advertising Bureau, Cable Advertising Bureau. Establishes minimum standards for electronic media ratings surveys. Commissions audits by CPA firms of the collection and processing of data gathered by audience measurement services, including A.C. Nielsen, Arbitron, Statistical Research Inc., and Mediafax.

***Media Sports Business.*** SNL Kagan, 40 Ragsdale Dr., Ste. 250 Monterey, CA 93940. Phone: (831)624-1536; Fax: (831)641-0961 • URL: http://www.kagan.com • Description: Discusses the economics of national and regional cable and pay TV sports. Includes semiannual census of cable and pay sports channels, coverage of values of sports media rights, and news of other developments in the field. **Remarks:** Also available via e-mail and fax.

***MediaFinder.*** Oxbridge Communications Inc., 186 5th Ave. New York, NY 10010. Phone: 800-955-0231 or (212)741-0231; Fax: (212)633-2938; Email: info@oxbridge.com • URL: http://www.oxbridge.com • $1,295 per year. Online database with 77,000 magazines, catalogs, newspapers, and journals.

***MediaMap/High-Tech Trade Show Report.*** Cision US Inc., 332 S Michigan Ave., Ste. 900 Chicago, IL 60604-4393. Phone: 866-639-5087; Email: info.us@cision.com • URL: http://us.cision.com • Annual. $495. Covers: 350 domestic and international high-tech trade shows. Entries include: Name, address, phone, fax; contact persons; show dates, focus and technology profile; exhibitor and attendee figures; attendee demographics; booth space rates.

***Mediaweek: The News Magazine of the Media.*** Nielsen Business Media Inc., 770 Broadway New York, NY 10003-9522. Phone: 866-890-8541 or (646)654-4500 or (646)654-5000; Fax: (646)654-5584 or (646)654-4500; Email: bmcomm@nielsen.com • URL: http://www.nielsenbusinessmedia.com • Published for advertising media buyers and managers.

***Medical & Health Care Books & Serials in Print.*** Grey House Publishing, 4919 Rte. 22 Amenia, NY 12501. Phone: 800-562-2139 or (518)789-8700; Fax: (518)789-0556; Email: books@greyhouse.com • URL: http://www.greyhouse.com • $645 Individuals Hardcover. Provides immediate access to the highly specialized publishing activity in the health sciences and allied health fields.

***Medical and Healthcare Marketplace Guide.*** IDD Inc., 1500 Walnut St., Ste. 1000 Philadelphia, PA 19102. Phone: 800-784-2332 or (215)875-1212; Fax: (215)735-3966; Email: info@dorlandhealth.com • Annual. $595.00. Two volumes. Provides market survey summaries for about 500 specific product and service categories (volume one: "Research Reports"). Contains profiles of nearly 5,500 pharmaceutical, medical product, and healthcare service companies (volume two: "Company Profiles").

***Medical Benefits.*** Wolters Kluwer Law and Business, 76 9th Ave., 7th Fl. New York, NY 10011-4962. Phone: 800-234-1660 or (212)771-0600; Fax: (800)901-9075 or (301)644-3550 • URL: http://www.wolterskluwerlb.com • Description: Focuses on key developments, statistics, and studies relating to the health care system. Covers eight major topic areas: cost containment, employee benefits, employee health/wellness, quality of care, delivery systems, government in health care, legal issues, and health care expenditure data.

***Medical Device and Diagnostic Industry.*** Canon Communications LLC, 11444 W Olympic Blvd., Suite 900 Los Angeles, CA 90064. Phone: (310)445-4200; Fax: (310)445-3799 or (310)445-4299; Email: mpmn@cancom.com • URL: http://www.cancom.com • Monthly. Focused on the medical technology industry.

***Medical Device Technology.*** Elsevier, Secondary Publishing Division, 650 Ave. of the Americas New York, NY 10011. Phone: 888-437-4636 or (212)633-3980; Fax: (212)633-3975; Email: t.reller@elsevier.com • URL: http://www.elseveier.com • $143.94 print and e-book; $119.95 print or e-book. Provides undergraduate engineering students with an introduction to commonly manufactured medical devices.

***Medical Economics.*** Advanstar Medical, 5 Paragon Dr. Montvale, NJ 07645-1742. Phone: 877-922-2022 or (973)944-7777; Fax: (973)847-5390; Email: customer_service@medec.com • URL: http://www.medec.com • Semimonthly. $109 /year. Covers the financial, economic, insurance, administrative, and other non-clinical aspects of private medical practice. Provides investment and estate planning advice.

***Medical Economics General Surgery-Orthopedic Surgery.*** Thomson Medical Economics, 5 Paragon Dr. Montvale, NJ 07645-1742. Phone: 800-526-4870 or (201)358-7200; Fax: (201)573-8999 or (201)722-2680; Email: customer.service@medec.com • URL: http://www.medec.com • Monthly. $65.00 per year. Provides information and advice on practice management (non-clinical) for surgeons. Formerly *Medical Economics for Surgeons.*

**Medical Group Management Association.** 104 Inverness Terr. E Englewood, CO 80112-5306. Phone: 877-275-6462 or (303)799-1111; Fax: (303)643-4439; Email: service@mgma.com • URL: http://www.mgma.com • Represents professionals involved in the management of medical group practices and administration of other ambulatory healthcare facilities. Provides products and services that includes education, benchmarking, surveys, national advocacy and networking opportunities for members.

***Medical Laser Report.*** PennWell Corp., 98 Spit Brook Rd. Nashua, NH 03062-5737. Phone: 800-225-0556 or (603)891-0123; Fax: (603)891-9294 • URL: http://www.pennwell.com • Description: Presents news on the medical laser industry, technology, research, and markets. Recurring features include news of research, business news and product introductions.

***The Medical Letter on Drugs and Therapeutics.*** Medical Letter, 145 Huguenot St., Ste. 312 New Rochelle, NY 10801-7537. Phone: 800-211-2769 or (914)235-0500; Fax: (914)632-1733; Email: custserv@medicalletter.org • URL: http://secure.medicalletter.org • Biweekly. $98 Individuals per year. Provides critical evaluation of new drugs, including effectiveness, toxicity, cost, and possible alternatives.

***Medical Malpractice Law and Strategy.*** ALM Media Properties LLC, 120 Broadway, 5th Fl. New York, NY 10271-1100. Phone: (212)457-9400; Fax: (646)417-7705; Email: customercare@alm.com • URL: http://www.alm.com • Monthly. $479 per year. Covers malpractice legal issues for lawyers representing physicians and for lawyers representing patients. Includes news of judicial, legislative, and medical developments affecting malpractice strategies. (A Law Journal Newsletter, formerly published by Leader Publications).

***Medical Marketing and Media.*** Haymarket Media, Inc., 7200 W. Camino Real, Suite 215 Boca Raton, FL 33433. Phone: 800-346-2015 or (407)368-9301; Fax: (407)368-7870 • URL: http://www.pmdcentral.com • Monthly. $148 U.S. 1-year subscription; $148 Canada 1-year subscription; $248 Other countries 1-year subscription. Contains articles on marketing, direct marketing, advertising media, and sales personnel for the healthcare and pharmaceutical industries.

*Medical Product Manufacturing News Buyers Guide*. Canon Communications LLC, 11444 W Olympic Blvd., Suite 900 Los Angeles, CA 90064. Phone: (310)445-4200; Fax: (310)445-3799 or (310)445-4299; Email: mpmn@cancom. com • URL: http://www.cancom.com • A directory of over 3,000 medical device and medical electronic equipment. Formerly *Medical Product Manufacturing News-Buyer's Guide and Designer's Sourcebook*.

*Medical Product Manufacturing News*. Canon Communications LLC, 11444 W Olympic Blvd., Suite 900 Los Angeles, CA 90064. Phone: (310)445-4200; Fax: (310)445-3799 or (310)445-4299; Email: mpmn@cancom.com • URL: http:// www.cancom.com • 5/year. Directed at manufacturers of medical devices and medical electronic equipment. Covers industry news, service news, and new products.

*Medical Quality Management Sourcebook*. Thomson Financial Inc., 195 Broadway New York, NY 10007-3100. Phone: (646)822-2000; Email: custserv@tfn.com • URL: http:// www.thomsonreuters.com • Annual. $295 Individuals. Covers: Clinical performance measurement and improvement systems, and organizations and individuals involved in patient satisfaction surveys. Database includes: Fact sheets, charts. Entries include: Company and individual name, address, phone, fax.

*Medical Reference Services Quarterly*. The Haworth Press Inc., 10 Alice St. Binghamton, NY 13904. Phone: 800-429-6784 or (607)722-5857; Fax: (607)771-0012 or (607)722-6362; Email: getinfo@haworthpress.com • URL: http:// www.haworthpressinc.com/store/product.asp?sku=J014 • Quarterly. Institutions, $275.00 per year. An academic and practical journal for medical reference librarians.

*Medical Research Centres: A World Directory of Organizations and Programmes*. Informa Group PLC, Informa House, 30-32 Mortimer St. London W1W 7RE, United Kingdom. Phone: 44 020 7017 5000 or 44 207 0175000; Fax: 44 020 7017 4286; Email: headoffice@informa.com • URL: http:// www.informa.com • Biennial. $470.00. Two volumes. Contains profiles of more than 7,000 medical research facilities around the world. Includes medical, dental, nursing, pharmaceutical, psychiatric, and surgical research centers.

**Medical Research Council of South Africa - Health Systems Research Unit**. PO Box 19070 Tygerberg 7505, South Africa. Phone: 27 21 9380454; Fax: 27 21 9380483; Email: cathy.mathews@mrc.ac.za • URL: http://www.mrc.ac.za/ healthsystems/healthsystems.htm • Health care services, systems, interventions, and policies.

**Medical Spa Society**. 60 E 56th St., 2nd Fl. New York, NY 10022. Phone: 888-MED-ISPA or (212)688-5882; Email: coordinator@medicalspasociety.com • URL: http://www. medicalspasociety.com • Seeks to raise and uphold the level of professionalism practiced throughout the medical spa industry. Promotes education, communication and standards of excellence for the medical spa profession. Encourages exchange of information and ideas that will further enhance the image and credibility of the medical spa industry.

*Medical Technology Stock Letter*. Medical Technology Stock Letter, PO Box 40460 Berkeley, CA 94704. Phone: (510)843-1857; Fax: (510)843-0901; Email: mtsl@bioinvest.com • URL: http://www.bioinvest.com • Description: Specializes in investments in biotechnology companies. Offers news of the industry and recommendations for buying, selling, and holding stocks. Recurring features include news of research, a model portfolio reflecting the editors' investment strategy, and columns titled Pulse of the Market and Industry Scan. **Remarks:** Also available through e-mail.

**Medical University of South Carolina - Center for Health Economics and Policy Studies**. CHP Research Bldg., 3rd Fl., Department of Health Sciences & Research, College of Health Professions Complex, 77 President St. Charleston, SC 29425. Phone: (843)792-3176; Fax: (843)792-1358; Email: lindrorc@musc.edu • URL: http://www.musc.edu/chp/cheps • Health economics and health policy.

*Medicare and Coordinated Care Plans*. Consumer Information Center, Department 59 Pueblo, CO 81009. • Free. Published by the U. S. Department of Health and Human Services. Contains detailed information on services to Medicare beneficiaries from health maintenance organizations (HMOs).

*Medicare & You Handbook*. Health Care Financing Administration U.S. Department of Health & Human Service, 200 Independence Ave. SW Washington, DC 20201. Phone: 877-696-6775 or (202)619-0257 • URL: http://www.os.dhhs.gov/ about/opdivs/hcfa.html • Irregular. Publication includes: Lists of Medicare carriers in individual states. Principal content includes discussion of what Medicare is, what its various options are, and what new benefits have been added recently.

*Medicare Compliance Alert*. UCG Holdings L.P., 11300 Rockville Pike, Suite 1100 Rockville, MD 20852-3030. Phone: 800-929-4824 or (301)816-8950 or (301)287-2700; Fax: (301)816-8945; Email: dhernan@ucg.com • URL: http:// www.ucg.com • $489 24 issues. Description: Procvides news and guidance to help keep health care practices on the right side of fraud and abuse laws and regulations.

*Medicare: Employer Health Plans*. Consumer Information Center, Department 59 Pueblo, CO 81009. • Free. Published by the U. S. Department of Health and Human Services. Explains the special rules that apply to Medicare beneficiaries who have employer group health plan coverage. (Publication No. 520-Y.).

*Medicare Explained*. Wolters Kluwer Law & Business CCH, 2700 Lake Cook Rd. Riverwoods, IL 60015. Phone: 888-224-7377 or (847)267-7000; Email: cust_serv@cch.com • URL: http://www.cchgroup.com • Annual. $67.95.

*Medicare Handbook*. U. S. Government Printing Office, 732 N Capitol St. NW Washington, DC 20401. Phone: 866-512-1800 or (202)512-1800 or (866)512-1800; Fax: (202)512-2104 or (202)512-2250; Email: contactcenter@gpo.gov • URL: http://www.gpo.gov • Annual. $3.00. Issued by the Health Care Financing Administration, U. S. Department of Health and Human Services. Provides information on Medicare hospital insurance and medical insurance, including benefits, options, and rights. Discusses the functions of Medigap insurance, managed care plans, peer review organizations, and Medicare insurance carriers. Formerly *Medicare Handbook*.

*Medicare: The Official U. S. Government Site for Medicare Information*. Centers for Medicare and Medicaid Services, Phone: (202)690-6726 • URL: http://www.medicare.gov • Web site provides extensive information on Medicare health plans, publications, fraud, nursing homes, top 20 questions and answers, etc. Includes access to the National Nursing Home Database, providing summary compliance information on "every Medicare and Medicaid certified nursing home in the country."Online searching is offered. Fees: Free.

**Mediphotonics Laboratory**. City College of City University of New York, 160 Convent Ave. New York, NY 10031. Phone: (212)650-7760; Fax: (212)650-5530 • URL: http://www. cuny.edu.

*Medium Companies of Europe*. Graham & Trotman Ltd., Sterling House, 66 Wilton Rd. London SW1V 1DE, United Kingdom. Phone: 71 8211123; Fax: 71 6305229 • Annual. $1,198 for set; $598 volume 1; $300 volume 2; $300 volume 3. Covers: Approximately 8,000 medium-sized companies in western Europe. Entries include: Company name, address, phone, telex, names and titles of key personnel, number of employees, financial data, subsidiary and branch names and locations, product/service. Companion to "Major Companies of Europe" (see separate entry).

*The MEED Middle East Financial Directory*. EMAP Business International, 33-39 Bowling Green Ln. London EC1R 0DA, United Kingdom. Phone: 44 20 74706200 or 44 1714300337; Fax: 44 71 74706641 • Annual. $120. Covers: 4,000 banks and financial institutions in the Middle East. Entries include: Company name, address, phone, telex, financial statistics, branch offices.

*MEEN Diagnostic and Invasive Technology*. Reilly Communications Group, 16 E Schaumburg Rd. Schaumburg, IL 60194-3551. Phone: (847)882-6336; Fax: (847)882-0631; Email: info@rcgpubs.com • URL: http://www.new.reillycomm.com/ contact.php • $90 Canada and Mexico; $120 Other countries. Bimonthly. Free to qualified personnel. Provides medical electronics industry news and new product information. Formerly *Medical Electronics and Equipment News*.

*Meeting and Conference Executives Alert*. MCEA, 554 Strawberry Hill Rd. Centerville, MA 02632-3037. Phone: (508)771-5200; Fax: (508)775-5658; Email: mcea@ mediaone.net • Monthly. $99.00 per year. Newsletter. Formerly *Meeting Planners Alert*.

*Meeting Facilities Directory*. InfoGroup Inc., 5711 S 86th Cir. Omaha, NE 68127-4146. Phone: (402)593-4500 • URL: http://www.infogroup.com • Annual. Number of listings: 6508. Entries include: Name, address, phone, size of advertisement, name of owner or manager, number of employees, year first in "Yellow Pages." Compiled from telephone company "Yellow Pages," nationwide.

*The Meeting Professional*. Meeting Professionals International, 3030 Lyndon B. Johnson Fwy., Ste. 1700 Dallas, TX 75234-2759. Phone: (972)702-3000; Fax: (972)702-3070; Email: feedback@mpiweb.org • URL: http://www.mpiweb.org • Monthly. Included in membership; $99 Nonmembers. Published for professionals in the meeting and convention industry. Contains news, features, and how-to's for domestic and international meetings management. Formerly *Meeting Manager*.

*Membership and Peer Network Directory*. Employee Morale and Recreation Association, PO Box 10517 Rockville, MD 20849. • URL: http://employeemorale.org • Annual. Lists more than 4,500 personnel managers, recreation directors and certified administrators in employee recreation, fitness and services. Formerly *National Employee Services and Recreation Association-Membership and Peer Network Directory*.

*Membership Directory and Business Guide for Huntsville and Madison County*. Chamber of Commerce of Huntsville/ Madison County, 225 Church St. Huntsville, AL 35801-5542. Phone: (256)535-2000; Fax: (256)535-2015; Email: info@ hsvchamber.org • URL: http://www.huntsvillealabamausa. com • Covers 2,100 businesses in Huntsville and Madison county.

*MENA Journal of Business Case Studies*. IBIMA Publishing, 34 E Germantown Pke., No. 327 Norristown, PA 19401. Email: contact@ibimapublishing.com • URL: http://www. ibimapublishing.com • Peer-reviewed journal publishing information on business and corporate activities in the Middle East and North Africa region.

**Mental Health America**. 2000 N Beauregard St., 6th Fl. Alexandria, VA 22311. Phone: 800-969-6642 or (703)684-7722; Fax: (703)684-5968 • URL: http://www. mentalhealthamerica.net • Addresses all aspects of mental health and mental illness and is dedicated to improving mental health, preventing mental disorders, and achieving victory over mental illnesses. Accomplishes its mission through advocacy, public education, research, and service in partnership with more than 340 affiliates across the country.

*Mental Health Law Reporter*. Business Publishers Inc., PO Box 17592 Baltimore, MD 21297-1592. Phone: 800-223-8720; Fax: (800)508-2592; Email: custserv@bpinews.com • URL: http://www.bpinews.com • Monthly. $290 Individuals; $372 Individuals 1 year; $297 Individuals internet sale price. Description: Provides news and coverage of court cases pertaining to legal issues affecting mental health professionals.

*Mental Measurements Yearbook*. University of Nebraska-Lincoln Buros Institute, 21 Teachers College Hall Lincoln, NE 68588-0348. Phone: 800-755-1105 or (402)472-6203 or (402)472-5146; Fax: (402)472-6207 • URL: http://buros.org • Biennial. $210. Includes timely, consumer-oriented test reviews, providing evaluative information to promote and encourage informed test selection.

*Mergent Bond Record and Annual Bond Record*. Mergent Inc., 60 Madison Ave., Fl. 6 New York, NY 10010. Phone: 888-411-0893 or (212)413-7700; Fax: (212)413-7670; Email: shirley.petersen@mergent.com • URL: http://www.mergent. com • Monthly. Formerly *Moody's Bond Record and Annual Bond Record*. Provides the most complete and accurate coverage available on corporate, government, municipal, industrial development/environmental control revenue and international bonds.

*Mergent Handbook of Common Stocks*. Mergent Inc., 60 Madison Ave., Fl. 6 New York, NY 10010. Phone: 888-411-0893 or (212)413-7700; Fax: (212)413-7670; Email: shirley. petersen@mergent.com • URL: http://www.mergent.com • Quarterly. Price on application. Facts, performance trends and financial summaries on nearly 1,000 New York Stock Exchange companies. Formerly *Moody's Handbook of Common Stocks*.

*Mergent Industrial Manual and News Reports*. Mergent Inc., 580 Kingsley Park Dr. Fort Mill, SC 29715. Phone: 800-937-1398 or (704)527-2700 or (704)559-7601; Fax: (704)559-6837 or (704)559-6960; Email: customerservice@mergent. com • URL: http://www.mergent.com • Annual. $2,095 including 'News Reports.' Covers: nearly 2,000 companies listed on the New York, American, or regional stock exchanges. Entries include: Company name, headquarters address, phone, names and titles of executive officers and directors, history, Standard Industrial Classification (SIC) code, Moody's rating, and financial and statistical data.

*Mergent International Manual and News Reports*. Mergent Inc., 60 Madison Ave., Fl. 6 New York, NY 10010. Phone: 888-411-0893 or (212)413-7700; Fax: (212)413-7670; Email: shirley.petersen@mergent.com • URL: http://www.mergent. com • Financial and other information about 13,000 companies in 100 countries. Formerly *Moody's International Manual and News Reports*.

*Mergent Municipal and Government Manual*. Mergent Inc., 60 Madison Ave., Fl. 6 New York, NY 10010. Phone: 888-411-0893 or (212)413-7700; Fax: (212)413-7670; Email: shirley. petersen@mergent.com • URL: http://www.mergent.com • Covers all U.S. taxing jurisdictions and agencies with total long-term rated debt of $25,000,000 or over.

*Mergent Online*. Mergent Inc., 580 Kingsley Park Dr. Fort Mill, SC 29715. Phone: 800-937-1398 or (704)527-2700 or (704)559-7601; Fax: (704)559-6837 or (704)559-6960; Email: customerservice@mergent.com • URL: http://www. mergent.com • Fee-based Web site provides detailed information on 20,000 publicly-owned companies in 100 foreign countries, as well as more than 10,000 corporations listed on the New York Stock Exchange, American Stock Exchange, NASDAQ, and U.S. regional exchanges. Searching is offered on many financial variables and text fields. Weekly updating. Formerly *FIS Online*.

*Mergent OTC Industrial Manual*. Mergent Inc., 60 Madison Ave., Fl. 6 New York, NY 10010. Phone: 888-411-0893 or (212)413-7700; Fax: (212)413-7670; Email: shirley. petersen@mergent.com • URL: http://www.mergent.com • Annual. $1,995 including 'News Reports.' Covers over 2,500 companies whose stock is traded over the counter. Includes biweekly *Moody's OTC Industrial News Report*.

*Mergent OTC Unlisted Manual*. Mergent, 5250 77 Center Dr. Charlotte, NC 28217. Phone: 800-342-5647 or (704)539-6945 or (704)527-2700; Fax: (704)559-6960; Email: customerservice@mergent.com • URL: http://www.mergent. com • Annual. $1,995.00 per year. Includes supplement *Moody's OTC Unlisted News Report*.

*Mergent's Annual Dividend Record*. Mergent Inc., 60 Madison Ave., Fl. 6 New York, NY 10010. Phone: 888-411-0893 or (212)413-7700; Fax: (212)413-7670; Email: shirley. petersen@mergent.com • URL: http://www.mergent.com • Annual. Provides detailed dividend data, including tax information, for 12,000 stocks and 18,000 mutual funds. Covers the most recent year. Formerly *Moody's Annual Dividend Record*.

*Mergent's Manuals*. Mergent Inc., 60 Madison Ave., Fl. 6 New York, NY 10010. Phone: 888-411-0893 or (212)413-7700; Fax: (212)413-7670; Email: shirley.petersen@mergent.com •

URL: http://www.mergent.com • Annual. Looseleaf supplements. Prices on application.

*Mergent's Public Utility Manual*. Mergent Inc., 60 Madison Ave., Fl. 6 New York, NY 10010. Phone: 888-411-0893 or (212)413-7700; Fax: (212)413-7670; Email: shirley. petersen@mergent.com • URL: http://www.mergent.com • Annual. $1,995.00. Updated weekly online. Contains financial and other information concerning publicly-held utility companies (electric, gas, telephone, water).

*Merger and Acquisition Sourcebook*. NVST Inc., 1100 Dexter Ave. N Seattle, WA 98109. Phone: 800-910-6878 or (206)676-3802; Fax: (206)273-7401; Email: info@nvst.com • URL: http://www.nvst.com • Annual. $450 Single issue discounted price. Publication includes: Profiles of companies most active in mergers and acquisitions in the previous year. Entries include: Company name, address, phone, financial data, history of transactions. Principal content of publication is summary and analysis of merger, acquisition, and divestiture activity in the previous year; company reorganizations; and terminated financial transactions.

*The Merger Yearbook*. Cambridge Corp., • Annual. $490 plus $5.00 shipping. Publication includes: About 15,000 mergers and joint ventures announced during preceding year, including lists of largest mergers, firms participating most frequently in acquisitions or joint ventures, active acquirers and divesters, acquisitions by foreign firms, and leveraged buyouts, mergers, and joint ventures in preceding year. Principal content of pubication is information on corporate mergers and acquisitions. Entries include: Company names, locations, and announced terms and prices; many listings include financial or other data.

*Merger Yearbook*. SourceMedia Inc., 1 State Street Plz., 27th Fl. New York, NY 10004. Phone: 800-221-1809 or (212)803-8200 or (212)803-8333; Fax: (212)843-9635 or (212)292-5216; Email: custserv@sourcemedia.com • URL: http://www.sourcemedia.com • Annual. $595.00. Provides detailed information on mergers and acquisitions announced or completed during the year. Includes many charts.

*Mergers & Acquisitions*. Glasser LegalWorks, 150 Clove Rd. Little Falls, NJ 07424. Phone: 800-308-1700 or (973)890-0008; Fax: (973)890-0042; Email: legalwks@aol.com • URL: http://www.glasserlegalworks.com • Looseleaf. $225.00, including CD-ROM version. Periodic Supplementation. Includes explanations of M & A legal procedures, with annotated forms. (Emerging Growth Companies Series.).

*Mergers & Acquisitions Magazine—Rosters*. MLR Publishing Co., Email: subscribe@iddis.com • Bimonthly. $70 per issue; $425 per year. Each issue includes a roster in three sections: "Mergers & Acquisitions," covering major deals concluded between American firms; "Foreign Investment in the U.S.," covering foreign firms which acquired companies in the United States; and "U.S. Investment Abroad," covering acquisitions by United States firms in other countries. Additional information on pending and completed deals, cancellations, and sell-offs is given in news sections. Entries include: Names and locations of participants, sales and net income of each, terms, lines of business of each participant, and effective date of transaction.

*Mergers & Acquisitions Report*. SourceMedia Inc., 1 State Street Plz., 27th Fl. New York, NY 10004. Phone: 800-221-1809 or (212)803-8200 or (212)803-8333; Fax: (212)843-9635 or (212)292-5216; Email: custserv@sourcemedia.com • URL: http://www.sourcemedia.com • Weekly. $1,295.00 per year. Newsletter. Covers pending and ongoing mergers, acquisitions, restructurings, and bankruptcies.

*Mergers & Acquisitions: The Dealmaker's Journal*. SourceMedia Inc., 1 State Street Plz., 27th Fl. New York, NY 10004. Phone: 800-221-1809 or (212)803-8200 or (212)803-8333; Fax: (212)843-9635 or (212)292-5216; Email: custserv@sourcemedia.com • URL: http://www.sourcemedia.com • Bimonthly. $475.00 per year. Provides articles on various aspects of M & A, including valuation, pricing, taxes, and strategy. Current M & A deals are listed and described.

*Mergerstat Quarterly Reports*. Houlihan Lokey Inc., 10250 Constellation Blvd., 5th Fl. Los Angeles, CA 90067. Phone: (310)553-8871; Fax: (310)553-2173; Email: info@hlhz.com • URL: http://www.hlhz.com • Quarterly. $100.00 per year. Newsletter. Provides details and analysis of recent corporate merger activity. Includes "Top deals year-to-date" and rankings of financial and legal advisors.

*Mergerstat Transaction Roster*. FactSet Mergerstat L.L.C., 2150 Colorado Ave., Ste. 150 Santa Monica, CA 90404. Phone: (310)315-3100; Email: info@mergerstat.com • URL: http://www.mergerstat.com • Annual. $299.00. A directory of all U. S. companies that were involved in merger and acquisition activity during the year covered. Includes details of each transaction.

*METADEX Materials Collection: Metals-Polymers-Ceramics*. Cambridge Scientific Abstracts L.P., 7200 Wisconsin Ave., Ste. 601 Bethesda, MD 20814. Phone: 800-843-7751 or (301)961-6700 or (301)961-6785; Fax: (301)961-6720 or (301)961-6708; Email: sales@proquest.com • URL: http://www.proquest.co.uk • Quarterly. Provides CD-ROM citations to the worldwide literature of materials science and metallurgy. Corresponds to *Metals Abstracts, Alloys Index, Steels Alert, Nonferrous Alert, Polymers/Ceramics/ Composites Alert*, and *Engineered Materials Abstracts*. (Formerly produced by ASM International.).

*Metal & Steel Traders of the World*. Metal Bulletin Ltd., Nestor House, Playhouse Yard London EC4V 5EX, United Kingdom. Phone: 44 20 7827 9977; Fax: 44 20 7827 6470; Email: editorial@metalbulletin.com • URL: http://www.metalbulletin.com • Annual. $995 Individuals. Covers: 2,000 steel traders worldwide, including exporters, importers, merchants, producers, sales companies, and agents. Entries include: Company name, address, phone, e-mail and web addresses where possible, executives, date founded, parent and subsidiary companies, products.

*Metal Bulletin*. Metal Bulletin Inc., 1250 Broadway, 26th Fl. New York, NY 10001-7781. Phone: 800-638-2525 or (212)213-6202 or (800)638-2525; Fax: (212)213-1870 or (212)213-6619; Email: sales@metbul.com • URL: http://www.metalbulletin.com • Daily. £1,395 1-year standard subscription. Provides news of international trends, prices, and market conditions for both steel and non-ferrous metal industries. (Published in England.).

*Metal Bulletin Monthly*. Metal Bulletin Inc., 1250 Broadway, 26th Fl. New York, NY 10001-7781. Phone: 800-638-2525 or (212)213-6202 or (800)638-2525; Fax: (212)213-1870 or (212)213-6619; Email: sales@metbul.com • URL: http://www.metalbulletin.com • Monthly. Edited for international metal industry business executives and senior technical personnel. Covers business, economic, and technical developments. (Published in England.).

*Metal Center News*. Sackett Business Media Inc., 1100 Jorie Blvd., Ste. 207 Oak Brook, IL 60522. Phone: (630)571-1067; Fax: (630)572-0689 • URL: http://www.metalcenternews.com • Monthly. $109 U.S. 1-year subscription (12 MCN magazine plus 1 annual directory); $125 Canada 1-year subscription (12 MCN magazine plus 1 annual directory); $179 Other countries 1-year subscription (12 MCN magazine plus 1 annual directory). The trade magazine of the metals distribution industry: the service centers that warehouse, process and distribute carbon and stainless steels, aluminum and copper and brass.

*Metal Finishing: Devoted Exclusively to Metallic Surface Treatments*. Elsevier, Secondary Publishing Division, 650 Ave. of the Americas New York, NY 10011. Phone: 888-437-4636 or (212)633-3980; Fax: (212)633-3975; Email: t.reller@elsevier.com • URL: http://www.elseveier.com • Monthly. Institutions, $190.00 per year. Includes annual *Metal Finishing Guidebook and Directory*.

*Metal Finishing Guidebook and Directory*. Elsevier, Secondary Publishing Division, 650 Ave. of the Americas New York, NY 10011. Phone: 888-437-4636 or (212)633-3980; Fax: (212)633-3975; Email: t.reller@elsevier.com • URL: http://www.elseveier.com • Included with subscription to Metal Finishing. Lists manufacturers and suppliers to the industry.

*Metal Powder Industries Federation*. 105 College Rd. E Princeton, NJ 08540. Phone: 888-546-8676 or (609)452-7700; Fax: (609)987-8523; Email: info@mpif.org • URL: http://www.mpif.org • Manufacturers of metal powders, powder metallurgy processing equipment and tools, powder metallurgy products, and refractory and reactive metals. Member associations are: Metal Injection Molding Association; Metal Powder Producers Association; Advanced Particulate Materials Association; Powder Metallurgy Equipment Association; Powder Metallurgy Parts Association; Refractory Metals Association. Promotes the science and industry of powder metallurgy and metal powder application through: sponsorship of technical meetings, seminars, and exhibits; establishment of standards; compilation of statistics; public relations; publications. Maintains speakers' bureau and placement service; conducts research.

*Metal Powder Report*. Elsevier, Secondary Publishing Division, 650 Ave. of the Americas New York, NY 10011. Phone: 888-437-4636 or (212)633-3980; Fax: (212)633-3975; Email: t.reller@elsevier.com • URL: http://www.elseveier.com • $759 Institutions. 11 times a year. Technical articles, company reports, up-to-date news and book reviews cover powder metallurgy worldwide.

*Metal Products: Industry Sector Profile*. Philippine-German Export Development Project Philippine Bureau of Export Trade Promotion, 6F Trade & Industry Bldg., 361 Sen. Gil Puyat Ave. Makati PH-1226, Philippines. Phone: 63 2 897 8199; Email: web@dti.dti.gov.ph • URL: http://www.dti.gov.ph • Publication includes: Companies exporting metal products from the Philippines. Entries include: Company name, address, phone, fax, name and title of contact, type of business, year established, subsidiary and branch names and locations, financial data, number of employees, government registrations, professional memberships, bank references, supply capability, export experience, business plan. Principal content of publication is an overview of the business environment and metal products industry in the Philippines.

*Metalforming Digest*. CSA, 7200 Wisconsin Ave. Bethesda, MD 20814. Phone: 800-843-7751 or (301)961-6700; Fax: (301)961-6720; Email: service@csa.com • URL: http://www.csa.com • Monthly. Price on application. Provides abstracts of the international literature of metal forming, including powder metallurgy, stamping, extrusion, forging, etc.

*Metallurgia, The Journal of Metals Technology, Metal Forming and Thermal Processing*. British Forging Industry Association. DMG World Media Ltd., Queensway House, 2

Queensway Red Hill RH1 1QS, United Kingdom. Phone: 44 1737 855527; Fax: (173)7 855470 • Monthly. $157.00 per year.

*Metallurgical and Materials Transactions A: Physical Metallurgy and Materials Science*. ASM International, 9639 Kinsman Rd. Materials Park, OH 44073-0002. Phone: 800-336-5152 or (440)338-5151; Email: memberservicecenter@asminternational.org • URL: http://www.asminternational.org • Monthly. $3,640 Members 1-year subscription. Formerly *Metallurgical Transactions A- Physical Metallurgy and Materials Science*. Publishes contributions on all aspects of physical metallurgy and materials science, with a special emphasis on relationships among the processing, structure, and properties of materials.

*Metallurgical and Materials Transactions B: Process Metallurgy and Materials Processing Science*. ASM International, 9639 Kinsman Rd. Materials Park, OH 44073-0002. Phone: 800-336-5152 or (440)338-5151; Email: memberservicecenter@asminternational.org • URL: http://www.asminternational.org • Bimonthly. $2,856 /year. Formerly *Metallurgical Transactions B: Process Metallurgy*. Focused on process metallurgy and materials processing science, contains only original, critically reviewed research on primary manufacturing processes, from extractive metallurgy to the making of a shape.

*Metals Abstracts*. CSA, 7200 Wisconsin Ave. Bethesda, MD 20814. Phone: 800-843-7751 or (301)961-6700; Fax: (301)961-6720; Email: service@csa.com • URL: http://www.csa.com • Monthly. $3,575.00 per year. Includes print and on-line editions.

*Meteorological & Geoastrophysical Abstracts (MGA)*. American Meteorological Society. American Meteorological Society, 45 Beacon St. Boston, MA 02108-3693. Phone: (617)227-2425 or (617)227-2426; Fax: (617)742-8718; Email: amsinfo@ametsoc.org • URL: http://www.ametsoc.org • Monthly. $1,605 print; $1,900 CD-ROM; $3,000 Web. Journal presenting abstrcts of current world literature in meteorology, climatology, aeronomy, planetary atmospheres, solar-terrestrial relations, hydrology, oceanography, glaciology.

*Metric Today*. U.S. Metric Association Inc., 10245 Andasol Ave. Northridge, CA 91325-1504. Phone: (818)363-5606; Fax: (818)363-5606; Email: valerie.antoine@verizon.net • Description: Provides news on metric system conversion in the U.S., Canada, and abroad. Covers metrication updates in industry, government, education, and consumer areas. Recurring features include news of members, metric book reviews, editorials, data on metric standards, and letters to the editor.

*Metro Atlanta Chamber of Commerce—Who's Who in Metro Atlanta Business*. Metro Atlanta Chamber of Commerce, 235 Andrew Young International Blvd. NW Atlanta, GA 30303-2718. Phone: (404)880-9000 • URL: http://www.metroatlantachamber.com • Covers: Over 5,000 member firms in Atlanta, Georgia. Entries include: Company or firm name, address, phone, name of contact, and description of products or services.

*Metro*. Bobit Business Media, 3520 Challenger St. Torrance, CA 90503. Phone: (310)533-2400; Fax: (310)533-2500; Email: info@lctmag.com • URL: http://www.bobit.com • Nine times a year. $40.00 per year. Subject matter is the management of public transportationsystems. Includes Factbook.

*Metro Business Review*. Metro Business Review, Box 12727 Jackson, MS 39236-2727. Phone: 888-529-2229; Fax: (601)956-4047 • Monthly. Professional journal covering local business.

*Metro Orlando International Business Directory*. Greater Orlando Chamber of Commerce, 75 S Ivanhoe Blvd. Orlando, FL 32804. Phone: (407)425-1234 or (407)835-2517; Fax: (407)839-5020 or (407)835-2500; Email: info@orlando.org • URL: http://www.orlando.org • Covers: about 400 central Florida, manufacturers, distributors, services, and support organizations involved in world trade. Entries include: Company name, address, phone, fax, telex, name of contact, product, and countries where the company does business.

*METROBusiness Magazine: The Entrepreneurial Spirit of Metropolitan Boston*. METROBusiness Magazine, 199 Newbury St. Danvers, MA 01923. Phone: (508)774-9434; Fax: (508)774-1632 • Bimonthly. $18; $3 Single issue. Magazine serving the business and professional community in metropolitan Boston.

*Metroplex Business Directory—Dallas Area*. Business Marketing Source, 2501 Ave. J, Ste. 120 Arlington, TX 76006-6227. Phone: (817)530-2500; Fax: (817)530-2525; Email: bmsinfo@bmsdata.com • URL: http://www.bmsdata.com • Covers: over 88,000 businesses in the Dallas, Texas area. Entries include: Company name, address, phone, names and titles of key personnel, number of employees, description, product/service, Standard Industrial Classification (SIC) code.

*Metroplex Business Directory—Tarrant Area*. Business Marketing Source, 2501 Ave. J, Ste. 120 Arlington, TX 76006-6227. Phone: (817)530-2500; Fax: (817)530-2525; Email: bmsinfo@bmsdata.com • URL: http://www.bmsdata.com • Annual. Covers: Approximately 47,500 businesses in Tarrant Area, Texas. Entries include: Company name, address, phone, names and titles of key personnel, number of employees, description of product/service, Standard Industrial Classification (SIC) code.

***Metroplex Technology Business Council—Membership Directory***. Metroplex Technology Business Council, 411 Belle Grove Dr. Richardson, TX 75080. Phone: (972)792-2850; Fax: (972)792-2825; Email: info@metroplextbc.org • URL: http://www.metroplextbc.org • Provides contact information for technology provider companies.

***Metropolitan Atlanta Manufacturing Directory***. Metro Atlanta Chamber of Commerce, 235 Andrew Young International Blvd. NW Atlanta, GA 30303-2718. Phone: (404)880-9000 • URL: http://www.metroatlantachamber.com • Biennial. $30 Members only available in PDF document sent via email; $40 Nonmembers. Covers: About 4,000 firms with Standard Industrial Classification (SIC) codes 20-39 in the Atlanta metropolitan area. Entries include: Company name, address, phone, names of principal executives, number of employees, product or service provided, SIC code, date established, market served.

***Metropolitan Home: Style for Our Generation***. Hachette Filipacchi Media U.S., Inc., 1633 Broadway New York, NY 10019. Phone: 800-289-9464 or (212)767-6000; Fax: (212)767-5600 or (212)767-5615; Email: soundandvision@hfmus.com • URL: http://www.hfmmag.com • Bimonthly. $17.94 per year.

***Metropolitan Toronto Business Journal***. The Toronto Region Board of Trade, 1 First Canadian Pl., 25th Fl. Toronto, ON, Canada M5X 1C1. Phone: (416)366-6811; Fax: (416)366-2444; Email: info@bot.com • URL: http://www.bot.com • Magazine serving the greater Toronto business community.

***Metropolitan Washington DC JobBank: The Job Hunter's Guide to Washington DC***. Adams Media Corp., 57 Littlefield St. Avon, MA 02322. Phone: 800-872-5627 or (508)427-7100; Fax: (508)427-6790 or (800)872-5628; Email: deskcopies@adamsmedia.com • URL: http://www.adamsmedia.com • $17.95 Individuals Paperback. Covers: 6,900 employers in Washington, D.C., Greater Baltimore, and Northern Virginia. Database includes: Information on the basics of job winning and writing resumes and cover letters; electronic job search information; 330 industry associations; 90 online career resources; 250 employment services. Entries include: Firm or organization name, address, local phone, toll-free phone, fax, recorded jobline, name and title of contact, description of organization, subsidiaries, other locations, names of management, hours, titles for common positions, educational backgrounds desired, company benefits, stock exchange listing, location of headquarters, training programs, internships, parent company, number of employees, revenues, email and URL address, projected number of hires.

***Metrosouth Business Review: Metropolitan Boston's Business Magazine***. • Monthly. Magazine serving the business and professional community throughout the southern suburbs of Boston.

***Metrowest Business Review: Metropolitan Boston's Business Magazine***. • Monthly. Magazine serving the business and professional community throughout the western suburbs of Boston.

***Mexican Buyers Guide***. Auto Care Association, 7101 Wisconsin Ave., Ste. 1300 Bethesda, MD 20814-3415. Phone: (301)654-6664; Fax: (301)654-3299; Email: info@autocare.org • URL: http://www.autocare.org • $50 Members; $100 Nonmembers. Covers: Approximately 450 dealers, distributors and wholesalers in Mexico interested in U.S. products. Entries include: Name, address, phone of companies, name and title of contact, names and titles of key personnel, type of business, company histories and geographical area served.

***Mexican Product Guide***. Todd Publications, PO Box 500 Millwood, NY 10546. Phone: 866-896-0916 or (914)373-4750; Fax: (914)373-4750; Email: toddpub@aol.com • URL: http://www.toddpublications.com • Biennial. $125. Covers: Over 5,000 Mexican importers and exporters. Entries include: Company name, address, phone, fax, telex.

***Mexico Business Forecast Report***. Telecommunications Insight, 85 Queen Victoria St. London EC4V 4AB, United Kingdom. Phone: 20 72 465100 or 44 20 7248 0468; Fax: 20 72 480467 or 44 20 7248 0467; Email: enquiries@telecomsinsight.com • URL: http://www.telecomsinsight.com • Quarterly. $1,195 Individuals Single user; $1,795 Individuals Up to 3 users. Business forecast report for Mexico.

***Mexico Business Journal***. Gulf Breeze Publishing Co., City of Gulf Breeze, 1070 Shoreline Dr. Gulf Breeze, FL 32561. Phone: (850)934-5100 • URL: http://www.cityofgulfbreeze.com • Weekly. Publication providing news and information on doing business in Mexico.

***Mexico Business Law Handbook***. International Business Publications, USA, PO Box 15343 Washington, DC 20003. Phone: (202)546-2103; Fax: (202)546-3275; Email: ibpusa@comcast.net • URL: http://ibpus.com • $99.95 Individuals hardcopy, e-book, CD-ROM. Covers: Information on basic business legislation, laws, export-import regulations, and contacts.

***Mexico Company Handbook***. Hoover's Inc., 5800 Airport Blvd. Austin, TX 78752-4204. Phone: 866-443-3939 or (512)374-4500 or (866)281-5969; Fax: (512)374-4501; Email: salesteam@hoovers.com • URL: http://www.hoovers.com • Annual. $49.95 plus $4.50 shipping. Covers: about 70 of Mexico's largest public companies and 8 mutual funds and investment advisors. Database includes: Profile of the Mexican economy, international trade, and investment climate; data on stock exchanges, investment advisors, and money managers. Entries include: Company name, address, phone, fax, year established, stock ticker symbol, names and titles of key personnel, number of employees, number of stockholders, bank references, auditor, company history, financial data, markets and competition, raw materials used and sources, names of major stockholders, affiliated companies.

***Mexico Government and Business Contacts Handbook***. International Business Publications, USA, PO Box 15343 Washington, DC 20003. Phone: (202)546-2103; Fax: (202)546-3275; Email: ibpusa@comcast.net • URL: http://ibpus.com • $99.95 Individuals hardcopy, e-book, CD-ROM. Covers: Strategic government and business information, export-import activity in the country, investment, business contacts and regulations.

***Mexico Investment and Business Guide***. International Business Publications, USA, PO Box 15343 Washington, DC 20003. Phone: (202)546-2103; Fax: (202)546-3275; Email: ibpusa@comcast.net • URL: http://ibpus.com • $99.95 Individuals hardcopy, e-book, CD-ROM. Covers: Strategic information on economy, business, export-import and investment climate, regulations and industrial development, banking, government, and opportunities. Entries include: Important business contacts and business travel.

**MGMA Center for Research**. 104 Inverness Ter. E Englewood, CO 80112-5306. Phone: 877-275-6462 or (303)799-1111; Fax: (303)784-6101; Email: dng@mgma.com • URL: http://www.mgma.com/cfr • Fields of research include medical group practice management. Formerly Center for Research in Ambulatory Health Care Administration.

***MGMA Connexion***. Medical Group Management Association, 104 Inverness Terr. E Englewood, CO 80112-5306. Phone: 877-275-6462 or (303)799-1111; Fax: (303)643-4439; Email: service@mgma.com • URL: http://www.mgma.com • 10/year. $95 Individuals /year; $175 Institutions /year. Formerly *Medical Group Management Journal*. Provides in-depth coverage of key industry topics and advice for group practice professionals.

***MH/RV Builders News: The Magazine for Builders of Manufactured-Mobile-Modular-Marine Homes and Recreational Vehicles***. Patrick Finn, editor. Dan Kamrow and Associates, Inc., P.O. Box 72367 Roselle, IL 60172. Phone: (747)891-8872 • Bimonthly. Controlled circulation.

***Michiana Business***. Indiana University South Bend Judd Leighton School of Business and Economics Bureau of Business and Economic Research, 1700 Mishawaka Ave. South Bend, IN 46634. Phone: (574)520-4208; Fax: (574)520-4866; Email: dagbetsi@iusb.edu • URL: http://www.iusb.edu/buse/academic_centers/bber/index.php • Quarterly.

***Michigan Business Directory***. InfoGroup Inc., 5711 S 86th Cir. Omaha, NE 68127-4146. Phone: (402)593-4500 • URL: http://www.infogroup.com • Annual. $795 for both print & CD-ROM. Covers: 416,857 businesses in Michigan. Entries include: Company name, address, phone, number of employees, name of owner or manager, sales volume. Compiled from telephone company 'Yellow Pages,' statewide. All states covered independently (see separate entries).

***Michigan Centennial Business Directory***. Historical Society of Michigan, 5815 Executive Dr. Lansing, MI 48911. Phone: 800-692-1828 or (517)324-1828; Fax: (517)324-4370; Email: hsm@hsmichigan.org • URL: http://www.hsmichigan.org • Irregular. Covers: over 500 firms that have been operating continuously in Michigan for at least 100 years; also includes list of about 15 business archives. Database includes: Map of Michigan. Entries include: For firms—Firm name, address, phone, date founded, name and title of chief executive officer. For archives—Facility name, address, date established, description of holdings.

***Michigan Exporters of Wood Products***. Forest Management Division of the Michigan Dept. of Natural Resources, • Irregular. Covers: Approximately 500 sawmills and manufacturers in Michigan that want to become involved in or are currently exporting their wood products. Entries include: Company name, address, phone, fax, telex, name and title of contact, number of employees, annual amount of wood purchased, principal products manufactured, species or material used, equipment, services, and specialty.

***Michigan Industrial Directory***. Dun & Bradstreet Inc., 103 JFK Pkwy. Short Hills, NJ 07078. Phone: 800-526-0651 or (973)921-5500 or (973)921-5000; Fax: (866)560-7035 or (512)794-7670; Email: info@dnb.com • URL: http://www.dnb.com • Annual. Covers: 20,100 Michigan manufacturing companies. Database includes: Statistical data, trade show calendar. Entries include: Company name, address, county, phone, fax, number of employees, names and titles of key executives, plant size, year established, parent company, annual sales, import and export information, Standard Industrial Classification (SIC) code, and product description.

***Michigan Site Network***. Michigan Economic Development Corporation, 300 N Washington Sq. Lansing, MI 48913. Phone: 888-522-0103 or (517)335-5975; Fax: (517)241-3689; Email: medcservices@michigan.org • URL: http://www.michiganbusiness.org • Database covers: Available buildings, land parcels, and brownfield sites in Michigan. Database includes: Name, address or location, facilities, transportation access; name, address, and phone of contact; locational maps; pictures.

**Michigan State University - Artificial Language Laboratory**. 405 Computer Ctr. East Lansing, MI 48824-1042. Phone: (517)353-5399 or (517)353-0870; Fax: (517)353-4766; Email: artlang@pilot.msu.edu • URL: http://www.msu.edu/unit/artlang/ • Research areas include speech analysis and synthesis by computer.

**Michigan State University College of Human Medicine - Office of Medical Education Research and Development**. E Fee Hall, Rm. A-202, 965 Fee Rd. East Lansing, MI 48824-1316. Phone: (517)353-2037 or (517)353-7791; Fax: (517)432-1798; Email: mavis@msu.edu • URL: http://omerad.msu.edu • Improvement in medical education and related service programs, through program evaluation, performance assessment, faculty development, and the application of technology to improve instruction.

**Michigan State University - Composite Materials and Structures Center**. 2100 Engineering Bldg. East Lansing, MI 48824-1226. Phone: (517)353-5466 or (517)353-4696; Fax: (517)432-1634; Email: rich@egr.msu.edu • URL: http://www.egr.msu.edu/cmsc/ • Studies polymer, metal, and ceramic based composites.

**Michigan State University - Institute for Food Laws and Regulations**. G.M. Trout Food Science and Human Nutrition Bldg., 469 Wilson Rd., Ste. 139 East Lansing, MI 48824. Phone: (517)355-8295; Fax: (517)432-1492; Email: iflr@msu.edu • URL: http://www.iflr.msu.edu • Conducts research on the food industry, including processing, packaging, marketing, and new products.

***Microcosm***. Dun & Bradstreet Inc., 103 JFK Pkwy. Short Hills, NJ 07078. Phone: 800-526-0651 or (973)921-5500 or (973)921-5000; Fax: (866)560-7035 or (512)794-7670; Email: info@dnb.com • URL: http://www.dnb.com • Microfiche. Covers: Over 150 separate editions list companies in local business areas throughout the U.S. Entries include: Company name, address, phone, number of employees, Standard Industrial Classification (SIC) code, sales volume, principal officer name and title, DUNS number.

**Microelectronics Laboratory**. c/o Mark Brenner, Manager, Ohio State University, 310 Caldwell Laboratory, 2015 Neil Ave. Columbus, OH 43210-1272. Phone: (614)292-2306; Fax: (614)292-7596 • URL: http://cleanroom.ece.ohio-state.edu

***Microform and Imaging Review***. R.R. Bowker L.L.C., 630 Central Ave New Providence, NJ 07974. Phone: 888-269-5372 or (908)286-1090; Email: info@bowker.com • URL: http://www.bowker.com • Quarterly. $198.00 per year. Evaluates scholarly micropublications for libraries. Includes articles on microform management. Text in German.

***Micrographics and Hybrid Imaging Systems Newsletter: Monthly Report for Busines Excutives Who Use of Market Microfilm Services and Hybrid Imaging Services and Equipment***. Microfilm Publishing Inc., PO Box 950 Larchmont, NY 10538. Phone: (914)834-3044; Fax: (914)834-3993; Email: mngreensht@aol.com • URL: http://www.micrographicsnews.com • Monthly. $198.00 per year. A report for business executives who use or market microfilm services and equipment. Formerly *Micrographics Newsletter*.

**Microkelvin Laboratory**. c/o Darlene Latimer, Dept. of Physics, 2273 New Physics Bldg. Gainesville, FL 32611. Phone: (352)392-9261; Fax: (352)392-3591 • URL: http://www.phys.ufl.edu/mkelvin • Focuses on electronic behavior changes in metals, insulators, and semiconductors at ultralow temperatures.

***Microprocessor Report: The Insiders' Guide to Microprocessor Hardware***. Reed Elsevier Group plc Reed Business Information, 360 Park Ave. S New York, NY 11010. Phone: (212)791-4208; Email: corporatecommunications@reedbusiness.com • URL: http://www.reedbusiness.com • 12 times a year. $695.00 per year. Newsletter. Covers the technical aspects of microprocessors from Intel, IBM, Cyrix, Motorola, and others.

***Microwave and Optical Technology Letters***. John Wiley and Sons, Inc., Journals Div., 111 River St. Hoboken, NJ 07030. Phone: 800-526-5368 or (201)748-6000; Fax: (201)748-6088; Email: consumers@wiley.com • URL: http://www.wiley.com • Monthly. Provides quick publication (3 to 6 month turnaround) of the most recent findings and achievements in high frequency technology, from RF to optical spectrum.

***Microwave Journal***. Horizon House Publications Inc., 685 Canton St. Norwood, MA 02062. Phone: 800-966-8526 or (781)769-9750; Fax: (781)769-5037; Email: mwj@mwjournal.com • URL: http://www.horizonhouse.com • Monthly. Source for the latest product announcements, industry news, catalogs, and vendor information for the RF and microwave industry.

***Microwaves and RF Product Data Directory***. Penton, 1166 Avenue of the Americas New York, NY 10036. Phone: (212)204-4200; Email: information@penton.com • URL: http://www.penton.com • Lists a large number of reputable, reliable firms specializing in the product categories under which they are listed.

***Mid-Atlantic Journal of Business***. Seton Hall University - W. Paul Stillman School of Business, 400 S Orange Ave. South Orange, NJ 07079. Phone: (973)761-9000; Email: thehall@shu.edu • URL: http://www.shu.edu • Biweekly. $39.95 Individuals print & online. Scholarly business journal for researchers and professionals.

***Mid-Missouri Business***. Network Publishing Corp., 312

Nebraska, Ste. C Columbia, MO 65201. Phone: (314)443-1311; Fax: (314)875-1149 • Monthly. $14.98 Individuals; $1.50 Single issue. Journal providing business information on central Missouri.

***Middle-East/Africa Kompass on Disc***. Kompass USA, Inc., 121 Whitney Ave. New Haven, CT 06510. Phone: (877)566-7277 or (203)503-6789; Fax: (203)503-6780; Email: mail@kompass-usa.com • URL: http://www.kompass.com • Annual. CD-ROM provides information on more than 140,000 companies in Algeria, Bahrain, Cyprus, Egypt, Lebanon, Mauritania, Morocco, Oman, Saudi Arabia, South Africa, Tunisia, and United Arab Emirates. Classification system covers approximately 50,000 products and services.

***Middle East and Africa Autos Directory***. Business Monitor International Ltd., Senator House, 85 Queen Victoria St. London EC4V 4AB, United Kingdom. Phone: 44 20 72480468; Fax: 44 20 72480467; Email: enquiry@businessmonitor.com • URL: http://www.businessmonitor.com • $995 Individuals CD; €780 Individuals CD. Covers: 1,483 top autos executives on 445 leading automotive companies from Algeria, Bahrain, Botswana, Egypt, Iran, Jordan, Kuwait, Lebanon, Libya, Morocco, Mozambique, Namibia, Oman, Qatar, Saudi Arabia, South Africa, Syria, Tunisia, Turkey, United Arab Emirates, Yemen, Zambia and Zimbabwe. Entries include: Parent company head offices, full company name, address, phone and fax numbers, email and website address, senior contact personnel, company description and profile, nationality, and ownership status.

***Middle East and Africa Food and Drink Directory***. Business Monitor International Ltd., Senator House, 85 Queen Victoria St. London EC4V 4AB, United Kingdom. Phone: 44 20 72480468; Fax: 44 20 72480467; Email: enquiry@businessmonitor.com • URL: http://www.businessmonitor.com • $995 Individuals CD; €780 Individuals CD. Covers: 1,553 top food and drink executives on 459 leading food and drink companies from Middle East and Africa. Entries include: Parent company head offices, full company name, address, phone and fax numbers, email and website address, senior contact personnel, company description and profile, nationality, and ownership status.

***Middle East and Africa Oil and Gas Directory***. Business Monitor International Ltd., Senator House, 85 Queen Victoria St. London EC4V 4AB, United Kingdom. Phone: 44 20 72480468; Fax: 44 20 72480467; Email: enquiry@businessmonitor.com • URL: http://www.businessmonitor.com • $975 Individuals CD; €780 Individuals CD. Covers: 1,126 top oil and gas executives on 424 leading oil and gas companies from Middle East and Africa. Entries include: Parent company head offices, full company name, address, phone and fax numbers, email and website address, senior contact personnel, company description and profile, nationality, and ownership status.

***Middle East and Africa Pharmaceuticals and Healthcare Directory***. Business Monitor International Ltd., Senator House, 85 Queen Victoria St. London EC4V 4AB, United Kingdom. Phone: 44 20 72480468; Fax: 44 20 72480467; Email: enquiry@businessmonitor.com • URL: http://www.businessmonitor.com • $975 Individuals CD; €780 Individuals CD. Covers: 2,032 top pharmaceutical executives on 615 leading pharmaceutical companies from Algeria, Bahrain, Botswana, Egypt, Greece, Iran, Jordan, Kuwait, Lebanon, Libya, Morocco, Mozambique, Namibia, Oman, Qatar, Saudi Arabia, South Africa, Syria, Tunisia, Turkey, UAE, Yemen, Zambia and Zimbabwe. Entries include: Parent company head offices, full company name, address, phone and fax numbers, email and website address, senior contact personnel, company description and profile, nationality, and ownership status.

***Middle East and Africa Telecommunications Directory***. Business Monitor International Ltd., Senator House, 85 Queen Victoria St. London EC4V 4AB, United Kingdom. Phone: 44 20 72480468; Fax: 44 20 72480467; Email: enquiry@businessmonitor.com • URL: http://www.businessmonitor.com • $995 Individuals CD; €780 Individuals CD. Covers: 1,402 top telecommunications executives on 450 leading telecommunications companies from Middle East and Africa. Entries include: Parent company head offices, full company name, address, phone and fax numbers, email and website address, senior contact personnel, company description and profile, nationality, and ownership status.

***Middle East and World Food Directory: An Essential Food Industry Resource***. CPH World Media s.a.r.l., Chouran Beirut, Lebanon. Phone: 961 1 748333; Fax: 961 1 352419; Email: info@cphworldmedia.com • URL: http://www.cphworldmedia.com • Covers: Major organizations participating in the food, beverage, packaging and catering industries in the Middle East and worldwide. Also includes a country report describing market needs, export-import figures, and forecasts of how these industries will develop.

***Middle East Countries Mineral Industry Handbook***. International Business Publications, USA, PO Box 15343 Washington, DC 20003. Phone: (202)546-2103; Fax: (202)546-3275; Email: ibpusa@comcast.net • URL: http://ibpus.com • $99.95 Individuals hardcopy, e-book, CD-ROM. Covers: Strategic information and contacts on mining resources and mineral industry on Middle East Countries.

***Middle East (Gulf) Business Directory***. NIIR Project Consultancy Services, 106 - E, Kamla Nagar New Delhi 110007, India. Phone: 91 11 23843955; Fax: 91 11 23841561; Email: npcs.india@gmail.com • URL: http://www.niir.org • $100 Individuals CD-ROM; Rs 1,686 Individuals CD-ROM. Covers: 20,000+ Middle East businesses. Entries include: Company name, full postal address, phone, fax, e-mail address (wherever available), website address (wherever available) as well as a listing of activities involved in or products dealt with.

**Middle East Investment Initiative**. 500 Eighth St. NW Washington, DC 20004. Phone: (202)799-4345; Fax: (202)799-5000 • URL: http://www.meiinitiative.org • Partners with public and private entities to offer specialized financial products in the Palestinian territories. Helps to revitalize the economy, stimulate economic activity and create jobs in the Middle East. Works to create risk insurance to address movement of products for Palestinian businesses.

**Middle East Librarians Association**. c/o Roberta L. Dougherty, Vice President/Program Chair, Yale University Library, PO Box 208240 New Haven, CT 06520-8240. Phone: (514)398-6787 • URL: http://www.mela.us • Librarians and others interested in aspects of librarianship that support the study or dissemination of information about the Middle East since the rise of Islam. Facilitates communication among members through meetings and publications. Improves the quality of area librarianship through the development of standards for the profession and education of Middle East library specialists. Compiles and disseminates information concerning Middle East libraries and collections and represents the judgment of the members in matters affecting them. Encourages cooperation among members and Middle East libraries, especially in the acquisition of materials and the development of bibliographic controls.

***The Middle Management of German Business***. Hoppenstedt Produktinformationen GmbH, Havelstrasse 9, Postfach 100139 D-64295 Darmstadt, Germany. Phone: 49 6151 1375444 or 49 6151 38 0; Fax: 49 6151 1375443 or 49 6151 380 360; Email: info@hoppenstedt.de • URL: http://www.hoppenstedt.com • Annual. $240. Covers 60,000 middle managers at 25,000 major German companies.

**Middle Tennessee State University - Business and Economic Research Center**. 1301 E Main St. Murfreesboro, TN 37132-0001. Phone: (615)898-2300 or (615)898-2610; Fax: (615)898-5045; Email: dpenn@mtsu.edu • URL: http://www.mtsu.edu • Various fields within business and economics.

**Middle Tennessee State University - Tennessee Center for Labor-Management Relations**. 1313 Old Ft. Pky., Ste. 300 Murfreesboro, TN 37129. Phone: (615)895-4166; Fax: (615)895-9389 • URL: http://www.tnlabormgmt.org • Steward training, leadership, supervisor training, labor-management cooperation, stress management, negotiation, health and safety, worker participation, mediation, alternate dispute resolution, and diversity.

***Middlesex Magazine & Business Review***. Middlesex Magazine & Business Review, 615 Main St. Cromwell, CT 06416. Phone: (203)635-1819; Fax: (203)632-7203; Email: ctbizmag@snet.net • Monthly. $20. Business journal/Consumer Mag.

***Midwest Stock Exchange Guide***. Wolters Kluwer Law & Business CCH, 2700 Lake Cook Rd. Riverwoods, IL 60015. Phone: 888-224-7377 or (847)267-7000; Email: cust_serv@cch.com • URL: http://www.cchgroup.com • Annual. $395 per year. Covers: members, associate members, and member organizations. Database includes: List of stocks and bonds traded on the exchange, arranged alphabetically by name of issuing company, trading code, trading post, and par value; rules of exchange. Entries include: Name, affiliation, address, date of admission to exchange.

**Midwestern State University - Bureau of Business and Government Research**. Dillard College of Business Administration, 3410 Taft Blvd. Wichita Falls, TX 76308. Phone: (940)397-4722; Fax: (940)397-4693; Email: john.martinez@mwsu.edu • URL: http://www.mwsu.edu/academics/business • North Texas and southwest U.S. economic and business research.

***Migration World: A Bimonthly Magazine Focusing on the Newest Immigrant and Refugee Groups; Policy and Legislation; Resources***. Center for Migration Studies, 27 Carmine St. New York, NY 10014-4423. Phone: (212)337-3080; Fax: (646)998-4625; Email: cms@cmsny.org • URL: http://cmsny.org • Bimonthly. $31 Individuals /year; $50 Institutions /year.

***The Milbank Quarterly: A Journal of Public Health and Health Care Policy***. Milbank Memorial Fund. Blackwell Publishing Inc., 350 Main St. Malden, MA 02148. Phone: 800-216-2522 or (781)388-8200; Fax: (781)388-8210; Email: journaladsusa@bos.blackwellpublishing.com • URL: http://www.blackwellpublishing.com • Quarterly. $268 Institutions print or online; $308 Institutions print and online; $95 Individuals print and online; $49 Students print and online. Devoted to scholarly analysis of significant issues in health and health care policy. It presents original research, policy analysis, and commentary from academics, clinicians, and policy makers. Formerly *Health and Society*.

***Military Grocer***. Downey Communications Inc., 4800 Montgomery Ln., Ste. 710 Bethesda, MD 20814-5341. Phone: (301)718-7600; Fax: (301)718-7604; Email: milgrocer@aol.com • Five times a year. $30.00 per year. Edited for managers and employees of supermarkets on military bases. (These are supermarkets administered by the Defense Commissary Agency.).

**Military Impacted Schools Association**. 6327 S 196th St. Omaha, NE 68135-3806. Phone: 800-291-6472 • URL: http://militaryimpactedschoolsassociation.org • Provides the educational needs of military families, including quality of life initiatives, community and school district support, and aid funding.

***Military Officer***. Military Officers Association, 201 N Washington St. Alexandria, VA 22314-2539. Phone: 800-234-6622 or (703)549-2311; Fax: (703)838-8179; Email: msc@moaa.org • URL: http://www.moaa.org • Monthly. Serves the overall military community.

**Military Officers Association of America**. 201 N Washington St. Alexandria, VA 22314-2537. Phone: 800-234-6622 or (703)549-2311; Email: msc@moaa.org • URL: http://www.moaa.org • Formerly The Retired Oficers Association.

***Military Retailing Directory***. Military Retailing Publisher, 270 Ross Ave. Melbourbe Beach, FL 32951. Phone: (407)952-9171 • Annual. Edited for use by military commissaries in making purchasing decisions. Lists sources of goods and sevices, with official military department and retail order numbers.

**Military Toxics Project**. PO Box 558 Lewiston, ME 04243. Phone: (207)783-5091; Fax: (207)783-5096; Email: mtp@miltoxproj.org • URL: http://meldi.snre.umich.edu/node/17588 • Promotes clean up of military pollution, safeguards transportation of hazardous materials, advances development of preventative solutions to toxic, radioactive pollution from military activities.

**Military Vehicle Preservation Association**. 3305 Blue Ridge Cut Off Independence, MO 64055-6101. Phone: 800-365-5798 or (816)833-6872; Fax: (816)833-5115; Email: hq@mvpa.org • URL: http://www.mvpa.org • Represents individuals and groups interested in the preservation, restoration, safe operation, maintenance, and enjoyment of historic military vehicles. Informs the public of the historical value of collectible military vehicles; serves as a clearinghouse for technical and historical information.

**Milk Industry Foundation**. International Dairy Foods Association, 1250 H St. NW, Ste. 900 Washington, DC 20005. Phone: (202)737-4332; Fax: (202)331-7820 • URL: http://www.idfa.org/about-idfa/boards-committees/milk-industry-foundation • Represents processors of fluid milk and milk products. Advocates before government and regulatory bodies on behalf of members.

***Milk Producers Directory***. InfoGroup Inc., 5711 S 86th Cir. Omaha, NE 68127-4146. Phone: (402)593-4500 • URL: http://www.infogroup.com • Annual. Number of listings: 1,964. Entries include: Name, address, phone, size of advertisement, name of owner or manager, number of employees, year first in "Yellow Pages." Compiled from telephone company "Yellow Pages," nationwide.

***Milking Machines—Wholesalers Directory***. InfoGroup Inc., 5711 S 86th Cir. Omaha, NE 68127-4146. Phone: (402)593-4500 • URL: http://www.infogroup.com • Annual. Number of listings: 956. Entries include: Name, address, phone, size of advertisement, name of owner or manager, number of employees, year first in "Yellow Pages." Compiled from telephone company "Yellow Pages," nationwide.

***Mill Valley Business Directory***. Mill Valley Chamber of Commerce, 85 Throckmorton Ave. Mill Valley, CA 94941. Phone: (415)388-9700; Email: info@millvalley.org • URL: http://www.millvalley.org • Covers: Businesses, information centers, and conferences in Mill Valley, CA.

***Miller European Accounting Guide***. Aspen Publishers, Inc., 7201 McKinney Cir. Frederick, MD 21704. Phone: 800-234-1660 or (301)698-7100 or (301)417-7500; Fax: (800)901-9075 or (301)695-7931; Email: customerservice@aspenpublisher.com • URL: http://www.aspenpublishers.com • Annual. $159.00. Presents analysis of accounting standards in 25 European and Eastern European countries.

***Miller's Antiques Shops, Fairs and Auctions***. Antique Collector's Club, Market Street Industrial Pk. Wappingers Falls, NY 12590. Phone: 800-225-5231 or (914)297-0003; Fax: (914)297-0068; Email: info@antiquecc.com • URL: http://www.antiquecc.com • Annual. $35 Individuals.

***Milling and Baking News***. Sosland Publishing Co., 4800 Main St., Ste. 100 Kansas City, MO 64112. Phone: (816)756-1000; Fax: (816)756-0494; Email: nwages@sosland.com • URL: http://www.sosland.com • Weekly. $135 print. News magazine for the breadstuffs industry.

***Milwaukee Christian Business Directory***. Red Letter Publishing, PO Box 272682 Fort Collins, CO 80527. Phone: 800-445-5614; Fax: (970)267-9669; Email: info@redletter.com • URL: http://www.christianbusinessdirectoryonline.com • Businesses, churches, organizations, and schools in Milwaukee, Wisconsin.

**Milwaukee School of Engineering - Fluid Power Institute**. 1025 N Broadway St. Milwaukee, WI 53202-3109. Phone: 800-332-6763 or (414)277-7191; Fax: (414)277-7470; Email: explore@msoe.edu • URL: http://www.msoe.edu/community/academics/labs/page/1917/fluid-power-institute • Fluid power and motion control evaluation and design of components and systems, including field troubleshooting, test stand design, mathematical modeling and simulation of components and systems, including, pumps, motors, cylinders, and valves, reliability assessments of fluid power components and systems, hydraulic fluids development and contamination control programs. Conducts performance and endurance tests on components and systems including pressure drop flowrate, fatigue, and dynamic response tests. Develops national and international industrial fluid power standards.

**Mind-Machine Interaction Research Center**. University of Florida, Electrical and Computer Engineering Dept., 300 Weil Hall Gainesville, FL 32611-6200. Phone: (352)392-6000; Fax: (352)392-9673; Email: info@eng.ufl.edu • URL: http://www.eng.ufl.edu.

*Mind the Gaps: Singapore Business in China*. Cengage Learning Inc., 20 Channel Center St. Boston, MA 02210. Phone: 800-487-8488 or (617)289-7700; Fax: (617)289-7844; Email: investors@cengage.com • URL: http://www.cengage.com • 2009. eBook. Published by Institute of Southeast Asian Studies. Provides analysis on how to be successful in China, especially for Singapore businessmen.

**Mineralogical Society of America**. 3635 Concorde Pkwy., Ste. 500 Chantilly, VA 20151-1110. Phone: (703)652-9950; Fax: (703)652-9951; Email: business@minsocam.org • URL: http://www.minsocam.org.

**The Minerals, Metals, and Materials Society**. 184 Thorn Hill Rd. Warrendale, PA 15086-7514. Phone: 800-759-4867 or (724)776-9000; Fax: (724)776-3770; Email: webmaster@tms.org • URL: http://www.tms.org/TMSHome.aspx • Members are metallurgists, metallurgical engineers, and materials scientists. Divisions include Light Metals and Electronic, Magnetic, and Photonic Materials. Formerly The Metallurigical Society.

*Mines Magazine*. Colorado School of Mines Alumni Association and the Colorado School of Mines, 1500 Illinois St. Golden, CO 80401. Phone: 800-446-9488 or (303)273-3000; Email: csmaa@mines.edu • URL: http://bulletin.mines.edu/services/csm_alumni_association • Quarterly. $50. A critical communication serving the Colorado School of Mines community.

*Minimize the Impact of Stress Claims on Your Business*. Chamber of Commerce and Industry Queensland, Phone: 61 1 300731988 • A$29.95 for members; A$34.95 for nonmembers.

**Mining and Metallurgical Society of America**. PO Box 810 Boulder, CO 80306-0810. Phone: (303)444-6032; Fax: (415)899-0262; Email: contactmmsa@mmsa.net • URL: http://www.mmsa.net • Works for the conservation of mineral resources, the advancement of mining and metallurgical industries, the better protection of mine investors and mine workers, the increase of scientific knowledge, and the encouragement of high professional ideals and ethics.

*Mining Engineering*. Society for Mining, Metallurgy, and Exploration, 12999 E Adam Aircraft Cir. Englewood, CO 80112. Phone: 800-763-3132 or (303)948-4200; Fax: (303)973-3845; Email: cs@smenet.org • URL: http://www.smenet.org • Monthly. $245 per year, includes full print and online access.

*The Mining Record*. Howell International Enterprises, PO Box 1630 Castle Rock, CO 80104-6130. Phone: 800-441-4748 or (303)663-7820; Fax: (303)663-7823; Email: questions@miningrecord.com • URL: http://www.miningrecord.com • Monthly. $85 Individuals second class mail; $115 Two years second class mail; $130 Individuals second class mail; 3 years; $122 Individuals first class mail; $132 Canada and Mexico air mail; $140 Other countries air mail. Description: Discusses a myriad of issues within the mining industry, particularly exploration, development, production, and milling.

*Mining Week*. National Mining Association, 101 Constitution Ave. NW, Ste. 500 E Washington, DC 20001-2133. Phone: (202)463-2600 or (202)463-2639; Fax: (202)463-2666; URL: http://www.nma.org • Weekly. 100 Nonmembers; Members Free. Covers legislative, business, research, and other developments of interest to the mining industry.

*Minnesota Airport Directory & Travel Guide*. Minnesota Department of Transportation, Office of Aeronautics, 222 E Plato Blvd. Saint Paul, MN 55107-1618. Email: aeroinfo.dot@state.mn.us • URL: http://www.dot.state.mn.us • Annual. Covers: Airports and public seaplane bases in Minnesota. Database includes: Information on approaches, ditches, lights, nearby rivers, elevation, latitude and longitude, storage facilities and repair potential. Entries include: Address and telephone number.

*Minnesota Business*. Tiger Oak Publications Inc., 900 S 3rd St. Minneapolis, MN 55415-1209. Phone: (612)548-3180; Fax: (612)548-3181 • URL: http://www.tigeroak.com • Business magazine.

*Minnesota Industries Guide*. Industries Guides Inc., 303 E Altamonte Dr. Altamonte Springs, FL 32716. Phone: (407)834-8181 • $95. Covers: Approximately 10,000 manufacturers in Minnesota. Entries include: Company name, address, phone.

*Minority and Women-Owned Business Resource Guide*. Dallas Regional Chamber, 500 N Akard St., Ste. 2600 Dallas, TX 75201. Phone: (214)746-6600; Email: information@dallaschamber.org • URL: http://www.dallaschamber.org • Annual. $15 Members; $30 Nonmembers. Covers: Minority and women-owned businesses in the greater Dallas area. Entries include: Company name, address, phone; business classification.

*Minority Business Entrepreneur*. Minority Business Entrepreneur, 3528 Torrance Blvd., Ste. 101 Torrance, CA 90503. Phone: (310)540-9398; Fax: (310)792-8263 • URL:

http://www.mbemag.com • Bimonthly. $25 Individuals print amd digital; $18 Individuals print only; $12 Individuals digital only. Reports on issues "critical to the growth and development of minority and women-owned firms." Provides information on relevant legislation and profiles successful women and minority entrepreneurs.

**Minority Professional Network**. PO Box 55399 Atlanta, GA 30308-5399. Phone: 888-676-6389 or (770)901-9323; Email: Support@MPNmail.com • URL: http://www.minorityprofessionalnetwork.com • Seeks to improve career counseling and placement services for minority college students.

*MIS Quarterly*. University of Minnesota, School of Management. MIS Research Center, Carlson School of Management, 321 19th Ave. S Minneapolis, MN 55455-0438. Phone: 877-625-6468 or (612)625-0027; Email: csom@umn.edu • URL: http://www.carlsonschool.umn.edu • Quarterly. $175 Individuals 1-year subscription within US (print); $350 Institutions 1-year subscription within US (print); $150 Students 1-year subscription within US (print); $200 Individuals 1-year subscription outside US (print); $425 Institutions 1-year subscription outside US (print); $175 Students 1-year subscription outside US (print); $100 online access (Individuals/Institurions).

*Mississauga Business Times*. Metroland News, 3145 Wolfedale Rd. Mississauga, ON, Canada L5C 3A9. Phone: (905)273-8111; Fax: (905)273-8109 • URL: http://www.mississauga.net • Monthly. Regional business magazine.

*Mississippi Business Directory*. InfoGroup Inc., 5711 S 86th Cir. Omaha, NE 68127-4146. Phone: (402)593-4500 • URL: http://www.infogroup.com • Annual. $795 for both print & CD-ROM. Covers: 114,788 businesses in Mississippi. Entries include: Company name, address, phone, number of employees, name of owner or manager, sales volume. Compiled from telephone company 'Yellow Pages,' statewide. All states covered independently (see separate entries).

*Mississippi News Media Directory*. News Media Directories, PO Box 316 Mount Dora, FL 32756. Phone: 800-749-6399; Fax: (866)586-7020; Email: newsmedia@comcast.net • Annual. $45 Individuals; $65 Individuals CD; $85 Individuals Combo-Directory and CD. Covers: Newspapers, periodicals, radio and television broadcasting stations, and press services operating in Mississippi. Entries include: Publisher or company name, address, phone, names and titles of key personnel, publication title, call letters, hours of operation, and frequency.

**Mississippi State University - Bureau of Educational Research and Evaluation**. PO Box 9710 Mississippi State, MS 39762. Phone: (662)325-3717; Fax: (662)325-8784; Email: rhr2@colled.msstate.edu • URL: http://www.msstate.edu.

**Mississippi State University - Division of Business Research**. 240 Darden/McCool Hall Mississippi State, MS 39762-5288. Phone: (662)325-3817; Fax: (662)325-8686; Email: jspencer@cobilan.msstate.edu • Business and economic affairs with particular reference to Mississippi. Serves as an information, advisory, and consulting agency on special research projects for local, state, and national governments and business.

**Mississippi State University - Social Science Research Center**. 1 Research Park, Ste. 103 Starkville, MS 39759. Phone: (662)325-7127; Fax: (662)325-7966; Email: arthur.cosby@ssrc.msstate.edu • URL: http://www.ssrc.msstate.edu • Economic and social issues in Mississippi, the southeastern region and the United States, particularly social and economic development, the family and children, rural health and health policy, community development, alcohol safety, homeland security, substance abuse, traffic safety, race relations, information-age societal monitoring, natural resources, social services, and crime, delinquency and justice. Research is conducted through three divisions: Family and Children Research Unit; Mississippi Alcohol Safety Education Program; and the Mississippi Health Policy Research Center and five laboratories: Evaluation and Decision Support Laboratory, Secure Data Laboratory, Monitor Laboratory, Survey Research Laboratory, and the Unit for Community and Environmental Studies.

**Missouri University of Science and Technology - Rock Mechanics and Explosives Research Center**. 1006 Kingshighway Rolla, MO 65409. Phone: 800-522-0938 or (573)341-4365 or (573)341-4111; Fax: (573)341-4368; Email: rockmech@mst.edu • URL: http://rockmech.mst.edu • Rock mechanics and explosives technology, including studies on applications of high-pressure water jets in cutting geologic material, ground support design, rock fracture mechanics, physical and computer modeling, static rock mechanics, dynamic rock mechanics, theory of waves in real earth materials, development of detonators, gun and rocket propellants, explosives research and development, shaped charges, and high-tech metal machining. Also studies design and behavior of excavations in salt and potash deposits, and performs field blasting experiments.

*MIT Sloan Management Review*. Sloan Management Review Association. Massachusetts Institute of Technology Department of Urban Studies and Planning Community Innovators Lab, Department of Urban Studies and Planning, Bldg./Rm. 9-419, 77 Massachusetts Ave. Cambridge, MA 02139. Phone: (617)253-3216; Fax: (617)258-6515; Email: colab-info@mit.

edu • URL: http://web.mit.edu/colab • Quarterly. $69. A business journal that bridges the gap between management research and practice.

*Mitchell Guide to New Jersey Foundations, Corporations and Their Managers*. Littman Associates, 23997 Cliff Dr. Ext. Worton, MD 21678. Fax: (410)778-7949 • Biennial. $135 postpaid; payment with order. Approximately 450 private foundations with minimum assets of $150,000 and grants in excess of $15,000 per year, and about 700 businesses in New Jersey with over 300 employees.

*Mix Magazine: Professional Recording, Sound, and Music Production*. Primedia Business Magazine and Media, 6400 Hollis St., Ste. 12 Emeryville, CA 94608. Phone: 800-795-5445 or (510)653-3307; Fax: (510)653-5142; Email: subs@primediabusiness.com • URL: http://www.primediabusiness.com • Monthly. $35.99 U.S. print and digital access; $46.99 Canada print and digital access; $56.99 Other countries print and digital access. Professional audio and music production periodical.

*MLO*. Thomson Medical Economics, 5 Paragon Dr. Montvale, NJ 07645-1742. Phone: 800-526-4870 or (201)358-7200; Fax: (201)573-8999 or (201)722-2680; Email: customer.service@medec.com • URL: http://www.medec.com • Monthly. Covers management, regulatory, and technical topics for clinical laboratory administrators.

*MLS: Marketing Library Services*. Information Today, Inc., 143 Old Marlton Pke. Medford, NJ 08055-8750. Phone: 800-300-9868 or (609)654-6266; Fax: (609)654-4309; Email: custserv@infotoday.com • URL: http://www.infotoday.com • $99.95 6 issues/year. Description: Tells librarians and information professionals how to actively market their services to gain clients and to justify their existence. Discusses marketing, communication skills, fundraising, promotional events, publicity, and advocacy. Recurring features include how-to articles, case studies, news, a Customer-Based Marketing column, and book reviews.

*Mobile PC*. Future Network USA, 150 North Hill Dr., Ste. 40 Brisbane, CA 94005. Phone: (415)468-4684; Fax: (415)468-4686; Email: btolinski@futurenetworkusa.com • URL: http://www.futurenetworkusa.com/ • Monthly. $20.00 per year. Provides information and detailed product reviews for consumers. Covers notebook/laptop computers, personal digital assistants (PDAs), wireless network equipment, cell phones, digital cameras, and other electronic products.

*Mobility*. Employee Relocation Council, 1717 Pennsylvania Ave., NW, Ste. 800 Washington, DC 20006-4665. Phone: (202)857-0857; Fax: (202)467-4012 • Monthly. $48 /year. Covers various aspects of the moving of corporate employees.

*Modern Brewery Age*. Business Journals Inc., 50 Day St. Norwalk, CT 06854. Phone: (203)853-6015; Fax: (203)852-8175; Email: macb@busjour.com • URL: http://www.busjour.com • Bimonthly. $125 Individuals. Magazine for the wholesale and brewing industry.

*Modern Bulk Transporter Buyers Guide*. Penton, 9800 Metcalf Ave. Overland Park, KS 66212. Phone: 866-748-4926 or (913)341-1300; Fax: (913)967-1905 or (913)967-1898; Email: corporatecustomerservice@penton.com • URL: http://www.penton.com • Contains key suppliers to the tank truck, tank container and storage terminal industries.

*Modern Bulk Transporter*. Primedia Business Magazines and Media, 4200 S Shepherd Dr., Ste. 200 Houston, TX 77098. Phone: 800-795-5445 or (713)523-8124; Fax: (713)523-8384; Email: subs@primediabusiness.com • URL: http://www.primediabusiness.com • Monthly. 50. Information for bulk logisitcs.

*Modern Casting*. American Foundry Society, 1695 N Penny Ln. Schaumburg, IL 60173. Phone: 800-537-4237 or (847)824-0181; Fax: (847)824-2174 or (847)824-7848; Email: jcall@afsinc.org • URL: http://www.afsinc.org • Monthly.

*Modern Casting-Buyer's Reference*. American Foundry Society, 1695 N Penny Ln. Schaumburg, IL 60173. Phone: 800-537-4237 or (847)824-0181; Fax: (847)824-2174 or (847)824-7848; Email: jcall@afsinc.org • URL: http://www.afsinc.org • About 1,700 manufacturers, suppliers, and distributors of foundry and metal casting equipment and products. Formerly *Modern Castings - Buyer's Guide*.

*Modern Estate Planning*. Matthew Bender and Company Inc., 1275 Broadway Albany, NY 12204-2638. Phone: 800-424-4200 or (518)487-3000; Fax: (518)487-3573 or (800)424-4200; Email: customer.support@lexisnexis.com • URL: http://www.matthewbender.com • $2,005 Print; $1,823 E-book. Covers estate, gift, and GST taxation.

*Modern Grocer*. GC Publishing Co., One University Plaza, Suite 200 Hackensack, NJ 07601. Phone: (201)488-1800; Fax: (201)488-7357 • URL: http://www.moderngrocer.com • Monthly. $50 Individuals. Magazine for food retailers, wholesalers, distributors, brokers, manufacturers, and packers in the metro New York and New Jersey marketing area. Formerly *Modern Grocer*.

*Modern Healthcare: The Newsmagazine for Adminstrators and Managers in Hospitals and Other Healthcare Institutions*. Crain Communications Inc., 150 N Michigan Ave. Chicago, IL 60601-7553. Phone: 800-678-9595 or (312)649-5200 or (312)649-5411; Fax: (312)280-3150 or (312)280-3174; Email: info@crain.com • URL: http://www.crain.com • $159 Premium Access (Web + Data + Digital Edition); $89 (Print or Digital Edition) + Daily Dose e-newsletter.

*Modern Jeweler*. Cygnus Business Media, 3 Huntington

Quadrangle, Ste. 301N Melville, NY 11747. Phone: 800-308-6397 or (631)845-2700; Fax: (631)845-2741 or (631)845-2798; Email: rich.reiff@cygnuspub.com • URL: http://www.cygnusb2b.com • Monthly. $60.00 per year. Edited for retail jewelers. Covers the merchandising of jewelry, gems, and watches. Supersedes in part *Modern Jeweler*.

*Modern Machine Shop*. Gardner Business Media, Inc., 6915 Valley Ave. Cincinnati, OH 45244-3029. Phone: 800-950-8020 or (513)527-8800; Fax: (513)527-8801; Email: orderbooks@gardnerweb.com • URL: http://www.gardnerweb.com • Monthly. $89 Individuals; $99 Canada; $200 Elsewhere includes airmail delivery. Lists products and services for the metalworking industry. Formerly *Modern Machine Shop CNC and Software Guide*.

*Modern Materials Handling Casebook Directory*. Reed Elsevier Group plc Reed Business Information, 360 Park Ave. S New York, NY 11010. Phone: (212)791-4208; Email: corporatecommunications@reedbusiness.com • URL: http://www.reedbusiness.com • Annual. Lists about 2,300 manufacturers of equipment and supplies in the materials handling industry. Supplement to *Modern Materials Handling*.

*Modern Materials Handling*. Reed Elsevier Group plc Reed Business Information, 360 Park Ave. S New York, NY 11010. Phone: (212)791-4208; Email: corporatecommunications@reedbusiness.com • URL: http://www.reedbusiness.com • 14 times a year. $99.90 per year. For managers and engineers who buy or specify equipment used to move, store, control and protect products throughout the manufacturing and warehousing cycles. Includes *Casebook Directory* and *Planning Guide*. Also includes *ADC News and Solutions*.

*Modern Metals*. Monthly. $85.00 per year. Covers management and production for plants that fabricate and finish metals of various kinds.

*Modern Paint and Coatings*. Chemical Week Associates, 2 Grand Central Tower, 140 E 45th St., 40th Fl. New York, NY 10017. Phone: 800-774-5733 or (212)884-9528 or (212)621-4900; Fax: (212)883-9514 or (212)884-9514; Email: webmaster@chemweek.com • URL: http://www.chemweek.com • Monthly. $52.00 per year. A comprehensive publication highlighting formulators and suppliers to the Paint, Coatings and Ink Industry.

*Modern Physician: Essential Business News for the Executive Physician*. Crain Communications Inc., 150 N Michigan Ave. Chicago, IL 60601-7553. Phone: 800-678-9595 or (312)649-5200 or (312)649-5411; Fax: (312)280-3150 or (312)280-3174; Email: info@crain.com • URL: http://www.crain.com • Monthly. $45.00. Edited for physicians responsible for business decisions at hospitals, clinics, HMOs, and other health groups. Includes special issues on managed care, practice management, legal issues, and finance.

*Modern Salon Magazine*. Vance Publishing Corp., 400 Knightsbridge Pkwy. Lincolnshire, IL 60069-3613. Phone: 800-255-5113 or (847)634-2600; Fax: (847)634-4342 or (847)634-4379; Email: info@vancepublishing.com • URL: http://www.vancepublishing.com • Monthly. The constant leader and voice of the salon industry since 1915, providing peer-based education, inspiration and collaboration for salon professionals.

*Modern Tire Dealer*. 3515 Massillon Rd., Ste. 350 Uniontown, OH 44685. Phone: (330)899-2200; Fax: (330)899-2209; Email: info@mtdealer.com • URL: http://www.mtdealer.com • Monthly. $65.00 per year. Serves independent tire dealers. Cover automotive service and dealership management topics.

*Modern Tire Dealer—Facts/Directory Issue*. Bobit Business Media, 3520 Challenger St. Torrance, CA 90503. Phone: (310)533-2400; Fax: (310)533-2500; Email: info@lctmag.com • URL: http://www.bobit.com • Annual. Publication includes: Directories of tire and car service suppliers, tire shop jobbers, and national and state associations. Entries include: Generally, listings show company or organization name, address, phone, names and titles of key personnel. Listings for manufacturers include products.

*Modern Tire Dealer: Facts/Directory*. Nielsen Business Media Inc., 770 Broadway New York, NY 10003-9522. Phone: 866-890-8541 or (646)654-4500 or (646)654-5000; Fax: (646)654-5584 or (646)654-4500; Email: bmcomm@nielsen.com • URL: http://www.nielsenbusinessmedia.com • Directories of tire and car service suppliers, tire shop jobbers, and national state associations.

*Modern Workers Compensation*. Thomson West, 610 Opperman Dr. Eagan, MN 55123. Phone: 800-328-9352 or (651)687-7000 • $1,137.81 Four volumes. Provides detailed coverage of workers' compensation law and procedure, including medical benefits, rehabilitation benefits, compensation costs, noncompensable injuries, etc.

*Molasses Market News*. Livestock and Seed Div., 801 Sangamon Ave. Springfield, IL 62794-9281. Phone: (217)782-4925; Fax: (217)785-5708; Email: custserv@infotoday.com • Description: Provides the market news on molasses and its import and export.

*Moldova Government and Business Contacts Handbook*. International Business Publications, USA, PO Box 15343 Washington, DC 20003. Phone: (202)546-2103; Fax: (202)546-3275; Email: ibpusa@comcast.net • URL: http://ibpus.com • $99.95 Individuals hardcopy, e-book, CD-ROM.

Covers: Strategic government and business information, export-import activity in the country, investment, business contacts and regulations.

*Moldova Industrial and Business Directory*. International Business Publications, USA, PO Box 15343 Washington, DC 20003. Phone: (202)546-2103; Fax: (202)546-3275; Email: ibpusa@comcast.net • URL: http://ibpus.com • Annual. $99.95 Individuals hardcopy, e-book, CD-ROM. Covers: Strategic industrial, investment and business contacts for conducting export-import and investment activity in the country. Contains strategic practical economic and business information.

**Molluscan Shellfish Institute**. c/o Lisa Wedding, National Fisheries Institute, 7918 Jones Branch Dr., Ste. 700 McLean, VA 22102. Phone: (703)752-8880; Fax: (703)752-7583 • URL: http://www.aboutseafood.com • A division of the National Fisheries Institute. Shellfish producers, processors, distributors, growers, and suppliers to the industry. Works to promote, protect, and advance the interests of the shellfish industry. Cooperates with federal, state, and municipal authorities in matters of legislation, sanitation standards, controls, and conservation.

**Monash University - Centre for Research in Accounting and Finance**. Wellington Rd., Bldg. 11E Clayton, VIC 3168, Australia. Phone: 61 3 99052389; Fax: 61 3 99055475; Email: kim.langfield-smith@buseco.monash.edu.au • URL: http://www.buseco.monash.edu.au/aaf/research/ • Accounting and finance.

**Monash University - Centre of Policy Studies - Impact Project**. Menzies Bldg., 11th Fl., Wellington Rd. Clayton, VIC 3800, Australia. Phone: 61 3 99052398; Fax: 61 3 99052426; Email: philip.adams@buseco.monash.edu.au • URL: http://www.monash.edu.au/policy/ • Economic modelling.

*The Monell Connection: From the Monell Chemical Senses Center, a Nonprofit Scientific Institute Devoted to Research on Taste and Smell*. Monell Chemical Senses Center, 3500 Market St. Philadelphia, PA 19104-3308. Phone: (267)519-4700 or (215)898-6666; Fax: (215)898-2084; Email: mcsc@monell.org • URL: http://www.monell.org • Three times a year. Free. Newsletter. Includes brief summaries of selected papers describing ongoing work of Monell scientists.

*Monetary Policy and Reserve Requirements Handbook*. U.S. Federal Reserve System Board of Governors Publications Services, 20th and Constitution Ave. NW Washington, DC 20551. Phone: (202)452-3244; Fax: (202)728-5886 • URL: http://www.federalreserve.gov • $75 U.S.; $100 Other countries. Includes regulations A and D.

*Money*. 1271 Avenue of the Americas New York, NY 10020-1393. Phone: 800-633-9970 or (212)522-1212; Fax: (212)522-1796; Email: cnnmoney@money.com • URL: http://www.money.cnn.com • 13 times a year. $19.95 per year. Covers all aspects of family finance; investments, careers, shopping, taxes, insurance, consumerism, etc.

*Money Fund Monitor*. iMoneyNet Inc., 1 Research Dr., Ste. 400A Westborough, MA 01581-5193. Phone: (508)616-6600; Fax: (508)616-5511 • URL: http://www.imoneynet.com • Provides daily and weekly performance information and rankings. Contact for pricing.

*Money Fund Report*. iMoneyNet Inc., 1 Research Dr., Ste. 400A Westborough, MA 01581-5193. Phone: (508)616-6600; Fax: (508)616-5511 • URL: http://www.imoneynet.com • Weekly. $1,095.00 per year. Looseleaf. Contains detailed information on about 1,000 U.S. money market funds, including portfolios and yields.

*Money Management Letter: Bi-Weekly Newsletter Covering the Pensions and Money Maagement Industry*. Institutional Investor Inc. Journals Group, 225 Park Ave. S New York, NY 10003. Phone: 800-437-9997 or (212)224-3570; Email: info@iijournals.com • URL: http://www.iijournals.com • Biweekly. $2,440.00 per year. Newsletter. Includes print and online editions. Edited for pension fund investment managers.

*Money Manager's Compliance Guide*. Thompson Publishing Group Inc., Government Information Services, Education Funding Research Council, 1725 K St. NW, Ste. 700 Washington, DC 20006. Phone: 800-677-3789 or (202)444-8741; Fax: (800)759-7179 or (202)296-1091; Email: service@thompson.com • URL: http://www.thompson.com • $739.00 per year. Two looseleaf volumes. Monthly updates and newletters. Edited for investment advisers and investment companies to help them be in compliance with governmental regulations, including SEC rules, restrictions based on the Employee Retirement Income Security Act (ERISA), and regulations issued by the Commodity Futures Trading Commission (CFTC).

*Money Market Directory of Pension Funds and Their Investment Managers*. Standard & Poors Money Market Directories, 320 E Main St. Charlottesville, VA 22902. Phone: 800-446-2810 or (434)977-1450; Fax: (434)979-9962 • URL: http://www.mmdaccess.com • Institutional funds and managers.

*Money Reporter: The Insider's Letter for Investors Whose Interest is More Interest*. MPL Communications Inc., 133 Richmond St. W, Ste. 700 Toronto, ON, Canada M5H 3M8. Phone: 800-804-8846 or (416)869-1177 or (416)869-2777; Fax: (416)869-0456 or (416)869-0616; Email: investors@mplcomm.com • URL: http://www.adviceforinvestors.com •

Semimonthly. $227 /year. Supplement available, *Monthly Key Investment*. Canadian interest-bearing deposits and investments.

*The Money Source Book*. Business Information Network Inc., 5400 LBJ Fwy., Ste. 3535 Dallas, TX 75240. Phone: (214)770-7959; Fax: (214)770-5040 • Annual. $24.95. Covers: Approximately 1,800 traditional and non-traditional sources of business capital, with emphasis on the south-central U.S. Entries include: Company or organization name, address, phone, name and title of contact, geographical area served, financial data, subsidiary and branch names and locations, eligibility requirements, prior 12 month loan/investment history, required client (customer) profiles.

*Money Sources for Small Business—How You Can Find Private, State, Federal, and Corporate Financing*. Puma Publishing Co., 1670 Coral Dr. Santa Maria, CA 93454. Phone: 800-255-5730 or (805)925-3216; Fax: (805)925-2656; Email: publications@pumapublishing.com • URL: http://www.pumapublishing.com • $19.95. Covers: sources of financing for small businesses. Entries include: Company or organization name, address, phone, name and title of contact, geographical area served, financial data.

*Money to Work II—Funding for Visual Artists*. Art Resources International, 5813 Nevada Ave. NW Washington, DC 20015. Phone: (202)363-6806 • Irregular. $8.95 plus $3.25 shipping. Covers: about 225 organizations offering grants for painters, sculptors, photographers, printmakers, and other visual and craft artists. Entries include: Organization name, description of grant, application and selection procedures.

*Moneyletter*. Agora Inc., 14 W Mt. Vernon Pl. Baltimore, MD 21201-5125. Phone: (410)783-8499; Email: csteam@agorapublishinggroup.com • URL: http://www.agora-inc.com • Description: Provides assertive, do-it-yourself, individual investors with a unique market timing system, specific buy and sell recommendations, and portfolio allocation advice on no-load mutual funds. Features updates on economic and financial market, fund profiles, and articles on non-mutual fund financial planning issues.

*The Moneypaper*. Temper of the Times Communications, Inc. Temper of the Times Communications Inc., 555 Theodore Fremd Ave., Ste B-103 Rye, NY 10585. Phone: 800-388-9993 or (914)381-5400; Fax: (914)381-7206; Email: moneypaper@aol.com • URL: http://www.temperofthetimes.com • Description: Contains strategies to minimize stock sales costs and articles on investing and market trends. Includes a summary of monthly financial news drawn from over 70 financial publications and advisory services. Recurring features include columns titled Summing Up, Market Outlook, and Stocktrack.

*Moneytalk*. Jean Kwiatowski, 334 Highlark Dr. Larksville, PA 18704. Phone: (717)287-6498 • Description: Provides suggestions for saving money through the use of coupons and refund offers. Recurring features include letters to the editor and news of research.

*Mongolia Industrial and Business Directory*. International Business Publications, USA, PO Box 15343 Washington, DC 20003. Phone: (202)546-2103; Fax: (202)546-3275; Email: ibpusa@comcast.net • URL: http://ibpus.com • $99.95 Individuals hardcopy, e-book, CD-ROM. Covers: Strategic and practical economic and business information. Entries include: Business contacts for conducting business activity in the country.

**Mongolian National Chamber of Commerce and Industry - Economic and Market Research Center**. Government Bldg. 11, Rm. 711, J. Sambuu St. 11 Ulaanbaatar, Mongolia. Phone: 976 11 327176; Fax: 976 324620; Email: chamber@mongolchamber.mn • URL: http://www.mongolchamber.mn/en/index.php • Economics, market research, trade and business promotion, consultancy, and training.

*Montana Business Directory*. InfoGroup Inc., 5711 S 86th Cir. Omaha, NE 68127-4146. Phone: (402)593-4500 • URL: http://www.infogroup.com • Annual. $375 both print & CD-ROM. Covers: 58,819 businesses in Montana. Entries include: Company name, address, phone, number of employees, name of owner or manager, sales volume. Compiled from telephone company "Yellow Pages," statewide. All states covered (see separate entries).

*Montana Manufacturers Directory*. Montana Department of Commerce Office of Trade and International Relations, 1424 9th Ave. Helena, MT 59620. Phone: (406)444-4392; Fax: (406)444-2903 • $50. Covers: Approximately 1,900 manufacturing firms in Montana. Entries include: Company name, address, phone, name of principal executive, number of employees, products or service provided.

**Montana State University, Bozeman - College of Agriculture - Montana Agricultural Experiment Station**. 202 Linfield Hall Bozeman, MT 59717. Phone: (406)994-3681; Fax: (406)994-6579 • URL: http://ag.montana.edu/maes.htm • Biological, physical, and social sciences as applied to agriculture, including research in agronomy, plant genetics and breeding, plant pathology, animal science, plant breeding and genetics, veterinary medicine, entomology, environmental sciences, microbiology, biochemistry, agricultural engineering, molecular biology, economics, and sociology.

*Monterey Peninsula Chamber of Commerce—Membership Directory & Business Referral Guide*. Monterey Peninsula Chamber of Commerce, 30 Ragsdale Dr., Ste. 200 Monterey,

CA 93940-7811. Phone: (831)648-5360; Fax: (831)649-3502; Email: info@montereychamber.com • URL: http://www.montereychamber.com • Annual. Contains business organizations and members of the association.

**Montford Point Marine Association.** PO Box 1070 Sharon Hill, PA 19079. Email: info@montfordpointmarines.org • URL: http://www.montfordpointmarines.com • Represents veterans and active members of all branches of the U.S. Armed Forces. Aims to support educational assistance programs, veterans programs and promotion of community services. Works to improve the social conditions of veterans, local families, youth and the growing population of senior citizens; named after Montford Point, New River, Camp Lejeune, NC, the only base in America used for the recruit or "Boot Camp" training of black Marines, 1942-49.

***Monthly Bibliography.*** United Nations Publications, c/o National Book Network, 15200 NBN Way Blue Ridge Summit, PA 17214. Phone: 888-254-4286 or (212)963-7680 or (212)963-8302; Fax: (800)338-4550; Email: unpublications@nbnbooks.com • URL: http://www.unp.un.org • Monthly. $180 per year. Text in English and French.

***Monthly Climatic Data for the World.*** U.S. National Climatic Data Center, Federal Bldg., 151 Patton Ave. Asheville, NC 28801-5001. Phone: (828)271-4800; Fax: (828)271-4010; Email: ncdc.orders@noaa.gov • URL: http://www.ncdc.noaa.gov • Monthly. Contains monthly mean temperature, pressure, precipitation, vapor pressure, and hours of sunshine for approximately 2,000 surface data collection stations worldwide and monthly mean upper air temperatures, dew point depressions, and wind velocities for approximately 500 observing sites.

***Monthly Commodity Price Bulletin.*** United Nations Publications, c/o National Book Network, 15200 NBN Way Blue Ridge Summit, PA 17214. Phone: 888-254-4286 or (212)963-7680 or (212)963-8302; Fax: (800)338-4550; Email: unpublications@nbnbooks.com • URL: http://www.unp.un.org • Monthly. $125.00 per year. Provides monthly average prices for the previous 12 months for a wide variety of commodities traded internationally.

***Monthly Payment Direct Reduction Loan Schedules.*** Financial Publishing Co., 1251 N Eddy St. Ste. 202 South Bemd, IN 46617-1478. Phone: 800-433-0090 or (219)247-3214; Fax: (574)243-6060 or (219)243-6060; Email: sales@financial-publishing.com • URL: http://www.financial-publishing.com • $75 13th edition. Loan amortization schedules, showing equal monthly payments necessary to amortize a loan of $1,000. Also shows the amount of interest and principal in each payment, and the balance outstanding at any time during the life of the loan.

***Monthly Price Review.*** Urner Barry Publications Inc., PO Box 389 Toms River, NJ 08754. Phone: (732)240-5330; Fax: (732)341-0891; Email: help@urnerbarry.com • URL: http://www.urnerbarry.com • Description: Provides daily price information and monthly averages on dairy, egg, and poultry products. **Remarks:** Subscription includes a supplement titled Annual Price Review.

***Monthly Product Announcement.*** U. S. Bureau of the Census, 4600 Silver Hill Rd. Washington, DC 20233-0001. Phone: (301)763-4636; Email: comments@census.gov • URL: http://www.census.gov • Monthly. Lists Census Bureau publications and products that became available during the previous month.

***Monthly Weather Review.*** American Meteorological Society, 45 Beacon St. Boston, MA 02108-3693. Phone: (617)227-2425 or (617)227-2426; Fax: (617)742-8718; Email: amsinfo@ametsoc.org • URL: http://www.ametsoc.org • Monthly. $1,600 Nonmembers online and print; $815 Nonmembers online only; $2,205 Members corporation and institution, online and print; $920 Members corporation and institution, online only. Peer-reviewed journal presenting original research and survey papers concerned with weather analysis and forecasting.

***Moody's Bank and Finance Manual.*** Mergent, 5250 77 Center Dr. Charlotte, NC 28217. Phone: 800-342-5647 or (704)539-6945 or (704)527-2700; Fax: (704)559-6960; Email: customerservice@mergent.com • URL: http://www.mergent.com • Annual. $1,750 Four volumes. Includes biweekly supplements in *Moody's Bank and Finance News Report.*

***Moody's Bond Survey.*** Moody's Investors Service Inc., 7 World Trade Center, 250 Greenwich St. New York, NY 10007-2140. Phone: 800-342-5647 or (212)553-1658 or (212)553-1653; Fax: (212)553-4820 or (212)553-0882; Email: clientservices@moodys.com • URL: http://www.moodys.com • Weekly (Mon.). Description: Presents statistical information and analysis of corporate, municipal, government, federal agency, and international bonds, preferred stock, and commercial paper. Includes ratings changes and withdrawals, calendars of recent and prospective bond offerings, and Moody's bond and preferred stock yield averages.

***Moody's Corporate Profiles.*** Moody's Investors Service Inc., 7 World Trade Center, 250 Greenwich St. New York, NY 10007-2140. Phone: 800-342-5647 or (212)553-1658 or (212)553-1653; Fax: (212)553-4820 or (212)553-0882; Email: clientservices@moodys.com • URL: http://www.moodys.com • Weekly. Database covers: more than 5,000 publicly held companies listed on the New York Stock Exchange or the American Stock Exchange or NMS companies traded on the National Association of Securities Dealers Automated Quotations. Database includes: Company name, address, phone, D-U-N-S number, Moody's number, stock exchange, ticker symbol, primary and secondary Standard Industrial Classification (SIC) codes and industries; line of business analysis, annual earnings and dividends per share and other financial and stock trading data for five-year period.

***Moody's Dividend Record and Annual Dividend Record.*** 60 Madison Ave., 6th Fl. New York, NY 10010. Phone: 800-342-5647 or (212)413-7601; Fax: (212)413-7777; Email: customerservice@mergent.com • URL: http://www.mergent.com • Semiweekly. $775.00 per year. Includes annual and cumulative supplement. Formerly *Moody's Dividend Record.*

***Moorpark Chamber of Commerce—Business Directory.*** Moorpark Chamber of Commerce, 18 High St. Moorpark, CA 93021. Phone: (805)529-0322; Fax: (805)529-5304; Email: info@moorparkchamber.com • URL: http://www.moorparkchamber.com • Annual. Business organizations in Moorpark, California.

***Morningstar American Depositary Receipts.*** Morningstar Inc., 22 W Washington St. Chicago, IL 60602. Phone: 800-735-0700 or (312)696-6000; Fax: (312)696-6001; Email: newsroom@morningstar.com • URL: http://www.corporate.morningstar.com • Biweekly. Looseleaf. Provides detailed profiles of 700 foreign companies having shares traded in the U. S. through American Depositary Receipts (ADRs).

***Morningstar FundInvestor.*** Morningstar Inc., 22 W Washington St. Chicago, IL 60602. Phone: 800-735-0700 or (312)696-6000; Fax: (312)696-6001; Email: newsroom@morningstar.com • URL: http://www.corporate.morningstar.com • Monthly. $135 Individuals 1-year subscription. Provides tables of statistical data and star ratings for leading mutual funds "The Morningstar 500" News of funds and financial planning advice for investors is also included.

***Morningstar Mutual Funds.*** Morningstar Inc., 22 W Washington St. Chicago, IL 60602. Phone: 800-735-0700 or (312)696-6000; Fax: (312)696-6001; Email: newsroom@morningstar.com • URL: http://www.corporate.morningstar.com • Twenty issues per year. $639 per year. Looseleaf service. Contains detailed information and risk-adjusted ratings on over 1,500 load and no-load, equity and fixed-income mutual funds. Annual returns are provided for up to 12 years for each fund.

***Morningstar.com: Your First Second Opinion.*** Morningstar Inc., 22 W Washington St. Chicago, IL 60602. Phone: 800-735-0700 or (312)696-6000; Fax: (312)696-6001; Email: newsroom@morningstar.com • URL: http://www.corporate.morningstar.com • Annual. $199 Premium membership. Web site provides a broad selection of information and advice on both mutual funds and individual stocks, including financial news and articles on investment fundamentals.

***Morocco Business Directory.*** Business Guide, PO Box 27669 Dubai, United Arab Emirates. Phone: 971 4 2651719; Fax: 971 4 2692151; Email: sales@africa-business.com • URL: http://www.africa-business.com • $250 Individuals. Covers: Over 245,000 business listings including wholesalers, importers, retailers, business houses, and agents in Morocco.

***Morocco Investment and Business Guide.*** International Business Publications, USA, PO Box 15343 Washington, DC 20003. Phone: (202)546-2103; Fax: (202)546-3275; Email: ibpusa@comcast.net • URL: http://ibpus.com • $99.95 Individuals hardcopy, e-book, CD-ROM. Covers: Strategic information on economy, business, export-import and investment climate, opportunities, industrial development, banking and government. Entries include: Business contacts and business travel.

***Mortgage and Real Estate Executives Report.*** Thomson West, 610 Opperman Dr. Eagan, MN 55123. Phone: 800-328-9352 or (651)687-7000 • Source of ideas and new updates. Covers the latest opportunities and developments.

***Mortgage-Backed Securities Letter.*** Securities Data Publishing, 395 Hudson, 3rd Fl., 40 W 57th St. New York, NY 10014. Phone: 888-605-3385 or (212)765-5311 or (212)333-9264; Fax: (646)822-3230 or (212)765-6123; Email: sdp@tfn.com • Description: Covers developments in the structured finance markets. Analyzes transactions and their collateral; follows litigation, refinancing opportunities, and market conditions.

**Mortgage Bankers Association.** 1919 M St. NW, 5th Fl. Washington, DC 20036. Phone: 800-793-6222 or (202)557-2700; Email: membership@mba.org • URL: http://www.mbaa.org • Principal lending and investor interests in the mortgage finance field, including mortgage banking firms, commercial banks, life insurance companies, title companies, and savings and loan associations. Seeks to improve methods of originating, servicing, and marketing loans of residential and income-producing properties through industry education and cooperation with federal agencies and the Congress. Holds clinics on all aspects of the mortgage finance business. Sponsors School of Mortgage Banking, and correspondence courses and web-based training on mortgage subjects for member personnel. Collects statistics and conducts research on the industry.

***Mortgage Banking Sourcebook.*** Mortgage Bankers Association, 1919 M St. NW, 5th Fl. Washington, DC 20036. Phone: 800-793-6222 or (202)557-2700; Email: membership@mba.org • URL: http://www.mbaa.org • $40 plus $4.95 shipping. Covers: federal, state, and private agencies and associations involved in the real estate finance industry. Database includes: Information on the mortgage banking industry, including sources of relevant information on regulations, legislation, tax & accounting procedures; definitions of industry jargon; educational programs; statistics & forecasts. Entries include: Organization name, address, phone, websites and fax numbers.

***Mortgage Banking: The Magazine of Real Estate Finance Managers and Employees.*** Mortgage Bankers Association, 1919 M St. NW, 5th Fl. Washington, DC 20036. Phone: 800-793-6222 or (202)557-2700; Email: membership@mba.org • URL: http://www.mbaa.org • Monthly. $45.00 per year.

**Mortgage Insurance Companies of America.** 1425 K St. NW, Ste. 210 Washington, DC 20005. Phone: (202)682-2683 or (202)393-5566; Fax: (202)842-9252; Email: doug@micadc.org • URL: http://www.micanews.com • U.S. and Australian mortgage insurance companies united to provide a forum for discussion of industrywide standards, and for representation before Congress and federal and state regulatory agencies that reviews housing-related legislation. Compiles statistics.

***Mortgage Loan Disclosure Handbook: A Step-by-Step Guide with Forms.*** Thomson West, 610 Opperman Dr. Eagan, MN 55123. Phone: 800-328-9352 or (651)687-7000 • Annual. $363.00. Covers disclosure requirements that lenders must meet under federal laws and regulations. Discusses the Truth-in-Lending Act, RESPA (Real Estate Settlement Procedures Act), the Equal Credit Opportunity Act, and the Fair Credit Reporting Act. (Real Property Law Series).

***Mortgage Servicing News: For Residential amd Commercial Servicers.*** SourceMedia Inc., 1 State Street Plz., 27th Fl. New York, NY 10004. Phone: 800-221-1809 or (212)803-8200 or (212)803-8333; Fax: (212)843-9635 or (212)292-5216; Email: custserv@sourcemedia.com • URL: http://www.sourcemedia.com • Monthly. $98.00 per year. Edited for personnel involved with processing and handling of mortgage loan payments and disbursements for such items as insurance and taxes.

***Mortgage Technology.*** SourceMedia Inc., 1 State Street Plz., 27th Fl. New York, NY 10004. Phone: 800-221-1809 or (212)803-8200 or (212)803-8333; Fax: (212)843-9635 or (212)292-5216; Email: custserv@sourcemedia.com • URL: http://www.sourcemedia.com • Eight times a year. $78.00 per year. Covers the use of computers, software, automation, and technology in the mortgage industry. Includes reviews of new hardware and software products.

***Mosby's GenRx (year).*** CME Inc., 2801 McGaw Ave. Irvine, CA 92614-5835. Phone: 800-933-2632 or (949)250-1008; Fax: (949)250-0445; Email: customer.service@cmellc.com • URL: http://www.cmellc.com • Quarterly. $250.00. CD-ROM contains detailed monographs for more than 45,000 generic and brand name prescription drugs. Includes color pill images and customizable patient education handouts.

***Moscow City Investment and Business Guide.*** International Business Publications, USA, PO Box 15343 Washington, DC 20003. Phone: (202)546-2103; Fax: (202)546-3275; Email: ibpusa@comcast.net • URL: http://ibpus.com • Annual. $99.95 Individuals hardcopy, e-book, CD-ROM. Covers: Strategic and business information, contacts, regulations and more. An ultimate guide for conducting investment, export-import activity in the Moscow City.

**Moscow International Business Association.** Office 505, Ilyinka d.5/2 109012 Moscow, Russia. Phone: 7 495 6200130; Fax: 7 495 6200552; Email: miba@mibas.ru • URL: http://www.mibas.ru • Strives to create an environment for Russian and foreign businessmen operating in Moscow. Boosts the Russian economy by helping businessmen engaged in productive endeavors.

**Mothers' Home Business Network.** PO Box 423 East Meadow, NY 11554. Phone: (516)997-7394; Fax: (516)997-0839; Email: momhomebiz@mhbn.com • URL: http://www.homeworkingmom.com • Mothers choosing to work at home so they can earn income, maintain careers, and remain the primary caretakers of their children. Offers advice and support services on how to begin a successful business at home; helps members communicate with others who have chosen the same career option. Provides information on home business products and services, including home furnishings, raw materials and office supplies, and publications. Consults with corporations and manufacturers on reaching the home-based market. Refers media to potential interviewees and writers specializing in home business topics.

**Motion Picture Association of America.** 1600 Eye St. NW Washington, DC 20006. Phone: (202)293-1966; Fax: (202)296-7410; Email: contactus@mpaa.org • URL: http://www.mpaa.org • Affiliated with Alliance of Motion Picture and Television Producers and the Motion Picture Association. Formerly Motion Picture Producers and Distributors of America.

***Motion Picture Credits Database.*** Academy of Motion Picture Arts and Sciences, 8949 Wilshire Blvd. Beverly Hills, CA 90211. Phone: (310)247-3000; Fax: (310)859-9619 • URL: http://www.oscars.org • Annual. $50. Gathered credits from films hoping to qualify for awards.

***The Motion Picture Guide Annual.*** CineBooks, 620 Ave. of the Americas New York, NY 10011. Phone: 800-521-8110 or (212)462-5000; Fax: (212)462-6009 or (212)462-6000 • URL: http://www.cinebooks.visualnet.com • Annual. $99.95. Provides detailed information on every domestic and foreign film released theatrically in the U. S. during the year covered. Includes annual Academy Award listings and film industry obituaries. Yearly volumes are available for older movies, beginning with the 1987 edition for films of 1986.

***Motion Picture TV and Theatre Directory: For Services and Products***. Motion Picture Enterprises Publications Inc., PO Box 276 Tarrytown, NY 10591-0276. Phone: (212)245-0969; Fax: (212)245-0974; Email: info@mpe.net • URL: http://www.mpe.net • Semiannual. $16.20. Companies providing products and services to the motion picture and television industries.

***Motion Systems Handbook***. Penton Media Inc., 1300 E 9th St. Cleveland, OH 44114-1501. Phone: (216)696-7000; Fax: (216)696-1752; Email: information@penton.com • URL: http://penton.com • Annual. $30.00.

***Motivation and Emotion***. Springer, 101 Philip Dr., Assinippi Pk. Norwell, MA 02061. Phone: (781)871-6600 or (781)681-0537; Fax: (781)878-0449 or (781)681-9045; Email: Yana.Lambert@springer.com • URL: http://www.springer-sbm.com • Publishes theoretical papers and original research reports either a basic or applied nature that focus on motivation and emotion.

***Motor Age: For the Professional Automotive Import and Domestic Service Industry***. Reed Elsevier Group plc Reed Business Information, 360 Park Ave. S New York, NY 11010. Phone: (212)791-4208; Email: corporatecommunications@reedbusiness.com • URL: http://www.reedbusiness.com • Monthly. $49.00 per year. Published for independent automotive repair shops and gasoline service stations.

**Motor and Equipment Manufacturers Association**. 10 Laboratory Dr. Research Triangle Park, NC 27709. Phone: (919)549-4800; Fax: (919)406-1465; Email: info@mema.org • URL: http://www.mema.org • Manufacturers of automotive and heavy-duty original equipment and aftermarket components, maintenance equipment, chemicals, accessories, refinishing supplies, tools, and service equipment united for research into all aspects of the automotive and heavy-duty markets. Provides manufacturer-oriented services and programs including marketing consultation for the automotive industry; federal and state legal, safety, and legislative representation and consultation; personnel services; manpower development workshops; international information.

***Motor Carrier Permit & Tax Update***. J.J. Keller and Associates Inc., 3003 W Breezewood Ln. Neehah, WI 54956-9611. Phone: (877)564-2333; Fax: (800)727-7516 • URL: http://www.jjkeller.com • Monthly. $219 1 year; print or online. Provides regular updates on changes to permitting and reporting requirements.

***MOTOR: Covering the World of Automotive Service***. Hearst Business Publishing Inc., 959 8th Ave. New York, NY 10019. Phone: (516)227-1300 or (212)297-9680; Fax: (212)286-9886 • URL: http://www.hearst.com • Monthly. Edited for professional automobile and light-truck mechanics. Includes industry news and market trends.

***Motor Trend***. PRIMEDIA Inc., 350 Fifth Ave., 59th Fl. New York, NY 10118. Phone: (212)601-1960 or (212)745-0100; Fax: (516)222-2357 or (212)745-0121; Email: information@primedia.com • URL: http://www.primediany.com • Monthly. $10 Individuals 12 issues; $18 Individuals 24 issues. Informs and entertains with features on the testing of both domestic and import cars, car care, motor sports coverage, sneak peeks at future vehicles, and auto-industry news.

***Motor Vehicle Regulation: State Capitals***. Wakeman/Walworth Inc., PO Box 7376 Alexandria, VA 22307-7376. Phone: 800-876-2545 or (703)768-9600; Fax: (703)768-9690; Email: newsletters@statecapitals.com • URL: http://statecapitals.com/ • 50 times a year. $245.00 per year; print and online editions, $350.00 per year. Formerly *From the State Capitals: Motor Vehicle Regulation*.

***Motorcycle & Powersports News Buyers Guide***. A.B. Publications Inc., 4130 Lien Rd. Madison, WI 53704. Phone: (608)249-0186 • URL: http://www.athleticbusinessconference.com • Provides information on companies related to the motorcycle business. Formerly *Motorcycle Product News Trade Directory*.

**Motorcycle Industry Council**. 2 Jenner St., Ste. 150 Irvine, CA 92618-3806. Phone: (949)727-4211; Fax: (949)727-3313 • URL: http://www.mic.org • Manufacturers and distributors of motorcycles and allied industries. Maintains liaison with state and federal governments. Operates collection of research documents, federal and state government documents, and trade publications. Compiles statistics.

***Motorcycle Product News***. Athletic Business Publications Inc., 4130 Lien Rd. Madison, WI 53704. Phone: 800-722-8764 or (608)249-0186; Fax: (608)249-1153; Email: editors@hardwoodfloorsmag.com • URL: http://www.athleticbusiness.com • Monthly. $55.00 per year. Edited for wholesalers and retailers of motorcycles and supplies.

***Motorcycle Shopper: The Source for Motorcycles, Parts, Accessories, Sidecars, Tools, Clubs, Events, and More***. Payne Corp., 1353 Herndon Ave. Deltona, FL 32725-9046. Phone: 800-982-4599 or (407)860-1989; Fax: (407)574-1014; Email: mshopper@iag.net • Monthly. $19.95 per year. Contains consumer advertisements for buying, selling, and trading motorcycles and parts.

***Motorcyclist***. PRIMEDIA Inc., 350 Fifth Ave., 59th Fl. New York, NY 10118. Phone: (212)601-1960 or (212)745-0100; Fax: (516)222-2357 or (212)745-0121; Email: information@primedia.com • URL: http://www.primediany.com • Monthly. $10.00 per year.

***Motorship Directory of Shipowners and Shipbuilders***. Reed Elsevier Group plc Reed Business Information, 360 Park Ave. S New York, NY 11010. Phone: (212)791-4208; Email: corporatecommunications@reedbusiness.com • URL: http://www.reedbusiness.com • Formerly *Directory of Shipowners and Shipbuilders*.

***The Mountain/Plains Business Journal***. Midlands Business Journal Publications, 1324 S 119th St. Omaha, NE 68144. Phone: (402)330-1760; Fax: (402)758-9315 • URL: http://www.mbj.com • Business publication covering regional business issues in Nebraska, Colorado, Iowa, Missouri, Kansas, Oklahoma, South Dakota, and Minnesota.

**Mountains and Plains Independent Booksellers Association**. 3278 Big Spruce Way Park City, UT 84098. Phone: (435)649-6079; Fax: (435)649-6105; Email: info@mountainsplains.org • URL: http://www.mountainsplains.org • Supports independent bookstores; promotes literacy and defends freedom of speech and of the press.

**Movement of French Businesses**. 55 Ave. Bosquet F-75330 Paris, France. Phone: 33 1 53591919; Fax: 33 1 45512044 • URL: http://archive.medef.com/main/core.php • Promotes French businesses.

***Movers Directory***. InfoGroup Inc., 5711 S 86th Cir. Omaha, NE 68127-4146. Phone: (402)593-4500 • URL: http://www.infogroup.com • Annual. Number of listings: 15,712. Entries include: Name, address, phone, size of advertisement, name of owner or manager, number of employees, year first in "Yellow Pages." Compiled from telephone company "Yellow Pages," nationwide.

***Moving a Business to Stow***. Stow-Munroe Falls Chamber of Commerce, 4301 Darrow Rd., Ste. 2450 Stow, OH 44224. Phone: (330)688-1579 or (330)697-1988; Fax: (330)688-6234; Email: smfcc@smfcc.com • URL: http://www.smfcc.com.

***Mozambique Business Law Handbook***. International Business Publications, USA, PO Box 15343 Washington, DC 20003. Phone: (202)546-2103; Fax: (202)546-3275; Email: ibpusa@comcast.net • URL: http://ibpus.com • $99.95 Individuals hardcover, e-book, CD-ROM. Covers: Information on basic business legislation, laws, business climate, export-import regulations, and contacts.

**MPA - The Association of Magazine Media**. 757 3rd Ave., 11th Fl. New York, NY 10017. Phone: (212)872-3700 or (212)872-3745; Email: mpa@magazine.org • URL: http://www.magazine.org • Members are publishers of consumer and other periodicals. Affiliated with American Society of Magazine Editors; Media Credit Association; Publishers Information Bureau. Formerly Magazine Publishers Association.

**MRA - The Management Association**. N19 W24400 Riverwood Dr. Waukesha, WI 53188. Phone: 800-488-4845 or (262)523-9090; Email: businesssolutions@mranet.org • URL: http://www.mranet.org • Aims to maximize performance of organizations and employees. Provides information and communications, training, transactional HR solutions, and high-level business and human resource consulting; members range in size from two employees to 10,000 and represent manufacturing service, healthcare, and finance.

***MS***. British American Tobacco Italia S.p.A., Via Amsterdam 147 00144 Rome, Italy. Phone: 39 06 52871; Fax: 39 06 52879020 • URL: http://www.batitalia.com • $14.95 Individuals Digital; $29.95 Digital and Print.

***MSDN Magazine***. UBM L.L.C., 600 Community Dr. Manhasset, NY 11030. Phone: (516)562-5000 or (512)562-5000; Fax: (212)378-2160 or (516)562-5036; Email: cmp@cmp.com • URL: http://www.cmp.com • Monthly. $25 U.S. 1-year subscription (online); $35 U.S. 1-year subscription (print); $60 Other countries 1-year subscription (print). Produced for professional software developers using Windows, MS-DOS, Visual Basic, and other Microsoft Corporation products. Incorporates *Microsoft Internet Developer*.

**MSPAlliance**. 1380 E Ave., Ste. 124-376 Chico, CA 95926-7349. Phone: (530)891-1340; Fax: (530)433-5707; Email: info@mspalliance.com • URL: http://www.mspalliance.com • Aims to promote the Managed Services Industry as a true and viable profession to the IT Business Consumer. Represents providers working together in a vendor-neutral manner to define and promote the Managed Services Industry. Educates consumers on the benefits of using Managed Service Providers.

**MTM Association for Standards and Research**. 1111 E Touhy Ave. Des Plaines, IL 60018. Phone: (847)299-1111; Fax: (847)299-3509; Email: webmaster@mtm.org • URL: http://www.mtm.org • Persons interested in the fields of industrial engineering, industrial psychology, and human engineering. Conducts research at accredited institutions on human motion (the physical movement of body and limb), with emphasis on examining: internal velocity, acceleration, tension, and control characteristics of a given motion under several conditions; external regularities of given groups of motion as they vary under several conditions of performance; the proper use of motion information in measuring, controlling, and improving manual activities. Also studies ergonomics and the effects of workplace environment on productivity. Provides information on fatigue, optimum methods of performance, the effect of practice on motion performance, and the use of motion information for determining allowances and predicting total performance time. Has developed computer programs for the application of Methods Time Measurement (MTM) and MTM-based work measurement systems. Conducts training courses and testing for certification of practitioners and instructors in all Association MTM Systems. Develops and makes available specialized productivity management services.

**Multi-Housing Laundry Association**. 1500 Sunday Dr., Ste. 102 Raleigh, NC 27607. Phone: (919)861-5579; Fax: (919)787-4916; Email: nshore@mla-online.com • URL: http://www.mla-online.com • Operating and supplier companies. Strives to provide tenants with professionally operated laundry facilities. Sponsors annual convention and trade show.

***Multi-Housing News***. Nielsen Business Media Inc., 770 Broadway New York, NY 10003-9522. Phone: 866-890-8541 or (646)654-4500 or (646)654-5000; Fax: (646)654-5584 or (646)654-4500; Email: bmcomm@nielsen.com • URL: http://www.nielsenbusinessmedia.com • Individuals and firms primarily engaged in the development, construction, planning and management of multi-housing.

***Multichannel News***. Reed Elsevier Group plc Reed Business Information, 360 Park Ave. S New York, NY 11010. Phone: (212)791-4208; Email: corporatecommunications@reedbusiness.com • URL: http://www.reedbusiness.com • 51 times a year. $139.00 per year. Covers the business, programming, market and technology concerns of cable television operators and their suppliers.

***Multimedia Schools: A Practical Journal of Technology for Education including Multimedia, CD-ROM, Online and Internet and Hardware in K-12***. Information Today, Inc., 143 Old Marlton Pke. Medford, NJ 08055-8750. Phone: 800-300-9868 or (609)654-6266; Fax: (609)654-4309; Email: custserv@infotoday.com • URL: http://www.infotoday.com • Six times a year. $39.95 per year. Edited for school librarians, media center directors, computer coordinators, and others concerned with educational multimedia. Coverage includes the use of CD-ROM sources, the Internet, online services, and library technology.

***Multinational Companies in Argentina***. Business Monitor International Ltd., Senator House, 85 Queen Victoria St. London EC4V 4AB, United Kingdom. Phone: 44 20 72480468; Fax: 44 20 72480467; Email: enquiry@businessmonitor.com • URL: http://www.businessmonitor.com • Annual. $995 Individuals CD-ROM. Covers: 4,470 senior executive contacts on 1,650 leading US, European and Asian multinational companies across 34 industry sectors in Argentina. Entries include: Full company name, address, phone and fax numbers, email and web addresses, and key contact names and titles.

***Multinational Companies in Bahrain***. Business Monitor International Ltd., Senator House, 85 Queen Victoria St. London EC4V 4AB, United Kingdom. Phone: 44 20 72480468; Fax: 44 20 72480467; Email: enquiry@businessmonitor.com • URL: http://www.businessmonitor.com • Annual. $995 Individuals CD-ROM. Covers: 2,040 senior executive contacts on 640 leading US, European and Asian multinational companies across 34 industry sectors in Bahrain. Entries include: Full company name, address, phone and fax numbers, email and web addresses, and key contact names and titles.

***Multinational Companies in Brazil***. Business Monitor International Ltd., Senator House, 85 Queen Victoria St. London EC4V 4AB, United Kingdom. Phone: 44 20 72480468; Fax: 44 20 72480467; Email: enquiry@businessmonitor.com • URL: http://www.businessmonitor.com • Annual. $995 Individuals CD-ROM. Covers: 9,520 senior executive contacts on 3,880 leading US, European and Asian multinational companies across 34 industry sectors in Brazil. Entries include: Full company name, address, phone and fax numbers, email and web addresses, and key contact names and titles.

***Multinational Companies in Chile***. Business Monitor International Ltd., Senator House, 85 Queen Victoria St. London EC4V 4AB, United Kingdom. Phone: 44 20 72480468; Fax: 44 20 72480467; Email: enquiry@businessmonitor.com • URL: http://www.businessmonitor.com • Annual. $995 Individuals CD-ROM. Covers: 3,530 senior executive contacts on 1,080 leading US, European and Asian multinational companies across 34 industry sectors in Chile. Entries include: Full company name, address, phone and fax numbers, email and web addresses, and key contact names and titles.

***Multinational Companies in Colombia***. Business Monitor International Ltd., Senator House, 85 Queen Victoria St. London EC4V 4AB, United Kingdom. Phone: 44 20 72480468; Fax: 44 20 72480467; Email: enquiry@businessmonitor.com • URL: http://www.businessmonitor.com • Annual. $995 Individuals CD-ROM. Covers: 2,200 senior executive contacts on 830 leading US, European and Asian multinational companies across 34 industry sectors in Colombia. Entries include: Full company name, address, phone and fax numbers, email and web addresses, and key contact names and titles.

***Multinational Companies in Egypt***. Business Monitor International Ltd., Senator House, 85 Queen Victoria St. London EC4V 4AB, United Kingdom. Phone: 44 20 72480468; Fax: 44 20 72480467; Email: enquiry@businessmonitor.com • URL: http://www.businessmonitor.com • Annual. $995 Individuals CD-ROM. Covers: 4,630 senior executive contacts on 1,520 leading US, European and Asian multinational companies across 37 industry sectors in Egypt. Entries include: full company name, address, phone and fax numbers, email and web addresses, and key contact names and titles.

***Multinational Companies in Estonia***. Business Monitor International Ltd., Senator House, 85 Queen Victoria St. London EC4V 4AB, United Kingdom. Phone: 44 20 72480468; Fax: 44 20 72480467; Email: enquiry@businessmonitor.com • URL: http://www.businessmonitor.com • Annual. $995 Individuals CD-ROM. Covers: 1,310 senior executive contacts on 400 leading US, European and Asian multinational companies across 34 industry sectors in Estonia. Entries include: Full company name, address, phone and fax numbers, email and web addresses, and key contact names and titles.

***Multinational Companies in Greece***. Business Monitor International Ltd., Senator House, 85 Queen Victoria St. London EC4V 4AB, United Kingdom. Phone: 44 20 72480468; Fax: 44 20 72480467; Email: enquiry@businessmonitor.com • URL: http://www.businessmonitor.com • Annual. $1,660 Individuals CD-ROM. Covers: 5,330 senior executive contacts on 2,070 leading US, European and Asian multinational companies across 34 industry sectors in Greece. Entries include: Full company name, address, phone and fax numbers, email and web addresses, and key contact names and titles.

***Multinational Companies in Hungary***. Business Monitor International Ltd., Senator House, 85 Queen Victoria St. London EC4V 4AB, United Kingdom. Phone: 44 20 72480468; Fax: 44 20 72480467; Email: enquiry@businessmonitor.com • URL: http://www.businessmonitor.com • Annual. $1,660 Individuals CD-ROM. Covers: 4,630 senior executive contacts on 1,450 leading US, European and Asian multinational companies 34 industry sectors in Hungary. Entries include: Full company name, address, phone and fax numbers, email and web addresses, and key contact names and titles.

***Multinational Companies in Iran***. Business Monitor International Ltd., Senator House, 85 Queen Victoria St. London EC4V 4AB, United Kingdom. Phone: 44 20 72480468; Fax: 44 20 72480467; Email: enquiry@businessmonitor.com • URL: http://www.businessmonitor.com • Annual. $995 Individuals CD-ROM. Covers: 2,910 senior executive contacts on 1,940 leading US, European and Asian multinational companies across 34 industry sectors in Iran. Entries include: Full company name, address, phone and fax numbers, email and web addresses, and key contact names and titles.

***Multinational Companies in Jordan, Lebanon & Syria***. Business Monitor International Ltd., Senator House, 85 Queen Victoria St. London EC4V 4AB, United Kingdom. Phone: 44 20 72480468; Fax: 44 20 72480467; Email: enquiry@businessmonitor.com • URL: http://www.businessmonitor.com • Annual. $1,110 Individuals. Covers: 3,860 senior executive contacts on 1,150 foreign company subsidiaries across 34 industry sectors in Jordan, Lebanon, and Syria. Entries include: Full company name, address, phone and fax numbers, email and web addresses, and key contact names and titles.

***Multinational Companies in Kuwait***. Business Monitor International Ltd., Senator House, 85 Queen Victoria St. London EC4V 4AB, United Kingdom. Phone: 44 20 72480468; Fax: 44 20 72480467; Email: enquiry@businessmonitor.com • URL: http://www.businessmonitor.com • $995 Individuals. Covers: 2,110 senior executive contacts on 610 leading US, European and Asian multinational companies across 34 industry sectors in Kuwait. Entries include: Full company name, address, phone and fax numbers, email and web addresses, and key contact names and titles.

***Multinational Companies in Latvia***. Business Monitor International Ltd., Senator House, 85 Queen Victoria St. London EC4V 4AB, United Kingdom. Phone: 44 20 72480468; Fax: 44 20 72480467; Email: enquiry@businessmonitor.com • URL: http://www.businessmonitor.com • Annual. $995 Individuals. Covers: 1,340 senior executive contacts on 460 leading US, European and Asian multinational companies across 34 industry sectors in Latvia. Entries include: Full company name, address, phone and fax numbers, email and web addresses, and key contact names and titles.

***Multinational Companies in Lithuania***. Business Monitor International Ltd., Senator House, 85 Queen Victoria St. London EC4V 4AB, United Kingdom. Phone: 44 20 72480468; Fax: 44 20 72480467; Email: enquiry@businessmonitor.com • URL: http://www.businessmonitor.com • Annual. $995 Individuals. Covers: 1,000 senior executive contacts on 450 leading US, European and Asian multinational companies across 34 industry sectors in Lithuania. Entries include: Full company name, address, phone and fax numbers, email and web addresses, and key contact names and titles.

***Multinational Companies in Macedonia***. Business Monitor International Ltd., Senator House, 85 Queen Victoria St. London EC4V 4AB, United Kingdom. Phone: 44 20 72480468; Fax: 44 20 72480467; Email: enquiry@businessmonitor.com • URL: http://www.businessmonitor.com • Annual. $1,110 Individuals USA. Covers: 900 senior executive contacts on 290 leading US, European and Asian multinational companies across 34 industry sectors in Macedonia. Entries include: Full company name, address, phone and fax numbers, email and web addresses, and key contact names and titles.

***Multinational Companies in Mexico***. Business Monitor International Ltd., Senator House, 85 Queen Victoria St. London EC4V 4AB, United Kingdom. Phone: 44 20 72480468; Fax: 44 20 72480467; Email: enquiry@businessmonitor.com • URL: http://www.businessmonitor.com • Annual. $995 Individuals. Covers: 5,990 senior executive contacts on 2,030 leading US, European and Asian multinational companies across 34 industry sectors in Mexico. Entries include: Full company name, address, phone and fax numbers, email and web addresses, and key contact names and titles.

***Multinational Companies in Peru***. Business Monitor International Ltd., Senator House, 85 Queen Victoria St. London EC4V 4AB, United Kingdom. Phone: 44 20 72480468; Fax: 44 20 72480467; Email: enquiry@businessmonitor.com • URL: http://www.businessmonitor.com • Annual. $995 Individuals. Covers: 2,260 senior executive contacts on 720 leading US, European and Asian multinational companies across 37 industry sectors in Peru. Entries include: Full company name, address, phone and fax numbers, email and web addresses, and key contact names and titles.

***Multinational Companies in Poland***. Business Monitor International Ltd., Senator House, 85 Queen Victoria St. London EC4V 4AB, United Kingdom. Phone: 44 20 72480468; Fax: 44 20 72480467; Email: enquiry@businessmonitor.com • URL: http://www.businessmonitor.com • Annual. $1,660 Individuals. Covers: 5,340 senior executive contacts on 2,030 leading US, European and Asian multinational companies across 37 industry sectors in Poland. Entries include: Full company name, address, phone and fax numbers, email and web addresses, and key contact names and titles.

***Multinational Companies in Qatar***. Business Monitor International Ltd., Senator House, 85 Queen Victoria St. London EC4V 4AB, United Kingdom. Phone: 44 20 72480468; Fax: 44 20 72480467; Email: enquiry@businessmonitor.com • URL: http://www.businessmonitor.com • Annual. $995 Individuals. Covers: 1,690 senior executive contacts on 640 leading US, European and Asian multinational across 34 industry sectors in Qatar. Entries include: Full company name, address, phone and fax numbers, email and web addresses, and key contact names and titles.

***Multinational Companies in Romania***. Business Monitor International Ltd., Senator House, 85 Queen Victoria St. London EC4V 4AB, United Kingdom. Phone: 44 20 72480468; Fax: 44 20 72480467; Email: enquiry@businessmonitor.com • URL: http://www.businessmonitor.com • Annual. $1,110 Individuals. Covers: 3,190 senior executive contacts on 1,190 leading US, European and Asian multinational companies across 34 industry sectors in Romania. Entries include: Full company name, address, phone and fax numbers, email and web addresses, and key contact names and titles.

***Multinational Companies in Russia***. Business Monitor International Ltd., Senator House, 85 Queen Victoria St. London EC4V 4AB, United Kingdom. Phone: 44 20 72480468; Fax: 44 20 72480467; Email: enquiry@businessmonitor.com • URL: http://www.businessmonitor.com • Annual. $1,660 Individuals. Covers: 6,150 senior executive contacts on 2,560 leading US, European and Asian multinational companies across 34 industry sectors in Russia. Entries include: Full company name, address, phone and fax numbers, email and web addresses, and key contact names and titles.

***Multinational Companies in Saudi Arabia***. Business Monitor International Ltd., Senator House, 85 Queen Victoria St. London EC4V 4AB, United Kingdom. Phone: 44 20 72480468; Fax: 44 20 72480467; Email: enquiry@businessmonitor.com • URL: http://www.businessmonitor.com • Annual. $1,660 Individuals. Covers: 6,730 senior executive contacts on 1,650 leading US, European and Asian multinational companies across 34 industry sectors in Saudi Arabia. Entries include: Full company name, address, phone and fax numbers, email and web addresses, and key contact names and titles.

***Multinational Companies in Serbia***. Business Monitor International Ltd., Senator House, 85 Queen Victoria St. London EC4V 4AB, United Kingdom. Phone: 44 20 72480468; Fax: 44 20 72480467; Email: enquiry@businessmonitor.com • URL: http://www.businessmonitor.com • Annual. $1,110 Individuals. Covers: 2,230 senior executive contacts on 760 leading US, European and Asian multinational companies across 34 industry sectors in Serbia. Entries include: Full company name, address, phone and fax numbers, email and web addresses, and key contact names and titles.

***Multinational Companies in Slovakia***. Business Monitor International Ltd., Senator House, 85 Queen Victoria St. London EC4V 4AB, United Kingdom. Phone: 44 20 72480468; Fax: 44 20 72480467; Email: enquiry@businessmonitor.com • URL: http://www.businessmonitor.com • Annual. $995 Individuals. Covers: 2,610 senior executive contacts on 830 leading US, European and Asian multinational companies across 34 industry sectors in Slovakia. Entries include: Full company name, address, phone and fax numbers, email and web addresses, and key contact names and titles.

***Multinational Companies in Slovenia***. Business Monitor International Ltd., Senator House, 85 Queen Victoria St. London EC4V 4AB, United Kingdom. Phone: 44 20 72480468; Fax: 44 20 72480467; Email: enquiry@businessmonitor.com • URL: http://www.businessmonitor.com • Annual. $1,110 Individuals. Covers: 2,290 senior executive contacts on 620 leading US, European and Asian multinational companies across 34 industry sectors in Slovenia. Entries include: Full company name, address, phone and fax numbers, email and web addresses, and key contact names and titles.

***Multinational Companies in Southern Africa***. Business Monitor International Ltd., Senator House, 85 Queen Victoria St. London EC4V 4AB, United Kingdom. Phone: 44 20 72480468; Fax: 44 20 72480467; Email: enquiry@businessmonitor.com • URL: http://www.businessmonitor.com • Annual. $1,110 Individuals. Covers: 2,960 senior executive contacts on 1,890 leading US, European and Asian multinational companies across 34 industry sectors in Southern Africa. Entries include: Full company name, address, phone and fax numbers, email and web addresses, and key contact names and titles.

***Multinational Companies in the Caribbean***. Business Monitor International Ltd., Senator House, 85 Queen Victoria St. London EC4V 4AB, United Kingdom. Phone: 44 20 72480468; Fax: 44 20 72480467; Email: enquiry@businessmonitor.com • URL: http://www.businessmonitor.com • Annual. $995 Individuals CDR. Covers: 7,000 senior executive contacts on 2,120 leading US, European and Asian multinational companies across 34 industry sectors in the Caribbean. Entries include: full company name, address, phone and fax numbers, email and web addresses, and key contact names and titles.

***Multinational Companies in the Philippines: Yearbook 2010***. Business Monitor International Ltd., Senator House, 85 Queen Victoria St. London EC4V 4AB, United Kingdom. Phone: 44 20 72480468; Fax: 44 20 72480467; Email: enquiry@businessmonitor.com • URL: http://www.businessmonitor.com • $995 Individuals CD. Covers: 4,910 senior executive contacts at 1,220 leading US, European and Asian multinational companies across 34 industry sectors in the Philippines. Entries include: Name, location, description, phone, ownership status and parentage.

***Multinational Companies in the UAE***. Business Monitor International Ltd., Senator House, 85 Queen Victoria St. London EC4V 4AB, United Kingdom. Phone: 44 20 72480468; Fax: 44 20 72480467; Email: enquiry@businessmonitor.com • URL: http://www.businessmonitor.com • Annual. $2,215 Individuals. Covers: 12,010 senior executive contacts on 3,970 leading US, European and Asian multinational companies across 34 industry sectors in United Arab Emirates. Entries include: Full company name, address, phone and fax numbers, email and web addresses, and key contact names and titles.

***Multinational Companies in Turkey***. Business Monitor International Ltd., Senator House, 85 Queen Victoria St. London EC4V 4AB, United Kingdom. Phone: 44 20 72480468; Fax: 44 20 72480467; Email: enquiry@businessmonitor.com • URL: http://www.businessmonitor.com • Annual. $1,660 Individuals. Covers: 5,960 senior executive contacts on 2,150 leading US, European and Asian multinational companies across 34 industry sectors in Turkey. Entries include: Full company name, address, phone and fax numbers, email and web addresses, and key contact names and titles.

***Multinational Companies in Ukraine***. Business Monitor International Ltd., Senator House, 85 Queen Victoria St. London EC4V 4AB, United Kingdom. Phone: 44 20 72480468; Fax: 44 20 72480467; Email: enquiry@businessmonitor.com • URL: http://www.businessmonitor.com • Annual. $1,110 Individuals. Covers: 2,420 senior executive contacts on 850 leading US, European and Asian multinational companies across 34 industry sectors in Ukraine. Entries include: Full company name, address, phone and fax numbers, email and web addresses, and key contact names and titles.

***Multinational Companies in Venezuela***. Business Monitor International Ltd., Senator House, 85 Queen Victoria St. London EC4V 4AB, United Kingdom. Phone: 44 20 72480468; Fax: 44 20 72480467; Email: enquiry@businessmonitor.com • URL: http://www.businessmonitor.com • Annual. $1,150 Individuals; $975 CD-ROM; $995 Individuals online. Covers: 1,658 senior executive contacts on 568 foreign company subsidiaries across 34 industry sectors in Venezuela. Entries include: Full company name, address, phone and fax numbers, email and web addresses, and key contact names and titles.

***Multinational Food & Drink Companies in Emerging Europe Directory***. Aroq Ltd., Seneca House, Buntsford Park Rd. Bromsgrove B60 3DX, United Kingdom. Phone: 44 1527 573600; Fax: 44 1527 577423 • URL: http://www.just-food.com • $577.46 with CD-ROM. Covers: 1,577 decision makers and 559 multinational food and drink companies in Europe.

***Multinational Monitor***. Essential Information, PO Box 19405 Washington, DC 20036. Phone: (202)387-8030; Fax: (202)234-5176; Email: monitor@essential.org • URL: http://www.essentialinformation.org • Monthly. $19.95 Individuals for new subscribers; $34.95 Individuals non profit orgs.; $44.95 Individuals business; $29.95 Canada and Mexico for new subscribers; $45 Canada and Mexico nonprofit orgs.; $55 Canada and Mexico business; $45 Out of country for new subscribers; $50 Out of country nonprofit orgs.; $60 Out of country business; $50 Two years. Tracks the activities of multinational corporations and their effects on the Third World, labor and the environment.

***Multistate Sales Tax Guide***. Wolters Kluwer Law & Business CCH, 2700 Lake Cook Rd. Riverwoods, IL 60015. Phone: 888-224-7377 or (847)267-7000; Email: cust_serv@cch.com • URL: http://www.cchgroup.com • Monthly. $1,349 /year. Looseleaf service. Nine volumes. Formerly *All State Sales Tax Reports*. Gives in-depth state sales tax law coverage on a wide variety of tax-related issues.

***Municipal Finance Journal***. Civic Research Institute, Po Box 585 Kingston, NJ 08528-0585. Phone: (609)683-4450; Fax: (609)683-7291; Email: order@civicresearchinstitute.com • URL: http://www.civicresearchinstitute.com • Quarterly. $359 Individuals Print and Online; $699 Institutions Print and Online. Recent tax and legal trends affecting both large and small state municipalities.

***Municipal Management Series***. International City/County Management Association, 777 N Capitol St. NE, Ste. 500 Washington, DC 20002-4201. Phone: (202)289-4262; Fax: (202)962-3500; Email: customerservices@icma.org • URL: http://icma.org/en/icma/home • 14 volumes. Various dates, 1968 to 1988. Finance, planning, training, public relations, and other subjects.

***Municipal Year Book***. Hemming Information Services, 32 Vauxhall Bridge Rd. London SW1V 2SS, United Kingdom. Phone: 44 207 79736400 or 71 9736400; Fax: 44 207 72335056 or 71 2335057; Email: info@hgluk.com • URL: http://www.hgluk.com • Annual. Covers: local authorities, central government, agencies and officials of the United Kingdom; associations, development organizations, libraries, museums, and other local authorities. Entries include: Name of authority or governing agency, address, phone, fax, names of elected councillors, officers, names and titles of key personnel, contacts, population, and pay.

***Municipal Yellow Book: Who's Who in the Leading City and County Governments and Local Authorities***. Leadership Directories Inc., 104 5th Ave. New York, NY 10011-6901. Phone: (212)627-4140; Fax: (212)645-0931; Email: info@leadershipdirectories.com • URL: http://www.leadershipdirectories.com • Annual. $465 /year. Lists approximately 30,000 key personnel in city and county departments, agencies, subdivisions, and branches.

***Murphy's Will Clauses: Annotations and Forms with Tax Effects***. Matthew Bender and Company Inc., 1275 Broadway Albany, NY 12204-2638. Phone: 800-424-4200 or (518)487-3000; Fax: (518)487-3573 or (800)424-4200; Email: customer.support@lexisnexis.com • URL: http://www.matthewbender.com • Semiannual. $2,071 book; $1,883 e-book. Five looseleaf volumes. Over 1,400 framed will and trust clauses.

***Mushroom Journal***. Mushroom Growers Association, Ketton Stamford PE9 3ZT, United Kingdom. Phone: 44 1780722074; Fax: 44 1780729006; Email: mel@mushjournal.fsnet.co.uk • Monthly. Membership.

***Mushroom News***. American Mushroom Institute, 1 Massachusetts Ave. NW, Ste. 800 Washington, DC 20001. Phone: (202)842-4344; Fax: (202)408-7763; Email: ami@mwmlaw.com • URL: http://www.americanmushroom.org • Monthly. $300 Individuals. Articles range from general interest to the latest technical innovations.

**Music Business Association**. 1 Eves Dr., Ste. 138 Marlton, NJ 08053. Phone: (856)596-2221; Fax: (856)596-7299 • URL: http://www.musicbiz.org • Serves the music and other prerecorded entertainment software industry as a forum for insight and dialogue; members include retailers, wholesalers, distributors, entertainment software suppliers, and suppliers of related products and services.

**Music Distributors Association**. 14070 Proton Rd., Ste. 100, LB 9 Dallas, TX 75244. Phone: (972)233-9107; Fax: (972)490-4219; Email: office@musicdistributors.org • URL: http://www.musicdistributors.org • International distributors and suppliers of musical instruments, sheet music, and allied merchandise; manufacturers of musical merchandise.

***Music Inc***. Maher Publications Inc., 102 N Haven Rd. Elmhurst, IL 60126. Phone: 800-554-7470 or (630)941-2030; Fax: (630)941-3210; Email: editor@downbeat.com • URL: http://www.downbeat.com • 11 times a year. $16.00. per year. Music and sound retailing. Formerly *Up Beat Monthly*.

***Music Index: A Subject-Author Guide to Music Periodical Literature***. Harmonie Park Press, 35675 Mound Rd. Sterling Heights, MI 48310-4727. Phone: 800-886-3080 or (586)979-2077; Fax: (586)979-1786; Email: egorzelski@yahoo.com • URL: http://www.harmonieparkpress.com • Quarterly. $2,195.00 per year. Annual cummulation. Supplement available: *Music Index Subject Heading List*. Guide to current periodicals. Entries are in language of country issuing the index.

***Music Journal***. Incorporated Society of Musicians, 4-5 Inverness Mews London W2 3JQ, United Kingdom. Phone: 44 20 72213499; Fax: 44 20 72433437; Email: membership@ism.org • URL: http://www.ism.org • Bimonthly. Contains news from our members, advice from our team, features and opinion pieces from experts in the music profession.

***Music Library Association Notes: Quarterly Journal of the Music Library Association***. Music Library Association, 8551 Research Way, Ste. 180 Middleton, WI 53562-3567. Phone: (608)836-5825; Fax: (608)831-8200; Email: mla@areditions.com • URL: http://www.musiclibraryassoc.org • Quarterly. Individuals, $70.00 per year; institutions, $80.00 per year. Indexes record reviews (classical).

***Music Reference Services Quarterly***. The Haworth Press Inc., 10 Alice St. Binghamton, NY 13904. Phone: 800-429-6784 or (607)722-5857; Fax: (607)771-0012 or (607)722-6362; Email: getinfo@haworthpress.com • URL: http://www.haworthpressinc.com/store/product.asp?sku=J014 • Quarterly. Institutions, $95.00 per year. An academic journal for music librarians.

***Music Technology Buyer's Guide***. United Entertainment Media, 460 Pk. Ave. S, 9th Fl. New York, NY 10016. Phone: (212)378-0400; Fax: (212)378-2160; Email: keyboard@uemedia.com • URL: http://www.mcsquared.com/brmscn.htm • $6.95. Annual. Lists more than 4,000 hardware and software music production products from 350 manufacturers. Includes synthesizers, MIDI hardware and software, mixers, microphones, music notation software, etc. Produced by the editorial staffs of *Keyboard* and *EQ* magazines.

***Music Trades***. Music Trades Corp., 80 W St. Englewood, NJ 07631. Phone: 800-423-6530 or (201)871-1965; Fax: (201)871-0455; Email: music@musictrades.com • URL: http://www.musictrades.com • Monthly. $16 Individuals; $23 Two years; $45 Other countries; $60 Two years foreign; $150 Individuals airmail. Music trade magazine. Includes *Purchaser's Guide to the Music Industries*.

***The Music Week International Directory***. CMP Information Ltd., Ludgate House, 245 Blackfriars Rd. London SE1 9UY, United Kingdom. Phone: 44 207 9215000 or 44 20 7940 8500; Fax: (740)7 7102; Email: enquiries@cmpinformation.com • URL: http://www.cmpi.biz/home • Annual. $80; $120. Covers: Music companies worldwide operating in over 20 sectors including record companies, distributors, publishers, manufacturers, promoters, and studios. Entries include: Name, address, phone, fax, e-mail address, and URL.

***Musical America International Directory of the Performing Arts***. UBM Global Trade, 400 Windsor Corporate Pk., 50 Millstone Rd., Ste. 200 East Windsor, NJ 08520-1415. Phone: 800-221-5488 or (609)371-7700 or (609)371-7701; Fax: (609)371-7885 or (609)371-7883; Email: customerservice@cbizmedia.com • URL: http://www.cbizmedia.com • Annual. $115.00. Covers United States and Canada.

***Musical Merchandise Review: Directory of Musical Instrument Dealers***. Larkin Publications, 50 Brook Rd. Needham, MA 02494. Phone: 800-964-5150 or (781)453-9310; Fax: (781)453-9389; Email: mprescott@larkinpublications.com • URL: http://www.mmrmagazine.com • Annual. $125.00. Lists retailers of musical instruments and supplies.

***Musical Merchandise Review: Music Industry Directory***. Larkin Publications, 50 Brook Rd. Needham, MA 02494. Phone: 800-964-5150 or (781)453-9310; Fax: (781)453-9389; Email: mprescott@larkinpublications.com • URL: http://www.mmrmagazine.com • Annual. $25.00. Lists about 1,500 manufacturers and distributors of musical instruments and supplies. Includes indexes to products and trade names.

***Mutual Fund Advisor: The Top Performing Mutual Funds***. The Mutual Fund Advisor Inc., 1 Sarasota Twr., Ste. 602 Sarasota, FL 34236. Phone: (941)954-5500 • Monthly. Price on application. Newsletter.

**Mutual Fund Education Alliance**. 100 NW Englewood Rd., No. 130 Kansas City, MO 64118. Phone: (816)454-9422; Fax: (816)454-9322; Email: mfeamail@mfea.com • URL: http://www.mfea.com • Formerly No-Load Mutual Fund Association.

***Mutual Fund Letter***. Investment Information Services Inc., 680 N Lake Shore Dr., Twr. Offices, No. 2038 Chicago, IL 60611. Phone: 800-362-6941 or (312)649-6940; Fax: (312)649-5537 • Monthly. $125.00 per year. Newsletter. Provides mutual fund recommendations.

***Mutual Fund Market News***. Dalbar Publishing Inc., Federal Reserve Plz., 30th Fl. Boston, MA 02210. Phone: (617)723-6400 • Description: Provides persons in the mutual fund industry with critical information, breaking news, industry developments, new product analyses, and changes in market share. Covers all major changes of distribution for mutual funds and related products, with emphasis on banks, broker/dealers, captive sales forces, corporate and nonprofit pensions, and direct markets. Recurring features include portfolio management strategies, letters to the editor, a calendar of events and conferences, reports of industry meetings, and columns titled Hot Off the Wire, On the Move, and Newly Registered Funds.

***Mutual Fund Profiles***. Standard & Poor's Financial Services L.L.C., 55 Water St. New York, NY 10041. Phone: 877-772-5436 or (212)438-2000; Fax: (212)438-1000; Email: questions@standardandpoors.com • URL: http://www.standardandpoors.com • Quarterly. $158.00 per year. Produced jointly with Lipper Analytical Services. Provides detailed information on approximately 800 of the largest stock funds and taxable bond funds. In addition, contains concise data on about 2,400 smaller funds and municipal bond funds.

***Mutual Fund Strategies***. Progressive Investing, Inc., P.O. Box 446 Burlington, VT 05402. Phone: (802)658-3515 • Monthly. $127.00 per year. Newsletter.

***Mutual Fund Trends***. Growth Fund Research Inc., 409 Kansas City St. Rapid City, SD 57701. Phone: 800-621-8322 or (605)341-1971 • Description: Provides high quality semi-log charts with multiple moving averages and relative strength line on approximately 180 top performing funds. Statistics include lows to current time and high to low. Market indicators with good records. Includes weekly telephone hot line.

***Mutual Funds Interactive***. Brill Editorial Services, Inc., Phone: (877)442-7455 • URL: http://www.brill.com • Web site provides specific information on individual funds in addition to general advice on mutual fund investing and 401(k) plans. Searching is provided, including links to moderated newsgroups and a chat page.

***Mutual Funds Update***. Thomson Financial Inc., 195 Broadway New York, NY 10007-3100. Phone: (646)822-2000; Email: custserv@tfn.com • URL: http://www.thomsonreuters.com • Monthly. $325.00 per year. Provides recent performance information and statistics for approximately 10,000 mutual funds and closed-end funds as compiled from the CDA/Wiesenberger database. Includes commentary and analysis relating to the mutual fund industry. Information is provided on new funds, name changes, mergers, and liquidations.

***MX—Business Strategies for Medical Technology Executives: Business Strategies for Medical Technology Executives***. UBM Canon, 2901 28th St., Ste. 100 Santa Monica, CA 90405-2975. Phone: (310)445-4200; Fax: (310)445-4299 • URL: http://www.ubmcanon.com • Semiannual. Free to qualified subscribers; $50 Single issue. Trade magazine covering medical device technology for executives in the industry.

***My Business***. Hammock Inc., 3322 W End Ave., Ste. 100 Nashville, TN 37203. Phone: (615)690-3400; Fax: (615)690-3401; Email: info@hammock.com • URL: http://www.hammock.com • Bimonthly. Business magazine.

***My Little Salesman Heavy Equipment Catalog; New and Used Equipment Guide***. My Little Salesman, 2898 Chad Dr. Eugene, OR 97401. Phone: 800-493-2295 or (541)341-4650; Fax: (541)342-3307 • URL: http://www.mylittlesalesman.com • Monthly.

***My Little Salesman Truck and Trailer Catalog***. My Little Salesman, 2898 Chad Dr. Eugene, OR 97401. Phone: 800-493-2295 or (541)341-4650; Fax: (541)342-3307 • URL: http://www.mylittlesalesman.com • Monthly. Products serving the trucking industry. Central and Western editions.

**My Own Business, Inc.** 13181 Crossroads Pkwy. N, Ste. 190 City of Industry, CA 91746. Phone: (562)463-1800; Fax: (562)463-1802; Email: support@myownbusiness.org • URL: http://www.myownbusiness.org • Educates small business owners by providing free coursework. Develops, produces, implements, updates and markets educational offerings through multiple delivery channels. Seeks to expand collaborations with companies, schools, the community and other institutions. Works to support the vital social and economic contributions of small businesses by nurturing entrepreneurship and helping individuals build their own business.

***MZM World Business Directory***. MZM Publications Publishing Promotion Co., PO Box 465 PL 81-705 Sopot, Poland. Phone: 58 55027306; Fax: 58 5513706; Email: mzmpublications@wp.pl • Irregular. $154 plus airmail. Covers: companies in 33 post-socialist countries involved in international trade and business: Albania, Armenia, Azerbaijan, Bosnia & Herzegovina, Bulgaria, Belorus, China, Croatia, Cuba, Czech Republic, Slovakia, Estonia, Georgia, former East Germany, Hungary, Kazakhstan, Kirghizia, Latvia, Lithuania, North Korea, Macedonia, Moldova, Mongolia, Poland, Romania, Russia, Kaliningrad Province of Russia, Slovenia, Tadzhikistan, Turkmenistan, Ukraine, Uzbekistan, Vietnam, and Yugoslavia. Entries include: Company name, address, phone, fax, telex, number of employees, year established, subsidiary companies, description.

***N A S D Manual***. National Association of Securities Dealers, Inc. Wolters Kluwer Law & Business CCH, 2700 Lake Cook Rd. Riverwoods, IL 60015. Phone: 888-224-7377 or (847)267-7000; Email: cust_serv@cch.com • URL: http://www.cchgroup.com • Quarterly. $452.00 per year. CD-Rom, $459.00.

***NABE News***. National Association for Business Economics, 1920 L St. NW, Ste. 300 Washington, DC 20036. Phone: (202)463-6223; Fax: (202)463-6239; Email: nabe@nabe.com • URL: http://www.nabe.com • Quarterly. Description: Concerned with business economics. Serves this professional Association of persons employed by private, institutional, or government concerns in the area of business-related economic analysis. Recurring features include results of the NABE quarterly outlook survey, featured articles of timely interest, reviews of seminars and annual meetings, news from local chapters and roundtables, and personal notes.

**NACE International: The Corrosion Society**. 1440 S Creek Dr. Houston, TX 77084-4906. Phone: 800-797-6223 or (281)228-6200 or (281)228-6223; Fax: (281)228-6300; Email: firstservice@nace.org • URL: http://www.nace.org • Serves as professional technical society dedicated to reducing the economic impact of corrosion, promoting public safety, and protecting the environment by advancing the knowledge of corrosion engineering and science. Conducts programs for technical training, sponsors technical conferences, and produces standards, publications, and software. Maintains certification program for engineers, technicians, and coating inspectors.

**NACHA: The Electronic Payments Association**. 13450 Sunrise Valley Dr., Ste. 100 Herndon, VA 20171. Phone: (703)561-1100; Fax: (703)787-0996; Email: abuse@nacha.org • URL: http://www.nacha.org • Automated Clearing House (ACH) association. Provides an interregional exchange for electronic debits and credits among ACHs and to establish and administer nationwide standards and operating rules for ACHs. Conducts national seminars and conferences on ACH operations and products; sponsors annual Payments and Electronic Commerce Institute; sponsors Accredited ACH Professional program. Sponsors national marketing campaign; compiles statistics.

**NADA Appraisal Guides**. National Automobile Dealers Association, 8400 Westpark Dr. McLean, VA 22102. Phone: 800-252-6232 or (703)821-7000; Fax: (703)821-7234; Email: help@nada.org • URL: http://www.nada.org • Prices and frequencies vary. Guides to prices of used cars, old used cars, motorcycles, mobile homes, recreational vehicles, and mopeds.

**NADA Marine Appraisal Guide**. National Automobile Dealers Association. N.A.D.A. Appraisal Guides, P.O. Box 7800 Costa Mesa, CA 92628-7800. Phone: 800-966-6232 or (714)556-8511; Fax: (714)556-8715 • 3/year. $140 Individuals.

**NAED National Education and Research Foundation**. 1181 Corporate Lake Dr. Saint Louis, MO 63132-1716. Phone: 888-791-2512 or (314)991-9000; Fax: (314)991-3060 • URL: http://www.naed.org • Established by the National Association of Electrical Distributors to provide electrical distributor and distributor-oriented manufacturers with the opportunity to become better business people by expanding their managerial skills. Designs and conducts seminars, workshops, conferences and home study materials covering all aspects of professional management in the electrical supply industry.

**NAEDA Buyer's Guide**. North American Equipment Dealers Association, 1195 Smizer Mill Rd. Fenton, MO 63026-3480. Phone: (636)349-5000; Fax: (636)349-5443; Email: naeda@naeda.com • URL: http://www.naeda.com • Annual. $35 print only. List of manufacturers and suppliers of agricultural, outdoor power equipment and construction equipment.

**NAEDA Equipment Dealer**. North American Equipment Dealers Association, 1195 Smizer Mill Rd. Fenton, MO 63026-3480. Phone: (636)349-5000; Fax: (636)349-5443; Email: naeda@naeda.com • URL: http://www.naeda.com • Monthly. $45 Individuals ground delivery; $150 Other countries mail. Covers power equipment for farm, outdoor, and industrial use. Formerly *Farm and Power Equipment Dealer*.

**NAFA Annual Reference Book**. NAFA Fleet Management Association, 125 Village Blvd., Ste. 200 Princeton, NJ 08540. Phone: (609)720-0882; Fax: (609)452-8004; Email: info@nafa.org • URL: http://www.nafa.org • Online. Automobile manufacturers' sales and leasing representatives throughout the country.

**NAFSA: Association of International Educators**. 1307 New York Ave. NW, 8th Fl. Washington, DC 20005-4701. Phone: 800-836-4994 or (202)737-3699; Fax: (202)737-3657; Email: inbox@nafsa.org • URL: http://www.nafsa.org • Members are individuals, organizations, and institutions involved with international educational interchange, including foreign student advisors, overseas educational advisers, foreign student admission officers, and U. S. students abroad. Formerly National Association for Foreign Student Affairs.

**NAFSA Newsletter**. • Description: Concerned with international educational interchange. Reports on English as a second language, foreign admissions, study abroad, foreign student advising, community programming, and other subjects. Recurring features include government news, book reviews, news of members, Association news, and columns titled News and Briefs and From the Front Lines of Advocacy.

**NAFTA Register**. Global Contact Inc., 383 Kings Hwy. N, Ste. 210 Cherry Hill, NJ 08034. Phone: (856)482-2011; Fax: (856)482-2066 • Annual. Covers: Companies within the NAFTA region interested in exporting their products/services. Entries include: Company name, address, phone, fax, e-mail and Internet addresses, name and title of contact, list of products/services offered.

**NAHB Home Innovation Research Labs**. 400 Prince George's Blvd. Upper Marlboro, MD 20774. Phone: 800-638-8556 or (301)249-4000; Fax: (301)430-6180 • URL: http://www.homeinnovation.com.

**NAIC News**. National Association of Insurance Commissioners, 1100 Walnut St., Ste. 1500 Kansas City, MO 64106-2277. Phone: (816)842-3600; Fax: (816)783-8175 • URL: http://www.naic.org • Monthly. $200.00 per year. Newsletter covering insurance legislation and regulation.

**Namibia Business Directory**. A.C. Braby (Pty) Ltd., 12 Caver-

sham Rd. Pinetown 3610, South Africa. Email: support@brabys.co.za • URL: http://www.brabys.com • Annual. Covers: Businesses in Namibia. Entries include: Company name, address, phone.

**Namibia Industrial and Business Directory**. International Business Publications, USA, PO Box 15343 Washington, DC 20003. Phone: (202)546-2103; Fax: (202)546-3275; Email: ibpusa@comcast.net • URL: http://ibpus.com • Annual. $99.95 Individuals hardcopy, e-book, CD-ROM. Covers: Strategic industrial, investment and business contacts for conducting export-import and investment activity in the country. Contains strategic practical economic and business information.

**Namibia Trade Directory**. Namibia Trade Directory, 5 Storch St. Windhoek, Namibia. Phone: 264 61 225665; Fax: 264 61 220410 • URL: http://www.namibiatradedirectory.com • Covers: Trade and industries in Namibia. Entries include: Addresses and contact persons.

**NAMIC Magazine**. National Association of Mutual Insurance Companies, 3601 Vincennes Rd. Indianapolis, IN 46268. Phone: (317)875-5250; Fax: (317)879-8408 • URL: http://www.namic.org • Quarterly. Specially packaged for property/casualty insurance executives, many of whom are members of the National Association of Mutual Insurance Companies (NAMIC). It is also designed to be of interest to underwriting, claims, and agency professionals; as well as insurance legislative contacts and management of other industry-related businesses.

**NAMM - The International Music Products Association**. 5790 Armada Dr. Carlsbad, CA 92008-4608. Phone: 800-767-6266 or (760)438-8001; Fax: (760)438-7327; Email: info@namm.org • URL: http://www.namm.org • Retailers of musical instruments and allied products, manufacturers, distributors, jobbers, wholesalers and publishers of print music. Holds several professional development seminars in various locations around the country and 2 major trade shows.

**NAN-Directorio Nacional Negocio a Negocio**. Yell Publicidad S.A., Av Manoteras 12 28050 Madrid, Spain. Phone: 34 913396001 • Annual. Covers: Approximately 230,000 business firms whose main activity is sales of products or services to the business to business sector in Spain.

**NARDA's Cost of Doing Business Survey**. North American Retail Dealers Association, 222 S Riverside Plz., Ste. 2100 Chicago, IL 60606. Phone: 800-621-0298 or (312)648-0649; Fax: (312)648-1212; Email: nardasvc@narda.com • URL: http://www.narda.com • $50 Members; $150 Nonmembers. Provides insight into revenue and costs, warranty information, expenses, and asset/liability information.

**NASDAQ-AMEX Market Group Fact Book**. NASD Media-Source, P.O. Box 9403 Gaithersburg, MD 20890-9403. Phone: (301)590-6142; Fax: (240)386-4838 • Annual. $20.00. Published by the American Stock Exchange, Inc. Contains statistical data relating to the American Stock Exchange. Also provides the address and phone number for each company listed on the Exchange. Formerly *American Stock Exchange Fact Book*.

**NASDAQ BX Guide**. Wolters Kluwer Law & Business CCH, 2700 Lake Cook Rd. Riverwoods, IL 60015. Phone: 888-224-7377 or (847)267-7000; Email: cust_serv@cch.com • URL: http://www.cchgroup.com • Annual. Covers: Members and member organizations, constitution & rules of the Exchange. Database includes: List of stocks and bonds admitted to trading on the exchange, arranged alphabetically by name of issuing company, and including description and class of stock or bond, trading code, trading post, and par value. Entries include: Name, affiliation, address, date of admission to exchange.

**NASDAQ PHLX Guide**. Wolters Kluwer Law & Business CCH, 2700 Lake Cook Rd. Riverwoods, IL 60015. Phone: 888-224-7377 or (847)267-7000; Email: cust_serv@cch.com • URL: http://www.cchgroup.com • Annual. $794 Individuals print. Covers: Members, associate members, and member organizations of the stock exchange in Philadelphia, Pennsylvania. Database includes: Directory and Constitution rules published for the Exchange. Entries include: Name, affiliation, address, date of admission to exchange.

**Nashville Business Journal**. American City Business Journals, Inc., 120 W Morehead St. Charlotte, NC 28202. Phone: (704)973-1000; Fax: (704)973-1001; Email: americancity@bizjournals.com • URL: http://www.acbj.com • Weekly. $91 Individuals print and digital. Regional business newspaper.

**Nashville Business Journal—Book of Lists**. Nashville Business Journals, 344 4th Ave. N Nashville, TN 37219. Phone: 800-486-3289 or (615)248-2222; Fax: (615)248-6246; Email: bizbooks@bizjournals.com • URL: http://www.nashville.bizjournals.com • $65 print only; $199.95 online only. Covers: About 700 major companies, foundations, government officials, utilities, news papers, radio and television stations, airlines, hospitals, financial institutions, shopping centers, resorts, and prominent individuals in the Nashville, Tennessee area. Entries include: Company, organization, or individual name, address, phone, names and titles of key personnel, financial data, products or services.

**Nashville Music Business Directory**. Nashville Area Chamber of Commerce, 211 Commerce St., Ste. 100 Nashville, TN 37201-1806. Phone: (615)743-3000; Fax: (615)743-3002 • URL: http://www.nashvillechamber.com • $15 Nonmembers; $7 Members. Lists record publisher, distributors, recording

companies, talent agencies and management companies in the Nashville music industry.

**NaSPA**. 7044 S 13th St. Oak Creek, WI 53154. Phone: (414)908-4945 or (414)768-8000; Fax: (414)768-8001; Email: customercare@naspa.com • URL: http://www.naspa.com • Members are systems programmers, communications analysts, database administrators, and other technical management personnel.

**National Aboriginal Capital Corporation Association**. 75 Albert St., Ste. 908 Ottawa, ON, Canada K1P 5E7. Phone: (613)688-0894; Fax: (613)688-0895 • URL: http://www.nacca.net • Assists Aboriginal Financial Institutions (AFIs) in promoting the growth and development of Aboriginal businesses. Provides products and services to AFIs and Aboriginal-focused organizations including institutional capacity-building, training, access to capital, advocacy, partnerships, and member services with quality and accountability.

**National Aboriginal Lands Managers Association**. 1024 Mississauga St. Curve Lake, ON, Canada K0L 1R0. Phone: 877-234-9813 or (705)657-7660; Fax: (705)657-7177; Email: info@nalma.ca • URL: http://www.nalma.ca • Advances the professional development and technical expertise in the field of land management. Provides a working environment to all First Nations Lands Managers. Creates opportunities for networking between land managers on land related issues. Creates a system that will assist First Nations interests in various land management functions.

**The National Academies - National Research Council**. 500 5th St. NW Washington, DC 20001. Phone: (202)334-2000 • URL: http://www.nationalacademies.org/nrc/ • Scientists, engineers, and other professionals serving pro bono on approximately 900 study committees. Serves as an independent adviser to the federal government on scientific and technical questions of national importance; is jointly administered by the National Academy of Sciences, National Academy of Engineering, and Institute of Medicine. Carries out objectives through conferences, technical committees, surveys, collection and analysis of scientific and technical data, and administration of public and private funds for research projects and fellowships.

**National Academy of Arbitrators**. NAA Operations Ctr., Ste. 412, 1 N Main St. Cortland, NY 13045. Phone: 888-317-1729 or (607)756-8363; Email: naa@naarb.org • URL: http://www.naarb.org • Labor-management arbitrators. Works to improve general understanding of the nature and use of arbitration as a means of settling labor disputes. Conducts research and educational programs.

**National Academy of Opticianry**. 8401 Corporate Dr., Ste. 605 Landover, MD 20785. Phone: 800-229-4828; Fax: (301)577-3880; Email: ctucker@nao.org • URL: http://www.nao.org • Offers review courses for national certification and state licensure examinations to members. Maintains speakers' bureau and Career Progression Program.

**National Accounts Statistics: Main Aggregates and Detailed Tables**. United Nations Publications, c/o National Book Network, 15200 NBN Way Blue Ridge Summit, PA 17214. Phone: 888-254-4286 or (212)963-7680 or (212)963-8302; Fax: (800)338-4550; Email: unpublications@nbnbooks.com • URL: http://www.unp.un.org • Annual.

**National Active and Retired Federal Employees Association**. 606 N Washington St. Alexandria, VA 22314. Phone: 800-627-3394 or (703)838-7760; Fax: (703)838-7785 • URL: http://www.narfe.org/departments/home/index.cfm • Formerly National Association of Retired Civil Employees.

**National Advertising Review Board**. 112 Madison Ave., 3rd fl. New York, NY 10016. Phone: (212)705-0115; Fax: (212)705-0136 • URL: http://www.asrcreviews.org/asrc-contact-us • Individuals from industry and the public. Sponsored by the National Advertising Review Council for the purpose of sustaining high standards of truth and accuracy in national advertising. Aims to maintain a self-regulatory mechanism that responds constructively to public complaints about national advertising and which significantly improves advertising performance and credibility.

**National Aeronautic Association**. Reagan Washington National Airport, Hangar 7, Ste. 202 Washington, DC 20001-6015. Phone: 800-644-9777 or (703)416-4888; Fax: (703)416-4877; Email: admin@naa.aero • URL: http://naa.aero • Persons interested in the progress and development of American general and military aviation. Supervises sporting aviation competitions and official world records in aeronautics and astronautics, model flying, gliding, soaring, parachuting, hang gliding, ballooning and helicopters.

**National Agri-Marketing Association**. 11020 King St., Ste. 205 Overland Park, KS 66210. Phone: (913)491-6500 or (815)422-0321; Fax: (913)491-6502; Email: agrimktg@nama.org • URL: http://www.nama.org • Persons engaged in agricultural marketing for manufacturers, advertising agencies and the media. Promotes the highest standards of agricultural marketing; provides for the exchange of ideas; encourages the study and better understanding of agricultural advertising, selling and marketing; works to broaden understanding of the economic importance of agriculture; encourages careers in agricultural marketing. Provides agri-marketing short courses.

**National Agricultural Aviation Association—Membership Directory**. National Agricultural Aviation Association, 1440

Duke St. Alexandria, VA 22314. Phone: (202)546-5722; Fax: (202)546-5726; Email: information@agaviation.org • URL: http://www.agaviation.org • Annual. Covers: Nearly 1300 executives, pilots, and supplier companies engaged primarily in aerial application. Entries include: For chapter and supplier company members—Name, spouse's name, company name, address, phone.

**National Air Carrier Association.** 1000 Wilson Blvd., Ste. 1700 Arlington, VA 22209. Phone: (703)358-8060; Fax: (703)358-8070 • URL: http://www.naca.cc • Represents U.S. certificated airlines specializing in low-cost scheduled and air charter operations. Assists members in the promotion of air transportation and serves as a liaison between members and U.S. government bodies that regulate air transportation.

***National Air Transportation Association—Aviation Resource and Membership Directory.*** National Air Transportation Association, 4226 King St. Alexandria, VA 22302. Phone: 800-808-6282 or (703)845-9000; Fax: (703)845-8176 • URL: http://www.nata.aero • Annual. $50 Nonmembers; $25 Members. Covers: More than 1,000 regular, associate, and affiliate members; regular members include airport service organizations, air taxi operators, and commuter airlines. Entries include: Company name, address, phone, fax number, name and title of contact.

***National Air Transportation Association Official Membership Directory.*** National Air Transportation Association, 4226 King St. Alexandria, VA 22302. Phone: 800-808-6282 or (703)845-9000; Fax: (703)845-8176 • URL: http://www.nata.aero • Annual. List more than 1,000 regular, associate, and affliate members; regular members include airport service organizations, air taxi operators, and commuter airlines.

**National Air Transportation Association.** 4226 King St. Alexandria, VA 22302. Phone: 800-808-6282 or (703)845-9000; Fax: (703)845-8176 • URL: http://www.nata.aero • Represents the interests of aviation businesses nationwide. Provides vital aviation services to the airlines, the military, and business/corporate/individual aircraft owners and operators; services includes fueling, maintenance, and flight instruction.

**National Alcohol Beverage Control Association.** 4401 Ford Ave., Ste. 700 Alexandria, VA 22302-1433. Phone: (703)578-4200; Fax: (703)820-3551; Email: nabca.info@nabca.org • URL: http://www.nabca.org • Formerly Joint Committee of the States to study Alcoholic Beverage Laws.

**National Alliance of Craftsmen Associations.** 816 Camaron St., Ste. 212 San Antonio, TX 78212. Phone: (210)271-9100; Fax: (210)212-9250 • Works to create and promote community empowerment, sustainability and growth through the development of employment, economic and educational opportunities in blighted communities. Concentrates on the barriers that perpetuate the underutilized, underemployed, unemployed, unskilled and underskilled community. Aims to build a stronger and healthier country one community at a time.

**National Alliance of Forest Owners.** 122 C St. NW, Ste. 630 Washington, DC 20001. Phone: (202)747-0759; Fax: (202)824-0770; Email: info@nafoalliance.org • URL: http://www.nafoalliance.org • Aims to protect and enhance the economic and environmental values of privately-owned forests through targeted policy advocacy at the national level. Focuses on issues for regulatory advocacy including climate change, renewable energy, environment, tax policy, land use, trade and market policy. Seeks public policies that shape environmental regulations, taxes, land use decisions, and timber and non-timber markets in ways that protect and grow forest values.

**National Alliance of Independent Crop Consultants.** 349 E Nolley Dr. Collierville, TN 38017. Phone: (901)861-0511; Fax: (901)861-0512; Email: jonesnaicc@aol.com • URL: http://www.naicc.org • Independent crop consultants and contract researchers united to promote agriculture and professionalism in the field. Seeks to: assist in the formation of state and national policies relating to agricultural production and of crop management philosophies; support agricultural crop producers by the most ecologically sound, environmentally safe, and economical means. Encourages members to expand their knowledge concerning crop management practices and techniques; participates in research in this area. Provides assistance in the formation of state and regional consultant organizations; offers referral system for members. Compiles statistics; sponsors educational programs.

***National Antique & Art Dealers Association of America—Membership Directory.*** National Antique and Art Dealers Association of America, 220 E 57th St. New York, NY 10022. Phone: (212)826-9707; Fax: (212)832-9493; Email: inquiries@naadaa.org • URL: http://www.naadaa.org • Continuous. Provides a list of members and their areas of specialization in the decorative arts.

**National Antique and Art Dealers Association of America.** 220 E 57th St. New York, NY 10022. Phone: (212)826-9707; Fax: (212)832-9493; Email: inquiries@naadaa.org • URL: http://www.naadaa.org • Art and antique dealers who handle antiques and works of art of the highest quality. Safeguards the interests of those who buy, sell, and collect antiques and works of art. Sponsors periodic exhibitions; maintains speakers' bureau.

**National Apartment Association.** 4300 Wilson Blvd., Ste. 400 Arlington, VA 22203. Phone: (703)518-6141; Fax: (703)248-9440; Email: webmaster@naahq.org • URL: http://www.naahq.org • Federation of 155 state and local associations of industry professionals engaged in all aspects of the multifamily housing industry, including owners, builders, investors, developers, managers, and allied service representatives. Provides education and certification for property management executives, on-site property managers, maintenance personnel, property supervisors, and leasing agents. Offers a nationwide legislative network concerned with governmental decisions at the federal, state, and local levels.

**National Architectural Accrediting Board.** 1101 Connecticut Ave. NW, Ste. 410 Washington, DC 20036. Phone: (202)783-2007; Fax: (202)783-2822; Email: info@naab.org • URL: http://www.naab.org • Formed by the American Institute of Architects, Association of Collegiate Schools of Architecture, and National Council of Architectural Registration Boards to stimulate the improvement of architectural education. Conducts continuing program of accreditation of programs of architecture. Compiles statistics; maintains library of 100 volumes of descriptions and self-evaluations of architecture schools.

**National Asphalt Pavement Association.** 5100 Forbes Blvd. Lanham, MD 20706. Phone: 888-468-6499 or (301)731-4748; Fax: (301)731-4621; Email: napa@hotmix.org • URL: http://www.hotmix.org • Manufacturers and producers of scientifically proportioned Hot Mix Asphalt for use in all paving, including highways, airfields, and environmental usages. Membership includes hot mix producers, paving contractors, equipment manufacturers, engineering consultants, and others. Supports research and publishes information on: producing, stockpiling, and feeding of the aggregate to the manufacturing facility; drying; methods of screening, storing, and proportioning in the manufacturing facility; production of the hot mix asphalt; transporting mix to paver; lay down procedure and rolling; general workmanship; and related construction practices and materials. Commits to product quality, environmental control, safety and health, and energy conservation. Conducts training programs on a variety of technical and managerial topics for industry personnel. Maintains speakers' bureau and Hot Mix Asphalt Hall of Fame.

***National Association for Business Economics Membership Directory.*** National Association for Business Economics, 1920 L St. NW, Ste. 300 Washington, DC 20036. Phone: (202)463-6223; Fax: (202)463-6239; Email: nabe@nabe.com • URL: http://www.nabe.com • Annual. Membership.

***National Association for Business Economics—Membership Directory.*** National Association for Business Economics, 1920 L St. NW, Ste. 300 Washington, DC 20036. Phone: (202)463-6223; Fax: (202)463-6239; Email: nabe@nabe.com • URL: http://www.nabe.com • Annual. Covers about 3,600 members internationally.

**National Association for Business Economics.** 1920 L St. NW, Ste. 300 Washington, DC 20036. Phone: (202)463-6223; Fax: (202)463-6239; Email: nabe@nabe.com • URL: http://www.nabe.com • Formerly National Association of Business Economists.

**National Association for Business Teacher Education.** 1914 Association Dr. Reston, VA 20191-1596. Phone: (703)860-8300; Fax: (703)620-4483; Email: nbea@nbea.org • URL: http://www.nabte.org • An institutional division of National Business Education Association. Represents colleges and universities with programs for the education of business teachers. Works to improve and advance business teacher education. Operates Business Education Research Foundation.

**National Association for College Admission Counseling.** 1050 N Highland St., Ste. 400 Arlington, VA 22201-2197. Phone: 800-822-6285 or (703)836-2222; Fax: (703)243-9375; Email: info@nacacnet.org • URL: http://www.nacacnet.org • Formerly National Association of College Admissions Counselors.

**National Association for Community College Entrepreneurship.** Bldg. 101-R, 1 Federal St. Springfield, MA 01105. Phone: (413)306-3131; Fax: (413)755-6101; Email: wolpert@nacce.com • URL: http://www.nacce.com • Establishes entrepreneurship education as a core offering to foster economic development through community colleges. Focuses on increasing economic development through entrepreneurship education and student business incubation at the community college level.

**National Association for Court Management.** National Center for State Courts, 300 Newport Ave. Williamsburg, VA 23185-4147. Phone: 800-616-6165 or (757)259-1841; Fax: (757)259-1520; Email: nacm@ncsc.org • URL: http://nacmnet.org • Court management professionals. Aims to foster communication among members. Conducts educational programs.

***National Association for Drama Therapy—Membership List.*** North American Drama Therapy Association, 44365 Premier Plz., Ste. 220 Ashburn, VA 20147. Phone: 888-416-7167 or (571)333-2991; Fax: (571)223-6440; Email: office@nadt.org • URL: http://www.nadt.org • Annual. Covers: About 400 registered drama therapists and NADT members. Entries include: Name, address, membership category.

**National Association for Equal Opportunity in Higher Education.** 209 3rd St. SE Washington, DC 20003. Phone: (202)552-3300; Fax: (202)552-3330 • URL: http://www.nafeo.org/community/index.php • Provides a unified framework representing historically and predominantly black universities and colleges and similarly situated institutions in their attempt to continue as viable forces in American society. Seeks to build a case for securing increased support from federal agencies, philanthropic foundations, and other sources, and to increase black leadership of educational organizations and membership on federal boards and commissions relating to education. Offers placement service. Maintains biographical data on member colleges/universities and presidents/chancellors. Compiles statistics on black graduates.

**National Association for Female Executives.** 2 Park Ave. New York, NY 10016. • URL: http://www.nafe.com • Represents and supports professional women and women business owners; provides resources and services through education, networking and public advocacy to empower members to achieve career success and financial security.

**National Association for Home Care and Hospice.** 228 7th St. SE Washington, DC 20003. Phone: (202)547-7424; Fax: (202)547-3540; Email: exec@nahc.org • URL: http://www.nahc.org • Promotes high standards of patient care in home care services. Members are durable medical providers, medical equipment and oxygen suppliers, mainly for home health care.

**National Association for Moisture Management.** 76 D St. Hull, MA 02045. Phone: (781)925-0354; Fax: (781)925-0650 • URL: http://na4mm.com • Educates and protects the consumer from problems associated with moisture. Works with state, federal and local officials to develop standards and practices in the moisture management industry. Offers continuing education programs for moisture management professionals.

**National Association for Printing Leadership.** 1 Meadowlands Plz., Ste. 1511 East Rutherford, NJ 07073. Phone: 800-642-6275 or (201)634-9600; Fax: (201)634-0324 or (201)986-2976; Email: jtruncale@napl.org • URL: http://www.napl.org • Text: Formerly National Association of Printers and Lithographers.

**National Association for Public Health Statistics and Information Systems.** 962 Wayne Ave., Ste. 701 Silver Spring, MD 20910. Phone: (301)563-6001; Fax: (301)563-6012; Email: hq@naphsis.org • URL: http://www.naphsis.org/Pages/home.aspx • Members are officials of state and local health agencies.

**National Association for Surface Finishing.** 1155 15th St. NW, Ste. 500 Washington, DC 20005. Phone: (202)457-8404 or (703)887-7235; Fax: (202)530-0659; Email: passante@nasf.org • URL: http://www.nasf.org • Members are management personnel of metal and plastic finishing companies. Finishing includes plating, coating, polishing, rustproofing, and other processes.

**National Association for the Advancement of Colored People.** 4805 Mt. Hope Dr. Baltimore, MD 21215. Phone: 877-NAACP-98 or (410)580-5777 or (410)580-5110; Email: actso@naacpnet.org • URL: http://www.naacp.org • Persons "of all races and religions" who believe in the objectives and methods of the NAACP. Works to achieve equal rights through the democratic process and eliminate racial prejudice by removing racial discrimination in housing, employment, voting, schools, the courts, transportation, recreation, prisons, and business enterprises. Offers referral services, tutorials, job referrals, and day care. Sponsors seminars; maintains law library. Sponsors the NAACP National Housing Corporation to assist in the development of low and moderate income housing for families. Compiles statistics.

**National Association for the Self-Employed.** PO Box 241 Annapolis Junction, MD 20701-0241. Phone: 800-232-6273; Email: advocacy@nase.org • URL: http://www.nase.org • Members are very small businesses and the self-employed. Acts as an advocacy group at the state and federal levels.

**National Association for the Specialty Food Trade.** 136 Madison Ave., 12th Fl. New York, NY 10016. Phone: (212)482-6440 or (212)921-1690; Fax: (212)921-1898 • URL: http://www.specialtyfood.com • Members are manufacturers, processors, importers, retailers, and brokers of specialty and gourmet food items.

**National Association for Uniformed Services.** 5535 Hempstead Way Springfield, VA 22151. Phone: 800-842-3451 or (703)750-1342; Email: info@naus.org • URL: http://www.naus.org • Members of the uniformed military services, active, retired or reserve, veteran, enlisted and officers, and their spouses or widows. Develops and supports legislation that upholds the security of the U.S., sustains the morale of the uniformed services, and provides fair and equitable consideration for all service people. Protects and improves compensation, entitlements, and benefits. Provides discount rates on travel, insurance, auto rentals, charge cards, prescription medicine, and legal services.

**National Association of Agricultural Contractors.** The Old Cart Shed, Easton Lodge Farm, Old Oundle Rd., Wansford Peterborough PE8 6NP, United Kingdom. Phone: 44 1780 784631; Fax: 44 1780 784933; Email: members@naac.co.uk • URL: http://www.naac.co.uk • Represents agricultural and amenity contractors in United Kingdom and their commercial and regulatory interests at the national level.

**National Association of Attorneys General.** 2030 M St. NW, 8th Fl. Washington, DC 20036-3306. Phone: (202)326-6000 or

(202)326-6027; Fax: (202)331-1427 • URL: http://www.naag.org • Attorneys general of the 50 states, District of Columbia, American Samoa, Guam, Puerto Rico, Virgin Islands, and Northern Mariana Islands. Sponsors legal education seminars on consumer protection, environmental protection, antitrust, corrections, insurance, charitable trusts and solicitations, and Supreme Court practice.

**National Association of Black Owned Broadcasters.** 1201 Connecticut Ave. NW, Ste. 200 Washington, DC 20036. Phone: (202)463-8970; Fax: (202)429-0657; Email: nabobinfo@nabob.org • URL: http://www.nabob.org • Black broadcast station owners; black formatted stations not owned or controlled by blacks; organizations having an interest in the black consumer market or black broadcast industry; individuals interested in becoming owners; and communications schools, departments and professional groups and associations. Represents the interests of existing and potential black radio and television stations. Works with the Office of Federal Procurement Policy to determine which government contracting major advertisers and advertising agencies are complying with government initiatives to increase the amount of advertising dollars received by minority-owned firms. Conducts lobbying activities; provides legal representation for the protection of minority ownership policies. Sponsors annual Communications Awards Dinner each March. Conducts workshops; compiles statistics.

**National Association of Blessed Billionaires.** Presbyterian Church of Mt. Vernon, 199 N Columbus Ave. Mount Vernon, NY 10553. Phone: (914)633-4417 or (347)933-3000; Email: nabb10m@aol.com • URL: http://blessedbillionaires.org • Aims to build self-esteem and good moral character among young people. Helps young men and women gain the skills they need to become successful and responsible adults. Provides a vehicle for inner-city youth to learn about and participate in the competitive market through leadership and entrepreneurial training. Conducts training on all aspects of business and money management.

**National Association of Boards of Pharmacy.** 1600 Feehanville Dr. Mount Prospect, IL 60056. Phone: (847)391-4406; Fax: (847)391-4502; Email: custserv@nabp.net • URL: http://www.nabp.net • Pharmacy boards of several states, District of Columbia, Puerto Rico, Virgin Islands, several Canadian provinces, the states of Victoria, Australia, and New South Wales, the Pharmaceutical Society of New Zealand, and the South African Pharmacy Council. Provides for inter-state reciprocity in pharmaceutic licensure based upon a uniform minimum standard of pharmaceutic education and uniform legislation; improves the standards of pharmaceutical education licensure and practice. Provides legislative information; sponsors uniform licensure examination; also provides information on accredited school and college requirements. Maintains pharmacy and drug law statistics.

**National Association of Broadcasters.** 1771 N St. NW Washington, DC 20036. Phone: 800-342-2460 or (202)429-5300 or (202)429-5490; Email: nab@nab.org • URL: http://www.nab.org • Formerly National Association of Radio and Television Broadcasters.

**National Association of Business Political Action Committees.** 101 Constitution Ave. NW, Ste. L-110 Washington, DC 20001-2115. Phone: (202)341-3780; Fax: (202)478-0342; Email: nabpac@nabpac.org • URL: http://www.nabpac.org • Political action professionals and government affairs representatives interested in campaign finance reform issues and innovations in political action committee management.

**National Association of Business Travel Agents.** 3699 Wilshire Blvd., Ste. 700 Los Angeles, CA 90010-2726. Phone: (213)382-3335 • Members specialize in corporate and business travel services.

**National Association of Certified Public Bookkeepers.** 140 N Union Ave., Ste. 240 Farmington, UT 84025-2954. Phone: 866-444-9989; Fax: (801)451-4688; Email: info@nacpb.org • URL: http://www.nacpb.org • Aims to protect the public interest by ensuring that only qualified individuals provide public bookkeeping services. Fosters the professional development of public bookkeepers. Offers certification programs in bookkeeping.

*National Association of Chain Drug Stores - Communications Directory.* National Association of Chain Drug Stores, 1776 Wilson Blvd., Ste. 200 Arlington, VA 22209. Phone: (703)549-3001; Fax: (703)836-4869; Email: contactus@nacds.org • URL: http://www.nacds.org • Annual. Membership. About 150 chain drug retailers and their 31,000 individual pharmacies; 900 supplier companies; state boards of pharmacy, pharmaceutical and retail associations, colleges of pharmacy; drug trade associations.

**National Association of Chain Drug Stores.** 1776 Wilson Blvd., Ste. 200 Arlington, VA 22209. Phone: (703)549-3001; Fax: (703)836-4869; Email: contactus@nacds.org • URL: http://www.nacds.org • Represents the concerns of community pharmacies in Washington, in state capitals, and across the country. Members are more than 210 chain community pharmacy companies. Collectively, community pharmacy comprises the largest component of pharmacy practice with over 107,000 FTE pharmacists.

**National Association of Chemical Distributors.** 1560 Wilson Blvd., Ste. 1100 Arlington, VA 22209. Phone: (703)527-6223; Fax: (703)527-7747; Email: nacdpublicaffairs@nacd.com • URL: http://www.nacd.com • Represents chemical

distributor companies that purchase and take title of chemical products from manufacturers. Promotes professionalism in the chemical distribution industry.

**National Association of Clean Air Agencies.** 444 N Capitol St. NW, Ste. 307 Washington, DC 20001. Phone: (202)624-7864; Fax: (202)624-7863; Email: 4cleanair@4cleanair.org • URL: http://www.cleanairworld.org • State, local and territorial air pollution program administrators and members of their staffs. Provides an opportunity for state and local officials who are responsible for implementing air pollution control programs established under the Clean Air Act to share air quality-related experiences and to discuss problems. Encourages communication and cooperation among federal, state, and local regulatory agencies.

**National Association of College Auxiliary Services.** 3 Boar's Head Ln., Ste B Charlottesville, VA 22903. Phone: (434)245-8425; Fax: (434)245-8453; Email: info@nacas.org • URL: http://www.nacas.org • Formerly Association of College Auxiliary Services.

**National Association of College Stores.** 500 E Lorain St. Oberlin, OH 44074. Phone: 800-622-7498 or (440)775-7777; Fax: (440)775-4769; Email: webteam@nacs.org • URL: http://www.nacs.org • Formerly College Bookstore Association.

**National Association of Commercial Finance Brokers.** Hamilton House, 1 Temple Ave. London EC4Y 0HA, United Kingdom. Phone: 44 20 74892056; Email: admin@nacfb.org.uk • URL: http://www.nacfb.org • Seeks to protect consumer from fraud and malpractice in the commercial finance industry. Raises professional standards of commercial finance brokers. Provides training, education and information.

**National Association of Concessionaires.** 180 N Michigan Ave., Ste. 2215 Chicago, IL 60601. Phone: (312)236-3858; Fax: (312)236-7809; Email: info@naconline.org • URL: http://www.naconline.org • Formerly Popcorn and Concessions Association.

**National Association of Container Distributors.** 800 Roosevelt Rd., Bldg. C-312 Glen Ellyn, IL 60137. Phone: (630)942-6585; Fax: (630)790-3095; Email: info@nacdmeetings.org • URL: http://www.nacd.net • Represents packaging distributors who supply bottles, lubes, pumps, sprayers, and related components. Services include warehousing and labeling.

**National Association of Convenience Stores.** 1600 Duke St., 7th Fl. Alexandria, VA 22314. Phone: 800-966-6227 or (703)684-3600; Fax: (703)836-4564; Email: nacs@nacsonline.com • URL: http://www.nacsonline.com • Members are small retail stores that sell a variety of food and nonfood items and that usually have extended hours of opening.

**National Association of Corporate Directors.** 2001 Pennsylvania Ave. NW, Ste. 500 Washington, DC 20006. Phone: (202)775-0509; Fax: (202)775-4857; Email: join@nacdonline.org • URL: http://www.nacdonline.org • Corporate directors and boards of directors; chief executive officers, presidents, accountants, lawyers, consultants, and other executives are members. Conducts research, surveys, and seminars.

**National Association of Corporate Treasurers.** 12100 Sunset Hills Rd., Ste. 130 Reston, VA 20190. Phone: (703)437-4377; Fax: (703)435-4390; Email: nact@nact.org • URL: http://www.nact.org • Members are corporate financial executives.

**National Association of Counties.** 25 Massachusetts Ave. NW, Ste. 500 Washington, DC 20001. Phone: 888-407-6226 or (202)393-6226; Fax: (202)393-2630; Email: naco@naco.org • URL: http://www.naco.org • Formerly National Association of County Human Services Administrators.

**National Association of County Collectors, Treasurers and Finance Officers.** PO Box 385 Stanton, NE 68779. Phone: (402)439-2223; Fax: (402)439-2262 • URL: http://www.nacctfo.org • Elected and appointed county treasurers, tax collectors and finance officers. Promotes improved and efficient operating and financial procedures in the financial administration of county tax revenue collection.

**National Association of County Park and Recreation Officials.** c/o Brenda Adams-Weyant, Association Manager, PO Box 74 Marienville, PA 16239. Phone: (814)927-8212; Fax: (814)927-6659 • URL: http://www.nacpro.org • Members are elected or appointed county government officials with parks and/or recreation advisory, administrative, or policy-making authority. Stimulates interest in county park and recreation resources and works to obtain more effective use of public and privately owned land and water areas.

**National Association of County Planners.** 440 1st St. NW, 8th Fl. Washington, DC 20001. Phone: (202)661-8807; Fax: (202)737-0480; Email: jdavenpo@naco.org • URL: http://www.countyplanning.org • Formerly National Association of County Planning Directors.

**National Association of Credit Management.** 8840 Columbia 100 Pkwy. Columbia, MD 21045-2158. Phone: (410)740-5560; Fax: (410)740-5574; Email: nacm_national@nacm.org • URL: http://www.nacm.org • Formerly National Institute of Credit.

**National Association of Criminal Defense Lawyers.** 1660 L St. NW, 12th Fl. Washington, DC 20036. Phone: (202)872-8600; Fax: (202)872-8690; Email: assist@nacdl.org • URL: http://www.nacdl.org • Formerly National Association of Defense Lawyers in Criminal Cases.

**National Association of Decorative Fabric Distributors.** 1 Windsor Cove, Ste. 305 Columbia, SC 29223-1833. Phone: 800-445-8629 or (803)765-0860; Email: info@nadfd.com •

URL: http://www.nadfd.com • Formerly National Association of Upholstery Fabric Distributors.

**National Association of Elevator Contractors.** 1298 Wellbrook Cir. Conyers, GA 30012. Phone: 800-900-6232 or (770)760-9660; Fax: (770)760-9714; Email: info@naec.org • URL: http://www.naec.org • Contractors who install and service elevators and lift equipment; suppliers of complete elevators and components.

**National Association of Entrepreneurial Parents.** PO Box 320722 Fairfield, CT 06825. Phone: (203)371-6212; Fax: (203)371-6212 • URL: http://www.en-parent.com • Seeks to assist "parents who are looking to balance work and family on their own terms." Facilitates networking among entrepreneurial parents; provides ad opportunities for members; organizes support groups for members; makes available discount programs and services to members.

**National Association of Environmental Professionals.** PO Box 460 Collingswood, NJ 08108. Phone: 866-251-9902 or (856)283-7816; Fax: (856)210-1619; Email: naep@bowermanagementservices.com • URL: http://www.naep.org • Promotes ethical practice, technical competency, and professional standards in the environment field. Provides access to the latest trends in environmental research, technology, law, and policy.

**National Association of Export Companies.** Grand Central Station New York, NY 10163. Phone: 877-291-4901; Fax: (646)349-9628; Email: director@nexco.org • URL: http://www.nexco.org • Established independent international trade firms, bilateral chambers of commerce, banks, law firms, accounting firms, trade associations, insurance companies, and product/service providers; export trading companies; export management companies. Promotes expansion of U.S. trade. Promotes the participation of members in international trade. Conducts educational programs.

**National Association of Farm Business Analysis Specialists.** PO Box 467 Camp Point, IL 62320. Phone: (217)593-7233; Fax: (217)593-7239 • URL: http://www.nafbas.org • Aims to advance comparative farm business analysis techniques. Provides opportunities for farm business analysis specialists to exchange ideas and methods. Encourages and promotes the professional competence of members.

**National Association of Federal Credit Unions.** 3138 10th St. N Arlington, VA 22201-2149. Phone: 800-336-4644; Email: fbecker@nafcu.org • URL: http://www.nafcu.org • Serves as federally-chartered credit unions. Offers legislative and regulatory advocacy, compliance assistance, training and professional development and a range of products. Provides information on the latest industry developments and proposed and final regulations. Represents members' interests before federal regulatory bodies and Congress. Compiles statistics and holds educational conferences.

**National Association of Financial and Estate Planning.** 515 E 4500 S, No. G-200 Salt Lake City, UT 84107. Phone: 800-454-2649; Fax: (877)890-0929 or (801)266-9900; Email: info@accuplan.net • URL: http://www.nafep.com • Represents financial and estate planners.

**National Association of Financial Services.** Tauentzienstrasse 12 D-10787 Berlin, Germany. Phone: 49 30 23003504 or 49 30 20454403; Fax: 49 30 23003562 or 49 30 20634759; Email: fifaeg@t-online.de • URL: http://www.fifa.de • Promotes the financial industry in Germany. Seeks to develop the field of financial services. Provides information on the financial industry.

**National Association of Flavors and Food-Ingredient Systems.** 3301 Rte. 66, Bldg. C, Ste. 205 Neptune, NJ 07753. Phone: (732)922-3218; Fax: (732)922-3590; Email: info@naffs.org • URL: http://www.naffs.org • Manufacturers of fruit and syrup toppings, flavors and stabilizers for the food industry. Formerly National Association of Fruits, Flavors and Syrups.

**National Association of Flight Instructors.** 3101 E Milham Ave. Portage, MI 49002. Phone: 866-806-6156; Email: nafi@nafinet.org • URL: http://www.nafinet.org • Flight instructors certified by the Federal Aviation Administration. Works to raise the professional standards of the flight instructor through education and organization. Serves as a central point for dissemination of knowledge, methodology, and new information relative to flight instruction. Supports improved legislation concerning pilot training, certification, and aviation regulations. Works with all segments of the industry for improvement of flight education, efficiency, and safety. Compiles statistics.

**National Association of Flour Distributors.** 5350 Woodland Pl. Canfield, OH 44406. Phone: (330)718-6563; Fax: (877)573-1230 • URL: http://www.thenafd.com • Affiliated with National Association of Wholesaler-Distributors.

**National Association of Government Employees.** 159 Burgin Pkwy. Quincy, MA 02169. Phone: 866-412-7762 or (617)376-0220 or (617)472-7566; Fax: (617)376-0285 or (617)472-7566; Email: membership@nage.org • URL: http://www.nage.org • Supersedes Federal Employees Veterans Association.

**National Association of Health and Educational Facilities Finance Authorities.** PO Box 906 Oakhurst, NJ 07755. Phone: 888-414-5713; Fax: (888)414-5713 • URL: http://www.naheffa.com • Serves the common interests and improves effectiveness of member authorities through communication, education, and advocacy, with emphasis on issues which directly influence the availability of or access to tax-exempt financing for healthcare facilities.

**National Association of Health Underwriters**. 1212 New York Ave. NW, Ste. 1100 Washington, DC 20005. Phone: (202)552-5060; Fax: (202)747-6820; Email: info@nahu.org • URL: http://www.nahu.org • Members are engaged in the sale of health and disability insurance. Formerly International Association of Health Underwriters.

**National Association of Home Based Businesses**. 5432 Price Ave. Baltimore, MD 21215. Phone: (410)367-5308 or (410)367-5309; Email: nahbb@msn.com • URL: http://www.usahomebusiness.com • Affiliated with International Association for Business Organizations and the Small Business Network.

**National Association of Home Builders - Systems Builder Council** . 1201 15th St. NW Washington, DC 20005. Phone: 800-368-5242 or (202)266-8200; Fax: (202)266-8400 • URL: http://www.nahb.org/reference_list.aspx?sectionID=815 • Formerly Home Manufacturers Councils of NAHB.

**National Association of Housing and Redevelopment Officials**. 630 Eye St. NW Washington, DC 20001-3736. Phone: 877-866-2476 or (202)289-3500; Fax: (202)289-8181; Email: nahro@nahro.org • URL: http://www.nahro.org • Formerly National Association of Housing Officials.

**National Association of Independent Insurance Adjusters**. 1880 Radcliff Ct. Tracy, CA 95376. Phone: (209)832-6962; Fax: (630)832-6964; Email: admin@naiia.com • URL: http://www.naiia.org • Claims adjusters and firms operating independently on a fee basis for all insurance companies. Originator of adjusters educational program administered by Insurance Institute of America.

**National Association of Independent Real Estate Brokers**. 7102 Mardyke Ln. Indianapolis, IN 46226. Phone: (317)547-4679; Email: director@nationalrealestatebrokers.org • URL: http://nationalrealestatebrokers.org • Aims to educate independent real estate brokers and real estate agents. Promotes the value of independent real estate brokers and real estate agents nationwide through national promotional campaigns. Works to introduce the general public to independent real estate brokers and real estate agents, their real estate companies and the benefits they offer.

**National Association of Independent Schools**. 1129 20th St. NW, Ste. 800 Washington, DC 20036-3425. Phone: (202)973-9700; Fax: (888)316-3862 or (202)973-9790; Email: info@nais.org • URL: http://www.nais.org • Independent elementary and secondary school members; regional associations of independent schools and related associations. Provides curricular and administrative research and services. Conducts educational programs; compiles statistics.

**National Association of Industrial and Office Properties**. 2201 Cooperative Way, Ste. 300 Herndon, VA 20171-3034. Phone: (703)904-7100; Fax: (703)904-7942 • URL: http://www.naiop.org • Members are owners and developers of business, industrial, office, and retail properties. Formerly The Association of Commercial Real Estate.

**National Association of Insurance and Financial Advisors**. 2901 Telestar Ct. Falls Church, VA 22042-1205. Phone: 877-866-2432; Email: membersupport@naifa.org • URL: http://www.naifa.org • Affiliated with Association for Advanced Life Underwriting. Formerly National Association of Life Underwriters.

**National Association of Insurance Commissioners**. 1100 Walnut St., Ste. 1500 Kansas City, MO 64106-2277. Phone: (816)842-3600; Fax: (816)783-8175 • URL: http://www.naic.org • Members are state officials involved in the regulation of insurance companies. Formerly National Convention of Insurance Commissioners.

**National Association of Investors Corporation**. PO Box 220 Royal Oak, MI 48068-0220. Phone: 877-275-6242 or (248)583-6242; Fax: (248)583-4880; Email: service@betterinvesting.org • URL: http://www.betterinvesting.org • Affiliated with Investment Education Institute. Formerly National Association of Investment Clubs.

**National Association of Manufacturers**. 733 10th St. NW, Ste. 700 Washington, DC 20001. Phone: 800-814-8468 or (202)637-3000; Fax: (202)637-3182; Email: manufacturing@nam.org • URL: http://www.nam.org • Manufacturers and cooperating non-manufacturers having a direct interest in or relationship to manufacturing. Represents industry's views on national and international problems to government. Maintains public affairs and public relations programs. Reviews current and proposed legislation, administrative rulings and interpretations, judicial decisions and legal matters affecting industry. Maintains numerous policy groups: Human Resources Policy; Small and Medium Manufacturers; Tax Policy; Resources & Environmental Policy; Regulation and Legal Reform Policy; International Economic Affairs. Affiliated with 150 local and state trade associations of manufacturers through National Industrial Council and 250 manufacturing trade associations through the Associations Council.

**National Association of Margarine Manufacturers**. 1156 15th St. NW, Ste. 900 Washington, DC 20005. Phone: (202)785-3232; Fax: (202)223-9741; Email: namm@kellencompany.com • URL: http://www.margarine.org • Margarine manufacturers, distributors and industry suppliers. Represents members' legislative and regulatory interests. Develops and disseminates information about margarine and margarine products to the public.

**National Association of Marine Services**. 5458 Wagon Master Dr. Colorado Springs, CO 80917. Phone: (719)573-5946; Fax: (719)573-5952; Email: nams@namsshipchandler.com • URL: http://www.namsshipchandler.com • Affiliated with International Ship Suppliers Association. Formerly National Associated Marine Suppliers.

**National Association of Minority Automobile Dealers**. 9745 Lottsford Rd., Ste. 150 Largo, MD 20774. Phone: (301)306-1614; Fax: (301)306-1493 • URL: http://www.namad.org • Automobile dealers. Acts as liaison between membership, the federal government, the community, and industry representatives; seeks to better the business conditions of its members on an ongoing basis. Serves as a confidential spokesperson for dealers. Offers business analysis, financial counseling, and short- and long-term management planning. Conducts research programs; compiles statistics.

**National Association of Minority Government Contractors**. PO Box 44609 Washington, DC 20026. Email: info@namgc.org • URL: http://www.namgc.org • Focuses on enhancing diversification in the workplace. Provides opportunities for the federal, state and local government sector to find key resources in order to engage in contracting opportunities. Provides members with networking, information and services which will connect them with federal, state and local government contracting opportunities.

**National Association of Mortgage Processors**. 1250 Connecticut Ave. NW, Ste. 200 Washington, DC 20036. Phone: 800-977-1197 or (202)261-6505; Fax: (202)318-0655; Email: contact@mortgageprocessor.org • URL: http://www.mortgageprocessor.org • Represents mortgage processors. Assists contract loan processors as well as in-house mortgage loan processors in all aspects of their businesses. Offers services such as training classes, blog cafe, community discussion, certification programs and download library.

**National Association of Mutual Insurance Companies**. 3601 Vincennes Rd. Indianapolis, IN 46268. Phone: (317)875-5250; Fax: (317)879-8408 • URL: http://www.namic.org • Affiliated with Crop Insurance Research Bureau and the Insurance Loss Control Association.

**National Association of Parliamentarians**. 213 S Main St. Independence, MO 64050-3808. Phone: 888-627-2929 or (816)833-3892; Fax: (816)833-3893; Email: hq@nap2.org • URL: http://www.parliamentarians.org • Represents persons interested in parliamentary procedure. Works to study, teach, promote, and disseminate the democratic principles of parliamentary law and procedure. Conducts examination and awards title of Registered Parliamentarian. Maintains referral service of Professional Registered Parliamentarians.

**National Association of Personal Financial Advisors**. 3250 N Arlington Heights Rd., Ste. 109 Arlington Heights, IL 60004. Phone: 888-333-6659 or (847)483-5400; Fax: (847)483-5415; Email: info@napfa.org • URL: http://www.napfa.org • Members are full-time financial planners who are compensated on a fee-only basis.

**National Association of Personnel Services**. 78 Dawson Village Way, Ste. 410-201 Dawsonville, GA 30534. Phone: (706)531-0060; Fax: (866)739-4750 • URL: http://www.naps360.org • Members are private employment agencies. Formerly National Association of Personnel Consultants.

**National Association of Pharmaceutical Sales Representatives**. 2020 Pennsylvania Ave. NW, Ste. 5050 Washington, DC 20006-1811. Phone: 800-284-1060; Email: contact@napsronline.org • URL: http://www.napsronline.org • Represents sales representatives, sales managers and sales trainers who work in the pharmaceutical industry. Provides Continuing Medical Education to members as well as candidates who wish to start a pharmaceutical sales career. Aims to educate, train, create standards and provide current information for professional pharmaceutical sales representatives as well as for individuals who want to gain entry into the industry.

**National Association of Photo Equipment Technicians**. c/o Worldwide Community of Imaging Associations, 2282 Springport Rd., Ste. F Jackson, MI 49202. Phone: 800-762-9287 or (517)788-8100; Fax: (517)788-8371 • URL: http://www.pmai.org/napet • Affiliated with Photo Marketing Association International.

**National Association of Plumbing, Heating, Cooling Contractors**. 180 S Washington St., Ste. 100 Falls Church, VA 22046. Phone: 800-533-7694 or (703)237-8100; Fax: (703)237-7442; Email: naphcc@naphcc.org • URL: http://www.phccweb.org • Federation of state and local associations of plumbing, heating, and cooling contractors. Seeks to advance sanitation, encourage sanitary laws, and generally improve the plumbing, heating, ventilating, and air conditioning industries. Conducts apprenticeship training programs, workshops, seminars, political action committee, educational and research programs.

**National Association of Power Engineers**. 1 Springfield St. Chicopee, MA 01013. Phone: (413)592-6273; Fax: (413)592-1998; Email: nape@powerengineers.com • URL: http://www.powerengineers.com • Professional society of power and stationary engineers; associate members are sales engineers and teachers of any phase of engineering. Areas of interest include air conditioning, compressed air, electric power, refrigeration, steam, and water. Promotes education in the power engineering areas. Secures and enforces engineers' license laws to prevent the destruction of life and property in the generation and transmission of power and for the conservation of fuel resources of the nation.

**National Association of Printing Ink Manufacturers**. 15 Technology Pkwy. S Peachtree Corners, GA 30092. Phone: (770)209-7289; Fax: (678)680-4920 • URL: http://www.napim.org • Formerly National Association of Printing Ink Makers.

**National Association of Private Enterprise**. Blvd. del Hipodromo 542 Col. San Benito San Salvador, El Salvador. Phone: 503 2209-8300; Fax: 503 2209-8317; Email: comunicaciones@anep.org.sv • URL: http://www.anep.org.sv • Promotes the enterprise sector of El Salvador.

**National Association of Produce Market Managers**. PO Box 1617 Garner, NC 27529-1617. Phone: (919)779-5258 • URL: http://www.napmm.org • Produce market managers and industrial produce dealers; associate members are county agents and state employees in agriculture. Seeks to improve market conditions.

**National Association of Professional Asian American Women**. 304 Oak Knoll Terr. Rockville, MD 20850. Phone: (301)785-8585; Email: napaw@comcast.net • URL: http://www.napaw.org • Represents the professional interests of Asian-American women. Promotes continued personal and professional development; works to enhance career opportunities. Encourages greater visibility of Asian-American women in public decision-making. Conducts educational programs.

**National Association of Professional Insurance Agents**. 400 N Washington St. Alexandria, VA 22314. Phone: (703)836-9340; Fax: (703)836-1279; Email: web@pianet.org • URL: http://www.pianet.com • Members are independent agents in various fields of insurance. Formerly National Association of Mutual Insurance Agents.

**National Association of Psychiatric Health System**. 900 17th St. NW, Ste. 420 Washington, DC 20006-2507. Phone: (202)393-6700; Fax: (202)783-6041; Email: naphs@naphs.org • URL: http://www.naphs.org • Formerly National Association of Private Psychiatric Hospitals.

**National Association of Quick Printers**. c/o Mitch Evans, Chairman, Mitch Evans Consulting, 8 Driftwood Cottage Ln. Daufuskie Island, SC 29915. Phone: (561)351-6950; Email: mitch@mitchevansconsulting.com • URL: http://napl.org/naqp • Independent printers and printing franchise businesses; industry suppliers. Seeks to bring recognition, improved quality, and increased profits to the entire quick printing field. Provides services to members; works to advance the collective interests of the printing industries at the national and international levels.

**National Association of Railroad Passengers**. 505 Capitol Ct. NE, Ste. 300 Washington, DC 20002-7706. Phone: (202)408-8362; Fax: (202)408-8287; Email: narp@narprail.org • URL: http://www.narprail.org • Users of rail passenger service, other concerned individuals, and organizations wishing to improve and expand rail passenger service. Seeks to increase public awareness and understanding of rail passenger service and its benefits. Works for fair and equal treatment for rail passenger service by government, in relation to other forms of transportation, and in the areas of defense transportation, mail transportation, taxation and user charges, and research and development expenditures. Seeks the establishment of a national transportation policy that includes rail passenger service as an essential element; initiates specific rail passenger improvements with appropriate government and transportation officials.

**National Association of Railway Business Women**. c/o Amy Schapp, Membership Chairperson, 5109 S 194th St. Omaha, NE 68135. Email: narbwinfo@narbw.org • URL: http://www.narbw.org • Formerly Railway Business Women's Association.

**National Association of Real Estate Appraisers**. 810 N Farrell Dr. Palm Springs, CA 92262. Phone: 877-743-6806; Fax: (760)327-5631; Email: info@narea-assoc.org • URL: http://www.narea-assoc.org • Real estate appraisers. Aims to make available the services of the most highly qualified real estate appraisers. Offers certification to members.

**National Association of Real Estate Brokers**. 9831 Greenbelt Rd. Lanham, MD 20706. Phone: (301)552-9340; Fax: (301)552-9216; Email: info@nareb.com • URL: http://www.nareb.com • Members of the real estate industry. Research, educational and certification programs include: Real Estate Management Brokers Institute; National Society of Real Estate Appraisers; Real Estate Brokerage Institute; United Developers Council. Encourages unity among those who are engaged in real estate. Promotes and maintains high standards of conduct. Protects the public against unethical, improper, or fraudulent practices connected with the real estate business. Conducts research; compiles statistics on productivity, marketing and development. Gives members license to use "Realtist" symbol. Sponsors educational seminars. Maintains Willis E. Carson Library.

**National Association of Real Estate Consultants**. 404 4th Ave. Lewiston, ID 83501. Phone: (208)746-7963; Fax: (208)746-4760 • URL: http://www.narec.com • Works to assist real estate professionals in reframing their focus as real estate consultants to better meet the needs of today's savvy consumer. Helps promote alternative or fee-for-service real estate business models.

**National Association of Real Estate Investment Trusts**. 1875 I St. NW, Ste. 600 Washington, DC 20006-5413. Phone: 800-

362-7348 or (202)739-9400; Fax: (202)739-9401; Email: baiken@nareit.com • URL: http://www.reit.com • Formerly National Association of Real Estste Investment Funds.

**National Association of Realtors**. 430 N Michigan Ave. Chicago, IL 60611-4087. Phone: 800-874-6500; Email: infocentral@realtors.org • URL: http://www.realtor.org • Federation of 54 state and territory associations and 1,860 local real estate boards whose members are real estate brokers and agents; terms are registered by the association in the U.S. Patent and Trademark Office and in the states. Promotes education, high professional standards and modern techniques in specialized real estate work such as brokerage, appraisal, property management, land development, industrial real estate, farm brokerage and counseling. Conducts research programs.

**National Association of Regulatory Utility Commissioners**. 1101 Vermont Ave. NW, Ste. 200 Washington, DC 20005-3553. Phone: (202)898-2200; Fax: (202)898-2213; Email: admin@naruc.org • URL: http://www.naruc.org • Formerly National Association of Railway and Utility Commissioners.

**National Association of Rocketry**. PO Box 407 Marion, IA 52302-0407. Phone: 800-262-4872; Fax: (319)373-8910; Email: nar-hq@nar.org • URL: http://www.nar.org • Model rockets. Formerly Model Missile Association.

**National Association of RV Parks and Campgrounds**. 9085 E Mineral Cir., Ste. 200 Centennial, CO 80112. Phone: (303)681-0401; Fax: (303)681-0426; Email: info@arvc.org • URL: http://www.arvc.org • Formerly National Campground Owners Association.

***National Association of Schools of Music—Directory***. National Association of Schools of Music, 11250 Roger Bacon Dr., Ste. 21 Reston, VA 20190-5248. Phone: (703)437-0700; Fax: (703)437-6312; Email: info@arts-accredit.org • URL: http://nasm.arts-accredit.org • Annual. $20 Individuals. Covers: Approximately 630 college and university departments of music and music conservatories accredited by the association. Entries include: School name, address, type of membership, description of music program, name of chief administrator, phone, degree or other study programs offered in music.

**National Association of Service Managers**. PO Box 250796 Milwaukee, WI 53225-6512. Phone: (414)466-6060 or (414)847-1200; Fax: (414)466-0840; Email: kenc@kencook.com • URL: http://www.nasm.com • Absorbed Service Managers of America.

**National Association of Settlement Purchasers**. c/o Susan Barnes, Association Administrator, 720 Collier Dr. Dixon, CA 95620. Phone: (707)888-2647; Email: susan@barnescompany.com • URL: http://www.nasp-usa.com • Finance companies that purchase structured settlements from individuals for a lump sum (structured settlements are received by individuals as redress for personal injury or other liability). Seeks to insure ethical practice in the trading of structured settlements; promotes advancement of the structured settlement purchasing industry. Serves as a clearinghouse on the purchase of structured settlements; lobbies for reform of regulations governing the trade in structured settlements.

**National Association of Small Business Contractors**. 700 12th St. NW, Ste. 700 Washington, DC 20005. Phone: 888-861-9290 • URL: http://www.nasbc.org • Serves and advances the interests of small business contractors. Seeks to establish opportunities for small business owners to meet with state and federal agencies, prime contractors, potential teaming partners and procurement experts. Strives to create a strong and respected voice for advocacy in support of small business' interests.

**National Association of Sporting Goods Wholesalers**. 1833 Centre Point Cir., Ste. 123 Naperville, IL 60563. Phone: (630)596-9006; Fax: (630)544-5055; Email: info@nasgw.org • URL: http://www.nasgw.org • Represents wholesalers and manufacturers of primarily fishing tackle and shooting equipment.

**National Association of State and Local Equity Funds**. 1970 Broadway, Ste. 250 Oakland, CA 94612. Phone: (510)444-1101; Fax: (510)444-1191; Email: info@naslef.org • URL: http://www.naslef.org • Promotes efficient management of state and local equity funds. Represents individuals, public and private corporations and professional associations with an interest in the tax credit program or an active involvement with a state or local equity fund. Fosters greater understanding of the Low Income Housing Tax Credit (LIHTC).

**National Association of State Aviation Officials**. Washington National Airport, Hangar 7, Ste. 218 Washington, DC 20001. Phone: (703)417-1883; Email: info@nasao.org • URL: http://www.nasao.org • Represents state aeronautics commissions or departments (including those in Guam and Puerto Rico) that promote, administer, and regulate aviation, and seek uniform aviation laws. Sponsors National Association of State Aviation Officials Center for Aviation Research and Education.

**National Association of State Boards of Accountancy**. 150 4th Ave. N, Ste. 700 Nashville, TN 37219-2417. Phone: 866-MY-NASBA or (615)880-4200; Fax: (615)880-4290; Email: cbtcpa@nasba.org • URL: http://nasba.org • Formerly Association of Certified Public Accountants.

**National Association of State Budget Officers**. Hall of the States Bldg., 444 N Capitol St. NW, Ste. 642 Washington, DC 20001-1556. Phone: (202)624-5382 or (202)624-8804; Fax: (202)624-7745; Email: nasbo-direct@nasbo.org • URL: http://www.nasbo.org • Budget directors, their deputies, and superior officers of the states and territories. Seeks to encourage study and research in state budgeting and promote cooperation and efficiency in budget programs. Conducts budget and legislative briefing every spring and four to five educational seminars each year.

**National Association of State Charity Officials**. c/o Alissa Gardenswartz, 1300 Broadway, 7th Fl. Denver, CO 80203. • URL: http://www.nasconet.org • Members are state officials responsible for the administration of charitable solicitation laws.

**National Association of State Departments of Agriculture**. 1156 15th St. NW, Ste. 1020 Washington, DC 20005. Phone: (202)296-9680; Fax: (202)296-9686; Email: nasda@nasda.org • URL: http://www.nasda.org • Directors of state and territorial departments of agriculture. Coordinates policies, procedures, laws, and activities between the states and federal agencies and Congress. Conducts research.

**National Association of State Directors of Veterans Affairs**. 107 S West St., Ste. 550 Alexandria, VA 22314. Phone: (334)242-5075; Fax: (334)353-5072 • URL: http://www.nasdva.us • Directors of veterans' affairs for state governments. Serves as medium for exchange of ideas among state veterans' officers. Maintains liaison with all congressionally chartered veterans' organizations.

**National Association of State Mental Health Program Directors**. 66 Canal Ctr. Plz., Ste. 302 Alexandria, VA 22314. Phone: (703)739-9333; Fax: (703)548-9517 • URL: http://www.nasmhpd.org • Promotes cooperation of state government agencies in delivery of services to people with severe mental illnesses; fosters the exchange of scientific and programmatic information in the administration of public mental health programs including treatment programs, community and hospital care of persons with mental illness, mental retardation, or substance abuse disorders. Monitors state and federal and congressional activities; gathers and analyzes information on organization, structure, funding, and programming of state government mental health programs. Operates under a cooperative agreement with the National Governors' Association.

**National Association of State Procurement Officials**. 201 E Main St., Ste. 1405 Lexington, KY 40507-2004. Phone: (859)514-9159; Fax: (859)514-9166; Email: headquarters@naspo.org • URL: http://www.naspo.org • Purchasing officials of the states and territories. Formerly National Association of State Purchasing Officials.

**National Association of Student Financial Aid Administrators**. 1101 Connecticut Ave. NW, Ste. 1100 Washington, DC 20036-4312. Phone: (202)785-0453; Fax: (202)785-1487; Email: web@nasfaa.org • URL: http://www.nasfaa.org • Serves as a national forum for matters related to student aid.

**National Association of Superintendents of U.S. Naval Shore Establishments**. 89 Pine Legde Dr. Wells, ME 04090. Phone: (207)646-7316; Email: admin@nasnse.org • URL: http://nasnse.org • Superintendents of production, maintenance, and public works branches of naval shore establishments. Promotes the general welfare of members professionally, intellectually, and socially; cultivates high standards of professional ethics.

**National Association of Supervisor of Business Education**. c/o Melissa Scott, Treasurer, 9890 S Maryland Pkwy., Ste. 221 Las Vegas, NV 89183. Phone: (702)486-6625 or (303)982-6654; Fax: (702)668-4321 • URL: http://www.nasbe.us • Acts as a representative voice for local supervisors of business and office education programs in public and private schools. Supports programs and activities in cooperation with the American Vocational Association and other business education organizations.

**National Association of Tax Professionals**. PO Box 8002 Appleton, WI 54914-8002. Phone: 800-558-3402; Fax: (800)747-0001; Email: natp@natptax.com • URL: http://www.natptax.com/Pages/default.aspx • Promotes high professional standards for tax practitioners. Formerly National Association for Tax Practitioners.

**National Association of Television Program Executives**. Phone: (310)857-1621 • URL: http://www.natpe.org • Formerly National Association of Television Program Executives.

**National Association of the Remodeling Industry**. PO Box 4250 Des Plaines, IL 60016. Phone: (847)298-9200; Fax: (847)298-9225; Email: info@nari.org • URL: http://www.nari.org • Represents remodeling contractors, manufacturers of remodeling/building products, lending institutions and wholesalers and distributors. Promotes the common business interests of those engaged in the home improvement and remodeling industries. Encourages ethical conduct, good business practices and professionalism in the remodeling industry. Conducts seminars, workshops and promotional programs and has developed an extensive certification program. Local chapters monitor legislations and regulations affecting the industry.

**National Association of Theatre Owners**. 750 1st St. NE, Ste. 1130 Washington, DC 20002. Phone: (202)962-0054; Fax: (202)962-0370; Email: nato@natodc.com • URL: http://www.natoonline.org • Owners, operators and executives of motion picture theaters. Provides services to assist theater owners in successfully operating their theaters including monitoring legislative and technological advancements; compiles statistics.

**National Association of Towns and Townships**. 1130 Connecticut Ave. NW, Ste. 300 Washington, DC 20036. Phone: 866-830-0008 or (202)454-3954 or (202)454-3950; Fax: (202)331-1598; Email: jimo@tfgnet.com • URL: http://www.natat.org • Provides technical and other assistance to officials of small communities.

**National Association of Video Distributors**. 16530 Ventura Blvd., Ste. 400 Encino, CA 91436. Phone: (818)385-1500; Fax: (818)385-1500 • URL: http://navdonline.org • Promotes the home video products industry. Conducts industry-wide programs in areas such as public, government, and industry relations.

**National Association of Waterfront Employers**. 919 18th St. NW, Ste. 901 Washington, DC 20006. Phone: (202)587-4800; Fax: (202)587-4888; Email: mto@nawe.us • URL: http://www.nawe.us • Formerly National Association of Stevedoves.

**National Association of Wheat Growers**. 415 2nd St. NE, Ste. 300 Washington, DC 20002. Phone: (202)547-7800; Email: wheatworld@wheatworld.org • URL: http://www.wheatworld.org • Federation of 19 state wheat growers associations. Represents wheat grower interest in educational, legislative, and regulatory projects and issues for wheat farmers in Washington, DC. Sponsors research and transportation, and leadership conferences; conducts seminars. Conducts charitable programs.

**National Association of Wholesaler-Distributors**. 1325 G St. NW, Ste. 1000 Washington, DC 20005. Phone: (202)872-0885; Fax: (202)785-0586; Email: naw@naw.org • URL: http://www.naw.org • Formerly National Association of Wholesalers.

**National Association of Women Artists**. 80 5th Ave., Ste. 1405 New York, NY 10011. Phone: (212)675-1616; Email: office@thenawa.org • URL: http://www.thenawa.org • Formerly Women's Art Club of the City of New York.

**National Association of Women Business Owners**. 601 Pennsylvania Ave. NW, South Bldg., Ste. 900 Washington, DC 20004. Phone: 800-556-2926; Fax: (202)403-3788; Email: national@nawbo.org • URL: http://www.nawbo.org • Formerly Association of Women Business Owners.

**National Association of Women in Construction**. 327 S Adams St. Fort Worth, TX 76104. Phone: 800-552-3506 or (817)877-5551; Fax: (817)877-0324; Email: nawic@nawic.org • URL: http://www.nawic.org • Seeks to enhance the success of women in the construction industry.

***National Association of Women Lawyers. President's Newsletter***. National Association of Women Lawyers, American Bar Ctr. MS 21.1, 321 N Clark St. Chicago, IL 60654-4714. Phone: (312)988-6186; Fax: (312)988-5100; Email: nawl@nawl.org • URL: http://www.nawl.org • Quarterly. Newsletter. Price on application.

**National Association of Women Lawyers**. American Bar Ctr. MS 21.1, 321 N Clark St. Chicago, IL 60654-4714. Phone: (312)988-6186; Fax: (312)988-5100; Email: nawl@nawl.org • URL: http://www.nawl.org • Membership is open to any person who is a member in good standing of the bar of any state or U.S. territory, any non-U.S. legal professional (attorney or judge), any prospective attorney currently attending law school, and any state or local bar or law school association with compatible objectives. Men are welcome and encouraged to join.

**National Association of Women MBAs**. Rice University, PO Box 2932 Houston, TX 77251-2932. Email: philana.kiely@mbawomen.org • URL: http://www.mbawomen.org • Provides networking opportunities for its members. Increases communication among graduate business schools regarding their initiatives to educate and support women in business.

**National Auctioneers Association**. 8880 Ballentine St. Overland Park, KS 66214. Phone: (913)541-8084; Fax: (913)894-5281 or (913)548-0932; Email: support@auctioneers.org • URL: http://www.auctioneers.org • Professional auctioneers. Provides continuing education classes for auctioneers, promotes use of the auction method of marketing in both the private and public sectors. Encourages the highest ethical standards for the profession.

**National Auto Auction Association**. 5320 Spectrum Dr., Ste. D Frederick, MD 21703. Phone: (301)696-0400; Fax: (301)631-1359; Email: naaa@naaa.com • URL: http://www.naaa.com • Owners/operators of wholesale automobile and truck auctions; associate members are car and truck manufacturers, insurers of checks and titles, car and truck rental companies, publishers of auto price guide books, and others connected with the industry. Maintains hall of fame.

***National Automatic Merchandising Association-Directory of Members***. National Automatic Merchandising Association, 20 N Wacker Dr., Ste. 3500 Chicago, IL 60606-3102. Phone: 888-337-8363 or (312)346-0370; Fax: (312)704-4140; Email: dgary@vending.org • URL: http://www.vending.org • Annual. Lists vending and food service management firms, along with vending machine manufacturers and distributors and producers of other equipment and food items.

**National Automatic Merchandising Association**. 20 N Wacker Dr., Ste. 3500 Chicago, IL 60606-3102. Phone: 888-337-8363 or (312)346-0370; Fax: (312)704-4140; Email: dgary@vending.org • URL: http://www.vending.org • Manufacturing and operating companies in the automatic vending machine industry; food service management firms; office coffee machine operators; suppliers of products and services. Compiles industry statistics.

**National Automobile Dealers Association**. 8400 Westpark Dr. McLean, VA 22102. Phone: 800-252-6232 or (703)821-7000; Fax: (703)821-7234; Email: help@nada.org • URL: http://www.nada.org • Franchised new car and truck dealers. Provides representation for franchised new car and truck dealers in the areas of government, industry, and public affairs. Offers management services and retirement and insurance programs to member dealers. Maintains National Automobile Dealers Charitable Foundation.

**National Bankers Association**. 1513 P St. NW Washington, DC 20005. Phone: (202)588-5432; Fax: (202)588-5443; Email: execdesk@nationalbankers.org • URL: http://www.nationalbankers.org • Minority banking institutions owned by minority individuals and institutions. Serves as an advocate for the minority banking industry. Organizes banking services, government relations, marketing, scholarship, and technical assistance programs. Offers placement services; compiles statistics.

**National Beauty Culturists' League**. 25 Logan Cir. NW Washington, DC 20005-3725. Phone: (202)332-2695; Fax: (202)332-0940; Email: nbcl@bellsouth.net • URL: http://www.nbcl.org • Beauticians, cosmetologists, and beauty products manufacturers. Encourages standardized, scientific, and approved methods of hair, scalp, and skin treatments. Offers scholarships and plans to establish a research center. Sponsors: National Institute of Cosmetology, a training course in operating and designing and business techniques. Maintains hall of fame; conducts research program.

**National Beer Wholesalers Association**. 1101 King St., Ste. 600 Alexandria, VA 22314-2944. Phone: 800-300-6417 or (703)683-4300; Fax: (703)683-8965; Email: info@nbwa.org • URL: http://www.nbwa.org • Independent wholesalers of malt beverages and affiliates of the malt beverage industry. Conducts specialized education programs.

**National Bicycle Dealers Association**. 3176 Pullman St., No. 117 Costa Mesa, CA 92626. Phone: (949)722-6909; Email: info@nbda.com • URL: http://nbda.com • Represents independent retail dealers who sell and service bicycles. Sponsors workshops and provides programs.

**National Black Business Council**. 600 Corporate Pointe, Ste. 1010 Culver City, CA 90230. Phone: (310)585-6222; Email: info@nbbc.org • URL: http://www.nbbc.org • Aims to create and advance black businesses; advocates for expansion of black business procurement.

**National Black Chamber of Commerce**. 4400 Jenifer St. NW, Ste. 331 Washington, DC 20015-2133. Phone: (202)466-6888; Fax: (202)466-4918; Email: info@nationalbcc.org • URL: http://www.nationalbcc.org • Works for the issues of economics and entrepreneurship in the African-American community.

**National Black MBA Association**. 1 E Wacker Ste. 3500 Chicago, IL 60601. Phone: (312)236-2622; Fax: (312)236-0390; Email: info@nbmbaa.org • URL: http://www.nbmbaa.org • Creates educational opportunities to form professional and economic growth of African-Americans. Develops partnerships to its members and provides educational programs to increase the awareness on business field.

***National Bond Summary***. OTC Markets Group Inc., 304 Hudson St., 3rd Fl. New York, NY 10013. Phone: 800-547-8682 or (212)896-4420 or (212)896-4400; Fax: (212)868-3848; Email: otcqx@otcmarkets.com • URL: http://www.otcqx.com • Monthly, with semiannual cumulations. $504.00 per year. Includes price quotes for both active and inactive issues, with transfer agents, market makers (brokers), capital changes, name changes, and other corporate information. Formerly published by the National Quotation Bureau.

***National Building Cost Manual***. Craftsman Book Co., 6058 Corte Del Cedro Carlsbad, CA 92011-1514. Phone: 800-829-8123 or (760)438-7828; Fax: (760)438-0398 • URL: http://www.craftsman-book.com • Annual. $63 Individuals.

**National Building Granite Quarries Association**. 1220 L St. NW, Ste. 100-167 Washington, DC 20005. Phone: 800-557-2848 • URL: http://www.nbgqa.com • Represents quarriers and manufacturers of building granites. Provides specifications for designers.

**National Bulk Vendors Association**. 1202 E Maryland Ave., Ste. 1K Phoenix, AZ 85014-1342. Phone: 888-628-2872; Fax: (480)302-5108; Email: admin@nbva.org • URL: http://www.nbva.info • Manufacturers, distributors, and operators of bulk vending merchandise and equipment.

**National Bureau of Certified Consultants**. c/o Peter A. Land Associates, Inc., 4210 Lomac St. Montgomery, AL 36106. Phone: (334)271-2639 • URL: http://www.peteland.com/cpcm.htm • Promotes adherence to high standards of ethics and practice in the field of management consulting. Works to improve management consulting curricula.

**National Bureau of Economic Research**. 1050 Massachusetts Ave. Cambridge, MA 02138-5398. Phone: (617)868-3900 or (617)253-6673; Fax: (617)868-2742; Email: info@nber.org • URL: http://www.nber.org • Conducts analyses of economic issues, including economic growth and fluctuations, productivity, financial institutions, money, international economic problems, taxation, government spending, labor studies, health, and American economic history.

***National Business Aircraft Association—Membership Directory***. National Business Aviation Association, 1200 G St. NW, Ste. 1100 Washington, DC 20005-3830. Phone: (202)783-9000; Fax: (202)331-8364; Email: info@nbaa.org • URL: http://www.nbaa.org • Periodic.

**National Business Aviation Association**. 1200 G St. NW, Ste. 1100 Washington, DC 20005-3830. Phone: (202)783-9000; Fax: (202)331-8364; Email: info@nbaa.org • URL: http://www.nbaa.org • Companies owning and operating aircraft for business use, suppliers, and maintenance and air fleet service companies. Compiles statistics; provides literature for researchers and students.

***National Business Directory***. Scott's Directories, 12 Concorde Pl., Ste. 800 Toronto, ON, Canada M3C 4J2. Phone: 800-668-2374 or (416)442-2122; Fax: (416)510-6870; Email: customercare@scottsdirectories.com • URL: http://www.scottsdirectories.com • Contains information on more than 308,000 individuals at more than 191,000 companies in Canada.

**National Business Education Association**. 1914 Association Dr. Reston, VA 20191-1596. Phone: (703)860-8300; Fax: (703)620-4483; Email: nbea@nbea.org • URL: http://www.nbea.org • Teachers of business subjects in secondary and postsecondary schools and colleges; administrators and research workers in business education; businesspersons interested in business education; teachers in educational institutions training business teachers; high school and college students preparing for careers in business.

***National Business Education Yearbook***. National Business Education Association, 1914 Association Dr. Reston, VA 20191-1596. Phone: (703)860-8300; Fax: (703)620-4483; Email: nbea@nbea.org • URL: http://www.nbea.org • Annual. $40 Individuals. Written by business education professionals with expertise in this ever-changing field. Refereed publication examines topical business education-related subjects.

**National Business Incubation Association**. 340 W State St., Unit 25 Athens, OH 45701-1565. Phone: (740)593-4331; Fax: (740)593-1996; Email: info@nbia.org • URL: http://www.nbia.org • Incubator developers and managers; corporate joint venture partners, venture capital investors; economic development professionals. (Incubators are business assistance programs providing business consulting services and financing assistance to start-up and fledgling companies.) Helps newly formed businesses to succeed. Educates businesses and investors on incubator benefits; offers specialized training in incubator formation and management. Conducts research and referral services; compiles statistics; maintains speakers' bureau; publishes information relevant to business incubation and growing companies.

**National Business Initiative**. Bldg. D, 3rd Fl., 32 Princess of Wales Terr., Sunnyside Office Park Johannesburg 2193, South Africa. Phone: 27 11 5446000; Fax: 27 11 4842754; Email: info@nbi.org.za • URL: http://www.nbi.org.za • Businesses. Promotes creation and maintenance of a social and economic climate conducive to the domestic development of South Africa. Conducts and assists programs in areas including education, economic growth and equity, enterprise, local government capacity building and transformation and public/private partnerships.

**National Business Officers Association**. 1400 L St. NW, Ste. 850 Washington, DC 20005. Phone: (202)407-7140 or (202)407-7141; Fax: (202)354-4944; Email: jeff.shields@nboa.net • URL: http://www.nboa.net • Independent school business officers. Helps members streamline business and strategic operations.

**National Cable and Telecommunications Association**. 25 Massachusetts Ave. NW, Ste. 100 Washington, DC 20001. Phone: (202)222-2300; Email: webmaster@ncta.com • URL: http://www.ncta.com • Affiliated with Motion Picture Association of America. Formerly National Cable Television Association.

**National Career Development Association**. 305 N Beech Cir. Broken Arrow, OK 74012. Phone: 866-367-6232 or (918)663-7060; Fax: (918)663-7058; Email: webeditor@ncda.org • URL: http://www.ncda.org • Represents professionals and others interested in career development or counseling in various work environments. Supports counselors, education and training personnel, and allied professionals working in schools, colleges, business/industry, community and government agencies, and in private practice. Provides publications, support for state and local activities, human equity programs, and continuing education and training for these professionals. Provides networking opportunities for career professionals in business, education, and government.

**National Catalog Managers Association**. Automotive Aftermarket Industry Association, 7101 Wisconsin Ave., Ste. 1300 Bethesda, MD 20814-3415. Phone: (301)654-6664; Fax: (301)654-3299; Email: ncma@aftermarket.org • URL: http://www.autocare.org/SegmentsDetail.aspx?id=594&gmssopc=1 • Individuals actively engaged in the management, preparation, production, and distribution of automotive product catalogs. Purposes are to: exchange practical and useful ideas in the creation, compilation, production and distribution of catalogs; raise standards of catalogs in automotive and related industries; create a better understanding of the current developments in the field of graphics; establish a professional and fraternal relationship with colleagues; improve professional recognition of the catalog specialist; promote high standards of ethics in the cataloging industry. Operates placement service.

**National Cattlemen's Beef Association**. 9110 E Nichols Ave., Ste. 300 Centennial, CO 80112. Phone: (303)694-0305; Fax: (303)694-2851; Email: information@beef.org • URL: http://www.beefusa.org • Represents 149 organizations of livestock marketers, growers, meat packers, food retailers, and food service firms. Conducts extensive program of promotion, education and information about beef, veal, and associated meat products. Conducts projects such as recipe testing and development, food demonstrations, food photography, educational service to colleges, experimental meat cutting methods, merchandising programs, and preparation of materials for newspapers, magazines, radio, and television.

**National Center for Employee Ownership**. 1736 Franklin St., 8th Fl. Oakland, CA 94612. Phone: (510)208-1300; Fax: (510)272-9510; Email: customerservice@nceo.org • URL: http://www.nceo.org • Association promotes an increased awareness and understanding of employee ownership of companies.

***National Center for Health Statistics: Monitoring the Nation's Health***. National Center for Health Statistics, Centers for Disease Control and Prevention. Phone: (301)458-4000; Email: nchsquery@cdc.gov • URL: http://www.cdc.gov/nchswww • Web site provides detailed data on diseases, vital statistics, and health care in the U. S. Includes a search facility and links to many other health-related Web sites. "Fastats A to Z" offers quick data on hundreds of topics from Accidents to Work-Loss Days, with links to Comprehensive Data and related sources. Frequent updates. Fees: Free.

**National Center for Housing Management**. 1801 Old Reston Ave., Ste. 203 Reston, VA 20190-3356. Phone: 800-368-5625; Email: service@nchm.org • URL: http://www.nchm.org • Purposes are to upgrade and professionalize the housing management industry through training, accreditation of firms, certification of individuals, research, technical assistance, and clearinghouse activities. Funded by performance contracts with federal, state, and local agencies, grants from foundations, and contracts with public and private management and mortgage servicing organizations. Provides training for all levels of housing management and currently awards certifications for occupancy specialists and maintenance managers. Offers technical assistance in compliance with the Fair Housing Act and Section 504 of the Rehabilitation Act of 1973.

**National Center for Manufacturing Sciences**. 3025 Boardwalk Ann Arbor, MI 48108-3230. Phone: 800-222-6267 or (734)995-0300; Fax: (734)995-1150 or (734)995-4004; Email: info@ncms.org • Research areas include process technology and control, machine mechanics, sensors, testing methods, and quality assurance.

**National Center for Policy Analysis**. 14180 Dallas Pkwy., Ste. 350 Dallas, TX 75254. Phone: (972)386-6272; Email: media@ncpa.org • URL: http://www.ncpa.org • Includes studies on medicare.

**National Center for Scientific Research - Institute for Research in the Sociology and Economics of Education**. University of Bourgogne, Pôle AAFE- Esplanade Erasme, BP 26513 F-21065 Dijon, France. Phone: 33 3 80395450; Fax: 33 3 80395479; Email: jean-francois.giret@u-bourgogne.fr • URL: http://iredu.u-bourgogne.fr • Economy, education and sociology.

**National Center for Scientific Research - Research Center for Medicine, Sciences, Health and Society**. CNRS UMR 8169-EHESS-Inserm U750, 7 rue Guy Môquet F-94801 Villejuif, France. Phone: 33 1 49583636; Fax: 33 1 49583438; Email: cermes@vjf.cnrs.fr • URL: http://cermes.vjf.inserm.fr • Health and medicine, including sociology, anthropology, economics, history and history of sciences.

**National Center for State Courts**. 300 Newport Ave. Williamsburg, VA 23185. Phone: 800-616-6164 or (757)259-1525 or (757)259-1826; Fax: (757)220-0449; Email: jcochet@ncsc.org • URL: http://www.ncsc.org • Provides assistance to state and local trial and appellate courts in improving their structure and administration. Furnishes consultant services; conducts national studies and projects; acts as a clearinghouse for exchange of information on court problems; coordinates activities of other organizations involved in judicial improvement, providing secretariat services for several. Conducts conferences and training courses. Compiles statistics on state court caseload and administrative operations. Research includes: appellate procedures, pretrial services, court delay, alternatives to incarceration, juvenile justice, rural court services, alternative dispute resolution, jury management, and sentencing and judicial information systems. Offers placement service.

**National Center on Nonprofit Enterprise**. 205 S Patrick St. Alexandria, VA 22314. Phone: (703)548-7978 or (757)214-5084; Fax: (501)637-2807; Email: richard@nationalcne.org • URL: http://www.nationalcne.org • Represents academic researchers, business leaders, consultants and non-profit practitioners supporting a comprehensive program of educational activities and services addressing economic and business decision-making issues facing the non-profit sector.

**National Certified Pipe Welding Bureau**. 1385 Piccard Dr. Rockville, MD 20850. Phone: 800-556-3653 or (301)869-5800; Fax: (301)990-9690 • URL: http://www.mcaa.org/ncpwb • Contractors in the piping field. Conducts research on development in the field of certified welding for the piping industry; establishes uniform welding procedures for pipe welding; provides for interchange of records of qualified welders.

**National Cheese Institute**. International Dairy Foods Association, 1250 H St. NW, Ste. 900 Washington, DC 20005-3952. Phone: (202)737-4332; Fax: (202)331-7820 • URL: http://www.idfa.org/about-idfa/boards-committees/national-cheese-institute • Represents manufacturers, processors, marketers, assemblers, and distributors of cheese and cheese products; advocates before government and regulatory bodies on behalf of members.

**National Chemical Credit Association**. 1100 Main St. Buffalo, NY 14209-2356. Phone: (716)887-9547; Fax: (716)878-0479 • URL: http://www.ncca1.org/document_1.html • Represents chemical companies. Aims to facilitate the exchange of commercial credit information among leaders of the chemical industry, as well as provide continual professional education to its members. Sponsors monthly educational programs at divisional meetings.

**National Chicken Council**. 1152 15th St. NW, Ste. 430 Washington, DC 20005-2622. Phone: (202)296-2622; Fax: (202)293-4005; Email: ncc@chickenusa.org • URL: http://www.nationalchickencouncil.org • Membership includes producers/processors of broiler chickens; distributors and allied industry. Sponsors National Chicken Cooking Contest and National Chicken Month. Compiles statistics; conducts generic promotion program for chicken; provides government relations services for member companies and the broiler industry.

**National Child Labor Committee**. 1501 Broadway, Ste. 1908 New York, NY 10036. Phone: (212)840-1801; Fax: (212)768-0963; Email: nclckapow@aol.com • URL: http://www.nationalchildlabor.org • Parent organization of National Committee on Employment of Youth and National Committee on the Education of Migrant Children. Provides direct and technical assistance to programs on youth-related issues, particularly education, job training, and employment.

**National Civic League**. 6000 E Evans Ave., Ste. 3-012 Denver, CO 80222. Phone: (303)571-4343 • URL: http://www.ncl.org • Community leaders, civic leaders, educators, public officials, civic organizations, libraries, nonprofits and businesses interested in community building, transforming democratic institutions and developing techniques of citizen action and participation. Serves as a clearinghouse for information on healthy communities, community renewal, local campaign, finance reform, All-American cities, city and county charters, election systems and techniques of citizen participation.

***National Civic Review***. National Civic League, Inc. Jossey-Bass, 989 Market St. San Francisco, CA 94103-1741. Phone: 800-225-5945 or (415)433-1740; Fax: (415)433-0499 or (415)951-8553; Email: jbsubs@jbp.com • URL: http://www.josseybass.com • Quarterly. $252 Institutions Online or Print only; $291 Institutions Print and Online; $64 Individuals Online or Print only; 71 Dh Individuals Print and Online. Presents civic strategies for improving local government operations and community life.

**National Clay Pipe Institute**. N6369 US Hwy. 12, Ste. A Elkhorn, WI 53121. Phone: (262)742-2904; Fax: (360)242-9094; Email: info@ncpi.org • URL: http://www.ncpi.org • Manufacturers of vitrified clay sewer pipe and fittings. Promotes use of clay pipe for sanitary sewer systems. Provides engineering advisory services; conducts scientific research; acts as government liaison.

**National Cleaners Association**. 252 W 29th St. New York, NY 10001-5271. Phone: 800-888-1622 or (212)967-3002; Fax: (212)967-2240; Email: info@nca-i.com • URL: http://www.nca-i.com • Members are dry cleaning establishments.

**National Club Association**. 1201 15th St. NW, Ste. 450 Washington, DC 20005. Phone: 800-625-6221 or (202)822-9822; Fax: (202)822-9808; Email: info@nationalclub.org • URL: http://www.nationalclub.org • Represents the business and legal interests of private clubs. Analyzes proposed laws and regulations affecting clubs; compiles statistics and economic data; drafts model legislation; and acts as a general center of information about club matters.

**National Coalition for Capital**. 1028 33rd St. NW, Ste. 200 Washington, DC 20007. Phone: (202)337-1661 • URL: http://www.nationalcoalitionforcapital.org • Represents leaders who support economic development and job creation through long-term access to capital for entrepreneurs and emerging companies. Serves as a resource for promising small and emerging companies, entrepreneurs, investors, economic developers and other stakeholders within the nation's emerging investment infrastructure.

**National Coffee Association of U.S.A.** 45 Broadway, Ste. 1140 New York, NY 10006. Phone: (212)766-4007; Fax: (212)766-5815; Email: info@ncausa.org • URL: http://www.ncausa.org • Formerly Associated Coffee Industries of America.

**National Committee for an Effective Congress**. 218 D St., SE, Fl. 3 Washington, DC 20003. Phone: (202)639-8300 • URL: http://www.ncec.org • Raises funds from private citizens and distributes them to its endorsed candidates for the United States Senate and House of Representatives.

**National Committee for Employer Support of the Guard and Reserve**. 4800 Mark Center Dr., Ste. 3E25 Alexandria, VA 22350-1200. Phone: 800-336-4590; Fax: (571)372-0705; Email: osd.esgritsupport@mail.mil • URL: http://www.esgr.mil • Provides free education, consultation, and if necessary, mediation for employers of guard and reserve members. Aims to ensure the national security. Promotes cooperation and understanding between reserve component members and their civilian employers and assists in the resolution of conflicts arising from an employee's military commitment. Operates with a network of almost 4,000 volunteers throughout 56 Committees located in each state, commonwealth, territory, and the District of Columbia. Operates an ombudsman program to assist in the informal resolution of employer-employee conflicts resulting from employee participation in the National Guard and Reserve.

**National Committee for Responsive Philanthropy**. 1331 H St. NW, Ste. 200 Washington, DC 20005-4706. Phone: (202)387-9177; Fax: (202)332-5084; Email: info@ncrp.org • URL: http://www.ncrp.org • Promotes charitable giving to new organizations working for social change or controversial issues. Formerly Committee for Responsive Philanthropy.

**National Committee on Uniform Traffic Laws and Ordinances**. 107 S West St., No. 110 Alexandria, VA 22314-2824. Phone: 800-807-5290; Fax: (540)465-5383; Email: twogen2@yahoo.com • URL: http://www.ncutlo.org • Formerly National Conference on Street and Highway Safety.

**National Committee to Preserve Social Security and Medicare**. 10 G St. NE, Ste. 600 Washington, DC 20002-4253. Phone: 800-966-1935 or (202)216-0420 or (202)216-8378; Fax: (202)216-0446; Email: memberservices@ncpssm.org • URL: http://www.ncpssm.org • Members are individuals concerned with Medicare and social security programs. Formerly National Committe to Preserve Social Security.

**National Community Development Association**. 522 21st St. NW, No. 120 Washington, DC 20006-5012. Phone: (202)293-7587; Fax: (202)887-5546 • URL: http://www.ncdaonline.org • Represents community development program directors. Supports the interests of Community Development Block Grant Programs as well as other community and economic development issues; disseminates information; operates workshops on various aspects of housing, economic, and community development.

**National Concrete Masonry Association**. 13750 Sunrise Valley Dr. Herndon, VA 20171. Phone: (703)713-1900; Fax: (703)713-1910; Email: info@ncma.org • URL: http://www.ncma.org • Manufacturers of concrete masonry units (concrete blocks), segmental retaining wall units and paving block; associate members are machinery, cement and aggregate manufacturers. Conducts testing and research on masonry units and masonry assemblies. Compiles statistics.

**National Confectioners Association of the U.S.** 1101 30th St. NW, Ste. 200 Washington, DC 20007. Phone: (202)534-1440; Fax: (202)337-0637; Email: info@candyusa.org • URL: http://www.candyusa.com/ • Affiliated with American Cocoa Research Institute and the Chocolate Manufacturers Associations of the U.S.A.

**National Confectioners Association**. 1101 30th St. NW, Ste. 200 Washington, DC 20007. Phone: (202)534-1440; Fax: (202)337-0637; Email: info@candyusa.org • URL: http://www.candyusa.com • Formerly Association of Cocoa and Chocolate Manufacturers of the U.S.

**National Confectionery Sales Association**. Spitfire House, 3135 Berea Rd. Cleveland, OH 44111. Phone: (216)631-8200; Fax: (216)631-8210; Email: info@candyhalloffame.org • URL: http://www.candyhalloffame.org • Salespersons, brokers, sales managers, wholesalers, and manufacturers in the candy industry. Maintains Candy Hall of Fame.

**National Conference of Bankruptcy Judges**. c/o Jeanne Sleeper, 954 La Mirada St. Laguna Beach, CA 92651-3751. Phone: (949)497-3673; Fax: (949)497-2523 • URL: http://www.ncbj.org • Represents active and former bankruptcy judges. Promotes improvements in law practice and administration of justice in U.S. bankruptcy courts; encourages uniformity in the administration of estates in bankruptcy.

**National Conference of Commissioners on Uniform State Laws**. 111 N Wabash Ave., Ste. 1010 Chicago, IL 60602-1917. Phone: (312)450-6600 or (312)450-6603; Fax: (312)450-6601 or (312)915-0187 • URL: http://www.uniformlaws.org • Judges, law school deans and professors, and practicing attorneys appointed by state governors. Promotes uniformity in state law on subjects where uniformity is deemed desirable and practicable. Also promotes uniformity of judicial decisions throughout the U.S. Drafts uniform and model acts on subjects suitable for interstate compact and subjects in which uniformity will make more effective the exercise of state powers and promote interstate cooperation.

**National Conference of Executives of the Arc**. 1825 K St. NW, Ste. 1200 Washington, DC 20006. Phone: 800-433-5255 or (202)534-3700; Fax: (202)534-3731; Email: info@thearc.org • URL: http://www.thearc.org/nce • Executives of the Arc. Promotes professional development of members; seeks to enhance the lives of people with mental retardation. Provides educational opportunities and professional support to Arc executives.

**National Conference of State Legislatures**. 7700 E 1st Pl. Denver, CO 80230-7143. Phone: (303)364-7700; Fax: (303)364-7800; Email: ncslnet-admin@ncsl.org • URL: http://www.ncsl.org • Affiliated with Council of State Governments.

**National Conference of State Liquor Administrators**. 543 Long Hill Rd. Gurnee, IL 60031. Phone: (847)721-6410 • URL: http://www.ncsla.org • State agencies administering liquor control laws and collecting beverage taxes under a license system rather than a state-controlled monopoly stores system.

**National Conference of State Social Security Administrators**. c/o Joe L. Lancaster, Jr., Secretary, PO Box 639 Frankfort, KY 40602-0639. Email: secretary@ncsssa.org • URL: http://www.ncsssa.org • Formerly Conference of State Social Security Administrators.

**National Conference on Citizenship**. 1100 17th St. NW, 12th Fl. Washington, DC 20036. Phone: (202)601-7096; Email: info@ncoc.net • URL: http://www.ncoc.net • Promotes citizenship activities and spirit of cooperation on part of all citizens. Leads annual Citizenship Day on September 17 to recognize youth reaching voting age and salutes foreign-born receiving citizenship through naturalization.

**National Conference on Weights and Measures**. 1135 M St., Ste. 110 Lincoln, NE 68508-2196. Phone: (402)434-4880; Fax: (402)434-4878; Email: info@ncwm.net • URL: http://www.ncwm.net • State and local weights and measures officials; representatives of manufacturers of weighing and measuring devices, trade associations, industry (users of devices), and representatives of federal government. Promotes uniformity in weights and measures laws, regulations, specifications and tolerances. Sponsored by National Institute of Standards and Technology.

***National Construction Estimator***. Craftsman Book Co., 6058 Corte Del Cedro Carlsbad, CA 92011-1514. Phone: 800-829-8123 or (760)438-7828; Fax: (760)438-0398 • URL: http://www.craftsman-book.com • Annual. $51.63 Individuals.

**National Consumer Law Center**. 7 Winthrop Sq. Boston, MA 02110-1245. Phone: (617)542-8010; Fax: (617)542-8028; Email: consumerlaw@nclc.org • URL: http://www.nclc.org • Serves as a specialized resource in consumer and energy law funded by federal, state, and foundation grants and donations. Lawyers provide research, technical consulting, and in-depth assistance to legal services, private lawyers, and state agencies throughout the nation. Defines recurring patterns in the problems of low-income consumers and develops a series of alternative solutions utilizing litigation, legislation, lawyer training, and development of new service delivery systems. Seeks consultants for an interdisciplinary approach to problems. Conducts analyses of weatherization and energy assistance programs for low-income homeowners, renters, and state and federal agencies.

**National Consumers League**. 1701 K St. NW, Ste. 1200 Washington, DC 20006. Phone: (202)835-3323; Fax: (202)835-0747; Email: info@nclnet.org • URL: http://www.nclnet.org • Identifies, protects, represents, and advances the economic and social interests of consumers and workers. Addresses issues including healthcare, food and drug safety, and consumer fraud. Promotes fairness and safety at the marketplace and in the workplace. Coordinates the Alliance Against Fraud in Telemarketing and the Child Labor Coalition. Administers the National Fraud Information Center and Internet Fraud Watch.

**National Contract Management Association**. 21740 Beaumeade Cir., Ste. 125 Ashburn, VA 20147. Phone: 800-344-8096 or (571)382-0082 or (703)448-9231; Fax: (703)448-0939; Email: wearelistening@ncmahq.org • URL: http://www.ncmahq.org • Professional individuals concerned with administration, procurement, acquisition, negotiation and management of contracts and subcontracts. Works for the education, improvement and professional development of members and nonmembers through national and chapter programs, symposia and educational materials. Offers certification in Contract Management (CPCM, CFCM, and CCCM) designations as well as a credential program. Operates speakers' bureau.

**National Cooperative Business Association**. 1401 New York Ave. NW, Ste. 1100 Washington, DC 20005. Phone: (202)638-6222; Fax: (202)638-1374 • URL: http://www.ncba.coop • Local, state, regional and national cooperative business organizations including farm supply, agricultural marketing, insurance, banking, housing, health care, consumer goods and services, student, worker, fishery and other cooperatives. Represents, strengthens and expands cooperative businesses. Programs include: supporting the development of cooperative businesses in the U.S.; developing and providing technical assistance to cooperatives in developing nations; representing American cooperatives in Washington, DC and abroad; promoting and developing commercial relations among the world's cooperatives. Supports the Cooperative Hall of Fame and the Cooperative Development Foundation.

**National Corn Growers Association**. 632 Cepi Dr. Chesterfield, MO 63005-1221. Phone: (636)733-9004; Fax: (636)733-9005; Email: corninfo@ncga.com • URL: http://www.ncga.com/home • Growers of corn. Furthers the use, proper marketing, legislative position, and efficient production of corn. Conducts research and educational programs. Sponsors National Yield Contest; compiles statistics.

**National Correctional Industries Association**. 1202 N Charles St. Baltimore, MD 21201. Phone: (410)230-3972; Fax: (410)230-3981; Email: info@nationalcia.org • URL: http://www.nationalcia.org • Professional correctional industry managers, supervisors, superintendents, and others employed in the industry. Seeks to improve the effectiveness of industrial programs as they relate to the correctional process by providing a forum for the development and exchange of ideas and by providing professional reaction and guidance concerning projected ideas and programs related to correctional industry trends. Compiles statistics.

**National Corrugated Steel Pipe Association**. 14070 Proton Rd., Ste. 100, LB 9 Dallas, TX 75244. Phone: (972)850-1907; Fax: (972)490-4219 • URL: http://www.ncspa.org • Represents firms fabricating corrugated steel drainage pipe and structures; steel mills; allied industries. Provides engineering service in design and installation of drainage products and systems. Conducts research programs.

**National Cotton Council of America**. 7193 Goodlett Farms Pkwy. Cordova, TN 38016. Phone: (901)274-9030; Fax: (901)725-0510 • URL: http://www.cotton.org • Delegates are from 19 cotton producing states.

**National Cottonseed Products Association**. 866 Willow Tree Cir. Cordova, TN 38018. Phone: (901)682-0800; Fax: (901)682-2856; Email: info@cottonseed.com • URL: http://www.cottonseed.com • Oil mills, refiners, dealers, brokers, chemists, and others interested in margarine, cooking fats, soaps, lubricants, cattle feed, and fertilizer. Maintains uniform trading rules covering the buying, selling, weighing, sampling, and analysis of cottonseed and its products; supports extensive research program to increase processing efficiency and to improve the quality and usefulness of cottonseed products. Conducts research programs and market development activities.

**National Council for Prescription Drug Programs**. 9240 E Raintree Dr. Scottsdale, AZ 85260-7518. Phone: (480)477-1000; Fax: (480)767-1042; Email: ncpdp@ncpdp.org • URL: http://www.ncpdp.org • Concerned with standardization of third party prescription drug programs.

**National Council for Public-Private Partnerships**. 2000 15th St. NW, Ste. 200 Washington, DC 20005. Phone: (202)962-0555; Fax: (202)289-7499; Email: ncppp@ncppp.org • URL: http://www.ncppp.org • Promotes private ownership of public services. Formerly Privitization Council, Inc.

**National Council of Agricultural Employers**. 8233 Old Courthouse Rd., Ste. 200 Vienna, VA 22182. Phone: (703)790-9039; Email: info@ncaeonline.org • URL: http://www.ncaeonline.org • Growers of agricultural commodities who employ hand labor for field crops; processors and handlers, farm and commodity organizations, and others whose business is related to labor-intensive farming in the U.S. Aims to improve the position and image of U.S. agriculture as an employer of labor and to facilitate and encourage the establishment and maintenance of an adequate force of agricultural employees. Serves as clearinghouse for exchange of information on labor supply, length of employment, and other conditions of work. Does not engage in recruitment, housing, supplying, or employment of agricultural workers, and does not represent its members or others in negotiating with labor unions or other organizations, or in agreeing to any contract relating to hours, wages, or working conditions. Keeps member abreast of national legislation affecting agricultural labor.

**National Council of Asian American Business Associations**. 475 N Whisman Rd., Ste. 200 Mountain View, CA 94043. Phone: (650)303-6164; Fax: (650)350-1545; Email: info@national-caaba.org • URL: http://www.national-caaba.org • Serve as the voice of Asian Pacific American business owners in the United States. Works to effect positive change in the areas of economic development, public contracting and private procurement, and public and fiscal policies that impact Asian Pacific American businesses and communities at large. Seeks to create opportunities in the social, political, and economic sectors for the Asian Pacific American business community.

**National Council of Chain Restaurants**. 325 7th St. NW, Ste. 1100 Washington, DC 20004. Phone: (202)783-7971; Fax: (202)737-2849; Email: info@nrf.com • URL: http://www. nccr.net • Major multiunit, multistate foodservice, restaurant and lodging companies in the United States.

**National Council of Commercial Plant Breeders**. c/o Ann Jorss, Secretary-Treasurer, 1701 Duke St., Ste. 275 Alexandria, VA 22314. Phone: (703)837-8140; Fax: (703)837-9365 • URL: http://www.nccpb.org • Commercial seed firms. Engages in plant research and breeding programs in order to develop and market new and improved seeds and plants. Promotes and seeks to protect the interests of private industry in seed development, processing, and marketing. Monitors legislative matters pertaining to the seed industry and public agency programs as they affect private firms engaged in plant breeding.

**National Council of Higher Education Resources**. 1100 Connecticut Ave. NW, Ste. 1200 Washington, DC 20036-4110. Phone: (202)822-2106; Fax: (202)822-2143; Email: info@ncher.us • URL: http://www.ncher.us • Attempts to coordinate federal, state, and private functions in the student loan program.

**National Council of Juvenile and Family Court Judges**. PO Box 8970 Reno, NV 89507-8970. Phone: (775)784-6012; Fax: (775)784-6628; Email: staff@ncjfcj.org • URL: http://www.ncjfcj.org • Judges with juvenile and family court jurisdiction and others with a professional interest in the nation's juvenile justice system. Works to further more effective administration of justice for young people through the improvement of juvenile and family court standards and

practices. Sponsors continuing education programs. Compiles and disseminates research data.

**National Council of Minorities in Energy**. 1725 I St. NW, Ste. 300 Washington, DC 20006. Phone: 866-663-9045; Fax: (866)663-8007; Email: contact@minoritiesinenergy.org • URL: http://www.minoritiesinenergy.org • Advocates for development and utilization of minority and women-owned businesses in the energy sector and energy-related industries across the United States and in international markets. Provides information regarding opportunities in the energy industry. Advocates on regulatory and legislative issues at the federal, state and local levels. Presents methodologies to help implement access to capital and credit facilitation.

**National Council of Private Enterprises - Panama**. Apartado 0816-07197, Zone 1 Panama City, Panama. Phone: 507 2 112672 or 507 2 112677; Fax: 507 2 112694; Email: conep1@cwpanama.net • URL: http://www.conep.org.pa • Promotes members' interest.

**National Council of Women of the United States**. 777 United Nations Plz. New York, NY 10017. Phone: (212)697-1278; Fax: (212)972-0164; Email: info@ncw-us.org • URL: http://www.ncwus.org • Works for the education, participation and advancement of women in all areas of society. Affiliated with International Council of Women.

**National Council on Alcoholism and Drug Dependence**. 217 Broadway, Ste. 712 New York, NY 10007. Phone: 800-622-2255 or (212)269-7797; Fax: (212)269-7510; Email: national@ncadd.org • URL: http://www.ncadd.org • Works for the prevention and treatment of alcoholism and other drug dependence through programs of public education, information and public policy advocacy.

**National Council on Crime and Delinquency**. 1970 Broadway, Ste. 500 Oakland, CA 94612. Phone: 800-306-6223; Email: info@nccdglobal.org • URL: http://nccdglobal.org • Promotes effective, humane, fair and economically sound solutions to family, community, and justice problems. Conducts research, promotes reform initiatives, and seeks to work with individuals, public and private organizations, and the media to prevent and reduce crime and delinquency.

**National Council on Economic Education**. 122 E 42nd St., Ste. 2600 New York, NY 10168. Phone: 800-338-1192 or (212)730-7007; Fax: (212)730-1793; Email: customerservice@councilforeconed.org • URL: http://www.councilforeconed.org • Formerly Joint Council in Economic Education.

**National Council on Problem Gambling**. 730 11th St. NW, Ste. 601 Washington, DC 20001. Phone: 800-522-4700 or (202)547-9204; Fax: (202)547-9206; Email: ncpg@ncpgambling.org • URL: http://www.ncpgambling.org • Advocates for programs and services to assist problem gamblers and their families. Formerly National Council on Compulsive Gambling.

**National Council on Public Polls**. 1425 Broad St., Ste. 7 Clifton, NJ 07013. Phone: 800-786-8000 or (973)857-8500; Fax: (973)857-8578; Email: info@ncpp.org • URL: http://www.ncpp.org • Members are public opinion polling organizations.

**National Court Reporters Association**. 8224 Old Courthouse Rd. Vienna, VA 22182-3808. Phone: 800-272-6272 or (703)556-6272; Fax: (703)556-6291; Email: president@ncrahq.org • URL: http://www.ncra.org • Represents Independent state, regional, and local associations. Verbatim court reporters who work as official reporters for courts and government agencies, as freelance reporters for independent contractors, and as captioners for television programming; retired reporters, teachers of court reporting, and school officials; student court reporters.

*National Credit Union Administration Rules and Regulations*. U. S. Government Printing Office, 732 N Capitol St. NW Washington, DC 20401. Phone: 866-512-1800 or (202)512-1800 or (866)512-1800; Fax: (202)512-2104 or (202)512-2250; Email: contactcenter@gpo.gov • URL: http://www.gpo.gov • Looseleaf. $130.00 for basic manual, including updates for an indeterminate period. Incorporates all amendments and revisions.

*National Customs Brokers and Forwarders Association of America Membership Directory*. National Customs Brokers and Forwarders Association of America, 1200 18th St. NW, No. 901 Washington, DC 20036. Phone: (202)466-0222; Fax: (202)466-0226; Email: staff@ncbfaa.org • URL: http://www.ncbfaa.org • Annual. $55.00. Lists about 600 customs brokers, international air cargo agents, and freight forwarders in the U.S.

**National Customs Brokers and Forwarders Association of America**. 1200 18th St. NW, No. 901 Washington, DC 20036. Phone: (202)466-0222; Fax: (202)466-0226; Email: staff@ncbfaa.org • URL: http://www.ncbfaa.org • Formerly Customs Brokers and Forwarders Association of America.

**National Defense Industrial Association**. 2111 Wilson Blvd., Ste. 400 Arlington, VA 22201. Phone: (703)522-1820 or (703)247-2548; Email: bprokuski@ndia.org • URL: http://www.ndia.org • Concerned citizens, military and government personnel, and defense-related industry workers interested in industrial preparedness for the national defense of the United States. Operates Technology Services that provides a forum for discussion of defense industry programs and issues. Conducts 55 technical meetings per year.

*National Defense Magazine: Business & Technology Journal*. National Defense Industrial Association, 2111 Wilson Blvd.,

Ste. 400 Arlington, VA 22201. Phone: (703)522-1820 or (703)247-2548; Email: bprokuski@ndia.org • URL: http://www.ndia.org • Monthly. $40 Individuals; $70 Two years; $45 Other countries surface mail; $80 Other countries 2 years; surface mail; $75 Other countries airmail; $140 Other countries 2 years; airmail. Magazine on the North American Defense Industry.

*National Defense: NDIA's Business and Technology Magazine*. National Defense Industrial Association, 2111 Wilson Blvd., Ste. 400 Arlington, VA 22201. Phone: (703)522-1820 or (703)247-2548; Email: bprokuski@ndia.org • URL: http://www.ndia.org • 10 times a year. $35.00 per year.

**National Defense Transportation Association**. 50 S Pickett St., Ste. 220 Alexandria, VA 22304-7296. Phone: (703)751-5011; Fax: (703)823-8761 • URL: http://www.ndtahq.com • Men and women in the field of transportation, travel logistics and related areas in the Armed Forces, federal government, private industry and the academic sector. Strives to foster a strong and efficient transportation system in support of national defense. Serves as link between government and industry on transportation matters. Operates a job placement service for members.

**National Democratic Institute for International Affairs**. 455 Massachusetts Ave. NW, 8th Fl. Washington, DC 20001-2783. Phone: 888-875-2887 or (202)728-5500; Fax: (202)728-5520; Email: contactndi@ndi.org • URL: http://www.ndi.org • Works to strengthen and expand democracy worldwide. Provides practical assistance to civic and political leaders advancing democratic values, practices and institutions. Works with democrats in every region of the world to build political and civic organizations, safeguard elections, and promote citizen participation, openness and accountability in government.

**National Development Council**. 708 Third Ave., Ste. 710 New York, NY 10017. Phone: (212)682-1106 or (859)578-4850; Fax: (212)573-6118; Email: training@nationaldevelopmentcouncil.org • URL: http://www.nationaldevelopmentcouncil.org • Brings innovative economic development financing programs to urban and rural communities interested in local business and industrial growth, commercial revitalization, and permanent job creation. Finances professionals' work with cities, counties, and states to: build permanent systems for developing financing; train local staff; structure and negotiate financing for development projects, local business development, and industrial expansion. Conducts intensive training program for economic development professionals with courses in business credit analysis, real estate financing, loan packaging, federal financing, and program management and implementation; has provided advice to congress and federal agencies that has helped create lending programs for job creation and small business investment; has initiated and managed presidential programs for Presidents Nixon, Ford, Carter, and Reagan.

*The National Dipper: The Magazine for Frozen Dessert Retailers*. 1028 W Devon Ave. Elk Grove Village, IL 60007. Phone: (847)301-8400; Fax: (847)301-8402 or (847)301-8402 • Bimonthly. $55.00 per year. Edited for ice cream store owners and managers. Includes industry news, new product information, statistics, and feature articles.

*National Directory for Employment in Education*. American Association for Employment in Education, 947 E Johnstown Rd., No. 170 Gahanna, OH 43230. Phone: (614)485-1111; Fax: (360)244-7802 or (614)485-9609; Email: execdir@aaee.org • URL: http://www.aaee.org/cwt/external/wcpages/index.aspx • Annual. $20 Nonmembers Processing fee $2; $10 Members processing fee $2. Covers: about 600 placement offices maintained by teacher-training institutions and 300 school district personnel officers and/or superintendents responsible for hiring profesional staff. Entries include: Institution name, address, phone, contact name, email address, and website.

*National Directory of Adult Day Care Centers*. Health Resources Publishing, 1913 Atlantic Ave., Ste. 200 Manasquan, NJ 08736. Phone: 800-516-4343 or (732)292-1100; Fax: (732)292-1111; Email: info@healthresourcesonline.com • URL: http://www.healthrespubs.com • Irregular. $145 Individuals. Covers: Over 3,200 centers and programs providing adult day care; 1,100 are described in detail. Database includes: Bibliography of resources; aging services suppliers' guide. Entries include: Center or program name, address, phone, director or coordinator name; detailed listings include programs, providing sponsor information, geographic area served, fees, number of clients and staff, hours and days of operation, client eligibility criteria, services and activities offered.

*The National Directory of Catalogs*. Oxbridge Communications Inc., 186 5th Ave. New York, NY 10010. Phone: 800-955-0231 or (212)741-0231; Fax: (212)633-2938; Email: info@oxbridge.com • URL: http://www.oxbridge.com • Annual. $995 Individuals print version; $1,195 Individuals CD-ROM single user; $1,995 Individuals print and CD-ROM. Describes over 12,000 United States and Canadian catalogs within 78 subject areas.

*National Directory of Corporate Distress Specialists*. Lustig Data Research Inc., 653 Arbuckle Ave. Woodmere, NY 11598-2701. Phone: (516)295-4165; Fax: (516)295-4165 • Annual. $245. Covers: 1,830 organizations and over 4,000 professionals providing 20 types of services in bankruptcies, workouts, turnarounds, and distressed securities investing, including attorneys, accountants, crisis managers, financial advisors, turnaround consultants, valuation experts, financing sources, investors, in-house workout officers, appraisers, auctioneers, liquidators, PR/crisis communications experts, real estate managers, etc. Entries include: Organization name, address, phone, fax, toll-free phone, year founded, parent company, department name, other offices, staff size, size of cases, types of representations, geographical area served, industry specializations, services offered, institutional clients, transaction history, party represented, key personnel, titles.

*National Directory of Corporate Giving.* • Annual. $195 Individuals. Provides information on nearly 4,400 company-sponsored foundations and corporate giving programs.

*National Directory of Corporate Public Affairs.* Columbia Books and Information Services, 8120 Woodmont Ave., Ste. 110 Bethesda, MD 20814. Phone: 888-265-0600 or (202)464-1662; Fax: (202)464-1775; Email: info@columbiabooks.com • URL: http://www.columbiabooks.com • Annual. $249 Individuals. Covers: About 17,000 corporations that have PACs foundations or other public affairs activities; over 14,000 corporate public affairs personnel. Database includes: List of contract lobbyists serving corporations at the state level; membership directory of the Public Affairs Council. Entries include: Company name, headquarters address, Washington, DC, address (if any), names of political action committees, PAC funds contributed, names of principal recipients; name of corporate foundation; total grants per year, assets; giving priorities; names and titles of public affairs personnel. For personnel—Name, title, affiliation, address, phone; if a lobbyist, where registered.

*National Directory of Drug and Alcohol Abuse Treatment Programs.* Substance Abuse and Mental Health Services Administration Data, Outcomes and Quality, 1 Choke Cherry Rd. Rockville, MD 20857. Phone: 877-SAM-HSA7 or (240)276-1250; Fax: (240)276-1260; Email: peter.delany@samhsa.hhs.gov • URL: http://www.samhsa.gov/data • Annual. Lists federal, state, local, and privately funded agencies administering or providing drug abuse and alcoholism treatment services. Formerly *National Directory of Drug Abuse and Alcoholism Treatment and Prevention Programs.*

*National Directory of HMOs.* America's Health Insurance Plans, 601 Pennsylvania Ave. NW, South Bldg., Ste. 500 Washington, DC 20004. Phone: (202)778-3200; Fax: (202)331-7487; Email: ahip@ahip.org • URL: http://www.ahip.org • Annual. $125.00. Includes names of key personnel and benefit options.

*National Directory of Law Enforcement Administrators.* National Public Safety Information Bureau, 601 Main St. Stevens Point, WI 54481. Phone: 800-647-7579 or (715)345-2772; Fax: (715)345-7288; Email: info@safetysource.com • URL: http://www.safetysource.com • Annual. $169.00. Lists a wide variety of law enforcement administrators and institutions, including city police departments, sheriffs, prosecutors, state agencies, federal agencies, correctional institutions, college campus police departments, airport police, and harbor police.

*National Directory of Minority-Owned Business Firms.* Business Research Services Inc., 7720 Wisconsin Ave., Ste. 213 Bethesda, MD 20814-3577. Phone: (301)229-5561; Fax: (301)229-6133; Email: brspubs@sba8a.com • URL: http://www.sba8a.com • $295 Individuals paperback; $295 National edition. Provides access to minority business enterprises. Detailed entries furnish up to 17 points of data about each firm, including complete address, contact name, minority type, date founded, certification status, trading area, business description, number of employees and sales volume.

*National Directory of Pension Funds That Invest in Real Estate Investments and Mortgages.* Communication Network International Inc., 3918 Ave. T Brooklyn, NY 11234-5028. Phone: (718)339-6245; Fax: (718)998-5915 • Irregular. $750 payment must accompany order. Covers: 1,300 pension funds. Entries include: Fund name, manager's name, address, phone, amount of investment.

*National Directory of Personnel Service Firms.* National Association of Personnel Services, 78 Dawson Village Way, Ste. 410-201 Dawsonville, GA 30534. Phone: (706)531-0060; Fax: (866)739-4750 • URL: http://www.naps360.org • Annual. Lists over 1,100 member private (for-profit) employment firms.

*National Directory of Woman-Owned Business Firms.* Business Research Services Inc., 7720 Wisconsin Ave., Ste. 213 Bethesda, MD 20814-3577. Phone: (301)229-5561; Fax: (301)229-6133; Email: brspubs@sba8a.com • URL: http://www.sba8a.com • Annual. $295 Individuals paperback. Covers more than 28,000 entries with up to 17 points of data about each firm. Each business listing is arranged first by SIC code and business description, then alphabetically by state, city and company name within the SIC category.

*National Distributors Select.* Scott's Directories, 12 Concorde Pl., Ste. 800 Toronto, ON, Canada M3C 4J2. Phone: 800-668-2374 or (416)442-2122; Fax: (416)510-6870; Email: customercare@scottsdirectories.com • URL: http://www.scottsdirectories.com • Annual. $224.75 Profiler (additional); $2,499 Prospector online (unlimited); $499 Pinpointer; $899 Profiler, online; $1,399 Prospector standard; $349.75 Prospector (additional). Covers: Over 59,000 wholesalers,

distributors, and wholesale agents of industrial products across Canada. Entries include: 34,500 company name, address, phone, description, brand names carried.

*National E-mail and Fax Directory.* Cengage Learning Inc., 20 Channel Center St. Boston, MA 02210. Phone: 800-487-8488 or (617)289-7700; Fax: (617)289-7844; Email: investors@cengage.com • URL: http://www.cengage.com • Annual. $265 Individuals. 2009. 23rd edition. A comprehensive "one stop" source of information on contact information — fax numbers, e-mail addresses, voice telephone numbers, and mailing addresses. Coverage spans over 151,000 major businesses, agencies and organizations in the United States.

**National Education Association.** 1201 16th St. NW Washington, DC 20036-3290. Phone: 800-229-4200 or (202)822-7200; Fax: (202)822-7974; Email: highered@nea.org • URL: http://www.nea.org • Professional organization and union of elementary and secondary school teachers, college and university professors, administrators, principals, counselors, and others concerned with education.

**National Electrical Contractors Association.** 3 Bethesda Metro Ctr., Ste. 1100 Bethesda, MD 20814. Phone: (301)657-3110; Fax: (301)215-4500 • URL: http://www.necanet.org • Contractors erecting, installing, repairing, servicing, and maintaining electric wiring, equipment, and appliances. Provides management services and labor relations programs for electrical contractors; conducts seminars for contractor sales and training. Conducts research and educational programs; compiles statistics. Sponsors honorary society, the Academy of Electrical Contracting.

**National Electrical Manufacturers Association.** 1300 N 17th St., Ste. 1752 Rosslyn, VA 22209. Phone: (703)841-3200 or (703)841-3272; Email: communications@nema.org • URL: http://www.nema.org • Aims to maintain and improve quality and reliability of products; insure safety standards in manufacture and use of products; organize and act upon members' interests in productivity, competition from overseas suppliers, energy conservation and efficiency, marketing opportunities, economic matters, and product liability. Develops product standards covering such matters as nomenclature, ratings, performance, testing, and dimensions; actively participates in regional and international standards process for electrical products; participates in developing National Electrical Code and National Electrical Safety Codes, and advocates their acceptance by state and local authorities; conducts regulatory and legislative analyses on issues of concern to electrical manufacturers; compiles and issues market data of all kinds, and statistical data on such factors as sales, new orders, unfilled orders, cancellations, production, and inventories.

**National Electronics Service Dealers Association.** 3608 Pershing Ave. Fort Worth, TX 76107-4527. Phone: 800-797-9197 or (817)921-9061; Fax: (817)921-3741; Email: mack@nesda.com • URL: http://www.nesda.com • Local and state electronic service associations and companies. Supplies technical service information on business management training to electronic service dealers. Offers certification and training programs through International Society of Certified Electronics Technicians. Conducts technical service and business management seminars.

**National Elevator Industry.** 1677 County, Rte. 64 Salem, NY 12865-0838. Phone: (518)854-3100; Fax: (518)854-3257; Email: info@neii.org • URL: http://www.neii.org • Serves as a trade association of the building transportation industry. Promotes safe building transportation for new and existing products and technologies, and adoption of the current codes by local government agencies.

*The National Estimator.* Society of Cost Estimating and Analysis, 101 S. Whiting St., Suite 201 Alexandria, VA 22304. Phone: (703)751-8069; Fax: (703)461-7328; Email: scea@sceaonline.net • URL: http://www.sceaonline.net • Quarterly. $30.00 per year. Covers government contract estimating.

**National Executive Service Corps.** 55 W 39th St., 12th Fl. New York, NY 10018. Phone: (212)269-1234; Fax: (212)269-0959; Email: info@nesc.org • URL: http://www.nesc.org • Provides management and business advisory services to nonprofit educational, health care, social services, cultural, and religious organizations. Supplies services through experienced and senior-leveled business people who act as volunteer management consultants.

**National Farmers Organization.** 528 Billy Sunday Rd., Ste. 100 Ames, IA 50010-2508. Phone: 800-247-2110; Email: nfo@nfo.org • URL: http://www.nfo.org • Nonpartisan organization of farmers who bargain collectively to obtain contracts with buyers, processors, and exporters for the sale of farm commodities. Works to continuously improve such contracts. Conducts educational programs; maintains speakers' bureau.

*National Farmers Union News.* National Farmers Union, 11900 E Cornell Ave. Aurora, CO 80014-3194. Phone: 800-347-1961 or (303)337-5500; Fax: (303)368-1390; Email: info@nfu.org • Description: Provides news, legislation, and tax information in relation to the farming industry.

**National Farmers Union.** 20 F St. NW, Ste. 300 Washington, DC 20001-6700. Phone: (202)554-1600; Fax: (202)554-1654 • URL: http://www.nfu.org • Farm families interested in agricultural welfare. Carries on educational, cooperative and legislative activities. Represents members' interests

especially in acquiring a more equitable share of the food dollar. Assists farm families in developing self-help institutions such as cooperatives.

**National Fastener Distributors Association.** 10842 Noel St., No. 107 Los Alamitos, CA 90720. Phone: 877-487-6332 or (714)484-7858; Fax: (562)684-0695; Email: nfda@nfda-fastener.org • URL: http://www.nfda-fastener.org • Marketers, distributors, manufacturers, and importers of the fastener industry (producers or distributors of screws, bolts, and nuts). Develops new uses for fasteners; collects and disseminates statistics and information for members; conducts membership performance surveys. Assists in the maintenance of sound and equitable relationships among members of the industry, the public, and government. Offers training and educational programs.

**National Federation of Advanced Information Services.** c/o Jill O'Neill, Director, 1518 Walnut St., Ste. 1004 Philadelphia, PA 19102-3403. Phone: (215)893-1561; Fax: (215)893-1564 • URL: http://nfais.org • Formerly National Federation of Abstracting and Indexing Services.

**National Federation of Federal Employees.** 805 15th St. NW, Ste. 500 Washington, DC 20005. Phone: (202)216-4420 or (202)216-4421; Fax: (202)898-1861; Email: cbythrow@nffe.org • URL: http://www.nffe.org • Independent. Opposes Social Security coverage for civil service workers. Conducts seminars on labor relations.

**National Federation of Independent Business.** 53 Century Blvd., Ste. 250 Nashville, TN 37214. Phone: (202)554-9000 or (615)874-5288; Email: web_membership@nfib.org • URL: http://www.nfib.com/ • Members are independent business and professional people.

**National Federation of Press Women.** 200 Little Falls St., Ste. 405 Falls Church, VA 22046. Phone: 800-780-2715 or (703)237-9804 or (703)534-2500; Fax: (703)237-9808; Email: presswomen@aol.com • URL: http://www.nfpw.org • Serves as federal of state associations of professional women and men in all phases of communications on a full-time or freelance basis. Seeks to: encourage the highest standards of professionalism in journalism; provide for exchange of ideas, knowledge, and experience. Offers specialized education programs.

**National Fenestration Rating Council.** 6305 Ivy Ln., Ste. 140 Greenbelt, MD 20770. Phone: (301)589-1776 or (785)862-1890; Fax: (301)589-3884; Email: info@nfrc.org • URL: http://www.nfrc.org • Individuals, organizations, and corporations interested in production, regulation, promotion, and development of technology related to fenestration products. Develops national voluntary energy performance rating system for fenestration products; coordinates certification and labeling activities to ensure uniform rating application. Promotes consumer awareness of fenestration ratings in an effort to encourage informed purchase of windows, doors, and skylights. Conducts efficiency testing. Maintains speakers' bureau; conducts educational and research programs.

*National Fire Codes.* National Fire Protection Association, 1 Batterymarch Park Quincy, MA 02169-7471. Phone: 800-344-3555 or (617)770-3000; Fax: (617)770-0700; Email: library@nfpa.org • URL: http://www.nfpa.org • Annual. $1,295 Individuals; $1,165.50 Members; $2,331 Two years; $2,097.90 Members 2 years. Features a compilation of over 300 fire codes, standards, recommended practices, manuals, and guides on fire protection.

**National Fire Protection Association.** 1 Batterymarch Park Quincy, MA 02169-7471. Phone: 800-344-3555 or (617)770-3000; Fax: (617)770-0700; Email: library@nfpa.org • URL: http://www.nfpa.org • Represents individuals from the fire service, business and industry, health care, educational and other institutions, and individuals in the fields of insurance, government, architecture, and engineering. Develops, publishes, and disseminates standards. Conducts fire safety education programs for the general public. Provides information on fire protection, prevention, and suppression; compiles annual statistics on causes and occupancies of fires, fire deaths, and fire fighter casualties. Provides field service by specialists on electricity, flammable liquids and gases, and marine fire problems. Sponsors National Fire Prevention Week each October and public education campaigns featuring Sparky the Fire Dog.

*National Fisherman.* Diversified Business Communications Inc., 121 Free St. Portland, ME 04101-3919. Phone: (207)842-5500 or (207)842-5600; Fax: (207)842-5503 or (207)842-5603; Email: custserv@divcom.com • URL: http://www.divbusiness.com • Monthly. $14.95 Individuals 1 year; $26.95 Two years. American fishing industry and boat building trade.

*National Five-Digit Zip Code and Post Office Directory.* United States Postal Service - National Customer Support Center, 475 L'Enfant Plaza SW, Rm. 4131 Washington, DC 20260-5601. Phone: 877-640-0724; Email: nadv1@email.usps.gov • URL: http://www.usps.com/nationalpremieraccounts/support.htm • Annual. Two volumes. Formerly National Zip Code and Post Office Directory.

*National Fluid Power Association—Reporter.* National Fluid Power Association, 3333 N Mayfair Rd., Ste. 211 Milwaukee, WI 53222-3219. Phone: (414)778-3344; Fax: (414)778-3361; Email: nfpa@nfpa.com • URL: http://www.nfpa.com • Description: Includes articles on the fluid power market, manufacturing, people and meetings. Also includes statistics.

**National Fluid Power Association**. 3333 N Mayfair Rd., Ste. 211 Milwaukee, WI 53222-3219. Phone: (414)778-3344; Fax: (414)778-3361; Email: nfpa@nfpa.com • URL: http://www.nfpa.com • Manufacturers of components such as fittings used in transmitting power by hydraulic and pneumatic pumps, valves, cylinders, filters, seals; the components are used in industrial and mobile machinery in the material-handling, automotive, railway, aircraft, marine, aerospace, construction, agricultural, and other industries. Works to develop: American National Standards Institute and International Organization for Standardization; fluid power technical standards; fluid power index (industry sales); management and marketing studies. Compiles statistics. Administers and serves as secretariat to several international project groups and other fluid power organizations.

**National Food Processors Association Research Foundation**. 1350 I (Eye) St. NW, Ste. 300 Washington, DC 20005. Phone: (202)639-5900; Fax: (202)639-5932; Email: nfpa@gmaonline.org • URL: http://www.gmaonline.org • Conducts research on food processing engineering, chemistry, microbiology, sanitation, preservation aspects, and public health factors.

**National Foreign Trade Council**. 1625 K St. NW, Ste. 200 Washington, DC 20006. Phone: (202)887-0278; Fax: (202)452-8160; Email: nftcinformation@nftc.org • URL: http://www.nftc.org • Manufacturers, exporters, importers, foreign investors, banks, transportation lines, and insurance, communication, law, accounting, service, and publishing firms. Works to promote and protect American foreign trade and investment. Areas of concern include the removal of arbitrary barriers to expansion of international trade and investment; a greater awareness by the government that this expansion is essential to the economic growth of the U.S.; the formation of a cohesive, consistent international economic policy.

**National Forensic League**. 125 Watson St. Ripon, WI 54971. Phone: (920)748-6206; Fax: (920)748-9478; Email: nfl@nflonline.org • URL: http://www.nationalforensicleague.org • High school honor society. Promotes the art of debate, oratory, interpretation, and extemporaneous speaking. Conducts educational and outreach programs; maintains speakers' bureau; maintains hall of fame; compiles statistics.

**National Foundation for Credit Counseling**. 2000 M St. NW, Ste. 505 Washington, DC 20036. Phone: (202)677-4300 • URL: http://www.nfcc.org • Supersedes Retail Credit Institute of America.

**National Foundation of Manufactured Home Owners**. 11 Moonrise Court Newport Beach, CA 92663-2103. Phone: (949)791-8302; Fax: (801)365-8205; Email: jsisker@yahoo.com • URL: http://www.mfghomeowners.net • Represents 20,000,000 owners of mobile/manufactured homes. Serves as a unified national voice for mobile/manufactured homeowners and to improve communications among members, and research problems homeowners can experience. Maintains resources, include extensive collection of material, clearinghouse of information, especially on the purchase, set-up and maintenance of homes.

***National Frozen and Refrigerated Foods Association Membership Directory***. National Frozen and Refrigerated Foods Association, 4755 Linglestown Rd., Ste. 300 Harrisburg, PA 17112. Phone: (717)657-8601; Fax: (717)657-9862; Email: info@nfraweb.org • URL: http://www.nfraweb.org • Annual. $195.00. Lists products, services and personnel.

**National Frozen and Refrigerated Foods Association**. 4755 Linglestown Rd., Ste. 300 Harrisburg, PA 17112. Phone: (717)657-8601; Fax: (717)657-9862; Email: info@nfraweb.org • URL: http://www.nfraweb.org • Absorbed Foodservice Organizations of Distributors. Formerly National Frozen Food Association.

**National Funeral Directors and Morticians Association**. 6290 Shannon Pkwy. Union City, GA 30291. Phone: 800-434-0958 or (770)969-0064; Fax: (770)969-0505 or (404)286-6573 • URL: http://www.nfdma.com • State, district and local funeral directors and embalmers associations and their members. Promotes ethical practices; encourages just and uniform laws pertaining to funeral directing and embalming industry.

**National Funeral Directors Association**. 13625 Bishops Dr. Brookfield, WI 53005-6607. Phone: 800-228-6332 or (262)789-1880; Fax: (262)789-6977; Email: nfda@nfda.org • URL: http://www.nfda.org • Federation of state funeral directors' associations with individual membership of funeral directors. Seeks to enhance the funeral service profession and promote quality services to the consumers. Conducts professional education seminars and home study courses. Compiles statistics.

***National Futures Association Manual***. National Futures Association, 300 S Riverside Plz., No. 1800 Chicago, IL 60606-6615. Phone: 800-621-3570 or (312)781-1300 or (312)781-1410; Fax: (312)781-1467; Email: information@nfa.futures.org • URL: http://www.nfa.futures.org • Quarterly. Price on application. Looseleaf service. Rules and regulations concerning commodity futures trading.

**National Futures Association**. 300 S Riverside Plz., No. 1800 Chicago, IL 60606-6615. Phone: 800-621-3570 or (312)781-1300 or (312)781-1410; Fax: (312)781-1467; Email: information@nfa.futures.org • URL: http://www.nfa.futures.org • Futures commission merchants; commodity trading advisors; commodity pool operators; brokers and their associated persons. Works to: strengthen and expand industry self-regulation to include all segments of the futures industry; provide uniform standards to eliminate duplication of effort and conflict; remove unnecessary regulatory constraints to aid effective regulation. Conducts member qualification screening, financial surveillance, and registration. Monitors and enforces customer protection rules and uniform business standards. Maintains information center. Arbitrates customer disputes; audits non-exchange member FCM's.

**National Glass Association**. 1945 Old Gallows Rd., Ste. 750 Vienna, VA 22182. Phone: 866-342-5642 or (703)442-4890; Fax: (703)442-0630 or (703)827-0557; Email: pjames@glass.org • URL: http://www.glass.org • Manufacturers, installers, retailers, distributors and fabricators of flat, architectural, automotive and specialty glass and metal products, mirrors, shower and patio doors, windows and tabletops. Provides informational, educational and technical services.

**National Golf Course Owners Association**. 291 Seven Farms Dr. Charleston, SC 29492. Phone: 800-933-4262 or (843)881-9956; Fax: (843)881-9958; Email: info@ngcoa.org • URL: http://www.ngcoa.org • Owners and operators of privately owned golf courses. Assist members to develop more productive, efficient, and profitable golf operations. Provides information on taxation, destination golf, community relations, environmental regulations, and marketing. Offers group purchasing opportunities. Conducts educational seminars. Compiles statistics.

**National Governors' Association**. Hall of the States, 444 N Capitol St. NW, Ste. 267 Washington, DC 20001-1512. Phone: (202)624-5300; Fax: (202)624-5313 • URL: http://www.nga.org/cms/home.html • Governors of the 50 states, Guam, American Samoa, the Virgin Islands, the Northern Mariana Islands, and Puerto Rico. Serves as vehicle through which governors influence the development and implementation of national policy and apply creative leadership to state problems. Keeps the federal establishment informed of the needs and perceptions of states. Through its Center for Best Practices, it provides a vehicle for sharing information on innovative programs among the states and providing technical assistance to governors on a wide range of issues.

**National Grain and Feed Association**. 1250 I St. NW, Ste. 1003 Washington, DC 20005. Phone: (202)289-0873; Fax: (202)289-5388; Email: ngfa@ngfa.org • URL: http://www.ngfa.org • Formerly Grain and Feed Dealers National Association.

**National Grange**. 1616 H St. NW Washington, DC 20006. Phone: 888-447-2643 or (202)628-3507; Fax: (202)347-1091; Email: info@nationalgrange.org • URL: http://www.nationalgrange.org • Rural family service organization with a special interest in agriculture. Promotes mission and goals through legislative, social, educational, community service, youth and member services programs. Sponsors needlework and stuffed toy contests.

**National Grants Management Association**. 2100 M St. NW, Ste. 170 Washington, DC 20037. Phone: (202)308-9443; Email: info@ngma.org • URL: http://netforum.avectra.com/eweb/StartPage.aspx?Site=ngma&WebCode=HomePage • Strengthens the relationship between grant-making agencies and grant recipients by empowering both sides with knowledge through training, seminars, workshops, and conferences. Focuses on federal, state, and local governments and private foundations that provide grants, grants-in-aid, cooperative agreements, and subsidies.

**National Grocers Association**. 1005 N Glebe Rd., Ste. 250 Arlington, VA 22201-5758. Phone: (703)516-0700; Fax: (703)516-0115; Email: feedback@nationalgrocers.org • URL: http://www.nationalgrocers.org • Independent food retailers; wholesale food distributors servicing 29,000 food stores. Promotes industry interests and works to advance understanding, trade and cooperation among all sectors of the food industry. Represents members' interests before the government. Aids in the development of programs designed to improve the productivity and efficiency of the food distribution industry. Offers services in areas such as store planning and engineering, personnel selection and training, operations and advertising. Sponsors seminars and in-house training. Maintains liaison with Women Grocers of America, which serves as an advisory arm.

**National Ground Water Association**. 601 Dempsey Rd. Westerville, OH 43081. Phone: 800-551-7379 or (614)898-7791; Fax: (614)898-7786; Email: ngwa@ngwa.org • URL: http://www.ngwa.org • Ground water drilling contractors; manufacturers and suppliers of drilling equipment; ground water scientists such as geologists, engineers, public health officials, and others interested in the problems of locating, developing, preserving, and using ground water supplies. Conducts seminars, and continuing education programs. Encourages scientific education, research, and the development of standards; offers placement services; compiles market statistics. Offers charitable program. Maintains speakers' bureau.

**National Guard Association of the United States**. 1 Massachusetts Ave. NW Washington, DC 20001-1401. Phone: (202)789-0031; Fax: (202)682-9358; Email: ngaus@ngaus.org • URL: http://www.ngaus.org • Active and Retired Officers and Warrant Officers of the Army National Guard and Air National Guard of the States, Commonwealth of Puerto Rico, the District of Columbia, Guam, and the Virgin Islands. Goals include: adequate national security and a strong Army National Guard and Air National Guard of the United States as components of the armed forces. Sponsors public affairs competition for National Guard personnel. Maintains the Museum of the National Guard, containing rare art and artifacts relating to the militia and National Guard.

**National Guard Executive Directors Association**. 3706 Crawford Ave. Austin, TX 78731. Phone: (512)454-7300; Fax: (512)467-6803 • URL: http://www.ngeda.org • Provides a forum for the exchange of information of common interest to members and the organizations they represent; encourages states to organize and maintain a National Guard association; participates in improving the operational readiness, training and image of the National Guard on both state and national levels.

**National Hair Society**. 39252 Winchester Rd., No. 107-383 Murrieta, CA 92563. Phone: (619)928-9750; Email: hsimon@nationalhairjournal.com • URL: http://www.nationalhairsociety.org • Represents hair management professionals. Offers information, education and networking pathways. Provides cross-marketing opportunities, seminars and workshops.

***National Hardwood Lumber Association Membership Directory***. National Hardwood Lumber Association, 6830 Raleigh La Grange Rd. Memphis, TN 38134-0518. Phone: 800-933-0318 or (901)377-1818; Fax: (901)382-6419 or (901)399-7581; Email: info@nhla.com • URL: http://www.nhla.com • Available on website. Members are hardwood lumber and veneer manufacturers, distributors, and users.

**National Hardwood Lumber Association**. 6830 Raleigh La Grange Rd. Memphis, TN 38134-0518. Phone: 800-933-0318 or (901)377-1818; Fax: (901)382-6419 or (901)399-7581; Email: info@nhla.com • URL: http://www.nhla.com • United States, Canadian and International hardwood lumber and veneer manufacturers, distributors and consumers. Inspects hardwood lumber. Maintains inspection training school. Conducts management and marketing seminars for the hardwood industry. Promotes research in hardwood timber management and utilization. Promotes public awareness of the industry.

***National Hardwood Magazine***. Miller Publishing Corp., 5175 Elmore Rd., Ste. 23 Memphis, TN 38184-0908. Phone: 800-844-1280 or (901)372-8280; Fax: (901)373-6180; Email: editor@millerpublishing.com • URL: http://www.millerpublishing.com • Monthly. $55 Individuals 1 year - US; $65 Individuals 1 year - Canada; $140 Other countries 1 year. Contains latest developments in the Hardwood Industry, both on the supplier side and in the marketplace.

**National Hay Association**. 151 Treasure Island Causeway, No. 2 Saint Petersburg, FL 33706. Phone: 800-707-0014 or (727)367-9702; Fax: (727)367-9608; Email: haynha@aol.com • URL: http://nationalhay.org • Hay shippers, dealers, brokers, producers, and others interested in the hay industry.

**National Health Policy Forum**. George Washington University, 2131 K St. NW, Ste. 500 Washington, DC 20037-1882. Phone: (202)872-1390; Fax: (202)862-9837; Email: nhpf@gwu.edu • URL: http://www.nhpf.org • Nonpartisan education program serving primarily senior federal legislative and executive branch health staff but also addressing the interests of state officials and their Washington representatives. Seeks to foster more informed government decision-making. Helps decision makers forge the personal acquaintances and understanding necessary for cooperation among government agencies and between government and the private sector.

**National Hispanic Corporate Council**. 1050 Connecticut Ave. NW, Fl. 10 Washington, DC 20036-5334. Phone: (202)772-1100; Fax: (202)772-3101; Email: info@nhcchq.org • URL: http://www.nhcchq.org • Corporate think tank serving Fortune 1000 companies and their representatives as a principal resource for information, expertise and counsel about Hispanic issues affecting corporate objectives, and to advocate for increased employment, leadership and business opportunities for Hispanics in corporate America.

***National Hog Farmer***. Primedia Business Magazines and Media, 7900 International Dr., Ste. 300 Minneapolis, MN 55425. Phone: 800-795-5445 or (925)851-9329 or (952)851-9329; Fax: (925)851-4601 or (952)851-4601; Email: subs@primediabusiness.com • URL: http://www.primediabusiness.com • Monthly. $39 Individuals 1 year; $78 Two years. Provides professional pork producers with breaking news, business management guidance, and timely production information needed to keep modern pork production systems competitive and profitable.

***National Home Center News: News and Analysis for the Home Improvement, Building Material Industry***. Lebhar-Friedman Inc., 425 Park Ave. New York, NY 10022. Phone: (212)756-5000 or (603)432-4077; Email: info@lf.com • URL: http://www.lf.com • 22 times a year. $99.00 per year. Includes special feature issues on hardware and tools, building materials, millwork, electrical supplies, lighting, and kitchens.

**National Honey Packers and Dealers Association**. 3301 Rte. 66, Ste. 205, Bldg. C Neptune, NJ 07753. Phone: (732)922-3008; Fax: (732)922-3590; Email: info@nhpda.org • URL: http://www.nhpda.org • Represents cooperative and independent processors, packers, and dealers of honey at either the wholesale or retail level. Offers members information on test-

SOURCES CITED

ing facilities for honey analysis. Consults with Department of Agriculture on research programs in the field of honey marketing.

**National Housing Conference**. 1900 M St. NW, Ste. 200 Washington, DC 20036. Phone: (202)466-2121; Fax: (202)466-2122 • URL: http://www.nhc.org • Housing authority officials, community development specialists, builders, bankers, lawyers, accountants, owners, residents, insurers, architects and planners, religious organizations, labor groups, and national housing and housing-related organizations. Mobilizes support for effective programs in housing and community development as well as affordable and accessible housing for all Americans. Holds educational programs.

**National Human Resources Association**. PO Box 5455 Manchester, NH 03108-5455. Phone: 866-523-4417; Fax: (603)718-3124; Email: info@humanresources.org • URL: http://www.humanresources.org • Represents human resource executives in business, industry, education and government. Established to expand and improve the professionalism of those in human resource management.

**National Hydropower Association**. 25 Massachusetts Ave. NW, Ste. 450 Washington, DC 20001. Phone: (202)682-1700; Fax: (202)682-9478; Email: help@hydro.org • URL: http://www.hydro.org • Represents hydrodevelopers, dam site owners, manufacturers, utilities and municipalities, individuals from the financial community (such as bankers, brokers, and investors), civil contracting firms, architects, engineering firms, and others actively involved in the promotion and development of hydropower. Promotes the development of hydroelectric energy. Participates in the regulatory process on issues such as simplified licensing procedures, purchase power rates, removal of regulatory barriers, and timely implementation of previously adopted legislation. Informs the government about the potential of hydropower and also monitors and drafts new legislation to government regulatory and legislative bodies.

**National Ice Cream Retailers Association**. 1028 W Devon Ave. Elk Grove Village, IL 60007. Phone: 866-303-6960 or (847)301-7500; Fax: (847)301-8402 • URL: http://www.nicra.org • Represents frozen dessert retailers that operate ice cream and frozen yogurt dipping stores or parlors. Provides free and frank exchange of information among members so that all may improve their operations, increase profits and prosper.

**National Immigration Forum**. 50 F St. NW, Ste. 300 Washington, DC 20001-1552. Phone: (202)347-0040; Fax: (202)347-0058 or (202)544-0004; Email: info@immigrationforum.org • URL: http://www.immigrationforum.org • Dedicated to extending and defending America's tradition as a nation of immigrants. Supports the reunification of families, the rescue and resettlement of refugees fleeing persecution, and the equitable treatment of immigrants under the law. Encourages immigrants to become U.S. citizens and promote cooperation and understanding between immigrants and other Americans.

**National Independent Automobile Dealers Association**. 2521 Brown Blvd. Arlington, TX 76006. Phone: 800-682-3837 or (817)640-3838 or (434)983-2073; Fax: (817)649-5866; Email: info@niada.com • URL: http://www.niada.com • Individuals, companies, or corporations licensed by their states as dealers to buy and sell used motor vehicles; associate members are businesses related to or associated with the buying or selling of motor vehicles. Gathers and disseminates information relative to the used car industry; represents used car dealers before regulatory and legislative bodies; provides educational and other programs to help used car dealers understand their responsibilities; works for the betterment of the automobile industry. Works closely with local and state independent automobile dealers' associations and others concerning dealers and the public. Maintains code of fair dealing for members. Conducts seminars, meetings, and professional training programs. Maintains speakers' bureau, services for children, and charitable programs. Sponsors competitions; compiles statistics.

**National Industrial Transportation League**. 1700 N Moore St., Ste. 1900 Arlington, VA 22209. Phone: (703)524-5011; Fax: (703)524-5017; Email: info@nitl.org • URL: http://www.nitl.org • Seeks to promote adequate national and international transportation; encourages the exchange of ideas and information concerning traffic and transportation; and cooperates with regulatory agencies and other transportation companies in developing an understanding of legislation.

**National Information Standards Organization**. 3600 Clipper Mill Rd., Ste. 302 Baltimore, MD 21211. Phone: (301)654-2512; Fax: (410)685-5278; Email: hreid@copyright.com • URL: http://www.niso.org • Identifies, develops, maintains, and publishes technical standards to manage information in the changing environment used by libraries, publishers, and information services. Supports open access to NISO standards. Standards available at website.

**National Institute for Automotive Service Excellence**. 101 Blue Seal Dr. SE, Ste. 101 Leesburg, VA 20175. Phone: 877-346-9327 or (703)669-6600; Fax: (703)669-6127; Email: asehelp@ase.com • URL: http://www.ase.com • A public interest organization which promotes high standards in automotive service and repair. Encourages effective training

programs for automobile mechanics/technicians. Affiliated with National Automotive Technicians Education Foundation.

**National Institute for Fitness and Sport**. 250 University Blvd. Indianapolis, IN 46202. Phone: (317)274-3432; Fax: (317)274-7408 • URL: http://www.nifs.org • Exercise physiology, sports medicine, and health and fitness education.

**National Institute of Food and Agriculture - Rural and Community Development Program**. Waterfront Ctr., 800 9th St. SW Washington, DC 20024. Phone: (202)401-2185; Fax: (202)730-9366; Email: phipple@nifa.usda.gov • URL: http://www.csrees.usda.gov/ruralcommunitydevelopment.cfm • Economic and rural community development.

**National Institute of Government Purchasing**. 151 Spring St. Herndon, VA 20170-5223. Phone: 800-367-6447 or (703)736-8900; Fax: (703)736-2818; Email: info@nigp.com • URL: http://www.nigp.org.

**National Institute of Oilseed Products**. 750 National Press Bldg., 529 14th St. NW Washington, DC 20045. Phone: (202)591-2461 or (202)785-3232; Fax: (202)223-9741; Email: niop@kellencompany.com • URL: http://www.oilseed.org • Shippers, brokers, growers, manufacturers, refiners, transportation, end users—anything to do with oilseeds. Establishes and maintains trading rules.

**National Institute of Senior Housing**. National Council on Aging, 1901 L St. NW, 4th Fl. Washington, DC 20036. Phone: (202)479-1200; Fax: (202)479-0735 • URL: http://www.ncoa.org • Members are organizations and individuals concerned with the housing needs of older persons. Provides information on the development and management of housing suitable for the elderly. Affiliated with National Council on Aging.

**National Institute of Standards and Technology - Advanced Technology Program - Economic Assessment Office**. 100 Bureau Dr., MS 4710 Gaithersburg, MD 20899-4710. Phone: (301)975-8978; Fax: (301)975-4776; Email: stephanie.shipp@nist.gov • URL: http://www.atp.nist.gov/eao/eao_main.htm • Seeks to evaluate how private-public partnerships in technology development interact with commercial markets and to assess their impact on the economy and society.

**National Institute of Statistics and Economic Studies - Center for Research in Economics and Statistics**. 15 Blvd. Gabriel Péri F-92245 Malakoff, France. Phone: 33 1 41176081; Fax: 33 1 41176029 • URL: http://www.insee.fr/en/insee-statistique-publique/default.asp?page=connaitre/genes.htm • Economic and social modeling; conception and implementation of statistical methods.

**National Institute on Disability and Rehabilitation Research - Self-Employment Technology Transfer**. 52 Corbin Hall, Rural Institute on Disabilities, University of Montana Missoula, MT 59812. Phone: 800-732-0320 or (406)268-2743; Fax: (406)243-4730; Email: nancy@ruralinstitute.umt.edu • URL: http://rtc.ruralinstitute.umt.edu/SelEm/RuSelfEm.htm • Vocational rehabilitation research, specifically, self-employment for people with disabilities.

**National Insulation Association**. 12100 Sunset Hills Rd., Ste. 330 Reston, VA 20190. Phone: (703)464-6422; Fax: (703)464-5896 • URL: http://www.insulation.org • Insulation contractors, distributors, and manufacturers.

*National Insurance Law Review*. NILS Publishing Co., 21625 Prairie St. Chatsworth, CA 91311. Phone: 800-423-5910 • URL: http://library-dialog.com • Quarterly. $95.00 per year. Contains insurance-related articles from major law reviews.

**National - Interstate Council of State Boards of Cosmetology**. c/o Debra Norton, Coordinator, 7622 Briarwood Cir. Little Rock, AR 72205. Phone: (501)227-8262; Fax: (501)227-8212 • URL: http://www.nictesting.org • Persons commissioned by 50 state governments as administrators of cosmetology laws and examiners of applicants for licenses to practice cosmetology.

**National Investor Relations Institute**. 225 Reinekers Ln., Ste. 560 Alexandria, VA 22314. Phone: (703)562-7700 or (703)506-3570; Fax: (703)562-7701 or (703)506-3571; Email: info@niri.org • URL: http://www.niri.org • Executives engaged in investor relations. Identifies the role of the investor relations practitioner; protects a free and open market with equity and access to investors of all kinds; improves communication between corporate management and shareholders, present and future. Holds professional development seminars and conducts research programs. Maintains placement service and speakers' bureau; compiles statistics.

*National Jeweler*. Nielsen Business Media Inc., 770 Broadway New York, NY 10003-9522. Phone: 866-890-8541 or (646)654-4500 or (646)654-5000; Fax: (646)654-5584 or (646)654-4500; Email: bmcomm@nielsen.com • URL: http://www.nielsenbusinessmedia.com • Bimonthly. $65.00 per year. For jewelry retailers.

*National JobBank*. Adams Media Corp., 57 Littlefield St. Avon, MA 02322. Phone: 800-872-5627 or (508)427-7100; Fax: (508)427-6790 or (800)872-5628; Email: deskcopies@adamsmedia.com • URL: http://www.adamsmedia.com • Annual. $475 Individuals payment with order. Covers: Over 20,000 employers nationwide. Entries include: Firm or organization name, address, local phone, toll-free phone, fax, contact name and title, description of organization, headquarters location, names of management, number of employees, other locations, subsidiaries, parent company, projected number of hires, training offered, internships, hours,

recorded jobline, typical titles for common positions, educational backgrounds desired, stock exchange (if listed), fringe benefits offered. Several state and regional volumes are available and described separately.

*National Journal: The Weekly on Politics and Government*. National Journal Group Inc., The Watergate, 600 New Hampshire Ave. NW Washington, DC 20037. Phone: 800-613-6701 or (202)739-8400; Fax: (202)833-8069; Email: service@nationaljournal.com • URL: http://www.nationaljournal.com • Weekly. $1,499 Individuals. Includes semiannual supplement *Capital Source*. A non-partisan weekly magazine on politics and government.

**National Kitchen and Bath Association**. 687 Willow Grove St. Hackettstown, NJ 07840. Phone: 800-843-6522; Fax: (908)852-1695; Email: feedback@nkba.org • URL: http://www.nkba.org • Formerly American Institute of Kitchen Dealers.

**National Latina Business Women Association**. 11664 National Blvd., Ste. 283 Los Angeles, CA 90064. Phone: 888-MY-NLBWA; Email: info@nlbwa.org • URL: http://nlbwa.org • Strives to promote, develop, and support the growth of Latina business owners and professionals. Seeks to create networking and mentoring opportunities for members.

*National Law Journal: The Weekly Newspaper for the Profession*. ALM Media Properties LLC, 120 Broadway, 5th Fl. New York, NY 10271-1100. Phone: (212)457-9400; Fax: (646)417-7705; Email: customercare@alm.com • URL: http://www.alm.com • Weekly. News and analysis of the latest developments in the law and the law profession.

**National Lawyers Guild - Military Law Task Force**. 730 N 1st St. San Jose, CA 95122. Phone: (619)463-2369 • URL: http://nlgmltf.org • Counselors, attorneys, and law students concerned with military, selective service, and veterans' law. Purposes are to: assist active-duty personnel, veterans, and those affected by selective service; provide educational and political work focused on these areas of law; offer research assistance in military and veterans law; support networking among attorneys and counselors. Operates speakers' bureau; offers informal referral services and educational materials.

**National Lawyers Guild**. 132 Nassau St., Rm. 922 New York, NY 10038. Phone: (212)679-5100; Fax: (212)679-2811 • URL: http://www.nlg.org • Lawyers, law students, legal workers, and jailhouse lawyers dedicated to seek economic justice, social equality, and the right to political dissent. Serves as national center for progressive legal work providing training programs to both members and nonmembers. Sponsors skills seminars in different areas of law. Maintains speakers' bureau and offers legal referrals.

**National League of Cities**. 1301 Pennsylvania Ave. NW, Ste. 550 Washington, DC 20004-1747. Phone: 877-827-2385 or (202)626-3000; Email: memberservices@nlc.org • URL: http://www.nlc.org • Formerly American Municipal Association.

**National Legal Aid and Defender Association**. 1901 Pennsylvania Ave. NW, Ste. 500 Washington, DC 20006. Phone: (202)452-0620; Fax: (202)872-1031; Email: info@nlada.org • URL: http://www.nlada100years.org • Legal aid offices and public defender organizations representing the indigent and individual members. Provides technical and management assistance to local organizations offering legal services to poor persons in civil or criminal cases and to state and local units of government. Advocates for federally funded high quality legal services with the public, media, congress, and members of the Executive branch. Offers litigation support through amicus curiae capability to organizations providing legal services. Serves as clearinghouse for information on the provision of legal aid and defender services to persons without means to pay lawyers' fees. Sponsors training program covering substantive law, management issues and litigation skills. Matches private law firms with impact cases to facilitate increased pro bono participation.

*National Library of Medicine*. National Institutes of Health, 9000 Rockville Pke. Bethesda, MD 20892. Phone: (301)496-4000; Email: nihinfo@od.nih.gov • URL: http://www.nih.gov • NLM Web site offers free access through MEDLINE ("PubMed") to about nine million references to articles appearing in some 4,000 biomedical journals, with abstracts. Search interfaces range from "simple keywords to advanced Boolean expressions." The NLM site offers many links to other sources of biomedical and technical information (the National Center for Biotechnology Information, for example). Fees: Free.

*National Locksmith*. National Publishing Company Inc., 1533 Burgundy Pkwy. Streamwood, IL 60107. Phone: (630)837-2044; Email: sales@thenationallocksmith.com • URL: http://www.thenationallocksmith.com • Monthly. $66 U.S. print and digital; $24.95 Other countries 1 year Digital magazine includes access to the digital Back issues 2009-2011. Source for automotive technology, safe opening techniques, electronic security.

**National Lubricating Grease Institute**. 249 SW Noel St., Ste. 249 Lees Summit, MO 64063-2241. Phone: (816)524-2500; Fax: (816)524-2504; Email: nlgi@nlgi.org • URL: http://www.nlgi.org • Companies manufacturing or selling all types of lubricating greases; suppliers to such companies; technical and educational organizations. Promotes research and testing for the development of better lubricating greases and improved grease lubrication engineering service to industry.

Collects and disseminates technical data; conducts forums and educational program. Operates the National Lubricating Grease Institute Research Fund.

**National Luggage Dealers Association**. 1817 Elmdale Ave. Glenview, IL 60026. Phone: (847)998-6869; Fax: (847)998-6884; Email: inquiry@nlda.com • URL: http://www.luggagedealers.com • Represents retailers of luggage, leather goods, gifts, and handbags. Buying group producing promotional materials.

**National Lumber and Building Material Dealers Association**. 2025 M St. NW, Ste. 800 Washington, DC 20036-3309. Phone: (202)367-1169; Fax: (202)367-2169; Email: info@dealer.org • URL: http://www.dealer.org • Formerly National Retail Lumber Dealers Association.

**National Mail Order Association**. 2807 Polk St. NE Minneapolis, MN 55418-2954. Phone: (612)788-1673; Email: info@nmoa.org • URL: http://www.nmoa.org • Provides education, information, and business contacts to those involved in direct marketing and mail order. Reports new and established product sources, ideas, techniques, developments, and services of value to mail marketers. Reviews and disseminates information on reports, government findings, new books and directories, mailing lists, and general data relating to developing maximum mail order sales.

*The National Managed Care Leadership Directory*. HealthQuest Publishers from MCOL, MCOL 1101 Standiford Ave., Ste. C-3 Modesto, CA 95350. Phone: (209)577-4888; Fax: (209)577-3557; Email: info@healthquestpublishers.com • URL: http://www.healthquestpublishers.com • $249 Individuals print; $595 Individuals CD-ROM; $215 Individuals PDF. Covers: 844 companies and 7,020 executive listings in the managed care industry including health plans, provider networks, PBMs, administrative organizations (quality improvement organizations, utilizations and disease management organizations, and TPAs) and specialty organizations (dental, vision and behavioral).

**National Management Association**. 2210 Arbor Blvd. Dayton, OH 45439. Phone: (937)294-0421; Email: nma@nma1.org • URL: http://www.nma1.org • Business and industrial management personnel; membership comes from supervisory level, with the remainder from middle management and above. Seeks to develop and recognize management as a profession and to promote the free enterprise system. Prepares chapter programs on basic management, management policy and practice, communications, human behavior, industrial relations, economics, political education, and liberal education. Maintains speakers' bureau and hall of fame. Maintains educational, charitable, and research programs. Sponsors charitable programs.

**National Marine Representatives Association**. PO Box 360 Gurnee, IL 60031. Phone: (847)662-3167; Fax: (847)336-7126; Email: info@nmraonline.org • URL: http://www.nmraonline.org • Works to serve the marine industry independent sales representatives and the manufacturers selling through representatives. Serves as industry voice, networking tool and information source promoting benefits of utilizing independent marine representatives for sales. Aims to assist manufacturers find the right marine sales reps for product lines.

**National Mining Association**. 101 Constitution Ave. NW, Ste. 500 E Washington, DC 20001-2133. Phone: (202)463-2600 or (202)463-2639; Fax: (202)463-2666 • URL: http://www.nma.org • Producers and sellers of coal and hardrock minerals, equipment manufacturers, distributors, equipment suppliers, other energy suppliers, consultants, utility companies, and coal transporters. Serves as liaison between the industry and federal government agencies. Keeps members informed of legislative and regulatory actions. Works with industry, consumers, and government agencies on mining industry issues. Seeks improved conditions for export of steam and metallurgical coal. Collects, analyzes, and distributes industry statistics; makes special studies of competitive fuels, coal and metal markets, production and consumption forecasts, and industry planning.

*National Minority and Women-Owned Business Directory*. Diversity Information Resources, 2105 Central Ave. NE Minneapolis, MN 55418. Phone: (612)781-6819; Fax: (612)781-0109; Email: info@diversityinforesources.com • URL: http://www.diversityinforesources.com • Annual. $169 Individuals print. Covers: Information regarding minority and women-owned business directories to acquaint major corporations and government purchasing agents with the products and services of minority and women-owned firms. Covers approximately 7000 minority-owned firms. Entries include: Company name, address, phone, fax, e-mail, Web site, number of employees, year established, products or services, certification status, minority identification, annual sales, NAICS code.

**National Minority Business Council**. 1633 Broadway, 30th Fl. New York, NY 10019. Phone: (347)289-7620 or (212)245-2652; Email: info@nmbc.org • URL: http://nmbc.org • Represents minority businesses in all areas of industry and commerce. Seeks to increase profitability by developing marketing, sales, and management skills in minority businesses. Acts as an informational source for the national minority business community. Includes programs such as: legal services plan that provides free legal services to members in such areas as sales contracts, copyrights, estate planning, and investment agreement; business referral service that develops potential customer leads; international trade assistance program that provides technical assistance in developing foreign markets; executive banking program that teaches members how to package a business loan for bank approval; procurement outreach program for minority and women business owners. Conducts continuing management education and provides assistance in teaching youth the free enterprise system.

**National Minority Supplier Development Council**. 1359 Broadway, 10th Fl., Ste. 1000 New York, NY 10018. Phone: (212)768-0430; Email: info@nmsdc.org • URL: http://www.nmsdc.org • Provides a direct link between its 3,500 corporate members and minority-owned businesses (Black, Hispanic, Asian and Native American) and increases procurement and business opportunities for minority businesses of all sizes.

**National Motor Freight Traffic Association**. 1001 N Fairfax St., Ste. 600 Alexandria, VA 22314. Phone: 866-411-6632 or (703)838-1810 or (703)683-6046; Fax: (703)683-6296; Email: customerservice@nmfta.org • URL: http://www.nmfta.org • Motor common carriers of general commodities. Represents interests of membership before the Surface Transportation Board, the Congress, the courts and state regulatory agencies.

**National Naval Officers Association**. PO Box 10871 Alexandria, VA 22310-0871. Phone: (703)231-8554 • URL: http://nnoa.memberclicks.net • Active, reserve, and retired Navy, Marine, and Coast Guard officers and students in college and military sea service programs. Promotes and assists recruitment, retention, and career development of minority officers in the naval service. Conducts specialized education; maintains counseling, referral, and mentorship. Makes available non-ROTC grants-in-aid. Sponsors competitions; operates charitable program.

**National Newspaper Association**. PO Box 7540 Columbia, MO 65205-7540. Phone: (573)777-4980; Fax: (573)777-4985 or (573)237-9808 • URL: http://nnaweb.org • Protects, promotes and enhances community newspapers. Represents community newspapers across America. Promotes quality journalism and business practices at its annual convention, through its various contests and awards and various other educational programs.

**National Notary Association**. 9350 DeSoto Ave. Chatsworth, CA 91313-2402. Phone: 800-876-6827 • URL: http://www.nationalnotary.org • Notaries public (officers empowered to witness the signing of documents, identify the signers, take acknowledgments, and administer oaths). Works to teach notaries public in the U.S. their duties, powers, limitations, liabilities, and obligations. Keeps members informed of changes in notary law; offers various services, supplies, and insurance plans to members. Maintains speakers' bureau.

*The National Notary*. National Notary Association, 9350 DeSoto Ave. Chatsworth, CA 91313-2402. Phone: 800-876-6827 • URL: http://www.nationalnotary.org • Bimonthly. $45 Members includes magazine & bulletin. Legal trade magazine.

*National Now Times*. National Organization for Women, 1100 H St. NW, Ste. 300 Washington, DC 20005-5488. Phone: (202)628-8669; Fax: (202)785-8576 • URL: http://now.org • Free to members.

**National Nurses in Business Association**. 8941 Atlanta Ave., Ste. 202 Huntington Beach, CA 92646. Phone: 877-353-8888 • URL: http://www.nnba.net • Promotes, supports, educates, and provides a comprehensive network for nurse entrepreneurs.

**National Ocean Industries Association**. 1120 G St. NW, Ste. 900 Washington, DC 20005. Phone: (202)347-6900; Fax: (202)347-8650; Email: rmyers@noia.org • URL: http://www.noia.org • Corporations organized to promote the common business interests of the offshore and ocean-oriented industries by: increasing public understanding of the ocean's use and its relation to the economy; encouraging interest in industrial, scientific, recreational, research, and educational activities in the field of ocean enterprise; encouraging the development and use of the resources of the ocean consistent with environmental practices and safeguards; encouraging compatible use of ocean resources; improving communication between industry and the federal government. Supports legislation and other governmental action favorable to the offshore and ocean industry and counsels against such action when it is not favorable. Seeks to expand the role of the free enterprise system in the development of ocean resources.

**National Oilseed Processors Association**. 1300 L St. NW, Ste. 1020 Washington, DC 20005-4168. Phone: (202)842-0463; Fax: (202)842-9126; Email: nopa@nopa.org • URL: http://www.nopa.org • Represents processors of oilseeds.

*National Onion Association—Newsletter*. National Onion Association, 822 7th St., Ste. 510 Greeley, CO 80631-3941. Phone: (970)353-5895; Fax: (970)353-5897; Email: info@onions-usa.org • URL: http://www.onions-usa.org • Quarterly. Description: Provides information on the onion industry.

**National Onion Association**. 822 7th St., Ste. 510 Greeley, CO 80631-3941. Phone: (970)353-5895; Fax: (970)353-5897; Email: info@onions-usa.org • URL: http://www.onions-usa.org • Growers, brokers, grower-shippers, shippers, suppliers, and support professionals engaged in the onion industry. Promotes the onion industry. Compiles monthly statistical report of stocks-on-hand, acreage, yield, and production of onions in the U.S. Lobbies issues of importance to national onion industry.

**National Optometric Association**. 5009 Beatties Ford Rd., Ste. 107, No. 278 Charlotte, NC 28216. Phone: 877-394-2020 or (704)918-1809; Email: mainoffice@natoptassoc.org • URL: http://nationaloptometricassociation.com • Represents optometrists dedicated to increasing awareness of the status of eye/vision health in the minority community and the national community at-large. Strives to make known the impact of the eye/vision dysfunction on the effectiveness and productivity of citizens and the academic proficiency of students. Conducts national minority recruiting programs, job placement, assistance programs for graduates, practitioners, and optometric organizations, and the promotion of delivery of care. Maintains speakers' bureau. Offers specialized education program.

**National Organization for Women**. 1100 H St. NW, Ste. 300 Washington, DC 20005-5488. Phone: (202)628-8669; Fax: (202)785-8576 • URL: http://now.org • Includes men and women seeking equality for women.

*National Packing News*. National Packing News, PO Box 829 Granby, MO 64844. Email: npnews@jscomm.net • Description: Discusses topics that affect the food processing industry in the nation, including production, marketing, new developments and products, new plants and plant expansions, and professional appointments. Recurring features include news of research, statistics, book reviews, and obituaries. **Remarks:** Incorporates the former Eastern Packing News and Western Packing News.

**National Park Hospitality Association**. 1200 G St. NW, Ste. 650 Washington, DC 20005. Phone: (202)682-9530; Fax: (202)682-9529 • URL: http://parkpartners.org • Represents private concessionaires operating in the U.S. national parks. Acts as liaison between members and the National Park Service and Congress.

**National Parking Association**. 1112 16th St. NW, Ste. 840 Washington, DC 20036. Phone: 800-647-7275 or (202)296-4336; Fax: (202)296-3102; Email: info@npapark.org • URL: http://www.npapark.org • Owners and operators of off-street parking facilities; architects, traffic engineers, equipment suppliers and manufacturers, colleges, universities, municipalities, airport authorities; others with an interest in downtown parking. Provides specialized education programs; offers scholarship program through the Parking Industry Institute.

*National Parliamentarian*. National Association of Parliamentarians, 213 S Main St. Independence, MO 64050-3808. Phone: 888-627-2929 or (816)833-3892; Fax: (816)833-3893; Email: hq@nap2.org • URL: http://www.parliamentarians.org • Quarterly. Provides readers with insightful, up-to-date information on parliamentary procedure and how it is applied to a variety of situations and needs.

**National Partnership for Women & Families**. 1875 Connecticut Ave. NW, Ste. 650 Washington, DC 20009. Phone: (202)986-2600; Fax: (202)986-2539; Email: info@nationalpartnership.org • URL: http://www.nationalpartnership.org • Formerly Women's Legal Defense Fund.

*National Pasta Association FYI Newsletter*. National Pasta Association, 750 National Press Bldg., 529 14th St. NW Washington, DC 20045. Phone: (202)591-2459; Fax: (202)591-2445; Email: info@ilovepasta.org • URL: http://www.ilovepasta.org • Weekly. Membership.

**National Pasta Association**. 750 National Press Bldg., 529 14th St. NW Washington, DC 20045. Phone: (202)591-2459; Fax: (202)591-2445; Email: info@ilovepasta.org • URL: http://www.ilovepasta.org • Manufacturers of pasta in the U.S. and suppliers to the industry. Seeks to improve manufacturer and supplier efficiency. Conducts agricultural and technical research programs. Sponsors U.S. pasta product public relations program and pasta/durum wheat technical course.

**National Pecan Shellers Association**. 1100 Johnson Ferry Rd., Ste. 300 Atlanta, GA 30342. Phone: (678)298-1189; Email: npsa@kellencompany.com • URL: http://www.ilovepecans.org • Shellers and processors of pecans. Promotes the welfare and interests of the pecan shelling and processing industry.

**National Pest Management Association International**. 10460 N St. Fairfax, VA 22030. Phone: 800-678-6722 or (703)352-6762; Fax: (703)352-3031; Email: npmateam@vaultcommunications.com • URL: http://www.pestworld.org • Represents firms engaged in control of insects, rodents, birds, and other pests, in or around structures, through use of insecticides, rodenticides, miticides, fumigants, and non-chemical methods. Provides advisory services on control procedures, new products, and safety and business administration practices. Promotes June as National Pest Control Month. Sponsors research, periodic technical and management seminars.

**National Petroleum Council**. 1625 K St. NW, Ste. 600 Washington, DC 20006. Phone: (202)393-6100; Fax: (202)331-8539; Email: info@npc.org • URL: http://www.npc.org • Advisory council to the Secretary of Energy on matters relating to oil and gas.

**National Pharmaceutical Association**. 107 Kilmayne Dr., Ste. C Cary, NC 27511. Phone: 877-215-2091; Fax: (919)469-5858; Email: npha@npha.net • URL: http://npha.net • State and local associations of professional minority pharmacists.

Provides a means whereby members may "contribute to their common improvement, share their experiences, and contribute to the public good."

**National Pharmaceutical Council**. 1717 Pennsylvania Ave. NW, Ste. 800 Washington, DC 20006. Phone: (202)827-2100; Fax: (202)827-0314; Email: info@npcnow.org • URL: http://www.npcnow.org • Pharmaceutical manufacturers producing high-quality prescription medication and other pharmaceutical products. Generates research; conducts specialized educational programs and forums.

**National Pork Producers Council**. 122 C St. NW, Ste. 875 Washington, DC 20001. Phone: (202)347-3600; Fax: (202)347-5265 • URL: http://www.nppc.org • Federation of state pork producer associations. Promotes the pork industry through research programs, consumer education, and lobbying activities. Compiles statistics; maintains speakers' bureau and hall of fame.

**National Ports and Waterways Institute**. University of New Orleans, 2300 Claredon Blvd., Ste. 300 Arlington, VA 22201. Phone: (703)276-7101; Fax: (703)276-7102; Email: npwi@seas.gwu.edu • URL: http://www.members.tripod.com/npwi.

**National Potato Council**. 1300 L St. NW, Ste. 910 Washington, DC 20005. Phone: (202)682-9456; Fax: (202)682-0333; Email: spudinfo@nationalpotatocouncil.org • URL: http://nationalpotatocouncil.org • Commercial potato growers. Takes action on national potato legislative, regulatory, and environmental issues.

**National Press Club**. National Press Bldg., 529 14th St. NW, 13th Fl. Washington, DC 20045. Phone: (202)662-7500 or (202)662-7505; Fax: (202)662-7512 • URL: http://press.org • Reporters, writers and news people employed by newspapers, wire services, magazines, radio and television stations and other forms of news media. Sponsors sports, travel and cultural events, rap sessions with news figures and authors and newsmaker breakfasts and luncheons. Offers monthly training.

**National Press Photographers Association**. 3200 Croasdaile Dr., Ste. 306 Durham, NC 27705-2588. Phone: (919)383-7246; Fax: (919)383-7261; Email: info@nppa.org • URL: http://www.nppa.org • Professional news photographers and others whose occupation has a direct professional relationship with photojournalism, the art of news communication by photographic image through publication, television film, or theater screen. Sponsors annual television-news film workshop and annual cross-country (five locations) short course. Conducts annual competition for news photos and for television-news film, and monthly contest for still clipping and television-news film.

**National Private Truck Council**. 950 N Glebe Rd., Ste. 2300 Arlington, VA 22203-4183. Phone: (703)683-1300 or (703)838-8816; Fax: (703)683-1217; Email: info@nptc.org • URL: http://www.nptc.org • Represents private motor carrier truck fleets and their suppliers.

**National Productivity and Competitiveness Council**. 4th Fl. Alexander House, Cybercity Ebene City, Mauritius. Phone: 230 4677700; Fax: 230 4673838; Email: natpro@intnet.mu • URL: http://www.npccmauritius.com • Generating consensus and building innovation capacity to move to a higher growth path. Hosts seminars and assemblies.

**National Productivity Council**. Utpadakta Bhavan, 5-6 Institutional Area, Lodhi Rd. New Delhi 110 003, Delhi, India. Phone: 91 11 24690331; Fax: 91 11 24615002; Email: npcinfo@npcindia.gov.in • URL: http://www.npcindia.gov.in • Represents professionals in the field of productivity. Promotes increased efficiency in all aspects of Indian economic activity. Conducts research, gathers and disseminates information.

**National Propane Gas Association**. 1899 L St. NW, Ste. 350 Washington, DC 20036-4623. Phone: (202)466-7200; Fax: (202)466-7205; Email: info@npga.org • URL: http://www.npga.org/i4a/pages/index.cfm?pageid=1 • Represents the propane industry, including small businesses and large corporations engaged in the retail marketing of propane gas and appliances, producers and wholesalers of propane gas and equipment, manufacturers and fabricators of propane gas cylinders and tanks, propane transporters, and manufacturer's representatives. Works to promote the safe and increased use of propane; advocates in Congress and federal regulatory agencies for favorable environment for production, distributing, and marketing of propane gas. Develops safety standards and training materials for the safe use and distribution of propane gas.

**National Property Management Association**. 4025 Tampa Rd., Ste. 1203 Oldsmar, FL 34677. Phone: (813)475-6998; Fax: (813)749-0812; Email: hq@npma.org • URL: http://www.npma.org • Aims to build leadership by educating, training and promoting standards of competency and ethical behavior in the asset management of personal property. Serves property professionals throughout the United States; members represent companies and organizations in both the public and private sectors, including scientific laboratories, universities, hospitals, public school systems, and local, state and federal government agencies.

***The National Provisioner: Serving Meat, Poultry, and Seafood Processors***. BNP Media, 2401 W Big Beaver Rd., Ste. 700 Troy, MI 48084. Phone: 800-952-6643 or (248)362-3700 or (847)763-9534; Fax: (248)362-5103 or (248)362-0317; Email: privacy@bnpmedia.com • URL: http://www.bnpmedia.com • Monthly. Free to qualified subscribers; $85.04 Individuals. *Buyer's Guide* available. Meat, poultry and seafood newsletter.

**National Ready Mixed Concrete Association**. 900 Spring St. Silver Spring, MD 20910. Phone: (240)485-1139 • URL: http://www.nrmca.org • Concrete plant manufacturers. Develops engineering standards with a view toward simplification and standardization of sizes, capacities, and other criteria associated with the manufacture of concrete plants. Performs services leading to higher quality concrete plant equipment.

***National Real Estate Index***. CB Richard Ellis Group Inc., 11150 Santa Monica Blvd., Ste. 1600 Los Angeles, CA 90025. Phone: 800-799-6523 or (310)405-8900; Fax: (302)655-5049; Email: carmen.cortes@cbre.com • URL: http://www.cbre.com • Price and frequency on application. Provides reports on commercial real estate prices, rents, capitalization rates, and trends in more than 65 metropolitan areas. Time span is 12 years. Includes urban office buildings, suburban offices, warehouses, retail properties, and apartments.

***National Real Estate Investor***. Penton, 9800 Metcalf Ave. Overland Park, KS 66212. Phone: 866-748-4926 or (913)341-1300; Fax: (913)967-1905 or (913)967-1898; Email: corporatecustomerservice@penton.com • URL: http://www.penton.com • Bimonthly. Magazine on commercial real estate investment, development and management. Includes annual *Directory*. Market surveys by city.

***National Real Estate Investor Sourcebook***. Primedia Business, 6151 Powers Ferry Rd. NW Atlanta, GA 30339. Phone: (770)955-2500 or (770)995-2500; Fax: (770)618-0204 • URL: http://www.primediabusiness.com • Annual. $79.95 payment must accompany order. List of about 7,000 companies and individuals in 18 real estate fields, including appraisers; asset managers; builders, contractors, and developers; communication services; corporate real estate managers; environmental consultants; equity investors; financial services; hospitality services; institutional advisors; pension funds; property managers; real estate brokers, agents, consultants, and counselors; software products and services; title insurance companies; related associations; and others.

**National Recreation and Park Association**. 22377 Belmont Ridge Rd. Ashburn, VA 20148-4501. Phone: 800-262-6772 or (703)858-0784; Email: customerservice@nrpa.org • URL: http://www.nrpa.org • Formerly National Conference on State Parks.

***The National Register of Fashion Accessories***. Marche Publishing, c/o Erika Fetter, Managing Dir., 333 S Grand Ave., 25th Fl. Los Angeles, CA 90071. Phone: 800-992-9892 or (213)995-5076; Fax: (213)995-5076; Email: golant@thenationalregister.com • URL: http://www.thenationalregister.com • $200 Individuals print; $400 Individuals print, CD; $250 Individuals CD; $150 Individuals online access; $500 Individuals online access, print, CD. Covers: Apparel accessory companies in the United States. Entries include: company name, address, phone, fax and toll free numbers, website and email addresses, officers, year established, brands, and affiliates.

***The National Register of Independent Sales Reps—Apparel and Accessories***. Marche Publishing, c/o Erika Fetter, Managing Dir., 333 S Grand Ave., 25th Fl. Los Angeles, CA 90071. Phone: 800-992-9892 or (213)995-5076; Fax: (213)995-5076; Email: golant@thenationalregister.com • URL: http://www.thenationalregister.com • $250 Individuals print; $500 Individuals print, CD; $625 Individuals print, online access, CD; $300 Individuals CD; $175 Individuals online access. Covers: 1,200 representatives throughout the United States and Canada. Entries include: Company name, address, phone and fax numbers, email address, year established, lines of business, origin of companies, and quote from reps.

**National Registration Center for Study Abroad**. 207 E Buffalo St., Ste. 610 Milwaukee, WI 53202-5712. Phone: (414)278-0631 or (414)278-7410; Fax: (414)271-8884; Email: study@nrcsa.com • URL: http://www.nrcsa.com • Members are foreign universities, foreign language institutions, and other institutions or organizations offering foreign study programs designed for North Americans.

**National Regulatory Research Institute**. 8611 2nd Ave., Ste. 2C Silver Spring, MD 20910. Phone: (301)588-5383 or (301)588-5384; Email: nrri.admin@nrri.org • URL: http://www.nrri.org • Electric, natural gas, water, and telephone utility regulation procedures. Specific topics include gas wellhead price deregulation, power pooling, gas marginal cost pricing, utility operating efficiency, regulatory incentives, retail wheeling, pricing wheeled power, funding nuclear decommissioning, measured rate telephone service, telecommunications competition, small water utility regulation, and electric utility subsidiaries.

**National Rehabilitation Information Center**. 8400 Corprate Dr., Ste. 500 Landover, MD 20785. Phone: 800-346-2742 or (301)459-5900; Fax: (301)459-4263; Email: naricinfo@heitechservices.com • URL: http://www.naric.com • Aims to improve delivery of information to the rehabilitation community. Disseminates the findings of programs funded by the National Institute on Disability and Rehabilitation Research; prepares custom bibliographies; helps locate answers to reference questions; searches for relevant materials in other commercially available databases.

**National Renderers Association**. 500 Montgomery St., Ste. 310 Alexandria, VA 22314. Phone: (703)683-0155; Fax: (571)970-2279; Email: renderers@nationalrenderers.com • URL: http://nationalrenderers.org • Producers of tallow and grease products (for use in soap and lubricants), and meat meal (for use in animal feeds), obtained as by-products of the meat-packing industry. Conducts research and educational programs; provides international and domestic market development services and legislative representation.

**National Research Council - Division of Behavioral and Social Science and Education - Center for Social and Economic Studies**. 500 5th St. NW, 11th Fl. Washington, DC 20001. Phone: (202)334-3730; Fax: (202)334-3829; Email: cses@nas.edu • URL: http://www7.nationalacademies.org/cses/ • Social and economic policy-related research, including racial dynamics in the U.S., urban issues, environmental decision-making, and international conflict resolution.

**National Research Council - Division on Engineering and Physical Sciences - National Materials and Manufacturing Board**. The National Academies, 500 5th St. NW Washington, DC 20001-2736. Phone: (202)334-3505; Fax: (202)334-3575; Email: nmmb@nas.edu • URL: http://sites.nationalacademies.org/DEPS/NMMB/index.htm • Represents members of the board and its committees and panels appointed by the chairman of the National Research Council; industry, universities, research institutes, and government. Promotes the advancement of materials science and engineering in the national interest. Conducts studies on materials problem, potential approaches, and policy issues.

**National Research Council Italy - Institute for Economic Research on Firms and Growth**. Via Bassini, 15 I-20131 Milan, Italy. Phone: 39 2 70643501; Fax: 39 2 23699530 • URL: http://www.ceris.cnr.it • Structural economic dynamics, technological change, and Schumpeterian economics.

**National Restaurant Association Educational Foundation**. 2055 L St. NW Washington, DC 20036. Phone: 800-424-5156; Email: scholars@nraef.org • URL: http://www.nraef.org • Serves as an educational foundation supported by the National Restaurant Association and all segments of the foodservice industry including restaurateurs, foodservice companies, food and equipment manufacturers, distributors and trade associations. Advances the professional standards of the industry through education and research. Offers video training programs, management courses and careers information. Conducts research and maintains hall of fame.

**National Restaurant Association**. 2055 L St. NW, Ste. 700 Washington, DC 20036. Phone: 800-424-5156 or (202)331-5900; Fax: (202)331-2429 • URL: http://www.restaurant.org • Represents restaurants, cafeterias, clubs, contract foodservice management, drive-ins, caterers, institutional food services and other members of the foodservice industry; also represents establishments belonging to non-affiliated state and local restaurant associations in governmental affairs. Supports foodservice education and research in several educational institutions. Is affiliated with the Educational Foundation of the National Restaurant Association to provide training and education for operators, food and equipment manufacturers, distributors and educators. Has 300,000 member locations.

**National Retail Federation**. 325 7th St. NW, Ste. 1100 Washington, DC 20004. Phone: 800-673-4692 or (202)783-7971 or (202)347-1932; Fax: (202)737-2849; Email: bookinquiries@nrf.com • URL: http://www.nrf.com • Represents state retail associations, several dozen national retail associations, as well as large and small corporate members representing the breadth and diversity of the retail industry's establishment and employees. Conducts informational and educational conferences related to all phases of retailing including financial planning and cash management, taxation, economic forecasting, expense planning, shortage control, credit, electronic data processing, telecommunications, merchandise management, buying, traffic, security, supply, materials handling, store planning and construction, personnel administration, recruitment and training, and advertising and display.

***National Retail Hardware Association Management Report: Cost of Doing Business Study***. North American Retail Hardware Association, 6325 Digital Way, Ste. 300 Indianapolis, IN 46278-1787. Phone: 800-772-4424 or (317)275-9400 or (317)290-0338; Fax: (317)275-9403 or (317)328-4354; Email: hwegeng@nrha.org • URL: http://www.nrha.org • Annual. Report provides information on business cost analysis.

**National Rifle Association of America**. 11250 Waples Mill Rd. Fairfax, VA 22030-7400. Phone: 800-672-3888 or (703)267-1614; Fax: (703)267-3913; Email: nfmstaff@nrahq.org • URL: http://www.nrahq.org • Target shooters, hunters, gun collectors, gunsmiths, police officers, and others interested in firearms. Promotes rifle, pistol, and shotgun shooting, hunting, gun collecting, home firearm safety, and wildlife conservation. Encourages civilian marksmanship. Educates police firearms instructors. Maintains national and international records of shooting competitions; sponsors teams to compete in world championships. Also maintains comprehensive collection of antique and modern firearms. Administers the NRA Political Victory Fund. Compiles statistics; sponsors research and education programs; maintains speakers' bureau and museum. Lobbies on firearms issues.

**National Roofing Contractors Association**. 10255 W Higgins Rd., Ste. 600 Rosemont, IL 60018-5607. Phone: (847)299-9070; Fax: (847)299-1183 • URL: http://www.nrca.net • Roofing, roof deck, and waterproofing contractors and industry-related associate members. Assists members to successfully satisfy their customers through technical support, testing and research, education, marketing, government relations, and consultation.

**National Rural Electric Cooperative Association**. 4301 Wilson Blvd. Arlington, VA 22203. Phone: (703)907-5500 or (703)907-5732; Fax: (703)907-5517; Email: michael.lynch@nreca.coop • URL: http://www.nreca.coop/Pages/default.aspx • Rural electric cooperative systems, public power districts and public utility districts in 46 states. Conducts activities such as: legislative representation; energy and regulatory; management institutes; professional conferences; training and consulting services; insurance and safety programs; international program; wage and salary surveys.

**National Rural Housing Coalition**. 1331 G St. NW, 10th Fl. Washington, DC 20005. Phone: (202)393-5229; Fax: (202)393-3034; Email: nrhc@ruralhousingcoalition.org • URL: http://ruralhousingcoalition.org • Advocates for improved government and private housing programs for people in small towns and rural areas. Develops informational and educational material; gives and coordinates testimony before congressional committees; seeks improved administrative procedures within the executive branch of the federal government. Lobbies for low-income rural housing and community facilities.

**National Rural Utilities Cooperative Finance Corp.** 20701 Cooperative Way Dulles, VA 20166. Phone: 800-424-2954 or (703)709-6700 or (703)467-1800; Fax: (703)467-5175; Email: publicrelations@nrucfc.coop • URL: http://www.nrucfc.coop.

**National Scholastic Press Association**. University of Minnesota, 2221 University Ave. SE, Ste. 121 Minneapolis, MN 55414-3074. Phone: (612)625-8335; Fax: (612)605-0072 or (612)626-0720; Email: info@studentpress.org • URL: http://www.studentpress.org/nspa • Represents publishers of high school newspapers, yearbooks, and magazines. Offers critical services for newspapers, yearbooks, and magazines.

**National School Boards Association**. 1680 Duke St. Alexandria, VA 22314-3493. Phone: (703)838-6722 or (703)838-6731; Fax: (703)683-7590; Email: info@nsba.org • URL: http://www.nsba.org • Federation of state school boards associations, the Board of Education of the District of Columbia and the Virgin Islands Board of Education. Advocates equity and quality education for primary and secondary public school children through legal counsel, research studies, legislative advocacy programs, and services for members, conferences, and magazines. Provides information on topics affecting K-12 public education and school policy. Maintains library and specialized clearinghouses.

**National School Supply and Equipment Association**. 8380 Colesville Rd., Ste. 250 Silver Spring, MD 20910. Phone: 800-395-5550 or (301)495-0240; Fax: (301)495-3330; Email: customerservice@nssea.org • URL: http://www.nssea.org • Absorbed Education Industries Association. Formerly National School Service Institute.

**National Science Foundation - Directorate for Social, Behavioral, and Economic Sciences - Division of Social and Economic Sciences**. 4201 Wilson Blvd., Rm. 995N Arlington, VA 22230. Phone: (703)292-8760; Fax: (703)292-9068; Email: jmumpowe@nsf.gov • URL: http://www.nsf.gov/div/index.jsp?div=SES • Economics, law and social science, political science, sociology, measurement methods and data improvement, decision, risk, and management science. The goal of the Division is to develop basic scientific knowledge of human social behavior, interaction, and decision-making, and of social and economic systems, organizations, and institutions. The Division also supports research on the human dimensions of global environmental change and research to improve the quality and the accessibility of social and economic data resources. In addition to research proposals, programs within the Division consider proposals for doctoral dissertation support, research conferences, the acquisition of specialized research and computing equipment, group international travel, and data collection.

***National Services Directory***. Dun & Bradstreet Inc., 103 JFK Pkwy. Short Hills, NJ 07078. Phone: 800-526-0651 or (973)921-5500 or (973)921-5000; Fax: (866)560-7035 or (512)794-7670; Email: info@dnb.com • URL: http://www.dnb.com • $495. Covers: Approximately 20,000 service companies in Canada. Entries include: Name, address, phone, fax.

**National Shellfisheries Association**. c/o Linda Kallansrude, 14 Carter Ln. East Quogue, NY 11942-4335. Phone: (631)653-6327; Fax: (631)653-6327; Email: secretariat@shellfish.org • URL: http://www.shellfish.org • Biologists, hydrographers, public health workers, shellfish producers, and fishery administrators. Encourages research on mollusks and crustaceans, with emphasis on those forms of economic importance known as shellfish.

**National Shoe Retailers Association**. 7386 N La Cholla Blvd. Tucson, AZ 85741-2305. Phone: 800-673-8446 or (520)209-1710; Fax: (520)209-5595; Email: info@nsra.org • URL: http://www.nsra.org • Proprietors of independent shoe stores and stores with major shoe departments. Provides business services and professional development programs including bankcard processing, shipping, freight discounts, free website listing, employee training; conducts research; monitors legislation.

**National Small Business Association**. 1156 15th St. NW, Ste. 1100 Washington, DC 20005. Phone: 800-345-6728 or (202)293-8830; Fax: (202)872-8543; Email: info@nsba.biz • URL: http://www.nsba.biz • Small businesses including manufacturing, wholesale, retail, service, and other firms. Works to advocate at the federal level on behalf of smaller businesses.

***National Small Business Journal: The information newspaper for small & growing businesses***. TWG Publishing Co., 1266 W Paces Ferry Rd., Ste. 522 Atlanta, GA 30327. Phone: 800-345-1959 or (404)605-0002; Fax: (404)355-3211 • $15 annual. Newspaper containing articles geared toward small businesses and their interests.

**National Society for Experiential Education**. 19 Mantua Rd. Mount Royal, NJ 08061-1006. Phone: (856)423-3427; Email: nsee@talley.com • URL: http://www.nsee.org • Members include representatives of internship programs. Formerly National Society for Internships and Experential Education.

***National Society for the Study of Education Yearbook***. National Society for the Study of Education. The University of Chicago Press, 11030 S Langley Ave. Chicago, IL 60628. Phone: 800-621-2736 or (773)702-7000 or (773)702-7700; Fax: (773)702-9756 or (773)702-7212; Email: custserv@press.uchicago.edu • URL: http://www.press.uchicago.edu • Annual. Membership. Two volumes per year.

**National Society of Accountants**. 1010 N Fairfax St. Alexandria, VA 22314. Phone: 800-966-6679 or (703)549-6400; Fax: (703)549-2984; Email: members@nsacct.org • URL: http://www.nsacct.org • Formerly *National Society of Public Accountants*.

**National Society of Hispanic MBAs**. 450 E John Carpenter Fwy. Irving, TX 75062. Phone: 877-467-4622 or (214)596-9338; Fax: (214)596-9325 • URL: http://www.nshmba.org • Hispanic MBA professional business network dedicated to economic and philanthropic advancement.

**National Society of Pershing Rifles**. 2 Spring Meadow Ln. Hockessin, DE 19707. Phone: (516)945-9299; Email: wwagne@optonline.net • URL: http://pershingriflessociety.org • Members range from military to civilian, male to female. Seeks to foster a spirit of friendship and cooperation among men and women in the military department and to maintain a highly efficient drill company.

***National Society of Public Accountants - Yearbook***. National Society of Accountants, 1010 N Fairfax St. Alexandria, VA 22314. Phone: 800-966-6679 or (703)549-6400; Fax: (703)549-2984; Email: members@nsacct.org • URL: http://www.nsacct.org • Annual. Free to members, government agencies and libraries; not available to others.

**National Society of Scabbard and Blade**. Oklahoma State University, 325 Thatcher Hall Stillwater, OK 74078. Phone: (405)377-4279; Fax: (405)377-2237; Email: memberships@scabbardandblade.org • URL: http://www.scabbardandblade.org • Honorary and recognition fraternity - men and women, military; advanced ROTC; junior ROTC, and all-Service. Maintains speakers' bureau.

***National Solid Waste Grants Database***. RCRA Research Library, EPA New England, 1 Congress St., Ste. 1100 Boston, MA 02114. Email: Friedman.Fred@epa.gov • Database covers: More than 500 grant and loan providers as well as venture capitalists interested in recycling, reuse and solid waste management. Database includes: Contact information for some Northeastern U.S. firms.

***National Solid Wastes Management Association: Member Companies***. National Waste and Recycling Association, 4301 Connecticut Ave. NW, Ste. 300 Washington, DC 20008-2304. Phone: 800-424-2869 or (202)244-4700; Fax: (202)966-4824; Email: info@wasterecycling.org • URL: http://wasterecycling.org • Annual. Lists waste management consulting firms. Available via website.

**National Speakers Association**. 1500 S Priest Dr. Tempe, AZ 85281. Phone: (480)968-2552; Email: info@gettingtothefinishline.com • URL: http://www.nsaspeaker.org • Professional speakers. Works to increase public awareness of the speaking profession, advance the integrity and visibility of professional speakers, and provide a learning and communication vehicle to professional speakers. Sponsors workshops, conventions, and labs.

**National Sporting Goods Association**. 1601 Feehanville Dr., Ste. 300 Mount Prospect, IL 60056. Phone: 800-815-5422; Fax: (847)391-9827; Email: info@nsga.org • URL: http://www.nsga.org • Provides services, education and information to assist member to profit in a competitive marketplace.

**National Sportscasters and Sportswriters Association**. PO Box 1545 Salisbury, NC 28145. Phone: (704)633-4275; Fax: (704)633-2027 • URL: http://nssafame.com • Members are sportswriters and radio/TV sportscasters.

***National Stock Summary***. OTC Markets Group Inc., 304 Hudson St., 3rd Fl. New York, NY 10013. Phone: 800-547-8682 or (212)896-4420 or (212)896-4400; Fax: (212)868-3848; Email: otcqx@otcmarkets.com • URL: http://www.otcqx.com • Monthly, with semiannual cumulations. $576.00 per year. Includes price quotes for both active and inactive issues, with transfer agents, market makers (brokers), capital changes, name changes, and other corporate information. Pink Sheets LLC also provides daily and weekly stock price services. Formerly published by the National Quotation Bureau.

**National Stone, Sand and Gravel Association**. 1605 King St. Alexandria, VA 22314-2726. Phone: 800-342-1415 or (703)525-8788 or (703)526-1098; Fax: (703)525-7782; Email: info@nssga.org • URL: http://www.nssga.org • Formerly National Stone Association.

**National Student Employment Association**. c/o June Hagler, Office Manager, 715 Northill Dr. Richardson, TX 75080. Phone: (972)690-8772; Fax: (972)767-5131; Email: nsea@nsea.info • URL: http://www.nsea.info • Directors, coordinators, and senior staff personnel of postsecondary educational institutions, including proprietary schools and corporate human resource directors, who are involved in student employment, internships, cooperative and experiential education, federal work-study, job location and development, and student placement. Answers problems associated with the management of student employment programs. Provides financial support for students in higher education. Creates and conducts training and professional development programs for higher education student employment professionals. Sponsors State Work Study Clearinghouse on state sponsored student employment programs. Compiles statistics. Conducts research programs. Provides legislative updates on current issues.

***National Survey of State Laws***. Cengage Learning Inc., 20 Channel Center St. Boston, MA 02210. Phone: 800-487-8488 or (617)289-7700; Fax: (617)289-7844; Email: investors@cengage.com • URL: http://www.cengage.com • 2007. eBook. 6th edition. Provides concise state-by-state comparisons of current state laws on a wide variety of topics. Includes references to specific codes or statutes. Inquire for pricing.

**National Swine Registry - United Duroc Swine Registry**. 2639 Yeager Rd. West Lafayette, IN 47996-2417. Phone: (765)463-3594; Fax: (765)497-2959; Email: nsr@nationalswine.com • URL: http://www.nationalswine.com • Promotes the Duroc swine breed in the U.S.

**National Tank Truck Carriers**. 950 N Glebe Rd., Ste. 520 Arlington, VA 22203. Phone: 800-441-1414 or (703)838-1960; Fax: (703)838-8860; Email: nttcstaff@tanktruck.org • URL: http://www.tanktruck.org • Common or contract "for-hire" tank truck carriers transporting liquid and dry bulk commodities, chemicals, food processing commodities, petroleum, and related products; allied industry suppliers. Promotes federal standards of construction, design, operation and use of tank trucks and equipment. Coordinates truck transportation system for shippers of bulk commodities. Secures improvements in tank specifications. Sponsors annual schools; conducts research.

***National Tax Association Proceedings of the Annual Conference on Taxation***. National Tax Association-Tax Institute of America, 725 15th St. NW, Ste. 600 Washington, DC 20005-2109. Phone: (202)737-3325 or (202)261-5577; Fax: (202)737-7308; Email: natltax@aol.com • URL: http://www.ntanet.org • Annual. Members, $85.00; individuals, $70.00; libraries, $90.00; corporations, $130.00.

**National Tax Association-Tax Institute of America**. 725 15th St. NW, Ste. 600 Washington, DC 20005-2109. Phone: (202)737-3325 or (202)261-5577; Fax: (202)737-7308; Email: natltax@aol.com • URL: http://www.ntanet.org.

***National Tax Journal***. National Tax Association-Tax Institute of America, 725 15th St. NW, Ste. 600 Washington, DC 20005-2109. Phone: (202)737-3325 or (202)261-5577; Fax: (202)737-7308; Email: natltax@aol.com • URL: http://www.ntanet.org • Quarterly. Membership. Topics of current interest in the field of taxation and public finance in the U.S. and foreign countries.

**National Taxpayers Union**. 108 N Alfred St. Alexandria, VA 22314-3053. Phone: (703)683-5700; Fax: (703)683-5722; Email: ntu@ntu.org • URL: http://www.ntu.org • Seeks to: reduce government spending; cut taxes; protect the rights of taxpayers. Claims to have helped generate federal budget cuts of over 120 billion dollars. Activities include research programs and an intense lobbying campaign in Washington, DC; has been a leader in the fights against government ventures such as: social security tax; guaranteed income; congressional and bureaucratic pay raises; federal subsidies; foreign aid; national health insurance. Works for a balanced federal budget/tax limitation constitutional amendment; federal pension reform; reduction of capital gains and personal income tax; social security reform. Has worked for airline deregulation; indexing of federal income tax, California's Proposition 13, Massachusetts Proposition 2 1/2, and other state tax cutting initiatives. Conducts annual voting study of congressmen and senators, rating their votes on spending and tax issues and presenting awards for best and worst records.

**National Tooling and Machining Association**. 1357 Rockside Rd. Cleveland, OH 44134-2776. Phone: 800-248-6862; Fax: (216)264-2840; Email: info@ntma.org • URL: http://www.ntma.org.

**National Tour Association**. 101 Prosperous Pl., Ste. 350 Lexington, KY 40509. Phone: 800-682-8886 or (859)264-6540; Fax: (859)264-6570; Email: questions@ntastaff.com • URL: http://www.ntaonline.com • Formerly National Tour Brokers Association.

***National Trade and Professional Associations Directory***. Columbia Books and Information Services, 8120 Woodmont Ave., Ste. 110 Bethesda, MD 20814. Phone: 888-265-0600 or (202)464-1662; Fax: (202)464-1775; Email: info@columbiabooks.com • URL: http://www.columbiabooks.com • Annual. $299. Provides key facts on approximately 7,800 trade associations, labor and professional organizations.

***National Trade Estimate Report on Foreign Trade Barriers (year)***. U. S. Government Printing Office, 732 N Capitol St. NW Washington, DC 20401. Phone: 866-512-1800 or (202)512-1800 or (866)512-1800; Fax: (202)512-2104 or (202)512-2250; Email: contactcenter@gpo.gov • URL: http://www.gpo.gov • Annual. $47. Issued by the Office of the United States Trade Representative. "Provides quantitative estimates of the impact of foreign practices on the value of United States exports.".

**National Treasury Employees Union**. 1750 H St. NW Washington, DC 20006-4600. Phone: (202)572-5500 • URL: http://www.nteu.org • Employees of the federal government. Conducts research and educational training programs. Sponsors Federal Employees Education and Assistance Fund.

***National Truck Equipment Association—Market Resource Guide***. National Truck Equipment Association, 37400 Hills Tech Dr. Farmington Hills, MI 48331-3414. Phone: 800-441-NTEA or (248)489-7090; Fax: (248)489-8590; Email: info@ntea.com • URL: http://www.ntea.com • Annual. $50 Nonmembers; $12 Members. Covers: Over 1,500 distributors who install commercial truck bodies and related equipment on chassis-cabs, truck body and equipment manufacturers, and associates. Entries include: Company name, address, phone, fax, e-mail, web site, name and title of contact; membership type and year began membership, products or services.

**National Truck Equipment Association**. 37400 Hills Tech Dr. Farmington Hills, MI 48331-3414. Phone: 800-441-NTEA or (248)489-7090; Fax: (248)489-8590; Email: info@ntea.com • URL: http://www.ntea.com • Serves as a trade group for commercial truck, truck body, truck equipment, trailer and accessory manufacturers and distributors. Advises members of current federal regulations affecting the manufacturing and installation of truck bodies and equipment; works to enhance the professionalism of management and improve profitability in the truck equipment business.

**National Turkey Federation**. 1225 New York Ave., Ste. 400 Washington, DC 20005. Phone: (202)898-0100; Fax: (202)898-0203; Email: info@turkeyfed.org • URL: http://www.eatturkey.com • Serves as the national advocate for all segments of the turkey industry. Provides services and conducts activities that increase demand for its members' products by protecting and enhancing their ability to profitably provide wholesome, high-quality, and nutritious products.

***National Underwriter***. • Weekly. Two editions: *Life* or *Health*. $86.00 per year, each edition.

***National Underwriter, Property and Casualty Edition***. • Weekly. $92.00 per year.

**National United States-Arab Chamber of Commerce**. 1023 15th St. NW, Ste. 400 Washington, DC 20005. Phone: (202)289-5920; Fax: (202)289-5938; Email: info@nusacc.org • URL: http://www.nusacc.org • Individuals, companies, corporations, and associations interested in commercial trade relations with the Arab world. Promotes business between the United States and the Arab world; encourages policies that promote better commercial relations. Conducts research and information services on commercial opportunities, export regulations, and conditions that affect the trade and investment climate. Sponsors trade delegations; holds seminars, conferences, and training sessions; acts as a central information center. Maintains relations with U.S. and Arab governments and agencies to develop, monitor, and recommend relevant legislation.

**National University of Singapore - Singapore Center for Applied and Policy Economics**. Department of Economics, AS2 No. 06-02, 1 Arts Link Singapore 117570, Singapore. Phone: 65 65166116; Fax: 65 67752646; Email: ecstabey@nus.edu.sg • URL: http://www.fas.nus.edu.sg/ecs/scape • Singapore and Asian macroeconomics and modeling, human resources and labor economics, public economics and social policy, and behavioral and experimental economics.

**National Urban League**. 120 Wall St. New York, NY 10005. Phone: (212)558-5300; Fax: (212)344-5332; Email: info@nul.org • URL: http://nul.iamempowered.com • Voluntary nonpartisan community service agency of civic, professional, business, labor, and religious leaders with a staff of trained social workers and other professionals. Aims to eliminate racial segregation and discrimination in the United States and to achieve parity for blacks and other minorities in every phase of American life. Works to eliminate institutional racism and to provide direct service to minorities in the areas of employment, housing, education, social welfare, health, family planning, mental retardation, law and consumer affairs, youth and student affairs, labor affairs, veterans' affairs, and community and minority business development. Maintains research department in Washington, DC.

**National Utilities Diversity Council**. 1017 L St. Sacramento, CA 95814. Phone: (916)492-9163; Fax: (916)473-9444; Email: mpl@cpuc.ca.gov • Promotes diversity in the utility industry in the areas of governance, employment, procurement, language access/customer service and philanthropy. Serves as a resource that promotes the inclusion of women, racial and ethnic minorities, service disabled veterans and other organized groups in utility corporate governance, philanthropy, employment, procurement, language access and customer service.

***National Venture Capital Association Yearbook***. Thomson Financial Inc., 195 Broadway New York, NY 10007-3100. Phone: (646)822-2000; Email: custserv@tfn.com • URL: http://www.thomsonreuters.com • Annual. $195.00. Provides a yearly review of the U.S. venture capital industry, including statistical data.

***National Verticals***. Scott's Directories, 12 Concorde Pl., Ste. 800 Toronto, ON, Canada M3C 4J2. Phone: 800-668-2374 or (416)442-2122; Fax: (416)510-6870; Email: customercare@scottsdirectories.com • URL: http://www.scottsdirectories.com • $1,395 Individuals CD-ROM (food and beverage) prospector; $1,895 Individuals CD-ROM (metal fabricating) prospector; $1,495 Individuals CD-ROM (machinery manufacturers) prospector; $895 Individuals CD-ROM (chemical and pharmaceutical) prospector; $795 Individuals CD-ROM (packaging industry) prospector; $2,195 Individuals CD-ROM (construction industry) prospector; $3,195 Individuals CD-ROM (exporters) prospector. Covers: Canadian industry-specific contacts and company profiles. Entries include: Complete business name, names and titles of executives and decision-makers, mailing and location addresses, phone and faxes, corporate email, products and/or services offered, annual estimated gross sales, year established, number of employees, ISO registration, North American industry classification standard (NAICS) codes, web site address.

***National Water Conditions***. U.S. Geological Survey - Water Resources Division, 12201 Sunrise Valley Dr. Reston, VA 20192. Phone: 888-275-8747 • URL: http://www.usgs.gov/water • Description: Describes the month's water conditions in the U.S. and Canada, compiling data on streamflow, ground water conditions, surface water, reservoirs, the flow of large rivers, water temperatures, and dissolved solids.

**National Water Resources Association**. 3800 N Fairfax Dr., Ste. 4 Arlington, VA 22203. Phone: (703)524-1544; Fax: (703)524-1548; Email: nwra@nwra.org • URL: http://www.nwra.org • Officers of irrigation districts, canal companies, businesses, and others interested in the development, control, conservation, and utilization of water resources in the reclamation states (17 western states). Conducts legislative tracking and provides updates.

**National Waterways Conference**. 1100 N Glebe Rd., Ste. 1010 Arlington, VA 22201. Phone: (703)224-8007 or (703)243-4090; Fax: (866)371-1390 or (703)243-4155; Email: amy@waterways.org • URL: http://www.waterways.org • Petroleum, coal, chemical, electric power, building materials, iron and steel, and grain companies; industrial development agencies, port authorities, and other governmental bodies; water carriers; companies which build, repair, service, or insure vessels; water resource development associations, banks, chambers of commerce, and individuals. Seeks to promote a better understanding of the public value of the American waterways system. Conducts research on the economics of water transportation; sponsors an educational program to point up the diverse benefits of efficient water transport; keeps members and other waterway proponents posted on developments affecting national waterways policy.

***National Wellness Institute—Member Directory***. National Wellness Institute, PO Box 827 Stevens Point, WI 54481-0827. Phone: 800-243-8694 or (715)342-2969; Fax: (715)342-2979; Email: nwi@nationalwellness.org • URL: http://www.nationalwellness.org • Covers: more than 1,600 health and wellness promotion professionals in corporations, hospitals, colleges, government agencies, universities, community organizations, schools (K-12), and consulting firms, and managed care. Entries include: Member name, address, and phone, fax, email.

**National Wellness Institute**. PO Box 827 Stevens Point, WI 54481-0827. Phone: 800-243-8694 or (715)342-2969; Fax: (715)342-2979; Email: nwi@nationalwellness.org • URL: http://www.nationalwellness.org • Aims to provide national leadership in the wellness movement; to assist professionals working in health and wellness promotion in all types of settings, and organizations with planning, development, implementation, and evaluation of wellness programs; and to assist in the development of high quality wellness products and services. Acts as clearinghouse on wellness information. Provides consultations; offers professional development conferences. Sponsors National Wellness Association.

**National Wildlife Federation**. 11100 Wildlife Center Dr. Reston, VA 20190. Phone: 800-822-9919 or (703)438-6000 • URL: http://www.nwf.org • Serves as a member-supported conservation group, with over four million members and supporters. Federation of state and territorial affiliates, associate members and individual conservationist-contributors. Seeks to educate, inspire and assist individuals and organizations of diverse cultures to conserve wildlife and other natural resources and to protect the earth's environment in order to achieve a peaceful, equitable and sustainable future. Encourages the intelligent management of the life-sustaining resources of the earth and promotes greater appreciation of wild places, wildlife and the natural resources shared by all. Publishes educational materials and conservation periodicals.

**National Women's Law Center**. 11 Dupont Cir. NW, Ste. 800 Washington, DC 20036-1209. Phone: (202)588-5180; Fax: (202)588-5185; Email: info@nwlc.org • URL: http://www.nwlc.org • Uses the law in all its forms: getting new laws on the books; litigating ground-breaking lawsuits all the way to the Supreme Court; and educating the public about how to make the law and public policies work for women and their families. "Takes on the issues that cut to the core of women's and girls' lives" in health, education, employment, and family economic security, with special priority given to the needs of low-income women and their families.

**National Women's Network**. c/o The Admin Center, 46 Beaumont Manor, Northumberland Blyth NE24 4LP, United Kingdom. Phone: 44 1670 618628 or 44 7855 746777 • URL: http://national-womens-network.co.uk • Professional women in England. Seeks to enhance the status of women. Provides a forum for women to develop social and professional contacts.

**National Writers Association**. 10940 S Parker Rd., No. 508 Parker, CO 80134. Phone: (303)841-0246; Fax: (303)841-2607; Email: natlwritersassn@hotmail.com • URL: http://www.nationalwriters.com • Professional full- or part-time freelance writers who specialize in business writing. Aims to serve as a marketplace whereby business editors can easily locate competent writing talent. Establishes communication among editors and writers.

**National Yang-Ming University - Research Center of Health and Welfare Policy**. Li-Nong St., No. 155, Section 2 Taipei 112, Taiwan. Phone: 886 2 28267000; Fax: 886 2 28205503; Email: ihw@ym.edu.tw • URL: http://www.ym.edu.tw/hwprc/engli.htm • Health and welfare policies of Taiwan.

**National Youth Employment Coalition**. 1836 Jefferson Pl. NW Washington, DC 20036. Phone: (202)659-1064; Fax: (202)659-0399; Email: nyec@nyec.org • URL: http://www.nyec.org • A network of over 180 community-based organizations, research organizations, public interest groups, policy analysis organizations, and others dedicated to promoting improved policies and practices related to youth employment/development, to help youth succeed in becoming lifelong learners, productive workers and self-sufficient citizens.

***Nation's Cities Weekly***. National League of Cities, 1301 Pennsylvania Ave. NW, Ste. 550 Washington, DC 20004-1747. Phone: 877-827-2385 or (202)626-3000; Email: memberservices@nlc.org • URL: http://www.nlc.org • Weekly. $96 Nonmembers; $149 Two years domestic nonmembers; $59 Individuals domestic members; $89 Individuals domestic members, 2 years; $128 Nonmembers; $213 Two years non-members; $59 for members; $96 for nonmembers in U.S.; $128 for nonmembers in Canada and Mexico; $183 for nonmembers in other foreign countries. Description: Presents news on the latest developments in Congress, the White House, federal agencies, and other public interest groups which may affect the nation's cities.

***Nations of the World: A Political, Economic and Business Handbook***. Grey House Publishing, 4919 Rte. 22 Amenia, NY 12501. Phone: 800-562-2139 or (518)789-8700; Fax: (518)789-0556; Email: books@greyhouse.com • URL: http://www.greyhouse.com • Annual. $180 Individuals softcover. Covers: Political, economic and business information for 231 nations and self-governing territories around the world. Database includes: Five regional chapters. Entries include: Key facts, political and economic issues, country profile, business information, maps, demographics, GDP figures, climate, chambers of commerce, media, travel information, and contact information for government offices.

***Nation's Restaurant News: The Newspaper of the Food Service Industry***. Lebhar-Friedman Inc., 425 Park Ave. New York, NY 10022. Phone: (212)756-5000 or (603)432-4077; Email: info@lf.com • URL: http://www.lf.com • $49.95 Individuals All access; $29.95 Individuals Digital and Print; $19.95 Individuals Digital access. 50 times a year.

**Native American Coalition for Healthy Alternatives**. 1038 E Tallent St. Rapid City, SD 57701. Phone: (605)877-4650 • URL: http://nacha501c.org • Strives to enhance the quality of life for the underrepresented by providing various services related to financial literacy.

**Native American Finance Officers Association**. 1101 30th St. NW, Ste. 500 Washington, DC 20007. Phone: (202)631-2003 • URL: http://www.nafoa.org • Improves the quality of financial and business management of Native American governments and businesses. Promotes tribal sovereignty through sound financial management. Develops scholarship training and internship program for Native American students and tribal employees.

**Natural Energy Services Association**. 17515 Spring Cypress Rd., Ste. C-327 Cypress, TX 77429-2688. Phone: (713)856-6525; Fax: (713)856-6199 • URL: http://www.nesanet.org.

***Natural Gas and Electricity: The Monthly Journal for Producers, Marketers, Pipels and End Users***. John Wiley & Sons Inc., 111 River St. Hoboken, NJ 07030-5774. Phone: 800-225-5945 or (201)748-6000; Fax: (201)748-6088; Email: info@wiley.com • URL: http://www.wiley.com • Monthly. $1,994 Institutions Online or Print only; $2,393 Institutions Print and Online; $924 Individuals Online only; $1,155 Individuals Print only; £1,020 Institutions Online only; £1,269 Institutions Print and Online; £1,057 Institutions Print only; £472 Individuals Online only; £626 Individuals Print only. Covers business, economic, regulatory, and high-technology news relating to the natural gas industry.

*Natural Gas Week.* Energy Intelligence Group, 5 E 37th St., 5th Fl. New York, NY 10016-2807. Phone: (212)532-1112; Fax: (212)532-4479; Email: customerservice@energyintel.com • URL: http://www.energyintel.com • Weekly. Covers natural gas economics, news, and analysis of gas/electric convergence.

**Natural Products Association.** 1773 T St. NW Washington, DC 20009. Phone: 800-966-6632 or (202)223-0101; Fax: (202)223-0250; Email: natural@npainfo.org • URL: http://www.npainfo.org • Represents retailers, wholesalers, brokers, distributors and manufacturers of natural, nutritional, dietetic foods, supplements, services and natural body and home care products.

*Natural Products Marketplace.* Virgo Publishing L.L.C., 3300 N Central Ave. Ste. 300 Phoenix, AZ 85012-2501. Phone: (480)990-1101; Fax: (480)990-0819 or (602)567-6852; Email: mikes@vpico.com • URL: http://www.vpico.com • Monthly. $50.00 per year. Covers all aspects of the vitamin and health supplement market, including new products. Includes an annual buyer's guide, an annual compilation of industry statistics, and annual guides to vitamins and herbs.

*The Natural Resources Journal.* University of New Mexico School of Law, 1 University of New Mexico, 1117 Stanford NE MSC11 6070 Albuquerque, NM 87131-0001. Phone: (505)277-2146; Fax: (505)277-9958 • URL: http://lawschool.unm.edu • Semiannual. Published by the University of New Mexico School of Law and is an international, interdisciplinary forum devoted to the study of natural and environmental resources.

*NAUMD News.* National Association of Uniform Manufacturers and Distributors, 6800 Jericho Tpke., Ste. 120 Syosset, NY 11791-4436. Phone: (516)393-5838; Fax: (516)393-5878 • URL: http://www.naumd.com • Description: Reports news that affects the uniform manufacturing and distributing industry. Also discusses Association programs and seminars, committee activities, and governmental trends and regulations.

*Nauru Business Law Handbook.* International Business Publications, USA, PO Box 15343 Washington, DC 20003. Phone: (202)546-2103; Fax: (202)546-3275; Email: ibpusa@comcast.net • URL: http://ibpus.com • $99.95 Individuals hardcopy, E-book and CD-ROM. Covers: Basic information on business laws and legislations, export-import regulations, business climate and contacts.

*Naval Affairs: In the Interest of the Enlisted Active Duty Reserve, and Retired Personnel of the U.S. Navy, Marine Corps and Coast Guard.* Fleet Reserve Association, 125 N West St. Alexandria, VA 22314-2709. Phone: 800-FRA-1924 or (703)683-1400; Email: news-fra@fra.org • URL: http://www.fra.org • Free to members; non-members, $7.00 per year.

*Naval Aviation News.* Chief of Naval Operations Bureau of Aeronautics. U. S. Government Printing Office, 732 N Capitol St. NW Washington, DC 20401. Phone: 866-512-1800 or (202)512-1800 or (866)512-1800; Fax: (202)512-2104 or (202)512-2250; Email: contactcenter@gpo.gov • URL: http://www.gpo.gov • Quarterly. $8 U.S. Single copy; $11.20 Other countries Single copy; $23 Individuals 1 year; $32.20 Other countries 1 year. Articles on all phases on Navy and Marine activity.

*Naval Engineers Journal.* American Society of Naval Engineers, 1452 Duke St. Alexandria, VA 22314. Phone: (703)836-6727; Fax: (703)836-7491; Email: asnehq@navalengineers.org • URL: http://www.navalengineers.org • Quarterly. $233 Individuals Print and Online; $202 Individuals Print or Online. Contains technical papers in the field of naval engineering. It also contains schedules of meetings, symposia, and other events, news, notes, and membership information.

**Naval Enlisted Reserve Association.** 6703 Farragut Ave. Falls Church, VA 22042-2189. Phone: 800-776-9020 • URL: http://www.nera.org • Enlisted personnel of the U.S. Naval Reserve, Marine Corps Reserve, and Coast Guard Reserve on active duty, inactive duty, or retired. Works to promote career enlisted service in the "sea-going" branches of the armed services; concerned with the readiness, training, morale, and well-being of all Reservists; obtains fair and proper recognition of the contributions made by Reservists to the national defense and to obtain protection and extension of benefits and entitlements for those Reservists who are currently serving and for those who have already served satisfactorily and have retired. Works with Congress and military leaders for legislation and proposals designed to improve and enhance the effectiveness of Reserve programs; also works to provide a communications link with the public.

**Naval Historical Foundation.** 1306 Dahlgren Ave. SE, Washington Navy Yard Washington, DC 20374-5109. Phone: 888-880-0102 or (202)678-4333; Fax: (202)889-3565; Email: nhfwny@navyhistory.org • URL: http://www.navyhistory.org • Dedicated to preserving and promoting the Navy's proud heritage, including the principal donation point for personal papers relating to naval history, a dynamic nationwide oral history program, a means for supporting the Navy's historical collections and programs, especially the Navy Museum. Provides historic research, and document and photo reproduction services.

**Naval Intelligence Professionals.** PO Box 11579 Burke, VA

22009-1579. Email: navintpro@aol.com • URL: http://www.navintpro.org • Active duty and former naval intelligence officers; enlisted personnel; civilian professionals; corporations. Objectives are to: improve naval intelligence operations; act as a clearinghouse for information on scientific and technical advances in naval intelligence; provide a forum for the exchange of ideas. Encourages readiness for those who would be involved in a national crisis mobilization.

*Naval Research Logistics: An International Journal.* John Wiley & Sons Inc., 111 River St. Hoboken, NJ 07030-5774. Phone: 800-225-5945 or (201)748-6000; Fax: (201)748-6088; Email: info@wiley.com • URL: http://www.wiley.com • 8/year. $2,868 Institutions Online or Print Only; $3,442 Institutions Print and Online; £1,465 Institutions Online Only; £1,913 Institutions Print and Online; £1,594 Institutions Print only. Peer-reviewed journal in operations research, applied statistics, and general quantitative modeling, with special interest in applications covering the full spectrum of logistics problems.

**Naval Reserve Association.** 1619 King St. Alexandria, VA 22314-2793. Phone: 877-628-9411; Fax: (866)683-3647 • URL: http://www.ausn.org • Naval officers on active or inactive duty or retired. Maintains involvement with legislation affecting U.S. Navy and Naval Reserve. Provides Naval Officer Promotion Record Reviews. Sponsors Naval Reserve Junior Officer of the Year Programs. Offers professional education; sponsors competitions; maintains speakers' bureau.

*Naval Review: Annual Review of World Seapower.* United States Naval Institute, 291 Wood Rd. Annapolis, MD 21402-1213. Phone: 800-223-8764 or (410)268-6110; Fax: (410)571-1703; Email: customer@usni.org • URL: http://www.usni.org • Annual. Price on application. Covers the previous year's events. May issue of *U.S. Naval Institute Proceedings.*

**Naval Sea Cadet Corps.** 2300 Wilson Blvd., Ste. 200 Arlington, VA 22201-5435. Phone: (703)243-6910; Fax: (703)243-3985 • URL: http://www.seacadets.org • Youths aged 11-17 years interested in the Navy, Marine Corps, Coast Guard, and Merchant Marines. Works to instill good citizenship and patriotism in youth. Encourages qualities such as personal neatness, loyalty, obedience, dependability, and responsibility to others. Offers courses in physical fitness and military drill, first aid, water safety, basic seamanship, and naval history and traditions.

**Navy Club of the United States of America Auxiliary.** c/o Andrew Murphy, Liason Officer, 194 Lepore Dr. Lancaster, PA 17602-2646. Phone: (717)392-4479 • URL: http://www.navyclubusa.org/auxiliary.htm • Women relatives of men who have served in the United States Navy, Marine Corps, Coast Guard, and component reserve services; women who are eligible in their own right for membership in the Navy Club of the United States of America. Provides assistance to the Navy Club; promotes fraternal love and sociability; encourages interest in the U.S. Navy and its history. Activities include veterans' service, rehabilitation programs, child welfare assistance, handicapped services, and overseas relief, memorials, and community service. Supports U.S. Navy special services. Maintains museum.

**Navy Club of the United States of America.** c/o Tom Minchin, National Executive Secretary, 304 Sarheim Rd. Harrisburg, PA 17112-2234. Phone: (717)884-1900; Email: ncusa1940@gmail.com • URL: http://www.navyclubusa.org • Persons who are, or have been, in the active service of the U.S. Navy, Naval Reserve, Marine Corps, Marine Corps Reserve, and Coast Guard. Promotes and encourages further public interest in the U.S. Navy and its history and to uphold the spirit and ideals of the U.S. Navy. Acts as public forum for members' views on national defense. Assists Navy Recruiting Command. Conducts charitable activities.

**Navy League of the United States.** 2300 Wilson Blvd., Ste. 200 Arlington, VA 22201-5424. Phone: 800-356-5760 or (703)528-1775; Fax: (703)528-2333 • URL: http://navyleague.org • Civilian organization that supports U.S. capability to keep the sea lanes open through a strong, viable Navy, Marine Corps, Coast Guard, and Merchant Marine. Seeks to awaken interest and cooperation of U.S. citizens in matters serving to aid, improve, and develop the efficiency of U.S. naval and maritime forces and equipment; acquires and disseminates information concerning the conditions of U.S. naval and maritime forces and equipment.

**Navy Retired Activities Branch.** OPNAV N170C, 5720 Integrity Dr. Millington, TN 38055-6220. Phone: 866-827-5672; Email: mill_retiredactivities@navy.mil • URL: http://www.public.navy.mil/bupers-npc/support/retired_activities/Pages/default.aspx • A program of the U.S. Department of the Navy. Assists Navy retirees and survivors with benefits and entitlement information. Maintains speakers' bureau.

*Navy Supply Corps Newsletter.* U. S. Government Printing Office, 732 N Capitol St. NW Washington, DC 20401. Phone: 866-512-1800 or (202)512-1800 or (866)512-1800; Fax: (202)512-2104 or (202)512-2250; Email: contactcenter@gpo.gov • URL: http://www.gpo.gov • Bimonthly. $31 U.S.; $43.40 Other countries; $10 U.S. Single copy; $14 Other countries Single copy. Newsletter issued by U. S. Navy Supply Systems Command. Provides news of Navy supplies and stores activities.

*Navy Times: Marine Corps, Navy, Coast Guard.* Gannett Government Media Corp., 6883 Commercial Dr. Springfield, VA 22159-0500. Phone: 800-368-5718 or (703)750-7400 • URL:

http://www.gannettgovernmentmedia.com • Weekly. $52.00 per year. In two editions: Domestic and International. *Supplement available.*

**NBFI and Modaraba Association of Pakistan.** 602, Progressive Ctr., 30-A, Blk. 6, PEHCS, Shahrah-e-Faisal Karachi 75400, Pakistan. Phone: 92 21 34389774; Fax: 92 21 34389775; Email: association@nbfi-modaraba.com.pk • URL: http://www.nbfi-modaraba.com.pk • Seeks to promote the Islamic way of business. Encourages public awareness of the role of modaraba in financing. Conducts surveys and analysis on the Islamic modes of business and finance. Safeguards and protects the interests of members.

*NCBA Membership Roster.* National Candy Brokers Association, 710 E Ogden Ave., Ste. 600 Naperville, IL 60563. Phone: (630)369-2406; Email: ncba@bonline.com • Annual. $25.00. Lists broker, manufacturer, and distributor members of the National Candy Brokers Association.

**NCSL International.** 2995 Wilderness Pl., Ste. 107 Boulder, CO 80301-5404. Phone: (303)440-3339 or (206)544-4885; Fax: (303)440-3384; Email: info@ncsli.org • URL: http://www.ncsli.org • Representatives of measurements standards and calibration laboratories; organizations with related interests. Seeks cost reduction or solution of problems, both technical and administrative, that besiege all measurement activities in the physical sciences, engineering, and technology. Conducts conferences and meetings for presentation of papers and discussions pertaining to technical and managerial problems, operating practices, and policies for measurement standards laboratories. Works with educational organizations to develop programs for training technical personnel and professional metrologists.

**NCTA: The Rural Broadband Association.** 4121 Wilson Blvd., Ste. 1000 Arlington, VA 22203. Phone: (703)351-2000 or (703)351-2030; Fax: (703)351-2001; Email: sbloomfield@ntca.org • URL: http://www.ntca.org • Members are telephone cooperatives and statewide associations.

*NDT and E International; The Independent Journal of Non-Destructive Testing.* Elsevier, Secondary Publishing Division, 650 Ave. of the Americas New York, NY 10011. Phone: 888-437-4636 or (212)633-3980; Fax: (212)633-3975; Email: t.reller@elsevier.com • URL: http://www.elseveier.com • 8/year. $1,315 Institutions.

*Nebraska Farmer.* Farm Progress Companies Inc., 255 38th Ave., Ste. P Saint Charles, IL 60174-5410. Phone: 800-441-1410 or (630)690-5600; Fax: (630)462-2869 or (630)462-4656; Email: wvogt@farmprogress.com • URL: http://www.farmprogress.com • $26.95 Individuals; $45 Two years.

*Negotiating to Settlement in Divorce.* Sanford N. Katz, editor. Wolters Kluwer Law and Business, 76 9th Ave., 7th Fl. New York, NY 10011-4962. Phone: 800-234-1660 or (212)771-0600; Fax: (800)901-9075 or (301)644-3550 • URL: http://www.wolterskluwerlb.com • $75.00. Looseleaf service. Periodic supplementation.

*Negotiation Journal: On the Process of Dispute Settlement.* Program on Negotiation. Blackwell Publishing Inc., 350 Main St. Malden, MA 02148. Phone: 800-216-2522 or (781)388-8200; Fax: (781)388-8210; Email: journaladsusa@bos.blackwellpublishing.com • URL: http://www.blackwellpublishing.com • Quarterly. $495 Individuals.

*Nelson Information's Directory of Institutional Real Estate.* Nelson Information, 195 Broadway New York, NY 10007. Phone: 800-333-6357 or (914)937-8400; Fax: (646)822-3000 or (914)937-8590; Email: nelson.support@thomson.com • Annual. 400. Includes real estate investment managers, service firms, consultants, real estate investment trusts (REITs), and various institutional investors in real estate. Formerly *Nelson's Directory of Real Estate Investments.*

*Nelson Information's Directory of Investment Managers.* Nelson Information, 195 Broadway New York, NY 10007. Phone: 800-333-6357 or (914)937-8400; Fax: (646)822-3000 or (914)937-8590; Email: nelson.support@thomson.com • Annual. $595.00. Three volumes. Provides information on 2,200 investment management firms, both U.S. and foreign.

*Nelson Information's Directory of Investment Research.* Nelson Information, 195 Broadway New York, NY 10007. Phone: 800-333-6357 or (914)937-8400; Fax: (646)822-3000 or (914)937-8590; Email: nelson.support@thomson.com • Annual. Covers: Over 7,000 firms; 14,000 public companies; and 9,000 analysts. Entries include: Name, address, phone, fax, names and titles of key personnel, five-year operating summary, description of business.

*Nelson Information's Directory of Pension Fund Consultants.* Nelson Information, 195 Broadway New York, NY 10007. Phone: 800-333-6357 or (914)937-8400; Fax: (646)822-3000 or (914)937-8590; Email: nelson.support@thomson.com • Annual. $995. Covers the pension plan sponsor industry. More than 325 worldwide consulting firms are described. Formerly *Nelson's Guide to Pension Fund Consultants.*

*Nelson Information's Directory of Plan Sponsors.* Nelson Information, 195 Broadway New York, NY 10007. Phone: 800-333-6357 or (914)937-8400; Fax: (646)822-3000 or (914)937-8590; Email: nelson.support@thomson.com • Annual. 610. Approximately 19,000 plan sponsors (corporate, union, public/government, endowment, foundation, and hospital) of investments (pensions, endowments) funds with assets over $10 million. Formerly *Nelson's Directory of Plan Sponsors and Tax-Exempt Funds.*

**Nerac Inc.** 1 Technology Dr. Tolland, CT 06084-3900. Phone:

(860)872-7000; Fax: (860)875-1749; Email: info@nerac.com • URL: http://www.nerac.com.

***Net Jobs***. Hoover's Inc., 5800 Airport Blvd. Austin, TX 78752-4204. Phone: 866-443-3939 or (512)374-4500 or (866)281-5969; Fax: (512)374-4501; Email: salesteam@hoovers.com • URL: http://www.hoovers.com • $12.95. Covers: Internet sites and online sources dealing with employment, including resume writing tips, interviewing advice, and classified listings. Entries include: Name, location/host.

***Netherlands Business Services Providers Leads***. Business Information Agency Inc. PlanetInform, 52 Tuscan Way, Ste. 202-181 Saint Augustine, VA 32092. Phone: (904)342-6124; Fax: (904)592-2632; Email: info@biasales.com • URL: http://www.biasales.com • Monthly. $231 Individuals mailing list; $484 Individuals sales list; $820 Individuals marketing list. Covers Netherlands' companies and all sub-industries that provide various services to commercial businesses, establishments, and organizations, including consulting, advertising and marketing services, and facilities maintenance.

***Netherlands Government and Business Contacts Handbook***. International Business Publications, USA, PO Box 15343 Washington, DC 20003. Phone: (202)546-2103; Fax: (202)546-3275; Email: ibpusa@comcast.net • URL: http://ibpus.com • $99.95 Individuals hardcopy, e-book, CD-ROM. Covers: Strategic government and business information, export-import activity in the country, investment, business contacts and regulations.

***Netherlands Industrial and Business Directory***. International Business Publications, USA, PO Box 15343 Washington, DC 20003. Phone: (202)546-2103; Fax: (202)546-3275; Email: ibpusa@comcast.net • URL: http://ibpus.com • Annual. $99.95 Individuals hardcover, e-book, CD-ROM. Covers: Detailed information on investment, export-import business opportunities, foreign economic assistance projects, government and business contacts.

**Netherlands Society for Industry and Trade**. Jan Van Nassaustraat 75 NL-2596 BP The Hague, Netherlands. Phone: 31 70 3141940; Fax: 31 70 3247515; Email: info@de-maatschappij.nl • URL: http://www.de-maatschappij.nl • Association of businesses and industries in the Netherlands. Promotes trade and investment. Conducts research.

***NetMag: Strategies and Solutions for the Network Professional***. UBM L.L.C., 600 Community Dr. Manhasset, NY 11030. Phone: (516)562-5000 or (512)562-5000; Fax: (212)378-2160 or (516)562-5036; Email: cmp@cmp.com • URL: http://www.cmp.com • 13 times a year. Free to qualified personnel. Incorporates *Data Communications*.

***Network Computing: Computing in a Network Environment***. UBM L.L.C., 240 W 35th St. New York, NY 10001. • URL: http://www.ubm.com • Semimonthly. Free to qualified personnel.

**Network for Teaching Entrepreneurship**. 120 Wall St., 18th Fl. New York, NY 10005. • URL: http://www.nfte.com • Devoted to teaching entrepreneurship education to low-income young people, ages 11 through 18.

***Network: Strategies and Solutions for the Network Professional***. UBM L.L.C., 600 Community Dr. Manhasset, NY 11030. Phone: (516)562-5000 or (512)562-5000; Fax: (212)378-2160 or (516)562-5036; Email: cmp@cmp.com • URL: http://www.cmp.com • 13 times a year. Free to qualified personnel. Covers network products and peripherals for computer professionals. Includes annual network managers salary survey and annual directory issue. Formerly *LAN: The Network Solutions Magazine*.

***Network World: The Newsweekly of Enterprise Network Computing***. Network World Inc., 492 Old Connecticut Path Framingham, MA 01701-9208. Phone: 800-622-1108 or (508)766-5301 or (508)460-3333; Fax: (508)460-1192; Email: adamato@nww.com • URL: http://www.networkworld.com • Weekly. $129.00 per year. Includes special feature issues on enterprise Internets, network operating systems, network management, high-speed modems, LAN management systems, and Internet access providers.

***Nevada Manufacturers Directory and Industrial Database***. Manufacturers' News Inc., 1633 Central St. Evanston, IL 60201-1569. Phone: (847)864-7000; Fax: (847)332-1100 • URL: http://www.manufacturersnews.com • Annual. $86 Individuals print; $305 Individuals database (EZ select full); $191 Individuals database (EZ select with 20 plus employees); $107 Individuals database (EZ select basic). Covers: 2,104 manufacturers in Nevada. Entries include: Company name, address, phone, names and titles of key personnel, year established, number of employees, plant square footage, services, Standard Industry Classification (SIC) code, parent and subsidiary company information, type of in-house computer system, URL, e-mail address.

***Nevada Manufacturers Register***. Harris InfoSource, 2057 E Aurora Rd. Twinsburg, OH 44087-1999. Phone: 800-888-5900 or (330)425-9000 or (973)921-5500; Fax: (800)643-5997 or (877)252-3375; Email: customerservice@harrisinfo.com • URL: http://www.harrisinfo.com • Annual. Covers: Approximately 2,800 manufacturers in Nevada plus names and titles of key executives. Entries include: Company name, address, parent name/location, telephone, fax and 800 numbers, Web site address (on CD-ROM only), number of employees, year established, annual revenue, plant size, business description, Standard Industrial Classification (SIC) codes, executive names/titles, public ownership, legal structure, import/export designators, female/minority ownership.

***New Bern Area Guide and Business***. New Bern Area Chamber of Commerce, 316 S Front St. New Bern, NC 28560. Phone: (252)637-3111; Fax: (252)637-7541; Email: marketing@newbernchamber.com • URL: http://www.newbernchamber.com • Annual. Covers businesses in New Bern/Craven County, NC.

***New Business Survival Package***. Greater Orlando Chamber of Commerce, 75 S Ivanhoe Blvd. Orlando, FL 32804. Phone: (407)425-1234 or (407)835-2517; Fax: (407)839-5020 or (407)835-2500; Email: info@orlando.org • URL: http://www.orlando.org • Annual. $49.99. Covers: taxing, licensing, registration, and zoning authorities and other contacts of interest to those starting new businesses in the Florida counties of Seminole, Orange, and Osceola. Database includes: Advice on starting a new business. Entries include: Agency name, address, phone.

***New Caledonia Industrial and Business Directory***. International Business Publications, USA, PO Box 15343 Washington, DC 20003. Phone: (202)546-2103; Fax: (202)546-3275; Email: ibpusa@comcast.net • URL: http://ibpus.com • Annual. $99.95 Individuals hardcopy, e-book, CD-ROM. Covers: Strategic industrial, investment and business contacts for conducting export-import and investment activity in the country. Contains strategic, practical economic and business information.

***New Directions for Higher Education***. Jossey-Bass, 989 Market St. San Francisco, CA 94103-1741. Phone: 800-225-5945 or (415)433-1740; Fax: (415)433-0499 or (415)951-8553; Email: jbsubs@jbp.com • URL: http://www.josseybass.com • $402 Institutions print + online; $335 Institutions print only; $98 Individuals print + online. Quarterly. Institutions, $311.00 per year; with online edition, $375.00 per year. Sample issue free to librarians.

***New England Business***. New England Business Corp., 20 Park Plz., Ste. 1120 Boston, MA 02116-4303. • Monthly. $29.95 Individuals. Business magazine.

***New England Journal of Medicine***. Massachusetts Medical Society, Waltham Woods Corporate Ctr., 860 Winter St. Waltham, MA 02451. Phone: 800-843-6356 or (781)893-4610; Fax: (781)893-8009; Email: info@massmed.org • URL: http://www.massmed.org • Weekly. $179 Individuals print and online; $149 Individuals online. The offical journal of the Massachusetts Medical Society.

***New Equipment Digest***. Intertec Publishing, 5 Penn Plz., 13th Fl. New York, NY 10001-1810. Phone: 800-795-5445 or (212)613-9700 or (212)204-4200; Fax: (212)613-9749 or (212)206-3622; Email: bethany.weaver@penton.com • URL: http://www.penton.com • Monthly. Magazine (tabloid) showcasing new or improved equipment, products, materials, and components. Formerly *Material Handling Engineering*.

***New Equipment Reporter: New Products Industrial News***. DeRoche Publications, 12 Del Italia Irvine, CA 92614. • Monthly. Controlled circulation.

***The New Hampshire Business and Professional Directory***. Tower Publishing Co., 588 Saco Rd. Standish, ME 04084. Phone: 800-969-8693 or (207)642-5400; Fax: (207)642-5463 or 800-264-3870; Email: info@towerpub.com • URL: http://www.towerpub.com • Annual. $95 Individuals plus $7 shipping fee per book; $165 Individuals CD-ROM. 27,409 New Hampshire professional and industrial firms.

***New Hampshire Manufacturers Register and Industrial Database***. Manufacturers' News Inc., 1633 Central St. Evanston, IL 60201-1569. Phone: (847)864-7000; Fax: (847)332-1100 • URL: http://www.manufacturersnews.com • Annual. $93 Individuals print; $355 Individuals database (EZ select full); $227 Individuals database (EZ select with 20 plus employees); $124 Individuals database (EZ select basic). Covers: 2,963 manufacturers in New Hampshire. Entries include: Company name, address, phone, names and titles of key personnel, year established, number of employees, plant square footage, services, Standard Industry Classification (SIC) code, parent and subsidiary company information, type of in-house computer system, URL, e-mail address.

***New Horizons***. Horticultural Research Institute, 1200 G St. NW, Ste. 800 Washington, DC 20005. Phone: (202)789-2900 or (202)695-2474; Fax: (202)789-1893 • URL: http://www.hriresearch.org • Semiannual. Description: Explores research of the science and art of nursery, retail garden center, and landscape plant production, marketing, and care.

***New Industries and Plant Expansions Reported in Wisconsin***. Wisconsin Department of Development Bureau of Information Services, 201 W Washington Ave. Madison, WI 53707. Phone: 800-HELP-BUS or (608)267-6876 or (608)266-3074; Fax: (608)267-0436 • URL: http://www.badger.state.wi.us • Annual. Covers: plant additions, new plants, branch plants, and relocated plants announced during the year to be built in Wisconsin; about 300 projects in recent edition. Entries include: Company name, city of new or expanded construction, type of project, square footage, type of facility (plant, office, etc.), number of workers to be added, product or service.

***The New Information Report: The International Industry Dossier***. Washington Researchers Ltd., 1655 N Fort Myer Dr., Ste. 800 Arlington, VA 22209. Phone: (703)312-2863; Fax: (703)527-4586; Email: research@researchers.com • URL: http://www.washingtonresearchers.com • Looseleaf service. $160.00 per year. Monthly updates. Formerly *The International Information Report*.

***New Jersey Business and Agency TTY/TDD Directory***. Scotch Plains Lions Club, • Annual. Covers more than 300 New Jersey businesses, government agencies, police departments, services for the handicapped (including qualified interpreters for the deaf), associations, schools, libraries, churches, and medical facilities equipped with devices which make them accessible by telephone to the hearing- and speech-impaired.

***New Jersey Business Source Book***. Research Communications, 6818 Oasis Pass, Ste. 101 Austin, TX 78731. Phone: (512)266-0067; Fax: (512)266-2696 • Annual. $495 Individuals book with CD; $159.95 Individuals book only. Covers: Sources of New Jersey business information, including 555 of the state's top employers, 798 trade and professional associations, and 170 NJ chambers of commerce. Database includes: Information on services available to the New Jersey business community and New Jersey web sites. Entries include: For companies—Name, address, phone, e-mail, URL, description names and titles of key personnel. For associations—Name, address, phone, number of members. For chambers of commerce—Name, address, phone, fax, e-mail.

***The New Jersey Corporate Guide***. Business Journal of New Jersey, • Annual. Covers: Approximately 1,000 of the largest public and private companies, financial institutions, leading firms in New Jersey and important out-of-state companies whose major operations are located in New Jersey. Entries include: Name, address, phone, fax, parent company, number of employees, sales volume, year founded, names and titles of executives. Public companies also include—5-year income statement, names and titles of officers and directors, subsidiaries, name of trade exchange and symbol, auditors, and number of shareholders.

***New Mexico Business Current Economic Report***. University of New Mexico Bureau of Business and Economic Research, Onate Hall, 303 Girard Blvd. NE, Ste. 116 Albuquerque, NM 87106. Phone: (505)277-2216; Fax: (505)277-7066; Email: lreynis@unm.edu • URL: http://bber.unm.edu • Monthly. $25 1 year.

**New Mexico Institute of Mining and Technology - Energetic Materials Research and Testing Center**. 801 Leroy Pl. Socorro, NM 87801. Phone: (575)835-5312; Fax: (575)835-5630; Email: webmaster@emrtc.nmt.edu • URL: http://www.emrtc.nmt.edu • Research areas include the development of industrial applications for explosives as energy sources.

***New Mexico International Trade Directory***. Proparaguay, Ayfra Bldg., Fl. 12 Asuncion, Paraguay. Phone: 595 21 208 276; Fax: 595 21 200 425; Email: ppy@proparaguay.gov.py • URL: http://www.proparaguay.gov.py • Annual. $10; Free controlled circulation. Covers: about 511 New Mexico firms seeking international trade. Database includes: Exportable products list. Entries include: Name of firm, address, phone, number of employees, name of contact, Standard Industrial Classification (SIC) code, product or service provided.

***New Orleans CityBusiness***. New Orleans CityBusiness, 1111 Veterans Blvd., Ste. 1440 Metairie, LA 70005. Phone: (504)834-9292; Fax: (504)832-3550; Email: mail@nopg.com • URL: http://www.neworleanscitybusiness.com • Weekly. $129 Individuals print + online; $199 Two years print + online; $239 Individuals 3 years, print + online; $99 Individuals online. Business newspaper (Tabloid).

***New Plant Report***. Conway Data Inc., 6625 The Corners Parkway, Ste. 200 Norcross, GA 30092-3334. Phone: (770)446-6996; Fax: (770)263-8825; Email: info@conway.com • URL: http://www.conway.com • Monthly. $1,800 All regions; $900 Eastern, Centraland Western region. Description: Covers new plants and plant expansions. Provides project location, company name, product to be manufactured or service performed, NAICS code, type of facility, stage of development, and (as available) number of employees, square footage, investment amount, and contact name. **Remarks:** Also available on disk and via e-mail.

**New Rules for Global Finance Coalition**. 2000 M St. NW, Ste. 720 Washington, DC 20036-3327. Phone: (202)277-9390; Fax: (202)280-1141 • URL: http://www.new-rules.org • Represents the interests of development, human rights, labor, environmental, and religious organizations and scholars. Aims to reform the global financial architecture to prevent financial crises. Works to stabilize the world economy, reduce poverty and inequality, uphold fundamental rights, and protect the environment.

**New South Wales Department of Primary Industries - Orange Agricultural Institute**. Forest Rd. Orange, NSW 2800, Australia. Phone: 61 2 63913800; Fax: 61 2 63913899; Email: david.michalk@dpi.nsw.gov.au • URL: http://www.dpi.nsw.gov.au/research/centres/orange • Animal health, including infectious and toxicity diseases; animal production, including sheep genetics, wool production, and vertebrate pests; plant production, including weed control and ecology, crops, pastures, and horticulture; agricultural scientific collections; plant protection, including entomology and plant pathology; biometrics; and economics.

***New Technical Books: A Selective List With Descriptive Annotations***. New York Public Library, Science and Technology Research Center, 5th Ave. and 42nd St. New York, NY 10018. Phone: (212)930-0573 or (212)930-0920; Fax: (212)869-7824 • Bimonthly. $30.00 per year.

***New Woman***. Endeavour House, 189 Shaftsbury Ave. London WC2H 8JG, United Kingdom. Phone: (020) 7859 8689; Email: emap@subscription.co.uk • URL: http://www.newwoman.co.uk • Monthly. $57.00 per year.

**New York Genealogical and Biographical Society**. 36 W 44th St., 7th Fl., Ste. 711 New York, NY 10036-8105. Phone: (212)755-8532; Fax: (212)754-4218; Email: pcampbell@nygbs.org • URL: http://www.newyorkfamilyhistory.org • Collects, preserves, and makes available to the public, information relating to genealogy, biography, and history, especially of the state of New York.

**New York Institute of Technology - Center for Energy, Environment and Economics**. Dept. of Energy Management, Harry Schure Hall, Rm. 116, Northern Blvd. Old Westbury, NY 11568-8000. Phone: (516)686-7990 or (516)686-7578; Fax: (516)686-7933; Email: ramundse@nyit.edu • URL: http://www.nyit.edu/engineering/centers/centers_energy_environment_economics • Established by the New York Institute of Technology as a major facility designed to disseminate information and conduct research into energy utilization and conservation, and to assist public, quasi-public, and private sector organizations in the practical use of present and future findings in the energy field. Conducts Master of Science in Energy Management and specialized professional certificate programs through NYIT's School of Engineering and Technology to provide interdisciplinary training in the technological, economic, sociological, and administrative skills required to implement new approaches to energy conversion and utilization.

***New York/New England & Eastern Canada Campground Guide***. Woodall Publications Corp., 2575 Vista Del Mar Dr. Ventura, CA 93001-3920. Email: info@woodallpub.com • URL: http://www.woodalls.com • Annual. $10.95 retail price; $4.95 discounted price. Covers: Campground site listings for New England states, including Maine, Connecticut, Massachusetts, New Hampshire, New York, Rhode Island, Vermont, and Ontario. Entries include: Site name, address, phone, facility description, driving directions, camping fees, attractions and seasonal events.

***New York No-Fault Arbitration Reports***. American Arbitration Association, 1633 Broadway, 10th Fl. New York, NY 10019. Phone: 800-778-7879 or (212)716-5800; Email: websitemail@adr.org • URL: http://www.adr.org • Description: Addresses developing laws under the no-fault law in the state of New York. Summarizes awards rendered under state-sponsored arbitration.

***New York Stock Exchange Guide***. Commerce Clearing House Inc., 4025 W Peterson Ave. Chicago, IL 60646-6085. Phone: 800-525-3335 or (312)583-8500; Fax: (773)866-3095 • Monthly. $485 per year, postpaid; payment with order. Covers: about 1,380 member companies listed as traders with the New York Stock Exchange, and exchange and floor officials. Entries include: Company name, address, date admitted, representatives.

**New York Stock Exchange Inc.** 11 Wall St. New York, NY 10005-1905. Phone: (212)656-3000 or (212)656-2060; Fax: (212)656-2126; Email: iec@nyse.com • URL: http://www.nyse.com • Aims to add value to the capital raising and asset management process by providing a cost effective, self regulated marketplace for the trading of financial instruments. Promotes confidence in, and understanding of, industry processes and serves as a forum for discussion of relevant national and international policy issues.

***The New York Times Biographical Service***. ProQuest L.L.C., 789 E Eisenhower Pkwy. Ann Arbor, MI 48106-1346. Phone: 800-521-0600 or (734)761-4700; Fax: (734)662-4554; Email: info@proquest.com • URL: http://www.proquest.com • Monthly. Price on application. Looseleaf service.

***New York Times Book Review***. The New York Times Co., 620 8th Ave. New York, NY 10018. Phone: 888-698-6397 or (212)556-7652; Fax: (212)556-3622 or (212)556-4603; Email: national@nytimes.com • URL: http://www.nytco.com • Weekly. $54.60 Individuals.

***The New York Times***. Gannett Co., Inc., 620 Eighth Ave. New York, NY 10018. Phone: 800-698-4637 or (212)556-7141 or (212)556-4306 • Mon.-Sun. (morn.). $5.85 Individuals; $3.10 Individuals Monday-Friday; $3.15 Individuals Sunday only; For information on pricing and ordering, e-mail steve.sidaway@chadwyck.co.uk. Provides personal finance expertise.

***New York University Annual Institute on Federal Taxation***. Melvin Cornfield. Matthew Bender and Company Inc., 1275 Broadway Albany, NY 12204-2638. Phone: 800-424-4200 or (518)487-3000; Fax: (518)487-3573 or (800)424-4200; Email: customer.support@lexisnexis.com • URL: http://www.matthewbender.com • Annual. $518 Individuals Book or Electronic version. Includes extensive index, table of revenue rulings, Code section reference table, table of Treasury regulations and more.

**New York University - Berkley Center for Entrepreneurial Studies**. NYU Stern School of Business, Ste. 7-150, KMC, 44 W 4th St. New York, NY 10012. Phone: (212)998-0070; Fax: (212)995-4211; Email: jeffrey.carr@stern.nyu.edu • URL: http://w4.stern.nyu.edu/berkley • Factors that promote entrepreneurship and lead to the creation of new wealth and business revenues; business venturing within established firms. Topics include the major pitfalls and obstacles to start-ups, securing of venture capital, psychology and sociology of entrepreneurship, valuation and management of new ventures, technological innovation and new product development, emerging and creative industries, and cross-cultural environments that stimulate entrepreneurship.

**New York University - Center for Experimental Social Science**. 19 W 4th St., 6th Fl. New York, NY 10012. Phone: (212)998-8952; Fax: (212)995-3932; Email: andrew.schotter@nyu.edu • URL: http://cess.nyu.edu • Social sciences, focusing on economic theory and/or the properties of proposed or existing economic, political, or social institutions.

**New York University Medical Center - Institute of Community Health and Research - Center for Health and Human Rights**. Bellevue C&D Bldg., Rm. 741, 462 1st Ave. New York, NY 10016. Phone: (212)562-8490; Fax: (212)562-4436 • URL: http://medicine.med.nyu.edu/dgim/sections/primary-care/health-and-human-rights-overview • Health policy related to human rights.

**New York University - Salomon Center for the Study of Financial Institutions**. Stern School of Business, 44 W 4th St., Ste. 9-160 New York, NY 10012. Phone: (212)998-0700; Fax: (212)995-4220; Email: mrichar0@stern.nyu.edu • URL: http://w4.stern.nyu.edu/salomon • Evaluates changing structure of financial instruments and markets and the use of these instruments and markets in financial intermediation and the management of risk by financial institutions and business corporations. Recent projects include modern portfolio management and the prudent man rule, role of financial futures and options in large financial institutions' investment portfolios, information and stock market efficiency, composition of individual investment portfolios, hedging and trading performance of new financial futures and options, new financial instruments, reforming Japan's financial markets, reconfiguration of the insurance industry, and restructuring the U.S. financial and insurance sectors.

**New York University - C.V. Starr Center for Applied Economics**. 19 W 4th St., 6th Fl. New York, NY 10012. Phone: (212)998-8936; Fax: (212)995-3932; Email: sydney.ludvigson@nyu.edu • URL: http://cvstarrnyu.org • Economic issues of social and economic consequence. Also develops analytical tools to facilitate economic decision making for the future.

***New Zealand Government and Business Contacts Handbook***. International Business Publications, USA, PO Box 15343 Washington, DC 20003. Phone: (202)546-2103; Fax: (202)546-3275; Email: ibpusa@comcast.net • URL: http://ibpus.com • $99.95 Individuals hardcopy, e-book, CD-ROM. Covers: Strategic government and business information, export-import activity in the country, investment, business contacts and regulations.

***New Zealand Industrial and Business Directory***. International Business Publications, USA, PO Box 15343 Washington, DC 20003. Phone: (202)546-2103; Fax: (202)546-3275; Email: ibpusa@comcast.net • URL: http://ibpus.com • Annual. $99.95 Individuals hardcopy, e-book, CD-ROM. Covers: Strategic industrial, investment and business contacts for conducting export-import and investment activity in the country.

**New Zealand Institute of Management**. Level 7, Lumley House, 3-11 Hunter St. Wellington 6140, New Zealand. Phone: 64 4 4958300; Email: enquiries@nzim.co.nz • URL: http://www.nzim.co.nz • Managers and managerial personnel. Promotes improved management of businesses in New Zealand. Conducts continuing professional education programs; maintains information center.

***New Zealand Trade Directory***. Current Pacific Ltd., Northcote Aucklannd 0748, New Zealand. Phone: 64 9 4801388; Fax: 64 9 4801387; Email: info@cplnz.com • URL: http://www.cplnz.com • Annual. $120 Individuals. Covers: More than 6,000 firms in New Zealand, including manufacturers, exporters, importers, distributors, food processors, banks and financial firms, tourism services, professional firms, trade promotion organizations, central and local governments, public libraries, tertiary and secondary education institutions, foreign government representations.

***Newbuildings Register***. IHS Global Ltd. Lloyd's Register—Fairplay Ltd., Lombard House, 3 Princess Way, Surrey Redhill RH1 1UP, United Kingdom. Phone: 44 1737 379000; Fax: 44 1737 379001; Email: marketing@ihs.com • URL: http://www.ihs.com • Monthly. £1,465 Individuals CD-ROM; $2,850 Individuals CD-ROM; €2,150 Individuals CD-ROM; £2,405 Individuals CD-ROM; network; $4,690 Individuals CD-ROM; network; €3,300 Individuals CD-ROM; network. Covers: Shipowners and builders of new commercial ships. Entries include: Name, address, phone.

***News from OECD***. Organisation for Economic Co-operation and Development Publications and Information Center, 2001 L St. NW, Ste. 650 Washington, DC 20036-4922. Phone: 800-456-6323 or (202)785-6323; Fax: (202)785-0350; Email: washington.contact@oecd.org • URL: http://www.oecd.org • Monthly.

***News Photographer: Dedicated to the Service and Advancement of News Photography***. National Press Photographers Association, 3200 Croasdaile Dr., Ste. 306 Durham, NC 27705-2588. Phone: (919)383-7246; Fax: (919)383-7261; Email: info@nppa.org • URL: http://www.nppa.org • Monthly. $48.00 per year.

***Newsbank***. NewsBank Inc., 5801 Pelican Bay Blvd., Ste. 600 Naples, FL 34108. Phone: 800-762-8182 or (802)875-2910; Fax: (239)263-3004; Email: sales@newsbank.com • URL: http://www.newsbank.com • Monthly. Price varies. Quarterly and annual cumulations. Index to articles of current interest from over 500 U.S. newspapers.

***Newsbreak***. Leather Industries of America, 3050 K St. NW, Ste. 400 Washington, DC 20007. Phone: (202)342-8497; Fax: (202)342-8583; Email: info@leatherusa.com • URL: http://www.leatherusa.com • Free to members and other qualified personnel. Reports on issues and events in the luggage industry.

***NewsInc.: The Business of the Newspaper Business***. The Cole Group, PO Box 719 Pacifica, CA 94044-0719. Phone: (650)557-9595 or (650)994-2100; Fax: (650)475-8479 or (650)557-9696; Email: admin@colegroup.com • URL: http://www.colegroup.com • Biweekly. $425 Individuals. Reports on trends in mass media, especially with regard to newspaper publishing. Articles on cable TV and other competitive media are included.

***Newsletter Publishing***. Entrepreneur Press, 2445 McCabe Way, Ste. 400 Irvine, CA 92614-6244. Phone: 800-864-6864 or (949)261-2325 or (949)622-7131; Fax: (949)261-7729 or (949)261-0234; Email: press@entrepreneur.com • URL: http://www.entrepreneurpress.com • Looseleaf. $59.50. A practical guide to starting a newsletter. Covers profit potential, start-up costs, market size evaluation, pricing, accounting, advertising, promotion, etc. (Start-Up Business Guide No. E1067.).

***Newsline: Research News from the U. S. Travel Data Center***. U.S. National Research Council, The National Academies, 500 5th St. NW Washington, DC 20001. Phone: (202)334-2000 • URL: http://www.nationalacademies.org/nrc • Monthly. $55.00 per year. Newsletter. Covers trends in the U. S. travel industry.

***Newsmakers***. Cengage Learning Inc., 20 Channel Center St. Boston, MA 02210. Phone: 800-487-8488 or (617)289-7700; Fax: (617)289-7844; Email: investors@cengage.com • URL: http://www.cengage.com • Annual. $314 Individuals. Four softbound issues and one hardbound annual. Biographical information on individuals currently in the news. Includes photographs. Formerly *Contemporary Newsmakers*. eBook also available. Contact for pricing.

***Newspaper Abstracts Ondisc***. ProQuest L.L.C., 789 E Eisenhower Pkwy. Ann Arbor, MI 48106-1346. Phone: 800-521-0600 or (734)761-4700; Fax: (734)662-4554; Email: info@proquest.com • URL: http://www.proquest.com • Monthly. $2,950.00 per year (covers 1989 to date; archival discs are available for 1985-88). Provides cover-to-cover CD-ROM indexing and abstracting of 19 major newspapers, including the *New York Times*, *Wall Street Journal*, *Washington Post*, *Chicago Tribune*, and *Los Angeles Times*.

***Newspaper Financial Executives Journal***. International Newspaper Financial Executives, 21525 Ridgetop Cir., Ste. 200 Sterling, VA 20166. Phone: (703)421-4060; Fax: (703)421-4068 • URL: http://www.infe.org • Quarterly. $100.00. Provides financially related information to newspaper executives.

**The Newspaper Guild**. 501 3rd St. NW Washington, DC 20001-2760. Phone: (202)434-7177; Fax: (202)434-1472; Email: guild@cwa-union.org • URL: http://www.newsguild.org • AFL-CIO; Canadian Labour Congress, and International Federation of Journalists. Sponsors Newspaper Guild International Pension Fund that provides retirement benefits to persons employed in the news industry.

***Newspapers Online***. BiblioData, PO Box 61 Needham Heights, MA 02494. Phone: (781)444-1154 or (781)444-1144; Fax: (781)449-4584; Email: ina@bibliodata.com • URL: http://www.bibliodata.com • Irregular. $99. Covers: Approximately 150 daily newspapers available online. Entries include: Name, address, phone, editor name, details on geographical area served; description; list of regional newsmaking companies/people/topics; circulation figures; electronic availability and coverage; electronic searching tips; name and phone of contact for database assistance.

***Nexis.com***. Lexis-Nexis Group, Phone: 800-227-4908 or (937)865-6800; Fax: (937)865-6909; Email: webmaster@prod.lexis-nexis.com • URL: http://www.nexis.com • Fee-based Web site offers searching of about 2.8 billion documents in some 30,000 news, business, and legal information sources. Features include a subject directory covering 1,200 topics in 34 categories and a Company Dossier containing information on more than 500,000 public and private companies. Boolean searching is offered.

***NFDA Directory of Members and Transportation Guide***. National Funeral Directors Association, 13625 Bishops Dr. Brookfield, WI 53005-6607. Phone: 800-228-6332 or (262)789-1880; Fax: (262)789-6977; Email: nfda@nfda.org • URL: http://www.nfda.org • Annual. $35 Members print; $125 Nonmembers. Covers 14,000 members of state funeral director associations affiliated with the National Funeral Directors Association. Formerly *National Funeral Directors Association-Membership Listing and Resources*.

***NFT Directory & Buying Guide***. BNP Media, 2401 W Big Beaver Rd., Ste. 700 Troy, MI 48084. Phone: 800-952-6643 or (248)362-3700 or (847)763-9534; Fax: (248)362-5103 or (248)362-0317; Email: privacy@bnpmedia.com • URL: http://www.bnpmedia.com • Annual. $35 Individuals. Covers: Floor covering manufacturers, distributors, retail groups and franchises, installation and technical training schools, sales agents, and products.

***NHLA Newsletter***. National Hardwood Lumber Association, 6830 Raleigh La Grange Rd. Memphis, TN 38134-0518. Phone: 800-933-0318 or (901)377-1818; Fax: (901)382-6419 or (901)399-7581; Email: info@nhla.com • URL: http://www.nhla.com • Monthly. Features hardwood products, industry trends, and legislation.

***NHMA Export Interest Directory***. International Housewares Association, 6400 Shafer Ct., Ste. 650 Rosemont, IL 60018. Phone: (847)292-4200; Fax: (847)292-4211 • URL: http://www.housewares.org • Covers: Approximately 300 member manufacturers that export housewares and small appliances. Products listed are at least 51% manufactured in the U.S. Entries include: Company name, address, phone, telex, fax, name and title of contact, geographical area served, products.

***Nicaragua Business Law Handbook***. International Business Publications, USA, PO Box 15343 Washington, DC 20003. Phone: (202)546-2103; Fax: (202)546-3275; Email: ibpusa@comcast.net • URL: http://ibpus.com • $99.95 Individuals hardcopy, e-book, CD-ROM. Covers: Information on basic business legislation, laws, business climate, foreign investments, export-import regulations, and contacts.

***Nichols Cyclopedia of Legal Forms Annotated***. Thomson West, 610 Opperman Dr. Eagan, MN 55123. Phone: 800-328-9352 or (651)687-7000 • Full set $7,451.00. Annual updates. Provides personal and business forms and alternative provisions for more than 230 law topics.

***Nigeria Business Directory***. Business Guide, PO Box 27669 Dubai, United Arab Emirates. Phone: 971 4 2651719; Fax: 971 4 2692151; Email: sales@africa-business.com • URL: http://www.africa-business.com • $250 Individuals. Covers: 47,500 business listings including wholesalers, importers, retailers, business houses, and agents in Nigeria.

***Nigeria Industrial and Business Directory***. International Business Publications, USA, PO Box 15343 Washington, DC 20003. Phone: (202)546-2103; Fax: (202)546-3275; Email: ibpusa@comcast.net • URL: http://ibpus.com • Annual. $99.95 Individuals hardcover; $99.95 Individuals CD-ROM; $99.95 Individuals e-book. Covers: Strategic industrial, investment and business contacts for conducting export-import and investment activity in the country.

***Nigerian Directory of Directors***. Asoms Biblio-Info Consult Publishers, 18 Kenyatta St. Enugu, Nigeria. Phone: 331827 • $5 Nigerian naira. Covers: directors of business firms in Nigeria. Entries include: Name of official, address, firm(s) for which a director.

***The Nikkei Weekly: Japan's Leading Business Newspaper***. Nikkei America, Inc., 1325 Ave. of the Americas, Ste. 2500 New York, NY 10019. Phone: (212)261-6200; Fax: (212)261-6208; Email: admin@nikkeiamerica.com • URL: http://www.nikkeiamerica.com • Weekly. $129 Individuals. A newspaper in English "dedicated to all aspects of Japanese business and its influence on people, markets and political trends around the world." Includes English versions of articles appearing in leading Japanese business newspapers, such as *Nihon Keizai Shimbun*, *Nikkei Marketing Journal* and *Nikkei Financial Daily*.

***The Nilson Report***. HSN Consultants Inc., 1110 Eugenia Pl., Ste. 100 Carpinteria, CA 93013-2080. Fax: (805)983-0792; Email: info@nilsonreport.com • Description: Provides information about the credit card industry.

***Nimmer on Copyright***. David Nimmer. Matthew Bender and Company Inc., 1275 Broadway Albany, NY 12204-2638. Phone: 800-424-4200 or (518)487-3000; Fax: (518)487-3573 or (800)424-4200; Email: customer.support@lexisnexis.com • URL: http://www.matthewbender.com • $3,087 book; $2,807 e-book. 10 looseleaf volumes. Periodic supplementation. Analytical and practical guide on the law of literary, musical, and artistic proprerty.

***904: Northeast Florida's Business & Executive Life Authority***. White Publishing Co., 1261 King St. Jacksonville, FL 32204. Fax: (904)389-3628; Email: mail@jacksonvillemag.com • URL: http://www.jacksonvillemag.com • Bimonthly. $9.04 Individuals; $16.95 Two years. Business periodical featuring business-related articles focusing on high-profile executives and business managers.

***9-1-1 Magazine: Public Safety Communications and Response***. Official Publications Inc., 18201 Weston Pl. Tustin, CA 92780. Phone: (714)544-7776 • Bimonthly. $29.95 per year. Covers technical information and applications for public safety communications personnel.

**Nine to Five: National Association of Working Women**. 207 E Buffalo St., Ste.211 Milwaukee, WI 53202. Phone: 800-522-0925 or (414)274-0925; Fax: (414)272-2870; Email: 9to5@9to5.org • URL: http://www.feminist.com/9to5.htm • Members are women office workers. Strives for the improvement of office working conditions for women and the elimination of sex and race discrimination.

***Nine to Five Newsletter***. 9 to 5, National Association of Working Women, 207 E Buffalo St., Ste. 211 Milwaukee, WI 53202-5758. Phone: 800-522-0925 or (414)274-0925; Fax: (414)272-2870; Email: 9to5@9to5.org • URL: http://www.9to5.org • 5/year. Members free; $25 Individuals. A newsletter dealing with the rights and concerns of women office workers.

**Ninety Nines, International Organization of Women Pilots**. 4300 Amelia Earhart Dr., Ste. A Oklahoma City, OK 73159.

Phone: 800-994-1929 or (405)685-7969; Fax: (405)685-7985; Email: 99s@ninety-nines.org • URL: http://www.ninety-nines.org • Licensed women pilots. Formerly Ninety-Nines International Women Pilots.

***Nisku Business Directory***. Nisku Business Association, Box 1041 Nisku, AB, Canada T9E 8A8. Phone: (780)955-7537; Fax: (780)955-7540; Email: nba@nisku.net • URL: http://www.nisku.org • Annual. Free to members; $30 Nonmembers book or CD. Lists companies located in Nisku Business Park and Edmonton International Airport.

***NLGI Spokesman***. National Lubricating Grease Institute, 249 SW Noel St., Ste. 249 Lees Summit, MO 64063-2241. Phone: (816)524-2500; Fax: (816)524-2504; Email: nlgi@nlgi.org • URL: http://www.nlgi.org • Bimonthly. $65 Members; $65 Nonmembers; $80 Canada nonmember; $109 Other countries nonmember. Bi-monthly. $65 per year. Information about the lubricating grease industry.

***NMA***. National Mining Association, Phone: (202)463-2600; Fax: (202)463-2666 • URL: http://www.nma.org • Web site provides information on the U. S. coal and mineral industries. Includes "Salient Statistics of the Mining Industry," showing a wide variety of annual data (six years) for coal and non-fuel minerals. Publications of the National Mining Association are described and links are provided to other sites. (National Mining Association formerly known as National Coal Association.) Fees: Free.

***The No-Load Fund Investor***. No-Load Fund Investor Inc., 410 Sawmill River Rd., Ste. 2060 Brentwood, TN 37024. Phone: 800-706-6364 or (914)693-7420; Fax: (914)693-8067; Email: noload@mleesmith.com • URL: http://www.sheldonjacobs.com • Description: Predicts which no-load and low-load funds will perform best overall in the coming year. Provides performance data for 995 no- and low-loads and recommends funds and analyzes promising new funds. Recurring features include a listing of the top 20 no-loads plus 18 model portfolios. **Remarks:** Published in conjuction with the Handbook for No-Load Investors.

***Noise Control Engineering Journal***. Institute of Noise Control Engineering, 100 E Washington St. Springfield, IL 62701. Phone: (217)528-9945; Fax: (283)654-6545 or (217)528-6545; Email: ibo@inceusa.org • URL: http://www.inceusa.org • Bimonthly. $90 Individuals.

***Noise Regulation Report: The Nation's Only Noise Control Publication***. Great Circle Communications LLC, 204 N Main St. Galena, MD 21635. Phone: 888-828-5437; Email: info@noisereport.com • URL: http://www.noisereport.com • Monthly. $487 Individuals. Covers federal and state rules and regulations for the control of excessive noise.

**Non Commissioned Officers Association of the United States of America**. 9330 Corporate Dr., Ste. 701 Selma, TX 78154-1257. Phone: 800-662-2620 or (210)653-6161; Fax: (210)637-3337 • URL: http://www.ncoausa.org • Noncommissioned and petty officers of the United States military serving in grades E1 through E9 from all five branches of the U.S. Armed Forces; includes active duty and retired personnel, members of the Reserve and National Guard components, and personnel who held the rank of NCO/PO at the time of separation from active duty under honorable conditions. Formed for patriotic, fraternal, social, and benevolent purposes. Offers veterans job assistance, legislative representation, and grants. Conducts charitable programs.

**Non-Ferrous Founders' Society**. 1480 Renaissance Dr., Ste. 310 Park Ridge, IL 60068. Phone: (847)299-0950; Fax: (847)299-3598; Email: nffstaff@nffs.org • URL: http://www.nffs.org • Manufacturers of brass, bronze, aluminum, and other nonferrous castings.

***Non-Ferrous Metal Data Yearbook***. American Bureau of Metal Statistics, PO Box 805 Chatham, NJ 07928. Phone: (973)701-2299; Fax: (973)701-2152; Email: info@abms.com • URL: http://www.abms.com • Annual. $405.00. Provides worldwide data on approximately about 200 statistical tables covering many nonferrous metals. Includes production, consumption, inventories, exports, imports, and other data.

**Non-Ferrous Metals Producers Committee**. 2030 M St. NW, Ste. 800 Washington, DC 20036. Phone: (202)466-7720; Fax: (202)466-2710 • URL: http://www.arcat.com/arcatcos/cos37/arc37679.cfm • Represents domestic copper, lead, and zinc producers. Promotes the interests of copper, lead, and zinc mining and metal industries in the U.S. with emphasis on tariffs, laws, regulations, and government policies affecting international trade and foreign imports.

***Non-Foods Management: The Annual Supermarket State of the Industry Report***. Millennium Media Corp., 267 Kentland Blvd., Suite 710 North Potomac, MD 20878. Phone: (301)865-8695; Fax: (301)865-8696 • Annual. $45.00. Written for top management and non-foods decision makers and executives at supermarkets.

***Non-Profit Legal and Tax Letter***. Organization Management Inc., 4289 Ellzey Dr. Ashburn, VA 20148-5026. Phone: (703)729-7052; Fax: (703)729-7053 • $235 Individuals. Covers fund raising, taxation, management, postal regulations, and other topics for nonprofit organizations.

***Non-Profit Organizations Directory***. InfoGroup Inc., 5711 S 86th Cir. Omaha, NE 68127-4146. Phone: (402)593-4500 • URL: http://www.infogroup.com • Annual. Number of listings: 80,335. Entries include: Name, address, phone, size of advertisement, name of owner or manager, number of employees, year first in "Yellow Pages." Compiled from

telephone company "Yellow Pages," nationwide.

***Non Store Marketing Report***. Maxwell Sroge Company Inc., 522 Forest Ave. Evanston, IL 60202-3005. Phone: (847)866-1890; Fax: (847)866-1899; Email: info@catalog-news.com • URL: http://www.catalog-news.com • Description: Source of analyses of key trends and key happeningsin the mail order, Internet, and interactive shopping business. order companies. Recurring features include an semiannual insert titled Trendwatch, which assesses the performance of publicly owned direct selling businesses, and company profiles on direct marketing businesses in the news.

***Nonferrous Castings***. U. S. Bureau of the Census, 4600 Silver Hill Rd. Washington, DC 20233-0001. Phone: (301)763-4636; Email: comments@census.gov • URL: http://www.census.gov • Annual. (Current Industrial Reports MA-33E.).

**Nonprofit Academic Centers Council**. 2121 Euclid Ave. Cleveland, OH 44115-2214. Phone: (216)687-9221 • URL: http://nonprofit-academic-centers-council.org • Provides leadership to strengthen existing centers and supports the establishment of new centers. Fosters collaboration among programs and centers. Develops creative approaches to researcher-practitioner collaborations.

**Nonprofit Australia**. c/o Netregistry Pty Ltd., PO Box 270 Sydney, NSW 2007, Australia. • URL: http://www.nonprofitaustralia.org.au • Improves the viability of nonprofit organizations for the benefit of Australian society. Increases the capabilities of nonprofit leadership teams and board members. Reduces the operating costs and increases the financial capacity of the sector. Develops targeted services and projects that provide new or improved solutions to the challenges faced by different sectors of Australian society.

***Nonprofit Counsel***. John Wiley and Sons, Inc., Journals Div., 111 River St. Hoboken, NJ 07030. Phone: 800-526-5368 or (201)748-6000; Fax: (201)748-6088; Email: consumers@wiley.com • URL: http://www.wiley.com • Monthly. $399 Institutions; $419 Institutions print edition.

***Nonprofit Issues***. Donald W. Kramer, PO Box 482 Dresher, PA 19025. Phone: 888-NP-ISSUE or (215)542-7547; Fax: (215)542-7548 • Description: Presents legal information for nonprofit executives and their professional advisors.

***Nonprofit Management and Leadership***. Jossey-Bass, 989 Market St. San Francisco, CA 94103-1741. Phone: 800-225-5945 or (415)433-1740; Fax: (415)433-0499 or (415)951-8553; Email: jbsubs@jbp.com • URL: http://www.josseybass.com • Quarterly. $160 Institutions.

***Nonprofit Management Resources Directory***. Global Ties U.S., 1420 K St. NW, Ste. 800 Washington, DC 20005. Phone: 800-523-8101 or (202)842-1414; Fax: (202)289-4625; Email: info@globaltiesus.org • URL: http://www.globaltiesus.org • Covers: Nonprofit organizations. Entries include: Name, address, phone, fax, email, and website address.

***The NonProfit Times: The Leading Business Publication For Nonprofit Management***. NPT Publishing Group Inc., 201 Littleton Rd., 2nd Fl. Morris Plains, NJ 07950. Phone: 800-535-8207 or (973)401-0202; Fax: (973)401-0404; Email: info@nptimes.com • URL: http://www.nptimes.com • $49.95 Individuals print; $19.95 Individuals digital only; $59.95 Individuals digital & print. Trade journal serving nonprofit organizations.

**Nonprofit VOTE**. 89 South St., Ste. 203 Boston, MA 02111-2750. Phone: (617)357-8683; Email: info@nonprofitvote.org • URL: http://www.nonprofitvote.org • Aims to expand the role of America's nonprofits in voting and elections. Provides resources and support to 501(c)(3) nonprofit voter participation initiatives that work year-round to increase the number of nonprofits integrating voter engagement activities into their ongoing work. Seeks to sustain the increasing voter participation in the country.

***Nonprofit World: The National Bi-Monthly Nonprofit Leadership and Management Journal***. Society for Nonprofit Organizations, PO Box 510354 Livonia, MI 48151. Phone: (734)451-3582; Fax: (734)451-5935; Email: info@snpo.org • URL: http://www.snpo.org • Bimonthly.

**Nonviolent Peaceforce**. 425 Oak Grove St. Minneapolis, MN 55403. Phone: (612)871-0005; Fax: (612)871-0006; Email: info@nonviolentpeaceforce.org • URL: http://www.nonviolentpeaceforce.org • Promotes the widespread implementation of effective nonviolent peacemaking in conflict areas around the world. Currently working to create the Nonviolent Peaceforce, an international organization to send hundreds and eventually thousands of trained peacemakers to work in areas of conflict at the invitation of local peacemakers or human rights workers. The Peace Force will be sent to conflict areas to prevent death and destruction, and protect human rights, thus creating the space for local groups to struggle nonviolently, enter into dialogue, and seek peaceful resolution.

***Nonwovens Industry: The International Magazine for the Nonwoven Fabrics and Disposable Soft Goods Industry***. Rodman Publications, 70 Hilltop Rd. Ramsey, NJ 07446. Phone: (201)825-2552; Fax: (201)825-0553; Email: happi@rodpub.com • URL: http://www.happi.com • Monthly. $48 Individuals.

**Nordic Financial Unions**. PO Box 720 S-101 34 Stockholm, Sweden. Phone: 46 8 6140300 or 46 8 6140302; Fax: 46 8 6113898 • URL: http://nordicfinancialunions.org • Bank and insurance employees' trade unions of Denmark, Finland, Iceland, Norway, and Sweden representing 165,000 individuals. Promotes the interests of bank and insurance employees in Scandinavia. Conducts biennial training course for shop stewards. Arranges conferences and meetings; training courses for shop stewards; carries out research, information, and lobbying activities; and has a system for economic assistance to member unions during labour conflicts.

***Nordic Stock Guide***. Delphi Economics AB, Hans Nilsson, 8 Bonn Pl. Weehawken, NJ 07087. Phone: (201)867-4303; Fax: (201)867-4666 • $34.95 plus $3.50 shipping. Covers: nearly 250 public companies in Denmark, Finland, Norway, and Sweden. Database includes: Interest rate histories, exchange rates, and commodities prices for each country. Entries include: Company name, address, phone, names and titles of key personnel, overview of company operations, stock and financial data for previous six years.

**North America Chinese Clean-tech and Semiconductor Association**. 809 Cuesta Dr., Ste. 208B Mountain View, CA 94040-3666. • URL: http://www.nacsa.com • Represents the interests of professionals dedicated to the advancement of Chinese professionals in high-tech industries. Strengthens networking among professionals. Fosters entrepreneurship among ethnic Chinese. Promotes the exchange in the global semiconductor and information technology industries.

**North American Agricultural Marketing Officials**. c/o Debra May, President, Florida Dept. of Agriculture and Consumer Services, 407 S Calhoun St. Tallahassee, FL 32399. Phone: (850)921-1727 • URL: http://www.naamo.org • Affiliated with National Association of Produce Market Managers and the National Association of State Departments of Argicutural. Formerly National Agricultural Marketing Officals.

**North American Association of Inventory Services**. PO Box 120145 Saint Paul, MN 55112. • URL: http://www.naais.com • Represents Independent inventory services; individuals interested in the inventory industry; individuals outside the industry who have performed notable service. Promotes activities aimed at enabling the inventory service to operate efficiently and maintain high standards of conduct. Provides a clearinghouse and medium for the benefit of owners of businesses and shops involving the utilization and maintenance of product inventories. Considers and deals with problems of operation and management, such as those associated with customer accounts and employment. Disseminates business information on the inventory service industry. Maintains speakers' bureau; compiles statistics.

**North-American Association of Uniform Manufacturers and Distributors**. 6800 Jericho Tpke., Ste. 120W Syosset, NY 11791. Phone: (516)393-5838; Fax: (516)393-5878 • URL: http://www.naumd.com • Formerly Uniform Manufacturers Exchange.

**North American Building Material Distribution Association**. 330 N Wabash Ave., Ste. 2000 Chicago, IL 60611. Phone: 888-747-7862 or (312)321-6845; Fax: (312)644-0310; Email: info@nbmda.org • URL: http://www.nbmda.org • Formerly National Building Material Distributors Association.

***North American Companies Manufacturing in Scotland***. Scottish Enterprise, Atrium Ct., 50 Waterloo St. Glasgow G2 6HQ, United Kingdom. Phone: 41 204 1111 or 41 2482700; Fax: 41 248 1600 or 41 2213217; Email: enquiries@scotent.co.uk • URL: http://www.scottish-enterprise.com • Covers: about 200 North American-owned companies in Scotland. Entries include: Company name, address, phone, telex, name and title of contact, number of employees, description of services.

**North American Die Casting Association**. 3250 N Arlington Heights Rd., Ste. 101 Arlington Heights, IL 60004. Phone: (847)279-0001; Fax: (847)279-0002; Email: nadca@diecasting.org • URL: http://www.diecasting.org • Represents producers of die castings and suppliers to the industry, product and die designers, metallurgists, and students. Develops product standards; compiles trade statistics on metal consumption trends; conducts promotional activities; provides information on chemistry, mechanics, engineering, and other arts and sciences related to die casting. Provides training materials and short, intensive courses in die casting. Maintains speakers' bureau.

***North American Directory of U.S. Importers and Canadian Importers***. Coble International, 1420 Steeple Chase Dover, PA 17315. Phone: (717)467-1835 • URL: http://www.importexporthelp.com • $285 print or CD-ROM; $325 print and CD-ROM. Covers: 19,000 importers in Canada and in the United States. Entries include: Name, address, phone, fax, primary contact person, list of products, e-mail addresses, and Web site.

**North American Equipment Dealers Association**. 1195 Smizer Mill Rd. Fenton, MO 63026-3480. Phone: (636)349-5000; Fax: (636)349-5443; Email: naeda@naeda.com • URL: http://www.naeda.com • Retailers of farm equipment, implements, light industrial equipment, outdoor power equipment and related supplies. Conducts programs on management training and governmental and trade relations.

**North American Export Grain Association**. 1250 I St. NW, Ste. 1003 Washington, DC 20005-3939. Phone: (202)682-4030; Fax: (202)682-4033; Email: info@naega.org • URL: http://www.naega.org • U.S. and Canadian exporters of grain and oilseeds from the United States.

**North American Home Furnishings Association**. 500 Giuseppe Ct., Ste. 6 Roseville, CA 95678. Phone: 800-422-3778 or (916)784-7677; Fax: (916)784-7697; Email: sbradley@nahfa.org • URL: http://www.nahfa.org • Provides business services to help retailers of home furnishings grow their businesses. Provides educational programs for retail sales managers and trainers, for middle management, for owners and executives, and for family businesses.

**North American Insulation Manufacturers Association**. 11 Canal Center Plz., Ste. 103 Alexandria, VA 22314. Phone: (703)684-0084; Fax: (703)684-0427 • URL: http://www.naima.org • Manufacturers of fiberglass, rock wool, and slag wool insulation products. Promotes energy efficiency and environmental preservation through the use of fiberglass, rock wool, and slag wool insulation products. Encourages safe production and use of insulation materials.

***North American Journal of Aquaculture***. American Fisheries Society, 5410 Grosvenor Ln. Bethesda, MD 20814. Phone: (301)897-8616; Fax: (301)897-8096; Email: main@fisheries.org • URL: http://fisheries.org • Quarterly. $419 Institutions print & online; $368 Institutions online only. Covers research and new developments relating to aquaculture.

***North American Journal of Fisheries Management***. American Fisheries Society, 5410 Grosvenor Ln. Bethesda, MD 20814. Phone: (301)897-8616; Fax: (301)897-8096; Email: main@fisheries.org • URL: http://fisheries.org • 6/year. $55 Individuals print, North America; $25 Individuals online, North America; $80 Individuals print and online, North America; $65 Out of country print; $90 Out of country print and online; $1,315 Institutions online only. Covers fisheries management trends and research.

**North American Meat Processors Association**. 1910 Association Dr. Reston, VA 20191. Phone: 800-368-3043 or (703)758-1900; Fax: (703)758-8001; Email: info@namp.com • URL: http://www.namp.com • Represents wholesalers of meats and meat products to hotels, restaurants, schools, hospitals, and institutions. Conducts technical seminars.

**North American Millers' Association**. 600 Maryland Ave. SW, Ste. 825 W Washington, DC 20024. Phone: (202)484-2200 or (202)554-1618; Fax: (202)488-7416; Email: generalinfo@namamillers.org • URL: http://www.namamillers.org • Grain milling companies that are processors of specially blended corn, wheat, and sorghum foods that are used primarily for overseas feeding programs. Millers of wheat, corn, oats, durum, and rye flour; members' mill 95 percent of total United States capacity.

**North American Retail Dealers Association**. 222 S Riverside Plz., Ste. 2100 Chicago, IL 60606. Phone: 800-621-0298 or (312)648-0649; Fax: (312)648-1212; Email: nardasvc@narda.com • URL: http://www.narda.com • Firms engaged in the retailing of electronic and electrical devices and components. Promotes and represents members' interests. Makes available services to members including: legal and technical consulting; employee screening; bank card processing; long-distance phone discounts; financial statements analysis; in-store promotion kits; customer check authorization. Advocates for members' interests before federal regulatory bodies; disseminates information on new regulations affecting members. Conducts educational programs.

**North American Retail Hardware Association**. 6325 Digital Way, Ste. 300 Indianapolis, IN 46278-1787. Phone: 800-772-4424 or (317)275-9400 or (317)290-0338; Fax: (317)275-9403 or (317)328-4354; Email: hwegeng@nrha.org • URL: http://www.nrha.org • Represents independent family-owned hardware/home improvement retailers. Sponsors correspondence courses in hardware and building materials retailing; conducts annual cost-of-doing-business study.

***North American Scrap Metals Directory***. Recycling Today Media Group, 4020 Kinross Lakes Pkwy., Ste. 201 Richfield, OH 44286-9084. Phone: 800-456-0707 or (330)523-5400; Fax: (330)659-0823 • URL: http://www.recyclingtoday.com • Annual. $95.20 Individuals discounted price; $119 Individuals list price. Covers: Suppliers of scrap metal materials in North America. Entries include: Contact information.

**North American Securities Administrators Association**. 750 1st St. NE, Ste. 1140 Washington, DC 20002-8034. Phone: (202)737-0900; Fax: (202)783-3571; Email: ri@nasaa.org • URL: http://www.nasaa.org • Represents the interests of the state, provincial and territorial securities administrators in the U.S., Canada, Mexico and Puerto Rico. Provides support to its members in government relations and with federal regulators, industry SROs and other groups.

**North American Security Products Organization**. 204 E St. NE Washington, DC 20002. Phone: (202)608-1322; Fax: (202)547-6348; Email: smc@naspo.info • URL: http://www.naspo.info • Aims to combat fraud within the areas of brand protection, finance and identity. Fosters the development of security risk management standards to reduce financial fraud, identify document fraud and dilution of brand integrity. Enables security product firms to classify and validate their ability to deliver high, medium or basic levels of security assurance throughout their operations.

**North American Trailer Dealers Association**. 111 2nd Ave. NE, Unit 1405 Saint Petersburg, FL 33701-3480. Phone: (727)360-0304; Fax: (727)231-8356; Email: info@natda.org • URL: http://natda.org • Supports the light and medium duty trailer dealers industry. Promotes financial strength, professional credibility and industry recognition for trailer dealers and manufacturers throughout the United States. Provides trailer dealers with benefits, programs and education.

***North Carolina Business Directory***. InfoGroup Inc., 5711 S 86th Cir. Omaha, NE 68127-4146. Phone: (402)593-4500 • URL: http://www.infogroup.com • Annual. $795 for both print & CD-ROM. Covers: 359,291 businesses in North Carolina. Entries include: Company name, address, phone, number of employees, name of owner or manager, sales volume. Compiled from telephone company 'Yellow Pages,' statewide. All states covered (see separate entries).

**North Carolina Department of Agriculture and Consumer Services - Border Belt Tobacco Research Station**. N Carolina State University, 86 Border Belt Dr. Whiteville, NC 28472-6828. Phone: (910)648-4703; Fax: (910)648-4858; Email: BorderBelt.ResSt@ncagr.gov • URL: http://www.ncagr.gov/research/bbtrs.htm • Tobacco breeding, variety testing, insect control, plant phenology, plant growth regulators, residues, plant physiology, fertilization, and methods development. Also studies corn, soybeans, and peanuts.

***North Carolina/South Carolina Industries Guide***. Industries Guides Inc., 303 E Altamonte Dr. Altamonte Springs, FL 32716. Phone: (407)834-8181 • $95. Covers: Approximately 14,000 manufacturers in North Carolina and South Carolina. Entries include: Company name, address, phone.

***North Houston Greenspoint Business***. Houston Intercontinental Chamber of Commerce, 12700 Northborough Houston, TX 77067. Phone: 855-839-4422 or (281)408-0866; Fax: (281)248-4388; Email: info@houstonicc.org • URL: http://houstonicc.org • Annual. Includes information on member firms.

***North Mobile Business***. Saraland Area Chamber of Commerce, 939 Hwy. 43 S Saraland, AL 36571. Phone: (251)675-4444; Fax: (251)675-2307 • URL: http://www.saralandchamber.com • Biennial. Lists businesses in Saraland/North Mobile, AL.

***North Shore Business Journal***. North Shore Chamber of Commerce, 5 Cherry Hill Dr., Ste. 100 Danvers, MA 01923-2568. Phone: (978)774-8565; Fax: (978)774-3418; Email: info@northshorechamber.org • URL: http://www.northshorechamber.org • Monthly. Includes information, updates of the chamber's events and other articles concerning North Shore Chamber of Commerce.

***Northeast Texas Buyers Guide to Minority Business***. Dallas/Fort Worth Minority Business Development Council, 8828 N Stemmons Fwy., 5th Fl., Ste. 550 Dallas, TX 75247. Phone: (214)630-0747; Fax: (214)637-2241; Email: admin@dfwmbdc.com • URL: http://www.dfwmsdc.com • Annual. Covers about 730 private firms offering professional, commercial, and industrial products and services, and in which more than 50% of company ownership is held by minority group members.

**Northeastern University - Center for the Study of Sport in Society**. Richards Hall, Ste. 350, 360 Huntington Ave. Boston, MA 02115. Phone: (617)373-4025; Fax: (617)373-8574; Email: sportinsociety@neu.edu • URL: http://www.northeastern.edu/sportinsociety • Research fields include sport sociology, sport journalism, and sport business.

***Northern Business Journal***. Northern Business Journal, 187 Cedar St. S Timmins, ON, Canada P4N 7G1. Phone: (705)268-5050; Fax: (705)268-7043 • URL: http://www.timminspress.com • Magazine presenting business articles related to northeastern Ontario, Canada.

***Northern California Business Directory and Buyers Guide***. Harris InfoSource, 2057 E Aurora Rd. Twinsburg, OH 44087-1999. Phone: 800-888-5900 or (330)425-9000 or (973)921-5500; Fax: (800)643-5997 or (877)252-3375; Email: customerservice@harrisinfo.com • URL: http://www.harrisinfo.com • Covers: 23,540 businesses in Northern California. Entries include: Company name, address, county, phone, fax, web site address (on CD-ROM only), number of employees, names and titles of key executives, plant size, year established, parent company, annual sales, import/export information, Standard Industrial Classification (SIC) code, and product description.

***Northern California Business Directory***. Harris InfoSource, 2057 E Aurora Rd. Twinsburg, OH 44087-1999. Phone: 800-888-5900 or (330)425-9000 or (973)921-5500; Fax: (800)643-5997 or (877)252-3375; Email: customerservice@harrisinfo.com • URL: http://www.harrisinfo.com • $175 for the print directory; $645 for the database.; $198 Members; $220 Nonmembers; $233 Members (with book and CD-ROM); $259 Nonmembers (with book and CD-ROM). Covers manufacturers, wholesalers and service businesses in the 45 counties north of San Luis Obispo, California. Entries include: Company profile, owners, names and titles of key personnel.

***Northern California High Technology***. Rich's Business Directories Inc., 1820 Gateway Blvd., Ste. 170 San Mateo, CA 94404. Phone: 800-969-7424 or (650)362-1020; Fax: (650)350-4084; Email: info@richsdata.com • URL: http://www.hightechdirectories.com • $935 Individuals database download; $470 Individuals print; $399 Individuals one year online subscription; $799 Individuals one year premium online subscription. Covers: Over 9,104 high technology firms in Northern California. Publication includes: Over 38,839 contact names. Entries include: Company name, address, web address, stock symbol, headquarters, year established, product type.

***The Northern Colorado Business Report***. The Northern Colorado Business Report, 141 S College Ave. Fort Collins, CO 80524-

2810. Phone: (970)221-5400; Fax: (970)221-5432; Email: publisher@ncbr.com • URL: http://www.ncbr.com/ • Biweekly. $44.97 Individuals; $79.97 Two years; $114.97 Individuals 3 years. Business newspaper.

***Northern Colorado Christian Business Directory***. Red Letter Publishing, PO Box 272682 Fort Collins, CO 80527. Phone: 800-445-5614; Fax: (970)267-9669; Email: info@redletter.com • URL: http://www.christianbusinessdirectoryonline.com • Businesses, churches, organizations, and schools in Northern Colorado.

***Northern Ireland Trade Directory***. Industrial Development Board for Northern Ireland Her Majesty's Stationary Office, 16 Arthur St. Belfast BT14 4JX, United Kingdom. Phone: 232 233233; Fax: 232 231328 • Annual. $33. Covers: Approximately 5,200 manufacturing companies in Northern Ireland. Entries include: Company name, address, phone, telex, name and title of contact, number of employees, description of product/service.

***Northern Kentucky Business Directory***. Christian Blue Pages, 521 Byers Rd., Ste. 102 Miamisburg, OH 45342. Phone: 800-860-2583 or (937)847-2583 • URL: http://www.christianbluepages.com • Annual. Christian-owned business enterprises in Northern Kentucky.

***The Northern Miner: Devoted to the Mineral Resources Industry of Canada***. Scott's Directories, 12 Concorde Pl., Ste. 800 Toronto, ON, Canada M3C 4J2. Phone: 800-668-2374 or (416)442-2122; Fax: (416)510-6870; Email: customercare@scottsdirectories.com • URL: http://www.scottsdirectories.com • Weekly. $114 per year.

**Northern Nut Growers Association**. PO Box 6216 Hamden, CT 06517-0216. Fax: (203)974-8502; Email: icomserve@aol.com • URL: http://www.northernnutgrowers.org • Consists of nut tree culturists, farmers, amateur and commercial nut tree growers, experiment station workers, horticultural teachers, scientists, nut tree breeders, nursery people, and foresters. Conducts visits to amateur and commercial orchards, experimental and research sites, nurseries and nut processing plants.

***Northern Saskatchewan Business Directory***. Economic Development Commission, 1328 Laronge Ave. La Ronge, SK, Canada S0J 1L0. Phone: 866-663-4065 or (306)425-4207; Fax: (306)425-4349; Email: sna@sna.gov.sk.ca • URL: http://www.northern.gov.sk.ca • Covers businesses, services, and goods in Saskatchewan's Northern Administration District.

***Northumberland Business Times***. Metroland Media Group, 3125 Wolfedale Rd. Mississauga, ON, Canada L5C 1W1. Phone: (905)279-0440 or (905)281-5656; Fax: (905)279-7763 or (905)279-5103 • URL: http://www.metroland.com/ • Monthly. Community newspaper bringing messages for and about local business.

**Northwest Farm Managers Association**. c/o North Dakota State University, Dept. 7000, 315 Morrill Hall Fargo, ND 58108-6050. Phone: (701)231-8944 • URL: http://www.ag.ndsu.edu/nwfm • Represents manager-operators of commercial farms and agriculturists interested in research in farm management, marketing, and agribusiness.

***Northwest Manitoba Business Directory***. Northwest Manitoba Business Directory, Box 892 Flin Flon, MB, Canada R8A 1N7. Phone: (204)472-3015; Email: natrp@sympatico.ca • Business directory covering businesses in Manitoba.

***Northwest Native American Business Directory***. ONABEN - Native American Business Network, 11825 SW Greenburg Rd., Ste. B-3 Tigard, OR 97223. Phone: 800-854-8289 or (503)968-1500; Fax: (503)968-1548 • URL: http://www.onaben.org • $19.95 Individuals. Covers: 350 native businesses, casinos, tribes, Native American chambers, and business associations in the Northwest.

***Northwestern Journal of International Law & Business***. Northwestern University School of Law Office of Legal Publications, 633 Clark St. Evanston, IL 60208. Phone: (847)491-3741 or (312)503-8649; Email: law-web@law.northwestern.edu • URL: http://www.law.northwestern.edu • 3/year. $40 Individuals; $50 Other countries; $15 Single issue; $18 Single issue international. Journal covering business law issues worldwide.

**Northwestern University - Center for Mathematical Studies in Economics and Management Sciences**. 580 Leverone Hall, Kellogg School of Management, 2001 Sheridan Rd. Evanston, IL 60208-2014. Phone: (847)491-3527; Fax: (847)491-2530; Email: cms-ems@northwestern.edu • URL: http://www.kellogg.northwestern.edu/research/math • Mathematical economics, mathematical programming, management science, and mathematical theory of economic organizations.

**Northwestern University - Center for Public Safety**. 1801 Maple Ave. Evanston, IL 60201-3149. Phone: 800-323-4011 or (847)491-5476; Fax: (847)491-5270; Email: nucps@northwestern.edu • URL: http://nucps.northwestern.edu • Police management, traffic law enforcement, criminal justice, accident investigation, and highway safety in all areas of traffic and transportation engineering, including highway and street design, traffic operations, use of computer tools, site development, and transit planning and operation.

**Northwestern University - Center for Retail Management**. Kellogg School of Management, 2001 Sheridan Rd. Evanston, IL 60208. Phone: (847)467-3600; Fax: (847)467-3620; Email: r-blattberg@kellogg.northwestern.edu • URL: http://www.kellogg.northwestern.edu/research/retail/ • Conducts research related to retail marketing and management.

**Northwestern University - Guthrie Center for Real Estate Research**. Kellogg School, 2001 Sheridan Rd., Rm. 401 Evanston, IL 60208. Phone: (847)491-3564; Fax: (847)491-5719; Email: tsm@kellogg.northwestern.edu • URL: http://www.kellogg.northwestern.edu/departments/real-estate/faculty-research/guthrie-center.aspx • Tax, real estate, and urban development and economics.

**Northwestern University - Media Management Center**. 1801 Maple Ave., Ste. 5316 Evanston, IL 60208-2101. Phone: (847)491-4900; Fax: (847)491-5619; Email: mediamanagement@mmc.northwestern.edu • URL: http://www.mediamanagementcenter.org • Research areas are related to various business aspects of the newspaper industry: management, marketing, personnel, planning, accounting, and finance. A joint activity of the J. L. Kellogg Graduate School of Management and the Medill School of Journalism.

**Northwestern University - Transportation Center**. 600 Foster St. Evanston, IL 60208-4055. Phone: (847)491-7287; Fax: (847)491-3090; Email: masmah@northwestern.edu • URL: http://transportation.northwestern.edu • Transportation, including information technology, air, rail, motor carrier, ocean and inland shipping, pipeline, telecommunications, and public transit. Focuses on the movement of materials, people, energy, and information. Emphasizes development of advanced models in logistics (vehicle routing, scheduling, inventory management, facility location), analyses of safety in the motor carrier and airline industries, evaluation of the impact of delivery restrictions in congested areas, use of advanced information technologies as competitive weapons in transportation management, studies of the impact of regulatory reform on industry economy, models of intercity travel behavior and suburban congestion, transportation planning.

***Norton Bankruptcy Law Adviser***. William L. Norton, Jr. Thomson West, 610 Opperman Dr. Eagan, MN 55123. Phone: 800-328-9352 or (651)687-7000 • Monthly. $598 Individuals.

***Norway Business Services Providers Leads***. Business Information Agency Inc. PlanetInform, 52 Tuscan Way, Ste. 202-181 Saint Augustine, VA 32092. Phone: (904)342-6124; Fax: (904)592-2632; Email: info@biasales.com • URL: http://www.biasales.com • Monthly. $134 Individuals mailing list; $283 Individuals sales list; $480 Individuals marketing list. Covers Norway's companies and all sub-industries that provide various services to commercial businesses, establishments, and organizations, including consulting, advertising and marketing services, and facilities maintenance.

***Norway Exports—Products and Services for Development***. The Export Council of Norway, Drammensveien 40 N-0253 Oslo, Norway. Phone: 47 2 926300; Fax: 47 2 926400 • Biennial. Covers: Products and services exported in Norway in a variety of lines of business, including financial and banking services, construction, mining, electricity, manufacturing and metals, electronics, training, surveying and mapping, wood processing, water supply and electricity. Entries include: Company name, address, phone, telex number, product/service.

***Norway's Top 10,000 Companies***. Dun & Bradstreet Inc., 103 JFK Pkwy. Short Hills, NJ 07078. Phone: 800-526-0651 or (973)921-5500 or (973)921-5000; Fax: (866)560-7035 or (512)794-7670; Email: info@dnb.com • URL: http://www.dnb.com • Covers: Approximately 15,000 companies in Norway. Entries include: Company name, address, phone, fax, telex, sales volume, rank, profit, SIC code, principal officer name and title, number of employees, export designation, equity capital.

**Norwegian Society of Financial Analysts**. PO Box 1276 VIKA N-0111 Oslo, Norway. Phone: 47 22 129210; Fax: 47 22 129211; Email: nff@finansanalytiker.no • URL: http://www.finansanalytiker.no • Financial analysts. Acts as a forum for exchange of technical information. Conducts educational programs.

***Not-for-Profit Entities - Best Practices in Presentation and Disclosure***. American Institute of Certified Public Accountants, 1211 Avenue of the Americas New York, NY 10036-8775. Phone: 888-777-7077 or (212)596-6200; Fax: (212)596-6213; Email: service@aicpa.org • URL: http://www.aicpa.org • $86.25 Nonmembers Print/Online; $69 Members Print/Online; $77 Nonmembers E-book; $62 Members E-book. Provides preparers and auditors with the tools they need to work through the process of creating and verifying the format and accuracy of their company or clients' financial statements.

***Not Too Small to Care: Small Businesses and Child Care***. Child Care Action Campaign, 24808 Deepdale Ave. Little Neck, NY 11362-1233. Phone: (212)239-0138; Fax: (212)268-6515 • URL: http://www.childcareaction.org • $15 for members; $25 for nonmembers. Profiles 29 small businesses that have implemented child care benefits: on-or-near-site child care centers, employee subsidies, and parental leave.

***NotiCen: Central American & Caribbean Affairs***. Latin America Data Base, University of New Mexico, 801 Yale Blvd. NE Albuquerque, NM 87131. Phone: (505)277-2961; Fax: (505)277-5989; Email: info@ladb.unm.edu • URL: http://ladb.unm.edu • An online newsletter covering economic, trade, political, and social issues in Central America. Time period is 1986 to date, with weekly updates. Inquire as to online cost and availability. Formerly EcoCentral.

***Novi Chamber of Commerce—Business Directory***. Novi Chamber of Commerce, 41875 W 11 Mile Rd., Ste. 201 Novi, MI 48375. Phone: (248)349-3743; Fax: (248)349-9719; Email: info@novichamber.com • URL: http://www.novichamber.com • Annual. Covers: Member businesses in Novi, Michigan.

**NPES-The Association for Suppliers of Printing and Publishing and Converting Technologies**. 1899 Preston White Dr. Reston, VA 20191-4326. Phone: (703)264-7200; Fax: (703)620-0994; Email: npes@npes.org • URL: http://www.npes.org • Formerly Association for Suppliers of Printing and Publishing and Converting Technologies.

**NPTA Alliance**. 330 N Wabash Ave., Ste. 2000 Chicago, IL 60611. Phone: 800-355-NPTA or (312)321-4092 or (631)777-2223; Fax: (312)673-6736; Email: npta@gonpta.com • URL: http://www.gonpta.com • Wholesale distributors and suppliers of paper, plastics and allied products.

**NSF International**. 789 N Dixboro Rd. Ann Arbor, MI 48113. Phone: 800-673-6275 or (734)769-8010; Fax: (734)769-0109; Email: info@nsf.org • URL: http://www.nsf.org • Specializes in the areas of public health and environmental quality focusing on water quality, food safety, indoor air health and the environment. Develops standards, operates product certification and listings programs for products that meet or exceed public health safety standards. Maintains a worldwide network of auditors who conduct unannounced inspections of manufacturer facilities to ensure compliance and to protect the integrity of the NSF Certification Mark. Provides special research and testing services to industry, government, and foundations.

***NSFRE-News***. Association of Fundraising Professionals, 4300 Wilson Blvd., Ste. 300 Arlington, VA 22203. Phone: 800-666-3863 or (703)684-0410; Fax: (703)684-0540; Email: afp@afpnet.org • URL: http://www.afpnet.org • Description: Covers tax-related issues affecting nonprofit organizations, conference and seminar information, educational opportunities, and chapter news.

***NSGA Now Magazine***. National Sporting Goods Association, 1601 Feehanville Dr., Ste. 300 Mount Prospect, IL 60056. Phone: 800-815-5422; Fax: (847)391-9827; Email: info@nsga.org • URL: http://www.nsga.org • Bimonthly. free for members; $50 for nonmembers. Bimonthy. Membership. Covers news and marketing trends for sporting goods retailers. Formerly *NSGA Sports Retailer*.

***NSPA Washington Reporter***. National Society of Accountants, 1010 N Fairfax St. Alexandria, VA 22314. Phone: 800-966-6679 or (703)549-6400; Fax: (703)549-2984; Email: members@nsacct.org • URL: http://www.nsacct.org • Monthly. Membership.

***NTIS Alerts: Agriculture & Food***. U.S. Department of Commerce National Technical Information Service, 5301 Shawnee Rd. Alexandria, VA 22312. Phone: 800-553-NTIS or (703)605-6050 or (703)605-6585; Email: info@ntis.gov • URL: http://www.ntis.gov • Biweekly. $130 per year. Covers agricultural economics, horticulture, fisheries, veterinary medicine, food technology, and related subjects.

***NTIS Alerts: Biomedical Technology & Human Factor Engineering***. U.S. Department of Commerce National Technical Information Service, 5301 Shawnee Rd. Alexandria, VA 22312. Phone: 800-553-NTIS or (703)605-6050 or (703)605-6585; Email: info@ntis.gov • URL: http://www.ntis.gov • Biweekly. $130 per year. Covers biotechnology, ergonomics, bionics, artificial intelligence, prosthetics, and related subjects.

***NTIS Alerts: Building Industry Technology***. U.S. Department of Commerce National Technical Information Service, 5301 Shawnee Rd. Alexandria, VA 22312. Phone: 800-553-NTIS or (703)605-6050 or (703)605-6585; Email: info@ntis.gov • URL: http://www.ntis.gov • Biweekly. $130 per year. Covers architecture, construction management, building materials, maintenance, furnishings, and related subjects.

***NTIS Alerts: Business & Economics***. U.S. Department of Commerce National Technical Information Service, 5301 Shawnee Rd. Alexandria, VA 22312. Phone: 800-553-NTIS or (703)605-6050 or (703)605-6585; Email: info@ntis.gov • URL: http://www.ntis.gov • Biweekly. $130 per year. Covers consumer affairs, minority enterprises, marketing and economics, international commerce, banking, and finance.

***NTIS Alerts: Communication***. U.S. Department of Commerce National Technical Information Service, 5301 Shawnee Rd. Alexandria, VA 22312. Phone: 800-553-NTIS or (703)605-6050 or (703)605-6585; Email: info@ntis.gov • URL: http://www.ntis.gov • Biweekly. $130 Individuals per year; domestic/foreign. Covers common carriers, satellites, radio/TV equipment, telecommunication regulations, and related subjects.

***NTIS Alerts: Computers, Control & Information Theory***. U.S. Department of Commerce National Technical Information Service, 5301 Shawnee Rd. Alexandria, VA 22312. Phone: 800-553-NTIS or (703)605-6050 or (703)605-6585; Email: info@ntis.gov • URL: http://www.ntis.gov • Biweekly. $130 per year. Covers computer hardware, software, control systems, pattern recognition, image processing, and related subjects.

***NTIS Alerts: Electrotechnology***. U.S. Department of Commerce National Technical Information Service, 5301 Shawnee Rd. Alexandria, VA 22312. Phone: 800-553-NTIS or (703)605-6050 or (703)605-6585; Email: info@ntis.gov • URL: http://

www.ntis.gov • Biweekly. $130 per year. Covers electronic components, semiconductors, antennas, circuits, optoelectronic devices, and related subjects.

***NTIS Alerts: Energy***. U.S. Department of Commerce National Technical Information Service, 5301 Shawnee Rd. Alexandria, VA 22312. Phone: 800-553-NTIS or (703)605-6050 or (703)605-6585; Email: info@ntis.gov • URL: http://www.ntis.gov • Biweekly. $130 per year. Covers electric power, batteries, fuels, geothermal energy, heating/cooling systems, nuclear technology, solar energy, energy policy, and related subjects.

***NTIS Alerts: Environmental Pollution & Control***. U.S. Department of Commerce National Technical Information Service, 5301 Shawnee Rd. Alexandria, VA 22312. Phone: 800-553-NTIS or (703)605-6050 or (703)605-6585; Email: info@ntis.gov • URL: http://www.ntis.gov • Biweekly. $130 per year. Covers the following categories of environmental pollution: air, water, solid wastes, radiation, pesticides, and noise.

***NTIS Alerts: Government Inventions for Licensing***. U.S. Department of Commerce National Technical Information Service, 5301 Shawnee Rd. Alexandria, VA 22312. Phone: 800-553-NTIS or (703)605-6050 or (703)605-6585; Email: info@ntis.gov • URL: http://www.ntis.gov • Biweekly. $130 per year. Covers a wide variety of industrial and technical areas.

***NTIS Alerts: Health Care***. U.S. Department of Commerce National Technical Information Service, 5301 Shawnee Rd. Alexandria, VA 22312. Phone: 800-553-NTIS or (703)605-6050 or (703)605-6585; Email: info@ntis.gov • URL: http://www.ntis.gov • Biweekly. $130 per year. Covers a wide variety of health care topics, including quality assurance, delivery organization, economics (costs), technology, and legislation.

***NTIS Alerts: Manufacturing Technology***. U.S. Department of Commerce National Technical Information Service, 5301 Shawnee Rd. Alexandria, VA 22312. Phone: 800-553-NTIS or (703)605-6050 or (703)605-6585; Email: info@ntis.gov • URL: http://www.ntis.gov • Biweekly. $130 per year. Covers computer-aided design and manufacturing (CAD/CAM), engineering materials, quality control, machine tools, robots, lasers, productivity, and related subjects.

***NTIS Alerts: Materials Sciences***. U.S. Department of Commerce National Technical Information Service, 5301 Shawnee Rd. Alexandria, VA 22312. Phone: 800-553-NTIS or (703)605-6050 or (703)605-6585; Email: info@ntis.gov • URL: http://www.ntis.gov • Biweekly. $130 per year. Covers ceramics, glass, coatings, composite materials, alloys, plastics, wood, paper, adhesives, fibers, lubricants, and related subjects.

***NTIS Alerts: Ocean Sciences and Technology***. U.S. Department of Commerce National Technical Information Service, 5301 Shawnee Rd. Alexandria, VA 22312. Phone: 800-553-NTIS or (703)605-6050 or (703)605-6585; Email: info@ntis.gov • URL: http://www.ntis.gov • Biweekly. $130 per year. Provides descriptions of government-sponsored research reports and software, with ordering information.

***NTIS Alerts: Transportation***. U.S. Department of Commerce National Technical Information Service, 5301 Shawnee Rd. Alexandria, VA 22312. Phone: 800-553-NTIS or (703)605-6050 or (703)605-6585; Email: info@ntis.gov • URL: http://www.ntis.gov • Biweekly. $130 per year. Covers air, marine, highway, inland waterway, pipeline, and railroad transportation.

***NTIS Database***. Ovid Technologies Inc., 333 7th Ave., 20th Fl. New York, NY 10001-5004. Phone: 800-950-2035 or (646)674-6300; Fax: (646)674-6301 or (647)674-6301; Email: sales@ovid.com • URL: http://www.ovid.com • Quarterly. $2,850.00 per year. Guide to over 2 million bibliographic entries. Compiled by the U.S. National Technical Information Service.

**Nuclear Energy Institute**. 1201 F St. NW, Ste. 1100 Washington, DC 20004-1218. Phone: (202)739-8000; Fax: (202)785-4019; Email: webmasterp@nei.org • URL: http://www.nei.org • Represents Electric utilities, manufacturers, industrial firms, research and service organizations, educational institutions, labor groups, and governmental agencies engaged in development and utilization of nuclear energy, especially nuclear-produced electricity, and other energy matters. Maintains speakers' bureau; compiles statistics and public attitude data.

***Nuclear Engineering International***. Wilmington Publishers Ltd., Wilmington House, Maidstone Rd., Wilmington Sidcup DA14 5HZ, United Kingdom. Email: energy@wilmington.co.uk • Monthly. $341.00 per year. Text in English; summaries in French and German.

***Nuclear Fuel***. Platts Global Energy, 2 Penn Plz., 25th Fl. New York, NY 10121-2298. Phone: 800-752-8878 or (212)904-3070 or (212)904-2977; Fax: (212)904-3070 or (212)904-4209; Email: support@platts.com • URL: http://www.platts.com • Biweekly. $3,270.00 per year. Newsletter.

**Nuclear Information and Records Management Association**. 10 Almas Rd. Windham, NH 03087-1105. Phone: (603)432-6476; Fax: (603)432-3024; Email: nirma@nirma.org • URL: http://www.nirma.org • Concerned with the maintenance of nuclear industry corporate records. Formerly Nuclear Records Management Association.

**Nuclear Information and Resource Service**. 6930 Carroll Ave., Ste. 340 Takoma Park, MD 20912. Phone: (301)270-6477; Fax: (301)270-4291; Email: nirsnet@nirs.org • URL: http://www.nirs.org • Promotes alternatives to nuclear power. Affiliated with World Information Service on Energy.

***Nuclear News***. American Nuclear Society, 555 N Kensington Ave. La Grange Park, IL 60526. Phone: 800-323-3044 or (708)352-6611; Fax: (708)352-0499; Email: nuclear@ans.org • URL: http://www.ans.org • Monthly. $510 Individuals online only; $580 Individuals print and online. Magazine focusing on applications of nuclear energy. Includes *Nuclear News Buyers Guide* and three special issues.

***Nuclear Plant Journal***. International Nuclear Power Industry. EQES Inc., 799 Roosevelt Rd., Ste. 6-208 Glen Ellyn, IL 60137-5925. Phone: (630)858-6161 • Bimonthly. $120.00 per year.

***Nuclear Power***. U. S. Government Printing Office, 732 N Capitol St. NW Washington, DC 20401. Phone: 866-512-1800 or (202)512-1800 or (866)512-1800; Fax: (202)512-2104 or (202)512-2250; Email: contactcenter@gpo.gov • URL: http://www.gpo.gov • Annual. Free. Lists government publications. GPO Subject Bibliography Number 200.

***Nuclear Science and Engineering: Research and Development Related to Peaceful Utilization of Nuclear Energy***. American Nuclear Society, 555 N Kensington Ave. La Grange Park, IL 60526. Phone: 800-323-3044 or (708)352-6611; Fax: (708)352-0499; Email: nuclear@ans.org • URL: http://www.ans.org • Nine times per year. Institutions, $1,725.00 per year. Includes online edition.

***Nuclear Standards News***. American Nuclear Society, 555 N Kensington Ave. La Grange Park, IL 60526. Phone: 800-323-3044 or (708)352-6611; Fax: (708)352-0499; Email: nuclear@ans.org • URL: http://www.ans.org • Semimonthly. Description: Provides current information on nuclear standards, U.S. Nuclear Regulatory Commission (NRC) regulations and licensing issues, and developments in the domestic and international nuclear standards field. Recurring features include a calendar of standards meetings and notices of pertinent publications.

**Nuclear Suppliers Association**. PO Box 1354 Westerly, RI 02891. Phone: (401)637-4224; Fax: (401)637-4822; Email: nsanews@charter.net • URL: http://www.nuclearsuppliers.org • Companies involved in the manufacture or distribution of products and services for the nuclear industry. Promotes nuclear power and the interests of the nuclear industry.

***Nuclear Technology***. American Nuclear Society, 555 N Kensington Ave. La Grange Park, IL 60526. Phone: 800-323-3044 or (708)352-6611; Fax: (708)352-0499; Email: nuclear@ans.org • URL: http://www.ans.org • Monthly. $2,260 Individuals print only; $2,337 Individuals online only; $2,490 Individuals print and online. Nuclear power; science and engineering.

***Nuclear Waste News: Generation-Packaging-Transportation-Processing-Disposal***. Business Publishers Inc., PO Box 17592 Baltimore, MD 21297-1592. Phone: 800-223-8720; Fax: (800)508-2592; Email: custserv@bpinews.com • URL: http://www.bpinews.com • Weekly. $867.00. per year. Newsletter.

***Nucleonics Week***. Platts Global Energy, 2 Penn Plz., 25th Fl. New York, NY 10121-2298. Phone: 800-752-8878 or (212)904-3070 or (212)904-2977; Fax: (212)904-3070 or (212)904-4209; Email: support@platts.com • URL: http://www.platts.com • Weekly. $3,000 basic; $3,650 enhanced access. Description: Provides an overview of all international developments relating to commercial nuclear power. Offers coverage of plant construction, low-level waste issues, government policies, plant performance, services, and decommissioning, as well as "comprehensive statistical coverage of plant production and the economics of nuclear power." Recurring features include a monthly listing of nuclear power electric generation worldwide. **Remarks:** Also available in electronic format.

***Numismatic News: The Complete Information Source for Coin Collectors***. Krause Publications Inc., 700 E State St. Iola, WI 54990-0001. Phone: 800-726-9966 or (715)445-2214 or (715)445-4612; Fax: (715)445-4087 • URL: http://www.krause.com • Weekly. $32.00 per year.

**Numismatics International**. PO Box 570842 Dallas, TX 75357-0842. • URL: http://www.numis.org • Numismatists, coin dealers, students, and numismatic authors in 35 countries. Works to: encourage and promote the science of numismatics; cultivate fraternal relations among collectors and numismatic students; encourage new collectors and foster the interest of youth in numismatics; stimulate and advance affiliations among collectors and kindred organizations; acquire, share, and disseminate numismatic knowledge including cultural and historical information on coins. Sponsors periodic lectures. Maintains coin collection.

***Nursery Business Retailer***. Brantwood Publications Inc., 2430 Estancia Blvd., Ste. 100 Clearwater, FL 33761-2644. Phone: (727)724-0020; Fax: (727)724-0021 • URL: http://www.interiorscape.com/ • Bimonthly. Price on application.

***Nursery Business Retailer—Top 100 Retailer Report***. Brantwood Publications Inc., 2430 Estancia Blvd., Ste. 100 Clearwater, FL 33761-2644. Phone: (727)724-0020; Fax: (727)724-0021 • URL: http://www.interiorscape.com/ • Annual. $15. Lists the largest 100 garden centers and retail nurseries based on sales.

***Nursing Economics: The Journal for Health Care Leaders***. Jannetti Publications Inc., E Holly Ave., Box 56 Pitman, NJ 08071-0056. Phone: (856)256-2300; Fax: (856)589-7463; Email: contact@ajj.com • URL: http://www.ajj.com • Bimonthly. Individuals, $80.00 per year; institutions, $100.00 per year.

***Nursing Home Regulations Manual***. Thompson Publishing Group Inc., Government Information Services, Education Funding Research Council, 1725 K St. NW, Ste. 700 Washington, DC 20006. Phone: 800-677-3789 or (202)444-8741; Fax: (800)759-7179 or (202)296-1091; Email: service@thompson.com • URL: http://www.thompson.com • $295.00 per year. Looseleaf service. Includes monthly updates, newsletters and internet access. Serves as a comprehensive guide to the Nursing Home Reform Act, federal regulations, resident assessment, deficiency findings, Medicare, Medicaid, Health Care Financing Administration (HCFA) policies, and related topics for nursing home and assisted living facility owners and managers.

***Nursing Homes: Long Term Care Management***. Medquest Communications, LLC, 3800 Lakeside Dr., No. 201 Cleveland, OH 44114. Phone: (216)391-9100; Fax: (216)391-9200 • Monthly. $95.00 per year. Covers business, finance, and management topics for nursing home directors and administrators.

***Nursing Management***. Springhouse Corp. Lippincott Williams & Wilkins, 2 Commerce Sq., 2001 Market St. Philadelphia, PA 19103. Phone: 800-638-3030 or (301)223-2300; Email: ronna.ekhouse@wolterskluwer.com • URL: http://www.lww.com • Monthly. Individuals, $83.00 per year; institutions, $397.00 per year. Non-clinical subject matter.

***Nutrition Abstracts and Reviews, Series A: Human and Experimental***. CABI Publishing North America, 38 Chauncey St., Ste. 1002 Boston, MA 02111. Phone: 800-552-3083; Email: cabi-nao@cabi.org • URL: http://www.cabi.org • Monthly. Institutions, $1,835.00 per year. Includes single site internet access. Published in England by CABI Publishing. Provides worldwide coverage of the literature.

***Nutrition Abstracts and Reviews, Series B: Livestock Feeds and Feeding***. CABI Publishing North America, 38 Chauncey St., Ste. 1002 Boston, MA 02111. Phone: 800-552-3083; Email: cabi-nao@cabi.org • URL: http://www.cabi.org • Monthly. Institutions, $1,180.00 per year. Online edition available, $1,215.00 per year. Published in England by CABI Publishing. Provides worldwide coverage of the literature.

***Nutrition Industry Executive***. Vitamin Retailer Magazine, Inc., 431 Cranbury Rd. East Brunswick, NJ 08816. Phone: (732)432-9600; Fax: (732)432-9288 • URL: http://www.vitaminretailer.com • 10 times a year. $50.00 per year. Edited for manufacturers of vitamins and other dietary supplements. Covers marketing, new products, industry trends, regulations, manufacturing procedures, and related topics. Includes a directory of suppliers to the industry.

***Nutrition Reviews***. International Life Science Institute, 1156 15th St. NW, Ste. 200 Washington, DC 20005-1743. Phone: (202)659-0074; Fax: (202)659-8654; Email: info@ilsi.org • URL: http://www.ilsi.org • Monthly. Individuals, $222.00 per year; institutions, $452.00 per year.

***Nutrition Today***. Lippincott Williams & Wilkins, 2 Commerce Sq., 2001 Market St. Philadelphia, PA 19103. Phone: 800-638-3030 or (301)223-2300; Email: ronna.ekhouse@wolterskluwer.com • URL: http://www.lww.com • Bimonthly. Individuals, $104.00 per year; institutions, $393.00 per year.

***The Nutshell***. Northern Nut Growers Association, PO Box 6216 Hamden, CT 06517-0216. Fax: (203)974-8502; Email: icomserve@aol.com • URL: http://www.northernnutgrowers.org • Quarterly. Description: Brings information to amateur and expert nut growers on cultural practices, new developments in propagation, and knowledge of new and better cultivars and where to get them. Contains supplements of reports on the latest practices, experiments in progress, and storage of nuts. Recurring features include letters to the editor, interviews, news of research, a calendar of events, reports of meetings, book reviews, and notices of publications available.

***NYU Stern School of Business***. • Office of Career Development section of website provides career resources for business graduates, along with resume databases arranged by classes. Many resources restricted to Stern students and alumni.

**Oak Ridge Institute for Science and Education**. 130 Badger Ave., OAB-44 Oak Ridge, TN 37831-0117. Phone: (865)576-3000 or (865)576-3146; Fax: (865)241-2923 or (615)576-9522; Email: communications@orau.org • URL: http://www.orise.orau.gov • Represents private, not-for-profit corporations and a consortium of 91 doctoral-granting colleges and universities. Serves the government, academia, and the private sector in important areas of science and technology. Manages and operates the Oak Ridge Institute for Science and Education (ORISE) for the U.S. Department of Energy. ORISE undertakes national and international programs in education, training, health, and the environment.

***Oakdale Business and Professional Association—Directory of Members***. Oakdale Business and Professional Association, c/o McNamara Co., 1330 E Hwy. 96 White Bear Lake, MN 55110. Email: info@obpa-mn.com • URL: http://www.obpa-mn.com • List of business members in Oakdale, Minnesota.

***Observer of Business and Politics***. Anthony Jasudasan, Tulsiani Chambers, 212 Nariman Point Mumbai 400 001, India. Phone: 91 022222247 • Daily. Newspaper focusing on business and economics.

***Occupational Earnings and Wage Trends in Metropolitan Areas***. U.S. Department of Labor Bureau of Labor Statistics, Postal

Square Bldg., 2 Massachusetts Ave. NE Washington, DC 20212. Phone: 800-877-8339 or (202)691-5200 or (202)606-5900; Fax: (202)691-6325; Email: blsdata_staff@bls.gov • URL: http://www.bls.gov • Three times a year.

***Occupational Health and Safety Letter.Towards Productivity and Peace of Mind***. Business Publishers Inc., PO Box 17592 Baltimore, MD 21297-1592. Phone: 800-223-8720; Fax: (800)508-2592; Email: custserv@bpinews.com • URL: http://www.bpinews.com • Biweekly. $317.00 per year.

***Occupational Injuries and Illnesses by Industry***. Bureau of Labor Statistics, U.S. Department of Labor. U. S. Government Printing Office, 732 N Capitol St. NW Washington, DC 20401. Phone: 866-512-1800 or (202)512-1800 or (866)512-1800; Fax: (202)512-2104 or (202)512-2250; Email: contactcenter@gpo.gov • URL: http://www.gpo.gov • Annual.

***Occupational Outlook Handbook***. Bureau of Labor Statistics, U.S. Department of Labor. U. S. Government Printing Office, 732 N Capitol St. NW Washington, DC 20401. Phone: 866-512-1800 or (202)512-1800 or (866)512-1800; Fax: (202)512-2104 or (202)512-2250; Email: contactcenter@gpo.gov • URL: http://www.gpo.gov • Biennial. $22 Individuals. Issued as one of the Bureau's Bulletin series and kept up to date by *Occupational Outlook Quarterly*.

***Occupational Outlook Quarterly***. U.S. Department of Labor Bureau of Labor Statistics, Postal Square Bldg., 2 Massachusetts Ave. NE Washington, DC 20212. Phone: 800-877-8339 or (202)691-5200 or (202)606-5900; Fax: (202)691-6325; Email: blsdata_staff@bls.gov • URL: http://www.bls.gov • Quarterly. $30 Two years; $15 Individuals; $42 Other countries 2 years; $6 Single issue; $8.40 Other countries single copy. Magazine providing occupational and employment information.

***Occupational Projections and Training Data***. U. S. Government Printing Office, 732 N Capitol St. NW Washington, DC 20401. Phone: 866-512-1800 or (202)512-1800 or (866)512-1800; Fax: (202)512-2104 or (202)512-2250; Email: contactcenter@gpo.gov • URL: http://www.gpo.gov • Biennial. $31.50. Issued by Bureau of Labor Statistics, U. S. Department of Labor. Contains projections of employment change and job openings over the next 15 years for about 500 specific occupations. Also includes the number of associate, bachelor's, master's, doctoral, and professional degrees awarded in a recent year for about 900 specific fields of study.

***Occupational Safety and Health Handbook: An Employer's Guide to OSHA Laws***. Matthew Bender and Company Inc., 1275 Broadway Albany, NY 12204-2638. Phone: 800-424-4200 or (518)487-3000; Fax: (518)487-3573 or (800)424-4200; Email: customer.support@lexisnexis.com • URL: http://www.matthewbender.com • $128. Periodic supplementation available. Covers inspections, violations, the citation process, ergonomics, hazards, equipment, and other topics relating to the law enforced by the federal Occupational Safety and Health Administration (OSHA).

***Occupational Therapy in Health Care: A Journal of Contemporary Practice***. The Haworth Press Inc., 10 Alice St. Binghamton, NY 13904. Phone: 800-429-6784 or (607)722-5857; Fax: (607)771-0012 or (607)722-6362; Email: getinfo@haworthpress.com • URL: http://www.haworthpressinc.com/store/product.asp?sku=J014 • Quarterly. $275.00 per year.

***Occupational Therapy in Mental Health: A Journal of Psychosocial Practice and Research***. The Haworth Press Inc., 10 Alice St. Binghamton, NY 13904. Phone: 800-429-6784 or (607)722-5857; Fax: (607)771-0012 or (607)722-6362; Email: getinfo@haworthpress.com • URL: http://www.haworthpressinc.com/store/product.asp?sku=J014 • Quarterly. Institutions, $385.00 per year.

***Ocean Development and International Law***. Taylor & Francis Group Journals, 325 Chestnut St., Ste. 800 Philadelphia, PA 19106-2608. Phone: 800-354-1420 or (215)625-8900; Fax: (215)625-2940; Email: customerservice@taylorandfrancis.com • URL: http://www.tandf.co.uk • Quarterly. $440 Individuals print; $812 Institutions online; $928 Institutions print and online. Peer-reviewed law journal.

***Ocean Engineering: An International Journal of Research and Development***. Elsevier, Secondary Publishing Division, 650 Ave. of the Americas New York, NY 10011. Phone: 888-437-4636 or (212)633-3980; Fax: (212)633-3975; Email: t.reller@elsevier.com • URL: http://www.elseveier.com • 18 times a year. Qualified personnel, $261.00 per year; institutions, $4,074.00 per year.

***Ocean Navigator: Marine Navigation and Ocean Voyaging***. Navigator Publishing L.L.C., 58 Fore St. Portland, ME 04101-4842. Phone: 866-918-6972 or (207)772-2466; Fax: (207)772-2879; Email: editors@oceannavigator.com • URL: http://www.navigatorpublishing.com • Bimonthly. $27.95 per year.

***Ocean Oil Weekly Report: News, Analysis, and Market Trends of the Worldwide Offshore Oil and Gas Industry***. PennWell Corp., Petroleum Div., 1700 W. Loop S., Suite 1000 Houston, TX 77027. Phone: 800-736-6935 or (713)621-9720; Email: petroleum@pennwell.com • URL: http://www.pennwell.com • Weekly. $495.00 per year. Newsletter with emphasis on the Gulf of Mexico offshore oil industry. Includes statistics.

***Oceanic Abstracts***. CSA, 7200 Wisconsin Ave. Bethesda, MD 20814. Phone: 800-843-7751 or (301)961-6700; Fax: (301)961-6720; Email: service@csa.com • URL: http://www.csa.com • Monthly. $1,645.00 per year. Includes print and online editions. Covers oceanography, marine biology, ocean shipping, and a wide range of other marine-related subject areas.

***OCREFO Creditreform Companies***. Verband der Vereine Creditreform e.V., Hellersbergstr. 12, Postfach 101553 D-41460 Neuss, Germany. Phone: 49 2131 109 0 or 49 2131 109 0; Fax: 49 2131 1098000 or 49 2131 109 8000; Email: creditrefom@verband.creditrefom.de • URL: http://www.creditreform.de • Quarterly. Database covers: over 20,000 profiles of companies registered in the new German states. Database includes: Company name, address, phone, legal status, year founded, registration data, owner, capital, management description, industry classification code, number of employees, annual sales.

***Ocular Surgery News***. SLACK Inc., 6900 Grove Rd. Thorofare, NJ 08086-9447. Phone: 877-307-5225 or (856)848-1000 or (609)848-1000; Fax: (856)848-6091 or (856)853-5991; Email: customerservice@slackinc.com • URL: http://www.slackinc.com • Biweekly. Individuals, $472.00 per year; institutions, $599.00 per year. Formerly *IOL & Ocular Surgery News*.

***OECD Catalogue of Publications***. Organization for Economic Cooperation and Development. Organisation for Economic Co-operation and Development Publications and Information Center, 2001 L St. NW, Ste. 650 Washington, DC 20036-4922. Phone: 800-456-6323 or (202)785-6323; Fax: (202)785-0350; Email: washington.contact@oecd.org • URL: http://www.oecd.org • Online only. No print edition.

***OECD Communications Outlook***. Organisation for Economic Co-operation and Development Publications and Information Center, 2001 L St. NW, Ste. 650 Washington, DC 20036-4922. Phone: 800-456-6323 or (202)785-6323; Fax: (202)785-0350; Email: washington.contact@oecd.org • URL: http://www.oecd.org • Biennial. Provides international coverage of yearly telecommunications activity. Includes charts, graphs, and maps.

***OECD Economic Outlook***. Organisation for Economic Co-operation and Development Publications and Information Center, 2001 L St. NW, Ste. 650 Washington, DC 20036-4922. Phone: 800-456-6323 or (202)785-6323; Fax: (202)785-0350; Email: washington.contact@oecd.org • URL: http://www.oecd.org • Semiannual. Price on application. $95.00 per year. Contains a wide range of economic and monetary data relating to the member countries of the Organization for Economic Cooperation and Development. Includes about 100 statistical tables and graphs, with 24-month forecasts for each of the OECD countries. Provides extensive review and analysis of recent economic trends.

***OECD Economic Survey of the United States***. Organisation for Economic Co-operation and Development Publications and Information Center, 2001 L St. NW, Ste. 650 Washington, DC 20036-4922. Phone: 800-456-6323 or (202)785-6323; Fax: (202)785-0350; Email: washington.contact@oecd.org • URL: http://www.oecd.org • Annual. €60.00.

***OECD Economic Surveys***. Organisation for Economic Co-operation and Development Publications and Information Center, 2001 L St. NW, Ste. 650 Washington, DC 20036-4922. Phone: 800-456-6323 or (202)785-6323; Fax: (202)785-0350; Email: washington.contact@oecd.org • URL: http://www.oecd.org • Annual. $26.00 each. These are separate, yearly reviews for each of the economies of the industrialized nations that comprise the OECD. Each edition includes forecasts, analyses, and detailed statistical tables for the country being surveyed. (The combined series, one annual volume for each nation, is available at $485.00.).

***OECD Iron and Steel Industry***. Organization for Economic Cooperation and Development. Organisation for Economic Co-operation and Development Publications and Information Center, 2001 L St. NW, Ste. 650 Washington, DC 20036-4922. Phone: 800-456-6323 or (202)785-6323; Fax: (202)785-0350; Email: washington.contact@oecd.org • URL: http://www.oecd.org • Annual. $34.00. Data for orders, production, manpower, imports, exports, consumption, prices and investment in the iron and steel industry in OECD member countries. Text in English and French.

***OECD Nuclear Energy Data***. Organization for Economic Cooperation and Development. Organisation for Economic Co-operation and Development Publications and Information Center, 2001 L St. NW, Ste. 650 Washington, DC 20036-4922. Phone: 800-456-6323 or (202)785-6323; Fax: (202)785-0350; Email: washington.contact@oecd.org • URL: http://www.oecd.org • Annual. $58.00. Produced by the OECD Nuclear Energy Agency. Provides a yearly compilation of basic statistics on electricity generation and nuclear power in OECD member countries. Text in English and French.

***OECD Observer***. Organisation for Economic Co-operation and Development Publications and Information Center, 2001 L St. NW, Ste. 650 Washington, DC 20036-4922. Phone: 800-456-6323 or (202)785-6323; Fax: (202)785-0350; Email: washington.contact@oecd.org • URL: http://www.oecd.org • Bimonthly. $101 Individuals print + online; €73 Individuals print + online; £57 Individuals print + online; ¥9,500 Individuals print + online. Magazine on economic affairs, science, and technology.

***OECD Oil and Gas Information***. Organisation for Economic Co-operation and Development Publications and Information Center, 2001 L St. NW, Ste. 650 Washington, DC 20036-4922. Phone: 800-456-6323 or (202)785-6323; Fax: (202)785-0350; Email: washington.contact@oecd.org • URL: http://www.oecd.org • Annual. Price varies. Data on oil and gas balances, supplies, consumption by end use sector and trade of OECD countries. Text in English and French.

***OECD Statistical Compendium***. Organization for Economic Cooperation and Development, 2001 L St. NW, Ste. 650 Washington, DC 20036-4922. Phone: 800-456-6323 or (202)785-6323; Fax: (202)785-0350; Email: washington.contact@oecd.org • URL: http://www.oecd.org • Semiannual. $1,905.00 per year for 1 to 10 users. CD-ROM contains more than 730,000 monthly, quarterly, and annual time series for OECD countries, 1960 to date. Includes fully searchable data on agriculture, food, economic indicators, national accounts, employment, energy, finance, industry, technology, and foreign trade. Results can be displayed in various forms.

***OECD Steel Market and Outlook***. Organization for Economic Cooperation and Development. Organisation for Economic Co-operation and Development Publications and Information Center, 2001 L St. NW, Ste. 650 Washington, DC 20036-4922. Phone: 800-456-6323 or (202)785-6323; Fax: (202)785-0350; Email: washington.contact@oecd.org • URL: http://www.oecd.org • Annual. Price varies.

***Oesterreich's Ten Thousand Groesste Unternehmen***. D & B - Schimmelpfeng Gesellschaft GmbH, Operning 3-5 A-1015 Vienna, Austria. Phone: 1 588 61 0 • Annual. $525. Covers: 11,000 Austrian companies. Entries include: Company name, address, phone, names and titles of key personnel, year founded, line of business, name and location of parent company, number of employees, year founded, SIC numbers, and sales volumes.

***Of Counsel: The Monthly Legal Practice Report***. Wolters Kluwer Law and Business, 76 9th Ave., 7th Fl. New York, NY 10011-4962. Phone: 800-234-1660 or (212)771-0600; Fax: (800)901-9075 or (301)644-3550 • URL: http://www.wolterskluwerlb.com • 12 times a year. $829.00 per year. Newsletter on the management, marketing, personnel, and compensation of law firms.

***OFERES***. Instituto Espanol de Comercio Exterior, Paseo de la Castellana, 14-16 E-28046 Madrid, Spain. Phone: 34 913 496100 or 1 3496100; Fax: 1 4316128; Email: buzonicex@icex.es • URL: http://www.icex.es • Weekly. Database covers: Approximately 100,000 export companies in Spain. Database includes: Company name, address, phone, fax, number of employees, export representative, languages, activity, current annual and total export volume, product sector, trademarks and brand names, trade partners.

***Oferta Exportable del Sector Textil de la Confeccion, Colombia***. The Export Promotion Fund, Proexpo, Centro Comercio Internacional, Calle 28, Numero 13A-15 Bogota, Colombia. Phone: 12 690777 • Covers: Textiles and clothing manufacturers in Columbia. Entries include: Company name, address, phone, number of employees, type of product exported, export capacity, name of contact person.

***Office—Czech Republic***. I.S.M.C. Information Systems and Marketing Contacts Ltd., Nam. Slobody 9, PO Box 47 81499 Bratislava, Slovakia. Phone: 421 7 265423783; Fax: 421 7 265422186; Email: ismc@ismc.sk • URL: http://www.ismc.sk • $75. Covers: Companies in the office furnishment and office equipment industries in the Czech Republic.

***Office Equipment, Stationery & Supplies, Packaging Importer Directory***. Biz Focus Company Ltd., 124 Soi Grand Village, Ladprao Rd., Wangthonglang Bangkok 10310, Thailand. Phone: 66 2 5395726; Fax: 66 2 5395726; Email: support@importerdata.com • URL: http://www.importerdata.com • $320 Individuals. Covers: 8,596 importers of accounting and invoicing machine, calculating machine, packaging and bottling machinery accessories, mailing and postal machinery and equipment, office machinery and equipment, and plastic articles for office use. Entries include: Company name, contact person, contact address, telephone number, fax number, e-mail, URL, and import products.

**Office for Sponsored Research**. Harvard University, Holyoke Ctr., Rm. 620, 1350 Massachusetts Ave. Cambridge, MA 02138. Phone: (617)495-5501; Fax: (617)496-2524 • URL: http://osp.fad.harvard.edu.

**Office of Academic Affairs, School of Public Health**. University of Michigan, 1415 Washington Heights Ann Arbor, MI 48109-2029. Phone: (734)764-5425; Fax: (734)763-5455; Email: nkjanz@umich.edu • URL: http://www.sph.umich.edu/ • Research fields include health care economics, health insurance, and long-term care.

***Office Products Analyst: A Monthly Report Devoted to the Analysis of Office Products***. Industry Analysts Inc., 50 Chestnut St., Ste. 900 Rochester, NY 14604. Phone: (585)232-5320; Fax: (585)454-5760; Email: info@industryanalysts.com • URL: http://www.industryanalysts.com • Monthly. $350.00 per year. Newsletter. Includes user ratings of office automation equipment.

***Office Products Dealer—Product Buying Guide and Industry Directory Issue***. Hitchcock Publishing Co., 191 S Gary Ave. Carol Stream, IL 60188-2024. Phone: (708)462-2292 • Annual. $15 plus $3.00 shipping. Publication includes: Lists of manufacturers, wholesalers, and distributors of furniture, machines, computer and word processing systems, and office products and equipment; manufacturers' representatives, and national industry associations that serve retail office products dealers.

***Office Products Representatives Alliance—Membership Directory***. Office Products Representatives Alliance, 301 N. Fairfax St. Alexandria, VA 22314. Phone: (703)549-9040; Fax: (703)683-7552; Email: info@nopanet.org • URL: http://www.bpia.org • Annual. $50 Nonmembers. Covers: nearly 120 independent office product and office furniture distribution firms. Entries include: Firm name, address, phone, product and service provided.

***Office Relocation Magazine***. ORM Group, 354 W. Lancaster Ave., c/o J. Barthelmess Haverford, PA 19041. Phone: (610)649-6565; Fax: (610)642-8020 • Bimonthly. $39.00 per year. Provides articles on the relocation of office facilities.

***Office Supplies Directory***. InfoGroup Inc., 5711 S 86th Cir. Omaha, NE 68127-4146. Phone: (402)593-4500 • URL: http://www.infogroup.com • Annual. Lists companies that offer office supplies and equipment.

***Office World News***. BUS Publications, 366 Ramtown Greenville Rd. Howell, NJ 07731-2789. Phone: (732)785-8300; Fax: (732)785-1347; Email: ownews@worldnet.att.net • URL: http://www.officeworldnews.com • Monthly. Free to qualified personnel; others, $50.00 per year. Formerly *Office Products News*.

***OfficePro***. Stratton Publishing and Marketing Inc., 5285 Shawnee Rd., Ste. 510 Alexandria, VA 22312-2334. Phone: (703)914-9200; Fax: (703)914-6777; Email: pubpros@strattonpub.com • URL: http://www.strattonpub.com • Nine times a year. $25.00 per year. Provides statistics and other information about secretaries and office trends. Formerly *Secretary*.

***The Official American International Toy Fair Directory***. Toy Industry Association, 1115 Broadway, Ste. 400 New York, NY 10010. Phone: (212)675-1141; Fax: (212)633-1429; Email: info@toyassociation.org • URL: http://www.toyassociation.org • Annual. Covers: About 1,500 toy, game, and holiday decoration manufacturers and their representatives. Entries include: Company name, address, phone, e-mail, fax, website, booth number or location at Toy Fair, products, name of representative.

***Official Board Markets: "The Yellow Sheet"***. Mark Arzoumanian. Advanstar Communications, 545 Boylston St. Boston, MA 02116. Phone: 888-527-7008 or (617)267-6500; Fax: (617)267-6900; Email: info@advanstar.com • URL: http://www.advanstar.com • Weekly. $160.00 per year. Covers the corrugated container, folding carton, rigid box and waste paper industries.

***Official E-mail and Fax Directory***. Todd Publications, PO Box 500 Millwood, NY 10546. Phone: 866-896-0916 or (914)373-4750; Fax: (914)373-4750; Email: toddpub@aol.com • URL: http://www.toddpublications.com • $150. Covers: 160,000 contacts at 50,000 U.S. companies, government agencies, and public and private institutions; includes manufacturers, professional service firms, media and publishing agencies, consultants, financial institutions, and government offices. Entries include: e-mail addresses.

***Official Export and Import Directory of Costa Rica***. Mercadeo Profesional, S.A., 1502-1002 Paseo de los Estudiantes San Jose, Costa Rica. Phone: 506 22965715; Fax: 506 22324871; Email: ventas@meprosa.com • URL: http://www.directorioscostarica.com • Annual. Covers: Export and import companies in Costa Rica.

***Official Gazette of the United States Patent and Trademark Office: Patents***. U. S. Government Printing Office, 732 N Capitol St. NW Washington, DC 20401. Phone: 866-512-1800 or (202)512-1800 or (866)512-1800; Fax: (202)512-2104 or (202)512-2250; Email: contactcenter@gpo.gov • URL: http://www.gpo.gov • Weekly. Contains the Patents, Patent Office Notices, and Designs issued each week (www.uspto.gov). Annual indexes are sold separately.

***Official Gazette of the United States Patent and Trademark Office: Trademarks***. U. S. Government Printing Office, 732 N Capitol St. NW Washington, DC 20401. Phone: 866-512-1800 or (202)512-1800 or (866)512-1800; Fax: (202)512-2104 or (202)512-2250; Email: contactcenter@gpo.gov • URL: http://www.gpo.gov • Weekly. $1,229.00 per year by first class mail. Contains Trademarks, Trademark Notices, Marks Published for Opposition, Trademark Registrations Issued, and Index of Registrants (www.uspto.gov).

***Offshore: Incorporating The Oilman***. PennWell Corp., Industrial Div., 1421 S Sheridan Rd. Tulsa, OK 74112. Phone: 800-331-4463 or (918)835-3161; Email: bid@pennwell.com • URL: http://www.pennwell.com • Monthly. $75.00 per year.

**Offshore Marine Service Association**. 935 Graver St., Ste. 2040 New Orleans, LA 70112. Phone: (504)528-9411; Fax: (504)528-9415 • URL: http://www.offshoremarine.org • Owners, operators, suppliers and crews of vessels servicing offshore oil and mineral installations. Seeks to advance the industry worldwide; monitors legislation and governmental regulations affecting the construction of offshore oil marine equipment and the operation of these specialized vessels, used primarily to supply and service offshore oil and gas operations worldwide. Conducts educational and personnel development and training programs; disseminates information on insurance and legal issues affecting offshore vessel operations. Maintains numerous committees representing all types of vessels engaged in the support of offshore installations.

**Ohio Aerospace Institute**. 22800 Cedar Point Rd. Cleveland, OH 44142. Phone: (440)962-3000; Fax: (216)962-3120 or (440)962-3120; Email: info@oai.org • URL: http://www.oai.org • Aerospace-related research, education, and technology transfers. Formerly Ohio Aerospace Institute.

***Ohio Industrial Directory***. Harris InfoSource, 2057 E Aurora Rd. Twinsburg, OH 44087-1999. Phone: 800-888-5900 or (330)425-9000 or (973)921-5500; Fax: (800)643-5997 or (877)252-3375; Email: customerservice@harrisinfo.com • URL: http://www.harrisinfo.com • Annual. $220 Individuals manufacturing price. Covers: 22,900 Ohio manufacturing companies. Database includes: Statistical data, trade show calendar. Entries include: Company name, address, county, phone, fax, number of employees, names and titles of key executives, plant size, year established, parent company, annual sales, import/export information, Standard Industrial Classification (SIC) code, and product description.

***Ohio Industries Guide***. Industries Guides Inc., 303 E Altamonte Dr. Altamonte Springs, FL 32716. Phone: (407)834-8181 • $95. Covers: Approximately 20,000 manufacturers in Ohio. Entries include: Company name, address, phone.

***Ohio Roster***. Edward Howard & Co., 1 Erieview Plz., 7th Fl. Cleveland, OH 44114-1715. Phone: (216)781-2400; Fax: (216)781-8810 • $12. Covers: the 200 largest manufacturers, retailers, service companies, transportation firms, public utilities, and financial institutions headquartered in Ohio whose stock is publicly traded. Database includes: Lists of the top 20 firms by revenue, assets, net income, and biggest sales gain. Entries include: Firm name, location, total revenues, net income, total assets, earnings per share, stock exchange on which traded.

**Ohio State University - Center for Health Outcomes, Policy and Evaluation Studies**. 280G Cunz Hall, 1841 Neil Ave. Columbus, OH 43210. Phone: (614)292-2129; Fax: (614)292-3572; Email: adembe@cph.osu.edu • URL: http://cph.osu.edu/hopes • Health care policy.

**Ohio State University - College of Education and Human Ecology - Center on Education and Training for Employment**. 1900 Kenny Rd. Columbus, OH 43210-1016. Phone: 800-848-4815 or (614)292-8008; Fax: (614)292-1260; Email: kelsey.28@osu.edu • URL: http://cete.osu.edu • Formerly National Center for Research in Vocational Education.

**Ohio State University - Fontana Corrosion Center**. 477 Watts Hall, 2041 College Rd. Columbus, OH 43210. Phone: (614)292-9857; Fax: (614)292-9857; Email: frankel.10@osu.edu • URL: http://www.matsceng.ohio-state.edu/frankel/FCC • Research areas include metal coatings and corrosion of alloys.

**Ohio State University - Gear and Power Transmission Research Laboratory**. Department of Mechanical and Aerospace Engineering, 201 W 19th Ave. Columbus, OH 43210. Phone: (614)292-4678 or (614)688-3952; Fax: (614)292-3163; Email: kahraman.1@osu.edu • URL: http://gearlab.org • Transmission error prediction for spur and helical gears, load distribution prediction, finite element modeling, vibration signal analysis, acoustic intensity measurements, and gear testing. Supports graduate student research.

**Ohio State University - Laboratory for Pest Control Application Technology**. Ohio Agricultural Research & Development Ctr., 1680 Madison Ave. Wooster, OH 44691. Phone: (330)263-3931; Fax: (330)263-3686; Email: downer.2@osu.edu • URL: http://www.oardc.ohio-state.edu/lpcat • Conducts pest control research in cooperation with the U. S. Department of Agriculture.

**Ohio State University - Jerome Lawrence and Robert E. Lee Theatre Research Institute**. 119 Thompson Library, 1858 Neil Ave. Mall Columbus, OH 43210-1230. Phone: (614)292-6614 or (614)292-9606; Fax: (614)688-8417; Email: theatreinst@osu.edu • URL: http://library.osu.edu/find/collections/theatre-research-institute • Theatrical activities in western Europe from 15th-19th centuries, especially festivals, theater architecture and machinery designs, costume designs, commedia dell'arte materials from 19th and 20th centuries, American and English promptbooks, and general theater and dance material from 19th, 20th and 21st centuries. Archives of American Theatre Companies and individual playwrights. Provides primary materials to students and scholars for research and publication, including doctoral work. Arranges exhibitions of materials.

**Ohio University - Avionics Engineering Center**. Russ College of Engineering and Technology, 131 McFarland Avionics Bldg. Athens, OH 45701. Phone: (740)593-1534 or (740)597-2657; Email: avionics@ohio.edu • URL: http://www.ohio.edu/avionics • Aeronautical electronics, including studies on aircraft navigational aids, propagation of very high frequency omnirange signals, weather radar systems, radio frequency interference, global positioning satellite (GPS) navigation, instrument landing system (ILS) technology, microwave landing system (MLS) technology, Loran-C navigation, navigation system air analyses, predictions of VHF communications coverage, datalink testing and analysis, UAVs, synthetic vision display research, and specialized computer equipment for flight data collection.

***Oil and Gas Asia Business Directory***. AP Energy Business Publications Private Ltd., 19 Kim Keat Rd., 04-06, Fu Tsu Bldg. Singapore 328804, Singapore. Phone: 65 622 23422 or 65 62223422; Fax: 65 622 25587 or 65 62225587; Email: eraj@safan.com • URL: http://petromin.safan.com • Annual. Drilling and production companies, pipeline contractors and operators, refinery, petrochemical and gas processing operators, equipment and service companies.

***Oil and Gas Investor***. Hart Energy, 1616 S Voss Rd., Ste. 1000 Houston, TX 77057-2627. Phone: 800-874-2544 or (713)260-6400 or (713)993-9320; Fax: (713)840-8585; Email: custserv@hartenergy.com • URL: http://www.hartenergy.com • Monthly. $297.00 per year.

***Oil and Gas Journal***. PennWell Corp., Industrial Div., 1421 S Sheridan Rd. Tulsa, OK 74112. Phone: 800-331-4463 or (918)835-3161; Email: bid@pennwell.com • URL: http://www.pennwell.com • Weekly. $84.00 per year.

***The Oil and Natural Gas Producing Industry in Your State***. Independent Petroleum Association of America. Petroleum Independent Publishers, Inc., 1201 15th St., NW, No. 300 Washington, DC 20005. Phone: (202)857-4722; Fax: (202)857-4799; Email: rcarter@ipaa.org • URL: http://www.ipaa.org • Annual. Free to members; non-members, $75.00. Statistical issue of *Petroleum Independent*.

***Oil Daily: Daily Newspaper of the Petroleum Industry***. Energy Intelligence Group, 5 E 37th St., 5th Fl. New York, NY 10016-2807. Phone: (212)532-1112; Fax: (212)532-4479; Email: customerservice@energyintel.com • URL: http://www.energyintel.com • Daily. Email, $1,595.00 per year; fax, $2,395.00 per year, online, $1,495.00 per year. Newspaper for the petroleum industry.

***Oil/Energy Statistics Bulletin: And Canadian Oil Reports***. Oil Statistics Company Inc., 595 Plymouth St. Whitman, MA 02382. Phone: (781)447-3965 or (781)447-6407; Fax: (781)447-3977; Email: oilstats@compuserve.com • Biweekly. $185.00 per year.

***Oil Express: Inside Report on Trends in Petroleum Marketing Without the Influence of Advertising***. UCG Holdings L.P., 11300 Rockville Pike, Suite 1100 Rockville, MD 20852-3030. Phone: 800-929-4824 or (301)816-8950 or (301)287-2700; Fax: (301)816-8945; Email: dhernan@ucg.com • URL: http://www.ucg.com • 50 times a year. $337.00 per year. Newsletter. Provides news of trends in petroleum marketing and convenience store operations. Includes *U.S. Oil Week's Price Monitor* (petroleum product prices) and *C-Store Digest* (news concerning convenience stores operated by the major oil companies) and *Fuel Oil Update*. Formerly *U.S. Oil Week*.

***Oil, Gas and Energy Quarterly***. Matthew Bender and Company Inc., 1275 Broadway Albany, NY 12204-2638. Phone: 800-424-4200 or (518)487-3000; Fax: (518)487-3573 or (800)424-4200; Email: customer.support@lexisnexis.com • URL: http://www.matthewbender.com • Quarterly. $474.00 per year. Covers latest tax ideas, techniques, and practice pointers in oil and gas taxation and accounting features.

***Oil, Gas and Petrochem Equipment***. PennWell Corp., Industrial Div., 1421 S Sheridan Rd. Tulsa, OK 74112. Phone: 800-331-4463 or (918)835-3161; Email: bid@pennwell.com • URL: http://www.pennwell.com • Monthly. $35.00 per year.

***Oil Market Intelligence***. Energy Intelligence Group, 5 E 37th St., 5th Fl. New York, NY 10016-2807. Phone: (212)532-1112; Fax: (212)532-4479; Email: customerservice@energyintel.com • URL: http://www.energyintel.com • Description: Provides analysis and statistics on worldwide oil markets and leading regional markets, including both the Atlantic Basin (Europe and the Americas) and Pacific Basins (East of Suez and the Far East). Covers futures and options markets and furnishes a monthly scorecard of prices for key products and crudes.

***The Oil Marketing Bulletin***. UCG Holdings L.P., 11300 Rockville Pike, Suite 1100 Rockville, MD 20852-3030. Phone: 800-929-4824 or (301)816-8950 or (301)287-2700; Fax: (301)816-8945; Email: dhernan@ucg.com • URL: http://www.ucg.com • Weekly. $695.00 per year. Newsletter. Marketing information service.

***Oil Price Information Service***. UCG Holdings L.P., 11300 Rockville Pike, Suite 1100 Rockville, MD 20852-3030. Phone: 800-929-4824 or (301)816-8950 or (301)287-2700; Fax: (301)816-8945; Email: dhernan@ucg.com • URL: http://www.ucg.com • Weekly. $545 Individuals; $150 regional editions. Quotes wholesale terminal prices for various petroleum products.

***The Oilman Weekly Newsletter***. PennWell Corp., Petroleum Div., 1700 W. Loop S., Suite 1000 Houston, TX 77027. Phone: 800-736-6935 or (713)621-9720; Email: petroleum@pennwell.com • URL: http://www.pennwell.com • Weekly. $1,990.00 per year. Newsletter. Provides news of developments concerning the North Sea and European oil and gas businesses. Each issue contains four pages of statistical data.

***Oklahoma Business Directory***. InfoGroup Inc., 5711 S 86th Cir. Omaha, NE 68127-4146. Phone: (402)593-4500 • URL: http://www.infogroup.com • Annual. $795 for both print & CD-ROM. Covers: 163,042 businesses in Oklahoma. Entries include: Company name, address, phone, number of employees, name of owner or manager, sales volume. Compiled from telephone company 'Yellow Pages,' statewide. All states covered (see separate entries).

***Oklahoma Directory of Manufacturers and Processors***. Dun & Bradstreet Inc., 103 JFK Pkwy. Short Hills, NJ 07078. Phone: 800-526-0651 or (973)921-5500 or (973)921-5000; Fax: (866)560-7035 or (512)794-7670; Email: info@dnb.com • URL: http://www.dnb.com • Annual. $100 Individuals. Covers: 5,000 Oklahoma manufacturers (Standard Industrial

Classification (SIC) codes 20-39). Entries include: Company name, address, phone, fax, name of principal executive, employment number, date established, Standard Industrial Classification (SIC) codes, list of products or services.

***Older Americans Report***. Business Publishers Inc., PO Box 17592 Baltimore, MD 21297-1592. Phone: 800-223-8720; Fax: (800)508-2592; Email: custserv@bpinews.com • URL: http://www.bpinews.com • Bimonthly. $449 Individuals; $349 internet sale. Description: Features brief articles on legislative, judicial, and federal agency activities concerning older Americans. Covers news of developments in such areas as Social Security, social services, Medicare, programs for retirement and pension funds, research projects, and the Older Americans Act. Recurring features include book reviews and a calendar of events.

***The Omaha Business Journal***. Midlands Business Journal Publications, 1324 S 119th St. Omaha, NE 68144. Phone: (402)330-1760; Fax: (402)758-9315 • URL: http://www.mbj.com • Monthly. Business publication covering local start-ups and entrepreneurs.

***Oman Chamber of Commerce and Industry—Industrial Directory***. Oman Chamber of Commerce and Industry, PO Box 1400 Ruwi 112, Oman. Phone: 968 24763700 or 96 824 707674; Fax: 968 24708497 or 96 824 708497; Email: occi@chamberoman.com • URL: http://www.chamberoman.com • 3 Omani Rial. Provides data on companies and industrial enterprises in the Sultanate and supporting institutions to invest in the industrial sector, investment incentives and facilities as well as available investment opportunities in all areas of economic activity.

***Oman Golden Key Directory***. International Institute of Trade Relation Promotion, Trade Information Centre of Iran, No. 7, 3rd Fl., Abbasie Bazar, Ferdowsi Sq. Tehran, Iran. Phone: 98 21 88833900; Fax: 98 21 88820697; Email: order@irangoldenkey.com • URL: http://www.goldenkeydirectory.com/about.html • £100 Individuals. Covers: 7,685 companies in Oman. Entries include: Company name, address, telephone, fax, products, services, Managing Director, and business activities.

***Oman Trade Directory***. Oman Chamber of Commerce and Industry, PO Box 1400 Ruwi 112, Oman. Phone: 968 24763700 or 96 824 707674; Fax: 968 24708497 or 96 824 708497; Email: occi@chamberoman.com • URL: http://www.chamberoman.com • 5 Omani Rial. Provides information about companies and economic institutions in Oman.

***OMB Watcher***. O M B Watch, 1742 Connecticut Ave., N.W. Washington, DC 20009. Phone: (202)234-8494; Fax: (202)234-8584 • Bimonthly. Individuals, $35.00 per year. Monitors operations of the federal Office of Management and Budget.

***On-Line Job Search Companion***. Hoover's Inc., 5800 Airport Blvd. Austin, TX 78752-4204. Phone: 866-443-3939 or (512)374-4500 or (866)281-5969; Fax: (512)374-4501; Email: salesteam@hoovers.com • URL: http://www.hoovers.com • $14.95. Covers: Online sources of employment opportunities. Database includes: Information on selecting a career path. Entries include: Name, location/host.

***On the Mhove***. Material Handling Industry, 8720 Red Oak Blvd., Ste. 201 Charlotte, NC 28217-3996. Phone: 800-345-1815 or (704)676-1190; Fax: (704)676-1199; Email: jnofsinger@mhia.org • URL: http://www.mhia.org • Quarterly. Free. Formerly *MHI News*.

***On Wall Street***. SourceMedia Inc., 1 State Street Plz., 27th Fl. New York, NY 10004. Phone: 800-221-1809 or (212)803-8200 or (212)803-8333; Fax: (212)843-9635 or (212)292-5216; Email: custserv@sourcemedia.com • URL: http://www.sourcemedia.com • Monthly. $96.00 per year. Edited for securities dealers. Includes articles on financial planning, retirement planning, variable annuities, and money management, with special coverage of 401(k) plans and IRAs.

***One-Hour Photo Processing Lab***. Entrepreneur Press, 2445 McCabe Way, Ste. 400 Irvine, CA 92614-6244. Phone: 800-864-6864 or (949)261-2325 or (949)622-7131; Fax: (949)261-7729 or (949)261-0234; Email: press@entrepreneur.com • URL: http://www.entrepreneurpress.com • Looseleaf. $59.50. A practical guide to starting a film developing and printing business. Covers profit potential, start-up costs, market size evaluation, owner's time required, site selection, lease negotiation, pricing, accounting, advertising, promotion, etc. (Start-Up Business Guide No. E1209.).

***100 Great Businesses and the Minds Behind Them***. Bolinda Publishing, 17 Mohr St. Tullamarine, VIC 3043, Australia. Phone: 61 3 93380666; Fax: 61 3 93351903; Email: info@bolinda.com • URL: http://www.bolinda.com • NZ$39.95 Individuals. Covers: Entrepreneurs and their collection of stories from Australia and around the world.

***One Hundred Highest Yields***. Bankrate Inc., 11760 US Hwy. 1, Ste. 200 North Palm Beach, FL 33408-3003. Phone: (561)630-2400; Fax: (561)625-4540; Email: bankratemail@bankratemail.com • URL: http://www.bankrate.com • Weekly. $124.00 per year. Newsletter. List CD's and money markets offered by federally insured banks. National coverage.

***101 Business Problems: Diagnosis and Remedy***. American CPE Inc., 826 Riviera Mansfield, TX 76063. Phone: 800-990-4273 or (817)477-0222; Fax: (817)473-4998; Email: director@americancpe.com • URL: http://www.americancpe.com • Contains detailed training information covering causes and solutions to more than 100 common business problems.

**100 Women in Hedge Funds**. 888C 8th Ave., No. 453 New York, NY 10019-8511. • URL: http://www.100womeninhedgefunds.org • Represents individuals who are professional women. Conducts educational programming, professional leverage initiatives and philanthropy. Provides fundraising and volunteer opportunities for members.

***The One-Person Library: A Newsletter for Librarians and Management***. Information Bridges International Inc., 477 Harris Rd. Cleveland, OH 44143-2537. Phone: (216)486-7443; Fax: (216)486-8810; Email: jsiess@ibi-opl.com • Monthly. $85.00 per year. Newsletter for librarians working alone or with minimal assistance. Contains reports on library literature, management advice, case studies, book reviews, and general information.

***1,000 China Leading Enterprises***. China Statistics Publishing House, 38 Yuetan Nanjie, Sanlihe Beijing 100826, China. • $200. Covers: 1,000 leading companies in China. Entries include: Company name and address, director, economic types, and sponsor unit, main economic indicators.

***1997 NAICS and 1987 SIC Correspondence Tables***. U. S. Census Bureau, Phone: 800-541-8345 or (301)457-4100 or (301)763-2713; Fax: (301)457-1296 or (301)457-3842; Email: naics@census.gov • URL: http://www.census.gov/epcd/www/naicstab.htm • Web site provides detailed tables for converting four-digit Standard Industrial Classification (SIC) numbers to the six-digit North American Industrial Classification System (NAICS) or vice versa: "1987 SIC Matched to 1997 NAICS" or "1997 NAICS Matched to 1987 SIC." Fees: Free.

***Online Business Link***. InfoGroup Inc., 5711 S 86th Cir. Omaha, NE 68127-4146. Phone: (402)593-4500 • URL: http://www.infogroup.com • Monthly. Database covers: More than 14 million United States businesses listed in "Yellow Pages" phone books nationwide, 551,000 manufacturers, and 4.3 million high-income consumers. Database includes: For businesses—Company name, address, phone, Standard Industrial Classification (SIC) code, brand and speciality information. For manufacturers—Company name, address, phone, name and title of chief officer, number of employees, sales volume, Standard Industrial Classification (SIC) code. For consumers—Name, address, phone, whether under or over 50 years of age. For company profiles—Company name, address, phone, Standard Industrial Classification (SIC) code, "Yellow Pages" category, as size, year listing first appeared in "Yellow Pages" (tracking began in 1985), franchise, brand or professional speciality. Business listings only were previously available under the title "Instant Yellow Page Service." A print version is available for each of the business categories listed in the "Yellow Pages" (use "Yellow Pages" categories to locate separate entries).

***Online Libraries and Microcomputers***. Information Intelligence Inc., PO Box 31098 Phoenix, AZ 85046. Phone: (602)996-2283; Email: rhuleatt@infointelligence.com • URL: http://www.infointelligence.com • Ten times a year. Individuals $43.75 per year; libraries. $62.50 per year. Newsletter. Covers library automation and electronic information (online, CD-ROM). Reviews or describes new computer hardware and software for library use.

***Online Marketplace***. Jupiter Communications, 627 Broadway, 2nd Fl. New York, NY 10012-2612. Phone: 800-488-4345 or (212)780-6060 or (917)534-6900; Fax: (212)780-6075 or (917)534-6800 • Description: Keeps abreast of the fast-emerging developments in the digital marketplace and emerging interactive technologies. Reports on players and devices to provide the "inside scoop" on this marketplace. Topics include screen phones, interactive television, and smart cards, to name a few. Recurring features include interviews, and columns titled Tool Watch, Site Watch, and News Digest.

***Online Newsletter***. Information Intelligence Inc., PO Box 31098 Phoenix, AZ 85046. Phone: (602)996-2283; Email: rhuleatt@infointelligence.com • URL: http://www.infointelligence.com • Description: Tracks developments in the fields of CD-ROM and online services. Contains news of online/CD-ROM developments and events, mergers and acquisitions, personnel movements, telecommunications and networks, new equipment and developments, microcomputer hardware and software, new and forthcoming databases, forthcoming meetings, and publications and user aids.

***Online Searcher***. Information Today, Inc., 143 Old Marlton Pke. Medford, NJ 08055-8750. Phone: 800-300-9868 or (609)654-6266; Fax: (609)654-4309; Email: custserv@infotoday.com • URL: http://www.infotoday.com • Bimonthly. $139 U.S. One year subscription; $154 Canada and Mexico One year subscription; $181 Other countries One year subscription (Outside North America). Covers a wide range of topics relating to online database searching.

***Online Searcher***. Information Today, Inc., 143 Old Marlton Pke. Medford, NJ 08055-8750. Phone: 800-300-9868 or (609)654-6266; Fax: (609)654-4309; Email: custserv@infotoday.com • URL: http://www.infotoday.com • Bimonthly. $139.00 per year. Edited for librarians, Webmasters, site designers, content managers, and others concerned with knowledge/information management. Includes critical reviews of Web sites, software, search engines, and information services. (Formerly published by Online, Inc.).

***Ontario Business***. Scott's Directories, 12 Concorde Pl., Ste. 800 Toronto, ON, Canada M3C 4J2. Phone: 800-668-2374 or (416)442-2122; Fax: (416)510-6870; Email: customercare@scottsdirectories.com • URL: http://www.scottsdirectories.com • Contains information on more than 130,000 individuals at more than 79,000 companies in Ontario, Canada.

***OPAC Directory: An Annual Guide to Internet-Accessible Online Public Access Catalogs***. Mecklermedia Corp., 475 Park Ave. S, 4th Fl. New York, NY 10016. Phone: (212)389-2000; Fax: (866)880-1429 or (212)725-4640; Email: info@webmediabrands.com • URL: http://www.webmediabrands.com • Annual. $70. Covers: Approximately 1,000 online public access catalogs (OPACs) and other locally mounted databases form hundreds of libraries worldwide. Database includes: Accessing Online Bibliographic Databases—annotated entries on over 700 Internet-accessible OPACs worldwide. Entries include: Description, access, search methods.

***Opening a Business in Stow***. Stow-Munroe Falls Chamber of Commerce, 4301 Darrow Rd., Ste. 2450 Stow, OH 44224. Phone: (330)688-1579 or (330)697-1988; Fax: (330)688-6234; Email: smfcc@smfcc.com • URL: http://www.smfcc.com.

***Operating Results of Independent Supermarkets***. Food Marketing Institute, 2345 Crystal Dr., Ste. 800 Arlington, VA 22202. Phone: (202)452-8444; Fax: (202)429-4519 • URL: http://www.fmi.org • Annual. Members, $50; non-members, $150. Includes data on gross margins, inventory turnover, expenses, etc.

***Operations Alert***. America's Community Bankers, 900 19th St. NW, Ste. 400 Washington, DC 20006. Phone: (202)857-3100; Fax: (202)296-8716; Email: partners@acbankers.org • URL: http://www.acbankers.org/ • Description: Reviews recent regulatory and product developments that affect community bank operations.

***Operations and Management, Guide/Safety Manual***. Helicopter Association International, 1920 Ballenger Ave. Alexandria, VA 22314-2898. Phone: 800-435-4976 or (703)683-4646; Fax: (703)683-4745; Email: rotor@rotor.org • URL: http://www.rotor.com • Annual.

***Operations Management***. Institutional Investor Inc. Journals Group, 225 Park Ave. S New York, NY 10003. Phone: 800-437-9997 or (212)224-3570; Email: info@iijournals.com • URL: http://www.iijournals.com • Weekly. $2,105.00 per year. Includes print and online editions. Newsletter. Edited for managers of securities clearance and settlement at financial institutions. Covers new products, technology, legalities, management practices, and other topics related to securities processing.

***Operations Research***. INFORMS, 5221 Research Park Dr., Ste. 200 Catonsville, MD 21228. Phone: 800-446-3676 or (443)757-3500; Fax: (433)757-3515; Email: informs@informs.org • URL: http://www.informs.org • Bimonthly. Individuals, $110.00 per year; institutions, $612.00 per year.

***Operations Research Letters***. Elsevier, Secondary Publishing Division, 650 Ave. of the Americas New York, NY 10011. Phone: 888-437-4636 or (212)633-3980; Fax: (212)633-3975; Email: t.reller@elsevier.com • URL: http://www.elsevier.com • 8 times a year. Institutions, $1,068.00 per year.

**Operative Plasterers and Cement Masons International Association**. 11720 Beltsville Dr., Ste. 700 Beltsville, MD 20705. Phone: (301)623-1000; Fax: (301)623-1032; Email: opcmiaintl@opcmia.org • URL: http://www.opcmia.org.

**Ophthalmic Research Institute**. 6110 Executive Blvd., Ste. 506 Rockville, MD 20852. Phone: (301)984-4735; Fax: (301)984-4737.

***Ophthalmology***. American Academy of Opthalmology. American Academy of Ophthalmology, 655 Beach St. San Francisco, CA 94109. Phone: (415)561-8500; Fax: (415)561-8533; Email: aaoe@aao.org • URL: http://www.aao.org • Monthly. $404 Individuals online or print; $668 Institutions online or print; $603 Other countries online or print; $882 Institutions, other countries online or print; $404 Canada online or print; $668 Institutions, Canada online or print. Journal publishing original, peer-reviewed reports of research in ophthalmology, including basic science investigations and clinical studies.

***Ophthalmology Times: All the Clinical News in Sight***. Advanstar Communications Inc., 2501 Colorado Ave., Ste. 280 Santa Monica, CA 90404. Phone: (310)857-7500; Fax: (310)857-7510; Email: info@advanstar.com • URL: http://www.advanstar.com • Semimonthly. $263 Individuals other countries; $200 Individuals U.S., Canada & Mexico; $20 Single issue U.S., Canada & Mexico. Magazine for ophthalmic community.

**Opportunities Industrialization Centers of America**. 1415 N Broad St., Ste. 227 Philadelphia, PA 19122-3323. Phone: 800-621-4642 or (215)236-4500; Fax: (215)236-7480; Email: info@oicofamerica.org • URL: http://www.oicofamerica.org • Network of employment and training programs. Serves disadvantaged and unskilled workers.

***Optical Engineering***. SPIE, PO Box 10 Bellingham, WA 98227-0010. Phone: 888-902-0894 or (360)685-5580 or (360)676-3290; Fax: (360)647-1445; Email: sdlinfo@spie.org • URL: http://spiedigitallibrary.org • Monthly. Members $45.00 per year; institutions, $815.00 per year. Technical papers and letters.

***Optical Fiber Technology: Materials, Devices, and Systems***. Elsevier, Secondary Publishing Division, 650 Ave. of the Americas New York, NY 10011. Phone: 888-437-4636 or (212)633-3980; Fax: (212)633-3975; Email: t.reller@

elsevier.com • URL: http://www.elseveier.com • Bimonthly. Individuals, $210.00 per year; institutions, $777.00 per year.

***Optical Goods Manufacturers Directory***. InfoGroup Inc., 5711 S 86th Cir. Omaha, NE 68127-4146. Phone: (402)593-4500 • URL: http://www.infogroup.com • Annual. Number of listings: 1,197. Entries include: Name, address, phone, size of advertisement, name of owner or manager, number of employees, year first in "Yellow Pages." Compiled from telephone company "Yellow Pages," nationwide.

***Optical Prism: Canada's Optical Business Magazine Since 1983***. Nusand Publishing Inc., 12 Tamerlane Ct. Toronto, ON, Canada M9B 6G4. Phone: (416)233-2487; Fax: (416)233-1746; Email: nusand@direct.com • 8/year. $45 Other countries; $90 Other countries air mail. An independent magazine providing practical information on practice management as well as coverage of Canada's optical industry to Canadian optometrists and their suppliers.

**Optical Sciences Center**. University of Arizona, 1630 E University Blvd. Tucson, AZ 85721. Phone: (520)621-6997; Fax: (520)621-9613 • URL: http://www.optics.arizona.edu.

***Optical Society of America Journal***. Optical Society of America, 2010 Massachusetts Ave. NW Washington, DC 20036-1023. Phone: 800-766-405A or (202)223-8130; Fax: (202)223-1096; Email: info@osa.org • URL: http://www.osa.org • Monthly. Part A, $2,173.00 per year; Part B, $2,173.00 per year.

**Optical Society of America**. 2010 Massachusetts Ave. NW Washington, DC 20036-1023. Phone: 800-766-405A or (202)223-8130; Fax: (202)223-1096; Email: info@osa.org • URL: http://www.osa.org • Persons interested in any branch of optics: research, instruction, optical applications, manufacture, distribution of optical equipment, and physiological optics. Sponsors topical meetings.

**Opticians Association of America**. 4064 E Fir Hill Dr. Lakeland, TN 38002. Phone: (901)388-2423; Fax: (901)388-2348; Email: oaa@oaa.org • URL: http://www.oaa.org • Formerly Guild of Prescription Opticians of America.

***Optics and Laser Technology***. Elsevier, Secondary Publishing Division, 650 Ave. of the Americas New York, NY 10011. Phone: 888-437-4636 or (212)633-3980; Fax: (212)633-3975; Email: t.reller@elsevier.com • URL: http://www.elseveier.com • Eight times a year. Institutions, $2,115.00 per year. Published in United Kingdom.

***Optics and Photonics News***. Optical Society of America, 2010 Massachusetts Ave. NW Washington, DC 20036-1023. Phone: 800-766-405A or (202)223-8130; Fax: (202)223-1096; Email: info@osa.org • URL: http://www.osa.org • Monthly. $99.00 per year. Includes print and online editions.

***Option Advisor***. Investment Research Institute Inc., 1259 Kemper Meadow Dr., Suite 100 Cincinnati, OH 45240. Phone: 800-448-2080 or (513)589-3800; Fax: (513)589-3810; Email: service@sir-inc.com • URL: http://www.schaeffersresearch.com • Monthly. $199.00 per year. Newsletter. Provides specific advice and recommendations for trading in stock option contracts (puts and calls).

***Optometric Management: The Business and Marketing Magazine for Optometry***. Boucher Communications, Inc., 1300 Virginia Dr. Fort Washington, PA 19034. Phone: (215)643-8000; Fax: (215)643-8099 • URL: http://www.boucher1.com • Monthly. $37.00 per year. Provides information and advice for optometrists on practice management and marketing.

***Orange County Business and Industrial Directory***. Orange County Business Council, 2 Park Plz., Ste. 100 Irvine, CA 92614-5904. Phone: (949)476-2242; Fax: (949)476-9240 • URL: http://www.ocbc.org • Number of listings: 5,000. Entries include: Company name, address, phone, names and titles of key personnel, line of business, number of employees.

***Orange County, New York Business Directory and Buyer's Guide***. Centers Composition, 5309 Pleasant Valley Rd. Pine Bush, NY 12566. Fax: (914)733-6788 • Number of listings: 11,000. Entries include: Company name, address, phone, name and title of contact, number of employees, type of business, product or service.

**Orders and Medals Society of America**. PO Box 540 Claymont, DE 19703-0540. • URL: http://www.omsa.org • Persons, including 300 members outside the U.S., interested in collecting and studying insignias of the orders of knighthood and merit, the decorations of valor and honor, the medals of distinction and service, and allied material and historical data.

***Oregon Manufacturers Directory and Industrial Database***. Manufacturers' News Inc., 1633 Central St. Evanston, IL 60201-1569. Phone: (847)864-7000; Fax: (847)332-1100 • URL: http://www.manufacturersnews.com • Annual. $114 Individuals print; $515 Individuals database (EZ select full); $335 Individuals database (EZ select with 20 plus employees); $180 Individuals database (EZ select basic). Covers: 6,835 manufacturers in Oregon. Entries include: Company name, address, phone, names and titles of key personnel, year established, number of employees, plant square footage, services, Standard Industry Classification (SIC) code, parent and subsidiary company information, type of in-house computer system, URL, e-mail address.

***Oregon Manufacturers Register***. Harris InfoSource, 2057 E Aurora Rd. Twinsburg, OH 44087-1999. Phone: 800-888-5900 or (330)425-9000 or (973)921-5500; Fax: (800)643-5997 or (877)252-3375; Email: customerservice@harrisinfo.com • URL: http://www.harrisinfo.com • Annual. Covers: Approximately 8,400 manufacturers plus key executives in Oregon. Entries include: Company, address, parent name/location, telephone, fax and 800 numbers, Web site address (on CD-ROM only), number of employees, year established, annual revenue, plant size, business description, Standard Industrial Classification (SIC) codes, executive names/titles, public ownership, legal structure, import/export designators, female/minority ownership.

***Oregon Wheat***. Oregon Wheat Growers League, 115 SE 8th St. Pendleton, OR 97801. Phone: (541)276-7330; Fax: (541)276-1723 • URL: http://www.owgl.org • Bi-monthly. Free to members; non-members, $15.00 per year. Deals with planting, weeds, and disease warnings, storage and marketing of wheat and barley. Specifically for Oregon growers.

**Organisation for Economic Co-Operation and Development**. 2, rue Andre Pascal F-75775 Paris, France. Phone: 33 1 45248200; Fax: 1 45248500; Email: webmaster@oecd.org • URL: http://www.oecd.org.

**Organization Design Forum**. 5016 E Mulberry Dr. Phoenix, AZ 85018-6525. Phone: (602)510-9105; Email: info@organizationdesignforum.org • URL: http://organizationdesignforum.org • Academics, practitioners, consultants, and human resource professionals. Works to promote the knowledge and practice of organizational design. Focuses on the effect organization structure and processes have on the performance of individuals, groups, and the organization itself. Offers basic and advanced training in organization design techniques.

**Organization for Competitive Markets**. PO Box 6486 Lincoln, NE 68506. Phone: (402)817-4443 • URL: http://www.competitivemarkets.com • Works for increased competition and protection for the agricultural marketplace. Works against "abuse of corporate power and consolidation of the agricultural market."

**Organization for Entrepreneurial Development**. 25 Pine St., Ste. 9 Rockaway, NJ 07866. Phone: 800-767-0999; Fax: (973)784-1099; Email: questions@oedglobal.org • URL: http://www.oedglobal.org • Offers educational and training programs that are focused on the entrepreneurial community. Collaborates with educators and educational institutions for the improvement of entrepreneurial skills and knowledge. Seeks to solicit the help and support of the business community at large in aiding the entrepreneurial community.

**Organization for the Promotion and Advancement of Small Telecommunications Companies**. 2020 K St. NW, 7th Fl. Washington, DC 20006. Phone: (202)659-5990; Email: mks@opastco.org • URL: http://www.opastco.org • Members are small telephone companies serving rural areas. Formerly Organization for the Protection and Advancement of Small Telephone Companies.

***Organizational Dynamics: A Quarterly Review of Organizational Behavior for Management Executives***. American Management Association, 1601 Broadway New York, NY 10019-7420. Phone: 877-566-9441 or (212)586-8100 or (518)891-5510; Fax: (212)903-8168 or (518)891-0368; Email: customerservice@amanet.org • URL: http://www.amanet.org • Quarterly. Individuals, $77.00 per year; institutions, $171.00 per year. Covers the application of behavioral sciences to business management.

**Organizational Systems Research Association**. Morehead State University, 150 University Blvd., Box 2478 Morehead, KY 40351-1689. Phone: (606)783-2718; Fax: (606)783-5025; Email: d.everett@moreheadstate.edu • URL: http://ais.site-ym.com/members/group_content_view.asp?group=89777&id=170352&terms=sigosra • Research areas include the analysis, design, and administration of office systems. Formerly Office Systems Research Association.

***Orient Trade Directory***. Selective Books International, 17195 Silver Pkwy., Ste. 236 Fenton, MI 48430. Fax: (248)927-0412 • URL: http://www.selectivebooksinc.com • $19.95 Individuals. Covers: Suppliers of over 4,000 products in Japan, Korea, Malaysia, China, India, Thailand, Indonesia and Singapore. Entries include: Photos, names, addresses, phones and fax.

**Oriental Rug Importers Association**. 100 Park Plaza Dr. Secaucus, NJ 07094. Phone: (201)866-5054; Fax: (201)866-6169; Email: oria@oria.org • URL: http://rugknot.com/oria-members-section/contact-about-us/ • Represents wholesalers and importers of Oriental rugs. Fosters ethical business practices and promotes the best interests of the Oriental Rug Trade in the United States and in countries that produce Oriental rugs.

***Oriental Rug Review***. Oriental Rug Auction Review Inc., P.O. Box 709 Meredith, NH 03253. Phone: (603)744-9191; Fax: (603)744-6933 • Bimonthly. $48.00 per year.

***Origination News: For Mortgage Brokers, Correspondents, Lenders, and Wholesalers***. SourceMedia Inc., 1 State Street Plz., 27th Fl. New York, NY 10004. Phone: 800-221-1809 or (212)803-8200 or (212)803-8333; Fax: (212)843-9635 or (212)292-5216; Email: custserv@sourcemedia.com • URL: http://www.sourcemedia.com • Monthly. $78.00 per year. Edited for executives responsible for the origination and subsequent sale of mortgage loans.

***Orion Blue Book—Copier***. Orion Research Corp., 14555 N Scottsdale Rd., Ste. 330 Scottsdale, AZ 85254. Phone: 800-844-0759 or (480)951-1114; Fax: (480)951-1117 or (800)375-1315 • Annual. $130 Individuals hardbound or CD. Publication includes: List of manufacturers of copiers and other office equipment. Entries include: Company name, address, phone. Principal content of publication is a listing of 3,091 office equipment products with the original retail value, value paid to customer on trade-in when in mint condition, and average value paid to customer on trade-in.

**Osaka University - Institute of Social and Economic Research**. 6-1 Mihogaoka Ibaraki 567-0047, Japan. Phone: 81 6 68798552; Fax: 81 6 68798584; Email: ogawa@iser.osaka-u.ac.jp • URL: http://www.iser.osaka-u.ac.jp • General economic theory, econometrics, experimental economics, and the Japanese economy.

***Osceola Business Journal***. St. Cloud Greater Osceola Chamber of Commerce, 1200 New York Ave. Saint Cloud, FL 34769-3742. Phone: (407)892-3671 or (407)791-5215; Fax: (407)892-5289; Email: info@stcloudflchamber.com • URL: http://stcloudflchamber.com/Content/index.aspx • Monthly.

***Osceola County Manufacturers/Industrial Business Directory***. Osceola Economic Alliance, 301 W Upton Ave. Reed City, MI 49677. Phone: (231)832-7397 • URL: http://www.osceola-county.org • Annual. Covers: Information on all Osceola County, Michigan, businesses.

***OSH-ROM: Occupational Safety and Health Information on CD-ROM***. SilverPlatter Information Inc., 100 River Ridge Dr. Norwood, MA 02062. Phone: 800-343-0064 or (781)769-2599; Fax: (781)769-8763; Email: sales@ovid.com • URL: http://www.silverplatter.com • Price and frequency on application. Produced in Geneva by the International Occupational Safety and Health Information Centre, International Labour Organization (www.ilo.org). Provides about two million citations and abstracts to the worldwide literature of industrial safety, industrial hygiene, hazardous materials, and accident prevention. Material is included from journals, technical reports, books, government publications, and other sources. Time span varies.

***OSHA Required Safety Training for Supervisors***. Occupational Safety and Health Administration. Business & Legal Resources, Inc., 141 Mill Rock Rd., E Old Saybrook, CT 06475. Phone: 800-454-0404 or (860)510-0100 or (800)727-5257; Fax: (860)510-7220 or (860)510-0100; Email: service@blr.com • URL: http://www.blr.com • Monthly. $99.00 per year. Newsletter. Formerly *Safetyworks for Supervisors*.

***Ottawa Business Journal (OBJ)***. InBusiness Media Network Inc., 5300 Canotek Rd., Unit 30 Ottawa, ON, Canada K1J 1A4. Phone: (613)744-4800; Fax: (613)744-8232; Email: jdonnelly@obj.ca • URL: http://www.sources.com/mnn/Ow9519.htm • Weekly (Mon.). $84.75 Individuals HST included; $169.50 Two years HST included. Local business magazine.

**Outdoor Advertising Association of America**. 1850 M St. NW, Ste. 1040 Washington, DC 20036. Phone: (202)833-5566; Fax: (202)833-1522; Email: nfletcher@oaaa.org • URL: http://www.oaaa.org • Firms owning, erecting and maintaining standardized poster panels and painted display advertising facilities. Absorbed Shelter Advertising Association.

***Outdoor Advertising Directory***. InfoGroup Inc., 5711 S 86th Cir. Omaha, NE 68127-4146. Phone: (402)593-4500 • URL: http://www.infogroup.com • Annual. Number of listings: 2,647. Entries include: Name, address, phone, size of advertisement, name of owner or manager, number of employees, year first in "Yellow Pages." Compiled from telephone company "Yellow Pages," nationwide.

**Outdoor Amusement Business Association**. 1035 S Semoran Blvd., Ste. 1045A Winter Park, FL 32792. Phone: 800-517-OABA or (407)681-9444; Fax: (407)681-9445; Email: oaba@oaba.org • URL: http://www.oaba.org • Represents executives and employees of carnivals and fairs; ride owners; independent food and games concessionaires; manufacturers and suppliers of equipment. Promotes and lobbies on behalf of the interests of the outdoor amusement industry; provides a center for dissemination of information.

**Outdoor Power Equipment Institute**. 341 S Patrick St. Alexandria, VA 22314. Phone: (703)549-7600 • URL: http://opei.org • Manufacturers of lawn mowers, garden tractors, snow throwers, utility vehicles, chainsaws, motor tillers, shredder/grinders, edger/trimmers, leaf vacuums, log splitters, stump cutters, chippers and sprayers, and major components. Compiles statistics and forecasting information; sponsors industry trade shows; produces comprehensive consumer education materials on safety and other industry issues; hosts' annual member meeting; represents members' interests on important legislative and regulatory issues.

***Outlook for Travel and Tourism***. U.S. Travel Association, 1100 New York Ave. NW, Ste. 450 Washington, DC 20005-3934. Phone: (202)408-8422; Fax: (202)408-1255; Email: feedback@ustravel.org • URL: http://www.ustravel.org • Annual. Members, $100.00; non-members, $175.00. Contains forecasts of the performance of the U. S. travel industry, including air travel, business travel, recreation (attractions), and accomodations.

***Outlook for United States Agricultural Trade***. U. S. Government Printing Office, 732 N Capitol St. NW Washington, DC 20401. Phone: 866-512-1800 or (202)512-1800 or (866)512-1800; Fax: (202)512-2104 or (202)512-2250; Email: contactcenter@gpo.gov • URL: http://www.gpo.gov •

Quarterly. $15.00 per year. Issued by the Economic Research Service, U. S. Department of Agriculture. (Situation and Outlook Reports.).

**Outsourcing Institute**. 6800 Jericho Tpke., Ste. 120W Syosset, NY 11791. Phone: (516)279-6850; Email: info@outsourcing.com • URL: http://www.outsourcing.com • Represents corporations making use of outside resources and services. Serves as a clearinghouse on the strategic use of outside resources. Conducts research, executive events, publications and educational programs.

***Outspokin'***. National Bicycle Dealers Association, 3176 Pullman St., No. 117 Costa Mesa, CA 92626. Phone: (949)722-6909; Email: info@nbda.com • URL: http://nbda.com • 10/year. Description: Offers bicycle retailing and management tips, and provides consumer survey results. Recurring features include Association and industry news.

***Outstanding Investor Digest: Perspectives and Activities of the Nation's Most Successful Money Managers***. Outstanding Investor Digest, Inc., 511 Ave. of the Americas, No. 282-G New York, NY 10011. Phone: (212)777-3330; Email: customer_support@oid.com • URL: http://oid.com • $395.00 for 10 issues. Newsletter. Each issue features interviews with leading money managers.

***Overseas and European Companies Manufacturing in Scotland***. Scottish Enterprise, Atrium Ct., 50 Waterloo St. Glasgow G2 6HQ, United Kingdom. Phone: 41 204 1111 or 41 2482700; Fax: 41 248 1600 or 41 2213217; Email: enquiries@scotent.co.uk • URL: http://www.scottish-enterprise.com • Covers: over 130 foreign owned companies, excluding North American owned, located in Scotland. Entries include: Company name, address, phone, telex, name and title of contact, number of employees, geographical area covered, description of services.

***Overseas Companies in Ireland***. Industrial Development Agency of Ireland, Wilton Park House, Wilton Pl. Dublin IR-2, Ireland. Phone: 353 1 6034000; Email: idaireland@ida.ie • URL: http://www.idaireland.com • Updated continuously; printed on request. Computer printout. About 1,000 overseas manufacturers and international service companies with operations in Ireland. Entries include: Name and address of parent company; name, address, phone of Irish filial company, description of product or service specialty.

***Owen's Worldwide Africa Business Directory***. Owen's Worldtrade Ltd., 18 Farndon Rd. Oxford OX2 6RT, United Kingdom. Fax: 865 310459 • Annual. $87.50. Covers: 12,000 manufacturers, importers, exporters; and travel, finance, transport other service firms; and government agencies and associations concerned with international trade in 21 African countries: Botswana, Burundi, Cameroon, Djibouti, Ethiopia, Gabon, Ivory Coast, Kenya, Liberia, Malawi, Nigeria, Rwanda, Senegal, Seychelles, Sierra Leone, Somalia, Sudan, Tanzania, Togo, Uganda, and Zimbabwe. Database includes: For each country, detailed information covering climate, currency, language, government, business days and hours, economy customs, etc. Entries include: Company or organization name, address, phone, telex, cable address; product, service, or line of business; some listings also include name of parent company.

***Owners and Officers of Private Companies***. Taft Group, 27500 Drake Rd. Farmington Hills, MI 48331-3535. Phone: 800-877-4253 or (248)699-4253 or (248)699-GALE; Fax: (800)414-5043 or (248)699-8061; Email: gale.salesassistance@thomson.com • URL: http://www.gale.com/taft • Annual. $320. Covers over 128,000 key executives who own and operate America's 48,000 private companies with annual sales over $3 million.

**Oxfam - America**. 226 Causeway St., 5th Fl. Boston, MA 02114. Phone: 800-77-OXFAM or (617)482-1211; Fax: (617)728-2594; Email: info@oxfamamerica.org • URL: http://www.oxfamamerica.org • Autonomous development and disaster assistance organization cooperating in a worldwide network known as Oxfam, a name derived from the Oxford Committee for Famine Relief, which began in England in 1942. Provides funds for self-help projects in the poorer countries of Asia, Africa, and the Americas. Emphasizes promoting economic and food self-reliance. Responds to emergency needs of political and natural disaster refugees by funding food, water resources, and medical aid programs. Supports development programs that address underlying causes of such disasters. Educates U.S. public about root causes of hunger; advocates for policy changes.

***OZ on Disc—Top 25,000***. Read Only Memory Proprietary Ltd., 125 Crystal St. Petersham, NSW 2049, Australia. Phone: 61 2 564 6700; Fax: 61 2 564 6480 • Quarterly. $4,950 per year. CD-ROM. Covers over 25,000 companies in Australia. Entries include: Company name, address, phone, fax, names and titles of key personnel, number of employees, Standard Industrial Classification (SIC) codes and descriptions, gross sales, related companies, banker.

***P-O-P Design (Point-of-Purchase): Products and News for High-Volume Pro ducers and Designers of Displays, Signs and Fixtures***. Hoyt Publishing, 7400 Skokie Blvd. Skokie, IL 60077. Phone: (847)675-7400; Email: getinfo@hoytpub.com • URL: http://www.p2pi.org • Nine times a year. $59.00 per year.

***Pacific Boating Almanac***. ProStar Publications, Inc., 8643 Hayden Place Culver City, CA 90232-2901. Phone: 800-481-6277 or (310)280-1010; Fax: (310)280-1025; Email: editor@prostarpublications.com • Annual. $24.95 Individuals. Three volumes. Volume one, *Pacific Northwest*; volume two, *Northern California and the Delta*; volume three *Southern California and Mexico*. Lists over 3,000 marine facilities serving recreational boating.

**Pacific Coast Paper Box Manufacturers' Association**. 201 N Union St., Ste. 220 Alexandria, VA 22314. Phone: (703)836-3300; Fax: (703)836-3290; Email: ben@paperbox.org • URL: http://www.paper-world.com/firmeninfo.php?sprache=uk&menue=10&keyfirma=1697536 • Represents folding carton and rigid carton manufacturers. Furthers the success and development of paperboard packaging in the territory west of the Rocky Mountains. Offers statistical, and labor data summary programs for members. Conducts technical and production seminars and employee training in plant and equipment operations. Sponsors student design-school competition.

**Pacific Coast Shellfish Growers Association**. 120 State Ave. NE, No. 142 Olympia, WA 98501. Phone: (360)754-2744; Fax: (360)754-2743; Email: pcsga@pcsga.org • URL: http://www.pcsga.org • Oyster, clam, mussel, scallop, geoduck growers, openers, packers and shippers in Alaska, California, Oregon, Washington, Hawaii and Mexico.

**Pacific International Center for High Technology Research**. 1440 Kapiolani Blvd., Ste. 1225 Honolulu, HI 96814. Phone: (808)943-9581; Fax: (808)943-9582; Email: info@pichtr.org • URL: http://www.pichtr.org • Desalination is included as a field of research.

***Pacific Magazine with Islands Business***. PacificBasin Communications, 1000 Bishop St., Ste. 405 Honolulu, HI 96813. Phone: (808)537-9500; Fax: (808)537-6455; Email: pmaddchange@pacificbasin.net • URL: http://www.honolulumagazine.com • Monthly. $15 Individuals; $55 Other countries airmail; $25 Two years. Magazine covering business in Hawaii.

***Pacific McGeorge Global Business and Development Law Journal***. University of the Pacific McGeorge School of Law, 3200 Fifth Ave. Sacramento, CA 95817. Phone: (916)739-7191 or (916)739-7105; Fax: (916)739-7301; Email: mcgeorge@pacific.edu • URL: http://www.mcgeorge.edu.

***PackagePrinting: For Printers and Converters of Labels, Flexible Packaging and Folding Cartons***. North American Publishing Co., 1500 Spring Garden St., Ste. 1200 Philadelphia, PA 19130-4069. Phone: (215)238-5300; Email: customerservice@napco.com • URL: http://www.napco.com • Monthly. Free to qualified personnel; others, $59.00 per year. Formerly *Package Printing and Converting*.

***Packaging Digest***. Reed Elsevier Group plc Reed Business Information, 360 Park Ave. S New York, NY 10010. Phone: (212)791-4208; Email: corporatecommunications@reedbusiness.com • URL: http://www.reedbusiness.com • 13 times a year. $119.90 per year.

**Packaging Machinery Manufacturers Institute**. 1191 Freedom Dr., Ste. 600 Reston, VA 20190. Phone: (571)612-3200; Fax: (703)243-8556 • URL: http://www.pmmi.org • Represents manufacturers of machinery used for all packaging operations including filling, capping, labeling, wrapping, cartoning, case loading, blister packaging, aerosol, check weighing, coding, counting, form-fill-seal, and bagging.

***Packaging Technology and Science***. John Wiley and Sons, Inc., Journals Div., 111 River St. Hoboken, NJ 07030. Phone: 800-526-5368 or (201)748-6000; Fax: (201)748-6088; Email: consumers@wiley.com • URL: http://www.wiley.com • Eight times a year. Individuals, $650.00 per year; institutions, $3,152.00 per year. Provides international coverage of subject matter. Published in England by John Wiley & Sons Ltd.

***The Packer: Devoted to the Interest of Commericial Growers, Packers, Shippers, Receivers and Retailers of Fruits, Vegetables and Other Products***. Vance Publishing Corp., Produce Div., 10901 W. 84th Terrace Lenexa, KS 66214-0695. Phone: 800-255-5113 or (913)438-8700; Fax: (913)438-0691 • URL: http://www.vancepublishing.com • Weekly. $65.00 per year. Supplements available: *Brand Directory and Fresh Trends, Packer's Produce Availability and Merchandising Guide* and *Produce Services Sourcebooks*.

***The Packer: The Business Newspaper of the Produce Industry***. Vance Publishing Corp., 400 Knightsbridge Pkwy. Lincolnshire, IL 60069-3613. Phone: 800-255-5113 or (847)634-2600; Fax: (847)634-4342 or (847)634-4379; Email: info@vancepublishing.com • URL: http://www.vancepublishing.com • Weekly. $99 Individuals; $139 Other countries. Newspaper on produce marketing.

***The Page***. Skillsoft Ireland Ltd., 500 Canal View Rochester, NY 14623. Phone: 800-434-3466 or (585)240-7500; Fax: (585)240-7760 or (585)292-4392; Email: info@elementk.com • URL: http://www.skillsoft.com • Description: Acts as a visual guide to McIntosh computer desktop publishing.

***Paint & Coatings Buyers Guide***. American Coatings Association, 1500 Rhode Island Ave. NW Washington, DC 20005. Phone: (202)462-6272; Fax: (202)462-8549 • URL: http://www.paint.org • $150. About 7,500 chemists, technicians, and supervisory production personnel in the decorative and protective coatings industry who are members of the 27 constituent societies of the federation.

***Paint and Coatings Industry***. BNP Media, 2401 W Big Beaver Rd., Ste. 700 Troy, MI 48084. Phone: 800-952-6643 or (248)362-3700 or (847)763-9534; Fax: (248)362-5103 or (248)362-0317; Email: privacy@bnpmedia.com • URL: http://www.bnpmedia.com • Monthly. Free to members, nonmembers, $55.00 per year. Includes annual *Raw Material and Equipment Directory and Buyers Guide*.

***Paint and Decorating Retailer***. Paint and Decorating Retailers Association, 1401 Triad Center Dr. Saint Peters, MO 63376-7353. Phone: (636)326-2636; Fax: (636)229-4750; Email: info@pdra.org • URL: http://www.pdra.org • Monthly. $45.00 per year. Formerly *Decorating Retailer*.

***Paint, Varnish, and Lacquer***. U. S. Bureau of the Census, 4600 Silver Hill Rd. Washington, DC 20233-0001. Phone: (301)763-4636; Email: comments@census.gov • URL: http://www.census.gov • Quarterly and annual. Provides data on shipments: value, quantity, imports, and exports. Includes paint, varnish, lacquer, product finishes, and special purpose coatings. (Current Industrial Reports, MQ-28F.).

**Painting and Decorating Contractors of America**. 2316 Millpark Dr. Maryland Heights, MO 63043. Phone: 800-332-7322 or (314)514-7322; Fax: (314)890-2068; Email: rbright@pdca.org • URL: http://www.pdca.org • Painting and wallcovering contractors.

***PAIS International***. ProQuest L.L.C., 789 E Eisenhower Pkwy. Ann Arbor, MI 48106-1346. Phone: 800-521-0600 or (734)761-4700; Fax: (734)662-4554; Email: info@proquest.com • URL: http://www.proquest.com • Monthly. $1,995.00 per year. Contains over 650,000 citations to the literature of contemporary social, political, and economic issues.

***PAIS International***. ProQuest L.L.C., 789 E Eisenhower Pkwy. Ann Arbor, MI 48106-1346. Phone: 800-521-0600 or (734)761-4700; Fax: (734)662-4554; Email: info@proquest.com • URL: http://www.proquest.com • Monthly. $850.00 per year; cumulations three times a year. Provides topical citations to the worldwide literature of public affairs, economics, demographics, sociology, and trade. Text in English; indexed materials in English, French, German, Italian, Portuguese and Spanish.

**Pakistan Agriculture and Dairy Farmers Association**. JK House, 32-W, Susan Rd., Madina Town Faisalabad, Pakistan. Phone: 92 41 8721956; Fax: 92 41 8712399; Email: info@padfapak.org • URL: http://www.padfapak.org • Represents trade, commerce, industry or services in agriculture and dairy farming in Pakistan. Encourages unity, mutual understanding and high ethical standards among its members. Supports a unified approach of policies affecting the interests of agriculture and dairy farming.

**Pakistan-Belgium Business Forum**. c/o Honorary Consulate of Belgium, A-9 Mohammad Ali Bogra Rd., Bath Island Karachi 75530, Pakistan. Phone: 92 21 35879876 or 92 21 35872941; Fax: 92 21 35861257; Email: pbbf1@cyber.net.pk • URL: http://www.pbbf.org • Promotes trade, commerce and economic cooperation between Pakistan and Belgium. Encourages mutual understanding and friendly relations of business communities. Fosters and organizes trade and investment delegations, trade fairs, exhibitions, symposia and lectures.

***Pakistan Export-Import and Business Directory***. International Business Publications, USA, PO Box 15343 Washington, DC 20003. Phone: (202)546-2103; Fax: (202)546-3275; Email: ibpusa@comcast.net • URL: http://ibpus.com • $99.95 Individuals paperback; $99.50 Individuals e-book; $99.95 Individuals CD-ROM. Covers: Information on strategic economic, investment, export-import, and business opportunities. Contains important export-import, government, and business contacts and more.

**Palladium Alliance International**. PO Box 81511 Billings, MT 59108. Phone: 877-473-7873; Email: info@luxurypalladium.com • URL: http://www.luxurypalladium.com • Represents experts who work with retailers, producers and manufacturers all over the world. Focuses on establishing palladium as a luxurious, precious and distinctive metal. Provides education, marketing and technical support and a vision for the advancement of palladium.

***Palm Beach Illustrated: The Best of Boca Raton to Vero Beach***. Palm Beach Media Group, PO Box 3344 Palm Beach, FL 33480. Phone: (561)659-0210; Fax: (561)659-1736 • URL: http://www.palmbeachmedia.com • 11 times a year. $39.95 per year. Includes *Palm Beach Social Observer*. Formerly *Illustrated*.

***Palos Verdes Peninsula Chamber of Commerce and Visitors' Center—Business Directory and Community Guide***. Palos Verdes Peninsula Chamber of Commerce and Visitors' Center, 707 Silver Spur Rd., Ste. 100 Rolling Hills Estates, CA 90274. Phone: (310)377-8111; Fax: (310)377-0614; Email: office@palosverdeschamber.com • URL: http://www.palosverdeschamber.com • Business organizations in Palos Verdes Hills, California.

***Panama Annual Directory***. U.S. Chamber of Commerce, 1615 H St. NW Washington, DC 20062-2000. Phone: 800-638-6582 or (202)463-5500 or (202)659-6000; Fax: (202)463-3129; Email: foundation@uschamber.com • URL: http://www.uschambersmallbusinessnation.com • Annual. $40 Individuals. Covers: 350 member companies of AmCham Panama. Entries include: Company name, address, phone.

***Panama Government and Business Contacts Handbook***. International Business Publications, USA, PO Box 15343 Washington, DC 20003. Phone: (202)546-2103; Fax: (202)546-3275; Email: ibpusa@comcast.net • URL: http://ibpus.com • $99.95 Individuals hardcopy, e-book, CD-ROM.

Covers: Strategic government and business information, export-import activity in the country, investment, business contacts and regulations.

***Panama Industrial and Business Directory***. International Business Publications, USA, PO Box 15343 Washington, DC 20003. Phone: (202)546-2103; Fax: (202)546-3275; Email: ibpusa@comcast.net • URL: http://ibpus.com • Annual. $99.95 Individuals hardcopy, e-book, CD-ROM. Covers: Strategic industrial, investment and business contacts for conducting export-import and investment activity in the country.

***Panama Investment and Business Guide***. International Business Publications, USA, PO Box 15343 Washington, DC 20003. Phone: (202)546-2103; Fax: (202)546-3275; Email: ibpusa@comcast.net • URL: http://ibpus.com • $99.95 Individuals hardcopy, e-book, CD-ROM. Covers: Strategic information on economy, business, export-import and investment climate, regulations and industrial development, banking, government, and opportunities. Entries include: Important business contacts and business travel.

***Panel World***. Hatton-Brown Publishers Inc., 225 Hanrick St. Montgomery, AL 36102. Phone: 800-669-5613 or (334)834-1170; Fax: (334)834-4525; Email: dianne@hattonbrown.com • URL: http://www.hattonbrown.net • Bimonthly. 28. Business magazine serving the worldwide veneer, plywood, and panel board industry. Formerly *Plywood and Panel World*.

***Paper Age***. Global Publications, 77 Waldron Ave. Glen Rock, NJ 07452-2830. Phone: (201)666-2262; Fax: (201)666-9046 • 10 times a year. $20.00 per year.

***Paper, Film and Foil Converter***. Primedia Business Magazines and Media, 330 N Wabash Ave., Suite 2300 Chicago, IL 60611. Phone: 800-795-5445 or (312)595-1080 or (312)726-2802; Fax: (312)595-0295 or (312)726-2574; Email: subs@primediabusiness.com • URL: http://www.primediabusiness.com • Monthly. $88.00 per year.

**Paper Industry Management Association**. 15 Technology Pkwy. S Norcross, GA 30092. Phone: (770)209-7230; Fax: (770)209-7359 • URL: http://www.pima-online.org • Professional organization of pulp, paper mill, and paper-converting production executives.

***Paper Manufacturers Directory***. InfoGroup Inc., 5711 S 86th Cir. Omaha, NE 68127-4146. Phone: (402)593-4500 • URL: http://www.infogroup.com • Annual. Number of listings: 1,832. Entries include: Name, address, phone, size of advertisement, name of owner or manager, number of employees, year first in "Yellow Pages." Compiled from telephone company "Yellow Pages," nationwide.

***Paper Money***. Society of Paper Money Collectors, PO Box 117060 Carrollton, TX 75011-7060. • URL: http://www.spmc.org • Bimonthly. Membership.

**Paper Shipping Sack Manufacturers' Association**. 5050 Blue Church Rd. Coopersburg, PA 18036. Phone: (610)282-6845; Fax: (610)282-1577; Email: admin@pssma.org • URL: http://www.pssma.com • Manufacturers of multi-wall (3-4-5-6 walls) paper shipping sacks designed for packaging and shipping products in domestic and export commerce.

***Paper Shredding Machines Directory***. InfoGroup Inc., 5711 S 86th Cir. Omaha, NE 68127-4146. Phone: (402)593-4500 • URL: http://www.infogroup.com • Updated continuously; printed on request. Number of listings: 700. Entries include: Name, address, phone, size of advertisement, name of owner or manager, number of employees, year first in "Yellow Pages." Compiled from telephone company "Yellow Pages," nationwide.

***Paperboard Packaging Council Member Directory***. Paperboard Packaging Council, 1350 Main St., Ste. 1508 Springfield, MA 01103-1628. Phone: (413)686-9191; Fax: (413)747-7777; Email: ben@paperbox.org • URL: http://www.paperbox.org • Annual.

**Paperboard Packaging Council**. 1350 Main St., Ste. 1508 Springfield, MA 01103-1628. Phone: (413)686-9191; Fax: (413)747-7777; Email: ben@paperbox.org • URL: http://www.paperbox.org • Represents manufacturers of paperboard packaging. Sponsors public relations activities, safety programs, and biannual human resource seminars. Conducts overall industry statistical studies, marketing surveys, product reviews, and labor relations and bargaining agreement studies. Provides active technical and production service.

***Paperboard Packaging Worldwide***. Advanstar Communications, 545 Boylston St. Boston, MA 02116. Phone: 888-527-7008 or (617)267-6500; Fax: (617)267-6900; Email: info@advanstar.com • URL: http://www.advanstar.com • Monthly. $39.00 per year.

**Parachute Industry Association**. 3833 W Oakton St. Skokie, IL 60076-3429. Phone: (847)674-9742; Fax: (847)674-9743 • URL: http://www.pia.com • Represents companies and individuals united by a common desire to improve business opportunities in the parachute industry. Develops technical, service and operating standards for parachute equipment, skydiving safety, and related aviation topics.

***Paraguay Business Law Handbook***. International Business Publications, USA, PO Box 15343 Washington, DC 20003. Phone: (202)546-2103; Fax: (202)546-3275; Email: ibpusa@comcast.net • URL: http://ibpus.com • $99.95 Individuals hardcopy, e-book, CD-ROM. Covers: Information on basic business legislation, laws, business climate, export-import regulations, and contacts.

**Paraguayan Industrial Union**. Av. Sacramento 945 Asuncion, Paraguay. Phone: 595 21 606988 • URL: http://www.uip.org.py • Promotes the economic and social development of Paraguay. Organizes conference and seminars.

**Parcel Shippers Association**. 1800 Diagonal Rd., Ste. 320 Alexandria, VA 22314. Phone: (571)257-7617; Fax: (571)257-7613; Email: psa@parcelshippers.org • URL: http://www.parcelshippers.org • Wholesalers, retailers, mail order houses, and other firms using parcel post service for distribution of products. Promotes the efficient and economical distribution of small package shipments.

***Parking Products & Services Directory: Parking Magazine***. National Parking Association, 1112 16th St. NW, Ste. 840 Washington, DC 20036. Phone: 800-647-7275 or (202)296-4336; Fax: (202)296-3102; Email: info@npapark.org • URL: http://www.npapark.org • Annual. $125 Individuals print and online; $165 Other countries print and online; 99 Individuals online. Covers: About 300 firms supplying products and services to the parking industry, including about 52 parking consultants. Entries include: Company name, address, phone, fax, product/service descriptions.

***Parking: The Magazine of the Parking Industry***. National Parking Association, 1112 16th St. NW, Ste. 840 Washington, DC 20036. Phone: 800-647-7275 or (202)296-4336; Fax: (202)296-3102; Email: info@npapark.org • URL: http://www.npapark.org • 10 times a year. $125.00 per year. Includes *Product and Services Directory*.

***Parliamentary Journal***. American Institute of Parliamentarians, 550M Ritchie Hwy., No. 271 Severna Park, MD 21146. Phone: 888-664-0428; Fax: (410)544-4640; Email: aip@aipparl.org • URL: http://www.aipparl.org • Quarterly. Journal presenting organizational problems and solutions that are parliamentary in nature.

***Partnership Houston: Membership Directory and Resource Guide***. Greater Houston Partnership, 1200 Smith, Ste. 700 Houston, TX 77002-4400. Phone: (713)844-3600; Fax: (713)844-0200; Email: ghp@houston.org • URL: http://www.houston.org • Annual. $40 Nonmembers print; $20 Members print; $125 Members CDR; $250 Nonmembers CDR. Covers: Over 1,700 member firms in the Houston, Texas area. Entries include: Firm name, address, phone, URL, name and title of contact, product or service provided, number of employees, line of business.

***Passenger Transport: The Weekly Newspaper of the Public Transportation Industry***. American Public Transportation Association, 1666 K St. NW, Ste. 1100 Washington, DC 20006. Phone: (202)496-4800; Fax: (202)496-4324; Email: info@apta.com • URL: http://www.apta.com • Weekly. $75 Individuals; $125 Two years; $87 Other countries. Covers current events and trends in mass transportation.

***Passport Newsletter***. Remy Publishing Co., 5819 S Blackstone Ave. Chicago, IL 60637-1855. Phone: (773)752-2142 • Monthly. $89.00 per year. Formerly *Passport*.

***Pasta Journal***. National Pasta Association, 750 National Press Bldg., 529 14th St. NW Washington, DC 20045. Phone: (202)591-2459; Fax: (202)591-2445; Email: info@ilovepasta.org • URL: http://www.ilovepasta.org • Bimonthly. $35.00 per year.

***Patent and Trademark Office Society Journal***. Patent and Trademark Office Society, PO Box 2089 Arlington, VA 22202. Phone: (571)270-3654 • URL: http://www.ptos.org/index.php • Individuals, $20.00 per year.

***Patent Law Basics***. Thomson West, 610 Opperman Dr. Eagan, MN 55123. Phone: 800-328-9352 or (651)687-7000 • $498.50 full set; $57 monthly. Covers Patent and Trademark Office applications, patent ownership, rights, protection, infringement, litigation, and other fundamentals of patent law.

***Patent Law Handbook***. Thomson West, 610 Opperman Dr. Eagan, MN 55123. Phone: 800-328-9352 or (651)687-7000 • Annual. $1,025 book-softbound; $85 monthly. Contains detailed information on patent law.

***Patent Strategy and Management***. ALM Media Properties LLC, 120 Broadway, 5th Fl. New York, NY 10271-1100. Phone: (212)457-9400; Fax: (646)417-7705; Email: customercare@alm.com • URL: http://www.alm.com • Monthly. $225.00 per year. Newsletter. Provides news of recent legal and business trends in the area of patent issuance and litigation. (A Law Journal Newsletter, formerly published by Leader Publications).

***Patent's Handbook: A Guide for Inventors and Researchers to Searching Patent Documents and Preparing and Making an Application***. McFarland & CPI, Publishers, 960 NC Hwy 88 W Jefferson, NC 28640. Phone: 800-253-2187 or (336)246-4460; Fax: (336)246-5018; Email: info@mcfarlandpub.com • URL: http://www.mcfarlandbooks.com • $39.95 Individuals softcover. Publication includes: List of information sources for researching patents and inventorship. Principal content of publication is an overview of the patent system in the United States. Database includes: Diagrams, facsimiles, appendix.

***PatentWeb***. Micropatent L.L.C., 250 Dodge Ave. East Haven, CT 06512-3360. Phone: 800-648-6787 or (203)466-5055; Fax: (203)466-5054; Email: info@micropat.com • URL: http://www.micropat.com • Over 50 million full-text records.

***Patuxtent Business Review***. Patuxent Publishing Co., 10750 Little Patuxent Pkwy. Columbia, MD 21044-3106. Phone: 877-886-1206 or (410)730-3990 or (301)725-2000; Fax: (410)992-5339 or (301)725-7344; Email: jquimby@patuxent.com • URL: http://www.patuxent.com • Monthly. Business newspaper covering Howard County and Laurel, MD.

***Payroll Management Guide***. Wolters Kluwer Law & Business CCH, 2700 Lake Cook Rd. Riverwoods, IL 60015. Phone: 888-224-7377 or (847)267-7000; Email: cust_serv@cch.com • URL: http://www.cchgroup.com • Weekly Monthly. $1,159 Individuals. Covers the basics of payroll management, including employer obligations, recordkeeping, taxation, unemployment insurance, processing of new employees, and government penalties.

***Paytech***. American Payroll Association, 660 N Main Ave., Ste. 100 San Antonio, TX 78205-1217. Phone: (210)226-4600 or (210)224-6406; Fax: (210)226-4027 or (210)224-6038; Email: APA@americanpayroll.org • URL: http://www.americanpayroll.org • Monthly. Membership. Covers the details and technology of payroll administration.

***PC Magazine: The Independent Guide to Personal Computing and the Internet***. Media Inc., 28 E. 28th St. New York, NY 10016-7930. Phone: 800-451-1032 or (212)503-3500; Fax: (212)503-4399; Email: info@ziffdavis.com • URL: http://www.ziffdavis.com • Biweekly. $49.97 per year.

***PC Register***. IHS Global Ltd. Lloyd's Register—Fairplay Ltd., Lombard House, 3 Princess Way, Surrey Redhill RH1 1UP, United Kingdom. Phone: 44 1737 379000; Fax: 44 1737 379001; Email: marketing@ihs.com • URL: http://www.ihs.com • £3,900 Individuals CD-ROM; single user; quarterly updates; $7,600 Individuals CD-ROM; single user; quarterly updates; €5,700 Individuals CD-ROM; single user; quarterly updates; £4,450 Individuals CD-ROM; single user; monthly updates; $10,210 Individuals CD-ROM; single user; monthly updates; €6,500 Individuals CD-ROM; single user; monthly updates; £5,900 Individuals CD-ROM; network quarterly updates; $11,500 Individuals CD-ROM; network quarterly updates; €8,700 Individuals CD-ROM; network quarterly updates; £21,445 Individuals 5 users monthly updates. Covers: Shipbuilder and owner information for over 170,000 vessels of 100 GT and above. Entries include: Name, address, phone.

***PC World: The No. 1 Source for Definitive How-to-Buy, How-to-Use Advice on Personal Computing Systems and Software***. IDG Communications Inc., 492 Old Connecticut Path Framingham, MA 01701. Phone: (508)872-0080 or (508)875-5000; Fax: (508)988-7888 • URL: http://www.idg.com/www/homenew.nsf/home?readform • Monthly. $29.90 per year.

**PCIA - The Wireless Infrastucture Association**. 500 Montgomery St., Ste. 500 Alexandria, VA 22314. Phone: (703)535-7492; Fax: (703)836-1608; Email: membership@pcia.com • URL: http://www.pcia.com • Promotes development of industry standards for mobile telephone systems. Also concerned with the advertising and marketing of mobile telephones. Formerly National Mobile Radio System.

***PCResource: The Hands-On Guide to Business and Personal Productivity***. IDG Communications Inc., 80 Elm St. Peterborough, NH 03458. Phone: (603)924-0100; Fax: (603)924-4066 • Monthly. Educational magazine for home and small business users of personal computers.

***PDR Drug Guide for Mental Health Professionals***. Thomson Medical Economics, 5 Paragon Dr. Montvale, NJ 07645-1742. Phone: 800-526-4870 or (201)358-7200; Fax: (201)573-8999 or (201)722-2680; Email: customer.service@medec.com • URL: http://www.medec.com • Annual. $39.95. Contains detailed profiles of more than 70 "common psychotropic drugs organized by brand name." Also contains information on the psychological side effects of about 1,000 other prescription drugs.

***PDR for Nutritional Supplements***. Medical Economics Co., Five Paragon Dr. Montvale, NJ 07645-1742. Phone: 800-442-6657 or (973)944-7777 or (973)944-9777; Fax: (973)847-5390 or (973)-944-5390; Email: customer.service@medec.com • URL: http://www.medec.com • $59.95 Individuals. Includes trade names, usage, adverse reactions, dosage, and other information about vitamins and minerals.

***PDR Guide to Drug Interactions, Side Effects, Indications***. American Medical Association. Medical Economics Co., Five Paragon Dr. Montvale, NJ 07645-1742. Phone: 800-442-6657 or (973)944-7777 or (973)944-9777; Fax: (973)847-5390 or (973)-944-5390; Email: customer.service@medec.com • URL: http://www.medec.com • Annual. $48.95. Includes a list of prescription drugs by "precise clinical situation.".

***PE Update***. Project Equality Inc., 7132 Main St. Kansas City, MO 64114-1406. Phone: (913)486-7010; Fax: (816)361-8997; Email: kirkp@projectequality.org • URL: http://www.projectequality.org • Quarterly. Membership. Formerly *Project Equality Update*.

***Peach-Times***. National Peach Council, 22 Triplett Ct. Dillsburg, PA 17019-9490. Phone: (717)329-8421 • URL: http://www.nationalpeachcouncil.org • Quarterly. Membership.

**Peanut and Tree Nut Processors Association**. PO Box 2660 Alexandria, VA 22301. Phone: (301)365-2521; Email: jhodges@ptnpa.org • URL: http://www.ptnpa.org • Formerly Peanut Butter Manufacturers and NutSalters Association.

***The Peanut Farmer: For Commercial Growers of Peanuts and Related Agribusiness***. SpecComm International Inc., 3101 Poplarwood Ct., Ste. 115 Raleigh, NC 27604. Phone:

(919)872-5040; Fax: (919)876-6531; Email: spec_circ@juno. com • URL: http://www.speccomm.com • Seven times a year. $15.00 per year.

*Peanut Journal and Nut World*. Virginia-Carolina Peanut Association. Peanut Journal Publishing Co., 2921 N Radcliffe Ln. Chesapeake, VA 23321-4551. Phone: (804)484-4804 • Monthly. $8.00 per year.

*Peanut Science*. American Peanut Research and Education Society, PO Box 15825 College Station, TX 77841. Phone: (979)845-8278 or (229)329-2949 • URL: http://www. apresinc.com • Semiannual. $9.00 per issue.

*Pecan South*. Texas Pecan Growers Association, 4348 Carter Creek Pkwy., Ste. 101 Bryan, TX 77802. Phone: (979)846-3285; Fax: (979)846-1752; Email: pecans@tpga.org • URL: http://www.tpga.org • Monthly. $18.00 per year.

**Peking University - Center for Healthy Aging and Family Studies**. China Ctr. for Economy Research Beijing 100871, China. Phone: 86 10 62756914; Fax: 86 10 62756843; Email: chafs@ccer.pku.edu.cn • URL: http://www.pku.edu.cn/ academic/ageing/english/indexe.htm • Healthy aging and inter-generational relationships within the family unit, as well as the economics of aging.

*Peninsula Business Journal*. Olympic View Publishing L.L.C., 147 W Washington St. Sequim, WA 98382-3337. Phone: 800-829-5810 or (360)683-3311; Fax: (360)683-6670 • URL: http://www.sequimgazette.com • Monthly. $9; $15 Out of area; $0.75 Single issue. Business journal serving Jefferson and Clallam Counties.

*PennSuburban Chamber of Commerce—Membership Directory*. PennSuburban Chamber of Commerce, 34 Susquehanna Ave. Lansdale, PA 19446. Phone: (215)362-9200; Fax: (215)362-0393; Email: info@northpenn.org • URL: http://www.pennsuburban.org • Annual. Covers: Over 900 member businesses and industries in Montgomery, Bucks, and Chester counties in Pennsylvania. Entries include: Company name, address, phone, names and titles of key personnel, number of employees, product or service provided.

*Pennsylvania Industrial Directory*. Dun & Bradstreet Inc., 103 JFK Pkwy. Short Hills, NJ 07078. Phone: 800-526-0651 or (973)921-5500 or (973)921-5000; Fax: (866)560-7035 or (512)794-7670; Email: info@dnb.com • URL: http://www. dnb.com • Annual. Covers: 22,600 manufacturing establishments in Pennsylvania. Database includes: Statistical data and trade show calendar. Entries include: Company name, address, county, phone, toll-free number, number of employees, names and titles of key executives, plant size, year established, parent company, annual sales, import/export information, SIC code, and product description.

*Pennsylvania Industries Guide*. Industries Guides Inc., 303 E Altamonte Dr. Altamonte Springs, FL 32716. Phone: (407)834-8181 • $95. Covers: Approximately 17,000 manufacturers in Pennsylvania. Entries include: Company name, address, phone.

**Pennsylvania State University - Applied Research Laboratory**. PO Box 30 State College, PA 16804-0030. Phone: (814)865-6531 or (814)865-6343; Fax: (814)865-3105; Email: lrh3@ psu.edu • URL: http://www.arl.psu.edu • Underwater acoustics, noise and vibration control, hydrodynamics and hydroacoustics, propulsors, guidance and control, signal processing, thermal power plants, engineering materials, systems engineering, modeling and simulation, manufacturing science, communications, information, electro-optics, navigation, condition-based maintenance, and visualization.

**Pennsylvania State University at Harrisburg - Economic Development Research and Training Center**. Church Hall, 777 W Harrisburg Pke. Middletown, PA 17057. Phone: (717)948-6117; Fax: (717)948-6306; Email: edrtc@psu.edu • URL: http://edrtc.hbg.psu.edu • Public policy, community development, economic development, economics, and economic impacts.

**Pennsylvania State University at Harrisburg - Institute of State and Regional Affairs - Pennsylvania State Data Center**. 777 W Harrisburg Pike Middletown, PA 17057-4898. Phone: (717)948-6336; Fax: (717)948-6754; Email: pasdc@psu.edu • URL: http://www.pasdc.hbg.psu.edu • Conducts research in environmental, general, and socioeconomic planning. Zoning is included.

**Pennsylvania State University - Beef Cattle and Sheep Research Center**. 324 Henning Bldg. University Park, PA 16802. Phone: (814)865-5893; Fax: (814)863-6042; Email: rswope@das.psu.edu • URL: http://www.das.cas.psu.edu/ • Animal science, including breeding selection, nutrition, and physiology of beef cattle and sheep; pasture management and intensive rotational grazing practices.

**Pennsylvania State University - Center for the Study of Higher Education**. 400 Rackley Bldg. University Park, PA 16802-3202. Phone: (814)865-9756 or (814)865-6346; Fax: (814)865-3638; Email: cshe@psu.edu • URL: http://www.ed. psu.edu/educ/cshe • Policy analysis of major trends, issues, and practices in higher education at the institutional, state, regional, and national levels. Research initiatives include postsecondary teaching, learning assessment, program review and evaluation, the impact of college on students, strategic and regional planning, organizational cultures, business-industry relationships with colleges and universities, and international higher education. Encourages interdisciplinary studies.

**Pennsylvania State University - College of Engineering -**

**Center for Acoustics and Vibration**. 229 Hammond Bldg. University Park, PA 16802. Phone: (814)863-0103 or (814)865-2761; Fax: (814)865-5965 or (814)863-7222; Email: gal4@psu.edu • URL: http://www.cav.psu.edu • Comprised of eight technical groups researching aspects of acoustics and vibration: Acoustic Characterization of Materials; Active Structures and Noise Control; Flow Induced Noise; Machinery Prognostics and Condition Monitoring; Propagation and Radiation; Quiet Product Design; Rotorcraft Acoustics and Dynamics; and Structural Vibration and Acoustics. and structural response induced by turbulent separation, noise control in automotive HVAC systems, and aeroacoustic radiation from automotive alternators. Materials Evaluation studies physical acoustics in composites and other advanced materials, acoustic microscopy and microstructural features, X-ray radiography to study residual stress, sensors for materials process monitoring and control, nondestructive evaluation of advanced materials, optical, fiberoptical and laser ultrasonic techniques for materials evaluation, and infrared thermography. Propagation and Radiation technical group researches generation and propagation of sound waves, response, fuzzy dynamics, mechanical and thermal internal fields, chains, belts, and gear vibrations, and chassis dynamics modeling.

**Pennsylvania State University - College of Engineering - Harold and Inge Marcus Department of Industrial and Manufacturing Engineering - Metal Casting Laboratory**. 221 Leonard Bldg. University Park, PA 16802. Phone: (814)863-7290 or (814)863-5640; Fax: (814)863-4745; Email: rcv2@psu.edu • URL: http://www.ie.psu.edu • Properties and processing of cast metals and alloys, dimensional control of castings, environmental solutions for the metal casting industry.

**Pennsylvania State University - Economic Research Institute of Erie**. Sam & Irene Black School of Business, 5091 Station Rd. Erie, PA 16563-1400. Phone: (814)898-7149; Fax: (814)898-6223; Email: k12@psu.edu • URL: http://128.118. 18.108 • Erie County, PA regional economy and its linkages to the national economy, including other issues related to local/metro economic development and regional economics.

**Pennsylvania State University - Institute for the Study of Business Markets**. 484 Business Bldg., Smeal College of Business University Park, PA 16802. Phone: (814)863-2782; Fax: (814)863-0413; Email: isbm@psu.edu • URL: http://isbm. smeal.psu.edu • Research areas include international distribution channels.

*The Penny Fortune Newsletter*. James M. Fortune, editor. Phoenix Communications Group Ltd., 3465 Hickory Hill Dr. Colorado Springs, CO 80906. Phone: (719)576-9200; Email: info@nbda.com • Description: Instructs small investors on how to invest modest sums of money every two weeks to build a portfolio of stocks and mutual funds.

*Pension and Employee Benefits: Code-ERISA and Regulations*. Wolters Kluwer Law & Business CCH, 2700 Lake Cook Rd. Riverwoods, IL 60015. Phone: 888-224-7377 or (847)267-7000; Email: cust_serv@cch.com • URL: http://www. cchgroup.com • $123.00. Two volumes.

*Pension and Profit Sharing Plans for Small or Medium Size Businesses*. Aspen Publishers, Inc., 7201 McKinney Cir. Frederick, MD 21704. Phone: 800-234-1660 or (301)698-7100 or (301)417-7500; Fax: (800)901-9075 or (301)695-7931; Email: customerservice@aspenpublisher.com • URL: http:// www.aspenpublishers.com • Monthly. $191.50 per year. Newsletter. Topics of interest and concern to professionals who serve small and medium size pension and profit sharing plans.

*Pension Facts*. American Council of Life Insurance, 101 Constitution Ave. NW Washington, DC 20001. Phone: (202)624-2000 • Biennial. Free.

*Pension Fund Litigation Reporter*. Andrews Publications, 175 Strafford Ave.. Bldg. 4, Suite 140 Wayne, PA 19087. Phone: 800-345-1101 or (610)225-0510 or (610)622-0510; Fax: (610)225-0501 or (610)622-0501; Email: customer@ andrewspub.com • URL: http://www.andrewspub.com • Semimonthly. $750.00 per year. Newsletter. Contains reports on legal cases involving pension fund fiduciaries (trustees).

*Pension Plan Fix-It Handbook*. Thompson Publishing Group Inc., Government Information Services, Education Funding Research Council, 1725 K St. NW, Ste. 700 Washington, DC 20006. Phone: 800-677-3789 or (202)444-8741; Fax: (800)759-7179 or (202)296-1091; Email: service@thompson. com • URL: http://www.thompson.com • Two looseleaf volumes. $529.00 per year. Two looseleaf volumes. Monthly updates and newsletters. Serves as a comprehensive guide to pension plan administration, taxation, and federal regulation. Includes both defined benefit and defined contribution plans.

*Pension Plan Guide*. Wolters Kluwer Law & Business CCH, 2700 Lake Cook Rd. Riverwoods, IL 60015. Phone: 888-224-7377 or (847)267-7000; Email: cust_serv@cch.com • URL: http:// www.cchgroup.com • Weekly. $2,225 Individuals CD-ROM; $2,175 Individuals print. Loose leaf series on pension plans. Formerly *Pension Plan Guide Summary*.

**Pension Research Council**. The Wharton School of the University of Pennsylvania, 3620 Locust Walk, 3000 Steinberg Hall - Dietrich Hall Philadelphia, PA 19104-6302. Phone: (215)898-7620; Fax: (215)573-3418; Email: prc@ wharton.upenn.edu • URL: http://www. pensionresearchcouncil.org • Research areas include various

types of private sector and public employee pension plans.

*Pension World—Real Estate Portfolio Manager Directory Issue*. Primedia Business, 6151 Powers Ferry Rd. NW Atlanta, GA 30339. Phone: (770)955-2500 or (770)995-2500; Fax: (770)618-0204 • URL: http://www.primediabusiness.com • Annual. $19.95 payment must accompany order. List of about 100 firms each currently managing real estate investments totalling at least $10 million for pension funds.

*Pensions and Investments: The Newspaper of Corporate and Institutional Investing*. Crain Communications Inc., 711 3rd Ave. New York, NY 10017. Phone: (212)210-0100; Email: info@crain.com • URL: http://www.crain.com • Biweekly. $325.00 per year. Formerly *Pensions and Investment Age*.

*People & Strategy*. HR People and Strategy, 1800 Duke St. Alexandria, VA 22314. Phone: 888-602-3270; Fax: (703)535-6490; Email: info@hrps.org • URL: http://www.hrps.org • Quarterly. $150 Nonmembers print only; $129 Members print only. Contains current theory, research and practice in strategic human resource management.

*People to People*. American Public Power Association, 1875 Connecticut Ave. NW, Ste. 1200 Washington, DC 20009-5715. Phone: 800-515-2772 or (202)467-2900; Fax: (202)467-2910; Email: info@publicpower.org • URL: http://www. publicpower.org • Description: Reports on public sector labor and personnel issues, especially those concerning the electric utility industry. Summarizes case studies in public labor relations.

*People's Republic of China Year Book*. Current Publications Ltd., 1503 Enterprise Bldg., 228-238 Queen's Rd. Central Hong Kong, China. Phone: 22 5434702; Fax: 22 8158396 • Annual. $98.00. Serves as the official yearbook of the People's Republic of China. Covers developments in various aspects of life in China, including the economy, industry, transportation, telecommunications, agriculture, technology, demographics, the legal system, health, and foreign relations. Includes many statistical tables and photographs. Text in Chinese.

*Performing Arts Forum*. International Society for the Performing Arts Foundation, 630 9th Ave., Ste. 213 New York, NY 10036. Phone: (212)206-8490; Fax: (212)206-8603; Email: info@ispa.org • URL: http://www.ispa.org • Description: Directed toward producers, managers, promoters, and representatives of artists and performing arts events in the U.S. and other countries. Discusses techniques and problems involved with the development and administration of the performing arts. Recurring features include items from readers, news of research, Society reports, and notes on members.

*Perfumer and Flavorist*. Allured Business Media, 336 Gundersen Dr., Ste. A Carol Stream, IL 60188-2403. Phone: (630)653-2155; Fax: (630)653-2192; Email: customerservice@allured. com • URL: http://www.allured.com • Monthly. $135.00 per year. Provides information on the art and technology of flavors and fragrances, including essential oils, aroma chemicals, and spices.

*Perishable Products Export Control Board—Export Directory*. Perishable Products Export Council Board, 45 Silwerboom Ave. Plattekloof 7500, South Africa. Phone: 27 21 9301134; Fax: 27 21 9367219 • URL: http://www.ppecb.com • Provides information and statistics of South African perishable export products.

**Personal Care Products Council**. 1620 L St. NW, Ste. 1200 Washington, DC 20036. Phone: (202)331-1770; Fax: (202)331-1969 • URL: http://www.personalcarecouncil.org • Formerly Cosmetic, Toiletry and Fragrance Association.

*Personal Finance*. KCI Communications Inc., 1750 Old Meadow Rd., Ste. 301 McLean, VA 22102. Phone: (703)394-1931; Fax: (703)905-8100; Email: service@kci-com.com • Description: Contains articles on subjects of interest to those investigating personal finance strategies. Provides news, information, and suggestions on investment decisions. Covers stock and growth stock activity, individual retirement accounts, market trends and developments, and real estate. Recurring features include columns titled Capsule Advisory and Answers to Your Money Questions.

*Personal Financial Planning Handbook: With Forms and Checklists*. Thomson Reuters Financial Unit, 200 W Madison Ave., Ste. 1200 Chicago, IL 60606. Phone: (312)288-6400; Email: TFOnlineRequests@thomson.com • URL: http:// thomsonreuters.com/products_services/financial • $360 book; $605 online. Looseleaf service. Biennial supplementation. Designed for professional financial planners, accountants, attorneys, insurance marketers, brokers, and bankers.

**Personal Injury Lawyers Marketing and Management Association**. 607 Briarwood Dr., Ste. 4 Myrtle Beach, SC 29572. Phone: 800-497-1890 or (843)361-1700; Fax: (866)859-8126; Email: info@pilmma.org • URL: http://www. pilmma.org • Represents personal injury lawyers and disability attorneys. Provides members with the necessary tools, information and education to help grow and manage a successful contingency-based injury and disability law practice. Seeks to fulfill the marketing and management needs of members by granting access to sources of credible information and educational events.

*Personal Strategies for Managing Stress*. American Management Association Extension Institute, 1601 Broadway New York, NY 10019. Phone: 800-262-9699 or (518)586-8100; Fax: (518)903-8168 • $139.00. Self-study course. Emphasis is on practical explanations, examples, and problem solving. Quizzes and a case study are included.

***Personen-Compass***. Compass-Verlag, Matznergasse 17 A-1141 Vienna, Austria. Phone: 43 1 981 16113; Fax: 43 1 981 16118; Email: herman.futter@compass.at • URL: http://www.compass.co.at • Annual. $1,250. Covers: over 19,000 principal executives of major Austrian companies. Entries include: Name, address, affiliations.

***Personnel Management: Communications***. Prentice Hall PTR, 1 Lake St. Upper Saddle River, NJ 07458. Phone: 800-227-1816 or (201)236-7676 or (201)236-7000; Fax: (800)445-6991 or (317)428-3343 • URL: http://phbusiness.prenhall.com • Looseleaf. Periodic supplementation. Price on application. Includes how to write effectively and how to prepare employee publications.

***Personnel Management: Compensation***. Prentice Hall PTR, 1 Lake St. Upper Saddle River, NJ 07458. Phone: 800-227-1816 or (201)236-7676 or (201)236-7000; Fax: (800)445-6991 or (317)428-3343 • URL: http://phbusiness.prenhall.com • Looseleaf. Periodic supplementation. Price on application.

***Personnel Management: Labor Relations Guide***. Prentice Hall PTR, 1 Lake St. Upper Saddle River, NJ 07458. Phone: 800-227-1816 or (201)236-7676 or (201)236-7000; Fax: (800)445-6991 or (317)428-3343 • URL: http://phbusiness.prenhall.com • Three looseleaf volumes. Periodic supplementation. Price on application.

***Personnel Management: Policies and Practices***. Prentice Hall PTR, 1 Lake St. Upper Saddle River, NJ 07458. Phone: 800-227-1816 or (201)236-7676 or (201)236-7000; Fax: (800)445-6991 or (317)428-3343 • URL: http://phbusiness.prenhall.com • Looseleaf. Periodic supplementation. Price on application.

***Personnel Psychology***. Personnel Psychology Inc., 1435 Cedar Ln. Bowling Green, OH 43402-1476. Phone: (419)352-1562; Email: ppsych@personnelpsychology.com • Quarterly. $98.00 per year. Publishes research articles and book reviews.

***Perspective***. Magna Publications Inc., 2718 Dryden Dr. Madison, WI 53704. Phone: 800-433-0499 or (608)246-3590 or (608)249-3590; Fax: (608)246-3597; Email: custserv@magnapubs.com • URL: http://www.magnapubs.com • Description: Provides administrators with guidelines for keeping their schools out of court. Examines current trends in law related to higher education, as well as past and future legal issues affecting students, faculty, administrators and the public. Recurring features include columns titled Key Case Review, Follow-Up, Resources, Legislative Note, Outside the Courts, Cross-Examination, and Cases Noted.

***The Perspective: Main Street Perspective (Business in the Southwest)***. Cheallaigh Shamrock, PO Box 190 Dodson, LA 71422. Phone: (318)628-8671; Fax: (318)628-8671; Email: journal@thepineywoods.com • URL: http://www.thepineywoods.com • Biweekly. Magazine.

***Peru Business Forecast Report***. Telecommunications Insight, 85 Queen Victoria St. London EC4V 4AB, United Kingdom. Phone: 20 72 465100 or 44 20 7248 0468; Fax: 20 72 480467 or 44 20 7248 0467; Email: enquiries@telecomsinsight.com • URL: http://www.telecomsinsight.com • Quarterly. $1,195 Individuals Single user; $1,795 Individuals Up to 3 users. Business forecast report for Peru.

***Peru Business Law Handbook***. International Business Publications, USA, PO Box 15343 Washington, DC 20003. Phone: (202)546-2103; Fax: (202)546-3275; Email: ibpusa@comcast.net • URL: http://ibpus.com • $99.95 Individuals hardcopy, e-book, CD-ROM. Covers: Information on basic business legislation, laws, business climate, export-import regulations, and contacts.

***Peru Government and Business Contacts Handbook***. International Business Publications, USA, PO Box 15343 Washington, DC 20003. Phone: (202)546-2103; Fax: (202)546-3275; Email: ibpusa@comcast.net • URL: http://ibpus.com • $99.95 Individuals hardcopy, e-book, CD-ROM. Covers: Strategic government and business information, export-import activity in the country, investment, business contacts and regulations.

***Peru Industrial and Business Directory***. International Business Publications, USA, PO Box 15343 Washington, DC 20003. Phone: (202)546-2103; Fax: (202)546-3275; Email: ibpusa@comcast.net • URL: http://ibpus.com • Annual. $99.95 Individuals hardcopy, e-book, CD-ROM. Covers: Strategic industrial, investment and business contacts for conducting export-import and investment activity in the country. Contains strategic, practical economic and business information.

***Peru Investment and Business Guide***. International Business Publications, USA, PO Box 15343 Washington, DC 20003. Phone: (202)546-2103; Fax: (202)546-3275; Email: ibpusa@comcast.net • URL: http://ibpus.com • Annual. $99.95 Individuals hardcopy, e-book, CD-ROM. Covers: Strategic and business information, contacts, regulations and more. An ultimate guide for conducting investment, export-import activity in the country.

***Pest Control***. Advanstar Communications, 545 Boylston St. Boston, MA 02116. Phone: 888-527-7008 or (617)267-6500; Fax: (617)267-6900; Email: info@advanstar.com • URL: http://www.advanstar.com • Monthly. $44.00 per year.

***Pest Control Technology***. Group Interest Enterprises. GIE Media, Inc., 5811 Canal Rd. Valley View, OH 44125. Phone: 800-456-0707 or (216)393-0300 or (216)93-0300; Fax: (216)525-0515 or (216)393-0300; Email: bharbison@gie.net • URL: http://www.giemedia.com • Monthly. $32.00 per year. Provides technical and business management information for pest control personnel.

***Pesticide Biochemistry and Physiology: An International Journal***. Elsevier, Secondary Publishing Division, 650 Ave. of the Americas New York, NY 10011. Phone: 888-437-4636 or (212)633-3980; Fax: (212)633-3975; Email: t.reller@elsevier.com • URL: http://www.elseveier.com • Nine times a year. Individuals, $487.00 per year; institutions, $1,819.00 per year; students, $89.00 per year.

***PestWeb: The Pest Control Industry Website***. Univar USA, Phone: 800-888-4897 or (425)889-3400; Email: webmaster@pestweb.com • URL: http://www.pestweb.com • Web site provides a wide variety of information on pest control products, manufacturers, associations, news, and education. Includes "Insects and Other Organisms," featuring details on 27 different kinds of pests, from ants to wasps. Online searching is offered. Fees: Free.

***Pet Age: The Magazine for the Professional Retailer***. Michelle Maskaly, editor. H.H. Backer Associates Inc., 18 S Michigan Ave., Ste. 1100 Chicago, IL 60603. Phone: (312)578-1818 or (312)663-4040; Fax: (312)578-1819 or (312)663-5676; Email: hhbacker@hhbacker.com • URL: http://www.hhbacker.com • Monthly. Free to qualified subscribers; $160 Other countries. Covers news and feature articles about human and animal relationships.

**Pet Food Institute**. 2025 M St. NW, Ste. 800 Washington, DC 20036-2422. Phone: (202)367-1120; Fax: (202)367-2120; Email: info@petfoodinstitute.org • URL: http://www.petfoodinstitute.org • Represents the manufacturers of 97% of the commercial pet food produced in the United States. Serves as the voice of the industry before legislative and regulatory bodies at both the federal and state levels.

***Pet Hospitals and Clinics Directory***. InfoGroup Inc., 5711 S 86th Cir. Omaha, NE 68127-4146. Phone: (402)593-4500 • URL: http://www.infogroup.com • Annual. Number of listings: 14,050. Entries include: Name, address, phone, size of advertisement, name of owner or manager, number of employees, year first in "Yellow Pages." Compiled from telephone company "Yellow Pages," nationwide.

**Pet Industry Distributors Association**. 3465 Box Hill Corporate Center Dr., Ste. H Abingdon, MD 21009. Phone: (443)640-1060; Fax: (443)640-1086; Email: pida@kingmgmt.org • URL: http://www.pida.org • Strives to enhance the well-being of the pet product wholesaler-distributor. Promotes partnerships between suppliers and customers. Fosters the human-companion animal bond.

**Pet Industry Joint Advisory Council**. 1146 19th St. NW, Ste. 350 Washington, DC 20036-3746. Phone: 800-553-7387 or (202)452-1525; Fax: (202)452-1516; Email: info@pijac.org • URL: http://www.pijac.org • Pet retailers, manufacturers and distributors; companion animal suppliers; pet industry trade associations. Works to monitor federal and state regulations and legislation affecting the industry. Sponsors research projects and industry-related educational programs.

***Pet Product News***. I-5 Publishing LLC, PO Box 6050 Mission Viejo, CA 92690. Phone: (949)855-8822; Fax: (949)855-3045 • URL: http://www.i5publishing.com • Free to qualified personnel; others, $118.00 per year. Supplement available *Pet Product News Buyer's Guide*.

***Pet Shop***. Entrepreneur Press, 2445 McCabe Way, Ste. 400 Irvine, CA 92614-6244. Phone: 800-864-6864 or (949)261-2325 or (949)622-7131; Fax: (949)261-7729 or (949)261-0234; Email: press@entrepreneur.com • URL: http://www.entrepreneurpress.com • $19.95. Looseleaf. $59.50. A practical guide to starting a pet store. Covers profit potential, start-up costs, market size evaluation, owner's time required, site selection, lease negotiation, pricing, accounting, advertising, promotion, etc. (Start-Up Business Guide No. E1007.).

***Peterson's Guide to Graduate Programs in Business, Education, Health, and Law***. Peterson's, 461 From Rd. Paramus, NJ 07652. Phone: 800-338-3282 or (609)896-1800 or (877)433-8277; Fax: (402)458-3042 or (609)896-4531; Email: custsvc@petersons.com • URL: http://www.petersons.com • Annual. $38.47 Individuals. Covers colleges and universities in the United States and Canada that offer more than 16,800 accredited graduate programs in business, education, health, and law.

***Peterson's Guide to MBA Programs: The Most Comprehensive Guide to U.S., Canadian, & International Business Schools***. Peterson's, 461 From Rd. Paramus, NJ 07652. Phone: 800-338-3282 or (609)896-1800 or (877)433-8277; Fax: (402)458-3042 or (609)896-4531; Email: custsvc@petersons.com • URL: http://www.petersons.com • $28.35 Individuals softcover. Covers: Over 4,000 U.S. accredited MBA programs worldwide. Entries include: Program name, address, phone.

***Petfood Industry***. Watt Publishing, 122 S Wesley Ave. Mount Morris, IL 61054-1497. Phone: (815)734-4171 • Bimonthly. $96.

***PetroChemical News: A Weekly News Service in English Devoted to the Worldwide Petrochemical Industry***. William F. Bland Co., 709 Turmeric Ln. Durham, NC 27713. Phone: (919)544-1717; Fax: (919)544-1999; Email: mbs@PetroChemical-News.com • URL: http://www.petrochemical-news.com • Weekly. $897. Report of current and significant news about the petrochemical business worldwide.

***Petroleum Abstracts***. University of Tulsa, 800 S Tucker Dr. Tulsa, OK 74104-3189. Phone: 800-247-8678 or (918)631-3080 or (918)594-8000; Fax: (918)631-3033; Email: info@osu-tulsa.okstate.edu • URL: http://www.utulsa.edu • 50 times a year. Service basis. Worldwide literature related to petroleum exploration and production.

***Petroleum-Energy Business News Index Elsevier Engineering Information, Inc.*** Elsevier, Secondary Publishing Division, 650 Ave. of the Americas New York, NY 10011. Phone: 888-437-4636 or (212)633-3980; Fax: (212)633-3975; Email: t.reller@elsevier.com • URL: http://www.elseveier.com • Monthly. Members, $475.00 per year; non-members, $950.00 per year.

**Petroleum Equipment Institute**. PO Box 2380 Tulsa, OK 74101-2380. Phone: (918)494-9696; Fax: (918)491-9895; Email: info@pei.org • URL: http://www.pei.org • Distributors and manufacturers of equipment used in service stations, bulk plants and other petroleum marketing operations.

**Petroleum Equipment Suppliers Association**. 1240 Blalock Rd., Ste. 110 Houston, TX 77055. Phone: (713)932-0168; Fax: (713)932-0497; Email: info@pesa.org • URL: http://www.pesa.org/index.php/home/c/home • Promotes improvement of the petroleum equipment, service, and supply industries. Represents members' interests; cooperates with the federal government in matters of national concern; gathers and disseminates information. Conducts educational programs.

***Petroleum Intelligence Weekly***. Energy Intelligence Group, 5 E 37th St., 5th Fl. New York, NY 10016-2807. Phone: (212)532-1112; Fax: (212)532-4479; Email: customerservice@energyintel.com • URL: http://www.energyintel.com • Description: Provides a "concise weekly summary and analysis of key developments in world oil and natural gas markets." Supplies highlights in petroleum news on an international scale. Concerned with OPEC (Organization of Petroleum Exporting Countries) and non-OPEC production levels, coverage of OPEC meetings and policy decisions, and quarterly demand and oil trade figures. Recurring features include analyses of emerging trends in oil and gas markets, notices of publications available, and columns titled Marketview (a weekly wrap-up of crude oil trading) and What's New Around the World (news briefs relating to the petroleum industry and market).

***Petroleum Management: The International Business Magazine for the Oil and Gas Industry***. Management Publishing Services, PO Box 55829 Houston, TX 77255-5829. Phone: (713)789-7887 • Monthly. $36. Trade magazine.

***Petroleum Marketing Monthly***. U. S. Government Printing Office, 732 N Capitol St. NW Washington, DC 20401. Phone: 866-512-1800 or (202)512-1800 or (866)512-1800; Fax: (202)512-2104 or (202)512-2250; Email: contactcenter@gpo.gov • URL: http://www.gpo.gov • Monthly. Current information and statistics relating to a wide variety of petroleum products. (Office of Oil and Gas, Energy Information Administration, U. S. Department of Energy.).

***Petroleum Statement, Annual Energy Report***. Energy Information Administration. U.S. Department of Energy, 1000 Independence Ave. SW Washington, DC 20585. Phone: (202)586-5000; Fax: (202)586-4403; Email: The.Secretary@hq.doe.gov • URL: http://energy.gov • Annual.

***Petroleum Supply Annual***. U. S. Government Printing Office, 732 N Capitol St. NW Washington, DC 20401. Phone: 866-512-1800 or (202)512-1800 or (866)512-1800; Fax: (202)512-2104 or (202)512-2250; Email: contactcenter@gpo.gov • URL: http://www.gpo.gov • Annual. $78.00. Two volumes. Produced by the Energy Information Administration, U. S. Department of Energy. Contains worldwide data on the petroleum industry and petroleum products.

***Petroleum Supply Monthly***. U. S. Government Printing Office, 732 N Capitol St. NW Washington, DC 20401. Phone: 866-512-1800 or (202)512-1800 or (866)512-1800; Fax: (202)512-2104 or (202)512-2250; Email: contactcenter@gpo.gov • URL: http://www.gpo.gov • Monthly. Produced by the Energy Information Administration, U. S. Department of Energy. Provides worldwide statistics on a wide variety of petroleum products. Covers production, supplies, exports and imports, transportation, refinery operations, and other aspects of the petroleum industry.

***Pew Research Center for the People and the Press***. Pew Charitable Trusts, Phone: (202)293-3126; Fax: (202)293-2569; Email: mailprc@people-press.org • URL: http://www.people-press.org • Free Web site includes public opinion poll "Reports by Topic." Five broad subject areas cover business, social issues, foreign policy, news media, and politics. Searching is offered within each of these broad areas, and there are links to other major sources of public opinion poll results ("FYI Other Polls").

***Pharma Business: The International Magazine of Pharmaceutical Business and Marketing***. Engel Publishing Partners, 828 A Newton-Yardley Rd. Newton, PA 18940. Phone: 800-431-1579 or (215)867-0044; Fax: (215)867-0053 • URL: http://www.englepub.com • Six times a year. $235.00 per year. Circulated mainly in European countries. Coverage includes worldwide industry news, new drug products, regulations, and research developments.

***The Pharma Letter***. The Pharma Letter, 39-43 Putney High St., Putney London SW15 1SP, United Kingdom. Phone: 44 208 780 6363; Email: enquiries@thepharmaletter.com • URL: http://www.thepharmaletter.com • Fifty times a year. $720.00

per year. Newsletter. Formerly *Marketletter*.

***Pharmaceutical and Medical Device Law Bulletin***. ALM Media Properties LLC, 120 Broadway, 5th Fl. New York, NY 10271-1100. Phone: (212)457-9400; Fax: (646)417-7705; Email: customercare@alm.com • URL: http://www.alm.com • Monthly. $199.00 per year. Newsletter. Edited for lawyers concerned with drug product or medical device litigation. Contains industry news items of special interest, reports on new products, legal case summaries, Food and Drug Administration actions, patent issues, and related news reports. (A Law Journal Newsletter, formerly published by Leader Publications).

***Pharmaceutical Engineering***. International Society for Pharmaceutical Engineering, 600 N Westshore Blvd., Ste. 900 Tampa, FL 33609-1114. Phone: (813)960-2105; Fax: (813)264-2816; Email: ask@ispe.org • URL: http://www.ispe.org • Bimonthly. Feature articles provide practical application and specification information on the design, construction, supervision and maintenance of process equipment, plant systems, instrumentation and pharmaceutical facilities.

***Pharmaceutical Executive: For Global Business and Marketing Leaders***. Advanstar Communications, 545 Boylston St. Boston, MA 02116. Phone: 888-527-7008 or (617)267-6500; Fax: (617)267-6900; Email: info@advanstar.com • URL: http://www.advanstar.com • Monthly. Covers fresh ideas about sales, regulations, finance, meetings and IT.

***Pharmaceutical Litigation Reporter: The National Journal of Record of Pharmaceutical Litigation***. Andrews Publications, 175 Strafford Ave., Bldg. 4, Suite 140 Wayne, PA 19087. Phone: 800-345-1101 or (610)225-0510 or (610)622-0510; Fax: (610)225-0501 or (610)622-0501; Email: customer@andrewspub.com • URL: http://www.andrewspub.com • Monthly. $775.00 per year. Newsletter. Reports on a wide variety of legal cases involving the pharmaceutical and medical device industries. Includes product liability lawsuits.

***Pharmaceutical Processing***. Advantage Business Media L.L.C., 100 Enterprise Dr., Ste. 600 Rockaway, NJ 07866-0912. Phone: (973)920-7000; Email: advantagecommunications@advantagemedia.com • URL: http://www.advantagebusinessmedia.com • 10/year. Includes *Buyers' Guide*. Formerly *Pharmaceutical and Cosmetic Equipment*.

***Pharmaceutical Representative***. McKnight's Long-Term Care News, 1 Northfield Plz., Ste. 521 Northfield, IL 60093-1216. Phone: 800-558-1703 or (847)784-8706 or (847)441-3700; Fax: (847)441-3701; Email: custserv@mcknights.com • URL: http://www.mcknights.com • Monthly. $37.95 per year. Edited for drug company salespeople and sales managers.

**Pharmaceutical Research and Manufacturers Association**. 950 F St. NW, Ste. 300 Washington, DC 20004. Phone: (202)835-3400 • URL: http://www.phrma.org • Formerly Pharmaceutical Manufacturers Association.

***Pharmaceutical Research Manufacturers Association Annual Fact Book***. Pharmaceutical Research and Manufacturers Association, 950 F St. NW, Ste. 300 Washington, DC 20004. Phone: (202)835-3400 • URL: http://www.phrma.org • Annual.

***Pharmaceutical Strategic Alliances: The Complete Drug and Biotech Alliances Reference Guide***. Windhover Information Inc., 10 Hoyt St. Norwalk, CT 06851. Phone: 800-332-2181 or (203)838-4401; Fax: (203)838-3214; Email: fdcwindhover.custcare@elsevier.com • URL: http://www.windhoverinfo.com • Annual. $2,495 Single issue volume XVII (print); $2,695 Single issue volume XVII (print and Adobe PDF); $2,495 Single issue volume XVII (Adobe PDF). Covers: Pharmaceutical industry strategic alliances, including joint ventures, research and development collaborations, marketing/licensing agreements, and equity investments. Entries include: Company name, address, phone, names and titles of key personnel, financial data, description of transaction, terms, valuations, product information including therapeutic categories, clinical phase of development, geographic marketing rights, statistical charts.

***Pharmaceutical Technology***. Advanstar Communications, 545 Boylston St. Boston, MA 02116. Phone: 888-527-7008 or (617)267-6500; Fax: (617)267-6900; Email: info@advanstar.com • URL: http://www.advanstar.com • Monthly. Practical hands on information about the manufacture of pharmaceutical products, focusing on applied technology.

**Pharmacology Research Laboratory**. c/o David Flockhart, Division Chief, Indiana University School of Medicine, Division of Clinical Pharmacology, 950 W Walnut St., Rm. 402 Indianapolis, IN 46202. Phone: (317)274-2810 or (317)274-2820 • URL: http://medicine.iupui.edu/clinpharm.

***Pharmacopeia of Herbs***. CME Inc., 2801 McGaw Ave. Irvine, CA 92614-5835. Phone: 800-933-2632 or (949)250-1008; Fax: (949)250-0445; Email: customer.service@cmellc.com • URL: http://www.cmellc.com • $149.00. Frequently updated CD-ROM provides searchable data on a wide variety of herbal medicines, vitamins, and amino acids. Includes information on clinical studies, contraindications, side-effects, phytoactivity, and 534 therapeutic use categories. Contains a 1,000 word glossary.

***Pharmacopeial Forum***. United States Pharmacopeial Convention, 12601 Twinbrook Pky. Rockville, MD 20852-1790. Phone: 800-227-8772 or (301)881-0666; Fax: (301)816-8299 or (301)816-8236; Email: custsvc@usp.org • URL: http://www.usp.org • Bimonthly. $469 Individuals. Journal on drug standards.

***Pharmacy Times: Practical Information for Today's Pharmacists***. Medical World Communications, 241 Forsgate Dr. Jamesburg, NJ 08831. Phone: (732)656-1140; Fax: (732)656-1142; Email: cms@skaininfo.com • URL: http://www.pharmacytimes.com • Monthly. $57 Individuals per year; $103 Institutions per year. Edited for pharmacists. Covers store management, new products, regulations, home health care products, managed care issues, etc.

**Phi Chi Theta**. 1508 E Beltline Rd., Ste. 104 Carrollton, TX 75006. Phone: (972)245-7202; Email: executivedirector@phichitheta.org • URL: http://www.phichitheta.org • Co-ed professional fraternity - business and economics. Maintains hall of fame; sponsors educational programs.

**Phi Gamma Nu**. 6745 Cheryl Ann Dr. Seven Hills, OH 44131-3720. Phone: (216)524-0019; Email: pgnexecutivedirector@gmail.com • URL: http://www.phigammanu.com • Professional fraternity - business administration and economics.

**Phi Theta Pi**. 6552 Bradford Dr. West Des Moines, IA 50266-2308. Phone: (515)440-2045 or (515)271-1540; Email: ptpfrat@mchsi.com • URL: http://www.phithetapi.org • Honorary fraternity of businessmen and women (includes faculty members).

***Philadelphia Business Journal—Book of Business Lists Issue***. Philadelphia Business Journal, 400 Market St., Ste. 1200 Philadelphia, PA 19106. Phone: (215)238-1450; Fax: (215)238-9489; Email: philadelphia@bizjournals.com • URL: http://www.philadelphia.bizjournals.com • Annual. $65 Individuals print edition; $199.95 Individuals data download; $169.95 Individuals CD. Publication includes: About 89 ranked lists (about 25 names per list) of major public and private businesses and organizations, including banks, brokers, construction companies, hospitals, schools, child-care centers, law firms, hotels, apartment complexes, office parks, architects, ad agencies, and employers in the Philadelphia area. Entries include: For organizations and institutions—Name, location, type of business or service, key personnel, financial facts.

***Philadelphia Business Journal***. Philadelphia Business Journal, 400 Market St., Ste. 1200 Philadelphia, PA 19106. Phone: (215)238-1450; Fax: (215)238-9489; Email: philadelphia@bizjournals.com • URL: http://www.philadelphia.bizjournals.com • Weekly. $105 Individuals print and digital; $105 Individuals digital. Regional and general business newspaper.

**Philatelic Foundation**. 341 W 38th St., 5th Fl. New York, NY 10018-9692. Phone: (212)221-6555; Fax: (212)221-6208; Email: philatelicfoundation@verizon.net • URL: http://www.philatelicfoundation.org • Educational institution chartered by New York State Department of Education for philatelic study and research. Offers philatelic slide programs as an educational aid for schools, organized youth groups, and stamp clubs. Renders opinions on stamps and other philatelic material. Prepares exhibitions for stamp shows.

***Philippine-European Business Directory***. European Chamber of Commerce of the Philippines, Axa Life Center, 19th Fl., Sen. Gil Puyat Ave., corner Tindalo St. Makati City 1200, Philippines. Phone: 63 2 8451324; Fax: 63 2 7596680; Email: info@eccp.com • URL: http://www.eccp.com • 2,600 ₱ Nonmembers hard copy; 2,670 ₱ Nonmembers hard copy (deliver within Philippines); 3,000 ₱ Nonmembers PDF copy; 2,565.89 ₱ Nonmembers courier charge to Netherlands; Free members only. Covers: 750 European business in the Philippines. Entries include: Contact details of each member.

***Philippine Review of Economics and Business***. University of the Philippines College of Business Administration, Diliman Quezon City 1128, Philippines. Phone: 63 29284571 • Semiannual. Journal covering research work and articles about Philippine economic and business conditions.

***Philippines Business Directory***. Philippine Editors and Publishers, PO Box 3199 Manila D-406, Philippines. • Annual. $75. Covers: 15,000 business and trade organizations, professional associations, civic groups, manufacturers, wholesalers, and distributors. Entries include: name, address, phone, telex.

***Philippines Business Forecast Report***. Telecommunications Insight, 85 Queen Victoria St. London EC4V 4AB, United Kingdom. Phone: 20 72 465100 or 44 20 7248 0468; Fax: 20 72 480467 or 44 20 7248 0467; Email: enquiries@telecomsinsight.com • URL: http://www.telecomsinsight.com • Quarterly. $1,195 Individuals Single user; $1,795 Individuals Up to 3 users. Business forecasting reports for the Phillipines.

***Philippines Business Law Handbook***. International Business Publications, USA, PO Box 15343 Washington, DC 20003. Phone: (202)546-2103; Fax: (202)546-3275; Email: ibpusa@comcast.net • URL: http://ibpus.com • $99.95 Individuals hardcopy, e-book, CD-ROM. Covers: Information on basic business legislation, laws and regulations affecting business, and contacts.

***Philippines Government and Business Contacts Handbook***. International Business Publications, USA, PO Box 15343 Washington, DC 20003. Phone: (202)546-2103; Fax: (202)546-3275; Email: ibpusa@comcast.net • URL: http://ibpus.com • $99.95 Individuals hardcopy, e-book, CD-ROM. Covers: Strategic government and business information, export-import activity in the country, investment, business contacts and regulations.

***Philippines Industrial and Business Directory***. International Business Publications, USA, PO Box 15343 Washington, DC 20003. Phone: (202)546-2103; Fax: (202)546-3275; Email: ibpusa@comcast.net • URL: http://ibpus.com • Annual. $99.95 Individuals hardcopy, e-book, CD-ROM. Covers: Strategic industrial, investment and business contacts for conducting export-import and investment activity in the country.

***Philippines Investment and Business Guide***. International Business Publications, USA, PO Box 15343 Washington, DC 20003. Phone: (202)546-2103; Fax: (202)546-3275; Email: ibpusa@comcast.net • URL: http://ibpus.com • $99.95 Individuals hardcopy, e-book, CD-ROM. Covers: Basic information on economy, export-import and investment climate, regulations and industrial development, banking, and government. Entries include: Important business contacts and business travel.

***PHL Bulletin***. National Institute of Packaging, Handling and Logistics Engineers, 5903 Ridgeway Dr. Grand Prairie, TX 75052. Phone: (937)269-5085 or (937)985-9375; Email: admin@niphle.com • URL: http://www.niphle.com • 6/year.

***Phone Communication Services Directory***. InfoGroup Inc., 5711 S 86th Cir. Omaha, NE 68127-4146. Phone: (402)593-4500 • URL: http://www.infogroup.com • Annual. Number of listings: 5473. Entries include: Name, address, phone, size of advertisement, name of owner or manager, number of employees, year first in "Yellow Pages." Compiled from telephone company "Yellow Pages," nationwide.

***PhoneDisc New York & New England***. PhoneDisc USA Corp., 5711 S 86th Cir. Omaha, NE 68127. Phone: 800-835-5856 or (402)593-4500; Fax: (402)331-5481; Email: info@phonedisc.com • URL: http://www.infousa.com • Monthly. CD-Rom. Database covers: Over 12 million residences and businesses in New York and New England. Database includes: Individual or company name, address, phone, Standard Industrial Classification (SIC) code. Includes residential, business, and government listings supplied by New York and New England telephone companies, along with independent telephone companies within the region.

***PhoneDisc QuickRef***. PhoneDisc USA Corp., 5711 S 86th Cir. Omaha, NE 68127. Phone: 800-835-5856 or (402)593-4500; Fax: (402)331-5481; Email: info@phonedisc.com • URL: http://www.infousa.com • Annual. $69. CD-Rom. Database covers: 100,000 businesses; state, federal, and local governments; libraries; colleges and universities; embassies; law firms; industrial manufacturers; associations; organizations, etc. Database includes: Company or organization name, address, phone, Standard Industrial Classification (SIC) code, annual sales, billings, number of employees. Information is extracted from the "National Directory of Addresses and Telephone Numbers" (see separate entry).

***Phonefacts***. United States Telecom Association, 607 14th St. NW, Ste. 400 Washington, DC 20005. Phone: (202)326-7300; Fax: (202)315-3603 • URL: http://www.ustelecom.org • Annual. Members, $5.00; non-members, $10.00. Presents basic statistics on the independent telephone industry in the U. S.

***Phonolog***. Muze, Inc., 304 Hudson St., 8th Floor New York, NY 10013. Phone: 800-456-7838 or (212)824-0300; Fax: (212)741-1246; Email: custsrv@muze.com • URL: http://www.muze.com • Annual. $550.00. 10 volumes. Provides detailed information on more than 370,000 titles of commercially available and out-of-print music recordings. Includes popular, jazz, and classical titles.

***Photo Copying Directory***. InfoGroup Inc., 5711 S 86th Cir. Omaha, NE 68127-4146. Phone: (402)593-4500 • URL: http://www.infogroup.com • Annual. Number of listings: 20,946. Entries include: Name, address, phone (including area code), size of advertisement, year first in "Yellow Pages," name of owner or manager, number of employees. Compiled from telephone company "Yellow Pages," nationwide.

***Photo Marketing***. Professional School Photographers Association International, 3000 Picture Pl. Jackson, MI 49201. Phone: 800-762-9287 or (517)788-8100; Fax: (517)788-8371; Email: m.bell@bellphoto.com • URL: http://www.pmai.org • Monthly. Membership.

**Photographic Society of America**. 8421 S Walker Ave., Ste. 104 Oklahoma City, OK 73139. Phone: 855-772-4636 or (405)843-1437; Email: hq@psa-photo.org • URL: http://www.psa-photo.org • Camera clubs; amateur, advanced amateur photographers. Sponsors competitions. Conducts slide and print contests, provides instruction slide sets, slide analysis, print portfolios, and other technical services.

**Photoimaging Manufacturers and Distributors Association**. 7600 Jericho Tpke., Ste. 301 Woodbury, NY 11797. Phone: (516)802-0895; Fax: (516)364-0140 • URL: http://www.pmda.com • Formerly Photographic Manufacturers and Distributors Association.

***Photonics Spectra***. Laurin Publishing Company Inc., 2 S St. Pittsfield, MA 01201-4949. Phone: 800-553-0051 or (413)499-0514; Fax: (413)442-3180; Email: photonics@laurin.com • URL: http://www.photonics.com • Monthly. Serves as a network among engineers, scientists and end users who develop, commercialize and buy photonics products. Provides both technical and practical information for every aspect of the global industry, integrating all segments of photonics.

***Photovoltaic Module Retail Businesses in the World***. Momentum Technologies L.L.C., PO Box 460813 Glendale, CO 80246.

Phone: (303)229-4841; Fax: (408)705-2031 • URL: http://www.mtt.com • Contains 811 directory listings of retail businesses throughout the world that supply photovoltaic modules and associated energy equipment. Includes business name, address, phone number, fax number, e-mail address, and web site address. Includes brief descriptions of product lines, services offered, and business type. Provides keyword search functions.

*Physical Fitness Center*. Entrepreneur Press, 2445 McCabe Way, Ste. 400 Irvine, CA 92614-6244. Phone: 800-864-6864 or (949)261-2325 or (949)622-7131; Fax: (949)261-7729 or (949)261-0234; Email: press@entrepreneur.com • URL: http://www.entrepreneurpress.com • Looseleaf. $59.50. A practical guide to starting a physical fitness center. Covers profit potential, start-up costs, market size evaluation, owner's time required, site selection, lease negotiation, pricing, accounting, advertising, promotion, etc. (Start-Up Business Guide No. E1172.).

**Physician Insurers Association of America**. 2275 Research Blvd., Ste. 250 Rockville, MD 20850. Phone: (301)947-9000; Fax: (301)947-9090 • URL: http://www.piaa.us • Members are cooperative physicians' professional liability insurers affiliated with state medical societies.

*Physicians & Computers*. Moorhead Publications Inc., 810 Waukegan Rd., Ste. 200 Lake Forest, IL 60045. Phone: (708)940-8333 or (847)615-8333; Fax: (708)615-8345 or (847)615-8345 • Monthly. $40.00 per year. Includes material on computer diagnostics, online research, medical and non-medical software, computer equipment, and practice management.

*Physicians' Desk Reference for Ophthalmology*. Medical Economics Co., Five Paragon Dr. Montvale, NJ 07645-1742. Phone: 800-442-6657 or (973)944-7777 or (973)944-9777; Fax: (973)847-5390 or (973)-944-5390; Email: customer.service@medec.com • URL: http://www.medec.com • Annual. $49.95. Provides detailed descriptions of ophthalmological instrumentation, equipment, supplies, lenses, and prescription drugs. Indexed by manufacturer, product name, product category, active drug ingredient, and instrumentation. Editorial discussion is included.

*Physicians' Desk Reference*. Medical Economics Co., Five Paragon Dr. Montvale, NJ 07645-1742. Phone: 800-442-6657 or (973)944-7777 or (973)944-9777; Fax: (973)847-5390 or (973)-944-5390; Email: customer.service@medec.com • URL: http://www.medec.com • Annual. $82.95. Generally known as "PDR." Provides detailed descriptions, effects, and adverse reactions for about 4,000 prescription drugs. Includes data on more than 250 drug manufacturers, with brand name and generic name indexes and drug identification photographs. Discontinued drugs are also listed.

*Physician's Marketing and Management*. AHC Media, 950 E Paces Ferry Rd. NE Atlanta, GA 30326. Phone: 800-688-2421 or (404)262-5476; Fax: (404)262-5560; Email: editorial_questions@ahcmedia.com • URL: http://www.ahcmedia.com • Monthly. Individuals, $299.00 per year; institutions, $323.00 per year. Newsletter. Formerly *Physician's Marketing*.

**Pi Omega Pi**. Box 9730 Mississippi State, MS 39762. Phone: (662)325-7528; Fax: (662)325-1837; Email: cforde@colled.msstate.edu • URL: http://catpages.nwmissouri.edu/m/oisbe/piomegapi • Purpose Honor society - men and women, business education.

*PICA Bulletin: News and Analysis for the Personal Communication Industry*. PCIA - The Wireless Infrastucture Association, 500 Montgomery St., Ste. 500 Alexandria, VA 22314. Phone: (703)535-7492; Fax: (703)836-1608; Email: membership@pcia.com • URL: http://www.pcia.com • Weekly. $550.00 per year.

*Picture Framing Magazine*. Hobby Publications, Inc., 83 South St., Ste. 307 Freehold, NJ 07728. Phone: (732)536-5160; Fax: (732)536-5761 • URL: http://www.hobbypub.com • Monthly. $20 per year. Published for retailers, wholesalers, and manufacturers of picture frames.

*Pimsleur's Checklists of Basic American Legal Publications*. American Association of Law Libraries. Fred B. Rothman and Co., 2350 N Forest Rd. Getzville, NY 14068-1296. Phone: 888-361-3255 or (303)979-5657; Fax: (303)979-0707 • URL: http://www.wshein.com • $295 Individuals 3 volumes Looseleaf. Authoritative bibliographic source in any library having an interest in our legal process.

**Pine Chemicals Association**. PO Box 17136 Fernandina Beach, FL 32035. Phone: (404)994-6267 • URL: http://www.pinechemicals.org • Represents manufacturers of chemical products (other than pulp, paper and paper products) produced by, or from, wood pulp industry products. Sponsors educational and management meetings. Collects statistical data.

*Pine Chemicals Review*. Kriedt Enterprises Ltd., 3803 Cleveland Ave. New Orleans, LA 70119. Phone: 888-884-4114 or (504)482-3914; Fax: (504)482-4205 • URL: http://www.louisianacookin.com/kriedt.htm • Bimonthly. $110 Individuals; $145 Other countries. Formerly *Forest Chemicals Review*.

*The Pink Sheet: Prescription Pharmaceuticals and Biotechnology*. Elsevier Business Intelligence, 5635 Fishers Ln., Ste. 6000 Rockville, MD 20852. Phone: 800-332-2181 or (240)221-4500 or (800)332-2181; Fax: (240)221-4400 or (301)656-3094; Email: fdc.customer.service@fdcreports.com

• URL: http://www.elsevierbi.com • 51 times a year. Institutions, $1,431.00 per year. Newsletter covering business and regulatory developments affecting the pharmaceutical and biotechnology industries. Provides information on generic drug approvals and includes a drug sector stock index.

*Pipe Line and Gas Industry: Crude Oil and Products Pipelines, Gas Transmission and Gas Distribution*. Gulf Publishing Co., 2 Greenway Plz., Ste. 1020 Houston, TX 77046-0208. Phone: 800-231-6275 or (713)529-4301 or (713)525-4626; Fax: (713)520-4433; Email: customerservices@gulfpub.com • URL: http://www.gulfpub.com • Monthly. Free to qualified personnel; others, $29.00 per year. International edition available.

**Pipe Line Contractors Association**. 1700 Pacific Ave., Ste. 4100 Dallas, TX 75201-4675. Phone: (214)969-2700; Email: plca@plca.org • URL: http://www.plca.org • Contractors of mainline cross-country pipeline. Associate members are equipment manufacturers, suppliers, and dealers. Represents the industry in labor negotiations.

*Pipeline and Gas Journal: Energy Construction, Transportation and Distribution*. Oildom Publishing Company of Texas Inc., 1160 Dairy Ashford Rd., Ste. 610 Houston, TX 77079. Phone: (281)558-6930; Fax: (281)558-7029; Email: ginfo@undergroundinfo.com • URL: http://www.oildompublishing.com • Monthly. $33.00 per year. Covers engineering and operating methods on cross-country pipelines that transport crude oil products and natural gas. Includes *Energy Management Report*. Incorporates *Pipeline*.

*Pit and Quarry*. Advanstar Communications, 641 Lexington Ave., 8th Fl. New York, NY 10022. Phone: 800-346-0085 or (212)951-6600; Fax: (212)951-6793; Email: info@advanstar.com • URL: http://www.advanstar.com • Monthly. Covers crushed stone, sand and gravel, etc.

*Pizzeria*. Entrepreneur Press, 2445 McCabe Way, Ste. 400 Irvine, CA 92614-6244. Phone: 800-864-6864 or (949)261-2325 or (949)622-7131; Fax: (949)261-7729 or (949)261-0234; Email: press@entrepreneur.com • URL: http://www.entrepreneurpress.com • Looseleaf. $59.50. A practical guide to starting a pizza shop. Covers profit potential, start-up costs, market size evaluation, owner's time required, site selection, lease negotiation, pricing, accounting, advertising, promotion, etc. (Start-Up Business Guide No. E1006.).

*Plan Sponsor*. Asset International, Inc., 125 Greenwich Ave. Greenwich, CT 06830. Phone: (203)629-5014; Fax: (203)629-5024 • Monthly. Edited for professional pension plan managers and executives. Defined contribution plans are emphasized.

**Plan Sponsor Council of America**. 20 N Wacker Dr., Ste. 3700 Chicago, IL 60606. Phone: (312)419-1863; Fax: (312)419-1864; Email: psca@psca.org • URL: http://www.psca.org • Members are business firms with profit sharing and/or 401(K) plans. Affiliated with the Profit Sharing/401(K) Education Foundation. Formerly Profit Sharing Council of America.

*Plane and Pilot*. Werner Publishing Corp., 12121 Wilshire Blvd., 12th Fl. Los Angeles, CA 90025. Phone: 800-283-4330 or (310)820-1500; Fax: (310)826-5008; Email: editors@planeandpilotmag.com • URL: http://www.wernerpublishing.com • 11/year. $14.97 per year.

*PlaNet Finance US*. 44 rue de Prony 75017 Paris, France. Email: contact@planetfinance.org • URL: http://www.planetfinance.org • Works to alleviate poverty through the development of microfinance. Seeks to support and strengthen the capacity of the microfinance sector. Raises public awareness of microfinancing.

*Planning*. American Planning Association, 205 N Michigan Ave., Ste. 1200 Chicago, IL 60601. Phone: (312)431-9100; Fax: (312)786-6700; Email: customerservice@planning.org • URL: http://www.planning.org • Monthly. Free members; $85 Nonmembers.

*Planning and Zoning News*. Planning & Zoning Center Inc., 715 N Cedar St., Ste. 2 Lansing, MI 48906-5275. Phone: (517)886-0555; Fax: (517)886-0564 • URL: http://www.pzcenter.com • Monthly. $185 per year. Newsletter on planning and zoning issues in the United States.

*Planning Cash Flow*. American Management Association Extension Institute, 1601 Broadway New York, NY 10019. Phone: 800-262-9699 or (518)586-8100; Fax: (518)903-8168 • Looseleaf. $139.00. Self-study course. Emphasis is on practical explanations, examples, and problem solving. Quizzes and a case study are included.

*Planning for Your Retirement: IRA and Keogh Plans*. Wolters Kluwer Law & Business CCH, 2700 Lake Cook Rd. Riverwoods, IL 60015. Phone: 888-224-7377 or (847)267-7000; Email: cust_serv@cch.com • URL: http://www.cchgroup.com • Annual.

*Planning Guide*. Ypsilanti Convention and Visitors Bureau, 106 W Michigan Ave. Ypsilanti, MI 48197. Phone: (734)483-4444 • URL: http://www.ypsilanti.org • Annual. Contains a resource guide for meetings.

*Planning Your Future: Resources on Careers and Higher Education*. AMIDEAST Publications, 1730 M St. NW, Ste. 1100 Washington, DC 20036-4505. Phone: 800-368-5720 or (202)776-9600; Fax: (202)776-7000; Email: inquiries@amideast.org • URL: http://www.amideast.org • Irregular. $29.95 Individuals first class mail; $13 Other countries international mail. Covers: over 1,000 printed and electronic sources of information on education and training for approximately 150 careers, including accredited programs,

nontraditional education, internships, and disabled student services. Entries include: Title name, date of publication, order address.

*Plant Engineering*. CFE Media LLC, 1111 W 22nd St., Ste. 250 Oak Brook, IL 60523. Phone: (630)571-4070; Fax: (630)214-4504 • URL: http://www.cfemedia.com/ • Monthly. $145; $180 Canada. Includes *Plant Engineering Product Supplier Guide*.

*Plant Science Bulletin*. St. Louis Univeristy Department of Biology, Macelwane Hall, 3507 Laclede Ave. Saint Louis, MO 63103. Phone: (314)977-3900; Fax: (314)977-3658; Email: custserv@magnapubs.com • URL: http://www.bio.slu.edu • Description: Carries news of this Association of plant scientists, with some issues including brief articles of more general interest in the field. Recurring features include notices of awards, meetings, courses, and study and professional opportunities; annotated lists of botanical books; and book reviews.

*Plant Services*. Putman Media Inc., 555 W Pierce Rd., Ste. 301 Itasca, IL 60143-2649. Phone: (630)467-1301 or (630)467-1300; Fax: (630)467-1120 or (630)467-1109; Email: controlroundup@putman.net • URL: http://www.putman.net • Monthly.

*Plant Shutdowns Monitor*. DataCenter, 1904 Franklin St., Ste. 900 Oakland, CA 94612. Phone: (510)835-4692; Fax: (510)835-3017; Email: datacenter@datacenter.org • URL: http://www.datacenter.org • Monthly. $450 per year for profit organizations; $340 per year for nonprofit organizations. Provides monthly listings of United States plant and business closures, layoffs, corporate downsizing and moves, organized by company involved; includes event location, industry, number of workers involved, explanatory notes.

*Plants, Sites, and Parks*. Reed Elsevier Group plc Reed Business Information, 360 Park Ave. S New York, NY 11010. Phone: (212)791-4208; Email: corporatecommunications@reedbusiness.com • URL: http://www.reedbusiness.com • Seven times a year. Free to qualified personnel; others, $43.90 per year. Covers economic development, site location, industrial parks, and industrial development programs.

*Plastics Digest on CD-ROM*. IHS Standards Store, 15 Inverness Way E Englewood, CO 80112. Phone: 800-854-7179 or (303)397-7956 or (303)792-2181; Fax: (303)397-2740 or (303)754-4033; Email: global@ihs.com • URL: http://global.ihs.com • Semiannual. CD-ROM index version (technical data only), $695.00 per year or $495.00 per disc. CD-ROM image version (technical data and specification sheet images), $1,295.00 per year or $995.00 per disc. Provides detailed information on the properties of 20,000 types of plastic, both current and obsolete. Time period is 1977 to date. Includes trade names and supplier names and addresses.

*Plastics Engineering*. Society of Plastics Engineers, 13 Church Hill Rd. Newtown, CT 06470. Phone: (203)775-0471; Fax: (203)775-8490; Email: info@4spe.org • URL: http://www.4spe.org • 10/year. $142 Nonmembers; $242 Nonmembers outside North America; $180 Institutions corporate library; $280 Institutions corporate library outside North America; included in membership dues; $160 /year for nonmembers. Plastics trade magazine.

*Plastics Hot Line: The Nation's Marketplace for Plastics Processing Equipment & Materials, Business and Employment Opportunities*. IMS L.L.C., 809 Central Ave., 2nd Fl. Fort Dodge, IA 50501. Phone: 888-247-2007 or (515)574-2248 • URL: http://www.industrymarketingsolutions.com/ • Monthly. Trade magazine.

**Plastics Institute of America**. 1 University Ave. Lowell, MA 01854. Phone: (978)934-2575; Fax: (978)934-3089; Email: contactus@plasticsinstitute.org • URL: http://www.plasticsinstitute.org • Serves as an educational and research organization supported on a cooperative basis by companies in the plastics and allied industries. Conducts fundamental research in plastics science and engineering and supports educational activities at the graduate school level in these fields. Provides comprehensive technical information to its members. Conducts a graduate level program of education for plastics scientists and engineers, in cooperation with major U.S. universities and colleges involved in polymer science and engineering.

*Plastics News*. Crain Communications, Inc., 1725 Merriman Rd., Suite 300 Akron, OH 44313-5283. Phone: 800-678-9595 or (330)836-9180; Email: info@crain.com • URL: http://www.crain.com • Weekly. $89 per year. Features articles regarding commercial, financial, legislative and market-related developments worldwide that affect North American plastic product manufacturers and their suppliers and customers.

**Plastics Pipe Institute**. 105 Decker Ct., Ste. 825 Irving, TX 75062. Phone: (469)499-1044; Fax: (469)499-1063 • URL: http://plasticpipe.org • Manufacturers of plastic pipe and fittings and suppliers of plastic pipe raw materials. Develops technical reports and promotes trade and user acceptance. Compiles statistics; offers research programs. Conducts periodic training seminar on plastic piping.

*Plastics Recognized Component Directory: Polymeric Materials, Processes, and Systems*. Underwriters Laboratories Inc., 333 Pfingsten Rd. Northbrook, IL 60062-2096. Phone: 877-854-3577 or (847)664-3035; Fax: (847)664-6243; Email: cec@us.ul.com • URL: http://www.ul.com/global/eng/pages/ • Annual. $220 Individuals electronic CD version. Covers: Companies that have qualified to use the UL recognized component marking on or in connection with materials that have been found to be in compliance with UL's requirements. Coverage includes foreign companies that manufacture for distribution in the U.S. Entries include: Company name, city, ZIP code, UL file number, type of product.

***Plastics Technology: The Only Magazine for Plastics Processors***. Nielsen Business Media Inc., 770 Broadway New York, NY 10003-9522. Phone: 866-890-8541 or (646)654-4500 or (646)654-5000; Fax: (646)654-5584 or (646)654-4500; Email: bmcomm@nielsen.com • URL: http://www.nielsenbusinessmedia.com • 13 times a year. Free to qualified personnel; others, $89.00 per year.

***Plastics Week: The Global Newsletter***. McGraw Hill Financial Inc., 1221 Avenue of the Americas New York, NY 10020-1095. Phone: (212)512-2000; Fax: (212)512-3840 • URL: http://www.mhfi.com • Weekly. $530.00 per year. Newsletter. Covers international trends in plastics production, technology, research, and legislation.

***Plating and Surface Finishing: Electroplating, Finishing of Metals, Organic Finishing***. American Electroplaters and Surface Finishers Society, 12644 Research Parkway Orlando, FL 32826-3298. Phone: 800-334-2052 or (407)281-6441; Fax: (407)281-6446; Email: editors@aesf.org • URL: http://www.aesf.org • Monthly. Members, $16.00 per year; non-members, $60.00 per year.

***Platt's Directory of Electric Power Producers and Distributors***. Platts Global Energy, 2 Penn Plz., 25th Fl. New York, NY 10121-2298. Phone: 800-752-8878 or (212)904-3070 or (212)904-2977; Fax: (212)904-3070 or (212)904-4209; Email: support@platts.com • URL: http://www.platts.com • Annual. $495 hardcopy; $1,500 mailing list and hardcopy; $2,500 statistical files. Over 3,500 investor-owned, municipal, rural cooperative and government electric utility systems in the U.S. and Canada. Formerly *Directory of Electric Power Producers and Distributors*.

***Platt's Metals Week***. Platts Global Energy, 2 Penn Plz., 25th Fl. New York, NY 10121-2298. Phone: 800-752-8878 or (212)904-3070 or (212)904-2977; Fax: (212)904-3070 or (212)904-4209; Email: support@platts.com • URL: http://www.platts.com • Weekly. $770 Individuals.

***Platt's Oilgram News***. The McGraw-Hill Companies Inc., PO Box 182604 Columbus, OH 43272. Phone: 877-833-5524 or (212)512-2000 or (212)904-2000; Fax: (614)759-3749 or (212)512-3840; Email: webmaster@mcgraw-hill.com • URL: http://www.mcgraw-hill.com • Daily. $3,990 basic; $6,080 enhanced access. Description: Monitors the latest developments in the politics and economics of petroleum. Covers exploration, production, supply and transportation, refining, and marketing. Recurring features include interviews, news of research, and reports of meetings. Coverage is global in scope.

***Platt's Oilgram Price Report: an International Daily Oil-Gas Price and Marketing Letter***. Platts Global Energy, 2 Penn Plz., 25th Fl. New York, NY 10121-2298. Phone: 800-752-8878 or (212)904-3070 or (212)904-2977; Fax: (212)904-3070 or (212)904-4209; Email: support@platts.com • URL: http://www.platts.com • Daily. $19,995 Individuals. Prices and marketing intelligence for petroleum products. Includes weekly statistical summaries. Worldwide coverage.

***Playthings: For Today's Merchandiser of Toys, Hobbies and Crafts***. Reed Elsevier Group plc Reed Business Information, 360 Park Ave. S New York, NY 11010. Phone: (212)791-4208; Email: corporatecommunications@reedbusiness.com • URL: http://www.reedbusiness.com • Monthly. $39.95 per year. Includes annual *Directory*. Covers the major toy and hobby categories, industry news and news products.

***PlugIn Datamation: Profit and Value from Information Technology***. EarthWeb, 23 Old Kings Highway Darien, CT 06820. Phone: (617)303-7906; Fax: (617)345-5486; Email: info@earthweb.com • URL: http://www.earthweb.com • Monthly. Price on application. Technical, semi-technical and general news covering EDP topics.

**Plumbing and Drainage Institute**. 800 Turnpike St., Ste. 300 North Andover, MA 01845. Phone: 800-589-8956 or (978)557-0720; Email: pdi@pdionline.org • URL: http://www.pdionline.org • Formerly Plumbing and Drainage Manufacturers Association.

***Plumbing Business Owner***. Cahaba Media Group, 1900 28th Ave. S Birmingham, AL 35209. Phone: (205)212-9402 • URL: http://www.cahabamedia.com/ • Monthly. Business magazine for plumbers.

***Plumbing Engineer—Product Directory Issue: Engineered Plumbing Systems Directory***. TMB Publishing Inc., 1838 Techny Ct. Northbrook, IL 60062. Phone: (847)564-1127 • URL: http://www.plumbingengineer.com • Monthly. $50 Individuals one year. Covers: Over 400 plumbing products from approximately 250 manufacturers. Database includes: List of American Society of Plumbing Engineers (ASPE) national officers, industry associations. Entries include: Company name, phone, fax, website, and e-mail; name of engineering contact with the firm.

***Plumbing Fixtures***. U. S. Bureau of the Census, 4600 Silver Hill Rd. Washington, DC 20233-0001. Phone: (301)763-4636; Email: comments@census.gov • URL: http://www.census.gov • Quarterly and annual. Provides data on shipments: value, quantity, imports, and exports. Includes both metal and plastic fixtures. (Current Industrial Reports, MQ-34E.).

***Plumbing Systems and Design***. American Society of Plumbing Engineers, 2980 S River Rd. Des Plaines, IL 60018. Phone: (847)296-0002; Fax: (773)695-9007; Email: info@aspe.org • URL: http://www.aspe.org • 10 times per year.

***Plunkett's Airline, Hotel, and Travel Industry Almanac***. Plunkett Research Ltd., 4102 Bellaire Blvd. Houston, TX 77025-1004. Phone: (713)932-0000; Fax: (713)932-7080; Email: customersupport@plunkettresearch.com • URL: http://www.plunkettresearch.com • Annual. $349.99. Contains profiles of 300 leading companies, including airlines, hotels, travel agencies, theme parks, cruise lines, casinos, and car rental companies.

***Plunkett's Automobile Industry Almanac***. Plunkett Research Ltd., 4102 Bellaire Blvd. Houston, TX 77025-1004. Phone: (713)932-0000; Fax: (713)932-7080; Email: customersupport@plunkettresearch.com • URL: http://www.plunkettresearch.com • $349.99 Individuals print + online; one-year subscription. Covers: 300 leading companies in the automotive industry. Entries include: Name, address, phone, fax, and key executives. Also includes analysis and information on trends, technology, and statistics in the field.

***Plunkett's Biotech and Genetics Industry Almanac***. Plunkett Research Ltd., 4102 Bellaire Blvd. Houston, TX 77025-1004. Phone: (713)932-0000; Fax: (713)932-7080; Email: customersupport@plunkettresearch.com • URL: http://www.plunkettresearch.com • Annual. $349.99 Individuals. Provides detailed profiles of 400 leading biotech corporations. Includes information on current trends and research in the field of biotechnology/genetics.

***Plunkett's Companion to the Almanac of American Employers: Mid-Size Firms***. Plunkett Research Ltd., 4102 Bellaire Blvd. Houston, TX 77025-1004. Phone: (713)932-0000; Fax: (713)932-7080; Email: customersupport@plunkettresearch.com • URL: http://www.plunkettresearch.com • Annual. $349.99 Individuals Printed Almanac & Online Tools. Covers: Approximately 500 rapidly growing mid-sized firms, defined as between 150 and 2,300 employees. Entries include: Name, address, phone, fax, and key executives.

***Plunkett's Consulting Industry Almanac***. Plunkett Research Ltd., 4102 Bellaire Blvd. Houston, TX 77025-1004. Phone: (713)932-0000; Fax: (713)932-7080; Email: customersupport@plunkettresearch.com • URL: http://www.plunkettresearch.com • $349.99 Individuals pint + online. Covers: Leading companies that provide consulting in areas including marketing, technology, management, manufacturing, and health care. Entries include: Name, address, phone, fax, and key executives. Also includes analysis and information on trends, technology, and statistics in the field.

***Plunkett's E-Commerce & Internet Business Almanac: Your Reference Source to All Facets of the Internet Business***. Plunkett Research Ltd., 4102 Bellaire Blvd. Houston, TX 77025-1004. Phone: (713)932-0000; Fax: (713)932-7080; Email: customersupport@plunkettresearch.com • URL: http://www.plunkettresearch.com • Biennial. $349.99 Individuals ebook, print and CD-ROM. Covers 400 of the largest companies working in all facets of e-commerce and Internet business, including Internet service providers, Web site operators, equipment and others.

***Plunkett's E-Commerce & Internet Business Almanac***. Plunkett Research Ltd., 4102 Bellaire Blvd. Houston, TX 77025-1004. Phone: (713)932-0000; Fax: (713)932-7080; Email: customersupport@plunkettresearch.com • URL: http://www.plunkettresearch.com • Contains comprehensive information on current trends and developments in electronic commerce and Internet business.

***Plunkett's E-Commerce and Internet Business Almanac***. Plunkett Research Ltd., 4102 Bellaire Blvd. Houston, TX 77025-1004. Phone: (713)932-0000; Fax: (713)932-7080; Email: customersupport@plunkettresearch.com • URL: http://www.plunkettresearch.com • Annual. $349.99. Contains detailed profiles of 250 large companies engaged in various areas of Internet commerce, including e-business Web sites, communications equipment manufacturers, and Internet service providers. Includes CD-ROM.

***Plunkett's Employers' Internet Sites with Careers Information***. Plunkett Research Ltd., 4102 Bellaire Blvd. Houston, TX 77025-1004. Phone: (713)932-0000; Fax: (713)932-7080; Email: customersupport@plunkettresearch.com • URL: http://www.plunkettresearch.com • Annual. $199.99. Includes diskette.

***Plunkett's Engineering and Research Industry Almanac: The Only Complete Guide to the Business of Research, Development, and Engineering***. Plunkett Research Ltd., 4102 Bellaire Blvd. Houston, TX 77025-1004. Phone: (713)932-0000; Fax: (713)932-7080; Email: customersupport@plunkettresearch.com • URL: http://www.plunkettresearch.com • Annual. $349.99 Individuals eBook, print and CD-ROM. Covers 500 of the largest companies involved in research, engineering and development in the biotech, electronics, aerospace and infotech industries.

***Plunkett's Engineering and Research Industry Almanac***. Plunkett Research Ltd., 4102 Bellaire Blvd. Houston, TX 77025-1004. Phone: (713)932-0000; Fax: (713)932-7080; Email: customersupport@plunkettresearch.com • URL: http://www.plunkettresearch.com • Annual. $349.99. Contains detailed profiles of major engineering and technology corporations. Includes CD-ROM.

***Plunkett's Financial Services Industry Almanac: The Only Complete Guide to the Technologies and Companies Changing the Way the World Banks, Invest and Borrows***. Plunkett Research Ltd., 4102 Bellaire Blvd. Houston, TX 77025-1004. Phone: (713)932-0000; Fax: (713)932-7080; Email: customersupport@plunkettresearch.com • URL: http://www.plunkettresearch.com • Annual. $249.99 plus $9.50 shipping (includes CD-ROM). Covers: 500 of the largest investment, banking, and financial companies. Entries include: Firm name, address, phone, fax; description; and leading executives with their titles, addresses, phone numbers, E-mail addresses, Web sites, and fax numbers.

***Plunkett's Food Industry Almanac***. Plunkett Research Ltd., 4102 Bellaire Blvd. Houston, TX 77025-1004. Phone: (713)932-0000; Fax: (713)932-7080; Email: customersupport@plunkettresearch.com • URL: http://www.plunkettresearch.com • $349.99 Individuals print + online. Covers: 340 leading companies in the global food industry. Entries include: Name, address, phone, fax, and key executives. Also includes analysis and information on trends, technology, and statistics in the field.

***Plunkett's On-Line Trading, Finance, and Investment Web Sites Almanac***. Plunkett Research Ltd., 4102 Bellaire Blvd. Houston, TX 77025-1004. Phone: (713)932-0000; Fax: (713)932-7080; Email: customersupport@plunkettresearch.com • URL: http://www.plunkettresearch.com • Annual. $149.99. Provides profiles and usefulness rankings of financial Web sites. Sites are rated from 1 to 5 for specific uses. Includes CD-ROM.

***Plunkett's Retail Industry Almanac: Complete Profiles on the Retail 500: The Leading Firms in Retail Stores, Services, Catalogs, and On-Line Sales***. Plunkett Research Ltd., 4102 Bellaire Blvd. Houston, TX 77025-1004. Phone: (713)932-0000; Fax: (713)932-7080; Email: customersupport@plunkettresearch.com • URL: http://www.plunkettresearch.com • Annual. $349.99 Individuals print. Covers: 500 of the largest retail stores, services, catalogs, and on-line sales companies. Entries include: Firm name, address, phone, fax; description; and leading executives with their titles, addresses, phone numbers, fax numbers, E-mail addresses, and Web sites.

***Plunkett's Telecommunications Industry Almanac: Your Reference Source to All Facets of the Telecom Business***. Plunkett Research Ltd., 4102 Bellaire Blvd. Houston, TX 77025-1004. Phone: (713)932-0000; Fax: (713)932-7080; Email: customersupport@plunkettresearch.com • URL: http://www.plunkettresearch.com • Biennial. $349.99 Individuals eBook, print and CD-ROM. Covers: 500 of the largest companies involved in telecommunications. Entries include: Name, address, phone, fax, names and titles of key personnel, subsidiary and branch names and locations, financial data, salaries and benefits, description of products/services, overview of company culture/activities.

***Plymouth County Business Review***. Plymouth County Development Council, 134 Court St. Plymouth, MA 02360. Phone: (508)747-0100; Fax: (508)747-3118; Email: admin@seeplymouth.com • URL: http://www.seeplymouth.com • Semiannual. $2 Free to qualified subscribers; $2 Single issue. Trade business review covering regional business trends and stories.

***PM Directory & Reference Issue: Plumbers Buyers Guide***. BNP Media, 2401 W Big Beaver Rd., Ste. 700 Troy, MI 48084. Phone: 800-952-6643 or (248)362-3700 or (847)763-9534; Fax: (248)362-5103 or (248)362-0317; Email: privacy@bnpmedia.com • URL: http://www.bnpmedia.com • Annual. Covers: Manufacturers, wholesalers, products, consultants, and manufacturers' representatives in the industries of plumbing, piping, and hydronic heating. Entries include: Contact name, company, address, phone, fax, and product descriptions.

***Podiatry Management***. Kane Communications Inc., 10 E Athens Ave., Ste. 208 Ardmore, PA 19003. Phone: (610)645-6940; Fax: (610)645-6943; Email: sounovmag@aol.com • URL: http://www.kanec.com • 9/year. $38. Non-clinical subject matter.

**Point-of-Purchase Advertising International**. 440 N Wells St., Ste. 740 Chicago, IL 60654. Phone: (312)863-2900; Fax: (312)229-1152; Email: info@popai.de • URL: http://www.popai.com • Producers and suppliers of point-of-purchase advertising signs and displays and national and regional advertisers and retailers interested in use and effectiveness of signs, displays and other point-of-purchase media. Conducts student education programs; maintains speakers' bureau.

***Poland Business Forecast Report***. Telecommunications Insight, 85 Queen Victoria St. London EC4V 4AB, United Kingdom. Phone: 20 72 465100 or 44 20 7248 0468; Fax: 20 72 480467 or 44 20 7248 0467; Email: enquiries@telecomsinsight.com • URL: http://www.telecomsinsight.com • Quarterly. $1,195 Individuals Single user; $1,795 Individuals Up to 3 users. Business forecast report for Poland.

***Poland Business Services Providers Leads***. Business Information Agency Inc. PlanetInform, 52 Tuscan Way, Ste. 202-181 Saint Augustine, VA 32092. Phone: (904)342-6124; Fax: (904)592-2632; Email: info@biasales.com • URL: http://www.biasales.com • Monthly. $160 Individuals mailing list; $336 Individuals sales list; $570 Individuals marketing list. Covers Polish companies and all sub-industries that provide various services to commercial businesses, establishments, and organizations, including consulting, advertising and marketing services, and facilities maintenance.

***Poland Government and Business Contacts Handbook***. International Business Publications, USA, PO Box 15343 Washington, DC 20003. Phone: (202)546-2103; Fax: (202)546-3275; Email: ibpusa@comcast.net • URL: http://ibpus.com • $99.95 Individuals hardcopy, e-book, CD-ROM. Covers: Strategic government and business information, export-import activity in the country, investment, business contacts and regulations.

***Poland Investment and Business Guide***. International Business Publications, USA, PO Box 15343 Washington, DC 20003. Phone: (202)546-2103; Fax: (202)546-3275; Email: ibpusa@comcast.net • URL: http://ibpus.com • $99.95 Individuals hardcopy, e-book, CD-ROM. Covers: Strategic information on economy, business, export-import and investment climate, opportunities, industrial development, banking and government. Entries include: Business contacts and business travel.

**Poland Ministry of Agriculture and Food Economy - Institute of Agricultural and Food Economics**. ul. Świetokrzyska 20 00-002 Warsaw, Poland. Phone: 48 22 5054444; Fax: 48 22 8271960; Email: andrzej.kowalski@ierigz.waw.pl • URL: http://www.ierigz.waw.pl • Agricultural and food policy, forecasting of agriculture and food economy development, farm and food industry economics, regional analyses, ownership transformations, analysis and prognosis of agricultural and food markets, and social transformation in agricultural and rural populations.

***Police Chief: Professional Voice of Law Enforcement***. International Association of Chiefs of Police, 44 Canal Center Plz., Ste. 200 Alexandria, VA 22314. Phone: 800-THE-IACP or (703)836-6767; Email: information@theiacp.org • URL: http://www.theiacp.org • Monthly. $30 per year; $47 Two years. Subject matter includes information on law enforcement technology and new products.

***Police Misconduct and Civil Rights Law Report***. National Lawyers Guild. Thomson West, 610 Opperman Dr. Eagan, MN 55123. Phone: 800-328-9352 or (651)687-7000 • Bimonthly. $297. Provides expert analysis ot the most current developments in police misconduct and civil rights law.

***Police Science and Technology Review***. Jane's Information Group, Inc., 110 N Royal St., Ste. 200 Alexandria, VA 22314-1651. Phone: 800-836-0297 or (703)683-3700; Fax: (703)836-0029 or (703)863-0029; Email: info.us@janes.con • URL: http://www.janes.com • Quarterly. $57.00 per year. Includes detailed information on technology relating to surveillance, forensics, and fingerprints.

***Police: The Law Enforcement Magazine***. Bobit Publications, 21061 S. Western Ave. Torrance, CA 90501. Phone: (310)533-2400; Fax: (310)533-2500; Email: info@policemag.com • URL: http://www.bobit.com • Monthly. $25 per year. Edited for law enforcement professionals. Includes information on new technology and equipment.

***Policy and Practice of Public Human Services***. American Public Human Services Association, 1133 19th St. NW, Ste. 400 Washington, DC 20036. Phone: (202)682-0100; Fax: (202)289-6555; Email: pubs@aphsa.org • URL: http://www.aphsa.org • Quarterly. $75 /year for nonmembers; $64 /year for members; $95 /year international. Contains articles, research reports, and book reviews about human services and public policy. Formerly *Public Welfare*.

**Polish Academy of Sciences - Institute of Economics**. Staszic Palace, 72 Nowy Świat St., Rm. 266 00-330 Warsaw, Poland. Phone: 48 22 6572707; Fax: 48 22 8267254; Email: inepan@inepan.waw.pl • URL: http://www.inepan.waw.pl/en • Economic theory and policy.

***Polish Business Directory***. Branzowy Katalog Firm-Ravi Sp., ul Mazowiecka 17 PL-50-412 Wroclaw, Poland. Phone: 71 44 67 11; Fax: 71 44 38 96 • Annual. Covers: More than 3,000 companies in Poland. Entries include: Company name, address, phone, name and title of contact, product/service.

***Polish Business Directory for Beginners***. MZM Publications Publishing Promotion Co., PO Box 465 PL 81-705 Sopot, Poland. Phone: 58 55027306; Fax: 58 5513706; Email: mzmpublications@wp.pl • $43 plus s&h. Covers: Polish commercial and diplomatic offices, hotels, publications, central institutions and organizations, advertising and marketing agencies, courts, banks, learning institutions, offices to rent, travel services and other services.

***Polish Companies***. Informationsvermittlungsagentur Waldemar Kubanski, Laubacher Str. 1A D-1000 Berlin, Germany. Phone: 30 8223125; Fax: 30 8223125 • Quarterly. Database covers: Polish companies. Entries include: Company name, address, phone, fax, industrial sector, legal status.

***Polish Industry Directory***. Branzowy Katalog Firm-Ravi Sp., ul Mazowiecka 17 PL-50-412 Wroclaw, Poland. Phone: 71 44 67 11; Fax: 71 44 38 96 • Annual. Covers: More than 10,000 companies in Poland, including leading Polish importers/exporters. Entries include: Company name, address, phone, product/service.

**Polish Private Equity Association**. ul. E Plater 53, 31 pietro 00-113 Warsaw, Poland. Phone: 48 22 4588430; Fax: 48 22 4588555; Email: psik@psik.org.pl • URL: http://www.ppea.org.pl • Promotes and develops the private equity and venture capital industry in Poland. Represents the interests of the Polish private equity and venture capital community in Poland and abroad. Keeps members informed about significant initiatives and proposed changes to the legal, tax and regulatory environment.

**Polish-U.S. Business Council**. Chamber of Commerce of the United States, 1615 H St. NW Washington, DC 20062-2000. Phone: 800-638-6582 or (202)659-6000; Email: press@uschamber.com • URL: http://www.uschamber.com • U.S. corporations involved in industry, agriculture, or services. Seeks to expand trade between the U.S. and Poland, and to encourage investment in Poland by U.S. firms.

***Political Risk Letter***. The PRS Group Inc., 5800 Heritage Landing Dr., Ste. E East Syracuse, NY 13057-9378. Phone: (315)431-0511; Fax: (315)431-0200; Email: custserv@prsgroup.com • URL: http://www.prsgroup.com • Monthly. Description: Offers concise political and economic forecasts for both 18 month and 5 year time spans. Provides country risk forecasts and analysis on 100 countries around the world and provides indepth coverage on 20 countries.

***Political Risk Yearbook***. The PRS Group Inc., 5800 Heritage Landing Dr., Ste. E East Syracuse, NY 13057-9378. Phone: (315)431-0511; Fax: (315)431-0200; Email: custserv@prsgroup.com • URL: http://www.prsgroup.com • Annual. Each volume covers a separate region of the world and assesses economic and political conditions as they relate to the risk of doing business.

***Polling Report: An Independent Survey of Trends Affecting Elections, Government, and Business***. Polling Report Inc., P.O. Box 42580 Washington, DC 20015-0580. Phone: (202)237-2000; Fax: (202)237-2001; Email: editor@pollingreport.com • URL: http://www.pollingreport.com • Biweekly. $195 Individuals. Reports on the results of a wide variety of public opinion polls.

***Pollution A to Z***. Cengage Learning Inc., 20 Channel Center St. Boston, MA 02210. Phone: 800-487-8488 or (617)289-7700; Fax: (617)289-7844; Email: investors@cengage.com • URL: http://www.cengage.com • 2003.Two volumes. Provides encyclopedic coverage of many aspects of environmental pollution, including air, water, noise, and soil. Inquire as to price and availability.

***Pollution Abstracts***. Cambridge Information Group, 7200 Wisconsin Ave., Ste. 601 Bethesda, MD 20814. Phone: 800-526-9537 or (301)961-6700; Fax: (301)961-6790 or (301)961-6720; Email: info@cambridgeinformationgroup.com • URL: http://www.cambridgeinformationgroup.com • Monthly. $1,390.00 per year. Includes print and online editions; with index, $1,515.00 per year.

***Pollution Engineering: Magazine of Environmental Control***. BNP Media, 2401 W Big Beaver Rd., Ste. 700 Troy, MI 48084. Phone: 800-952-6643 or (248)362-3700 or (847)763-9534; Fax: (248)362-5103 or (248)362-0317; Email: privacy@bnpmedia.com • URL: http://www.bnpmedia.com • Monthly. Covers the air, water, waste and remediation environmental concerns in the Pollution Control field.

**Pollution Probe Foundation**. 150 Ferrand Dr., Ste. 208 Toronto, ON, Canada M3C 3E5. Phone: 877-926-1907 or (416)926-1907; Fax: (416)926-1601; Email: pprobe@pollutionprobe.org • URL: http://www.pollutionprobe.org • Works to define environmental problems through research; seeks to raise public awareness of environmental issues through education; lobbies for environmental protection and remediation before government agencies and industrial associations. Focuses on smog and climate change, reduction and elimination of mercury in water, child health and the environment, indoor air quality, and water quality.

***Polymer Engineering and Science***. Society of Plastics Engineers, 13 Church Hill Rd. Newtown, CT 06470. Phone: (203)775-0471; Fax: (203)775-8490; Email: info@4spe.org • URL: http://www.4spe.org • Monthly. $822 Individuals; $2,157 Institutions. Contains proceedings of symposia on such diverse topics as polyblends, mechanics of plastics and polymer welding.

***The Polymer Library***. Rubber and Plastics Research Association of Great Britian. Smithers Rapra Technology, Shawbury Shrewsbury SY4 4NR, United Kingdom. Phone: 44 1939 250383 or 44 1939 250383; Fax: 44 1939 251118; Email: info@smithers.com • URL: http://www.rapra.net • Monthly. $2,700.00 per year. Up-to-date survey of current international information relevant to the rubber, plastics and associated industries.

**Polytechnic University - Center for Advanced Technology in Telecommunications**. 2 MetroTech Ctr., 9th Fl. Brooklyn, NY 11201. Phone: (718)260-3050; Fax: (718)260-3074; Email: info@catt.poly.edu • URL: http://catt.poly.edu • Research fields include active media for optical communication.

**Pontifical Catholic University of Peru - Center for Social, Economic, Political and Anthropological Research**. Av. Universitaria Cdra. 18, San Miguel Lima 32, Peru. Phone: 51 1 6262000; Fax: 51 1 6262815 • URL: http://cisepa.pucp.edu.pe • Social sciences, economy, sociology, anthropology and political sciences.

***Pool and Spa News: The National Trade Magazine for the Swimming Poool & Spa Industry***. DoveTale Publishers, 1 Thomas Cir. NW Washington, DC 20005. Phone: 877-275-8647 or (202)339-0744 or (202)452-0800; Fax: (202)785-1974 or (202)339-0749; Email: hwmicustomerservice@hanleywood.com • URL: http://www.hwmarketintelligence.com • Semimonthly. $19.97. Covers news, product information, business tips, technical information and design ideas for professionals in the pool and spa industry.

***Pool Table Equipment and Supplies Directory***. InfoGroup Inc., 5711 S 86th Cir. Omaha, NE 68127-4146. Phone: (402)593-4500 • URL: http://www.infogroup.com • Annual. Number of listings: 22,706. Entries include: Name, address, phone, size of advertisement, name of owner or manager, number of employees, year first in "Yellow Pages." Compiled from telephone company "Yellow Pages," nationwide.

**Popcorn Board**. 330 N Wabash Ave., Ste. 2000 Chicago, IL 60611. Phone: (312)644-6610; Email: info@popcorn.org • URL: http://www.popcorn.org • Represents companies engaged in popcorn processing and trade management activities as well as government relations. Provides a platform for discussion on the popcorn industry. Maintains hall of fame for retired members who have made contributions to the industry.

***Poptronics***. Gernsback Publications, Inc., 275 Marcus Blvd., Unit G Hauppauge, NY 11788-2022. Phone: (631)592-6720; Fax: (631)592-6723; Email: info@poptronics.com • URL: http://www.gernsback.com • Monthly. $19.99 per year. Incorporates *Electronics Now*.

**Population Action International**. 1300 19th St. NW, Ste. 200 Washington, DC 20036-1624. Phone: (202)557-3400; Fax: (202)728-4177; Email: pai@popact.org • URL: http://www.populationaction.org • Seeks to advance policies and programs that slow population growth in order to enhance the quality of life for all ages. Advocates expansion of voluntary family planning, other reproductive health services, and educational and economic opportunities for girls and women.

***Population and Development Review***. Blackwell Publishing Inc., 350 Main St. Malden, MA 02148. Phone: 800-216-2522 or (781)388-8200; Fax: (781)388-8210; Email: journaladsusa@bos.blackwellpublishing.com • URL: http://www.blackwellpublishing.com • Quarterly. $64. Includes print and online editions. *Supplement* available. Text in English; summaries in English, French and Spanish.

***Population and Vital Statistics Report***. United Nations Publications, c/o National Book Network, 15200 NBN Way Blue Ridge Summit, PA 17214. Phone: 888-254-4286 or (212)963-7680 or (212)963-8302; Fax: (800)338-4550; Email: unpublications@nbnbooks.com • URL: http://www.unp.un.org • Semiannual. $40.00 per year. Contains worldwide demographic statistics.

**Population Association of America**. 8630 Fenton St., Ste. 722 Silver Spring, MD 20910-3812. Phone: (301)565-6710; Fax: (301)565-7850; Email: lmbrown@popassoc.org • URL: http://www.populationassociation.org • Individuals interested in demography and its scientific aspects.

***Population Bulletin***. Population Reference Bureau, 1875 Connecticut Ave. NW, Ste. 520 Washington, DC 20009-5728. Phone: 800-877-9881; Fax: (202)328-3937; Email: popref@prb.org • URL: http://www.prb.org • Quarterly. $3.50 Single issue; Included in membership; $7 Nonmembers /copy. Covers population issues, country/regional studies, and health issues.

**Population Council** . 1 Dag Hammarskjold Plz. New York, NY 10017. Phone: 877-339-0500 or (212)339-0500 or (212)237-9434; Fax: (212)755-6052; Email: pubinfo@popcouncil.org • URL: http://www.popcouncil.org • Seeks to improve the well-being and reproductive health of current and future generations around the world. Helps achieve a humane, equitable, and sustainable balance between people and resources. Conducts research in three areas: HIV and AIDS; poverty, gender, and youth; and reproductive health.

**Population Reference Bureau**. 1875 Connecticut Ave. NW, Ste. 520 Washington, DC 20009-5728. Phone: 800-877-9881; Fax: (202)328-3937; Email: popref@prb.org • URL: http://www.prb.org • Gathers, interprets, and disseminates information on the facts and implications of national and world population trends.

***Pork: The Business Magazine for Professional Pork Producers***. Vance Publishing Corp., 400 Knightsbridge Pkwy. Lincolnshire, IL 60069-3613. Phone: 800-255-5113 or (847)634-2600; Fax: (847)634-4342 or (847)634-4379; Email: info@vancepublishing.com • URL: http://www.vancepublishing.com • Monthly. $50 Individuals; $65 Canada surface mail; $100 Other countries air mail delivery. Magazine on pork production and marketing.

**Portland Cement Association**. 5420 Old Orchard Rd. Skokie, IL 60077-1083. Phone: 800-868-6733 or (847)966-6200 or (202)408-9494; Fax: (847)966-8389; Email: info@cement.org • URL: http://www.cement.org • Companies in the U.S. and Canada. Seeks to improve and extend the uses of Portland cement and concrete through market promotion, research and development, educational programs, and representation with governmental entities. Conducts research on concrete technology and durability; concrete pavement design; load-bearing capacities, field performance, and fire resistance of concrete; transportation, building, and structural uses of concrete. Operates Construction Technology Laboratories, which conducts research and technical services in construction materials, products, and applications. Sponsors a public affairs program in Washington, DC.

***Ports and Terminals Guide***. IHS Global Ltd. Lloyd's Register—Fairplay Ltd., Lombard House, 3 Princess Way, Surrey Redhill RH1 1UP, United Kingdom. Phone: 44 1737 379000; Fax: 44 1737 379001; Email: marketing@ihs.com • URL: http://www.ihs.com • Biennial. $895 Individuals. Covers: Over 23,000 ports and service providers and details on over 10,000 ports. Also includes port conditions and news and ship index of 58,000 vessels. Database includes: Over 4,000 plans, maps, and port photographs. Entries include: For ports and service providers—Name, address, phone; for ports—location, general overview, load line zone, and maximum vessel size.

***Portugal Business Law Handbook***. International Business Publications, USA, PO Box 15343 Washington, DC 20003. Phone: (202)546-2103; Fax: (202)546-3275; Email: ibpusa@comcast.net • URL: http://ibpus.com • $99.95 Individuals hardcopy, e-book, CD-ROM. Covers: Information on basic business legislation, investment, tax, laws, export-import regulations, and contacts.

***Portugal Business Services Providers Leads***. Business Information Agency Inc. PlanetInform, 52 Tuscan Way, Ste. 202-181 Saint Augustine, VA 32092. Phone: (904)342-6124; Fax: (904)592-2632; Email: info@biasales.com • URL: http://www.biasales.com • Monthly. $113 Individuals mailing list; $238 Individuals sales list; $402 Individuals marketing list. Covers Portuguese companies and all sub-industries that provide services to commercial businesses, establishments, and organizations, including consulting, advertising and marketing services, and facilities maintenance.

***Portugal Government and Business Contacts Handbook***. International Business Publications, USA, PO Box 15343 Washington, DC 20003. Phone: (202)546-2103; Fax: (202)546-3275; Email: ibpusa@comcast.net • URL: http://ibpus.com • Annual. $99.95 Individuals hardcopy, e-book, CD-ROM. Covers: Information on strategic economic, investment, export-import, and business opportunities. Contains important export-import, government, and business contacts. Ultimate directory for conducting export-import operations in the country.

***Portugal Investment and Business Guide***. International Business Publications, USA, PO Box 15343 Washington, DC 20003. Phone: (202)546-2103; Fax: (202)546-3275; Email: ibpusa@comcast.net • URL: http://ibpus.com • $99.95 Individuals hardcopy, e-book, CD-ROM. Covers: Strategic information on economy, business, export-import and investment climate, opportunities, industrial development, banking and government. Entries include: Business contacts and business travel.

**Portuguese Chamber**. 11 Belgrave Sq., 4th Fl. London SW1X 8PP, United Kingdom. Phone: 44 20 72016638; Email: info@portuguese-chamber.org.uk • URL: http://www.portuguese-chamber.org.uk • Promotes business and commerce.

**Portuguese Confederation of Business and Services**. Av. Dom Vasco da Gama 29 P-1449-032 Lisbon, Portugal. Phone: 351 21 3031380 or 351 21 3929990; Fax: 351 21 3031401; Email: ccp@ccp.pt • URL: http://www.ccp.pt • Aims to strengthen the capacity of action of the industry.

***Postal Bulletin***. U. S. Government Printing Office, 732 N Capitol St. NW Washington, DC 20401. Phone: 866-512-1800 or (202)512-1800 or (866)512-1800; Fax: (202)512-2104 or (202)512-2250; Email: contactcenter@gpo.gov • URL: http://www.gpo.gov • Biweekly. $163. Issued by the United States Postal Service. Contains orders, instructions, and information relating to U. S. mail service.

***Postal Service***. U. S. Government Printing Office, 732 N Capitol St. NW Washington, DC 20401. Phone: 866-512-1800 or (202)512-1800 or (866)512-1800; Fax: (202)512-2104 or (202)512-2250; Email: contactcenter@gpo.gov • URL: http://www.gpo.gov • Annual. Free. Issued by the Superintendent of Documents. A list of government publications on mail services and the post office. (Subject Bibliography No. 169.).

***Postal World***. UCG Holdings L.P., 11300 Rockville Pike, Suite 1100 Rockville, MD 20852-3030. Phone: 800-929-4824 or (301)816-8950 or (301)287-2700; Fax: (301)816-8945; Email: dhernan@ucg.com • URL: http://www.ucg.com • Description: Disseminates information to help readers run a more efficient mail operation. "Discusses how to trim postage costs, speed delivery, improve mailroom productivity, and plan for rate increases." Recurring features include an annual salary survey and periodic special reports.

***Potato Abstracts***. CABI Publishing North America, 38 Chauncey St., Ste. 1002 Boston, MA 02111. Phone: 800-552-3083; Email: cabi-nao@cabi.org • URL: http://www.cabi.org • Quarterly. Institutions, $610.00 per year. Online edition available, $640.00 per year. Includes single site internet access. Published in England by CABI Publishing. Provides worldwide coverage of the literature.

**Potato Association of America**. University of Maine, 5719 Crossland Hall, Rm. 220 Orono, ME 04469-5719. Phone: (207)581-3042; Fax: (207)581-3015; Email: umpotato@maine.edu • URL: http://potatoassociation.org • Represents breeders, entomologists, horticulturists, plant pathologists, soil and fertilizer specialists, food technologists, producers, and handlers.

***Potato Grower of Idaho***. Harris Publishing Inc., 360 B St. Idaho Falls, ID 83402. Phone: 800-638-0135 or (208)524-7000; Fax: (208)522-5241; Email: customerservice@harrispublishing.com • URL: http://www.harrispublishing.com • Monthly. $24 per year.

***Potentials: Ideas and Products that Motivate***. Nielsen Business Media Inc., 770 Broadway New York, NY 10003-9522. Phone: 866-890-8541 or (646)654-4500 or (646)654-5000; Fax: (646)654-5584 or (646)654-4500; Email: bmcomm@nielsen.com • URL: http://www.nielsenbusinessmedia.com • Monthly. $59.00 per year. Covers incentives, premiums, awards, and gifts as related to promotional activities. Formerly *Potentials in Marketing*.

***Poultry Abstracts***. CABI Publishing North America, 38 Chauncey St., Ste. 1002 Boston, MA 02111. Phone: 800-552-3083; Email: cabi-nao@cabi.org • URL: http://www.cabi.org • Monthly. Institutions, $760.00 per year. Online edition available. Single site internet access, $735.00 per year. Published in England by CABI Publishing. Provides worldwide coverage of the literature.

***Poultry and Egg Marketing: The Bi-Monthly News Magazine of the Poultry Marketing Industry***. Poultry & Egg News Inc. Franklin Publishing, 345 Green St. NW Gainesville, GA 30503. Phone: (770)536-2476; Fax: (770)532-4894 • URL: http://www.poultryandeggnews.com • Bimonthly. Free to qualified personnel; others, $6.00 per year. Processing and marketing of eggs and poultry products.

**Poultry Science Association**. 1800 S Oak St., Ste. 100 Champaign, IL 61820-6974. Phone: (217)356-5285 or (217)356-3182; Fax: (217)398-4119; Email: psa@assochq.org • URL: http://www.poultryscience.org • Aims to advance the poultry industry. Promotes discovery, application and dissemination of knowledge. Creates a forum for the exchange of information among various segments of the poultry industry.

***Poultry Science***. Poultry Science Association, 1800 S Oak St., Ste. 100 Champaign, IL 61820-6974. Phone: (217)356-5285 or (217)356-3182; Fax: (217)398-4119; Email: psa@assochq.org • URL: http://www.poultryscience.org • Monthly. $540 Individuals online; $621 Individuals print and online; $540 Individuals /year; elsewhere; online; $655 Individuals /year; elsewhere; print and online; $45 Single issue. Contains articles on how to advance the scientific study of poultry.

***Poultry Times***. Poultry & Egg News Inc. Franklin Publishing, 345 Green St. NW Gainesville, GA 30503. Phone: (770)536-2476; Fax: (770)532-4894 • URL: http://www.poultryandeggnews.com • Biweekly. Directed to grow-out operations for the egg and poultry business.

***Poultry USA***. Watt Publishing, 122 S Wesley Ave. Mount Morris, IL 61054-1497. Phone: (815)734-4171 • Bimonthly. $28.00 per year. Incorporates *Broiler Industry*.

**Powder Coating Institute**. PO Box 2112 The Woodlands, TX 77380. Phone: 800-988-COAT or (936)597-5060; Fax: (936)597-5059; Email: pci-info@powdercoating.org • URL: http://www.powdercoating.org • Individuals and businesses that manufacture, sell, or develop powder coating materials and equipment. Promotes the application and use of powder coating technology among industrial finishers; disseminates information to both consumers and the industry on the value and performance of powder coating; supports educational programs in the industrial coating/finishing field; updates members, governmental departments, and regulatory agencies on the activities and developments concerning the manufacture, application, and proper handling of powder coatings. Presents technical papers at conferences of related organizations and prepares articles for the media on the powder coating industry.

***Powder Metallurgy***. Institute of Materials, Minerals and Mining. 1 Carlton House Terrace London SW1Y 5DB, United Kingdom. Phone: 20 7451 7300; Fax: (783)9 1702; Email: materials.world@iom3.org • URL: http://www.iom3.org • Five issues per year. $1048.00 per year.

***Powell Monetary Analyst***. Larson M. Powell, editor. Reserve Research Ltd., PO Box 4135 Portland, ME 04101. Phone: (207)774-4971 • Description: Offers investment advice concentrating on precious metals, gold coins, currencies, and mining stocks.

**Power and Communication Contractors Association**. 1908 Mt. Vernon Ave., 2nd Fl. Alexandria, VA 22301. Phone: 800-542-7222 or (703)212-7734; Fax: (703)548-3733; Email: info@pccaweb.org • URL: http://www.pccaweb.org • Contractors engaged in electrical power and communication line construction.

***Power Companies Directory***. InfoGroup Inc., 5711 S 86th Cir. Omaha, NE 68127-4146. Phone: (402)593-4500 • URL: http://www.infogroup.com • Annual. Number of listings: 6,906. Entries include: Name, address, phone, size of advertisement, name of owner or manager, number of employees, year first in "Yellow Pages." Compiled from telephone company "Yellow Pages," nationwide.

***Power Engineering International***. PennWell Corp., Industrial Div., 1421 S Sheridan Rd. Tulsa, OK 74112. Phone: 800-331-4463 or (918)835-3161; Email: bid@pennwell.com • URL: http://www.pennwell.com • Monthly.

***Power Equipment Trade***. Hatton-Brown Publishers Inc., 225 Hanrick St. Montgomery, AL 36102. Phone: 800-669-5613 or (334)834-1170; Fax: (334)834-4525; Email: dianne@hattonbrown.com • URL: http://www.hattonbrown.net • 10/year. Formerly *Chain Saw Age and Power Equipment Trade*.

***Power Generation Technology and Markets***. Pasha Publishing Inc., 1600 Wilson Blvd., Suite 600 Arlington, VA 22209. Phone: (703)816-8642; Fax: (703)528-7821 • Weekly. $790.00 per year. Newsletter. Formerly *Coal and Synfuels Technology*.

***Power***. The McGraw-Hill Companies Inc., PO Box 182604 Columbus, OH 43272. Phone: 877-833-5524 or (212)512-2000 or (212)904-2000; Fax: (614)759-3749 or (212)512-3840; Email: webmaster@mcgraw-hill.com • URL: http://www.mcgraw-hill.com • Description: Covers design, operation, construction, and maintenance of power plants for utilities, process industries, and manufacturers.

**Power-Motion Technology Representatives Association**. 5353 Wayzata Blvd., Ste. 350 Minneapolis, MN 55416-1300. Phone: 888-817-7872; Fax: (949)252-8096; Email: ptrahq@ptra.org • URL: http://www.ptra.org • Manufacturers and independent manufacturers representatives in the power transmission industry. Seeks to provide a channel of communication between manufacturers' independent representatives and their principals and other manufacturers within the industry by allowing interchange of sound business management ideas and by offering consultation on solving operational problems. Provides information and referral; compiles surveys. Offers training programs that include panels, table talk discussions and seminars on special topics.

**Power Tool Institute**. 1300 Sumner Ave. Cleveland, OH 44115-2851. Phone: (216)241-7333; Fax: (216)241-0105; Email: pti@powertoolinstitute.com • URL: http://www.powertoolinstitute.com • Represents manufacturers of portable and stationary tools, both electric and battery operated. Distributes publications and videos on power tool safety. Offers educational programs.

**Power Transmission Distributors Association**. 230 W Monroe St., Ste. 1410 Chicago, IL 60606-4802. Phone: (312)516-2100; Fax: (312)516-2101; Email: ptda@ptda.org • URL: http://www.ptda.org • Distributors and manufacturers of power transmission/motion and position control equipment. Maintains business management and continuing education resources; conducts educational programs; compiles statistics; sponsors industry summit; conducts research; cosponsors industry tradeshows.

***Powersports Business***. Ehlert Publishing Group Inc., 6420 Sycamore Ln. N, Ste. 100 Maple Grove, MN 55369-6013. Phone: 800-848-6247 or (763)383-4400; Fax: (763)383-4499 • URL: http://www.powersportsbusiness.com • $96 Other countries. Powersports trade magazine.

***PPI Detailed Report***. Periodical covering business. Bureau of Labor Statistics, U.S. Department of Labor. U. S. Government Printing Office, 732 N Capitol St. NW Washington, DC 20401. Phone: 866-512-1800 or (202)512-1800 or (866)512-1800; Fax: (202)512-2104 or (202)512-2250; Email: contactcenter@gpo.gov • URL: http://www.gpo.gov • Monthly. $55 Individuals.

***PR News***. Access Intelligence L.L.C., 4 Choke Cherry Rd., 2nd Fl. Rockville, MD 20850. Phone: 800-777-5006 or (301)354-2000 or (301)354-2101; Fax: (301)309-3847 or (801)365-2300; Email: info@accessintel.com • URL: http://www.accessintel.com/ • Weekly. $1,049 Individuals. Provides information and knowledge to handle any program with the best tools and insights at hand.

***The Practical Accountant: Providing the Competitive Edge***. SourceMedia Inc., 1 State Street Plz., 27th Fl. New York, NY 10004. Phone: 800-221-1809 or (212)803-8200 or (212)803-8333; Fax: (212)843-9635 or (212)292-5216; Email: custserv@sourcemedia.com • URL: http://www.sourcemedia.com • Monthly. $65.00 per year. Covers tax planning, financial planning, practice management, client relationships, and related topics.

***Practical Guide to Equal Employment Opportunity***. ALM Media Properties LLC, 120 Broadway, 5th Fl. New York, NY 10271-1100. Phone: (212)457-9400; Fax: (646)417-7705; Email: customercare@alm.com • URL: http://www.alm.com • $570 two volumes. Serves as a legal manual for EEO compliance. "Volume one analyzes discrimination on the basis of race, religion, sex, age, and physical handicaps including AIDS." Provides information relating to an employer's liability in cases of sexual harassment of employees, including same-sex harassment. Covers affirmative action and reverse discrimination issues. Volume two contains model affirmative action plans, a sample EEO compliance manual, checklists, and other documents. (Law Journal Press).

***Practical Guide to Foreign Direct Investment in the European Union: The Green Book***. Euroconfidentiel S. A., Rue de Rixensart 18 B-1332 Genval, Belgium. Phone: 32 02 652 02 84 or 32 2 6520284; Fax: (653) 01 80 or (653)0180; Email: nigel.hunt@skynet.be • URL: http://www.euroconfidential.com • Annual. $240.00. Provides coverage of national and EU business incentives. In addition to 70 charts and tables, includes EU country profiles of taxation, labor costs, and employment regulations.

***Practical Guide to Real Estate Taxation***. David F. Windish. Wolters Kluwer Law & Business CCH, 2700 Lake Cook Rd. Riverwoods, IL 60015. Phone: 888-224-7377 or (847)267-7000; Email: cust_serv@cch.com • URL: http://www.cchgroup.com • $150 1-4 Copies; $135 5-9 Copies; $121 10-24 Copies; $111 25 Copies. Date not set. Serves as a guide to the federal tax consequences of real estate ownership and operation. Covers mortgages, rental agreements, interest, landlord income, forms of ownership, and other tax-oriented topics.

***Practical Guide to the Occupational Safety and Health Act***. ALM Media Properties LLC, 120 Broadway, 5th Fl. New York, NY 10271-1100. Phone: (212)457-9400; Fax: (646)417-7705; Email: customercare@alm.com • URL: http://www.alm.com • $545 print + online + ebook; $515 ebook + online. Covers the practical aspects of doing business while complying with OSHA regulations. Covers inspections, enforcement, rights of employees, the possibility of criminal prosecution, and related issues. (Law Journal Press).

***The Practical Lawyer***. Committee on Continuing Professional

Education. American Law Institute - Committee on Continuing Professional Education, 4025 Chestnut St. Philadelphia, PA 19104. Phone: 800-253-6397 or (215)243-1600 or (215)243-1614; Fax: (215)243-1636 or (215)243-1664; Email: in-house@ali-aba.org • URL: http://www.ali.org • 6/year. $99 per year. Contains advice ondealing with the client's problem in commercial and corporate law, real estate, litigation, tax and estate planning.

***The Practical Real Estate Lawyer***. Committee on Continuing Professional Education. American Law Institute - Committee on Continuing Professional Education, 4025 Chestnut St. Philadelphia, PA 19104. Phone: 800-253-6397 or (215)243-1600 or (215)243-1614; Fax: (215)243-1636 or (215)243-1664; Email: in-house@ali-aba.org • URL: http://www.ali.org • Bimonthly. $99 per year. Frequently includes legal forms for use in real estate practice.

***The Practical Tax Lawyer***. Committee on Continuing Professional Education. American Law Institute - Committee on Continuing Professional Education, 4025 Chestnut St. Philadelphia, PA 19104. Phone: 800-253-6397 or (215)243-1600 or (215)243-1614; Fax: (215)243-1636 or (215)243-1664; Email: in-house@ali-aba.org • URL: http://www.ali.org • Quarterly. $89 Members per year; $99 Nonmembers per year. Contains advice on how to solve tax problems of every company's clients.

**Practising Law Institute**. 1177 Avenue of the Americas New York, NY 10036. Phone: 800-260-4754 or (212)824-5700; Fax: (212)824-5733; Email: info@pli.edu • URL: http://www.pli.edu • Provides through publications, videotapes, forums, and live and online seminars, training for lawyers throughout the country in new developments in the law and new legal techniques. Presents over 250 seminars annually.

***Practitioner's Guide to GAAS***. John Wiley & Sons Inc., 111 River St. Hoboken, NJ 07030-5774. Phone: 800-225-5945 or (201)748-6000; Fax: (201)748-6088; Email: info@wiley.com • URL: http://www.wiley.com • Annual. $105 paperback. Covers GAAS: Generally Accepted Auditing Standards, promulgated by the American Institute of Certified Public Accountants. (Includes CD-ROM.).

***Prague Business Journal***. New World Publishing Inc., Francouzska 4 120 00 Prague, Czech Republic. Phone: 42 246086501; Fax: 42 246086543; Email: info@pbj.cz • Weekly. $100 Individuals. English language business publication.

***Prairie Business Magazine***. Forum Communications Co., 101 5th St. N Fargo, ND 58102-4826. Phone: (701)235-7311; Fax: (701)241-5406; Email: inforum@fccinteractive.com • URL: http://www.in-forum.com • Magazine featuring business people and companies from North Dakota, Minnesota and South Dakota.

***Pratt's Guide to Venture Capital Sources***. Greenwood Electronic Media, c/o ABC-CLIO, 130 Cremona Dr. Santa Barbara, CA 93117. Phone: 800-368-6868 or (805)968-1911; Fax: (866)270-3856; Email: customerservice@abc-clio.com • URL: http://www.abc-clio.com • Annual. $249. Covers: Approximately 800 venture capital firms, principally in the United States; small business investment corporations (SBICs); corporate venture groups; and selected consultants and "deal men"; separate section for providers of professional services to venture capitalists. Database includes: Articles on raising venture capital. Entries include: Company name, address, phone, names of executives, investment preferences, and industry preferences.

**Precision Metalforming Association**. 6363 Oak Tree Blvd. Independence, OH 44131-2556. Phone: (216)901-8800; Fax: (216)901-9190; Email: pma@pma.org • URL: http://www.metalform.com • Represents the metalforming industry of North America; the industry that creates precision metal products using stamping, fabricating and other value-added processes. Its member companies include metal stampers, fabricators, spinners, slide formers and roll formers, as well as suppliers of equipment, materials and services to the industry. Members are located in 30 countries, with the majority found in North America; in 41 states of the United States as well as Canada and Mexico. Conducts technical and educational programs, compiles statistics, offers training systems, and provides legislative and regulatory assistance to members.

***Predictions: Specific Investment Forecasts and Recommendations from the World's Top Financial Experts***. Lee Euler, editor. Agora Inc., 14 W Mt. Vernon Pl. Baltimore, MD 21201-5125. Phone: (410)783-8499; Email: csteam@agorapublishinggroup.com • URL: http://www.agora-inc.com • Monthly. $78.00 per year. Newsletter.

***Prepared Foods***. BNP Media, 2401 W Big Beaver Rd., Ste. 700 Troy, MI 48084. Phone: 800-952-6643 or (248)362-3700 or (847)763-9534; Fax: (248)362-5103 or (248)362-0317; Email: privacy@bnpmedia.com • URL: http://www.bnpmedia.com • Monthly. Edited for food manufacturing management, marketing, and operations personnel.

***Preparing an Entrepreneurial Business Plan***. American CPE Inc., 826 Riviera Mansfield, TX 76063. Phone: 800-990-4273 or (817)477-0222; Fax: (817)473-4998; Email: director@americancpe.com • URL: http://www.americancpe.com • Contains detailed training and instructional information on preparing and writing entrepreneurial business plans for beginning businesses. Offers insight and guidance on the process of writing the business plan, what a business plan accomplishes for start-up entrepreneurs, and how business plans can be helpful at all stages in the business life cycle. Covers topics such as the definition of a business plan, what goes into a business plan, meshing the entrepreneurial process and business planning, preparing the first draft of the plan, financing a business, redrafting and revising business plans, reaching the final draft, and more. Offers self-paced courseware and learning materials designed to enhance users' skills, interpersonal development, and professional abilities.

***Prepress Bulletin***. Bessie Halfacre, editor. International Prepress Association, 600 Duke St., Ste. 420 Alexandria, VA 22314. Phone: (703)837-1070; Fax: (703)837-1072; Email: info@ipa.org • URL: http://www.ipa.org • Bimonthly. $20.00 per year. Provides management and technical information on the graphic arts prepress industry.

***Presentations: Technology and Techniques for Effective Communication***. Nielsen Business Media Inc., 770 Broadway New York, NY 10003-9522. Phone: 866-890-8541 or (646)654-4500 or (646)654-5000; Fax: (646)654-5584 or (646)654-4500; Email: bmcomm@nielsen.com • URL: http://www.nielsenbusinessmedia.com • Monthly. Free to qualified personnel; others, $69.00 per year. Covers the use of presentation hardware and software, including audiovisual equipment and computerized display systems. Includes an annual *Buyers Guide to Presentation Products*.

***The Presidency: The Magazine for Higher Education Leaders***. American Council on Education, 1 Dupont Cir. NW Washington, DC 20036. Phone: (202)939-9300 or (202)939-9420; Email: membership@ace.nche.edu • URL: http://www.acenet.edu • Quarterly. $70 Other countries; $40 Nonmembers; $30 Members. Magazine publishes articles on issues affecting higher education leadership; provides a forum for the presentation of ideas and information for college and university presidents. Formerly *Educational Record*.

***Presidential Studies Quarterly***. Center for the Study of the Presidency. Pine Forge Press, 2455 Teller Rd. Thousand Oaks, CA 91320-2234. Phone: 800-818-7243 or (805)499-4224 or (805)499-9774; Fax: (805)499-0871 or (805)583-2665; Email: sales@pfp.sagepub.com • URL: http://www.sagepub.com/sociologybooks • Quarterly. $559 Institutions print and online. Offers articles, features, review essays, and book reviews covering US Presidency.

***President's Club! Presidents of Computer and Telecommunications Companies Directory***. Ex-IBM Corp., 2713 Foxboro Dr. Garland, TX 75044. Phone: (214)557-6969; Email: ibmalumni@aol.com • URL: http://www.ibmalumni.com • $95 per issue. Covers: over 2,200 presidents of companies, organizations, or associations involved in the computer and telecommunications industries. Entries include: Company, organization, or association name, president's name, address, and phone.

***Prevention: The Magazine for Better Health***. Rodale Inc., 400 S 10th St. Emmaus, PA 18098-0001. Phone: 800-848-4735; Email: custservrwscp@rodale.com • URL: http://www.rodaleinc.com • Monthly. $24 Individuals.

***Prices and Earnings Around the Globe***. Union Bank of Switzerland, 299 Park Ave. New York, NY 10171. Phone: (212)715-3000 • Triennial. Free. Published in Zurich. Compares prices and purchasing power in 48 major cities of the world. Wages and hours are also compared.

***Prices of Agricultural Products and Selected Inputs in Europe and North America***. Economic Commission for Europe. United Nations Publications, c/o National Book Network, 15200 NBN Way Blue Ridge Summit, PA 17214. Phone: 888-254-4286 or (212)963-7680 or (212)963-8302; Fax: (800)338-4550; Email: unpublications@nbnbooks.com • URL: http://www.unp.un.org • Annual. $36 Individuals.

**Princeton University - Bendheim Center for Finance**. Department of Economics, 26 Prospect Ave. Princeton, NJ 08540-5296. Phone: (609)258-0770; Fax: (609)258-0771; Email: jessicab@princeton.edu • URL: http://www.princeton.edu/bcf • Research areas include securities markets, portfolio analysis, credit markets, and corporate finance. Emphasis is on quantitative and mathematical perspectives.

**Princeton University - Industrial Relations Section**. Firestone Library, A-18-J, 1 Washington Rd. Princeton, NJ 08544. Phone: (609)258-4040; Fax: (609)258-2907; Email: c6789@princeton.edu • URL: http://www.irs.princeton.edu • Fields of research include labor supply, manpower training, unemployment, and equal employment opportunity.

**Princeton University - Princeton Forrestal Center**. 105 College Rd. E Princeton, NJ 08540. Phone: (609)452-7720; Fax: (609)452-7485; Email: picus@picusassociates.com • URL: http://www.princetonforrestalcenter.com • Designed to create an interdependent mix of academia and business enterprise.

**Princeton University - Princeton Institute for International and Regional Studies**. Princeton University, 334 Aaron Burr Hall Princeton, NJ 08544-2001. Phone: (609)258-7497; Fax: (609)258-3988; Email: piirs@princeton.edu • URL: http://www.princeton.edu/piirs • International relations and world politics, including national defense and military policy, foreign policy, diplomacy and international political organization, comparative politics, political, social, and economic modernization, world order studies, U.S.-Japan relations, and economies of developing countries. Furthers research and publication on international relations at the University directed toward development of systematic, disciplined and comprehensive appraisals of varied aspects of international relations and world politics with special emphasis on U.S. foreign policy.

***Principles of Health and Hygiene in the Workplace***. Timothy J. Key and Michael A. Mueller. Lewis Publishers, 6000 Broken Sound Pky. NW, Ste. 300 Boca Raton, FL 33487. Phone: 800-272-7737 or (561)361-2532 or (561)994-0555; Fax: (561)989-9732 or (800)374-3401; Email: orders@crcpress.com • URL: http://www.crcpress.com • Date not set. $69.95.

**Print Alliance Credit Exchange**. 1100 Main St. Buffalo, NY 14209. Fax: (716)878-0479 • URL: http://www.gopace.com • Manufacturers or designers of business forms or graphic media, selling to dealers, distributors, office supply, copy stores, or end users. Promotes the collection, computation, and exchange of factual ledger experience information by members. Compiles statistics.

***Print: America's Graphic Design Magazine***. Krause Publications Inc., 700 E State St. Iola, WI 54990-0001. Phone: 800-726-9966 or (715)445-2214 or (715)445-4612; Fax: (715)445-4087 • URL: http://www.krause.com • Bimonthly. $57.00 per year. Emphasizes creative trends.

**Print Services and Distribution Association**. 330 N Wabash Ave., Ste. 2000 Chicago, IL 60611. Phone: 800-230-0175; Fax: (312)673-6880 • URL: http://www.psda.org • Independent distributors, manufacturers and suppliers to the forms, business printing and document management industries. Sponsors educational and channel marketing programs. Compiles statistics.

***Print Solutions—Buyers' Guide Issue***. Print Services and Distribution Association, 330 N Wabash Ave., Ste. 2000 Chicago, IL 60611. Phone: 800-230-0175; Fax: (312)673-6880 • URL: http://www.psda.org • Annual. $49 Individuals. Publication includes: List of about 600 suppliers of business forms and other business printing, such as ad specialties, barcoded forms & labels, commercial printing calendars, tags, cards, labels, and printed stationery. Entries include: name, address, phone, fax, capabilities, product/service.

***Print Solutions Magazine***. Document Management Industries Association, 433 E Monroe Ave. Alexandria, VA 22301. Phone: (703)836-6232; Fax: (703)836-2241; Email: dmia@printsolutionsmag.com • URL: http://www.dmia.org • Monthly. Members free; $99 Nonmembers.

***Printing Impressions***. North American Publishing Co., 1500 Spring Garden St., Ste. 1200 Philadelphia, PA 19130-4069. Phone: (215)238-5300; Email: customerservice@napco.com • URL: http://www.napco.com • *Master Specifier*.

**Printing Industries of America - Center for Technology and Research**. 200 Deer Run Rd. Sewickley, PA 15143-2600. Phone: 800-910-4283 or (412)741-6860; Fax: (412)741-2311; Email: printingind@printing.org • URL: http://www.printing.org/ctr • Affiliated with Printing Industries of America.

***Printing Industries of America Ratios***. Printing Industries of America - Center for Technology and Research, 200 Deer Run Rd. Sewickley, PA 15143-2600. Phone: 800-910-4283 or (412)741-6860; Fax: (412)741-2311; Email: printingind@printing.org • URL: http://www.printing.org/ctr • Annual. $750 Members Full Set (volume 1-16); $1,500 Nonmembers Full Set (volume 1-16). Annual financial benchmarking study.

***Printworld Directory of Contemporary Prints and Prices***. Printworld International Inc., PO Box 1957 West Chester, PA 19380. Phone: 800-788-9101 or (610)431-6654; Fax: (610)431-6653; Email: sales@printworlddirectory.com • URL: http://www.printworlddirectory.com/printworld • Irregular. $229 Individuals regular price; $269 Canada; $309 Other countries. Biographical data on 5,000 international artists in contemporary printmaking; thousands of galleries who handle prints and hundreds of print publishers, and 600,000 print/price listings.

***Prisoners in State and Federal Institutions***. Bureau of Justice Statistics, U.S. Department of Justice. U. S. Government Printing Office, 732 N Capitol St. NW Washington, DC 20401. Phone: 866-512-1800 or (202)512-1800 or (866)512-1800; Fax: (202)512-2104 or (202)512-2250; Email: contactcenter@gpo.gov • URL: http://www.gpo.gov • Annual.

***Private Asset Management***. Institutional Investor Inc. Journals Group, 225 Park Ave. S New York, NY 10003. Phone: 800-437-9997 or (212)224-3570; Email: info@iijournals.com • URL: http://www.iijournals.com • Biweekly. $2,335.00 per year. Newsletter. Includes print and online editions. Edited for managers investing the private assets of wealthy ("high-net-worth") individuals. Includes marketing, taxation, regulation, and fee topics.

**Private Equity CFO Association**. c/o RBS Citizens, 28 State St., 14th Fl. Boston, MA 02109. • URL: http://www.privateequitycfo.org • Provides networking opportunities for members to share best practices. Responds to and addresses industry and professional issues of current interest. Develops programs that will provide education to association members. Improves and strengthens the flow of information among members.

***Private Equity Week***. Thomson Financial Inc., 195 Broadway New York, NY 10007-3100. Phone: (646)822-2000; Email: custserv@tfn.com • URL: http://www.thomsonreuters.com • Weekly. $1,495.00 per year. Provides detailed information on both prospective and completed private equity transactions. Includes news, data, commentary, trends, developments, and analysis.

**Private Investigator**. Entrepreneur Press, 2445 McCabe Way, Ste. 400 Irvine, CA 92614-6244. Phone: 800-864-6864 or (949)261-2325 or (949)622-7131; Fax: (949)261-7729 or (949)261-0234; Email: press@entrepreneur.com • URL: http://www.entrepreneurpress.com • Looseleaf. $59.50. A practical guide to starting a private investigation agency. Covers profit potential, start-up costs, market size evaluation, pricing, accounting, advertising, promotion, etc. (Start-Up Business Guide No. E1320.).

**Private Label Buyer**. Stagnito Communcitions, Inc., 155 Pfingsten Rd., Ste. 205 Deerfield, IL 60015. Phone: (847)205-5660; Fax: (847)205-5680; Email: info@stagnito.com • URL: http://www.plnews.com • 8/year. Covers new private label product developments for chain stores. Formerly *Private Label News*.

**Private Label Directory**. E.W. Williams Publications Co., 2125 Center Ave., Ste. 305 Fort Lee, NJ 07024-5898. Phone: (201)592-7007 or (201)532-9290; Fax: (201)592-7171 or (201)779-8345; Email: philpl@ewwpi.com • URL: http://www.williamspublications.com • Annual. $75 U.S. and Canada; $125 Elsewhere; $75 Canada. Covers: Over 1,400 suppliers of food, health and beauty care, household supplies, general merchandise and service and supplies, with private and generic labels; international coverage. Entries include: Company name, address, phone, fax, e-mail, internet, names and titles of key personnel, products.

**Private Label International: The Magazine for Store Labels (Own Brands) and Generics**. E.W. Williams Publications Co., 2125 Center Ave., Ste. 305 Fort Lee, NJ 07024-5898. Phone: (201)592-7007 or (201)532-9290; Fax: (201)592-7171 or (201)779-8345; Email: philpl@ewwpi.com • URL: http://www.williamspublications.com • Semiannual. Edited for large chain store buyers and for manufacturers of private label products. Text in English; summaries in French and German.

**Private Label Manufacturers Association**. 630 3rd Ave. New York, NY 10017. Phone: (212)972-3131; Fax: (212)983-1382; Email: info@plma.com • URL: http://plma.com • Membership consists of manufacturers, brokers, suppliers, and consultants. Educates consumers on the quality and value of private label or store brand products; promotes private label industry. Compiles statistics; conducts research programs for members.

**Private Label: The Magazine for House Brands and Generics**. E.W. Williams Publications Co., 2125 Center Ave., Ste. 305 Fort Lee, NJ 07024-5898. Phone: (201)592-7007 or (201)532-9290; Fax: (201)592-7171 or (201)779-8345; Email: philpl@ewwpi.com • URL: http://www.williamspublications.com • Bimonthly. Edited for buyers of private label, controlled packer, and generic-labeled products. Concentrates on food, health and beauty aids, and general merchandise.

**Private Placement Letter: The Weekly for Privately Placed Fixed-Income Securities**. SourceMedia Inc., 1 State Street Plz., 27th Fl. New York, NY 10004. Phone: 800-221-1809 or (212)803-8200 or (212)803-8333; Fax: (212)843-9635 or (212)292-5216; Email: custserv@sourcemedia.com • URL: http://www.sourcemedia.com • Weekly. $1,495 per year. Newsletter. Provides information on private financing of debt and convertible securities.

**Private Power Executive**. Pequot Publishing Inc., PO Box 447 Southport, CT 06490. Phone: (203)259-1812 or (203)259-1112; Fax: (203)255-3313; Email: orders@gasturbineworld.com • URL: http://www.gtwbooks.com • Bimonthly. $90.00 per year. Covers private power (non-utility) enterprises, including cogeneration projects and industrial self-generation.

**Private Practice**. Congress of County Medical Societies (CCMS) Publishing Co., P.O. Box 1485 Shawnee, OK 74802-1485. • Monthly. $18.00 per year.

**Private Sector Council**. Partnership for Public Service, 1100 New York Ave. NW, Ste. 200 E Washington, DC 20005. Phone: (202)292-1020 or (202)775-9111; Fax: (202)775-8885 • URL: http://ourpublicservice.org/OPS/programs/psc • Serves as a nonpartisan, public service organization dedicated to improving the productivity, efficiency, and management of the federal government through a cooperative sharing of knowledge between the public and private sectors.

**Pro Audio Review: The Industry's Equipment Authority**. IMAS Publishing Group, 5827 Columbia Pke. Ste. 310 Falls Church, VA 22041. Phone: 800-336-3045 or (703)998-7600; Fax: (703)998-2966; Email: adsales@imaspub.com • URL: http://www.imaspub.com • Monthly. $24.95 /year. Provides critical product reviews of professional audio equipment and recording gear, including bench tests and user reports.

**PRO**. Braun de Mexico y Compania S.A. de C.V., Calle Vicente Guerrero 3, Local 7 54080 Mexico, Mexico. Phone: 52 55 5365 1660 • URL: http://www.braun.braun.com/in • 7/year. For owners and operators of lawn maintenance service firms. Includes annual *Product* issue.

**Pro Mujer**. 253 W 35th St., 11th Fl. New York, NY 10001. Phone: (646)626-7000; Fax: (212)904-1038; Email: communications@promujer.org • URL: http://promujer.org • Establishes microfinance organizations that provide financial and human development services for women. Provides business training and healthcare support.

**Probe Directory of Foreign Direct Investment in the United States**. Probe International, 225 Brunswick Ave. Toronto, ON, Canada M5S 2M6. Email: patriciaadams@probeinternational.org • URL: http://www.probeinternational.org • Triennial. $250. Covers: over 1,500 affiliate firms in the United States which are partially or totally owned by over 800 Japanese companies. Entries include: For U.S. companies—Company name, address, phone, subsidiary names, name of executive officer, foreign investor's name, line of business/product. For foreign investors—Company name, address, names of U.S. affiliates.

**Process Equipment Manufacturers Association**. 201 Park Washington Ct. Falls Church, VA 22046-4527. Phone: (703)538-1796; Email: info@pemanet.org • URL: http://www.pemanet.org • Represents North American process equipment companies. Maintains an organization of capital equipment manufacturers. Provides a social/business base where members can meet to share and exchange views on common interests.

**Process Industry Directory**. Telmo G. Mirat, PO Box 1493 1000 Buenos Aires, Argentina. Phone: 5412427912; Fax: 5412427912 • Annual. $95. Covers: Argentine manufacturers, importers, and exporters of raw materials, industrial chemicals, and products for the process industry.

**Processing**. Putman Media Inc., 555 W Pierce Rd., Ste. 301 Itasca, IL 60143-2649. Phone: (630)467-1301 or (630)467-1300; Fax: (630)467-1120 or (630)467-1109; Email: controlroundup@putman.net • URL: http://www.putman.net • 14 times a year. $54.00 per year. Emphasis is on descriptions of new products for all areas of industrial processing, including valves, controls, filters, pumps, compressors, fluidics, and instrumentation.

**Processors' and Growers' Research Organisation**. The Research Station, Great North Rd., Thornhaugh Peterborough PE8 6HJ, United Kingdom. Phone: 44 1780 782585; Fax: 44 1780 783993; Email: info@pgro.org • URL: http://www.pgro.org • Farmers, food processors, merchant seedsmen, agrochemical companies, higher education institutes and research stations. Provides research, evaluation and advice on the growing, harvesting and usage of different types of peas and beans. This includes the evaluation of new varieties, crop protection products and growing and harvesting techniques. Provides technical services including seed and soil testing and instrument calibration.

**Procurement Automated Source System**. U.S. Small Business Administration, 409 3rd St. SW Washington, DC 20416. Phone: 800-827-5722 or (202)205-8800 • URL: http://www.sba.gov • Annual. Online database. Database covers: More than 180,000 small businesses (including some 29,000 minority-owned, 44,000 woman-owned, and 51,000 veteran-owned businesses) seeking government procurement contracts. Database includes: Company name, address, phone, name and title of contact, employer identification number, number of employees, year established, geographical area served, whether veteran-, minority-, or woman-owned, whether interested in international trade, Standard Industrial Classification (SIC) code, Federal Supply Code (FSC), quality assurance information. Capability statement used by contracting officials of federal agencies and prime contractors to locate firms which can provide needed goods and services. For more info call: (800)231-PASS.

**Produce Merchandising: The Packer's Retailing and Merchandising Magazine**. Vance Publishing Corp., 400 Knightsbridge Pkwy. Lincolnshire, IL 60069-3613. Phone: 800-255-5113 or (847)634-2600; Fax: (847)634-4342 or (847)634-4379; Email: info@vancepublishing.com • URL: http://www.vancepublishing.com • Monthly. $35.00 per year. Provides information and advice on the retail marketing and promotion of fresh fruits and vegetalbe.

**Produce News**. Zim-mer Trade Publications Inc., 482 Hudson Ter. Englewood Cliffs, NJ 07632. Phone: (201)592-9100; Fax: (201)592-0809 • Weekly. $35.00 per year.

**Producers Directory**. Hollywood Creative Directory, • URL: http://www.ifilm.org • Covers: over 1,700 film and TV production companies, studios, networks, and TV shows, and over 7,700 creative executives within those companies. Majority of listings are located in Los Angeles and New York. Entries include: Company name, staff names and titles, address, phone, fax, e-mail address, web site address, company type, studio deals, and select credits.

**Producers Guild of America**. 8530 Wilshire Blvd., Ste. 400 Beverly Hills, CA 90211. Phone: (310)358-9020; Fax: (310)358-9520; Email: info@producersguild.org • URL: http://www.producersguild.org • Represents, protects and promotes the interests of members of the producing team in film, television and new media.

**Product Design and Development**. Advantage Business Media L.L.C., 100 Enterprise Dr., Ste. 600 Rockaway, NJ 07866-0912. Phone: (973)920-7000; Email: advantagecommunications@advantagemedia.com • URL: http://www.advantagebusinessmedia.com • 9/year.

**Product Development and Management Association**. 330 N Wabash Ave., Ste. 2000 Chicago, IL 60611. Phone: 800-232-5241 or (312)321-5145; Fax: (312)673-6885; Email: pdma@pdma.org • URL: http://www.pdma.org • Managers working in product innovation; teachers and researchers in the areas of product innovation management, product planning and development, and new product marketing; government regulators and facilitators involved in the product development process; product innovation consultants; market research firms; new product institutes; advertising agencies and media; testing companies; trade associations. Promotes improved product innovation management by drawing upon members' resources. Encourages research designed to make product innovation management more effective and efficient; Provides forum for the exchange of ideas and findings among universities, industry, government and related sectors.

**Product Distribution Law Guide**. Wolters Kluwer Law & Business CCH, 2700 Lake Cook Rd. Riverwoods, IL 60015. Phone: 888-224-7377 or (847)267-7000; Email: cust_serv@cch.com • URL: http://www.cchgroup.com • $199.00. Looseleaf service. Annual updates available. Covers the legal aspects of various methods of product distribution, including franchising.

**The Product Liability Alliance**. National Association of Wholesaler-Distributors, 1325 G St. NW, Ste. 1000 Washington, DC 20005. Phone: (202)872-0885; Fax: (202)785-0586; Email: naw@naw.org • Seeks enactment of federal product liability tort reform legislation. Supports and coordinates members' efforts in gaining passage of a product liability law. Coalition of trade associations, manufacturers, and nonmanufacturing product sellers. Works with the business community to develop suggestions and guidelines for such a law.

**Product Liability**. ALM Media Properties LLC, 120 Broadway, 5th Fl. New York, NY 10271-1100. Phone: (212)457-9400; Fax: (646)417-7705; Email: customercare@alm.com • URL: http://www.alm.com • $515. Covers product liability litigation as viewed by both the plaintiff and the defendant. Provides detailed discussion of pre-trial and trial procedures. (Law Journal Press).

**Product Liability Law and Strategy**. ALM Media Properties LLC, 120 Broadway, 5th Fl. New York, NY 10271-1100. Phone: (212)457-9400; Fax: (646)417-7705; Email: customercare@alm.com • URL: http://www.alm.com • Monthly. $475. Contains product liability verdict and settlement reports, legislative proposal analysis, and strategies for both the plaintiff's counsel and the defendant's counsel. (A Law Journal Newsletter, formerly published by Leader Publications).

**Product Safety Consultants Directory**. InfoGroup Inc., 5711 S 86th Cir. Omaha, NE 68127-4146. Phone: (402)593-4500 • URL: http://www.infogroup.com • Annual. Number of listings: 2,727. Entries include: Name, address, phone, size of advertisement, name of owner or manager, number of employees, year first in "Yellow Pages." Compiled from telephone company "Yellow Pages," nationwide.

**Product Safety Letter**. Washington Business Information Inc., 300 N Washington St., No. 200 Falls Church, VA 22046-3431. Phone: 888-838-5578 or (703)538-7600; Fax: (703)538-7676; Email: customerservice@fdanews.com • URL: http://www.fdanews.com • Description: Follows the actions of the Consumer Product Safety Commission and other regulatory agencies and monitors developments and trends in the manufacturing industry. Offers "inside information about major regulatory trends, actions, opinions, and ideas." Spotlights stringent new rules which affect the production and sale of many common items. Recurring features include news of research and reports of meetings.

**Production and Consumption**. Produccion y Consumo SACEFI, Ave. Boedo 822 1281 Buenos Aires, Argentina. Phone: 19 70019 • Annual. $100. Covers: Manufacturers and distributors of Argentine and foreign products, including factories, workshops, services, trademarks, transport, automotive, nautics, seacraft, and chambers of commerce. Entries include: Contact information.

**Production and Inventory Management Journal**. APICS, 8430 W Bryn Mawr Ave., Ste. 1000 Chicago, IL 60631. Phone: 800-444-2742 or (773)867-1777; Fax: (773)639-3000; Email: service@apics.org • URL: http://www.apics.org • Quarterly.

**Production and Operations Management**. Production and Operations Management Society, The University of Texas at Dallas, School of Management, 2601 N Floyd Rd. Richardson, TX 75080. Phone: (972)883-4047; Fax: (972)883-5834; Email: poms@utdallas.edu • URL: http://www.poms.org • Quarterly 6/year. $70 Individuals per year; $200 Libraries per year.

**Production and Operations Management Society**. The University of Texas at Dallas, School of Management, 2601 N Floyd Rd. Richardson, TX 75080. Phone: (972)883-4047; Fax: (972)883-5834; Email: poms@utdallas.edu • URL: http://www.poms.org • Members are professionals and educators in fields related to operations management and production.

**Production**. Gardner Business Media, Inc., 6915 Valley Ave. Cincinnati, OH 45244-3029. Phone: 800-950-8020 or (513)527-8800; Fax: (513)527-8801; Email: orderbooks@gardnerweb.com • URL: http://www.gardnerweb.com • Covers the latest manufacturing management issues. Discusses the strategic and financial implications of various tecnologies as they impact factory management, quality and competitiveness.

**Production Managers Association**. Ealing Studios, Ealing Green, Ealing London W5 5EP, United Kingdom. Phone: 44 20 87588699; Email: pma@pma.org.uk • URL: http://www.pma.org.uk • Professional organization representing over 180 production managers working in film, television and multimedia.

*Production Technology News*. Reed Elsevier Group plc Reed Business Information, 360 Park Ave. S New York, NY 11010. Phone: (212)791-4208; Email: corporatecommunications@reedbusiness.com • URL: http://www.reedbusiness.com • Monthly. $57.99 /year. Formerly *Metalworking Digest*. Premier resource for the latest information on new technology, services, systems and products.

**Productivity Association of Pakistan**. Natl. Productivity Organization, Ministry of Industries, Software Technology Park, 2nd Fl., Constitution Ave. Islamabad, Pakistan. Phone: 92 51 2823304 or 92 51 2823305; Fax: 92 51 2823309; Email: info@npo.gov.pk • URL: http://www.npo.gov.pk/productivity-association • Seeks to promote and increase productivity by utilizing the knowledge, experience, expertise and resources of members. Aims to strengthen networking activities with public and private sector organizations. Provides a platform for the exchange of information and knowledge that are of strategic importance to research and development.

*Products and Services to China*. Intervisual Advertising Ltd., 20 Dering St. London W1R 0LR, United Kingdom. Phone: 71 6296696; Fax: 71 7535496; Email: interviz@dial.pipex.com • Covers: Industries in China and Hong Kong. Database includes: Product/service, name, tradename. Entries include: Company name, location, phone, geographical area served, subsidiary and branch names and locations, description of product/services.

*Products Finishing*. Gardner Business Media, Inc., 6915 Valley Ave. Cincinnati, OH 45244-3029. Phone: 800-950-8020 or (513)527-8800; Fax: (513)527-8801; Email: orderbooks@gardnerweb.com • URL: http://www.gardnerweb.com • Monthly. Covers the latest news and trends of industrial plating, painting, powder coating, cleaning, pretreatment and mechanical finishing.

**Professional Association for Customer Engagement**. 8500 Keystone Crossing, Ste. 480 Indianapolis, IN 46240. Phone: (317)816-9336 • URL: http://paceassociation.com • Businesses involved in teleservices, telephone marketing sales, including suppliers, distributors, users, and hardware and software manufacturers; educators and teleservice businesses. Provides for the specific needs of the total telephone services community; assists in understanding and using telephone communications for marketing purposes; sponsors educational programs.

*Professional Builder—Annual Report of Housing's Giants*. Reed Elsevier Group plc Reed Business Information, 360 Park Ave. S New York, NY 11010. Phone: (212)791-4208; Email: corporatecommunications@reedbusiness.com • URL: http://www.reedbusiness.com • Annual. Publication includes: list of top 400 firms that started and closed the greatest number of housing construction units in the preceding year. Entries include: Company name, city, state, housing revenues, total revenues, units started, units sold.

*Professional Builder: Small Builders and Contractors Business Magazine*. Reed Elsevier Group plc Reed Business Information, 360 Park Ave. S New York, NY 11010. Phone: (212)791-4208; Email: corporatecommunications@reedbusiness.com • URL: http://www.reedbusiness.com • 11 times a year. $39.00 per year. Provides price and market forecasts on industrial products, components and materials. Office products, business systems and transportation. Includes supplement Luxury Homes. Formerly *Professional Builder and Remodeler*.

*Professional Carwashing and Detailing*. National Trade Publications Inc., 13 Century Hill Dr. Latham, NY 12110. Phone: (518)783-1281; Fax: (518)783-1386 • Monthly. Edited for owners, operators, and managers of automatic carwashes, custom hand carwash facilities, detail shops, and coin-operated, self-service carwashes.

**Professional Construction Estimators Association of America**. PO Box 680336 Charlotte, NC 28216. Phone: 877-521-7232 or (704)489-1494; Email: pcea@pcea.org • URL: http://www.pcea.org • Members are building and construction cost estimators.

*Professional Consulting Services: Industry Sector Profile*. Philippine-German Export Development Project Philippine Bureau of Export Trade Promotion, 6F Trade & Industry Bldg., 361 Sen. Gil Puyat Ave. Makati PH-1226, Philippines. Phone: 63 2 897 8199; Email: web@dti.dti.gov.ph • URL: http://www.dti.gov.ph • Publication includes: Companies exporting professional consulting services from the Philippines. Entries include: Company name, address, phone, fax, name and title of contact, type of business, year established, subsidiary and branch names and locations, financial data, number of employees, government registrations, professional memberships, bank references, supply capability, export experience, business plan. Principal content of publication is an overview of the business environment and professional consulting services industry in the Philippines.

**Professional Convention Management Association**. 35 E Wacker Dr., Ste. 500 Chicago, IL 60601-2105. Phone: 877-827-7262 or (312)423-7262; Fax: (312)423-7222; Email: deborah.sexton@pcma.org • URL: http://www.pcma.org • Represents the interests of meeting management executives from associations, non-profit organizations, corporations, independent meeting planning companies, and multi-management firms who recognize the importance of meetings to their organization. Provides education, research and advocacy to advance the meetings and hospitality industry.

Empowers members with the tools they need to succeed as meeting professionals and to promote the value of the industry to their organizations and the general public.

*Professional Corporations and Associations*. Berrien C. Eaton. Matthew Bender and Company Inc., 1275 Broadway Albany, NY 12204-2638. Phone: 800-424-4200 or (518)487-3000; Fax: (518)487-3573 or (800)424-4200; Email: customer.support@lexisnexis.com • URL: http://www.matthewbender.com • Semiannual. $3,211 ebook. Detailed information on forming, operating and changing a professional corporation or association.

**Professional Decorative Painters Association**. PO Box 13427 Denver, CO 80201-3427. Email: admin@pdpa.org • URL: http://www.pdpa.org • Promotes the advancement of professional decorative painting worldwide. Provides a forum for the industry's stakeholders, craftspersons, students, and manufacturers to improve the level of practice and relationship design in the field. Offers resources to foster growth and professionalism within the industry.

*Professional Financial Planning Directory*. InfoGroup Inc., 5711 S 86th Cir. Omaha, NE 68127-4146. Phone: (402)593-4500 • URL: http://www.infogroup.com • Annual. Number of listings: 14,191. Entries include: Name, address, phone, size of advertisement, name of owner or manager, number of employees, year first in "Yellow Pages." Compiled from telephone company "Yellow Pages," nationwide.

*Professional Freelance Writers Directory*. National Writers Association, 10940 S Parker Rd., No. 508 Parker, CO 80134. Phone: (303)841-0246; Fax: (303)841-2607; Email: natlwritersassn@hotmail.com • URL: http://www.nationalwriters.com • Annual. Database covers: About 200 professional members selected from the club's membership on the basis of significant articles or books, or production of plays or movies. Entries include: Name, address, phone (home and business numbers), special fields of writing competence, titles of books published by royalty firms, mention of contributions to specific magazines, journals, newspapers or anthologies, recent awards received, relevant activities and skills (photography, etc.).

**Professional Golfers' Association of America**. 100 Ave. of the Champions Palm Beach Gardens, FL 33418-3653. Phone: (561)624-8400 • URL: http://www.pga.com • Recruits and trains men and women to manage a variety of golf businesses, including golf clubs, courses, and tournaments. Sponsors PGA Championship, PGA Seniors' Championship, Ryder Cup Matches, PGA Grand Slam of Golf, Club Professional Championship, PGA Foundation, and Senior Club Professional Championship; PGA Junior Championship; PGA Assistants Championship. Conducts Professional Golf Management; certifies college programs in golf management at 14 universities. Sponsors winter tournament program for club professionals including tournaments held in south Florida. Offers complementary employment services for PGA members and employers, owns and operates PGA Golf Club and PGA Learning Center.

**Professional Landcare Network**. 950 Herndon Pkwy., Ste. 450 Herndon, VA 20170-5528. Phone: 800-395-2522 or (703)736-9666; Fax: (703)736-9668; Email: info@landcarenetwork.org • URL: http://www.landcarenetwork.org • Formerly Professional Lawn Care Association of America.

**Professional Lighting and Sign Management Companies of America**. 1100-H Brandywine Blvd. Zanesville, OH 43701-7303. Phone: (740)452-4541 • URL: http://plasmalighting.org • Represents independently owned service providers offering lighting and signage services, workmanship and expertise. Seeks to uphold the standards of practice within the lighting and sign management industry. Promotes and protects the interests of members.

*The Professional Manager*. Institute of Industrial Engineers, 3577 Parkway Ln., Ste. 200 Norcross, GA 30092. Phone: 800-494-0460 or (770)449-0460 or (770)449-0461; Fax: (770)441-3295 or (770)263-8532; Email: executiveoffices@iienet.org • URL: http://www.iienet2.org • Bimonthly. Free to members; non-members, $24.00 per year. Features articles on the latest problem-solving techniques and trends available to industrial managers. Formerly *Industrial Management*.

*Professional Negligence Law Reporter*. American Association for Justice, 777 6th St. NW, Ste. 200 Washington, DC 20001. Phone: 800-424-2725 or (202)965-3500; Fax: (202)625-7084; Email: membership@justice.org • URL: http://www.justice.org/cps/rde/xchg/justice/hs.xsl/default.htm • Description: Covers professional negligence cases, including verdicts, settlements, and court opinions. Coverage focuses on health care providers, accountants, lawyers, engineers, insurance brokers and nursing homes, among other areas. Recurring features include bylined articles, bibliographies, and indexes.

**Professional Numismatists Guild**. 28441 Rancho California Rd., Ste. 106 Temecula, CA 92590-3618. Phone: 800-375-4653 or (951)587-8300; Fax: (951)587-8301; Email: info@pngdealers.com • URL: http://www.pngdealers.com • Represents coin dealers who have been involved full-time in the profession for at least five years. Establishes, promotes, and defends ethics in the hobby of numismatics.

**Professional Organization of Women in the Arts**. 365 Bridge St., Ste. 7F Brooklyn, NY 11201. Email: powarts@gmail.com • URL: http://www.powarts.org • Promotes the advancement of women in the visual arts industry. Aims to educate,

empower and promote leadership among women employed in the visual arts. Serves as a medium for the communication and exchange of ideas between women in the visual arts industry.

*Professional Photographer*. Professional Photographers of America. 229 Peachtree St. NE, Ste. 2200 Atlanta, GA 30303. Phone: 800-786-6277 or (404)522-8600; Fax: (404)614-6405; Email: csc@ppa.com • URL: http://www.ppa.com • Monthly. $27.00 per year.

*Professional Pilot Magazine*. Queensmith Communications Corp., 30 S Quaker LN Ste. 300 Alexandria, VA 22314. Phone: (703)370-0606 • Monthly. $50 Individuals; $60 Canada and Mexico; $80 Other countries. Edited for career pilots in all areas of aviation: airline, corporate, charter, and military. Includes flying technique, avionics, navigation, accident analysis, career planning, corporate profiles, and business aviation news.

**Professional Reactor Operator Society**. PO Box 484 Byron, IL 61010-0484. Phone: 800-422-2725 or (815)234-8140; Fax: (800)422-2725; Email: theprosoffice@aol.com • URL: http://nucpros.com • Plenary members are licensed and certified nuclear reactor operators; associate members include equipment manufacturers and utility companies. Aims to develop a communication network between nuclear reactor operators and government agencies, Congress, and industry in order to promote safety and efficiency in nuclear facilities. Believes that the education, experience, and training of nuclear facility operators have not been fairly considered in the formation of regulations, guidelines, and decisions that affect their careers. Areas of concern include educational requirements and job stress. Plans to survey the views and concerns of members and other involved parties; also plans personal presentations of members' views, supported by scientific data, to persons in the decision-making process. Offers direct mailing service to members from advertisers and placement agencies. Compiles statistics.

*Professional Safety*. American Society of Safety Engineers, 1800 E Oakton St. Des Plaines, IL 60018. Phone: (847)699-2929; Fax: (847)768-3434; Email: customerservice@asse.org • URL: http://www.asse.org • Monthly. $60 U.S., Canada, and Mexico. Emphasis is on research and technology in the field of accident prevention.

**Professional School Photographers Association International**. 3000 Picture Pl. Jackson, MI 49201. Phone: 800-762-9287 or (517)788-8100; Fax: (517)788-8371; Email: m.bell@bellphoto.com • URL: http://www.pmai.org • Retailers of photo and video equipment, film, and supplies; firms developing and printing film. Maintains hall of fame. Compiles statistics; conducts research and educational programs.

**Professional Scripophily Trade Association**. PO Box 223795 Chantilly, VA 20153. Phone: 888-786-2576 or (703)579-4209; Fax: (703)995-4422; Email: bob@psta.com • URL: http://www.psta.com • Promotes the study and collection of scripophily for collectors, researchers, and for the interpretation and preservation of financial history. Helps support educational projects, programs, and seminars to help collectors and the general public gain a better understanding of scripophily, finance and business history.

**Professional Women Controllers**. PO Box 23924 Washington, DC 20024. Email: info@pwcinc.org • URL: http://www.pwcinc.org • Women controllers. Promotes the advancement of women within the financial industry. Represents members' interests; facilitates networking among women controllers; and makes available educational programs.

*Proff, the Business Finder*. Eniro Danmark A/S, Sydmarken 44A 2860 Soborg, Denmark. Phone: 45 88 38 38 00; Fax: 45 88 38 38 10 • URL: http://www.eniro.dk • Contains a directory for Denmark's business-to-business trade.

*ProFile Canada*. Micromedia ProQuest, 20 Victoria St. Toronto, ON, Canada M5C 2N8. Phone: 800-387-2689 or (416)362-5211; Fax: (416)362-6161; Email: info@micromedia.ca • URL: http://www.proquest.com • Quarterly. Database covers: Approximately 17,000 Canadian companies and organizations. Entries include: Legal company name, trade name, address, phone, fax, e-mail, URL, number of employees, benefits, pension information, and number of branches. Some listings include sales range, size of customer base, Standard Industrial Classification (SIC) code, import/export activity, Canadian Business 500 ranking, Financial Post 500 ranking, and key personnel.

*Profiles of Success*. International Health, Racquet and Sportsclub Association, 70 Fargo St. Boston, MA 02210. Phone: 800-228-4772 or (617)951-0055; Fax: (617)951-0056; Email: info@ihrsa.org • URL: http://www.ihrsa.org • Annual. Members, $249.95; non-members, $499.95. Provides detailed financial statistics for commercial health clubs, sports clubs, and gyms.

*Profiles of U. S. Hospitals*. Dorland Healthcare Information, 1500 Walnut St., Ste. 1000 Philadelphia, PA 19102. Phone: 855-225-5341; Fax: (301)287-2535; Email: chi@healthcare-info.com • URL: http://www.dorlandhealth.com • Annual. $299.00. Contains profiles of more than 6,000 community, teaching, children's, specialty, psychiatric, and rehabilitation hospitals. Emphasis is on 50 key financial and performance measures. Annual CD-ROM version with key word searching is available at $395.00.

*Profile's Stock Exchange Handbook*. Profile Media, PO Box 87254 Houghton 2041, South Africa. Phone: 27 11 7285510;

Fax: 27 11 7285845; Email: info@profile.co.za • URL: http://www.profile.co.za • Quarterly. R 155 Individuals. Covers: About 650 companies whose stock is traded on the Johannesburg, South Africa, stock exchange. Entries include: Company name, address, names and titles of key personnel, line of business, names of associated and subsidiary companies, capital, dates of dividend payments, five-year financial data, five-year comparison of high and low share prices and volumes traded.

***Profit Investor Portfolio: The International Magazine of Money and Style***. Profit Publications, Inc., 69-730 Highway 111, Suite 102 Rancho Mirage, CA 92270-9822. Phone: (619)202-1545; Fax: (619)202-1544 • URL: http://www.profitinc.com • Bimonthly. $29.95 per year. A glossy consumer magazine featuring specific investment recommendations and articles on upscale travel and shopping.

***Profit Sharing***. Plan Sponsor Council of America, 20 N Wacker Dr., Ste. 3700 Chicago, IL 60606. Phone: (312)419-1863; Fax: (312)419-1864; Email: psca@psca.org • URL: http://www.psca.org • Bimonthly. Membership.

***Profitable Investing***. Richard E. Band, editor. Profitable Investing, 7811 Montrose Rd. Potomac, MD 20854. Phone: (301)340-7788 • Description: Advises individuals seeking low-risk growth by providing : "a wealth of information." Discusses various stocks, mutual funds, interest income, and tax issues. Contains lists of best investments.

***Program: Electronic Library and Information Systems***. Emerald Group Publishing Ltd., Howard House, Wagon Ln. Bingley BD16 1WA, United Kingdom. Phone: 44 1274 777 700; Fax: 44 1274 785 201 • URL: http://www.emeraldinsight.com • Discusses computer applications for libraries.

***Progress in Aerospace Sciences: An International Journal***. Elsevier, Secondary Publishing Division, 650 Ave. of the Americas New York, NY 10011. Phone: 888-437-4636 or (212)633-3980; Fax: (212)633-3975; Email: t.reller@elsevier.com • URL: http://www.elseveier.com • $2,631 Individuals Print. Aerospace journal. Text in English, French and German.

***Progress in Materials Science: An International Review Journal***. Elsevier, Secondary Publishing Division, 650 Ave. of the Americas New York, NY 10011. Phone: 888-437-4636 or (212)633-3980; Fax: (212)633-3975; Email: t.reller@elsevier.com • URL: http://www.elseveier.com • $2,793 Individuals Print. Publishes authoritative reviews of recent advances in the science of materials and their exploitation in engineering.

***Progress in Oceanography***. Elsevier, Secondary Publishing Division, 650 Ave. of the Americas New York, NY 10011. Phone: 888-437-4636 or (212)633-3980; Fax: (212)633-3975; Email: t.reller@elsevier.com • URL: http://www.elseveier.com • $225 Individuals; $4,237 Institutions.

***Progress in Planning***. Elsevier, Secondary Publishing Division, 650 Ave. of the Americas New York, NY 10011. Phone: 888-437-4636 or (212)633-3980; Fax: (212)633-3975; Email: t.reller@elsevier.com • URL: http://www.elseveier.com • Eight times a year. $755.00 per year.

***Progressive Farmer***. Progressive Farmer, Inc., 2100 Lakeshore Dr. Birmingham, AL 35209. Phone: (205)877-6419; Fax: (205)877-6750; Email: jodie@progressivefarmer.com • URL: http://www.pathfinder.com/pf • Monthly. $16 per year. Includes supplement *Rural Sportsman*.

***Progressive Grocer Guidebook***. Trade Dimensions, 45 Danbury Rd. Wilton, CT 06897. Phone: 800-291-0410 or (203)563-3000; Fax: (203)563-3131; Email: info@tradedimensions.com • URL: http://www.tradedimensions.com • Annual. $375.00. Over 800 major chain and independent food retailers and wholesalers in the United States and Canada; also includes food brokers, rack jobbers, candy and tobacco distributors, and magazine distributors.

***Progressive Grocer***. Nielsen Business Media Inc., 770 Broadway New York, NY 10003-9522. Phone: 866-890-8541 or (646)654-4500 or (646)654-5000; Fax: (646)654-5584 or (646)654-4500; Email: bmcomm@nielsen.com • URL: http://www.nielsenbusinessmedia.com • 18 times a year. $129.00 per year. Formerly *Supermarket Business*.

***Progressive Grocer: The Magazine of Supermarketing***. Nielsen Business Media Inc., 770 Broadway New York, NY 10003-9522. Phone: 866-890-8541 or (646)654-4500 or (646)654-5000; Fax: (646)654-5584 or (646)654-4500; Email: bmcomm@nielsen.com • URL: http://www.nielsenbusinessmedia.com.

***Progressive Railroading***. Trade Press Media Group, 2100 W Florist Ave. Milwaukee, WI 53209. Phone: 800-727-7995 or (414)228-7701; Fax: (414)228-1134; Email: info@tradepress.com • URL: http://www.tradepress.com • Monthly. Provides feature articles, news, new product information, etc. Relative to the railroad and rail transit industry.

***Project Bait Business Magazine***. Black Awareness in Television, 30 Josephine St., 3rd Fl. Detroit, MI 48202-1810. Phone: (313)871-3333.

***Project Finance Monthly***. Infocast Inc., 6800 Owensmouth Ave., Ste. 300 Canoga Park, CA 91303. Phone: (818)888-4444; Fax: (818)888-4440; Email: service@rband.com • URL: http://www.infocastinc.com • Description: Provides information about the power industry. Includes industry news, financing, regulation, and contracts.

***Project Finance: The Magazine for Global Development***. American Educational Systems, PO Box 236 New York, NY

10024-0246. Phone: 800-431-1579; Email: aesbooks@aol.com • 11 times a year. $740.00 per year. Includes print and online editions. Provides articles on the financing of the infrastructure (transportation, utilities, communications, the environment, etc). Coverage is international. Supplements available *World Export Credit Guide* and *Project Finance Book of Lists*. Formed by the merger of *Infrastructure Finance* and *Project and Trade Finance*.

***Project Finance Yearbook***. Euromoney Institutional Investor P.L.C., 11 N Hill Colchester CO1 1DZ, United Kingdom. Phone: 44 1206 579591; Fax: 44 1206 560121; Email: yearbooks@euromoneyplc.com • URL: http://www.euromoney-yearbooks.com • $375 Individuals; £245 Individuals; €295 Individuals. Contains innovative project finance modelling, case studies of recent ground-breaking projects, advice on managing both country and project risk, legal and contractual problems and how they were solved. Covers: Approximately 3,000 companies involved in project finance worldwide. Entries include: Name, address, phone, fax, e-mail, names and titles of key personnel.

**Project Management Institute**. 14 Campus Blvd. Newtown Square, PA 19073-3299. Phone: 855-746-4849 or (610)356-4600; Fax: (610)482-9971; Email: customercare@pmi.org • URL: http://www.pmi.org • Corporations and individuals engaged in the practice of project management; project management students and educators. Seeks to advance the study, teaching and practice of project management. Establishes project management standards; conducts educational and professional certification courses; bestows Project Management Professional credential upon qualified individuals. Offers educational seminars and global congresses.

***Project Management Journal***. Project Management Institute, 14 Campus Blvd. Newtown Square, PA 19073-3299. Phone: 855-746-4849 or (610)356-4600; Fax: (610)482-9971; Email: customercare@pmi.org • URL: http://www.pmi.org • 6/year Quarterly. $465 Institutions; $505 Canada and Mexico institutions; $149 U.S., Canada, and Mexico; $165 U.S., Canada, and Mexico print and online. Contains technical articles dealing with the interests of the field of project management.

***Project Management Salary Survey***. Project Management Institute, 14 Campus Blvd. Newtown Square, PA 19073-3299. Phone: 855-746-4849 or (610)356-4600; Fax: (610)482-9971; Email: customercare@pmi.org • URL: http://www.pmi.org • Annual. $200.00. Gives compensation data for key project management positions in North America, according to job title, level of responsibility, number of employees supervised, and various other factors. Includes data on retirement plans and benefits.

**Project on Government Oversight**. 1100 G St. NW, Ste. 500 Washington, DC 20005-3806. Phone: (202)347-1122; Fax: (202)347-1116; Email: info@pogo.org • URL: http://www.pogo.org • Promotes accountability in government; monitors governmental agencies; exposes abuses of power, and waste and fraud committed by the government and its contractors.

**PROMAXBDA**. 1522e Cloverfield Blvd. Santa Monica, CA 90404. Phone: (310)788-7600; Fax: (310)788-7616 • URL: http://www.promaxbda.org • Advertising, public relations, and promotion managers of cable, radio, and television stations, systems and networks; syndicators. Seeks to: advance the role and increase the effectiveness of promotion and marketing within the industry, related industries, and educational communities. Conducts workshops and weekly fax service for members. Operates employment service. Maintains speakers' bureau, hall of fame, and resource center with print, audio, and visual materials.

***PROMO Annual SourceBook: The Only Guide to the $70 Billion Promotion Industry***. Primedia Business Magazines and Media, 11 River Bend Dr., S Stamford, CT 06907. Phone: 800-795-5445 or (203)358-9900 or (203)358-4159; Fax: (203)358-5811 or (203)358-5812; Email: kjoyce@primediabusiness.com • Annual. $49.95. Lists service and supply companies for the promotion industry. Includes annual salary survey and award winning campaigns.

***PROMO: Promotion Marketing Worldwide***. Primedia Business Magazines and Media, 11 River Bend Dr., S Stamford, CT 06907. Phone: 800-795-5445 or (203)358-9900 or (203)358-4159; Fax: (203)358-5811 or (203)358-5812; Email: kjoyce@primediabusiness.com • Monthly. $65.00 per year. Edited for companies and agencies that utilize couponing, point-of-purchase advertising, special events, games, contests, premiums, product samples, and other unique promotional items.

***Promotional Marketing***. Entrepreneur Press, 2445 McCabe Way, Ste. 400 Irvine, CA 92614-6244. Phone: 800-864-6864 or (949)261-2325 or (949)622-7131; Fax: (949)261-7729 or (949)261-0234; Email: press@entrepreneur.com • URL: http://www.entrepreneurpress.com • Looseleaf. $59.50. A practical guide to sales promotion and marketing for small businesses. (Start-Up Business Guide No. E1111.).

**Promotional Products Association International**. 3125 Skyway Cir. N Irving, TX 75038-3526. Phone: 888-426-7724 or (972)252-0404; Fax: (972)258-3004 or (972)258-3003; Email: membership@ppai.org • URL: http://www.ppai.org • Suppliers and distributors of promotional products including incentives, imprinted ad specialties, premiums, and executive gifts. Promotes industry contacts in 60 countries. Holds

executive development and sales training seminars. Conducts research and compiles statistics. Administers industry advertising and public relations program. Maintains speakers' bureau. Conducts trade shows, regional training, publishes educational resources.

***Promotional Products Business***. Promotional Products Association International, 3125 Skyway Cir. N Irving, TX 75038-3526. Phone: 888-426-7724 or (972)252-0404; Fax: (972)258-3004 or (972)258-3003; Email: membership@ppai.org • URL: http://www.ppai.org • Monthly. $58 /year for members; $72 /year for nonmembers; $70 Members in Canada and Mexico; $82 Nonmembers in Canada and Mexico; $75 Members international; $92 Nonmembers international; $48 Members; $60 Canada and Mexico members; $65 Other countries members; $62 Members for prospective members in U.S.; $74 Canada and Mexico for prospective members in Canada and Mexico; $79 Other countries for prospective members in other countries. Magazine covering news, trends, new products and business issues affecting the promotional products industry. Official magazine of the Promotional Products Assoc. International.

***Prompt***. Pasadena IBM User Group, 2303 Glen Canyon Rd. Altadena, CA 91001-3539. Phone: (818)791-1600; Fax: (818)791-1600; Email: 71333.130@compuserve.com • Monthly. Membership. Helps users of IBM compatibles understand their system.

***Proofs: The Magazine of Dental Sales***. PennWell Corp., Industrial Div., 1421 S Sheridan Rd. Tulsa, OK 74112. Phone: 800-331-4463 or (918)835-3161; Email: bid@pennwell.com • URL: http://www.pennwell.com • Contains information on dental trade shows, dental industry marketing, sales tools, and industry statistics.

***Properties***. Properties Magazine, Inc., PO Box 112127 Cleveland, OH 44111. Phone: 888-641-4241 or (216)251-0035; Fax: (216)251-0064 • URL: http://www.propertiesmag.com • Monthly. $24.95 Individuals; $34.95 Two years. News and features of interest to income property owners managers and related industries in Northeastern Ohio.

***Property-Casualty Insurance Facts***. Insurance Information Institute, 110 William St. New York, NY 10038. Phone: (212)346-5500; Email: members@iii.org • URL: http://www.iii.org • Annual. $22.50. Formerly *Insurance Facts*.

**Property Council of Australia**. 11 Barrack St., Level 1 Sydney, NSW 2000, Australia. Phone: 61 2 90331900; Fax: 61 2 90331967; Email: info@propertyoz.com.au • URL: http://www.propertyoz.com.au • Institutional investors, pension funds, property trusts, financial organizations, private investors, and developers. Represents the interests of the property sector in Australia. Seeks to increase property into an internationally competitive asset class. Participates in lobbying and advocacy activities. Offers educational programs. Conducts research; compiles statistics.

***Property Management Association—Directory***. Property Management Association, 7508 Wisconsin Ave., 4th Fl. Bethesda, MD 20814. Phone: (301)657-9200; Fax: (301)907-9326; Email: info@pma-dc.org • URL: http://www.pma-dc.org • Annual. $50 Nonmembers. Covers: Over 539 property managers and 336 related supplier firms. Entries include: For property managers—Name, firm name, address, phone, fax, specialty. For supplier firms—Company name, name of contact, address, phone, fax.

**Property Management Association**. 7508 Wisconsin Ave., 4th Fl. Bethesda, MD 20814. Phone: (301)657-9200; Fax: (301)907-9326; Email: info@pma-dc.org • URL: http://www.pma-dc.org • Property management professionals who own and operate multifamily residential, commercial, retail, industrial and other income-producing properties and firms that provide goods and services used in real property management. Works to enhance the interests and welfare of property owners, managers, supervisory employees and contractors involved in the management of multifamily residential and commercial property. Provides education and a forum for exchange of ideas on efficient methods of operation and progressive policies of management.

***Property Tax Alert***. State Taxation Institute, 4025 W Peterson Ave. Chicago, IL 60646-6085. Phone: 800-TELL-CCH; Fax: (773)866-3895 • Description: Features updates on property tax issues. Recurring features include a calendar of events and notices of publications available.

***ProQuest***. ProQuest L.L.C., 789 E Eisenhower Pkwy. Ann Arbor, MI 48106-1346. Phone: 800-521-0600 or (734)761-4700; Fax: (734)662-4554; Email: info@proquest.com • URL: http://www.proquest.com • Fee-based Web site providing Internet access to more than 3,000 periodicals, newspapers, and other publications. Many items are available full-text, with daily updates. Includes extensive corporate and financial information. Fees: Apply.

***ProSales Buyer's Guide***. DoveTale Publishers, 1 Thomas Cir. NW Washington, DC 20005. Phone: 877-275-8647 or (202)339-0744 or (202)452-0800; Fax: (202)785-1974 or (202)339-0749; Email: hwmicustomerservice@hanleywood.com • URL: http://www.hwmarketintelligence.com • Annual. Price on application. A directory of equipment for professional builders.

***ProSales: For Dealers and Distributors Serving the Professional Contractor***. DoveTale Publishers, 1 Thomas Cir. NW Washington, DC 20005. Phone: 877-275-8647 or (202)339-0744 or (202)452-0800; Fax: (202)785-1974 or (202)339-

0749; Email: hwmicustomerservice@hanleywood.com • URL: http://www.hwmarketintelligence.com • Includes special feature issues on selling, credit, financing, and the marketing of power tools.

***Protecting Trade Secrets, Patents, Copyrights, and Trademarks***. Robert C. Dorr and Christopher H. Munch. Aspen Publishers, Inc., 7201 McKinney Cir. Frederick, MD 21704. Phone: 800-234-1660 or (301)698-7100 or (301)417-7500; Fax: (800)901-9075 or (301)695-7931; Email: customerservice@aspenpublisher.com • URL: http://www.aspenpublishers.com • $165.00. Looseleaf service.

***Provider: For Long Term Care Professionals***. American Health Care Association, 1201 L St. NW Washington, DC 20005. Phone: (202)842-4444; Fax: (202)842-3860 • URL: http://www.ahcancal.org/Pages/Default.aspx • Monthly. Free to qualified long-term and post-acute care professionals.; $48 /year for nonmembers and libraries; $61 Canada and Mexico; $85 Other countries. Edited for medical directors, administrators, owners, and others concerned with extended care facilities and nursing homes. Covers business management, legal issues, financing, reimbursement, care planning, ethics, human resources, etc. Includes *Buyers' Guide*.

***Provincial Outlook***. Conference Board of Canada, 255 Smyth Rd. Ottawa, ON, Canada K1H 8M7. Phone: 866-711-2262 or (613)526-3280; Fax: (613)526-4857; Email: contactcboc@conferenceboard.ca • URL: http://www.conferenceboard.ca • Quarterly. Free to members; non-members, $2,500.00 per year. Contains detailed forecasts of economic conditions in each of the Canadian provinces.

***Provincial/Territorial Directories***. A.C. Braby (Pty) Ltd., 12 Caversham Rd. Pinetown 3610, South Africa. Email: support@brabys.co.za • URL: http://www.brabys.com • Annual. $35 Botswana ed.; $60 Cape Province ed.; $36 East Rand e.; $25 Lesotho ed.; $25 Natal ed.; $30 Orange Free State/Northern Cape ed.; $35 SWA/Nambia ed.; $25 Transkei ed.; $100 Transvaal ed.; $35 Zambia ed. Covers: Business listings in South Africa. Entries include: Company name, address, phone, telex number.

***The Prudent Speculator***. Al Frank Asset Management Inc., 32392 Coast Hwy., Ste. 260 Laguna Beach, CA 92651. Phone: 888-994-6827 or (949)497-7657; Fax: (949)499-3218; Email: info@alfrank.com • URL: http://www.alfrank.com • Description: Presents a fundamental approach to stock selection and buying strategies for long-term capital gains appreciation. Provides technical analysis to aid market timing for both speculators and conservative investors. Reviews editor's personal common stock portfolio in comparison with the Dow Jones Industrials and New York Stock Exchange Composite Index. Recurring features include a column titled Currently Recommended Stocks with follow-up reviews.

***Psychological Abstracts***. American Psychological Association, 750 First St. NE Washington, DC 20002-4242. Phone: 800-374-2721 or (202)336-5500 or (202)336-6013; Fax: (202)336-5812 or (202)336-5633; Email: journals@apa.org • URL: http://www.apa.org • Monthly. Members, $815.00 per year; individuals and institutions, $1,207.00 per year. Covers the international literature of psychology and the behavioral sciences. Includes journals, technical reports, dissertations, and other sources.

***Psychology and Marketing***. John Wiley and Sons, Inc., Journals Div., 111 River St. Hoboken, NJ 07030. Phone: 800-526-5368 or (201)748-6000; Fax: (201)748-6088; Email: consumers@wiley.com • URL: http://www.wiley.com • Monthly. $2,179 Institutions; $2,299 Institutions, Canada and Mexico; $2,401 Institutions, other countries institutions. Spots the latest social, economic, and cultural trends that affect marketing decisions.

***Psychology Today***. Sussex Publishers Inc., 49 21st St., 11th Fl. New York, NY 10010-6213. Phone: 800-234-8361 or (212)260-7210; Fax: (212)260-7566 or (212)260-7445 • $19.97 6 issues; $29.97 12 issues; $39.97 18 issues.

***Psychotropic Substances***. United Nations Publications, c/o National Book Network, 15200 NBN Way Blue Ridge Summit, PA 17214. Phone: 888-254-4286 or (212)963-7680 or (212)963-8302; Fax: (800)338-4550; Email: unpublications@nbnbooks.com • URL: http://www.unp.un.org • Annual. $50.00.

***Public Accounting Report: Competitive Intelligence for Accounting Firms***. Strafford Publications Inc., 590 Dutch Valley Rd. Atlanta, GA 30324-0729. Phone: 800-926-7926 or (404)881-1141; Fax: (404)881-0074; Email: custservice@straffordpub.com • URL: http://www.straffordpub.com • Presents news and trends affecting the accounting profession.

***Public Administration and Development: An International Journal of Training, Research and Practice***. John Wiley and Sons, Inc., Journals Div., 111 River St. Hoboken, NJ 07030. Phone: 800-526-5368 or (201)748-6000; Fax: (201)748-6088; Email: consumers@wiley.com • URL: http://www.wiley.com • 5/year. $2,038 Institutions. Focuses on administrative practice at the local, regional and national levels. International coverage. Published in England by John Wiley and Sons Ltd.

***Public Administration Review (PAR)***. American Society for Public Administration, 1301 Pennsylvania Ave. NW, Ste. 700 Washington, DC 20004-1716. Phone: (202)393-7878; Fax: (202)638-4952; Email: info@aspanet.org • URL: http://www.aspanet.org/public • Bimonthly. $539 Institutions U.S., print + online; £536 Institutions European, print + online; £1,050 Institutions, other countries print + online; $469 Institutions U.S., print or online; €591 Institutions European, print or online; £912 Institutions, other countries print or online; $90 /year. Serves governmental administrators, public officials, educators, research workers, and others interested in the public management profession. Includes online edition.

***Public Affairs Report***. University of California, Berkeley Institute of Governmental Studies, 109 Moses Hall, No. 2370 Berkeley, CA 94720-2370. Phone: (510)642-1473; Fax: (510)642-3020; Email: igs@berkeley.edu • URL: http://www.igs.berkeley.edu • Quarterly. Description: Publishes essays on emerging governmental and public policy issues of significance to public officials and citizens in both California and the nation. Covers such subjects as pollution, politics, finance, transportation, health and housing policy, and California-Mexico trade relations. Recurring features include bibliographies.

**Public Art Fund**. 1 E 53rd St. New York, NY 10022. Phone: (212)223-7800; Fax: (212)223-7801; Email: info@publicartfund.org • URL: http://www.publicartfund.org • Works with artists, architects, city planners, and community groups to explore and develop programs that bring art of both a temporary and permanent nature directly into the public environment. Provides public information and consultation on public art to governmental agencies, private businesses, and community groups, both in New York City and across the country.

***Public Assistance and Welfare Trends: State Capitals***. Wakeman/Walworth Inc., PO Box 7376 Alexandria, VA 22307-7376. Phone: 800-876-2545 or (703)768-9600; Fax: (703)768-9690; Email: newsletters@statecapitals.com • URL: http://statecapitals.com/ • 50 times a year. $245.00 per year; print and online editions, $350.00 per year. Newsletter. Formerly *From the State Capitals: Public Assistance and Welfare Trends*.

**Public Citizen**. 1600 20th St. NW Washington, DC 20009-1001. Phone: (202)588-1000; Email: member@citizen.org • URL: http://www.citizen.org • Formed by Ralph Nader to support the work of citizen advocates. Areas of focus include: consumer rights in the marketplace, safe products, a healthful environment and workplace, clean and safe energy sources, corporate and government accountability, and citizen empowerment. Methods for change include lobbying, litigation, monitoring government agencies, research, and public education including special reports, periodicals, expert testimony, and news media coverage. Acquires funding primarily through direct mail and also through payment for publications and court awards.

***Public Companies***. InfoGroup Inc., 5711 S 86th Cir. Omaha, NE 68127-4146. Phone: (402)593-4500 • URL: http://www.infogroup.com • Number of listings: 9,084. Entries include: Company name, address, phone, names and titles of key personnel, stock exchange symbol, Standard Industrial Classification (SIC) codes, annual sales, number of employees.

***Public Employee***. American Federation of State, County and Municipal Employees, 1625 L St. NW Washington, DC 20036-5687. Phone: (202)429-1000; Fax: (202)429-1293; Email: recruiting@afscme.org • URL: http://www.afscme.org • 8/year. Bimonthly. Membership. Newsletter. Formerly *Public Employee Magazine*.

***Public Employment***. Bureau of the Census, U.S. Department of Commerce. U. S. Government Printing Office, 732 N Capitol St. NW Washington, DC 20401. Phone: 866-512-1800 or (202)512-1800 or (866)512-1800; Fax: (202)512-2104 or (202)512-2250; Email: contactcenter@gpo.gov • URL: http://www.gpo.gov • Annual.

***Public Finance Review***. Pine Forge Press, 2455 Teller Rd. Thousand Oaks, CA 91320-2234. Phone: 800-818-7243 or (805)499-4224 or (805)499-9774; Fax: (805)499-0871 or (805)583-2665; Email: sales@pfp.sagepub.com • URL: http://www.sagepub.com/sociologybooks • Bimonthly. $1,223 Institutions print & e-access; $1,345 Institutions current volume print & all online content; $1,101 Institutions e-access; $1,223 Institutions e-access (all online content); $2,433 Institutions e-access (content through 1998); $1,199 Institutions print only; $181 Individuals print only; $220 Institutions single print; $39 Individuals single print. Public economy journal. Formerly *Public Finance Quarterly*.

***Public Human Services Directory***. American Public Human Services Association, 1133 19th St. NW, Ste. 400 Washington, DC 20036. Phone: (202)682-0100; Fax: (202)289-6555; Email: pubs@aphsa.org • URL: http://www.aphsa.org • Annual. $225 Individuals; $200 Members; $350 Institutions. Covers: Federal, state, territorial, county, and major municipal public human service agencies. Database includes: Information on all major human service programs, such as child welfare, child support enforcement, Medicaid eligibility and claims, interstate compacts, and other programs. Entries include: Agency name, address, phone, fax, e-mail address, web site address, names of key personnel, program area.

**Public Library Association; Technology Committee**. c/o American Library Association, 50 E Huron St. Chicago, IL 60611. Phone: 800-545-2433 or (312)280-5047; Fax: (312)280-5029 • URL: http://www.ala.org/pla/about/committees/pla-tech • Affiliated with the American Library Association. Formerly Public Libraries Division.

***Public Library Quarterly***. The Haworth Press Inc., 10 Alice St. Binghamton, NY 13904. Phone: 800-429-6784 or (607)722-5857; Fax: (607)771-0012 or (607)722-6362; Email: getinfo@haworthpress.com • URL: http://www.haworthpressinc.com/store/product.asp?sku=J014 • Quarterly. Institutions, $141.00 per year (print and online).

***Public Management: Devoted to the Conduct of Local Government***. International City/County Management Association, 777 N Capitol St. NE, Ste. 500 Washington, DC 20002-4201. Phone: (202)289-4262; Fax: (202)962-3500; Email: customerservices@icma.org • URL: http://icma.org/en/icma/home • 11/year. $46 U.S. for nonmembers; $155 Other countries for nonmembers; Included in membership.

***The Public Manager: The Journal for Practitioners***. Bureaucrat, Inc., 12007 Titian Way Potomac, MD 20854. Phone: (301)279-9445; Fax: (301)251-5872; Email: tnovo@aol.com • URL: http://www.thepublicmanager.org • Quarterly. $39 Members print and online; $79 Individuals print and online; $129 Institutions print and online. Formerly *Bureaucrat*.

***Public Opinion Quarterly***. American Association for Public Opinion Research. The University of Chicago Press, Journals Div., 1427 E 60th St. Chicago, IL 60637. Phone: 877-705-1878 or (773)702-7700; Email: subscriptions@press.uchicago.edu • URL: http://www.press.uchicago.edu/journals.html • Quarterly. $53 Individuals; $34 Students; $334 Institutions.

***Public Personnel Management***. International Personnel Management Association, 1617 Duke St. Alexandria, VA 22314. Phone: (703)549-7100; Fax: (703)684-0948; Email: publications@ipma-hr.org • URL: http://www.ipma-hr.org • Quarterly. $273 Institutions. Contains trends, case studies, and the latest research by top human resource scholars and industry experts.

***Public Power***. American Public Power Association, 1875 Connecticut Ave. NW, Ste. 1200 Washington, DC 20009-5715. Phone: 800-515-2772 or (202)467-2900; Fax: (202)467-2910; Email: info@publicpower.org • URL: http://www.publicpower.org • 8/year.

***Public Power Weekly***. American Public Power Association, 1875 Connecticut Ave. NW, Ste. 1200 Washington, DC 20009-5715. Phone: 800-515-2772 or (202)467-2900; Fax: (202)467-2910; Email: info@publicpower.org • URL: http://www.publicpower.org • Description: Reports on legislative, regulatory, judicial, and technical developments affecting local and state-owned electric utilities. Recurring features include employment notices and news briefs.

***Public Pulse: Roper's Authoritative Report on What Americans are Thinking, Doing, and Buying***. GfK SE, Nordwestring 101 90419 Nuremberg, Germany. Phone: 49 0911 395-0 or 49 911 395 0; Fax: 49 0911 395-2209 or 49 911 395 2209; Email: public.affairs@gfk.de • URL: http://www.gfk.de • Monthly. $297.00. Newsletter. Contains news of surveys of American attitudes, values, and behavior. Each issue includes a research supplement giving "complete facts and figures behind each survey question.".

***Public Relations***. Access Intelligence L.L.C., 4 Choke Cherry Rd., 2nd Fl. Rockville, MD 20850. Phone: 800-777-5006 or (301)354-2000 or (301)354-2101; Fax: (301)309-3847 or (801)365-2300; Email: info@accessintel.com • URL: http://www.accessintel.com/ • Biweekly. $397.00 per year. Newsletter on public relations and client communications for the healthcare industry. Incorporates (Healthcare PR and Marketing News).

***Public Relations Quarterly***. Hudson Associates, 44 W Market St. Rhinebeck, NY 12572. Phone: (845)876-2081; Fax: (845)876-2561; Email: hphudson@aol.com • URL: http://www.newsletter-clearinghse.com • Quarterly. $65.00 per year. Opinion articles and case studies on the theory and practice of public relations for and by leading practitioners and academicians.

***Public Relations Review: Journal of Research and Comment***. Elsevier, Secondary Publishing Division, 650 Ave. of the Americas New York, NY 10011. Phone: 888-437-4636 or (212)633-3980; Fax: (212)633-3975; Email: t.reller@elsevier.com • URL: http://www.elseveier.com • 5/year. $228 Individuals; $845 Institutions. Contains articles based on empirical research undertaken by professionals and academics in the field of public relations.

**Public Relations Society of America**. 33 Maiden Ln., 11th Fl. New York, NY 10038-5150. Phone: (212)460-1400; Fax: (212)995-0757 or (212)995-5024; Email: hq@prsa.org • URL: http://www.prsa.org • Absorbed American Public Relations Association and National Communication Council for Human Services.

***Public Relations Strategist: Issues and Trends That Affect Management***. Public Relations Society of America, 33 Maiden Ln., 11th Fl. New York, NY 10038-5150. Phone: (212)460-1400; Fax: (212)995-0757 or (212)995-5024; Email: hq@prsa.org • URL: http://www.prsa.org • Quarterly. $150 U.S.; $160 Canada; $170 Other countries. Provides public relations advice for corporate and government executives.

**Public Risk Management Association**. 700 S Washington St., Ste. 218 Alexandria, VA 22314. Phone: (703)528-7701; Fax: (703)739-0200; Email: info@primacentral.org • URL: http://www.primacentral.org • Public agency risk, insurance, human resources, attorneys, and/or safety managers from cities, counties, villages, towns, school boards, and other related areas. Provides an information clearinghouse and communications network for public risk managers to share resources, ideas, and experiences. Offers information on risk, insurance, and safety management. Monitors state and federal legislative actions and court decisions that deal with immunity, tort liability, and intergovernmental risk pools. Maintains library containing current reports from governmental units on their insurance procedures, self-insurance plans, and loss control and safety programs; and copies of policy statements, job descriptions, contractual arrangements, and indemnification clauses.

**Public Risk.** Public Risk Management Association, 700 S Washington St., Ste. 218 Alexandria, VA 22314. Phone: (703)528-7701; Fax: (703)739-0200; Email: info@primacentral.org • URL: http://www.primacentral.org • Monthly. $130 Individuals; $13.50 Single issue. Covers risk management for state and local governments, including various kinds of liabilities.

**Public Roads: A Journal of Highway Research and Development.** U. S. Government Printing Office, 732 N Capitol St. NW Washington, DC 20401. Phone: 866-512-1800 or (202)512-1800 or (866)512-1800; Fax: (202)512-2104 or (202)512-2250; Email: contactcenter@gpo.gov • URL: http://www.gpo.gov • Bimonthly. $31 U.S.; $43.40 Other countries. Contains articles relating to highway research, engineering, safety on the highways, surfacing, and other subjects.

**Public Utilities Fortnightly.** Public Utilities Reports Inc., 11410 Isaac Newton Sq., Ste. 220 Reston, VA 20190. Phone: 800-368-5001 or (703)847-7720; Fax: (703)847-0683; Email: radford@pur.com • URL: http://www.fortnightly.com • Monthly. $287 Individuals; $317 Other countries. Management magazine for utility executives in electric, gas, telecommunications and water industries.

**Public Works: City, County and State.** Public Works Journal Corp., 200 S Broad St. Ridgewood, NJ 07451. Phone: 800-524-2364 or (201)445-5800; Fax: (201)445-5170; Email: pw@pwmag.com • Monthly. Includes *Public Works Manual.*

**Public Works Manual.** Public Works Journal Corp., 200 S Broad St. Ridgewood, NJ 07451. Phone: 800-524-2364 or (201)445-5800; Fax: (201)445-5170; Email: pw@pwmag.com • Annual. $45. Publication includes: List of about 3,500 manufacturers and distributors of equipment, materials, services, computers, and software used in the design, construction, maintenance, and operation of streets and highways, water systems, wastewater and solid wastes processing, and recreation areas. Entries include: Company name, address, products. Principal content is technical articles on public works topics.

**Publications of the National Institute of Standards and Technology.** U. S. Government Printing Office, 732 N Capitol St. NW Washington, DC 20401. Phone: 866-512-1800 or (202)512-1800 or (866)512-1800; Fax: (202)512-2104 or (202)512-2250; Email: contactcenter@gpo.gov • URL: http://www.gpo.gov • Annual. Keyword and author indexes.

**Publishers' Auxiliary.** National Newspaper Association, PO Box 7540 Columbia, MO 65205-7540. Phone: (573)777-4980; Fax: (573)777-4985 or (573)237-9808 • URL: http://nnaweb.org.

**Publishers' Catalogues Home Page.** EBSCO Publishing Inc., 10 Estes St. Ipswich, MA 01938-2106. Phone: 800-653-2726 or (978)356-6500; Fax: (978)356-6565; Email: information@ebscohost.com • URL: http://www.ebscohost.com • Provides links to the Web home pages of about 1,700 U. S. publishers (including about 80 University presses) and publishers in 48 foreign countries. "International/Multinational Publishers" are included, such as the International Monetary Fund, the World Bank, and the World Trade Organization. Publishers are arranged in convenient alphabetical lists. Searching is offered. Fees: Free.

**Publishers' Catalogues.** Northern Lights Internet Solutions Ltd., 215 - 116 Research Dr. Saskatoon, SK, Canada S7N 3R3. Phone: (306)931-0020; Fax: (306)931-7667; Email: info2@lights.ca • URL: http://www.lights.ca • Covers: Publishing companies worldwide. Entries include: Company name, address, phone, fax, titles.

**Publishers-Directory & Guide Directory.** InfoGroup Inc., 5711 S 86th Cir. Omaha, NE 68127-4146. Phone: (402)593-4500 • URL: http://www.infogroup.com • Updated continuously; printed on request. Number of listings: 1,792. Entries include: Name, address, phone, size of advertisement, name of owner or manager, number of employees, year first in "Yellow Pages." Compiled from telephone company "Yellow Pages," nationwide.

**Publishers Directory.** Cengage Learning Inc., 20 Channel Center St. Boston, MA 02210. Phone: 800-487-8488 or (617)289-7700; Fax: (617)289-7844; Email: investors@cengage.com • URL: http://www.cengage.com • Annual. $756 Individuals print. Contains detailed information on more than 30,000 U.S. and Canadian publishers as well as small, independent presses.

**Publishers Information Bureau.** 810 7th Ave., 24th Fl. New York, NY 10019. Phone: (212)872-3700 or (212)872-3722; Email: weadie@magazine.org • URL: http://www.magazine.org • Measures the amount and type of advertising in magazines and reports this information monthly through printed and electronic formats; service prepared by TNSMI/Competitive Media Reporting (contracting agent).

**Publishers' International ISBN Directory.** Walter de Gruyter

GmbH & Co. KG, Genthiner Strasse 13 D-10785 Berlin, Germany. Phone: 49 302 60050; Fax: 49 302 6005251; Email: info@degruyter.com • URL: http://www.degruyter.de • Annual. Covers: About 620,000 publishers in the United States and 200 other countries, of which about 555,000 have been assigned International Standard Book Numbers (ISBNs) by one of 140 ISBN Group Agencies. Entries include: For publishers—Name, address, phone, fax, telex, e-mail, ISBN, group, and prefix numbers. For agencies—Name, address, phone, fax, e-mail, group number, names and titles of key personnel in charge of ISBN matters. Publication is a merger of "International ISBN Publishers' Directory" and "Publishers' International Directory.".

**Publishers Weekly: The International News Magazine of Book Publishing.** Reed Elsevier Group plc Reed Business Information, 360 Park Ave. S New York, NY 11010. Phone: (212)791-4208; Email: corporatecommunications@reedbusiness.com • URL: http://www.reedbusiness.com • Weekly. $20.95 print and online; monthly. The international news magazine of book publishing.

**PubList.com: The Internet Directory of Publications.** Bowes & Associates, Inc., Phone: (781)792-0999; Fax: (781)792-0988; Email: info@publist.com • URL: http://www.publist.com • "The premier online global resource for information about print and electronic publications." Provides online searching for information on more than 150,000 magazines, journals, newsletters, e-journals, and monographs. Database entries generally include title, publisher, format, address, editor, circulation, subject, and International Standard Serial Number (ISSN). Fees: Free.

**Pulp and Paper Canada.** Pulp and Paper Technical Association of Canada. Scott's Directories, 12 Concorde Pl., Ste. 800 Toronto, ON, Canada M3C 4J2. Phone: 800-668-2374 or (416)442-2122; Fax: (416)510-6870; Email: customercare@scottsdirectories.com • URL: http://www.scottsdirectories.com • Bimonthly. Contains accurate, technical information and news to assist those involved in the management and operation of Canada's pulp and paper industry.

**The Pulp and Paper Industry in OECD Member Countries.** Organization for Economic Cooperation and Development. Organisation for Economic Co-operation and Development Publications and Information Center, 2001 L St. NW, Ste. 650 Washington, DC 20036-4922. Phone: 800-456-6323 or (202)785-6323; Fax: (202)785-0350; Email: washington.contact@oecd.org • URL: http://www.oecd.org • Annual. $31.00. Presents annual data on production, consumption, capacity, utilization, and foreign trade. Covers 33 pulp and paper products in OECD countries. Text in English and French.

**Pulp and Paper International.** Paperloop, 4 Alfred Cir. Bedford, MA 01730. Phone: 866-271-8525 or (781)734-8900; Fax: (816)487-4550; Email: mkting@resourceinfo.com • URL: http://www.paperloop.com • Monthly. Contains latest business developments, operations techniques and technical innovations throughout the world.

**Pulp and Paper.** Paperloop, 4 Alfred Cir. Bedford, MA 01730. Phone: 866-271-8525 or (781)734-8900; Fax: (816)487-4550; Email: mkting@resourceinfo.com • URL: http://www.paperloop.com • 11 times a year. $135.00 per year.

**Pulp and Paper Week.** Paperloop, 4 Alfred Cir. Bedford, MA 01730. Phone: 866-271-8525 or (781)734-8900; Fax: (816)487-4550; Email: mkting@resourceinfo.com • URL: http://www.paperloop.com • Weekly. $1,450 /year.

**Pumps and Compressors.** U. S. Bureau of the Census, 4600 Silver Hill Rd. Washington, DC 20233-0001. Phone: (301)763-4636; Email: comments@census.gov • URL: http://www.census.gov • Annual. Provides data on value of manufacturers' shipments, quantity, exports, imports, etc. (Current Industrial Reports, MA-35P.).

**Purchasing People in Major Corporations.** Diversity Information Resources, 2105 Central Ave. NE Minneapolis, MN 55418. Phone: (612)781-6819; Fax: (612)781-0109; Email: info@diversityinforesources.com • URL: http://www.diversityinforesources.com • Annual. $175 Individuals /year (print and online); $90 Individuals print. Covers: Information regarding Diversity Information Resources. Lists corporate purchasing locations; listings include name of minority business program administrator, if that position exists.

**Purchasing: The Magazine of Total Supply Chain Management.** Reed Elsevier Group plc Reed Business Information, 360 Park Ave. S New York, NY 11010. Phone: (212)791-4208; Email: corporatecommunications@reedbusiness.com • URL: http://www.reedbusiness.com • 24 times a year. $109.90 per year. Includes *Guide and Directory.*

**Purdue University - Center for Urban and Industrial Pest Management.** Department of Entomology, 901 W State St. West Lafayette, IN 47907. Phone: (765)494-4564; Fax: (765)494-0535; Email: gbennett@purdue.edu • URL: http://extension.entm.purdue.edu/urban/home.html • Conducts research on the control of household and structural insect pests.

**Purdue University - Ray W. Herrick Laboratories.** School of Mechanical Engineering, 140 S Martin Jischke Dr. West Lafayette, IN 47907-2031. Phone: (765)494-2132; Fax: (765)494-0787; Email: rhlab@ecn.purdue.edu • URL: http://engineering.purdue.edu/Herrick/index.html • Mechanical engineering, including studies on heating, air conditioning, and refrigeration equipment and systems. engineering

acoustics, noise and vibration control (including vehicle and engine noise), sound quality, positive displacement compressor technology, mechanical reliability, precision measurements, mechanics of materials, tribology, noise control materials, electrohydraulic and engine controls, emissions, and automatic control.

**Purdue University - Robot Vision Laboratory.** Electrical Engineering Bldg., School of Electrical and Computer Engineering, 465 Northwestern Ave. West Lafayette, IN 47907-2035. Phone: (765)494-4600 or (765)494-3456; Fax: (765)494-6440; Email: kak@purdue.edu • URL: http://engineering.purdue.edu/RVL • Advanced automation with robotics and artificial intelligence, including studies in sensory feedback for intelligent robot manipulation and fundamental research in computer vision.

**Purdue University - Wood Research Laboratory.** Department of Forestry and Natural Resources, 175 Marsteller St. West Lafayette, IN 47907-2033. Phone: (765)494-3619; Fax: (765)496-1344; Email: chaviar@purdue.edu • URL: http://ag.purdue.edu/fnr/Pages/labwoodresearch.aspx • Use of wood and wood-base materials in engineered structures, ranging from furniture through residential and industrial/commercial building components; wood processing of wood and wood-base materials into furniture and cabinetry; structural applications of wood-base composites; and use, re-use, and care of wood in historic preservation and restoration. Research includes cross-disciplinary projects with engineering disciplines in simulation, machine vision and CAD.

**PVC Furniture Manufacturing.** Entrepreneur Press, 2445 McCabe Way, Ste. 400 Irvine, CA 92614-6244. Phone: 800-864-6864 or (949)261-2325 or (949)622-7131; Fax: (949)261-7729 or (949)261-0234; Email: press@entrepreneur.com • URL: http://www.entrepreneurpress.com • Looseleaf. $59.50. A practical guide to starting a business for the manufacture of plastic furniture. Covers profit potential, start-up costs, market size evaluation, owner's time required, site selection, lease negotiation, pricing, accounting, advertising, promotion, etc. (Start-Up Business Guide No. E1262.).

**Q Pages: WA Gay and Lesbian Business Directory.** Q Pages, PO Box 277 Bayswater, WA 6053, Australia. Phone: 61 8 93719877; Fax: 61 8 93704205 • URL: http://www.qpages.com.au • Gay and Lesbian-owned businesses in Western Australia.

**Qatar Golden Key Directory.** International Institute of Trade Relation Promotion, Trade Information Centre of Iran, No. 7, 3rd Fl., Abbasie Bazar, Ferdowsi Sq. Tehran, Iran. Phone: 98 21 88833900; Fax: 98 21 88820697; Email: order@irangoldenkey.com • URL: http://www.goldenkeydirectory.com/about.html • £100 Individuals. Covers: 10,256 companies in Qatar. Entries include: Company name, address, telephone, fax, products, services, Managing Director, and business activities.

**Qatari Businessmen Association.** PO Box 24475 Doha, Qatar. Phone: 974 443 53 120; Fax: 974 443 53 834; Email: qba@qataribusinessmen.org • URL: http://www.qataribusinessmen.org • Seeks to strengthen Qatar's business and economic growth. Supports and enhances the role of the private sector in the economy. Promotes private sectors' activities and establishes a channel of communication among Qatari businessmen. Acts as a catalyst for the promotion of diversified investment flows, modern entrepreneurial spirit and corporate development in Qatar.

**Qualitative Research Consultants Association—Membership Directory.** Qualitative Research Consultants Association, 1000 Westgate Dr., Ste. 252 Saint Paul, MN 55114. Phone: 888-674-7722 or (651)290-7491; Fax: (651)290-2266; Email: inquiries@qrca.org • URL: http://www.qrca.org • Annual. Covers: About 600 qualitative market and social researchers and consultants. Entries include: Company name, address, phone, name of contact, specialties, areas.

**Quality and Reliability Engineering International.** John Wiley and Sons, Inc., Journals Div., 111 River St. Hoboken, NJ 07030. Phone: 800-526-5368 or (201)748-6000; Fax: (201)748-6088; Email: consumers@wiley.com • URL: http://www.wiley.com • 8/year. $3,503 Institutions. Designed to bridge the gap between existing theoretical methods and scientific research on the one hand, and current industrial practices on the other. Published in England by John Wiley and Sons Ltd.

**Quality Bakers of America Cooperative Laboratory.** 1275 Glenlivet Dr., Ste. 100 Allentown, PA 18106. Phone: (203)531-7100; Fax: (203)531-1406; Email: info@qba.com • URL: http://www.qba.com.

**Quality Management Journal.** American Society for Quality, PO Box 3005 Milwaukee, WI 53201-3005. Phone: 800-248-1946 or (414)272-8575; Email: help@asq.org • URL: http://asq.org • Quarterly. $65 Members; $95 Members international; $99 Nonmembers; $119 Nonmembers international. Emphasizes research in quality control and management.

**Quality of Cotton Report.** Agricultural Marketing Service. U.S. Department of Agriculture, 1400 Independence Ave. SW Washington, DC 20250. Phone: 800-336-3747 or (202)720-2791 or (202)720-9904; Fax: (202)690-2164 or (202)720-6050; Email: fsis.outreach@usda.gov • URL: http://www.usda.gov • Weekly.

**Quality Progress.** American Society for Quality, PO Box 3005 Milwaukee, WI 53201-3005. Phone: 800-248-1946 or

(414)272-8575; Email: help@asq.org • URL: http://asq.org • Monthly. $70 Members; $116 Nonmembers international; $105 Members; $145 Nonmembers international. Covers developments in quality improvement throughout the world.

*Quantum PC Report for CPAs*. QNet, 5350 S. Roslyn St., Ste. 4000 Englewood, CO 80111. Phone: 800-325-8858; Email: info@quantum.org • URL: http://www.quantum.org • Monthly. $235.00 per year. Newsletter on personal computer software and hardware for the accounting profession.

*Quarry Management: The Monthly Journal for the Quarrying, Asphalt, Concrete and Recycling Industries*. QMJ Publishing Ltd., 7 Regent St. Nottingham NG1 5BS, United Kingdom. Phone: 44 115 9411315; Fax: 44 115 9484035; Email: mail@qmj.co.uk • URL: http://www.qmj.co.uk • Monthly. £45 Individuals; £81 Two years. Covers the latest news, issues, developments and advances in the quarry products sector.

*Quarterly Analysis of Failures*. Dun & Bradstreet Inc., 103 JFK Pkwy. Short Hills, NJ 07078. Phone: 800-526-0651 or (973)921-5500 or (973)921-5000; Fax: (866)560-7035 or (512)794-7670; Email: info@dnb.com • URL: http://www.dnb.com • Quarterly. $20.00.

*Quarterly Coal Report*. Energy Information Administration, U.S. Department of Energy. U. S. Government Printing Office, 732 N Capitol St. NW Washington, DC 20401. Phone: 866-512-1800 or (202)512-1800 or (866)512-1800; Fax: (202)512-2104 or (202)512-2250; Email: contactcenter@gpo.gov • URL: http://www.gpo.gov • Quarterly. $30.00 per year. Annual summary.

*Quarterly Financial Report for Manufacturing, Mining, Trade, and Selected Service Industries*. U.S. Federal Trade Commission and U.S. Securities and Exchange Commission. U.S. Census Bureau Foreign Trade Division, 4600 Silver Hill Rd. Washington, DC 20233-0001. Phone: 800-549-0595; Email: ftdwebmaster@census.gov • URL: http://www.census.gov/foreign-trade • Quarterly. Quarterly. Report on financial results of U.S. corporations.

*Quarterly Journal of Economics*. Harvard University, Dept. of Economics. The MIT Press, 55 Hayward St. Cambridge, MA 02142-1493. Phone: 800-356-0343 or (617)253-5646 or (617)253-5641; Fax: (617)258-6779 or (617)253-6779; Email: ewfaran@mit.edu • URL: http://mitpress.mit.edu • Quarterly. $70 Individuals; $37 Students; $646 Institutions. Covers all aspects of economics.

*Quarterly Journal of Finance and Accounting*. University of Nebraska at Lincoln College of Business Administration, PO Box 880405 Lincoln, NE 68588. Phone: 800-742-8800 or (402)472-9500; Fax: (402)472-5180; Email: dplowman2@unl.edu • URL: http://cba.unl.edu.

*Quarterly Labour Force Statistics*. Organization for Economic Cooperation and Development. Organisation for Economic Co-operation and Development Publications and Information Center, 2001 L St. NW, Ste. 650 Washington, DC 20036-4922. Phone: 800-456-6323 or (202)785-6323; Fax: (202)785-0350; Email: washington.contact@oecd.org • URL: http://www.oecd.org • Quarterly. $90.00 per year. Provides current data for OECD member countries on population, employment, unemployment, civilian labor force, armed forces, and other labor factors.

*Quarterly Mining Review*. National Mining Association, 101 Constitution Ave. NW, Ste. 500 E Washington, DC 20001-2133. Phone: (202)463-2600 or (202)463-2639; Fax: (202)463-2666 • URL: http://www.nma.org • Quarterly. $300.00 per year. Contains detailed data on production, shipments, consumption, stockpiles, and trade for coal and various minerals. (Publisher formerly National Coal Association.).

*Quarterly National Accounts*. Organisation for Economic Co-operation and Development Publications and Information Center, 2001 L St. NW, Ste. 650 Washington, DC 20036-4922. Phone: 800-456-6323 or (202)785-6323; Fax: (202)785-0350; Email: washington.contact@oecd.org • URL: http://www.oecd.org • Quarterly. $125.00 per year. National accounts data of OECD countries.

*Quarterly Operating Data of 68 Telephone Carriers*. Federal Communications Commission Wireless Telecommunications Bureau, 445 12th St. SW Washington, DC 20554. Phone: 877-480-3201; Fax: (866)418-0232; Email: fccinfo@fcc.gov • URL: http://wireless.fcc.gov • Quarterly.

*Quarterly Report on Companies whose Stocks are Quoted on the Stock Markets*. Bolsas de Comercio de Madrid, Bilbao, Barcelona, Valencia, Plz. Lealtad 1 E-28014 Madrid, Spain. Phone: 34 1 5891813; Fax: 34 1 5891813 • Quarterly. Covers: Companies on the stock exchange in Spain. Entries include: Company name, address, phone, financial and economic data.

*The Quarterly Review of Economics and Finance*. JAI Press, 100 Prospect St. Stamford, CT 06904. Phone: (203)323-9606; Fax: (203)357-8446; Email: order@jaipress.com • URL: http://www.jaipress.com • Quarterly. $142 Individuals; $760 Institutions. Publishes high quality manuscripts that cover topics in the areas of economics, financial economics and finance.

*Quebec Business*. Scott's Directories, 12 Concorde Pl., Ste. 800 Toronto, ON, Canada M3C 4J2. Phone: 800-668-2374 or (416)442-2122; Fax: (416)510-6870; Email: customercare@scottsdirectories.com • URL: http://www.scottsdirectories.com • Contains information on more than 74,000 individuals

at more than 42,000 Quebec companies.

**Queen's University at Kingston - Institute for Economic Research**. Department of Economics, 94 University Ave. Kingston, ON, Canada K7L 3N6. Phone: (613)533-2250; Fax: (613)533-6668; Email: admina@econ.queensu.ca • URL: http://www.econ.queensu.ca • Economics.

**Queen's University of Belfast - Finance and Economics Research Group**. Management School, Rm. 25. G07, 25 University Sq. Belfast BT7 1NN, United Kingdom. Phone: 44 28 90975126; Email: k.close@qub.ac.uk • URL: http://www.qub-efrg.com • Economic theory; econometrics; labor economics; microstructure finance; international finance; and financial institutions, including nonprofits.

**The Questers**. 210 S Quince St. Philadelphia, PA 19107-5534. Phone: (215)923-5183; Email: questers210@questers1944.org • URL: http://www.questers1944.org • Promotes the study and appreciation of antiques and objects of art and their historical backgrounds; aids in the restoration and preservation of historical places. Has donated several antique pieces to the White House and has contributed financially to historic houses, villages, and foundations. Sponsors annual scholarship at Columbia University for graduate studies in the field of architectural restoration.

*Qui Deade*. Bottin S.A., 5 rue Alfred de Vingy F-75008 Paris, France. Phone: 1 47 48 7575; Fax: 1 4748 7550; Email: bettinwebmaster@bottin.fr • Annual. Covers: 200,000 commercial and industrial entities and 4,000 products and services in France. Entries include: Company name, address, phone, product/service.

*Quick Frozen Foods International*. E.W. Williams Publications Co., 2125 Center Ave., Ste. 305 Fort Lee, NJ 07024-5898. Phone: (201)592-7007 or (201)532-9290; Fax: (201)592-7171 or (201)779-8345; Email: philpl@ewwpi.com • URL: http://www.williamspublications.com • Quarterly. $42.00 per year. Text in English, summaries in French and German.

*Quick Printing: The Information Source for Commercial Copy-shops and Printshops*. Cygnus Business Media, 3 Huntington Quadrangle, Ste. 301N Melville, NY 11747. Phone: 800-308-6397 or (631)845-2700; Fax: (631)845-2741 or (631)845-2798; Email: rich.reiff@cygnuspub.com • URL: http://www.cygnusb2b.com • Monthly.

*Quicken Business Law Partner*. Broderbund and The Learning Co., 1 Marthas Way Hiawatha, IA 52233-0100. Phone: (319)395-9626 • A computer software program that is capable of preparing up to 59 legal documents. The program allows the user to enter information either through the Interview method—in which documents are created based on answers to questions—or the typical Fill-in-the-Blank format. Quicken Business Law Partner prepares documents in 12 different categories, including Personal Information; Powers of Attorney; Consumer Letters; Credit Letters; Government Letters; Other Letters; Corporate Forms; Employment Forms; Small Claims Forms; Business Forms; Financial Forms; and Real Estate Forms. Business Law Partner is available on diskette or CD-ROM.

*Quill and Scroll*. International Honorary Society for High School Journalists. Quill and Scroll Society, University of Iowa, 100 Adler Journalism Bldg. Iowa City, IA 52242. Phone: (319)335-3457; Fax: (319)335-3989; Email: quill-scroll@uiowa.edu • URL: http://www.uiowa.edu • Quarterly. $17/year; $30 Two years. Devoted exclusively to the field of high school publications.

**Quill and Scroll Society**. University of Iowa, 100 Adler Journalism Bldg. Iowa City, IA 52242. Phone: (319)335-3457; Fax: (319)335-3989; Email: quill-scroll@uiowa.edu • URL: http://www.uiowa.edu • Honor Society high school journalism students recommended for membership by their schools. Seeks to reward individual achievements and to encourage individual initiative in high school journalism, creative writing, and allied fields. Provides information to editors, staffs, and advisers on all phases of publication work and supports news media evaluation service. Promotes research and conducts surveys through Quill and Scroll Foundation.

*Quill: The Magazine for Journalists*. Society of Professional Journalists, Eugene Pulliam National Journalism Center, 3909 N Meridian St. Indianapolis, IN 46208. Phone: (317)927-8000; Fax: (317)920-4789; Email: spj@spj.org • URL: http://www.spj.org • Bimonthly. $75 Individuals; Included in membership.

*Quoted Companies on the Brussels and Antwerp Stock Exchange*. DAFSA - Belgique S.A., Rue Gineste 11 B-1030 Brussels, Belgium. Phone: 2 2194460 • Annual. Covers: Companies with shares traded on the Antwerp and Brussels stock exchanges. Entries include: Company name, address, phone, officers, directors, executives, banks, brokers.

*R and D Contracts Monthly (Research and Development): A Continuously Up-dated Sales and R and D Tool For All Research Organizations and Manufacturers*. Government Data Publications Inc., 2300 M St. NW Washington, DC 20037. Phone: 800-275-4688 or (202)416-1761 or (718)627-0819; Fax: (718)998-5960; Email: gdp@govdata.com • URL: http://www.govdata.com • Monthly. $96.00 per year. Lists recently awarded government contracts. Annual *Directory* available.

*R & S Annual Directory*. Ricerche e Studi S.p.A. Mediobanca, Foro Buonaparte n. 10 20121 Milan, Italy. Phone: 99939 2 86462348; Fax: 99939 2 862267; Email: res@mbres.it • URL: http://www.mbres.it • Annual. €150 Individuals

European countries. Covers: Nearly 10,000 businesses forming part of 180 groups representing over a third of Italy's manufacturing industry. Database includes: Italian-English glossary. Entries include: Group name, address, phone, directors, details of shareholders, products, market shares, production facilities, sales and employees, financial data.

*R E Magazine*. National Rural Electric Cooperative Association, 4301 Wilson Blvd. Arlington, VA 22203. Phone: (703)907-5500 or (703)907-5732; Fax: (703)907-5517; Email: michael.lynch@nreca.coop • URL: http://www.nreca.coop/Pages/default.aspx • Monthly. $43 Members; $72 Nonmembers; $92 Other countries. News and information about the rural electric utility industry. Formerly *Rural Electrification*.

*RAB Co-op Directory*. Radio Advertising Bureau, 1320 Greenway Dr., Ste. 500 Irving, TX 75038-2587. Phone: 800-232-3131 or (972)753-6786 or (516)753-6782; Fax: (972)753-6727 or (212)753-6727; Email: efarber@rab.com • URL: http://www.rab.com • Annual. Database covers: Over 5,000 manufacturers that provide cooperative allowances for radio advertising. Database includes: Company name, address, name of contact, phone, fax, allowance, accrual rate, whether plan is administered by distributor, and expiration dates.

*Racine Area Manufacturers Directory*. • Annual. Covers: About 400 manufacturers in the Racine, Wisconsin, area. Entries include: Company name, address, phone, name of principal executive, number of employees, product or service provided, fax, and e-mail.

*Racine/Kenosha Christian Business Directory*. Red Letter Publishing, PO Box 272682 Fort Collins, CO 80527. Phone: 800-445-5614; Fax: (970)267-9669; Email: info@redletter.com • URL: http://www.christianbusinessdirectoryonline.com • Businesses, churches, organizations, and schools in Racine and Kenosha, Wisconsin.

*Racing Car Equipment (Manufacturers) Directory*. InfoGroup Inc., 5711 S 86th Cir. Omaha, NE 68127-4146. Phone: (402)593-4500 • URL: http://www.infogroup.com • Annual. Number of listings: 6,655. Entries include: Name, address, phone, size of advertisement, name of owner or manager, number of employees, year first in "Yellow Pages." Compiled from telephone company "Yellow Pages," nationwide.

**Radboud University Nijmegen - Faculty of Law - Business and Law Research Center**. Thomas van Aquinostraat 8 NL-6500 Nijmegen, Netherlands. Phone: 31 24 3615565; Fax: 31 24 3615662; Email: oor@jur.ru.nl • URL: http://www.ru.nl/law/businessandlawresearchcentre • Business and law.

**Radio Advertising Bureau**. 1320 Greenway Dr., Ste. 500 Irving, TX 75038-2587. Phone: 800-232-3131 or (972)753-6786 or (516)753-6782; Fax: (972)753-6727 or (212)753-6727; Email: efarber@rab.com • URL: http://www.rab.com • Includes radio stations, radio networks, station sales representatives, and allied industry services, such as producers, research firms, schools, and consultants. Calls on advertisers and agencies to promote the sale of radio time as an advertising medium. Sponsors program to increase professionalism of radio salespeople, awarding Certified Radio Marketing Consultant designation to those who pass examination. Sponsors regional marketing conferences. Conducts extensive research program into all phases of radio sales. Issues reports on use of radio by national, regional, and local advertisers. Speaks before conventions and groups to explain benefits of radio advertising. Sponsors Radio Creative Fund. Compiles statistics.

*Radio Facts: The Voice of Urban Culture*. RadioMan Publishing Inc., 595 Piedmont Ave., NE, Ste. 320 Studio City, CA 91604. Phone: (818)755-1611; Fax: (818)985-7386; Email: kevin.ross@radiofacts.com • URL: http://www.radiofacts.com • Annual. $50.00.

*Radio World*. IMAS Publishing Group, 5827 Columbia Pke. Ste. 310 Falls Church, VA 22041. Phone: 800-336-3045 or (703)998-7600; Fax: (703)998-2966; Email: adsales@imaspub.com • URL: http://www.imaspub.com • Biweekly. Free. Emphasis is on radio broadcast engineeri and equipment. Text in English, Portuguese and Spanish.

**Radiological Society of North America**. 820 Jorie Blvd. Oak Brook, IL 60523-2251. Phone: 800-381-6660 or (630)571-2670; Fax: (630)571-7837; Email: mwatson@rsna.org • URL: http://www.rsna.org • Members are radiologists and scientists. Includes a Technical Exhibits Committee and a Scientific Exhibits Committee. Formerly Western Roentgen Society.

**Radiology Business Management Association**. 10300 Eaton Pl., Ste. 460 Fairfax, VA 22030. Phone: 888-224-7262 or (703)621-3355; Fax: (703)621-3356 • URL: http://www.rbma.org • Provides education, resources and solutions to manage the business of radiology. Offers an online course in radiology coding.

*Ragan's Annual Report Review*. Lawrence Ragan Communications Inc., 316 N Michigan Ave., Ste. 400 Chicago, IL 60601. Phone: 800-878-5331 or (312)960-4100; Fax: (312)960-4106; Email: cservice@ragan.com • URL: http://www.ragan.com • Description: Provides business trends, tips, and tactics.

*Railroad Facts*. Association of American Railroads, 425 3rd St. SW Washington, DC 20024. Phone: (202)639-2100 or (202)639-2345; Fax: (202)639-2558; Email: media@aari.org • URL: http://www.aar.org • $5 Nonmembers; $20 Members. Annual.

*Railway Age*. Simmons-Boardman Publishing Corp., 345 Hudson St., 12th Fl. New York, NY 10014. Phone: 800-895-4389 or

(212)620-7200; Fax: (212)633-1165; Email: tjudge@rtands.com • URL: http://www.simmonsboardman.com • Monthly.

**Railway Engineering-Maintenance Suppliers Association**. 500 New Jersey Ave. NW, Ste. 400 Washington, DC 20001. Phone: (202)715-2921; Fax: (202)204-5753; Email: info@remsa.org • URL: http://www.remsa.org • Provides global business development opportunities to members. Works to transfer knowledge about markets, products and the industry to members and their customers. Supports government initiatives that advance the North American railroad industry.

**Railway Supply Institute**. 425 3rd St. SW, Ste. 920 Washington, DC 20024. Phone: (202)347-4664; Fax: (202)347-0047 • URL: http://rsiweb.org • Formerly Railway Progress Institute.

**Railway Systems Suppliers**. 9306 New LaGrange Rd., Ste. 100 Louisville, KY 40242. Phone: (502)327-7774; Fax: (502)327-0541; Email: rssi@rssi.org • URL: http://rssi.org • Corporations, partnerships, and individuals engaged in the manufacture, sale, and service of products, appliances, apparatus, and devices used in railway signals, controls, and communications; engineers and contractors engaged in construction or maintenance of any such product. Collects and disseminates information of interest to members.

***Railway Track and Structures***. Simmons-Boardman Publishing Corp., 345 Hudson St., 12th Fl. New York, NY 10014. Phone: 800-895-4389 or (212)620-7200; Fax: (212)633-1165; Email: tjudge@rtands.com • URL: http://www.simmonsboardman.com • Monthly.

**RAND - Center for Domestic and International Health Security**. 1200 S Hayes St. Arlington, VA 22202-5050. Phone: (703)413-1100; Email: globalhealth@rand.org • URL: http://www.rand.org/health/centers/healthsecurity • Health security at the global as well as community level. Research focuses on strengthening the U.S. public health system to address emerging challenges, supporting development of health systems in the global community, and advancing health in foreign policy.

**RAND - Center for Terrorism Risk Management Policy**. 1200 S Hayes St. Arlington, VA 22202-5050. Phone: (703)413-1100; Email: ctrmp@rand.org • URL: http://www.rand.org/multi/ctrmp.html • Terrorist threats and their affect on economic security. Research focuses on terrorism risk insurance, terrorism liability, compensation, security, and terrorism risk management.

**RAND Center for the Study of Aging**. 1776 Main St. Santa Monica, CA 90407-2138. Phone: (310)393-0411; Fax: (310)451-6923; Email: diana_malouf@rand.org • URL: http://www.rand.org/labor/aging • Relationships among institutional and socioeconomic factors, health, and financial well-being among the elderly.

**RAND - Labor and Population Program**. 1700 Main St. Santa Monica, CA 90407-2138. Phone: (310)393-0411 • URL: http://www.rand.org/labor • United States labor markets, demography of families and children, social welfare policy and family and child well being, social and economic functioning of the elderly, economic and social change in developing countries.

***Random Lengths: The Weekly Report on North American Forest Products Markets***. Random Lengths Publications, Inc., 450 Country Club Rd., Ste. 240 Eugene, OR 97441-6053. Phone: 888-686-9925 or (541)686-9925; Fax: (541)686-9629 or (800)874-7979; Email: rlmail@ripl.com • URL: http://www.randomlengths.com • Weekly. Information covering the wood products industry. Supplement available *Random Lengths Midweek Market Report*.

***Ranking the Banks***. American Banker/Bond Buyer Inc., 1 State St. Plz. 27 Fl. New York, NY 10004. Phone: 800-221-1809 or (212)803-8200 or (212)967-7000; Fax: (212)843-9600 or (212)843-9613; Email: custserv@americanbanker.com • URL: http://www.americanbanker.com • Annual. Price on application. Ranks domestic and foreign banks by 75 financial parameters.

***Rare Earth Bulletin***. Multi-Science Publishing Company Ltd., 5 Wates Way Brentwood CM15 9TB, United Kingdom. Phone: 44 1277224632; Fax: 44 1277223453; Email: info@multi-science.co.uk • URL: http://www.multi-science.co.uk • Bimonthly. Contains informative and concise summaries of scientific/technical papers, written in straightforward style by qualified experts.

***The Rauch Guide to the US Cosmetics and Toiletries Industry***. Impact Marketing Consultants Inc., PO Box 1226 Manchester Center, VT 05255. Phone: (802)362-2325; Fax: (802)362-3693; Email: comments@impactmarket.com • $895. Covers: Structure and current market information on cosmetics and toiletries industry.

***RCR and Global Wireless' International Database***. Crain Communications Inc., 1746 Cole Blvd. Golden, CO 80401-3208. Phone: (303)733-2500; Fax: (303)733-9941; Email: info@crain.com • URL: http://www.crain.com • Annual. $950; $300 per region. Covers: Worldwide cellular and PCS carriers.

***RCR Wireless News: The Newspaper for the Wireless Communications Industry***. Crain Communications, 777 E Speer Blvd. Denver, CO 80203-4214. Phone: 800-678-9595 or (303)733-2500; Email: info@crain.com • URL: http://www.crain.com • Weekly. $64.00 per year. Covers news of the wireless communications industry, including business and financial developments. Formerly *RCR*.

**Re:Gender**. 11 Hanover Sq. New York, NY 10005-2843. Phone: (212)785-7335; Email: regender@regender.org • URL: http://www.regender.org • Serves as a national network of organizations representing the academic community, policy makers, and others interested in women's issues. Works to bring institutional resources to bear on feminist research, policy analysis, and educational programs addressing legal, economic, and social inequities. Promotes collaborative research on issues affecting women; acts as clearinghouse. Houses the National Network of Women's Caucuses and Committees in the Disciplinary and Professional Associations.

***REACH: Review and Analysis of Companies in Holland***. Bureau van Dijk S.A., Ave. Louise, Louizalaan 250 B-1050 Brussels, Belgium. Phone: 32 2 6390606 or 32 2 639 06 06; Fax: 32 2 6488230 or 32 2 648 82 30; Email: brussels@bvdinfo.com • URL: http://www.bvdinfo.com • Bimonthly. Database covers: 150,000 company reports, including top 7,000 companies in Holland. Entries include: Company name, address, phone, fax, company history, description, historical annual accounts, financial ratios, directors and officers, names of holdings and subsidiaries, stock data.

***Readers' Guide to Periodical Literature***. EBSCO Publishing Inc., 10 Estes St. Ipswich, MA 01938-2106. Phone: 800-653-2726 or (978)356-6500; Fax: (978)356-6565; Email: information@ebscohost.com • URL: http://www.ebscohost.com • Provides indexing for over 400 periodicals dating back to 1983.

***Real Business***. Caspian Publishing, 198 King's Rd. London SW3 5XP, United Kingdom. Phone: 44 20 73687122 • Monthly. £40 Individuals; £50 Individuals Europe; £70 Individuals zone 1 & 2. Professional magazine covering business.

***Real Estate Advertisers Directory***. InfoGroup Inc., 5711 S 86th Cir. Omaha, NE 68127-4146. Phone: (402)593-4500 • URL: http://www.infogroup.com • Annual. Number of listings: 7,204. Entries include: Name, address, phone, size of advertisement, name of owner or manager, number of employees, year first in "Yellow Pages." Compiled from telephone company "Yellow Pages," nationwide.

***Real Estate Auctioneers Directory***. InfoGroup Inc., 5711 S 86th Cir. Omaha, NE 68127-4146. Phone: (402)593-4500 • URL: http://www.infogroup.com • Annual. Number of listings: 11,136. Entries include: Name, address, phone, size of advertisement, name of owner or manager, number of employees, year first in "Yellow Pages." Compiled from telephone company "Yellow Pages," nationwide.

***Real Estate Economics: Journal of the American Real Estate and Urban Economics Association***. The MIT Press, 55 Hayward St. Cambridge, MA 02142-1493. Phone: 800-356-0343 or (617)253-5646 or (617)253-5641; Fax: (617)258-6779 or (617)253-6779; Email: ewfaran@mit.edu • URL: http://mitpress.mit.edu • Quarterly. Covers a wide range of issues, from tax rules to brokers' commissions to corporate real estate including housing and urban economics, and the financial economics of real estate development and investment.

***Real Estate Finance and Investment***. Institutional Investor Inc. Journals Group, 225 Park Ave. S New York, NY 10003. Phone: 800-437-9997 or (212)224-3570; Email: info@iijournals.com • URL: http://www.iijournals.com • Weekly. $2,275.00 per year. Includes print and online editions. Newsletter for professional investors in commercial real estate. Includes information on financing, restructuring, strategy, and regulation.

***Real Estate Finance***. Institutional Investor Inc. Journals Group, 225 Park Ave. S New York, NY 10003. Phone: 800-437-9997 or (212)224-3570; Email: info@iijournals.com • URL: http://www.iijournals.com • Bimonthly. $350.00 per year. Covers real estate for professional investors. Provides information on complex financing, legalities, and industry trends.

***Real Estate Financing, with Forms on Disk***. ALM Media Properties LLC, 120 Broadway, 5th Fl. New York, NY 10271-1100. Phone: (212)457-9400; Fax: (646)417-7705; Email: customercare@alm.com • URL: http://www.alm.com • $560 print + online + ebook; $535 ebook + online. Includes forms on two diskettes. Covers loan modifications, wraparound mortgage loans, loans for condos, co-ops, and time shares, sale-leasebacks, installment sales, sales of mortgage loans, and various related topics. (Law Journal Press).

***Real Estate Forum***. 120 Broadway, 5th Fl. New York, NY 10271. Phone: (212)9457-9400; Fax: (646)822-5358; Email: jonathan.schein@scheinpublications.com • URL: http://www.almrealestatemediagroup.com • Ten times a year. $35.00 per year. Formerly *Better Buildings*.

***Real Estate Forum: America's Premier Real Estate Business Magazine***. Real Estate Media Inc., 520 8th Ave., 17th Fl. New York, NY 10018. Phone: (212)929-6900; Fax: (212)929-7124; Email: hoffman@remediainc.com • URL: http://www.remediainc.com/ • 10/year. Emphasis on corporate and industrial real estate.

***Real Estate Issues***. Counselors of Real Estate, 430 N Michigan Ave. Chicago, IL 60611-4089. Phone: (312)329-8427 or (312)329-8429; Fax: (312)329-8881; Email: info@cre.org • URL: http://www.cre.org • 3/year. $60 Individuals; $25 Single issue; $48 Nonmembers. Contains incisive, dynamic articles that respond to current trends and practices in the real estate industry.

***Real Estate Loans Directory***. InfoGroup Inc., 5711 S 86th Cir. Omaha, NE 68127-4146. Phone: (402)593-4500 • URL: http://www.infogroup.com • Annual. Number of listings: 74,550. Entries include: Name, address, phone, size of advertisement, name of owner or manager, number of employees, year first in "Yellow Pages." Compiled from telephone company "Yellow Pages," nationwide.

***Real Estate Review***. Thomson West, 610 Opperman Dr. Eagan, MN 55123. Phone: 800-328-9352 or (651)687-7000 • Gives inside information on the latest ideas in real estate. Provides advice from the leaders of the real estate field.

***Real Estate Software Directory and Catalog***. Z-Law Software Inc., 80 Upton Ave. Providence, RI 02940-4641. Phone: 800-526-5588 or (401)331-3002; Fax: (401)421-5334; Email: CS@z-law.com • URL: http://www.z-law.com • Semiannual. Publication includes: Listings of producers of real estate related software programs and ordering information. Principal content of publication is product name, description, specifications, requirements. Database includes: Applications for landlords, realtors, investors, property managers, lenders, contractors, attorneys, developers, and appraisers.

***Real Estate Tax Digest***. LexisNexis, 9443 Springboro Pke. Dayton, OH 45342. Phone: 800-227-4908 or (937)865-6800; Fax: (937)865-1211; Email: legalnotices@lexisnexis.com • URL: http://www.bender.com • Description: Features articles on and analyses of legislation, Treasury regulations, federal court and Tax Court decisions, Revenue Rulings, Revenue Procedures, and selected Letter Rulings of the Internal Revenue Service pertaining to federal taxation affecting real estate activities. Includes columns titled Special Topic, New Developments, Practitioner's Corner, and Inside Washington.

***Realtor Magazine***. National Association of Realtors, 430 N Michigan Ave. Chicago, IL 60611-4087. Phone: 800-874-6500; Email: infocentral@realtors.org • URL: http://www.realtor.org • Monthly. Free to members; non-members, $54.00 per year. Provides industry news and trends for realtors. Special features include Annual Compensation Survey, Annual Technology Survey, Annual All Stars, and The Year in Real Estate.

***Realtor Magazine: The Business tool for Real Estate Professionals***. National Association of Realtors, 430 N Michigan Ave. Chicago, IL 60611-4087. Phone: 800-874-6500; Email: infocentral@realtors.org • URL: http://www.realtor.org • Monthly. Included in membership; $56 Nonmembers U.S; $83 Nonmembers Canada; $103 Nonmembers International. Real estate magazine.

***Realty and Building***. Realty and Building Inc., 111 N Wabash, Ste. 1120 Chicago, IL 60602-2012. Phone: (312)467-1888; Fax: (312)467-0225 • Biweekly. $54.00 per year.

***Realty Stock Review***. 1875 I St. NW Wasington, DC 20006. Phone: (202)739-9400; Fax: (202)739-9401 • URL: http://www.reit.com • Semimonthly. $325.00 per year. Looseleaf service.

***ReCareering Newsletter: An Idea and Resource Guide to Second Career and Relocation Planning***. Publications Plus, Inc., 434 Ridge Rd. Wilimette, IL 60091-2471. Phone: (708)735-1981; Fax: (708)735-0046 • Monthly. $59.00 per year. Edited for "downsized managers, early retirees, and others in career transition after leaving traditional employment." Offers advice on second careers, franchises, starting a business, finances, education, training, skills assessment, and other matters of interest to the newly unemployed.

***Recommended Bank and Thrift Report***. BauerFinancial Inc., 2655 LeJeune Rd. Coral Gables, FL 33134-5832. Phone: 800-388-6686 or (305)445-9500; Fax: (800)230-9569; Email: customerservice@bauerfinancial.com • URL: http://www.bauerfinancial.com • Quarterly. $585.00 per year. Newsletter provides information on "safe, financially sound" commercial banks, savings banks, and savings and loan institutions. Various factors are considered, including tangible capital ratios and total risk-based capital ratios. (Six regional editions are also available at $150.00 per edition per year.).

***Record Retailing Directory***. • URL: http://www.billboard.com • Annual. $215 Individuals magazine. Covers: Over 5,000 independent and chain store record retailers (including audiobooks and online) in the U.S., American Samoa, Guam, and Puerto Rico. Entries include: For independents—Name, address, phone, store owner. For chain stores—Name, address, phone, fax, corporate management staff, number of outlets, year founded, corporate headquarters address and phone.

**Recording Industry Association of America**. 1025 F St. NW, 10th Fl. Washington, DC 20004. Phone: (202)775-0101 • URL: http://www.riaa.com • Formerly Record Industry Association of America.

***Recording Industry Sourcebook***. Cardinal Business Media, • Annual. $71.99 Individuals. Covers: 14,000 contacts in the music industry in over 65 categories, including record producers, publishers, promoters, attorneys, major and independent record labels, and music production facilities. Entries include: Name, address, phone, fax, name and title of contact, subsidiary and branch names and locations, background information, email, web address.

**Recreation Vehicle Dealers Association of North America**. 3930 University Dr. Fairfax, VA 22030-2515. Phone: (703)591-7130; Fax: (703)359-0152; Email: jnewhouse@rvda.org • URL: http://www.rvda.org.

***Recreation Vehicle Industry Association—Membership Directory and Industry Buyer's Guide***. Recreation Vehicle Industry Association, 1896 Preston White Dr. Reston, VA 20191. Phone: 800-336-0154 or (703)620-6003; Fax: (703)620-5071; Email: rvia@rvia.org • URL: http://www.rvia.org • Annual. Covers: Approximately 500 member recreation vehicle manufacturers, component parts suppliers, and associate firms; RV-related state and regional associations. Entries include: For businesses—Company name, address, phone, fax, name of contact, subsidiary and branch names and locations, product provided. For associations—Association name, address, phone.

**Recreation Vehicle Industry Association**. 1896 Preston White Dr. Reston, VA 20191. Phone: 800-336-0154 or (703)620-6003; Fax: (703)620-5071; Email: rvia@rvia.org • URL: http://www.rvia.org • Recreation vehicle manufacturers, manufacturers' representatives, and suppliers of accessories and equipment used by manufacturers. Seeks to provide a unified recreation vehicle organization for manufacturers and component parts suppliers of motor homes, travel trailers, fifth wheel trailers, horse trailer conversions, sport-utility trailers, truck campers and folding camping trailers. Promotes and represents the growth and concerns of the industry to federal and state government departments, the media, and the public. Collects shipment statistics, technical data, and consumer and media information. Monitors industry compliance with safety standards and the activities of federal and state governments that affect the RV industry. Provides legal and public relations services. Sponsors market research.

***Recruiting Trends: The Monthly Newsletter for the Recruiting Executive***. Kennedy Information Inc., 1 Phoenix Mill Ln., 3rd Fl. Peterborough, NH 03458. Phone: 800-531-0007 or (603)924-1006; Fax: (603)924-4460 or (603)924-4034; Email: customerservice@kennedyinfo.com • URL: http://www.kennedyinfo.com • Monthly. $179.00 per year.

***Recycling and Waste Management Guide to the Internet***. Government Institutes, 4501 Forbes Bvld., Ste. 200 Lanham, MD 20706. Phone: 800-462-6420 or (301)459-3366; Fax: (301)429-5748; Email: orders@rowman.com • URL: http://rowman.com • $72 Individuals. Covers: More than 350 web sites, discussion lists, and news groups on the internet covering waste management and recycling issues. Entries include: Site name, address, subject, site summary, contact name and e-mail.

***Recycling Today***. Group Interest Enterprises. GIE Media, Inc., 5811 Canal Rd. Valley View, OH 44125. Phone: 800-456-0707 or (216)393-0300 or (216)93-0300; Fax: (216)525-0515 or (216)393-0300; Email: bharbison@gie.net • URL: http://www.giemedia.com • Monthly. Serves the recycling industry in all areas.

***Red Book***. American Monument Association, 30 Eden Alley, Ste. 301 Columbus, OH 43215-2000. Phone: (614)461-5852; Fax: (614)461-1497 • Annual. $60. Covers: 7,000 retail monument dealers, suppliers of granite and marble, wholesalers, quarriers, funeral homes and cemeteries. Entries include: company; name, address, phone, fax; trade classification, names of owner or corporate officers and their titles. Available only to members of The American Monument Association.

***Redmond Business***. Greater Redmond Chamber of Commerce, 16210 NE 80th St. Redmond, WA 98052. Phone: (425)885-4014; Fax: (425)882-0996 • URL: http://redmond.patch.com • Monthly. Includes topical articles of issues affecting Redmond business community and information on sponsorship/promotional opportunities.

**Reference and User Services Association of the American Library Association**. 50 E Huron St. Chicago, IL 60611. Phone: 800-545-2433 or (312)280-4395; Fax: (312)280-5273; Email: rusa@ala.org • URL: http://www.ala.org/rusa • Affiliated with American Library Association. Formerly Reference and Adult Services Division of American Library Association.

***Reference and User Services Quarterly***. Reference and User Services Association of the American Library Association, 50 E Huron St. Chicago, IL 60611. Phone: 800-545-2433 or (312)280-4395; Fax: (312)280-5273; Email: rusa@ala.org • URL: http://www.ala.org/rusa • Quarterly. Included in membership; $65 Nonmembers /year. In addition to articles, includes reviews of databases, reference books, and library professional material. Formerly *RQ*.

***Reference Book of Corporate Managements***. Dun & Bradstreet Inc., 3 Sylvan Way Parsippany, NJ 07054-3896. Phone: 800-526-0651; Fax: (973)605-6911; Email: dnbmdd@dnb.com • URL: http://www.dnb.com • Annual. Libraries, $650.00 per year; others, $795.00 per year. Lease basis. Management executives at over 12,000 leading United States companies.

***Reference Book of Manufacturers***. Dun & Bradstreet Inc., 103 JFK Pkwy. Short Hills, NJ 07078. Phone: 800-526-0651 or (973)921-5500 or (973)921-5000; Fax: (866)560-7035 or (512)794-7670; Email: info@dnb.com • URL: http://www.dnb.com • Semiannual. Covers: over 400,000 U.S. manufacturers. Entries include: Company name, address, phone, line of business, branch offices, number of employees, year established, DUNS number, D&B credit rating.

***Reference Books Bulletin: A Compilation of Evaluations***. Mary Ellen Quinn, editor. Library and Information Technology Association, 50 E Huron St. Chicago, IL 60611-2795. Phone: 800-545-2433; Fax: (312)280-3257; Email: lita@ala.org • URL: http://www.ala.org/lita • *Booklist*.

***The Reference Librarian***. The Haworth Press Inc., 10 Alice St. Binghamton, NY 13904. Phone: 800-429-6784 or (607)722-5857; Fax: (607)771-0012 or (607)722-6362; Email: getinfo@haworthpress.com • URL: http://www.haworthpressinc.com/store/product.asp?sku=J014 • Semiannual. Institutions, $325.00 per year. Two volumes.

***Reference Modeling for Business Systems Analysis***. Cengage Learning Inc., 20 Channel Center St. Boston, MA 02210. Phone: 800-487-8488 or (617)289-7700; Fax: (617)289-7844; Email: investors@cengage.com • URL: http://www.cengage.com • 2007. eBook. Published by Information Science Reference. Covers all aspects of reference modeling, and provides foundations for model-driven systems development.

***Reference Reviews***. Information Today, Inc., 143 Old Marlton Pke. Medford, NJ 08055-8750. Phone: 800-300-9868 or (609)654-6266; Fax: (609)654-4309; Email: custserv@infotoday.com • URL: http://www.infotoday.com • Eight times a year. Price on application. Published in London by Aslib: The Association for Information Management. Incorporates *Aslib Book Guide*.

***Reference Source***. Sosland Publishing Co., 4800 Main St., Ste. 100 Kansas City, MO 64112. Phone: (816)756-1000; Fax: (816)756-0494; Email: nwages@sosland.com • URL: http://www.sosland.com • Annual. $45.00 per year. A statistical reference manual and specification guide for wholesale baking.

**The Refractories Institute**. PO Box 8439 Pittsburgh, PA 15218. Phone: (412)244-1880; Fax: (412)244-1881; Email: info@refractoriesinstitute.org • URL: http://www.refractoriesinstitute.org • Members are producers of fire brick and other refactory materials.

***Refractories***. U. S. Bureau of the Census, 4600 Silver Hill Rd. Washington, DC 20233-0001. Phone: (301)763-4636; Email: comments@census.gov • URL: http://www.census.gov • Annual. Provides data on value of manufacturers' shipments, quantity, exports, imports, etc. (Current Industrial Reports, MA-32C.).

**Refrigerating Engineers and Technicians Association**. PO Box 1819 Salinas, CA 93902. Phone: (831)455-8783; Fax: (831)455-7856; Email: info@reta.com • URL: http://www.reta.com • Formerly National Association Practical Refrigerating Engineers.

***Refrigeration, Air Conditioning, and Warm Air Heating Equipment***. U. S. Bureau of the Census, 4600 Silver Hill Rd. Washington, DC 20233-0001. Phone: (301)763-4636; Email: comments@census.gov • URL: http://www.census.gov • Annual. Provides data on quantity and value of shipments by manufacturers. Formerly *Air Conditioning and Refrigeration Equipment*. (Current Industrial Reports, MA-333M.).

***Refrigeration***. John W. Yopp Publications, Inc., P.O. Box 1147 Beaufort, SC 29901. Phone: 800-849-9677; Email: jcronley@jwyopp.com • URL: http://www.jwyopp.com • Monthly. $30.00 per year.

***Refundable Bundle***. PO Box 140 Centuck Station Yonkers, NY 10710. Phone: (914)472-2227; Email: info@refundlebundle.com • URL: http://www.refundlebundle.com • Bimonthly. $10.00 per year. Newsletter for grocery shoppers. Each issue provides details of new coupon and refund offers.

**Regional Airline Association**. 2025 M St. NW, Ste. 800 Washington, DC 20036-3309. Phone: (202)367-1170; Fax: (202)367-2170; Email: raa@raa.org • URL: http://www.raa.org • Regional air carriers engaged in the transportation of passengers, cargo, or mail on a scheduled basis; persons, companies and organizations engaged in pursuits related to commercial aviation; colleges and universities, state and local governments and state aviation associations. Responds to community, consumer and public needs for air transportation and aviation facilities and to help establish a healthy business, regulatory and legislative climate that enables members to profit through service to the nation and the flying public. Supports programs for improving safety and reliability of air transportation and air commerce; provides a forum for exchange of ideas and information.

***Regional Airline World***. Shephard Press Ltd., 111 High St. Burnham SL1 7JZ, United Kingdom. Phone: 44 1628 664334; Fax: (162)8 664075; Email: publishing@shephard.co.uk • URL: http://www.shephard.co.uk • 10 times a year. $130.00 per year. Covers the business, financial, and technical aspects of regional, short-haul, and commuter airline operations.

***Regional Business Directory***. Business Service Div. Birmingham Area Chamber of Commerce, 505 N 20th St. Birmingham, AL 35203. Phone: (205)324-2100; Fax: (205)324-2560 • URL: http://www.birminghamchamber.com • Covers: Approximately 4,000 businesses that are members of the area Chamber of Commerce. Entries include: Company name, address, phone, name and title of contact.

***Regional Industrial Buying Guide Series***. Thomas Regional Directory Company Inc., 5 Penn Plz. New York, NY 10001. Phone: 800-699-9822 or (212)695-0500; Fax: (212)290-7365; Email: contact@thomaspublishing.com • URL: http://www.thomaspublishing.com • Annual. Guides to manufacturers of industrial products within regions of a state or within contiguous portions of two or three states; the "Greater Allegheny Regional Industrial Buying Guide," for example, covers western Pennsylvania, northern West Virginia, and eastern Ohio. Guides also include listings for related industrial services, such as trucking, maintenance services, etc., and distributors and manufacturers' representatives. Guides now available cover eastern and western New England, greater New York City, upstate New York, northern New Jersey, greater Delaware Valley, greater Allegheny Valley, "Capital Cities" (Washington, DC, eastern Maryland, Delaware, eastern Virginia), north central tri-state area (Wisconsin/Illinois/Indiana), southern Michigan, northern Ohio, the Ohio Valley, north Texas/Oklahoma, Texas Gulf, North and South Carolina; northern California and southern California. Each includes 15,000-40,000 listings. Entries include: Company name, address, phone; product/service.

***Regional Official Guides: Tractors and Farm Equipment***. Iron Solutions, LLC, 660 Bakers Bridge Ave., Ste. 200 Franklin, TN 37067-6467. Phone: 877-266-4766; Email: sales@ironsolutions.com • URL: http://www.ironsolutions.com • Quarterly. Quarterly. Membership.

**Regional Science Association International**. University of Azores, Oficce 155-156, Rua Capitao Joao D'Avila, Angra do Heroismo 9700-042 Ponta Delgada, Portugal. • URL: http://www.regionalscience.org • Represents community of scholars interested in the regional impacts of national or global processes of economic and social change.

***Register of Arab Importers and Traders***. The Amalgamated Press, Narang House, 41 Ambalal Doshi Marg, Fort Mumbai 400 001, India. Phone: 91 22 2654184; Fax: 91 22 2641275 • Biennial. $150; $25; $40 airmail. Publication includes: Arab importers, exporters, distributors, wholesalers, agents, products, services, chambers of commerce, import/export trade associations, state trading organizations, boards of trade, consulates, embassies, high commissions, banks, hotels, travel, shipping and insurance companies, newspapers. Entries include: Company or organization name, address, phone. Principal content of publication is Geography, ports, econtomy, trade and travel in Algeria, Bahrain, Egypt, Iraq, Jordan, Kuwait, Lebanon, Libya, Mauritania, Morocco, Oman, Qatar, Saudi Arabia, Somalia, Sudan, Syria, Tunisia, United Arab Emirates, and Yemen.

***Register of Development Research Projects in Latin America***. OECD Publishing, 2, rue Andre Pascal F-75775 Paris, France. Phone: 33 1 45248200; Fax: 33 1 45248500; Email: news.contact@oecd.org • URL: http://www.oecd.org • Irregular. $75. Covers: 1,304 development research projects in 16 Latin American countries concerned with economic and social development, including economic policy, institutional framework, demography, labor, culture, and education. Entries include: Project title, institution name and address, researcher names, financial sponsor names and addresses, dates, description of project, planned output.

***Registered Representative***. Intertec Publishing, 5 Penn Plz., 13th Fl. New York, NY 10001-1810. Phone: 800-795-5445 or (212)613-9700 or (212)204-4200; Fax: (212)613-9749 or (212)206-3622; Email: bethany.weaver@penton.com • URL: http://www.penton.com • Monthly.

***Regulation: Cato Review of Business & Government***. Cato Institute, 1000 Massachusetts Ave. NW Washington, DC 20001-5403. Phone: (202)842-0200; Fax: (202)842-3490; Email: pr@cato.org • URL: http://www.cato.org • Quarterly. $20 Individuals; $35 Two years individuals; $50 Individuals 3 years; $40 Institutions and libraries; $70 Two years institutions and libraries; $100 Institutions 3 years; libraries and institutions. Magazine publishing articles on goverment regulation.

**Rehabilitation International**. 25 E 21st St., 4th Fl. New York, NY 10010. Phone: (212)420-1500; Fax: (212)505-0871; Email: ri@riglobal.org • URL: http://rehab-international.org • Formerly International Society for Rehabilitation of the Disabled.

***Release 1.0 Esther Dysons Monthly Report***. EDventure Holdings Inc., 104 5th Ave., 20th Fl. New York, NY 10011. Phone: (212)924-8800; Fax: (212)924-0240; Email: us@release1-0.com • URL: http://www.oreilly.com/ • Description: Reports on technology, communications, and the Internet. Reviews and analyzes the technology business. Recurring features include a calendar of events.

**Religious Conference Management Association**. 7702 Woodland Dr., Ste. 120 Indianapolis, IN 46278. Phone: (317)632-1888; Fax: (317)632-7909 • URL: http://www.rcmaweb.org.

***Relocation Journal and Real Estate News***. Mobility Services International, 124 High St. Newburyport, MA 01950. Phone: (978)463-0348; Email: diane@msimobility.com • URL: http://www.relojournal.com • Monthly. Free. Newsletter for real estate, building, financing and investing. Formed by the merger of *Real Estate News* and *Relocation Journal*.

***Remodeling: Excellence in Professional Remodeling***. DoveTale Publishers, 1 Thomas Cir. NW Washington, DC 20005. Phone: 877-275-8647 or (202)339-0744 or (202)452-0800; Fax: (202)785-1974 or (202)339-0749; Email: hwmicustomerservice@hanleywood.com • URL: http://www.hwmarketintelligence.com • Monthly. $44.95 per year. Covers new products, construction, management, and marketing for remodelers.

***Remodeling—Product Guide***. DoveTale Publishers, 1 Thomas Cir. NW Washington, DC 20005. Phone: 877-275-8647 or (202)339-0744 or (202)452-0800; Fax: (202)785-1974 or (202)339-0749; Email: hwmicustomerservice@hanleywood.com • URL: http://www.hwmarketintelligence.com • Annual. $10. Publication includes: List of more than 2,000 manufacturers and suppliers serving the remodeling contracting industry; list of industry-related associations. Entries include: For manufacturers and suppliers—Company name, address, phone, name and title of contact, product line, geographical area served. For associations—Association name, address, phone, director.

***Renewable Energy: An International Journal***. Elsevier, Secondary Publishing Division, 650 Ave. of the Americas New York, NY 10011. Phone: 888-437-4636 or (212)633-3980; Fax: (212)633-3975; Email: t.reller@elsevier.com • URL: http://www.elseveier.com • Monthly. $3,799 Institutions.

***Renewable Energy Businesses in the World***. Momentum Technologies L.L.C., PO Box 460813 Glendale, CO 80246. Phone: (303)229-4841; Fax: (408)705-2031 • URL: http://www.mtt.com • Contains more than 28,734 directory listings and associated contact data for renewable energy businesses and related companies in operation throughout the world. Includes company name, address, telephone number, fax number, e-mail address, and web site address. Provides description of business type, product types, and services provided. Searchable by location, business type, company name, and keyword.

**Renewable Natural Resources Foundation**. 5430 Grosvenor Ln. Bethesda, MD 20814-2142. Phone: (301)493-9101; Email: info@rnrf.org • URL: http://www.rnrf.org • Members are American Fisheries Society, American Geophysical Union, American Meteorological Society, American Society of Agronomy, American Society of Civil Engineers, Society of Landscape Architects, American Society for Photogrammetry and Remote Sensing, American Water Resources Association, Association of American Geographers, Humane Society of the United States, Society for Range Management, Society of Wood Science and Technology, Society of Environmental Toxicology and Chemistry, Soil and Water Conservation Society, Universities Council on Water Resources, and Wildlife Society. Concerned with renewable natural resources subjects and public policy alternatives. Develops 35-acre, forested Renewable Natural Resources Center, an office-park complex for natural resources and other nonprofit organizations.

**Rensselaer Polytechnic Institute - Paul J. and Kathleen M. Severino Center for Technological Entrepreneurship**. Pittsburgh Bldg., Lally School of Management, 110 8th St. Troy, NY 12180. Phone: (518)276-6842; Fax: (518)276-8661; Email: oconng@rpi.edu • URL: http://scte.rpi.edu • Technological entrepreneurship, including start-up companies to corporate venturing in Western economies and emerging markets.

**Rensselaer Polytechnic Institute**. Rensselaer Union, 110 8th St. Troy, NY 12180-3590. Phone: (518)276-6000 or (518)276-6344; Fax: (518)276-8728 or (518)276-4887; Email: ads@poly.rpi.edu • URL: http://www.rpi.edu • Serves as a conduit for research interactions between Rensselaer Polytechnic Institute and private companies.

***Rental***. Cygnus Business Media Inc., 1233 Janesville Ave. Fort Atkinson, WI 53538. Phone: 800-547-7377; Email: info@cygnus.com • URL: http://www.cygnus.com • Annual. Product rental management trade magazine.

***Rental Equipment Register***. Penton, 9800 Metcalf Ave. Overland Park, KS 66212. Phone: 866-748-4926 or (913)341-1300; Fax: (913)967-1905 or (913)967-1898; Email: corporatecustomerservice@penton.com • URL: http://www.penton.com • Monthly.

***Rental Management***. American Rental Association, 1900 19th St. Moline, IL 61265-4179. Phone: 800-334-2177 or (309)764-2475; Fax: (309)764-1533 • URL: http://www.ararental.org • Monthly. Covers all market segments of the equipment rental industry.

***Rep-Letter***. Manufacturers' Agents National Association, 6321 W Dempster St., Ste. 110 Morton Grove, IL 60053. Phone: 877-626-2776 or (949)859-4040; Fax: (949)855-2973; Email: mana@manaonline.org • URL: http://www.manaonline.org • Monthly. $37.50. A bound-in monthly feature of *Agency Sales Magazine*.

***Report on Business Corporate Database***. Globe Information Services Info Globe Online, 444 Front St. W Toronto, ON, Canada M5V 2S9. • URL: http://www.theglobeandmail.com • Weekly. Database covers: Current and historical information on over 3,000 Canadian companies, taken from their quarterly and annual reports. Database includes: Company name, address, phone, description of business, financial data, officers, general corporate information.

***Report on Electronic Commerce: Online Business, Financial and Consumer Strategies and Trends***. Wolters Kluwer Law and Business, 76 9th Ave., 7th Fl. New York, NY 10011-4962. Phone: 800-234-1660 or (212)771-0600; Fax: (800)901-9075 or (301)644-3550 • URL: http://www.wolterskluwerlb.com • Biweekly. $1,789.00 per year. Newsletter. Includes *Daily Multimedia News Service*. Incorporates *Interactive Services Report*.

***Report on Healthcare Information Management***. Capital Publications, Inc., 1101 King St., Suite 444 Alexandria, VA 22314. Phone: (703)683-4100; Fax: (703)739-6501 • Monthly. $358.00 per year. Newsletter. Covers management information sytems for hospitals and physicicans' groups.

***Report on the American Workforce***. U. S. Government Printing Office, 732 N Capitol St. NW Washington, DC 20401. Phone: 866-512-1800 or (202)512-1800 or (866)512-1800; Fax: (202)512-2104 or (202)512-2250; Email: contactcenter@gpo.gov • URL: http://www.gpo.gov • Annual. Issued by the U. S. Department of Labor (www.dol.gov). Appendix contains tabular statistics, including employment, unemployment, price indexes, consumer expenditures, employee benefits (retirement, insurance, vacation, etc.), wages, productivity, hours of work, and occupational injuries. Annual figures are shown for up to 50 years.

***Report***. Robinson and Associates, 1723 Jackson St. Santa Clara, CA 95050. Phone: (408)723-7311 • Monthly. $295.00 per year. Newsletter. Articles cover the artificial intelligence field. Formerly Artificial Intelligence Report.

***The Reporter***. Population Connection, 2120 L St. NW, Ste. 500 Washington, DC 20037. Phone: 800-767-1956 or (202)332-2200; Fax: (202)332-2302; Email: info@populationconnection.org • URL: http://www.populationconnection.org • Quarterly. Description: Reports on population growth and related social, environmental, and economic issues. Tracks legislative developments. Recurring features include interviews, news of research, book reviews, and regular columns.

**Reporters Committee for Freedom of the Press**. 1101 Wilson Blvd., Ste. 1100 Arlington, VA 22209. Phone: 800-336-4243 or (703)807-2100; Fax: (703)807-2109; Email: info@rcfp.org • URL: http://www.rcfp.org • Concerned with protecting freedom of information rights for the working press.

**Representative of German Industry and Trade**. 1776 I St. NW, Ste. 1000 Washington, DC 20006. Phone: (202)659-4777; Fax: (202)659-4779; Email: info@rgit-usa.com • URL: http://www.rgit-usa.com • Organizations representing 95% of private industry in Germany. Provides data concerning economic developments and the economic environment in Germany.

***Reproducible Copies of Federal Tax Forms and Instructions***. U. S. Government Printing Office, 732 N Capitol St. NW Washington, DC 20401. Phone: 866-512-1800 or (202)512-1800 or (866)512-1800; Fax: (202)512-2104 or (202)512-2250; Email: contactcenter@gpo.gov • URL: http://www.gpo.gov • Annual. $64 U.S. Looseleaf; $89.60 Other countries Looseleaf. Two looseleaf volumes issued by the Internal Revenue Service (www.irs.gov). "Contains the most frequently requested tax forms and instructions," prepared especially for libraries.

***Research Alert: A Bi-Weekly Report of Consumer Marketing Studies***. EPM Communications Inc., 19 W 21 St., Ste. 303 New York, NY 10010. Phone: 888-852-9467 or (212)941-0099; Fax: (212)941-1622; Email: info@epmcom.com • URL: http://www.epmcom.com • Biweekly. $389 /year. Provides descriptions (abstracts) of new, consumer market research reports from private, government, and academic sources. Includes sample charts and tables.

***Research Alert Yearbook: Vital Facts on Consumer Behavior and Attitudes***. EPM Communications Inc., 19 W 21 St., Ste. 303 New York, NY 10010. Phone: 888-852-9467 or (212)941-0099; Fax: (212)941-1622; Email: info@epmcom.com • URL: http://www.epmcom.com • Annual. $349 Individuals Single user (PDF) or Print; $444 Individuals Single user (PDF) and Print; $873 Individuals Multi-user (PDF); $249 Members Single user (PDF) or Print; $344 Members Single user (PDF) and Print; $623 Members Multi-user (PDF). Provides summaries of consumer market research from the newsletters *Research Alert, Youth Markets Alert*, and *Minority Markets Alert*. Includes tables, charts, graphs, and textual summaries for 41 subject categories. Sources include reports, studies, polls, and focus groups.

**Research and Development Associates for Military Food and Packaging Systems**. 16607 Blanco Rd., Ste. 501 San Antonio, TX 78232. Phone: (210)493-8024; Fax: (210)493-8036; Email: hqs@militaryfood.org • URL: http://militaryfood.org/newsite • Industrial firms, educational institutions and related groups engged in food, food service, distribution and container research and development.

***Research and Development: The Voice of the Research and Development Community***. Reed Elsevier Group plc Reed Business Information, 360 Park Ave. S New York, NY 11010. Phone: (212)791-4208; Email: corporatecommunications@reedbusiness.com • URL: http://www.reedbusiness.com • 13 times a year. $81.90 per year.

**Research and Engineering Council of NAPL**. 1 Meadowlands Plz., Ste. 1511 East Rutherford, NJ 07073. Phone: 800-642-6275 or (201)634-9600; Fax: (201)634-0324; Email: webmaster@napl.org • URL: http://napl.org.

***Research Centers Directory***. Cengage Learning Inc., 20 Channel Center St. Boston, MA 02210. Phone: 800-487-8488 or (617)289-7700; Fax: (617)289-7844; Email: investors@cengage.com • URL: http://www.cengage.com • Annual. $1,071 Individuals paperback. 2012. 42nd edition. Covers university, government, and other nonprofit research organizations established on a permanent basis to carry on continuing research programs in all areas of study; includes research institutes, laboratories, experiment stations, research parks, technology transfer centers, and other facilities and activities; coverage includes Canada. eBook also available.

**Research Foundation of CFA Institute**. c/o Walter V. Haslett, Jr., Executive Director, 477 Madison Ave., 21st Fl. New York, NY 10022. Phone: (856)780-5349; Email: info@cfainstitute.org • URL: http://www.cfainstitute.org/learning/foundation/Pages/index.aspx • Affiliated with Financial Analysts Federation.

***Research in Accounting Regulation***. Reed Elsevier Inc., 125 Park Ave., 23rd Fl. New York, NY 10017-5529. Phone: (212)309-8100; Fax: (212)309-8187; Email: newyork@reedelsevier.com • URL: http://www.reedelsevier.com • Irregular. Dates vary. Price varies. 15 volumes.

***Research in Corporate Social Performance and Policy: An Annual Compilation of Research***. Elsevier, Secondary Publishing Division, 650 Ave. of the Americas New York, NY 10011. Phone: 888-437-4636 or (212)633-3980; Fax: (212)633-3975; Email: t.reller@elsevier.com • URL: http://www.elseveier.com • Dates vary. $78.50. 15 volumes.

***Research in Domestic and International Agribusiness Management***. Elsevier, Secondary Publishing Division, 650 Ave. of the Americas New York, NY 10011. Phone: 888-437-4636 or (212)633-3980; Fax: (212)633-3975; Email: t.reller@elsevier.com • URL: http://www.elseveier.com • Dates vary. $73.25. 12 volumes.

***Research in Experimental Economics***. Elsevier, Secondary Publishing Division, 650 Ave. of the Americas New York, NY 10011. Phone: 888-437-4636 or (212)633-3980; Fax: (212)633-3975; Email: t.reller@elsevier.com • URL: http://www.elseveier.com • Dates vary. $84.00. Nine volumes. Supplement available *An Experiment in Non-Cooperative Oligopoly*.

***Research in Governmental and Nonprofit Accounting***. Elsevier, Secondary Publishing Division, 650 Ave. of the Americas New York, NY 10011. Phone: 888-437-4636 or (212)633-3980; Fax: (212)633-3975; Email: t.reller@elsevier.com • URL: http://www.elseveier.com • Dates vary. Price varies. 10 volumes.

***Research in International Business and Finance***. Elsevier, Secondary Publishing Division, 650 Ave. of the Americas New York, NY 10011. Phone: 888-437-4636 or (212)633-3980; Fax: (212)633-3975; Email: t.reller@elsevier.com • URL: http://www.elseveier.com • $347 Individuals Print. Publishes empirical and applied research on issues relating to International Business and International Finance.

***Research in Law and Economics: A Research Annual***. Richard O. Zerbe. Elsevier, Secondary Publishing Division, 650 Ave. of the Americas New York, NY 10011. Phone: 888-437-4636 or (212)633-3980; Fax: (212)633-3975; Email: t.reller@elsevier.com • URL: http://www.elseveier.com • Dates vary. $78.50. 20 volumes. Supplement available, *Economics of Nonproprietary Organizations*.

***Research in Marketing: An Annual Compilation of Research***. Jagdish N. Sheth, editor. Elsevier, Secondary Publishing Division, 650 Ave. of the Americas New York, NY 10011. Phone: 888-437-4636 or (212)633-3980; Fax: (212)633-3975; Email: t.reller@elsevier.com • URL: http://www.elseveier.com • Annual. Price on application.

***Research in Personnel and Human Resources Management***. Gerald D. Ferris, editor. Elsevier, Secondary Publishing Division, 650 Ave. of the Americas New York, NY 10011. Phone: 888-437-4636 or (212)633-3980; Fax: (212)633-3975; Email: t.reller@elsevier.com • URL: http://www.elseveier.com • Dates vary. $78.50. 21 volumes.

***Research in Philosophy and Technology***. Elsevier, Secondary Publishing Division, 650 Ave. of the Americas New York, NY 10011. Phone: 888-437-4636 or (212)633-3980; Fax: (212)633-3975; Email: t.reller@elsevier.com • URL: http://www.elseveier.com • Dates vary. Price varies. 21 volumes.

***Research in Population Economics***. Elsevier, Secondary Publishing Division, 650 Ave. of the Americas New York, NY 10011. Phone: 888-437-4636 or (212)633-3980; Fax: (212)633-3975; Email: t.reller@elsevier.com • URL: http://www.elseveier.com • Irregular. $90.25. Volumes 4-9.

***Research in Transportation Economics***. Elsevier, Secondary Publishing Division, 650 Ave. of the Americas New York, NY 10011. Phone: 888-437-4636 or (212)633-3980; Fax: (212)633-3975; Email: t.reller@elsevier.com • URL: http://www.elseveier.com • $727 Individuals Print. Covers a wide variety of topics relating to the economic aspects of transportation, government regulatory policies regarding transportation, and issues of concern to transportation industry planners.

***Research Journal of Business Management***. Academic Journals Inc., 224, 5th Ave., No. 2218 New York, NY 10001. Phone: 888-777-8532 • URL: http://www.academicjournalsinc.com • Peer-reviewed journal covering research in business management.

***Research on Technological Innovation, Management and Policy***. Richard S. Rosenbloom and Robert A. Burgelman, editors. Elsevier, Secondary Publishing Division, 650 Ave. of the Americas New York, NY 10011. Phone: 888-437-4636 or (212)633-3980; Fax: (212)633-3975; Email: t.reller@elsevier.com • URL: http://www.elseveier.com • Dates vary. Prices vary. Seven volumes.

***Research on Transport Economics***. Organisation for Economic Co-operation and Development Publications and Information Center, 2001 L St. NW, Ste. 650 Washington, DC 20036-4922. Phone: 800-456-6323 or (202)785-6323; Fax: (202)785-0350; Email: washington.contact@oecd.org • URL: http://www.oecd.org • Annual. Quarterly $138.00. Text in French.

***Research Reports***. American Institute for Economic Research, 250 Division St. Great Barrington, MA 01230-1000. Phone: 888-528-1216; Fax: (413)528-0103; Email: info@aier.org • URL: http://www.aier.org • Contains two or more current economic events in each issue.

***Research Strategies: A Journal of Library Concepts and Instruction***. Elsevier, Secondary Publishing Division, 650 Ave. of the Americas New York, NY 10011. Phone: 888-437-4636 or (212)633-3980; Fax: (212)633-3975; Email: t.reller@elsevier.com • URL: http://www.elseveier.com •

Quarterly. Individuals, $76.00 per year; institutions, $152.00 per year. Edited for librarians involved in bibliographic or library instruction.

**Researching Company Financial Information**. MarketResearch. com, 11200 Rockville Pke., Ste. 504 Rockville, MD 20852. Phone: 800-298-5699 or (240)747-3093; Fax: (240)747-3004; Email: customerservice@marketresearch.com • URL: http://www.marketresearch.com • $59 Individuals. Helps readers learn how to research and understand financial data from companies, as well as compile in-depth financial data on competitors in order to get a better picture of the competition. Publication includes: A directory of corporate financial info sources.

**Researching Markets, Industries, & Business Opportunities**. MarketResearch.com, 11200 Rockville Pke., Ste. 504 Rockville, MD 20852. Phone: 800-298-5699 or (240)747-3093; Fax: (240)747-3004; Email: customerservice@ marketresearch.com • URL: http://www.marketresearch.com • Irregular. $245. Publication includes: Lists of sources of business and market information. Entries include: Source name, address, phone, description. Principal content of publication is discussion of methods for studying markets and industries.

**Reserve Officers Association of the United States**. 1 Constitution Ave. NE Washington, DC 20002-5618. Phone: 800-809-9448 or (202)479-2200; Fax: (202)547-1641 • URL: http:// www.roa.org • Represents reserve members of the seven United States Uniformed Services-Army, Navy, Air Force, Marines, Coast Guard, Public Health Service, and National Oceanic and Atmospheric Administration Corps. Aims to "support and promote the development and execution of a military policy for the United States that will provide adequate National Security."

**Reserves of Crude Oil, Natural Gas Liquids and Natural Gas in the United States and Canada and United States Productive Capacity**. American Gas Association, 400 N Capitol St. NW Washington, DC 20001. Phone: (202)824-7000; Email: ggardner@aga.org • URL: http://www.aga.org • Annual. Price on application.

**Resident and Staff Physician**. Romaine Pierson Publishers Inc., 1065 Old Country Rd. Westbury, NY 11590. Phone: (516)997-0377; Fax: (516)997-0344 • Monthly. Individuals, $83.00 per year institutions, $149.00 per year; students, $50.00 per year.

**The Residential Specialist**. Council of Residential Specialists, 430 N Michigan Ave. Chicago, IL 60611. Phone: 800-462-8841 or (312)321-4400; Fax: (312)329-8851 • URL: http://crs.com • Bimonthly Quarterly. $29.95 Nonmembers; $54.95 Two years; $18 /year for members; $20 /year for nonmembers. Covers sales techniques, communication and brokerage management, residential sales associates and brokers.

**Resilient Floor Covering Institute**. 115 Broad St., Ste. 201 Lagrange, GA 30240. Phone: (706)882-3833; Fax: (706)882-3880 • URL: http://www.rfci.com • Supports the manufacturers of vinyl composition tile, solid vinyl tile, or sheet vinyl and rubber tile and people who use its products. Provides technical information and data regarding the resilient flooring industry.

**Resist**. 259 Elm St. Somerville, MA 02144. Phone: (617)623-5110; Email: resistinc@igc.org • URL: http://www.resistinc. org • Provides grants to small progressive groups in all parts of the country; has aided groups that have organized for reproductive rights for women, gay rights, nuclear disarmament, the rights of Third World people, and work for social and economic justice.

**Resistance Welding Manufacturing Alliance**. c/o Keila DeMoraes, 8669 Doral Blvd., Ste. 130 Doral, FL 33166. Phone: (305)443-9353; Email: rwma@aws.org • URL: http://www. aws.org/rwma • Manufacturers, suppliers, and users of resistance welding equipment and supplies. Conducts Resistance Welding School, an annual educational program. Compiles statistics. Offers VHS tape program on basics of resistance welding.

**Resort Management and Operations: The Resort Resource**. Finan Publishing, 533 Colebrook, Ste. A Saint Louis, MO 63119. Phone: (314)517-2466 or (314)961-6644; Fax: (314)961-4809; Email: pfinan@finan.com • URL: http:// www.finan.com • Bimonthly. Price on application. Edited for hospitality professionals at both large and small resort facilities.

**Resource and Energy Economics: A Journal Devoted to the Interdisciplinary Studies in the Allocation of Natural Resources**. Elsevier, Secondary Publishing Division, 650 Ave. of the Americas New York, NY 10011. Phone: 888-437-4636 or (212)633-3980; Fax: (212)633-3975; Email: t.reller@elsevier.com • URL: http://www.elseveier.com • Quarterly. $117 Individuals; $1,117 Institutions. Publishes papers that advance economic theory and empirical methods to gain novel insights into environmental problems.

**Resource Center Product Catalog**. Society for Nonprofit Organizations, PO Box 510354 Livonia, MI 48151. Phone: (734)451-3582; Fax: (734)451-5935; Email: info@snpo.org • URL: http://www.snpo.org • Included in subscription to *Nonprofit World*.

**Resource: LOMA's Magazine for Insurance and Financial Services Management**. LOMA, 2300 Windy Ridge Pkwy., Ste. 600 Atlanta, GA 30339-8443. Phone: (770)951-1770 or (770)984-3720; Fax: (770)984-6422; Email: askloma@loma.

org • URL: http://www.loma.org • Monthly. Included in membership; $75 Nonmembers; $100 Other countries. Contains news and information about industry operations and management.

**Resources, Conservation and Recycling**. Elsevier, Secondary Publishing Division, 650 Ave. of the Americas New York, NY 10011. Phone: 888-437-4636 or (212)633-3980; Fax: (212)633-3975; Email: t.reller@elsevier.com • URL: http:// www.elseveier.com • Monthly. $392 Individuals; $2,921 Institutions. Emphasizes the transformation processes involved in a transition toward more sustainable production and consumption systems.

**Resources in Education**. Educational Resources Information Center. U. S. Government Printing Office, 732 N Capitol St. NW Washington, DC 20401. Phone: 866-512-1800 or (202)512-1800 or (866)512-1800; Fax: (202)512-2104 or (202)512-2250; Email: contactcenter@gpo.gov • URL: http:// www.gpo.gov • Monthly. Reports on educational research.

**Resources Policy; The International Journal on the Economics, Planning and Use of Non-Renewable Resources**. Elsevier, Secondary Publishing Division, 650 Ave. of the Americas New York, NY 10011. Phone: 888-437-4636 or (212)633-3980; Fax: (212)633-3975; Email: t.reller@elsevier.com • URL: http://www.elseveier.com • Quarterly. $246 Individuals; $1,413 Institutions.

**Resources**. Resources for the Future, 1616 P St. NW Washington, DC 20036. Phone: (202)328-5000; Fax: (202)939-3460; Email: rffpress@rff.org • URL: http://www.rff.org • Description: Features articles on renewable resources, energy, climate, quality of the environment, and risk assessment and management. Recurring features include organizational news and book notices.

**Responsibilities of Corporate Officers and Directors Under Federal Securities Law**. Wolters Kluwer Law & Business CCH, 2700 Lake Cook Rd. Riverwoods, IL 60015. Phone: 888-224-7377 or (847)267-7000; Email: cust_serv@cch.com • URL: http://www.cchgroup.com • Annual. $132 paperback. Includes discussions of indemnification, "D & O" insurance, corporate governance, and insider liability.

**Responsibilities of Insurance Agents and Brokers**. Matthew Bender and Company Inc., 1275 Broadway Albany, NY 12204-2638. Phone: 800-424-4200 or (518)487-3000; Fax: (518)487-3573 or (800)424-4200; Email: customer.support@ lexisnexis.com • URL: http://www.matthewbender.com • Semiannual. $2,220 book; $2,018 e-book. Covers legal responsibilities of agents and federal tax consequences of insurance arrangements.

**Rest of the World Food Companies**. Datamonitor, Charles House, 108-110 Finchley Rd. London NW3 5JJ, United Kingdom. Phone: 44 20 7675 7000; Fax: 44 20 7675 7500; Email: euroinfo@datamonitor.com • $995. Covers: Food companies in countries outside of Europe, Asia, and the U.S. Entries include: Company name, address, phone, telex, names and titles of key personnel; number of employees; financial data, product/service, Standard Industrial Classification (SIC) code, production locations.

**Rest of the World Toiletry Index**. Datamonitor, Charles House, 108-110 Finchley Rd. London NW3 5JJ, United Kingdom. Phone: 44 20 7675 7000; Fax: 44 20 7675 7500; Email: euroinfo@datamonitor.com • $995. Covers: Companies involved in the toiletry and cosmetics industry in nations outside of Asia and North, Central, and South America. Entries include: Company name, address, phone, telex, names and titles of key personnel, number of employees; financial data, product/service, Standard Industrial Classification (SIC) code, production locations.

**Restatement of the Law**. American Law Institute - Committee on Continuing Professional Education, 4025 Chestnut St. Philadelphia, PA 19104. Phone: 800-253-6397 or (215)243-1600 or (215)243-1614; Fax: (215)243-1636 or (215)243-1664; Email: in-house@ali-aba.org • URL: http://www.ali. org • $131 hardbound. Multivolume set. Periodic supplementation. Price varies. Statements of the common law-an overview, clarification, and simplification of American law.

**Restaurant Facility Management Association**. 5600 Tennyson Pkwy., Ste. 280 Plano, TX 75024. Phone: (972)805-0905; Fax: (972)805-0906; Email: tracy@rfmaonline.com • URL: http://www.rfmaonline.com • Aims to promote the advancement of the restaurant facility management profession. Maintains professional and ethical standards among members. Provides networking to share knowledge and exchange information.

**Restaurant Hospitality**. Penton Media Inc., 1300 E 9th St. Cleveland, OH 44114-1501. Phone: (216)696-7000; Fax: (216)696-1752; Email: information@penton.com • URL: http://penton.com • Monthly.

**Restaurant Industry Operations Report**. National Restaurant Association, 2055 L St. NW, Ste. 700 Washington, DC 20036. Phone: 800-424-5156 or (202)331-5900; Fax: (202)331-2429 • URL: http://www.restaurant.org • Annual. $100 Members; $200 Nonmembers. Presents operating results as amounts per restaurant seat and as ratios to total sales.

**Restaurant Start-Up**. Entrepreneur Press, 2445 McCabe Way, Ste. 400 Irvine, CA 92614-6244. Phone: 800-864-6864 or (949)261-2325 or (949)622-7131; Fax: (949)261-7729 or (949)261-0234; Email: press@entrepreneur.com • URL: http://www.entrepreneurpress.com • $19.95. Looseleaf. $59.

50. A practical guide to starting a restaurant. Covers profit potential, start-up costs, market size evaluation, owner's time required, site selection, lease negotiation, pricing, accounting, advertising, promotion, etc. (Start-Up Business Guide No. E1279.).

**Restaurants and Institutions**. Reed Elsevier Group plc Reed Business Information, 360 Park Ave. S New York, NY 11010. Phone: (212)791-4208; Email: corporatecommunications@ reedbusiness.com • URL: http://www.reedbusiness.com • Semimonthly. $149.00 per year. Features news, new products, recipes, menu concepts and merchandising ideas from the most successful foodservice operations around the U.S.

**Resume Writing and Career Counseling**. Entrepreneur Press, 2445 McCabe Way, Ste. 400 Irvine, CA 92614-6244. Phone: 800-864-6864 or (949)261-2325 or (949)622-7131; Fax: (949)261-7729 or (949)261-0234; Email: press@ entrepreneur.com • URL: http://www.entrepreneurpress.com • Looseleaf. $59.50. A practical guide to starting a resume writing and career counseling service. Covers profit potential, start-up costs, market size evaluation, owner's time required, site selection, pricing, accounting, advertising, promotion, etc. (Start-Up Business Guide No. E1260.).

**Retail Ad World**. Visual Reference Publications Inc., 302 5th Ave., 6th Fl. New York, NY 10001. Phone: 800-251-4545 or (212)279-7000; Fax: (212)279-7014; Email: angie@ visualreference.com • URL: http://www.visualreference.com • Monthly. $299.00 per year. Weekly report on outstanding advertising by department stores, specialty stores and shopping centers with reprints of current advertising. Formerly *Retail Ad Week*.

**Retail Bakers of America**. 15941 Harlem Ave., No. 347 Tinley Park, IL 60477. Phone: 800-638-0924; Email: info@rbanet. com • URL: http://www.retailbakersofamerica.org • Independent and in-store bakeries, food service, specialty bakeries, suppliers of ingredients, tools and equipment; other. Provides information, management, production, merchandising and small business services.

**Retail Confectioners International**. 2053 S Waverly, Ste. C Springfield, MO 65804. Phone: 800-545-5381; Email: info@ retailconfectioners.org • URL: http://www. retailconfectioners.org • Manufacturing retail confectioners who make and sell their own candies through directly-owned retail candy shops; associates are suppliers to the industry. Provides education, promotion and legislative and information service. Monitors legislative activities that affect the industry at state and national levels. Holds comprehensive two-week course and one-week specialized course on retail candy making biennially.

**Retail Energy Supply Association**. PO Box 6089 Harrisburg, PA 17112. Phone: (717)566-5405; Email: tmccormick@resausa. org • URL: http://www.resausa.org • Represents the interests of retail energy suppliers. Promotes the development and furthering of retail energy markets in the United States. Sponsors social and networking opportunities for members.

**Retail Pharmacy Management**. McMahon Group, 545 W. 45th St., 8th Fl. New York, NY 10036. Phone: (212)957-5300; Fax: (212)957-7230; Email: dbron@mcmahonmed.com • URL: http://www.mcmahonmed.com • Monthly. $60.00 per year. Featues include product news for pharmacists and financial news for chain store executives. Formerly *Retail Pharmacy Management News*.

**Retail Shops Directory**. InfoGroup Inc., 5711 S 86th Cir. Omaha, NE 68127-4146. Phone: (402)593-4500 • URL: http://www. infogroup.com • Annual. Number of listings: 7,325. Entries include: Name, address, phone, size of advertisement, name of owner or manager, number of employees, year first in "Yellow Pages." Compiled from telephone company "Yellow Pages," nationwide.

**Retail Traffic**. Penton, 9800 Metcalf Ave. Overland Park, KS 66212. Phone: 866-748-4926 or (913)341-1300; Fax: (913)967-1905 or (913)967-1898; Email: corporatecustomerservice@penton.com • URL: http://www. penton.com • Monthly. $74. Provides coverage of all phases of the shopping center industry. Formerly *Shopping Center World*.

**Retail, Wholesale and Department Store Union**. 30 E 29th St. New York, NY 10016. Phone: (212)684-5300; Fax: (212)779-2809; Email: info@rwdsu.org • URL: http://www.rwdsu.info • Represents workers throughout the United States and Canada. Works in a wide variety of occupations that range from food processing, retail, manufacturing, service and healthcare.

**Retailing Today**. Robert Kahn and Associates, 3684 Happy Valley Rd. Lafayette, CA 94549-3040. Phone: (925)254-4434; Fax: (925)284-5612 • Description: Focuses on general merchandise, apparel, furniture, hardware, automotive, and food retailing. Offers "original research, comments on current trends and conditions, recommendations for company policy, and emphasis on ethical conduct in business.".

**Retailing Today: The Newspaper of Discount Retailing; The News Source for Power Retailing**. Lebhar-Friedman Inc., 425 Park Ave. New York, NY 10022. Phone: (212)756-5000 or (603)432-4077; Email: info@lf.com • URL: http://www.lf. com • Semimonthly. $119 Individuals; $228 Two years. Retailing business industry news and information.

**Retirement Benefits Tax Guide**. Wolters Kluwer Law & Business CCH, 2700 Lake Cook Rd. Riverwoods, IL 60015. Phone: 888-224-7377 or (847)267-7000; Email: cust_serv@cch.com

• URL: http://www.cchgroup.com • $199.00. Looseleaf service.

***Retirement Community Business***. Great River Publishing, Inc., 91 Windy Oaks Dr. Germantown, TN 38139-5207. Phone: 800-567-6912 or (901)624-5911; Fax: (901)624-5910 • Quarterly. $15.00 per year. Contains articles on management, marketing, legal concerns, development, construction, and other business-related topics.

***Retirement Letter: The Money Newsletter for Mature People***. Peter A. Dickinson, editor. Access Intelligence L.L.C., 4 Choke Cherry Rd., 2nd Fl. Rockville, MD 20850. Phone: 800-777-5006 or (301)354-2000 or (301)354-2101; Fax: (301)309-3847 or (801)365-2300; Email: info@accessintel.com • URL: http://www.accessintel.com/ • Monthly. $49.00 per year.

***Retirement Life***. Manpower Education Institute, 1835 Charles Ave. Lancaster, SC 29720-1512. Phone: (718)548-4200; Email: info@meipublishing.com • URL: http://www.manpower-education.org • Quarterly. Information for retirees.

***Retirement Plans Bulletin: Practical Explanations for the IRA and Retirement Plan Professional***. Universal Pensions Inc., 431 Golf Course Rd. N Brainerd, MN 56401. Phone: 800-346-3860 or (218)829-4781 or (218)825-0552; Fax: (218)825-5011 or (218)825-5010; Email: upi@upi-net.com • Monthly. $99.00 per year. Newsletter. Provides information on the rules and regulations governing qualified (tax-deferred) retirement plans.

**Retirement Research Foundation**. 8765 W Higgins Rd., Ste. 430 Chicago, IL 60631-4172. Phone: (773)714-8080; Fax: (773)714-8089; Email: info@rrf.org • URL: http://www.rrf.org • Works to promote aging and retirement issues. Supports efforts that improve care for the aging, and enable older adults to live at home or in residential settings that facilitate independent living.

***Reuse/Recycle***. Rowman & Littlefield Education, 4501 Forbes Blvd., Ste. 200 Lanham, MD 20706. Phone: 800-462-6420 or (301)459-3366; Fax: (301)429-5748 or (800)583-2665; Email: custserv@rowman.com • URL: http://www.rowmaneducation.com • Description: Contains information on "new processes, machinery, and uses for both industrial and municipal recycling." Publishes news of waste-to-energy and waste-to-materials processes, markets for recycled materials, recycling processing, plants, equipment and case history of successful projects and programs in the U.S. and Europe. Focuses on large-scale post-consumer, post-commercial and post-industrial waste recycling. Recurring features include a calendar of events.

***Revenue Statistics***. Organisation for Economic Co-operation and Development Publications and Information Center, 2001 L St. NW, Ste. 650 Washington, DC 20036-4922. Phone: 800-456-6323 or (202)785-6323; Fax: (202)785-0350; Email: washington.contact@oecd.org • URL: http://www.oecd.org • Annual. $65.00. Presents data on government revenues in OECD countries, classified by type of tax and level of government. Text in English and French.

***Review of Agricultural Entomology: Consisting of Abstracts of Reviews of Current Literature on Applied Entomology Throughout the World***. CABI Publishing North America, 38 Chauncey St., Ste. 1002 Boston, MA 02111. Phone: 800-552-3083; Email: cabi-nao@cabi.org • URL: http://www.cabi.org • Monthly. Institutions, $1,505.00 per year. Print and online edition, $1,505.00 per year. Published in England by CABI Publishing. Provides worldwide coverage of the literature. (Formerly *Review of Applied Entomology, Series A: Agricultural*.).

***Review of Economics and Business***. Kansai University Press, 3-3-35 Yamate-cho, Suita-shi Osaka 564-0073, Japan. • Semiannual. Journal covering economics.

***The Review of Economics and Statistics***. The MIT Press, 55 Hayward St. Cambridge, MA 02142-1493. Phone: 800-356-0343 or (617)253-5646 or (617)253-5641; Fax: (617)258-6779 or (617)253-6779; Email: ewfaran@mit.edu • URL: http://mitpress.mit.edu • 5/year. $567 Institutions Online; $662 Institutions Print and Online; $73 Individuals Online; $81 Individuals Print and Online; $39 Students Online; $43 Students Print and Online. Journal of applied economics, published some of the most important articles in empirical economics.

***Review of Financial Economics***. Elsevier, Secondary Publishing Division, 650 Ave. of the Americas New York, NY 10011. Phone: 888-437-4636 or (212)633-3980; Fax: (212)633-3975; Email: t.reller@elsevier.com • URL: http://www.elseveier.com • $623 /year. Publishes original research in finance.

***Review of Income and Wealth***. John Wiley & Sons Inc. Wiley-Blackwell, 9600 Garsington Rd. Oxford OX4 2DQ, United Kingdom. Phone: 44 1865 776868 or 44 186 5778054; Fax: 44 1865 714591 or 44 186 5471777; Email: customerservice@oxon.blackwellpublishing.com • URL: http://www.as.wiley.com/wileycda/brand/id-35.html • Quarterly. £397 Institutions print & online; $326 Institutions print & online; $295 Institutions print or online; £185 Institutions print or online; $397 Institutions, other countries print & online; $361 Institutions, other countries print or online. Association journal covering research on national and economic and social accounting as related to the measurement and analysis of income and wealth.

***Review of International Political Economy***. Taylor & Francis Ltd., 2 Park Sq., Milton Park Abingdon OX14 4RN, United Kingdom. Phone: 44 22 70176000 or 44 20 70176000; Fax: 44 22 70176699 or (701)76336; Email: info@e-elgar.co.uk • URL: http://www.taylorandfrancisgroup.com • 6/year. $884 Institutions Online; $241 Individuals Print. Includes articles on international trade, finance, production, and consumption.

***Review of Maritime Transport***. United Nations Conference on Trade and Development. United Nations Publications, c/o National Book Network, 15200 NBN Way Blue Ridge Summit, PA 17214. Phone: 888-254-4286 or (212)963-7680 or (212)963-8302; Fax: (800)338-4550; Email: unpublications@nbnbooks.com • URL: http://www.unp.un.org • Annual. $95.00.

***Review of Medical and Veterinary Entomology***. CAB International, Nosworthy Way Wallingford OX10 8DE, United Kingdom. Phone: 44 1491 832111; Fax: 44 1491 833508; Email: enquiries@cabi.org • URL: http://www.cabi.org • Monthly. 855 institutions; 885 print and online edition. Provides worldwide coverage of the literature. Formerly *Review of Applied Entomology, Series B: Medical and Veterinary*.

***Review of Scientific Instruments***. American Institute of Physics, 1 Physics Ellipse College Park, MD 20740-3843. Phone: 800-874-6383 or (301)209-3100; Fax: (516)576-2604; Email: aipinfo@aip.org • URL: http://www.aip.org • Monthly. $90 /year for members of AIP and its affiliates; $1,030 /year for nonmembers; $2,550 Members domestic, print & online; $84 Members online; $2,665 Members foreign surface. Includes information on scientific instruments, apparatus, and techniques.

***The Review of Securities and Commodities Regulations: An Analysis of Current Laws, Regulations Affecting the Securities and Futures Industries***. Standard & Poor's Financial Services L.L.C., 55 Water St. New York, NY 10041. Phone: 877-772-5436 or (212)438-2000; Fax: (212)438-1000; Email: questions@standardandpoors.com • URL: http://www.standardandpoors.com • 22 times a year. $350.00 per year.

***Review of Social Economy***. Association for Social Economics. Taylor & Francis Ltd., 2 Park Sq., Milton Park Abingdon OX14 4RN, United Kingdom. Phone: 44 22 70176000 or 44 20 70176000; Fax: 44 22 70176699 or (701)76336; Email: info@e-elgar.co.uk • URL: http://www.taylorandfrancisgroup.com • Quarterly. $152 Individuals Print and Online; $370 Institutions. Quarterly. Subject matter is concerned with the relationships between social values and economics. Includes articles on income distribution, poverty, labor, and class.

***Rhode Island Directory of Human Service Agencies & Government Agencies***. Travelers Aid Society of Rhode Island, 177 Union St. Providence, RI 02903. Phone: (401)521-2255 • URL: http://riroads.com/links/listdetail.cgi?Lookup=378039 • Biennial. Covers: about 1,200 public and private nonprofit human service agencies and organizations in Rhode Island. Entries include: Agency name, address, phone, name of contact or director; description of services; hours open; eligibility requirements; ages and geographic area served; fee for service; funding.

***RIA Federal Tax Handbook***. Thomson RIA, 195 Broadway New York, NY 10007-3100. Phone: 800-431-9025 or (212)367-6300 or (212)807-2298; Fax: (212)367-6305 or (212)337-4207; Email: ttacommunications@riag.com • URL: http://www.ria.thomson.com • Annual. $95.75 book or e-book. Provides quick and easy access to critical tax questions, the RIA Federal Tax Handbook offers comprehensive, insightful guidance on federal tax law, including the latest regulations, rulings, and revenue procedures as well as precise explanations about changes that could impact your business or your clients.

***RIC News***. Rare-Earth Information Center, Institute for Physical Research and Technology, Ames Laboratory, Iowa State University Ames, IA 50011-3020. Phone: (515)294-2272 or (515)294-5405; Fax: (515)294-3709; Email: ric@ameslab.gov • URL: http://www.external.ameslab.gov/RIC/index.html • Quarterly. Contains items of current interest concerning the science and technology of the rare earth.

***Rice Abstracts***. CABI Publishing North America, 38 Chauncey St., Ste. 1002 Boston, MA 02111. Phone: 800-552-3083; Email: cabi-nao@cabi.org • URL: http://www.cabi.org • Quarterly. Published in England by CABI Publishing. Provides worldwide coverage of the literature.

***Rice Farming***. Vance Publishing Corp., 400 Knightsbridge Pkwy. Lincolnshire, IL 60069-3613. Phone: 800-255-5113 or (847)634-2600; Fax: (847)634-4342 or (847)634-4379; Email: info@vancepublishing.com • URL: http://www.vancepublishing.com • Six times a year. $30.00 per year.

***Rice Journal: For Commerical Growers of Rice and Related Agribusiness***. SpecComm International Inc., 3101 Poplarwood Ct., Ste. 115 Raleigh, NC 27604. Phone: (919)872-5040; Fax: (919)876-6531; Email: spec_circ@juno.com • URL: http://www.speccomm.com • Seven times a year. $15.00 per year.

**Rice Millers' Association**. USA Rice Federation, 2101 Wilson Blvd., Ste. 610 Arlington, VA 22201. Phone: (703)236-2300; Fax: (703)236-2301; Email: riceinfo@usarice.com • URL: http://www.usarice.com/index.php?option=com_content&view=article&id=139&Itemid=441 • Represents independent and farmer-cooperative rice milling operators. Provides economic and statistical information on production, milling, and distribution of rice. Promotes research aimed at new uses for rice products and improvements in processing, packaging, storing, and distributing rice. Maintains liaison with U.S. and foreign government agencies, congress, and foreign buyers of U.S. rice.

**Rice University - Center for Computational Finance and Economic Systems**. Department of Statistics, MS-138 Houston, TX 77251-1892. Phone: (713)348-5839; Fax: (713)348-5476; Email: ensor@rice.edu • URL: http://www.cofes.rice.edu • Computational finance and economic systems, including credit risk management, pricing financial derivatives, emerging markets, energy markets, impact of politics on world finance, and risk fundamentals and integration of risk.

***Richard C. Young's Intelligence Report***. Access Intelligence L.L.C., 4 Choke Cherry Rd., 2nd Fl. Rockville, MD 20850. Phone: 800-777-5006 or (301)354-2000 or (301)354-2101; Fax: (301)309-3847 or (801)365-2300; Email: info@accessintel.com • URL: http://www.accessintel.com/ • Description: Provides information for "serious, conservative investors (buy and hold as opposed to active traders)." Features investing advice and recommendations for best funds, stocks, and bonds for current or retirement income.

***Richmond Business Directory***. City of Richmond Business and Development Division, 6911 No. 3 Rd. Richmond, BC, Canada V6Y 2C1. Phone: (604)276-4000 • URL: http://www.richmond.ca • Lists resident businesses with valid business license.

***RICO Business Disputes Guide***. Wolters Kluwer Law & Business CCH, 2700 Lake Cook Rd. Riverwoods, IL 60015. Phone: 888-224-7377 or (847)267-7000; Email: cust_serv@cch.com • URL: http://www.cchgroup.com • Contains information on pending U.S. Supreme Court RICO cases, as well as pending federal and state legislation.

***RICS Business***. Royal Institution of Chartered Surveyors, Parliament Sq. London SW1P 3AD, United Kingdom. Phone: 44 24 76868555 or 44 870 3331600; Fax: 44 20 73343811; Email: contactrics@rics.org • URL: http://www.rics.org • 10/year. Delivers news, features, analysis and interviews from the surveying profession.

**Rising Tide Capital**. 334 Martin Luther King Dr. Jersey City, NJ 07305. Phone: (201)432-4316; Fax: (201)432-3504; Email: info@risingtidecapital.org • URL: http://risingtidecapital.org • Strives to assist entrepreneurs and communities to build tough businesses that transform lives, strengthen families and create vibrant, sustainable neighborhoods. Works to build a replicable model for high-quality entrepreneurial development services that can be locally adopted in low-wealth communities and used as a catalyst for social and economic empowerment. Connects entrepreneurs to appropriate business financing.

***Risk and Insurance***. LRP Publications Library, lrp.com Technology Contacts, 747 Dresher Rd., Ste. 500 Horsham, PA 19044. Phone: 800-341-7874 or (215)784-0860 or (215)784-0910; Fax: (215)784-9639 or (215)784-0275; Email: techsup@lrp.com • URL: http://www.lrp.com • Monthly. Price on application. Topics include risk management, workers' compensation, reinsurance, employee benefits, and managed care.

**Risk and Insurance Management Society**. 1065 Ave. of the Americas, 13th Fl. New York, NY 10018. Phone: 800-713-7467 or (212)286-9292; Fax: (212)986-9716; Email: lists@rims.org • URL: http://www.rims.org • Formerly American Society of Insurance Management.

**Risk Management Association**. 1801 Market St., Ste. 300 Philadelphia, PA 19103-1613. Phone: (215)446-4000; Fax: (215)446-4101; Email: rmaar@rmahq.org • URL: http://www.rmahq.org • Commercial and savings banks, and savings and loan, and other financial services companies. Conducts research and professional development activities in areas of loan administration, asset management, and commercial lending and credit to increase professionalism.

***Risk Management***. Risk and Insurance Management Society. Risk and Insurance Management Society, 1065 Ave. of the Americas, 13th Fl. New York, NY 10018. Phone: 800-713-7467 or (212)286-9292; Fax: (212)986-9716; Email: lists@rims.org • URL: http://www.rims.org • 10/year. $115 Individuals; $199 Two years; $175 1st class/airmail rate. Magazine featuring analysis, insight, and news for corporate risk managers.

***Road & Track***. Hearst Magazines, 1271 Ave. of the Americas New York, NY 10020. Phone: (212)649-4115; Fax: (212)767-5612; Email: jdeval@hearst.com • URL: http://www.hearst.com • Monthly. $15 Individuals; $25 Two years. Automotive magazine.

***Road Construction and Safety***. U. S. Government Printing Office, 732 N Capitol St. NW Washington, DC 20401. Phone: 866-512-1800 or (202)512-1800 or (866)512-1800; Fax: (202)512-2104 or (202)512-2250; Email: contactcenter@gpo.gov • URL: http://www.gpo.gov • Annual. Free. Issued by the Superintendent of Documents. A list of government publications on highway construction and traffic safety. Formerly *Highway Construction, Safety and Traffic*. (Subject Bibliography No. 3.).

**The Road Information Program**. 3000 Connecticut Ave. NW, Ste. 208 Washington, DC 20008. Phone: (202)466-6706 • URL: http://www.tripnet.org • Conducts public education programs for the highway industry. Promotes transportation policies that relieve traffic congestion, improve air quality, make highway travel safer and enhance economic productivity.

***Roads & Bridges***. Scranton Gillette Communications Inc., 3030 W Salt Creek Ln., Ste. 201 Arlington Heights, IL 60005-5025. Phone: (847)391-1000; Fax: (847)390-0408; Email: hgillette@sgcmail.com • URL: http://www.scrantongillette.com • Monthly. Provides information on the planning/design, administration/management, engineering and contract execution for the road and bridge industry.

***Robb Report***. CurtCo Robb Media, 29160 Heathercliff Rd., Ste. 200 Malibu, CA 90265. Phone: (310)589-7700; Fax: (310)589-7701; Email: webfeedback@curtco.com • URL: http://robbreport.com • Monthly. $65 U.S. /year subscription (Online); $75 Canada /year subscription (Online); $105 Other countries /year subscription (Online). Consumer magazine featuring advertisements for expensive items-antique automobiles, boats, airplanes, large houses, etc.

***Robb Report Home Entertaining & Design***. CurtCo Robb Media, 29160 Heathercliff Rd., Ste. 200 Malibu, CA 90265. Phone: (310)589-7700; Fax: (310)589-7701; Email: webfeedback@curtco.com • URL: http://robbreport.com • Monthly. $65. Covers "high end" home theaters, audio, video, wireless home networks, and custom installations.

***Robb Report Motorcycling***. CurtCo Robb Media, 29160 Heathercliff Rd., Ste. 200 Malibu, CA 90265. Phone: (310)589-7700; Fax: (310)589-7701; Email: webfeedback@curtco.com • URL: http://robbreport.com • Semiannual. Price on application. Contains reviews of the "newest high-quality motorcycles.".

***Robb Report Worth: Wealth in Perspective***. CurtCo Robb Media, 29160 Heathercliff Rd., Ste. 200 Malibu, CA 90265. Phone: (310)589-7700; Fax: (310)589-7701; Email: webfeedback@curtco.com • URL: http://robbreport.com • Monthly. $54.95 per year. Glossy magazine featuring articles for the affluent on personal financial management, investments, estate planning, trusts, private bankers, taxes, travel, yachts, and lifestyle. Formerly *Worth: Financial Intelligence*.

**Robert Gordon University - Centre for Public Policy and Management**. Aberdeen Business School, Garthdee Rd. Aberdeen AB10 7QE, United Kingdom. Phone: 44 1224 263111; Fax: 44 1224 263434; Email: cppm@rgu.ac.uk • URL: http://www2.rgu.ac.uk/publicpolicy/cppm • Policy analysis, social administration, management, planning, law, economics and social science.

**Robotic Industries Association**. 900 Victors Way, Ste. 140 Ann Arbor, MI 48108. Phone: (734)994-6088; Fax: (734)994-3338; Email: webmaster@robotics.org • URL: http://www.robotics.org • Represents the interests of the robotics industry. Member companies include robot manufacturers, users, system integrators, component suppliers, research groups, and consulting firms. Sponsors the biennial International Robots and Vision Show, develops the ANSI/RIA national robot safety standard, collects and reports robotics industry statistics.

**Robotics International of the Society of Manufacturing Engineers**. 1 SME Dr. Dearborn, MI 48128. Phone: 800-733-4763 or (313)425-3000; Fax: (313)425-3400; Email: service@sme.org • URL: http://www.sme.org • Engineers, managers, educators and government officials in 50 countries working or interested in the field of robotics. Affiliated with the Society of Manufacturing Engineers.

**Rochester Institute of Technology - Chester F. Carlson Center for Imaging Science**. 54 Lomb Memorial Dr. Rochester, NY 14623. Phone: (585)475-5944; Fax: (585)475-5988; Email: baum@cis.rit.edu • URL: http://www.cis.rit.edu • Imaging sciences, including remote sensing, digital image processing, color science, optics, medical diagnostic imaging, visual perception, sensor development, printing technology, and astronomical imaging.

**Rochester Institute of Technology - Center for Integrated Manufacturing Studies**. Louise M. Slaughter Hall, Bldg. 78, 111 Lomb Memorial Dr. Rochester, NY 14623-5608. Phone: (585)475-5385 or (585)475-5101; Fax: (585)475-5250; Email: info@sustainability.rit.edu • URL: http://www.rit.edu/gis/research-centers/cims • Research areas include electronics, imaging, printing, and publishing.

***Rock Products: The Aggregate Industry's Journal of Applied Technology***. Primedia Business Magazines and Media, 330 N Wabash Ave., Suite 2300 Chicago, IL 60611. Phone: 800-795-5445 or (312)595-1080 or (312)726-2802; Fax: (312)595-0295 or (312)726-2574; Email: subs@primediabusiness.com • URL: http://www.primediabusiness.com • Monthly. $56.00 per year.

***Rocks & Minerals***. Routledge, 711 3rd Ave., 8th Fl. New York, NY 10017. Phone: 800-634-7064 or (212)216-7800; Fax: (212)564-7854 or (212)563-2269; Email: book.orders@tandf.co.uk • URL: http://www.routledge.com • Bimonthly. $213 Institutions print and online; $61 Individuals print and online. Six issues per year.

***Rocky Mountain Business Journal***. Rocky Mountain Business Journal, 2401 15th St., Ste. 350 Denver, CO 80202-1168. • Weekly (Mon.). $26 Individuals. Metro business journal.

**Thomas A. Roe Institute for Economic Policy Studies**. Heritage Foundation, 214 Massachusetts Ave. NE Washington, DC 20002-4999. Phone: (202)546-4400 or (202)675-1761; Fax: (202)546-8328; Email: info@heritage.org • URL: http://www.heritage.org • Concerned with the financing of Medicare.

***Roget's International Thesaurus***. Barbara A. Kipfer, editor. 10 E 53rd St. New York, NY 10022-5299. Phone: (212)207-7000 • URL: http://www.harpercollins.com • 2011. Seventh edition.

***Roller Rinks Directory***. InfoGroup Inc., 5711 S 86th Cir. Omaha, NE 68127-4146. Phone: (402)593-4500 • URL: http://www.infogroup.com • Annual. Number of listings: 2,944. Entries include: Name, address, phone, size of advertisement, name of owner or manager, number of employees, year first in "Yellow Pages." Compiled from telephone company "Yellow Pages," nationwide.

***Romania Business Services Providers Leads***. Business Information Agency Inc. PlanetInform, 52 Tuscan Way, Ste. 202-181 Saint Augustine, VA 32092. Phone: (904)342-6124; Fax: (904)592-2632; Email: info@biasales.com • URL: http://www.biasales.com • Monthly. $84 Individuals mailing list; $177 Individuals sales list; $300 Individuals marketing list. Covers Romanian companies and all sub-industries that provide various services to commercial businesses, establishments, and organizations, including consulting, advertising and marketing services, and facilities maintenance.

***Romania Investment and Business Guide***. International Business Publications, USA, PO Box 15343 Washington, DC 20003. Phone: (202)546-2103; Fax: (202)546-3275; Email: ibpusa@comcast.net • URL: http://ibpus.com • $99.95 Individuals hardcopy, e-book, CD-ROM. Covers: Detailed information on investment, export-import business opportunities, foreign economic assistance projects, government and business contacts.

***The Romanian Business Directory***. Topaz General Activities S.R. L., Splaiul Independentei 202 A R-77208 Bucharest, Romania. Phone: 40 1 613 9950; Fax: 40 1 312 0436 • Annual. $20. Covers: The most active companies and operators in the Romanian market, along with products and services. Entries include: Company business information.

**Romanian-U.S. Business Council**. 620 8th Ave. New York, NY 10018. Phone: (646)678-2905; Email: info@usrobc.org • URL: http://usrobc.org • Advocates American business interests with respect to U.S. Romanian trade and investments. Provides the American and Romanian business communities with a means of discussing bilateral trade and investment issues and the formulation of policy positions that will promote and expand economic relations between the two countries. Facilitates appropriate legislation and policies regarding trade between the U.S. and Romania. Has sponsored seminars on topics such as possibilities for cooperative commercial efforts in other countries and cooperation in energy development.

***Roofing Contractor—Single Ply Systems Index Issue***. BNP Media, 2401 W Big Beaver Rd., Ste. 700 Troy, MI 48084. Phone: 800-952-6643 or (248)362-3700 or (847)763-9534; Fax: (248)362-5103 or (248)362-0317; Email: privacy@bnpmedia.com • URL: http://www.bnpmedia.com • Annual. Publication includes: List of manufacturers of single ply roofing products. Entries include: Company name, address, phone, products.

***Roofing Service Consultants Directory***. InfoGroup Inc., 5711 S 86th Cir. Omaha, NE 68127-4146. Phone: (402)593-4500 • URL: http://www.infogroup.com • Annual. Number of listings: 1,225. Entries include: Name, address, phone, size of advertisement, name of owner or manager, number of employees, year first in "Yellow Pages." Compiled from telephone company "Yellow Pages," nationwide.

***Roofing, Siding, Insulation***. Advanstar Communications, 545 Boylston St. Boston, MA 02116. Phone: 888-527-7008 or (617)267-6500; Fax: (617)267-6900; Email: info@advanstar.com • URL: http://www.advanstar.com • Monthly. $44.00 per year.

***The Rose Sheet: Toiletries, Fragrances and Skin Care***. Elsevier Business Intelligence, 5635 Fishers Ln., Ste. 6000 Rockville, MD 20852. Phone: 800-332-2181 or (240)221-4500 or (800)332-2181; Fax: (240)221-4400 or (301)656-3094; Email: fdc.customer.service@fdcreports.com • URL: http://www.elsevierbi.com • 51 times a year. $1,910.00 online only. Newsletter. Provides industry news, regulatory news, market data, and a "Weekly Trademark Review" for the cosmetics industry.

***Rotor & Wing***. Access Intelligence L.L.C., 4 Choke Cherry Rd., 2nd Fl. Rockville, MD 20850. Phone: 800-777-5006 or (301)354-2000 or (301)354-2101; Fax: (301)309-3847 or (801)365-2300; Email: info@accessintel.com • URL: http://www.accessintel.com/ • Monthly. *World Helicopter Resources Rotor and Wing International*.

***Rough Notes***. The Rough Notes Company Inc., 11690 Technology Dr. Carmel, IN 46032-5600. Phone: 800-428-4384 or (317)582-1600; Fax: (317)816-1000 or (800)321-1909; Email: rnc@roughnotes.com • URL: http://www.roughnotes.com • Monthly. $25 Individuals.

***Route 422 Business Advisor***. TriCounty Area Chamber of Commerce, 152 High St., Ste. 360 Pottstown, PA 19464-5555. Phone: (610)326-2900; Fax: (610)970-9705 • URL: http://www.tricountyareachamber.com • Monthly. Magazine containing topics of interest to the business community of the Pottstown, PA area.

***Rowlett Business Directory***. Business Directories of Texas, 1774 Lake Breeze Rockwall, TX 75087. Phone: (972)722-6614 • URL: http://www.texasmediapros.com • List of businesses in Rowlett, Texas.

**Royal Agricultural Society of New Zealand**. PO Box 54 Woodend 7461, New Zealand. Phone: 64 3 3131004; Fax: 64 3 3131003 • URL: http://www.ras.org.nz • Promotes and rewards excellence in agribusiness in New Zealand.

***Rubber & Plastics News***. Crain Communications Inc., 77 Franklin St., Ste. 809 Boston, MA 02110-1510. Phone: (617)292-3385; Email: info@crain.com • URL: http://www.crain.com • Biweekly. $99 Individuals; $138 Individuals Canada; $140 Individuals foreign; $178 Two years; $251 Two years Canada; $255 Two years foreign. Written for rubber product manufacturers.

***Rubber Chemistry & Technology***. American Chemical Society - Rubber Division, 411 Wolf Ledges, Ste. 201 Akron, OH 44311. Phone: (330)972-7814; Fax: (330)972-5269 • URL: http://www.rubber.org • Four times per year.

***Rubber Statistical Bulletin***. International Rubber Study Group, 115 Heron House, 1st Fl., 109/115 Wembley Hill Rd. Wembley HA9 8DA, United Kingdom. Phone: 44 20 8900 5400; Fax: (890)3 2848; Email: irsg@rubberstudy.com • URL: http://www.rubberstudy.com • Quarterly. S$3,000.00 per year. S$1,500.00 per issue.

***Rubber World***. Lippincott, 1867 W. Market St. Akron, OH 44313. Phone: (330)864-2122; Fax: (330)864-5298; Email: jhl@rubberworld.com • URL: http://www.rubberworld.com • Monthly. $34 /year. Provides plant engineering personnel with the latest equipment and production technology.

***Runzheimer Mobility Report***. Runzheimer International, 1 Runzheimer Pkwy. Waterford, WI 53185-3599. Phone: 800-558-1702; Email: cls@runzheimer.com • URL: http://www.runzheimer.com • Monthly. $295.00 per year. Newsletter on the control of business travel costs.

***Runzheimer Reports on Relocation***. Runzheimer International, 1 Runzheimer Pkwy. Waterford, WI 53185-3599. Phone: 800-558-1702; Email: cls@runzheimer.com • URL: http://www.runzheimer.com • Monthly. $354.00 per year. Newsletter.

***Rural Cooperatives***. Rural Business Cooperative Service Cooperative Services Program, MS 3250, 1400 Independence SW Washington, DC 20250-3250. Phone: (202)720-7558; Fax: (202)720-4641; Email: chad.parker@wdc.usda.gov • URL: http://www.rurdev.usda.gov/LP_CoopPrograms.html • Bimonthly. 21. Issued by the U.S. Department of Agriculture. Contains articles on cooperatives in rural America. Formerly *Farmer Cooperatives*.

***Rural Transit Fact Book***. American Public Transportation Association, 1666 K St. NW, Ste. 1100 Washington, DC 20006. Phone: (202)496-4800; Fax: (202)496-4324; Email: info@apta.com • URL: http://www.apta.com • Annual. Serves as a national resource for statistics and information on rural transit in America.

***Russia Business Forecast Report***. Telecommunications Insight, 85 Queen Victoria St. London EC4V 4AB, United Kingdom. Phone: 20 72 465100 or 44 20 7248 0468; Fax: 20 72 480467 or 44 20 7248 0467; Email: enquiries@telecomsinsight.com • URL: http://www.telecomsinsight.com • Quarterly. $1,195 Individuals Single user; $1,795 Individuals Up to 3 users. Business forecast report for Russia.

***Russia Business Law Handbook***. International Business Publications, USA, PO Box 15343 Washington, DC 20003. Phone: (202)546-2103; Fax: (202)546-3275; Email: ibpusa@comcast.net • URL: http://ibpus.com • $99.95 Individuals hardcopy, e-book, CD-ROM. Covers: Information on business laws and climate, legislation, export-import regulations, and contacts.

***Russia Business Services Providers Leads***. Business Information Agency Inc. PlanetInform, 52 Tuscan Way, Ste. 202-181 Saint Augustine, VA 32092. Phone: (904)342-6124; Fax: (904)592-2632; Email: info@biasales.com • URL: http://www.biasales.com • Monthly. $101 Individuals mailing list; $212 Individuals sales list; $330 Individuals marketing list. Covers Russian companies and all sub-industries that provide various services to commercial businesses, establishments, and organizations, including consulting, advertising and marketing services, and facilities maintenance.

***Russia/CIS Exporters-Importers Directory***. Business Information Agency Inc. PlanetInform, 52 Tuscan Way, Ste. 202-181 Saint Augustine, VA 32092. Phone: (904)342-6124; Fax: (904)592-2632; Email: info@biasales.com • URL: http://www.biasales.com • Annual. $149 Individuals Paperback (plus shipping charge); $149 Individuals PDF version; $189 Individuals Both hard copy & PDF. Covers: 5,936 representatives of foreign firms and joint-venture companies in Russia. Entries include: Company name, location, detailed contact information, type of business, SIC codes, number of employees, year founded, legal status, and subsidiary indicators.

***Russia Defense Industry Directory***. International Business Publications, USA, PO Box 15343 Washington, DC 20003. Phone: (202)546-2103; Fax: (202)546-3275; Email: ibpusa@comcast.net • URL: http://ibpus.com • $99.95 Individuals hardcopy, e-book, CD-ROM. Covers: Strategic and practical information on government, national security, army, foreign and domestic politics, conflicts, relations with the US, international activity, economy, technology, mineral resources, culture, traditions, government and business contacts.

***Russia Industrial and Business Directory***. International Business

SOURCES CITED

Publications, USA, PO Box 15343 Washington, DC 20003. Phone: (202)546-2103; Fax: (202)546-3275; Email: ibpusa@comcast.net • URL: http://ibpus.com • Annual. $99.95 Individuals hardcopy, e-book, CD-ROM. Covers: Strategic industrial, investment and business contacts for conducting export-import and investment activity in the country.

***Russia Investment and Business Guide***. International Business Publications, USA, PO Box 15343 Washington, DC 20003. Phone: (202)546-2103; Fax: (202)546-3275; Email: ibpusa@comcast.net • URL: http://ibpus.com • $99.95 Individuals hardcopy, e-book, CD-ROM. Covers: Basic information on economy, export-import and investment climate, regulations and industrial development, banking, and government. Entries include: Important business contacts and business travel.

***Russia: Political and Economic Analysis and Business Directory***. Chamber World Network, c/o SCB Distributors, 15608 S New Center Dr. Gardena, CA 90248. Phone: 800-729-6423 or (310)532-9400; Fax: (310)532-7001 • $29.95. Publication includes: Directories of organizations, companies, and other agencies in or doing business in Russia, including Russian companies, joint ventures, firms from outside Russia accredited to do business there, banks, insurance companies, consulates and embassies, hotels. Database includes: Essays and tables on the economic and legal structure of Russia, including summaries of Russian law, statistics, and surveys of future trends. Entries include: For companies—Name, address, phone, annual sales, number of employees, products.

**Russian Academy of Entrepreneurship**. ul. Radio, 14 105005 Moscow, Russia. Phone: 7 495 6322425 or 7 495 6322426; Email: priem@rusacad.ru • URL: http://www.rusacad.ru • Works to help Russian businesses compete in a market economy. Conducts economic analysis.

**Russian Academy of Sciences - Central Economics and Mathematics Institute**. 47 Nakhimovsky prospect 117418 Moscow, Russia. Phone: 7 495 1291011; Fax: 7 495 7189615; Email: director@cemi.rssi.ru • URL: http://www.cemi.rssi.ru/en • Theoretical modeling and the development of mathematical, computer, and empirical methods for the study of the economic transition. Specific areas of research include the theory of the optimal functioning planned economies, the study of scientific-technical progress, methods of evaluating the economic efficiency of capital investment and of the location of manufacturing, the economics of natural resource use, general equilibrium and disequilibrium theory (including the incorporation of issues related to intellectual property), and decision making under uncertainty.

**Russian Academy of Sciences - Institute for International Economic and Political Studies**. Novocheryemushkinskaya, 42a 117418 Moscow, Russia. Phone: 7 499 1286780; Fax: 7 499 1208371; Email: omepi@mail.ru • URL: http://www.imepi-eurasia.ru/eng/kalendar.php • Theoretical principles and the practical problems of creating a post socialist economic order, including various aspects of foreign policy and foreign trade relations of Russia and of internal economic and political development of all post-communist countries.

**Russian Academy of Sciences - Institute of World Economy and International Relations**. 23 Profsoyuznaya St. 117997 Moscow, Russia. Phone: 7 499 1205236; Fax: 7 499 1206575; Email: imemoran@imemo.ru • URL: http://www.imemo.ru • Internationalization of production and capital, foreign trade, international monetary system, external debt, international relations, security and conflict management, arms control and disarmament, and economic political issues in Russia.

**Russian Association of Business Education**. Kronstadt Blvd. St., d. 37 B, Ste. 140 125499 Moscow, Russia. Phone: 7 499 9439302; Fax: 7 499 9439309; Email: office@rabe.ru • URL: http://www.rabe.ru • Aims to unite universities, institutes, business schools and other training centers in the field of business education. Trains, retrains and upgrades the qualifications of personnel engaged in developing Russian business. Participates in the elaboration of the strategy of business education development in Russia and CIS.

***Russian Business Magazine***. Vystavochno-Ekspertno-Marketingovaya i Zakupochnaya Programma: Luchshie Tovary i Uslugina Rynkakh Rossii, Bersenevskaya nab 20-2 103790 Moscow, Russia. Phone: 7 0952386486 • Bimonthly. $95 U.S. Magazine covering business in Russia.

***Russian Business White & Yellow Pages***. European Business Publications Inc., Box 891 Darien, CT 06820-9859. Phone: (203)656-2701 or (203)658-2701; Fax: (203)655-8332; Email: gale.customerservice@cengage.com • URL: http://www.curt.org/pdf/283.pdf • Covers: More than 25,000 major business companies, industrial enterprises and banks in Moscow, St. Petersburg and all 87 provinces of Russia and Worldwide. White Pages include Russian Federal Government information and contacts. Entries include: Name, address, phone, fax, line of business and product information.

***Russian Encyclopedia of Information and Telecommunications: Information on Information***. International Bureau for Information and Telecommunications, Leningradsky Ave. 80/2, p/b 44 125190 Moscow, Russia. Phone: 95 1588080; Fax: 95 1585665; Email: ieit@mbt.ru • $30. Covers: Approximately 1,500 organizations, 2,500 managers and senior employees in information and telecommunications in Russia. Also includes detailed descriptions of 1,700 electronic databases, 150 telecommunication networks, hosts, and their information resource. Entries include: Company, organization or personal name, address, phone, e-mail, website address, names and titles of key personnel, biographical data for individuals, number of employees, financial data, branch office or subsidiary names and addresses, products or services provided, key data, title of database.

***Russian Exporters and Importers—Firm Directory***. International Bureau for Information and Telecommunications, Leningradsky Ave. 80/2, p/b 44 125190 Moscow, Russia. Phone: 95 1588080; Fax: 95 1585665; Email: ieit@mbt.ru • Annual. $25. Covers: 4,300 leading Russian companies trading on the international market and their exports and imports product range. Entries include: Company name, address, phone, fax, geographical area served, products or services provided.

***Russian Nuclear Industry Business Opportunities Handbook***. International Business Publications, USA, PO Box 15343 Washington, DC 20003. Phone: (202)546-2103; Fax: (202)546-3275; Email: ibpusa@comcast.net • URL: http://ibpus.com • $99.95 Individuals. Strategic and business information on Russian nuclear industry, research on nuclear reactors, and contact information for major industrial and research facilities.

**Russian Venture Capital Association**. ORm. 209, Bldg. 12B, prospekt Engelsa 27 194156 Saint Petersburg, Russia. Phone: 7 812 3266180; Fax: 7 812 3266180; Email: rvca@rvca.ru • URL: http://www.rvca.ru • Promotes the development of the venture capital industry in Russia. Seeks to create a positive political and entrepreneurial environment for investment activities. Represents members' interests at the government level and in financial and industrial markets within the country and abroad.

***Rutgers Accounting Web***. Rutgers University Accounting Research Center, Phone: (973)353-5172; Fax: (973)353-1283 • URL: http://www.rutgers.edu/accounting • RAW Web site provides extensive links to sources of national and international accounting information, such as the Big Six accounting firms, the Financial Accounting Standards Board (FASB), SEC filings (EDGAR), journals, publishers, software, the International Accounting Network, and "Internet's largest list of accounting firms in USA." Searching is offered. Fees: Free.

**Rutgers University - Center for Negotiation and Conflict Resolution**. Bloustein School of Planning & Public Policy, 33 Livingston Ave. New Brunswick, NJ 08901-1985. Phone: (848)932-2896; Fax: (732)932-2493; Email: cncr@rci.rutgers.edu • URL: http://policy.rutgers.edu/CNCR • Seeks to expand and improve conflict resolution within a context that fosters greater theoretical understanding.

**Rutgers University - Center for Research in Regulated Industries**. Rutgers Business School, 1 Washington Park, Rm. 1104 Newark, NJ 07102-3122. Phone: (973)353-5761; Fax: (973)353-1348; Email: crri@business.rutgers.edu • URL: http://www.crri.rutgers.edu • Regulated industries, especially economics and finance of such institutions, governance mechanisms, and price structures.

**Rutgers University - Center for State Health Policy**. 112 Paterson St., 5th Fl. New Brunswick, NJ 08901-1913. Phone: (732)932-3105; Fax: (732)932-0069; Email: jcantor@ifh.rutgers.edu • URL: http://www.cshp.rutgers.edu/ • State health policy issues in New Jersey, including long-term care, access to health care, racial and ethnic health disparities, health care performance measurement, and pharmaceutical policy.

**Rutgers University - Eagleton Institute of Politics - Eagleton Center for Public Interest Polling**. 191 Ryders Ln. New Brunswick, NJ 08901. Phone: (732)932-9384; Fax: (732)932-6778; Email: redlawsk@rutgers.edu • URL: http://eagletonpoll.rutgers.edu • Provides survey research and program evaluation services.

**Rutgers University - Rutgers Accounting Research Center**. Rutgers Business School, Rm. 919, 1 Washington Park Newark, NJ 07102-3122. Phone: (973)353-5172; Fax: (973)353-1283; Email: miklosv@andromeda.rutgers.edu • URL: http://raw.rutgers.edu • Accounting theory and practice, especially digital accounting, continuous reporting and continuous audit.

***RV Business***. Affinity Group Inc., 2575 Vista del Mar Dr. Ventura, CA 93001. Phone: 800-234-3450 or (805)667-4100 or (805)667-4434; Fax: (805)667-4419 or (805)667-4484; Email: tlecs@magsserv.com • URL: http://www.goodsamclub.com • Monthly. Includes news about the entire recreational vehicle industry in the U.S.

***RV Business—RV Industry Directory Issue***. Affinity Group Inc., 2575 Vista del Mar Dr. Ventura, CA 93001. Phone: 800-234-3450 or (805)667-4100 or (805)667-4434; Fax: (805)667-4419 or (805)667-4484; Email: tlecs@magsserv.com • URL: http://www.goodsamclub.com • Annual. $19.95 Individuals 1-4 copies; $14.95 Individuals 5 or more copies. Publication includes: About 250 recreational vehicle manufacturers, 700 suppliers, and 600 distributors, wholesalers, manufacturers' representatives, and others in the industry; limited international coverage. Entries include: For manufacturers—Company name, address, phone, fax, names of key personnel, location of branch plants, types of vehicles made, brand names. For suppliers, and distributors—Company name, address, phone, fax, names of key personnel, products. For representatives—Company name, address, phone, fax, names and titles of key personnel, companies represented.

***The RVDA Membership Directory and Resource Guide***. Recreation Vehicle Dealers Association of North America, 3930 University Dr. Fairfax, VA 22030-2515. Phone: (703)591-7130; Fax: (703)359-0152; Email: jnewhouse@rvda.org • URL: http://www.rvda.org • Annual. Covers: Over 900 retail sales firms handling travel trailers, camping trailers, truck campers, and motor homes in the United States and Canada that are open for business twelve months of the year. Entries include: Company name, address, phone, and owner's or manager's name.

***Rwanda Investment and Business Guide***. International Business Publications, USA, PO Box 15343 Washington, DC 20003. Phone: (202)546-2103; Fax: (202)546-3275; Email: ibpusa@comcast.net • URL: http://ibpus.com • $99.95 Individuals hardcopy, e-book, CD-ROM. Covers: Strategic information on economy, business, export-import and investment climate, regulations and industrial development, banking, government, and opportunities. Entries include: Important business contacts and business travel.

**Rwanda Private Sector Federation**. PO Box 319 Kigali, Rwanda. Phone: 250 570650; Email: info@rpsf.org.rw • URL: http://www.psf.org.rw • Promotes and protects the interests of the Rwandan business community through lobbying and advocacy. Provides business development services that lead to sustainable economic growth and development. Facilitates a dialogue with the government on matters related to the improvement of business.

***Rx List: The Internet Drug Index***. WebMD Health Corp., 111 8th Ave. New York, NY 10011. Phone: (212)624-3700 • URL: http://www.wbmd.com • Web site features detailed information (cost, usage, dosage, side effects, etc.) from Mosby, Inc. for about 300 major pharmaceutical products, representing two thirds of prescriptions filled in the U. S. (3,700 other products are listed). The "Top 200" drugs are ranked by number of prescriptions filled. Keyword searching is provided. Fees: Free.

***S & P's Municipal Bond Book, with Notes, Commercial Paper, & IRBs***. Standard & Poor's Financial Services L.L.C., 55 Water St. New York, NY 10041. Phone: 877-772-5436 or (212)438-2000; Fax: (212)438-1000; Email: questions@standardandpoors.com • URL: http://www.standardandpoors.com • Bimonthly. $965.00 per year. Includes ratings and statistical information for about 20,000 municipal bonds, notes, commercial paper issues, and industrial revenue bonds (IRBs). The creditworthiness ("Rationales") of 200 selected municipalities and other issuers is discussed. Securities "under surveillance" by S & P are listed.

***SAE Handbook***. Society of Automotive Engineers, 400 Commonwealth Dr. Warrendale, PA 15096-0001. Phone: 877-606-7323 or (724)776-4841; Fax: (724)776-0790; Email: customerservice@sae.org • URL: http://www.sae.org • Annual. $425.00. Three volumes. Contains standards, recommended practices and information reports on ground vehicle design, manufacturing, testing and performance.

***SAEGIS Internet Search***. Thomson & Thomson, Phone: 800-692-8833 or (617)479-1600; Fax: (617)786-8273; Email: support@thomson-thomson.com • URL: http://www.thomson-thomson.com • Fee-based Web site provides extensive, common law screening of the World Wide Web for trademarks. Searches are performed offline, with final report delivered to user's "SAEGIS Inbox." Context of trademark within each relevant Web site is indicated, and links are provided.

***The Safe Deposit Bulletin***. New York State Safe Deposit Association, 150 Main St. Port Washington, NY 11050. Phone: (516)883-2390; Fax: (516)883-8429; Email: nys.safedeposit@yahoo.com • URL: http://www.nyssda.com • Description: Discusses topics on safe and sound business practice for safe deposit organizations. Recurring features include news of research, notices of publications available, a calendar of events, news of educational opportunities, Association news, current legal and regulatory changes, current practices and procedures and Q&A section.

***Safe Money Report***. Weiss Research Inc., 15430 Endeavour Dr. Jupiter, FL 33478-6402. Phone: 800-291-8545 or (561)627-3300; Fax: (561)625-6685; Email: wr@weissinc.com • URL: http://www.weissinc.com • Monthly. $99.00 per year. Newsletter. Provides financial advice and current safety ratings of various banks, savings and loan companies, insurance companies, and securities dealers.

***Safety and Health***. National Safety Council, 1121 Spring Lake Dr. Itasca, IL 60143-3201. Phone: 800-621-7615 or (630)285-1121; Fax: (630)285-1315; Email: info@nsc.org • URL: http://www.nsc.org • Monthly. Qualified professionals may receive free for one year.

***Sage Public Administration Abstracts***. EBSCO Publishing Inc., 10 Estes St. Ipswich, MA 01938-2106. Phone: 800-653-2726 or (978)356-6500; Fax: (978)356-6565; Email: information@ebscohost.com • URL: http://www.ebscohost.com • Titles include Journal of Public Economics, Public Administration, and Public Administratioin Review.

***SAGE Sourcebook of Modern Biomedical Devices Business Environments in a Global Market***. Cengage Learning Inc., 20 Channel Center St. Boston, MA 02210. Phone: 800-487-8488 or (617)289-7700; Fax: (617)289-7844; Email: investors@cengage.com • URL: http://www.cengage.com • 2007. eBook. Published by Sage Publications. A source of information that presents and quantifies the commercial success of numerous types of biomedical devices available in the global market.

***St. Agnes Traders Business Directory***. StAgnes-Traders.com, Little Meadows, Wheal Kitty, St. Agnes Cornwall TR5 0RL, United Kingdom. Phone: 44 777 9437106; Email: stagnestraders@gmail.com • URL: http://www.stagnes-traders.com • Covers: Businesses in Cornish village including the surrounding areas of Porthtowan, Mount Hawke, Blackwater, and Mithian.

***St. George Area Chamber of Commerce Business Directory***. St. George Area Chamber of Commerce, 97 E St. George Blvd. Saint George, UT 84770-2853. Phone: (435)628-1658; Fax: (435)628-5638 • URL: http://www.stgeorgechamber.com • Covers businesses, attractions, and history of the St. George, Utah, area.

***St. James Encyclopedia of Labor History Worldwide***. Cengage Learning Inc., 20 Channel Center St. Boston, MA 02210. Phone: 800-487-8488 or (617)289-7700; Fax: (617)289-7844; Email: investors@cengage.com • URL: http://www.cengage.com • $484. 2003. Two volumes. Cover 300 key events, national and international, that took place in labor history over the past 200 years. Includes illustrations, maps, a glossary, a bibliography, and indexes. St. James Press imprint. eBook also available. Inquire for pricing.

***St. John's Board of Trade Business Directory***. St. John's Board of Trade, PO Box 5127 Saint John's, NL, Canada A1C 5V5. Phone: (709)726-2961; Fax: (709)726-2003; Email: mail@bot.nf.ca • URL: http://www.bot.nf.ca • Annual. 900 business organizations in Newfoundland and Labrador.

**St. Joseph's University - Academy of Food Marketing**. 150 Mandeville Hall, 5600 City Ave. Philadelphia, PA 19131. Phone: (610)660-1600; Fax: (610)660-1604; Email: rhiggins@sju.edu • URL: http://www.sju.edu/academics/hsb/foodmarketing/academy • Food marketing from farm gate to table, including analysis and evaluation of concepts, precepts, and practices of the food industry in America and elsewhere. Conducts special studies on problems of food marketing in urban low-income areas, in-home electronic shopping, household buying behavior, national and international food consumption, and nutrient intake. Also seeks to improve efficiency in retail and wholesale operations, evaluates procedures for development of new products, examines aspects of consumer research, analyzes the effectiveness of coupons and in-store promotions, and investigates bulk foods and warehouse productivity.

***St. Louis Business Journal***. American City Business Journals, Inc., 120 W Morehead St. Charlotte, NC 28202. Phone: (704)973-1000; Fax: (704)973-1001; Email: americancity@bizjournals.com • URL: http://www.acbj.com • Weekly. $89 Individuals print + online. Business newspaper.

***St. Louis ComputerUser: A Business to Business Computing Publication***. Creative Publications Ltd., 11970 Borman Dr., Ste. 116 Saint Louis, MO 63146-4133. Phone: (314)991-1176; Fax: (314)991-7729 • Monthly. $12 Individuals. A business publication on computers and office technology.

***St. Paul Area Chamber of Commerce—Membership Directory and Business Resource Guide***. Saint Paul Area Chamber of Commerce, 401 N Robert St., Ste. 150 Saint Paul, MN 55101. Phone: (651)223-5000 or (651)265-2791; Email: info@saintpaulchamber.com • URL: http://www.saintpaulchamber.com • Annual. Covers: 2,100 members of the St. Paul Area Chamber of Commerce. Entries include: Company name, address, phone, name of principal executive, product or service provided, website address, e-mail address.

***St. Petersburg Business Guide***. Arguments and Facts Media Ltd., Hastings East Sussex TN34 2UX, United Kingdom. Phone: 01424442741; Fax: 01424442913; Email: 100104.1406@compuserve.com • Covers: Government agencies and companies of interest to individuals and firms conducting business in St. Petersburg, Russia; includes state and local government authorities, business organizations, financial and commercial services, consulting and legal services, customs offices, communications and transport services, advertising agencies, security firms, recruitment services, training specialists, and mass media outlets. Entries include: In general, agency or company name, address, phone, fax, description.

***St. Petersburg (Russia) Investment and Business Guide***. International Business Publications, USA, PO Box 15343 Washington, DC 20003. Phone: (202)546-2103; Fax: (202)546-3275; Email: ibpusa@comcast.net • URL: http://ibpus.com • Annual. $99.95 Individuals hardcopy, e-book, CD-ROM. Covers: Strategic and business information, contacts, regulations and more. An ultimate guide for conducting investment, export-import activity in the country.

***Salaries of Scientists, Engineers, and Technicians: A Summary of Salary Surveys***. Commission on Professionals in Science and Technology. CPST Publications, 1200 New York Ave. Washington, DC 20005. Phone: (202)326-7080; Fax: (202)842-1603 • Biennial. $100.00. A summary of salary surveys.

***Salem Area Chamber of Commerce Business Directory and Resource Guide***. Salem Area Chamber of Commerce, 1110 Commercial St. NE Salem, OR 97301-1020. Phone: (503)581-1466; Fax: (503)581-0972; Email: info@salemchamber.org • URL: http://www.salemchamber.org • Annual. Covers 1,250 businesses and organizations in Salem, OR.

***Sales and Marketing Management***. Nielsen Business Media Inc., 770 Broadway New York, NY 10003-9522. Phone: 866-890-8541 or (646)654-4500 or (646)654-5000; Fax: (646)654-5584 or (646)654-4500; Email: bmcomm@nielsen.com • URL: http://www.nielsenbusinessmedia.com • Monthly. $48.00 per year.

***Sales and Marketing Management Survey of Buying Power***. Nielsen Business Media Inc., 770 Broadway New York, NY 10003-9522. Phone: 866-890-8541 or (646)654-4500 or (646)654-5000; Fax: (646)654-5584 or (646)654-4500; Email: bmcomm@nielsen.com • URL: http://www.nielsenbusinessmedia.com • Annual. $150.00.

***Sales Prospector***. Sales Prospector, PO Box 185 Lake Bluff, IL 60044-0185. Phone: 800-752-4050 or (847)899-1271 • Description: Reports on planned construction of new plants, plant additions, shopping centers, commercial and institutional buildings, relocations, mergers, acquisitions, and government contracts to provide sales leads for salesmen and other businessmen. Provides name of company, location of construction, purpose, approximate dates of start and completion, name of contractor, architect, or developer, and estimate of amount of investment. Published in 28 separate editions each month for different areas of the country, plus two editions for Canada.

***Sales Representative Law Guide***. Wolters Kluwer Law & Business CCH, 2700 Lake Cook Rd. Riverwoods, IL 60015. Phone: 888-224-7377 or (847)267-7000; Email: cust_serv@cch.com • URL: http://www.cchgroup.com • $195.00 per year. Looseleaf service. Semiannual updates. Covers state laws on independent sales representation. Includes checklists and forms.

**Salk Institute for Biological Studies**. 10010 N Torrey Pines Rd. La Jolla, CA 92037. Phone: (858)453-4100; Fax: (858)453-8534 or (858)552-8534; Email: wrbrody@salk.edu • URL: http://www.salk.edu • Cellular and molecular biology and neuroscience with particular emphasis on cancer, molecular genetics, tumor virology, reproductive biology, neurobiology, neuroendocrinology, growth control, prebiotic chemistry, and neurotransmitter/neuroreceptor structure and function; research aimed toward the discovery of cause, prevention, control, and cure of disease.

**Salvadoran Association of Industrials**. Calle Roma y Liverpool, Col. Roma San Salvador, El Salvador. Phone: 503 2267-9200; Email: info@asi.com.sv • URL: http://industriaelsalvador.com • Promotes the industrial sector of El Salvador.

***SAM Advanced Management Journal***. Society for Advancement of Management. Society for Advancement of Management, 6300 Ocean Dr., OCNR 330, Unit 5807 Corpus Christi, TX 78412. Phone: 888-827-6077 or (361)825-3045; Fax: (361)825-5609; Email: moustafa.abdelsamad@tamucc.edu • URL: http://www.samnational.org • Quarterly. $64 Individuals one year; $117 Individuals two years; $169 Individuals three years; $30 Other countries airmail; $20 Other countries surface mail. Provides information on leading business topics for practicing managers.

***SAMPE Journal***. Society for the Advancement of Material and Process Engineering, 1161 Park View Dr., Ste. 200 Covina, CA 91724-3759. Phone: 800-562-7360 or (626)331-0616; Fax: (626)332-8929; Email: sampe@sampe.org • URL: http://www.sampe.org • Bimonthly. $125 Individuals print and online; $122 Individuals onlin only. Magazine covering materials and process engineering.

**Samuel Roberts Noble Foundation**. 2510 Sam Noble Pkwy. Ardmore, OK 73401. Phone: (580)223-5810 or (580)224-6230; Fax: (580)224-6265; Email: jacalaway@noble.org • URL: http://www.noble.org • Strives to promote agriculture, the ranching industry, and plant biology. Hosts the "Junior Beef Excellence Program."

**Samuel Zell and Robert Lurie Real Estate Center**. The Wharton School, University of Pennsylvania, Steinberg Hall-Dietrich Hall, 3620 Locust Walk, Ste. 1400 Philadelphia, PA 19104-6302. Phone: (215)898-9687; Fax: (215)573-2220; Email: frostr@wharton.upenn.edu • URL: http://realestate.wharton.upenn.edu.

***San Diego Business Journal***. San Diego Business Journal, 4909 Murphy Canyon Rd., Ste. 200 San Diego, CA 92123. Phone: (858)277-6359; Fax: (858)277-2149; Email: mdomine@sdbj.com • URL: http://www.sdbj.com • Weekly (Mon.). $99 Individuals; $180 Two years; $228 Individuals three years. Metropolitan business newspaper specializing in investigative and enterprise reporting on San Diego County businesses and related issues.

***San Diego County Business Directory***. Harris InfoSource, 2057 E Aurora Rd. Twinsburg, OH 44087-1999. Phone: 800-888-5900 or (330)425-9000 or (973)921-5500; Fax: (800)643-5997 or (877)252-3375; Email: customerservice@harrisinfo.com • URL: http://www.harrisinfo.com • Annual. $115 Individuals. Covers: Approximately 24,700 manufacturers, wholesalers, and service companies in San Diego County, California. Includes names of key executives. Entries include: Company name, address, parent name/location, telephone, fax and 800 numbers, Web site address (on CD-ROM only), number of employees, year established, annual revenue, plant size, business description, Standard Industrial Classification (SIC) codes, executive names/titles, public ownership, legal structure, import/export designators, female/minority ownership, and Thomas Guide Page and Grid Number.

***San Francisco Bay Area JobBank: The Job Hunter's Guide to Northern California***. Adams Media Corp., 57 Littlefield St. Avon, MA 02322. Phone: 800-872-5627 or (508)427-7100; Fax: (508)427-6790 or (800)872-5628; Email: deskcopies@adamsmedia.com • URL: http://www.adamsmedia.com • $17.95 Individuals Paperback. Covers: About 5,600 employers in the San Francisco Bay area and the Northern half of California including Oakland, Sacramento, San Jose, and Silicon Valley. Database includes: Information on the basics of job winning and writing resumes and cover letters; electronic job search information; 330 industry associations; 90 online career resources; 350 employment services. Entries include: Firm or organization name, address, local phone, toll-free phone, fax, e-mail, URL, recorded jobline, hours, description of organization, subsidiaries, other locations, number of employees, name and title of contact, headquarters location, typical titles for common positions, educational backgrounds desired, company benefits, stock exchange listing, training programs, internships, parent company, and number of employees, revenues, corporate headquarters, and number of projected hires.

***San Francisco Bay Area Silicon Valley International Business Directory***. San Francisco Chamber of Commerce, 235 Montgomery St., Ste. 760 San Francisco, CA 94104. Phone: (415)392-4520; Fax: (415)392-0485; Email: info@sfchamber.com • URL: http://www.sfchamber.com • $45 Members; $55 Nonmembers; $24 Members CD-ROM; $29 Nonmembers CD-ROM. Covers international businesses based in the San Francisco Bay/Silicon Valley area. Entries include contact details, parent companies, products and services.

***San Francisco Business Times***. American City Business Journals, Inc., 120 W Morehead St. Charlotte, NC 28202. Phone: (704)973-1000; Fax: (704)973-1001; Email: americancity@bizjournals.com • URL: http://www.acbj.com • Contains the full text of San Francisco Business Times, a business tabloid covering the San Francisco, California, area.

***San Francisco Business Times—Book of Lists***. San Francisco Business Times, 275 Battery St., Ste. 940 San Francisco, CA 94111. Phone: (415)989-2522; Fax: (415)398-2494; Email: eyoung@bizjournals.com • URL: http://www.bizjournals.com/sanfrancisco/ • Annual. $70 Individuals print; $199.95 Individuals electronic. A compilation of lists of the top 25 companies in various industries in the Bay Area.

***San Francisco Business—Top 51 Public Companies Issue***. San Francisco Chamber of Commerce, 235 Montgomery St., Ste. 760 San Francisco, CA 94104. Phone: (415)392-4520; Fax: (415)392-0485; Email: info@sfchamber.com • URL: http://www.sfchamber.com • Annual. $3 payment with order. Publication includes: List of 51 leading San Francisco Bay area public corporations (selected on the basis of sales). Entries include: Company name, address, phone, name of chief executive officer, current and prior year's rankings, line of business, sales, net assets, net income, net worth, number of employees.

***San Francisco County Business Directory***. Rich's Business Directories Inc., 1820 Gateway Blvd., Ste. 170 San Mateo, CA 94404. Phone: 800-969-7424 or (650)362-1020; Fax: (650)350-4084; Email: info@richsdata.com • URL: http://www.hightechdirectories.com • $215 Individuals; $450 Individuals database. Covers: 3,911 firms in San Francisco County. Entries include: Company name, address, phone, fax, year established, branch or headquarters, SIC code, and product type.

**San Jose State University - Institute for Social Responsibility, Ethics, and Education**. 1 Washington Sq. San Jose, CA 95192-0096. Phone: (408)924-5563; Fax: (408)924-4527; Email: lawrence.quill@sjsu.edu • URL: http://www.sjsu.edu/isree • Social responsibility, including professional and business ethics.

***San Marcos Chamber of Commerce Business & Relocation Directory***. San Marcos Chamber of Commerce, 904 W San Marcos Blvd., Ste. 10 San Marcos, CA 92078. Phone: (760)744-1270; Fax: (760)744-5230 • URL: http://www.sanmarcoschamber.com • Annual. $5.

***San Mateo County Business Directory***. Rich's Business Directories Inc., 1820 Gateway Blvd., Ste. 170 San Mateo, CA 94404. Phone: 800-969-7424 or (650)362-1020; Fax: (650)350-4084; Email: info@richsdata.com • URL: http://www.hightechdirectories.com • $199 Individuals online; $450 Individuals database. Covers: 2,963 firms in San Mateo County. Entries include: Company name, address, phone, fax, year established, branch or headquarters, SIC code, and product type.

***Sandwich Shop/Deli***. Entrepreneur Press, 2445 McCabe Way, Ste. 400 Irvine, CA 92614-6244. Phone: 800-864-6864 or (949)261-2325 or (949)622-7131; Fax: (949)261-7729 or (949)261-0234; Email: press@entrepreneur.com • URL: http://www.entrepreneurpress.com • Looseleaf. $59.50. A practical guide to starting a sandwich shop and delicatessen. Covers profit potential, start-up costs, market size evaluation, owner's time required, site selection, lease negotiation, pricing, accounting, advertising, promotion, etc. (Start-Up Business Guide No. E1156.).

***Sanger District Chamber of Commerce—Business Directory***. Sanger District Chamber of Commerce, 1789 Jensen Ave., Ste. B Sanger, CA 93657. Phone: (559)875-4575; Fax: (559)875-0745; Email: sangerchamber@gmail.com • URL:

http://www.sanger.org • Biennial. Covers 225 business organizations in Sanger, California.

***SANI.*** CERVED S.p.A., Via Appia Nuova, 696 I-00179 Rome, Italy. Phone: 6 780541; Fax: 6 780541 • Daily. Database covers: about 4 million Italian industrial, commercial, agricultural, and trade companies. Database includes: Company name, address, date and type of incorporation, incorporation capital, product/service, names and titles of key personnel. CERVED stands for Centri Elettronici Reteconnessi Valutazione Elaborazione Dati.

***Sanitary Maintenance.*** Trade Press Media Group, 2100 W Florist Ave. Milwaukee, WI 53209. Phone: 800-727-7995 or (414)228-7701; Fax: (414)228-1134; Email: info@tradepress.com • URL: http://www.tradepress.com • Monthly. Original publication serving the distributors and wholesalers of sanitary supplies.

***Santa Clara County Business Directory.*** Rich's Business Directories Inc., 1820 Gateway Blvd., Ste. 170 San Mateo, CA 94404. Phone: 800-969-7424 or (650)362-1020; Fax: (650)350-4084; Email: info@richsdata.com • URL: http://www.hightechdirectories.com • $219 Individuals online; $525 Individuals database. Covers: 5,745 firms in Santa Clara County. Entries include: Company name, address, phone, fax, year established, branch or headquarters, SIC code, and product type.

***Santa Monica Chamber of Commerce Business Profile and Membership Directory.*** Santa Monica Chamber of Commerce, 1234 6th St., Ste. 100 Santa Monica, CA 90401. Phone: (310)393-9825; Fax: (310)394-1868; Email: info@smchamber.com • URL: http://www.smchamber.com • Annual. Covers: Member businesses in Santa Monica, California.

***Sao Paulo Year Book: Amcham Yearbook Directory.*** American Chamber of Commerce for Brazil - Sao Paulo, Rua Da Paz, 1431 CEP 04713-001 Sao Paulo, Brazil. Phone: 55 11 30116000; Fax: 55 11 51803777; Email: vasco@amcham.com.br • URL: http://www.amcham.com.br • Annual. $500 Members; $1,500 Nonmembers. Covers: 5,450 member American and Brazilian firms and 20,000 individual members interested in developing trade and investment within and between the two countries; other American chambers of commerce, American organizations in Sao Paulo, government agencies, institutions, and associations. Database includes: Glossary of product terms in Portuguese; section on Brazilian business and economics; statistics. Entries include: For firms—Company name, address, phone, telex, fax, names and titles of key personnel, product/service, export and domestic sales, net worth, number of employees, registered capital, branches, affiliates abroad. For individual members—Name, title, company name, phone, home or office address, telex. For others—Name, address, phone.

***Satellite News.*** Access Intelligence L.L.C., 4 Choke Cherry Rd., 2nd Fl. Rockville, MD 20850. Phone: 800-777-5006 or (301)354-2000 or (301)354-2101; Fax: (301)309-3847 or (801)365-2300; Email: info@accessintel.com • URL: http://www.accessintel.com/ • Description: Provides business insights and analysis into the commercial satellite industry including new satellite applications, developing technologies, and unfolding partnerships. Recurring features include columns titled Satellite Spotlight, DBS News, Satellite News, Newsmaker Interiews, Satellite Circuit, and Satellite News Financial Ticker.

***Satellite News: The Monthly Newsletter Covering Management, Marketing Technology and Regulation.*** Access Intelligence L.L.C., 4 Choke Cherry Rd., 2nd Fl. Rockville, MD 20850. Phone: 800-777-5006 or (301)354-2000 or (301)354-2101; Fax: (301)309-3847 or (801)365-2300; Email: info@accessintel.com • URL: http://www.accessintel.com/ • 50 times a year. $1,097.00 per year. Newsletter. Covers business applications in space, including remote sensing and satellites. Incorporates (Space Business News).

***Satellite Week.*** Warren Communications News Inc., 2115 Ward Ct. NW Washington, DC 20037. Phone: 800-771-9202 or (202)872-9200; Fax: (202)318-8350 or (202)293-3435 • URL: http://www.warren-news.com • Weekly. Covers satellite broadcasting, telecommunications, and the industrialization of space.

***Saudi Arabia Business Forecast Report.*** Telecommunications Insight, 85 Queen Victoria St. London EC4V 4AB, United Kingdom. Phone: 20 72 465100 or 44 20 7248 0468; Fax: 20 72 480467 or 44 20 7248 0467; Email: enquiries@telecomsinsight.com • URL: http://www.telecomsinsight.com • Quarterly. $1,195 Individuals Single user; $1,795 Individuals Up to 3 users. Business forecast report for Saudi Arabia.

***Saudi Arabia Business Law Handbook.*** International Business Publications, USA, PO Box 15343 Washington, DC 20003. Phone: (202)546-2103; Fax: (202)546-3275; Email: ibpusa@comcast.net • URL: http://ibpus.com • $99.95 Individuals hardcopy, e-book, CD-ROM. Covers: Basic information on business laws and legislations, export-import regulations, business climate and contacts.

***Saudi Arabia Business Week.*** Saudi Arabia Business Week, PO Box 2894 Riyadh, Saudi Arabia. • Weekly. Business and economics magazine.

***Saudi Arabia Golden Key Directory.*** International Institute of Trade Relation Promotion, Trade Information Centre of Iran, No. 7, 3rd Fl., Abbasie Bazar, Ferdowsi Sq. Tehran, Iran. Phone: 98 21 88833900; Fax: 98 21 88820697; Email: order@irangoldenkey.com • URL: http://www.goldenkeydirectory.com/about.html • £100 Individuals. Covers: 37,309 companies in Saudi Arabia. Entries include: Company name, address, telephone, fax, products, services, Managing Director, and business activities.

***Saudi Arabia Industrial and Business Directory.*** International Business Publications, USA, PO Box 15343 Washington, DC 20003. Phone: (202)546-2103; Fax: (202)546-3275; Email: ibpusa@comcast.net • URL: http://ibpus.com • Annual. $99.95 Individuals hardcopy, e-book, CD-ROM. Covers: Strategic industrial, investment and business contacts for conducting export-import and investment activity in the country.

***Saudi Arabia Investment and Business Guide.*** International Business Publications, USA, PO Box 15343 Washington, DC 20003. Phone: (202)546-2103; Fax: (202)546-3275; Email: ibpusa@comcast.net • URL: http://ibpus.com • $99.95 Individuals hardcopy, e-book, CD-ROM. Covers: Strategic information on economy, business, export-import and investment climate, regulations and industrial development, banking, government, and opportunities. Entries include: Important business contacts and business travel.

***Saudi Industrial Development Fund—National Industries Directory.*** Saudi Industrial Development Fund, PO Box 4143 Riyadh 11149, Saudi Arabia. Phone: 966 1 4774002 or 966 01 477 4002; Fax: 966 01 479 0165; Email: info@sidf.gov.sa • URL: http://www.sidf.gov.sa/En/Pages/default.aspx • Covers: More than 2000 industrial plants in Saudi Arabia. Entries include: Name, address, phone, fax.

***Savannah Business Journal.*** Savannah Business Journal, 6203 Abercorn St., Ste. 103E Savannah, GA 31405. Phone: (912)233-5711 • Monthly. $15 Individuals. Business journal.

***The Savings Directory.*** Accuity Inc., 4709 W Golf Rd. Skokie, IL 60076. Phone: 800-321-3373 or (847)676-9600; Fax: (847)933-8101; Email: custserv@accuitysolutions.com • URL: http://www.accuitysolutions.com • Semiannual. $570 Individuals. Covers: Nearly 2,000 savings institutions and their 13,000 branch offices. Database includes: Lists of top 500 companies ranked by assets, deposits, and loans; savings institution routing numbers in numeric sequence; and discontinued or changed institution names. Entries include: Institution name, address, phone, fax, type, identification of mutual or stock ownership, type of insurance, routing number, number of employees, names and titles of key personnel, branch office locations, financial and operational data.

***Savings Institutions: Mergers, Acquisitions, and Conversions.*** ALM Media Properties LLC, 120 Broadway, 5th Fl. New York, NY 10271-1100. Phone: (212)457-9400; Fax: (646)417-7705; Email: customercare@alm.com • URL: http://www.alm.com • $560. Provides detailed information on the legal complexities of mergers and acquisitions involving savings institutions. (Law Journal Press).

***Savings Institutions—Top 200.*** Savings & Commerce Bankers-America, 111 E Wacker Dr. Chicago, IL 60601. Phone: (312)644-3100 • Annual. $5. Covers: 200 leading savings institutions as determined by their assets and savings. Entries include: Contact information.

***SBA Loan Guide.*** Entrepreneur Meida, Inc., 2445 McCabe Way Irvine, CA 92614. Phone: 800-421-2300 or (949)261-2325; Fax: (949)261-0234; Email: entmag@entrepreneur.com • URL: http://www.entrepreneur.com • Looseleaf. $59.50. A practical guide to obtaining loans through the Small Business Administration. (Start-Up Business Guide No. E1315.).

***SBA Loans: A Step-by-Step Guide.*** John Wiley & Sons Inc., 111 River St. Hoboken, NJ 07030-5774. Phone: 800-225-5945 or (201)748-6000; Fax: (201)748-6088; Email: info@wiley.com • URL: http://www.wiley.com • $27.95 Individuals paperback. Publication includes: A directory of Small Business Association field offices and a directory of services offered by the SBA. Principal content of publication is Step-by-step information of locating and securing a small business loan, including developing a business plan, researching finance options, recent lending statistics, eligibility requirements and other details.

***SBIC Directory and Handbook of Small Business Finance.*** International Wealth Success Inc., 5000 Windplay Dr., Ste. 4 El Dorado Hills, CA 95762. • Annual. $15 payment with order. Covers: over 400 small business investment companies (SBIC's) that lend money for periods from 5 to 20 years to small businesses. Entries include: Company name, address, amount and type of financing.

***Scandinavian Kompass on Disc.*** Kompass USA, Inc., 121 Whitney Ave. New Haven, CT 06510. Phone: (877)566-7277 or (203)503-6789; Fax: (203)503-6780; Email: mail@kompass-usa.com • URL: http://www.kompass.com • Semiannual. CD-ROM provides information on more than 120,000 companies in Denmark, Finland, Norway, and Sweden. Classification system covers approximately 50,000 products and services.

***Schmalenbach Business Review.*** Verlagsgruppe Handelsblatt GmbH, Kasernenstr. 67 D-40213 Dusseldorf, Germany. Phone: 49 211 887 0 or 49 211 8870; Fax: 49 211 887 2980 or 49 211 8872980; Email: info@vhb.de • URL: http://www.vhb.de • Quarterly. $135 Institutions; $31.30 Students; $67 Individuals; £65 Institutions; £32 Individuals; £15.10 Students; €91 Institutions; €45 Individuals; €21 Students.

***Scholarships, Fellowships & Loans.*** Cengage Learning Inc., 20 Channel Center St. Boston, MA 02210. Phone: 800-487-8488 or (617)289-7700; Fax: (617)289-7844; Email: investors@cengage.com • URL: http://www.cengage.com • $369 Individuals. 2013. $353.00. 30th edition. Describes more than 7,300 scholarships, fellowships, loans, and other educational funding sources available to U.S. and Canadian undergraduate and graduate students. eBook also available.

***School Bus Fleet.*** Bobit Business Media, 3520 Challenger St. Torrance, CA 90503. Phone: (310)533-2400; Fax: (310)533-2500; Email: info@lctmag.com • URL: http://www.bobit.com • Monthly. $25.00 per year. Includes *Factbook*.

***School Business Affairs.*** Association of School Business Officials. ASBO International, 11401 N Shore Dr. Reston, VA 20190-4200. Phone: 866-682-2729; Fax: (703)708-7060; Email: asboreq@asbointl.org • URL: http://www.asbointl.org • Monthly. Published 11 times per year. Available to members.

***School Business Affairs—Association of School Business Officials Official Membership Directory Issue.*** Association of School Business Officials International, 11401 N Shore Dr. Reston, VA 20190-4232. Phone: 866-682-2729 or (703)478-0405; Fax: (703)708-7060 or (703)478-0205; Email: asboreq@asbointl.org • URL: http://asbointl.org.

***School Business Magazine: Canada's Education Management Magazine.*** Momentum Media Management, 4040 Creditview Rd., Unit 11 Mississauga, ON, Canada L5C 3Y8. Fax: (905)813-7117 • Bimonthly. $15; $30 U.S.; $2.50 Single issue. Magazine for Canadian educators, executives, administrators, transportation, and operations personnel at schools, boards, colleges, and universities.

***School Enrollment, Social and Economic Characteristics of Students.*** U. S. Government Printing Office, 732 N Capitol St. NW Washington, DC 20401. Phone: 866-512-1800 or (202)512-1800 or (866)512-1800; Fax: (202)512-2104 or (202)512-2250; Email: contactcenter@gpo.gov • URL: http://www.gpo.gov • Annual. $2.50. Issued by the U. S. Bureau of the Census. Presents detailed tabulations of data on school enrollment of the civilian noninstitutional population three years old and over. Covers nursery school, kindergarten, elementary school, high school, college, and graduate school. Information is provided on age, race, sex, family income, marital status, employment, and other characteristics.

***School Law News.*** Wolters Kluwer Law and Business, 76 9th Ave., 7th Fl. New York, NY 10011-4962. Phone: 800-234-1660 or (212)771-0600; Fax: (800)901-9075 or (301)644-3550 • URL: http://www.wolterskluwerlb.com • Biweekly.

***School Library Journal.*** Media Source Inc., 7858 Industrial Pkwy. Plain City, OH 43064. Phone: 866-207-0310 or (614)873-7635 • URL: http://www.mediasourceinc.com • Monthly. $130.99 1 year subscription. Provides news, information and reviews for librarians and media specialists who serve children and young adults in school and public libraries.

**School Nutrition Association.** 120 Waterfront St., Ste. 300, National Harbor Oxon Hill, MD 20745-1142. Phone: 800-877-8822 or (301)686-3100; Fax: (301)686-3115; Email: servicecenter@schoolnutrition.org • URL: http://www.schoolnutrition.org • Persons engaged in school food service or related activities in public or private schools, preschools, colleges and universities. Seeks to encourage and promote the maintenance and improvement of the school food and nutrition program. Sponsors National School Lunch Week in October and National School Breakfast week in March. Distributes information on school food and nutrition programs and child nutrition legislation. Holds industry seminar, major city directors and supervisors' meeting, and annual national conference for school food service personnel. Maintains School Food Service Foundation, which conducts research and educational programs relating to child nutrition and encourages professional development of school food service personnel. Maintains hall of fame. Operates political action committee.

***School Planning & Management.*** Peter Li Inc., 2621 Dryden Rd., Ste. 300 Dayton, OH 45439-1600. Phone: 800-523-4625; Fax: (800)370-4450 • URL: http://www.peterli.com • Monthly. Contains articles about facility planning, safety and security, maintenance and operations, business, technology and finance issues.

***Schools—Business & Vocational Directory.*** InfoGroup Inc., 5711 S 86th Cir. Omaha, NE 68127-4146. Phone: (402)593-4500 • URL: http://www.infogroup.com • Annual. Covers over 5,000 businesses and vocations.

***Schools (Dancing) Directory.*** InfoGroup Inc., 5711 S 86th Cir. Omaha, NE 68127-4146. Phone: (402)593-4500 • URL: http://www.infogroup.com • Annual. Number of listings: 14,474. Entries include: Name, address, phone, size of advertisement, name of owner or manager, number of employees, year first in "Yellow Pages." Compiled from telephone company "Yellow Pages," nationwide.

***Science and Technology Almanac.*** Greenwood Publishing Group Inc., 88 Post Rd. W Westport, CT 06881. Phone: (203)226-3571; Fax: (203)222-1502; Email: orders@greenwood.com • URL: http://www.greenwood.com • $99.95 Individuals hardcover; £63 Individuals hardcover; €79 Individuals hardcover; A$108 Individuals hardcover. Provides the most comprehensive source for the significant science news of 2001 and for scientific information in general.

***Science & Technology Libraries.*** Routledge Journals Taylor & Francis Group, 270 Madison Ave. New York, NY 10016-0601. • URL: http://www.routledge.com • Quarterly. $121

Individuals online only; $129 Individuals print + online; $509 Institutions online only; $565 Institutions print + online; $130 Individuals print only. Peer-reviewed professional journal providing instructive material prepared for the science and technology librarian.

***Science Citation Index***. Thomson Reuters Intellectual Property and Science, 3501 Market St. Philadelphia, PA 19104-3302. Phone: 800-336-4474 or (215)386-0100; Fax: (215)386-2911; Email: general.info@thomsonreuters.com • URL: http://ip-science.thomsonreuters.com • Weekly. Includes *Source Index*, *Citation Index*, *Permuterm Subject Index*, and *Corporate Index*. Provides researchers, administrators, faculty, and students with quick, powerful access to the bibliographic and citation information they need to find research data, analyze trends, journals and researchers, and share their findings.

***Science et Technologie au Quebec***. Quebec Dans Le Monde, 404-1001, Church Rd. Sainte-Foy, QC, Canada G1V 4N5. Phone: (418)659-5540; Fax: (418)659-4143; Email: info@quebecmonde.com • URL: http://www.quebecmonde.com • Biennial. $52.95 Individuals. Covers: over 1,150 scientific associations, periodicals, research and development facilities, and research centers in Quebec. Entries include: Organization name, address, phone, fax, toll-free phone, description of services.

***Scientific Meetings***. Scientific Meetings Publications, 5214 Soledad Mountain Rd. San Diego, CA 92138. Phone: (858)270-2910; Fax: (858)270-2910; Email: scimeeting@access1.net • Quarterly. $85.00 per year. Provides information on forthcoming scientific, technical, medical, health, engineering and management meetings held throughout the world.

***The Scientist***. 1508 - 415 Madison Ave. New York, NY 10017. Phone: (705)528-6888; Fax: (215)387-7542; Email: info@the-scientist.com • URL: http://www.the-scientist.com • Biweekly. Individuals, $29.00 per year; institutions, $58.00 per year. Contains news for scientific, research, and technical personnel.

***Scotland's Top 500 Companies***. Jordans Ltd., 21 St. Thomas St. Bristol BS1 6JS, United Kingdom. Phone: 44 117 923 0600; Fax: 44 117 923 0063; Email: customerservices@jordans.co.uk • URL: http://www.jordans.co.uk • Annual. $55. Covers: Companies in Scotland. Entries include: Company name, address, phone, fax, type of activity, chief executives, sales figures, capital, profits, net cash flow.

***Scott Stamp Monthly***. Scott Publishing Company Inc., 911 Vandemark Rd. Sidney, OH 45365-8974. Phone: 800-572-6885 or (937)498-0802; Email: ssm@scottonline.com • URL: http://www.scottonline.com • Monthly. $19.99 per year.

***Scott's Business Suite***. Scott's Directories, 12 Concorde Pl., Ste. 800 Toronto, ON, Canada M3C 4J2. Phone: 800-668-2374 or (416)442-2122; Fax: (416)510-6870; Email: customercare@scottsdirectories.com • URL: http://www.scottsdirectories.com • $1,449 Individuals CD-ROM, pinpointer; $2,799 Individuals CD-ROM, profiler; $4,799 Individuals CD-ROM, prospector; $2,699 online, profiler; $4,599 online, prospector. Covers: 134,200+ manufacturers, manufacturers' sales offices, wholesalers, wholesale agents, and distributors operating in Greater Montreal, North and South Shore, Ontario, Greater Calgary, Edmonton and Greater Vancouver along with 245,000+ business contact names. Entries include: Company name, address, phone, fax, names and titles of key personnel, number of employees, parent companies, SIC, product, year established.

***Scott's Canadian Dental Directory***. Scott's Directories, 12 Concorde Pl., Ste. 800 Toronto, ON, Canada M3C 4J2. Phone: 800-668-2374 or (416)442-2122; Fax: (416)510-6870; Email: customercare@scottsdirectories.com • URL: http://www.scottsdirectories.com • Biennial. $259 Individuals Plus Applicable Taxes + S/H; $269 Individuals Web pinpointer; $599 Individuals Web profiler; $6,499 Individuals Web prospector. Covers: Approximately 18,000 dentists, dental suppliers, and dental laboratories and associations in Canada. Entries include: Name, address, phone, names and titles of key personnel, biographical data (for dentists), geographical area served.

***Scott's Canadian Pharmacists Directory***. Scott's Directories, 12 Concorde Pl., Ste. 800 Toronto, ON, Canada M3C 4J2. Phone: 800-668-2374 or (416)442-2122; Fax: (416)510-6870; Email: customercare@scottsdirectories.com • URL: http://www.scottsdirectories.com • Biennial. $229 Individuals Web pinpointer; $699 Individuals Web profiler; $1,499 Individuals Web prospector (unlimited); $2,999 Individuals Web prospector (unlimited). Covers: Approximately 18,000 pharmacists, university pharmacy faculty members, pharmacy suppliers, and drug and poison information centers in Canada, chain drug stores, independent. Entries include: Name, address, phone, names and titles of key personnel, biographical data (for pharmacists), geographical area served.

***Scott's Custom Solutions***. Scott's Directories, 12 Concorde Pl., Ste. 800 Toronto, ON, Canada M3C 4J2. Phone: 800-668-2374 or (416)442-2122; Fax: (416)510-6870; Email: customercare@scottsdirectories.com • URL: http://www.scottsdirectories.com • Covers: Details for 175,000+ companies and 275,000+ business contact names can be provided customized as per client requirements on the basis of specific geographies, specific products or services, specific job functions, size demographics. Entries include: Company name, address, phone, fax, names and titles of key personnel, number of employees, parent companies, SIC, product, year established.

***Scott's Directories: Greater Montreal and Laval Business Directory***. Scott's Directories, 12 Concorde Pl., Ste. 800 Toronto, ON, Canada M3C 4J2. Phone: 800-668-2374 or (416)442-2122; Fax: (416)510-6870; Email: customercare@scottsdirectories.com • URL: http://www.scottsdirectories.com • Annual. $229 Individuals. Covers: More than 18,000 manufacturers, distributors, wholesalers, manufacturers' representatives, contractors, transportation companies, financial institutions; legal, engineering, and architectural firms; real estate brokers, retail main offices, and special services related to industry in Montreal. Entries include: Name, postal code, phone, fax, executive names and titles, type of business or product produced, North American Standard Industrial Classification (NAICS) code, number of employees; code indicating line of business; year established.

***Scotts Valley Business Today***. Scotts Valley Chamber of Commerce, 360 Kings Village Rd. Scotts Valley, CA 95066. Phone: (831)438-1010; Fax: (831)438-6544; Email: info@scottsvalleychamber.com • URL: http://www.scottsvalleychamber.com • Monthly.

***Scrap***. Institute of Scrap Recycling Industries, 1615 L St. NW, Ste. 600 Washington, DC 20036-5610. Phone: (202)662-8500 or (202)626-8512; Fax: (202)626-0900; Email: robinwiener@isri.org • URL: http://www.isri.org • Bimonthly. $48 Individuals companies; $44 Libraries government & non-profit organizations; $57 Canada and Mexico first class; $152 Other countries; $80 Two years companies; $72 Libraries govt. & non profit organizations, 2 years; $94 Canada and Mexico 2 years; $251 Other countries airmail 2 years. Magazine for the scrap processing and recycling industry. Formerly *Scrap Processing and Recycling*.

***Screen Printing—Buyer's Guide Issue***. ST Media Group International Inc., 11262 Cornell Park Dr. Cincinnati, OH 45242. Phone: 800-421-1321 or (513)421-2050; Fax: (513)421-5144; Email: info@stmediagroup.com • URL: http://stmediagroup.com • Annual. Publication includes: List of about 500 manufacturers and distributors of products and equipment used in the screen printing industry. Database includes: Calendar of trade events; lists of industry associations, colleges and universities, reference guides. Entries include: Company name, address, phone; branch office locations, phone number, name of sales contact, product lines, geographic area served.

***Screen Printing—Distributor/Dealer Directory Section***. ST Media Group International Inc., 11262 Cornell Park Dr. Cincinnati, OH 45242. Phone: 800-421-1321 or (513)421-2050; Fax: (513)421-5144; Email: info@stmediagroup.com • URL: http://stmediagroup.com • Monthly. $5 per issue; $42 per year. Publication includes: Listings of over 135 dealers and distributors of screen printing equipment, materials, and services. Entries include: Company name, address, phone, fax, name and title of contact, geographical area served, and product/service.

***Scripta Materialia***. Acta Metallurgica, Inc. Elsevier, Secondary Publishing Division, 650 Ave. of the Americas New York, NY 10011. Phone: 888-437-4636 or (212)633-3980; Fax: (212)633-3975; Email: t.reller@elsevier.com • URL: http://www.elseveier.com • Semimonthly. $2,472 Institutions. Provides a forum for the rapid publication of short communications on the relationship between the structure and the properties of inorganic materials.

***Sea Technology Buyers Guide/Directory***. Email: oceanbiz@sea-technology.com • URL: http://www.sea-technology.com • Annual. $56 U.S. priority mail; $57 Canada first-class mail; $64 Other countries airmail printed. Covers: Manufacturing, service, research and development, engineering, construction, drilling, equipment lease and rental firms, and testing organizations providing goods and services to the oceanographic, offshore, marine sciences, and undersea defense industries. Eight informational sections. Entries include: Company name, contact information, executives' names, list of products and/or services.

***Sea Technology***. Compass Publications Inc., 1600 Wilson Blvd., Ste. 1010 Arlington, VA 22209. Phone: (703)524-3136; Fax: (703)841-0852 • URL: http://www.sea-technology.com • Monthly. $60 U.S. Marine industry's recognized authority for ocean design, engineering and application of equipment and services in the global ocean community.

***Sea-web Directory***. IHS Global Ltd. Lloyd's Register—Fairplay Ltd., Lombard House, 3 Princess Way, Surrey Redhill RH1 1UP, United Kingdom. Phone: 44 1737 379000; Fax: 44 1737 379001; Email: marketing@ihs.com • URL: http://www.ihs.com • $1,175 Individuals Online. Covers: Over entries including 178,000 companies in the shipping industry, 129,000 ship operators details and 52,000 contact names. Maritime organizations, ship brokers, marine insurance companies, and maritime schools are among the groups included. Entries include: Name, address, phone, fax.

***Seafood Business***. Diversified Business Communications Inc., 121 Free St. Portland, ME 04101-3919. Phone: (207)842-5500 or (207)842-5600; Fax: (207)842-5503 or (207)842-5603; Email: custserv@divcom.com • URL: http://www.divbusiness.com • $57 U.S.; $69 Canada; $99 Other countries. Edited for a wide range of seafood buyers, including distributors, restaurants, supermarkets, and institutions. Special issues feature information on specific products, such as salmon or lobster.

***Seafood Price-Current***. Urner Barry Publications Inc., PO Box 389 Toms River, NJ 08754. Phone: (732)240-5330; Fax: (732)341-0891; Email: help@urnerbarry.com • URL: http://www.urnerbarry.com • Semiweekly. $756 Individuals.

***Seapower***. Navy League of the United States, 2300 Wilson Blvd., Ste. 200 Arlington, VA 22201-5424. Phone: 800-356-5760 or (703)528-1775; Fax: (703)528-2333 • URL: http://navyleague.org • Monthly. $58 Nonmembers 1 year; $116 Nonmembers 2 years; $145 Nonmembers 1 year; other countries; $25 Nonmembers Active Duty Military/Schools & Libraries; Members included in membership dues; $5 Single issue U.S.; plus shipping fee; $14 Single issue other countries; plus shipping fee. Magazine covering America's seapower and the role of the sea services in defense.

***Search Engine Watch***. Internet.com Corp., Phone: (203)662-2800; Fax: (203)655-4686 • URL: http://www.searchenginewatch.com • Web site offers information on various aspects of search engines, including new developments, indexing systems, technology, ratings and reviews of major operators, specialty services, tutorials, news, history, "Search Engine EKGs," "Facts and Fun," etc. Online searching is provided. Formerly *A Webmaster's Guide to Search Engines*.

***Seattle Business Monthly***. Tiger Oak Publications Inc., 900 S 3rd St. Minneapolis, MN 55415-1209. Phone: (612)548-3180; Fax: (612)548-3181 • URL: http://www.tigeroak.com • Monthly. Business magazine.

***Seattle JobBank: The Job Hunter's Guide to Washington***. Adams Media Corp., 57 Littlefield St. Avon, MA 02322. Phone: 800-872-5627 or (508)427-7100; Fax: (508)427-6790 or (800)872-5628; Email: deskcopies@adamsmedia.com • URL: http://www.adamsmedia.com • $17.95 Individuals Paperback. Covers: About 4,800 employers in Washington state, including Spokane, Tacoma, and Bellevue. Database includes: Information on the basics of job winning and writing resumes and cover letters; regional employment outlook; 330 industry associations; 90 online career resources; 135 employment services. Entries include: Firm or organization name, address, local phone, toll-free phone, fax, e-mail, URL, description of organization, subsidiaries, name and title of contact, headquarters location, recorded jobline, typical titles for common positions, educational backgrounds desired, projected number of hires, company benefits, stock exchange listing, training programs, internships, parent company, number of employees, revenues.

***SEC Accounting Rules***. Wolters Kluwer Law & Business CCH, 2700 Lake Cook Rd. Riverwoods, IL 60015. Phone: 888-224-7377 or (847)267-7000; Email: cust_serv@cch.com • URL: http://www.cchgroup.com • $448.00. Looseleaf service.

***SEC Financial Reporting: Annual Reports to Shareholders, Form 10-K, and Quarterly Financial Reporting***. Matthew Bender and Company Inc., 1275 Broadway Albany, NY 12204-2638. Phone: 800-424-4200 or (518)487-3000; Fax: (518)487-3573 or (800)424-4200; Email: customer.support@lexisnexis.com • URL: http://www.matthewbender.com • Annual. $254.00. Looseleaf service. Coverage of aspects of financial reporting with GAAP disclosure and Regulation S-X preparation Step-by-step procedures for preparing information for Form 10-K and annual shareholders reports.

***SEC Handbook: Rules and Forms for Financial Statements and Related Disclosures***. Wolters Kluwer Law & Business CCH, 2700 Lake Cook Rd. Riverwoods, IL 60015. Phone: 888-224-7377 or (847)267-7000; Email: cust_serv@cch.com • URL: http://www.cchgroup.com • Annual. $59.00. Contains full text of rules and requirements set by the Securities and Exchange Commisssion for preparation of corporate financial statements.

***SEC News Digest***. U.S. Securities and Exchange Commission, Public Reference Room, 100 F St. NE Washington, DC 20549. Phone: (202)942-8088 • URL: http://www.sec.gov • Daily. Provides information on Commission actions.

***SEC Today***. Washington Service Bureau Inc., 1015 15th St. NW, 10th Fl. Washington, DC 20005-2605. Phone: 800-289-1057 or (202)842-7355 • URL: http://www.wsb.com • Daily. Includes the official *SEC News Digest* from the Securities and Exchange Commission and reports on public company filing activity.

***Secretarial/Word Processing Service***. Entrepreneur Press, 2445 McCabe Way, Ste. 400 Irvine, CA 92614-6244. Phone: 800-864-6864 or (949)261-2325 or (949)622-7131; Fax: (949)261-7729 or (949)261-0234; Email: press@entrepreneur.com • URL: http://www.entrepreneurpress.com • Looseleaf. $59.50. A practical guide to starting a secretarial and word processing business. Covers profit potential, start-up costs, market size evaluation, owner's time required, site selection, pricing, accounting, advertising, promotion, etc. (Start-Up Business Guide No. E1136.).

**Secretary of Agriculture and Supply - Institute of Food Technology**. Avda. Brasil 2880, Caixa Postal 139 13070-178 Campinas, SP, Brazil. Phone: 55 19 37431700; Fax: 55 19 37431799; Email: rh@ital.sp.gov.br • URL: http://www.ital.sp.gov.br • Food science, engineering and technology, including dehydrated foods, grain storage, juices and beverages, biotechnology, meat and meat products, post-harvest physiology of fruit and vegetable, food packaging, equipment design, flours and bakery products, milk and dairy products, marketing and economics, edible oils, seafood resources, and physical, chemical, biochemical, microbiological, and sensory evaluation of food products.

**Section of Ophthalmology and Visual Science**. University of Chicago, 5841 S Maryland Ave. - MC2114 Chicago, IL 60637. Phone: (773)702-3937; Fax: (773)702-1000; Email: jernest@midway.uchicago.edu • URL: http://surgery.uchicago.edu/specialties/ovs.

***Sectores***. Databank S.p.A., Via dei Piatti 11 I-20123 MilanO, Italy. Phone: 2 809556; Fax: 2 8056495; Email: info@databank.it • Annual. $1,300 per report. A series of reports on 100 industrial sectors in Spain. Each report includes a description of the industry, trends, size of market and market shares of individual companies, and financial data in addition to a list of names and addresses of industry suppliers.

***The Secured Lender***. Commercial Finance Association, 370 7th Ave., Ste. 1801 New York, NY 10001. Phone: (212)792-9390; Fax: (212)564-6053; Email: info@cfa.com • URL: http://www.cfa.com • Bimonthly. $35 Members domestic; $65 Nonmembers domestic; $62 Two years members; $105 Two years 2mbs. Bimonthly. Free to members.

**Securities and Exchange Commission - Office of Economic Analysis**. 100 F St. NE Washington, DC 20549. Phone: (202)942-8088; Fax: (202)942-9657; Email: help@sec.gov • URL: http://www.sec.gov/about/economic.shtml • Utilization of economic and empirical analyses in policy formulation, rule adoption, and post-adoption monitoring processes of the Securities and Exchange Commission. Emphasis is on evaluation of the impact of Commission regulations on capital markets and securities markets participants.

***Securities and Federal Corporate Law Report***. Thomson West, 610 Opperman Dr. Eagan, MN 55123. Phone: 800-328-9352 or (651)687-7000 • Features articles on securities and corporate law topics, providing highlights of significant cases, administrative policy, staff guidelines, and other important news and trends.

***Securities Arbitration Commentator***. Richard P. Ryder, P.O. Box 112 Maplewood, NJ 07040. Phone: (973)761-5880; Fax: (973)761-1504 • Monthly. $695.00 per year. Newsletter. Edited for attorneys and other professionals concerned with securities arbitration.

***Securities, Commodities, and Federal Banking: 1999 in Review***. Wolters Kluwer Law & Business CCH, 2700 Lake Cook Rd. Riverwoods, IL 60015. Phone: 888-224-7377 or (847)267-7000; Email: cust_serv@cch.com • URL: http://www.cchgroup.com • Irregular. $57.00. Summarizes the year's significant legal and regulatory developments.

***Securities Crimes***. Thomson West, 610 Opperman Dr. Eagan, MN 55123. Phone: 800-328-9352 or (651)687-7000 • Annual. $798 full set; $63 monthly. Analyzes the enfo of federal securities laws from the viewpoint of the defendant. Discusses Securities and Exchange Commission (SEC) investigations and federal sentencing guidelines. (Securities Law Series).

***Securities Industry Yearbook***. Securities Industry and Financial Markets Association, 120 Broadway, 35th Fl. New York, NY 10271-0080. Phone: (212)313-1350; Fax: (212)313-1324; Email: smg@sifma.org • URL: http://www.sifma.org • Annual. $110 Members; $150 Nonmembers. Covers: over 600 member securities firms, with about 480 of them covered in detail. Entries include: For firms covered in detail—Company name, name of parent company, address, phone, capital position and rank, number of offices and type, number of employees, area of specialization, names and titles of key personnel, number of registered representatives, departments with name of department head, dollar volume of underwriting and syndication by type, other financial data. For other firms—Company name, address, name of delegated liaison to the association.

***Securities Law Handbook***. Thomson West, 610 Opperman Dr. Eagan, MN 55123. Phone: 800-328-9352 or (651)687-7000 • $966 Individuals Book - softbound - Full set; $80 Individuals Monthly pricing. Provides in-depth coverage of basic and specialized issues, including types of offerings, registration, reporting, potential violations, and enforcement.

***Securities Law Review***. Thomson West, 610 Opperman Dr. Eagan, MN 55123. Phone: 800-328-9352 or (651)687-7000 • $1,144 Individuals Print; $90 Monthly pricing. Helps you stay on top of current critical thinking in securities regulation, as well as recent judicial, legislative and regulatory decisions.

***Securities: Public and Private Offerings, 2d***. William W. Prifti. Thomson West, 610 Opperman Dr. Eagan, MN 55123. Phone: 800-328-9352 or (651)687-7000 • Semiannual. $1,383 Individuals Binder/Looseleaf - Full Set; $110 Individuals Monthly pricing. How to issue securities. (Securities Law Series).

***Securities Regulation & Law Report***. Bloomberg BNA, 3 Bethesda Metro Center, Ste. 250 Bethesda, MD 20814-5377. Phone: 800-372-1033 or (703)341-3000; Fax: (800)253-0332; Email: customercare@bna.com • URL: http://www.bna.com • Weekly. Reports on developments in the regulation of securities and futures trading.

***Securities Technology Monitor***. SourceMedia Inc., 1 State Street Plz., 27th Fl. New York, NY 10004. Phone: 800-221-1809 or (212)803-8200 or (212)803-8333; Fax: (212)843-9635 or (212)292-5216; Email: custserv@sourcemedia.com • URL: http://www.sourcemedia.com • Newsletter covers securities dealing and processing, including regulatory compliance, shareholder services, human resources, transaction clearing, and technology.

***Securities Week***. McGraw-Hill Financial Services Co., 25 Broadway New York, NY 10004. Phone: 800-722-4726 or (212)512-2000; Fax: (212)509-8994; Email: info@accessintel.com • Description: Acts as a trade publication for Wall Street executives, publishing news stories on pertinent events and developments within the industry including those related to legislative and regulatory activity, major stock exchanges, investment banking and retail firms, institutional trading, and new products. Recurring features include reports on research departments and a column titled Financial Futures/Commodities Report.

**Security Analysis and Risk Management Association**. PO Box 100284 Arlington, VA 22210. Phone: (703)635-7906; Fax: (703)635-7935; Email: info@sarma.org • URL: http://sarma.org • Aims to further the development, standardization and professionalization of the security analysis and risk management discipline. Provides leadership, education and certification for security analysis and risk management professionals. Serves as a forum to share information, ideas and methodologies to improve the development and application of the security analysis and risk management profession.

***Security Director News: Business News for Security Practitioners***. HME News, PO Box 998 Yarmouth, ME 04096. Phone: (207)846-0600; Fax: (207)846-0657 • Monthly. Magazine for professional leaders in the security industry.

***Security Distributing and Marketing***. BNP Media, 2401 W Big Beaver Rd., Ste. 700 Troy, MI 48084. Phone: 800-952-6643 or (248)362-3700 or (847)763-9534; Fax: (248)362-5103 or (248)362-0317; Email: privacy@bnpmedia.com • URL: http://www.bnpmedia.com • 13 times a year. Covers applications, merchandising, new technology and management.

***Security Letter***. Security Letter Inc., 166 E 96th St., Ste. 3b New York, NY 10128-2512. Phone: (212)348-1553; Fax: (212)534-2957; Email: rmccrie@mindspring.com • Description: Contains "solution-oriented information on security and protection of assets from loss," particularly for executives concerned about the following: internal checks and controls, personnel practices, management of change, fraud and embezzlement, business crime trends, security, and urban terrorism. Recurring features include news of research, a calendar of events, semiannual FBI crime data, quarterly financial news of major companies in the security industry, book reviews, security and safety pointers, and a question-and-answer feature.

***Security Management***. ASIS International, 1625 Prince St. Alexandria, VA 22314. Phone: (703)519-6200; Fax: (703)519-6299; Email: asis@asisonline.org • URL: http://www.asisonline.org/Pages/default.aspx • Monthly. Members included in membership dues; $60 Nonmembers print and online. Included in membership. Articles cover the protection of corporate assets, including personnel property and information security.

***Security Owner's Stock Guide***. Standard & Poor's Financial Services L.L.C., 55 Water St. New York, NY 10041. Phone: 877-772-5436 or (212)438-2000; Fax: (212)438-1000; Email: questions@standardandpoors.com • URL: http://www.standardandpoors.com • Monthly. $125.00 per year.

***Security Systems Administration***. Cygnus Business Media Inc., 1233 Janesville Ave. Fort Atkinson, WI 53538. Phone: 800-547-7377; Email: info@cygnus.com • URL: http://www.cygnus.com • Monthly. $10.00 per year.

***Security Systems Directory***. InfoGroup Inc., 5711 S 86th Cir. Omaha, NE 68127-4146. Phone: (402)593-4500 • URL: http://www.infogroup.com • Annual. Number of listings: 2,295. Entries include: Name, address, phone, size of advertisement, name of owner or manager, number of employees, year first in "Yellow Pages." Compiled from telephone company "Yellow Pages," nationwide.

***Security: The Magazine for Buyers of Security Products, Systems and Service***. BNP Media, 2401 W Big Beaver Rd., Ste. 700 Troy, MI 48084. Phone: 800-952-6643 or (248)362-3700 or (847)763-9534; Fax: (248)362-5103 or (248)362-0317; Email: privacy@bnpmedia.com • URL: http://www.bnpmedia.com • Monthly. Security industry news and trends.

***Seed Abstracts***. CABI, Nosworthy Way, Oxfordshire Wallingford OX10 8DE, United Kingdom. Phone: 44 1491 832111; Fax: 44 1491 833508; Email: enquiries@cabi.org • URL: http://www.cabi.org • Available monthly in print; updated weekly online. Provides fully searchable abstracts.

***Seed Business Magazine***. Australian Seed Federation, Unit 1, 20 Napier Close Deakin, ACT 2600, Australia. Phone: 61 2 62826822; Fax: 61 2 62826922; Email: enquiry@asf.asn.au • URL: http://www.asf.asn.au • Quarterly.

***The Seed Technologist Newsletter***. Society of Commercial Seed Technologists, 653 Constitution Ave. NE Washington, DC 20002. Phone: (202)870-2412 or (605)688-4606; Email: scst@seedtechnology.net • URL: http://www.seedtechnology.net • 3/year. $35. Includes annual proceedings.

***Seed World***. Scranton Gillette Communications Inc., 3030 W Salt Creek Ln., Ste. 201 Arlington Heights, IL 60005-5025. Phone: (847)391-1000; Fax: (847)390-0408; Email: hgillette@sgcmail.com • URL: http://www.scrantongillette.com • *Seed Trade Buyer's Guide*.

**Seeds of Diversity Canada**. PO Box 36, Sta. Q Toronto, ON, Canada M4T 2L7. Phone: 866-509-7333 or (905)372-8983; Email: mail@seeds.ca • URL: http://www.seeds.ca • Promotes biodiversity of food crops through conservation, documentation, and use of open-pollinated plants. Teaches and encourages seed-saving of vegetables, fruits, and grains suitable for the diverse climates of Canada through magazines, member seed exchange, presentations, publications, and exhibits.

***Seibt - Umwelttechnikprodukte: Buyer's Guide for Environmental Technology***. Seibt Verlag GmbH, Havelstrasse 9 D-64295 Darmstadt, Germany. Phone: 49 6151 380140; Fax: 49 6151 380141; Email: info@seibt.com • URL: http://www.seibt.com • Semiannual. €33; €20 subscription. Database covers: German manufacturers, wholesalers, importers, exporters, and service firms that supply products for industry and international trade; German companies involved in the manufacturing and supply of medical and pharmaceutical equipment and supplies.

**Selected Independent Funeral Homes**. 500 Lake Cook Rd., Ste. 205 Deerfield, IL 60015. Phone: 800-323-4219; Fax: (847)236-9968 • URL: http://www.selectedfuneralhomes.org • Funeral directors. Aims to study, develop, and establish a standard of service for the benefit of its consumers. Provides a continuing forum for the exchange, development and dissemination of knowledge and information beneficial to members and the public.

***Selected Instruments and Related Products***. U.S. Department of Commerce U.S. Census Bureau, 4600 Silver Hill Rd. Washington, DC 20233. Phone: 800-923-8282 or (301)763-4636 or (301)763-3030; Fax: (301)457-4714 or (301)763-6239; Email: webmaster@census.gov • URL: http://www.census.gov/ • Annual. (Current Industrial Reports, MA-334B.).

***Selected Interest Rates***. U.S. Federal Reserve System Board of Governors Publications Services, 20th and Constitution Ave. NW Washington, DC 20551. Phone: (202)452-3244; Fax: (202)728-5886 • URL: http://www.federalreserve.gov • Weekly release, $20.00 per year.

***Selected Readings on Information Technology and Business Systems Management***. Cengage Learning Inc., 20 Channel Center St. Boston, MA 02210. Phone: 800-487-8488 or (617)289-7700; Fax: (617)289-7844; Email: investors@cengage.com • URL: http://www.cengage.com • 2009. eBook. Published by Information Science Reference. Focuses on key issues concerning technology in business. Contains selected readings in areas such as e-business, mobile marketing, and information resources management.

***Self***. Conde Nast Publications, 4 Times Sq. New York, NY 10036-6518. Phone: 800-289-9330 or (212)286-2860 or (212)286-3700; Fax: (212)286-6763 or (212)286-7093; Email: contact@condenast.com • URL: http://www.condenast.com • Monthly. $13 One year subscription. Provides content, tools and community for modern women.

***Self-Employed***. National Association for the Self-Employed, PO Box 241 Annapolis Junction, MD 20701-0241. Phone: 800-232-6273; Email: advocacy@nase.org • URL: http://www.nase.org • Bimonthly. Provides articles on marketing, management, motivation, accounting, taxes, and other topics for businesses having fewer than 15 employees.

**Self Storage Association of the United Kingdom**. Priestley House, The Gullet Nantwich CW5 5SZ, United Kingdom. Phone: 44 1270 623150; Email: admin@ssauk.com • URL: http://www.ssauk.com • Encourages members, of the Self Storage Industry, to operate their storage facilities to a recommended minimum standard. Encourages prospective self-storage operators to carry out a full research of the Industry before opening their facilities. Preserves high standards of conduct in its members and in the industry. Promotes the industry to the general public.

***Selling: The Front Line of Business***. Dartnell Corp., 2222 Sedwick Dr. Durham, NC 27713. Phone: (800)223-8720; Email: customerservice@dartnellcorp.com • URL: http://www.dartnellcorp.com • Monthly. $79 Individuals. Magazine covering information for sales professionals in all areas.

***Selling to Kids: News and Practical Advice on Successfully Marketing to Kids and Teens***. EPM Communications Inc., 19 W 21 St., Ste. 303 New York, NY 10010. Phone: 888-852-9467 or (212)941-0099; Fax: (212)941-1622; Email: info@epmcom.com • URL: http://www.epmcom.com • Biweekly. $495 per year. Includes market research information, news items, and case studies.

***Selling to Seniors***. Community Development Services, Inc. CD Publications, 8204 Fenton St. Silver Spring, MD 20910. Phone: 800-666-6380 or (301)588-6380; Fax: (301)588-6385; Email: info@cdpublications.com • URL: http://www.cdpublications.com • Monthly. $329.00 per year. Newsletter on effective ways to reach the "over 50" market.

***Sell's Products and Services Directory***. Miller Freeman UK Ltd., Miller Freeman House, Sovereign Way Tonbridge TN9 1RW, United Kingdom. Phone: 44 1732 364422; Fax: 44 1732 377137; Email: pbutler@unmf.com • Annual. $99 print. Covers: Approximately 60,000 firms in United Kingdom and Ireland, including over 8,900 suppliers of health care products, equipment, and services in the United Kingdom and industry associations. Entries include: Company name, address, phone, fax, telex, description of product/service, names and titles of key personnel.

***Sell's Scottish Directory***. Miller Freeman UK Ltd., Miller Freeman House, Sovereign Way Tonbridge TN9 1RW, United Kingdom. Phone: 44 1732 364422; Fax: 44 1732 377137; Email: pbutler@unmf.com • Annual. $30. Covers: 8,000 industrial and commercial firms in Scotland, including firms int he North Sea oil industry. Entries include: Company name, address, phone, telex number, type of business.

***SEMA News***. Specialty Equipment Market Association, 1575 S Valley Vista Dr. Diamond Bar, CA 91765-0910. Phone: (909)610-2030; Fax: (909)860-0184; Email: sema@sema.org • URL: http://www.sema.org • Monthly. Description: Covers the automotive specialty, performance equipment, and accessory sectors. Recurring features include news of government and legislative actions, new products, international markets, and member and Association activities.

***Semantic Web for Business: Cases and Applications***. Cengage Learning Inc., 20 Channel Center St. Boston, MA 02210. Phone: 800-487-8488 or (617)289-7700; Fax: (617)289-7844; Email: investors@cengage.com • URL: http://www.cengage.com • 2009. eBook. Published by Information Science Reference. Presents cases that illustrate the benefits of semantic seb technologies as applied to e-business and e-commerce scenarios. Covers topics such as business integration, organizational knowledge management, and semantic web services.

***Semantic Web Technologies and E-Business: Toward the Integrated Virtual Organization and Business Process Automation***. Cengage Learning Inc., 20 Channel Center St. Boston, MA 02210. Phone: 800-487-8488 or (617)289-7700; Fax: (617)289-7844; Email: investors@cengage.com • URL: http://www.cengage.com • 2007. eBook. Published by Information Science Reference. Presents research related to the application of semantic Web technologies, including semantic service-oriented architecture, semantic content management, and semantic knowledge sharing in e-business processes.

**Semiconductor Device Laboratory**. Department of Electrical and Computing Engineering, University of Virginia, 351 McCormick, Thornton Hall, Rm. C210 Charlottesville, VA 22904. Phone: (424)924-3960; Fax: (424)924-8818; Email: rcandler@ee.ucla.edu • URL: http://www.ece.virginia.edu.

***Semiconductor International—Semi Source***. Reed Elsevier Group plc Reed Business Information, 360 Park Ave. S New York, NY 11010. Phone: (212)791-4208; Email: corporatecommunications@reedbusiness.com • URL: http://www.reedbusiness.com • Annual. Publication includes: Lists of companies associated with the design, processing, assembly, packaging, and testing of semiconductor devices, integrated circuits, and hybrid circuits. Database includes: Specifications from industry equipment and material suppliers. Entries include: Company name, address, phone, fax, products.

***Semiconductor International: The Industry Sourcebook for Processing, Assembly and Testing***. Reed Electronics Group, 360 Park Ave., S New York, NY 10010. Phone: 800-446-6551 or (646)746-6400; Fax: (646)746-7028; Email: corporatecommunications@reedbusiness.com • URL: http://www.reedbusiness.com • Monthly. $131.99 per year. Devoted to processing, assembly and testing techniques.

**Semiconductor Research Laboratory**. Duke University, Dept. of Electrical and Computer Engineering Durham, NC 27708. Phone: (919)660-5252; Fax: (919)660-5293; Email: abrown@ee.duke.edu • URL: http://www.ee.duke.edu.

***Semiconductors, Printed Circuit Boards, and Other Electronic Components***. U. S. Bureau of the Census, 4600 Silver Hill Rd. Washington, DC 20233-0001. Phone: (301)763-4636; Email: comments@census.gov • URL: http://www.census.gov • Annual. Provides data on shipments: value, quantity, imports, and exports. (Current Industrial Reports, MA-36Q.).

***Seminar Promoting***. Entrepreneur Press, 2445 McCabe Way, Ste. 400 Irvine, CA 92614-6244. Phone: 800-864-6864 or (949)261-2325 or (949)622-7131; Fax: (949)261-7729 or (949)261-0234; Email: press@entrepreneur.com • URL: http://www.entrepreneurpress.com • Looseleaf. $59.50. A practical guide to starting a seminar promotion business. Covers profit potential, start-up costs, market size evaluation, owner's time required, site selection, pricing, accounting, advertising, promotion, etc. (Start-Up Business Guide No. E1071.).

***Seminars in Ultrasound, CT and MRI***. Elsevier Inc., 1600 John F. Kennedy Blvd., Ste. 1800 Philadelphia, PA 19103-2899. Phone: 800-523-1649 or (215)239-3900; Fax: (215)239-3990 or (215)238-7883; Email: custserv.ehs@elsevier.com • URL: http://www.elsevier.com • Bimonthly. $357 Individuals online + print; $179 Students online + print; $339 Other countries online + print; $234 Students, other countries online + print. Journal reviewing current techniques and equipment used in ultrasound, CT, and MRI.

***Senate Manual***. U. S. Government Printing Office, 732 N Capitol St. NW Washington, DC 20401. Phone: 866-512-1800 or (202)512-1800 or (866)512-1800; Fax: (202)512-2104 or (202)512-2250; Email: contactcenter@gpo.gov • URL: http://www.gpo.gov • Biennial. $57.00. Contains the standing rules, orders, laws, and resolutions affecting the Senate, as well as copies of historical U.S. documents, such as Jefferson's Manual, Declaration of Independence, Articles of Confederation, Constitution of the United States.

***Senegal Business Law Handbook***. International Business Publications, USA, PO Box 15343 Washington, DC 20003. Phone: (202)546-2103; Fax: (202)546-3275; Email: ibpusa@comcast.net • URL: http://ibpus.com • $99.95 Individuals hardcopy, e-book, CD-ROM. Covers: Information on basic business legislation, laws and regulations affecting business, business climate and contacts.

***Senior Day Care Center***. Entrepreneur Press, 2445 McCabe Way, Ste. 400 Irvine, CA 92614-6244. Phone: 800-864-6864 or (949)261-2325 or (949)622-7131; Fax: (949)261-7729 or (949)261-0234; Email: press@entrepreneur.com • URL: http://www.entrepreneurpress.com • Looseleaf. $59.50. A practical guide to starting a day care center for older adults (supervised environment for frail individuals). Covers profit potential, start-up costs, market size evaluation, owner's time required, site selection, lease negotiation, pricing, accounting, advertising, promotion, etc. (Start-Up Business Guide No. E1335.).

***The Sensible Sound***. 403 Darwin Dr. Snyder, NY 14226-4804. Phone: 800-695-8439 or (716)833-0930; Fax: (716)833-0929; Email: info@sensiblesound.com • URL: http://www.sensiblesound.com • Bimonthly. $29.00 per year. High fidelity equipment review.

***Sensor Technology: A Monthly Intgelligence Service***. Technical Insights, 605 Third Ave. New York, NY 10158-0012. Phone: 800-825-7550 or (212)850-8600; Fax: (212)850-8800; Email: insights@wiley.com • URL: http://www.wiley.com • Monthly. Institutions, $685.00 per year. Newsletter on technological developments relating to industrial sensors and process control.

***Sensors: Your Resource for Sensing, Communications, and Control***. Advanstar Communications, 545 Boylston St. Boston, MA 02116. Phone: 888-527-7008 or (617)267-6500; Fax: (617)267-6900; Email: info@advanstar.com • URL: http://www.advanstar.com • Monthly. $70.00 per year. Edited for design, production, and manufacturing engineers involved with sensing systems. Emphasis is on emerging technology.

***Serials Directory: An International Reference Book***. EBSCO Publishing Inc., 10 Estes St. Ipswich, MA 01938-2106. Phone: 800-653-2726 or (978)356-6500; Fax: (978)356-6565; Email: information@ebscohost.com • URL: http://www.ebscohost.com • Quarterly. $525. Covers: Over 185,000 current and ceased periodicals and serials worldwide. Entries include: Serial title, publisher, address, phone, price, ISSN; Library of Congress, Dewey Decimal, National Library of Medicine, and Universal Decimal classification numbers; CODEN designations, description of editorial content; whether publication is peer reviewed; name of advertising manager; registration at the Copyright Clearance Center. Other format availabilities (CD-Rom), indexing and abstracting information.

***Serials Directory***. EBSCO Publishing Inc., 10 Estes St. Ipswich, MA 01938-2106. Phone: 800-653-2726 or (978)356-6500; Fax: (978)356-6565; Email: information@ebscohost.com • URL: http://www.ebscohost.com • Contains data from more than 108,000 worldwide publishers.

***The Serials Librarian***. The Haworth Press Inc., 10 Alice St. Binghamton, NY 13904. Phone: 800-429-6784 or (607)722-5857; Fax: (607)771-0012 or (607)722-6362; Email: getinfo@haworthpress.com • URL: http://www.haworthpressinc.com/store/product.asp?sku=J014 • Quarterly. Two volumes.

***Serials Review***. Reed Elsevier N.V., Radarweg 29 1043 NX Amsterdam, Netherlands. Phone: 31 20 515 99 44; Fax: 31 20 515 99 00; Email: amstbkinfo@elsevier.com • URL: http://www.elsevier.nl • Quarterly. $288 Institutions all countries except Europe & Japan; Y34,100 Institutions Japan; €257 Institutions European countries; $105 Individuals all countries except Europe & Japan; Y12,600 Individuals Japan; €94 Individuals European countries. Journal primarily concerned with serials information and management. Occasionally contains topical reviews of serial literature.

***Services et Expertise—Conseil du Quebec***. Quebec Dans Le Monde, 404-1001, Church Rd. Sainte-Foy, QC, Canada G1V 4N5. Phone: (418)659-5540; Fax: (418)659-4143; Email: info@quebecmonde.com • URL: http://www.quebecmonde.com • Biennial. $63.95 Individuals. Covers: Approximately 1,600 organizations and consultants who provide business counsel. Entries include: name, address, phone.

**Seton Hill University's E-magnify**. Seton Hill University, 1 Seton Hill Dr., 3rd Fl., Administration Bldg. Greensburg, PA 15601. Phone: (724)830-4625; Fax: (724)834-7131; Email: info@e-magnify.com • URL: http://www.e-magnify.com • Promotes women and business ownership. Offers a variety of entrepreneurial resources, educational programs, advocacy initiatives and networking opportunities to women entrepreneurs. Works "to strengthen the economic impact of women business owners as a collective force and to advance their growth through innovative programming in entrepreneurship and new venture creation." Provides support, education and encouragement essential for the continued growth of women-owned businesses through its services.

***Sex Discrimination and Sexual Harassment in the Work Place***. ALM Media Properties LLC, 120 Broadway, 5th Fl. New York, NY 10271-1100. Phone: (212)457-9400; Fax: (646)417-7705; Email: customercare@alm.com • URL: http://www.alm.com • $565. Considers both sides: the point of view of employers and the point of view of employees filing complaints. Coverage includes sexual harassment statutes, the Family Medical Leave Act, the Equal Pay Act, "glass ceiling" issues, pregnancy discrimination, childcare issues, reinstatement after a leave, and other legal matters. (Law Journal Press).

***The Seybold Report***. Seybold Publications, 428e Baltimore Pke., PO Box 644 Media, PA 19063. Phone: 800-325-3830 or (610)565-2480; Fax: (610)565-4695 or (610)565-1858; Email: editors@seyboldreports.com • URL: http://www.seyboldreports.com • Semimonthly. $499 /year. The definitive and independent source of information about the technologies used for publishing and printing.

***Seychelles Business Law Handbook***. International Business Publications, USA, PO Box 15343 Washington, DC 20003. Phone: (202)546-2103; Fax: (202)546-3275; Email: ibpusa@comcast.net • URL: http://ibpus.com • $99.95 Individuals hardcopy, e-book, CD-ROM. Covers: Information on basic business legislation, property rights, laws, business climate, export-import regulations, taxation, banking and contacts.

***SFO: Stocks, Futures & Options***. W and A Publishing, PO Box 849 Cedar Falls, IA 50613. Phone: 800-927-8222; Fax: (319)266-0252 or (319)277-1562; Email: amy@traderpress.com • URL: http://www.w-apublishing.com • Subtitle: *Official Journal for Personal Investing in Stocks, Futures, and Options*. Covers mainly speculative techniques for stocks, commodity futures, financial futures, stock index futures, foreign exchange, short selling, and various kinds of options.

**Shandong University - Center for Health Management and Policy**. 44 Wenhua Xi Rd. Jinan 250012, Shandong, China. Phone: 86 531 8382692; Fax: 86 531 8382693; Email: qmeng@sdu.edu.cn • URL: http://www.chmp.sdu.edu.cn/Eng • Health economics, health policy analysis, and development of health management instruments.

**Shanghai Academy of Social Sciences - Institute of National Economy**. No. 7, Ln. 622, Huaihai Rd. Shanghai 200020, China. Phone: 86 21 53060606; Fax: 86 21 53063256; Email: jjs@sass.org.cn • URL: http://english.sass.org.cn/Institutions/?newsid=003700350039 • Economic issues, industry policy, development studies, regional studies, social issues.

***Shanghai Yellow Pages: Commercial/Industrial Directory***. China Yellow Pages Directories Co., Fortress Twr., Rm. 1204-5, 250 King's Rd., Hong Kong North Point, China. Phone: 8076807; Fax: 5032601 • Annual. $65. Covers: over 30,000 companies in Shanghai. Database includes: Lists of trade contacts in Hong Kong, Taiwan, Macau, and Singapore. Entries include: Company name, address, phone, fax, postal code.

***Sharjah Commercial Directory***. Express Print Publishers, PO Box 10263 Dubai, United Arab Emirates. Phone: 971 4 2857209; Fax: 971 4 2858084; Email: epsllc@eim.ae • URL: http://www.expgroup.com • Covers: Commercial industries in Sharjah. Entries include: Name, address, phone, fax.

***Sharjah Industrial Products Directory***. Express Print Publishers, PO Box 10263 Dubai, United Arab Emirates. Phone: 971 4 2857209; Fax: 971 4 2858084; Email: epsllc@eim.ae • URL: http://www.expgroup.com • Covers: Manufacturing firms operating in United Arab Emirates. Entries include: Company address, executives, and activities.

***Sheep Breeder***. Mead Livestock Services Inc., 1120 Wilkes Blvd. 65201 Columbia, MO 65205. Phone: (314)442-8257; Fax: (314)442-6588 • Monthly.

***Shelflife***. Library Binding Council, 4440 PGA Blvd., Ste. 600 Palm Beach Gardens, FL 33410. Phone: 800-837-7321 or (561)745-6821 • URL: http://www.lbibinders.org • Quarterly. $29 Individuals; $36 Other countries; $31 Canada.

***Shenzhen Yellow Pages: Commercial/Industrial Directory***. China Yellow Pages Directories Co., Fortress Twr., Rm. 1204-5, 250 King's Rd., Hong Kong North Point, China. Phone: 8076807; Fax: 5032601 • Annual. $65. Covers: over 20,000 Shenzhen companies. Database includes: Guide to investment in the Shenzhen area. Entries include: Company name, address, phone, fax, postal codes.

***Shingle Springs/Cameron Park Chamber of Commerce Business Directory***. Shingle Springs/Cameron Park Chamber of Commerce, PO Box 341 Shingle Springs, CA 95682. Phone: (530)677-8000; Fax: (530)676-8313; Email: info@sscpchamber.org • URL: http://www.sscpchamber.org • Complete business listings, shopping information, and history of the Shingle Springs and Cameron Park areas of California.

***Shoals Chamber of Commerce—Membership Directory and Business Reference Guide***. Shoals Chamber of Commerce, 20 Hightower Pl. Florence, AL 35630-4102. Phone: 877-764-4661 or (256)764-4661; Fax: (256)766-9017 • URL: http://www.shoalschamber.com • Annual. Covers 1,400 business organizations in Florence, Alabama.

***Shoe Factory Buyer's Guide***. Shoe Trades Publishing Co. Research Services, 241 Senneville Rd. Senneville, QC, Canada H9X 3X5. Phone: (514)457-8787; Fax: (514)457-5832; Email: books@shoetrades.com • URL: http://www.shoetrades.com • Annual. $59 Individuals. Covers: Over 600 suppliers and their representatives to the shoe manufacturing industries in the United States and Canada. Entries include: Company name, address, phone, fax, trade and brand names, list of products or services.

***Shoe Stats***. Footwear Distributors and Retailers of America, 1319 F St. NW, Ste. 700 Washington, DC 20004. Phone: (202)737-5660; Fax: (202)645-0789 or (202)638-2615; Email: info@fdra.org • URL: http://www.fdra.org • Annual. Free to members; non-members, $350.00; libraries, $225.00. Includes *Statistical Reporter*.

*SHOOT: The Leading Newsweekly for Commercial Production and Postproduction*. Nielsen Business Media Inc., 770 Broadway New York, NY 10003-9522. Phone: 866-890-8541 or (646)654-4500 or (646)654-5000; Fax: (646)654-5584 or (646)654-4500; Email: bmcomm@nielsen.com • URL: http:// www.nielsenbusinessmedia.com • Weekly. $125 /year. Covers animation, music, sound design, computer graphics, visual effects, cinematography, and other aspects of television and motion picture production, with emphasis on TV commercials.

*Shooting Industry*. Publishers Development Corp., 12345 World Trade Dr. San Diego, CA 92128. Fax: (858)605-0247; Email: subs@shootingindustry.com • URL: http://www. shootingindustry.com • Monthly. $45 Other countries. Magazine serving the firearms industry.

**Shop, Distributive, and Allied Employees' Association**. 53 Queen St., Level 6 Melbourne, VIC 3000, Australia. Phone: 61 3 86117000; Fax: 61 3 86117099 • URL: http://www.sda. org.au • Shopworkers in the retail and fast food industries. Promotes equal opportunity and equal treatment of all members regardless of race, creed, disability, sexual preference, or gender. Works to improve the terms and conditions of members' employment and to protect the interests of members.

*Shop Talk*. International Mobile Air Conditioning Association, 6410 Southwest Blvd., Ste. 212 Fort Worth, TX 76109-3920. Phone: (817)732-4600; Fax: (817)732-9610; Email: info@ imaca.org • URL: http://www.macsw.org/imaca.php • Monthly. $20 /year for domestic; $50 /year for international. Description: Carries news briefs on happenings in the motor vehicle air conditioning and installed accessories industry. Publishes technical as well as management-oriented articles and listings of manuals, technical services, and training opportunities available. Recurring features include reports of meetings, company and personnel news, reports on the Association's activities and professional interest groups, and monthly supplements on specific topics.

*Shopping Center and Store Leases*. Emanuel B. Halper. ALM Media Properties LLC, 120 Broadway, 5th Fl. New York, NY 10271-1100. Phone: (212)457-9400; Fax: (646)417-7705; Email: customercare@alm.com • URL: http://www.alm.com • $375 Individuals print; $400 Individuals PDF. Contains detailed information on supermarket and fast-food restaurants and includes an annotated sample lease form. Also provides expert guidance and insights on negotiating use and exclusive clauses, covering 26 distinct categories of tenants.

*Short Courses and Seminars—The Who's Who of Training in Canada*. Development Publications Inc., 152 Carlton St. Toronto, ON, Canada M3H 6A7. Phone: (416)972-1027; Fax: (416)967-0646 • Semiannual. $59. Covers: more than 3,000 business and management courses, seminars, and workshops offered in Canada on subjects such as accounting, communications, conflict management, human relations, and supervisory development. Each issue lists programs for the following six months. Entries include: Name of program, sponsors, location, date, fees.

*Short Story Writers*. Magill's Choice, 2 University Plz., Ste. 121 Hackensack, NJ 07601. Phone: 800-221-1592 or (201)968-9899 or (201)968-0500; Fax: (201)968-1411 or (201)968-0511; Email: csr@salempress.com • URL: http://salempress. com • $217 Individuals 3 volumes. Covers: 102 short story writers of the 19th and 20th centuries. Entries include: Writer name, principal works of short fiction, other literary forms produced, notable career and technical achievements related to the short story form, brief biography, glossary.

*Short-Term Energy Outlook: Quarterly Projections*. U. S. Government Printing Office, 732 N Capitol St. NW Washington, DC 20401. Phone: 866-512-1800 or (202)512-1800 or (866)512-1800; Fax: (202)512-2104 or (202)512-2250; Email: contactcenter@gpo.gov • URL: http://www. gpo.gov • Semiannual. Issued by Energy Information Administration, U. S. Department of Energy. Contains forecasts of U. S. energy supply, demand, and prices.

*SHOT Business*. Bonnier Corp., 460 N Orlando Ave., Ste. 200 Winter Park, FL 32789. Phone: (407)628-4802; Fax: (407)628-7061 • URL: http://www.bonniercorp.com • Magazine featuring shooting sports industry.

*Shutterbug*. Source Interlink Media L.L.C., 261 Madison Ave., 6th Fl. New York, NY 10016. Phone: (212)915-4000; Email: webmastersim@sourceinterlink.com • URL: http://www. sourceinterlinkmedia.com • Monthly. $17.95 Individuals; $32.95 Two years; $29.95 Canada; $41.95 Other countries. Articles about new equipment, test reports on film accessories, how-to articles, etc.

*Shuttle, Spindle & Dyepot*. Handweavers Guild of America, 1255 Buford Hwy., Ste. 211 Suwanee, GA 30024. Phone: (678)730-0010; Fax: (678)730-0836; Email: hga@ weavespindye.org • URL: http://www.weavespindye.org • Quarterly. Comprised of articles on fiber arts.

*SI: Special Issues*. Trip Wyckoff, editor. Hoover's Inc., 5800 Airport Blvd. Austin, TX 78752-4204. Phone: 866-443-3939 or (512)374-4500 or (866)281-5969; Fax: (512)374-4501; Email: salesteam@hoovers.com • URL: http://www.hoovers. com • Bimonthly. $149.95 per year. Newsletter. Serves as a supplement to *Directory of Business Periodical Special Issues*. Provides information on trade journal special issues and editorial calendars.

*SIA Snow Sports Directory*. SnowSports Industries America,

8377-B Greensboro Dr. McLean, VA 22102-3587. Phone: (703)556-9020; Fax: (703)821-8276; Email: siamail@ snowsports.org • URL: http://www.snowsports.org • Annual. Covers: 1,000 manufacturers, distributors, and suppliers of ski, snowboard, on-snow, and in-line skate apparel, equipment, and accessories who are members of SIA and who exhibit at the SIA show. Entries include: Company name, address, phone, names of management, sales representatives, and products (including trade or brand names).

*Sibbald Guide to Every Public and the Top 150 Private Companies in Oklahoma, Louisiana, and Arkansas*. Acorn Press Inc., 14 Springhill Randolph, NJ 07869-4313. Phone: (973)895-7299 • Annual. $80 per year, plus $5.00 shipping; payment must accompany order. Covers: 285 public and privately-held corporations and financial institutions in Oklahoma, Louisiana, and Arkansas. Entries include: Company name, address, phone, brief company history and description, names and titles of officers and directors; return on beginning equity, return on sales/revenues; condensed balance sheet, income statement for past five years, auditors, transfer agent, legal counsel, stock exchange.

*Sibbald Guide to Every Public and the Top 100 Private Companies in Missouri*. Acorn Press Inc., 14 Springhill Randolph, NJ 07869-4313. Phone: (973)895-7299 • Annual. $80 per year, plus $5.00 shipping; payment must accompany order. Covers: 205 public and privately-held corporations and financial institutions in Missouri. Entries include: Company name, address, phone; brief company history and description, names and titles of officers and directors; return on beginning equity, return on sales/revenues; condensed balance sheet, income statement for past five years, auditors, transfer agent, legal counsel, stock exchange.

*Sibbald Guide to the Texas Top 250 Public Companies and Top 250 Private Companies*. Acorn Press Inc., 14 Springhill Randolph, NJ 07869-4313. Phone: (973)895-7299 • Annual. $102.50 per year, plus $5.00 shipping; payment must accompany order. Covers: 500 public and privately-held corporations and financial institutions in Texas. Entries include: Company name, address, phone; brief company history and description, names and titles of officers and directors; return on beginning equity, return on sales/revenues; condensed balance sheet, income statement for past five years, auditors, transfer agent, legal counsel, stock exchange.

*Sibbald Guide to the Top 250 Public Companies and Top 250 Private Companies in Georgia, Florida, and the Carolinas*. Acorn Press Inc., 14 Springhill Randolph, NJ 07869-4313. Phone: (973)895-7299 • Annual. $102.50 per year, plus $5.00 shipping; payment must accompany order. Covers: 500 public and privately-held corporations and financial institutions in Georgia, Florida, and North and South Carolina. Entries include: Company name, address, phone; brief company history and description, names and titles of officers and directors; return on beginning equity, return on sales/revenues; condensed balance sheet, income statement for past five years, auditors, transfer agent, legal counsel, stock exchange.

*SIBD—The Business Directory for the Soviet Region*. FYI Information Resources for a Changing World, 1413 K St. NW Washington, DC 20005. Phone: (202)682-2394; Fax: (202)682-2399 • Annual. $240 plus $10.00 shipping. Covers: Approximately 6,500 independent, cooperative, and private business organizations from industry, agriculture, and service sectors in the 15 republics of the former Soviet Union. Database includes: List of 500 largest enterprises. Entries include: Company or organization name, address, phone, telex, names and titles of key personnel, number of employees, geographical area served, financial data, subsidiary and branch names and locations, description of product/service.

*Sierra Leone Investment and Business Guide*. International Business Publications, USA, PO Box 15343 Washington, DC 20003. Phone: (202)546-2103; Fax: (202)546-3275; Email: ibpusa@comcast.net • URL: http://ibpus.com • $99.95 Individuals hardcopy, e-book, CD-ROM. Covers: Guide for conducting business activity in the country. Entries include: Important business information, business travel, and contacts.

**Sigma Iota Epsilon**. c/o Dr. G. James Francis, President, Colorado State University, 213 Rockwell Hall Fort Collins, CO 80523. Phone: (970)491-6265 or (970)491-7200; Fax: (970)491-3522; Email: jim.francis@business.colostate.edu • URL: http://www.sienational.com • Honorary and professional fraternity for students in all management concentrations (business, construction management, etc.) Provides competitions, educational and charitable programs, and speakers' bureau on a local level. Student division of the Academy of Management.

*Signal Magazine—AFCEA Source Book Issue*. Email: signal@ afcea.org • URL: http://www.afcea.org/sourcebook • Annual. Publication includes: List of member companies concerned with communications, design, production, maintenance and operation of communications, electronics, command and control, computers, intelligence systems and imagery. Entries include: Company name, address, phone, names and titles of key personnel, financial keys, trade and brand names, products or services, affiliations, description of organizational purpose, objectives.

*Signs of the Times Magazine—Buyers' Guide Issue*. ST Media Group International Inc., 11262 Cornell Park Dr. Cincinnati, OH 45242. Phone: 800-421-1321 or (513)421-2050; Fax:

(513)421-5144; Email: info@stmediagroup.com • URL: http://stmediagroup.com • Annual. Publication includes: List of more than 600 manufacturers and distributors of equipment and supplies for the sign industry; trade associations, consultants, trade shows, and other related organizations. Entries include: For manufacturers and distributors— Company name, address, phone, name of sales contact; manufacturer listings also include product lines. For others— Organization name, address, phone; trade show listings include dates.

*Signs of the Times Magazine—Sign Erection and Maintenance Directory Section*. ST Media Group International Inc., 11262 Cornell Park Dr. Cincinnati, OH 45242. Phone: 800-421-1321 or (513)421-2050; Fax: (513)421-5144; Email: info@ stmediagroup.com • URL: http://stmediagroup.com • Monthly. Publication includes: List of over 750 companies that erect or maintain electrical signs. Entries include: Company name, address, phone, services.

*Signs of the Times Magazine—Sign Supply Distributors Directory Section*. ST Media Group International Inc., 11262 Cornell Park Dr. Cincinnati, OH 45242. Phone: 800-421-1321 or (513)421-2050; Fax: (513)421-5144; Email: info@ stmediagroup.com • URL: http://stmediagroup.com • Monthly. $39 per year -13 issues; $59 Canada Surface mail; $94 Canada 1st Class mail; $62 Other countries Surface mail; $60 Two years USA; $101 Two years Canada by surface mail; $171 Two years Canada by I class mail; $112 Two years Other countries by surface mail. Publication includes: List of more than 80 suppliers of products and services used by sign companies; all listings are paid. Entries include: Name of firm, address, phone, code indicating type of product.

*Signs of the Times*. ST Media Group International Inc., 11262 Cornell Park Dr. Cincinnati, OH 45242. Phone: 800-421-1321 or (513)421-2050; Fax: (513)421-5144; Email: info@ stmediagroup.com • URL: http://stmediagroup.com • 13 times a year. For designers and manufacturers of all types of signs. Features how-to-tips.

*The SIMBA Report on Directory Publishing*. SIMBA Information Inc., 60 Long Ridge Rd., Ste. 300 Stamford, CT 06902. Phone: (203)325-8193; Fax: (203)325-8975 • URL: http:// www.simbainformation.com • Monthly. Newsletter.

**Simon Fraser University - Centre for Policy Research on Science and Technology**. 8888 University Dr. Burnaby, BC, Canada V5A 1S6. Phone: (778)782-5114; Fax: (778)782-5239; Email: smith@sfu.ca • URL: http://www.sfu.ca/cprost/ • Focuses on the relationship between public policy and technology. Specific areas of public policy research include: innovation metrics, innovation policy; management of technological change; indicators of science and technology and innovation; disaster mitigation; and valuation of information services.

**Simon Fraser University - Centre for Research in Adaptive Behaviour in Economics**. Department of Economics, 8888 University Dr. Burnaby, BC, Canada V5A 1S6. Phone: (604)291-5603; Fax: (604)291-5944; Email: arifovic@sfu.ca • URL: http://www.sfu.ca/crabe • Behavioral economics.

*Simulation & Gaming: An International Journal of Theory, Design and Research*. Pine Forge Press, 2455 Teller Rd. Thousand Oaks, CA 91320-2234. Phone: 800-818-7243 or (805)499-4224 or (805)499-9774; Fax: (805)499-0871 or (805)583-2665; Email: sales@pfp.sagepub.com • URL: http://www.sagepub.com/sociologybooks • Quarterly. $156 Individuals; $1,159 Institutions. Served as a leading international forum for the exploration and development of simulation/gaming methodologies used in education, training, consultation, and research.

*Singapore Business Services*. International Enterprise Singapore, 230 Victoria St. Singapore 188024, Singapore. Phone: 65 63376628; Fax: 65 63376898; Email: enquiry@iesingapore. gov.sg • URL: http://www.iesingapore.gov.sg • Annual.

*Singapore Electronics Industry Directory*. Marshall Cavendish Business Information Private Ltd., Times Centre, 1 New Industrial Rd. Singapore 536196, Singapore. Phone: 65 6213 9300 or 65 6213 9288; Fax: 65 6285 0161 or 65 6284 4733; Email: bizinfo@sg.marshallcavendish.com • URL: http:// www.timesdirectories.com • $50 Individuals local. Covers: information on electronics manufacturers, traders, distributors, suppliers, and international purchasing offices. Entries include: corporate profiles, company listings and contacts.

*Singapore Electronics Trade Directory*. International Enterprise Singapore, 230 Victoria St. Singapore 188024, Singapore. Phone: 65 63376628; Fax: 65 63376898; Email: enquiry@ iesingapore.gov.sg • URL: http://www.iesingapore.gov.sg • Annual. S$81.55; S$100 Individuals print; S$80 Individuals CD; $140 Individuals Print and CD. Covers: Information and contacts of numerous manufacturers, traders, and other supporting service providers in the electronics industry.

*Singapore Exchange—Companies Handbook*. Singapore Exchange Ltd., 2 Shenton Way, 19-00 SGX Centre 1 Singapore 068804, Singapore. Phone: 65 6236 8888 or 65 6236-8888; Fax: 65 6535 3544 or 65 35-6994 • URL: http://www. sgx.com • Semiannual. $400 per year. Covers: companies whose stock is traded on the Singapore Exchange. Entries include: Company name, address, names and titles of key personnel, capital, history, line of business, products, three year comparison of financial data.

*Singapore Exporters Database*. NIIR Project Consultancy Services, 106 - E, Kamla Nagar New Delhi 110007, India.

Phone: 91 11 23843955; Fax: 91 11 23841561; Email: npcs.india@gmail.com • URL: http://www.niir.org • Rs 2,248 Individuals CD-ROM; $100 Individuals CD-ROM. Covers: 3,641 Singapore exporters. Entries include: Company name, full postal address, phone, fax, email (wherever available), website (wherever available), telex (wherever available).

***Singapore Government and Business Contacts Handbook***. International Business Publications, USA, PO Box 15343 Washington, DC 20003. Phone: (202)546-2103; Fax: (202)546-3275; Email: ibpusa@comcast.net • URL: http://ibpus.com • $99.95 Individuals hardcopy, e-book, CD-ROM. Covers: Strategic government and business information, export-import activity in the country, investment, business contacts and regulations.

***Singapore International Chamber of Commerce***. Singapore International Chamber of Commerce, John Hancock Twr., 6 Raffles Quay, No. 10-01 Singapore 048580, Singapore. Phone: 65 65000988; Fax: 65 62242785; Email: general@sicc.com.sg • URL: http://www.sicc.com.sg • Annual. Free members; $15 Nonmembers. Covers: Singapore Chamber of Commerce members. Entries include: Members' addresses and their type of business.

***Singapore International 100 Ranking***. International Enterprise Singapore, 230 Victoria St. Singapore 188024, Singapore. Phone: 65 63376628; Fax: 65 63376898; Email: enquiry@iesingapore.gov.sg • URL: http://www.iesingapore.gov.sg • S$30.60 local; S$56.05 foreign. Covers: Singapore's top 100 companies with largest revenue contributions from the markets of Africa, Americas, China, Europe, India, Middle East, North Asia, Oceania, Southeast Asia. Entries include: top 100 companies ranked by overseas revenue, top 10 companies ranked by market, and corporate profiles.

***Singapore Investment & Business Guide***. International Business Publications, USA, PO Box 15343 Washington, DC 20003. Phone: (202)546-2103; Fax: (202)546-3275; Email: ibpusa@comcast.net • URL: http://ibpus.com • $99.95 Individuals hardcopy, e-book, CD-ROM. Covers: Basic information on economy, export-import and investment climate, regulations and industrial development, banking, and government. Entries include: Important business contacts and business travel.

**Singapore Productivity Association**. 11 Eunos Rd. 8, No. 08-01 Singapore 408601, Singapore. Phone: 65 62783344; Fax: 65 62725095; Email: customersvc@spa.org.sg • URL: http://www.spa.org.sg • Promotes the active involvement of organizations and individuals in the productivity movement. Encourages the spread of productivity and techniques.

**Singapore Venture Capital and Private Equity Association**. 14 Robinson Rd., No. 07-02A, Far East Finance Bldg. Singapore 048545, Singapore. Phone: 65 6 2247001; Fax: 65 6 2246772; Email: info@svca.org.sg • URL: http://www.svca.org.sg • Promotes, develops, and maintains local venture capital and private equity industry as a source of equity finance. Represents the local venture capital industry in dealing with parties from other countries. Fosters interaction among members, investors, and investees.

***Sioux Falls Christian Business Directory***. Red Letter Publishing, PO Box 272682 Fort Collins, CO 80527. Phone: 800-445-5614; Fax: (970)267-9669; Email: info@redletter.com • URL: http://www.christianbusinessdirectoryonline.com • Businesses, churches, organizations, and schools in Sioux Falls, South Dakota.

***SIRENE***. France Institut National de la Statistique et des Etudes Economiques, 18, blvd. Adolphe Pinard F-75675 Paris, France. Phone: 1 45400614 • Daily. Database covers: Approximately 2.5 million French industrial and commercial firms. Entries include: Firm name, address, type of incorporation, national identification code, sector of activity, number of salaried employees, quarterly business volume.

***Site Selection and Industrial Development—Geo-Political Index Issue***. Conway Data Inc., 6625 The Corners Parkway, Ste. 200 Norcross, GA 30092-3334. Phone: (770)446-6996; Fax: (770)263-8825; Email: info@conway.com • URL: http://www.conway.com • Annual. $20 plus $2.00 shipping. Publication includes: List of state, county, and local governmental agencies which negotiate and administer inducements to industrial firms to locate new offices, plants, warehouses, or other facilities within their jurisdiction. Database includes: Tabulations of incentives, financing plans, etc., offered by state and local agencies. Entries include: Agency name, address, phone, name of principal executive, and indication of special services and incentives.

***Site Selection—Geo-Economic Index Issue***. Conway Data Inc., 6625 The Corners Parkway, Ste. 200 Norcross, GA 30092-3334. Phone: (770)446-6996; Fax: (770)263-8825; Email: info@conway.com • URL: http://www.conway.com • $20 plus $2.00 shipping. Publication includes: List of area development bodies, including state development agencies, city and county development offices, urban renewal agencies, port and airport agencies, railroads, utilities, banks, chambers of commerce, etc.; coverage includes Canada and over 50 other countries. Entries include: Group name, phone, name of contact.

***16 Million Businesses Phone Book***. Info U.S.A., 5711 S 86th Cir. Omaha, NE 68127-0347. Phone: (402)593-4595; Fax: (402)331-1505 • URL: http://www.infousa.com • Contains business information and phone numbers of U.S. and Canada businesses. Cross-referenced to search for company name or contact information. The database is available on CD-ROM.

***Skagway Business Directory***. Skagway Chamber of Commerce, PO Box 194 Skagway, AK 99840-0194. Phone: (907)983-1898; Fax: (907)983-2031; Email: chamber@aptalaska.net • URL: http://www.skagwaychamber.org • Annual. Covers: Comprehensive listing of area businesses.

***Sky and Telescope: The Essential Guide to Astronomy***. Sky Publishing Corp., 90 Sherman St. Cambridge, MA 02140. Phone: 800-253-0245 or (617)864-7360 or (617)864-1377; Fax: (617)864-6117; Email: info@skyandtelescope.com • URL: http://www.skyandtelescope.com • Monthly. $37.95 /year. Reports astronomy and space science for amateurs and professionals. Many "how to" features.

***SLA Annual Salary Survey***. Special Libraries Association, 331 S Patrick St. Alexandria, VA 22314-3501. Phone: (703)647-4900; Fax: (703)647-4901 • URL: http://www.sla.org • Annual. Members, $75.00; non-members, $150.00. Provides data on salaries for special librarians in the U. S. and Canada, according to location, job title, industry, budget, and years of experience.

***SLAM—Trade Yearbook of Africa***. SLAM Trade Year Book of Africa, Apartado Postal 14013 E-29080 Madrid, Spain. • Annual. $60. Covers: Approximately 400,000 industrial and commercial companies in Africa. Entries include: Company name, address, phone, line of business, product/service, trademarks.

**Slovak Academy of Sciences - Institute of Economic Research**. Šancová No. 56 811 05 Bratislava, Slovakia. Phone: 421 2 52498214; Fax: 421 2 52495106; Email: milan.sikula@savba.sk • URL: http://www.ekonom.sav.sk • Macroeconomics, microeconomics, international economics, economic integration into the EU, economic analysis, and economic modeling.

**Slovak Venture Capital Association**. Stefanikova 6a 811 05 Bratislava, Slovakia. Phone: 421 2 754414356; Fax: 421 2 754431180; Email: slovca@slovca.sk • URL: http://www.slovca.sk • Provides information for people seeking capital for new and existing enterprises. Represents the interests of members before the government and other related institutions/agencies. Encourages the highest standards of business practice.

***Slovenia Business Services Providers Leads***. Business Information Agency Inc. PlanetInform, 52 Tuscan Way, Ste. 202-181 Saint Augustine, VA 32092. Phone: (904)342-6124; Fax: (904)592-2632; Email: info@biasales.com • URL: http://www.biasales.com • Monthly. $84 Individuals mailing list; $177 Individuals sales list; $300 Individuals marketing list. Covers Slovenian companies and all sub-industries that provide various services to commercial businesses, establishments, and organizations, including consulting, advertising and marketing services, and facilities maintenance.

***Sludge Newsletter: The Newsletter on Municipal Wastewater and Biosolids***. Business Publishers Inc., PO Box 17592 Baltimore, MD 21297-1592. Phone: 800-223-8720; Fax: (800)508-2592; Email: custserv@bpinews.com • URL: http://www.bpinews.com • Biweekly. $409.00 per year. per year. Newsletter. Monitors sludge management developments in Washington and around the country.

***Small Business Administration. Annual Report***. U. S. Government Printing Office, 732 N Capitol St. NW Washington, DC 20401. Phone: 866-512-1800 or (202)512-1800 or (866)512-1800; Fax: (202)512-2104 or (202)512-2250; Email: contactcenter@gpo.gov • URL: http://www.gpo.gov • Annual. Two volumes.

**Small Business Administration - Office of Technology**. 409 3rd St. SW Washington, DC 20416. Phone: (202)205-6450; Fax: (202)481-1518; Email: edsel.brown@sba.gov • URL: http://archive.sba.gov/aboutsba/sbaprograms/sbir/index.html • Provides policy for the Small Business Innovation Research Program (SBIR). SBIR is a federal procurement system that provides qualified small business concerns with opportunities to compete for federal research and development awards. Also oversees the Small Business Technology Transfer (STTR) Program. STTR coordinates cooperative research and development activities between small business STTR awardee, nonprofit research institutions, or federally funded research and development centers.

***The Small Business Advisor***. Small Business Advisors Inc., 11 Franklin Ave. Hewlett, NY 11557. Phone: (516)374-1387; Fax: (720)294-3202; Email: joe@smallbusinessadvice.com • URL: http://www.smallbusinessadvice.com • Monthly. $45 print or soft copy. Seeks to help emerging growth companies increase profits. Considers small business issues, including marketing sales, finance, taxes, organizing, competition, management, and human resources. Recurring features include letters to the editor, interviews, and columns titled Info Bank, In the Mail Box, Taxes, Human Resources, Marketing, Insurance, and Law. Remarks: Publication suspended in 1980; resumed publication Fall 1993.

***Small Business Barometer***. Small Business Association of Michigan, 120 N Washington Sq., Ste. 1000 Lansing, MI 48933. Phone: 800-362-5461; Fax: (517)482-4205; Email: websupport@sbam.org • URL: http://www.sbam.org • Contains surveys of Michigan business owners and reports on their economic outlook.

***Small Business Controller***. Thomson RIA, 195 Broadway New York, NY 10007-3100. Phone: 800-431-9025 or (212)367-6300 or (212)807-2298; Fax: (212)367-6305 or (212)337-4207; Email: ttacommunications@riag.com • URL: http://www.ria.thomson.com • Quarterly. $76 Individuals. Source for technical information in accounting and financial management. For financial managers in growing and emerging businesses.

***Small Business Exchange***. Canadian Auto Review, 926 Natoma St. San Francisco, CA 94103-2515. Phone: (415)256-4111 • Semimonthly. $92.50 -220; $3 -5 single issue. Trade newspaper.

**Small Business Innovation Research Program - Small Business Technology Transfer Program**. Germantown Bldg., SC-29, 1000 Independence Ave. SW Washington, DC 20585. Phone: (301)903-5707; Fax: (301)903-5488; Email: sbir-sttr@science.doe.gov • URL: http://science.energy.gov/sbir • Private sector commercialization of energy-related innovations derived from Federal research and development; technological innovation; the use small business to meet Federal research and development needs; Phase I funding up to $100,000 for a period of approximately nine months; further funding (up to $750,000 for not more than 24 months) to continue development of promising programs initiated in Phase I; and, finally, follow-on funding for commercial applications of the research or development pursued by small business with nonfederal capital, or alternatively, follow-on non-SBIR federal contracts for products or processes desired by the government. to $100,000 for a period of approximately six months; further funding (up to $750,000 for not more than 24 months) to continue development of promising programs initiated in Phase I; and, finally, follow-on funding for commercial applications of the research or development pursued by small business with nonfederal capital, or alternatively, follow-on non-SBIR federal contracts for products or processes desired by the government.

***Small Business Investment Company Directory and Handbook***. International Wealth Success Inc., 24 Canterbury Rd. Rockville Centre, NY 11570-1310. Phone: 800-323-0548 or (516)766-5850; Fax: (516)766-5919; Email: admin@iwsmoney.com • URL: http://www.iwsmoney.com • $20 Individuals. Gives tips from the U.S. Small Business Administration (SBA) on obtaining financing and on small business financial management and explains how SBICs work. Covers: Over 400 small business investment companies interested in investing in various businesses.

**Small Business Investor Alliance**. 1100 H St. NW, Ste. 610 Washington, DC 20005. Phone: (202)628-5055; Email: membership@sbia.org • URL: http://www.sbia.org • Affiliated with Small Business Investor Alliance.

***Small Business Opportunities***. Harris Publications Inc., 1115 Broadway New York, NY 10010. Phone: (212)807-7100; Fax: (212)924-8416 or (212)924-2352; Email: subscriptions@harris-pub.com • URL: http://www.harris-pub.com • Monthly. 14.97. Source for entrepreneurs and small business owners.

***Small Business Preferential Subcontracts Opportunities Monthly***. Government Data Publications Inc., 2300 M St. NW Washington, DC 20037. Phone: 800-275-4688 or (202)416-1761 or (718)627-0819; Fax: (718)998-5960; Email: gdp@govdata.com • URL: http://www.govdata.com • Monthly. $84 Individuals per year. Companies whose government contracts exceed $1,000,000 in value for construction; $500,000 for others.

***Small Business Reference Guide***. Bluechip Books, 134 Main St. Putney Stratford, CT 06497. Phone: (203)375-1233 • Irregular. $14.95. Covers: over 350 firms, associations, and government agencies offering products and services of assistance to small businesses. Entries include: Organization name, address, phone; most listings also include description of services, products, or activities.

***Small Business Resource Center***. Cengage Learning Inc., 20 Channel Center St. Boston, MA 02210. Phone: 800-487-8488 or (617)289-7700; Fax: (617)289-7844; Email: investors@cengage.com • URL: http://www.cengage.com • Covers all major areas of starting and operating a business including financing, management, marketing, human resources, franchising, accounting and taxes.

***The Small Business Resource Guide***. National Black Chamber of Commerce, 4400 Jenifer St. NW, Ste. 331 Washington, DC 20015-2133. Phone: (202)466-6888; Fax: (202)466-4918; Email: info@nationalbcc.org • URL: http://www.nationalbcc.org.

***Small Business Retirement Savings Advisor***. U. S. Department of Labor, Phone: (202)219-8921 • URL: http://www.dol.gov/elaws/pwbaplan.htm • Web site provides "answers to a variety of commonly asked questions about retirement saving options for small business employers." Includes a comparison chart and detailed descriptions of various plans: 401(k), SEP-IRA, SIMPLE-IRA, Payroll Deduction IRA, Keogh Profit-Sharing, Keogh Money Purchase, and Defined Benefit. Searching is offered. Fees: Free.

**Small Business Service Bureau**. 554 Main St. Worcester, MA 01615-0014. Phone: 800-343-0939; Email: info@sbsb.com • URL: http://www.sbsb.com • Represents businesses with less than 100 employees. Offers planning and strategy programs to aid businesspersons in starting, improving, or expanding small businesses. Disseminates guides, manuals and other materials on small business operations. Offers trade assistance to the People's Republic of China.

***Small Business Sourcebook***. Cengage Learning Inc., 20 Channel

Center St. Boston, MA 02210. Phone: 800-487-8488 or (617)289-7700; Fax: (617)289-7844; Email: investors@cengage.com • URL: http://www.cengage.com • Annual. $747 Individuals print. Contains over 340 profiles on small businesses as well as nearly 100 small business topics.

***Small Business Sources of Capital Handbook***. Metro Atlanta Chamber of Commerce, 235 Andrew Young International Blvd. NW Atlanta, GA 30303-2718. Phone: (404)880-9000 • URL: http://www.metroatlantachamber.com • $8. Covers: Sources of capital available to small businesses in the metropolitan Atlanta area. Entries include: Source name, address, phone, description.

***Small Business Tax News***. Inside Mortgage Finance Publications, 7910 Woodmont Ave., Ste. 1000 Bethesda, MD 20814. Phone: 800-570-5744 or (301)951-1240; Fax: (301)656-1709 • URL: http://www.insidemortgagefinance.com • Monthly. $139 Online; $149 Print. Contains latest news on tax changes, as well as detailed analysis of guidances from the IRS.

***The Small Business Tax Review***. A/N Group Inc., 17 Scott Dr. Melville, NY 11747. Phone: (631)549-4090; Fax: (631)385-9858; Email: angroup@pb.net • URL: http://www.smbiz.com • Description: Reports tax news on such topics as new laws, court cases, IRS rulings, fringe benefits, and business and individual taxes, with emphasis on smaller businesses. Advises on financial planning and technical aspects of small business management.

**Small Firms Association**. Confederation House, 84-86 Lower Baggot St. Dublin 2, Dublin, Ireland. Phone: 353 1 6051500 or 353 1 6051602; Fax: 353 1 353 1 6381602; Email: info@sfa.ie • URL: http://www.sfa.ie • Represents the small enterprises in Ireland. Provides economic, commercial, employee relations and social affairs advice and assistance.

***Small Law Firm Economic Survey***. Incisive Legal Intelligence, 2 Campus Blvd., Ste. 200 Newtown Square, PA 19073-3243. Phone: 888-782-7297 or (212)457-4994 or (610)886-2000; Fax: (646)822-5384 or (610)359-0467; Email: incisivesurveys@incisivemedia.com • Annual. $395.00. Provides aggregate data (benchmarks) on the economics, finances, billing, and staffing of law offices in the U. S. having "less than 12 lawyers.".

***Smart Computing***. Sandhills Publishing Co., 120 W. Harvest Dr. Lincoln, NE 68521. Phone: 800-331-1978 or (402)479-2181; Fax: (402)479-2195; Email: feedback@sandhills.com • URL: http://www.sandhills.com/ • Monthly. $29.00 per year. Provides basic computer advice "in plain English." Includes reviews of hardware and software.

***Smart TV and Sound: Interactive Television and DVD-MP3-Internet Audio and Video-Satellite Television***. York Publishing Inc., 1350 E 9th St. Chico, CA 95928. Phone: 800-284-3226 or (530)891-8410; Fax: (530)891-8443; Email: customerservice@videomaker.com • URL: http://www.videomaker.com • Semiannual. $14.97 per year. Consumer magazine covering WebTV, PC/TV appliances, DVD players, "Smart TV," and other topics relating to interactive television, the Internet, and multimedia. Formerly *Smart TV*.

***Smart/Utilize Catalog Index***. Property Management Systems Corp., 2800 28th St., Ste. 109 Santa Monica, CA 90405-6204. Phone: 800-755-3968 or (310)450-2566; Fax: (310)450-1311; Email: sales@assetsmart.com • URL: http://www.assetsmart.com • Bimonthly. Database covers: about 20,000 manufacturers of over 250,000 models of electronic, computer, office, and machine tool equipment; limited international coverage. Database includes: Company name, address, phone, subsidiary and branch names and locations, description of products with model number and performance specifications, trade/brand names, merger/buyout audit trail.

***SmartMoney: The Wall Street Journal Magazine of Personal Business***. The Hearst Corp., 300 W 57th St. New York, NY 10019. Phone: (212)649-2000; Fax: (212)765-2639; Email: corpcommunications@hearst.com • URL: http://www.hearst.com • Monthly. $10 Individuals 12 issues; $18 Individuals 24 issues; $24 Individuals 36 issues; $25 Other countries 12 issues; $33 Individuals 24 isssues; $39 Individuals 36 issues. Magazine featuring practical and imaginative ideas for investing, spending and saving. Includes *Stock Trader's Almanac*.

***SMI and SME Business Directory: The Official Business Directory of SMI Association of Malaysia***. Tourism Publications Corporation Sdn. Bhd., Wisma Chinese Chamber, 5th Fl., 258 Jln. Ampang 50450 Kuala Lumpur, Malaysia. Phone: 60 3 42512288; Fax: 60 3 42578868; Email: info@tpcsb.com • URL: http://www.tpcsb.com • $69.90 Individuals; S$45 Individuals; $60 Other countries. Aims to develop the potential of SMIs/SMEs and to enable them to evolve according to the demands of the new economy.

***Smokeshop***. 26 Broadway, Fl. 9M New York, NY 10004. Phone: (212)391-2060; Fax: (212)827-0945; Email: circulation@lockwoodpublications.com • URL: http://www.lockwoodpublications.com • Bimonthly. $24.00 per year.

***SMPTE Motion Imaging Journal***. Society of Motion Picture and Television Engineers, 3 Barker Ave., 5th Fl. White Plains, NY 10601. Phone: (914)761-1100; Fax: (914)761-3115; Email: smpte@smpte.org • URL: http://www.smpte.org • Monthly. $125 Nonmembers; Included in membership; $130 Individuals. Peer-reviewed journal containing articles pertaining to new developments in motion picture and television technology; standards and recommended practices; general news of the industry. Formerly *SMPTE Journal*.

***Snack Food and Wholesale Bakery: The Magazine That Defines the Snack Food Industry***. BNP Media, 2401 W Big Beaver Rd., Ste. 700 Troy, MI 48084. Phone: 800-952-6643 or (248)362-3700 or (847)763-9534; Fax: (248)362-5103 or (248)362-0317; Email: privacy@bnpmedia.com • URL: http://www.bnpmedia.com • Monthly. Monthly. Free to qualified personnel; others, $85.06 per year. Provides information for producers of pretzels, potato chips, cookies, crackers, nuts, and other snack foods. Includes *Annual Buyers Guide* and *State of Industry Report*.

***Snips***. BNP Media, 2401 W Big Beaver Rd., Ste. 700 Troy, MI 48084. Phone: 800-952-6643 or (248)362-3700 or (847)763-9534; Fax: (248)362-5103 or (248)362-0317; Email: privacy@bnpmedia.com • URL: http://www.bnpmedia.com • Monthly. $18.00 per year. Provides information for heating, air conditioning, sheet metal and ventilating contractors, wholesalers, manufacturers representatives and manufacturers.

***Soap and Cosmetics***. Cygnus Business Media, 3 Huntington Quadrangle, Ste. 301N Melville, NY 11747. Phone: 800-308-6397 or (631)845-2700; Fax: (631)845-2741 or (631)845-2798; Email: rich.reiff@cygnuspub.com • URL: http://www.cygnusb2b.com • Monthly. $60.00 per year. Formerly *Soap, Cosmetics, Chemical Specialties*.

**SOAS, University of London - Centre for Development Policy and Research**. Russell Sq., Thornhaught St. London WCIH 0XG, United Kingdom. Phone: 44 20 798984316; Fax: 44 20 74363844 • URL: http://www.soas.ac.uk/cdpr • Economies in transition, stabilization and structural adjustment programs, illicit drugs and development, development assistance.

**SOAS, University of London - Japan Research Centre**. Russell Sq., Thornhaught St. London WC1H 0XG, United Kingdom. Phone: 44 207 8984892; Fax: 44 207 8984489; Email: centres@soas.ac.uk • URL: http://www.soas.ac.uk/jrc • Japan, including its anthropology, art and archaeology, economics, geography, gender and sexuality, history, imperialism, language and literature, law, linguistics, media, music, politics, religion and sociology.

**Social Democrats, U.S.A.** PO Box 16161 Pittsburgh, PA 15242. Email: info@socialistcurrents.org • URL: http://www.socialdemocrats.org • Serves as political action and education organization of young people, students, and trade unionists. Supports Independent and Democratic liberal-labor candidates for public office. Seeks realignment of the major political parties in the U.S. Maintains speakers' bureau. Supports "greater democratic decision-making over the social forces that control our everyday economic lives." Recommends democratic economic planning to ease pains of the economic crisis and to allocate resources in the public interest. Favors public aid to education and increased public investment in such areas as national health care, mass transit, low-cost housing, and new sources of energy. Supports trade unionism. Believes in foreign policy that supports democratic movements and governments.

***Social Implications and Challenges of E-Business***. Cengage Learning Inc., 20 Channel Center St. Boston, MA 02210. Phone: 800-487-8488 or (617)289-7700; Fax: (617)289-7844; Email: investors@cengage.com • URL: http://www.cengage.com • 2007. eBook. Published by Information Science Reference. Explores the profound social implications and challenges of e-business, investigates how the rapid development of the Internet and e-business shapes, and is shaped, by various social forces; and highlights the enormous difficulties and challenges involved in applying e-business technologies and principles in public services and other non-business activities.

***Social Sciences Abstracts***. EBSCO Publishing Inc., 10 Estes St. Ipswich, MA 01938-2106. Phone: 800-653-2726 or (978)356-6500; Fax: (978)356-6565; Email: information@ebscohost.com • URL: http://www.ebscohost.com • Provides indexing from 1983 and abstracting from 1994 of more than 750 periodicals covering economics, area studies, community health, public administration, public welfare, urban studies, and many other topics related to the social sciences.

***Social Sciences Citation Index***. Thomson Reuters Corp., 3 Times Sq. New York, NY 10036. Phone: 800-336-4474 or (646)223-4000 or (646)822-2000; Email: general.info@thomsonreuters.com • URL: http://www.thomsonreuters.com • Weekly. Product is accessed via *Web of Science*.

***Social Sciences Index Retrospective: 1907-1983***. EBSCO Publishing Inc., 10 Estes St. Ipswich, MA 01938-2106. Phone: 800-653-2726 or (978)356-6500; Fax: (978)356-6565; Email: information@ebscohost.com • URL: http://www.ebscohost.com • Indexing for 1,000,000 articles. Coverage includes international index and social sciences and humanities index.

**Social Security Administration - Office of Research, Evaluation, and Statistics**. 6401 Security Blvd. Baltimore, MD 21235. Phone: (410)965-2841 • URL: http://www.ssa.gov/policy/about/ORES.html • Social security programs. Activities include: conducting policy studies mandated by Congress; conducting policy studies intended to support the legislative development process, such as research on the relationship between social security and the U.S. economy, descriptions of the effects of specific program provisions, and analysis of the role of social security in providing for the economic security of the aged and disabled; tabulating basic statistics on the beneficiary population from administrative records and surveys; maintaining and enhancing databases used to conduct these activities; evaluating the effectiveness of enacted legislation, legislative proposals, and current law provisions, and providing statistical and methodological support to aid other SSA components.

***Social Security & Medicare Facts***. • Annual. $110.00.

***Social Security Benefits, Including Medicare***. Wolters Kluwer Law & Business CCH, 2700 Lake Cook Rd. Riverwoods, IL 60015. Phone: 888-224-7377 or (847)267-7000; Email: cust_serv@cch.com • URL: http://www.cchgroup.com • Annual. $11.00.

***Social Security Bulletin***. Social Security Administration. U. S. Government Printing Office, 732 N Capitol St. NW Washington, DC 20401. Phone: 866-512-1800 or (202)512-1800 or (866)512-1800; Fax: (202)512-2104 or (202)512-2250; Email: contactcenter@gpo.gov • URL: http://www.gpo.gov • Quarterly. $27.00 per year. Annual statistical supplement.

***Social Security Explained***. Wolters Kluwer Law & Business CCH, 2700 Lake Cook Rd. Riverwoods, IL 60015. Phone: 888-224-7377 or (847)267-7000; Email: cust_serv@cch.com • URL: http://www.cchgroup.com • Annual. $37.00.

***Social Security Handbook***. U. S. Government Printing Office, 732 N Capitol St. NW Washington, DC 20401. Phone: 866-512-1800 or (202)512-1800 or (866)512-1800; Fax: (202)512-2104 or (202)512-2250; Email: contactcenter@gpo.gov • URL: http://www.gpo.gov • Annual. $53.00. Issued by the Social Security Administration (www.ssa.gov). Provides detailed information about social security programs, including Medicare, with brief descriptions of related programs administered by agencies other than the Social Security Administration.

***Social Security Manual***. • Annual. $22.95.

***Social Security Online: The Official Web Site of the Social Security Administration***. U. S. Social Security Administration, Phone: 800-772-1213 or (410)965-7700 • URL: http://www.ssa.gov • Web site provides a wide variety of online information relating to social security and Medicare. Topics include benefits, disability, employer wage reporting, personal earnings statements, statistics, government financing, social security law, and public welfare reform legislation.

***Social Security Practice Guide***. Matthew Bender and Company Inc., 1275 Broadway Albany, NY 12204-2638. Phone: 800-424-4200 or (518)487-3000; Fax: (518)487-3573 or (800)424-4200; Email: customer.support@lexisnexis.com • URL: http://www.matthewbender.com • Irregular. $1,839 Individuals Book; $1,672 Individuals Electronic version; $2,143 Individuals CD-ROM. Periodic supplementation. Complete, practical guide on all substantive and procedural aspects of social security practice. Prepared under the supervision of the National Organization of Social Security Claimants' Representatives (NOSSCR).

***Social Security Programs Throughout the World***. U. S. Government Printing Office, 732 N Capitol St. NW Washington, DC 20401. Phone: 866-512-1800 or (202)512-1800 or (866)512-1800; Fax: (202)512-2104 or (202)512-2250; Email: contactcenter@gpo.gov • URL: http://www.gpo.gov • Annual. $35.70 Individuals International List price - paperback; $25.50 Individuals USA List price - paperback. Issued by the Social Security Administration (www.ssa.gov). Presents basic information on more than 170 social security systems around the world.

***Social Trends & Indicators USA***. Monique D. Magee, editor. Cengage Learning Inc., 20 Channel Center St. Boston, MA 02210. Phone: 800-487-8488 or (617)289-7700; Fax: (617)289-7844; Email: investors@cengage.com • URL: http://www.cengage.com • Includes data on labor, economics, the health care industry, crime, leisure, population, education, social security, and many other topics. Sources include various government agencies and major publications. Inquire for pricing.

**Social Venture Network**. PO Box 29221 San Francisco, CA 94129-0221. Phone: (415)561-6501; Fax: (415)561-6435; Email: svn@svn.org • URL: http://www.svn.org • Aims to build a just and sustainable world through business. Promotes new models and leadership for socially and environmentally sustainable business through initiatives, information services and forums.

**Society for Advancement of Management**. 6300 Ocean Dr., OCNR 330, Unit 5807 Corpus Christi, TX 78412. Phone: 888-827-6077 or (361)825-3045; Fax: (361)825-5609; Email: moustafa.abdelsamad@tamucc.edu • URL: http://www.samnational.org • Represents management executives in industry commerce, government, and education. Fields of interest include management education, policy and strategy, MIS, international management, administration, budgeting, collective bargaining, distribution, incentives, materials handling, quality control, and training.

***Society for Historians of American Foreign Relations Newsletter***. Society for Historians of American Foreign Relations, Ohio State University, Dept. of History, 106 Dulles Hall, 230 W 17th Ave. Columbus, OH 43210-1367. Phone: (614)292-1951; Fax: (614)292-2282; Email: shafr@osu.edu • URL: http://www.shafr.org • Quarterly. $15.00 per year.

**Society for Information Management**. 15000 Commerce Pkwy., Ste. C Mount Laurel, NJ 08054. Phone: 800-387-9746; Fax: (856)439-0525; Email: sim@simnet.org • URL: http://www.simnet.org • Provides a diverse membership with a sound infrastructure to pool insights resulting to access to international IT perspectives, continuing education opportunities and an elite network of peer resources through programs designed exclusively for the information management executive. Aims to support IT leaders by increasing the knowledge base of members and associates; giving back to local communities; being the voice of the IT community on critical issues and developing the next generation of effective IT leaders.

**Society for Judgment and Decision Making.** PO Box 3061110 Tallahassee, FL 32306-1110. Phone: (850)644-8231; Fax: (850)644-8234; Email: gbc@rci.rutgers.edu • URL: http://www.sjdm.org • Individuals interested in the study of decision-making. Promotes research and scholarship in the field. Conducts research and educational programs; gathers and disseminates information. Facilitates cooperation between members and researchers and scholars in related fields.

**Society for the Study of Social Problems.** University of Tennessee, 901 McClung Tower Knoxville, TN 37996-0490. Phone: (865)689-1531; Fax: (865)689-1534 • URL: http://www.sssp1.org • An interdisciplinary community of scholars, activists, practitioners, and students endeavoring to create greater social justice through social research. Members are often social scientists working in colleges and universities, in non-profit organizations and in other applied and policy settings.

***Society of Actuaries Yearbook.*** Society of Actuaries, 475 N Martingale Rd., Ste. 600 Schaumburg, IL 60173. Phone: (847)706-3500; Fax: (847)706-3599; Email: feedback@soa.org • URL: http://www.soa.org • Annual. The yearbook houses information from each department within the SOA. Background information, bylaws, statements and other governing documents, recipients of awards and past officer listings are all easily accessible.

**Society of Air Force Physicians.** PO Box 64 Devine, TX 78016-0064. Phone: (830)665-4048; Fax: (830)665-9658; Email: safp2002@aol.com • URL: http://www.acponline.org/about_acp/chapters/usaf • Air Force internists, family practitioners, and specialists in emergency medicine, dermatology, allergy/immunology, and neurology. Seeks to foster advancement of the art and science of medicine in the Air Force; encourage clinical and laboratory investigation; disseminate information.

**Society of Certified Credit Executives.** ACA International, 4040 W 70th St. Minneapolis, MN 55435. Phone: (952)926-6547; Fax: (952)926-1624; Email: aca@acainternational.org • URL: http://www.acainternational.org • A division of the International Credit Association. Credit executives who have been certified through SCCE's professional certification programs. Seeks to improve industry operations while expanding the knowledge of its members. Maintains placement service.

**Society of Corporate Secretaries and Governance Professionals.** 240 W 35th St., Ste. 400 New York, NY 10001. Phone: (212)681-2000; Fax: (212)681-2005 • URL: http://www.governanceprofessionals.org • Corporate secretaries, assistant secretaries, officers and executives of corporations and others interested in corporate practices and procedures. Conducts surveys and research. Sponsors educational programs for members. Maintains a central information and reference service.

**Society of Financial Service Professionals.** 19 Campus Blvd., Ste. 100 Newtown Square, PA 19073-3239. Phone: 800-392-6900 or (610)526-2500; Fax: (610)527-1499; Email: info@financialpro.org • URL: http://www.financialpro.org • Represents the interests of financial advisers. Fosters the development of professional responsibility. Assists clients to achieve personal and business-related financial goals. Offers educational programs, online professional resources and networking opportunities.

**Society of Insurance Financial Management.** PO Box 9001 Mount Vernon, NY 10552. Phone: (914)966-3180; Fax: (914)966-3264; Email: sifm@cinn.com • URL: http://www.sifm.org • Represents insurance company officers and employees in financial management departments. Provides a timely forum for discussing current insurance industry issues relating to financial accounting and reporting, reinsurance, taxation, regulatory developments and other relevant topics.

***Society of Leather Technologists and Chemists Journal.*** Society of Leather Technologies and Chemists, c/o Mrs. Pat Potter, 8 Copper Leaf Close, Moulton Northampton NN3 7HS, United Kingdom. Fax: 44 1924 460864; Email: office@sltc.org • URL: http://www.sltc.org • Bimonthly. Bimonthly. $75.00 per year. Scientific, technical, historical and commercial papers on leather and allied industries. Contains papers covering all topics of associated interest with other sections devoted to news of new products/processes, news of members, meeting reports, notes on relevant publications and our own Axel's Agony Column which deals with topical subjects.

**Society of Manufacturing Engineers - Computer and Automated Systems Techincal Group.** 1 SME Dr. Dearborn, MI 48121. Phone: 800-733-4763 or (313)425-3000; Fax: (313)425-3400; Email: service@sme.org • URL: http://www.arcat.com/arcatcos/cos37/arc37031.html • Sponsored by the Society of Manufacturing Engineers. Formerly Computer and Automated Systems Association.

**Society of Manufacturing Engineers.** One SME Dr. Dearborn, MI 48121. Phone: 800-733-4763 or (313)425-3000; Fax: (313)425-3400; Email: service@sme.org • URL: http://www.sme.org • Professional society of manufacturing engineers, practitioners and management executives concerned with manufacturing technologies for improved productivity. Seeks to advance the science of manufacturing through the continuing education of manufacturing engineers, practitioners and management. Conducts expositions, international seminars and clinics.

**Society of Medical Banking Excellence.** The Medical Banking Project, 401 Pond View Ct. Franklin, TN 37064. Phone: (615)794-2009; Fax: (615)468-7606; Email: info@mbproject.org • Seeks to advance the creation of digital infrastructures to be used to test and implement EDI processing techniques and analytics in medical payment channels.

**Society of Medical Consultants to the Armed Forces.** c/o Kevin G. Berry, Councilor, 5009 Overlea Ct. Bethesda, MD 20816. Phone: (301)320-0847 • URL: http://www.smcaf.org • Professional society of physicians and surgeons who have been in active military service and who have acted as consultants to the Surgeons General of the Army, Navy, or Air Force. Preserves and encourages the association of civilian consultants and military medical personnel and assists in the development and maintenance of the highest standards of medical practice in the Armed Forces.

**Society of Military Orthopaedic Surgeons.** 110 W Rd., Ste. 227 Towson, MD 21204. Phone: 866-494-1778; Fax: (410)494-0515; Email: info@somos.org • URL: http://www.somos.org • Orthopedic surgeons who have served in the active or reserve military. Seeks to stimulate scholarly contribution by military medical residents; act as clearinghouse; provides opportunities for consultation with and contributions of surgeons who are retired from the military; furthers the continuing education of orthopedic surgeons and residents. Presents scientific papers at annual meeting.

**Society of Military Otolaryngologists - Head and Neck Surgeons.** PO Box 923 Converse, TX 78109. Email: spearce@att.net • URL: http://www.miloto.org • Otolaryngologists, head and neck surgeons and residents in training of the U.S. Army, Air Force, Navy, and former active duty members. Purposes are to further the social and professional contacts of military otolaryngologists and to advance the science and art of the field.

**Society of Quantitative Analysts.** PO Box 6 Rutledge, MO 63563. Phone: 800-918-7930; Email: sqa@sqa-us.org • URL: http://www.sqa-us.org • Works for the application of new and innovative techniques in finance, with particular emphasis on the use of quantitative techniques in investment and risk management. Sponsors a half-day program in the fall and a Fuzzy Day seminar in the spring on an exploratory topic.

**Society of the Fifth Division.** c/o Bobby Moody-Kirsten, President, 2124 3 & 21 Rd. Easley, SC 29642-8350. Phone: (864)859-9952 • URL: http://www.societyofthefifthdivision.com • Works to perpetuate and memorialize the valiant acts and patriotic deeds of the Fifth Division.

**Society of the 3rd Infantry Division.** c/o Kathleen M. Daddato, Membership Chairperson, 22511 N River Rd. Alva, FL 33920-3358. Phone: (239)728-2475 • URL: http://www.warfoto.com/3rdiv.htm • Past and present members of the 3rd Infantry Division of the U.S. Army and attached and supporting units; families of veterans of the division. Fosters and strengthens associations and friendships formed during service with the Third Infantry Division. Honors the Third Infantry Division War Dead and perpetuates their memory. Encourages and achieves the mutual benefit and support resulting from a close and cooperative alliance between the Society and the Third Infantry Division, U.S. Army. Supports the government of the United States. Assists in the maintenance of monuments dedicated to the Third Infantry Division. Organizes and conducts wreath laying and memorial ceremonies.

***Sociological Abstracts.*** ProQuest L.L.C., 789 E Eisenhower Pkwy. Ann Arbor, MI 48106-1346. Phone: 800-521-0600 or (734)761-4700; Fax: (734)662-4554; Email: info@proquest.com • URL: http://www.proquest.com • Monthly. A compendium of non-evaluative abstracts covering the field of sociology and related disciplines.

***Sock Shop.*** Entrepreneur Press, 2445 McCabe Way, Ste. 400 Irvine, CA 92614-6244. Phone: 800-864-6864 or (949)261-2325 or (949)622-7131; Fax: (949)261-7729 or (949)261-0234; Email: press@entrepreneur.com • URL: http://www.entrepreneurpress.com • Looseleaf. $59.50. A practical guide to starting a store that sells stockings of various kinds. Covers profit potential, start-up costs, market size evaluation, owner's time required, site selection, lease negotiation, pricing, accounting, advertising, etc. (Start-Up Business Guide No. E1340.).

***Soft Drink Letter.*** Whitaker Newsletters Inc., 313 S Ave. Fanwood, NJ 07023-0192. Phone: 800-359-6049 • Description: Covers news pertaining to the beverage industry with emphasis on soft drinks, mixers, and bottled water. Includes reports on new products and federal/state regulations, interviews with leading industry executives, marketing trends, and advertising and marketing research.

***Soft-Letter: Trends and Strategies in Software Publishing.*** UCG Technologies, 11300 Rockville Pike, Ste. 1100 Rockville, MD 20852-3030. Phone: (301)287-2718; Fax: (301)924-3944; Email: jtarter@softletter.com • URL: http://www.softletter.com • Monthly. $399 Individuals 1 year; $689 Individuals 2 years - 24 issues; $869 Individuals 3 years - 36 issues. Newsletter on the software industry, including new technology and financial aspects.

***Software Development.*** Miller Freeman Inc., 600 Harrison St. San Francisco, CA 94107. Phone: (415)905-2200; Fax: (415)905-2232 or (415)356-3480; Email: kgates@mfi.com • URL: http://www.telehealthmag.com • Monthly. $39.00 per year. Edited for professional software developers and managers.

***Software Digest: The Independent Comparative Ratings Report for PC and LAN Software.*** NSTL, 670 Sentry Pky, 2nd Fl. Blue Bell, PA 19422. Phone: 800-257-2402 or (610)832-8400; Fax: (610)941-9952 • URL: http://www.nstl.com • 12 times a year. $450.00 per year. Critical evaluations of personal computer software.

***Software Economics Letter: Maximizing Your Return on Corporate Software.*** Computer Economics Inc., 2082 Business Center Dr., Ste. 240 Irvine, CA 92612-1164. Phone: (949)831-8700; Fax: (949)442-7688; Email: info@computereconomics.com • URL: http://www.computereconomics.com • Monthly. $395.00 per year. Newsletter for information systems managers. Contains data on business software trends, vendor licensing policies, and other corporate software management issues.

***Software Magazine.*** Wiesner Publishing, Inc., 7009 S. Potomac St., Suite 200 Englewood, CA 80112. Phone: 800-669-5613 or (303)397-7600; Fax: (303)397-7619 • URL: http://www.softwaremaqazine.com • Monthly. Free to qualified personnel; others, $42.00 per year.

***Software Store.*** Entrepreneur Press, 2445 McCabe Way, Ste. 400 Irvine, CA 92614-6244. Phone: 800-864-6864 or (949)261-2325 or (949)622-7131; Fax: (949)261-7729 or (949)261-0234; Email: press@entrepreneur.com • URL: http://www.entreneurpress.com • Looseleaf. $59.50. A practical guide to opening a computer software retail establishment. Covers profit potential, start-up costs, market size evaluation, owner's time required, site selection, lease negotiation, pricing, accounting, advertising, promotion, etc. (Start-Up Business Guide No. E1261.).

***SOHO Journal.*** National Association for the Cottage Industry, PO Box 14460 Chicago, IL 60614. Phone: (312)472-8116; Fax: (312)880-2409 • Members, $25.00 per year; libraries, $35.00 per year. Newsletter on home businesses. Formerly *Mind Your Own Business at Home*.

***Soil Science: An Interdisciplinary Approach to Soils Research.*** Lippincott Williams & Wilkins, 2 Commerce Sq., 2001 Market St. Philadelphia, PA 19103. Phone: 800-638-3030 or (301)223-2300; Email: ronna.ekhouse@wolterskluwer.com • URL: http://www.lww.com • Monthly. Monthly. Individuals, $182.00 per year; institutions, $336.00 per year.

**Solar Energy and Energy Conversion Laboratory.** University of Florida, Dept. of Mechanical Engineering, 231 MAE-A Gainesville, FL 32611. Phone: (352)392-0961; Fax: (352)392-7303; Email: solar@cimar.me.ufl.edu • URL: http://www.mse.ufl.edu.

***Solar Energy Businesses in the World.*** Momentum Technologies L.L.C., PO Box 460813 Glendale, CO 80246. Phone: (303)229-4841; Fax: (408)705-2031 • URL: http://www.mtt.com • Contains detailed directory listings and contact information for more than 16,302 solar energy businesses in operation throughout the world. Includes business name, address, phone and fax numbers, and online contact addresses. Includes brief descriptions of product lines, services offered, and business type. Covers businesses manufacturing, selling, or distributing solar electric power systems, solar heating systems, photovoltaic modules, solar water pumping systems, and more. Searchable by product, location, business type, company name, and keyword.

***Solar Energy: International Journal for Scientists, Engineers and Technologists Energy and Its Application.*** International Solar Energy Society. Elsevier, Secondary Publishing Division, 650 Ave. of the Americas New York, NY 10011. Phone: 888-437-4636 or (212)633-3980; Fax: (212)633-3975; Email: t.reller@elsevier.com • URL: http://www.elseveier.com • 4,168 Institutions.

***Solar Energy.*** U. S. Government Printing Office, 732 N Capitol St. NW Washington, DC 20401. Phone: 866-512-1800 or (202)512-1800 or (866)512-1800; Fax: (202)512-2104 or (202)512-2250; Email: contactcenter@gpo.gov • URL: http://www.gpo.gov • Annual. Free. Lists government publications. GPO Subject Bibliography Number 9.

***Solid State and Superconductivity Abstracts.*** Cambridge Scientific Abstracts L.P., 7200 Wisconsin Ave., Ste. 601 Bethesda, MD 20814. Phone: 800-843-7751 or (301)961-6700 or (301)961-6785; Fax: (301)961-6720 or (301)961-6708; Email: sales@proquest.com • URL: http://www.proquest.co.uk • Monthly. Covers chemistry, physics, metallurgy, resonance, materials, measurement, and superconductivity theories, applications, and problem areas. Formerly *Solid State Abstracts Journal*.

**Solid-State Device and Materials Research Laboratory.** School of Electrical and Computer Engineering, Purdue University, 465 Northwestern Ave. West Lafayette, IN 47907. Phone: (765)494-3540; Fax: (765)494-6441; Email: miller@ecn.purdue.edu • URL: http://www.ece.purdue.edu.

***Solid State Technology.*** PennWell Corp., Advanced Technology Div., 98 Spit Brook Rd. Nashua, NH 03062-5737. Phone: 800-225-0556 or (603)891-0123; Fax: (603)891-9294; Email: atd@pennwell.com • URL: http://www.pennwell.com •

8/year. $258 Individuals; $360 Canada; $434 Other countries; $130 Individuals online only. Covers the technical and business aspects of semiconductor and integrated circuit production. Includes *Buyers Guide*.

***Solid Waste Report: Resource Recovery-Recycling-Collection-Disposal***. Business Publishers Inc., PO Box 17592 Baltimore, MD 21297-1592. Phone: 800-223-8720; Fax: (800)508-2592; Email: custserv@bpinews.com • URL: http://www.bpinews.com • Weekly. $627.00 per year. Newsletter. Covers regulation, business news, technology, and international events relating to solid waste management.

***Solomon Islands Business Law Handbook***. International Business Publications, USA, PO Box 15343 Washington, DC 20003. Phone: (202)546-2103; Fax: (202)546-3275; Email: ibpusa@comcast.net • URL: http://ibpus.com • $99.95 Individuals hardcopy, e-book, CD-ROM. Covers: Information on basic business legislation, laws, business climate, export-import regulations, and contacts.

***Solomon Islands Investment and Business Guide***. International Business Publications, USA, PO Box 15343 Washington, DC 20003. Phone: (202)546-2103; Fax: (202)546-3275; Email: ibpusa@comcast.net • URL: http://ibpus.com • $99.95 Individuals hardcopy, e-book, CD-ROM. Covers: Strategic and business information, contacts, regulations and more. An ultimate guide for conducting investment, export-import activity in the country.

***Solutions! The Official Publication of TAPPI and PIMA***. Technical Association of the Pulp & Paper Industry, 15 Technology Pkwy. S, Ste. 115 Peachtree Corners, GA 30092-8200. Phone: 800-332-8686 or (770)446-1400; Fax: (770)446-6947; Email: outreach@tappi.org • URL: http://www.tappi.org • Monthly. Membership. Formerly *TAPPI Journal*.

***Somalia Business Law Handbook***. International Business Publications, USA, PO Box 15343 Washington, DC 20003. Phone: (202)546-2103; Fax: (202)546-3275; Email: ibpusa@comcast.net • URL: http://ibpus.com • $99.95 Individuals hardcopy, e-book, CD-ROM. Covers: Information on basic business legislation, laws and climate, export-import regulations, and contacts.

***Somalia—Productive Sectors of the Economy***. Indigo Publications, 142, rue Montmartre F-75002 Paris, France. Phone: 33 1 4488 2610 or 1 4488 2610; Fax: 33 1 4488 2615 or 1 4488 2615; Email: info@indigo-net.com • URL: http://www.indigo-net.com • Irregular. $500. Covers: Major companies in Somalia, including government services, state and private entities. Entries include: Company name, address, phone, managers, production figures.

***Somerset County Chamber of Commerce Business Directory***. Somerset County Chamber of Commerce, 601 N Center Ave. Somerset, PA 15501. Phone: (814)445-6431 or (814)445-1548; Fax: (814)443-4313; Email: info@somersetcountychamber.com • URL: http://www.somersetcountychamber.com • Covers: Area businesses.

***Sonoma County International Trade Directory***. Sonoma County Economic Development Board, c/o Ben Stone, Director, 141 Stony Cir., Ste. 110 Santa Rosa, CA 95401. Phone: (707)565-7170; Fax: (707)565-7231 • URL: http://www.sonoma-county.org/edb • Irregular. $5 plus $2.00 shipping. Covers: Approximately 100 government agencies, banks, foreign consulates, and international chambers of commerce located in Sonoma County, California that provide international trade assistance. Database includes: Publications on the topic, guide to overseas communications, pertinent government regulations. Entries include: Company or organization name, address, phone, names and titles of key personnel.

***Sound and Communications***. Testa Communications, 25 Willowdale Ave. Port Washington, NY 11050-3716. Phone: (516)767-2500; Fax: (516)767-9335; Email: testa@testa.com • URL: http://www.testa.com • Monthly. $15.00 per year. A business, news and technical journal for contractors, consultants, engineers and system managers who design, install and purchase sound and communications equipment. Provides important industry information, also serves as a communicator for the various elements that comprise this strong and dynamic market.

***Sound and Vibration Buyer's Guide***. PO Box 40416 Bay Village, OH 44140. Phone: (440)835-0101; Fax: (440)835-9303; Email: sv@mindspring.com • URL: http://www.sandvmag.com • Annual. Free to qualified personnel. Lists of manufacturers of products for noise and vibration control, dynamic measurements instrumentation, and dynamic testing equipment.

***Sound and Vibration***. Sound and Vibration, 27101 E Oviatt Rd. Bay Village, OH 44140. Phone: (440)835-0101; Fax: (440)835-9303; Email: info@sandv.com • URL: http://www.sandv.com/home.htm • Monthly. Free to qualified subscribers United States; $60 Other countries 12 issues - 1 year; $25 Canada 12 issues - 1 year. Monthly. Free to qualified personnel; others, $60.00 per year.

***Sound & Vision: Home Theater- Audio- Video-MultimediaMovies- Music***. Bonnier AB, Kungsgatan 49 SE-113 90 Stockholm, Sweden. Phone: 46 08 736 40 00; Fax: 46 08 736 40 31; Email: info@bonnier.se • URL: http://www.bonnier.se • 10/year. $12.97 10 issues; $22.97 20 issues. Popular magazine providing explanatory articles and critical reviews of equipment and media (CD-ROM, DVD, etc.). Supplement available *Stereo Review's Sound and Vision Buyers Guide*. Replaces *Stereo Review* and *Video Magazine*.

***The SOURCE: Commercial Buildings Products Guide***. Stamats Business Media, 615 5th St. SE Cedar Rapids, IA 52406-1888. Phone: 800-553-8878; Fax: (319)364-4278; Email: info@stamatsbusinessmedia.com • URL: http://www.stamatsbusinessmedia.com/ • Annual. Lists sources of surface materials, furniture, lighting, etc., for interior designers. Formerly the annual buyers guide.

***Source Directory of Indian, Eskimo, and Aleut Owned-and-Operated Arts and Crafts Businesses***. U.S. Indian Arts and Crafts Board, Rm. 4004-MIB Washington, DC 20240. Phone: (202)208-3773 • Irregular. Covers over 250 Native American-owned businesses specializing in arts and crafts products.

***Sourcebook of Criminal Justice Statistics***. U. S. Government Printing Office, 732 N Capitol St. NW Washington, DC 20401. Phone: 866-512-1800 or (202)512-1800 or (866)512-1800; Fax: (202)512-2104 or (202)512-2250; Email: contactcenter@gpo.gov • URL: http://www.gpo.gov • Annual. $56.00. Issued by the Bureau of Justice Statistics, U. S. Department of Justice (www.usdoj.gov/bjs). Contains both crime data and corrections statistics.

***The Sourcebook of Franchise Opportunities***. QSU Publishing, PO Box 546436 Surfside, FL 33154. Phone: 866-225-3122; Fax: (703)359-8462; Email: news@qsuonline.com • URL: http://www.qsuonline.com • Annual. $35. Covers: Over 3,000 franchising opportunities. Entries include: Franchisor name, address, phone, and profiles are included for approximately 1,000.

***Sourcebooks America CD-ROM***. CACI Marketing Systems, 1100 N Glebe Rd. Arlington, VA 22201-5781. Phone: 800-292-2224 or (703)841-7800; Fax: (703)841-7882 or (703)243-6272 • URL: http://www.caci.com • Annual. $1,250.00. Provides the CD-ROM version of *The Sourcebook of ZIP Code Demographics: Census Edition* and *The Sourcebook of County Demographics: Census Edition*.

***SourceGuide to Food Industry Information***. London Business School Information Service, Sussex Pl., Regents Park London NW1 4SA, United Kingdom. Phone: 71 2625050 or 44 20 7723 3404; Fax: 71 7061897 or 44 20 7706 1897; Email: infoserve@london.edu • URL: http://www.bestofbiz.com • $50. Covers: Sources of information on the food industry available in the U.K., with some international coverage; includes statistics sources, directories, trade journals, trade associations, and online databases. Entries include: Source name, address, phone, type of data available, price.

***SourceGuide to Industrial Market Data***. London Business School Information Service, Sussex Pl., Regents Park London NW1 4SA, United Kingdom. Phone: 71 2625050 or 44 20 7723 3404; Fax: 71 7061897 or 44 20 7706 1897; Email: infoserve@london.edu • URL: http://www.bestofbiz.com • $100. Covers: Directories, yearbooks, journals, statistical sources, market reports, trade and research associations, libraries and information services, and databases that provide data on 14 industrial market sectors in the U.K. Entries include: Source name, address, phone, description, evaluation.

***SourceGuide to Management Information***. London Business School Information Service, Sussex Pl., Regents Park London NW1 4SA, United Kingdom. Phone: 71 2625050 or 44 20 7723 3404; Fax: 71 7061897 or 44 20 7706 1897; Email: infoserve@london.edu • URL: http://www.bestofbiz.com • $50. Covers: Sources of published and unpublished information on management issues available worldwide, including journals, databases and other electronic sources, abstracting and indexing services, reference works, academic working papers, and other relevant materials. Entries include: Source name, address, phone, description.

***SourceGuide to Market Share and Business Ranking Tables***. London Business School Information Service, Sussex Pl., Regents Park London NW1 4SA, United Kingdom. Phone: 71 2625050 or 44 20 7723 3404; Fax: 71 7061897 or 44 20 7706 1897; Email: infoserve@london.edu • URL: http://www.bestofbiz.com • $100. Covers: Key U.K., Pan European, and international business ranking and market share information published in 1989 or later and available in U.K. commercial libraries; includines newspapers, journals, directories, and databases. Entries include: Source name, address, phone, description.

***Sources of Free Business Information***. Kogan Page, Limited, 120 Pentonville Rd. London N1 9JN, United Kingdom. Phone: 44 20 72780433 or (440) 2072780433; Fax: 44 20 78376348 or (783)76348; Email: kpinfo@kogan-page.co.uk • URL: http://www.kogan-page.co.uk/ • Irregular. $12.95 hardback; $6.95 paperback. Covers: Free business information and how to obtain it, including taxation, business finance, grants and incentives, exporting and overseas business, general economic and business information, small business advice, legal matters, computers, and investment. Entries include: Providers of information name, address, phone.

***South Africa Business Directory***. Business Guide, PO Box 27669 Dubai, United Arab Emirates. Phone: 971 4 2651719; Fax: 971 4 2692151; Email: sales@africa-business.com • URL: http://www.africa-business.com • $250 Individuals. Covers: 32,600 business listings including wholesalers, importers, retailers, business houses, and agents in South Africa.

***South Africa Business Forecast Report***. Telecommunications Insight, 85 Queen Victoria St. London EC4V 4AB, United Kingdom. Phone: 20 72 465100 or 44 20 7248 0468; Fax: 20 72 480467 or 44 20 7248 0467; Email: enquiries@telecomsinsight.com • URL: http://www.telecomsinsight.com • Quarterly. $1,195 Individuals Single user; $1,795 Individuals Up to 3 users. Business forecast report for South Africa.

**South Africa China Business Association**. 5 Dongzhimen Wai Dajie Beijing 100600, China. Email: secretary@sacba-prc.org • URL: http://www.sacba-prc.org • Strives to strengthen and grow social and business ties between South Africa and China. Promotes social interaction and cultural understanding between South Africa and China through the facilitation of interactive events.

***South Africa Industrial and Business Directory***. International Business Publications, USA, PO Box 15343 Washington, DC 20003. Phone: (202)546-2103; Fax: (202)546-3275; Email: ibpusa@comcast.net • URL: http://ibpus.com • Annual. $99.95 Individuals hardcopy, e-book, CD-ROM. Covers: Strategic industrial, investment and business contacts for conducting export-import and investment activity in the country.

***South Africa National Classified Directory***. A.C. Braby (Pty) Ltd., 12 Caversham Rd. Pinetown 3610, South Africa. Email: support@brabys.co.za • URL: http://www.brabys.com • Annual. Covers: Government and businesses in South Africa. Database includes: Maps.

**South African Venture Capital and Private Equity Association**. PO Box 1140 Houghton 2041, South Africa. Phone: 27 11 2680041; Fax: 27 11 2680527; Email: info@savca.co.za • URL: http://www.savca.co.za • Promotes the venture capital and private equity profession in Southern Africa. Develops and stimulates professional and transactional venture capital and private equity investments.

***South America: A Directory and Sourcebook***. Euromonitor International Business Reference Div., 224 S Michigan Ave., Ste. 1500 Chicago, IL 60604. Phone: (312)922-1115; Fax: (312)922-1157; Email: insight@euromonitorintl.com • URL: http://www.euromonitor.com • $390. Covers: major companies in South America; international and national organizations and statistical agencies, trade journals, electronic databases, consultants, market research firms, research centers, trade associations, trade unions, libraries, and other information sources. Database includes: Overview and statistical tables summarizing the economies of South America and the individual countries. Entries include: For companies—Name, address, phone, fax, telex, line of business, chief executive, number of employees, sales, products, outlets. For others—Organization name or publication title, address, phone, telex, fax, names and titles of key personnel, description of activities or contents.

***South America Mineral Industry Handbook***. International Business Publications, USA, PO Box 15343 Washington, DC 20003. Phone: (202)546-2103; Fax: (202)546-3275; Email: ibpusa@comcast.net • URL: http://ibpus.com • $99.95 Individuals hardcopy, e-book, CD-ROM. Covers: Strategic information and contacts on mining resources and mineral industry on South America.

***South Asian Journal of Global Business Research***. Emerald Group Publishing Ltd., Howard House, Wagon Ln. Bingley BD16 1WA, United Kingdom. Phone: 44 1274 777 700; Fax: 44 1274 785 201 • URL: http://www.emeraldinsight.com • Peer-reviewed journal publishing articles on business and management issues facing multinational and local organizations within South Asia.

***South Carolina Business Directory***. InfoGroup Inc., 5711 S 86th Cir. Omaha, NE 68127-4146. Phone: (402)593-4500 • URL: http://www.infogroup.com • Annual. $795 for both print & CD-ROM. Covers: 172,002 businesses in South Carolina. Entries include: Company name, address, phone, number of employees, name of owner or manager, sales volume. Compiled from telephone company 'Yellow Pages,' statewide. All states covered (see separate entries).

***South Carolina Business Journal***. South Carolina Chamber of Commerce, 1301 Gervais St., Ste. 1100 Columbia, SC 29201. Phone: (803)799-4601; Fax: (803)779-6043; Email: grassroots@scchamber.net • URL: http://www.scchamber.net • Monthly. $25. Business newspaper.

***South Carolina Chamber of Commerce Business Directory & Resource Guide***. South Carolina Chamber of Commerce, 1301 Gervais St., Ste. 1100 Columbia, SC 29201. Phone: (803)799-4601; Fax: (803)779-6043; Email: grassroots@scchamber.net • URL: http://www.scchamber.net • Covers: Member businesses, chambers of commerce, and professional and trade associations in South Carolina.

***South Carolina Industrial Directory***. South Carolina Department of Commerce, 1201 Main St., Ste. 1600 Columbia, SC 29201-3200. Phone: 800-868-7232 or (803)737-0400; Email: info@sccommerce.com • URL: http://sccommerce.com • Annual. Covers: nearly 4,000 industrial companies throughout South Carolina. Entries include: Company name, address, phone, parent company (if applicable), plant address, names of principal executives, whether firm exports or imports, number of employees, product or service provided, Standard Industrial Classification (SIC) code, NAICS code, email, and web addresses.

***South Carolina Investment and Business Guide***. International Business Publications, USA, PO Box 15343 Washington, DC 20003. Phone: (202)546-2103; Fax: (202)546-3275; Email: ibpusa@comcast.net • URL: http://ibpus.com • $99.95 Individuals hardcopy, e-book, CD-ROM. Covers: Strategic and business information, contacts, regulations and more. An ultimate guide for conducting investment, export-import activity in the country.

***South Carroll Business Association—Directory***. South Carroll Business Association, PO Box 1401 Sykesville, MD 21784. • URL: http://www.southcarroll.org • Covers local business owners and managers in South Caroll county.

***South-Central American International Business Directory of Importers***. Coble International, 1420 Steeple Chase Dover, PA 17315. Phone: (717)467-1835 • URL: http://www.importexporthelp.com • $285 print or CD-ROM; $325 print and CD-ROM. Covers: 23,000 importers from the West Indies, Nicaragua, Mexico, Honduras, Guyana, El Salvador, Uruguay, Paraguay, Brazil, Guatemala, Belize, Colombia, Costa Rica, Puerto Rico, Dominican Republic, Chile, Haiti, Bahamas, Jamaica, Panama, Peru, Bolivia, Ecuador, Venezuela and Argentina. Entries include: Name, address, phone, fax, primary contact person, list of products, e-mail addresses, and Web site.

***South Central High Technology Firms***. Rich's Business Directories Inc., 1820 Gateway Blvd., Ste. 170 San Mateo, CA 94404. Phone: 800-969-7424 or (650)362-1020; Fax: (650)350-4084; Email: info@richsdata.com • URL: http://www.hightechdirectories.com • $199 Individuals 1 year premium online; $99 Individuals 1 year online; $215 Individuals database download. Covers: Approximately 2,221 high tech research, manufacturing, and development firms in south central United States (Arkansas, Louisiana, and Oklahoma). Entries include: Company name, address, phone, names and titles of key personnel, year established, number of employees, type of ownership, annual sales volume, product service provided, SIC code.

***South East Business***. Evegate Publishing Ltd., South East Business, Spicer House, Lympne Business Park, Hythe Kent CT21 4LR, United Kingdom. Phone: 44 1303 233885; Fax: 44 1303 239517 • URL: http://www.southeastbusiness.net • Monthly. £40 Individuals; £57 Elsewhere. Professional magazine covering local business news.

***South Florida Business Journal***. The Business Journals, 120 W. Morehead St., Ste. 400 Charlotte, NC 28202. Phone: (704)973-1000; Fax: (704)973-1001; Email: info@bizjournals.com • URL: http://www.bizjournals.com/ • $91 Individuals. Newspaper covering business in Miami, Fort Lauderdale, and West Palm Beach.

***South Shore Business Journal***. Mariner Newspapers, 254 2nd Ave. Needham, MA 02494. Phone: (781)837-3500; Fax: (781)837-4540 • URL: http://www.tomonline.com • Monthly. Tabloid covering business news in Plymouth and Norfolk counties.

***South Sound Christian Business Directory***. Red Letter Publishing, PO Box 272682 Fort Collins, CO 80527. Phone: 800-445-5614; Fax: (970)267-9669; Email: info@redletter.com • URL: http://www.christianbusinessdirectoryonline.com • Businesses, churches, organizations, and schools in Seattle South Sound.

***Southeast Asia's Chinese Businesses in an Era of Globalization***. Cengage Learning Inc., 20 Channel Center St. Boston, MA 02210. Phone: 800-487-8488 or (617)289-7700; Fax: (617)289-7844; Email: investors@cengage.com • URL: http://www.cengage.com • 2009. eBook. Published by Institute of Southeast Asian Studies. Addresses the rise of China and its impacts on Southeast Asia's economies and businesses, especially on those of ethnic Chinese.

***Southeastern Fisheries Association***. 1118-B Thomasville Rd. Tallahassee, FL 32303. Phone: (850)224-0612; Fax: (850)222-3663; Email: info@sfaonline.org • URL: http://www.sfaonline.org/ • Producers, distributors and suppliers of seafood in the South Atlantic and Gulf of Mexico areas. Disseminates information on legislation, both proposed and implemented, that affects fishermen in that area. Promotes and represents commercial fishermen's interests in legislative, industrial and environmental matters. Provides HAACP training onsite.

***Southern Africa Institute for Management Services***. PO Box 7045, Centurion Tshwane 0046, South Africa. Phone: 27 79 4979183; Fax: 27 86 5587183; Email: saimas@global.co.za • URL: http://www.saimas.org.za • Maintains professional standards for the management services practice. Seeks to improve professional expertise. Promotes the education and training of persons who enter, or intend to enter the field of management services.

***Southern California Business Directory and Buyers Guide***. Dun & Bradstreet Inc., 103 JFK Pkwy. Short Hills, NJ 07078. Phone: 800-526-0651 or (973)921-5500 or (973)921-5000; Fax: (866)560-7035 or (512)794-7670; Email: info@dnb.com • URL: http://www.dnb.com • Annual. $220 Individuals. Covers: 174,700 Southern California businesses. Database includes: Statistical data, trade show calendar. Entries include: Company name, address, county, phone, fax, number of employees, names and titles of key executives, plant size, year established, parent company, annual sales, import/export information, Standard Industrial Classification (SIC) code, and product description.

***Southern California Business Directory***. Harris InfoSource, 2057 E Aurora Rd. Twinsburg, OH 44087-1999. Phone: 800-888-'5900 or (330)425-9000 or (973)921-5500; Fax: (800)643-5997 or (877)252-3375; Email: customerservice@harrisinfo.com • URL: http://www.harrisinfo.com • Profiles 32,000 top companies in the 13 Southern California counties and lists the

names and titles of 81,412 CEOs, owners, and key executives. The listings include company name and address; telephone, fax, and toll-free numbers; Web site email addresses; number of employees; annual sales; products and services; SIC codes; export/import indicators; and primary bank.

***Southern Lumberman***. Hatton-Brown Publishers Inc., 225 Hanrick St. Montgomery, AL 36102. Phone: 800-669-5613 or (334)834-1170; Fax: (334)834-4525; Email: dianne@hattonbrown.com • URL: http://www.hattonbrown.net • Monthly. $23.00 per year. Controlled circulation. A magazine for the sawmill industry.

***Southern Methodist University - Geothermal Laboratory***. Heroy Hall, Rm. 235, Department of Earth Sciences, 3225 Daniel Ave. Dallas, TX 75205. Phone: (214)768-2749; Email: blackwel@smu.edu • URL: http://smu.edu/geothermal • Temperature history of sedimentary basins, geothermal regime of North America, and geothermal systems in the Western U.S., especially, Nevada, the Cascade Range and the Snake River Plains. Oil and Gas well conversion to geothermal energy production.

***Southern Ulster County Chamber of Commerce Business Directory***. Southern Ulster County Chamber of Commerce, PO Box 320 Highland, NY 12528. Phone: (845)691-6070; Fax: (845)691-9194; Email: info@southernulsterchamber.org • URL: http://www.southernulsterchamber.org • Annual. Covers bsinesses and local organizations in southern Ulster County, NY.

***Southern U.S. Trade Association***. 701 Poydras St., Ste. 3725 New Orleans, LA 70139. Phone: (504)568-5986; Fax: (504)568-6010; Email: susta@susta.org • URL: http://www.susta.org • The Southern U.S. Trade Association (SUSTA) promotes the export of high-value food and agricultural products internationally. SUSTA works closely on an individual basis with its export company members to develop and expand their share of agricultural export markets through partnering with the Department of Agriculture to provide southern U.S. companies discounted booth space at international trade exhibitions, and inbound and outbound trade missions. SUSTA facilitates the MAP Branded Program that reimburses up to 50% of certain international marketing and promotion expenses, including eligible tradeshows, instore displays, and required label changes.

***Southwest Case Research Association***. Augusta State University, Knox School of Accountancy, Hull College of Business, 2500 Walton Way Augusta, GA 30904-2200. Phone: (706)667-4541 • URL: http://www.swcrahome.org • Promotes research, writing, and publication of decision-based cases for graduate and undergraduate business studies.

***Southwestern Financial Directory: 11th Fed, Dallas***. Accuity Inc., 4709 W Golf Rd. Skokie, IL 60076. Phone: 800-321-3373 or (847)676-9600; Fax: (847)933-8101; Email: custserv@accuitysolutions.com • URL: http://www.accuitysolutions.com • Semiannual. $400 Individuals. Holding companies, head offices and branches of every commercial bank, Savings & Loan, and credit union over $5 million in the states of Arkansas, Louisiana, New Mexico, Oklahoma, and Texas.

***Souvenirs, Gifts & Novelties Magazine—Buyer's Guide Issue***. Kane Communications Inc., 10 E Athens Ave., Ste. 208 Ardmore, PA 19003. Phone: (610)645-6940; Fax: (610)645-6943; Email: sounovmag@aol.com • URL: http://www.kanec.com • Annual. Publication includes: List of 1,000 manufacturers, wholesalers, and importers of souvenirs, gifts, apparel, toys, jewelry novelty, and candle items. Entries include: Company name, address, phone, products, whether firm is manufacturer, wholesaler, or importer.

***Soviet Trade Directory***. Flegon Press, 37B New Cavendish St. London W1M 8JR, United Kingdom. Phone: 44 181 752 1296; Fax: 44 181 752 1296 • $200. Covers: Over 20,000 listings of ex-Soviet plants, factories, and enterprises in all branches of industry. Entries include: Company name and address.

***Soya and Oilseed Bluebook***. Soyatech, Inc., Seven Pleasant St. Bar Harbour, ME 04609. Phone: 800-424-7692 or (207)288-4969; Fax: (207)288-5264; Email: data@soyatech.comm • URL: http://www.soyatech.com • Annual. $70.00. Includes quarterly *Bluebook Update*. Formerly *Soya Bluebook Plus*. Contains more than 3,300 company listings and references to over 400 individual products, supplies, equipment systems or services.

***Soybean Abstracts***. CABI Publishing North America, 38 Chauncey St., Ste. 1002 Boston, MA 02111. Phone: 800-552-3083; Email: cabi-nao@cabi.org • URL: http://www.cabi.org • Weekly. Searchable database of soybean research. Provides worldwide coverage of the literature.

***Space Institute - University of Tennessee***. B.H. Goethert Pky;, MS01 Tullahoma, TN 37388-9700. Phone: (931)393-7213; Fax: (931)393-7211; Email: tmccay@utsi.edu • URL: http://www.utsi.edu.

***Space Sciences: Macmillan Science Library***. Cengage Learning Inc., 20 Channel Center St. Boston, MA 02210. Phone: 800-487-8488 or (617)289-7700; Fax: (617)289-7844; Email: investors@cengage.com • URL: http://www.cengage.com • $690 Individuals. 2012. $629.00. Four volumes. Includes business and economic aspects of aerospace technology. (Macmillan Reference USA imprint, Macmillan Science Library). eBook also available.

***Spain: A Directory and Sourcebook***. Euromonitor International

Business Reference Div., 224 S Michigan Ave., Ste. 1500 Chicago, IL 60604. Phone: (312)922-1115; Fax: (312)922-1157; Email: insight@euromonitorintl.com • URL: http://www.euromonitor.com • $390. Publication includes: Lists of major companies and sources of information regarding to consumer markets in Spain. Database includes: Statistics. Entries include: Company or organization name, address, phone, telex, names and titles of key personnel, description. Principal content of publication is an overview of issues affecting Spain.

***Spain Business Law Handbook***. International Business Publications, USA, PO Box 15343 Washington, DC 20003. Phone: (202)546-2103; Fax: (202)546-3275; Email: ibpusa@comcast.net • URL: http://ibpus.com • $99.95 Individuals hardcopy, e-book, CD-ROM. Covers: Information on basic business legislation, tax, investment, laws, export-import regulations, and contacts.

***Spain Business Services Providers Leads***. Business Information Agency Inc. PlanetInform, 52 Tuscan Way, Ste. 202-181 Saint Augustine, VA 32092. Phone: (904)342-6124; Fax: (904)592-2632; Email: info@biasales.com • URL: http://www.biasales.com • Monthly. $230 Individuals mailing list; $485 Individuals sales list; $820 Individuals marketing list. Covers Spanish companies and all sub-industries that provide various services to commercial businesses, establishments, and organizations, including consulting, advertising and marketing services, and facilities maintenance.

***Spain Government and Business Contacts Handbook***. International Business Publications, USA, PO Box 15343 Washington, DC 20003. Phone: (202)546-2103; Fax: (202)546-3275; Email: ibpusa@comcast.net • URL: http://ibpus.com • $99.95 Individuals hardcopy, e-book, CD-ROM. Covers: Strategic government and business information, export-import activity in the country, investment, business contacts and regulations.

***Spain Industrial and Business Directory***. International Business Publications, USA, PO Box 15343 Washington, DC 20003. Phone: (202)546-2103; Fax: (202)546-3275; Email: ibpusa@comcast.net • URL: http://ibpus.com • Annual. $99.95 Individuals hardcopy, e-book, CD-ROM. Covers: Strategic industrial, investment and business contacts for conducting export-import and investment activity in the country.

***Spain-Portugal Mergers and Acquisitions Directory***. S.p.A., Lagasca 27-1-E E-28001 Madrid, Spain. Phone: 349 1 5759350; Fax: 349 1 5759962; Email: 101363.1076@compuserve.com • Biennial. Covers: 200 banks, brokers, auditors, lawyers of the mergers and acquisitions sector with the names of the principals in Spain and Portugal. Entries include: Company name, names and titles of key personnel, number of employees, financial data, branch office name and address, description, services provided.

***Spain's 30,000 Top Companies***. Dun & Bradstreet Inc., 103 JFK Pkwy. Short Hills, NJ 07078. Phone: 800-526-0651 or (973)921-5500 or (973)921-5000; Fax: (866)560-7035 or (512)794-7670; Email: info@dnb.com • URL: http://www.dnb.com • Annual. $385. 15,000 companies in Spain with annual sales of at least $500,000.

***Spanish-American Commercial Directory***. IBAR, Apartado Postal 14013 E-29080 Madrid, Spain. • Triennial. $60. Covers: More than 350,000 businesses in Spain, Portugal, and Latin-American countries, as well as companies in African, Asia, Australia, Canada, and Europe interested in conducting business with Latin-American countries. Entries include: Company name, address, phone.

***Spanish Business Directory***. INFOT Inc., PO Box 2052 Rockville, MD 20847. Phone: 866-838-2619 • URL: http://www.infotusa.com • $72.25 CD-ROM; additional $125 for MS Access format. Covers: 86,807 selected businesses from the Spanish-speaking countries. Entries include: Name, physical address, email and website addresses, telephone and fax number, business description etc.

***Spanish Confederation of Business Organisations***. Calle Diego de Leon, 50 E-28006 Madrid, Spain. Phone: 34 91 5663400; Fax: 34 91 5622562; Email: ceoe@ceoe.es • URL: http://www.ceoe.es • Represents the Spanish business community in all sectors, including agriculture, industry and services.

***Sparks Chamber of Commerce—Business Directory***. Sparks Chamber of Commerce, 1420 Scheels Dr., Ste. E108 Sparks, NV 89434. Phone: (775)636-9560; Fax: (775)337-3038; Email: info@sparkschamber.org • URL: http://cityofsparks.us/visiting/reno-sparks-chamber-commerce • Covers 1,500 business members in Spark, Nevada.

***The Special Event Magazine***. Penton, 1166 Avenue of the Americas New York, NY 10036. Phone: (212)204-4200; Email: information@penton.com • URL: http://www.penton.com • Monthly. $48.00 per year. Edited for professionals concerned with parties, meetings, galas, and special events of all kinds and sizes. Provides practical ideas for event planning. Formerly *Special Events*.

***Special Interest Autos***. Watering Inc., Special Interest Publications, PO Box 904 Bennington, VT 05201. Phone: (802)442-3101; Fax: (802)447-1561; Email: hmnmail@hemmings.com • URL: http://www.hemmings.com • Bimonthly. $19.95 per year.

***Special Situations Newsletter: In-Depth Survey of Under-Valued Stocks***. Charles Howard Kaplan, 26 Broadway, Suite 200 New York, NY 10004-1703. Phone: 800-756-1811 or (201)418-4411; Fax: (201)418-5085 • Monthly. $75.00 per year. Newsletter. Principal content is "This Month's Recommendation," a detailed analysis of one special situation stock.

***Specialty Advertising***. Entrepreneur Press, 2445 McCabe Way, Ste. 400 Irvine, CA 92614-6244. Phone: 800-864-6864 or (949)261-2325 or (949)622-7131; Fax: (949)261-7729 or (949)261-0234; Email: press@entrepreneur.com • URL: http://www.entrepreneurpress.com • Looseleaf. $59.50. A practical guide to starting a business dealing in advertising specialties. Covers profit potential, market size evaluation, start-up costs, pricing, accounting, advertising, promotion, etc. (Start-Up Business Guide No. E1292.).

***Specialty Baker's Voice***. Specialty Bakery Owners of America, 1568 Ralph Ave. Brooklyn, NY 11236-3129. Phone: (212)227-7754 • Monthly. $25.00 per year.

***Specialty Coffee Retailer: The Coffee Business Monthly***. RCM Enterprises Inc., 2233 University Ave. W, Ste. 410 Saint Paul, MN 55114-1600. Phone: 800-451-9278 or (651)523-0666; Fax: (612)473-7068 • Monthly. $5 Single issue; $36 Canada; $45 US; $95 Other countries. Magazine reporting on new products, equipment, trends and management techniques for retail specialty coffee businesses.

***Specialty Fabrics Review Buyer's Guide***. Industrial Fabrics Association International, 1801 County Rd. B W Roseville, MN 55113-4061. Phone: 800-225-4324 or (651)222-2508; Fax: (651)631-9334; Email: generalinfo@ifai.com • URL: http://www.ifai.com • Annual. $69 U.S. two years; $79 Canada two years; $169 Other countries two years. Guide to services, products, and supplies for the specialty fabric industry.

***Specialty Fabrics Review***. Industrial Fabrics Association International, 1801 County Rd. B W Roseville, MN 55113-4061. Phone: 800-225-4324 or (651)222-2508; Fax: (651)631-9334; Email: generalinfo@ifai.com • URL: http://www.ifai.com • Monthly. $69 Two years /year in U.S.; $79 Two years /year in Canada and Mexico; $169 Two years /year outside U.S. Magazine covering the technical and industrial fabrics industries.

***Spectra***. National Communication Association, 1765 N St. NW Washington, DC 20036. Phone: (202)464-4622 or (202)467-4868; Fax: (202)464-4600 or (202)872-1331; Email: nkidd@natcom.org • URL: http://www.natcom.org • Description: Discusses forensics, interpretation, interpersonal communication, rhetoric and public address, communication theory, mass media, theater, speech and language sciences, and job advertising. Recurring features include official business of the Association, news briefs concerning members, and notices of available materials.

***Spectrum: Journal of State Government***. Chief Officers of State Library Agencies, 201 E Main St., Ste. 1405 Lexington, KY 40507. Phone: 800-800-1910 or (859)514-9151 or (859)244-8000; Fax: (859)514-9166 or (859)244-8001; Email: lsingler@amrms.com • URL: http://www.cosla.org • Quarterly. $49.99 Individuals; $15.99 Single issue. State government journal. Formerly *Journal of State Government*.

***Sport, Business and Management***. Emerald Group Publishing Ltd., Howard House, Wagon Ln. Bingley BD16 1WA, United Kingdom. Phone: 44 1274 777 700; Fax: 44 1274 785 201 • URL: http://www.emeraldinsight.com • Peer-reviewed journal covering the development of coherent, high-quality body of work in sport, business and management.

***Sport Business***. Sport Business International, 104 Blackfriars Foundry, 156 Blackfriars Rd. London SE1 8EN, United Kingdom. Phone: 44 2077217229 • Monthly. $270 Individuals. Professional magazine covering the business of sports worldwide.

***Sporting Goods Business: The National Newsmagazine of the Sporting Goods Industry***. Nielsen Business Media Inc., 770 Broadway New York, NY 10003-9522. Phone: 866-890-8541 or (646)654-4500 or (646)654-5000; Fax: (646)654-5584 or (646)654-4500; Email: bmcomm@nielsen.com • URL: http://www.nielsenbusinessmedia.com • 16 times a year. Free to qualified personnel; others, $65.00 per year. The national news magazine of the sporting goods industry.

***Sporting Goods Store***. Entrepreneur Press, 2445 McCabe Way, Ste. 400 Irvine, CA 92614-6244. Phone: 800-864-6864 or (949)261-2325 or (949)622-7131; Fax: (949)261-7729 or (949)261-0234; Email: press@entrepreneur.com • URL: http://www.entrepreneurpress.com • Looseleaf. $59.50. A practical guide to starting a retail sporting goods business. Covers profit potential, start-up costs, market size evaluation, owner's time required, site selection, lease negotiation, pricing, accounting, advertising, promotion, etc. (Start-Up Business Guide No. E1286.).

***Sports Industry News: Management and Finance, Regulation and Litigation, Media and Marketing***. Gamepoint Publishing, PO Box 946 Camden, ME 04843. Phone: (207)236-8346 • Weekly. $244.00 per year. Newsletter. Covers ticket promotions, TV rights, player contracts, concessions, endorsements, etc.

***Sports Trend***. Shore Communications Inc., 4 Merritt Ln. Westport, CT 06880-1421. Phone: (203)293-8511 or (203)226-9488; Fax: (203)663-8259; Email: inquiries@shore.com • URL: http://www.shore.com • Monthly. $60 Individuals; $40 Institutions. Magazine serving sporting goods retailers and mass merchandisers with sporting goods departments; covering products related to every major sport.

***Spotlight***. World Affairs Council of Northern California, 312 Sutter St., Ste. 200 San Francisco, CA 94108. Phone: (415)293-4600; Fax: (415)982-5028; Email: info@worldaffairs.org • URL: http://www.worldaffairs.org • Description: Includes one major and 30-40 brief annotated reviews of books on international relations, world politics, and economics. Includes transcripts of council programs.

***Spray Technology and Marketing: The Magazine of Spray Pressure Packaging***. Industry Publications Inc., 3621 Hill Rd. Parsippany, NJ 07054. Phone: (973)331-9545 or (973)331-9545610; Fax: (973)331-9547 or (973)331-9537; Email: info@spraytechnology.com • URL: http://www.spraytechnology.com • Monthly. $30.00 per year. Formerly *Aerosol Age*.

***Springfield and Urbana Business Directory***. Christian Blue Pages, 521 Byers Rd., Ste. 102 Miamisburg, OH 45342. Phone: 800-860-2583 or (937)847-2583 • URL: http://www.christianbluepages.com • Annual. Christian-owned business enterprises in Springfield and Urbana area, Ohio.

***Springfield Christian Business Directory***. Red Letter Publishing, PO Box 272682 Fort Collins, CO 80527. Phone: 800-445-5614; Fax: (970)267-9669; Email: info@redletter.com • URL: http://www.christianbusinessdirectoryonline.com • Businesses, churches, organizations, and schools in Springfield, Illinois.

***SRC Green Book of 5 Trend 35-Year Charts***. Securities Research Co., 400 Talcott Ave. Watertown, MA 02472-2700. Phone: 877-388-4502 or (781)235-0900; Fax: (617)235-9684; Email: src@babson.com • URL: http://www.babson.com • Annual. $150.00. Chart book presents statistical information on the stocks of 400 leading companies over a 35-year period. Each full page chart is in semi-log format to avoid visual distortion. Also includes charts of 12 leading market averages or indexes and 39 major industry groups.

***SRDS Interactive Advertising Source***. Kantar Media SRDS, 1700 Higgins Rd., 5th Fl. Des Plaines, IL 60018-5610. Phone: 800-851-7737 or (847)375-5000; Email: next@srds.com • URL: http://next.srds.com • Quarterly. $569.00 per year. Provides descriptive profiles, rates, audience, personnel, etc., for producers of various forms of interactive or multimedia advertising: online/Internet, CD-ROM, interactive TV, interactive cable, interactive telephone, interactive kiosk, and others.

***Sri Lanka Journal of Tea Science***. Tea Research Institute of Sri Lanka, St. Coombs Talawakale, Sri Lanka. Phone: 94 5258385; Email: info@tri.lk • URL: http://www.tri.lk • Semiannual. $20; $20. Journal covering the tea industry. Text in English. Formerly *Tea Quarterly*.

***SSA Publications on CD-ROM***. U. S. Government Printing Office, 732 N Capitol St. NW Washington, DC 20401. Phone: 866-512-1800 or (202)512-1800 or (866)512-1800; Fax: (202)512-2104 or (202)512-2250; Email: contactcenter@gpo.gov • URL: http://www.gpo.gov • Monthly. Provides updated text of three Social Security Administration publications: *Program Operations Manual; Social Security Handbook; and Social Security Rulings*.

***Stamp Collector***. Krause Publications Inc., 700 E State St. Iola, WI 54990-0001. Phone: 800-726-9966 or (715)445-2214 or (715)445-4612; Fax: (715)445-4087 • URL: http://www.krause.com • Biweekly. $32.98 per year. Newspaper.

***Stamp Exchangers Directory***. Levine Publications, Box 9090 Trenton, NJ 08650. • Annual. $35. Covers: over 1000 people who are interested in exchanging stamps, coins, and other collectibles with Americans; international coverage. Entries include: Name, address, item collected.

***Stamps: The Weekly Magazine of Philately***. American Publishing Co. of New York, 85 Canisteo St. Hornell, NY 14843. Phone: (607)324-2212; Fax: (607)324-1753 • Weekly. $23.50 per year.

***Standard and Poor's Bond Guide***. Standard & Poor's Financial Services L.L.C., 55 Water St. New York, NY 10041. Phone: 877-772-5436 or (212)438-2000; Fax: (212)438-1000; Email: questions@standardandpoors.com • URL: http://www.standardandpoors.com • Monthly. $239.00 per year.

***Standard & Poor's Corporation Records***. Standard & Poor's Financial Services L.L.C., 55 Water St. New York, NY 10041. Phone: 877-772-5436 or (212)438-2000; Fax: (212)438-1000; Email: questions@standardandpoors.com • URL: http://www.standardandpoors.com • Covers: Over 12,000 publicly-owned companies. Entries include: Corporation name, address, detailed descriptions of background, financial structure, and securities.

***Standard & Poor's Corporations***. Dialog OnDisc, 11000 Regency Parkway, Suite 10 Cary, NC 27511. Phone: 800-334-2564 or (919)462-8600; Fax: (919)468-9890; Email: ondisc@dialog.com • URL: http://products.dialog.com/products/ondisc/ • Monthly. Price on application. Produced by Standard & Poor's. Contains three CD-ROM files: Executives, Private Companies, and Public Companies, providing detailed information on more than 70,000 business executives, 55,000 private companies, and 12,000 publicly-traded corporations.

***Standard and Poor's Daily Stock Price Records***. Standard & Poor's Financial Services L.L.C., 55 Water St. New York, NY 10041. Phone: 877-772-5436 or (212)438-2000; Fax: (212)438-1000; Email: questions@standardandpoors.com • URL: http://www.standardandpoors.com • Quarterly. $420 New York Stock Exchange; $441 American Stock Exchange; $530 NASDAQ.

***Standard and Poor's Dividend Record***. Standard & Poor's Financial Services L.L.C., 55 Water St. New York, NY 10041. Phone: 877-772-5436 or (212)438-2000; Fax: (212)438-1000; Email: questions@standardandpoors.com • URL: http://www.standardandpoors.com • Offers detailed data to track and process payments and corporate actions. Covers more than 26,000 equity securities, including an extensive list of more than 16,000 open and closed end funds. Daily. $825.00 per year.

***Standard & Poor's 500 Directory***. Index Products & Services Standard & Poor's Corp., 55 Water St. New York, NY 10041. Fax: (212)438-2000 • Annual. Covers: The 500 companies included in the Standard & Poor's 500 Stock Index. Database includes: Derivative product information including futures, options, options on futures. Entries include: Company name, address, phone, fax, profile.

***Standard & Poor's Industry Surveys***. Standard & Poor's Financial Services L.L.C., 55 Water St. New York, NY 10041. Phone: 877-772-5436 or (212)438-2000; Fax: (212)438-1000; Email: questions@standardandpoors.com • URL: http://www.standardandpoors.com • Semiannual. $1,800.00. Two looseleaf volumes. Includes monthly *Supplements*. Provides detailed, individual surveys of 52 major industry groups. Each survey is revised on a semiannual basis. Also includes "Monthly Investment Review" (industry group investment analysis) and monthly "Trends & Projections" (economic analysis).

***Standard & Poor's MarketScope***. Standard & Poor's Financial Services L.L.C., 55 Water St. New York, NY 10041. Phone: 877-772-5436 or (212)438-2000; Fax: (212)438-1000; Email: questions@standardandpoors.com • URL: http://www.standardandpoors.com • Daily. Covers: Over 7,000 companies in the 'Reference Section' of Standard and Poors database, inculding all NYSE and ASE listed companies and 3,500 NASDAQ listed companies. Database covers: Over 7,000 companies in the 'Reference Section' of Standard and Poors database, including all NYSE and ASE listed companies and 3,500 NASDAQ listed companies. Database includes: Company name, phone, background information, current and historical financial information, earnings and dividend projections (for 1,1 00 major companies). No addresses or locations are given."Action Section," which details financial investment information, including stock market commentaries, company news and analyses, specific buy and sell recommendations on stocks, interest, and exchange rate information.

***Standard and Poor's Ratings Handbook***. Standard & Poor's Financial Services L.L.C., 55 Water St. New York, NY 10041. Phone: 877-772-5436 or (212)438-2000; Fax: (212)438-1000; Email: questions@standardandpoors.com • URL: http://www.standardandpoors.com • Monthly. $275.00 per year. Newsletter. Provides news and analysis of international credit markets, including information on new bond issues. Formerly *Credit Week International Ratings*.

***Standard & Poor's Register of Corporations, Directors and Executives***. Standard & Poor's Financial Services L.L.C., 55 Water St. New York, NY 10041. Phone: 877-772-5436 or (212)438-2000; Fax: (212)438-1000; Email: questions@standardandpoors.com • URL: http://www.standardandpoors.com • Annual. Covers: over 55,000 public and privately held corporations in the United States, including names and titles of over 400,000 officials (Volume 1); 70,000 biographies of directors and executives (Volume 2). Database includes: In Volume 3, lists of new executives, new companies, a corporate "Family Tree," Standard & Poor's 500 composite stock indices, and obituaries. Entries include: For companies—Name, address, phone, names of principal executives and accountants; primary bank, primary law firm, number of employees, estimated annual sales, outside directors, Standard Industrial Classification (SIC) code, product or service provided. For directors and executives—Name, home and principal business addresses, date and place of birth, fraternal organization memberships, business affiliations.

***Standard and Poor's Semi-Weekly Called Bond Record***. Standard & Poor's Financial Services L.L.C., 55 Water St. New York, NY 10041. Phone: 877-772-5436 or (212)438-2000; Fax: (212)438-1000; Email: questions@standardandpoors.com • URL: http://www.standardandpoors.com • Semiweekly. $1,175.00 per year.

***Standard & Poor's SmallCap 600 Guide***. McGraw Hill Financial Inc., 1221 Avenue of the Americas New York, NY 10020-1095. Phone: (212)512-2000; Fax: (212)512-3840 • URL: http://www.mhfi.com • Monthly. $24.95. Contains detailed profiles of the companies included in Standard & Poor's SmallCap 600 Index of stock prices. Includes income and balance sheet data for up to 10 years, with growth and stability rankings for 600 small capitalization corporations.

***Standard & Poor's Statistical Service. Current Statistics***. Standard & Poor's Financial Services L.L.C., 55 Water St. New York, NY 10041. Phone: 877-772-5436 or (212)438-2000; Fax: (212)438-1000; Email: questions@standardandpoors.com • URL: http://www.standardandpoors.com • Monthly. $688.00 per year. Includes 10 *Basic Statistics* sections, *Current Statistics Supplements* and *Annual Security Price Index Record*.

***Standard & Poor's Stock Reports: NASDAQ and Regional Exchanges***. Standard & Poor's Financial Services L.L.C., 55 Water St. New York, NY 10041. Phone: 877-772-5436 or (212)438-2000; Fax: (212)438-1000; Email: questions@standardandpoors.com • URL: http://www.standardandpoors.com • Irregular. $1,100.00 per year. Looseleaf service.

Provides two pages of financial details and other information for each corporation included.

*Standard & Poor's Stock Reports: New York Stock Exchange.* Standard & Poor's Financial Services L.L.C., 55 Water St. New York, NY 10041. Phone: 877-772-5436 or (212)438-2000; Fax: (212)438-1000; Email: questions@standardandpoors.com • URL: http://www.standardandpoors.com • Irregular. $1,295.00 per year. Looseleaf service. Provides two pages of financial details and other information for each corporation with stock listed on the N. Y. Stock Exchange.

*Standard Business Forms for the Entrepreneur.* Entrepreneur Press, 2445 McCabe Way, Ste. 400 Irvine, CA 92614-6244. Phone: 800-864-6864 or (949)261-2325 or (949)622-7131; Fax: (949)261-7729 or (949)261-0234; Email: press@entrepreneur.com • URL: http://www.entrepreneurpress.com • Looseleaf. $59.50. A practical collection of forms useful to entrepreneurial small businesses. (Start-Up Business Guide No. E1319.).

*Standard Directory of Advertisers: The Advertiser Red Book.* LexisNexis, 9443 Springboro Pke. Dayton, OH 45342. Phone: 800-227-4908 or (937)865-6800; Fax: (937)865-1211; Email: legalnotices@lexisnexis.com • URL: http://www.bender.com • Annual. $1,399 Individuals classified 2010; $1,399 Individuals geographical edition 2010; $1,599 Individuals classified with supplements 2010. Covers over 14,000 U.S. and Canadian companies that place over $200,000 worth of national and/or regional advertising.

*Standard Highway Signs, as Specified in the Manual on Uniform Traffic Control Devices.* U. S. Government Printing Office, 732 N Capitol St. NW Washington, DC 20401. Phone: 866-512-1800 or (202)512-1800 or (866)512-1800; Fax: (202)512-2104 or (202)512-2250; Email: contactcenter@gpo.gov • URL: http://www.gpo.gov • Looseleaf. $153.00. Issued by the U. S. Department of Transportation (www.dot.gov). Includes basic manual, with updates for an indeterminate period. Contains illustrations of typical standard signs approved for use on streets and highways, and provides information on dimensions and placement of symbols.

*Standard Periodical Directory.* Oxbridge Communications Inc., 186 5th Ave. New York, NY 10010. Phone: 800-955-0231 or (212)741-0231; Fax: (212)633-2938; Email: info@oxbridge.com • URL: http://www.oxbridge.com • Annual. $1,995 Individuals print version; $995 Individuals digital edition; $1,995 Individuals single user CD-ROM; $2,995 Individuals print and CD-ROM. Covers: 63,000 magazines, journals, newsletters, directories, house organs, association publications, etc., in the United States and Canada. Entries include: Publication current and former title; publisher name, address, phone; names and titles of key personnel; circulation and advertising rates; description of contents; ISSN, year founded, frequency; subscription rates, print method, page size, number of pages.

*Standards Engineering.* Standards Engineering Society, 1950 Lafayette Rd. Portsmouth, NH 03801. Phone: (603)926-0750; Fax: (603)610-7101; Email: admin@ses-standards.org • URL: http://www.ses-standards.org • Bimonthly. $45.00 per year.

*Stanford Business.* Stanford University Stanford Graduate School of Business, 655 Knight Way Stanford, CA 94305-7298. Phone: (650)723-2146; Email: gsb_info@gsb.stanford.edu • URL: http://www.gsb.stanford.edu • Quarterly. $10 U.S. and Canada; $12 Other countries; $14 Other countries faster delivery. Magazine for business school alumni.

*Stanford Journal of Law, Business and Finance.*

**Stanford University - Center for Integrated Systems.** Paul G. Allen Bldg., MS 4070, 420 Via Palou Mall Stanford, CA 94305-4070. Phone: (650)725-3621; Fax: (650)725-0991; Email: rdasher@cis.stanford.edu • URL: http://cis.stanford.edu • Research programs include manufacturing science, design science, computer architecture, semiconductor technology, and telecommunications.

**Stanford University - Center for Primary Care and Outcomes Research.** 117 Encina Commons Stanford, CA 94305-6019. Phone: (650)736-0815; Fax: (650)723-1919; Email: garber@stanford.edu • URL: http://healthpolicy.stanford.edu • Clinical practice and public health, including medical technology assessment, advancement of primary care policy and practice, clinical decision making and practice guideline development, patient safety and quality of care, and medical outcomes.

**Stanford University - Edward L. Ginzton Laboratory.** Spilker Engineering and Applied Sciences, 348 Via Pueblo Mall Stanford, CA 94305. Phone: (650)724-2765; Fax: (650)725-2533; Email: solgaard@stanford.edu • URL: http://www.stanford.edu/group/ginzton • Research fields include low-temperature physics and superconducting electronics.

**Stanford University - W.W. Hansen Experimental Physics Laboratory.** 452 Lomita Mall Stanford, CA 94305-4085. Phone: (650)724-7667; Fax: (650)725-8311; Email: nchristiansen@stanford.edu • URL: http://www.stanford.edu/group/hepl • Conducts large-scale cryogenic research.

**Stanford University - Information Systems Laboratory.** 350 Serra Mall, Department of Electrical Engineering Stanford, CA 94305-9510. Phone: (650)723-3473; Fax: (650)723-8473; Email: abbas@ee.stanford.edu • URL: http://isl.stanford.edu • Research fields include speech coding and recognition.

**Stanford University - Space, Telecommunications and Radioscience Laboratory.** David Packard Electrical & Engineering Bldg., Rm. 356, Department of Electrical Engineering, 350 Serra Mall Stanford, CA 94305-9515. Phone: (650)723-4994; Fax: (650)723-9251; Email: inan@nova.stanford.edu • URL: http://nova.stanford.edu • Radio and radar astronomy, ionospheric physics, high frequency and very low frequency (whistler) propagation, tropospheric sensing and propagation, communication satellite system analysis, telecommunications, environmental monitoring oceanscatter, computer simulation of propagation, satellite measurements, planetary exploration, space plasma physics, signal processing, and telescience.

**Stanford University - Stanford Center for International Development.** Gunn/SIEPR Bldg., 366 Galvez St. Stanford, CA 94305-6015. Phone: (650)725-8730; Fax: (650)725-6069; Email: nhope@stanford.edu • URL: http://scid.stanford.edu • Economic policy problems facing developing countries and countries with economies in transition.

**Stanford University - Stanford Institute for Economic Policy Research.** John A. & Cynthia Fry Gunn Bldg., 366 Galvez St. Stanford, CA 94305-6015. Phone: (650)725-1874; Fax: (650)723-8611; Email: shoven@stanford.edu • URL: http://siepr.stanford.edu • Economic policy issues facing the United States and other countries. Research is conducted through three centers and six programs, focusing on such areas as macroeconomics, regulation, energy economics, policy reform in developing countries, economic growth and technology, tax and budget policy, government and finance.

**Stanford University - Stanford Research Park.** Real Estate Office, Ste. 200, 3160 Porter Dr. Palo Alto, CA 94304. Phone: (650)497-9797; Fax: (650)724-5059; Email: tgriego@stanford.edu • URL: http://lbre.stanford.edu/realestate/research_park • Links research resources of Stanford University with private enterprise.

**Stanford University - Structures and Composites Laboratory.** William F. Durand Bldg., Rm. 054, Department of Aeronautics and Astronautics, 496 Lomita Mall Stanford, CA 94305. Phone: (650)723-3524; Fax: (650)725-3377; Email: fkchang@stanford.edu • URL: http://structure.stanford.edu • Flight vehicle structures and composite materials.

**Stanford University - U.S.-Asia Technology Management Center.** School of Engineering, 450 Serra Mall Stanford, CA 94305. Phone: (650)724-0096; Fax: (650)725-9974; Email: rdasher@stanford.edu • URL: http://asia.stanford.edu • Business and technology trends in advanced electronics, information technology, supply chain management, entrepreneurship in Asia, optoelectronics, nanotechnologies, semiconductor chips, packaging, etc.

*Stanger Report: A Guide to Partnership Investing.* Robert A. Stanger & Company Inc., 1129 Broad St., Ste. 201 Shrewsbury, NJ 07702. Phone: (732)389-3600; Fax: (732)389-1751 • URL: http://www.rastanger.com • Quarterly. $447 Individuals Annual. Includes overall statistics on the size of the current market, quarterly fundraising, current distribution rates and coverage and latest valuation reports for closed non-traded REITs, market updates on new registrations, newly-effective issues and fund closings, secondary market transactions, and more.

*Start-Up and Emerging Companies: Planning, Financing, and Operating the Successful Business, with Forms on Disk.* ALM Media Properties LLC, 120 Broadway, 5th Fl. New York, NY 10271-1100. Phone: (212)457-9400; Fax: (646)417-7705; Email: customercare@alm.com • URL: http://www.alm.com • $925 print + online + ebook; $875 online + ebook. Covers a wide variety of business and legal topics relating to new enterprises. Provides information on venture financing, formation of corporations, tax laws, limited liability companies, employee benefits, contracts, and accounting. Includes a CD-ROM containing more than 75 sample legal forms, clauses, agreements, organizational resolutions, and checklists. (Law Journal Press).

*Start Up and Run Your Own Business.* Cengage Learning Inc., 20 Channel Center St. Boston, MA 02210. Phone: 800-487-8488 or (617)289-7700; Fax: (617)289-7844; Email: investors@cengage.com • URL: http://www.cengage.com • 2010. eBook. Published by Kogan Page. Offers a complete information resource for those looking to set up their own business, including raising finance, taxation, IT, market research and employment issues.

*Start-Up Business Guides.* Entrepreneur Press, 2445 McCabe Way, Ste. 400 Irvine, CA 92614-6244. Phone: 800-864-6864 or (949)261-2325 or (949)622-7131; Fax: (949)261-7729 or (949)261-0234; Email: press@entrepreneur.com • URL: http://www.entrepreneurpress.com • Looseleaf. $59.50 each. Practical guides to starting a wide variety of small businesses.

*Starting a Business from Home.* Cengage Learning Inc., 20 Channel Center St. Boston, MA 02210. Phone: 800-487-8488 or (617)289-7700; Fax: (617)289-7844; Email: investors@cengage.com • URL: http://www.cengage.com • 2009. eBook. Published by Kogan Page. Offers information about running a profitable and successful business from your own home with particular emphasis on opportunities provided by the internet.

*Starting a Successful Business.* Cengage Learning Inc., 20 Channel Center St. Boston, MA 02210. Phone: 800-487-8488 or (617)289-7700; Fax: (617)289-7844; Email: investors@cengage.com • URL: http://www.cengage.com • 2009.

eBook. Published by Kogan Page. Covers topics such as franchises, marketing, publicity, e-business, financial management, business law, recruitment, taxation, insurance, business planning and development.

*Starting a Successful Small Business.* Kogan Page, Limited, 120 Pentonville Rd. London N1 9JN, United Kingdom, Phone: 44 20 72780433 or (440) 2072780433; Fax: 44 20 78376348 or (783)76348; Email: kpinfo@kogan-page.co.uk • URL: http://www.kogan-page.co.uk/ • Irregular. $8.99. Publication includes: List of organizations of assistance to those starting small businesses. Entries include: Organization name, address. Principal content of publication is a discussion of how to set up a successful small business, including marketing, finances, legal questions, employment, and insurance.

*Starting an Online Business for Dummies.* John Wiley & Sons Inc., 111 River St. Hoboken, NJ 07030-5774. Phone: 800-225-5945 or (201)748-6000; Fax: (201)748-6088; Email: info@wiley.com • URL: http://www.wiley.com • $24.99 Individuals paperback. Covers: Information needed to get an online business off the ground: identifying a market need, choosing a Web hosting service, securing transactions, and attracting customers.

*State and Business in Russia.* Maximov Publications, 12, Rozhdestvenka St. 107103 Moscow, Russia. Phone: 7 495 7270260; Fax: 7 495 7270261 or (495) 7270261; Email: info@maximov.com • URL: http://www.maximov.com • Semiannual. Updated twice per year. Covers nearly 100,000 figures in Russian government and business. Available in multiple formats.

*State and Local Communications Report.* Wolters Kluwer Law and Business, 76 9th Ave., 7th Fl. New York, NY 10011-4962. Phone: 800-234-1660 or (212)771-0600; Fax: (800)901-9075 or (301)644-3550 • URL: http://www.wolterskluwerlb.com • Biweekly. $645.00 per year. Newsletter. Formerly *Telecommunications Week.*

*State Capitals.* Wakeman/Walworth Inc., PO Box 7376 Alexandria, VA 22307-7376. Phone: 800-876-2545 or (703)768-9600; Fax: (703)768-9690; Email: newsletters@statecapitals.com • URL: http://statecapitals.com/ • Irregular. Prices may vary. A group of 39 newsletters, with each publication having its own subtitle and topic of relevance to state government.

*State Government News: The Monthly Magazine Covering All Facets of State Government.* Chief Officers of State Library Agencies, 201 E Main St., Ste. 1405 Lexington, KY 40507. Phone: 800-800-1910 or (859)514-9151 or (859)244-8000; Fax: (859)514-9166 or (859)244-8001; Email: lsingler@amrms.com • URL: http://www.cosla.org • Monthly. $39.00 per year.

*State Guard Association of the United States.* 36 Thorn Oak, Ste. 200 Dove Canyon, CA 92679. Phone: (949)888-5792; Fax: (949)888-4799; Email: info@sgaus.org • URL: http://www.sgaus.org • Active and retired officers and enlisted personnel of State Defense Forces (SDF) including State Guard, State Military Reserve, National Reserve, Defense Force, Guard Reserve, and other militia. Promotes the SDF in states where they exist; lobbies on behalf of SDF before state and federal governments; fosters exchange among states to keep members abreast of changes in laws pertaining to the SDF. Seeks to educate the public and disseminates information on the history and mission of the militia and to advocate a viable state militia system.

*State Income Tax Alert.* State Taxation Institute, 4025 W Peterson Ave. Chicago, IL 60646-6085. Phone: 800-TELL-CCH; Fax: (773)866-3895 • Description: Features updates on state income tax issues. Recurring features include a calendar of events, book reviews, and news of educational opportunities.

*State Legislative Report.* National Conference of State Legislatures, 7700 E 1st Pl. Denver, CO 80230-7143. Phone: (303)364-7700; Fax: (303)364-7800; Email: ncslnet-admin@ncsl.org • URL: http://www.ncsl.org • Description: Contains briefings on topics of state legislative concerns covering a broad range of policy issues.

*State Legislatures.* National Conference of State Legislatures, 7700 E 1st Pl. Denver, CO 80230-7143. Phone: (303)364-7700; Fax: (303)364-7800; Email: ncslnet-admin@ncsl.org • URL: http://www.ncsl.org • Description: Provides a national perspective on government and policy in the each state. Features articles on public policy issues.

*The State of Food and Agriculture.* Bernan Associates, 15200 NBN Way Blue Ridge Summit, PA 17214. Phone: 800-865-3457 or (301)459-7666; Fax: (301)459-6988 or (800)865-3450; Email: customercare@bernan.com • URL: http://www.bernan.com • Annual. $75. Published by the Food and Agriculture Organization of the United Nations (FAO). A yearly review of world and regional agricultural and food activities. Includes tables and graphs. Text in English.

*State of the World (year).* Worldwatch Institute, 1400 16th St. NW, Ste. 430 Washington, DC 20036. Phone: (202)745-8092; Fax: (202)478-2534; Email: worldwatch@worldwatch.org • URL: http://www.worldwatch.org • Annual. $22.00. Provides yearly analysis of factors influencing the global environment.

*State of Washington Supervisor of Banking—Annual Report.* Division of Banking Washington State Department of Financial Institutions, 150 Israel Rd., SW Tumwater, WA 98501. Phone: 877-746-4334 or (360)902-8703; Fax: (360)664-2258; Email: dcs@dfi.wa.gov • URL: http://www.dfi.wa.gov • Covers: About 100 state-chartered commercial banks and trust companies, savings banks, and alien banks. Database includes: Composite financial statements for each type of institution, and changes of location for banks, trust companies, and consumer loan offices. Entries include: For banks and trust companies—total assets, deposits.

**State-Owned Companies in Finland.** Advisory Committee on State-Owned Cos., Aleksanterinkatu 4 SF-00100 Helsinki, Finland. Phone: 0 1603583; Fax: 0 1603666 • Annual. Covers: about 13 government-owned manufacturing companies in Finland. Entries include: Company name, address, phone, telex, names and titles of key personnel, number of employees, financial data, subsidiary and branch names and locations.

**State Tax Actions.** National Conference of State Legislatures, 444 North Capitol St. NW, Ste. 515 Washington, DC 20001. Phone: (202)624-5400 or (212)624-5400; Fax: (202)737-1069; Email: ncslnet-admin@ncsl.org. • URL: http://www.ncsl.org • Annual. $35 Individuals List price. Summarizes yearly tax changes by type and by state. Features state-by-state-details about tax actions taken during regular and special legislative sessions.

**State Tax Notes.** Tax Analysts, 400 S Maple Ave., Ste. 400 Falls Church, VA 22046. Phone: 800-955-2444 or (703)533-4400; Fax: (703)533-4444; Email: cservice@tax.org • URL: http://www.tax.org • Weekly. $949.00 per year, including annual CD-ROM. Newsletter. Covers tax developments in all states. Provides state tax document summaries and citations.

**State University of New York at Buffalo - Buffalo Human Rights Center.** 710 John Lord O'Brian Hall, School of Law, North Campus Buffalo, NY 14260-1100. Phone: (716)645-2257; Email: buffalohrc@gmail.com • URL: http://wings.buffalo.edu/law/BHRC • Human rights issues around the globe. The group focuses primarily on economic, cultural and social rights, as well as the relationships between labor, trade, and human rights.

**State Wildlife Laws Handbook.** Government Institutes, 4501 Forbes Bvld., Ste. 200 Lanham, MD 20706. Phone: 800-462-6420 or (301)459-3366; Fax: (301)429-5748; Email: orders@rowman.com • URL: http://rowman.com • $127 Individuals cloth. Publication includes: Listing of state fish and wildlife agencies. Entries include: Name, address, phone. Principal content of publication is an analysis of wildlife management and protection laws for all fifty states.

**The States and Small Business: A Directory of Programs and Activities.** U.S. Small Business Administration - Office of Advocacy, 409 3rd St. SW Washington, DC 20416. Phone: (202)205-6533; Fax: (202)205-6928; Email: advocacy@sba.gov • URL: http://www.sba.gov/advocacy • Irregular. $21. Covers: over 750 state government small business offices, legislative committees, small business conferences. Entries include: Agency name, address, phone; name and title of contact; description of activities; summary of small business legislation, etc.

**The Statesman's Yearbook: Statistical and Historical Annual of the States of the World.** St. Martin's Press, Macmillan Publishers, 175 5th Ave. New York, NY 10010. Phone: (646)307-5151; Fax: (212)598-9173; Email: enquiries@stmartins.com • URL: http://us.macmillan.com/SMP.aspx • Annual. £220 Individuals Hardcover. presents a political, economic and social account of every country of the world together with facts and analysis.

**Statistical Abstract of Latin America.** University of California, Los Angeles, School of Law, 405 Hilgard Ave. Los Angeles, CA 90095-1476. Phone: (310)206-4841 or (310)825-4321 • URL: http://www.law.ucla.edu/home/Default.aspx • Annual. $325.00. Two volumes.

**Statistical Abstract of the United States.** U. S. Government Printing Office, 732 N Capitol St. NW Washington, DC 20401. Phone: 866-512-1800 or (202)512-1800 or (866)512-1800; Fax: (202)512-2104 or (202)512-2250; Email: contactcenter@gpo.gov • URL: http://www.gpo.gov • Annual. $44.00. Issued by the U. S. Bureau of the Census.

**Statistical Annual: Grains, Options on Agricultural Futures.** Chicago Board of Trade, 141 W Jackson Blvd. Chicago, IL 60604-2901. Phone: 800-331-3332 or (312)435-3758 or (312)435-3500; Fax: (312)341-3392 or (312)435-7152; Email: info@cmegroup.com • URL: http://www.cbot.com • Annual. Includes historical data on Wheat Futures, Options on Wheat Futures, Corn Futures, Options on Corn Futures, Oats Futures, Soybean Futures, Options on Soybean Futures, Soybean Oil Futures, Soybean Meal Futures.

**Statistical Annual: Interest Rates, Metals, Stock Indices, Options on Financial Futures, Options on Metals Futures.** Chicago Board of Trade, 141 W Jackson Blvd. Chicago, IL 60604-2901. Phone: 800-331-3332 or (312)435-3758 or (312)435-3500; Fax: (312)341-3392 or (312)435-7152; Email: info@cmegroup.com • URL: http://www.cbot.com • Annual. Includes historical data on GNMA CDR Futures, Cash-Settled GNMA Futures, U. S. Treasury Bond Futures, U. S. Treasury Note Futures, Options on Treasury Note Futures, NASDAQ-100 Futures, Major Market Index Futures, Major Market Index MAXI Futures, Municipal Bond Index Futures, 1,000-Ounce Silver Futures, Options on Silver Futures, and Kilo Gold Futures.

**Statistical Bulletin of the International Office of Cocoa, Chocolate and Sugar Confectionary.** International Confectionery Association, Rue Defacqz 1 B-1000 Brussels, Belgium. Phone: 32 2 32 2 5391800; Fax: 32 2 32 2 5391575;

Email: caobisco@caobisco.eu • URL: http://www.codexalimentarius.org/members-observers/observers/detail/en/c/14558 • Annual.

**Statistical Indicators for Asia and the Pacific.** United Nations Publications, c/o National Book Network, 15200 NBN Way Blue Ridge Summit, PA 17214. Phone: 888-254-4286 or (212)963-7680 or (212)963-8302; Fax: (800)338-4550; Email: unpublications@nbnbooks.com • URL: http://www.unp.un.org • Quarterly. Quarterly. $80.00 per year. Provides data on economic and demographic trends in the region. Text in English.

**Statistical Information on the Financial Services Industry.** American Bankers Association, 1120 Connecticut Ave. NW Washington, DC 20036. Phone: 800-226-5377 or (202)663-5268; Fax: (202)828-5053; Email: custserv@aba.com • URL: http://www.aba.com • Annual. Members, $150.00; non-members, $275.00. Presents a wide variety of data relating to banking and financial services, including consumer economics, personal finance, credit, government loans, capital markets, and international banking.

**Statistical Reports.** National Alcohol Beverage Control Association, 4401 Ford Ave., Ste. 700 Alexandria, VA 22302-1433. Phone: (703)578-4200; Fax: (703)820-3551; Email: nabca.info@nabca.org • URL: http://www.nabca.org • Monthly. Price on application. Includes quarterly and annual cumulations.

**Statistical Theory and Method Abstracts.** International Association for Official Statistics, PO Box 24070 2490 AB The Hague, Netherlands. Phone: 31 70 3375737; Fax: 31 70 3860025; Email: stephen.penneck@ons.gsi.gov.uk • URL: http://www.isi-web.org • Available as a component of Zentralblatt MATH (ZBMATH), referred to as STMA-Z. Contact for pricing.

**Statistical Yearbook for Asia and the Pacific.** United Nations Publications, c/o National Book Network, 15200 NBN Way Blue Ridge Summit, PA 17214. Phone: 888-254-4286 or (212)963-7680 or (212)963-8302; Fax: (800)338-4550; Email: unpublications@nbnbooks.com • URL: http://www.unp.un.org • Annual. $90.00. Includes 56 countries of the region. Contains data on national accounts, trade, industry, banking, wages, consumption, population, and other economic and demographic subjects. Text in English and French.

**Statistical Yearbook for Latin America and the Caribbean. •** Annual. $79.00. Issued by the Economic Commission for Latin America and the Caribbean. Includes a wide variety of economic, industrial, and trade data for Latin American nations. Text in English and Spanish.

**Statistical YearBook of the Electric Power Industry.** Edison Electric Institute, 701 Pennsylvania Ave. NW Washington, DC 20004-2696. Phone: 800-334-5453 or (202)508-5000; Fax: (800)525-5562; Email: eblume@eei.org • URL: http://www.eei.org/Pages/default.aspx • Annual. $550 print or pdf; 270 Members.

**Statistical Yearbook.** United Nations Publications, c/o National Book Network, 15200 NBN Way Blue Ridge Summit, PA 17214. Phone: 888-254-4286 or (212)963-7680 or (212)963-8302; Fax: (800)338-4550; Email: unpublications@nbnbooks.com • URL: http://www.unp.un.org • Annual. $125.00. Contains statistics for about 200 countries on a wide variety of economic, industrial, and demographic topics. Compiled by United Nations Statistical Office.

**Statistics Canada!.** Statistics Canada, 150 Tunney's Pasture Driveway Ottawa, ON, Canada K1A 0T6. Phone: 800-263-1136; Email: infostats@statcan.gc.ca • URL: http://www.statcan.gc.ca • Web site in English and French provides basic statistical information relating to economic and social conditions in Canada: "The Land," "The People," "The Economy," "The State." Includes daily news, latest indicators, products and services, and links to other sites. Keyword searching is provided. Fees: Free.

**Statistics Canada.** 150 Tunney's Pasture Driveway Ottawa, ON, Canada K1A 0T6. Phone: 800-263-1136; Email: infostats@statcan.gc.ca • URL: http://www.statcan.gc.ca • Issues compilations of census data and other facts relating to Canadian business, finance, industry, economics, and society in general. Statistics Canada is the country's national statistical agency, required to collect data according to the Statistics Act.

**Statistics of Income Bulletin.** U. S. Government Printing Office, 732 N Capitol St. NW Washington, DC 20401. Phone: 866-512-1800 or (202)512-1800 or (866)512-1800; Fax: (202)512-2104 or (202)512-2250; Email: contactcenter@gpo.gov • URL: http://www.gpo.gov • Quarterly. $44. Current data compiled from tax returns relating to income, assets, and expenses of individuals and businesses. (U. S. Internal Revenue Service).

**Statistics of Income: Corporation Income Tax Returns.** U.S. Internal Revenue Service. U. S. Government Printing Office, 732 N Capitol St. NW Washington, DC 20401. Phone: 866-512-1800 or (202)512-1800 or (866)512-1800; Fax: (202)512-2104 or (202)512-2250; Email: contactcenter@gpo.gov • URL: http://www.gpo.gov • Annual.

**Statistics of Paper, Paperboard and Wood Pulp.** American Forest and Paper Association, 1101 K St., NW, Ste. 700 Washington, DC 20005. Phone: (202)463-2700; Fax: (202)463-2785;

Email: info@afandpa.org • URL: http://www.afandpa.org • Annual. $395.00. Formerly *Statistics of Paper and Paperboard.*

**Statistics of World Trade in Steel.** United Nations Economic Commission for Europe. • Annual. $90.00.

**Statistics on International Trade in Services.** Organization for Economic Cooperation and Development. Organisation for Economic Co-operation and Development Publications and Information Center, 2001 L St. NW, Ste. 650 Washington, DC 20036-4922. Phone: 800-456-6323 or (202)785-6323; Fax: (202)785-0350; Email: washington.contact@oecd.org • URL: http://www.oecd.org • Annual. $126.00. Presents a compilation and assessment of data on OECD member countries' international trade in services. Covers four major categories for 20 years: travel, transportation, government services, and other services.

**Statistics on Occupational Wages and Hours of Work and on Food Prices.** International Labor Organization, 1828 L St. NW, Ste. 600 Washington, DC 20036. Phone: (202)653-7652 or (202)617-3952; Fax: (202)653-7687 or (202)617-3960; Email: washington@ilo.org • URL: http://www.ilo.org • Annual. Provides international data on wages and hours for 159 occupations within 49 industries. Includes retail prices for 93 food items.

**Statistics Sources.** Cengage Learning Inc., 20 Channel Center St. Boston, MA 02210. Phone: 800-487-8488 or (617)289-7700; Fax: (617)289-7844; Email: investors@cengage.com • URL: http://www.cengage.com • $874 Individuals. 2012. $836.00. 37th edition. Lists sources of statistical information for more than 20,000 topics.

**Steam Electric Market Analysis.** National Mining Association, 101 Constitution Ave. NW, Ste. 500 E Washington, DC 20001-2133. Phone: (202)463-2600 or (202)463-2639; Fax: (202)463-2666 • URL: http://www.nma.org • Monthly. Free to members; non-members, $300.00 per year. Covers 400 major electric power plants, with detailed data on coal consumption and stockpiles. Shows percent of power generated by fuel type. (Publisher formerly National Coal Association.).

**Steel Mill Products.** U.S. Department of Commerce U.S. Census Bureau, 4600 Silver Hill Rd. Washington, DC 20233. Phone: 800-923-8282 or (301)763-4636 or (301)763-3030; Fax: (301)457-4714 or (301)763-6239; Email: webmaster@census.gov • URL: http://www.census.gov/ • Annual. (Current Industrial Reports MA-33B).

**Steel Times International.** Quartz Business Media Ltd., Westgate House, 120/130 Station Rd., Redhill Surrey RH1 1ET, United Kingdom. Phone: 44 1737 855000; Fax: 44 1737 855475 • Bimonthly. £168 Individuals; £302 Two years; £240 Other countries; £432 Two years overseas. Includes *Iron and Steel Directory.*

**Step-By-Step Electronic Design: The How-To Newsletter for Electronic Designers.** Dynamic Graphics Inc., 6000 N Forest Park Dr. Peoria, IL 61614-3556. Phone: 888-698-8545 or (309)688-8800 or (309)688-2300; Fax: (309)688-8809 or (309)688-3075; Email: service@dgusa.com • Monthly. $48.00 per year.

**Step Inside Design: The World of Design from Inside Out.** Dynamic Graphics Inc., 6000 N Forest Park Dr. Peoria, IL 61614-3556. Phone: 888-698-8545 or (309)688-8800 or (309)688-2300; Fax: (309)688-8809 or (309)688-3075; Email: service@dgusa.com • Bimonthly. $42.00 per year. Formerly *Step-by-Step Graphics.*

**Stereophile: For the High Fidelity Stereo Perfectionist.** PRIMEDIA Inc., 350 Fifth Ave., 59th Fl. New York, NY 10118. Phone: (212)601-1960 or (212)745-0100; Fax: (516)222-2357 or (212)745-0121; Email: information@primedia.com • URL: http://www.primediany.com • Monthly. $12.97 Individuals 12 issues; $23.97 Individuals 24 issues. Offers authoritative reviews, informed recommendations, helpful advice, and controversial opinions, all stemming from the revolutionary idea that audio components should be judged on how they reproduce music.

**Stock Artists Alliance.** 229 Peachtree St., Ste. 2200 Atlanta, GA 30303. Phone: 888-722-1334; Fax: (404)614-6405; Email: admin@stockartistsalliance.org • URL: http://www.stockartistsalliance.org • Aims to support and protect the business interests of professional stock photographers worldwide. Provides information resources and promotes the use of equitable business models, fair contracts and ethical practices at all levels of the stock industry. Strengthens solidarity among stock artists.

**Stock Brokers Bible: Directory of Public Companies.** Wall Street Financial Services Inc., PO Box 162 Richmond, MI 48062. Phone: (810)749-9151; Fax: (810)749-6668 • Semiannual. $28.95. Covers: about 9,000 publicly traded companies in the U.S.; major broker dealers, mutual funds, and trusts. Entries include: Company name, address, phone, Standard Industrial Classification (SIC) code, exchange on which company is traded, ticker symbol.

**The Stock Exchange of Hong Kong—Fact Book.** The Stock Exchange of Hong Kong Corporate Communications Department, 12/F One International Finance Ctr., 1 Harbour View St., Central Hong Kong, China. Phone: 852 25221122; Fax: 852 22953106; Email: info@hkex.com.hk • URL: http://www.hkex.com.hk • Annual. Publication includes: List of companies listed on the Stock Exchange of Hong Kong. Principal content of publication is stock price index movement, trading value and volume, market capitalization, dividend yields and P/E ratios, and listed companies' activities and statistical records. Principal content of publication is a picture of the Hong Kong stock market for the year.

***The Stock Exchange of Hong Kong—List of Exchange Participants and Holders of Stock Exchange Trading Rights***. The Stock Exchange of Hong Kong Corporate Communications Department, 12/F One International Finance Ctr., 1 Harbour View St., Central Hong Kong, China. Phone: 852 25221122; Fax: 852 22953106; Email: info@hkex.com.hk • URL: http://www.hkex.com.hk • Quarterly. $134. Covers: Hong Kong stock exchange, including lists of exchange participants, holders of stock exchange trading rights, dealing directors, options exchange participants, and registered branch offices. Entries include: Name, address, phone.

**Stockholm School of Economics - Center for Entrepreneurship and Business Creation**. Saltmätargatan 13-17 SE-113 83 Stockholm, Sweden. Phone: 46 8 7369355; Email: info@hhs.se • URL: http://www.hhs.se/cebc/Pages/default.aspx • Entrepreneurship, business creation, and economic change.

**Stockholm School of Economics - Department of Accounting - Center for Accounting and Managerial Finance**. PO Box 6501 SE-113 83 Stockholm, Sweden. Phone: 46 8 7369000; Fax: 46 8 318186; Email: info@hhs.se • URL: http://www.economicresearch.se/amf • Accounting theory, management accounting, financial accounting, and financial markets.

**Stockholm School of Economics - Economic Research Institute**. PO Box 6501 SE-113 83 Stockholm, Sweden. Phone: 46 8 7369000; Fax: 46 8 316270; Email: filip.wijkstrom@hhs.se • URL: http://www.hhs.se/EFI/Pages/default.aspx • Organization and management, economic psychology, marketing, accounting, control and corporate finance, finance, economics, economic statistics, and law.

***Stocks, Bonds, Bills, and Inflation Classic Yearbook***. Ibbotson Associates, 225 N. Michigan Ave., Suite 700 Chicago, IL 60601-7676. Phone: 800-758-3557 or (312)616-1620; Fax: (312)616-0404 • Annual. $185. Provides detailed data from 1926 to the present on inflation and the returns from various kinds of financial investments, such as small-cap stocks and long-term government bonds.

***Stocks, Bonds, Options & Derivatives: Symbol Book***. American Stock Exchange Inc., 86 Trinity Pl. New York, NY 10006-1818. Phone: 866-422-2639 or (212)306-1000 or (212)306-1472 • URL: http://www.amex.com • Quarterly. $8 per edition; $30 four editions. Covers: Ticker symbols, corporate names, cusip numbers, and other information on stocks, bonds, options, and derivative products listed on the American Stock Exchange.

***STOR-TELE***. AffarsData, News Line Group, Ynglingagatan 2 S-113 47 Stockholm, Sweden. Phone: 46 8 5175 7734 or 8 7365919; Fax: 46 8 736 5555 or 8 7231390; Email: information.se@bisnode.com • URL: http://www.ad.se • Database covers: Approximately 100,000 Swedish companies. Database includes: Company name, address, phone, products and services.

***Stores***. National Retail Federation. NRF Enterprises Inc., 325 7th St. NW, Ste. 1100 Washington, DC 20004. Phone: 800-673-4692 or (202)783-7971 or (202)626-8101; Fax: (202)737-2849 or (202)626-8191 • URL: http://www.nrf.com • Monthly. Individuals $49.00 per year; institutions, $120.00 per year.Offers an insider's view of the entire retail industry by featuring the latest trends, hottest ideas, current technologies and consumer attitudes.

***Storm Data***. U.S. National Climatic Data Center, Federal Bldg., 151 Patton Ave. Asheville, NC 28801-5001. Phone: (828)271-4800; Fax: (828)271-4010; Email: ncdc.orders@noaa.gov • URL: http://www.ncdc.noaa.gov • Monthly. Contains a chronological listing, by state, of hurricanes, tornadoes, thunderstorms, hail, floods, drought conditions, lightning, high winds, snow, temperature extremes and other weather phenomena.

***Stow-Munroe Falls Chamber of Commerce Member Business Directory***. Stow-Munroe Falls Chamber of Commerce, 4301 Darrow Rd., Ste. 2450 Stow, OH 44224. Phone: (330)688-1579 or (330)697-1988; Fax: (330)688-6234; Email: smfcc@smfcc.com • URL: http://www.smfcc.com.

***Strategic Finance***. Institute of Management Accountants, 10 Paragon Dr., Ste. 1 Montvale, NJ 07645-1774. Phone: 800-638-4427 or (201)573-9000; Email: ima@imanet.org • URL: http://www.imanet.org • Monthly. Included in membership; $220 Nonmembers; $18 Individuals each - back issue. Provides articles on corporate finance, cost control, cash flow, budgeting, corporate taxes, and other financial management topics.

***Strategic Health Care Marketing***. Health Care Communications, 11 Heritage Ln. Rye, NY 10580. Phone: (914)967-6741; Fax: (914)967-3054; Email: healthcomm@aol.com • URL: http://www.strategichealthcare.com • Monthly. 299 Individuals. Description: Provides news and analysis on health care services marketing, and business development. Covers strategies and techniques used by marketing innovators. Recurring features include interviews, news of research, a calendar of events, reports of meetings, and notices of publications available.

***Strategic Management Journal***. John Wiley and Sons, Inc., Journals Div., 111 River St. Hoboken, NJ 07030. Phone: 800-526-5368 or (201)748-6000; Fax: (201)748-6088; Email: consumers@wiley.com • URL: http://www.wiley.com • $2,992 Institutions; $3,591 Institutions Print and Online. Original refereed material concerned with all aspects of strategic management. Devoted to the development and improvement of both theory and practice. Provides international coverage.

**Strategic Planning Institute**. PO Box 447 Newton Center, MA 02459-0004. Phone: (617)491-9200; Fax: (617)491-9200 or (617)491-1634; Email: spi@pimsonline.com • URL: http://www.pimsonline.com/ • Conducts research in business information and strategy.

**Strategic Planning Society**. New Bond House, 124 New Bond St. London W1S 1DX, United Kingdom. Phone: 44 845 0563663; Email: members@sps.org.uk • URL: http://www.sps.org.uk • Corporations, educational institutions, and small companies and firms; executives, planners, government officials, and interested individuals. Promotes strategic planning in private, public, and governmental organizations. Seeks to: create and maintain networks for decision makers and planners; develop improved techniques for strategic planning; provide resources of knowledge and experience to aid businesses with planning problems; address political, economic, and social issues facing planners. Has established special interest and regional groups. Maintains Speaker's Bureau.

***Strategic Sales Negotiations***. American Management Association Extension Institute, 1601 Broadway New York, NY 10019. Phone: 800-262-9699 or (518)586-8100; Fax: (518)903-8168 • $1,895 Members (2) days seminar; $2,095 Nonmembers (2) days seminar. Details tools and techniques of successful negotiation.

***Strategize Magazine: tomorrow's ideas for today's business***. Avenir Publishing Inc., 180 N Wabash, Ste. 725 Chicago, IL 60601. Phone: (312)577-7200; Fax: (312)263-0952; Email: sales@avenirpublishing.com • URL: http://www.avenirpublishing.com • Bimonthly. Magazine for business improvement and innovation.

***strategy business***. 101 Park Ave. New York, NY 10178. Phone: (212)551-6222; Fax: (212)551-6732; Email: editors@strategy-business.com • URL: http://www.strategy-business.com • Quarterly. $38.00 per year.

***Strathalbyn District Commerce Association—Business Directory***. Strathalbyn District Commerce Association, PO Box 645 Strathalbyn, SA 5255, Australia. Phone: 61 8 85368366 • Covers local businesses in Strathalbyn, South Australia.

**Stratis Health**. 2901 Metro Dr., Ste. 400 Bloomington, MN 55425-1525. Phone: 877-787-2847 or (952)854-3306; Fax: (952)853-8503; Email: info@stratishealth.org • URL: http://www.stratishealth.org • Physicians interested in ensuring the availability of quality health care at reasonable costs. Evaluates health care services at hospitals, retirement homes, and other facilities. Develops health care standards for hospitals and offers consultation services to operators of health care facilities to improve efficiency in services. Conducts research and development on latest treatments and medical technologies. Tests new medical technologies.

***Stress and Health***. John Wiley and Sons, Inc., Journals Div., 111 River St. Hoboken, NJ 07030. Phone: 800-526-5368 or (201)748-6000; Fax: (201)748-6088; Email: consumers@wiley.com • URL: http://www.wiley.com • $1,204 Institutions, other countries print; €778 Institutions print; £616 Institutions print. A forum for discussion of all aspects of stress, which affect the individual in both health and disease. Provides international coverage. Formerly *Stress Medicine*.

***Student Aid News: The Independent Biweekly News Service on Student Financial Assistance Programs***. Wolters Kluwer Law and Business, 76 9th Ave., 7th Fl. New York, NY 10011-4962. Phone: 800-234-1660 or (212)771-0600; Fax: (800)901-9075 or (301)644-3550 • URL: http://www.wolterskluwerlb.com • Biweekly. $383.00 per year. Newsletter on federal student aid programs.

***The Student Guide: Financial Aid***. U.S. Dept. of Education - Federal Student Aid Information Center, PO Box 84 Washington, DC 20044-0084. Phone: 800-433-3243 or (319)337-5665; Email: FederalStudentAidCustomerService@ed.gov • URL: http://www.studentaid.ed.gov • Annual. Describes financial aid for college and vocational school students. Available online.

***Studies in American Humor***. American Humor Studies Association, Averett University, 316 Frith Hall Danville, VA 24541. Phone: (434)791-7242 • URL: http://americanhumorstudiesassociation.wordpress.com • Annual.

***Studio Photography and Design***. Cygnus Business Media Inc., 1233 Janesville Ave. Fort Atkinson, WI 53538. Phone: 800-547-7377; Email: info@cygnus.com • URL: http://www.cygnus.com • Monthly. Free to qualified personnel; others, $60.00 per year. Incorporates *Commercial Image*.

***Subject Bibliography: Art and Artists***. U. S. Government Printing Office, 732 N Capitol St. NW Washington, DC 20401. Phone: 866-512-1800 or (202)512-1800 or (866)512-1800; Fax: (202)512-2104 or (202)512-2250; Email: contactcenter@gpo.gov • URL: http://www.gpo.gov • Annual. Free. Lists books, pamphlets, periodicals, and other government publications on art-related topics. (Subject Bibliography No. SB-107.).

***Subject Bibliography Index: A Guide to U.S. Government Information***. U. S. Government Printing Office, 732 N Capitol St. NW Washington, DC 20401. Phone: 866-512-1800 or (202)512-1800 or (866)512-1800; Fax: (202)512-2104 or (202)512-2250; Email: contactcenter@gpo.gov • URL: http://www.gpo.gov • Annual. Free. Issued by the Superintendent of Documents. Lists currently available subject bibliographies by title and by topic. Each *Subject Bibliography* describes government books, periodicals, posters, pamphlets, and subscription services available for sale from the Government Printing Office.

***Subject Guide to Books in Print***. Grey House Publishing, 4919 Rte. 22 Amenia, NY 12501. Phone: 800-562-2139 or (518)789-8700; Fax: (518)789-0556; Email: books@greyhouse.com • URL: http://www.greyhouse.com • Annual. $880. Six volumes.

***Subsidiaries of German Firms in the U.S.*** German American Chamber of Commerce, 75 Broad St., 21st Fl. New York, NY 10004. Phone: (212)974-8830; Fax: (212)974-8867; Email: info@gaccny.com • URL: http://www.gaccny.com • Annual. $100 Members; $120 Nonmembers. Covers: Over 3,500 German firms and subsidiaries in the U.S. Entries include: Name, address, phone, and telex of American firm; name and address of German parent company; percentage of German participation; number of employees; type of company (manufacturer, sales agent, etc.); and products.

***The Successful Benefits Communicator***. Lawrence Ragan Communications Inc., 316 N Michigan Ave., Ste. 400 Chicago, IL 60601. Phone: 800-878-5331 or (312)960-4100; Fax: (312)960-4106; Email: cservice@ragan.com • URL: http://www.ragan.com • Description: Offers ideas, techniques, and tips for those who communicate benefits information.

***Successful Cost Control Strategies for CEOs, Managers, and Administrators***. Siefer Consultants Inc., PO Box 1384 Storm Lake, IA 50588. Phone: (712)660-1026; Email: info@siefer.com • URL: http://www.siefer.com • Monthly. $279.00 per year. Newsletter. Provides a variety of ideas on business budgeting and controlling company expenses. Formerly *Employee Cost Control Strategies for CEOs, Managers, and Administrators*.

***Successful Dealer***. Kona Communications Inc., 707 Lake Cook Rd. Deerfield, IL 60015. Phone: (847)498-3180; Fax: (847)498-3197 • Bimonthly. $50.00 per year. For truck and heavy duty equipment dealers.

***Successful Meetings: The Authority on Meetings and Incentive Travel Management***. Nielsen Business Media Inc., 770 Broadway New York, NY 10003-9522. Phone: 866-890-8541 or (646)654-4500 or (646)654-5000; Fax: (646)654-5584 or (646)654-4500; Email: bmcomm@nielsen.com • URL: http://www.nielsenbusinessmedia.com • Monthly. Monthly. $79.00 per year.

***Sudan Business Directory***. Business Guide, PO Box 27669 Dubai, United Arab Emirates. Phone: 971 4 2651719; Fax: 971 4 2692151; Email: sales@africa-business.com • URL: http://www.africa-business.com • $150 Individuals. Covers: 1,200 business listings including wholesalers, importers, retailers, business houses, and agents in Sudan.

**Sudanese Chambers of Industries Association**. PO Box 2565 Khartoum, Sudan. Phone: 249 1 83471717; Fax: 249 1 83471720; Email: sec.general@sudanindustry.org • URL: http://sudanindustry.org • Represents businessmen from the private industrial sector. Participates in trade agreements, workers' legislation and decision making in issues regarding the industry as well as the economy of Sudan. Encourages local and foreign investment in the industrial sector.

***Sugar and Sweetener Situation and Outlook***. U. S. Government Printing Office, 732 N Capitol St. NW Washington, DC 20401. Phone: 866-512-1800 or (202)512-1800 or (866)512-1800; Fax: (202)512-2104 or (202)512-2250; Email: contactcenter@gpo.gov • URL: http://www.gpo.gov • Three times per year. $18.00 per year. Issued by Economic Research Service, U. S. Department of Agriculture. Provides current statistical information on supply, demand, and prices.

***Sugar Bulletin***. American Sugar Cane League of the U.S.A., 206 E Bayou Rd. Thibodaux, LA 70301. Phone: (985)448-3707; Fax: (985)448-3722 • URL: http://www.amscl.org • Monthly. Monthly. Free to members; non-members, $15.00 per year.

***Sugar Journal: Covering the World's Sugar Industry***. Kriedt Enterprises Ltd., 3803 Cleveland Ave. New Orleans, LA 70119. Phone: 888-884-4114 or (504)482-3914; Fax: (504)482-4205 • URL: http://www.louisianacookin.com/kriedt.htm • Monthly. $50 U.S. 12 issues; $85 Other countries 12 issues; $15 Single issue back issue. A monthly technical publication designed to inform sugar beet and cane farms, factories, and refineries throughout the world about the latest developments in the sugar industry.

***Sugar Producer: Representing the Sugar Beet Industry in the United States***. Harris Publishing Inc., 360 B St. Idaho Falls, ID 83402. Phone: 800-638-0135 or (208)524-7000; Fax: (208)522-5241; Email: customerservice@harrispublishing.com • URL: http://www.harrispublishing.com • 9/year. $20 Individuals; $90 Other countries. Seven times a year. $10.95 per year. Supplies sugar beet growers with information to assist them in production of quality sugar beet crops.

***Sugar y Azucar***. RUSPAM Communications Inc., 452 Hudson Ter. Englewood Cliffs, NJ 07632-2922. Phone: (201)871-9200 • Monthly. $75.00 per year. Text in English and Spanish.

***Suggested State Legislation (SSL)***. Chief Officers of State Library Agencies, 201 E Main St., Ste. 1405 Lexington, KY 40507. Phone: 800-800-1910 or (859)514-9151 or (859)244-8000;

Fax: (859)514-9166 or (859)244-8001; Email: lsingler@amrms.com • URL: http://www.cosla.org • Annual. A source of legislative ideas and drafting assistance for state government officials.

***Sulphur: Covers All Aspects of World Sulphur and Sulphuric Acid Industry***. British Sulphur Publishing, 31 Mount Pleasant London WC1X 0AD, United Kingdom. Phone: 44 20 79032000 or 44 20 7837 5600; Fax: 44 20 78370976 or (783)7 0292; Email: customer.services@crugroup.com • URL: http://www.cruonline.crugroup.com/ • Bimonthly. $520.00 per year.

***Sultanate of Oman Telephone Directory***. Tele-Gulf Directory Publication WLL, PO Box 3030 Ruwi 112, Oman. Phone: 605815; Fax: 605825 • Annual. Covers: businesses in Oman; separate editions in English and Arabic. Entries include: Company name, address, phone.

***Summary of Commentary on Current Economic Conditions by Federal Reserve District***. Board of Governors of the Federal Reserve System, Phone: (202)452-3000; Fax: (202)452-3819 • URL: http://www.federalreserve.gov/publications.htm • 8/year. Free Web site provides current "anecdotal information" eight times a year on economic conditions within each of the 12 Federal Reserve Districts, plus an extensive national *Summary*. Text is based on the opinions of bank officials, business executives, economists, financial market experts, and others. Typically contains views of consumer spending, manufacturing, services, credit, employment, prices, wages, and the economy in general. Usually referred to as the Beige Book.

***Summary of Health Information for International Travel***. U.S. Department of Health and Human Services, 200 Independence Ave. SW Washington, DC 20201. Phone: 877-696-6775 • URL: http://www.hhs.gov • Biweekly. Formerly *Weekly Summary of Health Information for International Travel*.

***Summary of International Travel to the United States***. International Trade Administration, Tourism Industries. U.S. Department of Commerce, 1401 Constitution Ave. NW Washington, DC 20230. Phone: 800-782-8872 or (202)482-2000 or (202)482-6607; Email: TheSec@doc.gov • URL: http://www.commerce.gov • Monthly. Quarterly and annual versions available. Provides statistics on air travel to the U.S. from 90 countries. Formerly *Summary and Analysis of International Travel to the United States*.

***Summary of Labor Arbitration Awards***. American Arbitration Association, 1633 Broadway, 10th Fl. New York, NY 10019. Phone: 800-778-7879 or (212)716-5800; Email: websitemail@adr.org • URL: http://www.adr.org • Monthly. Periodical covering private sector arbitration decisions and collective bargaining issues.

***Summary of Sanitation Inspections of International Cruise Ships***. Centers for Disease Control and Prevention, 1600 Clifton Rd. Atlanta, GA 30333. Phone: 800-232-4636 or (404)639-3311 or (404)639-1819; Fax: (404)639-8628; Email: cdcinfo@cdc.gov • URL: http://www.cdc.gov • Biweekly. Apply. "All passenger cruise ships arriving at U. S. ports are subject to unannounced inspection.to achieve levels of sanitation that will minimize the potential for gastrointestinal disease outbreaks on these ships." Individual ships are listed, with sanitation rating and date of inspection. (CDC Document No. 510051.).

***Summers on Oil and Gas***. Thomson West, 610 Opperman Dr. Eagan, MN 55123. Phone: 800-328-9352 or (651)687-7000 • Annual. $1,101 Individuals book - hardbound - full set; $75 Individuals. Legal aspects of the petroleum industry.

***Sunday Telegraph Business Finance Directory***. Graham & Trotman Ltd., Sterling House, 66 Wilton Rd. London SW1V 1DE, United Kingdom. Phone: 71 8211123; Fax: 71 6305229 • Annual. $219. Covers: 900 institutions providing financial services for businesses and sources of financial advice. Entries include: Institution name, address, phone, telex number, contact name, requirements, conditions.

***Superconductor and Cyroelectronics***. WestTech, 5478 Wilshire Blvd., Ste. 205 Los Angeles, CA 90036-4225. Phone: (323)937-1211 • Quarterly. $22.00 per year.

***Superconductor Week: The Newsletter of Record in the Field of Superconductivity***. WestTech, 5478 Wilshire Blvd., Ste. 205 Los Angeles, CA 90036-4225. Phone: (323)937-1211 • $450 Individuals Internet Only; $556 Individuals Internet and Print; $275 Individuals First timer - Internet only; $335 Individuals First timer - Internet and Print; $245 Individuals Back issues; $24 Single issue; $16 Individuals individual article. Covers applications of superconductivity and cryogenics, including new markets and products.

***Supermarket News: The Industry's Weekly Newspaper***. Fairchild Publications, 750 Third Ave. New York, NY 10017. Phone: 800-360-1700 or (212)630-4600 or (212)630-4000; Fax: (212)630-3675 or (212)630-4015; Email: hillary_kribben@condenast.com • URL: http://www.fairchildmediakit.com • Weekly. Individuals, $196.00 per year; retailers, $45.00 per year; manufacturers, $89.00 per year.

***Supply Chain Systems: The Resource for Supply Chain Automation***. Helmers Publishing, Inc., 174 Concord St. Peterborough, NH 03458. Phone: (603)924-9631; Fax: (603)924-7408; Email: dandrews@helmers.com • URL: http://www.scs-mag.com • Monthly. Free to qualified personnel; others, $55.00 per year. Covers trends in automatic identification technology and management. Formerly *ID Systems7*.

**Support Services Alliance**. 2457 State Rte. 7, Ste. 1 Cobleskill, NY 12043. Phone: 800-909-2772; Email: info@ssamembers.com • URL: http://www.ssamembers.com • Represents small businesses (less than 50 employees), the self-employed, and associations of such individuals. Provides services and programs such as group purchasing discounts, health coverage, legislative advocacy, and business and financial support services.

**Supporting Emotional Needs of the Gifted**. PO Box 488 Poughquag, NY 12570. Phone: (845)797-5054; Fax: (866)728-4990; Email: office@sengifted.org • URL: http://www.sengifted.org.

***Surface Coating Resin Index***. European Resin Manufacturers' Association, Minerva House, Ufford Rd., Bainton Stamford PE9 3BB, United Kingdom. Phone: 44 161 7990592; Fax: 44 161 8501589; Email: info@erma.org.uk • URL: http://www.erma.org.uk • Triennial. $5. Covers: Manufacturers, products and trade names of surface coating resins in the United Kingdom. Entries include: Manufacturer name, address, phone, products, trade names.

***The Surface Treatment & Finishing of Aluminium & its Alloys***. Finishing Publications Ltd., 105 Whitney Dr. Stevenage SG1 4BL, United Kingdom. Phone: 44 1438745115; Fax: 44 1438906306; Email: office@finpubs.com • URL: http://finishingpublications.com • $390 6th Edition. Over 12,000 abstracts. Collection of almost 12,000 abstracts from 1960 to date, relating to the surface treatment of aluminium, incl. papers, patents, books.

***Surgical Products***. Advantage Business Media L.L.C., 100 Enterprise Dr., Ste. 600 Rockaway, NJ 07866-0912. Phone: (973)920-7000; Email: advantagecommunications@advantagemedia.com • URL: http://www.advantagebusinessmedia.com • Monthly. $41.90 per year. Covers new Technology and products for surgeons and operation rooms.

***SurgiStrategies: Business Solutions for the ASC***. Virgo Publishing L.L.C., 3300 N Central Ave. Ste. 300 Phoenix, AZ 85012-2501. Phone: (480)990-1101; Fax: (480)990-0819 or (602)567-6852; Email: mikes@vpico.com • URL: http://www.vpico.com • $45 Individuals; $65 Canada; $80 Other countries. Magazine featuring Ambulatory Surgery Centers industry.

***Surplus Record: Machinery and Equipment Directory***. Surplus Record Inc., 20 N Wacker Dr., Ste. 2400 Chicago, IL 60606. Phone: 800-622-5449 or (312)372-9077; Fax: (312)372-6537; Email: surplus@surplusrecord.com • URL: http://www.surplusrecord.com • Monthly. $33.00 per year. Lists over 46,000 items of used and surplus machine tools, chemical processing and electrical equipment.

***Survey and Analysis of Employee Relocation Policies and Costs***. Runzheimer International, 1 Runzheimer Pkwy. Waterford, WI 53185-3599. Phone: 800-558-1702; Email: cls@runzheimer.com • URL: http://www.runzheimer.com • Annual. Based on surveys of relocation administrators.

***Survey of Advanced Technology: A Strategic Analysis of Today's Leading-edge Information Technologies***. I.T. Works, Technology Park 3 9052 Ghent, Belgium. Phone: 32 09 241 5613; Fax: (241) 5656; Email: custserv@compecon.com • URL: http://www.itworks.be • Annual. $795.00. Surveys the corporate use (or neglect) of advanced computer technology. Topics include major technology trends and emerging technologies.

***Survey of Business Travelers***. U.S. Travel Association, 1100 New York Ave. NW, Ste. 450 Washington, DC 20005-3934. Phone: (202)408-8422; Fax: (202)408-1255; Email: feedback@ustravel.org • URL: http://www.ustravel.org • Biennial. Members, $100.00 per year; non-members, $175.00 per year.

***Survey of Business***. University of Tennessee College of Business Administration, Center for Business & Economic Research, Glocker Hall, Ste. 100 Knoxville, TN 37996-4170. Phone: (615)974-5441; Fax: (615)974-3100 • Quarterly. Magazine for Tennessee business professionals about current economic and socio-economic trends in the state.

***Survey of Current Business***. Bureau of Economic Analysis Office of Regional Economic Accounts, 1441 L St. NW Washington, DC 20230. Phone: (202)606-9605 • URL: http://www.bea.gov/regional/index.htm • Monthly.

***Survey of Current Business***. U. S. Government Printing Office, 732 N Capitol St. NW Washington, DC 20401. Phone: 866-512-1800 or (202)512-1800 or (866)512-1800; Fax: (202)512-2104 or (202)512-2250; Email: contactcenter@gpo.gov • URL: http://www.gpo.gov • Monthly. $29 Individuals; $40.60 Other countries. Publication containing economic analyses of business.

***Survey of Current Business***. U. S. Government Printing Office, 732 N Capitol St. NW Washington, DC 20401. Phone: 866-512-1800 or (202)512-1800 or (866)512-1800; Fax: (202)512-2104 or (202)512-2250; Email: contactcenter@gpo.gov • URL: http://www.gpo.gov • Published by Bureau of Economic Analysis, U. S. Department of Commerce. Presents a wide variety of business and economic data.

***Survey of Industries in Texarkana—Arkansas/Texas***. Texarkana Chamber of Commerce, 819 N State Line Ave. Texarkana, TX 75501. Phone: (903)792-7191; Fax: (903)793-4304; Email: chamber@texarkana.org • URL: http://www.texarkana.org • Quarterly. $2. Covers: Approximately 120 Texarkana manufacturers, processors, and sales agencies. Entries include: Company name, address, phone, number of employees, name of contact person, and products/services.

***Survey of Industry Activity***. Equipment Leasing and Finance Association, 1825 K St. NW, Ste. 900 Washington, DC 20006. Phone: (202)238-3400; Fax: (202)238-3401 • URL: http://www.elfaonline.org • Annual. Provides financial and statistical data on the equipment leasing industry. Price on application.

***Survey of Law Firm Economics: A Management and Planning Tool***. ALM Media Properties LLC, 120 Broadway, 5th Fl. New York, NY 10271. Phone: 877-256-2472 or (212)457-9400; Fax: (646)417-7705; Email: customercare@alm.com • URL: http://www.alm.com • Annual. Provides aggregate economic statistics and financial data (benchmarks) relating to the legal profession in the U. S. Includes income, expenses, hourly rates, billable hours, compensation, staffing, data by states, and trends. Most information is arranged by region, firm size, years of experience, and other factors.

***Survey of Mortgage Lending Activity***. U.S. Department of Housing and Urban Development, 451 7th St. SW Washington, DC 20410. Phone: 800-245-2691 or (202)708-1112; Fax: (202)708-9981; Email: helpdesk@huduser.org • URL: http://www.hud.gov • Monthly.

***Survey of Pharmaceutical Enterprises in China***. Xinhua Publishing House, Xuanwumen Xi Dajie Beijing 100803, China. Phone: 1 3073897 or 86 010 6307 1114; Fax: 3073880 or 86 010 6307 5134; Email: english@xinhuanet.com • URL: http://www.xinhuanet.com • $30. Covers: pharmaceutical companies in China. Entries include: Company name, address, description, including product information and management.

***Survey Research***. University of Illinois at Chicago - Survey Research Laboratory, 412 S Peoria St., 6th Fl. Chicago, IL 60607. Phone: (312)996-5300; Fax: (312)996-3358 or (312)413-3358; Email: tjohnson@srl.uic.edu • URL: http://www.srl.uic.edu • 3/year. $15 Individuals; $60 Institutions. Description: Contains "descriptions of current survey research projects by academic and not-for-profit survey research organizations; news from survey research centers; descriptions of recent methodological publications on survey research."; Recurring features include news of research and columns titled Current Research, Personnel Notes, and New Methodological Publications.

***Surveying and Land Information Systems: Devoted to the Advancement of the Sciences of Surveying and Mapping***. American Congress on Surveying and Mapping, 5119 Pegasus Ct., Ste. Q Frederick, MD 21704. Phone: (240)439-4615 or (240)632-9716; Fax: (240)439-4952 or (240)632-1321; Email: curtis.sumner@acsm.net • URL: http://www.acsm.net • Quarterly. Free to members; non-members, $110.00 per year. Formerly *Surveying and Mapping*.

**Sustainable Buildings Industry Council**. 1090 Vermont Ave. NW, Ste. 700 Washington, DC 20005. Phone: (202)289-7800; Fax: (202)289-1092; Email: nibs@nibs.org • URL: http://www.nibs.org/?page=sbic • Works to advance the design, affordability, energy performance, and environmental soundness of commercial, institutional, and residential buildings nationwide. Offers professional training, consumer education, and energy analysis tools. Provides accurate, easy-to-use guidelines, software, and general information about energy conservation measures, energy efficient equipment and appliances, daylighting, and sustainable architecture. Active in presenting workshops and seminars geared toward improving building energy performance in cities and towns throughout the nation.

**Sustainable Fishery Advocates**. 303 Potrero St., Ste. 201 Santa Cruz, CA 95060. Phone: (831)427-1707; Fax: (309)213-4688; Email: t.ish@sustainablefishery.org • URL: http://www.sustainablefishery.org • Aims to improve the sustainability and financial performance of seafood retailers, distributors and producers. Provides innovative, market-based tools to promote the health and recovery of ocean ecosystems. Supports sustainability in the seafood industry through environmentally responsible business practices.

**Sustainable Food Trade Association**. 49 Race St. New Castle, VA 24127-6397. Phone: (413)624-6678; Email: info@sustainablefoodtrade.org • URL: http://www.sustainablefoodtrade.org • Works to foster sustainable business practices in the organic food trade. Collaborates with businesses in the organic and natural foods trade to align their day-to-day business practices with sustainability principles. Provides education, research, and networking for industry leaders to create opportunities for cross-supply chain innovation and best practices.

***Sveriges Handelskalender***. Telenor Foretagsinformation, AB, POB 30211, Sveavagen 84 S-10425 Stockholm, Sweden. Phone: 46 08 587 13100; Fax: 46 08 587 13100 • Annual. $960. Covers: Approximately 16,000 commercial companies in Sweden. Entries include: Company name, address, phone, business data.

***Swansea Business Directory***. Burrows Publishing Ltd., 106 Stafford Rd. Wallington SM6 9AY, United Kingdom. Phone: 44 20 87733000; Email: generalservices@burrows.co.uk • URL: http://www.burrows.co.uk • $27 Individuals with CD-

ROM; $20 Individuals within the city and county of Swansea. Covers over 2,000 local companies trading in the city and county of Swansea, U.K.

***Swap Meet Magazine***. Forum Publishing Co., 383 E Main St. Centerport, NY 11721. Phone: 800-635-7654 or (631)754-5000; Fax: (631)754-0630; Email: forumpublishing@aol.com • URL: http://www.forum123.com • Monthly. $29.97 Individuals 1 year (12 issues); $59.94 Two years. Covers: Over 5,000 manufacturers and importers of jewelry, electronics, clothing, cosmetics, watches, novelties, and other items that are sold to merchandise retailers and flee market vendors at wholesale prices. Entries include: Company name, address, phone, products or services.

***SWE***. Anne Perusek, editor. Society of Women Engineers, 203 N La Salle St., Ste. 1675 Chicago, IL 60601. Phone: 877-SWE-INFO or (312)596-5223; Fax: (312)596-5252; Email: hq@swe.org • URL: http://societyofwomenengineers.swe.org • Bimonthly. Members, $10.00 per year; non-members, $20.00 per year. Covers technical articles, continuing development, career guidance and recruitment and product advertising. Formerly *U.S. Woman Engineer*.

***Sweden Business Law Handbook***. International Business Publications, USA, PO Box 15343 Washington, DC 20003. Phone: (202)546-2103; Fax: (202)546-3275; Email: ibpusa@comcast.net • URL: http://ibpus.com • $99.95 Individuals hardcopy, e-book, CD-ROM. Covers: Information on business laws and climate, investment, tax, export-import regulations, and contacts.

***Sweden Business Services Providers Leads***. Business Information Agency Inc. PlanetInform, 52 Tuscan Way, Ste. 202-181 Saint Augustine, VA 32092. Phone: (904)342-6124; Fax: (904)592-2632; Email: info@biasales.com • URL: http://www.biasales.com • Monthly. $220 Individuals mailing list; $464 Individuals sales list; $784 Individuals marketing list. Covers Swedish companies and all sub-industries that provide various services to commercial businesses, establishments, and organizations, including consulting, advertising and marketing services, and facilities maintenance.

***Sweden Government and Business Contacts Handbook: Trade, Investment & Business Development Contacts***. International Business Publications, USA, PO Box 15343 Washington, DC 20003. Phone: (202)546-2103; Fax: (202)546-3275; Email: ibpusa@comcast.net • URL: http://ibpus.com • $99.95 Individuals hardcopy,e-book,cd-rom. Covers: Strategic government and business information, export-import activity in the country, investment, business contacts and regulations.

***Sweden in America***. Swedish-American Chamber of Commerce, 570 Lexington Ave., 20th Fl. New York, NY 10022. Phone: (212)838-5530; Fax: (212)755-7953 • URL: http://www.saccny.org • Annual. $110. Covers: companies in the U.S. with ties to Sweden. Entries include: Company name, address, phone, fax, telex, number of employees, description of product/service.

***Sweden Industrial and Business Directory***. International Business Publications, USA, PO Box 15343 Washington, DC 20003. Phone: (202)546-2103; Fax: (202)546-3275; Email: ibpusa@comcast.net • URL: http://ibpus.com • Annual. $99.95 Individuals hardcopy, e-book, CD-ROM. Covers: Strategic industrial, investment and business contacts for conducting export-import and investment activity in the country. Contains strategic, practical economic and business information.

**Swedish Business Association of Singapore**. No. 05-01 Triple One Somerset, 111 Somerset Rd. Singapore 238164, Singapore. Phone: 65 67345009; Email: swedbiz@singnet.com.sg • URL: http://www.sbas.org.sg • Aims to promote the development of commerce between Singapore and Sweden.

***Swedish Chamber of Commerce—Trade Directory***. Swedish Chamber of Commerce, Sweden House, 5 Upper Montagu St. London W1H 2AG, United Kingdom. Phone: 44 20 72248001; Fax: 44 20 72248884; Email: info@scc.org.uk • URL: http://www.scc.org.uk • Annual. Covers: 400 member companies representing Swedish, British and European companies.

***Swedish Industrial Directory***. Sveriges Industrieforbund, Storgatan 10, Postfack 5501 S-114 85 Stockholm, Sweden. Phone: 46 87838000 • Annual. $400. Covers: Manufacturing companies in Sweden. Entries include: Manufacturer name, address, phone.

***Swedish Related Companies in the United States***. Swedish-American Chamber of Commerce, 570 Lexington Ave., 20th Fl. New York, NY 10022. Phone: (212)838-5530; Fax: (212)755-7953 • URL: http://www.saccny.org • Annual. $24.90 Members; $34.90 Individuals; $24.90 Students. Covers: Swedish-related companies in the U.S. and their parent companies; lists more than 700 companies in the US; chambers of commerce, trade offices, embassies and consulates, information offices, and tourist offices. Entries include: Name of parent company, address, phone, telex, fax, name of United States subsidiary, address, phone, name and title of key executive, products.

**Swedish Trade Council**. 150 N Michigan Ave., Ste. 1950 Chicago, IL 60601. Phone: (312)781-6222; Fax: (312)276-8606; Email: usa@swedishtrade.se • URL: http://www.swedishtrade.se/english • Promotes Swedish exports and assists American companies in contacting Swedish suppliers. Performs market developments studies and research, partner searches, and project management.

**Sweet and Fortified Wine Association**. PO Box 193 Applegate, CA 95703. Phone: (916)258-7115; Email: sweetandfortified@sbcglobal.net • URL: http://sweetandfortifiedwine.org • Aims to expand and develop the market for sweet and fortified wines. Provides a forum for industry partners and the general public to share ideas and information on sweet and fortified wines. Advocates for responsible consumption of alcoholic beverages.

***Swimming Pool/Spa Age—Product Directory***. Primedia Business, 6151 Powers Ferry Rd. NW Atlanta, GA 30339. Phone: (770)955-2500 or (770)995-2500; Fax: (770)618-0204 • URL: http://www.primediabusiness.com • Annual. $47.95 payment must accompany order. Covers: about 2,000 manufacturers of swimming pool and spa equipment and supplies, and suppliers of services for the industry; manufacturers of spas and hot tubs; distributors and manufacturers' representatives; and pool industry associations. Entries include: Company or association name, address, phone, name and title of contact, branch offices.

**Swiss-Argentine Chamber of Commerce**. Av. Leandro N Alem 1074, Piso 10 C1001AAS Buenos Aires, Argentina. Phone: 54 11 43117187; Email: info@suiza.org.ar • URL: http://www.suiza.org.ar/select_lang.php • Promotes businesses between Argentina and Switzerland.

**Swiss Business Association Singapore**. c/o Embassy of Switzerland, 1, Swiss Club Link Singapore 288162, Singapore. Phone: 65 67220799 • URL: http://www.swissbusiness.org.sg • Assists Swiss companies established in Singapore in conducting, sponsoring or promoting any activity that will benefit its members. Promotes the interests of members related to trade. Encourages the growth of the Swiss trade by promoting investment, finance, commerce and industry.

***Swiss Foundry and Metalworks***. Verlag fur Internationale Wirtschaftsliteratur Ltd., Box 28 CH-8047 Zurich, Switzerland. Phone: 1 4926130 or 41 1 492 61 30; Fax: 41 1 401 05 45; Email: Angela.Wall@was.rep.admin.ch • Biennial. $60. Covers: Manufacturers, associations, and importers in the metal, iron, foundry and metal working industries. Entries include: Company or association name, address, phone.

**Swiss Malaysian Business Association**. c/o Embassy of Switzerland, 16 Persiaran Madge 55000 Kuala Lumpur, Malaysia. Phone: 60 3 21629889; Fax: 60 3 21418410; Email: info@smba.org.my • URL: http://www.myswiss.org • Promotes and fosters bilateral trade, services and investment between Switzerland and Malaysia. Assists potential new Swiss companies in establishing their headquarters in Malaysia. Maintains and improves close trading, commercial and other links between Malaysia and Switzerland. Provides a forum for members in exchanging information and identifying and discussing issues of common interests regarding economic, industrial and commercial objectives.

**Swiss Management Association**. Zeltweg 48 8032 Zurich, Switzerland. Phone: 41 44 2022325; Fax: 41 44 2699001; Email: office@smg.ch • URL: http://www.smg.ch • Acts as an umbrella association of personalities from economy, science, administration; deals with and takes into transdisciplinary consideration the complex terms related to decision making; promotes exchange of capabilities and knowledge, ideas and questions, and experience and aims of leadership and management.

**SwissCham Australia**. 46 Market St., Ste. 303 Sydney, NSW 2000, Australia. Phone: 61 2 92621511; Fax: 61 2 92901928 • URL: http://www.swisscham.com.au • Represents Swiss business interests in Australia.

***Switchboard***. Switchboard, Inc., Phone: (508)898-8000; Fax: (508)898-1755; Email: webmaster@switchboard.com • URL: http://www.switchboard.com • Web site provides telephone numbers and street addresses for more than 100 million business locations and residences in the U. S. Broad industry categories are available. Fees: Free.

***Switzerland Business Services Providers Leads***. Business Information Agency Inc. PlanetInform, 52 Tuscan Way, Ste. 202-181 Saint Augustine, VA 32092. Phone: (904)342-6124; Fax: (904)592-2632; Email: info@biasales.com • URL: http://www.biasales.com • Monthly. $219 Individuals mailing list; $460 Individuals sales list; $780 Individuals marketing list. Covers Swiss companies and all sub-industries that provide various services to commercial businesses, establishments, and organizations, including consulting, advertising and marketing services, and facilities maintenance.

***Switzerland Industrial and Business Directory***. International Business Publications, USA, PO Box 15343 Washington, DC 20003. Phone: (202)546-2103; Fax: (202)546-3275; Email: ibpusa@comcast.net • URL: http://ibpus.com • Annual. $99.95 Individuals hardcopy, e-book, CD-ROM. Covers: Strategic industrial, investment and business contacts for conducting export-import and investment activity in the country.

***Synthetic Organic Chemicals: United States Production and Sales***. International Trade Commission. U. S. Government Printing Office, 732 N Capitol St. NW Washington, DC 20401. Phone: 866-512-1800 or (202)512-1800 or (866)512-1800; Fax: (202)512-2104 or (202)512-2250; Email: contactcenter@gpo.gov • URL: http://www.gpo.gov • Annual.

***Syria Business Law Handbook***. International Business Publications, USA, PO Box 15343 Washington, DC 20003. Phone: (202)546-2103; Fax: (202)546-3275; Email: ibpusa@comcast.net • URL: http://ibpus.com • $149.95 Individuals. Covers: Basic information on business, laws, export-import, business climate, regulations, and contacts.

***Syria Golden Key Directory***. International Institute of Trade Relation Promotion, Trade Information Centre of Iran, No. 7, 3rd Fl., Abbasie Bazar, Ferdowsi Sq. Tehran, Iran. Phone: 98 21 88833900; Fax: 98 21 88820697; Email: order@irangoldenkey.com • URL: http://www.goldenkeydirectory.com/about.html • £100 Individuals. Covers: 27,614 companies in Syria. Entries include: Company name, address, telephone, fax, products, services, Managing Director, and business activities.

***Sys Admin: The Journal for Unix System Administrators***. UBM L.L.C., 600 Community Dr. Manhasset, NY 11030. Phone: (516)562-5000 or (512)562-5000; Fax: (212)378-2160 or (516)562-5036; Email: cmp@cmp.com • URL: http://www.cmp.com • Monthly. $39.00 per year. Provides technical information for managers of Unix systems.

***Systems User***. Caulfield Publishing Ltd., 308 E Van Buren St. Janesville, WI 53545-4047. Phone: (608)754-8580; Fax: (608)754-7904 • Monthly. $62.00 per year.

***T and D Magazine***. ASTD, 1640 King St. Alexandria, VA 22314-2746. Phone: 800-628-2783 or (703)683-8100; Fax: (703)683-1523; Email: customercare@astd.org • URL: http://www.astd.org • Monthly. Free to members; non-members, $85.00 per year.

***T H E Journal***. Ed Warnshuis Ltd., 17501 17th St., Suite 230 Tustin, CA 92680-3670. Phone: (714)730-4011; Fax: (714)730-3739; Email: eedwards@thejournal.com • URL: http://www.thejournal.com • 11 times a year. $29.00 per year. For educators of all levels.

***T W I C E: This Week in Consumer Electronics***. Reed Elsevier Group plc Reed Business Information, 360 Park Ave. S New York, NY 11010. Phone: (212)791-4208; Email: corporatecommunications@reedbusiness.com • URL: http://www.reedbusiness.com • 29 times a year. $129.90 per year. Contains marketing and manufacturing news relating to a wide variety of consumer electronic products, including video, audio, telephone, and home office equipment.

***TableBase™***. Cengage Learning Inc., 20 Channel Center St. Boston, MA 02210. Phone: 800-487-8488 or (617)289-7700; Fax: (617)289-7844; Email: investors@cengage.com • URL: http://www.cengage.com • Contains tabular data on companies, industries, products, and demographics on more than 90 global industries.

***Tables of Redemption Values for United States Savings Bonds, Series EE and Series E***. U. S. Government Printing Office, 732 N Capitol St. NW Washington, DC 20401. Phone: 866-512-1800 or (202)512-1800 or (866)512-1800; Fax: (202)512-2104 or (202)512-2250; Email: contactcenter@gpo.gov • URL: http://www.gpo.gov • Semiannual. $14 U.S. single copy; $19.60 Other countries single copy. Issued by the Public Debt Bureau, U. S. Treasury Department.

***Tack'n Togs Merchandising: The Monthly Business Magazine for Equine Retailers***. Farm Progress Companies Inc., 255 38th Ave., Ste. P Saint Charles, IL 60174-5410. Phone: 800-441-1410 or (630)690-5600; Fax: (630)462-2869 or (630)462-4656; Email: wvogt@farmprogress.com • URL: http://www.farmprogress.com • Monthly. International trade magazine for marketers of products for horse and rider.

***Tacoma-Pierce County Business Directory***. Tacoma-Pierce County Chamber of Commerce, 950 Pacific Ave., Ste. 300 Tacoma, WA 98402. Phone: (253)627-2175; Fax: (253)597-7305; Email: info@tacomachamber.org • URL: http://www.tacomachamber.org • Annual. included in membership dues; $19.95 for nonmembers.

***Taft Monthly Portfolio***. Taft Group, 27500 Drake Rd. Farmington Hills, MI 48331-3535. Phone: 800-877-4253 or (248)699-4253 or (248)699-GALE; Fax: (800)414-5043 or (248)699-8061; Email: gale.salesassistance@thomson.com • URL: http://www.gale.com/taft • Monthly. $75.00 per year. New ideas and proven techniques used by universitites, hospitals and other nonprofit organizations to raise philanthropic gifts. Formerly *FRI Monthly Portfolio*.

***TAGA Newsletter***. Technical Association of the Graphic Arts, 200 Deer Run Rd. Sewickley, PA 15143. Phone: (412)259-1706; Fax: (412)741-2311 • URL: http://www.printing.org/taga • Description: Disseminates information in the graphic arts industry to members which is international in scope. Recurring features include interviews, news of research, reports of meetings, news of educational opportunities, and standards updates.

**Tailhook Association**. 9696 Businesspark Ave. San Diego, CA 92131-1643. Phone: 800-322-4665 or (858)689-9223; Fax: (858)578-8839 • URL: http://www.tailhook.net • Individuals who have been designated as Naval Aviators or Naval Flight Officers and have made carrier landings; other individuals who have made carrier landings or who have the background and interest to support the objectives of the association. Seeks to foster, develop, study, and support U.S. aircraft carriers and aircrews, and their role in the nation's defense system.

**Taipei Business Association in Singapore**. No. 06-07 SCCCI Bldg., 47 Hill St. Singapore 179365, Singapore. Phone: 65 63383916; Fax: 65 63383930; Email: tpebiz@singnet.com.sg • URL: http://www.tbas.org.sg.

***Taiwan Business Directory***. China Credit Information Service

Ltd., 5F, No. 57, Tung Hsing Rd. Taipei, Taiwan. Phone: 886 2 87683266; Fax: 886 2 87682033; Email: service@ccis.com.tw • URL: http://www.credit.com.tw/creditonline/ • Annual. $160 Individuals. Covers 30,000 manufacturing, service, and trading companies in Taiwan.

***Taiwan Government and Business Contacts Handbook***. International Business Publications, USA, PO Box 15343 Washington, DC 20003. Phone: (202)546-2103; Fax: (202)546-3275; Email: ibpusa@comcast.net • URL: http://ibpus.com • $99.95 Individuals hardcopy, e-book, CD-ROM. Covers: Strategic government and business information, export-import activity in the country, investment, business contacts and regulations.

***Taiwan Industrial and Business Directory***. International Business Publications, USA, PO Box 15343 Washington, DC 20003. Phone: (202)546-2103; Fax: (202)546-3275; Email: ibpusa@comcast.net • URL: http://ibpus.com • Annual. $99.95 Individuals hardcopy, e-book, CD-ROM. Covers: Strategic industrial, investment and business contacts for conducting export-import and investment activity in the country.

***Taiwan Industrial Pages***. INFOT Inc., PO Box 2052 Rockville, MD 20847. Phone: 866-838-2619 • URL: http://www.infotusa.com • $46.75 CD-ROM; additional $167.50 for MS Access format. Covers: 100,882 Taiwan manufacturers, factories, plants, exporters, and importers. Entries include: Email and website addresses, telephone and fax number, business titles, address, number of employees, capital, and industry.

**Taiwan Private Equity and Venture Capital Association**. Rm. 133, 10th Fl., No. 133, Sect. C, Minsheng E Rd., Songshan Dist. Taipei 105, Taiwan. Phone: 886 2 25450075; Fax: 886 2 25452752; Email: public@tvca.org.tw • URL: http://www.tvca.org.tw • Promotes awareness of the venture capital industry in Taiwan and its importance to the economy. Provides networking opportunity among members. Acts as a liaison between members and the government in order to update members of relevant investment regulations. Establishes professional venture capital information center in Taiwan in order to provide members with relevant local and international industry information. Promotes relevant business laws and regulations and economic policies.

***Taiwan Product Guide***. Todd Publications, PO Box 500 Millwood, NY 10546. Phone: 866-896-0916 or (914)373-4750; Fax: (914)373-4750; Email: toddpub@aol.com • URL: http://www.toddpublications.com • Biennial. $125. Covers: More than 6,000 Taiwan exporters. Database includes: Taiwan government agencies and essential services available. Entries include: Company name, address, phone, fax, telex.

***Tajikistan Industrial and Business Directory***. International Business Publications, USA, PO Box 15343 Washington, DC 20003. Phone: (202)546-2103; Fax: (202)546-3275; Email: ibpusa@comcast.net • URL: http://ibpus.com • Annual. $99.95 Individuals hardcopy, e-book, CD-ROM. Covers: Strategic industrial, investment and business contacts for conducting export-import and investment activity in the country.

***The Take-Charge Assistant***. American Management Association, 1601 Broadway New York, NY 10019-7420. Phone: 877-566-9441 or (212)586-8100 or (518)891-5510; Fax: (212)903-8168 or (518)891-0368; Email: customerservice@amanet.org • URL: http://www.amanet.org • Monthly. Description: Features career and professional guidance, tips, and problem solving.

***Taking Stocks: A Snapshot of Portland Metro-Area Public Companies***. The Business Journal, 851 SW 6th Ave., Ste. 500 Portland, OR 97204. Phone: (503)274-8733; Fax: (503)219-3450 • URL: http://www.bizjournals.com • Annual. Covers: About 75 public firms that are either based in Portland, Oregon, or have a strong presence there. Entries include: Firm address, phone, names, and titles of executive officers, board of directors, products or services, significant stockholders, financial data.

**Tampa Bay Rare Fruit Council International**. 39320 North Ave. Zephyrhills, FL 33542. Email: tampa.bay.rfci@gmail.com • URL: http://www.rarefruit.org • Individuals in 34 countries interested in propagating and raising tropical fruit plants. Formerly Rare Fruit Council.

***The Tan Sheet: Nonprescription Pharmaceuticals and Nutritionals***. Elsevier Business Intelligence, 5635 Fishers Ln., Ste. 6000 Rockville, MD 20852. Phone: 800-332-2181 or (240)221-4500 or (800)332-2181; Fax: (240)221-4400 or (301)656-3094; Email: fdc.customer.service@fdcreports.com • URL: http://www.elsevierbi.com • Weekly. $1,220.00 per year. Newsletter covering over-the-counter drugs and vitamin supplements. Emphasis is on regulatory activities of the U. S. Food and Drug Administration (FDA).

***Tanker Register***. Clarkson Research Studies, St. Magnus House, 3 Lower Thames St. London EC3R 6HE, United Kingdom. Phone: 44 20 73340000; Fax: 44 20 76264189; Email: crs@clarksons.com • URL: http://www.clarksons.com • Annual. $522 Individuals; £290 Individuals; €377 Individuals. Covers: More than 5,820 tankers and combined carriers throughout the world having deadweight tonnage exceeding 10,000, and their owners and managers. Entries include: Ship name, owner or manager, where registered, when and where built, tonnage, draft, capacity, engines, etc.

***Tanzania Business Directory***. Business Guide, PO Box 27669 Dubai, United Arab Emirates. Phone: 971 4 2651719; Fax: 971 4 2692151; Email: sales@africa-business.com • URL: http://www.africa-business.com • $250 Individuals. Covers: 23,000 business listings including wholesalers, importers, retailers, business houses, and agents in Tanzania.

***Tanzania Business Law Handbook***. International Business Publications, USA, PO Box 15343 Washington, DC 20003. Phone: (202)546-2103; Fax: (202)546-3275; Email: ibpusa@comcast.net • URL: http://ibpus.com • $99.95 Individuals hardcopy, e-book, CD-ROM. Covers: Basic information on business, laws, export-import, business climate, regulations, and contacts.

***Tanzania Investment and Business Guide***. International Business Publications, USA, PO Box 15343 Washington, DC 20003. Phone: (202)546-2103; Fax: (202)546-3275; Email: ibpusa@comcast.net • URL: http://ibpus.com • $99.95 Individuals hardcopy, e-book, CD-ROM. Covers: Strategic information on economy, opportunities, export-import and investment climate, regulations and industrial development, banking, and government. Entries include: Business contacts and business travel.

***Tape/Disc Business***. Access Intelligence L.L.C., 2700 Westchester Ave., Ste. 107 Purchase, NY 10577. Phone: 800-800-5474 or (914)251-4705 or (212)621-4900; Fax: (914)251-7107 or (212)621-4800; Email: clientservices@pbimedia.com • Monthly. $74; $10 Single issue. Magazine for dealers, manufacturers, and users of magnetic and optical media.

***Target Marketing: The Leading Magazine for Integrated Database Marketing***. North American Publishing Co., 1500 Spring Garden St., Ste. 1200 Philadelphia, PA 19130-4069. Phone: (215)238-5300; Email: customerservice@napco.com • URL: http://www.napco.com • Monthly. $65.00 per year. Dedicated to direct marketing excellence. Formerly *Zip Target Marketing*.

**Tasmanian Chamber of Commerce and Industry**. 309 Liverpool St. Hobart, TAS 7000, Australia. Phone: 61 3 62363600; Fax: 61 3 62311278; Email: admin@tcci.com.au • URL: http://www.tcci.com.au • Represents businesses in Tasmania, Australia.

***Taunton's Fine Homebuilding***. Taunton Press Inc., 63 S Main St. Newtown, CT 06470. Phone: 800-477-8727 or (203)426-8171; Fax: (203)426-3434 or (203)549-0747; Email: booksales@taunton.com • URL: http://www.taunton.com • Eight issues per year $37.95. Special interest magazine written by builders for builders - professional and homeowners. Formerly *Fine Homebuilding*.

***Tax Administrators News***. Federation of Tax Administrators, 444 N Capitol St. NW, Ste. 348 Washington, DC 20001. Phone: (202)624-5890; Fax: (202)624-7888 • URL: http://www.taxadmin.org/fta/default.html • Description: Focuses on state tax legislation and administration. Covers research results and federal legislation that affects state taxation. Recurring features include state-by-state news of tax changes and innovations in administration, announcements of conferences and meetings, profiles of state revenue commissioners, and special sections on motor fuel taxes and technology in tax administration.

***Tax-Advantaged Securities Law Report***. Robert J. Haft. Thomson West, 610 Opperman Dr. Eagan, MN 55123. Phone: 800-328-9352 or (651)687-7000 • Description: Devotes each issue to one or two articles on federal or major state law concerning tax-advantaged securities. Presents explanation and analysis of new decisions, laws, rulings, and regulations. Gives practical advice and cautions for selected tax investments.

***The Tax Adviser***. American Institute of Certified Public Accountants, 1211 Avenue of the Americas New York, NY 10036-8775. Phone: 888-777-7077 or (212)596-6200; Fax: (212)596-6213; Email: service@aicpa.org • URL: http://www.aicpa.org • Monthly. $106.25 Individuals; $85 Members. Newsletter about federal tax issues.

***The Tax Directory***. Tax Analysts, 400 S Maple Ave., Ste. 400 Falls Church, VA 22046. Phone: 800-955-2444 or (703)533-4400; Fax: (703)533-4444; Email: cservice@tax.org • URL: http://www.tax.org • Quarterly. $499 Individuals both volumes, web, CD or print; $599 Individuals both volumes plus CD-ROM; $774 Individuals both volumes plus web. Updated quarterly on CD-ROM and in print; updated continually online. Covering federal, state, and international tax officials, tax practitioners, and corporate tax executives.

***The Tax Executive***. Tax Executives Institute, 1200 G St. NW, Ste. 300 Washington, DC 20005-3814. Phone: (202)638-5601; Fax: (202)638-5607; Email: asktei@tei.org • URL: http://www.tei.org • Bimonthly. $22 Single issue; $120 Individuals; $110 Institutions; $145 Other countries; $135 Institutions, other countries; Included in membership.

***Tax Guide for Small Business***. U.S. Department of the Treasury, Internal Revenue Service. U. S. Government Printing Office, 732 N Capitol St. NW Washington, DC 20401. Phone: 866-512-1800 or (202)512-1800 or (866)512-1800; Fax: (202)512-2104 or (202)512-2250; Email: contactcenter@gpo.gov • URL: http://www.gpo.gov • Annual. $11 Individuals USA List price; $15.40 Other countries. Contains tax information for small business owners.

***Tax Management Compensation Planning Journal***. BNA Tax Management, 1231 25th St., NW Washington, DC 20037. Phone: 800-223-7270 or (202)785-7191; Fax: (202)785-7195; Email: customercare@bna.com • URL: http://www.bnatax.com • Monthly. $426.00 per year. Formerly *Compensation Planning Journal*.

***Tax Management International Forum***. Bloomberg BNA, 3 Bethesda Metro Center, Ste. 250 Bethesda, MD 20814-5377. Phone: 800-372-1033 or (703)341-3000; Fax: (800)253-0332; Email: customercare@bna.com • URL: http://www.bna.com • Quarterly. $370.00 per year.

***Tax Management International Journal: A Monthly Professional Review of Current International Tax Developments***. BNA Tax Management, 1231 25th St., NW Washington, DC 20037. Phone: 800-223-7270 or (202)785-7191; Fax: (202)785-7195; Email: customercare@bna.com • URL: http://www.bnatax.com • Monthly. $426.00 per year. Semiannual *Index*.

***Tax Management Weekly Report***. Tax Management Inc., 1250 23rd St. NW Washington, DC 20037-1164. Phone: 800-223-7270 or (202)785-7195; Fax: (202)833-7297; Email: tm@bna.com • URL: http://www.bnatax.com • Weekly. Description: Covers developments affecting taxation and the tax aspects of accounting. Includes summaries of federal cases including the U.S. Tax Court, synopses of IRS general counsel and technical advice memoranda, analysis of selected IRS revenue rulings, procedures and private letter rulings, and status reports of Treasury Department actions on pending regulations. Covers topics in financial planning, including memoranda on current financial and tax planning strategies.

***Tax Notes: The Weekly Tax Service***. Tax Analysts, 400 S Maple Ave., Ste. 400 Falls Church, VA 22046. Phone: 800-955-2444 or (703)533-4400; Fax: (703)533-4444; Email: cservice@tax.org • URL: http://www.tax.org • Weekly. Weekly. $1,699.00 per year. Includes an *Annual* and compilations of previous years. Newsletter. Covers "tax news from all federal sources," including congressional committees, tax courts, and the Internal Revenue Service. Each issue contains "summaries of every document that pertains to federal tax law," with citations. Commentary is provided.

***Tax Planning for Corporations and Shareholders: Forms***. Matthew Bender and Company Inc., 1275 Broadway Albany, NY 12204-2638. Phone: 800-424-4200 or (518)487-3000; Fax: (518)487-3573 or (800)424-4200; Email: customer.support@lexisnexis.com • URL: http://www.matthewbender.com • Annual. $422 Individuals Book or electronic version. Includes expertly crafted forms for such transactions as forming a new corporation, S corporation elections and revocations, and more.

***Tax Planning for Highly Compensated Individuals***. RIA Group, 395 Hudson St. New York, NY 10014. Phone: (212)367-6300; Fax: (212)367-6314 • $235.00. Looseleaf service. Biennial supplementation.

***Tax Policy and the Economy***. The MIT Press, 55 Hayward St. Cambridge, MA 02142-1493. Phone: 800-356-0343 or (617)253-5646 or (617)253-5641; Fax: (617)258-6779 or (617)253-6779; Email: ewfaran@mit.edu • URL: http://mitpress.mit.edu • Annual. $25. Reviews "issues in the current tax debate.".

***Tax Practice***. Tax Analysts, 400 S Maple Ave., Ste. 400 Falls Church, VA 22046. Phone: 800-955-2444 or (703)533-4400; Fax: (703)533-4444; Email: cservice@tax.org • URL: http://www.tax.org • Weekly. $199.00 per year. Newsletter. Covers news affecting tax practitioners and litigators, with emphasis on federal court decisions, rules and regulations, and tax petitions. Provides a guide to Internal Revenue Service audit issues.

***Tax Preparation Service***. Entrepreneur Press, 2445 McCabe Way, Ste. 400 Irvine, CA 92614-6244. Phone: 800-864-6864 or (949)261-2325 or (949)622-7131; Fax: (949)261-7729 or (949)261-0234; Email: press@entrepreneur.com • URL: http://www.entrepreneurpress.com • Looseleaf. $59.50. A practical guide to starting a business for the preparation of income tax returns. Covers profit potential, start-up costs, market size evaluation, owner's time required, site selection, lease negotiation, pricing, accounting, advertising, promotion, etc. (Start-Up Business Guide No. E2332.).

***Tax Year in Review***. Wolters Kluwer Law & Business CCH, 2700 Lake Cook Rd. Riverwoods, IL 60015. Phone: 888-224-7377 or (847)267-7000; Email: cust_serv@cch.com • URL: http://www.cchgroup.com • Annual. Covers the year's "major new legislative and regulatory changes.".

***Taxation and Revenue Policies: State Capitals***. Wakeman/Walworth Inc., PO Box 7376 Alexandria, VA 22307-7376. Phone: 800-876-2545 or (703)768-9600; Fax: (703)768-9690; Email: newsletters@statecapitals.com • URL: http://statecapitals.com/ • 50 times a year. $345.00 per year; print and online edition, $490.00 per year. Formerly *From the State Capitals: Taxation and Revenue Policies*.

***Taxation of Securities Transactions***. Matthew Bender and Company Inc., 1275 Broadway Albany, NY 12204-2638. Phone: 800-424-4200 or (518)487-3000; Fax: (518)487-3573 or (800)424-4200; Email: customer.support@lexisnexis.com • URL: http://www.matthewbender.com • Semiannual. $653. Looseleaf service. Covers taxation of a wide variety of securities transactions, including those involving stocks, bonds, options, short sales, new issues, mutual funds, dividend distributions, foreign securities, and annuities.

***Taxes on Parade***. Wolters Kluwer Law & Business CCH, 2700 Lake Cook Rd. Riverwoods, IL 60015. Phone: 888-224-7377 or (847)267-7000; Email: cust_serv@cch.com • URL: http://www.cchgroup.com • Weekly. $129.00 per year. Newsletter.

***Taxes-Property: State Capitals***. Wakeman/Walworth Inc., PO Box

7376 Alexandria, VA 22307-7376. Phone: 800-876-2545 or (703)768-9600; Fax: (703)768-9690; Email: newsletters@statecapitals.com • URL: http://statecapitals.com/ • 50 times a year. $345.00 per year; print and online edition, $490.00. Formerly *From the State Capitals: Taxes-Property*.

***Taxes: The Tax Magazine***. Wolters Kluwer Law & Business CCH, 2700 Lake Cook Rd. Riverwoods, IL 60015. Phone: 888-224-7377 or (847)267-7000; Email: cust_serv@cch.com • URL: http://www.cchgroup.com • Monthly. $420 Individuals. Provides its readers with cogent, innovative and practice-oriented analyses of federal, state and international tax issues.

***Taxi and Livery Management***. International Taxicab and Livery Association, 3849 Farragut Ave. Kensington, MD 20895-2004. Phone: (301)946-5701; Fax: (301)946-4641; Email: itla@itla-info.org • URL: http://www.taxinetwork.com • Quarterly. $16.00 per year.

***TAXNET.PRO***. Carswell, Phone: 800-387-5164 or (416)609-3800; Fax: (416)298-5082; Email: orders@carswell.com • URL: http://www.carswell.com/taxnetpro.asp • Fee-based Web site provides complete coverage of Canadian tax law and regulation, including income tax, provincial taxes, accounting, and payrolls. Daily updates. Base price varies according to product.

***Taylors Corporate Birmingham & West Midlands***. Vincent Taylor & Co., 13 Manor Pl. Edinburgh EH3 7DR, United Kingdom. Phone: 131 225 5155; Fax: 131 2259513 • Annual. $20. Covers: Approximately 800 major companies in Birmingham and the West Midlands of England. Entries include: Company name, address, phone, names and titles of key personnel, number of employees, geographical area served, financial data, description of services, products provided.

***Taylors Corporate North of England***. Vincent Taylor & Co., 13 Manor Pl. Edinburgh EH3 7DR, United Kingdom. Phone: 131 225 5155; Fax: 131 2259513 • Annual. $20. Covers: Approximately 800 major companies and agencies in the North of England. Entries include: Company name, address, phone, names and titles of key personnel, number of employees, geographical area served, financial data, description of services, products provided.

***Taylors Corporate Scotland***. Vincent Taylor & Co., 13 Manor Pl. Edinburgh EH3 7DR, United Kingdom. Phone: 131 225 5155; Fax: 131 2259513 • Annual. $20. Covers: Approximately 850 major company entities and government agencies involved in the development of business in Scotland. Entries include: Company name, address, phone, names and titles of key personnel, number of employees, geographical area served, financial data, description of services, products provided.

***Taylors Corporate South Africa***. Vincent Taylor & Co., 13 Manor Pl. Edinburgh EH3 7DR, United Kingdom. Phone: 131 225 5155; Fax: 131 2259513 • Annual. $120. Covers: Approximately 400 companies and agencies involved in the development of business in South Africa. Entries include: Company name, address, phone, names and titles of key personnel, number of employees, geographical area served, financial data, description of services, products provided.

***tC teleCommunication: Magazine for Business, Technical and Politics***. tC teleCommunication Publishing Group Ltd., Am Buschhof 8 D-53227 Bonn, Germany. Phone: 49 228 970970; Fax: 49 228 9709775; Email: redaktion@behoerdenspaegel.de • Monthly. €61.03 Individuals; €2.50 Single issue. Journal covering economic and political events in the telecommunications market in Germany and worldwide.

***Tea and Coffee Trade Journal***. Lockwood Publications Inc., 26 Broadway, Fl. 9M New York, NY 10004. Phone: (212)391-2060; Fax: (212)827-0945; Email: operations@lockwoodpublications.com • URL: http://www.lockwoodpublications.com • Monthly. $49 Individuals; $59 Canada and Mexico; $89 Other countries Surface Mail; $129 Other countries Air Mail. Current trends in coffee roasting and tea packing industry.

***Teaching Business & Economics***. Economics and Business Education Association, The Forum, 277 London Rd. Burgess Hill RH15 9QU, United Kingdom. Phone: 44 1444 240150; Fax: 44 1444 240101; Email: office@ebea.org.uk • URL: http://www.ebea.org.uk/ebea • 3/year. Publication covering business education.

***Team Leader***. LRP Publications Library, lrp.com Technology Contacts, 747 Dresher Rd., Ste. 500 Horsham, PA 19044. Phone: 800-341-7874 or (215)784-0860 or (215)784-0910; Fax: (215)784-9639 or (215)784-0275; Email: techsup@lrp.com • URL: http://www.lrp.com • Description: Keeps business team leaders up to date on team-leading techniques and provides solutions to team-oriented issues.

**Team Success**. 5050 Laguna Blvd., Ste. 112-415 Elk Grove, CA 95758-4151. Phone: (916)629-4229; Email: admin@teamsuccessinc.com • URL: http://www.teamsuccessinc.org • Promotes the education and improvement of youth throughout the United States. Seeks to improve the social development, life skills, employability, social skills and entrepreneurship abilities of youth. Assists the community by providing business related workshops, mentoring and job assistance.

***Teamwork: Your Personal Guide to Working Successfully with People***. Dartnell Corp., 350 Hiatt Dr. Palm Beach Gardens, FL 33418. Phone: 800-341-7874 or (561)622-6520; Fax: (561)622-2423; Email: custserv@lrp.com • URL: http://www.dartnellcorp.com • Monthly. $249 Individuals Print and Online - Annual; $179 Individuals Online only. Offers your employees practical tips and techniques that help them work together as a cohesive unit, improve relations with other teams, and motivate themselves.

***Tech Directions—Annual Buyers' Guide: A Directory of Suppliers***. Prakken Publications Inc., 2851 Boardwalk Dr. Ann Arbor, MI 48104. Phone: 800-530-9673 or (734)975-2800; Fax: (734)975-2787 • URL: http://www.techdirections.com • Annual. Publication includes: Directory of manufacturers and suppliers of equipment and materials to industrial and vocational/technical schools, community colleges, and universities. Entries include: Company name, address, phone, fax, logo, e-mail, web address, product descriptions.

**TechAmerica**. 1001 19th St. N, 20th Fl. Arlington, VA 22209. Phone: (202)682-9110; Fax: (202)682-9111; Email: database@techamerica.org • URL: http://www.techamerica.org • A division of the Information Technology Association of America; software companies involved in the development or marketing of software for personal, midrange, and mainframe computers. Promotes the software industry and addresses specific problems of the industry. Represents the industry before various governmental units; provides educational programs to members; conducts research and makes available legal services. Develops standards.

**TechAssure Association**. 1550 17th St., Ste. 600 Denver, CO 80202. Phone: (888)208-8670 • Provides training and education services for risk management professionals that specialize in technology, life sciences and digital media industries. Works with insurance companies to customize policy forms and to improve the underwriting process. Encourages members to share best practices and to discuss ideas and experiences.

***Technical Analysis of Stocks & Commodities: The Traders Magazine***. Technical Analysis Inc., 4757 California Ave. SW Seattle, WA 98116-4499. Phone: 800-832-4642 or (206)938-0570; Fax: (206)938-1307; Email: editor@traders.com • URL: http://www.traders.com • $89.99 Individuals Annual; $6.99 Single issue. 13 times a year. Covers use of personal computers for stock trading, price movement analysis by means of charts, and other technical trading methods.

**Technical Analysis Society of St. Lucia**. PO Box 1764 Castries 00110-5000, Saint Lucia. • URL: http://www.tasstlucia.com • Promotes technical analysis for the study and self-directed investments in the financial markets. Fosters excellence in the theory and practice of technical analysis. Provides a local forum for St. Lucian traders and investors to share ideas, news, and experiences.

***Technical Communication***. Society for Technical Communication, 9401 Lee Hwy., Ste. 300 Fairfax, VA 22031. Phone: (703)522-4114; Fax: (703)522-2075 • URL: http://www.stc.org • Quarterly. Includes articles about the practical application of technical communication.

***Technical Education News***. Glencoe/McGraw-Hill, PO Box 543 Blacklick, OH 43004-0544. Phone: 800-334-7344; Fax: (614)755-5682; Email: customerservice@mcgraw-hill.com • URL: http://www.mheonline.com • Semiannual. Free to qualified personnel.

***Technical Services in the United Kingdom***. Financial Times Healthcare, Maple House, 149 Tottenham Court Rd. London W1P 9LL, United Kingdom. Phone: 171 896 2066; Fax: 171 896 2213; Email: lizg@pearson-pro.com • Irregular. $400. Covers: 2,000 public and private companies offering technical services and facilities for hire in the United Kingdom. Entries include: Company name, address, phone, type of service, facilities.

***Technical Services Quarterly: New Trends in Computers, Automation, and Advanced Technologies in the Technical Operation of Libraries and Information Centers***. The Haworth Press Inc., 10 Alice St. Binghamton, NY 13904. Phone: 800-429-6784 or (607)722-5857; Fax: (607)771-0012 or (607)722-6362; Email: getinfo@haworthpress.com • URL: http://www.haworthpressinc.com/store/product.asp?sku=J014 • Quarterly. Institutions, $375.00 per year.

***Technical Trends: The Indicator Accuracy Service***. Technical Trends Inc., P.O. Box 792 Wilton, CT 06897. Phone: 800-736-0229 or (203)762-0229; Fax: (203)761-1504 • URL: http://www.capecod.net/techtrends • 40 times a year. $147.00 per year. Technical investment newsletter.

***TECHniques***. Informix Software, 16011 College Blvd. Lenexa, KS 66215-0998. Phone: (913)599-7100 • Eight times a year. Free to members; non-members, $45.00 per year. Formerly Vocational Educational Journal.

***Technological Forecasting and Social Change: An International Journal of the Dragon Project***. Elsevier, Secondary Publishing Division, 650 Ave. of the Americas New York, NY 10011. Phone: 888-437-4636 or (212)633-3980; Fax: (212)633-3975; Email: t.reller@elsevier.com • URL: http://www.elseveier.com • Nine times a year. Individuals, $131.00 per year; institutions, $839.00 per year.

***Technology and Learning: The Leading Magazine of Electronic Education***. UBM L.L.C., 600 Community Dr. Manhasset, NY 11030. Phone: (516)562-5000 or (512)562-5000; Fax: (212)378-2160 or (516)562-5036; Email: cmp@cmp.com • URL: http://www.cmp.com • Eight times a year. $29.95 per year. Covers all levels of computer/electronic education, from elementary to college. Formerly *Classroom Computer Learning*.

**Technology Based Learning and Research**. Arizona State University, College of Education Phoenix, AZ 85069. Phone: (602)543-6358; Fax: (602)543-6900; Email: ps@asu.edu • URL: http://tblr.asu.edu • Research activities are related to computer literacy.

***Technology Forecasts and Technology Surveys***. Technology Forecasts, 205 S. Beverly Dr.,, Suite 208 Beverly Hills, CA 90212. Phone: (310)273-3486; Fax: (310)858-8272 • Monthly. $192.00 per year. Newsletter. Information on major breakthroughs in advanced technologies along with forecasts of effects on future applications and markets.

***Technology in Society: An International Journal***. Elsevier, Secondary Publishing Division, 650 Ave. of the Americas New York, NY 10011. Phone: 888-437-4636 or (212)633-3980; Fax: (212)633-3975; Email: t.reller@elsevier.com • URL: http://www.elseveier.com • Quarterly. Individuals, $233.00 per year; institutions, $981.00 per year.

***Technology Law Alert: Monthly Newsletter Covering Computer-Related Law and Tax Issues***. Roditti Reports Corp., 954 Lexington Ave., Ste. 283 New York, NY 10021-5013. Phone: (212)879-3322; Fax: (212)879-4496 • URL: http://www.computerlawandtax.com • Monthly. $297.00 per year. Newsletter. Formerly *Computer Law and Tax Report*.

***Technology Review: MITs National Magazine of Technology and Policy***. Massachusetts Institute of Technology Department of Urban Studies and Planning Community Innovators Lab, Department of Urban Studies and Planning, Bldg./Rm. 9-419, 77 Massachusetts Ave. Cambridge, MA 02139. Phone: (617)253-3216; Fax: (617)258-6515; Email: colab-info@mit.edu • URL: http://web.mit.edu/colab • Ten times a year. $30.00 per year. Examines current technological issues facing society.

***Technology Transfer Highlights***. Argonne National Laboratory Industrial Technology Development Div., 9700 S Cass Ave. Lemont, IL 60439. Phone: 800-627-2596 or (630)252-2000; Email: partners@anl.gov • URL: http://www.anl.gov • Description: Provides information on federally-developed technology available for transfer and commercialization.

**Techsolve Inc.** 6705 Steger Dr. Cincinnati, OH 45237. Phone: 800-345-4482 or (513)948-2000; Fax: (513)948-2109 or (800)345-4482; Email: perkins@techsolve.org • URL: http://www.techsolve.org • Fields of research include quality improvement, computer-aided design, artificial intelligence, and employee training.

***TechTrends: For Leaders in Education and Training***. Association for Educational Communications and Technology, 320 W 8th St., Ste. 101 Bloomington, IN 47404. Phone: 877-677-2328 or (812)335-7675; Fax: (812)335-7678; Email: aect@aect.org • URL: http://www.aect.org/newsite • Bimonthly. $65.00 per year.

**Tel Aviv University - Eitan Berglas School of Economics - Foerder Institute for Economic Research**. Berglas Bldg., Rm. 123, Ramat Aviv 69978 Tel Aviv, Israel. Phone: 972 3 6409255; Fax: 972 3 6405815; Email: fersht@post.tau.ac.il • URL: http://econ.tau.ac.il/research/foerder.asp?theSubject=research • All fields of economics.

**Tel Aviv University - Interdisciplinary Center for Technology Analysis and Forecasting**. Ramat Aviv 69978 Tel Aviv, Israel. Phone: 972 3 6407571; Email: tsofer@eng.tau.ac.il • URL: http://ictaf.tau.ac.il/index.asp?lang=eng • Center assists decision makers through forecasting studies on issues of national interest as well as high-tech strategy, and translates findings into short-term decisions. Areas of interest include systems analysis, chemistry, economics, physics, mechanical engineering, electronics, operations research, sociology, statistics, business administration, production engineering, information science, science policy, high-tech strategy, urban planning, space and remote sensing.

***Telco Business Report: Executive Briefings on the Bell Operating Companies, Regional Holding Companies and Independent Telcos***. Briefings Publishing Group, 1101 King St., Ste. 110 Alexandria, VA 22314. Phone: 800-722-9221 or (703)518-2343; Fax: (703)684-2136 • 26 times a year. $759.00 per year. Newsletter. Covers long-distance markets, emerging technologies, strategies of Bell operating companies, and other telephone business topics.

***TelCor America Classified Directory***. TelCor America, PO Box 40206 Cleveland, OH 44140. Phone: (216)835-5850 • Continuous. Database covers: All types of businesses in the United States. Database includes: Company name, address, phone; product/service; geographical area served. The telephone number for accessing the computer is (216)835-4550.

***Telecom Business***. Primedia Business Magazines, PO Box 66010 Houston, TX 77266. Phone: 800-880-0368 or (713)523-8124; Fax: (713)523-8384; Email: inquiries@prismb2b.com • URL: http://www.primediabusiness.com • Monthly. Professional magazine covering the telecommunications industry for carriers, resellers and next generation networks.

***Telecommunications***. 555 Huehl Rd. Northbrook, IL 60062. Phone: (847)564-8900; Fax: (847)564-1203; Email: tc@omeda.com • URL: http://www.omeda.com • Monthly. Free to qualified personnel; others, $145.00 per year. International coverage.

***Telecommunications Directory***. Cengage Learning Inc., 20 Channel Center St. Boston, MA 02210. Phone: 800-487-8488 or (617)289-7700; Fax: (617)289-7844; Email: investors@cengage.com • URL: http://www.cengage.com • Annual. $993 Individuals. Two volumes: North America and International. Cover national and international voice and data communications networks, electronic mail services, teleconferencing facilities and services, facsimile services, Internet access providers, videotex and teletext operations, transactional services, local area networks, audiotex services, microwave systems/networkers, satellite facilities, and others involved in telecommunications, including related consultants, advertisers/marketers; associations, regulatory bodies, and publishers. Available as eBook.

***Telecommunications Export Guide***. North American Telecommunications Association, 2000 M St. NW, Ste. 550 Washington, DC 20036. Phone: 800-538-6282 or (202)296-9800; Fax: (202)296-4993 • Irregular. $103. Publication includes: List of about 135 foreign telecommunications agencies, and federal and state government agencies concerned with exports in the United States, including Department of Commerce district offices, port authorities, and small business administration field offices. Entries include: For foreign agencies—Name of the official telecommunications agency, address, U.S. representative, customs requirements, type of electrical current, technical data and statistics. For U.S. agencies—Name, address.

**Telecommunications Industry Association**. 1320 N Courthouse Rd., Ste. 200 Arlington, VA 22201. Phone: (703)907-7700; Fax: (703)907-7727; Email: gseiffert@tiaonline.org • URL: http://www.tiaonline.org • Serves the communications and IT industry, with proven strengths in standards development, domestic and international public policy, and trade shows. Facilitates business development and opportunities and a competitive market environment; provides a forum for member companies, the manufacturers and suppliers of products and services used in global communications. Represents the communications sector of the Electronic Industries Alliance.

***Telecommunications Policy***. Elsevier, Secondary Publishing Division, 650 Ave. of the Americas New York, NY 10011. Phone: 888-437-4636 or (212)633-3980; Fax: (212)633-3975; Email: t.reller@elsevier.com • URL: http://www.elseveier.com • 11/year. $1,973 Institutions.

***Telecommunications Regulation: Cable, Broadcasting, Satellite, and the Internet***. Matthew Bender and Company Inc., 1275 Broadway Albany, NY 12204-2638. Phone: 800-424-4200 or (518)487-3000; Fax: (518)487-3573 or (800)424-4200; Email: customer.support@lexisnexis.com • URL: http://www.matthewbender.com • Semiannual. $1,747; $1,588. Four looseleaf volumes. Covers local, state, and federal regulation, with emphasis on the Telecommunications Act of 1996. Includes regulation of television, telephone, cable, satellite, computer communication, and online services. Formerly *Cable Television Law*.

***Telecommunications Reports***. 76 9th Ave., 7th Fl. New York, NY 10011. Phone: 800-234-1660 or (212)771-0600; Fax: (212)771-0732; Email: customerservice@tr.com • URL: http://www.tr.com • Twice monthly. $2,039.00 per year.

***TeleCommunicator***. Association of TeleServices International, 222 S Westmonte Dr., Ste. 101 Altamonte Springs, FL 32714. Phone: 866-896-ATSI; Fax: (407)774-6440; Email: admin@atsi.org • URL: http://www.atsi.org • Bimonthly. Description: Contains news concerning telephone company, legislative and governmental actions, and Association activities.

***Telecommuting, Teleworking, and Alternative Officing***. Gil Gordon Associates, Phone: (732)329-2266; Fax: (732)329-2703 • URL: http://www.gilgordon.com • Web site includes "About Telecommuting" (questions and answers), "Worldwide Resources" (news groups, publications, conferences), and "Technology" (virtual office, intranets, groupware). Other features include monthly updates and an extensive list of telecommuting/telework related books. Fees: Free.

***Teleconferencing Business Magazine: Annual Directory of Teleconferencing Products & Services***. Business Teleconferencing, 18 Hudson Rd. Garden City, NY 11530. Phone: 888-222-4764 or (516)775-4247; Fax: (516)775-0849 • Annual. $36. Magazine for news on the industry of teleconferencing.

***Telecons***. Applied Business Telecommunications, 2300 Territorial Rd. Saint Paul, MN 55114. Phone: (651)643-6595; Fax: (651)643-6596; Email: service@abcominc.com • URL: http://www.abcominc.com • Bimonthly. $30.00 per year. Topics include teleconferencing, videoconferencing, distance learning, telemedicine, and telecommuting.

***Telehealth Buyer's Guide***. Miller Freeman Inc., 600 Harrison St. San Francisco, CA 94107. Phone: (415)905-2200; Fax: (415)905-2232 or (415)356-3480; Email: kgates@mfi.com • URL: http://www.telehealthmag.com • Annual. $10.00. Lists sources of telecommunications and information technology products and services for the health care industry.

***Telemarketer***. Actel Marketing, 163 Third Ave., Suite 303 New York, NY 10003. Phone: (212)674-2545 • Semimonthly. $285.00 per year. Newsletter.

***Telemarketing Law Guide***. Wolters Kluwer Law & Business CCH, 2700 Lake Cook Rd. Riverwoods, IL 60015. Phone: 888-224-7377 or (847)267-7000; Email: cust_serv@cch.com • URL: http://www.cchgroup.com • Contains detailed information on federal do-not-call legislation, various state laws, court decisions, and penalties.

***Telematics and Informatics: An International Journal on Telecommunications and Internet Technology***. Elsevier, Secondary Publishing Division, 650 Ave. of the Americas New York, NY 10011. Phone: 888-437-4636 or (212)633-3980; Fax: (212)633-3975; Email: t.reller@elsevier.com • URL: http://www.elseveier.com • Four times a year. Institutions, $938.00 per year.

***Telephone Answering Service***. Entrepreneur Press, 2445 McCabe Way, Ste. 400 Irvine, CA 92614-6244. Phone: 800-864-6864 or (949)261-2325 or (949)622-7131; Fax: (949)261-7729 or (949)261-0234; Email: press@entrepreneur.com • URL: http://www.entrepreneurpress.com • Looseleaf. $59.50. A practical guide to starting a telephone answering service. Covers profit potential, start-up costs, market size evaluation, owner's time required, pricing, accounting, advertising, promotion, etc. (Start-Up Business Guide No. E1148).

***The Telephone Industry Directory***. Access Intelligence L.L.C., 4 Choke Cherry Rd., 2nd Fl. Rockville, MD 20850. Phone: 800-777-5006 or (301)354-2000 or (301)354-2101; Fax: (301)309-3847 or (801)365-2300; Email: info@accessintel.com • URL: http://www.accessintel.com/ • $249 U.S., Canada, and Mexico; $289 Other countries. Covers: 7,000 companies and 14,000 contacts in the telephone industry.

***Telephone Management Strategist***. Buyers Laboratory L.L.C., 20 Railroad Ave. Hackensack, NJ 07601. Phone: (201)488-0404; Fax: (201)488-0461; Email: info@bertl.com • URL: http://www.buyerslab.com • Monthly. $125.00 per year. Newsletter. Information on business telecommunications.

***Telephone Selling Report: Providing Proven Sales Ideas You Can Use***. Art Sobczak, editor. Business by Phone Inc., 13254 Stevens St. Omaha, NE 68137. Phone: 800-326-7721 or (402)895-9399; Fax: (402)896-3353; Email: arts@businessbyphone.com • URL: http://businessbyphone.com • Bimonthly. $69.00 per year. Newsletter. How-to newsletter providing proven ideas, tips, and techniques for telephone prospecting and selling.

***Telephony: Intelligence for the Broadband Economy***. Primedia Business Magazines and Media, 330 N Wabash Ave., Suite 2300 Chicago, IL 60611. Phone: 800-795-5445 or (312)595-1080 or (312)726-2802; Fax: (312)595-0295 or (312)726-2574; Email: subs@primediabusiness.com • URL: http://www.primediabusiness.com • Biweekly. $114.00 per year.

***Teleselekt***. Austrian Federal Economic Chamber, Wiedner Hauptstrasse 63 A-1045 Vienna, Austria. Phone: 43 5 90900 or 43 5 909005678; Email: office@wko.at • URL: http://www.wko.at • Semiannual. Database covers: 10,000 Austrian exporters and importers and 18,000 products. Entries include: Company name and address, management, number of employees, turnover, shares, commodities, services, and product information.

***TeleTrends***. International Telework Association Council, 8403 Colesville Rd., Ste. 865 Silver Spring, MD 20910. Phone: (301)650-2322; Email: info@workfromanywhere.com • URL: http://www.telecommute.org • Quarterly. Newsletter. Price on application.

***Television and Cable Factbook***. Warren Communications News Inc., 2115 Ward Ct. NW Washington, DC 20037. Phone: 800-771-9202 or (202)872-9200; Fax: (202)318-8350 or (202)293-3435 • URL: http://www.warren-news.com • Annual. $595. Commercial and noncommercial television stations and networks.

***Television Digest with Consumer Electronics***. Warren Communications News Inc., 2115 Ward Ct. NW Washington, DC 20037. Phone: 800-771-9202 or (202)872-9200; Fax: (202)318-8350 or (202)293-3435 • URL: http://www.warren-news.com • Weekly. $944.00 per year. Newsletter featuring new consumer entertainment products utilizing electronics. Also covers the television broadcasting and cable TV industries, with corporate and industry news.

***Television International Magazine***. TVI Publishing, P.O. Box 8471 University City, CA 91618-8471. Phone: (213)462-1099; Email: tvi@smartgo.com • URL: http://www.tvinews.com • Bimonthly. $42.00 per year.

***Television Quarterly***. Academy of Television Arts and Sciences, 5220 Lankershim Blvd. North Hollywood, CA 91601. Phone: (818)754-2800 • URL: http://www.emmys.com • Quarterly. Individuals, $30.00 per year; students, $22.00 per year.

***Television Week***. Crain Communications Inc., 711 3rd Ave. New York, NY 10017. Phone: (212)210-0100; Email: info@crain.com • URL: http://www.crain.com • Weekly. $119.00 per year. Formerly *Electronic Media*.

***Temporary Help Service***. Entrepreneur Press, 2445 McCabe Way, Ste. 400 Irvine, CA 92614-6244. Phone: 800-864-6864 or (949)261-2325 or (949)622-7131; Fax: (949)261-7729 or (949)261-0234; Email: press@entrepreneur.com • URL: http://www.entrepreneurpress.com • Looseleaf. $59.50. A practical guide to starting an employment agency for temporary workers. Covers profit potential, start-up costs, market size evaluation, owner's time required, site selection, lease negotiation, pricing, accounting, advertising, promotion, etc. (Start-Up Business Guide No. E1189.).

**Tennessee Agricultural Experiment Station - University of Tennessee, Knoxville**. 103 Morgan Hall Knoxville, TN 37996-4506. Phone: (865)974-4520; Fax: (865)974-6451; Email: AgResearch@tennessee.edu • URL: http://taes.tennessee.edu.

***Tennessee Business Services Directory***. Nashville Area Chamber of Commerce, 211 Commerce St., Ste. 100 Nashville, TN 37201-1806. Phone: (615)743-3000; Fax: (615)743-3002 • URL: http://www.nashvillechamber.com • $121 Members; $132 Nonmembers. Covers: 7,500 Tennessee businesses in the service industry with 20 employees and in the restaurant industry with 50 employees. Entries include: Name, address, phone, and fax.

***Tennis Industry***. Tennis Industry Association, 117 Executive Ctr., 1 Corpus Christie Pl. Hilton Head Island, SC 29928. Phone: 866-686-3036 or (843)686-3036; Fax: (843)686-3078; Email: info@tennisindustry.org • URL: http://www.tennisindustry.org • Bimonthly. $22.00 per year. Edited for retailers serving the "serious tennis enthusiast." Provides news of apparel, rackets, equipment, and court construction.

**Territorial Newspapers**. 3280 E Hemisphere Loop, Ste. 180 Tucson, AZ 85706. Phone: (520)294-1200; Fax: (520)294-4040 or (520)295-4076 • URL: http://www.azbiz.com.

***Test and Measurement World: The Magazine for Quality in Electronics***. Reed Electronics Group, 360 Park Ave., S New York, NY 10010. Phone: 800-446-6551 or (646)746-6400; Fax: (646)746-7028; Email: corporatecommunications@reedbusiness.com • URL: http://www.reedbusiness.com • 15 times a year. $93.99 per year.

***Tests: A Comprehensive Reference for Assessments in Psychology, Education and Business***. Pro-Ed Inc., 8700 Shoal Creek Blvd. Austin, TX 78757-6897. Phone: 800-897-3202 or (512)451-3246; Fax: (512)451-8542 or (800)397-7633; Email: general@proedinc.com • URL: http://www.proedinc.com • Irregular. $108 Individuals Hardcover; $77 Individuals Softcover. Covers over 200 publishers of over 2,000 psychological, educational, aptitude, and business tests.

***Tests***. Cengage Learning Inc., 20 Channel Center St. Boston, MA 02210. Phone: 800-487-8488 or (617)289-7700; Fax: (617)289-7844; Email: investors@cengage.com • URL: http://www.cengage.com • 2008. $105.00. 6th edition. List nearly 200 publishers for over 2,000 tests. Published by Pro-Ed Inc.

***Tests in Print***. Linda L. Murphy and others. University of Nebraska-Lincoln Buros Institute of Mental Measurements, 21 Teachers College Hall Lincoln, NE 68588-0484. Phone: 800-755-1105 or (402)472-6203; Fax: (800)526-2617; Email: pressmail@unl.edu • URL: http://www.unl.edu/buros • Price varies. Two volumes. Lists over 4,000 testing instruments.

**Texas A&M AgriLife Research Center - Sonora - Texas A & M University**. 7887 US Highway 87 N San Angelo, TX 76901. Phone: (325)653-4576; Fax: (325)655-7791 • URL: http://sanangelo.tamu.edu/satellite-stations/sonora.

**Texas A&M University - Agribusiness, Food, and Consumer Economics Research Center**. Department of Agricultural Economics, 600 John Kimbrough Blvd., Ste. 371, 2124 TAMU College Station, TX 77843-2124. Phone: (979)845-5911; Fax: (979)845-6378; Email: afcerc@tamu.edu • URL: http://afcerc.tamu.edu • Marketing of Texas and U.S. agricultural products. Areas include domestic and foreign market opportunities, marketing policies and strategies, international competitiveness of Texas and the U.S. in the production and marketing of traditional bulk and high value/value-added products, impact of new technologies on markets and prices, efficiency of market information systems, market structure and performance, and consumer survey research.

**Texas A&M University - Center for Retailing Studies**. Wehner Bldg., Ste. 201, Mays Business School, 4112 TAMU College Station, TX 77843-4112. Phone: (979)845-0325; Fax: (979)845-5117 or (979)845-5230; Email: c-bridges@mays.tamu.edu • URL: http://www.crstamu.org • Research areas include retailing issues and consumer economics.

**Texas A&M University - College of Agriculture and Life Sciences - Department of Wildlife and Fisheries Sciences - Aquacultural Research and Teaching Facility**. 210 Nagle Hall College Station, TX 77843. Phone: (979)272-3422 or (979)845-7471; Fax: (979)845-3786 or (979)845-7103; Email: d-gatlin@tamu.edu • URL: http://wfsc.tamu.edu/facilities/aquacultural-research-and-teaching-facility • Warm water aquaculture, including basic and applied studies in nutrition, bioenergetics, environmental physiology, and developmental biology. Species of interest include channel catfish, crawfish, tilapia, red drum, hybrid striped bass, and largemouth bass.

**Texas A&M University - Texas Transportation Institute**. 3135 TAMU College Station, TX 77843-3135. Phone: (979)845-1713; Fax: (979)845-9356; Email: dennis-c@tamu.edu • URL: http://tti.tamu.edu • Concerned with all forms and modes of transportation. Research areas include transportation economics, highway construction, traffic safety, public transportation, and highway engineering.

***Texas Business Magazine***. • Monthly. Magazine on Texas industry, commerce, and finance.

***Texas Industrial Expansion***. University of Texas at Austin IC2 Institute Bureau of Business Research, 2815 San Gabriel St. Austin, TX 78705. Phone: (512)475-8900; Fax: (512)475-8903; Email: bkellison@ic2.utexas.edu • URL: http://ic2.utexas.edu/bbr • Monthly. $60. Covers: New and expanding manufacturing facilities in Texas in Standard Industrial Classifications (SIC) 1321, 1477, 2011-3999, 4911. Entries include: Company name, address, phone, name of principal executive square footage and cost of project when available, number of employees, products or services.

***Texas Real Estate Business***. France Publications Inc., 3500 Piedmont Rd., Ste. 415 Atlanta, GA 30305. Phone: (404)832-8262; Fax: (404)832-8260; Email: jerry@francepublications.com • URL: http://www.francepublications.com/contact.html • Monthly. $64 Individuals; $110 Two years. Magazine that covers the latest news, developments and trends in commercial real estate in Texas.

**Texas Tech University - Center for Communications Research**. College of Mass Communications Lubbock, TX 79409-3082. Phone: (806)834-3117; Fax: (806)742-1085; Email: p.muhlberger@ttu.edu • URL: http://www.depts.ttu.edu/comc/ccr/index.php • Public opinion and consumer surveys, communication experiments, economic and policy studies, and television/radio production and testing, including studies on communication immunization and functions, and television personality and viewers' preference.

**Texas Tech University - Center for Healthcare Innovation, Education and Research**. Rawls College of Business Administration Lubbock, TX 79409. Phone: (806)742-1236; Fax: (806)742-3434; Email: tim.huerta@ttu.edu • URL: http://chier.ba.ttu.edu/index.asp • Interdisciplinary approaches to studying healthcare safety issues and addition of electronic medical records.

**Texas Transportation Institute, Systems Planning - Texas A & M University**. 3135 TAMU College Station, TX 77843-3135. Phone: (979)845-6002 or (979)845-9356; Fax: (979)945-6008; Email: k-turnbull@tamu.edu • URL: http://www.tti.tamu.edu.

***Textile Hi-Lights***. American Textile Manufacturers Institute, 1130 Connecticut Ave. NW Washington, DC 20036-3954. Phone: (202)862-0500; Fax: (202)862-0570 • URL: http://www.textileweb.com/storefronts/amertextile.html • Quarterly. $125.00 per year. Monthly *Supplements*.

***Textile Horizons: Providing Essential Reading for All Present and Future Decision Makers in Textiles and Fashion Worldwide***. World Textile Publications Ltd., Perkins House, One Longlands St., c/o Keith Higgenbottom Bradford BD1 2TP, United Kingdom. Phone: 44 1274 378800; Fax: (127)4 378811; Email: info@worldtextile.com • URL: http://www.worldtextile.com • Bimonthly. $115.00 per year.

**Textile Materials Technology**. Philadelphia University, 4201 Henry Ave. Philadelphia, PA 19144. Phone: (215)951-2700; Fax: (215)951-2651; Email: admissions@philau.edu • URL: http://www.philau.edu/textilemat • Many research areas, including industrial and nonwoven textiles.

***Textile Month***. Reed Business Information, Quadrant House, The Quadrant Surrey SM2 5AS, United Kingdom. Phone: 44 20 86523500 or 1 6618904; Fax: 44 20 86528932; Email: webmaster@rbi.co.uk • URL: http://www.reedbusiness.com • Biennial. $4. Covers: United Kingdom companies representing overseas manufacturers of textile machinery. Entries include: Company name, address, phone, telex, key personnel, overseas contacts, types of machinery handled.

***Textile Research Journal***. TRI/Princeton, 601 Prospect Ave. Princeton, NJ 08542. Phone: (609)430-4820 • URL: http://www.triprinceton.org • Monthly. Individuals, $325.00 per year; college and university libraries, $500.00 per year.

***Textile Technology Index™***. EBSCO Publishing Inc., 10 Estes St. Ipswich, MA 01938-2106. Phone: 800-653-2726 or (978)356-6500; Fax: (978)356-6565; Email: information@ebscohost.com • URL: http://www.ebscohost.com • Monthly. $545 Individuals. Includes indexing and abstracts for more than 470 periodicals.

***Textile World***. Billian Publishing Inc., 2100 RiverEdge Pkwy., Ste. 1200 Atlanta, GA 30328. Phone: 800-800-5668 or (770)955-5656; Fax: (770)952-0669; Email: info@billian.com • URL: http://www.billian.com • Monthly. Free to qualified personnel.

***Textile World Blue Book***. RentPath Inc., 3585 Engineering Dr., Ste. 100 Norcross, GA 30092-2831. Phone: 800-216-1423 or (678)421-3000 • URL: http://www.rentpath.com • Annual. $160.00. Provides information on more than 5,200 textile mills in the U.S., Canada, and Mexico, including number of employees and names of about 17,000 key personnel. Also provides data on 2,500 suppliers of equipment and products for textile mills. Also known as *Official North American Textile World Blue Book*, formerly *Textile Red Book*.

***Thai-American Business (T-AB)***. American Chamber of Commerce in Thailand, GPF Witthayu Tower A, 7th Fl., 93/1 Wireless Rd., Lumpini, Pathumwan Bangkok 10330, Thailand. Phone: 66 22541041; Fax: 66 22511605; Email: service@amchamthailand.com • URL: http://www.amchamthailand.com • Annual. Business and Economics journal.

***Thai Business Groups: A Unique Guide to Who Owns What***. Brooker Group Public Company Ltd., The Trendy Office Bldg., 26th Fl., 10/190-193 Soi Sukhumvit 13, Sukhumvit Rd., Klong Toey Nua, Wattana Bangkok 10110, Thailand. Phone: 66 2 21687100; Fax: 66 2 21681711; Email: info@brookergroup.com • URL: http://www.brookergroup.com • Annual. 10,700 &baht; Individuals; $340 Individuals. Covers: 150 top family business groups in Thailand. Entries include: Contact addresses, key executives of major companies, history and background of the top Thailand business families.

**Thai Venture Capital Association**. 19/1 Bldg. 2, King Chamnanaksorn, Phaholyothin Rd., Phayathai Bangkok 10400, Thailand. Phone: 66 2 6617898; Fax: 66 2 6617899; Email: tvca@venturecapital.or.th • URL: http://www.venturecapital.or.th • Promotes venture capital and private equity businesses in Thailand. Supports and assists members in all problems related to venture capital businesses, including negotiations with any foreign parties. Promotes closer working relationships among members in order to exchange ideas and opinions regarding technical knowledge, news, economic research and financial information.

***Thailand Business Forecast Report***. Telecommunications Insight, 85 Queen Victoria St. London EC4V 4AB, United Kingdom. Phone: 20 72 465100 or 44 20 7248 0468; Fax: 20 72 480467 or 44 20 7248 0467; Email: enquiries@telecomsinsight.com • URL: http://www.telecomsinsight.com • Quarterly. $1,195 Individuals Single user; $1,795 Individuals Up to 3 users. Business forecasting report for Thailand.

***Thailand Business Law Handbook***. International Business Publications, USA, PO Box 15343 Washington, DC 20003. Phone: (202)546-2103; Fax: (202)546-3275; Email: ibpusa@comcast.net • URL: http://ibpus.com • $99.95 Individuals hardcopy, e-book, CD-ROM. Covers: Information on business laws and regulations, business, investments, tax and contacts.

***Thailand Export-Import Yellow Pages***. Teleinfo Media Company Ltd., 25th-28th Fl., Vanit Bldg. 2, 1126/2 New Phetchaburi Rd., Khwaeng Makkasan, Khet Ratchathewi Bangkok 10400, Thailand. Phone: 66 22628888; Fax: 66 22628899; Email: info@larka.fr • URL: http://www.teleinfomedia.net • Covers: Updated information for exporters and importers in Thailand. Entries include: Company information and contact details.

***Thailand Investment: A Directory of Companies Promoted by the Board of Investment***. Cosmic Group of Cos., 4th Fl., Phyathai Bldg., 31 Phyathai Rd., Rajthevi Bangkok 10400, Thailand. Phone: 662 2453850; Fax: 662 2461710; Email: cosmic@loxinfo.co.th • Annual. $60 plus shipping charges. Covers: Approximately 3,600 companies in Thailand that are promoted by the Thailand Board of Investment. Database includes: Information on doing business in Thailand. Entries include: Company name, address, phone.

***Thailand Investment and Business Guide***. International Business Publications, USA, PO Box 15343 Washington, DC 20003. Phone: (202)546-2103; Fax: (202)546-3275; Email: ibpusa@comcast.net • URL: http://ibpus.com • $99.95 Individuals hardcopy, e-book, CD-ROM. Covers: Basic information on economy, export-import and investment climate, regulations and industrial development, banking, and government. Entries include: Important business contacts and business travel.

***Thailand Product Guide***. Todd Publications, PO Box 500 Millwood, NY 10546. Phone: 866-896-0916 or (914)373-4750; Fax: (914)373-4750; Email: toddpub@aol.com • URL: http://www.toddpublications.com • $95. Covers: Over 1,500 Thailand exporters. Entries include: Company name, address, phone, fax, telex.

***Thailand Showcase: A Buyers' Guide***. Cosmic Group of Cos., 4th Fl., Phyathai Bldg., 31 Phyathai Rd., Rajthevi Bangkok 10400, Thailand. Phone: 662 2453850; Fax: 662 2461710; Email: cosmic@loxinfo.co.th • Annual. $48 plus shipping charges. Covers: More than 3,000 companies in Thailand engaged in exporting their goods. Database includes: Overview of the Thailand economy. Entries include: Company name, address, phone.

***Thailand: The MFC Investment Handbook***. Hoover's Inc., 5800 Airport Blvd. Austin, TX 78752-4204. Phone: 866-443-3939 or (512)374-4500 or (866)281-5969; Fax: (512)374-4501; Email: salesteam@hoovers.com • URL: http://www.hoovers.com • Annual. $46.95 plus $3.50 shipping. Covers: over 340 companies listed on the Stock Exchange of Thailand; 23 unit trusts. Entries include: Company name, address, phone, fax, stock symbol, company overview, price per share, trading volume, net income, capital, financial ratios, foreign holdings, limits on foreign ownership, list of major shareholders, names and titles of key personnel.

***the Journal of Business, Entrepreneurship, and the Law***.

***Theatre Journal***. Association for Theatre in Higher Education. Johns Hopkins University Press, 2715 N Charles St. Baltimore, MD 21218-4363. Phone: 800-537-5487 or (410)516-6900 or (800)537-5487; Fax: (410)516-6968 or (410)516-6998; Email: jrnlcirc@press.jhu.edu • URL: http://www.press.jhu.edu • Quarterly. $81 Individuals print (2 years); $165 Institutions; $160 Institutions print (2 years); $45 Individuals print; $320 Institutions print (2 years); $50 Individuals electronic access. Quarterly. Individuals, $35.00 per year; institutions, $108.00 per year. Contains material on theatre history, theatre news, and reviews of books and plays.

***The Theatre Listing: A Directory of Professional Theatre in Canada***. Professional Association of Canadian Theatres, 215 Spadina Ave., Ste. 555 Toronto, ON, Canada M5T 2C7. Phone: 800-263-7228 or (416)595-6455; Fax: (416)595-6450; Email: info@pact.ca • URL: http://www.pact.ca • Covers: Over 300 English-language professional theatres in Canada. Entries include: Theatre name, address, phone, fax, e-mail, internet sites, contacts, key personnel, budget, mandates, facilities, submissions, repertoire, play development and other programs, affiliations.

**Thermophysical Properties Research Laboratory**. 3080 Kent Ave. West Lafayette, IN 47906. Phone: (765)463-1581; Fax: (765)463-5235; Email: tprlinqr@tprl.com • URL: http://www.tprl.com • Studies the thermophysical properties of materials from cryogenic to very high temperatures.

***TheStreet.com: Your Insider's Look at Wall Street***. TheStreet.com, Inc., Phone: 800-562-9571 or (212)321-5000; Fax: (212)321-5016 • URL: http://www.thestreet.com • Daily. Iconoclastic advice and comment on the stock market, but premium service displays a more comprehensive selection of news and analysis.

***33 Metalproducing: For Primary Producers of Steel, Aluminum, and Copper-Base Alloys***. Penton Media Inc., 1300 E 9th St. Cleveland, OH 44114-1501. Phone: (216)696-7000; Fax: (216)696-1752; Email: information@penton.com • URL: http://penton.com • Monthly. $65.00 per year. Covers metal production technology and methods and industry news. Includes a bimonthly *Nonferrous Supplement*.

***Thomas Register of American Manufacturers***. Thomas Publishing Company L.L.C., 5 Penn Plz. New York, NY 10001. Phone: (212)695-0500; Fax: (212)290-7362; Email: contact@thomaspublishing.com • URL: http://www.thomaspublishing.com • Annual. More than 168,000 manufacturing firms are listed in this 34 volume set. Volumes 1-23 list the firms under 68,000 product headings. Thomas Register is enhanced with over 8,000 manufacturers' catalogs and is available in print, CD-ROM, DVD or online. Logistics Guide, a reference manual for freight and shipping sourcing.

***Thomas Register Online***. Thomas Publishing Company L.L.C., 5 Penn Plz. New York, NY 10001. Phone: (212)695-0500; Fax: (212)290-7362; Email: contact@thomaspublishing.com • URL: http://www.thomaspublishing.com • Provides concise information on approximately 194,000 U. S. companies, mainly manufacturers, with over 50,000 product classifications. Indexes over 115,000 trade names. Information is updated semiannually. Inquire as to online cost and availability.

***Thomson World Bank Directory: International Edition***. Accuity Inc., 4709 W Golf Rd. Skokie, IL 60076. Phone: 800-321-3373 or (847)676-9600; Fax: (847)933-8101; Email: custserv@accuitysolutions.com • URL: http://www.accuitysolutions.com • Annual. $685 Individuals. Covers: Over 10,000 international banks and their branches in around 200 countries around the globe, including the top 1,000 U.S. Banks. Entries include: Institution name, address, phone, fax, key banking officers by functional title, directors, data established, expanded statement of condition, including a profit and loss account and historic performance ratios.

***Thornton Guide to Hong Kong Companies***. Hoover's Inc., 5800 Airport Blvd. Austin, TX 78752-4204. Phone: 866-443-3939 or (512)374-4500 or (866)281-5969; Fax: (512)374-4501; Email: salesteam@hoovers.com • URL: http://www.hoovers.com • Semiannual. $69.95. Covers: More than 500 companies in Hong Kong. Database includes: Introduction to the Hong Kong capital market. Entries include: Name, address, phone, fax, stock codes and sector of business, board of directors, major shareholders, financial data, description of business activities.

***Thornton Guide to the Companies of Singapore and Malaysia***. Hoover's Inc., 5800 Airport Blvd. Austin, TX 78752-4204. Phone: 866-443-3939 or (512)374-4500 or (866)281-5969; Fax: (512)374-4501; Email: salesteam@hoovers.com • URL: http://www.hoovers.com • Semiannual. $69.95. Covers: Nearly 250 companies in Singapore and nearly 500 companies in Malaysia. Database includes: Overview of the Stock Exchange of Singapore and the Kuala Lumpur Stock Exchange. Entries include: Name, address, phone, fax, stock codes and sector of business, board of directors, major shareholders, financial data, description of business activities.

***3W Register of Chinese Business***. 3W International Digital Publishing, 43 Michaelson Dr. Mount Laurel, NJ 08054-1355. • Biennial. $298. Covers: Approximately 31,000 Chinese companies in a variety of industries, including textile and garment, electronics and computer, mechanical and metallurgical, chemical and materials, construction and construction materials, service, wholesale trade and food, and agriculture, engineering, and management service. Entries include: Company name, address, phone, fax, telex, cable number, names and titles of key personnel, ownership information, financial data, date founded, number of employees, stock availability, imports, exports, product/service, Standard Industrial Classification (SIC) codes.

***Thunder Bay Business***. North Superior Publishing Inc., 1145 Barton St. Thunder Bay, ON, Canada P7B 5N3. Phone: (807)623-2348; Fax: (807)623-7515; Email: nspinc@tbaytel.net • URL: http://www.northsuperiorpublishing.com • Monthly. Trade magazine.

***The Thunderbird Guide to International Business Resources on the World Wide Web***. Wiley Publishing Group, 10475 Crosspoint Blvd. Indianapolis, IN 46256. Phone: 800-434-3422 or (317)572-3000; Fax: (317)572-4000 • URL: http://www.wiley.com • $57.95 Individuals Paperback. Covers: Web sites for political and economic developments that affect trade worldwide. Derived from a study by Dean's Global Information and Technology at Thunderbird (American Graduate School of International Management). Entries include: country, category (country information, business, business topics, government resources, information providers), title, URL, and description.

***Thunderbird International Business Review***. Thunderbird American Graduate School of International Management. John Wiley and Sons, Inc., Journals Div., 111 River St. Hoboken, NJ 07030. Phone: 800-526-5368 or (201)748-6000; Fax: (201)748-6088; Email: consumers@wiley.com • URL: http://www.wiley.com • Bimonthly. $937 Institutions print only; $997 Institutions, Canada and Mexico print only; $1,048 Institutions, other countries print only; $289 Other countries print; $289 U.S., Canada, and Mexico print. Journal on international business and commerce for academic scholars, business and government executives, and trade specialists. Formerly *International Executive*.

***TIA Directory and Desk Reference***. Telecommunications Industry Association, 1320 N Courthouse Rd., Ste. 200 Arlington, VA 22201. Phone: (703)907-7700; Fax: (703)907-7727; Email: gseiffert@tiaonline.org • URL: http://www.tiaonline.org • Lists manufacturers and suppliers of interconnect telephone equipment. Formerly *Multimedia Telecommunications Sourcebook*.

***Tianjin Yellow Pages: Commercial/Industrial Directory***. China Yellow Pages Directories Co., Fortress Twr., Rm. 1204-5, 250 King's Rd., Hong Kong North Point, China. Phone: 8076807; Fax: 5032601 • $65. Covers: over 20,000 companies in the Tianjin area. Database includes: Investment information. Entries include: Company, name, address, phone.

***Tile and Decorative Surfaces: The Voice of America's Tile Market***. Dialysis Inc., 18 Penthouse E 41st St. New York, NY 10017. Phone: (212)376-7722; Fax: (212)376-7723; Email: ashleepub@aol.com • URL: http://www.ashlee.com • Monthly. $50.00 per year.

***Tile Design and Installation***. BNP Media, 2401 W Big Beaver Rd., Ste. 700 Troy, MI 48084. Phone: 800-952-6643 or (248)362-3700 or (847)763-9534; Fax: (248)362-5103 or (248)362-0317; Email: privacy@bnpmedia.com • URL: http://www.bnpmedia.com • Quarterly. $55.00 per year. Formerly *Tile World*.

**Tile Roofing Institute**. 23607 Hwy. 99, Ste. 2C Edmonds, WA 98026. Phone: (425)778-6162; Fax: (425)771-9588; Email: info@tileroofing.org • URL: http://www.tileroofing.org • Members are producers of clay and concrete tile roofing. Formerly National Tile Roofing Manufacturers Association.

***Timber Bulletin***. Economic Commission for Europe. United Nations Publications, c/o National Book Network, 15200 NBN Way Blue Ridge Summit, PA 17214. Phone: 888-254-4286 or (212)963-7680 or (212)963-8302; Fax: (800)338-4550; Email: unpublications@nbnbooks.com • URL: http://www.unp.un.org • Irregular. $30. Contains international statistics on forest products, including price, production, and foreign trade data.

***Timber Harvesting***. Hatton-Brown Publishers Inc., 225 Hanrick St. Montgomery, AL 36102. Phone: 800-669-5613 or (334)834-1170; Fax: (334)834-4525; Email: dianne@hattonbrown.com • URL: http://www.hattonbrown.net • 10 times a year. $40.00 per year.

***Timber Harvesting—Logger's Resource Guide***. Hatton-Brown Publishers Inc., 225 Hanrick St. Montgomery, AL 36102. Phone: 800-669-5613 or (334)834-1170; Fax: (334)834-4525; Email: dianne@hattonbrown.com • URL: http://www.hattonbrown.net • Annual. Publication includes: List manufacturers and distributors of equipment used in harvesting and handling timber, logging trade organizations and trade associations. Entries include: Firm name, division or subsidiary name, address, fax, phone, e-mail, website, year company established, names and titles of key personnel.

***Time Table of Business, Politics and Media***. Etronica, 15332 Antioch St., Ste. 438 Pacific Palisades, CA 90272. Phone: (310)356-6568; Fax: (310)231-3682; Email: info@etronica.com • A computer-readable database containing more than 6200 stories tracing the quest for wealth, power, and knowledge through history from the Trojan Horse to Desert Storm. Entries feature voiceover narration providing a political context, pictures, graphics and animations, zoom-in maps, bibliographic references, pertinent quotes, portraits, and portions of significant documents.

***The Times 1,000: The Indispensable Annual Review of the World's Leading Industrial and Financial Companies***. Times Books Ltd., 77/85 Fulham Palace Rd., Hammersmith London W6 8JB, United Kingdom. Phone: 81 7417070; Fax: 81 3074813 • Annual. $32.50. Covers: 1,000 leading companies in the United Kingdom; 1,000 leading companies in Europe; leading firms in the United States, Canada, Australia, South Africa, Ireland, Hong Kong, and Japan. Entries include: For all companies—Company name and address. For British firms—Company name, names of chairman and managing director, sales, profits, capital, number of employees, and ranks and ratios. Listings for other firms vary in detail.

***Tin International***. Tin Magazines Ltd., Kingston Lane Uxbridge UB8 3PJ, United Kingdom. • Monthly. $215.00 per year. News and analysis for the international tin industry.

***Tire and Rim Association Year Book***. Tire and Rim Association, 175 Montrose West Ave., Ste. 150 Copley, OH 44321. Phone: (330)666-8121; Fax: (330)666-8340; Email: tra@us-tra.org • URL: http://www.us-tra.org • $119 Individuals. Contains all TRA Standards and related information approved by the Association for tires, rims and allied parts for ground vehicles.

***Tire Business***. Crain Communications, Inc., 1725 Merriman Rd., Suite 300 Akron, OH 44313-5283. Phone: 800-678-9595 or (330)836-9180; Email: info@crain.com • URL: http://www.crain.com • Bi-weekly. $79.00 per year. Edited for independent tire retailers and wholesalers.

***Tire Review—Sourcebook & Directory Issue***. Babcox, 3550 Embassy Pkwy. Akron, OH 44333. Phone: (330)670-1234; Fax: (330)670-0874 • URL: http://www.babcox.com • Annual. Publication includes: About 850 suppliers of tires, repair equipment, and automotive service supplies and equipment to tire dealers and retreaders. Entries include: Company name, address, phone, name and title of contact, products, brand names, email and website addresses.

***Tire Review: The Authority on Tire Dealer Profitability***. Babcox Publications Inc., 3550 Embassy Pkwy. Akron, OH 44333-8318. Phone: (330)670-1234; Fax: (330)670-0874; Email: info@babcox.com • URL: http://www.babcox.com • Monthly. $64.00. Includes *LiftGuide, Custom Wheel and Tire Style Guide, Sourcebook and Directory and NTDRA Show*.

***Titanium: A Statistical Review***. International Titanium Association, 11674 Huron St., Ste. 100 Northglenn, CO 80234. Phone: (303)404-2221; Fax: (303)404-9111; Email: ita@titanium.org • URL: http://www.titanium.org • Annual. Members free; $75.

***Titanium Newsletter***. Titanium Development Association, 4141 Arapahoe Ave., Ste. 100 Boulder, CO 80303. Phone: (303)443-7515; Fax: (303)443-4406 • Description: Presents news on the titanium industry. Covers corporate and Association activities, personnel changes, and legislative news. Recurring features include news of research, news of members, a calendar of events, product information, and columns titled Ti News Pipeline and Ti Reference Library.

***Title News***. American Land Title Association, 1828 L St. NW, Ste. 705 Washington, DC 20036-5104. Phone: 800-787-2582 or (202)296-3671; Fax: (202)223-5843 or (800)329-2582; Email: service@alta.org • URL: http://www.alta.org • Monthly. Description: Provides information for title companies and property investors.

***TMA Tobacco Tax Guide: Summaries of Key Provisions of Tobacco Tax Laws, All Tobacco Products, All States***. Tobacco Merchants Association of the U.S., 231 Clarksville Rd. Princeton, NJ 08543-8019. Phone: (609)275-4900; Fax: (609)275-8379; Email: tma@tma.org • URL: http://www.tma.org • Looseleaf service. Members, $750.00 per year; nonmembers, $2,250.00 per year. Quarterly updates.

***The Toastmaster: For Better Listening, Thinking, Speaking***. Suzanne Frey, editor. Toastmasters International, PO Box 9052 Mission Viejo, CA 92690-9052. Phone: (949)858-8255 or (949)835-1300; Fax: (949)858-1207; Email: tminfo@toastmasters.org • URL: http://www.toastmasters.org • Monthly. Membership. Provides information and "how-to" articles on communication and leadership.

***Tobacco Abstracts***. North Carolina State University North Carolina Agricultural Research Service, 201 Patterson Hall, Box 7643 Raleigh, NC 27695-7643. Phone: (919)515-2717; Fax: (919)515-7745; Email: david_monks@ncsu.edu • URL: http://harvest.cals.ncsu.edu/ncars/index.cfm?pageID=1599 • Monthly. Bimonthly.

***Tobacco-Cigarette News***. International Press Cutting Service, P.O. Box 121 Allahabad 211 001, India. Phone: 91 532 622392 • Weekly. $85.00 per year. Formerly *Tobacco News*.

***Tobacco International***. Lockwood Publications Inc., 26 Broadway, Fl. 9M New York, NY 10004. Phone: (212)391-2060; Fax: (212)827-0945; Email: operations@lockwoodpublications.com • URL: http://www.lockwoodpublications.com • Weekly. $32.00 per year.

***Tobacco Market Review***. U.S. Department of Agriculture - Agricultural Marketing Service, Rm. 3071-S, Ag Stop 0201, 1400 Independence Ave., SW Washington, DC 20250. Phone: (800)333-4636; Email: amsadministratoroffice@ams.usda.gov. • URL: http://www.ams.usda.gov/AMSv1.0 • Annual.

***Tobacco Reporter: Devoted to All Segments of the International Tobacco Trade Processing, Trading, Manufacturing***. SpecComm International Inc., 3101 Poplarwood Ct., Ste. 115 Raleigh, NC 27604. Phone: (919)872-5040; Fax: (919)876-6531; Email: spec_circ@juno.com • URL: http://www.speccomm.com • Monthly. $36.00 per year.

***Tobacco Retailers Almanac***. International Premium Cigar and Pipe Retailers, No. 4 Bradley Park Ct., Ste. 2-H Columbus, GA 31904-3637. Phone: (706)494-1143; Fax: (706)494-1893; Email: info@ipcpr.org • URL: http://www.ipcpr.org • Annual. Lists virtually every tobacco related product available (including cigars, cigarettes, pipes, tobacco, lighters and gift items).

***Tobe Report***. Tobe Associates Inc., 463 7th Ave., Ste. 202 New York, NY 10018-7604. Phone: (212)867-8677; Fax: (212)867-8662; Email: tobe@tobereport.com • URL: http://www.tobereport.com • Monthly. Edited for fashion retailers. Provides detailed information and analysis relating to current trends in the women's, children's, and men's apparel and accessories markets.

***Today's Chemist at Work***. American Chemical Society, 1155 16th St. NW Washington, DC 20036. Phone: 800-227-5558 or (202)872-4600; Email: help@acs.org • URL: http://www.acs.org • Monthly. Institutions, $200.00 per year; others, price on application. Provide pracrtical information for chemists on day-to-day operations. Product coverage includes chemicals, equipment, apparatus, instruments, and supplies.

***Today's Facility Manager: The Magazine of Facilities-Interior Planning Team***. Group C Media Inc., 44 Apple St., Ste. 3 Tinton Falls, NJ 07724. Phone: 800-524-0337 or (732)842-7433; Fax: (732)758-6634; Email: lconnor@groupc.com • URL: http://www.facilitycity.com • Monthly. $30.00 per year. Covers office design, furnishings, and furniture, including open plan systems. Formerly *Business Interiors*.

***Today's Insurance Professionals***. International Association of Insurance Professionals, 8023 E 63rd Pl., Ste. 540 Tulsa, OK 74133. Phone: 800-766-6249 or (918)294-3700; Fax: (918)294-3711 • URL: http://naiw.site-ym.com • Quarterly. $15 Individuals; $5 Single issue; $15 /year for nonmembers in U.S.; $25 /year for nonmembers outside U.S. Provides advice on professional and personal development in the insurance business. Formerly *Today's Insurance Woman*.

***Today's Top 100 Service Providers***. Coordinated Service Inc., 20 Ct. St. Groton, MA 01450. Phone: (978)456-9699; Fax: (978)456-9599 • $99. Covers: The top 100 customer service providers in the U.S. Entries include: Company name, address, phone, fax, contacts, years in business, equipment serviced, geographical locations covered, other services offered.

**Tohoku University - Center for Northeast Asian Studies**. Kawauchi 41, Aoba-ku Sendai 980-8576, Japan. Phone: 81 22 7956009; Fax: 81 22 7956010; Email: contasia@cneas.tohoku.ac.jp • URL: http://field.cneas.tohoku.ac.jp/index_e.html • Area studies in the Northeast Asian region, including East Asia, North Asia and Japan, particularly culture, society, economy, history, resources and the environment.

***Toll-Free Phone Book USA: A Directory of Toll-Free Numbers for Businesses and Organizations Nationwide***. Omnigraphics Inc., PO Box 31-1640 Detroit, MI 48231. Phone: (313)961-1340; Fax: (313)961-1383; Email: customerservice@omnigraphics.com • URL: http://www.omnigraphics.com • Annual. $175 Individuals softcover; $193 Individuals List Price. Approximately 45,000 toll-free numbers for major companies, associations, educational institutions, travel providers, and government agencies in the U.S.

***Tollways***. International Bridge, Tunnel and Turnpike Association, 1146 19th St. NW, Ste. 600 Washington, DC 20036-3725. Phone: (202)659-4620; Fax: (202)659-0500; Email: carnold@ibtta.org • URL: http://www.IBTTA.org • Monthly. Description: Focuses on trends, developments, and news about the worldwide toll industry for members.

***Tonga Business Law Handbook***. International Business Publications, USA, PO Box 15343 Washington, DC 20003. Phone: (202)546-2103; Fax: (202)546-3275; Email: ibpusa@comcast.net • URL: http://ibpus.com • $99.95 Individuals hardcopy, E-book and CD-ROM. Covers: Basic information on business laws and legislations, export-import regulations, business climate and contacts.

***Tools of the Trade Annual Buyers Guide***. DoveTale Publishers, 1 Thomas Cir. NW Washington, DC 20005. Phone: 877-275-8647 or (202)339-0744 or (202)452-0800; Fax: (202)785-1974 or (202)339-0749; Email: hwmicustomerservice@hanleywood.com • URL: http://www.hwmarketintelligence.com • Annual. Price on application. A directory of tools for the construction industry.

***Top Careers for Business Graduates***. InfoBase Holdings Inc., 132 W 31st., 17 Fl. New York, NY 10001-3406. Phone: (212)967-8800; Fax: (800)678-3633; Email: info@infobasepublishing.com • URL: http://www.ferguson.infobasepublishing.com • $14.95 Individuals Paperback. Covers: What it takes to transform a major in business into a job that pays well, is expected to grow, offers a sense of security and opportunity for advancement, and is likely to provide a sense of job satisfaction.

***Top European Companies Database***. European Business Press Group N.V., Research Park Zellik B-1731 De Haak, Belgium. Phone: 2 4675780; Fax: 2 4675079 • Annual. Diskette. Covers 500 major companies in Europe. Entries include: Company name, address, phone, names and titles of key personnel, financial data.

***Top Executive Compensation***. The Conference Board, 845 3rd Ave. New York, NY 10022-6601. Phone: (212)759-0900 or (212)339-0345; Fax: (212)980-7014 or (212)836-9740; Email: membership@conferenceboard.org • URL: http://www.conference-board.org • Annual. $395 Nonmembers. Provides data on compensation of highest paid executives in major corporations.

***The Top 500 Design Firms Sourcebook***. McGraw Hill Financial Inc., 1221 Avenue of the Americas New York, NY 10020-1095. Phone: (212)512-2000; Fax: (212)512-3840 • URL: http://www.mhfi.com • Annual. Lists 500 leading architectural, engineering and speciality design firms selected on basis of annual billings. Formerly *ENR Directory of Design Firms*.

***Top 500 MBS Investors***. Inside Mortgage Finance Publications Inc., 7910 Woodmont Ave., Ste. 1000 Bethesda, MD 20814-7019. Phone: 800-570-5744 or (301)951-1240; Fax: (301)656-1709; Email: service@imfpubs.com • URL: http://www.imfpubs.com • $500. Database covers: The top 500 thrift, commercial bank, and federal credit unions in terms of their mortgage-related securities holdings. Entries include: Name, address, phone.

***Top Global 500 Companies in China***. SinoMedia Ltd., 1408 Golden Bell Plz., 98 Huaihai Zhong Lu Shanghai 200021, China. Phone: 86 21 5187 9633; Fax: 86 21 5385 8953; Email: ads@chinaeconomicreview.com • URL: http://www.sinomedia.net • Annual. $200 Individuals. Covers: 500 companies in China including 4,500 contacts, 4,400 offices and 1,700 email addresses. Entries include: Manager's names, telephone, profiles of the top global 50 enterprises.

***Top 900 Blue Chip Indian Companies Database***. NIIR Project Consultancy Services, 106 - E, Kamla Nagar New Delhi 110007, India. Phone: 91 11 23843955; Fax: 91 11 23841561; Email: npcs.india@gmail.com • URL: http://www.niir.org • Rs 3,147 Individuals CD-ROM; $200 Individuals CD-ROM. Covers: 900 Blue chip Indian companies. Entries include: Company name, name of CEO, postal address, city, state, pin code, phone, fax and the stock exchanges on which they are listed.

***Top 1,000 Food & Drink Companies in Asia-Pacific***. Datamonitor, Charles House, 108-110 Finchley Rd. London NW3 5JJ, United Kingdom. Phone: 44 20 7675 7000; Fax: 44 20 7675 7500; Email: euroinfo@datamonitor.com • $995. Covers: 1,000 leading food and drink companies in Asia and the Pacific. Entries include: Company name, address, phone, telex, names and titles of key personnel, number of employees; financial data, product/service, Standard Industrial Classification (SIC) code, production locations.

***Top 1,000 Food & Drink Companies in Latin America***. Datamonitor, Charles House, 108-110 Finchley Rd. London NW3 5JJ, United Kingdom. Phone: 44 20 7675 7000; Fax: 44 20 7675 7500; Email: euroinfo@datamonitor.com • $995. Covers: 1,000 leading food and drink companies in Latin America. Entries include: Company name, address, phone, telex, names and titles of key personnel, number of employees; financial data, product/service, Standard Industrial Classification (SIC) code, production locations.

***Top 1,000 Food & Drink Companies in the U.S.*** Datamonitor, Charles House, 108-110 Finchley Rd. London NW3 5JJ, United Kingdom. Phone: 44 20 7675 7000; Fax: 44 20 7675 7500; Email: euroinfo@datamonitor.com • $995. Covers: 1,000 leading food and drink companies in the U.S. Entries include: Company name, address, phone, telex, names and titles of key personnel, number of employees; financial data, product/service, Standard Industrial Classification (SIC) code, production locations.

***Top 1000 Performing Companies in Asia Pacific***. Dun & Bradstreet Singapore Pte. Ltd., 20 Harbour Dr., PSA Vista 06-02 Singapore 117612, Singapore. Phone: 65 65656161; Fax: 65 67784627; Email: csc@dnb.com.sg • URL: http://www.icdnb.com.sg • $299.60 local; $353.10 foreign. Covers: top 1000 performing companies in Asia Pacific, profiles of the Local top 50 companies, and payment trend analysis in the Asia Pacific region.

***Top Romanian Companies***. Chamber of Commerce and Industry of Romania, Bd. Octavian Goga nr. 2, Sector 3 R-030982 Bucharest, Romania. Phone: 40 21 3190114 or 40 21 3190118; Email: ccir@ccir.ro • URL: http://www.ccir.ro • Annual. $20. Covers: 600 of the most efficient Romanian companies ranked by size, field of activity, turnover rate, profit margin, development effort, and turnover per employee. Entries include: Company name, address, profile, contact person.

***Top 30 U.S. Business Media***. • URL: http://www.infocomgroup.com • Semiannual. $49. More than 900 editors, reporters, producers, and bookers at 30 major business media outlets.

***Top 22,000 Businesses in the People's Republic of China***. China Books, 360 Swift Ave., Ste. 48 South San Francisco, CA 94080. Phone: (800)818-2017; Fax: (650)872-7808; Email: info@chinabooks.com • URL: http://www.chinabooks.com • $360 cloth. Covers: Leading 22,000 businesses in China, including manufacturing, foods, apparel, paper, chemicals, and real estate industries. Entries include: Name, address, phone, executive names, number of employees, profits.

***Toronto Business Journal***. Toronto Business Journal, 8 King St. E, Ste. 710 Toronto, ON, Canada M5C 1B5. Phone: 866-410-6660 or (416)368-1886; Fax: (416)368-1889 • Weekly. Free; $93 By mail. Newspaper covering local business.

**Total Attorneys**. 25 E Washington St., Ste. 510 Chicago, IL 60602. Phone: 877-349-1307; Email: solutions@totalattorneys.com • URL: http://www.totalattorneys.com • Focuses on the advancement of attorneys, paralegals and other legal support staff. Offers solo practitioners and small law firms the tools, training and network needed to collaborate with peers, connect with experts and find better work-life balance. Coordinates workshops and conferences, educational resources, legal tools, affinity partnerships and community forums.

***Total Quality Management & Business Excellence***. Routledge, 711 3rd Ave., 8th Fl. New York, NY 10017. Phone: 800-634-7064 or (212)216-7800; Fax: (212)564-7854 or (212)563-2269; Email: book.orders@tandf.co.uk • URL: http://www.routledge.com • Monthly. $929 Individuals print only; $2,503 Institutions online only; $929 Individuals print and online; $2,861 Institutions print and online. Peer-reviewed journal general business publication.

***Tourism Economics: The Business and Finance of Tourism and Recreation***. IP Publishing Ltd., 258 Belsize Rd. London NW6 4BT, United Kingdom. Phone: 44 20 73161870; Fax: 44 20 76249994; Email: jedmondson@ippublishing.com • URL: http://www.ippublishing.com • Bimonthly. $530 Institutions; €510 Institutions in Europe; £348 Institutions, other countries. Journal covering the business and finance aspects of the tourism and recreation industry.

***Tourism Policy and International Tourism in OECD Member Countries***. Organisation for Economic Co-operation and Development Publications and Information Center, 2001 L St. NW, Ste. 650 Washington, DC 20036-4922. Phone: 800-456-6323 or (202)785-6323; Fax: (202)785-0350; Email: washington.contact@oecd.org • URL: http://www.oecd.org • Annual. $50.00. Reviews developments in the international tourism industry in OECD member countries. Includes statistical information.

***Town and Country***. The Hearst Corp., 300 W 57th St. New York, NY 10019. Phone: (212)649-2000; Fax: (212)765-2639; Email: corpcommunications@hearst.com • URL: http://www.hearst.com • Monthly. $24.00 per year.

***Toxline***. National Library of Medicine, 8600 Rockville Pke. Bethesda, MD 20894. Phone: 888-346-3656 or (301)594-5983 or (301)402-2808; Fax: (301)402-1384 or (301)496-2809; Email: contact@nachc.com • URL: http://www.nlm.nih.gov • Weekly. Abstracting service covering human and animal toxicity studies, 1965 to present (older studies available in *Toxback* file). Weekly updates. Inquire as to online cost and availability.

***Toy Trader Year Book***. Turret-Wheatland Ltd., Penn Pl. Rickmansworth WD3 1SN, United Kingdom. Phone: 92 377 7000 • Annual. Covers: Toy and toy supplier manufacturers, importers, wholesalers, retailers, and agents in the U.K. Entries include: Company name, address, phone, products, brand names.

***Toyo Keizai Company Information***. Toyo Keizai Inc., 1-2-1 Nihonbashi Hongokucho, Chuo-ku Tokyo 103-8345, Japan. Phone: 81 3 32465551 or 3 32465580; Fax: 81 3 32790332 or 3 32424067; Email: info@toyokeizai.co.jp • URL: http://www.toyokeizai.co.jp/english • Daily. Database covers: Japanese companies.

***Toys & Games—Buyer's Guide Issue***. Chelsie Communications Inc., 61 Alness St., Ste. 216 North York, ON, Canada M3J 2H2. Phone: (416)663-9229; Fax: (416)663-2353; Email: cantoymag@bellnet.ca • URL: http://www.toysandgamesmag.com • Annual. Publication includes: List of about 400 Canadian manufacturers and distributors of toys and games for children; trade associations, trade show organizers, and licensors. Entries include: For manufacturers and distributors—Company name, address, phone, key officials, branches, name of firm represented, key to line of business. For associations—Name, address, phone, contact name, property/show represented.

***TPG Briefing on Local Exchange Statistics***. Warren Communication News, 2115 Ward Court, N. W. Washington, DC 20037. Phone: 800-771-9202 or (202)872-9200; Fax: (202)293-3435; Email: customerservice@warren-news.com • URL: http://www.warren-news.com • Annual. $325.00. Contains statistics on local telephone companies: revenues, expenses, debt, income, advertising, access lines, network usage, etc. Provides "Current Information on Major Competitors.".

***Trade-a-Plane***. 174 4th St. Crossville, TN 38555. Phone: 800-337-5263 or (931)484-5137; Fax: (931)484-5232; Email: subs@trade-a-plane.com • URL: http://www.trade-a-plane.com • 36 issues per year. $36.00 per year. Subject matter is aircraft for sale or trade.

***Trade and Development Report (TDR)***. United Nations Conference on Trade and Development, Palais des Nations, 8-14, Av. de la Paix CH-1211 Geneva, Switzerland. Phone: 41 22 9171234 or 41 22 9172142; Fax: 41 22 9170057 or 41 22 9070195; Email: unctadinfo@unctad.org • URL: http://www.unctad.org • Annual. Yearly overview of trends in international trade, including an analysis of the economic and trade situation in developing countries. Published by the United Nations Conference on Trade and Development (UNCTAD).

***Trade and Employment in Developing Countries***. Anne O. Krueger, editor. The University of Chicago Press, 11030 S Langley Ave. Chicago, IL 60628. Phone: 800-621-2736 or (773)702-7000 or (773)702-7700; Fax: (773)702-9756 or (773)702-7212; Email: custserv@press.uchicago.edu • URL: http://www.press.uchicago.edu • $20 volume 3, 1983; $55 volume 2, 1982. (National Bureau of Economic Research Project Report Series).

***Trade Channel***. Trade Channel Europe, Nieuw Guineastraat 30 2022 PA Haarlem, Netherlands. Phone: 31 626 906 467; Email: info@tradechannel.com • URL: http://etradechannel.net • Monthly. 88. Features export "offers" and import "wants." Worldwide coverage. Technical products and consumer products. Formerly *Export Channel*.

***Trade Dimensions' Market Scope: The Desktop Guide to Supermarket Share***. Trade Dimensions, 55 Greens Farms Rd., Ste. 2 Westport, CT 06880-6149. Phone: 800-291-0410 or (203)222-5750; Fax: (203)222-5701; Email: tradedimensions@tradedimensions.com • Annual. Covers: Market share for over 1,400 supermarket chains and wholesalers. Entries include: Company name, location, number of stores in the area, market share. Syndicated market areas include 52 AC Nielsen Scantrack markets, all 64 IRI InfoScan markets, all 205 DMAs (Designated Market Areas) and 100 MSAs (government-defined), plus 48 Trade Dimensions markets.

***Trade Directory for Istanbul***. Istanbul Chamber of Commerce, Resadiye Caddesi TR-34112 Istanbul, Turkey. Phone: 90 212 4556000; Fax: 90 212 5131565; Email: ito@ito.org.tr • URL: http://www.ito.org.tr • Annual. Covers: Exporters, importers, commission agents, and building contractors in Istanbul.

***Trade Directory of Mexico***. Hoover's Inc., 5800 Airport Blvd. Austin, TX 78752-3812. Phone: 800-486-8666 or (512)374-4500; Fax: (512)374-4501 • URL: http://www.hoovers.com • Annual. $99.95. Published by IMF Editora. Contains profiles of 6,000 Mexican companies involved in foreign trade. Includes profile of Mexico and of the individual states.

***Trade Directory of Nigeria***. World Trade Center of Nigeria, Western House, 8th Fl., 8/10 Broad St. Lagos, Nigeria. Phone: 234 1 8103570; Email: info@wtcnlagos.org • URL: http://www.wtcnlagos.org • Triennial. Covers: Trade-related information for import/export companies, manufacturers, government representatives, lawyers, accountants, and interested individuals in Nigeria.

***Trade Directory of the Former Soviet Union***. Flegon Press, 37B New Cavendish St. London W1M 8JR, United Kingdom. Phone: 44 181 752 1296; Fax: 44 181 752 1296 • Biennial. $300. Covers: over 60,000 plants, factories, and other companies in all branches of industry in the former Soviet Union. Entries include: Company name, address, phone, telex, subsidiary and branch names and locations, description of product/service, number of employees.

***Trade Directory of Western Sweden***. Goteborg and Western Sweden Chamber of Commerce, POB 5253 S-40225 Goteborg, Sweden. Phone: 46 31 835900; Fax: 46 31 835936; Email: info@handelskammaren.net • URL: http://www.handelskammaren.net • Biennial. $300; $50. Covers: Companies, wholesalers, importers/exporters, and manufacturers in Goteborg and the western Sweden Chamber of Commerce area. Entries include: Company name, address, phone, telex number, line of business.

***Trade Directory of Yugoslavia***. Privredni Pregled, Marsala Birjuzova 3 Belgrad, Serbia. Phone: 11 62 30 45 • Annual. $150. Covers: Trading and manufacturing entities and products, chambers of commerce, and other economic organizations. Entries include: Name, address, phone, products.

***Trade Policy Agenda***. U. S. Government Printing Office, 732 N Capitol St. NW Washington, DC 20401. Phone: 866-512-1800 or (202)512-1800 or (866)512-1800; Fax: (202)512-2104 or (202)512-2250; Email: contactcenter@gpo.gov • URL: http://www.gpo.gov • Annual. $45.00. Lists U. S. trade agreements "that afford increased foreign market access or reduce foreign barriers.".

***Trade Policy Reviews***. Bernan Press, PO Box 191 Blue Ridge Summit, PA 17214. Phone: 800-865-3457 or (301)459-7666; Fax: (301)459-6988; Email: customercare@bernan.com • URL: http://www.bernan.com • Annual. Each review describes "trade policies, practices, and macroeconomic situations." Prepared by the Trade Policy Review Board of the World Trade Organization.

***Trade Secret Protection in an Information Age***. Gale R. Peterson. Glasser LegalWorks, 150 Clove Rd. Little Falls, NJ 07424. Phone: 800-308-1700 or (973)890-0008; Fax: (973)890-0042; Email: legalwks@aol.com • URL: http://www.glasserlegalworks.com • Looseleaf. $149.00, including sample forms on disk. Periodic supplementation available. Covers trade secret law relating to computer software, online databases, and multimedia products. Explanations are based on more than 1,000 legal cases. Sample forms on disk include work-for-hire examples and covenants not to compete.

***Trade Secrets***. ALM Media Properties LLC, 120 Broadway, 5th Fl. New York, NY 10271-1100. Phone: (212)457-9400; Fax: (646)417-7705; Email: customercare@alm.com • URL: http://www.alm.com • $520. Covers the legal protection of trade secrets, including information on the Economic Espionage Act of 1996. Includes a CD-ROM with samples of applicable legal forms. (Law Journal Press).

***Trade Show Center***. Global Sources/Trade Media Holdings Ltd., Phone: (656)574-2800; Email: service@globalsources.com • URL: http://www.globalsources.com/TRADESHW/TRDSHFRM.HTM • Free Web site provides current, detailed information on more than 1,000 major trade shows worldwide, including events in the U. S., but with an emphasis on "Asia and Greater China." Searching is offered by product, supplier, country, and month of year. Includes links to "Trade Information.".

***Trade Shows Worldwide***. Cengage Learning Inc., 20 Channel Center St. Boston, MA 02210. Phone: 800-487-8488 or (617)289-7700; Fax: (617)289-7844; Email: investors@cengage.com • URL: http://www.cengage.com • 2013. $645.00. 31st edition. Provides detailed information from over 75 countries on more than 10,000 trade shows and exhibitions. Separate sections are provided for trade shows/exhibitions, for sponsors/organizers, and for services, facilities, and information sources. Indexing is by date, location, subject, name, and keyword.

***Trade Unions of the World***. Cengage Learning Inc., 20 Channel Center St. Boston, MA 02210. Phone: 800-487-8488 or (617)289-7700; Fax: (617)289-7844; Email: investors@cengage.com • URL: http://www.cengage.com • $160 Individuals. Covers trade union centers, international affiliations of trade unions, and major organizations outside of the trade union centers.

***Tradeline Exclusive Reports***. Tradeline Inc., 115 Orinda Way Orinda, CA 94563. Phone: (925)254-1744; Fax: (925)254-1093 • URL: http://www.tradelineinc.com • Monthly. $120.00 per year. Newsletter. Covers the planning, design, construction, and renovation of of a variety of corporate facilities. Formerly *FM Data Monthly*.

***Trademark Manual of Examining Procedure***. U. S. Government Printing Office, 732 N Capitol St. NW Washington, DC 20401. Phone: 866-512-1800 or (202)512-1800 or (866)512-

1800; Fax: (202)512-2104 or (202)512-2250; Email: contactcenter@gpo.gov • URL: http://www.gpo.gov • $70 Individuals looseleaf binding; $98 Other countries. Covers "practices and procedures" relating to the processing of applications to register trademarks in the U. S. Patent and Trademark Office.

*The Trademark Reporter*. International Trademark Association, 655 3rd Ave., 10th Fl. New York, NY 10017-5617. Phone: (212)642-1700 or (212)768-9887; Fax: (212)768-7796 or (212)687-8267; Email: info@inta.org • URL: http://www.inta.org • Bimonthly. $80 Members; included in membership dues; $50 /year for libraries, school and government agency. Contains articles on trademark developments, trademark law, and the use of trademarks.

*The Trademarker Reporter*. International Trademark Association, 655 3rd Ave., 10th Fl. New York, NY 10017-5617. Phone: (212)642-1700 or (212)768-9887; Fax: (212)768-7796 or (212)687-8267; Email: info@inta.org • URL: http://www.inta.org • Bimonthly. Publishes works of high-quality legal scholarship by trademark practitioners and professionals, academic faculty and law students.

*TRADEMARKSCAN - Federal*. EBSCOhost, • Updated weekly. Contains information for more than 5 million records.

*Trademarkscan—International Register*. Thomson CompuMark Americas, 500 Victory Rd. North Quincy, MA 02171-3139. Phone: 800-692-8833 or (617)479-1600; Fax: (800)543-1983 or (617)786-8381; Email: compumark.us@thomson.com • URL: http://trademarks.thomsonreuters.com/?cid=98 • Semimonthly. Database covers: Over 445,000 active registered trademarks on file at the World Intellectual Property Organization. Also included are inactive records from the last 3 years. Entries include: Trademark word and/or design reference, current status, international class(es), description of product/service, registration number, publication details, owner name/location.

*TRADEMARKSCAN: International Register*. Thomson Compu-Mark Americas, 500 Victory Rd. North Quincy, MA 02171-3139. Phone: 800-692-8833 or (617)479-1600; Fax: (800)543-1983 or (617)786-8381; Email: compumark.us@thomson.com • URL: http://trademarks.thomsonreuters.com/?cid=98 • Supplies current information on more than 400,000 trademarks registered with the World Intellectual Property Organization. Updates are monthly. Inquire as to online cost and availability. (TRADEMARKSCAN also maintains extensive databases for individual countries: Canada, U. K., Germany, Italy, France, and others.).

*TRADEMARKSCAN: U. S. Federal*. Thomson CompuMark Americas, 500 Victory Rd. North Quincy, MA 02171-3139. Phone: 800-692-8833 or (617)479-1600; Fax: (800)543-1983 or (617)786-8381; Email: compumark.us@thomson.com • URL: http://trademarks.thomsonreuters.com/?cid=98 • Provides information on more than two million trademarks registered and pending at the U. S. Patent and Trademark Office. Time period is 1884 to date for active trademarks, with updates twice a week. Graphic images are show. Inquire as to online cost and availability.

*TRADEMARKSCAN: U. S. State*. Thomson CompuMark Americas, 500 Victory Rd. North Quincy, MA 02171-3139. Phone: 800-692-8833 or (617)479-1600; Fax: (800)543-1983 or (617)786-8381; Email: compumark.us@thomson.com • URL: http://trademarks.thomsonreuters.com/?cid=98 • Contains information on more than 970,000 trademarks registered with the Office of the Secretary of State in all 50 states and in Puerto Rico. Time period is 1900 to date for active trademarks, with weekly updates. Inquire as to online cost and availability.

*TRADEMARKSCAN - U.S. State*. EBSCOhost, • Updated weekly. Provides information for more than 1.4 million trademarks registered with the Office of the Secretary of State in all 50 states and in Puerto Rico.

*Traders Magazine*. SourceMedia Inc., 1 State Street Plz., 27th Fl. New York, NY 10004. Phone: 800-221-1809 or (212)803-8200 or (212)803-8333; Fax: (212)843-9635 or (212)292-5216; Email: custserv@sourcemedia.com • URL: http://www.sourcemedia.com • Monthly. $60.00 per year. Edited for institutional buy side and sell side equity traders. Covers industry news, market trends, regulatory developments, and personnel news. Serves as the official publication of the Security Traders Association.

*Tradeshow and Exhibit Manager*. Goldstein & Associates, 1150 Yale St., Ste. 12 Santa Monica, CA 90403. Phone: (310)828-1309; Fax: (310)829-1169 • Bimonthly. $80.00 per year. Edited for exhibit, tradeshow, and exposition managers. Covers design trends, site selection, shipping problems, industry news, etc. Supplement available *Tradeshow Directory*.

*Tradeshow Week: Since 1971, the Only Weekly Source of News and Statistics on the Tradeshow Industry*. Reed Elsevier Group plc Reed Business Information, 360 Park Ave. S New York, NY 11010. Phone: (212)791-4208; Email: corporatecommunications@reedbusiness.com • URL: http://www.reedbusiness.com • 50 times a year. $419.00 per year; includes 18 *Supplements* and 7 *Websites*. Edited for corporate and association trade show and exhibit managers. Includes show calendars and labor rates.

*Trading Cycles*. R.E. Andrews, editor. Andrews Publications, Inc., 156 Shadow Creek Lane Paso Robles, CA 93446-1922.

Phone: (408)778-2925 • Monthly. $97.99 per year. Newsletter. Technical investment newsletter. Formerly *Andrews Trading Cycles*.

*Trado Asian & African Directory*. Trado Publications Private Ltd., C-6 Safdarjung Development Area, Community Ctr. New Delhi 110016, India. • Annual. $115 airmail postpaid. Covers: manufacturers, exporters, and importers in Bahrain, Bangladesh, Canary Islands, Cyprus, Ethiopia, Hong Kong, India, Iran, Iraq, Japan, Jordan, Kenya, Kuwait, Liberia, Libya, Malta, Malawi, Mauritius, Nigeria, Philippines, Saudi Arabia, Sierra Leone, Singapore, Malaysia, Somalia, South Yemen, Sri Lanka, Sudan, Syria, Tanzania, Thailand, United Arab Emirates, and Zambia.

*Traffic Engineering and Control: The International Journal of Traffic Management and Transportation Planning*. Printerhall Ltd., 29 Newman St. London W1P 3PE, United Kingdom. Phone: 44 171 636 3956 or 44 171 6363956; Fax: 44 171 436 7016 or (171) 4367016 • Monthly. $120.00 per year. Provides authoritative articles on planning, engineering and management of highways for safe and efficient operation.

*Traffic World: The Logistics News Weekly n*. Journal of Commerce, Inc., 2 Penn Plz. E Newark, NJ 07105. Phone: (973)776-8660 • URL: http://www.joc.com • Weekly. $174.00 per year.

*Trailer Body Builders Buyers Guide*. Primedia Business Magazines and Media, 4200 S Shepherd Dr., Ste. 200 Houston, TX 77098. Phone: 800-795-5445 or (713)523-8124; Fax: (713)523-8384; Email: subs@primediabusiness.com • URL: http://www.primediabusiness.com • Annual. Controlled circulation. List of 8,000 products used by original equipment manufacturers of truck trailers and truck bodies.

*Trailer Life*. Good Sam Club. Affinity Group Inc., T L Enterprises, 2575 Vista Del Mar Dr. Ventura, CA 93001. Phone: 800-825-6861 or (805)667-4100; Fax: (805)667-4484 or (805)667-4379; Email: info@trailerlife.com • URL: http://www.rv.net • Monthly. $15.97 /year.

*Trailer Life Campground and RV Services Directory*. Trailer Life Publishing Company Inc. PO Box 6888 Englewood, CO 80155-6888. Phone: 877-2096655 or (805)667-4100; Fax: (805)667-4301 • Annual. $19.95. Describes and rates over 18,000 RV campgrounds, service centers and tourist attractions.

*The Training Manager's Yearbook*. AP Information Services Ltd., c/o Wilmington Publishing & Information Ltd., 6-14 Underworld St. London N1 7JQ, United Kingdom. Phone: 44 20 75498708; Fax: 44 20 74908238; Email: info@apinfo.co.uk • URL: http://www.apinfo.co.uk • Annual. £239 Individuals /year. Covers: Training managers in 8,750 organizations in the United Kingdom; profiles of over 4,500 suppliers and advisors to training managers in the United Kingdom. Entries include: For organizations—Name, address, phone, fax, e-mail, contact, history, names and titles of key personnel.

*Training: The Magazine of Covering the Human Side of Business*. Nielsen Business Media Inc., 770 Broadway New York, NY 10003-9522. Phone: 866-890-8541 or (646)654-4500 or (646)654-5000; Fax: (646)654-5584 or (646)654-4500; Email: bmcomm@nielsen.com • URL: http://www.nielsenbusinessmedia.com • Monthly. $78.00 per year.

*Trains; The Magazine of Railroading*. Kalmbach Publishing Co., 21027 Crossroads Cir. Waukesha, WI 53187-1612. Phone: 800-533-6644 or (262)796-8776 or (414)796-8776; Fax: (262)796-1615 or (414)798-6468; Email: customerservice@kalmbach.com • URL: http://corporate.kalmbach.com • Monthly. $39.95 per year.

*Transdex Index*. ProQuest L.L.C., 789 E Eisenhower Pkwy. Ann Arbor, MI 48106-1346. Phone: 800-521-0600 or (734)761-4700; Fax: (734)662-4554; Email: info@proquest.com • URL: http://www.proquest.com • Provides access to materials originally published outside the United States and translated into English.

*Transform: Reinventing Business with Content and Collaboration Technologies*. UBM L.L.C., 600 Community Dr. Manhasset, NY 11030. Phone: (516)562-5000 or (512)562-5000; Fax: (212)378-2160 or (516)562-5036; Email: cmp@cmp.com • URL: http://www.cmp.com • Monthly. $25.00 per year. Emphasis is on descriptions of new imaging products. Formerly *Imaging and Document Solutions*.

*Transitions Abroad: The Guide to Learning, Living, and Working Overseas*. Transitions Abroad Publishing, 18 Hulst Rd. Amherst, MA 01002. Phone: 800-293-0373 or (413)256-3414; Fax: (413)256-0373; Email: senioreditor@transitionsabroad.com • URL: http://www.transitionsabroad.com • Bimonthly. Provides practical information and advice on foreign education and employment. Supplement available *Overseas Travel Planner*.

*Transkei Business Directory*. A.C. Braby (Pty) Ltd., 12 Caversham Rd. Pinetown 3610, South Africa. Email: support@brabys.co.za • URL: http://www.brabys.com • Annual. R 30 payment must accompany order. Covers: businesses in Transkei. Entries include: Company name, address, phone.

**Transmission Rebuilders Network International**. 6501 E Greenway Pkwy., Ste. 103/298 Scottsdale, AZ 85254-2065. Phone: 888-582-8764; Email: info@trannybuilder.com • URL: http://www.trannybuilder.com • Advances the science of rebuilding automatic transmissions and the art of managing a transmission shop. Serves as a forum for the members to share and exchange ideas on automatic transmissions.

Provides training, support and technical information based on the needs, trends and opportunities of the transmission/powertrain industry.

*Transnational Corporations and Labor: A Directory of Resources*. WorldViews, 3693 S Bay Bluffs Dr. Cedar, MI 49621. Phone: (231)228-7116; Fax: (253)540-2583 or (231)540-2583; Email: worldviews@igc.org • URL: http://worldviews.igc.org/ • $12.95 plus $2.00 shipping. Covers: sources for books, periodicals, pamphlets, audiovisuals, and other educational resources on transnational corporations and labor issues; names of resources with annotations and ordering information. Entries include: Organization name, address, phone, titles of print and audio/visual material. Part of a 10 volume series (updated in "Third World Resources"), each volume covering single region or issue.

**Transparency, Consciousness and Citizenship**. CLN 202, Bloco B, Sala 101 70832-525 Brasilia, DF, Brazil. Phone: 55613218085; Fax: 55 55613216333; Email: mail@tcc-brasil.org.br • URL: http://www.tcc-brasil.org.br • Corporations, organizations, and individuals interested in reducing fraud and corruption in international business transactions. Seeks to: raise public awareness of anticorruption measures; influence legislation regulating international business transactions. Formulates standards of integrity to govern international business dealings; maintains network of businesses agreeing to adhere to these standards. Conducts anticorruption and antifraud programs. Sponsors research and educational activities.

**Transparency International Anti-corruption Center** . Aygestan 9th St., House 6 0025 Yerevan, Armenia. Phone: 374 2 10569910 or 374 2 10553069; Fax: 374 2 10571399; Email: info@transparency.am • URL: http://transparency.am • Represents corporations, organizations and individuals interested in reducing fraud and corruption in international business transactions. Raises public awareness of anticorruption measures and influences legislation regulating international business transactions. Formulates standards of integrity to govern international business dealings. Conducts anti-corruption and antifraud programs.

**Transparency International - Argentina**. Piedras 547 1070 Buenos Aires, Argentina. Phone: 54 11 43314925; Fax: 54 11 43314925; Email: comunicacion@poderciudadano.org • URL: http://www.poderciudadano.org.ar • Corporations, organizations, and individuals interested in reducing fraud and corruption in international business transactions. Seeks to raise public awareness of anticorruption measures and influence legislation regulating international business transactions. Formulates standards of integrity to govern international business dealings and maintains network of businesses agreeing to adhere to these standards. Conducts anticorruption and antifraud programs. Sponsors research and educational activities.

**Transparency International - Australia**. PO Box 41 Melbourne, VIC 3130, Australia. Phone: 61 3 98770369; Fax: 61 3 98771628; Email: tioz@transparency.org.au • URL: http://www.transparency.org.au • Corporations, organizations, and individuals interested in reducing fraud and corruption in international business transactions. Seeks to: raise public awareness of anticorruption measures; influence legislation regulating international business transactions. Formulates standards of integrity to govern international business dealings; maintains network of businesses agreeing to adhere to these standards. Conducts anticorruption and antifraud programs. Sponsors research and educational activities.

**Transparency International - Azerbaijan**. Jafar Jabbarli St. 16, Apt. 7 AZ1001 Baku, Azerbaijan. Phone: 994 12 4978170; Fax: 994 12 5962038; Email: info@transparency.az • URL: http://transparency.az • Represents corporations, organizations and individuals interested in reducing fraud and corruption in international business transactions. Raises public awareness of anticorruption measures and influences legislation regulating international business transactions. Formulates standards of integrity to govern international business dealings. Conducts anticorruption and antifraud programs.

**Transparency International - Bangladesh**. House 141, Blk. E, Rd. 12, Banani Dhaka 1213, Bangladesh. Phone: 880 2 9887884 or 880 2 8826036; Fax: 880 2 9884811; Email: info@ti-bangladesh.org • URL: http://www.ti-bangladesh.org • Corporations, organizations, and individuals interested in reducing fraud and corruption in international business transactions. Seeks to: raise public awareness of anticorruption measures; influence legislation regulating international business transactions. Formulates standards of integrity to govern international business dealings; maintains network of businesses agreeing to adhere to these standards. Conducts anticorruption and antifraud programs. Sponsors research and educational activities.

**Transparency International - Bosnia and Herzegovina**. Gajeva 2 78000 Banja Luka, Bosnia and Herzegovina. Phone: 387 51 216928; Fax: 387 51 216369; Email: info@ti-bih.org • URL: http://www.ti-bih.org • Represents corporations, organizations and individuals interested in reducing fraud and corruption in international business transactions. Raises public awareness of anticorruption measures and influences legislation regulating international business transactions.

Formulates standards of integrity to govern international business dealings. Conducts anticorruption and antifraud programs.

**Transparency International - Brazil**. Rua Francisco Leitao 339, cj 122 05414-025 Sao Paulo, SP, Brazil. Phone: 55 11 30623436; Fax: 55 11 30623436; Email: tbrasil@transparencia.org.br • URL: http://www.transparencia.org.br • Represents corporations, organizations and individuals interested in reducing fraud and corruption in international business transactions. Raises public awareness of anticorruption measures and influences legislation regulating international business transactions. Formulates standards of integrity to govern international business dealings. Conducts anticorruption and antifraud programs.

**Transparency International - Brussels**. E Jacqmainlaan 135 B-1000 Brussels, Belgium. Phone: 32 2 5090031; Email: info@transparencybelgium.be • URL: http://www.transparencybelgium.be • Corporations, organizations, and individuals interested in reducing fraud and corruption in international business transactions. Seeks to raise public awareness of anticorruption measures and influence legislation regulating international business transactions. Formulates standards of integrity to govern international business dealings and maintains network of businesses agreeing to adhere to these standards. Conducts anticorruption and antifraud programs. Sponsors research and educational activities.

**Transparency International - Bulgaria**. PO Box 72 Sofia, Bulgaria. Phone: 359 2 9867713 or 359 2 9867920; Fax: 359 2 9867834; Email: mbox@transparency.bg • URL: http://www.transparency.bg • Represents corporations, organizations and individuals interested in reducing fraud and corruption in international business transactions. Raises public awareness of anti-corruption measures and influences legislation regulating international business transactions. Formulates standards of integrity to govern international business dealings. Conducts anti-corruption and anti-fraud programs.

**Transparency International - Burundi**. c/o ABUCO, Ave. du 28 Novembre, No. 4611/C Bujumbura, Burundi. Phone: 257 237686; Email: abuco@ymail.com • URL: http://www.burunditransparence.org • Aims to promote good governance and fight against corruption. Seeks to raise public awareness of anti-corruption measures and influence legislation regulating international business transactions. Formulates standards of integrity to govern international business dealings.

**Transparency International - Cameroon**. Nouvelle Route Bastos, rue 1.839 Yaounde, Cameroon. Phone: 237 33156378; Email: transparency@ti-cameroon.org • URL: http://www.ti-cameroon.org • Aims to promote good governance and fight against corruption. Works with coalitions of individuals and organizations to prevent corruption and reform the systems. Fosters dialogue with the government and companies.

**Transparency International - Canada**. Business Ethics Office - N211, Schulich School of Business, York University, 4700 Keele St. Toronto, ON, Canada M3J 1P3. Phone: (416)488-3939; Fax: (416)483-5128; Email: ti-can@transparency.ca • URL: http://www.transparency.ca • Represents corporations, organizations and individuals interested in reducing fraud and corruption in international business transactions. Raises public awareness of anticorruption measures and influences legislation regulating international business transactions. Formulates standards of integrity to govern international business dealings. Conducts anticorruption and antifraud programs.

**Transparency International - Chile**. Avda. Providencia 1017, Providencia Santiago, Chile. Phone: 56 2 2364507; Fax: 56 2 2364507; Email: chiletransparente@chiletransparente.cl • URL: http://www.chiletransparente.cl • Represents corporations, organizations and individuals interested in reducing fraud and corruption in international business transactions. Raises public awareness of anticorruption measures and influences legislation regulating international business transactions. Formulates standards of integrity to govern international business dealings. Conducts anticorruption and antifraud programs.

**Transparency International - Colombia**. Carrera 45, No. 93-61, Barrio la Castellana Bogota, Colombia. Phone: 57 1 6100822; Fax: 57 1 6373603; Email: transparencia@transparenciacolombia.org.co • URL: http://www.transparency.org/whoweare/contact#O_nc_colombia • Represents corporations, organizations and individuals interested in reducing fraud and corruption in international business transactions. Raises public awareness of anticorruption measures and influences legislation regulating international business transactions. Formulates standards of integrity to govern international business dealings. Conducts anticorruption and antifraud programs.

**Transparency International - Costa Rica**. 800 metros oeste del Restaurante Tony Romas, Urbanizacion Trejos Montealegre San Jose, Costa Rica. Phone: 506 40340929; Email: crintegra@gmail.com • URL: http://www.transparency.org/whoweare/contact#O_nc_costarica • Represents corporations, organizations and individuals interested in reducing fraud and corruption in international business transactions. Raises public awareness of anti-corruption measures and influences legislation regulating international business transactions. Formulates standards of integrity to govern international business dealings. Conducts anti-corruption and antifraud programs.

**Transparency International - Croatia**. Ilica 35 CT-10000 Zagreb, Croatia. Phone: 385 1 4830653; Fax: 385 1 4830654; Email: ti-croatia@transparency.hr • URL: http://www.transparency.hr • Represents corporations, organizations and individuals interested in reducing fraud and corruption in international business transactions. Raises public awareness of anticorruption measures and influences legislation regulating international business transactions. Formulates standards of integrity to govern international business dealings. Conducts anticorruption and antifraud programs.

**Transparency International - Czech Republic**. Sokolovska 260/143 CZ-180 00 Prague, Czech Republic. Phone: 420 2 24240895 or 420 2 24240897; Email: info@transparency.cz • URL: http://www.transparency.cz • Represents corporations, organizations and individuals interested in reducing fraud and corruption in international business transactions. Raises public awareness of anticorruption measures and influences legislation regulating international business transactions. Formulates standards of integrity to govern international business dealings. Conducts anticorruption and antifraud programs.

**Transparency International - Denmark**. c/o Mellemfolkeligt Samvirke, Faelledvej 12 DK-2200 Copenhagen, Denmark. Email: sekretariatet@transparency.dk • URL: http://transparency.dk • Represents corporations, organizations and individuals interested in reducing fraud and corruption in international business transactions. Raises public awareness of anti-corruption measures and influences legislation regulating international business transactions. Formulates standards of integrity to govern international business dealings. Conducts anti-corruption and antifraud programs.

**Transparency International - Dominican Republic**. Calle Wenceslao Alvarez, No. 8 Santo Domingo, Dominican Republic. Phone: (809)685-6200; Fax: (809)685-6631; Email: info@pciudadana.org • URL: http://www.pciudadana.org • Aims to promote good governance and fight against corruption. Seeks to raise public awareness of anti-corruption measures and influence legislation regulating international business transactions. Formulates standards of integrity to govern international business dealings.

**Transparency International - Estonia**. Telliskivi 60a 10412 Tallinn, Estonia. Phone: 372 56678118; Email: info@transparency.ee • URL: http://www.transparency.ee • Seeks to highlight the appearance of corruption in the public and private sector. Strengthens cooperation between the institutions and private persons concerned with the fight against corruption. Analyzes the risks of corruption and proposes legislative amendments related to transparency, accountability and corruption.

**Transparency International - Ethiopia**. PO Box 27847 Addis Ababa, Ethiopia. Phone: 251 11 6621596 or 251 11 6555508 • URL: http://transparencyethiopia.org • Aims to promote good governance and fight against corruption. Seeks to raise public awareness of anti-corruption measures and influence legislation regulating international business transactions. Formulates standards of integrity to govern international business dealings.

**Transparency International - Fiji**. 72 Pratt St. Suva, Fiji. Phone: 679 3304702; Fax: 679 3303533; Email: oa@transparencyfiji.org • URL: http://www.transparencyfiji.org • Represents corporations, organizations and individuals interested in reducing fraud and corruption in international business transactions. Raises public awareness of anti-corruption measures and influences legislation regulating international business transactions. Formulates standards of integrity to govern international business dealings. Conducts anti-corruption and antifraud programs.

**Transparency International - France**. 14, passage Dubail F-75010 Paris, France. Phone: 33 1 84169565; Email: contact@transparence-france.org • URL: http://www.transparence-france.org • Represents corporations, organizations and individuals interested in reducing fraud and corruption in international business transactions. Raises public awareness of anti-corruption measures and influences legislation regulating international business transactions. Formulates standards of integrity to govern international business dealings. Conducts anti-corruption and antifraud programs.

**Transparency International - Georgia**. 26, Rustaveli Ave. 0108 Tbilisi, Republic of Georgia. Phone: 995 32 2921403; Fax: 995 32 2920251; Email: info@transparency.ge • URL: http://www.transparency.ge • Represents corporations, organizations and individuals interested in reducing fraud and corruption in international business transactions. Raises public awareness of anti-corruption measures and influences legislation regulating international business transactions. Formulates standards of integrity to govern international business dealings. Conducts anti-corruption and antifraud programs.

**Transparency International - Germany**. Alte Schoenhauser Str. 44 D-10119 Berlin, Germany. Phone: 49 30 5498980; Fax: 49 30 54989822; Email: office@transparency.de • URL: http://www.transparency.de • Dedicates itself to curbing corruption in all its forms and increasing government accountability. Develops standards of integrity to govern national and international business dealings; seeks to raise public awareness of anticorruption measures and influences the government to strengthen anticorruption laws. Maintains information and documentation center; undertakes publicity campaigns; works in networks with other organizations with similar focus; most of the program work is done by volunteers.

**Transparency International - Greece**. Thetidos 4 GR-11528 Athens, Greece. Phone: 30 210 7224940; Fax: 30 210 7224947; Email: tihellas@otenet.gr • URL: http://www.transparency.gr • Represents corporations, organizations and individuals interested in reducing fraud and corruption in international business transactions. Raises public awareness of anticorruption measures and influences legislation regulating international business transactions. Formulates standards of integrity to govern international business dealings. Conducts anticorruption and antifraud programs.

**Transparency International - Haiti**. PO Box 16136 Petionville, Haiti. Phone: 509 37017089; Fax: 509 25137089; Email: heritagehaiti@yahoo.com • URL: http://www.transparency.org • Aims to promote good governance and fight against corruption. Seeks to raise public awareness of anti-corruption measures and influence legislation regulating international business transactions. Formulates standards of integrity to govern international business dealings.

**Transparency International - Hungary**. Falk Miksa u. 30th 4th em. 2 1055 Budapest, Hungary. Phone: 36 1 2699534; Fax: 36 1 2699535; Email: info@transparency.hu • URL: http://www.transparency.org • Represents corporations, organizations and individuals interested in reducing fraud and corruption in international business transactions. Raises public awareness of anti-corruption measures and influences legislation regulating international business transactions. Formulates standards of integrity to govern international business dealings. Conducts anti-corruption and anti-fraud programs.

**Transparency International - India**. Qr.No.- 4, Lajpat Bhawan, Lajpat Nagar - IV New Delhi 110 024, Delhi, India. Phone: 91 11 26460826; Fax: 91 11 26460824; Email: tiindia.newdelhi@gmail.com • URL: http://www.transparencyindia.org • Represents corporations, organizations and individuals interested in reducing fraud and corruption in international business transactions. Raises public awareness of anticorruption measures and influences legislation regulating international business transactions. Formulates standards of integrity to govern international business dealings. Conducts anticorruption and antifraud programs.

**Transparency International - Indonesia**. Jl. Senayan Bawah No. 17 12180 Jakarta, Indonesia. Phone: 62 21 7208515; Fax: 62 21 7267815; Email: info@ti.or.id • URL: http://www.transparency.org • Represents corporations, organizations and individuals interested in reducing fraud and corruption in international business transactions. Raises public awareness of anticorruption measures and influences legislation regulating international business transactions. Formulates standards of integrity to govern international business dealings. Conducts anticorruption and antifraud programs.

**Transparency International - Initiative Madagascar**. Lot 11 M 98 B, Antsakaviro Antananarivo 101, Madagascar. Phone: 261 2 2265357; Email: transparency.mg@moov.mg • URL: http://www.transparency.org/whoweare/contact/org/nc_madagascar • Represents corporations, organizations and individuals interested in reducing fraud and corruption in international business transactions. Raises public awareness of anticorruption measures and influences legislation regulating international business transactions. Formulates standards of integrity to govern international business dealings. Conducts anticorruption and antifraud programs.

**Transparency International - Ireland**. The Capel Bldg., Ste. 109 Dublin 7, Dublin, Ireland. Phone: 353 1 8719433; Email: info@transparency.ie • URL: http://transparency.ie • Aims to promote good governance and fight against corruption. Seeks to raise public awareness of anti-corruption measures and influence legislation regulating international business transactions. Provides anti-corruption tools, strategies and programs.

**Transparency International - Israel**. PO Box 39874 IL-61398 Tel Aviv, Israel. Phone: 972 3 6409176; Fax: 972 3 6409176; Email: shvil@ti-israel.org • URL: http://www.ti-israel.org • Represents corporations, organizations and individuals interested in reducing fraud and corruption in international business transactions. Raises public awareness of anti-corruption measures and influences legislation regulating international business transactions. Formulates standards of integrity to govern international business dealings. Conducts anti-corruption and antifraud programs.

**Transparency International - Italy**. Via Zamagna 19 I-20148 Milan, Italy. Phone: 39 2 40093560; Fax: 39 2 406829; Email: info@transparency.it • URL: http://www.transparency.org • Represents corporations, organizations and individuals interested in reducing fraud and corruption in international business transactions. Raises public awareness of anticorruption measures and influences legislation regulating international business transactions. Formulates standards of integrity to govern international business dealings. Conducts anticorruption and antifraud programs.

**Transparency International - Kazakhstan**. Karasai Batyr 85, 4th Fl., Office 41 050026 Almaty, Kazakhstan. Phone: 7 327 2726981; Fax: 7 327 2726981 • URL: http://www.

transparencykazakhstan.org • Represents corporations, organizations and individuals interested in reducing fraud and corruption in international business transactions. Raises public awareness of anticorruption measures and influences legislation regulating international business transactions. Formulates standards of integrity to govern international business dealings. Conducts anticorruption and antifraud programs.

**Transparency International - Kenya**. ACK Garden House, 3rd Fl., Wing D, 1st Ngong Ave. off Bishops Rd. Nairobi, Kenya. Phone: 254 2 2727763 or 254 2 2730324; Fax: 254 2 2729530; Email: transparency@tikenya.org • URL: http://www.tikenya.org • Represents corporations, organizations and individuals interested in reducing fraud and corruption in international business transactions. Raises public awareness of anticorruption measures and influences legislation regulating international business transactions. Formulates standards of integrity to govern international business dealings. Conducts anticorruption and antifraud programs.

**Transparency International - Korea**. 1006 Pierson Bldg., 89-27 Sinmunno 2-ga, Jongno-Gu Seoul 110-762, South Korea. Phone: 82 2 7176211; Fax: 82 2 7176210; Email: ti@ti.or.kr • URL: http://ti.or.kr/xe • Represents corporations, organizations and individuals interested in reducing fraud and corruption in international business transactions. Raises public awareness of anti-corruption measures and influences legislation regulating international business transactions. Formulates standards of integrity to govern international business dealings. Conducts anti-corruption and antifraud programs.

**Transparency International - Lithuania**. Didzioji St. 5 LT-01128 Vilnius, Lithuania. Phone: 370 5 2126951; Fax: 370 5 2121687; Email: info@transparency.lt • URL: http://www.transparency.org • Represents corporations, organizations and individuals interested in reducing fraud and corruption in international business transactions. Raises public awareness of anticorruption measures and influences legislation regulating international business transactions. Formulates standards of integrity to govern international business dealings. Conducts anticorruption and antifraud programs.

**Transparency International - Malaysia**. Wisma Pantai, Plz. Pantai, Ste. B-11-1, No. 5 Jalan 4/83A, Off Jalan Pantai Baru 59200 Kuala Lumpur, Malaysia. Phone: 60 3 22840630; Fax: 60 3 22840690; Email: admin@transparency.org.my • URL: http://www.transparency.org • Represents corporations, organizations and individuals interested in reducing fraud and corruption in international business transactions. Raises public awareness of anticorruption measures and influences legislation regulating international business transactions. Formulates standards of integrity to govern international business dealings. Conducts anticorruption and antifraud programs.

**Transparency International - Moldova**. 98, 31-August 1989 St., Rm. 205 MD-2004 Chisinau, Moldova. Phone: 373 2 2203484 or 373 2 2203485; Fax: 373 2 2237876; Email: office@transparency.md • URL: http://www.transparency.md • Represents corporations, organizations and individuals interested in reducing fraud and corruption in international business transactions. Raises public awareness of anticorruption measures and influences legislation regulating international business transactions. Formulates standards of integrity to govern international business dealings. Conducts anticorruption and antifraud programs.

**Transparency International - Mongolia**. Bldg. of Zorig Foundation, 2nd Fl., Peace Ave. 17, Sukhbaataar District Ulan Bator, Mongolia. Phone: 976 1 70154250; Fax: 976 1 70154250 • URL: http://www.transparency.org/country#MNG_Chapter • Represents corporations, organizations and individuals interested in reducing fraud and corruption in international business transactions. Raises public awareness of anticorruption measures and influences legislation regulating international business transactions. Formulates standards of integrity to govern international business dealings. Conducts anticorruption and antifraud programs.

**Transparency International - Nepal**. Newplaza, Pulalisadak Kathmandu, Nepal. Phone: 977 1 436462 or 977 1 420412; Email: trans@tinepal.org • URL: http://www.tinepal.org • Represents corporations, organizations and individuals interested in reducing fraud and corruption in international business transactions. Raises public awareness of anti-corruption measures and influences legislation regulating international business transactions. Formulates standards of integrity to govern international business dealings. Conducts anti-corruption and antifraud programs.

**Transparency International - New Zealand**. Lambton Quay Wellington, New Zealand. Email: mpetrie@ihug.co.nz • URL: http://www.transparency.org/whoweare/contact#O_nc_newzealand • Represents corporations, organizations and individuals interested in reducing fraud and corruption in international business transactions. Raises public awareness of anti-corruption measures and influences legislation regulating international business transactions. Formulates standards of integrity to govern international business dealings. Conducts anti-corruption and antifraud programs.

**Transparency International - Nigeria**. No. 11B Otukpo St., Gimbiya St., Area 11, Off Onitsha Crescent, Garki Abuja, Nigeria. Email: info@ti-nigeria.org • URL: http://www.transparency.org/content/view/full/337/(filter)/n • Represents

corporations, organizations and individuals interested in reducing fraud and corruption in international business transactions. Raises public awareness of anticorruption measures and influences legislation regulating international business transactions. Formulates standards of integrity to govern international business dealings. Conducts anticorruption and antifraud programs.

**Transparency International - Pakistan**. 5-C, 2nd Fl., Khayaban-e-Ittehad, Phase VII, D.H.A. Karachi, Pakistan. Phone: 92 21 5390408 or 92 21 5390409; Fax: 92 21 5390410; Email: ti.pakistan@gmail.com • URL: http://www.transparency.org.pk • Aims to raise public awareness of the effects of bribery and corruption. Encourages the government, government departments, municipalities, civic agencies and private-sector organizations to establish and implement laws, policies and anti-corruption programs. Enhances public transparency and accountability in administrative, financial and business transactions.

**Transparency International - Papua New Guinea**. PO Box 591 Port Moresby, Papua New Guinea. Phone: 675 3202188; Fax: 675 3202189 • URL: http://www.transparencypng.org.pg • Aims to combat corruption. Promotes openness, honesty and accountability in public and private dealings. Encourages research and analysis of the extent and effect of corruption in Papua New Guinea. Raises awareness of the presence and adverse effects of dishonest and corrupt practices.

**Transparency International - Philippine Chapter**. Philippine International Convention Center, Rm. S-370, CCP Complex Pasay City 1000, Philippines. Phone: 63 2 5529188; Fax: 63 2 5529188; Email: transparencyinternational_ph@yahoo.com • URL: http://www.transparency.org • Represents corporations, organizations and individuals interested in reducing fraud and corruption in international business transactions. Raises public awareness of anticorruption measures and influences legislation regulating international business transactions. Formulates standards of integrity to govern international business dealings. Conducts anticorruption and antifraud programs.

**Transparency International - Poland**. ul. Ordynacka 9, pok. 33 00-364 Warsaw, Poland. Phone: 48 22 8289243; Email: ti@transparency.pl • URL: http://www.transparency.pl • Represents corporations, organizations and individuals interested in reducing fraud and corruption in international business transactions. Raises public awareness of anti-corruption measures and influences legislation regulating international business transactions. Formulates standards of integrity to govern international business dealings. Conducts anti-corruption and antifraud programs.

**Transparency International - Romania**. 21 Nicolae Balcescu Blvd., 2nd Fl., Sector 1 010044 Bucharest, Romania. Phone: 40 21 3177170; Fax: 40 21 3177172; Email: office@ransparency.org.ro • URL: http://www.transparency.org.ro • Represents corporations, organizations and individuals interested in reducing fraud and corruption in international business transactions. Raises public awareness of anticorruption measures and influences legislation regulating international business transactions. Formulates standards of integrity to govern international business dealings. Conducts anticorruption and antifraud programs.

**Transparency International - Russia**. Nikoloyamskaya ul. 6 109240 Moscow, Russia. Phone: 7 95 9150019; Fax: 7 95 9150019; Email: info@transparency.org.ru • URL: http://www.transparency.org.ru • Represents corporations, organizations and individuals interested in reducing fraud and corruption in international business transactions. Raises public awareness of anticorruption measures and influences legislation regulating international business transactions. Formulates standards of integrity to govern international business dealings. Conducts anticorruption and antifraud programs.

**Transparency International - Slovakia**. Bajkalska 25 827 18 Bratislava, Slovakia. Phone: 421 2 53417207; Fax: 421 2 53417207; Email: tis@transparency.sk • URL: http://www.transparency.sk • Represents corporations, organizations and individuals interested in reducing fraud and corruption in international business transactions. Raises public awareness of anticorruption measures and influences legislation regulating international business transactions. Formulates standards of integrity to govern international business dealings. Conducts anticorruption and antifraud programs.

**Transparency International - Solomon Islands**. PO Box 1665 Honiara, Solomon Islands. Email: tsi@solomon.com.sb • URL: http://www.transparency.org • Aims to promote good governance and fight against corruption. Seeks to raise public awareness of anti-corruption measures and influence legislation regulating international business transactions. Formulates standards of integrity to govern international business dealings.

**Transparency International - South Africa**. Methodist House, 114 Rissik St., Braamfontein 2017, South Africa. Phone: 27 11 4037746; Fax: 27 11 4034966 • URL: http://www.tisa.org.za • Corporations, organizations, and individuals interested in reducing fraud and corruption in international business transactions. Seeks to raise public awareness of anticorruption measures and to influence legislation regulating international business transactions. Formulates standards of integrity to govern international business dealings; maintains network of businesses agreeing to adhere to these

standards. Conducts anticorruption and antifraud programs. Sponsors research and educational activities.

**Transparency International - Sri Lanka**. No. 6, 37th Ln., Off Queens Rd. Colombo 3, Sri Lanka. Fax: 94 112 506419; Email: tisl@tisrilanka.org • URL: http://www.tisrilanka.org • Represents corporations, organizations and individuals interested in reducing fraud and corruption in international business transactions. Raises public awareness of anticorruption measures and influences legislation regulating international business transactions. Formulates standards of integrity to govern international business dealings. Conducts anticorruption and antifraud programs.

**Transparency International - Sweden**. Linnegatan 14, 6 tr S-114 47 Stockholm, Sweden. Phone: 46 8 7914040; Email: info@transparency-se.org • URL: http://www.transparency-se.org • Represents corporations, organizations and individuals interested in reducing fraud and corruption in international business transactions. Raises public awareness of anti-corruption measures and influences legislation regulating international business transactions. Formulates standards of integrity to govern international business dealings. Conducts anti-corruption and antifraud programs.

**Transparency International - Switzerland**. Schanzeneckstrasse 25, Postfach 8509 CH-3001 Bern, Switzerland. Phone: 41 31 3823550; Fax: 41 31 3825044; Email: info@transparency.ch • URL: http://www.transparency.ch/de/index.php?navid=1 • Corporations, organizations, and individuals interested in reducing fraud and corruption in international business transactions. Seeks to raise public awareness of anti-corruption measures and to influence legislation regulating international business transactions. Formulates standards of integrity to govern international business dealings; maintains network of businesses agreeing to adhere to these standards. Conducts anti-corruption and antifraud programs. Sponsors research and educational activities.

**Transparency International - Taiwan**. PO Box 6-16 Mucha Taipei 11699, Taiwan. Phone: 886 2 22362204; Fax: 886 2 22363325; Email: tict@tict.org.tw • URL: http://www.transparency.org • Represents corporations, organizations and individuals interested in reducing fraud and corruption in international business transactions. Raises public awareness of anticorruption measures and influences legislation regulating international business transactions. Formulates standards of integrity to govern international business dealings. Conducts anticorruption and antifraud programs.

**Transparency International - Thailand**. Centre for Philanthropy and Civil Society, 118 Seri-Thai Rd., Bankapi Bangkok 10240, Thailand. Phone: 66 2 3777206; Fax: 66 2 3747399 • URL: http://www.transparency-thailand.org • Represents corporations, organizations, and individuals interested in reducing fraud and corruption in international business transactions. Seeks to raise public awareness of anticorruption measures and influence legislation regulating international business transactions. Formulates standards of integrity to govern international business dealings and maintains network of businesses agreeing to adhere to these standards. Conducts anticorruption and antifraud programs. Sponsors research and educational activities.

**Transparency International - Turkey**. Niyazi Bey Apt., No. 30, D:5 Sisli Istanbul, Turkey. Phone: 90 212 240 52 81; Fax: 90 212 240 52 81; Email: info@seffaflik.org • URL: http://www.seffaflik.org/index_en.asp • Corporations, individuals, organizations interested in reducing fraud and corruption in Turkish government, business and society. Seeks to raise public awareness of anticorruption measures and to influence legislation regulating transparency and good governance. Formulates standards of integrity in all sectors; maintains network of businesses agreeing to adhere to these standards. Conducts anticorruption and antifraud programs. Sponsors research and educational activities.

**Transparency International - Uganda**. Plot 3 Martyrs Ln., Ntinda Kampala, Uganda. Phone: 256 414 255836; Fax: 256 414 341546; Email: info@tiuganda.org • URL: http://tiuganda.org • Aims to promote good governance and fight against corruption. Seeks to raise public awareness of anti-corruption measures and influence legislation regulating international business transactions. Formulates standards of integrity to govern international business dealings.

**Transparency International - UK**. 32-36 Loman St. London SE1 0EH, United Kingdom. Phone: 44 20 7922-7906; Email: info@transparency.org.uk • URL: http://www.transparency.org.uk • Corporations, organizations, and individuals interested in reducing corruption in international business transactions. Eliminates corruption, particularly its corrosive impact on development in poorer countries and corruption's role in worsening poverty, increasing political instability and undermining the rule of law and democracy. Aims to encourage business to adopt commercial practices that are ethical. Formulates standards of integrity to govern international business dealings; maintains network of businesses agreeing to adhere to these standards. Priority areas are: construction and engineering sector; corruption in the official arms trade; money laundering in the UK; transparency in the extractive industries and reform of the UK law of corruption. Conducts anticorruption programs. Undertakes research and educational activities.

**Transparency International - Ukraine**. 17, Egorova St., Off. 4 25006 Kirovograd, Ukraine. Phone: 380 522 272754; Fax:

380 522 321553; Email: info@ti-ukraine.org • URL: http://www.transparency.org • Represents corporations, organizations and individuals interested in reducing fraud and corruption in international business transactions. Raises public awareness of anti-corruption measures and influences legislation regulating international business transactions. Formulates standards of integrity to govern international business dealings. Conducts anti-corruption and antifraud programs.

**Transparency International - Vanuatu**. PO Box 355 Port Vila, Vanuatu. Phone: 678 25715; Fax: 678 25716; Email: transparency@vanuatu.com.vu • URL: http://www.transparencyvanuatu.org • Represents corporations, organizations and individuals interested in reducing fraud and corruption in international business transactions. Raises public awareness of anticorruption measures and influences legislation regulating international business transactions. Formulates standards of integrity to govern international business dealings. Conducts anticorruption and antifraud programs.

**Transparency International - Zambia**. Stand No. 3880, Kwacha Rd., Olympia Park Lusaka, Zambia. Phone: 260 1 290080; Fax: 260 1 293649; Email: tizambia@zamnet.zm • URL: http://www.transparency.org/whoweare/contact#O_nc_zambia • Represents corporations, organizations and individuals interested in reducing fraud and corruption in international business transactions. Raises public awareness of anti-corruption measures and influences legislation regulating international business transactions. Formulates standards of integrity to govern international business dealings. Conducts anti-corruption and antifraud programs.

**Transparency International - Zimbabwe**. 96 Central Ave., Causeway Harare, Zimbabwe. Phone: 263 4 793246 or 263 4 793277; Email: tiz@transparency.org.zw • URL: http://www.transparency.org.zw • Corporations, organizations, and individuals interested in reducing fraud and corruption in international business transactions. Seeks to raise public awareness of anti-corruption measures and influence legislation regulating international business transactions. Formulates standards of integrity to govern international business dealings and maintains network of businesses agreeing to adhere to these standards. Conducts anti-corruption and antifraud programs. Sponsors research and educational activities.

**Transparency Maldives**. MF Bldg., 7th Fl., Chaandhanee Magu Male, Maldives. Phone: 960 3304017; Fax: 960 3006062; Email: office@transparencymaldives.org • URL: http://www.transparencymaldives.org • Promotes collaboration, awareness and other initiatives to improve governance and eliminate corruption. Encourages discussion on transparency, accountability and the fight against corruption. Seeks to engage stakeholders from all sectors to raise awareness on corruption.

**Transparency Mauritius**. TN Tower, 6th Fl., St. Georges St. Port Louis, Mauritius. Phone: 230 2130796; Fax: 230 2130795; Email: transparency.mauritius@gmail.com • URL: http://www.transparency.org • Represents corporations, organizations and individuals interested in reducing fraud and corruption in international business transactions. Raises public awareness of anti-corruption measures and influences legislation regulating international business transactions. Formulates standards of integrity to govern international business dealings. Conducts anti-corruption and antifraud programs.

***Transport Topics***. American Trucking Associations, 950 N Glebe Rd., Ste. 210 Arlington, VA 22203-4181. Phone: (703)838-1700; Email: media@trucking.org • URL: http://www.truckline.com • Description: Covers news of the trucking transportation industry.

***Transportation and Distribution: Integrating Logistics in Supply Chain Management***. Penton Media Inc., 1300 E 9th St. Cleveland, OH 44114-1501. Phone: (216)696-7000; Fax: (216)696-1752; Email: information@penton.com • URL: http://penton.com • Monthly. Free to qualified personnel; others, $50.00 per year. Essential information on transportation and distribution practices in domestic and international trade.

***Transportation Builder***. American Road and Transportation Builders Association. Heartland Custom Publishers Group, 1003 Central Ave. Fort Dodge, IA 50501. Phone: 800-247-2000 or (515)955-1600; Fax: (800)247-2000 • Monthly. $50.00 per year.

***Transportation Business***. Baxter Publications Inc., 310 Dupont St. Toronto, ON, Canada M5R 1V9. Phone: (416)968-7252; Fax: (416)968-2377; Email: baxgroup@baxter.net • URL: http://www.baxter.net • Biweekly. Publication covering all aspects of the transportation industry.

***Transportation Journal***. American Society of Transportation and Logistics, 8430 W Bryn Mawr Ave., Ste. 1000 Chicago, IL 60631. Phone: (773)355-4900; Fax: (773)355-4888; Email: info@astl.org • URL: http://www.astl.org • Quarterly. $128 Individuals print or online; $258 Institutions print or online; $256 Two years print or online; individuals.; $516 Two years print or online; institutions. Covers research findings and original writings on transportation, logistics, and related fields.

***The Transportation Leader—Buyer's Guide Issue***. Taxicab, Limousine and Paratransit Association, 3200 Tower Oaks Blvd., Ste. 220 Rockville, MD 20852. Phone: (301)984-5700 or (301)946-5701; Fax: (301)984-5703 or (301)946-4641; Email: info@tlpa.org • URL: http://www.tlpa.org • Annual. Publication includes: List of manufacturers of taxicabs, minibuses, vans, limousines, parts, service equipment, wheelchair lifts, communications systems; also includes consultants, insurance agencies, advertising services, propane or natural gas systems; dealers in used vehicles, two-way radios, and meters; and other companies servicing the for-hire vehicle fleet industry (taxicabs, limousines, vans, and minibuses). Entries include: Company name, address, phone, contact person, and brief description of product or service.

***Transportation Quarterly: An Independent Journal for Better Transportation Policy***. Eno Transportation Foundation, 1710 Rhode Island Ave. NW Washington, DC 20036. Phone: (202)879-4700; Fax: (202)879-4719 • URL: http://www.enotrans.com • Quarterly. $55.00 per year. To qualify a written request must be submitted.

***Transportation Research Information Services ((TRIS))***. Transportation Research Board, Highway Research Information, The National Academies, 500 5th St. NW Washington, DC 20001. Phone: (202)334-2934; Email: cbaker@nas.edu • URL: http://www.trb.org • Part of the TRID database, which contains more than 900,000 research records.

***Transportation Research Part E: Logistics and Transportation Review***. University of British Columbia Centre for Transportation Studies. Elsevier, Secondary Publishing Division, 650 Ave. of the Americas New York, NY 10011. Phone: 888-437-4636 or (212)633-3980; Fax: (212)633-3975; Email: t.reller@elsevier.com • URL: http://www.elseveier.com • Bimonthly. Individuals, $213.00 per year; institutions, $897.00 per year.

***Transportation Science***. INFORMS, 5221 Research Park Dr., Ste. 200 Catonsville, MD 21228. Phone: 800-446-3676 or (443)757-3500; Fax: (433)757-3515; Email: informs@informs.org • URL: http://www.informs.org • Quarterly. Individuals, $155.00 per year. Includes print and online editions. Institutions, $221.00 per year. Includes print and online editions.

***Transportation Telephone Tickler***. Journal of Commerce Group, 2 Penn Pl. E Newark, NJ 07105-2257. Phone: (973)776-8660; Email: joc@halldata.com • URL: http://www.joc.com • Annual. $199 Individuals free shipping and handling. Covers: 24,000 companies and agents in North American port districts which provide transportation services ranging from air freight forwarding to warehousing. Published in a four-volume national edition and 7 regional editions. Entries include: Company name, headquarters and branch addresses, phone and fax numbers, names of key personnel, e-mail and web addresses.

***TransWorld Business***. Bonnier Corp., 460 N Orlando Ave., Ste. 200 Winter Park, FL 32789. Phone: (407)628-4802; Fax: (407)628-7061 • URL: http://www.bonniercorp.com • Magazine featuring board-sports news and information.

***Travel Agency***. Entrepreneur Press, 2445 McCabe Way, Ste. 400 Irvine, CA 92614-6244. Phone: 800-864-6864 or (949)261-2325 or (949)622-7131; Fax: (949)261-7729 or (949)261-0234; Email: press@entrepreneur.com • URL: http://www.entrepreneurpress.com • Looseleaf. $59.50. A practical guide to starting a travel agency. Covers profit potential, start-up costs, market size evaluation, owner's time required, site selection, lease negotiation, pricing, accounting, advertising, promotion, etc. (Start-Up Business Guide No. E1154.).

***Travel Agent: The National Newsweekly Magazine of the Travel Industry***. Advanstar Communications, 545 Boylston St. Boston, MA 02116. Phone: 888-527-7008 or (617)267-6500; Fax: (617)267-6900; Email: info@advanstar.com • URL: http://www.advanstar.com • 51 times a year. 250.00 per. year.

***Travel and Leisure***. American Express Publishing Corp., 1120 Ave. of The Americas, 11th Fl. New York, NY 10036-6700. Phone: 888-461-6180 or (212)382-5600; Fax: (212)382-5878 or (212)768-1568; Email: aepc@customersvc.com • URL: http://www.amexpub.com • Monthly. $39.00 per year. In three regional editions and one demographic edition.

***Travel and Tourism***. U. S. Government Printing Office, 732 N Capitol St. NW Washington, DC 20401. Phone: 866-512-1800 or (202)512-1800 or (866)512-1800; Fax: (202)512-2104 or (202)512-2250; Email: contactcenter@gpo.gov • URL: http://www.gpo.gov • Annual. Free. Issued by the Superintendent of Documents. A list of government publications on the travel industry and tourism. Formerly *Mass Transit, Travel and Tourism*. (Subject Bibliography No. 302.).

***The Travel Book: Guide to the Travel Guides***. The Scarecrow Press Inc., 4501 Forbes Blvd., Ste. 200 Lanham, MD 20706-4346. Phone: 800-462-6420 or (301)459-3366; Fax: (301)429-5748; Email: custserv@rowman.com • URL: http://www.scarecrowpress.com • Covers: Travel guides from throughout the world.

***Travel Law***. ALM Media Properties LLC, 120 Broadway, 5th Fl. New York, NY 10271-1100. Phone: (212)457-9400; Fax: (646)417-7705; Email: customercare@alm.com • URL: http://www.alm.com • $555. Emphasis is on the legal rights of travelers, including a consideration of class action suits. Includes such matters as tour operator liability, hotel responsibilities, overbooking by airlines, and frequent-flyer issues. (Law Journal Press).

***Travel Management Daily***. Cahners Business Information, 500 Plaza Dr. Secaucus, NJ 07094. Phone: (201)902-7788; Fax: (201)902-1991; Email: tmdsecaucus@cahners.com • Description: E-mail and internet publication which offers news and advice for those who work in the travel industry.

***Travel Manager's Executive Briefing***. American Business Publishing C/0 Health Resources Publishing, 1913 Atlantic Ave., Ste. F4 Manasquan, NJ 08736. Fax: (732)292-1111; Email: info@healthresourcesonline.com • URL: http://www.healthrespubs.com • Description: Follows developments in the field of travel and expense cost control. Recurring features include news of discounted air fares, car rentals, and hotel bills; case histories of other companies cutting costs; travel alternatives, phone savings, planning for meetings; and trends in government legislation affecting business travel costs.

***Travel Smart: Pay Less, Enjoy More***. Dunan Communications, Inc., PO Box 397 Dobbs Ferry, NY 10522. Phone: 800-327-3633 or (914)693-8300 • Monthly. $39.00 per year. Newsletter. Provides information and recommendations for travelers. Emphasis is on travel value and opportunities for bargains. Incorporates *Joy of Travel*.

***Travel Trade News Edition: The Business Paper of the Travel Industry***. Travel Trade Publications, 15 W. 44th St., 6th Fl. New York, NY 10036. Phone: (212)730-6600; Fax: (212)730-7137; Email: travelcat@aol.com • URL: http://www.traveltrade.com • Weekly. $10.00 per year. Formerly *Travel Trade*.

***Travel Weekly***. Northstar Travel Media L.L.C., 100 Lighting Way, 2nd Fl. Secaucus, NJ 07094. Phone: 800-742-7076 or (201)902-2000 or (201)902-1800; Fax: (201)902-2045 or (201)319-1947; Email: secausushelpdesk@ntmllc.com • URL: http://www.northstartravelmedia.com • Weekly. $266.00 per year. Includes cruise guides, a weekly "Business Travel Update," and special issues devoted to particular destinations and areas. Edited mainly for travel agents and tour operators.

***Travelware***. Business Journals Inc., 50 Day St. Norwalk, CT 06854. Phone: (203)853-6015; Fax: (203)852-8175; Email: macb@busjour.com • URL: http://www.busjour.com • Seven times a year. $32.00. Formerly *Luggage and Travelware*.

***Travelware Suppliers Directory***. Business Journals Inc., 50 Day St. Norwalk, CT 06854. Phone: (203)853-6015; Fax: (203)852-8175; Email: macb@busjour.com • URL: http://www.busjour.com • Annual. $20 postpaid; payment with order. Covers: 500 manufacturers and importers that supply hardware, leather, fabrics, and other components to the luggage and leather goods industry (SIC 3161). Entries include: Company name, address, phone, fax, telex, name of principal executive, sales offices/showrooms/reps, email, URL.

***Treasury and Risk Management***. Wicks Business Information, 363 Reef Rd. Fairfield, CT 06430. Phone: (203)255-4990; Fax: (203)255-4353; Email: info@wickbusinessinfo.com • URL: http://www.wicksbusinessinfo.com • 10 times a year. $64.00 per year. Covers risk management tools and techniques. Incorporates *Treasury*.

***Treasury Bulletin***. U. S. Government Printing Office, 732 N Capitol St. NW Washington, DC 20401. Phone: 866-512-1800 or (202)512-1800 or (866)512-1800; Fax: (202)512-2104 or (202)512-2250; Email: contactcenter@gpo.gov • URL: http://www.gpo.gov • Quarterly. $51 List Price. Issued by the Financial Management Service, U. S. Treasury Department. Provides data on the federal budget, government securities and yields, the national debt, and the financing of the federal government in general.

***Treasury Manager's Report: Strategic Information for the Financial Executive***. Access Intelligence L.L.C., 4 Choke Cherry Rd., 2nd Fl. Rockville, MD 20850. Phone: 800-777-5006 or (301)354-2000 or (301)354-2101; Fax: (301)309-3847 or (801)365-2300; Email: info@accessintel.com • URL: http://www.accessintel.com/ • Biweekly. $630.00. Newsletter reporting on legal developments affecting the operations of banks, savings institutions, and other financial service organizations. Formerly *Financial Services Law Report*.

***Trends in Mutual Fund Activity***. Investment Company Institute, 1401 H St. NW, Ste. 1200 Washington, DC 20005. Phone: (202)326-5800 or (202)371-5413; Fax: (202)326-5986; Email: chris@ici.org • URL: http://www.ici.org • Monthly. free for members; $400 Nonmembers per year. Contains statistical tables showing fund industry sales, redemptions, assets, cash, and other data.

***Trends in the Hotel Industry: U.S.A. Edition***. PKF Consulting Corp., 50 California St., 19th Fl. San Francisco, CA 94111. Phone: (415)788-3102; Fax: (415)433-7844; Email: thomas.callahan@pkfc.com • URL: http://www.pkfc.com • Annual. $350 online. Provides detailed financial analysis of hotel operations in the U. S. (PKF is Pannell Kerr Forster.).

***The Trends Journal: The Authority on Trends Management***. Gerald Celente, editor. Trends Research Institute, PO Box 660 Rhinebeck, NY 12572-0660. Phone: 800—ON-TREND or (845)876-6700; Fax: (845)758-5252; Email: joneill@trendsresearch.com • URL: http://www.trendsresearch.com/ • Quarterly. $185.00 per year. Newsletter. Provides forecasts on a wide variety of economic, social, and political topics. Includes "Hot Trends to Watch.".

***Tri-Cities Christian Business Directory***. Red Letter Publishing, PO Box 272682 Fort Collins, CO 80527. Phone: 800-445-5614; Fax: (970)267-9669; Email: info@redletter.com • URL: http://www.christianbusinessdirectoryonline.com • Businesses, churches, organizations, and schools in Tri-Cities, Washington.

***The Tri-County Business Advocate***. Arcade Area Chamber of

Commerce, 684 W Main St. Arcade, NY 14009. Phone: (585)492-2114; Fax: (585)492-5103 • URL: http://www.arcadechamber.org • Quarterly. Contains latest news and events about Arcade Area Chamber of Commerce.

***Tri-State Directory of Export Management and Trading Companies***. National Association of Export Cos., 205 Bergen Tpke., Apt. 2L Ridgefield Park, NJ 07660-2369. Phone: (201)814-0336; Fax: (201)440-1216 • Irregular. Free to members; $20 Nonmembers. Covers: 700 export management and trading companies in Connecticut, New Jersey, and New York who are National Association of Export Companies (NEXCO) members. Entries include: Company name, address, phone, fax, contact name, product specialty.

***Triad Business News***. Triad Business News, 5601 Roanne Way, Ste. 113 Greensboro, NC 27409. Phone: 800-287-1094 or (336)854-3001; Fax: (336)854-3013 • Weekly. $36; $48 Out of state. Business publication.

***Trial***. American Association for Justice, 777 6th St. NW, Ste. 200 Washington, DC 20001. Phone: 800-424-2725 or (202)965-3500; Fax: (202)625-7084; Email: membership@justice.org • URL: http://www.justice.org/cps/rde/xchg/justice/hs.xsl/default.htm • Monthly. $89 Individuals.

***Trial Lawyers Quarterly***. New York State Trial Lawyers Association, 132 Nassau St., Ste. 200 New York, NY 10038. Phone: (212)349-5890; Fax: (212)608-2310; Email: info@nystla.org • URL: http://www.nystla.org • Quarterly. $50.00 per year.

***Triangle Business Journal's Book of Lists***. Greater Raleigh Chamber of Commerce, 800 S Salisbury St. Raleigh, NC 27601-2202. Phone: (919)664-7000; Fax: (919)664-7097; Email: mail@raleighchamber.org • URL: http://www.raleighchamber.org • $45 Members; $45 Nonmembers. Provides 25 listings for 75 different business sectors in Raleigh and Durham area including advertising agencies, architects, banks, real estate agencies, hotels, accountants, and golf courses.

***Triangle***. Florida Citrus Mutual, 411 E Orange St. Lakeland, FL 33801. Phone: (863)682-1111; Fax: (863)682-1074; Email: info@flcitrusmutual.com • URL: http://flcitrusmutual.com • Description: Contains items of interest to citrus growers, including statistical data, market information, ongoing scientific research, and action by various government agencies. Recurring features include weather forecasts, market information, production statistics, news of research, a calendar of events, and reports of meetings.

***Tribology International; The Practice and Technology of Lubrication, Wear Prevention and Friction Control***. Elsevier, Secondary Publishing Division, 650 Ave. of the Americas New York, NY 10011. Phone: 888-437-4636 or (212)633-3980; Fax: (212)633-3975; Email: t.reller@elsevier.com • URL: http://www.elseveier.com • Monthly. Qualified personnel, $173.00 per year; institutions, $1,528.00 per year.

***Trinidad & Tobago—American Chamber of Commerce—Membership Directory***. U.S. Chamber of Commerce, 1615 H St. NW Washington, DC 20062-2000. Phone: 800-638-6582 or (202)463-5500 or (202)659-6000; Fax: (202)463-3129; Email: foundation@uschamber.com • URL: http://www.uschambersmallbusinessnation.com • Annual. $80 Individuals. Covers: Companies in the U.S. and Trinidad and Tobago and individuals interested in the development of trade within and between the two countries. Entries include: For firms—Company name, address, phone, fax, telex, cable address, names and titles of key personnel, line of business, subsidiary and branch names and locations, locations of plants or branch offices, product/service information. For individuals—Name, title, affiliation, address.

***Trinidad and Tobago Investment and Business Guide***. International Business Publications, USA, PO Box 15343 Washington, DC 20003. Phone: (202)546-2103; Fax: (202)546-3275; Email: ibpusa@comcast.net • URL: http://ibpus.com • $99.95 Individuals hardcopy, E-book and CD-ROM. Covers: Strategic and information on economy, business, export-import activity, investment climate, opportunities, industrial development, banking and government. Entries include: Business contacts, regulations, etc.

***TRIS: Transportation Research Information Service***. The National Academies National Research Council, 500 5th St. NW Washington, DC 20001. Phone: (202)334-2000 • URL: http://www.nationalacademies.org/nrc/ • Contains abstracts and citations to a wide range of transportation literature, 1968 to present, with monthly updates. Includes references to the literature of air transportation, highways, ships and shipping, railroads, trucking, and urban mass transportation. Formerly *TRIS-ON-LINE*. Inquire as to online cost and availability.

***Troubled and Problematic Bank and Thrift Report***. BauerFinancial Inc., 2655 LeJeune Rd. Coral Gables, FL 33134-5832. Phone: 800-388-6686 or (305)445-9500; Fax: (800)230-9569; Email: customerservice@bauerfinancial.com • URL: http://www.bauerfinancial.com • Quarterly. $225.00 per year. Newsletter provides information on seriously undercapitalized ("Troubled") banks and savings institutions, as defined by a federal Prompt Corrective Action Rule. "Problematic" banks and thrifts are those meeting regulatory capital levels, but showing negative trends.

**Troy State University - Center for Business and Economic Services**. Sorrell College of Business Troy, AL 36082. Phone: (334)670-3524; Fax: (334)670-3636; Email: jkervin@trojan.troyst.edu • URL: http://troy.troy.edu/cbes/index.html • Business and economics, including feasibility studies, market research, economic projections, cost analyses, accounting and budgeting models, and similar projects.

***Truck Cover and Tarp Association Membership Directory***. Industrial Fabrics Association International, 1801 County Rd. B W Roseville, MN 55113-4061. Phone: 800-225-4324 or (651)222-2508; Fax: (651)631-9334; Email: generalinfo@ifai.com • URL: http://www.ifai.com • Annual. Publication includes: Listings of member companies that manufacture and supply material, equipment or services to the truck cover and tarpaulin industry. Entries include: name, address, phone, fax of company and names and titles of key personnel, along with descriptions of services and products.

***Truck Frame & Axle Repair Association—Membership Directory***. Truck-frame & Axle Repair Association, 3741 Enterprise Dr. SW Rochester, MN 55902. Phone: 800-232-8272; Fax: (866)529-0380 • URL: http://www.taraassociation.com • Biennial. Covers: About 150 regular and associate members that repair heavy-duty truck equipment or supply the industry. Database includes: Map showing locations of members. Entries include: Firm name, address, phone, key personnel, coding to indicate specialties.

***Truck Trailers***. U. S. Bureau of the Census, 4600 Silver Hill Rd. Washington, DC 20233-0001. Phone: (301)763-4636; Email: comments@census.gov • URL: http://www.census.gov • Monthly Annual. Provides data on shipments of truck trailers and truck trailer vans: value, quantity, imports, and exports. (Current Industrial Reports, M37L.).

***Trust Administration and Taxation***. Matthew Bender and Company Inc., 1275 Broadway Albany, NY 12204-2638. Phone: 800-424-4200 or (518)487-3000; Fax: (518)487-3573 or (800)424-4200; Email: customer.support@lexisnexis.com • URL: http://www.matthewbender.com • Semiannual. $1,857 Individuals Book; $1,688 Individuals Electronic version. A well-documented, practical text on the establishment, administration and taxation of trusts, covering revocable living trusts, charitable remainder trusts, and more.

**Trust Companies' Association of Japan**. Nippon Kaikan, 6th Fl., 2-6-2, Otemachi Chiyoda, Tokyo 100-0004, Japan. Phone: 81 3 3241-7135; Fax: 81 3 3241-7200 • URL: http://www.shintaku-kyokai.or.jp • Works on the promotion, protection, and advancement of the interests of closed-ended investment trust companies and their shareholders by influencing developments in legislation and practice affecting investors, companies and the stock market, by political lobbying and by promotion of their merits, in particular to private investors and independent financial advisers.

***Trust Department Administration and Operations***. Matthew Bender and Company Inc., 1275 Broadway Albany, NY 12204-2638. Phone: 800-424-4200 or (518)487-3000; Fax: (518)487-3573 or (800)424-4200; Email: customer.support@lexisnexis.com • URL: http://www.matthewbender.com • Semiannual. $726 Individuals Book or Electronic version. Covers every aspect of setting up a trust department, day-to-day administration, asset management, operations, marketing, and internal management. A procedural manual, training guide and idea source.

***Trust Letter***. American Bankers Association, 1120 Connecticut Ave. NW Washington, DC 20036. Phone: 800-226-5377 or (202)663-5268; Fax: (202)828-5053; Email: custserv@aba.com • URL: http://www.aba.com • Monthly. Description: Contains updates of national legislation and regulation that impacts the trust and investment businesses. Reports on significant industry happenings, important research, and provides coverage of ABA legislative/regulatory testimony and committee activities, especially in the areas of taxation, securities, and employee benefits.

***Trust Management Update***. American Bankers Association, 1120 Connecticut Ave. NW Washington, DC 20036. Phone: 800-226-5377 or (202)663-5268; Fax: (202)828-5053; Email: custserv@aba.com • URL: http://www.aba.com • Bimonthly. $95.00 per year.

***Trustee: The Magazine for Hospital Governing Boards***. American Hospital Association, Health Forum L.L.C., 155 N Wacker Dr., Ste. 400 Chicago, IL 60606. Phone: 800-821-2039 or (312)893-6800; Fax: (312)422-4500 • URL: http://www.healthforum.com • 10 times a year. $55.00 per year. Emphasis is on community health care.

***Trusts and Estates***. RentPath Inc., 3585 Engineering Dr., Ste. 100 Norcross, GA 30092-2831. Phone: 800-216-1423 or (678)421-3000 • URL: http://www.rentpath.com • Monthly. $139.00 per year. Includes annual *Directory*.

***TRW Business Credit Profiles***. Experian Information Solutions Inc., 475 Anton Blvd. Costa Mesa, CA 92626-7037. Phone: 866-256-4468 or (714)830-7000; Email: privacy@experian.com • URL: http://www.experian.com • Provides credit history (trade payments, payment trends, payment totals, payment history, etc.) for public and private U. S. companies. Key facts and banking information are also given. Updates are weekly. Inquire as to online cost and availability.

***TRW Trade Payment Guide***. TRW Business Credit Services, 505 City Pkwy. W, 10th Fl. Orange, CA 92868. Phone: (714)385-7000 • Quarterly. Database covers: About 2,500,000 credit active business locations. Database includes: Company name, address, phone; Standard Industrial Classification (SIC) code; public record filings indicator; TRW days beyond terms credit store/history.

***Tucson Business Digest***. Thompson Publications Ltd., 6651 N Campbell, No. 105 Tucson, AZ 85718. • Monthly. $24 Individuals. Business magazine covers news and information for the Tucson business community.

**Tufts University - Tufts Center for the Study of Drug Development**. 75 Kneeland St., Ste. 1100 Boston, MA 02111. Phone: (617)636-2170; Fax: (617)636-2425; Email: csdd@tufts.edu • URL: http://csdd.tufts.edu • Provides strategic information to help drug developers, regulators, and policy makers improve the quality and efficiency of pharmaceutical development, review, and utilization; focuses on: research & development, economic, and performance issues; regulatory policies and initiatives; biotechnology product development; drug development operational processes; public policy, healthcare financing, and law.

***Tulane Maritime Law Journal***. Tulane University School of Law, 6329 Freret St. New Orleans, LA 70118. Phone: (504)865-5959; Fax: (504)865-8878 • URL: http://www.law.tulane.edu • Semiannual. $28.00 per year. Formerly *Maritime Lawyer*.

***Tulsa Chamber Membership Directory***. • Covers Tulsa Metro Chamber of Commerce membership roster.

***Tulsa***. Information Services, 600 S. College, Harwell 101 Tulsa, OK 74104. Phone: 800-247-8678 or (918)631-2297; Fax: (918)599-9361 • Worldwide literature in the petroleum and natural gas areas, 1965 to present. Inquire as to online cost and availability. Includes petroleum exploration patents. Updated weekly.

***Tulsa Metropolitan Chamber Business Directory and Buyer's Guide***. Mary Brett & Associates/Image Publishing, 2530 E 71st St., No. D Tulsa, OK 74136-5577. • Covers: about 3,500 companies; federal, state, and local government agencies and officials, schools, and associations in the greater Tulsa, Oklahoma area. Entries include: Company, institution, organization, or individual name, address, phone.

***Tunnel Business Magazine: Covering the North American Tunneling Market***. Benjamin Media Inc., 1770 Main St. Peninsula, OH 44264. Phone: (330)467-7588; Email: info@benjaminmedia.com • URL: http://www.benjaminmedia.com • Free in United States and Canada; $99 Other countries; $10 Single issue. Magazine featuring tunnel construction and engineering in North America.

***Turkey Business Forecast Report***. Telecommunications Insight, 85 Queen Victoria St. London EC4V 4AB, United Kingdom. Phone: 20 72 465100 or 44 20 7248 0468; Fax: 20 72 480467 or 44 20 7248 0467; Email: enquiries@telecomsinsight.com • URL: http://www.telecomsinsight.com • Quarterly. $1,195 Individuals Single user; $1,795 Individuals Up to 3 users. Business forecast report for Turkey.

**Turkey Farmers of Canada**. Bldg. 1, Ste. 202, 7145 W Credit Ave. Mississauga, ON, Canada L5N 6J7. Phone: (905)812-3140; Fax: (905)812-9326; Email: info@tfc-edc.ca • URL: http://www.turkeyfarmersofcanada.ca • Turkey processors (3) and representatives of provincial turkey producers' organizations (8). Promotes a healthy business climate for turkey processors and growers. Sets national turkey production and supply levels. Conducts marketing programs; gathers and disseminates industry information; represents members before government agencies.

***Turkey Government and Business Contacts Handbook***. International Business Publications, USA, PO Box 15343 Washington, DC 20003. Phone: (202)546-2103; Fax: (202)546-3275; Email: ibpusa@comcast.net • URL: http://ibpus.com • $99.95 Individuals hardcopy, e-book, CD-ROM. Covers: Strategic government and business information, export-import activity in the country, investment, business contacts and regulations.

***Turkey Industry and Trade Directory***. AGT Research Development & Information Corporation Inonu Caddesi, Haci Hanim Sok, Derya Ste. 8/8 TR-80090 Istanbul, Turkey. Phone: 11 451385 • Annual. $112. Covers: 14,500 producers, marketers, foreign trade investment service companies, representatives, authorized sellers, and wholesalers in Turkey.

***Turkey Investment and Business Guide***. International Business Publications, USA, PO Box 15343 Washington, DC 20003. Phone: (202)546-2103; Fax: (202)546-3275; Email: ibpusa@comcast.net • URL: http://ibpus.com • $99.95 Individuals hardcopy, E-book and CD-ROM. Covers: Detailed information on investment, export-import business opportunities, foreign economic assistance projects, government and business contacts.

**Turkish American Business Connection**. 2784 Homestead Rd., No. 118 Santa Clara, CA 95051. Phone: (408)404-5208; Fax: (408)404-5208; Email: info@tabc-us.org • URL: http://www.tabc-us.org • Brings together Turkish-American entrepreneurs, professionals and business people. Advances the interests of Turkish-American businessmen, entrepreneurs and professionals from all industries. Promotes professional networking opportunities for and among its members.

***Turkish Business Directory***. London Business Guide, 146-148 Oxford St. London W1D 1NB, United Kingdom. Phone: 44 844 5043309; Fax: 44 844 5047660 • URL: http://www.londonbusinessguide.org • Covers: 25,000 companies and businesses in United Kingdom and Europe.

***Turkmenistan Government and Business Contacts Handbook***. International Business Publications, USA, PO Box 15343 Washington, DC 20003. Phone: (202)546-2103; Fax: (202)546-3275; Email: ibpusa@comcast.net • URL: http://ibpus.com • $99.95 Individuals hardcopy, e-book, CD-ROM.

Covers: Strategic government and business information, export-import activity in the country, investment, business contacts and regulations.

**Turku School of Economics and Business Administration - Business Research and Development Center**. PO Box 110 FIN-20521 Turku, Finland. Phone: 358 2 4814548; Fax: 358 2 4814268; Email: antti.paasio@tse.fi • URL: http://www.tukkk.fi/brdc/default.asp • Economy, business, small business, management, entrepreneurship, communications, marketing and development.

**Turnaround Management Association**. 150 N Wacker Dr., Ste. 1900 Chicago, IL 60606. Phone: (312)578-6900; Fax: (312)578-8336; Email: info@turnaround.org • URL: http://www.turnaround.org/Default.aspx • Practitioners (interim managers, consultants, corporate managers and professional advisors), academics, students, attorneys and judges, commercial lenders and legislative personnel. Promotes the image and credibility of the turnaround profession; fosters professional development and networking opportunities for turnaround executives; serves as a clearinghouse of information and research pertinent to the profession. Conducts networking forums; offers educational and credentialing programs.

***Turnkey Offers from India***. EEPC India, c/o Bhaskar Sarkar, Executive Director/Secretary, 11, Tolstoy Marg, Vandha, 4th Fl. New Delhi 110001, India. Phone: 91 11 23353353; Fax: 91 11 23310920; Email: eecpto@eecpindia.net • URL: http://www.eepcindia.org • Biennial. Covers: Companies in India involved in international projects.

***The TV Guide***. Gemstar-TV Guide International, 1211 Avenue of the Americas New York, NY 10036. Phone: 800-866-1400 or (610)293-8500; Fax: (610)688-6216 • URL: http://www.tvguide.com • Weekly. $46.28 per year.

***TV Technology***. IMAS Publishing Group, 5827 Columbia Pke. Ste. 310 Falls Church, VA 22041. Phone: 800-336-3045 or (703)998-7600; Fax: (703)998-2966; Email: adsales@imaspub.com • URL: http://www.imaspub.com • Biweekly. $75.00 per year. International coverage available.

***21.C: Scanning the Future: A Magazine of Culture, Technology, and Science***. International Publishers Distributors, P.O. Box 200029, Riverfront Plaza Station Newark, NJ 07102-0301. Phone: 800-545-8398 or (973)643-7500; Fax: (973)643-7676 • URL: http://www.21c.com • Quarterly. $24.00 per year. Contains multidisciplinary articles relating to the 21st century.

***21st Century Economics: A Reference Handbook***. Cengage Learning Inc., 20 Channel Center St. Boston, MA 02210. Phone: 800-487-8488 or (617)289-7700; Fax: (617)289-7844; Email: investors@cengage.com • URL: http://www.cengage.com • 2010. eBook. Published by Sage Publications. Covers traditional economic theory as well as challenges that face the nation in an economy with unemployment issues, failures of major businesses and industries, and continued dependence on oil with its wildly fluctuating prices.

***21st Century Management: A Reference Handbook***. Cengage Learning Inc., 20 Channel Center St. Boston, MA 02210. Phone: 800-487-8488 or (617)289-7700; Fax: (617)289-7844; Email: investors@cengage.com • URL: http://www.cengage.com • 2008. eBook. Published by Sage Pubications. Highlights the topics, issues, questions and debates that any student obtaining a degree in the field of management must master to be effective in today's business world.

***Twin Plant News: The Magazine of the Maquiladora Industry***. Nibbe, Hernandez and Associates Inc., 725 S Mesa Hills El Paso, TX 79912. Phone: 866-955-2323 or (915)532-1567; Fax: (915)544-7556 • Monthly. $85.00 per year. Focuses on Mexican labor laws, taxes, economics, industrial trends, and culture. Industries featured include electronic components, plastics, automotive supplies, metals, communications, and packaging.

***TwinWest Chamber of Commerce—Membership Directory & Business Guide***. TwinWest Chamber of Commerce, 10700 Old County Road 15, Ste. 170 Plymouth, MN 55441. Phone: (763)450-2220; Fax: (763)450-2221; Email: info@twinwest.com • URL: http://www.twinwest.com • Annual. Cvers 1,000 businesses and industries ranging from nationally and internationally renowned corporations and industrially driven manufacturers, to home-based businesses and companies involved in the service and professional sectors.

***The 2,000 Top Spanish Companies***. Fomento de la Produccion, Casanova 57 E-08011 Barcelona, Spain. Phone: 34 3 2530697 • URL: http://www.fomenweb.com • Annual. $15. Covers: 2,000 leading companies in Spain. Entries include: Company name, address, phone, telex number, sales, ranking.

***Tyne & Wear Chamber Regional Business Directory***. Ten Alps Publishing, Trelawney House, Chestergate Macclesfield SK11 6DW, United Kingdom. Phone: 44 1625 613000; Fax: (162)5 511446; Email: info@ft.com • URL: http://www.tenalpscommunications.com/ • Covers: businesses in Tyne and Wear, England. Entries include: Company name, address, phone, telex, fax, description of products or services.

***UAE Commercial Directory***. Federation of UAE Chamber of Commerce & Industry, PO Box 3014 Abu Dhabi, United Arab Emirates. Phone: 971 2 6214144; Fax: 971 2 6339210; Email: info@fcciuae.ae • URL: http://www.fcciuae.ae • Annual. Provides information on UAE diplomatic missions abroad, Chambers of Commerce and Industry, and lists of business establishments. Entries include: Addresses of government institutions.

***UAE Golden Key Directory***. International Institute of Trade Relation Promotion, Trade Information Centre of Iran, No. 7, 3rd Fl., Abbasie Bazar, Ferdowsi Sq. Tehran, Iran. Phone: 98 21 88833900; Fax: 98 21 88820697; Email: order@irangoldenkey.com • URL: http://www.goldenkeydirectory.com/about.html • £100 Individuals. Covers: 237,564 companies in United Arab Emirates. Entries include: Company name, address, telephone, fax, products, services, managing director, and business activities.

***UAE Industrial Directory***. Federation of UAE Chamber of Commerce & Industry, PO Box 3014 Abu Dhabi, United Arab Emirates. Phone: 971 2 6214144; Fax: 971 2 6339210; Email: info@fcciuae.ae • URL: http://www.fcciuae.ae • Aims to widen the industrial channels and provide all the available services in order to help industrialists, business men and investors in different fields and to consolidate trust and provide suitable ambience for cooperation between industrialists and consumers. Covers: Industrial firms and companies operating in UAE. Entries include: Company name and address.

**UAW - Community Action Program**. Solidarity House, 8000 E Jefferson Ave. Detroit, MI 48214. Phone: 800-243-8829 or (313)926-5000; Email: uaw@uaw.org • URL: http://www.uaw.org/page/uaw-community-action-program • Serves as a program of the International Union, United Automobile, Aerospace and Agricultural Implement Workers of America. Informs UAW members through political education programs on topics including lobbying, the relationship between collective bargaining and the ballot box, and voluntary fundraising for political contributions. Maintains speakers' bureau; compiles statistics.

***UCC Bulletin***. Thomson West, 610 Opperman Dr. Eagan, MN 55123. Phone: 800-328-9352 or (651)687-7000 • Monthly. $560.00 per year. Newsletter. Includes case summaries of recent UCC decisions.

**UCLA Film and Television Archive-Research and Study Center**. University of California, Los Angeles, 46 Powell Library Los Angeles, CA 90095. Phone: (310)206-5388; Fax: (310)206-5392; Email: arsc@cinema.ucla.edu • URL: http://www.cinema.ucla.edu • Research areas include animation.

***Uganda Business Directory***. Business Guide, PO Box 27669 Dubai, United Arab Emirates. Phone: 971 4 2651719; Fax: 971 4 2692151; Email: sales@africa-business.com • URL: http://www.africa-business.com • $250 Individuals. Covers: 11,000 business listings including wholesalers, importers, retailers, business houses, and agents in Uganda.

***UK Coal***. Organisation for Economic Co-operation and Development Publications and Information Center, 2001 L St. NW, Ste. 650 Washington, DC 20036-4922. Phone: 800-456-6323 or (202)785-6323; Fax: (202)785-0350; Email: washington.contact@oecd.org • URL: http://www.oecd.org • Annual. $200. A yearly report on world coal market trends and prospects.

***U.K. Directory of Talent Management***. Executive Grapevine International Ltd., Rosanne House, Pkwy., Hertfordshire Welwyn Garden City AL8 6HG, United Kingdom. Phone: 44 1707 351451; Fax: 44 1707 390143; Email: info@askgrapevine.com • URL: http://www.executive-grapevine.com • $239 Individuals. Covers: 700 top U.K. executive recruitment and interim management providers and over 3,000 consultant biographies. Entries include: Company profile, consultant biographies, salary range of assignments, function, fees, and major clients.

***The UK/USA Investment Directory & Business Resource***. BritishAmerican Business Inc. of New York and London, 52 Vanderbilt Ave., 20th Fl. New York, NY 10017. Phone: (212)661-4060; Fax: (212)661-4074; Email: nyinfo@babinc.org • URL: http://www.babinc.org • Biennial. $149. Covers: Over 6,000 British and American companies and their approximately 4,000 subsidiaries in the United Kingdom and the United States. Entries include: Parent company name, address, phone, fax; name of British subsidiary in the United States, address, phone, fax; percentage of business British or American owned, number of staff, product or service provided, Standard Industrial Classification (SIC) code.

***Ukraine Government and Business Contacts Handbook***. International Business Publications, USA, PO Box 15343 Washington, DC 20003. Phone: (202)546-2103; Fax: (202)546-3275; Email: ibpusa@comcast.net • URL: http://ibpus.com • Annual. $99.95 Individuals hardcopy, E-book and CD-ROM. Covers: Strategic industrial, investment and business contacts for conducting export-import and investment activity in the country.

***Ukraine Top 100 Exporters***. IIA Sistema-Reserve, ul. Aviatstionnaya, 25 320017 Dnepropetrovsk, Ukraine. Phone: 562 441368; Fax: 562 441368 • Annual. $75. Covers: 100 exporting companies in Ukraine, with partial listing for approximately 20 other exporting companies. Entries include: Company name, address, phone, fax, telex, names and titles of key personnel, number of employees, financial data, description of product/service, import purchases planned.

***ULI Market Profiles: North America***. Urban Land Institute, 1025 Thomas Jefferson St. NW, Ste. 500 W Washington, DC 20007. Phone: 800-321-5011 or (202)624-7000; Fax: (202)624-7140; Email: customerservice@uli.org • URL: http://www.uli.org • Annual. Members, $249.95; nonmembers, $299.95. Provides real estate marketing data for residential, retail, office, and industrial sectors. Covers 76 U. S. metropolitan areas and 13 major foreign metropolitan areas.

***Ulrich's International Periodicals Directory Online***. Bowker Electronic Publishing, 630 Central Ave. New Providence, NJ 07974. Phone: 888-269-5372 or (908)464-6800; Fax: (908)665-3528 • $2,175 Individuals hardcover. Includes over 275,000 periodicals currently published worldwide and publications discontinued. Corresponds to *Ulrich's International Periodcals Directory, Irregular Serials and Annuals, Bowker International Serials Database Update*, and *Sources of Serials*.

***Ulrich's Periodicals Directory: International Periodicals Information Since 1932***. R.R. Bowker L.L.C., 630 Central Ave New Providence, NJ 07974. Phone: 888-269-5372 or (908)286-1090; Email: info@bowker.com • URL: http://www.bowker.com • Annual. $1,260 Individuals Hardcover, 4 volumes. Covers: Nearly 200,000 current periodicals and newspapers published worldwide. Entries include: In main list—Publication title; Dewey Decimal Classification number, Library of Congress Classification Number (where applicable), CODEN designation (for sci-tech serials), British Library Document Supply Centre shelfmark number, country code, ISSN; subtitle, language(s) of text, year first published, frequency, subscription prices, sponsoring organization, publishing company name, address, phone, fax, e-mail and website addresses, editor and publisher names; regular features (reviews, advertising, abstracts, bibliographies, trade literature, etc. ), indexes, circulation, format, brief description of content; availability of microforms and reprints; whether refereed; CD-ROM availability with vendor name; online availability with service name; services that index or abstract the periodical, with years covered; advertising rates and contact; right and permissions contact name and phone; availability through document deliver.

***Ulrichsweb.com***. R.R. Bowker L.L.C., 630 Central Ave New Providence, NJ 07974. Phone: 888-269-5372 or (908)286-1090; Email: info@bowker.com • URL: http://www.bowker.com • Web site provides fee-based access to about 250,000 serials records from the *Ulrich's International Periodicals Directory* database. Includes periodical evaluations from *Library Journal* and *Magazines for Libraries*. Monthly updates.

***The Ultimate Directory of Film Technicians: A Necrology of Dates and Places of Births and Deaths of More than 9,000 Producers, Directors, Screenwriters, Composers, Cinematographers.*.** The Scarecrow Press Inc., 4501 Forbes Blvd., Ste. 200 Lanham, MD 20706-4346. Phone: 800-462-6420 or (301)459-3366; Fax: (301)429-5748; Email: custserv@rowman.com • URL: http://www.scarecrowpress.com • $70 Individuals Hardback; £44.95 Individuals Hardback. Covers: Film technicians from the beginning of the film industry to the present, including executives, producers, directors, screenwriters, cinematographers, set and costume designers, composers, art directors, choreographers, publicists, and editors. Entries include: Birth and death dates and career information.

***Ultrasonic Imaging, An International Journal***. Dynamedia of America Inc., 205 S Hoover Blvd., Ste. 102 Tampa, FL 33609. Phone: 800-875-7851 or (813)287-8177 • URL: http://www.dynagang.com • Quarterly. $325.00 per year.

***Ultrasonics: The World's Leading Journal Covering the Science and Technology of Ultrasound***. Elsevier, Secondary Publishing Division, 650 Ave. of the Americas New York, NY 10011. Phone: 888-437-4636 or (212)633-3980; Fax: (212)633-3975; Email: t.reller@elsevier.com • URL: http://www.elseveier.com • 10 times a year. Institutions, $131.00 per year; institutions, $1,461.00 per year.

***Ultrasound in Medicine and Biology (UMB)***. Elsevier, Secondary Publishing Division, 650 Ave. of the Americas New York, NY 10011. Phone: 888-437-4636 or (212)633-3980; Fax: (212)633-3975; Email: t.reller@elsevier.com • URL: http://www.elseveier.com • Monthly. Institutions, $1,305.00 per year.

***UN Chronicle***. United Nations Pulications, PO Box 960 Herndon, VA 20172. Phone: (703)661-1571; Fax: (703)996-1010 • URL: http://unp.un.org • 11 times a year. $25.00 per year. Editions in English, French and Spanish.

***UNCTAD Commodity Yearbook***. United Nations Conference on Trade and Development. United Nations Publications, c/o National Book Network, 15200 NBN Way Blue Ridge Summit, PA 17214. Phone: 888-254-4286 or (212)963-7680 or (212)963-8302; Fax: (800)338-4550; Email: unpublications@nbnbooks.com • URL: http://www.unp.un.org • Contains statistics on trade, production and consumption of commodities, as well as special tables showing the most important exporting and importing countries.

***UNCTAD Handbook of Statistics***. United Nations Conference on Trade and Development, DC2-1120, United Nations New York, NY 10017. Phone: (212)963-0027; Email: unctadny1@un.org • URL: http://www.unctad.org • $130 Individuals Book with CD-Rom; $65 Individuals Softcopy. Database covers: Statistical data relevant to the analysis of international trade, investment and development, for individual countries and for economic and trade groupings. It presents reference statistics on international merchandise trade, trade and commodity price indices, structure of international trade by region, structure of international trade by product, international trade in services, international finance, indicators of development, special studies.

*UNCTAD-Trade Analysis and Information System*. United Nations Conference on Trade and Development, DC2-1120, United Nations New York, NY 10017. Phone: (212)963-0027; Email: unctadny1@un.org • URL: http://www.unctad.org • Database covers: Indicators of trade control measures (tariff, para-tariff and non-tariff measures), as well as imports by suppliers at each harmonized system 6-digit level for over 160 countries. It also provides country notes of trade regimes for some 40 developing countries, describing market access conditions according to the UNCTAD coding system of Trade control measures.

*Undercar Digest—Buyer's Guide Issue: The Sourcebook*. MD Publications Inc., 3057 E Cairo St. Springfield, MO 65802. Phone: 800-274-7890 or (417)866-3917; Fax: (417)866-2781; Email: mdickemann@mdpublications.com • URL: http://www.mdpublications.com • Annual. $10 Individuals. Publication includes: List of automotive aftermarket manufacturers and suppliers of mufflers, exhaust pipes, brakes, chassis, steering, suspension, driveline, shop equipment and tools, and other products. Entries include: Company name, address, phone, fax, name and title of contact, products.

*Understanding Workers Compensation: A Guide for Safety and Health Professionals*. Government Institutes, 4501 Forbes Bvld., Ste. 200 Lanham, MD 20706. Phone: 800-462-6420 or (301)459-3366; Fax: (301)429-5748; Email: orders@rowman.com • URL: http://rowman.com • $72 Individuals Paperback; £44.95 Individuals Paperback. Publication includes: Listing of state and provincial workers compensation administrators. Database includes: Sample forms, checklists, U.S. Chamber of Commerce analysis. Entries include: Name, address, phone. Principal content of publication is explanation of the Workers Compensation System.

*Unemployment Insurance Weekly Claims Report*. U.S. Department of Labor, Employment and Training Administration, Frances Perkins Bldg., 200 Constitution Ave., NW Washington, DC 20210. Phone: 866-487-2365; Email: etapagemaster@dol.gov • URL: http://www.doleta.gov • Weekly.

*Unfinished Business*. Unfinished Furniture Association, PO Box 520 Spofford, NH 03462. Phone: 800-487-8321 or (518)832-7939; Email: ufa@unfinishedfurniture.org • URL: http://www.unfinishedfurniture.org • Bimonthly.

*Uniform Crime Reports for the United States*. Federal Bureau of Investigation, U.S. Department of Justice. U. S. Government Printing Office, 732 N Capitol St. NW Washington, DC 20401. Phone: 866-512-1800 or (202)512-1800 or (866)512-1800; Fax: (202)512-2104 or (202)512-2250; Email: contactcenter@gpo.gov • URL: http://www.gpo.gov • Annual. $45.

**Uniformed Services Academy of Family Physicians**. 1503 Santa Rosa Rd., Ste. 207 Richmond, VA 23229. Phone: (804)968-4436; Fax: (804)968-4418; Email: admin@vafp.org • URL: http://www.usafp.org • Family physicians, teachers of family medicine, medical students, and residents in the armed services, public health service, or Indian health service. Sponsors continuing education program. Sponsors educational programs.

*UNIMA*. 10, Cours Aristide Briand, BP 402 F-08107 Charleville-Mezieres, France. Phone: 33 324 328563; Fax: 33 324 327692; Email: sgi@unima.org • URL: http://www.unima.org/en/home • Agricultural contractors, farm workers, farmers, farm equipment manufacturers, and other providers of support and services to agricultural industries. Seeks to advance the interests of agribusinesses. Represents members' commercial and regulatory interests at the national level.

*Union Labor Report*. Bloomberg BNA, 3 Bethesda Metro Center, Ste. 250 Bethesda, MD 20814-5377. Phone: 800-372-1033 or (703)341-3000; Fax: (800)253-0332; Email: customercare@bna.com • URL: http://www.bna.com • Biweekly. Description: Covers legal, legislative, and regulatory developments and trends affecting management and labor in the workplace.

**Union of Finance Personnel in Europe**. Friedrichstrasse 169/170 D-10117 Berlin, Germany. Phone: 49 30 206256600; Fax: 49 30 206256601 • URL: http://www.finanzpersonal-europa.de/pages/default/impressum.php • Promotes the finance industry in Europe. Protects the legal, economic, and professional interests of European finance personnel.

**Union of Shop, Distributive and Allied Workers**. 188 Wilmslow Rd. Manchester M14 6LJ, United Kingdom. Phone: 44 161 2242804 or 44 161 2492400; Fax: 44 161 2572566; Email: enquiries@usdaw.org.uk • URL: http://www.usdaw.org.uk • Shopworkers in the distributive and allied trades. Seeks to improve the terms and conditions and to protect the interests of members. Works to promote equal opportunities and equal treatment for all members and oppose discrimination on grounds of sex, race, ethnic origin, disability, sexual orientation or religion.

*Unique Homes: The Global Resource of Luxury Real Estate*. Unique Homes, Inc., 2020 Santa Monica Blvd., Ste. 460 Santa Monica, CA 90404. Phone: 800-732-4092 or (310)453-0500; Fax: (310)453-0511 • URL: http://www.uniquehomes.com • Six times a year. $29.97 per year. Homes for sale.

**United Abrasives Manufacturers Association**. 30200 Detroit Rd. Cleveland, OH 44145-1967. Phone: (440)899-0010; Fax: (440)892-1404; Email: contact@uama.org • URL: http://www.uama.org • Formerly *Coated Abrasives Manufacturers Institute*.

**United Agribusiness League**. 54 Corporate Park Irvine, CA 92606-5105. Phone: 800-223-4590 or (949)975-1424; Fax: (949)975-1573 or (949)975-1671; Email: marketing@aul.org • URL: http://www.ual.org • Agricultural industries and businesses. Promotes the development and common interest of the agricultural industry. Works to coordinate members' activities to advance agribusiness in general; provides services and benefits to enable members to realize greater productive efficiency. Serves as a clearinghouse on international agribusiness. Provides employee health care plans and other insurance to agribusinesses.

*United Arab Emirates Business Forecast Report*. Telecommunications Insight, 85 Queen Victoria St. London EC4V 4AB, United Kingdom. Phone: 20 72 465100 or 44 20 7248 0468; Fax: 20 72 480467 or 44 20 7248 0467; Email: enquiries@telecomsinsight.com • URL: http://www.telecomsinsight.com • Quarterly. $1,195 Individuals Single user; $1,795 Individuals Up to 3 users. Business forecast report for the United Arab Emirates.

*United Arab Emirates Government and Business Contacts Handbook*. International Business Publications, USA, PO Box 15343 Washington, DC 20003. Phone: (202)546-2103; Fax: (202)546-3275; Email: ibpusa@comcast.net • URL: http://ibpus.com • $99.95 Individuals hardcopy, e-book, CD-ROM. Covers: Strategic government and business information, export-import activity in the country, investment, business contacts and regulations.

*United Arab Emirates Industrial and Business Directory*. International Business Publications, USA, PO Box 15343 Washington, DC 20003. Phone: (202)546-2103; Fax: (202)546-3275; Email: ibpusa@comcast.net • URL: http://ibpus.com • Annual. $99.95 Individuals hardcopy, E-book and CD-ROM. Covers: Strategic industrial, investment and business contacts for conducting export-import and investment activity in the country.

*United Kingdom Business Finance Directory*. Graham & Trotman Ltd., Sterling House, 66 Wilton Rd. London SW1V 1DE, United Kingdom. Phone: 71 8211123; Fax: 71 6305229 • Annual. $265. Covers: 1,500 financial institutions, banks, insurance companies, accountants, investment brokers, and job hunters in the United Kingdom. Entries include: Company name, address, phone, fax, telex number.

**United Kingdom Forum for Organisational Health**. c/o Mary Manolias, Secretary, 43 Pemberton Rd., Surrey East Molesey KT8 9LG, United Kingdom. Phone: 44 20 89793344; Email: mary.manolias@talktalk.net • URL: http://www.ukfoh.org.uk • Professionals who share a common interest in the healthy development of organisations and includes occupational health physicians and nurses, researchers, counselors, personnel managers, general managers and occupational psychologists. Promotes the development and maintenance of the psychosocial health of organisations and of the individual within the workplace. Believes that people are the most critical resource in any organisation, supports humanisation of the workplace and recognition of ways in which individual creativity and growth contribute to organisational effectiveness.

**United Kingdom Science Park Association**. Chesterford Research Park, Little Chesterford, Essex Saffron Walden CB10 1XL, United Kingdom. Phone: 44 1799 532050; Fax: 44 1799 532049; Email: info@ukspa.org.uk • URL: http://www.ukspa.org.uk • Supports and encourages the startup, incubation and development of innovation led, high growth, knowledge-based businesses. Provides opportunity for larger and international businesses to develop specific and close interactions with a particular centre of knowledge creation for mutual benefit.

*United Kingdom's 10,000 Largest Companies*. William Snyder Publishing Associates, Five Mile Dr. Oxford OX2 8HT, United Kingdom. Phone: 44 1865 513186; Fax: 44 1865 311015; Email: snyderpub@aol.com • Annual. $250. Covers: top 10,000 companies in the United Kingdom, ranked by turnover. Database includes: Financial and statistical business information on each company. Entries include: Company name, address, phone, name of director, number of employees, financial data, year established, International Standard Industrial Classification (ISIC) code, parent company.

*United Nations Disarmament Yearbook*. United Nations Publications, c/o National Book Network, 15200 NBN Way Blue Ridge Summit, PA 17214. Phone: 888-254-4286 or (212)963-7680 or (212)963-8302; Fax: (800)338-4550; Email: unpublications@nbnbooks.com • URL: http://www.unp.un.org • Annual. $55 Individuals.

*United Nations Document Index*. United Nations Publications, c/o National Book Network, 15200 NBN Way Blue Ridge Summit, PA 17214. Phone: 888-254-4286 or (212)963-7680 or (212)963-8302; Fax: (800)338-4550; Email: unpublications@nbnbooks.com • URL: http://www.unp.un.org • Quarterly. Annual cumulation. Text in English.

**United Nations Framework Convention on Climate Change**. PO Box 260124 D-53153 Bonn, Germany. Phone: 49 228 8151000; Fax: 49 228 8151999; Email: secretariat@unfccc.

int • URL: http://unfccc.int/2860.php • Member countries united to stabilize greenhouse gas concentrations in the atmosphere at a level that would prevent dangerous anthropogenic interference with the climate system. Works to achieve this goal within a time-frame sufficient to allow ecosystems to adapt naturally to climate change, to ensure that food production is not threatened, and to enable economic development to proceed in a sustainable manner.

**U.S. Armor Association**. PO Box 607 Fort Knox, KY 40121-0607. Phone: (502)942-8624; Fax: (502)942-6219 • URL: http://www.cavalryandarmor.com • U.S. Army officers, noncommissioned officers, enlisted men, and veterans of all components. Disseminates professional knowledge of military art and science, especially mobile ground warfare.

**United States Army Warrant Officers Association**. 462 Herndon Pkwy., Ste. 207 Herndon, VA 20170-5235. Phone: (703)742-7727; Fax: (703)742-7728 • URL: http://www.usawoa.org • Active duty, National Guard, Reserve, and retired U.S. Army warrant officers. Promotes the technical and social welfare of warrant officers. Recommends Army improvement programs. Circulates professional information among warrant officers. Stimulates patriotism, devotion to duty, and comradeship among members.

*U.S. Banker*. SourceMedia Inc., 1 State Street Plz., 27th Fl. New York, NY 10004. Phone: 800-221-1809 or (212)803-8200 or (212)803-8333; Fax: (212)843-9635 or (212)292-5216; Email: custserv@sourcemedia.com • URL: http://www.sourcemedia.com • Monthly. $65.00 per year. Edited for bank executives and managers. Covers a wide variety of banking and financial topics.

*The U.S. Beer Market: Impact Databank Review and Forecast*. M. Shanken Communications Inc., 387 Park Ave. S New York, NY 10016. Phone: 800-227-1617 or (212)684-4224; Fax: (212)481-1540 or (212)481-0721; Email: mmorgenstern@mshanken.com • URL: http://www.mshanken.com • Annual. Price varies. Includes industry commentary and statistics.

*The U.S. Beer, Spirits and Wine Market: Impact Databank Market Review and Forecast*. M. Shanken Communications Inc., 387 Park Ave. S New York, NY 10016. Phone: 800-227-1617 or (212)684-4224; Fax: (212)481-1540 or (212)481-0721; Email: mmorgenstern@mshanken.com • URL: http://www.mshanken.com • Annual. Price varies. Includes industry commentary and statistics.

**U.S. Bureau of Labor Statistics - Office of Prices and Living Conditions**. 2 Massachusetts Ave. NE. Rm. 3120 Washington, DC 20212. Phone: (202)691-5200; Fax: (202)691-7890; Email: greenless.john@bls.gov • URL: http://www.bls.gov/bls/inflation.htm • Prices in retail and primary markets; conducts research to improve the measurement of price change. Areas of interest include consumer price indexes; producer price indexes; export and import price indexes for U.S. foreign trade; and consumer expenditures, income, assets, and liabilities of all U.S. families. Office comprises: the Consumer Expenditure Surveys Division; Consumer Prices and Price Indexes Division, which provides measures of price change for a specified market basket of consumer goods and services; Industrial Prices and Price Indexes Division, which provides measures of change in prices received by producers at the level of the first commercial transaction for many commodities and some services; International Prices Division, which measures change in the prices of commodities and some services imported to and exported from the United States; Price and Index Number Research Division; and Price Statistical Methods Division.

**U.S. Bureau of Labor Statistics - Office of Productivity and Technology - Foreign Labor Statistics Division**. 2 Massachusetts Ave. NE, Ste. 2150 Washington, DC 20212-0001. Phone: (202)691-5654; Fax: (202)691-5679 • URL: http://www.bls.gov/fls/ • Labor conditions and developments abroad. Research involves the development of internationally comparable economic-statistical measures covering the labor force and unemployment, productivity, and labor costs. This information is used to assess current economic trends abroad that may affect U.S. performance; inform government and private officials of foreign developments that might affect U.S. policy; review foreign experience for possible application domestically; aid in the appraisal of U.S. competitiveness in foreign and domestic markets; and provide labor information to individuals, corporations, labor unions, and others concerned with foreign investment and development.

*U.S. Business Advisor*. Small Business Administration, Phone: (202)205-6600; Fax: (202)205-7064 • URL: http://www.sba.gov • Web site provides "a one-stop electronic link to all the information and services government provides for the business community." Covers about 60 federal agencies that exist to assist or regulate business. Detailed information is provided on financial assistance, workplace issues, taxes, regulations, international trade, and other business topics. Searching is offered. Fees: Free.

*U.S. Census Bureau Catalog and Guide*. U. S. Government Printing Office, 732 N Capitol St. NW Washington, DC 20401. Phone: 866-512-1800 or (202)512-1800 or (866)512-1800; Fax: (202)512-2104 or (202)512-2250; Email: contactcenter@gpo.gov • URL: http://www.gpo.gov • Annual. Lists publications and electronic media products currently available from the U. S. Bureau of the Census, along with some out of print items. Includes comprehensive title and subject indexes. Formerly *Bureau of the Census Catalog*.

**U.S. Census Bureau Demographic Programs - Demographic Surveys Division.** 4600 Silver Hill Rd. Washington, DC 20233. Phone: (301)763-2071 • URL: http://www.census.gov/aboutus/sur_demo.html • Survey and data collection on demographics in such areas as income, education, health, employment, unemployment, crime, expenditures, and housing. Division is also responsible for contracting with other federal agencies for survey work to be completed by divisions in the Bureau.

**U.S. Census Bureau Demographic Programs - Social, Economic and Housing Statistics Division.** 4600 Silver Hill Rd. Washington, DC 20233. Phone: (301)763-3234 or (301)763-6443; Email: david.s.johnson@census.gov • URL: http://www.census.gov/newsroom/releases/archives/bios/david_johnson_bio.html • Physical, economic, and social characteristics of housing; household income, poverty, and labor force characteristics, including health insurance coverage. Division collects and analyzes housing data from the Decennial Census of Housing, American Community Survey, American Housing Survey, Quarterly Housing Vacancy Survey, and Survey of Market Absorption, and socioeconomic data from the Decennial Census of Population, American Community Survey, Current Population Survey, and Survey of Income and Program Participation.

***U.S. Census Bureau: The Official Statistics.*** U. S. Bureau of the Census. Phone: (301)763-4636 or (301)763-4100; Fax: (301)763-4794; Email: webmaster@census.gov • URL: http://www.census.gov/prod/www/abs/mfg-prof.html • Web site is "Your Source for Social, Demographic, and Economic Information." Contains "Current U. S. Population Count," "Current Economic Indicators," and a wide variety of data under "Other Official Statistics." Keyword searching is provided. Fees: Free.

***United States Census of Agriculture.*** U.S. Department of Agriculture National Agricultural Statistics Service, 1400 Independence Ave. SW Washington, DC 20250. Phone: 800-727-9540; Email: nass@nass.usda.gov • URL: http://www.nass.usda.gov • Quinquennial. Provides uniform, comprehensive farming and ranching operations data for every U.S. state and county, including production expenses, market value of products, and operator characteristics.

***United States Census of Construction Industries.*** U.S. Department of Commerce U.S. Census Bureau, 4600 Silver Hill Rd. Washington, DC 20233. Phone: 800-923-8282 or (301)763-4636 or (301)763-3030; Fax: (301)457-4714 or (301)763-6239; Email: webmaster@census.gov • URL: http://www.census.gov/ • Quinquennial. Results presented in reports, tape, and CD-ROM files.

***United States Census of Governments.*** Bureau of the Census, U.S. Department of Commerce. U. S. Government Printing Office, 732 N Capitol St. NW Washington, DC 20401. Phone: 866-512-1800 or (202)512-1800 or (866)512-1800; Fax: (202)512-2104 or (202)512-2250; Email: contactcenter@gpo.gov • URL: http://www.gpo.gov • Quinquennial.

***United States Census of Manufactures.*** U.S. Department of Commerce U.S. Census Bureau, 4600 Silver Hill Rd. Washington, DC 20233. Phone: 800-923-8282 or (301)763-4636 or (301)763-3030; Fax: (301)457-4714 or (301)763-6239; Email: webmaster@census.gov • URL: http://www.census.gov/ • Quinquennial. Results presented in reports, tape, CD-ROM, and Diskette files.

***United States Census of Mineral Industries.*** Bureau of the Census, U.S. Department of Commerce. U. S. Government Printing Office, 732 N Capitol St. NW Washington, DC 20401. Phone: 866-512-1800 or (202)512-1800 or (866)512-1800; Fax: (202)512-2104 or (202)512-2250; Email: contactcenter@gpo.gov • URL: http://www.gpo.gov • Quinquennial.

***United States Census of Population and Housing.*** Bureau of the Census, U.S. Department of Commerce. U. S. Government Printing Office, 732 N Capitol St. NW Washington, DC 20401. Phone: 866-512-1800 or (202)512-1800 or (866)512-1800; Fax: (202)512-2104 or (202)512-2250; Email: contactcenter@gpo.gov • URL: http://www.gpo.gov • Quinquennial.

***United States Census of Retail Trade.*** U.S. Department of Commerce U.S. Census Bureau, 4600 Silver Hill Rd. Washington, DC 20233. Phone: 800-923-8282 or (301)763-4636 or (301)763-3030; Fax: (301)457-4714 or (301)763-6239; Email: webmaster@census.gov • URL: http://www.census.gov/ • Quinquennial.

***United States Census of Service Industries.*** U.S. Department of Commerce U.S. Census Bureau, 4600 Silver Hill Rd. Washington, DC 20233. Phone: 800-923-8282 or (301)763-4636 or (301)763-3030; Fax: (301)457-4714 or (301)763-6239; Email: webmaster@census.gov • URL: http://www.census.gov/ • Quinquennial. Various reports available.

***United States Census of Transportation.*** Bureau of the Census, U.S. Department of Commerce. U. S. Government Printing Office, 732 N Capitol St. NW Washington, DC 20401. Phone: 866-512-1800 or (202)512-1800 or (866)512-1800; Fax: (202)512-2104 or (202)512-2250; Email: contactcenter@gpo.gov • URL: http://www.gpo.gov • Quinquennial.

***United States Census of Wholesale Trade.*** Bureau of the Census, U.S. Department of Commerce. U. S. Government Printing Office, 732 N Capitol St. NW Washington, DC 20401. Phone: 866-512-1800 or (202)512-1800 or (866)512-1800; Fax: (202)512-2104 or (202)512-2250; Email: contactcenter@gpo.gov • URL: http://www.gpo.gov • Quinquennial.

**U.S. Chamber of Commerce.** 1615 H St. NW Washington, DC 20062-2000. Phone: 800-638-6582 or (202)463-5500 or (202)659-6000; Fax: (202)463-3129; Email: foundation@uschamber.com • URL: http://www.uschambersmallbusinessnation.com • National federation of business organizations and companies. Membership includes chambers of commerce, trade and professional associations, and companies. Determines and makes known to the government the recommendations of the business community on national issues and problems affecting the economy and the future of the country. Works to advance human progress through an economic, political, and social system based on individual freedom and initiative. Informs, trains, equips, and encourages members to participate in policy-making at federal, state, and local levels and in legislative and political action at the national level. Produces First Business, a daily business-oriented news broadcast; and It's Your Business, a weekly television debate program. Operates the American Business Network (BizNet), through which the group maintains a video production studio to produce and syndicate programs. Conducts continuing education program for business executives, including satellite seminars and Institutes for Organization Management (courses to improve management skills of chamber of commerce and association executives). Maintains speakers' bureau; compiles statistics; conducts research programs.

***U.S.-China Business Services Directory.*** U.S.-China Business Council, 1818 N St. NW, Ste. 200 Washington, DC 20036. Phone: (202)429-0340; Fax: (202)775-2476; Email: info@uschina.org • URL: http://www.uschina.org • Irregular. $35. Covers: more than 900 companies in the U. S., Hong Kong, and China providing business services to China, such as consulting firms, architectural and construction engineering firms, freight forwarding companies, and law firms. Entries include: Company name, address, phone, telex, name and title of contact, subsidiary and branch names and locations, description of products or services.

**United States-China Chamber of Commerce.** 55 W Monroe St., Ste. 630 Chicago, IL 60603. Phone: (312)368-9911; Fax: (312)368-9922; Email: info@usccc.org • URL: http://www.usccc.org • Members are individuals interested in improving trade between the U. S. and the People's Republic of China.

**United States Christian Chamber of Commerce.** 2201 Main St., Ste. 400 Dallas, TX 75201-4418. Phone: (214)801-5419 • URL: http://www.usccc1.org • Represents Christian-led businesses, churches, ministry and para-church organizations, schools and individuals. Promotes Christian business ownership and organizational leadership in the United States of America. Fosters the development of biblically-based operating standards for Christian-led businesses, churches, schools and ministries.

***United States Coast Guard Marine Safety Council Proceedings.*** U.S. Department of Homeland Security U.S. Coast Guard, 2100 2nd St. SW Washington, DC 20593. Phone: 800-323-7233 or (202)372-2100 or (202)372-4411; Fax: (202)372-4960 • URL: http://www.uscg.mil • Bimonthly.

***United States Code Annotated: Crimes and Criminal Procedures.*** Thomson West, 610 Opperman Dr. Eagan, MN 55123. Phone: 800-328-9352 or (651)687-7000 • $3,125.00. 15 volumes. Annual cumulation. Arranged in parallel fashion to *United States Code*. Gives abstracts of relevant federal and state court decisions pertaining to each section of the code. Supplemented by annual pocket parts.

***United States Code.*** U.S. Congress. U. S. Government Printing Office, 732 N Capitol St. NW Washington, DC 20401. Phone: 866-512-1800 or (202)512-1800 or (866)512-1800; Fax: (202)512-2104 or (202)512-2250; Email: contactcenter@gpo.gov • URL: http://www.gpo.gov • Continual supplements. Price varies. Permanent and general public law of the United States from 1789 to the codification date.

***U.S. Copyrights.*** DIALOG, 11000 Regency Pkwy., Ste. 400 Cary, NC 27511. Phone: 800-334-2564 or (919)462-8600; Fax: (919)468-9890 • URL: http://www.dialog.com • Provides access to registration details for all active copyright registrations on file at the U. S. Copyright Office since 1978. Contains information on initial registration, renewal, assignments, and ownership status. Weekly updates. Inquire as to online cost and availability.

**United States Council for International Business.** 1212 Avenue of the Americas New York, NY 10036. Phone: (212)354-4480 or (212)703-5046; Fax: (212)575-0327; Email: info@uscib.org • URL: http://www.uscib.org • Serves as the U.S. National Committee of the International Chamber of Commerce. Enables multinational enterprises to operate effectively by representing their interests to intergovernmental and governmental bodies and by keeping enterprises advised of international developments having a major impact on their operations. Serves as: U.S. representative to the International Organization of Employers; national affiliate to the U.S.A. Business and Industry Advisory Committee to the BIAC. Operates ATA Carnet export service, which enables goods to be shipped overseas duty-free for demonstration and exhibition. Sponsors seminars and luncheon briefings.

**U.S. Council of Better Business Bureaus.** 3033 Wilson Blvd., Ste. 600 Arlington, VA 22201. Phone: (703)276-0100 • URL: http://www.bbb.org • Promotes ethical relationships between businesses and the public through self-regulation, consumer and business education, and service excellence.

***U.S. Custom House Guide.*** UBM Global Trade, 400 Windsor Corporate Pk., 50 Millstone Rd., Ste. 200 East Windsor, NJ 08520-1415. Phone: 800-221-5488 or (609)371-7700 or (609)371-7701; Fax: (609)371-7885 or (609)371-7883; Email: customerservice@cbizmedia.com • URL: http://www.cbizmedia.com • Annual. $899 Individuals online access. Publication includes: List of ports having customs facilities, customs officials, port authorities, chambers of commerce, embassies and consulates, foreign trade zones, and other organizations; related trade services. Entries include: For each principal port—Name of organization or agency, address, phone, fax, names and titles of key personnel; description and limitations of port facilities. For service firms—Company name, address, phone, fax. Principal content is U.S. tariff schedules and customs regulations, and a "How to Import" manual.

**U.S. Customs and Border Protection - Office of Field Operations - Laboratories and Scientific Services Division - Research Laboratory.** 7501 Boston Blvd., Ste. 113 Springfield, VA 22153. Phone: (703)921-7200; Fax: (703)921-7155; Email: cbp.labresearch@dhs.gov • URL: http://www.cbp.gov/xp/cgov/import/operations_support/labs_scientific_svcs/ • Provides technical services in support of the U.S. Customs mission in tariff and trade and in enforcement. Principal area of interest is analytical chemistry (instrumentation and methodology). Laboratory supports a field laboratory system, with affiliated laboratories in New York City, Savannah, New Orleans, Los Angeles, San Francisco, Chicago, and San Juan.

**U.S. Department of Agriculture Agricultural Research Service - National Soil Dynamics Laboratory.** c/o Henry Allen Torbert, Scientist, 411 S Donahue Dr. Auburn, AL 36832-5806. Phone: (334)844-3979 • URL: http://www.ars.usda.gov/main/site_main.htm?modecode=64-20-05-00.

***U.S. Dept. of Commerce—U.S. Exporters' Yellow Pages.*** Office of Export Trading Company Affairs, U.S. Department of Commerce, International Trade Administration, 1401 Constitution Ave. NW Washington, DC 20230. Email: oetca@ita.doc.gov • URL: http://www.ita.doc.gov • Annual. Covers: over 27,000 firms, including export trading companies, export management companies, bankers, attorneys, freight forwarders, and manufacturers interested in international trade. Publication is produced but not sold through the U.S. Department of Commerce/International Trade Administration. To obtain copies and information, contact the U.S. Commerce Department Export Assistance Center in your state.

**U.S. Department of Energy - Bioenergy Feedstock Development Program - Oak Ridge National Laboratory.** 1 Bethel Valley Rd. Oak Ridge, TN 37831-6006. Phone: 800-541-1625 or (865)574-4160; Fax: (865)574-0595 or (865)574-2232; Email: ighotline@hq.doe.gov • URL: http://www.ornl.gov.

**U.S. Department of Energy - National Nuclear Security Administration - Los Alamos National Security, LLC - Los Alamos National Laboratory.** PO Box 1663 Los Alamos, NM 87545. Phone: (505)667-5061 or (505)667-7000; Fax: (505)667-2997 or (505)665-4411; Email: mcmillan1@lanl.gov • URL: http://www.lanl.gov • Nuclear, high-energy, plasma, low temperature, and cryogenic physics, earth and space sciences, engineering and environmental sciences, life sciences, inorganic chemistry, metallurgy, cryogenic engineering, molecular biology, mesons, mathematics, biomedicine, energy, and national security, including research and development programs relating to nuclear and thermonuclear weapons, use of nuclear energy for production of power, energy lasers, controlled release of thermonuclear energy, and thermionic conversion.

**U.S. Department of Energy - Office of Energy Efficiency and Renewable Energy - Industrial Technologies Program - Industrial Assessment Center.** School of Engineering, San Francisco State University, 1600 Holloway Ave. San Francisco, CA 94132. Phone: (415)338-6218 or (415)338-7736; Fax: (415)338-3086; Email: iac@sfsu.edu • URL: http://www.sfsu.edu/iac • Research areas include multimedia, computerized experimental arts processes, and digital sound.

***United States Department of State Indexes of Living Costs Abroad, Quarters Allowances, and Hardship Differentials.*** U. S. Government Printing Office, 732 N Capitol St. NW Washington, DC 20401. Phone: 866-512-1800 or (202)512-1800 or (866)512-1800; Fax: (202)512-2104 or (202)512-2250; Email: contactcenter@gpo.gov • URL: http://www.gpo.gov • Quarterly. Provides data on the difference in living costs between Washington, DC and each of 160 foreign cities.

**U.S. Department of the Treasury - Alcohol and Tobacco Tax and Trade Bureau - Scientific Services Division - Compliance Laboratory.** 490 N Wiget Ln. Walnut Creek, CA 94598. Phone: (513)684-3356; Email: compliance.laboratory@ttb.gov • URL: http://www.ttb.gov/ssd/compliance_monitoring_lab.shtml • Monitoring of regulatory compliance of both beverage and nonbeverage alcohol products.

**U.S. Department of the Treasury - Office of International Affairs - Office of Risk and Research Analysis.** 1500 Pennsylvania Ave. NW Washington, DC 20220. Phone: (202)622-2000; Fax: (202)622-6415 • URL: http://www.

treasury.gov/about/organizational-structure/offices/International-Affairs/Pages/rra.aspx • Global economy, crisis prevention and financial vulnerabilities, and financial markets.

**U.S.-English.** 2000 L St. NW, Ste. 702 Washington, DC 20036. Phone: 800-787-8216 or (202)833-0100; Fax: (202)833-0108; Email: info@usenglish.org • URL: http://www.us-english.org • Aims to preserve the common bond by making English the official language of government in the U.S. Promotes opportunities for people living here to learn English.

**U.S. Environmental Protection Agency - Office of Research and Development.** 1200 Pennsylvania Ave. NW, MC 8101R Washington, DC 20460. Phone: (202)564-6620 or (202)564-6825; Email: kadeli.lek@epa.gov • URL: http://www2.epa.gov/aboutepa/about-office-research-and-development-ord • Provides research support and management and production of technical information.

*United States Equal Employment Opportunity Commission Annual Report: Job Patterns for Minorities and Women in Private Industry.* U.S. Equal Employment Opportunity Commission, 131 M St., NE Washington, DC 20507. Phone: (202)663-4900; Fax: (202)663-4494; Email: info@eeoc.gov • URL: http://www.eeoc.gov • Annual.

*United States Export Administration Regulations.* U.S. Government Printing Office, 732 N Capitol St. NW Washington, DC 20401. Phone: 866-512-1800 or (202)512-1800 or (866)512-1800; Fax: (202)512-2104 or (202)512-2250; Email: contactcenter@gpo.gov • URL: http://www.gpo.gov • $199 U.S. Looseleaf. Includes supplements.; $278.60 Other countries Looseleaf. Includes supplements. Includes basic manual and supplementary bulletins for one year. Issued by the Bureau of Export Administration, U.S. Department of Commerce (www.doc.gov). Consists of export licensing rules and regulations.

**U.S. Export Directory.** Reed Business Information, Quadrant House, The Quadrant Surrey SM2 5AS, United Kingdom. Phone: 44 20 86523500 or 1 6618904; Fax: 44 20 86528932; Email: webmaster@rbi.co.uk • URL: http://www.reedbusiness.com • Annual. $235. Covers: Exporting companies in the U.S. Entries include: Company name, address, telecommunication information, overseas agents and subsidiaries.

**U.S. Exports of Merchandise.** U.S. Bureau of the Census, Foreign Trade Division, 4600 Silver Hill Rd. Washington, DC 20233-0800. Phone: 800-923-8282 or (301)763-4636; Fax: (301)457-3842 • URL: http://www.census.gov/foreign-trade/reference/products/catalog/impDVD.html • Monthly and quarterly data. Provides export data in the most extensive detail available, including product, quantity, value, shipping weight, country of destination, customs district of exportation, etc.

**U.S. Firms in Germany.** German American Chamber of Commerce, 75 Broad St., 21st Fl. New York, NY 10004. Phone: (212)974-8830; Fax: (212)974-8867; Email: info@gaccny.com • URL: http://www.gaccny.com • Annual. $100. Covers: Over 700 U.S. companies located in Germany. Entries include: Company name, address, phone in Germany, company name, address, phone of their American parent company.

**U.S. Food and Drug Administration - Center for Drug Evaluation and Research - Office of Prescription Drug Promotion.** Bldg. 51, Rm. 3200, 10903 New Hampshire Ave. Silver Spring, MD 20993-0002. Phone: (301)796-1200; Fax: (301)847-8445; Email: thomas.abrams@fda.hhs.gov • URL: http://www.fda.gov/AboutFDA/CentersOffices/OfficeofMedicalProductsandTobacco/CDER/ucm090142.htm • Industry-wide marketing practices of the pharmaceutical industry and improvement of drug communications between FDA, health professionals, and the public. Specific research areas include prescription drugs, marketing practices, and health communications.

*United States Foreign Trade Sanctions Handbook.* International Business Publications, USA, PO Box 15343 Washington, DC 20003. Phone: (202)546-2103; Fax: (202)546-3275; Email: ibpusa@comcast.net • URL: http://ibpus.com • $99.95 Individuals paperback. Covers: United States trade sanctions for selected countries.

**U.S. Glass, Metal, and Glazing.** AutoGlass Repair and Replacement Key Communications Inc., PO Box 569 Garrisonville, VA 22463. Phone: (540)720-5584; Fax: (540)720-5687 • URL: http://www.usglassmag.com • Monthly. $35.00 per year. Edited for glass fabricators, glaziers, distributors, and retailers. Special feature issues are devoted to architectural glass, mirror glass, windows, storefronts, hardware, machinery, sealants, and adhesives. Regular topics include automobile glass and fenestration (window design and placement).

*United States Government Annual Report, Fiscal Year.* U.S. Government Printing Office, 732 N Capitol St. NW Washington, DC 20401. Phone: 866-512-1800 or (202)512-1800 or (866)512-1800; Fax: (202)512-2104 or (202)512-2250; Email: contactcenter@gpo.gov • URL: http://www.gpo.gov • Annual. Issued by the Financial Management Service, U.S. Treasury Department (www.fms.treas.gov). Contains the official report on the receipts and outlays of the federal government. Presents budgetary results at the summary level.

*U.S. Government Books: Publications for Sale by the Government Printing Office.* U.S. Government Printing Office, 732 N Capitol St. NW Washington, DC 20401. Phone: 866-512-1800 or (202)512-1800 or (866)512-1800; Fax: (202)512-2104 or (202)512-2250; Email: contactcenter@gpo.gov • URL: http://www.gpo.gov • Quarterly. Free. Describes best selling government documents and "new titles that reflect today's news and consumer issues.".

*U.S. Government Information Catalog of New and Popular Titles.* U.S. Government Printing Office, 732 N Capitol St. NW Washington, DC 20401. Phone: 866-512-1800 or (202)512-1800 or (866)512-1800; Fax: (202)512-2104 or (202)512-2250; Email: contactcenter@gpo.gov • URL: http://www.gpo.gov • Irregular. Free. Includes recently issued and popular publications, periodicals, and electronic products.

*U.S. Government Information for Business.* U.S. Government Printing Office, 732 N Capitol St. NW Washington, DC 20401. Phone: 866-512-1800 or (202)512-1800 or (866)512-1800; Fax: (202)512-2104 or (202)512-2250; Email: contactcenter@gpo.gov • URL: http://www.gpo.gov • Annual. Free. A selected list of currently available publications, periodicals, and electronic products on business, trade, labor, federal regulations, economics, and other topics. Also known as *Business Catalog.*

*United States Government Manual.* Office of the Federal Register, c/o The National Archives & Records Administration, 8601 Adelphi Rd. College Park, MD 20740-6001. Phone: 866-272-6272 or (301)837-0482; Fax: (301)837-0483; Email: request.schedule@nara.gov • URL: http://www.archives.gov/federal-register/index.html • Annual. $29 Individuals. Provides information on the agencies of the executive, judicial, and legislative branches of the Federal government. Contains a section on terminated or transferred agencies. Database includes: Includes boards, commissions, committees and quasi-official agencies and organizations in which US participates.

*U.S. Government Subscriptions.* U.S. Government Printing Office, 732 N Capitol St. NW Washington, DC 20401. Phone: 866-512-1800 or (202)512-1800 or (866)512-1800; Fax: (202)512-2104 or (202)512-2250; Email: contactcenter@gpo.gov • URL: http://www.gpo.gov • Quarterly. Free. Includes agency and subject indexes.

*U.S. Housing Markets.* DoveTale Publishers, 1 Thomas Cir. NW Washington, DC 20005. Phone: 877-275-8647 or (202)339-0744 or (202)452-0800; Fax: (202)785-1974 or (202)339-0749; Email: hwmicustomerservice@hanleywood.com • URL: http://www.hwmarketintelligence.com • Monthly. $345.00 per year. Includes eight interim reports. Provides data on residential building permits, apartment building completions, rental vacancy rates, sales of existing homes, average home prices, housing affordability, etc. All major U.S. cities and areas are covered.

*U.S. Immigration and Migration Reference Library.* Cengage Learning Inc., 20 Channel Center St. Boston, MA 02210. Phone: 800-487-8488 or (617)289-7700; Fax: (617)289-7844; Email: investors@cengage.com • URL: http://www.cengage.com • 2004. $378.00. Five volumes. Includes *Almanac* (2 vols.), *Biographies* (2 vols.), and *Primary Sources*. Provides detailed history and information relating to U.S. immigration from "earliest times" to the present. (U-X-L imprint). eBook also available.

*United States Immigration Laws, General Information.* U.S. Immigration and Naturalization Service. U.S. Government Printing Office, 732 N Capitol St. NW Washington, DC 20401. Phone: 866-512-1800 or (202)512-1800 or (866)512-1800; Fax: (202)512-2104 or (202)512-2250; Email: contactcenter@gpo.gov • URL: http://www.gpo.gov • Irregular.

*U.S. Importers Product Guide.* Todd Publications, PO Box 500 Millwood, NY 10546. Phone: 866-896-0916 or (914)373-4750; Fax: (914)373-4750; Email: toddpub@aol.com • URL: http://www.toddpublications.com • Biennial. $195. Covers: Approximately 10,000 United States import companies. Entries include: Name, address, phone, fax, name and title of contact, description of product/service.

*U.S. Imports of Merchandise.* U.S. Bureau of the Census, Foreign Trade Division, 4600 Silver Hill Rd. Washington, DC 20233-0800. Phone: 800-923-8282 or (301)763-4636; Fax: (301)457-3842 • URL: http://www.census.gov/foreign-trade/reference/products/catalog/impDVD.html • Monthly. $2,400 per year. Provides import data in the most extensive detail available, including product, quantity, value, shipping weight, country of origin, customs district of entry, rate provision, etc.

*U.S. Income Tax Treaties with Foreign Countries Handbook.* International Business Publications, USA, PO Box 15343 Washington, DC 20003. Phone: (202)546-2103; Fax: (202)546-3275; Email: ibpusa@comcast.net • URL: http://ibpus.com • $99.95 Individuals hardcopy, E-book and CD-ROM. Covers: US income tax treaties with Australia, Austria, Barbados, Belgium, Canada, China, Cyprus, Czech Republic, Denmark, Denmark, Egypt, Estonia, and Finland.

*United States Industrial and Business Directory.* International Business Publications, USA, PO Box 15343 Washington, DC 20003. Phone: (202)546-2103; Fax: (202)546-3275; Email: ibpusa@comcast.net • URL: http://ibpus.com • Annual. $99.95 Individuals hardcopy, E-book and CD-ROM. Covers:

Detailed information on investment, export-import business opportunities, foreign economic assistance projects, government and business contacts.

*U.S. Industrial Directory.* Reed, 1100 Summer St. Stamford, CT 06905. Phone: (203)328-2500; Fax: (203)328-2530 • Annual. $179 per set. Publication consists of three volumes, of which the "Telephone/Address Section" provides name, address, phone, fax, local sales offices and distributors for over 52,000 companies. Other volumes comprise the "Product Sections," with listings of suppliers categorized by product and service.

*U.S. Industrial Outlook: An Almanac of Industry, Technology, and Services.* Reference Press Inc., 6448 Hwy. 290 E, Ste. E-104 Austin, TX 78723. Phone: 800-486-8666 or (512)454-7778; Fax: (512)454-9401; Email: orders@hoovers.com • Annual. $27.95. Covers: Nearly 200 service and manufacturing industries. Database includes: Tables, rankings, forecasts, projections. Entries include: Description.

*U.S. Industry and Trade Outlook.* U.S. Department of Commerce National Technical Information Service, 5301 Shawnee Rd. Alexandria, VA 22312. Phone: 800-553-NTIS or (703)605-6050 or (703)605-6585; Email: info@ntis.gov • URL: http://www.ntis.gov • Annual. Produced by the International Trade Administration, U.S. Department of Commerce, in a "public-private" partnership with DRI/McGraw-Hill and Standard & Poor's. Provides basic data, outlook for the current year, and "Long-Term Prospects" (five-year projections) for a wide variety of products and services. Includes high technology industries. Formerly *U.S. Industrial Outlook.*

*United States International Air Travel Statistics.* U.S. Department of Transportation, Center for Transportation Information, Kendall Square Cambridge, MA 02142. Phone: (617)494-2000; Fax: (617)494-2497 • Provides detailed statistics on air passenger travel between the U.S. and foreign countries for both scheduled and charter flights. Time period is 1975 to date, with monthly updates. Inquire as to online cost and availability.

**U.S. International Trade Commission - Minerals, Metals, Machinery, and Miscellaneous Manufacturers Division.** 500 E St. SW Washington, DC 20436. Phone: (202)205-3418; Fax: (202)205-2217; Email: brookhart@usitc.gov • URL: http://www.usitc.gov • Survey data related to international trade matters, including international competitiveness of U.S. industries, especially iron and steel products, industrial minerals and nonferrous metals, machinery and general manufactured products.

*U.S. Investments in Germany: A Listing of American Subsidiaries in Germany.* American Chamber of Commerce in Germany, Charlottenstrasse 42 10117 Berlin, Germany. Phone: 49 30 28878921; Fax: 49 30 28878929; Email: amcham-berlin@amcham.de • URL: http://www.amcham.de • €150 Individuals print; €540 Individuals CD-ROM; €120 Members print; €432 Members CD-ROM. Covers: Approximately 3,000 German subsidiaries of U.S. Firms. Entries include: Company address, management details, and SIC code.

*U.S. Japan Business News.* U.S. Japan Business News, 312 E 1st St., Ste. 300 Los Angeles, CA 90012. Phone: (213)626-5001; Fax: (213)613-1187; Email: la@usjbnews.com • Weekly. $78 Individuals; $150 Two years. Japanese language business newspaper.

*United States Law Week: A National Survey of Current Law.* Bloomberg BNA, 3 Bethesda Metro Center, Ste. 250 Bethesda, MD 20814-5377. Phone: 800-372-1033 or (703)341-3000; Fax: (800)253-0332; Email: customercare@bna.com • URL: http://www.bna.com • Weekly. $1,152.00 per year. Covers U.S. Supreme Court proceedings and gives full text of decisions. Also provides detailed reports on important legislative and regulatory actions.

*U.S. List.* American Chamber of Commerce in Austria, Porzellangasse 39/7 A-1090 Vienna, Austria. Phone: 43 1 3195751; Fax: 43 1 3195151; Email: office@amcham.at • URL: http://www.amcham.at • Biennial. €80 Members; €100 Nonmembers; €120 Members per CD-ROM; €150 Nonmembers per CD-ROM. Covers: About 360 U.S. subsidiaries and affiliated companies located in Austria. Entries include: U.S. Parent company name and address, Austrian subsidiary or affiliated company name, address, phone, fax, managing director, line of business, e-mail, Internet-homepage address, kind of relationship.

**United States Marine Corps Drill Instructors Association.** PO Box 5117 Parris Island, SC 29905. Phone: (828)757-0968 • URL: http://www.parrisislanddi.org • Present and former U.S. Marine Corps drill instructors. Fosters a spirit of comradery through social and recreational activities. Promotes the welfare of elderly, disabled, and needy veterans; sponsors patriotic, charitable, and educational programs. Maintains living memorial monument fund; conducts blood drives and active participants' toys 4 tots.

*U.S. Master Bank Tax Guide.* Wolters Kluwer Law & Business CCH, 2700 Lake Cook Rd. Riverwoods, IL 60015. Phone: 888-224-7377 or (847)267-7000; Email: cust_serv@cch.com • URL: http://www.cchgroup.com • Annual. $389.95 Individuals book-softcover; $389.95 Individuals ebook. Summarizes and explains federal tax rules affecting financial institutions.

*U.S. Master Depreciation Guide.* Wolters Kluwer Law & Business CCH, 2700 Lake Cook Rd. Riverwoods, IL 60015. Phone: 888-224-7377 or (847)267-7000; Email: cust_serv@

cch.com • URL: http://www.cchgroup.com • Annual. $97.50 Institutions 1 - 4; $89.02 Institutions 5 - 9; $79.48 Institutions 10 -. Contains explanations of ADR (asset depreciation range), ACRS (accelerated cost recovery system), and MACRS (modified accelerated cost recovery system). Includes the historical background of depreciation.

***U.S. Master Employee Benefits Guide***. Wolters Kluwer Law & Business CCH, 2700 Lake Cook Rd. Riverwoods, IL 60015. Phone: 888-224-7377 or (847)267-7000; Email: cust_serv@cch.com • URL: http://www.cchgroup.com • Annual. $102.50 Individuals. Explains federal tax and labor laws relating to health care benefits, disability benefits, workers' compensation, employee assistance plans, etc.

***U.S. Master Estate and Gift Tax Guide***. Wolters Kluwer Law & Business CCH, 2700 Lake Cook Rd. Riverwoods, IL 60015. Phone: 888-224-7377 or (847)267-7000; Email: cust_serv@cch.com • URL: http://www.cchgroup.com • Annual. $103 Quantity: 1 - 4; $92.97 Quantity: 5 - 9; $83.99 Quantity: 10 -. Covers federal estate and gift taxes, including generation-skipping transfer tax plans. Includes tax tables and sample filled-in tax return forms.

***U.S. Master Multistate Corporate Tax Guide***. Wolters Kluwer Law & Business CCH, 2700 Lake Cook Rd. Riverwoods, IL 60015. Phone: 888-224-7377 or (847)267-7000; Email: cust_serv@cch.com • URL: http://www.cchgroup.com • Annual. $136.75 Quantiy: 1 - 4; $122.43 Quantiy: 5 - 9; $109.18 Quantiy: 10 - 24; $97.53 Quantiy: 25. Provides corporate income tax information for 47 states, New York City, and the District of Columbia.

***U.S. Master Pension Guide***. Wolters Kluwer Law & Business CCH, 2700 Lake Cook Rd. Riverwoods, IL 60015. Phone: 888-224-7377 or (847)267-7000; Email: cust_serv@cch.com • URL: http://www.cchgroup.com • Annual. $99.95 1 - 4 (quantity); $97.95 5 - 9 (quantity); $93.95 10 - 24 (quantity); $90.95 25 - (quantity). Explains IRS rules and regulations applying to 401(k) plans, 403(k) plans, ESOPs (employee stock ownership plans), IRAs, SEPs (simplified employee pension plans), Keogh plans, and nonqualified plans.

***U.S. Master Property Tax Guide***. Wolters Kluwer Law & Business CCH, 2700 Lake Cook Rd. Riverwoods, IL 60015. Phone: 888-224-7377 or (847)267-7000; Email: cust_serv@cch.com • URL: http://www.cchgroup.com • Annual. $130.90 Quantity: 1 -4; $117.81 Quantity: 5 - 9; $106.03 Quantity: 10 - 24; $96.87 Quantity: 25. Provides state-by-state coverage of "key property tax issues and concepts," including exemptions, assessments, taxpayer remedies, and property tax calendars.

***U.S. Master Sales and Use Tax Guide***. Wolters Kluwer Law & Business CCH, 2700 Lake Cook Rd. Riverwoods, IL 60015. Phone: 888-224-7377 or (847)267-7000; Email: cust_serv@cch.com • URL: http://www.cchgroup.com • Annual. $129.95 1 - 4 (quantity); $113.26 5 - 9 (quantity); $104.91 10 - 24 (quantity); $93.59 25 - (quantity). Contains concise information on sales and use taxes in all states and the District of Columbia.

***U.S. Master Tax Guide***. Wolters Kluwer Law & Business CCH, 2700 Lake Cook Rd. Riverwoods, IL 60015. Phone: 888-224-7377 or (847)267-7000; Email: cust_serv@cch.com • URL: http://www.cchgroup.com • Annual. $93.50.

***U.S. Mayor***. United States Conference of Mayors, 1620 Eye St. NW Washington, DC 20006-4005. Phone: (202)293-7330; Fax: (202)293-2352; Email: info@usmayors.org • URL: http://www.usmayors.org • Description: Provides a national forum for issues that affect cities in the U.S. Contains ideas in public programs and coverage of innovative projects. Recurring features include letters to the editor, interviews, a calendar of events, and reports of meetings.

***United States National Credit Union Administration NCUA Quarterly***. National Credit Union Administration Office of Small and Disadvantaged Business Utilization, 1775 Duke St. Alexandria, VA 22314-3428. Phone: 800-778-1030 or (703)518-6300 or (703)518-6320; Fax: (703)518-6661 or (703)518-6409; Email: boardmail@ncua.gov • URL: http://www.ncua.gov.

**United States Naval Institute**. 291 Wood Rd. Annapolis, MD 21402-1213. Phone: 800-223-8764 or (410)268-6110; Fax: (410)571-1703; Email: customer@usni.org • URL: http://www.usni.org • Regular, reserve, and retired professionals in the Navy, Marine Corps, and Coast Guard; civilians interested in the advancement of the knowledge of sea power and in advancing professional, literary, and scientific knowledge in the naval and maritime services. Conducts oral history and color print program.

***U.S. 1 Business Directory: Your Source for Business in Central New Jersey***. U.S. 1 Publishing Corp., 12 Roszel Rd. Princeton, NJ 08540. Phone: (609)452-7000; Fax: (609)452-0033; Email: info@princetoninfo.com • URL: http://www.princetoninfo.com • Annual. $18.95; $23.95 delivery. Covers: Approximately 5,500 business to business listings in 212 categories in such areas as computer science, pharmaceuticals, R & D, architecture, advertising agencies, accounting, law firms, warehouses, consultants in the central New Jersey area. Entries include: Company name, address, phone, fax, number of employees, financial data, descriptions of product/service, e-mail, home page addresses, year founded, and revenue range.

**U.S.-Pakistan Business Council**. 1615 H St. NW Washington, DC 20062. Phone: (202)463-5732; Fax: (202)822-2491; Email: uspbc@uschamber.com • URL: http://www.uspakistan.org • Fosters awareness of business opportunities in Pakistan. Increases U.S. foreign direct investment in Pakistan. Brings together Pakistani and American business leaders for discussions on business conditions and policy related issues. Provides a forum for dialogue on key economic, commercial, and other relevant issues of interest to American companies doing or planning to do business in Pakistan.

***United States Patent and Trademark Office***. U. S. Department of Commerce, Phone: 800-786-9199 or (703)308-4357; Fax: (703)305-7786; Email: help@mbda.gov • URL: http://www.uspto.gov • Web site provides extensive information about patents and trademarks, with advanced search facilities for specific documents or names. "Special Pages" are available for "How to Search," "Trademarks-Logos-Brands," "Inventor Resources," and other topics. A complete fee schedule is available for filing applications, appeals, copies, etc.

***U.S. Patents Fulltext***. DIALOG, 11000 Regency Pkwy., Ste. 400 Cary, NC 27511. Phone: 800-334-2564 or (919)462-8600; Fax: (919)468-9890 • URL: http://www.dialog.com • Contains complete text of patents issued by the U. S. Patent and Trademark Office since 1971. Weekly updates. Inquire as to online cost and availability.

**United States Personal Chef Association**. 7680 Universal Blvd., Ste. 550 Orlando, FL 32819-8959. Phone: 800-995-2138; Email: info@uspca.com • URL: http://www.uspca.com • Promotes the personal chef; committed in advancing the profession of the personal chef as a legitimate career choice in the culinary arts field; ensures the credibility of the personal chef with the industry-wide implementation of Educational Standards of Knowledge.

***U.S. Pharmacist***. Jobson Publishing L.L.C., 100 Avenue of the Americas New York, NY 10013. Phone: (212)274-7000; Fax: (212)431-0500 • URL: http://www.jobson.com/ • Monthly. $25 Individuals U.S.; $65 Students U.S.; $130 Canada; $130 Individuals Europe; $76 Other countries; $115 Two years U.S.; $160 Two years Canada; $230 Two years Europe; $230 Two years other countries. Covers a wide variety of topics for independent, chain store, hospital, and other pharmacists.

***United States Pharmacopeia National Formulary***. United States Pharmacopeial Convention, 12601 Twinbrook Pky. Rockville, MD 20852-1790. Phone: 800-227-8772 or (301)881-0666; Fax: (301)816-8299 or (301)816-8236; Email: custsvc@usp.org • URL: http://www.usp.org • Annual. $850. Contains standards for (chemical and biological drug substances, dosage forms, and compounded preparations), excipients, medical devices, and dietary supplements.

***United States Postal Service: Make Your Mark***. U.S. Postal Service, Phone: (202)268-2000; Email: webmaster@email.usps.com • URL: http://www.usps.com • Web site contains detailed information on U. S. mail services and post offices, including ZIP codes, postage rates, stamps, addressing, Express Mail tracking, and consumer postal information in general. Links are provided to the State Department for passport procedures and to the IRS for tax forms.

***U.S. Postal Service Revenue and Cost Analysis Report***. United States Postal Service, 475 W L'enfant Plz. SW Washington, DC 20260-0004. Phone: 800-275-8777 or (202)268-2500 or (202)268-2000; Fax: (202)268-4860 or (202)268-2304 • URL: http://www.usps.com • Annual.

***U.S. Rail News***. Business Publishers Inc., PO Box 17592 Baltimore, MD 21297-1592. Phone: 800-223-8720; Fax: (800)508-2592; Email: custserv@bpinews.com • URL: http://www.bpinews.com • Description: Reports developments in all aspects of the rail transportation industry. Covers topics such as deregulation, mergers and acquisitions, labor relations, and financial management. Recurring features include news briefs and a calendar of related conferences and meetings.

***U.S. Real Estate Register***. Barry Inc., PO Box 551 Wilmington, MA 01887-0551. Phone: (978)658-0441; Email: sales@barryinc.com • URL: http://www.barryinc.com • Annual. $95 Individuals. Covers: Real estate departments of large national companies, industrial economic/development organizations, utilities, real estate brokers, and railroads involved in commercial and industrial real estate development. Entries include: Company or organization name, address; many listings include name of contact.

***U.S. Residential Real Estate Investment Guide for Foreigners***. International Business Publications, USA, PO Box 15343 Washington, DC 20003. Phone: (202)546-2103; Fax: (202)546-3275; Email: ibpusa@comcast.net • URL: http://ibpus.com • $99.95 Individuals hardcopy, E-book and CD-ROM. Covers: basic and contact information for buying and selling real estate in the US.

***U.S. Securities and Exchange Commission***. 100 F St. NE Washington, DC 20549. Phone: 800-732-0330 or (202)942-8088; Fax: (202)942-9634; Email: webmaster@sec.gov • URL: http://www.sec.gov • SEC Web site offers free access through EDGAR to text of official corporate filings, such as annual reports (10-K), quarterly reports (10-Q), and proxies. (EDGAR is "Electronic Data Gathering, Analysis, and Retrieval System.") An example is given of how to obtain executive compensation data from proxies. Text of the daily *SEC News Digest* is offered, as are links to other government sites, non-government market regulators, and U. S. stock exchanges. Search facilities are extensive. Fees: Free.

***United States Securities and Exchange Commission Annual Report***. U. S. Government Printing Office, 732 N Capitol St. NW Washington, DC 20401. Phone: 866-512-1800 or (202)512-1800 or (866)512-1800; Fax: (202)512-2104 or (202)512-2250; Email: contactcenter@gpo.gov • URL: http://www.gpo.gov • Annual. The Commission maintains a Web site at www.sec.gov.

**U.S. Small Business Administration - Office of Advocacy - Research and Statistics - Office of Economic Research**. 409 3rd St., 7th Fl. Washington, DC 20416. Phone: (202)205-6533 or (202)205-6973; Fax: (202)206-6928 or (202)205-6928; Email: advocacy@sba.gov • URL: http://www.sba.gov/advo/research • Economic research and analysis pertaining to small business economic issues and statistics. Of particular interest are projects that are policy-oriented to develop alternative approaches to solving small business problems. Proposals may be submitted by any individual or firm (including small businesses).

***United States Statutes at Large***. U.S. Office of the Federal Register. U. S. Government Printing Office, 732 N Capitol St. NW Washington, DC 20401. Phone: 866-512-1800 or (202)512-1800 or (866)512-1800; Fax: (202)512-2104 or (202)512-2250; Email: contactcenter@gpo.gov • URL: http://www.gpo.gov • Annual. Congressional acts and presidential proclamations issued during the Congressional session. For all laws in force at a specific date, refer to *United States Code*.

***U.S. Supreme Court Bulletin***. Wolters Kluwer Law & Business CCH, 2700 Lake Cook Rd. Riverwoods, IL 60015. Phone: 888-224-7377 or (847)267-7000; Email: cust_serv@cch.com • URL: http://www.cchgroup.com • Monthly and on each decision day while the Court is in session.

***U.S. Survey of Business Expectations***. Dun & Bradstreet Inc., 103 JFK Pkwy. Short Hills, NJ 07078. Phone: 800-526-0651 or (973)921-5500 or (973)921-5000; Fax: (866)560-7035 or (512)794-7670; Email: info@dnb.com • URL: http://www.dnb.com • Quarterly. $40. A survey of 3,000 U. S. business executives as to their expectations for next quarter's sales, profits, prices, inventories, employment, exports, and new orders.

***United States Timber Production, Trade, Consumption, And Price Statistics***. Forest Service. U.S. Department of Agriculture, 1400 Independence Ave. SW Washington, DC 20250. Phone: 800-336-3747 or (202)720-2791 or (202)720-9904; Fax: (202)690-2164 or (202)720-6050; Email: fsis.outreach@usda.gov • URL: http://www.usda.gov • Annual.

**U.S. Travel Association**. 1100 New York Ave. NW, Ste. 450 Washington, DC 20005-3934. Phone: (202)408-8422; Fax: (202)408-1255; Email: feedback@ustravel.org • URL: http://www.ustravel.org • Conducts economic, statistical, and market research relating to the U. S. travel industry. Affiliated with the Travel Industry Association of America.

**U.S.-Vietnam WTO Coalition**. 1101 17th St. NW, Ste. 411 Washington, DC 20036. Phone: (202)289-1912; Fax: (202)289-0519; Email: vncoalition@usasean.org • URL: http://www.usvtc.org/coalition.asp • Represents American companies, farm groups, trade associations, veterans associations and public interest organizations supportive of Vietnam's accession to the World Trade Organization and the attainment of full U.S.-Vietnam normalization.

***United States Waterborne Exports and General Imports***. U.S. Department of Commerce U.S. Census Bureau, 4600 Silver Hill Rd. Washington, DC 20233. Phone: 800-923-8282 or (301)763-4636 or (301)763-3030; Fax: (301)457-4714 or (301)763-6239; Email: webmaster@census.gov • URL: http://www.census.gov/ • Quarterly and annual.

***The U.S. Wine Market: Impact Databank Review and Forecast***. M. Shanken Communications Inc., 387 Park Ave. S New York, NY 10016. Phone: 800-227-1617 or (212)684-4224; Fax: (212)481-1540 or (212)481-0721; Email: mmorgenstern@mshanken.com • URL: http://www.mshanken.com • Annual. $845.00. Includes industry commentary and statistics.

***United Way Annual Report***. United Way Worldwide, 701 N Fairfax St. Alexandria, VA 22314-2045. Phone: (703)836-7112 or (703)519-0092; Fax: (703)519-0097 or (703)683-7846; Email: gallagher@uww.unitedway.org • URL: http://www.unitedway.org • Annual.

***The Universal Healthcare Almanac: A Complete Guide for the Healthcare Professional - Facts, Figures, Analysis***. Silver & Cherner, Ltd., 10221 N. 32nd St., Suite D Phoenix, AZ 85028-3849. Phone: (602)996-2220; Fax: (602)996-2330; Email: uhaeditor@aol.com • $195.00 per year. Looseleaf service. Quarterly updates. Includes a wide variety of health care statistics: national expenditures, hospital data, health insurance, health professionals, vital statistics, demographics, etc. Years of coverage vary, with long range forecasts provided in some cases.

**Universitat Pompeu Fabra - Research Center in Financial Economics and Accounting**. Ramon Trias Fargas, 25-27 E-08005 Barcelona, Spain. Phone: 34 93 5421619; Fax: 34 93 5421746; Email: xavier.freixas@upf.edu • URL: http://www.crefc.upf.edu • Financial economics, accounting, and business.

**University at Albany, State University of New York - Nelson A. Rockefeller Institute of Government**. 411 State St. Albany, NY 12203-1003. Phone: (518)443-5522; Fax: (518)443-5788; Email: thomas.gais@rockinst.suny.edu • URL: http://www.rockinst.org • Public policy issues, including economic development, education, public finance, environment, governance, criminal justice, health, human services, information management, faith-based social service programs, and other issues facing New York and the nation.

***University Business: Solutions for Today's Higher Education***. Educational Media L.L.C., 488 Main Ave. Norwalk, CT 06851-1008. Phone: (203)663-0100; Fax: (203)663-0149; Email: fcassone@promediagrp.com • URL: http://www.universitybusiness.com • 10 times a year. $60.00 per year. Edited for college administrators, including managers of business services, finance, computing, and telecommunications. Includes information on relevant technological advances.

***University District Business News***. Greater University Chamber of Commerce, 4710 University Way NE, Ste. 144 Seattle, WA 98105. Phone: (206)527-4417; Email: administrator@udistrictchamber.org • URL: http://www.udistrictchamber.org • Monthly.

**University of Adelaide - Centre for International Economic Studies**. School of Economics Adelaide, SA 5005, Australia. Phone: 61 8 83134712; Fax: 61 8 82231460; Email: kym.anderson@adelaide.edu.au • URL: http://www.adelaide.edu.au/cies • International economics and closely related disciplines with relevance to the Asia-Pacific region and the global trading system, including programs on China and Indonesia; macroeconomic, monetary, and financial issues; environmental and resource economics; wine.

**University of Adelaide - South Australian Centre for Economic Studies**. Rundle Mall, 3rd Fl., Nexus 10, 10 Pulteney St. Adelaide, SA 5000, Australia. Phone: 61 8 83035555; Fax: 61 8 83034916 • URL: http://www.adelaide.edu.au/saces • Economic issues.

**University of Akron - Buchtel College of Arts and Sciences - Institute of Bioscience and Social Research**. Polsky Bldg. 520, 225 S Main St. Akron, OH 44325-1915. Phone: (330)972-6765; Fax: (330)972-8675; Email: wilder@uakron.edu • URL: http://www.uakron.edu/ibsr • Healthcare policy and services.

**University of Alabama - Alabama State Data Center**. Box 870221 Tuscaloosa, AL 35487-0221. Phone: (205)348-6191; Email: asdc@cba.ua.edu • URL: http://cber.cba.ua.edu/asdc • Makes census data (1980- ) available for research and other uses at the University and throughout the state. Maintains both census and other varied technical documentation.

**University of Alabama at Birmingham - Center for Labor Education and Research**. 1044 11th St. S. Birmingham, AL 35294-4500. Phone: (205)934-2101 or (205)856-8030; Fax: (205)975-5087 or (205)856-8044; Email: csturgis@uab.edu • URL: http://www.jeffstateonline.com/clear • Labor issues, including studies on collective bargaining, arbitration, occupational safety and health, confined space rescue, labor law, trade union organization and administration, and workplace topics of individual faculty interest.

**University of Alabama at Birmingham - Lister Hill Center for Health Policy**. Ryals Public Health Bldg., 1665 University Blvd. Birmingham, AL 35294-0022. Phone: (205)975-9007; Fax: (205)934-3347; Email: morrisey@uab.edu • URL: http://www.soph.uab.edu/index.php?q=listerhill • Health policy research, focusing on health care markets and managed care, maternal and child health, management in public health organizations, aging policy, and outcomes research.

**University of Alabama - Culverhouse College of Commerce and Business Administration - Center for Business and Economic Research**. Box 870221 Tuscaloosa, AL 35487. Phone: (205)348-6191; Fax: (205)348-2951; Email: uacber@cba.ua.edu • URL: http://www.cber.cba.ua.edu • Business and economics, revenue forecasting, and employment in Alabama; estimates of population in Alabama counties; and investigations of state and regional economies. Engaged in construction and maintenance of annual econometric model for the state.

**University of Alabama - Enterprise Integration Laboratory**. Culverhouse College of Commerce & Business Administration Tuscaloosa, AL 35487-0226. Phone: (205)348-5525; Fax: (205)348-6327; Email: dhale@cba.ua.edu • URL: http://old.cba.ua.edu/mis/research/eil • Sharing, managing, controlling, and coordinating business data, work practices, and networks.

**University of Alberta - Institute for Public Economics**. 8-14 HM Tory, Department of Economics Edmonton, AB, Canada T6G 2H4. Phone: (780)492-3406; Fax: (780)492-3300; Email: rascah@ualberta.ca • URL: http://www.ipe.ualberta.ca • Public economics, including the public sector and its influence on the economy and society.

**University of Amsterdam - Center for Nonlinear Dynamics in Economics and Finance**. Department of Economics & Econometrics, Roetersstraat 11 1018 Amsterdam, Netherlands. Phone: 31 20 5254217; Fax: 31 20 5254349; Email: c.h.hommes@uva.nl • URL: http://www1.fee.uva.nl/cendef • Nonlinear dynamics in economics and finance.

**University of Arizona - Eller College of Management - Economic and Business Research Center**. McClelland Hall, Rm. 103, 1130 Helen St. Tucson, AZ 85721-0108. Phone: (520)621-2155 or (520)621-2109; Fax: (520)621-2150; Email: ebrlib@eller.arizona.edu • URL: http://ebr.eller.arizona.edu • Regional economic forecasting, economic data collection and analysis, econometric and input-output impact models, policy-analytic studies, and international economic research. Assists individuals and groups interested in Arizona economy and aids public and private organizations with their research and planning activities.

**University of Arizona - Udall Center for Studies in Public Policy**. 803 E 1st St. Tucson, AZ 85719. Phone: (520)626-4393; Fax: (520)626-3664; Email: udallctr@u.arizona.edu • URL: http://udallcenter.arizona.edu • Multidisciplinary public policy research in the areas of natural resources and the environment, economic development, health care, and the effects of science and technology on public policy. Special emphasis is on U.S.-Mexico border environmental institutions and policy, American Indian policy and environmental conflict resolution in the Western U.S.

**University of Arkansas at Little Rock - Institute for Economic Advancement**. 2801 S University Ave. Little Rock, AR 72204-1099. Phone: (501)569-8519; Fax: (501)569-8538; Email: jlyoungquist@ualr.edu • URL: http://www.aiea.ualr.edu • Business and economics, industrial development, labor statistics, demographics, government and taxes, economic development and U.S. census.

**University of Arkansas for Medical Sciences - Arkansas Center for Health Improvement**. Victory Bldg., Ste. 300, 1401 W Capitol Little Rock, AR 72201. Phone: (501)526-2244; Fax: (501)526-2252 • URL: http://www.achi.net • Policies that improve the health of the citizens of Arkansas.

**University of Auckland - Centre for Mental Health Research**. Bldg. 505, Level 2, Faculty of Medical and Health Sciences, 85 Park Rd., Private Bag 92019 Auckland 1142, New Zealand. Phone: 64 9 3737599; Fax: 64 9 3677158; Email: b.mckenna@auckland.ac.nz • URL: http://www.fmhs.auckland.ac.nz/son/cmhr • Mental health policy, services, workforce and clinical practice.

**University of Bath - School of Management - Centre for Business Organisations and Society**. Bath BA2 7AY, United Kingdom. Phone: 44 1225 384974 • URL: http://www.bath.ac.uk/cbos • Relationship between corporations and the societies in which they operate, the ethical position of modern corporations in different societal contexts, and the study of corporate social responsibility as a strategic phenomenon.

**University of Brighton - School of Applied Social Science - Social Science Policy and Research Centre**. Mayfield House, Falmer Brighton BN1 9PH, United Kingdom. Phone: 44 1273 643980; Fax: 44 1273 643496; Email: marian.barnes@brighton.ac.uk • URL: http://www.brighton.ac.uk/sass/research/ • Health and social policy issues, including neighborhood renewal, community participation, social exclusion, interagency working, health and social care, the social services workforce, third sector concerns, policing and criminal justice, transport and the environment, housing, and youth concerns.

**University of Bristol - Centre for Market and Public Organisation**. 2 Priory Rd. Bristol BS8 1TX, United Kingdom. Phone: 44 117 3310799; Fax: 44 117 3310705; Email: simon.burgess@bristol.ac.uk • URL: http://www.bristol.ac.uk/cmpo • Reform of activities on the boundaries of the state, regulation, privatization, and incentives in the public sector.

**University of British Columbia - Centre for Health Services and Policy Research**. 201-2206 E Mall Vancouver, BC, Canada V6T 1Z3. Phone: (604)822-4969; Fax: (604)822-5690; Email: mbarer@chspr.ubc.ca • URL: http://www.chspr.ubc.ca • Pharmaceuticals, primary health care, patterns of health and health care utilization, and data and infrastructure development.

**University of British Columbia - Centre for Labour and Empirical Economic Research**. Department of Economics, 997-1873 E Mall Vancouver, BC, Canada V6T 1Z1. Phone: (604)822-4870; Fax: (604)822-5915; Email: cleer2@interchange.ubc.ca • URL: http://www.econ.ubc.ca/cleer/ • Labor markets and other sectors of the economy.

***University of Calcutta Business Studies***. University of Calcutta, Senate House, 87/1 College St. Kolkata 700 073, India. Phone: 91 33 22410071; Email: admin@caluniv.ac.in • URL: http://www.caluniv.ac.in/ • Semiannual. $20; $4 Other countries. Publication on business and economic studies.

**University of Calgary - Institute of Professional Communication**. Social Sciences 110, 2500 University Dr. NW Calgary, AB, Canada T2N 1N4. Phone: (403)220-7255; Fax: (403)220-6716; Email: cmsopcza@ucalgary.ca • URL: http://www.ipc.ucalgary.ca/ • Professional communication.

**University of Calgary - Latin American Research Centre**. Social Sciences 004, 2500 University Dr. NW Calgary, AB, Canada T2N 1N4. Phone: (403)210-3929; Fax: (403)282-8606; Email: larc@ucalgary.ca • URL: http://larc.ucalgary.ca • Geography, archaeology, literature, business in Latin America.

**University of California at Berkeley - Center for Environmental Design Research**. 390 Wurster Hall, MC 1839 Berkeley, CA 94720-1839. Phone: (510)642-2896; Fax: (510)643-5571; Email: cedr@ced.berkley.edu • URL: http://ced.berkeley.edu/research/center-for-environmental-design-research.

**University of California, Berkeley - Institute for Business Innovation**. F402 Haas School of Business, No. 1930 Berkeley, CA 94720-1930. Phone: (510)642-4041; Fax: (510)642-2826; Email: teece@haas.berkeley.edu • URL: http://businessinnovation.berkeley.edu • Research areas include a wide range of business management functions.

**University of California, Berkeley - Institute for Research on Labor and Employment**. 2521 Channing Way, No. 5555 Berkeley, CA 94720-5555. Phone: (510)643-8140 or (510)642-1705; Fax: (510)642-6432; Email: mreich@econ.berkeley.edu • URL: http://www.irle.berkeley.edu • Employment and training systems in the United States, Japan, and Europe; green economy; high performance workplaces; labor-management relations, organizational behavior, wages and related problems, economic security programs, labor market and labor mobility, social and industrial psychology, comparative developmental studies, labor history, and occupational health. Conduct interdisciplinary research program.

**University of California, Berkeley - Institute of Business and Economic Research**. 371 Stephens Hall, Haas School of Business, UCB MC 1922 Berkeley, CA 94720-1922. Phone: (510)642-1922; Fax: (510)642-5018 or (510)642-1420; Email: iber@haas.berkeley.edu • URL: http://iber.berkeley.edu • Research fields are business administration, economics, finance, real estate, and international development.

**University of California, Berkeley - Institute of Urban and Regional Development**. 316 Wurster Hall, MC 1870 Berkeley, CA 94720-1870. Phone: (510)642-4874; Fax: (510)643-9576; Email: iurd@berkeley.edu • URL: http://iurd.berkeley.edu • Research topics include the effects of changing economic trends in urban areas.

**University of California, Berkeley - School of Public Health - Center for Health and Public Policy Studies**. 50 University Hall, No. 7360 Berkeley, CA 94720-7360. Phone: (510)643-1675; Fax: (510)643-2340; Email: chpps@berkeley.edu • URL: http://chpps.berkeley.edu • Issues in health policy and politics that affect California and the nation.

**University of California - California Agricultural Experiment Station**. 1111 Franklin St., Rm. 6402 Oakland, CA 94607-5200. Phone: (510)987-0036 or (510)987-0060; Fax: (510)465-2659 or (510)451-2317; Email: steve.nation@ucop.edu • URL: http://ucanr.org/AES.shtml • Plant and animal biology, agricultural engineering and economics, soils, and water, including basic and applied studies directed toward solving problems of agriculture involved in production, storage, and transportation of over 300 commodities produced in California. Studies problems relating to forestry, human welfare and nutrition, pest management, mosquito control, and outdoor recreation. Operates on a statewide basis, with main units on Berkeley, Davis, and Riverside campuses of the University and ten research and extension centers throughout the state.

**University of California Cooperative Extension, Riverside County**. 21150 Box Springs Rd., Ste. 202 Moreno Valley, CA 92557-8718. Phone: (951)683-6491; Fax: (951)788-2615; Email: ceriverside@ucdavis.edu • URL: http://ceriverside.ucanr.edu • Agriculture, food safety, food preservation, consumer economics, and human nutrition. Provides assistance in the development and dissemination of information about the public's supply of food and fiber and seeks to educate the public on the wide use of natural resources.

**University of California, Davis - Center for Healthcare Policy and Research**. 2103 Stockton Blvd. Sacramento, CA 95817. Phone: (916)734-2818; Fax: (916)734-8731 • URL: http://www.ucdmc.ucdavis.edu/chsrpc • Public health policy, including causes and prevention of adverse health outcomes, quality of care, physician-patient interaction, and cost effectiveness.

**University of California, Los Angeles - Anderson Forecast**. Gold Hall, Ste. B302, 110 Westwood Plz. Los Angeles, CA 90095. Phone: (310)825-1623; Fax: (310)206-9940; Email: eleamer@anderson.ucla.edu • URL: http://uclaforecast.com • Development and continuous revision of complex econometric models for the U.S., California, and subregions of the state, using these models to project short-run and long-range forecasts and to conduct impact studies, including evaluating the effects of alternative governmental policies. Provides econometric model for California to on-line users through a time-sharing firm.

**University of California, Los Angeles - Center for Health Policy Research**. 10960 Wilshire Blvd., Ste. 1550 Los Angeles, CA 90024. Phone: (310)794-0909; Fax: (310)794-2686; Email: healthpolicy@ucla.edu • URL: http://healthpolicy.ucla.edu/Pages/home.aspx • Cost-effectiveness of health programs and services and their effects on health of communities and consumers; policy analysis and develops policy tools that address issues of health promotion and disease prevention.

**University of California, Los Angeles - Institute for the Study of Educational Entrepreneurship**. Moore Hall, Box 951521 Los Angeles, CA 90095. Phone: (310)825-2297; Email: isee@gseis.ucla.edu • URL: http://isee.gseis.ucla.edu • Relationships between private for-profit, private not-for-profit, and public organizations and their potential to advance public education reform.

**University of California, Los Angeles - Latin American Center**. 10349 Bunche Hall Los Angeles, CA 90095. Phone: (310)825-4571; Fax: (310)206-6859; Email: latinamctr@international.ucla.edu • URL: http://www.international.ucla.edu/lai.

**University of California, Los Angeles - Molecular Biology Institute**. Paul D. Boyer Hall, Box 951570, 611 Charles E Young Dr. E Los Angeles, CA 90095-1570. Phone: (310)825-1018; Fax: (310)206-7286; Email: arispe@mcdb.ucla.edu •

URL: http://www.mbi.ucla.edu • Supports, encourages, and facilitates university-wide research and training in molecular biology, with emphasis on molecular genetics; protein and nucleic acid synthesis, properties, and function; cell biology; molecular medicine.

**University of California, Los Angeles - Social Sciences Grant Support**. 2134 Rolfe Hall Los Angeles, CA 90095-1484. Phone: (310)825-0711; Fax: (310)206-4453; Email: aortega@ucla.edu • URL: http://www.issr.ucla.edu • Basic and policy studies on a broad spectrum of contemporary sociological, psychological, political, and economic problems and community issues. Encourages collaborative research between faculty in various social science departments of the University, as well as cooperative projects involving members of professional schools of the University and faculty of the School. Sponsors the following interdisciplinary research programs: Center for American Politics and Public Policy; Center for the Study of Urban Poverty; and Center for Social Theory and Comparative History.

**University of California, Los Angeles - Richard S. Ziman Center for Real Estate**. Gold Hall, Ste. B100, 110 Westwood Plz. Los Angeles, CA 90095-1481. Phone: (310)206-9424 or (213)825-3977; Fax: (310)267-5391 or (310)206-5455; Email: stuart.gabriel@anderson.ucla.edu • URL: http://www.anderson.ucla.edu/centers/ziman • Secondary mortgage markets, housing finance, growth management, infrastructure, corporate finance issues, and development industry.

**University of California, Riverside - Air Pollution Research Center**. 205 Fawcett Laboratory Riverside, CA 92521. Phone: (951)827-4191 or (909)787-5124; Fax: (951)827-5004 or (909)787-5004; Email: roger.atkinson@ucr.edu • URL: http://www.aprc.ucr.edu • Atmospheric chemistry and the effects of pollutants on plant systems and modeling of photochemical smog formation to yield information relevant to the development of rational and cost-effective air pollution control strategies. Research program includes studies of chemical and physical transformations of pollutants in the atmosphere, chemical composition and related mutagenicity of gaseous and particulate organic pollutants, spectroscopic identification and measurement of atmospheric constituents, effects of pollutants on agricultural crops, definition of tolerance levels for specified plant species and description of symptom expression of plants, modeling atmospheric transformations of pollutants, and translation of research results into models suitable for direct application to control strategies by state and federal agencies and public officials.

**University of California, San Diego - Center for Energy Research**. 9500 Gilman Dr., MC 0417 La Jolla, CA 92093-0417. Phone: (858)534-6527 or (858)534-4285; Fax: (858)534-7716; Email: faw@ames.ucsd.edu • URL: http://cer.ucsd.edu • Stable, secure, and affordable energy supplies that have minimal impact on the environment.

**University of California, San Diego - Scripps Institution of Oceanography**. 9500 Gilman Dr., MC 0210 La Jolla, CA 92093-0210. Phone: (858)534-3624; Fax: (858)534-5306; Email: scrippsnews@ucsd.edu • URL: http://scripps.ucsd.edu • Marine sciences, focusing on physical, chemical, biological, geological, and geophysical studies.

**University of California, San Francisco - Institute for Health and Aging**. UCSF Box 0646 San Francisco, CA 94143-0646. Phone: (415)476-9483; Fax: (415)476-3915; Email: wendy.max@ucsf.edu • URL: http://nursing.ucsf.edu/iha • Aging health policy issues and policy alternatives; state discretionary policies in long-term care, social services, and income maintenance; private sector involvement in supporting health and social services for the elderly; effects of intergovernmental relations and state and federal fiscal conditions on services to the elderly; coordination between state and local aging programs and health planning, financing, and regulatory programs; special health and social service needs of the low-income, isolated elderly; enrollment of the elderly in health maintenance and social/health organizations; gender issues; Alzheimer's disease resources and program evaluation; AIDS; international alcohol; health promotion and injury and disease prevention; disability statistics; and health status of the elderly, with special emphasis on selected acute and chronic health conditions.

**University of California, San Francisco - Institute for Health Policy Studies**. 3333 California St., Ste. 265 San Francisco, CA 94118. Phone: (415)476-5255; Fax: (415)476-0705; Email: claire.brindis@ucsf.edu • URL: http://healthpolicy.ucsf.edu • Health policy and health services research.

**University of California, San Francisco - Francis I. Proctor Foundation for Research in Ophthalmology**. 95 Kirkham St. San Francisco, CA 94143-0944. Phone: (415)476-1442; Fax: (415)476-2521; Email: todd.margolis@ucsf.edu • URL: http://proctor.ucsf.edu • Infectious and inflammatory diseases of the eye with particular emphasis on chlamydial infections, trachoma, herpetic eye infections, dry eye conditions, and uveitis.

**University of California, San Francisco - Rosalind Russell Medical Research Center for Arthritis**. 350 Parnassus Ave., Ste. 600 San Francisco, CA 94117. Phone: (415)476-1141; Fax: (415)476-3526; Email: rrac@medicine.ucsf.com • URL: http://www.rosalindrussellcenter.ucsf.edu • Arthritis and its probable causes, focusing on immunology, immunogenetics, and inflammation. Examines health services and policy and educational approaches and methods for arthritis patients and health professionals.

**University of California, Santa Barbara - Institute for Social, Behavioral, and Economic Research - Center on Police Practices and Community**. 2201 N Hall Santa Barbara, CA 93106-2150. Phone: (805)901-4439; Fax: (805)893-7995; Email: mca@coppac.ucsb.edu • URL: http://www.coppac.ucsb.edu/ • Relationships between law enforcement and society.

**University of Central Florida - Center for Research and Education in Optics and Lasers**. College of Optics & Photonics, 4000 Central Florida Blvd. Orlando, FL 32816-2700. Phone: (407)823-6800; Fax: (407)823-6880; Email: creol@creol.ucf.edu • URL: http://www.creol.ucf.edu • Photonics, nanophotonics, biophotonics, optical switching, nonlinear optics fiber optics, laser propagation, waveguides, growth of nonlinear and laser host materials, optical scattering, laser-produced plasmas, free electron lasers, opto-electronics, quantum electronics, optical sensors, correlation techniques, laser-induced damage, optical power limiting, ultra-fast phenomena (femtosecond laser interactions), nonlinear optical spectroscopy, diffractive optics, liquid crystal optics, spatial solitons, image understanding, thin film optics, X-ray lasers, diode pumped lasers, micro-lasers, and classical optics. Applications include the following: optical telecommunications, new laser sources, detection, surveillance, reconnaissance, command and control, counter and counter-counter measures, intelligence collection, and the development of improved optical components, sensor protection, optical computing, and medical lasers.

**University of Central Florida - Transportation Systems Institute**. Department of Civil, Environmental, and Construction Engineering, 12800 Pegasus Dr., Ste. 211 Orlando, FL 32816-2450. Phone: (407)823-2988; Fax: (407)823-3315; Email: haitham.al-deek@ucf.edu • URL: http://tsi.cecs.ucf.edu • Research areas include mass transportation systems.

**University of Chicago - Booth School of Business - Center for Research in Security Prices**. 105 W Adams St., Ste. 1700 Chicago, IL 60603. Phone: (312)263-6400; Fax: (312)263-6430; Email: subscriptions@crsp.chicagobooth.edu • URL: http://www.crsp.com • Historical financial data.

**University of Chicago - Center for Population Economics**. 5807 S Woodlawn Ave. Chicago, IL 60637. Phone: (773)702-7709; Fax: (773)702-2901; Email: rwf@cpe.uchicago.edu • URL: http://www.cpe.uchicago.edu • Analysis of long-term structural changes in the economy at the microeconomic level, including studies on the economics of mortality in North America (1650-1910), nutrition, labor welfare, labor productivity, distribution of wealth, economic mobility, patterns and determinants of internal migration, and savings and investments by households.

**University of Chicago Graduate School of Business - Center for Decision Research**. 5807 S Woodlawn Ave. Chicago, IL 60637. Phone: (773)702-4877; Fax: (773)834-9134; Email: vicki.drozd@chicagobooth.edu • URL: http://research.chicagobooth.edu/cdr.

**University of Chicago - George J. Stigler Center for the Study of the Economy and the State**. Booth School of Business, 5807 S Woodlawn Ave. Chicago, IL 60637. Phone: (773)702-7519; Fax: (773)834-9134; Email: robert.topel@chicagogsb.edu • URL: http://research.chicagobooth.edu/economy • Effects of legal and political institutions on economic activity, including studies on the growth of government, income redistribution policies of governments, and regulation of utilities, insurance, and water resources.

**University of Chicago**. 947 E 58th St., MC0926 Chicago, IL 60637-5416. Phone: (773)702-6371 or (773)702-1234; Fax: (773)702-1216 or (773)702-7222; Email: info@ssa.uchicago.edu • URL: http://pps.bsd.uchicago.edu/.

**University of Cincinnati - Center for Health and Environmental Research**. Department of Communication, 601A Teachers College Cincinnati, OH 45221-0184. Phone: (513)556-4001; Fax: (513)556-0899; Email: depoe@uc.edu • URL: http://asweb.artsci.uc.edu/communication/checr/about/index.html • Communication processes and practices in environmental and health policy contexts, in order to enhance the understanding and quality of communication processes and practices among citizen, industry, and government participants in environmental and health policy formation and implementation. The center's research agenda includes the design, analysis, and evaluation of informational and persuasive messages and campaigns produced by and addressed to individuals and institutions which pertain to environmental and human health risk contexts and controversies; the analysis and evaluation of communication processes within environmental and health-related organizations; and the design, facilitation, and evaluation of processes of stakeholder involvement in risk-based decision-making.

**University of Cincinnati - Institute for the Study of Health**. PO Box 670840 Cincinnati, OH 45267-0840. Phone: (513)558-2756; Fax: (513)558-2744; Email: ronnie.horner@uc.edu • URL: http://www.healthinstitute.uc.edu/Templates/Home.cfm • Health policy and health services, especially cost effectiveness and health outcomes.

**University of Colorado at Boulder - Center for Economic Analysis**. Department of Economics, 256 UCB Boulder, CO 80309-0256. Phone: (303)492-8024; Fax: (303)492-8960; Email: teresa.decandia@colorado.edu • Economics.

**University of Colorado at Boulder - Institutions Program**. Institute of Behavioral Science Bldg. 2, 487 UCB Boulder, CO 80309-0487. Phone: (303)492-8147; Fax: (303)492-3609; Email: edward.greenberg@colorado.edu • URL: http://www.colorado.edu/IBS/pec/ • Political economy, class and stratification, structures of international relations, and national, class, and group conflict.

**University of Colorado at Denver - Center for Nonprofit Leadership and Research**. PO Box 173364 Denver, CO 80217-3364. Phone: (303)352-3800 or (303)315-2089; Fax: (303)315-2229; Email: lisa.carlson@cudenver.edu • URL: http://www.ucdenver.edu/about/centers-institutes/Pages/default.aspx • Conducts research on public sector issues. Provides leadership training for public, private, and nonprofit managers, offers facilitation and technical assistance services.

**University of Connecticut - Center for Public Health and Health Policy - Health Policy Group**. 99 Ash St., 2nd Fl., MC 7160 East Hartford, CT 06108. Phone: (860)282-8578; Fax: (860)282-8505; Email: meberle@uchc.edu • URL: http://www.publichealth.uconn.edu/policy-analysis.html • Health policy, including prevention, health promotion and primary care.

**University of Connecticut - Connecticut Center for Economic Analysis**. 2100 Hillside Rd., U-1240 Storrs, CT 06269-1240. Phone: (860)486-0614; Fax: (860)486-0889; Email: fred.carstensen@uconn.edu • URL: http://ccea.uconn.edu • Economic analysis, including state and local finance, economic impact, policy analysis, cluster analysis, assessment of fiscal structure, dynamic REMI forecasting, econometrics, bench-marketing, labor, and health economics.

**University of Connecticut - School of Medicine - Department of Community Medicine and Health Care - Center for International Community Health Studies**. MC 6325, 263 Farmington Ave. Farmington, CT 06030-6325. Phone: (860)679-1570; Fax: (860)679-5464; Email: schensul@nso2.uchc.edu • URL: http://www.commed.uchc.edu/cichs • The health of underprivileged people in the U.S. and abroad, emphasizing international primary health care and community health, including international health policy, urban health in developing and developed countries, maternal and child health, health programs and problems in Peru, Sri Lanka, Kenya, Mauritius, and Connecticut, effects of economic development on health, and the role of the hospital in the developing world. Facilitates international health research for faculty and graduate students through consultation on grant proposals, networking with international contacts, advocating for researchers within international agencies, and establishing foreign research and educational placements.

**University of Cyprus - Center for Banking and Financial Research**. School of Economics & Management Nicosia 1678, Cyprus. Phone: 357 2 2892496; Fax: 357 2 2892421; Email: hermes@ucy.ac.cy • URL: http://www.ucy.ac.cy/hermes/en • Computational finance and economics.

**University of Delaware - Center for Composite Materials**. 202 Composites Manufacturing Science Lab Newark, DE 19716-3144. Phone: (302)831-8149; Fax: (302)831-8525; Email: gillespie@udel.edu • URL: http://www.ccm.udel.edu • Development of core competencies in composites science and engineering, including textile preforming, liquid molding (resin transfer molding, vacuum-assisted resin infusion), thermoplastic processing, joining, interphase science, sensing and control, multifuctional materials, cost modeling, and application of composites to civil infrastructure. Major programs include a national testbed for intelligent VARTM processing.

**University of Delaware - Center for Energy and Environmental Policy**. 278 Graham Hall Newark, DE 19716. Phone: (302)831-8405; Fax: (302)831-3098; Email: jbbyrne@udel.edu • URL: http://ceep.udel.edu • Energy, environmental, and technology policy issues focusing on social, political, and economic dimensions of technology, and natural resource use. Center research and graduate study is informed by theories and concepts drawn from the fields of political economy and environment, technology, and society. Of particular interest are analyses of climate change, sustainable development, energy and environmental policy, environmental justice, water and energy conservation, renewable energy policies, energy and environmental issues in developing nations, and environmental planning.

**University of Delaware - College of Agriculture and Natural Resources - Delaware Water Resources Center**. 531 S College Ave. Newark, DE 19716. Phone: (302)831-2191 or (302)831-2698; Fax: (302)831-3651 or (302)831-6758; Email: jtsims@udel.edu • URL: http://ag.udel.edu/dwrc • Water and other resources that affect water, including basic and practical studies on supply, use, conservation, and reuse of water. Also studies wastewater reclamation, economic, governmental, and other social aspects of water resource development, groundwater flow, and water use efficiency in agriculture. Established under Water Resources Research Act of 1964, Public Law 88-379; authorized currently under Water Research Act of 1984, Public Law 98-242, to conduct and coordinate research activities to assure the state and surrounding region of a supply of water sufficient in quantity and quality to meet requirements of its expanding population and economy. Assists in training of scientists for research on water resources problems.

**University of East Anglia - School of Environmental Sciences - Centre for Social and Economic Research on the Global Environment**. Norwich NR4 7TJ, United Kingdom. Phone: 44 1603 593224; Fax: 44 1603 591327; Email: i.bateman@uea.ac.uk • URL: http://www.cserge.ac.uk • Environmental issues, including biodiversity, climate change, coastal zone management, environmental resource valuation, sustainable development, tropical forests, waste management and life cycle assessment, and water and wetlands.

**University of Edinburgh - Arts and Humanities Research Council - Research Centre for Studies in Intellectual Property and Technology Law**. School of Law, Old College, S Bridge Edinburgh EH8 9YL, United Kingdom. Phone: 44 131 6502014; Fax: 44 131 6506317; Email: itandip@ed.ac.uk • URL: http://www.law.ed.ac.uk/ahrc/aboutus.aspx • Intellectual property, copyright, patents, technology, commerce, society, information technology, genetics, and medical jurisprudence and ethics.

**University of Essex - Institute for Social and Economic Research - European Centre for Analysis in the Social Sciences**. Wivenhoe Park Colchester CO4 3SQ, United Kingdom. Phone: 44 1206 872957; Fax: 44 1206 873151; Email: stephenj@essex.ac.uk • URL: http://www.iser.essex.ac.uk/research/ecass • European social and economic change.

**University of Exeter - Business School - Centre for Innovation and Service Research**. Streatham Ct., Rennes Dr. Exeter EX4 4PU, United Kingdom. Phone: 44 1392 722557; Fax: 44 1392 723210 • URL: http://business-school.exeter.ac.uk/research/areas/centres/isr • Design, analysis and management of business processes, including the analysis of process flows, capacity, resource utilization, and throughput analyses.

**University of Florida - Center for Exercise Science**. PO Box 118208 Gainesville, FL 32611. Phone: (352)294-1713; Fax: (352)392-0316; Email: spowers@hhp.ufl.edu • URL: http://apk.hhp.ufl.edu/index.php/departments-centers/center-for-exercise-science-ces • Studies fitness as it relates to the general population and as it relates to athletic performance.

**University of Florida - Center for Intelligent Machines and Robotics**. Department of Mechanical Engineering Gainesville, FL 32611. Phone: (352)392-9461; Fax: (352)392-1071; Email: ccrane@ufl.edu • URL: http://cimar.mae.ufl.edu/CIMAR/index.html • Robotics and artificial intelligence, including studies in industrial robotics, nuclear reactor maintenance, interactive animated display of man-controlled and autonomous robots, light machinery, hazardous area manipulation, and human augmentation.

**University of Florida - College of Engineering - Department of Electrical & Computer Engineering - Photonics Research Laboratory**. 216 Larsen Hall Gainesville, FL 32611-6200. Phone: (352)392-0911 or (352)392-9265; Fax: (352)392-8671; Email: rakov@ece.ufl.edu • URL: http://old.ece.ufl.edu/research/labs/photonics.html • Integrated optics, optoelectronic integration, high-speed electro-optic guided-wave modulators, modulators with linearized transfer curves, wavelength-selective filters, waveguide structures in ferroelectric crystals with domain reversals, waveguide lasers/amplifiers.

**University of Florida - Engineering and Industrial Experiment Station**. 300 Weil Hall, College of Engineering Gainesville, FL 32611-6550. Phone: (352)392-6000; Fax: (352)392-9673; Email: caber@eng.ufl.edu • URL: http://www.eng.ufl.edu • Research fields include chemical, civil, electrical, industrial, mechanical, and other types of engineering.

**University of Florida - Fredric G. Levin College of Law - Center for Governmental Responsibility**. 309 Vill. Dr. Gainesville, FL 32611. Phone: (352)273-0835; Fax: (352)392-1457 • URL: http://www.law.ufl.edu/academics/centers/cgr • Research fields include family law.

**University of Florida - Institute for Child Health Policy**. 1329 SW 16th St. Gainesville, FL 32608. Phone: (352)265-7220; Fax: (352)265-7221 • URL: http://ichp.ufl.edu • Child health policy and family and child health care delivery issues, including development of an equitable and comprehensive child health policy model for states; development of case management programs for children with special health care needs; development of health care financing strategies, including school enrollment-based health insurance; and comprehensive program development and health services research and evaluation.

**University of Florida - Public Policy Research Center**. 204 Matherly Hall, Department of Economics, Warrington College of Business Administration Gainesville, FL 32611-7140. Phone: (352)392-3904; Fax: (352)392-7860; Email: sapping@ufl.edu • URL: http://warrington.ufl.edu/centers/pprc • Public policy on antitrust, regulation, taxation, education, and other government policy.

**University of Florida - Transportation Research Center**. 512 Weil Hall Gainesville, FL 32611. Phone: 800-226-1013 or (352)392-9537 or (352)392-7575; Fax: (352)392-3394 or (352)392-3224; Email: elefter@ce.ufl.edu • URL: http://trc.ce.ufl.edu • Traffic operations, traffic simulation, traffic signal control, congestion pricing, network modeling, optimization, transportation planning, land use planning, older driver issues.

**University of Florida - Tropical Research and Education Center**. 18905 SW 280th St. Homestead, FL 33031. Phone: (305)246-7000; Fax: (305)246-7003; Email: hom@gnv.ifas.ufl.edu • URL: http://trec.ifas.ufl.edu • Production of tropical and subtropical fruits and winter-grown vegetables, including studies in horticulture, pathology, entomology, plant breeding, soils, irrigation, plant nutrition, and tissue culture.

**University of Georgia - Selig Center for Economic Growth**. c/o Dr. Jeffrey M. Humphreys, Director, 110 E Clayton St. Athens, GA 30602. Phone: (706)542-4085; Email: jhumphre@uga.edu • URL: http://www.terry.uga.edu/about/centers-institutes/selig • Economics and business conditions, including studies of county income, economic forecasting, and gross state product. Conducts statistical studies on Georgia and neighboring states.

**University of Graz - Institute of Public Economics**. Universitätsstrasse 15/E4 A-8010 Graz, Austria. Phone: 43 316 3803460; Fax: 43 316 3809530; Email: richard.sturn@uni-graz.at • URL: http://www.uni-graz.at/fwiwww/2010/Frontpage/index.html • Economic aspects of cultural policy in Austria.

**University of Guelph - Ontario Public Interest Research Group-Guelph**. 1 Trent Ln. Guelph, ON, Canada N1G 2W1. Phone: (519)824-2091; Fax: (519)824-8990; Email: opirg@uoguelph.ca • URL: http://www.opirgguelph.org/index.php?mode=2&linkID=1&l=0 • Social, political, economic and environmental issues of public concern.

**University of Hawaii at Manoa - Hawaii Natural Energy Institute**. 1680 E West Rd., Post 109 Honolulu, HI 96822. Phone: (808)956-8890; Fax: (808)956-2336; Email: hnei@hawaii.edu • URL: http://www.hnei.hawaii.edu • Research areas include geothermal, wind, solar, hydroelectric, and other energy sources.

**University of Helsinki - Research Unit of Economic Structures and Growth**. Department of Economics, 4th Fl., Faculty of Social Sciences, Arkadiankatu 7 (PL 17) 00014 Helsinki, Finland. Phone: 358 9 19128718; Fax: 358 9 19128742; Email: erkki.koskela@helsinki.fi • URL: http://www.valt.helsinki.fi/raka/about.htm • Economics, including labor, resource and industrial economics and taxation.

**University of Hertfordshire - Group for Research in Organisational Evolution**. Business School, de Havilland Campus Hatfield AL10 9AB, United Kingdom. Phone: 44 1707 284800; Fax: 44 1707 284870; Email: g.m.hodgson@herts.ac.uk • URL: http://www.herts.ac.uk/research/ssahri/research-areas/business-management/groe • Institutional economics, including research in subfields such as the economics of property rights and economics and law.

**University of Hong Kong - Hong Kong Institute of Economics and Business Strategy**. Faculty of Business & Economics, Pokfulam Rd. Hong Kong, China. Phone: 86 852 25489300; Fax: 86 852 25483223; Email: info@hiebs.hku.hk • URL: http://www.hiebs.hku.hk • Economic policy and business strategy in Hong Kong and its role in China and the Asia-Pacific region.

**University of Hong Kong - School of Economics and Finance - Hong Kong Center for Economic Research**. Pokfulam Rd. Hong Kong, China. Phone: 86 852 25478313; Fax: 86 852 25486319; Email: hkcer@econ.hku.hk • URL: http://www.hku.hk/hkcer • Economic issues and economic policy.

**University of Houston - Center for Public Policy**. 306 McElhinney Hall Houston, TX 77204-5035. Phone: (713)743-3970; Fax: (713)743-3978; Email: jgranato@uh.edu • URL: http://www.uh.edu/hcpp • Economic, political, sociological, related to public policy issues, including studies in regional economics and demographics. Provides assistance to a variety of research undertaken by University faculty and initiates and sponsors surveys. Primary focus is on the eight county areas surrounding Houston.

**University of Houston - Health Law and Policy Institute**. 100 Law Ctr. Houston, TX 77204-6060. Phone: (713)743-2101; Fax: (713)743-2117; Email: healthlaw@uh.edu • URL: http://www.law.uh.edu/healthlaw • Health issues affecting the state and nation, including health law and policy, occupational injury and illness, nonfinancial barriers to health care, and family violence and the health care system.

**University of Idaho - Center for Business Development and Entrepreneurship**. College of Business & Economics Moscow, ID 83844-3161. Phone: 800-960-3033; Fax: (208)885-8939; Email: dansmith@uidaho.edu • URL: http://www.cbehome.uidaho.edu/default.aspx?pid=32593 • Business and economics, including studies on market and labor force, regional economics.

**University of Illinois at Chicago - Electronic Visualization Laboratory**. Department of Computer Science, Rm. 1120, MC 152, 851 S Morgan St. Chicago, IL 60607-7053. Phone: (312)996-3002; Fax: (312)413-7585; Email: spiff@uic.edu • URL: http://www.evl.uic.edu • Research areas include computer graphics, virtual reality, multimedia, and interactive techniques.

**University of Illinois at Chicago - Institute for Health Research and Policy - Center for Health Services Research**. Westside Research Office Bldg., Rm. 560 CU3, 1747 W Roosevelt Rd., MC 275 Chicago, IL 60608. Phone: (312)996-1062; Fax: (312)996-5356; Email: jzwanzig@uic.edu • URL: http://ihrp.uic.edu/center/center-health-services-research • New health care technologies, medical informatics, health manpower, observation unit medicine in the hospital emergency room, and performance of preventive through tertiary healthcare delivery at the systems, program, and specific intervention levels. Studies focus on access, appropriateness, acceptability, cost, safety, availability, effectiveness, benefits, and overall quality of healthcare. Specific topics include clinical decision-making, health information management, psychological and social sciences, and public health policy analysis.

**University of Illinois at Chicago - Survey Research Laboratory**. 412 S Peoria St., 6th Fl. Chicago, IL 60607. Phone: (312)996-5300; Fax: (312)996-3358 or (312)413-3358; Email: tjohnson@srl.uic.edu • URL: http://www.srl.uic.edu • Research areas include survey methodology and sampling techniques.

**University of Illinois at Springfield - Center for State Policy and Leadership**. Public Affairs Ctr., Rm. 409, 1 University Plz., MS PAC 409 Springfield, IL 62703-5407. Phone: (217)206-8417; Fax: (217)206-6542; Email: draci2@uis.edu • URL: http://cspl.uis.edu • Public problems and policies, focusing on applied research on the Illinois government, the judicial system, and state administrative agencies. Specific areas of study include social services, health policy, Illinois budgeting, public law and administrative rule making, law and public policy, patronage, capital punishment, abortion, and campaign and school financing. Also evaluates the effectiveness of government programs.

**University of Illinois at Urbana-Champaign - Bureau of Economic and Business Research**. 430 Wohlers Hall, Office of Research, College of Business, 1206 S 6th St. Champaign, IL 61820. Phone: (217)333-2330; Fax: (217)333-7410; Email: lhuff@uiuc.edu • URL: http://business.illinois.edu/research • Economics and business, including studies in business expectations, health economics, forecasting and planning, innovation, entrepreneurship, consumer behavior, poverty problems, small business operations and problems, investment and growth, productivity, research methodology, organizational behavior, and international business and banking.

**University of Illinois at Urbana-Champaign - Center for Cement Composite Materials**. 2129 Newmark Civil Engineering Laboratory, 205 Mathews Ave. Urbana, IL 61801. Phone: (217)333-2544 or (217)333-6900; Fax: (217)265-8040; Email: lstruble@uiuc.edu • URL: http://ccm.cee.uiuc.edu • Concrete, cement, and their constituent materials, including comprehensive interdisciplinary studies of advanced cement-based materials. Center works with high-performance materials such as DSP cements, MDF cements, and magnesium phosphate cements. Expertise includes electron microscopy, rheology, computer-based modeling, fracture, cement chemistry, and microstructure characterization.

**University of Illinois at Urbana-Champaign - Center for International Education and Research in Accounting**. 320 Wohlers Hall, 1206 S 6th St. Champaign, IL 61820. Phone: (217)333-4545; Fax: (217)244-6565; Email: ciera@uiuc.edu • URL: http://www.cba.uiuc.edu.

**University of Illinois at Urbana-Champaign - Office of Real Estate Research**. 140A Wohlers Hall, 1206 S 6th St. Champaign, IL 61820. Phone: (217)333-2278; Fax: (217)244-3102; Email: orer@illinois.edu • URL: http://business.illinois.edu/orer • Ongoing and contract studies on real estate issues, including appraisal and valuation, marketing and brokerage, environmental issues, land markets, municipal finance, property management, real estate investment, real estate financial markets, tenure choice, law, and public policy issues such as property rights, rent control, taxation, eminent domain, impact fees, etc.

**University of Indonesia - Faculty of Economics - Demographic Institute**. Gedung A, Lantai 2 & 3 16424 Depok, Indonesia. Phone: 62 21 7872911; Fax: 62 21 7872909 • URL: http://www.ld-feui.org • Demography, population, and development studies, including fertility, mortality, migration and urbanization, labor-force, health economics, human resources, and the economic environment.

**University of Iowa - Law, Health Policy and Disability Center**. 280-1 Boyd Law Bldg. Iowa City, IA 52242-1113. Phone: (319)335-8469; Fax: (319)335-9764; Email: helen-schartz@uiowa.edu • URL: http://disability.law.uiowa.edu • Legal, health policy and employment issues facing persons with disabilities.

**University of Iowa - McGladrey Institute of Accounting Education and Research**. 108 John Pappajohn Business Bldg., Henry B. Tippie College of Business Iowa City, IA 52242-1994. Phone: 800-553-4692 or (319)335-0958 or (319)335-0862; Fax: (319)335-1956; Email: mark-penno@uiowa.edu • URL: http://tippie.uiowa.edu/accounting/mcgladrey/index.cfm • Accounting, auditing, and financial reporting by public and private organizations.

**University of Iowa - Office of the Vice President for Research and Economic Development - Public Policy Center - Health Policy Research Program**. 209 S Quadrangle, 310 S Grand Ave. Iowa City, IA 52242-1192. Phone: (319)335-6867; Fax: (319)335-6801 • URL: http://ppc.uiowa.edu/health • Effects of policy initiatives and government activities on the cost, access, and quality of health care.

**University of Karachi - Applied Economics Research Center**. PO Box 8403 Karachi 75270, Pakistan. Phone: 92 21 99261541; Fax: 92 21 99261545; Email: aerc@cyber.net.pk • URL: http://www.aerc.edu.pk • Applied economics, focusing on the areas of urban and regional economics, agriculture, human resource development, poverty, health, public finance, nutrition and environment, and women's issues.

**University of Kent at Canterbury - Centre for Health Services**

Studies. Cornwallis Bldg., George Allen Wing Canterbury CT2 7NF, United Kingdom. Phone: 44 1227 824057; Fax: 44 1227 827868; Email: s.peckham@kent.ac.uk • URL: http://www.kent.ac.uk/chss • Recuperative care; aged in more care; health needs assessment for prisons; integrated health and social care for older persons, including issues, problems and solutions; stroke and rehabilitation, identification and management of risks of everyday life.

**University of Kent at Canterbury - School of Economics - Centre for European, Regional and Transport Economics.** Keynes College Canterbury CT2 7NP, United Kingdom. Phone: 44 1227 823642; Fax: 44 1227 827784 • URL: http://www.kent.ac.uk/economics/research/certe • Economics of Europe and the European Union, particularly on continuing work on aspects of transport and the regional development of the European Union, especially the role of transport infrastructure, building on the success of the Channel Tunnel Research Unit over the period 1986-93.

**University of Kentucky - Center for Applied Energy Research.** 2540 Research Park Dr. Lexington, KY 40511-8479. Phone: (859)257-0305; Fax: (859)257-0220; Email: rodney.andrews@uky.edu • URL: http://www.caer.uky.edua • Technical and environmental problems related to the use of coal for energy. Other areas of study include synthetic fuels and alternative energies such as biomass and solid waste conversion. Conducts joint research projects with coal companies, utilities, high technology industries, and government agencies to help bring new developments into practical application.

**University of Kentucky - College of Agriculture, Food and Environment - Kentucky Tobacco Research and Development Center.** Cooper & University Drs. Lexington, KY 40546-0236. Phone: (859)257-5798; Fax: (859)323-1077; Email: ochamb@uky.edu • URL: http://www2.ca.uky.edu/ktrdc/index.html • Application of biotechnology for the development of new crops based on tobacco and other plants. Development of new medicinal and industrial applications for plant natural products. Development of new crops from native plants and adaptation of existing crops for more efficient production of plant-made pharmaceuticals, plant-made industrial products, and plant natural products.

**University of Leeds - Faculty of Medicine and Health - Leeds Institute of Cancer and Pathology - Epidemiology and Biostatistics Section.** Cancer Genetics Bldg., St. James's University Hospital Leeds LS9 7TF, United Kingdom. Phone: 44 113 2064573 • URL: http://medhealth.leeds.ac.uk/info/920/epidemiology_and_biostatistics • Public health, health services and health policy.

**University of Liège - Center for Social Economy.** Bd du Rectorat, 3, Bat B33 Bte 4 4000 Liège, Belgium. Phone: 32 4 3662751; Fax: 32 4 3662851; Email: j.defourny@ulg.ac.be • URL: http://www.ces.ulg.ac.be • Social economy, focusing on conceptual approaches in industrialized countries, profiles and issues in developing countries, statistics on associations, the volunteer sector, public contracts and North-South relations.

**University of Liège - International and Interregional Economics Service.** Department of Economics, Blvd. du Rectorat, 7, Batiment B31, btc. 9 B-4000 Liège, Belgium. Phone: 32 4 3662965; Fax: 32 4 3662981; Email: jgazon@ulg.ac.be • URL: http://www.ecoint.hec.ulg.ac.be • Regional and urban economics, real estate, and international economics.

**University of London - Centre for the History of Science, Technology and Medicine.** Department of Humanities, Imperial College, S Kensington Campus London SW7 2AZ, United Kingdom. Phone: 44 20 75945220; Fax: 44 20 75949353; Email: a.warwick@imperial.ac.uk • URL: http://www3.imperial.ac.uk/historyofscience • History of science, technology, and medicine.

**University of Louisville - Department of Urban and Public Affairs - Urban Studies Institute.** 426 W Bloom St. Louisville, KY 40208. Phone: (502)852-2435; Fax: (502)852-7386; Email: upa@louisville.edu • URL: http://usi.louisville.edu • Social policy and economics.

**University of Maine - Canadian-American Center.** 154 College Ave. Orono, ME 04473. Phone: (207)581-4220; Fax: (207)581-4223; Email: hornsby@maine.edu • URL: http://www.umaine.edu/canam/ • Research areas include Canadian-American business, economics, and trade.

**University of Manchester - Centre on Regulation and Competition.** Harold Hankins Bldg., Precinct Ctr., Institute for Development Policy & Management, School of Environment & Development, Oxford Rd. Manchester M13 9QH, United Kingdom. Phone: 44 161 2752798; Fax: 44 161 2750808; Email: paul.cook@manchester.ac.uk • URL: http://www.competition-regulation.org.uk/ • Economic regulation and policy; regulatory impact assessment; competition, innovation and development; competition policy and development; institutional innovation in regulatory governance; regulations, politics and poverty.

**University of Manitoba - Faculty of Medicine - Department of Community Health Sciences - Manitoba Centre for Health Policy.** 408-727 McDermot Ave. Winnipeg, MB, Canada R3E 3P5. Phone: (204)789-3819; Fax: (204)789-3910; Email: info@cpe.umanitoba.ca • URL: http://umanitoba.ca/faculties/medicine/units/community_health_sciences/departmental_units/mchp • Health of Manitobans, focusing on health services, population and public health, and social determinants of health.

**University of Maryland at Baltimore - Center for Vaccine Development.** 685 W Baltimore St., Rm. 480 Baltimore, MD 21201-1509. Phone: (410)706-5328; Fax: (410)706-6205; Email: mlevine@medicine.umaryland.edu • URL: http://medschool.umaryland.edu/CVD • Bacterial diseases, parasitic diseases, viral diseases, novel delivery systems, combination vaccines and public health and policy.

**University of Maryland at College Park - Center for Automation Research.** A.V. Williams Bldg. 115, Rm. 4413 College Park, MD 20742-3275. Phone: (301)405-4526; Fax: (301)314-9115; Email: lsd@umiacs.umd.edu • URL: http://www.cfar.umd.edu • Automation, including computer vision, graphics, robotics, and perceptual interfaces.

**University of Maryland at College Park - Center for Global Business Education.** 2410 Van Munching Hall, Robert H. Smith School of Business College Park, MD 20742-1815. Phone: (301)405-0200; Fax: (301)314-9526; Email: lbarnard@rhsmith.umd.edu • URL: http://www.rhsmith.umd.edu/global • Global business and management.

**University of Maryland at College Park - Center for International Economics.** 3105 Tydings Hall, Department of Economics College Park, MD 20742. Phone: (301)405-3548; Fax: (301)405-3542; Email: mendozae@econ.umd.edu • URL: http://www.econ.umd.edu/about/centers/CIE • International economics.

**University of Maryland at College Park - International Communications and Negotiations Simulations.** 0145 Tydings Hall, Department of Government & Politics College Park, MD 20742. Phone: (301)405-4172; Fax: (301)314-9301; Email: dfridl@umd.edu • URL: http://www.icons.umd.edu • Focuses on the critical connections between international issues and the perspectives that different cultures bring to negotiations. Also teaches cross cultural negotiation and develops international economic, environmental, and political scenarios/curriculum materials for university and high school students.

**University of Maryland, Baltimore County - Maryland Institute for Policy Analysis and Research.** 428 Public Policy Bldg., 1000 Hilltop Cir. Baltimore, MD 21250. Phone: (410)455-1080; Fax: (410)455-1084; Email: mipar_info@umbc.edu • URL: http://www.umbc.edu/mipar/ • Significant issues of public policy, including public welfare, public housing, emergency health services, health policy, computers and information management, juvenile justice, family literacy, minority contracting programs, and childcare.

**University of Maryland - Institute for Governmental Service and Research.** 4321 Hartwick Rd., Ste. 208 College Park, MD 20742-3225. Phone: (301)405-4905; Fax: (301)314-9258; Email: bgr@bgr.umd.edu • URL: http://www.igsr.umd.edu/about_IGSR/history.php.

**University of Massachusetts at Amherst - Political Economy Research Institute.** Gordon Hall, Ste. A, 418 N Pleasant St. Amherst, MA 01002. Phone: (413)545-6355; Fax: (413)577-0261; Email: gepstein@econs.umass.edu • URL: http://www.peri.umass.edu • Human and ecological well-being in both advanced and developing economies. Areas of interest include globalization and macroeconomics, labor markets and living wages; and development, peace building, and the environment.

**University of Massachusetts at Amherst - West Experiment Station - Soil and Plant Tissue Testing Laboratory.** 682 N Pleasant St. Amherst, MA 01003. Phone: (413)545-2311; Fax: (413)545-1931; Email: veneman@psis.umass.edu • URL: http://soiltest.umass.edu • Soil and plant tissue.

**University of Massachusetts at Worcester - Medical School - Center for Health Policy and Research.** 333 South St. Shrewsbury, MA 01545. Phone: (508)856-3124; Fax: (508)856-6100; Email: chpr@umassmed.edu • URL: http://chpr.umassmed.edu • Health policy.

**University of Melbourne - Faculty of Business and Economics - Melbourne Institute of Applied Economic and Social Research.** Business and Economics Bldg., Level 5, 111 Barry St. Melbourne, VIC 3010, Australia. Phone: 61 3 83442100; Fax: 61 3 83442111; Email: melb-inst-director@unimelb.edu.au • URL: http://www.melbourneinstitute.com • Economic performance, including business cycles, economic growth, performance and dynamics of Australian enterprises and social economics, including unemployment and labor markets, taxation, welfare, income distribution, poverty, development of social indicators.

**University of Michigan - Center for Statistical Consultation and Research.** 3550 Rackham, 915 E Washington St. Ann Arbor, MI 48109-1070. Phone: (734)764-7828; Fax: (734)647-2440; Email: cscar@umich.edu • URL: http://cscar.research.umich.edu • Statistical analysis and statistical computing techniques. Provides statistical consulting service and data analysis for graduate students and faculty of the University. Also provides statistical software support.

**University of Michigan - Collaboratory for Research on Electronic Work.** School of Information N, Rm. 2226, 1075 Beal Ave. Ann Arbor, MI 48109-2112. Phone: (734)764-6131; Fax: (734)647-8045; Email: finholt@umich.edu • URL: http://www.crew.umich.edu/about.html • Concerned with the design and use of computer-based tools for thinking and planning in the professional office.

**University of Michigan Energy Institute** . Michigan Memorial Phoenix Laboratory, 2301 Bonisteel Blvd. Ann Arbor, MI 48109-2100. Phone: (734)763-7401; Fax: (734)763-9232; Email: umichenergy@umich.edu • URL: http://www.energy.umich.edu • Conducts research in peaceful uses of nuclear energy.

**University of Michigan - Erb Institute for Global Sustainable Enterprise.** Dana Bldg., 440 Church St. Ann Arbor, MI 48109-1234. Phone: (734)647-9799; Fax: (734)647-8551; Email: tplyon@umich.edu • URL: http://erb.umich.edu • Understanding the complex dynamics of coupled human and natural systems in relation to economic activity. Research addresses four questions: how can dynamic interactions between nature and society, including lags and inertia, be incorporated into emerging models and conceptualizations that integrate the Earth system, human development, and sustainability; how are long-term trends in environment and development, including consumption and population, reshaping nature-society interactions in ways relevant to sustainability; what systems of incentive structures, including markets, rules, norms, and scientific information, can most effectively improve social capacity to guide interactions between nature and society toward more sustainable trajectories; and how can today's operational systems for monitoring and reporting on environmental and social conditions be integrated and extended to prove guidance for efforts to navigate a transition toward sustainability.

**University of Michigan - Health Management Research Center.** 1015 E Huron St. Ann Arbor, MI 48104-1688. Phone: (734)763-2462; Fax: (734)763-2206; Email: hmrc-contact@umich.edu • URL: http://www.hmrc.umich.edu • Examines the relationships between lifestyle behaviors, quality of life, organizational productivity, and health care costs.

**University of Michigan - Institute for Social Research - Inter-University Consortium for Political and Social Research.** 330 Packard St. Ann Arbor, MI 48104. Phone: 888-741-7242 or (734)615-8400 or (734)615-7652; Fax: (734)647-8200; Email: netmail@icpsr.umich.edu • URL: http://www.icpsr.umich.edu/icpsrweb/landing.jsp • Cooperative partnership among institutions of higher education represented by libraries and departments of political science, history, sociology, and related disciplines concerned with the systematic study of political and social behavior. Seeks to facilitate research in the social sciences by: developing a major data repository providing access to basic research materials; conducting an advanced training program providing formal course work in methodology, research techniques, and substantive fields for advanced graduate students and faculty; stimulating new research projects; consulting in computer support needs. Makes available technical facilities to scholars from member institutions. Data repository holdings include survey, election, census, and roll call data, representing nations throughout the world.

**University of Michigan - Research Seminar in Quantitative Economics.** Lorch Hall, Rm. M116, Department of Economics, 611 Tappan St. Ann Arbor, MI 48109. Phone: (734)764-2567; Fax: (734)763-1307; Email: rsqe-admin@umich.edu • URL: http://www.rsqe.econ.lsa.umich.edu • Development and application of econometric techniques to matters of public policy, also construction of large economy-wide and state-wide econometric models for forecasting and policy analysis.

**University of Michigan - Stephen M. Ross School of Business - Office of Tax Policy Research.** 701 Tappan St., Rm. R5380 Ann Arbor, MI 48109-1234. Phone: (734)763-3068; Fax: (734)763-4032; Email: jslemrod@umich.edu • URL: http://www.bus.umich.edu/OTPR/ • Tax policy, including compliance, capital gains, reform, international taxation, and income dynamics.

**University of Michigan - Transportation Research Institute.** 2901 Baxter Rd. Ann Arbor, MI 48109-2150. Phone: (734)764-6504; Fax: (734)936-1081; Email: umtri-director@umich.edu • URL: http://www.umtri.umich.edu • Research areas include highway safety, transportation systems, and shipbuilding.

**University of Minnesota - Corrosion Research Center.** 112 Amundson Hall, 421 Washington Ave. Minneapolis, MN 55455. Phone: (612)625-0014 or (612)625-1313; Fax: (612)626-7246; Email: dshores@umn.edu • URL: http://www.cems.umn.edu/research/crc • Research areas include the effect of corrosion on high technology materials and devices.

**University of Minnesota - Division of Health Policy and Management.** School of Public Health, MMC 729, 420 Delaware St. SE Minneapolis, MN 55455-0392. Phone: (612)624-6151; Fax: (612)624-2196; Email: mosco001@umn.edu • URL: http://www.sph.umn.edu/hpm • Fields of research include health insurance, consumer choice of health plans, quality of care, and long-term care.

**University of Minnesota, Duluth - Center for Economic Development.** 11 E Superior St., Ste. 210 Duluth, MN 55802. Phone: 888-387-4594 or (218)726-7298; Fax: (218)726-6338; Email: umdced@d.umn.edu • URL: http://www.umdced.com • Economic development and innovation, including management training and innovation commercialization.

**University of Minnesota - Hubert H. Humphrey Institute of Public Affairs.** 301 19th Ave. S Minneapolis, MN 55455. Phone: (612)625-0669 or (612)626-8910; Fax: (612)625-

3513 or (612)626-6351; Email: jbatwood@umn.edu • URL: http://www.hhh.umn.edu • Studies strategic management in both the private and the public sectors.

**University of Minnesota - Minnesota Population Center.** 50 Willey Hall, 225 - 19th Ave. S Minneapolis, MN 55455. Phone: (612)624-5818; Fax: (612)626-8375; Email: mpc@umn.edu • URL: http://www.pop.umn.edu • Historical demography, population geography, economics, public health, and family and life course demography.

**University of Mississippi - Center for Pharmaceutical Marketing and Management.** Faser Hall Rms. 128-136, School of Pharmacy University, MS 38677. Phone: (662)915-5352 or (662)915-5948; Fax: (662)915-5262; Email: benb3@olemiss.edu • URL: http://www.pharmacy.olemiss.edu/cpmm • Proprietary and in-house marketing and management studies relating to pharmaceutical products, including formulary decision factors, generic substitution, reimbursement issues, medication compliance and consumer preferences. Conducts mail surveys, telephone interviews, focus groups, internet surveys, consumer reaction panels, and surveys of professionals at national and state meetings.

**University of Missouri—Columbia - Business Research and Information Development Group.** 410 S 6th St., 200 Engineering N Columbia, MO 65211. Phone: (573)882-8855; Fax: (573)884-4297; Email: schmidtdc@missouri.edu • URL: http://www.bridg.org • Entrepreneurship, small business development and growth.

**University of Missouri—Kansas City - Center for Economic Information.** 210 Haag Hall, Department of Economics, 5211 Rockhill Rd. Kansas City, MO 64110. Phone: (816)235-2832; Fax: (816)235-2834; Email: eatonp@umkc.edu • URL: http://cei.umkc.edu • Provides local, regional, and national information and analysis to economic decision-makers in the Kansas City metropolitan area.

**University of Missouri—St. Louis - Center for Business and Industrial Studies.** 220 Express Scripts Hall, 1 University Dr. Saint Louis, MO 63121-4499. Phone: (314)516-6108 or (314)516-5451; Email: ldsmith@umsl.edu • URL: http://www.umsl.edu/divisions/business/ncbis/index.html • Research fields include inventory and management control. Specific projects also include development of computer software for operations in public transit systems.

**University of Montana - Bureau of Business and Economic Research.** Gallagher Business Bldg., 32 Campus Dr., Rm. 6840 Missoula, MT 59812-6840. Phone: (406)243-4831 or (406)243-5113; Fax: (406)243-2086 or (406)248-2086 • URL: http://www.bber.umt.edu • Business, economics, and other social sciences, including regional economic analysis and forecasting emphasizing Montana and the northern Rocky Mountain region, forest industry analysis and data collection, survey research, and public opinion surveys. Provides Montana business community with statistical data and interpretation and disseminates general information on economic conditions and prospects in the state.

**University of Navarra - International Research Center on Organizations.** IESE Business School, Camino del Cerro del Águila, 3 E-28023 Madrid, Spain. Phone: 34 91 2113000; Fax: 34 91 3572913; Email: info@iese.edu • URL: http://www.iese.edu/en/Research/CentersandChairs/Centers/IRCO/Homeirco/IRCOInternationalResearchCenterforOrganizations.asp • Business, strategic management of human resources in organizations, management models, international human relations, and leadership and motivation.

**University of Nebraska—Lincoln - Agricultural Research Division.** 207 Agricultural Hall Lincoln, NE 68583-0704. Phone: (402)472-2045; Fax: (402)472-9071; Email: aclutter2@unl.edu.

**University of Nebraska—Omaha - Nebraska Business Development Center.** Mammel Hall, Ste. 200, College of Business Administration, 6708 Pine St. Omaha, NE 68182. Phone: (402)554-2521; Fax: (402)554-3473; Email: rbernier@unomaha.edu • URL: http://nbdc.unomaha.edu • Sustainable development, technology commercialization, management education, market research, marketing plans, strategic planning, financial planning, cash flow budgeting, capital budgeting, loan packaging, and rural development.

**University of New Brunswick - Canadian Research Institute for Social Policy.** Keirstead Hall, Ste. 300 Fredericton, NB, Canada E3B 5A3. Phone: (506)447-3178; Fax: (506)447-3427; Email: crisp@unb.ca • URL: http://www.unb.ca/research/institutes/crisp • Social policy in Canada, especially policy affecting education, child care, and health.

**University of New England - Center for Health Policy, Planning and Research.** Linnell Hall, 716 Stevens Ave. Portland, ME 04103. Phone: (207)221-4560; Fax: (207)523-1914; Email: rdeprez@une.edu • URL: http://www.une.edu/chppr • Healthcare improvement initiatives in communities, health systems, regions and countries, especially for patients with chronic medical conditions.

**University of New Hampshire - College of Health and Human Services - New Hampshire Institute for Health Policy and Practice.** Hewitt Hall, Ste. 202, 4 Library Way Durham, NH 03824. Phone: (603)862-5031; Fax: (603)862-4457 • URL: http://chhs.unh.edu/ihpp • Health policy and practice for the citizens of New Hampshire, focusing on community health, Medicaid policy, and adolescent health.

**University of New Hampshire - International Private Enterprise Center.** Peter T. Paul College of Business & Economics, 10 Garrison Ave. Durham, NH 03824. Phone: (603)862-3354; Fax: (603)862-3383; Email: frk@christa.unh.edu • URL: http://paulcollege.unh.edu/international-private-enterprise-center • Public policy and managerial strategies to enhance private sector economic growth.

**University of New Mexico - Institute of Public Law.** 1117 Stanford NE, MSC11 6070, 1 University of New Mexico Albuquerque, NM 87131-0001. Phone: (505)277-5006; Fax: (505)277-7064; Email: lambert@law.unm.edu • URL: http://lawschool.unm.edu/ipl/index.php • Public law and policy analysis.

**University of New Orleans - Division of Business and Economic Research.** 315 Kirshman Hall, College of Business Administration, 2000 Lakeshore Dr. New Orleans, LA 70148. Phone: (504)280-6240; Fax: (504)280-6094; Email: jspeyrer@uno.edu • URL: http://www.uno.edu/coba/DBER/index.aspx • Business, economic, and demographic characteristics and trends at local, state, and national levels. Also studies local economic forecasting and tourism.

**University of New South Wales - Centre for Clinical Governance Research.** AGSM Bldg., Level 1, Faculty of Medicine Sydney, NSW 2052, Australia. Phone: 61 2 93853861; Fax: 61 2 96634926; Email: j.braithwaite@unsw.edu.au • URL: http://www.aihi.unsw.edu.au/ccgr • Role of clinicians in health care delivery and why and how this is being affected by changes in the social, legal, economic, organizational, informational and political contexts of health service organizations.

**University of Newcastle upon Tyne - Cultures, Imperialism and Accounting Practice Research Group.** Ridley Bldg., Business School Newcastle upon Tyne NE1 7RU, United Kingdom. Phone: 44 191 2227586; Email: s.s.k.davie@newcastle.ac.uk • URL: http://www.ncl.ac.uk/niassh/ciap/index.htm • History of accounting across cultures and its relation to economics, politics, and society.

**University of North Carolina at Chapel Hill - Carolina Population Center.** University Sq., CB 8120, 123 W Franklin St. Chapel Hill, NC 27516-2524. Phone: (919)966-2157 or (919)966-2152; Fax: (919)966-6638; Email: pmorgan@unc.edu • URL: http://www.cpc.unc.edu • Coordinates on a University-wide basis, an interdisciplinary program in population research and research training. Activities encompass social, behavioral and health sciences, including anthropology, biostatistics, city and regional planning, economics, epidemiology, family medicine, geography, health behavior and education, maternal and child health, nutrition, obstetrics and gynecology, political science, psychology, health policy and administration, sociology, business administration, and journalism. Serves as a link between the university and related institutions and agencies in the U.S. and abroad.

**University of North Carolina at Chapel Hill - Odum Institute for Research in Social Science.** Davis Library, 2nd Fl., CB 3355 Chapel Hill, NC 27599. Phone: (919)962-3061; Fax: (919)962-2875; Email: carsey@unc.edu • URL: http://www.odum.unc.edu/odum/home2.jsp • Sociology, anthropology, psychology, political science, city and regional planning, journalism, economics, history, geography, religion, education, business administration, library science, law, public health, survey methodology, digital archives and curation, and social work.

**University of Northern Iowa - College of Social and Behavioral Sciences - Center for Social and Behavioral Research.** 2304 College St. Cedar Falls, IA 50614-0402. Phone: (319)273-2105; Fax: (319)273-3104; Email: gene.lutz@uni.edu • URL: http://www.uni.edu/csbr/ • Geography, history, home economics, political science, psychology, sociology, anthropology, criminology, social work, and public policy, including studies on adolescents, adult education, airline passengers, airports, educational needs assessment, elderly, environmental impact assessment, highways, human services needs assessment, outdoor recreation, radio listening habits, substance abuse, and television viewing habits. Performs feasibility studies on proposed projects such as sports complexes and auditoriums. Conducts special surveys for groups, organizations, localities, regions, and social aggregates.

**University of Oklahoma - Mewbourne College of Earth and Energy - Energy Institute of the Americas.** Sarkeys Energy Ctr., Rm. 1510, 100 E Boyd Norman, OK 73019-1006. Phone: (405)325-4753 or (405)325-3821; Fax: (405)325-3180 or (405)325-6621; Email: ywalschap@ou.edu • URL: http://www.ou.edu/content/mcee/international_programs/energy_instituteoftheamericas.html • Energy resources and related environmental issues in the Americas. Recognizing the interdependence of the Americas with respect to energy resources, development, technology and supply, the institute engages in activities that promote energy sector growth that is economically and environmentally sound. The institute also seeks to further greater hemispheric self-sufficiency through dependable and competitively priced energy, expand national, integrated economies and increase the quality of life for the peoples of the Americas.

**University of Oklahoma - Michael F. Price College of Business - Center for Economic and Management Research.** 307 W Brooks, Ste. 4 Norman, OK 73019. Phone: (405)325-3611; Fax: (405)325-7688; Email: pricecollege@ou.edu • URL: http://www.ou.edu/price/cemr.html • Business and economic problems, including studies on business conditions, energy demand, utilization of human resources, economic development, and business trends in the state. Conducts feasibility analyses, market surveys, impact studies, production analyses, socioeconomic statistical analyses and estimates, and compilation and interpretation of economic data. Develops new techniques of data analysis and maintains an extensive database.

**University of Oregon - Solar Energy Center.** Department of Physics, 1274 University of Oregon Eugene, OR 97403-1274. Phone: (541)346-4745 or (541)346-3656; Fax: (541)346-5861 • URL: http://uocatalog.uoregon.edu/graduatestudies/research%20institutes%20and%20centers • Solar resource monitoring and assessment, and analysis of climate in terms of architectural response.

**University of Oslo - Ragnar Frisch Centre for Economic Research.** Gaustadalléen 21 N-0349 Oslo, Norway. Phone: 47 22958810; Fax: 47 22958825; Email: oddbjorn.raaum@frisch.uio.no • URL: http://www.frisch.uio.no/ • Applied economics.

**University of Oxford - Centre for Socio-Legal Studies.** Manor Rd. Oxford OX1 3UQ, United Kingdom. Phone: 44 1865 284220; Fax: 44 1865 284221; Email: fernanda.pirie@csls.ox.ac.uk • URL: http://www.csls.ox.ac.uk • Law and society, including studies on government, regulation, family law, business law, dispute resolution, public international law, media studies.

**University of Oxford - Centre for the Study of African Economies.** Department of Economics, Manor Rd. Oxford OX1 3UQ, United Kingdom. Phone: 44 1865 271084; Fax: 44 1865 281447; Email: paul.collier@economics.ox.ac.uk • URL: http://www.csae.ox.ac.uk • African economies, developing economies.

**University of Oxford - Department of Education - Centre on Skills, Knowledge and Organisational Performance.** 15 Norham Gardens Oxford OX2 6PY, United Kingdom. Phone: 44 1865 611030; Fax: 44 1865 611031; Email: skope@education.ox.ac.uk • URL: http://www.skope.ox.ac.uk • Link between acquisition and use of skills and knowledge, product market strategies, and economic development.

**University of Oxford - St. Antony's College - Asian Studies Centre.** 62 Woodstock Rd. Oxford OX2 6JF, United Kingdom. Phone: 44 1865 274559; Fax: 44 1865 274559; Email: rachel.murphy@sant.ox.ac.uk • URL: http://www.sant.ox.ac.uk/asian • Politics, economics, history, anthropology and international relations of East, Southeast, Northeast and South Asia.

**University of Pennsylvania - Center for Analytical Research in Economics and the Social Sciences.** 3718 Locust Walk Philadelphia, PA 19104-6297. Phone: (215)898-5735 • URL: http://economics.sas.upenn.edu/research • Economic theory and related mathematics.

**University of Pennsylvania - Center for Bioethics.** c/o Dr. Arthur L. Caplan, Director, 3401 Market St. Philadelphia, PA 19104-3318. Fax: (215)573-3036 • URL: http://www.pennmedicine.org/lung/research/centers-institutes/center-for-bioethics.html • Works as an interdisciplinary unit of the University of Pennsylvania Health System; seeks to advance scholarly and public understanding of ethical, legal, social and public policy issues in healthcare. Conducts research aimed at improving the practice and delivery of medical care. Offers degree programs. Maintains speakers' bureau.

**University of Pennsylvania - Center for Human Resources.** 204 Steinberg Hall/Dietrich Hall, The Wharton School, 3620 Locust Walk Philadelphia, PA 19104-6302. Phone: (215)898-5606; Fax: (215)898-5908; Email: cappelli@wharton.upenn.edu • URL: http://chr.wharton.upenn.edu • U.S. and international manpower issues, labor-management relations, human resources management and related areas.

**University of Pennsylvania - Leonard Davis Institute of Health Economics.** Colonial Penn Ctr., 3641 Locust Walk Philadelphia, PA 19104-6218. Phone: (215)898-5611 or (215)898-1657; Fax: (215)898-0229; Email: polsky@mail.med.upenn.edu • URL: http://ldi.upenn.edu • Research fields include health care management and cost-quality trade-offs.

**University of Pennsylvania - S.S. Huebner Foundation.** 3000 Steinberg Hall-Dietrich Hall, 3620 Locust Walk Philadelphia, PA 19104-6302. Phone: (215)898-9631; Fax: (215)573-2218; Email: huebner_foundation@wharton.upenn.edu • URL: http://www.huebnergeneva.org/huebner • Awards grants for research in various areas of insurance.

**University of Pennsylvania - Institute for Law and Economics.** 3501 Sansom St. Philadelphia, PA 19104. Phone: (215)898-7719; Fax: (215)573-2025; Email: mwachter@law.upenn.edu • URL: http://www.law.upenn.edu/academics/institutes/ile • Applies economic analysis in law to major policy issues affecting business and government, including economic analysis of common law doctrine, taxation and tax policy, public finance, labor market regulation, antitrust, financial institutions, and commercial law and industrial organization. Jointly conducts programs with the Law and Wharton Schools and the Department of Economics.

**University of Pennsylvania - Office of Research Services.** 3451 Walnut St., Rm. P-221 Philadelphia, PA 19104-6205. Phone: (215)898-7293; Fax: (215)898-9708; Email: epeloso@upenn.edu • URL: http://www.upenn.edu/researchservices • Administers extramurally sponsored research for all departments and research units of the University and handles processing of research applications, financial reporting, and indirect cost proposal preparation.

**University of Pennsylvania - School of Nursing - Center for Health Outcomes and Policy Research**. Fagin Hall, Rm. 387, 418 Curie Blvd. Philadelphia, PA 19104-4217. Phone: (215)898-5673; Email: laiken@nursing.upenn.edu • URL: http://www.nursing.upenn.edu/chopr/Pages/default.aspx • Health care and workforce organization, financing, and outcomes; and public policies that influence nursing and health care delivery nationally and internationally.

**University of Pennsylvania - Wharton School - SEI Center for Advanced Studies in Management**. 700 Jon M. Huntsman Hall, 3730 Walnut St. Philadelphia, PA 19104-6340. Phone: (215)898-8267 or (215)898-6848; Email: windj@wharton.upenn.edu • URL: http://seicenter.wharton.upenn.edu • Conducts interdisciplinary management studies.

**University of Pennsylvania - The Wharton School - Rodney L. White Center for Financial Research**. 3254 Steinberg Hall-Dietrich Hall Philadelphia, PA 19104-6367. Phone: (215)898-7616; Fax: (215)573-8084; Email: rlwctr@finance.wharton.upenn.edu • URL: http://rodneywhitecenter.wharton.upenn.edu • Research areas include financial management, money markets, real estate finance, and international finance.

**University of Pittsburgh - Business, Government, and Society Research Institute**. School of Business, Mervis Hall Pittsburgh, PA 15260. Phone: (412)648-1555; Fax: (412)648-1693; Email: mitnick@pitt.edu.

**University of Quebec at Montreal - Centre for Interdisciplinary Research on Science and Technology**. Succursale Centre-Ville, C.P. 8888 Montreal, QC, Canada H3C 3P8. Phone: (514)987-4018; Fax: (514)987-7726; Email: doray.pierre@uqam.ca • URL: http://www.cirst.uqam.ca • Economics, management, policy, and history of science and technology.

**University of Quebec at Trois-Rivieres - Research Institute for Small and Medium-Sized Enterprises**. Pavillon Desjardins-Hydro-Quebec, 3351, Blvd. des Forges Trois-Rivieres, QC, Canada G9A 5H7. Phone: (819)376-5235; Fax: (819)376-5138; Email: inrpme@uqtr.ca • URL: http://oraprdnt.uqtr.uquebec.ca/pls/public/gscw030?owa_no_site=861 • Small business and entrepreneurship, including management, strategy, finance, operation, marketing, information systems innovation, regional sciences, and economics.

**University of Reading - Centre for International Business History**. Henley Business School, Whiteknights Reading RG6 6UD, United Kingdom. Phone: 44 118 3785435; Fax: 44 118 3784029; Email: p.m.scott@henley.ac.uk • URL: http://www.henley.reading.ac.uk/research/research-centres/the-centre-for-international-business-history • Empirical research on the past of business to concepts and theories developed in economics, management, and other disciplines.

**University of Rhode Island - Air Pollution Research Laboratory**. 121 Wales Hall Kingston, RI 02881. Phone: (401)874-2535; Fax: (401)874-2355 • URL: http://ww2.uri.edu.

**University of Rhode Island - Research Center in Business and Economics**. College of Business Administration, 7 Lippitt Rd. Kingston, RI 02881. Phone: (401)874-2549; Fax: (401)874-4825; Email: rcbe@etal.uri.edu • URL: http://www.cba.uri.edu/research/rcbe/ • Services research activities of faculty members of the College in fields of accounting, business law, economics, finance, insurance, management, marketing, and quantitative analysis. Conducts survey research, economic analyses, and business-related research projects on a contract basis.

**University of Rochester - Bradley Policy Research Center**. 305 Schlegel Hall, William E Simon Graduate School of Business Rochester, NY 14627. Phone: (585)275-3316 or (585)275-2668; Fax: (585)275-0095; Email: sue.north@simon.rochester.edu • URL: http://www.simon.rochester.edu/faculty—research/research-center-and-conferences/bradley-policy-research-center/index.aspx • Corporate control and corporate takeovers are among the research areas covered.

**University of Rochester - Institute of Optics**. Wilmot Bldg., 275 Hutchison Rd. Rochester, NY 14627-0186. Phone: (585)275-2322; Fax: (585)244-4936; Email: xi-cheng.zhang@rochester.edu • URL: http://www.optics.rochester.edu • Fourier optics, quantum optics, electro- and acousto-optics, geometrical optics, optoelectronics, fiber optics, image processing, image-forming systems, holography, optical processing, laser engineering, ultra-high resolutive dye laser spectroscopy, integrated optics, automatic lens design, testing, and fabrication, optical and electronic properties of solids, thin films, gradient index optics, and nonlinear optics.

**University of St. Gallen - Institute for Business Ethics**. Tannenstrasse 19 CH-9000 Saint Gallen, Switzerland. Phone: 41 71 2242644; Fax: 41 71 2242881; Email: ethik@unisg.ch • URL: http://www.iwe.unisg.ch • Economic ethics, including normative fundamentals of economics as a scientific discipline, crisis reflection of economics in industrial societies, business ethics, political philosophy, and sociology.

**University of St. Gallen - Swiss Institute for International Economics and Applied Economic Research**. Bodanstrasse 8 CH-9000 Saint Gallen, Switzerland. Phone: 41 71 2242340; Fax: 41 71 2242298; Email: gabriela.schmid@unisg.ch • URL: http://www.siaw.unisg.ch • Applied economics, economic policy, and international economics.

**University of San Diego - Center for Public Interest Law**. School of Law, 5998 Alcalá Park San Diego, CA 92110. Phone: (619)260-4806; Fax: (619)260-4753 • URL: http://www.cpil.org • State regulation of business, professions, and trades, including the Public Utilities Commission, Department of Insurance, Medical Board of California, and the State Bar.

**University of Saskatchewan - International Centre for Northern Governance and Development**. Kirk Hall, Rm. 234, 117 Science Pl. Saskatoon, SK, Canada S7N 5C8. Phone: (306)966-1665; Fax: (306)966-7780 • URL: http://artsandscience.usask.ca/icngd/ • Governance and development in three areas: capacity building for legal and judicial reform, knowledge development on market economy and social development interrelationships, and policy analysis for good governance.

**University of South Carolina at Columbia - College of Arts and Sciences - Institute for Public Service and Policy Research**. 1600 Hampton St., Rm. 402 Columbia, SC 29208. Phone: (803)777-4566 or (803)777-4568; Fax: (803)777-4575; Email: roldendi@mailbox.sc.edu • URL: http://www.ipspr.sc.edu • State and local government, with special emphasis on South Carolina, urban policy, public finance and health policy.

**University of Southern California - Information Sciences Institute**. 4676 Admiralty Way, Ste. 1001 Marina del Rey, CA 90292. Phone: (310)822-1511; Fax: (310)823-6714; Email: vcomms@usc.edu • URL: http://www.isi.edu/home • Research fields include online information and computer science, with emphasis on the World Wide Web.

**University of Southern California - Integrated Media Systems Center**. 306 Powell Hall of Engineering, 3737 Watt Way Los Angeles, CA 90089-0272. Phone: (213)740-8945; Fax: (213)740-2539; Email: shahabi@usc.edu • URL: http://imsc.usc.edu • Media areas for research include education, mass communication, and entertainment.

**University of Southern California - Tlargi Rubber Technology Foundation**. Los Angeles, CA 90089-1211. Phone: (213)740-2225; Fax: (213)740-8053; Email: salove@almaak.usc.edu.

**University of Stellenbosch - Faculty of Arts and Social Sciences - Department of Philosophy - Center for Applied Ethics**. Private Bag X1 Matieland 7602, South Africa. Phone: 27 21 8082055; Fax: 27 21 8083556 • URL: http://sun025.sun.ac.za/portal/page/portal/Arts/Departments/philosophy/cae • Bioethics, environmental and business ethics.

**University of Stockholm - Institute for International Economic Studies**. S-106 91 Stockholm, Sweden. Phone: 46 8 162000; Fax: 46 8 161443; Email: harry.flam@iies.su.se • URL: http://www.iies.su.se • International economics, macroeconomics, public finance, industrial organization.

**University of Strathclyde - Fraser of Allander Institute**. Sir William Duncan Bldg., 130 Rottenrow Glasgow G4 0GE, United Kingdom. Phone: 44 141 5483958; Fax: 44 141 5485776; Email: fraser@strath.ac.uk • URL: http://www.strath.ac.uk/fraser • Scottish economy, including studies in regional economics, input-output analysis, econometric modeling, labor economics, and economic development. Institute's goals include: analysis and forecasting of short-term trends in the Scottish economy; long-term analysis of prospective trends in the Scottish economy (Medium Term Model); applied computable general equilibrium modeling; compilation, updating, and maintenance of the Scottish Economic Data Bank; and portfolio of applied economics research projects.

**University of Sydney - Effective Healthcare Australia**. Victor Coppleson Bldg. D02 Sydney, NSW 2006, Australia. Phone: 61 2 93514378; Fax: 61 2 93515204; Email: grubin@med.usyd.edu.au • URL: http://www.eha.usyd.edu.au/ • Clinical and public health care improvement and health care policy in the Asia Pacific region.

**University of Sydney - George Institute for Global Health**. Missenden Rd. Sydney, NSW 2050, Australia. Phone: 61 2 96570300; Fax: 61 2 96570301; Email: info@georgeinstitute.org.au • URL: http://www.georgeinstitute.org/ • Chronic disease and injury, particularly involving the heart and vascular system; epidemiology and biostatistics; injury prevention and trauma care; mental health; and medical policy and practice.

**University of Tennessee at Knoxville - Municipal Technical Advisory Service Library**. 600 Henley St., Ste. 120 Knoxville, TN 37996-4105. Phone: (865)974-0411; Fax: (865)974-0423; Email: steve.thompson@tennessee.edu • URL: http://www.mtas.tennessee.edu/web2012.nsf/Web/Home • Research areas include municipal finance, police administration, and public works.

**University of Tennessee at Knoxville - Waste Management Research and Education Institute**. Energy, Environment & Resources Ctr., 311 Conference Ctr. Bldg. Knoxville, TN 37996-4134. Phone: (865)974-4251 or (865)974-1000; Fax: (865)974-1838; Email: barkenbu@utk.edu • URL: http://eerc.ra.utk.edu/WMREI.html • Research fields include chemical, nuclear, and solid waste management, especially waste policy and environmental biotechnology studies.

**University of Tennessee at Tullahoma - Center for Laser Applications**. 411 B.H. Goethert Pkwy. Tullahoma, TN 37388. Phone: (931)393-7466; Fax: (931)454-2271; Email: hof@utsi.edu • URL: http://cla.utsi.edu • In addition to

research, provides technical assistance relating to the industrial use of lasers.

**University of Texas at Austin - Applied Research Laboratories**. PO Box 8029 Austin, TX 78713-8029. Phone: (512)835-3200; Fax: (512)835-3259; Email: webcontactUs@arlut.utexas.edu • URL: http://www.arlut.utexas.edu • Sonar systems, underwater acoustics, satellite tracking, high accuracy positioning using satellite systems, industrial acoustics, biomedical acoustics, network security, information assurance, digital communications, electromagnetic security systems.

**University of Texas at Austin - Artificial Intelligence Laboratory**. Department of Computer Science, 2317 Speedway, 2.302 Austin, TX 78712. Phone: (512)471-9565; Fax: (512)471-8885; Email: porter@cs.utexas.edu • URL: http://www.cs.utexas.edu/ai-lab • Artificial intelligence, physics problem solving, automatic programming, natural language understanding, neural networks, automatic theorem proving, machine learning, logical foundations of artificial intelligence, qualitative reasoning, and robotics.

**University of Texas at Austin - Bureau of Economic Geology**. 10100 Burnet Rd. Austin, TX 78758-4445. Phone: (512)471-1534; Fax: (512)471-0140; Email: scott.tinker@beg.utexas.edu • URL: http://www.beg.utexas.edu • Energy, the environment, hydrogeology, geologic mapping, and coastal studies.

**University of Texas at Austin - Center for Aeromechanics Research**. WRW 201B, Mail Code C060, Department of Aerospace Engineering and Engineering Mechanics, Cockrell School of Engineering Austin, TX 78712-1085. Phone: (512)471-3110 or (512)471-5962; Fax: (512)471-3788; Email: varghese@mail.utexas.edu • URL: http://research.ae.utexas.edu/car • Aeroelasticity and structural dynamics; control of flexible structures; flight structures; supersonic and hypersonic shock-induced separated flows; turbulence; combustion; transient chemically reacting flow models for the study of glow discharges and semiconductor process plasmas; plasma thrusters; micro-plasma discharges; rarefied and non-equilibrium flows; low density planetary atmospheres; optical diagnostics and laser-based sensor development.

**University of Texas at Austin - Center for Health and Social Policy**. Lyndon B. Johnson School of Public Affairs Austin, TX 78713-8925. Phone: (512)232-3423; Email: cheinrich@austin.utexas.edu • URL: http://www.utexas.edu/lbj/chasp • Health and social policy.

**University of Texas at Austin - Center for Transportation Research**. 1616 Guadalupe St., Ste. 4.202, MC D9300 Austin, TX 78701. Phone: (512)232-3100; Fax: (512)232-3153; Email: bhat@mail.utexas.edu • URL: http://www.utexas.edu/research/ctr • Coordinates and develops highway, air, rail, pipeline, waterway, intermodal and transportation policy, and mass transportation research activities at the University. Emphasizes improvement of local and state transportation, including studies on optimizing traffic flow, transportation planning and policy, computer methods of structural design, foundation design, alternative fuels, multi-modal transportation investment, pavement design, drainage, dynamics of highway loading, safety, and highway structures. Operates a cooperative research program with the Texas Department of Transportation.

**University of Texas at Austin - Geotechnical Engineering Center**. Department of Civil, Architectural and Environmental Engineering, Cockrell School of Engineering, 1 University Station, C1792 Austin, TX 78712-0280. Phone: (512)232-3682; Fax: (512)471-6548; Email: k.stokoe@mail.utexas.edu • URL: http://www.ce.utexas.edu/dept/area/geotech/index.html • Areas of research include offshore complexes.

**University of Texas Medical Branch at Galveston - Institute for the Medical Humanities**. 301 University Blvd. Galveston, TX 77555-1311. Phone: (409)772-2376; Fax: (409)772-5640; Email: davicker@utmb.edu • URL: http://imh.utmb.edu • History of professional medical ethics, phenomenology of aging, iconography of the life cycle, confidentiality in the doctor-patient relationship, women in medicine, ethics of research in clinical medicine, and empathy in medical practice.

**University of Texas—Houston Health Science Center - School of Public Health - Center for Health Promotion and Prevention Research**. 7000 Fannin, Ste. 2056D Houston, TX 77030. Phone: (713)500-9609; Fax: (713)500-9602; Email: susan.tortolero@uth.tmc.edu • URL: http://sph.uth.edu/chppr • Fields of study include worksite health promotion. Formerly Center for Health Promotion Research and Development.

**University of the West Indies - Sir Arthur Lewis Institute of Social and Economic Studies**. St. Augustine Campus Saint Augustine, Trinidad and Tobago. Phone: (868)662-2002; Fax: (868)645-6329; Email: patrick.watson@sta.uwi.edu • URL: http://sta.uwi.edu/salises • Social and economic problems of the Caribbean. Focuses on issues relating to manpower, economic development, political sciences, public administration, migration, demography, women and development, and human resource development.

**University of Tokyo - Institute of Social Science**. 7-3-1 Hongo, Bunkyo-ku Tokyo 113-0033, Japan. Phone: 81 3 58414904; Fax: 81 3 58414905; Email: webmaster@iss.u-tokyo.ac.jp • URL: http://www.iss.u-tokyo.ac.jp • Comparative contemporary law, politics, economics, and societies.

**University of Toledo - International Business Institute**. 2801 W

Bancroft St., 2044 Stranahan Hall Toledo, OH 43606-3328. Phone: 800-586-5336 or (419)530-2068; Fax: (419)530-2101; Email: thomas.sharkey@utoledo.edu • URL: http://www.utoledo.edu/business/ibi/index.html • International business, exporting, foreign direct investment, international marketing, and comparative management.

**University of Toronto - Ontario Tobacco Research Unit.** 33 Russell St. Toronto, ON, Canada M5S 2S1. Phone: (416)595-6888; Fax: (416)595-6068; Email: info@otru.org • URL: http://otru.org • Tobacco control, including epidemiology of tobacco use and cessation, tobacco and youth, gender issues in tobacco use, ethnicity and tobacco use, economic factors in tobacco use, tobacco policy attitudes, policy and program evaluation, community interventions, and environmental tobacco smoke.

**University of Toronto - Robotics and Automation Laboratory.** Department of Mechanical Engineering, 5 King's College Rd. Toronto, ON, Canada M5S 3G8. Phone: (416)978-5745; Fax: (416)978-7753; Email: golden@mie.utoronto.ca • URL: http://www.mie.utoronto.ca/labs/ral.

**University of Utah - Center for Public Policy and Administration.** 260 S Central Campus Dr., Rm. 214 Salt Lake City, UT 84112-9154. Phone: (801)581-6781; Email: robinson@cppa.utah.edu • URL: http://cppa.utah.edu • Local and state government finance, organization, and administration; public policy research on education, health, environment, transportation, resources, energy; Western regional policy issues and regional governance.

**University of Vermont - Canadian Studies Program.** Wheeler House, Rm. 309, 94 University Pl. Burlington, VT 05405. Phone: (802)656-8451 or (802)656-1096; Fax: (802)656-8518; Email: paul.martin@uvm.edu • URL: http://www.uvm.edu/global/canadian • Research areas include Canadian corporate strategies, telecommunications, and natural resources.

**University of Victoria - Centre for Global Studies - Canadian Institute for Climate Studies.** 3800 Finnerty Rd., Sedgewick Bldg., Sta. C173 Victoria, BC, Canada V8P 1A1. Phone: (250)721-8800; Fax: (250)472-4830 • URL: http://www.uvic.ca/research/centres/globalstudies • Corporations, societies, companies, universities, government departments, and individuals with an interest in climate. Seeks to further the understanding of the climate system, its variability, and potential for change and the application of that understanding to decision-making, both in the public and private sectors. Manages climate related research initiatives; provides advice and consultation to those whose decisions are sensitive to variations in climate; and provides climate scenario data, maps, and background materials.

**University of Virginia - McIntire School of Commerce Foundation - Center for Growth Enterprises.** 125 Ruppel Dr. Charlottesville, VA 22903. Phone: (434)924-7063 • URL: http://www.commerce.virginia.edu/centers/growthenterprises/Pages/default.aspx • Strategic, finance, and management issues associated with growth companies, including closely held firms, venture capital/private equity, mature industries, real estate/asset-intensive firms, and non-financial performance measures.

**University of Warwick - Centre for Education and Industry.** CEDAR, Rm. WE145 Coventry CV4 7AL, United Kingdom. Phone: 44 24 76523909; Fax: 44 24 76524472; Email: geoff.lindsay@warwick.ac.uk • URL: http://www2.warwick.ac.uk/fac/soc/cei • Advisory teaching and consultation in national and international education in business partnership and collaboration.

**University of Warwick - Warwick Institute for Employment Research.** Social Sciences Bldg. Coventry CV4 7AL, United Kingdom. Phone: 44 24 76523284; Email: r.m.lindley@warwick.ac.uk • URL: http://www2.warwick.ac.uk/fac/soc/ier • Economics and social behavior, policy analysis, and forecasting. Subjects of research include: macroeconomic, industrial and spatial aspects of employment determination and their policy implications; economy/labor market relations; labor market behavior and policy; links between labor market and population change, educational developments, and household behavior, and related policy issues; and relevant international comparative studies.

**University of Western Australia - Centre for Health Services Research.** School of Population Health, 35 Stirling Hwy. Crawley, WA 6009, Australia. Phone: 61 8 64881307; Fax: 61 8 64881188; Email: david.preen@uwa.edu.au • URL: http://www.sph.uwa.edu.au/research/chsr • Health services policy and practice, focusing on the inequalities in health care, preventable inpatient time, best practices in surgical and procedural care, clinical safety and post-implementation surveillance.

**University of Wisconsin-Madison - Cast Metals Laboratory.** University of Wisconsin-Madison, Dept. of Materials Science & Engineering, 276 Materials Science & Engineering Bldg., 1509 University Ave. Madison, WI 53706-1595. Phone: (608)262-3732 or (608)262-2562; Fax: (608)262-8353; Email: msaedept@engr.wisc.edu • URL: http://www.engr.wisc.edu/mse.

**University of Wisconsin - Madison - Center for Climatic Research.** 1225 W Dayton St. Madison, WI 53706-1695. Phone: (608)262-2839; Fax: (608)263-4190; Email: jww@geography.wisc.edu • URL: http://ccr.aos.wisc.edu.

**University of Wisconsin - Madison - College of Agricultural and Life Sciences - Wisconsin Agricultural Experiment Station.** 212 Agricultural Hall, 1450 Linden Dr. Madison, WI 53706. Phone: (608)261-1432; Fax: (608)265-9534; Email: waes@cals.wisc.edu • URL: http://www.cals.wisc.edu/waes.

**University of Wisconsin - Madison - Wisconsin Historical Society - Wisconsin Center for Film and Theater Research.** 816 State St. Madison, WI 53706-1417. Phone: (608)264-6466 or (608)264-6467; Fax: (608)264-6472; Email: askmovies@wisconsinhistory.org • URL: http://www.wisconsinhistory.org/Content.aspx?dsNav=N:4294963828-4294963805&dsRecordDetails=R:CS4075 • Studies the performing arts in America, including theater, cinema, radio, and television.

**University of Wisconsin—Madison - Center for Communication Research.** Department of Communication Arts, College of Letters & Science, 821 University Ave. Madison, WI 53706. Phone: (608)262-2543; Fax: (608)262-9953; Email: xenos@wisc.edu • URL: http://ccr.commarts.wisc.edu • Media effects, including prosocial programming's effects on children, the effects of media violence on children's aggression and fears, and aging and media use. Political communication, including the framing of issues, political advertising, and the representation of nation-states on TV. Interpersonal communication, including group processes, information sharing, and group memory. Conflict and miscommunication.

**University of Wisconsin—Madison - Center for Cooperatives.** 427 Lorch St. Madison, WI 53706-1503. Phone: (608)262-3981; Fax: (608)262-3251; Email: hueth@wisc.edu • URL: http://www.uwcc.wisc.edu • Cooperative action to meet the economic and social needs of people.

**University of Wisconsin—Madison - Center for Health System Research and Analysis.** WARF Bldg., 11th Fl., 610 Walnut St. Madison, WI 53726-2397. Phone: (608)263-5722; Fax: (608)263-4523; Email: jim_robinson@chsra.wisc.edu • URL: http://www.chsra.wisc.edu • Five major research areas: quality assessment and improvement, long term care, public health policy and program evaluation, consumer decision making, and patient education and support.

**University of Wisconsin—Madison - Center for Quality and Productivity Improvement.** 3130 Engineering Centers Bldg., 1550 Engineering Dr. Madison, WI 53706. Phone: (608)263-2520; Fax: (608)263-1425; Email: carayon@ie.engr.wisc.edu • URL: http://cqpi.engr.wisc.edu • Research areas include quality management and industrial engineering.

**University of Wisconsin—Madison - College of Agricultural and Life Sciences - Food Research Institute.** Microbial Sciences Bldg., 1550 Linden Dr. Madison, WI 53706. Phone: (608)263-7777; Fax: (608)263-1114; Email: czuprync@svm.vetmed.wisc.edu • URL: http://fri.wisc.edu • Food microbiology and toxicology, with emphasis on practical problems of food producers and distributors, including studies on foodborne diseases; food safety, preservation, processing, handling, spoilage, quality, and allergens; mycotoxins; heat induced mutagens in food; and anti-carcinogens in food.

**University of Wisconsin—Madison - Mass Communications Research Center.** 5115 Vilas Hall, 821 University Ave. Madison, WI 53706. Phone: (608)262-3690 or (608)263-3381; Fax: (608)262-1361; Email: dshah@wisc.edu • URL: http://mcrc.journalism.wisc.edu • Mass communication, including mass media institutions, processes and effects generally and in a number of specific contexts. Current research specializations include political communication, communication campaigns, health communication, uses and effects of new communication technologies, cognitive and attention processes, advertising and persuasion, history of mass communication, framing, minorities, international and intercultural communication, community, geographic contexts, risk and science communication, and methodological studies.

**University of Wisconsin—Madison - Medical Electronics Laboratory.** 1300 University Ave., Rm. 80 Madison, WI 53706. Phone: (608)262-1326; Email: yee@physiology.wisc.edu • URL: http://www.mel.wisc.edu • Develops electronic instrumentation for medical and biological research.

**University of Wisconsin—Madison - Medical Instrumentation Laboratory.** 1550 Engineering Dr. Madison, WI 53706. Phone: (608)263-1574; Fax: (608)265-9239; Email: webster@engr.wisc.edu • URL: http://www.engr.wisc.edu • Research subjects include medical electrodes, medical amplifiers, bioimpedance techniques, and miniature tactile pressure sensors.

**University of Wisconsin—Madison - Molecular and Environmental Toxicology Center.** 1300 University Ave., 1530 MSC Madison, WI 53706. Phone: (608)263-4580; Fax: (608)262-5245; Email: bradfield@oncology.wisc.edu • URL: http://metc.med.wisc.edu/metc • Formerly Environmental Toxicology Center.

**University of Wisconsin—Madison - Social Systems Research Institute.** William H. Sewell Social Science Bldg., Rm. 6470, Department of Economics, 1180 Observatory Dr. Madison, WI 53706. Phone: (608)262-0446; Fax: (608)263-3876; Email: ssri@wisc.edu • URL: http://www.econ.wisc.edu/archive • Econometrics, industrial organization, international economics, labor economics, macroeconomics, public economics and economic theory.

**University of Wisconsin—Milwaukee - Center for Urban Transportation Studies.** PO Box 784 Milwaukee, WI 53201. Phone: (414)229-5787; Fax: (414)229-6958; Email: cuts@csd.uwm.edu • URL: http://www4.uwm.edu/cuts • Transportation engineering and planning, mass transit, outreach, and technology transfer. Studies include alternative methods of organizing transportation planning; transit sensitive land use design; highway projects effects on land use; intelligent transportation systems; investigations of transport improvement, evaluation, and methodologies through private financing; the use of microcomputers for transportation planning; improved methods of transport management; and transit innovations.

**University of Wisconsin—Milwaukee - Center for Urban Initiatives and Research.** Engelmann Hall, Rm. B50, 2033 E Hartford Ave. Milwaukee, WI 53211. Phone: (414)229-5916; Fax: (414)229-3884; Email: cuir@uwm.edu • URL: http://www4.uwm.edu/cuir • Public policy with emphasis on metropolitan governance and economic revitalization, urban education, technological innovation and transfer, state and metropolitan public policy, health care organization and policy, employment and manpower, and housing and urban development. Also studies gangs and drug use in Midwestern cities.

**University of Wisconsin—Milwaukee - International Business Center.** Sheldon B. Lubar School of Business Milwaukee, WI 53201. Phone: (414)229-6260; Fax: (414)229-5999; Email: vkp@uwm.edu • URL: http://www4.uwm.edu/business/research/ibc.cfm • International business.

**University of Wollongong - Centre for Social Marketing Research.** Bldg. 19, Rm. 1034a, Faculty of Commerce, Northfields Ave. Wollongong, NSW 2522, Australia. Phone: 61 2 42215994; Fax: 61 2 42213257; Email: csmr@uow.edu.au • URL: http://www.uow.edu.au/commerce/smm/mark/academics/UOW010679.htm • Social marketing, including commercial marketing, nonprofit marketing, and issues of corporate social responsibility.

**University of York - Centre for Experimental Economics.** Department of Economics & Related Studies York YO10 5DD, United Kingdom. Phone: 44 1904 433788; Fax: 44 1904 1433759 • URL: http://www.york.ac.uk/economics/research/research-clusters/experimental-economics • Experimental investigations of economic behavior, particularly under risk and uncertainty (both exogenous and endogenous).

**University of York - Institute for Research in the Social Sciences.** Heslington York YO10 5DD, United Kingdom. Phone: 44 1904 321290; Fax: 44 1904 321281; Email: hdj1@york.ac.uk • URL: http://www.york.ac.uk/iriss • Health economics, social policy, housing policy, and social work.

***Up Here Business.*** Up Here Publishing, No. 800-4920 52nd St. Yellowknife, NT, Canada X1A 3T1. Phone: 800-661-0861 • URL: http://www.uphere.ca • Monthly. $28.29 Individuals canada, digital subscription; $41.70 Individuals usa; $47.70 Individuals international; $50.86 Two years canada; $65.40 Two years usa; $71.40 Two years international. Magazine featuring Northern Canada's business community.

**W.E. Upjohn Institute for Employment Research.** 300 S Westnedge Ave. Kalamazoo, MI 49007-4686. Phone: 888-227-8569 or (269)343-5541; Fax: (269)343-7310; Email: communications@upjohn.org • URL: http://www.upjohninstitute.org • Research fields include unemployment, unemployment insurance, worker's compensation, labor productivity, profit sharing, the labor market, economic development, earnings, training, and other areas related to employment.

***Uptown San Diego Examiner: Business News.*** Uptown Examiner Group, 3930 Oregon St., Ste. 110 San Diego, CA 92104. Phone: (619)955-8960; Fax: (619)955-8962 • URL: http://uptownexaminer.com/ • Semiweekly (Wed. and Fri.). $35 Individuals; $40 Out of area. Community newspaper.

***Urban Affairs Review.*** Pine Forge Press, 2455 Teller Rd. Thousand Oaks, CA 91320-2234. Phone: 800-818-7243 or (805)499-4224 or (805)499-9774; Fax: (805)499-0871 or (805)583-2665; Email: sales@pfp.sagepub.com • URL: http://www.sagepub.com/sociologybooks • Bimonthly. $1,241 Institutions print & e-access; $1,365 Institutions current volume print & all online content; $1,117 Institutions e-access; $1,241 Institutions e-access (all online content); $3,134 Institutions e-access (content through 1998); $1,216 Institutions print only; $170 Individuals print only; $223 Institutions single print; $37 Individuals single print. Urban studies journal. Formerly *Urban Affairs Quarterly*.

***Urban Land: News and Trends in Land Development.*** Urban Land Institute, 1025 Thomas Jefferson St. NW, Ste. 500 W Washington, DC 20007. Phone: 800-321-5011 or (202)624-7000; Fax: (202)624-7140; Email: customerservice@uli.org • URL: http://www.uli.org • Monthly.

***Urban Studies Abstracts.*** EBSCO Publishing Inc., 10 Estes St. Ipswich, MA 01938-2106. Phone: 800-653-2726 or (978)356-6500; Fax: (978)356-6565; Email: information@ebscohost.com • URL: http://www.ebscohost.com • Quarterly. $967 Institutions print only; $261 Individuals print only; $266 Institutions single print; $85 Individuals single print. Coverage includes community development, urban affairs, urban history.

***Urban Transport News: Management-Funding Terrorism-Ridership-Technology.*** Business Publishers Inc., PO Box 17592 Baltimore, MD 21297-1592. Phone: 800-223-8720; Fax: (800)508-2592; Email: custserv@bpinews.com • URL:

http://www.bpinews.com • 25 times a year. $437.00 per year. Newsletter. Provides current news from Capitol Hill, the White House, the Dept. of Transportation, as well as transit operations and industries across the country.

***Urethanes Technology***. Crain Communications Ltd., 4th Fl., 26 Dingwall Rd. Croydon CR0 9XF, United Kingdom. Phone: 44 20 82539600 or 44 207 253 9600; Email: info@crain.com • URL: http://www.crain.co.uk • Bimonthly. £79 Individuals printed issues by post; £103 Individuals electronic edition; £120 Individuals issues by post and electronic edition; $108 Individuals. Covers the international polyurethane industry.

***Uruguay Government and Business Contacts Handbook***. International Business Publications, USA, PO Box 15343 Washington, DC 20003. Phone: (202)546-2103; Fax: (202)546-3275; Email: ibpusa@comcast.net • URL: http://ibpus.com • Annual. $99.95 Individuals hardcopy, e-book, CD-ROM. Covers: Strategic government and business information, export-import activity in the country, investment, business contacts and regulations.

***Uruguay Industrial and Business Directory***. International Business Publications, USA, PO Box 15343 Washington, DC 20003. Phone: (202)546-2103; Fax: (202)546-3275; Email: ibpusa@comcast.net • URL: http://ibpus.com • Annual. $99.95 Individuals hardcopy, E-book and CD-ROM. Covers: Strategic industrial, investment and business contacts for conducting export-import and investment activity in the country.

***Uruguay Investment & Business Guide***. International Business Publications, USA, PO Box 15343 Washington, DC 20003. Phone: (202)546-2103; Fax: (202)546-3275; Email: ibpusa@comcast.net • URL: http://ibpus.com • $99.95 Individuals hardcopy, E-book and CD-ROM. Covers: Strategic information on economy, business, export-import and investment climate, regulations and industrial development, banking, government, and opportunities. Entries include: Important business contacts and business travel.

***USA Business Database***. The Data Supplier, 9107 Wilshire Blvd., Ste. 450 Beverly Hills, CA 90210. Phone: 888-930-3282; Fax: (818)221-0295; Email: contactus@thedatasupplier.com • URL: http://www.thedatasupplier.com • Contains contact information for more than 13.6 million companies in the United States. Includes business name, full contact information, NAICS/SIC codes, year founded, number of employees, annual sales, parent and subsidiary companies, and other data.

***USA Business Email Database***. The Data Supplier, 9107 Wilshire Blvd., Ste. 450 Beverly Hills, CA 90210. Phone: 888-930-3282; Fax: (818)221-0295; Email: contactus@thedatasupplier.com • URL: http://www.thedatasupplier.com • Contains e-mail addresses for more than 4 million companies in the United States. Also includes business name, address, telephone and fax numbers, Web site, and category/SIC.

***USA Food Manufacturers Directory***. Business Information Agency Inc. PlanetInform, 52 Tuscan Way, Ste. 202-181 Saint Augustine, VA 32092. Phone: (904)342-6124; Fax: (904)592-2632; Email: info@biasales.com • URL: http://www.biasales.com • Annual. $149 Individuals Hard copy or PDF; $189 Hard copy and PDF. Covers: 2,500 American food manufacturers of meat and meat products, bakery, beverages, and dairy products, along with 1,000 food manufacturers in Asia and Europe. Entries include: Company name, location, industry description, manufacturing indicator, contact information, SIC codes, number of employees, type of business, year founded, legal status, and subsidiary indicators.

***USA/France Business and Culture Update***. Integrated Information Technologies, 3 Church Cir., Ste. 211 Annapolis, MD 21401. Fax: (410)280-1617 • Monthly. $190 per year (12 issues). Publication includes: List of organizations or sources providing information to businesses wishing to enter markets in France. Entries include: Name, address, phone, fax, description of products/services offered. Principal content of publication is a newsletter providing general information on the French business and cultural climate.

***USA Major Manufacturers Directory***. Business Information Agency Inc. PlanetInform, 52 Tuscan Way, Ste. 202-181 Saint Augustine, VA 32092. Phone: (904)342-6124; Fax: (904)592-2632; Email: info@biasales.com • URL: http://www.biasales.com • Annual. $199 Individuals Hard copy or PDF; $249 Both hard copy and PDF. Covers: 4,000 industrial and consumer product manufacturers in the U.S.A. Entries include: Company name, location, contact information, SIC codes, number of employees, type of business, year founded, legal status, and subsidiary indicators.

***USA Trade***. U.S. Department of Commerce, 1401 Constitution Ave. NW Washington, DC 20230. Phone: 800-782-8872 or (202)482-2000 or (202)482-6607; Email: TheSec@doc.gov • URL: http://www.commerce.gov • Monthly. $650.00 per year. Provides over 150,000 trade-related data series on CD-ROM. Includes full text of many government publications. Specific data is included on national income, labor, price indexes, foreign exchange, technical standards, and international markets. Website address is www.stat-usa.gov/.

***USACC Business Directory***. Unites States-Azerbaijan Chamber of Commerce, 1212 Potomac St., NW Washington, DC 20007. Phone: (202)333-8702; Fax: (202)333-8703 • URL: http://www.usacc.org • Annual. Included in membership; $50 Nonmembers. Covers: Government, business, and international organizations in the United States and Azerbaijan. Entries include: Contact information.

***USAN and the USP Dictionary of Drug Names***. United States Pharmacopeial Convention, 12601 Twinbrook Pky. Rockville, MD 20852-1790. Phone: 800-227-8772 or (301)881-0666; Fax: (301)816-8299 or (301)816-8236; Email: custsvc@usp.org • URL: http://www.usp.org • Annual. 348. Adopted names, brand names, compendial and other generic names, CAS Registry Numbers, molecular weights, and other information.

***USDA***. U.S. National Institute of Standards and Technology, 100 Bureau Dr. Gaithersburg, MD 20899-1070. Phone: 800-877-8339 or (301)975-6478 or (202)720-2791; Fax: (301)975-8295; Email: inquiries@nist.gov • URL: http://www.nist.gov • The USDA home page has six sections: News and Information; What's New; About USDA; Agencies; Opportunities; Search and Help. Keyword searching is offered from the USDA home page and from various individual agency home pages. Agencies are the Economic Research Service, Agricultural Marketing Service, National Agricultural Statistics Service, National Agricultural Library, and about 12 others. Updating varies. Fees: Free.

***Used Book Store***. Entrepreneur Press, 2445 McCabe Way, Ste. 400 Irvine, CA 92614-6244. Phone: 800-864-6864 or (949)261-2325 or (949)622-7131; Fax: (949)261-7729 or (949)261-0234; Email: press@entrepreneur.com • URL: http://www.entrepreneurpress.com • Looseleaf. $59.50. A practical guide to starting a used book store. Covers profit potential, start-up costs, market size evaluation, owner's time required, site selection, lease negotiation, pricing, accounting, advertising, promotion, etc. (Start-Up Business Guide No. E1117.).

***Used Car Dealer***. National Independent Automobile Dealers Association, 2521 Brown Blvd. Arlington, TX 76006. Phone: 800-682-3837 or (817)640-3838 or (434)983-2073; Fax: (817)649-5866; Email: info@niada.com • URL: http://www.niada.com • Monthly. Included in membership; $80 /year for nonmembers; $125 Individuals. Association magazine for dealers who buy and sell used cars.

***Used-Car Rental Agency***. Entrepreneur Press, 2445 McCabe Way, Ste. 400 Irvine, CA 92614-6244. Phone: 800-864-6864 or (949)261-2325 or (949)622-7131; Fax: (949)261-7729 or (949)261-0234; Email: press@entrepreneur.com • URL: http://www.entrepreneurpress.com • Looseleaf. $59.50. A practical guide to starting a used-car rental business. Covers profit potential, start-up costs, market size evaluation, owner's time required, site selection, lease negotiation pricing, accounting, advertising, promotion, etc. (Start-Up Business Guide No. E1108.).

***Used Car Sales***. Entrepreneur Press, 2445 McCabe Way, Ste. 400 Irvine, CA 92614-6244. Phone: 800-864-6864 or (949)261-2325 or (949)622-7131; Fax: (949)261-7729 or (949)261-0234; Email: press@entrepreneur.com • URL: http://www.entrepreneurpress.com • Looseleaf. $59.50. A practical guide to getting started in the business of selling used cars. Covers profit potential, start-up costs, market size evaluation, owner's time required, site selection, lease negotiation, pricing, accounting, advertising, etc. (Start-Up Business Guide No. E2330.).

***Used Equipment Directory***. Penton, 1166 Avenue of the Americas New York, NY 10036. Phone: (212)204-4200; Email: information@penton.com • URL: http://www.penton.com • Monthly. $35 Individuals 1 year, 3rd class mail, (12 issues); $35 Individuals 2 year, 3rd class mail, (24 issues); $50 Individuals 1 year, 1st class mail, (12 issues); $90 Individuals 2 years, 1st class mail, (24 issues). Publication includes: List of 800 dealers in used metalworking, electrical, power, process, and material handling equipment, woodworking and machine tools. Entries include: Company name, address, phone; principal executive; types of equipment handled; description of machinery offered. Principal content is approximately 75,000 paid listings of used equipment for sale, classified by type.

***Utah Major Employers Guide***. • URL: http://www.edcutah.org/majorEmployersGuide.php • Biennial. $50 Individuals for investors; $85 Individuals non-investors. Covers: More than 900 companies in 29 counties in Utah that have 100 or more full-time employees. Entries include: Company name, address, phone, fax, contact names, names and titles of key personnel, year established, type of operation, Standard Industrial Classification (SIC) code, product/service, county, number of full-time employees, website addresses.

***Utah Manufacturers Directory and Industrial Database***. Manufacturers' News Inc., 1633 Central St. Evanston, IL 60201-1569. Phone: (847)864-7000; Fax: (847)332-1100 • URL: http://www.manufacturersnews.com • Annual. $102 Individuals print; $428 Individuals database (EZ select full); $291 Individuals database (EZ select with 20 plus employees); $150 Individuals database (EZ select basic). Covers: 4,504 manufacturers in Utah. Entries include: Company name, address, phone, names and titles of key personnel, year established, number of employees, plant square footage, services, Standard Industry Classification (SIC) code, parent and subsidiary company information, type of in-house computer system, URL, e-mail address.

***Utah Manufacturers Register***. Harris InfoSource, 2057 E Aurora Rd. Twinsburg, OH 44087-1999. Phone: 800-888-5900 or (330)425-9000 or (973)921-5500; Fax: (800)643-5997 or (877)252-3375; Email: customerservice@harrisinfo.com • URL: http://www.harrisinfo.com • Annual. Covers: Approximately 4,600 manufacturers in Utah, plus names of key executives. Entries include: Company name, address, parent name/location, telephone, fax and 800 numbers, Web site address (on CD-ROM only), number of employees, year established, annual revenue, plant size, business description, Standard Industrial Classification (SIC) codes, executive names/titles, public ownership, legal structure, import/export designators, female/minority ownership.

**Utah State University - Bee Biology and Systematics Laboratory**. 5310 Old Main Hill Logan, UT 84322-5310. Phone: (435)797-2524; Fax: (435)797-0461 • URL: http://www.loganbeelab.usu.edu.

**Utah State University - Department of Animal, Dairy and Veterinary Sciences - Caine Dairy Center**. 4300 S Hwy. 91 Wellsville, UT 84339. Phone: (435)245-6067; Fax: (435)245-7680; Email: john.wallentine@usu.edu • URL: http://advs.usu.edu/htm/about-advs/facilities/caine-dairy-farm • Breeding, feeding, physiology, and management of dairy cattle.

***Utilities Industry Litigation Reporter: National Coverage of the Many Types of Litigation Stemming From the Transmission and Distribution of Energy By Publicly and Privately Owned Utilities***. Andrews Publications, 175 Strafford Ave., Bldg. 4, Suite 140 Wayne, PA 19087. Phone: 800-345-1101 or (610)225-0510 or (610)622-0510; Fax: (610)225-0501 or (610)622-0501; Email: customer@andrewspub.com • URL: http://www.andrewspub.com • Monthly. $775.00 per year. Newsletter. Reports on legal cases involving the generation or distribution of energy.

***Utility Automation***. PennWell Corp., Industrial Div., 1421 S Sheridan Rd. Tulsa, OK 74112. Phone: 800-331-4463 or (918)835-3161; Email: bid@pennwell.com • URL: http://www.pennwell.com • 10 times a year. $69.00 per year; schools and public libraries, $10.00 per year. Covers new information technologies for electric utilities, including automated meter reading, distribution management systems, and customer information systems.

***Utility Business***. Penton, 9800 Metcalf Ave. Overland Park, KS 66212. Phone: 866-748-4926 or (913)341-1300; Fax: (913)967-1905 or (913)967-1898; Email: corporatecustomerservice@penton.com • URL: http://www.penton.com • Monthly. Trade magazine covering the utility industry for executives, managers and others in the electric, gas, water and telecommunications utility business.

**Utility Industry Group**. Southern California Edison Co., Bldg. 3-2 MD3, 4910 Rivergrade Rd. Irwindale, CA 91706. Phone: (626)543-6291; Fax: (626)302-5332 • URL: http://www.uig.org • Represents the interests of the utility industry including distribution companies, energy suppliers, service providers and their customers, supply chain participants and other interested parties. Promotes effective implementation of electronic commerce to standards committees, governmental bodies and other appropriate organizations involved in the standards setting process. Provides a forum for the exchange of ideas and solutions related to electronic commerce and its influence on the business needs of the utility industry.

**Utility Supply Management Alliance**. PO Box 6608 Pine Bluff, AR 71611. Phone: (913)768-7005; Fax: (913)397-0901; Email: parbuckle4@comcast.net • URL: http://www.usma.com • Reduces overall supply chain costs by providing a forum for utilities and suppliers. Advocates for aggressive and responsible leadership, responsiveness to customer needs and continuous improvement in supply chain management. Improves the service and profitability of utilities and suppliers.

**UWC: Strategic Services on Unemployment and Workers' Compensation**. 910 17th St. NW, Ste. 1070 Washington, DC 20006. Phone: (202)223-8902; Fax: (202)783-1616; Email: info@uwcstrategy.org • URL: http://www.uwcstrategy.org • Works to serve the business community by promoting Unemployment Insurance (UI) and Workers' Compensation (WC) programs that provide fair benefits to workers at affordable cost to employers and the community.

***Uzbekistan Government and Business Contacts Handbook***. International Business Publications, USA, PO Box 15343 Washington, DC 20003. Phone: (202)546-2103; Fax: (202)546-3275; Email: ibpusa@comcast.net • URL: http://ibpus.com • $99.95 Individuals hardcopy, e-book, CD-ROM. Covers: Strategic government and business information, export-import activity in the country, investment, business contacts and regulations.

***Uzbekistan Industrial and Business Directory***. International Business Publications, USA, PO Box 15343 Washington, DC 20003. Phone: (202)546-2103; Fax: (202)546-3275; Email: ibpusa@comcast.net • URL: http://ibpus.com • $99.95 Individuals hardcopy, E-book and CD-ROM. Covers: Strategic and practical economic and business information. Entries include: Business contacts for conducting business activity in the country.

***Vacation Study Abroad: The Complete Guide to Summer and Short-Term Study***. Institute of International Education, IIE New York City, 809 United Nations Plz. New York, NY 10017-3503. Phone: (212)883-8200 or (212)984-5412; Fax: (212)984-5452; Email: membership@iie.org • URL: http://www.iie.org • Annual. Covers: More than 2,200 college-level and adult education summer and short-term courses sponsored by the United States and foreign colleges, language schools, and private and public organizations. Courses run from as briefly as two weeks to three months. Entries include: Name of institution or other sponsor, inclusive dates, subjects offered, orientation information, language of instruction, whether United States college credit is offered and how much, related travel, housing, costs, scholarships, work-study or internship opportunities, deadline, phone, fax, e-mail, website and address for application.

**Valacta.** 555 boul. des Anciens-Combattants Sainte-Anne-de-Bellevue, QC, Canada H9X 3R4. Phone: (514)459-3030; Fax: (514)459-3020; Email: service.clientele@valacta.com • URL: http://www.valacta.com.

***Value Line Convertible Data Base***. Value Line Inc., 220 E 42nd St., 6th Fl. New York, NY 10017-5806. Email: vlcr@valueline.com • URL: http://www.valueline.com • Provides online data for about 600 convertible bonds and other convertible securities: price, yield, premium, issue size, liquidity, and maturity. Information is current, with weekly updates. Inquire as to online cost and availability.

***The Value Line Investment Survey***. Value Line Inc., 220 E 42nd St., 6th Fl. New York, NY 10017-5806. Email: vlcr@valueline.com • URL: http://www.valueline.com • Weekly. $598 U.S. /year; $698 Canada and Mexico /year; $1,020 Other countries /year. Provides detailed information and ratings for 1,700 stocks actively-traded in the U. S.

***Value of Construction Put in Place***. U.S. Bureau of the Census. U. S. Government Printing Office, 732 N Capitol St. NW Washington, DC 20401. Phone: 866-512-1800 or (202)512-1800 or (866)512-1800; Fax: (202)512-2104 or (202)512-2250; Email: contactcenter@gpo.gov • URL: http://www.gpo.gov • Monthly.

***Value Retail News: The Journal of Outlet and Off-Price Retail and Development***. Off-Price Specialists, Inc. Value Retail News, 2519 N McMullen Booth Rd., Ste. 510-356 Clearwater, FL 33761-2137. • URL: http://www.valueretailnews.com • Monthly. $99 Members; $144 Nonmembers; $175 Nonmembers other countries. Provides news of the off-price and outlet store industry. Emphasis is on real estate for outlet store centers.

**Vanderbilt University - First Amendment Center.** 1207 18th Ave. S Nashville, TN 37212. Phone: (615)727-1600; Fax: (615)727-1319; Email: info@fac.org • URL: http://www.firstamendmentcenter.org • Research fields include mass communication and technological change, including mass media and the public trust.

***Vanity Fair***. Conde Nast Publications, 4 Times Sq. New York, NY 10036-6518. Phone: 800-289-9330 or (212)286-2860 or (212)286-3700; Fax: (212)286-6763 or (212)286-7093; Email: contact@condenast.com • URL: http://www.condenast.com • Monthly. $18.00 per year.

***Vankirk's International Venture Capital Directory***. Online Publishing Inc., 2800 Shirlington Rd., Ste. 804 Arlington, VA 22206. Phone: 800-257-2947 or (703)379-9200; Fax: (703)824-5699 • Semiannual. $245. Covers: more than 350 companies and organizations providing capital to business ventures outside the U.S. Database includes: Articles on working with venture capitalists, trends and statistics, and how to develop an effective business plan; glossary. Entries include: Organization name, address, phone, fax, names and titles of key personnel, preferred stage of funding; preferred industries, geographic preference, minimum and maximum amounts invested, preferred size of investment, total capital under management, current activity level, total of recently made investments, compensation method, type of organization, year founded, staff size, trade association memberships, affiliated organizations and funds, corporate description.

***Vankirk's Venture Capital Directory***. Online Publishing Inc., 2800 Shirlington Rd., Ste. 804 Arlington, VA 22206. Phone: 800-257-2947 or (703)379-9200; Fax: (703)824-5699 • Semiannual. $245. Covers: over 1,000 sources of venture capital in the U.S. Database includes: Articles on working with venture capitalists, venture capital trends, and developing a business plan; statistics. Entries include: Organization name, address, phone, fax, name and title of contact, preferred stage of funding (start-up, acquisition, leveraged buyout, etc.), industry preference, geographic preference (mid-Atlantic, U.S., global, etc.), type of investments (debt, equity, etc), minimum and maximum initial investments, preferred size of investment, amount of capital under management, current activity level, total value of recent investments, compensation method, type of organization, year founded, number of employees, trade association memberships, affiliated organizations and funds, description.

***Vankirk's Venture Capital Investments Profiled***. Online Publishing Inc., 2800 Shirlington Rd., Ste. 804 Arlington, VA 22206. Phone: 800-257-2947 or (703)379-9200; Fax: (703)824-5699 • Semiannual. $245. Covers: more than 1,200 investments made by over 110 venture capital firms. Database includes: Statistics; glossary. Entries include: Investing firm name, address, phone, fax, names and titles of key personnel; recipient firm's name, location, description of product or service, amount of funding provided, stage of funding; industry, type of investment (debt, equity, etc.).

***Vapor Trail's Boating News and International Yachting and Cruiser and Manufacturers Report***. Gemini Productions, Ltd., 8962 Bainford Dr. Huntington Beach, CA 92646. Phone: (714)833-8003 • Monthly. $24.00 per year.

***Variety International Film Guide***. Peter Cowie, editor. Silman-James Press, 3624 Shannon Rd. Los Angeles, CA 90027.

Phone: 877-757-2665 or (323)661-9922; Fax: (323)661-4442 or (323)661-9933; Email: silmanjamespress@earthlink.net • URL: http://www.silmanjamespress.com • Annual. $24.95. Covers the "who, what, where, and when of the international film scene." Includes information from 70 countries on film festivals, top-grossing films, awards, schools, etc.

***Variety: The International Entertainment Weekly***. Reed Elsevier Group plc Reed Business Information, 360 Park Ave. S New York, NY 11010. Phone: (212)791-4208; Email: corporatecommunications@reedbusiness.com • URL: http://www.reedbusiness.com • Weekly. $199 Individuals print + online; $299 Other countries print + online. Contains national and international news of show business, with emphasis on motion pictures and television. Includes *Market* and *Special Focus* issues.

***Vault Guide to the Top Business Services Employers***. Vault.com Inc., 132 W 31st St., 17th Fl. New York, NY 10001-3406. Phone: 800-535-2074; Fax: (212)366-6117; Email: customerservice@vault.com • URL: http://www.vault.com • $19.95 Individuals Online; $19.95 Members Gold. Covers: Top business service companies in United States. Entries include: Company name, contact person, location, address, phone and fax numbers, zip code, statistics, hiring process and email.

**Vecova Centre for Disability Services and Research.** 3304 - 33rd St. NW Calgary, AB, Canada T2L 2A6. Phone: (403)284-1121; Fax: (403)284-1146; Email: info@vecova.ca • URL: http://vecova.ca • Associated with University of Calgary.

***Vegetables and Specialties Situation and Outlook***. U. S. Government Printing Office, 732 N Capitol St. NW Washington, DC 20401. Phone: 866-512-1800 or (202)512-1800 or (866)512-1800; Fax: (202)512-2104 or (202)512-2250; Email: contactcenter@gpo.gov • URL: http://www.gpo.gov • Three times a year. Issued by the Economic Research Service of the U. S. Department of Agriculture. Provides current statistical information on supply, demand, and prices.

***Vehicle Leasing***. Entrepreneur Press, 2445 McCabe Way, Ste. 400 Irvine, CA 92614-6244. Phone: 800-864-6864 or (949)261-2325 or (949)622-7131; Fax: (949)261-7729 or (949)261-0234; Email: press@entrepreneur.com • URL: http://www.entrepreneurpress.com • Looseleaf. $59.50. A practical guide to starting an automobile leasing business. Covers profit potential, start-up costs, market size evaluation, owner's time required, site selection, lease negotiation, pricing, accounting, advertising, promotion, etc. (Start-Up Business Guide No. E2329.).

***VenCap Data Quest***. Reference Press Inc., 6448 Hwy. 290 E, Ste. E-104 Austin, TX 78723. Phone: 800-486-8666 or (512)454-7778; Fax: (512)454-9401; Email: orders@hoovers.com • $89.95 Eastern version; $89.95 Western version; $149.95 Both versions. Diskette. Contains over 750 venture capital firms in the eastern and western U.S. Entries include: Company name, address, phone, fax, officers, partners, type of fund, number of years providing funding, dollars under management, industries covered and geographical preferences, preferred low- and high-average investments, preferred maturity stages, and product description of portfolio companies.

***Vending Machines***. U. S. Bureau of the Census, 4600 Silver Hill Rd. Washington, DC 20233-0001. Phone: (301)763-4636; Email: comments@census.gov • URL: http://www.census.gov • Annual. Provides data on value of manufacturers' shipments, quantity, exports, imports, etc. (Current Industrial Reports, MA-35U.).

***Vending Times Census of the Industry***. Vending Times Inc., 55 Maple Ave., Ste. 102 Rockville Centre, NY 11570. Phone: (516)442-1850 or (212)302-4700; Fax: (516)442-1849 or (212)221-3311; Email: subscriptions@vendingtimes.net • URL: http://www.vendingtimes.com • Annual. $50 U.S. and Canada.

***Vending Times: Vending-Feeding-Coffee Service-Music and Games***. Vending Times Inc., 55 Maple Ave., Ste. 102 Rockville Centre, NY 11570. Phone: (516)442-1850 or (212)302-4700; Fax: (516)442-1849 or (212)221-3311; Email: subscriptions@vendingtimes.net • URL: http://www.vendingtimes.com • Monthly. $50 Individuals; $150 Other countries. Incorporates *V-T Music and Games*.

***Vendor Guide: How to Do Business with the States***. National Association of State Procurement Officials, 201 E Main St., Ste. 1405 Lexington, KY 40507-2004. Phone: (859)514-9159; Fax: (859)514-9166; Email: headquarters@naspo.org • URL: http://www.naspo.org • Annual. $60.

***Venezuela Business Law Handbook***. International Business Publications, USA, PO Box 15343 Washington, DC 20003. Phone: (202)546-2103; Fax: (202)546-3275; Email: ibpusa@comcast.net • URL: http://ibpus.com • $99.95 Individuals hardcopy, e-book, CD-ROM. Covers: Basic information on business laws and legislations, export-import regulations, business climate and contacts.

***Venezuela Company Handbook***. Hoover's Inc., 5800 Airport Blvd. Austin, TX 78752-4204. Phone: 866-443-3939 or (512)374-4500 or (866)281-5969; Fax: (512)374-4501; Email: salesteam@hoovers.com • URL: http://www.hoovers.com • $29.95 plus $3.50 shipping. Covers: major Venezuelan companies listed on the Caracas Stock Exchange. Database includes: Profile of Venezuela's economy, including information on privatization and accounting rules. Entries include:

Company name, address, phone, fax, year established, stock ticker symbol, names and titles of key personnel, number of employees, number of stockholders, bank references, auditor, company history, financial data, markets and competition, raw materials used and sources, names of major stockholders, affiliated companies.

***Venezuela Industrial and Business Directory***. International Business Publications, USA, PO Box 15343 Washington, DC 20003. Phone: (202)546-2103; Fax: (202)546-3275; Email: ibpusa@comcast.net • URL: http://ibpus.com • Annual. $99.95 Individuals hardcopy, E-book and CD-ROM. Covers: Strategic industrial, investment and business contacts for conducting export-import and investment activity in the country.

**Venezuelan-American Chamber of Commerce and Industry.** PO Box 5181 Caracas 1010-A, Venezuela. Phone: 58 212 2630833; Fax: 58 212 2631829 • URL: http://www.venamcham.org • Promotes business and commercial relations between the U.S. and Venezuela. Represents members' interests in areas of public policies and legislation. Strives to create a climate favorable to the growth of companies in Venezuela.

**Venezuelan Confederation of Industries.** Ave. Araure (Principal de Chuao) Caracas 1061, Venezuela. Phone: 58 212 991-2116; Fax: 58 212 991-7737; Email: conindustria@conindustria.org • URL: http://www.conindustria.org • Represents the interests of the industrial regions and productive sectors in Venezuela.

***The Venture Capital Directory on CD-ROM***. Infon Corp., 555 Bryant St., Ste. 347 Palo Alto, CA 94301-1704. Phone: 800-654-6366 or (650)330-1344 • Covers: over 500 venture capital firms and over 2,000 investors. Entries include: venture capital firms—investment size, location, and industry; investors—education and experience.

***Venture Capital Journal***. Thomson Venture Economics, 195 Broadway New York, NY 10007. Phone: 888-989-8373 or (646)822-2000; Fax: (646)822-3230; Email: ThomsonONEBankerSupportUS@tfn.com • URL: http://www.ventureeconomics.com • Description: Hard news, analysis and data on the North American private equity market.

***Venture Capital Report Guide to Venture Capital in Europe***. Pitman Publishing, 128 Long Acre London WC2E 9AN, United Kingdom. Phone: 44 0 207 447 2000; Fax: 44 0 207 447 2170 • $125. Covers: over 500 European venture capital firms, companies supplying funds for research and development, banks with venture capital divisions, organizations disbursing government funds, and venture capital associations. Entries include: Company profile, size of investment, industry and geographic preferences, number of executives, time-table for investments, fees. Covers 960.

***Vermont Business Phone Book***. Manufacturers' News Inc., 1633 Central St. Evanston, IL 60201-1569. Phone: (847)864-7000; Fax: (847)332-1100 • URL: http://www.manufacturersnews.com • Covers: about 850 industrial firms in Vermont. Entries include: Company name, address, phone, number of employees, name of chief executive officer, products imported and exported.

***Vermont Business***. Vermont Chamber of Commerce, 751 Granger Rd. Barre, VT 05641. Phone: (802)223-3443; Fax: (802)223-4257; Email: info@vtchamber.com • URL: http://www.vtchamber.com • Annual.

***Vermont Manufacturers Register and Industrial Database***. Manufacturers' News Inc., 1633 Central St. Evanston, IL 60201-1569. Phone: (847)864-7000; Fax: (847)332-1100 • URL: http://www.manufacturersnews.com • Annual. $82 Individuals print; $277 Individuals database (EZ select full); $162 Individuals database (EZ select with 20 plus employees); $97 Individuals database (EZ select basic). Covers: 1,698 manufacturers in Vermont. Entries include: Company name, address, phone, names and titles of key personnel, year established, number of employees, plant square footage, services, Standard Industry Classification (SIC) code, parent and subsidiary company information, type of in-house computer system, URL, e-mail address.

***Vero Beach Christian Business Association—Directory***. Vero Beach Christian Business Association, PO Box 650242 Vero Beach, FL 32965-0242. Email: info@vbcba.org • URL: http://www.vbcba.org • Covers Christian business leaders in Vero Beach, Florida.

***Vertical File Index: Guide to Pamphlets and References to Current Topics***. H.W. Wilson Co., 950 University Ave. Bronx, NY 10452-4224. Phone: 800-367-6770 or (718)588-8400 or (718)558-8400; Fax: (718)590-1617 or (800)590-1617; Email: custserv@hwwilson.com • URL: http://www.hwwilson.com • 11 times a year. $115.00 per year. A subject and title index to selected pamphlet material.

***Vertiflite***. AHS International, 217 N Washington St. Alexandria, VA 22314-2538. Phone: 855-247-4685 or (703)684-6777; Fax: (703)739-9279; Email: staff@vtol.org • URL: http://www.vtol.org • Bimonthly. $135 Nonmembers inside US; $165 Nonmembers outside US; $40 Single issue member; $50 Single issue nonmember; Included in membership.

**Veterans Health Administration - Health Services Research and Development Service - Houston Center for Quality of Care and Utilization Studies - Health Policy and Quality Division.** Veterans Affairs Medical Ctr. (152), 2002 Holcombe Blvd. Houston, TX 77030. Phone: (713)794-8623;

Fax: (713)748-7359; Email: laura.petersen@va.gov • URL: http://www.hsrd.houston.med.va.gov/health-policy-quality.htm • Effects of local, state, and federal government policies on the health of populations, access to care, efficiency of care and the quality of health care.

***Veterinary Economics: Business Solutions for Practicing Veterinarians***. Thomson Veterinary Healthcare Communications, 8033 Flint Lenexa, KS 66214. Phone: 800-255-6864 or (913)492-4300; Fax: (913)492-4157; Email: ve@vetmedpub.com • URL: http://www.vetmetpub.com • Monthly. Free to qualified subscribers; $42 Individuals. Provides business management and financial articles for veterinarians.

***VFW Magazine: Ensuring Rights, Recognition, and Remembrance***. Remembrance, 406 W. 34th St. Kansas City, MO 64111. Phone: (816)756-3390; Fax: (816)968-1149; Email: info@vfw.org • URL: http://www.vfw.org • 11/year. Members free; $15 Nonmembers. Events and general features.

***Via Satellite***. Access Intelligence L.L.C., 4 Choke Cherry Rd., 2nd Fl. Rockville, MD 20850. Phone: 800-777-5006 or (301)354-2000 or (301)354-2101; Fax: (301)309-3847 or (801)365-2300; Email: info@accessintel.com • URL: http://www.accessintel.com/ • Monthly. $49 Individuals. Covers the communications satellite industry.

***Vickers On-Line***. Vickers Stock Research Corp., 61 Broadway St., Ste. 1700 New York, NY 10006. Phone: 800-645-5043 or (516)945-0020; Email: sales@vickers-stock.com • URL: http://www.vickers-stock.com • Provides detailed online information relating to insider trading and the securities holdings of institutional investors. Daily updates. Inquire as to online cost and availability.

***Vickers Weekly Insider Report***. Vickers Stock Research Corp., 61 Broadway St., Ste. 1700 New York, NY 10006. Phone: 800-645-5043 or (516)945-0020; Email: sales@vickers-stock.com • URL: http://www.vickers-stock.com • Description: Reports on stock insider transactions and maintains portfolios based on insider buy signals-96 up 68%.

**Victoria University - Centre for Strategic Economic Studies**. PO Box 14428 Melbourne, VIC 8001, Australia. Phone: 61 3 99191340; Fax: 61 3 99191350; Email: bruce.rasmussen@vu.edu.au • URL: http://www.cfses.com • Long term economic, social, and technological issues. Center has 3 prime areas of regional focus: Australia, the OECD countries, and East Asia, with special reference to China and Indonesia. Current programs include Growth Trade and Development; Technology, Innovation, and Industrial Change; Governance and Regional Economics; Sustainable Development and the Environment; and Inequality and Work.

**Victorian Employers' Chamber of Commerce and Industry**. 486 Albert St. Melbourne, VIC 3002, Australia. Phone: 61 3 86625333; Fax: 61 3 86625462; Email: vecci@vecci.org.au • URL: http://www.vecci.org.au • Represents businesses in Victoria, Australia.

***Video and Television***. Orion Research Corp., 14555 N Scottsdale Rd., Ste. 330 Scottsdale, AZ 85254. Phone: 800-844-0759 or (480)951-1114; Fax: (480)951-1117 or (800)375-1315 • Annual. $144 Individuals. Quotes retail and wholesale prices of used video and TV equipment. Original list prices and years of manufacture are also shown.

***Video Business***. Chilton Publications, 250 Hudson St., Frnt. 4 New York, NY 10014-4504. Phone: (212)887-8400; Fax: (212)887-8585 • Weekly. Magazine for retailers of prerecorded video software and related goods and services.

***Video Investor***. SNL Kagan, 40 Ragsdale Dr., Ste. 250 Monterey, CA 93940. Phone: (831)624-1536; Fax: (831)641-0961 • URL: http://www.kagan.com • Description: Reports videocassette industry developments, including sales statistics and forecasts. Provides news of related conventions and events and focuses on sales and rentals of film product, performance of retail outlets, market shares of suppliers and distributors, the sale of chains and outlets, hardware revenues and sales, and laser disk technologies. **Remarks:** Also available via e-mail and fax.

***Video Librarian: The Video Review Magazine***. Video Librarian, 3435 NE Nine Boulder Dr. Poulsbo, WA 98370. Phone: 800-692-2270 or (360)626-1259; Fax: (360)626-1260; Email: vidlib@videolibrarian.com • URL: http://www.videolibrarian.com • Bimonthly. $64; $99 print and online. Edited for public and school libraries. Each issue includes reviews of hundreds of video DVDs or cassettes, in various subject areas.

***Video Technology News***. Access Intelligence L.L.C., 4 Choke Cherry Rd., 2nd Fl. Rockville, MD 20850. Phone: 800-777-5006 or (301)354-2000 or (301)354-2101; Fax: (301)309-3847 or (801)365-2300; Email: info@accessintel.com • URL: http://www.accessintel.com/ • Description: Reports on video technologies from a business point of view. Provides industry analyses and forecasts, reports on new products and emerging media trends. Covers legal and regulatory developments. **Remarks:** Incorporates the former FutureHome Technology News, merged December 1992.

***Videocassette Rental Store***. Entrepreneur Press, 2445 McCabe Way, Ste. 400 Irvine, CA 92614-6244. Phone: 800-864-6864 or (949)261-2325 or (949)622-7131; Fax: (949)261-7729 or (949)261-0234; Email: press@entrepreneur.com • URL: http://www.entrepreneurpress.com • Looseleaf. $59.50. A practical guide to starting a videocassette rental store. Covers profit potential, start-up costs, market size evaluation, owner's time required, site selection, lease negotiation, pricing, accounting, advertising, promotion, etc. (Start-Up Business Guide No. E1192.).

***Videolog***. Muze, Inc., 304 Hudson St., 8th Floor New York, NY 10013. Phone: 800-456-7838 or (212)824-0300; Fax: (212)741-1246; Email: custsrv@muze.com • URL: http://www.muze.com • Annual. $250.00. Five volumes. Provides detailed information on more than 170,000 VHS and DVD video titles. Includes a "Directory of Stars and Directors" and 13 category sections.

***Vietnam Business Forecast Report***. Telecommunications Insight, 85 Queen Victoria St. London EC4V 4AB, United Kingdom. Phone: 20 72 465100 or 44 20 7248 0468; Fax: 20 72 480467 or 44 20 7248 0467; Email: enquiries@telecomsinsight.com • URL: http://www.telecomsinsight.com • Quarterly. $1,195 Individuals Single user; $1,795 Individuals Up to 3 users. Business forecast report for Vietnam.

***Vietnam Business Law Handbook***. International Business Publications, USA, PO Box 15343 Washington, DC 20003. Phone: (202)546-2103; Fax: (202)546-3275; Email: ibpusa@comcast.net • URL: http://ibpus.com • $99.95 Individuals hardcopy, E-book and CD-ROM. Covers: Information on basic business legislation, laws, business climate, export-import regulations, taxation, banking and contacts.

***Vietnam: Business Opportunities and Risks***. China Books, 360 Swift Ave., Ste. 48 South San Francisco, CA 94080. Phone: (800)818-2017; Fax: (650)872-7808; Email: info@chinabooks.com • URL: http://www.chinabooks.com • A$5. Publication includes: Business contacts in Vietnam. Database includes: Maps, charts, and a bibliography. Entries include: Name, address, phone. Principal content of publication is information on the business environment, forms of foreign investment, laws, taxes, and investment regulations in Vietnam.

***Vietnam Business***. Vietnam Trade Information Center Ministry of Trade, 46 Ngo Nguyen St. Hanoi, Vietnam. Phone: 84 48259772 • Semimonthly. $15,000. Provides information for foreign traders and investors.

***Vietnam Investment and Business Guide***. International Business Publications, USA, PO Box 15343 Washington, DC 20003. Phone: (202)546-2103; Fax: (202)546-3275; Email: ibpusa@comcast.net • URL: http://ibpus.com • $99.95 Individuals hardcopy, E-book and CD-ROM. Covers: Strategic and business information, contacts, regulations and more. An ultimate guide for conducting investment, export-import activity in the country.

**Villgro**. 3rd Flr., IIT Madras Research Park, Kanagam Rd., Taramani Chennai 600113, Tamil Nadu, India. Phone: 91 44 66630400; Email: info@villgro.org • URL: http://www.villgro.org • Promotes the spirit of innovation; encourages experimentation, nurtures the creativity of rural innovators.

***Virginia Business Directory***. InfoGroup Inc., 5711 S 86th Cir. Omaha, NE 68127-4146. Phone: (402)593-4500 • URL: http://www.infogroup.com • Annual. $795 for both print & CD-ROM. Covers: 297,373 businesses in Virginia. Entries include: Company name, address, phone, number of employees, name of owner or manager, sales volume. Compiled from telephone company 'Yellow Pages,' statewide. All states covered (see separate entries).

**Virginia Commonwealth University - Virginia Center for Urban Development**. 919 W Franklin St. Richmond, VA 23284-3061. Phone: (804)828-7528; Fax: (804)828-6838; Email: bkinsey@vcu.edu • URL: http://www.vcu.edu/cppweb/urban • Economics, including impact analysis and forecasting.

***Virginia Industrial Directory***. Florida Chamber of Commerce, PO Box 11309 Tallahassee, FL 32302-3309. Phone: (850)521-1200; Email: info@flchamber.com • URL: http://www.flchamber.com • Annual. $105 Members; $115 Nonmembers. Covers: over 6,000 manufacturing and mining firms. Entries include: Company name, address, phone, names and titles of key personnel, number of employees, product/service provided, headquarters address (if different). Separate list of firms with foreign affiliations gives parent company, country, and product only.

***Virginia Peninsula Regional Business Directory***. Virginia Peninsula Chamber of Commerce, 21 Enterprise Pkwy., Ste. 100 Hampton, VA 23666. Phone: (757)262-2000; Fax: (757)262-2009; Email: info@vpcc.org • URL: http://www.virginiapeninsulachamber.com • Annual. $25 Individuals. Covers: Over 2,500 business leaders and chamber members.

***Virtual Reality Annual International Symposium***. IEEE - Computer Society, 2001 L St. NW, Ste. 700 Washington, DC 20036-4928. Phone: 800-272-6657 or (202)371-0101 or (714)821-8380; Fax: (202)728-9614 or (714)821-4010; Email: help@computer.org • URL: http://www.computer.org • Annual.

**The Viscardi Center**. 201 I.U. Willets Rd. Albertson, NY 11507-1599. Phone: (516)465-1400; Email: info@abilitiesonline.org • URL: http://www.viscardicenter.org • Formerly National Center for Disability Services.

**Vision Council - Optical Lab Division**. 225 Reinekers Ln., Ste. 700 Alexandria, VA 22314. Phone: 866-826-0290 or (703)548-4560; Fax: (703)548-4580; Email: info@thevisioncouncil.org • URL: http://www.thevisioncouncil.org/ola • Represents independent, wholesale ophthalmic laboratories and suppliers serving the ophthalmic field.

***Visons***. Unified Abrasives Manufacturers' Association - Grain Committee, 30200 Detroit Rd. Cleveland, OH 44145-1967. Phone: (440)899-0010; Fax: (440)892-1404; Email: contact@uama.org • URL: http://www.uama.org • Irregular. Newsletter. Price on application.

***Visual Merchandising & Store Design—Buyers' Guide Issue***. ST Media Group International Inc., 11262 Cornell Park Dr. Cincinnati, OH 45242. Phone: 800-421-1321 or (513)421-2050; Fax: (513)421-5144; Email: info@stmediagroup.com • URL: http://stmediagroup.com • Annual. Publication includes: Over 1,300 manufacturers and distributors of retail display equipment and products; nearly 600 store design, lighting, and visual merchandising firms; related trade and professional associations. Database includes: Calendar of events. Entries include: For manufacturers and service firms—Company name, address, phone, name and title of contact, number of employees, sales volume, products. Similar data given for associations.

***Vital Signs: The Trends That Are Shaping Our Future (year)***. Worldwatch Institute, 1400 16th St. NW, Ste. 430 Washington, DC 20036. Phone: (202)745-8092; Fax: (202)478-2534; Email: worldwatch@worldwatch.org • URL: http://www.worldwatch.org • Annual. $19.95. Provides access to selected indicators showing social, economic, and environmental trends throughout the world. Includes data relating to food, energy, transportation, finance, population, and other topics.

***Vital Statistics of the United States***. Public Health Service, U.S. Dept. of Health and Human Services. Bernan Press, PO Box 191 Blue Ridge Summit, PA 17214. Phone: 800-865-3457 or (301)459-7666; Fax: (301)459-6988; Email: customercare@bernan.com • URL: http://www.bernan.com • Biennial. $110.

***Vital Statistics of the United States: Life Tables***. U. S. Government Printing Office, 732 N Capitol St. NW Washington, DC 20401. Phone: 866-512-1800 or (202)512-1800 or (866)512-1800; Fax: (202)512-2104 or (202)512-2250; Email: contactcenter@gpo.gov • URL: http://www.gpo.gov • Annual. $64. Produced by the National Center for Health Statistics, Public Health Service, U. S. Department of Health and Human Services. Provides detailed data on expectation of life by age, race, and sex. Historical data is shown annually from the year 1900. (Vital Statistics, volume 2.).

***VNU Business Media***. ADWEEK Media, 770 Broadway St. New York, NY 10003. • URL: http://www.vnubusinessmedia.com • Annual. $100.00. Presents cost, circulation, and audience statistics for various mass media segments, including television, radio, magazines, newspapers, telephone yellow pages, and cinema.

***Vocational Education and Training Abstracts***. Taylor & Francis Ltd., 2 Park Sq., Milton Park Abingdon OX14 4RN, United Kingdom. Phone: 44 22 70176000 or 44 20 70176000; Fax: 44 22 70176699 or (701)76336; Email: info@e-elgar.co.uk • URL: http://www.taylorandfrancisgroup.com • Annual. £926 Institutions print + online; $1,622 Institutions print + online; £833 Institutions online; $1,460 Institutions online; £284 Individuals; $482 Individuals; €1,293 Institutions print and online; €1,164 Institutions online only; €383 Individuals. Journal providing information needs of those engaged in technical or vocational education.Published in England. Formerly *Technical Education Abstracts*.

***Vows: The Bridal and Wedding Business Journal***. Grimes and Associates, 24 Daisy St. Ladera Ranch, CA 92694. Phone: (949)388-4848; Fax: (949)388-8448; Email: info@vowsmagazine.com • URL: http://www.vowsmagazine.com • Bimonthly. $30 Individuals; $52 Two years; $55 Elsewhere. Trade journal for bridal and wedding professionals.

***Wabash Business Directory***. Wabash Area Chamber of Commerce, 210 S Wabash St. Wabash, IN 46992-3132. Phone: (260)563-1168; Fax: (260)563-6920; Email: info@wabashchamber.org • URL: http://www.wabashchamber.org • Covers businesses and industrial businesses in Wabash, Indiana. Entries include contact details.

***Wageweb: Salary Survey Data On-Line***. HRPDI: Human Resources Programs Development and Improvement, Phone: (804)363-1792; Fax: (804)594-3721; Email: salaries@wageweb.com • URL: http://www.wageweb.com • Web site provides salary information for more than 170 benchmark positions, including (for example) 29 information management jobs. Data shows average minimum, median, and average maximum compensation for each position, based on salary surveys. Fees: Free for national salary data; $169.00 per year for more detailed information (geographic, organization size, specific industries).

***Wake Forest Journal of Business and Intellectual Property Law***. Wake Forest University School of Law, Reynolda Sta. Winston-Salem, NC 27109. Phone: (336)758-5437 or (336)758-5435; Fax: (336)758-3930; Email: admissions@law.wfu.edu • URL: http://law.wfu.edu.

***Walden's ABC Guide***. Walden-Mott Corp., 225 N Franklin Tpke. Ramsey, NJ 07446. Phone: (201)818-8630; Fax: (201)818-8720 • URL: http://www.walden-mott.com/ • Annual. $245 Individuals full online access and free print edition. Covers: Over 10,000 firms which manufacture, convert, and sell paper products and their suppliers. Entries include: Company name, address, phone, names of executives, and products and services offered.

***Wales Business Directory***. Kemps Publishing Ltd., 11 The Swan Courtyard, Charles Edward Rd. Yardley B26 1BU, United Kingdom. Phone: 44 121 7654144 or (441)21 7654144; Fax:

44 121 7063491 or (441)21 7063491; Email: enquiries@kempspublishing.co.uk • URL: http://www.kempspublishing.co.uk • Annual. $18. Covers: Members of the Chambers of Commerce of Cardiff, Chester, North Wales, Neath, Newport, Gwent, Port Talbot, and Swansea and local businesses. Entries include: Company name, address, phone, member name.

***Walker's Manual of Community Bank Stocks***. Walker's Manual Inc., 92 W Main St. Freehold, NJ 07728-2133. Phone: (732)431-6614; Email: info@walkersmanual.com • URL: http://www.walkersmanual.com • $95. Covers 502 community banks in the United States—community banks are financed with less than $10 million and usually serve a limited geographic area.

***Walker's Manual of Western Corporations***. Walker's Manual Inc., 92 W Main St. Freehold, NJ 07728-2133. Phone: (732)431-6614; Email info@walkersmanual.com • URL: http://www.walkersmanual.com • Annual. $380 base edition; $480 including updates. Covers: over 1,500 publicly owned corporations headquartered in Alaska, Arizona, California, Colorado, Hawaii, Idaho, Montana, Nevada, New Mexico, Oregon, Utah, Washington, and Wyoming. Entries include: Company name, address, phone, description of business; names of executives and directors with shareholdings of each; number of employees, brand names or product lines, financial data and common share data covering five years, capitalization, number of shareholders, sales and management statements, income and balance sheet information for five years.

***The Wall Street Digest***. Donald H. Rowe The Wall Street Digest, 2 N Tamiami Trl. Sarasota, FL 34236. Phone: 800-785-5050 or (941)954-5500; Fax: (941)364-8447; Email: subscribe@wallstreetdigest.com • Description: Covers major investment areas, including stocks and bonds; foreign currencies; gold, silver, and other precious metals; real estate; tax shelters; and estate planning. Recurring features include "a digest of the month's best" investment and financial seminars, newsletter reviews, and statistics.

***Wall Street Journal Guide to the Top Business Schools***. Simon and Schuster Inc., 1230 Ave. Of The Americas New York, NY 10020. Phone: 800-223-2336 or (212)698-7000 • URL: http://www.simonandschuster.com • Annual. $11.99. Rankings are based on surveys of recruiters of MBA graduates. Includes detailed descriptions of the leading U.S. business schools and information for applicants.

***Wall Street Journal Interactive Edition***. Dow Jones & Co., Inc., 1211 Avenue of the Americas New York, NY 10036. Phone: 800-369-5663; Email: service@dowjones.com • URL: http://new.dowjones.com • Fee-based Web site providing online searching of worldwide information from *The Wall Street Journal*. Includes "Company Snapshots," "The Journal's Greatest Hits," "Index to Market Data," "Journal Links," etc. Financial price quotes are available. Fees: $49.00 per year; $29.00 per year to print subscribers.

***Wallis & Futuna Investment & Business Guide***. International Business Publications, USA, PO Box 15343 Washington, DC 20003. Phone: (202)546-2103; Fax: (202)546-3275; Email: ibpusa@comcast.net • URL: http://ibpus.com • $99.95 Individuals hardcopy, E-book and CD-ROM. Covers: Basic information on economy, export-import and investment climate, regulations and industrial development, banking, and government. Entries include: Important business contacts and business travel.

**WAM International: Women Advancing Microfinance**. 402 Constitution Ave. NE Washington, DC 20002. Phone: (202)547-4546; Email: wam.international.president@gmail.com • URL: http://waminternational.org • Promotes the advancement of women working in the microfinance industry. Seeks to extend economic opportunities to women globally and encourages active participation of women in management and governance roles.

***Wansbeck Business Directory***. Wansbeck Business Forum, Arch Centre for Enterprise, Lintonville Enterprise Park Ashington NE63 9JZ, United Kingdom. Phone: 44 1670 528400; Email: info@wansbeckbusiness.co.uk • URL: http://www.wansbeckbusiness.co.uk • Covers businesses within Wansbeck Area in United Kingdom.

***Ward's AutoInfoBank***. Ward's Communications, 3000 Town Ctr., Ste. 2750 Southfield, MI 48075-1245. Phone: (248)357-0800 or (248)799-2647; Fax: (248)357-0810; Email: wards@wardsauto.com • URL: http://www.wardsauto.com • Provides weekly, monthly, quarterly, and annual statistical data from 1980 to date for U. S. and imported cars and trucks. Covers production, shipments, sales, inventories, optional equipment, etc. Updating varies by series. Inquire as to online cost and availability.

***Ward's Automotive Reports***. Ward's Communications, 3000 Town Ctr., Ste. 2750 Southfield, MI 48075-1245. Phone: (248)357-0800 or (248)799-2647; Fax: (248)357-0810; Email: wards@wardsauto.com • URL: http://www.wardsauto.com • Description: Reports "vital statistical information and exclusive news of critical interest" to the automotive industry. **Remarks:** Subscription includes Ward's Automotive Yearbook. Ward's Communications, Inc. is a subsidiary of Intertec Publishing Corp.

***Ward's Automotive Yearbook***. Ward's Communications, 3000 Town Ctr., Ste. 2750 Southfield, MI 48075-1245. Phone: (248)357-0800 or (248)799-2647; Fax: (248)357-0810; Email: wards@wardsauto.com • URL: http://www.

wardsauto.com • Annual. $570 Single issue 2010 edition; $895 Single issue 2010 edition and CD-ROM set; $580 Single issue 2011 edition; $910 Single issue 2011 edition and CD-ROM set; $590 Single issue 2012 edition; $925 Single issue 2012 edition and CD-ROM set; $610 Single issue 2013 edition; $940 Single issue 2013 edition and CD-ROM set; $1,540 Individuals full year; $1,590 Other countries full year. Comprehensive statistical information on automotive production, sales, truck data and suppliers. Included with subscription to *Ward's Automotive Reports*.

***Ward's Business Directory of U.S. Private and Public Companies***. Cengage Learning Inc., 20 Channel Center St. Boston, MA 02210. Phone: 800-487-8488 or (617)289-7700; Fax: (617)289-7844; Email: investors@cengage.com • URL: http://www.cengage.com • Annual. Edition 56, 8-vol. set, $4,485.00 (includes inter-edition supplement ). Some individual volumes also sold separately.; $3,627 Individuals five-volume set; $3,205 Individuals four-volume set; $1,697 Individuals volumes 5, 6, or 7; $1,149 Individuals volume 8. Eight volumes. Ward's contains basic information on about 115,000 business firms, of which 90 percent are private companies. Volumes available individually.

***Warehouse Management's Guide to Public Warehousing***. Reed Elsevier Group plc Reed Business Information, 360 Park Ave. S New York, NY 11010. Phone: (212)791-4208; Email: corporatecommunications@reedbusiness.com • URL: http://www.reedbusiness.com • Annual. $55.00. List of general merchandise,contract and refrigerated warehouses.

***Warehousing Distribution Directory***. UBM Global Trade, 400 Windsor Corporate Pk., 50 Millstone Rd., Ste. 200 East Windsor, NJ 08520-1415. Phone: 800-221-5488 or (609)371-7700 or (609)371-7701; Fax: (609)371-7885 or (609)371-7883; Email: customerservice@cbizmedia.com • URL: http://www.cbizmedia.com • Semiannual. Publication includes: List of about 800 warehousing and consolidation companies and firms offering trucking, trailer on flatcar, container on flatcar, and piggyback carrier services. Entries include: Name of firm, address, phone, name and title of contact, services, insurance provided, bank references, territory covered, restrictions, number of staff, and branches or subsidiaries with their locations.

***Warman's Antiques & Collectibles Price Guide***. Krause Publications Inc., 700 E State St. Iola, WI 54990-0001. Phone: 800-726-9966 or (715)445-2214 or (715)445-4612; Fax: (715)445-4087 • URL: http://www.krause.com • Annual. $20 Individuals Paperback. Covers: Over 50,000 antiques and collectibles, plus listings for collector's clubs. Database includes: 1,500 color photos. Entries include: Description, price.

***Warman's Antiques and Collectibles Price Guide***. Krause Publications Inc., 700 E State St. Iola, WI 54990-0001. Phone: 800-726-9966 or (715)445-2214 or (715)445-4612; Fax: (715)445-4087 • URL: http://www.krause.com • Annual. $20 Individuals. Manufacturer profiles, key events, current status, collector's clubs, museums, resources available for Americana and collectibles.

***Warner Business Association—Business Directory***. Warner Business Association, PO Box 301 Warner, NH 03278. Phone: (603)456-3330 • URL: http://kearsargechamber.org • List of businesses, artists, and artisans in Warner, New Hampshire.

***Warren's Forms of Agreements***. Matthew Bender and Company Inc., 1275 Broadway Albany, NY 12204-2638. Phone: 800-424-4200 or (518)487-3000; Fax: (518)487-3573 or (800)424-4200; Email: customer.support@lexisnexis.com • URL: http://www.matthewbender.com • Biennial. $2,368 print; $2,153 E-book. 8-volume set. A compact source of forms that business transaction lawyers are most frequently asked to document.

***Warshaw Collection of Business Americana, ca. 1724-1977***. Smithsonian Institution National Museum of American History Archives Center, West Wing, 1st Fl., 14th and Constitution Ave. NW Washington, DC 20560. Phone: (202)633-3270; Email: archivescenter@si.edu • URL: http://sirismm.si.edu/siris/SIASC/archives_center.htm • Contains bibliographic and cataloguing references to items from the Warshaw Collection of Business Americana held in the collections of the Smithsonian Institution's National Museum of American History.

***Washington: A Comprehensive Directory of the Key Institutions and Leaders in t he National Capitol Area***. Columbia Books Inc., 1350 New York Ave. NW, Ste. 207 Washington, DC 20005. Phone: (202)737-3777 • Annual. $149.00. Provides information on about 5,000 Washington, DC key businesses, government offices, non-profit organizations, and cultural institutions, with the names of about 25,000 principal executives. Includes Washington media, law offices, foundations, labor unions, international organizations, clubs, etc.

***The Washington Agricultural Record***. Washington Agricultural Record, Box 25001, Georgetown Sta. Washington, DC 20007. Phone: (202)333-8190; Fax: (202)337-3809 • Description: Focuses on Washington farm issues and developments, reporting international congressional and United States Department of Agriculture (U.S.D.A.) news and international agricultural developments.

***Washington Drug Letter***. Washington Business Information Inc., 300 N Washington St., No. 200 Falls Church, VA 22046-3431. Phone: 888-838-5578 or (703)538-7600; Fax: (703)538-7676; Email: customerservice@fdanews.com •

URL: http://www.fdanews.com • Description: Focuses on regulation and legislation affecting prescription and proprietary drugs. Monitors Food & Drug Administration (FDA) actions and new drug applications, manufacturing procedures, advertising and labeling, compliance cases, research, and testing rules.

***Washington Information Directory***. CQ Press, 2300 N St. NW, Ste. 800 Washington, DC 20037. Phone: 866-427-7737 or (202)729-1900; Email: customerservice@cqpress.com • URL: http://www.cqpress.com • Annual. $175 Individuals print cloth, standing order. Covers: 10,000 governmental agencies, congressional committees, and non-governmental associations considered competent sources of specialized information. Entries include: Name of agency, committee, or association; address, phone, fax, and Internet; annotation concerning function or activities of the office; and name of contact.

***Washington International Arts Letter***. Allied Business Consultants Inc., 317 Fairchild St. Iowa City, IA 52245-2115. • Description: Publishes information about cultural developments; personalities in the arts; and the workings and actions of the National Endowments of the Arts and Humanities, Congress, and federal offices as they affect this field. Recurring features include announcements of jobs, scholarships, grants, and other forms of assistance available in the arts and humanities; bibliographies; publications reviews; and listings of names and addresses of businesses and organizations that contribute to the arts.

***Washington Manufacturers Directory and Industrial Database***. Manufacturers' News Inc., 1633 Central St. Evanston, IL 60201-1569. Phone: (847)864-7000; Fax: (847)332-1100 • URL: http://www.manufacturersnews.com • Annual. $118 Individuals print; $554 Individuals database (EZ select full); $366 Individuals database (EZ select with 20 plus employees); $194 Individuals database (EZ select basic). Covers: 7,834 manufacturers in Washington State. Entries include: Company name, address, phone, names and titles of key personnel, year established, number of employees, plant square footage, services, Standard Industry Classification (SIC) code, parent and subsidiary company information, type of in-house computer system, URL, e-mail address.

***Washington Manufacturers Register***. Harris InfoSource, 2057 E Aurora Rd. Twinsburg, OH 44087-1999. Phone: 800-888-5900 or (330)425-9000 or (973)921-5500; Fax: (800)643-5997 or (877)252-3375; Email: customerservice@harrisinfo.com • URL: http://www.harrisinfo.com • Annual. Covers: 12,600 manufacturers in Washington state, plus names of key executives. Entries include: Company name, address, parent name/location, telephone, fax and 800 numbers, Web site address (on CD-ROM only), number of employees, year established, annual revenue, plant size, business description, Standard Industrial Classification (SIC) codes, executive names/titles, public ownership, legal structure, import/export designators, female/minority ownership.

**Washington State University - Agricultural Research Center**. PO Box 646240 Pullman, WA 99164-6240. Phone: (509)335-4563; Fax: (509)335-6751; Email: agresearch@wsu.edu • URL: http://arc.wsu.edu • Agriculture and food safety, including economics; biological systems engineering; agronomy and soils; animal sciences; human development; food science and human nutrition; apparel; merchandising; interior design; rural sociology; entomology; natural resource management; horticulture and landscape architecture; plant pathology; veterinary science; plant and animal biotechnology; wood materials; and low-input sustainable agriculture. Performs forage, seed, and minor pesticide testing.

**Washington University in St. Louis - Center for Health Policy**. Simon Hall, CB 1133, 1 Brookings Dr. Saint Louis, MO 63130. Phone: (314)935-8767; Fax: (314)935-9199; Email: peckw@wustl.edu • URL: http://healthpolicy.wustl.edu • Health policy, including disparities in access to care and insurance, healthcare costs, medical workforce shortages, and inefficiencies and errors in provision of medical services.

**Washington University in St. Louis - Center for Security Technologies**. 1 Brookings Dr., Box 1127 Saint Louis, MO 63130. Phone: (314)935-4767; Fax: (314)935-7500; Email: rsi@wustl.edu • URL: http://www.cst.wustl.edu/ • Systems that provide judgment and control critical to the security of people, objects, and intellectual assets, while considering key factors such as privacy, public policy, and economic impact.

**Washington University in St. Louis - Weidenbaum Center on the Economy, Government, and Public Policy**. CB 1027, 1 Brookings Dr. Saint Louis, MO 63130-4899. Phone: (314)935-5630; Fax: (314)935-5688; Email: smith@wustl.edu • URL: http://wc.wustl.edu • Effects of public policy on the American business system, including international trade, government regulation of business, federal taxing, and spending, international regulation, capital formation, federal credit activity, and corporate governance.

***Waste Age Buyers' Guide***. RentPath Inc., 3585 Engineering Dr., Ste. 100 Norcross, GA 30092-2831. Phone: 800-216-1423 or (678)421-3000 • URL: http://www.rentpath.com • Annual. Manufacturers of equipment and supplies for the waste management industry.

***Waste Business West***. CHMM Inc., 951 Denison St., Unit 4 Markham, ON, Canada L3R 3W9. Phone: 888-701-1111 or (905)305-6155; Fax: (905)305-6255 • Bimonthly. Magazine for waste-industry.

***Waste Treatment System Businesses in the World***. Momentum Technologies L.L.C., PO Box 460813 Glendale, CO 80246. Phone: (303)229-4841; Fax: (408)705-2031 • URL: http://www.mtt.com • Contains 250 directory listings of businesses throughout the world that manufacture or sell waste treatment systems and associated components. Includes business name, address, phone number, fax number, e-mail address, and web site address. Provides brief descriptions of product lines, services offered, and business type. Includes information on manufacturers, component makers, wholesalers, retailers, system designers, system installers, trade associations, and more. Searchable by location, business type, company name, and keyword.

***Waste Treatment Technology News***. BCC Research, 70 New Canaan Ave. Norwalk, CT 06850. Phone: 866-285-7216 or (203)750-9783; Fax: (203)229-0087; Email: info@bccresearch.com • URL: http://www.bccresearch.com • Description: Profiles existing and developing industrial waste treatment techniques. Follows governmental action such as Superfund legislation and EPA (Environmental Protection Agency) activities. Focuses on the research and development of waste treatment technologies, listing recent patents in the field. Recurring features include news of research.

***The Watch Repairer's Manual***. Henry B. Fried. American Watchmakers-Clockmakers Institute, 701 Enterprise Dr. Harrison, OH 45030. Phone: 866-367-2924 or (513)367-9800; Fax: (513)367-1414; Email: info@awci.com • URL: http://www.awci.com • $35.00. 1986. Fourth revised edition.

***Water and Environment Manager***. Chartered Institution of Water and Environmental Management. Terence Dalton Ltd., Arbons House, Water St. Lavenham CO10 9RN, United Kingdom. Phone: 44 1787 249290; Fax: (178)7 248267; Email: postmaster@lavenhambroup.co.uk • 10 times a year. $90.00 per year. Formerly *Chartered Institution of Water and Environmental Management Newsletter*.

***Water Conditioning & Purification—Buyers Guide Issue***. Publicom Inc., 2800 E Fort Lowell Rd. Tucson, AZ 85716. Phone: (520)323-6144; Fax: (520)323-7412; Email: info@wcponline.com • URL: http://www.wcponline.com • Continuous. Publication includes: List of about 800 manufacturers and suppliers in the water treatment and purification industry. Entries include: Company name, address, phone, name of contact, line of business.

***Water Desalination Report***. Maria C. Smith, PO Box 10 Tracys Landing, MD 20779-0010. Phone: (301)261-5010; Fax: (301)261-5010; Email: info@bccresearch.com • Description: Concentrates on the activities of government and industry worldwide concerning the desalination of seawater and brackish water. Discusses such topics as problems with water supply and reuse, resource planning, and pollution control. Reports on federal budgets, regulation, new and future programs, opportunities in business, and research. Recurring features include book reviews and a schedule of activities.

***Water Filtering and Purification System Businesses in the World***. Momentum Technologies L.L.C., PO Box 460813 Glendale, CO 80246. Phone: (303)229-4841; Fax: (408)705-2031 • URL: http://www.mtt.com • Contains 322 directory listings and contact information of businesses providing water filtering and purification systems throughout the world. Includes business name, address, phone number, fax number, e-mail address, and web site address. Provides brief descriptions of product lines, services offered, and business type. Includes information on manufacturers, component makers, wholesalers, retailers, system designers, system installers, trade associations, and more. Searchable by location, business type, company name, and keyword.

***The Waterlow Stock Exchange Yearbook***. Macmillan Publishers Ltd., The Macmillan Bldg., 4 Crinan St. London N1 9XW, United Kingdom. Phone: 44 020 7833 4000 or 44 20 78434000; Fax: 44 020 7843 4640 or 44 20 78434640 • URL: http://www.macmillan.co.uk • Annual. $400 Individuals; $200 Individuals charity rate; 50% discount. Covers: firms whose stock is traded on the London Stock Exchange; worldwide coverage. Entries include: Company name, address, registrars, directors, auditors, bankers, date registered on the exchange, line of business, capital, loan capital, additional financial data.

***Waterway Guide—The Yachtman's Bible***. Argus Press Inc., • $36.95 postpaid. Covers: inland and coastal waterways in the eastern half of the United States; published in three editions. Northern edition covers coastal waterways from the Delaware Bay to the U.S.-Canadian border; plus New York canals, Champlain Waterways, and St. Lawrence River; Middle Atlantic edition covers waterways from the Chesapeake Bay to the Florida-Georgia line; Southern edition covers intracoastal waterways from the Florida-Georgia line to the Texas-Mexico border and the Bahamas. Entries include: Name of marine facility, location, navigation information and courses, points of interest, anchorages.

***The Way We Work: An Encyclopedia of Business Culture***. Cengage Learning Inc., 20 Channel Center St. Boston, MA 02210. Phone: 800-487-8488 or (617)289-7700; Fax: (617)289-7844; Email: investors@cengage.com • URL: http://www.cengage.com • 2010. eBook. Published by Greenwood Publishing Group. Explores in over 150 A-Z entries, the origins and impact of the concepts, ideas, fads and themes that have become part of the business vernacular, shedding light on the dynamic ways in which business and society both influence and reflect each other.

**Wayne State University - College of Nursing - Office of Health Research**. Cohn Bldg., Rm. 319, 5557 Cass Ave. Detroit, MI 48202. Phone: (313)577-4135; Fax: (313)577-5777; Email: n.artinian@wayne.edu • URL: http://www.nursing.wayne.edu/faculty/health-research.php • Studies innovation in health care organization and financing.

***Wearables Business***. Penton, 9800 Metcalf Ave. Overland Park, KS 66212. Phone: 866-748-4926 or (913)341-1300; Fax: (913)967-1905 or (913)967-1898; Email: corporatecustomerservice@penton.com • URL: http://www.penton.com • Trade magazine covering the wearable segment of the promotional products industry for distributors.

***Weather Almanac***. Cengage Learning Inc., 20 Channel Center St. Boston, MA 02210. Phone: 800-487-8488 or (617)289-7700; Fax: (617)289-7844; Email: investors@cengage.com • URL: http://www.cengage.com • 2004. eBook. 11th edition. Weather records for 108 major U.S. cities and a climatic overview of the country. Contact for pricing.

***Web Site Source Book: A Guide to Major U.S. Businesses, Organizations, Agencies, Institutions, and Other Information Resources on the World Wide Web***. Omnigraphics Inc., PO Box 31-1640 Detroit, MI 48231. Phone: (313)961-1340; Fax: (313)961-1383; Email: customerservice@omnigraphics.com • URL: http://www.omnigraphics.com • Annual. $185 Individuals paperback; $204 Individuals List Price. Covers: Over 99,000 websites for businesses, organizations, agencies, and institutions. Entries include: Name, address, phone, fax, toll-free phone number, and URL addresses.

***WebFinance***. SourceMedia Inc., 1 State Street Plz., 27th Fl. New York, NY 10004. Phone: 800-221-1809 or (212)803-8200 or (212)803-8333; Fax: (212)843-9635 or (212)292-5216; Email: custserv@sourcemedia.com • URL: http://www.sourcemedia.com • Semimonthly. $995.00 per year. Newsletter (also available online at www.webfinance.net). Covers the Internet-based provision of online financial services by banks, online brokers, mutual funds, and insurance companies. Provides news stories, analysis, and descriptions of useful resources.

***Weekly Board of Trade, Cotton Exchange***. New York Cotton Exchange, 4 World Trade Ctr. New York, NY 10048. Phone: (212)748-4000 • URL: http://www.nyce.com • Weekly. $100.00 per year.

***Weekly Business Failures***. Dun & Bradstreet Inc., 103 JFK Pkwy. Short Hills, NJ 07078. Phone: 800-526-0651 or (973)921-5500 or (973)921-5000; Fax: (866)560-7035 or (512)794-7670; Email: info@dnb.com • URL: http://www.dnb.com • Weekly. $445.00 per year.

***The Weekly Corporate Growth Report***. NVST Inc., 1100 Dexter Ave. N Seattle, WA 98109. Phone: 800-910-6878 or (206)676-3802; Fax: (206)273-7401; Email: info@nvst.com • URL: http://www.nvst.com • Weekly. Publication includes: Current acquisition and merger transactions. Entries include: Buyer and seller names and locations, annual sales and net income for each, seller's net worth and price-earnings ratio, and purchase price, including terms and various ratios.

***Weekly Petroleum Status Report***. Energy Information Administration. U. S. Government Printing Office, 732 N Capitol St. NW Washington, DC 20401. Phone: 866-512-1800 or (202)512-1800 or (866)512-1800; Fax: (202)512-2104 or (202)512-2250; Email: contactcenter@gpo.gov • URL: http://www.gpo.gov • Weekly. Current statistics in the context of both historical information and selected prices and forecasts.

***Weiss Ratings Guide to Life and Annuity Insurers***. Weiss Ratings, Inc., 15430 Endeavor Dr. Jupiter, FL 33478-6400. Phone: 877-934-7778 • URL: http://www.weissratings.com • Quarterly. Rates life insurance companies for overall safety and financial stability.

***Welcome to the Foundation Center***. Foundation Center, Phone: (212)620-4230 or (212)807-3679; Fax: (212)807-3677; Email: mfn@fdncenter.org • URL: http://www.fdncenter.org • Web site provides a wide variety of information about foundations, grants, and philanthropy, with links to philanthropic organizations. "Grantmaker Information" link furnishes descriptions of available funding.

***Weldasearch***. TWI World Centre for Materials Joining Technology, Granta Park, Great Abington Cambridge CB21 6AL, United Kingdom. Phone: 44 1223 899000; Fax: 44 1223 892588; Email: twi@twi.co.uk • URL: http://www.twi-global.com • Contains abstracts of international welding literature, 1967 to date. Inquire as to online cost and availability.

***Welding Research Council Yearbook***. Welding Research Council, PO Box 201547 Shaker Heights, OH 44122. Phone: (216)658-3847; Fax: (216)658-3854; Email: mprager@forengineers.org • URL: http://forengineers.org/welding-research-council • Annual. Lists the objectives and long-range plans of the Council and committee membership.

***Wer Liefert Was? Central Europe: Business-to-Business Directory***. Wer liefert was GmbH, Normannenweg 16-20 D-20537 Hamburg, Germany. Phone: 49 40 254400 or 49 40 254 400; Fax: 49 40 25440100 or 49 40 254 40 100; Email: info@wlw.de • URL: http://www.wlw.de • Annual. Database covers: Over 45,000 companies in the Czech Republic, Slovenia, Slovakia, and Croatia. Entries include: Name, address, phone, fax, description of products/services offered.

***Wer Liefert Was? Online***. Wer liefert was GmbH, Normannenweg 16-20 D-20537 Hamburg, Germany. Phone: 49 40 254400 or 49 40 254 400; Fax: 49 40 25440100 or 49 40 254 40 100; Email: info@wlw.de • URL: http://www.wlw.de • Database covers: Products and services from over 307,356 companies in Germany, Austria, Switzerland, the Netherlands, Belgium, Luxembourg, the Czech Republic, Slovakia, Slovenia, Croatia, the UK, France, and Italy. Entries include: Company name, address, phone, product/service, managers, ISO certification, e-mail/internet address.

***West Lincoln Business Directory***. West Lincoln Chamber of Commerce, PO Box 555 Smithville, ON, Canada L0R 2A0. Phone: (905)957-1606; Fax: (905)957-4628 • URL: http://www.westlincolnchamber.com • Covers 1,200 businesses in West Lincoln, Canada.

**West Virginia University - College of Business and Economics - Center for Chinese Business**. PO Box 6025 Morgantown, WV 26506-6025. Phone: (304)293-7885; Fax: (304)293-3274 • URL: http://www.be.wvu.edu/chinese_business • Emerging market economy in China.

***Western Cape Business Register***. Intratex Holdings, 12 Caversham Rd. Pinetown 3610, South Africa. Phone: 27 31 7174000; Fax: (717)4001; Email: webmaster@brabys.com • Covers: businesses and residences in the Cape Peninsula area of South Africa. Entries include: Company or personal name, address, phone.

***Western European Countries Mineral Industry Handbook***. International Business Publications, USA, PO Box 15343 Washington, DC 20003. Phone: (202)546-2103; Fax: (202)546-3275; Email: ibpusa@comcast.net • URL: http://ibpus.com • $99.95 Individuals Hardbound. Covers: strategic information and contacts on mining and mineral industry of the Western European countries.

***Western Farmer-Stockman***. Farm Progress Companies Inc., 255 38th Ave., Ste. P Saint Charles, IL 60174-5410. Phone: 800-441-1410 or (630)690-5600; Fax: (630)462-2869 or (630)462-4656; Email: wvogt@farmprogress.com • URL: http://www.farmprogress.com • Monthly. $26.95 Individuals 1-year subscription. Formerly *Montana Farmer*.

***Western Grower and Shipper: The Business Magazine of the Western Product Industry***. Western Growers Association. 17620 Fitch St. Irvine, CA 92614. Phone: (949)863-1000; Fax: (949)863-9028; Email: ddewees@wga.com • URL: http://www.wga.com • Monthly. $18.00 per year.

***Western Growers Association—Membership Directory***. Western Growers Association, 17620 Fitch St. Irvine, CA 92614-6032. Phone: 800-333-4942 or (949)863-1000; Fax: (949)863-9028; Email: info@wga.com • URL: http://www.wga.com • Annual. Covers: 2,700 growers, shippers, packers, brokers, and distributors of fruits, vegetables, nuts, and allied industries in California and Arizona. Entries include: Company name, address, phone and fax, names of executives, list of commodities.

***Western Lumber Export Buyers Guide***. Western Wood Products Association, 1500 SW 1st Ave., Ste. 870 Portland, OR 97201. Phone: (503)224-3930; Fax: (503)224-3934; Email: info@wwpa.org • URL: http://www2.wwpa.org • Annual. Covers: Approximately 75 producers of softwood lumber products for overseas markets. Entries include: Company name, address, phone, telex, name and title of contact, subsidiary and branch names and locations, description of products and services.

***Western Manufacturers Database Prospect System***. Harris InfoSource, 2057 E Aurora Rd. Twinsburg, OH 44087-1999. Phone: 800-888-5900 or (330)425-9000 or (973)921-5500; Fax: (800)643-5997 or (877)252-3375; Email: customerservice@harrisinfo.com • URL: http://www.harrisinfo.com • $3,125. Database covers: Manufacturers covering the western U.S. Entries include: Company number of employees, annual sales, plant size, year established, names and titles for up to 10 executives, SIC codes.

**Western Payments Alliance**. 300 Montgomery St., Ste.400 San Francisco, CA 94104. Phone: (415)433-1230; Fax: (415)433-1370; Email: info@wespay.org • URL: http://www.wespay.org • Represents financial institutions and others involved in payments systems in the U.S.

***Western Real Estate Business: Connecting Real Estate in the West***. France Publications Inc., 3500 Piedmont Rd., Ste. 415 Atlanta, GA 30305. Phone: (404)832-8262; Fax: (404)832-8260; Email: jerry@francepublications.com • URL: http://www.francepublications.com/contact.html • Monthly. $67 Individuals; $116 Two years. Magazine that covers the latest news, developments and trends in commercial real estate in the western states.

***Western Sahara Business Law Handbook***. International Business Publications, USA, PO Box 15343 Washington, DC 20003. Phone: (202)546-2103; Fax: (202)546-3275; Email: ibpusa@comcast.net • URL: http://ibpus.com • $99.95 Individuals hardcopy, E-book and CD-ROM. Covers: Information on business laws and climate, legislation, export-import regulations, and contacts.

***Western States Exporters and Importers Database***. Harris InfoSource, 2057 E Aurora Rd. Twinsburg, OH 44087-1999. Phone: 800-888-5900 or (330)425-9000 or (973)921-5500; Fax: (800)643-5997 or (877)252-3375; Email: customerservice@harrisinfo.com • URL: http://www.harrisinfo.com • $445. Covers: 11,500 exporting and 5,000 importing companies in Alaska, Arizona, California, Colorado, Hawaii, Idaho, Montana, New Mexico, Nevada, Oregon, Utah, Washington, and Wyoming. Entries include:

Company name, address, phone, fax, toll-free, names and titles of key personnel, number of employees, geographical area served, financial data, descriptions of product/service, Standard Industrial Classification (SIC) code, year established, annual revenues, plant size, legal structure, export/import information.

***Western Union Directory and Buyer's Guide***. Western Union Directory Services, 13022 Hollenberg Dr. Bridgeton, MO 63044. Fax: (314)739-7316 • Publication includes: Yellow Pages Buyers' Guide list of businesses under classified business headings. Entries include: Company name, address, phone, telex, and EasyLink numbers. Principal content of publication is a listing of more than 200,000 US subscribers to Western Union Telex, EasyLink, and Worldcom; 60,000 subscribers in Canada and Mexico.

**Western Washington University - Center for Canadian-American Studies**. Canada House 201, 516 High St. Bellingham, WA 98225-9110. Phone: (360)650-3728 or (360)650-3000; Fax: (360)650-3995; Email: donald.alper@wwu.edu • URL: http://www.wwu.edu/canam • Research areas include Canadian business and economics.

**Western Washington University - Center for Economic and Business Research**. Parks Hall 326, MS 9074, College of Business & Economics, 516 High St. Bellingham, WA 98225. Phone: (360)650-3909; Fax: (360)650-7688; Email: hart. hodges@wwu.edu • URL: http://www.cbe.wwu.edu/cebr/index.shtml • Acts as grant agent for the College of Business and Economics and contracts research for the local area.

***Westlaw Business Law Practitioner***. Thomson Reuters Westlaw, 610 Opperman Dr. Eagan, MN 55123. Phone: 800-344-5008 or (651)687-7000; Fax: (651)687-5827; Email: west. customer.service@thomson.com • Contains comprehensive and current online resources, by practice and jurisdiction, for legal research in business and commercial pursuits.

***Westlaw Journal Entertainment Industry***. Thomson Reuters Westlaw, 610 Opperman Dr. Eagan, MN 55123. Phone: 800-344-5008 or (651)687-7000; Fax: (651)687-5827; Email: west.customer.service@thomson.com • Monthly. *Sports and Entertainment Litigation Reporter*. Provides concise, unbiased coverage of litigation involving such issues as breach of contract, First Amendment, invasion of privacy, unfair competition, misappropriation of funds, and copyright and trademark issues.

***Westlaw Journal Securities Litigation & Regulation***. Thomson Reuters Westlaw, 610 Opperman Dr. Eagan, MN 55123. Phone: 800-344-5008 or (651)687-7000; Fax: (651)687-5827; Email: west.customer.service@thomson.com • $3,563.52 full set. Provides coverage of shareholder lawsuits against public companies.

***Westlaw Journal Tobacco Industry***. Thomson Reuters Westlaw, 610 Opperman Dr. Eagan, MN 55123. Phone: 800-344-5008 or (651)687-7000; Fax: (651)687-5827; Email: west. customer.service@thomson.com • $2,988.96. Reports on major lawsuits brought against tobacco companies.

***West's Encyclopedia of American Law***. Cengage Learning Inc., 20 Channel Center St. Boston, MA 02210. Phone: 800-487-8488 or (617)289-7700; Fax: (617)289-7844; Email: investors@cengage.com • URL: http://www.cengage.com • 2004. eBook. Second edition. Covers a wide variety of legal topics for the general reader. Inquire for pricing.

***West's Legal Forms***. Thomson West, 610 Opperman Dr. Eagan, MN 55123. Phone: 800-328-9352 or (651)687-7000 • Annual. 4,975 Multivolume set. Selection of customizable forms suitable for drafting a wide range of legal documents. Includes detailed commentary, analysis, checklists, and library references to the Key Number System.

***What to Buy for Business***. Dagens Industri, Box 3177 S-103 63 Stockholm, Sweden. • Monthly. General business publication.

***What's New in Advertising and Marketing***. Special Libraries Association - Advertising and Marketing Div., c/o John Patton, Suffolk Cooperative Library System, 627 N Sunrise Service Rd. Bellport, NY 11713. Phone: (516)286-1600; Fax: (516)286-1647; Email: scla@suffolk.lib.ny.us • URL: http://scla.net/main/resources • Quarterly. Non-profit organizations, $20.00 per year; corporations, $30.00 per year. Lists and briefly describes a wide variety of free or inexpensive material relating to advertising, marketing, and media.

***Wheat, Barley and Triticale Abstracts***. CABI, Nosworthy Way, Oxfordshire Wallingford OX10 8DE, United Kingdom. Phone: 44 1491 832111; Fax: 44 1491 833508; Email: enquiries@cabi.org • URL: http://www.cabi.org • Updated weekly. Published in England by CABI Publishing. Provides worldwide coverage of the literature of wheat, barley, and rye.

***Which Airline & Business Travel Update***. BMI Publications Ltd., Suffolk House, George St. Croydon CR9 1SR, United Kingdom. Phone: 44 20 86497233; Fax: 44 20 86497234; Email: enquiries@bmipublishing.co.uk • URL: http://www.bmipublications.com • Semiannual. Consumer magazine covering airline services for business travelers.

***Which Business CD-ROM?***. Bowker-Saur, Maypole House, Maypole Rd. East Grinstead RH19 1HV, United Kingdom. Phone: 44 1342 330100; Fax: 44 1342 330198; Email: customer.services@bowker-saur.co.uk • Annual. $259 plus $30.00 shipping. Publication includes: List of major CD-ROM publishers in the field of business; coverage includes the U.K. and Europe, with limited U.S. listings. Principal content of publication is information significant CD-ROM

titles in various business fields, such as company directories, company accounts, mergers/acquisitions, business news, legislation/regulations, market research, industries, economics and finance, international trade, and business management literature. Entries include: Publisher name, address, phone.

***Which European Database?***. K.G. Saur Verlag KG, Mies-van-der-Rohe-Strasse 1 D-80807 Munich, Germany. Phone: 49 490 89 769020; Email: info@degruyter.com • URL: http://www.degruyter.com/browse?publisher=KGS • Annual. $299 plus $15.00 shipping. Publication includes: List of leading business databases available throughout Europe. Entries include: Database name, description.

***White Collar Crime: Business and Regulatory Offenses***. ALM Media Properties LLC, 120 Broadway, 5th Fl. New York, NY 10271-1100. Phone: (212)457-9400; Fax: (646)417-7705; Email: customercare@alm.com • URL: http://www.alm.com • $740 print + online + ebook; $540 online + ebook. Covers such legal matters as criminal tax cases, securities fraud, computer crime, mail fraud, bank embezzlement, criminal antitrust activities, extortion, perjury, the criminal liability of corporations, and RICO (Racketeer Influenced and Corrupt Organization Act). (Law Journal Press).

***White Paper on American Business in China***. American Chamber of Commerce - People's Republic of China, The Office Park, Tower AB, 6th Fl., No. 10 Jintongxi Rd. Beijing 100020, China. Phone: 86 10 85190800; Fax: 86 10 85190899; Email: amcham@amchamchina.org • URL: http://www.amchamchina.org • Annual.

***Who Audits the UK?***. Public Relations Consultants Association, 17-23 Willow Pl., 1st Fl. London SW1P 1JH, United Kingdom. Phone: 44 20 72336026; Fax: 44 20 78284797 • URL: http://www.prca.org.uk • Irregular. $46. Covers: Information on the auditing of 2,000 companies and organizations in the UK. Entries include: Company name, address, phone.

***Who Belongs to Whom: Capital Links in German Companies***. Commerzbank AG, Kaiserplatz 60311 Frankfurt am Main, Germany. Phone: 49 069 136-20; Fax: 49 069 28 53 89; Email: info@commerzbank.com • URL: http://www.commerzbank.de • Semiannual. Covers: about 11,000 German companies and their domestic and foreign shareholders. Database includes: Glossary of German technical terms, translated in English, French, Italian, and Spanish. Entries include: Company name, trade or industry code number, capital, names of principal shareholders, partners, investors, and percentage of stock owned.

***Who Knows About Foreign Industries and Markets***. MarketResearch.com, 11200 Rockville Pke., Ste. 504 Rockville, MD 20852. Phone: 800-298-5699 or (240)747-3093; Fax: (240)747-3004; Email: customerservice@marketresearch.com • URL: http://www.marketresearch.com • Annual. $85. Covers: 2,500 U.S. experts and authorities on international trade. Entries include: Name and telephone number.

***Who Knows What: The Essential Business Resource Book***. Henry Holt and Co., 175 5th Ave. New York, NY 10010-7703. Phone: 888-330-8477 or (646)307-5095 or (800)488-5233; Fax: (212)633-0748; Email: publicity@hholt.com • URL: http://www.henryholt.com • $45. Covers: Approximately 5,500 businesses, special libraries, government agencies, and other organizations in the U.S. that have access to information in over 500 business-related subject areas. Entries include: Company or organization name, address, phone, fax, name and title of contact, description of services and projects.

***Who Knows Who: Networking through Corporate Boards***. Who Knows Who Publishers, 568 62nd St., Unit - A Oakland, CA 94609. Phone: (510)601-1556 • Annual. $165. Publication includes: List of over 1,000 companies noted by either Fortune magazine or Forbes magazine, or both; over 120 major foundations. Entries include: Company or foundation name, address, phone, boards of directors. Principal content of publication is lists of the companies and their boards of directors showing relationships among the companies by showing which of the board members sit on several of the companies' boards, i.e. interlocking directorates.

***Who Owns Corporate America***. Taft Group, 27500 Drake Rd. Farmington Hills, MI 48331-3535. Phone: 800-877-4253 or (248)699-4253 or (248)699-GALE; Fax: (800)414-5043 or (248)699-8061; Email: gale.salesassistance@thomson.com • URL: http://www.gale.com/taft • Annual. $285. Covers: nearly 75,000 officers, directors, and 10% principal stockholders who own securities registered with the Securities and Exchange Commission. Entries include: Name, company, stock symbol, number of shares held, date of last stock transaction, class of security held, type of ownership, relationship of stockholder to the company, market value of holdings.

***Who Owns What in World Banking***. Public Relations Consultants Association, 17-23 Willow Pl., 1st Fl. London SW1P 1JH, United Kingdom. Phone: 44 20 72336026; Fax: 44 20 78284797 • URL: http://www.prca.org.uk • Biennial. $350 airmail postpaid. Covers: about 225 leading multinational and consortium banks and their subsidiaries and affiliated banks. Entries include: Name of bank, location, financial data, percentage held by parent company, subsidiaries and affiliates and whether they are domestic or international.

***Who Owns Whom***. Dun & Bradstreet Inc., 103 JFK Pkwy. Short

Hills, NJ 07078. Phone: 800-526-0651 or (973)921-5500 or (973)921-5000; Fax: (866)560-7035 or (512)794-7670; Email: info@dnb.com • URL: http://www.dnb.com • Annual. Covers: In four regional volumes, approximately 320,000 company affiliates and subsidiaries of more than 23,000 companies in Australia and the Far East, North America, the United Kingdom and Ireland, and Continental Europe. Entries include: Ultimate parent and country, parent name, address, phone, place of incorporation, Standard Industrial Classification (SIC) code, trade investments, direct subsidiaries.

***Who Owns Whom—North America***. Dun & Bradstreet Inc., 103 JFK Pkwy. Short Hills, NJ 07078. Phone: 800-526-0651 or (973)921-5500 or (973)921-5000; Fax: (866)560-7035 or (512)794-7670; Email: info@dnb.com • URL: http://www.dnb.com • Annual. Covers: Parent companies located in the U.S., Canada, South America, and the West Indies and their foreign and domestic subsidiaries; 66,000 parent companies, 200,000 subsidiaries. Parents with international investments only are shown in the United States section. Entries include: Parent company name, address, phone, industrial classification, direct subsidiary names, and country of incorporation.

***Wholesale Commodity Report***. The Financial Times, Inc., 1330 Ave. of the Americas New York, NY 10019. Phone: 800-628-8088 or (212)641-6544; Fax: (212)641-6515; Email: uscirculation@ft.com • URL: http://www.ft.com • Weekly.

***The Wholesaler—Directory of Manufacturers Representatives Issue***. TMB Publishing Inc., 1838 Techny Ct. Northbrook, IL 60062. Phone: (847)564-1127 • URL: http://www.plumbingengineer.com • Annual. $50 Individuals hardcopy or CD-ROM. Publication includes: 2,000 manufacturers' representatives handling plumbing, heating, piping, air conditioning, and refrigeration products. Entries include: Representative's name or firm name, address, phone, fax, territory, and lines carried.

***The Wholesaler—'The Wholesaling 100' Issue***. TMB Publishing Inc., 1838 Techny Ct. Northbrook, IL 60062. Phone: (847)564-1127 • URL: http://www.plumbingengineer.com • Annual. $50 Individuals print or CD-ROM. Publication includes: Ranks 100 leading wholesalers of plumbing, heating, air conditioning, refrigeration equipment, and industrial pipe, valves and fittings. Entries include: Company name, address, phone, fax, names and titles of key personnel, number of employees, business breakdown (percentage).

***Who's Who Among African Americans***. Cengage Learning Inc., 20 Channel Center St. Boston, MA 02210. Phone: 800-487-8488 or (617)289-7700; Fax: (617)289-7844; Email: investors@cengage.com • URL: http://www.cengage.com • Annual. 357. Includes biographical details on over 20,000 notable African Americans. eBook also available. Contact for pricing.

***Who's Who Among Business Printing Independents***. Print Services and Distribution Association, 330 N Wabash Ave., Ste. 2000 Chicago, IL 60611. Phone: 800-230-0175; Fax: (312)673-6880 • URL: http://www.psda.org • Annual. Covers: about 2,400 member independent manufacturers and distributors of business forms; coverage is international. Database includes: Calendar of events; description of events and seminars. Entries include: Company name, address, phone, names of executives, financial keys, branch offices or subsidiaries, member services.

***Who's Who: An Annual Biographical Dictionary***. St. Martin's Press, Macmillan Publishers, 175 5th Ave. New York, NY 10010. Phone: (646)307-5151; Fax: (212)598-9173; Email: enquiries@stmartins.com • URL: http://us.macmillan.com/SMP.aspx • Annual. $330.00. Over 29,000 prominent individuals worldwide, but with emphasis on the United Kingdom.

***Who's Who Greater Norwalk Business Directory***. Greater Norwalk Chamber of Commerce, 101 East Ave. Norwalk, CT 06852. Phone: (203)866-2521; Fax: (203)852-0583; Email: info@norwalkchamberofcommerce.com • URL: http://www.norwalkchamberofcommerce.com • Annual. $525 Individuals employees. Businesses, community phone numbers, and regional information about the greater Norwalk, CT area.

***Who's Who in Alexandria Business***. Alexandria Chamber of Commerce, 801 N Fairfax St., Ste. 402 Alexandria, VA 22314. Phone: (703)549-1000; Fax: (703)549-1001; Email: info@alexchamber.com • URL: http://www.alexchamber.com • Annual. Covers businesses in Alexandria, Virginia.

***Who's Who in America***. Marquis Who's Who L.L.C., 300 Connell Dr., Ste. 2000 Berkeley Heights, NJ 07922. Phone: 800-473-7020 or (908)673-1000 or (908)673-1010; Fax: (908)673-1179; Email: customerservice@marquiswhoswho.com • URL: http://www.marquiswhoswho.com • Annual. $789.00. Two volumes. Contains over 90,000 concise biographies, with a Geographic/Professional Index.

***Who's Who in American Art***. Marquis Who's Who L.L.C., 300 Connell Dr., Ste. 2000 Berkeley Heights, NJ 07922. Phone: 800-473-7020 or (908)673-1000 or (908)673-1010; Fax: (908)673-1179; Email: customerservice@marquiswhoswho.com • URL: http://www.marquiswhoswho.com • Biennial. $297. Lists over 14,000 people active in visual arts.

***Who's Who in American Education***. Marquis Who's Who L.L.C., 300 Connell Dr., Ste. 2000 Berkeley Heights, NJ 07922. Phone: 800-473-7020 or (908)673-1000 or (908)673-1010; Fax: (908)673-1179; Email: customerservice@marquiswhoswho.com • URL: http://www.marquiswhoswho.

com • Biennial. $159.95. Contains over 27,000 concise biographies of teachers, administrators, and other individuals involved in all levels of American education.

***Who's Who in American Law***. Marquis Who's Who L.L.C., 300 Connell Dr., Ste. 2000 Berkeley Heights, NJ 07922. Phone: 800-473-7020 or (908)673-1000 or (908)673-1010; Fax: (908)673-1179; Email: customerservice@marquiswhoswho. com • URL: http://www.marquiswhoswho.com • Biennial. $345 Individuals. Contains over 23,000 concise biographies of American lawyers, judges, and others in the legal field.

***Who's Who in American Politics***. Marquis Who's Who L.L.C., 300 Connell Dr., Ste. 2000 Berkeley Heights, NJ 07922. Phone: 800-473-7020 or (908)673-1000 or (908)673-1010; Fax: (908)673-1179; Email: customerservice@ marquiswhoswho.com • URL: http://www.marquiswhoswho. com • Biennial. $349 Individuals. Contains about 27,000 biographical sketches of local, state, and national elected or appointed individuals.

***Who's Who in Art***. Cengage Learning Inc., 20 Channel Center St. Boston, MA 02210. Phone: 800-487-8488 or (617)289-7700; Fax: (617)289-7844; Email: investors@cengage.com • URL: http://www.cengage.com • Biennial. $190 Individuals cloth bound. Contains about 3,000 brief biographies of artists, designers, curators, critics, and other art-related individuals. International coverage, with British emphasis. Published by Hilmarton Manor Press.

***Who's Who in Asian Banking & Finance***. Bibliotheque: Worldwide, 11 Petria Irvine, CA 92606. Phone: (949)786-3913; Fax: (949)786-8918 • URL: http://www. bibliothequeworldwide.com • Annual. $210 plus $7.50 shipping. Covers: 1,851 prominent and influential bankers and investors and 1,552 banks and financial institutions in Asia. Entries include: For individuals—Name, address, phone, fax, current job title and function, other professional, educational, and personal background details. For companies—Name, address, phone, fax, names and titles of key personnel.

***Who's Who in Association Management***. ASAE: The Center for Association Leadership, 1575 I St. NW Washington, DC 20005-1103, Phone: 888-950-ASAE or (202)371-0940; Fax: (202)371-8315; Email: mbrshpsec@asaenet.org • URL: http://www.asaecenter.org • Annual. $160. Lists paid executives who are members of the association and suppliers of products and services to the association.

***Who's Who in Athens Magazine***. Image Marketing Inc., 217 Briarwood Cir. 35613 Athens, Greece. Phone: 25 6 6034848; Fax: 25 6 6034848; Email: gloria@jamiecooper.com • URL: http://www.whoswhoinathens.com • Semiannual. Covers: Individuals and businesses in Athens, AL.

***Who's Who in British Economics: A Directory of Economists in Higher Education, Business and Government***. Edward Elgar Publishing Inc., The William Pratt House, 9 Dewey Ct. Northampton, MA 01060-3815. Phone: (413)584-5551; Fax: (413)584-9933; Email: info@e-elgar.co.uk • URL: http:// www.e-elgar.co.uk • £106.20 Individuals hardback. Covers: Professional economists in the United Kingdom. Entries include: Name, address, biographical data, select bibliography of works, description of main area of work.

***Who's Who in Business***. Bixby Metro Chamber of Commerce, 10441 S Regal Blvd., Ste. 104 Bixby, OK 74008. Phone: (918)366-9445; Fax: (918)366-9443; Email: info@ bixbychamber.com • URL: http://www.bixbychamber.com • Annual. included in membership dues; $20 for nonmembers; $20 Individuals per package. Covers businesses in Marion County, FL.

***Who's Who in Canadian Business***. University of Toronto Press Inc., 10 St. Mary St., Ste. 700 Toronto, ON, Canada M4Y 2W8. Phone: 800-565-9523 or (416)978-2239 or (416)595-5100; Fax: (416)978-4738 or (416)596-5155; Email: info@ utpress.utoronto.ca • URL: http://www.utpress.utoronto.ca • Annual. $192.95 Individuals plus shipping charges; €120. Covers: About 5,400 corporate and entrepreneurial leaders, each with a detailed biography and contact information. Biographies include such information as current employment, address, education, career history, publications, favorite charities and honors. Entries include: Name, degree(s), position, and title; office address, phone, fax, e-mail, and URL; personal, education, and career data; memberships, affiliations, and other interests.

***Who's Who in Chicago Business***. Crain Communications Inc., 150 N Michigan Ave. Chicago, IL 60601-7553. Phone: 800-678-9595 or (312)649-5200 or (312)649-5411; Fax: (312)280-3150 or (312)280-3174; Email: info@crain.com • URL: http://www.crain.com • $249 Individuals Excel format. Covers 800 civic, professional, and cultural leaders in Chicago.

***Who's Who in Export***. Indian Export Trade Journal, 212 Arun Chambers, Tardeo Rd. Mumbai 400 034, India. • Biennial. $25; $20.

***Who's Who in Finance and Business***. Marquis Who's Who L.L. C., 300 Connell Dr., Ste. 2000 Berkeley Heights, NJ 07922. Phone: 800-473-7020 or (908)673-1000 or (908)673-1010; Fax: (908)673-1179; Email: customerservice@ marquiswhoswho.com • URL: http://www.marquiswhoswho. com • Biennial. $349 Individuals. Provides over 21,000 concise biographies of business leaders in all fields.

***Who's Who in Governmental Research***. Governmental Research Association, c/o Center for Governmental Research, 1 S

Washington St., Ste. 400 Rochester, NY 14614. Phone: (205)870-2482 or (205)726-2482; Fax: (205)726-2900 • URL: http://www.graonline.org • Annual. $50. Lists information on governmental research organization throughout the country.

***Who's Who in International Business Education and Research***. Edward Elgar Publishing Inc., The William Pratt House, 9 Dewey Ct. Northampton, MA 01060-3815. Phone: (413)584-5551; Fax: (413)584-9933; Email: info@e-elgar.co.uk • URL: http://www.e-elgar.co.uk • $256.50 Individuals hardbound. Covers: 150 individuals in international business education and research. Entries include: Biographical data and professional data, career summary, URL.

***Who's Who in Metal Forming and Fabricating***. Fabricators and Manufacturers Association International, 833 Featherstone Rd. Rockford, IL 61107-6301. Phone: 888-394-4362 or (815)399-8700 • URL: http://www.fmanet.org • Annual. $200 for nonmembers; included in membership dues. Lists members of the Fabricators and Manufacturers Association (FMA), International; and members of the Tube and Pipe Association. Includes five indexes. Formerly *FMA Member Resource Directory*.

***Who's Who in Metro Atlanta Business: Membership Directory & Buyers Guide***. Metro Atlanta Chamber of Commerce, 235 Andrew Young International Blvd. NW Atlanta, GA 30303-2718. Phone: (404)880-9000 • URL: http://www. metroatlantachamber.com • Annual. $35 Individuals. Covers: Over 7,000 member firms. Database includes: Chamber of commerce history, business facts and figures, annual report and initiatives for Metro Atlanta Chamber. Entries include: Company name, line of business, address, phone, names of key personnel and their URL addresses.

***Who's Who in Packaging***. Institute of Packaging Professionals, 1833 Centre Point Cr., Ste. 123 Naperville, IL 60563-0114. Phone: (630)544-5050; Fax: (630)544-5055; Email: info@ iopp.org • URL: http://www.iopp.org • Annual. Covers information on the packaging industry. Formerly *Who's Who and What's What in Packaging*.

***Who's Who in Science and Engineering***. Marquis Who's Who L.L.C., 300 Connell Dr., Ste. 2000 Berkeley Heights, NJ 07922. Phone: 800-473-7020 or (908)673-1000 or (908)673-1010; Fax: (908)673-1179; Email: customerservice@ marquiswhoswho.com • URL: http://www.marquiswhoswho. com • Biennial. $249.00. Provides concise biographical information on 33,545 prominent engineers and scientists. International coverage, with geographical and professional indexes.

***Who's Who in the Securities Industry***. Economist Publishing Co., 111 N Wabash Ave., Ste. 1120 Chicago, IL 60602-2012. Fax: (312)467-0225 • Annual. $15.00. Lists about 1,000 investment bankers.

***Who's Who in the World***. Marquis Who's Who L.L.C., 300 Connell Dr., Ste. 2000 Berkeley Heights, NJ 07922. Phone: 800-473-7020 or (908)673-1000 or (908)673-1010; Fax: (908)673-1179; Email: customerservice@marquiswhoswho. com • URL: http://www.marquiswhoswho.com • Annual. $324.00. Provides biographical profiles of about 35,000 prominent individuals. International coverage.

***Who's Who in World Petrochemicals and Plastics***. Reed Elsevier Group plc Reed Business Information, 360 Park Ave. S New York, NY 11010. Phone: (212)791-4208; Email: corporatecommunications@reedbusiness.com • URL: http:// www.reedbusiness.com • Annual. $175.00. Names, addresses, telephone numbers, and company affiliations of individuals active in the petrochemical business. Formerly *Who's Who in World Petrochemicals*.

***Who's Who Membership Directory***. Personal Care Product Council, 1620 L St. NW, Ste. 1200 Washington, DC 20036. Phone: (202)331-1770; Fax: (202)331-1969; Email: membership@personalcarecouncil.org • URL: http://www. personalcarecouncil.org • Annual. Available on website. Lists 600 member companies, with key personnel, products, and services.

***Who's Who of American Women***. Marquis Who's Who L.L.C., 300 Connell Dr., Ste. 2000 Berkeley Heights, NJ 07922. Phone: 800-473-7020 or (908)673-1000 or (908)673-1010; Fax: (908)673-1179; Email: customerservice@ marquiswhoswho.com • URL: http://www.marquiswhoswho. com • Biennial. $305.00. Provides over 30,444 biographical profiles of important women, including individuals prominent in business, finance, and industry.

***Who's Who of Britain's Business Elite***. Who's Who Publications, Comino House, Furlong Rd. Bourne End SL8 5AQ, United Kingdom. Phone: 44 628 811611; Fax: 44 628 552112; Email: info@whoswho.co.uk • URL: http://www. whoswho.co.uk • $59. Includes Boards of Directors involved in the most established and successful companies in the U.K.

***Who's Who of Colombian-American Business***. Colombian-American Chamber of Commerce - Bogota, Calle 98, No. 22-64, Of. 1209 Bogota, Colombia. Phone: 57 15877828 • URL: http://www.amchamcolombia.com.co • Annual. $75. Covers industrial, commercial, financial, tourist, and other service companies in Bogota, Cali, Cartagena, and Medellin.

***Who's Who of European Business and Industry***. Triumph Books Inc., 814 N Franklin St. Chicago, IL 60610. Phone: 800-888-4741 or (312)337-0747; Fax: (312)280-5470 or (312)337-5985; Email: orders@ipgbook.com • URL: http://www. triumphbooks.com • Covers: over 9,500 European business

executives (volume 1) and over 1,400 companies (volume 2). Entries include: For executives—Name, biographical data. For companies—Name, address, phone, profile.

***Wichita Business Journal***. The Business Journals, 120 W. Morehead St., Ste. 400 Charlotte, NC 28202. Phone: (704)973-1000; Fax: (704)973-1001; Email: info@bizjournals.com • URL: http://www.bizjournals.com • Weekly. $91 Individuals /year, print and online; $4.99 Single issue PDF. Business newspaper.

***Wichita Christian Business Directory***. Red Letter Publishing, PO Box 272682 Fort Collins, CO 80527. Phone: 800-445-5614; Fax: (970)267-9669; Email: info@redletter.com • URL: http://www.christianbusinessdirectoryonline.com • Businesses, churches, organizations, schools and professionals in Wichita, Kansas.

***Will County Business Directory***. Manufacturers' News Inc., 1633 Central St. Evanston, IL 60201-1569. Phone: (847)864-7000; Fax: (847)332-1100 • URL: http://www.manufacturersnews. com • Biennial. $41. Approximately 1,212 manufacturing and related service companies in Will County, Illinois.

***Williston on Contracts***. Richard A. Lord. Thomson West, 610 Opperman Dr. Eagan, MN 55123. Phone: 800-328-9352 or (651)687-7000 • $3,224.20 Full Set. Encyclopedic coverage of contract law.

***Wilson Business Abstracts Online***. H.W. Wilson Co., 950 University Ave. Bronx, NY 10452-4224. Phone: 800-367-6770 or (718)588-8400 or (718)558-8400; Fax: (718)590-1617 or (800)590-1617; Email: custserv@hwwilson.com • URL: http://www.hwwilson.com • Indexes and abstracts 600 major business periodicals, plus the *Wall Street Journal* and the business section of the *New York Times*. Indexing is from 1982, abstracting from 1990, with the two newspapers included from 1993. Updated weekly. Inquire as to online cost and availability. (*Business Periodicals Index* without abstracts is also available online.)

***The Wilson Guide to Internet Experts***. H.W. Wilson Co., 950 University Ave. Bronx, NY 10452-4224. Phone: 800-367-6770 or (718)588-8400 or (718)558-8400; Fax: (718)590-1617 or (800)590-1617; Email: custserv@hwwilson.com • URL: http://www.hwwilson.com • $54.99. Covers: Noted authorities in the Internet industry. Entries include: Biographical details, office address and phone number, e-mail and Web site addresses, current projects, specialties.

***Wilson Social Sciences Abstracts Online***. H.W. Wilson Co., 950 University Ave. Bronx, NY 10452-4224. Phone: 800-367-6770 or (718)588-8400 or (718)558-8400; Fax: (718)590-1617 or (800)590-1617; Email: custserv@hwwilson.com • URL: http://www.hwwilson.com • Provides online abstracting and indexing of more than 500 periodicals covering area studies, community health, public administration, public welfare, urban studies, and many other social science topics. Time period is 1994 to date for abstracts and 1983 to date for indexing, with updates weekly. Inquire as to online cost and availability.

***WILSONDISC: Library Literature and Information Science Index***. H.W. Wilson Co., 950 University Ave. Bronx, NY 10452-4224. Phone: 800-367-6770 or (718)588-8400 or (718)558-8400; Fax: (718)590-1617 or (800)590-1617; Email: custserv@hwwilson.com • URL: http://www. hwwilson.com • Quarterly. Includes unlimited access to the online version of *Library Literature*. Provides CD-ROM indexing of about 400 periodicals, covering a wide range of topics having to do with libraries, library management, and the information industry.

***WilsonWeb Periodicals Databases***. H.W. Wilson Co., 950 University Ave. Bronx, NY 10452-4224. Phone: 800-367-6770 or (718)588-8400 or (718)558-8400; Fax: (718)590-1617 or (800)590-1617; Email: custserv@hwwilson.com • URL: http://www.hwwilson.com • Web sites provide fee-based access to *Wilson Business Full Text, Applied Science & Technology Full Text, Biological & Agricultural Index, Library Literature & Information Science Full Text*, and *Readers' Guide Full Text, Mega Edition*. Daily updates.

***Wilton Manors Business Association—Directory***. Wilton Manors Business Association, PO Box 24332 Fort Lauderdale, FL 33307-4332. • URL: http://www. wiltonmanorsbusinessassociation.com • Covers 200 businesses in Wilton Manors.

***Wind Energy Businesses in the World***. Momentum Technologies L.L.C., PO Box 460813 Glendale, CO 80246. Phone: (303)229-4841; Fax: (408)705-2031 • URL: http://www.mtt. com • Contains directory listings and contact information for more than 2600 businesses involved with wind energy and related subjects throughout the world. Includes business name, address, phone number, fax number, e-mail address, and web site address. Includes brief descriptions of product lines, services offered, and business type. Covers manufacturers, wholesalers, retailers, installers, and more. Searchable by location, business type, company name, and keyword.

**Window and Door Manufacturers Association**. 2025 M St. NW, Ste. 800 Washington, DC 20036-3309. Phone: (202)367-1157; Email: wdma@wdma.com • URL: http://www.wdma. com • Members are manufacturers of wooden door and window products. Absorbed Ponderosa Pine Woodwork Association. Formerly National Wood Window and Door Association.

***Window Fashions Magazine: Design and Education Magazine***. Grace McNamara Publishing, Inc., 4215 White Bear

Parkway, Suite 100 Saint Paul, MN 55110-7635. Phone: (651)293-1544; Fax: (651)653-4308; Email: barb@gracemcnamara.com • URL: http://www.gwmcnamara.com • Monthly. $39.00 per year. A directory of suppliers, manufacturers, and fabricators of vertical blinds, soft shades, curtains, draperies, and other window treatment items. Appears as a regular feature of *Window Fashions Magazine* and covers a different product category each month.

*Window Washing Service*. Entrepreneur Press, 2445 McCabe Way, Ste. 400 Irvine, CA 92614-6244. Phone: 800-864-6864 or (949)261-2325 or (949)622-7131; Fax: (949)261-7729 or (949)261-0234; Email: press@entrepreneur.com • URL: http://www.entrepreneurpress.com • Looseleaf. $59.50. A practical guide to starting a window cleaning business. Covers profit potential, start-up costs, market size evaluation, owner's time required, pricing, accounting, advertising, promotion, etc. (Start-Up Business Guide No. E1012.).

*Windows in Financial Services*. 162 Fifth Ave., Suite 1015 New York, NY 10010. Phone: (212)206-9393; Fax: (212)206-9778 • URL: http://www.windowsfs.com • Quarterly. $39.00 per year. Covers information technology applications and products for Microsoft Windows users in the financial sector.

*Windows NT Server Concise*. Jerry Dixon and J. Scott Reeves. New Riders Publishing, 201 W 103rd St. Indianapolis, IN 46290-1907. Phone: 800-428-5331 • URL: http://www.pearson.com • Date not set. $19.99.

*Wine Business Monthly: The Industry's Leading Publication for Wineries and Growers*. New World Wine Communications Inc., 110 W Napa St. Sonoma, CA 95476. Phone: (707)939-0822; Fax: (707)939-0833; Email: info@winebusiness.com • URL: http://www.winebusiness.com/company/contactus.cfm • Monthly. $39 Individuals; $49 Canada; $89 Other countries; $58 Two years in US; $90 Two years Canada; $160 Other countries two years. Trade magazine for the wine industry.

*Wine Enthusiast*. 333 N Bedford Rd. Mount Kisco, NY 10549. Phone: 800-829-5901 or (914)345-8463; Fax: (914)218-9186; Email: mvataj@wineenthusiast.net • URL: http://www.wineenthusiast.com • 13 times a year. $29.95 per year. Covers domestic and world wine. Formerly *Wine Times*.

*Wines and Vines: Annual Directory/Buyer's Guide*. Wines & Vines, 65 Mitchell Blvd., Ste. A San Rafael, CA 94903. Phone: (415)453-9700; Email: info@winesandvines.com • URL: http://www.winesandvines.com • Annual. $95.00. List of wineries and wine bottlers in the United States, Canada, and Mexico; also lists industry suppliers.

*Winning New Business*. Cengage Learning Inc., 20 Channel Center St. Boston, MA 02210. Phone: 800-487-8488 or (617)289-7700; Fax: (617)289-7844; Email: investors@cengage.com • URL: http://www.cengage.com • 2009. eBook. Published by Kogan Page. Offers information to those who seek the skills of successful selling but lack the training - or the courage - to sell effectively.

*Wire & Cable Technology Buyer's Guide*. Initial Publications Inc., 1867 W Market St., Ste. C3 Akron, OH 44305. Phone: (330)864-2122; Fax: (330)686-9563; Email: buyersguide@wiretech.com • URL: http://www.wiretech.com • Annual. $50. Lists 2,300 companies by over 1,200 product categories.

*Wire Journal International Reference Guide*. Wire Journal Inc., 1570 Boston Post Rd. Guilford, CT 06437. Phone: (203)453-2777; Fax: (203)453-8384 • URL: http://www.wirenet.org • Annual. Free to members; $140 Nonmembers. Covers: Manufacturers and suppliers of steel and nonferrous rods, strip, wire, wire products, electrical wire and cable, fiber optics, and machinery and equipment to the industry (SIC 33). Entries include: Company name, address, phone, fax, e-mail and website addresses, year established, number of employees, names of executives, trade and brand names, product indices and geographical cross reference.

*Wired News*. Lycos Inc., 400-2 Totten Pond Rd. Waltham, MA 02451-2053. Phone: (781)370-2700 or (415)276-8400; Fax: (781)370-2600 or (415)276-8500; Email: press@lycos.com • URL: http://www.lycos.com • Provides summaries and full-text of "Top Stories" relating to the Internet, computers, multimedia, telecommunications, and the electronic information industry in general. These news stories are placed in the broad categories of Politics, Business, Culture, and Technology. Affiliated with *Wired* magazine. Fees: Free.

*Wireless Data News*. Access Intelligence L.L.C., 4 Choke Cherry Rd., 2nd Fl. Rockville, MD 20850. Phone: 800-777-5006 or (301)354-2000 or (301)354-2101; Fax: (301)309-3847 or (801)365-2300; Email: info@accessintel.com • URL: http://www.accessintel.com/ • Description: Provides analysis of technology, applications, marketing, and competition in the mobile communications industry. Scope is international. Recurring features include news of research.

*Wisconsin Beverage Business*. Illinois Beverage Media Inc., 2260 Bracken Ln. Northfield, IL 60093. Phone: (847)441-7776; Fax: (847)441-7796 • Monthly. $15 Individuals; $4 Single issue. Trade magazine for the bar and package beverage alcohol industry.

*Wisconsin Business Directory*. InfoGroup Inc., 5711 S 86th Cir. Omaha, NE 68127-4146. Phone: (402)593-4500 • URL: http://www.infogroup.com • Annual. $520 both print & CD-ROM. Covers: 256,558 businesses in Wisconsin. Entries include: Company name, address, phone, number of employees, name of owner or manager, sales volume. Compiled from telephone company "Yellow Pages," statewide. All states covered (see separate entries).

*Wisconsin Business Services Directory*. Wisconsin Manufacturers & Commerce Foundation, 501 E Washington Ave. Madison, WI 53703-2944. Phone: 800-328-2567 or (608)258-3400; Fax: (608)258-3413; Email: mem@wmc.org • URL: http://www.wmc.org • Annual. $199 Individuals. Covers: Over 10,700 business service companies with 25 or more employees in Wisconsin. Entries include: Company name, address, phone, fax, number of employees, SIC codes, names and titles of key personnel, services offered, product descriptions, ownership status, import/export activity, parent company.

*Wisconsin Exporters' Directory*. Wisconsin Department of Commerce, 201 W Washington Ave. Madison, WI 53703-7970. Phone: (608)266-1018; Fax: (608)264-6151; Email: webfeedback@commerce.state.wi.us • URL: http://www.commerce.state.wi.us/ • Irregular. Covers: about 1,400 Wisconsin firms that export or are interested in exporting. Entries include: Company name, address, telex, names and titles of key personnel, product and service, Standard Industrial Classification (SIC) code.

*Wisconsin Industries Guide*. Industries Guides Inc., 303 E Altamonte Dr. Altamonte Springs, FL 32716. Phone: (407)834-8181 • $95. Covers: Approximately 10,000 manufacturers in Wisconsin. Entries include: Company name, address, phone.

*Wisconsin Manufacturers Directory*. Wisconsin Manufacturers & Commerce Foundation, 501 E Washington Ave. Madison, WI 53703-2944. Phone: 800-328-2567 or (608)258-3400; Fax: (608)258-3413; Email: mem@wmc.org • URL: http://www.wmc.org • Annual. $177 Individuals. Covers: Approximately 12,300 manufacturers in Wisconsin. Entries include: Company name, address, phone, fax, number of employees, SIC codes, names and titles of key personnel, import/export activity, product descriptions, ownership status, parent company.

*Wisconsin Medical Directory*. Jola Publications, 2933 N 2nd St. Minneapolis, MN 55411. Phone: 866-565-2782 or (612)529-5001; Fax: (612)521-2289 or (612)605-4645; Email: medical@jolapub.com • URL: http://www.jolapub.com • Annual. $25 Individuals. Covers: Approximately 15,000 doctors, hospitals, clinics, nursing homes, and other selected health care providers in Wisconsin. Entries include: Doctor or facility name, address, phone, fax, doctors' UPINS.

*Wisconsin Minority-Owned Business Directory*. Wisconsin Department of Commerce, 201 W Washington Ave. Madison, WI 53703-7970. Phone: (608)266-1018; Fax: (608)264-6151; Email: webfeedback@commerce.state.wi.us • URL: http://www.commerce.state.wi.us/ • Annual. Covers approximately 750 non-retail minority firms.

*Wisconsin Services Directory*. Harris InfoSource, 2057 E Aurora Rd. Twinsburg, OH 44087-1999. Phone: 800-888-5900 or (330)425-9000 or (973)921-5500; Fax: (800)643-5997 or (877)252-3375; Email: customerservice@harrisinfo.com • URL: http://www.harrisinfo.com • Annual. $98 members/libraries; $139 Nonmembers. Covers: 16,000 business service companies in Wisconsin and over 24,000 key contact personnel. Entries include: Company name, address, phone, fax, name and title of contact, names and titles of key personnel, number of employees, geographical area served, financial data, subsidiary and branch names and locations, product/service, Standard Industrial Classification (SIC) code, computer used, year established, import/export information, web and e-mail address, first month of fiscal year, export countries.

*Wise Giving Guide*. Better Business Bureau - Wise Giving Alliance, 3033 Wilson Blvd., Ste. 600 Arlington, VA 22201. Phone: (703)276-0100; Fax: (703)525-8277; Email: info@bbb.org • URL: http://www.bbb.org • Three times per year. Full year available via contribution. Evaluates national charities against a set of standards concerning management, government and budget.

*WISE International Business Directory*. World Institute of Scientology Enterprises, 6331 Hollywood Blvd., Ste. 701 Los Angeles, CA 90028. Phone: 800-935-WISE or (323)960-3540; Fax: (323)960-3549; Email: info@wise.org • URL: http://www.wise.org • Covers: Business people who use L. Ron Hubbard management technology. Entries include: Contact information.

*Wollombi Valley—Business Directory*. Greater Wollombi Communities Alliance Inc., Wollombi General Store Wollombi, NSW 2325, Australia. Phone: 61 2 49983388; Fax: 61 2 49983149 • URL: http://wollombi.nsw.au • Covers businesses in Wollombi Valley Region.

*The Woman's Consultants Directory*. CAE Consultants Inc., 41 Travers Ave. Yonkers, NY 10705-1648. Phone: (914)963-3695; Fax: (914)376-5011 • URL: http://www.municipalnets.com • Annual. $75. Covers: About 3,000 women consultants in every line of business. Entries include: Consultant name, address, phone, fax, line of business, description.

Women Against Military Madness. 4200 Cedar Ave. S, Ste. 3 Minneapolis, MN 55407. Phone: (612)827-5364; Fax: (612)827-6433; Email: wamm@mtn.org • URL: http://www.worldwidewamm.org • Advocates for a radical shift in the nation's priorities away from militarism, military spending, arms trade, military intervention and the militarization of schools.

*Women and the Law*. Carol H. Lefcourt, editor. Thomson West, 610 Opperman Dr. Eagan, MN 55123. Phone: 800-328-9352 or (651)687-7000 • Annual. $691.60 Individuals book -

softbound. Covers such topics as employment discrimination, pay equity (comparable worth), sexual harassment in the workplace, property rights, and child custody issues.

Women Business Owners. 9594 1st Ave. NE, No. 274 Seattle, WA 98115-2012. Phone: (206)575-3232; Email: info@womenbusinessowners.org • URL: http://www.womenbusinessowners.org • Aims to empower, educate and enhance the lives of children and women business owners throughout the world. Provides programs and workshops on educating future entrepreneurs. Works to develop and encourage entrepreneurship, achievement and success in business.

Women Chiefs of Enterprises International. c/o Julie Ankers, President, Level 6 276 Pitt St. Sydney, NSW 2000, Australia. Phone: 61 2 92675220; Fax: 61 2 92674202 • URL: http://www.wcei.com.au • Represents women entrepreneurs in Australia. Encourages innovation in the development of entrepreneurial skills. Creates opportunities for business development.

*Women Directors of the Top Corporate 1,000*. National Women's Economic Alliance Foundation, 808 17th St. NW, Ste. 600 Washington, DC 20006. Phone: (202)393-5257; Fax: (202)887-0905 • Annual. $100. Covers: about 600 women serving on the boards of Fortune 1,000 corporations; compiled from surveys of Fortune 500 Industrial and Fortune 500 Service corporations and the Corporate Yellow Book. Entries include: Name, title, company name, address, corporate boards on which serves.

Women Entrepreneurs of Canada. 720 Spadina Ave., Ste. 202 Toronto, ON, Canada M5S 2T9. Phone: 866-207-4439 or (416)921-5050; Fax: (416)929-5256; Email: wec@wec.ca • URL: http://www.wec.ca • Addresses the need of women entrepreneurs and supports their growth and development. Provides meaningful networking opportunities to connect with peers as well as the larger business community, government and the international business community. Builds entrepreneurship acumen and business leadership capacity.

*Women in Business*. The ABWA Company Inc., 9100 Ward Pky. Kansas City, MO 64114-0728. Phone: 800-228-0007; Email: abwa@abwa.org • URL: http://www.abwa.org • Bimonthly. Women's business magazine.

Women in Housing and Finance. 400 N Washington St., Ste. 300 Alexandria, VA 22314. Phone: (703)683-4742; Fax: (703)683-0018; Email: whf@whfdc.org • URL: http://www.whfdc.org • Professionals employed in the fields of housing or finance. Provides women finance professionals with the opportunity for continued professional development through interaction with others with similar interests. Promotes educational development of women in housing and finance; provides members with services and benefits to help them attain higher levels of expertise. Sponsors social events for members; holds receptions for congressional and regulatory leaders; conducts monthly luncheon and programs featuring speakers from federal agencies, Congress and the private sector. Sponsors career development workshops. Activities are concentrated in the Washington, DC, area.

Women in Management. PO Box 6690 Elgin, IL 60121-6690. Email: wimfoxvalley@gmail.com • URL: http://www.wimonline.org • Supports network of women in professional and management positions that facilitate the exchange of experience and ideas. Promotes self-growth in management; provides speakers who are successful in management; sponsors workshops and special interest groups to discuss problems and share job experiences.

Women Organizing for Change in Agriculture and Natural Resource Management. 1775 K St. NW, Ste. 410 Washington, DC 20006. Phone: (202)331-9099; Fax: (202)331-9366 • URL: http://www.wocan.org • Builds leadership among women and men in agriculture and natural resource management towards gender equality. Seeks to empower women as leaders and agents in adapting to, mitigating and reducing the adverse effects of climate change. Creates global awareness campaigns on the impact of climate change in women. Conducts and publishes gender-specific climate change research.

*Women Studies Abstracts*. Springer ScienceBusiness Media LLC, 233 Spring St. New York, NY 10013-1578. Phone: (212)460-1500 or (732)445-2280; Fax: (212)460-1575; Email: trans@transactionpub.com • URL: http://www.springer.com • Quarterly. Covers significant research in women's studies.

*Women's Accessories Store*. Entrepreneur Press, 2445 McCabe Way, Ste. 400 Irvine, CA 92614-6244. Phone: 800-864-6864 or (949)261-2325 or (949)622-7131; Fax: (949)261-7729 or (949)261-0234; Email: press@entrepreneur.com • URL: http://www.entrepreneurpress.com • Looseleaf. $59.50. A practical guide to starting a women's clothing accessories shop. Covers profit potential, start-up costs, market size evaluation, owner's time required, site selection, lease negotiation, pricing, accounting, advertising, promotion, etc. (Start-Up Business Guide No. E1333.).

*Women's Apparel Shop*. Entrepreneur Press, 2445 McCabe Way, Ste. 400 Irvine, CA 92614-6244. Phone: 800-864-6864 or (949)261-2325 or (949)622-7131; Fax: (949)261-7729 or (949)261-0234; Email: press@entrepreneur.com • URL: http://www.entrepreneurpress.com • Looseleaf. $59.50. A practical guide to starting a women's clothing store. Covers profit potential, start-up costs, market size evaluation, owner's time required, site selection, lease negotiation, pricing, accounting, advertising, promotion, etc. (Start-Up Business Guide No. E1107.).

***Women's Health Concerns Sourcebook***. Omnigraphics Inc., PO Box 31-1640 Detroit, MI 48231. Phone: (313)961-1340; Fax: (313)961-1383; Email: customerservice@omnigraphics.com • URL: http://www.omnigraphics.com • Irregular. $85 Individuals Hardcover; $95 Individuals List price. Publication includes: Resources on women's health issues. Entries include: Publication name, address. Principal content of publication is articles on specific health issues, definitions, symptoms, risks, treatment, and answers to frequently asked questions.

**Women's High Tech Coalition**. c/o MaryClare Fitzgerald, Chief Executive Officer, Dutko Grayling, 100 M St. SE, No. 500 Washington, DC 20003. Phone: (202)479-7141 • URL: http://www.womenshightech.org • Provides resources and opportunities for professional women in the technology industry. Works to create an atmosphere that generates sincere discussions and access to industry leaders both in the private and public sector.

***Wood & Wood Products—Laminating Users Guide Issue***. Laminating Materials Association, 116 Lawrence St. Hillsdale, NJ 07642-2730. Phone: (201)664-2700; Fax: (201)666-5665 • URL: http://www.arcat.com/arcatcos/cos37/arc37367.cfm • Annual. Publication includes: List of approximately 150 manufacturers and importers of decorative overlays, wood substrates, adhesives, laminating equipment, and laminated products. Entries include: Company name, address, phone, name and title of contact.

***Wood Digest-Showcase***. Cygnus Business Media Inc., 1233 Janesville Ave. Fort Atkinson, WI 53538. Phone: 800-547-7377; Email: info@cygnus.com • URL: http://www.cygnus.com • Monthly. Publication includes: List of suppliers of materials, machinery, tools, and services for woodworking, cabinetry, casegoods, and furniture manufacturing processes (SIC 24, 25, 37, and 39). Entries include: Company name, phone number, photograph of product, services.

***Wood Technology-Equipment Catalog and Buyers' Guide***. UBM L.L.C., 600 Community Dr. Manhasset, NY 11030. Phone: (516)562-5000 or (512)562-5000; Fax: (212)378-2160 or (516)562-5036; Email: cmp@cmp.com • URL: http://www.cmp.com • Annual. $55.00. Formerly *Forest Industries-Lumber Review and Buyers' Guide*.

***Woodall's Canada Campground Guide***. Woodall Publications Corp., 2575 Vista Del Mar Dr. Ventura, CA 93001-3920. Email: info@woodallpub.com • URL: http://www.woodalls.com • $8.96 Individuals discounted; $9.95 Individuals retail price. Covers: Campground site listings for all Canadian provinces. Entries include: Site name, address, phone, facility description, driving directions, camping fees, attractions and seasonal events.

***Woodall's Far West Campground Guide***. Woodall Publications Corp., 2575 Vista Del Mar Dr. Ventura, CA 93001-3920. Email: info@woodallpub.com • URL: http://www.woodalls.com • Annual. $4.95 Individuals; $10.95 retail price. Covers: Campground site listings for the Far West U.S., including Alaska, Arizona, California, Idaho, Nevada, Oregon, Washington, and British Columbia, Mexico, and the Yukon. Entries include: Site name, address, phone, facility description, driving directions, camping fees, attractions and seasonal events.

***Woodall's Frontier West/Great Plains & Mountain Region Campground Guide***. Woodall Publications Corp., 2575 Vista Del Mar Dr. Ventura, CA 93001-3920. Email: info@woodallpub.com • URL: http://www.woodalls.com • $4.95 Individuals; $9.95 Individuals retail price. Covers: Campground site listings for Arkansas, Kansas, Missouri, New Mexico, Oklahoma, Texas, and Mexico. Entries include: Site name, address, phone, facility description, driving directions, camping fees, attractions and seasonal events.

***Woodall's Great Lakes Campground Guide***. Woodall Publications Corp., 2575 Vista Del Mar Dr. Ventura, CA 93001-3920. Email: info@woodallpub.com • URL: http://www.woodalls.com • Annual. $4.95 Individuals; $10.95 Individuals retail price. Covers: Campground site listings for Great Lakes states, including Illinois, Indiana, Iowa, Michigan, Minnesota, Ohio, and Wisconsin. Entries include: Site name, address, phone, facility description, driving directions, camping fees, attractions and seasonal events.

***Woodall's Mid-Atlantic Campground Guide***. Woodall Publications Corp., 2575 Vista Del Mar Dr. Ventura, CA 93001-3920. Email: info@woodallpub.com • URL: http://www.woodalls.com • Annual. $4.95 Individuals; $10.95 retail price. Covers: Campground site listings for Mid-Atlantic states, including Delaware, District of Columbia, Maryland, New Jersey, Pennsylvania, Virginia, and West Virginia. Entries include: Site name, address, phone, facility description, driving directions, camping fees, attractions and seasonal events.

***Woodall's South Campground Guide***. Woodall Publications Corp., 2575 Vista Del Mar Dr. Ventura, CA 93001-3920. Email: info@woodallpub.com • URL: http://www.woodalls.com • Annual. $10.95 Individuals Retail price; $4.95 Individuals Discounted. Covers: Campground site listings for the 9 Southern U.S. states, including Alabama, Florida, Georgia, Kentucky, Louisiana, Mississippi, North Carolina, South Carolina, and Tennessee. Entries include: Site name, address, phone, facility description, driving directions, camping fees, attractions and seasonal events.

**Worcester Polytechnic Institute - Center for Economic and Policy Dynamics**. Department of Social Science & Policy Studies, 100 Institute Rd. Worcester, MA 01609-2280. Phone: (508)831-5583; Fax: (508)831-5896; Email: doyle@wpi.edu • URL: http://www.wpi.edu/Academics/Depts/SSPS/Research/cepd.html • Economics and public policy.

**Worcester Polytechnic Institute - Department of Computer Science - Image Science Research Group**. 100 Institute Rd. Worcester, MA 01609-2280. Phone: (508)831-5671 or (508)831-5357; Fax: (508)831-5776; Email: matt@wpi.edu • URL: http://web.cs.wpi.edu/Research/isrg/ • Areas of research include image processing, computer graphics, and computational vision.

**Worcester Polytechnic Institute - Economics, Policy, and Law Research Group**. Department of Social Science & Policy Studies, 100 Institute Rd. Worcester, MA 01609-2280. Phone: (508)831-5234; Fax: (508)831-5892; Email: epl@wpi.edu • URL: http://web.cs.wpi.edu/Research/trg/ • Economics, policy, and law.

**Work for Progress**. 1543 Wazee St., Ste. 440 Denver, CO 80202-1450. Phone: (303)623-4900; Fax: (720)306-3699; Email: info@workforprogress.org • URL: http://www.workforprogress.org • Focuses on strengthening organizations that work for social change. Recruits job-seekers to work with the nation's nonprofit organizations and progressive campaigns for social justice, consumer protection and the environment. Helps activist-minded jobseekers to connect with progressive campaigns and organizations that are working across the country on progressive issues.

**The Work Foundation**. Peter Runge House, 3 Carlton House Ter. London SW1Y 5DG, United Kingdom. Phone: 44 870 1656700 or 44 20 79763565; Email: customercentre@theworkfoundation.com • URL: http://www.theworkfoundation.com • Works to improve the quality and productivity of U.K. work life, offers clients innovative solutions through research, consultancy, leadership and coaching programs.

***Workboat***. Diversified Business Communications Inc., 121 Free St. Portland, ME 04101-3919. Phone: (207)842-5500 or (207)842-5600; Fax: (207)842-5503 or (207)842-5603; Email: custserv@divcom.com • URL: http://www.divbusiness.com • Monthly. Provides in-depth reporting on topics including offshore services, shipbuilding and repair, port security, marine electronics, environmental regulations and more.

***Workers' Compensation Law Bulletin***. Quinlan Publishing Co., Marine Industrial Park, 23 Drydock Ave. 6th Fl. Boston, MA 02210-2387. Phone: 800-229-2084 or (617)542-0048; Fax: (617)345-9646; Email: info@quinlan.com • URL: http://www.quinlan.com • Description: Summarizes in layman's terms recent court cases deriving from the worker compensation law, with specific identification of cases and brief explanations of the court decisions.

***Workers' Compensation Monitor***. LRP Publications Library, lrp.com Technology Contacts, 747 Dresher Rd., Ste. 500 Horsham, PA 19044. Phone: 800-341-7874 or (215)784-0860 or (215)784-0910; Fax: (215)784-9639 or (215)784-0275; Email: techsup@lrp.com • URL: http://www.lrp.com • Description: Suggests ways to reduce workers' compensation costs and improve your return-to-work programs. Provides proven solutions your colleagues have implemented to resolve their challenges. Keeps readers up-to-date on the latest developments in national workers' compensation issues including benefits, insurance coverage, legislative reform and costs.

**Workflow Management Coalition**. 759 CJC Hwy., Ste. No. 363 Cohasset, MA 02025-2115. Phone: (781)719-9209; Fax: (781)735-0491; Email: nathaniel@wfmc.org • URL: http://www.wfmc.org • Represents adopters, developers, consultants, analysts, university and research groups engaged in workflow and Business Process Management (BPM). Seeks to expand the BPM market by promoting the business value of process management. Strives to decrease the risk of using BPM and workflow products through interoperability standards.

***Working Options***. Association of Part-Time Professionals, 701 W. Broad St., No. 400 Falls Church, VA 22046. Phone: (703)532-8961 or (703)532-8962; Fax: (703)532-9096 or (703)734-7405; Email: lemans@erols.com • URL: http://www/aptp.org • Bimonthly. Description: Advocates alternative work schedules, particularly part-time employment for professionals. Topics include job sharing, older workers, personnel policies, employee benefits, insurance, chapter news, and legislative news. Also provides how-to information on part-time employment and profiles employees and employers who have used flexible work schedules and part-time employment to their advantage. Recurring features include news about the Association and a column titled Point of View, the Executive Director's Corner and Members' Mail Box.

***Working Papers of the College of Business and Economics***. University of Kentucky Center for Business and Economic Research, 335-BA Gatton College of Business & Economics Lexington, KY 40506-0034. Phone: (859)257-7675; Fax: (859)257-7671; Email: cber@uky.edu • URL: http://cber.uky.edu.

***Working Press of the Nation***. R.R. Bowker L.L.C., 630 Central Ave New Providence, NJ 07974. Phone: 888-269-5372 or (908)286-1090; Email: info@bowker.com • URL: http://www.bowker.com • Annual. $530.00. $295.00 per volume. Three volumes: (1) *Newspaper Directory*; (2) *Magazine and Internal Publications Directory*; (3) *Radio and Television Directory*. Includes names of editors and other personnel.

***Working Solo: The Real Guide to Freedom & Financial Success with Your Own Business, 2nd Edition***. Portico Press, • URL: http://wiley.com • $21.95 Individuals paperback. Covers: Over 1,000 solo business opportunities, as well as a resource section on publications, organizations, and other essential contacts for solo professionals.

***Working USA: The Journal of Labor and Society***. M.E. Sharpe Inc., 80 Business Park Dr. Armonk, NY 10504. Phone: 800-541-6563 or (914)273-1800; Fax: (914)273-2106; Email: info@mesharpe.com • URL: http://www.mesharpe.com • Quarterly. $160.00 per year to institutions; $45.00 to individuals. Provides a wide range of material on employment, labor markets, societal issues, and present-day labor unions.

***Workplace Substance Abuse Advisor***. LRP Publications Library, lrp.com Technology Contacts, 747 Dresher Rd., Ste. 500 Horsham, PA 19044. Phone: 800-341-7874 or (215)784-0860 or (215)784-0910; Fax: (215)784-9639 or (215)784-0275; Email: techsup@lrp.com • URL: http://www.lrp.com • Description: Reviews federal, state, and local laws and regulations concerning alcohol and drug use, testing, and policies. Discusses significant court decisions. Contains information on the drug enforcement budgets at all levels of government. Examines employee assistance plans and other educational programs designed to help substance abusers.

***World Agricultural Economics and Rural Sociology Abstracts (WAERSA)***. CABI, Nosworthy Way, Oxfordshire Wallingford OX10 8DE, United Kingdom. Phone: 44 1491 832111; Fax: 44 1491 833508; Email: enquiries@cabi.org • URL: http://www.cabi.org • Monthly. Print and online available. Published in England by CABI Publishing. Provides worldwide coverage of the literature.

***The World Almanac and Book of Facts***. The World Almanac and Book of Facts, 512 7th Ave., 22nd Fl. New York, NY 10018. Phone: 800-322-8755 or (212)967-8800; Fax: (800)678-3633; Email: custserv@factsonfile.com • URL: http://www.worldalmanac.com • Annual. $11.95.

**World Association for Small and Medium Enterprises**. Plot No. 4, Institutional Area, Sector 16A Noida 201301, Uttar Pradesh, India. Fax: 91 120 4216283; Email: bds@wasmeinfo.org • URL: http://www.wasmeinfo.org • Works to undertake research programmes and incisive studies on various issues of small businesses; arranges placement of counsellors, specialists and trainers to facilitate flow of knowledge and expertise in specific fields.

***World Banking Abstracts***. Institution of European Finance. John Wiley & Sons Inc. Wiley-Blackwell, 9600 Garsington Rd. Oxford OX4 2DQ, United Kingdom. Phone: 44 1865 776868 or 44 186 5778054; Fax: 44 1865 714591 or 44 186 5471777; Email: customerservice@oxon.blackwellpublishing.com • URL: http://www.as.wiley.com/wileycda/brand/id-35.html • Bimonthly. Provides worldwide coverage of articles appearing in over 400 financial publications.

***World Business Directory***. NIIR Project Consultancy Services, 106 - E, Kamla Nagar New Delhi 110007, India. Phone: 91 11 23843955; Fax: 91 11 23841561; Email: npcs.india@gmail.com • URL: http://www.niir.org • Rs 2,248 Individuals CD-ROM; $200 Individuals CD-ROM. Covers: More than 300,000 worldwide businesses. Entries include: Company name, postal address, city, state, pin code, phone, fax and the emails.

***World Business Intelligence: Economic & Political Financial Analysts from Rundt's New York***. S.J. Rundt & Associates Inc., PO Box 1572 Montclair, NJ 07042. Phone: (973)731-7502; Fax: (973)731-7503; Email: info@rundtsintelligence.com • URL: http://www.rundtsintelligence.com • $885 Individuals. Magazine featuring information on international trade, country risk analyses, currencies, and political, financial, and economic intelligence. Formerly *Rundt's Weekly Intelligence*.

***World Buyers' Guide to Unusual & Innovative Products***. Emir Publications, Katong Singapore, Singapore. Phone: 2951414; Fax: 7433307; Email: zachko@pacific.net.sg • Biennial. $20. Covers: manufacturers and suppliers of unusual merchandise worldwide for mail order dealers, gift stores, novelty dealers, catalog businesses, importers, and opportunity seekers. Entries include: Name of firm, address, cable address, telex, fax, products.

***World Chamber of Commerce Directory***. 1717 Madison Ave., Ste. 3 Loveland, CO 80538. Phone: (970)663-3231; Fax: (970)663-6187; Email: worldchamberdirectory@compuserve.com • URL: http://www.worldchamberdirectoryonline.com • Annual. $50.00.

**World Cocoa Foundation**. 1411 K St. NW, Ste. 502 Washington, DC 20005. Phone: (202)737-7870; Fax: (202)737-7832; Email: wcf@worldcocoa.org • URL: http://www.worldcocoafoundation.org • Supported by manufacturers of cocoa and chocolate products. Encourages educational and research projects in the cultivation of more cacao of better quality; strives to improve economic conditions of cacao farmers by increasing yields on farms and reducing the per unit production cost. Projects include: research on life history and control of insects attacking cacao; studies on principal cacao diseases; germ plasma assembly and testing; breeding for yield and disease resistance; and physiology. Sponsors exchanges of personnel and training fellowships. Disseminates information.

**World Confederation of Productivity Science**. c/o Linda Carbone, Executive Secretary, 500 Sherbrooke St. W, Ste. 900 Montreal, QC, Canada H3A 3C6. Email: secretariat@wcps.info • URL: http://www.wcps.info • Fraternal association of manufacturing and commercial enterprises and employees, government agencies, professional institutions, and researchers. Goals are to promote productivity science, advance management techniques, and improve the quality of working life and environment.

***World Cosmetics and Toiletries Marketing Directory***. Cengage Learning Inc., 20 Channel Center St. Boston, MA 02210. Phone: 800-487-8488 or (617)289-7700; Fax: (617)289-7844; Email: investors@cengage.com • URL: http://www.cengage.com • 2010. $475.00. 6th edition. Published by Euromonitor. Provides detailed descriptions of the world's cosmetics and toiletries companies. Includes consumers market research data.

***World Crude Oil Data***. Energy Intelligence Group, 5 E 37th St., 5th Fl. New York, NY 10016-2807. Phone: (212)532-1112; Fax: (212)532-4479; Email: customerservice@energyintel.com • URL: http://www.energyintel.com • Annual. An overview covers "The Inner Workings of Crude Oil Markets," including a glossary of terms. Reference sections contain detailed profiles of 44 "key producing countries," legal terms, crude oil sales contracts, prices, and other information.

***World Database of Business Information Sources on the Internet***. Euromonitor International Business Reference Div., 224 S Michigan Ave., Ste. 1500 Chicago, IL 60604. Phone: (312)922-1115; Fax: (312)922-1157; Email: insight@euromonitorintl.com • URL: http://www.euromonitor.com • $690. Covers: Over 35,000 business information sources worldwide, including 12,000 organizations, 13,000 publications, 2,000 exhibitions, and 700 online databases. Entries include: Source name, contact information, description.

***World Database of Consumer Brands and Their Owners***. Euromonitor International Business Reference Div., 224 S Michigan Ave., Ste. 1500 Chicago, IL 60604. Phone: (312)922-1115; Fax: (312)922-1157; Email: insight@euromonitorintl.com • URL: http://www.euromonitor.com • Annual. $995. Covers: Descriptive information on the owning companies of approximately 56,000 brands across 1,000 consumer sectors in 85 countries.

***World Databases in Company Information***. K.G. Saur Verlag KG, Mies-van-der-Rohe-Strasse 1 D-80807 Munich, Germany. Phone: 49 490 89 769020; Email: info@degruyter.com • URL: http://www.degruyter.com/browse?publisher=KGS • Covers: Electronically published databases and their vendors, worldwide.

***World Development Report***. World Bank Group, 1818 H St. NW Washington, DC 20433. Phone: 800-831-0463 or (202)473-1000; Fax: (202)477-6391; Email: books@worldbank.org • URL: http://www.worldbank.org • Annual. Covers history, conditions, and trends relating to economic globalization and localization. Includes selected data from *World Development Indicators* for 132 countries or economies. Key indicators are provided for 78 additional countries or economies.

***World Directory of Business Information Sources***. Euromonitor International Business Reference Div., 224 S Michigan Ave., Ste. 1500 Chicago, IL 60604. Phone: (312)922-1115; Fax: (312)922-1157; Email: insight@euromonitorintl.com • URL: http://www.euromonitor.com • $700 Individuals U.S.D. Covers: National and international Web sites of interest to business researchers, provided by trade associations, magazines, government agencies, private research firms and others.

***World Directory of Business Websites***. Euromonitor P.L.C., 60-61 Britton St. London EC1M 5UX, United Kingdom. Phone: 44 20 7251 8024; Fax: 44 20 7608 3149; Email: info@euromonitor.com • URL: http://www.euromonitor.com • A handbook of consumer market size data. It provides volume and value sales statistics (1999-2004) for more than 330 consumer products from 13 European countries.

***World Directory of Clothing, Garments and Apparel Importers***. World-Wide Market-Link, 16 Sandmore Garth, Town Ln., Thackley Bradford BD10 8PW, United Kingdom. • Irregular. $35; $70. Covers: 1,500 apparel importers in 27 countries. Entries include: Company name, address, phone, products.

***World Directory of Cosmetics, Beauty Supplies, and Toiletries Importers***. World-Wide Market-Link, 16 Sandmore Garth, Town Ln., Thackley Bradford BD10 8PW, United Kingdom. • Irregular. $35; $70. Covers: 800 importers and wholesaler of cosmetics, beauty supplies an toiletries in 30 countries. Entries include: Company name, address, phone, products.

***World Directory of Hides, Skins & Raw Leather Importers***. World-Wide Market-Link, 16 Sandmore Garth, Town Ln., Thackley Bradford BD10 8PW, United Kingdom. • Irregular. $35; $70. Covers: 400 leather importers and wholesalers in the U.S. and Canada, the United Kingdom, Australia, Austria, Belgium, Denmark, Finland, France, West Germany, Greece, Holland, Italy, Israel, Japan, Spain, Sweden, and Switzerland. Entries include: Company name, address, phone, products handled.

***World Directory of Industrial Information Sources***. United Nations Publications, c/o National Book Network, 15200 NBN Way Blue Ridge Summit, PA 17214. Phone: 888-254-4286 or (212)963-7680 or (212)963-8302; Fax: (800)338-4550; Email: unpublications@nbnbooks.com • URL: http://www.unp.un.org • $40 Individuals. Covers: Industrial information sources for the most appropriate sources of technology and equipment. It contains profiles of information providers such as information and documentation centers, banks, training institutes, development agencies and manufacturers associations that are prepared to provide entrepreneurs in developing countries with answers to their industrial needs.

***World Directory of Manufactured Fiber Producers***. Fiber Economics Bureau, 1530 Wilson Blvd., Ste. 690 Arlington, VA 22209. Phone: (703)875-0676; Fax: (703)875-0675; Email: ddezan@afma.org • URL: http://www.fibereconomics.com • Annual. $395 CD-ROM, 2014 issue. Provides information on 2,000 fiber producers in 75 countries. (Fiber Economics Bureau is a subsidiary of the American Fiber Manufacturers Association.).

***World Directory of Marketing Information Sources***. Euromonitor International Business Reference Div., 224 S Michigan Ave., Ste. 1500 Chicago, IL 60604. Phone: (312)922-1115; Fax: (312)922-1157; Email: insight@euromonitorintl.com • URL: http://www.euromonitor.com • Irregular. $590; $650 Individuals U.S.D. Covers: 6,000 market research organizations, libraries and information services, information databases, business and marketing associations, business and marketing journals, statistical offices, chambers of commerce, embassies, and foreign trade departments in Europe. Entries include: Organization, agency, or association name, contact name and address, type of data offered, publications.

***World Directory of Non-Official Statistical Sources***. Euromonitor International Business Reference Div., 224 S Michigan Ave., Ste. 1500 Chicago, IL 60604. Phone: (312)922-1115; Fax: (312)922-1157; Email: insight@euromonitorintl.com • URL: http://www.euromonitor.com • $750 Individuals U.S.D. Covers: Over 2,800 titles, serials, and statistical data services produced by associations, business schools, trade journals, market research companies, banks, insurance companies, employers' organizations, and building societies in the world. Entries include: Source title, publisher or producer name, address, phone, fax, description.

***World Directory of Toys & Games***. World-Wide Market-Link, 16 Sandmore Garth, Town Ln., Thackley Bradford BD10 8PW, United Kingdom. • Irregular. $35; $70. Covers: 1,700 toy and game importers and wholesalers in 60 countries. Entries include: Company name, address, phone.

***World Directory of Trade and Business Association***. Euromonitor Publications Ltd., 60-61 Britton St. London EC1M 5UX, United Kingdom. Phone: 44 20 72518024; Fax: 44 20 76083149; Email: info@euromonitor.com • URL: http://www.euromonitor.com • $750 Individuals. Covers: publication and membership details of each association. Entries include: full contact details of trade and business associations world wide.

***World Directory of Trade and Business Journals***. Euromonitor International Business Reference Div., 224 S Michigan Ave., Ste. 1500 Chicago, IL 60604. Phone: (312)922-1115; Fax: (312)922-1157; Email: insight@euromonitorintl.com • URL: http://www.euromonitor.com • $590; $750 Individuals. Covers: international consumer and industrial trade journals. Entries include: title, publisher address, coverage, language, frequency, readership, cost, and circulation.

***World Directory of Trade Promotion Organizations and Other Foreign Trade Bodies***. International Trade Centre, Palais des Nations CH-1211 Geneva, Switzerland. Phone: 41 22 7300234; Fax: 41 22 7300577 • URL: http://www.intracen.org • Annual. $50 Free to developing countries/economies in transition; $20 to developed countries. Covers: over 1,200 international trade promotion organizations and other foreign trade bodies involved in international trade, including ministries, trade promotion organizations, import promotion offices, chambers of commerce in principal business centers and/or federations of chambers of commerce, trade associations, operational trade pointes, and selected regional and inter-regional organizations. Entries include: Organization name, address, phone, fax, telex, e-mail, URL, and codes description of services provided when available.

***World Drug Report***. United Nations Publications, c/o National Book Network, 15200 NBN Way Blue Ridge Summit, PA 17214. Phone: 888-254-4286 or (212)963-7680 or (212)963-8302; Fax: (800)338-4550; Email: unpublications@nbnbooks.com • URL: http://www.unp.un.org • Annual. $60 Individuals print; $30 Individuals pdf. Issued by the United Nations Office for Drug Control and Crime Prevention. Includes maps, graphs, charts, and tables.

***World Economic and Social Survey: Trends and Policies in the World Economy***. United Nations Publications, c/o National Book Network, 15200 NBN Way Blue Ridge Summit, PA 17214. Phone: 888-254-4286 or (212)963-7680 or (212)963-8302; Fax: (800)338-4550; Email: unpublications@nbnbooks.com • URL: http://www.unp.un.org • Annual. $55.00. Includes discussion and "an extensive statistical annex of economic, trade, and financial indicators, incorporating current data and forecasts.".

***World Economic Factbook***. Cengage Learning Inc., 20 Channel Center St. Boston, MA 02210. Phone: 800-487-8488 or (617)289-7700; Fax: (617)289-7844; Email: investors@cengage.com • URL: http://www.cengage.com • Annual. $475 Individuals E-book. Published by Euromonitor International. Presents key economic facts and figures for each of 204 countries worldwide, including details of chief industries, export-import trade, currency, political risk, household expenditures, and the economic situation in general.

***World Economic Outlook Reports***. International Monetary Fund, 700 19th St. NW Washington, DC 20431. Phone: (202)623-7000 or (202)623-6220; Fax: (202)623-4661; Email: insinfo@imf.org • URL: http://www.imf.org/institute • Semiannual. $110. Provides key insights into how to view unprecedented global imbalances, respond to capital account crises caused by abrupt shifts in global asset allocations, and evaluate the opportunities for all member countries, especially low-income countries, to grow.

***World Economic Prospects***. Cengage Learning Inc., 20 Channel Center St. Boston, MA 02210. Phone: 800-487-8488 or (617)289-7700; Fax: (617)289-7844; Email: investors@cengage.com • URL: http://www.cengage.com • 2010. $650.00. 8th edition. Published by Euromonitor International. Ranks countries by specific economic characteristics, such as gross domestic product (GDP) per capita and short term growth prospects. Discusses the economic situation, prospects, and market potential of each of the countries.

***World Economic Situation and Prospects***. United Nations Publications, c/o National Book Network, 15200 NBN Way Blue Ridge Summit, PA 17214. Phone: 888-254-4286 or (212)963-7680 or (212)963-8302; Fax: (800)338-4550; Email: unpublications@nbnbooks.com • URL: http://www.unp.un.org • Annual. $42 Individuals print; $21 Individuals pdf. Serves as a supplement and update to the UN *World Economic and Social Survey*.

***World Employment Report***. International Labor Organization, 1828 L St. NW, Ste. 600 Washington, DC 20036. Phone: (202)653-7652 or (202)617-3952; Fax: (202)653-7687 or (202)617-3960; Email: washington@ilo.org • URL: http://www.ilo.org • Contains detailed information on the world employment situation and world employment trends.

***World Energy and Nuclear Directory***. Specialist Journals, 345 Park Ave., S New York, NY 10010-1707. Phone: (212)726-9333; Fax: (212)696-0052; Email: sjsupport@nature.com • URL: http://www.nature.com • Biennial. $385.00. Lists 5,000 public and private, international research and development organizations functioning in a wide variety of areas related to energy.

**World Energy Cities Partnership**. 901 Bagby Houston, TX 77002. Phone: (832)393-0829; Email: matthew.shailer@houstontx.gov • URL: http://www.energycities.org • Collaborates and assists cities around the world to support the local energy sectors. Encourages exchange of petroleum industry knowledge and economic and infrastructure development strategies. Provides a network of industry support services and resources.

***World Financial System***. Financial Times Healthcare, Maple House, 149 Tottenham Court Rd. London W1P 9LL, United Kingdom. Phone: 171 896 2066; Fax: 171 896 2213; Email: lizg@pearson-pro.com • Irregular. $165. Publication includes: Descriptions of 56 international economic organizations, including monetary, developmental, trade, and petroleum organizations. Database includes: Essays on international monetary relations from 1944 to 1992, including summaries of events, conferences, and important documents. Entries include: Name, address, name of chief executive, background, functions, member countries, structure, operations, description of activities, conferences, etc.

***World Food Marketing Directory***. Euromonitor International Business Reference Div., 224 S Michigan Ave., Ste. 1500 Chicago, IL 60604. Phone: (312)922-1115; Fax: (312)922-1157; Email: insight@euromonitorintl.com • URL: http://www.euromonitor.com • £325 Individuals; $475 Individuals; €375 Individuals. Covers: Over 2,000 retailers and wholesalers, 1,500 manufacturers, over 2,000 international and European organizations, statistical agencies, trade journals and associations, databases, and trade fairs in the grocery and food industries worldwide. Entries include: Company name, address, phone, telex, names of parent company and subsidiaries, number of employees, financial data, products and brand names handled; retailers and wholesalers include type of outlet, names and titles of key personnel.

***World Futures Studies Federation Membership Directory***. World Futures Studies Federation, c/o Marianne Rugard Jarvstrat, Sec. Gen., De Lavalsgatan 6 Trollhattan, Sweden. Phone: 46 709 906923; Email: secretariat@wfsf.org • URL: http://www.wfsf.org/ • Annual. Publication includes: List of over 700 member individuals and 60 institutions with an interest in the study of the world's future. Entries include: Name, address, phone, fax, e-mail.

***World Gas Handbook***. Energy Intelligence Group, 5 E 37th St., 5th Fl. New York, NY 10016-2807. Phone: (212)532-1112; Fax: (212)532-4479; Email: customerservice@energyintel.com • URL: http://www.energyintel.com • Annual. Contains the gas industry structure, policies, markets, and production data for each of about 50 countries. Also includes detailed profiles of 56 major gas producers.

**World Health Organization - Regional Office for Europe**. Marmorvej 51 DK-2100 Copenhagen, Denmark. Phone: 45 45

337000; Fax: 45 45 337001; Email: postmaster@euro.who.int • URL: http://www.euro.who.int • Works to ensure that WHO programs effectively meet the particular public health needs of Europe; serves as a liaison between national and local public health agencies and the WHO.

***World Investment Report***. United Nations Publications, c/o National Book Network, 15200 NBN Way Blue Ridge Summit, PA 17214. Phone: 888-254-4286 or (212)963-7680 or (212)963-8302; Fax: (800)338-4550; Email: unpublications@nbnbooks.com • URL: http://www.unp.un.org • Annual. Concerned with foreign direct investment, economic development, regional trends, transnational corporations, and globalization.

***World Labour Report***. International Labour Office. 1828 L St. NW, Ste. 600 Washington, DC 20036-5121. Phone: (202)653-7652; Fax: (202)653-7687; Email: ilopubs@tascol.com • URL: http://www.ilo.org • Irregular. Price varies. International coverage. Reviews significant recent events and labor policy developments in the following areas: employment, human rights, labor relations, and working conditions.

***World Leading Global Brand Owners***. Euromonitor International Business Reference Div., 224 S Michigan Ave., Ste. 1500 Chicago, IL 60604. Phone: (312)922-1115; Fax: (312)922-1157; Email: insight@euromonitorintl.com • URL: http://www.euromonitor.com • $1,495 Individuals Hardcopy. Covers: Profiles of the top 200 multinationals worldwide operating in key consumer markets. Entries include: Detailed corporate and financial information and analysis, information on the global market share and significant subsidiaries, strengths, weaknesses, opportunities and threats, main brands, product range, and full operational data.

***World M&A Network***. NVST Inc., 1100 Dexter Ave. N Seattle, WA 98109. Phone: 800-910-6878 or (206)676-3802; Fax: (206)273-7401; Email: info@nvst.com • URL: http://www.nvst.com • Monthly Quarterly. $395 U.S.; $425 Out of country; $395 Members annual membership; $39.50 Members month-to-month membership. Lists companies for sale, companies seeking to purchase other companies, and sources of acquisition financing.

***World Market Share Reporter***. Cengage Learning Inc., 20 Channel Center St. Boston, MA 02210. Phone: 800-487-8488 or (617)289-7700; Fax: (617)289-7844; Email: investors@cengage.com • URL: http://www.cengage.com • $572 Individuals. Compilation of global market share data from periodical literature. Covers nearly 1,670 entries in 360 geographic worldwide locations of companies and products and services.

***World Migration Report***. United Nations Publications, c/o National Book Network, 15200 NBN Way Blue Ridge Summit, PA 17214. Phone: 888-254-4286 or (212)963-7680 or (212)963-8302; Fax: (800)338-4550; Email: unpublications@nbnbooks.com • URL: http://www.unp.un.org • Annual. $39.00. Analyzes major trends in world migration, including individual country profiles.

***World of Information Business & Economic Europe Review***. Kogan Page, Limited, 120 Pentonville Rd. London N1 9JN, United Kingdom. Phone: 44 20 72780433 or (440) 2072780433; Fax: 44 20 78376348 or (783)76348; Email: kpinfo@kogan-page.co.uk • URL: http://www.kogan-page.co.uk/ • Covers: Tourist and business information, including airlines, banks, hotels, ministries and associations in Europe. Entries include: Address.

***World Online Markets***. Jupitermedia Corp., 23 Old Kings Hwy. S Darien, CT 06820. Phone: 800-488-4345 or (203)662-2800; Fax: (203)655-4686; Email: ameckler@jupitermedia.com • URL: http://www.webmediabrands.com • Annual. $1,895.00. Market research report. Provides broad coverage of worldwide Internet and online information business activities, including country-by-country data. Includes company profiles and five-year forecasts or trend projections.

***World Opinion Update***. Survey Research Consultants International, Inc. Survey Research Consultants International Inc., 156 Bulkley St. Williamstown, MA 01267. Phone: (413)458-5338 • Description: Gives tabular results of recent public opinion polls conducted in many countries on international public affairs subjects: sociological, political, economic, military, and religious. Recurring features include statistics.

***World Patent Information***. European Commission BEL. Elsevier, Secondary Publishing Division, 650 Ave. of the Americas New York, NY 10011. Phone: 888-437-4636 or (212)633-3980; Fax: (212)633-3975; Email: t.reller@elsevier.com • URL: http://www.elseveier.com • Quarterly. $1,030 Institutions up to 5 authorized users. Contains papers concerned with all aspects of Industrial Property information and documentation.

**World Presidents Organization**. 600 E Las Colinas Blvd., Ste. 1000 Irving, TX 75039. Phone: 800-773-7976 or (972)587-1500 or (972)587-1618; Fax: (972)587-1611; Email: membership@ypowpo.org • URL: http://www.wpo.org • Corporate executives, all of whom are former members of the Young Presidents' Organization. Functions as a graduate school for former members of YPO. Strives to provide high quality program content and to keep members well-informed on major topics through contact with the world's leading authorities. Conducts seminars.

***World Press Encyclopedia***. Cengage Learning Inc., 20 Channel Center St. Boston, MA 02210. Phone: 800-487-8488 or (617)289-7700; Fax: (617)289-7844; Email: investors@cengage.com • URL: http://www.cengage.com • 2003. $572.00. Second edition. Two volumes. Comprehensive essays cover the background and economic framework of newspapers and other news media in about 200 countries. Covers relevant legal issues, censorship, government relations, education in journalism, status of news agencies, cable, Internet, and other media topics. eBook also available.

***World Radio TV Handbook: The Directory of Global Broadcasting***. World Radio TV Handbook, PO Box 290 Oxford OX2 7FT, United Kingdom. Fax: 44 1865 514405; Email: sales@wrth.com • URL: http://www.wrth.com • Annual. Covers: 25,000 radio and television stations worldwide; national regulatory bodies. Database includes: Maps; essays on international broadcasting, list of English-language broadcasts. Entries include: For stations—Name, frequency, address, phone, telex, name and title of contact and key personnel, description of programming. For agencies—Name, address, phone.

***World Surface Coatings Abstracts (Online)***. Paint Research Association of Great Britain, Waldegrave Rd. Teddington TW11 8LD 4, United Kingdom. Phone: 44 20 86144800; Fax: (894)34705 • Indexing and abstracting of the literature of paint and surface coatings, 1976 to present. Monthly updates. Inquire as to online cost and availability.

***World Surface Coatings Abstracts***. PRA Coatings Technology Centre, 14 Castle Mews, High St. Hampton TW12 2NP, United Kingdom. Phone: 44 20 84870800; Fax: 44 20 84870801 • URL: http://www.pra-world.com • Monthly. Available in print or online.

***World Textile Abstracts***. Elsevier, Secondary Publishing Division, 650 Ave. of the Americas New York, NY 10011. Phone: 888-437-4636 or (212)633-3980; Fax: (212)633-3975; Email: t.reller@elsevier.com • URL: http://www.elsevier.com • $2,609 Institutions, other countries; ¥309,000 Institutions Japan; €2,334 Institutions European countries and Iran. Digests of articles published in the world's textile literature. Includes subscription to *World Textile Digest*.

***World Textiles***. Elsevier, Secondary Publishing Division, 650 Ave. of the Americas New York, NY 10011. Phone: 888-437-4636 or (212)633-3980; Fax: (212)633-3975; Email: t.reller@elsevier.com • URL: http://www.elseveier.com • Provides abstracting and indexing from 1970 of worldwide textile literature (periodicals, books, pamphlets, and reports). Includes U. S., European, and British patent information. Updating is monthly. Inquire as to online cost and availability.

***World Trade Almanac***. Hoover's Inc., 5800 Airport Blvd. Austin, TX 78752-4204. Phone: 866-443-3939 or (512)374-4500 or (866)281-5969; Fax: (512)374-4501; Email: salesteam@hoovers.com • URL: http://www.hoovers.com • $86.95. Publication includes: Lists of embassies and consulates, trade organizations, chambers of commerce, world trade centers, industrial associations, trade fair sponsors, domestic and international banks, and major business service providers for 120 countries of the world. Entries include: Name, address, phone. Principal content of publication is country profiles.

***World Trade Analyzer***. Statistics Canada, International Trade Division, Ottawa, ON, Canada K1A OT6. Phone: 800-263-1136 or (514)283-8300; Email: infostats@statcan.gc.ca • URL: http://www.statcan.ca • $4,000. Annual. CD-ROM provides 20 years of export-import data for 800 commodities traded by the 180 member countries of the United Nations.

***World Trade Association International Business Directory***. San Francisco Chamber of Commerce, 235 Montgomery St., Ste. 760 San Francisco, CA 94104. Phone: (415)392-4520; Fax: (415)392-0485; Email: info@sfchamber.com • URL: http://www.sfchamber.com • Annual. $12.50. Covers: Members of the San Francisco Chamber of Commerce engaged in import or export activities. Entries include: Company name, address, phone, commodities, countries imported from or exported to, services.

**World Trade Center Nigeria**. Western House, 8th Fl., 8/10 Broad St. Lagos, Lagos, Nigeria. Phone: 234 1 8103570; Email: info@wtcnlagos.org • URL: http://www.wtcnlagos.org • Works to improve the business climate in Nigeria by pushing ideas that would make the working environment more conducive for international trade and investment. Facilitates trade and investment by disseminating information and match-making foreign business persons with their appropriate local counterparts.

***World Trade Organization Dispute Settlement Decisions: Bernan's Annotated Reporter***. Bernan Press, PO Box 191 Blue Ridge Summit, PA 17214. Phone: 800-865-3457 or (301)459-7666; Fax: (301)459-6988; Email: customercare@bernan.com • URL: http://www.bernan.com • 3/year. $320 2 volume set. Contains all World Trade Organization Panel Reports and Appellate Decisions since the establishment of the WTO in 1995. Includes such cases as "The Importation, Sale, and Distribution of Bananas."

***World Trade Organization Trade Policy Review***. Bernan Press, PO Box 191 Blue Ridge Summit, PA 17214. Phone: 800-865-3457 or (301)459-7666; Fax: (301)459-6988; Email: customercare@bernan.com • URL: http://www.bernan.com • Annual. $95. provides detailed trade information for each of 40 countries. Includes search capabilities, hypertext links, charts, tables, and graphs.

***World Trade Review: Economics, Law, International Institutions***. Cambridge University Press, 32 Ave. of the Americas New York, NY 10013-2473. Phone: 800-872-7423 or (212)924-3900 or (212)337-5048; Fax: (212)691-3239; Email: newyork@cambridge.org • URL: http://www.cambridge.org/us • Three times a year. Individuals, $48.00 pr year; institutions, $200.00 per year. Published in conjunction with the World Trade Organization (www.wto.org). Covers "issues of relevance to the multilateral trading system.".

***The World Trade System***. Cartermill International, Maple House, 149 Tottenham Ct. Rd. London W1P 9LL, United Kingdom. Phone: 44 171 896 2424; Fax: 44 171 896 2449; Email: lizg@pearson-pro.com • $165. Publication includes: List of national and international trade organizations. Entries include: Organization name, address, phone, contact information. Principal content of publication is information on and analysis of world trade activity.

***World Trademark Law and Practice***. Matthew Bender and Company Inc., 1275 Broadway Albany, NY 12204-2638. Phone: 800-424-4200 or (518)487-3000; Fax: (518)487-3573 or (800)424-4200; Email: customer.support@lexisnexis.com • URL: http://www.matthewbender.com • $1,864 print; $1,646 E-book. Five looseleaf volumes. Periodic supplementation. A guide to international trademark practice with detailed coverage of 35 major jurisdictions and summary coverage for over 100.

***World Watch: Working for a Sustainable Future***. Worldwatch Institute, 1400 16th St. NW, Ste. 430 Washington, DC 20036. Phone: (202)745-8092; Fax: (202)478-2534; Email: worldwatch@worldwatch.org • URL: http://www.worldwatch.org • Bimonthly. $25.00 per year. Emphasis is on environmental trends, including developments in population growth, climate change, human behavior, the role of government, and other factors.

***World Wide Importers Register International Buyers Directory***. NIIR Project Consultancy Services, 106 - E, Kamla Nagar New Delhi 110007, India. Phone: 91 11 23843955; Fax: 91 11 23841561; Email: npcs.india@gmail.com • URL: http://www.niir.org • Rs 6,742 Individuals; $250 Individuals. Covers: 45,000 entries of importing firms in Europe, America, Middle East, Asia/Pacific, South/Central America and Africa. Entries include: Indian missions/embassies, e-mail, phone, fax and complete address to facilitate exporters.

**WorldatWork**. 14040 N Northsight Blvd. Scottsdale, AZ 85260. Phone: 866-816-2962 or (480)922-2020 or (480)951-9191; Fax: (480)483-8352 or (866)816-2962; Email: customerrelations@worldatwork.org • URL: http://www.worldatwork.org • Dedicated to knowledge leadership in compensation, benefits and total rewards, focusing on disciplines associated with attracting, retaining and motivating employees. Offers CCP, CBP, and GRP certification and education programs, conducts surveys, research and provides networking opportunities.

***Worldmark Encyclopedia of National Economies***. Cengage Learning Inc., 20 Channel Center St. Boston, MA 02210. Phone: 800-487-8488 or (617)289-7700; Fax: (617)289-7844; Email: investors@cengage.com • URL: http://www.cengage.com • 2002. $572.00. Four volumes. Covers both the current and historical development of the economies of 200 foreign nations. Includes analysis and statistics. Also available as eBook.

***The World's Major Companies***. Euromonitor International Business Reference Div., 224 S Michigan Ave., Ste. 1500 Chicago, IL 60604. Phone: (312)922-1115; Fax: (312)922-1157; Email: insight@euromonitorintl.com • URL: http://www.euromonitor.com • $550. Covers: Approximately 4,000 major multinational companies. Entries include: Company name, address, phone, telex, names and titles of key personnel, number of employees, financial data, subsidiary and branch names and locations, description.

***World's Major Multinationals***. Euromonitor International Business Reference Div., 224 S Michigan Ave., Ste. 1500 Chicago, IL 60604. Phone: (312)922-1115; Fax: (312)922-1157; Email: insight@euromonitorintl.com • URL: http://www.euromonitor.com • Covers: List of major multinational companies. Entries include: Company name, address, phone; performance analysis; list of subsidiaries; market share; net profit and turnover; leading brands; and merger and acquisition information.

***Worldscope Fundamentals***. Thomson Reuters Corp., 3 Times Sq. New York, NY 10036. Phone: 800-336-4474 or (646)223-4000 or (646)822-2000; Email: general.info@thomsonreuters.com • URL: http://www.thomsonreuters.com • Daily. Database covers: profiles, company financial statement data, ratios, and stock performance of approximately 20,000 companies listed on leading stock exchanges worldwide. Database includes: Company name, address, phone, names and titles of key personnel, products, number of employees, major shareholders, geographic and product segment, financial data.

***Worldtariff Guidebook on Customs Tariff Schedules of Import Duties***. Worldtariff Division, Morse Agri-Energy Associates, 220 Montgomery St., Suite 432 San Francisco, CA 94104. Phone: 800-556-9334 or (415)391-7501; Fax: (415)391-7537 • Looseleaf. Over 60 volumes. Prices vary. Consists generally of volumes for individual countries and volumes for broad classes of products, such as clothing. (Country volumes are typically $500.00 each.).

***Worldwide Business Collaborations—Consultants News and Business Opportunities***. International Press Cutting Service,

PO Box 121 Allahabad 211 001, India. Phone: 91 0532622392 • Weekly. $715; $85 Other countries. Publication spotlighting international business opportunities and openings.

***Worldwide Business Contact Name Email Database***. The Data Supplier, 9107 Wilshire Blvd., Ste. 450 Beverly Hills, CA 90210. Phone: 888-930-3282; Fax: (818)221-0295; Email: contactus@thedatasupplier.com • URL: http://www.thedatasupplier.com • Contains e-mail addresses for more than 2.8 million business contacts around the world. Also includes contact name, business name, address, telephone and fax numbers, and Web site.

***Worldwide Business Database***. The Data Supplier, 9107 Wilshire Blvd., Ste. 450 Beverly Hills, CA 90210. Phone: 888-930-3282; Fax: (818)221-0295; Email: contactus@thedatasupplier.com • URL: http://www.thedatasupplier.com • Contains contact information for more than 32.6 million companies around the world. Includes business name, full contact information, year founded, number of employees, products and services, type of business, income, and other data.

***Worldwide ERC***. 4401 Wilson Blvd., Ste. 510 Arlington, VA 22203. Phone: (703)842-3400; Fax: (703)527-1552; Email: customercare@worldwideerc.org • URL: http://www.worldwideerc.org/Pages/index.aspx • Members are major corporations seeking efficiency and minimum disruption when employee transfers take place. Formerly Employee Relocation Real Estate Advisory Council.

***Worldwide Magnetics Industry Directory***. Webcom Communications Corp., 7355 E Orchard Rd., Ste. 100 Englewood, CO 80111. Phone: 800-803-9488 or (720)528-3770; Fax: (720)528-3771; Email: general@webcomcommunications.com • URL: http://www.webcomcommunications.com • $195 Individuals hardcopy; $225 Individuals PDF version; $575 Individuals CD-ROM. Covers: 2,400 companies that manufacture, distribute, and assemble materials and equipment in the magnetic industry worldwide. Includes industry-wide listing of magnetic manufacturers and distributors as well as suppliers of parts, components, systems and supplies used in the manufacture and aftermarket service of the magnet and materials industry. Information on over 4,800 personnel involved in the industry.

***Worldwide Offshore Petroleum Directory***. PennWell Corp., Petroleum Div., 1700 W. Loop S., Suite 1000 Houston, TX 77027. Phone: 800-736-6935 or (713)621-9720; Email: petroleum@pennwell.com • URL: http://www.pennwell.com • Annual. $135.00. Lists about 5,800 companies.

***Worldwide Tax Daily***. Tax Analysts, 400 S Maple Ave., Ste. 400 Falls Church, VA 22046. Phone: 800-955-2444 or (703)533-4400; Fax: (703)533-4444; Email: cservice@tax.org • URL: http://www.tax.org • Weekly. $999 Individuals. Provides "news and in-depth reports on a variety of international tax topics." Summarizes tax statutes, regulations, rulings, court decisions, and treaties from various countries of the world.

***Worldwide Trade Secrets Law***. Melvin Jager, author. Thomson West, 610 Opperman Dr. Eagan, MN 55123. Phone: 800-328-9352 or (651)687-7000 • Annual. $2,560 3 volume looseleaf (Full set). Covers the pure trade secret license, the pure patent license, hybrid patents, and trade secret licenses.

***Worldwide Tradeshow Schedule***. Glahe International, Inc., PO Box 2460 Washington, DC 20013. Phone: (202)659-4557; Fax: (202)457-0776 • Covers: Approximately 200 international trade fairs in all major industrial sectors worldwide. Entries include: Organization name, address, phone, telex, name and title of contact, description of event.

***Writers' and Artists' Yearbook: A Directory for Writers, Artists, Playwrights, Writers for Film, Radio and Television, Photographers and Composers***. Midpoint Trade Books, 1263 Southwest Blvd. Kansas City, KS 66103-1901. Phone: (212)727-0190; Fax: (212)727-0195 • URL: http://www.midpointtrade.com • Annual. $25.00. A worldwide guide to markets for various kinds of writing and artwork. Published in England by A O C Black. Formerly *International Writers' and Artists' Yearbook*.

***Writers Directory***. InfoGroup Inc., 5711 S 86th Cir. Omaha, NE 68127-4146. Phone: (402)593-4500 • URL: http://www.infogroup.com • Updated continuously; printed on request. Number of listings: 2,400. Entries include: Name, address, phone, size of advertisement, name of owner or manager, number of employees, year first in "Yellow Pages." Compiled from telephone company "Yellow Pages," nationwide.

***Writer's Guide to Book Editors, Publishers, and Literary Agents, Who They Are, What They Want, and How to Win Them Over***. Prima Publishing Inc., 3300 Lava Ridge Ct. Roseville, CA 95661. Phone: 800-632-8676 or (916)787-7000 or (916)632-4400; Fax: (916)787-7001 or (916)787-7003; Email: websupportlife@primpub.com • URL: http://www.primapublishing.com • Annual. $27.95; with CD-ROM, $49.95. Directory for authors includes information on publishers' response times and pay rates.

***Writer's Market: Where & How to Sell What You Write***. North Light Books, 10151 Carver Rd., Ste. 200 Blue Ash, OH 45242-4760. Phone: (513)531-2690; Email: contact_us@fwmedia.com • URL: http://www.fwmedia.com • Annual. $19.79 Individuals paperback. Covers: Over 3,500 buyers of books, articles, short stories, plays, gags, verse, fillers, and other original written material. Includes book and periodical publishers, greeting card publishers, play producers and

publishers, audiovisual material producers, syndicates, and contests and awards. Database includes: Interviews with editors and writers and advice on writing, freelancing, and marketing. Entries include: Name and address of buyer, phone, payment rates, editorial requirements, reporting time, how to break in.

***Writing Effective Business Plans***. Entrepreneur Press, 2445 McCabe Way, Ste. 400 Irvine, CA 92614-6244. Phone: 800-864-6864 or (949)261-2325 or (949)622-7131; Fax: (949)261-7729 or (949)261-0234; Email: press@entrepreneur.com • URL: http://www.entrepreneurpress.com • Looseleaf. $49.50. A step-by-step guide. Includes a sample business plan.

***www.BusinessLaw.gov***. U.S. Small Business Administration, 409 3rd St. SW Washington, DC 20416. Phone: 800-827-5722 or (202)205-8800 • URL: http://www.sba.gov • Web site provides information on legal and regulatory issues for small businesses. It offers access to critical information on topics from advertising to zoning, including laws on hiring and managing employees. The site allows businesses to apply for licenses or permits, e-file tax returns, and confer with other business owners.

***Wyoming Business Directory***. InfoGroup Inc., 5711 S 86th Cir. Omaha, NE 68127-4146. Phone: (402)593-4500 • URL: http://www.infogroup.com • Annual. $375 both print & CD-ROM. Covers: 33,514 businesses in Wyoming. Entries include: Company name, address, phone, number of employees, name of owner or manager, sales volume. Compiled from telephone company "Yellow Pages," statewide. All states covered (see separate entries).

***Wyoming Directory of Manufacturing and Mining***. Wyoming Business Council, 214 W 15th St. Cheyenne, WY 82002-0240. Phone: 800-262-3425 or (307)777-2800 or (307)777-7284; Fax: (307)777-2837 or (307)777-2838; Email: info.wbc@wyo.gov • URL: http://www.wyomingbusiness.org • Biennial. $15; Free to non-profit organizations. Covers: About 790 companies in mining and manufacturing; state and local organizations and government agencies that provide business assistance. Entries include: For businesses—Name of firm, address, phone, name of key executive, product or activity, parent company (if any), codes for number of employees and geographic scope, Standard Industrial Classification (SIC) code. For organizations and agencies—Name of agency or organization, address, phone, contact name or official.

***Wytheville Chamber of Commerce Business Directory***. Wytheville-Wythe-Bland Chamber of Commerce, 150 E Monroe St. Wytheville, VA 24382. Phone: (276)223-3365; Fax: (276)223-3412; Email: chamber@wytheville.org • URL: http://www.wwbchamber.com • Covers: List of members. Entries include: name, address, phone.

***Wytheville-Wythe-Bland Chamber of Commerce Business Directory***. Wytheville-Wythe-Bland Chamber of Commerce, 150 E Monroe St. Wytheville, VA 24382. Phone: (276)223-3365; Fax: (276)223-3412; Email: chamber@wytheville.org • URL: http://www.wwbchamber.com • Annual. Contains complete list of member's addresses and phone numbers.

***Xiamen Yellow Pages: Commercial/Industrial Directory***. China Yellow Pages Directories Co., Fortress Twr., Rm. 1204-5, 250 King's Rd., Hong Kong North Point, China. Phone: 8076807; Fax: 5032601 • Annual. $65. Covers: over 15,000 companies in the Xiamen area. Database includes: Investment information. Entries include: Company name, address, phone, fax, postal code.

**Yale University - Cowles Foundation for Research in Economics**. PO Box 208281 New Haven, CT 06520-8281. Phone: (203)432-3702; Fax: (203)432-6167; Email: donald.andrews@yale.edu • URL: http://cowles.econ.yale.edu • Development and application of mathematical and statistical methods in economics and related social sciences.

***Yancey County Business Directory***. Yancey County/Burnsville Chamber of Commerce, 106 W Main St. Burnsville, NC 28714. Phone: (828)682-7413; Email: info@yanceychamber.com • URL: http://www.yanceychamber.com • Periodic.

***Yearbook***. Association of Government Accountants, 2208 Mt. Vernon Ave. Alexandria, VA 22301-1314. Phone: 800-AGA-7211 or (703)684-6931; Fax: (703)548-9367; Email: agamembers@agacgfm.org • URL: http://www.agacgfm.org • Annual.

***Yearbook of Agriculture***. U.S. Department of Agriculture. U. S. Government Printing Office, 732 N Capitol St. NW Washington, DC 20401. Phone: 866-512-1800 or (202)512-1800 or (866)512-1800; Fax: (202)512-2104 or (202)512-2250; Email: contactcenter@gpo.gov • URL: http://www.gpo.gov • Annual.

***Yearbook of the Athens Stock Exchange***. Athens Stock Exchange, 110 Athinon Ave. 10442 Athens, Greece. Phone: 302 10 3366385; Fax: 302 10 3366286; Email: information_services@helex.gr • URL: http://www.ase.gr • Annual. €20 plus postage. Covers: About 196 companies quoted on the Athens Stock Exchange; list of stockbrokers. Database includes: List of business loans available, with description and financial data; financial statistics. Entries include: For companies—Name, address, phone, telex, year established, year first listed, line of business, number of shareholders, board of directors, number of employees, financial data. For brokers—Name, address, phone.

***Yearbook of the International Law Commission***. United Nations, Department of Public Information, Grand Central Sta. New

York, NY 10163-5850. Phone: (212)963-1516 or (212)963-4475; Fax: (212)963-1381 or (212)963-7055; Email: inquiries@un.org • URL: http://www.devbusiness.com • Annual.

***Yearbook of the Lebanese Joint-Stock Companies***. Publitec Publications, Gedeon House, 139-141 John Kennedy St. Beirut, Lebanon. Phone: 961 1 495401; Fax: 961 1 493330; Email: publitecpublications@hotmail.com • URL: http://www.whoswhointhearabworld.info • Annual. $120. Covers: Lebanese and foreign companies operating in Lebanon, including companies working in the fields of insurance, banking, commerce, industry, real estate, transport, finance, holdings, and offshore. Entries include: Contact information.

***Yearbook of the Lebanese Limited Liability Companies***. Publitec Publications, Gedeon House, 139-141 John Kennedy St. Beirut, Lebanon. Phone: 961 1 495401; Fax: 961 1 493330; Email: publitecpublications@hotmail.com • URL: http://www.whoswhointhearabworld.info • Annual. $120. Covers: Lebanese limited liability companies, including insurance companies, commerce, industry, real estate, transport, and finance. Entries include: Contact information.

***Yellow Pages Industry Sourcebook***. Communications Trends Inc., 5871 Glenridge Dr. NE, Ste. 140 Atlanta, GA 30328-5306. Phone: (404)843-8717; Fax: (404)801-0028 • Annual. $295. Publication includes: Company listings. Entries include: Company name, address, phone, description, officer names, financial data, key customers, national accounts.

***Yellow Pages Moscow***. Deutsche Telekom Medien GmbH, Wiesenhuttenstrasse 18 D-60329 Frankfurt, Germany. Phone: 69 26 820101 or 49 69 26820; Fax: 69 26 821101 or 49 69 26821101; Email: info@detemedien.de • URL: http://www.detemedien.de • Annual. Covers: Approximately 70,000 commercial telephone subscribers in Moscow. Entries include: Name, address, phone, product/service.

***Yemen Business Law Handbook***. International Business Publications, USA, PO Box 15343 Washington, DC 20003. Phone: (202)546-2103; Fax: (202)546-3275; Email: ibpusa@comcast.net • URL: http://ibpus.com • $99.95 Individuals hardcopy, E-book and CD-ROM. Covers: Information on basic business legislation, laws and climate, export-import regulations, and contacts.

**Yemeni Businessmen Club**. PO Box 15539 Sana'a, Yemen. Phone: 967 1 440360 or 967 1 444910; Fax: 967 1 440207; Email: ybc-yemen@yemen.net.ye • URL: http://www.ybc-yemen.com • Seeks to strengthen links between members and to develop their institutions and contribute to the overall development process. Implements programs and activities by trust and a spirit of cooperation. Works to strengthen links between members.

***Yonsei Business Review***. Yonsei University Industrial Management Research Centre, College of Business and Economics, 134 Sinchon-Dong, Sudaemoon-ku Seoul, South Korea. Phone: 82 23920192 • Semiannual. $8,000. Business and economics journal.

***York County Regional Chamber of Commerce Business Directory***. York County Regional Chamber of Commerce, 116 E Main St. Rock Hill, SC 29731. Phone: (803)324-7500; Fax: (803)324-1889; Email: info@yorkcountychamber.com • URL: http://www.yorkcountychamber.com • Covers: Information on all York County, New York, businesses.

**Young Presidents' Organization**. 600 E Las Colinas Blvd., Ste. 1000 Irving, TX 75039. Phone: 800-773-7976 or (972)587-1500; Fax: (972)587-1611; Email: askypo@ypo.org • URL: http://www.ypo.org • Presidents or chief executive officers of corporations with minimum of 50 employees; each member must have been elected president before his/her 40th birthday and must retire by June 30th the year after his/her 50th birthday. Assists members in becoming better presidents through education and idea exchange. Conducts courses for members and spouses, in business, arts and sciences, world affairs, and family and community life, during a given year at various locations, including graduate business schools.

**Young Women Social Entrepreneurs**. 6006 Colton Blvd. Oakland, CA 94611. Phone: (415)378-4417; Email: sara@ywse.org • URL: http://www.ywse.org • Serves women, primarily ages 25-40, with socially conscious agenda who are founders and leaders within businesses, non-profits, and government organizations. Aims to promote young women entrepreneurs by providing training and development, access to resources, and networking opportunities.

***Your Federal Income Tax***. U.S. Department of the Treasury, Internal Revenue Service. U. S. Government Printing Office, 732 N Capitol St. NW Washington, DC 20401. Phone: 866-512-1800 or (202)512-1800 or (866)512-1800; Fax: (202)512-2104 or (202)512-2250; Email: contactcenter@gpo.gov • URL: http://www.gpo.gov • Annual. $23 U.S.; $32.20 Other countries. Layman's guide to income tax preparation.

***Youth Markets Alert***. EPM Communications Inc., 19 W 21 St., Ste. 303 New York, NY 10010. Phone: 888-852-9467 or (212)941-0099; Fax: (212)941-1622; Email: info@epmcom.com • URL: http://www.epmcom.com • Description: Features information and research results related to young consumers from elementary school through high school.

**Youth Venture**. 1700 N Moore St., Ste. 2000 Arlington, VA 22209. Phone: (703)527-8300; Fax: (703)527-8383; Email: yvinfo@youthventure.org • URL: http://www.youthventure.org • Works to empower young people to create and launch their own enterprises in order to take greater responsibility for their lives and communities.

*Yritys-Suomi CD*. Helsinki Media, Blue Book, Hoylaamotie 1 D FIN-00040 Helsinki, Finland. Phone: 358 9 1201 or 0 1205971; Fax: 358 9 1205599 or 0 1205999; Email: info@ bluebook.fi • URL: http://www.sanoma.com/contact-us/ sanoma-media-finland • Biennial. Database covers: Information on 170,000 companies from other Blue Book directories.

*Yugoslavia Export-Import Directory*. Yugoslaviapublic, Kneza Mihailova 10 YU-10000 Belgrade, Serbia. • Annual. Covers: Foreign trade organizations, products, services in Yugoslavia. Entries include: Name, address, phone.

*Yugoslavia (Serbia) Government and Business Contacts Handbook*. International Business Publications, USA, PO Box 15343 Washington, DC 20003. Phone: (202)546-2103; Fax: (202)546-3275; Email: ibpusa@comcast.net • URL: http://ibpus.com • Annual. $99.95 Individuals hardcopy, e-book, CD-ROM. Covers: Strategic government and business information, export-import activity in the country, investment, business contacts and regulations.

*Yugoslavia (Serbia) Industrial and Business Directory*. International Business Publications, USA, PO Box 15343 Washington, DC 20003. Phone: (202)546-2103; Fax: (202)546-3275; Email: ibpusa@comcast.net • URL: http:// ibpus.com • Annual. $99.95 Individuals hardcopy, E-book and CD-ROM. Covers: Strategic industrial, investment and business contacts for conducting export-import and investment activity in the country.

*Yunnan Yellow Pages*. China Yellow Pages Directories Co., Fortress Twr., Rm. 1204-5, 250 King's Rd., Hong Kong North Point, China. Phone: 8076807; Fax: 5032601 • Annual. Covers: Over 20,000 companies in Yunnan Province, Taiwan. Database includes: An investment guide containing Yunnan's policies, rules and procedures for investment plus a compilation of product and service advertisements. Entries include: Company name, address, phone.

*Zacks Analyst Directory*. Zacks Investment Research Inc., 111 N Canal St., Ste. 1101 Chicago, IL 60606. Phone: 800-767-3771 or (312)630-9880; Fax: (312)630-9898; Email: support@zacks.com • URL: http://www.zacks.com • Updated daily. Lists stockbroker investment analysts and gives the names of major U.S. corporations covered by those analysts.

*Zacks Analyst Guide*. Zacks Investment Research Inc., 111 N Canal St., Ste. 1101 Chicago, IL 60606. Phone: 800-767-3771 or (312)630-9880; Fax: (312)630-9898; Email: support@zacks.com • URL: http://www.zacks.com • Ranks analysts within more than 70 industry groups.

*Zacks Earnings Estimates*. Zacks Investment Research Inc., 111 N Canal St., Ste. 1101 Chicago, IL 60606. Phone: 800-767-3771 or (312)630-9880; Fax: (312)630-9898; Email: support@zacks.com • URL: http://www.zacks.com • Provides online earnings projections for about 6,000 U. S. corporations, based on investment analysts' reports. Data is mainly from 200 major brokerage firms. Time span varies according to online provider, with daily or weekly updates. Inquire as to online cost and availability.

**Zambia Union of Financial Institutions and Allied Workers**. Luangwa House, Cairo Rd. Lusaka, Zambia. Phone: 260 211 222105; Fax: 260 211 231364; Email: zufiaw@zamnet.zm • URL: http://www.africaefuture.org/zufiaw • Exists to improve the material conditions of members and their families. Aims to strive for equality between all men and women in the sharing of all national wealth and world leisure.

*Zoning and Planning Deskbook, 2d*. Katherine Kmiec Turner and Douglas W. Kmiec, authors. Thomson West, 610 Opperman Dr. Eagan, MN 55123. Phone: 800-328-9352 or (651)687-7000 • Annual. $530.60 book - softbound; full set. Emphasis is on legal issues. Examines the latest developments in land use control, discussing procedural and substantive considerations, remedies, strategies, and state and federal litigation.

*Zoning and Planning Law Handbook*. Patricia Salkin. Thomson West, 610 Opperman Dr. Eagan, MN 55123. Phone: 800-328-9352 or (651)687-7000 • Annual. $601.30. Assembles the insights and guidance offered by the country's leading authorities in zoning law, land use planning, and conservation.

**Zurich Chamber of Commerce**. Selnaustrasse 32 CH-8022 Zurich, Switzerland. Phone: 41 44 2174050 or 41 44 2174040; Fax: 41 44 2174051; Email: direktion@zurichcci.ch • URL: http://www.zurichcci.ch • Keeps members up-to-date on economically relevant political and legal issues. Collects opinions during hearings on the drafting of new laws. Maintains documentation to provide economic information, informs members about import regulations, and provides educational courses on international trading formalities. Represents Swiss interests abroad, particularly in the International Chamber.

CPSIA information can be obtained
at www.ICGtesting.com
Printed in the USA
FFOW04n1124180315
11949FF